MIDDLE AND JUNIOR HIGH CORE COLLECTION

ELEVENTH EDITION

CORE COLLECTION SERIES

FORMERLY
STANDARD CATALOG SERIES

CHRISTI SHOWMAN FARRAR, GENERAL EDITOR

CHILDREN'S CORE COLLECTION
MIDDLE AND JUNIOR HIGH CORE COLLECTION
SENIOR HIGH CORE COLLECTION
PUBLIC LIBRARY CORE COLLECTION: NONFICTION
PUBLIC LIBRARY CORE COLLECTION: FICTION

MIDDLE AND JUNIOR HIGH CORE COLLECTION

ELEVENTH EDITION

EDITED BY

EVE-MARIE MILLER

LIZA OLDHAM

AND

CHRISTI SHOWMAN FARRAR

H. W. Wilson

A Division of EBSCO Information Service, Inc.

Ipswich, Massachusetts

2014

GREY HOUSE PUBLISHING

Printed in the United States of America

ISBN 978-0-8242-1229-2

Abridged Dewey Decimal Classification and Relative Index, Edition 15 is © 2004-2012 OCLC Online Computer Library Center, Inc. Used with Permission. DDC, Dewey, Dewey Decimal Classification, and WebDewey are registered trademarks of OCLC.

Middle and Junior High Core Collection, 2014, published by Grey House Publishing, Inc., Amenia, NY, under exclusive license from EBSCO Information Services, Inc.

A catalog record for this title is available from the Library of Congress.

PRINTED IN THE UNITED STATES OF AMERICA

TABLE OF CONTENTS

PREFACE

MIDDLE AND JUNIOR HIGH CORE COLLECTION is a selective list of books recommended for young people in grades five through nine, together with professional aids for librarians and library media specialists. The Core Collections are also available in electronic format via EBSCOhost, updated weekly.

What's new in this Edition?

A new feature is the identification of titles that are considered "most highly recommended". These titles constitute a short list of the essential books in a given category or on a given subject. There are often a number of recommended titles on a single subject, such as biographies of Abraham Lincoln, and the Short List designation helps a user who wants only one or two. A star (★) at the start of an entry indicates that a book is a "most highly recommended" title.

This edition includes more than 10,000 book titles, over 2,000 more than the 10th edition. Of these 10,000 titles, over 4,000 titles are new since the 10th edition. There are broad revisions in the areas of computers, math, and the sciences. An expanded list of works for the librarian or media specialist includes bibliographies and other resources for the selection and evaluation of materials; library management and programming; library building design; and the use of the Internet in instruction.

History

JUNIOR HIGH SCHOOL LIBRARY CATALOG, first published in 1965, was developed to address the unique needs of younger adolescents. It developed from the STANDARD CATALOG FOR HIGH SCHOOL LIBRARIES, which was subsequently modified in scope and renamed SENIOR HIGH SCHOOL LIBRARY CATALOG. With the seventh edition in 1995, the title of the Catalog was changed from JUNIOR HIGH SCHOOL LIBRARY CATALOG to MIDDLE AND JUNIOR HIGH SCHOOL CATALOG to reflect the prevalence of middle school programs and the extension of coverage to grades five and six. With the ninth edition in 2009, the title was changed to MIDDLE AND JUNIOR HIGH CORE COLLECTION to emphasize the function of the database in establishing and maintaining the solid core of a library, which can be expanded in many ways, according to the library's individual needs.

Scope

All books listed are published in the United States, or published in Canada or the United Kingdom and distributed in the United States. All titles were available for purchase at the time of printing.

The Core Collection excludes the following: non-English-language materials, with the exception of bilingual materials, dictionaries, and similar items; works of adult fiction other than books originally written for adults but read by young people or books widely used in the curriculum; textbooks; and books about individual computer programs or versions of programs, and other topics that quickly become outdated. This volume includes a generous selection of graphic novels, even though a more comprehensive collection of recommended graphic novels can be found in GRAPHIC NOVELS CORE COLLECTION on EBSCOhost.

Preparation

Books included in this edition were selected by experienced librarians representing public library systems and academic libraries across the United States who also act as a committee of advisors on library policy and trends. The names of participating librarians and their affiliations are listed in the Acknowledgments.

Organization

The Core Collection is organized into two parts: the Classified Collection; and an Author, Title, and Subject Index.

Part 1. Classified Collection. This is arranged according to the Dewey Decimal Classification. Within classes, arrangement is by main entry, with complete bibliographical and cataloging information given for each book. The classified arrangement, along with the descriptive and critical annotations, provides a useful guide to book selection. Entries include such information as price and ISBN to facilitate acquisitions.

Part 2. Author, Title, and Subject Index. This is a comprehensive key to the Classified List with entries for authors, titles, and subjects.

ACKNOWLEDGMENTS

H. W. Wilson and EBSCO Information Services express special gratitude to the following librarians who both advised the company in editorial matters and assisted in the selection and weeding of titles for this Core Collection:

Advisory Board

Betty Carter
Texas Woman's University
Denton, Texas

Priscille Dando
Robert E. Lee High School
Springfield, Virginia

Gail de Vos
University of Alberta
Edmonton, Alberta, Canada

Vicki Emery
Lake Bradock Secondary School
Burke, Virginia

Laura Harrington
North Andover High School
North Andover, Massachusetts

Pam Spencer Holley
Library Consultant
Hallwood, Virginia

Angela Leeper
University of Richmond
Richmond, Virginia

Gregory Lum
Jesuit High School
Portland, Oregon

John Peters
Children's Literature Specialist
Bronx, New York

Heather Campbell Shock
West Virginia Library Commission
Charleston, West Virginia

Linda Ward-Callaghan
Joliet Public Library
Joliet, Illinois

DIRECTIONS FOR USE OF THE CORE COLLECTION

USES OF THE COLLECTION

MIDDLE AND JUNIOR HIGH CORE COLLECTION is designed to serve a number of purposes:

As an aid in purchasing. The Core Collection is designed to assist in the selection and ordering of titles. Annotations are provided for each title along with information concerning the publisher, ISBN, price, and availability. Since Part 1, Classified Collection, is arranged according to the Dewey Decimal Classification, the Core Collection may be used to identify parts of the library collection that should be updated or strengthened. In evaluating the suitability of a work each library will want to consider the special character of the school and community it serves.

As an aid to the reader's advisor. The work of the reader's advisor is furthered by the information about sequels and companion volumes and the descriptive and critical annotations in the Classified Collection, and by the subject access in the Index.

As an aid in verification of information. For this purpose full bibliographical data are provided in the Classified Collection. Entries also include recommended subject headings based upon *Sears List of Subject Headings* and a suggested classification derived from the *Abridged Dewey Decimal Classification and Relative Index*. Notes describe editions available, awards, publication history, and other titles in the series.

As an aid in curriculum support. The classified approach, subject indexing, and annotations are helpful in identifying materials appropriate for classroom use.

As an aid in collection maintenance. Information about titles available on a subject facilitates decisions to rebind, replace, or discard items. If a book has been deleted from the Core Collection in this edition because it is no longer in print, that deletion is not intended as a sign that the book is no longer valuable or that it should necessarily be weeded from the collection.

As an instructional aid. The Core Collection is useful in courses that deal with literature and book selection for young people.

ORGANIZATION

The Core Collection consists of two parts: a Classified Collection, and an Author, Title, and Subject Index.

Part 1. Classified Collection

The Classified Collection is arranged with nonfiction books first, classified according to the Dewey Decimal Classification in numerical order from 000 to 999. Individual biographies are classed at 92 and follow the 920s (collective biography). Fiction books (Fic) follow the nonfiction. Short story collections (S C) follow fiction. The information supplied for each book includes bibliographic description, suggested subject headings, an annotation, and frequently, an evaluation from a quote source.

An Outline of Classification, which serves as a table of contents for the Classified Collection, is reproduced below. It should be noted that many topics can be classified in more than one discipline. If a particular title is not found where it might be expected, the Index should be consulted to determine if it is classified elsewhere.

Within classes, works are arranged alphabetically under main entry, usually the author. Works of individual biography are arranged alphabetically under the biography's subject.

Each listing consists of a full bibliographical description. Prices, which are always subject to change, have been obtained from the publisher, when available, and are as current as possible. Entries include recommended subject headings derived from the *Sears List of Subject Headings,* a suggested classification number from the *Abridged Dewey Decimal Classification and Relative Index,* a brief description of the contents, and, whenever possible, an evaluation from a quoted source. The following is an example of a typical entry and a description of its components:

★**Gourley, Catherine, 1950-**
    Flappers and the new American woman; perceptions of women from 1918 through the 1920s. Twenty-first Century Books 2008 144p il (Images and issues of women in the twentieth century) lib bdg $38.60
    Grades 7 8 9 10   **305.4**
      1. Women—United States—History 2. United States—History—1919-1933
      ISBN 978-0-8225-6060-9; 0-8225-6060-7
      LC 2001-8530

    This describes images of women in the United States from 1918- through the 1920s.
    "The sparkling and engaging [text is] generously expanded by numerous, well-placed black-and-white photographs and period reproductions. ...Great for research or browsing." SLJ
    Includes bibliographical references

The star at the start of the entry indicates this is a "most highly recommended" title. The name of the author, Catherine Gourley, is given in conformity with *Anglo-American Cataloguing Rules, 2nd edition,* 2002 revision. The title of the book is *Flappers and the new American woman; perceptions of women from 1918 through the 1920s.* The book was published by Twenty-first Century Books in 2008.

The book has 144 pages and contains illustrations. It is published in the "Images and issues of women in the twentieth century" series, in a library binding, and sells for $38.60. (Prices given were current when the Collection went to press.) The book is recommended for any of the following grade levels: 7 8 9 10.

At the end of the last line of type in the body entry is the figure 305.4 in bold face type. This is the classification number derived from the fifteenth edition of the *Abridged Dewey Decimal Classification.* The number 305.4 is the classification number for "Women".

The numbered terms "1. Women—United States—History" and "2. United States—History—1919-1933" are recommended subject headings for this book based on *Sears List of Subject Headings.*

The ISBN (International Standard Book Number) is included to facilitate ordering. The Library of Congress control number is provided when available.

Following are three notes supplying additional information about the book. The first is a description of the book's content. The second is a critical note from *School Library Journal*. Such annotations are useful in evaluating books for selection and in determining which of several books on the same subject is best suited for the individual reader. The final note describes special features, in this case a bibliography. Notes are also made to describe sequels and companion volumes, editions available, awards, and publication history.

Part 2. Author, Title, and Subject Index

The Index is a single alphabetical list of all the books entered in the Core Collection. Each book is entered under author; title (if distinctive); and subject. The classification number, displayed in boldface type, is the key to the location of the main entry for the book in the Classified Collection.

Appropriate added entries are made for joint authors and editors. "See" references are made from forms of names or subjects that are not used as headings. "See also" references are made to related or more specific headings.

The following are examples of Index entries for the book cited above:

Author	**Gourley, Catherine, 1950-**	
	Flappers and the new American woman	**305.4**
Title	**Flappers** and the new American woman. Gourley, C.	**305.4**
Subject	**Women—United States—History**	
	Gourley, C. Flappers and the new American woman	
		305.4

Standards Used

Anglo-American Cataloguing Rules, 2nd ed., 2002 revision, 2005 update. Chicago: American Library Association, 2005.

Dewey, Melvil. *Abridged Dewey Decimal Classification and Relative Index.* 15th ed. Edited by Joan S. Mitchell, et al. Dublin, Ohio: OCLC, 2012.

McCarthy, Susan and Joseph Miller, eds. *Sears List of Subject Headings.* 20th ed. New York: The H. W. Wilson Company, 2010.

OUTLINE OF CLASSIFICATION

Reproduced below is the Second Summary of the Dewey Decimal Classification. * As Part 1 of this Core Collection is arranged according to this classification, the outline will serve as a table of contents for it. Please note, however, that the inclusion of this outline is not to be considered a substitute for consulting the Dewey Decimal Classification itself.

000 Computer science, knowledge & systems
010 Bibliographies
020 Library & information sciences
030 Encyclopedias & books of facts
040 [Unassigned]
050 Magazines, journals & serials
060 Associations, organizations & museums
070 News media, journalism & publishing
080 Quotations
090 Manuscripts & rare books

100 Philosophy
110 Metaphysics
120 Epistemology
130 Parapsychology & occultism
140 Philosophical schools of thought
150 Psychology
160 Logic
170 Ethics
180 Ancient, medieval & eastern philosophy
190 Modern western philosophy

200 Religion
210 Philosophy & theory of religion
220 The Bible
230 Christianity & Christian theology
240 Christian practice & observance
250 Christian pastoral practice & religious orders
260 Christian organization, social work & worship
270 History of Christianity
280 Christian denominations
290 Other religions

300 Social sciences, sociology & anthropology
310 Statistics
320 Political science
330 Economics
340 Law
350 Public administration & military science
360 Social problems & social services
370 Education
380 Commerce, communications & transportation
390 Customs, etiquette & folklore

400 Language
410 Linguistics
420 English & Old English languages
430 German & related languages
440 French & related languages
450 Italian, Romanian & related languages
460 Spanish & Portuguese languages
470 Latin & Italic languages
480 Classical & modern Greek languages
490 Other languages

500 Science
510 Mathematics
520 Astronomy
530 Physics
540 Chemistry
550 Earth sciences & geology
560 Fossils & prehistoric life
570 Life sciences; biology
580 Plants (Botany)
590 Animals (Zoology)

600 Technology
610 Medicine & health
620 Engineering
630 Agriculture
640 Home & family management
650 Management & public relations
660 Chemical engineering
670 Manufacturing
680 Manufacture for specific uses
690 Building & construction

700 Arts
710 Landscaping & area planning
720 Architecture
730 Sculpture, ceramics & metalwork
740 Drawing & decorative arts
750 Painting
760 Graphic arts
770 Photography & computer art
780 Music
790 Sports, games & entertainment

800 Literature, rhetoric & criticism
810 American literature in English
820 English & Old English literatures
830 German & related literatures
840 French & related literatures
850 Italian, Romanian & related literatures
860 Spanish & Portuguese literatures
870 Latin & Italian literatures
880 Classical & modern Greek literatures
890 Other literatures

900 History
910 Geography & travel
920 Biography & genealogy
930 History of ancient world (to ca. 499)
940 History of Europe
950 History of Asia
960 History of Africa
970 History of North America
980 History of South America
990 History of other areas

* Reproduced from Edition 15 of the Abridged Dewey Decimal Classification and Relative Index, published in 2012, by permission of OCLC Online Computer Library Center, Inc., owner of copyright.

MIDDLE AND JUNIOR HIGH CORE COLLECTION
ELEVENTH EDITION
CLASSIFIED COLLECTION

000   COMPUTER SCIENCE, KNOWLEDGE & SYSTEMS

001.4   Research; statistical methods

Cefrey, Holly
Researching people, places, and events. Rosen Central 2010 48p il (Digital and information literacy) lib bdg $26.50
Grades: 5 6 7 8   **001.4**
1. Research 2. Report writing 3. Internet research
ISBN 978-1-4358-5317-1 lib bdg; 1-4358-5317-2 lib bdg
LC 2008-46785
Describes researching people, places, and events on the Internet, including using primary and secondary sources, evaluating source material, and avoiding plagiarism
"Colorful photos, diagrams, and sidebars and [a] lively [text creates an] appealing, user-friendly [presentation]. . . . Students and teachers will find [this title] useful in keeping up-to-date on and utilizing online resources and today's technology in a rapidly changing digital world." SLJ
Includes glossary and bibliographical references

The **Nobel** book of answers; the Dalai Lama, Mikhail Gorbachev, Shimon Peres, and other Nobel Prize winners answer some of life's most intriguing questions for young people. edited by Bettina Stiekel; translated by Paul De Angelis and Elisabeth Kaestner. Atheneum Bks. for Young Readers 2003 254p $14.95
Grades: 5 6 7 8   **001.4**
1. Nobel Prizes 2. Questions and answers 3. Children's questions and answers
ISBN 0-689-86310-1
LC 2003-8721
"Will I soon have a clone? Why are leaves green? Why are some people rich and others poor? Why does 1 + 1 = 2? Why is there war? What is love? Nobel Prize winners honored for their work for peace and in science, economics, medicine, and literature speak to children about elemental issues. . . . Most of these intellectuals do an amazing job of explaining complex ideas. . . . This will be especially welcome as a discussion opener in science and social studies classrooms." Booklist

Randolph, Ryan P.
New research techniques; getting the most out of search engine tools. [by] Ryan Randolph. Rosen

Central 2011 48p il (Digital and information literacy) lib bdg $27.95; pa $11.75
Grades: 5 6 7 8   **001.4**
1. Internet resources 2. Internet searching 3. Web search engines
ISBN 978-1-4488-1321-6 lib bdg; 1-4488-1321-2 lib bdg; 978-1-4488-2292-8 pa; 1-4488-2292-0 pa
LC 2010016912
Explains new research techniques and tools that are available for online searching. Among the topics covered are browser tools and search engine toolbars, browser add-ons, Web mashups, e-mail and text alerts, RSS feeds and readers, Boolean operators, and refining research results.
"Color illustrations, large fonts, clearly defined subheadings, and easy to read content encourage access to copious information. . . . Teachers and librarians should find this . . . to be a highly versatile teaching tool." Libr Media Connect
Includes glossary and bibliographical references

Valenza, Joyce Kasman
★ **Power** research tools; learning activities & posters. illustrated by Emily Valenza. American Library Association 2003 113p il pa $55
Grades: Adult Professional   **001.4**
1. Research 2. Report writing 3. Internet resources 4. Internet searching 5. Report writing -- Study and teaching 6. Internet searching -- Study and teaching 7. Information retrieval -- Study and teaching 8. Research -- Methodology -- Study and teaching 9. Electronic information resource literacy -- Study and teaching
ISBN 0-8389-0838-1
LC 2002-8972
A collection of "lessons, rubrics, graphic organizers, and curriculum designed to help students become successful users of information. Beginning with the first steps of research, the development of a thesis, the material progresses logically through the succeeding steps, covering Boolean operators; search tools and strategies; subject and keyword searching; ethics; plagiarism; documenting and citing resources; creating source and note cards; the process of writing the paper; and quoting, paraphrasing, and summarizing. . . . This is an invaluable resource for teaching information skills in any subject area, in middle school or high school." SLJ

Worek, Michael
The **Nobel** Prize; the story of Alfred Nobel and the most famous prize in the world. Firefly 2010 79p il $19.95
Grades: 7 8 9 10   **001.4**
1. Chemists 2. Inventors 3. Nobel Prizes 4.

Philanthropists 5. Manufacturing executives
ISBN 978-1-55407-711-3; 1-55407-711-7

"Starting with a biography of Alfred Nobel, this current (to 2009) title is thorough, well-written, and interesting. The text is broken down by discipline—science, literature, peace, and economics. The works of each Nobel laureate . . . are explained. Photographs pepper the book, and time lines of awards and an extensive index complete the text. This is a fine effort, especially useful for reports." SLJ

001.9   Controversial knowledge

Allen, Judy

Unexplained. Kingfisher 2006 144p il $19.95

Grades: 5 6 7 8   **001.9**
1. Parapsychology 2. Curiosities and wonders
ISBN 978-0-7534-5950-8; 0-7534-5950-7

This addresses such topics as ghosts, psychic phenomena, superstitions, mysterious natural phenomena, alleged monsters, disappearances, secrets and mysteries of ancient history, and possible extraterrestrials.

"A seamless combination of absorbing fact-filled text and stunning visuals in an investigation of mysteries that continue to baffle, tantalize, and spark endless debate." SLJ
Includes glossary

Allman, Toney

Are extraterrestrials a threat to mankind? ReferencePoint Press 2011 80p il (Extraterrestrial life) $28.95

Grades: 5 6 7 8   **001.9**
1. Extraterrestrial beings
ISBN 1-60152-170-7; 978-1-60152-170-5
LC 2010046621

This "captures the subject's inherent allure, while maintaining a serious . . . tone. Kids . . . will . . . learn about the compounds necessary for life and their availability on other planets, the microbial threat of extraterrestrial life, and communication with other life forms. The solid text also includes theories about what (and who) might be out there. . . . The book's computer-generated illustrations . . . take advantage of its subject with a couple of images of scary ETs. . . . [This is a] well-sourced volume." Booklist
Includes bibliographical references

Ape-men; Kelly Wand, book editor. Greenhaven Press/Thomson/Gale 2006 174p (Fact or fiction?) $29.95

Grades: 6 7 8 9   **001.9**
1. Yeti 2. Monsters 3. Sasquatch
ISBN 0-7377-1892-7; 978-0-7377-1892-8
LC 2005046293

"Five essays offer proof of the existence of large apelike creatures around the world, while another five refute it. In an epilogue, readers are guided through the process of analyzing the arguments critically. Materials for further research include a fairly good selection of monographs, periodical articles, and three annotated Web sites." SLJ
Includes bibliographical references

Bardhan-Quallen, Sudipta

The **real** monsters; written by Sudipta Bardhan-Quallen; illustrated by Josh Cochran. Sterling 2008 88p il (Mysteries unwrapped) pa $5.95

Grades: 5 6 7 8   **001.9**
1. Ghosts 2. Monsters
ISBN 978-1-4027-3776-3 pa; 1-4027-3776-9 pa
LC 2009275635

Investigates whether ghosts, werewolves, vampires, mummies, zombies and other such monsters exist

The book has "an ample number of clear black-and-white and full-color photographs and illustrations. . . . Perfect for libraries that need a boost or an update to their scary-story collections." SLJ
Includes bibliographical references

Barton, Chris

Can I see your I.D.? true stories of false identities. illustrated by Paul Hoppe. Dial Books for Young Readers 2011 121p il $16.99

Grades: 6 7 8 9   **001.9**
1. Identity (Psychology) 2. Impostors and imposture 3. Impersonation
ISBN 978-0-8037-3310-7; 0-8037-3310-0
LC 2010-11878

"In 10 impeccably crafted profiles, Barton . . . shares the stories of individuals—many just teenagers—who adopted false identities for amusement, profit, or survival. . . . Barton reveals the motivations behind and the consequences of each deception. The use of second-person narration is very effective, allowing readers to assume the identities of each individual. Barton's prose captures the daring, ingenuity, and quick thinking required of each imposter. . . . Hoppe contributes dynamic comic book style panel art." Publ Wkly
Includes bibliographical references

Emmer, Rick

Kraken; fact or fiction? Chelsea House 2010 108p il (Creature scene investigation) $35.00

Grades: 5 6 7 8   **001.9**
1. Squids
ISBN 978-0-7910-9780-9
LC 2009011467

Describes the sea monster known as the kraken, presents evidence of the existence of giant squids and their relatives, and discusses how the kraken is portrayed historically and in popular culture.
Includes glossary and bibliographical references

Gee, Joshua

Encyclopedia horrifica; the terrifying truth! about vampires, ghosts, monsters, and more. Scholastic Inc. 2007 129p il $14.99

Grades: 4 5 6 7   **001.9**
1. Ghosts 2. Monsters 3. Vampires
ISBN 978-0-439-92255-5; 0-439-92255-0
LC 2007061733

A visual reference contains true stories of such creatures as vampires, aliens, werewolves, and ghosts, accompanied by photographic evidence, eyewitness accounts, and original interviews.

"Each topic is replete with color illustrations and photos and is accompanied by a light, readable text that tries to separate fact from fiction." Voice Youth Advocates
Includes bibliographical references

Halls, Kelly Milner
★ **Tales** of the cryptids; mysterious creatures that may or may not exist. by Kelly Milner Halls, Rick Spears, Roxyanne Young; [illustrated by Rick Spears] Darby Creek 2006 72p il map $18.95
Grades: 4 5 6 7   **001.9**
1. Monsters
ISBN 1-58196-049-2
This considers the existence of creatures such as Bigfoot, the Loch Ness Monster, Marozi of Kenya, the Orangpendek of Sumatra, and the Thylacine of Tasmania.
"The conversational text makes for fun reading, and a plethora of pictures . . . will prove enticing." SLJ

Kallen, Stuart A.
Crop circles. ReferencePoint Press 2010 104p il (The mysterious & unknown) $25.95
Grades: 4 5 6 7   **001.9**
1. Crop circles
ISBN 978-1-60152-103-3; 1-60152-103-0
LC 2009034368
In an attempt to explain the phenomenon of crop circles, "Kallen reaches back to a 1678 account of a 'mowing devil' before considering numerous potential culprits: plasma vortexes, psychokenesis, UFOs, the military, and even wallabies stoned on opium. Equal time is spent between cereologists (those who study these formations) and plain old hoaxsters—and both are equally interesting." Booklist
Includes bibliographical references

Matthews, Rupert
Disappearances. QEB Pub. 2010 32p il map (Unexplained) lib bdg $28.50
Grades: 4 5 6 7   **001.9**
1. Parapsychology 2. Missing persons
ISBN 978-1-59566-855-4; 1-59566-855-1
LC 2010014190
This discusses some mysterious disappearances such as the lost colony of Roanoke, the Mary Celeste, disappearances on Mt. Everest, vanishing lighthousemen, and the Maya.
"This well-written and thoughtfully designed [book] features [an] engrossing [topic]. . . . Though the pages are profusely illustrated with large, well-reproduced photographs and drawings, the layout is not cluttered. This [book] just might inspire kids to seek out more in-depth materials." SLJ
Includes glossary and bibliographical references

Strange animals. QEB Pub. 2011 30p il (Unexplained) lib bdg $28.50
Grades: 4 5 6 7   **001.9**
1. Monsters
ISBN 978-1-59566-856-1; 1-59566-856-X
LC 2010017915
This discusses the possible existence of cryptids such as Bigfoot, the Loch Ness monster, the Bunyip, sea monsters, the Orang Pendek, and the Marozi.

"This well-written and thoughtfully designed [book] features [an] engrossing [topic]. . . . Though the pages are profusely illustrated with large, well-reproduced photographs and drawings, the layout is not cluttered. This [book] just might inspire kids to seek out more in-depth materials." SLJ
Includes glossary and bibliographical references

Miller, Ron
Is the end of the world near? from crackpot predictions to scientific scenarios. Twenty-First Century Books 2011 120p il $35.00
Grades: 6 7 8 9 10   **001.9**
1. End of the world
ISBN 0-7613-7396-9; 978-0-7613-7396-4
LC 2010051963
"The author devotes most of his presentation to a selective tally of our possible ends, from religious and pseudo-scientific predictions (including the supposed Mayan apocalypse 'scheduled' for December 21, 2012) to an array of more feasible pandemics, ecological breakdowns, nuclear conflagrations, supervolcanoes, and other natural catastrophes. . . . He also tucks in references to prominent end-of-days novels and films, and takes his eschatological narrative to the universe-ending 'Big Crunch' before closing on a perversely optimistic note. Capped with generous annotated lists of multimedia resources and illustrated throughout with dramatic photographed or digitally rendered disasters." SLJ
Includes bibliographical references

Nardo, Don
Martians; by Don Nardo. KidHaven Press 2008 48p il (Monsters) lib bdg $26.20
Grades: 4 5 6 7   **001.9**
1. Popular culture 2. Extraterrestrial beings
ISBN 978-0-7377-3639-7 lib bdg; 0-7377-3639-9 lib bdg
LC 2007-30616
"Nardo walks readers through everything from early astronautical observations of the Red Planet to Martians in the movies and on television. His writing is clear, informative and often humorous." SLJ
Includes glossary and bibliographical references

Stewart, Gail
UFOs; by Gail B. Stewart. ReferencePoint Press 2007 96p il (The mysterious & unknown) lib bdg $24.95
Grades: 6 7 8 9   **001.9**
1. Unidentified flying objects
ISBN 978-1-60152-030-2; 1-60152-030-1
This book "combines numerous stories of [UFO] sightings with historical and scientific details about investigations, providing a balanced view of a controversial topic. . . . Colorful illustrations and appealing design will encourage readers." SLJ
Includes bibliographical references

001.94   Mysteries

Hawkins, John

   Atlantis and other lost worlds; by John Hawkins. PowerKids Press 2012 32 p. col. ill. (Mystery Hunters) (library) $25.25; (paperback) $10.60

Grades: 4 5 6 7   **001.94**
   1. Extinct cities 2. Cities & towns 3. Atlantis (Legendary place)
   ISBN 1448864291; 9781448864294; 9781448864416; 9781448864423

                                         LC 2011021292

This book by John Hawkins is part of the Mystery Hunters series and focuses on lost and legendary cities. "The sunken city of Atlantis is a popular myth, and is just one of the many myths of lost worlds featured in this . . . volume. This book explores the history behind these . . . stories. It presents readers with evidence that lost worlds are real and evidence that they are all made up, so that they can gather the information and make up their own minds." (Publisher's note)

004   Computer science; computer programming, programs, data; special computer methods

Flath, Camden

   Tomorrow's enterprising scientists; computer software designers and specialists. Mason Crest Publishers 2010 64p il (New careers for the 21st century: finding your role in the global renewal) lib bdg $22.95

Grades: 7 8 9 10   **004**
   1. Vocational guidance 2. Computer software industry
   ISBN 978-1-4222-1822-8 lib bdg; 1-4222-1822-8 lib bdg

                                         LC 2010019187

"Chapters identify and emphasize specific careers—important strengths, necessary aptitudes and interests, education and training, projected earnings, closely related occupations, type of work environment, and predictions for the future of the field. . . . Color photos have a small role amid the many statistics, figures, graphs and charts that support and supplement the . . . [text]." SLJ
   Includes bibliographical references

Hollander, Barbara Gottfried

   The **next** big thing; developing your digital business idea. Barbara Gottfried Hollander. 1st ed. Rosen Pub. 2013 64 p. col. ill. (Digital entrepreneurship in the age of apps, the web, and mobile devices) (library) $31.95; (paperback) $12.95

Grades: 8 9 10 11 12   **004**
   1. Entrepreneurship 2. Internet industry 3. New products 4. Electronic commerce 5. New business enterprises
   ISBN 1448869269; 9781448869268; 9781448869312; 9781448869718

                                         LC 2012003029

This book is part of the Digital Entrepreneurship in the Age of Apps, the Web, and Mobile Devices series and fo-cuses on digital businesses. "These how-to titles lead teens through building a digital business. Each volume uses real-world examples from current Internet companies such as Facebook, Twitter, and Netflix to explain the various steps involved in building a website, blog, app, etc." (School Library Journal)
   Includes bibliographical references and index.

Lohr, Steve

   Digital revolutionaries; the men and women who brought computing to life. Flash Point 2009 165p il pa $11.99

Grades: 5 6 7 8   **004**
   1. Computer industry 2. Computers -- History
   ISBN 978-1-59643-532-2 pa; 1-59643-532-1 pa

"This text will be a fascinating read for students who are curious about the development of the technology present in every aspect of their lives and the many people behind it. The five chapters are written in a lively, conversational voice. Lohr describes how many independent and creative thinkers helped to develop computers as we know them to-day. His history includes topics from software programs to animation, from FORTRAN to BASIC, and from Bill Gates to Steve Jobs, bringing technology to life along the way. . . . A positive, upbeat, and enlightening read." SLJ
   Includes bibliographical references

Snedden, Robert

   Who invented the computer? Arcturus Pub. 2011 46p il (Breakthroughs in science and technology) lib bdg $32.80

Grades: 5 6 7 8   **004**
   1. Computers -- History
   ISBN 978-1-84837-678-6; 1-84837-678-2

                                         LC 2010011017

This is "divided into easy to read short chapters with large, colorful photographs and graphics on every page. . . . The added inserts provide additional information to engage readers and help them connect with the scientific details." Libr Media Connect
   Includes glossary and bibliographical references

Wilkinson, Colin

   Mobile platforms; getting information on the go. Rosen Pub. 2011 48p il (Digital and information literacy) lib bdg $26.50; pa $11.75

Grades: 5 6 7 8   **004**
   1. Cellular telephones 2. Wireless communication systems
   ISBN 978-1-4488-1320-9 lib bdg; 1-4488-1320-4 lib bdg; 978-1-4488-2291-1 pa; 1-4488-2291-2 pa

                                         LC 2010023682

Though this "title is a broad overview of a sometimes-complex subject, the detail is significant. . . . Touches of blue enhance the clean design. . . . [This] offers very current explanations of smart phones and apps, with plenty of information that will be new even to tech-savvy kids." Booklist
   Includes bibliographical references

004.6 Interfacing and communications

Cornwall, Phyllis

Online etiquette and safety. Cherry Lake Pub. 2010 32p il (Super smart information strategies) lib bdg $27.07

Grades: 3 4 5 6   **004.6**

   1. Etiquette 2. Internet -- Social aspects 3. Internet -- Security measures

   ISBN 978-1-60279-956-1 lib bdg; 1-60279-956-3 lib bdg

LC 2010002023

This "teaches valuable lessons on why it's important to be responsible online citizens despite the misleading anonymity of the Web and offers tips on how to deal with cyberbullies and other online dangers." Booklist

Includes bibliographical references

Grayson, Robert

Managing your digital footprint. Rosen Central 2011 48p il (Digital and information literacy) lib bdg $26.50; pa $11.75

Grades: 5 6 7 8   **004.6**

   1. Internet 2. Etiquette 3. Right of privacy

   ISBN 978-1-4488-1319-3 lib bdg; 1-4488-1319-0 lib bdg; 978-1-4488-2290-4 pa; 1-4488-2290-4 pa

LC 2010025746

Though this "title is a broad overview of a sometimes-complex subject, the detail is significant. . . . Touches of blue enhance the clean design. . . . [This] discusses the permanence of impulsively posted material online, contrasting it with more retro forms of self-expression, such as keeping a paper diary." Booklist

Includes bibliographical references

Mooney, Carla

Online predators. ReferencePoint Press 2011 96p il (Issues in the digital age) $28.95

Grades: 7 8 9 10 11 12   **004.6**

   1. Cyberbullying 2. Computer crimes 3. Child sexual abuse 4. Internet -- Safety measures

   ISBN 1-60152-193-6; 978-1-60152-193-4

LC 2011020180

"Packed with frightening cases of online attacks by sexual predators, financial predators, and bullies, this detailed, up-to-date, highly readable guide is a warning to young people—and adults—about Internet-based crime and identity theft. . . . Computer-savvy teens will especially welcome the coverage of emerging careers in cybersecurity and forensics. . . . A clean design with color photos and extensive back matter . . . further add to this title's appeal." Booklist

Includes bibliographical references

Sandler, Corey

Living with the Internet and online dangers. Facts on File 2010 ix, 165p il (Teen's guides) $34.95; pa $14.95

Grades: 6 7 8 9   **004.6**

   1. Computer security 2. Internet and teenagers 3. Internet -- Security measures

   ISBN 978-0-8160-7874-5; 0-8160-7874-2; 978-0-8160-7875-2 pa; 0-8160-7875-0 pa

LC 2009023137

"Sandler acknowledges the importance of the Internet, cell phones, and digital devices for communication but also wants to inform readers about safety and security. Chapters cover social networking, shopping, online job hunting, file-sharing, email scams and Internet fraud, online drugstores, and online meeting and dating. The author also addresses protecting one's identity, viruses, cell phones, IMs and text messaging, wireless security, and helping friends cope with Internet and online dangers. Written in an informative and respectful manner, this book is sure to be useful for teens' informational reading." SLJ

Includes glossary and bibliographical references

004.67 Wide-area networks

Brasch, Nicolas

The **Internet**; Nicolas Brasch. Smart Apple Media 2011 32 p. col. ill., map (library) $28.50

Grades: 5 6 7 8   **004.67**

   1. Internet

   ISBN 159920567X; 9781599205670

LC 2009054445

Brasch "provides much worthwhile information. He discusses recent history and current tools and suggests where this know-how might be headed in the near future. He differentiates between the Internet and the World Wide Web; clarifies how search engines, web pages, blogs, and e-mail work; explains instant messaging, tweeting, and voice-over Internet protocol (VOIP); and distinguishes between Web 2.0 and Web 3.0 technology. . . . Topics are discussed in heavily illustrated double-page spreads containing numerous sidebars, web links, definitions, and diagrams. . . . The text reads smoothly, and pages have a clean, inviting look." Booklist

005 Computer programming, programs, data

Orr, Tamra

Creating multimedia presentations. Rosen Central 2010 48p il (Digital and information literacy) lib bdg $26.50

Grades: 5 6 7 8   **005**

   1. Multimedia 2. Presentation software

   ISBN 978-1-4358-5319-5 lib bdg; 1-4358-5319-9 lib bdg

LC 2008-54736

Describes how to create a multimedia presentation, including adding graphs, images, sounds, and video, and how to integrate these elements to form an informative presentation

"Colorful photos, diagrams, and sidebars and [a lively text creates an] appealing, user-friendly [presentation]. . . . Students and teachers will find [this title] useful in keeping up-to-date on and utilizing online resources and today's technology in a rapidly changing digital world." SLJ

Includes glossary and bibliographical references

005.1092   Computer programmers

Henderson, Harry
   Larry Page and Sergey Brin; information at your fingertips. author, Harry Henderson. Chelsea House 2012 134 p. (Trailblazers in science and technology) (library) $35
Grades: 7 8 9 10 11 12   005.1092
   1. Web search engines 2. Webmasters -- United States -- Biography   3. Businesspeople -- United States -- Biography   4. Computer programmers -- United States -- Biography 5. Internet programming -- United States -- Biography   6. Telecommunications engineers -- United States -- Biography
   ISBN 1604136766; 9781604136760
                          LC 2011032584
   This book, by Harry Henderson, is a biography of the founders of the Internet company Google Inc. as part of the "Trailblazers in Science and Technology" series. "When . . . Larry Page and Sergey Brin collaborated on the search engine Google, they didn't realize that their invention would soon become so ingrained in Web culture that its name would be used as a verb." (Publisher's note)
   Includes bibliographical references and index

005.8   Data security

Hunter, Nick
   Internet safety; Nick Hunter. Heinemann Library 2012 56 p. col. ill. lib bdg $33.50 pa $9.99
Grades: 6 7 8 9 10   005.8
   1. Internet users 2. Internet -- Safety measures 3. Computer crimes -- Prevention
   ISBN 9781432948719; 9781432962050
                          LC 2010046905
   "...Discusses types of crime, cyber bullying, phishing, and scams and viruses, ending with ways to protect yourself. Statistics and websites provide information for both individual research and for educators wishing to lead discussion on the topic... Good choices for student research and debate." SLJ
   Includes bibliographical references (p. 54-55) and index

006.3   Artificial intelligence

Henderson, Harry
   Artificial intelligence; mirrors for the mind. Chelsea House 2007 190p il (Milestones in discovery and invention) $35
Grades: 7 8 9 10 11 12   006.3
   1. Artificial intelligence
   ISBN 0-8160-5749-4; 978-0-8160-5749-8
                          LC 2006-16639
   This book includes "portraits of the men and women in the vanguard of this innovative field. Subjects include Alan Turing, who made the connection between mathematical reasoning and computer operations; Allen Newell and Herbert Simon, who created a program that could reason like a human being; Pattie Maes, who developed computerized

agents to help people with research and shopping; and Ray Kurzweil, who, besides inventing the flatbed scanner and a reading machine for the blind, has explored relationships between people and computers that may exceed human intelligence." Publisher's note
   Includes glossary and bibliographical references

Pearce, Q. L.
   Artificial intelligence. Lucent Books 2011 112p il (Technology 360) $33.45
Grades: 7 8 9 10   006.3
   1. Robots 2. Artificial intelligence
   ISBN 978-1-4205-0384-5; 1-4205-0384-7
                          LC 2011006362
   This offers "clean design with clear explanations of sometimes-complicated scientific subjects. . . . Artificial Intelligence covers the history of how people have tried to teach machines to think and move, concluding with a chapter on the ethics surrounding AI. . . . A strong [title] for report writers and students with a serious interest in technology and its inventions." Booklist
   Includes glossary and bibliographical references

006.7   Multimedia systems

Fontichiaro, Kristin
   Podcasting 101. Cherry Lake Pub. 2010 32p il (Super smart information strategies) lib bdg $27.07
Grades: 3 4 5 6   006.7
   1. Podcasting
   ISBN 978-1-60279-953-0 lib bdg; 1-60279-953-9 lib bdg
                          LC 2010004533
   "A knockout resource for media-fair projects, Podcasting 101 doles out page after page of useful information, from the equipment required to content ideas for those who might need a creative spark to tips for structuring and adding effects to a successful podcast." Booklist
   Includes bibliographical references

Kling, Andrew A.
   Web 2.0. Lucent Books 2011 128p il map (Technology 360) $33.45
Grades: 7 8 9 10   006.7
   1. Internet 2. Online social networks
   ISBN 978-1-4205-0171-1; 1-4205-0171-2
                          LC 2010028893
   This offers "clean design with clear explanations of sometimes-complicated scientific subjects. . . . The history of the Internet and how people interact with it is the focus in Web 2.0, which discusses groundbreaking sites from Napster to Facebook, with a concluding chapter that tries to foresee the future. . . . A strong [title] for report writers and students with a serious interest in technology and its inventions." Booklist
   Includes bibliographical references

Rowell, Rebecca

YouTube; the company and its founders. ABDO Pub. Co. 2011 112p il (Technology pioneers) lib bdg $32.44

Grades: 5 6 7 8   **006.7**
   1. Internet
   ISBN 978-1-61714-813-2 lib bdg; 1-61714-813-X lib bdg; 978-1-61758-971-3 e-book
                                   LC 2010043379

This is an introduction to YouTube and its founders.

"Written in a clear, linear fashion, this series offers vivid, well-researched details about the development of technological advancements considered essential in today's society. . . . Readers who are interested in technology and inventions will be thoroughly engrossed." SLJ

Includes glossary and bibliographical references

Selfridge, Benjamin

A **teen's** guide to creating Web pages and blogs; [by] Benjamin Selfridge, Peter Selfridge, and Jennifer Osburn. Prufrock Press 2009 148p il pa $16.95

Grades: 5 6 7 8 9 10   **006.7**
   1. Weblogs 2. Internet and teenagers 3. Web sites -- Design
   ISBN 978-1-59363-345-5; 1-59363-345-9
                                   LC 2008-40044

First published 2004 by Zephyr Press with title: Kid's guide to creating Web pages for home and school

"This guide begins with basic step-by-step information about HTML, fonts, images, lists, and tables. . . . The book's last half introduces more advanced techniques, such as JavaScript, functions, loops, and applications like Flash and Instant Messenger. . . . Illustrated, with references and a glossary, this attractive paperback has lots of practical content." Voice Youth Advocates

Includes glossary and bibliographical references

Truesdell, Ann

Wonderful wikis; by Ann Truesdell. Cherry Lake Publishing 2013 32 p. (Information explorer) (library) $28.50; (paperback) $14.21

Grades: 4 5 6 7   **006.7**
   1. Wikis (Computer science)
   ISBN 1610804805; 9781610804806; 9781610806541
                                   LC 2012001758

This juvenile nonfiction book, by Ann Truesdell, as part of the publisher's "Explorer Library" series, presents a profile and guidelines for school children to make use of wikis online for educational purposes. Topics addressed include definitions of what a wiki is, how to contribute to them properly, and what ways they are most useful.

Includes bibliographical references and index

011   Bibliographies and catalogs

★ **Recommended** reference books for small and medium-sized libraries and media centers, Vol.

30; Shannon Graff Hysell, associate editor. 2010 ed; Libraries Unlimited 2010 344p $75

Grades: Adult Professional   **011**
   1. Best books 2. Reference books 3. Reference books -- Reviews 4. Reference books -- Bibliography
   ISBN 978-1-59884-592-1

Annual. First published 1981

Each annual volume includes reviews of about 550 titles chosen by the editor as the most valuable reference titles published during the previous year.

011.6   General bibliographies and catalogs of works for young people and people with disabilities; for specific types of libraries

Barnhouse, Rebecca

The **Middle** Ages in literature for youth; a guide and resource book. Scarecrow Press 2004 183p (Literature for youth) pa $30

Grades: Adult Professional   **011.6**
   1. Reference books 2. Middle Ages -- Bibliography 3. Middle Ages 4. Children's literature -- Bibliography 5. Young adult literature -- Bibliography
   ISBN 0-8108-4916-X
                                   LC 2004-74

"Searchable by subject, title, location, or author, this is a comprehensive guide to books about the period. Each chapter presents a topic, such as Vikings or Crusades, and then gives annotated lists of both fiction and nonfiction titles. Added features include classroom activities such as creative-writing prompts, medieval measurements using tools from the time period, and math involving computations using Roman numerals. . . . Professional sources for educators round out this useful bibliography." SLJ

Gillespie, John Thomas

Classic teenplots; a booktalk guide to use with readers ages 12-18. [by] John T. Gillespie and Corinne J. Naden. Libraries Unlimited 2006 348p (Children's and young adult literature reference series) $55

Grades: Adult Professional   **011.6**
   1. Book talks 2. Teenagers -- Books and reading
   ISBN 1-59158-312-8
                                   LC 2006017624

"Prefaced by a brief guide to booktalking are one hundred entries for in-print classic titles for teens, taken from the out-of-print Juniorplots and Seniorplots series. Additional titles have been added to round out the eight theme/genre-based sections, which include topics such as Teenage Life and Concerns, Historical Fiction and Other Lands, and Important Nonfiction. . . . This excellent resource offers from sixteen to twenty titles per section." Voice Youth Advocates

Includes bibliographical references

★ The **children's** and young adult literature handbook; a research and reference guide. Libraries Unlimited 2005 393p (Children's and young adult literature reference series) $55

Grades: Adult Professional   **011.6**
1. Reference books 2. Children's literature --
Bibliography 3. Young adult literature -- Bibliography
4. Children's literature -- History and criticism 5.
Young adult literature -- History and criticism
ISBN 1-56308-949-1
"This reference should meet the needs of librarians,
teachers, and scholars." Choice

Matthew, Kathryn I.
Neal-Schuman guide to recommended children's
books and media for use with every elementary subject; by Kathryn I. Matthew and Joy L. Lowe. 2nd
ed; Neal-Schuman Publishers 2010 356p pa $75
Grades: Adult Professional   **011.6**
1. Best books 2. Books and reading 3. Children --
Books and reading 4. Audiovisual materials -- Catalogs
5. Children's literature -- Bibliography
ISBN 978-1-55570-688-3; 1-55570-688-6
                                            LC 2010014082
First published 2002
"Listing more than 1,000 books, videos, software, CDs,
and Web sites up through early 2010, this book offers elementary (and middle-school) librarians a wonderful collection-development and collaboration tool. Each chapter
covers one elementary subject area. . . . The chapters are
broken down into narrower topics; each section covers the
book and media choices plus ideas for exploring many of the
resources listed. Each chapter begins with relevant national
standards and ends with teacher resources and references
including books, professional organizations, and Web sites.
The annotated listings are arranged by grade level from pre–
K up through middle school and include full bibliographic
information." Booklist
Includes bibliographical references

Matulka, Denise I.
Picture this; picture books for young adults: a
curriculum-related annotated bibliography. Greenwood Press 1997 xx, 267p $39.95
Grades: Adult Professional   **011.6**
1. Reference books 2. Young adult literature 3.
Picture books -- Bibliography 4. Teenagers -- Books
and reading 5. Young adult literature -- Bibliography
ISBN 0-313-30182-4
                                            LC 97-2234
"This bibliography introduces 424 titles. . . . It is organized according to curriculum-content areas—the arts,
health, literature, mathematics, science, and social sciences
and history. Each annotation lists bibliographic information,
summarizes the book, discusses artistic style and mediums
employed, suggests companion titles, and provides ideas for
classroom use." SLJ
Includes bibliographical references

Meese, Ruth Lyn
Family matters; adoption and foster care in children's literature. Libraries Unlimited 2010 147p pa
$35
Grades: Adult Professional   **011.6**
1. Adoption in literature 2. Adoption -- Bibliography
3. Foster home care -- Bibliography 4. Children's

literature -- Bibliography
ISBN 978-1-59158-782-8 pa; 1-59158-782-4 pa
                                            LC 2009040750
"Meese's goal is to help adults, particularly educators,
select high-quality children's books about adoption and
foster care and to raise awareness about the unique issues
that adoptees often face. . . . Charts, Venn diagrams, and extensive annotations supplement the annotated list of books
for children in kindergarten through grade eight. Meese explains her rationale for choosing these books so that readers
have the tools to evaluate other selections." SLJ
Includes bibliographical references

Nieuwenhuizen, Agnes
Right book, right time; 500 great books for teen-
agers. Allen & Unwin 2008 355p il pa $19.95
Grades: 7 8 9 10 11 12 Adult Professional   **011.6**
1. Best books 2. Reference books 3. Teenagers
-- Books and reading 4. Young adult literature --
Bibliography
ISBN 978-174114-883-1; 174114-883-9
"This Australian reader's guide offers detailed annota-
tions of 200 recent young adult and adult books divided into
twelve thematic sections ranging from 'Actions, Adventure
& Crime' to 'When You Want to Laugh.' . . . Titles from
Australia intermingle with books from the UK and the U.S.
. . . With its open format and direct address to the reader,
this will be a useful reference for those YAs looking to expand their reading horizons, but enterprising YA librarians
will also find this a useful new dimension for expanding or
promoting a collection. Interspersed with the annotations
are essays championing a variety of literatures ranging from
graphic novels to chick-lit." Bull Cent Child Books
Includes bibliographical references

Reid, Rob
Reid's read-alouds; selections for children and
teens. American Library Association 2009 xiii, 121p
pa $45
Grades: Adult Professional   **011.6**
1. Books and reading 2. Children -- Books and
reading 3. Children's reading -- Projects 4. Young
adults -- Books and reading 5. Children's literature --
Bibliography 6. Young adult literature -- Bibliography
ISBN 978-0-8389-0980-5 pa; 0-8389-0980-9 pa
                                            LC 2008045376
"Reid has collected 200 titles published between 2000
and 2008 that have both readability and general kid appeal.
The titles are organized alphabetically by author, and the
book includes subject and age-level indexes. Each selection
has a cursory summary, grade-level range, and a suggestion
for a 10-minute read-aloud, which either provides an introduction to the main characters or a glimpse into the story. . . .
This last part is what makes the book so useful." SLJ
Includes bibliographical references

Reid's read-alouds 2; modern day classics from
C.S. Lewis to Lemony Snicket. American Library
Association 2011 160p lib bdg $33.50 pa $9.99
Grades: Adult Professional   **011.6**
1. Books and reading 2. Children's literature --

Bibliography 3. Young adult literature -- Bibliography
ISBN 0-8389-1072-6; 978-0-8389-1072-6

LC 2010028985

"The very successful first edition of Reid's Read-Alouds (ALA, 2009) profiled children's and young adult books published between the years 2000 and 2008. This companion volume showcases 200 strong titles that were published from 1950 to 1999. Reid offers a variety of genres and age levels, and a good balance between male and female protagonists. . . . The focus is on books that are great to read to groups of young people. Each entry includes a brief plot summary, suggested grade level, and Reid's signature '10 Minute Selections,' which are engaging episodes from the books that can be read in one sitting. These alone make the book a valuable resource." SLJ

Includes bibliographical references

Safford, Barbara Ripp

Guide to reference materials for school library media centers; 6th ed; Libraries Unlimited 2010 236p $60

Grades: Adult Professional   **011.6**

1. Instructional materials centers 2. Children's reference books 3. School libraries -- Catalogs 4. Reference books -- Bibliography
ISBN 978-1-59158-277-9; 1-59158-277-6

LC 2009-51190

First edition by Christine Gehrt Wynar published 1973 with title: Guide to reference books for school media centers

"This volume has been updated to include web-based reference offerings as well as listings of older sources, provided that their content is still valid. . . . This title profiles resources recommended for use by school librarians for collection management, readers' advisory, teaching, general reference materials, the social sciences and humanities, and science and technology. This volume is an excellent starting point for new school librarians, as well as for those who are building a library from scratch." SLJ

Includes bibliographical references

Schon, Isabel

Recommended books in Spanish for children and young adults, 2004-2008. Scarecrow Press 2009 414p $55

Grades: Adult Professional   **011.6**

1. Reference books 2. Children's literature, Spanish 3. Young adult literature, Spanish 4. Spanish literature -- Bibliography 5. Children's literature -- Bibliography 6. Young adult literature -- Bibliography 7. Children's literature, Spanish American 8. Young adult literature, Spanish American 9. Latin American literature -- Bibliography 10. Children's literature -- Translations into Spanish 11. Young adult literature -- Translations into Spanish
ISBN 978-0-8108-6386-6; 0-8108-6386-3

LC 2008-33390

"Schon evaluates 1231 reference books, fiction, and nonfiction. . . . Entries are arranged alphabetically by author and include a grade level for each book. . . . Schon examines and recommends materials based on the quality of the Spanish language, literary appeal, and the versatility of the translators, paying special attention to the effective use of Peninsular Spanish or the Spanish from the Americas. This annotated bibliography will help selectors in public libraries and media centers to develop existing Spanish-language collections." SLJ

Spiegel, Carol

Book by book; an annotated guide to young people's literature with peacemaking and conflict resolution themes. Educators for Social Responsibility 2010 186p pa $35

Grades: Adult Professional   **011.6**

1. Peace -- Bibliography 2. Peace 3. Conflict management -- Bibliography 4. Children's literature -- Bibliography 5. Young adult literature -- Bibliography 6. Conflict management
ISBN 978-0-942349-93-1 pa; 0-942349-93-8 pa

"More than 900 books for preschool through high school have been organized by title into two sections, picture and chapter books; described; and assigned behavioral headings. Thematic clusters include making connections, emotional literacy, caring and effective communication, cultural competence and social responsibility, and conflict management and responsible decision making. . . . Useful especially in elementary and middle schools where character education is part of the curriculum without the explicit mandate." SLJ

Welch, Rollie James

A **core** collection for young adults; 2nd ed; Neal-Schuman Publishers 2011 416p (Teens @ the library series) pa $80

Grades: Adult Professional   **011.6**

1. Young adults' libraries 2. Teenagers -- Books and reading 3. Young adult literature -- Bibliography
ISBN 978-1-55570-692-0; 1-55570-692-4

LC 2010-46693

First published 2003 under the authorship of Patrick Jones

Provides information meant to be a practical manual for developing collections that appeal to teens. Includes a guide to more than 100 "Best" lists, tips for maintaining a core collection, and selection tips for major YA genres.

"The book is a wide-reaching resource that introduces literature with appeal to young adults to an audience new to library work with teens." Voice Youth Advocates

Includes bibliographical references

Young Adult Library Services Association

The **official** YALSA awards guidebook; compiled and edited by Tina Frolund for the Young Adult Library Services Association. Neal-Schuman Publishers 2008 171p pa $55

Grades: Adult Professional   **011.6**

1. Reference books 2. Young adults' libraries 3. Teenagers -- Books and reading 4. Young adult literature -- Awards 5. Young adult literature -- Bibliography
ISBN 978-1-55570-629-6; 1-55570-629-0

LC 2008-17584

This "volume offers one-stop shopping for an overview of the Alex, Printz, and Edwards awards. In addition to annotated bibliographies of winners and honor books, the title includes acceptance speeches for the Printz and Edwards awards and award interviews from YALSA starwarts

Mary Arnold, Michael Cart, and Betty Carter." Bull Cent
Child Books

Includes bibliographical references

011.62   Works for young people

Wright, Cora M.

★ **More** hot links; linking literature with the
middle school curriculum. Libraries Unlimited 2002
212p tab pa $33.95

Grades: Adult Professional   **011.62**

   1. Reference books 2. Books and reading 3. Children's
literature 4. Children's literature -- Bibliography
5. School libraries -- Relations with teachers and
curriculum 6. Middle school students -- Books and
reading -- United States

   ISBN 1-56308-942-4

                     LC 2002-11278

   "This companion to . . . Hot Links by the same author
provides . . . annotations for an additional 300+ fiction and
nonfiction books . . . that support and enhance the middle
school curriculum." Publisher's note

   Includes bibliographical references

016   Bibliographies and catalogs of works on specific subjects

Al-Hazza, Tami Craft

★ **Books** about the Middle East; selecting and
using them with children and adolescents. [by] Tami
Craft Al-Hazza and Katherine T. Bucher. Linworth
Pub. 2008 168p pa $39.95

Grades: Adult Professional   **016**

   1. Reference books 2. Children's literature --
Bibliography 3. Young adult literature -- Bibliography

   ISBN 978-1-58683-285-8; 1-58683-285-9

                     LC 2007-40149

   "This book examines the body of literature about the
diverse groups of people who inhabit the Middle East, and
it also explores a variety of ways in which this literature
can be used. . . . It fills a huge gap and should not be overlooked. This powerhouse book will be tremendously helpful
to media specialists, educators, and public librarians." Voice
Youth Advocates

   Includes bibliographical references

Crew, Hilary S.

Women engaged in war in literature for youth;
a guide to resources for children and young adults.
Scarecrow Press 2007 303p (Literature for youth)
pa $51

Grades: Adult Professional   **016**

   1. Women soldiers 2. Reference books 3. Women and
war 4. War -- Bibliography 5. Women -- Bibliography
6. Children's literature -- Bibliography 7. Young adult
literature -- Bibliography

   ISBN 978-0-8108-4929-7; 0-8108-4929-1

                     LC 2006-101112

"Crew's guide to print and online sources documents
women's roles in wars over the centuries and throughout the
world, divided by time periods. . . . This is a great addition
for libraries looking for a way to move Women's Studies
beyond the month of March." SLJ

   Includes bibliographical references

Fichtelberg, Susan

★ **Encountering** enchantment; a guide to speculative fiction for teens. Libraries Unlimited 2007
328p (Genreflecting advisory series) $48

Grades: Adult Professional   **016**

   1. Reference books 2. Fantasy fiction -- Bibliography
3. Science fiction -- Bibliography 4. Young adult
literature -- Bibliography

   ISBN 1-59158-316-0; 978-1-59158-316-5

                     LC 2006-33739

   "This useful guide should be in every YA collection." SLJ

   Includes bibliographical references

Garcha, Rajinder

The **world** of Islam in literature for youth; a
selective annotated bibliography for K-12. [by] Rajinder Garcha, Patricia Yates Russell. Scarecrow
Press 2006 xx, 221p (Literature for youth) pa $35

Grades: Adult Professional   **016**

   1. Best books 2. Reference books 3. Islam in literature
4. Islam -- Bibliography 5. Islam 6. Children's
literature -- Bibliography 7. Young adult literature --
Bibliography

   ISBN 978-0-8108-5488-8; 0-8108-5488-0

                     LC 2005-26645

   "This highly useful bibliography fills a conspicuous gap
in a much-needed cultural area." Voice Youth Advocates

   Includes bibliographical references

Hall, Susan

Using picture storybooks to teach literary devices; recommended books for children and young
adults. Libraries Unlimited 2007 282p (Using picture books to teach) pa $42

Grades: Adult Professional   **016**

   1. Literature -- Study and teaching

   ISBN 978-1-59158-493-3 pa; 1-59158-493-0 pa

   "This fourth volume of the series, . . . gives teachers
and librarians the . . . tool to teach literary devices in grades
K–12. With this volume, the author has added: colloquialism; counterpoint; solecism; archetype; and others to the list
of devices. The entries have been reorganized to include all
the information under the book listing itself. Each entry includes an annotation, a listing of curricular tie-ins for the
book and the art style used, and a listing and explanation of
all the literary devices taught by that title." Publisher's note

   Includes bibliographical references

Halsall, Jane

Visual media for teens; creating and using a
teen-centered film collection. [by] Jane Halsall and
R. William Edminster. Libraries Unlimited 2009
xxii, 158p (Libraries Unlimited professional guides
for young adult librarians) pa $40

Grades: Adult Professional **016**
1. Young adults' libraries 2. Libraries and motion pictures 3. Motion pictures -- Catalogs
ISBN 978-1-59158-544-2; 1-59158-544-9
LC 2009-20300
"This is an excellent guide for librarians interested in building a popular film collection to satisfy their teen audiences. It offers professionals an organized look at current films that have young adult appeal and provides analysis of the importance of such a collection." SLJ
Includes filmographies and bibliographical references

Herald, Diana Tixier
Teen genreflecting 3; a guide to reading interests. Libraries Unlimited 2011 xxiv, 377p (Genreflecting advisory series) $48
Grades: Adult Professional **016**
1. Reference books 2. Fiction genres 3. Teenagers -- Books and reading 4. Young adult literature -- Bibliography
ISBN 978-1-59158-729-3; 1-59158-729-3
LC 2010-40791
First published 1997 with title: Teen genreflecting
"The chapters and subchapters provide a brief overview of the topic and are organized by genre, subgenre, or an overall theme. Each entry is annotated and includes a concise subject list, and some entries include a list of read-alikes. Herald also includes books written for children and those for adults that have teen appeal. . . . Herald suggests using this volume to identify read-alikes, to beef up genre collections, and for library staff to familiarize themselves with the literature. . . . A worthy addition to reference or professional-development collection." SLJ
Includes bibliographical references

Mosley, Shelley
The **suffragists** in literature for youth; the fight for the vote. [by] Shelley Mosley, John Charles. The Scarecrow Press, Inc. 2006 326p (Literature for youth) pa $45
Grades: Adult Professional **016**
1. Suffragists 2. Reference books 3. Women -- Suffrage -- Bibliography 4. Women -- Suffrage -- United States 5. Children's literature -- Bibliography 6. Young adult literature -- Bibliography
ISBN 978-0-8108-5372-0 pa; 0-8108-5372-8 pa
LC 2006-17542
"This book would be a tremendous resource to any library or classroom collection." Voice Youth Advocates
Includes bibliographical references

Rabey, Melissa
Historical fiction for teens; a genre guide. Libraries Unlimited 2011 324p (Genreflecting advisory series) $45
Grades: Adult Professional **016**
1. Teenagers -- Books and reading 2. Historical fiction -- Bibliography 3. Young adult literature -- Bibliography
ISBN 978-1-59158-813-9; 1-59158-813-8
LC 2010041101
This "includes more than 300 novels popular with teen readers. Limited to titles written for grades 5 and up, from

1975 to 2010 (with some notable exceptions), the book is divided by regions, time periods, and subgenres. . . . This volume would be especially useful for readers' advisory and for browsing in school and public libraries." Booklist
Includes bibliographical references

Rosen, Philip
Bearing witness; a resource guide to literature, poetry, art, music, and videos by Holocaust victims and survivors. [by] Philip Rosen and Nina Apfelbaum. Greenwood Press 2002 210p $52.95
Grades: Adult Professional **016**
1. Reference books 2. Holocaust, 1933-1945 -- Bibliography 3. Holocaust, Jewish (1939-1945) -- Video catalogs 4. Holocaust, Jewish (1939-1945), in art -- Catalogs 5. Holocaust, Jewish (1939-1945), in literature -- Bio-bibliography 6. Holocaust, Jewish (1939-1945) -- Personal narratives -- Bio-bibliography 7. Holocaust, Jewish (1939-1945) -- Songs and music -- Bibliography -- Catalogs
ISBN 0-313-31076-9
LC 00-69153
"This volume will be valuable to all who are researching the Holocaust. Its strength lies in the inclusion of materials not often found elsewhere." Booklist
Includes bibliographical references

Thomas, Rebecca L.
Popular series fiction for middle school and teen readers; a reading and selection guide. [by] Rebecca L. Thomas and Catherine Barr. 2nd ed; Libraries Unlimited 2009 710p (Children's and young adult literature reference series) $65
Grades: Adult Professional **016**
1. Reference books 2. Children's literature -- Series 3. Monographic series -- Bibliography 4. Young adults' literature -- Series 5. Children's literature -- Bibliography 6. Young adult literature -- Bibliography
ISBN 978-1-59158-660-9
LC 2008-38125
First published 2005
"The authors have identified nearly 2,200 in-print series . . . (including manga, Cine-Manga, and illustrated novels) that will appeal to readers in grades 6-12. Entries are arranged by the series title and contain author, most recent publisher, grade level, notation for availability of accelerated-reader resources, genre, a descriptive three- to five-sentence annotation, and a list of individual titles in the series, arranged by publication date." Booklist
Includes bibliographical references

Wadham, Rachel
This is my life; a guide to realistic fiction for teens. [by] Rachel L. Wadham. Libraries Unlimited 2010 431p (Genreflecting advisory series) $55
Grades: Adult Professional **016**
1. Teenagers -- Books and reading 2. Social problems 3. Young adult literature -- Bibliography
ISBN 978-1-59158-942-6; 1-59158-942-8
LC 2010-24074

This "surveys contemporary realistic fiction for young adults (middle through high school). Wadham . . . annotates some 1,300 titles published for young adults between 1999 and 2009. Arranged by theme, titles represent real-life issues of broad interest (friendship, love, family, work) as well as specific issues faced in 'problem novels' (pregnancy, homelessness, eating disorders, crime and violence, abuse, drugs and alcohol, death, racism). Annotations include plot summaries, availability in audio, awards, grade-level designations, and subject keywords. . . . This is a useful tool for its intended audience of librarians and instructors seeking issue-related fiction." Booklist

Includes bibliographical references

Walter, Virginia A.

★ **War** & peace; a guide to literature and new media, grades 4-8. [by] Virginia A. Walter. Libraries Unlimited 2007 276p (Children's and young adult literature reference series) pa $40

Grades: Adult Professional   **016**
1. Reference books 2. War -- Bibliography 3. Peace -- Bibliography 4. War 5. Children's literature -- Bibliography 6. Young adult literature -- Bibliography
ISBN 1-59158-271-7 pa; 978-1-59158-271-7 pa
     LC 2006030671

"Walter addresses the issue of war—and peace—by examining the information needs of children and how we as professionals can meet them. . . . The bulk of the book is the annotated listing of resources that is divided topically. . . . The well-annotated bibliography includes books, DVDs, Web sites, and CDs, as well as suggestions for using the materials. . . . This book should be a 'must purchase.'" SLJ

Includes bibliographical references

Wee, Patricia Hachten

World War II in literature for youth; a guide and resource book. [by] Patricia Hachten Wee, Robert James Wee. Scarecrow Press 2004 391p (Literature for youth) pa $48

Grades: Adult Professional   **016**
1. Reference books 2. World War, 1939-1945 -- Bibliography 3. Children's literature -- Bibliography 4. Young adult literature -- Bibliography 5. World War, 1939-1945
ISBN 0-8108-5301-9
     LC 2004-11087

This "offers more than 3,000 annotated bibliographies for resources on the Second World War. Entries are arranged according to well-thought-out subjects and cover multiple genres (biographies, memoirs, fiction, eyewitness accounts, technical reports, etc.) and formats (monographs, reference sets, periodicals, Web sites, CDs, videos, DVDs). Annotations are succinct but informative and include both positive and negative comments." Booklist

Includes bibliographical references

Wesson, Lindsey Patrick

Green reads; best environmental resources for youth, K-12. Libraries Unlimited 2009 219p (Children's and young adult literature reference series) $50

Grades: Adult Professional   **016**
1. Reference books 2. Ecology 3. Children's literature -- Bibliography 4. Young adult literature -- Bibliography 5. Environmental protection -- Bibliography 6. Environmental protection 7. Conservation of natural resources -- Bibliography 8. Conservation of natural resources
ISBN 978-1-59158-834-4; 1-59158-834-0
     LC 2009-17353

"This well-organized bibliography offers 450 annotated resources that can be integrated into the classroom to introduce students to environmental concepts. The five chapters focus on global warming, pollution, the Earth's resources, recycling, and conservation. Subchapters follow a uniform organization, including fiction; DVDs and CDs; nonfiction; seminal works, which are labeled 'Recycled Favorites'; and a storytime lesson plan with a variety of activities including songs and tactile learning activities. . . . This reference will delight educators and professionals interested in making students aware of environmental issues and to help youngsters rediscover the outside and natural worlds around them." SLJ

Includes bibliographical references

020   Library and information sciences

Fontichiaro, Kristin

Go straight to the source. Cherry Lake Pub. 2010 32p il (Super smart information strategies) lib bdg $27.07

Grades: 3 4 5 6   **020**
1. Research 2. Information resources 3. History -- Sources
ISBN 978-1-60279-640-9 lib bdg; 1-60279-640-8 lib bdg
     LC 2009028057

"The appealing layout includes manageable paragraphs, a variety of engaging illustrations, and examples that clearly guide reader through each topic. . . . [This] provides an excellent introduction to primary sources and will create enthusiasm in readers for examining old photographs and ads." SLJ

Includes glossary and bibliographical references

Lanning, Scott

Concise guide to information literacy; Scott Lanning. Libraries Unlimited 2012 xii, 99 p.p (paperback) $35

Grades: Adult Professional   **020**
1. Research 2. Information literacy 3. LANGUAGE ARTS & DISCIPLINES -- Literacy 4. LANGUAGE ARTS & DISCIPLINES -- Library & Information Science -- General
ISBN 1598849492; 9781598849493
     LC 2011049229

This book "takes the reader through the entire research process, from selecting a topic to evaluating the final project. . . . Topics covered include categories and types of information and how to conduct both print and online searches, how to evaluate information, the research process, and the final project is also included, along with a chapter on utilizing librarians. Charts and graphs help illustrate the research process." (Library Media Connection)

Includes bibliographical references (pages 91-93) and index

McCain, Mary Maude

Dictionary for school library media specialists; a practical and comprehensive guide. [by] Mary Maude McCain and Martha Merrill. Libraries Unlimited 2001 219p pa $42

Grades: Adult Professional   **020**

1. Reference books 2. Terms and phrases 3. Terminology 4. School librarianship 5. Library science -- Dictionaries 6. School libraries -- Dictionaries 7. Instructional materials centers -- Dictionaries

ISBN 1-56308-696-4

LC 01-16506

"The book defines more than 375 terms. There are two types of definitions—shorter glossary descriptions (capital outlay, reboot) and longer, more detailed treatments (poetry, proximity operators). See references (especially from acronyms and abbreviations) and see also references facilitate use." Booklist

021   Relationships of libraries, archives, information centers

York, Sherry

Booktalking authentic multicultural literature; fiction and history for young readers. Linworth Pub. 2009 112p pa $39.95

Grades: Adult Professional   **021**

1. Book talks 2. Young adult literature 3. Multicultural education 4. Multiculturalism in literature 5. Youth -- Books and reading 6. Ethnic groups in literature 7. Teenagers -- Books and reading 8. Multiculturalism -- Bibliography 9. Ethnic groups 10. Young adult literature -- Bibliography 11. American literature -- Minority authors 12. Multiculturalism

ISBN 978-1-58683-300-8 pa; 1-58683-300-6 pa

LC 200843798

This title "highlights 101 contemporary books by a variety of U.S. authors. Arranged alphabetically by title, entries include the cultural background of author, illustrator, and translator; their Web sites when available; reading and interest levels; genre; related titles; and the single-paragraph booktalk itself. Over 20 ethnic groups are represented. . . . Librarians will find this book helpful in expanding their collections to reflect our global society." SLJ

021.2   Relationships with the community

Gillespie, Kellie M.

Teen volunteer services in libraries. VOYA Books 2004 133p il (VOYA guides) pa $26.95

Grades: Adult Professional   **021.2**

1. Libraries 2. Volunteer work 3. Teenage volunteer workers in libraries 4. Teenage volunteer workers in

libraries -- United States -- Case studies

ISBN 0-8108-4837-6

LC 2003-17932

"If you are even considering starting a teen volunteer program, you must read this book. If you already have one in your library, this volume still has much to offer." SLJ

Includes bibliographical references

Langemack, Chapple

The **author** event primer; how to plan, execute and enjoy author events. Libraries Unlimited 2007 188p pa $35

Grades: Adult Professional   **021.2**

1. Authors 2. Libraries and community 3. Author-library relations 4. Program planning -- Handbooks, manuals, etc.

ISBN 978-1-59158-302-8 pa; 1-59158-302-0 pa

LC 2006032405

"Langemack gives practical guidance that will be useful to experienced and novice planners on how to host an author event. She covers everything, from reasons for having author visits to carrying off 'the really big do,' with humor and experience. The text is supplemented with charts; sample event proposals, fact sheets, letters, forms, and emails. . . . This book will be an invaluable source." Libr Media Connect

Includes bibliographical references

Squires, Tasha

Library partnerships; making connections between school and public libraries. Information Today, Inc. 2009 203p pa $39.50

Grades: Adult Professional   **021.2**

1. Public libraries 2. School libraries 3. Library cooperation 4. Libraries and schools 5. Libraries and students

ISBN 978-1-57387-362-8; 1-57387-362-4

LC 2008-51647

"Squires's confident advice can get beleaguered librarians through . . . difficulties and into mutually productive partnerships." Voice Youth Advocates

Includes bibliographical references

021.7   Promotion of libraries, archives, information centers

Cole, Sonja

Booktalking around the world; great global reads for ages 9-14. Libraries Unlimited 2010 155p pa $35

Grades: Adult Professional   **021.7**

1. Book talks 2. Ethnology 3. Geography 4. World history 5. Children's literature -- Bibliography

ISBN 1-59884-613-2 pa; 978-1-59884-613-3 pa; 978-1-59884-614-0 ebook

LC 2010036580

"In this authoritative and highly readable text, [Cole] presents booktalks and reading lists of interest to children. The titles chosen are set in Africa, Asia, Europe, the Americas, Australia, New Zealand and the South Pacific Islands, and the Arctic and Antarctic. Each booktalk contains an enticing description of the book, bibliographic information, interest and reading levels, and awards. Those that have videos available are noted." SLJ

Includes bibliographical references

Flowers, Helen F.

Public relations for school library media programs; 500 ways to influence people and win friends for your school library media center. Neal-Schuman 1998 158p pa $55

Grades: Adult Professional   **021.7**

1. School libraries 2. Libraries -- Public relations 3. School libraries -- Public relations 4. Public relations of libraries -- School libraries 5. School libraries -- Public relations -- United States 6. Instructional materials centers -- Public relations -- United States

ISBN 978-1-55570-320-2 pa; 1-55570-320-8 pa

LC 98-11470

"Writing with a sense both of purpose and of humor, Flowers turns a book of excellent lists into a good, entertaining read." Voice Youth Advocates

Includes bibliographical references

Imhoff, Kathleen R.

Library contests; a how-to-do-it manual. [by] Kathleen R.T. Imhoff, Ruthie Maslin. Neal-Schuman Publishers 2007 182p il (How-to-do-it manuals for librarians) pa $55

Grades: Adult Professional   **021.7**

1. Contests 2. Libraries and community 3. Advertising -- Libraries 4. Libraries -- Public relations

ISBN 1-55570-559-6 pa; 978-1-55570-559-6 pa

LC 2006-33177

"This comprehensive book covers planning, implementing, and evaluating contests of all kinds, for all kinds of libraries. It addresses setting budgets and schedules, choosing prizes and judges, establishing rules, promoting the contest, and evaluating it once it is over. . . . The authors . . . cover potential negatives as well as positives in plain language. . . . The illustrations are informative." SLJ

Includes bibliographical references

Keane, Nancy J.

The **tech**-savvy booktalker; a guide for 21st-century educators. [by] Nancy J. Keane and Terence W. Cavanaugh. Libraries Unlimited 2009 162p il pa $35

Grades: Adult Professional   **021.7**

1. Book talks 2. Information technology

ISBN 978-1-59158-637-1 pa; 1-59158-637-2 pa

LC 2008-38988

"Keane offers a way to enhance booktalks with technology and to invite students to explore new ways to talk about books using Web 2.0 tools. The volume is divided into 11 chapters from booktalking concepts to more advanced uses of technology including scanners, digital cameras, computer software, and audio recording. Also included are chapters on software programs such as PowerPoint and iMovie as well as Internet sites such as YouTube and Amazon. The sequence of chapters is designed to allow easy access to information for both novice and experienced computer users. . . . This

excellent resource shows ways to use existing technology to augment booktalks and to expand the experience beyond the classroom." SLJ

Includes bibliographical references

Langemack, Chapple

★ The **booktalker's** bible; how to talk about the books you love to any audience. [by] Chapple Langemack. Libraries Unlimited 2003 199p pa $30

Grades: Adult Professional   **021.7**

1. Book talks

ISBN 1-56308-944-0

LC 2003-47543

"This book reminds readers that booktalks . . . are an effective way to present books and can be aimed at all types of settings . . . and age groups. It explains why booktalks are needed, tells how to hold one, and offers tips for a fail-safe presentation. Each chapter provides practical examples and closes with additional reading. Appendixes include sample talks and ideas for titles as well as other helpful resources." Booklist

Includes bibliographical references

Mahood, Kristine

Booktalking with teens. Libraries Unlimited 2010 289p (Libraries Unlimited professional guides for young adult librarians) pa $45

Grades: Adult Professional   **021.7**

1. Book talks 2. Teenagers -- Books and reading 3. Young adult literature -- Bibliography

ISBN 978-1-59158-714-9; 1-59158-714-X

LC 2009-49893

This "provides advice about preparing, developing, writing, performing and justifying booktalks. . . . Mahood's expertise and enthusiasm are contagious and challenge all of us who work with youth to be as inspiring while sharing books as she is." Booklist

Includes bibliographical references

Phillips, Susan P.

Great displays for your library step by step. McFarland & Co. 2008 234p il pa $45

Grades: Adult Professional   **021.7**

1. Libraries -- Exhibitions

ISBN 978-0-7864-3164-9; 0-7864-3164-4

LC 2007-47450

"Phillips' enthusiasm, creativity, and breadth of personal interests are evident throughout this book. . . . This text will inspire readers to locate and showcase the treasures in their own collections." SLJ

Includes bibliographical references

022   Administration of physical plant

Bolan, Kimberly

Teen spaces; the step-by-step library makeover. 2nd ed; American Library Association 2009 225p il pa $40

Grades: Adult Professional   **022**

1. Young adults' libraries 2. Public libraries -- Planning

3. Young adults' library services 4. Young adults' libraries -- Administration 5. Architecture and building -- Color, decoration, etc.
ISBN 978-0-8389-0969-0
LC 2008-26621
First published 2003
"An essential guide for any library planning a teen-space project. . . . After an introductory chapter on teens and their needs within a library, all aspects of teen areas are explained. From the analysis and planning to design and decoration, Bolan outlines the steps to take and the pitfalls to avoid. . . . This book truly is a guide to step-by-step library makeovers." SLJ
Includes bibliographical references

025.04 Information storage and retrieval systems

Alcorn, Louise E.
Wireless networking; a how-to-do-it manual for librarians. [by] Louise E. Alcorn, Maryellen Mott Allen. Neal-Schuman Publishers 2006 201p (How-to-do-it manuals for librarians) pa $65
Grades: Adult Professional   **025.04**
1. Library information networks 2. Wireless communication systems
ISBN 1-55570-478-6 pa; 978-1-55570-478-0 pa
LC 2004053760
"This practical reference provides timely, appropriate guidance on how and why libraries should go wireless. The authors present data and ideas on standards, transfer rates, equipment costs and options, planning and implementation, technical and project-management concerns, and site surveys. Common issues such as marketing, compatibility with existing networks, privacy and security options, and trouble-shooting and maintenance are also covered." Booklist
Includes bibliographical references

Barnett, Diana
Putting it all together; teaching the research process. Upstart 2009 74p pa $17.95
Grades: Adult Professional   **025.04**
1. Research 2. Information literacy
ISBN 978-1-932146-99-8 pa; 1-932146-99-7 pa
"This well-organized and to-the-point title focuses on practical application of the AASL standards of information literacy for student learning in middle and high schools. The research process is broken down into eight integrated steps, with teacher modeling ideas and printable student exercises for each one. . . . An excellent starting point for teaching research." SLJ

Bell, Suzanne S.
Librarian's guide to online searching; 2nd ed.; Libraries Unlimited, an imprint of ABC-CLIO, LLC 2012 286 p. il (paperback) $55
Grades: Adult Professional   **025.04**
1. Internet searching 2. Librarians -- Training of
ISBN 9781610690355; 1610690354
LC 200835924

First published 2006
This book, the second edition by Suzanne S. Bell, looks at online searching and "covers everything from Boolean searching to using specific topic-based databases. Bell also includes a variety of screen captures from many of the databases she discusses. . . . The final chapter guides librarians in how to use the searching knowledge they have in order to teach others." (Voice of Youth Advocates)
This "online searching guide will be invaluable to anyone starting out or looking for a refresher course on this topic. In clear concise language, the author covers everything from Boolean searching to using specific topic-based databases. . . . This easy-to-use manual, written with just a touch of humor and not a drop of condescension, is sure to be embraced by librarians of all skill levels." Voice Youth Advocates
Includes bibliographical references

Berger, Pam
★ **Choosing** Web 2.0 tools for learning and teaching in a digital world; [by] Pam Berger and Sally Trexler; foreword by Joyce Valenza. Libraries Unlimited 2010 221p il map pa $40
Grades: Adult Professional   **025.04**
1. Web 2.0 2. Internet in education 3. Internet searching -- Study and teaching 4. Information literacy -- Study and teaching
ISBN 978-1-59158-706-4; 1-59158-706-9
LC 2009-54069
"This guide offers a plethora of ideas for incorporating digital learning into schools in an accessible and reader-friendly manner." Voice Youth Advocates
Includes glossary and bibliographical references

Jaeger, Paul T.
★ **Public** libraries and internet service roles; measuring and maximizing Internet services. [by] Charles R. McClure and Paul T. Jaeger. American Library Association 2009 112p il map $65
Grades: Adult Professional   **025.04**
1. Internet 2. Public libraries 3. Libraries and the Internet 4. Internet -- Public libraries 5. Librarianship -- Social aspects 6. Public libraries -- Social aspects 7. Public libraries -- Aims and objectives
ISBN 978-0-8389-3576-7; 0-8389-3576-1
LC 2008-26622
The authors "summarize the existing research on the meanings of social roles and expectations of public libraries and the results of studies detailing those roles and expectations in relation to the Internet. . . . Their book raises our awareness of some very critical issues and is required reading for anyone who cares about public libraries." Booklist
Includes bibliographical references

Managing the Internet controversy; edited by Mark L. Smith. Neal-Schuman 2000 226p (Neal-Schuman net-guide series) pa $49.95
Grades: Adult Professional   **025.04**
1. Internet 2. Information society 3. Intellectual freedom 4. Information technology 5. Library information networks 6. Censorship -- Internet 7. Internet -- Censorship 8. Information retrieval -- Social aspects 9. Internet -- Access control -- United States

10. Internet access for library users -- United States 11. Information technology -- Social aspects -- United States
ISBN 1-55570-395-X

LC 00-62516

This is a "compilation of 12 essays. . . . Topics range from the historical and philosophical underpinnings of intellectual freedom to strategies for building public support for library policies to handling media interviews. Although the core of the discussion is the Internet and the concerns raised by its widespread use in libraries, the end product is a seminar on the key issues of library management. . . . Thought-provoking analysis by respected library professionals coupled with practical tools for addressing difficult issues makes this a valuable resource for school and public librarians." Book Rep

Includes bibliographical references

Pascaretti, Vicki

Team up online; by Vicki Pascaretti and Sara Wilkie. Cherry Lake Pub. 2010 32p il (Super smart information strategies) lib bdg $27.07

Grades: 3 4 5 6   **025.04**

1. Internet research 2. Wikis (Computer science)
ISBN 978-1-60279-644-7 lib bdg; 1-60279-644-0 lib bdg

LC 2009027082

"The appealing layout includes manageable paragraphs, a variety of engaging illustrations, and examples that clearly guide readers through each topic. . . . [This] introduces collaboration by using a garden analogy: plant, dig, garden, and ponder. It also insists on adequate privacy safeguards and discusses online tools such as wikis that will help students work together." SLJ

Includes glossary and bibliographical references

Porterfield, Jason

Conducting basic and advanced searches. Rosen Central 2010 48p il (Digital and information literacy) lib bdg $26.50

Grades: 5 6 7 8   **025.04**

1. Internet resources 2. Internet searching
ISBN 978-1-4358-5316-4 lib bdg; 1-4358-5316-4 lib bdg

LC 2008-46783

Describes how to conduct both basic and advanced searches on the Internet, from the basics of online search engines, boolean search terms, and evaluating the content of search results

"Colorful photos, diagrams, and sidebars and [a] lively [text creates an] appealing, user-friendly [presentation]. . . . Students and teachers will find [this title] useful in keeping up-to-date on and utilizing online resources and today's technology in a rapidly changing digital world." SLJ

Includes glossary and bibliographical references

Rabbat, Suzy

Find your way online. Cherry Lake Pub. 2010 32p il (Super smart information strategies) lib bdg $27.07

Grades: 3 4 5 6   **025.04**

1. Internet searching
ISBN 978-1-60279-639-3 lib bdg; 1-60279-639-4 lib bdg

LC 2009024549

"The appealing layout includes manageable paragraphs, a variety of engaging illustrations, and examples that clearly guide readers through each topic. . . . [This] begins with keywords, narrowing the search, and search engines. Then it shows students how to 'drill down' using subject directories and databases." SLJ

Scheeren, William O.

Technology for the school librarian; theory and practice. Libraries Unlimited 2010 223p il $50

Grades: Adult Professional   **025.04**

1. School libraries 2. Digital libraries 3. Information technology 4. Libraries -- Special collections
ISBN 978-1-59158-900-6; 1-59158-900-2

LC 2009-51922

"This title provides information on the practical aspects of technology in the school library as well as the theoretical framework to spark continued learning. Sharing actual case studies as well as practical tips on technology implentation and terminology, this title will be a valuable resource to any school librarian." Libr Media Connect

Includes bibliographical references

Truesdell, Ann

Find the right site. Cherry Lake Pub. 2010 32p il (Super smart information strategies) lib bdg $27.07

Grades: 3 4 5 6   **025.04**

1. Internet searching
ISBN 978-1-60279-638-6 lib bdg; 1-60279-638-6 lib bdg

LC 2009027083

"The appealing layout includes manageable paragraphs, a variety of engaging illustrations, and examples that clearly guide readers through each topic. . . . [This] is an excellent introduction to Web site evaluation and related pitfalls." SLJ

Includes glossary and bibliographical references

025.042   World Wide Web

Bodden, Valerie

Using the Internet; Valerie Bodden. Creative Education 2012 48 p. (Research for writing) $35.65

Grades: 8 9 10 11 12   **025.042**

1. Internet resources 2. Internet searching 3. Internet in education 4. Internet research 5. Computer network resources 6. Electronic information resource literacy
ISBN 160818207X; 9781608182077

LC 2011040493

This book is part of the Research for Writing series and focuses on using the Internet for research. The titles within the series "explain information such as the difference between qualitative and quantitative data, how to evaluate sources (both in print and online), and the importance of reference librarians." (School Library Journal)

Includes bibliographical references and index.

Devine, Jane

Going beyond Google again; strategies for using and teaching the Invisible Web. Jane Devine and Francine Egger-Sider. Amer Library Assn 2013 160 p. (paperback) $70.00

Grades: Adult Professional **025.042**

1. Internet in education 2. Internet searching -- Study and teaching

ISBN 1555708986; 9781555708986

LC 2013010867

This book is a follow-up volume to book "Going Beyond Google" by Jane Devine and Francine Egger-Sider, "which placed teaching the Invisible Web into information literacy programs. [This volume] expands on the teaching foundation laid in the first book and continues to document the Invisible Web's existence and evolution, and suggests ways of teaching students to use it." (Publisher's note)

Includes bibliographical references and index

Harris, Frances Jacobson

★ **I** found it on the Internet; coming of age online. Frances Jacobson Harris. 2nd ed. American Library Association 2010 xi, 234 p.p ill. (paperback) $45

Grades: Adult Professional **025.042**

1. Internet searching 2. Internet in education 3. Internet and teenagers 4. Young adults' libraries 5. Internet/Social aspects

ISBN 0838910661; 9780838910665

LC 2010013644

This book is an "analysis of the fundamental differences in how teens . . . and adults . . . view information and communication. . . . The book opens with a description of the current state of library affairs, wherein information retrieval has become primarily a computerized event and the collision between information technology and communication technology has literally forged a new, merged reality that Harris terms ICT (information community technology)." (School Library Journal)

This is an "analysis of the fundamental differences in how teens (for whom the Internet is a primary language) and adults (who will always be second-language learners) view information and communication." SLJ

Includes bibliographical references and index.

025.1   Administration

Anderson, Cynthia

Write grants, get money; [by] Cynthia Anderson and Kathi Knop. 2nd ed.; Linworth Pub. 2008 128p pa $44.95

Grades: Adult Professional **025.1**

1. Grants-in-aid

ISBN 978-1-58683-303-9 pa; 1-58683-303-0 pa

LC 2008-22038

First published 2002

"This practical, grant writing manual will prove invaluable to both novice and experienced grant writers. Written clearly and concisely, this title outlines the grant writing process step by step, from generating ideas to the nuts and bolts of writing an effective proposal. . . . Multiple appendices provide a plethora of supplemental information such as resources on grant writing, Web sites, awards and contests, listservs for media specialists, and a sample grant proposal format. . . . This book makes grant writing as simple as its title." Libr Media Connect

Includes glossary and bibliographical references

Curzon, Susan Carol

Managing change; a how-to-do-it manual for librarians. rev ed.; Neal-Schuman Publishers 2005 129p (How-to-do-it manuals for librarians) pa $55

Grades: Adult Professional **025.1**

1. Libraries -- Administration 2. Personnel -- Administration 3. Libraries -- Human resource management 4. Administration -- Handbooks, manuals, etc.

ISBN 1-55570-553-7

LC 2005-22846

First published 1989

"The real-world approach makes the book a valuable addition to the professional collection." Booklist

Includes bibliographical references

Farmer, Lesley S. Johnson

Neal-Schuman technology management handbook for school library media centers; by Lesley S. Johnson Farmer and Marc E. McPhee. Neal-Schuman Publishers 2010 289p il pa $59.95

Grades: Adult Professional **025.1**

1. School libraries 2. Instructional materials centers

ISBN 978-1-55570-659-3; 1-55570-659-2

LC 2010-9301

"This informative, well-researched text is perfect for those in the early stages of integrating technology into their programs. The first chapter begins with an overview of the impact technology has had on society and defines technology and its role in the library, including past, present, and possible future changes, as well as managerial roles of the librarian. Other chapters examine planning for management, assessing, researching, developing a technology plan, acquiring all types of tech resources, and managing the physical space to accommodate equipment and networking." SLJ

Includes bibliographical references

The **frugal** librarian; thriving in tough economic times. edited by Carol Smallwood. American Library Association 2011 277p il $42.00

Grades: Adult Professional **025.1**

1. Library finance 2. Libraries and community 3. Libraries -- United States

ISBN 0-8389-1075-0; 978-0-8389-1075-7

LC 2010034317

"The thirty-four chapters in Smallwood's collection address a myriad of issues faced by libraries and librarians when times get tough and money is tight. Written by practicing librarians from academic, public, and school libraries, the concise essays are easy to read, sometimes personal, and highly practical. . . . This issue is certainly timely, but in reality, sound management and creative budgeting never vanish from the library environment. The table of contents and descriptive title chapters, coupled with the index, allow for ease of use for the browser. This inexpensive volume from ALA will be particularly helpful to public and academic librarians." Voice Youth Advocates

Includes bibliographical references

Fullner, Sheryl Kindle

The **shoestring** library. Linworth Publishing 2010 139p il pa $30

Grades: Adult Professional   **025.1**
1. Library finance
ISBN 978-1-58683-520-0 pa; 1-58683-520-3 pa
LC 2010-718

"The book is divided into two sections. 'Library Management for Tough Times' has hints for taking advantage of free continuing-education opportunities, using volunteers, networking, and more. 'The Physical Plant' contains suggestions for sprucing up the library at little or no cost (for example: request mismatched or clearance paints from paint stores; then get students to do the painting)." (Booklist)

"Every librarian will find plenty of new ideas, insights, and inspiration from the wealth of suggestions found here." Libr Media Connect

Harvey, Carl A.

★ **No** school library left behind; leadership, school improvement, and the media specialist. [by] Carl A. Harvey II. Linworth Pub. 2008 106p pa $39.95

Grades: Adult Professional   **025.1**
1. School libraries 2. Instructional materials centers 3. Libraries -- Administration
ISBN 978-1-58683-233-9; 1-58683-233-6
LC 2007-42178

"The content [of this book] constitutes a crash course in school improvement, covering definitions, history, legislation, research, best practices, assessment, profiles of accreditation associations, and most importantly, a strong rationale for why media specialists should lead the way in school improvement efforts. . . . Of major interest to novice and seasoned practitioners, this guide is timely and relevant." Libr Media Connect

Includes bibliographical references

Lushington, Nolan

Libraries designed for kids. Neal-Schuman Publishers 2008 173p il pa $85

Grades: Adult Professional   **025.1**
1. Children1s libraries 2. Young adults' libraries 3. Libraries -- Administration
ISBN 978-1-55570-631-9
LC 2008-32537

"Lushington's guide will be invaluable to librarians and boards of trustees as they consider renovating, expanding, or creating new service areas for children and teens. . . . Lushington guides the planning team through creating the library program utilizing demographics and community input, which will help with determining the size of the facility. However, the largest sections of the book focus on design considerations to both enhance the user's experience and to most efficiently organize and supervise the collection and facility." SLJ

Includes bibliographical references

MacDonell, Colleen

★ **Essential** documents for school libraries; 2nd ed.; Linworth 2010 xxiv, 156p il $50

Grades: Adult Professional   **025.1**
1. Libraries -- Administration
ISBN 978-1-58683-400-5
LC 2010-21241

First published 2004

"Each chapter begins with why the documents are needed, followed by practical advice for writing the documents, and examples of how the documents make an effective change in the library media program." Libr Media Connect [review of 2004 edition]

Includes bibliographical references

Marek, Kate

Organizational storytelling for librarians; using stories for effective leadership. American Library Association 2011 105p pa $50

Grades: Adult Professional   **025.1**
1. Leadership 2. Storytelling 3. Communication 4. Administration
ISBN 978-0-8389-1079-5; 0-8389-1079-3
LC 2010033485

"This professional offering teaches librarians to use storyteling as an effective leadership tool. . . . Marek has written a clear and thorough introduction to organizational storytelling for librarians. Carefully researched, the book includes notes at the end of each chapter. A comprehensive resource list encourages further study. Controlling one's own story and the story of one's library is a useful skill, especially during times of budgetary turbulence. Individual librarians and library leaders need to be able to convey personal and shared values effectively; this title provides a wealth of information on the topic." Voice Youth Advocates

Includes bibliographical references

Martin, Barbara Stein

★ **Fundamentals** of school library media management; a how-to-do-it manual. [by] Barbara Stein Martin and Marco Zannier. Neal-Schuman Publishers 2009 172p il (How-to-do-it manuals for librarians) pa $59.95

Grades: Adult Professional   **025.1**
1. School libraries 2. Instructional materials centers 3. School libraries -- Administration 4. Administration -- Handbooks, manuals, etc.
ISBN 978-1-55570-656-2; 1-55570-656-8
LC 2009-7930

This book "contains useful information to help school librarians manage a myriad of tasks and roles. . . . [The authors] have created a book that is helpful, accessible, and full of down-to-earth, concrete examples." Booklist

Includes bibliographical references

McGhee, Marla W.

The **principal's** guide to a powerful library media program; a school library for the 21st century. [by] Marla W. McGhee and Barbara A. Jansen. 2nd ed.; Linworth 2010 xxviii, 149p pa $45

Grades: Adult Professional **025.1**
1. School libraries 2. Instructional materials centers 3. School superintendents and principals
ISBN 978-1-58683-526-2 pa; 1-58683-526-2 pa; 978-1-58683-527-9 ebook

LC 2010-21243

First published 2005
"With focused and well-organized topics from understanding the research and standards to supporting and sustaining them through collaborative processes, this . . . offers a great deal of concrete information. . . . This book gives administrators a clear idea of what is required in the media center and the role of the librarian as a specialist. . . . An excellent choice for the professional media specialist's or principal's shelf." SLJ
Includes bibliographical references

Independent school libraries; perspectives on excellence. Dorcas Hand, editor. Libraries Unlimited 2010 369p il (Libraries Unlimited professional guides in school librarianship) pa $45
Grades: Adult Professional **025.1**
1. Private schools 2. School libraries
ISBN 978-1-59158-803-0 pa; 1-59158-803-0 pa; 978-1-59158-812-2 ebook

LC 2010-14567

"Twenty-one essays by prominent independent school librarians both address the current state of independent school librarianship in the United States and offer suggestions for the future. Pieces cover the library's role in the school, statistical comparisons, staffing, advocacy, assessment, technology, information commons, collaboration, college preparation, programming, traditions, collection development, minors' rights, budgeting, facilities, accreditation, and disaster planning. . . . Librarians from all schools will find a wealth of information here." Voice Youth Advocates
Includes bibliographical references

★ **School** library management; [edited by] Judi Repman and Gail Dickinson. 6th ed.; Linworth Pub. 2007 200p il pa $44.95
Grades: Adult Professional **025.1**
1. School libraries 2. Libraries -- Administration
ISBN 978-1-58683-296-4; 1-58683-296-4

LC 2006-103468

First published 1987 with title: School library management notebook
"This collection of more than 35 articles written for Library Media Connection from 2003 to 2006 is a virtual treasure trove for library media specialists. . . . The book covers the very practical everyday issues such as scheduling and overdues, and also provides invaluable information on data gathering, facilities planning, professional development, the role of the library in the world of standardized testing, the technological future of libraries, and much more." SLJ
Includes bibliographical references

Tips and other bright ideas for elementary school libraries. Volume 4 Kate Vande Brake, editor. Linworth 2010 134p Volume 4 pa $35
Grades: Adult Professional **025.1**
1. Elementary school libraries 2. Libraries --

Administration
ISBN 978-1-58683-416-6 pa; 1-58683-416-9 pa; 978-1-58683-417-3 ebook

LC 2010011049

This title includes "fun and informative management advice from fellow librarians. All of it has been taken from 2006-2009 Library Media Connection magazine. . . . [The introduction] reviews some of the many jobs and responsibilities in a librarian's day. Section one includes management hints to help maximize effectiveness, followed by sections on working with students, teaching skills, . . . working with teachers, technology, reading promotion, public relations, and working with helpers." SLJ

025.2   Acquisitions and collection development

Baumbach, Donna
★ **Less** is more; a practical guide to weeding school library collections. American Library Association 2006 194p il pa $32
Grades: Adult Professional **025.2**
1. Libraries -- Collection development 2. Discarding of books, periodicals, etc. 3. School libraries -- Collection development
ISBN 978-0-8389-0919-5; 0-8389-0919-1

LC 2006-7490

"This outstanding, easy-to-use guide makes weeding realistic and achievable. . . . This is an indispensable resource for every school library." Booklist
Includes bibliographical references

Brenner, Robin E.
★ **Understanding** manga and anime. Libraries Unlimited 2007 335p il pa $40
Grades: Adult Professional **025.2**
1. Anime 2. Manga -- Study and teaching 3. Libraries -- Collection development 4. Libraries -- Special collections -- Graphic novels
ISBN 978-1-59158-332-5; 1-59158-332-2

LC 2007-9773

The author "provides thorough explanations of manga and anime vocabulary, potential censorship issues because of cultural disparities, and typical Manga conventions. . . . No professional collection could possibly be complete without this all-inclusive and exceptional work." Voice Youth Advocates

Fagan, Bryan D.
Comic book collections for libraries; [by] Bryan D. Fagan and Jody Condit Fagan; foreword by Stan Sakai; cover art by Derek Steed. Libraries Unlimited 2011 162p pa $45; e-book $45
Grades: Adult Professional **025.2**
1. Graphic novels 2. Comic books, strips, etc. 3. Graphic novels -- Bibliography 4. Graphic novels -- History and criticism 5. Comic books, strips, etc. -- Bibliography 6. Comic books, strips, etc. -- History and criticism 7. Libraries -- Special collections -- Graphic

novels
ISBN 978-1-59884-511-2 pa; 1-59884-511-X pa;
978-1-59884-512-9 e-book

LC 2010052532

"Armed with this book, librarians should feel confident about knowledgeably creating and maintaining a successful comic-book collection." SLJ

Includes bibliographical references

Fletcher-Spear, Kristin

Library collections for teens: manga and graphic novels; [by] Kristen Fletcher-Spear and Merideth Jenson-Benjamin. Neal-Schuman Publishers 2010 175p pa $55

Grades: Adult Professional   **025.2**

1. Graphic novels 2. Young adults' libraries 3. Comic books, strips, etc. 4. Graphic novels -- Bibliography 5. Graphic novels -- History and criticism 6. Libraries -- Special collections -- Graphic novels

ISBN 1-55570-745-9; 978-1-55570-745-3

LC 2010040895

"This informative, comprehensive handbook is perfect for any librarian, whether new to graphic novels and manga or already familiar with the format. The first chapter explains how to use the book. . . . The chapter then goes on to give a brief history of graphic novels and manga for those interested in gaining a better understanding of their evolution. Other topics featured include the literacy benefits of graphic novels, how to create and maintain a collection and selection policy, and how to develop programming with graphic novels as the focus. The last chapter lists recommended books by genre. . . . This all-inclusive guide will enable librarians to better serve teens through a more diverse collection." SLJ

Includes glossary and bibliographical references

Franklin, Patricia

School library collection development; just the basics. Claire Gatrell Stephens and Patricia Franklin. Libraries Unlimited 2012 x, 71 p.p ill. (Just the basics) (paperback) $35

Grades: Adult Professional   **025.2**

1. School libraries 2. Libraries -- Collection development 3. Collection management (Libraries) -- United States 4. School libraries -- Collection development -- United States

ISBN 1598849433; 9781598849431

LC 2012016990

This book, by Claire Gatrell Stephens and Patricia Franklin, discusses collection development for school librarians. This volume offers a "manual that explains the fundamentals of purchasing, developing, and managing a collection. Containing information useful to anyone from a paraprofessional working under the guidance of a certified school librarian to a newcomer to the field to a certified media specialist, this book covers all of the basics through best practices." (Publisher's note)

Gallaway, Beth

★ **Game** on! gaming at the library. Neal-Schuman Publishers 2009 306p il pa $55

Grades: Adult Professional   **025.2**

1. Video games 2. Video games and children 3. Video games and teenagers 4. Multimedia library services 5. Electronic games -- Collections 6. Libraries -- Special collections

ISBN 978-1-55570-595-4; 1-55570-595-2

LC 2009-14110

"An essential guide for any librarian who plans on embracing the video-game phenomenon, or at the very least, understanding it. . . . [The chapters] are well organized and contain an abundance of practical information. The sections on selection, collection, and circulation of video games include relevant advice on policy, cataloging, marketing, storage, and displays. . . . The annotated list of video games for a core collection is wonderful for selection purposes." SLJ

Includes bibliographical references

Goldsmith, Francisca

The **readers'** advisory guide to graphic novels. American Library Association 2010 124p (ALA readers' advisory series) pa $45

Grades: Adult Professional   **025.2**

1. Graphic novels 2. Graphic novels -- Bibliography 3. Libraries -- Special collections -- Graphic novels

ISBN 978-0-8389-1008-5; 0-8389-1008-4

LC 2009-25239

"After dispelling the two main myths that ghettoize graphic novels—they are just for adolescents and they are far less complex than texts without pictures—Goldsmith emphasizes that GNs are a format and not a genre. She suggests active and passive ways to offer readers' advisory (RA) from face-to-face encounters with patrons to book displays and book groups and offers guidance on helping established GN readers to find new titles they might enjoy. . . . All in all it is a valuable and quite readable resource that belongs in every library's professional collection." Voice Youth Advocates

Includes glossary and bibliographical references

Graphic novels beyond the basics; insights and issues for libraries. Martha Cornog and Timothy Perper, editors. Libraries Unlimited 2009 xxx, 281p il pa $45

Grades: Adult Professional   **025.2**

1. Graphic novels -- History and criticism 2. Comic books, strips, etc. -- History and criticism 3. Libraries -- Special collections -- Graphic novels

ISBN 978-1-59158-478-0; 1-59158-478-7

LC 2009-16189

Editors Cornog and Perper have collected essays by experts Robin Brenner, Francisca Goldsmith, Trina Robbins, Michael R. Lavin, Gilles Poitras, Lorena O'English, Michael Niederhausen, Erin Byrne, and Cornog herself, all about graphic novels in libraries. Topics covered range from the appeal of superheroes to manga, the appeal of comics to women and girls, anime, independent comics, dealing with challenges to the material, and more. Appendices provide resource information on African American-interest graphic novels, Latino-Interest graphic novels, LGBT-interest graphic novels, religious-themed graphic novels, a bibliography of books about graphic novels in libraries, and online resources.

"Whether you are serious about the genre, interested in the history, or looking for ammunition, this book should be on your shelf. The wealth of knowledge and research

that went into these essays is impressive, and reading this book will put you on the road to becoming an expert." Libr Media Connect
Includes bibliographical references

Herald, Nathan

Graphic novels for young readers; a genre guide for ages 4-14. Libraries Unlimited 2011 188p (Genreflecting advisory series) $40
Grades: Adult Professional   025.2
  1. Graphic novels   2. Graphic novels -- Bibliography
ISBN 1-59884-395-8; 978-1-59884-395-8
                                   LC 2010044947
"Librarians looking to beef up their graphic-novel collections will do well to get their hands on this valuable volume. The annotated entries are laid out in eight chapters organized by major genre, and from action and adventure to educational. Within chapters, the titles, 600 in all, are arranged alphabetically into popular subgenres such as superheroes, mythology, sports, and many more. . . . The intended audience for each title is clear, with bold icons providing an age range. Herald's writing style lends personality to what could easily be a dry overview. . . . A thorough, well-organized, one-stop shop for quality graphic novels." SLJ
Includes bibliographical references

Lukenbill, W. Bernard

Community resources in the school library media center; concepts and methods. [by] W. Bernard Lukenbill. Libraries Unlimited 2004 195p il $45
Grades: Adult Professional   025.2
  1. School libraries 2. Libraries and community 3. Internet in school libraries 4. School libraries -- Collection development 5. Community resources -- Information services
ISBN 978-1-59158-110-9; 1-59158-110-9
                                   LC 2004-48926
"This text outlines organizational strategies for managing community resources. . . . Lukenbill includes information such as agency directories, telementoring numbers, historical documents, museum exhibits, photos, and volunteer pools. Expanding the concept of the vertical file, the author presents ideas for developing, managing, marketing, and accessing electronic photo archives, Web site links, school documents, and bulletin boards. One chapter addresses sensitive community information, censorship, privacy, and terrorism concerns. . . . A definitive tool for developing community-resource collections." SLJ

Mayer, Brian

Libraries got game; aligned learning through modern board games. [by] Brian Mayer and Christopher Harris. American Library Association 2010 134p il pa $45
Grades: Adult Professional   025.2
  1. Board games 2. Libraries -- Special collections
ISBN 978-0-8389-1009-2; 0-8389-1009-2
                                   LC 2009-26839
"This is a valuable resource for K-12 librarians interested in building curriculum-aligned 'designer' game collections. The authors . . . explain how specific games enhance language-arts, social-studies, and math units, and build literacy skills. The two chapters devoted to promoting and justifying the inclusion of games in the library are well documented and a wonderful source to have to convince skeptical administrators. Suggestions for building a core collection, which highlights top recommended games for elementary school, middle school, and high school; a list of game publishers; a list of games discussed; and a glossary of terminology are included." SLJ
Includes bibliographical references

Reichman, Henry

★ **Censorship** and selection; issues and answers for schools. 3rd ed; American Library Association 2001 223p pa $37
Grades: Adult Professional   025.2
  1. Censorship 2. Academic freedom 3. School libraries
ISBN 0-8389-0798-9
                                   LC 00-67657

First published 1988
"Reichman's manual provides sound practical advice on how to handle this complex and emotionally charged subject." Voice Youth Advocates
Includes bibliographical references

Scales, Pat R.

★ **Protecting** intellectual freedom in your school library; scenarios from the front lines. [by] Pat R. Scales for the Office for Intellectual Freedom. American Library Association 2009 148p (Intellectual freedom front lines) pa $55
Grades: Adult Professional   025.2
  1. School libraries 2. Intellectual freedom
ISBN 978-0-8389-3581-1; 0-8389-3581-8
                                   LC 2008-39893

"Scales uses court opinions, federal and state laws, and ALA documents to offer solutions for responding to infringements. A broad range of potential scenarios—from challenges to materials in both the library and the classroom, the legality of film rating systems, using computerized reading programs as selection tools and labeling books by reading levels, policies for interlibrary loans and reserves to confidentiality of children's and teens' circulation records—are covered. . . . This resource should be in every school library's professional collection." Voice Youth Advocates
Includes bibliographical references

★ **Intellectual** freedom manual; 8th ed; American Library Association 2010 xxii, 439 p. $65
Grades: Adult Professional   025.2
  1. Intellectual freedom -- United States -- Handbooks, manuals, etc. 2. Libraries -- Censorship -- United States -- Handbooks, manuals, etc.
ISBN 0838935907; 9780838935903
                                   LC 2010016157
"All libraries should have a copy of this book to use when writing or revising policies; indispensable." Libr J

025.3   Bibliographic analysis and control

★ **Cataloging** correctly for kids; an introduction to the tools. edited by Sheila S. Intner, Joanna F. Fountain, and Jean Weihs. 5th ed.; Association for Library Collections and Technical Services, American Library Association 2011 224p pa $55

Grades: Adult Professional   **025.3**
1. Cataloging 2. Reference books 3. Children's literature -- Cataloging
ISBN 978-0-8389-3589-7 pa; 0-8389-3589-3 pa
LC 2010012945

First published 1989 by the Cataloging for Children's Materials Committee

Among the topics discussed are: guidelines for standardized cataloging for children; how children search; using AACR2 and MARC 21; copy cataloging; using RDA; Sears List of Subject Headings; LC Children's headings; sources for Dewey numbers; cataloging nonbook materials; authority control; how the CIP program helps children; cataloging for kids in the academic library; cataloging for non-English-speaking children and preliterate children; automating the children's catalog; vendors of cataloging for children's materials.

Includes bibliographical references

Oliver, Chris

★ **Introducing** RDA; a guide to the basics. Chris Oliver. American Library Association 2010 vii, 117 p.p ill. (paperback) $45

Grades: Adult Professional   **025.3**
1. Cataloging 2. Resource description & access -- Handbooks, manuals, etc. 3. Cataloging/Standards 4. Descriptive cataloging/Standards
ISBN 083893594X; 9780838935941
LC 2010021719

This book looks at Resource Description and Access (RDA), the cataloging standard that's replacing Anglo-American Cataloguing Rules (AACR). "Through numerous examples, [Chris] Oliver compares and contrasts RDA and AACR. He also discusses RDA background and its connection to the Functional Requirements for Bibliographic Records (FRBR) and Functional Requirements for Authority Data (FRAD) models and international standards." (Library Journal)

This is "a useful guide that provides a clear explanation of what RDA is all about. . . . Highly recommended for novice and experienced catalogers." Libr J

Includes bibliographical references (p. 105-109) and index.

025.4   Subject analysis and control

★ **Sears** list of subject headings; Joseph Miller, editor; Susan McCarthy, associate editor. 20th ed; H.W. Wilson Co. 2010 liii, 847p $150

Grades: Adult Professional   **025.4**
1. Reference books 2. Subject headings
ISBN 978-0-8242-1105-9; 0-8242-1105-7
LC 2010-5731

First published 1923 with title: List of subject headings for small libraries, by Minnie Earl Sears

"The Sears List of Subject Headings delivers a core list of key headings, together with patterns and examples to guide the cataloger in creating additional headings as required. It features: agreement with the Dewey Decimal Classification system to ensure that subject headings conform with library standards; [a] thesaurus-like format; accompanying list of canceled and replacement headings; and legends within the list that identify earlier forms of headings; scope notes accompanying . . . headings where clarification of the specialized use of a term may be required." Publisher's note

Includes bibliographical references

025.5   Services for users

American Association of School Librarians
Standards for the 21st-century learner in action. American Association of School Librarians 2009 120p pa $39

Grades: Adult Professional   **025.5**
1. Information literacy 2. Libraries -- Standards
ISBN 978-0-8389-8507-6 pa; 0-8389-8507-6 pa

"Standards in Action attempts to expand upon AASL's Standards for the 21st Century Learner by providing benchmarks and action examples. The original document was a nine-page brochure that outlined nine common beliefs, four learning standards, four strands, and indicators under each strand. It was an excellent starting point, but the addition of benchmarks at grades two, five, eight, ten, and twelve helps flesh out the original vision. . . . School libraries should own a copy of this professional, which has a role within any program." Voice Youth Advocates

Includes glossary and bibliographical references

Foundations for effective school library media programs; Ken Haycock, editor. Libraries Unlimited 1999 331p hardcover o.p. pa $52

Grades: Adult Professional   **025.5**
1. School libraries 2. Bibliographic instruction 3. Instructional materials centers 4. School librarianship 5. School libraries -- United States 6. Library orientation for school children -- United States
ISBN 1-56308-720-0; 1-56308-368-X pa
LC 98-40343

Explores the role of library media specialists in school improvement, curriculum design, collaboration with teachers, and building information literacy. Articles discuss learning theories, flexible scheduling, new technologies, and thematic units

Includes bibliographical references

Grassian, Esther S.

Information literacy instruction; theory and practice. [by] Esther S. Grassian and Joan R. Kaplowitz. 2nd ed; Neal-Schuman Publishers 2009 xxvii, 412p pa $75

Grades: Adult Professional **025.5**

1. Information literacy 2. Information literacy -- Study and teaching 3. Information retrieval -- Study and teaching 4. Bibliographic instruction -- College and university students

ISBN 978-155570-666-1; 1-55570-666-5

LC 2009-23647

First published 2001

This "is designed for anyone involved in the creation and management of information literacy programming. Sixteen well-written chapters, organized into five sections, provide both theory and practical applications, with the emphasis on the practical. . . . Several extras appear in the accompanying CD-ROM. . . . A timely, thorough, and endlessly useful must-have title for librarians, teaching librarians, and library schools." Booklist

Includes bibliographical references

Harper, Meghan

Reference sources and services for youth. Neal-Schuman Publishers 2011 307p $65

Grades: Adult Professional **025.5**

1. School libraries 2. Children's libraries 3. Young adults' libraries 4. Reference services (Libraries)

ISBN 978-1-55570-641-8; 1-55570-641-X

LC 2011004987

"The concept of school and public library collaboration is thoroughly explored in this excellent volume on providing reference services. The chapter on information literacy includes web links with information about standards, models, instruction and assessment, rubrics, web quests, graphic organizers, evaluation tools, and assessment. Additional chapters provide a discussion of online resources, government resources for youth, evaluation and marketing reference services, and managing them." SLJ

Includes bibliographical references

Intner, Carol F.

Homework help from the library; in person and online. American Library Association 2011 202p il pa $47

Grades: Adult Professional **025.5**

1. Homework 2. Library resources 3. Libraries and students

ISBN 978-0-8389-1046-7; 0-8389-1046-7

LC 2010042096

"Building on the concept that information services and education converge with homework help, the author sketches in the history of youth services and current learning theories. She offers practical suggestions for needs assessment and determining a guiding philosophy. Speaking to the public librarian, Intner outlines the points to consider in designing a homework help program and training staff. Possible workshop topics include an overview of student needs and available resources, creating a comfortable and inviting space, considering the needs of different ages, understanding youth culture, and responding to various learning styles. . . .

Youth librarians will want this comprehensive and practical guide within easy reach. " Voice Youth Advocates

Includes bibliographical references

Lanning, Scott

Essential reference services for today's school media specialists; [by] Scott Lanning and John Bryner. 2nd ed.; Libraries Unlimited 2010 141p il pa $45

Grades: Adult Professional **025.5**

1. School libraries 2. Reference services (Libraries)

ISBN 978-1-59158-883-2; 1-59158-883-9

LC 2009-39375

"The content focuses on core reference skills, electronic resources, and leadership. The first few chapters discuss information literacy, evaluation of resources, the role of print resources, and the reference interview. These are followed by chapters on the library catalog, electronic resources, and the Web as a reference tool. Finally, there are several chapters dealing with the teacher-librarians' instructional and leadership roles. The authors use a very accessible tone while providing the basics." Booklist

Includes bibliographical references

Lenburg, Jeff

The **Facts** on File guide to research; 2nd ed; Facts on File 2010 xxxvi, 720p (Facts on File library of language and literature) $50; pa $18.95

Grades: 8 9 10 11 12 **025.5**

1. Research 2. Reference books 3. Information resources

ISBN 978-0-8160-8121-9; 0-8160-8121-2; 978-0-8160-8122-6 pa; 0-8160-8122-0 pa

LC 2009-48200

First published 2005

This guide includes "lists of thousands of resources and explains general research methods and proper citation of sources. . . . [It features] discussions of Google and other search engines, subject-specific keyword search strategies, a cautionary note about Wikipedia, and . . . more." Publisher's note

Includes bibliographical references

Smith, Susan S.

★ **Web**-based instruction; a guide for libraries. [by] Susan Sharpless Smith. 3rd ed.; American Library Association 2010 236p il pa $65

Grades: Adult Professional **025.5**

1. Bibliographic instruction 2. Library information networks 3. Computer-assisted instruction 4. Web sites -- Design

ISBN 978-0-8389-1056-6; 0-8389-1056-4

LC 2010-6452

First published 2001

This book covers "tools and trends, including current browsers, access methods, hardware, and software. [The author] also supplies tips to secure project funding and provides strategic guidance for all types of libraries." Publisher's note

Includes bibliographical references

Tallman, Julie I.

Making the writing and research connection with the I-search process; a how-to-do-it manual. [by] Julie I. Tallman, Marilyn Z. Joyce. 2nd ed.; Neal-Schuman Publishers 2006 xx, 167p il (How-to-do-it manuals for librarians) pa $55

Grades: Adult Professional   **025.5**
    1. Research 2. Libraries 3. Report writing 4. Young adults' libraries 5. Bibliographic instruction
    ISBN 1-55570-534-0; 978-1-55570-534-3
                LC 2005-32473

First published 1997
This volume "covers the I-Search process for middle and high-school students and . . . includes a detailed explanation of I-Search in the context of content units. Although it is useful for the media specialist and teacher who are familiar with I-Search, novices will also find valuable information. . . . The accompanying CD-ROM contains all of the figures found in the book (templates, handouts, etc.), which can be reproduced and adapted." Booklist
Includes bibliographical references

Wichman, Emily T.

Librarian's guide to passive programming; easy and affordable activities for all ages. Emily T. Wichman. Libraries Unlimited Inc. 2012 xvii, 152 p.p ill. (pbk. : acid-free paper) $40

Grades: Professional   **025.5**
    1. Librarians 2. Library finance 3. Library services 4. LANGUAGE ARTS & DISCIPLINES -- Study & Teaching 5. Libraries -- Activity programs -- United States 6. LANGUAGE ARTS & DISCIPLINES -- Library & Information Science -- General
    ISBN 159884895X; 9781598848953; 9781598848960
                LC 2011045419

In her book, author Emily T. Wichman discusses library budget cuts, and how "librarians are seeking new ways to stretch their programming dollars and maximize staff resources. Passive programming allows libraries to inexpensively showcase their services while inviting visitors of all ages to enjoy the value that libraries bring to the community." (Publisher's note)
Includes bibliographical references and index.

025.8   Maintenance and preservation of collections

Halsted, Deborah D.

Disaster planning; a how-to-do-it manual for librarians with planning templates on CD-ROM. Neal-Schuman Publishers 2005 xx, 247p il (How-to-do-it manuals for librarians) pa $85

Grades: Adult Professional   **025.8**
    1. Disaster relief 2. Accidents -- Prevention 3. Disasters -- Handbooks, manuals, etc. 4. Library resources -- Conservation and restoration
    ISBN 1-55570-486-7
                LC 2003-65152

"Step-by-step instructions discuss creating a working disaster team, establishing a communications strategy, iden-

tifying relief and recovery agencies, developing response plans, and examining issues of cutting-edge library security. . . . This valuable resource is an important addition to most professional collections." Booklist
Includes bibliographical references

027   General libraries, archives, information centers

Trumble, Kelly

The **Library** of Alexandria; illustrated by Robina MacIntyre Marshall. Clarion Bks. 2003 72p il maps $17

Grades: 5 6 7 8   **027**
    1. Ancient civilization
    ISBN 0-395-75832-7
                LC 2003-150

An introduction to the largest and most famous library in the ancient world, discussing its construction in Alexandria, Egypt, its vast collections, rivalry with the Pergamum Library, famous scholars, and destruction by fire
This is a "well-organized and thorough resource." SLJ
Includes bibliographical references (p. 68-69) and index

027.6   Libraries for special groups and organizations

Alire, Camila

★ **Serving** Latino communities; a how-to-do-it manual for librarians. [by] Camila Alire, Jacqueline Ayala. 2nd ed; Neal-Schuman Publishers 2007 229p il (How-to-do-it manuals for librarians) pa $59.95

Grades: Adult Professional   **027.6**
    1. Libraries and Hispanic Americans 2. Public libraries -- Services to Hispanic Americans
    ISBN 978-1-55570-606-7; 1-55570-606-1
                LC 2007-7783

First published 1998
"The information covered helps library staff understand the needs of their library's Latino community; develop successful programs and services; obtain funding for projects and programs; prepare staff to work more effectively with Latinos; establish partnerships with relevant external agencies and organizations; improve collection development; and perform effective outreach and public relations. . . . There are few resources widely available on this topic and none as complete." Libr Media Connect
Includes bibliographical references

Lerch, Maureen T.

Serving homeschooled teens and their parents. Libraries Unlimited 2004 242p (Libraries Unlimited professional guides for young adult librarians) pa $39

Grades: Adult Professional   **027.6**
    1. Home schooling 2. Young adults' libraries 3. Libraries and education 4. Home schooling -- United States 5. Libraries -- Services to parents 6. Libraries and families -- United States 7. Public libraries --

Services to parents 8. Libraries and education -- United States 9. Libraries and teenagers -- United States 10. Public libraries -- Services to teenagers -- United States
ISBN 0-313-32052-7

LC 2004-46518

"After introductory chapters that dispel many myths about homeschooling and delve into adolescent psychology, the two experts give sound advice and great examples for service plan creation, collection development, programming, and promotion of services." Libr Media Connect

Includes bibliographical references

027.62 Libraries for specific age groups

Alessio, Amy

A **year** of programs for teens 2; [by] Amy J. Alessio and Kimberly A. Patton. American Library Association 2011 151p pa $45

Grades: Adult Professional   **027.62**

1. Young adults' libraries 2. Teenagers -- Books and reading

ISBN 978-0-8389-1051-1; 0-8389-1051-3

LC 2010013661

"The authors offer great suggestions to public and school librarians who either need more ideas or to those who just want to spice up their current routines. The book includes plenty of real-life examples and variety. Part one offers ideas for core programming—those that can be scheduled on a regular basis. The authors give great advice for starting monthly clubs as well as introducing or revamping reading programs. Great book lists and ideas for displays are included, and passive activities like puzzles and quizzes round out this section. The second section lays out a year's worth of possible programming, with multiple options for each month." SLJ

Includes bibliographical references

A **year** of programs for teens. American Library Association 2007 159p il pa $35

Grades: Adult Professional   **027.62**

1. Young adults' libraries 2. Teenagers -- Books and reading 3. Young adults' library services -- Activity projects

ISBN 0-8389-0903-5; 978-0-8389-0903-4

LC 2006-13758

"Following an overview of the planning component of successful teen programming, this guide is presented as a calendar of ideas for each month of the year. Each month offers three to four programs with the preparation time, the length of the program, the recommended number of teen participants, age range, a shopping list, the setup required, variations or extra activities, and resources. . . . Librarians working with teens will find plenty of fresh ideas here." Booklist

Includes bibliographical references

Anderson, Sheila B.

Extreme teens; library services to nontraditional young adults. Libraries Unlimited 2005 xxiii, 175p (Libraries Unlimited professional guides for young adult librarians) pa $36

Grades: Adult Professional   **027.62**

1. Young adults' libraries 2. Libraries and teenagers 3. Teenagers -- Books and reading 4. Young adults' reading -- Projects 5. Librarians -- Social responsibilities 6. Public libraries -- Collection development 7. Young adults' libraries -- Activity programs 8. Young adults' library services -- Activity projects 9. Young adults -- Reading -- Study and teaching -- Activities and projects

ISBN 1-59158-170-2

LC 2005016076

"This accessible manual offers practical advice on working with 'extreme teens,' young adults who, because of their sexuality, educational circumstances, or living situations, tend to be underserved by traditional public library services. Individual sections discuss definitions of various populations, service specifications for subgroups, collection development, and promotional programs. Additional features include statistics, scenarios, cited sources, and lists of recommended print and electronic resources, both fiction and nonfiction." Booklist

Includes bibliographical references

Braafladt, Keith

Technology and literacy; 21st century library programming for children and teens. by Jennifer Nelson and Keith Braafladt. American Library Association 2012 129 p. (alk. paper) $50.00

Grades: Adult Professional   **027.62**

1. Library services 2. Literacy programs 3. Literature and technology 4. Children's libraries -- Activity programs 5. Scratch (Computer program language) 6. Computer literacy -- Study and teaching 7. Technological literacy -- Study and teaching 8. Young adults' libraries -- Activity programs

ISBN 0838911080; 9780838911082

LC 2011035104

This book by Jennifer Nelson presents a "guide for creating and implementing technology-based programming in public libraries. . . . Beginning chapters explain and present a plan for offering such programs, providing steps on how to execute them. . . . The author explains the value of this type of programming and the process involved with adoption, and covers planning, gathering support from both administration and staff, marketing . . . managing time, etc." (School Library Journal)

Includes bibliographical references and index.

Braun, Linda W.

Risky business; taking and managing risks in library services for teens. [by] Linda W. Braun, Hillias Jack Martin, and Connie Urquhart for the Young Adult Library Services Association. American Library Association 2010 151p $55.00

Grades: Adult Professional   **027.62**

1. Young adults' libraries 2. Risk-taking (Psychology) 3. Teenagers -- Books and reading 4. Libraries -- Collection development

ISBN 0-8389-3596-6; 978-0-8389-3596-5

LC 201005995

"This thought-provoking title will pique awareness and present some 'ah ha!' moments. It involves a degree of risk to provide exemplary library services to young adults in terms of collection building, programming, and technology. This book encourages librarians to take the necessary risks and describes factors to consider in different situations. . . . Of particular interest are chapters devoted to developing a mature, appealing, high-interest YA collection. This section alone makes the book a worthwhile addition." SLJ

Includes bibliographical references

Brehm-Heeger, Paula

Serving urban teens. Libraries Unlimited 2008 229p (Libraries Unlimited professional guides for young adult librarians) pa $40

Grades: Adult Professional   **027.62**

1. Young adults' libraries 2. Teenagers -- Books and reading 3. Young adults' library services 4. Public libraries -- Metropolitan areas

ISBN 978-1-59158-377-6; 1-59158-377-2

LC 2007045415

This book "begins with definitions and a brief history of library services to urban teens, followed by a description of issues concerning this special group. The remaining chapters detail every aspect of making positive connections with teens, from training staff—the entire library staff—to making space, developing the collection, designing programs, and developing partnerships within the community. . . . It is not only the mission of libraries but also in their self-interest to capture the minds and hearts of youth while they can. This book provides the tools to accomplish the job." Voice Youth Advocates

Includes bibliographical references

Burek Pierce, Jennifer

Sex, brains, and video games; a librarian's guide to teens in the twenty-first century. American Library Association 2008 130p pa $35

Grades: Adult Professional   **027.62**

1. Adolescence 2. Young adults' libraries 3. Teenagers -- United States 4. Young adults' library services

ISBN 978-0-8389-0951-5; 0-8389-0951-5

LC 2007-21926

"This guide provides new and reevaluated ideas and insights about the sociological, neurological, emotional, and sexual perspectives of adolescence. The author's purpose is to assist librarians as they try to engage teens through relevant and attractive responses to their recreational, informational, and technological needs and interests. . . . It is filled with a great deal of pertinent and thought-provoking advice and information." SLJ

Includes bibliographical references

Cannon, Tara C.

Cooler than fiction; a planning guide for teen nonfiction booktalks. [by] Jill S. Jarrell and Tara C. Cannon. McFarland & Company, Inc., Publishers 2011 189p il pa $45

Grades: Adult Professional   **027.62**

1. Book talks 2. Young adults' libraries 3. Teenagers -- Books and reading

ISBN 978-0-7864-4886-9; 0-7864-4886-5

LC 2010040710

"This wonderful professional resource for teen librarians and school media specialists focuses on the art of booktalk-

ing with a twist. . . . The authors' take on talking up nonfiction books to teens is refreshing and creative and shows their love of reading and teens. Each title receives a summary, along with extra discussion questions and activities for awesome interactive appeal. Each chapter groups an assortment of nonfiction titles into unique categories like 'Funny, Gross, and Disturbing,' 'Food and Crafts,' 'Knowing Your World,' 'Science,' and 'History.'. . . This book is a much-needed tool for public librarians serving teens, as well as school media specialists, to develop excellent booktalking programs and partnerships while getting more teens to read and fun have doing so. It is a must-have for professional collections in public and school libraries." Voice Youth Advocates

Includes bibliographical references

Colston, Valerie

Teens go green! tips, techniques, tools, and themes for YA programming. Valerie Colston. Libraries Unlimited 2012 xiii, 142 p.p ill. (acid-free paper) $40

Grades: Professional   **027.62**

1. School libraries -- Activity projects 2. Environmental education -- Activity projects 3. Libraries and teenagers -- United States 4. Environmental education -- Activity programs -- United States 5. Young adults' libraries -- Activity programs -- United States

ISBN 1591589290; 1591589304; 9781591589297; 9781591589303

LC 2011029006

This book is a reference resource "for librarians or high school teachers looking for low-cost, environmentally themed art projects and programs that teens will relate to and find fun. In Part 1, the author explains the needs for these programs, offers tips for teaching them, and suggests ways to expand teen involvement in the library. Part 2 provides dozens of . . . art project ideas that demonstrate how simple teaching green teen art projects can be." (Publisher's note)

"...A nice resource to have on hand for librarians whose community is ecominded or for those who want affordable programming options to consult." Booklist

Includes bibliographical references and index

Flowers, Sarah

Evaluating teen services and programs; Sarah Flowers. Neal-Schuman, an imprint of the American Library Association 2012 xv, 119 p.p (pbk.) $49.95

Grades: Professional   **027.62**

1. Library services 2. Young adults' libraries 3. Libraries -- United States 4. Libraries and teenagers -- United States 5. Young adults' libraries -- Evaluation -- United States

ISBN 1555707939; 9781555707934

LC 2012015105

Author Sarah Flowers presents "a guide that provides basic information to help teen/youth services librarians, library directors, library school students studying teen services, and middle/high school librarians examine all aspects of their teen programs and services to determine where improvement is needed. Find out what you need to develop goals and objectives for evaluation, and learn how to collect the data that will give you a realistic picture of your library's strengths and weaknesses." (Publisher's note)

Includes bibliographical references and index

Young adults deserve the best; YALSA's competencies in action. [by] Sarah Flowers for the Young Adult Library Services Association. American Library Association 2011 126p pa $45

Grades: Adult Professional   **027.62**

  1. Librarians 2. Young adults' libraries 3. Young adults' librarians -- Qualifications 4. Young adults' library services -- Aims and objectives

  ISBN 978-0-8389-3587-3; 0-8389-3587-7

           LC 2010-14148

This "guide to the professional competencies developed by the Young Adult Library Services Association of ALA aims to 'outline the skills, the knowledge, and the philosophy that should be a part of the makeup of every librarian who serves teens.' Flowers begins by elaborating on and demonstrating how to execute the YALSA competencies. From there she discusses how to advocate for a teen-services department when none exists. The final section is a compilation of various resources, including the Library Bill of Rights and ALA interpretations of them with regard to labels and rating systems, Internet activity, ethics, and nonprint materials.. . . The information is presented in a clear, concise, and conversational manner, making this resource both easy to navigate and a pleasure to read." SLJ

Includes bibliographical references

Follos, Alison M. G.

  Reviving reading; school library programming, author visits, and books that rock! [by] Alison M. G. Follos; foreword by Jack Gantos. Libraries Unlimited 2006 xx, 143p bibl pa $32

Grades: Adult Professional   **027.62**

  1. Books and reading 2. Children's libraries 3. Young adults' libraries 4. School libraries -- Activity projects 5. School libraries -- Relations with teachers and curriculum

  ISBN 1-59158-356-X

           LC 2006017616

This is an "idea-packed manual on innovative literacy programs for elementary, middle, and high-school students. . . . Three sections address why, how, and what needs to be done to instill lifelong reading habits in children and young adults. . . . This realistic and reasonable guide is recommended for school and public library professional collections." Booklist

  Includes bibliographical references

Gorman, Michele

  Connecting young adults and libraries; a how-to-do-it manual. [by] Michele Gorman and Tricia Suellentrop. 4th ed; Neal-Schuman Publishers Inc. 2009 xxxiii, 450p il (How-to-do-it manuals for librarians) pa $85

Grades: Adult Professional   **027.62**

  1. Young adults' libraries 2. Procedure manuals 3. Libraries and teenagers 4. Teenagers -- Books and reading 5. Young adults -- Books and reading 6. Young

adult literature -- Bibliography 7. Young adults' library services -- Administration

  ISBN 978-1-55570-665-4

           LC 2009-17657

First published 1992 under the authorship of Patrick Jones

  "This useful, comprehensive handbook on how to best serve young adult library patrons is a must-have for any librarian's professional library. . . . All key topics are covered here—customer service (affirming the fact that young adults are our customers), information literacy, collection development, booktalking, outreach, programming, technology, and more. Each chapter is well organized and includes background on the topic, suggestions to improve services, useful ideas, advice, sources, and works cited. . . . [This] is an excellent professional resource." Voice Youth Advocates

  Includes bibliographical references

Hardesty, Constance

  The **teen**-centered writing club; bringing teens and words together. Libraries Unlimited 2008 174p il (Libraries Unlimited professional guides for young adult librarians) pa $40

Grades: Adult Professional   **027.62**

  1. Creative writing 2. Young adults' libraries 3. English language -- Composition and exercises 4. Young adults' library services -- Activity projects

  ISBN 978-1-59158-548-0; 1-59158-548-1

           LC 2008-11519

"Hardesty encourages librarians to listen to teens and assist them in their search for identity through the written word. . . . From starting a club and the writing activities to share, to grand finales and how to evaluate the program's effectiveness, the author details all the information needed to create such a club. Particularly useful are chapters on the four roles of facilitators, creating a nonfiction writing club, and how to take your efforts online. Many handouts are included, a boon to any busy librarian. An appendix includes resources for publishing. All this information is laid out in a straightforward, positive manner. An essential resource for planning or presenting writing clubs." SLJ

  Includes bibliographical references

Honnold, RoseMary

  ★ **More** teen programs that work. Neal-Schuman Publishers 2005 xxi, 245p il (Teens @ the library series) $49.95

Grades: Adult Professional   **027.62**

  1. Young adults' libraries 2. Teenagers -- Books and reading 3. School libraries -- Activity projects

  ISBN 1-55570-529-4

           LC 2004-19032

"Full of practical and excellent information, this is a definite choice for any library that wants to expand its programming for teens." SLJ

  Includes bibliographical references

Jones, Ella W.

  Start-to-finish YA programs; hip-hop symposiums, summer reading programs, virtual tours, poetry slams, teen advisory boards, term paper clinics, and more! Neal-Schuman Publishers 2009 217p il pa $75

Grades: Adult Professional   **027.62**
1. Cultural programs   2. Young adults' libraries 3.
Libraries and teenagers 4. Young adults -- Books and
reading 5. Young adults' libraries -- Activity programs
6. Young adults' library services -- Activity projects
ISBN 978-1-55570-601-2; 1-55570-601-0
                                       LC 2008-50853

"Jones's creativity, twenty-five years of experience, and
her genuine love for teenagers is obvious in the meticulous
and creative programming ideas and materials. This valuable resource will be appreciated by librarians in public and
school settings." Voice Youth Advocates
Includes bibliographical references

Kan, Katharine
★ **Sizzling** summer reading programs for young
adults; [by] Katharine L. Kan for the Young Adult
Library Services Association. 2nd ed.; American Library Association 2006 110p il pa $30
Grades: Adult Professional   **027.62**
1. Young adults' libraries 2. Teenagers -- Books and
reading 3. Young adults' reading -- Projects 4. Young
adults -- Reading -- Study and teaching -- Activities and
projects
ISBN 0-8389-3563-X
First published 1998

This "presents more than 50 summer reading programs
that have been used successfully with preteens and teenagers. . . . Submissions represent a cross section of themes,
incentives, activities and budgets. . . . Children and young
adult services librarians will find a wealth of practical,
hands-on information." Booklist

Koelling, Holly
Classic connections; turning teens on to great
literature. Libraries Unlimited 2004 xxi, 405p (Libraries Unlimited professional guides for young adult
librarians) pa $40
Grades: Adult Professional   **027.62**
1. Teenagers -- Books and reading
ISBN 1-59158-072-2
                                       LC 2004-48644

"The book is divided into two sections: Laying the
Groundwork and Making it Happen. The first section covers
the essential elements that define a book as a classic, reviews
adolescent development and reading habits, and discusses
what types of classics have teen appeal. The second section
contains a discussion of collection development, readers'
advisory, programming, booktalking, and promotion of the
classics. . . . It is a valuable book for anyone trying to connect teens to classic literature." Voice Youth Advocates
Includes bibliographical references

Kunzel, Bonnie Lendermon
The **teen**-centered book club; readers into leaders. [by] Bonnie Kunzel and Constance Hardesty.
Libraries Unlimited 2006 xxi, 211p (Libraries Unlimited professional guides for young adult librarians)
pa $40
Grades: Adult Professional   **027.62**
1. Young adults' libraries 2. Book clubs (Discussion

groups) 3. Book discussion groups 4. Teenagers --
Books and reading 5. Young adults' library services --
Activity projects
ISBN 1-59158-193-1

"Two experienced youth-services librarians introduce
the idea of teen-centered book clubs. . . . In clear prose supported by research, the authors cover every aspect of the
program, from assessing the needs of the library and teens to
conducting successful meetings to evaluating activities. . . .
An excellent reference." SLJ
Includes bibliographical references

Ludwig, Sarah
Starting from scratch; building a teen library
program. Libraries Unlimited 2011 xiv, 202p pa
$40; ebook $40
Grades: Adult Professional   **027.62**
1. Young adults' libraries
ISBN 978-1-59884-607-2 pa; 1-59884-607-8 pa;
978-1-59884-608-9 ebook; 1-59884-608-6 ebook
                                       LC 2011020103

This book offers a practical, comprehensive guide to creating a successful, vibrant, and youth-centered teen services
program with limited resources.

"Ludwig provides plenty of real-world advice and ideas.
. . . This well-written and helpful book will be invaluable to
both new and seasoned teen librarians as well as those thinking about pursuing a career working with teens." SLJ
Includes bibliographical references

Mahood, Kristine
A **passion** for print; promoting reading and
books to teens. Libraries Unlimited 2006 239p il
(Libraries Unlimited professional guides for young
adult librarians) pa $40
Grades: Adult Professional   **027.62**
1. Young adults' libraries 2. Young adults -- Reading 3.
Teenagers -- Books and reading 4. Publicity -- Young
adults' library services
ISBN 1-59158-146-X; 978-1-59158-146-8
                                       LC 2006-3716

"Beginning with research on reading, Mahood moves
on to merchandising principles; developing teen collections,
spaces, and Web sites; and finally to booktalking, readers'
advisory, and events scheduling. The author's enthusiasm
and experience, coupled with citing current studies, other
professional books, articles, and Web sites, make her suggestions appealing and attainable. She provides everything
from lists of YA genres to easy design principles for displays to suggestions for questions to ask for better readers'
advisory." Booklist

Martin, Hillias J.
★ **Serving** lesbian, gay, bisexual, transgender,
and questioning teens; a how-to-do-it manual for librarians. [by] Hillias J. Martin, Jr., James R. Murdock. Neal-Schuman Publishers 2007 267p bibl
(How-to-do-it manuals for librarians) pa $55
Grades: Adult Professional   **027.62**
1. Gay men 2. Lesbians 3. Bisexuality 4.
Transsexualism 5. Young adults' libraries 6. Libraries

and teenagers 7. Young adults' library services 8. Libraries and sexual minorities 9. Public libraries -- Services to homosexuals

ISBN 978-1-55570-566-4; 1-55570-566-9

LC 2006-39469

"This volume offers abundant useful guidance not only for reaching the target audience, but also for planning and promoting library services to teens in general. . . . The tone is friendly and largely free of jargon. . . . All librarians should turn to this book for pertinent insight on the needs of 5 to 10 percent of the teen population." SLJ

Includes bibliographical references

Miller, Donna P.

Crash course in teen services. Libraries Unlimited 2008 128p (Crash course) pa $30

Grades: Adult Professional   **027.62**

1. Young adults' libraries 2. Procedure manuals 3. Young adults' library services

ISBN 978-1-59158-565-7; 1-59158-565-1

LC 2007-32758

"Designed for public librarians new to teen service, the book offers advice on relating to teens and creating teen-friendly space as well as tips on teen-centered reference, collection development, readers' advisory, programming, and 'the three Ps': professional resources, professional development, and public relations." Booklist

Includes bibliographical references

Ott, Valerie A.

Teen programs with punch; a month-by-month guide. Libraries Unlimited 2006 282p il (Libraries Unlimited professional guides for young adult librarians) pa $40

Grades: Adult Professional   **027.62**

1. Young adults' libraries 2. Teenagers -- Books and reading 3. Young adults' library services -- Activity projects

ISBN 1-59158-293-8

LC 2006012775

"Ott has gathered together less-than-conventional program ideas arranged by month. She provides clear instructions, lists of supplemental materials, promotional ideas, reading lists, costs, and suggested grade levels for each one. For librarians with limited budgets, and who may be pressed for time, there are quick and easy ideas that cost little or no money. . . . Many of the programs are designed to draw underserved populations, such as goths, GLBTQ teens, and vegetarians, into the library. . . . This highly informative guide would make a great addition to any YA librarian's professional collection." SLJ

Includes bibliographical references

Rankin, Virginia

★ The **thoughtful** researcher; teaching the research process to middle school students. Libraries Unlimited 1999 211p il (Information literacy series) $37.00

Grades: Adult Professional   **027.62**

1. Research 2. School libraries 3. Bibliographic instruction 4. Library orientation for middle school students -- United States 5. Bibliographic instruction

-- Elementary and high school students

ISBN 1-56308-698-0

LC 98-55916

Rankin "offers concrete suggestions (and 16 reproducible handouts) for researching a topic, generating questions, planning a project, managing time, searching for information, evaluating sources, note taking, mastering thinking skills, selecting a presentation format, and assessing the product and the process. . . . A must-have resource for school libraries serving grades 5-9, this will be welcomed by classroom teachers and teacher-librarians." Booklist

Includes bibliographical references

Reid, Rob

★ **What's** black and white and Reid all over? something hilarious happened at the library. Rob Reid. American Library Association 2012 xii, 175 p.p (softbound) $45

Grades: Professional   **027.62**

1. Storytelling 2. Children's libraries 3. Storytelling -- United States 4. Wit and humor, -- Bibliography 5. Children's libraries -- Activity programs -- United States

ISBN 0838911471; 9780838911471

LC 2011043233

This book presents "10 humorous story programs -- five aimed at preschoolers and five for school-aged children. . . . Each one provides read-aloud suggestions and movement activities. There are also . . . storytelling tips that include everything from how to hold the book to what props to use. . . . Reid also includes an additional list of titles that can be substituted, jokes, call-and-response chants, short storybooks, songs, and musical activities." (School Library Journal)

"Those new to interactive book talking will appreciate his instructions for hamming up particular titles. Seasoned users will be grateful for the flexibility Reid provides to tailor programs to the tastes, time slots, and collection at hand." VOYA

Includes bibliographical references and index

Sima, Judy

Raising voices; creating youth storytelling groups and troupes. [by] Judy Sima, Kevin Cordi. Libraries Unlimited 2003 xxviii, 241p pa $32.50

Grades: Adult Professional   **027.62**

1. Storytelling 2. Children's stories

ISBN 1-56308-919-X

LC 2003-47631

This offers a "blueprint for beginning and sustaining a successful group or troupe of storytellers from grades 4 to 12. . . . The book includes reproducible forms that will save a lot of work and lists of valuable resources. . . . Raising Voices is the complete, and essential, handbook for this special group of storytellers." SLJ

Includes bibliographical references

Simpson, Martha Seif

Bringing classes into the public library; a handbook for librarians. [by] Martha Seif Simpson and Lucretia I. Duwel. McFarland & Co. 2007 175p il pa $45

Grades: Adult Professional   **027.62**

1. Public libraries 2. Children's libraries 3. Libraries

and schools 4. Young adults' libraries
ISBN 978-0-7864-2806-9 pa; 0-7864-2806-6 pa
LC 2006037527

"This handbook articulates the reasons and defines a
strategy for promoting a program of class visits to the public
library, and provides . . . instructions and . . . templates to
assist librarians in initiating an organized program of class
visits." Publisher's note

Teaching Generation M; a handbook for librarians
and educators. edited by Vibiana Bowman Cvet-
kovic and Robert J. Lackie. Neal-Schuman Publishers 2009 368p il pa $85
Grades: Adult Professional   **027.62**
1. Technology 2. Information literacy 3. Educational
technology 4. Internet and teenagers 5. Young adults'
libraries 6. Technology and youth 7. Libraries and
teenagers
ISBN 978-1-55570-667-8; 1-55570-667-3
LC 2009-17658

"This professional handbook tackles three important
topics—who is the millennial generation, what kind of
world do millennials live in, and what can we do to teach
them? Chapter topics include media literacy, the information search process, Facebook, YouTube, Google, and Wikipedia, gaming, webcomics, mobile technology, cooperative
learning, screencasting, and the new generation of research
papers. . . . In-text citations make this book more of a resource than a pleasure read, but it is a must-read for non-
M-generation librarians new to young adult services and for
those new teachers or anyone wanting to understand Web
2.0." Voice Youth Advocates
Includes bibliographical references

Tuccillo, Diane
Teen-centered library service; putting youth
participation into practice. [by] Diane P. Tuccillo.
Libraries Unlimited 2010 xxii, 259p il (Libraries
Unlimited professional guides for young adult librar-
ians) pa $45
Grades: Adult Professional   **027.62**
1. School libraries 2. Young adults' libraries
ISBN 978-1-59158-765-1; 1-59158-765-4
LC 2009-45692

This offers "guidelines to YA librarians for getting teens
to play a part in their libraries. . . . The book begins with
a description of this philosophy and places it into context
within the history of YA librarianship. Each chapter then
deals with specifics: teen advisory groups, writing and performance ideas, ways to meld teens and technology, ideas
for community outreach, ways to combine teen and adult
library groups, ideas to involve teens who are only around
for limited time, and a chapter on assessing your YA participation. . . . This well-organized title is aimed at public librarians and might also be useful to show administrators how
important YA services are to the library as a whole." SLJ
Includes bibliographical references

Urban teens in the library; research and practice.
edited by Denise E. Agosto and Sandra Hughes-

Hassell. American Library Association 2010
208p bibl il pa $60
Grades: Adult Professional   **027.62**
1. Internet and teenagers 2. Young adults' libraries
3. Libraries and teenagers 4. Teenagers -- Books and
reading 5. Young adults' library services 6. Libraries
and socio-economic problems
ISBN 978-0-8389-1015-3; 0-8389-1015-7
LC 2009-25147

"This work does much to explain who urban teens are
and what they need from their libraries. The authors examine the existing research—some of which they have performed—that provides a wealth of data for public and school
libraries." SLJ
Includes bibliographical references

Walter, Virginia A.
Twenty-first-century kids, twenty-first-century librarians. American Library Association 2010 104p
pa $45
Grades: Adult Professional   **027.62**
1. Librarians 2. Children's libraries 3. Young adults'
libraries
ISBN 978-0-8389-1007-8 pa; 0-8389-1007-6 pa
LC 2009016972

"This volume more than updates Walter's 2001 Children
and Libraries; it revisits the nature of children, addressing
social changes and encouraging a new generation of children's librarians. Chapter 1 provides a fine history about
U.S. library services to children, primarily in public libraries. Subsequent chapters detail six enduring core values of
children's library services and add two emerging themes: the
need for information (and information literacy) and collaboration. Walter's main contribution lies in her description of
five models of children relative to the library: as reader, as
a child of the information age, as a community member, as
global, and as an empowered person. Another chapter focuses on management principals. . . . Walter's core values
are worth reading and implementing." Booklist
Includes bibliographical references

Welch, Rollie James
The **guy**-friendly YA library; serving male teens.
Libraries Unlimited 2007 xxi, 196p (Libraries Un-
limited professional guides for young adult librarians)
pa $40
Grades: Adult Professional   **027.62**
1. Young adults' libraries 2. Boys -- Books and reading
3. Teenagers -- Books and reading
ISBN 978-1-59158-270-0; 1-59158-270-9
LC 2006-102882

"The first chapter offers key components for quality service for teen males, while the second chapter explains the
characteristics and developmental issues of this population.
The book emphasizes reading, with three chapters dedicated
to male teen reading habits, topics of interest, and detailed
genre coverage. . . . The sixth chapter deals with programming and also explains how the establish an effective teen
advisory board. . . . The seventh chapter covers school visits and emphasizes the importance of booktalks. The eighth
chapter discusses creating a teen area in the library." Booklist
Includes bibliographical references

027.8 School libraries

Adams, Helen R.

★ **Ensuring** intellectual freedom and access to information in the school library media program. Libraries Unlimited 2008 xxi, 254p il map pa $40
Grades: Adult Professional   **027.8**
1. Censorship 2. School libraries 3. Freedom of information
ISBN 978-1-59158-539-8; 1-59158-539-2
        LC 2008-16753
This is "an extremely helpful guide for dealing with intellectual-freedom and information-access issues. In chapters geared to school situations and covering topics including selection of resources, the First Amendment, privacy, challenges to resources, the Internet, and access for students with disabilities, Adams offers background on the topic and bulleted lists of strategies for dealing with the issue. . . . This is a book that every school librarian needs to keep handy and share with administrators, colleagues, and parents." Booklist
Includes bibliographical references

Baule, Steven M.

Facilities planning for school library and technology centers; 2nd ed.; Linworth Pub. 2007 134p il pa $39.95
Grades: Adult Professional   **027.8**
1. School libraries -- Design and construction 2. Instructional materials centers -- Design and construction
ISBN 978-1-58683-294-0; 1-58683-294-8
        LC 2006-34179
First published 1992
The author "provides information on how to put together a planning team; how to perform a needs assessment for the library media center or technology lab; how to create bid documents and specification charts; how to develop time lines; and how to plan to move into the new facility once construction is complete. . . . Anyone who is going to build or renovate a facility will want this book." Booklist
Includes bibliographical references

Bishop, Kay

The **collection** program in schools; concepts, practices, and information sources. 4th ed. Libraries Unlimited 2007 xx, 269p il (Library and information science text series) pa $50; $65
Grades: Adult Professional   **027.8**
1. School libraries 2. Libraries -- Collection development 3. School libraries -- Collection development 4. Children's literature -- Bibliography of bibliographies 5. Young adult literature -- Bibliography of bibliographies
ISBN 1-59158-360-8 pa; 1-59158-583-X; 978-1-59158-360-8 pa; 978-1-59158-583-1
        LC 2007-9005
First published 1988 under the authorship of Phyllis J. Van Orden
"Media specialists who read this book will be renewed in their quest for excellence in their collections. . . . The book covers A-Z: Acquisitions, Evaluation, Ethical Issues, Inventory, Procedure Manual, Selection, Special Groups of Students, Weeding, etc. . . . This is a must purchase for every school library media center." Libr Media Connect
Includes bibliographical references

Bush, Gail

Tales out of the school library; developing professional dispositions. [by] Gail Bush and Jami Biles Jones; foreword by Theodore R. Sizer. Libraries Unlimited 2010 135p il pa $40
Grades: Adult Professional   **027.8**
1. Librarians 2. School libraries
ISBN 978-1-59158-832-0; 1-59158-832-4
        LC 2009-46648
This book "answers the question, how should school librarians conduct themselves in their teaching, communicating, and leading roles in light of the AASL Standards for the 21st-Century Learner? In addition, what factors make an exemplary school librarian who will not only inspire students, but also nurture needed dispositions in them? . . . Readers are introduced to three fictional, yet very realistic school librarians in a series of thought-provoking vignettes that focus on instructional strategies, information literacy, assessment, literacy and reading, diversity, intellectual freedom, communication, advocacy, collaboration, resiliency, leadership, and professional ethics. Each chapter connects to the AASL standards and includes follow-up and discussion questions. All school librarians aiming to become reflective practitioners who model professional dispositions should read this unique book." SLJ
Includes bibliographical references

Buzzeo, Toni

The **collaboration** handbook. Linworth Pub. 2008 132p il pa $42.95
Grades: Adult Professional   **027.8**
1. School libraries
ISBN 978-1-58683-298-8 pa; 1-58683-298-0 pa
        LC 2008-18119
"In this succinct guide, Buzzeo paints a picture of how media specialists can use instructional collaboration to transform a media program and increase student achievement. . . . Those new to the field will appreciate the step-by-step approach to increasing collaboration, while experienced media specialists will likely benefit most from the chapters on data-driven collaboration and assessment. The book concludes with a substantial amount of information on how to overcome common barriers to collaboration, the role of advocacy, and the importance of integrating new technologies into collaborative projects." SLJ
Includes bibliographical references

Church, Audrey P.

★ **Leverage** your library program to help raise test scores; a guide for library media specialists, principals, teachers, and parents. Linworth Pub. 2003 123p il pa $39.95
Grades: Adult Professional   **027.8**
1. School libraries 2. Instructional materials centers 3. School libraries -- United States 4. Teacher-librarians -- United States 5. Academic achievement -- United States 6. Information literacy -- United States 7. Libraries and education -- United States 8. Media programs

(Education) -- United States 9. Instructional materials centers -- United States
ISBN 1-58683-120-8

LC 2003-40080

"In chapter one, recent research on school libraries is provided and briefly explains the results in layman terms. This is followed by a chapter each for the administrators, teachers, and parents that describes what each needs to know about the library and librarian's roles. A chapter is included for the librarian on what they need to do. The final chapter pulls the book together with perspectives from principals and librarians . . . This book can serve as a means to start a dialog with the administration and at the same time as a reference book for the school librarian." Libr Media Connect

Includes bibliographical references

★ **Curriculum** connections through the library; edited by Barbara K. Stripling and Sandra Hughes-Hassell. Libraries Unlimited 2003 xxi, 229p (Principles and practice series) pa $37.50
Grades: Adult Professional   **027.8**
1. School libraries 2. School librarian participation in curriculum planning 3. School libraries -- Relations with teachers and curriculum
ISBN 1-56308-973-4

LC 2003-54628

The editors have chosen "essays that sample existing scholarship and direct professionals in ways to affect curriculum, collections, and collaboration across disciplines and to aid students who must perform under the scrutiny of the national standards movement. The book contains some suggestions for joint projects, but primarily promotes open-ended, inquiry-based learning. . . . The writing is clear and purposeful. . . . A stimulating choice for practicing librarians and students of library science." SLJ

Includes bibliographical references

Doll, Carol Ann
The **resilient** school library; [by] Carol A. Doll and Beth Doll. Libraries Unlimited 2010 123p il pa $40
Grades: Adult Professional   **027.8**
1. School libraries 2. Academic achievement
ISBN 978-1-59158-639-5; 1-59158-639-9

LC 2010-21570

"The premise of the research provided in this informative text is that school library media specialists have the opportunity to play a major role in promoting resiliency through library programming and services for at-risk students. . . . The content of this comprehensive and interesting text provides examples; a planning template to follow; and supplementary graphs, charts, and tables." SLJ

Includes bibliographical references

Downs, Elizabeth
The **school** library media specialist's policy & procedure writer. Neal-Schuman Publishers 2009 195p pa $75
Grades: Adult Professional   **027.8**
1. School libraries 2. School libraries -- Administration

3. School libraries -- Policy statements
ISBN 978-1-55570-621-0; 1-55570-621-5

LC 2009-35177

"School library media specialists who need policies or procedures will surely find what they are looking for in this thorough book. Downs lays the foundation by describing necessary forms and policies for a school library media center, then provides a variety of examples and templates. The book includes mission statements, goals and objectives, budgeting, facilities use, circulation, collection development, disaster management, weeding, copyright, ILL, ethics, and accessibility policies." SLJ

Erikson, Rolf
Designing a school library media center for the future; [by] Rolf Erikson and Carolyn Markuson. 2nd ed; American Library Association 2007 117p il pa $45
Grades: Adult Professional   **027.8**
1. School libraries -- Design and construction 2. Architecture and building -- School libraries 3. Instructional materials centers -- Design and construction
ISBN 978-0-8389-0945-4; 0-8389-0945-0

LC 2006-37644

First published 2000

"The first chapter offers an overview of the various steps involved in any project. Succeeding chapters cover technology planning, space allocations, furniture and placement, lighting and acoustics, ADA requirements, specifications, and bids." Booklist

Includes bibliographical references

Farmer, Lesley S. Johnson
Collaborating with administrators and educational support staff; [by] Lesley S. J. Farmer. Neal-Schuman Publishers 2007 217p (Best practices for school library media professionals) pa $65
Grades: Adult Professional   **027.8**
1. School libraries 2. Instructional materials centers 3. Schools -- Administration 4. School management and organization 5. School libraries -- Relations with teachers and curriculum 6. School libraries -- Relations with principals and superintendents
ISBN 978-1-55570-572-5; 1-55570-572-3

LC 2006-11171

"Farmer begins by exploring how schools work, the role of the library media specialist, and the background on collaboration. She then discusses, in some depth, how to work with different levels of administrators and key service personnel, such as technology directors, reading specialists, special-education educators, pupil services personnel, and physical health and co-curricular personnel. Farmer concludes with ways of measuring the impact of collaboration and improving literacy, and provides suggestions for becoming a collaborative leader. This book is a must for school districts and a school library media specialists' personal collections." SLJ

Includes bibliographical references

Grimes, Sharon

★ **Reading** is our business; how libraries can foster reading comprehension. American Library Association 2006 155p il pa $35

Grades: Adult Professional   **027.8**

1. School libraries 2. Books and reading 3. Reading comprehension 4. School libraries -- Activity projects 5. Children's reading -- Educational aspects 6. Children -- Reading -- Educational aspects

ISBN 0-8389-0912-4

LC 2005028263

Grimes "led a school-wide research study with classroom teachers to transform the reading program at Lansdowne Elementary School in Baltimore. The study resulted in dramatic and measurable gains in student reading achievement. This book can be used as a toolkit to duplicate those results. Grimes's work is informed by solid educational research in the field of reading comprehension. The text is lively and clearly written, accessible to teachers and librarians." SLJ

Includes bibliographical references

Harada, Violet H.

Assessing for learning; librarians and teachers as partners. [by] Violet H. Harada and Joan M. Yoshina. 2nd ed.; Libraries Unlimited 2010 242p il pa $45

Grades: Adult Professional   **027.8**

1. School libraries 2. Instructional materials centers

ISBN 978-1-59884-470-2; 1-59884-470-9

First published 2055 with title: Assessing learning

"Using assessment tools familiar to the classroom teacher, the authors show how to use them in the library setting. Starting with the challenges that face 21st century schools, the rationale for schools as learning organizations is laid out. The tools for assessment are the main points of this title and include checklists, rubrics, rating scales, conferences, logs, personal correspondence, exit passes, graphic organizers, and student portfolios. . . . The tools for better instruction and assessment of learning need to be used by all educators, and this title provides examples and models for all librarians." Libr Media Connect

Includes bibliographical references

Hughes-Hassell, Sandra

School reform and the school library media specialist; [by] Sandra Hughes-Hassell and Violet H. Harada. Libraries Unlimited 2007 xxiii, 204p il (Principles and practice series) pa $40

Grades: Adult Professional   **027.8**

1. School libraries 2. Educational change 3. School libraries -- Relations with teachers and curriculum

ISBN 978-1-59158-427-8; 1-59158-427-2

LC 2007-16437

"This volume covers critical issues impacting school libraries today and offers practical solutions to meet these challenges. Written by leaders in the field such as Pam Berger, Carol Gordon, Barbara Stripling, and Ross Todd, the articles expound on implications of No Child Left Behind legislation, 21st-century literacy requirements, population diversity, and professional growth. . . . This volume will empower current and future school librarians as they embrace its guidelines." SLJ

Johnson, Doug

School libraries head for the edge; rants, recommendations, and reflections. Linworth Pub. 2010 196p pa $35

Grades: Adult Professional   **027.8**

1. School libraries

ISBN 978-1-58683-392-3; 1-58683-392-8

LC 2009-22053

"Eighty long-running 'Head for the Edge' columns in Library Media Connection and its predecessor, Technology Connection, are collected here, in topical clusters dealing with professional issues relevant to both veterans and newbies. . . . The columns are reflective, conversational, and characteristically humorous. . . . Chapters end with quotes, questions, and self-evaluative reflection that readers will be inspired to mirror. For all practitioners." SLJ

Morris, Betty J.

★ **Administering** the school library media center; 5th ed.; Libraries Unlimited 2010 580p il $75; pa $60

Grades: Adult Professional   **027.8**

1. School libraries 2. Instructional materials centers

ISBN 978-1-59158-685-2; 1-59158-685-2; 978-1-59158-689-0 pa; 1-59158-689-5 pa

LC 2010015939

First published 1973 under the authorship of John T. Gillespie and Diana L. Spirt with title: Creating a school media program

"This updated edition provides a comprehensive and current examination of the multiple and varied jobs media specialists do to manage today's school library media centers. . . . Sample job description statements, media center budgets, and budget justification tools are thorough and valuable references. Morris addresses the proactive and visible leadership role that today's media specialists must take on to remain viable and support student learning. . . . The title supports concepts on current standards. It is a forward thinking text for new or future library media specialists and a realistic, functional reference for practitioners." Libr Media Connect

Includes bibliographical references

Ray, Virginia Lawrence

School wide book events; how to make them happen. [by] Virginia Lawrence Ray. Libraries Unlimited 2003 133p pa $28

Grades: Adult Professional   **027.8**

1. School libraries 2. Books and reading 3. Reading promotion 4. Children -- Books and reading 5. School libraries -- Activity programs 6. Language arts (Elementary) -- Activity programs

ISBN 978-1-59158-038-6 pa; 1-59158-038-2 pa

LC 2003-47724

"The author's intent is to present ideas on how to celebrate reading across grade levels and curriculum, involving teachers, administration, faculty, and students both in preparation and actual activities. She proposes that school libraries have a Book Event for the whole school. . . . All events require simple resources and are easy to follow even for school systems with extremely limited budgets." SLJ

Includes bibliographical references

Schuckett, Sandy

Political advocacy for school librarians; you have the power! Linworth Pub. 2004 128p pa $39.95

Grades: Adult Professional   027.8

1. Lobbying 2. School libraries 3. Libraries and community

ISBN 1-58683-158-5

LC 2004-4869

"Schuckett motivates and explicitly details an exciting 'how-to' of political lobbying at all levels—from the school site and local board all the way to the national level. . . . School librarians need political clout, and Schuckett shows us how to get it." SLJ

Includes bibliographical references

Stephens, Claire Gatrell

Library 101; a handbook for the school library media specialist. [by] Claire Gatrell Stephens and Patricia Franklin. Libraries Unlimited 2007 233p il pa $35

Grades: Adult Professional   027.8

1. School libraries 2. Instructional materials centers 3. Procedure manuals 4. Libraries -- Handbooks, manuals, etc.

ISBN 978-1-59158-324-0; 1-59158-324-1

LC 2007-18420

"This handbook provides information for brand-new and inexperienced librarians preparing for a first job in a school library media center. Articles are divided into four subcategories covering day-to-day operations (library organization, circulation policies, media management, scheduling, staffing, and media center arrangement); collaboration with teachers; collection development and management; and equipment." Booklist

Includes bibliographical references

Valenza, Joyce Kasman

★ **Power** tools recharged; 125+ essential forms and presentations for your school library information program. illustrated by Emily Valenza. American Library Association 2004 various paging il pa $55

Grades: Adult Professional   027.8

1. School libraries 2. Libraries -- Public relations 3. School libraries -- Marketing 4. School libraries -- Activity programs 5. School libraries -- Administration -- Forms 6. Media programs (Educational) -- Administration -- Forms

ISBN 0-8389-0880-2

LC 2004-5853

First published 1998 with title: Power tools

This offers a compilation of customizable, reproducible forms and handouts for school library administration and assessment, teaching information literacy, making presentations. Included are such items as templates for a gift book program, letters to parents and faculty members, a checklist of tasks, library equipment sign-out forms, and a reading interest survey.

Includes bibliographical references

Van Deusen, Jean Donham

Enhancing teaching and learning; a leadership guide for school library media specialists. [by] Jean Donham. rev. ed.; Neal-Schuman Publishers 2008 353p il pa $65

Grades: Adult Professional   027.8

1. School libraries 2. Instructional materials centers 3. School libraries -- Aims and objectives

ISBN 978-1-55570-647-0; 1-55570-647-9

LC 2008-23321

First published 1998

"This title is well-written, well-researched, and informative. Donham masterfully weaves together current AASL standards and the real world of today's media specialist." Voice Youth Advocates

Includes bibliographical references

Woolls, E. Blanche

The **school** library media manager; [by] Blanche Woolls. 4th ed; Libraries Unlimited 2008 279p il (Library and information science text series) $55; pa $45

Grades: Adult Professional   027.8

1. School libraries 2. Instructional materials centers 3. School libraries -- Administration

ISBN 978-1-59158-648-7; 1-59158-648-8; 978-1-59158-643-2 pa; 1-59158-643-7 pa

LC 2008-18081

First published 1994

Provides information "for teaching the administration of school library media centers. . . . Readers learn how to choose a credential program, how to find the requirements for working in each of the 50 states, what to do when looking for and choosing a job, and how to survive the first week in that new position. . . . Sections also cover: collaborating with teachers, how to write a proposal, and how to accept leadership responsibilities, including the role of a media specialist in the legislative process." Publisher's note

Includes bibliographical references

028   Reading and use of other information media

Ross, Val

You can't read this; forbidden books, lost writing, mistranslations, & codes. Tundra Books 2006 140p il $19.95

Grades: 7 8 9 10   028

1. Books -- Censorship 2. Books and reading -- History 3. Ciphers 4. Young adult literature -- Works 5. Prohibited books 6. Books and reading -- History

ISBN 0-88776-732-X

The author "offers a unique historical survey based around a broadly interpreted theme: the power of reading. The chronologically arranged chapters touch on censorship, literacy, and the influence of political texts. . . . The accounts are fascinating, and Ross is an accomplished storyteller who brings history right into the present. Scattered

black-and-white photos and art illustrate this timely, power-ful text." Booklist
Includes bibliographical references

028.1   Reviews

Baxter, Kathleen A.
★ **From** cover to cover; evaluating and review-ing children's books. rev ed.; Collins 2010 229p $14.99
Grades: Adult Professional   028.1
1. Books -- Reviews 2. Children's literature -- History and criticism
ISBN 978-0-06-077757-9; 0-06-077757-5
First published 1997
The author addresses the distinctions between evaluation and review, and what makes a good children's book. She dis-cusses categories of children's books including nonfiction; traditional literature (folktales, myths, legends, etc.); poetry, verse, rhymes, and songs; picture books; easy readers and transitional books; and fiction. She then describes the pro-cess of writing a review.
This is a "very complete resource that will continue to be the venerable reference tool and required reading for educa-tion and library-science students, youth librarians, teachers, and anyone else interested in kids, reading, and children's literature." SLJ

★ **Into** focus; understanding and creating middle school readers. editors: Kylene Beers, Barbara G. Samuels. Christopher-Gordon Pubs. 1998 xx, 490p il pa $44.95
Grades: Adult Professional   028.1
1. Reading   2. Reading (Middle school) 3. Literature -- Study and teaching 4. Reading (Middle school) --Handbooks, manuals, etc 5. Middle school students --Books and reading -- Handbooks, manuals, etc
ISBN 0-926842-64-1
In this "handbook, 24 experts from the fields of reading theory, library science, response theory, children's literature, and middle school philosophy present strategies, describe programs, and provide lists that foster academic success and a lifelong love of reading." SLJ
Includes bibliographical references

Naidoo, Jamie Campbell
★ **Rainbow** family collections; selecting and using children's books with lesbian, gay, bisexual, transgender, and queer content. Jamie Campbell Nai-doo. Libraries Unlimited, an imprint of ABC-CLIO, LLC 2012 xvii, 260 p.p ill. (hardback) $50
Grades: Professional   028.1
1. Libraries and sexual minorities 2. Sexual minorities in literature 3. EDUCATION -- Professional Development 4. Libraries and sexual minorities -- United States 5. Libraries -- Special collections -- Sexual minorities   6. Children's libraries -- Collection development -- United States 7. Children's libraries -- Services to minorities -- United States 8. Children of sexual minority parents -- Books and reading 9. LANGUAGE

ARTS & DISCIPLINES -- Library & Information Science -- School Media 10. LANGUAGE ARTS & DISCIPLINES -- Library & Information Science -- Collection Development
ISBN 1598849603; 9781598849608
LC 2012008362
This book by Jamie Campbell Naidoo "highlight[s] titles for children from infancy to age 11" featuring lesbian, gay, bisexual, transgender, and queer content. It "supplies a syn-opsis of the title's content, lists awards it has received, cites professional reviews, and provides suggestions for librarians considering acquisition. The book also provides a brief his-torical overview of LGBTQ children's literature along with the major book awards for this genre." (Publisher's note)
Includes bibliographical references and index

Schall, Lucy
Value-packed booktalks; genre talks and more for teen readers. Libraries Unlimited 2011 261p pa $45; e-book $45
Grades: Adult Professional   028.1
1. Book talks   2. Fiction genres 3. Values --Bibliography 4. Teenagers -- Books and reading 5. Young adult literature -- Bibliography
ISBN 978-1-59884-735-2 pa; 978-1-59884-736-9 e-book
LC 2010053243
"This volume provides an in-depth break-down of nearly 100 books in a variety of categories. Each selection features a title summary, suggested page numbers for read-aloud moments, a sample booktalk, invaluable connections to the school curriculum, and related works. Each category, such as 'Problem Solving: Mystery' and 'Heritage: Historical Books,' also includes several helpful subcategories, includ-ing 'Loyalty' and 'Equality.' . . . While this book will prove to be a useful tool, it should be used in tandem with other guides that include more classics." SLJ
Includes bibliographical references

Young Adult Library Services Association
★ **Best** books for young adults; edited by Holly Koelling; foreword by Betty Carter. 3rd ed; Ameri-can Library Association 2007 346p il pa $42
Grades: Adult Professional   028.1
1. Best books 2. Reference books   3. Teenagers -- Books and reading 4. Young adult literature --Bibliography
ISBN 978-0-8389-3569-9; 0-8389-3569-9
LC 2007-26009
First published 1994 under the editorship of Betty Carter
This "is a classic, standard resource for collection build-ing and on-the-spot readers' advisory. . . . Absolutely indis-pensable for school and public libraries." Booklist
Includes bibliographical references

028.5   Reading and use of other information media by young people

Barr, Catherine
Best books for middle school and junior high readers; grades 6-9. [by] Catherine Barr and John T.

Gillespie. 2nd ed; Libraries Unlimited 2009 1242p (Children's and young adult literature reference series) lib bdg $85

Grades: Adult Professional   **028.5**
1. Books and reading   2. Teenagers -- Books and reading 3. Children's literature -- Bibliography 4. Young adult literature -- Bibliography
ISBN 978-1-59158-573-2 lib bdg; 1-59158-573-2 lib bdg

LC 2008-50755
First published 2004
"This guide to books for readers in grades six through nine lists approximately 15,000 titles, now including those published from 2004 through 2008. Titles were selected primarily on the basis of reviews in Booklist, School Library Journal, VOYA, and other review journals. Arrangement is first by subject or genre and then alphabetically by author. In addition to author and title, each listing contains reading level, publication data, a brief annotation, Dewey decimal classification number, and citations for reviews. . . . Best Books titles are valuable collection-development tools for school and public libraries." Booklist

Bartel, Julie
Annotated book lists for every teen reader; the best from the experts at YALSA-BK. [by] Julie Bartel and Pam Spencer Holley for the Young Adult Library Services Association. Neal-Schuman Publishers 2011 270p pa $65

Grades: Adult Professional   **028.5**
1. Best books   2. Teenagers -- Books and reading 3. Young adult literature -- Bibliography 4. Young adult literature -- Stories, plots, etc.
ISBN 1-55570-658-4; 978-1-55570-658-6

LC 2010-33312
"Bartel and Holley have scoured the YALSA-BK archives to find more than 1100 books with broad teen readership. While the book's primary purpose is for readers' advisory, the authors also suggest it will be useful in creating displays as well as igniting creativity. . . . The scope is wide ranging with a good mix of standards, classics, and newer titles. With a highly appropriate title, this volume hits the mark." SLJ
Includes bibliographical references

Baxter, Kathleen A.
Gotcha again for guys! more nonfiction books to get boys excited about reading. [by] Kathleen A. Baxter and Marcia Agness Kochel. Libraries Unlimited 2010 248p il pa $35

Grades: Adult Professional   **028.5**
1. Book talks   2. Boys -- Books and reading 3. Boys 4. Children's literature -- Bibliography
ISBN 978-1-59884-376-7 pa; 1-59884-376-1 pa; 978-1-59884-377-4 e-book

LC 2010036577
This "highlights books published mainly between 2007 and 2009. Twelve chapters cover themes such as sports, animals, gross/disgusting stuff, mysteries/disasters, and machines. Each one features anywhere from a few to two dozen ready-to-use booktalks, most aimed at grades 3-8, along with

extensive bibliographies (not annotated) of other titles that have received good reviews in Booklist, Horn Book Guide, and School Library Journal. New to this volume are enlightening interviews with male authors such as Kadir Nelson, Nic Bishop, and Seymour Simon, whose books are featured in the text. The introduction also lists ideas for promoting books to boys in public libraries and school media centers." SLJ
Includes bibliographical references

Gotcha good! nonfiction books to get kids excited about reading. [by] Kathleen A. Baxter and Marcia Agness Kochel. Libraries Unlimited 2008 259p pa $35

Grades: Adult Professional   **028.5**
1. Books and reading   2. Children's literature -- Bibliography 3. Young adult literature -- Bibliography
ISBN 978-1-59158-654-8 pa; 1-59158-654-2 pa

LC 2008010350
"In addition to annotations for over 1000 nonfiction titles, [the authors] profile eight prolific authors and provide fun top-10 features for the various subjects covered. . . . The titles chosen are truly high quality, relevant, and up-to-date, with suggested ages provided, most ranging from grades three through eight. . . . A must-have for all librarians who want to get kids excited about nonfiction." SLJ
Includes bibliographical references

Bilz, Rachelle Lasky
Life is tough; guys, growing up, and young adult literature. [by] Rachelle Lasky Bilz. Scarecrow Press 2004 xiii, 153p (Scarecrow studies in young adult literature) $45

Grades: Adult Professional   **028.5**
1. Boys -- Books and reading 2. Young adult literature -- Bibliography
ISBN 0-8108-5055-9; 978-0-8108-5055-2

LC 2004-8439
"Bilz focuses on books that can help boys mature into resourceful, well-adjusted young men. She begins with an overview of classic tales of heroism in which strong male protagonists like Robin Hood, King Arthur, and Robinson Crusoe not only exhibit their steely strengths, but share, too, their fears and doubts along the way. Her lists of contemporary treatments and read-alikes of each of these tales will be particularly helpful to educators seeking thematic bridges between old and new. . . . This is a useful bibliography for anyone who wants to place books in the paths of boys as beacons toward meaningful manhood." SLJ

Bodart, Joni Richards
Radical reads 2; working with the newest edgy titles for teens. Scarecrow Press 2010 479p pa $45
Grades: Adult Professional   **028.5**
1. Teenagers -- Books and reading 2. Young adult literature -- Bibliography
ISBN 978-0-8108-6908-0; 0-8108-6908-X

LC 2009-25724
Bodart "offers insight into writing book reports and booktalks that secondary school English teachers and library media specialists can share with students. . . . The detailed book entries include citations with suggested reading and

interest levels designated by middle school, younger high school, and older high school. Also included are subject areas, character descriptions, a booktalk and booktalk ideas, a list of major themes and ideas, book report ideas, risks, strengths, awards, and full-text reviews. The entries' detail will be an asset in readers' advisory and a quick resource to check the content and reviews for a title that is being questioned." Voice Youth Advocates

Includes bibliographical references

Booth, Heather

★ **Serving** teens through readers' advisory. American Library Association 2007 159p (ALA readers' advisory series) pa $36

Grades: Adult Professional   **028.5**

1. Young adults' libraries 2. Reader guidance 3. Young adults' reading 4. Teenagers -- Books and reading 5. Young adult literature -- Bibliography
ISBN 0-8389-0930-2; 978-0-8389-0930-0

LC 2006-36134

"The first few chapters discuss teen reading habits and why readers' advisory for this group is different and also provide 'tips for the generalist' who may not be an expert in teen fiction. Other chapters cover elements of the readers' advisory interaction . . . and survey the appropriate books. Two unique chapters offer well-thought-out and practical advice on making reading-related homework assignments less painful for staff and students as well as suggestions for providing readers' advisory services to teens through their parents or other adults. . . . [This] is essential reading for all readers' advisors and any library staff who work with teens." Booklist

Includes bibliographical references

Bromann, Jennifer

★ **Booktalking** that works. Neal-Schuman 2001 155p (Teens @ the library series) pa $35

Grades: Adult Professional   **028.5**

1. Book talks 2. Young adults' libraries 3. Reading promotion 4. Teenagers -- Books and reading 5. Public libraries -- Services to teenagers 6. Young adults' libraries -- Activity programs 7. Young adults' library services -- Activity projects
ISBN 1-55570-403-4

LC 2001-18340

"Practical, smart, hip, and irreverent. . . . A fun read that will encourage you to find your own personal style." Booklist

Includes bibliographical references

More booktalking that works. Neal-Schuman 2005 145p (Teens @ the library series) pa $49.95

Grades: Adult Professional   **028.5**

1. Book talks 2. Young adults' libraries 3. Teenagers -- Books and reading 4. Young adults' library services -- Activity projects
ISBN 1-55570-525-1

LC 2005-2326

"Bromann has expanded on her previous booktalking title, Booktalking That Works (Neal-Schuman, 2001), with additional practical advice based on added years of experience. . . . The first part of this book is arranged in a question-and-answer format covering various aspects of booktalking,

from creating and presenting booktalks to choosing books and developing hooks for reluctant readers. This section includes a list of the top-20 types of books to booktalk and 10 very brief quick talks. The second section offers 200 booktalks of varying length and covering several fiction and nonfiction genres that she encourages librarians to adapt for personal use. . . . School and public librarians will find many helpful hints, whether they are novice or veteran booktalkers." Booklist

Brooks, Wanda M.

Embracing, evaluating, and examining African American children's and young adult literature; edited by Wanda M. Brooks, Jonda C. McNair; foreword by Rudine Sims Bishop. Scarecrow Press 2008 251p pa $45

Grades: Adult Professional   **028.5**

1. African Americans in literature 2. Children -- Books and reading 3. Children's literature -- History and criticism 4. Young adult literature -- History and criticism 5. American literature -- African American authors -- History and criticism
ISBN 978-0-8108-6027-8 pa; 0-8108-6027-9 pa

LC 2007025703

"Brooks and McNair have compiled 12 scholarly studies about the use of books by and about African-American children and young adults in classrooms across the United States. Selections include a detailed textual analysis of the work of Arna Bontemps and Langston Hughes; a sociolinguistic perspective on readers' response to books containing African-American Vernacular English; and a detailed study of the books used as classroom read-alouds by teachers in rural schools, which found that only three percent were about African Americans. While each study is complete in and of itself, the text as a whole gives a broad picture of what is currently being done in this field, both in K-12 classrooms and college classes that emphasize children's literature." SLJ

Includes bibliographical references

Cart, Michael

★ **Young** adult literature: from romance to realism; rev ed.; American Library Association 2010 242p pa $60

Grades: Adult Professional   **028.5**

1. Teenagers -- Books and reading 2. Young adults' literature -- History 3. Young adult literature -- History and criticism
ISBN 978-0-8389-1045-0; 0-8389-1045-9

LC 2010-13674

A revised edition of: From romance to realism: 50 years of growth and change in young adult literature, published 1996 by HarperCollins Pub.

"This updated and expanded second edition of Cart's already lively and comprehensive history of young adult literature (1996) is an essential resource. It is divided into two sections ('That Was Then' and 'This Is Now'), and the author once again discusses the history and current moment to offer a broad and loving overview of the rich literature. . . . Highly accessible and thorough, the text is a staple for any study of the canon." SLJ

Includes bibliographical references

Collins, Joan

Motivating readers in the middle grades; [by] Joan Collins. Linworth Pub. 2008 128p il pa $36.95

Grades: Adult Professional   **028.5**

1. Middle schools 2. Youth -- Books and reading
ISBN 978-1-58683-297-1; 1-58683-297-2

LC 2007-51426

"This workbook describes three six-week projects for inciting reading motivation in grades six through eight, developed by Massachusetts middle school educators. . . . This resource is supremely teacher-friendly; projects are presented by grade with concise rationales, instructions, suggestions, and caveats. Suggested novels are annotated, varied, and age appropriate." Voice Youth Advocates

Includes bibliographical references

Cox Clark, Ruth E.

Tantalizing tidbits for middle schoolers; quick booktalks for the busy middle school and jr. high library media specialist. [by] Ruth E. Cox Clark. Linworth Pub. 2005 140p pa $36.95

Grades: Adult Professional   **028.5**

1. Book talks 2. Books and reading 3. Children's literature -- Bibliography 4. Young adult literature -- Bibliography
ISBN 1-58683-195-X

LC 2005013159

"In the first sections, the author provides information on annual recommended reading lists and children's book awards and describes different booktalking techniques. Section 5, the heart of the book, offers 75 booktalk examples. For each, the author provides bibliographic information, subjects and genres, references to pertinent reading lists and awards, and interest levels. This information is followed by a brief annotation, a booktalk, a page reference for an excerpt to read, a curriculum connection, and a list of similar books. A list of themes and an index of the books and authors mentioned conclude the volume, which is highly recommended for librarians, teachers, and students." Booklist

★ **Dear** author; letters of hope. edited by Joan F. Kaywell; with an introduction by Catherine Ryan Hyde. Philomel Books 2007 222p $14.99

Grades: 8 9 10 11 12   **028.5**

1. Authors, American 2. Teenagers -- Books and reading 3. Books and reading 4. Authors and readers
ISBN 978-0-399-23705-8; 0-399-23705-4

LC 2006-21050

"Chris Lynch, Nancy Garden, and Christopher Paul Curtis and are just a few of the well-known authors who respond to real teens' letters in this powerful compilation. Not mere fan mail, the selections speak about teens' gravest concerns—bullying, derailed friendships, racism, date rape, incest, illness, divorce, and more—and they describe how the authors' books helped them face the heartaches. . . . For some readers, this dialogue between writers and readers will be inspiring; for those harboring their own wounding secrets, it may be lifesaving." Booklist

Includes bibliographical references

Diamant-Cohen, Betsy

Booktalking bonanza; ten ready-to-use multimedia sessions for the busy librarian. American Library Association 2009 240p il pa $40

Grades: Adult Professional   **028.5**

1. Book talks 2. Books and reading
ISBN 978-0-8389-0965-2; 0-8389-0965-5

LC 2008-15371

"This volume is a collection of scripts for multimedia-enriched booktalks. After an introductory chapter that explains the reasoning for this approach, 10 scripts are outlined. Books, music, video, and Web sites are included for each one. The programs are geared toward elementary-aged children, although suggestions for adapting them for a middle or high school audience are included." SLJ

Includes bibliographical references

Embracing, evaluating, and examining African American children's and young adult literature; edited by Wanda M. Brooks, Jonda C. McNair; foreword by Rudine Sims Bishop. Scarecrow Press 2008 251p pa $45

Grades: Adult Professional   **028.5**

1. African Americans in literature 2. Children -- Books and reading 3. Children's literature -- History and criticism 4. Young adult literature -- History and criticism 5. American literature -- African American authors -- History and criticism
ISBN 978-0-8108-6027-8 pa; 0-8108-6027-9 pa

LC 2007025703

"Brooks and McNair have compiled 12 scholarly studies about the use of books by and about African-American children and young adults in classrooms across the United States. Selections include a detailed textual analysis of the work of Arna Bontemps and Langston Hughes; a sociolinguistic perspective on readers' response to books containing African-American Vernacular English; and a detailed study of the books used as classroom read-alouds by teachers in rural schools, which found that only three percent were about African Americans. While each study is complete in and of itself, the text as a whole gives a broad picture of what is currently being done in this field, both in K-12 classrooms and college classes that emphasize children's literature." SLJ

Includes bibliographical references

Fraser, Elizabeth

Reality rules! a guide to teen nonfiction reading interests. Libraries Unlimited 2008 246p (Genreflecting advisory series) $50.00

Grades: Adult Professional   **028.5**

1. Reference books 2. Teenagers -- Books and reading 3. Young adult literature -- Bibliography
ISBN 9781591585633

LC 2007-51063

"This guide focuses on titles created for teens and those with strong teen appeal. The author covers more than 500 titles published since 2000, also including benchmarks and perennial classics." Publisher's note

Includes bibliographical references

Gilmore, Barry

★ **Speaking** volumes; how to get students discussing books, and much more. Heinemann 2006 128p pa $17.95

Grades: Adult Professional   **028.5**
1. Books and reading
ISBN 978-0-325-00915-5 pa; 0-325-00915-5 pa
     LC 2005-28371

"Gilmore provides practical, hands-on methods to involve students in oral and written classroom conversations that encourage reflection and ultimately polished, coherent expression. . . . Both new and seasoned discussion leaders will want a copy for repeated reference." Voice Youth Advocates

Includes bibliographical references

Handbook of research on children's and young adult literature; edited by Shelby A. Wolf . . . [et al.] Routledge 2010 555p $295; pa $119.95

Grades: Adult Professional   **028.5**
1. Children's literature -- History and criticism   2. Young adult literature -- History and criticism
ISBN 978-0-415-96505-7; 0-415-96505-5; 978-0-415-96506-4 pa; 0-415-96506-3 pa; 978-0-203-84354-3 e-book
     LC 2010-16339

"The book examines readers, texts, and cultural contexts of children's literature and across the three intersecting disciplines of Education, English, and Library and Information Science, in an effort to model a multidisciplinary approach to children's literature research. Thirty-seven scholarly articles, by figures such as Eliza Dresang, Rudine Sims Bishop, and Roderick McGillis . . . are counterpointed by responses that often provide more personal perspectives, including insights from noted authors such as Lois Lowry, M. T. Anderson, and Markus Zusak." Bull Cent Child Books

Honnold, RoseMary

The **teen** reader's advisor. Neal-Schuman Publishers 2006 491p (Teens @ the library series) pa $75

Grades: Adult Professional   **028.5**
1. Young adults' libraries   2. Teenagers -- Books and reading   3. Young adult literature -- Bibliography
ISBN 1-55570-551-0
     LC 2006-12640

"The first part deals with the challenges of working with teens, from developing a rapport and dealing with the more conservative adults in their lives, to marketing a YA collection to its audience. The author's descriptions of the major awards and lists relating to the literature as well as the list of print and online reader's advisory resources are sure to be helpful. Part two consists of subject and genre lists. Each one has at least 10 titles. The annotations are excellent." SLJ

Includes bibliographical references

Jones, Patrick

★ **Connecting** with reluctant teen readers; tips, titles, and tools. [by] Patrick Jones, Maureen L. Hartman, Patricia Taylor. Neal-Schuman Publishers 2006 xxi, 314p $59.95

Grades: Adult Professional   **028.5**
1. Young adults' libraries   2. Teenagers -- Books and reading   3. Young adult literature -- Bibliography
ISBN 1-55570-571-5; 978-1-55570-571-8
     LC 2006-12355

"Well written and well researched, this practical hands-on guide to defining and wooing reluctant readers is a must-read for librarians and teachers who work with adolescents. It is divided into three parts: 'Tips That Work,' 'Titles That Work,' and 'Tools That Work.'" SLJ

Includes bibliographical references

Kajder, Sara B.

Bringing the outside in; visual ways to engage reluctant readers. [by] Sara B. Kajder; foreword by Linda Rief. Stenhouse Publishers 2006 105p il $18.50

Grades: Adult Professional   **028.5**
1. Reading
ISBN 1-57110-401-1; 978-1-57110-401-4
     LC 2005056415

"Teachers, especially those working with at-risk students, will be thankful for hands-on methods to engage teens through technology." Voice Youth Advocates

Includes bibliographical references

Keane, Nancy J.

101 great, ready-to-use book lists for children; Nancy J. Keane. Libraries Unlimited, an imprint of ABC-CLIO, LLC 2012 xiv, 246 p.p (paperback) $45

Grades: Adult Professional   **028.5**
1. Best books   2. Children -- Books and reading   3. School libraries -- Book lists   4. Children's libraries -- Book lists   5. Children's literature -- Bibliography   6. Children -- Books and reading -- United States
ISBN 1610690834; 9781610690836
     LC 2011051429

Includes bibliographical references and index

101 great, ready-to-use book lists for teens; Nancy J. Keane. Libraries Unlimited, an imprint of ABC-CLIO, LLC 2012 xiv, 263 p.p (paperback) $40; (ebook) $40

Grades: Adult Professional   **028.5**
1. Book selection   2. Books and reading   3. Young adult literature -- Bibliography   4. High school libraries -- Book lists   5. Teenagers -- Books and reading -- United States
ISBN 1610691342; 9781610691345; 9781610691352
     LC 2011051428

This book offers a "compilation of YA [Young Adult] materials . . . published prior to August 2011. The book is divided . . . into themed lists such as 'Genres,' 'Readalikes,' and 'Teaching Literary Elements.' The themes . . . include . . . topics such as 'Romance,' 'Autism & Asperger's Syndrome,' 'Different Belief Systems,' and 'Crossing the Border.' Each entry includes the title, author, publisher, publication date, page numbers, an annotation, Lexile level when available, and interest level by grade or age range." (School Library Journal)

Includes bibliographical references and index

★ **Booktalking** across the curriculum: the middle years. Libraries Unlimited 2002 217p il pa $30

Grades: Adult Professional   028.5
1. Book talks 2. Books and reading 3. Book talks -- United States 4. Content area reading -- United States 5. Reading (Middle school) -- United States 6. Children's literature -- Study and teaching (Middle school) -- United States
ISBN 1-56308-937-8

LC 2002-12171

"The booktalks are well written, easy to use, and encourage critical thinking." Libr Media Connect

Includes bibliographical references

The **big** book of teen reading lists; 100 great, ready-to-use book lists for educators, librarians, parents, and teens. Libraries Unlimited 2006 297p pa $35

Grades: Adult Professional   028.5
1. Teenagers -- Books and reading 2. Young adult literature -- Bibliography
ISBN 1-59158-333-0; 978-1-59158-333-2

LC 2006-17627

"Keane has produced another great resource for teachers, librarians, and students, especially reluctant readers." SLJ

Includes bibliographical references

Knowles, Elizabeth
Boys and literacy; practical strategies for librarians, teachers, and parents. [by] Elizabeth Knowles and Martha Smith. Libraries Unlimited 2005 xxi, 164p il pa $35

Grades: Adult Professional   028.5
1. Reading interests 2. Boys -- Books and reading 3. Children's literature -- Bibliography 4. Young adult literature -- Bibliography
ISBN 1-59158-212-1

"Boys don't seem to like to read. . . . This book briefly explores the research about this situation, outlines strategies to reverse this trend, and lists books within genres that boys enjoy reading. . . . The best part of the book is the author section. . . . For each author covered, there is a complete list of books, contact information, . . . and Web sites. . . . This is a wonderful resource for teachers and parents to begin working on improving literacy with boys." Booklist

Krashen, Stephen D.
★ The **power** of reading; insights from the research. by Stephen D. Krashen. 2nd ed; Libraries Unlimited 2004 199p bibl diag tab $25

Grades: Adult Professional   028.5
1. Reading 2. Literacy 3. Books and reading 4. Children -- Reading
ISBN 1-59158-169-9 pa

LC 2004-44207

First published 1993

The author presents research for "the argument that free voluntary reading (FVR) is the most effective tool available for increasing literacy. . . . Some of the topics he explores include the research surrounding second language acquisition, reading rewards and incentives programs, and some of today's popular 'electronic reading products.'" Publisher's note

Includes bibliographical references

Larson, Jeanette C.
Bringing mysteries alive for children and young adults; [by] Jeanette Larson. Linworth Pub. 2004 134p il pa $39.95

Grades: Adult Professional   028.5
1. Interdisciplinary approach in education 2. Children -- Books and reading 3. Activity programs in education 4. Teenagers -- Books and reading 5. Children's literature -- Bibliography 6. Children's libraries -- Activity programs 7. Children -- Books and reading -- United States 8. Teenagers -- Books and reading -- United States 9. Detective and mystery stories -- Study and teaching
ISBN 1-58683-012-0

LC 2003-22064

"Larson offers a thorough introduction to the genre and discusses why teachers and librarians should use it in language-arts plans. She provides multiple suggestions for integrating mysteries into the classroom curriculum or special programs, discussing the different types of mysteries and making suggestions for each category...The book has excellent ideas for beginning as well as seasoned professionals." SLJ

Includes bibliographical references

Lukenbill, W. Bernard
Biography in the lives of youth; culture, society, and information. Libraries Unlimited 2006 251p il pa $45

Grades: Adult Professional   028.5
1. Biography 2. Children's libraries 3. Young adults' libraries 4. Children -- Books and reading 5. Teenagers -- Books and reading 6. Biography 7. Children's literature -- Non-fiction 8. School libraries -- Activity projects 9. Children's reading -- Psychological aspects 10. Children -- Reading -- Psychological aspects 12. Young adults -- Reading -- Psychological aspects
ISBN 1-59158-284-9

LC 2006007466

"Reflecting on the different and varied uses of biography depending on the age, interests, and developmental needs of students, Lukenbill breaks the genre down into the different types of biographies and how they have changed over time. He includes author and literature suggestions throughout the text and concludes with an extensive bibliography of selection aids, including books and periodicals, for locating recommended titles." SLJ

Includes bibliographical references

McDaniel, Deanna
Gentle reads; great books to warm hearts and lift spirits, grades 5-9. [by] Deanna J. McDaniel. Li-

braries Unlimited 2008 318p (Children's and young adult literature reference series) $45

Grades: Adult Professional   **028.5**
1. Children's literature -- Bibliography 2. Young adult literature -- Bibliography
ISBN 978-1-59158-491-9

LC 2008018878

This includes "500 recommended titles. Here readers will find books with divorce, drug use, attempted suicides, and more but they all meet the criteria the author has set by being either inspiring, heartwarming, or in some way uplifting. . . . Arranged by genres, the entries include full bibliographic information, an annotation, and a description of why the book fits the 'gentle criteria.'" SLJ
Includes bibliographical references

Nilsen, Alleen Pace

★ **Literature** for today's young adults; [by] Alleen Pace Nilsen, Kenneth L. Donelson. 8th ed; Allyn and Bacon/Pearson 2008 xx, 491p il $122.20

Grades: Adult Professional   **028.5**
1. Books and reading 2. Young adult literature -- History and criticism
ISBN 978-0-205-59323-1; 0-205-59323-2

LC 2008-2625

First published 1980

This is an "introduction to young adult literature framed within a literary, historical, and social context. The authors provide teachers with criteria for evaluating books of all genres, from poetry and nonfiction to mysteries, science fiction, and graphic novels. . . . [It also includes coverage of] issues such as pop culture and mass media." Publisher's note
Includes bibliographical references

Quick and popular reads for teens; edited by Pam Spencer Holley for the Young Adult Library Services Association. American Library Association 2009 228p pa $45

Grades: Adult Professional   **028.5**
1. Teenagers -- Books and reading 2. Young adult literature -- Bibliography
ISBN 978-0-8389-3577-4; 0-8389-3577-X

LC 2008-49691

"This practical guide pulls together the Quick Picks for the Reluctant Young Adult Reader lists and the Popular Paperbacks for Young Adults lists created by the Young Adult Library Services Association (YALSA), a division of the American Library Association (ALA) from 1999 to 2008. . . . [The editor] assembles the lists into separate Nonfiction and Fiction categories, with an additional chapter containing Theme-Oriented Booklists that is useful for putting together displays, bookmarks, or readers' advisory. . . . This essential tool for librarians will help them find that popular book to turn a reluctant reader into a teen who appreciates the enjoyment one comes from reading." Voice Youth Advocates
Includes bibliographical references

Saccardi, Marianne

Books that teach kids to write; [by] Marianne C. Saccardi. Libraries Unlimited 2011 150p pa $30; e-book $30

Grades: Adult Professional   **028.5**
1. Creative writing 2. Books and reading 3. Literature -- Study and teaching
ISBN 978-1-59884-451-1 pa; 978-1-59884-452-8 e-book

LC 2011001866

"Divided into sections such as 'Making Stories Unique,' 'Creating Memorable Characters,' and 'Putting Passion and Voice into Nonfiction Writing,' this book gives countless recommendations for teaching various skills. Saccardi offers short, annotated summaries of mentor texts and describes how they can be used to model good writing techniques. . . . After reading this resource, educators will have a long wish list of materials to purchase." SLJ
Includes bibliographical references

Schall, Lucy

Genre talks for teens; booktalks and more for every teen reading interest. Libraries Unlimited 2009 309p pa $40

Grades: Adult Professional   **028.5**
1. Book talks 2. Teenagers -- Books and reading
ISBN 978-1-59158-743-9; 1-59158-743-3

LC 2008-54984

"Schall has chosen about 100 books published since 2003 for inclusion in this volume. . . . Each book includes a summary, a booktalk, a read-aloud/reader response sampling, supporting learning activities, and related works. Books are keyed by theme, reading level, and audience. . . . Because of its varied ways to engage readers and its current coverage, the book is a welcome addition." Booklist
Includes bibliographical references

Silvey, Anita

500 great books for teens. Houghton Mifflin Co. 2006 397p $26

Grades: Adult Professional   **028.5**
1. Teenagers -- Books and reading 2. Young adult literature -- Bibliography
ISBN 978-0-618-61296-3; 0-618-61296-3

LC 2006-3350

"Silvey selects and annotates five hundred titles for young adults, arranging them loosely in twenty-one chapters by genre and/or area of interest, from 'Adventure and Survival' to 'War and Conflict.' Each book is coded for either younger (12-14) or older (14-18) teens and gets a couple hundred words or so. . . . The selections are both sturdy and wide-ranging." Horn Book
Includes bibliographical references

Sullivan, Edward T.

Reaching reluctant young adult readers; a handbook for librarians and teachers. Scarecrow Press 2002 121p $24.50

Grades: Adult Professional   **028.5**
1. Teenagers -- Books and reading 2. Reading promotion -- United States 3. Young adult literature -- Bibliography 4. Reading (Middle school) -- United States 5. Preteens -- Books and reading -- United States 6. Teenagers -- Books and reading -- United States
ISBN 0-8108-4343-9

LC 2002-21219

"Sullivan explains his concern over the preponderance of 'aliterate' (able to read, but choosing not to) young adults. He defines young adult readers as those between the ages of 10 and 15. . . . He places responsibility for the problem on teachers, librarians, and parents and then offers strategies to reverse the trend. The bulk of the book concentrates on overlooked resources including fiction series and short stories, comics and graphic novels, nonfiction, magazines, picture books, and audiobooks. . . . A bibliography of professional resources completes the practical information provided. . . . A valuable tool to combat the nonreader." Booklist

Includes bibliographical references

Sullivan, Michael

★ **Connecting** boys with books 2; closing the reading gap. American Library Association 2009 119p il pa $40

Grades: Adult Professional   **028.5**

1. School libraries 2. Children's libraries 3. Young adults' libraries 4. Reading promotion 5. Boys -- Books and reading 6. Reading -- Sex differences 7. Teenage boys -- Books and reading 8. Children's libraries -- Activity programs 9. Young adults' libraries -- Activity programs

ISBN 978-0-8389-0979-9 pa; 0-8389-0979-5 pa

     LC 2008-34925

"A must-read for all librarians and media specialists." SLJ

Includes bibliographical references (p. 105-110)

Serving boys through readers' advisory. American Library Association 2010 152p (ALA readers' advisory series) pa $48

Grades: Adult Professional   **028.5**

1. Reference services (Libraries) 2. Boys -- Books and reading 3. Boys

ISBN 978-0-8389-1022-1; 0-8389-1022-X

     LC 2009-26841

"This volume was created to give a general direction when helping most boys select books. . . . Sullivan challenges us to throw out our preconceived notions about how to conduct such an interview. Methods of performing indirect readers' advisory with parents and teachers are included. The excellent booktalks for elementary, middle school, and high school boys alone make this a worthwhile purchase." SLJ

Includes bibliographical references

Temple, Charles A.

Children's books in children's hands; an introduction to their literature. [by] Charles Temple, Mariam Martinez, Junko Yokota; with contributions by Evelyn B. Freeman. 3rd ed.; Pearson Allyn and Bacon 2006 xxv, 630p il $129.33

Grades: Adult Professional   **028.5**

1. Books and reading 2. Children's literature -- History and criticism

ISBN 0-205-42043-5; 978-0-205-42043-8

     LC 2006272616

First published 1998

Part I covers the intellectual development of children, literary elements of children's literature, and reader response criticism. Part II surveys the literature by genre. Part III shows how to create a literature-based classroom through

activities, classroom libraries, and book discussions. Appendices list award-winning titles, professional organizations, publishers, children's periodicals and Web sites. This edition has been updated to include coverage of such topics as technology in the classroom, visual literacy, and the influence of the No Child Left Behind Act of 2000 on reading instruction in the public schools.

Includes bibliographical references

Trelease, Jim

★ The **read**-aloud handbook; 6th ed.; Penguin Books 2006 xxvi, 340p il pa $15

Grades: Adult Professional   **028.5**

1. Books and reading 2. Picture books for children 3. Children's literature -- Bibliography

ISBN 0-14-303739-0

     LC 2006-41773

First published 1982

This handbook explains the importance of reading aloud to children, offers guidance on how to set up a read-aloud atmosphere in the home or classroom and suggests 1,500 titles for reading aloud.

Includes bibliographical references

Zbaracki, Matthew D.

Best books for boys; a resource for educators. foreward by Jon Scieszka. Libraries Unlimited 2008 189p il (Children's and young adult literature reference series) $50.00

Grades: Adult Professional   **028.5**

1. Best books 2. Reading interests 3. Boys -- Books and reading 4. Boys 5. Children's literature -- Bibliography 6. Young adult literature -- Bibliography

ISBN 1-59158-599-6; 978-1-59158-599-2

     LC 2007-51065

"Good source notes guide readers to additional writings on the topic and speak to the author's significant research in his field. Nicely indexed by author, title, and subject, this [is an] easy-to-navigate resource." Voice Youth Advocates

Includes bibliographical references

028.7   Use of books and other information media as sources of information

Callison, Daniel

★ The **blue** book on information age inquiry, instruction and literacy; [by] Daniel Callison and Leslie Preddy. Libraries Unlimited 2006 643p il pa $45

Grades: Adult Professional   **028.7**

1. Information literacy 2. Bibliographic instruction 3. Media literacy -- Study and teaching 4. Information literacy -- Study and teaching

ISBN 978-1-59158-325-7; 1-59158-325-X

     LC 2006-23645

A revised edition of Key Words, Concepts and Methods for Information Age Instruction, published 2003 by LMS Associates

"Part 1 introduces the concepts of information inquiry, providing foundational documents and exploring search and use models, information literacy, standards, the instructional role of library media specialists, online inquiry learning, and resource management. Part 2 offers concrete examples of inquiry applied to the middle-school student research process and supplies reproducible pages for classroom use. Part 3 discusses and defines 51 key terms. Entries here are several pages in length and include citations and references. Indispensable for all school media specialists, this book will also appeal to other readers, who will be impressed by its well-organized design, thoroughness, and practicality." Booklist

Includes bibliographical references

Riedling, Ann Marlow

Learning to learn; a guide to becoming information literate in the 21st century. 2nd ed.; Neal-Schuman Publishers 2006 148p il pa $35

Grades: Adult Professional   **028.7**

1. Research 2. Internet resources 3. Internet searching 4. Information literacy

ISBN 978-1-55570-556-5; 1-55570-556-1

LC 2006-13721

First published 2002

This is a "guide to the research/learning process. Chapters lead researchers step-by-step through the information maze to find what they are looking for. Numerous URLs and exercises are included, as is material on copyright, plagiarism, and basic citation styles. . . . The section on evaluating Web sites is particularly valuable. As an added bonus, all mentioned sites are updated and hyperlinked at the publisher's Web site. This is a practical guide for all librarians, but particularly for those teaching research skills." SLJ [review of 2002 edition]

Includes bibliographical references

030   General encyclopedic works

Anderson, Jennifer Joline

Wikipedia; the company and its founders. ABDO Pub. Co. 2011 112p il (Technology pioneers) lib bdg $34.22

Grades: 5 6 7 8   **030**

1. Electronic encyclopedias 2. Wikis (Computer science)

ISBN 978-1-61714-812-5 lib bdg; 1-61714-812-1 lib bdg; 978-1-61758-970-6 e-book

LC 2010037886

This is an introduction to Wikipedia and its founders.

"Written in a clear, linear fashion, this series offers vivid, well-researched details about the development of technological advancements considered essential in today's society. . . . Readers who are interested in technology and inventions will be thoroughly engrossed." SLJ

Includes glossary and bibliographical references

The **world** almanac and book of facts 2013; edited by Sarah Janssen. World Almanac Books 2012 1007 p. (paperback) $12.99

Grades: 6 7 8 9 10 11 12 Adult   **030**

1. Almanacs 2. Geography 3. Popular culture

ISBN 160057162X; 9781600571626

This book is a world almanac and book of facts for 2013. "There is a version of the book for kids—that one features Justin Bieber and a cute frog on the cover. The adult version shows actress Anne Hathaway and a wounded Syrian rebel (in separate frames)." The facts are from a wide range of genres, from popular culture, politics, and geography. (Publishers Weekly)

031   General encyclopedic works in specific languages and language families

DK Publishing, Inc.

DK children's illustrated encyclopedia; 7th ed.; DK Pub. 2010 600p il map $34.99

Grades: 4 5 6 7   **031**

1. Encyclopedias and dictionaries

ISBN 978-0-7566-5759-8; 0-7566-5759-8

LC 2010279636

First published 1991 with title: Random House children's encyclopedia; a revised edition of Dorling Kindersley's children's illustrated encyclopedia 6th ed. published 2006

A highly illustrated one-volume encyclopedia containing entries ranging from Abolitionist movement to Zoos.

"This handsome revision features more than 3000 photographs, maps, time lines, and illustrations. . . . The attractive format encourages browsing." SLJ

Turner, Tracey

World of the weird. Firefly Books 2009 144p il $14.95

Grades: 5 6 7 8   **031**

1. Curiosities and wonders

ISBN 978-1-55407-481-5; 1-55407-481-9

"A first-rate browsing item, from the bicycle-riding frog on the front cover to the recipe for chocolate-covered crickets at the end. . . . Turner presents barrages of snippets on extreme sports ('chessboxing'), uncommon maladies ('exploding head syndrome'), oddball festivals, bizarre beliefs ('Eating stolen bacon is a cure for constipation.' Do tell!), strange creatures real or otherwise, supernatural phenomena and . . . more. . . . Illustrated with photos that are often startling but never gory or gross, this compact page-turner will light up the imaginations of motivated young readers and jaded nonreaders alike." Kirkus

The **Kingfisher** children's encyclopedia. Kingfisher 2012 480 p. (hardcover) $29.99

Grades: 3 4 5 6 7 8   **031**

1. Encyclopedias and dictionaries

ISBN 075346814X; 9780753468142

The entries in this updated children's encyclopedia "range from one to four pages in length each, feature full-color illustrations and photos and subheadings in a large, easy-to-read font and sidebars and fact boxes of thought-provoking information." Topics include "continents and countries, technology, transportation, animal and plant life, religion, and space." (School Library Journal)

★ The **World** Book Encyclopedia. World Book, Inc. 2013 22v col. ill. (hardcover) set $1,422
Grades: 4 5 6 7 8 9 10 11 12 Adult   **031**
1. Curiosities and wonders 2. Encyclopedias and dictionaries 3. Reference books
ISBN 0716601133; 9780716601135
LC 2012024690
First published 1917-1918 by Field Enterprises. Frequently revised

This 2013 encyclopedia "engages more than 4,000 scholars and experts as contributors, reviewers, and consultants" and includes "more than 25,000 . . . photographs and illustrations." The "22-volume World Book Encyclopedia set includes thousands of articles covering" a variety of topics including "Pixar Animation Studios, rhythm and blues, National September 11 Memorial and Museum, magnetism, Adélie penguin, prime number," and the Cold War. (Publisher's note)

031.02   Books of miscellaneous facts

Aronson, Marc
For boys only; the biggest, baddest book ever. [by] Marc Aronson [and] H.P. Newquist. Feiwel and Friends 2007 157p il map $14.95
Grades: 4 5 6 7   **031.02**
1. Boys 2. Curiosities and wonders 3. Boys 4. Handbooks, vade-mecums, etc.
ISBN 978-0-312-37706-9; 0-312-37706-1
LC 2007-32847
"In a tone both light and humorous, Newquist and Aronson aim to please by assembling a tantalizing miscellany—codes, puzzles, best lists, brief history and science facts, instructions for making fake blood and playing Ultimate Frisbee. . . . This offers lots of good fun." Booklist

Farndon, John
Do not open; written by John Farndon. DK Publishing 2007 256p il $24.99
Grades: 4 5 6 7   **031.02**
1. Curiosities and wonders
ISBN 978-0-7566-3205-2; 0-7566-3205-6
LC 2007300131
This encyclopedic tome catalogues "the mysterious and unusual. . . . Flaps, foldout pages and varied styles of illustration—from photomontage to digital cartoons and more conventional line art—keep the book visually fresh and ably complement the subject matter. . . . Taking in everything from weird weather like St. Elmo's fire and raining frogs to possible locations of Atlantis, the book incites curiosity—and expansively rewards it." Publ Wkly

Iggulden, Conn
The **dangerous** book for boys; [by] Conn Iggulden, Hal Iggulden. Collins 2007 270p il map $24.95
Grades: 4 5 6 7   **031.02**
1. Boys 2. Amusements 3. Recreation 4. Curiosities and wonders 5. Fathers and sons 6. Handbooks, vade-mecums, etc.
ISBN 0-06-124358-2; 978-0-06-124358-5
LC 2006-491918
"This eclectic collection addresses the undeniable boy-appeal of certain facts and activities. Dozens of short chapters, in fairly random order, cover a wide range of topics in conversational prose. Simple instructions for coin tricks and paper airplanes alternate with excerpts from history such as Famous Battles and facts about ancient wonders of the world and astronomy. . . . Tongue-in-cheek humor emerges throughout." SLJ

Kane, Joseph Nathan
Famous first facts; a record of first happenings, discoveries, and inventions in American history. [by] Joseph Nathan Kane, Steven Anzovin, & Janet Podell. 6th ed.; Wilson, H.W. 2006 1307p il $185
Grades: 5 6 7 8 9 10 11 12 Adult   **031.02**
1. Reference books 2. Encyclopedias and dictionaries
ISBN 978-0-8242-1065-6; 0-8242-1065-4
LC 2006-3096
First published 1933
Over 7500 entries cover first occurences in American history, organized into 16 chapters each divided into sections. Sections are alphabetically organized, and individual entries are organized chronologically within each section. Includes five indexes: subject index, index by years, index by days, index to personal names, and geographical index

"Besides serving as an essential ready-reference source, the book is also fun to read out loud to colleagues—when was bubble gum first manufactured in the U.S.? When was the spray can introduced?" Booklist

The **World** almanac for kids. World Almanac il maps pa $13.99 hc $24.95
Grades: 4 5 6 7   **031.02**
1. Almanacs 2. Reference books
Annual. First published 1995 for 1996
This volume contains information on animals, art, religion, sports, books, law, language, science and computers. Includes a section of full-color maps and flags. Illustrated throughout with pictures, diagrams, and charts

050   General serial publications

Botzakis, Stergios
Pretty in print; questioning magazines. by Stergios Botzakis. Fact Finders 2007 32p il (Media literacy) lib bdg $22.60; pa $7.95
Grades: 4 5 6 7   **050**
1. Periodicals 2. Publishers and publishing
ISBN 978-0-7368-6764-1 lib bdg; 0-7368-6764-3 lib bdg; 978-0-7368-7860-9 pa; 0-7368-7860-2 pa
LC 2006021443
This is "written in a breezy style and [has] plenty of popping colors and photos. . . . Useful and attractive." SLJ
Includes bibliographical references

070.1 Documentary media, educational media, news media

Garner, Joe

We interrupt this broadcast; the events that stopped our lives--from the Hindenburg explosion to the Virginia Tech shooting. [foreword by Walter Cronkite; afterword by Brian Williams; narrated by Bill Kurtis] 10th anniversary ed.; Sourcebooks MediaFusion 2008 194p il $49.95

Grades: 7 8 9 10 11 12 Adult **070.1**
    1. Disasters 2. Broadcast journalism 3. Television broadcasting of news
    ISBN 978-1-4022-1319-9; 1-4022-1319-0
                    LC 2008-20015
First published 1998
This book and 3 CD set "documents, in text, audio and black-and-white photographs, the moments when history, for better or for worse (though usually for worse), was made in an instant. . . . In addition to the CDs' reports and sound bites dramatically introduced and explained . . . each event gets about four pages of coverage, with an efficient summary and at least half a dozen photos. . . . These are the kinds of moments that still shock and amaze. This moving book is 'a tribute of sorts' to the events that defined eras, the journalists who reported on them and the media television, radio that made us all witnesses." Publ Wkly

070.4 Journalism

Bausum, Ann

★ Muckrakers; how Ida Tarbell, Upton Sinclair, and Lincoln Steffens helped expose scandal, inspire reform, and invent investigative journalism. by Ann Bausum; foreword by Daniel Schorr. National Geographic 2007 111p il $21.95; lib bdg $32.90

Grades: 6 7 8 9 **070.4**
    1. Authors 2. Novelists 3. Historians 4. Journalism 5. Journalists 6. Essayists 7. Biographers 8. Social reformers 9. Socialist leaders 10. Writers on politics 12. Investigative reporting
    ISBN 978-1-4263-0137-7; 1-4263-0137-5; 978-1-4263-0138-4 lib bdg; 1-4263-0138-3 lib bdg
                    LC 2007-11391
This describes "muckrakers, 20th-century journalists who investigated corruption and called for reform. . . . The well-captioned, black-and-white illustrations, mainly photos, are sometimes reproduced with a sepia tone. . . . Clearly written, this offers a very readable and informative introduction to American muckrakers." Booklist
Includes bibliographical references

Reeves, Diane Lindsey

TV journalist; [by] Diane Lindsey Reeves. Ferguson 2007 64p il (Virtual apprentice) $29.95

Grades: 6 7 8 9 **070.4**
    1. Vocational guidance 2. Television broadcasting of news
    ISBN 978-0-8160-6753-4; 0-8160-6753-8
                    LC 2006-36570

This book about becoming a TV journalist is "written with engaging language capable of drawing even reluctant readers into the prose. . . . Pop quizzes, information boxes, quotes from famous people in the field, and on-the-job description make these books highly attractive to the target audience." Libr Media Connect

Sullivan, George

Journalists at risk; reporting America's wars. [by] George Sullivan. Twenty-First Century Books 2006 128p il (People's history) lib bdg $26.60

Grades: 5 6 7 8 **070.4**
    1. War 2. Journalism
    ISBN 0-7613-2745-2
                    LC 2003015855
Discusses the role of reporters during war time, including the risks they take and the censorship they face, and how their jobs have changed with each conflict since the Civil War.
"As a case study in the fluidity of First Amendment rights in wartime, it's thought-provoking reading." Booklist
Includes bibliographical references

070.5 Publishing

Todd, Mark

Whatcha mean, what's a zine? the art of making zines and mini comics. [by] Mark Todd + Esther Peal Watson; with contributions by more than 20 creators of Indie-comics and magazines. Houghton Mifflin 2006 110p il pa $12.99

Grades: 7 8 9 10 **070.5**
    1. Desktop publishing 2. Comic books, strips, etc. 3. Zines 4. Underground periodicals
    ISBN 978-0-618-56315-9; 0-618-56315-6
                    LC 2005-55026
"A zine is a mini-magazine or homemade comic about any topic of the creator's choice, designed for maximum creativity and expression. The authors present a history of self-publishing. . . . Other topics include ideas for zine subjects; copying, binding, and printing tips, including easy-to-understand silk-screening and gocco instruction. . . . Throughout, technical terms are deftly used and advice is dispensed in an accessible, rousing format that includes comics, drawings, and cut-and-paste zine techniques. This well-designed and entertaining resource is sure to find an audience among hip, artistic, and do-it-yourself enthusiasts." SLJ

070.92 Biography regardless of area, region, place

Bankston, John

Nellie Bly; journalist. John Bankston. Chelsea House 2011 155 p. ill. (hc) $35.00

Grades: 7 8 9 10 **070.92**
    1. Women journalists 2. Journalists -- United States -- Biography 3. Women journalists -- United States --

Biography
ISBN 1604139080; 9781604139082

LC 2011000040

This book offers a biography journalist Elizabeth Co-chrane, better known as Nellie Bly. An angry letter she wrote in response to a newspaper article about the role of women "earned her a job and a new name: Nellie Bly. As her alter ego, she gave a voice to women who worked in factories and were being treated in asylums. And she would travel around the world faster than anyone ever had. By the time she was 25, Nellie Bly was the most famous reporter in the world." (Google Books)

Includes bibliographical references (p. 144-147) and index

Hunter-Gault, Charlayne

To the mountaintop! my journey through the civil rights movement Charlayne Hunter-Gault. Roaring Brook Press 2012 v, 198 p.p ill $22.99

Grades: 6 7 8 9 10 11 12   **070.92**
1. Colleges and universities 2. Women political activists 3. African Americans -- Civil rights 4. African American journalists -- Biography 5. Journalists -- United States -- Biography 6. Civil rights movements -- Southern States -- History -- 20th century 7. African Americans -- Civil rights -- Southern States -- History -- 20th century
ISBN 9781596436053

LC 2011020894

This book is written by Charlayne "Hunter-Gault . . . [who along with her] classmate Hamilton Holmes . . . [was one of] the first African Americans to be admitted to the University of Georgia, Athens. . . . [It] recalls the turbulent years from 1959, when she was first approached to challenge the system by seeking admission, through two years of legal battles for her admission to be finalized, through the campus protests and challenges unleashed by her actual enrollment, to graduation and her full-time position in 1965 at the 'New Yorker.' Organized by year, Hunter-Gault's personal experiences are set within the context of the larger civil rights movement." (Bulletin of the Center for Children's Books)

Includes bibliographical references and index

081   General collections in specific languages and language families

Hudson, Wade

★ **Powerful** words; more than 200 years of ex-traordinary writing by African Americans. illustrated by Sean Qualls; foreword by Marian Wright Edel-man. Scholastic Nonfiction 2004 178p il $19.95

Grades: 5 6 7 8   **081**
1. Quotations 2. African Americans 3. Speeches, addresses, etc 4. African Americans -- History 5. African Americans -- Biography 6. American literature -- African American authors   7. African Americans -- Quotations 8. African Americans -- History -- Sources 9. Speeches, addresses, etc., American -- African American authors
ISBN 0-439-40969-1

LC 2003-42792

A collection of speeches and writings by African Ameri-cans, with commentary about the time period in which each person lived, information about the speaker/writer, and pub-lic response to the words.

"Short enough to hold attention, the selections . . . are also long enough to show the writers' tone and style. Many sensitive full-page portraits are included. . . . This well-de-signed volume will be an excellent addition to many library collections." Booklist

Includes bibliographical references

098   Prohibited works, forgeries, hoaxes

Scales, Pat R.

Teaching banned books; 12 guides for young readers. American Library Association 2001 134p pa $28

Grades: Adult Professional   **098**
1. School libraries 2. Books -- Censorship 3. Children's literature -- Study and teaching
ISBN 0-8389-0807-1

LC 01-22340

"Scales knows her material inside out. She also knows how to inspire others to take up this cause and gives them an effective handbook to do just that." Booklist

Includes bibliographical references

100   PHILOSOPHY

100   Philosophy, parapsychology and occultism, psychology

Law, Stephen

Really, really big questions; about the weird, the wonderful, and everything else. illustrated by Nis-hant Choksi. Kingfisher 2009 62p il $16.99

Grades: 5 6 7 8   **100**
1. Philosophy
ISBN 978-0-7534-6309-3; 0-7534-6309-1

An introduction to philosophy which uses clear analo-gies to explore some of life's biggest moral and scientific questions, including the origins of the universe and the meaning of life

"Through a combination of vibrant colors; hip, retro illustrations; and interesting quotes, Law has produced a stimulating work for young minds that is sure to spark con-versation and, of course, more questions." SLJ

130   Parapsychology and occultism

Steiger, Brad

Gale encyclopedia of the unusual and unex-plained; [by] Brad E. Steiger and Sherry Hansen Steiger. Thomson/Gale 2003 3v il map set $205

Grades: 7 8 9 10 11   **130**
1. Occultism 2. Supernatural 3. Parapsychology 4.

Reference books 5. Occultism -- Encyclopedias 6. Supernatural -- Encyclopedias
ISBN 0-7876-5382-9

LC 2003-3995

"These volumes cover broad concepts from 'Afterlife Mysteries' to 'Invaders from Outer Space.'. . . [This is] an encyclopedia for believers. The volumes are meant to 'explore and describe the research of those who take such phenomena seriously.'. . . The work covers material of interest to a large segment of the public in a way that is clear and readable." Booklist

Includes bibliographical references

133 Specific topics in parapsychology and occultism

★ **Paranormal** phenomena: opposing viewpoints; Mary E. Williams, book editor. Greenhaven Press/Thomson Gale 2003 205p il (Opposing viewpoints series) lib bdg $21.95; pa $14.96
Grades: 7 8 9 10   133
1. Ghosts 2. Future life 3. Parapsychology 4. Extrasensory perception 5. Unidentified flying objects
ISBN 0-7377-1238-4 lib bdg; 0-7377-1237-6 pa

LC 2002-66461

Replaces the edition published 1997 under the editorship of Paul A. Winters

"Four chapters of four to six essays each offer opinions on the reality of ghosts, psychic ability, extraterrestrial life, UFO's, near-death experiences, reincarnation, and changing concepts of eternal life. Each essay is preceded by an introduction, which poses questions to be answered in the article." SLJ

Includes bibliographical references

133.1 Apparitions

Gudgeon, Christopher

Ghost trackers; the unreal world of ghosts, ghost-hunting, and the paranormal. by Chris Gudgeon; foreword by Joe MacLeod. Tundra Books 2010 75p il pa $14.95
Grades: 4 5 6 7   133.1
1. Ghosts 2. Parapsychology
ISBN 978-0-88776-950-4; 0-88776-950-0

"Gudgeon thoroughly discusses all things ghostly. Chapters take on the history of sightings, scientists and paranormal research, haunted places around the world, and ghost tracking. . . . Side boxes offer other assorted information, and photographs and illustrations, some quite eerie, are sprinkled throughout. The writing is clear and the subject is presented in an evenhanded manner." SLJ

Hawes, Jason

Ghost hunt; chilling tales of the unknown. [by] Jason Hawes & Grant Wilson; with Cameron Dokey. Little Brown & Co. 2010 218p il $16.99

Grades: 4 5 6 7 8 9   133.1
1. Ghosts
ISBN 978-0-316-09959-2; 0-316-09959-7

"This collection of stories is based on case files from The [Atlantic] Paranormal Society, TAPS, founded by Hawes and Wilson. Each of the eight selections describes the sightings and paranormal activity from the perspective of the observer, then describes how members of TAPS researched, set up equipment, and discovered explanations for what happened. . . . The stories have enough elements of the unknown to make them spine-tingling, but they are more mystery than horror. . . . The easy-to-read format and subject matter will keep even the most reluctant of readers interested." SLJ

Ghost hunt 2; more chilling tales of the unknown. by Jason Hawes and Grant Wilson; with Cameron Dokey. Little Brown & Co. 2011 297p il $16.99
Grades: 4 5 6 7 8   133.1
1. Ghosts
ISBN 978-0-316-09958-5; 0-316-09958-9

"From ghostly spirits roaming Alcatraz to glowing red eyes in the woods, The Atlantic Paranormal Society (aka the popular reality television series Ghost Hunters) is back with a compilation of even more chilling and terrifying tales. Selections include a restless spirit terrorizing a house-sitting victim through her dreams, ghosts reappearing in the O.K. Corral in Tombstone, AZ, and a saddened ghost revisiting a lighthouse where her family was eradicated long ago." SLJ

Matthews, Rupert

Ghosts and spirits. QEB Pub. 2011 32p il (Unexplained) lib bdg $28.50
Grades: 4 5 6 7   133.1
1. Ghosts 2. Apparitions
ISBN 978-1-59566-857-8; 1-59566-857-8

LC 2010014205

This discusses stories about ghosts and poltergeists.

"This well-written and thoughtfully designed [book] features [an] engrossing [topic]. . . . Though the pages are profusely illustrated with large, well-reproduced photographs and drawings, the layout is not cluttered. This [book] just might inspire kids to seek out more in-depth materials." SLJ

Includes glossary

Stefoff, Rebecca

Ghosts and spirits; [by] Rebecca Stefoff. Marshall Cavendish Benchmark 2007 94p il (Secrets of the supernatural) lib bdg $32.79
Grades: 5 6 7 8   133.1
1. Ghosts
ISBN 978-0-7614-2634-9 lib bdg; 0-7614-2634-5 lib bdg

LC 2006031652

This is a history of beliefs in ghosts and spirits throughout the world, including haunted houses, spiritualism, hoaxes, and investigations into paranormal phenomena.

"Nearly every other page has an illustration. . . . The text is accessible." Libr Media Connect

Includes glossary and bibliographical references

Wetzel, Charles

Haunted U.S.A. written by Charles Wetzel; illustrated by Josh Cochran. Sterling 2008 86p il (Mysteries unwrapped) pa $5.95

Grades: 5 6 7 8   **133.1**

1. Ghosts

ISBN 978-1-4027-3735-0 pa; 1-4027-3735-1 pa

LC 2007045905

"Wetzel tells stories of haunted America from the White House to Hollywood. Although some of the places and people mentioned, such as the Amityville house and Rudolph Valentino, might be unfamiliar to younger readers, the selections are still good ghost stories. . . . [The book has] an ample number of clear black-and-white and full-color photographs and illustrations. . . . Perfect for libraries that need a boost or an update to their scary-story collections." SLJ

Includes bibliographical references

133.3   Divinatory arts

Stefoff, Rebecca

Prophets and prophecy; [by] Rebecca Stefoff. Marshall Cavendish Benchmark 2007 79p il (Secrets of the supernatural) lib bdg $32.79

Grades: 5 6 7 8   **133.3**

1. Prophets 2. Prophecies

ISBN 978-0-7614-2638-7 lib bdg; 0-7614-2638-8 lib bdg

LC 2007008779

This is a history of prophecy and fortune-telling from ancient times to the present, discussing such topics as tarot cards, the Oracle of Delphi, astrology, fate, Nostradamus, Jean Dixon, omens, and the I Ching.

"Nearly every other page has an illustration. . . . The text is accessible." Libr Media Connect

Includes glossary and bibliographical references

133.4   Demonology and witchcraft

Black magic and witches; Tamara L. Roleff, book editor. Greenhaven Press 2003 127p (Fact or fiction) $29.95; pa $21.20

Grades: 6 7 8 9   **133.4**

1. Magic 2. Witchcraft

ISBN 0-7377-1318-6; 0-7377-1319-4 pa

LC 2002-378

Explores both sides of the question of whether or not witchcraft is destructive, looking at issues related to the Harry Potter books, wiccans serving in the military, and the validity of magic

"This is a useful introduction to current debate over witchcraft." SLJ

Includes bibliographical references

Hirschmann, Kris

Demons. ReferencePoint Press 2011 80p il (Monsters and mythical creatures) $26.95

Grades: 5 6 7 8   **133.4**

1. Demonology

ISBN 978-1-60152-147-7; 1-60152-147-2

LC 2010029905

"Beginning with an introduction that explains the origins of the devilish creatures, the book discusses demon-like entities throughout cultures and religions. . . . The book's visuals, which include contemporary photos of ceremonies and artists' rendering of demons, can be quite startling. Excellent sidebars . . . cover topics such as the number of exorcists in the Catholic Church." Booklist

Includes bibliographical references

Kerns, Ann

Wizards and witches. Lerner Publications 2010 48p il (Fantasy chronicles) lib bdg $27.93

Grades: 4 5 6 7   **133.4**

1. Witches

ISBN 978-0-8225-9983-8 lib bdg; 0-8225-9983-X lib bdg

LC 2008050757

"The explanations and history behind . . . witches [and wizards] . . . will provide satisfaction for readers who want to know more about these familiar characters from myth, fantasy, and folk and fairy tales. Brief and concise." SLJ

Includes bibliographical references

Schanzer, Rosalyn

★ **Witches!** the absolutely true tale of disaster in Salem. National Geographic Society 2011 144p il $16.95; lib bdg $27.99

Grades: 6 7 8 9   **133.4**

1. Witchcraft 2. Witches

ISBN 978-1-4263-0869-7; 1-4263-0869-8; 978-1-4263-0870-3 lib bdg; 1-4263-0870-1 lib bdg; 978-1-4263-0888-8 e-book

LC 2011012989

"With text that flows like a dramatic novel, Schanzer brings readers into the famous Salem trials, asking them to ponder the motivations of the accusers and the tribulations of the accused. Black-and-white ink prints and red accents are wonderfully evocative and set an appropriately horrific tone." SLJ

150   Psychology

Fullick, Ann

★ **Understanding** health and behavior. Heinemann Library 2009 56p il (Why science matters) lib bdg $32.86; pa $9.49

Grades: 7 8 9 10   **150**

1. Health 2. Human behavior 3. Animal behavior 4. Health behavior

ISBN 978-1-4329-1840-8 lib bdg; 1-4329-1840-0 lib bdg; 978-1-4329-1853-8 pa; 1-4329-1853-2 pa

LC 2008-14349

This book discusses various behaviors, including reactions to hunger and social interactions, observations of people and animals in laboratories and natural environments, the role of nature and nurture on the development of humans and animals, and the effects of exercise, diet, and drug use

"The layout is bright and engaging. . . . This book should be engaging to its target readers and will provide them with a behavioral perspective on topics that will be both relevant and critically important to them throughout their teen and adult years." Sci Books & Films

Includes glossary and bibliographical references

Gardner, Robert

★ **Health** science projects about psychology; [by] Robert Gardner and Barbara Gardner Conklin. Enslow Pubs. 2002 112p il (Science projects) $26.60

Grades: 7 8 9 10 **150**

1. Psychology 2. Science projects
ISBN 0-7660-1439-8

LC 2001-3425

Uses science projects to explore such areas of psychology as personality, emotions, perception, learning, memory, and parapsychology

"Schools with psychology classes should find this title helpful as well as schools whose students participate in science fair competitions." Book Rep

Includes bibliographical references

Kincher, Jonni

Psychology for kids vol. 1: 40 fun tests that help you learn about yourself; [by] Jonni Kincher; [edited by Julie Bach and Pamela Espeland] updated ed.; Free Spirit Pub. Inc. 2008 132p il pa $21.95

Grades: 6 7 8 9 **150**

1. Personality 2. Psychological tests
ISBN 978-1-57542-283-1

LC 2008020660

First published 1990

"Are you an extrovert or an introvert? An optimist or a pessimist? Can you predict the future? Are you creative? Left-brained or right-brained? What body language do you speak? Do you have ESP? Based on . . . psychological concepts, these 40 . . . tests help kids explore their interests and abilities." Publisher's note

Includes bibliographical references

Psychology for kids vol. 2: 40 fun experiments that help you learn about others. Free Spirit Pub. 2008 132p il pa $21.95

Grades: 6 7 8 9 **150**

1. Psychology
ISBN 978-1-57542-284-8

LC 2008020663

First published 1995

"Are people more logical or emotional? How do people make judgments? Do males and females see things differently? Can we shape other people's behavior? Are we more alike or more different? Based on science and . . . psychological concepts and research, 40 . . . experiments make it fun for kids to learn about what makes people tick." Publisher's note

Includes bibliographical references

152.1 Sensory perception

Jackson, Donna M.

Phenomena; secrets of the senses. Little, Brown and Company 2008 174p il $16.99

Grades: 6 7 8 9 **152.1**

1. Senses and sensation 2. Young adult literature -- Works 3. Extrasensory perception
ISBN 978-0-316-16649-2; 0-316-16649-9

LC 2008-31215

"Students with an interest in the weird and unusual will find this book fascinating. It begins with an introduction to human senses and continues with chapters devoted to phenomena such as the 'sixth sense,' synesthesia, and intuition. One of the most interesting sections discusses animals that use their senses in unusual ways. . . . The black-and-white illustrations and photographs are plentiful enough to make the text accessible to reluctant readers. Accurate, entertaining nonfiction." SLJ

Includes glossary and bibliographical references

152.14 Visual perception

Vry, Silke

Trick of the eye; art and illusion. Prestel 2010 89p il $14.95

Grades: 4 5 6 **152.14**

1. Art appreciation 2. Optical illusions
ISBN 978-3-7913-7026-2; 3-7913-7026-X

"From the Parthenon to the Mona Lisa to the Op-Art of the 1960s, images and text reveal the many ways our eyes play tricks on us. Perception of size and color is discussed using standard optical illusions, but this book includes much more. Anecdotes, such as the story of dueling Greek painters Zeuxis and Parrhasius, and unique reproductions, like portraits with altered facial features, lend excitement. The author has taken an interactive approach, filling the pages with questions, puzzles, and project ideas. . . . Text explains the images, which are large and clear. The broad range of styles represented and the fun of the interactive approach will no doubt appeal to young art lovers and curious kids alike." SLJ

Wick, Walter

★ **Walter** Wick's optical tricks; by Walter Wick. 10th anniversary edition; Cartwheel Books 2008 43p il $14.99

Grades: 4 5 6 7 **152.14**

1. Optical illusions
ISBN 978-0-439-85520-4; 0-439-85520-9

First published 1998

Presents a series of optical illusions and explains what is seen.

The author "has produced a stunning picture book of optical illusions. With crystal-clear photographs, he creates a series of scenes that fool the eye and the brain." Booklist [review of 1998 ed.]

152.4 Emotions

Andrews, Linda Wasmer

Emotional intelligence. Franklin Watts 2004 80p il (Life balance) $19.50

Grades: 5 6 7 8 9   **152.4**
1. Emotions
ISBN 0-531-12335-9
                                                   LC 2003-19772

"This book explains that the ability to manage one's emotions and to understand those of others is important for success in life. . . . This title will help young people to understand themselves and others better, and the tools for managing relationships and one's own emotions will promote maturity and development of social skills." SLJ

Includes glossary and bibliographical references

DiConsiglio, John

Out of control; how to handle anger--yours and everyone else's. Franklin Watts 2008 112p il (Scholastic choices) lib bdg $22.50

Grades: 7 8 9 10   **152.4**
1. Anger
ISBN 978-0-531-18846-0 lib bdg; 0-531-1-8846-9 lib bdg
                                                   LC 2007008648

This book has "a magazine-like feel to [it], with glossy pages, lots of photos and graphics, an eye-catching layout with sidebars and boxes, and even tests and quizzes. There is solid content behind the slick facade, though. [The book] delves into the physical and emotional roots of anger, exploring the differences between healthy and unhealthy reactions, and discussing anger-management techniques." Voice Youth Advocates

Includes glossary and bibliographical references

Guarino, Robert

Me and my feelings; what emotions are and how we can manage them. written by Robert Guarino; illustrated by Jeff Jackson; foreword by Robert Ornstein. Hoopoe Books 2011 162p il pa $15.99

Grades: 7 8 9 10   **152.4**
1. Emotions
ISBN 978-1-933779-71-3; 1-933779-71-3

This "title devotes a chapter each to the 'primary' emotions—fear, anger, sadness, happiness, surprise, and disgust—and how to handle them, along with an easy-to-understand discussion. . . . 'Secondary' emotions like pride, jealousy, and love are briefly explored in a separate section. With cartoonlike illustrations throughout, interesting situations, and concise scientific explanations, the book offers a wealth of information in an accessible format." SLJ

Tym, Kate

Coping with your emotions; [by] Kate Tym and Penny Worms. Raintree 2005 48p il (Get real) $29.93

Grades: 6 7 8 9   **152.4**
1. Emotions
ISBN 1-4109-0575-6
                                                   LC 2004-8069

"Chapters consist of a spread presenting an overview of a topic such as depression . . . followed by three case studies about teens dealing with the problem. On the same page, three 'experts' . . . offer advice. . . . The advice of professionals lends credibility to the information presented. . . . Sure to appeal to readers looking for advice." SLJ

Inlcudes glossary and bibliographical references

153.1 Memory and learning

Hudmon, Andrew

★ **Learning** and memory. Chelsea House Publishers 2005 136p il (Gray matter) $32.95

Grades: 8 9 10 11 12   **153.1**
1. Brain 2. Memory 3. Psychology of learning
ISBN 0-7910-8638-0
                                                   LC 2005-11699

This "volume provides fascinating insights into various processes involved in how we learn different things in different ways. Particularly enlightening is the section differentiating explicit memory (learning facts) and implicit memory (learning processes) . . . The [book features] colorful historical photos and illustrations, process models, and shaded insets." SLJ

Includes bibliographical references

153.4 Thought, thinking, reasoning, intuition, value, judgment

Watanabe, Ken

No problem! an easy guide to getting what you want. illustrated by Elwood H. Smith; adapted by Sarah L. Thomson. Viking 2010 70p il $16.99; pa $9.99

Grades: 4 5 6   **153.4**
1. Problem solving
ISBN 978-0-670-01203-9; 0-670-01203-3; 978-0-670-01254-1 pa; 0-670-01254-8 pa

Adaptation of: Problem solving 101, published 2009 for adults

"This little gem explains how to approach intimidating goals or jobs by breaking them down into simple tasks. Realistic scenarios such as finding money for a big purchase or choosing a high school are approached with data-driven evaluation tools. The author defines the steps involved along with terms such as hypothesis, logic trees, matrixes, and evaluation charts." SLJ

153.8 Will (Volition)

Bachel, Beverly K.

★ **What** do you really want? how to set a goal and go for it! A guide for teens. Free Spirit 2000 134p il pa $12.95

Grades: 7 8 9 10 11 12   **153.8**
1. Success 2. Motivation (Psychology)
ISBN 1-57542-085-6
                                                   LC 00-57286

The book discusses various ways for teenagers to set goals, build support networks, keep themselves motivated in the process and reap the harvest of their successes

Bachel's "helpful advice is well supported by quotations from teens who have tried some of the techniques, and simple, appealing graphics keep things light. . . . Back matter includes goal-setting resources and some helpful organizations and Web sites." Booklist

Sobel, David

What's the catch? how to avoid getting hooked and manipulated. illustrated by Jeff Jackson; foreword by Robert Ornstein. Hoopoe Books 2011 138p il pa $15.99

Grades: 7 8 9 10   **153.8**
    1. Mass media 2. Advertising 3. Persuasion (Psychology)
    ISBN 978-1-933779-78-2; 1-933779-78-2

This "is a guide for teens to understand how they are influenced by parents, peers, and the media, often without knowing it. Chapters explain advertising methods and their effect on consumers, and a discussion of Internet safety is included. . . . Although [this] clearly written, well-organized [book] could be read independently, [it includes] questions for discussion and classroom activities, making [it an] excellent [resource] for group discussions." SLJ

153.9   Intelligence and aptitudes

Armstrong, Thomas

You're smarter than you think; a kid's guide to multiple intelligences. edited by Jennifer Brannen. Free Spirit 2003 186p il pa $15.95

Grades: 7 8 9 10 11 12   **153.9**
    1. Intellect 2. Learning strategies 3. Multiple intelligences
    ISBN 1-57542-113-5
                          LC 2002-2687

"A self-help book that's clear, concise, and fun to peruse." SLJ

Includes bibliographical references

155.45   Exceptional children; children by social and economic levels, by ethnic or national group

Fonseca, Christine

101 success secrets for gifted kids; the ultimate guide. Prufrock Press 2011 xi, 191p pa $14.95

Grades: 4 5 6 7 8   **155.45**
    1. Gifted children
    ISBN 978-1-59363-544-2; 1-59363-544-3
                      LC 2011004912

"Fonseca explains what it means to be labeled 'gifted,' how to cope in school, and how to interact with friends and family. Information is delivered in a friendly, conversational manner with firsthand advice from gifted kids and their parents. The myriad tips include how to deal with stress, how to complete homework assignments effectively, how to be respectful of others, how to accept oneself, and even how to deal with bullies. All are incredibly useful." SLJ

Includes bibliographical references

155.5   Psychology of young people twelve to twenty

Hugel, Bob

I did it without thinking; true stories about impulsive decisions that changed lives. Franklin Watts 2008 112p il (Scholastic choices) lib bdg $27; pa $8.95

Grades: 6 7 8 9 10   **155.5**
    1. Decision making 2. Adolescent psychology 3. Risk-taking (Psychology)
    ISBN 978-0-531-13868-7 lib bdg; 0-531-13868-2 lib bdg; 978-0-531-20526-6 pa; 0-531-20526-6 pa
                    LC 2008-690

Teenagers give their stories of impulsive decisions, their reasons for making them, and the consequences—whether good or bad.

This book is "colorful and compact, with . . . an appealing layout. . . . The stories, while not overly preachy, are brief and generally upbeat. . . . [The] book has excellent black-and-white photographs of a diverse array of teens." SLJ

Includes glossary and bibliographical references

Saval, Malina

The secret lives of boys; inside the raw emotional world of male teens. Basic Books 2009 257p $25.95

Grades: Adult Professional   **155.5**
    1. Boys -- Psychology 2. Emotions in adolescence 3. Teenage boys -- Psychology 4. Teenage boys -- United States
    ISBN 978-0-465-00254-2; 0-465-00254-4
                  LC 2008-49703

The author "sought to find out if teen boys really were seriously at risk, and to offer, if possible, a more nuanced portrayal of young males. On both counts, she has succeeded. Through in-depth interviews and research, she portrays the lives of 10 young males. . . . It is a fascinating take on the subject, written in a clear and lively style with a useful index and interesting endnotes that can lead to further exploration." SLJ

Includes bibliographical references

155.9   Environmental psychology

De la Bedoyere, Camilla

Balancing work and play. Amicus 2010 46p il (Healthy lifestyles) lib bdg $32.80

Grades: 7 8 9 10 11 12   **155.9**
    1. Stress (Psychology)
    ISBN 978-1-60753-083-1; 1-60753-083-X

This book is "well-written and satisfyingly informative. . . . [The] magazine-like format includes numerous sidebars, color photos, and charts." SLJ

Includes glossary

Gootman, Marilyn E.

★ **When** a friend dies; a book for teens about grieving & healing. edited by Pamela Espeland. Rev. and updated ed.; Free Spirit Pub. 2005 118p pa $9.95

Grades: 7 8 9 10   **155.9**
   1. Death 2. Bereavement
   ISBN 1-57542-170-4
                               LC 2005-447

First published 1994

This offers "information on subjects including: How can I stand the pain? How should I be acting? What is 'normal'? What if I can't handle my grief on my own? and How can I find a counselor or a therapist? Interspersed throughout the book . . . are quotes by teenagers who have experienced grief. . . . Quotes from well-known writers and philosophers give insight into the grieving process and healing." SLJ

Harmon, Dan

Frequently asked questions about overscheduling and stress; [by] Daniel E. Harmon. Rosen Pub. 2010 64p il (FAQ: teen life) lib bdg $29.25

Grades: 7 8 9 10   **155.9**
   1. Stress (Psychology)
   ISBN 978-1-4358-3514-6; 1-4358-3514-X
                             LC 2009-17825

"Common stressors such as multi-tasking and over-filling one's schedule are discussed, along with how too much stress can cause damage to one's body. Suggestions are made on how to rethink scheduling and de-stress one's life. . . . This is a good resource for teens struggling to understand what is happening to themselves or to their friends." Voice Youth Advocates

Includes glossary and bibliographical references

Myers, Edward

★ **When** will I stop hurting? teens, loss, and grief. illustrations by Kelly Adams. Scarecrow Press 2004 159p il (It happened to me) $34.50

Grades: 7 8 9 10   **155.9**
   1. Bereavement 2. Loss (Psychology) 3. Grief in adolescence 4. Loss (Psychology) in adolescence 5. Bereavement in adolescence -- Psychological aspects
   ISBN 0-8108-4921-6
                             LC 2003-23698

This book "will be extremely helpful for teens struggling to understand their emotions following the loss of a loved one. Grieving is well explained and the individual nature of grief is stressed." Libr Media Connect

Includes bibliographical references

Phillips, Tracy A.

Losing someone you love; dealing with death and dying. Enslow Publishers 2009 104p il (Issues in focus today) lib bdg $31.93

Grades: 7 8 9 10   **155.9**
   1. Death 2. Bereavement
   ISBN 978-0-7660-3067-1 lib bdg; 0-7660-3067-9 lib bdg
                             LC 2008042872

"The final chapters are most helpful, detailing typical responses and reactions to grief as well as how to find support and to be supportive. . . . Bold subheads, interior color photos, and pull quotes break up the text. . . . Keep this title on the assignment shelf." SLJ

Includes glossary and bibliographical references

Simons, Rae

Survival skills; how to handle life's catastrophes. Mason Crest Publishers 2009 128p il (Survivors: ordinary people, extraordinary circumstances) lib bdg $24.95

Grades: 5 6 7 8   **155.9**
   1. Life skills 2. Survival skills
   ISBN 978-1-4222-0456-6 lib bdg; 1-4222-0456-1 lib bdg
                             LC 2008-50320

"Begins with a brief and accessible discussion of the psychology of stress and its role in adolescence, and offers twelve pieces of advice for overcoming difficult experiences and catastrophes. . . . [This book features] important, and sometimes complex, information in an easy-to-read format, offering high gloss photographs, marginal glossary notes, concept definitions, a bibliography, and further reading recommendations." Voice Youth Advocates

Includes glossary and bibliographical references

158   Applied psychology

Amblard, Odile

Friends forever? why your friendships are so important. by Odile Amblard; illustrated by Andree Prigent; edited by Andrea Bussell. Amulet Books 2008 112p il (Sunscreen) $9.95

Grades: 5 6 7 8   **158**
   1. Friendship 2. Interpersonal relations
   ISBN 978-0-8109-9480-5; 0-8109-9480-1
                             LC 2007-43138

"The importance of friendship is stressed in the opening of Friends Forever?, followed by brief discussions on the types of friendships and how they are formed and maintained. . . . The tone of the [book] is breezy and light without being flippant. The [author] never [talks] down to the teen reader." Voice Youth Advocates

Andrews, Linda Wasmer

Meditation; [by] Linda Wasmer Andrews. F. Watts 2004 79p (Life balance) $19.50; pa $6.95

Grades: 5 6 7 8   **158**
   1. Meditation
   ISBN 0-531-12219-0; 0-531-16609-0 pa
                             LC 2003-7153

"Andrews emphasizes that meditation is not a flaky practice, or a particularly religious one, but one that's designed to reduce stress and help individuals manage their lives. Four chapters explain the why and how of meditating. . . . [This offers] solid, easy-to-understand information" SLJ

Includes bibliographical references

Auderset, Marie-Josee

Walking tall; how to build confidence and be the best you can be. by Marie-Jose Auderset; illustrated by Gaetan de Seguin; edited by N.B. Grace. Amulet Books 2008 112p il (Sunscreen) $9.95

Grades: 5 6 7 8   **158**

   1. Self-confidence

   ISBN 978-0-8109-9479-9; 0-8109-9479-8

                         LC 2007-43416

This "addresses issues of self-confidence and section one deals with feelings of high and low self-esteem, acceptance of oneself, and body image issues. It includes an exercise to help the reader realize her strengths and use that realization to build self-confidence. . . . The tone of the [book] is breezy and light without being flippant. The [author] never [talks] down to the teen reader." Voice Youth Advocates

Includes bibliographical references

Bezdecheck, Bethany

Relationships; 21st-century roles. Rosen Pub. 2010 112p il (A young woman's guide to contemporary issues) lib bdg $31.95

Grades: 7 8 9 10   **158**

   1. Family 2. Friendship 3. Interpersonal relations

   ISBN 978-1-4358-3540-5; 1-4358-3540-9

                         LC 2009-12065

"Facts are shared in a conversational tone, creating the sense of a chat with a big sister. . . . [Though] designed for personal reading and browsing, the data provided are accurate and also lend themselves to use in reports. This . . . will be of great interest." SLJ

Includes glossary and bibliographical references

Canfield, Jack

Chicken soup for the teenage soul [I-IV] [by] Jack Canfield, Mark Victor Hansen, Kimberly Kirberger. Health Communications 1997 4v il hardcover o.p. v1 pa $14.95; v2 pa $9.99; v3 pa $14.95; v4 pa $14.95

Grades: 7 8 9 10 11 12   **158**

   1. Emotions 2. Interpersonal relations

   ISBN 1-55874-468-1 [I]; 1-55874-463-0 [I pa]; 1-55874-615-3 [II]; 1-55874-616-1 [II pa]; 1-55874-761-3 [III]; 0-7573-0233-5 [IV]

These books cover "teenage subjects running the gamut from love, family ties, and self-esteem to developing values and life crises, such as a death in the family. . . . Teenagers not only helped select the poems, stories, and accounts that have been included but also have written some of them . . . with a few contributions by well-known people, including Sandra Cisneros, Helen Keller, and Robert Fulghum. . . . This isn't a religious book, but it is an inspirational and motivational one, sometimes funny, sometimes poignant." Booklist [review of 1997 volume]

Includes bibliographical references

Chicken soup for the teenage soul's the real deal; school: cliques, classes, clubs, and more. [compiled by] Jack Canfield, Mark Victor Hansen,

Deborah Reber. Health Communications 2005 292p pa $12.95

Grades: 7 8 9 10   **158**

   1. Emotions 2. Interpersonal relations

   ISBN 0-7573-0255-6

                        LC 2005046051

"The stories included here were submitted by students and are based on their own experiences. Almost every page includes a fun fact, a statistic, or a quiz." SLJ

Crist, James J.

What to do when you're sad & lonely; a guide for kids. [by] James J. Crist. Free Spirit Pub. 2006 124p il pa $9.95

Grades: 4 5 6 7   **158**

   1. Solitude 2. Depression (Psychology)

   ISBN 978-1-57542-189-6 pa; 1-57542-189-5 pa

                        LC 2005021794

"Advising his audience to read this book and work through negative feelings with an adult, Crist describes sad and lonely feelings, distinguishes them from more serious conditions such as depression, and then suggests 'Blues Busters' and ways to ask for help. . . . Crist's clear explanations and simple techniques . . . are relevant for both children and adults." Voice Youth Advocates

Includes bibliographical references

★ **What** to do when you're scared & worried; a guide for kids. [by] James Crist. Free Spirit Pub. 2004 128p il pa $9.95

Grades: 4 5 6 7   **158**

   1. Fear 2. Worry

   ISBN 1-57542-153-4

"Part one deals with normal anxiety, offering detailed steps for developing 10 coping mechanisms. Expert help is needed to deal with the more serious problems discussed in Part two (e.g., phobias, separation anxiety, obsessive-compulsive disorder). Throughout, the author provides information, case histories, and coping skills in a manner that is both reassuring and encouraging. . . . Illustrations lighten the tone of the subject matter." SLJ

Includes bibliographical references

Fox, Annie

Be confident in who you are; [by] Annie Fox. Free Spirit Pub. 2008 92p il (Middle school confidential) pa $9.95

Grades: 5 6 7 8   **158**

   1. Self-confidence

   ISBN 978-1-57542-302-9; 1-57542-302-2

                        LC 2008-4754

"The book contains quizzes, is chock-full of helpful hints, and lists other resources to help readers increase their self-esteem. Kindt's cartoons include several great panels that move the teens' story forward. The graphic-novel-like design will make this self-help tool stand out and appeal to fans of that format." SLJ

Real friends vs. the other kind. Free Spirit Pub. 2009 90p il $9.99

Grades: 5 6 7 8   **158**
1. Friendship 2. Interpersonal relations
ISBN 1-57542-319-7 pa; 978-1-57542-319-7 pa
LC 2008031368

"Jack, Abby, Mateo, Jen, Chris, and Michelle are the middle school students of various ethnicities who take readers through this slim, interactive guide. Chapters cover such topics as friendship dilemmas, so-called friends, when friendships aren't working, crushes, and making new friends. Each chapter opens with a scene played out by the students in cartoon panels. Next, bits of text, along with a multitude of side boxes, address the topic at hand. . . . Lists of questions are offered, along with the answers. There's a lot packed into this colorful title that falls somewhere between self-help and peer advice." SLJ

★ **Too** stressed to think? a teen guide to staying sane when life makes you crazy. by Annie Fox and Ruth Kirschner; edited by Elizabeth Verdick. Free Spirit Pub. 2005 163p il pa $14.95
Grades: 7 8 9 10   **158**
1. Stress (Psychology)
ISBN 1-57542-173-9
LC 2005018484

"This well-organized, upbeat book discusses what stress is and how it affects the body and brain, talks about tools to reduce and control it, and gives suggestions for recognizing the myriad situations that can trigger stress at home and at school and seeking help when necessary. Best of all, each one of these scenarios includes information on how the situation might be addressed." SLJ
Includes bibliographical references

Hantman, Clea

30 days to finding and keeping sassy sidekicks and BFFs; a friendship manual. [by] Clea Hantman. Delacorte Press 2009 176p pa $7.99
Grades: 8 9 10 11 12   **158**
1. Friendship
ISBN 978-0-385-73623-7; 0-385-873623-1
LC 2007-51599

"In an easy-to-read style, Hantman begins at the beginning with how to initiate a friendship and includes ideas for parties, clubs, and just simple approachability and kindness. . . . She addresses ways to work through problems with female friends, whether the issue is boyfriend stealing, depression, or competition. . . . Hantman's sense of humor and youthfulness will make this book appealing to female readers. . . . This book should prove very popular with its intended audience." Voice Youth Advocates

30 days to getting over the dork you used to call your boyfriend; a heartbreak handbook. by Clea Hantman. Delacorte Press 2008 161p il pa $7.99
Grades: 8 9 10 11 12   **158**
1. Loss (Psychology)
ISBN 978-0-385-73549-0 pa; 0-385-73549-9 pa
LC 2007005945

"Hautman outlines a thirty-day process to help teens get through the five stages of a break-up—denial, anger, bargaining, depression, and acceptance. . . . Each day involves exercises to help put events, one's ex, and oneself in perspective. Each day also has a song of the day, which high-lights the day's theme, and a bonus inspirational haiku. . . . The process and activities are helpful and even fun." Voice Youth Advocates

Harris, Ashley Rae

★ **Cliques,** crushes & true friends; developing healthy relationships. ABDO Pub. Co. 2009 112p il (Essential health: strong, beautiful girls) lib bdg $22.95
Grades: 6 7 8 9   **158**
1. Friendship 2. Interpersonal relations 3. Girls -- Psychology
ISBN 978-1-60453-099-5; 1-60453-099-5
LC 2008-12103

This guide to healthy relationships covers the social world of adolescent girls.

"Each chapter tells a personal narrative, with a consulting doctor giving insight and making suggestions. The topics are well selected, the design is attractive, and the stories feature girls from a variety of cultures." Booklist
Includes glossary and bibliographical references

★ **Girl** in the mirror; understanding physical changes. ABDO Pub. 2009 112p il (Essential health: strong, beautiful girls) lib bdg $22.95
Grades: 6 7 8 9   **158**
1. Puberty 2. Self-esteem
ISBN 978-1-60453-100-8; 1-60453-100-2
LC 2008-11903

This features fictional narratives paired with firsthand advice from a licensed psychologist to help preteen and teen girls feel comfortable with their changing bodies and know that they are not alone. Situations include developing early and "late-bloomers".
Includes glossary and bibliographical references

Jones, Jami Biles

Bouncing back; dealing with the stuff life throws at you. [by] Jami L. Jones. Franklin Watts 2007 112p il (Choices) lib bdg $22.50; pa $8.95
Grades: 6 7 8 9 10 11 12   **158**
1. Personality 2. Problem solving
ISBN 0-531-12404-5 lib bdg; 978-0-531-12404-8 lib bdg; 0-531-17730-0 pa; 978-0-531-17730-3 pa
LC 2004018426

"The image of a bouncing ball is used effectively throughout this book to discuss the concept of resiliency in the context of adjusting to life's problems. Each chapter begins with a short vignette of a teen facing a stressful situation and ends by reminding readers of the story and hypothesizing solutions. . . . The advice given is psychologically sound, the writing is clear and easy to read, the pages are visually appealing, and photos show teens of both genders and various racial backgrounds." SLJ
Includes glossary and bibliographical references

Kreiner, Anna

Everything you need to know about creating your own support system. Rosen Pub. Group 1996 64p il (Need to know library) lib bdg $25.25

Grades: 7 8 9 10 **158**
1. Interpersonal relations
ISBN 0-8239-2215-4

LC 95-10753

Discusses how teenagers can create their own support system, a group of people in their lives to whom they feel connected and who can help them build skills and solve problems

This offers "valuable information in easily understood language, illustrated with appealing black-and-white and full-color photographs with a nice mix of genders and ethnic groups." SLJ

Includes glossary and bibliographical references

McIntyre, Thomas
★ The **behavior** survival guide for kids; how to make good choices and stay out of trouble. [by] Thomas McIntyre. Free Spirit Pub. 2003 167p pa $14.95
Grades: 5 6 7 8 **158**
1. Interpersonal relations 2. Problem children
ISBN 1-57542-132-1

LC 2003-4565

"The author provides skills and activities to learn and practice so that new behaviors can replace those that have resulted in getting students into trouble. . . . Those motivated to make better choices for how they behave in school or with friends and family will find much to help them." Voice Youth Advocates

Moss, Wendy
Being me; a kid's guide to boosting confidence and self-esteem. by Wendy L. Moss. Magination Press 2010 112p il $14.95; pa $9.95
Grades: 5 6 7 8 **158**
1. Self-esteem 2. Self-confidence
ISBN 978-1-4338-0883-8; 1-4338-0883-8; 978-1-4338-0884-5 pa; 1-4338-0884-6 pa

LC 2010014384

"Moss encourages her young audience to concentrate on two areas: focusing on inner self-esteem and building social confidence. Through procedure and practice . . . Moss reminds kids that real confidence doesn't come from being the smartest, prettiest, or the most popular one in the room but from the comfort one has with him- or herself. . . . Moss' offering gives great tips for the truly interested." Booklist

Orr, Tamra
★ **Beautiful** me; finding personal strength & self acceptance. ABDO Pub. 2009 112p il (Essential health: Strong, beautiful girls) lib bdg $22.95
Grades: 6 7 8 9 **158**
1. Self-esteem 2. Depression (Psychology)
ISBN 978-1-60453-098-8; 1-60453-098-7

LC 2008-11902

"The topics are well selected, the design is attractive, and the stories feature girls from a variety of cultures." Booklist
Includes glossary and bibliographical references

Owens, L. L.
★ **Frenemies**; dealing with friend drama. content consultant, Robyn J. A. Silverman. ABDO Pub. 2010 112p il (Essential health: strong, beautiful girls) lib bdg $32.79
Grades: 6 7 8 9 **158**
1. Friendship 2. Interpersonal relations 3. Girls -- Psychology
ISBN 978-1-60453-750-5; 1-60453-750-7

LC 2009-2132

In this book about friendships "each chapter tells a personal narrative, with a consulting doctor giving insight and making suggestions. The topics are well selected, the design is attractive, and the stories feature girls from a variety of cultures." Booklist

Perrier, Pascale
Flying solo; how to soar above your lonely feelings, make friends, and find the happiest you. by Pascale Perrier with Erin Zimring; illustrated by Klaas Verplancke. Amulet Books 2007 112p il pa $9.95
Grades: 5 6 7 8 **158**
1. Solitude 2. Friendship
ISBN 978-0-8109-9281-8 pa; 0-8109-9281-7 pa

LC 2006023609

"A self-help book with solid, practical advice. The text is divided into three sections or, as they are called here, phases: 'Why do I feel alone?,' 'How to stop feeling lonely,' and 'Finding solitude.' Each section has a series of subsections with quick discussions of mini-topics designed to hold readers' attention while imparting the necessary information. For the most part, the presentation is clear, understandable, and immediate. . . . The cartoon drawings are colorfully bright and match the text in its attempt to keep the tone light." SLJ

Piquemal, Michel
When life stinks; how to deal with your bad moods, blues, and depression. [by] Michel Piquemal with Melissa Daly; illustrated by Olivier Tossan; [translated by Jane Moseley] Amulet Books 2004 112p il pa $9.95
Grades: 7 8 9 10 **158**
1. Teenagers 2. Depression (Psychology)
ISBN 0-8109-4932-6

LC 2004-13001

"The pleasing use of blocks of color and cartoon illustrations enhances the text. . . . Using the common-sense suggestions provided, readers will more successfully navigate the turmoil of adolescence." SLJ
Includes bibliographical references

Romain, Trevor
★ **Cliques,** phonies & other baloney. Free Spirit 1998 129p il pa $9.95
Grades: 7 8 9 10 **158**
1. Friendship 2. Social groups 3. Interpersonal relations 4. Cliques (Sociology)
ISBN 1-57542-045-7

LC 98-36248

Discusses cliques, what they are and their negative aspects, and gives advice on forming healthier relationships and friendships

"With a sense of ease and lighthearted humor . . . the author serves up solid advice in friendly, reassuring prose." SLJ

Includes bibliographical references

Taylor, Julie

The **girls'** guide to friends; straight talk on making close pals, creating lasting ties, and being an all-around great friend. Three Rivers Press (NY) 2002 222p pa $12

Grades: 7 8 9 10   **158**

1. Friendship

ISBN 0-609-80857-5

LC 2002-18123

Explores the comforts and confusions of friendship, discussing the different kinds of friends, keeping in touch with friends, mixing romance and friendship, the impact of friendship, saving a friendship, and more

"In her practical guide, journalist Taylor maintains the format and bouncy voice of teen-oriented magazines, with slang, cutesy wordplay, and plenty of how-tos." Booklist

Webber, Diane

Your space; dealing with friends and peers. F. Watts 2008 112p il (Scholastic choices) lib bdg $27; pa $8.95

Grades: 6 7 8 9   **158**

1. Friendship 2. Peer pressure

ISBN 978-0-531-18849-1 lib bdg; 0-531-18849-3 lib bdg; 978-0-531-14774-0 pa; 0-531-14774-6 pa

LC 2007006579

Provides advice and tips for teenagers on making and maintaining worthwhile friendships, evaluating friendships and clique behavior, handling peer pressure, bullying, and staying safe on the Internet.

Includes bibliographical references

170   Ethics (Moral philosophy)

Weinstein, Bruce D.

★ **Is** it still cheating if I don't get caught? [by] Bruce Weinstein; illustrations by Harriet Russell. Roaring Brook 2009 160p il pa $12.95

Grades: 8 9 10 11 12   **170**

1. Ethics 2. Teenagers

ISBN 978-1-59643-306-9; 1-59643-306-X

"This appealing guide speaks to the ethical dilemmas that all young people experience in their daily lives, and it should prompt considerable conversation and reflection." Kirkus

174   Occupational ethics

★ **Ethics** in school librarianship; a reader. edited by Carol Simpson. Linworth Pub. 2003 164p pa $44.95

Grades: Adult Professional   **174**

1. School libraries 2. Librarians -- Ethics 3. School

librarians -- Professional ethics 4. Library science -- Moral and ethical aspects 5. School libraries -- Moral and ethical aspects

ISBN 1-58683-084-8

LC 2003-7956

This is a compilation of "articles dealing with the ethical aspects of collection development, access, confidentiality, technology, intellectual freedom, intellectual property, administration, Internet use, and professional relationships. . . . School librarians and administrators would do well to have this thought and discussion-provoking book on hand." SLJ

Includes bibliographical references

Hartman, Eve

Science ethics and controversies; [by] Eve Hartman and Wendy Meshbesher. Raintree 2009 48p il (Sci-hi: life science) $31.43; pa $8.99

Grades: 5 6 7 8   **174**

1. Science -- Ethical aspects

ISBN 978-1-4109-3330-0; 1-4109-3330-X; 978-1-4109-3338-6 pa; 1-4109-3338-5 pa

LC 2009003475

In this introduction to science ethics and controversies "clear language, embedded definitions, and interesting examples illustrate abstract concepts through both text and well-chosen photographs. . . . [It] discusses topics such as global warming and animal research, and their implications for decision-making by scientists, policy makers, and voters. Because so many issues are raised in this book, it will be especially useful as a research starter in both science and social-studies classes. . . . [The] book also includes suggested activities to test ideas as well as a thorough glossary and a Webliography." SLJ

Includes glossary and bibliographical references

174.2   Medical and health professions

Altman, Linda Jacobs

★ **Bioethics**; who lives, who dies, and who decides? Enslow Publishers 2006 112p il (Issues in focus today) lib bdg $23.95

Grades: 7 8 9 10 11 12   **174.2**

1. Bioethics 2. Medical ethics

ISBN 0-7660-2546-2; 978-0-7660-2546-2

LC 2006-07002

This "provides an overview of the big moral issues brought about by breakthroughs in biotechnology. Altman is fair to all sides, whether the passionate argument is about abortion, the cloning of animals, assisted suicide, artificial life support, or organ transplants. . . . The readable style and clear, abundantly illustrated design will stimulate debate." Booklist

Includes glossary and bibliographical references

Boskey, Elizabeth

America debates genetic DNA testing. Rosen Central 2008 64p il (America debates) lib bdg $29.25

Grades: 7 8 9 10   **174.2**
1. Genetic screening
ISBN 978-1-4042-1926-7 lib bdg; 1-4042-1926-9
lib bdg
LC 2006-102516

The issues "are debated in a clear, concise manner. . . . Color photographs and boxed information highlighted in red break up the [text]." SLJ
Includes glossary and bibliographical references

Freedman, Jeri
   America debates stem cell research. Rosen Central 2008 64p il map (America debates) lib bdg $29.25
Grades: 7 8 9 10   **174.2**
1. Stem cell research
ISBN 978-1-4042-1928-1 lib bdg; 1-4042-1928-5
lib bdg
LC 2007-1036

This book is an "overview of the issues surrounding stem cells and their potential to revolutionize medicine and provide cures, with a focus on the use of embryonic stem cells. The ethical and moral debates over how cells are obtained, the definition of 'personhood,' and various religious perspectives are explored, as well as how politics play a part in the discussion of this issue. It includes a look at stem cell research around the world." Publisher's note
Includes glossary and bibliographical references

Lovegrove, Ray
   Health; ethical debates in modern medicine. Black Rabbit Books 2008 46p il map (Dilemmas in modern science) lib bdg $34.25
Grades: 7 8 9 10   **174.2**
1. Medical ethics
ISBN 978-1-59920-095-8; 1-59920-095-3
LC 2007-35690

This title is "easy to navigate as evocative photographs, charts, and sidebars help break down complicated arguments into manageable parts for easy digestion." SLJ
Includes glossary and bibliographical references

Marzilli, Alan
   Stem cell research and cloning. Chelsea House 2007 144p il (Point/counterpoint) lib bdg $35
Grades: 7 8 9 10   **174.2**
1. Cloning 2. Stem cell research
ISBN 978-0-7910-9230-5 lib bdg; 0-7910-9230-5
lib bdg
LC 2006017148

"This book explores the legal and political ramifications of the debates about [stem cell research and cloning], including federal funding for stem cell research, privately funded research, and the government's role in limiting scientific inquiry." Publisher's note
Includes bibliographical references

Schafer, Susan
   Cloning. M.E. Sharpe 2009 88p il (Genetics: the science of life) $38.95

Grades: 6 7 8 9   **174.2**
1. Cloning
ISBN 978-0-7656-8138-6; 0-7656-8138-2
LC 2008-8115

This discusses what cloning is, how it works, its ethics and future.
   "Chock-full of information. . . . Interest is maintained through countless fascinating examples. . . . Illustrations and color photographs enhance [the text]." SLJ
Includes bibliographical references

Uschan, Michael V., 1948-
   Forty years of medical racism; the Tuskegee experiments. Lucent Books 2005 112p il map (Lucent library of Black history) lib bdg $28.70
Grades: 8 9 10 11 12   **174.2**
1. Syphilis 2. Human experimentation in medicine 3. African Americans -- Health and hygiene
ISBN 1-59018-486-6

This is an account of "the Tuskegee Study of Untreated Syphilis in the Negro Male. . . . Halftone photographs of participants and of the persons who designed, conducted, or criticized the project supplement the text. Informational sidebars provide additional descriptions and photographs of some of the damage done by untreated syphilis." SLJ
Includes bibliographical references

176   Ethics of sex and reproduction

Cloning; William Dudley, book editor. Greenhaven Press 2005 112p il (Writing the critical essay) $26.20
Grades: 7 8 9 10   **176**
1. Cloning
ISBN 0-7377-3196-6

This presents essays representing various points of view on the ethics of cloning and includes questions designed to aid the reader in analyzing each essay.
Includes bibliographical references

178   Ethics of consumption

Kerr, Jim
   ★ **Food**; ethical debates on what we eat. Smart Apple Media 2009 46p il map (Dilemmas in modern science) lib bdg $34.25
Grades: 7 8 9 10   **178**
1. Food industry 2. Genetic engineering 3. Food supply 4. Food industry and trade 5. Agricultural productivity
ISBN 978-1-59920-094-1; 1-59920-094-5
LC 2007-39651

This title is "easy to navigate as evocative photographs, charts, and sidebars help break down complicated arguments into manageable parts for easy digestion." SLJ
Includes glossary and bibliographical references

179   Other ethical norms

Belanger, Jeff

    What it's like; to climb Mount Everest, blast off into space, survive a tornado, and other extraordinary stories. Sterling Pub. Co. 2010 136p il pa $9.95

Grades: 5 6 7 8   **179**

    1. Courage 2. Anecdotes 3. Adventure and adventurers

    ISBN 978-1-4027-6711-1; 1-4027-6711-0

                           LC 2009040875

    "This illustrated collection presents short, first-person accounts of high-octane adventures—and, in some cases, personal disasters—by the people who actually experienced them. . . . The stories are told in present-tense, straightforward language, filled in with many pertinent and fascinating details. . . . The exciting action and the entries' short length will draw reluctant readers, as will the many color photographs, which are imaginatively laid out. This attractive package will be an easy sell." Booklist

Cheating; Stefan Kiesbye, book editor. Greenhaven Press 2010 107p (Social issues firsthand) $31.80

Grades: 7 8 9 10   **179**

    1. Ethics 2. Honesty 3. Cheating (Education)

    ISBN 978-0-7377-5009-6; 0-7377-5009-X

                           LC 2010000920

    "The 13 entries in this book were written from the perspective of those who have cheated, for example, an 'economic hit man,' and those who have observed cheating, such as college professors. The selections are organized in several sections, including the school setting, the workplace, and sports. A list of organizations is included. This collection is particularly interesting because of the use of the personal narrative, and it is a good addition for libraries." SLJ

    Includes bibliographical references

Judson, Karen

    ★ **Animal** testing. Marshall Cavendish Benchmark 2006 144p il (Open for debate) lib bdg $37.07

Grades: 7 8 9 10   **179**

    1. Animal rights 2. Animal experimentation

    ISBN 0-7614-1882-2

    This presents a history of animal testing, arguments for and against the use of animals in product safety testing, biomedical research, and education, and describes animal rights organizations and alternatives to animal testing.

Ravilious, Kate

    Power; ethical debates about resources and the environment. Black Rabbit Books 2009 46p il map (Dilemmas in modern science) lib bdg $29.25

Grades: 7 8 9 10   **179**

    1. Conservation of natural resources 2. Natural resources -- Management

    ISBN 978-1-59920-096-5; 1-59920-096-1

                           LC 2007-35691

    This title is "easy to navigate as evocative photographs, charts, and sidebars help break down complicated arguments into manageable parts for easy digestion." SLJ

    Includes glossary and bibliographical references

Factory farming; Debra A. Miller, book editor. Greenhaven Press 2010 183p (Current controversies) lib bdg $38.50; pa $26.75

Grades: 8 9 10 11 12   **179**

    1. Livestock industry

    ISBN 978-0-7377-4909-0 lib bdg; 0-7377-4909-1 lib bdg; 978-0-7377-4910-6 pa; 0-7377-4910-5 pa

                           LC 2009053380

    "This solid volume looks at the economics, ethics, environmental impact, and future of factory farming. The issues are explored through diverse pro and con articles that have been edited for brevity, highlighting various points in the discussion surrounding the large-scale production and slaughter of animals for food. . . . This is a valuable addition to collections needing information on the state of modern food production." SLJ

    Includes bibliographical references

179.7   Respect and disrespect for human life

Death and dying; Jane Langwith, book editor. Greenhaven Press 2008 128p il (Introducing issues with opposing viewpoints) lib bdg $33.70

Grades: 7 8 9 10   **179.7**

    1. Death 2. Bereavement 3. Future life 4. Right to die 5. Terminal care -- Ethical aspects

    ISBN 978-0-7377-3974-9; 0-7377-3974-6

    Presents essays covering different viewpoints on death, including the role of religion in death, the possibility of the afterlife, and whether physicians should assist in the process of dying.

    Includes bibliographical references

Euthanasia: opposing viewpoints; Carrie L. Snyder, book editor. Greenhaven Press 2006 269p il (Opposing viewpoints series) lib bdg $34.95; pa $23.70

Grades: 7 8 9 10   **179.7**

    1. Euthanasia

    ISBN 0-7377-2933-3 lib bdg; 0-7377-2934-1 pa

                           LC 2005-55110

    "The four chapters explore whether euthanasia is ethical, if it should be legalized, if legalization would lead to involuntary killing, and under what circumstances, if any, doctors should assist in suicide." Booklist [review of 2000 edition]

    Includes bibliographical references

Rebman, Renee C.

    Euthanasia and the right to die; a pro/con issue. Enslow Pubs. 2002 64p il (Hot pro/con issues) lib bdg $27.93

Grades: 7 8 9 10   **179.7**

    1. Euthanasia 2. Right to die

    ISBN 0-7660-1816-4

                           LC 2001-5251

    The author discusses "the right to die by choice rather than by nature. . . . Rebman steps into the debate by asking what is a 'good death.' . . . She goes on to offer a variety of possible answers without bias, and she paints a historic picture of the controversy and how technology has complicated our definitions of life and death. . . . Objectivity makes this a good reference." Booklist

Includes bibliographical references and index

Stefoff, Rebecca

The **right** to die. Marshall Cavendish Benchmark 2009 126p il (Open for debate) lib bdg $29.95

Grades: 7 8 9 10 **179.7**

1. Suicide 2. Euthanasia 3. Right to die 4. Medical ethics

ISBN 978-0-7614-2948-7 lib bdg; 0-7614-2948-4 lib bdg

LC 2008000361

This presents arguments for and against euthanasia and assisted suicide in ancient and modern times

Includes bibliographical references

181   Eastern philosophy

Whitfield, Susan

Philosophy and writing. Sharpe Focus 2009 80p il map (Inside ancient China) $34.95

Grades: 7 8 9 10 **181**

1. Chinese literature 2. Chinese philosophy

ISBN 978-0-7656-8168-3; 0-7656-8168-4

LC 2008-31167

"Whitfield covers religion and philosophy [of ancient China] and how they have been passed down using various precursors to books and printing. . . . [This is illustrated with] fine and frequent color photographs and reproductions. Readers will be rewarded . . . with clear, accessible writing, peppered liberally with entertaining stories from history." SLJ

Includes glossary and bibliographical references

183   Sophistic, Socratic, related Greek philosophies

Lim, Jun

Socrates; the public conscience of Golden Age Athens. by Jun Lim. 1st ed. Rosen Pub. 2006 112 p. col. ill., col. map (Library of Greek philosophers) (library) $34.60

Grades: 5 6 7 8 **183**

1. Philosophers

ISBN 1404205640; 9781404205642

LC 2005012259

This book by Jun Lim is part of the Library of Greek Philosophers series and looks at Socrates. "This series introduces students to the great philosophers and mathematicians who helped shape the intellectual world in modern times." Examples are given "of the kinds of knowledge these men taught to their students. The early years, travels, and education of each man are told, and the contributions to society are detailed in the context of the times." (Library Media Connection)

Includes bibliographical references (p. 107-108) and index.

200   RELIGION

200   Religion

Breuilly, Elizabeth

★ **Religions** of the world; the illustrated guide to origins, beliefs, traditions & festivals. [by] Elizabeth Breuilly, Joanne O'Brien, Martin Palmer; consultant editor, Martin E. Marty. rev ed; Facts on File 2005 160p il map $29.95

Grades: 7 8 9 10 **200**

1. Religions

ISBN 0-8160-6258-7

LC 2005051101

First published 1997

This "is a valuable resource, covering the beliefs and practices of 10 major religions and lavishly illustrated with color photos, maps, diagrams, and charts." SLJ

Includes bibliographical references

Buller, Laura

A **faith** like mine; a celebration of the world's religions . . . seen through the eyes of children. DK Pub. 2005 80p il maps $19.99

Grades: 4 5 6 7 **200**

1. Religions

ISBN 0-7566-1177-6

"Buller introduces Hinduism, Islam, Judaism, Christianity, Buddhism, and Sikhism through the eyes of children. . . . The amount of information is adequate and straightforward and focuses on aspects of the religion that would appeal to children. The clear, vibrant photographs are especially inviting." SLJ

The **encyclopedia** of world religions; Robert S. Ellwood, general editor; Gregory D. Alles, associate editor. Rev. ed.; Facts on File 2006 514p il map (Facts on File library of religion and mythology) $50

Grades: 7 8 9 10 11 12 **200**

1. Reference books 2. Religions -- Encyclopedias

ISBN 978-0-8160-6141-9; 0-8160-6141-6

LC 2005-56750

First published 1998

This encyclopedia "covers all the major and minor religions of the world, including the religions of the ancient world; the major religions practiced around the world today; religions of contemporary indigenous peoples; definitions of religious symbols and ideas; key leaders and thinkers; and terms and definitions." Publisher's note

Includes bibliographical references

Hackney Blackwell, Amy

Lent, Yom Kippur, and other Atonement days. Chelsea House 2009 112p il (Holidays and celebrations) $40

Grades: 6 7 8 9   **200**
1. Lent 2. Yom Kippur 3. Religious holidays
ISBN 978-1-60413-100-0; 1-60413-100-4

LC 2009010109

This "presents a welcome worldview of various atonement days, headlined by Lent, Yom Kippur, and the Buddhist holiday Rains Retreat. . . . Each gets an introduction to its associated religion, a brief history of the holiday, and a rundown of the significant days, rituals, and practices of observation. Then, readers are treated to a trip around the world . . . to investigate the unique ways in which different cultures observe similar holidays. The layout is text-dominated but dotted with colorful quality photos and a few informational insets. A good choice to help explain the significance behind holidays, . . . illuminating the many similarities lurking behind cultural and religious differences." Booklist
Includes glossary and bibliographical references

Langley, Myrtle
    Religion; written by Myrtle Langely; special photography by Ellen Howden . . . [et al.] Rev. ed.; DK Pub. 2005 72p il (DK eyewitness books) $15.99; lib bdg $19.99
Grades: 4 5 6 7   **200**
1. Religion
ISBN 978-0-7566-1087-6; 0-7566-1087-7; 978-0-7566-1088-3 lib bdg; 0-7566-1088-5 lib bdg

LC 2005-278287

First published 1996 by Knopf

Introduces the history, philosophies, and rituals of various world religions including Hinduism, Buddhism, Shintoism, Zoroastrianism, and Christianity.

"Text consists of comprehensive, elucidative captions for the eye-catching, full-color photographs, drawings, and reproductions of paintings clustered on the pages. . . . This is a superb, succinct overview of the founders, tenets, and ways of worship of the world's major religions." SLJ

Murphy, Larry
    ★ **African**-American faith in America; [by] Larry G. Murphy. Facts on File 2003 128p il (Faith in America) $30
Grades: 7 8 9 10   **200**
1. African Americans -- Religion
ISBN 0-8160-4990-4

LC 2002-28593

"In-depth coverage of diverse religious worship practiced among African Americans is presented. Murphy examines popular Christian religions, but also explores Judaism, Islam, Buddhism, and more. The well-written account begins with the religious experiences of the first Africans in America, moves to the establishment of pioneer religious institutions, and culminates with a chapter on the current status of diverse congregations. . . . Students will find ample material on well-known historical figures and current leaders" SLJ
Includes bibliographical references

Osborne, Mary Pope
    ★ **One** world, many religions; the ways we worship. Knopf 1996 86p il map $19.95

Grades: 4 5 6 7   **200**
1. Islam 2. Taoism 3. Judaism 4. Buddhism 5. Hinduism 6. Religions 7. Christianity 8. Confucianism 9. Religions
ISBN 0-679-83930-5

LC 96-836

"The presentation is notable for its respect to each group, succinctness, and clarity. . . . The artful, full-page, color and black-and-white photographs tell much of the story." SLJ
Includes glossary and bibliographical references

National Geographic concise history of world religions; an illustrated time line. edited by Tim Cooke. National Geographic 2011 352 p. col. ill. (hardcover) $40.00
Grades: 8 9 10 11 12 Adult   **200**
1. Ethics 2. World history 3. Religious institutions 4. Religions -- Encyclopedias 5. Religion -- History -- Chronology 6. Religions 7. Religion and ethics 8. Religions -- History
ISBN 1426206984; 9781426206986

LC 2011276808

This book "continues the 'Concise History' series with [a] . . . take on major religions and lesser-known faiths of all times and nations." It offers a "global perspective on the history of faith in the Americas, Europe, Asia and Oceania, and Africa and the Middle East. . . . 50 feature essays explore in detail the origins, development and influence of faith." (Publisher's Note)
Includes bibliographical references (p. 343-344) and index

What do you believe? religion and faith in the world today. DK Pub. 2011 96p il map $16.99
Grades: 4 5 6 7   **200**
1. Religions 2. Philosophy
ISBN 978-0-7566-7228-7; 0-7566-7228-7

"This extensive guidebook covers the beliefs and history of the world's major religions. Focusing in particular on Buddhism, Christianity, Hinduism, Islam, Judaism, and Sikhism, the book also explores atheism and agnosticism, indigenous belief systems, East Asian religions, philosophy, and morality. . . . The graphically bold format—which mixes photographs, cartoons, and sidebars—will keep kids' attention, whether they are seeking truth, knowledge, or more to ponder." Publ Wkly

200.9   History, geographic treatment, biography

Braude, Ann
    ★ **Women** and American religion; Jon Butler & Harry S. Stout, general editors. Oxford University Press 2000 141p il (Religion in American life) lib bdg $28
Grades: 7 8 9 10   **200.9**
1. Women -- Religious life 2. Women and religion -- United States -- History
ISBN 0-19-510676-8

LC 99-32968

Braude discusses "how women from various groups, including African Americans, immigrants, and social crusaders, shaped the face of religion in the U.S. . . . Included are individuals such as colonist Margaret Winthrop and African American preacher Jarena Lee, as well as religious leaders such as Mary Baker Eddy and Mother Elizabeth Seaton. Black-and-white illustrations and historical engravings pepper the text." Booklist

Includes bibliographical references

Fridell, Ron

Religious fundamentalism. Marshall Cavendish Benchmark 2009 144p il (Open for debate) $29.95

Grades: 7 8 9 10   **200.9**

1. Islam 2. Christianity 3. Religious fundamentalism
ISBN 978-0-7614-2945-6; 0-7614-2945-X

         LC 2008000364

This examines religious fundamentalism in Christianity and Islam.

Includes bibliographical references

★ **Religion** in America: opposing viewpoints; David Haugen and Susan Musser, book editors. Greenhaven Press 2011 237p il (Opposing viewpoints series) $39.70; pa $27.50

Grades: 8 9 10 11 12   **200.9**

ISBN 978-0-7377-4988-5; 0-7377-4988-1; 978-0-7377-4989-2 pa; 0-7377-4989-X pa

         LC 2010016975

This volume explores the topics relating to religion in the United States by presenting varied expert opinions that examine many of the different aspects that comprise these issues.

Includes bibliographical references

201 Specific aspects of religion

Glick, Susan

War and peace; by Susan Glick. Lucent Books 2004 112p il map (Discovering mythology) $28.70

Grades: 6 7 8 9   **201**

1. War 2. Peace 3. Mythology 4. War -- Mythology 5. Peace -- Mythology
ISBN 1-56006-903-1

         LC 2004-6290

This examines the meaning and cultural significance behind the myths concerning war and peace in ancient world cultures

Includes bibliographical references

Hamilton, Virginia

★ **In** the beginning; creation stories from around the world; told by Virginia Hamilton; illustrated by Barry Moser. Harcourt Brace Jovanovich 1988 161p il hardcover o.p. pa $20

Grades: 5 6 7 8   **201**

1. Creation 2. Mythology
ISBN 0-15-238740-4; 0-15-238742-0 pa

         LC 88-6211

A Newbery Medal honor book, 1989

"Hamilton has gathered 25 creation myths from various cultures and retold them in language true to the original. Images from the tales are captured in Moser's 42 full-page illustrations, tantalizing oil paintings that are rich with somber colors and striking compositions. Included in the collection are the familiar stories (biblical creation stories, Greek and Roman myths), and some that are not so familiar (tales from the Australian aborigines, various African and native American tribes, as well as from countries like Russia, China, and Iceland). At the end of each tale, Hamilton provides a brief commentary on the story's origin and originators." Booklist

Includes bibliographical references

Kallen, Stuart A.

Shamans; by Stuart A. Kallen. Lucent Books 2004 112p il (Mystery library) $28.70

Grades: 6 7 8 9   **201**

1. Shamanism
ISBN 1-59018-628-1

         LC 2004-12665

"The methods employed by shamans to visit the realm of spirits in order to learn how to effect cures are described in some detail. . . . Activities of Siberian and North, Central, and South American shamans receive the most attention. Chinese, Australian aboriginal, Greenlander, ancient Greek, and a few other practitioners are mentioned. . . . Halftone photographs make textual descriptions real while numerous shaded sidebars offer considerable supplementary material. . . . This title provides a varied, understandable introduction to the spiritual side of many human cultures." SLJ

Includes bibliographical references

Mass, Wendy

Gods and goddesses. Lucent Bks. 2002 112p (Discovering mythology) $27.45

Grades: 6 7 8 9   **201**

1. Mythology 2. Gods and goddesses 3. Gods 4. Goddesses
ISBN 1-56006-852-3

         LC 2001-5775

Examines the origins and nature of Egyptian, Hindu, Celtic, Greek, Roman, Viking, and Aztec gods and goddesses as revealed in the mythologies of these cultures

"This is a good overview for study of mythology that may spark interest in further study." Book Rep

Includes bibliographical references

McIntosh, Kenneth

★ **When** religion & politics mix; how matters of faith influence political policies. by Kenneth McIntosh, M.Div., and Marsha McIntosh. Mason Crest Publishers 2005 112p il (Religion and modern culture) $22.95

Grades: 7 8 9 10   **201**

1. Religion and politics 2. Church and state -- United States
ISBN 1-59084-971-X; 978-1-59084-971-2

         LC 2005-3057

This is an "overview of where U.S. voters stand on the relevance of religion in their personal and public lives. The book explores topics such as abortion, same-sex marriage, and stem cell research, and it compares religious views in the U.S. with Canada's more secular perspectives. . . . [The book provides] a lucid perspective on different beliefs within and beyond various religions." Booklist

Includes bibliographical references

★ **U-X-L** encyclopedia of world mythology. UXL 2009 5v il set $314

Grades: 7 8 9 10 11 12   **201**
1. Reference books 2. Mythology -- Encyclopedias
ISBN 978-1-41443-030-0; 1-41443-030-2

LC 2008-12696

"In A-Z format, the set provides more than 300 entries for five content areas: characters, deities, myths, themes, and cultures. . . . The entries generally range from three to four pages. . . . Recommended for middle- and high-school libraries." Booklist

World mythology; the illustrated guide. Roy Willis, general editor. Oxford University Press 2006 311p il map pa $22.50

Grades: 8 9 10 11 12   **201**
1. Mythology
ISBN 0-19-530752-6; 978-0-19-530752-8

LC 2005-30779

First published 1993 by Holt & Co.

This book describes "the myths of Egypt, the Middle East, India, China, Tibet, Mongolia, Japan, Greece, Rome, the Celtic lands, Northern and Eastern Europe, the Arctic, North and South America, Mesoamerica, Africa, Australia, Oceania, and Southeast Asia." Libr J [review of 1993 edition]

Includes bibliographical references

204   Religious experience, life, practice

Philip, Neil

★ **In** the house of happiness; a book of prayers and praise. selected by Neil Philip; illustrated by Isabelle Brent. Clarion Bks. 2003 un il $17

Grades: 6 7 8 9   **204**
1. Prayers
ISBN 0-618-23481-0

LC 2002-10269

A collection of short prayers from major religions—Christianity, Judaism, Hinduism, Buddhism, and Islam—along with tribal chants, folk rhymes, and poems of praise and devotion

"The beautiful art encourages readers to pick up the book. Brent, who was inspired by the Book of Hours, lavishly employs illumination to highlight her pictures of nature. . . . This book offers the opportunity for quiet moments of reflection in a lovely setting." Booklist

209   Sects and reform movements

Stein, Stephen J.

Alternative American religions. Oxford Univ. Press 1999 156p il (Religion in American life) lib bdg $28

Grades: 7 8 9 10   **209**
1. Cults 2. Sects 3. Cults -- United States -- History
4. Sects -- United States -- History
ISBN 0-19-511196-6

LC 99-42370

Examines various alternative religions, or New Religious Movements, that have existed in the United States from colonial times through the twentieth century and from the perspectives of both insiders and outsiders

"The tone throughout is nonjudgmental and the emphasis is on people and their ideas. Black-and-white photos and reproductions add information and perspective to the presentation." SLJ

220   Bible

Atkinson, Peter

The **Lion** encyclopedia of the Bible; illustrated by Peter Dennis. Lion 2009 127p il map $19.99

Grades: 7 8 9 10 11 12   **220**
1. Reference books
ISBN 978-0-7459-6010-4; 0-7459-6010-3

Taking a chronological approach to the story line of the Bible, this resource integrates and explores the Bible's historical, geographical, and social origins. It also overviews the different types of writing found within the texts and shows how they relate to Christian beliefs.

This is "thematically immense but skillfully distilled in presentation. . . . Complex and potentially confusing material is explained succinctly. . . . Maps and colorful and dramatic drawings, paintings, and photographs appear throughout. . . . With its inviting format and unaffected writing, this is a welcome resource." SLJ

Brown, Alan

The **Bible** and Christianity; by Alan Brown. Smart Apple Media 2003 30p il (Sacred texts) $27.10

Grades: 5 6 7 8   **220**
1. Christianity 2. Bible (as subject)
ISBN 1-58340-243-8

LC 2003-41645

Explains how the Old and New Testaments came to be part of the Bible used by Christians and discusses some of the important messages found in the holy scriptures.

"Colorful strips of symbolic patterns adorn the pages and accent the informative text boxes. . . . The clear captioned . . . illustrations (photos and historical art) provide additional background." Horn Book Guide

Includes glossary

220.3   Encyclopedias and topical dictionaries

Oxford University Press

The **Oxford** companion to the Bible; edited by Bruce M. Metzger, Michael D. Coogan. Oxford Univ. Press 1993 xxi, 874p il map $70

Grades: 8 9 10 11 12 Adult **220.3**
1. Reference books 2. Bible (as subject) -- Dictionaries
ISBN 0-19-504645-5

LC 93-19315
This volume "contains more than 700 signed entries treating the formation, transmission, circulation, sociohistorical situation, interpretation, theology, uses, and influence of the Bible." Libr J

220.5 Modern versions and translations

Bible

The **Bible**: Authorized King James Version; with an introduction and notes by Robert Carroll and Stephen Prickett. Oxford University Press 2008 lxxiv, 1039, 248, 445p il map (Oxford world's classics) pa $18.95
Grades: 5 6 7 8 9 10 11 12 Adult **220.5**
ISBN 978-0-19-953594-1

LC 2008-273825
This Oxford World's Classics version first published 1997
The authorized or King James Version originally published 1611.
Includes bibliographical references

Good news Bible; today's English version. American Bible Soc. 2006 1563p $10.99
Grades: 8 9 10 11 12 Adult **220.5**
ISBN 978-1-58516-154-6; 1-58516-154-3
"Begun in 1964 with the Gospel of Mark, The New Testament was completed in 1966, with rev. eds. in 1971 and 1976. The whole Bible was published in 1976. An extremely popular, inexpensive translation using contemporary American English. . . . Especially useful for youth or lay Bible study as well as for private reading." Bollier. Lit of Theology

The **Holy** Bible; containing the Old and New Testaments with the Apocryphal/Deuterocanonical books: New Revised Standard Version. Oxford University Press 1989 xxi, 996, 298, 284p map $29.99
Grades: 5 6 7 8 9 10 11 12 Adult **220.5**
ISBN 0-19-528330-9; 978-0-19-528330-3

LC 90-222105
"Intended for public reading, congregational worship, private study, instruction, and meditation, it attempts to be as literal as possible while following standard American English usage, avoids colloquialism, and prefers simple, direct terms and phrases." Sheehy. Guide to Ref Books. 10th edition. suppl

The **New** American Bible; translated from the original languages with critical use of all the ancient sources including the revised Psalms and the revised New Testament. authorized by the Board of Trustees of the Confraternity of Christian Doctrine and approved by the Administrative Committee Board of the National Conference of Catholic Bishops and the United States Catholic Conference. Oxford University Press 2006 xxiii, 1514p $39.99

Grades: 8 9 10 11 12 Adult **220.5**
ISBN 978-0-19-528904-6; 0-19-528904-8
First published 1970 by Kenedy
"Roman Catholic version based on modern English translations; replaces the Douay edition." N Y Public Libr Book of How & Where to Look It Up

The **new** Jerusalem Bible; [general editor: Henry Wansbrough] Doubleday 1985 2108p map $45; pa $29.95
Grades: 7 8 9 10 11 12 Adult **220.5**
ISBN 0-385-14264-1; 978-0-385-14264-9; 0-385-24833-4 pa; 978-0-385-24833-4 pa

LC 85-16070
First published in this format 1966 with title: The Jerusalem Bible
"Derives from the French version edited at the Dominican Ecole Biblique de Jerusalem and known as 'La Bible de Jerusalem.' The introductions and notes are 'a direct translation from the French, though revised and brought up to date in some places' but translation of the Biblical text goes back to the original languages." Guide to Ref Books. 11th edition

220.9 Geography, history, chronology, persons of Bible lands in Bible times

Lottridge, Celia Barker

Stories from Adam and Eve to Ezekiel; retold from the Bible. by Celia Barker Lottridge; illustrated by Gary Clement. Douglas & McIntyre/Groundwood 2004 192p il $24.95
Grades: 4 5 6 7 **220.9**
1. Bible stories
ISBN 0-88899-490-7
"Lottridge uses her storyteller's ear to bring ancient stories from the Hebrew Bible to a young audience, tailoring them to make them more age appropriate. . . . The numerous, well-drawn ink-and-watercolor illustrations are reminiscent of Warwick Hutton's work. Some pictures . . . are quite spectacular." Booklist

Murphy, Claire Rudolf

★ **Daughters** of the desert; stories of remarkable women from Christian, Jewish, and Muslim traditions. [by] Claire Rudolf Murphy . . . [et al.] SkyLight Paths Pub. 2003 178p $19.95
Grades: 7 8 9 10 **220.9**
1. Bible stories 2. Women in the Bible 3. Women in the Qur'an 4. Women in the Koran 5. Women in the Bible -- Biography
ISBN 1-89336-172-1

LC 2002-153821
"Using sacred writings as their basis, the five women authors have reshaped the stories of such individuals as Sarah, Mary Magdalene, Eve, and Khadiji, the wife of Mohammed. . . . The stories are short and simply told, but they are intriguing and invite discussion." Booklist
Includes bibliographical references

Tubb, Jonathan N.

Bible lands. Dorling Kindersley 2000 63p il map (DK eyewitness books) $15.99; lib bdg $19.99

Grades: 4 5 6 7   **220.9**

1. Bible (as subject) -- Antiquities

ISBN 0-7894-5770-9; 0-7694-6579-5 lib bdg

Photographs and text document life in Biblical times, surveying the clothing, food, and civilizations of a wide variety of cultures, including the Israelites, Babylonians, Persians, and Romans.

221.9   Geography, history, chronology, persons of Old Testament lands in Old Testament times

Ward, Elaine M.

Old Testament women; [by] Elaine Ward. Enchanted Lion 2004 32p il (Art revelations) $18.95

Grades: 5 6 7 8   **221.9**

1. Bible stories 2. Women in the Bible

ISBN 1-59270-011-X

These Old Testament stories about women include "explanatory paragraphs, sidebars, and captions by the author. Art masterpieces . . . illustrate each story. . . . The captions provide background on the artist and the significance of each painting or mosaic. . . . The 18 women . . . include Rachel, Leah, Ruth, and Bathsheba. . . . Bosch, Botticelli, and Poussin are among the painters whose work appears here. . . . Visually stunning." SLJ

222   Historical books of Old Testament

Bible/O.T./Pentateuch

The **Torah**: the five books of Moses; a new translation of the Holy Scriptures according to the Masoretic text; first section. Jewish Publication Society 1963 393p $20; pa $15

Grades: 8 9 10 11 12 Adult   **222**

ISBN 0-8276-0015-1; 0-8276-0680-X pa

This "translation of Genesis, Exodus, Leviticus, Numbers, and Deuteronomy was prepared . . . to present a version of the Bible that takes into account modern insights and knowledge of ancient times. . . . Of chief value to persons of the Jewish religion but of interest to Bible scholars of any religion." Booklist

The **contemporary** Torah; a gender-sensitive adaptation of the JPS translation. revising editor, David E.S. Stein; consulting editors, Adele Berlin, Ellen Frankel, and Carol L. Meyers. Jewish Publication Society 2006 xlii, 412p $28

Grades: 8 9 10 11 12 Adult   **222**

ISBN 0-8276-0796-2; 978-0-8276-0796-5

LC 2006-40608

A modern adaptation of the Jewish Publication Society's translation of the Torah. "In places where the ancient audience probably would not have construed gender as pertinent to the text's plain sense, the editors changed words into gender-neutral terms; where gender was probably understood to be at stake, they left the text as originally translated, or even introduced gendered language where none existed before. They made these changes regardless of whether words referred to God, angels, or human beings." Publisher's note

Feiler, Bruce S.

★ **Walking** the Bible; an illustrated journey for kids through the greatest stories ever told. by Bruce Feiler; illustrated by Sasha Meret. HarperCollinsPublishers 2004 108p il map $16.99; lib bdg $17.89

Grades: 5 6 7 8   **222**

1. Authors 2. Journalists 3. Bible (as subject) 4. Travel writers

ISBN 0-06-051117-6; 0-06-051118-4 lib bdg

LC 2003-15861

The author describes his journey through places mentioned in the Old Testament

"In this version of his adult book with the same title (Morrow, 2001), Feiler largely succeeds in slimming rather than dumbing down his account of his trip across the 10,000-mile setting of the earliest Bible stories. The author's unpretentious . . . tone and astute pacing help make the volume accessible, and his sincerity is palpable." SLJ

Fischer, Chuck

★ **In** the beginning: the art of Genesis; a pop-up book. by Chuck Fischer. Little, Brown 2008 un il $35

Grades: 5 6 7 8   **222**

1. Bible stories 2. Religious art 3. Pop-up books

ISBN 978-0-316-11842-2; 0-316-11842-7

LC 2007045411

Fischer "presents an impressive, three-dimensional view of the Book of Genesis. . . . Fischer and his collaborators offer a Garden of Eden scene executed in an artistic style that recalls ancient tile work; a huge Noah's Ark landed atop a mountain; and a Tower of Babel impressively high. . . . The text, more commentary than story, is hidden in inset mini-books and is accompanied by reproductions of biblical masterpieces. . . . This book becomes more amazing as the pages are turned." Booklist

223   Poetic books of Old Testament

Bible/O.T./Ecclesiastes

★ **To** every thing there is a season; verses from Ecclesiastes. illustrations by Leo and Diane Dillon. Blue Sky Press (NY) 1998 un il $16.95

Grades: 4 5 6 7 8   **223**

1. Jesus Christ

ISBN 0-590-47887-7

LC 97-35124

Presents that selection from Ecclesiastes which relates that everything in life has its own time and season

"The Dillons compellingly convey the relevance of the Ecclesiastes verse throughout history, via a stunning array of artwork that embraces motifs from cultures the world over." Publ Wkly

226 Gospels and Acts

Connolly, Sean
New Testament miracles; 1st American ed; Enchanted Lion Books 2004 32p il (Art revelations) $18.95
Grades: 7 8 9 10   **226**
   1. Christian art 2. Miracles -- Christianity
   ISBN 1-59270-012-8

                LC 2003-49414
"The 12 miracles discussed . . . include Jesus healing the man born blind, Jesus raising Lazarus from the dead, and the conversion of Paul. Each one is told from verses in the four Gospels or the Book of Acts, with explanatory paragraphs, sidebars, and captions by the author. Art masterpieces . . . illustrate each story. Works by El Greco, Rembrandt, Tintoretto, and Witz, among others, are featured. . . . Visually stunning." SLJ

230 Christianity

Hale, Rosemary Drage
Christianity. Rosen Pub. 2010 112p il (Understanding religions) lib bdg $31.95
Grades: 7 8 9 10   **230**
   1. Christianity
   ISBN 978-1-4358-5621-9; 1-4358-5621-X

                LC 2009-10295
This book about Christianity "discusses origins and historical development; aspects of the divine; sacred texts, persons, space, and time; ethical principles; death and the afterlife; and society and religion." SLJ
Includes glossary and bibliographical references

Martin, Michael J.
Champion of freedom; Dietrich Bonhoeffer. by Michael Martin. Morgan Reynolds Pub. 2012 144 p. ill. (some col.) (hbk.) $28.95
Grades: 7 8 9 10 11 12   **230**
   1. Clergy 2. Theologians
   ISBN 1599351692; 9781599351698

                LC 2010049095
This book looks at "Dietrich Bonhoeffer [who in 1943] was arrested and imprisoned by the Gestapo for crimes [against] the government. . . . [This] German Lutheran Pastor was integrally involved in the plot to assassinate Adolf Hitler. During his two years of imprisonment, Bonhoeffer manages extreme circumstances, including interrogation and isolation, but is able to protect both himself and his co-conspirators through careful rhetorical practices. How does a pastor and a loyal German justify his involvement in the plot? . . . How could a pastor who penned a book titled Ethics, ethically justify his actions? This book considers some of those questions and is for theologians, ethicists, and rhetoricians as it examines the intersection of faith, politics, and classic rhetorical theory. (Amazon.com)
Includes bibliographical references (p. 140) and index.

Nardo, Don
Christianity. Compass Point Books 2010 48p il map (World religions) lib bdg $27.99
Grades: 5 6 7 8   **230**
   1. Christianity
   ISBN 978-0-7565-4237-5 lib bdg; 0-7565-4237-5 lib bdg

                LC 2009-15811
"The colorful, attractive layout includes high-quality reproductions of photographs, maps, and paintings. Students who are new to religious studies, as well as those doing reports, will find that this . . . meets their needs." SLJ
Includes glossary and bibliographical references

Self, David
★ Christianity; [by] David Self. World Almanac Library 2005 48p il map (Religions of the world) lib bdg $30
Grades: 5 6 7 8   **230**
   1. Christianity
   ISBN 0-8368-5866-2

                LC 2005041712
This is a summary of the Christian religion including history, beliefs, worship, festivals, practice, and current disagreements.
"Wonderfully colorful in images, language, and fact. . . . [This is] enumerated with full-color photographs on every page, charts, maps, and tables." SLJ
Includes bibliographical references

232.9 Family and life of Jesus

Bible/N.T.
★ Jesus; his life in verses from the King James Holy Bible. art by Gennady Spirin. Marshall Cavendish Children 2010 un il $21
Grades: 5 6 7 8   **232.9**
   ISBN 978-0-7614-5630-8; 0-7614-5630-9

                LC 2009005956
"In an unusual project, a tempera painting by Spirin has been digitally dissected to create individual images for this picture book that portrays 13 events from the life of Jesus. . . . Details from the larger work illustrate key moments—including the Annunciation, Jesus' baptism, and the raising of Lazarus, among others—beside passages from the King James Bible (Jesus' words are printed in red). The result is an elegant, large-format volume that offers a reverent and arresting visual interpretation of biblical events." Publ Wkly

Lottridge, Celia Barker
Stories from the life of Jesus; retold from the Bible by Celia Barker Lottridge; illustrated by Linda Wolfsgruber. Doulgas & McIntyre 2004 140p il $24.95
Grades: 4 5 6 7   **232.9**
   1. Bible stories
   ISBN 0-88899-497-4
A retelling of selected events from the life of Christ based on biblical accounts

This is an "exceptional collection. . . . Each story is retold in three or four pages of clear, concise prose that is meant to be read aloud. . . . Each selection is enhanced by dramatic and atmospheric, mixed-media illustrations that are executed in warm earth tones." SLJ

270 History, geographic treatment, biography of Christianity; Church history; Christian denominations and sects

Nardo, Don

The **birth** of Christianity. Morgan Reynolds Pub. 2011 112p il (World religions and beliefs) lib bdg $28.95

Grades: 7 8 9 10   **270**

    1. Christianity 2. Church history
    ISBN 978-1-59935-145-2; 1-59935-145-5
                LC 2010038443

This covers the beginnings of Christianity "in an impartial way. The [context] in which the [religion] developed [is] explained, offering insight into how [Christianity] came to be and introducing major concepts from the [religion]." SLJ

Includes glossary and bibliographical references

274 Christianity by specific continents, countries, localities in modern world

Hinds, Kathryn, 1962-

★ The **church**; Kathryn Hinds. Marshall Cavendish Benchmark 2008 80 p. ill. (library) $34.21

Grades: 6 7 8 9 10 11 12   **274**

    1. Church of England
    ISBN 0761425454; 9780761425458
                LC 2007009392

This describes the role of the Church of England in Elizabethan society, discussing the church's role in the community, the roles of men and women in the church, the church's role in life stages, and holy days.

This offers "good-quality, full-color reproductions. . . . The attractive, open format and the engaging presentation of the subject matter, combined with documented primary-source quotations and sidebars . . . will appeal to both researchers and those who are just interested in learning more about this period." SLJ

Includes bibliographical references (p. 75-76) and index.

Schomp, Virginia

The **church**. Marshall Cavendish Benchmark 2010 80p il (Life in Victorian England) lib bdg $34.21

Grades: 6 7 8 9   **274**

    1. Church of England
    ISBN 978-1-60870-031-8 lib bdg; 1-60870-031-3 lib bdg
                LC 2010006901

Describes the role of religion in the lives of Victorians, including how it influenced the way they lived, how they observed special occasions, and how they coped with the many changes and challenges of their times

This "is clearly written, thorough, and informative. The visually rich layout includes photographs and paintings from the time period, full-page illustrations, and attention-grabbing sidebars. Most appealing are the primary source quotations, which are plentiful and relevant." Libr Media Connect

Includes glossary and bibliographical references

280 Denominations and sects of Christian church

Brown, Stephen F.

Catholicism & Orthodox Christianity; by Stephen F. Brown and Khaled Anatolios. 3rd ed.; Chelsea House 2009 144p il (World religions) $40

Grades: 7 8 9 10 11 12   **280**

    1. Catholic Church 2. Orthodox Eastern Church
    ISBN 978-1-60413-106-2; 1-60413-106-3
                LC 2008-43046

First published 2002 by Facts and File

This "traces the roots of [Catholicism and Orthodox Christianity] from the early Christian churches to today. The historical passage of the Catholic and Orthodox faiths is recounted, from the original teachings of Jesus Christ to the separation of the Eastern and Western Churches to recent attempts at reconciliation." Publisher's note

Includes glossary and bibliographical references

Protestantism; 3rd ed.; Chelsea House 2009 144p il map (World religions) $40

Grades: 7 8 9 10 11 12   **280**

    1. Protestantism
    ISBN 978-1-60413-112-3; 1-60413-112-8
                LC 2008-29659

First published 1991 by Facts on File

This "explores the origins, customs, and history of Protestantism, from its beginnings in the Middle Ages to its role in today's world. Current issues, such as the development of new religious denominations, its stance on abortion, the ordination of gays and women, and the relationship between religion and politics, are explored within the framework of the fundamental moral tenets of the faith." Publisher's note

Includes glossary and bibliographical references

Noll, Mark A.

★ **Protestants** in America; general editors, Jon Butler and Harry S. Stout. Oxford University Press 2000 155p il (Religion in American life) lib bdg $28

Grades: 7 8 9 10   **280**

    1. Protestant churches 2. Protestant churches -- History
    3. Protestant churches -- United States -- History
    ISBN 0-19-511034-X
                LC 00-27271

Discusses the origins of Protestantism, the diversity of Protestant churches in the United States, and the role of Protestants in American life from colonial times to the present

"This volume is especially valuable for its discussion of the church in the African-American community and its coverage of smaller sects, like the Shakers. The many black-

and-white photographs and reproduction add immensely to the text." SLJ

Includes bibliographical references

289.3   Latter-Day Saints (Mormons)

Bial, Raymond

Nauvoo; Mormon city on the Mississippi River. [by] Raymond Bial. Houghton Mifflin Co. 2006 44p il map $17

Grades: 5 6 7 8   **289.3**
1. Mormons 2. Church of Jesus Christ of Latter-day Saints
ISBN 978-0-618-39685-6; 0-618-39685-3
LC 2005027528

"Bial introduces readers to a city that was established by the Church of Jesus Christ of Latter Day Saints in 1839. . . . This effectively written account provides a sympathetic but balanced introduction to Mormon beliefs. . . . Excellent color photographs grace almost every page." SLJ

Book of Mormon

★ The **Book** of Mormon; another testament of Jesus Christ. [translated by Joseph Smith, Jr.] Doubleday 2004 586p $24.95

Grades: 8 9 10 11 12 Adult   **289.3**
1. Mormons 2. Church of Jesus Christ of Latter-day Saints
ISBN 0-385-51316-X
LC 2004-51982
First published 1830

"Based on golden plates which Joseph Smith claimed were revealed to him, and which he unearthed from Cumorah Hill, New York, this book is roughly similar in structure to the Bible. . . . Emphasized are the doctrines of pre-existence, perfection, the afterlife, and Christ's second coming." Haydn. Thesaurus of Book Dig

Bushman, Claudia L.

★ **Mormons** in America; [by] Claudia Lauper Bushman and Richard Lyman Bushman. Oxford Univ. Press 1998 142p il (Religion in American life) $28

Grades: 7 8 9 10   **289.3**
1. Mormons 2. Church of Jesus Christ of Latter-day Saints 3. Mormon Church -- United States
ISBN 0-19-510677-6
LC 98-18605

Chronicles the history of the Church of Jesus Christ of Latter-Day Saints beginning in America in the early 1800s and continuing to the present day throughout the world

"A solid resource for libraries. Illustrated with historical material and black-and-white photos. Time line and bibliography appended." Booklist

Includes bibliographical references

292   Classical religion (Greek and Roman religion)

Bryant, Megan E.

Oh my gods! a look-it-up guide to the gods of mythology. Franklin Watts 2009 128p il map (Mythlopedia) lib bdg $39; pa $13.95

Grades: 4 5 6 7   **292**
1. Gods and goddesses 2. Classical mythology
ISBN 978-1-60631-026-7 lib bdg; 1-60631-026-7 lib bdg; 978-1-60631-058-8 pa; 1-60631-058-5 pa
LC 2009-17169

Presents a guide to Greek mythology, providing profiles of gods and goddesses along with information on monsters, heroes, and the underworld.

"The book is organized around entries on major gods and titans, each with vital stats and a Top 10 Things to Know about Me, followed by a few highlights from their lore and sidebars that delve into their cultural relevance. Illustrations abound, from embellished stock images to original cartoons, and the pastel-heavy color scheme may entice readers otherwise resistant to the grays and ivories that tend to dominate classicism." Booklist

Includes glossary and bibliographical references

She's all that! a look-it-up guide to the goddesses of mythology. Franklin Watts 2009 128p il map (Mythlopedia) lib bdg $39; pa $13.95

Grades: 4 5 6 7   **292**
1. Gods and goddesses 2. Classical mythology
ISBN 978-1-60631-027-4 lib bdg; 1-60631-027-5 lib bdg; 978-1-60631-059-5 pa; 1-60631-059-3 pa
LC 2009-17168

Presents a guide to Greek mythology, providing profiles of goddesses and the myths surrounding them.

This "spices things up with sassy artwork, a pastel color scheme, and an OMG sensibility. . . . Aside from the heaps of information coming from all angles on just about every page, . . . [this] book also contains a decent family tree, a rudimentary star chart, and lists of further reading. . . . For kids unconvinced that anything so old and gray could have any bearing on their lives, . . . [this provides] a feisty . . . guide to the many cultural references lingering from antiquity." Booklist

Includes glossary and bibliographical references

Daly, Kathleen N.

Greek and Roman mythology, A to Z; [by] Kathleen N. Daly; revised by Marian Rengel. 3rd ed.; Chelsea House Publishers 2009 162p il (Mythology A to Z) lib bdg $45

Grades: 8 9 10 11 12   **292**
1. Classical mythology
ISBN 978-1-60413-412-4; 1-60413-412-7
LC 2009-8243
First published 1992 by Facts on File

Alphabetically listed entries identify and explain the characters, events, important places, and other aspects of Greek and Roman mythology

"The format is accessible, making the book useful for school assignments, as well as enjoyable for general reading. Each entry provides a clear definition, and retells the stories associated with the character or place. The broad coverage, ample cross-references, and extensive index enable readers to recognize the many connections and interrelationships between characters and myths." SLJ [review of 1992 edition]

Includes bibliographical references

Evans, Hestia

The **mythology** handbook; a course in ancient Greek myths. by Hestia Evans; edited by Dugald A. Steer and Clint Twist. Candlewick Press 2009 71p il map $12.99

Grades: 4 5 6 7   **292**

1. Classical mythology

ISBN 978-0-7636-4291-4

"This follow-up to Mythology (Candlewick, 2007) again uses the voice of a fictional 19th-century scholar. Here, Lady Hestia Evans offers a guide to elements of Greek myth for her two children, providing information in 'lessons' . . . with exercises based on each topic. Some of the activities encourage students to do further research . . . while others suggest that they draw new monsters, write hymns with the Muses' help, or design a new pentathlon for the Olympics. Mazes and a word search (using Greek letters) are also included. . . . The activities are engaging, and the illustrations of creatures and maps of the ancient world will add to the knowledge of even more experienced myth fans." SLJ

Fleischman, Paul

★ **Dateline**: Troy; [by] Paul Fleischman; collages by Gwen Frankfeldt & Glenn Morrow. new updated ed.; Candlewick Press 2006 80p il $18.99

Grades: 7 8 9 10   **292**

1. Trojan War

ISBN 978-0-7636-3083-6; 0-7636-3083-7

First published 1996

A retelling of the story of the Trojan War illustrated with collages featuring newspaper clippings of modern events from World War I through the Iraq War

Hamilton, Edith

Mythology; illustrated by Steele Savage. Little, Brown 1942 497p il $27.95; pa $13.95

Grades: 8 9 10 11 12 Adult   **292**

1. Trojan War 2. Norse mythology 3. Gods and goddesses 4. Classical mythology 5. Perseus (Greek mythology) 6. Theseus (Greek mythology) 7. Odysseus (Greek mythology) 8. Argonauts (Greek mythology) 9. Aeneas (Legendary character) 10. Hercules (Legendary character)

ISBN 0-316-34114-2; 0-316-34151-7 pa

A retelling of Greek, Roman and Norse myths

McCaughrean, Geraldine

★ **Hercules**; retold by Geraldine McCaughrean. Cricket Books 2005 142p il (Heroes) $16.95

Grades: 5 6 7 8   **292**

1. Classical mythology 2. Hercules (Legendary character)

ISBN 978-0-8126-2737-4; 0-8126-2737-7

LC 2005004524

First published 2003 by Oxford University Press

This is a retelling of the twelve labors of Hercules including his battles with the Cretan Bull, the many-headed Hydra, the Nemean Lion, and the three-headed guardian of hell, Cerberus.

"This volume does a creditable job of making Hercules a dimensional character whose struggles against fate and the vindictiveness of the gods arouse readers' sympathy. . . . McCaughrean enlivens the familiar story with arresting imagery." SLJ

★ **Odysseus**; retold by Geraldine McCaughrean. Cricket Books 2004 148p il (Heroes) $16.95

Grades: 5 6 7 8   **292**

1. Classical mythology 2. Odysseus (Greek mythology) 3. Young adult literature -- Works 4. Mythology, Greek 5. Odysseus (Greek mythology)

ISBN 978-0-8126-2721-3; 0-8126-2721-0

LC 2004-10734

"With mounting suspense, wild action, and simple, rhythmic prose, this dramatic retelling of Homer's classic makes a gripping read-aloud as well as an exciting introduction to the story." Booklist

★ **Perseus**; retold by Geraldine McCaughrean. Cricket Books 2005 118p il (Heroes) $16.95

Grades: 5 6 7 8   **292**

1. Classical mythology 2. Perseus (Greek mythology)

ISBN 978-0-8126-2735-0; 0-8126-2735-0

This "makes a thrilling read-aloud. . . . McCaughrean blends the colloquial and contemporary into the heroic quest." Booklist

Mitchell, Adrian, 1941-

★ **Shapeshifters**; tales from Ovid's Metamorphoses. retold by Adrian Mitchell; illustrated by Alan Lee. Frances Lincoln Children's 2010 143p il $22.95

Grades: 7 8 9 10   **292**

1. Classical mythology

ISBN 1-84507-536-6; 978-1-84507-536-1

This is a "marvelous re-creation of myth from Ovid. . . . The language is simple and contemporary, moving from rhyme to free verse to prose and back again. . . . All of these stories explore mystery: the origins of flowers, mountains, lakes. Pygmalion, Persephone, Midas and Arachne all appear here . . . [Lee] makes men and women, gods and beasts, sea, sky and leaf shimmer." Kirkus

Nardo, Don

The **Greenhaven** encyclopedia of Greek and Roman mythology; Don Nardo, author; Barbette Spaeth, consulting editor. Greenhaven Press 2002 304p il (Greenhaven encyclopedia of) lib bdg $76.20

Grades: 7 8 9 10   **292**

1. Classical mythology

ISBN 0-7377-0719-4

LC 2001-40864

This is an overview of classical mythology, its heroes, and its influence on the history of Western civilization

Includes bibliographical references

Otfinoski, Steven

All in the family; a look-it-up guide to the in-laws, outlaws, and offspring of mythology. F. Watts 2009 128p il (Mythlopedia) lib bdg $39; pa $13.95

Grades: 4 5 6 7   **292**

1. Classical mythology

ISBN 978-1-60631-025-0 lib bdg; 1-60631-025-9 lib bdg; 978-1-60631-057-1 pa; 1-60631-057-7 pa

    LC 2009-20999

"Jam-packed with trivia, brief profiles, god and goddess relationships, stories, 'Top 10 Things to Know About Me' facts, and entertaining illustrations, this title explores 20 heroes and mortals of classic Greek mythology. The selections include the well-known Achilles, Heracles, Odysseus, and Pandora and the more obscure Meleager, Orion, Atalanta, and Bellerophon; each one is given lively treatment. . . . The lighthearted style and humorous collage and cartoon illustrations may draw even the most reluctant of readers. " SLJ

Includes glossary and bibliographical references

Rylant, Cynthia

The **beautiful** stories of life; six Greek myths, retold. illustrated by Carson Ellis. Harcourt 2009 71p il $16

Grades: 5 6 7 8   **292**

1. Classical mythology   2. Mythology, Greek

ISBN 978-0-15-206184-5; 0-15-206184-3

    LC 2007-34808

"Rylant retells the stories of Pandora, Persephone, Orpheus, Pygmalion, Narcissus, and Psyche in this trim, handsome book. Written in a modern style with an old-fashioned feel, the selections sit well with other titles in the genre. . . . Accompanied by full-page black-and-white illustrations and sprinkled with decorations, the whole package is nicely done." SLJ

Schomp, Virginia

The **ancient** Greeks; [by] Virginia Schomp. Marshall Cavendish Benchmark 2007 96p il map (Myths of the world) lib bdg $22.95

Grades: 6 7 8 9   **292**

1. Classical mythology

ISBN 978-0-7614-2547-2

    LC 2006028375

"With [its] beautiful illustrations, high-quality production, and focus on source material, the [book] should whet the interest of readers." SLJ

Includes glossary and bibliographical references

The **ancient** Romans; [by] Virginia Schomp. Marshall Cavendish Benchmark 2008 96p il map (Myths of the world) lib bdg $23.93

Grades: 6 7 8 9   **292**

1. Classical mythology

ISBN 978-0-7614-3094-0; 0-7614-3094-6

    LC 2008007083

"A retelling of several key ancient Roman myths, with background information describing the history, geography, belief systems, and customs of ancient Rome." Publisher's note

Includes glossary and bibliographical references

Turnbull, Ann

★ **Greek** myths; retold by Ann Turnbull; illustrated by Sarah Young. Candlewick Press 2011 165p il $18.99

Grades: 5 6 7 8 9 10   **292**

1. Classical mythology   3. Mythology, Greek

ISBN 0-7636-5111-7; 978-0-7636-5111-4

    LC 2010-39178

Turnbull divides sixteen Greek myths "under three headings: Earth, the Heavens, and the Underworld; Monsters and Heroes; Gods and Mortals. . . . Grades five to ten." (Bull Cent Child Books)

"Sixteen Greek myths . . . are retold here with stylistic grace well matched to beautiful visual presentation. . . . Turnbull narrates with . . . vibrancy. . . . Sarah Young's mixed-media artwork—regal, yet sensuous compositions in richly textured earthtones touch[ed] with gold—is sufficiently representational to assist younger readers with context clues, and sufficiently elegant and sophisticated to satisfy seasoned readers." Bull Cent Child Books

293   Germanic religion

Daly, Kathleen N.

Norse mythology A to Z; [by] Kathleen N. Daly; revised by Marian Rengel. 3rd ed.; Chelsea House 2009 128p il map (Mythology A to Z) lib bdg $45

Grades: 8 9 10 11 12   **293**

1. Reference books   2. Norse mythology -- Dictionaries

ISBN 978-1-60413-411-7; 1-60413-411-9

    LC 2009-13338

First published 1991

Alphabetically listed entries identify and explain the characters, events, and important places of Norse mythology

Includes bibliographical references

Porterfield, Jason

Scandinavian mythology; [by] Jason Porterfield. Rosen Pub. Group 2008 64p il map (Mythology around the world) lib bdg $29.95

Grades: 5 6 7 8   **293**

1. Norse mythology

ISBN 978-1-4042-0740-0 lib bdg; 1-4042-0740-6 lib bdg

    LC 2005037508

The author describes the history of "the Scandinavian nations, introducing concepts and characters central to Norse myths. . . . The most remarkable part of [this book] . . . is the respect [it shows] for the mythological customs, treating them throughout with the same care that writers of books on major religions might offer. The illustrations show both ancient and modern incarnations of the deities and heroes described in the [text]." SLJ

Includes glossary and bibliographical references

Schomp, Virginia

The **Norsemen**; [by] Virginia Schomp. Marshall Cavendish Benchmark 2007 96p il map (Myths of the world) lib bdg $22.95

Grades: 6 7 8 9   **293**
1. Norse mythology
ISBN 978-0-7614-2548-9
LC 2007002772
"With [its] beautiful illustrations, high-quality production, and focus on source material, the [book] should whet the interest of readers." SLJ
Includes bibliographical references

294   Religions of Indic origin

Mann, Gurinder Singh
Buddhists, Hindus, and Sikhs in America; [by] Gurinder Singh Mann, Paul David Numrich & Raymond B. Williams. Oxford University Press 2001 158p il (Religion in American life) hardcover o.p. pa $12.95
Grades: 7 8 9 10   **294**
1. Sikhism 2. Buddhism 3. Hinduism 4. Asian Americans -- Religion 5. Immigrants -- Religious life -- United States
ISBN 0-19-512442-1; 0-19-533311-X pa
LC 2001-45151
Presents the basic tenets of these three Asian religions and discusses the religious history and experience of their practitioners after immigration to the United States
"Solid information, a large selection of historical and contemporary photographs, interesting readings from primary sources, and accounts from school-age Buddhists, Hindus, and Sikhs combine to make this is a valuable resource." Booklist
Includes bibliographical references

Ollhoff, Jim
Indian mythology. ABDO Pub. 2012 32 p. il map lib bdg $27.07
Grades: 5 6 7 8   **294**
1. Hinduism 2. Indic mythology
ISBN 978-1-61714-722-7; 1-61714-722-2
LC 2010041628
'This book offers information about Indian mythology, answering questions such as "Who is Devi? What is Ganesha? Why are myths so important in our lives? Myths are a rich source of history. People use them to make sense of our world. Even before myths were written down, people told and retold the stories of the gods and goddesses of their homeland. Readers of Indian Mythology will learn the history of myths, as well as their deeper meaning." (Publisher's note)
"Ollhoff writes in a clear and engaging fashion, presenting complex issues in a way that will be easy for youngsters to grasp. . . . The photographs and reproductions of art tie directly to the [text]." SLJ

294.3   Buddhism

Demi
★ **Buddha**. Holt & Co. 1996 un il $21.95

Grades: 4 5 6   **294.3**
1. Philosophers 2. Buddhist leaders 3. Buddhism 4. Children's literature -- Works -- Grades two through six
ISBN 0-8050-4203-2
LC 95-16906
Demi "uses clear, uncomplicated storytelling to present complex philosophical concepts. . . . The gilded illustrations (based, according to the jacket, on 'Indian, Chinese, Japanese, Burmese, and Indonesian paintings, sculptures, and sutra illustrations') are delicate, yet the colors and composition are bold, with central figures and action cascading beyond the careful borders." Bull Cent Child Books

★ The **Dalai** Lama; a biography of the Tibetan spiritual and political leader. Henry Holt & Co. 1998 un il $18.95
Grades: 4 5 6 7   **294.3**
1. Buddhism 2. Buddhist leaders 3. Political leaders 4. Nobel laureates for peace 5. Dalai Lamas -- Biography
ISBN 0-8050-5443-X
LC 97-30654
In this biography of the Buddhist spiritual leader, Demi "uses straightforward prose and fluid, eastern-influenced art—small pen-and-ink and watercolor images with fine, intricate detail. . . . Told with respect and devotion, this is an inspirational picture-book biography." Horn Book

Eckel, Malcolm David
Buddhism. Rosen Pub. 2010 112p il (Understanding religions) lib bdg $31.95
Grades: 7 8 9 10   **294.3**
1. Buddhism
ISBN 978-1-4358-5619-6; 1-4358-5619-8
LC 2009-10083
Subjects covered in this book include "buddhas and bodhisattvas, Zen meditation, Tantric scriptures, pilgrimage, temples, and festivals and rites." Publisher's note
Includes glossary and bibliographical references

Ganeri, Anita
★ **Buddhism**; [by] Anita Ganeri. World Almanac Library 2006 48p il map (Religions of the world) lib bdg $30.60
Grades: 5 6 7 8   **294.3**
1. Buddhism
ISBN 0-8368-5865-4
LC 2005041708
The author "presents a survey of Buddhist history, beliefs, sacred texts, festivals, and lifecycle events. . . . There is discussion of the art and folk literature associated with the religious tradition. Colorful photographs, illustrations, and art reproductions appear throughout." SLJ
Includes bibliographical references

Gedney, Mona
★ The **life** and times of Buddha. Mitchell Lane Pubs. 2005 48p il map (Biography from ancient civilizations) lib bdg $19.95
Grades: 5 6 7 8   **294.3**
1. Philosophers 2. Buddhist leaders
ISBN 1-58415-342-3

A biography of Siddhartha Gautama, who became known as Buddha

This "offers a fluid and lively retelling of the basic story, including insight into the broader context of the times, an introduction to the teachings of [Buddha], and a recounting of the facts that most believers would assent to." SLJ

Includes bibliographical references

Lee, Jeanne M.

I once was a monkey; stories Buddha told. Farrar, Straus & Giroux 1999 un il $16

Grades: 4 5 6 7   **294.3**

1. Jataka stories 2. Jataka stories, English
ISBN 0-374-33548-6

LC 98-17651

A retelling of six Jatakas, or birth stories, which illustrate some of the central tenets of Buddha's teachings, such as compassion, honesty, and thinking clearly before acting

"The appealing character of the monkey will pull children into the tales, which convey lessons in a direct yet gentle way that is never preachy. The accompanying linocut illustrations are lovely." Booklist

Nardo, Don

Buddhism. Compass Point Books 2009 48p il map (World religions) lib bdg $27.99

Grades: 5 6 7 8   **294.3**

1. Buddhism
ISBN 978-0-7565-4236-8 lib bdg; 0-7565-4236-7 lib bdg

LC 2009-11453

"The colorful, attractive layout includes high-quality reproductions of photographs, maps, and paintings. Students who are new to religious studies, as well as those doing reports, will find that this . . . meets their needs." SLJ

Includes glossary and bibliographical references

Wangu, Madhu Bazaz

Buddhism; 4th ed.; Chelsea House 2009 144p il (World religions) $40

Grades: 7 8 9 10 11 12   **294.3**

1. Buddhism
ISBN 978-1-60413-105-5; 1-60413-105-5

LC 2008-51265

First published 1993 by Facts on File

This "tells the story of Buddhism's origins and its development into three major schools of thought—and presents the particular beliefs and practices of those schools of Buddhism. . . . [This] title explores the concept of the 'socially engaged Buddhist,' the growth and practice of Buddhism in America, and the recent revival of Buddhism in Asia." Publisher's note

Includes glossary and bibliographical references

Winston, Diana

★ **Wide** awake: a Buddhist guide for teens. Perigee Bk. 2003 290p pa $13.95

Grades: 7 8 9 10 11 12   **294.3**

1. Buddhism
ISBN 0-399-52897-0

LC 2002-192666

"Switching between anecdotes of her own journey in Buddhism and advice on how teens can apply the Buddha's teachings to their lives, Winston offers a personal and thoughtful introduction to Buddhist thought and practice." Booklist

294.5   Hinduism

Ganeri, Anita

The **Ramayana** and Hinduism. Smart Apple Media 2003 30p il (Sacred texts) $27.10

Grades: 5 6 7 8 9   **294.5**

1. Hinduism
ISBN 1-58340-242-X

LC 2003-42352

Explains the history and practices of the religion of Hinduism, especially as revealed through its sacred book, the Ramayana

Narayanan, Vasudha

Hinduism. Rosen Pub. 2010 112p il (Understanding religions) lib bdg $31.95

Grades: 7 8 9 10   **294.5**

1. Hinduism
ISBN 978-1-4358-5620-2; 1-4358-5620-1

LC 2009-11026

This book about Hinduism "discusses origins and historical development; aspects of the divine; sacred texts, persons, space, and time; ethical principles; death and the afterlife; and society and religion." SLJ

Includes glossary and bibliographical references

Plum-Ucci, Carol

Celebrate Diwali; [by] Carol Plum-Ucci. Enslow Publishers 2008 128p il map (Celebrate holidays) $31.93

Grades: 5 6 7 8   **294.5**

1. Divali
ISBN 978-0-7660-2778-7; 0-7660-2778-3

LC 2006028106

This describes the history, cultural significance, customs, symbols and celebrations around the world of the Hindu holiday of Diwali.

"Captioned photographs, maps, drawings, and sidebars combine with accessible text to present a thorough discussion of [Diwali]. . . . This . . . is a useful resource." Horn Book Guide

Includes glossary and bibliographical references

Rasamandala Das

★ **Hinduism**. World Almanac Library 2006 48p il map (Religions of the world) $30.60

Grades: 5 6 7 8   **294.5**

1. Hinduism
ISBN 0-8368-5867-0

Hinduism is "explored in an accessible introductory manner, including information on [its] history, teachings, religious practices, culture and lifestyle, and the [faith's role] in today's global society. Vibrant full-color photographs are appropriately placed within the [text]. Ideal for . . . school reports or for general interest." SLJ

Includes bibliographical references

Rosinsky, Natalie M.

Hinduism. Compass Point Books 2009 48p il map (World religions) lib bdg $27.99

Grades: 5 6 7 8   **294.5**

1. Hinduism

ISBN 978-0-7565-4238-2 lib bdg; 0-7565-4238-3 lib bdg

LC 2009-9349

"The colorful, attractive layout includes high-quality reproductions of photographs, maps, and paintings. Students who are new to religious studies, as well as those doing reports, will find that this . . . meets their needs." SLJ

Includes glossary and bibliographical references

Schomp, Virginia

Ancient India. Marshall Cavendish Benchmark 2009 96p il (Myths of the world) lib bdg $34.21

Grades: 6 7 8 9   **294.5**

1. Buddhism 2. Hindu mythology 3. Indic mythology

ISBN 978-0-7614-4213-4 lib bdg; 0-7614-4213-8 lib bdg

LC 2008034952

"The language is straightforward but has enough variation in sentence structure to keep the reading lively. . . . Liberally illustrated with large and vibrant reproductions of artwork in diverse media, the [book reflects] the grace and opulence of [this] ancient [culture] as well as the more vividly grotesque expressions of imagination." SLJ

Includes glossary and bibliographical references

Wangu, Madhu Bazaz

Hinduism; 4th ed.; Chelsea House 2009 144p il (World religions) $40

Grades: 7 8 9 10 11 12   **294.5**

1. Hinduism

ISBN 978-1-60413-108-6; 1-60413-108-X

LC 2008-43047

First published 1991 by Facts on File

This describes the history of Hinduism, its customs, beliefs, and rites of passage, the Hindu nationalist movement in India, Hinduism and the interfaith movement, and Hinduism and the environmental movement.

Includes glossary and bibliographical references

294.6   Sikhism

Singh, Nikky-Guninder Kaur

Sikhism; 3rd ed.; Chelsea House 2009 144p il (World religions) $40

Grades: 7 8 9 10 11 12   **294.6**

1. Sikhism

ISBN 978-1-60413-114-7; 1-60413-114-4

LC 2008-29662

First published 1993 by Facts on File

This "describes the basic tenets of Sikhism, examines the recent move toward greater political independence with-

in the Indian nation, and covers issues of cultural adaptation, persecution, and subsequent education now taking place in the West." Publisher's note

Includes glossary and bibliographical references

295   Zoroastrianism (Mazdaism, Parseeism)

Hartz, Paula

Zoroastrianism; by Paula R. Hartz. 3rd ed.; Chelsea House 2009 144p il (World religions) $40

Grades: 7 8 9 10 11 12   **295**

1. Zoroastrianism

ISBN 978-1-60413-116-1; 1-60413-116-0

LC 2008-35811

First published 1999 by Facts on File

This "analyzes how [Zoroastrianism] has a crucial place in religious history and continues to maintain a devoted following today." Publisher's note

Includes glossary and bibliographical references

Schomp, Virginia

The **ancient** Persians. Marshall Cavendish Benchmark 2009 96p il (Myths of the world) lib bdg $34.21

Grades: 6 7 8 9   **295**

1. Poets 2. Zoroastrianism

ISBN 978-0-7614-4218-9 lib bdg; 0-7614-4218-9 lib bdg

LC 2009011876

"The language is straightforward but has enough variation in sentence structure to keep the reading lively. . . . Liberally illustrated with large and vibrant reproductions of artwork in diverse media, the [book reflects] the grace and opulence of [this] ancient [culture] as well as the more vividly grotesque expressions of imagination." SLJ

Includes glossary and bibliographical references

296   Judaism

Buxbaum, Shelley M.

Jewish faith in America; {by} Shelley M. Buxbaum, Sara E. Karesh. Facts on File 2003 128p il (Faith in America) $30

Grades: 7 8 9 10   **296**

1. Judaism 2. Jews -- United States 3. Jews -- United States -- History 4. Judaism -- United States -- History

ISBN 0-8160-4986-6

LC 2002-29392

"Thoroughly researched and heavily illustrated." Libr Media Connect

Includes glossary and bibliographical references

Ehrlich, Carl S.

Judaism. Rosen Pub. 2010 112p il (Understanding religions) lib bdg $31.95

Grades: 7 8 9 10   **296**

1. Judaism

ISBN 978-1-4358-5622-6; 1-4358-5622-8

LC 2009-10055

This "book provides students with an overview of the great religious tradition of Judaism. Readers learn about the covenant with God, the Bible, the Mishnah, and the Talmud. They also read about sects, messianic movements, mysticism, and the Kabbalah. Rabbinical systems of law and custom are covered as are various principles and practices, holy days, and contemporary movements in Judaism." Publisher's note

Includes glossary and bibliographical references

Keene, Michael

★ **Judaism**; [by] Michael Keene. World Almanac Library 2006 48p il map (Religions of the world) lib bdg $30.60

Grades: 5 6 7 8   **296**

1. Judaism

ISBN 0-8368-5869-7

LC 2005041734

This "volume presents fundamental beliefs and faith foundations, current status and practices of [Judaism] around the globe, and a time line of historically significant events. . . . The [book is] enumerated with full-color photographs on every page, charts, maps, and tables. . . . [This title] will enhance the education of diverse populations." SLJ

Includes bibliographical references

Morrison, M. A.

Judaism; by Martha A. Morrison and Stephen F. Brown. 4th ed.; Chelsea House 2009 144p il (World religions) $40

Grades: 7 8 9 10 11 12   **296**

1. Judaism

ISBN 978-1-60413-110-9; 1-60413-110-1

LC 2008-29657

First published 1991 by Facts on File under the authorship of Fay Carol Gates

This "presents the basic beliefs of the Jewish religious heritage and highlights the different manners in which these traditions can be upheld. Both Orthodox Judaism and the religious practices and movements within Reformed Judaism, including Reform Judaism, Conservative Judaism, and Reconstructionist Judaism, are explored." Publisher's note

Includes glossary and bibliographical references

Rosinsky, Natalie M.

Judaism. Compass Point Books 2009 48p il map (World religions) lib bdg $27.99

Grades: 5 6 7 8   **296**

1. Judaism

ISBN 978-0-7565-4240-5 lib bdg; 0-7565-4240-5 lib bdg

LC 2009-15813

"The colorful, attractive layout includes high-quality reproductions of photographs, maps, and paintings. Students who are new to religious studies, as well as those doing reports, will find that this . . . meets their needs." SLJ

Includes glossary and bibliographical references

296.03

The **Oxford** dictionary of the Jewish religion; editor in chief, Adele Berlin. 2nd ed. Oxford University Press 2011 xxiv, 934 p.p (hardcover) $195

Grades: 8 9 10 11 12 Adult   **296.03**

1. Judaism -- Dictionaries 2. Judaism -- Encyclopedias

ISBN 0199730040; 9780199730049; 9780199759279

LC 2010035774

This book, by Maxine Grossman, edited by Adele Berlin, presents an updated, second edition of its original 1997 publication. It "focuses on recent and changing rituals in the Jewish community. . . . Nearly 200 internationally renowned scholars have created a new edition that incorporates updated bibliographies, biographies of 20th-century individuals who have shaped the recent thought and history of Judaism, and an index with alternate spellings of Hebrew terms." (Publisher's note)

Includes bibliographical references and index.

296.1   Sources

Chaikin, Miriam

★ **Angels** sweep the desert floor; Bible legends about Moses in the wilderness. illustrated by Alexander Koshkin. Clarion Bks. 2002 102p il $19

Grades: 4 5 6 7   **296.1**

1. Prophets 2. Bible stories 3. Jewish legends 4. Legends, Jewish 5. Biblical characters 6. Midrash 7. Angels (Judaism)

ISBN 0-395-97825-4

LC 2001-47501

A collection of eighteen stories based on the Bible which tell how angels respond to God's commands to ease the way for Moses and the Israelites as they cross the wilderness after being freed from slavery in Egypt

"The full-page watercolor, tempera, and gouache illustrations have a fanciful formality that complements the narrative. Capable of exciting the creative, as well as the spiritual imagination, these wonderful stories make great read-alouds." SLJ

Includes bibliographical references

Pinsker, Marlee

In the days of sand and stars; illustrated by François Thisdale. Tundra Books 2006 87p il $22.95

Grades: 5 6 7 8   **296.1**

1. Bible stories 2. Jewish legends 3. Women in the Bible

ISBN 978-0-88776-724-1; 0-88776-724-9

This is a collection of stories from the Midrash about women including Eve, Naamah, Sarai, Sarah, Rebecca, Leah, Rachel, Dina, and Yocheved.

"Pinsker works like a musician, playing with words instead of notes, but the result is just as lilting and lyrical. The stories are matched by unusual illustrations. Thisdale blends traditional artwork with digital technology. Pieces of photographs mix with ancient elements, giving the pictures a fresh, compelling look." Booklist

296.4   Traditions, rites, public services

Kimmel, Eric A.

★ **Wonders** and miracles; a Passover companion. illustrated with art spanning three thousand years; written and compiled by Eric A. Kimmel. Scholastic Press 2004 136p il $18.95

Grades: 4 5 6 7   **296.4**

1. Passover
ISBN 0-439-07175-5

LC 2002-4732

Presents the steps performed in a traditional Passover Seder, plus stories, songs, poetry, and pictures that celebrate the historical significance of this holiday to Jews all over the world.

"The marvelous selection of art—paintings, photographs, artifacts, and illustrations from historical Haggadahs—illuminates each step in the service. . . . Both the presentation of information and the overall design attest to the careful and loving attention given to every detail. This inviting, handsome, and informative compendium should find a place of honor in every library." SLJ

Includes bibliographical references

Metter, Bert

Bar mitzvah, bat mitzvah; the ceremony, the party, and how the day came to be. by Bert Metter; illustrated by Joan Reilly. Clarion Books 2007 un il $16; pa $5.95

Grades: 4 5 6 7   **296.4**

1. Bar mitzvah 2. Bat mitzvah
ISBN 978-0-618-76772-4; 0-618-76772-X; 978-0-618-76773-1 pa; 0-618-76773-8 pa

LC 2006032942

The author "describes a typical ceremony and explains how this custom began for boys during the Middle Ages and how it was adapted for girls beginning in 1922. He also discusses the recent custom of adult bar and bat mitzvahs and celebratory parties. The writing is clear and concise; ink illustrations . . . help break up the text." Booklist

Includes bibliographical references

297   Islam, Babism, Bahai Faith

Alkouatli, Claire

Islam. Marshall Cavendish 2006 143p il (World religions) lib bdg $39.93

Grades: 7 8 9 10   **297**

1. Islam
ISBN 978-0-7614-2120-7 lib bdg; 0-7614-2120-3 lib bdg

LC 2005026862

This offers a "fine, well-detailed overview of the second largest religion in the world." Booklist

Includes glossary and bibliographical references

Aslan, Reza, 1972-

No god but God; the origins and evolution of Islam. Delacorte Press 2011 166p $16.99; lib bdg $19.99

Grades: 7 8 9 10   **297**

1. Islam -- History
ISBN 0-385-73975-3; 0-385-90805-9 lib bdg; 978-0-385-73975-7; 978-0-385-90805-4 lib bdg

LC 2010020408

Adaptation of: No god but God: the origins, evolution, and future of Islam, published 2006 by Random House for adults

"Packing in a formidable amount of research, legend, and critical analysis, Aslan condenses his adult book of the same name to create a concise introduction to Islam. By breaking up chapters with clear subheadings, maintaining a conversational tone, and incorporating numerous anecdotes that both inform and entertain, Aslan makes 15 centuries of religious history digestible without oversimplifying complex material. . . . This welcome addition to Islamic studies provides a valuable context for reflection about the origins of issues facing Muslims and their neighbors today." Publ Wkly

Barnard, Bryn

★ The **genius** of Islam; how Muslims made the modern world. Alfred A. Knopf 2011 37p il map $17.99; lib bdg $20.99

Grades: 4 5 6 7   **297**

1. Islamic civilization 2. Islam -- History
ISBN 978-0-375-84072-2; 0-375-84072-9; 978-0-375-94072-9 lib bdg; 0-375-94072-3 lib bdg

LC 2010-12777

This is a "concise and eloquent exploration of the far-reaching influence of Islam over the centuries. Each spread is devoted to a different subject (writing, Arabic numerals, architecture, astronomy, agriculture), while captioned spot art homes in on specific inventions and innovations (the zither, the astrolabe, advanced medical knowledge)." Publ Wkly

Includes bibliographical references

Demi

★ **Muhammad**; written and illustrated by Demi. Margaret K. McElderry Bks. 2003 un il $19.95

Grades: 4 5 6 7   **297**

1. Islam 2. Prophets 3. Islamic leaders 4. Writers on religion
ISBN 0-689-85264-9

LC 2002-2985

"With dramatic scenes extending past the borders of the intricately patterned frames, the art will be a continual source of interest for young people. . . . [An] excellent retelling of the Prophet's life that combines beauty and scholarship." Booklist

Includes bibliographical references

Gordon, Matthew

Islam; by Matthew S. Gordon. 4th ed. Chelsea House 2009 144 p. col. ill., map (World religions) (library) $40.00

Grades: 7 8 9 10 11 12   **297**

1. Islam
ISBN 978-1-60413-109-3; 1-60413-109-8

LC 2008035810

First published 1991 by Facts on File

This describes the founding of Islam and its spread, The Koran, Hadith, and Islamic law, branches of Islam and their basic beliefs, Muslim customs and rituals, the pattern of Islamic life, and the place of Islam in the modern world.

Includes bibliographical references (p. 138-139) and index.

Hafiz, Dilara

★ The **American** Muslim teenager's handbook; by Dilara Hafiz, Imran Hafiz, and Yasmine Hafiz. [new ed.]; Atheneum Books for Young Readers 2009 168p il pa $11.99

Grades: 7 8 9 10 11 12   **297**

1. Islam 2. Muslims -- United States 3. Teenagers -- Religious life

ISBN 978-1-4169-8578-5; 1-4169-8578-6

A revised edition of the title first published 2007 by Acacia Pub.

"Casual, colloquial, joking, contemporary, and passionate, this interactive handbook by two Arizona teens and their mom talks about their faith, about what it is like to be both proud Americans and proud Muslims, and about misunderstandings and stereotypes. . . . There are also step-by-step guides on how to pray, how to read the Qur'an, and how to fast at Ramadan. Muslim and non-Muslim teens alike will be caught by the candor, the humor, and the call for interfaith dialogue and tolerance." Booklist

Includes bibliographical references

Hinds, Kathryn, 1962-

★ **Faith**; [by] Kathryn Hinds. Marshall Cavendish Benchmark 2008 96p il map (Life in the Medieval Muslim world) lib bdg $23.95

Grades: 6 7 8 9 10   **297**

1. Middle Ages 2. Medieval civilization 3. Islam -- History

ISBN 978-0-7614-3092-6 lib bdg; 0-7614-3092-X lib bdg

LC 2008019268

"Richly illustrated with art reproductions, maps, photos, and ornate Islamic border designs, [this] . . . will entice visual learners." Libr Media Connect

Includes glossary and bibliographical references

Illustrated dictionary of the Muslim world; [editor, Felicity Crowe and others] Marshall Cavendish Reference 2010 192p il (Muslim world) $85.64

Grades: 7 8 9 10   **297**

1. Reference books 2. Islam -- Dictionaries 3. Islamic civilization -- Dictionaries

ISBN 978-0-7614-7929-1; 0-7614-7929-5

LC 2010008613

Contains hundreds of short entries on Islamic concepts, religious practices, historical events and personalities, geographical places, and fact files of nations with large Muslim populations.

"Attractive trim on the pages, colorful fonts, quality illustrations, and framed (often illustrated) sideboxes create a pleasing layout. Excellent for assignments." SLJ

Includes glossary and bibliographical references

Is **Islam** a religion of war or peace? Jann Einfeld, book editor. Greenhaven Press 2005 108p (At issue) hardcover o.p. pa $19.95

Grades: 7 8 9 10   **297**

1. Islam 2. Terrorism 3. War -- Religious aspects 4. Terrorism -- Religious aspects

ISBN 0-7377-3099-4 lib bdg; 0-7377-3100-1 pa

LC 2004-59678

"Eleven opinions are presented here. The book begins with Osama bin Laden's justification for his attacks on Americans. The portrayal of Islam as a predominantly peaceful religion by President George W. Bush is countered by evangelist Pat Robertson. Additional perspectives are offered by Islamic scholars, a former Muslim, a female Muslim reformer, and a rabbi who is an expert on Islam." SLJ

Includes bibliographical references

Islam in America; Laura K. Egendorf, book editor. Greenhaven Press 2006 112p (At issue) lib bdg $28.70; pa $19.95

Grades: 7 8 9 10 11 12   **297**

1. Islam 2. Muslims -- United States

ISBN 0-7377-2727-6 lib bdg; 0-7377-2728-4 pa

LC 2005046317

The selections in this collection "treat such subjects as whether American Muslims support terrorist groups and whether or not they experience discrimination. The pieces on African-American Muslims and the growing popularity of Islam among Hispanic Americans are particularly interesting." SLJ

Includes bibliographical references

Islamic beliefs, practices, and cultures. Marshall Cavendish Reference 2010 352p il (Muslim world) lib bdg $114.21

Grades: 7 8 9 10   **297**

1. Islamic civilization 2. Islam -- Customs and practices

ISBN 978-0-7614-7926-0; 0-7614-7926-0

LC 2010008611

"Attractive trim on the pages, colorful fonts, quality illustrations, and framed (often illustrated) sideboxes create a pleasing layout. Excellent for assignments." SLJ

Luxenberg, Alan

Radical Islam. Mason Crest 2009 64p il (World of Islam) lib bdg $22.95

Grades: 7 8 9 10 11 12   **297**

1. Islam 2. Radicalism

ISBN 978-1-4222-0536-5 lib bdg; 1-4222-0536-3 lib bdg

Luxenberg "describes Islam's historical background, its rise to world prominence, its decline, the factions that have arisen, and the move of some toward radicalism. . . . In examing specific radical arms (and their leaders), the book suggests ways for U.S. leaders to interpret intentions and future implications. . . . The book . . . would be a good addition for world-religion collections." Booklist

Includes glossary and bibliographical references

Modern Muslim societies. Marshall Cavendish Reference 2010 416p il (Muslim world) lib bdg $114.21

Grades: 7 8 9 10   **297**

1. Islam -- Customs and practices

ISBN 978-0-7614-7927-7; 0-7614-7927-9

LC 2010008612

"Attractive trim on the pages, colorful fonts, quality illustrations, and framed (often illustrated) sideboxes create a pleasing layout. Excellent for assignments." SLJ

Nardo, Don

The **birth** of Islam. Morgan Reynolds Pub. 2011 112p (World religions and beliefs) lib bdg $28.95

Grades: 7 8 9 10   **297**

1. Islamic civilization 2. Islam -- History

ISBN 978-1-59935-146-9; 1-59935-146-3

LC 2010038442

This covers the beginnings of Islam "in an impartial way. The [context] in which the [religion] developed [is] explained, offering insight into how [Islam] came to be and introducing major concepts the [religion]." SLJ

Includes glossary and bibliographical references

Raatma, Lucia

Islam. Compass Point Books 2010 48p il map (World religions) lib bdg $27.99

Grades: 5 6 7 8   **297**

1. Islam

ISBN 978-0-7565-4239-9 lib bdg; 0-7565-4239-1 lib bdg

LC 2009-15812

"The colorful, attractive layout includes high-quality reproductions of photographs, maps, and paintings. Students who are new to religious studies, as well as those doing reports, will find that this . . . meets their needs." SLJ

Includes glossary and bibliographical references

297.1   Islam

Koran

The **meaning** of the glorious Koran; an explanatory translation by Marmaduke Pickthall; with an introduction by William Montgomery Watt. A.A. Knopf 1992 xxiv, 693p il $22

Grades: 7 8 9 10 11 12 Adult   **297.1**

ISBN 0-679-41736-2; 978-0-679-41736-1

LC 92-52928

This translation first published 1930

"The sacred scripture of Islam, regarded by Muslims as the Word of God, and except in sura I.—which is a prayer to God—and some few passages in which Muhammad or the angels speak in the first person, the speaker throughout is God." Ency Britannica

297.122

Abdel Haleem, M. A. S.

The **Qur'an**; English translation and parallel Arabic text. M. A. S. Abdel Haleem. Oxford University Press 2010 xxxix, 624 p.p (hardcover) $45

Grades: 7 8 9 10 11 12 Adult   **297.122**

ISBN 019957071X; 9780199570713

LC 2010281328

This book, by M. A. S. Abdel Haleem, offers an English translation of the Qur'an with Arab text presented in parallel. "This translation is written in contemporary language . . ., set page-for-page against the most widespread traditional calligraphic Arabic text. . . . Furthermore, Haleem includes notes that explain geographical, historical, and personal allusions as well as an index in which Qur'anic material is arranged into topics for easy reference." (Publisher's note)

"Because the Koran stresses its Arabic nature, devout Muslims believe that only an Arabic version is the actual Koran and insist that its translation cannot be more than an approximate interpretation. . . Yet anyone wishing to understand Islamic civilization and global affairs may find this Koran very useful. . . . Highly recommended." LJ

Includes bibliographical references and index

297.3   Islamic worship

Jeffrey, Laura S.

Celebrate Ramadan; [by] Laura S. Jeffrey. Enslow Publishers 2007 112p il (Celebrate holidays) lib bdg $31.93

Grades: 5 6 7 8   **297.3**

1. Islam 2. Ramadan 3. Id al-Adha

ISBN 978-0-7660-2774-9 lib bdg; 0-7660-2774-0 lib bdg

LC 2006028107

"This book opens by introducing a contemporary Muslim, Bushra, who celebrated Ramadan as a girl growing up in England [and] later immigrated to the United States. . . . An informative chapter surveys the history, beliefs, and practices of Islam. . . . The remainder of the book offers a detailed discussion of Ramadan, prayer, and spiritual awareness, and of l'Id al Fitr. . . . Punctuated by sidebars and illustrated with color photos, this clearly written book offers a good overview of how the holidays of Islam are celebrated." Booklist

Includes glossary and bibliographical references

297.9   Babism and Bahai Faith

Hartz, Paula

Baha'i Faith; 3rd ed.; Chelsea House 2009 144p il (World religions) $40

Grades: 7 8 9 10 11 12   **297.9**

1. Bahai Faith

ISBN 978-1-60413-104-8; 1-60413-104-7

LC 2008043045

First published 2002 by Facts and File

This "explores all aspects of the Baha'i faith, from the original teachings of its founder, Baha'u'llah, to the modern-day communities that exist in 236 countries and territories throughout the world." Publisher's note

Includes glossary and bibliographical references

299 Religions not provided for elsewhere

Harpur, James

  Celtic myth; a treasury of legends, art, and history. [by] James Harpur. M.E. Sharpe 2008 96p il (The world of mythology) $35.95

Grades: 8 9 10 11 12   299

  1. Celtic mythology 2. Celtic civilization

  ISBN 978-0-7656-8102-7

LC 2007006015

"With lots of heroic adventures and exciting, sometimes gruesome detail, Harpur retells stories of the Irish and Welsh Celts and weaves in facts about their culture and the history of their struggle for dominence. The dense text is broken up with beautiful, color images on every page, including paintings and photos of the settings, sculptures, weapons, and other artifacts." Booklist

Includes glossary and bibliographical references

Hinds, Kathryn, 1962-

  ★ **Religion**; by Kathryn Hinds. Marshall Cavendish Benchmark 2007 vii, 72 p.p col. ill., col. maps (Life in ancient Egypt) (library) $8.66

Grades: 6 7 8 9   299

  1. Egyptian mythology

  ISBN 9780761421863; 0761421866

LC 2006011086

"Describes the role of religion in ancient Egypt during the New Kingdom period, from about 1550 BCE to about 1070 BCE, including the diverse gods and goddesses the people worshipped, their creation myths, and the role of priesthood." Publisher's note

Includes bibliographical references (p. 67-68) and index.

Kramer, Ann

  Egyptian myth; a treasury of legends, art, and history. M. E. Sharpe 2008 96p il map (The world of mythology) $35.95

Grades: 5 6 7 8   299

  1. Egyptian art 2. Egyptian mythology

  ISBN 978-0-7656-8105-8; 0-7656-8105-6

LC 2007005876

This "handsomely designed [book is] illustrated with works of art from the culture. [It] is a well-organized presentation that includes information and tales about the gods and the pharoahs as well as magical stories and legends, providing an excellent introduction to this fascinating culture." SLJ

Includes glossary and bibliographical references

Matson, Gienna

  Celtic mythology A to Z; [by] Gienna Matson. Facts on File 2004 114p il map (Mythology A to Z) $40

Grades: 8 9 10 11 12 Adult   299

  1. Celtic mythology

  ISBN 0-8160-4890-8

LC 2004-47111

"This title is an excellent introduction to the mythology of Celtic cultures and should be in most public and school libraries." Booklist

Includes bibliographical references

Schomp, Virginia

  The **ancient** Egyptians; [by] Virginia Schomp. Marshall Cavendish Benchmark 2007 95p il map (Myths of the world) lib bdg $22.95

Grades: 6 7 8 9   299

  1. Egyptian mythology

  ISBN 978-0-7614-2549-6

LC 2006037686

"With [its] beautiful illustrations, high-quality production, and focus on source material, the [book] should whet the interest of readers." SLJ

Includes glossary and bibliographical references

Taylor, Rodney Leon

  Confucianism; Rodney L. Taylor. Chelsea House Publishers 2004 151p il (Religions of the world)

299

  1. Confucianism

  ISBN 0-7910-7857-4

LC 2003-23920

"Taylor discusses the elements of Confucian tradition in culture and in the arts as well as its specification of differing roles for men, women, and children in society. He devotes one chapter to significant developments through the centuries and another to the place of the tradition's ancient practices and ideas in the world today. Full-page sidebars feature selections from Confucian writings and teachings, which serve to both break up and add flavor to the long sections of text." SLJ

299.5 Religions of East and Southeast Asian origin

Demi

  ★ The **legend** of Lao Tzu and the Tao te ching. Margaret K. McElderry Books 2007 un il $21.99

Grades: 4 5 6 7   299.5

  1. Taoism 2. Philosophers

  ISBN 1-4169-1206-1; 978-1-4169-1206-4

LC 2005029695

"This is the legend of Lao Tzu . . . who may or may not have founded Taoism, one of the greatest religions of the world. Demi's elegant picture-book introduction to the legendary Chinese philosopher . . . combines nuggets of his purported life with 20 verses from the Tao Te Ching. . . . The narrative and graceful paintings are contained in a gold circular frame on each parchment shaded page." SLJ

Hartz, Paula

  Daoism; by Paula R. Hartz. 3rd ed.; Chelsea House 2009 144p il (World religions) $40

Grades: 7 8 9 10 11 12   **299.5**
1. Taoism
ISBN 978-1-60413-115-4; 1-60413-115-2
LC 2008-35809
First published 1993 by Facts on File with title: Taoism
This "traces the history of Daoism and explains its basic thoughts, traditions, and practices. It also details the Daoist movement worldwide and how the limitations of consumerism are leading a younger generation to search for their own spiritual harmony." Publisher's note
Includes glossary and bibliographical references

Shinto; by Paula R. Hartz. 3rd ed.; Chelsea House 2009 144p il (World religions) $40
Grades: 7 8 9 10 11 12   **299.5**
1. Shinto
ISBN 978-1-60413-113-0; 1-60413-113-6
LC 2008-29661
First published 1997 by Facts on File
This "examines the basic tenets of Shinto, its evolution in response to other religious influences, and how the original Shinto religion—rooted in an agrarian society—survives in contemporary Japan." Publisher's note
Includes glossary and bibliographical references

Helft, Claude
Chinese mythology; stories of creation and invention. [by] Claude Helft; illustrations by Chen Jiang Hong; translated from the French by Michael Hariton and Claudia Bedrick. 1st American ed.; Enchanted Lion Books 2007 78p il $14.95
Grades: 7 8 9 10   **299.5**
1. Chinese mythology
ISBN 978-1-59270-074-5; 1-59270-074-8
LC 2007031297
"This slim book offers high visual interest along with concise introductions to an important body of myths. Helft deftly organizes what can be confusing anecdotes about gods who often occupy themselves with governing and making war. . . . Interleaved pages describe a dozen cultural items (jade, yin/yang, dragons, etc.). . . . Full-page and vignette illustrations in traditional style with strong ink lines emphasize vitality and movement. Chen's evocative and richly colored paintings add value to this compact collection." SLJ

Kallen, Stuart A.
Shinto. Lucent Bks. 2002 128p il map (Religions of the world) lib bdg $27.45
Grades: 6 7 8 9   **299.5**
1. Shinto
ISBN 1-56006-988-0
LC 2001-6120
Discusses historical origins, the teachings, practices, and the spread of Shinto into modern times
Includes glossary and bibliographical references

Levin, Judith
Japanese mythology; [by] Judith Levin. The Rosen Pub. Group 2008 64p il map (Mythology around the world) $29.95

Grades: 5 6 7 8   **299.5**
1. Shinto 2. Buddhism 3. Japanese mythology
ISBN 978-1-4042-0736-3; 1-4042-0736-8
LC 2005035279
This "presents not only an introduction to Shinto and Buddhist beliefs, but also Japanese history and mythology in general. . . . The most remarkable part of [this book] . . . is the respect [it shows] for the mythological customs, treating them throughout with the same care that writers of books on major religions might offer. The illustrations show both ancient and modern incarnations of the deities and heroes." SLJ
Includes glossary and bibliographical references

Roberts, Jeremy
Chinese mythology A to Z; 2nd ed.; Chelsea House 2009 172p il (Mythology A to Z) lib bdg $45
Grades: 8 9 10 11 12   **299.5**
1. Chinese mythology
ISBN 978-1-60413-436-0; 1-60413-436-4
LC 2009-10176
First published 2004
"Coverage includes: Buddhist deities and legendary characters; animal stories, such as the fox legends; important locations, such as shrines and sacred places; [and] allegorical figures, such as the Jade Emperor, the Rain Master, and the Lord of the Granary." Publisher's note
Includes bibliographical references

299.6   Religions originating among Black Africans and people of Black African descent

Lugira, Aloysius Muzzanganda
African traditional religion; by Aloysius M. Lugira. 3rd ed.; Chelsea House 2009 144p il map (World religions) $40
Grades: 7 8 9 10 11 12   **299.6**
1. Africa -- Religion
ISBN 978-1-60413-103-1; 1-60413-103-9
LC 2008-51188
First published 1999 by Facts on File with title: African religion
"The African continent is home to more than 6,000 different ethnic and cultural groups, each with its own religious traditions. Yet these many traditions have much in common. . . . [This book] offers a . . . perspective on the beliefs that are a permanent part of Africa's history and future." Publisher's note
Includes glossary and bibliographical references

Lynch, Patricia Ann
African mythology, A to Z; revised by Jeremy Roberts. 2nd ed.; Chelsea House 2010 xxiv, 149p il map (Mythology A to Z) lib bdg $45
Grades: 8 9 10 11 12   **299.6**
1. African mythology
ISBN 978-1-60413-415-5; 1-60413-415-1
LC 2009-33612
First published 2004

This is a "reference to the deities, places, events, animals, beliefs, and other subjects that appear in the myths of various African peoples." Publisher's note

Includes bibliographical references

Schomp, Virginia

The **ancient** Africans; [by] Virginia Schomp. Marshall Cavendish Benchmark 2009 96p il map (Myths of the world) $23.95

Grades: 6 7 8 9   **299.6**

1. African mythology 2. Ethnology -- Africa

ISBN 978-0-7614-3099-5; 0-7614-3099-7

LC 2008011695

"A retelling of several ancient African myths, with background information describing the history, geography, belief systems, and customs of various peoples of Africa." Publisher's note

Includes bibliographical references

299.7   Religions of North American native origin

Hartz, Paula

Native American religions; [by] Paula R. Hartz. 3rd ed.; Chelsea House 2009 144p il (World religions) $40

Grades: 7 8 9 10 11 12   **299.7**

1. Native Americans -- Religion

ISBN 978-1-60413-111-6; 1-60413-111-X

LC 2008051197

First published 1997 by Facts on File

This "presents the history of the Native American religions, starting from their roots as tribal religions, and then details the detrimental effects of European colonization, the annihilation of the Native Americans that threatened the religions, and their sudden restoration in the 20th century." Publisher's note

Includes glossary and bibliographical references

Martin, Joel

★ **Native** American religion. Oxford University Press 1999 157p il (Religion in American life) $28

Grades: 7 8 9 10   **299.7**

1. Native Americans -- Religion 2. Indians of North America -- Religion

ISBN 0-19-511035-8

LC 98-50155

An "examination of religious life and practices from ancient times through the Colonial period and the Western Expansion, and into the 20th century. Martin acknowledges the importance of religion in all aspects of Native American daily life and explores some of the differences among the various cultures. He also addresses the impact of the arrival of Europeans on spiritual life." SLJ

Includes bibliographical references

300   SOCIAL SCIENCES, SOCIOLOGY & ANTHROPOLOGY

302.23   Media (Means of communication)

Adams, Simon

Politics. Amicus 2010 43p il (Media power) lib bdg $21.95

Grades: 6 7 8 9   **302.23**

1. Politics 2. Journalism 3. Mass media

ISBN 978-1-60753-114-2; 1-60753-114-3

LC 2009051449

"Each chapter spread incorporates captioned photographs with sharp, insightful text. . . . The excellent photographs exemplify how to make a dramatic impact without sensationalizing the subject." SLJ

Includes glossary and bibliographical references

Anderson, Judith

Crime. Amicus 2010 45p il (Media power) lib bdg $21.95

Grades: 6 7 8 9   **302.23**

1. Crime 2. Journalism 3. Mass media

ISBN 978-1-60753-113-5; 1-60753-113-5

LC 2009051452

"Each chapter spread incorporates captioned photographs with sharp, insightful text. . . . The excellent photographs exemplify how to make a dramatic impact without sensationalizing the subject." SLJ

Includes glossary and bibliographical references

War and conflict. Amicus 2010 43p il (Media power) $21.95

Grades: 6 7 8 9   **302.23**

1. War 2. Journalism 3. Mass media

ISBN 978-1-60753-116-6; 1-60753-116-X

LC 2009051532

"Each chapter spread incorporates captioned photographs with sharp, insightful text. . . . The excellent photographs exemplify how to make a dramatic impact without sensationalizing the subject." SLJ

Includes glossary and bibliographical references

Heneghan, Judith

Celebrity and fame. Amicus 2010 43p il (Media power) lib bdg $21.95

Grades: 6 7 8 9   **302.23**

1. Mass media 2. Celebrities 3. Journalistic ethics

ISBN 978-1-60753-112-8; 1-60753-112-7

LC 2009051451

"Each chapter spread incorporates captioned photographs with sharp, insightful text. . . . The excellent photographs exemplify how to make a dramatic impact without sensationalizing the subject." SLJ

Includes glossary and bibliographical references

Marcovitz, Hal

Bias in the media. Lucent Books 2010 112p il (Hot topics) lib bdg $32.45

Grades: 5 6 7 8   302.23
1. Journalism 2. Mass media
ISBN 978-1-4205-0224-4 lib bdg; 1-4205-0224-7
lib bdg
LC 2009048285

"Young researchers are ill-equipped to judge the integrity of media, much less distinguish between conservative or liberal points of view. Marcovitz's thorough text not only gives them an in-depth look at bias in the news, but also leaves them with knowledge that will help them discern such slants in the future. . . . This text needs to be introduced to kids, perhaps in the context of a current-events class. Discussion questions are included. A comprehensive, useful book." SLJ

Includes bibliographical references

Mass media: opposing viewpoints; Roman Espejo, book editor. Greenhaven Press/Gale Cengage Learning 2010 250p (Opposing viewpoints series) $39.70; pa $27.50
Grades: 8 9 10 11 12   302.23
1. Mass media
ISBN 978-0-7377-4530-6; 0-7377-4530-4; 978-0-7377-4531-3 pa; 0-7377-4531-2 pa
LC 2009023849

A compendium of viewpoints—both pro and con—on several issues relating to the role and regulation of media in American society.

Includes bibliographical references

302.3   Social interaction within groups

Bullying; Beth Rosenthal, book editor. Greenhaven Press 2008 120p il (Introducing issues with opposing viewpoints) lib bdg $33.70
Grades: 7 8 9 10   302.3
1. Bullies
ISBN 978-0-7377-3801-8; 0-7377-3801-4
LC 2007-32382

"Topics covered in this book range from the causes of bullying, what role society plays in encouraging bullying, the roles of TV and/or video games in violence and bullying, the responsibility of parents, the value of anti-bullying programs, and the ways that the behavior can be reduced. . . . Articles are presented in a pro/con format; 'active reading' questions preface each viewpoint and are designed to help students focus on the main points and to read carefully. Full-color photos and other graphics appear throughout." SLJ

Includes bibliographical references

Dear bully; seventy authors tell their stories. edited by Carrie Jones and Megan Kelley Hall. HarperTeen 2011 369p $17.99; pa $9.99
Grades: 7 8 9 10 11 12   302.3
1. Bullies
ISBN 978-0-06-206098-3; 0-06-206098-8; 978-0-06-206097-6 pa; 0-06-206097-X pa
LC 2011010166

"In brief, true stories about bullying victims, perpetrators, and bystanders, 70 children's authors look back at what was often the hell of growing up, especially in junior high. .

. . This timely collection is an excellent resource, especially for group discussion." Booklist

DiPiazza, Francesca Davis
Friend me! six hundred years of social networking in America. by Francesca Davis DiPiazza. Twenty-First Century Books 2012 112 p.
Grades: 6 7 8 9   302.3
1. Social networking -- History 2. Social groups -- United States -- History 3. Community life -- United States -- History 4. United States -- Social life and customs -- History 5. Communities -- United States -- History 6. Social networks -- United States -- History
ISBN 0761358692; 9780761358695
LC 2011021268

This book's title "makes [it] appear to be about the recent phenomena of electronic social networks. However, the subtitle is a clue that the scope includes so much more. The whole of the American history of socializing is covered, beginning with the Iroquois and their method of weaving beads into wampum belts. Early religious groups, colonial coffeehouses, broadsides, secret gatherings of slaves, circuit riders, telegraphs, mail orders, and groups such as the YMCA and NAACP are profiled as examples of social networking. Today's online communities (Facebook, Twitter, blogs, e-mail, etc.) are touched upon with the supposition that face-to-face socializing is still important." (Booklist)

Includes bibliographical references and index

Ellis, Deborah
★ **We** want you to know; kids talk about bullying. Coteau Books 2010 120p il $19.95; pa $15.95
Grades: 5 6 7 8 9 10   302.3
1. Bullies 2. Bullying
ISBN 978-1-55050-417-0; 1-55050-417-7; 978-1-55050-463-7 pa; 1-55050-463-0
"As part of her work with an anti-bullying campaign in her local Canadian community, Ellis interviewed young people between the ages of 9 and 19 about their experiences. In honest, straightforward prose, she shares their stories, many as targets and some as perpetrators or bystanders. . . . Each story is written from the first-person point of view, some with real names and photos, providing an intimacy and immediacy that are critical with these kinds of issues. Readers will find at least one or two stories they can relate to, and educators should be able to use many of the narratives to jumpstart conversation." SLJ

Includes bibliographical references

Golus, Carrie
Take a stand! what you can do about bullying. illustrated by Jack Desrocher. Lerner Publications Co. 2009 64p il (Health zone) lib bdg $30.60
Grades: 5 6 7 8   302.3
1. Bullies
ISBN 978-0-8225-7554-2; 0-8225-7554-X
LC 2007-49659

This offers advice about stopping bullying.

"The format is beyond lively, with lots of color, cartoons, and an informal writing style, but it manages to present sometimes frightening material in a non-threatening and browsable way." Booklist

Includes glossary and bibliographical references

Hillstrom, Laurie Collier

Online social networks. Lucent Books 2010 96p il (Technology 360) $32.45

Grades: 8 9 10 11 12   **302.3**

1. Online social networks

ISBN 978-1-4205-0167-4; 1-4205-0167-4

LC 2009045044

This book explores "the early development and advances of [online social network] technology, its impact on society both positive and negative, and the importance it plays in our lives. . . . [It] begins with the history of the Internet. It explains the early purpose of the ARPANET, its expansion, the changes from text-based to the graphic interface of the World Wide Web, email communication, the features of some of the first social sites, and the differentiating characteristics of MySpace, Facebook, and Twitter. . . . Numerous color photos, diagrams, 'Bits & Bytes' boxes as well as many other additional text boxes create appeal and provide beneficial informative and complementary material to aid in understanding the technical details of the [text]." SLJ

Includes glossary and bibliographical references

Kevorkian, Meline

101 facts about bullying; what everyone should know. [by] Meline Kevorkian and Robin D'Antona. Rowman & Littlefield Pub. 2008 148p $32.95

Grades: Adult Professional   **302.3**

1. Bullies

ISBN 978-1-57886-849-0; 1-57886-849-1

"A user-friendly, accessible, and well-organized resource. . . . The format will lend itself well to group discussions and give teachers and others who work with young people a solid basis upon which to explore the issues surrounding this prevalent problem." SLJ

Lusted, Marcia Amidon

Social networking: MySpace, Facebook, & Twitter. ABDO Pub. Co. 2011 112p il (Technology pioneers) lib bdg $34.22

Grades: 5 6 7 8   **302.3**

1. Online social networks

ISBN 978-1-61714-811-8 lib bdg; 1-61714-811-3 lib bdg; 978-1-61758-969-0 e-book

LC 2010037885

This is an introduction to social networking sites, MySpace, Facebook, and Twitter.

"Written in a clear, linear fashion, this series offers vivid, well-researched details about the development of technological advancements considered essential in today's society. . . . Readers who are interested in technology and inventions will be thoroughly engrossed." SLJ

Includes glossary and bibliographical references

Shapiro, Ouisie

Bullying and me; schoolyard stories. illustrated by Steven Vote. Albert Whitman & Company 2010 un il $16.99

Grades: 4 5 6 7   **302.3**

1. Bullies

ISBN 978-0-8075-0921-0; 0-8075-0921-3

LC 2010000754

"Thirteen individuals, including some adults, who have been bullied at school share their painful experiences. . . . Vote's full-color portraits sensitively depict the faces at the receiving end of abuse. . . . An educational psychologist specifically addresses each individual's dilemma, but the book's strength lies in the honestly conveyed in the personal stories." Publ Wkly

Solomon, Laura

Doing social media so it matters; a librarian's guide. American Library Association 2011 65p pa $37

Grades: Adult Professional   **302.3**

1. Online social networks 2. Libraries and community

ISBN 978-0-8389-1067-2; 0-8389-1067-X

LC 2010034319

"This slim manual is packed with useful advice. Solomon, a library services manager for the Ohio Public Information Network, sprinkles her account with real-world examples of the power of libraries leveraging social media. She makes a strong case for establishing social-media accounts. . . . Discussions about branding, social capital, and other strategies for success are especially important. Wrapping up with chapters on statistics and whether the investment of time and effort is worthwhile, Solomon gives libraries the knowledge they need to proceed on their own." SLJ

Includes bibliographical references

302.302   Computer applications

Schwartz, Heather E.

Safe social networking; by Heather E. Schwartz. Capstone Press 2013 32 p. col. ill. (Fact finders. Tech safety smarts) (library) $26.65

Grades: 4 5 6 7   **302.302**

1. Online social networks 2. Internet -- Security measures 3. Social networking 4. Social networks 5. Online social networks -- Security measures

ISBN 1429699434; 9781429699433; 9781620658024

LC 2012026027

This children's resource book, by Heather E. Schwartz, is part of the publisher's "Fact Finders" series, providing guidance for young children to safely use and navigate online social media. "If a strange person asks to be your online friend, do you know what to do? . . . This book is here to help! Learn tech-savvy ways to keep your social networking sites safe sites without taking away all the fun!" (Publisher's note)

Includes bibliographical references (p. 31) and index.

302.34   Social interaction in primary groups

Bazelon, Emily

★ **Sticks** and stones; defeating the culture of bullying and rediscovering the power of character and

empathy. by Emily Bazelon. Random House 2013
viii, 386 p.p ill. (hardcover) $27
Grades: Adult Professional   **302.34**
  1. Bullies 2. Adolescence 3. Social media 4. Bullying
5. Bullying in schools 6. Bullying -- Prevention 7.
Bullying in schools -- Prevention
  ISBN 0812992806; 9780679644002; 9780812992809
                  LC 2012022773
This book, by Emily Bazelon, discusses teen culture in
the U.S., focusing on bullying. "Being a teenager has never
been easy, but in recent years, with the rise of the Internet
and social media, it has become exponentially more challenging. . . . Bazelon defines what bullying is and, just as
important, what it is not. She explores when intervention is
essential and when kids should be given the freedom to fend
for themselves. She also dispels persistent myths." (Publisher's note)
"While less prescriptive than other books on the topic,
very useful FAQs are included, as are resource lists for readers. Masterfully written, Bazelon's book will increase understanding, awareness, and action." Pub Wkly
Includes bibliographical references and index

Strauss, Susan L.
  ★ **Sexual** harassment and bullying; a guide to
keeping kids safe and holding schools accountable.
Susan L. Strauss. Rowman & Littlefield Publishers
2012 290 p. (cloth : alk. paper) $34.95
Grades: Adult Professional   **302.34**
  1. Bullies 2. Social media 3. Sexual harassment 4.
Bullying 5. Bullying -- Prevention 6. Sexual harassment
in education 7. Sexual harassment -- Prevention
  ISBN 1442201622; 9781442201620
                  LC 2011031731
In this book, "[Susan L.] Strauss draws on her experiences as consultant, former high-school teacher, and parent of a child who was sexually harassed to advise parents,
teachers, and other adults on how to protect children" from
bullying and harassment. She gives definitions of bullying
and harassment, "offers a particular focus on the kind of harassment of gay, bisexual, and transgendered students," and
examines "how social media . . . have ramped up bullying
and harassment." (Booklist)
Includes bibliographical references and index.

Vicious; true stories by teens about bullying. edited
by Hope Vanderberg. Free Spirit Pub. Inc. 2012
167 p. (Real teen voices) (paperback) $11.99
Grades: 6 7 8   **302.34**
  1. Bullies 2. Teenagers' writings 3. Bullying -- Case
studies 4. Self-esteem in adolescence -- Case studies
5. Aggressiveness in adolescence -- Case studies 6.
Interpersonal conflict in adolescence -- Case studies
  ISBN 1575424134; 9781575424132
                  LC 2012015908
This book is a collection of "autobiographical essays"
from teenagers involved with the New York-based organization Youth Communication in which they detail "their
struggles with bullies, anger about bad home situations and
unfair treatment, and pressure to conform or be successful."
(School Library Journal)
Includes bibliographical references and index

303.3   Coordination and control

Tarshis, Thomas Paul
  Living with peer pressure and bullying. Facts on
File 2010 167p (Teen's guides) $34.95; pa $14.95
Grades: 6 7 8 9   **303.3**
  1. Bullies 2. Peer pressure 3. Adolescent psychology
  ISBN 978-0-8160-7914-8; 0-8160-7914-5; 978-0-
8160-7915-5 pa; 0-8160-7915-3 pa
                LC 2009024521
"Tarshis examines topics such as peer pressure, managing difficult situations, the risks and rewards of telling the
truth, mental-health problems, cyberbullying, and finding
and paying for medical care. Each chapter begins with a
personal account about a teen facing the chapter topic; includes explanations presented in clear language, at times
accompanied by questionnaires and explanatory charts; and
ends with 'What You Need to Know,' which summarizes the
main ideas. [This book is an] important [addition] for most
libraries." SLJ
Includes glossary and bibliographical references

Webber, Diane
  Totally tolerant; spotting and stopping prejudice.
[by] Diane Webber and Laurie Mandel. Franklin
Watts 2008 112p il (Scholastic choices) lib bdg
$27; pa $8.95
Grades: 5 6 7 8   **303.3**
  1. Prejudices 2. Toleration
  ISBN 978-0-531-13867-0 lib bdg; 0-531-13867-4 lib
bdg; 978-0-531-20525-9 pa; 0-531-20525-8 pa
                LC 2007-51873
This book about tolerance contains "vignettes and
quotes from teens. . . . Statistics, quizzes, historical photos
that illustrate prejudice in the 1950s and even recent news
stories such as the Jena Six are peppered throughout for a
professional perspective. The young reader is also motivated
to think critically and use other tools such as journaling or
volunteering to create change in their own lives. . . . Plenty
of photos accompany . . . [this] book, and words are defined
not only in a glossary but used clearly in context as well,
providing a great introduction to the topic for the beginning
reader." Voice Youth Advocates
Includes glossary and bibliographical references

303.4   Social change

Harris, Ashley Rae
  ★ **Txt** me l8r; using technology responsibly.
content consultant, Robyn J. A. Silverman. ABDO
Pub. Co. 2010 112p il (Essential health: strong,
beautiful girls) $34.22
Grades: 6 7 8 9   **303.4**
  1. Technology 2. Information technology 3.
Technological innovations 4. Internet -- Social aspects
  ISBN 978-1-60453-754-3; 1-60453-754-X
                LC 2009-2138
Using personal narratives, with a consulting doctor
giving insight and making suggestions, this discusses the
responsible use of technology and the dangers of over-

use of cell phones, social websites, texting, and other online communication.

"The topics are well selected, the design is attractive, and the stories feature girls from a variety of cultures." Booklist

Includes bibliographical references

Hill, Laban Carrick

★ **America** dreaming; how youth changed America in the sixties. Little, Brown & Company 2007 165p il pa $12.99

Grades: 6 7 8 9 10   **303.4**

1. Social change 2. Youth movement 3. Baby boom generation 4. Nineteen sixties 5. Social change -- United States

ISBN 978-0-316-00904-1; 0-316-00904-0; 978-0-316-07148-2 pa; 0-316-07148-X pa

LC 2006-27898

"An excellent textbook for the children and, probably, grandchildren of baby boomers who want to know what the youth culture of the time as all about." NY Times Book Rev

Includes bibliographical references

The Internet: opposing viewpoints; James D. Torr, book editor. Greenhaven Press 2005 204p il (Opposing viewpoints series) lib bdg $34.95; pa $23.70

Grades: 8 9 10 11 12   **303.4**

1. Internet

ISBN 0-7377-2941-4 lib bdg; 0-7377-2942-2 pa

LC 2004-59699

"The authors in this volume examine the diverse effects of the Internet revolution—and suggest ways in which the technology can be harnessed for the better." Publisher's note

Includes bibliographical references

Solway, Andrew

Communication; the impact of science and technology. Gareth Stevens Pub. 2010 64p il (Pros and cons) lib bdg $35

Grades: 5 6 7 8   **303.4**

1. Communication 2. Telecommunication 3. Information technology

ISBN 978-1-4339-1986-2 lib bdg; 1-4339-1986-9 lib bdg

LC 2009-12435

An "active layout that features color photographs, maps, graphs or charts on every spread, this . . . [book] has much to offer. . . . It conveniently outlines the range of views . . . . helping students to learn how to view both sides of [the] issue[s]." SLJ

Includes glossary and bibliographical references

Turney, Jon

Technology; ethical debates about the application of science. Smart Apple Media 2009 46p il (Dilemmas in modern science) $34.25

Grades: 7 8 9 10   **303.4**

1. Technology 2. Science -- Ethical aspects 3. Science

ISBN 978-1-59920-097-2; 1-59920-097-X

LC 2007-35692

This title is "easy to navigate as evocative photographs, charts, and sidebars help break down complicated arguments into manageable parts for easy digestion." SLJ

Includes glossary and bibliographical references

303.48   Causes of change

Changemakers; rebels and radicals who changed US history. edited by Michele Bollinger and Dao X. Tran. Haymarket Books 2012 210 p. (alk. paper) $19.95

Grades: 6 7 8   **303.48**

1. Change 2. Radicalism 3. Social justice 4. Social movements -- United States 5. Social reformers -- United States -- Biography

ISBN 1608461564; 9781608461561

LC 2012034044

This book, edited by Michele Bollinger and Dao X Tran, "offers a 'people's history' version of the individuals who have shaped [the U.S.] for middle school students. In the place of founding fathers, presidents, and titans of industry, are profiles of those who . . . fought for social justice in America: Tecumseh, Harriet Tubman, Mark Twain, César Chávez, Rachel Carson, Harvey Milk, Henry Wallace, and many more." (Publisher's note)

Gentry, Sarah E.

Living with the Internet; Samuel C. McQuade, III and Sarah Gentry. Chelsea House Publishers 2011 152 p. (Cybersafety) $39.95

Grades: 7 8 9 10 11 12   **303.48**

1. Internet forums 2. Internet -- Social aspects 3. Internet -- Safety measures 4. Online social networks

ISBN 1604136979; 9781604136975

LC 2011005646

"Backed by recent statistics and facts, this straightforward series educates teens about online safety." Booklist

Includes bibliographical references and index

Kenschaft, Lori

Lydia Maria Child; the quest for racial justice. Oxford Univ. Press 2002 126p il (Oxford portraits) lib bdg $24

Grades: 7 8 9 10   **303.48**

1. Authors 2. Novelists 3. Suffragists 4. Abolitionists 5. Women authors 6. Essayists 7. Authors, American 8. Authors, American -- 19th century -- Biography 9. Women abolitionists -- United States -- Biography 10. Women social reformers -- United States -- Biography

ISBN 0-19-513257-2

LC 2001-52339

A biography of the popular writer who, in the mid-nineteenth century, gave up her literary success to fight for the abolition of slavery, for women's rights, and for the fair treatment of American Indians

"This well-done book will give young people an opportunity to learn more about one woman and the ideals for which she stood." SLJ

Includes bibliographical references

Scandiffio, Laura

People who said no; courage against oppression. Laura Scandiffio. Annick Press 2012 168 p. $24.95

Grades: 5 6 7   **303.48**

1. Demonstrations 2. Protest movements 3. Civil disobedience 4. Resistance to government

ISBN 1554513839; 9781554513833

This book, by Laura Scandiffio, profiles activists who broke the law to protest injustices. "Sometimes it's okay to ignore the rules or break the law. . . . This . . . book features people who did just that: Sophie and Hans Scholl . . . and Andrei Sakharov. . . . Also included are Helen Suzman, . . . Aung San Suu Kyi, . . . and the people of Egypt, who recently brought down the repressive government of Hosni Mubarak." (Publisher's note)

303.6   Conflict and conflict resolution

Drew, Naomi

★ The **kids'** guide to working out conflicts; how to keep cool, stay safe, and get along. Naomi Drew. Free Spirit Pub. 2004 146p il pa $13.95

Grades: 6 7 8 9   **303.6**

1. Conflict management 2. Interpersonal relations 3. Conflict (Psychology) 4. Fighting (Psychology) 5. Interpersonal conflict

ISBN 1-57542-150-X

LC 2003-21108

Describes common forms of conflict, the reasons behind conflicts, and various positive ways to deal with and defuse tough situations at school, at home, and in the community without getting physical.

"In clean, respectful language, [the author] offers youth a highly doable eight-step plan to overcome anger issues. . . . The thoughtful encouraging tone of this important book . . . embraces children all along the conflict spectrum, from tortured victims of bullying to those who endure sustained stress and from moderate levels of conflict to full-blown bullies. . . . Highly recommended." Voice Youth Advocates

Includes bibliographical references

Ellis, Deborah

★ **Off** to war; voices of soldiers' children. Groundwood Books/House of Anansi Press 2008 175p il $15.95; pa $9.95

Grades: 5 6 7 8   **303.6**

1. Children and war 2. Iraq War, 2003-2011 3. Iraq War, 2003- 4. Children of military personnel

ISBN 978-0-88899-894-1; 0-88899-894-5; 978-0-88899-895-8 pa; 0-88899-895-3 pa

The wars in Iraq and Afghanistan have impacted the children of soldiers—men and women who have been called away from their families to fight in a faraway war. In their own words, some of these children describe how their experience has marked and shaped their lives

"Accessible and utterly readable. . . . The book is an excellent resource for opening discussions about the current events." SLJ

Includes glossary and bibliographical references

Engle, Dawn

PeaceJam; a billion simple acts of peace. written by Ivan Suvanjieff and Dawn Gifford Engle. Puffin Books 2008 194p il pa $16.99

Grades: 5 6 7 8 9   **303.6**

1. Peace 2. Youth

ISBN 978-0-14-241234-3 pa; 0-14-241234-1 pa

LC 2008-24865

"This visually impressive and well-organized book would work well as a reference tool, how-to handbook, or promotional device for classroom altruistic activities or civil service clubs. Each stand-alone chapter uses a Nobel Peace Laureate as the catalyst for a particular crisis, introduces the reader to a courageous young person who has been inspired to help with a specific problem, and ends with a list of ten very 'doable' suggestions of ways that every concerned citizen can help. The resources listed in the back of the book are extensive and current. An excellent addition to the text is a snappy thirty-minute DVD that could serve as a book talk, review tool or promotional device." Voice Youth Advocates

Gottfried, Ted

★ The **fight** for peace; a history of antiwar movements in America. 21st Century Bks. 2006 136p il (People's history) $26.60

Grades: 7 8 9 10   **303.6**

1. War 2. Peace 3. Pacifism

ISBN 0-7613-2932-3

"Gottfried starts out by explaining that a group in Connecticut rallied together in 2003 to peacefully protest the war against Iraq. . . . Then the author discusses the antiwar movement during the Civil War and proceeds through history, beginning with the ancient Greek play Lysistrata. . . . The pictures, political cartoons, and quotes are an excellent addition. . . . This is a book that can be read for general interest as well as for reports." SLJ

Includes bibliographical references

Judson, Karen

★ **Resolving** conflicts; how to get along when you don't get along. Enslow Pubs. 2005 112p il (Issues in focus today) $31.93

Grades: 7 8 9 10 11 12   **303.6**

1. Conflict management

ISBN 0-7660-2359-1

LC 2004-28119

The author "describes different kinds of conflicts and how they can be resolved, with a special focus on teens and building their conflict-resolution skills and understanding." Publisher's note

Includes bibliographical references

Mara, Wil

Civil unrest in the 1960s; riots and their aftermath. Marshall Cavendish Benchmark 2009 127p il (Perspectives on) lib bdg $27.95

Grades: 8 9 10 11 12   **303.6**

1. Riots

ISBN 978-0-7614-4025-3; 0-7614-4025-9

LC 2008-24673

This book describes "the turbulent decade that bore witness to the Civil Right[s] Movement, the divisive Vietnam War, and various other movements concerning women, gays, and the environment. . . . The potency of [this title] lies in the excellent arrangement of numerous well-chosen sidebars and photos, and fluent, concise prose." SLJ

Includes bibliographical references

O'Brien, Anne Sibley

After Gandhi; one hundred years of nonviolent resistance. [by] Anne Sibley O'Brien and Perry Edmond O'Brien. Charlesbridge 2009 181p il map $15.95

Grades: 7 8 9 10   303.6

1. Nonviolence 2. Passive resistance 3. Essayists 4. Pacifists 5. Memoirists 6. Political leaders 7. Civil rights activists 8. Nobel laureates for peace 9. Social reformers -- Biography 10. Political activists -- Biography 11. Nonviolence 12. Nonviolence -- History -- 20th century

ISBN 978-1-58089-129-5; 1-58089-129-2

LC 2008-10660

"Using Gandhi as its starting point, this large-format book traces the history of nonviolent resistance by looking at significant adherents from 1908 to 2003 including Martin Luther King, Jr., Nelson Mandela, Charles Perkins, César Chávez, Aung San Suu Kyi, Vaclav Havel, and Wangari Maathi and groups such as the student activists of Tiananmen Square and the Madres de Plaza de Mayo (Mothers of the Disappeared) in Argentina. . . . The handsome design and striking black-and-white illustrations are strong visuals that complement the story of nonviolent resistance in action." Booklist

Includes bibliographical references

Senker, Cath

Violence. Smart Apple Media 2010 46p il (Voices) lib bdg $34.25

Grades: 7 8 9 10 11 12   303.6

1. Violence

ISBN 978-1-59920-280-8 lib bdg; 1-59920-280-8 lib bdg

LC 2008050432

This book about violence "addresses the causes, possible solutions, and outlooks, both good and bad, of . . . [the] issue. Each brief chapter covers basic questions, answered with a simple definition or explanation, then supported by pertinent quotes and statistics from well-known experts and organizations. Color photographs, sidebars, graphs, and charts pull the content together in a busy but cohesive presentation. . . . Students assigned research on . . . [the topic] will appreciate the quotes and statistics plus commentary that address the . . . [issue] from several angles." Libr Media Connect

Includes glossary

Weinberg, Leonard

★ **What** is terrorism? [by] Leonard Weinberg and William Eubank. Chelsea House Publishers 2006 104p il (The roots of terrorism) lib bdg $35

Grades: 7 8 9 10   303.6

1. Terrorism

ISBN 0-7910-8305-5

LC 2005027569

This "gives a history of terrorism from its early beginnings through current events. This volume describes the actions and goals of numerous terrorist groups. . . . This . . . has a great deal of information. . . . The glossy pages show off an eye-pleasing color format with neat sections and well-placed pictures." Voice Youth Advocates

Includes bibliographical references

304.6   Population

Altman, Linda Jacobs

Genocide; the systematic killing of a people. rev. and expanded; Enslow Publishers 2009 128p il map (Issues in focus today) lib bdg $31.93

Grades: 6 7 8 9   304.6

1. Genocide

ISBN 978-0-7660-3358-0 lib bdg; 0-7660-3358-9 lib bdg

LC 2007050697

First published 1995

This is written in "short accessible chapters." Horn Book Guide

Includes glossary and bibliographical references

Barber, Nicola

Coping with population growth; Nicola Barber. Raintree 2011 48 p. col. ill.

Grades: 4 5 6 7   304.6

1. Population 2. Population -- Environmental aspects

ISBN 9781410942968; 9781410943033

LC 2010052702

"Barber examines the pressures exerted on the environment and global resources due to population growth... Color photographs add interest, and helpful diagrams effectively convey statistical concepts." Horn Book

Includes bibliographical references (p. 46-47) and index

Bellamy, Rufus

Population growth. Amicus 2010 44p il map (Sustaining our environment) lib bdg $31.35

Grades: 6 7 8 9   304.6

1. Population 2. Overpopulation 3. Environmental protection

ISBN 978-1-60753-137-1 lib bdg; 1-60753-137-2 lib bdg

LC 2009-30032

Discusses how population expansion taxes our resources and poses a threat to the environment.

"The tone is refreshingly optimistic with its examples of specific steps being taken to reduce harm to the environment. Sidebars highlight case studies and campaigns from around the world and from the individual to the national levels. Clear, informative captions accompany the excellent selection of color photographs, charts and graphs." SLJ

Includes glossary

January, Brendan

★ **Genocide**; modern crimes against humanity. Twenty-First Century Books 2007 160p il map lib bdg $31.93

Grades: 8 9 10 11 12   **304.6**

1. Genocide
ISBN 978-0-7613-3421-7 lib bdg; 0-7613-3421-1 lib bdg

LC 2005032850

"January gives young readers a sensitive, solid framework with which to comprehend multiple facets of genocide, from etymology of the term to acknowledging deniers of the Holocaust. The slim volume devotes chapters to separate examples of genocide, historic and contemporary: Armenians of the Ottoman Empire, European Jews, Cambodians, Tutsis of Rwanda, Muslims of Bosnia, and tribes of Darfur. . . . . This outstanding book sparks thoughtful inquiry." Voice Youth Advocates

Includes bibliographical references

Perl, Lila

Genocide; stand by or intervene? Marshall Cavendish Benchmark 2010 127p il (Controversy!) lib bdg $25.95

Grades: 8 9 10 11 12   **304.6**

1. Genocide
ISBN 978-0-7614-4900-3; 0-7614-4900-0

This book "examines the U.N.'s efforts to define and make the crime of genocide punishable under international law. . . . [It] is suggested for libraries that need updated books covering 21st-century events." SLJ

Springer, Jane

★ **Genocide**. Groundwood Books 2006 144p (Groundwork guides) hardcover o.p. pa $9.95

Grades: 8 9 10 11 12   **304.6**

1. Genocide
ISBN 978-0-88899-681-7; 0-88899-681-0; 978-0-88899-682-4 pa; 0-88899-682-9 pa

"This disturbing history of mass ethnic killings across the world examines the why, when, where, and how genocide takes place. . . . In a lucid, informal text, Springer ably documents particular crimes against humanity, including the transatlantic slave trade, the slaughter of America's Native peoples, the Turkish massacre of the Armenians, the Nanking massacre, the Holocaust, and the Khmer Rouge slaughter in Cambodia." Booklist

304.8   Movement of people

Andryszewski, Tricia

★ **Walking** the earth; a history of human migration. [by] Tricia Andryszewski. Twenty-First Century Books 2007 80p il map lib bdg $27.23

Grades: 5 6 7 8   **304.8**

1. Population 2. Prehistoric peoples 3. Immigration and emigration
ISBN 978-0-7613-3458-3 lib bdg; 0-7613-3458-0 lib bdg

LC 2005033430

"Copious sepia-toned visuals, including drawings, photographs, maps, and charts, create an attractive and accessible presentation of complex material." SLJ

Includes bibliographical references

Daniels, Roger

American immigration; a student companion. Oxford Univ. Press 2000 303p (Oxford student companions to American history) lib bdg $60

Grades: 7 8 9 10   **304.8**

1. Immigrants -- United States 2. Immigrants -- United States -- Encyclopedias
ISBN 0-19-511316-0

LC 00-56673

"This resource would be ideal for young adults seeking brief overviews of particular ethnic groups." Voice Youth Advocates

Includes bibliographical references

Ellis Island Oral History Project

I was dreaming to come to America; memories from the Ellis Island Oral History Project. selected and illustrated by Veronica Lawlor; foreword by Rudolph W. Giuliani. Viking 1995 38p il hardcover o.p. pa $6.99

Grades: 4 5 6 7   **304.8**

1. Immigrants -- Biography
ISBN 0-670-86164-2; 0-14-055622-2 pa

LC 95-1281

In their own words, coupled with hand-painted collage illustrations, immigrants recall their arrival in the United States. Includes brief biographies and facts about the Ellis Island Oral History Project

"There is a flavor of Chagall in the peasant figures dancing above the ship or hopping ashore near the turreted towers of the huge building on Ellis Island. The elegant rendering offers a timeless view of this significant journey that is at once personal and universal." Horn Book

Hammerschmidt, Peter A.

History of American immigration. Mason Crest Publishers 2009 64p il (Major American immigration) lib bdg $22.95; pa $9.95

Grades: 6 7 8 9   **304.8**

1. Immigrants -- United States
ISBN 978-1-4222-0613-3 lib bdg; 1-4222-0613-0 lib bdg; 978-1-4222-0680-5 pa; 1-4222-0680-7 pa

LC 2008-28222

"Hammerschmidt's book makes a point of mentioning the importation of slaves as one way in which people came to the United States. . . . Both legal and illegal immigration are given a reasonable amount of space. . . . Overall the coverage is solid. . . . [This] accessible [book] will primarily be used for reports, but [is a] good [choice] to round out a collection on immigration and citizenship topics." SLJ

Includes glossary and bibliographical references

Ollhoff, Jim

Exploring immigration. ABDO Pub. Co. 2011 32p il (Your family tree) $18.95

Grades: 4 5 6 7 **304.8**
1. Genealogy 2. Immigrants
ISBN 978-1-61613-463-1; 1-61613-463-1
LC 2009050807
This book about immigration is "great . . . for kids interested in genealogy. [It does] a wonderful job of presenting the fundamentals of genealogical research in a clear and exciting manner. . . . Understanding and properly using primary documents is stressed throughout. . . . [An] attractive, spacious [layout]; full-color, sharp images; clearly labeled diagrams; and scattered maps add information and appeal." SLJ
Includes glossary

Senker, Cath
Immigrants and refugees; Cath Senker. Smart Apple Media 2012 46 p. (Mapping global issues) (library) $35.65
Grades: 6 7 8 **304.8**
1. Internal migration 2. Immigration and emigration 3. Refugees 4. Immigrants
ISBN 1599205092; 9781599205090
LC 2011000248
This "entry in the Mapping Global Issues series tracks movement of people throughout the world as they search for a better life, whether fleeing from poverty or war, and goes into surprising detail about the methods by which they move. Beginning with sub-Saharan Africa, this title reminds readers of the amount of in-country migration that occurs. . . . Frequent large maps outline migration patterns regionally and globally." (Booklist)
Includes bibliographical references (p. 45) and index

Walker, Paul Robert
A **nation** of immigrants. Kingfisher 2012 32 p. (All About America)
Grades: 2 3 4 5 6 **304.8**
1. United States -- History 2. Immigrants -- United States
ISBN 0753466716; 0753467135; 9780753466711; 9780753467138
This book, part of the "All About America" series, "covers the role immigration played in the development of the United States." Features include "text, . . . illustrations, a one-paragraph introduction on the contents page that summarizes the scope of the book, and translation of period costs to current dollar values. . . . Each spread is busy with illustrations, engravings, and photos, all with captions." (School Library Journal)

305   Groups of people

Stewart, Sheila
Growing up in religious communities. Mason Crest 2009 64p il (The changing face of modern families) $22.95
Grades: 6 7 8 9 **305**
1. Family 2. Religious communities
ISBN 978-1-4222-1500-5; 1-4222-1500-8

This describes some of the unique challenges facing families in religious communities, which may be set apart from others by what they wear, their rituals, what they are not allowed to eat or do, or else by not mixing at all with those outside the community, but which may have their own strengths.
"Colorful photographs and sidebars appear throughout. [This book is a] good [introduction] to the study of sociology and interpretation of data." SLJ
Includes bibliographical references

305.23   Young people

Bedell, J. M.
Teens in Pakistan. Compass Point Books 2009 96p il map (Global connections) lib bdg $33.26
Grades: 6 7 8 9 **305.23**
1. Teenagers
ISBN 978-0-7565-4043-2; 0-7565-4043-7
LC 2008-38332
Discusses the similarities and differences of teenagers in Pakistan.
Includes glossary

Burton, Bonnie
Girls against girls; why we are mean to each other and how we can change. Zest Books 2009 128p il pa $12.95
Grades: 7 8 9 10 **305.23**
1. Bullies 2. Girls -- Psychology
ISBN 978-0-9790173-6-0; 0-9790173-6-X
This guide for teenage girls explains why girls can sometimes be mean to each other, what to do if you are a victim of bullying, and the importance of treating other girls with respect.
This offers "excellent coping techniques. . . . Burton never talks down to her readers, nor does she pull her punches. Readers will respond to the author's clear respect for the painful nature of the problem." Booklist

★ The **Courage** to be yourself; true stories by teens about cliques, conflicts, and overcoming peer pressure. edited by Al Desetta with Educators for Social Responsibility. Free Spirit Pub. 2005 145p pa $13.95
Grades: 7 8 9 10 11 12 **305.23**
1. Teenagers
ISBN 1-57542-185-2
LC 2005-5173
"There is certainly some value in hearing teens of many ethnicities and orientations speaking plainly about being fat, or being from India in a school full of blond, blue-eyed folk, or being Arab after 9/11." Booklist
Includes bibliographical references

Dalton, David
Living in a refugee camp; Carbino's story. World Almanac Lib. 2005 48p il map (Children in crisis) $30

Grades: 6 7 8 9   **305.23**
1. Refugees
ISBN 0-8368-5960-X
"Carbino was 11 when he left his Sudanese village to go to school in Ethiopia; 14 years passed before he returned. Now 28, he recounts the story of his life in his homeland, then being marched from one place to another, living in camps, making friends only to see them killed, and finally returning home, where he is a translator for Doctors Without Borders. . . . [This is] attractively designed. . . . Well written and informative." SLJ

Donovan, Sandra, 1967-
Teens in Thailand; by Sandy Donovan. Compass Point Books 2009 96p il map (Global connections) lib bdg $33.26
Grades: 6 7 8 9   **305.23**
1. Teenagers
ISBN 978-0-7565-4046-3; 0-7565-4046-1
LC 2008-35714
Uncovers the challenges, pastimes, customs and culture of teens in Thailand.
Includes glossary and bibliographical references

Edge, Laura Bufano, 1953-
From jazz babies to generation next; the history of the American teenager. by Laura B. Edge. Twenty-First Century Books 2011 112p il (People's history) lib bdg $33.26
Grades: 6 7 8 9 10   **305.23**
1. Teenagers -- United States
ISBN 978-0-7613-5868-8; 0-7613-5868-4
LC 2010031144
Traces the history of teenagers in the United States, including their influence on the economy, fashion, and entertainment.
"The writing is smooth, informative, and interesting. Although the subject matter may not translate directly into a report topic, it does provide sociocultural, historical, and political overviews of the 1900s. Almost every two-page spread contains a photograph." Voice Youth Advocates
Includes bibliographical references

Farrell, Courtney
Children's rights. ABDO Pub. 2010 112p il (Essential issues) lib bdg $22.95
Grades: 7 8 9 10   **305.23**
1. Child labor 2. Child sexual abuse
ISBN 978-1-60453-952-3; 1-60453-952-6
LC 2009-29938
The text is "well-written, providing examples that put a human face to each problem. Quotes and facts are clearly attributed, and their sources are noted in the extensive back matter. . . . . . . [This] will be of great assistance to students writing reports." SLJ
Includes glossary and bibliographical references

Freedman, Russell
Children of the Great Depression. Clarion Books 2005 118p il lib bdg $20

Grades: 4 5 6 7   **305.23**
1. Great Depression, 1929-1939 2. Children -- United States 3. Depressions -- 1929 4. Children -- United States -- History 5. Children -- United States -- Social conditions
ISBN 0-618-44630-3
LC 2005-06506
"This stirring photo-essay combines . . . unforgettable personal details with a clear historical overview of the period and black-and-white photos by Dorothea Lange, Walker Evans, and many others." Booklist

Howard, Helen
Living as a refugee in America; Mohammed's story. text by Helen Howard; accompanied by interview in the words of Mohammed Nazari; interview conducted by Amy De Leal. World Almanac Library 2005 48p il map (Children in crisis) lib bdg $30.60
Grades: 6 7 8 9   **305.23**
1. Refugees 2. Afghan Americans
ISBN 0-8368-5959-6
LC 2005045251
"Mohammed, 15, is an Afghan who escaped the Taliban with his mother and two sisters; his father fled earlier. After briefly living in Iran and Turkey, they settled in St. Louis, MO. The teen remembers little of his early life as he was only six or seven when he left his homeland, but he describes his experiences before coming to America. . . . [This is] attractively designed. . . . Well written and informative." SLJ
Includes bibliographical references

Mangan, Tricia
How to feel good; 20 things teens can do. by Tricia Mangan. Magination Press 2012 125 p. (pbk. : alk. paper) $12.95
Grades: 8 9 10 11 12   **305.23**
1. Teenagers 2. Life skills 3. Adolescent psychology 4. Teenagers -- Life skills guides
ISBN 1433810409; 9781433810404
LC 2011020623
This book offers advice to teenagers in areas of psychological health in order "to feel good about . . . [themselves] and . . . [their] abilities. For teens, new relationships and experiences are happening all around them, and can make them feel overwhelmed and stressed. Being confident and secure can seem miles away. . . . [This book] provides interactive exercises and questions to help teens recognize and understand why they feel the way they do and to change hurtful thought patterns and habits. With these 20 . . . steps, teens can use this book to learn how to be confident and happy with themselves." (Publisher's note)
"With a gentle, firm but never condescending tone . . . clinical psychologist Mangan leads anxious teens through the A's (activating events), B's (beliefs), and C's (consequences) of taking control of spiraling and self-defeating moods." Booklist

Muharrar, Aisha
★ **More** than a label; why what you wear and who you're with doesn't define who you are. Free Spirit 2002 144p il pa $13.95

Grades: 7 8 9 10   **305.23**
1. Brand name products 2. Adolescent psychology 3. Fashion merchandising 4. Clothing trade -- Trademarks
ISBN 1-57542-110-0

LC 2001-7386

Drawn from a survey of more than one thousand teenagers, first-person stories help to address the problems inherent in labeling people

"The enthusiastic, conversational tone will make the compassionate message very acceptable to teen readers." Booklist

Includes bibliographical references

Musolf, Nell

Teens in Greece. Compass Point Books 2009 96p il map (Global connections) lib bdg $33.26
Grades: 6 7 8 9   **305.23**
1. Teenagers
ISBN 978-0-7565-4040-1; 0-7565-4040-2

LC 2008-35713

Discusses the similarities and differences of teenagers in Greece.
Includes glossary

Smith, David J.

This child, every child; a book about the world's children. written by David J. Smith; illustrated by Shelagh Armstrong. Kids Can Press 2011 36p il (CitizenKid) $18.95
Grades: 4 5 6 7   **305.23**
1. Children
ISBN 978-1-55453-466-1; 1-55453-466-6

This title "takes a global look at the lives of contemporary children. Balancing statistics with fictional profiles of kids, Smith's concise narrative focuses on such topics as families, homes, health, work, war, and play. Each spread contains accessible summaries of articles from 1989's United Nations Convention on the Rights of the Child, underscoring the disparity between many children's lives and that document's vision and goals. . . . Rendered in acrylics with digital textures, Armstrong's gauzy paintings sometimes span multiple cultures in a single illustration . . . reinforcing the universal nature of children's needs." Publ Wkly

Smith-Llera, Danielle

Teens in Argentina. Compass Point Books 2009 96p il map (Global connections) lib bdg $33.26
Grades: 6 7 8 9   **305.23**
1. Teenagers
ISBN 978-0-7565-4037-1; 0-7565-4037-2

LC 2008-35712

Discusses the similarities and differences of teenagers in Argentina.
Includes glossary and bibliographical references

Wilson, Janet

One peace; true stories of young activists. written and illustrated by Janet Wilson. Orca Book Publishers 2008 43p il $19.95
Grades: 4 5 6 7   **305.23**
1. Peace 2. Children and war 3. Pacifists 4. Children

and peace
ISBN 978-1-55143-892-4; 1-55143-892-5

"The stories of young people who have been refugees from war, injured by land mines, or learned about the consequences of violence through other means are interspersed with children's poems, quotes, artwork, and photographs. The brief, powerful accounts document how these children ages 8 to 15 worked for or became symbols of peace." SLJ

305.235   Young people twelve to twenty

Donovan, Sandra, 1967-

Teens in Morocco; by Sandy Donovan. Compass Point Books 2008 96 p. col. ill., col. maps (Global connections) (library) $33.99
Grades: 7 8 9 10   **305.235**
1. Teenagers 2. Teenagers -- Morocco -- Social conditions 3. Teenagers -- Morocco -- Social life and customs
ISBN 075653402X; 9780756534028

LC 2007032692

Uncovers the challenges, pastimes, customs and culture of teens in Morocco

"Information is solid, giving readers an informed and realistic view of life in that country. A historical timeline is included, and suggestions for other nonfiction and fiction titles for further reading." Voice Youth Advocates

Includes bibliographical references (p. 92-93) and index.

Ellis, Deborah

Kids of Kabul; living bravely through a never-ending war. Deborah Ellis. Groundwood Books 2012 143 p. $15.95
Grades: 6 7 8 9 10 11 12   **305.235**
1. Interviews 2. Children -- Afghanistan
ISBN 1554981816; 9781554981816

This book is a collection of interviews with Afghani children who "mostly don't remember the Taliban's fall more than a decade ago, but they can't help but be shaped by the damage the Taliban did to their country. . . . One girl is imprisoned for fleeing a forced child marriage, while another's mother is a member of Parliament; one boy's damaged by a landmine, and another's proud to be a Scout. . . . [I]ntroductions to each young person provide historical, legal and social context." (Kirkus Reviews)

Jukes, Mavis

★ The **guy** book; an owner's manual for teens: safety, maintenance, and operating instructions for teens. Crown 2002 152p il hardcover o.p. pa $12.95
Grades: 7 8 9 10   **305.235**
1. Boys 2. Puberty 3. Adolescence 4. Sex education 5. Teenage boys 6. Sex instruction for boys 7. Sex instruction for boys 8. Sex instruction for teenagers 9. Interpersonal relations in adolescence
ISBN 0-679-99028-3 lib bdg; 0-679-89028-9 pa

LC 2001-47073

Provides information for boys on changes that occur in their bodies during puberty and offering advice on sexual topics, nutrition, drugs, girls, and more.

"In a jokey premise that will appeal to teens, the book follows the format of a car owner's manual with a retro look. . . . Much of this information is available in other sources, but the added sense of fun will make this a first choice for a lot of young men." Booklist

Includes bibliographical references

Lilly, Alexandra

Teens in Turkey; by Alexandra Lilly. Compass Point Books 2008 96 p. ill., maps (library) $33.99

Grades: 7 8 9 10   **305.235**
1. Teenagers 2. Teenagers -- Turkey -- Social conditions 3. Teenagers -- Turkey -- Social life and customs
ISBN 9780756534141; 0756534143

LC 2007033090

Uncovers the challenges, pastimes, customs and culture of teens in Turkey

"Information is solid, giving readers an informed and realistic view of life in that country. A historical time line is included, and suggestions for other nonfiction and fiction titles for further reading." Youth Voice Advocates

ncludes bibliographical references (p. 90-91) and index.

Shandler, Sara

Ophelia speaks; adolescent girls write about their search for self. HarperPerennial 1999 285p pa $12.95

Grades: 7 8 9 10   **305.235**
1. Girls 2. Adolescence 3. Youths' writings, American 4. Body image in adolescence -- United States 5. Self-esteem in adolescence -- United States 6. Teenage girls -- United States -- Physiology 7. Teenage girls -- United States -- Psychology
ISBN 0-06-095297-0

LC 99-13534

"Shandler collected writings from adolescent girls all over the country on topics that include sexuality, eating disorders, feminism, family dynamics, and friendship; their words, framed by Shandler's own reflections, are riveting and revealing." Libr J

305.3   People by gender or sex

Male and female roles: opposing viewpoints; Karen Miller, book editor. Greenhaven Press 2010 229p (Opposing viewpoints series) lib bdg $39.70; pa $27.50

Grades: 8 9 10 11 12   **305.3**
1. Gender role 2. Sex role
ISBN 978-0-7377-4528-3 lib bdg; 0-7377-4528-2 lib bdg; 978-0-7377-4529-0 pa; 0-7377-4529-0 pa
LC 2009-19788

A series of essays that expresses various perspectives on the individual roles of men and women.

Includes bibliographical references

305.4   Women

Bausum, Ann

★ **With** courage and cloth; winning the fight for a woman's right to vote. by Ann Bausum. National Geographic 2004 111p il $21.95; lib bdg $32.90

Grades: 6 7 8 9   **305.4**
1. Women -- Suffrage   2. Women -- United States -- History 3. Women -- Suffrage -- United States
ISBN 0-7922-7647-7; 0-7922-6996-9 lib bdg

LC 2004-1191

This is a history of the movement for women's suffrage in the United States.

"Vintage photographs, some never before published, depict key figures in the movement speaking, protesting, parading, picketing, and going to jail. Bausum's careful research is evident throughout, with sources thoroughly cited and a text studded with original source quotations." SLJ

Bingham, Jane

Women at war; the progressive era, World War I and women's suffrage, 1900-1920. Chelsea House 2011 il (A cultural history of women in America) $35

Grades: 5 6 7 8   **305.4**
1. World War, 1914-1918 2. Women -- Employment 3. Women -- Social conditions 4. Women -- United States -- History
ISBN 978-1-6041-3932-7; 1-6041-3932-3

LC 2010044828

An "eye-catching [layout] with good use of color, photographs, and informative sidebars, many of which use primary-source quotations, are the highlights of [this] appealing [volume]. . . . After a succinct overview of contemporary events, the chapters describe women's lives at home, at work, in education, in politics, in the arts, and their role in the general culture. . . . [This book] explores the changing role of women during the Progressive Era, the impact of World War I on their lives, and the struggle for voting rights." SLJ

Includes glossary and bibliographical references

Coppens, Linda Miles

★ **What** American women did, 1789-1920; a year-by-year reference. McFarland & Co. 2001 259p il hardcover o.p. pa $49.95

Grades: 7 8 9 10   **305.4**
1. Women -- Social conditions 2. Women -- United States -- History 3. Women -- United States -- Social conditions -- 18th century 4. Women -- United States -- Social conditions -- 19th century 5. Women -- United States -- Social conditions -- 20th century
ISBN 0-7864-0899-5; 0-7864-3245-4 pa

LC 00-64010

"A chronological account of women's accomplishments in the areas of domesticity, work, education, religion, the arts, law and politics, and reform efforts. . . . This work will prove useful for students wishing to gain a better perspective of history, particularly social history, as it pertained to women." SLJ

Includes bibliographical references

Coster, Patience

A **new** deal for women; the expanding roles of women, 1938-1960. Chelsea House 2011 64p il (A cultural history of women in America) $35

Grades: 5 6 7 8   **305.4**

1. Feminism 2. Women -- Social conditions 3. Women -- United States -- History

ISBN 978-1-6041-3934-1; 1-6041-3934-X

LC 2010045959

An "eye-catching [layout] with good use of color, photographs, and informative sidebars, many of which use primary-source quotations, are the highlights of [this] appealing [volume]. . . . After a succinct overview of contemporary events, the chapters describe women's lives at home, at work, in education, in politics, in the arts, and their role in the general culture. . . . New opportunities for women were a part of the New Deal and World War II and together changed American culture—these topics are explored [this] volume covering the years 1938-1960." SLJ

Includes glossary and bibliographical references

Gorman, Jacqueline Laks

The **modern** feminist movement; sisters under the skin, 1961-1979. Chelsea House 2011 il (A cultural history of women in America) $35

Grades: 5 6 7 8   **305.4**

1. Feminism 2. Women -- Social conditions 3. Women -- United States -- History

ISBN 978-1-6041-3935-8; 1-6041-3935-8

LC 2010045990

An "eye-catching [layout] with good use of color, photographs, and informative sidebars, many of which use primary-source quotations, are the highlights of [this] appealing [volume]. . . . After a succinct overview of contemporary events, the chapters describe women's lives at home, at work, in education, in politics, in the arts, and their role in the general culture. . . . [This book] delves into the years of protest and quest for equal rights." SLJ

Includes glossary and bibliographical references

Gourley, Catherine

★ **Flappers** and the new American woman; perceptions of women from 1918 through the 1920s. Twenty-First Century Books 2008 144p il (Images and issues of women in the twentieth century) lib bdg $38.60

Grades: 7 8 9 10   **305.4**

1. Women -- United States -- History

ISBN 978-0-8225-6060-9; 0-8225-6060-7

LC 2006-28983

This describes images of women in the United States from 1918 through the 1920s.

"The sparkling and engaging [text is] generously expanded by numerous, well-placed black-and-white photographs and period reproductions. . . . Great for research or browsing." SLJ

Includes bibliographical references

★ **Gibson** girls and suffragists; perceptions of women from the turn of the century through 1918. Twenty-First Century Books 2008 144p il (Images

and issues of women in the twentieth century) lib bdg $38.60

Grades: 7 8 9 10   **305.4**

1. Women -- United States -- History 2. Women -- United States -- History -- 20th century 3. Women -- United States -- Social life and customs 4. Women -- United States -- Social conditions -- 20th century

ISBN 978-0-8225-7150-6; 0-8225-7150-1

LC 2007-1689

This describes the images of women in United States at the beginning of the twentienth century.

"The sparkling and engaging [text is] generously expanded by numerous, well-placed black-and-white photographs and period reproductions. . . . Great for research or browsing." SLJ

Includes bibliographical references

★ **Gidgets** and women warriors; perceptions of women in the 1950s and 1960s. by Catherine Gourley. Twenty-First Century Books 2008 144p il (Images and issues of women in the twentieth century) $38.60

Grades: 7 8 9 10   **305.4**

1. Nineteen fifties 2. Nineteen sixties 3. Women -- United States -- History 4. Women -- United States -- History -- 20th century 5. Popular culture -- United States -- History -- 20th century 6. Women -- United States -- Social conditions -- 20th century

ISBN 978-0-8225-6805-6; 0-8225-6805-5

LC 2006036103

This "examines women after World War II. Chapters explore varied aspects of the lives of white women as teens, consumers, wives, mothers, and burgeoning activists. . . . Most images and discussions of minority women are confined to the chapter on the Civil Rights movement. . . . Text is accessible and interesting for teens fascinated with women's history." Youth Voice Advocates

Includes bibliographical references (p. 132-139)

★ **Rosie** and Mrs. America; perceptions of women in the 1930s and 1940s. Twenty-First Century Books 2008 144p il (Images and issues of women in the twentieth century) lib bdg $38.60

Grades: 7 8 9 10   **305.4**

1. Women -- United States -- History

ISBN 978-0-8225-6804-9; 0-8225-6804-7

LC 2006-28984

This describes images of women in the United States in the 1930s and 1940's.

"The sparkling and engaging [text is] generously expanded by numerous, well-placed black-and-white photographs and period reproductions. . . . Great for research or browsing." SLJ

Includes bibliographical references

Macdonald, Fiona

Women in 19th-century Europe. Bedrick Bks. 1999 48p il (Other half of history) $17.95

Grades: 5 6 7 8   **305.4**

1. Women -- Europe 2. Women -- Social conditions 3. Women -- Europe -- History -- 19th century 4. Women

-- Europe -- History -- 19th century
ISBN 0-87226-565-X

LC 98-42170

Examines the reality of women's lives in Europe during the 1800s and how change slowly occurred

"The pages are a panorama of illustrations from black-and-white woodcuts to line drawings and full-color reproductions, each accompanied by a succinct caption. . . . A delight to browse, and should lead readers to more extensive exploration." SLJ

Includes glossary and bibliographical references

Marsico, Katie

Women's right to vote; America's suffrage movement. Marshall Cavendish Benchmark 2010 112p il (Perspectives on) $39.93

Grades: 7 8 9 10   305.4
1. Women -- Suffrage 2. Women -- United States -- History
ISBN 978-0-7614-4980-5; 0-7614-4980-9

This discusses the history of the women's suffrage movement in the United States.

This "well-written [book begins] with [an overview] and some historical background, and then [proceeds] chronologically to the current decade. . . . Marsico engages readers especially well, particularly when recounting the tenuous hours before the 19th Amendment ratification vote in Tennessee. It is evident that . . . [the author has] done [her] research. [The book contains] information that is perhaps less well-known to student researchers, including . . . the treatment of imprisoned suffragists. Black-and-white and color photographs along with some period cartoons place readers in the time period, and sidebars interspersed throughout present issues that aren't easily covered within the main [text]." SLJ

Includes bibliographical references

Miller, Brandon Marie

Good women of a well-blessed land; women's lives in colonial America. Lerner Pubs. 2003 96p il (People's history) $31.93

Grades: 6 7 8 9   305.4
1. Women -- United States -- History 2. Women -- United States -- History -- 17th century 3. Women -- United States -- History -- 18th century
ISBN 0-8225-0032-9

LC 2002-8902

A social history of the American colonial period with a focus on the daily lives of women, including European immigrants, Native Americans, and slaves

"The well-written account offers enough solid information to give readers a good sense of the period and enough fascinating detail to keep them interested." Booklist

Includes bibliographical references

Mills, J. Elizabeth

Expectations for women; confronting stereotypes. Rosen Pub. 2010 112p il (A young woman's guide to contemporary issues) lib bdg $31.95

Grades: 7 8 9 10   305.4
1. Women 2. Body image 3. Self-perception
ISBN 978-1-4358-3543-6; 1-4358-3543-3

LC 2009-14429

"Facts are shared in a conversational tone, creating the sense of a chat with a big sister. . . . [Though] designed for personal reading and browsing, the data provided are accurate and also lend themselves to use in reports. This . . . will be of great interest." SLJ

Includes glossary and bibliographical references

Schomp, Virginia

★ **American** voices from the women's movement. Marshall Cavendish Benchmark 2007 138p il (American voices from--) lib bdg $37.07

Grades: 6 7 8 9 10 11 12   305.4
1. Feminism 2. Women's rights 3. Women -- United States -- History
ISBN 978-0-7614-2171-9 lib bdg; 0-7614-2171-8 lib bdg

LC 2006-5800

"Describes the history of the women's rights movement in the United States, from colonial times to the present day, through the use of primary resources such as letters, diary entries, official government documents, newspaper articles, historical art, and photographs." Publisher's note

Includes glossary and bibliographical references

Senker, Cath

Strength in numbers; industrialization and political activism, 1861-1899. Chelsea House 2011 64p il (A cultural history of women in America) $35

Grades: 7 8 9 10   305.4
1. Feminism 2. Women's rights 3. Women -- United States -- History
ISBN 978-1-60413-931-0; 1-60413-931-5

LC 2010045964

This is a history of American women from 1861-1899.

This book offers a "comprehensive, vivid, and thought-provoking [look] at the struggles and triumphs of . . . the women who [participated] in shaping our nation. Through succinct, informative text, [this] heavily illustrated volume incorporates the history of three major groups of people: the Natives, European settlers, and African slaves. Featured quotes from books, articles, letters, and speeches bring the history to life." SLJ

Includes glossary and bibliographical references

Stearman, Kaye

Feminism; [by] Kaye Stearman. Raintree 2004 64p il (Ideas of the modern world) lib bdg $32.79

Grades: 7 8 9 10   305.4
1. Feminism 2. Feminism -- History
ISBN 0-7398-6415-7

LC 2003-2068

"Stearman discusses the history of women's rights with connections made to other political movements such as abolitionism and temperance. . . . The author looks at new interpretations of feminism and issues such as sweatshop labor, countries with controversial social laws against women's rights, and female genital mutilation. [This book has] a balance of ideas and nonjudgmental language. Black-and-white and full-color photos appear throughout." SLJ

Includes bibliographical references

Women of today; contemporary issues and conflicts, 1980-present. [by] Kaye Stearman and Patience Coster. Chelsea House 2011 64p il (A cultural history of women in America) $35

Grades: 5 6 7 8 **305.4**

1. Feminism 2. Women -- United States 3. Women -- Social conditions

ISBN 978-1-6041-3936-5; 1-6041-3936-6

LC 2010046014

An "eye-catching [layout] with good use of color, photographs, and informative sidebars, many of which use primary-source quotations, are the highlights of [this] appealing [volume]. . . . After a succinct overview of contemporary events, the chapters describe women's lives at home, at work, in education, in politics, in the arts, and their role in the general culture. . . . [This book] highlights women's achievements, including U.S. Supreme Court justices, Speaker of the U.S. House of Representatives, and presidential candidates." SLJ

Includes glossary and bibliographical references

Swisher, Clarice

Women of the roaring twenties; [by] Clarice Swisher. Lucent Books 2006 112p il (Women in history) $28.70

Grades: 7 8 9 10 **305.4**

1. Women -- United States -- History

ISBN 1-59018-363-0

LC 2004-23410

This "account draws on diaries, letters, and journals to tell the story of women in the 1920s—coeds and housewives, laborers and professionals, writers and activists. . . . The clear prose and occasional photos will hold readers." Booklist

Includes bibliographical references

Taschek, Karen

Daughters of liberty; the American Revolution and the Early Republic, 1775-1827. Chelsea House 2011 64p il (A cultural history of women in America) $35

Grades: 7 8 9 10 **305.4**

1. Women -- United States -- History

ISBN 978-1-60413-928-0; 1-60413-928-5

LC 2010033717

This is a history of women in America from 1775-1827.

This book offers a "comprehensive, vivid, and thought-provoking [look] at the struggles and triumphs of . . . the women who [participated] in shaping our nation. Through succinct, informative text, [this] heavily illustrated volume incorporates the history of three major groups of people: the Natives, European settlers, and African slaves. Featured quotes from books, articles, letters, and speeches bring the history to life." SLJ

Includes glossary and bibliographical references

VanMeter, Larry A.

Women win the vote; the hard-fought battle for women's suffrage. Enslow Publishers 2009 128p il map (America's living history) lib bdg $31.93

Grades: 5 6 7 8 **305.4**

1. Women -- Suffrage 2. Women -- United States -- History

ISBN 978-0-7660-2940-8 lib bdg; 0-7660-2940-9 lib bdg

LC 2008024900

"Archival photographs, maps, and sidebars combine with . . . informative [text]." Horn Book Guide

Includes glossary and bibliographical references

Woolf, Alex, 1964-

Finding an identity; early America and the Colonial Period, 1492-1774. Chelsea House 2011 64p il (A cultural history of women in America) $35

Grades: 7 8 9 10 **305.4**

1. Women -- United States -- History

ISBN 978-1-6041-3927-3; 1-6041-3927-7

LC 2010029225

This is a history of women in America from 1492-1774.

This book offers a "comprehensive, vivid, and thought-provoking [look] at the struggles and triumphs of . . . the women who [participated] in shaping our nation. Through succinct, informative text, [this] heavily illustrated volume incorporates the history of three major groups of people: the Natives, European settlers, and African slaves. Featured quotes from books, articles, letters, and speeches bring the history to life." SLJ

Includes glossary and bibliographical references

305.8 Ethnic and national groups

★ The **African** American almanac; Christopher A. Brooks, editor; foreword by Benjamin Jealous. 11th ed; Gale Cengage Learning 2011 1601p il map $297

Grades: 8 9 10 11 12 Adult **305.8**

1. Reference books 2. African Americans

ISBN 978-1-4144-4547-2

First edition under the editorship of Harry A. Ploski published 1967 by Bellwether with title: The Negro almanac. Periodically revised. Editors vary

"Reference covering the cultural and political history of Black Americans. Includes generous amount of statistical information and biographies of Black Americans, both historical and contemporary." N Y Public Libr. Book of How & Where to Look It Up

The **Black** experience in America; from civil rights to the present. edited by Jeff Wallenfeldt. Britannica Educational Pub. 2010 230p il (African American history and culture) lib bdg $45

Grades: 8 9 10 11 12 **305.8**

1. African Americans -- History 2. African Americans -- Civil rights

ISBN 978-1-61530-146-1; 1-61530-146-1

LC 2010-14639

This "is notable for the depth and breadth of its coverage. Beginning with WWII events that led to integration, the book, illustrated with black-and-white photos, chronologically follows the history of the civil rights movement as well as introducing black influences on literature, sports, and music. . . . It's hard to find a single-volume title that covers so much." Booklist

Includes glossary and bibliographical references

Bolden, Tonya

★ **Tell** all the children our story; memories and mementos of being young and Black in America. Abrams 2001 128p il $24.95

Grades: 5 6 7 8   305.8

1. Race relations 2. African Americans 3. African American children 4. African Americans -- History 5. African American children -- History 6. African American children -- Social conditions

ISBN 0-8109-4496-0

LC 2001-1353

"This compilation of the African American experience, from colonial times through the twentieth century, reads and looks like a family scrapbook. . . . Photographs, excerpts from diaries and memoirs, and reproductions of artwork by black artists such as Charles Altson beautifully bring the story of each generation to life. Bolden vibrantly delivers her historical message through a contemporary perspective." Booklist

Includes bibliographical references

Discrimination: opposing viewpoints; Jacqueline Langwith, book editor. Greenhaven Press 2008 247p il (Opposing viewpoints series) $36.20; pa $24.95

Grades: 8 9 10 11 12   305.8

1. Minorities 2. Discrimination 3. Affirmative action programs

ISBN 978-0-73773-739-4; 0-73773-739-5; 978-0-73773-740-0 pa; 0-73773-740-9 pa

LC 2007-933224

This covers the topic of discrimination "in pro and con articles written by experts in the field or journalists with relevant experience. Clearly written, well researched, and far reaching, Discrimination explores the problem in its many forms." SLJ

Includes bibliographical references

Doak, Robin S.

Struggling to become American; [by] Robin Doak. Chelsea House 2007 106p il map (Latino American history) $35

Grades: 5 6 7 8   305.8

1. Latinos (U.S.) 2. Hispanic Americans 3. Immigrants -- United States

ISBN 0-8160-6443-1; 978-0-8160-6443-4

LC 2006017140

"Topics such as U.S. policy decisions regarding Puerto Rico and Cuba, racism experienced by immigrants and those who became American when the U.S. Mexican border shifted in 1848, Latino culture in the United States, and the repatriation of Mexicans during the Great Depression are covered in a reasonable amount of detail. Plenty

of captioned photographs, political cartoons, and colorful subheads and informational sidebars keep the book visually interesting." SLJ

Includes bibliographical references

Engelbert, Phillis

American civil rights: biographies; Betz Des Chenes, editor. U.X.L 1999 xl, 203p il $60

Grades: 8 9 10 11 12   305.8

1. Civil rights 2. Civil rights movements -- United States -- History 3. Civil rights workers -- United States -- Biography 4. Minorities -- Civil rights -- United States -- History

ISBN 0-7876-3173-6

LC 99-20497

This collection of biographies of major civil rights figures, includes sidebars covering related events and issues

Includes bibliographical references

Gustaitis, Joseph Alan

Chinese Americans. Marshall Cavendish Benchmark 2009 80p il map (New Americans) lib bdg $35.64

Grades: 5 6 7 8   305.8

1. Chinese Americans 2. Immigrants -- United States

ISBN 978-0-7614-4303-2 lib bdg; 0-7614-4303-7 lib bdg

LC 2009003170

This describes the history of Chinese communities in America.

"Consistent in content, and providing a mix of facts and personal accounts, this . . . will be [a] . . . very useful addition to the collection." Libr Media Collect

Includes glossary and bibliographical references

Haskins, James

★ The **rise** of Jim Crow; by James Haskins and Kathleen Benson; with Virginia Schomp. Marshall Cavendish Benchmark 2008 80p il (Drama of African-American history) lib bdg $23.95

Grades: 5 6 7 8   305.8

1. African Americans -- History 2. African Americans -- Segregation

ISBN 978-0-7614-2640-0

"Provides a history of the decades of poverty, oppression, and terror that African Americans suffered under the system of segregation in the United States, from the end of the Reconstruction era through the early decades of the twentieth century." Publisher's note

Includes glossary and bibliographical references

Hernandez, Roger E.

1898 to World War II. Marshall Cavendish Benchmark 2009 78p il (Hispanic America) lib bdg $34.21

Grades: 4 5 6 7   305.8

1. Hispanic Americans -- History

ISBN 978-0-7614-4176-2 lib bdg; 0-7614-4176-X lib bdg

LC 2008041140

"Provides comprehensive information on the history of the Spanish coming to the United States, focusing on the time from 1898 to the start of World War II." Publisher's note
Includes glossary and bibliographical references

Horst, Heather A.

Jamaican Americans; [by] Heather A. Horst and Andrew Garner; series editor, Robert D. Johnston. Chelsea House 2007 144p il map (The new immigrants) lib bdg $27.95
Grades: 7 8 9 10 11 12   **305.8**
  1. West Indian Americans 2. Immigrants -- United States
  ISBN 0-7910-8790-5; 978-0-7910-8790-9
                                   LC 2006-25904
The "chatty narrative style may engage readers." Horn Book Guide
Includes bibliographical references

Horton, James Oliver

Landmarks of African American history. Oxford University Press 2004 207p (American landmarks) $30
Grades: 8 9 10 11 12   **305.8**
  1. Historic sites 2. African Americans -- History 3. African Americans -- Monuments 4. Historic sites -- United States
  ISBN 0-19-514118-0
                                    LC 2004-2798
"Horton discusses 13 historic places, beginning with Jamestown, VA, and ending with the Woolworth department store in Greensboro, NC, the site of the first student sit-in in 1960. Clearly written and well organized, the text enriches the study of African-American history, providing a context and a look at its artifacts. . . . Well-placed illustrations of archival and current photographs and maps make for an attractive presentation." SLJ
Includes bibliographical references

It's not all black and white; multiracial youth speak out. St. Stephen's Community House. Annick Press 2012 109 p. $12.95
Grades: 8 9 10 11 12   **305.8**
  1. Prejudices 2. Minority youth 3. Identity (Psychology) 4. Racially mixed people
  ISBN 1554513804; 9781554513802
In this collection of "poems, interviews, and short essays, a group of young people describe being biracial, multiracial, or of mixed race. . . . Themes include navigating mixed-race relationships, dealing with prejudice and the assumptions people make based on appearances, and working through identity confusion to arrive at a strong and positive sense of self." (Publisher's note)

Katz, William Loren

Black Indians; a hidden heritage. Atheneum Pubs. 1986 198p il $17.95; pa $10
Grades: 8 9 10 11 12   **305.8**
  1. Native Americans 2. African Americans
  ISBN 0-689-31196-6; 0-689-80901-8 pa
                                    LC 85-28770

Traces the history of relations between blacks and American Indians, and the existence of black Indians, from the earliest foreign landings through pioneer days.
The author "has provided a valuable addition to titles on American Indians. Excellent for assignments, it contains important information many history instructors may be unaware of. His sections on black Indians and the Seminoles of Florida and their views about living together are particularly good." Child Book Rev Serv
Includes bibliographical references

Keedle, Jayne

Americans from the Caribbean and Central America. Marshall Cavendish Benchmark 2009 80p il map (New Americans) lib bdg $35.64
Grades: 5 6 7 8   **305.8**
  1. Caribbean Americans 2. Central American Americans 3. Immigrants -- United States
  ISBN 978-0-7614-4302-5 lib bdg; 0-7614-4302-9 lib bdg
                                   LC 2009003171
This title looks at Caribbean and Central American "communities in America today, detailing earlier generations of immigrants and current arrivals who are making new lives, changing the American culture, and looking to the future. [The] title includes many full-color photos, maps, and charts. . . . The [book does] a good job of helping readers to understand the differences between undocumented and documented immigrants and describe the citizenship process. The topics of racism, stereotypes, and other issues related to integration into American society are sensitively covered." SLJ
Includes glossary and bibliographical references

Mexican Americans. Marshall Cavendish Benchmark 2009 80p il map (New Americans) lib bdg $35.64
Grades: 5 6 7 8   **305.8**
  1. Mexican Americans 2. Immigrants -- United States
  ISBN 978-0-7614-4307-0 lib bdg; 0-7614-4307-X lib bdg
                                   LC 2008052101
This describes the history of Mexican Americans
"Consistent in content, and providing a mix of facts and personal accounts, this . . . will be [a] . . . very useful addition to the collection." Libr Media Collect
Includes glossary and bibliographical references

West African Americans. Marshall Cavendish Benchmark 2009 80p il map (New Americans) lib bdg $35.64
Grades: 5 6 7 8   **305.8**
  1. African Americans 2. Africans -- United States 3. Immigrants -- United States
  ISBN 978-0-7614-4313-1 lib bdg; 0-7614-4313-4 lib bdg
                                   LC 2008055753
This title looks at West African "communities in America today, detailing earlier generations of immigrants and current arrivals who are making new lives, changing the American culture, and looking to the future. [The] title includes many full-color photos, maps, and charts. . . . [The

book does] a good job of helping readers to understand the differences between undocumented and documented immigrants and describe the citizenship process. The topics of racism, stereotypes, and other issues related to integration into American society are sensitively covered." SLJ

Includes glossary and bibliographical references

Masoff, Joy

★ The **African** American story; the events that shaped our nation--and the people that changed our lives. Five Ponds 2007 95p il map $26.50
Grades: 4 5 6 7   **305.8**
1. African Americans -- History
ISBN 978-0-9727156-9-0

This "covers the history of the African people in America from the 1400s to the present. Historical photographs, archival documents, maps, and a fact-filled time line provide a visually stimulating introduction to the subject. . . . Masoff provides a tremendous amount of material in an exciting, appealing title that is useful for browsing, introductory lessons, quick reference, and beginning research." SLJ

Includes bibliographical references

Miller, Calvin Craig

Backlash; race riots in the Jim Crow Era. Calvin Craig Miller. Morgan Reynolds Pub. 2012 128 p. $28.95
Grades: 8 9 10 11 12   **305.8**
1. Racism -- History 2. Riots -- United States 3. African Americans -- History 4. Cities and towns -- United States 5. United States -- Race relations -- History 6. United States -- Race relations 7. African Americans -- Crimes against 8. Riots -- United States -- History -- 20th century 9. African Americans -- Crimes against -- History -- 20th century
ISBN 1599351838; 9781599351834
               LC 2011005673

This book details the history of "violence against African Americans in the Jim Crow era. . . . In cities, without the protection of secrecy, violence manifested itself in white mob attacks against black communities. This . . . [book] recognizes seven of the worst attacks that occurred in cities across the United States. Starting with the 1898 riot in Wilmington, North Carolina, in which white supremacists overturned an elected government . . . and killed 30 blacks, the . . . text goes on to cover similar events in Atlanta, Springfield, East St. Louis, Chicago, Tulsa, and Detroit. In each case, [Calvin Craig] Miller notes numerous similarities, including rage among working-class whites over competition with blacks for jobs and affordable housing, and rumors fueled by racist media." (Booklist)

Includes bibliographical references (p. 123-124) and index

Ochoa, George

Atlas of Hispanic-American history; [by] George Ochoa and Carter Smith. Rev ed; Facts on File 2008 250p il map (Facts on File library of American history) $95; pa $21.95

Grades: 7 8 9 10   **305.8**
1. Reference books 2. Hispanic Americans -- History
ISBN 978-0-8160-7092-3; 978-0-8160-7736-6 pa
               LC 2008-20664
First published 2001

This reference chronicles the "cultural, historical, political, and social experiences of Hispanic Americans through the years. . . . [It] examines Spanish, Native American, and African influences and how they combine in different ways to form the varied cultures of Hispanic America." Publisher's note

Includes bibliographical references

Park, Ken

Americans from India and other South Asian countries. Marshall Cavendish Benchmark 2009 80p il map (New Americans) lib bdg $35.64
Grades: 5 6 7 8   **305.8**
1. Asian Americans 2. Immigrants -- United States 3. East Indians -- United States
ISBN 978-0-7614-4305-6 lib bdg; 0-7614-4305-3 lib bdg
               LC 2009002599

This title looks at Indian and other South Asian "communities in America today, detailing earlier generations of immigrants and current arrivals who are making new lives, changing the American culture, and looking to the future. [The] title includes many full-color photos, maps, and charts.. . . The [book does] a good job of helping readers to understand the differences between undocumented and documented immigrants and describe the citizenship process. The topics of racism, stereotypes, and other issues related to integration into American society are sensitively covered." SLJ

Includes glossary and bibliographical references

Perl, Lila

To the Golden Mountain; the story of the Chinese who built the transcontinental railroad. Benchmark Bks. 2002 112p il music (Great journeys) lib bdg $32.79

                   305.8
1. Chinese -- United States 2. Railroads -- United States 3. Alien labor, Chinese -- United States -- History -- 19th century 4. Railroad construction workers -- United States -- History -- 19th century
ISBN 0-7614-1324-3
               LC 2001-6241

"More than the story of Chinese workers' contributions to building the transcontinental railroad, this book is also a brief history of China's contacts with the West, focusing on the financial despair that drove many men to emigrate, beginning in the 1840s. The anti-Chinese sentiment that rose in California after their success in the gold rush is discussed, as is life in the Chinatowns that were established." SLJ

Includes bibliographical references

Petrillo, Valerie

A **kid's** guide to Latino history; more than 70 activities. Chicago Review Press 2009 214p il pa $14.95

Grades: 4 5 6 7 **305.8**
1. Hispanic Americans -- History
ISBN 978-1-55652-771-5 pa; 1-55652-771-3 pa
LC 2008040433
"This big, lively overview examines the history of Latinos in the U.S. . . . The chatty, informative text, presented in readable, spacious layouts, will draw kids with lots of fun, illustrated instructions for related activities. . . . The accessible facts and the individual portraits of notable authors, athletes, entertainers, and politicians portray Latinos' rich contribution to U.S. heritage, and kids will want to talk about the well-presented issues." Booklist
Includes bibliographical references

Race relations: opposing viewpoints; Karen Miller, book editor. Greenhaven Press 2011 204p il (Opposing viewpoints series) lib bdg $39.70; pa $26.50
Grades: 8 9 10 11 12 **305.8**
ISBN 978-0-7377-4986-1 lib bdg; 0-7377-4986-5 lib bdg; 978-0-7377-4987-8 pa; 0-7377-4987-3 pa
LC 2010028939
Articles in this anthology present opposing views on the nature of race, the impact of society and the government on race relations, and what the future holds.
Includes bibliographical references

Radzilowski, John
Ukrainian Americans; [by] John Radzilowski. Chelsea House 2006 128p il map (The new immigrants) lib bdg $27.95
Grades: 7 8 9 10 11 12 **305.8**
1. Ukrainian Americans
ISBN 978-0-7910-8789-3 lib bdg; 0-7910-8789-1 lib bdg
LC 2006-15644
"In addition to profiles on notable Ukrainian Americans, such as actor Jack Palance and Hall of Fame NHL goaltender Terry Sawchuk, . . . [this book provides an] introduction to the history, culture, religion, and experiences of this immigrant group." Publisher's note
Includes glossary and bibliographical references

Rangaswamy, Padma
Indian Americans; [by] Padma Rangaswamy. Chelsea House 2007 158p il map (The new immigrants) lib bdg $27.95
Grades: 7 8 9 10 11 12 **305.8**
1. East Indian Americans 2. Immigrants -- United States 3. East Indians -- United States
ISBN 0-7910-8786-7
LC 2006-8384
The author traces the history of new immigrants from India "from the early days of the Punjabi pioneers in California to the triumphs of the 'dot-com generation.'" Publisher's note
Includes bibliographical references

Rodger, Marguerite
Racism and prejudice; [by] Marguerite Rodger and Jessie Rodger. Crabtree Pub. Co. 2010 48p il (Straight talk about. . .) lib bdg $29.27; pa $9.95
Grades: 7 8 9 10 **305.8**
1. Racism 2. Prejudices
ISBN 978-0-7787-2129-1 lib bdg; 0-7787-2129-9 lib bdg; 978-0-7787-2136-9 pa; 0-7787-2136-1 pa
LC 2010019132
The authors "cover topics ranging from overt racism to homophobia to the treatment of people with mental and physical disabilities. They discuss the history of hate and include personal accounts from those who've dealt with being stereotyped. The book is well laid out and easy to read. . . . Readers will appreciate the relevant photos of teens, the quotes, and the honest writing style." SLJ
Includes glossary

Rubin, Susan Goldman
★ **L'chaim!** to Jewish life in America! [by] Susan Goldman Rubin. Harry N. Abrams 2004 176p il map $24.95
Grades: 7 8 9 10 **305.8**
1. Jews -- United States 2. Jews -- United States -- History
ISBN 0-8109-5035-9
LC 2004-5848
This is an "exceptionally attractive package, packed with quotes, personal stories, and photos of art from The Jewish Museum. . . . The art is gorgeous, and Rubin . . . writes with clarity and enthusiasm." Booklist
Includes bibliographical references

Sanna, Ellyn
We shall all be free; survivors of racism. Mason Crest Publishers 2009 128p il (Survivors: ordinary people, extraordinary circumstances) lib bdg $24.95
Grades: 7 8 9 10 **305.8**
1. Racism 2. Minorities 3. Prejudices
ISBN 978-1-4222-0458-0; 1-4222-0458-8
LC 2008-50326
"Sanna covers racism of all kinds, including genocide in parts of Africa; the deplorable conditions of Native Americans; anti-Semitism; racism against the Roma, better known as Gypsies, and against African Americans; and the conditions faced by some immigrants. . . . [This title exposes] the underbelly of society, explaining terms that might be unfamiliar and providing multiple examples of the issues." SLJ
Includes bibliographical references

Schomp, Virginia
★ **Marching** toward freedom; by Virginia Schomp. Marshall Cavendish Benchmark 2008 80p il (Drama of African-American history) lib bdg $23.95
Grades: 5 6 7 8 **305.8**
1. African Americans -- History
ISBN 978-0-7614-2643-1
"Explores the period between 1929 and 1954 in African-American history, when the 'New Negro' emerged, proud of

his or her racial heritage and determined to topple the barriers to black advancement." Publisher's note

Includes glossary and bibliographical references

Schroeder, Michael J.

★ **Mexican** Americans; [by] Michael J. Schroeder. Chelsea House 2007 150p il map (The new immigrants) lib bdg $27.95

Grades: 6 7 8 9   **305.8**

    1. Mexican Americans 2. Immigrants -- United States

    ISBN 0-7910-8785-9

                          LC 2006008380

"Focused primarily on the achievements and hardships of Mexican American immigrants since the passage of the Immigration and Naturalization Services Act in 1965, this book . . . offers important historical understanding of how U.S. immigration issues and policies have evolved over the past few decades." Booklist

Includes bibliographical references

Szulhan, Rebecca

Contemporary achievements. Weigl Publishers 2009 48p il (African American history) lib bdg $29.05; pa $10.95

Grades: 6 7 8 9   **305.8**

    1. African Americans -- History 2. African Americans -- Biography

    ISBN 978-1-59036-884-8 lib bdg; 1-59036-884-3 lib bdg; 978-1-59036-885-5 pa; 1-59036-885-1 pa

                          LC 2008-42473

"Combines short biographies and quick facts about academics, athletics, politics and literature. . . . This . . . is fabulous for students interested in or researching history. Glossy pictures, quick facts, techonology links, and sidebars of information interrupt the text, giving readers interesting and important information without overwhelming them." Voice Youth Advocates

Includes glossary and bibliographical references

Thomas, William David

Korean Americans. Marshall Cavendish Benchmark 2009 80p il (New Americans) lib bdg $35.64

Grades: 5 6 7 8   **305.8**

    1. Korean Americans 2. Immigrants -- United States

    ISBN 978-0-7614-4306-3 lib bdg; 0-7614-4306-1 lib bdg

                          LC 2008054846

This describes the history of Korean Americans

"Consistent in content, and providing a mix of facts, and personal accounts, this . . . will be [a] . . . very useful addition to the collection." Libr Media Connect

Includes glossary and bibliographical references

Wachtel, Alan

Southeast Asian Americans. Marshall Cavendish Benchmark 2009 80p il map (New Americans) lib bdg $35.64

Grades: 5 6 7 8   **305.8**

    1. Asian Americans 2. Immigrants -- United States

    ISBN 978-0-7614-4312-4 lib bdg; 0-7614-4312-6 lib bdg

                          LC 2008055752

This title looks at Southeast Asian "communities in America today, detailing earlier generations of immigrants and current arrivals who are making new lives, changing the American culture, and looking to the future. [The] title includes many full-color photos, maps, and charts. . . . The books [does] a good job of helping readers to understand the differences between undocumented and documented immigrants and describe the citizenship process. The topics of racism, stereotypes, and other issues related to integration into American society are sensitively covered." SLJ

Includes glossary and bibliographical references

Weiss, Gail Garfinkel

Americans from Russia and Eastern Europe. Marshall Cavendish Benchmark 2009 80p il (New Americans) lib bdg $35.64

Grades: 5 6 7 8   **305.8**

    1. Russian Americans 2. East European Americans 3. Immigrants -- United States

    ISBN 978-0-7614-4310-0 lib bdg; 0-7614-4310-X lib bdg

                          LC 2008046350

This title looks at Russian and Eastern European "communities in America today, detailing earlier generations of immigrants and current arrivals who are making new lives, changing the American culture, and looking to the future. [The] title includes many full-color photos, maps, and charts. . . . The [book does] a good job of helping readers to understand the differences between undocumented and documented immigrants and describe the citizenship process. The topics of racism, stereotypes, and other issues related to integration into American society are sensitively covered." SLJ

Includes glossary and bibliographical references

Worth, Richard

1950s to 1960s. Marshall Cavendish Benchmark 2009 79p il (Hispanic America) lib bdg $34.21

Grades: 4 5 6 7   **305.8**

    1. Hispanic Americans -- History

    ISBN 978-0-7614-4177-9 lib bdg; 0-7614-4177-8 lib bdg

                          LC 2008-28195

"Provides comprehensive information on the history of the Spanish coming to the United States, focusing on the decades of the 1950s and 1960s." Publisher's note

Includes glossary and bibliographical references

Wright, Simeon

Simeon's story; an eyewitness account of the kidnapping of Emmett Till. [by] Simeon Wright; with Herb Boyd. Lawrence Hill Books 2010 144p il map $19.95

Grades: 6 7 8 9 10   **305.8**

    1. Racism 2. Children 3. Lynching 4. Trials (Homicide) 5. Murder victims 6. African Americans

-- Mississippi
ISBN 978-1-55652-783-8; 1-55652-783-7

LC 2009-33631

"Simeon Wright was 12 years old when his cousin Emmett 'Bobo' Till came from Chicago to visit relatives in Mississippi. . . . One hot August night in 1955, Till whistled at a white female store clerk, setting off a chain of events that left an indelible mark not only on our nation's history, but also on the cousin who witnessed Till's gaffe and eventual kidnapping. Wright's story is chilling, and his honest account will hook readers from the beginning." SLJ

305.896   Africans and people of African descent

Osborne, Linda Barrett

★ **Miles** to go for freedom; segregation and civil rights in the Jim Crow years. by Linda Barrett Osborne. Abrams Books for Young Readers 2011 118 p. $24.95
Grades: 6 7 8   **305.896**
1. United States -- History 2. United States -- Race relations 3. African Americans -- Segregation 4. African Americans -- Civil rights 5. African Americans -- Segregation -- History -- 20th century 6. African Americans -- Civil rights -- History -- 20th century 7. Civil rights movements -- United States -- History -- 20th century
ISBN 9781419700200

LC 2011022854

In this book, the "companion volume to 'Traveling the Freedom Road' (2009), Osborne . . . offers a[n] . . . overview of African American history, focusing here on both the South and the North during the late nineteenth-century through the mid-twentieth century. . . . Period images, including photos of public events, such as lynchings; magazine illustrations; and prints fill every double-page spread. After the first section on the South, the following section about the North focuses on the Great Migration, exploring not only the reasons why African Americans left but also the often chilly reception they received when they arrived. The final short section about the nation as a whole ends with the triumph of Brown v. Board of Education." (Booklist)
Includes bibliographical references and index

306   Culture and institutions

Bales, Kevin

Slavery today; [by] Kevin Bales and Becky Cornell. Groundwood Books 2008 141p il (Groundwork guides) $18.95; pa $10
Grades: 7 8 9 10   **306**
1. Slavery 2. Slave labor
ISBN 978-0-88899-772-2; 0-88899-772-8; 978-0-88899-773-9 pa; 0-88899-773-6 pa

"Easy to read and extremely engaging, the work traces the existence and occurrence of slavery in modern factories, jungles, and farms around the world, and discusses prostitution and strategies for ending slavery in the global market. . . . Students will find this book of great use for research papers, but it is also highly readable for personal enrichment. The language used is not complicated, the prose is understandable, and the personal narratives are passionate, even when describing awful, inhumane acts." Libr Media Connect
Includes bibliographical references

Bowling, beatniks, and bell-bottoms; pop culture of 20th-century America. Sara Pendergast and Tom Pendergast, editors. U.X.L 2002 5v il set $250
Grades: 8 9 10 11 12 Adult   **306**
1. Popular culture -- United States 2. Popular culture -- United States -- History -- 20th century -- Miscellanea
ISBN 0-7876-5675-5

LC 2002-1829

The editors "track trends in American popular culture through 750 entries arranged chronologically by decade over five volumes. Within decades, entries are divided into nine major areas: 'Commerce,' 'Fashion,' 'Film and Theater,' 'Food and Drink,' 'Music,' 'Print Culture,' 'Sports and Games,' Television and Radio,' and 'The Way We Lived'. . . . Informative, entertaining, and clearly presented." Libr J
Includes bibliographical references

Brownell, Richard

American counterculture of the 1960s. Lucent Books 2010 96p il (World history) lib bdg $33.45
Grades: 6 7 8 9   **306**
1. Counter culture 2. Demonstrations -- United States
ISBN 978-1-4205-0263-3; 1-4205-0263-8

LC 2010010503

This is an introduction to the counterculture of the 1960s, including personal stories and important personalities.

This "shines as it provides a contemporaneous writing as well as work by scholars that offer plenty of drama—and lots of facts too. . . . [It also] provides a solid time line, plenty of photographs, sourced quotes, and a list of books and websites for further investigation. Excellent for reports and research." Booklist
Includes bibliographical references

306.3   Economic institutions

Lester, Julius

★ **From** slave ship to freedom road; paintings by Rod Brown. Dial Bks. 1998 40p il hardcover o.p. pa $6.99
Grades: 5 6 7 8   **306.3**
1. Slavery -- United States 2. Afro-Americans -- Social conditions 3. Slavery -- United States -- History 4. Slavery -- United States -- Pictorial works
ISBN 0-8037-1893-4; 0-14-056669-4 pa

LC 96-44422

"Lester's impassioned questions grow from his visceral response to Brown's narrative paintings. . . . The combination of history, art, and commentary demands interaction." Booklist

Murphy, Jim

★ **Gone** a-whaling; the lure of the sea and the hunt for the great whale. Clarion Bks. 1998 208p il $18

Grades: 7 8 9 10   **306.3**
1. Whaling 2. Whaling -- History 3. Boy whalers
-- History
ISBN 0-395-69847-2

LC 97-13051

"Murphy makes history fascinating and immediate with
a lively, engrossing narrative that both informs and entertains." Voice Youth Advocates
Includes glossary and bibliographical references

306.4   Specific aspects of culture

Palad, Thea
★ **Mixed** messages; interpreting body image &
social norms. ABDO Pub. Co. 2009 112p il (Essential health: strong, beautiful girls) lib bdg $22.95
Grades: 6 7 8 9   **306.4**
1. Self-esteem 2. Self-acceptance 3. Girls --
Psychology
ISBN 978-1-60453-102-2 lib bdg; 1-60453-102-9
lib bdg

LC 2008-19351

This features fictional narratives paired with firsthand
advice from a licensed psychologist to help preteen and teen
readers better understand the countless media messages that
are presented to them daily. Topics include body image, stereotypes, and feeling comfortable in one's own skin.
"The topics are well selected, the design is attractive, and
the stories feature girls from a variety of cultures." Booklist
Includes glossary and bibliographical references

306.7   Sexual relations

Burningham, Sarah O'Leary
Boyology; a teen girl's crash course in all things
boy. illustrations by Keri Smith. Chronicle Books
2009 167p il pa $12.99
Grades: 6 7 8 9 10   **306.7**
1. Dating (Social customs) 2. Interpersonal relations 3.
Boys -- Psychology
ISBN 978-0-8118-6436-7; 0-8118-6436-7

LC 2008-5277

"Adolescent girls seeking a deeper understanding of
the opposite sex will appreciate this appealing, entertaining
guide full of useful facts and sound advice. Burningham . .
. explores a wide range of subjects, including how to determine which 'breed' of boy you're dealing with, first dates
and the rules of the dating game, setting boundaries, peer
conflicts and pressures, dealing with parents, the difference
between having a boyfriend and boy friends and coping with
the inevitable breakup." Kirkus

Feinstein, Stephen
Sexuality and teens; what you should know
about sex, abstinence, birth control, pregnancy, and
stds. Enslow Publishers 2010 104p il (Issues in
focus today) lib bdg $31.93
Grades: 7 8 9 10   **306.7**
1. Youth -- Sexual behavior   2. Teenagers -- Sexual

behavior
ISBN 978-0-7660-3312-2; 0-7660-3312-0

LC 2009-1373

"This text provides a well-balanced look at sexual attitudes and behaviors as they relate to today's youth. . . . The
book could be useful for basic report and debate information
or as a jumping-off point for class discussions." SLJ
Includes glossary and bibliographical references

Forssberg, Manne
★ **Sex** for guys; translated by Maria Lundin.
Groundwood Books/House of Anansi 2007 142p il
(Groundwork guides) $15.95; pa $9.95
Grades: 7 8 9 10 11 12   **306.7**
1. Sex education
ISBN 978-0-88899-770-8; 978-0-88899-771-5 pa

This "will prove invaluable to guys bombarded with less
sensitive and comprehensive media messages. . . . This is a
witty, sane treatment of the things that drive guys crazy—a
must read for teens with questions." Bull Cent Child Books
Includes bibliographical references

306.76   Sexual orientation, transgenderism,
intersexuality

★ The **Full** spectrum; a new generation of writing
about gay, lesbian, bisexual, transgender, questioning, and other identities. edited by David
Levithan & Billy Merrell. Knopf 2006 272p il
hardcover o.p. pa $9.95
Grades: 8 9 10 11 12   **306.76**
1. Gay men 2. Lesbians 3. Gender role 4.
Homosexuality 5. Sex role 6. Gay youth 7. Gender
identity 8. Sexual orientation
ISBN 0-375-93290-9; 0-375-83290-4 pa

LC 2005-23435

"The 40 contributions to this invaluable collection about
personal identity have two things in common: all are nonfiction and all are by writers under the age of 23. Beyond that,
diversity is the order of the day, and the result is a vivid
demonstration of how extraordinarily broad the spectrum
of sexual identity is among today's gay, lesbian, bisexual,
transgender, and questioning youth. . . . Insightful, extraordinarily well written, and emotionally mature, the selections
offer compelling, dramatic evidence that what is important
is not what we are but who we are." Booklist

Huegel, Kelly
★ **GLBTQ**; the survival guide for gay, lesbian,
bisexual, transgender, and questioning teens. rev
& updated 2nd ed.; Free Spirit Pub. 2011 229p il
$15.99
Grades: 7 8 9 10 11 12   **306.76**
1. Lesbianism 2. Bisexuality 3. Homosexuality 4.
Transsexualism
ISBN 1-57542-363-0; 978-1-57542-363-0

LC 2010-48196

First published 2003

Describes the challenges faced by gay, lesbian, bisexual, and transgendered teens, offers practical advice, real-life experiences, and accessible resources and support groups.

"The information . . . [this] provides for GLBTQ teens makes it a valuable addition to any high school or public library collection." Voice Youth Advcocates

Includes bibliographical references

Marcus, Eric

What if someone I know is gay? answers to questions about what it means to be gay and lesbian. by Eric Marcus. Rev. and updated 1st Simon Pulse ed Simon & Schuster 2008 183 p. (prebind) $17.99; (paperback) $9.99

Grades: 7 8 9 10 11 12   **306.76**

1. Homosexuality

ISBN 9781435285101; 9781416949701

First published in 2000 by Price/Stern/Sloan

"The content . . . stands strong, and readers will appreciate Marcus's gentle tone and the careful candor that he uses to describe the sometimes-rocky LGB experience. Helpful information about gay-straight alliances and marriage and partnership issues are all addressed." SLJ

Includes bibliographical references.

Sanna, Emily

Gay believers; homosexuality and religion. Mason Crest Publishers 2010 64p il (Gallup's guide to modern gay, lesbian, and transgender lifestyle) $22.95; pa $9.95

Grades: 8 9 10 11 12   **306.76**

1. Religions 2. Homosexuality

ISBN 978-1-4222-1749-8; 978-1-4222-1868-6 pa

LC 2010012747

This discusses homosexuality in Christianity, Judaism, Islam, Hinduism, and Buddhism.

"The advice is solid. . . . The [book is] easy to read, up-to-date, and [includes] personal stories that many readers will relate to." SLJ

Includes bibliographical references

Seba, Jaime

Coming out; telling family and friends. Mason Crest Publishers 2010 64p il (Gallup's guide to modern gay, lesbian, and transgender lifestyle) $22.95; pa $9.95

Grades: 8 9 10 11 12   **306.76**

1. Homosexuality

ISBN 978-1-4222-1745-0; 978-1-4222-1865-5 pa

LC 2010017052

This discusses revealing one's homosexuality to friends and family.

"The advice is solid. . . . The [book is] easy to read, up-to-date, and [includes] personal stories that many readers will relate to." SLJ

Includes bibliographical references

Gallup guides for youth facing persistent prejudice; by Jaime Seba. Mason Crest Publishers 2013 64 p. col. ill., photographs (library) $22.95

Grades: 5 6 7 8   **306.76**

1. LGBT people -- Civil rights 2. Homophobia 3. Gay youth -- United States 4. Homophobia -- United States 5. Sexual minorities -- Civil rights -- United States

ISBN 1422224678; 9781422224670

LC 2012017108

This book by Jaime Seba on the LGBT community "discusses the history of prejudice toward this group, the laws that protect people against discrimination-and what you can do to fight the prejudice you find in the world." (Publisher's note)

As part of the "Gallup Guides for Youth Facing Persistent Prejudice" series, it "emphasiz[es] recent violence and other problems, such as bullying and depression, which are, unfortunately, still routine for many LGBT youth." (Booklist)

Includes bibliographical references (p. 62) and index.

Homosexuality around the world; safe havens, cultural challenges. by Jaime A. Seba. Mason Crest Publishers 2011 64 p. ill. (chiefly col.) (hardcover) $22.95; (paperback) $9.95

Grades: 6 7 8 9 10   **306.76**

1. Gay rights 2. Homosexuality 3. Depression, Mental 4. Gays 5. Gay rights 6. Gays -- Legal status, laws, etc.

ISBN 1422217531; 1422218724; 9781422217535; 9781422218723

LC 2010017917

This book looks at global views on homosexuality. Readers can "explore different countries and learn about their cultural attitudes toward lesbian, gay, bisexual, and transgender people, as gay men and women from around the globe share their personal stories and experiences. Find out how American policies compare with our North American neighbors, Canada and Mexico, [and] discover how gay equal rights are beginning to emerge in places such as India and South Africa." (Publisher's note)

Includes bibliographical references (p. 60-61) and index.

306.8   Marriage and family

Fields, Julianna

Gay and lesbian parents. Mason Crest 2009 64p il map (The changing face of modern families) $22.95

Grades: 6 7 8 9   **306.8**

1. Gay parents

ISBN 978-1-4222-1495-4; 1-4222-1495-8

This describes the challenges facing gay and lesbian parents.

This is "informative [and] nonjudgmental. . . . Including color photos, plentiful sidebars, and interesting headline stories, the accessible [text presents] real-life experiences and numerous supporting facts, definitions, graphs, charts, and statistics." SLJ

Includes glossary and bibliographical references

Multiracial families. Mason Crest Publishers 2010 64p il (The changing face of modern families) lib bdg $22.95

Grades: 6 7 8 9   **306.8**
1. Family 2. Interracial marriage 3. Racially mixed people
ISBN 978-1-4222-1494-7 lib bdg; 1-4222-1494-X lib bdg

This describes the challenges that multi-racial families face.

This is "informative [and] nonjudgmental. . . . Including color photos, plentiful sidebars, and interesting headline stories, the accessible [text presents] real-life experiences and numerous supporting facts, definitions, graphs, charts, and statistics." SLJ

Includes glossary and bibliographical references

Fox, Annie
What's up with my family? illustrated by Matt Kindt. Free Spirit 2010 90p il (Middle school confidential) pa $9.99
Grades: 6 7 8 9   **306.8**
1. Family
ISBN 978-1-57542-333-3 pa; 1-57542-333-2 pa

"Using a magazine-style format that is part graphic novel and part nonfiction advice, Fox helps teens work out family problems like sibling rivalry, blended families, overprotective parents, and dealing with loss. . . . The book is full of tips on strengthening family relationships while working through the challenges every family faces. . . . This short, readable book will attract even reluctant readers with the format and give practical advice for all teens on improving family life." Voice Youth Advocates

Lynette, Rachel
★ **What** makes us a family? living in a nontraditional family. content consultant, Robyn J. A. Silverman. ABDO Pub. Co. 2009 112p il (Essential health: strong beautiful girls) lib bdg $32.79
Grades: 6 7 8 9   **306.8**
1. Family
ISBN 978-1-60453-756-7 lib bdg; 1-60453-756-6 lib bdg
                         LC 2009004416

"The topics are well selected, the design is attractive, and the stories feature girls from a variety of cultures." Booklist

The **sibling** slam book; what it's really like to have a brother or sister with special needs. Woodbine House 2005 152p il pa $15.95
Grades: 6 7 8 9   **306.8**
1. Siblings 2. Handicapped children
ISBN 1-890627-52-6

"This multifaceted vehicle for eliciting some unique and many universal emotions is designed specifically for siblings of special-needs children. An adolescent mainstay, the slam book is the chosen venue for encouraging the venting of opinions, hopes, fears, frustrations, and triumphs. Comments by 81 young people display the recurring theme of optimism, complicated by hard work, dedication, resentment, and fierce protection, all as by-products of love." SLJ

Simons, Rae
Blended families. Mason Crest 2009 64p il (The changing face of modern families) lib bdg $22.95
Grades: 6 7 8 9   **306.8**
1. Stepfamilies
ISBN 978-1-4222-1492-3 lib bdg; 1-4222-1492-3 lib bdg

"Colorful photographs and sidebars appear throughout. [This book is a] good [introduction] to the study of sociology and interpretation of data." SLJ

Includes glossary and bibliographical references

Grandparents raising kids. Mason Crest Publishers 2010 64p il (The changing face of modern families) lib bdg $22.95
Grades: 6 7 8 9   **306.8**
1. Grandparents 2. Child rearing
ISBN 978-1-4222-1496-1 lib bdg; 1-4222-1496-6 lib bdg

This describes the challenges facing families in which children are raised by their grandparents.

"There are questions directed at the reader to encourage deeper consideration of their opinions and synthesis of the knowledge they have gained from the book. . . . This . . . would be very helpful for students writing reports or simply seeking information." SLJ

Teen parents. Mason Crest 2009 64p il (The changing face of modern families) lib bdg $22.95
Grades: 6 7 8 9   **306.8**
1. Teenage mothers 2. Teenage fathers
ISBN 978-1-4222-1491-6 lib bdg; 1-4222-1491-5 lib bdg

This describes the challenges facing teen parents.

This is "informative [and] nonjudgmental. . . . Including color photos, plentiful sidebars, and interesting headline stories, the accessible [text presents] real-life experiences and numerous supporting facts, definitions, graphs, charts, and statistics." SLJ

Includes glossary and bibliographical references

Stewart, Sheila
What is a family? Mason Crest 2009 64p il (The changing face of modern families) lib bdg $22.95
Grades: 6 7 8 9   **306.8**
1. Family
ISBN 978-1-4222-1528-9 lib bdg; 1-4222-1528-8 lib bdg

This discusses traditional and non-traditional families, including single-parent families, blended families, gay or lesbian-parent families, and grandparents raising grandchildren and addresses questions such as: 'Are non-traditional families new?' 'What makes some families strong, while others struggle?' and 'Are some families so non-traditional that they can't really even be considered families?'

"Colorful photographs and sidebars appear throughout. [This book is a] good [introduction] to the study of sociology and interpretation of data." SLJ

Includes glossary and bibliographical references

Winchester, Elizabeth

Sisters and brothers; the ultimate guide to understanding your siblings and yourself. [by] Elizabeth Siris Winchester. Franklin Watts 2008 112p il (Scholastic choices) lib bdg $27; pa $8.95

Grades: 6 7 8 9 10   306.8

1. Family 2. Siblings

ISBN 978-0-531-13870-0 lib bdg; 0-531-13870-4 lib bdg; 978-0-531-20528-0 pa; 0-531-20528-2 pa

LC 2007-51871

Real-life stories from teenagers about interacting with siblings, whether blood, adopted, foster, or step.

"Colorful and compact, with [an] attractive cover [and] . . . excellent black-and-white photographs of a diverse array of teens." SLJ

Includes glossary and bibliographical references

Worth, Richard

Frequently asked questions about teen fatherhood. Rosen Pub. 2010 64p il (FAQ: teen life) lib bdg $29.25

Grades: 7 8 9 10   306.8

1. Teenage fathers

ISBN 978-1-4358-5325-6; 1-4358-5325-3

LC 2008-51938

"While conversational, [this volume is] surprisingly helpful—even emotive. . . . [This book greets] its intended audience with encouragement and aplomb. Dealing with feelings of disbelief and blame quickly segue into preparing for a birth, staying in school, and considering part-time jobs. Adoption and abortion are given only brief mentions." Booklist

Includes glossary and bibliographical references

306.84   Types of marriage and relationships

Spilsbury, Louise

Same-sex marriage; Louise Spilsbury. Rosen Central 2012 48 p. col. ill. lib bdg $29.25 pa $11.75

Grades: 7 8 9 10   306.84

1. Same-sex marriage

ISBN 1448870135; 9781448860203; 9781448870134; 9781448870141

LC 2011032847

This book by Louise Spilsbury "[d]iscusses the legal debate of same-sex marriage, including the history of the gay rights movement, the arguments both in support and opposition of same-sex marriage, and how same-sex marriage is treated around the world." (WorldCat)

Includes bibliographical references and index

Sterngass, Jon

Same sex marriage; Jon Sterngass. Marshall Cavendish Benchmark 2012 143 p. ill. (chiefly col.) (Controversy!) (library) $37.07; (ebook) $37.07

Grades: 8 9 10 11 12   306.84

1. Current events 2. Same-sex marriage 3. Same-sex

marriage -- United States

ISBN 1608704904; 9781608704903; 9781608706426 pdf

LC 2010046435

This book is part of the Controversy! series and looks at same-sex marriage. The series "tackles issues that are prevalent in today's society. Each book provides a history of the subject, in detail, before delving into specific controversial areas. . . . At the end of each book, a timeline is given, as well as notes from each chapter, further information sources, websites (accurate at the time of printing), a bibliography, and an index." (Voice of Youth Advocates)

Includes bibliographical references (p. 122-136) and index

306.874   Parent-child relationship

Buscemi, Karen

Split in two; keeping it together when your parents live apart. Karen Buscemi. Zest 2009 120 p. ill. (paperback) $12.95

Grades: 7 8 9 10 11 12   306.874

1. Children of divorced parents

ISBN 0980073219; 9780980073218

LC 2008936059

"Provides advice to children of divorced parents on living in two homes simultaneously, including how to organize during moves, managing different lifestyles, and coping with the emotional stress of separation." Publisher's note

"Written in a casual, genuine tone, the substantive chapters begin with valuable questions that help kids assess whether their basic needs for privacy and comfort are met in each household. . . . Like the text, Mucha's quirky cartoon illustrations find humor in the complicated situations and feelings, adding further appeal to this hip, reassuring guide filled with straightforward, honest advice." Booklist

Littlefield, Bruce

My two moms; lessons of love, strength, and what makes a family. by Zach Wahls; with Bruce Littlefield. Gotham Books 2012 xix, 233 p.p ill. (hardcover) $26; (paperback) $16

Grades: 7 8 9 10 11 12   306.874

1. Same-sex marriage 2. Children of gay parents 3. Gay rights -- United States 4. Lesbian mothers -- United States 5. Same-sex marriage -- United States 6. Children of gay parents -- United States

ISBN 1592407137; 1592407633; 9781592407132; 9781592407637

LC 2011053087

In this book, "[Zach] Wahls writes about growing up as the son of gay parents in the heartland. In January 2011, the author, then a student at the University of Iowa, testified before the Iowa House Judiciary Committee as they considered a state constitutional amendment to ban same-sex marriage. . . . The speech was aimed at dismantling the myth that kids are damaged by having gay parents . . . Here the author expands on his speech, discussing the values that his parents helped to instill in him." (Kirkus)

306.89   Separation and divorce

Bingham, Jane

  Why do families break up? Raintree 2005 48p il (Exploring tough issues) lib bdg $31.43

Grades: 4 5 6 7   **306.89**

  1. Divorce

  ISBN 0-7398-6683-4

                      LC 2003-20285

  "This book looks at the reasons people divorce and discusses the stages a family goes through when a marriage breaks up. It also considers how different family members struggle with the painful effects, and the benefits of counseling. Case studies, quotes, and color photos personalize the issues, and fact boxes provide a few statistics. . . . Libraries needing self-help information for young people dealing with divorce will find Bingham's volume a useful addition." SLJ

  Includes bibliographical references

Trueit, Trudi Strain

  Surviving divorce; teens talk about what helps and what hurts. [by] Trudi Strain Trueit. 1st ed.; Scholastic 2007 112p il (Choices) lib bdg $22.50; pa $8.95

Grades: 6 7 8 9   **306.89**

  1. Divorce

  ISBN 0-531-12368-5 lib bdg; 978-0-531-12368-3 lib bdg; 0-531-16726-7 pa; 978-0-531-16726-7 pa

                    LC 2004018423

  This "is an inviting guide to the facts and feelings of parental divorce. Personal stories and photos of kids begin each chapter, and frequent statistics and quizzes will help readers assess their feelings and put them into context. The solid advice is well presented, as are the messages that readers are not alone and that there are many ways to seek help." Booklist

  Includes glossary and bibliographical references

306.9   Institutions pertaining to death

Noyes, Deborah

  ★ **Encyclopedia** of the end; mysterious death in fact, fancy, folklore, and more. Houghton Mifflin Co. 2008 143p il $25

Grades: 7 8 9 10 11 12   **306.9**

  1. Death 2. Reference books 3. Funeral rites and ceremonies

  ISBN 978-0-618-82362-8; 0-618-82362-X

                    LC 2008-1872

  "This stylish A-to-Z encounter with all things related to death and dying shows Noyes . . . at her liveliest. . . . The author offers a broad illumination of spiritual, historical and biological aspects of death. Photos, paintings and engravings in homage to 'the end' make the book dynamic visually, too." Publ Wkly

Thornhill, Jan

  I found a dead bird; the kids' guide to the cycle of life & death. Maple Tree Press 2006 64p il $21.95; pa $9.95

Grades: 4 5 6   **306.9**

  1. Death 2. Bereavement 3. Life cycles (Biology)

  ISBN 1-897066-70-8; 1-897066-71-6 pa

  Explores the cycle of life and death, and how the process is necessary in nature, while also commenting on how death effects people personally, and the skills they use to cope with such a trauma when it occurs.

  "This straightforward, no holds barred approach to the subject will captivate children. Chock-full of color photographs, the well-designed book contains boxes with tidbits of information on a wide variety of topics, such as death of a species, human destruction, plant decomposition, trapped in time, and learning from death." SLJ

307   Communities

Anderson, Judith

  ★ **Looking** at settlements; by Judith Anderson. Smart Apple Media 2007 il map (Geography skills) $22.95

Grades: 6 7 8 9   **307**

  1. Human settlements

  ISBN 978-1-59920-052-1; 1-59920-052-X

                  LC 2006036142

  "The text is easy to follow. . . . The examples given in the text that involve places are almost always accompanied by excellent photographs. . . . Maps, block diagraoms, tables, and graphs are clearly presented and easy to interpret." Sci Books Films

  Includes glossary and bibligraphical references

Dyer, Hadley

  Watch this space; designing, defending and sharing public space. written by Hadley Dyer; illustrated by Marc Ngui. Kids Can Press 2010 80p il $18.95

Grades: 5 6 7 8   **307**

  1. Public spaces

  ISBN 978-1-55453-293-3

  This book aims to "introduce youth to what public space is, why it is important and how best to use it. It also underscores the need to create, preserve and protect public space. Readers will learn what makes successful public spaces work, the ins and outs of sharing and designing them, [and] the issues surrounding teenagers in public spaces." (Publisher's note)

307.2   Movement of people to, from, within communities

Harris, Laurie Lanzen

  The **great** migration north, 1910-1970; by Laurie Lanzen Harris. Omnigraphics, Inc. 2012 xvi, 241 p.p

Grades: 7 8 9 10 11 12   **307.2**

  1. Internal migration 2. African Americans -- History 3. United States -- History -- 20th century 4. African Americans -- Migrations -- History -- 20th century 5. Rural-urban migration -- United States -- History -- 20th

century
ISBN 0780811860; 9780780811867

LC 2011033540

This historical survey by Laurie Lanzen Harris "explains the social and economic factors that drove the African-American exodus out of the rural South to the industrial cities of the North during the first half of the twentieth century. The book also details the transformative impact of this migration on U.S. industry, culture, and race relations, as well as the daily experiences of the men, women, and children who built new lives for themselves in New York, Chicago, Philadelphia, Detroit, and other cities of the North. Finally, it explains how this multi-generational flight from oppression to opportunity changed the internal dynamics of African-American families and communities across America." (Publisher's note)

Includes bibliographical references and index.

307.7 Specific kinds of communities

Laidlaw, Jill A.

Cities; by Jill Laidlaw. Amicus 2011 44p il map (Sustaining our environment) lib bdg $31.35
Grades: 6 7 8 9   307.7
1. Urban ecology 2. Sustainable architecture 3. Renewable energy resources 4. Cities and towns
ISBN 978-1-60753-135-7 lib bdg; 1-60753-135-6 lib bdg

LC 2009040708

"The tone is refreshingly optimistic with its examples of specific steps being taken to reduce harm to the environment. Sidebars highlight case studies and campaigns from around the world and from the individual to the national levels. Clear, informative captions accompany the excellent selection of color photographs, charts and graphs." SLJ

Includes glossary

Lorinc, John

Cities. Groundwood Books/House of Anansi Press 2008 144p (Groundwork guides) $18.95; pa $10
Grades: 7 8 9 10 11 12   307.7
1. Urbanization 2. Cities and towns
ISBN 978-0-88899-820-0; 0-88899-820-1; 978-0-88899-819-4 pa; 0-88899-819-8 pa

"This packed, highly readable [title] . . . does an excellent job of tracing urban history worldwide, raising the big social, political, and economic issues of poverty, migration, conservation, public health, crime, transportation, and much more, always rooted in specific examples of the problems and riches of city life." Booklist

Includes bibliographical references

307.76 Urban communities

Collier, Christopher

The **rise** of the cities, 1820-1920; [by] Christopher Collier, James Lincoln Collier. Benchmark Bks.

(Tarrytown) 2001 95p il maps (Drama of American history) lib bdg $31.36
Grades: 6 7 8 9   307.76
1. Cities and towns -- United States 2. Urbanization -- United States -- History 3. Cities and towns -- United States -- History 4. City and town life -- United States -- History
ISBN 0-7614-1051-1

LC 99-38409

This "traces the development, problems, and increasing prominence of cities in America between 1820 and 1920. Illustrations, many in color, include period photographs and engravings as well as maps and charts. . . . Highly readable and informative." Booklist

Includes bibliographical references

Spilsbury, Richard

Towns and cities; by Richard Spilsbury. Heinemann Library 2012 64 p. (The impact of environmentalism) (library) $35.00; (paperback) $9.99
Grades: 6 7 8   307.76
1. Environmental protection 2. City planning 3. Cities and towns 4. Urban ecology (Sociology)
ISBN 1432965190; 9781432965198; 9781432965259

LC 2012001039

This book by Richard Spilsbury is part of the Impact of Environmentalism series and looks at cities and towns. The series provides "a global overview of environmentalism from different, often overlapping, perspectives." This entry "supplies insights into sustainable urbanization, including information about solar-energy efforts in cities worldwide." (School Library Journal)

Includes bibliographical references and index.

317.3 Statistics collections -- United States

Proquest Statistical Abstract of the United States 2013; ProQuest LLC. 1st ed. Rowman & Littlefield Pub Inc 2012 xvi, 1025 p.p (hardcover) $179
Grades: 8 9 10 11 12 Adult   317.3
1. Almanacs 2. United States -- Census
ISBN 159888591X; 9781598885910

This almanac, published by ProQuest, offers statistical summaries of Census data and socio-demographic information of the United States as of 2013. This annually compiled work "is the best-known statistical reference publication in the country. . . . As a carefully selected collection of statistics on the social, political, and economic conditions of the United States, it is a snapshot of America and its people." (Publisher's note)

320 Political science (Politics and government)

Anderson, Jodi Lynn

★ **Americapedia**; taking the dumb out of freedom. [by] Jodi Anderson, Daniel Ehrenhaft, Andisheh Nouraee. Walker Books for Young Readers 2011 240p il $24.99; pa $16.99

Grades: 7 8 9 10   **320**
1. Citizenship 2. World politics
ISBN 978-0-8027-9792-6; 0-8027-9792-X; 978-0-
8027-9793-3 pa; 0-8027-9792-X pa
LC 2010-38028
"This examination of the state of the union uses edgy
humor to discuss pertinent matters in the worlds of politics,
international relations, religion, and culture. Bullet points,
footnotes, sidebars, and tongue-in-cheek graphics . . . lighten
heady topics like nuclear proliferation and the Israel-Pales-
tine conflict. Despite the irreverent tone . . . discussions of
such topics as the stem cell debate, global warming, and ger-
rymandering remind readers of the seriousness behind the
issues." Publ Wkly
Includes bibliographical references

Bukovac, Matthew
   Failed states; unstable countries in the 21st century. Rosen Pub. 2011 64p il map (In the news) lib
bdg $29.95; pa $12.95
Grades: 7 8 9 10   **320**
1. Financial crises
ISBN 978-1-4358-9447-1 lib bdg; 1-4358-9447-2 lib
bdg; 978-1-4488-1679-8 pa; 1-4488-1679-3 pa
LC 2009045686
This book "tackles in simple terms what exactly constitute a failed state and how a country lands in such a predicament. Further chapters cover countries presently in the
media, including Iraq, Somalia, and Pakistan, among others. . . . With numerous photos, concise and manageable
chapters, and a glossary, . . . [this book provides] an excellent background for students with an interest in social sciences or a jumping off point for school assignments." Voice
Youth Advocates
Includes glossary and bibliographical references

320.01   Philosophy and theory

The **politics** book; Big ideas simply explained. edited by Rebecca Warren and Kate Johnsen; illus-
trated by James Graham. 1st American ed. DK
Pub. 2013 352 p. ill. (some col.) (Big ideas
simply explained) (hardcover) $25.00
Grades: 8 9 10 11 12 Adult   **320.01**
1. Political philosophy
ISBN 1465402144; 9781465402141
LC 2012533724
This book, part of the Big Ideas Simply Explained series, looks at political philosophy. "More than 100 political
philosophers, among them Confucius, Plato, Machiavelli,
Mary Wollstonecraft, Karl Marx, Ito Hirobumi, Emiliano
Zapata, Jomo Kenyatta, and Mao Zedong, are covered in
seven chronological sections ranging from 'Ancient Politi-
cal Thought' to 'Postwar Politics.'" (Library Journal)

320.4   Structure and functions of government

Encyclopedia of American government; consulting
editor, Joseph M. Bessette; project editor, R. Kent

Rasmussen. Salem Press 1998 4v il maps set
$221
Grades: 8 9 10 11 12 Adult   **320.4**
1. Reference books 2. United States -- Politics and
government
ISBN 0-89356-117-7
LC 98-28986
"Two hundred alphabetically arranged essays make up
this . . . set that covers the basics of American government.
Well-written, illuminating articles range from broad subjects
such as Federalism to more specific topics such as 'Iron
Triangles' and reflect an awareness for gender and minority
issues." SLJ
Includes bibliographical references

Han, Lori Cox
   Handbook to American democracy; Lori Cox
Han and Tomislav Han. Facts On File 2011 224 p.
hc $220.00
Grades: 8 9 10 11 12 Adult   **320.4**
1. United States -- History 2. Democracy -- United
States -- History 3. United States -- Politics and
government
ISBN 0816078548; 9780816078547
LC 2011005185
The authors "address the foundations of American de-
mocracy and the three branches of American government.
The books introduce offices, history, and issues in eight
chapters each (e.g., 'The Founding Fathers and the American
Revolution,' 'How Congress Is Organized,' and 'Vice Presi-
dents, Presidential Advisers, and America's First Ladies').
The material is complemented by black-and-white photos
and sidebars on legal cases, laws and legislation, statistics,
maps, biographies of major figures such as Henry VIII, and
other primary materials, and chapters close with a summary.
. . . [The volumes] each include an individual glossary, index, selected bibliography, and table of contents." (Libr J)
Includes bibliographical references and index

320.5   Political ideologies

Fleming, Thomas
   Socialism. Marshall Cavendish Benchmark 2007
143p il (Political systems of the world) lib bdg
$39.93
Grades: 7 8 9 10 11 12   **320.5**
1. Socialism
ISBN 978-0-7614-2632-5; 0-7614-2632-9
LC 2006-33048
"There is solid information here." SLJ
Includes bibliographical references

320.52   Conservatism

Novak, Amy
   Glenn Beck; by Amy Novak. Lucent Books
2011 112 p. col. ill. (People in the news) (hbk.)
$33.95

Grades: 6 7 8 9   **320.52**
1. Radio broadcasting 2. Conservatism -- United States
3. Conservatives -- United States -- Biography 4. Radio
personalities -- United States -- Biography 5. Television
personalities -- United States -- Biography
ISBN 1420506056; 9781420506051

LC 2011005084

This book offers a biography of Conservative radio and
television personality Glenn Beck by author Amy Novak. It
is part of the "People in the News" series, which "profiles the
lives and careers of some of today's most prominent newsmakers. Whether covering contributions and achievements
or notorious deeds, books in this series examine why these
well-known individuals garnered public attention." (Publisher's note)

Includes bibliographical references (p. 103-105)
and index

321   Systems of governments and states

Davidson, Tish
★ **Theocracy**; Tish Davidson. Mason Crest
2013 64 p. col. ill. (Major forms of world govern-
ment) (library) $22.95; (ebook) $28.95
Grades: 6 7 8 9 10   **321**
1. Theocracy 2. Political science
ISBN 1422221431; 9781422221433; 9781422294604
LC 2012027863

This book, by Tish Davidson, as part of the publisher's
"Major Forms of World Government" series, "examines
theocratic governments, from ancient Egypt to present-day
Iran. It explores how different theocracies arose, how their
leaders maintained authority, and what it was like for ordinary people living under religious rule." (Publisher's note)

Includes bibliographical references and index.

Perl, Lila
Theocracy. Marshall Cavendish Benchmark
2007 158p il (Political systems of the world) lib
bdg $27.95
Grades: 7 8 9 10 11 12   **321**
1. Theocracy
ISBN 978-0-7614-2631-8
LC 2006-26055

"Gives an overview of theocracy as a political system,
including and historical discussion of theocratic regimes
throughout the world." Publisher's note

Includes bibliographical references

Stefoff, Rebecca
Monarchy. Marshall Cavendish Benchmark
2007 143p il (Political systems of the world) lib
bdg $27.95
Grades: 7 8 9 10 11 12   **321**
1. Monarchy
ISBN 978-0-7614-2630-1
LC 2006-26384

"Discusses monarchies as a political system, and details
the history of monarchies throughout the world." Publisher's note

Includes bibliographical references

321.8   Democratic government

Lansford, Tom
Democracy. Marshall Cavendish Benchmark
2007 143p il (Political systems of the world) lib
bdg $27.95
Grades: 7 8 9 10 11 12   **321.8**
1. Democracy
ISBN 978-0-7614-2629-5
LC 2006-25351

"Gives an overview of democracy as a political system,
including an historical discussion of democracies throughout the world." Publisher's note

Includes bibliographical references

Laxer, James
Democracy. Groundwood Books 2009 143p
(Groundwork guides) $18.95; pa $10
Grades: 8 9 10 11 12   **321.8**
1. Democracy 2. Globalization 3. Economic policy
ISBN 978-0-88899-912-2; 0-88899-912-7; 978-0-
88899-913-9 pa; 0-88899-913-5 pa

This title "stands out for its accessible introduction to
historical and contemporary democracy across the globe.
Laxer skillfully supports his arguments with examples and
avoids pat definitions." Booklist

Includes bibliographical references

321.9   Authoritarian government

Fridell, Ron
Dictatorship. Marshall Cavendish Benchmark
2007 144p il (Political systems of the world) lib
bdg $27.95
Grades: 7 8 9 10 11 12   **321.9**
1. Dictators
ISBN 978-0-7614-2627-1
LC 2006-23121

"Discusses dictatorships as a political system, and details the history of dictatorships throughout the world." Publisher's note

Includes bibliographical references

322.4   Political action groups

Bartoletti, Susan Campbell
★ **They** called themselves the K.K.K. the birth
of an American terrorist group. Houghton Mifflin
2010 172p il map $19
Grades: 7 8 9 10   **322.4**
1. Racism 2. White supremacy movements 3.
Reconstruction (1865-1876) 5. Racism -- United States

6. Hate groups -- United States
ISBN 0-618-44033-X; 978-0-618-44033-7

LC 2009-45247

"In this comprehensive, accessible account, . . . [the author] draws from documentary histories, slave narratives, newspapers, congressional testimony, and other sources to chronicle the origins and proliferation of the Ku Klux Klan against the charged backdrop of Reconstruction politics and legislation. . . . The author lives up to her introductory promise to avoid censoring racist language and images, and includes some horrifying descriptions of lynchings and murders perpetuated during KKK raids. . . . Her account of attending a Klan meeting while researching the book is chilling to the core." Publ Wkly

Includes bibliographical references

323   Civil and political rights

Bausum, Ann

★ **Marching** to the mountaintop; how poverty, labor fights, and civil rights set the stage for Martin Luther King, Jr.'s final hours. by Ann Bausum. National Geographic 2012 104 p. hc $19.95 lib bdg $28.90

Grades: 7 8 9 10   **323**

1. Memphis (Tenn.) -- History 2. African Americans -- Civil rights 3. Strikes -- United States -- History 4. African Americans -- Economic conditions 5. Sanitation Workers Strike, Memphis, Tenn., 1968 6. Labor movement -- Tennessee -- Memphis -- History -- 20th century 7. African Americans -- Tennessee -- Memphis -- Social conditions -- 20th century
ISBN 1426309392; 1426309406; 9781426309397; 9781426309403

LC 2011024661

"In this . . . [book about] the 1968 Memphis Sanitation Workers Strike, [author Ann] Bausum . . . handles both the labor action itself—born of institutionalized racial injustice within the public works system and the tragic deaths of two African-American workers in a faulty compactor—and what would be the final civil rights action of Dr. King's storied career. . . . She . . . [covers] the African-American workers who accepted . . . dangerous sanitation jobs, and . . . the ploys to cut back their already minimal pay. . . . [T]he focus shifts to follow King's involvement, as he hoped the national focus on labor injustice would draw attention to his broader plans for an attack on poverty itself as the next great civil rights issue." (Bulletin of the Center for Children's Books)

Includes bibliographical references (p. 100-102) and index

Civil liberties; Lauri S. Friedman, book editor. Greenhaven Press 2010 144p il map (Introducing issues with opposing viewpoints) lib bdg $34.70

Grades: 7 8 9 10 11 12   **323**

1. Terrorism 2. Civil rights 3. National security
ISBN 978-0-7377-4732-4; 0-7377-4732-3

LC 2009-51887

This book "of pro/con essays . . . [is] intended to stimulate discussion of critical social issues and to open readers' minds to divergent opinions. Civil Liberties includes discussions of the Patriot Act, the rights of Muslims and Arab Americans, and racial profiling. . . . Active-reading questions preface the essays, which are followed by directions for evaluating the arguments presented. Color photos and other graphics throughout enliven the reading experience." SLJ

Includes bibliographical references

Fradin, Judith Bloom

The **power** of one; Daisy Bates and the Little Rock Nine. by Judith Bloom Fradin & Dennis Brindell Fradin. Clarion Books 2004 178p il $19

Grades: 7 8 9 10   **323**

1. School integration 2. Civil rights activists
ISBN 0-618-31556-X

LC 2004-4618

This is a biography of Daisy Bates. Born in a small town in rural Arkansas, Bates was a journalist and activist. In 1957 she mentored the nine black students who were integrated into Central High School in Little Rock, Arkansas

"This compelling biography clearly demonstrates that one person can indeed make a difference." SLJ

Includes bibliographical references

Icenoggle, Jodi

Schenck v. United States and the freedom of speech debate. Enslow Pubs. 2005 128p il (Debating Supreme Court decisions) lib bdg $26.60

Grades: 7 8 9 10   **323**

1. Freedom of speech
ISBN 0-7660-2392-3

In the "case of Schenck v. United States, the Supreme Court held that people who opposed World War I were not allowed to use their free speech rights to interfere with the draft. . . . [In this book the author] explains the different arguments that have been used for and against free speech." Publisher's note

Includes glossary and bibliographical references

National Geographic Society (U.S.)

★ **Every** human has rights; a photographic declaration for kids. based on the United Nations Universal Declaration of Human Rights; with poetry from the ePals community; foreword by Mary Robinson. National Geographic 2009 30p il $26.90

Grades: 4 5 6 7 8   **323**

1. Human rights
ISBN 978-1-4263-0511-5; 1-4263-0511-7

"On the sixtieth anniversary of the Universal Declaration of Human Rights, this full-color photo-essay combines prize-winning poems by young people with beautiful photographs from all over the world. . . . The stirring pictures will stimulate classroom discussion about the declaration, which is quoted in full at the back." Booklist

Stewart, Gail

Human rights in the Middle East; by Gail B. Stewart. Lucent Books 2004 112p il map (Lucent library of conflict in the Middle East) $28.70

Grades: 6 7 8 9   **323**
1. Human rights 2. Human rights -- Middle East
ISBN 1-59018-488-2

LC 2004-10836

This discusses such human rights issues in the Middle East as the forced labor of children, discrimination against women and ethnic minorities, torture and executions, and censorship.

Includes bibliographical references

323.1   Civil and political rights of nondominant groups

Archer, Jules

★ **They** had a dream; the civil rights struggle from Frederick Douglass to Marcus Garvey to Martin Luther King and Malcolm X. Viking 1993 258p il (Epoch biographies) hardcover o.p. pa $7.99
Grades: 6 7 8 9   **323.1**
1. Clergy 2. Slaves 3. Authors 4. Abolitionists 5. Memoirists 6. Nonfiction writers 7. Writers on politics 8. Black Muslim leaders 9. Civil rights activists 10. Nobel laureates for peace 11. African Americans -- Biography 12. African Americans -- Civil rights 13. African Americans -- Biography 14. African Americans -- Civil rights
ISBN 0-14-034954-5 pa

LC 92-40071

Traces the progression of the civil rights movement and its effect on history through biographical sketches of four prominent and influential African Americans: Frederick Douglass, Marcus Garvey, Martin Luther King, Jr., and Malcolm X

"This discussion of the contributions of four pivotal civil rights activists is balanced and substantive." Publ Wkly

Includes bibliographical references

Aretha, David

Freedom Summer. Morgan Reynolds Pub. 2007 128p (The civil rights movement) lib bdg $27.95
Grades: 7 8 9 10 11 12   **323.1**
1. African Americans -- Civil rights
ISBN 978-1-59935-059-2; 1-59935-059-9

LC 2007-23815

This "discusses the collaborative strategies black and white Americans . . . devised to dismantle the restrictive, often violent measures used in the South to prevent most African Americans from voting. . . . [This title is] visually appealing with generous white space around the [text]. Throughout, mostly black-and-white historical photos . . . enhance the [narrative]. Also adding impact are numerous dramatic accounts by participants in the struggle." SLJ

Includes bibliographical references

Montgomery bus boycott. Morgan Reynolds Pub. 2009 128p il (The civil rights movement) $28.95

Grades: 7 8 9 10   **323.1**
1. African Americans -- Civil rights
ISBN 978-1-59935-020-2; 1-59935-020-3

LC 2008-18679

"The wrenching consequences of Rosa Parks's decision that sparked the Civil Rights Movement are depicted in this well-written book. Descriptions of civil rights activism dating back to 1865 . . . provide historical context and a sense of the fervor surrounding discrimination and segregation. The facts of the boycott are documented with supportive news articles, relevant quotations, moving individual stories, and significant court cases. . . . [Photographs] depict significant figures and document incidents such as meetings and carpooling to avoid buses." SLJ

Includes bibliographical references

Sit-ins and freedom rides. Morgan Reynolds Pub. 2009 128p il lib bdg $28.95
Grades: 5 6 7 8   **323.1**
1. African Americans -- Civil rights
ISBN 978-1-59935-098-1 lib bdg; 1-59935-098-X lib bdg

LC 2008039600

"Aretha opens with an introduction to the four college students who orchestrated the famous sit-in at Woolworth's in Greensboro, NC, in 1960. He follows that with chapters that describe slavery, Reconstruction, and Jim Crow in terms of how they set the stage for the resistance efforts. . . . [The book] offers insight into to workings of the protests at the grassroots level. Individual anecdotes interspersed thoughout the detailed narrative provide personal and effective accounts that go beyond mere facts. Black-and-white and some color photographs appear on almost every page." SLJ

Includes bibliographical references

Bausum, Ann

★ **Freedom** Riders; John Lewis and Jim Zwerg on the front lines of the civil rights movement. by Ann Bausum; forewords by Freedom Riders Congressman John Lewis and Jim Zwerg. National Geographic 2006 79p il por $18.95; lib bdg $28.90
Grades: 5 6 7 8   **323.1**
1. Members of Congress 2. Civil rights activists 3. African Americans -- Civil rights
ISBN 0-7922-4173-8; 0-7922-4174-6 lib bdg

LC 2005012947

"Bausum's narrative style, fresh, engrossing, and at times heart-stopping, brings the story of the turbulent and often violent dismantling of segregated travel alive in vivid detail. The language, presentation of material, and pacing will draw readers in and keep them captivated." SLJ

Includes bibliographical references

Boerst, William J.

Marching in Birmingham. Morgan Reynolds Pub. 2008 112p il map (The civil rights movement) $27.95
Grades: 7 8 9 10 11 12   **323.1**
1. Clergy 2. Nonfiction writers 3. Civil rights activists 4. Nobel laureates for peace 5. African Americans --

Civil rights
ISBN 978-1-59935-055-4; 1-59935-055-6
LC 2007-26640

This "focuses on Alabama and the organized efforts by both black and white Americans to end local-government-sanctioned segregation and inequality. [This title is] visually appealing with generous white space around the [text]. Throughout, mostly black-and-white historical photos . . . enhance the [narrative]. Also adding impact are numerous dramatic accounts by participants in the struggle." SLJ

Includes bibliographical references

Bowers, Rick

★ The **spies** of Mississippi; the true story of the spy network that tried to destroy the Civil Rights Movement. National Geographic 2010 120p il $16.95; lib bdg $26.90

Grades: 7 8 9 10   **323.1**
1. African Americans -- Civil rights 2. African Americans -- Civil rights
ISBN 978-1-4263-0595-5; 1-4263-0595-8; 978-1-4263-0596-2 lib bdg; 1-4263-0596-6 lib bdg
LC 2009-18944

"Bowers draws upon archival material, supplemented with his own extensive research, to document the activities of the Mississippi State Sovereignty Commission, a Civil Rights-era state agency that disseminated segregationist propaganda and used Soviet-style methods to spy upon, harass, and harm those who challenged white supremacy. . . . This book's unique perspective will help students understand the previously unknown history of the despicable actions of Mississippi leaders who opposed civil rights and the silent citizens who supported their activities." SLJ

Includes bibliographical references

Brimner, Larry Dane

Birmingham Sunday. Calkins Creek 2010 48p il $17.95

Grades: 5 6 7 8   **323.1**
1. Bombings 2. Hate crimes 3. Racism 4. Young adult literature -- Works 5. African Americans -- Civil rights 6. Hate crimes -- Birmingham (Ala.) 7. African Americans -- Civil rights 8. Bombings -- Alabama -- Birmingham
ISBN 1590786130; 9781590786130
LC 2009035716

"This moving photo-essay covers much more than just an account of the Birmingham, Alabama, Baptist Church bombing that killed four young girls in 1963. The detailed text, illustrated with black-and-white photos on every spacious double-page spread, sets the shocking assassination of the children within a general overview of both the racist segregation of the times and the struggle against it." Booklist

★ **Black** & white; the confrontation of Reverend Fred L. Shuttlesworth and Eugene Bull O'Connor. Calkins Creek 2011 109p il $16.95

Grades: 7 8 9 10 11 12   **323.1**
1. Clergy 2. Police officials 3. Civil rights activists 4. Organization officials 5. African Americans -- Civil rights
ISBN 1-59078-766-8; 978-1-59078-766-3

"Reverend Fred L. Shuttlesworth led the civil rights struggle for equality in Birmingham, Alabama. . . . Eugene 'Bull' Connor, backed by the Ku Klux Klan, became a symbol of racist hatred and violence against Shuttlesworth. With a spacious design that includes archival pictures and primary-source documents on almost every page, this accessible photo-essay recounts the events in three sections, which focus first on the preacher, then on the commisioner, and finally, on their confrontation. . . . Never simplistic in his depictions, Brimner shows the viewpoints from all sides. . . . A penetrating look at elemental national history." Booklist

Includes bibliographical references

Bullard, Sara

Free at last; a history of the Civil Rights Movement and those who died in the struggle. introduction by Julian Bond. Oxford Univ. Press 1993 112p il map $28; pa $12.95

Grades: 8 9 10 11   **323.1**
1. African Americans -- Civil rights
ISBN 0-19-508381-4; 0-19-509450-6 pa
LC 92-38174

An illustrated history of the civil rights movement, including a timeline and profiles of forty people who gave their lives in the movement

Includes bibliographical references

Civil rights; Jill Karson, book editor. Greenhaven Press 2003 238p il map (Great speeches in history series) lib bdg $33.70; pa $22.45

Grades: 7 8 9 10   **323.1**
1. Speeches 2. African Americans -- Civil rights 3. African Americans -- Civil rights -- History -- 20th century -- Sources 4. Civil rights movements -- United States -- History -- 20th century -- Sources
ISBN 0-7377-1593-6 lib bdg; 0-7377-1594-4 pa
LC 2002-32209

"A collection of the speeches of well-known individuals who participated in or supported the American Civil Rights Movement from early pioneers through the 1960s up until today. Selections from Frederick Douglass, Malcolm X, Fannie Lou Hamer, Jesse Jackson, and Nelson Mandela emphasize the power of oratory to inform, persuade, and make an impact." SLJ

Includes bibliographical references

Cooper, John

Season of rage; Hugh Burnett and the struggle for civil rights. [by] John Cooper. Tundra Books 2005 71p il pa $9.95

Grades: 7 8 9 10   **323.1**
1. Race discrimination 2. Carpenters 3. Civil rights activists 5. Civil rights
ISBN 0-88776-700-1

"Cooper has chosen the small town of Dresden, Ontario, to paint a picture of what life was like for black Canadians in the middle of the last century. One Sunday in the early 1930s, when 12-year-old Hugh Burnett and his younger brother had a hankering for ice cream, they entered a restaurant. The boys were told that they would have to eat in the kitchen. . . . The event in the restaurant sparked a lifelong crusade for Burnett, who spearheaded the formation of the

National Unity Association. . . . A number of archival photos enhance the text. . . . An eye-opening story." SLJ

Cruz, Barbara

Triumphs and struggles for Latino civil rights. Enslow Pubs. 2008 128p il map (From many cultures, one history) lib bdg $31.93

Grades: 6 7 8 9   **323.1**
1. Civil rights 2. Latinos (U.S.) 3. Hispanic Americans
ISBN 978-0-7660-2804-3 lib bdg; 0-7660-2804-6 lib bdg

The author "describes the long journey of Latinos in the United States, from the founding of the oldest city on the American mainland at St. Augustine, Florida, to the continued struggle for civil rights today." Publisher's note

Includes glossary and bibliographical references

Des Chenes, Betz

American civil rights: primary sources; [compiled by] Phillis Engelbert; edited by Betz Des Chenes. U.X.L 1999 xl, 200p il $58

Grades: 8 9 10 11 12   **323.1**
1. Civil rights 2. Civil rights movements -- United States -- History -- Sources 3. Minorities -- Civil rights -- United States -- History -- Sources
ISBN 0-7876-3170-1

LC 99-27167

Presents fifteen documents, including speeches, autobiographical texts, and proclamations, related to the civil rights movement and arranged by category under economic rights, desegregation, and human rights

"The uniqueness of this set lies in the range of people covered. Students will find it an excellent resource for reports and interesting reading." Booklist

Includes bibliographical references

Finlayson, Reggie

We shall overcome; the history of the American civil rights movement. Lerner Publs. 2003 96p il (People's history) lib bdg $25.26

Grades: 6 7 8 9   **323.1**
1. African Americans -- Civil rights 2. African Americans -- Civil rights -- History -- 20th century 3. Civil rights movements -- United States -- History -- 20th century
ISBN 0-8225-0647-5

LC 2002-954

Uses the words of spirituals and other music of the time to frame a discussion of the civil rights movement in the United States, focusing on specific people, incidents, and court cases

The author "ably places events in their historical context and tells a linear, inspiring story of the crucial era. Compelling black-and-white photos . . . bring the events up close." Booklist

Includes bibliographical references

Freedman, Russell

★ **Freedom** walkers; the story of the Montgomery bus boycott. Holiday House 2006 114p il $18.95

Grades: 4 5 6 7   **323.1**
1. Clergy 2. Historians 3. College teachers 4. Nonfiction writers 5. Civil rights activists 6. Nobel laureates for peace 7. Boycotts 8. African Americans -- Civil rights 9. Civil rights movements -- Alabama -- Montgomery
ISBN 978-0-8234-2031-5; 0-8234-2031-0

LC 2006-41148

This account of the Montgomery bus boycott of 1955 focuses on Jo Ann Robinson, Claudette Colvin, Rosa Parks, Martin Luther King, and other participants.

This offers "expertly paced text, balanced but impassioned. . . . The narrative arc is compelling; well-captioned black-and-white photographs enhance the impact." Horn Book

Includes bibliographical references

Hynson, Colin

The **civil** rights movement. Arcturus 2010 48p il (Timelines) lib bdg $34.25

Grades: 5 6 7 8   **323.1**
1. African Americans -- Civil rights
ISBN 978-1-84837-638-0 lib bdg; 1-84837-638-3 lib bdg

LC 2009051261

"This title offers a succinct overview of the civil rights movement in the U.S., beginning with the country's first-ever Civil Rights Act, signed by Congress in 1866. The picture-book-sized format is dynamic: each neatly laid-out spread combines short, informative paragraphs with a time line of landmark dates; well-chosen boxed quotes and archival images; and cross-referenced notes that link to related spreads and help students synthesize the events into a bigger historical picture." Booklist

Includes glossary and bibliographical references

Johnson, Troy R.

Red power; the Native American civil rights movement. [by] Troy R. Johnson. Chelsea House 2007 112p il (Landmark events in Native American history) lib bdg $35

Grades: 7 8 9 10   **323.1**
1. Native Americans -- Civil rights
ISBN 978-0-7910-9341-2 lib bdg; 0-7910-9341-7 lib bdg

LC 2006102264

This "describes and defines what has come to be known as the American Indian Movement. . . . Early resistance . . . is summarized briefly and includes a chapter on the massacre at Wounded Knee Creek in 1890. The remaining six chapters focus on pivotal events such as the murders at Pine Ridge Reservation, the occupations of Alcatraz in 1969 and Wounded Knee in 1973, and the subsequent changes in government policy toward Native self-governance. . . . [This book is an excellent [tool] for first-time researchers and history buffs alike." SLJ

Includes bibliographical references

Kallen, Stuart A.

Women of the civil rights movement; [by] Stuart A. Kallen. Lucent Books 2005 112p il map (Women in history) $28.70

Grades: 7 8 9 10　　　**323.1**
1. Women -- Biography 2. African Americans -- Civil rights
ISBN 1-59018-569-2

LC 2004023822

"Kallen spotlights the unsung women who played a significant role in the Civil Rights movement. Short chapters are divided into various aspects of the struggle, including organizations, protests, education, voting rights, political office, radicals, and creative expression. Upclose black-and-white photographs and vignettes highlight key people." SLJ
Includes bibliographical references

Kasher, Steven
The **civil** rights movement: a photographic history, 1954-68; [by] Steven Kasher; foreword by Myrlie Evers-Williams. Abbeville Press 1996 255p il $45; pa $29.95
Grades: 8 9 10 11 12 Adult　　　**323.1**
1. African Americans -- Civil rights 2. African Americans -- Civil rights -- Pictorial works
ISBN 0-7892-0123-2; 0-7892-0656-0 pa

LC 96-4337

"This book contains images by more than 50 photographers, whose images were borrowed from photo agencies, galleries, and private collections. Ten accompanying essays break the Civil Rights movement into chronological periods. Kasher's research, writing, and photo selection are impeccable and engaging." Libr J
Includes bibliographical references

King, Martin Luther
The **words** of Martin Luther King, Jr. selected by Coretta Scott King. Newmarket Press 1983 112p il $15.95; pa $11.95
Grades: 8 9 10 11 12 Adult　　　**323.1**
1. African Americans -- Civil rights
ISBN 0-937858-28-5; 1-55704-483-X pa

LC 83-17306

This "volume of selections from Dr. King's speeches and writings . . . focuses on seven areas of his concerns: 'The Community of Man, Racism, Civil Rights, Justice and Freedom, Faith and Religion, Nonviolence, and Peace'"
Publisher's note
Includes bibliographical references

Linda Brown, you are not alone; the Brown v. Board of Education decision: a collection. Jump at the Sun/Hyperion Books for Children 2003 114p il $15.99
Grades: 5 6 7 8　　　**323.1**
1. School integration 2. African Americans -- Civil rights 3. African Americans -- Civil rights -- History
ISBN 0-7868-0821-7

A collection of personal reflections, stories and poems of 10 well-known children's authors, such as Jerry Spinelli, Eloise Greenfield, Lois Lowry, Michael Cart, and Katherine Paterson, who were themselves young people in 1954 when the Supreme Court handed down the decision to desegregate public schools.
The authors' "personal reminiscences capture a spectrum of powerfully expressed emotions. . . . James's closely

focused, lifelike pastel illustrations feature striking portraits and memorable images." Publ Wkly

Living through the Civil Rights Movement; Charles George, book editor. Greenhaven Press 2007 117p il (Living through the Cold War) lib bdg $32.35
Grades: 7 8 9 10　　　**323.1**
1. African Americans -- Civil rights
ISBN 978-0-7377-2919-1 lib bdg; 0-7377-2919-8 lib bdg

LC 2006017184

"This title does an excellent job of chronicling the movement by using primary-source documents. Excerpts from speeches by government officials, such as Lyndon Baines Johnson, George Wallace, and John F. Kennedy, appear as well as speeches or statements from Malcolm X, Martin Luther King, Jr., and Stokely Carmichael." SLJ
Includes bibliographical references

Malaspina, Ann
The **ethnic** and group identity movements; earning recognition. Chelsea House 2007 176p il map (Reform movements in American history) lib bdg $30
Grades: 6 7 8 9 10　　　**323.1**
1. Minorities 2. Civil rights 3. Multiculturalism 4. Social movements
ISBN 978-0-7910-9571-3; 0-7910-9571-1

LC 2007-21721

"Malaspina explains how leaders within the Asian, disability, Chicano, senior, gay, American Indian, and Muslim communities drew on models of the successful civil and women's rights movements to build group identity and improve the social and political treatment of their members. . . . Illustrations include black-and-white and color photos and period art." SLJ
Includes bibliographical references

Marsico, Katie
The **Montgomery** bus boycott; milestone of the civil rights movement. Marshall Cavendish Benchmark 2011 111p il (Perspectives on) lib bdg $39.93
Grades: 8 9 10 11 12　　　**323.1**
1. African Americans -- Civil rights
ISBN 978-1-60870-447-7; 1-60870-447-5

LC 2010033906

This title offers "excellent, thorough, and accurate information for reports or for general reading. . . . [It] explores the way that the boycott and resulting Supreme Court decision ruling that segregation of Montgomery's bus system was unconstitutional led to the beginning of the Civil Rights Movement while relaying the risks taken by those who participated in and supported the boycott." SLJ
Includes bibliographical references

Mayer, Robert H.
★ **When** the children marched; the Birmingham civil rights movement. Enslow Publishers 2008 176p il map (Prime) $34.60

Grades: 7 8 9 10   **323.1**
1. African American children   2. African Americans -- Civil rights
ISBN 978-0-7660-2930-9; 0-7660-2930-1
                          LC 2007-25590

"Children played a significant role in Birmingham's crucial civil rights struggle, and this stirring history of the movement, with many photos, news reports, and quotes from all sides, emphasizes the connections between the young people's power and that of the big leaders. . . . From the cover picture of police escorting African American children to jail, the numerous photos of youth in nonviolent confrontation—marching, attacked by dogs and fire hoses, crammed in prisons—will draw readers with their gripping drama." Booklist

Includes glossary and bibliographical references

McClaurin, Irma

★ The **civil** rights movement; by Irma McClaurin. Marshall Cavendish Benchmark 2008 80p il (Drama of African-American history) lib bdg $23.95
Grades: 5 6 7 8   **323.1**
1. African Americans -- Civil rights
ISBN 978-0-7614-2642-4

"Covers the struggle of African Americans to gain their civil rights, from Brown v. Board of Education in 1954 through the turbulent Sixties." Publisher's note

McWhorter, Diane

A **dream** of freedom; the Civil Rights Movement from 1954 to 1968. foreword by Reverend Fred Shuttlesworth. Scholastic Nonfiction 2004 160p il $19.95
Grades: 5 6 7 8   **323.1**
1. African Americans -- Civil rights   2. African Americans -- Civil rights -- History
ISBN 0-439-57678-4

The author discusses "the national civil rights movement from Brown v. the Board of Education to the assassination of Martin Luther King Jr. . . . This account is both factual and personal. She discusses her feelings as a white child in the South, and she focuses in on the many ways in which both white and black children were involved in the movement. . . . The breadth and depth of McWhorter's book is exemplary." Booklist

Nardo, Don

Birmingham 1963; how a photograph rallied Civil Rights support. Compass Point 2011 64p il (Captured history) lib bdg $33.99
Grades: 6 7 8 9   **323.1**
1. Documentary photography   2. Photojournalists   3. African Americans -- Civil rights
ISBN 978-0-7565-4398-3; 0-7565-4398-3

This book about Charles Moore's 1963 photograph of young African American civil rights protesters being blasted with a fire hose places the photo "in historical context, profiles the photographer, describes the conditions under which it was taken, and analyzes both its immediate and its continuing impact. The [text includes] ample background infor-

mation and details and [is] enhanced by large photos and sidebars." SLJ

Includes glossary and bibliographical references

Partridge, Elizabeth

★ **Marching** for freedom; walk together, children, and don't you grow weary. Viking 2009 72p il $19.99
Grades: 6 7 8 9 10 11 12   **323.1**
1. African Americans -- Civil rights   2. Civil rights movements   3. African American children   4. African Americans -- Civil rights
ISBN 978-0-670-01189-6; 0-670-01189-4
                        LC 2009-9696
Boston Globe-Horn Book Award: Nonfiction (2010)

An examination of the march from Selma to Montgomery in 1965 led by Dr. Martin Luther King, Jr., this book focuses on the children who faced terrifying violence in order to walk alongside him in their fight for freedom and the right to vote.

This is a "stirring photo-essay. . . . The vivid text is filled with quotes collected from Partridge's personal interviews with adults who remember their youthful experiences. . . . Filled with large black-and-white photos, every spread brings readers up close to the dramatic, often violent action." Booklist

Includes bibliographical references

Sharp, Anne Wallace

A **dream** deferred; the Jim Crow era. [by] Anne Wallace Sharp. Lucent Books 2005 112p il (Lucent library of Black history) lib bdg $22.96
Grades: 7 8 9 10   **323.1**
1. African Americans -- Civil rights
ISBN 1-59018-700-8
                        LC 2005002799

This title "about the Jim Crow Era, organized chronologically from Reconstruction through the Brown v. Board of Education decision, emphasizes the devastating and demoralizing effect of Jim Crow laws on the black community, and the eventual organized response that became the birth of the civil rights movement. . . . The black-and-white photographs and drawings that accompany the text are well captioned and clearly reproduced. This is a straightforward overview that will prove invaluable for homework assignments on the origins of the civil rights movement." Booklist

Includes bibliographical references

Sirimarco, Elizabeth

★ **American** voices from the civil rights movement. Benchmark Books 2004 xxi, 134p (American voices from--) lib bdg $34.21
Grades: 6 7 8 9   **323.1**
1. African Americans -- Civil rights   2. African Americans -- Civil rights -- History -- Sources   3. Civil rights movements -- United States -- History -- Sources
ISBN 0-7614-1697-8
                        LC 2003-7952

Presents the history of the civil rights movement in the United States, from Reconstruction to the late 1960s, through excerpts from letters, newspaper articles, speeches, songs, and poems of the time.

This "excellent [resource stands] out . . . because [it deals] strictly with primary sources, [contains] topnotch illustrations, and [enables] students to grasp the concepts without being overwhelmed." SLJ

Includes glossary and bibliographical references

Turck, Mary

★ **Freedom** song; young voices and the struggle for civil rights. [by] Mary C. Turck. Chicago Review Press 2009 146p il pa $18.95

Grades: 7 8 9 10   323.1

1. African American music 2. African Americans -- Civil rights

ISBN 978-1-55652-773-9; 1-55652-773-X

LC 2008-29673

"The book is divided into chapters that represent the history of the Civil Rights Movement. 'Sunday of Song,' 'Singing in the Churches,' and 'South Africa,' for example, contain information about the factual events while including how the evolution of the music captured the mood and sentiment of the time. The importance of music in the lives of African Americans is described in depth. . . . The accompanying CD allows students to internalize the words and their emotional impact as they listen. Overall, this informative and well-written book is an excellent addition to any collection." SLJ

Includes bibliographical references

Walsh, Frank

The **Montgomery** bus boycott. World Almanac Library 2003 48p il map (Landmark events in American history) lib bdg $26.60; pa $11.95

Grades: 5 6 7 8   323.1

1. African Americans -- Civil rights 2. Segregation in transportation -- Alabama -- Montgomery -- History -- 20th century 3. African Americans -- Civil rights -- Alabama -- Montgomery -- History -- 20th century

ISBN 0-8368-5375-X lib bdg; 0-8368-5403-9 pa

LC 2002-36020

Describes how the black community of Montgomery, Alabama, staged the 1955 boycott to end segregation on public buses and discusses that struggle in the context of the Civil Rights Movement

"Brief but informative. . . . [The book is] heavily illustrated with well-chosen and carefully placed archival photographs and . . . reproductions of historical documents." SLJ

Includes glossary and bibliographical references

Wexler, Sanford

The **civil** rights movement; an eyewitness history. introduction by Julian Bond. Facts on File 1993 356p il maps (Eyewitness history series) $75

Grades: 7 8 9 10   323.1

1. African Americans -- Civil rights 2. African Americans -- Civil rights

ISBN 0-8160-2748-X

LC 92-28674

Uses speeches, articles, and other writings of those involved to trace the history of the civil rights movement in the United States, primarily from 1954 to 1965

"This very readable source deserves a place in every public and middle and high school library, though it may fit better in the circulating collection." Booklist

Includes bibliographical references

Williams, Juan

Eyes on the prize: America's civil rights years, 1954-1965; [by] Juan Williams with the Eyes on the prize production team; introduction by Julian Bond. Viking 1987 300p il hardcover o.p. pa $20

Grades: 7 8 9 10   323.1

1. African Americans -- Civil rights

ISBN 0-670-81412-1; 0-14-009653-1 pa

LC 86-40271

"Highly recommended both as a socio-historical document and as a heartfelt, poignant remembrance of a movement and its activists." Booklist

Includes bibliographical references

Williams, Mary E.

Civil rights; edited by Mary E. Williams. Greenhaven Press 2002 94p il (Examining issues through political cartoons) lib bdg $24.95; pa $16.20

Grades: 7 8 9 10   323.1

1. Affirmative action programs 2. African Americans -- Civil rights -- Cartoons and caricatures 3. African Americans -- Civil rights -- History -- Caricatures and cartoons 4. Civil rights movements -- United States -- History -- Caricatures and cartoons 5. Minorities -- Civil rights -- United States -- History -- Caricatures and cartoons

ISBN 0-7377-1100-0 lib bdg; 0-7377-1099-3 pa

LC 2001-55743

The author provides "readers with an overview of African Americans' struggle for those rights enjoyed by other citizens and of the historical role of the political cartoon. . . . Four chapters ('The Struggle for Justice,' 'Has the Civil Rights Movement Benefited Minorities?' 'How Has Affirmative Action Affected Civil Rights?' and 'What Is the Legacy of the Civil Rights Movement?') examine three to six cartoons each. All are reproduced in the book, and information about the artist is provided." SLJ

Includes bibliographical references

323.119

Levinson, Cynthia Y.

We've got a job; the 1963 Birmingham Children's March. written by Cynthia Levinson. Peachtree Publishers 2012 176 p. $19.95

Grades: 6 7 8 9   323.119

1. Political activists 2. African American youth 3. African Americans -- Civil rights 4. Birmingham (Ala.) -- Race relations 5. Civil rights demonstrations -- Alabama 6. African American youth -- Alabama -- Birmingham -- History -- 20th century 7. Civil rights movements -- Alabama -- Birmingham -- History -- 20th century 8. African American students -- Alabama -- Birmingham -- History -- 20th century 9. African Americans -- Civil rights -- Alabama -- Birmingham --

History -- 20th century
ISBN 9781561456277

LC 2011031738

YALSA Award for Excellence in Nonfiction for Young Adults Finalist (2013)

In this book, "[c]overing the history of the Birmingham Children's March from inception to full impact, [author Cynthia Y.] Levinson traces the stories of four young people between the ages of 9 and 15 in 1963. Audrey Hendricks, Washington Booker III, Arnetta Streeter, and James Stewart came from very different segments of the city's black community, but all risked their lives and spent time in jail to fight for their freedom." (School Library Journal)

323.3 Civil and political rights of other social groups

Serres, Alain

I have the right to be a child; author, Alain Serres; illustrator, Aurélia Fronty; translator, Helen Mixter. Groundwood Books 2012 48 p. $18.95

Grades: 3 4 5 6 7   323.3
1. Treaties 2. Human rights 3. Children -- Civil rights
ISBN 1554981492; 9781554981496

In this children's book, "a young narrator describes what it means to be a child with rights -- from the right to food, water and shelter, to the right to go to school, to the right to be free from violence, to the right to breathe clean air, and much more. The book emphasizes that these rights belong to every child on the planet. . . . A brief afterword explains that the rights outlined in the book come from the Convention on the Rights of the Child." (Publisher's note)

323.44 Freedom of action (Liberty)

Carson, Brian

Understanding your right to freedom from searches; [by] Brian Carson and Catherine Ramen. Rosen Pub. 2011 160p il (Personal freedom & civic duty) lib bdg $33.25

Grades: 6 7 8 9   323.44
1. Searches and seizures
ISBN 978-1-44884-670-2; 1-44884-670-6

LC 2010044135

This "offers a balanced, engagingly lucid summary of the legal history behind the Fourth Amendment to the U.S. Constitution and the reasoning behind a number of subsequent Supreme Court rulings that have helped to define the amendment's ambiguous wording. . . . This survey will leave readers with both a greater understanding of how the amendment's interpretation has developed over time and an enhanced appreciation of the entire Constitution's vital significance in our lives." Booklist

Includes bibliographical references

Dougherty, Terri

Freedom of expression and the Internet. Lucent Books 2010 112p il map $33.45

Grades: 7 8 9 10   323.44
1. Copyright 2. Freedom of speech 3. Intellectual freedom 4. Internet -- Social aspects
ISBN 978-1-4205-0227-5; 1-4205-0227-1

LC 2010-1547

"This book explores the parameters of freedom of speech and the responsibility that accompanies it, explaining as well the difference between the presentation of fact and opinion. The remainder of the volume is devoted to child-protection policies, concerns about anonymity, copyright issues, trademark violations, 'School Speech and Cyberbullies,' and 'International Free Speech.' The text is well organized and clearly written, outlining the issues in such a way as to be understandable to teens. Color photos, sidebars, discussion questions, and a list of organization contacts are included. This is a good source for report writers." SLJ

Includes bibliographical references

Senker, Cath

Privacy and surveillance; Cath Senker. Rosen Central 2012 48 p. (Ethical debates) pa $11.75 lib bdg $29.25

Grades: 7 8 9 10   323.44
1. Right of privacy 2. Electronic surveillance 3. Privacy, Right of 4. Privacy, Right of -- Case studies 5. Electronic surveillance -- Case studies
ISBN 1448870119; 9781448860227; 9781448870110; 9781448870127

LC 2011028565

This book by Cath Senker, part of the Ethical Debates series, "[d]iscusses the controversies regarding privacy and surveillance, including the ethical aspects of electronic surveillance of citizens by the government, security of identity over the Internet, and students under surveillance at schools." (WorldCat)

Includes bibliographical references and index

323.6 Citizenship and related topics

Maury, Rob

Citizenship; rights and responsibilities. Mason Crest Publishers 2009 64p il (Major American immigration) lib bdg $22.95; pa $9.95

Grades: 6 7 8 9   323.6
1. Citizenship
ISBN 978-1-4222-0618-8 lib bdg; 1-4222-0618-1 lib bdg; 978-1-4222-0685-0 pa; 1-4222-0685-8 pa

LC 2008-28223

Presents the rights and responsibilities held by United States citizens, and describes the U.S. naturalization process.

"The chapters are short and easy to read, the sidebars are informative, and the chronology is helpful." Voice Youth Advocates

Includes glossary and bibliographical references

Raatma, Lucia

Citizenship; by Lucia Raatma. Children's Press 2012 64 p. ill. (chiefly col.), col. map (Cornerstones of freedom) (library) $30; (paperback) $8.95

Grades: 4 5 6   **323.6**
1. Citizenship -- United States
ISBN 0329917374; 0531230643; 0531281647;
9780329917371; 9780531230640; 9780531281642
LC 2011031340
This book on citizenship by Lucia Raatma "covers everything from basic facts about naturalization to debates over hot issues such as gun control." It is part of the "Cornerstones of Freedom" series for students in grades 4 to 6. Included are "a two-page map of 'What Happened Where?'; a two-page epilogue; glossary-style identifications of significant people; a page of primary sources; a bibliography of books; a glossary; and an index plus author bio." (Booklist)
Includes bibliographical references (p. 61) and index.

324   The political process

Morris-Lipsman, Arlene
Presidential races; campaigning for the White House. Rev. ed.; Twenty-First Century Books 2012 112p il (People's history) lib bdg $33.26
Grades: 6 7 8 9 10   **324**
1. Presidents -- United States -- Election
ISBN 978-0-7613-7395-7; 0-7613-7395-0
LC 2011001304
First published 2007
Describes how election campaigns for the office of president of the United States have changed from the time of George Washington to the Obama vs. McCain campaign of 2008.
Includes bibliographical references

Steele, Philip
Vote. DK Pub. 2008 72p il (Eyewitness books) $15.99
Grades: 4 5 6 7 8   **324**
1. Elections
ISBN 978-0-7566-3382-0; 0-7566-3382-6
"Engaging visual material and a wealth of assorted facts trace the history of voting and its impact on human rights, politics, and other related areas. The first half moves chronologically from ancient Greece to modern times, with current information into the 21st century. Later sections look at political structures, election logistics, and even nongovernmental elections (including trade unions, the Oscars, and Britain's Pop Idol). Several high-quality photographs and reproductions appear on each spread. . . . The book does a nice job of pulling together an impressive array of topics, events, and ideas within the broad concept of global suffrage. The book comes with a poster-size wall chart and a clip-art CD with downloadable images of many of the illustrations." SLJ

The **Election** of 2000 and the administration of George W. Bush; editor, Arthur M. Schlesinger, Jr.; associate editors, Fred L. Israel & Jonathan H. Mann. Mason Crest Publs. 2003 128p il (Major presidential elections and the administrations that followed) lib bdg $24.95
Grades: 7 8 9 10   **324**
1. Governors 2. Presidents 3. Baseball executives 4.

Children of presidents 5. Energy industry executives 6. Presidents -- United States -- Election -- 2000
ISBN 1-59084-365-7
LC 2002-13397
A discussion of the presidential election of 2000 and the subsequent administration of George W. Bush, based on source documents
"An exemplary, evenhanded discussion of the election and of the Bush administration, through the Trade Bill of 2002." SLJ
Includes bibliographical references

324.6   Election systems and procedures; suffrage

Aretha, David
Selma and the Voting Rights Act. Morgan Reynolds Pub. 2007 128p il (The civil rights movement) lib bdg $27.95
Grades: 7 8 9 10 11 12   **324.6**
1. African Americans -- Suffrage 2. African Americans -- Civil rights
ISBN 978-1-59935-056-1; 1-59935-056-4
LC 2007-24655
The author discusses "mid-1960s Alabama and the black struggle to exercise the constitutional right to vote. Even those who know the story of the famous protest marches will be interested in the details here. . . . There are quotes from and photos of the famous as well as the unknown, as well as excerpts from speeches and news photos." Booklist
Includes bibliographical references

Hollihan, Kerrie Logan
Rightfully ours; how women won the vote : 21 activities. Kerrie Logan Hollihan. 1st ed. Chicago Review Press 2012 xiii, 130 p.p ill. (some col.) (paperback) $16.95
Grades: 4 5 6 7 8   **324.6**
1. Women -- Suffrage 2. Women -- United States -- History 3. Suffragists -- United States -- History 4. Women's rights -- United States -- History 5. Women -- Suffrage -- United States -- History 6. Women's rights -- Study and teaching -- Activity programs -- United States 7. Women -- Suffrage -- Study and teaching -- Activity programs -- United States
ISBN 1883052890; 9781883052898
LC 2012006044
This book is an "account of the struggle for women's suffrage. The first three chapters focus on notable activists Lucy Stone, Elizabeth Cady Stanton, and Susan B. Anthony. [Kerrie Logan] Hollihan recounts how this battle was inexorably tied to the antislavery movement and the role played by women of color in both movements, including Harriett Tubman, Sojourner Truth, and Ida Wells-Barnett." (School Library Journal)
Includes bibliographical references (p. 121-124) and index

Marzilli, Alan
Election reform; 2nd ed.; Chelsea House 2010 119p il map (Point-counterpoint) lib bdg $35

Grades: 7 8 9 10   **324.6**
  1. Politics 2. Elections -- United States 3. Campaign funds -- United States
  ISBN 978-1-60413-691-3; 1-60413-691-X
LC 2009-51401
First published 2004
This book "examines ongoing debates over voting rights and election laws and asks how the United States might reach the ideal of 'one person, one vote.'" Publisher's note
Includes bibliographical references

Monroe, Judy
  The **Susan** B. Anthony women's voting rights trial; a headline court case. Enslow Pubs. 2002 112p il (Headline court cases) lib bdg $26.60
Grades: 7 8 9 10   **324.6**
  1. Suffragists 2. Abolitionists 3. Women -- Suffrage 4. Women -- Suffrage -- United States -- History -- 19th century 5. Women -- Suffrage -- New York (State) -- History -- 19th century 6. Election law -- United States -- Criminal provisions -- History -- 19th century
  ISBN 0-7660-1759-1
LC 2001-4528
Examines the efforts to gain the right for women in the United States to vote, focusing on the trial of Susan B. Anthony for illegally voting in the presidential election in 1872
"Simple syntax, insightful quotes, and logical organization make the information easily accessible." SLJ
Includes glossary and bibliographical references

Senker, Cath
  Women claim the vote; the rise of the women's suffrage movement, 1828-1860. Chelsea House 2011 64p il (A cultural history of women in America) $35
Grades: 7 8 9 10   **324.6**
  1. Feminism 2. Women -- Suffrage 3. Women -- United States -- History
  ISBN 978-1-60413-930-3; 1-60413-930-7
LC 2010045960
This is a history of the women's suffrage movement in America from 1828-1860 .
This book offers a "comprehensive, vivid, and thought-provoking [look] at the struggles and triumphs of . . . the women who [participated] in shaping our nation. Through succinct, informative text, [this] heavily illustrated volume incorporates the history of three major groups of people: the Natives, European settlers, and African slaves. Featured quotes from books, articles, letters, and speeches bring the history to life." SLJ
Includes glossary and bibliographical references

325   International migration and colonization

Anderson, Dale
  Arriving at Ellis Island. World Almanac Library 2002 48p il map (Landmark events in American history) lib bdg $26.60; pa $11.95
Grades: 5 6 7 8   **325**
  ISBN 0-8368-5337-7 lib bdg; 0-8368-5351-2 pa
LC 2002-24627

Discusses immigration to the United States during the nineteenth and early twentieth centuries and describes the small island in New York harbor that served as the point of entry for millions of immigrants from 1892 to 1954
The "design is attractive, with drawings, maps, paintings, and photos; primary sources, such as excerpts from diaries, letters, and newspapers, support and enhance the [text]. . . . Informative, competently written." Booklist
Includes glossary and bibliographical references

Bausum, Ann
  ★ **Denied,** detained, deported; stories from the dark side of American immigration. National Geographic 2009 111p il $21.95; lib bdg $32.90
Grades: 6 7 8 9 10 11 12   **325**
  1. Essayists 2. Anarchists 3. Memoirists 4. Writers on politics 5. Family planning advocates 6. Immigrants -- United States
  ISBN 978-1-4263-0332-6; 1-4263-0332-7; 978-1-4263-0333-3 lib bdg; 1-4263-0333-5 lib bdg
"This volume deals frankly with the more troubling aspects of United States immigration policy. The author chose the stories of three immigrants. . . . Twelve-year-old German-Jew Herb Karliner was denied entry to the United States at the border when he attempted to escape Nazi Germany. Sixteen-year-old Japanese-American Mary Matsuda was detained with the rest of her family during World War II. Labor-activist Emma Goldman was deported for her 'un-American' views. . . . The themes of the three stories are unified by the introduction and conclusion, which deal with Chinese immigration during the late 19th century and the history of immigration across the southern border of the United States, respectively. Photographs throughout will help students relate to the narrative. . . . This is an interesting and readable book." SLJ
Includes bibliographical references

Bial, Raymond
  Ellis Island; coming to the land of liberty. Houghton Mifflin Books for Children 2009 56p il $18
Grades: 4 5 6 7   **325**
  1. Immigrants -- United States
  ISBN 978-0-618-99943-9; 0-618-99943-4
LC 2008-36794
"Bial examines the history of the famed immigration station. . . . He looks at the socio-historical roots of the mass exodus to America and provides a detailed look at the immigrant experience from ship to shore, with Ellis Island in between. Primary-source quotes and period photos pair eloquently with the modern narrative voice and color photographs of the museum exhibits. . . . The generously sized period photos and Bial's museum shots tell a vivid and poignant tale." SLJ
Includes bibliographical references

Conway, Lorie
  Forgotten Ellis Island; the extraordinary story of America's immigrant hospital. [by] Lorie Conway. 1st Smithsonian Books ed.; Smithsonian Books/Collins 2007 185p il map $26.95

Grades: 7 8 9 10 11 12   325
1. Hospitals 2. Immigrants -- Health and hygiene
ISBN 978-0-06-124196-3; 0-06-124196-2
LC 2007022913
"Conway details the medical inspection that immigrants went through after disembarking and shows how thousands of people were treated at the island's hospitals, sometimes against their will. . . . Each chapter contains dozens of interesting archival photographs and large blocks of quotes from doctors and immigrants. . . . [The book] will add depth to any report on U.S. immigration." SLJ
Includes bibliographical references

Fields, Julianna
First-generation immigrant families.   Mason Crest 2009 64p il map (The changing face of modern families) $22.95
Grades: 6 7 8 9   325
1. Family 2. Immigrants -- United States
ISBN 978-1-4222-1499-2; 1-4222-1499-0
This describes the unique set of challenges facing first-generation immigrant families as they live with two cultures and, often, two languages.
"Colorful photographs and sidebars appear throughout. [This book is a] good [introduction] to the study of sociology and interpretation of data." SLJ

Meltzer, Milton
★ Bound for America; the story of the European immigrants. Benchmark Bks. 2002 112p il (Great journeys) $32.79
Grades: 5 6 7 8   325
1. Immigrants -- United States
ISBN 0-7614-1227-1
LC 00-51875
This history of immigration to the United States focuses on Europeans who arrived in the late 19th and early 20th century
Includes bibliographical references

Nakaya, Andrea C.
Immigration. ReferencePoint Press 2010 104p il (Compact research. Current issues) $25.95
Grades: 8 9 10 11 12   325
1. Immigrants -- United States
ISBN 978-1-60152-095-1; 1-60152-095-6
LC 2009-23404
After an overview of immigration, this addresses such questions as "'How Should the United States Address the Issue of Illegal Immigration?' [and offers] thorough and balanced answers incorporating viewpoints from both ends of the pro/con spectrum. The 'Primary Source Quotes' and 'Facts and Illustrations' sections allow readers to zero in on information that would be particularly helpful in supporting arguments." SLJ
Includes bibliographical references

Sandler, Martin W.
Island of hope; the story of Ellis Island and the journey to America. Scholastic Nonfiction 2004 144p il $18.95

Grades: 5 6 7 8   325
1. Immigrants -- United States
ISBN 0-439-53082-2
LC 2003-54448
Relates the story of immigration to America through the voices and stories of those who passed through Ellis Island, from its opening in 1892 to the release of the last detainee in 1954.
"This engagingly written, inspirational account will give children, particularly immigrants or descendants of immigrants, some sharp insight into the trials and triumphs of their predecessors." Booklist
Includes bibliographical references

Solway, Andrew
Graphing immigration. Raintree 2010 32p il (Real world data) $28.21; pa $7.99
Grades: 4 5 6 7   325
1. Statistics 2. Graphic methods 3. United States -- Immigration and emigration
ISBN 978-1-4329-2617-5; 1-4329-2617-9; 978-1-4329-2626-7 pa; 1-4329-2626-8 pa
LC 2009001185
"A line graph in [this] title shows the estimated number of illegal immigrants in the U.S. from 1980 to 2005. Arguments about costs and benefits of all kinds of immigrants include a pie chart that shows where immigrants in the U.S. come from and pairs thoughts on why people migrate with a discussion of costs and benefits. . . . The clear design, with lots of full-color photos and sidebars, will encourage browsers as much as the up-to-date examples and the clear directions for remaining 'chart smart.'" Booklist
Includes glossary and bibliographical references

Stefoff, Rebecca
★ American voices from a century of immigration: 1820-1924. Marshall Cavendish Benchmark 2006 115p (American voices from--) lib bdg $37.07
Grades: 6 7 8 9   325
1. Immigrants -- United States
ISBN 978-0-7614-2172-6 lib bdg; 0-7614-2172-6 lib bdg
LC 2005035963
"Describes the diverse peoples who came to the United States from 1820, when records began to be kept, to 1924, when the gates were nearly closed to immigrants. The reactions of Americans to the new arrivals, laws that were passed, and the experiences of the immigrants themselves are covered through the use of primary sources." Publisher's note
Includes glossary and bibliographical references

326   Slavery and emancipation

Altman, Linda Jacobs
The politics of slavery; fiery national debates fueled by the slave economy. foreword by series advisor Henry Louis Gates. Enslow 2004 128p il map (Slavery in American history) lib bdg $26.60

Grades: 7 8 9 10 **326**
1. Slavery -- United States
ISBN 0-7660-2150-5

LC 2003-26532

"Altman relates the beginning of 'the peculiar institution' and the constitutional, historical, and political issues and figures surrounding it from 1619 to the ratification of the Thirteenth Amendment in 1865. . . . [This book] will be useful in American-history collections." SLJ

Bial, Raymond
The **Underground** Railroad. Houghton Mifflin 1995 48p il map hardcover o.p. pa $6.95
Grades: 4 5 6 7 **326**
1. Underground railroad 2. Slavery -- United States 3. Slaves
ISBN 0-395-69937-1; 0-395-97915-3 pa

LC 94-19614

"Although the text covers ground often trodden by other works on this popular subject, Bial's shots of places and things which now appear tidy and innocent conjure spirits of desperate freedom-seekers as handily as do more detailed narratives." Bull Cent Child Books
Includes bibliographical references

Cloud Tapper, Suzanne
Voices from slavery's past; yearning to be heard. foreword by series advisor Henry Louis Gates. Enslow Publishers 2004 128p il map (Slavery in American history) lib bdg $26.60
Grades: 7 8 9 10 **326**
1. Clergy 2. Slaves 3. Authors 4. Geologists 5. Abolitionists 6. African Americans 7. Domestics 8. Memoirists 9. Slaveholders 10. College teachers 11. Newspaper editors 12. Slavery -- History 13. Slavery -- United States 14. African Americans -- Biography 15. Slavery -- United States -- History 16. Slaves -- United States -- Biography 17. Slaveholders -- United States -- Biography
ISBN 0-7660-2157-2

LC 2003-25134

This profiles escaped slave Henry Bibb, slave trader John Newton, captured African Olauda Equiano, racist scientist Joseph Le Conte, slave mistress Letitia Burwell, escaped slave Harriet Jacobs, and abolitionists William Lloyd Garrison and Frederick Douglass
This title is "consistently solid, with many informative period photographs and drawings, excerpts from primary-source documents, and strong back matter." SLJ
Includes glossary and bibliographical references

The **Complete** history of American slavery; James Miller, book editor. Greenhaven Press 2001 642p il map (Complete history of) lib bdg $123.75
Grades: 7 8 9 10 **326**
1. Slavery -- United States 2. African Americans -- History
ISBN 0-7377-0424-1

LC 00-39332

This anthology includes more than 90 entries and "begins with the Atlantic slave trade and ends with the Civil War, with entries by Frederick Douglass, Nat Turner,

Mary Chestnut, and many others. It is organized into 16 chapters on a number of topics, including a fascinating discussion of whether the Underground Railroad actually existed." Booklist
Includes bibliographical references

DeFord, Deborah H.
★ **Life** under slavery; [by] Deborah H. DeFord. Chelsea House 2006 112p il map (Slavery in the Americas) $35
Grades: 6 7 8 9 **326**
1. Slavery -- United States
ISBN 978-0-8160-6135-8; 0-8160-6135-1

LC 2005034651

This describes the treatment of slaves in the United States, life expectancies, entertainments, and family lives of slaves, and the cultural elements introduced into the New World by enslaved Africans.
"Clearly written, accessible, and well organized . . . [this] is illustrated with black-and-white drawings, period photographs, and explanatory text boxes." SLJ
Includes bibliographical references

Edwards, Judith
Abolitionists and slave resistance; breaking the chains of slavery. foreword by Henry Louis Gates. Enslow Publishers 2004 128p il map (Slavery in American history) lib bdg $26.60
Grades: 7 8 9 10 **326**
1. Abolitionists 2. Slave insurrections 3. Antislavery movements 4. Slavery -- United States 5. Abolitionists -- United States -- History 6. Slave insurrections -- United States -- History 7. Antislavery movements -- United States -- History
ISBN 0-7660-2155-6

LC 2003-13457

"Edwards examines the growth of the abolition movement and provides examples of some of the ways slaves themselves protested, including theft, work slowdowns, and destruction of property. Rebellions, runaways, and the Underground Railroad are also covered. The sensitive and respectful approach leads to an understanding of the social issues that remain as a legacy of slavery in American society today." SLJ
Includes bibliographical references

Eskridge, Ann E.
Slave uprisings and runaways; fighting for freedom and the Underground Railroad. foreword by series advisor Henry Louis Gates. Enslow 2004 128p il map (Slavery in American history) lib bdg $26.60
326
1. Slavery 2. Fugitive slaves 3. African Americans 4. Underground railroad 5. Slave insurrections 6. Slavery -- United States 7. Underground Railroad 8. Slavery -- United States -- History 9. Slave insurrections -- United States 10. Slaves -- United States -- Biography 11. Fugitive slaves -- United States -- History
ISBN 0-7660-2154-8

LC 2003-26533

This history of slave rebellions and escapes covers such topics as Nat Turner, John Brown, Harriet Tubman,

Frederick Douglass, The Fugitive Slave Act, and The Underground Railroad.

Includes bibliographical references

Fradin, Dennis B.

Bound for the North Star; true stories of fugitive slaves. [by] Dennis Brindell Fradin. Clarion Bks. 2000 206p il $20

Grades: 7 8 9 10   326

1. Abolitionists 2. Underground railroad 3. Slavery -- United States 4. Abolitionists -- United States 5. Fugitive slaves -- United States 6. Antislavery movements -- United States

ISBN 0-395-97017-2

LC 00-29052

"Fradin here draws on more than 16 slaves' personal experiences to show what slavery was like: the unrelenting racism; the physical brutality, including rape and flogging; the anguish of family separation. . . . The narrative is direct, with no rhetoric or cover-up. . . . This is painful reading about legal racist cruelty and those who resisted it." Booklist

Includes bibliographical references

Fradin, Judith Bloom

★ **5,000** miles to freedom; Ellen and William Craft's flight from slavery. [by] Judith Bloom Fradin and Dennis Brindell Fradin. National Geographic 2006 96p il $19.95; lib bdg $29.90

Grades: 5 6 7 8 9 10   326

1. Slaves 2. Memoirists 3. Slavery -- United States 5. Fugitive slaves

ISBN 0-7922-7885-2; 0-7922-7886-0 lib bdg

"In 1848, light-skinned Ellen Craft, dressed in the clothing of a rich, white man, assumed the identity of Mr. William Johnson and, escorted by his black slave, William, traveled by railroad and boat to reach the North. With the passage of a more stringent Fugitive Slave Law in 1850, the couple . . . decided to travel to England. . . . In 1869, they returned to the United States, opening a school and operating a farm in Georgia. . . . This lively, well-written volume presents the events in their lives in an exciting, page-turner style that's sure to hold readers attention. Black-and-white photographs, illustrations, and reproductions enhance the text." SLJ

Includes bibliographical references

Gann, Marjorie

★ **Five** thousand years of slavery; [by] Marjorie Gann and Janet Willen. Tundra Books 2011 168p il map $27.95

Grades: 7 8 9 10   326

1. Slavery 3. Slavery -- History

ISBN 978-0-88776-914-6; 0-88776-914-4

"This well-researched global survey introduces readers to slavery practices, customs, suffering, uprisings, and revolts as well as antislavery efforts from ancient Greece and Rome to today's world. . . . Informative documentary photos and factually rich sidebars enhance the text. . . . [This is a] groundbreaking title." SLJ

Includes bibliographical references

Gold, Susan Dudley

United States v. Amistad; slave ship mutiny. Marshall Cavendish Benchmark 2006 144p il (Supreme Court milestones) lib bdg $39.93

Grades: 7 8 9 10   326

1. Slavery -- United States

ISBN 978-0-7614-2143-6; 0-7614-2143-2

This is an account of the 1841 Supreme Court case involving the mutiny aboard the slave ship Amistad and the circumstances which surrounded it.

Includes bibliographical references

Grant, Reg

Slavery; real people and their stories of enslavement. DK Pub. 2009 191p il $24.99

Grades: 7 8 9 10   326

1. Slavery

ISBN 978-0-7566-5169-5; 0-7566-5169-7

"This encyclopedic guide to the subject of slavery highlights its history from Mesopotamia through the Atlantic slave trade and into the present day. . . . Photographs, time lines, quotations from historical figures and paintings create a diverse panorama of information. . . . As thorough as it is socially pertinent." Publ Wkly

Grayson, Robert

The **Amistad**. ABDO Pub. 2011 112p il (Essential events) lib bdg $23.95

Grades: 7 8 9 10 11 12   326

1. Slave trade

ISBN 978-1-61714-761-6; 1-61714-761-3

LC 2010044662

This "is dramatic history, focusing on the 1839-40 trial of the kidnapped Africans who rebelled on the slave ship from Cuba and were captured and tried in the U.S. on charges of piracy. Were the Africans property? . . . The spacious . . . design is inviting, with many color illustrations and screens, and the extensive back matter includes a detailed time line, glossary, bibliography and source notes." Booklist

Includes glossary and bibliographical references

Hulm, David

United States v. the Amistad; the question of slavery in a free country. Rosen Pub. Group 2004 64p il (Supreme Court cases through primary sources) lib bdg $29.25

Grades: 7 8 9 10   326

1. Slavery -- United States 2. Trials (Mutiny) -- United States 3. Fugitive slaves -- Legal status, laws, etc -- United States

ISBN 0-8239-4013-6

LC 2003-5938

This is an account of the mutiny aboard the slave ship Amistad and the court cases which followed.

This "deserves a place in every library. . . . Copious and well-chosen primary source documents give extra value to this [book]. . . . Each document adds human drama to the already engaging text." Lib Media Connect

Includes glossary and bibliographical references

McKissack, Patricia C.

★ **Rebels** against slavery; by Patricia C. McKissack and Fredrick McKissack. Scholastic 1996 181p il $15.95

Grades: 5 6 7 8   326
  1. Slavery -- United States 2. Slaves 3. Slavery -- United States
  ISBN 0-590-45735-7

LC 94-41089

A Coretta Scott King honor book for text, 1997

The authors "explore slave revolts and the men and women who led them, weaving a tale of courage and defiance in the face of tremendous odds. Readers learn not only about Nat Turner and Denmark Vesey, but also about Cato, Gabriel Prosser, the maroons, and the relationship between escaped slaves and Seminole Indians. The activities of abolitionists are described as well. The authors' careful research, sensitivity, and evenhanded style reveal a sad, yet inspiring story of the will to be free." SLJ

McNeese, Tim

The **rise** and fall of American slavery; freedom denied, freedom gained. foreword by series advisor Dr. Henry Louis Gates, Jr. Enslow Publishers 2004 128p il map (Slavery in American history) lib bdg $26.60

Grades: 7 8 9 10   326
  1. Antislavery movements 2. Slavery -- United States 3. Slavery -- United States -- History 4. African Americans -- History -- To 1863 5. Slavery -- United States -- History 6. African Americans -- History -- To 1863 7. Antislavery movements -- United States -- History
  ISBN 0-7660-2156-4

LC 2003-13459

This is a history of American slavery from colonial times to emacipation.

"Drawing on personal slave narratives as well as the commentary and analysis of eminent scholars, {this title} . . . {brings} immediacy and depth to crucial events and {assesses} their lasting impact on America's economy, politics, and culture. . . . The documentation is exemplary." Booklist

Includes bibliographical references (p. 124-125) and index

Nardo, Don

The **Atlantic** slave trade; [by] Don Nardo. Thomson/Gale 2008 104p il (Lucent library of black history) lib bdg $32.45

Grades: 6 7 8 9   326
  1. Slavery 2. Slave trade
  ISBN 978-1-4205-0007-3 lib bdg; 1-4205-0007-4 lib bdg

LC 2007-22999

"Nardo examines [slave trade and] its impact on West Africa, its implication for the economic and social health of the entire African continent, the role that black Africans played in the sale of their countrymen, and the continuing shadow slavery still casts over this country's race relations.

. . . Include[s] extensive bibliographies, period illustrations, and primary-source documents." SLJ

Includes bibliographical references

Sharp, S. Pearl

★ The **slave** trade and the middle passage; by S. Pearl Sharp with Virginia Schomp. Marshall Cavendish Benchmark 2007 70p il map (Drama of African-American history) lib bdg $34.21

Grades: 5 6 7 8   326
  1. Slavery 2. Slave trade
  ISBN 978-0-7614-2176-4 lib bdg; 0-7614-2176-9 lib bdg

LC 2006005321

"Traces the history of the transatlantic slave trade and the development of slavery in the New World." Publisher's note

Includes glossary and bibliographical references

Sirimarco, Elizabeth

★ **American** voices from the time of slavery. Marshall Cavendish Benchmark 2007 114p (American voices from--) lib bdg $37.07

Grades: 6 7 8 9   326
  1. Slavery -- United States 2. African Americans -- History
  ISBN 978-0-7614-2169-6 lib bdg; 0-7614-2169-6 lib bdg

LC 2005025854

"Describes the history of slavery in the United States—from the landing of the first enslaved Africans to the close of the Civil War—through various primary source documents, such as slave narratives, advertisements, newspaper accounts, official documents and laws, plus contemporary art and photos." Publisher's note

Includes glossary and bibliographical references

Slavery; James D. Torr, book editor. Greenhaven Press 2004 240p map (Opposing viewpoints in world history) hardcover o.p. pa $22.45

Grades: 8 9 10 11 12   326
  1. Slavery -- United States
  ISBN 0-7377-1705-X; 0-7377-1706-8 pa

LC 2003-44812

This book offers "perspectives on American slavery through a selection of primary sources. The excerpts, culled from speeches, pamphlets, and scholarly texts, are divided into four sections that cover moral issues, slave resistance, abolitionists, and events that led to the Civil War. . . . The entries that are included . . . will greatly enhance students' understanding of the issues. . . . An important, useful addition to the high-school history curriculum." Booklist

Includes bibliographical references

Tackach, James

★ The **abolition** of American slavery. Lucent Bks. 2002 112p il maps (World history series) lib bdg $27.45

Grades: 7 8 9 10   326
  1. Abolitionists 2. Slavery -- History 3. Antislavery movements 4. Slavery -- United States 5. Slavery -- United States -- History 6. Antislavery movements --

United States -- History
ISBN 1-59018-002-X

LC 2001-5301

Discusses the introduction of slaves into American society, the beginnings of the abolitionist movement, the national conflict over slavery and the resulting Civil War, emancipation of the slaves, and slavery's legacy

"There is a good deal of information packed into the brief text and both report writers and general readers will be well served. The book is illustrated with archival photographs and reproductions of prints and broadsides." SLJ

Includes bibliographical references

Thomas, Velma Maia

Lest we forget; the passage from Africa to slavery and emancipation. Crown 1997 32p il $29.95

Grades: 7 8 9 10   **326**

1. Slave trade 2. Slavery -- United States 3. African Americans -- History
ISBN 0-609-60030-3

LC 96-54240

"By combining highly effective and readable text with photographs, news clippings, drawings, and facsimilies of documents, Thomas shares with her readers the details of virtually every aspect of slave life. . . . Throughout the assortment of pop-out and pull-out replicas, points are raised that will lead to classroom discussion." SLJ

Worth, Richard

Slave life on the plantation; prisons beneath the sun. Enslow Publishers 2004 128p il (Slavery in American history) lib bdg $26.60

Grades: 7 8 9 10   **326**

1. Plantation life 2. Slavery -- United States 3. Southern States -- Social conditions 4. Slavery -- Southern States -- History 5. Plantation life -- Southern States -- History 6. Slaves -- Southern States -- Social conditions
ISBN 0-7660-2152-1

LC 2003-24291

"Worth frames his account within the sweep of history, but his focus is on daily life—the work, the hardship (especially the breakup of family life), punishment, and resistance—and he discusses the relationship between owners and slaves, the importance of cotton, and African American culture. [This title includes] several stirring page-long slave narratives as well as black-and-white drawings and photos. The documentation is exemplary." Booklist

Includes glossary and bibliographical references

The **slave** trade in America; cruel commerce. foreword by series advisor Dr. Henry Louis Gates, Jr. Enslow Publishers 2004 128p il map (Slavery in American history) lib bdg $26.60

Grades: 7 8 9 10   **326**

1. Slave trade 2. Slave trade -- History 3. Slavery -- United States 4. Slave trade -- Africa -- History 5. Slave trade -- United States -- History
ISBN 0-7660-2151-3

LC 2003-12079

This is a history of the slave trade in America from colonial times to emancipation

This "clearly written, well-researched {book presents} solid coverage of the subject." SLJ

Includes glossary and bibliographical references

327   International relations

Collier, Christopher

★ The **United** States in the Cold War: 1945-1989; [by] Christopher Collier, James Lincoln Collier. Benchmark Bks. 2001 95p il maps (Drama of American history) $31.36

Grades: 6 7 8 9   **327**

1. Cold war 2. Arms race 3. Korean War, 1950-1953 4. Vietnam War, 1961-1975 5. World politics -- 1945-1991
ISBN 0-7614-1317-0

LC 00-68010

The author discusses such topics as the Berlin Wall, the Korean and Vietnam Wars, the arms race, and other conflicts between the United States and the Soviet Union and other communist countries

This is written in "engaging narrative style . . . [and is] easy to read and informative." Book Rep

Includes bibliographical references

Renehan, Edward J.

The **Monroe** doctrine; the cornerstone of American foreign policy. [by] Edward J. Renehan Jr. Chelsea House 2007 122p il map (Milestones in American history) lib bdg $35

Grades: 7 8 9 10   **327**

1. Monroe Doctrine
ISBN 0-7910-9353-0 lib bdg; 978-0-7910-9353-5 lib bdg

LC 2006034126

This description of the Monroe Doctrine is "accessible, lively. . . . Many quotations, sidebars, art reproductions, and maps support the [text]. Excerpts from primary source materials also help give readers a sense of time and place." Horn Book Guide

Includes bibliographical references

327.12   Espionage and subversion

Earnest, Peter

The **real** spy's guide to becoming a spy; by Peter Earnest and Suzanne Harper, in association with the Spy Museum. Abrams Books for Young Readers 2009 144p il $16.95

Grades: 4 5 6 7   **327.12**

1. Spies 2. Espionage 3. Intelligence service
ISBN 978-0-8109-8329-8; 0-8109-8329-X

LC 2009-00518

"This guide, written by the executive director of the International Spy Museum, gives readers a glimpse at how spies work. Along with descriptions of the different types of intelligence officers and agencies and the tasks they perform, the text includes brief stories of spies in action." Horn Book Guide

Goodman, Michael E.

The **KGB** and other Russian spies; Michael E. Goodman. Creative Education 2012 48 p. col. ill. (library) $35.65

Grades: 6 7 8 9   **327.12**

1. Spies 2. Russia 3. Espionage, Soviet 4. Spies -- Soviet Union 5. Intelligence service -- Soviet Union
ISBN 1608182274; 9781608182275

LC 2011035790

This book is part of the Spies Around the World series and focuses on Russian spies. "Each title contains an introduction to that particular country's spying apparatus plus chapters covering origins and famous individuals, and an explanation of this shadowy occupation. Each table of contents lists eight special features under the 'Evolution of Espionage' heading, where a particular event or spy-related item is highlighted." (Library Media Connection)

Includes bibliographical references (p. 47) and index

The **SIS** and other British spies; Michael E. Goodman. Creative Education 2012 48 p. ill. (library) $35.65

Grades: 6 7 8 9   **327.124**

1. Intelligence service 2. Spies 3. Espionage, British 4. Spies -- Great Britain 5. Intelligence service -- Great Britain
ISBN 1608182290; 9781608182299

LC 2011035791

This book is part of the Spies Around the World series and focuses on the British SIS and other British spies. "Each title contains an introduction to that particular country's spying apparatus plus chapters covering origins and famous individuals, and an explanation of this shadowy occupation. Each table of contents lists eight special features under the 'Evolution of Espionage' heading, where a particular event or spy-related item is highlighted." (Library Media Connection)

Includes bibliographical references (p. 47) and index

Janeczko, Paul B.

The **dark** game; true spy stories. Candlewick Press 2010 248p il $16.99

Grades: 5 6 7 8   **327.12**

1. Espionage
ISBN 978-0-7636-2915-1; 0-7636-2915-4

"From Benedict Arnold and Mata Hari to the lesser-known Elizabeth Van Lew and Juan Pujol, Janeczko delves into [spies'] stories with delicious detail, drawing readers into a world of intrigue and danger. Did you ever wonder why invisible ink works? How a code breaker deciphers a message? Or whether dentistry could affect a secret agent's success? The answers to these questions and more can be found here. Each chapter covers a historical era and chronicles the maturation of spying, while primary-source photographs are interspersed throughout, lending an authentic feel to each section." SLJ

Mitchell, Susan K.

Spies and lies; famous and infamous spies. Enslow Publishers 2011 48p il (The secret world of spies) lib bdg $23.93

Grades: 4 5 6   **327.12**

1. Spies 2. Espionage
ISBN 978-0-7660-3713-7

LC 2010044126

Includes glosssary and bibliographical references

"Archival photographs, sidebars, and multiple fact-filled features (sidebars, text boxes, etc.) combine with accessible texts to present a thorough (albeit busy) introduction to the history and current enterprise of spies and spying." Horn Book

Spies, double agents, and traitors. Enslow Publishers 2011 48p il (The secret world of spies) lib bdg $23.93

Grades: 4 5 6   **327.12**

1. Spies 2. Espionage
ISBN 978-0-7660-3711-3

LC 2010006178

Discusses double agents and traitors throughout history, such as Benedict Arnold, Dusan Popov, Kim Philby, and Robert Hanssen, and includes information on becoming a spy catcher (counterintelligence agent).

Includes glossary bibliographical references

Spy gizmos and gadgets. Enslow Publishers 2011 48p il (The secret world of spies) lib bdg $23.93

Grades: 4 5 6   **327.12**

1. Espionage 2. Electronic surveillance
ISBN 978-0-7660-3710-6

LC 2010006177

Discusses different gadgets used by spies, such as invisible ink, hidden cameras, small guns made to look like ordinary objects, and bugs, and includes career information.

Includes glossary and bibliographical references

327.1273   CIA (Intelligence agency)

Goodman, Michael E.

The **CIA** and other American spies; Michael E. Goodman. Creative Eduation 2012 48 p. ill. (Spies around the world) (library) $35.65

Grades: 6 7 8 9   **327.1273**

1. Intelligence service -- United States 2. United States -- Central Intelligence Agency 3. Espionage, American 4. Spies -- United States
ISBN 1608182266; 9781608182268

LC 2011035789

This book is part of the Spies Around the World series. "Focused more on the histories of spying organizations, each title looks at a different agency, making references to popular culture (e.g., the work of the CIA is compared to the 'Bourne' trilogy) and showing the difference between reality and movies. While not adding career how-to's, the volumes showcase famous spies from history, going back to the origins of each agency, as well as 'Tools of the Trade' and major cases." (School Library Journal)

Includes bibliographical references and index

330 Economics

Hlinka, Michael

Follow Your Money; Who Gets It, Who Spends It, Where Does It Go? by Kevin Sylvester and Michael Hlinka; illustrated by Kevin Sylvester. Annick Press 2013 56 p. col. ill. (paperback) $14.95; (hardcover) $24.95

Grades: 5 6 7 8   **330**
1. Pricing 2. Money
ISBN 1554514800; 1554514819; 9781554514809; 9781554514816

This book by Kevin Sylvester and Michael Hlinka answers the questions "what happens to your money after you hand it to the cashier? Who actually pockets it or puts it into the bank? Was the price you paid fair? Why do things cost what they do? Kids will also discover the trail their money takes through advertising, banks [and] charitable giving. [It is an] introduction to the . . .people and companies that we influence and are influenced by when we pay for a product or service." (Publisher's note)

Hollander, Barbara

Money matters; an introduction to economics. [by] Barbara Gottfried Hollander. Heinemann Library 2010 56p il map (The global marketplace) $33.50

Grades: 6 7 8 9   **330**
1. Money 2. Economics
ISBN 978-1-4329-3929-8; 1-4329-3929-7
LC 2010003996

This introduction to economics covers "a wealth of material in concise paragraphs with pertinent sub-headings. . . . [It includes] excellent photos, charts, maps, and tables that help with the understanding of some sophisticated concepts." SLJ
Includes glossary and bibliographical references

Outman, James L.

Industrial Revolution: biographies; [by] James L. Outman, Elisabeth M. Outman. U.X.L 2003 218p il (Industrial revolution reference library) $55

Grades: 8 9 10 11 12   **330**
1. Inventors 2. Industrial revolution 3. Capitalists and financiers 4. Industrialists 5. Industrial revolution 6. Inventors -- Biography 7. Industrialists -- Biography 8. Capitalists and financiers -- Biography
ISBN 0-7876-6514-2
LC 2002-155421

"The 25 essays in [this volume] provide biographical information with an emphasis on each person's contribution or impact on the Industrial Revolution. . . . More than 50 black-and-white photographs complement the text. . . . This is an excellent adjunct to American and world history units and classes on economics and labor movements." Booklist
Includes bibliographical references

The **Statesman's** Yearbook 2014; The Politics, Cultures and Economies of the World. edited by Barry Turner. 150th ed. Palgrave Macmillan 2013 1608 p. (hardcover) $325

Grades: 8 9 10 11 12 Adult   **330**
1. Almanacs 2. Geopolitics
ISBN 0230377696; 9780230377691

This reference book "presents a political, economic and social account of every country of the world together with facts and analysis. The 2014 edition includes revised and updated biographical profiles of all current leaders," "revised economic overviews for every country," and a "chronology of key political events from April 2010 to March 2011." (Publisher's note)

330.9 Economic situation and conditions

Arnold, James R.

The **industrial** revolution; [by] James R. Arnold and Roberta Weiner. Grolier 2005 10v il map set $299

Grades: 5 6 7 8   **330.9**
1. Reference books 2. Industrial revolution
ISBN 0-7172-6031-3
LC 2004-54243

"The Industrial Revolution spanned several centuries and continents, and this set covers developments and their impact in a well-organized fashion. . . . The set is copiously illustrated, with a variety of art reproductions, diagrams, and historical photographs. . . . With worldwide scope and coverage from the 18th century through the early 1900s, this is more comprehensive than single-volume histories, while the logical structure and appealing layout make it accessible to a wide range of students." SLJ
Includes glossary and bibliographical references

Brezina, Corona

America's recession; the effects of the economic downturn. Rosen Pub. 2011 64p il (Headlines!) lib bdg $29.25

Grades: 7 8 9 10   **330.9**
1. Recessions 2. Global Financial Crisis, 2008-2009 3. Economic policy -- United States
ISBN 978-1-4488-1296-7; 1-4488-1296-8
LC 2010016915

This "volume addresses the . . . topic of America's economic recession. Beginning with the housing boom that peaked in 2006, Brezina discusses predatory lending and other causes, then government efforts to combat recession. She also addresses topics such as foreclosure and unemployment, concluding with possible patterns of recovery. Good organization, clear writing, captioned photos, and sidebars deliver the information clearly." Horn Book Guide
Includes glossary and bibliographical references

Doak, Robin S.

Black Tuesday; prelude to the Great Depression. by Robin S. Doak. Compass Point Books 2008 96p il map (Snapshots in history) lib bdg $31.93

Grades: 6 7 8 9   **330.9**
1. Stock market crash, 1929 2. Great Depression, 1929-

1939
ISBN 978-0-7565-3327-4 lib bdg; 0-7565-3327-9
lib bdg

LC 2007004911

This "explains how the decade's economic boom and un-regulated markets created the speculative bubble that burst when the stock market crashed in 1929. Doak concludes that growing investor panic and inadequate government response to the crash contributed to the Great Depression. . . . [The text incorporates] primary-source material and [includes] numerous period photos and political cartoons." SLJ

Grant, R. G.

Why did the Great Depression happen? Gareth Stevens Pub. 2010 il map (Moments in history) lib bdg $31.95; pa $14.05

Grades: 6 7 8 9 **330.9**
1. Stock market crash, 1929 2. Great Depression, 1929-1939
ISBN 978-1-4339-4169-6 lib bdg; 1-4339-4169-4; 978-1-4339-4170-2 pa; 1-4339-4170-8 pa

LC 2010012461

This "explains the before, during and after of [the Great Depression] in a clear, unbiased manner. . . . Sidebars include meticulously cited eyewitness quotes or extra insight on particularly important events. Even more information is contained in the maps, period photographs, and well-placed captions that grace every page." SLJ

Includes glossary and bibliographical references

Heinrichs, Ann

★ The **great** recession. Children's Press 2011 il (Cornerstones of freedom) lib bdg $30; pa $8.95

Grades: 4 5 6 7 **330.9**
1. Recessions 2. Financial crises 3. Economic policy -- United States
ISBN 978-0-531-25035-8 lib bdg; 0-531-25035-0 lib bdg; 978-0-531-26560-4 pa; 0-531-26560-9 pa

LC 2011010824

This "offers simplified but not simplistic explanations of the current great recession's course and immediate causes. The . . . design has . . . visually stimulating pages that combine big color photos, boxed side essays, and blocks of large text with bright-red headers and highlights. In simple language and a judicious, matter-of-fact tone, Heinrichs describes the origins and growth of the housing bubble and the trade in mortgage-backed securities that magnified the effects of its eventual collapse; summarizes the federal government's palliative measures; surveys the effects of hard times on general patterns of living and spending; and notes the creation of a 'Generation R,' for whom high unemployment and financial insecurity are likely to become ways of life." Booklist

Includes bibliographical references

Lange, Brenda

The **Stock** Market Crash of 1929; the end of prosperity. [by] Brenda Lange. Chelsea House 2007 114p il (Milestones in American history) lib bdg $35

Grades: 7 8 9 10 **330.9**
1. Stock market crash, 1929 2. Great Depression, 1929-

1939
ISBN 0-7910-9354-9 lib bdg; 978-0-7910-9354-2 lib bdg

LC 2006038868

This describes the Stock Market Crash of October 29, 1929, also known as Black Tuesday, and its consequences.

This is "accessible, lively. . . . Many quotations, sidebars, art reproductions, and maps support the [text]. Excerpts from primary source materials also help give readers a sense of time and place." Horn Book Guide

Includes bibliographical references

Mooney, Carla

The **Industrial** Revolution; investigate how science and technology changed the world with 25 projects. illustrated by Jen Vaughn. Nomad Press 2011 120p il (Build it yourself) $21.95; pa $15.95

Grades: 4 5 6 7 **330.9**
1. Industrial revolution
ISBN 978-1-936313-81-5; 1-936313-81-2; 978-1-936313-80-8; 1-936313-80-4 pa

This "gives on overview of the era known as the Industrial Revolution as well as the consequences, good and bad, of each new development upon the average citizen. Topics covered include the transformation of textiles from home-spun to manufactured, the birth of labor unions, advances in transportation and communication, the inventions of Thomas Edison, and brief profiles of 'Captains of Industry,' such as Carnegie, Vanderbilt, and Rockefeller. Each chapter ends with enticing projects related to the topic. . . . The crisp, clear format, featuring ample black-and-white sketches and diagrams and pleasingly arranged type in a large font, is in sync with the straightforward text." Booklist

Outman, James L.

Industrial Revolution: almanac; [by] James L. Outman, Elisabeth M. Outman. U.X.L 2003 242p il (Industrial revolution reference library) $55

Grades: 8 9 10 11 12 **330.9**
1. Reference books 2. Industrial revolution
ISBN 0-7876-6513-4

LC 2002-155422

"This is an excellent adjunct to American and world history units and classes on economics and labor movements." Booklist

Includes bibliographical references

Industrial Revolution: primary sources; [by] James L. Outman, Elisabeth M. Outman. U.X.L 2003 212p il (Industrial revolution reference library) $55

Grades: 8 9 10 11 12 **330.9**
1. Reference books 2. Industrial revolution 3. Industrial revolution -- Sources
ISBN 0-7876-6515-0

LC 2002-155420

"This is an excellent adjunct to American and world history units and classes on economics and labor movements." Booklist

Includes bibliographical references

330.973   Economic conditions -- United States

Staton, Hilarie N.

The **Industrial** Revolution. Kingfisher 2012 32 p. ill. (some col.), col. maps

Grades: 3 4 5 6   **330.973**
1. Industrial revolution 2. United States -- History
ISBN 0753466708; 0753467127; 9780753466704; 9780753467121

This book is a "survey of the growth of industries in this country from the Colonial period to the post–World War II era." Also included are "narrative-overview blocks, boxed side observations and . . . captions" with "contemporary prints or . . . photos." Other "entries in the All About America series deal . . . with 'Explorers, Trappers, and Pioneers,' 'A Nation of Immigrants' and 'Stagecoaches and Railroads.'" (Kirkus)

Includes bibliographical references (p. 31) and index.

331.3   Labor force by personal attributes

Bartoletti, Susan Campbell

★ **Growing** up in coal country. Houghton Mifflin 1996 127p il $17; pa $7.95

Grades: 5 6 7 8   **331.3**
1. Child labor 2. Coal mines and mining 3. Immigrants 4. Coal miners 5. Pennsylvania -- History 6. Children -- Employment -- United States
ISBN 0-395-77847-6; 0-395-97914-5 pa

LC 96-3142

This is an "account of working and living conditions in Pennsylvania coal towns. The first half of the volume . . . {describes} various duties in the mines, from jobs performed by the youngest boys to the tasks of adult miners, while the second half describes the company village, common customs and recreational activities, and the accidents and diseases that frequently beset the workers. Preceding each chapter and within the text {are} quotes from personal interviews with miners, as well as taped interviews and transcripts." (Horn Book)

"With compelling black-and-white photographs of children at work in the coal mines of northeastern Pennsylvania about 100 years ago, this handsome, spacious photo-essay will draw browsers as well as students doing research on labor and immigrant history." Booklist

Includes bibliographical references

Burgan, Michael

★ **Breaker** boys; how a photograph helped end child labor. Compass Point Books 2011 64p il (Captured history) lib bdg $33.99; pa $8.95

Grades: 6 7 8 9   **331.3**
1. Photographers 2. Coal mines and mining 3. Documentary photography 4. Child labor -- United States
ISBN 978-0-7565-4439-3 lib bdg; 0-7565-4439-4; 978-0-7565-4510-9 pa; 0-7565-4510-2 pa

LC 2011003316

This book explains how Lewis Hine's photographs of children who worked in coal mines in Pennsylvania helped lead to the passage of child labor laws.

This "is model nonfiction. . . . The design is fresh and inviting, the writing clear, and the back matter . . . is useful and extensive. An all-around winner." Booklist

Includes glossary and bibliographical references

Chambers, Catherine

Living as a child laborer; Mehboob's story. by Catherine Chambers. World Almanac Library 2006 48p il (Children in crisis) lib bdg $30

Grades: 6 7 8 9   **331.3**
1. Poverty 2. Child labor
ISBN 0-8368-5958-8

LC 2005045250

This focuses on a young Indian boy named Mehboob subjected to child labor.

This includes "numerous full-color photographs. . . . The material is basically accurate, clearly written, and thought provoking." SLJ

Includes bibliographical references

Freedman, Russell

★ **Kids** at work; Lewis Hine and the crusade against child labor. with photographs by Lewis Hine. Clarion Bks. 1994 104p il $20; pa $9.95

Grades: 5 6 7 8   **331.3**
1. Child labor 2. Photographers 3. Children -- Employment 4. Labor -- United States 5. Documentary photography
ISBN 0-395-58703-4; 0-395-79726-8 pa

LC 93-5989

Freedman "does an outstanding job of integrating historical photographs with meticulously researched and highly readable prose." Publ Wkly

Includes bibliographical references

Gifford, Clive

Child labor. Smart Apple Media 2010 46p il (Voices) lib bdg $34.25

Grades: 7 8 9 10 11 12   **331.3**
1. Child labor
ISBN 978-1-59920-279-2 lib bdg; 1-59920-279-4 lib bdg

LC 2008-50429

The "text offers statistics, graphs, quotations (from politicians and scientists to children and laborers), and many photographs to make clear how . . . [child labor affects] the world today. An eye to how the issue affects young people— and how young people can help—is also a priority. . . . [This] book is quick to read and stocked with quotations and statistics that will assist in research as well as general interest." Voice Youth Advocates

Includes glossary and bibliographical references

331.4   Women workers

Colman, Penny

★ **Rosie** the riveter; women working on the home front in World War II. Crown 1995 120p il hardcover o.p. pa $10.99

Grades: 5 6 7 8   **331.4**
1. Women -- Employment   2. World War, 1939-1945 -- United States   3. World War, 1939-1945 -- Women 4. World War, 1939-1945 -- War work
ISBN 0-517-59790-X; 0-517-88567-0 pa

LC 94-3614

"A thoughtfully prepared look at women's history and wartime society, this dynamic book is characterized by extensive research." Horn Book
Includes bibliographical references

331.6   Workers by ethnic and national origin

Ouellette, Jeannine
A **day** without immigrants; rallying behind America's newcomers. by Jeannine Ouellette. Compass Point Books 2008 96p il map (Snapshots in history) $31.93
Grades: 6 7 8 9   **331.6**
1. Migrant labor   2. Illegal aliens   3. Immigrants -- United States
ISBN 978-0-7565-2498-2 lib bdg; 0-7565-2498-9 lib bdg

LC 2007004679

This book "uses the rallies of May 1, 2006 to address issues about immigration, both legal and illegal. . . . [This] volume includes a minimal glossary, a helpful time line, and suggestions for further reading." Voice Youth Advocates
Includes glossary and bibliographical references

331.7   Labor by industry and occupation

Barter, James
A **worker** on the transcontinental railroad. Lucent Bks. 2003 112p il map (Working life) $27.45
Grades: 6 7 8 9   **331.7**
1. Railroad engineering   2. Railroads -- History   3. Railroad construction workers -- History -- 19th century 4. Railroads -- United States -- History -- 19th century 5. Railroad construction workers -- United States -- History -- 19th century
ISBN 1-59018-247-2

LC 2002-9883

This presents a history of the construction of the Union Pacific and Central Pacific railroads focusing on the lives and labor of the construction workers
Includes bibliographical references

Farrell, Courtney
Green jobs. ABDO Pub. 2011 112p il (Inside the industry) lib bdg $34.22
Grades: 8 9 10 11 12   **331.7**
1. Occupations   2. Vocational guidance   3. Environmental protection
ISBN 978-1-61714-801-9; 1-61714-801-6

LC 2010039122

"This book contains an interesting overview of jobs that fall beneath the 'green' umbrella. Farrell writes in clear prose about the wide range of career opportunities that stu-

dents with environmental interests can pursue. She focuses on four fields: green architect, organic farmer, professional conservationist, and alternative-energy expert." SLJ
Includes glossary and bibliographical references

Hopkinson, Deborah
★ **Up** before daybreak; cotton and people in America. Scholastic Nonfiction 2005 120p il $18.99
Grades: 5 6 7 8   **331.7**
1. Cotton   2. Working class   3. Textile industry   4. Textile industry -- History   5. Cotton trade   7. Cotton growing 8. Cotton picking 9. Slavery -- United States
ISBN 0-439-63901-8

LC 2005-8128

"From the industrial revolution to the 1950s demise of the Lowell cotton mills, Hopkinson discusses the history and sociology of king cotton, frequently emphasizing the children who labored under slave masters, endured dead-end mill jobs, or helped sharecropping parents claw out a living. . . . Stories of real people . . . sharply focus the dramatic history, as do arresting archival photos of stern youngsters manipulating hoes, cotton sags, or bobbins." Booklist

J.G. Ferguson Publishing Company
Encyclopedia of careers and vocational guidance; 15th ed.; Ferguson 2010 5v il set $249.95
Grades: 8 9 10 11 12 Adult   **331.7**
1. Reference books   2. Occupations -- Encyclopedias   3. Vocational guidance -- Encyclopedias
ISBN 978-0-8160-8313-8; 0-8160-8313-4

LC 2010-17724

First published 1967
"These five volumes contain more than 700 . . . [articles] on careers in nearly 100 industries. Each three to five-page entry provides a concise and engaging profile of fields like accounting, animal care, computers, the environment, publishing, sales, and the visual arts. Included in each job entry are an overview, a history, a description, requirements, employers, advancement, earnings, work environment, outlook, and more." Libr J [review of 2008 edition]
Includes bibliographical references

United States/Dept. of Labor
Young person's occupational outlook handbook; 5th ed; Jist Works 2005 319p il $19.95
Grades: 6 7 8 9   **331.7**
1. Occupations   2. Reference books   3. Vocational guidance
ISBN 1-59357-125-9

LC 2004-13091

This "career reference includes 277 jobs employing 88 percent of the workforce. . . . Each entry includes a short description of duties and working conditions; suggested academic preparation; hands-on activites simulating actual job aspects; related personal habits and preferences or sources for further investigation; and additional related jobs. . . . The book is a strong starting point for student research." Voice Youth Advocates

331.702   Choice of vocation

Loy, Jessica

    When I grow up; a young person's guide to interesting & unusual occupations. Jessica Loy. Holt 2008 37 p. $16.95

Grades: 4 5 6   **331.702**
    1. Vocational guidance
    ISBN 0805077170; 9780805077179
                        LC 2007938930

    This juvenile book, by Jessica Loy, explores fourteen unusual professional careers. "What do you want to be when you grow up? Consider all your options. How about being a game designer. . . ? Or, if you like chocolate, you could become a chocolatier. . . . The choices are endless. So come read about . . . unusual and satisfying work. . . . Maybe some of these career paths will inspire ideas of your own." (Publisher's note)
    Includes bibliographical references

331.8   Labor unions, labor-management bargaining and disputes

Baker, Julie

    The **Bread** and Roses strike of 1912. Morgan Reynolds Pub. 2007 160p il (American workers) $27.95

Grades: 6 7 8 9 10   **331.8**
    1. Strikes 2. Textile industry -- History
    ISBN 978-1-59935-044-8; 1-59935-044-0
                        LC 2006101826

    A history of the 1912 strike of textile workers in Lawrence, Massachusetts.
    "Baker's style is readable, and the well-chosen, well-reproduced photos make the subject all the more real." SLJ
    Includes bibliographical references

Laughlin, Rosemary

    The **Ludlow** massacre of 1913-14; [by] Rosemary Laughlin. 1st ed.; Morgan Reynolds Pub. 2006 144p il (American workers) lib bdg $27.95

Grades: 6 7 8 9   **331.8**
    1. Strikes 2. Coal mines and mining 3. Labor movement -- History
    ISBN 978-1-931798-86-0; 1-931798-86-9
                        LC 2005030050

    "In the autumn of 1913, coal miners working for the Colorado Fuel and Iron Company walked off the job, demanding recognition of their union. This . . . chronicles the long strike that frequently erupted into armed combat between the Colorado state militia and the miners. Vivid portraits are presented of the protagonists in the struggle. . . . Laughlin presents the facts with a storyteller's flair, supplemented by frequent quotes, period photographs, and engravings that show what life was like for the miners." Booklist
    Includes bibliographical references

    The **Pullman** strike of 1894; [by] Rosemary Laughlin. Morgan Reynolds Pub. 2006 144p il (American workers) lib bdg $27.95

Grades: 6 7 8 9   **331.8**
    1. Strikes 2. Labor movement 3. Railroads -- History 4. Labor movement -- History
    ISBN 978-1-931798-89-1; 1-931798-89-3
                        LC 2005028637

    First published 2000 in the series Great events

    This "tells the story of the strike and explains its long-term effects on the labor movement and the nation. The author examines the arguments made by labor and management and explains how the strike affected all of those involved. . . . [This is] a good choice for report material on industrialization, labor history, or the Gilded Age." SLJ
    Includes bibliographical references

Skurzynski, Gloria

    Sweat and blood; a history of U.S. labor unions. Twenty-First Century Books 2008 112p il (People's history) lib bdg $31.93

Grades: 7 8 9 10   **331.8**
    1. Labor unions 2. Working class
    ISBN 978-0-8225-7594-8; 0-8225-7594-9
                        LC 2007-50270

    This "begins with the roots of unionization in colonial America, cruises through the frenzy of industrialization in the twentieth century, and ends in the present day. . . . The period prints and photographs are well chosen to highlight and comment on the text. Classes studying any part of the industrial or social history of this country will be well served by this valuable resource." Booklist
    Includes bibliographical references

Whitelaw, Nancy

    The **Homestead** Steel Strike of 1892; [by] Nancy Whitelaw. 1st ed.; Morgan Reynolds Pub. 2006 144p il (American workers) lib bdg $27.95

Grades: 6 7 8 9   **331.8**
    1. Strikes 2. Steel industry 3. Philanthropists 4. Homestead Strike, 1892 5. Art collectors 6. Labor movement -- History 7. Metal industry executives
    ISBN 978-1-931798-88-4; 1-931798-88-5
                        LC 2005027113

    This is the story of the 1892 strike against the Homestead Steel company owned by Andrew Carnegie and Henry Clay Frick which led to bloodshed and a breaking of the union.
    "This is a riveting story told in 11 well-written, lively chapters, with well-placed, good-quality reproductions and drawings throughout the text." SLJ
    Includes bibliographical references

331.892   Strikes

Bartoletti, Susan Campbell

    ★ **Kids** on strike! Houghton Mifflin 1999 208p il $20; pa $8.95

Grades: 5 6 7 8   **331.892**
    1. Strikes 2. Child labor 3. Centenarians 4. Labor leaders 5. Child labor -- History 6. Strikes and lockouts -- History 7. Child labor -- United States -- History 8.

Strikes and lockouts -- United States -- History
ISBN 0-395-88892-1; 0-618-36923-6 pa

LC 98-50575

Describes the conditions and treatment that drove workers, including many children, to various strikes, from the mill workers strikes in 1828 and 1836 and the coal strikes at the turn of the century to the work of Mother Jones on behalf of child workers

"This well-researched and well-illustrated account creates a vivid portrait of the working conditions of many American children in the 19th and early 20th centuries." SLJ

Includes bibliographical references

332.024   Personal finance

Blatt, Jessica

The **teen** girl's gotta-have-it guide to money; getting smart about making it, saving it, and spending it. by Jessica Blatt with Variny Paladino; illustrated by Cynthia Frenette. Watson-Guptill Publications 2008 96p il pa $8.95

Grades: 7 8 9 10   **332.024**
1. Personal finance 2. Teenagers -- Employment
ISBN 978-0-8230-1727-0; 0-8230-1727-3

LC 2007-25948

Explains to teenage girls how to budget their money, save, invest and create business plans.

"This is a great little reference guide for teenage girls to peruse and learn about money matters. . . . This is an important addition to any collection." KLIATT

Bochner, Rose

The **new** totally awesome money book for kids (and their parents) [by] Arthur Bochner & Rose Bochner; foreword by Adriane G. Berg. 3rd ed., rev & updated.; Newmarket Press 2007 189p il pa $9.95

Grades: 4 5 6 7   **332.024**
1. Personal finance
ISBN 978-1-55704-738-0

LC 2006038930

First published 1993 with title: The totally awesome money book for kids (and their parents)

An introduction to money for kids including the basics of saving, investing, working, and taxes.

"Using an easy and comfortable style that young people will find unthreatening, the book presents a wealth of information. . . . The cute illustrations are also fun." Voice Youth Advocates

Includes bibliographical references

Bostick, Nan

Managing Money. Saddleback Educational Pub. 2012 120 p. ill. $16.95

Grades: 8 9 10 11 12   **332.024**
1. Life skills 2. Banks and banking 3. Household budgets 4. Teenagers -- Personal finance 5. Economics -- Handbooks, manuals, etc. 6. Adult education 7. Finance, Personal 8. Life skills--Handbooks, manuals,

etc.
ISBN 1616516593; 9781616516598

This book is a part of the "Life Skills Handbooks" series. "With the text split into four main topics—controlling your spending, banking basics, buying now and paying later, and improving your budgeting skills—young adults get a comprehensive look at the world of personal finance. . . . When it comes to sticking to a budget, teens are encouraged to keep their needs and wants in sharp focus. There's even a chapter devoted to unexpected purchases and variable spending. . . . There are also helpful hints for paying those expenses without credit cards. Credit-card debt, loans, and spending more than one earns are issues that are addressed . . . . Basic advice, such as how to write out a check and read a bank statement, is included." (Booklist) Index.

Chatzky, Jean

Not your parents' money book; making, saving, and spending your own money. [by Jean Sherman Chatzky]; illustrated by Erwin Haya. Simon & Schuster Books for Young Readers 2010 162p il pa $12.99

Grades: 5 6 7 8   **332.024**
1. Money 2. Personal finance
ISBN 978-1-4169-9472-5 pa; 1-4169-9472-6 pa

LC 2010008840

"Written in a light, somewhat jocular tone and sprinkled with amusing but eye-opening and conversation-starting quotes from 12, 13, and 14-year-olds, this book is sure to hold readers' attention. The content includes how you get money, via allowances and jobs, and notes the difference between cash-only and paychecks. Tracking typical teen expenditures, both long-term and short, is juxtaposed against keeping money in checking, savings, and money-market accounts. . . . Chatzky's presentation is engaging. . . . Cartoons appear on almost every page, adding humor and some additional material." SLJ

Includes bibliographical references

Hall, Alvin

★ **Show** me the money; [by] Alvin Hall. DK 2008 96p il $15.99

Grades: 4 5 6   **332.024**
1. Money 2. Personal finance
ISBN 978-0-7566-3762-0; 0-7566-3762-7

"Four main sections cover the history of money, expenses/income, the basics of economics, and the world of work and business. Brief profiles of eight wealthy entrepreneurs and their paths to prosperity and eight significant economists and their theories are included. The lively writing features real-life examples that will be meaningful to students and is presented in a balanced, nonjudgmental style that encourages them to decide for themselves among the various ideas concerning economic policies. . . . Color photos and graphics excel at conveying the concepts presented and represent diversity well." SLJ

Includes glossary

Holyoke, Nancy

A **smart** girl's guide to money; how to make it, save it, and spend it. illustrated by Ali Douglass. Pleasant Co. 2006 95p il pa $9.95

Grades: 4 5 6 7   332.024
1. Personal finance 2. Money
ISBN 1-59369-103-3

This "offers advice on earning, saving, and spending money. Holyoke addresses topics such as feelings about money, launching a business, becoming a smart shopper, and investing. . . . The text is upbeat and informal. . . . This book is an engaging introduction to personal economics." Booklist

Morrison, Jessica

Saving. Weigl Publishers 2009 32p il (Everyday economics) lib bdg $26; pa $9.95

Grades: 5 6 7   332.024
1. Saving and investment
ISBN 978-1-60596-647-2 lib bdg; 1-60596-647-9 lib bdg; 978-1-60596-648-9 pa; 1-60596-648-7 pa
LC 2009018567

This "informative [book introduces savings in] U.S. economic theory and practices using everyday language and real-life examples. [It] includes history, a brief annotated chronology, sidebar and intext explanations of terminology, and helpful diagrams. . . . With brief paragraphs; large, captioned photographs; ample margins; and well-organized graphics, the [book's] design makes economics accessible without sacrificing content. . . . [This is] easy to navigate and full of solid information and interesting facts." SLJ
Includes glossary

Peterson, Judy Monroe

First budget smarts. Rosen Pub. 2010 64p il (Get smart with your money) lib bdg $29.95; pa $12.95

Grades: 7 8 9 10 11 12   332.024
1. Personal finance 2. Household budgets 3. Budget
ISBN 978-1-4358-5273-0 lib bdg; 1-4358-5273-7 lib bdg; 978-1-4358-5552-6 pa; 1-4358-5552-3 pa
LC 2008-40549

This book offers advice on budgeting for teens, with examples of such expenses as music downloads, pizza, and gas.
This offers "practical information and advice. . . . The writing is accessible. . . . The [book is] heavily illustrated with large, clear, up-to-date photographs of teens." SLJ
Includes glossary and bibliographical references

Roderick, Stacey

Centsibility; the Planet Girl guide to money. [by] Stacey Roderick and Ellen Warwick; illustrated by Monika Melnychuk. Kids Can Press 2008 80p il (Planet girl) $12.95

Grades: 5 6 7 8   332.024
1. Personal finance 2. Money
ISBN 978-1-55453-208-7

"This book presents handy methods for managing money. . . . Chapters are broken down into subsections . . . which are peppered with quizzes and craft projects to keep readers engaged. . . . The book's sound advice is both practical and approachable." Horn Book Guide

Wiseman, Blaine

Budgeting. Weigl Publishers 2009 32p il (Everyday economics) lib bdg $26; pa $9.95

Grades: 5 6 7   332.024
1. Budget
ISBN 978-1-60596-643-4 lib bdg; 1-60596-643-6 lib bdg; 978-1-60596-644-1 pa; 1-60596-644-4 pa
LC 2009018439

This "informative [book introduces budgeting in] U.S. economic theory and practices using everyday language and real-life examples. [It] includes history, a brief annotated chronology, sidebar and intext explanations of terminology, and helpful diagrams. . . . With brief paragraphs; large, captioned photographs; ample margins; and well-organized graphics, the [book's] design makes economics accessible without sacrificing content. . . . [This is] easy to navigate and full of solid information and interesting facts." SLJ
Includes glossary

332.1   Banks

Casil, Amy Sterling

Why banks fail. Rosen Pub. 2011 80p il (Real world economics) lib bdg $30.60

Grades: 7 8 9 10   332.1
1. Bank failures 2. Banks and banking
ISBN 978-1-4358-9462-4; 1-4358-9462-6
LC 2009041635

This "is fascinating, well written, and accessible. The primary focus is our recent sub-prime mortgage debacle and how these mortgages alone caused the massive bank failures around the world of the last decade. This text is lucid and keeps such concepts as 'contagious' bank runs and 'cascading' bank failures easy for students to understand." SLJ
Includes glossary and bibliographical references

Connolly, Sean

Banks and banking. Amicus 2010 46p il (World economy explained) lib bdg $34.25

Grades: 7 8 9 10   332.1
1. Financial crises 2. Banks and banking
ISBN 978-1-60753-077-0 lib bdg; 1-60753-077-5 lib bdg
LC 2009021077

"Complex concepts like lending, earning, and charging interest are presented simply and with clear examples. Lively photos and 'Personal Account' asides bring home the ramifications for individuals of big-bank collapses." SLJ
Includes glossary and bibliographical references

Fischer, James

Banking basics. Mason Crest Publishers 2010 64p il (Junior library of money) $22.95; pa $9.95

Grades: 6 7 8 9   332.1
1. Banks and banking
ISBN 978-1-4222-1761-0; 1-4222-1761-2; 978-1-4222-1880-8 pa; 1-4222-1880-5 pa
LC 2010021814

This offers a history of banking and describes how banks operate.
This title presents "solid information and [has] eye-catching and relevant illustrations. . . . [The book is] clearly

written, making understandable connections between daily life and financial concepts." SLJ
Includes glossary and bibliographical references

332.4 Money

Brezina, Corona
How deflation works. Rosen Pub. 2011 80p il (Real world economics) lib bdg $30.60
Grades: 7 8 9 10   **332.4**
 1. Deflation (Finance)
 ISBN 978-1-4358-9465-5; 1-4358-9465-0
                                    LC 2009045292
This "discusses the possible correlations between a recession and deflation, expanding at length about why deflation, expanding at length about why deflation is ultimately unhealthy for the economy." SLJ
Includes bibliographical references

Cribb, Joe
 ★ **Money**; written by Joe Cribb. rev ed; DK Pub. 2005 72p il (DK eyewitness books) lib bdg $15.99
Grades: 4 5 6 7   **332.4**
 1. Money
 ISBN 0-7566-1389-2
 First published 1990 by Knopf
Examines, in text and photographs, the symbolic and material meaning of money, from shekels, shells, and beads to gold, silver, checks, and credit cards. Also discusses how coins and banknotes are made, the value of money during wartime, and how to collect coins

Simons, Rae
 All about money; the history, culture, and meaning of modern finance. Mason Crest Publishers 2010 64p il $22.95; pa $9.95
Grades: 6 7 8 9   **332.4**
 1. Money 2. Economics
 ISBN 978-1-4222-1760-3; 1-4222-1760-4; 978-1-4222-1879-2 pa; 1-4222-1879-1 pa
                                    LC 2010021818
This describes the history currency and how money is used in various economic systems.
This title presents "solid information and [has] eye-catching and relevant illustrations. . . . [The book is] clearly written, making understandable connections between daily life and financial concepts." SLJ
Includes glossary and bibliographical references

332.6 Investment

Connolly, Sean
 The **stock** market. Amicus 2010 46p il (World economy explained) lib bdg $34.25
Grades: 7 8 9 10   **332.6**
 1. Stocks 2. Stock exchanges 3. Financial crises
 ISBN 978-1-60753-082-4; 1-60753-082-4
                                    LC 2009-29073

"Explains the functions and history of the Stock Market and its involvement with the 2007 credit crunch." Publisher's note
Includes glossary

Furgang, Kathy
 How the stock market works. Rosen Pub. 2011 80p il (Real world economics) lib bdg $30.60
Grades: 7 8 9 10   **332.6**
 1. Stocks 2. Stock exchanges
 ISBN 978-1-4358-9466-2; 1-4358-9466-9
                                    LC 2009045687
This "includes a history of Wall Street and discusses the ups and downs of the stock market and its impact on people's everyday lives in a general and accessible manner for students." SLJ
Includes glossary and bibliographical references

Healey, Aaron
 Making the trade; stocks, bonds, and other investments. Heinemann Library 2011 56p il (The global marketplace) lib bdg $33.50
Grades: 6 7 8 9   **332.6**
 1. Investments 2. Stock exchanges 3. Saving and investment
 ISBN 978-1-4329-3931-1; 1-4329-3931-9
                                    LC 2010004094
This title covers "a wealth of material in concise paragraphs with pertinent subheadings. . . . [The book] reinforces the concept of balancing stock investments with an umbrella-versus-suntan-lotion example that has the great subtext of suggesting stock investment can be as risky as the weather." SLJ
Includes glossary and bibliographical references

Morrison, Jessica
 Investing. Weigl Publishers 2009 32p il (Everyday economics) lib bdg $26; pa $9.95
Grades: 5 6 7   **332.6**
 1. Investments
 ISBN 978-1-60596-649-6 lib bdg; 1-60596-649-5 lib bdg; 978-1-60596-650-2 pa; 1-60596-650-9 pa
                                    LC 2009018568
This explains the advantages of investing money, how to read a stock report, interest, and the types of investments provided by different companies.
This "informative [book introduces] U.S. economic theory and practices using everyday language and real-life examples. . . . [This is] easy to navigate and full of solid information and interesting facts." SLJ
Includes glossary

Thompson, Helen
 Investing money. Mason Crest Publishers 2010 64p il (Junior library of money) $22.95; pa $9.95
Grades: 6 7 8 9   **332.6**
 1. Money 2. Personal finance 3. Saving and investment
 ISBN 978-1-4222-1766-5; 1-4222-1766-3; 978-1-4222-1885-3 pa; 1-4222-1885-6 pa
                                    LC 2010027815
This title presents "solid information and [has] eye-catching and relevant illustrations. . . . Investing Money

includes a 'risk/reward' pyramid and touches on diversified investments with a nice piggy-bank analogy about hiding your full piggy banks in different spots around the house in case of disaster or theft. . . . [The book is] clearly written, making understandable connections between daily life and financial concepts." SLJ

Includes glossary and bibliographical references

Understanding the stock market. Mason Crest Publishers 2010 64p il (Junior library of money) $22.95; pa $9.95

Grades: 6 7 8 9   **332.6**
     1. Investments 2. Stock exchanges
     ISBN 978-1-4222-1773-3; 1-4222-1773-6; 978-1-4222-1892-1 pa; 1-4222-1892-9 pa
                   LC 2010028431

This is an introduction to how the stock market works, including concepts such as shares, investing, The Dow Jones Industrial Average, bull markets and bear markets, and the stock market's effect on the economy.

This title presents "solid information and [has] eye-catching and relevant illustrations. . . . [It is] clearly written, making understandable connections between daily life and financial concepts." SLJ

Includes glossary and bibliographical references

332.64   Exchange of securities and commodities; speculation

Blumenthal, Karen

     Six days in October; the stock market crash of 1929. Atheneum Bks. for Young Readers 2002 156p il $17.95

Grades: 7 8 9 10   **332.64**
     1. Great Depression, 1929-1939 2. Stock Market Crash, 1929
     ISBN 0-689-84276-7
                   LC 2001-46360

A comprehensive review of the events, personalities, and mistakes behind the Stock Market Crash of 1929, featuring photographs, newspaper articles, and cartoons of the day

"This fast-paced, gripping . . . account of the market crash of October 1929 puts a human face on the crisis." Publ Wkly

Includes bibliographical references

332.7   Credit

Byers, Ann

     First credit cards and credit smarts. Rosen Pub. 2010 64p il (Get smart with your money) lib bdg $29.95; pa $12.95

Grades: 7 8 9 10 11 12   **332.7**
     1. Credit cards 2. Consumer credit
     ISBN 978-1-4358-5271-6 lib bdg; 1-4358-5271-0 lib bdg; 978-1-4358-5548-9 pa; 1-4358-5548-5 pa
                   LC 2008-54969

This offers advice on managing credit, including topics such as credit scores, interest, and money management.

This offers "practical information and advice. The writing is accessible. . . . [The book is] heavily illsutrated with large, clear, up-to-date photographs of teens." SLJ

Includes glossary and bibliographical references

Tomljanovic, Tatiana

     Borrowing. Weigl Pubs. 2009 32p il (Everyday economics) lib bdg $26; pa $9.95

Grades: 5 6 7   **332.7**
     1. Credit
     ISBN 978-1-60596-645-8 lib bdg; 1-60596-645-2 lib bdg; 978-1-60596-646-5 pa; 1-60596-646-0 pa
                   LC 2009018444

This "informative [book introduces borrowing in] U.S. economic theory and practices using everyday language and real-life examples. [It] includes history, a brief annotated chronology, sidebar and intext explanations of terminology, and helpful diagrams. . . . With brief paragraphs; large, captioned photographs; ample margins; and well-organized graphics, the [book's] design makes economics accessible without sacrificing content. . . . [This is] easy to navigate and full of solid information and interesting facts." SLJ

Includes glossary

333.7   Natural resources and energy

Cunningham, Kevin

     Soil. Morgan Reynolds Pub. 2010 111p il (Diminishing resources) $28.95

Grades: 8 9 10 11 12   **333.7**
     1. Soils 2. Soil conservation
     ISBN 978-1-59935-114-8; 1-59935-114-5
                   LC 2009-10487

"The first chapter of Soil discusses how depletion of this resource began as far back as the Neolithic age, and the book continues through time, closing with today's efforts to conserve soil in places such as Iceland. In addition to being great research resources, [this title is] interesting enough for pleasure reading. [It contains] beautiful, full-page photographs, as well as a helpful time line." SLJ

Includes bibliographical references

Gazlay, Suzy

     Managing green spaces; careers in wilderness and wildlife management. Crabtree 2010 64p il (Green-collar careers) lib bdg $30.60; pa $10.95

Grades: 4 5 6 7   **333.7**
     1. Wildlife 2. Wilderness areas 3. Vocational guidance 4. Conservation of natural resources 5. Environmental protection -- Vocational guidance
     ISBN 978-0-7787-4855-7 lib bdg; 0-7787-4855-3 lib bdg; 978-0-7787-4866-3 pa; 0-7787-4866-9 pa
                   LC 2009-28145

"Passions often lead to professions, as this upbeat title . . . shows. . . . There is inevitable overlap among the categories: government-run parks and forestry, outdoor adventure, science, and wildlife sanctuaries. The browsable format, combining many crisp color photos with blocks of narrative texts and sidebars featuring specific ecoprofessionals, will easily lead students through the survey of nature-focused careers." Booklist

Rockliff, Mara

★ **Get** real. Running Press 2010 112p il pa $10.95

Grades: 6 7 8 9 10   **333.7**
1. Consumer education 2. Consumption (Economics)
ISBN 978-0-7624-3745-0; 0-7624-3745-6

This book "points out plenty of practical ways for kids to impact their world by making different choices about what food to eat, what clothes to wear, how often to replace a cell phone, and more. . . . Nicely designed, the book has colorful graphic elements on many pages, including photographs and eye-catching digital images incorporating photos. . . . A clearly written guide for reader who want to translate social and environmental awareness into action." Booklist
Includes filmography and bibliographical references

Conserving the environment; John Woodward and Jennifer Skancke, book editors. Greenhaven Press 2007 248p il (Current controversies) lib bdg $32.20; pa $24.95

Grades: 7 8 9 10 11 12   **333.7**
1. Environmental protection 2. Biological diversity
ISBN 978-0-7377-2476-9 lib bdg; 0-7377-2476-5 lib bdg; 978-0-7377-2477-6 pa; 0-7377-2477-3 pa
LC 2005055071

"This volume examines the degree to which the environment is in jeopardy, whether global warming should be addressed, the role of the government vis-à-vis conservation, and how society can protect the environment. The first two chapters present affirmative and negative responsive essays. Chapters three and four invoke timely topics such as the Clear Skies Act, drilling in the Arctic National Wildlife Refuge, renewal of the Endangered Species Act, the cost of renewable energy, organic farming, and fuel-efficient vehicles vs. SUVs. . . . The essays are accessible, divided into subtopics, and useful for reports and debates." SLJ
Includes bibliographical references

333.72   Conservation and protection

Bailey, Jacqui

What's the point of being green? [illustrated by Jan McCafferty] Barron's Educational Series 2010 96p il map pa $12.99

Grades: 4 5 6 7   **333.72**
1. Environmental movement 2. Environmental protection
ISBN 978-0-7641-4427-1 pa; 0-7641-4427-8 pa

"This colorful book outlines in lively, conversational prose the reasons that kids should be concerned about the future of our planet. Each short chapter covers different environmental challenges and discusses ways that children can work toward improving the situation. . . . A cartoon teen appears on each page and directly addresses readers. There are also ample color photos and diagrams. The layout is dynamic with text and illustrations placed at odd angles and in a variety of bold fonts. Kids will find this book incredibly informational, fun to read, and full of great ideas." SLJ
Includes bibliographical references

Dell, Pamela

Protecting the planet; environmental activism. Compass Point Books 2010 64p il (Green generation) lib bdg $31.99; pa $6.95

Grades: 5 6 7 8 9   **333.72**
1. Environmental movement 2. Environmental protection
ISBN 978-0-7565-4248-1 lib bdg; 0-7565-4248-0 lib bdg; 978-0-7565-4295-5 pa; 0-7565-4295-2 pa
LC 2009-8782

"The cover design, layout, and graphics feel hip and of the moment. The clear writing is easy to understand and includes many concrete examples of environmentally friendly practices. . . . [A] good choice[s] for both leisure reading and reports." SLJ
Includes glossary and bibliographical references

Fuoco, Gina Dal

Earth. Compass Point Books 2009 40p il (Mission: science) lib bdg $26.60

Grades: 4 5 6   **333.72**
ISBN 978-0-7565-4070-8 lib bdg; 0-7565-4070-4 lib bdg
LC 2008-37575

Discusses the basic parts systems (atmosphere, hydrosphere, and geosphere) of Earth and how important it is to protect Earth's resources
Includes glossary

The **green** movement; Debra A. Miller, book editor. Greenhaven Press 2010 219p (Current controversies) lib bdg $39.70; pa $27.50

Grades: 7 8 9 10   **333.72**
1. Environmental movement
ISBN 978-0-7377-4913-7 lib bdg; 0-7377-4913-X lib bdg; 978-0-7377-4914-4 pa; 0-7377-4914-8 pa
LC 2010003354

"This book presents varying opinions concerning the [green] movement. Proponents view green efforts as necessary to guarantee a sustainable future and advocate for current change in this direction. . . . Opponents view these opinions as merely hype and offer counter perspectives. Readers are given a balanced view of the subject through pro and con arguments presented in a question-and-response format. . . . A useful purchase for school and public libraries." SLJ
Includes bibliographical references

Green, Jen

Conservation; Jen Green. Heinemann Library 2012 64 p. (The impact of environmentalism) (hb) $35

Grades: 6 7 8   **333.72**
1. Environmental movement 2. Biodiversity conservation 3. Conservation of natural resources 4. Environmentalism 5. Conservation of natural resources
ISBN 1432965166; 9781432965167; 9781432965228
LC 2012000824

This book by Jen Green is part of the series "The Impact of Environmentalism". It "addresses biodiversity and efforts to assist endangered animals" and "looks at the way changing ideas about the environment and sustainability have affected our attitudes to conservation, and will do so in the future." (Booklist)

Includes bibliographical references and index.

Hirshfield, Lynn

Girls gone green. Puffin Books 2010 192p il pa $11.99

Grades: 6 7 8 9 10   **333.72**

1. Social action 2. Environmental movement 3. Environmental protection

ISBN 978-0-14-241406-4 pa; 0-14-241406-9 pa

"This volume is packed with ideas and suggestions for living green. Chapters describe the work of beauty entrepreneurs, animal-rights advocates, educators, artists, grocers, scientists, and engineers. Women and girls of various backgrounds share their stories of how they are making the world a better place. . . . Bright colors and copious photographs highlight the lively layout." SLJ

Includes bibliographical references

Kelsey, Elin

★ **Not** your typical book about the environment; illustrated by Clayton Hammer. Owlkids 2010 64p il $22.95; pa $10.95

Grades: 4 5 6 7   **333.72**

1. Environmental protection 2. Ecology 3. Sustainable living

ISBN 978-1-897349-79-3; 1-897349-79-3; 978-1-897349-84-7 pa; 1-897349-84-X pa

Written to allay children's fears about the environment, this book shows how smart technologies, innovative ideas, and a growing commitment to alternative lifestyles are exploding around the world, creating a future that will be brighter than we sometimes might think. Includes profiles of unexpected personalities.

"Imaginative, comic-booklike illustrations add to a lively layout that will keep readers moving from one paragraph to the next, and funny wordplay prevents the facts from becoming overwhelming or dry. . . . This hilarious, information-packed work is an excellent addition." SLJ

Kriesberg, Daniel A.

Think green, take action; books and activities for kids. illustrated by Kathleen A. Price. Libraries Unlimited 2010 136p il pa $30; e-book $30

Grades: Adult Professional   **333.72**

1. Environmental sciences -- Study and teaching 2. Environmental sciences

ISBN 978-1-59884-378-1 pa; 1-59884-378-8 pa; 978-1-59884-379-8 e-book

LC 2010014409

"A resource for teaching environmental understanding and activism through stewardship, this book outlines teaching strategies for ages 6-10, provides resources for understanding environmental concerns for ages 10-13, and promotes action and growth for ages 13+. Chapters focus on local ecology, endangered species, resource depletion, and pollution. Extensive annotated bibliographies of both recent and older fiction and nonfiction selections . . . supplement the activities." SLJ

Includes bibliographical references

Leardi, Jeanette

Making cities green. Bearport Pub. 2009 32p il (Going green) lib bdg $25.27

Grades: 4 5 6 7   **333.72**

1. Urban ecology 2. Renewable energy resources

ISBN 978-1-59716-961-5 lib bdg; 1-59716-961-7 lib bdg

LC 2009-19166

"Color photographs (most full page) and a few diagrams accompany the informative text[s]. . . . Overall, the [book] . . . is user-friendly and covers topics that are not easily found elsewhere." SLJ

Includes glossary and bibliographical references

McKay, Kim

True green kids; 100 things you can do to save the planet. [by] Kim McKay and Jenny Bonnin. National Geographic 2008 143p il $15.95

Grades: 4 5 6 7   **333.72**

1. Environmental protection 2. Environmentalism 3. Recycling (Waste, etc.) 4. Environmental responsibility 4. Conservation of natural resources

ISBN 978-1-4263-0442-2; 1-4263-0442-0

Presents an overview of global warming and describes 100 simple ways to be more environmentally friendly in the bedroom, in the house, at school, and on vacation.

"Accompanied by attractive, up-to-date pictures in a lively design, the one hundred suggestions are direct . . . and generally practical." Horn Book Guide

Includes glossary

Molland, Judy

Get out! 150 easy ways for kids & grown-ups to get into nature and build a greener future. Free Spirit Pub. 2009 119p il pa $10.99

Grades: 5 6 7 8   **333.72**

1. Environmental movement 2. Environmental protection

ISBN 978-1-57542-335-7 pa; 1-57542-335-9 pa

LC 2009017352

"This handy reference book is filled with nifty ideas to live green and save the Earth. . . . The 150 ideas are simple and direct. Suggestions range from recycling bottles and shoes, to toy exchanges, to building owl and bat boxes. This book can be used by classroom teachers across the curriculum as a source for activities and is sure to inspire budding environmentalists." SLJ

Nagle, Jeanne

Living green; [by] Jeanne Nagle. Rosen Pub. 2009 64p il (In the news) lib bdg $21.95

Grades: 7 8 9 10   **333.72**

1. Environmental protection

ISBN 978-1-43585037-8; 1-435-85037-8

"Accessible and up-to-date. . . . Living Green presents theories of climate change and short biographies of green pioneers before examining the role of government and NGOs in environmental protection, as well as basic, earth-friendly lifestyle changes that individuals can make. Throughout, Nagle addresses the controversies that surround issues, encouraging readers to take a wide, nuanced view." Booklist

Petronis, Lexi

47 things you can do for the environment. Zest 2011 128p il pa $10.99

Grades: 6 7 8 9   **333.72**

1. Environmental protection

ISBN 978-0-9827322-1-2; 0-9827322-1-X

"Divided into categories revolving around habits at home, school, in the community, or on the road, [this book] offers such suggestions as shopping at vintage or second-hand stores, eating less meat, donating old cellphones, and carpooling. Each green venture is followed by concrete ideas . . . that encourage direct action. Cheerful cartoon spot art underscores the positive tone." Publ Wkly

Power Scott, Jennifer

Green careers; you can make money and save the planet. Lobster Press 2010 240p il pa $16.95

Grades: 8 9 10 11 12   **333.72**

1. Vocational guidance   2. Environmental protection   3. Ecology -- Vocational guidance   4. Environmental protection -- Vocational guidance

ISBN 978-1-897550-18-2; 1-897550-18-9

"Written in a breezy, conversational style, this book recounts the stories of 30 young people who are working in environmental jobs. . . . They are eco-entrepreneurs, urban activists, green architects, organic gardeners, animal caretakers, artists, and fashion designers. . . . These inspirational stories are sure to spark interest and creative thinking." SLJ

Raatma, Lucia

Green living; no action too small. Compass Point Books 2009 64p il (Green generation) lib bdg $31.99; pa $6.95

Grades: 5 6 7 8 9   **333.72**

1. Environmental movement   2. Environmental protection

ISBN 978-0-7565-4245-0 lib bdg; 0-7565-4245-6 lib bdg; 978-0-7565-4293-1 pa; 0-7565-4293-6 pa

LC 2009-8779

Shows children how can they make a difference. From fighting global warming to protecting wildlife, this book contains the information young environmentalists need to change the world

"The cover design, layout, and graphics feel hip and of the moment. The clear writing is easy to understand and includes many concrete examples of environmentally friendly practices. . . . [A] good [choice] for both leisure reading and reports." SLJ

Includes glossary and bibliographical references

Rapp, Valerie

Protecting Earth's land; by Valerie Rapp. Lerner Publications 2009 72p il map (Saving our living Earth) lib bdg $30.60

Grades: 5 6 7 8   **333.72**

1. Environmental protection

ISBN 978-0-8225-7559-7 lib bdg; 0-8225-7559-0 lib bdg

LC 2008-3549

"Provides a thorough, interesting discussion of multiple aspects of [land protection], including historical origins, the current situation, and potential solutions. . . . Photos from around the world accompany discussions. . . . [This is a] solid choice to replace outdated books." SLJ

Includes glossary and bibliographical references

★ **Recycle** this book; 100 top children's book authors tell you how to go green. edited by Dan Gutman. Yearling 2009 267p pa $5.99

Grades: 5 6 7 8   **333.72**

1. Authors   2. Recycling   3. Environmental protection

ISBN 978-0-385-73721-0 pa; 0-385-73721-1 pa

LC 2008-10800

"This lively collection of brief essays (and a poem) by 100 outstanding children's and young adult authors teaches through example. Each selection highlights a small step (or steps) taken by the writer toward a greener Earth. . . . The essays also provide insight into the lives and thoughts of many familiar and beloved authors such as Laurie Halse Anderson, Ralph Fletcher, Gary Schmidt, Lois Lowry, Susan Patron, and Rick Riordan. Several pages of Web sites offer a starting point for action and information. Highly useful for classroom and family discussions and science-project ideas." SLJ

Reilly, Kathleen M.

Planet Earth; 25 environmental projects you can build yourself. Nomad Press 2008 122p il (Projects you can build yourself) $21.95; pa $14.95

Grades: 4 5 6 7   **333.72**

1. Science projects   2. Environmental sciences   3. Environmental education   4. Recycling (Waste, etc.)

ISBN 978-1-934670-05-7; 1-934670-05-7; 978-1-934670-04-0 pa; 1-934670-04-9 pa

"Both comprehensive and approachable, this title . . . combines explanations of science concepts and environmental issues with hands-on projects. . . . Elementary- and middle-school students will find the succinct overview of the facts very useful, and they'll welcome the clearly presented projects." Booklist

Ride, Sally K.

Mission: save the planet; things you can do to help fight global warming. [by] Sally Ride and Tam O'Shaughnessy; illustrated by Andrew Arnold. Roaring Brook Press 2009 61p il (Sally Ride science) pa $7.99

Grades: 5 6 7 8   **333.72**

1. Environmental protection   2. Global warming   3. Climatic changes

ISBN 978-159643-379-3 pa; 1-59643-379-5 pa

LC 2009-29254

"The first chapter in this slim volume discusses our energy use, dependence on fossil fuels, and the environmental impact of these practices. The remaining chapters are packed with facts and suggestions on reducing our carbon footprint. . . . The authors' background in science education is evident, as the writing style is clear, precise, and kid-friendly. Black-and-white cartoon illustrations provide excellent visuals for many of the recommendations." SLJ

Rohmer, Harriet

★ **Heroes** of the environment; true stories of people who are helping to protect our planet. illustrated by Julie McLaughlin. Chronicle Books 2009 109p il map $16.99

Grades: 4 5 6   333.72
   1. Environmentalists
   ISBN 978-0-8118-6779-5; 0-8118-6779-X
                        LC 2009004366

"Engaging graphics and clear writing combine to provide a compelling reading experience." Sci Books Films

Sivertsen, Linda

Generation green; the ultimate teen guide to living an eco-friendly life. written by Linda Sivertsen and Tosh Sivertsen. Simon Pulse 2008 248p pa $10.99

Grades: 5 6 7 8   333.72
   1. Environmental movement
   ISBN 978-1-4169-6122-2; 1-4169-6122-4

"A thorough yet accessible manual on green living. . . . The book's incisive voice, using teen idioms, is accessible to those who have little or no background in environmental issues, yet the standards within will likewise engage readers already committed to being green. . . . [This book is] unique, for its central focus is not to explain the science behind current environmental challenges, but rather to reveal how young people can work to solve those problems in their everyday lives." SLJ

Includes bibliographical references

Smalley, Carol Parenzan

Green changes you can make around your home. Mitchell Lane Publishers 2010 47p il (Tell your parents) lib bdg $21.50

Grades: 4 5 6 7   333.72
   1. Environmental movement 2. Environmental protection
   ISBN 978-1-58415-764-9 lib bdg; 1-58415-764-X lib bdg
                        LC 2009-4527

This book that explains how to be environmentally friendly "offers numerous facts and statistics, all of which are cited. . . . Chapters cover present-day issues and . . . are interspersed with full-color photographs and short 'Did You Know' trivia boxes. . . . Back matter includes detailed resource lists and 'Try This!' experiments." SLJ

Includes glossary and bibliographical references

Strange, Cordelia

Environmental science & protection; keeping our planet green. Mason Crest Publishers 2011 64p il map (New careers for the 21st century: finding your role in the global renewal) lib bdg $22.95; pa $9.95

Grades: 7 8 9 10   333.72
   1. Vocational guidance 2. Environmental sciences 3. Environmental protection
   ISBN 978-1-4222-1813-6 lib bdg; 1-4222-1813-9 lib bdg; 978-1-4222-2034-4 pa; 1-4222-2034-6 pa
                        LC 2010011418

"Chapters identify and emphasize specific careers–important strengths, necessary aptitudes and interests, education and training, projected earnings, closely related occupations, type of work environment, and predictions for the future of the field. . . . Color photos have a small role amid the many statistics, figures, graphs and charts that support and supplement the . . . [text]." SLJ

Includes bibliographical references

Try this at home; planet-friendly projects for kids. Jackie Farquhar, D.I.Y. editor. Owlkids 2009 93p il pa $10.95

Grades: 5 6 7 8   333.72
   1. Environmental protection 2. Environmental education
   ISBN 978-2-89579-192-8 pa; 2-89579-192-9 pa

"Many of these projects are unique or innovative, featuring ideas like growing your own pizza ingredients and making a foosball game out of recycled corks, clothespins, and plastic fruit baskets. One of the best projects provides tips on making sure a bike is road ready, offering advice on checking the cables, gears, and oiling the chain. The book also includes sections designed to increase environmental awareness, including information on carbon footprint and 'eco all-stars.' Interactive elements, like a game board, should appeal to children. Illustrations are hip collages of full-color photographs and cartoons." SLJ

Includes bibliographical references

333.73   Land

Casper, Julie Kerr

Lands; taming the wilds. Chelsea House 2007 226p il (Natural resources) $39.50

Grades: 8 9 10 11 12   333.73
   1. Land use
   ISBN 978-0-8160-6356-7; 0-8160-6356-7
                        LC 2006-37262

This "addresses human impacts on all types of landscapes and how people can become responsible caretakers of these vital repositories of nature's bounty." Publisher"s note

Includes bibliographical references

Desonie, Dana

Geosphere; the land and its uses. Chelsea House 2008 200p il map (Our fragile planet) $35

Grades: 7 8 9 10   333.73
   1. Land use 2. Human influence on nature
   ISBN 978-0-8160-6217-1; 0-8160-6217-X
                        LC 2007-25453

Outlines the causes and effects of the human impact on the environment, discussing such topics as agriculture, mining, energy production, urbanization, and overpopulation, and describes ways to achieve sustainable environmental practices.

Includes glossary and bibliographical references

333.75 Forest lands

Casper, Julie Kerr
Forests; more than just trees. Chelsea House Publishers 2007 194p il map (Natural resources) $39.50
Grades: 8 9 10 11 12   **333.75**
    1. Forests and forestry
    ISBN 978-0-8160-6355-0; 0-8160-6355-9
                     LC 2006100042
This "focuses on the importance of all types of forests, why it is necessary to protect and conserve these natural resources, and what people can do to maintain healthy forest ecosystems." Publisher's note
Includes bibliographical references

Littlewood, Antonia
Rain forest destruction; Peter and Antonia Littlewood. Smart Apple Media 2012 46 p. col. ill., col. maps (Mapping global issues) (library) $35.65
Grades: 6 7 8   **333.75**
    1. Rain forests 2. Forest conservation 3. Deforestation 4. Rain forest ecology 5. Rain forest conservation
    ISBN 1599205122; 9781599205120
                     LC 2011017067
This book is part of the Mapping Global Issues series and it focuses on rainforest destruction. "Colorful layouts with numerous maps and graphs dominate this series, which provides an international perspective on important issues. Brief chapters frame problems, discuss their causes, and suggest possible solutions, using maps to illustrate the locations and extent of threats." (School Library Journal)
Includes bibliographical references (p. 45) and index

Stenstrup, Allen
Forests. Morgan Reynolds Pub. 2009 112p il (Diminishing resources) lib bdg $28.95
Grades: 8 9 10 11 12   **333.75**
    1. Forest conservation 2. Forests and forestry
    ISBN 978-1-59935-116-2; 1-59935-116-1
                     LC 2009-31025
"This highly readable [book] provides a unique viewpoint on the utilization of natural resources, as scientific and environmental concerns are discussed from a historical perspective. . . . [It contains] beautiful, full-page photographs, as well as a helpful time line." SLJ
Includes bibliographical references

333.76 Rural lands

Morris, Neil
The **landscape**; Neil Morris. Heinemann Library 2012 64 p. (The impact of environmentalism) (library) $35.00; (paperback) $9.99
Grades: 6 7 8   **333.76**
    1. Landscape protection 2. Environmental movement 3. Landscape changes 4. Landscape assessment 5. Landscapes -- Environmental aspects
    ISBN 1432965247; 9781432965181; 9781432965242
                     LC 2012001036

This book by Neil Morris is part of the "Impact of Environmentalism" series. It "looks at the way changing ideas about the environment and sustainability have affected our attitudes to the landscape, and will do so in the future." (Publisher's note)
"Visual evidence shows how lands have been changed by human activities." The "book also discusses . . . efforts by humankind to protect the environment and create sustainable smaller environments." (School Library Journal)
Includes bibliographical references and index

333.78 Recreational and wilderness areas

McHugh, Erin
National Parks; A Kid's Guide to America's Parks, Monuments and Landmarks. Erin McHugh; Art by Neal Aspinall, Doug Leen, and Brian Maebius. Black Dog & Leventhal Publishers 2012 128 p. col. ill., col. map (hbk.) $19.95; (hbk.) $19.95
Grades: 4 5 6   **333.78**
    1. National parks and reserves -- United States
    ISBN 157912884X; 9781579128845
This book, "arranged alphabetically by state . . . tours more than 75 U.S. parks, monuments, and landmarks, from the rocky shores of Maine's Acadia National Park to the ancient redwood groves of Northern California. Also included is a removable, fold-out collector map to house" the commemorative quarters from the America the Beautiful series. (Publisher's note)

333.79 Energy

Bailey, Gerry
Out of energy. Gareth Stevens 2011 48p il (Planet SOS) lib bdg $31.95; pa $14.05
Grades: 4 5 6   **333.79**
    1. Energy resources 2. Renewable energy resources
    ISBN 978-1-4339-4978-4 lib bdg; 1-4339-4978-4 lib bdg; 978-1-4339-4979-1 pa; 1-4339-4979-2 pa
                     LC 2010032889
This book "has separate chapters on fossil fuels, renewable energy, nuclear energy, and more. The many large, colorful photos will engage readers and assist them in understanding the important concepts introduced." SLJ
Includes glossary

Ballard, Carol
From steam engines to nuclear fusion; discovering energy. [by] Carol Ballard. Heinemann Library 2007 64p il (Chain reactions) lib bdg $34.29
Grades: 6 7 8 9   **333.79**
    1. Energy resources
    ISBN 1-4034-9554-8 lib bdg; 978-1-4034-9554-9 lib bdg
                     LC 2006049785
"Ballard traces the history of the scientific community's understanding of energy and how that has been applied to everyday life. Beginning with an explanation of what energy is, the discussion touches on topics such as steam power,

electricity, radioactivity, quantum theory, relativity, and nuclear power. . . . Illustrations, many in color, include period portraits of scientists and photos of equipment, as well as a few diagrams." Booklist

Includes glossary and bibliographical references

Bowden, Rob, 1973-

Energy sources; the impact of science and technology. Gareth Stevens Pub. 2010 64p il (Pros and cons) lib bdg $35

Grades: 5 6 7 8   333.79

1. Energy resources

ISBN 978-1-4339-1987-9 lib bdg; 1-4339-1987-7 lib bdg

LC 2009-12434

"Looks at how scientific and technological advances in recent decades have dramatically altered the way we live—and examines both positive and negative impacts of these changes." Publisher's note

Includes glossary and bibliographical references

Brezina, Corona

Jobs in sustainable energy. Rosen Pub. 2010 80p il (Green careers) lib bdg $30

Grades: 5 6 7 8   333.79

1. Vocational guidance 2. Renewable energy resources

ISBN 978-1-4358-3569-6 lib bdg; 1-4358-3569-7 lib bdg

LC 2009021855

This "well-conceived [introduction focuses] on various jobs in [sustainable energy], the education and experience required, and expected earnings. The [book is] well organized, making it easy to gain an overview of the major aspects of the work. . . . [This book] will make [a] good [addition] to career collections. Photographs from the field and website and contact information for professional organizations add value." SLJ

Includes glossary and bibliographical references

Caduto, Michael J.

★ **Catch** the wind, harness the sun; 22 supercharged science projects for kids. Storey Pub. 2011 223p il $26.95; pa $16.95

Grades: 5 6 7 8   333.79

1. Energy conservation 2. Renewable energy resources 3. Science -- Experiments

ISBN 978-1-60342-971-9; 1-60342-971-9; 978-1-60342-794-4 pa; 1-60342-794-5 pa; 1603427945 pa; 1603429719; 9781603427944 pa; 9781603429719

LC 2010051169

"The eco-themed activities that Caduto lays out here are only the beginning, as he embeds them in short but clear explanations of relevant scientific facts, profiles of young eco-activitists, provocative follow-up questions, photos and cartoon spot art aplenty, folktales, and other enhancements." Booklist

Flath, Camden

Careers in green energy; fueling the world with renewable resources. Mason Crest Publishers 2010 64p il map (New careers for the 21st century: find-

ing your role in the global renewal) lib bdg $22.95; pa $9.95

Grades: 7 8 9 10   333.79

1. Vocational guidance 2. Renewable energy resources

ISBN 978-1-4222-1812-9 lib bdg; 1-4222-1812-0 lib bdg; 978-1-4222-2033-7 pa; 1-4222-2033-8 pa

LC 2010020683

"Chapters identify and emphasize specific careers—important strengths, necessary aptitudes and interests, education and training, projected earnings, closely related occupations, type of work environment, and predictions for the future of the field. . . . Color photos have a small role amid the many statistics, figures, graphs and charts that support and supplement the . . . [text]." SLJ

Includes bibliographical references

Fridell, Ron

Earth-friendly energy; by Ron Fridell. Lerner Publications 2009 72p il map (Saving our living earth) lib bdg $30.60

Grades: 5 6 7 8   333.79

1. Environmental movement 2. Renewable energy resources

ISBN 978-0-8225-7563-4 lib bdg; 0-8225-7563-9 lib bdg

LC 2007-35923

"Provides a thorough, interesting discussion of multiple aspects of [Earth-friendly energy], including historical origins, the current situation, and potential solutions. . . . Photos from around the world accompany discussions. . . . [This is a] solid choice to replace outdated books." SLJ

Includes glossary and bibliographical references

Friedman, Lauri S.

Energy alternatives; Lauri S. Friedman, book editor. Greenhaven Press 2011 154p il map (Introducing issues with opposing viewpoints) $36.82

Grades: 7 8 9 10   333.79

1. Renewable energy resources

ISBN 978-0-7377-5198-7; 0-7377-5198-3

LC 2011000872

Essays examine both sides of the questions raised about energy alternatives.

This is is an "excellent [resource] both for student research and for personal interest." Booklist

Includes bibliographical references

Gardner, Robert

Energy; green science projects about solar, wind, and water power. Enslow Publishers 2011 128p il (Team Green science projects) lib bdg $31.93

Grades: 6 7 8 9 10   333.79

1. Energy resources 2. Science projects 3. Science -- Experiments

ISBN 978-0-7660-3643-7; 0-7660-3643-X

This book offers science experiments about energy resources and energy conservation.

"Gardner provides plenty of information, well-designed experiments, and demonstrations, and then shares brief science-fair ideas. . . . Experiments and demonstrations are presented with clear step-by-step instructions and occasional illustrations and represent a wide range of complexity." SLJ

Includes glossary and bibliographical references

Gunderson, Jessica

The **energy** dilemma. Creative Education 2010 48p il (Earth issues) lib bdg $34.25

Grades: 6 7 8 9 10   **333.79**

1. Pollution 2. Energy resources 3. Power resources

ISBN 978-1-58341-980-9 lib bdg; 1-58341-980-2 lib bdg

LC 2009-28048

"Unfamiliar words are printed in bold type and defined in the glossary for students. . . . Written in a straightforward manner, with photographs that are clearly captioned, . . . [this] is a welcome addition for libraries." Libr Media Connect

Includes glossary and bibliographical references

Kallen, Stuart A.

Renewable energy research. ReferencePoint Press 2010 96p il (Inside science) lib bdg $26.95

Grades: 7 8 9 10   **333.79**

1. Renewable energy resources

ISBN 978-1-60152-129-3; 1-60152-129-4

LC 2010-18102

This "offers the necessary information for stellar reports. Politics, debates, and ethical concerns are briefly and fairly mentioned, but the . . . [book concentrates] on consistent, documented, and well-balanced scientific coverage. The human stories sprinkled throughout will help kids identify with both scientists and patients." SLJ

Includes bibliographical references

Laidlaw, Jill A.

Energy; by Jill Laidlaw. Amicus 2011 44p il map (Sustaining our environment) lib bdg $31.35

Grades: 6 7 8 9   **333.79**

1. Energy resources 2. Renewable energy resources

ISBN 978-1-60753-136-4 lib bdg; 1-60753-136-4 lib bdg

LC 2009-29985

"The tone is refreshingly optimistic with its examples of specific steps being taken to reduce harm to the environment. Sidebars highlight case studies and campaigns from around the world and from the individual to the national levels. Clear, informative captions accompany the excellent selection of color photographs, charts and graphs." SLJ

Includes glossary

Miller, Debra A.

Energy production and alternative energy; Michael E. Miller consulting editor. Greenhaven Press 2011 123p il map (Confronting global warming) lib bdg $37.10

Grades: 7 8 9 10 11 12   **333.79**

1. Electric power 2. Renewable energy resources

ISBN 978-0-7377-5106-2; 0-7377-5106-1

LC 2010024976

Discusses the world's history of energy production and consumption, and explains how alternative energy sources

may help with the coming fossil fuel energy crisis and protecting the worldwide environment.

"Presented in a scholarly design that will appeal to older readers. . . . The illustrations and pictures support the text, and the graphics and sidebars are well placed." Libr Media Connect

Includes glossary and bibliographical references

Rau, Dana Meachen

Alternative energy beyond fossil fuels. Compass Point Books 2010 64p il (Green generation) lib bdg $31.99; pa $6.95

Grades: 5 6 7 8 9   **333.79**

1. Energy resources 2. Renewable energy resources 3. Fossil fuels 4. Power resources

ISBN 978-0-7565-4247-4 lib bdg; 0-7565-4247-2 lib bdg; 978-0-7565-4289-4 pa; 0-7565-4289-8 pa

LC 2009-08778

"This great little book introduces the topics of fossil fuel usage, the limited nature of fossil fuels, and alternative energy options. It is particularly praiseworthy for its refreshingly objective, but still enthusiastic, presentations on solar, wind, geothermal, hydro, and biomass energy. . . . Interesting, well-written, and appropriately illustrated, the book is entertaining enough for general reading, but factual enough for use as a science text." Sci Books Films

Includes glossary and bibliographical references

Rigsby, Mike

Doable renewables; 16 alternative energy projects for young scientists. Chicago Review Press 2010 196p il pa $16.95

Grades: 6 7 8 9 10   **333.79**

1. Renewable energy resources 2. Science -- Experiments

ISBN 978-1-56976-343-8 pa; 1-56976-343-7 pa

LC 2010019520

This is a "collection of science-oriented projects, focused . . . on renewable energy sources. From a windmill . . . to a human-powered LED light that relies on a hand-cranked generator, this activities range in complexity and skill, but all use simple technology to show basic and fascinating processes." Booklist

Sobey, Ed

Solar cell and renewable energy experiments. Enslow Publishers 2011 128p il (Cool science projects with technology) lib bdg $31.93

Grades: 6 7 8 9   **333.79**

1. Renewable energy resources 2. Science -- Experiments

ISBN 978-0-7660-3305-4; 0-7660-3305-8

LC 2010027430

This explains what solar cells do and how they work, how wind and water power electronics, and offers experiments in renewable energy.

Includes glossary and bibliographical references

Solway, Andrew

Renewable energy sources. Raintree 2010 48p il (Sci-hi: Earth and space science) lib bdg $31.43; pa $8.99

Grades: 4 5 6 7   **333.79**

1. Renewable energy resources

ISBN 978-1-4109-3351-5 lib bdg; 1-4109-3351-2 lib bdg; 978-1-4109-3361-4 pa; 1-4109-3361-X pa

LC 2009-3535

"Multiple colorful sidebars and large and small diagrams and photographs will help students to grasp the fundamentals being discussed, and the easy but interesting science experiments will act as further reinforcements." SLJ

Includes glossary and bibliographical references

Thaddeus, Eva

Powering the future; new energy technologies. with illustrations by Catherine Paplin. University of New Mexico Press 2010 125p il map (Worlds of wonder) $24.95

Grades: 6 7 8 9 10   **333.79**

1. Renewable energy resources

ISBN 978-0-8263-4901-9; 0-8263-4901-3

LC 2009044300

The author tackles "environmental issues with depth and rigor, attuned to both current events and the concerns of today's teens. . . . The excellent [text is] enhanced by color photographs and diagrams that further explain scientific ideas." Horn Book Guide

Includes glossary

333.8   Subsurface resources

Gardner, Timothy

Oil. Morgan Reynolds Pub. 2009 111p il (Diminishing resources) lib bdg $28.95

Grades: 8 9 10 11 12   **333.8**

1. Petroleum 2. Energy conservation 3. Greenhouse effect

ISBN 978-1-59935-117-9; 1-59935-117-X

LC 2009-10245

This book about oil "will draw activists, but even readers who do not think they care that much will find the facts devastating. Quotes from authoritative sources . . . about both the historic overview and the contemporary crisis accompany full-color double-page photos that show what is happening now. . . . [The book] discusses in detail the role of the Middle East, the effects of America's addiction to cars, and always, the current focus on global warming." Booklist

Includes bibliographical references

Gorman, Jacqueline Laks

Fossil fuels. Gareth Stevens Pub. 2009 48p il map (What if we do nothing?) lib bdg $31

Grades: 5 6 7 8   **333.8**

1. Coal 2. Petroleum 3. Environmental protection 4. Fossil fuels

ISBN 978-1-4339-0087-7 lib bdg; 1-4339-0087-4 lib bdg

LC 2008-29214

This "examines a potential crisis, its historical causes, scientific background, and possible outcome if no action is taken. . . . [The book] makes the connection between climate change and the use of polluting energy sources, and the Kyoto Protocol's plans for the reduction of globe-warming emissions are considered. . . . Full-color photographs, charts, and maps help illustrate some of the ideas and problems." SLJ

Includes glossary and bibliographical references

Hartman, Eve

Fossil fuels; [by] Eve Hartman and Wendy Meshbesher. Raintree 2010 48p il map (Sci-hi: Earth and space science) lib bdg $31.43; pa $8.99

Grades: 4 5 6 7   **333.8**

1. Coal 2. Oils and fats

ISBN 978-1-4109-3350-8 lib bdg; 1-4109-3350-4 lib bdg; 978-1-4109-3360-7 pa; 1-4109-3360-1 pa

LC 2009-3548

"Multiple colorful sidebars and large and small diagrams and photographs will help students to grasp the fundamentals being discussed, and the easy but interesting science experiments will act as further reinforcements." SLJ

Includes glossary and bibliographical references

Mooney, Carla

Oil spills and offshore drilling. ReferencePoint Press 2011 96p il map (Compact research: energy and the environment) lib bdg $26.95

Grades: 7 8 9 10 11 12   **333.8**

1. Oil spills 2. Offshore oil well drilling

ISBN 978-1-60152-141-5; 1-60152-141-3

LC 2010037325

This volume has "up-to-date information with frequent references to . . . the Deepwater Horizon disaster in the Gulf of Mexico. . . . [It] asks if the U.S. needs to drill offshore, if it's an environmental risk, if regulations are adequate, and discusses the future of offshore drilling. . . . Each chapter is followed by a section of primary-source quotes espousing pro and con views. . . . [This is a] first-rate ready-reference [book] and excellent to use in teaching research with primary documents." SLJ

Includes bibliographical references

White, Nancy

Using Earth's underground heat. Bearport Pub. 2009 32p il (Going green) lib bdg $25.27

Grades: 4 5 6 7   **333.8**

1. Geothermal resources

ISBN 978-1-59716-963-9 lib bdg; 1-59716-963-3 lib bdg

LC 2009-15119

"Color photographs (most full page) and a few diagrams accompany the informative text[s]. . . . Overall, the [book] . . . is user-friendly and covers topics that are not easily found elsewhere." SLJ

Includes glossary and bibliographical references

333.9   Other natural resources

Dobson, Clive
Wind power; 20 projects to make with paper.
Firefly Books 2010 96p il $24.95; pa $12.95
Grades: 5 6 7 8   **333.9**
1. Wind power 2. Paper crafts
ISBN 978-1-55407-659-8; 1-55407-659-5; 978-1-
55407-749-6 pa; 1-55407-749-4 pa
"In this informative craft book, a celebration of wind and
of innovative efforts to harness its energy, Dobson describes
the geometric and aerodynamic principles behind windmills,
sails, and wind turbines, then implements these concepts
via 20 paper projects, ranging from a two-blade pinwheel
to a dramatic 'Squirrel Cage' turbine. . . . Readers should
gain a more palpable understanding of the subject matter by
building and watching the graceful compositions function."
Publ Wkly

333.91   Water and lands adjoining bodies of water

Currie, Stephen
Hydropower. ReferencePoint Press 2011 96p
il map (Compact research: energy and the environment) $26.95
Grades: 7 8 9 10 11 12   **333.91**
1. Hydroelectric power plants 2. Renewable energy
resources
ISBN 978-1-60152-122-4; 1-60152-122-7
LC 2010017393
This volume has "up-to-date information with frequent
references to the Three Gorges Dam in China. . . . [It] poses
questions concerning the possibility of reducing dependency
on fossil fuels, the impact of hydropower on the environment, how developing countries can benefit from its use, and
if the oceans represent the future of hydropower. . . . [This
volume is a] first-rate ready-reference [book] and excellent
to use in teaching research with primary documents." SLJ
Includes bibliographical references

Kaye, Cathryn Berger
★ Going blue; a teen guide to saving our oceans
& waterways. by Cathryn Berger Kaye; with Philippe
Cousteau and Earth Echo International. Free Spirit
Pub. 2010 151p il map pa $14.95
Grades: 6 7 8 9 10   **333.91**
1. Marine ecology 2. Marine pollution 3. Environmental
protection
ISBN 978-1-57542-348-7; 1-57542-348-0
LC 2010-16589
Teaches young people about the Earth's water crisis and
provides practical suggestions on how readers can identify
water-related needs in the community and transform their
ideas into action.
"This valuable how-to manual is suitable for an individual student, a family, a youth group, or a school wishing to
protect our precious resource of water. This upbeat treasure
will challenge anyone interested in environmental activism,

whether water related or not. It is a must for any library serving youth." Voice Youth Advocates
Includes bibliographical references

Laidlaw, Jill A.
Water; by Jill Laidlaw. Amicus 2011 44p il
map (Sustaining our environment) lib bdg $31.35
Grades: 6 7 8 9   **333.91**
1. Water 2. Water supply
ISBN 978-1-60753-140-1; 1-60753-140-2
LC 2009028258
This book looks at key environmental and social issues
that are linked with water and highlights what is being done
to try to make water sustainable for all.
"The tone is refreshingly optimistic with its examples
of specific steps being taken to reduce harm to the environment. Sidebars highlight case studies and campaigns from
around the world and from the individual to the national
levels. Clear, informative captions accompany the excellent
selection of color photographs, charts and graphs." SLJ
Includes glossary

333.95   Biological resources

Guerive, Gaelle
Extraordinary endangered animals; by Sandrine
Silhol & Gaelle Guérive; illustrated by Marie Douce-
dame. Abrams 2011 157p il $24.95
Grades: 5 6 7 8   **333.95**
1. Endangered species
ISBN 978-1-4197-0034-7; 1-4197-0034-0
"Detailed, large-scale photographs and intricate drawings depict 35 endangered species from around the globe,
including the California condor, the sea otter, the golden
lion tamarin, and the sawfish. Silhol and Guérive describe
the habitat, behavior, and endangered status of each animal,
while sidebars place each in human context, implicating our
role in their endangerment. . . . Honest but not downbeat,
this informative collection encourages readers to take action
before these species disappear." Publ Wkly

Kurlansky, Mark, 1948-
The world without fish; how could we let this
happen? illustrations by Frank Stockton. Workman
Pub. 2011 183p il $16.95
Grades: 5 6 7 8 9 10   **333.95**
1. Water pollution 2. Commercial fishing
ISBN 978-0-7611-5607-9; 0-7611-5607-0
LC 2011-15516
"Brief sections in graphic-novel format follow a young
girl, Ailat, and her father over a couple of decades as the
condition of the ocean grows increasingly dire, eventually an
orange, slimy mess mostly occupied by jellyfish and leather-
back turtles. At the end, Ailat's young daughter doesn't even
know what the word fish means. This is juxtaposed against
nonfiction chapters with topics including types of fishing
equipment and the damage each causes, a history of the destruction of the cod and its consequences, the international
politics of the fishing industry and the effects of pollution
and global warming. . . . Depressing and scary yet grimly
entertaining." Kirkus

Littlewood, Peter

Endangered species; Peter Littlewood. Smart Apple Media 2012 46 p. col. ill., col. maps (Mapping global issues) (library binding) $35.65

Grades: 6 7 8   333.95

1. Endangered species

ISBN 1599205076; 9781599205076

LC 2011017064

This book by Peter Littlewood, part of the Mapping Global Issues series, offers "coloured photos, maps and diagrams. Throughout the book there are numerous case studies which give detailed information about issues, for example, . . . why some people think that Giant Panda's are beyond saving." (School Librarian)

Includes bibliographical references (p. 45) and index

Mackay, Richard

The **atlas** of endangered species; Rev and updated; University of California Press 2009 128p il map pa $19.95

Grades: 6 7 8 9   333.95

1. Endangered species 2. Endangered ecosystems

ISBN 978-0-520-25862-4 pa; 0-520-25862-2 pa

First published 2002 in the United Kingdom

Catalogs the inhabitants of a wide variety of ecosystems, including forests, mangroves, and coral reefs. It examines the major threats to biodiversity, from loss of habitat to hunting, and describes the steps being taken toward conservation.

"More than 40 topics, among them 'Human Environmental Impact,' 'Temperate Forests,' 'Dolphins and Whales,' and 'Conserving Domestic Breeds,' are presented on double-page spreads containing full-color maps, charts, graphs, small photographs, and text. The presentation is clear and attractive." Booklist

Includes bibliographical references

Mills, Andrea

Animals like us; written and edited by Andrea Mills. DK Pub. 2005 79p il map $19.99

Grades: 5 6 7 8   333.95

1. Rare animals 2. Endangered species 3. Wildlife conservation

ISBN 978-0-7566-1008-1; 0-7566-1008-7

LC 2005299478

Colorful introduction to animals around the world details physical attributes, geographic distribution, and habitat.

"Captivating digital photo layouts are interspersed with 'fact files' that point out loss of habitat and dwindling animal populations." Horn Book Guide

Salmansohn, Pete, 1947-

Saving birds; heroes around the world. [by] Pete Salmansohn and Stephen W. Kress. Tilbury House 2003 39p il $16.95; pa $7.95

Grades: 5 6 7 8   333.95

1. Endangered species 2. Wildlife conservation 3. Birds -- Protection

ISBN 0-88448-237-5; 0-88448-276-6 pa

LC 2002-6710

Profiles adults and children working in six habitats around the world to save wild birds, some of which are on the brink of extinction.

"As a teaching aid, this volume is an exceptional supplement. The six articles relating the heroic rescue of the endangered birds are accurate and enhanced by appropriate color photographs." Sci Books Films

Sheehan, Sean

Endangered species; by Sean Sheehan. Gareth Stevens Pub. 2009 48p il map (What if we do nothing?) lib bdg $31

Grades: 5 6 7 8   333.95

1. Endangered species

ISBN 978-1-4339-0086-0 lib bdg; 1-4339-0086-6 lib bdg

LC 2008029167

"Using intelligent, focused text; an open design; vivid photos; and excellent maps, [this] book demands attention." Booklist

Includes bibliographical references

Walker, Niki

Biomass; fueling change. [by] Niki Walker. Crabtree Pub. 2007 32p il (Energy revolution) lib bdg $19.95; pa $8.95

Grades: 5 6 7 8   333.95

1. Biomass energy

ISBN 978-0-7787-2914-3 lib bdg; 0-7787-2914-1 lib bdg; 978-0-7787-2928-0 pa; 0-7787-2928-1 pa

LC 2006016035

This "book presents a range of historical uses of the various forms of biomass, from charcoal smelters in ancient Egypt to ethanol-fueled lanterns in the 19th century and gasifiers during World War II. Vivid color photographs with informative captions extend the [text]." SLJ

Includes glossary

Endangered oceans: opposing viewpoints; Louise I. Gerdes, book editor. Greenhaven Press 2009 234p il (Opposing viewpoints series) lib bdg $38.50; pa $26.75

Grades: 8 9 10 11 12   333.95

1. Marine ecology 2. Marine pollution 3. Environmental policy

ISBN 978-0-7377-4210-7 lib bdg; 978-0-7377-4211-4 pa

LC 2008-36462

Articles in this anthology cover such topics as overfishing and loss of coral reefs, government policies to protect ocean life, sustainable fishing, and the effects of human activities on marine mammals.

Includes bibliographical references

Reptiles and amphibians; edited by Tim Harris. Brown Bear Books 2012 64 p. (Facts at your fingertips: endangered animals) (library binding) $35.65

Grades: 5 6 7 8   333.95

1. Reptiles 2. Amphibians 3. Endangered species 4.

Rare reptiles 5. Rare amphibians
ISBN 1936333368; 9781936333363

LC 2010053968

This book "profiles a global sampling of reptiles and amphibians in various degrees of endangerment . . . . Twenty-one species are described in . . . detail that includes information on their classification, distribution, physical characteristics, habitat, diet, and reproduction." The book is part of "the 'Facts at Your Fingertips: Endangered Animals' series, which profiles various groups of endangered species from all parts of the planet." (National Science Teachers Association)

Includes bibliographical references and index

Should drilling be permitted in the Arctic National Wildlife Refuge? David M. Haugen, book editor. Greenhaven Press 2008 92p (At issue) lib bdg $29.95; pa $21.20

Grades: 7 8 9 10 11 12   333.95
1. Oil well drilling
ISBN 978-0-7377-3930-5 lib bdg; 0-7377-3930-4 lib bdg; 978-0-7377-3931-2 pa; 0-7377-3931-2 pa

LC 2007-51383

"This collection of essays, . . . examines the current issue of drilling for oil in the Arctic National Wildlife Refuge (ANWR). . . . Having these essays collected into one volume makes this book a valuable option for young adults in speech and debate activities. Additional strengths are the list of organizations to contact and a bibliography of recent books and articles on this hot topic." Booklist

Includes bibliographical references

335.4   Marxian systems

McIntosh, J. S.

Escape and evasion; by Jack Montana. Mason Crest Publishers 2011 il (Special forces: protecting, building, teaching and fighting) lib bdg $22.95

Grades: 6 7 8 9   335.4
1. Survival skills 2. Military art and science
ISBN 978-1-4222-1840-2; 1-4222-1840-6

LC 2010020680

The book covers all the essential skills of an undercover soldier. Infiltration by land, sea, and air are described in detail. The unique physical demands of night fighting are explained. Tracking techniques are also revealed.

"The well-chosen color photographs help make this series a fun armchair experience for military enthusiasts as well as a good resource for reports and for males considering military careers." Booklist

Includes bibliographical references

336.2   Taxes

La Bella, Laura

How taxation works. Rosen Pub. 2011 80p il (Real world economics) lib bdg $30.60

Grades: 7 8 9 10   336.2
1. Taxation -- United States
ISBN 978-1-4358-9463-1; 1-4358-9463-4

LC 2009047165

This describes how taxation works.

Includes glossary and bibliographical references

338   Production

Rankin, Kenrya

Start it up; the complete guide to turning your passions into pay. [illustrated by Eriko Takada and Marissa Fiend] Zest Books 2011 155p il pa $14.95

Grades: 7 8 9 10 11 12   338
1. Entrepreneurship 2. Business enterprises
ISBN 978-0-9819733-5-7; 0-9819733-5-3

"Combining a conversational style with a systematic approach, [this book] walks teens through starting their own business. . . . Rankin gives a good overview of such difficult concepts as start-up and operating costs and asks readers to consider potentially overlooked topics like the pros and cons of publicizing prices and things to consider when working with family and friends." Booklist

338.1   Specific kinds of industries

Green, Jen

Food and farming; Jen Green. 1st ed. Heinemann Library 2012 64 p. (The impact of environmentalism) (hardcover) $35

Grades: 6 7 8 9 10   338.1
1. Environmental movement 2. Agriculture -- Environmental aspects 3. Food supply 4. Environmentalism
ISBN 1432965174; 9781432965174; 9781432965235

LC 2012001033

This book by Jen Green is part of the Impact on Environmentalism series. In "discussing the impact of the environmental movement on food and farming, Green also explores controversies surrounding modern agriculture and its distribution practices. A brief history of farming . . . leads to a discussion of more recent trends, including high-yield varieties of crops, monoculture, genetically modified foods, pesticides, water management, factory farming, organic farming, [and] fair trade." (Booklist)

Pollan, Michael

★ The **omnivore's** dilemma; the secrets behind what you eat. adapted by Richie Chevat. Young readers ed.; Dial Books 2009 298p il $17.99

Grades: 5 6 7 8 9 10   338.1
1. Food supply 2. Food chains (Ecology) 3. Food habits 4. Food preferences 5. Sustainable agriculture
ISBN 978-0-8037-3415-9; 0-8037-3415-8

LC 2009-9283

Adapted from: The omnivore's dilemma: a natural history of four meals, published 2006 by Penguin Press

"Adopting the role of food detective, the author 'peers behind the curtain' of the modern food industry and finds that the industrial approach to the food chain imperils our health and planet. The four sections of the volume describe differing types of meals: industrial; industrial organic; local sustainable; and hunted, gathered and found. Clear organization and lively writing rooted in fascinating examples make this accessible and interesting." Kirkus

Includes bibliographical references

338.5   General production economics

Brezina, Corona

How stimulus plans work. Rosen Pub. 2011 80p il (Real world economics) lib bdg $30.60

Grades: 7 8 9 10   **338.5**
    1. Recessions 2. Economic policy -- United States
    ISBN 978-1-4358-9464-8; 1-4358-9464-2
                        LC 2009045557

This "gives a simple yet comprehensive summary of a complex and expansive topic. It makes the point that all economies are cyclical and that recessions may be caused by different events. It covers deficits and Roosevelt's New Deal and Obama's stimulus plan at length, as well as the Marshall Plan and Japan's response to its recession of the 1990s." SLJ

Includes glossary and bibliographical references

Hollander, Barbara

Booms, bubbles, and busts; the economic cycle. [by] Barbara Gottfried Hollander. Heinemann Library 2010 56p il map (The global marketplace) lib bdg $33.50

Grades: 6 7 8 9   **338.5**
    1. Business cycles 2. Financial crises
    ISBN 978-1-4329-3932-8; 1-4329-3932-7
                        LC 2010004095

This title about the economic cycle covers "a wealth of material in concise paragraphs with pertinent subheadings. . . . [It] includes an informative time line from 2001 to 2009. . . and . . . excellent photos, charts, maps, and tables that help with the understanding of some sophisticated concepts." SLJ

Includes glossary and bibliographical references

338.6   Organization of production

Bezdecheck, Bethany

Bailout! government intervention in business. Rosen Pub. 2011 64p il (In the news) lib bdg $29.95; pa $12.95

Grades: 7 8 9 10   **338.6**
    1. Bankruptcy 2. Corporations 3. Industrial policy -- United States
    ISBN 978-1-4358-9449-5 lib bdg; 1-4358-9449-9 lib bdg; 978-1-4488-1681-1 pa; 1-4488-1681-5 pa
                        LC 2009052247

This " succinctly and objectively covers corporate bailouts and includes a history of government intervention in business dating back to 1970, when the government provided the Penn Central Transportation Company with $700 million to pay its creditors. . . . With numerous photos, concise and manageable chapters, and a glossary, . . . [this provides]

an excellent background for students with an interest in social sciences or a jumping off point for school assignments." Voice Youth Advocates

Includes glossary and bibliographical references

338.7   Business enterprises

Buckley, A. M.

Pixar; the company and its founders. ABDO Pub. Co. 2011 112p il (Technology pioneers) lib bdg $34.22

Grades: 5 6 7 8   **338.7**
    1. Animated films 2. Computer animation
    ISBN 978-1-61714-810-1 lib bdg; 1-61714-810-5 lib bdg; 978-1-61758-968-3 e-book
                        LC 2010044831

An introduction to Pixar Animation Studios and its founders.

"Written in a clear, linear fashion, this series offers vivid, well-researched details about the development of technological advancements considered essential in today's society. . . . Readers who are interested in technology and inventions will be thoroughly engrossed." SLJ

Includes glossary and bibliographical references

Ehrenhaft, Daniel

Larry Ellison; sheer nerve. 21st Cent. Bks. (Brookfield) 2001 80p il (Techies) lib bdg $23.93

Grades: 6 7 8 9   **338.7**
    1. Businessmen 2. Businesspeople 3. Computer software industry 4. Computer software executives 5. Businessmen -- United States -- Biography 6. Computer software industry -- United States
    ISBN 0-7613-1962-X
                        LC 2001-27167

This is a profile of the computer software executive who founded the Oracle Corporation

This "will appeal not only to report writers, but also to recreational readers." SLJ

Includes bibliographical references

Marc Andreessen; Web warrior. 21st Cent. Bks. (Brookfield) 2001 77p il (Techies) lib bdg $23.90

Grades: 6 7 8 9   **338.7**
    1. Internet 2. Businessmen 3. Businesspeople 4. Computer programmers 5. Computer software executives 6. Internet
    ISBN 0-7613-1964-6
                        LC 00-57710

This offers "a breezy style, short length, large font, numerous photographs, and attractive page design." Voice Youth Advocates

Includes bibliographical references

Firestone, Mary

Nintendo; the company and its founders. ABDO Pub. Co. 2011 112p il (Technology pioneers) lib bdg $34.22

Grades: 5 6 7 8   338.7

1. Video games

ISBN 978-1-61714-809-5 lib bdg; 1-61714-809-1 lib bdg; 978-1-61758-967-6 e-book

LC 2010044664

This is an introduction to the Nintendo video game company and its founders.

"Written in a clear, linear fashion, this series offers vivid, well-researched details about the development of technological advancements considered essential in today's society. . . . Readers who are interested in technology and inventions will be thoroughly engrossed." SLJ

Includes glossary and bibliographical references

Gitlin, Marty

EBay; the company and its founder. ABDO Pub. Co. 2011 112p il (Technology pioneers) lib bdg $34.22

Grades: 5 6 7 8   338.7

1. Auctions 2. Executives 3. Businesspeople 4. Internet marketing 5. Software engineers 6. Internet executives

ISBN 978-1-61714-807-1 lib bdg; 1-61714-807-5 lib bdg; 978-1-61758-965-2 e-book

LC 2010044663

This is an introduction to eBay internet auction site and its founder, Pierre Omidyar.

"Written in a clear, linear fashion, this series offers vivid, well-researched details about the development of technological advancements considered essential in today's society. . . . Readers who are interested in technology and inventions will be thoroughly engrossed." SLJ

Includes glossary and bibliographical references

Hamen, Susan E.

Google; the company and its founders. ABDO Pub. Co. 2011 112p il (Technology pioneers) lib bdg $34.22

Grades: 5 6 7 8   338.7

1. Computer industry 2. Web search engines 3. Computer scientists 4. Internet executives 5. Information technology executives

ISBN 978-1-61714-808-8; 1-61714-808-3

LC 2010037884

This book about Google and its founders "provides a compact, direct, well-researched, and relevant explanation of how Sergey Brin, Larry Page, and their brand have changed the world. . . . This title presents just the right amount of background on the two men . . . before it moves into more thorough explorations of how the founders' creation has grown far beyond providing basic Web searching. . . . Dynamically designed with clear and colorful photographs, sidebars, and wide margins, this is at once a dual biography, Internet history, and business primer." Booklist

Includes bibliographical references

Segall, Grant

John D. Rockefeller; anointed with oil. Oxford University Press 2000 125p il (Oxford portraits) $28

Grades: 7 8 9 10   338.7

1. Philanthropists 2. Capitalists and financiers 3.

Energy industry executives 4. Businessmen -- United States -- Biography 5. Industrialists -- United States -- Biography 6. Philanthropists -- United States -- Biography 7. Capitalists and financiers -- United States -- Biography

ISBN 0-19-512147-3

LC 00-44616

"Included in the biography are some primary documents, such as letters, photos, and cartoons, as well as references to some of the other giants of industry, such as Flagler, Carnegie, and Gould." Book Rep

Includes bibliographical references

338.9   Economic development and growth

Belmont, Helen

★ **Planning** for a sustainable future; [by] Helen Belmont. Smart Apple Media 2008 46p il map (Geography skills) $22.95

Grades: 6 7 8 9   338.9

1. City planning 2. Human ecology

ISBN 978-1-59920-051-4; 1-59920-051-1

LC 2006100028

"The text is easy to follow. . . . The examples given in the text that involve places are almost always accompanied by excellent photographs. . . . Maps, block diagrams, tables, and graphs are clearly presented and easy to interpret." Sci Books Films

Includes glossary and bibliographical references

339.4   Factors affecting income and wealth

Thompson, Helen

Cost of living. Mason Crest Publishers 2010 63p il (Junior library of money) $22.95; pa $9.95

Grades: 6 7 8 9   339.4

1. Prices 2. Personal finance 3. Cost and standard of living

ISBN 978-1-4222-1762-7; 1-4222-1762-0; 978-1-4222-1866-2 pa; 1-4222-1866-X pa

LC 2010029402

This defines the cost of living as the amount of money a person needs to spend on housing, food, transportation, clothing, and other items that people need to live and explains how it can go up and down based on the conditions in the economy, and depending on where you live.

This title presents "solid information and [has] eye-catching and relevant illustrations. . . . [The book is] clearly written, making understandable connections between daily life and financial concepts." SLJ

Includes glossary and bibliographical references

341.242   European regional organizations

Ponsford, Simon

The **European** Union today; [by] Simon Ponsford. Sea-to-Sea Publications 2009 48p il (Today) lib bdg $32.80

Grades: 4 5 6   **341.242**

1. European federation
ISBN 978-1-59771-124-1 lib bdg; 1-59771-124-1 lib bdg

LC 2008-4573

This "is a good choice for readers who may be a bit hazy, for instance, on the organization's structure and purpose— not to mention the significant differences between the European Council, the Council of the European Union, and the Council of Europe. [The book is] well stocked with color photos, fact boxes, and statistics." SLJ

Includes glossary

341.6   Law of war

Kenney, Karen Latchana

Korematsu v. the United States; World War II Japanese-American internment camps. by Karen Latchana Kenney; content consultant Richard D. Friedman. ABDO Pub. Co. 2013 160 p. ill. (some col.) (library) $35.64

Grades: 8 9 10 11 12   **341.6**

1. Korematsu v. United States (Supreme Court case) 2. Japanese Americans -- Evacuation and relocation, 1942-1945
ISBN 1617834734; 9781617834738

LC 2012001277

This book by Karen Latchana Kenney is part of the Landmark Supreme Court Cases series and focuses on the case of Korematsu v. the United States. It "looks at the historical impact of World War II and the internment of Japanese American citizens out of fear and hysteria following the bombing of Pearl Harbor." (School Library Journal)

Includes bibliographical references (p. 146-154) and index.

342   Branches of law; laws, regulations, cases; law of specific jurisdictions, areas, socioeconomic regions

Anderson, Wayne

Plessy v. Ferguson; legalizing segregation. Rosen Pub. Group 2004 64p il (Supreme Court cases through primary sources) lib bdg $29.25

Grades: 6 7 8 9   **342**

1. Shoemakers 2. Discrimination in public accommodations 3. Segregation -- Law and legislation 4. Segregation in transportation -- Law and legislation -- Louisiana -- History
ISBN 0-8239-4011-X

LC 2002-154574

This examines the Supreme Court case that challenged a state's right to allow separate but equal railroad accommodations for different races.

This "deserves a place in every library. . . . Copious and well-chosen primary source documents give value to this [book]. . . . Each document adds human drama to the already engaging text." Lib Media Connect

Includes glossary and bibliographical references

Axelrod-Contrada, Joan

Plessy v. Ferguson; separate but unequal. Marshall Cavendish Benchmark 2009 143p il (Supreme Court milestones) $29.95

Grades: 7 8 9 10   **342**

1. Shoemakers 2. Discrimination in public accommodations 3. Segregation -- Law and legislation
ISBN 978-0-7614-2951-7; 0-7614-2951-4

LC 2007031606

Looks at the 1896 Supreme Court case that tested the constitutionality of laws in the South that enforced racial segregation in train travel, and discusses the impact of the verdict which provided a legal cover for racial discrimination throughout the United States.

Includes bibliographical references

The **Constitutional** Convention; Richard Haesly, book editor. Greenhaven Press 2002 240p il maps (History firsthand) lib bdg $34.95; pa $23.70

Grades: 7 8 9 10   **342**

1. Constitutional history -- United States 2. Constitutional history -- United States -- Sources 3. Constitutional conventions -- United States -- History -- Sources
ISBN 0-7377-1072-1 lib bdg; 0-7377-1071-3 pa

LC 2001-23832

This is a "study of the historical and political events that led up to the ratification of the U.S. Constitution. Using accounts and opinions by actual delegates and other prominent figures such as Patrick Henry and Thomas Jefferson, Haesly outlines the concepts of the Declaration of Independence, the Articles of Confederation, and the Constitution/Bill of Rights. The volume is enlivened by personal stories of those who lived through and influenced the events depicted, and includes discussions on slavery and the nature of the presidency. . . . Well suited for reports." SLJ

Includes bibliographical references

Feinberg, Barbara Silberdick

The **Articles** of Confederation; the first constitution of the United States. 21st Cent. Bks. (Brookfield) 2002 110p il maps lib bdg $24.90

Grades: 7 8 9 10   **342**

1. Constitutional history 2. Constitutional history -- United States
ISBN 0-7613-2114-4

LC 2001-27441

"Feinberg introduces the history and text of 'The Articles of Confederation and Perpetual Union,' the constitution that guided the U.S. government from 1776 to 1787. . . . Attractively laid out, this solid choice includes many black-and-white illustrations, including portrait paintings, engravings, and maps." Booklist

Includes bibliographical references

★ **Free** speech; John Boaz, book editor. Greenhaven Press 2006 221p (Current controversies) lib bdg $34.95; pa $23.70

Grades: 1 2 8 9 10 11   342

1. Freedom of speech

ISBN 0-7377-2204-5 lib bdg; 978-0-7377-2204-8 lib bdg; 0-7377-2205-3 pa

LC 2005-46225

"This volume explores the challenges facing free speech post September 11, 2001, including the Patriot Act, commercial free speech, and consolidation of the media." Publisher's note

Includes bibliographical references

Freedman, Russell

★ **In** defense of liberty; the story of America's Bill of Rights. Holiday House 2003 196p il $24.95

Grades: 5 6 7 8 9   342

1. Civil rights

ISBN 0-8234-1585-6

LC 2002-191918

Describes the origins, applications of, and challenges to the ten amendments to the United States Constitution that comprise the Bill of Rights

"This excellent study of the continually evolving meaning and interpretation of the Bill of Rights . . . is an essential purchase for all libraries." SLJ

Includes bibliographical references

Fridell, Ron

U.S. v. Eichman; flag burning and free speech. Marshall Cavendish Benchmark 2009 144p il (Supreme Court milestones) $29.95

Grades: 7 8 9 10   342

1. Freedom of speech 2. Flags -- Law and legislation

ISBN 978-0-7614-2953-1; 0-7614-2953-0

LC 2007022595

This examines the Supreme Court case regarding the Flag Protection Act of 1989.

Includes bibliographical references

Furgang, Kathy

The **Ninth** Amendment; rights retained by the people. Rosen Central 2011 64p il (Amendments to the United States Constitution: The Bill of Rights) $29.25; pa $12.95

Grades: 5 6 7 8   342

1. Civil rights 2. Constitutional law -- United States

ISBN 978-1-4488-1264-6; 1-4488-1264-X; 978-1-4488-2310-9 pa; 1-4488-2310-2 pa

LC 2010020091

This book about the Ninth Amendment to the U.S. Constitution is "well-written, objective and informative. . . . [It discusses] the historical reasons for [the] amendment, its basis in British and American common law, and the statutory and case law that shaped its implementation and development. . . . While primarily useful for reports, [this book] will also give students perspective on current events." SLJ

Includes glossary and bibliographical references

Gold, Susan Dudley

New York Times Co. v. Sullivan; freedom of the press or libel? [by] Susan Dudley Gold. Marshall Cavendish Benchmark 2006 144p il (Supreme Court milestones) lib bdg $39.93

Grades: 7 8 9 10   342

1. Freedom of the press

ISBN 978-0-7614-2145-0; 0-7614-2145-9

LC 2005033983

This is an account of the 1960 Supreme Court case involving a libel suit against the New York Times by Alabama politician L. B. Sullivan claiming false statements were made about police treatment of civil rights protesters.

Includes bibliographical references

The **Pentagon** papers; national security or the right to know. by Susan Dudley Gold. Benchmark Books 2004 144p il lib bdg $25.95

Grades: 7 8 9 10   342

1. Freedom of the press 2. Freedom of the press -- United States 3. Vietnamese Conflict, 1961-1975 -- United States 4. Security classification (Government documents) -- United States

ISBN 0-7614-1843-1

LC 2004-8583

An examination of the Supreme Court decision regarding the New York Times decision to publish articles about United States government's "secret war" in Cambodia and Vietnam

"The format of the [book] makes [it] easy to read and understand. [A] valuable [resource] for reports." SLJ

Includes bibliographical references

Roberts v. Jaycees; women's rights. Marshall Cavendish Benchmark 2009 144p il (Supreme Court milestones) $29.95

Grades: 7 8 9 10   342

1. Sex discrimination

ISBN 978-0-7614-2952-4; 0-7614-2952-2

LC 2007043021

First published 1984 by Twenty-First Century Books with title: Roberts v. U.S. Jaycees

This examines the Supreme Court case regarding sex discrimination against women members of the the the Jaycees organization.

Includes bibliographical references

Tinker v. Des Moines; free speech for students. [by] Susan Dudley Gold. Marshall Cavendish Benchmark 2006 143p il (Supreme Court milestones) lib bdg $39.93

Grades: 7 8 9 10   342

1. Freedom of speech 2. Pacifists 3. Computer programmers 4. Vietnam War, 1961-1975 -- Protest movements

ISBN 978-0-7614-2142-9; 0-7614-2142-4

LC 2005029838

This is an account of the Supreme Court case which dealt with the rights of students to protest against the U.S. involvement in the Vietnam War.

Includes bibliographical references

Worcester v. Georgia; American Indian rights. Marshall Cavendish Benchmark 2009 144p il (Supreme Court milestones) $29.95

Grades: 7 8 9 10　　　　　　　　　　　　　**342**

1. Cherokee Indians 2. Translators 3. Missionaries 4. Native Americans -- Civil rights

ISBN 978-0-7614-2956-2; 0-7614-2956-5

LC 2007050437

This describes the 1832 Supreme Court case of missionary Samuel Worcester against the State of Georgia, which arrested him for not obtaining a permit to work on Cherokee Indian tribal lands, and discusses the history of Cherokee relations with the U.S. government, including the Trail of Tears.

Includes bibliographical references

Haynes, Charles C.

First freedoms; a documentary history of the First Amendment Rights in America. [by] Charles C. Haynes, Sam Chaltain, Susan M. Glisson. Oxford University Press 2005 255p il $40

Grades: 8 9 10 11 12　　　　　　　　　　　**342**

1. Freedom of speech 2. Freedom of religion 3. Freedom of the press 4. Constitutional history -- United States

ISBN 978-0-19-515750-5; 0-19-515750-8

LC 2005-31880

This is "an excellent resource for all libraries, as well as enjoyable reading for history buffs." SLJ

Jones, Molly

The **First** Amendment; freedom of speech, the press, and religion. Rosen Central 2011 64p il (Amendments to the United States Constitution: The Bill of Rights) lib bdg $29.25; pa $12.95

Grades: 5 6 7 8　　　　　　　　　　　　　**342**

1. Freedom of speech 2. Freedom of religion 3. Freedom of the press

ISBN 978-1-4488-1252-3 lib bdg; 1-4488-1252-6 lib bdg; 978-1-4488-2302-4 pa; 1-4488-2302-1 pa

LC 2010023234

This book about the First Amendment to the U.S. Constitution is "well-written, objective and informative. . . . [It discusses] the historical reasons for [the] amendment, its basis in British and American common law, and the statutory and case law that shaped its implementation and development. . . . While primarily useful for reports, [this book] will also give students perspective on current events." SLJ

Includes glossary and bibliographical references

Krull, Kathleen

A **kid's** guide to America's Bill of Rights; curfews, censorship, and the 100-pound giant. illustrated by Anna DiVito. Avon Bks. 1999 226p il $15.99

Grades: 4 5 6 7　　　　　　　　　　　　　**342**

1. Civil rights 2. Constitutional amendments -- United States

ISBN 0-380-97497-5

LC 99-17324

"After describing how the first 10 amendments came to be added to the Constitution, the book considers each one from a historical point of view, examining Supreme Court cases and famous challenges, and explaining in what ways each amendment applies to children and teenagers. Anna Divito's cartoonlike drawings add a visually appealing touch." Booklist

Includes bibliographical references

McKissack, Patricia C.

To establish justice; citizenship and the Constitution. [by] Patricia McKissack and Arlene Zarembka. Alfred A. Knopf 2004 154p il map $18.95; lib bdg $22.99

Grades: 7 8 9 10　　　　　　　　　　　　　**342**

1. Discrimination -- Law and legislation

ISBN 0-679-89308-3; 0-679-99308-8 lib bdg

LC 2003-27929

The authors "examine issues of justice and equality in American history by focusing on the Supreme Court's role in defining rights of minority groups and citizens. . . . This book covers a broad spectrum of cases, and the authors do a fine job of providing the history, background, and events surrounding each Supreme Court decision." SLJ

Naden, Corinne J.

Dred Scott; person or property? [by] Corinne J. Naden and Rose Blue. Benchmark Books 2004 128p il (Supreme Court milestones) lib bdg $25.95

Grades: 7 8 9 10　　　　　　　　　　　　　**342**

1. Slaves 2. Slavery -- United States 3. Slavery -- Law and legislation -- United States -- History 4. Slavery -- United States -- Legal status of slaves in free states

ISBN 0-7614-1841-5

LC 2003-25568

The is an account of the 1857 Supreme Court decision regarding Dred Scott, who sued for his freedom from slavery

The authors "sandwich a clear account of the case's course, arguments, and participants between summaries of prior and subsequent historical events and an analysis of the decision's place in Supreme Court history. Illustrated with images of documents and oil portraits and supplemented by boxed essays." Booklist

Includes bibliographical references

Orr, Tamra

The **Tenth** Amendment; limiting federal powers. Rosen Central 2011 64p il (Amendments to the United States Constitution: The Bill of Rights) lib bdg $29.25; pa $12.95

Grades: 5 6 7 8　　　　　　　　　　　　　**342**

1. Federal government 2. State rights

ISBN 978-1-4488-1265-3 lib bdg; 1-4488-1265-8 lib bdg; 978-1-4488-2311-6 pa; 1-4488-2311-0 pa

LC 2010021852

This book about the Tenth Amendment to the U.S. Constitution is "well-written, objective and informative. . . . [It discusses] the historical reasons for [the] amendment, its basis in British and American common law, and the statutory and case law that shaped its implementation and development. . . . While primarily useful for reports, [this book] will also give students perspective on current events." SLJ

Includes glossary and bibliographical references

Patrick, John J.

The **Bill** of Rights; a history in documents. Oxford Univ. Press 2003 205p il map (Pages from history) lib bdg $32.95

Grades: 7 8 9 10   **342**
  1. Civil rights 2. Civil rights -- United States -- History
  ISBN 0-19-510354-8
                                                   LC 2002-6294
Uses contemporary documents to explore the history of the first ten amendments to the U.S. Constitution, the British traditions on which they were based, and their impact on American society

"This attractive and informative volume will be a valuable resource for most collections." SLJ

Includes bibliographical references

Pendergast, Tom

Constitutional amendments: from freedom of speech to flag burning; [by] Tom Pendergast, Sara Pendergast, and John Sousanis; Elizabeth Shaw Grunow, editor. U.X.L 2001 3v set $165

Grades: 7 8 9 10   **342**
  1. Civil rights 2. Constitutional law -- United States
  ISBN 0-7876-4865-5
                                                   LC 00-67236
"Presentation is very clear. . . . This is definitely a set that belongs in school and public libraries." Booklist

Includes glossary and bibliographical references

Phillips, Tracy A.

Hazelwood v. Kuhlmeier and the school newspaper censorship debate; debating Supreme Court decisions. Enslow Publishers 2006 112p il (Debating Supreme Court decisions) lib bdg $26.60

Grades: 7 8 9 10   **342**
  1. Censorship 2. Freedom of the press 3. Students -- Law and legislation
  ISBN 0-7660-2394-X
                                                 LC 2005034655
This discusses the Supreme Court case involving the censorship of a high school newspaper in Hazelwood Missouri.

This is "objectively and clearly written and would be useful for reports." SLJ

Includes bibliographical references

Porterfield, Jason

The **Third** Amendment; the right to privacy in the home. Rosen Central 2011 64p il (Amendments to the United States Constitution: The Bill of Rights) lib bdg $29.25; pa $12.95

Grades: 5 6 7 8   **342**
  1. Right of privacy
  ISBN 978-1-4488-1256-1 lib bdg; 1-4488-1256-9 lib bdg; 978-1-4488-2304-8 pa; 1-4488-2304-8 pa
                                                 LC 2010015855

This book about the Third Amendment to the U.S. Constitution is "well-written, objective and informative. . . . [It discusses] the historical reasons for [the] amendment, its basis in British and American common law, and the statutory and case law that shaped its implementation and development. . . . While primarily useful for reports, [this book] will also give students perspective on current events." SLJ

Includes glossary and bibliographical references

Racial discrimination; Mitchell Young, book editor.

Greenhaven Press 2006 183p il (Issues on trial) lib bdg $34.95

Grades: 8 9 10 11 12   **342**
  1. Hate crimes 2. Segregation 3. Race discrimination 4. Affirmative action programs
  ISBN 0-7377-2787-X; 978-0-7377-2787-6
                                                 LC 2005-55092
This anthology examines four major court cases involving racial discrimination: Plessy v. Ferguson (1896), Brown v. Board of Education (1954), Wisconsin v. Mitchell (1993), and Grutter v. Bollinger (2003).

Includes bibliographical references

Ritchie, Donald A.

★ **Our** Constitution. Oxford University Press 2006 255p il map $40

Grades: 7 8 9 10   **342**
  1. Constitutional history -- United States
  ISBN 978-0-19-522385-9; 0-19-522385-3
                                                 LC 2005031885
This "volume begins with five chapters of background (Why have a constitution? How has it changed?) and then goes on to discuss the preamble, articles, and amendments, using a What It Says (word for word) and What It Means format. Every spread contains photos, reproductions, and sidebars, all of which invite students to read and understand this living document. . . . This is an excellent, well-documented addition for most libraries." SLJ

Includes glossary and bibliographical references

Sergis, Diana K.

Bush v. Gore; controversial presidential election case. Diana K. Sergis. Enslow Publishers 2003 128p il (Landmark Supreme Court cases) $26.60

Grades: 7 8 9 10   **342**
  1. Governors 2. Presidents 3. Vice-presidents 4. Conservationists 5. Senators 6. Baseball executives 7. Members of Congress 8. Children of presidents 9. Presidential candidates 10. Nobel laureates for peace 11. Energy industry executives 12. Presidents -- United States -- Election -- 2000 13. Contested elections -- United States
  ISBN 0-7660-2095-9
                                                 LC 2002-154646
An account of the Supreme Court decision which decided the outcome of the 2000 presidential election.

"Hewing closely to the legal aspects of the contest, the book nevertheless gives some of the atmosphere surrounding the decision, maintaining a balanced tone without avoiding the tough questions." Horn Book Guide

Includes bibliographical references

Stearman, Kaye

Freedom of information; Kaye Stearman. Rosen Central Pub. 2012 48 p. (pbk.) $11.75

Grades: 7 8 9 10   **342**

1. Secrecy 2. Political ethics 3. United States -- Politics and government 4. Freedom of information -- United States

ISBN 1448860199; 1448870089; 1448870100; 9781448860197; 9781448870080; 9781448870103

LC 2011034070

Author Kaye Stearman presents "explanations of how freedom of information laws work and how they have been framed in different countries. . . . Most countries' laws contain limits on disclosure, and there are many debates about where the lines should be drawn. . . . Chapters explore the debate about how these laws should be applied so that they work well for both government officials and the public." (Publisher's note)

Includes bibliographical references and index.

Stefoff, Rebecca

U.S. v. Nixon; the limits of presidential privilege. Marshall Cavendish Benchmark 2009 127p il (Supreme Court milestones) lib bdg $29.95

Grades: 7 8 9 10   **342**

1. Presidents 2. Vice-presidents 3. Watergate Affair, 1972-1974 4. Senators 5. Nonfiction writers 6. Members of Congress

ISBN 978-0-7614-2955-5 lib bdg; 0-7614-2955-7 lib bdg

LC 2007031607

This examines the Supreme Court regarding the Watergate scandal.

Includes bibliographical references

Van Zee, Amy

Dred Scott v. Sandford; slavery and freedom before the American civil war. by Amy Van Zee; content consultant, Earl Maltz. ABDO Pub. Co. 2013 160 p. ill. (some col.) (Landmark Supreme Court cases) (hbk. : alk. paper) $35.64

Grades: 8 9 10 11 12   **342**

1. Slavery -- United States 2. Slavery -- Law and legislation -- United States -- History -- 19th century

ISBN 1617834726; 9781617834721

LC 2012001276

This book is part of the Landmark Supreme Court Cases Series. This title focuses on Dred Scott v. Sandford and explains how "the origins of slavery in the United States in regard to societal acceptance and black inferiority, deeply ingrained throughout the growth and development of the country, played a major role in every aspect of the developing nation with the continuing struggle between both sides of the issue." (School Library Journal)

Includes bibliographical references (p. 146-153) and index

Vile, John R.

The **United** States Constitution; questions and answers. Greenwood Press 1998 316p il $39.95

Grades: 8 9 10 11 12   **342**

1. Constitutional law 2. Constitutional law -- United States 3. Constitutional law -- United States -- Miscellanea 4. Constitutional law -- United States -- Popular works

ISBN 0-313-30643-5

LC 97-32008

The author examines each section of the U.S. Constitution "and provides a question-and-answer format that allows for easy explanation of a complicated document. The amendments are addressed in detail. . . . The book is easy to read and well laid out." Book Rep

Includes bibliographical references

343   Military, defense, public property, public finance, tax, commerce (trade), industrial law

Streissguth, Thomas

Clay v. United States and how Muhammad Ali fought the draft; [by] Tom Streissguth. Enslow Pubs. 2006 112p il (Debating Supreme Court decisions) lib bdg $26.60

Grades: 7 8 9 10   **343**

1. Boxers (Persons) 2. Draft -- Law and legislation

ISBN 0-7660-2393-1

Describes the trial of Muhammad Ali, the first three-time boxing Heavyweight Champion of the world, for refusing to serve in the Vietnam War.

344   Labor, social service, education, cultural law

Anderson, Wayne

★ **Brown** v. Board of Education; the case against school segregation. Rosen Pub. Group 2004 64p il (Supreme Court cases through primary sources) lib bdg $29.95

Grades: 6 7 8 9   **344**

1. Clergy 2. Segregation in education 3. Welders 4. Railroad workers 5. Civil rights activists 6. Discrimination in in education -- Law and legislation -- United States

ISBN 0-8239-4009-8

LC 2003-219

This is a discussion of the Supreme Court decision which ended racial segregation in public schools.

This "deserves a place in every library. . . . Copious and well-chosen primary source documents give extra value to this [book]. . . . Each document adds human drama to the already engaging text." Lib Media Connect

Includes glossary and bibliographical references

Axelrod-Contrada, Joan

Reno v. ACLU; internet censorship. Marshall Cavendish Benchmark 2006 144p il (Supreme Court milestones) lib bdg $39.93

Grades: 7 8 9 10   **344**

1. Obscenity (Law) 2. Freedom of speech 3. Internet

-- Law and legislation
ISBN 978-0-7614-2144-3; 0-7614-2144-0

This is an account of the 1996 Supreme Court case in which the American Civil Liberties Union challenged the law which made it a crime to send "patently offensive" material over the internet to anyone under the age of 18.

Includes bibliographical references

Bodden, Valerie

Environmental law. Creative Education 2011 48p il (Earth issues) lib bdg $23.95

Grades: 6 7 8 9   **344**
   1. Environmental law
   ISBN 978-1-58341-981-6; 1-58341-981-0

"Unfamiliar words are printed in bold type and defined in the glossary for students. . . . Written in a straightforward manner, with photographs that are clearly captioned, . . . [this] is a welcome addition for libraries." Libr Media Connect

Includes glossary and bibliographical references

Chmara, Theresa

Privacy and confidentiality issues; a guide for libraries and their lawyers. American Library Association 2009 98p pa $40

Grades: Adult Professional   **344**
   1. Library services 2. Right of privacy 3. Libraries -- Law and legislation
   ISBN 978-0-8389-0970-6; 0-8389-0970-1
                  LC 2008-34902

"This slim title is a must read. Chmara, a First Amendment attorney and litigation expert, clarifies privacy and confidentiality issues such as requests or subpoenas for patron-use records (both book and Internet), hostile-work-environment issues, state and federal privacy and confidentiality statutes, and minors' First Amendment rights and rights to privacy." Booklist

Includes bibliographical references

Donnelly, Karen J.

Cruzan v. Missouri; the right to die. by Karen Donnelly. Rosen Pub. Group 2004 64p il (Supreme Court cases through primary sources) lib bdg $29.25

Grades: 6 7 8 9   **344**
   1. Metalworkers 2. Accident victims 3. Right to die -- Law and legislation
   ISBN 0-8239-4014-4
                  LC 2002-156162

This "deserves a place in every library. . . . Copious and well-chosen primary source documents give extra value to this [book]. . . . Each document adds human drama to the already engaging text." Lib Media Connect

Includes glossary and bibliographical references

Fridell, Ron

Cruzan v. Missouri and the right to die debate; debating Supreme Court decisions. Enslow Publishers 2005 128p il (Debating Supreme Court decisions) lib bdg $26.60

Grades: 7 8 9 10   **344**
   1. Metalworkers 2. Accident victims 3. Right to die

-- Law and legislation
ISBN 0-7660-2356-7
                  LC 2004-20028

This examines both sides of the debate concerning assisted suicide and related Supreme Court decisions.

Includes glossary and bibliographical references

Gerber, Larry

The **Second** Amendment; the right to bear arms. Rosen Central 2011 64p il (Amendments to the United States Constitution: The Bill of Rights) lib bdg $29.25; pa $12.95

Grades: 5 6 7 8   **344**
   1. Gun control
   ISBN 978-1-4488-1253-0 lib bdg; 1-4488-1253-4 lib bdg; 978-1-4488-2303-1 pa; 1-4488-2303-X pa
                  LC 2010015854

This book about the Second Amendment to the U.S. Constitution is "well-written, objective and informative. . . . [It discusses] the historical reasons for [the] amendment, its basis in British and American common law, and the statutory and case law that shaped its implementation and development. . . . While primarily useful for reports, [this book] will also give students perspective on current events." SLJ

Includes glossary and bibliographical references

Gold, Susan Dudley

Brown v. Board of Education; separate but equal? by Susan Dudley Gold. Benchmark Books 2004 143p il (Supreme Court milestones) lib bdg $25.95

Grades: 6 7 8 9   **344**
   1. Clergy 2. Segregation in education 3. Welders 4. Railroad workers 5. Civil rights activists
   ISBN 0-7614-1842-3
                  LC 2004-5866

An overview of the Supreme Court decision which struck down racial segregation in schools.

"The format of the [book] makes [it] easy to read and understand. [A] valuable [resource] for reports." SLJ

Roe v. Wade; a woman's choice? by Susan Dudley Gold. Benchmark Books 2004 144p il (Supreme Court milestones) lib bdg $25.95

Grades: 6 7 8 9   **344**
   1. District attorneys 2. Pro-choice activists 3. Abortion -- Law and legislation 4. Trials (Abortion) -- United States 5. Abortion -- Law and legislation -- United States
   ISBN 0-7614-1839-3
                  LC 2003-25567

An overview of the Supreme Court decision which made abortion legal.

"The format of the [book] makes [it] easy to read and understand. [A] valuable [resource] for reports." SLJ

Includes bibliographical references

Vernonia School District v. Acton; drug testing in the schools. Marshall Cavendish Benchmark 2005 141p il (Supreme Court milestones) lib bdg $37.07

Grades: 7 8 9 10   **344**
1. Drug testing 2. Students -- Law and legislation
ISBN 0-7614-1941-1

"Describes the historical context of the Vernonia School District versus Acton case, detailing the claims made by both sides and the outcome and including excerpts from the Supreme Court justices' decisions and revelant sidebars." Publisher's note

Includes bibliographical references

Hayhurst, Chris

Jobs in environmental law. Rosen Pub. 2010 80p il (Green careers) lib bdg $30.60
Grades: 7 8 9 10   **344**
1. Environmental law 2. Vocational guidance
ISBN 978-1-4358-3567-2 lib bdg; 1-4358-3567-0 lib bdg

LC 2009025276

This "offers broad descriptions of the work of lawyers, paralegals, and legal secretaries and the professional requirements and mindset necessary to succeed in this field. Environmental police officers, lobbyists, and regulations and communications specialists are also included. . . . [This] slim [title is] well organized and [contains] informatively captioned color photos." SLJ

Includes glossary and bibliographical references

Kowalski, Kathiann M.

The **Earls** case and the student drug testing debate; debating Supreme Court decisions. Enslow Publishers 2006 128p il (Debating Supreme Court decisions) lib bdg $26.60
Grades: 7 8 9 10   **344**
1. Students 2. Drug testing 3. Students -- Law and legislation
ISBN 0-7660-2478-4

LC 2005034654

This is an account of the Supreme Court case involving Lindsay Earls, a high school student in Oklahoma who was subjected to a random drug test.

This is "objectively and clearly written and would be useful for reports." SLJ

Includes glossary and bibliographical references

Mountjoy, Shane

Engel v. Vitale; school prayer and the establishment clause. Chelsea House 2007 128p il (Great Supreme Court decisions) lib bdg $30
Grades: 7 8 9 10   **344**
1. Church and state 2. Religion in the public schools
ISBN 0-7910-9241-0; 978-0-7910-9241-5

LC 2006-7328

This describes the 1962 Supreme Court case which ruled that official prayers in public schools were unconstitutional.

"Excellent period photos, magazine covers, and portraits of historical figures are closely cued to the [text]. . . . Handsomely packaged, accessible." SLJ

Includes glossary and bibliographical references

Perl, Lila

Cruzan v. Missouri; the right to die? Marshall Cavendish Benchmark 2007 143p il (Supreme Court milestones) $27.95
Grades: 7 8 9 10   **344**
1. Metalworkers 2. Accident victims 3. Right to die -- Law and legislation
ISBN 978-0-7614-2581-6; 0-7614-258-0

LC 2006-25740

"Perl discusses Nancy Cruzan's parents quest for her right to die following an auto accident and her resulting vegetative state. Highlights include the discussion of religious arguments, physician-assisted suicide, and the cases of Karen Ann Quinlan and Terry Schiavo. . . . Additional information is presented in sidebars. Occasional black-and-white photos add interest." SLJ

Includes bibliographical references

345   Criminal law

Aaseng, Nathan

You are the juror. Oliver Press (Minneapolis) 1997 160p (Great decisions) lib bdg $18.95
Grades: 6 7 8 9   **345**
1. Jury 2. Trials
ISBN 1-88150-840-4

LC 96-53046

The reader assumes the role of a juror in eight famous trials of the twentieth century: the Lindbergh kidnapping, Sullivan v. New York Times, the Chicago Seven, Patty Hearst's trial for armed robbery, and others

"For each case, the author presents just enough information for readers to assume the role of juror, with three options from which to choose. He then reveals the actual results and analyzes the consequences. This format balances the passions of those on all sides of these cases and allows Aaseng to present controversial views in a palatable way." SLJ

Includes bibliographical references

Aretha, David

The **trial** of the Scottsboro boys. Morgan Reynolds Pub. 2007 128p il (The civil rights movement) lib bdg $27.95
Grades: 7 8 9 10 11 12   **345**
1. Trials 2. Scottsboro case 3. African Americans -- Civil rights
ISBN 978-1-59935-058-5; 1-59935-058-0

LC 2007-23818

This describes the case of nine young black men between the ages of 13 and 20 who were accused of rape in the 1930s in Alabama by two white women and were sentenced to death.

"Aretha writes clearly, with objectivity and compassion." SLJ

Includes bibliographical references

Brezina, Corona

The **Fifth** Amendment; double jeopardy, self-incrimination, and due process of law. Rosen Central 2011 64p il (Amendments to the United States

Constitution: The Bill of Rights) lib bdg $29.25; pa $12.95

Grades: 5 6 7 8   **345**
  1. Criminal procedure
  ISBN 978-1-4488-1260-8 lib bdg; 1-4488-1260-7 lib bdg; 978-1-4488-2306-2 pa; 1-4488-2306-4 pa
                       LC 2010018820
This book about the Fifth Amendment to the U.S. Constitution is "well-written, objective and informative. . . . [It discusses] the historical reasons for [the] amendment, its basis in British and American common law, and the statutory and case law that shaped its implementation and development. . . . While primarily useful for reports, [this book] will also give students perspective on current events." SLJ
  Includes glossary and bibliographical references

Burgan, Michael

  The **Scopes** trial; faith, science, and American education. Marshall Cavendish Benchmark 2010 112p il (Perspectives on) $39.93

Grades: 7 8 9 10   **345**
  1. Geologists 2. Science teachers 3. Evolution -- Study and teaching
  ISBN 978-0-7614-4981-2; 0-7614-4981-7
  An account of the trial of John T. Scopes, prosecuted in 1925 for teaching evolution.
  This "well-written [book begins] with [an overview] and some historical background, and then [proceeds] chronologically to the current decade. . . . Burgan presents both sides with respect and objectivity. . . . It is evident that . . . the author [has] done [his] research. [The book contains] information that is perhaps less well-known to student researchers, including the preliminary events leading up to the Scopes trial. . . . Black-and-white and color photographs along with some period cartoons place readers in the time period, and sidebars interspersed throughout present issues that aren't easily covered within the main [text]." SLJ

Cates, David

  The **Scottsboro** boys; by David Cates. ABDO Pub. Co. 2012 112 p. ill. $34.22

Grades: 6 7 8 9   **345**
  1. Scottsboro case 2. Civil rights -- United States -- History 3. Trials (Rape) -- Alabama -- Scottsboro 4. Scottsboro Trial, Scottsboro, Ala., 1931 5. African Americans -- Civil rights -- History
  ISBN 161783310X; 9781617833106
                       LC 2011036128
This book "tells the story of the nine African American teenagers accused of raping two white women on a train in Scottsboro, Alabama in 1931, covering the arrests and . . . legal proceedings." The book "explores the history of America at the time of the trials, the accounts of the nine men on trial regarding their train ride from Tennessee to Alabama, their sentences, and the effects of this event on society." (Publisher's notes)
  "These titles are excellent introductions to these important topics, particularly for developing an analytical framework for debate." SLJ
  Includes bibliographical references (p. 104-109) and index

Cohen, Laura

  The **Gault** case and young people's rights; debating Supreme Court decisions. Enslow Publishers, Inc. 2006 128p il (Debating Supreme Court decisions) lib bdg $26.60

Grades: 7 8 9 10   **345**
  1. Juvenile courts 2. Children -- Law and legislation
  ISBN 0-7660-2476-8
                       LC 2006001741
Examines the 1967 Supreme Court Case in which the court ruled that juvenile courts cannot deprive children of certain rights guaranteed by the Constitution.
  This is "objectively and clearly written and would be useful for reports." SLJ
  Includes bibliographical references

Coleman, Wim

  Racism on trial; From the Medgar Evers murder case to 'Ghosts of Mississippi' [by] Wim Coleman and Pat Perrin. Enslow Publishers 2009 112p il (Famous court cases that became movies) lib bdg $31.93

Grades: 5 6 7 8   **345**
  1. Lynching 2. Trials (Homicide) 3. Murderers 4. White supremacists 5. Civil rights activists
  ISBN 978-0-7660-3059-6; 0-7660-3059-8
                       LC 2008-21483
"Examines the Byron De La Beckwith murder trials, including the mistrials and his eventual conviction, key figures in the case, and the inspiration for the movie Ghosts of Mississippi." Publisher's note
  Includes glossary and bibliographical references

Fireside, Bryna J.

  The **trial** of the police officers in the shooting death of Amadou Diallo; a headline court case. Bryna J. Fireside. 1st ed; Enslow Publishers 2004 128p il (Headline court cases) lib bdg $19.95

Grades: 7 8 9 10   **345**
  1. Trials 2. Police brutality 3. Peddlers 4. Murder victims 5. Police brutality -- New York (State) -- New York 6. Trials (Manslaughter) -- New York (State) -- New York
  ISBN 0-7660-2166-1
                       LC 2004-7139
"Without wasting a word, this fast-paced, balanced text, which reads like a mystery, dives right into the events." Booklist
  Includes bibliographical references and index

Fridell, Ron

  Gideon v. Wainwright; the right to free counsel. Marshall Cavendish Benchmark 2006 144p il (Supreme Court milestones) lib bdg $39.93

Grades: 7 8 9 10   **345**
  1. Legal aid
  ISBN 978-0-7614-2146-7; 0-7614-2146-7
This describes the Supreme Court case which established the right to free counsel.
  Includes bibliographical references

Miranda law; the right to remain silent. [by] Ron Fridell. 1st ed.; Marshall Cavendish Benchmark 2006 144p il (Supreme Court milestones) lib bdg $37.07

Grades: 7 8 9 10   345

1. Criminals 2. Right to counsel

ISBN 0-7614-1942-X

LC 2005001156

"Describes the historical context of the Miranda versus Arizona Supreme Court case, detailing the claims made by both sides as well as the outcome, and including excerpts from the Supreme Court justices' decisions and relevant sidebars." Publisher's note

Includes bibliographical references

Galiano, Dean

The **Fourth** Amendment; unreasonable search and seizure. Rosen Central 2011 64p il (Amendments to the United States Constitution: The Bill of Rights) lib bdg $29.25; pa $12.95

Grades: 5 6 7 8   345

1. Searches and seizures

ISBN 978-1-4488-1259-2 lib bdg; 1-4488-1259-3 lib bdg; 978-1-4488-2305-5 pa; 1-4488-2305-6 pa

LC 2010017394

This book about the Fourth Amendment to the U.S. Constitution is "well-written, objective and informative. . . . [It discusses] the historical reasons for [the] amendment, its basis in British and American common law, and the statutory and case law that shaped its implementation and development. . . . While primarily useful for reports, [this book] will also give students perspective on current events." SLJ

Includes glossary and bibliographical references

Hinds, Maurene J.

Furman v. Georgia and the death penalty debate; [by] Maurene J. Hinds. Enslow Publishers 2005 128p il (Debating Supreme Court decisions) lib bdg $26.60

Grades: 7 8 9 10   345

1. Capital punishment

ISBN 0-7660-2390-7

LC 2004-18943

The author "examines the arguments on both sides of the [death penalty] debate, and she shows how the courts—especially the Supreme Court—have played a part in the evolution of capital punishment in the United States." Publisher's note

Includes glossary and bibliographical references

Jacobs, Thomas A.

★ **They** broke the law, you be the judge; true cases of teen crime. edited by Al Desetta. Free Spirit Pub. 2003 213p il pa $15.95

Grades: 7 8 9 10   345

1. Crime 2. Juvenile courts 3. Administration of justice 4. Administration of criminal justice 5. Juvenile delinquents 6. Justice, Administration of 7. Juvenile delinquents -- United States 8. Juvenile justice,

Administration of -- United States

ISBN 1-57542-134-8

LC 2003-4814

"An excellent introduction to how juvenile justice works, this will be a great resource for classroom and group discussions." Booklist

Includes bibliographical references

Jarrow, Gail

The **printer's** trial; the case of John Peter Zenger and the fight for a free press. [by] Gail Jarrow. 1st ed.; Calkins Creek Books 2006 102p il $18.95

Grades: 7 8 9 10   345

1. Trials 2. Freedom of the press 3. Printers 4. Newspaper editors 5. Newspaper executives

ISBN 978-1-59078-432-7; 1-59078-432-4

LC 2006000772

"This volume presents the 1735 trial of New York printer John Peter Zenger. The discussion begins with a good summary of Zenger's legal battle and why it matters, followed by a helpful, annotated list of participants and an intelligent discussion that acknowledges the limits of research based on those printed records that have survived." Booklist

Includes bibliographical references

Kelly-Gangi, Carol

Miranda v. Arizona and the rights of the accused; debating Supreme Court decisions. [by] Carol Kelly-Gangi. Enslow Publishers 2006 128p il (Debating Supreme Court decisions) lib bdg $26.60

Grades: 7 8 9 10   345

1. Criminals 2. Right to counsel

ISBN 0-7660-2477-6

LC 2006011737

This discusses the Supreme Court case involving a suspect's rights while being questioned by police.

Includes bibliographical references

Pellowski, Michael

The **O.J.** Simpson murder trial; a headline court case. [by] Michael J. Pellowski. Enslow Pubs. 2001 112p il (Headline court cases) lib bdg $26.60

Grades: 6 7 8 9   345

1. Football players 2. Trials (Homicide) 3. Sportscasters 4. Trials (Murder) -- California -- Los Angeles 5. Murder -- California -- Los Angeles -- Investigation

ISBN 0-7660-1480-0

LC 00-11907

"This book provides background information, the cases for the prosecution and for the defense, and a follow-up to one of the most controversial murder trials of all time. . . . The author presents the elements of the investigation in an objective manner. . . . Excerpts of public opinion and legal analysis are included as well as a page of questions to be used as springboard for discussion. . . . Well done and worthy of shelf space." SLJ

Includes glossary and bibliographical references

Roza, Greg

The **Eighth** Amendment; preventing cruel and unusual punishment. Rosen Central 2011 64p il

(Amendments to the United States Constitution: The Bill of Rights) lib bdg $29.25; pa $12.95

Grades: 5 6 7 8   **345**

1. Punishment
ISBN 978-1-4488-1263-9 lib bdg; 1-4488-1263-1 lib bdg; 978-1-4488-2309-3 pa; 1-4488-2309-9 pa
LC 2010015857

This book about the Eighth Amendment to the U.S. Constitution is "well-written, objective and informative. . . . [It discusses] the historical reasons for [the] amendment, its basis in British and American common law, and the statutory and case law that shaped its implementation and development. . . . While primarily useful for reports, [this book] will also give students perspective on current events." SLJ

Includes glossary and bibliographical references

Shea, Therese

The **Sixth** Amendment; the rights of the accused in criminal cases. Rosen Central 2011 64p il (Amendments to the United States Constitution: The Bill of Rights) lib bdg $29.25; pa $12.95

Grades: 5 6 7 8   **345**

1. Criminal procedure
ISBN 978-1-4488-1261-5 lib bdg; 1-4488-1261-5 lib bdg; 978-1-4488-2307-9 pa; 1-4488-2307-2 pa
LC 2010021318

This book about the Sixth Amendment to the U.S. Constitution is "well-written, objective and informative. . . . [It discusses] the historical reasons for [the] amendment, its basis in British and American common law, and the statutory and case law that shaped its implementation and development. . . . While primarily useful for reports, [this book] will also give students perspective on current events." SLJ

Includes glossary and bibliographical references

Sorensen, Lita

The **Scottsboro** Boys Trial; a primary source account. Rosen Pub. Group 2004 64p il (Great trials of the 20th century) lib bdg $29.25

Grades: 8 9 10 11 12   **345**

1. Trials 2. Scottsboro case 3. African Americans -- Civil rights 4. Trials (Rape) -- Alabama -- Scottsboro 5. Scottsboro Trial, Scottsboro, Ala., 1931 6. African Americans -- Civil rights -- History
ISBN 0-8239-3975-8
LC 2002-153356

An account of the 1931 trial in which African American youths were charged with rape.

This is "packed with information. . . . [An] attractive, intelligent offering." SLJ

Includes bibliographical references

Stefoff, Rebecca

Furman v. Georgia; debating the death penalty. Marshall Cavendish Benchmark 2007 127p il (Supreme Court milestones) lib bdg $27.95

Grades: 7 8 9 10   **345**

1. Capital punishment
ISBN 978-0-7614-2583-0; 0-7614-2583-7
LC 2007-582

"Stefoff shows how Furman's murder case, guilty verdict, and death sentence went through the process of appeals to the final decision. Discussions of the history of the death penalty and the use of the electric chair, gas chamber, and lethal injection contribute insight into the controversy and complexities of the case. . . . Additional information is presented in sidebars. Occasional black-and-white and color photos add interest." SLJ

Includes bibliographical references

VanMeter, Larry A.

Miranda v. Arizona; the rights of the accused. Chelsea House 2007 112p il (Great Supreme Court decisions) lib bdg $30

Grades: 7 8 9 10   **345**

1. Criminals 2. Right to counsel
ISBN 0-7910-9259-3; 978-0-7910-9259-0
LC 2006-7578

This discusses the case in which the Supreme Court ruled that suspects must be informed of their rights to remain silent and the right to counsel when they are being questioned by the police.

"Excellent period photos, magazine covers, and portraits of historical figures are closely cued to the [text]. Reproductions of primary documents, including Ernesto Miranda's signed confession, greatly enhance the presentation of the [case]. . . . Handsomely packaged, accessible." SLJ

Includes glossary and bibliographical references

Wormser, Richard

Defending the accused; stories from the courtroom. Watts 2001 127p $25

Grades: 7 8 9 10   **345**

1. Lawyers 2. Criminal procedure 3. Administration of criminal justice 4. Public defenders 5. Justice, Administration of 6. Defense (Criminal procedure) 7. Public defenders -- United States 8. Defense (Criminal procedure) -- United States
ISBN 0-531-11378-7
LC 00-33036

Presents case histories that illustrate the role of and techniques used by defense lawyers in the American judicial system

"The writing is lively and accessible. . . . This solid introduction to the subject will stimulate class discussion." SLJ

Includes glossary and bibliographical references

345.73 Criminal justice -- United States

Margulies, Philip

★ The **devil** on trial; witches, anarchists, atheists, communists, and terrorists in America's courtrooms. by Phillip Marguiles and Maxine Rosaler. Houghton Mifflin Co. 2008 218 p. ill., ports $22

Grades: 7 8 9 10 11 12   **345.73**

1. Lawyers 2. Trials -- History 3. Administration of criminal justice -- United States 4. Diplomats 5. Trials -- United States 6. Criminal justice, Administration of -- Social aspects -- United States 7. Discrimination in

criminal justice administration -- United States -- History

ISBN 061871717X; 9780618717170

LC 2008001870

The authors examine cases such as the Scopes 'monkey' trial, the two trials of Alger Hiss trials, and the witch trials in Salem, Mass. Glossary. Bibliography. Index. "Grades seven to ten." (Bull Cent Child Books)

The authors "examine five highly emotional court cases, each of which served as a litmus test for the health of America's justice system at the time it occurred. . . . Each chapter gives historical context of the court proceeding, describes its progression in some detail, and comments on the political and intellectual aftermath. . . . [This is] a highly relevant and riveting book." SLJ

Includes bibliographical references (p. [203] - 207) and index

346   Private law

Butler, Rebecca P.

★ **Copyright** for teachers & librarians in the 21st century. Neal-Schuman Publishers 2011 274p il pa $70

Grades: Adult Professional   **346**

1. Copyright 2. Fair use (Copyright)

ISBN 978-1-55570-738-5

LC 2011012600

First published 2004 with title: Copyright for teachers and librarians

"Library educator Rebecca Butler explains fair use, public domain, documentation and licenses, permissions, violations and penalties, policies and ethics codes, citations, creation and ownership, how to register copyrights, and gives tips for staying out of trouble." Publisher's note

Includes bibliographical references

Gold, Susan Dudley

Loving v. Virginia; lifting the ban against interracial marriage. Marshall Cavendish Benchmark 2007 143p il (Supreme Court milestones) lib bdg $27.95

Grades: 7 8 9 10   **346**

1. Construction workers 2. Civil rights activists 3. Interracial marriage -- Law and legislation

ISBN 978-0-7614-2586-1 lib bdg; 0-7614-2586-1 lib bdg

LC 2006-35955

"Gold looks at the issue of interracial marriage, brought to the forefront in 1958 with the arrest of a couple living in Virginia. She discusses the history of interracial-marriage laws, the impact of the 14th amendment, civil rights issues, and the couple's struggle to have their case heard in the Supreme Court. . . . Additional information is presented in sidebars. Occasional black-and-white and color photos add interest." SLJ

Includes bibliographical references

Jacobs, Thomas A.

What are my rights? 95 questions and answers about teens and the law. rev. ed; Free Spirit Pub. 2006 199p il pa $14.95

Grades: 7 8 9 10 11 12   **346**

1. Youth -- Law and legislation

ISBN 1-57542-028-7

LC 97-8599

First published 1997

This "presents answers to questions about laws that affect teens, encouraging youths to understand both their rights and responsibilities in order to make sound decisions. The book is organized into chapters on family, school, work, teens and their bodies, growing up, criminal behavior, and the legal system. . . . An accessible, current resource." SLJ

Includes bibliographical references

Popek, Emily

Copyright and digital ethics. Rosen Central 2011 48p il (Digital and information literacy) lib bdg $26.50; pa $11.75

Grades: 5 6 7 8   **346**

1. Ethics 2. Internet 3. Copyright

ISBN 978-1-4488-1323-0 lib bdg; 1-4488-1323-9; 978-1-4488-2294-2 pa; 1-4488-2294-7 pa

LC 2010027018

Though this "title is a broad overview of a sometimes-complex subject, the detail is significant. . . . Touches of blue enhance the clean design. . . . [This] explains concepts like fair use and tries to persuade readers of the damage done by digital piracy and plagiarism." Booklist

Includes bibliographical references

Riley, Gail Blasser

Internet piracy; [by] Gail Riley. Marshall Cavendish Benchmark 2010 111p il (Controversy!) lib bdg $25.95

Grades: 8 9 10 11 12   **346**

1. Copyright 2. Internet -- Law and legislation

ISBN 978-0-7614-4902-7; 0-7614-4902-7

LC 2009-50574

This "discusses copyright protection, theft of intellectual property, and the rise of online piracy of software, movies, and music. The book addresses the debate between those who push for freedom of information and those who want to crack down on violators. With rapid changes in technology and legislation, [this book is] recommended for all libraries seeking quality and current materials on [this topic]." SLJ

Includes bibliographical references

346.03   Torts (Delicts)

Sergis, Diana K.

Cipollone v. Liggett Group; suing tobacco companies. Enslow Pubs. 2001 128p (Landmark Supreme Court cases) lib bdg $26.60

Grades: 7 8 9 10   **346.03**

1. Trials 2. Liability (Law) 3. Tobacco industry 4. Trials (Products liability) -- United States 5. Tobacco -- Products liability -- United States

ISBN 0-7660-1343-X

LC 00-9787

"This volume focuses on the Supreme Court case concerning whether or not cigarette companies are protected from litigation by warning labels mandated by federal law. The text contains clear and useful background information on previous cases, explanations of the legal issues, and a discussion of repercussions of the case." Horn Book Guide

Includes glossary and bibliographical references

346.04   Property

Crews, Kenneth D.

★ **Copyright** law for librarians and educators; creative strategies and practical solutions. with contributions from Dwayne K. Buttler . . . [et al.] 2nd ed; American Library Association 2012 xii, 192 p.p ill. (alk. paper) $57

Grades: Adult Professional   **346.04**

1. Copyright 2. Sound recordings 3. Fair use (Copyright) 4. Copyright -- United States 5. Fair use (Copyright) -- United States 6. Teachers -- United States -- Handbooks, manuals, etc 7. Librarians -- United States -- Handbooks, manuals, etc

ISBN 0838910920; 9780838910924

LC 2011027604

First published 2000 with title: Copyright essentials for librarians and educators

The author "addresses 18 areas of copyright in 5 parts. He begins with the scope of protectable works as well as works without copyright protection. Next, he discusses the rights of ownership, including duration and exceptions. He then explains fair use and its related guidelines. Part 4 focuses on the TEACH Act, Section 108, and responsibilities and liabilities. Lastly, Crews examines special issues such as the Digital Millennium Copyright Act." Booklist

Includes bibliographical references and index.

346.73   Private law -- United States

Russell, Carrie

Complete copyright for K-12 librarians and educators; Carrie Russell. American Library Association 2012 xi, 173 p.p ill. (chiefly col.) (alk. paper) $50

Grades: Professional   **346.73**

1. Copyright 2. Fair use (Copyright) 3. Segregation -- Law and legislation 4. Copyright -- United States 5. Fair use (Copyright) -- United States 6. Librarians -- Legal status, laws, etc. -- United States 7. School libraries -- Law and legislation -- United States

ISBN 0838910831; 9780838910832

LC 2012016674

This book by Carrie Russell "is designed as a resource for educators, offering guidance for providing material to students while carefully observing copyright law. The book offers detailed advice on distinctive issues of intellectual property in the school setting; explores scenarios often encountered by educators . . . and precisely defines 'fair use,' by showing readers exactly what's possible within the law." (Education Digest)

Includes bibliographical references and index

347   Procedure and courts

Brannen, Daniel E.

★ **Supreme** Court drama; cases that changed America. [by] Daniel E. Brannen & Richard Clay Hanes; Elizabeth M. Shaw, editor. U.X.L 2001 4v il set $215

Grades: 7 8 9 10   **347**

1. Constitutional law -- United States 2. Constitutional law -- United States -- Cases

ISBN 0-7876-4877-9

LC 00-56380

"This set will be an especially useful reference when students need to retrieve concise information on Supreme Court cases." Book Rep

Includes glossary and bibliographical references

Furgang, Kathy

The **Seventh** Amendment; the right to a jury trial. Rosen Central 2011 64p il (Amendments to the United States Constitution: The Bill of Rights) lib bdg $29.25; pa $12.95

Grades: 5 6 7 8   **347**

1. Jury

ISBN 978-1-4488-1262-2 lib bdg; 1-4488-1262-3 lib bdg; 978-1-4488-2308-6 pa; 1-4488-2308-0 pa

LC 2010017696

This book about the Seventh Amendment to the U.S. Constitution is "well-written, objective and informative. . . . [It discusses] the historical reasons for [the] amendment, its basis in British and American common law, and the statutory and case law that shaped its implementation and development. . . . While primarily useful for reports, [this book] will also give students perspective on current events." SLJ

Includes glossary and bibliographical references

Panchyk, Richard

Our Supreme Court; a history with 14 activities. Chicago Review Press 2006 195p il $16.95

Grades: 7 8 9 10   **347**

1. Constitutional law -- United States

ISBN 978-1-55652-607-7; 1-55652-607-5

LC 2006009018

"The history and evolution of the court and how it works are discussed in the first chapter. Thematic sections follow, covering such topics as free speech, privacy, and civil rights, with significant decisions included. . . . This a solid work that makes a complex and important subject accessible to students." SLJ

Includes bibliographical references

347.73   Civil procedure and courts of the United States

Jost, Kenneth

★ The **Supreme** Court A to Z; Kenneth Jost. 5th ed. CQ Press 2012 xvii, 668 p.p ill. (hardcover : alk. paper) $125.00

Grades: 8 9 10 11 12 Adult   347.73
1. United States. Supreme Court -- Encyclopedias
ISBN 1608717445; 9781608717446

LC 2012000642

This book by Kenneth Jost "offers . . . information about the Supreme Court, including its history, traditions, organization, dynamics, and personalities. The entries in The Supreme Court A to Z are arranged alphabetically and are . . . cross-referenced to related information. This volume also has a detailed index, reference materials on Supreme Court nominations, a seat chart of the justices, the U.S. Constitution, online sources of decisions, and a bibliography." (Publisher's note)

Includes bibliographical references (p. 617-630) and index.

The **Supreme** Court justices; illustrated biographies, 1789-2012. edited by Clare Cushman, the Supreme Court Historical Society; foreword by Chief Justice John G. Roberts, Jr. 3rd ed. CQ Press, an imprint of SAGE Publications 2013 xx, 562 p.p ill., ports. (hardcover) $135
Grades: 8 9 10 11 12 Adult   347.73
1. Judges -- Biography 2. Judges -- United States -- Biography
ISBN 1608718328; 9781608718320

LC 2012031502

This book, edited by Clare Cushman, is "a single-volume reference profiling every Supreme Court justice from John Jay through Elena Kagan. An original essay on each justice paints a . . . picture of his or her individuality as shaped by family, education, pre-Court career, and the times in which he or she lived. Each biographical essay also presents the major issues on which the justice presided. Essays are arranged in the order of the justices' appointments." (Publisher's note)

"Written by leading constitutional scholars, the well-researched essays are arranged in chronological order of the justices' appointment to the Court. The volume includes a revised bibliography organized by individual justices, and a thorough index. . . . Recommended." Choice

Includes bibliographical references (pages 516-538) and index.

355 Military science

Barker, Geoff P.
War; [by] Geoff Barker. Smart Apple Media 2010 46p il (Voices) lib bdg $34.25
Grades: 7 8 9 10 11 12   355
1. War
ISBN 978-1-59920-2785; 1-59920-278-6

LC 2009-5418

This discusses "today's headline conflicts in Iraq, Afghanistan, and Gaza, as well as a look back at World War I, the bombing of Hiroshima and Nagasaki, and the fighting in Kosovo, Eritrea, and Cambodia. Ongoing issues include the role of child soldiers, WMDs, and the number of civilian deaths. The . . . blend of current political debate with witnesses' close-up experiences told through photos, narratives,

and quotes will draw browsers, and many will go on to find out more." Booklist

Includes glossary and bibliographical references

Brownlie, Ali
Why do people fight wars? [by] Ali Brownlie & Chris Mason. Raintree Steck-Vaughn Pubs. 2002 48p il (Exploring tough issues) lib bdg $25.69
Grades: 6 7 8 9   355
1. War 2. Military history 3. National security 4. Peacekeeping forces
ISBN 0-7398-4961-1

LC 2001-48372

Explores issues related to war, such as causes, types, results, and peacekeeping efforts, illustrated by examples of armed conflicts throughout history and throughout the world

This "does an excellent job of giving students a solid background and well-written explanation of [the subject]." Voice Youth Advocates

Includes glossary and bibliographical references

Chapman, Caroline
★ **Battles** & weapons: exploring history through art; [by] Caroline Chapman. Two-Can 2007 64p il (Picture that!) $19.95
Grades: 5 6 7 8   355
1. War in art 2. Military history 3. Military art and science
ISBN 978-1-58728-588-2

LC 2006033229

"High quality reproductions of paintings, murals, sculptures, and artifacts show military customs and equipment over the centuries. . . . The lively, informative text creates a 'you are there' sense that will engage even reluctant readers." SLJ

Includes bibliographical references

Chrisp, Peter
Warfare; by Peter Chrisp. Lucent Books 2004 48p il map (Medieval realms) $28.70
Grades: 6 7 8 9   355
1. Military history 2. Medieval civilization 3. Knights and knighthood
ISBN 1-59018-537-4

LC 2003-18308

This briefly describes wars and warfare in the Middle Ages, including the Norman invasions, the Crusades, knighthood and chivalry, the Hundred Years War, the campaign of Crécy, the Black Prince's War, and the Wars of the Roses

Inlcudes glossary and bibliographical references

Dolan, Edward F.
Careers in the U.S. Army. Marshall Cavendish Benchmark 2009 79p il (Military service) lib bdg $24.25
Grades: 6 7 8 9   355
1. Vocational guidance
ISBN 978-0-7614-4206-6 lib bdg; 0-7614-4206-5 lib bdg

LC 2008027821

Discusses service in the U.S. Army, including training, educational benefits, and career opportunities.

"Young people interested in exploring a career in [the U. S. Army] will find solid information. . . . Colored photographs, acronyms, Web sites, and a detailed index will add to the appeal." Booklist

Includes bibliographical references

Gravett, Christopher

Going to war in Viking times. Watts 2001 32p il (Armies of the past) lib bdg $24.50; pa $6.95

Grades: 4 5 6   **355**

1. Vikings 2. Military history 3. Naval art and science 4. Military history, Medieval 5. Naval art and science -- History -- To 1500

ISBN 0-531-14592-1 lib bdg; 0-531-16353-9 pa

LC 00-42642

This describes the weaponry, dress, transportation, and military and naval strategies of Viking times

This volume is "wonderfully attractive, highly visual, and historically accurate." Book Rep

Includes glossary

Park, Louise

The **Japanese** samurai; [by] Louise Park and Timothy Love. Marshall Cavendish Benchmark 2010 32p il map (Ancient and medieval people) lib bdg $28.50

Grades: 4 5 6   **355**

1. Samurai 2. Military art and science -- History

ISBN 978-0-7614-4448-0 lib bdg; 0-7614-4448-3 lib bdg

LC 2009-3573

This title has "a simple and elegant design with the proper balance of quality writing and quantity of information. . . . Handy time lines, well-chosen photos of ruins and artifacts, quality illustrations, inset 'Quick Facts', and 'What You Should Know About' features will grab reluctant readers and captivate even those with short attention spans." SLJ

Includes glossary

The **Pharaohs'** armies; by Louise Park and Timothy Love. Marshall Cavendish Benchmark 2009 32p il map (Ancient and medieval people) lib bdg $28.50

Grades: 4 5 6   **355**

1. Military art and science -- History

ISBN 978-0-7614-4451-0 lib bdg; 0-7614-4451-3 lib bdg

This title has "a simple and elegant design with the proper balance of quality writing and quantity of information. . . . Handy time lines, well-chosen photos of ruins and artifacts, quality illustrations, inset 'Quick Facts', and 'What You Should Know About' features will grab reluctant readers and captivate even those with short attention spans." SLJ

Includes glossary

Solway, Andrew

Graphing war and conflict. Raintree 2010 32p il (Real world data) $28.21; pa $7.99

Grades: 4 5 6 7   **355**

1. Graphic methods 2. Military history

ISBN 978-1-4329-2620-5; 1-4329-2620-9; 978-1-4329-2629-8 pa; 1-4329-2629-2 pa

LC 2009001188

This "uses graphs and charts to talk about global conflicts between 1990 and 2005, from guerilla warfare and civil war to nuclear attacks, with a special section on terrorism, including 9/11 and suicide bombers. . . . The clear design, with lots of full-color photos and sidebars, will encourage browsers as much as the up-to-date examples and the clear directions for remaining 'chart smart.'" Booklist

Includes glossary and bibliographical references

War: opposing viewpoints; Louise Gerdes, book editor. Greenhaven Press 2005 239p il (Opposing viewpoints series) lib bdg $34.95; pa $23.70

Grades: 8 9 10 11 12   **355**

1. War 2. Intervention (International law) 3. Military policy -- United States

ISBN 0-7377-2591-5 lib bdg; 0-7377-2592-3 pa

LC 2004-54283

In this anthology the authors "debate controversies surrounding the causes and conduct of war, including under what circumstances war is justified, how prisoners and civilians should be treated, and what measures, if any, will prevent wars." Publisher's note

Includes bibliographical references

355.02   War and warfare

Benoit, Peter

The **nuclear** age; by Peter Benoit. Children's Press 2012 64 p. ill. (chiefly col.), col. map (Cornerstones of freedom) (library) $30.00; (paperback) $8.95

Grades: 4 5 6   **355.02**

1. Nuclear weapons -- History

ISBN 0531230627; 0531281620; 9780531230626; 9780531281628

LC 2011031341

This book by Peter Benoit, part of the "Cornerstones of Freedom" series, "offers comprehensive coverage of all concepts related to the nuclear age beginning in the late 1800s through current times. . . . Four chapters highlight issues that emerge--birth of the new age, cold war, atom's legacy and human dilemma." Topics include "the atomic bomb, [Adolf] Hitler versus allies, international competitions, precautions, peaceful pursuits and cleaner sources of energy." (Children's Literature)

Includes bibliographical references (p. 61) and index.

355.1   Military life and customs

Hart, Joyce

Frequently asked questions about being part of a military family. Rosen Pub. 2009 64p il (FAQ: teen life) lib bdg $29.25

Grades: 6 7 8 9   **355.1**
1. Family life 2. Military personnel
ISBN 978-1-4358-5328-7 lib bdg; 1-4358-5328-8
lib bdg

     LC 2008055612

"While conversational, [this volume is] surprisingly helpful—and even emotive. [This] starts big: who's in the military, what are the branches, etc. Mostly, though, this is mentor-to-friend reassurance." Booklist

Includes glossary and bibliographical references

355.4   Military operations

Durman, Laura
    Siege; by Laura Durman. Arcturus Pub. 2012 32 p. col. ill. (Knights and castles) (library) $28.50
Grades: 4 5 6   **355.4**
1. Middle Ages 2. Military art and science 3. Sieges 4. Castles 5. Siege warfare
ISBN 1848585624; 9781848585621

     LC 2011051446

This book by Laura Durman is part of the Knights and Castles series and looks at sieges. In "two-page spreads filled with photos, staged reenactments, diagrams, and line drawings, Durman . . . outlines how both sides prepared and fared in a siege. Chapters on castle defense, defense tactics, and personal protection" are included as is an "in-depth look at the precision and force at work with such siege machines as the trebuchet, mangonel, battering ram, and belfry." (Children's Literature)

Includes bibliographical references (p. 31) and index.

Grayson, Robert
    Military. Marshall Cavendish Benchmark 2010 62p il (Working animals) lib bdg $28.50
Grades: 4 5 6 7   **355.4**
1. Animals -- War use
ISBN 978-1-60870-164-3 lib bdg; 1-60870-164-6 lib bdg

"Attractively designed and packed with information. . . . The composition of each page is attractively set up with well-selected and reproduced stock and historical photos." SLJ

Includes glossary and bibliographical references

McIntosh, J. S.
    Urban warfare; by Jack Montana. Mason Crest Publishers 2011 64p il (Special forces: protecting, building, teaching and fighting) lib bdg $22.95
Grades: 6 7 8 9   **355.4**
1. Urban warfare
ISBN 978-1-4222-1844-0; 1-4222-1844-9

     LC 2010024704

Introduces readers to the special tactics used by elite military forces for self-defense in urban settings.

"The well-chosen color photographs help make this series a fun armchair experience for military enthusiasts as well as a good resource for reports and for males considering military careers." Booklist

Includes bibliographical references

355.8   Military equipment and supplies

Byam, Michele
    Arms & armor; written by Michéle Byam. rev ed; DK Pub. 2004 72p il (DK eyewitness books) $15.99
Grades: 4 5 6 7   **355.8**
1. Armor 2. Weapons
ISBN 0-7566-0654-3

     LC 2004-558979

First published 1988 by Knopf

A photo essay examining the design, construction, and uses of hand weapons and armor from a Stone Age axe to the revolvers and rifles of the Wild West

Sullivan, Edward T.
    The **ultimate** weapon; the race to develop the atomic bomb. Holiday House 2007 182p il $24.95
Grades: 6 7 8 9   **355.8**
1. Atomic bomb 2. Young adult literature -- Works 3. Atomic bomb -- United States -- History 4. Atomic bomb -- History
ISBN 978-0-8234-1855-8; 0-8234-1855-3

     LC 2005-50330

This history of the Manhattan Project "effectively distills the science behind the development of the atomic bomb into understandable terms that turns the human story behind the project into compelling drama." Booklist

Includes bibliographical references

Vander Hook, Sue
    The **Manhattan** Project. ABDO Pub. 2011 112p il map (Essential events) lib bdg $23.95
Grades: 7 8 9 10 11 12   **355.8**
1. Atomic bomb
ISBN 978-1-61714-767-8; 1-61714-767-2

     LC 2010041429

This describes the project that developed the first atomic bomb, and discusses the political, social, and technical issues pertaining to it.

Includes glossary and bibliographical references

356   Specific kinds of military forces and warfare

Earl, C. F.
    Army Rangers; by Gabrielle Vanderhoof and C.F. Earl. Mason Crest Publishers 2011 96p il (Special forces: protecting, building, teaching and fighting) lib bdg $22.95
Grades: 6 7 8 9   **356**
1. United States -- Army
ISBN 978-1-4222-1838-9; 1-4222-1838-4

     LC 2010023795

This describes the Army Rangers unit and its history, training, weapons, modern missions.

"The well-chosen color photographs help make this series a fun armchair experience for military enthusiasts as well as a good resource for reports and for males considering military careers." Booklist

Includes bibliographical references

Green Berets. Mason Crest Publishers 2011 64p il (Special forces: protecting, building, teaching and fighting) lib bdg $22.95

Grades: 6 7 8 9   **356**

1. United States -- Army

ISBN 978-1-4222-1841-9; 1-4222-1841-4

LC 2010025293

This is an overview of the training, duties, and characteristics of Green Beret personnel.

"The well-chosen color photographs help make this series a fun armchair experience for military enthusiasts as well as a good resource for reports and for males considering military careers." Booklist

Includes bibliographical references

Haney, Eric L.

Inside Delta Force; the story of America's elite counterterrorist unit. Delacorte Press 2006 246p il hardcover o.p. pa $17

Grades: 8 9 10 11 12   **356**

1. Soldiers 2. Veterans 3. Security consultants

ISBN 0-385-73251-1; 0-385-33936-4 pa

LC 2004-30945

"In this adaptation of an adult book, Retired Command Sergeant Major Haney relates a . . . story of the 1977 founding of the ultrasecret counterterrorist unit of the U.S. Army known as Delta Force. . . . Better stock up on copies; you won't want to ration this one." Booklist

McIntosh, J. S.

Elite forces selection; by Jack Montana. Mason Crest Publishers 2011 64p il (Special forces: protecting, building, teaching and fighting) lib bdg $22.95

Grades: 6 7 8 9   **356**

1. United States -- Armed forces

ISBN 978-1-4222-1839-6; 1-4222-1839-2

LC 2010016871

This describes how special forces are selected and trained.

"The well-chosen color photographs help make this series a fun armchair experience for military enthusiasts as well as a good resource for reports and for males considering military careers." Booklist

Includes bibliographical references

358   Air and other specialized forces and warfare; engineering and related services

Marcovitz, Hal

Biological & chemical warfare. ABDO Pub. Co. 2010 112p il (Essential issues) lib bdg $22.95

Grades: 7 8 9 10   **358**

1. Chemical warfare 2. Biological warfare

ISBN 978-1-60453-951-6; 1-60453-951-8

LC 2009-29947

The text is "well-written, providing examples that put a human face to each problem. Quotes and facts are clearly attributed, and their sources are noted in the extensive back matter. . . . Sidebars provide further information, or, more compellingly, offer stories about those touched by the topic. . . . [This] will be of great assistance to students writing reports." SLJ

Includes glossary and bibliographical references

358.4   Air forces and warfare

Dolan, Edward F.

Careers in the U.S. Air Force. Marshall Cavendish Benchmark 2009 80p il (Military service) lib bdg $24.95

Grades: 6 7 8 9   **358.4**

1. Vocational guidance 2. United States -- Air Force

ISBN 978-0-7614-4205-9 lib bdg; 0-7614-4205-7 lib bdg

LC 2008039820

"Dolan gives the history of the Air Force and a description of its aircraft. . . . He discusses requirements for joining, years of service, enlistment and training, and salary and benefits. Dolan uses straightforward language to present the facts and does not glamorize service in the Air Force. . . . Young people interested in exploring a career [in the Air Force] will find solid information." Booklist

Includes bibliographical references

Schwartz, Heather E.

Women of the U.S. Air Force; aiming high. Capstone Press 2011 32p (Women in the U.S. Armed Forces) lib bdg $26.65

Grades: 4 5 6 7   **358.4**

1. Women air pilots 2. Women in the armed forces 3. United States -- Air Force

ISBN 978-1-4296-5449-4; 1-4296-5449-X

LC 2010040749

Describes the past, present, and future of women in the U.S. Air Force.

The book has "a snappy design and eye-catching photographs, and the [text is] written with struggling readers in mind. The content is engaging, the material is worthy, and the [package is] attractive." SLJ

Includes glossary and bibliographical references

Vanderhoof, Gabrielle

Air Force. Mason Crest Publishers 2011 64p il (Special forces: protecting, building, teaching and fighting) lib bdg $22.95

Grades: 6 7 8 9   **358.4**

1. United States -- Air Force

ISBN 978-1-4222-1837-2; 1-4222-1837-6

LC 2010019186

"The well-chosen color photographs help make this series a fun armchair experience for military enthusiasts as well as a good resource for reports and for males considering military careers." Booklist

Includes bibliographical references

359 Sea forces and warfare

Dolan, Edward F.
Careers in the U.S. Navy. Marshall Cavendish Benchmark 2009 80p il (Military service) lib bdg $24.95
Grades: 6 7 8 9   **359**
   1. Vocational guidance 2. United States -- Navy
   ISBN 978-0-7614-4210-3 lib bdg; 0-7614-4210-3
   lib bdg
                     LC 2008035919
Discusses service in the U.S. Navy, including training, educational benefits, and career opportunities.
"Young people interested in exploring a career in [the U. S. Navy] will find solid information. . . . Colored photographs, acronymns, Web sites, and a detail index will add to the appeal." Booklist
Includes bibliographical references

Llanas, Sheila Griffin
Women of the U.S. Navy; making waves. Capstone Press 2011 32p il (Women in the U. S. Armed Forces) lib bdg $26.65
Grades: 4 5 6 7   **359**
   1. Sailors 2. Women in the armed forces 3. United States -- Navy
   ISBN 978-1-4296-5448-7; 1-4296-5448-1
                     LC 2010040801
This book explains "how women's roles in the U.S. [Navy] have evolved over the years. [The] volume starts with an account of one specific servicewoman and then delves into her branch's history. [The book has] a snappy design and eye-catching photographs, and the [text is] written with struggling readers in mind. The content is engaging, the material is worthy, and the [package is] attractive." SLJ
Includes glossary and bibliographical references

359.009

Templin, Stephen
  ★ **I** am a SEAL Team Six warrior; memoirs of an American soldier. Howard E. Wasdin and Stephen Templin. 1st ed. St. Martin's Griffin 2012 $7.99 vi, 182 p.p. ill.
Grades: 8 9 10 11 12   **359.009**
   1. Snipers -- United States -- Biography
   ISBN 1250016436; 9781250016430
                     LC 2012376658
This book offers an "[a]bridged, . . . young-readers version of an ex-SEAL sniper's account ('SEAL Team Six,' 2011) of his training and combat experiences in Operation Desert Storm and the first Battle of Mogadishu. . . . In later chapters he retraces his long, difficult physical and emotional recovery from serious wounds received during the 'Black Hawk Down' operation, his increasing focus on faith and family after divorce and remarriage and his second career as a chiropractor." (Kirkus Reviews)
Includes bibliographical references (p. [181]-182).

359.8 Naval equipment and supplies

Myers, Walter Dean, 1937-
USS Constellation; pride of the American navy. Holiday House 2004 86p il $16.95
Grades: 5 6 7 8   **359.8**
   1. Warships 2. United States -- Navy
   ISBN 0-8234-1816-2
                     LC 2003-56764
This "book traces the history of the USS Constellation, which was built as a frigate, launched in 1797, and initially charged with battling privateers that threatened U.S. trade with Europe. She was rebuilt as a sloop in 1854 and, in 1999, restored to her 1854 glory and docked in Baltimore Harbor. . . . The volume features an attractive design and many black-and-white reproductions of period photographs, drawings, paintings, and documents. . . . A unique addition to American history collections." Booklist
Includes glossary and bibliographical references

359.9 Specialized combat forces; engineering and related services

Dolan, Edward F.
Careers in the U.S. Marine Corps. Marshall Cavendish Benchmark 2009 80p il (Military service) lib bdg $24.95
Grades: 6 7 8 9   **359.9**
   1. Vocational guidance 2. United States -- Marine Corps
   ISBN 978-0-7614-4209-7 lib bdg; 0-7614-4209-X
   lib bdg
                     LC 2008039818
Discusses service in the U.S. Marine Corps, including training, educational benefits, and career opportunities.
"Young people interested in exploring a career in [the U. S. Marine Corps] will find solid information. . . . Colored photographs, acronyms, Web sites, and detailed index will add to the appeal." Booklist
Includes bibliographical references

Gray, Judy Silverstein
The **U.S.** Coast Guard and military careers; [by] Judy Silverstein Gray. Enslow Publishers 2007 128p il (The U.S. Armed Forces and military careers) lib bdg $31.93
Grades: 6 7 8 9   **359.9**
   1. Vocational guidance 2. United States -- Coast Guard 3. Coast Guard
   ISBN 978-0-7660-2493-9 lib bdg; 0-7660-2493-8
   lib bdg
                     LC 2006001744
This offers a history of the U.S. Coast Guard, describes what the Coast Guard does and outlines career opportunities.
Includes glossary and bibliographical references

McIntosh, J. S.
Marines; by Jack Montana. Mason Crest Publishers 2011 64p il (Special forces: protecting, building, teaching and fighting) lib bdg $22.95

Grades: 6 7 8 9   **359.9**
  1. United States -- Marine Corps
  ISBN 978-1-4222-1842-6; 1-4222-1842-2
                  LC 2010020681
Briefly describes the history, training, and missions of the United States Marine Corps.

"The well-chosen color photographs help make this series a fun armchair experience for military enthusiasts as well as a good resource for reports and for males considering military careers." Booklist
Includes bibliographical references

Navy SEALs; by Jack Montana. Mason Crest Publishers 2011 96p il (Special forces: protecting, building, teaching and fighting) lib bdg $22.95
Grades: 6 7 8 9   **359.9**
  1. United States -- Navy
  ISBN 978-1-4222-1843-3; 1-4222-1843-0
                  LC 2010021842
This describes the history of the Navy SEALs, their training and selection, their survival tactics and modern missions around the world.

"The well-chosen color photographs help make this series a fun armchair experience for military enthusiasts as well as a good resource for reports and for males considering military careers." Booklist
Includes bibliographical references

361.2   Social action

Drake, Jane
  Yes you can! your guide to becoming an activist. [by] Jane Drake & Ann Love. Tundra Books 2010 136p pa $12.95
Grades: 7 8 9 10   **361.2**
  1. Social action
  ISBN 978-0-88776-942-9; 0-88776-942-X pa
"Young people who want to effect change are guided by a sequence of nine steps and inspirational examples of grassroots activism. . . . Each step, or chapter, includes a story, strategies, skills, and a time line of milestones and setbacks. . . . The style is conversational and the tone offers realistic encouragement to teens looking to solve problems. . . . This title will primarily serve as a how-to, although the time lines, an accessible index, and factual information about anti-smoking campaigns, recycling, and children's rights make it a useful historical perspective of activism." SLJ

Halpin, Mikki
  ★ **It's** your world--if you don't like it, change it; activism for teenagers. Simon Pulse 2004 305p pa $8.99
Grades: 7 8 9 10   **361.2**
  1. Social action
  ISBN 0-689-87448-0
"Animal rights, racism, war protest, AIDS, school violence and bullying, women's rights, and promoting tolerance are among the topics covered here. Halpin provides basic information about each one and then makes myriad suggestions for action at home, in the community, the 'five-minute

activist,' etc. The ideas are easy to implement. . . .This is an important book that will empower any young adult who would like to make a difference." SLJ
Includes bibliographical references

Zeiler, Freddi
  A **kid's** guide to giving; illustrated by Ward Schumaker. InnovativeKids 2006 205p il pa $9.99
Grades: 7 8 9 10   **361.2**
  1. Charity
  ISBN 1-58476-489-9
"In this inspiring and motivating book, Zeiler challenges teens to make a difference by contributing to charitable causes. Her enthusiastic, personal appeal offers advice on selecting a charity and deciding whether to donate money, useful items, or time." SLJ

361.3   Social work

Flath, Camden
  Social workers; finding solutions for tomorrow's society. Mason Crest Publishers 2011 64p il (New careers for the 21st century: finding your role in the global renewal) lib bdg $22.95; pa $9.95
Grades: 7 8 9 10   **361.3**
  1. Social work 2. Vocational guidance
  ISBN 978-1-4222-1821-1 lib bdg; 1-4222-1821-X lib bdg; 978-1-4222-2042-9 pa; 1-4222-2042-7 pa
                  LC 2010017920
"Chapters identify and emphasize specific careers—important strengths, necessary aptitudes and interests, education and training, projected earnings, closely related occupations, type of work environment, and predictions for the future of the field. . . . Color photos have a small role amid the many statistics, figures, graphs and charts that support and supplement the . . . [text]." SLJ
Includes bibliographical references

Gay, Kathlyn
  ★ **Volunteering**; the ultimate teen guide. Scarecrow Press 2004 127p il (It happened to me) $37.50; pa $14.95
Grades: 7 8 9 10   **361.3**
  1. Volunteer work
  ISBN 0-8108-4922-4; 978-0-8108-4922-8; 0-8108-5833-9 pa; 978-0-8108-5833-6 pa
                  LC 2004-8174
"This is a useful tool in that it provides a one-stop resource for teens interested in locating volunteer opportunities." SLJ
Includes bibliographical references

Karnes, Frances A.
  Empowered girls; a girl's guide to positive activism, volunteering, and philanthropy. [by] Frances Karnes A. & Kristen R. Stephens. Prufrock Press 2005 191p pa $14.95
Grades: 6 7 8 9   **361.3**
  1. Social action 2. Volunteer work 3. Charity organization
  ISBN 1-59363-163-4

"Those looking to get involved in service projects will find this an inspiring and motivational guide." SLJ

Includes bibliographical references

Marcovitz, Hal

Teens & volunteerism. Mason Crest 2005 112p il (Gallup Youth Survey) $22.95

Grades: 7 8 9 10   **361.3**

1. Volunteer work

ISBN 1-59084-877-2

LC 2004004827

This is "based on the findings of the Gallup Youth Survey (a 20-year ongoing survey of teens). . . . [It] covers the gamut of issues surrounding [volunteerism and youth], focusing on mandatory vs. optional community service in high school and college, military service, political community service, and activism. [The book is] well documented." SLJ

Includes bibliographical references

O'Neal, Claire

Volunteering in your school. Mitchell Lane Publishers 2011 47p (How to help: a guide to giving back) lib bdg $29.95

Grades: 4 5 6   **361.3**

1. Volunteer work

ISBN 978-1-58415-920-9; 1-58415-920-0

LC 2010011982

This suggests ways in which young people can volunteer to do such tasks as participating in a clean-up day, setting up a recycling center, or planting a garden to enhance and contribute to the school community.

This "well-organized [book] will encourage children to contribute to the world around them. [The] title is filled with examples of volunteer opportunities that can be accomplished with some adult involvement and supervision to guide, steer, and maintain focus so that youngsters will have varied and successful experiences." SLJ

Includes bibliographical references

Ways to help in your community. Mitchell Lane 2010 47p il (How to help: a guide to giving back) lib bdg $29.95

Grades: 4 5 6   **361.3**

1. Community life 2. Volunteer work

ISBN 978-1-58415-921-6 lib bdg; 1-58415-921-9 lib bdg

This "well-organized [book] will encourage children to contribute to the world around them. [The] title is filled with examples of volunteer opportunities that can be accomplished with some adult involvement and supervision to guide, steer, and maintain focus so that youngsters will have varied and successful experiences. . . . [The book] offers specific examples and steps for making a neighborhood safer, organizing yard sales, spending time with an elderly person, helping at a soup kitchen, or offering to do storyhours at a library." SLJ

Includes bibliographical references

361.7   Private action

Reusser, Kayleen

Celebrities giving back. Mitchell Lane Publishers 2011 47p (How to help: a guide to giving back) lib bdg $29.95

Grades: 4 5 6   **361.7**

1. Charities 2. Celebrities 3. Philanthropists

ISBN 978-1-58415-922-3 lib bdg; 1-58415-922-7 lib bdg

LC 2010014904

"Reusser writes about 17 people, including Bono and his interest in eliminating world hunger and poverty, President Carter's dreams of building homes for the homeless, and charitable works by Rihanna, Shakira, Tony Hawk, and others." SLJ

Includes bibliographical references

361.9   History, geographic treatment, biography

Slavicek, Louise Chipley, 1956-

Jane Addams. Chelsea House 2011 126 p. ill (some col.) (Women of achievement) lib bdg $35

Grades: 6 7 8 9   **361.9**

1. Authors 2. Philanthropists 3. Essayists 4. Pacifists 5. Social welfare leaders 6. Nobel laureates for peace

ISBN 978-1-60413-907-5; 1-60413-907-2

LC 2011000038

Details on her role in "found[ing] the pioneering settlement house, Hull House, where she and a dedicated staff of volunteers, most of them college-educated women like herself, lived and worked among some of Chicago's most destitute residents" are also presented. (Publisher's note)

This book "traces [Jane] Addams' life and considerable accomplishments in social welfare, labor reform, and women's suffrage . . . [and] portrays Addams' difficult path to good education and her determination to use her life well." It is "supplemented with sidebars and illustrations . . . [and] includes a chronology, notes for the many quotes, a source bibliography, and lists of recommended books and websites." (Booklist)

Includes bibliographical references and index.

362   Specific social problems and services

Ingram, Scott

Want fries with that? obesity and the supersizing of America. Franklin Watts 2006 128p il $26

Grades: 7 8 9 10   **362**

1. Obesity 2. Eating customs 3. Convenience foods

ISBN 0-531-16756-9

LC 2005-5619

This is an "exploration of the physical phenomenon of obesity and its emotional and social ramifications. The text is packed with information on specific dangers such as increased risks of diabetes, cancer, and other health problems. The author casts a critical eye on the effect of advertising and the availability of fast food, both in and out of school, and covers recent state legislation seeking to inform parents of diagnoses of obesity in their children." SLJ

Includes glossary and bibliographical references

362.1 People with illnesses and disabilities

Dreyer, ZoAnn

Living with cancer; ZoAnn Dreyer. Facts On File 2008 202p $34.95

Grades: 8 9 10 11 12 **362.1**
1. Cancer
ISBN 978-0-8160-6484-7

LC 2007-10675

"Although written for teens with these conditions, these titles will have more general appeal... Material in both titles is presented in a straightforward manner." SLJ

Includes bibliographical references (p. 192-194) and index.

Farrell, Courtney

Mental disorders. ABDO Pub. Co. 2010 112p il (Essential issues) lib bdg $22.95

Grades: 7 8 9 10 **362.1**
1. Mental illness
ISBN 978-1-60453-956-1; 1-60453-956-9

LC 2009-29942

"This title examines the world's critical issues surrounding mental disorders. Readers will learn the historical background of mental disorders, leading up to the current and future impact on society." Publisher's note

Includes glossary and bibliographical references

Fleischman, John

★ **Phineas** Gage: a gruesome but true story about brain science. Houghton Mifflin 2002 86p il $16; pa $8.95

Grades: 5 6 7 8 9 **362.1**
1. Railroad workers 2. Brain -- Wounds and injuries 3. Brain damage -- Complications 4. Personality disorders -- Etiology 5. Brain damage -- Patients -- United States -- Biography
ISBN 0-618-05252-6; 0-618-49478-2 pa

LC 2001-39253

"The author deftly introduces readers to a diverse range of relevant scientific history as well as more specific beliefs that influenced the medical establishment's understanding of Gage, then goes on to examine subsequent neurological discoveries that have changed and enhanced our understanding of Gage's fate. The book's present-tense narrative is inviting and intimate, and the text is crisp and lucid." Bull Cent Child Books

Includes glossary and bibliographical references

Jones, Molly

Health care for everyone. Rosen Pub. 2011 64p il (Headlines!) lib bdg $29.95

Grades: 7 8 9 10 **362.1**
1. Medical care 2. Health insurance
ISBN 978-1-4488-1290-5; 1-4488-1290-9

LC 2010024137

This book "begins with President Obama's 2010 [health care] legislation then discusses problems within the industry. . . . Good organization, clear writing, captioned photos, and sidebars deliver the information cleanly." Horn Book Guide

Includes glossary and bibliographical references

Libal, Autumn

Social discrimination and body size; too big to fit? Mason Crest Publishers 2006 104p il (Obesity: modern-day epidemic) $23.95

Grades: 7 8 9 10 **362.1**
1. Obesity 2. Body image 3. Discrimination
ISBN 978-1-59084-949-1; 1-59084-949-3

LC 2004-27863

Explains "the effects social discrimination based on body size have on individuals and society." Publisher's note

Includes bibliographical references

Naden, Corinne J.

Patients' rights; [by] Corinne Naden. Marshall Cavendish Benchmark 2008 144p il (Open for debate) lib bdg $27.95

Grades: 7 8 9 10 **362.1**
1. Medical care
ISBN 978-0-7614-2576-2; 0-7614-2576-4

LC 2006-21786

This book maintains a "balanced tone while providing an abundance of examples and factual information. Many captioned color photos enhance the text." SLJ

Includes bibliographical references

Parks, Peggy J., 1951-

HPV. ReferencePoint Press 2009 104p il map (Compact research. Diseases and disorders) $25.95

Grades: 7 8 9 10 11 12 **362.1**
1. Papillomaviruses
ISBN 978-1-60152-070-8; 1-60152-070-0

LC 2008-44026

Presents an overview of the causes, symptoms, and various types of the Human Papillomavirus; and provides information on available vaccines, health risks of genital HPV, and organizations and advocacy groups.

This book "is a timely overview of the most prevalent sexually transmitted disease among female teens today." Booklist

Includes bibliographical references

Winick, Judd

Pedro & me; friendship, loss, & what I learned. Henry Holt and Co. 2009 187p il pa $16.99

Grades: 7 8 9 10 11 12 **362.1**
1. Graphic novels 2. Television personalities 3. Biographical graphic novels 4. AIDS patients 5. AIDS activists 6. Friendship -- Graphic novels 7. AIDS (Disease) -- Graphic novels
ISBN 978-0-8050-8964-6

First published 2000

2001 Robert F. Sibert Honor Book for informational books for youth

In this "volume—part graphic novel, part memoir—professional cartoonist Winick pays tribute to his Real World housemate and friend Pedro Zamora, an AIDS activist who died of the disease in 1994." Publ Wkly

Fast food; Lauri S. Friedman, book editor. Greenhaven Press 2010 122p il map (Introducing issues with opposing viewpoints) $34.70
Grades: 7 8 9 10 11 12   **362.1**
1. Obesity 2. Restaurants 3. Convenience foods
ISBN 978-0-7377-4733-1; 0-7377-4733-1
LC 2009-51963
This is a collection of essays arguing various viewpoints about fast foods and their effects on health, and whether or not fast food restaurants should be banned, taxed, or regulated.
This "contains some fascinating arguments, including the central question of whether or not fast food makes people fat and sick. Active-reading questions preface the essays, which are followed by directions for evaluating the arguments presented. Color photos and other graphics throughout enliven the reading experience." SLJ
Includes bibliographical references

Terminal illness: opposing viewpoints; Andrea C. Nakaya, book editor. Greenhaven Press 2005 204p il (Opposing viewpoints series) lib bdg $34.95; pa $23.70
Grades: 8 9 10 11 12   **362.1**
1. Marijuana 2. Euthanasia 3. Right to die 4. Terminal care
ISBN 0-7377-2963-5 lib bdg; 0-7377-2964-3 pa
LC 2004-60595
"The authors of this anthology present various opinions on the best way to care for the terminally ill and their friends and family, including a debate on the role of euthanasia." Publisher's note
Includes bibliographical references

What can I do now?: Health care. Ferguson 2007 222p $29.95
Grades: 8 9 10 11 12   **362.1**
1. Medicine 2. Vocational guidance
ISBN 0-8160-6031-2; 978-0-8160-603-1
LC 2006030410
"This volume offers an overview of the health-care industry, a look at different careers, ideas for getting experience, and additional resources. . . . The layout is attractive, the font a good size, and the information accessible. . . . An excellent addition." SLJ

362.196   Specific conditions

Therrien, Patricia
An **enemy** within; overcoming cancer and other life-threatening diseases. by Patty Therrien. Mason Crest Publishers 2009 128 p. col. ill. (library) $24.95
Grades: 7 8 9 10   **362.196**
1. Terminally ill 2. Cancer -- Patients 3. Cancer in children -- Patients -- Biography 4. Catastrophic illness

-- Patients -- Biography
ISBN 1422204502; 9781422204504
LC 2008033776
This book offers a collection of "stories of courageous young people and how their lives have changed due to such a diagnosis [which] are told from their own viewpoint." The volume "includes full-color photographs, table of contents, for further reading and for more information sections, bibliography, index, and author and consultant profiles." (Publisher's note)
Includes bibliographical references (p. 125) and index.

362.2   People with mental illness and disabilities

Flath, Camden
21st-century counselors; new approaches to mental health & substance abuse. Mason Crest Publishers 2011 64p il (New careers for the 21st century: finding your role in the global renewal) lib bdg $22.95
Grades: 7 8 9 10   **362.2**
1. Counseling 2. Vocational guidance 3. Drug abuse counseling
ISBN 978-1-4222-1825-9 lib bdg; 1-4222-1825-2 lib bdg
LC 2010021812
"Chapters identify and emphasize specific careers—important strengths, necessary aptitudes and interests, education and training, projected earnings, closely related occupations, type of work environment, and predictions for the future of the field. . . . Color photos have a small role amid the many statistics, figures, graphs and charts that support and supplement the . . . [text]." SLJ
Includes bibliographical references

Mental illness: opposing viewpoints; Mary E. Williams, book editor. Greenhaven Press 2007 238p (Opposing viewpoints series) lib bdg $36.20; pa $24.95
Grades: 8 9 10 11 12   **362.2**
1. Mental illness
ISBN 0-7377-2947-3 lib bdg; 978-0-7377-2947-4 lib bdg; 0-7377-2948-1 pa; 978-0-7377-2948-1 pa
LC 2006-20106
"This collections of articles, written by individuals with differing opinions and from varying backgrounds, analyzes issues relevant to mental health and public policy." SLJ
Includes bibliographical references

362.28   Suicide

Galas, Judith C.
★ The **power** to prevent suicide; a guide for teens helping teens. [by] Richard E. Nelson, Judith C. Galas; foreword by Bev Cobain; edited by Pamela Espeland. Updated ed; Free Spirit 2006 115p pa $13.95
Grades: 7 8 9 10 11 12   **362.28**
1. Suicide
ISBN 1-57542-206-9; 978-1-57542-206-0

First published 1994

"The authors' premise is that, as trusted and caring friends, YAs have a special role in the prevention of suicide among their peers, and discuss what to do if they observe the danger signals. . . . This book provides clear, practical information and advice." SLJ

Marcovitz, Hal
Suicide. ABDO Pub. Co. 2010 112p il (Essential issues) lib bdg $22.95
Grades: 7 8 9 10   **362.28**
1. Suicide
ISBN 978-1-60453-958-5; 1-60453-958-5
     LC 2009-30354
This is "well-written, providing examples that put a human face to each problem. Quotes and facts are clearly attributed, and their sources are noted in the extensive back matter. . . . Sidebars provide further information, or, more compellingly, offer stories about those touched by the topic. . . . [This] will be of great assistance to students writing reports." SLJ
Includes glossary and bibliographical references

Suicide: opposing viewpoints; Jacqueline Langwith, book editor. Greenhaven Press 2008 268p (Opposing viewpoints series) lib bdg $38.50; pa $26.75
Grades: 8 9 10 11 12   **362.28**
1. Suicide 2. Euthanasia
ISBN 978-0-7377-4012-7 lib bdg; 0737740124 lib bdg; 978-0-7377-4013-4 pa; 0-7377-4013-2 pa
     LC 2008-1007
The articles in this anthology cover topics such as suicide among teens and other types of people, what causes suicide, assisted suicide, and how suicide can be prevented.
Includes bibliographical references

362.29   Substance abuse

Axelrod-Contrada, Joan
The **facts** about drugs and society. Marshall Cavendish Benchmark 2008 143p il (Drugs) $27.95
Grades: 7 8 9 10 11 12   **362.29**
1. Drugs
ISBN 978-0-7614-2674-5
This discusses drugs in relation to history, pop culture, risk factors, gender, the brain, the law, treatment and prevention.
This is "well-organized, attractively illustrated, current, and highly informative." Sci Books Films

Barter, James
Hallucinogens. Lucent Bks. 2002 112p il (Drug education library) lib bdg $27.45
Grades: 7 8 9 10   **362.29**
1. Drug abuse 2. Hallucinogens 3. Hallucinogenic drugs 4. Hallucinogenic plants
ISBN 1-56006-915-5
     LC 2001-5776

Discusses the development of hallucinogens, their use for spiritual, medicinal, and recreational purposes, and the laws governing their use
"This intelligently written, objective title provides students with detailed information." SLJ
Includes bibliographical references and index

Berne, Emma Carlson
Methamphetamine. ReferencePoint Press 2007 102p il map (Compact research) $24.95
Grades: 8 9 10 11 12   **362.29**
1. Drug abuse 2. Methamphetamine
ISBN 978-1-60152-004-3; 1-60152-004-2
     LC 2006032206
"Berne explores whether methamphetamine usage in the U.S. has reached epidemic proportions, its dangers, the link between addiction and crime, and abuse prevention." SLJ
Includes bibliographical references

Bjornlund, Lydia
Marijuana; by Lydia Bjornlund. ReferencePoint Press 2012 136 p. (Compact research series) (hardcover) $27.95
Grades: 7 8 9 10 11 12   **362.29**
1. Marijuana 2. Drug education 3. Medical botany 4. Drugs -- Physiological effect 5. Drugs -- Law and legislation -- United States 6. Marijuana -- United States 7. Marijuana -- Law and legislation -- United States
ISBN 160152160X; 9781601521606
     LC 2011007743
This book on marijuana is a part of the Compact Research: Drugs series and "focus[es] on three types of information: "objective single-author narratives, opinion-based primary source quotations, and facts and statistics." What this translates to on the page is an overview of the topic and an in-depth chapter-by chapter discussion of the points raised in the overview." Lydia Bjornlund "looks at questions such as whether marijuana is a dangerous drug, whether it should be legalized, and the most pressing dilemma: Should the drug be readily available for medical use?" (Booklist)
Includes bibliographical references and index.

Bjornlund, Lydia D.
Teen smoking. Reference Point Press 2010 104p il (Compact research. Current issues) $25.95
Grades: 8 9 10 11 12   **362.29**
1. Smoking
ISBN 978-1-60152-098-2; 1-60152-098-0
     LC 2009-28008
This addresses the following questions: How serious a problem is teen smoking?; Who is to blame for teen smoking?; How should teen smoking be regulated?; How can we prevent teen smoking?
"The straightforward presentation of serious subject matter, graphics, and easy access to facts . . . [make this book] excellent . . . for reports and debates." SLJ

Breguet, Amy
Vicodin, OxyContin, and other pain relievers; [by] Amy E. Breguet. Chelsea House 2008 112p il (Junior drug awareness) $30

Grades: 6 7 8 9   362.29
1. Narcotics 2. Analgesics 3. Drug abuse
ISBN 978-0-7910-9700-7; 0-7910-9700-5
                                    LC 2007032350
This describes the effects of Vicodin and OxyContin and
other pain relievers, how they are used and abused, and how
to get help for addiction.
Includes glossary and bibliographical references

Cobb, Allan B.
  Heroin. Chelsea House Publishers 2009 109p il
(Junior drug awareness) lib bdg $30
Grades: 6 7 8 9   362.29
1. Heroin 2. Drug abuse
ISBN 978-0-7910-9749-6 lib bdg; 0-7910-9749-8
lib bdg
                                    LC 2007043662
This "describes the uses and abuses of [heroin]. . . . The
reasons people might take drugs, their dangers, signs of ad-
diction, and treatment options are covered. . . . The content is
reliable and comprehensive." Horn Book Guide
Includes glossary and bibliographical references

Egendorf, Laura K.
  Performance-enhancing drugs. Reference point
2007 96p il (Compact research) lib bdg $24.95
Grades: 8 9 10 11 12   362.29
1. Drugs 2. Athletes -- Drug use
ISBN 978-1-60152-003-6 lib bdg; 1-60152-003-4
lib bdg
This "well-organized [volume presents] general information that report writers, particularly reluctant readers,
will find useful. Brightly colored illustrated facts and statistics charts invite perusal. Thought-provoking questions
introduce most of the chapters. . . . [This book] covers
ethical issues and dangers in usage, effectiveness of testing, and prevention. . . . Primary-source quotes are well
documented." SLJ

Freedman, Jeri
  Professional wrestling; steroids in and out of
the ring. Rosen Central 2009 48p il (Disgraced!
the dirty history of performance-enhancing drugs in
sports) lib bdg $26.50
Grades: 5 6 7 8   362.29
1. Steroids 2. Wrestling 3. Athletes -- Drug use
ISBN 978-1-4358-5305-8 lib bdg; 1-4358-5305-9
lib bdg
                                    LC 2009-1041
Discusses professional wrestlers who died relatively
young due to steroid use, the reason why it is common in
professional wrestling, efforts at control, the effects of
the drugs, related scandals, and steroids in other types
of wrestling
  "Amazing statements from athletes giving reasons why
they took illegal drugs are good for discussion topics. . . .
Concludes with thoughts regarding future additional legislation. [A] useful [update]." SLJ
Includes glossary and bibliographical references

Gottfried, Ted
  Marijuana; by Ted Gottfried with Lisa Harkrad-
er. Marshall Cavendish Benchmark 2010 32p il
(Drug facts) $19.95
Grades: 4 5 6 7   362.29
1. Marijuana
ISBN 978-0-7614-4351-3; 0-7614-4351-7
                                    LC 2008-52761
"Provides clear explanations about effects, followed by
diagrams of the body to clarify the specific organs/body sys-
tems that suffer the most damage. . . . An excellent starting
point." SLJ
Includes glossary

  ★ The **facts** about marijuana. Benchmark Books
2004 109p il (Drugs) lib bdg $37.07
Grades: 6 7 8 9   362.29
1. Marijuana
ISBN 0-7614-1806-7
                                    LC 2004-5578
The author describes the effects of marijuana use, varying opinions about legalization, marijuana laws, and drug
testing in schools.
Includes glossary and bibliographical references

Ingram, Scott
  Marijuana; [by] W. Scott Ingram. Chelsea
House 2008 110p il (Junior drug awareness) lib
bdg $30
Grades: 6 7 8 9   362.29
1. Marijuana 2. Drug abuse
ISBN 978-0-7910-9695-6 lib bdg; 0-7910-9695-5
                                    LC 2007-24826
This "provides useful, balanced, and comprehensive in-
formation." Horn Book Guide
Includes glossary and bibliographical references

Klosterman, Lorrie
  The **facts** about drug dependence to treatment.
Marshall Cavendish Benchmark 2008 126p il
(Drugs) lib bdg $31.94
Grades: 7 8 9 10 11 12   362.29
1. Drug abuse
ISBN 978-0-7614-2676-9
                                    LC 2007-8780
This discusses the beginnings of drug dependence, its
costs, first steps to recovery, rehabilitation, and lifetime free-
dom from drugs.
  This is "well-organized, attractively illustrated, current,
and highly informative." Sci Books Films
Includes glossary and bibliographical references

Koellhoffer, Tara
  Ecstasy and other club drugs; [by] Tara Koellhoffer. Chelsea House 2008 120p il (Junior drug
awareness) $30
Grades: 6 7 8 9   362.29
1. Drug abuse 2. Ecstasy (Drug)
ISBN 978-0-7910-9697-0; 0-7910-9697-1
                                    LC 2007017789

This describes the effects of Ecstasy (MDMA), GHB, Rohypnol, Ketamine, LSD, and other drugs, why people take them, and addiction and treatment.

This "provides useful, balanced, and comprehensive information." Horn Book Guide

Includes glossary and bibliographical references

Inhalants and solvents; [by] Tara Koellhoffer. Chelsea House 2008 112p il (Junior drug awareness) lib bdg $30

Grades: 6 7 8 9   **362.29**
1. Inhalant abuse
ISBN 978-0-7910-9698-7 lib bdg; 0-7910-9698-X lib bdg

                                    LC 2007024824

This "provides useful, balanced, and comprehensive information." Horn Book Guide

Includes glossary and bibliographical references

Kreske, Damian P.

How to say no to drugs. Chelsea House Publishers 2008 112p il (Junior drug awareness) lib bdg $30

Grades: 6 7 8 9   **362.29**
1. Drug abuse
ISBN 978-0-7910-9699-4 l; 0-7910-9699-8

                                    LC 2007043664

This "explains how drug use affects the body and can lead to addiction, as well as how young people can avoid peer pressure to use drugs. The book also includes the personal stories of teenagers who have gone through treatment to repair the damage their drug use did." Publisher's note

Includes glossary and bibliographical references

Landau, Elaine

Meth; America's drug epidemic. [by] Elaine Landau. Twenty-First Century Books 2007 120p il lib bdg $30.60

Grades: 7 8 9 10   **362.29**
1. Drug abuse 2. Methamphetamine
ISBN 978-0-8225-6808-7

                                    LC 2006030923

"This excellent exposé explains the facts about methamphetamine: its effects upon addicts, the impact of the drug's widespread manufacture and use upon society as a whole, and the efforts of government and law enforcement to curtail its spread." Booklist

Includes bibliographical references

LeVert, Suzanne

Ecstasy; by Suzanne LeVert with Jeff Hendricks. Marshall Cavendish Benchmark 2010 32p il (Drug facts) $19.95

Grades: 4 5 6 7   **362.29**
1. Drug abuse 2. Designer drugs 3. Ecstasy (Drug)
ISBN 978-0-7614-4349-0; 0-7614-4349-5

                                    LC 2008-52753

"Provides clear explanations about effects, followed by diagrams of the body to clarify the specific organs/body systems that suffer the most damage. . . . An excellent starting point." SLJ

Includes glossary

Steroids; by Suzanne LeVert with Jim Whiting. Marshall Cavendish Benchmark 2010 32p il (Drug facts) $19.95

Grades: 4 5 6 7   **362.29**
1. Steroids 2. Sports -- Corrupt practices
ISBN 978-0-7614-4352-0; 0-7614-4352-5

                                    LC 2008-52752

"Provides clear explanations about effects, followed by diagrams of the body to clarify the specific organs/body systems that suffer the most damage. . . . An excellent starting point." SLJ

Includes glossary

★ The **facts** about LSD and other hallucinogens; [by] Suzanne LeVert. Marshall Cavendish Benchmark 2005 96p il (Drugs) lib bdg $42.79; pa $6.99

Grades: 7 8 9 10   **362.29**
1. Drug abuse 2. LSD (Drug) 3. Hallucinogens
ISBN 978-0-7614-1974-7 lib bdg; 0-7614-1974-8 lib bdg; 978-0-7614-3596-9 pa; 0-7614-3596-4 pa

                                    LC 2005-3948

This "useful [volume is] attractively packaged and will be of interest to report writers and general readers. [Text] and photos do an excellent job of showing how [this] group of drugs affects the body." SLJ

Includes glossary and bibliographical references

★ The **facts** about cocaine; [by] Suzanne LeVert. Marshall Cavendish Benchmark 2005 96p il map (Drugs) lib bdg $42.79; pa $6.99

Grades: 7 8 9 10   **362.29**
1. Cocaine 2. Drug abuse
ISBN 978-0-7614-1973-0 lib bdg; 0-7614-1973-X lib bdg; 978-0-7614-3593-8 pa; 0-7614-3593-X pa

                                    LC 2005-1313

Describes how cocaine affects the mind and body, the dangers of cocaine abuse, cocaine and the law, and how to deal with addiction.

Includes glossary and bibliographical references

★ The **facts** about ecstasy; [by] Suzanne LeVert. Benchmark Books 2004 96p il (Drugs) lib bdg $12.79; pa $6.99

Grades: 6 7 8 9   **362.29**
1. Ecstasy (Drug)
ISBN 978-0-7614-1807-8 lib bdg; 0-7614-1807-5 lib bdg; 978-0-7614-3588-4 pa; 0-7614-3588-3 pa

                                    LC 2004-9341

The author describes the drug MDMA, commonly known as ecstasy, and how it is abused, its health risks, the laws against it, and how to recover from the habit

Inlcudes glossary and bibliographical references

★ The **facts** about heroin; [by] Suzanne LeVert. Marshall Cavendish Benchmark 2005 95p il (Drugs) lib bdg $42.79; pa $6.99

Grades: 7 8 9 10   362.29
1. Heroin 2. Drug abuse
ISBN 978-0-7614-1975-4 lib bdg; 0-7614-1975-6 lib
bdg; 978-0-7614-3595-2 pa; 0-7614-3595-6 pa
                                        LC 2005001728
"Describes the history, characteristics, legal status, and
abuse of the drug Heroin." Publisher's note
Includes glossary and bibliographical references

★ The **facts** about nicotine; [by] Suzanne Le-
Vert. Marshall Cavendish Benchmark 2007 112p il
(Drugs) lib bdg $42.79
Grades: 6 7 8 9   362.29
1. Smoking 2. Tobacco
ISBN 978-0-7614-2244-0 lib bdg; 0-7614-2244-7
                                        LC 2006002405
This describes the effects of nicotine and smoking on the
mind and body, the tobacco industry and the law, and how
live free of smoke and nicotine.
Includes glossary and bibliographical references

★ The **facts** about steroids; [by] Suzanne Le-
Vert. Benchmark Books 2004 96p il (Drugs) lib
bdg $42.79
Grades: 6 7 8 9   362.29
1. Steroids 2. Athletes -- Drug use
ISBN 978-0-7614-1808-5 lib bdg; 0-7614-1808-3
lib bdg
                                        LC 2004-11852
The author "discusses the effects of steroids on the body,
health risks, the law, prevention, and treatment. The medicinal use of steroids is very briefly mentioned. . . . [This title
has a] readable, well-organized [text], and good use of color,
graphics, photographs, tables, diagrams, and labels helps to
spark readers' interest." SLJ
Includes glossary and bibliographical references

Menhard, Francha Roffe
★ The **facts** about amphetamines; [by] Francha
Roffé Menhard. 1st ed.; Marshall Cavendish Benchmark 2005 96p il (Drugs) lib bdg $42.79
Grades: 6 7 8 9   362.29
1. Drug abuse 2. Amphetamines
ISBN 978-0-7614-1972-3 lib bdg; 0-7614-1972-1
lib bdg
                                        LC 2005001142
This "useful [volume is] attractively packaged and will
be of interest to report writers and general readers. [Text]
and photos do an excellent job of showing how [this] group
of drugs affects the body." SLJ
Includes glossary and bibliographical references

★ The **facts** about inhalants; [by] Francha Roffe
Menhard. Benchmark Books 2004 92p il (Drugs)
lib bdg $42.79
Grades: 6 7 8 9   362.29
1. Solvent abuse
ISBN 978-0-7614-1809-2 lib bdg; 0-7614-1809-1
lib bdg
                                        LC 2004-11858
The author "addresses the types of inhalants, the history,
dangers, effects, available help for abuse of these drugs,

and the laws regulating them. . . . [This title has a] readable,
well-organized [text], and good use of color, graphics, photographs, tables, diagrams, and labels helps to spark readers'
interest." SLJ
Includes glossary and bibliographical references

Merino, Noel
Smoking; Noël Merino, book editor. Greenhaven
Press 2010 143p il (Introducing issues with oppos-
ing viewpoints) $35.75
Grades: 8 9 10 11 12   362.29
1. Smoking 2. Tobacco habit
ISBN 978-0-7377-5101-7; 0-7377-5101-0
                                        LC 2010-26766
Replaces the edition published 2006 under the editorship
of Laurie S. Friedman
"The articles in this anthology expose multiple sides of . .
. [the smoking] debate." Publisher's note
Includes bibliographical references

Naff, Clay Farris
Nicotine and tobacco; by Clay Farris Naff. ReferencePoint Press, Inc. 2007 110p il (Compact research) $24.95
Grades: 8 9 10 11 12   362.29
1. Smoking 2. Tobacco habit
ISBN 978-1-60152-006-7; 1-60152-006-9
                                        LC 2006033962
This "well-organized [volume presents] general information that report writers, particularly reluctant readers, will
find useful. Brightly colored illustrated facts and statistics
charts invite perusal. Thought-provoking questions introduce most of the chapters. . . . [This book] addresses the
dangers of smoking and chewing tobacco and of exposure
to secondhand smoke, why young people use tobacco, and
how numbers can be reduced. Primary-source quotes are
well documented." SLJ
Includes bibliographical references

Porterfield, Jason
Doping; athletes and drugs. [by] Jason Porterfield. 1st ed.; Rosen Pub. 2008 64p il (In the news)
$29.95
Grades: 5 6 7 8   362.29
1. Steroids 2. Drug abuse 3. Athletes -- Drug use
ISBN 978-1-4042-1917-5; 1-4042-1917-X
                                        LC 2007015919
"Overview of the sports and sports figures most of-
ten connected with drug scandals, why athletes resort to
drug use, the different types of drugs used for physical
enhancement, and the methods used to police doping. . . .
[This] short [volume is] packed full of information." Voice
Youth Advocates
Includes glossary and bibliographical references

Major League Baseball; the great steroid scandals. Rosen Central 2010 48p il (Disgraced! the
dirty history of performance-enhancing drugs in
sports) lib bdg $26.50

Grades: 5 6 7 8   362.29
1. Baseball 2. Steroids 3. Athletes -- Drug use
ISBN 978-1-4358-5302-7 lib bdg; 1-4358-5302-4
lib bdg

LC 2008-55581

Discusses drug abuse by professional baseball players, with an emphasis on the widespread use of steroids since the late 1980s, revelations of the extent of the problem, and the effects of steroids on the players and on the game and its records

"Amazing statements from athletes giving reasons why they took illegal drugs are good for discussion topics. . . . Concludes with thoughts regarding future additional legislation. [A] useful [update]." SLJ

Includes glossary and bibliographical references

Powell, Jillian

Alcohol and drug abuse; by Jillian Powell; health consultant, John G. Samanich. Gareth Stevens Pub. 2009 48p il (Emotional health issues) lib bdg $31
Grades: 6 7 8 9   362.29
1. Alcoholism 2. Drug abuse
ISBN 978-0-8368-9199-7; 0-8368-9199-6

LC 2008-5459

First published 2008 in the United Kingdom

This book about alcohol and drug abuse has "clear language and explanations. . . . [It is] suitable for fact-finding missions, but the abundant graphics and case studies are likely to draw in browsers as well. Throughout, unfamiliar vocabulary is highlighted in bold and explained in context and in the glossary. . . . Fact boxes and case study sidebars add information." SLJ

Includes glossary and bibliographical references

Schaefer, Adam

Steroids; [by] A.R. Schaefer. Cherry Lake Pub. 2009 32p il (Health at risk) lib bdg $27.07
Grades: 4 5 6 7   362.29
1. Steroids 2. Athletes -- Drug use
ISBN 978-1-60279-287-6 lib bdg; 1-60279-287-9
lib bdg

LC 2008017502

This describes how steroids affect the body and what sports groups are doing to halt their use.

"Great for reports or reluctant readers." Booklist

Includes bibliographical references

Sommers, Annie Leah

College athletics; steroids and supplement abuse. Rosen Pub. Group 2010 48p il (Disgraced! the dirty history of performance-enhancing drugs in sports) lib bdg $26.50
Grades: 5 6 7 8   362.29
1. Steroids 2. College sports 3. Athletes -- Drug use 4. Sports -- Corrupt practices
ISBN 978-1-4358-5303-4 lib bdg; 1-4358-5303-2
lib bdg

LC 2008-55408

Discusses efforts to enhance performance in sports, the use of steroids and supplements by college athletes, including the case of football player Tommy Chaikin, college players as role models, and the influence of the NCAA

"Amazing statements from athletes giving reasons why they took illegal drugs are good for discussion topics. . . . Concludes with thoughts regarding future additional legislation. Useful updates." SLJ

Includes glossary and bibliographical references

Sommers, Michael A.

The **NFL**; steroids and human growth hormone. Rosen Central 2010 48p il (Disgraced! the dirty history of performance-enhancing drugs in sports) lib bdg $26.50
Grades: 5 6 7 8   362.29
1. Football 2. Steroids 3. Athletes -- Drug use
ISBN 978-1-4358-5304-1 lib bdg; 1-4358-5304-0
lib bdg

LC 2008-56131

Discusses the uses of performance enhancing drugs, particularly anabolic steroids, by professional football players, their effects on the players and the sport, and the successes and failures of efforts to control their use

"Amazing statements from athletes giving reasons why they took illegal drugs are good for discussion topics. . . . Concludes with thoughts regarding future additional legislation. [A] useful [update]." SLJ

Includes glossary and bibliographical references

Sterngass, Jon

Steroids. Marshall Cavendish Benchmark 2011 112p il (Controversy!) lib bdg $25.95
Grades: 8 9 10 11 12   362.29
1. Steroids
ISBN 9780761449034; 0761449035

Discusses what steroids are, how they are used in sports, how they can be used in other areas, and the debate surrounding them.

This is "written in clear, sophisticated language and will serve well . . . for research papers or debates." Voice Youth Advocates

Includes bibliographical references

Warburton, Lianne

Amphetamines and other stimulants; [by] Lianne Warburton and Diana Callfas. Chelsea House 2008 120p il (Junior drug awareness) lib bdg $30
Grades: 6 7 8 9   362.29
1. Drug abuse 2. Stimulants 3. Amphetamines
ISBN 978-0-7910-9712-0 lib bdg; 0-7910-9712-9
lib bdg

LC 2007018860

This "provides useful, balanced, and comprehensive information." Horn Book Guide

Includes glossary and bibliographical references

West, Krista

Cocaine and crack; [by] Krista West. Chelsea House Publishers 2008 119p il map (Junior drug awareness) lib bdg $30

Grades: 6 7 8 9   **362.29**
1. Cocaine 2. Drug abuse 3. Crack (Drug)
ISBN 978-0-7910-9704-5 lib bdg; 0-7910-9704-8
lib bdg

LC 2007024971

This "provides useful, balanced, and comprehensive information." Horn Book Guide
Includes glossary and bibliographical references

Steroids and other performance-enhancing drugs.
Chelsea House 2009 118p il (Junior drug awareness) lib bdg $30
Grades: 6 7 8 9   **362.29**
1. Steroids
ISBN 978-0-7910-9748-9 lib bdg; 0-7910-9748-X
lib bdg

LC 2008-14062

"The content is reliable and comprehensive." Horn
Book Guide
Includes glossary and bibliographical references

Addiction: opposing viewpoints; Christina Fisanick,
book editor. Greenhaven Press 2009 228p il
(Opposing viewpoints series) lib bdg $39.70; pa
$27.50
Grades: 8 9 10 11 12   **362.29**
1. Alcoholism 2. Drug abuse
ISBN 978-0-7377-4352-4 lib bdg; 0-7377-4352-2 lib
bdg; 978-0-7377-4351-7 pa; 0-7377-4351-4 pa

LC 2008-53997

Articles in this anthology discuss the nature of addiction,
including how addictions can be prevented and treated.
Includes bibliographical references

Drugs, alcohol, and tobacco; learning about addictive behavior. Rosalyn Carson-DeWitt, editor in
chief. Macmillan Ref. USA 2003 3v set $295
Grades: 7 8 9 10   **362.29**
1. Reference books 2. Drug abuse -- Encyclopedias
3. Alcoholism -- Encyclopedias 5. Tobacco habit --
Encyclopedias 6. Substance abuse -- Encyclopedias 7.
Compulsive behavior -- Encyclopedias 8. Teenagers --
Substance use -- Encyclopedias
ISBN 0-02-865756-X

LC 2002-9270

Based on the Encyclopedia of drugs, alcohol & addictive
behavior, 2nd edition, published 2001
"The 190 alphabetically arranged articles range from
one to six pages in length and yield a comprehensive look at
the nature of, treatments for, and social issues surrounding
addictive substances and behaviors. Topics include specific
drugs, diagnoses, treatments, legal and social implications,
drug trafficking, cultural pressures, and related compulsive
behaviors." SLJ
Includes bibliographical references

Let's clear the air: 10 reasons not to start smoking;
with a foreword by Christy Turlington; [illus-

trations by Deanne Staffo] Lobster Press 2007
192p il pa $14.95
Grades: 5 6 7 8   **362.29**
1. Smoking
ISBN 978-1-897073-66-7 pa; 1-897073-66-6 pa

"Young people ranging in ages from 9 to 14 offer sound
arguments for not taking up cigarettes. . . . Interspersed
throughout the accessible text are boxes and sidebars with
facts and statistics, photos, and spot art. . . . The antismoking
message here is all the more effective coming directly from
a diverse group of young people." Booklist

Tobacco and smoking: opposing viewpoints; Susan
Hunnicutt, book editor. Greenhaven Press 2009
222p il (Opposing viewpoints series) lib bdg
$39.70; pa $27.50
Grades: 8 9 10 11 12   **362.29**
1. Smoking 2. Tobacco habit 3. Tobacco industry
ISBN 978-0-7377-4242-8 lib bdg; 0-7377-4242-9 lib
bdg; 978-0-7377-4243-5 pa; 0-7377-4243-7 pa

LC 2008-28546

Articles in this anthology discuss topics such as smokeless tobacco, teen smoking, government regulation of smoking, and tobacco advertising.
Includes bibliographical references

Tobacco information for teens; health tips about the
hazards of using cigarettes, smokeless tobacco,
and other nicotine products: including facts about
nicotine addiction, nicotine delivery systems, secondhand smoke, health consequ. edited by Karen
Bellenir. 2nd ed.; Omnigraphics 2010 440p il
(Teen health series) $69
Grades: 7 8 9 10 11 12   **362.29**
1. Smoking 2. Tobacco habit
ISBN 978-0-7808-1153-9; 0-7808-1153-4

LC 2010023716

First published 2007
"Provides basic consumer health information for teens
on tobacco use, addiction, and related diseases, along with
tips for quitting smoking. Includes index and resource information." Publisher's note
Includes bibliographical references

362.292   Alcohol

Aretha, David
On the rocks; teens and alcohol. by David
Aretha. Franklin Watts 2007 144p il pa $17.95
Grades: 6 7 8 9   **362.292**
1. Alcoholism 2. Teenagers -- Alcohol use
ISBN 0-531-16792-5 pa; 978-0-531-16792-2 pa

LC 2005024291

"Basic facts about drinking in America, teen usage, and
warning signs of alcoholism are presented in this readable,
unbiased text. The effects of alcoholism on families, the dangers of binge drinking, and the successes and failures of solutions and strategies to solve these issues are discussed." SLJ
Includes bibliographical references

Bjornlund, Lydia D.

Alcohol; [by] Lydia Bjornlund. Cherry Lake Pub. 2009 32p il (Health at risk) lib bdg $27.07

Grades: 4 5 6 7   **362.292**
   1. Alcohol 2. Alcoholism
   ISBN 978-1-60279-280-7 lib bdg; 1-60279-280-1 lib bdg
                                 LC 2008017495

This describes the effects of alcohol, the dangers of driving drunk, how to get help, and how to make good choices. "Great for reports or reluctant readers." Booklist

Includes bibliographical references

Gottfried, Ted

Alcohol; by Ted Gottfried with Katherine Follett. Marshall Cavendish Benchmark 2010 32p il (Drug facts) $19.95

Grades: 4 5 6 7   **362.292**
   1. Alcoholism 2. Drinking of alcoholic beverages 3. Alcohol -- Physiological effect
   ISBN 978-0-7614-4348-3; 0-7614-4348-7
                                 LC 2008-52751

"Provides clear explanations about effects, followed by diagrams of the body to clarify the specific organs/body systems that suffer the most damage. . . . An excellent starting point." SLJ

Includes glossary

★ The **facts** about alcohol; [by] Ted Gottfried. Benchmark Books 2004 111p il (Drugs) lib bdg $2.79; pa $6.99

Grades: 6 7 8 9   **362.292**
   1. Alcoholism 2. Drinking of alcoholic beverages 3. Youth -- Alcohol use 4. Teenagers -- Alcohol use 5. Alcoholism -- United States 6. Youth -- Alcohol use -- United States 7. Drinking of alcoholic beverages -- United States
   ISBN 978-0-7614-1805-4 lib bdg; 0-7614-1805-9 lib bdg; 978-0-7614-3587-7 pa; 0-7614-3587-5 pa
                                 LC 2004-5388

The author "includes historical aspects of alcohol and society, including humans' first experimentations with fermentation, Prohibition, and the temperance movement; related laws and legislation; and definition, causes, treatment, and effects. . . . [This title has a] readable, well-organized [text], and good use of color, graphics, photographs, tables, diagrams, and labels helps to spark readers' interest." SLJ

Includes glossary and bibliographical references

Smith, Terri Peterson

Alcohol. Chelsea House Publishers 2008 110p il (Junior drug awareness) lib bdg $30

Grades: 6 7 8 9   **362.292**
   1. Alcoholism
   ISBN 978-0-7910-9764-9 lib bdg; 0-7910-9764-1 lib bdg
                                 LC 2008014066

This "describes the uses and abuses of [alcohol]. . . . The reasons people [drink alcohol, its] dangers, signs of addiction, and treatment options are covered. . . . The content is reliable and comprehensive." Horn Book Guide

Includes glossary and bibliographical references

Youngerman, Barry

The **truth** about alcohol; Robert N. Golden, general editor; Fred L. Peterson, general editor; Barry Youngerman, principal author; Heath Dingwell, contributing author; Richelle Rennegarbe, adviser. 2nd ed.; Facts on File 2010 230p (Truth about series) $35

Grades: 8 9 10 11 12   **362.292**
   1. Alcoholism 2. Teenagers -- Alcohol use
   ISBN 978-0-8160-7639-0; 0-8160-7639-1
                               LC 2009-53476
   First published 2004

This discusses such topics as binge drinking, underage drinking, the prevalence of drinking on college campuses, drunken driving, dealing with alcohol abuse in the family, alcohol advertising and counter-advertising, and seeking help for an alcohol problem.

Includes glossary and bibliographical references

★ **Teen** alcoholism; Laura K. Egendorf, book editor. Greenhaven Press 2001 138p (Contemporary issues companion) lib bdg $22.96; pa $14.96

Grades: 8 9 10 11 12   **362.292**
   1. Alcoholism 2. Teenagers -- Alcohol use 3. Alcoholism -- United States 4. Teenagers -- Alcohol use -- United States
   ISBN 0-7377-0683-X lib bdg; 0-7377-0682-1 pa
                                 LC 00-68181

A collection of essays on such topics as the risk factors of teen alcoholism, the effects of parental drinking, social pressures, and advertising on teen drinking, and the dangers of alcohol abuse

The editor includes "an entire chapter of personal essays from people who have actually struggled with teen alcoholism or seen effects on a friend or family member. This chapter alone is worth the entire volume. . . . The rest of the book, which includes charts and sometimes staggering facts, will help in standard research." Booklist

Includes bibliographical references

362.4 People with physical disabilities

Lambert, Joseph

The **Center** for Cartoon Studies presents Annie Sullivan and the trials of Helen Keller; by Joseph Lambert; with an introduction by TK. Disney Hyperion Books 2012 $17.99 96 p.

Grades: 5 6 7   **362.4**
   1. Women authors -- Biography 2. Handicapped -- Graphic novels 3. Female friendship -- Graphic novels 4. Graphic novels 5. Women -- United States -- History 6. Women -- United States -- Biography 7. Female friendship -- United States -- History
   ISBN 9781423113362
                                 LC 2011036324

This nonfiction graphic novel about Annie Sullivan and Helen Keller "focuses on the trials both Annie and Helen struggle with in their lives," particularly the incident when Helen was accused of plagiarism in her story 'The Frost King' and interrogated at the Perkins Institution. "Helen's perspective is . . . communicated in dialogue-free black panels in which she is represented as only a gray silhouette" by author/illustrator Joseph Lambert. (Kirkus) Bibliography.

Martin, Claudia

Helpers. Marshall Cavendish Benchmark 2010 64p il (Working animals) lib bdg $28.50

Grades: 4 5 6 7   **362.4**

1. Animals and the handicapped

ISBN 978-1-60870-163-6 lib bdg; 1-60870-163-8 lib bdg

"Attractively designed and packed with information. . . . The composition of each page is attractively set up with well-selected and reproduced stock and historical photos." SLJ

Thornton, Denise

Physical disabilities; the ultimate teen guide. Scarecrow Press 2007 162p il (It happened to me) $42

Grades: 7 8 9 10 11 12   **362.4**

1. Physically handicapped

ISBN 978-0-8108-5300-3; 0-8108-5300-0

LC 2006-29235

"Thornton interviewed hundreds of young people to help readers understand disabilities from a personal viewpoint. She divides this very broad subject into eight areas—school, technologies and tools, getting around, sports, the arts, relationships, independence, and advocacy. In each section, she includes personal stories plus essential information helpful to the disabled. . . . Well-organized and helpful." SLJ

Includes bibliographical references

362.5   Poor people

Fields, Julianna

Kids growing up without a home. Mason Crest 2009 64p il (The changing face of modern families) $22.95

Grades: 6 7 8 9   **362.5**

1. Homeless persons

ISBN 978-1-4222-1498-5; 1-4222-1498-2

This describes the challenges facing homeless families. This is "informative [and] nonjudgmental. . . . Including color photos, plentiful sidebars, and interesting headline stories, the accessible [text presents] real-life experiences and numerous supporting facts, definitions, graphs, charts, and statistics." SLJ

Gifford, Clive

Poverty. Smart Apple Media 2010 46p il (Voices) lib bdg $34.25

Grades: 7 8 9 10 11 12   **362.5**

1. Poverty

ISBN 978-1-59920-277-8; 1-59920-277-8

LC 2008-50431

This book "focuses on poor countries and also the poor in rich countries, addressing poverty's causes, the role of welfare and foreign aid, and always, the hardships individuals in need face day to day. . . . [The] blend of current political debate with witnesses' close-up experiences told through

photos, narratives, and quotes will draw browsers, and many will go on to find out more." Booklist

Includes glossary and bibliographical references

The **Homeless**: opposing viewpoints; Jennifer A. Hurley, book editor. Greenhaven Press 2002 186p (Opposing viewpoints series) lib bdg $34.95; pa $23.70

Grades: 8 9 10 11 12   **362.5**

1. Homeless persons

ISBN 0-7377-0750-X lib bdg; 0-7377-0749-6 pa

LC 2001-23916

Replaces the edition published 1995 under the editorship of Tamara L. Roleff

This collection of essays addresses the causes and seriousness of homelessness and possible remedies

Includes bibliographical references

Inner-city poverty; Tamara L. Roleff, book editor. Greenhaven Press 2002 176p (Contemporary issues companion) $22.45; pa $16.96

Grades: 8 9 10 11 12   **362.5**

1. Poverty 2. Inner cities 3. Public welfare 4. Poor -- United States 5. Poverty -- United States 6. Urban poor -- United States 7. Inner cities -- United States 8. Public welfare -- United States

ISBN 0-7377-0841-7; 0-7377-0840-9 pa

LC 2002-23639

"A number of writers contributed to this collection of articles about the severity of the urban poverty dilemma. All aspects of the problem are clearly presented. Proposed solutions are suggested. The effectiveness of these solutions in dealing with the urban poor is discussed. Several personal accounts shed illuminating perspectives on living the life of the inner city poor." Libr Media Connect

Includes bibliographical references

Kowalski, Kathiann M.

★ **Poverty** in America; causes and issues. Enslow Pubs. 2003 128p il (Issues in focus) lib bdg $26.60

Grades: 8 9 10 11 12   **362.5**

1. Poor 2. Poverty 3. Poor -- United States 5. Poverty -- United States

ISBN 0-7660-1945-4

LC 2002-156034

Explores the issues of poverty in the United States through real-life stories of poor people and the agencies and organizations available to help them

"Kowalski tackles a tough topic and makes balanced sense of it. . . . Well organized, this book provides fundamental information and perspectives for vital classroom discussion." SLJ

Includes bibliographical references

Lusted, Marcia Amidon

Poverty. ABDO Pub. Co. 2010 112p il map (Essential issues) lib bdg $22.95

Grades: 7 8 9 10   **362.5**
1. Poverty
ISBN 978-1-60453-957-8; 1-60453-957-7
LC 2009-30333
The text is "well-written, providing examples that put a human face to each problem. Quotes and facts are clearly attributed, and their sources are noted in the extensive back matter. . . . Sidebars provide further information, or, more compellingly, offer stories about those touched by the topic. . . . [This] will be of great assistance to students writing reports." SLJ
Includes glossary and bibliographical references

Mason, Paul, 1967-
★ **Poverty**; [by] Paul Mason. Heinemann Library 2006 48p il map (Planet under pressure) lib bdg $31.43
Grades: 4 5 6 7   **362.5**
1. Poverty
ISBN 1-4034-7743-4
LC 2005017166
"Mason presents common factors for poverty worldwide, such as lack of money and education, as well as natural disasters. He also addresses the effects of outsourcing jobs from wealthier countries to poorer ones and how poverty affects environment. The book should make the global situation clearer. [This has] numerous quality color visuals, and sidebars. Up-to-date and informative." SLJ
Includes bibliographical references

Poverty; David M. Haugen and Matthew J. Box, book editors. Greenhaven Press 2006 108p il (Social issues firsthand) lib bdg $28.70
Grades: 8 9 10 11 12   **362.5**
1. Poverty 2. Poor -- United States
ISBN 0-7377-2899-X
LC 2005-45120
These "16 accounts from poverty's gritty trenches evaporate easy assumptions about the poor, and reveal the obstacles faced by stricken individuals and families hampered by catch-22 social policies, entrenched racial inequities, and logistics such as cleaning up for an interview." Booklist
Includes bibliographical references

Senker, Cath
Poverty; [by] Cath Senker. World Almanac Library 2007 48p il (What if we do nothing?) lib bdg $30.60; pa $11.95
Grades: 5 6 7 8   **362.5**
1. Poor 2. Poverty
ISBN 978-0-8368-7757-1 lib bdg; 978-0-8368-8157-8 pa
LC 2006030447
"After discussing patterns of poverty, each chapter raises specific 'What would you do?' questions, with brief suggested answers at the back of the book. Whether the issue is increased taxation of the wealthy, cancellation of unpayable debts, improving primary health care, or more, student activists will want to talk about it, and social-studies teachers will find this a strong curriculum title." Booklist
Includes bibliographical references

Poverty and hunger; Cath Senker. Smart Apple Media 2012 46 p. col. ill., col. maps (library) $35.65
Grades: 6 7 8   **362.5**
1. Hunger 2. Poverty 3. Poor 4. Food security
ISBN 1599205114; 9781599205113
LC 2011017066
This book is part of the Mapping Global Issues series and it focuses on poverty and hunger. "Colorful layouts with numerous maps and graphs dominate this series, which provides an international perspective on important issues. Brief chapters frame problems, discuss their causes, and suggest possible solutions, using maps to illustrate the locations and extent of threats." (School Library Journal)
Includes bibliographical references (p. 45) and index.

362.7   Young people

★ **Adoption**; David M. Haugen and Matthew J. Box, book editors. Greenhaven Press 2005 108p (Social issues firsthand) lib bdg $28.70
Grades: 8 9 10 11 12   **362.7**
1. Adoption
ISBN 0-7377-2881-7
LC 2005-46075
"The book explores such diverse issues as gay adoptive parents, open and transracial adoptions, the search for and reunion with birthparents, custody battles, and more. The editors have done an excellent job of selecting 16 lively, articulate, and poignant essays by birthparents, adoptive parents, and adoptees, all offering different perspectives on the process." SLJ
Includes bibliographical references

Adoption: opposing viewpoints; Mary E. Williams, book editor. Greenhaven Press 2006 226p il (Opposing viewpoints series) lib bdg $34.95; pa $23.70
Grades: 7 8 9 10   **362.7**
1. Adoption
ISBN 0-7377-3301-2 lib bdg; 978-0-7377-3301-3 lib bdg; 0-7377-3302-0 pa; 978-0-7377-3302-0 pa
LC 2006-43350
This anthology addresses such topics as "whether adoption should be encouraged; conflicting views on transracial, international, and gay parent adoptions; whose rights are most in need of protection—adoptive or birth parents or those of adoptees; as well as what government policies should be implemented." SLJ
Includes bibliographical references

★ **Child** and youth security sourcebook; edited by Chad T. Kimball. Omnigraphics 2003 646p il (Security reference series) $68
Grades: 8 9 10 11 12   **362.7**
1. School violence 2. Safety education 3. Youth -- Health and hygiene
ISBN 0-7808-0613-1
LC 2002-45010

This is an "examination of safety and security issues in the lives of children and teenagers geared toward parents, teachers, and students. . . . The nine sections discuss how to protect young people from school crime and violence, physical/sexual/emotional abuse and neglect, drug use and abuse, gangs, Internet sex offenders, and mental and emotional health risks. . . . This successful blend of clear writing, quality research, and meticulous attention to detail conveys much of the information through user-friendly outlines, checklists, and lists of key points. . . . An essential purchase for all libraries serving youth." SLJ

Includes bibliographical references

Ellis, Deborah

Our stories, our songs; African children talk about AIDS. Fitzhenry & Whiteside 2005 104p il $18.95

Grades: 6 7 8 9   **362.7**

1. Orphans 2. AIDS (Disease)

ISBN 1-55041-913-7

"In the summer of 2003, Ellis traveled to Malawi and Zambia and met with children and teens whose lives have been touched by AIDS. In short, autobiographical vignettes, the young people, many of whom are orphans or living on the street, discuss their families, their favorite pastimes, their fears, and their dreams. . . . Ellis presents the stories in a matter-of-fact and compassionate manner that maintains the children's dignity. . . . An impressive offering whose chilling accounts remain with readers long after the book is finished." SLJ

Fields, Julianna

Foster families. Mason Crest 2009 64p il (The changing face of modern families) $22.95

Grades: 6 7 8 9   **362.7**

1. Foster home care

ISBN 978-1-4222-1497-8; 1-4222-1497-4

This describes the challenges facing foster families.

This is "informative [and] nonjudgmental. . . . Including color photos, plentiful sidebars, and interesting headline stories, the accessible [text presents] real-life experiences and numerous supporting facts, definitions, graphs, charts, and statistics." SLJ

Gordon, Sherri Mabry

Beyond bruises; the truth about teens and abuse. Enslow 2009 128p il (Issues in focus today) lib bdg $31.93

Grades: 7 8 9 10   **362.7**

1. Date rape 2. Invective 3. Child abuse 4. Domestic violence

ISBN 978-0-7660-3064-0; 0-7660-3064-4

               LC 2008-12273

"Discusses the various types of abuse teenagers face, including both domestic and dating abuse, the impact abuse has on teens, and several ways to help teens who suffer from some form of abuse." Publisher's note

Includes glossary and bibliographical references

Hynson, Colin

Living on the street; Hamilton's story. [by] Colin Hynson. World Almanac Library 2006 48p il (Children in crisis) lib bdg $30

Grades: 6 7 8 9   **362.7**

1. Homeless persons 2. Homeless

ISBN 0-8368-5961-8

               LC 2005047521

This is the story of a homeless boy in Rio, Brazil named Hamilton Correia Rodrigues

"The material is basically accurate, clearly written, and thought provoking." SLJ

Includes bibliographical references

Jocelyn, Marthe

A home for foundlings. Tundra Books 2005 128p il pa $15.95

Grades: 7 8 9 10   **362.7**

1. Abandoned children

ISBN 0-88776-709-5

"Black-and-white reproductions of early admission documents and ledgers as well as period photographs and engravings appear throughout. This is a useful resource." SLJ

Lanchon, Anne

All about adoption; how to deal with the questions of your past. illustrated by Monike Czarnecki; edited by Tucker Shaw. Abrams/Amulet 2006 104p il (Sunscreen) pa $9.95

Grades: 7 8 9 10   **362.7**

1. Adoption

ISBN 0-8109-9227-2

"This guide covers an adopted child's traditional worries and concerns, such as establishing identity and living with overprotective parents. It also addresses such squirm-worthy issues as the fear of abandonment, racist comments, and discussing birth parents with adoptive parents. . . . Originally published in France, this handsomely designed self-help title . . . provides practical advice and reassurance for adopted teens and their families." Booklist

Includes bibliographical references

McAlpine, Margaret

Working with children. Gareth Stevens Pub 2005 64p il (My future career) lib bdg $26

Grades: 6 7 8 9   **362.7**

1. Teaching 2. Child care 3. Child development 4. Vocational guidance

ISBN 0-8368-4241-3

               LC 2004-45226

This describes seven occupations related to children, including a description of the job and the responsibilities, qualifications, and best personality type for each one.

"The writing is clear and interesting, and the [book is] visually well organized." SLJ

Includes bibliographical references

Medina, Sarah

Abuse and neglect; by Sarah Medina; health consultant, John G. Samanich. G. Stevens Pub. 2009 48p il (Emotional health issues) lib bdg $31

Grades: 6 7 8 9   **362.7**
  1. Child abuse 2. Child sexual abuse
ISBN 978-0-8368-9198-0 lib bdg; 0-8368-9198-8
lib bdg

              LC 2008-5458

First published 2008 in the United Kingdom
This book about abuse has "clear language and explanations. . . . [It is] suitable for fact-finding missions, but the abundant graphics and case studies are likely to draw in browsers as well. Throughout, unfamiliar vocabulary is highlighted in bold and explained in context and in the glossary. . . . Fact boxes and case study sidebars add information." SLJ
Includes glossary and bibliographical references

Pregnancy; William Dudley, book editor. Greenhaven Press 2001 191p il (Teen decisions) lib bdg $33.70; pa $22.45
Grades: 7 8 9 10   **362.7**
  1. Teenage pregnancy 2. Youth -- Sexual behavior
ISBN 0-7377-0492-6 lib bdg; 0-7377-0491-8 pa

              LC 00-32162

"This volume features the stories of teens who chose adoption, abortion, or parenthood, and the advice they offer to others." Publisher's note
Includes bibliographical references

Reef, Catherine
  Alone in the world; orphans and orphanages in America. by Catherine Reef. Clarion Books 2005 135p il $18
Grades: 6 7 8 9   **362.7**
  1. Orphans 2. Orphanages 3. Orphans -- United States -- History
ISBN 0-618-35670-3

              LC 2004-20179

This is a history of orphanages "in the U.S. beginning in 1729, when a place for girls was founded in New Orleans. . . . [The author] ends with a discussion of the challenges the U.S. faces today in caring for growing numbers of homeless, abused, or neglected children. Illustrated with archival photographs and reproductions." SLJ
Includes bibliographical references

Saul, Laya
  Ways to help disadvantaged youth. Mitchell Lane Publishers 2011 47p (How to help: a guide to giving back) lib bdg $29.95
Grades: 4 5 6   **362.7**
  1. Poor 2. Social action
ISBN 978-1-58415-918-6; 1-58415-918-9

              LC 2010006536

This "well-organized [book] will encourage children to contribute to the world around them. [This] title is filled with examples of volunteer opportunities that can be accomplished with some adult involvement and supervision to guide, steer, and maintain focus so that youngsters will have varied and successful experiences. . . . [The book] suggests tutoring, having a toy or food drive, etc." SLJ
Includes bibliographical references

Simons, Rae
  Adoptive parents. Mason Crest Publishers 2009 64p il map (The changing face of modern families) $22.95
Grades: 6 7 8 9   **362.7**
  1. Adoption
ISBN 978-1-4222-1502-9; 1-4222-1502-4

              LC 2009026372

This discusses some the questions facing adoptive parents such as 'What role do birth families play? Are they going to be a part of the child's life?' and 'What do you tell the child about his birth and adoption?'
"Colorful photographs and sidebars appear throughout. These books are good introductions to the study of sociology and interpretation of data." SLJ
Includes bibliographical references

Stewart, Sheila
  A **house** between homes; kids in the foster care system. by Sheila Stewart and Camden Flath. Mason Crest Publishers 2010 48p il lib bdg $19.95; pa $7.95
Grades: 3 4 5 6   **362.7**
  1. Foster home care
ISBN 978-1-4222-1692-7 lib bdg; 1-4222-1692-6 lib bdg; 978-1-4222-1905-8 pa; 1-4222-1905-4 pa

              LC 2010012756

"The prose is respectable in its dialogue, character development, and pacing... This series will be well placed in a school media center, as well as in any institution that serves high-risk children." SLJ

★ **Strong** at the heart; how it feels to heal from sexual abuse. [compiled] by Carolyn Lehman. Farrar, Straus & Giroux 2005 156p il $18
Grades: 8 9 10 11 12   **362.7**
1. Rape 2. Incest 3. Child sexual abuse
ISBN 0-374-37282-9

              LC 2004-56280

This "gathers 11 personal stories by young men and women who experienced rape, molestation, or incest and found healing through speaking out about their abuse. . . . Clearly and candidly written, the narratives recounted here include sufficient details of abuse to be authentic, but never titillating. . . . An attractive, accessible format and black-and-white portraits throughout personalize the presentation." SLJ

Warren, Andrea
  Orphan train rider; one boy's true story. Houghton Mifflin 1996 80p il hardcover o.p. pa $7.95
Grades: 4 5 6 7   **362.7**
  1. Orphans 2. Adoption 3. Abandoned children
ISBN 0-395-69822-7; 0-395-91362-4 pa

              LC 94-43688

"Between 1854 and 1930, more than 200,000 orphaned and abandoned children from the cities of the eastern seaboard were 'placed out' to new homes and families in the midwest and western states. . . . {This is an} account of the 'orphan-train' phenomena, and of one man's story of how it affected his life. . . . The chapters alternate information about the largest agency, the Children's Aid Society, and its history, with the story of Lee Nailling, from whom the author has gathered the facts of his own childhood journey to Texas and his eventual reunion, late in life, with some of his long-lost siblings." (SLJ)

Includes bibliographical references

362.73   Institutional and related services

Warren, Andrea

  We rode the orphan trains. Houghton Mifflin 2001 132p il $18; pa $8.95

Grades: 4 5 6 7   **362.73**

  1. Orphans 2. Orphan trains 3. Orphans -- United States -- Biography

  ISBN 0-618-11712-1; 0-618-11712-1 pa

                          LC 00-47279

"This is powerful nonfiction for classroom and personal reading and for discussion." Booklist

Includes bibliographical references

362.82   Families

Stewart, Sheila

  When Daddy hit Mommy; by Sheila Stewart and Rae Simons. Mason Crest Publishers 2011 48p il lib bdg $19.95; pa $7.95

Grades: 3 4 5   **362.82**

  1. Child abuse 2. Domestic violence

  ISBN 978-1-4222-1696-5 lib bdg; 1-4222-1696-9 lib bdg; 978-1-4222-1909-6 pa; 1-4222-1909-7 pa

                        LC 2010029346

Zehr, Howard

  What will happen to me? by Howard Zehr and Lorraine Stutzman Amstutz; portraits by Howard Zehr. Good Books 2010 94p il pa $14.95

Grades: 7 8 9 10   **362.82**

  1. Children of prisoners

  ISBN 978-1-56148-689-2

                        LC 2010-12419

This discusses issues facing "children of incarcerated parents. . . . In part one, the statements from the children interviewed are accompanied by full-color photo portraits. What comes through is that they all love their parents unequivocally, but here it is tangible and poignant both in their words and faces. . . . Part two offers advice for caregivers and includes 10 questions often asked by children whose parents are in jail." SLJ

Includes bibliographical references

  ★ **Domestic** violence: opposing viewpoints; Mike Wilson, book editor. Greenhaven Press 2008 217p (Opposing viewpoints series) lib bdg $39.70; pa $27.50

Grades: 8 9 10 11 12   **362.82**

  1. Domestic violence

  ISBN 978-0-7377-4206-0 lib bdg; 0-7377-4206-2 lib bdg; 978-0-7377-4207-7 pa; 0-7377-4207-0 pa

                        LC 2008-28517

Articles in this anthology discuss domestic violence, including its causes and possible remedies.

Includes bibliographical references

362.87   Displaced persons

Nelson, Sheila

  In defense of our country; survivors of military conflict. by Sheila Stewart with Joyce Zoldak. Mason Crest Publishers 2009 128p il map (Survivors: ordinary people, extraordinary circumstances) lib bdg $24.95

Grades: 7 8 9 10   **362.87**

  1. War 2. Soldiers 3. Ethnic relations 4. Military history

  ISBN 978-1-4222-0452-8 lib bdg; 1-4222-0452-9 lib bdg

                        LC 2008-50556

The title "looks at wars in Africa, Southeast Asia, Eastern Europe, and the Middle East, though plenty of inset boxes cover other topics such as trench warfare in World War I, the Red Cross, and the American Civil War. . . . [This book] will be valued for . . . [its] ability to generate empathy for survivors and their strengths and resilience in difficult situations." SLJ

Includes bibliographical references

362.88   Victims of war

Bickerstaff, Linda

  Violence against women; public health and human rights. Rosen Pub. 2010 112p il (A young woman's guide to contemporary issues) lib bdg $31.95

Grades: 7 8 9 10   **362.88**

  1. Violence 2. Abused women

  ISBN 978-1-4358-3539-9; 1-4358-3539-5

                        LC 2009-12062

"Facts are shared in a conversational tone, creating the sense of a chat with a big sister. . . . [Though] designed for personal reading and browsing, the data provided are accurate and also lend themselves to use in reports." SLJ

Includes glossary and bibliographical references

Landau, Elaine

  ★ **Date** violence; [by] Elaine Landau. Franklin Watts 2004 80p (Life balance) $20.50; pa $6.95

Grades: 5 6 7 8   **362.88**

  1. Violence 2. Date rape 3. Dating (Social customs)

  ISBN 0-531-12214-X; 0-531-16613-9 pa

                        LC 2003-19480

"Landau helps those who are new to dating to distinguish between healthy and unhealthy relationships by providing understandable warning signs of emotional, physical, and sexual abuse. . . . This book will help young people make informed decisions and more wisely navigate the emotionally charged, confusing issues associated with adolescent relationships." SLJ

Includes glossary and bibliographical references

Simons, Rae

Gender danger; survivors of rape, human trafficking, and honor killings. by Rae Simons with Joyce Zoldak. Mason Crest Publishers 2009 128p il (Survivors: ordinary people, extraordinary circumstances) lib bdg $24.95

Grades: 7 8 9 10 **362.88**

1. Rape 2. Violence 3. Sex crimes 4. Abused women 5. Women -- Social conditions

ISBN 978-1-4222-0451-1; 1-4222-0451-0

LC 2008-50322

The author discusses "the issues faced by women in this and other cultures. The book looks at rape as a weapon of war, honor killings, female circumcision, and the complex and often dangerous world of transgender individuals." SLJ

Includes bibliographical references

362.883 Rape

Wilkins, Jessica

Date rape. Crabtree Pub. 2011 48p il (Straight talk about . . .) $29.27; pa $9.95

Grades: 7 8 9 10 **362.883**

1. Date rape

ISBN 978-0-7787-2128-4; 0-7787-2128-0; 978-0-7787-2135-2 pa; 0-7787-2135-3 pa

LC 2010-16397

This book about date rape "also spends a good deal of its pages covering dating violence, both verbal and physical, which girls don't always understand to be problematic. . . . The information . . . is strong and far reaching." Booklist

363 Other social problems and services

Esherick, Joan

The **FDA** and psychiatric drugs; how a drug is approved. by Joan Esherick. Mason Crest Publishers 2004 128p il (Psychiatric disorders) $24.95

363

1. Psychotropic drugs 2. Drug approval -- United States 3. Psychotropic drugs -- Testing -- Law and legislation -- United States

ISBN 1-590-84578-1

LC 2003-2387

Describes how a psychiatric drug is approved for use by the FDA, as well as some historical background on the agency.

This "solidly written and attractively designed [title offers] complex psychiatric information and drug treatments in an understandable and readable manner." SLJ

Includes bibliographical references and index

363.1 Public safety programs

Aronson, Marc

★ **Trapped**; how the world rescued 33 miners from 2,000 feet below the Chilean desert. Atheneum 2011 144p il $16.99

Grades: 4 5 6 7 **363.1**

1. Rescue work 2. Gold mines and mining 3. Copper mines and mining 4. Mine accidents -- Chile

ISBN 1-4169-1397-1; 978-1-4169-1397-9

LC 2011000777

This title is about thirty-three miners trapped in a copper-gold mine in San Jose, Chile and how experts from around the world, from drillers, to astronauts, to submarine specialists, came together to make their remarkable rescue possible.

This is "a riveting, in-depth recounting of the events that held the world rapt. . . . Twelve short chapters with photos and diagrams keep the story well-paced." Publ Wkly

Includes bibliographical references

Ballard, Carol

Food safety. Gareth Stevens Pub. 2010 48p il (What if we do nothing?) lib bdg $31

Grades: 7 8 9 10 **363.1**

1. Food poisoning 2. Food contamination

ISBN 978-1-4339-1982-4 lib bdg; 1-4339-1982-6 lib bdg

LC 2008-52284

This describes the precautions taken by food producers, retailers, and food safety organizations to guard against food-borne illnesses from such causes as pesticides, microbes, pollution, and chemical additives.

"Meaningful illustrations include color photos and text-enhancing charts. . . . [This is] well written and useful for reports." SLJ

Includes glossary and bibliographical references

Bennie, Paul

The **great** Chicago fire of 1871; [by] Paul Bennie. Chelsea House 2008 128p il (Great historic disasters) $35

Grades: 7 8 9 10 **363.1**

1. Fires -- Chicago (Ill.)

ISBN 978-0-7910-9638-3; 0-7910-9638-6

LC 2007-36550

"On October 8, 1871, a fire started in the O'Learys' barn in Chicago. . . . [This occurence] brought about lasting changes in fire prevention and building codes. . . . [This book], which [describes] the [disaster] and [its] aftermath in detail, [is] well written and informative. . . . [This is] first-rate for reports and general browsing." SLJ

Includes bibliographical references

Chernobyl; David Erik Nelson, book editor. Greenhaven Press 2010 220p il map (Perspectives on modern world history) $38.50

Grades: 8 9 10 11 12 **363.1**

1. Chernobyl Nuclear Accident, Chernobyl, Ukraine, 1986

ISBN 978-0-7377-4555-9; 0-7377-4555-X

LC 2009-27203

"This volume contains a wealth of relevant information representing many viewpoints of the current discussions surrounding the 1986 disaster at the Chernobyl nuclear power plant in Ukraine, which led to an official death toll of 56 people. Each article, skillfully drawn from multinational secondary sources, provides researchers with an admirable base for reports." SLJ

Includes glossary and bibliographical references

Lace, William W.

The **Hindenburg** disaster of 1937. Chelsea House Publishers 2008 120p il (Great historic disasters) lib bdg $35

Grades: 6 7 8 9 10   363.1

1. Aircraft accidents

ISBN 978-0-7910-9739-7; 0-7910-9739-0

LC 2008004890

On May 6, 1937, the celebrated airship Hindenburg caught fire during its landing in Lakehurst, New Jersey, killing 36 people. This describes the disaster and its aftermath.

The book covers its topic "thoroughly and [includes] high-quality photographs and occasional sidebars. Lace's account of the airship has a good deal of intrigue and drama and could be useful for reports or recreational reading." SLJ

Includes glossary and bibliographical references

Lusted, Marcia Amidon

The **Chernobyl** Disaster. ABDO Pub. 2011 112p il (Essential events) lib bdg $23.95

Grades: 7 8 9 10 11 12   363.1

1. Nuclear power plants 2. Chernobyl Nuclear Accident, Chernobyl, Ukraine, 1986

ISBN 978-1-6171-4763-0; 1-6171-4763-X

LC 2010045019

This describes "the technology and engineering detail of how a nuclear power plant generates electricity and why it is dangerous, as well as the politics of why the disaster happened. . . . The spacious . . . design is inviting, with many color illustrations and screens, and the extensive back matter includes a detailed time line, glossary, bibliography and source notes." Booklist

Includes glossary and bibliographical references

The **Three** Mile Island nuclear disaster; by Marcia Amidon Lusted. ABDO Pub. Company 2012 112 p. il (Essential events) $34.22

Grades: 6 7 8   363.1

1. Nuclear energy 2. Nuclear power plants 3. Nuclear power plants -- Accidents

ISBN 1617833118; 9781617833113

LC 2011036182

This children's educational book by Marcia Amidon Lusted "examines an important historic event—the Three Mile Island nuclear disaster near Middletown, Pennsylvania. . . . [It] explores the history of nuclear power in the United States, how a nuclear plant works, details of the emergency at Metropolitan Edison Company's nuclear power plant, handling of the disaster by the Nuclear Regulatory Commission, President Jimmy Carter's visit to Three Mile Island, the investigation into the disaster, and the effects of this event on society. Features include a table of contents, glossary, se-

lected bibliography, Web links, source notes, and an index, plus a timeline and essential facts." (Publisher's note)

Includes glossary and bibliographical references.

Mara, Wil

The **Chernobyl** disaster; legacy and impact on the future of nuclear energy. Marshall Cavendish Benchmark 2010 112p il (Perspectives on) $39.93

Grades: 7 8 9 10   363.1

1. Chernobyl Nuclear Accident, Chernobyl, Ukraine, 1986

ISBN 978-0-7614-4984-3; 0-7614-4984-1

"Briefly outlines the nuclear disaster in an easy-to-read format. It examines the nuclear crisis from the moment it occurred to the fallout afterwards. The volume begins with a moment-by-moment account of the disaster itself. Color illustrations of the reactor provide a detailed explanation of the process behind its failure. . . . This is a recommended addition to any school or public library." Voice Youth Advocates

Mayell, Mark

Tragedies of space exploration. Lucent Books 2004 112p il (Manmade disasters) $27.45

Grades: 5 6 7 8   363.1

1. Astronautics 2. Space vehicle accidents 3. Astronautics -- History 4. Astronautics -- Accidents

ISBN 1-59018-508-0

LC 2003-15618

Analyzes the inherent risks and dangers of human space exploration, from those that affect the health of astronauts to those that result in shuttle explosions, and examines ways of reducing safety-related incidents.

"Behind-the-headlines details are fresh and thought-provoking. . . . Halftone photographs and clear drawings speak to the reality of these events. . . . [This is] rich in content and detail." SLJ

Includes bibliographical references

Mintzer, Richard

The **National** Transportation Safety Board; {by} Rich Mintzer. Chelsea House 2002 64p il (Your government—how it works) lib bdg $20.75

Grades: 6 7 8 9   363.1

1. Traffic accidents 2. Traffic safety -- United States 3. Transportation accidents -- United States

ISBN 0-7910-6794-7

LC 2002-44

Describes the workings and history of the National Transportation Safety Board as part of the United States government, including how it investigates transportation accidents and makes safety recommendations

Includes glossary and bibliographical references

Parks, Peggy J., 1951-

Drunk driving. ReferencePoint Press 2009 96p il (Compact research. Current issues) lib bdg $25.95

Grades: 7 8 9 10   363.1

1. Drunk driving

ISBN 978-1-60152-072-2; 1-60152-072-7

LC 2008-48499

This "title has an overview of [drunk driving] as well as topic-specific chapters such as 'Who Drives Drunk?' and 'How Should Drunk Drivers Be Punished?' It offers differing ideas on questions that have more than one answer. The colorful graphs and charts contain current information." SLJ

Includes bibliographical references

Sherman, Jill

The **Hindenburg** disaster. ABDO Pub. Co. 2010 112p il (Essential events) lib bdg $34.22

Grades: 6 7 8 9   **363.1**

1. Airships 2. Aircraft accidents

ISBN 978-1-60453-944-8; 1-60453-944-5

LC 2009-30427

This book offers "vivid detail as well as historical and political context. . . . Recounting the [Hindenburg] crash, Sherman captures readers' attention with an opening chapter devoted to the actual crash. She then paints a full picture of the invention of the zeppelin and its uses and development. The author then works her way back to a full description of the crash and a discussion of the theories around its cause. [This title has] pertinent sidebars with primary source material. Archival photos add to the dramatic [narrative]." SLJ

Includes bibliographical references

Vogt, Gregory

Disasters in space exploration; Gregory L. Vogt. rev ed; Millbrook Press 2003 79p il lib bdg $25.90

Grades: 6 7 8 9   **363.1**

1. Space vehicle accidents

ISBN 0-7613-2895-5

LC 2003-10864

First published 2001

Examines the failed missions, accidents, and destroyed vehicles of various world space programs, including the explosion of the space shuttle Columbia in 2003

"The writing is interesting and succinct without leaving out any of the details. Brimming with clearly reproduced full-color and black-and-white photographs." SLJ

Includes bibliographical references

363.11   Occupational and industrial hazards

Scott, Elaine

★ **Buried** alive! how 33 miners survived 69 days deep under the Chilean desert. Elaine Scott. Houghton Mifflin Harcourt 2012 80 p. col. ill., col. maps (hardcover) $17.99; (ebook) $17.99

Grades: 4 5 6 7 8   **363.11**

1. Miners 2. Disasters 3. Industrial accidents 4. San José Mine Accident, Chile, 2010 5. Mine rescue work -- Chile -- Copiapó Region   6. Gold mines and mining -- Accidents -- Chile -- Copiapó Region 7. Copper mines and mining -- Accidents -- Chile -- Copiapó Region

ISBN 0547707789; 9780547707785; 9780547691787

LC 2011025945

Author Elaine Scott chronicles the events that took place "[o]n August 5, 2010, [when] a copper mine in Chile collapsed, trapping 33 miners nearly half a mile underground . . . [The author] describes the choices the miners' strong leader advised that prolonged their survival long enough to

be rescued and the creative solutions that effected that rescue. They drilled through over 2,000 feet of especially hard rock, delivered supplies to the trapped men through a tiny bore hole and then invented a way to carry the men, one at a time, to the surface in a very small capsule." (Kirkus)

Includes bibliographical references (p. 78) and index.

363.17   Hazardous materials

Kops, Deborah

The **Great** Molasses Flood; Boston, 1919. Deborah Kops. Charlesbridge 2012 102 p. $19.95

Grades: 6 7 8 9   **363.17**

1. Molasses 2. Industrial accidents 3. Boston (Mass.) -- History 4. Floods -- Massachusetts -- Boston -- History -- 20th century 5. Industrial accidents -- Massachusetts -- Boston -- History -- 20th century 6. Alcohol industry -- Accidents -- Massachusetts -- Boston -- History -- 20th century 7. Molasses industry -- Accidents -- Massachusetts -- Boston -- History -- 20th century

ISBN 1580893481; 9781580893480; 9781580893497

LC 2011000655

This historical survey by Deborah Kops follows the events of "January 15, 1919 . . . an unseasonable warm day in Boston, Massachusetts, and a day that would go down in history. One minute it was business as usual on the waterfront and the next - KABOOM! A large tank holding molasses exploded, sending shards of metal hundreds of feet away, collapsing buildings, and coating the harborfront community with a thick layer of sticky-sweet sludge." (Publisher's note)

"The combination of the sepia-toned photographs, the use of brown to highlight the chapter headings, and the choice of cream-colored paper gives this book a rich, elegant quality while staying consistent with the subject matter." Booklist

363.2   Police services

Allman, Toney

★ The **medical** examiner. Gale 2006 104p il (Crime scene investigations) lib bdg $31.20

Grades: 7 8 9 10   **363.2**

1. Forensic sciences 2. Medical jurisprudence

ISBN 1-59018-912-4

Discusses what medical examiners do.

This "book has fascinating, factual information and quotes taken from interviews with professionals. . . . [This] well-organized [title has] clear subheadings, tables of statistics, and well-chosen color photos." SLJ

Arroyo, Sheri L.

How crime fighters use math; math curriculum consultant: Rhea A. Stewart. Chelsea Clubhouse 2010 32p il (Math in the real world) lib bdg $28

Grades: 4 5 6   **363.2**

1. Mathematics 2. Vocational guidance 3. Criminal

investigation
ISBN 978-1-60413-602-9 lib bdg; 1-60413-602-2
lib bdg

LC 2009-23330

"The layout for [this] slim [title] is bright and colorful with a photograph and a 'You Do the Math' problem to solve and large, easy-to-read text on every spread. An answer key is included in the back matter, along with a page detailing the career choices and the educational requirements. [It] touches on crime-scene grids, the importance of shoe prints in tracking a criminal, cracking secret codes, and more. . . . [This title] would be useful to supplement lessons on mathematics. [It] will also appeal to students wanting to learn more about math as it relates to specific careers." SLJ

Includes glossary and bibliographical references

Ballard, Carol

At the crime scene! collecting clues and evidence. Enslow Publishers 2009 48p il (Solve that crime!) lib bdg $23.93

Grades: 5 6 7 8   **363.2**

1. Forensic sciences 2. Criminal investigation
ISBN 978-0-7660-3373-3 lib bdg; 0-7660-3373-2
lib bdg

LC 2008-33306

This "title boasts in-depth information, sidebars detailing events of true crime, and activities that will increase understanding. . . . Photographs are colorful, well-captioned, and related to the text." SLJ

Includes glossary and bibliographical references

Crime under the microscope! in the forensics lab. Enslow Publishers 2009 48p il (Solve that crime!) lib bdg $23.93

Grades: 5 6 7 8   **363.2**

1. Forensic sciences 2. Criminal investigation
ISBN 978-0-7660-3374-0 lib bdg; 0-7660-3374-0
lib bdg

LC 2008-33307

This describes how forensics solves crimes in the laboratory

This "title boasts in-depth information, sidebars detailing events of true crime, and activities that will increase understanding. . . . Photographs are colorful, well-captioned, and related to the text." SLJ

Includes glossary and bibliographical references

Crimebusting! identifying criminals and victims. Enslow Publishers 2010 48p il lib bdg $23.93

Grades: 5 6 7 8   **363.2**

1. Criminals -- Identification
ISBN 978-0-7660-3375-7 lib bdg; 0-7660-3375-9
lib bdg

LC 2008-34803

This "title boasts in-depth information, sidebars detailing events of true crime, and activities that will increase understanding. . . . Photographs are colorful, well-captioned, and related to the text." SLJ

Bell, Suzanne

Encyclopedia of forensic science; foreword by Barry A.J. Fisher; preface by Robert C. Shaler. rev ed; Facts on File 2008 402p il (Facts on File science library) $85

Grades: 8 9 10 11 12 Adult   **363.2**

1. Reference books 2. Forensic sciences 3. Forensic sciences -- Encyclopedias
ISBN 978-0-8160-6799-2; 0-8160-6799-6

LC 2008-5862

First published 2003

"In addition to explaining the science of forensics, Bell . . . reviews various disciplines related to forensic science, among them entomology, odontology, and psychology. Other entries cover professional organizations, government agencies, famous names in the field of forensics, evidence, and legal issues. . . . With its clear language and brief entries [this] volume will provide readers with a nuts-and-bolts understanding of the real world of forensic science." Booklist [review of 2003 edition]

Includes bibliographical references

Fakes and forgeries. Facts On File 2008 108p il (Essentials of forensic science) $35

Grades: 7 8 9 10 11 12   **363.2**

1. Fraud 2. Forgery
ISBN 978-0-8160-5514-2; 0-8160-5514-9

LC 2008-4502

This is a "fascinating introduction to how scientists identify fraudulent copies, from signatures to oil paintings. . . . Bell moves from examples of the crime that date back to ancient Mesopotamian civilizations all the way through to today's high-tech counterfeiting cases." Booklist

Includes glossary and bibliographical references

Denega, Danielle

Skulls and skeletons; true life stories of bone detectives. Franklin Watts 2007 64p il map (24/7: Science behind the scenes) lib bdg $26; pa $7.95

Grades: 6 7 8 9   **363.2**

1. Forensic sciences 2. Forensic anthropology
ISBN 978-0-531-12064-4 lib bdg; 0-531-12064-3 lib bdg; 978-0-531-17527-9 pa; 0-531-17527-8 pa

LC 2006-21229

Explains how forensic anthropologists figure out a victim's profile and examines three case studies in which forensic anthropologists help identify the victims.

Includes glossary and bibliographical references

Dolan, Edward F.

Careers in the U.S. Coast Guard. Marshall Cavendish Benchmark 2008 80p il (Military service) lib bdg $24.95

Grades: 6 7 8 9   **363.2**

1. Vocational guidance
ISBN 978-0-7614-4207-3 lib bdg; 0-7614-4207-3
lib bdg

LC 2008039819

Discusses service in the U.S. Coast Guard, including training, educational benefits, and career opportunities.

"Young people interested in exploring a career in [the U. S. Coast Guard] will find solid information. . . . Colored photographs, acronyms, Web sites, and detailed index will add to the appeal." Booklist

Includes bibliographical references

Evans, Colin

★ **Crime** lab. Chelsea House 2011 134p il (Law enforcement agencies) lib bdg $35

Grades: 6 7 8 9 **363.2**

1. Forensic sciences 2. Criminal investigation

ISBN 978-1-60413-612-8; 1-60413-612-X

LC 2010043271

This describes the work of crime labs from the 19th century to the present, including the technology used such as ballistics, toxicology, atomic evidence, radio carbon dating, DNA, and fingerprints.

"The Law Enforcement Agencies series is as formidable as the various groups it introduces. Solidly and comprehensively researched. . . . An attractive design, plenty of photos, and solid back matter complete each package. Extremely useful for students and appealing for browsers." Booklist

Includes bibliographical references

Evidence. Chelsea House 2010 132p il (Criminal justice) lib bdg $35

Grades: 6 7 8 9 **363.2**

1. Forensic sciences 2. Criminal investigation

ISBN 978-1-60413-615-9 lib bdg; 1-60413-615-4 lib bdg

The author "describes with authority how varieties of direct and circumstantial evidence . . . are gathered and analyzed. . . . He explains how crime-scene reconstructions, autopsies, and careful observation—as well as traces of blood, skin, poison, carpet fiber, and other substances—played central roles in obtaining convictions. . . . This makes a compelling introduction to a perennially popular topic." Booklist

★ **Interpol**. Chelsea House Publishers 2011 112p il (Law enforcement agencies) lib bdg $35

Grades: 6 7 8 9 **363.2**

1. Law enforcement 2. Criminal investigation

ISBN 978-1-60413-613-5; 1-60413-613-8

LC 2010048099

This is a history of Interpol from 1914 to the present, covering some of its international cases.

Includes bibliographical references

★ **New** York Police Department. Chelsea House Publishers 2011 120p il (Law enforcement agencies) lib bdg $35

Grades: 6 7 8 9 **363.2**

1. Law enforcement 2. Police -- New York (N.Y.)

ISBN 978-1-60413-614-2; 1-60413-614-6

LC 2010049866

This is a history of the New York City Police Department from 1800 to the present, covering such topics as The Mafia, fingerprints, The Son of Sam, police corruption, John Gotti, and the attacks of September 11, 2001.

Includes bibliographical references

Gardner, Robert

Forensic science projects with a crime lab you can build; [by] Robert Gardner. Enslow Publishers 2007 128p il (Build-a-lab! science experiments) $23.95

Grades: 6 7 8 9 **363.2**

1. Science projects 2. Forensic sciences 3. Criminal investigation

ISBN 978-0-7660-2806-7; 0-7660-2806-2

LC 2006039026

Describes how to build a crime lab out of everyday materials so that things like fingerprints and handwriting can be analyzed.

"Gardner creatively handles the challenging task of assembling activities that connect strongly with his often grisly theme. . . . While the forensics information will draw students' interest, the potential dangers may lead some recommenders to set this aside for use in classrooms, where adult supervision can be ensured." Booklist

Includes bibliographical references

Graham, Ian

Forensic technology. Smart Apple Media 2011 il (New technology) lib bdg $34.25

Grades: 4 5 6 7 **363.2**

1. Forensic sciences 2. Criminal investigation

ISBN 978-1-599-20532-8; 1-599-20532-7

LC 2010044238

Describes the technology used by forensic scientists to gather and analyze evidence from crime scenes.

This "offers a fine overview for reports, and its attractive design may also entice middle-grade readers to learn more." Booklist

Gray, Leon

Virtual crime! solving cybercrime. Enslow Publishers 2009 48p il (Solve that crime!) lib bdg $23.93

Grades: 5 6 7 8 **363.2**

1. Computer crimes

ISBN 978-0-7660-3376-4 lib bdg; 0-7660-3376-7 lib bdg

LC 2008-33308

This "title boasts in-depth information, sidebars detailing events of true crime, and activities that will increase understanding. . . . Photographs are colorful, well-captioned, and related to the text." SLJ

Includes glossary and bibliographical references

Harris, Elizabeth Snoke

★ **Crime** scene science fair projects. Lark Books 2006 112p il $25.95

Grades: 6 7 8 9 10 **363.2**

1. Science projects 2. Forensic sciences 3. Criminal investigation

ISBN 1-57990-765-2

LC 2006-16803

"Harris begins with an explanation of forensic science and how it's applied in the everyday world, followed by a discussion of how to plan for a successful project. The projects involve lie detection, lifting fingerprints, recovering data from burned documents, and so on. . . . The author's concise, lively style will even engage students who aren't fond of reading nonfiction." SLJ

Harris, Nathaniel

Crime fighting; the impact of science and technology. Gareth Stevens Pub. 2010 64p il (Pros and cons) lib bdg $35

Grades: 5 6 7 8   **363.2**

     1. Criminal investigation

     ISBN 978-1-4339-1985-5 lib bdg; 1-4339-1985-0 lib bdg

                 LC 2009-12433

An "active layout that features color photographs, maps, graphs or charts on every spread, this . . . [book] has much to offer. . . . It conveniently outlines the range of views . . . helping students to learn how to view both sides of [the] issue[s]." SLJ

Includes glossary and bibliographical references

Innes, Brian

DNA and body evidence. Sharpe Focus 2008 96p il (Forensic evidence) $39.95

Grades: 7 8 9 10 11 12   **363.2**

     1. Forensic sciences 2. DNA fingerprinting 3. Criminal investigation

     ISBN 978-0-7656-8115-7

                 LC 2007-6749

This "book begins with the history of DNA and fluid analysis, continues with DNA fingerprinting and gathering evidence, and highlights landmark usage of DNA evidence as well as its routine uses in both the judicial and penal systems. . . . The [book is] comprehensive enough for students with prior knowledge of forensics but approachable for beginners. . . . [It weaves] technical terms and anecdotal evidence into a seamless presentation." SLJ

Includes glossary and bibliographical references

Fingerprints and impressions. Sharpe Focus 2008 96p il (Forensic evidence) $39.95

Grades: 7 8 9 10 11 12   **363.2**

     1. Fingerprints 2. Forensic sciences 3. Criminal investigation

     ISBN 978-0-7656-8114-0

                 LC 2007-6751

This "covers the origins of fingerprinting and the analysis and usage of fingerprinting data and concludes with its use as admissible evidence in court. . . . [The book is] comprehensive enough for students with prior knowledge of forensics but approachable for beginners. . . . [It weaves] technical terms and anecdotal evidence into a seamless presentation." SLJ

Includes glossary and bibliographical references

Joyce, Jaime

Bullet proof! the evidence that guns leave behind. [by] Jaime Joyce. Franklin Watts 2007 64p il map (24/7, science behind the scenes) lib bdg $27; pa $7.95

Grades: 5 6 7 8   **363.2**

     1. Firearms 2. Forensic sciences 3. Criminal investigation

     ISBN 0-531-11820-7 lib bdg; 978-0-531-11820-7 lib bdg; 0-531-15455-6 pa; 978-0-531-15455-7 pa

                 LC 2006005718

"Joyce explores the field of forensic firearms analysis, including the facts and figures behind the science of ballistics, real-life case studies of historical and contemporary crimes involving gun violence, and information for young people interested in pursuing ballistics as a career path. . . . Photographs, sidebars, maps, and other graphic elements are used liberally to enliven and build upon the narrative." SLJ

Includes glossary and bibliographical references

Kops, Deborah

★ **Racial** profiling. Marshall Cavendish Benchmark 2006 127p il (Open for debate) lib bdg $39.93

Grades: 7 8 9 10   **363.2**

     1. Law enforcement 2. Racial profiling in law enforcement 3. Racial profiling 4. War on terrorism 5. Japanese Americans -- Evacuation and relocation, 1942-1945

     ISBN 978-0-7614-2298-3; 0-7614-2298-6

This is "well organized and . . . clearly and plainly written." SLJ

Includes bibliographical references

Lane, Brian

Crime and detection; written by Brian Lane. Dorling Kindersley 2005 61p il (DK eyewitness books) $15.99

Grades: 4 5 6 7   **363.2**

     1. Crime 2. Forensic sciences 3. Criminal investigation

     ISBN 0-7566-1386-8

     First published 1998 by Knopf

Explores the many different methods used to solve crimes, covering such topics as criminal, detectives, and forensics

Mezzanotte, Jim

Police. Marshall Cavendish Benchmark 2010 64p il (Working animals) lib bdg $28.50

Grades: 4 5 6 7   **363.2**

     1. Animals in police work

     ISBN 978-1-60870-166-7 lib bdg; 1-60870-166-2 lib bdg

                 LC 2010007006

Describes animals, such as dogs and horses, which work with police in such areas as search-and-rescue, tracking criminals, and sniffing out explosives

"Attractively designed and packed with information. . . . The composition of each page is attractively set up with well-selected and reproduced stock and historical photos." SLJ

Newton, Michael

★ **Bomb** squad. Chelsea House Publishers 2010 127p il (Law enforcement agencies) lib bdg $35

Grades: 6 7 8 9   **363.2**

     1. Bombs 2. Police

     ISBN 978-1-60413-624-1; 1-60413-624-3

                 LC 2010022102

"Solidly and comprehensively researched. . . . Bomb Squad shows that explosives have always been a means of striking terror throughout history. The volume covers the making and defusing of bombs, nuclear devices, and headline-making acts of terror. . . . An attractive design, plenty of photos, and solid back matter complete [the] package. Extremely useful for students and appealing for browsers." Booklist

Includes bibliographical references

★ **Drug** Enforcement Administration. Chelsea House Publishers 2011 128p il (Law enforcement agencies) lib bdg $35

Grades: 6 7 8 9   363.2

1. Drug traffic 2. Drugs -- Law and legislation

ISBN 978-1-60413-641-8; 1-60413-641-3

LC 2010036940

This describes the work of the Drug Enforcement Administration, including some of its cases concerning marijuana, cocaine, heroin, and methamphetamine.

"The Law Enforcement Agencies series is as formidable as the various groups it introduces. Solidly and comprehensively researched. . . . An attractive design, plenty of photos, and solid back matter complete each package. Extremely useful for students and appealing for browsers." Booklist

Includes bibliographical references

★ **SWAT** teams. Chelsea House Publishers 2010 127p il (Law enforcement agencies) lib bdg $35

Grades: 6 7 8 9   363.2

1. Police 2. Law enforcement

ISBN 978-1-60413-625-8; 1-60413-625-1

LC 2010026511

This describes the work of SWAT (Special Weapons and Tactics) teams in law enforcement, including missions ranging from hostage rescue and apprehension of violent felons to drug raids and natural-disaster relief. The book traces the history of special police teams worldwide, examining their techniques, tools, successes, and failures.

Includes bibliographical references

★ **U.S.** marshals. Chelsea House Publishers 2011 128p il (Law enforcement agencies) lib bdg $35

Grades: 6 7 8 9   363.2

1. Law enforcement

ISBN 978-1-60413-627-2; 1-60413-627-8

LC 2010038195

This describes the U. S. Marshals Service, its history, and its work in fighting counterfeiting, in court security, the Witness Security Program, and fugitive investigations.

"The Law Enforcement Agencies series is as formidable as the various groups it introduces. Solidly and comprehensively researched. . . . An attractive design, plenty of photos, and solid back matter complete each package. Extremely useful for students and appealing for browsers." Booklist

Includes bibliographical references

Orr, Tamra

Racial profiling. ABDO Pub. Co. 2010 112p il (Essential viewpoints) lib bdg $32.79

Grades: 7 8 9 10   363.2

1. Racial profiling in law enforcement 2. Racial profiling

ISBN 978-1-60453-535-8; 1-60453-535-0

LC 2008-34915

"This timely book covers racial profiling as practiced in the United States since the terrorist attacks of 9/11, when it

has come to center on young men of Middle Eastern extraction. . . . Orr presents arguments for and against the practice in focused, clearly written essays that will help students become informed. . . . There are plenty of color photographs. This book will enhance most collections." SLJ

Includes bibliographical references

Owen, David

Police lab; how forensic science tracks down and convicts criminals. Firefly Bks. 2002 128p il $19.95; pa $9.95

Grades: 7 8 9 10   363.2

1. Forensic sciences 2. Criminal investigation

ISBN 1-55297-620-3; 1-55297-619-X pa

LC 2002-512986

The author explains "how forensics experts gather, analyze, and assess data on forgery, poisoning, suicides, explosions, and murder by fire, water, suffocation, and various weapons. Detailed descriptions of the forensics process are always put into historical context, with brief, gripping summaries of many famous cases and historical events. . . . An exciting, enlightening read." Booklist

Includes glossary

Perritano, John

Science beats crime. Marshall Cavendish Benchmark 2010 48p il (Cool science) lib bdg $28.50

Grades: 5 6 7 8   363.2

1. Forensic sciences 2. Criminal investigation

ISBN 978-1-60870-078-3 lib bdg; 1-60870-078-X lib bdg

LC 2009053774

"Perritano briefly traces the history of forensic science, . . . discusses different subspecialities, such as toxicology and forensic anthropology, and then gets into the good stuff—fingerprinting, DNA profiling, ballistics, splatter patterns, even a gross-out spread of how studying maggots can determine time of death. Interspersed throughout are real-life case studies. . . . This solid, amply illustrated, and easy-reading introduction to forensic science ends with a look at the future of the field." Booklist

Includes glossary and bibliographical references

Rainis, Kenneth G.

★ **Blood** & DNA evidence; crime-solving science experiments. science consultant, Brian Gestring. Enslow Publishers 2006 104p il (Forensic science projects) lib bdg $31.93

Grades: 7 8 9 10   363.2

1. Forensic sciences 2. DNA fingerprinting 3. Bloodstains 4. Forensic genetics 5. DNA fingerprinting 6. Forensic hematology

ISBN 0-7660-1958-6

LC 2005029214

This "invites readers to complete scientific experiments that emulate the solution to actual murders. . . . Following each real-life scenario, the book provides a checklist of materials and a step-by-step experiment to get the same results as the detectives. . . . The format is easy to follow, the scenarios intriguing, and the experiments complex enough for real science buffs to feel challenged." Booklist

Includes glossary and bibliographical references

★ **Forgery**; crime-solving science experiments. Enslow Pub, Inc. 2006 128p il (Forensic science projects) lib bdg $31.93

Grades: 7 8 9 10   **363.2**

1. Forgery 2. Forensic sciences

ISBN 0-7660-1961-6

           LC 2005029212

This describes how forgeries are detected and offers activities

Includes glossary and bibliographical references

★ **Hair,** clothing and tire track evidence; crime-solving science experiments. [by] Kenneth G. Rainis. Enslow Publishers, Inc. 2006 128p il (Forensic science projects) lib bdg $31.93

Grades: 7 8 9 10   **363.2**

1. Forensic sciences

ISBN 0-7660-2729-5

           LC 2005037399

This describes how hair, clothing and tire tracks are used in solving crimes and offers activities in forensic science.

Includes glossary and bibliographical references

Ricciuti, Edward R.

★ **Federal** Bureau of Investigation. Chelsea House Publishers 2010 144p il (Law enforcement agencies) lib bdg $35

Grades: 6 7 8 9   **363.2**

1. Criminal investigation

ISBN 978-1-60413-636-4; 1-60413-636-7

"Solidly and comprehensively researched. . . . Federal Bureau of Investigation is a broad and deep look at the agency from its inception. Many of its most famous cases, including the Rosenbergs' arrest, terror cases, and the fight against organized crime, are discussed. Common criticisms, such as the overreach of the agency (J. Edgar Hoover in particular) are included. . . . An attractive design, plenty of photos, and solid back matter complete [the] package. Extremely useful for students and appealing for browsers." Booklist

Includes bibliographical references

Ryan, Bernard

★ The **Secret** Service. Chelsea House Publishers 2010 128p il (Law enforcement agencies) lib bdg $35

Grades: 6 7 8 9   **363.2**

ISBN 978-1-60413-623-4; 1-60413-623-5

This describes the work of The Secret Service including protecting the president, other key government figures, and visiting foreign leaders, investigating financial fraud and protecting crowds, buildings, and locations from potential threats.

"The Law Enforcement Agencies series is as formidable as the various groups it introduces. Solidly and comprehensively researched. . . . An attractive design, plenty of photos,

and solid back matter complete each package. Extremely useful for students and appealing for browsers." Booklist

Includes bibliographical references

Schindler, Howard

Science sleuths; solving mysteries using scientific inquiry. [by] Howard Schindler and Dennis Mucenski. Prufrock Press Inc. 2010 vii, 195p il pa $19.95

Grades: Adult Professional   **363.2**

1. Forensic sciences 2. Science -- Methodology

ISBN 978-1-59363-397-4 pa; 1-59363-397-1 pa

           LC 2009042622

"This professional resource uses [the] field [of forensics] to develop skills in scientific inquiry. The book features three activities in which students, working in groups or individually, analyze the evidence presented to them to solve a case. The activities are keyed to national standards for scientific inquiry. The tasks for 3-4 days of activities, culminating in a final essay, assist the teacher in planning the solution. . . . This is a most valuable resource for the science teacher of grades 6-9." Voice Youth Advocates

Includes bibliographical references

Spilsbury, Richard

Counterfeit! stopping fakes and forgeries. Enslow Publishers 2009 48p il (Solve that crime!) lib bdg $23.93

Grades: 5 6 7 8   **363.2**

1. Fraud 2. Forgery

ISBN 978-0-7660-3378-8 lib bdg; 0-7660-3378-3 lib bdg

           LC 2008-33310

This "title boasts in-depth information, sidebars detailing events of true crime, and activities that will increase understanding. . . . Photographs are colorful, well-captioned, and related to the text." SLJ

Includes glossary and bibliographical references

Stefoff, Rebecca

Crime labs. Marshall Cavendish Benchmark 2010 95p il (Forensic science investigated) $23.95

Grades: 6 7 8 9 10   **363.2**

1. Forensic sciences 2. Graphologists 3. Criminologists

ISBN 978-0-7614-4140-3; 0-7614-4140-9

           LC 2010-10536

The "titles in the Forensic Science Investigated series stand out not only for their thorough overviews of how forensic science is practiced today but also for their fascinating historical perspectives. . . . Crime labs introduces nineteenth-century Frenchman Edmond Locard, creator of the world's first forensic lab." Booklist

Includes bibliographical references

Criminal profiling. Marshall Cavendish Benchmark 2010 93p il (Forensic science investigated) $23.95

Grades: 6 7 8 9   **363.2**

1. Physicians 2. Criminal investigation 3.

Criminologists 4. Writers on medicine
ISBN 978-0-7614-4141-0; 0-7614-4141-7

LC 2010010535

The "titles in the Forensic Science Investigated series stand out not only for their thorough overviews of how forensic science is practiced today but also for their fascinating historical perspectives. . . . Criminal Profiling spotlights early criminologists, such as Cesare Lombroso, who believed that criminal instincts manifested in physical features." Booklist

Includes bibliographical references

Forensic anthropology. Marshall Cavendish Benchmark 2010 95p il (Forensic science investigated) $19.95

Grades: 6 7 8 9   **363.2**
1. Forensic anthropology 2. Criminal investigation
ISBN 978-0-7614-4142-7; 0-7614-4142-5

LC 2010010534

The "titles in the Forensic Science Investigated series stand out not only for their thorough overviews of how forensic science is practiced today but also for their fascinating historical perspectives. . . . Forensic Anthropology starts off with a riveting account of scientists who cracked an 1849 Harvard murder case by finding clues among the victim's remains." Booklist

Includes bibliographical references

Stewart, Gail
Bombings; by Gail B. Stewart. Thomson/Gale 2006 104p il (Crime scene investigations series) $28.70

Grades: 7 8 9 10   **363.2**
1. Bombings 2. Criminal investigation
ISBN 1-59018-620-6

LC 2005026125

An examination of criminal investigations of bombings. This scrutinizes "current, highly publicized criminal cases that young readers will recognize. . . . Case studies are accompanied by actual, clearly labeled, color case photos showing just enough to fascinate the reader without unneeded gore." Voice Youth Advocates

Includes bibliographical references

K-9 police units; by Gail B. Stewart. Lucent Books 2010 104p il (Crime scene investigations) lib bdg $32.45

Grades: 7 8 9 10   **363.2**
1. Working dogs 2. Animals in police work
ISBN 978-1-4205-0137-7 lib bdg; 1-4205-0137-2 lib bdg

LC 2009-27456

This describes "the rigorous selection and training process of both dog and handler. Also discussed are the many different types of applications for these brave animals, as well as the bond of mutual trust that is required between the police officer and his canine companion while working in true life-and-death situations. . . . [This] should not only be a popular addition to any collection but will also go a long way in setting the record straight regarding who does what within a criminal investigation." Voice Youth Advocates

Includes bibliographical references

★ **Police** brutality; by Gail B. Stewart. Lucent Books 2005 112p il (Lucent overview series) $28.70

Grades: 7 8 9 10   **363.2**
1. Police brutality
ISBN 1-59018-190-5

LC 2004-21489

This discusses the use of force by police, the causes and effects of police brutality, racism and the police, and possible solutions to the problem.

Includes bibliographical references

Townsend, John
Famous forensic cases. Amicus 2011 32p il (Amazing crime scene science) $19.95

Grades: 4 5 6 7   **363.2**
1. Forensic sciences 2. Criminal investigation
ISBN 978-1-60753-169-2; 1-60753-169-0

In this book "readers will find a straight presentation of fascinating information. Loosely organized by era, the book opens with a history of fingerprinting . . . which focuses on the 1920s and 1930s. Other topics include hair science in the 1950s, voiceprints in the 1970s, and recent advancements in DNA forensics. Scatter throughout are case studies. . . . This entry features an eye-catching layout, plenty of sidebars, and well-chosen photos. . . . Kids will go for this one." Booklist

Walker, Pamela
Forensic science experiments; [by] Pamela Walker, Elaine Wood. Facts on File 2009 150p il (Facts on File science experiments) $35

Grades: 7 8 9 10   **363.2**
1. Forensic sciences 2. Science -- Experiments
ISBN 978-0-8160-7804-2; 0-8160-7804-1

LC 2008-39900

This "contains 20 experiments that allow students to actively engage in scientific inquiry. Projects are presented in a uniform format, with an introduction to the topic, time requirements (35 minutes to 2 weeks), a materials list, numbered procedures, and several analysis questions. . . . The experiments themselves are timely and fascinating. . . . In [this book], a banana autopsy, blood-spatter inquiry, and 'Glitter as Trace Evidence' will hook CSI fans. Despite detailed instructions, close teacher supervision is a must." SLJ

Includes glossary and bibliographical references

Webber, Diane
Do you read me? famous cases solved by handwriting analysis! [by] Diane Webber. Franklin Watts 2007 64p il map (24/7, science behind the scenes) lib bdg $27; pa $7.95

Grades: 5 6 7 8   **363.2**
1. Graphology 2. Forensic sciences
ISBN 978-0-531-12066-8 lib bdg; 0-531-12066-X lib bdg; 978-0-531-15456-4 pa; 0-531-15456-4 pa

LC 2006006797

"Cases such as the infamous Lindbergh kidnapping and the discovery of Hitler's lost diaries are used to explore how handwriting can be used to solve a mystery. Subsequent sections tackle questions such as the validity of handwriting analysis as well as explore some of the nuances of the science." Voice Youth Advocates

Includes glossary and bibliographical references

Weir, William

★ **Border** patrol. Chelsea House 2010 125p il (Law enforcement agencies) lib bdg $35

Grades: 6 7 8 9   **363.2**

1. Smuggling 2. Illegal aliens

ISBN 978-1-60413-635-7; 1-60413-635-9

LC 2010030051

"Solidly and comprehensively researched. . . . Border Patrol takes on a topic much in the news. The hottest issues of border control are all examined: drugs, bandits, and smuggling of goods and people. There is also great information on the technology used, as well as a levelheaded discussion on the terror threat presented by illegal immigrants. . . . An attractive design, plenty of photos, and solid back matter complete [the] package. Extremely useful for students and appealing for browsers." Booklist

Includes glossary and bibliographical references

Worth, Richard

★ **Los** Angeles Police Department. Chelsea House Publishers 2011 128p il (Law enforcement agencies) lib bdg $35

Grades: 6 7 8 9   **363.2**

1. Law enforcement 2. Police -- Los Angeles (Calif.)

ISBN 978-1-60413-656-2; 1-60413-656-1

LC 2010040906

This is a history of the Los Angeles Police Department from the early days of California to the present, including such cases as The Sleepy Lagoon Murder and the Zoot Suit Riots, The Black Dahlia murder, the Watts riots, and the Charles Manson case.

"The Law Enforcement Agencies series is as formidable as the various groups it introduces. Solidly and comprehensively researched. . . . An attractive design, plenty of photos, and solid back matter complete each package. Extremely useful for students and appealing for browsers." Booklist

Includes bibliographical references

Yancey, Diane

Tracking serial killers; by Diane Yancey. Thomson/Gale 2007 104p il (Crime scene investigations) $32.45

Grades: 7 8 9 10   **363.2**

1. Homicide 2. Forensic sciences 3. Criminal investigation

ISBN 978-1-59018-985-6; 1-59018-985-X

LC 2007006813

Presents the forensic techniques that are used in the investigations of serial killers and that aid in their apprehension, including such processes as psychological and DNA profiling, analyses of biological evidence, and the coordinated use of national databases.

"Reluctant readers will be fascinated." SLJ

Includes bibliographical references

Young, Karen Romano

Crime scene science; 20 projects and experiments about clues, crimes, criminals, and other mys-

terious things. illustrations by David Goldin. National Geographic 2009 80p il (Science fair winners) $12.95; lib bdg $24.90

Grades: 6 7 8 9   **363.2**

1. Science projects 2. Forensic sciences 3. Criminal investigation

ISBN 978-1-4263-0521-4; 1-4263-0521-4; 978-1-4263-0522-1 lib bdg; 1-4263-0522-2 lib bdg

LC 2009-20387

This is a "collection of 20 science fair show-stoppers. . . . Significantly deeper than most science-fair tutorials. . . . High-interest topics abound: footprint casting, crime scene mapping, lie detection, and even compelling tricks like decoding those weird little bars the postal service stamps onto letters." Booklist

Includes bibliographical references

363.25   Detection of crime (Criminal investigation)

MacLeod, Elizabeth

Bones Never Lie; How Forensics Helps Solve History's Mysteries. Elizabeth MacLeod. Firefly Books Ltd 2013 iv, 156 p.p (hardcover) $24.95

Grades: 4 5 6 7 8   **363.25**

1. Forensic sciences -- Encyclopedias

ISBN 1554514835; 9781554514830

This children's book, by Elizabeth MacLeod, explores how through "forensics--the scientific way of examining physical evidence--we now know what killed Napoleon and whether Anastasia survived the massacre of the Russian royal family. Seven intriguing stories about historical royal figures whose demise was suspicious, and hard scientific facts about crime-solving techniques make each event seem like an episode of CSI rather than a history lesson." (Publisher's note)

"In real life, forensics can be slow and tedious, but MacLeod invests these high-profile deaths with considerable vim and drama. A good selection of staged and archival photographs and artwork accompany the stories. A fully fleshed and crisply told story of forensics at its romantic best." Kirkus

363.3   Other aspects of public safety

Cunningham, Kevin

Wildfires. Morgan Reynolds Pub. 2009 112p il (Extreme threats) lib bdg $28.95

Grades: 7 8 9 10   **363.3**

1. Wildfires

ISBN 978-1-59935-120-9; 1-59935-120-X

LC 2009-25709

This book about wildfires has "black-and-white and color photographs on almost every page. . . . Frequent sidebars, covering as much as a spread, discuss peripheral and often unusual information. The conclusion . . . explains what scientists are doing, or what they anticipate doing, to ameliorate the threat." SLJ

Includes glossary and bibliographical references

Media violence: opposing viewpoints; David Haugen and Susan Musser, book editors. Greenhaven Press 2009 232p il (Opposing viewpoints series) lib bdg $37.40; pa $25.95
Grades: 8 9 10 11 12   363.3
1. Violence 2. Mass media
ISBN 978-0-7377-4218-3 lib bdg; 978-0-7377-4219-0 pa
LC 2008-30355
This anthology "begins with articles that probe the scope and severity of the phenomenon and then moves on to sections about how violence in the media should be regulated, the effects of violence in the news, and cyberbullying." Booklist
Includes bibliographical references

363.31   Censorship

Gottfried, Ted
★ Censorship. Benchmark Books 2005 143p il (Open for debate) $37.07
Grades: 7 8 9 10   363.31
1. Censorship
ISBN 0-7614-1883-0
This discusses censorship issues in regard to such topics as pornography, the internet, motion pictures, politics, and literature.
Includes bibliographical references

Steffens, Bradley
★ Censorship; by Bradley Steffens. Lucent Books 2004 112p il (Lucent overview series) $27.45
Grades: 7 8 9 10   363.31
1. Censorship
ISBN 1-59018-187-5
LC 2004-10852
Discusses the history of censorship, what is and is not protected under the First Amendment, and regulations and standards for the Internet
"Interestingly written chapters are short but comprehensive. Well-chosen illustrations add visual interest and provide additional information." SLJ
Includes bibliographical references

363.32   Social conflict

Bedell, J. M.
Combating terrorism. Compass Point Books 2010 48p il (Terrorism) lib bdg $27.99
Grades: 6 7 8 9   363.32
1. Terrorism
ISBN 978-0-7565-4309-9 lib bdg; 0-7565-4309-6 lib bdg
LC 2009-38908
"The style stays consistently clear and strightforward throughout , and the tone remains objective. A well-designed layout, with plenty of white space and well-placed sidebars, adds to the acessibility. . . . A great choice." SLJ
Includes glossary and bibliographical references

Burgan, Michael
Terrorist groups. Compass Point Books 2010 48p il (Terrorism) lib bdg $27.99
Grades: 6 7 8 9   363.32
1. Terrorism 2. Terrorists
ISBN 978-0-7565-4311-2 lib bdg; 0-7565-4311-8 lib bdg
Discusses terrorist groups such as al-Qaida, the Colombian FARC, and the Palestinian PFLP.
"The style stays consistenly clear and straightforward throughout, and the tone remains objective. A well-designed layout, with plenty of white space and well-placed sidebars, adds to the accessibility. . . . A great choice." SLJ
Includes glossary and bibliographical references

Can the War on Terrorism be won? David Haugen and Susan Musser, book editors. Greenhaven Press 2007 109p (At issue: National security) $29.95; pa $21.20
Grades: 6 7 8 9   363.32
1. Terrorism 2. War on terrorism
ISBN 978-0-7377-1973-4; 978-0-7377-1974-1 pa
LC 2006039099
This "gathers 13 excerpted articles and speeches. . . . Readers encounter a spectrum of opinions about the War on Terror. . . . Each extract is headed with a straightforward title . . . and prefaced with a helpful abstract. Capped by an extensive reading list and annotated list of organizations, this is a strong option for assignment or debate-team research." Booklist
Includes bibliographical references

Fremont-Barnes, Gregory
Rescue at the Iranian Embassy; the most daring SAS raid. Rosen Pub. 2011 64p il map (The most daring raids in history) lib bdg $29.25
Grades: 7 8 9 10   363.32
1. Great Britain -- Army 2. Iran -- History -- 1979-
ISBN 978-1-4488-1869-3; 1-4488-1869-9
LC 2010029625
First published 2009 in the United Kingdom with title: Who dares wins
On May 5, 1980, the world watched as the SAS performed a daring raid on the Iranian Embassy in London. The raid was a huge success for the SAS, rescuing nineteen hostages with near-perfect military execution, although two were killed by the terrorists.
This book is "packed with facts, covering the details of the action, the people involved, and the tools used, in engaging prose. The authors cite their sources thoroughly. . . . Diagrams, photos, . . . and maps make the action easy to follow and provide visual context for the raids. . . . This . . . is sure to find a large readership." SLJ
Includes glossary and bibliographical references

Friedman, Lauri S.
Terrorist attacks. ReferencePoint Press 2008 128p il map (Compact research. Current issues) lib bdg $24.95

Grades: 7 8 9 10 11 12   **363.32**
1. Terrorism
ISBN 978-1-60152-022-7; 1-60152-022-0
LC 2007-9907
This "introduces theories as to why people carry out terrorist attacks, how they are executed, and how the attacks might be prevented. . . . [The] volume includes people and groups associated with the issue, a chronology of events, related organizations, and suggestions for further research. Chapters open and end with an array of quotes that argue for or against a particular argument or aspect of the issue, complete with full citation." SLJ
Includes glossary and bibliographical references

Gupta, Dipak K.
★ **Who** are the terrorists? Chelsea House 2006 116p il map (The roots of terrorism) lib bdg $35
Grades: 7 8 9 10   **363.32**
1. Islam 2. Terrorism
ISBN 0-7910-8306-3
LC 2005021627
This "volume discusses the world history as well as the groups and individuals behind today's headlines. . . . Gupta emphasizes that equating Islam with the barbaric acts of a few terrorists is like making the burning crosses of the Ku Klux Klan the essence of Christianity. He also points out the role of the American invasion of Iraq and the images from Abu Ghraib. . . . This is sure to spark vehement group discussion." Booklist
Includes bibliographical references

Katz, Samuel M.
Against all odds; counterterrorist hostage rescues. by Samuel M. Katz. Lerner Publications 2005 72p il (Terrorist dossiers) lib bdg $26.60
Grades: 7 8 9 10   **363.32**
1. Police 2. Hostages 3. Terrorism
ISBN 0-8225-1567-9
LC 2004-6215
"Katz presents the history and politics behind high-profile hostage rescues and highlights the work of groups such as the Sayeret Mat'kal of Israel, the Groupe d' Intervention de la Gendarmerie Nationale (GIGN) in France, the Dutch Bijzondere Bijstands Eenheid (BBE) and Grenzschutzgruppe 9 (GSG-9) of Germany, Britain's Special Air Service (SAS), Italy's Nucleo Operativo Centrale di Sicurezza (NOCS), Fuerza de Operaciones Especiales (FOE) in Peru, and Russia's Alpha Group. . . . A useful addition for reports." SLJ
Includes bibliographical references

Landau, Elaine
★ **Suicide** bombers; foot soldiers of the terrorist movement. Twenty-First Century Books 2007 120p lib bdg $31.93
Grades: 7 8 9 10   **363.32**
1. Terrorism 2. Suicide bombers
ISBN 978-0-7613-3470-5; 0-7613-3470-X
LC 2005033422
"The author studies several individual examples of young people who are recruited into or choose to become human sacrifices, and the convoluted path that leads them

to their final, grisly end. Landau . . . does an excellent job of dissecting the complex history, motives, and philosophies that feed the culture of the suicide bomber. . . . Compelling and easy to follow." Voice Youth Advocates
Includes bibliographical references

Nardo, Don
The **history** of terrorism. Compass Point Books 2010 48p il (Terrorism) lib bdg $27.99
Grades: 6 7 8 9   **363.32**
1. Terrorism
ISBN 978-0-7565-4310-5 lib bdg; 0-7565-4310-X lib bdg
Discusses the use of terrorism throughout history, and examines the individuals and groups who have resorted to violent actions in order to generate fear
"The style stays consistently clear and straightforward throughout, and the tone remains objective. A well-designed layout, with plenty of white space and well-placed sidebars, adds to the accessibility. . . . A great choice." SLJ
Includes glossary and bibliographical references

Terrorism; an opposing viewpoints guide. Stephen Currie, book editor. Greenhaven Press 2006 111 p. ill. (chiefly col.) (Opposing viewpoints series) (library) $33.75
Grades: 8 9 10 11 12   **363.32**
1. Terrorism 2. Authorship
ISBN 9780737732061; 0737732067
LC 2005049314
This title "makes use of the . . . Opposing Viewpoints format (with selections that argue crucial issues from many sides), adding exercises, suggestions, and models for students' writing. More than half the book is published articles from alternative viewpoints, and the vital contemporary questions (Are terrorist attacks inevitable? Is the threat of terrorism exaggerated? etc.) will spark debate and discussion." Booklist
Includes bibliographical references (p. 104-106) and index.

Tougas, Shelley
What makes a terrorist? Compass Point Books 2010 48p il (Terrorism) lib bdg $27.99
Grades: 6 7 8 9   **363.32**
1. Terrorism 2. Terrorists
ISBN 978-0-7565-4312-9 lib bdg; 0-7565-4312-6 lib bdg
Discusses terrorism and the traits of terrorists.
"The style stays consistently clear and straightforward throughout, and the tone remains objective. A well-designed layout, with plenty of white space and well-placed sidebars, adds to the accessibility. . . . A great choice." SLJ
Includes glossary and bibliographical references

363.33   Control of firearms

Atkin, S. Beth
★ **Gunstories**; life-changing experiences with guns. interviews and photographs by S. Beth Atkin.

HarperCollins Publishers 2006 245p il $16.99; lib bdg $17.89

Grades: 7 8 9 10 11 12   363.33
  1. Firearms
  ISBN 0-06-052659-9; 0-06-052660-2 lib bdg
                                        LC 2005-2076
"This book should be useful for students involved in the debate about guns in our culture as well as for those with a general interest in the subject." SLJ

★ **Guns** and violence; Laura K. Egendorf, book editor. Greenhaven Press 2005 202p (Current controversies) lib bdg $34.95; pa $23.70

Grades: 8 9 10 11 12   363.33
  1. Violence 2. Gun control
  ISBN 0-7377-2206-1 lib bdg; 0-7377-2207-X pa
                                        LC 2004-52287
Presents differing viewpoints on the seriousness of gun violence, whether or not gun control reduces crime and its constitutionality, the effectiveness of gun ownership as self defense, and what measures would reduce gun violence
  Includes bibliographical references

363.34 Disasters

Bailey, Gerry
  Fragile planet. Gareth Stevens Pub. 2011 48p il map (Planet SOS) lib bdg $31.95; pa $14.05

Grades: 4 5 6   363.34
  1. Natural disasters
  ISBN 978-1-4339-4974-6 lib bdg; 1-4339-4974-1 lib bdg; 978-1-4339-4975-3 pa; 1-4339-4975-X pa
                                        LC 2010032886
This "well-designed [book]. . . . discusses natural events and disasters, such as avalanches, earthquakes, floods, hurricanes, lightning, volcanoes, and windstorms. . . . The many large, colorful photos will engage readers and assist them in understanding the important concepts introduced." SLJ
  Includes glossary

Butts, Edward
  SOS: stories of survival; true tales of disaster, tragedy, and courage. by Ed Butts. Tundra Books 2007 119p il pa $12.95

Grades: 6 7 8 9   363.34
  1. Disasters   2. Natural disasters 3. Survival after airplane accidents, shipwrecks, etc.
  ISBN 978-0-88776-786-9 pa
"Butts writes with taut excitement about 13 devastating events—floods, fires, explosions, mountain slides, and more—from the 1891 Canadian Springhill Mine Disaster and the Triangle Shirtwaist Fire to Chernobyl, the Tsunami of 2004, and Hurricane Katrina. . . . The personal eyewitness accounts and occasional archival photos dramatize the cataclysmic events." Booklist
  Includes bibliographical references

Engelbert, Phillis
  Dangerous planet; the science of natural disasters. U.X.L 2001 3v il maps set $165

Grades: 6 7 8 9   363.34
  1. Natural disasters
  ISBN 0-7876-2848-4
                                        LC 98-54422
"The science is accurate, and the technical terms are explained well. The illustrations are clear and well placed." Booklist
  Includes bibliographical references

Fradin, Judith Bloom
  ★ **Droughts**; [by] Judy & Dennis Fradin. National Geographic 2008 48p il map (Witness to disaster) $16.95; lib bdg $20.90

Grades: 4 5 6 7   363.34
  1. Droughts
  ISBN 978-1-4263-0339-5; 1-4263-0339-4; 978-1-4263-0340-1 lib bdg; 1-4263-0340-8 lib bdg
                                        LC 2008020424
"This book examines the lessons from the Dust Bowl droughts for farmers, including the importance of topsoil. The history of droughts around the world compares impacts on a wide variety of societies. The final chapter looks at the latest tools and technologies developed to help us survive future droughts." Publisher's note
  Includes glossary and bibliographical references

Garbe, Suzanne
  The **Worst** wildfires of all time; by Suzanne Garbe. Capstone Press 2013 32 p. ill. (chiefly col.), col. maps (library) $27.32

Grades: 4 5 6 7   363.34
  1. Wildfires 2. Natural disasters
  ISBN 1429684186; 9781429684187
                                        LC 2011053150
This book by Suzanne Garbe is part of the Epic Disasters series and looks at the worst wildfires of all time. "These uncontrolled fires can strike in the blink of an eye and spread just as quickly. Put out the flames and read about the worst wildfires in history." The series allows readers to "witness the destructive power of hurricanes, earthquakes, and more." (Publisher's note)
  Includes bibliographical references and index.

Karwoski, Gail
  Tsunami; the true story of an April Fools' Day disaster. [by] Gail Langer Karwoski; illustrated by John MacDonald. Darby Creek Pub. 2006 64p il $17.95

Grades: 4 5 6 7   363.34
  1. Tsunamis
  ISBN 1-58196-944-1
The author "opens with a description of the tsunami waves that struck the northern coast of the Hawaiian Islands in 1946, destroying a school and sweeping many children and adults out to sea. The book goes on to provide broader information about tsunamis, from scientific understanding of how they occur to ongoing efforts at early warning systems. . . . Clearly written and informative." Booklist

Langley, Andrew

Hurricanes, tsunamis, and other natural disasters; [by] Andrew Langley. Kingfisher 2006 63p il map (Kingfisher knowledge) $12.95

Grades: 5 6 7 8   363.34

1. Natural disasters

ISBN 978-0-7534-5975-1; 0-7534-5975-2

LC 2005027200

This briefly describes such natural disasters as hurricanes, tsunamis, avalanches, brush fires, earthquakes, floods, tornadoes, drought and famine, pandemics, with many color illustrations and maps

"This book presents a high-interest topic in an attractively designed format that features colorful, eye-catching graphics and a solidly written text." Booklist

Includes glossary and bibliographical references

Markle, Sandra

Rescues! Millbrook Press 2006 88p il map lib bdg $25.26

Grades: 4 5 6 7   363.34

1. Rescue work 2. Survival after airplane accidents, shipwrecks, etc.

ISBN 978-0-8225-3413-6 lib bdg; 0-8225-3413-4 lib bdg

LC 2005-09707

"From the collapse of a Pennsylvania coal mine in 2002 to the tsunami that struck 11 countries in 2004 to Hurricane Katrina in 2005, the 11 disasters Markle describes are straight from news headlines. In this full-color photo-essay, she uses individual experiences of rescue and survival to bring each drama close." Booklist

Includes bibliographical references

Miller, Debra A.

Hurricane Katrina; devastation on the Gulf Coast. by Debra A. Miller. Lucent Books 2006 104p il map (Overview series) $28.70

Grades: 7 8 9 10   363.34

1. Hurricane Katrina, 2005

ISBN 1-59018-936-1

LC 2005030656

"This readable account of the hurricane and the subsequent flood stresses the effect of the disaster on the survivors, quoting them frequently. In addition to the storm itself, the author covers the response, the damage, the hurricanes effect on New Orleans's residents, and prospects for their future, including the cost, responsibility, and viability of rebuilding." SLJ

Includes bibliographical references

Miller, Mara

Hurricane Katrina strikes the Gulf Coast; disaster & survival. [by] Mara Miller. Enslow Publishers 2006 48p il map (Deadly disasters) $23.93

Grades: 4 5 6 7   363.34

1. Hurricanes 2. Rescue work 3. Hurricane Katrina, 2005

ISBN 0-7660-2803-8

LC 2005030989

"Miller begins with an account of the development of Hurricane Katrina as it struck Florida and then threatened the Gulf Coast. She discusses the subsequent flooding of New Orleans, the damage it caused, rescue and recovery attempts, and planning for the aftermath of future hurricanes. The author includes a clear scientific description of hurricanes, defining key terms. Color photos and graphics help explain concepts such as the structure of a hurricane, Katrina's path, and the conditions endured by the victims." SLJ

Includes glossary and bibliographical references

Palser, Barb

★ Hurricane Katrina; aftermath of disaster. Compass Point Books 2007 96p il map (Snapshots in history) lib bdg $31.93

Grades: 7 8 9 10   363.34

1. Hurricanes 2. Disaster relief 3. Hurricane Katrina, 2005

ISBN 978-0-7565-2101-1 lib bdg; 0-7565-2101-7 lib bdg

LC 2006009119

This describes the impact of the hurricane which struck New Orleans and the Gulf coast in 2005 and subsequent relief and rebuilding efforts

"An unusually handsome design and a brisk, information-packed narrative make this . . . volume . . . an outstanding acquisition for libraries." Booklist

Includes glossary and bibliographical references

Pietras, Jamie

Hurricane Katrina; [by] Jamie Pietras. Chelsea House 2008 128p il map (Great historic disasters) $35

Grades: 7 8 9 10   363.34

1. Hurricane Katrina, 2005

ISBN 978-0-7910-9639-0; 0-7910-9639-4

LC 2007036551

"This book details the meteorological, political, and social circumstances that came together so fatally during 2005's Hurricane Katrina. Mostly objective, the writing is occasionally peppered with commentary on the local and federal governments' missteps and inaction following the storm and ensuing floods. Gripping photographs support the text." Horn Book Guide

Includes glossary and bibliographical references

Reilly, Kathleen M.

Natural disasters; investigate Earth's most destructive forces. by Kathleen M. Reilly; illustrated by Tom Casteel. Nomad Press 2012 121 p. (paperback) $15.95

Grades: 4 5 6 7   363.34

1. Weather 2. Natural disasters

ISBN 1619301466; 9781619301467

In this book, "spiraling winds, surging waters, eruptions, blazing forests, and chilling snows are discussed." Topics include "the MMS Scale and the Enhanced Fujita Scale." In addition to an "explanation of each type of phenomenon, safety tips, historical incidences, pen-and-ink line drawings, and correlative projects using simple materials are included." (School Library Journal)

Robson, David

Disaster response. ReferencePoint Press 2009 96p il map (Compact research. Current issues) lib bdg $25.95

Grades: 7 8 9 10   **363.34**

1. Disaster relief

ISBN 978-1-60152-081-4; 1-60152-081-6

LC 2009-2283

"Robson covers disasters ranging from manmade to weather-related and bioterrorism. . . . Hurricane Katrina is discussed in the overview and leads into chapters that question the ability of the United States to handle natural disasters and how it can be improved. . . . Colorful graphs and up-to-date statistics are included. [This title] would be [a] great [addition] for students needing print materials to help with research projects, and for those who require some kind of first-person account included in their research." SLJ

Includes bibliographical references

Rusch, Elizabeth

Eruption! volcanoes and the science of saving lives. text by Elizabeth Rusch; illustrated by Tom Uhlman. Houghton Mifflin Harcourt 2013 76 p. col. ill. (hardcover) $18.99

Grades: 5 6 7 8   **363.34**

1. Disaster response and recovery 2. Volcanoes 3. Natural disasters 4. Volcanic eruptions

ISBN 0547503504; 9780547503509

LC 2012034055

This book by Elizabeth Rusch contains "photographs and sidebars [which] reveals the perilous . . . life-saving work of an international volcano crisis team (VDAP) and the sleeping giants they study, from Colombia to the Philippines, from Chile to Indonesia. [It presents a] stunning account of volcanologists Andy Lockhart, John Pallister, and their group of scientists who risk their lives, investigating deadly volcanoes that remain constant threats to people around the world." (Publisher's note)

Includes bibliographical references (pages 74-75) and index.

Sanna, Ellyn

Nature's wrath; surviving natural disasters. Mason Crest Publishers 2009 128p il map (Survivors: ordinary people, extraordinary circumstances) lib bdg $24.95

Grades: 7 8 9 10   **363.34**

1. Natural disasters 2. Hurricane Katrina, 2005 3. Indian Ocean earthquake and tsunami, 2004

ISBN 978-1-4222-0454-2 lib bdg; 1-4222-0454-5 lib bdg

LC 2008-33334

Describes how natural disasters have decimated areas and lives, and how people have worked to reclaim their lives in the aftermath

"Supplemented by fact boxes, large color photos, and color-blocked vocabulary, . . . [this book is] . . . visually appealing as well as informational." SLJ

Includes bibliographical references

Saul, Laya

Ways to help after a natural disaster; by Laya Saul. Mitchell Lane Publishers 2011 47 p. col. ill. (library) $29.95

Grades: 4 5 6   **363.34**

1. Volunteer work 2. Disaster relief

ISBN 1584159170; 9781584159179

LC 2010006538

"This focuses on various activities in which children can participate to help families be prepared in the event of a natural disaster or in its aftermath, when citizens experience the devastating results. The brief sections on teaching preparedness include advice for putting together supply kits and a sample list for collecting emergency numbers. The bulk of the information is sound, practical, commonsense recommendations. . . . Included are simple measures, such as offering emotional support, as well as those that are more complicated, such as organizing drives for collecting blood or food and clothing. The design is inviting, with text appealingly laid out and offset by blocks of color." Booklist

Includes bibliographical references and index.

Stefoff, Rebecca

Forensics and modern disasters. Marshall Cavendish Benchmark 2010 95p il (Forensic science investigated) $23.95

Grades: 6 7 8 9 10   **363.34**

1. Disasters 2. Forensic sciences 3. Criminal investigation

ISBN 978-0-7614-4144-1; 0-7614-4144-1

LC 2010-10533

The "titles in the Forensic Science Investigated series stand out not only for their thorough overviews of how forensic science is practiced today but also for their fascinating historical perspectives. . . . Forensics and Modern Disasters dives directly into contemporary practices and shows how techniques . . . have helped identify victims of large-scale tragedies, including 9/11." Booklist

Includes bibliographical references

363.4 Controversies related to public morals and customs

Blumenthal, Karen

★ **Bootleg**; murder, moonshine, and the lawless years of Prohibition. Roaring Brook Press 2011 154p il $18.99

Grades: 8 9 10 11 12   **363.4**

1. Temperance 2. Prohibition 3. Alcholic beverage industry 4. Prohibition -- United States

ISBN 978-1-59643-449-3; 1-59643-449-X

LC 2010032687

The author "offers a highly readable, well-shaped look at the Eighteenth Amendment. . . . She provides concise, clearly written insights into the seeds of temperance movements in the late eighteenth century. . . . The section on Al Capone will satisfy readers hungry for the gangster-warfare side of Prohibition. A closing chapter makes an argument that despite the mostly disastrous results, there were bright points to Prohibition. . . . Plenty of archival images lend to

the book's pleasant design, and an ample bibliography and source notes close out this top-notch resource." Booklist
   Includes bibliographical references

Hill, Jeff
   Prohibition. Omnigraphics 2004 xxv, 201p il (Defining moments) $38
   Grades: 7 8 9 10   **363.4**
   1. Prohibition
   ISBN 0-7808-0768-5
                             LC 2004-22643
   This book provides an "historical analysis of the Prohibition era (1920-33), including the politics of the Eighteenth Amendment; the Mob wars; the roles played by important public figures, from mobster Al Capone to Prohibition activist Carry Nation to President Warren Harding; and much more. . . . With a detailed glossary, a chronology, and an annotated bibliography, this is an important curriculum resource on the social and political history of an era." Booklist
   Includes glossary and bibliographical references

Pornography: opposing viewpoints; Helen Cothran, book editor. Greenhaven Press 2002 186p il (Opposing viewpoints series) lib bdg $34.95; pa $23.70
   Grades: 8 9 10 11   **363.4**
   1. Internet 2. Censorship 3. Pornography
   ISBN 0-7377-0761-5 lib bdg; 0-7377-0760-7 pa
                             LC 2001-16036
   This collection of essays "addresses both sides of the following questions: 'Is Pornography Harmful?' 'Should Pornography Be Censored?' 'How Should Internet Pornography Be Regulated?' 'What Should Be the Feminist Stance on Pornography?'" SLJ
   Includes bibliographical references

Worth, Richard
   Teetotalers and saloon smashers; the temperance movement and prohibition. Enslow Publishers 2009 128p il map (America's living history) lib bdg $31.93
   Grades: 5 6 7 8   **363.4**
   1. Temperance 2. Prohibition
   ISBN 978-0-7660-2908-8 lib bdg; 0-7660-2908-5 lib bdg
                             LC 2008-13905
   "Discusses the temperance movement in American history, including important figures in the movement, the history of temperance, and the period of Prohibition in the United States." Publisher's note
   Includes glossary and bibliographical references

363.45   Drug traffic

Harris, Nathaniel
   Drug trafficking. Gareth Stevens Pub. 2010 48p il (What if we do nothing?) lib bdg $31

Grades: 7 8 9 10   **363.45**
   1. Drug abuse 2. Drug traffic
   ISBN 978-1-4339-1981-7 lib bdg; 1-4339-1981-8 lib bdg
                             LC 2008-52495
   This "explains how drugs are grown, created, and distributed, and the problems individuals face when they become addicted. Meaningful illustrations include color photos and text-enhancing charts. . . . [This title is] well written and useful for reports." SLJ
   Includes glossary and bibliographical references

Sherman, Jill
   Drug trafficking. ABDO Pub. Co. 2010 112p il (Essential issues) lib bdg $22.95
   Grades: 7 8 9 10   **363.45**
   1. Drug abuse 2. Drug traffic
   ISBN 978-1-60453-953-0; 1-60453-953-4
                             LC 2009-29935
   This is "well-written, providing examples that put a human face to each problem. Quotes and facts are clearly attributed, and their sources are noted in the extensive back matter. . . . [This] will be of great assistance to students writing reports." SLJ
   Includes glossary and bibliographical references

363.46   Abortion

★ **Abortion**: opposing viewpoints; David Haugen, Susan Musser, and Kacy Lovelace, book editors. Greenhaven Press 2010 206p (Opposing viewpoints series) lib bdg $39.70; pa $27.50
   Grades: 8 9 10 11 12   **363.46**
   1. Abortion
   ISBN 978-0-7377-4747-8 lib bdg; 0-7377-4747-1 lib bdg; 978-0-7377-4748-5 pa; 0-7377-4748-X pa
                             LC 2009-41649
   Provides opposing viewpoints on the topic of abortion.
   Includes bibliographical references

The **abortion** controversy; Lucinda Almond, book editor. Greenhaven Press 2007 199p (Current controversies) $36.20; pa $24.95
   Grades: 8 9 10 11 12   **363.46**
   1. Abortion
   ISBN 978-0-7377-3273-3; 0-7377-3273-3; 978-0-7377-3274-0 pa; 0-7377-3274-1 pa
                             LC 2007-4509
   Replaces the edition published 2001 under the editorship of Lynette Knapp
   "With vehement arguments from all sides of the abortion debate this . . . includes essays by a range of today's writers and activists. . . . The range of viewpoints represented here will spark passionate responses from teens." Booklist
   Includes bibliographical references

Haney, Johannah
   The **abortion** debate; understanding the issues. Enslow Publishers 2009 112p il (Issues in focus today) lib bdg $31.93

Grades: 6 7 8 9   363.46
  1. Abortion
  ISBN 978-0-7660-2916-3 lib bdg; 0-7660-2916-6
  lib bdg

             LC 2008013900
  "Examines the debate over abortion, discussing both the pro-life and pro-choice sides of the argument, the history and laws on abortion in the United States, and finding a middle ground on the issue." Publisher's note
  Includes bibliographical references

363.5   Housing

Rubel, David
  If I had a hammer; building homes and hope with Habitat for Humanity. with a foreword by Jimmy Carter. Candlewick Press 2009 148p il $19.99
Grades: 6 7 8 9 10   363.5
  1. Housing 2. Social action 3. Voluntarism 4. Low-income housing
  ISBN 978-0-7636-4701-8; 0-7636-4701-2
             LC 2009025691
  "Technology and faith are the subjects in this hands-on account of Habitat for Humanity, the organization that helps create safe, decent housing for those in need in the U.S. and across the globe. . . . The book's open design, with clear type on thick, quality paper, includes many color photos. . . . The text's details about the essentials of providing shelter, fresh water, electricity, and effective sewage systems for all combine into a powerful message that will inspire many readers." Booklist

363.6   Public utilities and related services

Bowden, Rob, 1973-
  Water supply; our impact on the planet. Raintree Steck-Vaughn Pubs. 2003 64p il (21st century debates) lib bdg $28.56
Grades: 6 7 8 9   363.6
  1. Water supply
  ISBN 0-7398-5506-9
             LC 2002-151938
  The author packs "in a dense amount of data, made accessible by the attractive page design, full-color photos, sidebars, and boxes that extend the scope of {the} volume." Booklist
  Includes bibliographical references

Brown, Cynthia Light
  Discover National Monuments, National Parks; natural wonders. illustrated by Blair Shedd. Nomad Press 2009 106p il (Discover your world) pa $19.95
Grades: 5 6 7 8   363.6
  1. National parks and reserves
  ISBN 978-1-9346702-8-6 pa; 1-9346702-8-6 pa
  "With an inviting, browsable design and a chatty style, this large-sized volume . . . covers 15 national monuments and parks in the U.S. that celebrate and protect natural phe-

nomena . . . The science will excite readers, with detailed explanations of tectonic plates, radiometric dating, and dendrochronology." Booklist

Burgan, Michael
  Not a drop to drink; water for a thirsty world. Peter H. Gleick, consultant. National Geographic 2008 64p il map (National Geographic investigates) $17.95
Grades: 4 5 6 7   363.6
  1. Water 2. Water supply 3. Climatic changes
  ISBN 978-1-4263-0360-9; 1-4263-0360-2
  Explores the important connections between human activity and the water cycle and shows how researchers are working to understand such issues as how climate change affects water supplies and how the oceans can help solve the water crisis.

Workman, James G.
  Water. Morgan Reynolds Pub. 2009 111p il (Diminishing resources) lib bdg $28.95
Grades: 8 9 10 11 12   363.6
  1. Water supply 2. Water conservation
  ISBN 978-1-59935-115-5; 1-59935-115-3
             LC 2009-28708
  This discussion of world water supply and conservation "will draw activists, but even readers who do not think they care that much will find the facts devastating. Quotes from authoritative sources—environmentalists, scientists, and survivors—about both the historic overview and the contemporary crisis accompany full-color double-page photos that show what is happening now. . . . The discussion ranges from the pros and cons of dams to the price of bottled water." Booklist
  Includes bibliographical references

363.7   Environmental problems

Albee, Sarah
  Poop happened! a history of the world from the bottom up. illustrated by Robert Leighton. Walker 2010 170p il lib bdg $20.89; pa $15.99
Grades: 4 5 6 7   363.7
  1. Feces 2. Toilets 3. Sanitation 4. Refuse and refuse disposal
  ISBN 978-0-8027-9825-1 lib bdg; 0-8027-9825-X lib bdg; 978-0-8027-2077-1 pa; 0-8027-2077-3 pa
  "Albee deposits a heaping history of human sanitation—or rather lack thereof— and its effects. . . . She pumps out a steady stream of comments on the miasmic effects of urbanization, waste disposal, and the roles of (not) bathing in ancient Greece, Rome, medieval Europe, . . . and the 'Reeking Renaissance.' She then digs into the gradual adoption of better practices in the nineteenth century. . . . The cartoon illustrations feature sludgy green highlights." Booklist

Bellamy, Rufus
  Tourism. Amicus 2010 44p il map (Sustaining our environment) lib bdg $31.35

Grades: 6 7 8 9   363.7
1. Tourist trade
ISBN 978-1-60753-138-8 lib bdg; 1-60753-138-0
lib bdg

LC 2009-28236

"The tone is refreshingly optimistic with its examples
of specific steps being taken to reduce harm to the environment. Sidebars highlight case studies and campaigns from
around the world and from the individual to the national
levels. Clear, informative captions accompany the excellent
selection of color photographs, charts and graphs." SLJ
Includes glossary

Waste and pollution. Amicus 2010 44p il map
(Sustaining our environment) lib bdg $31.35
Grades: 6 7 8 9   363.7
1. Pollution 2. Waste products 3. Industrial waste 4.
Refuse and refuse disposal
ISBN 978-1-60753-139-5 lib bdg; 1-60753-139-9
lib bdg

LC 2009-40709

Introduces problems associated with pollution and waste
disposal and how we may be able to ease the bad effects on
the environment.

"The tone is refreshingly optimistic with its examples
of specific steps being taken to reduce harm to the environment. Sidebars highlight case studies and campaigns from
around the world and from the individual to the national
levels. Clear, informative captions accompany the excellent
selection of color photographs, charts and graphs." SLJ
Includes glossary

Berne, Emma Carlson

Global warming and climate change. ReferencePoint Press 2008 112p il (Compact research)
$24.95
Grades: 8 9 10 11 12   363.7
1. Greenhouse effect 2. Climate -- Environmental
aspects
ISBN 978-1-60152-019-7; 1-60152-019-0

LC 2007-8371

This discusses global warming and climate change, its
consequences and controversies and possible solutions.

"Useful for reports. . . . [This] presents pertinent questions with appropriate and well-documented quotations from
a variety of viewpoints and basic facts and diagrams." SLJ
Includes bibliographical references

Bridges, Andrew

Clean air. Roaring Brook Press 2009 40p il
(Sally Ride science) pa $7.99
Grades: 5 6 7 8   363.7
1. Air pollution 2. Greenhouse effect
ISBN 978-1-59643-576-6 pa; 1-59643-576-3 pa
This is a "well-written, engaging book. . . . The [book's]
best feature is the conversational tone that simply and clearly conveys important, and sometimes complicated, scientific
concepts. Illustrations and layout are well done, and include
colorful photographs and charts. Excellent." SLJ

Bryan, Nichol

Bhopal; chemical plant accident. World Almanac
Library 2004 48p il map (Environmental disasters)
hardcover o.p. lib bdg $29.27
Grades: 5 6 7 8   363.7
1. Bhopal Union Carbide Plant Disaster, Bhopal, India,
1984 2. Chemical industry -- Accidents
ISBN 0-8368-5503-5 lib bdg; 0-8368-5510-8 pa

LC 2003-49718

Presents an account of the 1984 chemical accident at the
Union Carbide plant in Bhopal, India, and its aftermath
Includes glossary and bibliographical references

Danube; cyanide spill. by Nichol Bryan. World
Almanac Library 2004 48p il map (Environmental
disasters) lib bdg $29.27; pa $11.95
Grades: 5 6 7 8   363.7
1. Chemical spills 2. Water pollution 3. Chemical
spills -- Environmental aspects 4. Water -- Pollution
-- Danube River Watershed 5. Gold mines and mining
-- Environmental aspects 6. Cyanides -- Environmental
aspects -- Danube River Watershed 7. Heavy metals
-- Environmental aspects -- Danube River Watershed 8.
Chemical spills -- Environmental aspects -- Danube River
Watershed 9. Gold mines and mining -- Environmental
aspects -- Romania -- Baia Mare
ISBN 0-8368-5505-1 lib bdg; 0-8368-5512-4 pa

LC 2003-57694

Discusses the disastrous year 2000 overflow of a Romanian reservoir that held heavy metals and cyanide, pouring
the deadly mix into rivers that feed the Danube and killing
all living creatures in its path.
Includes glossary and bibliographical references

Love Canal; pollution crisis. World Almanac Li-
brary 2004 48p il map (Environmental disasters)
hardcover o.p. lib bdg $29.27
Grades: 5 6 7 8   363.7
1. Pollution 2. Chemical plants -- Waste disposal --
Environmental aspects -- New York (State) -- Niagara
Falls
ISBN 0-8368-5508-6 lib bdg; 0-8368-5515-9 pa

LC 2003-57162

Traces the history and eventual cleanup of the ecological
disaster known as Love Canal, which resulted from building
a neighborhood over a chemical dumpsite that poisoned the
environment and endangered the health of residents.

This is "well-illustrated. . . . [It does] a fine job of placing
[the] disaster within a larger context by including detailed
background about America's industrial and environmental
history; quotes from eyewitnesses, politicians, and journalists; and clear explanations of the changes in policy that [the]
disaster instigated." Booklist
Includes glossary and bibliographical references

Byrnes, Patricia

Environmental pioneers. Oliver Press (Minneapolis) 1998 160p il (Profiles) lib bdg $19.95
Grades: 7 8 9 10   363.7
1. Authors 2. Governors 3. Cartoonists 4. Naturalists
5. Conservationists 6. Environmentalists 7. Senators

8. Feminists 9. Centenarians 10. College teachers 11. Marine biologists 12. State legislators 13. Writers on nature 14. Writers on science 15. Organization officials 16. Environmentalists -- United States -- Biography
ISBN 1-881508-45-5

LC 97-30233

Profiles people who have been influential in the environmental movement: John Muir, Jay Norwood "Ding" Darling, Rosalie Edge, Aldo Leopold, Olaus and Margaret Murie, Rachel Carson, David Brower, and Gaylord Nelson

"Unlike most authors of books on this topic for a young audience, Byrnes is an experienced environmental writer, and takes an affectionate tone in describing her subjects." SLJ

Includes bibliographical references

Cherry, Lynne

★ **How** we know what we know about our changing climate; scientists and kids explore global warming. by Lynne Cherry and Gary Braasch; with a foreword by David Sobel. Dawn Publications 2008 66p il $18.95; pa $11.95

Grades: 4 5 6 7   363.7
    1. Greenhouse effect   2. Climate -- Environmental aspects 3. Earth sciences 4. Global warming 5. Climatic changes
    ISBN 978-1-58469-103-7; 0-1-58469-103-4; 978-1-58469-130-3 pa; 1-58469-130-1 pa

LC 2007-37255

"The can-do emphasis helps to make the topic less depressing, and the intriguing color photographs are thoughtful and upbeat." Booklist

Collard, Sneed

Global warming; a personal guide to causes and solutions. Lifelong Learning 2011 62p il $18

Grades: 6 7 8 9   363.7
    1. Greenhouse effect 2. Climate -- Environmental aspects
    ISBN 978-0-97853677-0

"After a quick introduction and opening discussion of the basics and impacts of global warming, Collard identifies the causes, challenges, and related issues and examines the complex issue of what needs to be done. He suggests various solutions and gives global examples to support his arguments. His knowledgeable and persuasive tone convinces readers that change is necessary and achievable. . . . The informative text is broken into columns, making the extra-wide-page format easy to read. More than eight pages of references give students many further-research options. . . . An excellent resource for reports and debates." SLJ

David, Laurie

★ The **down**-to-earth guide to global warming; [by] Laurie David and Cambria Gordon. Orchard Books 2007 112p il map pa $15.99

Grades: 4 5 6 7   363.7
    1. Greenhouse effect   2. Climate -- Environmental aspects 3. Global warming
    ISBN 978-0-439-02494-5 pa; 0-439-02494-3 pa

LC 2006-35705

The authors "put forth the basics on global warming, climate change, and how readers can green up the environment. They temper the book's often troubling subject matter with kid-friendly humor, some celebrity shout-outs, and explanations of the scientific underpinnings. An amply illustrated layout, featuring attention-grabbing sidebars, dramatic photos, and diagrams, will sustain reader interest." Booklist

Includes bibliographical references

Davies, Nicola

Gaia warriors; urgent; the fight is on! with an afterword by James Lovelock. Candlewick Press 2011 192p il $14.99

Grades: 5 6 7 8   363.7
    1. Gaia hypothesis 2. Environmental protection 3. Greenhouse effect 4. Climate -- Environmental aspects 5. Climatic changes
    ISBN 978-0-7636-4808-4; 0-7636-4808-6

LC 2010-40126

This "offers a dynamic overview of global warming's causes and concerns. Davies . . . devotes half the book to exciting profiles of individuals . . . who are working to slow climate change. . . . They include scientists, rock musicians, food distributors, architects, and youth organizers, and their broad variety reinforces the sense that every creative individual effort matters. Highly browsable layouts combine color photos and quotes printed in varied, eye-catching fonts. . . . [This has a] humorous, conversational tone." Booklist

Includes glossary

Delano, Marfe Ferguson

★ **Earth** in the hot seat; bulletins from a warming world. National Geographic 2009 63p il (Preserve our planet) $19.95; lib bdg $28.90

Grades: 5 6 7 8   363.7
    1. Greenhouse effect   2. Climate -- Environmental aspects 3. Global warming 4. Climatic changes 5. Greenhouse effect, Atmospheric   6. Conservation of natural resources
    ISBN 978-1-4263-0434-7; 1-4263-0434-X; 978-1-4263-0435-4 lib bdg; 1-4263-0435-8 lib bdg

LC 2008029317

"This book lays out . . . the evidence for global warming and the part that human activity plays in it. Five chapters lay out the signs and evidences of a warming world. . . . Subsequent chapters of the book are devoted to what humankind can expect in a warming world and steps that must be taken to avert catastrophe for humans and the planet. . . . The illustrative photos are fully up to National Geographic high standards. This [is a] fine book, reasonably priced and carefully researched." Voice Youth Advocates

Includes bibliographical references

Dorion, Christiane

Pollution. Gareth Stevens Pub. 2010 48p il (What if we do nothing?) lib bdg $31

Grades: 7 8 9 10   363.7
    1. Pollution 2. Environmental protection
    ISBN 978-1-4339-1984-8 lib bdg; 1-4339-1984-2 lib bdg

LC 2008-52494

This "title covers the main sources of air, water, and ground pollution and offers some suggestions for reducing it. . . . Meaningful illustrations include color photos and text-enhancing charts. . . . [This title is] well written and useful for reports." SLJ

Includes glossary and bibliographical references

The **environment**: opposing viewpoints; Louise I. Gerdes, book editor. Greenhaven Press 2009 224p il (Opposing viewpoints series) $39.70; pa $27.50
Grades: 8 9 10 11 12   **363.7**
1. Environmental sciences
ISBN 978-0-7377-4362-3; 978-0-7377-4361-6 pa
LC 2008-55846

This collection of essays offers varying viewpoints on environmental pollution and protection.

Includes bibliographical references

Evans, Kate
Weird weather; everything you didn't want to know about climate change but probably should find out. [with an introduction by George Monbiot] Groundwood Books 2007 95p il $15.95; pa $9.95
Grades: 8 9 10 11 12   **363.7**
1. Graphic novels 2. Weather -- Graphic novels 3. Greenhouse effect -- Graphic novels 4. Climate -- Environmental aspects -- Graphic novels
ISBN 978-0-88899-838-5; 978-0-88899-841-5 pa

First published 2006 in the United Kingdom with title: Funny weather

This book, in graphic novel format, presents "the history of global warming, likely outcomes of current pollution patterns, and what can be done if we hope to survive as a species. Cleverly, the narrative unfolds through the voices of three main characters: an outraged young idealist, a scientist fascinated by the challenges of the situation, and a greedy consumer who is only interested in himself. Accessible and entertaining, this book will be adored by science teachers. . . . Important reading for secondary students and adults." SLJ

Includes bibliographical references

Farrell, Courtney
The **Gulf** of Mexico oil spill. ABDO Pub. 2011 112p il (Essential events) lib bdg $23.95
Grades: 7 8 9 10 11 12   **363.7**
1. Gulf of Mexico oil spill, 2010
ISBN 978-1-61714-765-4; 1-61714-765-6
LC 2010044976

This describes the political, social, and technical issues concerning the 2010 oil spill in the Gulf of Mexico.

Includes glossary and bibliographical references

Fridell, Ron
Protecting Earth's water supply; by Ron Fridell. Lerner Publications Co. 2009 72p il (Saving our living Earth) lib bdg $30.60

Grades: 5 6 7 8   **363.7**
1. Water pollution 2. Water conservation
ISBN 978-0-8225-7557-3 lib bdg; 0-8225-7557-4 lib bdg
LC 2007-35924

"Provides a thorough, interesting discussion of multiple aspects of [water supply protection], including historical origins, the current situation, and potential solutions. . . . Photos from around the world accompany discussions. . . . [This is a] solid choice to replace outdated books." SLJ

Includes glossary and bibliographical references

Geiger, Beth
Clean water. Roaring Brook Press 2009 40p il (Sally Ride science) pa $7.99
Grades: 5 6 7 8   **363.7**
1. Water supply 2. Water pollution
ISBN 978-1-59643-577-3 pa; 1-59643-577-1 pa

This is a "well-written, engaging book. . . . The [book']s best feature is the conversational tone that simply and clearly conveys important, and sometimes complicated, scientific concepts. Illustrations and layout are well done, and include colorful photographs and charts. Excellent." SLJ

★ **Global** warming: opposing viewpoints; David Haugen, Susan Musser, and Kacy Lovelace, book editors. Greenhaven Press 2010 249p il map (Opposing viewpoints series) $39.70; pa $27.50
Grades: 8 9 10 11 12   **363.7**
1. Greenhouse effect
ISBN 978-0-7377-4631-0; 0-7377-4631-9; 978-0-7377-4632-7 pa; 0-7377-4632-7 pa
LC 2009-38723

"Explores whether global warming is a real phenomenon or a myth, addressing possible causes like carbon dioxide, deforestation, melting permafrost, and livestock agriculture. Examines the effects of global warming on the polar ice caps, polar bears and human health, and discusses some proposed strategies to mitigate the impact." Publisher's note

Includes bibliographical references

Gore, Al
Our choice; how we can solve the climate crisis. [text adapted by Richie Chevat] Young readers ed.; Puffin Books 2009 207p il map $24.99; pa $16.99
Grades: 6 7 8 9 10   **363.7**
1. Human ecology 2. Environmental policy 3. Environmental protection 4. Greenhouse effect
ISBN 978-0-670-01248-0; 0-670-01248-3; 978-0-14-240981-7 pa; 0-14-240981-2 pa
LC 2010-455157

"This colorful, well-designed volume presents the climate crisis in an easy-to-understand format. Covering many aspects of this complex problem, it addresses the effects of pollution on the environment, the search for alternative energy sources, and offers suggestions for conserving power and reducing the impact of human habitation on the planet. . . . Although the urgency of the current global situation is stressed, the chapters are also laced with hope. Suggestions for change offer positive steps that anyone can take to reduce his carbon footprint, and extend a call to unite globally to save the planet for future generations." Voice Youth Advocates

★ An **inconvenient** truth; the crisis of global warming. adapted for young readers by Jane O'Connor. rev ed.; Viking 2007 191p il map $23; pa $16

Grades: 5 6 7 8   **363.7**

1. Greenhouse effect   2. Climate -- Environmental aspects 3. Global warming 4. Greenhouse effect, Atmospheric

ISBN 978-0-670-06271-3; 978-0-670-06272-0 pa

Adapted from the title for adults published 2006 by Rodale Press

This explains what global warming is, what causes it, and explains how to take action to stop this crisis.

This is illustrated with "easy-to-grasp graphics and revealing before-and-after photos. . . . O'Connor rephrases Gore's arguments in briefer, simpler language without compromising their flow." SLJ

Gunderson, Jessica

Global warming. Creative Education 2011 48p il (Earth issues) lib bdg $23.95

Grades: 6 7 8 9 10   **363.7**

1. Climate 2. Greenhouse effect

ISBN 978-1-58341-982-3; 1-58341-982-9

"An examination of the causes and potential effects of increasing global temperatures, exploring how humans and natural phenomena are involved, as well as how people can contribute to a healthier planet." Publisher's note

Includes glossary and bibliographical references

Hanel, Rachael

Climate fever; stopping global warming. Compass Point Books 2010 64p il (Green generation) lib bdg $31.99; pa $6.95

Grades: 5 6 7 8 9   **363.7**

1. Greenhouse effect 2. Climate -- Environmental aspects

ISBN 978-0-7565-4246-7 lib bdg; 0-7565-4246-4 lib bdg; 978-0-7565-4291-7 pa; 0-7565-4291-X pa

LC 2009-11448

"The cover design, layout, and graphics feel hip and of the moment. The clear writing is easy to understand and includes many concrete examples of environmentally friendly practices. . . . [A] good choice[s] for both leisure reading and reports." SLJ

Includes glossary and bibliographical references

Henningfeld, Diane Andrews

Health and disease; Michael E. Mann, consulting editor. Greenhaven Press 2011 136p il map (Confronting global warming) lib bdg $37.10

Grades: 7 8 9 10 11   **363.7**

1. Weather 2. Environmentally induced diseases 3. Greenhouse effect

ISBN 978-0-7377-4858-1; 0-7377-4858-3

LC 2010014227

"Presented in a scholarly design that will appeal to older readers. . . . The illustrations and pictures support the text, and the graphics and sidebars are well placed." Libr Media Connect

Includes glossary and bibliographical references

Hirschmann, Kris

Pollution. Kidhaven Press 2004 48p il (Our environment) lib bdg $23.70

Grades: 5 6 7 8   **363.7**

1. Pollution

ISBN 0-7377-1563-4

This briefly describes the sources and effects of air and water pollution and refuse disposal and suggests possible solutions

Includes glossary and bibliographical references

Hodge, Susie

Global warming. New Forest Press 2010 64p il map (Cutting-edge science) lib bdg $34.25

Grades: 7 8 9 10   **363.7**

1. Greenhouse effect 2. Climate -- Environmental aspects

ISBN 978-1-84898-320-5; 1-84898-320-4

This book covers "the topical science [issue] of climate change. . . . [It] includes contemporary scientific findings, the more stable science underlying the [issue], and the social [context]. The color photographs throughout are mainly stock images. Sidebars profile scientists in action or delve deeper into the research methods and studies producing this information." Horn Book Guide

Includes bibliographical references

Jakab, Cheryl

Waste management. Marshall Cavendish Benchmark 2010 32p il map (Environment in focus) lib bdg $28.50

Grades: 4 5 6   **363.7**

1. Refuse and refuse disposal

ISBN 978-1-60870-093-6; 1-60870-093-3

"The layout gives each topic the look of a file folder, with the first spread going to a case-study problem and the second going to a 'Toward a Sustainable Future' case-study solution. . . . Photos bring home the heartbreaking litter, human-waste treatment plants, etc." Booklist

Includes glossary

Johnson, Rebecca L.

Understanding global warming; by Rebecca L. Johnson. Lerner Publications 2009 72p il map (Saving our living Earth) lib bdg $30.60

Grades: 5 6 7 8   **363.7**

1. Greenhouse effect 2. Climate -- Environmental aspects

ISBN 978-0-8225-7561-0 lib bdg; 0-8225-7561-2 lib bdg

LC 2007-48358

"Provides a thorough, interesting discussion of multiple aspects of [global warming], including historical origins, the current situation, and potential solutions. . . . Photos from around the world accompany discussions. . . . [This is a] solid choice to replace outdated books." SLJ

Includes glossary and bibliographical references

Macgillivray, Alex

Understanding Rachel Carson's Silent Spring. Rosen Pub. 2011 128p il (Words that changed the world) lib bdg $31.95

Grades: 7 8 9 10   **363.7**

1. Authors 2. Insect pests 3. Conservationists 4. Pesticides and wildlife 5. College teachers 6. Marine biologists 7. Writers on nature 8. Writers on science 9. Pesticides -- Environmental aspects

ISBN 978-1-4488-1670-5; 1-4488-1670-X

LC 2010-9260

"This focused title examines Rachel Carson's Silent Spring, zeroing in on the content and enduring impact of the watershed 1962 work. . . . The text begins with a brief introduction to Carson and her times before moving into an analysis of the text and its indictment of pesticide use, . . . the immediate postpublication response, and its hugely influential legacy today. . . . A useful supplement to environmental-science units, this will easily support student research." Booklist

Includes glossary and bibliographical references

Marcovitz, Hal

How serious a threat is climate change? ReferencePoint Press 2011 96p il (In controversy) lib bdg $26.95

Grades: 7 8 9 10   **363.7**

1. Environmental protection 2. Greenhouse effect

ISBN 978-1-60152-142-2; 1-60152-142-1

LC 2010033916

Discusses the scientific evidence for climate change, what countries around the world are doing to combat it, and why some people are skeptical.

"The author presents substantial amounts of information in a readable, student-friendly manner. Useful for reports." SLJ

Includes bibliographical references

Is offshore oil drilling worth the risks? ReferencePoint Press 2011 96p il (In controversy) lib bdg $26.95

Grades: 7 8 9 10   **363.7**

1. Oil spills 2. Offshore oil well drilling

ISBN 978-1-60152-143-9; 1-60152-143-X

LC 2010037854

Discusses the issues surrounding offshore oil drilling.

"The author presents substantial amounts of information in a readable, student-friendly manner. Useful for reports." SLJ

Includes bibliographical references

McCutcheon, Chuck

What are global warming and climate change? answers for young readers. University of New Mexico Press 2010 103p il map (Worlds of wonder) $24.95

Grades: 6 7 8 9 10   **363.7**

1. Greenhouse effect 2. Climate -- Environmental aspects

ISBN 978-0-8263-4745-9; 0-8263-4745-2

The author tackles "environmental issues with depth and rigor, attuned to both current events and the concerns of today's teens. . . . The excellent [text is] enhanced by color photographs and diagrams that further explain scientific ideas." Horn Book Guide

Mileham, Rebecca

Global pollution. New Forest Press 2010 64p il map (Cutting-edge science) lib bdg $34.25

Grades: 7 8 9 10   **363.7**

1. Pollution

ISBN 978-1-84898-322-9; 1-84898-322-0

This book covers "the topical science [issue] of . . . pollution. . . . [It] includes contemporary scientific findings, the more stable science underlying the [issue], and the social [context]. The color photographs throughout are mainly stock images. Sidebars profile scientists in action or delve deeper into the research methods and studies producing this information." Horn Book Guide

Inlcudes bibliographical references

Miller, Debra A.

Garbage and recycling. Lucent Books 2009 112p il map (Hot topics) $32.45

Grades: 7 8 9 10   **363.7**

1. Recycling 2. Refuse and refuse disposal

ISBN 978-1-4205-0147-6; 1-4205-0147-X

LC 2009-18371

This is a "standout survey of what happens to what we throw away and how those decisions affect the globe. . . . This overview offers a balance of viewpoints in its clear comparison of traditional methods of waste management with more sustainable technologies, such as recycling and new landfill techniques. . . . [Sidebars] make for compelling reading, while numerous color photos, charts, and maps will further attract readers' attention." Booklist

Includes bibliographical references

Miller, Malinda

Tomorrow's transportation; green solutions for air, land & sea. Mason Crest Publishers 2011 64p il (New careers for the 21st century: finding your role in the global renewal) lib bdg $22.95

Grades: 7 8 9 10   **363.7**

1. Transportation 2. Vocational guidance

ISBN 978-1-4222-1824-2 lib bdg; 1-4222-1824-4 lib bdg

LC 2010021833

"Chapters identify and emphasize specific careers–important strengths, necessary aptitudes and interests, education and training, projected earnings, closely related occupations, type of work environment, and predictions for the future of the field. . . . Color photos have a small role amid the many statistics, figures, graphs and charts that support and supplement the . . . [text]." SLJ

Includes bibliographical references

Morris, Neil

★ **Global** warming. World Almanac Library 2007 48p il (What if we do nothing?) lib bdg $22.95; pa $11.95

Grades: 5 6 7 8   **363.7**
1. Greenhouse effect 2. Climate -- Environmental aspects
ISBN 978-0-8368-7755-7 lib bdg; 0-8368-7755-1 lib bdg; 978-0-8368-155-4 pa; 0-8368-8155-9 pa
LC 2006-30444
This "boasts an attractive format, with large pages that allow room for pictures, excellent charts and graphs, as well as a thoughtful, clear discussion of the topic." Booklist
Includes bibliographical references

Nardo, Don
Climate crisis; the science of global warming. by Don Nardo. Compass Point Books 2009 47p il map (Headline science) lib bdg $27.93; pa $7.95
Grades: 5 6 7   **363.7**
1. Greenhouse effect 2. Climate -- Environmental aspects
ISBN 978-0-7565-3571-1 lib bdg; 0-7565-3571-9 lib bdg; 978-0-7565-3948-1 pa; 0-7565-3948-X pa
LC 2008-7259
"Color photos and graphics provide visual information; a timeline is helpful to find fast facts, and the Facthound Web site provides students with additional information." Libr Media Connect
Includes glossary and bibliographical references

Oil spill; disaster. Scholastic Press 2010 31p il pa $5.99
Grades: 4 5 6 7 8   **363.7**
1. Oil spills 2. Gulf of Mexico oil spill, 2010
ISBN 978-0-545-31776-4; 0-545-31776-2
Explores the immediate and future consequences of the Gulf of Mexico oil spill in April 2010, when the offshore oil rig Deepwater Horizon exploded, causing major environmental and economical damage along the Gulf coast of the United States.
"While text and color photographs convey the extent of the devastation to the Gulf, the book also highlights some innovative attempts to clean up oil spills and profiles two middle school students, who researched cleaning up oil in their own neighborhood." Publ Wkly

Oxlade, Chris
Climate change. Smart Apple Media 2010 44p il map (Science in the news) lib bdg $34.25
Grades: 6 7 8 9   **363.7**
1. Greenhouse effect
ISBN 978-1-59920-319-5 lib bdg; 1-59920-319-7 lib bdg
LC 2008-41437
The narrative "move[s] smoothly, occasionally pausing for the definition of a term. [The title] boast[s] plenty of attractive photos, and a clean layout allows the information to be easily consumed. . . . Provides the information that younger teens need." SLJ
Includes glossary

Parker, Steve, 1952-
Population. QEB Pub. 2010 32p il (QEB changes in . . .) lib bdg $28.50

Grades: 3 4 5 6   **363.7**
1. Human ecology 2. Human influence on nature
ISBN 978-1-59566-774-8 lib bdg; 1-59566-774-1 lib bdg
LC 2008-56070
"The information is presented in brief paragraphs and sidebars. Suggestions for kids to help improve the planet are sprinkled throughout. . . . Students will enjoy this appealing layout and the information can spark further research on the topic[s]. . . . Either digitally or on paper, students could make fantastic presentations using a similar design." Libr Media Connect
Includes glossary

Pollution: opposing viewpoints; Louise I. Gerdes, book editor. Greenhaven Press 2011 262p il (Opposing viewpoints series) lib bdg $39.70; pa $26.50
Grades: 8 9 10 11 12   **363.7**
1. Pollution
ISBN 978-0-7377-5231-1 lib bdg; 0-7377-5231-9 lib bdg; 978-0-7377-5232-8 pa; 978-0-7377-5232-7 pa
LC 2010-51681
"The authors in this . . . anthology debate several controversial questions, including whether various forms of pollution continue to be a serious problem, whether pollution poses a public health threat, and what policies and programs will best reduce pollution." Publisher's note
Includes bibliographical references

Rapp, Valerie
Protecting Earth's air quality; by Valerie Rapp. Lerner Publications 2009 72p il map (Saving our living Earth) lib bdg $30.60
Grades: 5 6 7 8   **363.7**
1. Air pollution
ISBN 978-0-8225-7558-0 lib bdg; 0-8225-7558-2 lib bdg
LC 2008-907
"Provides a thorough, interesting discussion of multiple aspects of [protecting Earth's air quality], including historical origins, the current situation, and potential solutions. . . . Photos from around the world accompany discussions. . . . [This is a] solid choice to replace outdated books." SLJ
Includes glossary and bibliographical references

Robinson, Matthew
America debates global warming; crisis or myth? Rosen Central 2008 64p il (America debates) lib bdg $29.25
Grades: 5 6 7 8 9 10 11 12   **363.7**
1. Greenhouse effect 2. Climate -- Environmental aspects
ISBN 978-1-4042-1925-0 lib bdg; 1-4042-1925-0 lib bdg
LC 2007-10931
This "is especially effective in laying out the information in a simple, logical format." SLJ
Includes glossary and bibliographical references

Scarborough, Kate

★ **Nuclear** waste. Bridgestone Bks. 2003 32p il (Our planet in peril) lib bdg $22.60

Grades: 5 6 7 8   **363.7**

    1. Nuclear energy 2. Radioactive waste disposal 3. Radioactive wastes

    ISBN 0-7368-1362-4

                  LC 2002-10139

"Chapters introduce topics such as . . . 'What is nuclear power?' through brief paragraphs of information. Numerous colorful photographs, graphs, and diagrams with informative captions add details on each spread." SLJ

    Includes glossary and bibliographical references

Silverstein, Alvin

    Global warming; by Alvin Silverstein, Virginia Silverstein, Laura Silverstein Nunn. rev. ed.; Twenty-First Century Books 2009 112p il (Science concepts, second series) $31.93

Grades: 5 6 7 8   **363.7**

    1. Greenhouse effect 2. Climate -- Environmental aspects

    ISBN 978-0-7613-3935-9; 0-7613-3935-3

    First published 2003

    Includes bibliographical references

Stille, Darlene R.

The **greenhouse** effect; warming the planet. Compass Point Books 2006 48p il map (Exploring science) $26.60

Grades: 7 8 9 10   **363.7**

    1. Greenhouse effect 2. Climate -- Environmental aspects 3. Climatology 4. Global warming 5. Greenhouse effect, Atmospheric

    ISBN 978-0-7565-1956-8; 0-7565-1956-X

                  LC 2006-06763

"The book provides a brief, yet thorough, explanation and overview of the greenhouse effect. . . . The text . . . is straightforward and clearly written. The illustrations and diagrams . . . further clarify the explanations in the text." Sci Books Films

    Includes glossary and bibliographical references

Townsend, John

    Predicting the effects of climate change. Heinemann Library 2009 56p il map (Why science matters) $31.43; pa $9.49

Grades: 6 7 8 9   **363.7**

    1. Greenhouse effect 2. Climate -- Environmental aspects 3. Climatic changes

    ISBN 978-1-4329-1839-2; 1-4329-1839-7; 978-1-4329-1852-1 pa; 1-4329-1852-4 pa

                  LC 2008-14309

Provides an overview of climate change, discussing evidence, causes, and effects, and examines what can be done to stop its progression.

This book "would be a good addition to middle school libraries." Sci Books Films

    Includes filmography, glossary and bibliographical references

Wilcox, Charlotte

Earth-friendly waste management; by Charlotte Wilcox. Lerner 2009 72p il (Saving our living Earth) lib bdg $30.60

Grades: 5 6 7 8   **363.7**

    1. Recycling 2. Refuse and refuse disposal

    ISBN 978-0-8225-7560-3 lib bdg; 0-8225-7560-4 lib bdg

                  LC 2008-1883

"Provides a thorough, interesting discussion of multiple aspects of [waste management], including historical origins, the current situation, and potential solutions. . . . Photos from around the world accompany discussions. . . . [This is a] solid choice to replace outdated books." SLJ

    Includes glossary and bibliographical references

Recycling. Lerner Publications 2008 48p il (Cool science) lib bdg $26.60

Grades: 4 5 6   **363.7**

    1. Salvage 2. Recycling

    ISBN 978-0-8225-6768-4 lib bdg; 0-8225-6768-7 lib bdg

                  LC 2006102423

"This book explains the many amazing ways people use science to recycle garbage into great things." Publisher's note

    Includes glossary and bibliographical references

363.73   Pollution

Solway, Andrew

    Transportation; by Andrew Solway. Heinemann Library 2013 64 p. (The impact of environmentalism) (library) $35.00; (paperback) $9.99

Grades: 6 7 8   **363.73**

    1. Environmental movement 2. Transportation -- Environmental aspects 3. Pollution 4. Environmentalism

    ISBN 1432965204; 9781432965204; 9781432965266

                  LC 2012001043

This book Andrew Solway is part of the "Impact of Environmentalism" series. It "discusses global warming, climate change, and energy alternatives such as biofuels and renewable energies." It "also discusses the history of human activities and its environmental impact, and efforts by humankind to protect the environment and create sustainable smaller environments. Sidebars and full-color photos appear throughout." (School Library Journal)

    Includes bibliographical references and index.

363.738   Pollutants

Global warming; Debra A. Miller, book editor. Greenhaven Press 2008 189 p. (Current controversies) (library) $40.95; (paperback) $28.45

Grades: 8 9 10 11 12   **363.738**

    1. Greenhouse effect

    ISBN 9780737740707; 9780737740714; 073774071X; 0737740701

                  LC 2008001004

"Controversies covered in this volume include . . . [global warming's] causes, potential threats, and the possible actions society can take to reduce its effects. For each question considered, opposing opinions are showcased in the form of articles, reports, and essays authored by a variety of individuals including journalists, scientists, and policymakers. . . . This book will be an excellent choice for teens writing a pro/con paper, as both sides of the issues are clearly delineated." SLJ

Includes bibliographical references (p. 173-178) and index.

363.8   Food supply

Barker, Geoff P.

Hunger; by Geoff Barker. Smart Apple Media 2010 46p il (Voices) lib bdg $34.25

Grades: 7 8 9 10 11 12   **363.8**

1. Famines 2. Food relief

ISBN 978-1-59920-281-5 lib bdg; 1-59920-281-6 lib bdg

LC 2008-50430

This book about hunger "addresses the causes, the possible solutions, and outlooks, both good and bad, of . . . [the] issue. Each brief chapter covers basic questions, answered with a simple definition or explanation, then supported by pertinent quotes and statistics from well-known experts and organizations. Color photographs, sidebars, graphs and charts pull the content together in a busy but cohesive presentation. . . . Students . . . will appreciate the quotes and statistics plus commentary that addresses the . . . [issue] from several angles." Libr Media Connect

Includes glossary

Morris, Neil

Do you know where your food comes from? [by] Neil Morris. Heinemann Library 2006 56p il (Making healthy food choices) $32.86; pa $9.49

Grades: 6 7 8 9   **363.8**

1. Nutrition 2. Food industry

ISBN 978-1-4034-8575-5; 1-4034-8575-5; 978-1-4034-8581-6 pa; 1-4034-8581-X pa

LC 2006003973

This "not only teaches adolescents about how and where food is produced but also about how to make sensible food choices. Also addressed are issues that move beyond personal health (such as the environmental impact of limiting 'food miles,' the distance foods travel from where they are produced to where they are consumed). Straightforward paragraphs are nicely supported by colorful fact boxes and sidebars, covering information as diverse as the world's top producers of milk and the omega-3 content of various fish. An attractive layout and full-color photos enhance the content." Booklist

363.9   Population problems

McLeish, Ewan

Overcrowded world. Gareth Stevens Pub. 2009 48p il map (What if we do nothing?) lib bdg $31

Grades: 5 6 7 8   **363.9**

1. Overpopulation

ISBN 978-1-4339-0088-4 lib bdg; 1-4339-0088-2 lib bdg

LC 2008029182

"Using intelligent, focused text; an open design; vivid photos; and excellent maps, [this] book demands attention." Booklist

Includes bibliographical references

364   Criminology

Somervill, Barbara A.

Graphing crime. Raintree 2010 32p il (Real world data) $28.21; pa $7.99

Grades: 4 5 6 7   **364**

1. Crime 2. Statistics 3. Graphic methods

ISBN 978-1-4329-2623-6; 1-4329-2623-3; 978-1-4329-2632-8 pa; 1-4329-2632-2 pa

LC 2009001292

This "discusses juvenile offenders, drug money, terrorism, and more, and teaches readers how to evaluate statistics in the various charts, such as the difference between crimes committed and crimes reported, or between total numbers and rate per population. . . . The clear design, with lots of full-color photos and sidebars, will encourage browsers as much as the up-to-date examples and the clear directions for remaining 'chart smart.'" Booklist

Includes glossary and bibliographical references

Townsend, John

Crime through time. Raintree 2006 48p il (Painful history of crime) lib bdg $31.43

Grades: 6 7 8 9   **364**

1. Crime -- History

ISBN 1-4109-2051-8

This "looks at violations of the law from ancient times to the present, giving insight into criminals, types of crime, and methods of solving it. . . . The subject, format, and presentation of material in [this book] will inform students, including reluctant readers." SLJ

Includes bibliographical references

364.1   Criminal offenses

Blackwood, Gary L.

Gangsters. Benchmark Bks. 2002 72p il (Bad guys) lib bdg $29.93

Grades: 4 5 6   **364.1**

1. Criminals 2. Gangsters 3. Gangsters -- United States -- Biography 4. Gangsters -- United States -- History -- 20th century

ISBN 0-7614-1016-3

LC 00-57154

This profiles Monk Eastman, James Colosimo, Al Capone, Clyde Barrow, John Dillinger, and Alvin Karpis

"Useful for research and pleasure reading. . . . There is an attractive mix of illustrations, photos, maps, and reproductions." Book Rep

Includes glossary and bibliographical references

Fooks, Louie

The **drug** trade; the impact on our lives. [by] Louie Fooks. Raintree 2003 64p il (21st century debates) lib bdg $32.79

Grades: 6 7 8 9   **364.1**

1. Drug traffic 2. Drugs and crime

ISBN 0-7398-6033-X

                      LC 2003-3593

This "looks at global drug production and trafficking, types of illegal drugs, who uses them, and possible solutions. The book includes information about drug crops and the economic implications that make it difficult for governments around the world to control their sale and abuse. . . . Color photographs are plentiful and color-keyed boxes include opposing viewpoints, facts, and topics to debate." SLJ

Hanel, Rachael

Identity theft. Marshall Cavendish Benchmark 2011 143p il (Controversy!) lib bdg $25.95

Grades: 8 9 10 11 12   **364.1**

1. Identity theft

ISBN 978-0-7614-4901-0; 0-7614-4901-9

"Hanel explores types of identity theft, common scams, and prevention, which is a contentious point. Many argue that governmental proposals to secure data are invading people's privacy and civil liberties. . . . With rapid changes in technology and legislation, [this book is] recommended for all libraries seeking quality and current materials on [this topic]." SLJ

What is a **hate** crime? Roman Espejo, book editor. Greenhaven Press 2002 106p (At issue) lib bdg $28.70; pa $19.95

Grades: 7 8 9 10   **364.1**

1. Hate crimes

ISBN 0-7377-0813-1 lib bdg; 0-7377-0812-3 pa

                      LC 2001-23817

This presents a range of opinions about hate crimes from a variety of sources

Includes bibliographical references

Haugen, Brenda

The **Great** Train Robbery; history-making heist. Compass Point Books 2011 96p il (True crime) lib bdg $33.99

Grades: 6 7 8 9   **364.1**

1. Thieves 2. Railroads

ISBN 978-0-7565-4360-0; 0-7565-4360-6

                  LC 2010017722

This is an account of the Great Train Robbery of 1963. Its loot was, at that time, the largest amount of cash ever stolen in Britain.

"The chapters are short and will keep students engaged." Libr Media Connect

Includes bibliographical references

Jacobs, Thomas A.

★ **Teen** cyberbullying investigated; where do your rights end and consequences begin? Free Spirit Pub. 2010 195p il pa $15.99

Grades: 7 8 9 10 11 12   **364.1**

1. Bullies 2. Computer crimes

ISBN 978-1-57542-339-5; 1-57542-339-1

                      LC 2009-43293

This title deals with the "topic of online teen harassment, by both teens and by adults. The author, a former judge, focuses on recent landmark court cases, many of them still pending, and in an informal, interactive style, each chapter discusses one case in detail, bringing together the rights of the victim as well as those of the perpetrator." Booklist

Includes glossary and bibliographical references

Johnson, Julie

Why do people join gangs? Raintree Steck-Vaughn Pubs. 2001 48p il (Exploring tough issues) lib bdg $29.93

Grades: 6 7 8 9   **364.1**

1. Gangs 2. Bullies 3. Gangs -- United States

ISBN 0-7398-3236-0

                      LC 00-51750

This attempts to explain the attraction of gangs with sections on bullying, rites and rituals, gang mentality, and drug and protection rackets

"Concise and well written, this book provides an overview of the problem, focusing on the United States, but discussing other countries as well." SLJ

Includes glossary and bibliographical references

Kaminker, Laura

Everything you need to know about dealing with sexual assault. Rosen Pub. Group 1998 64p il (Need to know library) lib bdg $17.95

Grades: 6 7 8 9   **364.1**

1. Rape 2. Dating violence 3. Acquaintance rape 4. Young women -- Crimes against 5. Rape -- United States 6. Acquaintance rape -- United States 7. Young women -- Crimes against -- United States

ISBN 0-8239-2837-3

                      LC 98-7048

Discusses the myths and facts surrounding sexual assault and rape, the physical and psychological consequences, suggests ways to stay safe, and explains what to do if sexually assaulted

Includes glossary and bibliographical references

MacNee, Marie J.

Outlaws, mobsters & crooks; from the Old West to the Internet. edited by Jane Hoehner. U.X.L 1998 5v il v1-3 set $225; v4 & v5 ea $83

Grades: 8 9 10 11 12   **364.1**

1. Reference books 2. Criminals -- Dictionaries

ISBN 0-7876-2803-4 v1-3; 0-7876-6482-0 v4; 0-7876-6483-9 v5

                      LC 98-14861

Presents the lives of seventy-five North American criminals including the nature of their crimes, their motivations, and information relating to the law officers who challenged them

"Browsers and researchers alike will make good use of this enjoyable reference set due to its fact-filled content and peek into the lives of such a wide variety of outlaws." Voice Youth Advocates

Marcovitz, Hal

Gangs. ABDO Pub. Co. 2010 112p il (Essential issues) lib bdg $22.95

Grades: 7 8 9 10   **364.1**

1. Gangs

ISBN 978-1-60453-954-7; 1-60453-954-2

LC 2009-29862

The text is "well-written, providing examples that put a human face to each problem. . . . [This] will be of great assistance to students writing reports." SLJ

Includes glossary and bibliographical references

Marsico, Katie

The **Texas** polygamist raid; religious freedom versus child welfare. Marshall Cavendish Benchmark 2011 128p il (Perspectives on) $39.93

Grades: 8 9 10 11 12   **364.1**

1. Polygamy 2. Child welfare 3. Religious fundamentalism

ISBN 978-1-60870-449-1; 1-60870-449-1

LC 2010016038

Provides comprehensive information on the Texas polygamist raid and the differing perspectives accompanying it.

This title offers "excellent, thorough, and accurate information for reports or for general reading. . . . [It] contrasts child welfare with the importance of freedom of religion." SLJ

Includes bibliographical references

Miller, Debra A.

Political corruption; by Debra A. Miller. Lucent Books 2007 112p il (Hot topics) $32.45

Grades: 7 8 9 10   **364.1**

1. Political corruption

ISBN 978-1-59018-982-5; 1-59018-982-5

LC 2007007793

This "offers a historical overview of political misdeeds and current efforts to curb them. Miller knows her [subject] and offers enough intrigue to hold readers' attention. Sidebars and relevant photos appear throughout." Horn Book Guide

Includes bibliographical references

Olson, Kay Melchisedech

The **D.B.** Cooper hijacking; vanishing act. Compass Point Books 2011 96p il (True crime) lib bdg $33.99

Grades: 6 7 8 9   **364.1**

1. Criminals 2. Missing persons 3. Hijacking of airplanes

ISBN 978-0-7565-4359-4; 0-7565-4359-2

LC 2010006550

This is an account of the hijacking of a Boeing 727 in November of 1971 by a man known as D.B. Cooper, who

was carrying $200,000 and a briefcase he said contained a bomb. No trace of the man has ever been found.

Includes bibliographical references

Roleff, Tamara L.

Hate groups; by Tami Roleff. Greenhaven Press 2001 112p il (Opposing viewpoints digests) $29.95; pa $19.95

Grades: 8 9 10 11 12   **364.1**

1. Hate crimes 2. White supremacy movements 3. Hate groups 4. Hate crimes -- United States 5. Hate groups -- United States

ISBN 0-7377-0677-5; 0-7377-0676-7 pa

LC 00-12170

This book "poses three basic questions about hate groups and hate speech (Are these groups a problem? Should hate speech be restricted? Are hate crimes laws necessary?) before unveiling documented pro and con essays that explore each question's complexities. Roleff's crisp, journalistic writing combines anecdotes and facts in a dense, but easily readable style." Booklist

Includes bibliographical references

Schroeder, Andreas

★ **Scams!** ten stories that explore some of the most outrageous swindlers and tricksters of all time. Annick Press 2004 154p (True stories from the edge) $18.95; pa $7.95

Grades: 5 6 7 8   **364.1**

1. Fraud 2. Swindlers and swindling

ISBN 1-55037-853-8; 1-55037-852-X pa

This is a "collection of stories about forgers, con artists, and other individuals who duped the public for fame, money, love, or power. . . . Schroeder's lively narration with undocumented dialogue breathes life into characters whom readers can't help but marvel at for their sheer ingenuity. . . . Schroeder's page-turning stories are suspenseful." SLJ

Includes bibliographical references

Swift, Richard

★ **Gangs**; Richard Swift. Groundwood 2011 144 p. (Groundwork guides) pa $10.00 hc $18.95

Grades: 7 8 9 10 11 12   **364.1**

1. Gangs 2. Ethnic groups 3. Urban sociology 4. Crime -- History

ISBN 088899978X pa; 0888999798; 9780888999788 pa; 9780888999795

"This riveting volume, which is both comprehensive and concise, explores a complex and potentially controversial issue. Swift frames the issue against the gross social inequities that create gangs and discusses the factors that contribute to their existence, such as racism, poverty, drug use and trafficking, lack of jobs, crumbling global economies, etc. . . . Despite its conveniently compact size, the book is packed with information. . . . This interesting and accessible volume is an essential purchase." SLJ

364.15   Offenses against the person

Blackwood, Gary L.
Highwaymen. Benchmark Bks. 2002 72p il (Bad guys) lib bdg $29.93
Grades: 4 5 6   **364.15**
1. Thieves 2. Robbers and outlaws 3. Brigands and robbers -- Europe -- History 4. Brigands and robbers -- United States -- History
ISBN 0-7614-1017-1
LC 99-86663
Describes the lives and careers of such European and American highwaymen as Claude Duval, Mary Frith, and Joseph Thompson Hare
"Well written and well designed. . . . {This book is} illustrated with reproductions of period artwork, documents, and photographs." Booklist
Includes glossary and bibliographical references

Outlaws. Benchmark Bks. 2002 72p il (Bad guys) lib bdg $29.93
Grades: 4 5 6   **364.15**
1. Thieves 2. Robbers and outlaws 3. Outlaws -- United States -- Biography 4. Outlaws -- United States -- History -- 19th century
ISBN 0-7614-1015-5
LC 00-57161
This profiles seven outlaws of the Old West including Joaquin Murieta, Jesse James, John Wesley Hardin, Billy the Kid, Black Bart, Pearl Hart, and Henry Starr
"Vivid photographs, reproductions, and illustrations effectively complement the text. . . . Entertaining and informative reading." SLJ
Includes glossary and bibliographical references

Broyles, Janell
Frequently asked questions about hate crimes; Barbara Dunkell, Janell Broyles. Rosen Pub. 2012 64 p. col. ill. (FAQ: teen life) (library) $31.95
Grades: 7 8 9 10 11 12   **364.15**
1. Hate crimes 2. Discrimination 3. Hate crimes -- United States
ISBN 1448855624; 9781448855629
LC 2011015910
This book, which looks at hate crimes, is part of the FAQ: Teen Life series, which "focuses on a wide variety of timely, high-interest issues for adolescents. . . . Each title provides excellent contextual information about the topic, dispels common myths, and answers key questions concerning each issue. The authors also provide lists of vital questions to ask teachers, guidance counselors, and other specialists." (Voice of Youth Advocates)
Includes bibliographical references and index

Draper, Allison Stark
The **assassination** of Malcolm X. Rosen Pub. Group 2002 64p il (Library of political assassinations) lib bdg $26.50
Grades: 5 6 7 8   **364.15**
1. Black Muslims 2. Black Muslim leaders 3. Civil rights activists 4. African Americans -- Biography 5.

African American Muslims -- Biography
ISBN 0-8239-3542-6
LC 2001-3323
"Draper confronts the important issues with exceptional candor and clarity, including the ongoing controversy of who ordered the murder." Booklist
Includes glossary and bibliographical references

364.152   Homicide

Aretha, David
The **murder** of Emmett Till. Morgan Reynolds Pub. 2007 160p il (The civil rights movement) lib bdg $27.95
Grades: 7 8 9 10 11 12   **364.152**
1. Children 2. Lynching 3. Murder victims 4. African Americans -- Civil rights
ISBN 978-1-59935-057-8; 1-59935-057-2
LC 2007-26250
"The heinous murder of Emmett Till galvanized the civil rights movement and raised the nation's awareness of the extreme racism in the South. . . . This title . . . details the events surrounding Till's murder, the trial and acquittal of his killers, and the nation's racial climate before and after this milestone in civil rights history." Booklist
Includes bibliographical references

Crowe, Chris
Getting away with murder: the true story of the Emmett Till case. Phyllis Fogelman Bks. 2003 128p il map $18.99
Grades: 7 8 9 10   **364.152**
1. Racism 2. Children 3. Lynching 4. Trials (Homicide) 5. Murder victims
ISBN 0-8037-2804-2
LC 2002-5736
This is the story of "the black 14-year-old from Chicago who was brutally murdered while visiting relatives in the Mississippi Delta in 1954. . . . The gruesome, racially motivated crime and the court's failure to convict the white murderers was a powerful national catalyst for the civil rights movement. . . . Crowe's powerful, terrifying account does justice to its subject in bold, direct telling, supported by numerous archival photos and quotes from those who remember." Booklist
Includes bibliographical references

Faryon, Cynthia J.
Guilty of being weird; the story of Guy Paul Morin. Cynthia J. Faryon. James Lorimer & Co. 2013 144 p. (Lorimer Real Justice) (hardcover) $18.95
Grades: 7 8 9 10 11 12   **364.152**
1. False accusation
ISBN 1459400933; 9781459400931
This book, by Cynthia J. Faryon, is part of the "Lorimer Real Justice" series. "At twenty-four, Guy Paul Morin was considered a bit strange. . . . So when the nine-year-old girl next door went missing, the police were convinced that Morin was responsible. . . . This book tells his story, showing

how the justice system not only failed to help an innocent young man, but conspired to convict him." (Publisher's note)

"Structured like a data log, each chapter covers a specific date. . . . Teens interested in CSI can turn a critical eye to badly executed procedures and biased criminal investigation. . . . However, the choppy organization by date and the differences between the Canadian and American legal system will limit the book's appeal." SLJ

Haugen, Brenda

The **Black** Dahlia; shattered dreams. Compass Point Books 2010 96p il (True crime) lib bdg $33.99

Grades: 6 7 8 9   **364.152**

1. Homicide 2. Murder victims

ISBN 978-0-7565-4358-7; 0-7565-4358-4

LC 2010011206

This is an account of the 1947 the murder of aspiring actress Elizabeth Short, who became known as the Black Dahlia.

Includes bibliographical references

★ The **Zodiac** killer; terror and mystery. Compass Point Books 2010 96p il lib bdg $33.99

Grades: 6 7 8 9   **364.152**

1. Homicide 2. Criminal investigation

ISBN 978-0-7565-4357-0 lib bdg; 0-7565-4357-6 lib bdg

LC 2010-11205

"The serial killer who terrorized California in the late 1960s and early 1970s—he called himself Zodiac—is the subject of this heart-stopper of a book. . . . Haugen goes briskly through the details with a curt efficiency well suited for teen readers. . . . Photographs are few, but the reproductions of Zodiac's letters pack a punch, and sidebars . . . add to the overall strong design. Zodiac was never captured, but Haugen's conclusions on his impact are savvy." Booklist

Houser, Aimee

Tragedy in Tucson; the Arizona shooting rampage. by Aimee Houser. ABDO Pub. Co. 2012 112 p. col. ill., col. map (hc) $34.22

Grades: 6 7 8 9 10   **364.152**

1. Gun control 2. Schizophrenia 3. Murder -- Arizona -- Tucson 4. Mental health laws -- United States 5. Firearms and crime -- Arizona -- Tucson 6. Firearms -- Social aspects -- United States

ISBN 1617833126; 9781617833120

LC 2011038452

This book "examines . . . the shooting of Representative Gabrielle Giffords and 18 others in Tucson, Arizona." It "explores the man behind the shooting, Jared Loughner, and his history of mental illness, the disease schizophrenia, Giffords's rise in politics, [and] the political climate in America, including the hot button issue of health-care reform, Giffords's fight for her life, and the effects of this event on society. Also discussed are the gun laws in America." (Publisher's note)

"..These titles are excellent introductions to these important topics, particularly for developing an analytical framework for debate." SLJ

Includes bibliographical references (p. 104-109, 112)

and index

Mackay, Jenny

The **Columbine** School shooting. Lucent Books 2010 96p il (Crime scene investigations) lib bdg $32.45

Grades: 7 8 9 10   **364.152**

1. School shootings

ISBN 978-1-4205-0138-4; 1-4205-0138-0

LC 2009-36532

Discusses the Columbine High School Massacre in Littleton, Colorado, on April 20, 1999, focusing on the crime itself as well as the tools and techniques used to process the scene. Also features crime stats, facts versus fiction sections, full-color photos and more.

This book is "both interesting and easily readable . . . [and includes] vivid color photography, charts, graphs, sidebar commentaries, highlighted facts (including career information), an annotated bibliography, and an index. . . . [This] should not only be a popular addition to any collection but will also go a long way in setting the record straight regarding who does what within a criminal investigation." Voice Youth Advocates

Includes bibliographical references

Marsico, Katie

The **Columbine** High School massacre; murder in the classroom. Marshall Cavendish Benchmark 2010 128p il (Perspectives on) lib bdg $39.93

Grades: 7 8 9 10   **364.152**

1. School shootings

ISBN 978-0-7614-4985-0; 0-7614-4985-X

LC 2009020590

This "is a well-written examination of this violent school shooting and the controversies it inspired. The roles of society and the controversial effects of violent video games are discussed, as well as the evolution of school security. . . . The title provides a complete and concise examination of the issue at hand, from its occurrence to the impact on society. It also contains a timeline of events and well-chosen illustrations. This is a recommended addition to any school or public library." Voice Youth Advocates

Includes bibliographical references

Robson, David

The **murder** of Emmett Till. Lucent Books 2010 104p il (Crime scene investigations) lib bdg $32.45

Grades: 7 8 9 10   **364.152**

1. Racism 2. Children 3. Homicide 4. Murder victims 5. African Americans -- Mississippi

ISBN 978-1-4205-0213-8; 1-4205-0213-1

LC 2009-33485

"Explores the 1955 landmark case of egregious racial injustice that is largely credited with igniting a nationwide social movement against segregation, bigotry, and hate crime. . . . [This book is] both interesting and easily readable . . . [and includes] vivid color photography, charts, graphs, sidebar commentaries, highlighted facts (including career information), an annotated bibliography, and an index. . . . [This] should not only be a popular addition to any collection but will also go a long way in setting the record straight

regarding who does what within a criminal investigation."
Voice Youth Advocates

Includes bibliographical references

Uschan, Michael V., 1948-

Lynching and murder in the deep South; [by] Michael V. Uschan. Lucent Books 2007 104p il map (Lucent library of Black history) $32.45

Grades: 8 9 10 11 12   **364.152**
1. Lynching 2. African Americans -- Civil rights
ISBN 1-59018-845-4

LC 2005037807

"Uschan deals honestly with this important historical topic . . . that occurred from the end of Reconstruction through the 1920s, '30s, and into the '40s and '50s. Writing in clear and telling prose, the author chronicles the horrific history of this practice in the South, why it was so pervasive, and how it was eventually brought to an end. This is a book that fills a gap. . . . Black-and-white photos and reproductions appear throughout." SLJ

Includes bibliographical references

Worth, Richard

Massacre at Virginia Tech; disaster & survival. [by] Richard Worth. Enslow Publishers 2008 48p il map (Deadly disasters) $23.93

Grades: 4 5 6 7   **364.152**
1. Students 2. School violence 3. Virginia Tech (Blacksburg, Va.) shootings, 2007 4. Murderers
ISBN 978-0-7660-3274-3; 0-7660-3274-4

LC 2007025592

Examines the tragic school shooting at Virginia Tech University, detailing the horrifying massacre, the lives of the killer and victims, and the sociological problems surrounding school shootings.

"The sequence of events, profiles of pertinent figures, and related topics such as gun control are all discussed. Photographs of the killer, victims, and survivors lend chilling immediacy." Horn Book Guide

Includes glossary and bibliographical references

364.16   Offenses against property

Blackwood, Gary L.

Swindlers. Benchmark Bks. 2002 72p il (Bad guys) lib bdg $29.93

Grades: 4 5 6   **364.16**
1. Swindlers and swindling 2. Swindlers and swindling -- History 3. Swindlers and swindling -- Biography
ISBN 0-7614-1031-7

LC 00-57153

"Swindlers traces the concept of cheating to the biblical story of Jacob and Esau but focuses on historical personages such as William Henry Ireland, an English forger of Shakespearean plays; Soapy Smith, a con artist of the American West; and Joseph 'Yellow Kid' Weil, a swindler on a grand scale. Well written and well designed. . . . Illustrated with reproductions of period artwork, documents, and photographs." Booklist

Includes glossary and bibliographical references

Guillain, Charlotte

Great art thefts; by Charlotte Guillain. Capstone Raintree 2013 48 p. col. ill. (Treasure hunters) (library) $29.33; (paperback) $8.99

Grades: 5 6 7 8   **364.16**
1. Theft -- History 2. Art thefts
ISBN 1410949583; 9781410949516; 9781410949585

LC 2012012759

This book by Charlotte Guillain, part of the Treasure Hunters series, looks at art thefts. "After . . . introductions that lay foundations so children will understand why thieves might want to steal art or treasure hunters take such risks, each volume contains chapters that follow the discovery and/or quests for objects such as 'Roman Riches' or locations such as the legendary city of Troy." (School Library Journal)

Includes bibliographical references and index.

Hynson, Colin

Cyber crime; by Colin Hynson. Smart Apple Media 2012 44 p. col. ill. (Inside crime) (library) $35.65

Grades: 7 8 9 10   **364.16**
1. Computer crimes 2. Computer crimes -- Prevention
ISBN 1599203960; 9781599203966

LC 2010043232

This book, part of the Crime and Detection Series, focuses on cyber crime. "These titles examine the diversity of crimes committed around the world. Each . . . illustrated, oversized volume has a photograph or reproduction on every spread, many times taking up a full page." Andrew Grant-Adamson "looks at hackers, viruses, and computer crimes that have come to light in the age of the Internet." (School Library Journal)

Includes bibliographical references (p. 43) and index

Juettner, Bonnie

Blackmail and bribery; by Bonnie Juettner. Lucent Books 2009 104 p. col. ill. (Crime scene investigations) (hardcover) $35.45

Grades: 7 8 9 10   **364.16**
1. Bribery 2. Forensic sciences 3. Extortion 4. White collar crimes
ISBN 1420500686; 9781420500684

LC 2008025864

This book, part of the Crime Scene Investigations series, focuses on blackmail and bribery. This series "unveils the tools and techniques used by today's (and yesterday's) professionals. . . . Each title focuses on a particular type of crime, and includes features like crime stats, facts versus fiction sections, full-color photos and more." (Publisher's note)

Includes bibliographical references (p. 92-95) and index.

364.3   Offenders

Stemple, Heidi E. Y.

Bad girls; sirens, Jezebels, murderesses, thieves, and other female villains. Jane Yolen and Heidi E. Y. Stemple; illustrated by Rebecca Guay. Charlesbridge 2012 176 p. (reinforced for library use) $18.95

Grades: 6 7 8 9 10 11 12   **364.3**
1. Women criminals 2. Criminals -- Biography 3. Femmes fatales -- Biography 4. Women murderers -- Biography 5. Female offenders -- Biography
ISBN 1580891853; 9781580891851

LC 2012000783

This book, by Jane Yolen and Heidi E. Stemple, illustrated by Rebecca Guay, examines the history of "twenty-six . . . notorious women. Each bad girl has a rotten reputation, but there are two sides to every tale. Decide whether Tituba was really a conspiring witch or just a humble housemaid. Analyze the evidence stacked for and against Lizzie Borden. And what made the brazen Cleopatra so dishonorable . . . or honorable?" (Publisher's note)

Includes bibliographical references and index

364.6   Penology

Gerber, Larry
Torture. Rosen Pub. 2011 64p il (Headlines!) lib bdg $29.95
Grades: 7 8 9 10   **364.6**
1. Torture
ISBN 978-1-4488-1291-2; 1-4488-1291-7

LC 2010018898

This book "looks at the history and modern practice of torture, ending with discussion of Abu Ghraib and Guantanamo. Good organization, clear writing, captioned photos, and sidebars deliver the information cleanly." Horn Book Guide
Includes glossary and bibliographical references

Kerrigan, Michael
The **history** of punishment; [by] Michael Kerrigan. Mason Crest Publishers 2003 96p il (Crime and detection) $22.95
Grades: 7 8 9 10   **364.6**
1. Punishment 2. Punishment -- History
ISBN 1-59084-386-X

LC 2003-488

This covers punishment "from the beginning of time, taking into account secular and religious laws and rules of conduct, and the various means people have employed to punish those who violate the laws, including corporal punishment, imprisonment, capital punishment, and rehabilitation efforts. . . . [This book provides] no-nonsense, straightforward, gritty information, accompanied by good-quality, full-color photos, reproductions, and illustrations." SLJ

Torture; Lauri S. Friedman, book editor. Greenhaven Press 2011 147p il (Introducing issues with opposing viewpoints) $36.75
Grades: 7 8 9 10   **364.6**
1. Torture
ISBN 978-0-7377-5203-8; 0-7377-5203-3

LC 2011005638

This is an "excellent [resource] both for student research and for personal interest. . . . Torture discusses the ethics of state-approved torture, particularly of terrorism suspects, and covers the Geneva Conventions, the death penalty, and whether torture produces good information." Booklist
Includes bibliographical references

Townsend, John
Punishment and pain; [by] John Townsend. Raintree 2006 48p il (Painful history of crime) lib bdg $31.43; pa $8.90
Grades: 6 7 8 9   **364.6**
1. Punishment
ISBN 1-4109-2054-2 lib bdg; 1-4109-2059-3 pa

LC 2005012517

This "shows the painful consequences of crime through torture and death, from the 1500s to the present. . . . The subject, format, and presentation of material in [this book] will inform students, including reluctant readers." SLJ
Includes bibliographical references

364.66   Capital punishment

The **death** penalty: opposing viewpoints; Diane Andrews Henningfeld, book editor; Bonnie Szumski, publisher; Helen Cothran, managing editor. Greenhaven Press 2006 223p il (Opposing viewpoints series) hardcover o.p. pa $23.70
Grades: 8 9 10 11 12   **364.66**
1. Capital punishment
ISBN 0-7377-2929-5; 0-7377-2930-9 pa

LC 2005-52743

"Powerful people and organizations contribute essays to the death-penalty debate. Supreme Court Justice Antonin Scala argues that the death penalty is just, and his former colleague, Sandra Day O'Connor, debates whether juveniles should be exempt from it. This nonbiased, comprehensive look at one of today's most difficult issues will be helpful for students writing persuasive essays and for debate groups." SLJ
Includes bibliographical references

Kuklin, Susan
★ **No** choirboy; murder, violence, and teenagers on death row. Henry Holt and Co. 2008 212p il $17.95
Grades: 8 9 10 11 12   **364.66**
1. Capital punishment 2. Juvenile delinquency 3. Death row inmates 4. Juvenile delinquents 5. Juvenile justice, Administration of
ISBN 978-0-8050-7950-0; 0-8050-7950-5

LC 2007-46940

"The book opens with candid interviews that introduce three inmates, all of them teenagers when they committed their crimes. . . . This eye-opening account will likely open minds. . . . The book concludes with solid back matter—notes, glossary, bibliography, and index." Horn Book
Includes glossary and bibliographical references

365   Penal and related institutions

America's prisons: opposing viewpoints; Noah Berlatsky, book editor. Greenhaven Press 2010 224p il map (Opposing viewpoints series) $39.70; pa $27.50

Grades: 8 9 10 11 12   **365**

1. Prisons -- United States

ISBN 978-0-7377-4956-4; 0-7377-4956-3; 978-0-7377-4957-1 pa; 0-7377-4957-1 pa

LC 2009-50927

"This collection of opposing viewpoints provides students an opportunity to weigh the merits of arguments that support or oppose the operation of America's prisons." Publisher's note

Includes bibliographical references

Edge, Laura Bufano

Locked up; a history of the U.S. prison system. by Laura B. Edge. Twenty-First Century Books 2009 112p il (People's history) lib bdg $31.93

Grades: 6 7 8 9 10   **365**

1. Prisons -- United States

ISBN 978-0-8225-8750-7; 0-8225-8750-5

LC 2008-26883

"Using primary resources, photographs, and solid research, Edge has written a well-organized and engaging history of our prison system. . . . This book can serve as an excellent resource for reports." SLJ

Includes bibliographical references

Lock, Joan

Famous prisons; [by] Joan Lock. Mason Crest Publishers 2003 96p il (Crime and detection) $22.95

Grades: 7 8 9 10   **365**

1. Prisons

ISBN 1-59084-380-0

LC 2003-477

"Lock takes readers on a tour of famous U.S. prisons . . . as well as one in England . . . and another in Ireland. . . . She includes a history of each one, and the conditions over time, as well as interesting stories about each prison, and some of its famous inmates. . . . [The book provides] no-nonsense, straightforward, gritty information, accompanied by good-quality, full-color photos, reproductions, and illustrations." SLJ

Includes bibliographical references

Rabiger, Joanna

Daily prison life; [by] Joanna Rabiger. Mason Crest Publishers 2003 96p il (Crime and detection) $22.95

Grades: 7 8 9 10   **365**

1. Prisons 2. Prisoners

ISBN 1-59084-384-3

LC 2003-364

"Rabiger concentrates on the U.S. prison system and gives readers a closeup and grimly realistic view of living in one. . . . [This book provides] no-nonsense, straightforward, gritty information, accompanied by good-quality, full-color photos, reproductions, and illustrations." SLJ

Includes bibliographical references

Townsend, John

Prisons and prisoners; [by] John Townsend. Raintree 2006 48p il (Painful history of crime) lib bdg $31.45; pa $8.90

Grades: 6 7 8 9   **365**

1. Prisons 2. Prisoners

ISBN 1-4109-2053-4 lib bdg; 1-4109-2058-5 pa

LC 2005012516

This "looks at the history of [prisons] and the reforms that have taken place over the years from the days of the medieval castle dungeon to modern Supermax prisons. . . . The subject, format, and presentation of material in [this book] will inform students, including reluctant readers." SLJ

Includes bibliographical references

369.463   Girl Scouts and Girl Guides

Wadsworth, Ginger

★ **First** Girl Scout; Ginger Wadsworth. Clarion Books 2012 xiii, 210p ill. $17.99

Grades: 7 8 9 10 11 12   **369.463**

1. Biography 2. Girl Scouts 3. Philanthropists 4. Scout leaders

ISBN 978-0-547-24394-8; 0-547-24394-4

LC 2011009642

"This well-documented biography introduces readers to the founder of the Girl Scouts. . . . Low's personality really comes to life through the details in the narrative. Wadsworth shows readers that this remarkable woman was a skilled leader and hostess in spite of having suffered severe hearing loss that made conversation difficult. . . . The attractive book design features chapter headings that look like Girl Scout badges, and most spreads include period photos or reproductions of primary-source documents. Exemplary nonfiction." SLJ

Includes bibliographical references (p. 201-204) and index.

370.15   Educational psychology

Wilson, David

★ **Strategies** for evaluation; forming judgments about information for classroom, homework, and test success. [by] David Wilson. Rosen Pub. Group 2006 48p il (The library of higher order thinking skills) lib bdg $25.25; pa $11.95

Grades: 5 6 7 8   **370.15**

1. Critical thinking 2. Evaluation

ISBN 1-4042-0473-3 lib bdg; 1-4042-0656-6 pa

LC 2004030620

"In an effort to help students improve their ability to think critically, this slim, colorful volume discusses how to evaluate and form judgments about information so that one can be successful in the classroom, with homework, and on tests. . . . While the information is basic, the book is easy to read for students who need some help learning how to tap into those higher-order thinking skills." SLJ

Includes bibliographical references

370.2   Miscellany

The **Handbook** of private schools; an annual descriptive survey of independent education. 89th ed; Sargent Pubs. 2008 1296p il map $99

Grades: Adult Professional   **370.2**

1. Reference books 2. Private schools -- Directories 3. Education -- United States -- Directories

ISBN 978-0-87558-165-1; 0-87558-165-X

Annual. First published 1915 with title: Handbook of the best private schools of the United States and Canada

"Describes more than 1,700 boarding and day schools, providing information on age and grade ranges, whether co-educational or for boys or girls, enrollment, faculty size and background, academic orientation and curriculum, and where graduates attend college. 'Features classified' section lists institutions offering military programs, elementary boarding divisions, programs for students with learning differences, international and bilingual schools, and schools with more than 500 or fewer than 100 students." Guide to Ref Books. 11th edition

370.71   Education

McKeown, Rosalyn

Into the classroom; a practical guide for starting student teaching. Rosalyn McKeown. University of Tennessee Press 2011 xv, 165 p.p (pbk.) $14.95

Grades: Adult Professional   **370.71**

1. Teaching 2. Student teaching 3. Student teaching -- United States

ISBN 1572338164; 9781572338166

LC 2011011282

This book offers suggestions to those "just starting out in a secondary school classroom. . . . After exploring the pitfalls of inexperience and providing . . . guidance on maintaining order in the classroom, [Rosalyn] McKeown focuses on teaching skills. She advises readers on writing objectives and lesson plans, creating interesting ways to start and end class, introducing variety into the classroom, lecturing, asking meaningful questions, and using visual aids." (Amazon. com)

Includes bibliographical references and index.

371.1   Schools and their activities

Harada, Violet H.

Inquiry learning through librarian-teacher partnerships; [by] Violet H. Harada and Joan M. Yoshina. Linworth Pub. 2004 172p il pa $39.95

Grades: Adult Professional   **371.1**

1. Teaching teams 2. School libraries 3. Questioning 4. Teaching teams -- United States 5. School libraries -- United States 6. Curriculum planning -- United States

ISBN 1-58683-134-8

LC 2004-662

"The authors describe what happens in an inquiry-based classroom and library media center and show teachers/librarians how to develop a curriculum that incorporates es-

sential questions and important habits of mind, all aligned with content standards. . . . The volume contains everything a teacher-librarian team would need to create, teach, research, and assess major interdisciplinary units." SLJ

Includes bibliographical references

Miller, Malinda

Tomorrow's teachers; urban leadership, empowering students & improving lives. Mason Crest Publishers 2011 64p il (New careers for the 21st century: finding your role in the global renewal) lib bdg $22.95

Grades: 7 8 9 10   **371.1**

1. Teaching 2. Vocational guidance 3. Academic achievement

ISBN 978-1-4222-1823-5 lib bdg; 1-4222-1823-6 lib bdg

LC 2010021832

"Chapters identify and emphasize specific careers–important strengths, necessary aptitudes and interests, education and training, projected earnings, closely related occupations, type of work environment, and predictions for the future of the field. . . . Color photos have a small role amid the many statistics, figures, graphs and charts that support and supplement the . . . [text]." SLJ

Includes bibliographical references

371.2   School administration; administration of student academic activities

Odden, Allan R.

Improving student learning when budgets are tight; Allan R. Odden. Corwin 2012 xxi, 184 p.p $36.95

Grades: Adult Professional   **371.2**

1. Schools -- Finance 2. Academic achievement 3. Schools -- Administration 4. School budgets -- United States 5. School improvement programs -- United States

ISBN 1452217084; 9781452217086

LC 2011045908

This book by Allan R. Odden "offers a comprehensive framework to enhance student achievement in good times and in bad. . . . Odden outlines a school improvement action plan focused sharply on student learning and then shows how to target resources to implement each strategy in that plan. . . . Educators will find a wide range of real-life examples of schools and districts that have implemented these strategies and significantly improved student learning." (Publisher's note)

Includes bibliographical references and index

371.3   Methods of instruction and study

Crane, Beverley E.

Using WEB 2.0 tools in the K-12 classroom. Neal-Schuman Publishers 2009 189p il $64.95

Grades: Adult Professional   **371.3**

1. Web 2.0 2. Internet in education 3. Education --

Curricula
ISBN 1-55570-653-3; 978-1-55570-653-1
LC 2008-46167
"This excellent resource should be widely appealing to teachers, librarians, and school media specialists." Voice Youth Advocates
Includes glossary and bibliographical references

Fox, Janet S.
★ **Get** organized without losing it; by Janet S. Fox; edited by Pamela Espeland. Free Spirit Pub. 2006 105p il (Laugh & learn) pa $8.95
Grades: 5 6 7 8   **371.3**
1. Life skills 2. Study skills 3. Time management
ISBN 978-1-57542-193-3 pa; 1-57542-193-3 pa
LC 2005032809
"In this handbook for students, Fox uses humor to provide practical, easy-to-follow ideas for organizing desks, backpacks, and lockers; managing time for homework and after school activities; planning long-term projects; and taking better notes. . . . Fox writes in a conversational style. . . . Humorous illustrations complement the text." Voice Youth Advocates
Includes bibliographical references

Green, Julie
Write it down. Cherry Lake Pub. 2010 32p il (Super smart information strategies) lib bdg $27.07
Grades: 3 4 5 6   **371.3**
1. Note-taking
ISBN 978-1-60279-645-4 lib bdg; 1-60279-645-9 lib bdg
LC 2009024741
"The appealing layout includes manageable paragraphs, a variety of engaging illustrations, and examples that clearly guide readers through each topic. . . . Effective note taking and highlighting are the focus of [this book], but the book also suggests using sticky notes and creating diagrams and charts." SLJ
Includes glossary and bibliographical references

Greenberg, Michael
Painless study techniques; illustrations by Michele Earle-Bridges. Barron's Educational Series 2009 234p il pa $9.99
Grades: 6 7 8 9 10   **371.3**
1. Study skills
ISBN 978-0-7641-4059-4 pa; 0-7641-4059-0 pa
LC 2008-42609
"This book provides helpful information on topics such as time management, homework organization, note taking, creating outlines, studying for tests and quizzes, grammar, and writing a research paper. Greenberg breaks down each main topic into smaller, more manageable subtopics, giving examples to help illustrate his ideas. . . . Greenberg's writing style is clear and interesting. . . . A solid resource for most libraries." SLJ
Includes bibliographical references

Johnson, Steve
Digital tools for teaching; 30 e-tools for collaborating, creating, and publishing across the curriculum. Maupin House Pub. 2011 152p $23.95
Grades: Adult Professional   **371.3**
1. Internet in education 2. Computer-assisted instruction
ISBN 978-1-934338-84-1; 1-934338-84-2
LC 2010037430
"Considering the vast number of e-tools now available, . . . Johnson does an excellent job of sorting through them, listing his top choices, and even including ideas for using them. The book is divided into two parts. Part one provides information on today's tech-driven student, the importance of utilizing new technology, ways to start using the technology, and how to assess student products. Part two describes the e-tools, giving the following for each: a brief overview, how to get started, ways to use the tool in the classroom, and any other issues that need to be considered. . . . [This] provides a wealth of information in a user-friendly, practical format that would benefit all educators regardless of grade level or content area." Voice Youth Advocates
Includes bibliographical references

November, Alan C.
Empowering students with technology; 2nd ed.; Corwin Press 2010 115p il pa $25.95
Grades: Adult Professional   **371.3**
1. Internet in education 2. Computer-assisted instruction
ISBN 978-1-4129-7425-7; 1-4129-7425-9
LC 2009-43649
First published 2001 by Skylight Professional Development
"Discusses the relationship of technology to today's learning environment and the potential for technology to encourage students to learn collaboratively. This . . . edition emphasizes current topics such as information literacy, global connectivity, and the educational applications of utilities such as digital cameras and cell phones. The book's usefulness is as a reasource for teachers and librarians to consult in creating, planning, and assisting with school projects in all subjects." Libr Media Connect
Includes bibliographical references

Richardson, Will
Blogs, wikis, podcasts, and other powerful Web tools for classrooms; 3rd ed.; Corwin 2010 171p il pa $31.95
Grades: Adult Professional   **371.3**
1. Weblogs 2. Podcasting 3. Internet in education 4. Online social networks 5. Wikis (Computer science) 6. Teaching -- Aids and devices
ISBN 978-1-4129-7747-0; 1-4129-7747-9
LC 2009-51376
First published 2006
"The book is well-written and comprehensive. The author's engaging writing style will instill confidence in readers that they will be able to easily integrate the same technologies with the same results in their classrooms. Readers will not want to stop reading this eye-opening and inspirational book. It is jam-packed with proven ideas, and individuals,

especially educators, will want to try out these technologies." Libr Media Connect

Includes bibliographical references

Teehan, Kay

Wikis; the educator's power tool. Linworth 2010 78p il pa $30

Grades: Adult Professional   **371.3**
1. Internet in education 2. Electronic encyclopedias 3. Wikis (Computer science) 4. Computer-assisted instruction
ISBN 978-1-58683-530-9 pa; 1-58683-530-0 pa; 978-1-58683-531-6 e-book; 1-58683-531-9 e-book
       LC 2010020285

"This book breaks down three types of wikis: library wikis, which are usually content and link-to-content focused; reciprocal wikis, which are collaborative in nature; and student-produced wikis that are developed to share projects and research. . . . There is also a wiki to complement the guidelines in the book. This is a simple to use quick-start guide and a great resource for school technology teachers and librarians." Libr Media Connect

Includes bibliographical references

371.5   School discipline and related activities

Beaudoin, Marie-Nathalie

Responding to the culture of bullying and disrespect; new perspectives on collaboration, compassion, and responsibility. [by] Marie-Nathalie Beaudoin, Maureen Taylor. rev 2nd ed.; Corwin Press 2009 281p il $76.95; pa $36.95

Grades: Adult Professional   **371.5**
1. Bullies 2. School discipline
ISBN 978-1-4129-6853-9; 1-4129-6853-4; 978-1-4129-6854-6 pa; 1-4129-6854-2 pa
       LC 2008-55933

First published 2004 with title: Breaking the culture of bullying and disrespect

"This profound resource explores the behaviors that cultivate a culture of bullying and disrespect. . . . Concrete solutions to issues are offered, and the authors make sure to load this title with practical suggestions for affecting change. They delve into ways to work directly with young people to better address their concerns. . . . This purchase is essential for any educator, counselor, or parent. It should be a staple of the school library reference collection because the information provided should be used daily. It will be a title that can be referenced for years to come and will help with adults struggling to overcome bullying." Voice Youth Advocates

Includes glossary and bibliographical references

Bott, C. J.

More bullies in more books. Scarecrow Press 2009 197p il pa $35

Grades: Adult Professional   **371.5**
1. Bullies 2. Reference books 3. Bullying in schools 4. Children's literature -- Bibliography 5. Young adult

literature -- Bibliography
ISBN 978-0-8108-6654-6 pa; 0-8108-6654-4 pa
       LC 2009-923

This "offers more than 350 annotated titles published since 2000 to create awareness of the many types of harassment and bullying. . . . Although the text is written for educators and librarians for use in classroom settings, the information is equally helpful for parents, caregivers, and public librarians." SLJ

Includes bibliographical references

Myers, Jill J.

Responding to cyber bullying; an action tool for school leaders. [by] Jill J. Myers, Donna S. McCaw, Leaunda S. Hemphill. Corwin Press 2011 195p pa $33.95

Grades: Adult Professional   **371.5**
1. Bullies 2. Cyberbullying 3. School violence
ISBN 978-1-4129-9484-2; 1-4129-9484-5
       LC 2010040679

"The book's introduction addresses the nature of 'digital generation' students. The problem of cyberbullying is introduced in light of the generational reality. The book covers decisions made to resolve real-life situations, practical principles about censorship, and the capacity and limitations of school authority. Included is a matrix that serves as a decision-making tool for administration. This resource is a healthy blend of the theoretical and practical." Libr Media Connect

Includes bibliographical references

371.58   Specific discipline problems

★ **Bully**; an action plan for teachers and parents to combat the bullying crisis. edited by Lee Hirsch and Cynthia Lowen; with Dina Santorelli. Perseus Books Group 2012 viii, 295 p.p ill. $15.99

Grades: Adult Professional   **371.58**
1. Bullies 2. Bullying 3. Bullying -- Prevention 4. Cyberbullying -- Prevention 5. Bullying in schools -- Prevention
ISBN 1602861846; 1602861854; 9781602861848; 9781602861855

       LC 2012289039

"This companion book to the documentary film Bully was edited by filmmaker [Lee]Hirsch and writer/producer [Cynthia] Lowen, with contributing chapters by a number of celebrities, authors, experts, government officials, and educators. Part homage to the film, part resource, the book interweaves the stories of children who have been bullied with practical information and advice for parents and other readers." (Publishers Weekly)

Includes bibliographical references (p. 281-289) and index

371.7   Student welfare

Flath, Camden

Therapy jobs in educational settings; speech, physical, occupational & audiology. Mason Crest Publishers 2010 64p il (New careers for the 21st century: finding your role in the global renewal) lib bdg $22.95; pa $9.95

Grades: 7 8 9 10   371.7

1. Speech therapy 2. Physical therapy 3. Vocational guidance 4. Occupational therapy
ISBN 978-1-4222-1826-6 lib bdg; 1-4222-1826-0 lib bdg; 978-1-4222-2047-4 pa; 1-4222-2047-8 pa

LC 2010021727

"Chapters identify and emphasize specific careers—important strengths, necessary aptitudes and interests, education and training, projected earnings, closely related occupations, type of work environment, and predictions for the future of the field. . . . Color photos have a small role amid the many statistics, figures, graphs and charts that support and supplement the . . . [text]." SLJ

Includes bibliographical references

Hester, Joseph P.

★ **Public** school safety; a handbook, with a resource guide. McFarland & Co. 2003 200p pa $35

Grades: Adult Professional   371.7

1. School violence 2. Education -- Government policy 3. School violence -- United States 4. School violence -- United States -- Prevention
ISBN 0-7864-1483-9

LC 2003-2511

This "begins by discussing a number of important government reports that have identified the problems and causes of youth violence and some ideas for combating it. . . . The myriad strategies involving the community, parents, and teachers are discussed and both ineffective and effective programs are evaluated. . . . This is a solid and thorough guide." SLJ

Includes bibliographical references

McPherson, Stephanie Sammartino

Stressed out in school? learning to deal with academic pressure. Enslow Publishers 2009 112p il (Issues in focus today) lib bdg $31.93

Grades: 7 8 9 10   371.7

1. Students 2. Stress (Psychology)
ISBN 978-0-7660-3069-5 lib bdg; 0-7660-3069-5 lib bdg

LC 2008-40339

"Examines the stress and academic pressure students of all ages encounter, including early education, homework, standardized tests, college applications, peer pressure, and alternative learning styles." Publisher's note

Includes glossary and bibliographical references

Parks, Peggy J., 1951-

School violence. ReferencePoint Press 2008 104p il map (Compact research. Current issues) $25.95

Grades: 8 9 10 11 12   371.7

1. School violence
ISBN 978-1-60152-057-9; 1-60152-057-3

LC 2008-18372

The introduction "looks at the prevalence of [school violence]; causes such as bullying and gangs; the influence of the media, including online sources, on behavior; and the roles of alcohol and drugs, etc. The '. . . at a glance' spread and 'Overview' prepare readers for the more detailed information to come and provide facts about safety issues. Each of four chapters then addresses both sides of a question, followed by four pages of quotes and a section of colorful graphs, charts, and illustrations." SLJ

Includes bibliographical references

Schier, Helga

The **causes** of school violence; by Helga Schier. ABDO Publishing 2008 112 p. ill. (chiefly col.) (library) $34.22

Grades: 7 8 9 10   371.7

1. School violence
ISBN 160453060X; 9781604530605

LC 2007031920

This book is part of the Essential Viewpoints series and looks at the causes of school violence. The series "examines critical debates occurring today, including the legislation that has shaped the issue as well as the numerous sides of each argument. Color photos, detailed maps, and informative sidebars accompany" the text. (Publisher's note)

Includes bibliographical references (p. 102-103) and index.

Simons, Rae

Students in danger; survivors of school violence. Mason Crest Publishers 2009 128p il (Survivors: ordinary people, extraordinary circumstances) lib bdg $24.95

Grades: 7 8 9 10   371.7

1. Bullies 2. School violence 3. School shootings
ISBN 978-1-4222-0455-9 lib bdg; 1-4222-0455-3 lib bdg

LC 2008-50333

"This book is dedicated to explaining the psychology of school violence through real-life examples and stories. . . . It also discusses bullying as another, and often overlooked, form of school violence. . . . [This book features] important, and sometimes complex information in an easy-to-read format, offering high gloss photographs, marginal glossary notes, concept definitions, a bibliography, and further reading recommendations." Voice Youth Advocates

Includes glossary and bibliographical references

Student drug testing; Patty Jo Sawvel, book editor. Greenhaven Press 2007 136p il (Issues that concern you) lib bdg $33.70

Grades: 7 8 9 10 11 12   371.7

1. Drug testing 2. Youth -- Drug use 3. Students -- Civil rights
ISBN 0-7377-2424-2 lib bdg; 978-0-7377-2424-0 lib bdg

LC 2006043352

"This title compiles articles and essays that take opposing viewpoints on the issues of teen drug testing. A range of opinions is introduced, from students and educators to journalists, government officials, and experts specializing in this topic. . . . Color illustrations are attractive and effective in emphasizing points, and cartoons add humor and interest. . . . A well-rounded presentation." SLJ

Includes bibliographical references

371.8 Students

Tym, Kate

School survival; a guide to taking control of your life. [by] Kate Tym and Penny Worms. Raintree 2005 48p il (Get real) $29.93

Grades: 7 8 9 10   **371.8**

1. Schools 2. Peer pressure 3. Socialization
ISBN 1-4109-0577-2

               LC 2004-8070

"Chapters consist of a spread presenting an overview of a topic such as . . . peer pressure, followed by three case studies about teens dealing with the problem. On the same page, three 'experts' . . . offer advice. . . . The advice of professionals lends credibility to the information presented. . . . [This volume is] sure to appeal to readers looking for advice." SLJ

371.82 Specific groups of students; schools for specific groups of students

Mortenson, Greg

Three cups of tea; one man's mission to promote peace--one school at a time. [by] Greg Mortenson and David Oliver Relin; adapted for young readers by Sarah Thomson. Dial Books for Young Readers 2009 209p il $16.99; pa $8.99

Grades: 4 5 6 7   **371.82**

1. Humanitarian intervention 2. Mountaineers 3. Humanitarians 4. Schools -- Pakistan 5. Schools -- Afghanistan 6. Humanitarian assistance
ISBN 978-0-8037-3392-3; 0-8037-3392-5; 978-0-14-241412-5 pa; 0-14-241412-3 pa

Based on Three cups of tea: one man's mission to fight terrorism and build nations one school at a time, published 2006 by Viking for adults

"In 1993, while climbing one of the world's most difficult peaks, Mortenson became lost and ill, and eventually found aid in the tiny Pakistani village of Korphe. He vowed to repay his generous hosts by building a school; his efforts have grown into the Central Asia Institute. . . . Retold for middle readers, the story remains inspirational and compelling. . . . Illustrated throughout with b&w photos, it also contains two eight-page insets of color photos." Publ Wkly

371.826

Cahill, Sean

LGBT youth in America's schools; Jason Cianciotto and Sean Cahill. The University of Michigan Press 2012 236 p. (pbk. : alk. paper) $30

Grades: Adult Professional   **371.826**

1. Bullies 2. Gay youth 3. Discrimination 4. Schools -- Administration 5. Gay students -- United States 6. Sexual minorities -- Education 7. Lesbian students -- United States 8. Bisexual students -- United States 9. Homosexuality and education -- United States 10. Transgender youth -- Education -- United States
ISBN 0472031406; 9780472028320; 9780472031405; 9780472118229

               LC 2011045478

In this book, "[Jason] Cianciotto and [Sean] Cahill use statistics and real-life anecdotes to show the pervasiveness of gender- and sexual orientation-based harassment in American schools, and argue for institutional reform and policy changes. . . . [R]esearch shows that . . . more young people are coming out . . . while still technically a minor, and thus subject to the rules of their educational institutions, and increasingly the abuse of their peers, teachers, and school administrators." (Publishers Weekly)

Includes bibliographical references and index.

371.9 Special education

Brinkerhoff, Shirley

Why can't I learn like everyone else? youth with learning disabilities. by Shirley Brinkerhoff. Mason Crest Publishers 2004 127p il (Youth with special needs) $24.95; pa $14.95

Grades: 5 6 7 8   **371.9**

1. Learning disabilities 2. Learning disabled youth -- Education -- United States
ISBN 1-59084-730-X; 1-42220-432-0 pa

               LC 2003-18438

"Charlie Begay, an eighth-grade Navajo student in New Mexico who cannot read due to dyslexia, describes his personal journey of embarrassment, frustration, and low self-esteem. Following the fictional narrative is factual material about learning disabilities, covering terminology, possible signs, diagnosis, the law, coping strategies, and success stories." SLJ

Includes bibliographical references

Kent, Deborah

Athletes with disabilities. Watts 2003 63p il (Watts library) hardcover o.p. lib bdg $24

Grades: 4 5 6 7   **371.9**

1. Athletes 2. Sports for the handicapped 3. People with disabilities 4. Sports for people with disabilities 5. Athletes with disabilities -- Biography
ISBN 0-531-12019-8 lib bdg; 0-531-16664-3 pa

               LC 2002-8883

Explores the people and events involved in sports competitions for people with disabilities and discusses people with disabilities who play professional sports

"Information is effectively conveyed through clear, straightforward prose and accounts of individual athletes. . . . [This is] informative, often inspirational and thought-provoking." Booklist

Includes bibliographical references

Paquette, Penny Hutchins

★ **Learning** disabilities; the ultimate teen guide. [by] Penny Hutchins Paquette, Cheryl Gerson Tuttle. Scarecrow Press 2003 301p il (It happened to me) lib bdg $32.50; pa $17.95

Grades: 7 8 9 10   **371.9**

1. Learning disabilities   2. Learning disabilities -- Handbooks, manuals, etc 3. Learning disabled teenagers -- Education -- United States -- Handbooks, manuals, etc
ISBN 0-8108-4261-0 lib bdg; 0-8108-5643-3 pa
LC 2002-17588

"Far more detailed than similiar books from other publishers." Voice Youth Advocates

Includes bibliographical references

Parks, Peggy J., 1951-

Learning disabilities. ReferencePoint Press 2009 96p il (Compact research. Diseases and disorders) lib bdg $25.95

Grades: 7 8 9 10   **371.9**

1. Learning disabilities
ISBN 978-1-60152-077-7; 1-60152-077-8
LC 2009-13445

"Parks explains what learning disabilities are and discusses the causes and overcoming them. The book's strength is that it explains how learning disabilities differ from other types of disorders. . . . Teens will find the overall organization of [this] succinct and easy-to-read [book] useful and attractive." SLJ

Includes bibliographical references

Stanley, Jerry

Children of the Dust Bowl; the true story of the school at Weedpatch Camp. Crown 1992 85p il map hardcover o.p. pa $9.95

Grades: 5 6 7 8   **371.9**

1. Migrant labor   2. Great Depression, 1929-1939   3. Education -- Social aspects
ISBN 0-517-88094-6; 0-517-58782-3 pa
LC 92-393

Describes the plight of the migrant workers who traveled from the Dust Bowl to California during the Depression and were forced to live in a federal labor camp and discusses the school that was built for their children

"Stanley's text is a compelling document. . . . The story is inspiring and disturbing, and Stanley has recorded the details with passion and dignity." Booklist

Includes bibliographical references

371.91   Students with physical disabilities

Hauser, Peter C.

★ **How** deaf children learn; what parents and teachers need to know. Marc Marschark Peter C. Hauser. Oxford University Press 2012 156 p. $26.50

Grades: Adult Professional   **371.91**

1. Teaching 2. Deaf children 3. Elementary education 4. Deaf -- Education 5. Deaf -- Means of communication
ISBN 0195389751; 9780195389753
LC 2011012553

This book is "about teaching deaf children. Written primarily for parents and teachers of deaf or hard-of-hearing children, this work covers general information about their education, gives insights into their cognitive development, and provides steps to their school success. The authors also discuss issues such as the value of cochlear implants and the debate over signing vs. speaking." (Library Journal)

Includes bibliographical references.

371.95   Gifted students

Karnes, Frances A.

★ **Competitions** for talented kids; win scholarships, big prize money, and recognition. [by] Frances A. Karnes & Tracy L. Riley. Prufrock Press 2005 245p pa $17.95

Grades: 7 8 9 10 11 12   **371.95**

1. Contests 2. Gifted children
ISBN 1-59363-156-1

"Featuring more than 140 competitions focused on a wide range of academic subjects, studio arts, performing arts, leadership, and service learning, this volume encourages students to seek scholarships, prize money, and recognition for their talents." Booklist

Includes bibliographical references

372   Specific levels of education

Brooks-Young, Susan

Teaching with the tools kids really use; learning with Web and mobile technologies. Corwin 2010 137p pa $26.95

Grades: Adult Professional   **372**

1. Web 2.0 2. Teachers -- Training
ISBN 978-1-4129-7275-8 pa; 1-4129-7275-2 pa
LC 2009-43856

"In this book, we see how technology can be used, but we also see the reponsiblity of the educator to make sure it is done appropriately, so 21st-century skills are addressed. The author addresses technologies and applications, and also discusses their ethical uses and how to think ahead to make adjustments for the future. . . . This book will be incredibly useful for those who are unsure about Web 2.0 tools, want to explore their possibilities, and would like to educate themselves further about usage in their own schools." Libr Media Connect

Includes bibliographical references

Gates, Pamela

Cultural Journeys; Multicultural Literature for Elementary and Middle School Students. Rowman & Littlefield Pub Inc 2010 258 p. (paperback) $29.95

Grades: Adult Professional **372**
1. Best books 2. Multicultural literature
ISBN 144220687X; 9781442206878

This book looks at multicultural literature for elementary and middle school students. The first chapter asks "the question of 'why.' Why use multicultural literature? . . . The 'why' is further developed as the chapter continues with a definition of multicultural literature." The seventh chapter looks at "works that challenge stereotypes and go beyond the common one-dimensional diversity theme." (Alberta Journal of Educational Research)

Lukenbill, W. Bernard

Health information in a changing world; practical approaches for teachers, schools, and school librarians. [by] W. Bernard Lukenbill and Barbara Froling Immroth. Libraries Unlimited 2010 244p il $45

Grades: Adult Professional **372**
1. Health education 2. Youth -- Health and hygiene 3. Health -- Information services
ISBN 978-1-59884-398-9; 1-59884-398-2
LC 2010-7505

"This is quite an impressive book and a real treasure for any professional involved with health education, whether for the classroom, public health, or personal counseling." Voice Youth Advocates
Includes bibliographical references

Mackey, Bonnie

A **librarian's** guide to cultivating an elementary school garden; [by] Bonnie Mackey and Jennifer Mackey Stewart. Linworth Pub. 2009 124p il pa $39.95

Grades: Adult Professional **372**
1. Gardening 2. School libraries -- Activity projects
ISBN 978-1-58683-328-2 pa; 1-58683-328-6 pa
LC 2008-34963

"Its unusual topic makes this book a standout." Libr Media Connect
Includes bibliographical references

372.4 Reading

Bernadowski, Carianne

Research-based reading strategies in the library for adolescent learners; [by] Carianne Bernadowski and Patricia Liotta Kolencik. Libraries Unlimited 2010 108p il pa $40

Grades: Adult Professional **372.4**
1. Reading 2. School libraries
ISBN 978-1-58683-347-3; 1-58683-347-2
LC 2009-21198

"This book explains six proven strategies—question/answer, think-alouds, reciprocal teaching, anticipation guides,

questioning the author, and SQR3 (survey, question, read, recite, and review)—for reading comprehension and three strategies (Semantic Feature Analysis, word maps/journals, and Frayer Models/word sorts) for vocabulary building. . . . Although the strategies are standard approaches, weaving in librarian roles makes this book useful for librarians who serve teens." Booklist
Includes bibliographical references

Teaching literacy skills to adolescents using Coretta Scott King Award winners. Libraries Unlimited 2009 136p il pa $35

Grades: Adult Professional **372.4**
1. Coretta Scott King Award 2. African Americans in literature 3. Teenagers -- Books and reading
ISBN 978-1-58683-337-4; 1-58683-337-5
LC 2009-15279

"The book includes award-winning book selections and Coretta Scott King Honor Books. It is a showcase for African-American authors' works, and helps educators working with adolescent students and their reading needs. . . . Each chapter covers one title and contains an annotation, grade level discussion starters, writing prompts, pre-reading activities, literary strategies for reading, post-reading activities, additional information about the author, and additional resources. This book would be a great professional resource, and a must have for those educators that teach adolescents." Libr Media Connect
Includes bibliographical references

Moreillon, Judi

Collaborative strategies for teaching reading comprehension; maximizing your impact. [by] Judi Moreillon. American Library Association 2007 170p il $38

Grades: Adult Professional **372.4**
1. Reading comprehension
ISBN 978-0-8389-0929-4; 0-8389-0929-9
LC 2006036132

This "begins by emphasizing the importance of collaboration between classroom teachers and teacher-librarians. . . . The bulk of the book focuses on seven reading comprehension strategies and how to teach them. . . . Overall this book is a cut above other 'how-to' books with its plethora of suggestions and resources for teachers and librarians." Voice Youth Advocates
Includes glossary and bibliographical references

372.6 Language arts (Communication skills)

Cavanaugh, Terence W.

Bookmapping; lit trips and beyond. [by] Terence W. Cavanaugh, Jerome Burg. International Society for Technology in Education 2011 228p il pa $34.95

Grades: Adult Professional **372.6**
1. Audiovisual education 2. Literature -- Study and teaching 3. Maps -- Study and teaching -- Activities

and projects
ISBN 978-1-56484-283-1; 1-56484-283-5

LC 2010051664

This book "provides ideas on how teachers can use elements from different disciplines in their own classrooms. . . . Other information includes using Google Earth, sources for images, Bing maps, information on creating your own bookmaps, instruction for bookmaps done individually and in cooperation with another teacher's class or classes, how to set up mapping in the classroom, and exploring existing bookmaps available on the Web. . . . This book should be in the professional collection of every middle and high school library, preferably in every classroom." Voice Youth Advocates

Includes bibliographical references

Chatton, Barbara

Using poetry across the curriculum; learning to love language. 2nd ed; Libraries Unlimited 2010 241p pa $40

Grades: Adult Professional   **372.6**

1. Poetry -- Study and teaching
ISBN 978-1-59158-697-5; 1-59158-697-6

LC 2009-36711

First published 1993

"With the emphasis in most schools on improving literacy, fluency, and reading and writing test scores, this book is extremely valuable. Sections are divided into various curricula areas. Each section begins with the national standards for that discipline, then a few paragraphs explain how the poetry in the extensive listing can be used. . . . Because all teachers must incorporate writing into their teaching, having relevant poetry for their curriculum and ideas on how to use it, will make this book popular." Libr Media Connect

Includes bibliographical references

Hamilton, Martha

Children tell stories; teaching and using storytelling in the classroom. [by] Martha Hamilton and Mitch Weiss. 2nd ed.; Richard C. Owen Publishers 2005 xx, 264p il pa $29.95

Grades: Adult Professional   **372.6**

1. Storytelling
ISBN 978-1-57274-663-3 pa; 1-57274-663-7 pa

LC 2005021667

First published 1990

"Combining enthusiasm and inspiration with practical tips, handouts, and resources, Hamilton and Weiss offer a comprehensive second edition that will be useful to both novice and experienced tellers. . . . The accompanying high-quality DVD shows children and adults telling stories, gives Web links, and includes 25 stories to download and print." SLJ

Includes bibliographical references

Hopkins, Lee Bennett

★ **Pass** the poetry, please! 3rd ed; HarperCollins Pubs. 1998 277p $25; pa $5.99

Grades: Adult Professional   **372.6**

1. Poetry -- Study and teaching
ISBN 0-06-027746-7; 0-06-446199-8 pa

LC 98-19617

First published 1972
"This a must-purchase." SLJ
Includes bibliographical references

Hostmeyer, Phyllis

Storytelling and QAR strategies; [by] Phyllis Hostmeyer and Marilyn Adele Kinsella. Libraries Unlimited 2010 123p pa $30

Grades: Adult Professional   **372.6**

1. Storytelling
ISBN 978-1-59884-494-8 pa; 1-59884-494-6 pa; 978-1-59884-495-5 e-book

LC 2010036576

"The authors, both storytellers with backgrounds in education and library work, present 18 stories based on six aspects of character development. These selections, which include folktales, fables, and myths, are just right for youngsters in third through eighth grades. Each one is followed by telling tips, a story path, and questions using the QAR (Question-Answer Relationships) model." SLJ

Includes bibliographical references

Literacy development in the storytelling classroom; Sherry Norfolk, Jane Stenson, and Diane Williams, editors. Libraries Unlimited 2009 342p il $40

Grades: Adult Professional   **372.6**

1. Storytelling 2. Language arts
ISBN 978-1-59158-694-4; 1-59158-694-1

LC 2009-11550

"This excellent essay collection connects storytelling to music, poetry, art, social studies, math, science, and physical education and provides sample stories and hands-on lesson plans for preschool through middle school-plus classrooms. Opening articles use research and anecdotal experience to tell why a multiple sensory activity like storytelling trumps teach-to-the-test exercises. Chapters two through five present the 'how-to' and for each lesson, include the appropriate national standards met, objectives, materials, instructional plans, some adaptations, assessments, and bibliography. The extensive suggested resource section includes book, non-book, professional, and student materials. . . . It is a fascinating collection with useful, creative surprises for classrooms and library programs." Voice Youth Advocates

Includes bibliographical references

Miller, Donalyn

★ **The book** whisperer; awakening the inner reader in every child. [by] Donalyn Miller; foreword by Jeff Anderson. Jossey-Bass 2009 227p $24.95

Grades: Adult Professional   **372.6**

1. Books and reading
ISBN 978-0-4703-7227-2; 0-4703-7227-3

LC 2008055666

Donalyn Miller's approach to reading promotion "is simple yet provocative: affirm the reader in every student, allow students to choose their own books, carve out extra reading time, model authentic reading behaviors, discard time-worn reading assignments such as book reports and comprehension worksheets, and develop a classroom library filled with high-interest books. . . . Miller provides many tips for teachers and parents and includes a useful list of ultimate reading suggestions picked by her students. This outstanding contribution to the literature is highly recommended." Libr J

Includes bibliographical references

Monnin, Katie

Teaching graphic novels; practical strategies for the secondary ELA classroom. Maupin House Pub. 2010 xx, 236p il pa $24.95

Grades: Adult Professional   372.6

1. Literacy 2. Graphic novels -- Study and teaching 3. English language -- Study and teaching

ISBN 978-1-934338-40-7 pa; 1-934338-40-0 pa

LC 2009040723

"Responding to the growth of all forms of graphic novels and nonfiction, Monnin advocates using the material that students willingly read to improve literacy, not just in reading classrooms but also as part of the English/Language Arts curriculum. . . . The examples and book titles will be a help to teachers unfamiliar with graphic novels and suggestions for comparison units using a graphic novel with a traditional novel will support those more at ease with conventional selections. The appendixes alone are worth the cost of the book. This should be in the professional collections of all secondary school libraries." SLJ

Includes bibliographical references

Roth, Rita

The **story** road to literacy; [by] Rita Roth. Teacher Ideas Press 2006 176p il pa $30

Grades: Adult Professional   372.6

1. Immigrants 2. Language arts 3. Children of immigrants 4. English language -- Study and teaching 5. Children's reading -- Educational aspects 6. Children -- Reading -- Educational aspects

ISBN 1-59158-323-3

LC 2005030835

"Roth advances the idea that using traditional literature with students who are learning English will help them acquire critical communication skills while tying unfamiliar new places to familiar elements of their own heritages. The author provides practical, ready-to-use lesson plans, story samples, and suggested activities." SLJ

Includes bibliographical references

372.62   Written and spoken expression

★ **Breakfast** on Mars and 37 Other delectable Essays; Edited by Rebecca Stern and Brad Wolfe. Roaring Brook Press 2013 xii, 211p.p ill. (hardcover) $16.99

Grades: 6 7 8 9 10 11 12   372.62

1. American essays 2. Authorship -- Handbooks, manuals, etc. 3. Essay -- Authorship 4. English language -- Composition and exercises -- Study and teaching (Elementary) 5. English language -- Composition and exercises -- Study and teaching (Middle school)

ISBN 1596437375; 9781596437371

LC 2012040918

This book is a collection of essays meant for middle- and high-school students. "Thirty-eight short essays . . . come from Sloane Crosley, Sarah Prineas, Ned Vizzini,

Scott Westerfeld, Rita Williams-Garcia, and more. Assigned a genre (personal, persuasive, etc.) and topic ('What made your upbringing unique?' 'What makes someone or something "cool"?'), the contributors write essays [meant to] inspire and entertain." (Publishers Weekly)

"This handy volume fills a gap. Thirty-eight essays for young readers by contemporary writers demonstrate that "essays can be just as enjoyable to read as fiction"...An important collection that ought to become a staple in writing classes." Kirkus

Ellis, Sarah

From reader to writer; teaching writing through classic children's books. Douglas & McIntyre 2000 176p hardcover o.p. pa $14.95

Grades: Adult Professional   028

1. Poets 2. Artists 3. Authors 4. Novelists 5. Dramatists 6. Librarians 7. Theologians 8. Illustrators 9. Mathematicians 10. Creative writing 11. Children's literature 12. Editors 13. Essayists 14. Linguists 15. Satirists 16. Biographers 17. Philologists 18. Travel writers 19. Fantasy writers 20. Literary critics 21. Children's authors 22. Nonfiction writers 23. Writers on science 24. Short story writers 25. Young adult authors 26. Science fiction writers 27. Children -- Books and reading 28. Rhetoric -- Study and teaching 29. Children's literature -- Study and teaching

ISBN 0-88899-372-2; 0-88899-440-0 pa

The author discusses the work of seventeen British, Canadian and American authors of children's literature. "With each classic book, there's a 'sneak preview' (i.e., booktalk), a suggested read-aloud, exercises to help students and adult writers find their own stories, and a short annotated bibliography of related children's books." Booklist

372.63   Spelling and handwriting

Cunha, Stephen F.

How to ace the National Geographic Bee; official study guide. by Stephen F. Cunha. 4th ed. National Geographic 2012 127 p. ill., maps (library) $18.90; (paperback) $9.95

Grades: 4 5 6 7 8   372.63

1. Maps 2. Geography 3. Examinations -- Study guides 4. Contests 5. Geography -- Competitions 6. School contests -- United States 7. Geography -- Competitions -- United States

ISBN 1426309856; 1426309864; 9781426309854; 9781426309861

LC 2012419185

This book "is a study guide to prepare the reader for test questions in geographic trivia. . . . The book then separates into six distinct chapters. It begins with defining geography and giving the reader an overall understanding of how the bee is conducted. Chapter 3 . . . defines the various types of maps and how they should be interpreted and also explains map features and landforms." (Voice of Youth Advocates)

Includes bibliographical references (p. 109-117).

372.64   Literature appreciation

Pellowski, Anne

The **storytelling** handbook; a young people's collection of unusual tales and helpful hints on how to tell them. illustrated by Martha Stoberock. Simon & Schuster Bks. for Young Readers 1995 129p il hardcover o.p. pa $7.99

Grades: Adult Professional   **372.64**
1. Storytelling
ISBN 0-689-80311-7; 978-1-4169-7598-4 pa; 1-4169-7598-5 pa

LC 95-2991

This work "addresses the young person who wants to tell stories in a public setting. It is similar in format to many adult books on storytelling how-tos, with sections on getting started and selecting and preparing stories, as well as a selection of sample tales. Pellowski's notes are extensive and will be very useful to novices looking for ways to research stories." Booklist

Includes bibliographical references

373   Secondary education

Somerlott, Robert

The **Little** Rock school desegregation crisis in American history. Enslow Pubs. 2001 128p il (In American history) lib bdg $26.60

Grades: 7 8 9 10   **373**
1. School integration 2. Segregation in education 3. African Americans -- Education 4. School integration -- Arkansas -- Little Rock -- History -- 20th century 5. Afro-American students -- Arkansas -- Little Rock -- History -- 20th century 6. Afro-Americans -- Civil rights -- Arkansas -- Little Rock -- History -- 20th century
ISBN 0-7660-1298-0

LC 00-11444

This book discusses the desegregation of Central High School in Little Rock Arkansas in 1957

This is a "well-researched and well-documented account. . . . Somerlott clearly captures the courage of the students and their families in the face of violent threats. He also presents a broader view of the impact of this event on the city of Little Rock, the state of Arkansas, and the nation." SLJ

Includes bibliographical references

373.1   Organization and activities in secondary education

Braun, Linda W.

★ **Teens,** technology, and literacy; or, Why bad grammar isn't always bad. Libraries Unlimited 2007 105p il pa $30

Grades: Adult Professional   **373.1**
1. Literacy 2. Information technology 3. Bibliographic instruction 4. Computer-assisted instruction 5. Social networks 6. Teenagers -- Books and reading 7. Microcomputers -- Children's use 8. Information

retrieval -- Social aspects
ISBN 1-59158-368-3; 978-1-59158-368-4

LC 2006-31714

"Braun shows teachers, administrators, and librarians how to incorporate today's technologies into the development of literacy skills. The author backs up the grammar used in IMs and text messaging by explaining how these technologies promote better literacy in the classroom. . . . This book is a must for most collections." SLJ

Includes bibliographical references

Elliott, Kathleen

How to prepare for the SSAT/ISEE, Secondary School Admissions Test/Independent School Entrance Exam. Barron's 2005 358p pa $16.95

Grades: 6 7 8 9   **373.1**
1. High schools -- Entrance requirements
ISBN 0-76412-900-7 pa; 978-0-76412-900-1 pa

LC 2004061121

This "manual prepares students to pass either the Secondary School Admissions Test or the Independent School Entrance Exam, tests that are nationally administered as admission requirements by many private secondary schools. Students will find practice and review exercises in verbal skills, reading comprehension, analogies, essay writing, and mathematics, with review material designed to help students pinpoint areas where they need more intensive study. Two practice SSAT exams and two practice ISEE exams are included." Publisher's note

Erlbach, Arlene

The **middle** school survival guide; illustrations by Helen Flook. Walker & Co. 2003 150p il pa $8.95

Grades: 5 6 7 8   **373.1**
1. Schools 2. Teenagers 3. Life skills 4. Middle schools 5. Adolescent psychology 6. Preteens -- Life skills guides 7. Teenagers -- Life skills guides 8. Middle school students -- Life skills guides
ISBN 0-8027-8852-1

LC 2002-34784

A guidebook to help deal with changes in school, families, social lives, and bodies that come during the middle school years, with specific advice for a variety of situations

"Erlbach's advice is sound, but the real gems are the quotes from kids. There are some explicit content and frank discussion, with Erlbach using the same no-nonsense language whether covering drugs, sexual harassment, crushes, cheating, oral sex, or pregnancy. . . . Strong, and well-delivered, often necessary medicine." Booklist

Gagliardi, Tina

★ **School** survival; keeping your cool at school. ABDO Pub. Co. 2009 112p il (Essential health: strong, beautiful girls) lib bdg $22.95

Grades: 6 7 8 9   **373.1**
1. Education -- Social aspects
ISBN 978-1-60453-104-6 lib bdg; 1-60453-104-5 lib bdg

LC 2008-11904

This features fictional narratives paired with firsthand advice from a licensed psychologist to help preteen and teen girls find new ways to face everyday challenges at school. Situations include handling test anxiety, and dealing with bullies.

"The topics are well selected, the design is attractive, and the stories feature girls from a variety of cultures." Booklist

Includes glossary and bibliographical references

Glasser, Debbie

New kid, new scene; a guide to moving and switching schools. by Debbie Glasser and Emily Schenck. Magination Press 2012 112p il $14.95; pa 9.95

Grades: 5 6 7 8   373.1

1. Moving 2. Students

ISBN 978-1-4338-1039-8; 1-4338-1039-5; 978-1-4338-1038-1 pa; 1-4338-1038-7 pa

LC 2011013608

"Students making the transition to new schools, new communities, or new homes will always experience a bit of anxiety, and this self-help book offers practical advice on how to make those changes smoother. The ideas and suggestions are sound and practical. . . . The eye-catching layout will keep students flipping through the pages." SLJ

Katz, Eric D.

High school's not forever; [by] Jane Bluestein and Eric Katz. HCI Teens 2005 302p il pa $12.95

Grades: 7 8 9 10 11 12   373.1

1. High school students

ISBN 0-7573-0256-4

LC 2005-50232

"Culled from the responses of some 2000 high and post-high school students, this title gives voice to young people who have lived through the experience and who offer both affirming and cautionary tales as they attempted to navigate the uncertain seas of friendship, depression, academic achievement, drugs, and sexuality. . . . There is no question that this book will enhance most YA collections." SLJ

Includes bibliographical references

Serritella, Judy

Look again! appealing bulletin board ideas for secondary students. Linworth Pub. 2002 160p pa $36.95

Grades: Adult Professional   373.1

1. Bulletin boards 2. Bulletin boards in libraries 3. Teenagers -- Books and reading 4. High school students -- Books and reading

ISBN 1-58683-053-8

LC 2002-16181

"Basic practical tips suggest ways to liven up board displays, for example, by using three-dimensional materials such as corrugated cardboard or wallpaper. Ideas focus on providing students with information they need, as well as on promoting reading and library services." Book Rep

Includes bibliographical references

375   Curricula

Bishop, Kay

Connecting libraries with classrooms; the curricular roles of the media specialist. 2nd. ed.; Linworth 2011 122p pa $45

Grades: Adult Professional   375

1. Librarians 2. School libraries 3. Instructional materials centers

ISBN 978-1-59884-599-0; 1-59884-599-3

LC 2010051623

This book provides an . . . exploration of the topics that are currently relevant in K-12 curricula, including the school librarian's role in dealing with these issues, collaborating with teachers, and connecting to classrooms.

"Kay Bishop's book covers a wide range of topics and issues within the school library field. . . . Collaborative planning between classroom teacher, principal, students, and the community is also addressed. This material will be a welcome addition to the Library Media Specialist's arsenal of resources to stay current and involved." Libr Media Connect

Includes bibliographical references

Nichols, Beverly

Managing curriculum and assessment; a practitioner's guide. [by] Beverly Nichols . . . [et al.] Linworth Publishing 2006 170p pa $49.95

Grades: Adult Professional   375

1. Evaluation 2. Education -- Curricula

ISBN 1-58683-216-6

LC 2006003202

"This is a guide by practitioners who give advice on how to respond to the laws and requirements of No Child Left Behind. It is an invaluable resource that provides new insights. . . . There are three sections to the guide with an accompanying CD that contains everything in the book and more. . . . This guide is loaded with examples and is a must have for your professional library." Libr Media Connect

Includes bibliographical references

379   Public policy issues in education

Magoon, Kekla

Today the world is watching you; the Little Rock Nine and the fight for school integration, 1957. Twenty-First Century Books 2011 160p il map lib bdg $38.60

Grades: 6 7 8 9   379

1. School integration 2. Segregation in education 3. African Americans -- Education

ISBN 978-0-7613-5767-4; 0-7613-5767-X

LC 2010028443

On September 4, 1957, nine African American teenagers made their way toward Central High School in Little Rock, Arkansas. Armed soldiers of the Arkansas National Guard blocked most of them at the edge of campus. The three students who did make it onto campus faced an angry mob. But the U.S. Supreme Court had ruled in 1955 that school segregation—that is, separate schools for black children and white children—was unconstitutional.

"Well-paced and engaging, the book is broken up into manageable chapters and gives background information on racial tensions in America starting with slavery. The information is carefully documented. . . . Black-and-white photographs and text boxes give additional information and context. . . . An ideal purchase for research purposes." SLJ

Includes glossary and bibliographical references

Miller, Mara

School desegregation and the story of the Little Rock Nine; [by] Mara Miller. Enslow Publishers 2008 128p il map (From many cultures, one history) lib bdg $31.93

Grades: 6 7 8 9   379

1. School integration 2. Segregation in education 3. African Americans -- Education

ISBN 978-0-7660-2835-7; 0-7660-2835-6 lib bdg

LC 2007023376

"Through the 1950s, segregation was a way of life in the Deep South. But in 1957, after the U.S. Supreme Court ruling in the case of Brown v. Board of Education, nine courageous African-American students, the Little Rock Nine, prepared to integrate Central High School in Little Rock, Arkansas." Publisher's note

Includes glossary and bibliographical references

Sharp, Anne Wallace

Separate but equal; the desegregation of America's schools. [by] Anne Wallace Sharp. Lucent Books 2007 104p il (Lucent library of black history) $28.70

Grades: 7 8 9 10   379

1. School integration 2. Segregation in education 3. African Americans -- Education

ISBN 1-59018-953-1; 978-1-59018-953-5

LC 2006008269

"This simple and direct overview begins with the ban against educating slaves and the efforts of Prudence Crandall to provide black girls with schooling in Connecticut in 1832. Following a history of segregation, the major battles to desegregate public schools in the North and in the South, as well as those to desegregate universities and colleges, are highlighted. The violent white backlash that occurred in both Southern and Northern states in the 1960s and '70s is also covered." SLJ

Includes bibliographical references

Stokes, John

★ Students on strike; Jim Crow, civil rights, Brown, and me; a memoir. by John A. Stokes with Lois Wolfe, and Herman J. Viola. National Geographic 2008 127p il $15.95; lib bdg $23.90

Grades: 4 5 6 7   379

1. Segregation in education 2. African Americans -- Education

ISBN 978-1-4263-0153-7; 1-4263-0153-7; 978-1-4263-0154-4 lib bdg; 1-4263-0154-5 lib bdg

"In 1951, a group of African-American high school students in Prince Edward County, VA, went on strike to protest the substandard conditions in their segregated schools. They eventually became plaintiffs in a lawsuit that was one of the

five that were part of the 1954 Brown decision . . . Fear of retribution and lingering bitterness has kept the strike leaders silent, but Stokes, who was among them, has decided that the story of the strike and its aftermath need to be told. . . . Stoke's inspiring story reveals an almost completely unreported part of one of the most important court cases of the 20th century." SLJ

Tougas, Shelley

★ Little Rock girl 1957; how a photograph changed the fight for integration. Compass Point Books 2011 64p il (Captured history) lib bdg $33.99; pa $8.95

Grades: 6 7 8 9   379

1. Students 2. School integration 3. Documentary photography 4. Segregation in education 5. Photojournalists 6. African Americans -- Education

ISBN 978-0-7565-4440-9 lib bdg; 0-7565-4440-8; 978-0-7565-4512-3 pa; 0-7565-4512-9 pa

LC 2010054303

This explains how Will Counts' 1957 photograph of an African American student, Elizabeth Eckford, attempting to enter the all-white Central High School in Little Rock, Arkansas while surrounded by an angry mob, helped focus national attention on racial segregation.

This "is model nonfiction. . . . The design is fresh and inviting, the writing clear, and the back matter . . . is useful and extensive. An all-around winner." Booklist

Includes glossary and bibliographical references

Walker, Paul Robert

★ Remember Little Rock; the time, the people, the stories. by Paul Robert Walker. National Geographic 2008 61p il map $17.95; lib bdg $27.90

Grades: 5 6 7 8 9   379

1. School integration 2. Segregation in education 3. African Americans -- Education

ISBN 978-1-4263-0402-6; 1-4263-0402-1; 978-1-4263-0403-3 lib bdg; 1-4263-0403-X lib bdg

LC 2008-24959

"The story of the battle to integrate Central High School in 1957 Little Rock, Arkansas, is presented through photographs and firsthand accounts from those who were there. . . . The multitude of eyewitness accounts, the poignant photographs, and the contextual background make this text a must-have addition to any classroom or library." Voice Youth Advocates

Includes bibliographical references

379.2   Specific policy issues in public education

Aretha, David

With all deliberate speed; court-ordered busing and American schools. David Aretha. Morgan Reynolds Pub. 2012 128 p. ill. (some col.) (The civil rights movement) (lib. bdg.) $28.95

Grades: 7 8 9 10   379.2

1. School integration 2. Busing (School integration) 3. Boston (Mass.) -- Race relations 4. Busing for school integration 5. School integration -- History 6. Busing

for school integration -- History 7. School integration -- United States -- History 8. Busing for school integration -- United States -- History
ISBN 1599351811; 1599352176; 9781599351810; 9781599352176

LC 2011019530

This book, part of the "Civil Rights Movement" series, "details the slow, painful, unpopular, and often ineffective process of integrating public schools by busing students outside their neighborhoods in the decades following the 1954 landmark Brown v. Board of Education decision. In addition to a detailed account of experiences in Boston, [David] Aretha includes specific information on busing in numerous large and small metropolitan areas around the country." (Booklist)

Includes bibliographical references (p. 122-124) and index

381   Commerce (Trade)

Freese, Susan M.
Craigslist; the company and its founder. ABDO Pub. Co. 2011 112p il (Technology pioneers) lib bdg $34.22

Grades: 5 6 7 8   **381**
1. Advertising 2. Businessmen 3. Internet marketing 4. Online social networks 5. Webmasters 6. Software engineers
ISBN 978-1-61714-806-4 lib bdg; 1-61714-806-7 lib bdg; 978-1-61758-964-5 e-book

LC 2010042448

This is an introduction to Craigslist and its founder, Craig Newmark.

"Written in a clear, linear fashion, this series offers vivid, well-researched details about the development of technological advancements considered essential in today's society. . . . Readers who are interested in technology and inventions will be thoroughly engrossed." SLJ

Includes glossary and bibliographical references

Gilbert, Sara
The **story** of Wal-Mart. Creative Education 2011 48p il (Built for success) lib bdg $23.95

Grades: 6 7 8 9   **381**
1. Retail trade 2. Retail executives
ISBN 978-1-60818-064-6; 1-60818-064-6

LC 2010031370

A look at the origins, leaders, growth, and operations of Wal-Mart, the discount retailing company whose first store opened in 1962 and which today is one of the largest corporations in the world.

This book is "written in a lively style, yet with a minimum of fuss. . . . The slim, gleaming format, well-chosen photos, and the effort to explore what makes a company successful today [makes this title] unique." Booklist

Includes bibliographical references

★ The **story** of eBay. Creative Education 2011 46p il (Built for success) $23.95

Grades: 6 7 8 9   **381**
1. Corporations
ISBN 978-1-60818-062-2; 1-60818-062-X

LC 2010031226

A look at the origins, leaders, growth, and holdings of eBay, the online auction and shopping company that was founded in 1995 and today sells a multitude of collectibles and other consumer products.

This book is "written in a lively style, yet with a minimum of fuss. . . . The slim, gleaming format, well-chosen photos, and the effort to explore what makes a company successful today [makes this title] unique." Booklist

Includes bibliographical references

382   International commerce (Foreign trade)

Gifford, Clive
The **arms** trade. Chrysalis Education 2004 61p il (World issues) $29.95

Grades: 7 8 9 10   **382**
1. Defense industry 2. Firearms industry
ISBN 1-59389-154-7
"This book packs in copious information from a well-rounded perspective. . . . Very effective color photos . . . add a startling and engrossing element." Booklist

Includes glossary and bibliographical references

Major, John S.
The **Silk** Route; 7,000 miles of history. illustrated by Stephen Fieser. HarperCollins Pubs. 1995 32p il maps hardcover o.p. pa $6.99

Grades: 4 5 6 7   **382**
1. Trade routes
ISBN 0-06-443468-0

LC 92-38169

"The pictures and short segments make the book a teaching tool as well as a resource when learning about China and its silk industry." Child Book Rev Serv

384   Communications

Henderson, Harry
★ **Communications** and broadcasting; from wired words to wireless Web. rev ed.; Facts on File 2006 201p il (Milestones in discovery and invention) $35

Grades: 7 8 9 10 11 12   **384**
1. Telecommunication
ISBN 0-8160-5748-6; 978-0-8160-5748-1

LC 2006-5577

First published 1997

This is a "look at the development and interconnection of [the following] scientific ideas: electromagnetism, leading to the telegraph and telephone; Maxwell's wave theory, leading to radio and television; and communications and information theory, from Claude Shannon to the World Wide Web and beyond. In addition, there are . . . portraits of the inventors themselves." Publisher's note

Includes glossary and bibliographical references

384.5   Wireless communication

Byers, Ann

Communications satellites. Rosen Pub. Group 2003 58p il (Library of satellites) lib bdg $26.50

Grades: 4 5 6 7   384.5

    1. Artificial satellites in telecommunication

    ISBN 0-8239-3851-4

LC 2002-7527

This discusses the history, development, and applications of communications satellites

"Clear and topical photographs enliven the [presentation]. While packed with information, the [text is] easy to read." SLJ

Includes bibliographical references

385   Railroad transportation

Gimpel, Diane

The **transcontinental** railroad. ABDO Pub. Co. 2011 112p il (Essential events) lib bdg $23.95

Grades: 7 8 9 10 11 12   385

    1. Railroads -- History

    ISBN 978-1-61714-768-5; 1-61714-768-0

LC 2010044830

Describes how and why the Transcontinental Railroad was built and tells how it affected the westward expansion of settlers.

Includes glossary and bibliographical references

Landau, Elaine

The **transcontinental** railroad; [by] Elaine Landau. Franklin Watts 2005 63p il (Watts library) $25.50

Grades: 5 6 7 8   385

    1. Frontier and pioneer life 2. Railroads -- History

    ISBN 0-531-12326-X

LC 2005000914

"Landau describes how people traveled prior to the building of the railroads and how the concept of Manifest Destiny influenced the development of the railroads. . . . Black-and-white and color illustrations, maps, sidebars, and time lines enhance the well-organized [text]." SLJ

Includes bibliographical references

McMahon, Peter

Ultimate trains. Kids Can Press 2010 40p il (Machines of the future) $16.95

Grades: 4 5 6 7   385

    1. Railroads 2. Science -- Experiments

    ISBN 978-1-55453-366-4; 1-55453-366-X

"In simple engaging text and illustrations, McMahon and Mora present a brief history of [railroads]. Integral to the book are five experiments children can create. . . . Each experiment ties in well with a particular type of train, features clear instructions, and offers safety precautions." Booklist

Includes glossary

Murphy, Jim

★ **Across** America on an emigrant train. Clarion Bks. 1993 150p il hardcover o.p. pa $10.95

Grades: 5 6 7 8   385

    1. Poets 2. Authors 3. Novelists 4. Authors, Scottish 5. Essayists 6. Travel writers 7. Short story writers 8. Railroads -- History 9. Railroads -- United States 10. United States -- Description   11. United States -- Immigration and emigration

    ISBN 0-395-63390-7; 0-395-76483-1 pa

LC 92-38650

"Murphy presents a forthright and thoroughly engrossing history of the transcontinental railway, with entries from Robert Louis Stevenson's 1879 journal as he rode cross country. It's also an inviting introduction to Stevenson, with a romance in the bargain." SLJ

Includes bibliographical references

Renehan, Edward J.

The **Transcontinental** Railroad; the gateway to the West. [by] Edward J. Renehan, Jr. Chelsea House 2007 120p il (Milestones in American history) lib bdg $35

Grades: 7 8 9 10   385

    1. Railroads -- History

    ISBN 0-7910-9351-4 lib bdg; 978-0-7910-9351-1 lib bdg

LC 2006-38870

This history of the transcontinental railroad is "accessible, lively. . . . Many quotations, sidebars, art reproductions, and maps support the [text]. Excerpts from primary source materials also help give readers a sense of time and place." Horn Book Guide

Includes bibliographical references

Zimmermann, Karl R.

★ **All** aboard! passenger trains around the world. [by] Karl Zimmermann; photography by the author. Boyds Mills Press 2006 48p il $19.95

Grades: 5 6 7 8   385

    1. Railroads 2. Railroads -- Passenger-cars

    ISBN 1-59078-325-5

LC 2005-24990

Zimmermann "has traveled by train across six continents, and his beautiful, big color photos appear on every double-page spread of this enthusiastic account, which blends history, geography, business, and engineering with his personal focus." Booklist

★ **Steam** locomotives; whistling, chugging, smoking iron horses of the past. Boyds Mills Press 2004 48p il $19.95

Grades: 4 5 6 7   385

    1. Locomotives 2. Steam engines

    ISBN 1-59078-165-1

"In this photo-essay, Zimmermann shares his excitement for steam locomotives with young readers, tracing the development of the early engines and their impact on the history of the U.S. He includes a clear explanation . . . of how a steam engine works. The photographs, some archival and some from the present day, are excellent. . . . The engaging text clearly imparts the author's enthusiasm and love for the subject." SLJ

Includes glossary

386   Inland waterway and ferry transportation

Bial, Raymond

The **canals**. Benchmark Bks. 2002 56p il map (Building America) lib bdg $27.07

Grades: 6 7 8 9   **386**

1. Canals 2. Canals -- United States

ISBN 0-7614-1336-7

LC 00-65078

This describes the history of canals in America from colonial times to the 19th century

This book is "marked by strong research, clear writing, good organization, and very handsome color photographs." Booklist

Includes glossary and bibliographical references

Coleman, Wim

The **amazing** Erie Canal and how a big ditch opened up the West; [by] Wim Coleman & Pat Perrin. MyReportLinks.com Books 2006 128p il map (The wild history of the American West) lib bdg $33.27

Grades: 6 7 8 9   **386**

1. Canals

ISBN 1-59845-017-4

LC 2005029389

This book "shares a brief, informative history of canals; the geographic need for the Erie Canal; and an explanation of how its creation impacted American commerce and history. . . . Throughout the text, illustrations of Web pages invite readers to search online for more detailed information. The book's text is clear, and the format is attractive, with excellent black-and-white photos and color illustrations on nearly every page." Booklist

Includes bibliographical references

Roop, Peter

River roads west; America's first highways. [by] Peter and Connie Roop. Calkins Creek 2007 64p il map $19.95

Grades: 6 7 8 9   **386**

1. Canals 2. Rivers 3. Transportation -- History

ISBN 1-59078-430-8; 978-1-59078-430-3

"The role of transportation in national history has seldom been more clearly delineated than in this meticulous treatment. Spanning prehistory to the 19th century, the sparkling text, inflected with wry humor, focuses sequentially on the Hudson River and Erie Canal, the Ohio, Mississippi, Missouri, Rio Grande, and the Colorado Rivers, and the Columbia River." SLJ

Includes bibliographical references

387.1   Ports

House, Katherine L.

Lighthouses for kids; history, science, and lore with 21 activities. [by] Katherine L. House. Chicago Review Press 2008 118p il pa $14.95

Grades: 4 5 6 7 8   **387.1**

1. Lighthouses

ISBN 978-1-55652-720-3 pa; 1-55652-720-9 pa

LC 2007-27093

"This book is noteworthy for the way in which the activities are related to the information in the text. . . . Readers learn about the challenges of building . . . [lighthouses], inventions to make them more reliable, and how lighthouses function as historical relics today." SLJ

Includes glossary and bibliographical references

387.2   Ships

Zimmermann, Karl R.

Ocean liners; crossing and cruising the seven seas. photographs by the author. Boyds Mills Press 2008 48p il $17.95

Grades: 5 6 7 8   **387.2**

1. Ocean liners 2. Ocean travel

ISBN 978-1-59078-552-2; 1-59078-552-5

LC 2007049323

This is "a comprehensive overview of ships from sail to steam to diesel, from the important modes of transportation to the modern resorts at sea. The information is organized in chapters about the history and development of the ships, the star ships of the Atlantic crossings and the conversion to modern cruising. . . . All is accompanied by photographs taken over the years by the author and supplemented by historic drawings, photos and documents. . . . A fascinating voyage." Kirkus

Includes glossary

387.7   Air transportation

Parker, Steve

By air. Marshall Cavendish Benchmark 2011 32p il (Future transport) $28.50

Grades: 4 5 6   **387.7**

1. Aeronautics 2. Forecasting

ISBN 1608707776; 9781608707775

LC 2011000998

"Beginning with a speculative illustration featuring people of the future traveling through the air in carlike personal jets, this title . . . offers a fascinating look at prototypes for all sorts of aircraft, from small planes to passenger airliners to lighter-than-air vehicles. . . . The various possibilities for future aircraft are covered in double-page spreads that are well laid out and easy to digest. Illustrated with plenty of striking, digitally enhanced color pictures, this will probably be of equal interest to those doing reports and browsers." Booklist

Includes bibliographical references

388 Transportation

Harris, Joseph
  Transportation; the impact of science and technology. Gareth Stevens Pub. 2010 64p il (Pros and cons) lib bdg $35
  Grades: 5 6 7 8   **388**
  1. Transportation 2. Transportation -- History
  ISBN 978-1-4339-1990-9 lib bdg; 1-4339-1990-7 lib bdg
                                    LC 2009-12437
  An "active layout that features color photographs, maps, graphs or charts on every spread, this . . . [book] has much to offer. . . . It conveniently outlines the range of views . . . helping students to learn how to view both sides of [the] issue[s]." SLJ
  Includes glossary and bibliographical references

Mulder, Michelle
  Pedal it! how bicycles are changing the world. Michelle Mulder. Orca Book Publishers 2013 48 p. (Footprints) (hardcover) $19.95
  Grades: 3 4 5 6 7 8   **388**
  1. Cycling 2. Bicycles
  ISBN 1459802195; 9781459802193
                                    LC 2012953464
  This book, by Michelle Mulder, "celebrates the humble bicycle--from the very first boneshakers to the sleek racing bikes of today, from handlebars to spokes to gear sprockets--and shows you why and how bikes can make the world a better place. Not only can bikes be used to power computers and generators, they can also reduce pollution, promote wellness and get a package across a crowded city--fast!" (Publisher's note)

388.4 Local transportation

Reis, Ronald A.
  The **New** York City subway system. Chelsea House 2009 136p il (Building America: then and now) lib bdg $35
  Grades: 6 7 8 9   **388.4**
  1. Subways 2. Transportation -- History
  ISBN 978-1-60413-046-1 lib bdg; 1-60413-046-6 lib bdg
                                    LC 2008-25550
  This is a history of New York City's subway system
  Includes glossary and bibliographical references

Sandler, Martin W.
  ★ **Secret** subway; the fascinating tale of an amazing feat of engineering. National Geographic 2009 96p il map $17.95; lib bdg $26.90
  Grades: 5 6 7 8   **388.4**
  1. Subways 2. Inventors 3. Magazine editors 4. Subways -- New York (N.Y.)
  ISBN 978-1-4263-0462-0; 1-4263-0462-5; 978-1-4263-0463-7 lib bdg; 1-4263-0463-3 lib bdg
                                    LC 2008-39831

"Sandler takes an in-depth look at the building of New York's first subway. . . . [He] writes about the subway in a well-put-together book with interesting information, great pictures, and a compelling true story." Voice Youth Advocates
  Includes bibliographical references

391 Customs

Bailey, Diane
  Tattoo art around the world. Rosen Pub. 2011 64p il (Tattooing) lib bdg $30.60; pa $12.95
  Grades: 7 8 9 10   **391**
  1. Tattooing
  ISBN 978-1-4488-4618-4 lib bdg; 1-4488-4618-8 lib bdg; 978-1-4488-4622-1 pa; 1-4488-4622-6 pa
                                    LC 2010048428
  This book "discusses how different cultures have used tattoos. . . . The design and the reading level are accessible without talking down to the audience, so this is a good choice for enticing reluctant readers with an interest in body art." Booklist
  Includes bibliographical references

Baker, Patricia
  Fashions of a decade, The 1940s. Chelsea House Publishers 2006 64p il $35
  Grades: 7 8 9 10 11 12   **391**
  1. Costume
  ISBN 0-8160-6720-1; 978-0-8160-6720-6
                                    LC 2006-49934
  First published 1992
  Chronicles clothing trends of the 1940s and the influence of World War II on styles of dress, availability of many fabrics, and the new ideas of "designers at war"
  Includes glossary and bibliographical references

  Fashions of a decade, The 1950s. Chelsea House Publishers 2006 64p il $35
  Grades: 7 8 9 10 11 12   **391**
  1. Costume
  ISBN 0-8160-6721-X; 978-0-8160-6721-3
                                    LC 2006-50142
  First published 1992
  Surveys the fads, fashions, trends, and cultural and intellectual preoccupations of the 1950s
  Includes glossary and bibliographical references

Behnke, Alison
  The **little** black dress and zoot suits; Depression and wartime fashions from the 1930s to 1950s. Twenty-First Century Books 2011 64p il (Dressing a nation: the history of U.S. fashion) $31.93
  Grades: 7 8 9 10   **391**
  1. Fashion 2. Clothing and dress
  ISBN 0-7613-5892-7; 978-0-7613-5892-3
                                    LC 2010035444
  This "covers a time of rapid change in the American fashion industry, from an era of frugal thriftiness necessary in the face of the Great Depression and WWII to one in-

formed by a brand-new youth culture, movie stars, and post-war leisure time. . . . There's plenty for fashion-savy readers to digest. . . . The book's sharp, bold, rather tidy design features eye-catching art from the period. . . . . [This is an] engaging title." Booklist

Includes bibliographical references

Bix, Cynthia Overbeck

Petticoats and frock coats; revolution and Victorian Age fashions from the 1770s to the 1860s. Twenty-First Century Books 2011 64p il (Dressing a nation: the history of U.S. fashion) lib bdg $31.93

Grades: 7 8 9 10   **391**

   1. Fashion 2. American national characteristics 3. Clothing and dress -- History

ISBN 978-0-7613-5888-6; 0-7613-5888-9

                            LC 2010053384

This is a history of fashion in the U.S. from the 1770s to the 1860s.

Includes bibliographical references

Bliss, John

Preening, painting, and piercing; body art. Raintree 2010 32p il (Culture in action) lib bdg $29

Grades: 5 6 7 8   **391**

   1. Body art 2. Cosmetics 3. Tattooing 4. Theatrical makeup

ISBN 978-1-4109-3924-1; 1-4109-3924-1

                            LC 2009051182

"This book covers different looks achieved through makeup, body painting, tattoos, and piercing. Photographs, advertisements, paintings, and artifacts show a variety of cultures and time periods and help readers see the huge changes in the fashion of physical appearance. . . . The author does a good job of explaining that some cultures have negative stereotypes of tattooed people being criminals and some piercing can be dangerous to people with allergies. Fun activities are included. . . . This book . . . is well written and has few biases." SLJ

Includes glossary and bibliographical references

Carnegy, Vicky

Fashions of a decade, The 1980s. Chelsea House Publishers 2006 64p il $35

Grades: 7 8 9 10 11 12   **391**

   1. Costume

ISBN 978-0-8160-6724-4; 0-8160-6724-4

                            LC 2006-49458

First published 1992

A pictorial survey chronicling the international clothing fashions of the 1980s

This "provides an accessible overview of the decade, placing fashion trends within their appropriate political and historical contexts. . . . Browsers and fashion design students alike will be intrigued." Booklist

Includes glossary and bibliographical references

Clancy Steer, Deirdre

The **1980s** and 1990s. Chelsea House 2009 64p il (Costume & fashion source books) $35

Grades: 6 7 8 9   **391**

   1. Costume -- History 2. Fashion -- History 3. Clothing and dress -- History

ISBN 978-1-60413-386-8; 1-60413-386-4

                            LC 2009-6700

This describes how gender, occasion, class, and social clime affected fashion during the 1980s and 1990s.

This is written "in a clear, engaging style. . . . [The] volume is profusely and gorgeously illustrated with period paintings and photographs, movie and TV stills, design sketches, and photographs from period reenactments. Each illustration is captioned with intriguing, relevant facts that enhance the text." SLJ

Includes glossary and bibliographical references

Connikie, Yvonne

Fashions of a decade, The 1960s. Chelsea House Publishers 2006 64p il $35

Grades: 7 8 9 10 11 12   **391**

   1. Costume

ISBN 0-8160-6722-8; 978-0-8160-6722-0

First published 1992

A pictorial survey chronicling the international fashions of the 1960s

This is "not for serious students of fashion, but will be fun for browsers and those interested in an introduction to the concept of clothing design in the context of contemporary events." SLJ

Includes glossary and bibliographical references

Costantino, Maria

Fashions of a decade, The 1930s. Chelsea House Publishers 2006 64p il $35

Grades: 7 8 9 10 11 12   **391**

   1. Costume

ISBN 0-8160-6719-8; 978-0-8160-6719-0

                            LC 2006-49933

First published 1992

Chronicles trends in 1930s styles such as lower hemlines and broader shoulders; the introduction of synthetic fabrics; and new views of fitness, health, and personal beauty

Includes glossary and bibliographical references

Elgin, Kathy

Elizabethan England. Chelsea House 2009 64p il (Costume & fashion source books) $35

Grades: 6 7 8 9   **391**

   1. Costume -- History 2. Fashion -- History 3. Clothing and dress -- History

ISBN 978-1-60413-379-0; 1-60413-379-1

                            LC 2008-47258

This describes how gender, occasion, class, and social clime affected fashion in Elizabethan England.

This is written "in a clear, engaging style. . . . [The] volume is profusely and gorgeously illustrated with period paintings and photographs, movie and TV stills, design sketches, and photographs from period reenactments. Each illustration is captioned with intriguing, relevant facts that enhance the text." SLJ

Includes glossary and bibliographical references

The **medieval** world. Chelsea House 2009 64p il (Costume & fashion source books) $35

Grades: 6 7 8 9   **391**

1. Medieval civilization 2. Costume -- History 3. Fashion -- History 4. Clothing and dress -- History

ISBN 978-1-60413-378-3; 1-60413-378-3

LC 2008-47259

This describes how gender, occasion, class, and social clime affected clothing and dress during the Middle Ages.

This is written "in a clear, engaging style. . . . [The] volume is profusely and gorgeously illustrated with period paintings and photographs, movie and TV stills, design sketches, and photographs from period reenactments. Each illustration is captioned with intriguing, relevant facts that enhance the text." SLJ

Includes glossary and bibliographical references

Gerber, Larry

Getting inked; what to expect when you get a tattoo. Rosen Pub. 2011 64p il (Tattooing) lib bdg $30.60; pa $12.95

Grades: 7 8 9 10   **391**

1. Tattooing

ISBN 978-1-4488-4616-0 lib bdg; 978-1-4488-4621-4 pa

LC 2010045970

This book "details how to find a competent tattoo artist, what the inking process is like, and how to care for the tattoo afterward. . . . Illustrations . . . are of high quality. . . . The design and the reading level are accessible without talking down to the audience, so this is a good choice for enticing reluctant readers with an interest in body art." Booklist

Includes bibliographical references

Graydon, Shari

In your face; the culture of beauty and you. Annick 2004 176p il hardcover o.p. pa $14.95

Grades: 7 8 9 10   **391**

1. Body image 2. Personal appearance

ISBN 1-55037-857-0; 1-55037-856-2 pa

The author "looks at fashion across time and cultures, and analyzes the underlying messages in today's focus . . . on thinness, long nails, and high heels. Along the way, she warns both young men and women of the very real dangers of eating disorders, plastic surgery, liposuction, and other body-image 'solutions.' . . . Graydon will make readers laugh as well as think about the issues." Booklist

Includes bibliographical references

Havelin, Kate

Buckskin dresses and pumpkin breeches; colonial fashions from the 1580s to 1760s. Twenty-First Century Books 2011 64p il (Dressing a nation: the history of U.S. fashion) lib bdg $31.93

Grades: 7 8 9 10   **391**

1. Native Americans -- History 2. Clothing and dress -- History

ISBN 978-0-7613-5887-9; 0-7613-5887-0

LC 2011001176

This is a history of Colonial U.S. fashion from 1580s to 1760s.

Includes bibliographical references

Hoopskirts, Union blues, and Confederate grays; Civil War fashions from 1861 to 1865. Twenty-First Century Books 2011 64p il (Dressing a nation: the history of U.S. fashion) lib bdg $31.93

Grades: 7 8 9 10   **391**

1. Fashion 2. Clothing and dress -- History

ISBN 978-0-7613-5889-3; 0-7613-5889-7

LC 2010048808

This is a history of fashion in the U.S. from 1861 to 1865.

Includes bibliographical references

Herald, Jacqueline

Fashions of a decade, The 1920s. Chelsea House Publishers 2006 64p il $35

Grades: 7 8 9 10 11 12   **391**

1. Costume

ISBN 0-8160-6718-X; 978-0-8160-6718-3

LC 2006-49932

First published 1992

Surveys the fads, fashions, trends, and cultural and intellectual preoccupations of the 1920s

"Students interested in fashion and societal changes, as well as those in need of a good outline reference, will find this volume . . . helpful." Booklist

Includes glossary and bibliographical references

Fashions of a decade, The 1970s. Chelsea House Publishers 2006 64p il $35

Grades: 7 8 9 10 11 12   **391**

1. Costume

ISBN 0-8160-6723-6; 978-0-8160-6723-7

LC 2006-46807

First published 1992

This volume in the series looks at how the fashions of the 1970s reflected the social, historical and cultural events of that decade

This "includes chapters on 'Black is Beautiful,' 'Dressed to Clash,' 'Trash Culture,' etc. . . . An abundance of full-color and black-and-white illustrations and photographs amplify the text with generally appropriate placement and captions." SLJ

Includes glossary and bibliographical references

Krohn, Katherine E.

Calico dresses and buffalo robes; American West fashions from the 1840s to the 1890s. Twenty-first Century Books 2011 64p il (Dressing a nation: the history of U.S. fashion) lib bdg $31.93

Grades: 7 8 9 10   **391**

1. Native Americans -- History 2. Clothing and dress -- History 3. Frontier and pioneer life -- West (U.S.)

ISBN 978-0-7613-5890-9; 0-7613-5890-0

LC 2011003036

This is a history of clothing and dress in the American West from the 1840s to 1890s.

Includes bibliographical references

Kyi, Tanya Lloyd

★ The **blue** jean book; the story behind the seams. Annick Press 2005 79p il $24.95; pa $12.95

391

1. Jeans (Clothing)
ISBN 1-55037-917-8; 1-55037-916-X pa

"Kyi traces the history of these pants from the early life of Levi Strauss and the patented riveted pocket to the stiff competition and controversy of production in our modern world. . . . History and social issues are intertwined to show how activities, jobs, and the economy influence the development and production of clothing. . . . This is an enjoyable read for anyone wishing to know more about this fashion item and an excellent resource for an introduction to product development and economy." SLJ

Mason, Paul, 1967-

★ **Body** piercing and tattooing. Heinemann Lib. 2003 56p il (Just the facts) lib bdg $25.64

Grades: 6 7 8 9 **391**

1. Tattooing 2. Body piercing
ISBN 1-4034-0817-3

LC 2002-10936

Describes the history of body piercing and tattooing, as well as what motivates people to get a piercing or a tattoo, how to care for them, problems that can arise, and legal issues surrounding them

"The writing is clear and frank. . . . Students will find much to like and make use of in [this book]." Libr Media Connect

Includes glossary and bibliographical references

McEvoy, Anne

The **1920s** and 1930s. Chelsea House 2009 64p il (Costume & fashion source books) $35

Grades: 6 7 8 9 **391**

1. Fashion -- History 2. Clothing and dress -- History
ISBN 978-1-60413-383-7; 1-60413-383-X

LC 2009-1236

This describes how gender, occasion, class, and social clime affected fashion during the 1920s and 1930s.

This is written "in a clear, engaging style. . . . [The] volume is profusely and gorgeously illustrated with period paintings and photographs, movie and TV stills, design sketches, and photographs from period reenactments. Each illustration is captioned with intriguing, relevant facts that enhance the text." SLJ

Includes glossary and bibliographical references

The **American** West. Chelsea House 2009 64p il (Costume & fashion source books) $35

Grades: 6 7 8 9 **391**

1. Native American costume 2. Frontier and pioneer life 3. Costume -- History 4. Fashion -- History 5. Clothing and dress -- History
ISBN 978-1-60413-382-0; 1-60413-382-1

LC 2008-47261

A look at what was worn by pioneers and settlers as well as Native Americans as the West opened up.

This is written "in a clear, engaging style. . . . [The] volume is profusely and gorgeously illustrated with period paintings and photographs, movie and TV stills, design

sketches, and photographs from period reenactments. Each illustration is captioned with intriguing, relevant facts that enhance the text." SLJ

Includes glossary and bibliographical references

Fashions of a decade, The 1990s. Chelsea House Publishers 2006 64p il $35

Grades: 7 8 9 10 11 12 **391**

1. Costume
ISBN 0-8160-6725-2; 978-0-8160-6725-1

LC 2006-41268

First published 1992

A pictorial survey of the 1990s fashion trends

"Fashions of a Decade: The 1990s recounts the history of fashion as it threaded its way through this exciting era. From silk walking shorts to bike leathers to layered minidresses to stretch-velvet jumpsuits, the 1990s represented a period of fun, innovative styles that could be sold at affordable prices for the average person. This revised, full-color volume covers everything readers would want to know about this fashionable topic." Publisher's Note

Includes glossary and bibliographical references

Nagle, Jeanne

Why people get tattoos and other body art. Rosen 2011 64p il (Tattooing) lib bdg $30.60; pa $12.95

Grades: 7 8 9 10 **391**

1. Tattooing
ISBN 978-1-4488-4617-7 lib bdg; 978-1-4488-4620-7 pa

LC 2011000276

This book "explains the appeal of tattoos for a wide variety of people as a way of expressing themselves aesthetically, religiously, or for other reasons. Illustrations . . . are of high quality. . . . The design and the reading level are accessible without talking down to the audience, so this is a good choice for enticing reluctant readers with an interest in body art." Booklist

Includes bibliographical references

Pendergast, Sara

Fashion, costume, and culture; clothing, headwear, body decoration, and footwear through the ages. [by] Sara Pendergast and Tom Pendergast. U.X.L 2004 5v il set $275

Grades: 6 7 8 9 **391**

1. Fashion 2. Clothing and dress 3. Costume -- History
ISBN 0-7876-5417-5

This set "surveys how people have covered and adorned themselves through the ages and around the world. . . . There are 430 entries in all, ranging from a paragraph or two to a page. . . . The work is notable for its organization, breadth of coverage, and attractive design. Strongly recommended for school and public libraries." Booklist

Platt, Richard

They wore what?! the weird history of fashion and beauty. [by] Richard Platt. Two-Can 2007 48p il $16.95; pa $9.95

Grades: 4 5 6   **391**

  1. Personal appearance 2. Fashion -- History
ISBN 978-1-58728-582-0; 1-58728-582-7; 978-1-
58728-584-4 pa; 1-58728-584-3 pa

                       LC 2006039159

Published in the United Kingdom with title: Would you
believe in 1500, platform shoes were outlawed?

  "Busy, colorful pages recount the historical, social, and
political sides of clothing, hair, hats, and shoes, from legal
and moral issues such as wearing fur to dangerous practices
like cinched waists and bound feet. . . . Ever-fluctuating
ideas of beauty and body image are also explored." Horn
Book Guide

  Includes glossary and bibliographical references

Rooney, Anne

  The **1950s** and 1960s. Chelsea House 2009 64p
il (Costume & fashion source books) $35

Grades: 6 7 8 9   **391**

  1. Costume -- History 2. Fashion -- History 3. Clothing
and dress -- History
ISBN 978-1-60413-385-1; 1-60413-385-6

                       LC 2008-47260

This describes how gender, occasion, class, and social
clime affected fashion during the 1950s and 1960s

  This is written "in a clear, engaging style. . . . [The]
volume is profusely and gorgeously illustrated with period
paintings and photographs, movie and TV stills, design
sketches, and photographs from period reenactments. Each
illustration is captioned with intriguing, relevant facts that
enhance the text." SLJ

  Includes glossary and bibliographical references

Rowland-Warne, L.

  Costume; written by L. Rowland-Warne; [spe-
cial photography, Liz McAulay] Dorling Kindersley
2000 63p il (DK eyewitness books) $15.99; lib
bdg $19.99

Grades: 4 5 6 7   **391**

  1. Costume 2. Clothing and dress 3. Fashion -- History
ISBN 0-7894-5586-2; 0-7894-6584-1 lib bdg

First published 1992 by Knopf

  Photographs and text document the history and meaning of clothing, from loincloths to modern children's clothes

Spalding, Frank

  Erasing the ink; getting rid of your tattoo. Rosen
Pub. 2011 64p il (Tattooing) lib bdg $30.60; pa
$12.95

Grades: 7 8 9 10   **391**

  1. Skin 2. Tattooing
ISBN 978-1-4488-4615-3 lib bdg; 978-1-4488-4619-
1 pa

                       LC 2010045920

This book "focuses . . . on the negatives of getting a tattoo and the difficulties of removing them. . . . Illustrations . .
. are of high quality. . . . The design and the reading level are
accessible without talking down to the audience, so this is a
good choice for enticing reluctant readers with an interest in
body art." Booklist

  Includes bibliographical references

Steer, Deirdre Clancy

  Colonial America; [by] Deirdre Clancy Steer and
Amela Baksic. Chelsea House 2009 64p il (Costume & fashion source books) $35

Grades: 6 7 8 9   **391**

  1. Costume -- History 2. Fashion -- History 3. Clothing
and dress -- History
ISBN 978-1-60413-380-6; 1-60413-380-5

A look at what kinds of clothing people in colonial
America wore.

  This is written "in a clear, engaging style. . . . [The]
volume is profusely and gorgeously illustrated with period
paintings and photographs, movie and TV stills, design
sketches, and photographs from period reenactments. Each
illustration is captioned with intriguing, relevant facts that
enhance the text." SLJ

Taschek, Karen

  The **Civil** War. Chelsea House 2009 64p il
(Costume & fashion source books) $35

Grades: 6 7 8 9   **391**

  1. Costume -- History 2. Fashion -- History 3. Clothing
and dress -- History
ISBN 978-1-60413-381-3; 1-60413-381-3

                       LC 2008-47262

A look at the clothing and styles on both sides of the
Civil War.

  This is written "in a clear, engaging style. . . . [The]
volume is profusely and gorgeously illustrated with period
paintings and photographs, movie and TV stills, design
sketches, and photographs from period reenactments. Each
illustration is captioned with intriguing, relevant facts that
enhance the text." SLJ

  Includes glossary and bibliographical references

  ★ **Fashions** of a decade [series] Chelsea House Publishers 2006 8v il set $280

Grades: 7 8 9 10 11 12   **391**

  1. Costume
ISBN 0-8160-7059-8; 978-0-8160-7059-6

First published 1991-1992

This set describes clothing styles of the 20th century in
the context of world events, social movements, and cultural
movements of each decade.

  "These titles provide colorful and fascinating information. . . . Attractive black-and-white illustrations, color
photos, reproductions, sketches from magazines and newspapers, and fact boxes enhance and bring to life these lively
and accessible texts." SLJ

393   Death customs

Colman, Penny

  ★ **Corpses,** coffins, and crypts; a history of
burial. Holt & Co. 1997 212p il $17.95

Grades: 7 8 9 10   **393**

  1. Death 2. Burial 3. Funeral rites and ceremonies 4.
Death -- Social aspects
ISBN 0-8050-5066-3

                       LC 97-7842

Documents the burial process throughout the centuries and in different cultures.

The author "is both candid and detailed in her handling of the gruesome nitty-gritty. . . . Many of the photographs in the liberally illustrated text are from her own explorations, and all are captioned, some in great detail. . . . She's filled her sensitive, solid book with answers to questions people often need and want to know but are too reluctant to ask." Booklist

Includes glossary and bibliographical references

Deem, James M.

★ **Bodies** from the ice; melting glaciers and the recovery of the past. Houghton Mifflin 2008 58p il map $17

Grades: 5 6 7 8 9 10   393
1. Mummies 2. Glaciers 3. Ice mummies
ISBN 978-0-618-80045-2; 0-618-80045-X
LC 2008-01868

A Sibert Medal honor book, 2009

This describes the discovery of human remains preserved in glaciers in the Alps, the Andes, The Himalayas, and other places around the world and what can be learned from them

"Full-color photographs, reproductions, and maps are clearly captioned; grand images of glaciated mountain peaks span entire pages, and detailed pictures of recovered objects . . . are presented. . . . [This] is a fantastic resource. Deem superbly weaves diverse geographical settings, time periods, and climate issues into a readable work that reveals the increasing interdisciplinary dimensions of the sciences." SLJ

Includes bibliographical references

Greene, Meg

Rest in peace; a history of American cemeteries. Twenty-First Century Books 2008 112p il map (People's history) lib bdg $30.60

Grades: 8 9 10 11 12   393
1. Burial 2. Cemeteries
ISBN 978-0-8225-3414-3 lib bdg; 0-8225-3414-2 lib bdg
LC 2007022093

"This account of cemeteries in the U.S. offers a sweeping history . . . as well as plenty of noteworthy details, illustrated throughout with black-and-white photos shaded in sepia tones. . . . This book . . . presents many aspects of an unusual topic." Booklist

Includes bibliographical references

Halls, Kelly Milner

Mysteries of the mummy kids. Darby Creek Pub. 2007 72p il map $18.95

Grades: 4 5 6 7   393
1. Mummies 2. Human remains (Archaeology)
ISBN 978-1-58196-059-4; 1-58196-059-X

"Halls presents an eerily fascinating exploration of mummified children and teens found in South and North America, Europe, and Asia. . . . The writing style is plain yet absorbing, presenting scientific and historical information in simple terms." Voice Youth Advocates

Includes bibliographical references

Knapp, Ron

Mummy secrets uncovered. Enslow Publishers 2011 48p il (Bizarre science) lib bdg $23.93

Grades: 5 6 7 8   393
1. Mummies
ISBN 978-0-7660-3670-3; 0-7660-3670-7
LC 2010000976

First published 1996 with title: Mummies

This describes mummies such as the Iceman found in the Italian Alps in 1991, King Tut of Egypt, the people of Pompeii killed by the eruption of Mount Vesuvius, Tollund Man found in Denmark in 1950, and the Ice Maiden found in the Siberian Steppes.

"Aimed at reluctant readers, [this title is] sure to disgust and delight in equal measure. . . . [The title] will pique interest and get kids lining up at the reference desk looking for more. The text is complemented by illustrations and magnified photos of things that you would hope never to see." SLJ

Includes glossary and bibliographical references

Malam, John

Mummies; foreword by Ron Beckett and Gerald Conlogue. Kingfisher 2003 63p il (Kingfisher knowledge) $11.95

Grades: 5 6 7 8   393
1. Mummies
ISBN 0-7534-5623-0
LC 2003-44630

"Malam covers Egyptian mummies; the discovery of a variety of preserved bodies throughout history and the world in bogs, deserts, and ice; animal mummies; and mummies today. [The title includes] stunning, captioned photos and illustrations that emphasize the many intriguing factual details in the text." SLJ

Includes glossary and bibliographical references

Markle, Sandra

★ **Outside** and inside mummies. Walker & Co. 2005 40p il $17.95; lib bdg $18.85

Grades: 4 5 6 7   393
1. Mummies
ISBN 0-8027-8966-8; 0-8027-8967-6 lib bdg
LC 2004-66128

"Markle explores a global smorgasbord of mummy varieties, both those created by human procedures and those caused by nature. Crisp (if gruesome) color photos accompany the readable, informative text, which discusses not only the mummification process, but also the cutting-edge technologies used by forensic anthropologists and others to study the mummies themselves." SLJ

Includes glossary

Perl, Lila

Mummies, tombs, and treasure; secrets of ancient Egypt. drawings by Erika Weihs. Clarion Bks. 1987 120p il lib bdg $16; pa $8.95

Grades: 4 5 6 7   393
1. Mummies 2. Funeral rites and ceremonies 3. Tombs
ISBN 0-89919-407-9 lib bdg; 0-395-54796-2 pa
LC 86-17646

This "book is attractive, readable, plentifully illustrated with drawings and black-and-white photographs. . . . Phonetic pronunciations throughout make this easily accessible." Appraisal

Includes bibliographical references

Robson, David

The **mummy**. ReferencePoint Press 2011 80p il (Monsters and mythical creatures) $27.95

Grades: 6 7 8 9   **393**

1. Mummies

ISBN 978-1-60152-182-8; 1-60152-182-0

LC 2011022437

This is "an ideal starting point for young researchers interested in the weird, mysterious, and paranormal. Using fleet, descriptive prose to communicate the impressively researched (and sourced) information, [this] medium-length [work manages] to rope in just about everything, from folklore to history to pop culture. . . . The Mummy begins with the seminal 1932 Boris Karloff film before backtracking into the worldwide 'mummy lust' that began with the 1922 discovery of King Tut's tomb and and the subsequent curses and legends. . . . The illustrations are fine and varied, the sidebars always illuminating, and the back matter robust." Booklist

Includes bibliographical references

Sloan, Christopher

Mummies. National Geographic 2010 48p il (National Geographic Kids) $17.95; lib bdg $26.90

Grades: 4 5 6 7   **393**

1. Mummies

ISBN 978-1-4263-0695-2; 1-4263-0695-4; 978-1-4263-0696-9 lib bdg; 1-4263-0696-2 lib bdg

LC 2010-08498

"A gratifyingly grisly album of choice photos accompanies Sloan's lucid, informative text as he describes not only the mummification processes but also individual mummies produced whether by intent or by chance. From the dried Beauty of Krorän in China to the bundled Lady of Cao in a Peruvian pyramid or the familiar Boy King Tut in Egypt, a global variety is offered to fascinated readers. . . . [This is a] well-written, heavily illustrated glimpse into the world of after-death preservation, either by accident or design." SLJ

Includes glossary and bibliographical references

394.1   Eating, drinking; using drugs

Augustin, Byron

The **food** of Mexico. Marshall Cavendish Benchmark 2011 il (Flavors of the world) $21.95

Grades: 4 5 6 7   **394.1**

1. Mexican cooking 2. Festivals -- Mexico

ISBN 978-1-6087-0237-4

LC 2010013830

"Sidebars highlight foods, places, and other information. How food plays a part in family life, as well as in festivals and religious holidays, is covered at great length." SLJ

Includes bibliographical references

Kras, Sara Louise

The **food** of Italy. Marshall Cavendish Benchmark 2011 64p il (Flavors of the world) $21.95

Grades: 4 5 6 7   **394.1**

1. Italian cooking 2. Festivals -- Italy

ISBN 978-1-6087-0236-7

LC 2010021542

This explores the culture, traditions, and festivals of Italy through its food.

Includes bibliographical references

Kummer, Patricia K.

The **food** of Thailand. Marshall Cavendish Benchmark 2011 64p il (Flavors of the world) $21.95

Grades: 4 5 6 7   **394.1**

1. Thai cooking 2. Festivals -- Thailand

ISBN 978-1-6087-0238-1

LC 2010023508

This explores the culture, traditions, and festivals of Thailand through its food.

Includes bibliographical references

Orr, Tamra

The **food** of Greece; [by] Tamra B. Orr. Marshall Cavendish Benchmark 2011 64p il (Flavors of the world) $21.95

Grades: 4 5 6 7   **394.1**

1. Greek cooking 2. Festivals -- Greece 3. Greece -- Social life and customs

ISBN 978-1-6087-0235-0; 978-1-6087-0688-4 e-book

LC 2010035820

This explores the culture, traditions, and festivals of Greece through its food.

Includes bibliographical references

The **food** of China; [by] Tamra B. Orr. Marshall Cavendish Benchmark 2011 il (Flavors of the world)

Grades: 4 5 6 7   **394.1**

1. Chinese cooking 2. Festivals -- China

ISBN 1-608-70234-0; 978-1-608-70234-3; 978-1-608-70687-7 e-book

LC 2010039293

This explores the culture, traditions, and festivals of China through its food.

"Numerous high-quality, close-up color photos of outdoor vegetable markets, food in various stages of preparation, and families gathering around the table will keep readers engaged (and hungry) throughout the accessible and enlightening food tour." Booklist

Includes bibliographical references

Schlosser, Eric

★ **Chew** on this; everything you don't want to know about fast food. by Eric Schlosser and Charles Wilson. Houghton Mifflin Co. 2006 304p il $16; pa $9.99

Grades: 6 7 8 9 10   **394.1**

1. Eating habits 2. Food industry 3. Convenience foods 4. Junk food 5. Fast food restaurants 6. Food

industry and trade
ISBN 0-618-71031-0; 0-618-59394-2 pa
LC 2005-27527

"An adaptation of Schlosser's Fast Food Nation (Houghton, 2001), Chew on This covers the history of the fast-food industry and delves into the agribusiness and animal husbandry methods that support it. . . . Equally disturbing is his revelation of the way that the fast-food giants have studied childhood behavior and geared their commercials and free toy inclusions to hook the youngest consumers. The text is written in a lively, layout-the-facts manner. Occasional photographs add bits of visual interest." SLJ

Silverstein, Alvin

Chocolate ants, maggot cheese, and more; the yucky food book. by Alvin and Virginia Silverstein and Laura Silverstein Nunn; illustrated by Gerald Kelley. Enslow Publishers 2010 48p il (Yucky science) lib bdg $23.93

Grades: 4 5 6 7   **394.1**
  1. Eating customs
ISBN 978-0-7660-3315-3 lib bdg; 0-7660-3315-5 lib bdg
LC 2009012283

"Written in an engaging and conversational style and full of revolting descriptions and entertaining cartoon illustrations . . . [this is] sure to turn even the strongest stomach. An introduction . . . puts 'yucky' in perspective, reminding kids that our world is diverse and that everyone has a different definition of repulsive." SLJ

Includes glossary and bibliographical references

Whitman, Sylvia

What's cooking? the history of American food. Lerner Publs. 2001 88p il (People's history) lib bdg $22.60

Grades: 5 6 7 8   **394.1**
  1. Food 2. Food supply 3. Food habits 4. Food -- History 6. Food supply -- United States -- History
ISBN 0-8225-1732-9
LC 00-9168

A look at food in the United States from colonial times to the present, describing what we have eaten, where it came from, and how it reflected events in American history

"The text is very accessible, and there are many interesting black-and-white photographs. . . . Intriguing as well as informative." Booklist

Includes bibliographical references

394.12   Eating and drinking

Mogren, Molly

Andrew Zimmern's field guide to exceptionally weird, wild, & wonderful foods; an intrepid eater's digest. by Andrew Zimmern. 1st ed. Feiwel & Friends 2012 197 p. ill. (paperback) $14.99; (hardcover) $19.99

Grades: 5 6 7   **394.12**
  1. Food 2. Cooking
ISBN 0312606613; 125001929X; 9780312606619; 9781250019295
LC 2012289475

This book is a "guide to world cuisine." The authors Andrew Zimmern and Molly Mogren "focus on 40 unusual foodstuffs including cockroaches, guinea pigs, headcheese, lutefisk, turducken, and Twinkies. Recipes, interviews, and a great many facts . . . lead to . . . digressions, including suggestions on how to survive a zombie outbreak . . . and a time line of popular dances, following a discussion of eating 'dancing' (live) shrimp." (Publishers Weekly)

394.2   Special occasions

Heath, Alan

Windows on the world; multicultural festivals for schools and libraries. Scarecrow Press 1995 392p il hardcover o.p. pa $47.95

Grades: Adult Professional   **394.2**
  1. Festivals 2. Multiculturalism 3. Ethnic groups 4. Program planning -- Handbooks, manuals, etc. 5. Children's library services -- Activity projects 6. Libraries -- Services to children -- Activities and projects
ISBN 0-8108-2880-4; 0-8108-3958-X pa
LC 94-10032

This guide "promotes reading through thematic festive activities centered around diverse cultural celebrations. Students explore varied art forms, from sculpture, print-making, batik, and puppetry to drama, music, dancing, cooking, and writing. . . . The book is profusely illustrated with photographs, diagrams, activity sheets, maps, bulletin board ideas, and . . . instructions for arts and crafts projects." Publisher's note

Includes bibliographical references

394.26   Holidays

Bowler, Gerald

The **world** encyclopedia of Christmas; [by] Gerry Bowler. McClelland & Stewart 2000 257p il hardcover o.p. pa $12.95

Grades: 8 9 10 11 12   **394.26**
  1. Reference books 2. Christmas -- Encyclopedias
ISBN 0-7710-1531-3; 0-7710-1535-6 pa

This "provides more than 1,000 entries on worldwide secular and religious Christmas practices expressed in song, literature, events, film, arts, and trivia and is aimed at young adult and adult readers as well as researchers. Entries are primarily descriptive, but a number of them, especially those on films, contain critical commentary. . . . The book is enticing reading with its many descriptions of exotic customs and its blend of the ancient and the modern. It is written well and concisely." Booklist

Breuilly, Elizabeth

Festivals of the world; the illustrated guide to celebrations, customs, events, and holidays. [by]

Elizabeth Breuilly, Joanne O'Brien, Martin Palmer. Checkmark Bks. 2002 160p il maps $29.95

Grades: 6 7 8 9   **394.26**

1. Festivals 2. Reference books 3. Religious holidays 4. Fasts and feasts

ISBN 0-8160-4481-3

LC 2001-59876

The religions featured include Judaism, Christianity, Islam, Hinduism, Buddhism, Sikhism, Taoism, and Zoroastrianism

"A unique approach to holidays, organized by religion rather than alphabet, marks this thoughtful reference book. The introduction relates world festivals to the universal human search for meaning, and offers thematic relationships between seemingly disparate events. . . . Beautiful full-color photographs, diagrams, and maps bring the celebrations to life, and informative text boxes offer additional facts. . . . This book deserves to be in every reference collection." SLJ

Includes glossary and bibliographical references

Colman, Penny

Thanksgiving; the true story. [by] Penny Colman. Henry Holt 2008 149p il $18.95

Grades: 5 6 7 8   **394.26**

1. Thanksgiving Day

ISBN 978-0-8050-8229-6; 0-8050-8229-8

LC 2007046943

"Drawing on historical research and the results of a written questionaire, Colman first retraces the growth of Thanksgiving as a national holiday and then surveys the wide range of customs and mouthwatering comestibles associated with the celebration. Both tracks are illuminating. . . . A selection of old photos and prints illustrate this engagingly presented [title]." Booklist

Includes bibliographical references

Henderson, Helene

Patriotic holidays of the United States; an introduction to the history, symbols, and traditions behind the major holidays and days of observance. by Helene Henderson; foreword by Matthew Dennis. Omnigraphics 2006 408p il map $63

Grades: 7 8 9 10 11 12   **394.26**

1. Holidays 2. Patriotism

ISBN 0-7808-0733-2

LC 2005024870

"Henderson defines patriotic holidays as those dealing with aspects of democratic civic rights, responsibilities, and values consistent with the ideals laid out in the nation's founding documents. . . . The book begins with a fascinating look at patriotism. Along with several definitions and views on it, the author explores different symbols of the U.S., including those of political parties, the cornucopia, the eagle, and the flag. She then considers each holiday in alphabetical order, describing any customs, songs, and foods associated with it; the history behind the observance; and a sampling of activities and observances around the country. . . . The volume also contains almost 100 pages of useful primary documents related to holidays, including The Mayflower Compact; The Declaration of Independence; flag laws; and excerpts from diaries, letters, and speeches." SLJ

Includes bibliographical references

★ **Holidays**, festivals, and celebrations of the world dictionary; detailing more than 3,000 observances from all 50 states and more than 100 nations: a compendious reference guide to popular, ethnic, religious, national, and ancient holidays. . . edited by Cherie D. Abbey. 4th ed.; Omnigraphics 2010 1323p $144

Grades: 8 9 10 11 12 Adult   **394.26**

1. Reference books 2. Holidays -- Dictionaries 3. Festivals -- Dictionaries

ISBN 978-0-7808-0994-9

LC 2009-41138

First edition published 1994 compiled by Sue Ellen Thompson and Barbara W. Carlson

"A comprehensive dictionary that describes more than 3,000 holidays and festivals celebrated around the world. Features both secular and religious events from many different cultures, countries, and ethnic groups. Includes contact information for events; multiple appendices with background information on world holidays; extensive bibliography; multiple indexes." Publisher's note

Jeffrey, Laura S.

Celebrate Martin Luther King, Jr., Day; [by] Laura S. Jeffrey. Enslow 2006 104p il (Celebrate holidays) lib bdg $31.93

Grades: 5 6 7 8   **394.26**

1. Clergy 2. Martin Luther King Day 3. Nonfiction writers 4. Civil rights activists 5. Nobel laureates for peace 6. African Americans -- Civil rights

ISBN 0-7660-2492-X

LC 2005028110

This offers a brief introduction to the life of Martin Luther King and the Civil Rights movement in the United States and how Martin Luther King Day became a holiday and is celebrated.

Includes glossary and bibliographical references

Celebrate Tet; [by] Laura S. Jeffrey. Enslow Publishers 2008 104p il map (Celebrate holidays) lib bdg $31.93

Grades: 5 6 7 8   **394.26**

1. Vietnamese New Year

ISBN 978-0-7660-2775-6 lib bdg; 0-7660-2775-9 lib bdg

LC 2006031922

"Captioned photographs, maps, drawings, and sidebars combine with an accessible text to present a thorough discussion of the Vietnamese New Year celebration. Jeffrey discusses the holiday's legendary origins and ancient traditions along with people's modern-day observances." Horn Book Guide

Includes glossary and bibliographical references

Marks, Diana F.

Let's celebrate today; calendars, events, and holidays. illustrated by Donna L. Farrell. 2nd ed; Libraries Unlimited 2003 340p il pa $38.95

Grades: Adult Professional **394.26**
1. Holidays 2. Calendars 3. Festivals
ISBN 1-59158-060-9

LC 2003-47723

First published 1998

This is a "day-by-day calendar . . . for planning . . . activities and classroom units based on national and international holidays, multicultural and historic events, famous firsts, inventions, birthdays of important individuals (including authors), and more. The entries are annotated and include contact information and Web site addresses to facilitate further research and learning. In addition, three suggested learning activities are provided for each day of the year." Publisher's note

Includes bibliographical references

Mattern, Joanne
Celebrate Christmas; [by] Joanne Mattern. Enslow Publishers 2007 112p il (Celebrate holidays) lib bdg $31.93
Grades: 5 6 7 8 **394.26**
1. Christmas
ISBN 978-0-7660-2776-3 lib bdg; 0-7660-2776-7 lib bdg

LC 2006025258

The author "devotes several pages to the origins of Christmas, first as a pagan holiday, then as a celebration of Jesus' birth, and its evolution into the holiday as it is observed today. Symbols of Christmas, important people, and traditions from around the world are explored, and there is a fair amount of discussion about the commercialization of the holiday. . . . Full-color photos and reproductions appear throughout. There is plenty here for reports." SLJ

Includes glossary and bibliographical references

Celebrate Cinco de Mayo; [by] Joanne Mattern. Enslow Pub. 2006 104p il map (Celebrate holidays) lib bdg $31.93
Grades: 5 6 7 8 **394.26**
1. Cinco de Mayo
ISBN 0-7660-2579-9

LC 2005028107

This describes the history of Cinco de Mayo and how it is celebrated.

Includes glossary and bibliographical references

Rajtar, Steve
United States holidays and observances; by date, jurisdiction, and subject, fully indexed. McFarland & Co. 2003 165p $45
Grades: 11 12 Adult **394.26**
1. Holidays 2. Festivals 3. Holidays -- United States 4. Special days -- United States
ISBN 0-7864-1446-4

LC 2002-154293

This "concentrates on observances and holidays established by statute in the U.S. and American Samoa, District of Columbia, Guam, the Northern Mariana Islands, Puerto Rico, and the U.S. Virgin Islands. In addition, UN-designated holidays are included. . . . The text is arranged by month, and chapters for each month are divided into 'Observances with Variable Dates' and 'Observances with Fixed Dates.'

Each entry identifies the observance as federal or specific to a state and offers a description that ranges in length from three or four lines to a quarter page. . . . [This] would be a good addition to ready-reference desks in public libraries and information centers in schools." Booklist

395 Etiquette (Manners)

Aboukhair, Rachel
The **grumpy** girl's guide to good manners. New Chapter Pub. 2011 93p il pa $14.95
Grades: 6 7 8 9 **395**
1. Etiquette
ISBN 978-0-9827918-4-4; 0-9827918-4-4

"In this hilarious and satirical memoir, written when the author was 16, readers meet Rachel, a uncooperative teen whose mother decreed a week of etiquette lessons in the middle of the Texas desert. What follows is an account of the 15-year-old's trials: a cousin who never stops talking about her ex-boyfriend and instructions on how to hold silverware, apply makeup, dress properly, walk in high heels, and dance with a boy. . . . Occasional bullet point tips are offered on such topics as manicuring nails and a proper handshake. Readers will enjoy the author's conversational style and sympathize with her plight, and, who knows, they just might learn a few manners along the way." SLJ

Post, Peggy
Emily Post's The guide to good manners for kids; by Peggy Post & Cindy Post Senning. HarperCollins 2004 144p il $15.99; lib bdg $16.89
Grades: 4 5 6 7 **395**
1. Etiquette
ISBN 0-06-057196-9; 0-06-057197-7 lib bdg

LC 2003-26426

This offers advice on etiquette at home, at school, and other places, including letter writing and on-line communication, table manners, phone answering, and behavior at social gatherings, and public places.

"The writing is clear, friendly, and sometimes clever. . . . The advice is consistently practical and simple." SLJ

Emily Post's table manners for kids. Collins 2009 96p $15.99
Grades: 4 5 6 7 **395**
1. Etiquette
ISBN 978-0-06-111709-1; 0-06-111709-9

LC 2008010655

"This deceptively slim guide teems with advice about everything from meal courses to table settings, from the art of conversation to dining out. The tone is measured and mildly proscriptive, offset by Bjorkman's amusing cartoons. . . . A strength: the excellent troubleshooting for specific concerns, such as eating fondue and using chopsticks." Kirkus

Senning, Cindy Post
Emily Post prom and party etiquette. Collins 2010 134p il $15.99

Grades: 7 8 9 10 11 12   **395**
1. Parties 2. Etiquette
ISBN 978-0-06-111713-8; 0-06-111713-7

LC 2009-2795

"Covering parties and special occasions like prom, homecoming, quinceañera, and graduation, the authors have developed a modern set of rules for navigating today's more relaxed social customs with finesse and confidence. Myriad issues are tackled, from how to rent a tuxedo and who pays for what on prom night to table settings and crafting the perfect thank-you note, with important points highlighted. The comprehensive guide gives proper respect to religious occasions and thoughtfully explains how to determine from an invitation whether bringing a date is acceptable or not. Witty line drawings complement the text." SLJ

Teen manners; from malls to meals to messaging and beyond. by Cindy Post Senning and Peggy Post. 1st ed.; Collins 2007 134p il $15.99; lib bdg $16.89
Grades: 7 8 9 10   **395**
1. Etiquette
ISBN 978-0-06-088198-6; 0-06-088198-4; 978-0-06-088199-3 lib bdg; 0-06-088199-2 lib bdg

LC 2007010991

This offers advice on etiquette in personal relationships, in communication, dining, school, getting a job or getting into college, parties and dating, and other social situations.

395.1 Etiquette for people by gender or sex; for age groups

Dougherty, Karla
★ The **rules** to be cool; etiquette and netiquette. Enslow Pubs. 2001 64p il (Teen issues) lib bdg $22.60
Grades: 7 8 9 10   **395.1**
1. Etiquette 2. Etiquette for children and teenagers
ISBN 0-7660-1607-2

LC 00-10311

"Dougherty approaches good manners as a means of showing respect and consideration for others, thereby prompting reciprocation and easing social relationships and situations. . . . Always practical and low-key, the tips and attitudes emphasize kindness and courtesy as a way of life." SLJ
Includes bibliographical references

Packer, Alex J.
★ **How** rude! the teenagers' guide to good manners, proper behavior, and not grossing people out. Free Spirit 1997 465p il pa $19.95
Grades: 7 8 9 10   **395.1**
1. Etiquette 4. Teenagers -- Life skills guides
ISBN 1-57542-024-4

LC 97-13015

This guide to etiquette for teenagers covers such areas as sex etiquette, toilet etiquette, net etiquette (cyberspace behavior) as well as the correct way to answer invitations and standard protocols for life in a "proper" society

"This volume not only uses humor to make the subject palatable but also makes good sense in terms of most young people's everyday lives." Booklist
Includes bibliographical references

398 Folklore

Allen, Judy
Fantasy encyclopedia; 1st ed.; Kingfisher 2005 144p il $19.95
Grades: 4 5 6 7   **398**
1. Fairies 2. Mythical animals
ISBN 0-7534-5847-0

LC 2004-29475

"This highly visual presentation introduces readers to fantasy characters within their habitats and genres. . . . More than 50 types of characters are arranged in nine chapters covering topics such as 'The Little People,' 'Mysterious Animals,' and 'Ghosts and Spirits.' . . . Student fans of the fantasy genre will find this tool exceedingly browsable, and school and public libraries will want to purchase reference and circulating copies." Booklist
Includes glossary

Curran, Robert
The **zombie** handbook; an essential guide to zombies and more importantly, how to avoid them. Barron's 2011 80p il $14.99
Grades: 6 7 8 9   **398**
1. Zombies
ISBN 978-0-7641-6409-5; 0-7641-6409-0
"This compact book does a good job of introducing zombies: what they are, how they look, where you find them. . . . The text is highly readable, the interspersed artwork is creepy and plentiful." Booklist

Etingoff, Kim
Howling at the moon; vampires & werewolves in the New World. Mason Crest Publishers 2011 63p il (The making of a monster: vampires & werewolves) lib bdg $22.95; pa $9.95
Grades: 7 8 9 10   **398**
1. Vampires 2. Werewolves
ISBN 978-1-4222-1805-1 lib bdg; 1-4222-1805-8 lib bdg; 978-1-4222-1958-4 pa; 1-4222-1958-5 pa

LC 2010022670

Explores New World variants of myths and folklore about werewolves and vampires.
"The writing is engaging and accessible, and peppered easily with teen vernacular. . . . Large, clear photographs and period and contemporary drawings appear on every other page or so. . . . First-rate entertainment." SLJ
Includes glossary and bibliographical references

The **science** of the beast; the facts behind the fangs. Mason Crest Publishers 2011 63p il (The making of a monster: vampires & werewolves) lib bdg $22.95; pa $9.95

Grades: 7 8 9 10 **398**
1. Vampires 2. Werewolves
ISBN 978-1-4222-1808-2 lib bdg; 1-4222-1808-2 lib bdg; 978-1-4222-1961-4 pa; 1-4222-1961-5 pa
LC 2010023660
Describes medical conditions and other observable phenomena that may have influenced early belief in vampires and werewolves.
"The writing is engaging and accessible, and peppered easily with teen vernacular. . . . Large, clear photographs and period and contemporary drawings appear on every other page or so. . . . First-rate entertainment." SLJ
Includes glossary and bibliographical references

Indovino, Shaina Carmel
Transylvania and beyond; vampires & werewolves in old Europe. Mason Crest Publishers 2011 63p il (The making of a monster: vampires & werewolves) lib bdg $22.95; pa $9.95
Grades: 7 8 9 10 **398**
1. Vampires 2. Werewolves
ISBN 978-1-4222-1809-9 lib bdg; 1-4222-1809-0 lib bdg; 978-1-4222-1962-1 pa; 1-4222-1962-3 pa
LC 2010021831
Explores European variants of myths and folklore about werewolves and vampires.
"The writing is engaging and accessible, and peppered easily with teen vernacular. . . . Large, clear photographs and period and contemporary drawings appear on every other page or so. . . . First-rate entertainment." SLJ
Includes glossary and bibliographical references

Kallen, Stuart A.
Vampire history and lore. ReferencePoint Press 2010 80p il (The vampire library) lib bdg $26.95
Grades: 7 8 9 10 **398**
1. Vampires
ISBN 978-1-60152-132-3; 1-60152-132-4
LC 2010005866
Explores vampire beliefs from the blood sucking beasts of ancient times to the immortal teen heartthrobs of the twenty first century.
"Energetic and surprisingly educational, this lively [book] seizes upon a zeitgeist topic and takes it as far as possible." Booklist

Werewolves. Reference Point Press 2010 104p il (The mysterious & unknown) $25.95
Grades: 4 5 6 7 **398**
1. Werewolves
ISBN 978-1-60152-097-5; 1-60152-097-2
Describes the history and lore surrounding the topic of werewolves, examining how the shape-shifting beast has been feared by various cultures around the world, and its continuing influence on popular culture
This is "surprisingly exhaustive. . . . Breakout summaries and quotes enliven the layout. . . . There is . . . plenty of creepy stuff to scrutinize." Booklist
Includes bibliographical references

The **sphinx**; part of the Monsters and mythical creatures series. by Stuart A. Kallen. ReferencePoint Press 2012 80 p. ill. (chiefly col.) (Monsters and mythical creatures series) (hardback) $27.95
Grades: 4 5 6 7 8 **398**
1. Sphinxes (Mythology)
ISBN 1601522223; 9781601522221
LC 2011026636
This book, part of the "Monsters and Mythical Creatures" series. It "reveals the significant symbolic role this creature has played in human civilization from ancient Egypt through classical Greece and the Renaissance into the twenty-first century. . . . The ancient mythical creature has been an inspiration for artists, writers, architects, scholars, and theologians for millennia." (Publisher's note)
"Children will get a well-rounded look at the featured subjects and how they have evolved into the creatures that still fascinate many today." SLJ
Includes bibliographical references and index

Kelly, Sophia
What a beast! a look-it-up guide to the monsters and mutants of mythology. Scholastic 2010 128p il map (Mythlopedia) lib bdg $39; pa $13.95
Grades: 4 5 6 7 **398**
1. Monsters 2. Classical mythology
ISBN 978-1-60631-028-1 lib bdg; 1-60631-028-3 lib bdg; 978-1-60631-060-1 pa; 1-60631-060-7 pa
LC 2009-20998
Describes some of the creatures and monsters in Greek mythology.
This "spices things up with sassy artwork, a pastel color scheme, and an OMG sensibility. . . . [This title is] loaded with information on the inspired methods with which various nasty creatures could put an end to bothersome heroes. Aside from the heaps of information coming from all angles on just about every page, . . . [the] book also contains a decent family tree, a rudimentary star chart, and lists of further reading. . . . For kids unconvinced that anything so old and gray could have any bearing on their lives, . . . [this book provides] a feisty . . . guide to the many cultural references lingering from antiquity." Booklist
Includes glossary and bibliographical references

Knudsen, Shannon
Fairies and elves. Lerner 2010 48p il (Fantasy chronicles) lib bdg $27.93
Grades: 4 5 6 7 **398**
1. Fairies
ISBN 978-0-8225-9979-1 lib bdg; 0-8225-9979-1 lib bdg
LC 2008050207
"The explanations and history behind . . . fairies [and elves] . . . will provide satisfaction for readers who want to know more about these familiar characters from myth, fantasy, and folk and fairy tales. Brief and concise." SLJ
Includes bibliographical references

Losure, Mary
The **Fairy** Ring, or, Elsie and Frances Fool the World; Mary Losure. Candlewick Press 2012 184 p. ill. $16.99

Grades: 5 6 7 8   **398**
1. Deception 2. Fairies 3. Fairies -- England
ISBN 9780763656706; 0763656704

LC 2011046081

This book offers explores an event that occurred "[t] owards the end of World War I, [when] two girls in Yorkshire took photographs that purported to capture the fairies they regularly saw, and these pictures . . . became a national sensation when . . . Sir Arthur Conan Doyle . . . championed them as authentic. . . . [The] book . . . conveys the widening of the ripples from the event and . . . the impulses behind the creation of the photographs." (Bulletin of the Center for Children's Books)

Martin, Nicholas
Fighting the fangs; a guide to vampires and werewolves. Mason Crest Publishers 2011 63p il (The making of a monster: vampires & werewolves) lib bdg $22.95; pa $9.95
Grades: 7 8 9 10   **398**
1. Vampires 2. Werewolves
ISBN 978-1-4222-1804-4 lib bdg; 1-4222-1804-X lib bdg; 978-1-4222-1957-7 pa; 1-4222-1957-7 pa

LC 2010025187

A guide to identifying and defeating vampires and werewolves.
"The writing is engaging and accessible, and peppered easily with teen vernacular. . . . Large, clear photographs and period and contemporary drawings appear on every other page or so. . . . First-rate entertainment." SLJ
Includes glossary and bibliographical references

Nelson, Sheila
The **psychology** of our dark side; humans' love affair with vampires & werewolves. by Sheila Stewart. Mason Crest Publishers 2011 63p il (The making of a monster: vampires & werewolves) lib bdg $22.95; pa $9.95
Grades: 7 8 9 10   **398**
1. Vampires 2. Werewolves 3. Superstition
ISBN 978-1-4222-1807-5 lib bdg; 1-4222-1807-4 lib bdg; 978-1-4222-1960-7 pa; 1-4222-1960-7 pa

LC 2010025294

Explores some of the reasons that many people, both past and present, are fascinated by vampires and werewolves.
"The writing is engaging and accessible, and peppered easily with teen vernacular. . . . Large, clear photographs and period and contemporary drawings appear on every other page or so. . . . First-rate entertainment." SLJ
Includes glossary and bibliographical references

Regan, Sally
The **vampire** book. DK Pub. 2009 93p il $19.99
Grades: 5 6 7 8   **398**
1. Vampires
ISBN 978-0-7566-5551-8; 0-7566-5551-X
"This guide covers the origins and evolution of vampires throughout history, giving a worldwide perspective on legends, mythology, and lore, from African tales of terror to blood-drinking witches of Southeast Asia. It also covers

vampires in literature, film, and television. . . . The vivid colors in the often full-page art leap from the pages, and the bold font demands attention." SLJ

Robson, David
Encounters with vampires. ReferencePoint Press 2010 80p il (Vampire library) lib bdg $26.95
Grades: 7 8 9 10   **398**
1. Vampires
ISBN 978-1-6015-2133-0; 1-6015-2133-2

LC 2010-10100

The author "lays out both folklore and real-world reports of bloodsucking beings. Expanding beyond familiar Transylvanian tales and stories of vampires in strictly human form, the author's survey is global, from the Malaysian langsuyar, believed to be responsible for many newborn deaths, to the red-eyed, monstrous Latin American chupacabra, notorious for preying on livestock. . . . Young vampire-fiction fans will find much to ponder here, while the accounts of contemporary murders with purported vampire links may emerge as the most chilling and grisly." Booklist
Includes bibliographical references

Sanna, Emily
Pop monsters; the modern-day craze for vampires and werewolves. Mason Crest Publishers 2011 63p il (The making of a monster: vampires & werewolves) lib bdg $22.95; pa $9.95
Grades: 7 8 9 10   **398**
1. Vampires 2. Werewolves
ISBN 978-1-4222-1806-8 lib bdg; 1-4222-1806-6 lib bdg; 978-1-4222-1959-1 pa; 1-4222-1959-3 pa

LC 2010025186

Describes the current phenomenon of vampires and werewolves in popular culture, from books, television, and movies, to computer games.
"The writing is engaging and accessible, and peppered easily with teen vernacular. . . . Large, clear photographs and period and contemporary drawings appear on every other page or so. . . . First-rate entertainment." SLJ
Includes glossary and bibliographical references

Stewart, Gail
Vampires: do they exist? [by] Gail B. Stewart. ReferencePoint Press 2010 80p il (The vampire library) $26.95
Grades: 7 8 9 10   **398**
1. Vampires
ISBN 978-1-60152-110-1; 1-60152-110-3
Examines the legends about the forms vampires can take, how they feed on the living, and the dangers of encountering them.
"Energetic and surprisingly educational, this lively [book] seizes upon a zeitgeist topic and takes it as far as possible." Booklist

Vande Velde, Vivian
Tales from the Brothers Grimm and the Sisters Weird. Harcourt Brace & Co. 1995 128p il hardcover o.p. pa $5.95

Grades: 7 8 9 10 **398**

1. Fairy tales 2. Short stories

ISBN 0-15-200220-0; 0-15-205572-X pa

LC 94-26341

This collection presents alternative versions of such familiar fairy tales as Rumpelstiltskin, Hansel and Gretel, and The Princess and the Pea

"Vande Velde challenges readers' notions of good, bad, and ugly. . . . Modern references and sensibilities . . . add to the humor (often the gallows variety). Entertaining and provocative, these selections make good read-alouds and can be used to spark discussion or creative writing exercises." SLJ

Myths and legends. Macmillan Lib. Ref. USA 2000
436p (Macmillan profiles) $95

Grades: 7 8 9 10 **398**

1. Reference books 2. Folklore -- Dictionaries 3. Mythology -- Dictionaries

ISBN 0-02-865376-9

LC 99-51558

This volume "contains informative, accurate, and detailed information." SLJ

398.2 Folk literature

American Indian myths and legends; selected and edited by Richard Erdoes and Alfonso Ortiz. Pantheon Bks. 1984 527p il hardcover o.p. pa $18

Grades: 8 9 10 11 12 Adult **398.2**

1. Native Americans -- Folklore 2. Native Americans -- Religion 3. Indians of North America -- Folklore 4. Indians of North America -- Religion

ISBN 0-394-74018-1

LC 84-42669

"This volume comprises 160 tales of native folklore and myth ranging from one geographical end of our continent to the other. The book is organized according to type of myth. . . . Erdoes and Ortiz seek to keep Indian myth intact and pure through their retellings, using, as often as possible, primary sources." Booklist

Includes bibliographical references

The **August** House book of scary stories; spooky tales for telling out loud. edited by Liz Parkhurst. August House 2009 144p $15.95

Grades: 4 5 6 7 8 **398.2**

1. Folklore 2. Storytelling 3. Short stories 4. Horror fiction

ISBN 978-0-87483-915-9; 0-87483-915-7

LC 2009008711

An anthology of spooky stories drawn from folklore, local history, and the storytellers' imaginations, and divided into the categories "Just Desserts and Lessons Learned," "Ghostly Guardians," "Dark Humor," "Urban Legends and Jump Tales," and "Fearless Females."

"Each of these 20 chilling tales is meant to be told out loud and includes author notes about how to maximize the spooky effect. Middle schoolers will relish reading and sharing these tales, hoping to creep each other out." SLJ

Baynes, Pauline

Questionable creatures; a bestiary. [by] Pauline Baynes. Eerdmans Books for Young Readers 2006 47p il $18

Grades: 4 5 6 7 **398.2**

1. Bestiaries 2. Mythical animals

ISBN 978-0-8028-5284-7; 0-8028-5284-X

LC 2005033658

"Baynes introduces readers to the creatures and myths found in medieval bestiaries and explains how the books were made and how they were viewed by the general public. The rest of the volume details the commonly held beliefs that both peasants and scholars embraced about specific animals. . . . Baynes's detailed gouache and colored-pencil illustrations . . . are done in the style of medieval illuminations. . . . The artist shows great respect for the early bestiary creators while also giving the stories relevance for modern readers." SLJ

Includes bibliographical references

Bedard, Michael

The **painted** wall and other strange tales; selected and adapted from the Liao-chai of Pu Sung-ling by Michael Bedard. Tundra Books 2003 109p $16.95

Grades: 7 8 9 10 **398.2**

1. Folklore -- China

ISBN 0-88776-652-8

"Known as the Liao-chai, these . . . stories were first collected by a scholar named Pu Sung-ling. . . . Wildly popular in China but little known in the West, they draw on the supernatural or unusual to cast their spell. . . . The stories are short and accessible to reluctant readers." SLJ

Bennett, Adelaide

Ancient werewolves and vampires; the roots of the teeth. Mason Crest Publishers 2011 63p il (The making of a monster: vampires & werewolves) lib bdg $22.95; pa $9.95

Grades: 7 8 9 10 **398.2**

1. Vampires 2. Werewolves

ISBN 978-1-4222-1802-0 lib bdg; 1-4222-1802-3 lib bdg; 978-1-4222-1955-3 pa; 1-4222-1955-0 pa

LC 2010023796

Explores the earliest tales and folklore about werewolves and vampires.

"The writing is engaging and accessible, and peppered easily with teen vernacular. . . . Large, clear photographs and period and contemporary drawings appear on every other page or so. . . . First-rate entertainment." SLJ

Includes glossary and bibliographical references

Global legends and lore; vampires and werewolves around the world. Mason Crest Publishers 2011 63p il (The making of a monster: vampires & werewolves) lib bdg $22.95; pa $9.95

Grades: 7 8 9 10 **398.2**

1. Vampires 2. Werewolves

ISBN 978-1-4222-1810-5 lib bdg; 1-4222-1810-4 lib bdg; 978-1-4222-1963-8 pa; 1-4222-1963-1 pa

LC 2010025778

Presents legends about vampires and werewolves from around the world.

"The writing is engaging and accessible, and peppered easily with teen vernacular. . . . Large, clear photographs and period and contemporary drawings appear on every other page or so. . . . First-rate entertainment." SLJ

Includes glossary and bibliographical references

Blackwood, Gary L.

Legends or lies? Marshall Cavendish Benchmark 2006 72p il (Unsolved history) lib bdg $34.21

Grades: 4 5 6 7   **398.2**

1. Legends

ISBN 978-0-7614-1891-7 lib bdg; 0-7614-1891-1 lib bdg

Describes several legends that have intrigued people for centuries: the lost civilization of Atlantis, the Amazons, King Arthur, St Brendon, Pope Joan, and El Dorado

This collection "of tidbits about lingering mysteries of the past . . . [offers] more substance than most. . . . [It offers] a full-page illustration opening each chapter; reproductions, many in color; and a generously spaced format." SLJ

Includes glossary and bibliographical references

Boughn, Michael

Into the world of the dead; astonishing adventures in the underworld. Annick Press 2006 56p il lib bdg $24.95; pa $12.95

Grades: 5 6 7 8   **398.2**

1. Death -- Folklore 2. Future life -- Folklore

ISBN 1-55037-959-3 lib bdg; 1-55037-958-5 pa

"Boughn retells stories from many cultures on every continent except South America, including quite a few from Mesoamerica, Asia, Africa, and Oceania. Readers will find heroes who have traveled to and returned from the underworld as well as the gods and monsters who dwell there. Full-color and black-and-white illustrations, including reproductions, photos, and plenty of graphics of skulls, appear on every page. . . . This is a book that many young people may find appealing." SLJ

Brown, Dee Alexander

Dee Brown's folktales of the Native American; retold for our times. Holt & Co. 1993 174p pa $12

Grades: 7 8 9 10   **398.2**

1. Native Americans -- Folklore

ISBN 0-8050-2607-X

LC 93-12449

First published 1979 by Holt, Rinehart & Winston with title: Teepee tales of the American Indian

This is a collection of 36 folktales from Native American tribes, including the Seneca, Hopi, Navaho, Creek, Cheyenne, Cherokee, and Blackfoot, grouped by themes such as tricksters and magicians, heroes and heroines, and ghost stories

Includes bibliographical references

Bryan, Ashley

★ **Ashley** Bryan's African tales, uh-huh. Atheneum Bks. for Young Readers 1998 198p $22

Grades: 4 5 6   **398.2**

1. Tales -- Africa 2. Folklore -- Africa

ISBN 0-689-82076-3

LC 97-77743

This volume combines three previously published titles: The ox of the wonderful horns and other African folktales (1971), Beat the story-drum, pum-pum (1980), Lion and the ostrich chicks and other African folktales (1986)

This collection of African folktales is "told with Bryan's distinctive rhythmic word patterns and filled with humor, life lessons, and the antics of trickster Ananse. . . . Quality reproductions of the original woodcuts enrich this handsome volume." Horn Book Guide

Burns, Batt

★ The **king** with horse's ears and other Irish folktales; [by] Batt Burns; illustrated by Igor Oleynikov. Sterling Pub. Co. 2009 96p il (Folktales of the world) $14.95

Grades: 4 5 6 7   **398.2**

1. Fairy tales 2. Folklore -- Ireland

ISBN 978-1-4027-3772-5; 1-4027-3772-6

LC 2007035258

"These 13 Irish tales retold by storyteller Burns follow fairies and warriors, heroes and clever thieves. . . . The stories are cleanly retold in contemporary, accessible language, and each is introduced with a short paragraph providing cultural or other information. . . . Oleynikov's paintings have a rough texture that suits the energy of the retellings and adds to the lively tone. This is a hearty collection, handsomely produced with Celtic-knot borders and gouache full-page and spot illustrations." Booklist

Includes glossary

Chase, Richard

The **Jack** tales; told by R.M. Ward and his kindred in the Beech Mountain section of western North Carolina and by other descendants of Council Harmon (1803-1896) elsewhere in the southern mountains; with three tales from Wise County, Virginia; set down from these sources and edited by Richard Chase; with an appendix compiled by Herbert Halpert; and illustrated by Berkeley Williams, Jr. Houghton Mifflin 2003 216p il pa $7.95

Grades: 5 6 7 8 Adult Professional   **398.2**

1. Folklore -- Southern States

ISBN 978-0-618-34692-9 pa; 0-618-34692-9 pa

LC 2003276676

First published 1943

A collection of folk tales from the southern Appalachians that center on a single character, the irrepressible Jack

"Humor, freshness, colorful American background, and the use of one character as a central figure in the cycle mark these 18 folk tales, told here in the dialect of the mountain country of North Carolina. A scholarly appendix by Herbert Halpert, giving sources and parallels, increases the book's value as a contribution to American folklore. Black-and-white illustrations in the spirit of the text." Booklist

Includes bibliographical references

Currie, Stephen

African American folklore. Lucent Books 2008 104p il (Lucent Library of Black History) $32.45
Grades: 7 8 9 10 **398.2**
1. African Americans -- Folklore
ISBN 978-1-4205-0082-0; 1-4205-0082-1
LC 2008020201
Examines African American folklore in context so that readers will understand the connection between black history and the broad sweep of America's story.
The book is "highly accessible and [provides] cultural context to help readers understand [the] topic. . . . [The] book includes captioned color and black-and-white photographs and reproductions on every spread. Well-organized and clearly written." SLJ
Includes bibliographical references

Curry, Jane Louise

Hold up the sky: and other Native American tales from Texas and the Southern Plains; illustrated by James Watts. Margaret K. McElderry Bks. 2003 159p il $17.95
Grades: 4 5 6 7 **398.2**
1. Folklore -- Southern States 2. Native Americans -- Folklore
ISBN 0-689-85287-8
LC 2002-16519
Retells twenty-six tales from Native Americans whose traditional lands were in Texas and the Southern Plains, and provides a brief introduction to the history of each tribe
"Curry has carefully researched and sensitively retold tales from fourteen Native American nations. Attractive pencil drawings enhance the stories." Horn Book Guide
Includes bibliographical references

DiPrimio, Pete

The **sphinx**. Mitchell Lane Publishers 2010 48p il map (Monsters in myth) lib bdg $29.95
Grades: 4 5 6 7 **398.2**
1. Sphinxes (Mythology)
ISBN 978-1-58415-931-5; 1-58415-931-6
LC 2010006560
This describes the mythic Sphinx that has appeared in both Egyptian and Greek myth.
This book is "thorough and respectful of a number of ancient and modern sources and [bends] over backward to navigate often contradictory, interlinked legends. . . . A number of paintings and photos break up the otherwise text-heavy pages, and copious chapter notes and reading suggestions conclude. This is by no means entry-level stuff, but for kids handy with the basics and ready to delve deeper, [this book] will be of great use." Booklist
Includes glossary and bibliographical references

Eastman, Mary Huse

★ **Index** to fairy tales; including folklore, legends, and myths in collections. Scarecrow Press 1985 4v
Grades: Adult Professional **398.2**
1. Fairy tales 2. Reference books 3. Legends -- Indexes 4. Folklore -- Indexes 5. Mythology -- Indexes

Volumes covering 1949-1972 and 1973-1977 first published by Faxon 1973 and 1979 respectively
"Although this is an essential reference book for the children's department, it is also a valuable source for the location of much folklore and fairy-tale material and should be available in adult book collections as well." Ref Sources for Small & Medium-sized Libr. 6th edition

English folktales; edited by Dan Keding and Amy Douglas. Libraries Unlimited 2005 231p il map (World folklore series) $35
Grades: Adult Professional **398.2**
1. Folklore -- Great Britain
ISBN 1-59158-260-1
LC 2005016075
"This collection of more than 50 English folktales contains a variety of stories arranged by common themes: The Fool in All His Glory, Wily Wagers and Tall Tales, Dragons and Devils, etc. The work of 22 storytellers is represented and their tellings are lively and inflected with the rhythms and speech of the regions from which their stories emanate. It is a delightful compendium for storytellers." SLJ

Forest, Heather

Wisdom tales from around the world; retold by Heather Forest. August House 1996 156p $28; pa $17.95
Grades: 7 8 9 10 **398.2**
1. Folklore
ISBN 0-87483-478-3; 0-87483-479-1 pa
LC 96-31141
A collection of traditional stories from around the world, reflecting the cumulative wisdom of Sufi, Zen, Taoist, Buddhist, Jewish, Christian, African, and Native American cultures
"Forest retells folktales, proverbs, and parables in a thoughtful and satisfying style that amuses as it deftly imparts lessons for living." SLJ
Includes bibliographical references

Gavin, Jamila

Tales from India; illustrated by Amanda Hall. Candlewick Press 2011 88p il $19.99
Grades: 5 6 7 8 **398.2**
1. Hindu mythology 2. Folklore -- India
ISBN 0-7636-5564-3; 978-0-7636-5564-8
LC 2010047651
"Gavin, . . . presents 10 classic Hindu stories, accompanied by Hall's lush and elegant gouache illustrations. . . . . Readers should be drawn toward the valor, action, and dramatic transformations in these powerful tales." Publ Wkly

Hamilton, Virginia

★ The **people** could fly: American Black folktales; told by Virginia Hamilton; illustrated by Leo and Diane Dillon. 2009 178p il $24.99; pa $13
Grades: 5 6 7 8 **398.2**
1. African Americans -- Folklore
ISBN 978-0-394-86925-4; 0-394-86925-7; 978-0-679-84336-8 pa; 0-679-84336-1 pa
A reissue of the title first published 1985

Coretta Scott King honor book for illustration, 1986

The author "has been successful in her efforts to write these tales in the Black English of the slave storytellers. Her scholarship is unobtrusive and intelligible. She has provided a glossary and notes concerning the origins of the tales and the different versions in other cultures. Handsomely illustrated." NY Times Book Rev

Includes bibliographical references

Harris, John

Strong stuff; Herakles and his labors. fierce words by John Harris; powerful art by Gary Baseman. J. Paul Getty Museum 2005 un il map $16.95

Grades: 4 5 6 7   398.2

1. Classical mythology   2. Hercules (Legendary character)

ISBN 0-89236-784-9

LC 2004-7904

This is a "simplified version of the 12 labors of Hercules (Herakles as the Greeks called him). . . . Each labor is allotted a spread with bright and bold illustrations featuring Herakles locked in mortal combat with the monster of the moment, accompanied by a chatty, humorous commentary." SLJ

Hausman, Gerald

Horses of myth; [by] Gerald and Loretta Hausman; pictures by Robert Florczak. Dutton Children's Books 2004 100p il $12

Grades: 4 5 6 7   398.2

1. Folklore 2. Horses -- Folklore

ISBN 0-525-46964-8

LC 2002-40809

"These five tales each feature a different type of horse, remarkable for both its individuality and the qualities representative of its breed. . . . Florczak's illustrations adapt characteristics appropriate to the locations and time periods of each selection's origins. . . . This is an attractive volume, useful to teachers and librarians for read-alouds and of interest to horse-loving youngsters." SLJ

Hayes, Joe

Dance, Nana, dance; Cuban folktales in English and Spanish. retold by Joe Hayes; illustrated by Mauricio Trenard Sayago. Cinco Puntos Press 2008 128p il $20.95

Grades: 5 6 7 8 9   398.2

1. Folklore -- Cuba   2. Bilingual books -- English-Spanish

ISBN 978-1-933693-17-0; 1-933693-17-7

LC 2007-38295

A collection of stories from Cuban folklore, representing the cultures of Spain, Africa, and the Caribbean.

"Each tale is accompanied by a full-page illustration that is colorful and contributes to the text. This book is a great addition to folktale and Spanish language collections. Students will enjoy these stories that could easily be incorporated into the curriculum." Libr Media Connect

Helbig, Alethea

Myths and hero tales; a cross-cultural guide to literature for children and young adults. [by] Alethea K. Helbig and Agnes Regan Perkins. Greenwood Press 1997 288p $49.95

Grades: 8 9 10 11 12 Adult   398.2

1. Reference books 2. Tales 3. Mythology -- Bibliography 4. Mythology

ISBN 0-313-29935-8

LC 97-8778

"Brief, incisive critical reviews of 189 books, published between 1985 and 1996, that contain 1455 myths and hero tales form the heart of this . . . sourcebook. Scholarly accuracy and literary quality are the authors' chief criteria for inclusion, but they also comment trenchantly on illustrations. Indexes list stories by writer, tale type, culture, character and place name, grade level, title, or illustrator." SLJ

Hirschmann, Kris

Medusa. ReferencePoint Press 2011 80p il (Monsters and mythical creatures) $27.95

Grades: 6 7 8 9   398.2

1. Medusa (Greek mythology)

ISBN 978-1-60152-181-1; 1-60152-180-4

LC 2011020993

This is "an ideal starting point for young researchers interested in the weird, mysterious, and paranormal. Using fleet, descriptive prose to communicate the impressively researched (and sourced) information, [this] medium-length [work manages] to rope in just about everything, from folklore to history to pop culture. . . . Medusa goes into the monster's roots in Greek storytelling before delving more deeply into Homer's Iliad, the story of Perseus, and the Gorgan's appearance in art, theater, opera, and more. . . . The illustrations are fine and varied, the sidebars always illuminating, and the back matter robust." Booklist

Includes bibliographical references

Horowitz, Anthony

Death and the underworld; illustrated by Thomas Yeates. Kingfisher 2011 133p il (Legends) $9.99

Grades: 6 7 8   398.2

1. Folklore 2. Death -- Folklore 3. Future life -- Folklore

ISBN 978-07534-6542-4; 0-7534-6542-6

This retells classic myths and legends of afterlife.

"Balancing the heroic and the macabre, these dryly humorous, sometimes gory retellings hold particular appeal for reluctant readers. The conversational language also lends itself well to reading aloud. Black-and-white illustrations provide occasional breaks in the text while adding visual interest." Horn Book Guide

Heroes and villains; illustrated by Thomas Yeates. Kingfisher 2011 165p il (Legends) $9.99

Grades: 6 7 8   398.2

1. Folklore

ISBN 978-0-7534-6546-2; 0-7534-6546-9

This retells classic myths and legends of heroes and villains.

"Balancing the heroic and the macabre, these dryly humorous, sometimes gory retellings hold particular appeal for reluctant readers. The conversational language also lends itself well to reading aloud. Black-and-white illustrations provide occasional breaks in the text while adding visual interest." Horn Book Guide

Houston, James A.

James Houston's Treasury of Inuit legends. Harcourt 2006 268p $18; pa $8.95

Grades: 5 6 7 8   398.2

1. Inuit -- Folklore

ISBN 978-0-15-205924-8; 978-0-15-205930-9 pa

LC 2006043577

"This collection includes four previously published stories: 'Tiktaliktak' (1965), 'The White Archer' (1967), 'Akavak' (1968), and 'Wolf Run' (1971). Noted artist Houston lived among the Inuit people for fourteen years and brought their culture to life through his books and artwork." Horn Book Guide

Jaffe, Nina

The **cow** of no color: riddle stories and justice tales from around the world; [by] Nina Jaffe and Steve Zeitlin; pictures by Whitney Sherman. Holt & Co. 1998 159p il $17

Grades: 4 5 6 7   398.2

1. Folklore

ISBN 0-8050-3736-5

LC 98-14167

In each of these stories, collected from around the world, a character faces a problem situation which requires that he make a decision about what is fair or just

"Sherman's black-and-white line drawings have a stark gracefulness that complements the tales' form and structure; the tales themselves are simply told with little embellishment." Bull Cent Child Books

Includes bibliographical references

Krasno, Rena

Cloud weavers; ancient Chinese legends. [by] Rena Krasno and Yeng-Fong Chiang; illustrations from the collection of Yeng-Fong Chiang. Pacific View Press 2003 96p il $22.95

Grades: 5 6 7 8   398.2

1. Tales -- China 2. Folklore -- China

ISBN 1-881896-26-9

LC 2002-35911

Presents legends and tales from China, including ancient folktales, stories that reflect Chinese traditions and virtues, historical tales, and selections from literature

This collection "provides a showcase for some remarkable pieces of Chinese calendar art and advertising posters from the 1920s and 1930s. . . . Prefaces provide cultural insight for some stories, and the brisk retellings weave important background unobtrusively into the narrative." Booklist

Lester, Julius

★ **Uncle** Remus, the complete tales; with a new introduction. as told by Julius Lester; illustrated by Jerry Pinkney. 1999 xxi, 686p il lib bdg $35

Grades: 4 5 6 7   398.2

1. Animals -- Folklore 2. African Americans -- Folklore

ISBN 0-8037-2451-9

LC 99-17121

Reprint in one volume of works originally published separately, 1987-1994

Lester retells stories of the trickster rabbit from African American folklore collected by Joel Chandler Harris

"This is a landmark collection. . . . Lester's retellings are sharp and flavorful and grounded in the here and now." [review of book 1] Booklist

Livo, Norma J.

Folk stories of the Hmong; peoples of Laos, Thailand, and Vietnam. [by] Norma J. Livo and Dia Cha. Libraries Unlimited 1991 135p il $26

Grades: 8 9 10 11 12 Adult   398.2

1. Hmong Americans

ISBN 0-87287-854-6

LC 91-370

This is a collection of folktales of the Hmong people of Asia which also includes a description of Hmong history and culture, with 16 pages of color photographs of Hmong dress and needlework

Includes bibliographical references

Marshall, James Vance

Stories from the Billabong; retold by James Vance Marshall; illustrated by Francis Firebrace. Frances Lincoln Children's Books 2009 61p il $19.95

Grades: 3 4 5 6   398.2

1. Aboriginal Australians -- Folklore 2. Legends -- Australia 3. Australian aborigines 4. Mythology, Australian aboriginal

ISBN 978-1-84507-704-4; 1-84507-704-0

"With the help of Aboriginal storytellers who have collected the tales and myths of their people, Marshall has assembled 10 fascinating stories of the Dreamtime. . . . Each selection is beautifully told and is illustrated by a traditional artist who uses the distinctive symbols and colors of the Aboriginal people. . . . This is an engaging, colorful book that belongs in most libraries." SLJ

Martin, Rafe

★ The **world** before this one; a novel told in legend. with paper sculpture by Calvin Nicholls. Levine Bks. 2002 195p il hardcover o.p. pa $5.99

Grades: 4 5 6 7   398.2

1. Seneca Indians -- Folklore 2. Seneca mythology 3. Tales -- New York (State)

ISBN 0-590-37976-3; 978-0-590-37980-9 pa; 0-590-37980-1 pa

LC 2001-23403

"Written in the style of a novel, this collection of 14 Seneca tales is presented through the retelling of one central story into which all of the others are artfully woven. . . . Martin offers sources for the tales along with an introductory note by Seneca Elder Peter Jemison. Each chapter includes a painstakingly detailed white paper sculpture of a character (often an animal) from one of the stories." SLJ

McCaughrean, Geraldine

★ The **epic** of Gilgamesh; retold by Geraldine McCaughrean; illustrated by David Parkins. Eerdmans Bks. for Young Readers 2003 95p il $18

Grades: 5 6 7 8　　　　　　　　　　　　**398.2**

1. Folklore -- Iraq

ISBN 0-8028-5262-9

LC 2003-1086

A retelling, based on seventh-century B.C. Assyrian clay tablets, of the wanderings and adventures of the god king, Gilgamesh, who ruled in ancient Mesopotamia (now Iraq) in about 2700 B.C., and of his faithful companion, Enkidu

This is "clearly a telling for our time, but one that honors its source. Parkins captures the epic's primitive power and universal emotions in rough, broadly rendered portraits." Horn Book

McKinley, Robin

★ The **outlaws** of Sherwood. Greenwillow Bks. 1988 282p hardcover o.p. pa $14

Grades: 8 9 10 11 12　　　　　　　　　　**398.2**

1. Robin Hood (Legendary character)　3. Folklore -- England

ISBN 0-688-07178-3; 0-441-01325-2 pa

LC 88-45227

"McKinley takes a fresh look at a classic, changing some of the events or deviating from standard characterization to gain new dimensions. Her afterword explains her artistic compromise with myth and history, her wish to write a version that is 'historically unembarrassing.' With a few exceptions, she has done that admirably, creating a story that has pace and substance and style, and that is given nuance and depth by the characterization." Bull Cent Child Books

Menchu, Rigoberta

The **secret** legacy; [by] Rigoberta Menchu with Dante Liano; pictures by Domi; translated by David Unger. Groundwood Books/House of Anansi Press 2008 64p il $19.95

Grades: 4 5 6 7 8　　　　　　　　　　　**398.2**

1. Mayas -- Folklore 2. Folklore -- Guatemala

ISBN 978-0-88899-896-5; 0-88899-896-1

"On her first day watching over her Mayan grandfather's cornfields, young Ixkem is invited by the b'e'n , spirits in the form of small humans, to visit them underground. They feed her generously and she tells them stories that explain Mayan customs and include bits of folklore. . . . The Mexican artist Domi has provided bright paintings in a naturalistic, folk-art style. The lyrical translation preserves the storyteller's voice." SLJ

Mhlophe, Gcina

African tales; a Barefoot collection. written by Gcina Mhlophe; illustrated by Rachel Griffin. Barefoot Books 2009 95p il map $19.99

Grades: 5 6 7 8　　　　　　　　　　　　**398.2**

1. Folklore -- Africa

ISBN 1-84686-118-7; 978-1-84686-118-5

LC 2008028042

"Each of these eight tales is preceded by information and interesting facts about the country from which it originated.

A basic map of Africa helps orient readers to the location of the various countries represented. Extensive source notes are appended. . . . There are many choices that could be read aloud or told using a call-and-response format. The book design . . . is a feast for the eyes. Griffin employs a collage technique using colored beads, sewn fabric, and textured papers, and incorporates them into shapes and faces of animals and humans. . . . This compilation contains a wealth of information and will enhance folklore collections." SLJ

Includes bibliographical references

Mitton, Tony

The **storyteller's** secrets; illustrated by Peter Bailey. David Fickling Books 2010 118p il $15.99

Grades: 4 5 6　　　　　　　　　　　　　**398.2**

1. Folklore

ISBN 978-0-385-75190-2; 0-385-75190-7

"In a handsome volume profusely illustrated with a mix of silhouettes and vigorous line drawings, Mitton presents verse renditions of European tales and legends. . . . Written in ballad-style quatrains with unforced, natural sounding rhymes and cadences, the stories offer enthralling, easy-to-follow plots with clear themes. . . . Mitton links all of his selections with prose encounters between two marveling children and a mysterious old Storyteller. . . . This gathering will cast the same sort of profound spell on readers and listeners." Booklist

Monte, Richard

The **mermaid** of Warsaw; and other tales from Poland. illustrated by Paul Hess. Frances Lincoln 2011 105p il pa $8.95

Grades: 4 5 6 7　　　　　　　　　　　　**398.2**

1. Folklore -- Poland

ISBN 978-1-84780-164-7; 1-84780-164-1

"A gratifying and unusual collection of folktales from Poland. There are a number of good stock characters in these pages: beautiful princesses who get themselves into trouble, warty-nosed ogres, . . . buffoons who overstep themselves or commit one-too-many deadly sins. There are also talking trees, dark forests, miraculous springs and . . . monsters. . . . The tales are told . . . in an unwavering voice, with portent enough to keep an audience listening close, and Hess' artwork has the right spidery look and sinister atmosphere. . . . That the locales are ancient and real gives the whole collection added wallop." Kirkus

Morpurgo, Michael

★ **Beowulf**; illustrated by Michael Foreman. Candlewick Press 2006 92p il $17.99

Grades: 5 6 7 8　　　　　　　　　　　　**398.2**

1. Folklore -- Europe 2. Monsters -- Folklore

ISBN 978-0-7636-3206-9; 0-7636-3206-6

"Morpurgo retells the classic story of the courageous young warrior . . . who used his brute strength to save the neighboring Danes, then his own kinsmen, by slaying two horrible monsters, a sea serpent, and a massive dragon. . . . Many attractive full-page watercolor and pastel paintings illustrate important action-filled scenes. . . . This is a fine retelling." SLJ

Sir Gawain and the Green Knight; as told by Michael Morpurgo; illustrated by Michael Foreman. Candlewick Press 2004 114p il $18.99

Grades: 5 6 7 8   **398.2**

1. Arthurian romances 2. Gawain (Legendary character) 3. Arthurian romances -- Adaptations 4. Gawain (Legendary character) -- Legends

ISBN 0-7636-2519-1

LC 2003-65527

The quest of Sir Gawain for the Green Knight teaches him a lesson in pride, humility, and honor

"Morpurgo's sprightly writing brings out all the humor as well as the horror of the original tale, and Foreman's profuse, evocative watercolor-and-pastel illustrations highlight the drama in each scene." SLJ

Napoli, Donna Jo, 1948-

★ **Treasury** of Greek mythology; classic stories of gods, goddesses, heroes & monsters. National Geographic Society 2011 191p il map $24.95; lib bdg $33.90

Grades: 5 6 7 8   **398.2**

1. Greek mythology

ISBN 978-1-4263-0844-4; 1-4263-0844-2; 978-1-4263-0845-1 lib bdg; 1-4263-0845-0 lib bdg

LC 2011024327

"Napoli presents 25 tales introducing the major players of the Greek pantheon along with an assortment of celebrated heroes and mortals. . . . At once eloquent and elemental, these lyrically written portraits deftly detail each character's origins, realm of power, and legendary story lines. Filled with sensual imagery, the language is poetic, yet balanced by amusing asides and wry observations that add a contemporary, almost conversational accessibility. . . . Stunning stylized paintings featuring luminous colors, rich patterns, and star-infused motifs add depth and drama to the text. . . . Interesting sidebars appear throughout, providing historical, scientific, and cultural information." SLJ

Norman, Howard

★ **Between** heaven and earth; bird tales from around the world. illustrated by Leo & Diane Dillon. Harcourt 2004 78p il lib bdg $22

Grades: 4 5 6 7   **398.2**

1. Folklore 2. Birds -- Folklore

ISBN 0-15-201982-0

LC 2003-7874

A collection of folktales from around the world, all of which have a bird as a main character

This is "a collection of stories that are rich in cultural references from the lands of their origins. . . . The Dillons' luminous watercolor-and-pencil illustrations, detailed with patterns drawn from each tale's culture of origin, will draw readers and listeners back to the stories." Booklist

Oberman, Sheldon

★ **Solomon** and the ant; and other Jewish folktales. retold by Sheldon Oberman; introduction and commentary by Peninnah Schram. Boyds Mills Press 2006 165p $19.95

Grades: 5 6 7 8   **398.2**

1. Jews -- Folklore

ISBN 1-59078-307-7

LC 2005020115

"This collection of 43 traditional Jewish stories is authoritative as well as immensely entertaining. . . . The stories, from both Ashkenazi and Sephardic traditions, are arranged more or less chronologically—from biblical days through the talmudic period to more contemporary times. There are legends, medieval fables, trickster tales, and more. . . . The stories, wonderful for storytelling and sharing, are accessible even to listeners younger than the target audience, and the notes and commentary will provide older children with context and history." Booklist

Includes bibliographical references

Ollhoff, Jim

Japanese mythology. ABDO Pub. 2011 32p il (The world of mythology) lib bdg $27.07

Grades: 5 6 7 8   **398.2**

1. Japanese mythology

ISBN 978-1-61714-723-4

LC 2010042019

'This book offers information about Japanese mythology, answering questions such as "Who is Hachiman? What is the Seven Gods of Fortune? Why are myths so important in our lives? Myths are a rich source of history. People use them to make sense of our world. Even before myths were written down, people told and retold the stories of the gods and goddesses of their homeland. Readers of Japanese Mythology will learn the history of myths, as well as their deeper meaning." (Publisher's note)

"Ollhoff writes in a clear and engaging fashion, presenting complex issues in a way that will be easy for youngsters to grasp. . . . The photographs and reproductions of art tie directly to the [text]." SLJ

Olson, Arielle North

Ask the bones: scary stories from around the world; selected and retold by Arielle North Olson and Howard Schwartz; illustrated by David Linn. Viking 1999 145p il hardcover o.p. pa $5.99

Grades: 4 5 6 7   **398.2**

1. Folklore

ISBN 0-670-87581-3; 0-14-230140-X pa

LC 98-19108

A collection of scary folktales from countries around the world including China, Russia, Spain, and the United States

"David Linn's bone-chilling black-and-white illustrations . . . will stay with the reader long after the book is closed. Excellent for reading aloud, this collection will satisfy even jaded genre fans." Booklist

Includes bibliographical references

More bones; scary stories from around the world. selected and retold by Arielle North Olson and Howard Schwartz; illustrated by E.M. Gist. Viking 2008 162p il $15.99

Grades: 4 5 6 7   **398.2**

1. Folklore

ISBN 978-0-670-06339-0; 0-670-06339-8

"This tour of the world's shadowy corners is full of dark wizards, unkind witches, and other untrustworthy creatures. . . . The 22 tales, as retold by Olson and Schwartz, give a vivid glimpse into unfamiliar, unnerving territory. . . . The atmospheric illustrations, while not intricately detailed, are somewhat startling in their imagery." Booklist

Orr, Tamra

The **monsters** of Hercules. Mitchell Lane Publishers 2011 48p il map (Monsters in myth) lib bdg $29.95

Grades: 4 5 6 7   **398.2**

1. Monsters 2. Hercules (Legendary character)

ISBN 978-1-58415-927-8; 1-58415-927-8

LC 2010028764

This book about the monsters of Hercules is "thorough and respectful of a number of ancient and modern sources and [bends] over backward to navigate often contradictory, interlinked legends. . . . A number of paintings and photos break up the otherwise text-heavy pages, and copious chapter notes and reading suggestions conclude. This is by no means entry-level stuff, but for kids handy with the basics and ready to delve deeper, [this book] will be of great use." Booklist

Includes glossary and bibliographical references

The **sirens**. Mitchell Lane Publishers 2011 48p il map (Monsters in myth) lib bdg $29.95

Grades: 4 5 6 7   **398.2**

1. Sirens (Mythology)

ISBN 978-1-58415-930-8; 1-58415-930-8

LC 2010026965

This book examines the various stories that surround the myths of the Sirens.

This book is "thorough and respectful of a number of ancient and modern sources and [bends] over backward to navigate often contradictory, interlinked legends. . . . A number of paintings and photos break up the otherwise text-heavy pages, and copious chapter notes and reading suggestions conclude. This is by no means entry-level stuff, but for kids handy with the basics and ready to delve deeper, [this book] will be of great use." Booklist

Includes glossary and bibliographical references

Philip, Neil

★ **Celtic** fairy tales; retold with an introduction by Neil Philip; illustrated by Isabelle Brent. Viking 1999 137p il $21.99

Grades: 4 5 6 7   **398.2**

1. Fairy tales 2. Celts -- Folklore 3. Folklore -- Great Britain

ISBN 0-670-88387-5

LC 98-50081

An illustrated collection of twenty stories from many Celtic regions, including "The Battle of the Birds," "Finn MacCool and the Scotch Giant," and "The Ship that Went to America."

"There's a mix of the almost familiar and nicely exotic in this collection, which is lavishly illustrated with a glowing full-page painting for each tale and Celtic motifs on every page." Booklist

Pyle, Howard

The **merry** adventures of Robin Hood; [by] Howard Pyle; illustrated by Scott McKowen. Sterling Pub. 2004 335p il (Sterling unabridged classics) $9.95

Grades: 8 9 10 11 12   **398.2**

1. Robin Hood (Legendary character) 2. Folklore -- Great Britain

ISBN 978-1-4027-1456-6; 1-4027-1456-4

LC 2004016213

Recounts the legend of Robin Hood, who plundered the king's purse and poached his deer and whose generosity endeared him to the poor.

The **story** of King Arthur and his knights; written and illustrated by Howard Pyle. Scribner 1984 312p il $22.95

Grades: 8 9 10 11   **398.2**

1. Arthurian romances 2. Kings

ISBN 0-684-14814-5

LC 84-50167

A reissue of the title first published 1903

This is an account of the times "when Arthur, son of Uther-Pendragon, was Overlord of Britain and Merlin was a powerful enchanter, when the sword Excalibur was forged and won, when the Round Table came into being." Publisher's note

The **story** of Sir Launcelot and his companions. Dover Publications 1991 340p il pa $13.95

Grades: 8 9 10 11 12   **398.2**

1. Arthurian romances 2. Lancelot (Legendary character)

ISBN 0-486-26701-6

LC 90-22326

A reissue of the title first published 1907 by Scribner

This third book of the series follows "Sir Launcelot's adventures as he rescues Queen Guinevere from the clutches of Sir Mellegrans, does battle with the Worm of Corbin, wanders as a madman in the forest and is finally returned to health by the Lady Elaine." Best Sellers

The **story** of the Grail and the passing of Arthur. Dover Publications 1992 258p il pa $12.95

Grades: 8 9 10 11 12   **398.2**

1. Arthurian romances 2. Kings 3. Grail

ISBN 0-486-27361-X

LC 92-29058

A reissue of the title first published 1910 by Scribner

This fourth volume of the series follows the adventures of Sir Geraint, Galahad's quest for the holy Grail, the battle between Launcelot and Gawaine, and the slaying of Mordred

The **story** of the champions of the Round Table; written and illustrated by Howard Pyle. Dover Publications 1968 328p il pa $11.95

Grades: 8 9 10 11 12   **398.2**

1. Arthurian romances

ISBN 0-486-21883-X

A reissue of the title first published 1905 by Scribner

"Pyle's second volume of Arthurian legends will be of interest to motivated students of literature and history, as well as useful in professional collections for comparisons and source work. In spite of the archaic language . . . the narrative depth and graphic force . . . will draw in readers." Booklist

Rapunzel and other magic fairy tales; selected and illustrated by Henriette Sauvant; translated by Anthea Bell. Trafalgar Square 2008 157p il $15.95

Grades: 5 6 7 8   **398.2**
1. Folklore 2. Fairy tales
ISBN 1-4052-2702-8

"Sauvant has selected 14 tales of German, English, and French origin, many of them written down by the Grimm brothers. While most of them are familiar . . . others will be unknown to most readers. . . . The illustrations, which range in size from tiny fillers to full-page and double-page pictures, appear to be painted in watercolor or acrylic on a textured surface. While some are painted in classic fairy-tale style, others are best described as surreal. . . . The sophistication of both stories and artwork makes this collection most suitable for older readers." SLJ

Raven, Nicky
★ **Beowulf**; a tale of blood, heat, and ashes. retold by Nicky Raven; illustrated by John Howe. 1st U.S. ed.; Candlewick Press 2007 72p il $18.99

Grades: 7 8 9 10 11 12   **398.2**
1. Folklore -- Europe 2. Monsters -- Folklore
ISBN 978-0-7636-3647-0; 0-7636-3647-9
LC 2007027094

A modern, illustrated retelling of the Anglo-Saxon epic about the heroic efforts of Beowulf, son of Ecgtheow, to save the people of Heorot Hall from the terrible monster, Grendel.

This is "a gripping rendition of the Anglo-Saxon epic. . . . Raven takes some liberties that add welcome nuance to the story. . . . Howe's artwork . . . is . . . spectacular, easily capturing the heroic grandeur and horrific gruesomeness of the tale." Booklist

Rumford, James
★ **Beowulf**; a hero's tale retold. Houghton Mifflin Company 2007 un il $17

Grades: 4 5 6 7   **398.2**
1. Folklore -- Europe 2. Monsters -- Folklore
ISBN 0-618-75637-X; 978-0-618-75637-7

A simplified and illustrated retelling of the exploits of the Anglo-Saxon warrior, Beowulf, and how he came to defeat the monster Grendel, Grendel's mother, and a dragon that threatened the kingdom.

"Superb on all counts—from the elegant bookmaking to the vigorous, evocative prose . . . to the pen-and-ink and watercolor illustrations that strikingly recall the work of Edmund Dulac." Horn Book

San Souci, Robert
★ **Cut** from the same cloth; American women of myth, legend, and tall tale. collected and told by Robert D. San Souci; illustrated by Brian Pinkney; introduction by Jane Yolen. Philomel Bks. 1993 140p il hardcover o.p. pa $6.99

Grades: 4 5 6 7   **398.2**
1. Tall tales 2. Women -- Folklore 3. Folklore -- United States
ISBN 0-399-21987-0; 0-698-11811-1 pa
LC 92-5233

A collection of fifteen stories about legendary American women from Anglo-American, African American, and Native American folklore

"San Souci's language is vigorous and action verbs abound; Pinkney's black-and-white block prints match the strength of the telling. The inclusion of notes on the sources and a general bibliography make this an academic resource as well as a good collection of rolicking stories." Child Book Rev Serv

★ A **terrifying** taste of short & shivery; thirty creepy tales. retold by Robert D. San Souci; illustrated by Lenny Wooden. Delacorte Press 1998 159p il $14.95; pa $10.95

Grades: 4 5 6 7   **398.2**
1. Folklore 2. Ghost stories 3. Tales 4. Ghosts -- Folklore
ISBN 0-385-32635-1; 0-385-32255-0 pa
LC 98-5551

"Drawing on urban legends, myths, folktales, and ghost stories from around the world and across time, the reteller serves up 30 tales of the supernatural that range from eerie to downright scary. . . . Suspenseful, accessible, and energetic, the tales are uniformly brief and gripping." SLJ

Includes bibliographical references

Sanna, Ellyn
★ **Latino** folklore and culture; stories of family, traditions of pride. [by] Ellyn Sanna. Mason Crest Publishers 2005 112p il (Hispanic heritage) $22.95

Grades: 7 8 9 10   **398.2**
1. Folklore -- Latin America 2. Latin Americans -- Social life and customs
ISBN 1-59084-932-9
LC 2004024248

This "book begins with a description of the place of folklore in culture and the differences between the terms Latino and Hispanic. Specific folktales, such as the many versions of 'La Llorona,' and dominant themes, such as machismo, strong women, and religion, are described in subsequent chapters. . . . [This is] an excellent resource both for students researching Latino arts for reports and for general readers." SLJ

Includes bibliographical references

Schwartz, Alvin, 1927-1992
★ **More** scary stories to tell in the dark; collected from folklore and retold by Alvin Schwartz; illustrated by Brett Helquist. Reillustrated Harper Trophy ed Harper 2010 111 p. ill. (hardcover) $15.99

Grades: 4 5 6 7   **398.2**
1. Ghost stories 2. Horror fiction 3. Folklore -- United

States
ISBN 9780060835217; 0060835214

LC 2010922248

Originally published in 1984 by Lippincott, with illustrations by Stephen Gammell.

This volume contains stories of ghosts, murders, graveyards and other horrors.

"Helquist's new illustrations for Schwartz's classic [collection] of ghost stories inhabit an altogether more benign universe than the nightmarish Stephen Gammell originals. [This edition is] handsome and accessible, ceding the stories themselves pride of place." Horn Book Guide

Includes bibliographical references (pages 105-111).

★ **Scary** stories 3; more tales to chill your bones. collected from folklore and retold by Alvin Schwartz; drawings by Stephen Gammell. HarperCollins Pubs. 1991 115p il music $15.99; lib bdg $16.89; pa $5.99

Grades: 4 5 6 7   **398.2**

1. Ghost stories 2. Horror fiction 3. Folklore -- United States 4. Folklore
ISBN 0-06-021794-4; 0-06-021795-2 lib bdg; 0-06-440418-8 pa

LC 90-47474

Traditional and modern-day stories of ghosts, haunts, superstitions, monsters, and horrible scary things

"The book is well paced and continually captivates, surprises, and entices audiences into reading just one more page. Gammell's gauzy, cobwebby, black-and-white pen-and-ink drawings help to sustain the overall creepy mood." SLJ

Includes bibliographical references

Schwartz, Howard

The **day** the Rabbi disappeared: Jewish holiday tales of magic; retold by Howard Schwartz; illustrated by Monique Passicot. Viking 2000 80p il hardcover o.p. pa $9.95

Grades: 4 5 6 7   **398.2**

1. Jews 2. Folklore 3. Tales 4. Jews -- Folklore 5. Jewish holidays -- Fiction 6. Fasts and feasts -- Judaism
ISBN 0-670-88733-1; 0-8276-0757-1 pa

LC 99-42061

Retellings of twelve traditional tales from Jewish folklore featuring elements of magic and relating to holidays, including Rosh Hodesh, Sukkot, Tu bi-Shevat, and Shabbat

"Schwartz follows these brief, clear, and simply told tales with rich and highly readable notes about the history of the holiday, the importance of the rabbi, and the sources of the story." Horn Book

Shelby, Anne

The **adventures** of Molly Whuppie and other Appalachian folktales; [by] Anne Shelby; illustrations by Paula McArdle. The University of North Carolina Press 2007 88p il $14.95

Grades: 4 5 6 7   **398.2**

1. Folklore -- Appalachian Mountains
ISBN 978-0-8078-3163-2

LC 2007013789

A collection of Appalachian folktales featuring Molly Whuppie and her adventures.

"Shelby has captured the language of Appalachia. . . . Her adaptations are true to the traditional folktales. . . . Young readers and listeners will make these stories their own and enjoy retelling them." SLJ

Includes bibliographical references

Stewart, Gail

Trolls. ReferencePoint Press 2011 80p il (Monsters and mythical creatures) $27.95

Grades: 6 7 8 9   **398.2**

1. Trolls
ISBN 978-1-60152-183-5; 1-60152-183-9

LC 2011016391

This is "an ideal starting point for young researchers interested in the weird, mysterious, and paranormal. Using fleet, descriptive prose to communicate the impressively researched (and sourced) information, [this] medium-length [work manages] to rope in just about everything, from folklore to history to pop culture. . . . Trolls [twines] together the various strands of Norse legends into a coherent, readable, eye-opening narrative that begins in the ninth century and ends with Harry Potter. . . . The illustrations are fine and varied, the sidebars always illuminating, and the back matter robust." Booklist

Includes bibliographical references

Talk that talk: an anthology of African-American storytelling; edited by Linda Goss & Marian E. Barnes. Simon & Schuster 1989 521p hardcover o.p. pa $32.95

Grades: 8 9 10 11 12 Adult   **398.2**

1. African Americans -- Folklore
ISBN 0-671-67167-7; 0-671-67168-5 pa

LC 89-10582

The selections included range "from slave stories and the animal legends of Brer Rabbit and Brer Fox to the comedy monologues of Dick Gregory and rap routines. . . . Interspersed throughout are brief sections of commentary and analysis." Booklist

Includes bibliographical references

Tarnowska, Wafa'

★ **Arabian** nights; written by Wafa' Tarnowska; illustrated by Carole Hénaff. Barefoot Books 2010 125p il $24.99

Grades: 5 6 7 8   **398.2**

1. Fairy tales 2. Arabs -- Folklore
ISBN 978-1-84686-122-2; 1-84686-122-5

LC 2008028159

"With bright, lush, stylized acrylic illustrations, this collection of eight stories from A Thousand and One Nights is designed for reading aloud. . . . Throughout, the spacious paintings capture the sense of the supernatural in daily life, including magical images of people taking flight above city, trees, and desert." Booklist

Taylor, C. J.

Peace walker; the legend of Hiawatha and Tekanawita. Tundra Books 2004 45p il $15.95

Grades: 6 7 8 9   398.2
    1. Indian leaders 2. Iroquois Indians -- Folklore
    ISBN 0-88776-547-5
    "The events surrounding the collaboration of two chiefs, the Onandaga Hiawatha and Tekanawita of the Mohawk, to upset the tyrant Atotarho are related simply and abound with graphic details of Native life. . . . Each chapter includes one full-page illustration done in acrylic on canvas in a slightly naive style. . . . The writing is eloquent and poetically rhythmic." SLJ

Tchana, Katrin Hyman
    ★ **Changing** Woman and her sisters; stories of goddesses from around the world. retold by Katrin Hyman Tchana; illustrated by Trina Schart Hyman. Holiday House 2006 80p il $18.95
Grades: 5 6 7 8   398.2
    1. Folklore 2. Gods and goddesses   4. Goddesses
    ISBN 978-0-8234-1999-9; 0-8234-1999-1
                                              LC 2005-52504
    An illustrated collection of traditional tales which feature goddesses from different cultures, including Navajo, Mayan, and Fon. Notes explain each goddess's place in her culture, the reason for the book, and how the illustrations were developed
    "This large, handsome volume assembles well-chosen, well-told stories. . . . Hyman . . . contributed distinctive portrayals of the goddesses using a technique that melded photographs and found materials into full-page ink and acrylic paintings." Booklist
    Includes bibliographical references

Thomas, Joyce Carol
    ★ The **skull** talks back and other haunting tales; collected by Zora Neale Hurston; adapted by Joyce Carol Thomas; illustrated by Leonard Jenkins. HarperCollins 2004 56p $15.99; lib bdg $16.89
Grades: 4 5 6 7   398.2
    1. Authors 2. Novelists 3. Dramatists 4. Short stories 5. Horror fiction 6. Memoirists 7. Folklorists 8. Horror tales 9. Horror stories 10. Short story writers 11. Hurston, Zora Neale, 1891-1960 -- Adaptations 12. African Americans -- Folklore
    ISBN 0-06-000631-5; 0-06-000634-X lib bdg
                                              LC 2003-22215
    "Using a direct style that loses none of the colloquial immediacy of the original voices, Thomas has done a great job of retelling six of Hurston's supernatural tales, and Jenkins' monochromatic collages and silhouettes capture the delicious, shivery glow of skeletons and graveyards." Booklist

Tingle, Tim
    Spirits dark and light; supernatural tales from the five civilized tribes. [by] Tim Tingle. August House 2006 192p $15.95
Grades: 6 7 8 9   398.2
    1. Supernatural -- Fiction 2. Native Americans -- Folklore
    ISBN 0-87483-778-2
                                              LC 2006042709

"Choctaw storyteller Tingle tells 25 deliciously scary tales collected from the five major Native American tribes of the southeastern U.S.the Cherokee, Chickasaw, Choctaw, Creek, and Seminole. . . . For each tribe, Tingle begins with background on history, culture, and folklore. The language is clear and informal, and the dialogue is immediate." Booklist

Walking the Choctaw road. Cinco Puntos Press 2003 142p il $24.95; pa $10.95
Grades: 7 8 9 10   398.2
    1. Choctaw Indians -- Folklore 2. Folklore -- Southern States
    ISBN 0-938317-74-1; 0-938317-73-3 pa
                                              LC 2003-1069
    A collection of stories of the Choctaw people, including traditional lore arising from beliefs and myths, historical tales passed down through generations, and personal stories of contemporary life
    "Sophisticated narrative devices and some subtle character nuances give these stories a literary cast, but the author's evocative language, expert pacing, and absorbing subject matter will rivet readers and listeners both." Booklist

Tracy, Kathleen
    Cerberus. Mitchell Lane Publishers 2011 48p il map (Monsters in myth) lib bdg $29.95
Grades: 4 5 6 7   398.2
    1. Classical mythology
    ISBN 978-1-58415-924-7; 1-58415-924-3
                                              LC 2010026968
    This describes myths of Cerberus, Hades three-headed watchdog who guarded the gates of the Greek Underworld.
    This book is "thorough and respectful of a number of ancient and modern sources and [bends] over backward to navigate often contradictory, interlinked legends. . . . A number of paintings and photos break up the otherwise text-heavy pages, and copious chapter notes and reading suggestions conclude. This is by no means entry-level stuff, but for kids handy with the basics and ready to delve deeper, [this book] will be of great use." Booklist
    Includes glossary and bibliographical references

    ★ **Trickster**: Native American tales; a graphic collection. edited by Matt Dembicki. Fulcrum 2010 231p il pa $22.95
Grades: 5 6 7 8   398.2
    1. Graphic novels 2. Folklore -- Graphic novels 3. Native Americans -- Folklore
    ISBN 978-1-55591-724-1 pa; 1-55591-724-0 pa
                                              LC 2009-49668
    "More than 40 storytellers and cartoonists have contributed to this original and provocative compendium of traditional folklore presented in authentic, colorful, and engaging sequential art. The stories are drawn from a variety of Native peoples across North America, and so the trickster character appears variously as Rabbit, a raccoon, Coyote, and in other guises; landscapes, clothing and rhythms of speech and action also vary in keeping with distinct traditions. Realistic, impressionistic, painterly, and cartoon styles of art are employed to echo and announce the tone of each tale and telling style, making this a rich visual treasure as well as cultural trove." SLJ

Valentino, Serena

How to be a werewolf; the claws-on guide for the modern lycanthrope. Candlewick Press 2011 144p il $14.99

Grades: 7 8 9 10   **398.2**

1. Werewolves

ISBN 978-0-7636-5387-3; 0-7636-5387-X

LC 2010039173

"This handbook is divided into three distinct segments: 'Unleashing Your Wild Side,' 'The Stylish Lycanthrope,' and 'Moonlight Mystery.' Each chapter quizzes readers or is full of helpful tips to advise them on their path toward lycanthropy. The guide sheds light on understanding your werewolf self, hunting strategies and lunar charts, living quarters, party recipes, and music to howl by. The volume . . . includes research on werewolf legends and lore as well as movies, TV shows, comics, games, books, and further study. An entertaining read full of color photos and illustrations that add to the book's charm." SLJ

Yep, Laurence, 1948-

★ The **rainbow** people; [retold by] Laurence Yep; illustrated by David Wiesner. Harper & Row 1989 194p il hardcover o.p. pa $6.99

Grades: 4 5 6 7   **398.2**

1. Folklore -- China

ISBN 0-06-026760-7; 0-06-026761-5; 0-06-440441-2 pa

LC 88-21203

"Twenty Chinese folktales, selected and retold by Yep from those collected in the 1930s in the Oakland Chinatown as part of a WPA project. . . . The tales, while drawn from the depicting Chinese culture, present a variety of familiar motifs and types: wizards and saints, shape changing and magical objects, pourquoi tales and lessons. An 'Afterword' provides suggestions for further reading on Chinese folktales. This is an excellent introduction to Chinese and Chinese-American folklore." SLJ

Includes bibliographical references

Yolen, Jane

★ **Mightier** than the sword; world folktales for strong boys. collected and told by Jane Yolen; with illustrations by Raul Colón. Silver Whistle/Harcourt 2003 112p il $19

Grades: 4 5 6 7   **398.2**

1. Folklore

ISBN 0-15-216391-3

LC 2002-9886

A collection of folktales from around the world which demonstrate the triumph of brains over brawn

Yolen's "versions of these stories are lively, expressively written, ready for reading aloud or telling, and illustrative of her point." SLJ

Includes bibliographical references

African folktales; traditional stories of the black world. selected and retold by Roger D. Abraha-

ms. Pantheon Bks. 1983 354p il (Pantheon fairy tale & folklore library) hardcover o.p. pa $18

Grades: 8 9 10 11 12 Adult   **398.2**

1. Folklore -- Africa

ISBN 0-394-72117-9 pa

LC 83-2474

This collection contains almost one hundred tales gleaned from the storytelling traditions of Africa, south of the Sahara

Includes bibliographical references

398.209   History, geographic treatment, biography

Delacre, Lulu

Golden tales; myths, legends, and folktales from Latin America. [retold by] Lulu Delacre. Scholastic 1996 73p hardcover o.p. pa $5.99

Grades: 5 6 7 8   **398.209**

1. Folklore -- Latin America 2. Native Americans -- Folklore 3. Indians -- Folklore

ISBN 0-439-24398-X pa

LC 94-36724

This includes 12 "stories from four native cultures (Taino, Zapotec, Muisca, and Quechua), including pourquoi tales, legends of the conquistadores, and folktales from before and after the age of Columbus. . . . [The author's] . . . retellings are done in a clear and confident voice and are accompanied by her robust, colorful oil paintings. . . . This impressively presented and referenced collection will inspire readers and tellers alike." Booklist

Includes bibliographical references

O'Connor, George

Hades. First Second 2012 76p col. ill. (Olympians) $9.99

Grades: 4 5 6   **398.209**

1. Graphic novels 2. Greek mythology 3. Persephone (Greek deity) 4. Mother-daughter relationship 5. Hades (Greek deity) -- Comic books, strips, etc.

ISBN 9781596434349

LC 2011017563

In this book, a "tempestuous mother-daughter relationship makes up the centerpiece of [author and illustrator George] O'Connor's . . . Olympian portrait. Snatched down to the Underworld in the wake of a screaming fight with her mother Demeter, . . . raging adolescent Kore (meaning, generically 'The Maiden') initially gives her quiet, gloomy captor Hades a hard time too. After grabbing the opportunity to give herself a thorough makeover and changing her name to Persephone ('Bringer of Destruction'), though, she takes charge of her life--so surely that, when offered the opportunity to return to her remorseful mom, she lies about having eaten those pomegranate seeds so she can spend half of each year as Queen of the Dead." (Kirkus)

Includes bibliographical references.

Ollhoff, Jim

Middle Eastern Mythology; by Jim Ollhoff. ABDO Publishing Company 2011 32p il (The world of mythology) lib bdg $27.07

Grades: 5 6 7 8   **398.209**

1. Mythology 2. Middle East 3. Children -- Books and reading 4. Mythology -- Middle East
ISBN 1617147257; 9781617147258; 1-61714-725-7; 978-1-61714-725-8

LC 2010042977

This describes the history of myths of the Middle East, their meaning, and their gods and goddesses including Mithra, Mot, the Mesopotamian goddess Ishtar, and the Canaanite thunder god, Baal.

"Ollhoff writes in a clear and engaging fashion, presenting complex issues in a way that will be easy for youngsters to grasp. . . . The photographs and reproductions of art tie directly to the [text]." SLJ

Smith, Charles R., 1969-

The **mighty** 12; superheroes of Greek myth. by Charles R. Smith, Jr.; illustrated by P. Craig Russell. 1st ed. Little, Brown 2008 48 p. col. ill. (hardcover) $16.99; (paperback) $7.99

Grades: 5 6 7 8   **398.209**

1. Gods and goddesses 2. Classical mythology
ISBN 031601043X; 9780316010436 out of print; 9780316073660; 0316073660

LC 2007048729

"Future students of Homer get a handy checklist of musclebound Greek gods in this combo of mythology, comics and loose rhyme. . . . Smith and Russell make the pairing of classical material and a comics-like format look completely natural, with a gee-why-didn't-we-think-of-that simplicity." Publ Wkly

Includes bibliographical references (p. 48).

398.21   Tales and lore on a specific topic

Beauty and the beast

Beauties and beasts; by Betsy Hearne; illustrated by Joanne Caroselli. Oryx Press 1993 179p il (Oryx multicultural folktale series) pa $33.95

Grades: 8 9 10 11 12 Adult   **398.21**

1. Folklore 2. Mythology 3. Fairy tales 4. Folk literature
ISBN 0-89774-729-1

LC 93-16

"Professionals will be very grateful for this sensitively written, thoughtful, and accessible interpretive collection." J Youth Serv Libr

Includes bibliographical references

398.24   Tales and lore of plants and animals

Hirschmann, Kris

The **werewolf**; by Kris Hirschmann. ReferencePoint Press 2012 80 p. (hardback) $27.95

Grades: 4 5 6 7 8   **398.24**

1. Werewolves
ISBN 160152238X; 9781601522382

LC 2011036347

This book on werewolves "examines these legendary creatures . . . describing their bodies, their behavior, and their monstrous transformations. It also goes snout to snout with some of history's most infamous real-life werewolves and discusses the many books and films these encounters have inspired." (Publisher's note)

"Children will get a well-rounded look at the featured subjects and how they have evolved into the creatures that still fascinate many today." SLJ

Includes bibliographical references and index

Nigg, Joe

Wonder beasts; tales and lore of the phoenix, the griffin, the unicorn, and the dragon. Libraries Unlimited 1995 160p il $27.50

Grades: 7 8 9 10   **398.24**

1. Dragons 2. Unicorns 3. Animals -- Folklore
ISBN 1-56308-242-X

LC 94-46797

The author "has compiled material ranging from Herodotus, Ovid, Pliny the Elder, to Chinese and Native American folk tales, and fantasies by Edith Nesbit. Each entry is carefully documented and a reference list at the end provides dozens of full citations for those who'd like to delve deeper. Wonder Beasts will be useful to students who are researching myth and folklore, and to librarians and scholars who are looking for a comprehensive source list on the topic." Voice Youth Advocates

398.25   Ghost stories

Schwartz, Alvin, 1927-1992

★ **Scary** stories to tell in the dark; collected from folklore by Alvin Schwartz; edited by Rachel Abrams; illustrated by Brett Helquist. Newly illustrated ed. Harper 2010 113 p. ill. (paperback) $5.99; (hardcover) $16.99

Grades: 4 5 6 7   **398.25**

1. Ghost stories 2. Horror fiction 3. Folklore -- United States
ISBN 9780060835200; 0060835192; 0060835206; 9780060835194

Stories of ghosts and witches, "jump" stories, scary songs, and modern-day scary stories.

"Helquist's new illustrations for Schwartz's classic [collection] of ghost stories inhabit an altogether more benign universe than the nightmarish Stephen Gammell originals. [This edition is] handsome and accessible, ceding the stories themselves pride of place." Horn Book Guide

398.8   Rhymes and rhyming games

Bodden, Valerie

Nursery rhymes. Creative Education 2010 32p il (Poetry basics) $28.50

Grades: 5 6 7 8   398.8
   1. Nursery rhymes
ISBN 978-1-58341-778-2; 1-58341-778-8
                         LC 2008009157

   This book describes nursery rhymes' "history, characteristics, and variations. Many examples are provided as well as ideas for how children can write their own pieces. The information is accessible, and the writing is sufficiently lively to engage readers. The well-designed pages feature a variety of art reproductions from different literary eras and some photographs." Horn Book Guide

   Includes glossary and bibliographical references

400   LANGUAGE

401   Philosophy and theory

Lunge-Larsen, Lise

   ★ **Gifts** from the gods; written by Lise Lunge-Larsen; illustrated by Gareth Hinds. Houghton Mifflin Harcourt/Childrens 2011 90p. $18.99

Grades: 4 5 6 7   401
   1. Vocabulary 2. Classical mythology
ISBN 978-0-547-15229-5; 0-547-15229-9
                         LC 2010031635

   In this book "[Lise] Lunge-Larsen and [Gareth] Hinds explain what words like echo, grace, hypnotize, and janitor have in common, tracing the origins of common words and expressions to Greek and Roman myths. Readers may know that 'arachnid' derives from the story of Arachne and that modern-day 'sirens' have mythical antecedents, but this collection . . . [also explains] the roots of 'nemesis' (the goddess of justice) or 'tantalize,' after doomed Tantalus. Lunge-Larsen provides additional context, including dictionary definitions, and quotes from children's literature. Hinds incorporates graphic novel–style elements into his . . . illustrations, including dialogue balloons and filmic perspectives." (Publishers Weekly)

411   Writing systems of standard forms of languages

Donoughue, Carol

   The **story** of writing; [by] Carol Donoughue. Firefly Books 2007 48p il map $19.95

Grades: 4 5 6 7   411
   1. Writing -- History 2. Alphabet -- History
ISBN 978-1-55407-306-1; 1-55407-306-5

   This is an "introduction to the history of the Roman alphabet. . . . Beginning sections about early civilizations' alphabets, starting with Sumerian cuniforms, include a you-are-there narrative. . . . Later spreads cover European illuminated manuscripts and the development of printing technology. A final section [covers] Chinese characters. . . . Numerous carefully chosen color photos of artifacts . . . greatly enhance the book's appeal." Booklist

   Includes bibliographical references

Robb, Don

   ★ **Ox,** house, stick; the history of our alphabet. illustrated by Anne Smith. Charlesbridge 2007 48p il $16.95; pa $7.95

Grades: 4 5 6 7   411
   1. Writing -- History 2. Alphabet -- History 4. English language -- Alphabet
ISBN 978-1-57091-609-0; 978-1-57091-610-6 pa
                         LC 2005-06015

   "Robb traces the history of each letter from its origin to its modern appearance in the Roman alphabet. He explains the birth of writing in pictogram form and the eventual transition to written symbols that stand for sounds. . . . Smith's whimsical paintings are a fitting companion to Robb's lighthearted text." SLJ

418   Standard usage (Prescriptive linguistics)

Ostenson, Jonathan W.

   Integrating young adult literature through the common core standards; Rachel L. Wadham and Jonathan W. Ostenson. Libraries Unlimited, an imprint of ABC-CLIO, LLC 2013 x, 260 p.p (paperback) $45

Grades: Adult Professional   418
   1. Reading   2. Reading (Secondary) 3. Reading comprehension 4. Teenagers -- Books and reading -- United States 5. Language arts (Secondary) -- Standards -- United States 6. Young adult literature -- Study and teaching (Secondary)
ISBN 1610691180; 9781610691185
                         LC 2012036269

   This text "examines the various components to be considered when determining the complexity of YA texts. The book is divided into two sections with the first part dealing with the various elements that make texts complex and the second section providing specific instructional suggestions for integrating the CCSS [common core standards] with YAL [young adult literature]." (New England Reading Association Journal)

   Includes bibliographical references and indexes

419   Sign languages

Butterworth, Rod R.

   The **Perigee** visual dictionary of signing; an A-to-Z guide to over 1,350 signs of American Sign Language. [by] Rod R. Butterworth and Mickey Flodin. rev & expanded 3rd ed; Berkley Pub. Group 1995 478p il pa $15.95

Grades: 8 9 10 11 12 Adult   419
   1. Sign language 2. Reference books 3. Sign language -- Dictionaries
ISBN 0-399-51952-1
                         LC 95-1380

First published 1983

   This guide to American Sign Language features more than 1,350 alphabetically arranged signs with directions on how to form them. Illustrations show precise hand positions and movements. Includes memory aids

Costello, Elaine
Random House Webster's American Sign Language dictionary: unabridged. Random House Reference 2008 xxxii, 1200p $55

Grades: 8 9 10 11 12 Adult **419**
1. Reference books 2. Sign language -- Dictionaries
ISBN 978-0-375-42616-2; 0-375-42616-7

First published 1994 with title: Random House American Sign Language dictionary

This dictionary includes "over 5,600 signs for the novice and experienced user alike. It includes complete descriptions of each sign, plus full-torso illustrations. There is also a subject index for easy reference as well as alternate signs for the same meaning." Publisher's note

Gallaudet University
★ The **Gallaudet** dictionary of American Sign Language; Clayton Valli, editor in chief; illustrated by Peggy Swartzel Lott, Daniel Renner, and Rob Hills. Gallaudet University Press 2005 xli, 558p il $49.95

Grades: 8 9 10 11 12 Adult **419**
1. Reference books 2. Sign language -- Dictionaries
ISBN 1-56368-282-6; 978-1-56368-282-7
LC 2005-51129

"This is a very valuable language resource for parents, students, and teachers learning ASL as a first language and as a second language." Choice
Includes bibliographical references

Sternberg, Martin L. A.
★ **American** Sign Language; a comprehensive dictionary. illustrated by Herbert Rogoff. Unabridged; HarperCollins Pubs. 1998 xxi, 983p il $60; pa $24

Grades: 8 9 10 11 12 Adult **419**
1. Sign language 2. Reference books 3. Sign language -- Dictionaries
ISBN 0-06-271608-5; 0-06-273634-5 pa
LC 98-26649

First published 1981

Arranged alphabetically, this dictionary features 7,000 sign entries, with cross-references and more than 12,000 illustrations
Includes bibliographical references

Warner, Penny
Signing fun; American sign language vocabulary, phrases, games & activities. illustrated by Paula Gray. Gallaudet Univ. Press 2006 225p il pa $19.95

Grades: 4 5 6 7 8 **419**
1. Sign language
ISBN 1-56368-292-3

"This book is a great resource for readers who want to learn more signs, or for teachers and librarians looking for fun ways to share them with kids." SLJ

420 Specific languages

Dubosarsky, Ursula
The **word** snoop; illustrated by Tohby Riddle. Dial Books 2009 246p il $16.99

Grades: 5 6 7 8 **420**
1. English language -- History
ISBN 978-0-8037-3406-7; 0-8037-3406-9
LC 2009-8306

First published 2008 in Australia with title: The word spy

A tour of the English language from the beginning of the alphabet in 4000 BC to modern text messaging and emoticons

"Short chapters, clear explanations, and humorous examples bring the subject to life, while word puzzles and coded messages at the end of each section invite reader participation. The attractive design adds to the appeal." Booklist

421 Writing system, phonology, phonetics of standard English

Truss, Lynne
Eats, shoots & leaves; the zero tolerance approach to punctuation. Gotham Books 2004 xxvii, 209p $19.95; pa $12

Grades: 8 9 10 11 12 Adult **421**
1. Punctuation 2. English language -- Punctuation
ISBN 1-59240-087-6; 1-59240-203-8 pa
LC 2004-40646

First published 2003 in the United Kingdom

The author "dissects common errors that grammar mavens have long deplored (often, as she readily points out, in isolation) and makes . . . arguments for increased attention to punctuation correctness. . . . Truss serves up delightful, unabashedly strict and sometimes snobby little book, with cheery Britishisms ('Lawks-a-mussy!') dotting pages that express a more international righteous indignation." Publ Wkly
Includes bibliographical references

422 Etymology of standard English

Baker, Rosalie F.
In a word; 750 words and their fascinating stories and origins. by Rosalie Baker; illustrated by Tom Lopes. Cobblestone Pub. 2003 221p il $17.95

Grades: 5 6 7 8 **422**
1. English language -- Etymology
ISBN 0-8126-2710-5
LC 2003-25582

"The entries in this book discuss the meanings and derivations of 750 words and phrases. . . . While exploring word origins, Baker also touches on interesting facets of European history and Greek mythology. The jaunty illustrations are reproduced in black and shades of gray. . . . This informative book fosters an appreciation for the richness of the English language." Booklist

Gorrell, Gena K.

Say what? the weird and mysterious journey of the English language. Tundra Books 2009 146p il pa $10.95

Grades: 7 8 9 10 11 12   **422**

1. English language -- Etymology

ISBN 978-0-88776-878-1; 0-88776-878-4

"Gorrell takes readers on a quick and amusing historical tour of the English language, looking at how it has been influenced by Latin, Old English, French, and German. . . . This clever and funny book also integrates explanations for tricky grammar and spelling problems as part of the historical explanation for our changing language. Readers are not only given examples of malapropisms but also a list of several words that are often confused. . . . Supplementary materials including a time line and a large number of illustrations will make this book a valuable addition to both public and school libraries." Voice Youth Advocates

Hitchings, Henry

The **secret** life of words; how English became English. Farrar, Straus and Giroux 2008 440p $27

Grades: 8 9 10 11 12 Adult   **422**

1. English language -- Etymology 2. English language -- Lexicography -- History

ISBN 978-0-374-25410-0; 0-374-25410-9

LC 2008-26055

"Hitchings here provides a colorful, thematic history of the English language. Treating borrowings and coinages as psychological windows to history, the author takes the reader on a tour of the lexicon from Anglo-Saxon to the present day and shows how new words answer linguistic needs. . . . Hitchings treats the reader to some 3,000 word histories. . . . With 90-plus pages of notes, sources, and useful indexes, this is a fine choice for libraries and a 'smorgasbord' for language aficionados." Choice

Includes bibliographical references

More word histories and mysteries; from aardvark to zombie. from the editors of the American Heritage dictionaries. Houghton Mifflin 2006 288p il pa $12.95

Grades: 8 9 10 11 12 Adult   **422**

1. Reference books 2. English language -- Etymology

ISBN 978-0-618-71681-4; 0-618-71681-5

LC 2006020835

This "emphasizes the huge number of source languages from which English draws its vast vocabulary—from Sanskrit to French and beyond. The introductory pages give the reader a brief overview of the methods and aims of etymology and a potted history of the origins of English. . . . The editors then present an alphabetical listing of words and their etymology. Each of the 300-plus entries is about half a page to a page long and briefly outlines the origins of the word, its use, and the evolution of its meaning. . . . The book's informative yet informal writing style would appeal to the amateur enthusiast, and accessibility is further enhanced by a useful glossary of linguistic terms." Libr J

Morris, William

Morris dictionary of word and phrase origins; [by] William and Mary Morris; foreword by Isaac Asimov. 2nd ed; Harper & Row 1988 669p $38

Grades: 8 9 10 11 12 Adult   **422**

1. English language -- Etymology 2. English language -- Terms and phrases 3. English language -- Etymology -- Dictionaries

ISBN 0-06-015862-X

LC 87-45651

Original three volume edition published 1962-1971; one volume edition first published 1977

"Traces the origins of several thousand words and phrases commonly used in the English language, including slang terms and clichés not usually found in more formal works. Entries are listed alphabetically by the first word in the phrase, with an index at the end." Ref Sources for Small & Medium-sized Libr. 6th edition

Word histories and mysteries; from abracadabra to Zeus. from the editors of the American Heritage dictionaries. Houghton Mifflin Co. 2004 xvi, 348p il pa $12.95

Grades: 8 9 10 11 12 Adult   **422**

1. Reference books 2. English language -- Etymology

ISBN 978-0-618-45450-1; 0-618-45450-0

LC 2004014798

"The 400 alphabetically arranged entries here illustrate the diversity from which the English language draws its vocabulary, particularly from the prehistoric base that linguists call Proto-Indo-European. As a result, the editors aim to demonstrate links between the ancient base and modern English. . . . An overall quality resource." Libr J

423   Dictionaries of standard English

Little, Brown & Co. Inc.

★ **Bartlett's** Roget's thesaurus. Little, Brown 1996 xxxii, 1415p $21.95; pa $16.95

Grades: 8 9 10 11 12 Adult   **423**

1. Americanisms 2. Reference books 3. English language -- Synonyms and antonyms

ISBN 0-316-10138-9; 0-316-73587-6 pa

LC 96-18343

This thesaurus "reflects the current state of American English, including terminology from the worlds of composers and television, with such sub-categories as 'Living Things,' 'The Arts,' 'Feelings.' But what really makes the book a joy to use is the tremendously useful lists—everything from phobias to styles and periods of furniture." Am Libr

McCutcheon, Marc

★ The **Facts** on File student's thesaurus. Facts on File 2005 592p $60

Grades: 6 7 8 9   **423**

1. Reference books 2. English language -- Synonyms and antonyms

ISBN 0-8160-6038-X

LC 2004061966

This provides synonyms and antonyms for more than 9,000 words listed in alphabetical order

Princeton Language Institute

Roget's 21st century thesaurus in dictionary form; the essential reference for home, school, or office. edited by the Princeton Language Institute; Barbara Ann Kipfer, head lexicographer. 3rd ed; Bantam Dell 2005 962p $15; pa $5.99

Grades: 8 9 10 11 12 Adult   423
1. Reference books 2. English language -- Synonyms and antonyms
ISBN 0-385-33895-3; 0-440-24269-X pa
First published 1992

This thesaurus, cross referencing each word with the same concept, provides 500,000 synonyms and antonyms in a dictionary format and includes recently coined and common slang terms and commonly used foreign terms.

Terban, Marvin

★ **Scholastic** dictionary of idioms; new & updated; Scholastic 2006 298p il pa $19.85

Grades: 4 5 6 7   423
1. Reference books 2. English language -- Idioms
ISBN 978-0-439-77083-5 pa; 0-439-77083-1 pa
First published 1996

This "introduction to American slang and phrase origins identifies and defines more than six hundred commonly used idioms, complementing the entries with . . . sample sentences and . . . illustrations." Publisher's note

★ The **American** Heritage student dictionary; Updated ed.; Houghton Mifflin 2007 xx, 1068p il $19.95

Grades: 6 7 8 9   423
1. Reference books 2. English language -- Dictionaries
ISBN 978-0-618-70149-0; 0-618-70149-4
LC 2006277388

First published 1977 with title: The American Heritage school dictionary

Contains more than 65,000 entries, including hundreds of notes on usage, word histories, accompanied by 2000 color photo and illustrations.

The **Merriam-Webster** dictionary of synonyms and antonyms. Merriam-Webster 1992 443p pa $4.99

Grades: 8 9 10 11 12 Adult   423
1. Reference books 2. English language -- Synonyms and antonyms
ISBN 0-87779-906-7
LC 93-119503

First published 1942 with title: Webster's dictionary of synonyms

"This synonym dictionary is an outstanding work. . . . Synonyms and similar words, alphabetically arranged, are carefully defined, discriminated, and illustrated with thousands of quotations. The entries also include antonyms and analogous words." Nichols. Guide to Ref Books for Sch Media Cent. 4th edition

Merriam-Webster's school thesaurus. Merriam-Webster 1994 690p $15.95

Grades: 7 8 9 10   423
1. Reference books 2. English language -- Synonyms and antonyms
ISBN 0-87779-178-3

First published 1978 with title: Webster's student thesaurus

This alphabetically arranged volume includes more than 43,000 synonyms, antonyms, idiomatic phrases, related words, and contrasted words

★ **Merriam-Webster's** visual dictionary. Merriam-Webster, Inc. 2012 1112 p. (hbk.) $39.95

Grades: 6 7 8 9 10 11 12 Adult   423
1. English language -- Dictionaries
ISBN 0877791511; 9780877791515

This visual dictionary, edited by Jean-Claude Corbeil, has "more than 8,000 highly detailed, full-color illustrations, organized by subject in specialized fields from all aspects of life, . . . [and] nearly 25,000 . . . technical and everyday terms with clear, concise definitions. . . . Themes include a wide variety of fields: astronomy, the earth, human beings, the animal kingdom, plants and gardening, . . . food, arts and architecture, . . . sports and games" and more. (Publisher's note)

★ **Random** House Webster's unabridged dictionary; 2nd ed.; Random House 2005 xxvi, 2230p il map $59.95

Grades: 8 9 10 11 12 Adult   423
1. Reference books 2. English language -- Dictionaries
ISBN 0-375-42599-3

First published 1966 with title: The Random House dictionary of the English language

This dictionary contains over 315,000 entries. A new-words section and an essay on the growth of English are included. 2,400 spot maps and illustrations complement the text

Roget's II; the new thesaurus. by the editors of The American Heritage Dictionaries. 3rd ed.; Houghton Mifflin 2003 1200p $21

Grades: 8 9 10 11 12 Adult   423
1. Reference books 2. English language -- Synonyms and antonyms
ISBN 0-618-25414-5
First published 1980

The work uses a dictionary format, with words and numbered definitions on the left column of a page, and corresponding numbered synonyms, near-synonyms, antonyms and near-antonyms on the right column.

Roget's international thesaurus; 6th ed; HarperResource 2001 xxv, 1248p $20.95; pa $16.95

Grades: 8 9 10 11 12 Adult   423
1. Reference books 2. English language -- Synonyms and antonyms
ISBN 0-06-273693-0; 0-06-093544-8 pa
LC 2002-276277

First copyright edition published 1911 with title: The standard thesaurus of English words and phrases classified and arranged so as to facilitate the expression of ideas and assist in literary composition

This edition includes 330,000 words and phrases organized into 1,075 categories and a pinpoint reference system that directs the user from a comprehensive index to the numbered category of the right word. Cross-references throughout lead to other categories. Also included are supplemental word lists that supply the names of things which have no synonyms (measurements, wines, state mottoes) as well as quotations that amplify the meanings of selected words

Scholastic dictionary of synonyms, antonyms, and homonyms. Scholastic Reference 2001 220p pa $5.99

Grades: 7 8 9 10 11 12   **423**

1. Reference books 2. English language -- Homonyms 3. English language -- Synonyms and antonyms
ISBN 0-439-25415-9

LC 2001-278627

A revised edition of Webster's synonyms, antonyms, homonyms, published 1962

"Most of the book is dedicated to the dictionary of synonyms and antonyms; the final 25 pages or so list homonyms. This is good for browsing or for a writer's quick reference." KLIATT

427   Historical and geographic variations, modern nongeographic variations of English

Dictionary of American slang; Barbara Ann Kipfer, editor; Robert L. Chapman, founding editor. 4th ed., fully rev. and updated; Collins 2007 592p $45

Grades: 8 9 10 11 12 Adult   **427**

1. Americanisms 2. Reference books 3. English language -- Slang -- Dictionaries
ISBN 978-0-06-117646-3; 0-06-117646-X

First published 1960 by Crowell. Variant title: New dictionary of American slang

This dictionary of American slang terms "features pronunciation guides, word origins, examples of appropriate usage as well as a . . . highlighting system that lets you know which terms should be used with caution, and never in polite company." Publisher's note

428   Standard English usage (Prescriptive linguistics)

Bacon, Pamela S.

100 + literacy lifesavers; a survival guide for librarians and teachers K-12. [by] Pamela S. Bacon and Tammy K. Bacon. Libraries Unlimited 2009 363p il pa $40

Grades: Adult Professional   **428**

1. Reading 2. Teaching teams
ISBN 978-1-59158-669-2 pa; 1-59158-669-0 pa

LC 2008-45514

"This wonderful professional resource's focus is mainly school librarians and teachers, but it could be used by pub-

lic librarians to generate ideas for educational programs. . . . This book is an insightful tool that provides the skills and plans for successful collaboration and evaluation of literacy efforts between teachers and librarians." Voice Youth Advocates

Includes glossary and bibliographical references

Budzik, Mary

Punctuation: the write stuff! [created by Basher; written by Mary Budzik] Kingfisher 2010 64p il (Basher basics) pa $7.99

Grades: 4 5 6 7   **428**

1. Punctuation
ISBN 978-0-7534-6420-5 pa; 0-7534-6420-9 pa

"This slim volume uses catchy graphic design and an informal narrative to spark interest in the subject. In a presentation reminiscent of manga and Saturday-morning cartoons, each punctuation mark is introduced as a unique character who conveys his job through chatty dialogue. . . . The book explains the various uses of each mark and some basics of sentence structure." SLJ

Includes glossary

Fogarty, Mignon

Grammar girl presents the ultimate writing guide for students; with illustrations by Erwin Haya. Henry Holt and Co. 2010 294p il $19.99; pa $12.99

Grades: 6 7 8 9 10   **428**

1. Rhetoric 2. Report writing 3. English language -- Grammar
ISBN 978-0-8050-8943-1; 0-8050-8943-8; 978-0-8050-8944-8 pa; 0-8050-8944-6 pa

LC 2010011699

"This text is evenly divided into five sections: parts of speech, sentence structure, punctuation, usage, and a final segment on how readers can improve their writing. Fogarty's style mimics her podcasts with pithy but helpful rules and advice laced with examples. Pop quizzes and cartoon illustrations are also included. Libraries should purchase this book for reference use if nothing else, but budding writers will find it invaluable." SLJ

Includes bibliographical references

Fuhrken, Charles

What every middle school teacher needs to know about reading tests (from someone who has written them) Charles Fuhrken. Stenhouse Publishers 2012 vii, 237 p.p ill. (pbk. : alk. paper) $24

Grades: Adult Professional   **428**

1. Achievement tests 2. Examinations -- Study guides 3. Educational tests and measurements 4. Reading (Middle school) -- Ability testing
ISBN 1571108858; 1571109455; 9781571108852; 9781571109453

LC 2011037287

This book's author, "Charles Fuhrken, has spent years working with several major testing companies and contributing to the reading assessments of various testing programs.' He "offers . . . strategies to help students perform well on test day." Particular focus is given to "information about reading tests, including . . . preparation materials, samples of the most frequently assessed reading standards, and . . . core-reading activities." (Publisher's note)

Includes bibliographical references and index.

O'Conner, Patricia T.

Woe is I Jr; the junior grammarphobes' guide to better English in plain English. [by] Patricia O'Conner; drawings by Tom Stiglich. G.P. Putnam's Sons 2007 152p il $16.99

Grades: 4 5 6 7 8   **428**

1. English language -- Usage 2. English language -- Grammar

ISBN 978-0-399-24331-8

     LC 2006020575

An adaptation of Woe is I, published 2003 for adults by Riverhead Books

The author "covers pronouns, plurals, possessives, verb usage, subject-verb agreement, capitalization, and punctuation with jargon-free explanations and entertaining examples. . . . She knows her subject, can convey her message with wit and ease, and does it all in a compact, easy-to-read format." SLJ

Ostler, Rosemarie

Dewdroppers, waldos, and slackers; a decade-by-decade guide to the vanishing vocabulary of the twentieth century. Oxford University Press 2003 239p il hardcover o.p. pa $23

Grades: 8 9 10 11 12   **428**

1. Americanisms 2. Reference books 3. English language -- Slang 4. English language -- Obsolete words 5. English language -- 20th century -- Slang -- Dictionaries 6. English language -- United States -- Slang -- Dictionaries 7. English language -- 20th century -- Glossaries, vocabularies, etc 8. English language -- United States -- Glossaries, vocabularies, etc

ISBN 978-0-19-516146-5; 0-19-516146-7; 978-0-19-518254-5 pa; 0-19-518254-5 pa

     LC 2003-8302

"This reference work is not simply a slang dictionary. Along with definitions . . . Ostler includes in each decade's chapter both brief discussions of relevant cultural topics and a few photos. These short, often humorous essays are a way to provide examples for the terms defined. . . . Ostler's work is fun for browsing; it offers a unique presentation of recent cultural history." Libr J

Includes bibliographical references

Terban, Marvin

★ **Scholastic** dictionary of spelling; rev ed; Scholastic Reference 2006 272p il pa $9.99

Grades: 4 5 6   **428**

1. Spellers 2. Reference books

ISBN 978-0-439-76421-6; 0-439-76421-1

First published 1998

This spelling dictionary gives instructions for looking up a word the reader does not know how to spell, offers more than 150 memory tricks to correct commonly misspelled words, explains general spelling rules and their exceptions, and includes sections such as "The Four Longest Words in the English Language" and "The Spelling Words That Made

Kids Champions." To aid pronunciation, each word is divided into syllables with the accented syllable in boldface.

Scholastic guide to grammar; [by] Marvin Terban as Professor Grammar. Scholastic Inc. 2011 255p il pa $9.99

Grades: 4 5 6 7   **428**

1. English language -- Grammar

ISBN 978-0-545-35669-5; 0-545-35669-5

This guide to English language grammar covers the parts of speech, sentences and paragraphs, spelling, capitalization, punctuation, communicating ideas through vocabulary, homonyms, homophones, homographs, figures of speech, alliteration, hyperbole, similes, personification, and idioms, and includes a thesaurus.

L is for lollygag; quirky words for a clever tongue. Chronicle Books 2008 125p $12.99

Grades: 4 5 6 7   **428**

1. Vocabulary

ISBN 978-0-8118-6021-5; 0-8118-6021-3

     LC 2007021061

"Budding and accomplished wordsmiths will delight in this specialized dictionary showcasing oft-overlooked gems of the English language. . . . Each definition is related with humor, sometimes including word origination and listing equally interesting synonyms. . . . Black-and-white engravings juxtaposed with cartoons in Picassoesque profile give an old-fashioned yet offbeat air to this unusual compendium." SLJ

Includes bibliographical references

433   Dictionaries of standard German

Betteridge, Harold T.

Cassell's German-English, English-German dictionary. Websters New World 1978 1580p $27

Grades: 8 9 10 11 12 Adult   **433**

1. Reference books 2. German language -- Dictionaries

First compiled 1888 by Elizabeth Weir and published by Heath. Periodically revised. Previous American editions published by Funk & Wagnalls with title: The New Cassell's German dictionary

This dictionary incorporates "many new words and usages. Gives phonetic transcriptions of headwords. One of the most useful bilingual dictionaries." Guide to Ref Books. 11th edition

443   Dictionaries of standard French

Girard, Denis

Cassell's French dictionary; French-English, English-French. completely revised by Denis Girard with the assistance of Gaston Dulong, Oliver Van Oss, and Charles Guinness. Wiley 2002 762, 655p thumb-indexed $24.95

Grades: 8 9 10 11 12 Adult   **443**

1. Reference books 2. French language -- Dictionaries

ISBN 0-02-522620-7

First published 1920 with title: Cassell's French-English, English-French dictionary. Previous American editions published by Funk & Wagnalls with title: The New Cassell's French dictionary

"New words including colloquialisms, slang, American English and French-Canadian terms [are included]. . . . There are also sections on French verbs and French and English abbreviations. Reliable, standard dictionary. A first choice." N Y Public Libr. Ref Books for Child Collect. 2d edition

453   Dictionaries of standard Italian

Cassell's Italian dictionary; Italian-English, English-Italian. compiled by Piero Rebora, with the assistance of Francis M. Guercio and Arthur L. Hayward. Wiley 2002 xxi, 1128p thumb-indexed $24.95

Grades: 8 9 10 11 12 Adult   **453**
1. Reference books 2. Italian language -- Dictionaries
ISBN 0-02-522540-5
First published 1958 in the United Kingdom with title: Cassell's Italian-English, English-Italian dictionary. Previous United States editions published by Funk & Wagnalls

"A general dictionary of the Italian language as currently written and spoken." Ref Sources for Small & Medium-sized Libr. 5th edition

463   Dictionaries of standard Spanish

Gooch, Anthony
  Cassell's Spanish-English, English-Spanish dictionary; completely revised by Anthony Gooch, Angel Garcia de Paredes. Wiley 2002 xxv, 1109p $22.95

Grades: 8 9 10 11 12 Adult   **463**
1. Reference books 2. Spanish language -- Dictionaries
ISBN 0-02-522910-9
Previously published in 1978 by Macmillan
This dictionary emphasizes the Spanish of Latin America, and includes both classical and literary Spanish as well as the language of the modern Spanish-speaking world.

473   Dictionaries of classical Latin

Simpson, D. P.
  Cassell's Latin dictionary; Latin-English, English-Latin. by D. P. Simpson. Macmillan 1977 883p thumb-indexed $24.95

Grades: 8 9 10 11 12 Adult   **473**
1. Reference books 2. Latin language -- Dictionaries
ISBN 0-02-522580-4
LC 77-7670
First published 1854. This edition first published 1959. Previous United States editions published by Funk & Wagnalls with title: Cassell's New Latin dictionary

"Cassell's incorporates current English idiom and Latin spelling into the traditional presentation of classical Latin. The 30,000 entries include generic terms, geographical and

proper nouns. Etymological notes and illustrative quotations are provided within entries." Wynar. Guide to Ref Books for Sch Media Cent. 3d edition

493   Non-Semitic Afro-Asiatic languages

Giblin, James
  The **riddle** of the Rosetta Stone; key to ancient Egypt. [by] James Cross Giblin. Crowell 1990 85p il hardcover o.p. pa $7.99

Grades: 5 6 7 8   **493**
1. Hieroglyphics 2. Egyptian language
ISBN 0-06-446137-8 pa
LC 89-29289
Describes how the discovery and deciphering of the Rosetta Stone unlocked the secret of Egyptian hieroglyphics

"Suspense keeps the reader glued to this fine piece of nonfiction as the mystery of hieroglyphs is slowly unraveled. . . . The author has done a masterful job of distilling information, citing the highlights, and fitting it all together in an interesting and enlightening look at a puzzling subject." Horn Book

Includes bibliographical references

500   SCIENCE

500   Natural sciences and mathematics

★ The **big** idea science book; incredible concepts that show how science works in the real world. editor, Matilda Gollon; consultant, Lisa Burke. DK Pub. 2010 304p il $29.99

Grades: 4 5 6 7   **500**
1. Science
ISBN 978-0-7566-6287-5; 0-7566-6287-7
LC 2010-281143
"Aimed at grabbing readers' general interest in science, this lively overview is split into sections on life, earth, and physical science; within each category, specific subjects are plainly labeled for easy reference. . . . Full-color photographs, drawings, and diagrams further inform, and readers can visit an interactive Web site for more exploration. For breadth of material and clarity, it's hard to beat." Publ Wkly

Bryson, Bill
  A **really** short history of nearly everything. Delacorte Press 2009 169p il $19.99

Grades: 4 5 6 7   **500**
1. Science
ISBN 978-0-385-73810-1; 0-385-73810-2
A newly illustrated, abridged and adapted edition of A short history of nearly everything, published 2003 by Broadway Books for adults; this edition first published in the United Kingdom 2008

Bryson "whirls through mind-numbing notions such as the creation of the universe and the life span of an atom with good cheer and accessible, even exciting, writing. The two-page spreads meander their way through the various recesses of science with a combination of explanatory prose, historical anecdotes, wry asides, and illustrations that range from helpful to comical." Booklist

Currie, Stephen

African American inventors; Stephen Currie. Lucent Books 2010 104 p. ill. (some col.) (hardcover) $36.10

Grades: 6 7 8 9 10 **500**

1. Inventions 2. African American inventors 3. Inventions -- United States -- History 4. African American inventors -- Biography

ISBN 1420501216; 9781420501216

LC 2009038456

This book is part of the Lucent Library of Black History and focuses on African-American Inventors and Inventions. "Each volume in the Lucent Library of Black History examines an event or time period of particular significance in African American history. . . . Each chapter contains sidebars that highlight relevant personalities and events. Numerous photos and illustrations" are included. (Publisher's note)

Includes bibliographical references (p. 93-98) and index.

Hillman, Ben

How weird is it; a freaky book all about strangeness. Scholastic 2009 47p il $15.99

Grades: 5 6 7 8 **500**

1. Science 2. Curiosities and wonders

ISBN 978-0-439-91868-8; 0-439-91868-5

LC 2008-09787

Strange but facinating facts about everyday things that turn out to be extraordinary.

"Humor adds interest to the random but readable text. Large, vivid computer-manipulated photographs illustrate the information." Horn Book Guide

Murphy, Glenn

Why is snot green; and other extremely important questions (and answers) Roaring Brook Press 2009 236p il pa $9.95

Grades: 4 5 6 7 **500**

1. Science 2. Technology

ISBN 978-1-59643-500-1 pa; 1-59643-500-3 pa

"Conservation, evolution, technology, animal life, space travel, physics, and much more are discussed in this lively science book. . . . [This offers] chatty questions and answers . . . with text that is compelling, never intimidating, and sometimes deliberately outrageous. . . . Children will have fun browsing the spacious pages and sharing what they read with adults." Booklist

O'Meara, Stephen James

Are you afraid yet? the science behind scary stuff; written by Stephen James O'Meara; illustrated by Jeremy Kaposy. Kids Can Press 2009 78p il $17.95; pa $9.95

Grades: 5 6 7 8 **500**

1. Science 2. Supernatural

ISBN 978-1-55453-294-0; 1-55453-294-9; 978-1-55453-295-7 pa; 1-55453-295-7 pa

"This book cleverly weaves together the supernatural and the scientific in an entertaining read that answers questions about ghosts, UFOs, vampires, werewolves, and how long a decapitated head can remain conscious. Examples depicting such things in classical fiction and popular movies are seamlessly interjected between the factual explanations. Each page is filled with detailed black-and-white illustrations, emphasizing the sometimes-humorous, yet often-macabre descriptions." SLJ

Richardson, Gillian

Kaboom! explosions of all kinds. Annick Press 2009 83p il $22.95; pa $12.95

Grades: 4 5 6 7 **500**

1. Science 2. Explosions

ISBN 978-1-55451-204-1; 1-55451-204-2; 978-1-55451-203-4 pa; 1-55451-203-4 pa

"With comic-style sound-effect headings and fact boxes galore, Kaboom! highlights the supercharged of the natural and manmade worlds, from astronomy, geology, biology, herbology, and entomology to chemistry, mechanics, pyrotechnics, and art. Text is broken into asymmetrical panels for bite-size explanations. Some explosions are captured in sequence and detail with historical and high-speed photography and illustrations in comic-style panel frames. . . . Kaboom! is an engrossing attention-getter, effectively tapping the sensationalism of all types of blasts." SLJ

Williams, Brian

Science across cultures. Raintree 2010 48p il (Sci-hi: Earth and space science) lib bdg $31.34; pa $8.99

Grades: 6 7 8 9 **500**

1. Science 2. Scientists

ISBN 978-1-4109-3353-9 lib bdg; 1-4109-3353-9 lib bdg; 978-1-4109-3363-8 pa; 1-4109-3363-6 pa

LC 2009-13461

"This . . . makes science high impact and electric. . . . There are full-color pictures and eye-popping illustrations on quality paper. With no white spaces, every page is an attention-grabbing feast of color and design. Information is dispensed in large type with key words in bold. Interesting facts appear in pop-up balloons making this book an enjoyable read." Libr Media Connect

Includes glossary and bibliographical references

Wollard, Kathy

How come? in the neighborhood; illustrated by Debra Solomon. Workman Pub. 2007 292p il pa $12.95

Grades: 5 6 7 **500**

1. Science

ISBN 978-0-7611-4429-8

"Wollard explains hundreds of phenomena commonly encountered at home, at school, or in the yard—from boiling water to blushing, from why a yo-yo comes back to how the body makes and uses fat. Even taking on such knotty issues as whether the chicken or the egg came first, she answers each query with a specific, closely reasoned answer, animated by lively turns of phrase and intriguing observations. . . . Decorated with small, comical line drawings and supplemented by a healthy list of relevant Web sites, this volume will draw both browsers and serious-minded students like bugs to a porch light." Booklist

YES mag (Periodical)

Hoaxed! fakes & mistakes in the world of science. by the editors of YES mag; illustrated by Howie Woo. Kids Can Press 2009 48p il lib bdg $16.95; pa $8.95

Grades: 5 6 7 8   **500**

1. Fraud 2. Science 3. Fraud in science 4. Errors, Scientific

ISBN 978-1-55453-206-3 lib bdg; 1-55453-206-X lib bdg; 978-1-55453-207-0 pa; 1-55453-207-8 pa

"Piltdown man, Richard Meinertzhagen the light-fingered bird collector, 'Stone Age' Tasaday in the Philippines, crop circles in England, cold fusion energy and UFOs in Roswell, N.M., are the fakes and mistakes described in this lively introduction to fraud in science. The breezy text opens with a clear description of the scientific process of hypothesis, experiment, publication in professional magazines and replication of results before proceeding to the many colorful fakes exposed." Kirkus

Includes index.

500.5   Space sciences

Parks, Peggy J., 1951-

Space research. ReferencePoint Press 2010 96p il (Inside science) $26.95

Grades: 8 9 10 11 12   **500.5**

1. Astronautics 2. Space sciences

ISBN 978-1-60152-111-8; 1-60152-111-1

LC 2009-48159

"Parks piles on the research, digging deep into interstellar study, programs that reach into space, and what it all means to the common person, never shying away from detail and onerous proper nouns. . . . The color layout features plenty of photos, boxes, and charts, while Parks delivers a surprisingly spry text." Booklist

Includes bibliographical references

500.8   Groups of people

Thimmesh, Catherine

The **sky's** the limit; stories of discovery by women and girls. illustrated by Melissa Sweet. Houghton Mifflin 2002 73p il hardcover o.p. pa $7.95

Grades: 5 6 7 8   **500.8**

1. Science 2. Women scientists 3. Women in science 4. Science -- Miscellanea

ISBN 0-618-07698-0; 0-618-49489-8 pa

LC 2001-39111

"The lively design and the mixed-media collage artwork is a creative delight, and the intricate ink-and-watercolor borders, inventive paintings, and childlike pictures will draw readers in. The best thing about the book, however, is Thimmesh's sparkling writing style. . . . Report writers will appreciate this, but the book will also charm browsers." Booklist

Includes bibliographical references

502   Miscellany

Murphy, Glenn

How loud can you burp? more extremely important questions (and answers!) Roaring Book Press 2009 284p il pa $10.99

Grades: 4 5 6 7   **502**

1. Science 2. Questions and answers

ISBN 978-1-59643-506-3 pa; 1-59643-506-2 pa

"'Why does pollen give you hay fever?' 'Why don't big metal ships just sink?' These are but a couple of the questions that Murphy received on the Web site he set up to solicit inquiries from kids. Written in an informal, question-and-answer format, he delivers serious scientific information in an easygoing, humorous manner, with several pages dedicated to each topic. . . . A few line drawings break up the text and sidebars highlight interesting facts or are, at times, simply funny. . . . This is an entertaining, accessible approach to science that's sure to appeal to science buffs and general browsers alike." SLJ

502.8   Auxiliary techniques and procedures; apparatus, equipment, materials

Kramer, Stephen

★ **Hidden** worlds: looking through a scientist's microscope; photographs by Dennis Kunkel. Houghton Mifflin 2001 57p il (Scientists in the field) $16; pa $5.95

Grades: 4 5 6 7   **502.8**

1. Microscopes 2. Microscopists

ISBN 0-618-05546-0; 0-618-35405-0 pa

LC 00-58083

This book takes a "look at the work of a microscopist. Kunkel works with microscopes to explore science. . . . This book contains many of his photos, most taken with electron microscopes. . . . Several opening pages, along with the front and back endpapers, are visually dazzling. The heart of the book, though, is what readers learn about how Kunkel produces these images, and to what uses scientists put them. . . . This title offers a wealth of scientific information along with an insightful look at the world of an individual scientist." SLJ

Includes bibliographical references

Levine, Shar

★ The **ultimate** guide to your microscope; [by] Shar Levine & Leslie Johnstone. Sterling Pub. 2008 143p il pa $9.95

Grades: 5 6 7 8 9   **502.8**

1. Microscopes 2. Microscopy

ISBN 978-1-4027-4329-0 pa; 1-4027-4329-7 pa

LC 2006-100967

"Through this fun and inviting book, readers can begin to explore the world using a microscope. Students are encouraged to learn the basics in the two first chapters and then undertake the 41 hands-on activities in the next eight chapters. Activities are presented in manageable one or two-page uniformly formatted modules." SLJ

503 Dictionaries, encyclopedias, concordances

Jakab, Cheryl

★ The **encyclopedia** of junior science; [by] Cheryl Jakab, David Keystone. Chelsea Clubhouse 2009 10v il map set $230

Grades: 4 5 6 7   **503**

  1. Reference books 2. Science -- Encyclopedias

  ISBN 978-1-60413-554-1 set; 1-60413-554-9 set

              LC 2008-38113

"This set introduces students to basic science concepts. Approximately 270 entries are arranged alphabetically. . . . The writing is basic, and much of the information is presented in the form of charts and bulleted lists. . . . This set would be useful for school and public libraries seeking a science encyclopedia." Booklist

The **Kingfisher** science encyclopedia; general editor, Charles Taylor. 3rd ed. Kingfisher 2011 vii, 488 p.p ill. (some col.) (hardcover) $34.99

Grades: 5 6 7 8   **503**

  1. Science -- Encyclopedias 2. Science

  ISBN 0753466880; 9780753466889

              LC 2011047026

This book is a science encyclopedia edited by Charles Taylor. The book is arranged thematically and "most topics are presented on . . . two-page spreads, with relevant charts, timelines, and other illustrations surrounding the text. In the bottom right corner of the spread is a 'See Also Pages' box that directs readers to related topics with their page numbers." (Voice of Youth Advocates)

Topical chapters present "basic surveys of physics, geology, chemistry, biology, anatomy, the environment, and space. . . . Articles are generally, though not rigidly, confined to a spread each, and all have see-also references. . . . The illustrations are a plus; they are crisply reproduced, finely detailed, and labeled, enhancing the text rather than competing with it." SLJ

The **new** book of popular science. Scholastic Library Pub. 2008 6v il set $399

Grades: 7 8 9 10 11 12   **503**

  1. Reference books 2. Science -- Encyclopedias 3. Technology -- Encyclopedias

  ISBN 978-0-7172-1226-2

              LC 2007-41858

First published 1924 with title: The book of popular science. Frequently revised

The information in this set is classified under such broad categories as astronomy and space science, computers and mathematics, earth sciences, energy, environmental sciences, physical sciences, general biology, plant life, animal life, mammals, human sciences and technology.

Includes bibliographical references

507.8 Use of apparatus and equipment in study and teaching

Bardhan-Quallen, Sudipta

Last-minute science fair projects; when your Bunsen's not burning but the clock's really ticking. Sterling Pub. 2006 112p il $19.95

Grades: 5 6 7 8   **507.8**

  1. Science projects 2. Science -- Experiments

  ISBN 978-1-4027-1690-4; 1-4027-1690-7

              LC 2005-34455

"The introduction goes through a stripped-down summary of things to consider in choosing a project . . . a description of what to include in the project report, and some tips on presentation. . . . The description of each project is succinct and specific, with question, hypothesis, materials, and procedures clearly outlined." Sci Books Films

Bonnet, Robert L.

46 science fair projects for the evil genius. McGraw-Hill 2009 194p il (Evil genius series) pa $19.95

Grades: 6 7 8 9   **507.8**

  1. Science projects 2. Science -- Experiments

  ISBN 978-0-07-160027-9; 0-07-160027-2

              LC 2008008078

Provides instructions and plans for science projects across various disciplines, including physics, astronomy, energy, environmental science and economics.

Cobb, Vicki

See for yourself; more than 100 amazing experiments for science fairs and school projects. illustrated by Dave Klug. 2nd ed; Skyhorse Pub. 2010 192p il pa $14.95

Grades: 4 5 6 7   **507.8**

  1. Science -- Experiments

  ISBN 978-1-61608-083-9; 1-61608-083-3

              LC 2010020800

First published 2001 by Scholastic

This is an "accessible and often intriguing collection of activities and experiments. . . . The experiments are grouped by their source of inspiration: humans, the supermarket, the toy store, drugstore, and hardware and stationery stores. . . . Cartoon-style illustrations are . . . in full color." SLJ

★ **We** dare you! hundreds of science bets, challenges, and experiments you can do at home. [by] Vicki Cobb and Kathy Darling. Skyhorse Pub. 2007 321p il hardcover o.p. pa $14.94

Grades: 4 5 6 7   **507.8**

  1. Science -- Experiments 2. Scientific recreations

  ISBN 978-1-60239-225-0; 1-60239-225-0; 978-1-60239-775-0 pa; 1-60239-775-9 pa

              LC 2007-51236

"Divided into chapters with titles such as 'The Human Wonder,' 'Fluid Feats,' 'Energy Entrapments,' and 'Mathematical Duplicity,' this volume has more than 200 experiments with clear how-to instructions. All of the projects are doable and the science behind them is explained in a kid-accessible manner. . . . Black-and-white line drawings add humor and clarify instructions. This is a great resource for teachers, parents, and budding scientists—and for any youngster who can't resist a challenge." SLJ

Includes bibliographical references

Connolly, Sean

The **book** of potentially catastrophic science; 50 experiments for daring young scientists. Workman Pub. 2010 305p il $13.95

Grades: 5 6 7 8   **507.8**

1. Science -- Experiments

ISBN 0-7611-5687-9; 978-0-7611-5687-1

LC 2010-07044

This book presents thirty-four experiments. "Each chapter starts with a brief outline of the scientific advances of the time, followed by a clarification of the science and then one or more hands-on experiments to illustrate the object or concept presented. " (Sci Books Films)

"This volume approaches science historically, spotlighting certain periods, processes, individuals, discoveries, and inventions. Each of the 34 chapters includes a discussion and one or two related activities, such as making a Stone Age tool, creating an earthquake in Jell-O, building a parachute for an egg drop, and extracting a banana's DNA. Safety concerns are addressed for each project, and adult help will be necessary to complete some of the experiments successfully. . . . Connolly's writing is engaging, and the historical approach works well, offering kids a quick introduction to science history and the opportunity to explore certain ideas along the way." Booklist

Gardner, Robert

Light, sound, and waves science fair projects; revised and expanded using the scientific method. Enslow Publishers 2010 160p il (Physics science projects using the scientific method) lib bdg $34.60

Grades: 7 8 9 10   **507.8**

1. Light 2. Sound 3. Waves 4. Science projects 5. Science -- Experiments

ISBN 978-0-7660-3416-7 lib bdg; 0-7660-3416-X lib bdg

LC 2009006493

First published 2004 with title: Light, sound, and waves science fair projects using sunglasses, guitars, CDs, and other stuff

"Explains how to use the scientific method to conduct several science experiments about light, sound, and waves. Includes ideas for science fair projects." Publisher's note

Includes bibliographical references

Planet Earth science fair projects; revised and expanded using the scientific method. Enslow Publishers 2010 160p il (Earth science projects using the scientific method) lib bdg $34.60

Grades: 7 8 9 10   **507.8**

1. Earth sciences 2. Science projects 3. Science -- Experiments 4. Geology 5. Astronomy

ISBN 978-0-7660-3423-5 lib bdg; 0-7660-3423-2 lib bdg

LC 2009-26546

A revised edition of Planet Earth Science Fair Projects Using the Moon, Stars, Beach Balls, Frisbees, and Other Far-out Stuff, published 2005

"Explains how to use the scientific method to conduct several science experiments about earth science. Includes ideas for science fair projects." Publisher's note

Includes bibliographical references

Goodstein, Madeline

Ace your sports science project; great science fair ideas. [by] Madeline Goodstein, Robert Gardner, and Barbara Gardner Conklin. Enslow Publishers 2009 128p il (Ace your physics science project) lib bdg $31.93

Grades: 5 6 7 8   **507.8**

1. Sports 2. Physics 3. Science projects 4. Science -- Experiments

ISBN 978-0-7660-3229-3 lib bdg; 0-7660-3229-9 lib bdg

LC 2008-4689

"Presents several science experiments and project ideas dealing with the physics of sports." Publisher's note

Includes bibliographical references

Goal! science projects with soccer. Enslow Publishers 2009 104p il (Score! Sports science projects) lib bdg $31.93

Grades: 5 6 7 8   **507.8**

1. Motion 2. Soccer 3. Force and energy 4. Science projects 5. Science -- Experiments

ISBN 978-0-7660-3106-7 lib bdg; 0-7660-3106-3 lib bdg

LC 2008-2999

"Introductions include information about the history of the sport, safety steps to follow, and the scientific method. . . . Detailed diagrams help clarify many of the directions." SLJ

Includes glossary and bibliographical references

Graham, Ian

Science rocks! written by Ian Graham; additional text by Dr. Mike Goldsmith; step illustrations by Dan Wright. DK Pub. 2011 144p il $19.99

Grades: 6 7 8 9   **507.8**

1. Science -- Experiments

ISBN 978-0-7566-7198-3; 0-7566-7198-1

"Physics, chemistry, biology, and human physiology are the subjects covered in this huge, lavishly illustrated volume, packed with detailed suggestions for experiments to perform at home, at school, and for science-fair projects. The tone is relaxed but never cute, and the browsable design blends how-to with explanations of the forces at play." Booklist

Harris, Elizabeth Snoke

Save the Earth science experiments; science fair projects for eco-kids. [illustrator, Orrin Lundgren] Lark Books 2008 112p il $19.95

Grades: 4 5 6   **507.8**

1. Science projects 2. Environmental protection 3. Science -- Experiments

ISBN 978-1-60059-322-2; 1-60059-322-4

LC 2008017826

This describes science fair projects such as how to harness energy with windmills, make a biogas generator, create alternative fuels, and recycle paper

Margles, Samantha

Mythbusters science fair book. Scholastic 2011 128p il pa $9.99

Grades: 4 5 6 7   **507.8**
   1. Science projects 2. Science -- Experiments
   ISBN 978-0-545-23745-1; 0-545-23745-9

This offers "50 original ideas for science fair projects or long, boredom-riddled summer days. Much like the popular television program on which it's based, the book stays true to the scientific method. . . . Divided into chapters on chemical reactions, temperature, energy and force, and more, the two- to three-page experiments on busily designed pages feature easy step-by-step procedures." Booklist

Newcomb, Rain

Smash it! crash it! launch it! 50 mind-blowing, eye-popping science experiments. [by] Rain Newcomb & Bobby Mercer. Lark Books 2006 80p il $14.95

Grades: 4 5 6 7   **507.8**
   1. Science -- Experiments 2. Physics
   ISBN 978-1-57990-795-2; 1-57990-795-4
                                         LC 2006-05518

"Science teachers will find entertaining ways to impress their students with Newton's laws if they're willing to break a few eggs as described in this engaging book. The study of physics becomes appealing when combined with marshmallow catapults, potato popguns, and water-balloon launchers. The authors provide a brief explanation of the physical principles involved and emphasize that cleanup is required on some of the messier projects. . . . Humorous cartoon illustrations and sketchy templates supplement the descriptions of how to set up the projects. Typical household ingredients like straws, pop bottles, fruits, and lots of eggs are the materials required." SLJ

VanCleave, Janice Pratt

Janice VanCleave's engineering for every kid; easy activities that make learning science fun. Jossey-Bass 2007 205p il (Science for every kid series) pa $14.95

Grades: 4 5 6 7   **507.8**
   1. Engineering 2. Science projects 3. Science -- Experiments 4. Engineering -- Experiments
   ISBN 978-0-471-47182-0 pa; 0-471-47182-8 pa
                                         LC 2006-10540

Explains some of the basic physical principles of engineering, accompanied by activities that illustrate those principles

Vickers, Tanya M.

Teen science fair sourcebook; winning school science fairs and national competitions. Enslow Publishers 2009 160p il lib bdg $34.60

Grades: 7 8 9 10   **507.8**
   1. Science projects 2. Science -- Exhibitions 3. Science

-- Experiments
   ISBN 978-0-7660-2711-4; 0-7660-2711-2
                                         LC 2008-30779

"The book is clearly written, and its page design, which includes the occasional photo, is colorful. . . . A useful resource for highly motivated students." Booklist

Includes glossary and bibliographical references

Walker, Pamela

Environmental science experiments; [by] Pamela Walker, Elaine Wood. Facts on File 2010 153p il (Facts on File science experiments) $35

Grades: 7 8 9 10   **507.8**
   1. Environmental science 2. Science -- Experiments
   ISBN 978-0-8160-7805-9; 0-8160-7805-X
                                         LC 2008-53715

This "contains 20 experiments that allow students to actively engage in scientific inquiry. Projects are presented in a uniform format, with an introduction to the topic, time requirements (35 minutes to 2 weeks), a materials list, numbered procedures, and several analysis questions. . . . Line drawings, colorful images, and data tables enhance instructions. . . . The experiments themselves are timely and fascinating. [The book] includes high-interest investigations into what people throw away, the safety of reusing water bottles, and a 'bottled versus tap water' taste test." SLJ

Includes glossary and bibliographical references

Williams, Jennifer

★ **Oobleck,** slime, & dancing spaghetti; twenty terrific at-home science experiments inspired by favorite children's books. by Jennifer Williams. Bright Sky Press 2009 192 p. ill. (paperback) $14.95

Grades: 4 5 6   **507.8**
   1. Science -- Experiments
   ISBN 1933979348; 9781933979342
                                         LC 2009000876

"Using children's literature as a springboard, this title provides a series of science experiments designed to explore concepts and ideas that spring from various stories. At the beginning of each chapter, a children's book is nicely summarized. The author then explains a related science concept, suggests discussion questions that connect the experiment to the story, and offers ideas for taking the project further. This is serious science. . . . The experiments do a really wonderful job of emphasizing the importance of observation and data collection. The writing is relatively clear. . . . This book is great choice for home use and science units." SLJ

Includes bibliographical references.

Young, Karen Romano

Junkyard science; 20 projects and experiments about junk, garbage, waste, things we don't need anymore, and ways to recycle or reuse it--or lose it. illustrations by David Goldin. National Geographic 2010 80p il (Science fair winners) $24.90; pa $12.95

Grades: 3 4 5 6   **507.8**
   1. Recycling 2. Environmental sciences 3. Science -- Experiments
   ISBN 978-1-4263-0690-7; 1-4263-0690-3; 978-1-4263-0689-1 pa; 1-4263-0689-X pa

This volume provides "outlines for science fair projects in the . . . environmental . . . sciences. The procedures include just enough structure to help novice experimenters get started. . . . Well-placed questions encourage creativity and further thinking. [The] volume includes humorous cartoon spot illustrations and a section on preparing presentations." Horn Book Guide

Science activities for all students; edited by Aviva Ebner. Facts on File 2009 2v il loose-leaf $370

    Grades: Adult Professional   **507.8**

    1. Science projects 2. Science -- Experiments

    ISBN 978-0-8160-7396-2 loose-leaf; 0-8160-7396-1 loose-leaf

LC 2008043827

Replaces Science Projects for All Students and More Science Projects for All Students, published 1998 and 2002 respectively

These "binders enable students in grades 4 through 9 with developmental or physical challenges to join their classmates in . . . hands-on [science] activities. There are 60 experiments in each binder—designed to be as inclusive as possible—in the areas of basic skills, Earth science, weather, space science, life science, and physical science. Each binder is also enhanced by approximately 250 black-and-white line illustrations." Publisher's note

Includes glossary and bibliographical references

508   Natural history

Art, Henry Warren

    Woodswalk; peepers, pikas, and exploding puff balls. [by] Henry W. Art and Michael W. Robbins. Storey Books 2003 122p il map $21.95; pa $14.95

    Grades: 4 5 6   **508**

    1. Seasons 2. Nature study 3. Forest plants 4. Forest animals

    ISBN 1-58017-477-9; 1-58017-452-3 pa

"This inviting introduction to forests describes the sights, sounds, and smells that await young explorers. The accessible text details the wonders of each season in both eastern and western locales, while full-color photos depict the flora and fauna that inhabit these intriguing environments." SLJ

Baker, Stuart

    In the Antarctic. Marshall Cavendish Benchmark 2009 32p il map (Climate change) lib bdg $19.95

    Grades: 5 6 7 8   **508**

    1. Greenhouse effect

    ISBN 978-0-7614-4438-1 lib bdg; 0-7614-4438-6 lib bdg

LC 2009-5766

The book about climate change in the Antarctic "is perfectly organized for students. . . . Unique layout features serve as signposts and will help focus readers' attention. . . . [The book] features an outstanding chart of possible effects of global warming on the area in question, listing 'Possible Event', 'Predicted Result', and 'Impact' in short, bulleted statements." SLJ

    Includes glossary

In the tropics. Marshall Cavendish Benchmark 2010 32p il map (Climate change) lib bdg $19.95

    Grades: 5 6 7 8   **508**

    1. Greenhouse effect

    ISBN 978-0-7614-4440-4 lib bdg; 0-7614-4440-8 lib bdg

LC 2009-5768

The book about climate change in the Tropics "is perfectly organized for students. . . . Unique layout features serve as signposts and will help focus readers' attention. . . . [The book] features an outstanding chart of possible effects of global warming on the area in question, listing 'Possible Event', 'Predicted Result', and 'Impact' in short, bulleted statements." SLJ

    Includes glossary

Bardhan-Quallen, Sudipta

    Nature science experiments; what's hopping in a dust bunny? illustrated by Edward Miller. Sterling 2010 64p il (Mad science) $12.95

    Grades: 4 5 6   **508**

    1. Nature study 2. Science -- Experiments 3. Biology

    ISBN 978-1-4027-2412-1; 1-4027-2412-8

"The first chapter of this attractive book, 'The Stuff of Life,' jumps right in by outlining the materials needed and the step-by-step process to follow to collect and isolate DNA by rinsing one's mouth out with salt water. . . . Youngsters can turn to the table of contents or detailed index to choose experiments based on interest and availability of resources. . . . The chapters on bacteria and protists include color photomicrographs of the organisms, and amusing cartoon illustrations appear throughout. This exploration of the natural world will spark readers' interest in experimenting and questioning results." SLJ

Burnie, David

    The **Kingfisher** nature encyclopedia; rev ed.; Kingfisher 2010 320p il $27.99

    Grades: 4 5 6 7   **508**

    1. Nature 2. Natural history 3. Reference books

    ISBN 978-0-7534-6503-5; 0-7534-6503-5

First published 2004 with title: The Kingfisher illustrated nature encyclopedia

"Organized into three sections—the first on our planet's origin and the evolution of life, the second surveying the five biotic kingdoms, the third taking closer looks at 14 biomes . . .—each spread offers a topical discussion that ranges in scope from 'Seasons and Weather' or 'How Fungi Feed' to 'Protozoans' and 'Tropical Forests.' Color photos on every page add visual interest while playing supporting roles to information presented in captions and columns of lucid, not heavily technical narrative text. . . . This is a first-rate overview of its topic." SLJ

Chin, Jason

    ★ **Island**; a story of the Galapagos. Jason Chin. 1st ed. Roaring Brook Press 2012 40 p. (alk. paper) $16.99

    Grades: 3 4 5 6   **508**

    1. Birds 2. Droughts 3. Reptiles 4. Natural history

-- Galapagos Islands
ISBN 1596437162; 9781596437166
LC 2011033797
The author, Jason Chin, explains "how species of reptiles and birds on the Galapagos have evolved. He begins with the birth of the islands themselves, a process in which volcanic eruptions punch successive holes in the Earth's surface as tectonic plates move over them, [and] the adaptations of the islands' animals.... [Chin also provides information on the] droughts [that] become more common [due to the] climate and geology." (Publishers Weekly)
Includes bibliographical references and index.

Hamilton, Neil A.
Scientific exploration and expeditions; from the age of discovery to the twenty-first century. [by] Neil Hamilton. M.E. Sharpe 2011 2v il map set $165
Grades: 7 8 9 10 11 12   508
1. Reference books 2. Scientific expeditions
ISBN 978-0-7656-8076-1; 0-7656-8076-9
LC 2010-12118
"Hamilton's 115 entries in this set describe the courses and discoveries of significant scientific expeditions from the early 15th century to mid 2009. . . . The presentations are systematic, carefully detailed, not exclusively Eurocentric, and when appropriate, skeptical. The currency of information and focus on science will make this work particularly useful." SLJ
Includes bibliographical references

Lynch, Wayne
The **Everglades**; text and photographs by Wayne Lynch. NorthWord Books for Young Readers 2007 64p il (Our wild world: ecosystems) $16.95; pa $8.95
Grades: 4 5 6 7   508
1. Natural history -- Florida 2. Natural history -- Florida -- Everglades
ISBN 978-1-55971-970-4; 1-55971-970-2; 978-1-55971-971-1 pa; 1-55971-971-0 pa
LC 2006-101497
This "provides an up-close look at the fascinating flora and fauna of the world-famous Everglades. . . . Lynch . . . smoothly pairs engaging prose with numerous color photographs that capture the beauty of the region in both sweeping panorama and close-up detail." Booklist

Wadsworth, Ginger
John Burroughs; the sage of Slabsides. Clarion Bks. 1997 95p il $16.95
Grades: 5 6 7 8   508
1. Authors 2. Naturalists 3. Writers on nature
ISBN 0-395-77830-1
LC 95-48400
A photobiography of the naturalist, ornithologist, author, poet, teacher, and pioneer of the conservation movement who lived and worked in his rustic cabin in the Catskill Mountains
"The pictures are mostly informal and candid, taken from personal collections, with a few studio portraits interspersed. Written with a familiar, almost intimate tone, the text is liberally sprinkled with quotes from Burroughs's publications." SLJ
Includes bibliographical references

Wood, A. J.
Charles Darwin and the Beagle adventure; countries visited during the voyage round the world of HMS Beagle under the command of Captain Fitzroy, Royal Navy, including extracts from the works of Charles Darwin. written by A.J. Wood & Clint Twist. Candlewick Press 2009 un il map $19.99
Grades: 4 5 6 7 8   508
1. Evolution 2. Naturalists 3. Travel writers 4. Writers on science 5. Natural history 6. Evolution (Biology)
ISBN 978-0-7636-4538-0; 0-7636-4538-9
LC 2009-921214
"This beautifully illustrated large-format book immediately appeals to both the eye and the mind. Imitating a 19th-century scrapbook to a certain extent, including various pull-outs . . . the book draws the young reader in. . . . Included are copious quotes from Darwin's journals and other writings, as well as reproductions . . . of numerous 19th-century engravings, drawings, and watercolors, some from the Beagle voyage itself. . . . Integrated into the 19th-century material are modern illustrations and well-written narratives relating background information, the story of the Beagle's voyage . . . and notes on Darwin's life and work. . . . This volume provides an excellent introduction to Darwin and his accomplishments." Sci Books Films

Woods, Michael
Seven natural wonders of Africa; by Michael Woods and Mary B. Woods. Twenty-First Century Books 2009 80p il map (Seven natural wonders) lib bdg $33.26
Grades: 5 6 7 8   508
1. Curiosities and wonders 2. Natural history -- Africa
ISBN 978-0-8225-9071-2; 0-8225-9071-9
LC 2008-21867
This book "takes seven noteworthy wonders in [Africa] and spotlights them in separate chapters. The text introduces each one from a historical perspective, and beautiful color photographs offer inviting views, while maps, sidebars, and featured quotes add variety to the pages. [This book] looks at mountain gorillas, the Nile, Victoria Falls, the Sahara Desert, Mount Kilimanjaro, the Seychelles Islands and the Serengeti Plain." Booklist
Includes bibliographical references

Seven natural wonders of Asia and the Middle East; by Michael Woods and Mary B. Woods. Twenty-First Century Books 2009 80p il (Seven natural wonders) lib bdg $33.26
Grades: 5 6 7 8   508
1. Curiosities and wonders 2. Natural history -- Asia 3. Natural history -- Middle East
ISBN 978-0-8225-9073-6; 0-8225-9073-5
LC 2008027605
Chapters in this book describe Mount Everest, the Gobi Desert, Mount Fuji, Sumatra rain forests, the Dead Sea, Cap-

padocia, and the Chocolate Hills, including historical perspectives and color photographs.

Includes bibliographical references

Seven natural wonders of Australia and Oceania; by Michael Woods and Mary B. Woods. Twenty-First Century Books 2009 80p il (Seven natural wonders) lib bdg $33.26

Grades: 5 6 7 8   508
1. Curiosities and wonders 2. Natural history -- Australia
ISBN 978-0-8225-9074-3 lib bdg; 0-8225-9074-3 lib bdg
LC 2008014003

Chapters in this book describe the Australian outback, Aoraki/Mount Cook, Mount Kilauea, the Bungle Bungles, the Tasmanian wilderness, Bora Bora, and New Caledonia, including historical perspectives and color photographs.

Includes bibliographical references

Seven natural wonders of Central and South America; by Michael Woods and Mary B. Woods. Twenty-First Century Books 2009 80p il map (Seven natural wonders) lib bdg $33.26

Grades: 5 6 7 8   508
1. Curiosities and wonders 2. Natural history -- South America 3. Natural history -- Central America
ISBN 978-0-8225-9070-5 lib bdg; 0-8225-9070-0 lib bdg
LC 2008027203

This book "takes seven noteworthy wonders in [Central and South America] . . . and spotlights them in separate chapters. The text introduces each one from a historical perspective, and beautiful color photographs offer inviting views, while maps, sidebars, and featured quotes add variety to the pages. . . . [This book] discusses Angel Falls, the Amazon River, the Atacama Desert, the Galápagos Islands, the Montecristo Cloud Forest, Poás Volcano, and the Andes Mountains." Booklist

Includes glossary and bibliographical references

Seven natural wonders of Europe; by Michael Woods and Mary B. Woods. Twenty-First Century Books 2009 80p il (Seven natural wonders) lib bdg $33.26

Grades: 5 6 7 8   508
1. Curiosities and wonders 2. Natural history -- Europe
ISBN 978-0-8225-9072-9 lib bdg; 0-8225-9072-7 lib bdg
LC 2008027604

Chapters in this book describe Loch Ness, Westmann Islands, Lake Baikal, Black Forest, Mons Klint, Fjords of Norway, and The Alps, including historical perspectives and color photographs.

Includes bibliographical references

Seven natural wonders of North America; by Michael Woods and Mary B. Woods. Twenty-First Century Books 2009 80p il map (Seven natural wonders) lib bdg $33.26

Grades: 5 6 7 8   508
1. Curiosities and wonders 2. Natural history -- North America
ISBN 978-0-8225-9069-9; 0-8225-9069-7
LC 2008021864

This book "takes seven noteworthy wonders in [North America] . . . and spotlights them in separate chapters. The text introduces each one from a historical perspective, and beautiful color photographs offer inviting views, while maps, sidebars, and featured quotes add variety to the pages. . . . [This book] takes readers to Dinosaur Provincial Park, Pacific Rim National Park, the redwood forests, Niagara Falls, the Grand Canyon, Yellowstone National Park, and the Paricutin Volcano." Booklist

Includes glossary and bibliographical references

509   History, geographic treatment, biography

Blanchard, Anne
★ **Arab** science and invention in the golden age; [illustrated by Emmanuel Cerisier; translated by R.M. Brent] Enchanted Lion Books 2008 65p il map $19.95

Grades: 6 7 8 9   509
1. Arab civilization 2. Science -- History 3. Inventions 4. Islamic Empire -- Civilization
ISBN 978-1-59270-080-6; 1-59270-080-2
LC 2008-26431

"The Muslim world led an amazing scientific revolution for hundreds of years with breakthroughs in math, geography, physics, astronomy, and medicine. This large-size, attractive volume packs in a wealth of information about the rise and fall of the immense empire. . . . The open format, with lots of boxed inserts and detailed illustrations on each double-page spread, is dense with information." Booklist

Includes glossary and bibliographical references

Eamer, Claire
Before the World Was Ready; Stories of Daring Genius in Science. by Claire Eamer. Firefly Books Ltd 2013 125 p. (paperback) $14.95

Grades: 5 6 7 8   509
1. Inventions 2. Scientists
ISBN 1554515351; 9781554515356

This book looks at eight scientists and inventors. "Alfred Wegener struggled to convince geologists that the ground beneath our feet is moving. . . . Nikola Tesla's futuristic ideas about electricity were dismissed. Charles Darwin delayed publishing his controversial theory of evolution for decades." Also included are Charles Babbage, Ada Lovelace, Rachel Carson, and George Cayley. (Publisher's note)

Hakim, Joy
★ The **story** of science: Aristotle leads the way. Smithsonian Books 2004 282p (Story of science) $24.95

Grades: 8 9 10 11 12   509
1. Ancient civilization 2. Science -- History
ISBN 1-58834-160-7

"Hakim has interwoven creation myths, history, physics, and mathematics to present a seamless, multifaceted view of the foundation of modern science. . . . The entire volume is beautifully organized." SLJ

Includes bibliographical references

★ The **story** of science: Einstein adds a new dimension. Smithsonian Books 2007 468p il (Story of science) $27.95

Grades: 8 9 10 11 12   509

1. Cosmology 2. Physicists 3. Quantum theory 4. Science -- History 5. Nobel laureates for physics

ISBN 978-1-58834-162-4; 1-58834-162-3

LC 2007-14096

Hakim delivers a "brisk, intellectually challenging account of the development of quantum theory and modern cosmology. . . . She introduces a teeming cast of deep thinkers who . . . delivered a series of brilliant experiments and insights. . . . Supplemented by a digestible resource list and a generous assortment of illustrations." Booklist

Includes bibliographical references

★ The **story** of science: Newton at the center. Smithsonian Books 2005 463p (Story of science) $24.95

Grades: 8 9 10 11 12   509

1. Physics 2. Astronomy 3. Science -- History

ISBN 1-58834-161-5

LC 2004-58465

This "is an account of the history of astronomy and physics from c.1500 to 1900."

"Teachers will find anecdotal information to enliven their lessons; browsers will be fascinated by the sidebars and captioned illustrations that enhance the text or show related information." SLJ

Includes bibliographical references

Jackson, Donna M.

★ **Extreme** scientists; exploring nature's mysteries from perilous places. Houghton Mifflin Harcourt 2009 63p il (Scientists in the field) $18

Grades: 5 6 7 8   509

1. Botanists 2. Explorers 3. Scientists 4. Spelunkers 5. Meteorologists 6. Microbiologists 7. College teachers

ISBN 978-0-618-77706-8; 0-618-77706-7

LC 2008-36796

This volume "profiles three scientists working far out in the field. Hurricane hunter Paul Flaherty, . . . Hazel Barton, a microbiologist specializing in single-cell organisms living in extreme conditions, . . . [and] ecologist and college professor Steve Sillett, who . . . climbs into the canopies to study redwoods. While the clearly written text includes vivid passages about the dangers these scientists face, it goes on to discuss what drives them to pursue their subjects and what they have discovered along the way. . . . The many excellent color photos portray these adventures as scientists intently focused on their work." Booklist

Includes glossary and bibliographical references

Moser, Diane

The **birth** of science: ancient times to 1699; [by] Ray Spangenburg and Diane Kit Moser. Facts on File 2004 256p (History of science) $35

Grades: 7 8 9 10   509

1. Science -- History

ISBN 0-8160-4851-7

LC 2003-19470

First published 1993 with title: The history of science from the ancient Greeks to the scientific revolution

Discusses major scientists as well as scientific knowledge and discoveries from ancient times through the seventeenth century

"Very well written and thoroughly understandable, the book succeeds hugely in its objective to introduce the development of science in an interesting fashion to the intended audience without patronizing or oversimplifying." Sci Books Films [review of 1993 edition]

Includes glossary and bibliographical references

Mullins, Lisa

Science in the Renaissance; [by] Lisa Mullins. Crabtree Pub. 2009 32p pa $8.95; lib bdg $26.60

Grades: 6 7 8 9   509

1. Science 2. Renaissance

ISBN 978-0-7787-4614-0 pa; 0-7787-4614-3 pa; 978-07787-4594-5 lib bdg; 0-7787-4594-5 lib bdg

LC 2008-52602

"Ideal introductions to concepts, people, and events of the Renaissance... succinct and thorough." SLJ

Reynolds, Moira Davison

American women scientists; 23 inspiring biographies, 1900-2000. McFarland & Co. 1999 149p il hardcover o.p. pa $24.95

Grades: 7 8 9 10   509

1. Women scientists 2. Women scientists -- United States 3. Women scientists -- United States -- History -- 20th century

ISBN 0-7864-0649-6; 0-7864-2161-4 pa

LC 99-14603

"Four-to-six page profiles of 23 of the century's premier women scientists, representing a wide variety of disciplines. The entries are arranged chronologically beginning with Cornelia Clapp (1849-1934) and ending with Mary Good (1931-). . . . Each entry includes a black-and-white portrait." SLJ

Includes bibliographical references

Spangenburg, Ray

Science frontiers, 1946 to the present; [by] Ray Spangenburg and Diane Kit Moser. Facts on File 2004 272p (History of science) $35

Grades: 7 8 9 10   509

1. Science -- History

ISBN 0-8160-4855-X

LC 2003-24290

First published 1994 with title: The history of science from 1946 to the 1990s

The authors provide "descriptions of complex scientific theories and lines of research in the latter part of the 20th century—but only in the natural sciences: physics (new particles, lasers, and superconductors), astronomy (quasars, black holes, cosmology, dark matter, planetary geology, and SETI), geology (evolution, plate tectonics, and environmental change), and biology (DNA, biotechnology, the human genome, and retroviruses)." Sci Books Films [review of 1994 edition]

Includes glossary and bibliographical references

509.2   Scientists

Baxter, Roberta

John Dalton and the development of atomic theory; by Roberta Baxter. Morgan Reynolds Pub. 2012 144 p. ill. (library) $28.95

Grades: 7 8 9 10 11 12   **509.2**
1. Atomic theory 2. Chemists -- Great Britain -- Biography
ISBN 1599351226; 9781599351223; 9781599352763
LC 2010038610

This children's nonfiction book, by Roberta Baxter, is part of the "Profiles in Science" series, profiling the 19th-century physicist and chemist John Dalton and his contributions to the development of atomic theory. Topics include a profile of his personal life, his work researching atomic theory at the turn of the 19th century, and the legacy of his theories after his death.

"The reading level is high, some of the more advanced scientific concepts are not adequately illustrated, and the author assumes reader familiarity with British currency, history, and geography. . . . [T]his title should be considered as a supplementary choice for secondary readers who possess a basic understanding of chemistry and need report material on Dalton or his revolutionary work." SLJ

Includes bibliographical references

Davidson, Tish

African American scientists and inventors; by Tish Davidson. Mason Crest Publishers 2013 64 p. ill. (some col.) (Major Black contributions from Emancipation to civil rights) (library) $22.95

Grades: 4 5 6   **509.2**
1. African American inventors 2. African American scientists 3. African American inventors -- Biography 4. African American scientists -- Biography
ISBN 1422223752; 9781422223758
LC 2011051942

This book by Tish Davidson profiles African American scientists and inventors. "Some of them were elementary school dropouts. Others became medical doctors or college professors. Some were famous, while some toiled in obscurity. . . . Lewis Latimer devised a manufacturing process that made electric lights affordable for ordinary people. Charles Drew did pioneering work in blood storage, helping save countless lives. Garrett Woods figured out how to send messages from moving trains." (Publisher's note)

Includes bibliographical references (pages 60-61) and index.

Di Domenico, Kelly

Women scientists who changed the world; by Kelly Di Domenico. Rosen Pub. 2012 106 p. col. ill. (library) $34.60

Grades: 5 6 7 8   **509.2**
1. Women scientists -- Biography 2. Women in science -- Biography
ISBN 1448859999; 9781448859993
LC 2011032120

In this collective biography by Kelly Di Domenico, "readers meet eleven women scientists, whose research and discoveries are outstanding in their fields. . . . Readers are introduced to each scientist's life and work, including the obstacles each woman had to overcome to achieve success. Profiles include biologist Rachel Carson, orangutan researcher Birute Galdikas, and Nobel Prize-winning biochemist Ada Yonath." (Publisher's note)

Includes bibliographical references (p. 101) and index.

Miles, Liz

Louis Pasteur; by Liz Miles. Raintree 2009 48 p. ill. (chiefly col.) (Great scientists) (library) $32.00

Grades: 4 5 6   **509.2**
1. Science -- History -- 19th century 2. Scientists -- France -- Biography 3. Microbiologists -- France -- Biography
ISBN 141093229X; 9781410932297
LC 2007050125

This book by Liz Miles is part of the Leveled Biographies series and looks at Louis Pasteur. "What is Pasteurization? How has Pasteur's work helped treat many diseases? The 'Leveled Biographies' series offers leveled, high-interest nonfiction in a range of text genres. Each title tells the story of one memorable life, using pictures, maps, sidebars, and engaging text to make each person's story come alive." (Publisher's note)

Includes bibliographical references (p. 46) and index.

Ottaviani, Jim

Primates; The Fearless Science of Jane Goodall, Dian Fossey, and Biruté Galdikas. Jim Ottaviani; illustrated by Maris Wicks. First Second 2013 133 p. (hardcover) $19.99

Grades: 5 6 7 8   **509.2**
1. Scientists -- Biography
ISBN 1596438657; 9781596438651

This nonfiction graphic novel, by Jim Ottaviani, illustrated by Maris Wicks, presents an "account of the three greatest primatologists of the last century: Jane Goodall, Dian Fossey, and Biruté Galdikas. These three ground-breaking researchers were all students of the great Louis Leakey, and each made profound contributions to primatology--and to our own understanding of ourselves." (Publisher's note)

509.4   History of science in Europe

Nardo, Don

The **scientific** revolution; by Don Nardo. Lucent Books 2011 104 p. ill. (World history series) (library) $34.95

Grades: 6 7 8 9   509.4
 1. Science -- History 2. Discoveries in science -- Europe
 ISBN 1420506137; 9781420506136
                                            LC 2011006556

This book by Don Nardo is part of the World History series and looks at the Scientific Revolution. The series entries offer an "overview of an important historical event or period. The series is designed both to acquaint readers with the basics of history and to make them aware that their lives and their own historical era are an intimate part of the ongoing human saga." (Publisher's note)

Includes bibliographical references (p. 96-98) and index.

509.56   History of science in the Islamic Empire

Romanek, Trudee

Science, medicine, and math in the early Islamic world; Trudee Romanek. Crabtree Pub. Company 2012 48 p. (reinforced library binding : alk. paper) $30.60

Grades: 4 5 6 7   509.56
 1. Science -- History 2. Medicine -- History 3. Mathematics -- History 4. Islamic civilization 5. Science -- Islamic Empire -- History
 ISBN 0778721701; 9780778721703; 9780778721772; 9781427195630; 9781427198402
                                            LC 2012000077

This children's educational book, by Trudee Romanek, describes "the scientific contributions of the early Islamic empires to science, medicine, and mathematics. . . . This . . . book explores their public hospitals, libraries, and universities; their achievements in mathematics and astronomy, and the pursuit of alchemy; Arabic numbers; optics; music and musical instruments; poetry; and education." (Publisher's note)

510   Mathematics

Bazin, Maurice

★ **Math** and science across cultures; activities and investigations from the Exploratorium. [by] Maurice Bazin, Modesto Tamez, and the Exploratorium Teacher Institute. New Press 2002 176p il maps pa $19.95

Grades: Adult Professional   510
 1. Science 2. Mathematics 3. Science -- Study and teaching 4. Mathematics -- Study and teaching
 ISBN 1-56584-541-2
                                            LC 00-136455

This book provides "activities that integrate geography, math, and science into a multicultural curriculum. . . . Each topic provides a hands-on, minds-on activity that enriches

thinking skills and the application-research-based process." Sci Books Films

Includes bibliographical references

Henderson, Harry

Mathematics: powerful patterns in nature and society. Facts on File 2007 170p il (Milestones in discovery and invention) $35

Grades: 7 8 9 10 11 12   510
 1. Mathematics
 ISBN 0-8160-5750-8; 978-0-8160-5750-4
                                            LC 2006-24680

"Some mathematicians have discovered relatively simple yet exceedingly powerful patterns that yield insight into aspects of natural and human behavior. . . . [This book] presents 10 essays that profile the minds behind such patterns, many of which have surfaced in recent popular culture." Publisher's note

Includes glossary and bibliographical references

Lee, Cora

The **great** number rumble; [a story of math in surprising places] [by] Cora Lee & Gillian O'Reilly; illustrations by Virginia Gray. Annick Press 2007 104p il $24.95; pa $14.95

Grades: 4 5 6   510
 1. Mathematics
 ISBN 978-1-55451-032-0; 1-55451-032-5; 978-1-55451-031-3 pa; 1-55451-031-7 pa

"When the schools in Jeremy's town ban math, there are loud cheers from the kids. . . . But Jeremy's best friend Sam, a self-proclaimed mathnik, sets out to prove that math is not only important, but fun. In the chapters that follow, Sam reveals math's presence in everyday places, including sports (types of triangles determine how a bike functions), art (artist M.C. Escher combined math patterns with imagination), even in nature (ants instinctively calculate dead reckoning—a navigation tool also used by astronauts). . . . In the end, Jeremy, his teachers, and even the Director of Education have to admit that school minus math equals all sorts of trouble." (Publisher's note)

"Interspersed with the story line are one-page biographies of Pythagoras, Archimedes, Hypatia of Alexandria, Sophie Germain, Charles Ludwig Dodgson, Srinivasa Ramanujan, and Andrew Wiles. Sidebars with Jeremy's thoughts on chaos theory, cash prizes for new prime numbers, laws of probability, and palindrome numbers add to the information. Full-color cartoons, diagrams, and photos appear throughout." SLJ

McKellar, Danica

★ **Math** doesn't suck; how to survive middle school math without losing your mind or breaking a nail. [by] Danica McKellar. Hudson Street Press 2007 297p il $23.95

Grades: 5 6 7 8   510
 1. Mathematics
 ISBN 978-1-59463-039-2; 1-59463-039-9
                                            LC 2007017091

This "covers some of the most basic ideas of middle-grade math, including concepts relating to fractions, decimals, and ratios, making each comprehensible, interesting, and fun. Using real-world constructions, such as tangled necklaces, boyfriends, and pizza, concepts are thoroughly explained." Voice Youth Advocates

Salvadori, Mario George

★ **Math** games for middle school; challenges and skill-builders for students at every level. [by] Mario Salvadori and Joseph P. Wright. Chicago Review Press 1998 168p il pa $16.95

Grades: 6 7 8 9   **510**
    1. Mathematics 2. Games in mathematics education 3. Mathematics -- Study and teaching 4. Mathematics -- Problems, exercises, etc 5. Mathematics -- Study and teaching (Middle school)
    ISBN 1-55652-288-6

                                  LC 97-51422
Uses explanations, word problems, and games to cover some mathematical topics that middle school students need to know, including the invention of numerical notations, basic arithmatical operations, measurements, geometry, graphs, and probability

512   Algebra

Caron, Lucille

Pre-algebra and algebra smarts! [by] Lucille Caron, Philip M. St. Jacques. Enslow Publishers 2011 64p il (Math smarts!) lib bdg $27.93

Grades: 6 7 8   **512**
    1. Algebra 2. Mathematics
    ISBN 978-0-7660-3938-4

                          LC 2011006928
This helps re-inforce classroom learning of important pre-algebra and algebra skills such as positive and negative rational numbers, absolute value, and solving equations
Includes bibliographical references

Schwartz, Richard Evan

You can count on monsters; the first 100 numbers and their characters. A.K. Peters 2010 un il pa $24.95

Grades: 5 6 7 8   **512**
    1. Counting 2. Prime numbers 3. Factoring (Mathematics) 4. Factor tables 5. Numbers, Prime
    ISBN 978-1-56881-578-7 pa; 1-56881-578-6 pa
                         LC 2009-38661
"This hybrid math/art book is both ambitious and imaginative. An introductory section explains the colored-dot configurations and factor trees for numbers 1 to 100, which appear on the verso of each spread. These factor trees are 'all the way grown out' to the lowest common factors, or prime numbers. On the opposite page is a monster scene that represents the number. Schwartz has created a creature for each prime number. . . . Thus, the monster for 5 is a five-featured, five-pointed star, and the 13 monster sports a pink-and-white eye-patch with 13 segments. . . . Readers will need patience and an open, undaunted mind to deconstruct the monster scenes. This is a book for math lovers who want to have some fun. Challenge these students to create their own prime monsters and combinations." SLJ

513   Arithmetic

Caron, Lucille

Fraction and decimal smarts! [by] Lucille Caron, Philip M. St. Jacques. Enslow Publishers 2011 64p il (Math smarts!) lib bdg $27.93

Grades: 5 6 7 8   **513**
    1. Fractions 2. Decimal fractions
    ISBN 978-0-7660-3936-0

                          LC 2011008382
"This clearly written series provides definitions and examples of many concepts... examples are realistic and appropriate for the target age group." SLJ
Includes bibliographical references

Percent and ratio smarts! [by] Lucille Caron, Philip M. St. Jacques. Enslow Publishers 2011 64p il (Math smarts!) lib bdg $27.93

Grades: 5 6 7 8   **513**
    1. Fractions 2. Ratios (Statistics)
    ISBN 978-0-7660-3940-7

                          LC 2011008164
This helps re-inforce classroom learning of important percent and ratio skills including reducing ratios, the golden rectangle, and the meaning of percents
Includes bibliographical references

Julius, Edward H.

Arithmetricks; 50 easy ways to add, subtract, multiply, and divide without a calculator. illustrations by Dale M. Gladstone. Wiley 1995 142p il pa $12.95

Grades: 7 8 9 10   **513**
    1. Arithmetic
    ISBN 0-471-10639-9

                          LC 94-41836
This book "offers fifty ways to do simple arithmetic calculations in one's head. . . . Each trick is covered on two facing pages. The first page presents the problem and gives two examples of how to use the trick. The facing page has a black and white cartoon and extra exercises to practice. The correct answers are given at the end of the book. This would be a fun book for mathematically inclined Middle-Schoolers and up. Math teachers will enjoy using this book for extra-curricular activities." Appraisal

516   Geometry

Caron, Lucille

Geometry smarts! [by] Lucille Caron, Philip M. St. Jacques. Enslow Publishers 2011 64p il (Math smarts!) lib bdg $27.93

Grades: 5 6 7 8   **516**
    1. Geometry
    ISBN 978-0-7660-3935-3

                          LC 2011008384
This helps re-inforce classroom learning of geometry skills such as points, lines, planes, triangles, circles, quadrilaterals, perimeter, area, and circumference
Includes bibliographical references

Sullivan, Navin

Area, distance, and volume; [by] Navin Sullivan. Marshall Cavendish Benchmark 2007 44p il (Measure up!) lib bdg $20.95

Grades: 4 5 6 7   **516**

  1. Geometry 2. Measurement

  ISBN 978-0-7614-2323-2 lib bdg; 0-7614-2323-0 lib bdg

          LC 2006026394

An "engaging and informative [title]. . . . An excellent blend of photographs, charts, and diagrams complements the [text]." SLJ

Includes glossary and bibliographical references

516.2   Euclidean geometry

Blatner, David

  ★ **Joy** of [pi] Walker and Co. 1997 129p il hardcover o.p. pa $12

Grades: 8 9 10 11 12   **516.2**

  1. Numbers 2. Geometry

  ISBN 0-8027-1332-7; 0-8027-7562-4 pa

"Why does an irrational number impel rational people to do irrational things—like calculating pi to several billion digits? That's what's happening with a pair of characters in Blatner's delightful excursion through the history of pi. . . . Even numerically challenged readers will find Blatner's tale immensely appealing, both for the graphic layout, in day-glo colors, no less, and for the amusing and informative anecdotes Blatner relates." Booklist

Green, Dan

Algebra & geometry; anything but square. illustrated by Simon Basher. Kingfisher 2011 128p il (Basher science) $14.99; pa $8.99

Grades: 4 5 6   **516.2**

  1. Algebra 2. Geometry

  ISBN 978-0-7534-6627-8; 978-0-7534-6597-4 pa

Wingard-Nelson, Rebecca

Trigonometry smarts! Enslow Publishers 2012 64p il (Math smarts!) lib bdg $27.93

Grades: 5 6 7 8   **516.2**

  1. Trigonometry

  ISBN 978-0-7660-3944-5

          LC 2011006492

This helps re-inforce classroom learning of important trigonometry topics such as square roots, the Pythagorean Theorem, tangents, radians, and degrees.

Includes bibliographical references

519.2   Probabilities

Wingard-Nelson, Rebecca

Graphing and probability word problems; no problem! Enslow Publishers 2010 64p il (Math busters word problems) lib bdg $27.93

Grades: 6 7 8 9   **519.2**

  1. Mathematics 2. Problem solving

  ISBN 978-0-7660-3372-6; 0-7660-3372-4

          LC 2010003281

This offers ways to tackle word math problems with graphing and probability using real world examples.

520   Astronomy and allied sciences

Aguilar, David A.

  ★ **Planets,** stars, and galaxies; a visual encyclopedia of our universe. written and illustrated by David A. Aguilar; contributing writers Christine Pulliam & Patricia Daniels. National Geographic 2007 191p il $24.95; lib bdg $38.90

Grades: 5 6 7 8 9 10 11 12   **520**

  1. Galaxies 2. Astronomy

  ISBN 978-1-4263-0170-4; 1-4263-0170-7; 978-1-4263-0171-1 lib bdg; 1-4263-0171-5 lib bdg

          LC 2007061234

"This text introduces readers to the most current information available about the universe. Information is presented is a clear and easy-to-understand manner. . . . The book features bright, eye-catching illustrations that Aguilar created on his computer. In addition, there are many vibrant photographs in the book that were taken by cameras here on Earth as well as by satellites and telescopes." Booklist

Includes glossary and bibliographical references

Boerst, William J.

Johannes Kepler; discovering the laws of celestial motion. Morgan Reynolds 2003 144p il maps (Renaissance scientists) lib bdg $23.95

Grades: 7 8 9 10   **520**

  1. Astronomers 2. Mathematicians

  ISBN 1-88384-698-6

          LC 2003-708

A biography of Johannes Kepler, the seventeenth-century German astronomer and mathematician who formulated the three laws of planetary motion

"Boerst not only offers a good portrait of the astronomer and his work but also shows the effects of the contentious political and religious forces that created upheaval in his society and made scholarship anything but a safe haven. The well-designed pages feature excellent color illustrations." Booklist

Includes bibliographical references

The **Facts** on File dictionary of astronomy; edited by John Daintith, William Gould. 5th ed.; Facts on File 2006 550p il (Facts on File science library) $59.50

Grades: 7 8 9 10 11 12   **520**

  1. Reference books 2. Astronomy -- Dictionaries

  ISBN 0-8160-5998-5; 978-0-8160-5998-0

          LC 2006-40860

First published 1979 under the editorship of Valerie Illingworth

This dictionary includes "more than 3,700 entries . . . that reflect all aspects of astronomy, together with associated

terms in spectroscopy, photometry, and particle physics."
Publisher's note
Includes bibliographical references

Gardner, Robert
  Ace your space science project; great science fair
ideas. [by] Robert Gardner and Madeline Goodstein.
Enslow Publishers 2009 128p il (Ace your science
project) lib bdg $31.93
  Grades: 5 6 7 8   **520**
    1. Space sciences 2. Science projects 3. Science --
Experiments
    ISBN 978-0-7660-3230-9 lib bdg; 0-7660-3230-2
lib bdg
                                          LC 2008-04688
  "Informative, practical, and not without dry wit, this is
a good bet for replacing older books of science projects related to astronommy." Booklist
  Includes bibliographical references

Garlick, Mark A.
  Atlas of the universe. Simon & Schuster Books
for Young Readers 2008 128p il map (Insiders)
$19.99
  Grades: 5 6 7 8   **520**
    1. Astronomy 2. Cosmology
    ISBN 978-1-4169-5558-0; 1-4169-5558-5
  "Seamlessly commingling luscious, color space photographs and dramatic, sharply detailed digital imagery, this
tour of the universe earns high marks for visual impact. It's
not too shabby in breadth of coverage either." SLJ

Gater, Will
  The **practical** astronomer; [by] Will Gater and
Anton Vamplew; consultant Jacqueline Mitton. DK
Pub. 2010 256p il map pa $19.95
  Grades: 7 8 9 10 11 12   **520**
    1. Astronomy 2. Astronomy -- Observers' manuals
    ISBN 978-0-7566-6210-3; 0-7566-6210-9
                                          LC 2010-281460
  "This beautifully illustrated volume is a valuable and
accurate guide to observing and understanding the wide
variety and essential characteristics of fascinating astronomical objects that are visible from Earth. . . . [It enables]
the reader to learn about coordinate systems; solar system
motions; the nature of light; and how to use the eye, bin-
oculars, telescopes, cameras, and astronomical atlases and
catalogues to explore the heavens directly and efficiently."
Sci Books Films

Green, Dan
  Astronomy; out of this world! illustrated by Simon Basher. Kingfisher 2009 128p il pa $8.95
  Grades: 5 6 7 8   **520**
    1. Astronomy
    ISBN 978-0-7534-6290-4 pa; 0-7534-6290-7 pa
  "Basher has created a portrait gallery of personified
planets, comets, space probes, galaxies, several kinds of
stars, and an array of other celestial bodies in a hyper-cute,
pastel cartoon style. . . . Along with short bulleted lists of
additional information, each figure offers a fact-based self-

description. . . . Green's astro-narrative is both accurate and
spiced with seldom-mentioned details." SLJ
  Includes glossary

Jankowski, Connie
  Space exploration. Compass Point Books 2009
40p il (Mission: science) lib bdg $26.60
  Grades: 4 5 6   **520**
    1. Astronomy
    ISBN 978-0-7565-3958-0 lib bdg; 0-7565-3958-7
lib bdg
                                          LC 2008-7722
  Discusses outer space exploration and examines future
possibilities such as a permanent space station, colonies in
space, and journeys outside the solar system
  Includes glossary

Lippincott, Kristen
  Astronomy; written by Kristen Lippincott. rev.
ed.; DK Pub. 2008 72p il map (DK eyewitness
books) $15.99
  Grades: 4 5 6 7   **520**
    1. Astronomy
    ISBN 978-0-7566-3767-5; 0-7566-3767-8
                                          LC 2008-276037
  First published 1994
  This covers a history of astronomy and telescopes, the
planets and stars, galaxies, and modern research.

  ★ **NightWatch**: a practical guide to viewing the
universe; foreword by Timothy Ferris; illustrations by Adolf Schaller, Victor Costanzo, Roberta
Cooke, Glenn LeDrew; principal photography by
Terence Dickinson. 4th ed.; Firefly Books 2006
192p il $35
  Grades: 8 9 10 11 12   **520**
    1. Astronomy
    ISBN 978-1-55407-147-0; 1-55407-147-X
                                          LC 2006-491527
  First published 1983
  This "handbook for amateur astronomers combines a
text both meaty and hard to put down with a great array of
charts, boxes, tables, and dazzling full-color photos of the
sky." SLJ [review of 1998 edition]
  Includes bibliographical references

Silverstein, Alvin
  ★ The **universe**; by Alvin & Virginia Silverstein
& Laura Silverstein Nunn. rev. ed.; Twenty-First
Century Books 2009 112p il (Science concepts,
second series) lib bdg $31.93
  Grades: 6 7 8 9   **520**
    1. Universe 2. Astronomy
    ISBN 978-0-7613-3937-3; 0-7613-3937-X
                                          LC 2007052245
  First published 2003
  This book explores the universe and its elements, in-
cluding the Milky Way, the solar system, the stars, and other
astronomical bodies.

"Authoritative, objective, and broadly based. . . . Beautifully designed and well illustrated." SLJ [review of 2003 edition]

Includes bibliographical references

Space: a visual encyclopedia. DK Pub. 2010 254p il $24.99

Grades: 5 6 7 8   **520**
1. Astronomy 2. Astronautics 3. Space sciences
ISBN 978-0-7566-6277-6; 0-7566-6277-X

"Any reader wishing to gain a fair introductory understanding of astronomy in one concise book will find much satisfaction in this work. An abundance of fascinating information is contained within these pages, and the format is such that excellent and attractive related photographs and diagrams directly accompany the text. . . . The book is very well organized and very well written." Sci Books & Films

Sparrow, Giles
Cosmic! the ultimate 3-D guide to the universe. [author, Giles Sparrow; paper engineer, Richard Ferguson] DK Publishing 2008 un il $24.99

Grades: 5 6 7 8   **520**
1. Astronomy 2. Cosmology 3. Toy and movable books 4. Pop-up books
ISBN 978-0-7566-4021-7; 0-7566-4021-0
LC 2008-300768

This book "traces the history of the universe beginning with the Big Bang, discussing the structure of the solar system, planets, stars, galaxies, how the Hubble telescope functions, and the spaceships used in space exploration." Publisher's note

Walker, Pamela
★ **Space** and astronomy experiments; [by] Pamela Walker, Elaine Wood. Facts on File 2010 xx, 152p il (Facts on File science experiments) $35

Grades: 7 8 9 10 11 12   **520**
1. Astronomy 2. Space sciences 3. Science -- Experiments
ISBN 978-0-8160-7809-7; 0-8160-7809-2
LC 2009-32825

This book "presents experiments designed to foster understanding of space science and astronomy. Geared to middle and high-school students and their teachers, the 20 experiments convey basic astronomy principles, draw from historic experiments, or explore new technologies. . . . Schools and libraries where students and teachers are looking for science experiments on space and astronomy will find this volume a useful addition to the collection." Booklist

Includes glossary and bibliographical references

Ward, D. J.
Seven wonders of space phenomena; by D.J. Ward. Twenty-First Century Books 2011 80 p. ill. (chiefly col.) (library) $33.26

Grades: 5 6 7 8   **520**
1. Universe 2. Astronomy 3. Astronomy -- Miscellanea
ISBN 0761354522; 9780761354529
LC 2010028447

This book by D.J. Ward looks at "space phenomena, such as dark matter, dark energy, and the beginning of the universe. Read what astronomers and space scientists have discovered about these amazing wonders—and what they have yet to learn." (Publisher's note)

Includes bibliographical references (p. 76-78) and index.

Yount, Lisa
Modern astronomy; expanding the universe. Facts on File 2006 204p il (Milestones in discovery and invention) $35

Grades: 7 8 9 10 11 12   **520**
1. Astronomy 2. Astronomers 3. Astronomy -- History
ISBN 0-8160-5746-X; 978-0-8160-5746-7
LC 2005-25113

This book profiles "12 men and women whose research and work in new technologies brought about a revolution in the understanding of time and space during the 20th century." Publisher's note

Includes glossary and bibliographical references

520.78   Astronomy -- Experiments

VanCleave, Janice Pratt, 1942-
Step-by-step science experiments in astronomy; by Janice VanCleave. Rosen Pub. 2013 80 p. col. ill. (Janice Vancleave's first-place science fair projects) (library) $33.25; (paperback) $14.15

Grades: 5 6 7 8   **520.78**
1. Astronomy 2. Science -- Experiments 3. Science projects 4. Astronomy -- Experiments
ISBN 1448869781; 9781448869787; 9781448884612
LC 2012000715

This book by Janice VanCleave presents 22 science experiments in astronomy for children. "Van Cleave states the basic goal of the experiments, followed by a list of necessary materials. . . . Step-by-step instructions are . . . accompanied by diagrams where needed. The results section states exactly what is expected to happen and the 'Why?' section explains in accessible terms why those specific results were achieved." (School Library Journal)

Includes bibliographical references (p. 77-78) and index

520.9   Astronomy -- History

Carson, Mary Kay
★ **Beyond** the solar system; exploring galaxies, black holes, alien planets, and more : a history with 21 activities. by Mary Kay Carson. Chicago Review Press 2013 vii, 127 p.p col. ill. (paperback) $18.95

Grades: 5 6 7 8   **520.9**
1. Creative activities 2. Astronomy -- History
ISBN 1613745443; 9781613745441
LC 2012046330

In this book, "Mary Kay Carson traces the evolution of humankind's astronomical knowledge, from the realization that we are not at the center of the universe to recent telescopic proof of planets orbiting stars outside our solar system. . . . This book contains 21 hands-on projects to further explore the subjects discussed" as well as "minibiographies of famous astronomers, a time line of major scientific discoveries . . .[and] a glossary of technical terms." (Publisher's note)

Includes bibliographical references (p. 121) and index.

520.92 Astronomers

Yount, Lisa

Edward Pickering and his women "computers" analyzing the stars. Lisa Yount. Chelsea House 2011 130 p. (Trailblazers in science and technology) (library) $35

Grades: 7 8 9 10 11 12   **520.92**

1. Women astronomers 2. Pickering, Edward C. (Edward Charles), 1846-1919 3. Physicists -- United States -- Biography 4. Astronomers -- United States -- Biography

ISBN 1604136642; 9781604136647

LC 2011002792

This book, by Lisa Yount, is part of the "Trailblazers in Science and Technology" series. "In the 42 years that Edward Pickering directed the Harvard College Observatory, he and his team of women 'computers' made strides in promoting the new field of astrophotography. . . . The advances these women made under Pickering's direction broadened the window of professional opportunity for women as well as our greater understanding of the universe." (Publisher's note)

Includes bibliographical references and index

522 Techniques, procedures, apparatus, equipment, materials

Cole, Michael D.

Eye on the universe; the incredible hubble space telescope. Michael D. Cole. Enslow Publishers 2013 48 p. $23.93

Grades: 4 5 6 7 8   **522**

1. Hubble Space Telescope 2. Outer space -- Exploration 3. Astronomy -- Research 4. Astronautics in astronomy

ISBN 0766040771; 9780766040779

LC 2011047074

This book looks at the Hubble Space Telescope. "Orbiting high above Earth, the Hubble Telescope captures . . . wonders of space. . . . Photographs are relayed back to Earth, allowing scientists and astronomers to study parts of space that were once completely unknown. Michael D. Cole explores the . . . journey of launching this telescope into space and how it has unlocked many of the . . . mysteries in the universe." (Publisher's note)

Includes bibliographical references and index

DeVorkin, David H.

Hubble imaging space and time; [by] David Devorkin & Robert W. Smith. Smithsonian National Air and Space Museum in association with National Geographic 2008 223p il $50

Grades: 8 9 10 11 12 Adult   **522**

1. Astronomy 2. Hubble Space Telescope

ISBN 978-1-4262-0322-0; 1-4262-0322-5

LC 2008018242

"This handsome volume celebrates the technological and scientific breakthroughs that have made the Hubble such a resounding success. The full, up-to-date story is told in glorious photographs and the equally sparkling commentary of Hubble experts DeVorkin and Smith. . . . The authors cover the people, science, and aesthetics of the stellar Hubble era. Not only are the telescope's contributions to science beyond quantification, DeVorkin and Smith aver, the images the Hubble has gathered have also had profound effects on our imagination and spiritual growth." Booklist

Includes bibliographical references

Gardner, Robert

Astronomy projects with an observatory you can build; [by] Robert Gardner. Enslow Publishers 2007 128p il (Build-a-lab! science experiments) lib bdg $31.93

Grades: 7 8 9 10   **522**

1. Astronomy 2. Science projects 3. Science -- Experiments

ISBN 978-0-7660-2808-1 lib bdg; 0-7660-2808-9 lib bdg

LC 2006032807

This describes the scientific method and offers instructions in building an observatory and projects in observing Earth, the moon, the sun, the stars, and the planets.

"The digitally rendered diagrams are helpful in clarifying the written directions. [This volume is] involving and entertaining." SLJ

Includes bibliographical references

Matloff, Gregory L.

More telescope power; all new activities and projects for young astronomers. with drawings by C. Bangs. Wiley 2002 118p il pa $12.95

                                                              522

1. Astronomy 2. Telescopes 3. Science -- Experiments 4. Astronomy -- Experiments 5. Telescopes -- Experiments

ISBN 0-471-40985-5

LC 2001-46738

Presents various astronomy activities using a telescope, including constructing a simple telescope, tracking satellites, and sketching details of the moon

This "book is well-written, interesting, and suitable for anyone who wants to learn more about astronomy." Book Rep

Includes glossary and bibliographical references

Scott, Elaine

★ **Space,** stars, and the beginning of time; what the Hubble telescope saw. Clarion Books 2011 66p il $17.99

Grades: 5 6 7 8   **522**

1. Astronomy 2. Hubble Space Telescope 3. Outer space -- Exploration

ISBN 0-547-24189-5; 978-0-547-24189-0

LC 2010-08040

This book examines data collected from the Hubble Space Telescope. Index. "Grades four to eight." (Bull Cent Child Books)

This examines "some of the data that has been collected over the two decades of the Hubble Telescope's operation. Opening chapters discuss the satellite's instrumentation and its 2009 repairs, and then the real fun begins with sections on calculating the age of the universe and its speed of expansion; the nature of dark matter, dark energy, and black holes; star formation; and planet formation, particularly outside our solar system. . . . Gasp-worthy photographs should fire up the most sluggish imaginations." Bull Cent Child Books

523 Specific celestial bodies and phenomena

Pasachoff, Jay M.

A **field** guide to the stars and planets; 4th ed; Houghton Mifflin 2000 578p il map (Peterson field guide series) $30; pa $19

Grades: 8 9 10 11 12 Adult   **523**

1. Stars 2. Astronomy 3. Astronomy -- Observers' manuals

ISBN 0-395-93432-X; 0-395-93431-1 pa

LC 99-27354

First published 1964 under the authorship of Donald H. Menzel and Jay M. Pasachoff

This guide contains 24 monthly sky maps, 54 atlas charts, information and numerous color photographs from NASA and other sources, and time-sensitive material through 2010

Includes bibliographical references

523.1 The universe, galaxies, quasars

Fleisher, Paul

★ The **big** bang; by Paul Fleisher. Twenty-First Century Books 2006 80p il (Great ideas of science) lib bdg $27.93

Grades: 6 7 8 9   **523.1**

1. Big bang theory 3. Cosmology

ISBN 0-8225-2133-4

LC 2005001234

Explains how scientists' observations of the stars led to the development of the big bang theory, a theory of how our universe was formed.

"The book offers a few interesting analogies and includes 22 color diagrams, photos, and informational sidebars. A solid addition for introductory reports." SLJ

Includes bibliographical references

Goldsmith, Mike

Universe; journey into deep space. Mike Goldsmith; illustrated by Mark A. Garlick. Kingfisher 2012 48 p. (hardcover) $17.99

Grades: 4 5 6 7   **523.1**

1. Universe 2. Astronomy 3. Outer space

ISBN 075346876X; 9780753468760

This book, by Mike Goldsmith, illustrated by Mark A. Garlick, profiles "some of the Universe's most intriguing places, and along the way . . . [describes] the amazing his-

tory of the Cosmos. A series of . . . spreads give . . . snapshots of distant galactic locations as the reader journeys . . . from red cold Mars (3 light minutes away) to a massive Supernova (10,000 light years away) and beyond." (Publisher's note)

523.2 Planetary systems

Aguilar, David A.

★ **13** planets; the latest view of the solar system. National Geographic 2011 60p il $16.95; lib bdg $25.99

Grades: 5 6 7 8   **523.2**

1. Planets 2. Solar system

ISBN 9781426307706; 1426307705; 9781426307713 lib bdg; 1426307713 lib bdg

LC 2010032510

Updated and revised edition of: 11 planets: A new view of the Solar System (2008)

Profiles each of the planets in Earth's solar system, including Pluto, Ceres, Eris, Haumea, MakeMake, the sun, the Oort cloud, comets, and more.

"Aguilar offers an amended volume reflecting the findings of the International Astronomical Union, which currently classifies eight objects in the solar system as planets and, with the addition of Haumea and Makemake, five as dwarf planets. . . . Aguilar has not only added sections on Haumea and Makemake, he has also used this opportunity to rewrite portions of the text and captions throughout the book and, in some cases, to substitute new illustrations or improve old ones for the new volume. The result is a more readable, more accurate, and more handsome edition of the previous work." Booklist

Includes bibliographical references and index.

Benson, Michael

★ **Beyond**; a solar system voyage. Abrams Books for Young Readers 2009 121p il $19.95

Grades: 5 6 7 8 9 10   **523.2**

1. Astronomy 2. Solar system

ISBN 0-8109-8322-2; 978-0-8109-8322-9

LC 2008-22297

This book presents the solar system from the perspective of the space probes sent there. Sci Books Films

"The book's focus is the exploration of the solar system by space probes, with many full-page photos. . . . The author skillfully blends lively narrative with the photos to contribute to the excitement of the explorations. . . . It is an inexpensive but valuable addition for any library." Voice Youth Advocates

Includes glossary and bibliographical references

Carson, Mary Kay

Exploring the solar system; a history with 22 activities. by Mary Kay Carson. Chicago Review Press 2008 vii, 168 p.p ill. (paperback) $17.95

Grades: 4 5 6 7   **523.2**

1. Astronomy 2. Solar system

ISBN 1556527152; 9781556527159

This book by Mary Kay Carson is a "mix of facts, history, and hands-on activities [about the solar system]. Beginning with a two-page table of contents with chapters arranged as planets in our solar system and an introductory time line, the author takes readers on a historical journey of what was known and/or discovered in each of eight time periods." (School Library Journal)

Greathouse, Lisa E.

Solar system. Compass Point Books 2009 40p il (Mission: science) lib bdg $26.60

Grades: 4 5 6   **523.2**

1. Solar system

ISBN 978-0-7565-4071-5 lib bdg; 0-7565-4071-2 lib bdg

LC 2008-35728

Introduces the solar system and the specific characteristics of its planets

Includes glossary

Tourville, Amanda Doering

Exploring the solar system. Rourke Pub. 2010 48p il (Let's explore science) $32.79; pa $9.95

Grades: 4 5 6 7   **523.2**

1. Solar system

ISBN 978-1-61590-323-8; 1-61590-323-2; 978-1-61590-562-2 pa; 1-61590-562-6 pa

LC 2010009910

This "moves from basic definitions . . . to more technical information, such as the formula for calculating the speed of light. Also included is up-to-date coverage of Pluto's demotion from planet to plutoid, as well as a section on dwarf planets. . . . In [this] title, well-chosen boxed examples, abundant color photos, diagrams, and an appended glossary add interest and support the engaging [text]." Booklist

Includes glossary and bibliographical references

Wittenstein, Vicki Oransky

Planet hunter; Goeff Marcy and the search for other earths. Boyds Mills Press 2010 48p il $17.95

Grades: 5 6 7 8   **523.2**

1. Extrasolar planets 2. Life on other planets 3. Astrophysicists 4. College teachers 5. Young adult literature -- Works 6. Biography, Individual 7. Life on other planets 8. Children's literature -- Works -- Grades two through six

ISBN 978-1-59078-592-8; 1-59078-592-4

"The profound thrill of searching for (and finding!) planets orbiting stars other than our own is deftly captured in this profile of Geoff Marcy, one of the great hunt's most successful practitioners. Matched to big, sharp color photos of scientists (mostly) at work and compelling speculative views of exotic suns and landscapes, Wittenstein's matter-of-fact narrative first introduces readers to Marcy and his team on the night shift . . . at the W. M. Keck Observatory atop Hawaii's Mauna Kea. . . . This handsomely packaged introduction is just the ticket for turning earthbound (for now) children into budding skywatchers." SLJ

Includes glossary and bibliographical references

523.3   Specific parts of solar system

Carlowicz, Michael J.

The **moon**; [by] Michael Carlowicz. Abrams 2007 240p il $19.95

Grades: 8 9 10 11   **523.3**

1. Moon 2. Moon -- Exploration

ISBN 978-0-8109-9307-5; 0-8109-9307-4

LC 2006102611

A collection of photographs celebrate the moon, its influence on Earth and society, and the scientific expeditions to the satellite

Includes bibliographical references

Simon, Seymour

★ The **moon**; rev ed.; Simon & Schuster Bks. for Young Readers 2003 un il $17.95

Grades: 4 5 6 7   **523.3**

1. Moon 2. Moon -- Exploration

ISBN 0-689-83563-9

LC 2001-31303

First published 1984 by Four Winds Press

A basic introduction to Earth's closest neighbor, its composition, and man's missions to it

"The digitally remastered color photographs in this update are incredible. . . . The text has undergone minimal change. . . . The facts remain true and relevant, and the writing reflects the graphics: beautiful. This is a must-have for astronomy sections." SLJ

523.4   Planets, asteroids, trans-Neptunian objects of solar system

Bjorklund, Ruth

Venus. Marshall Cavendish Benchmark 2009 64p il (Space!) lib bdg o.p.; ebook $33

Grades: 4 5 6 7   **523.4**

1. Solar system

ISBN 978-0-7614-4251-6; 9780761445616

LC 2009014665

"Describes Venus, including its history, its composition, and its role in the solar system." Publisher's note

Includes glossary and bibliographical references

Capaccio, George

Jupiter. Marshall Cavendish Benchmark 2009 64p il (Space!) lib bdg $22.95

Grades: 4 5 6 7   **523.4**

1. Jupiter (Planet)

ISBN 978-0-7614-4244-8 lib bdg; 0-7614-4244-8 lib bdg; 9780761445555

LC 2008037276

"Describes Jupiter, including its history, its composition, and its role in the solar system." Publisher's note

Includes glossary and bibliographical references

Mars. Marshall Cavendish Benchmark 2010 64p il (Space!) lib bdg $22.95

Grades: 4 5 6 7   **523.4**
1. Mars (Planet)
ISBN 978-0-7614-4247-9 lib bdg; 0-7614-4247-2 lib bdg; 9780761445579

LC 2008037280

Describes Mars, including its history, its composition, and its role in the solar system
Includes glossary and bibliographical references

Colligan, L. H.
Mercury. Marshall Cavendish Benchmark 2009 64p il (Space!) lib bdg $22.95
Grades: 4 5 6 7   **523.4**
1. Mercury (Planet)
ISBN 0-7614-4239-1 lib bdg; 9780761442394 lib bdg; 9780761445517

LC 2008037278

"Describes Mercury, including its history, its composition, and its role in the solar system." Publisher's note
Includes glossary and bibliographical references

Hicks, Terry Allan
Saturn. Marshall Cavendish Benchmark 2010 64p il (Space!) lib bdg $22.95
Grades: 4 5 6 7   **523.4**
1. Saturn (Planet)
ISBN 978-0-7614-4249-3 lib bdg; 0-7614-4249-9 lib bdg; 9780761445593

LC 2008037453

"Describes Saturn, including its history, its composition, and its role in the solar system." Publisher's note
Includes glossary and bibliographical references

Jones, Thomas D.
★ **Planetology**; unlocking the secrets of the solar system. [by] Tom Jones and Ellen Stofan. National Geographic 2008 217p il $35
Grades: 7 8 9 10 11 12   **523.4**
1. Planets 2. Astrogeology 3. Planetology 4. Planets -- Geology
ISBN 978-1-4262-0121-9; 1-4262-0121-4

LC 2008-10726

"This beautifully produced book provides an introduction to comparative planetology for a general audience. The large-format volume focuses on comparing and contrasting different processes that shape and form the primary planets in the solar system. . . . The writing is crisp and clear, and the choice of imagery and examples is very strong." Choice
Includes bibliographical references

Miller, Ron
Mars; [by] Ron Miller. Twenty-First Century Books 2006 95p il (Worlds beyond) lib bdg $27.90
Grades: 7 8 9 10   **523.4**
1. Mars (Planet)
ISBN 0-7613-2362-7

LC 2003-10139

Chronicles the discovery and explorations of the planet Mars and discusses each of its moons, its place in the solar system, and more.

"Chock full of stunning photographs and illustrations. . . . Written clearly and concisely. . . . A valuable resource." Voice Youth Advocates
Includes bibliographical references

Seven wonders of the gas giants and their moons. Twenty-First Century Books 2011 80p il (Seven wonders) lib bdg $33.26
Grades: 5 6 7 8   **523.4**
1. Planets 2. Outer planets
ISBN 978-0-7613-5449-9 lib bdg; 0-7613-5449-2 lib bdg; 9780761372813

LC 2010-15558

This book describes seven phenomena about the outer planets of the solar system and their moons, including the great red spot of Jupiter and the underground sea of Europa. Index. "Grades five to eight." (Sci Books Films)
This "celebrates the most unique features of Jupiter, Saturn, Uranus and Neptune, including companion moons and Saturn's mysterious rings. . . . [This] volume makes basic concepts clear in lively, energetic language that, along with the mesmerizing color photos and artists' renderings of space, will easily captivate a young audience, while up-to-date examples, including discoveries made in the last five years, will only increase the sense of immediacy and excitement." Booklist
Includes glossary and bibliographical references

Seven wonders of the rocky planets and their moons. Twenty-First Century Books 2011 80p il (Seven wonders) lib bdg $33.26
Grades: 4 5 6   **523.4**
1. Planets 2. Inner planets
ISBN 978-0-7613-5448-2 lib bdg; 0-7613-5448-4 lib bdg; 9780761372837

LC 2010-15553

This book shows "views of features on Mercury, Venus, Earth (and its moon), and Mars. Sci Books Films
This "compares the fascinating diversity of Earth's land masses with those on Mars, Venus and Mercury. . . . [This] volume makes basic concepts clear in lively, energetic language that, along with the mesmerizing color photos and artists' renderings of space, will easily captivate a young audience, while up-to-date examples, including discoveries made in the last five years, will only increase the sense of immediacy and excitement." Booklist
Includes glossary and bibliographical references

Nardo, Don
Asteroids and comets. Morgan Reynolds Pub. 2009 112p il (Extreme threats) lib bdg $28.95
Grades: 7 8 9 10   **523.4**
1. Comets 2. Asteroids
ISBN 978-1-59935-121-6; 1-59935-121-8

LC 2009-26295

This book covers "evidence of impacts, types of impactors, giant impacts and mass extinctions, recent impacts and near misses, the current and future danger of near-earth-objects (NEOs), and scientific research on how to address the threat. . . . Features high-gloss pages in mottled green, full-color pictures, and informative sidebars. . . . [It is] well written, nicely designed, and interesting." Voice Youth Advocates

Includes glossary and bibliographical references

Poynter, Margaret

Doomsday rocks from space. Enslow Publishers 2011 48p il (Bizarre science) lib bdg $23.93

Grades: 5 6 7 8   523.4

1. Comets 2. Asteroids 3. Meteorites

ISBN 978-0-7660-3673-4; 0-7660-3673-1

LC 2009053601

First published 1996 with title: Killer asteroids

"Aimed at reluctant readers, [this title is] sure to disgust and delight in equal measure. . . . [The title] will pique interest and get kids lining up at the reference desk looking for more. The text is complemented by illustrations and magnified photos of things that you would hope never to see." SLJ

Includes glossary and bibliographical references

Scott, Elaine

When is a planet not a planet? the story of Pluto. Clarion Books 2007 43p il $17

Grades: 3 4 5 6   523.4

1. Planets

ISBN 978-0-618-89832-9; 0-618-89832-8

"Scott takes the 2006 downgrading of Pluto from planet to dwarf planet as a teachable moment for discussing questions such as how the number of planets has changed through the centuries, what can be called a planet, and how scientists come to conclusions—and occasionally change their minds. . . . Beautifully designed, the book includes many well-captioned, color illustrations, from period portraits to NASA images to artist's conceptions." Booklist

Sherman, Josepha

Asteroids, meteors, and comets. Marshall Cavendish Benchmark 2009 64p il (Space!) lib bdg $22.95

Grades: 4 5 6 7   523.4

1. Comets 2. Meteors 3. Asteroids

ISBN 978-0-7614-4252-3 lib bdg; 0-7614-4252-9 lib bdg

LC 2008037281

This stands out for its "clear, accurate [presentation] of basic facts punctuated by lively turns of phrase and, sometimes, details not commonly found in the plethora of similar tours of the solar system and beyond." SLJ

Includes glossary and bibliographical references

Neptune. Marshall Cavendish Benchmark 2009 63p il (Space!) lib bdg $22.95

Grades: 4 5 6 7   523.4

1. Neptune (Planet)

ISBN 978-0-7614-4246-2 lib bdg; 0-7614-4246-4 lib bdg;

LC 2008037279

"Describes Neptune, including its history, its composition, and its role in the solar system." Publisher's note

Includes glossary and bibliographical references

Uranus. Marshall Cavendish Benchmark 2010 63p il (Space!) lib bdg $22.95

Grades: 4 5 6 7   523.4

1. Astronomers 2. Uranus (Planet)

ISBN 978-0-7614-4248-6 lib bdg; 0-7614-4248-0 lib bdg; 9780761445586

LC 2008037274

"Describes Uranus, including its history, its composition, and its role in the solar system." Publisher's note

Includes glossary and bibliographical references

Spangenburg, Ray

A **look** at Mercury; [by] Ray Spangenburg and Kit Moser. Watts 2003 110p il map (Out of this world) lib bdg $33.50; pa $14.95

Grades: 6 7 8 9   523.4

1. Mercury (Planet)

ISBN 0-531-11928-9 lib bdg; 0-531-16673-2 pa

LC 2002-8508

Describes the discovery and observation of the planet nearest the sun, Mercury, including the findings of the Mariner 10 fly-by mission of 1974-75

Includes glossary and bibliographical references

Sparrow, Giles

Destination Uranus, Neptune, and Pluto. PowerKids Press 2010 32p il lib bdg $23.95; pa $10

Grades: 3 4 5 6   523.4

1. Uranus (Planet) 2. Neptune (Planet) 3. Pluto (Dwarf planet)

ISBN 978-1-4358-3446-0 lib bdg; 978-1-4358-3463-7 pa

LC 2009-2985

Examines the outer planets, and discusses their moons, interiors, atmospheres, locations, and exploration.

Tabak, John

A **look** at Neptune. Watts 2003 107p il (Out of this world) lib bdg $33.50; pa $14.95

Grades: 6 7 8 9   523.4

1. Neptune (Planet)

ISBN 0-531-12267-0 lib bdg; 0-531-15584-6 pa

LC 2002-2023

Describes the discovery and observation of the planet Neptune and what has been learned about it, particularly from the Voyager spacecraft mission

Overall this "conveys the material well. Outstanding color photos contribute to the content." SLJ

Includes glossary and bibliographical references

Tyson, Neil De Grasse

The **Pluto** files; the rise and fall of America's favorite planet. W.W. Norton 2009 194p il $23.95; pa $15.95

Grades: 8 9 10 11 12 Adult   523.4

1. Astrophysicists 2. Museum administrators 3. Classification of sciences 4. Pluto (Dwarf planet)

ISBN 978-0-393-06520-6; 0-393-06520-0; 978-0-393-33732-7 pa; 0-393-33732-4 pa

LC 2008-40436

An exploration of the controversy surrounding Pluto and its planet status from an astrophysicist at the heart of the controversy.

The author "uses an engaging mix of facts, photographs, cartoons, illustrations, songs, e-mails, and humor to explain what's up (and down) with Pluto." Christ Sci Monit

Includes bibliographical references

523.43   Mars

Rusch, Elizabeth
★ The **mighty** Mars rovers; the incredible adventures of Spirit and Opportunity. by Elizabeth Rusch. Houghton Mifflin Books for Children 2012 79 p. ill. (chiefly col.) (hardcover) $18.99
Grades: 4 5 6   **523.43**
    1. Mars probes 2. Mars (Planet) -- Exploration 3. Astronautics 5. Roving vehicles (Astronautics)
    ISBN 054747881X; 9780547478814
                       LC 2011012159

In this book, "[Elizabeth] Rusch covers not only the scientific aspects of Mars exploration but also the personalities of the people who made it happen, and profiles the rovers themselves, Spirit and Opportunity." She looks at "the behind-the-scenes efforts of launching a scientific mission." Also included are "[f]ull-color photographs," a glossary, and a list of further resources. (School Library Journal)

Includes bibliographical references (p. 76), discography (p. 78), filmograophy (p. 78), and index.

523.45   Jupiter

Miller, Ron
Jupiter. 21st Cent. Bks. (Brookfield) 2002 72p il (Worlds beyond) lib bdg $27.90
Grades: 5 6 7 8   **523.45**
    1. Jupiter (Planet)
    ISBN 0-7613-2356-2
                       LC 2001-36790

Chronicles the discovery and explorations of the planet Jupiter and discusses each of its moons, its place in the solar system, and more

Illustrated "with a mix of NASA photos and big, amazingly realistic, digitally produced, color images." SLJ

Includes glossary and bibliographical references

523.46   Saturn

Miller, Ron
Saturn; Ron Miller. Twenty-First Century Books 2003 80p ill. (library) $27.93
Grades: 5 6 7 8   **523.46**
    1. Saturn (planet)
    ISBN 9780761323600; 0761323600

Chronicles the discovery and exploration of the planet Saturn and discusses its rings and moons, its place in the solar system, and more.

"Concepts are explained clearly, and helpful diagrams and carefully chosen illustrations assist understanding." SLJ

Includes bibliographical references

523.5   Meteors, solar wind, zodiacal light

Koppes, Steven N.
Killer rocks from outer space; asteroids, comets, and meteorites. Lerner Publications Co. 2004 112p il (Discovery!) $26.60
Grades: 6 7 8 9   **523.5**
    1. Comets 2. Asteroids 3. Meteorites
    ISBN 0-8225-2861-4
                       LC 2003-10077

Describes the role that collisions with meteors, comets, and asteroids have played in the history of Earth and other planets in the solar system and examines what is being done to protect Earth from future collisions

"A catchy title, colorful cover, and well-written and interesting information combine to make this unusual science book one that students will find to be very readable and extremely useful for research projects. . . . This book will find many readers and should inspire students to further study astronomy." Lib Media Connect

Includes bibliographical references

Spangenburg, Ray
Meteors, meteorites, and meteoroids; [by] Ray Spangenburg and Kit Moser. Watts 2002 112p il (Out of this world) $33.50; pa $14.95
Grades: 6 7 8 9   **523.5**
    1. Meteors 2. Meteorites 3. Meteoroids
    ISBN 0-531-11925-4; 0-531-15567-6 pa
                       LC 2002-17

Explores the mysteries of rocks that travel vast distances through space, sometimes passing through Earth's atmosphere and sometimes landing on the surface

This "includes scientific facts and personal touches that give the text warmth. The conversational style makes for easy reading and high interest. The illustrations are accurate and colorful and significantly provide understanding to the text." Book Rep

Includes glossary and bibliographical references

523.7   Sun

Capaccio, George
The **sun**. Marshall Cavendish Benchmark 2009 64p il (Space!) lib bdg $22.95
Grades: 4 5 6 7   **523.7**
    1. Sun
    ISBN 978-0-7614-4242-4 lib bdg; 0-7614-4242-1 lib bdg
                       LC 2008037275

This stands out for its "clear, accurate [presentation] of basic facts punctuated by lively turns of phrase and, sometimes, details not commonly found in the plethora of similar tours of the solar system and beyond." SLJ

Includes glossary and bibliographical references

Spangenburg, Ray

The **sun**; [by] Ray Spangenburg and Kit Moser. Watts 2001 63p il map (Watts library) $24.50; pa $8.95

Grades: 4 5 6   **523.7**
1. Sun
ISBN 0-531-11767-7; 0-531-13991-3 pa
LC 00-39924

This describes the sun "beginning with a historical account of its formation and discovery. About half of [the] book focuses on modern exploration . . . using earth-based and space-based telescopes and spacecraft. . . . [This book is] well illustrated with both diagrams and photographs . . . [and] difficult concepts are presented in an easy-to-understand fashion." Sci Books Films

Includes glossary and bibliographical references

523.8 Stars

Abramson, Andra Serlin

Inside stars; by Andra Serlin Abramson and Mordecai-Mark Mac Low. Sterling Children's Books 2011 48p il (Inside . . .) $16.95; pa $9.95

Grades: 5 6 7 8   **523.8**
1. Stars
ISBN 978-1-4027-7709-7; 1-4027-7709-4; 978-1-4027-8162-9 pa; 1-4027-8162-8 pa
LC 2011283564

Presents an illustrated overview of stars, including information on how they affect the Earth, how scientists study them, how they are classified, how they form and die, and specific information about our star, the Sun.

"On full but not crowded-looking pages, the captions, vocabulary words and digestible blocks of text are set into and around an engagingly diverse mix of cutaway views, digital paintings and eye-widening deep-space photographs. . . . There's plenty here to stimulate both random browsers and confirmed young sky watchers." Kirkus

Includes bibliographical references

Aguilar, David A.

Super stars; the biggest, hottest, brightest, and most explosive stars in the Milky Way. National Geographic 2010 48p il $16.95; lib bdg $27.90

Grades: 4 5 6 7   **523.8**
1. Stars 2. Supergiant stars
ISBN 978-1-4263-0601-3; 1-4263-0601-6; 978-1-4263-0602-0 lib bdg; 1-4263-0602-4 lib bdg
LC 2009-37124

"Pairing dramatic space art with souped-up prose, Aguilar introduces more than a dozen types of stars and stellar phenomena. . . . Aside from the occasional alien or interstellar spacecraft set against glowing star fields, the information in both pictures and texts sticks to the facts, accurately reflecting current knowledge without ever coming close to turning into a dry recitation of data. . . . [This is an] unusually exuberant ticket to ride for young sky watchers and armchair space travelers." SLJ

Includes glossary and bibliographical references

Croswell, Ken

★ The **lives** of stars. Boyds Mills Press 2009 72p il $19.95

Grades: 5 6 7 8   **523.8**
1. Stars 2. Astronomy
ISBN 978-1-59078-582-9; 1-59078-582-7
LC 2008033913

"Extensive, detailed information about stars is coupled with amazing colorful photographs, many from the Hubble Space Telescope, in this stunning book. Packed with facts about the stars and their life cycle, the text often relates them to situations or objects familiar to readers." SLJ

Includes glossary

DeCristofano, Carolyn Cinami

★ A **black** hole is not a hole; Carolyn Cinami DeCristofano; Illustrated by Michael Carroll. Charlesbridge 2012 v, 74 p.p col ill. (reinforced for library use) $18.95

Grades: 4 5 6 7   **523.8**
1. Stars 2. Universe 3. Black holes (Astronomy)
ISBN 9781570917837; 9781570917844
LC 2010022764

In this non-fiction children's book, Carolyn Cinami DeCristofano discusses black holes. "Covering the life cycles of stars; the formation of black holes and weird optical and physical effects associated with them; more recent revelations of super-sized black holes at the centers of galaxies; and the general effects of mass on space, light, and matter, she presents a . . . picture of the strange structure and stranger physics of black holes." (Booklist)

Jackson, Ellen B.

★ The **mysterious** universe; supernovae, dark energy, and black holes. text by Ellen Jackson; photographs and illustrations by Nic Bishop. Houghton Mifflin 2008 60p il (Scientists in the field) $18

Grades: 5 6 7 8   **523.8**
1. Supernovas 2. Black holes (Astronomy) 3. Astronomy
ISBN 978-0-618-56325-8; 0-618-56325-3
LC 2007-41165

This "follows prominent astronomer Alex Filippenko and associates from the Keck Observatory in Hawaii to the Lick Observatory in California on a hunt for supernovae and related large-scale astronomical phenomena. . . . Along with depicting the scientists, the images also include massive telescopes and photos or digital simulations of galaxies, exploding stars, and other astronomical phenomena." SLJ

Includes glossary and bibliographical references

Mack, Gail

The **stars**. Marshall Cavendish Benchmark 2009 64p il (Space!) lib bdg $32.79

Grades: 4 5 6 7   **523.8**
1. Stars 2. Galaxies
ISBN 978-0-7614-4250-9 lib bdg; 0-7614-4250-2 lib bdg
LC 2009014655

This stands out for its "clear, accurate [presentation] of basic facts punctuated by lively turns of phrase and, sometimes, details not commonly found in the plethora of similar tours of the solar system and beyond." SLJ

Includes glossary and bibliographical references

Miller, Ron

Seven wonders beyond the solar system. Twenty-First Century Books 2011 80p il (Seven wonders) lib bdg $33.26

Grades: 5 6 7 8   **523.8**
1. Extrasolar planets
ISBN 978-0-7613-5454-3; 0-7613-5454-9
                    LC 2010028446

This "discusses how stars and galaxies form and how scientists search for 'the most Earthlike planet,' as well as the noteworthy nebulae, pulsars, and superclusters. . . . [This] volume makes basic concepts clear in lively, energetic language that, along with the mesmerizing color photos and artists' renderings of space, will easily captivate a young audience, while up-to-date examples, including discoveries made in the last five years, will only increase the sense of immediacy and excitement." Booklist

Includes glossary and bibliographical references

Ridpath, Ian

The **monthly** sky guide; Ian Ridpath; illustrated by Wil Tirion. 9th ed. Cambridge University Press 2012 71 p. col. ill. (paperback) $17.99

Grades: 8 9 10 11 12 Adult   **523.8**
1. Astronomy 2. Stars -- Atlases 3. SCIENCE -- Astronomy 4. Stars -- Identification 5. Stars -- Observers' manuals
ISBN 1107683157; 9781107683150
                    LC 2012033599

This book, the ninth edition of Ian Ridpath and Wil Tirion's guide to the night sky, "is updated with planet positions and forthcoming eclipses to the end of the year 2017. It contains twelve chapters describing the main sights visible in each month of the year, providing" information for anyone "wanting to identify prominent stars, constellations, star clusters, nebulae and galaxies; to watch out for meteor showers . . . or to follow the movements of the four brightest planets." (Publisher's note)

Includes bibliographical references and index.

525   Earth (Astronomical geography)

Bell, Trudy E.

Earth's journey through space; by Trudy E. Bell. Chelsea House Publishers 2008 80p il (Scientific American) lib bdg $30

Grades: 5 6 7 8   **525**
1. Astronomy
ISBN 978-0-7910-9050-3 lib bdg; 0-7910-9050-7 lib bdg
                    LC 2007032351

The author "describes in some detail just how our planet's axial tilt, rotation, and orbital path were discovered and measured, as well as how external forces affect all three. She then goes on to explain how scientists use parallax and other physical effects to determine distances and movements in

our galaxy and the universe at large. . . . In general, the old prints, modern space photos, and clear digital images are well chosen to clarify and enhance the presentation." SLJ

Includes bibliographical references

Hicks, Terry Allan

Earth and the moon. Marshall Cavendish Benchmark 2009 64p il (Space!) lib bdg $22.95

Grades: 4 5 6 7   **525**
1. Earth 2. Moon
ISBN 978-0-7614-4254-7 lib bdg; 0-7614-4254-5 lib bdg
                    LC 2009014663

"Describes Earth and its Moon, including their history, their composition, and their roles in the solar system." Publisher's note

Includes glossary and bibliographical references

Miller, Ron

Earth and the moon. 21st Cent. Bks. (Brookfield) 2003 96p il (Worlds beyond) lib bdg $25.90

Grades: 5 6 7 8   **525**
1. Young adult literature -- Works 2. Children's literature -- Works -- Grades two through six 3. Earth 4. Moon
ISBN 0-7613-2358-9
                    LC 2001-8479

Chronicles the origin, evolution, and exploration of the Earth and the Moon, and discusses their composition, their place in our solar system, and more

This is illustrated "with a mix of NASA photos and wide-angle, computer-generated art. . . . Students with a serious interest in the physical history of the Earth and its moon will be engrossed by his account of our planet's first few billion years, the Moon's probable origin, and the rise of life." SLJ

Includes glossary and bibliographical references

Ride, Sally K.

Mission: planet Earth; our world and its climate--and how humans are changing them. [by] Sally Ride & Tam O'Shaughnessy. Roaring Brook Press 2009 80p il map (Sally Ride science) $19.95

Grades: 5 6 7 8   **525**
1. Climate -- Environmental aspects 2. Global warming 3. Climatic changes 4. Nature -- Effect of human beings on
ISBN 978-1-59643-310-6; 1-59643-310-8
                    LC 2009-29253

"This environmental-science primer introduces a range of important concepts necessary to understand climate change and global warming. Topics include the carbon cycle, water cycle, long-range carbon emissions data, biological evidence of climate change, and much more. The authors have an extensive background in science education, and their text exhibits an excellent balance of concept thoroughness with ease of comprehension. Attractive photographs and colorful graphics, including many charts and diagrams, are incorporated throughout." SLJ

Simon, Seymour

★ **Earth**: our planet in space; rev ed; Simon & Schuster Bks. for Young Readers 2003 un il $17.95

Grades: 4 5 6 7   **525**
1. Earth
ISBN 0-689-83562-0

LC 2001-31304

First published 1984 by Four Winds Press
This describes the relationship between the Earth, the sun, and the moon and explains the seasons, day and night, the atmosphere, and changes in the planet's surface. Illustrated with photographs taken from space

526.9   Surveying

Anderson, Judith
★ **Ways** to do surveys; [by] Judith Anderson. Smart Apple Media 2008 32p il map (Geography skills) $22.95
Grades: 6 7 8 9   **526.9**
1. Surveying
ISBN 978-1-59920-053-8; 1-59920-053-8

LC 2006036140

"The text is easy to follow. . . . The examples . . . are almost always accompanied by excellent photographs. . . . Maps, block diagrams, tables, and graphs are clearly presented and easy to interpret." Sci Books Films
Includes glossary and bibliographical references

529   Chronology

Farndon, John
Time. Benchmark Bks. 2003 32p il (Science experiments) lib bdg $24.21
Grades: 5 6 7 8   **529**
1. Time 2. Experiments 3. Science -- Experiments 4. Time measurements -- Experiments
ISBN 0-7614-1470-3

LC 2002-4846

Includes glossary

Formichelli, Linda
Timekeeping; Explore the History and Science of Telling Time With 15 Projects. by Linda Formichelli, W. Eric Martin; illustrated by Sam Carbaugh. Independent Pub Group 2012 128 p. (hardcover) $21.95
Grades: 4 5 6 7 8   **529**
1. Time 2. Science -- Experiments
ISBN 1619301369; 9781619301368
This juvenile activity book, by Linda Formichelli, W. Eric Martin, with illustrations by Sam Carbaugh, is part of the "Build It Yourself" series. It teaches "the cultural history of time" through providing several activities and projects such as "making a shadow clock, tracking time like an ancient Egyptian, using a protractor to create a sundial, measuring time with water, and making a candle clock." (Publisher's note)

Jenkins, Martin
The **time** book; a brief history from lunar calendars to atomic clocks. illustrated by Richard Holland. Candlewick Press 2009 57p il map lib bdg $18.99

Grades: 4 5 6 7   **529**
1. Time 2. Calendars 3. Clocks and watches 6. Time measurements
ISBN 978-0-7636-4112-2 lib bdg; 0-7636-4112-X lib bdg

LC 2008-19706

"Conversational text, whimsical mixed-media artwork, and elegant book design combine to present an informative and entertaining romp through time." SLJ

Kagayame, Johnny
Discovering the construct of time; [by] Johnny Kagayame, Josepha Sherman. Rosen Pub. 2011 112p il (The scientist's guide to physics) $34.60
Grades: 7 8 9 10   **529**
1. Time 2. Calendars 3. Space and time 4. Clocks and watches
ISBN 1448847036; 9781448847037

LC 2010042035

"Beginning with a brief discussion of the concept of time and its meaning in different cultures, this book presents the history of time measurement. . . . A section of the chapter 'Time in Modern Times' introduces Einstein's theories of relativity. . . . Illustrated chiefly with clearly reproduced color photos, this volume provides an accessible, basic introduction to its subject." Booklist
Includes glossary and bibliographical references

Kummer, Patricia K.
★ The **calendar**; by Patricia K. Kummer. Franklin Watts 2005 80p il (Inventions that shaped the world) $30.50; pa $9.95
Grades: 4 5 6 7   **529**
1. Calendars
ISBN 0-531-12340-5; 0-531-16720-8 pa

LC 2004-6914

This "book presents the origins and history of the calendar. . . . The illustrations include clear reproductions of period paintings, engravings, and drawings as well as photos of artifacts, sculpture, and contemporary scenes. . . . A good basic introduction." Booklist
Includes bibliographical references

Sullivan, Navin
Time; [by] Navin Sullivan. Marshall Cavendish Benchmark 2007 48p il (Measure up!) lib bdg $20.95
Grades: 4 5 6 7   **529**
1. Time 2. Calendars 3. Clocks and watches
ISBN 978-0-7614-2321-8 lib bdg; 0-7614-2321-4 lib bdg
This is "engaging and informative. . . . The excellent blend of photographs, charts, and diagrams complements the [text]." SLJ
Includes glossary and bibliographical references

530 Physics

Baxter, Roberta

The **particle** model of matter. Raintree 2009 48p il (Sci-hi: physical science) lib bdg $31.43; pa $8.99

Grades: 4 5 6 7   530

1. Atoms 2. Matter

ISBN 978-1-4109-3244-0 lib bdg; 978-1-4109-3259-4 pa

LC 2008030582

This takes a look at atoms, the building blocks of matter. It describes the different kinds of atoms, the particles that make up an atom, and the different states that matter can take

Includes bibliographical references

Bonnet, Robert L.

Home run! science projects with baseball and softball. [by] Robert L. Bonnet and Dan Keen. Enslow Publishers 2009 104p il (Score! Sports science projects) lib bdg $31.93

Grades: 5 6 7 8   530

1. Motion 2. Baseball 3. Force and energy 4. Science projects 5. Science -- Experiments

ISBN 978-0-7660-3365-8 lib bdg; 0-7660-3365-1 lib bdg

LC 2008-3005

"In addition to colorful, digital drawings illustrating the projects, a few photos and period prints also brighten the pages. . . . [This] will appeal to those looking for fresh science-project ideas." Booklist

Includes glossary and bibliographical references

Christianson, Gale E.

Isaac Newton and the scientific revolution. Oxford Univ. Press 1996 155p il (Oxford portraits in science) lib bdg $28

Grades: 7 8 9 10   530

1. Physicists 2. Scientists 3. Mathematicians 4. Writers on science 6. Science -- History

ISBN 0-19-509224-4

LC 96-13179

Explores the life and scientific contributions of the famed English mathematician and natural philosopher

This book "reads easily and with a pleasant and comfortable flow. Structured around pivotal moments in Newton's life, the book is an excellent reference for biographical data on the great English scientist; in addition, it affords a fine historical perspective of the scientific revolution." Sci Books Films

Includes bibliographical references

Farndon, John

Experimenting with physics. Marshall Cavendish Benchmark 2009 112p il (Experimenting with science) $35.64

Grades: 7 8 9 10   530

1. Physics 2. Science -- Experiments

ISBN 978-0-7614-3929-5; 0-7614-3929-3

LC 2008017568

"Explores and explains physics concepts—including energy, motion, simple machines, gravity, flight, electricity, and magnetism—and provides experiments to aid in understanding physics." Publisher's note

Gardner, Robert

Ace your physical science project; great science fair ideas. [by] Robert Gardner, Madeline Goodstein, and Thomas R. Rybolt. Enslow Publishers 2009 128p il (Ace your physics science project) lib bdg $31.93

Grades: 5 6 7 8   530

1. Physics 2. Science projects 3. Science -- Experiments

ISBN 978-0-7660-3225-5 lib bdg; 0-7660-3225-6 lib bdg

LC 2008-29637

"Dozens of . . . science activities are presented with background information, step-by-step instructions, and suggestions for extending to the science fair level. . . . Color illustrations and important safety information are included." Horn Book Guide

Includes bibliographical references

Science fair projects about the properties of matter; revised and expanded using the scientific method. Enslow Publishers 2010 160p il (Physics science projects using the scientific method) lib bdg $34.60

Grades: 7 8 9 10   530

1. Matter 2. Science projects 3. Science -- Experiments

ISBN 978-0-7660-3417-4 lib bdg; 0-7660-3417-8 lib bdg

LC 2009014804

First published 2004 with title: Science fair projects about the properties of matter using marbles, water, balloons, and more

"Explains how to use the scientific method to conduct several science experiments about the properties of matter. Includes ideas for science fair projects." Publisher's note

Includes bibliographical references

Slam dunk! science projects with basketball; [by] Robert Gardner and Dennis Shortelle. Enslow Publishers 2009 104p il (Score! sports science projects) lib bdg $31.93

Grades: 5 6 7 8   530

1. Physics 2. Basketball 3. Science projects 4. Science -- Experiments

ISBN 978-0-7660-3366-5 lib bdg; 0-7660-3366-X lib bdg

LC 2008-24879

"Introductions include information about the history of the sport, safety steps to follow, and the scientific method. . . . Detailed diagrams help clarify many of the directions." SLJ

Includes glossary and bibliographical references

Goodstein, Madeline

Wheels! science projects with bicycles, skateboards, and skates. Enslow Publishers 2009 104p il (Score! sports science projects) lib bdg $31.93

Grades: 5 6 7 8 9 10   530

1. Wheels 2. Physics 3. Science projects 4. Science

-- Experiments
ISBN 978-0-7660-3107-4 lib bdg; 0-7660-3107-1
lib bdg

LC 2008-24880

"Introductions include information about the history of the sport, safety steps to follow, and the scientific method. . . . Detailed diagrams help clarify many of the directions." SLJ
Includes glossary and bibliographical references

Green, Dan

Physics; why matter matters! [by] Dan Green; Simon Basher, illustrator. Kingfisher 2008 128p il pa $8.95

Grades: 5 6 7 8 **530**

1. Physics
ISBN 978-0-7534-6214-0 pa; 0-7534-6214-1 pa

LC 2007-31805

This "introduces the elements of physics as anthropomorphic, cartoon-style characters. . . . Each of the groupings begins with an introduction and each concept is given its own spread that shows the cartoon figure and describes its 'personality.' The information is presented in a chatty and conversational tone. . . . Along with the narrative, which is written in the first person from the concept's point of view, other key facts are presented. This book would be handy as a supplement to a physics curriculum." SLJ
Includes glossary

Hartman, Eve

Light and sound; [by] Eve Hartman and Wendy Meshbesher. Raintree 2008 48p il (Sci-hi: physical science) lib bdg $22; pa $8.99

Grades: 5 6 7 8 **530**

1. Light 2. Sound
ISBN 978-1-4109-3378-2 lib bdg; 1-4109-3378-4 lib bdg; 978-1-4109-3383-6 pa; 1-4109-3383-0 pa

LC 2009-3506

A "compelling read for both browsers and science buffs. . . . Information is clearly presented and flows smoothly. . . . A treasure trove of information." SLJ
Includes glossary and bibliographical references

Lee, Cora

The **great** motion mission; a surprising story of physics in everyday life. illustrated by Steve Rolston. Annick Press 2009 114p il $24.95; pa $14.95

Grades: 4 5 6 **530**

1. Physics
ISBN 978-1-55451-185-3; 1-55451-185-2; 978-1-55451-184-6 pa; 1-55451-184-4 pa

"This book is a combination of narrative and concepts about physics. . . . Jeremy and his friends are distraught when the local summer fair is canceled in order to host a physics conference. While Jeremy helps his uncle campaign to save the fair, his new neighbor, Aubrey, sets out to prove that physics isn't only necessary, but also fun. The text is chatty and accessible to students. Topics include 'Physics and Sight,' 'Physics and Sound,' and 'Physics in Motion.' Each chapter profiles a featured physicist, from Albert Einstein to Richard Feynman. . . . Cartoon illustrations help to explain concepts such as the water cycle and wave patterns. Photographs are scattered throughout, and boxed areas high-

light specific topics. This title would be especially useful for students wanting a good introduction to physics." SLJ
Includes glossary and bibliographical references

Matter; edited by Andrea R. Field. 1st ed. Britannica Educational Pub. in association with Rosen Educational Services 2013 77 p. ill. (some col.) (Introduction to physics) (library) $31.70

Grades: 7 8 9 10 **530**

1. Matter 2. Physics
ISBN 1615308393; 9781615308392

LC 2011052216

This book by Andrea R. Field is part of the Introduction to Physics series and focuses on Matter. The entry "covers the basic properties and states of matter; its relationship to energy, including Einstein's theory of special relativity; and physicists' quandaries with dark matter and antimatter." (Booklist)
Includes bibliographical references (p. 73) and index.

Morgan, Sally

From Greek atoms to quarks; discovering atoms. by Sally Morgan. Heinemann Library 2007 64p il (Chain reactions) lib bdg $34.29

Grades: 6 7 8 9 **530**

1. Atoms 2. Matter
ISBN 978-1-4034-9551-8 lib bdg; 1-4034-9551-3 lib bdg

LC 2006037044

"Morgan tells the story of the atom, including its discovery, structure, power, and future in subatomic particles. . . . Archival and full-color photos and reproductions appear on nearly every page." SLJ
Includes glossary and bibliographical references

The **science** of physics; edited by Andrea Field. Britannica Educational Pub. 2012 80 p. (Introduction to physics) (library binding) $31.70

Grades: 7 8 9 10 **530**

1. Physics
ISBN 1615306765; 9781615306763

LC 2011026548

This children's book, edited by Andrea R. Field, is part of the Introduction to Physics series. It "surveys some of the major branches of physics, the laws, and theories significant to each. Also chronicled are some of the historical milestones in the field by such great minds as Galileo and Isaac Newton." (Publisher's note)
Includes bibliographical references and index

Silverstein, Alvin

Matter; by Alvin Silverstein, Virginia Silverstein, Laura Silverstein Nunn. Twenty-First Century Books 2009 112p il (Science concepts) lib bdg $31.93

Grades: 5 6 7 8 **530**

1. Matter
ISBN 978-0-8225-7515-3 lib bdg; 0-8225-7515-9 lib bdg

LC 2007049493

This is a "simple and straightforward [discussion] of the [subject]. The layout . . . is attractive and inviting, with full-color photographs and/or diagrams on almost every spread. In addition, the authors make good use of fact boxes. . . . [This] discusses the states of matter, the elements, chemical reactions, and more. [This title] will interest browsers and provide ample information for reports." SLJ

Includes glossary and bibliographical references

Sullivan, Navin

Weight. Marshall Cavendish Benchmark 2007 48p il (Measure up!) lib bdg $20.90

Grades: 4 5 6 7   **530**

1. Gravity 2. Weights and measures
ISBN 978-0-7614-2324-9 lib bdg; 0-7614-2324-9 lib bdg

"Examples using familiar objects and excellent full-color graphics help to bring concepts to life." SLJ

Includes glossary and bibliographical references

Weir, Jane

Matter. Compass Point Books 2009 40p il (Mission: science) lib bdg $26.60

Grades: 4 5 6   **530**

1. Matter
ISBN 978-0-7565-4069-2 lib bdg; 0-7565-4069-0 lib bdg

LC 2008-37624

An introduction to the scientific concept of matter, including elements, atoms, and molecules

Includes glossary

530.092

Baxter, Roberta

Ernest Rutherford and the birth of the atomic age; by Roberta Baxter. Morgan Reynolds Pub. 2011 112p ill. (Profiles in science) (library) $28.95

Grades: 7 8 9 10 11 12   **530.092**

1. Nuclear physics 2. Nuclear physics -- History 3. Physicists -- New Zealand -- Biography
ISBN 1599351714; 9781599351711; 9781599352756

LC 2010049096

This children's nonfiction book, by Roberta Baxter, is part of the "Profiles in Science" series, profiling the nuclear physicist Ernest Rutherford. Topics include a profile of his life as a child growing up in New Zealand, his work researching physics in Canada, his Nobel Prize, and the legacy of his work after his death.

"This is a well-rounded portrait of the 20th century's greatest experimental scientists. Baxter not only explains Rutherford's major accomplishments . . . in lucid but not oversimplified terms, but she also paints a vivid picture of an ambitious but not egotistical man with a big personality and close family ties. Enlightening diagrams and plenty of photographs . . . add solid visual elements. . ." SLJ

Includes bibliographical references and index

Pohlen, Jerome

Albert Einstein and relativity for kids; his life and ideas with 21 activities and thought experiments.

Jerome Pohlen. Chicago Review Press 2012 xv, 126 p.p (pbk.) $16.95

Grades: 5 6 7   **530.092**

1. Physicists 2. Relativity (Physics) 3. Physicists -- Biography 4. Relativity (Physics) -- Experiments 5. Science & Nature -- Experiments & Projects
ISBN 161374028X; 9781613740286

LC 2012021342

This biography of physicist Albert Einstein "includes the science, politics, and people that surrounded the" scientist. "Einstein's role in the development of the atomic bomb is included along with an explanation of how nuclear fission works. His humanitarian efforts, including his regret at being the instigator behind the bomb are described along with his marriages, his relationships with his children, his eccentricities, and his scientific shortcomings." (School Library Journal)

Includes bibliographical references (page 117) and index

530.11   Relativity theory

Whiting, Jim

Space and time; Jim Whiting; photographs by Getty Images; folio illustration, Alex Ryan. 1st ed. Creative Education 2013 48 p. col. ill., col. maps (library) $35.65

Grades: 4 5 6 7   **530.11**

1. Physics 2. Space and time 3. Relativity (Physics)
ISBN 1608181928; 9781608181926

LC 2011040146

This book, by Jim Whiting, explores the concepts of space and time as part of the "Mysteries of the Universe" series. It appeals "to report writers and serious astronomy students. Each book carefully examines the history behind attempts to unravel explanations for the subjects, going back to Anaxagoras's work on energy in 450 B.C. all the way up to the contemporary findings of Stephen Hawking." (School Library Journal)

Includes bibliographical references (p. 46-47) and index.

530.4   States of matter

Claybourne, Anna

The **nature** of matter; [by] Anna Claybourne. Gareth Stevens Pub. 2007 48p il (Gareth Stevens vital science: physical science) lib bdg $26.60; pa $11.95

Grades: 4 5 6 7   **530.4**

1. Matter
ISBN 978-0-8368-8088-5 lib bdg; 978-0-8368-8097-7 pa

LC 2006033732

This describes uses for matter and what happens when it changes from one form to another, the basic physical laws and properties of matter, and the various ways in which we control how matter behaves.

This is "straightforward and clear. . . . The layout is bright and colorful, with photographs and illustrations on almost every page." SLJ

Includes glossary and bibliographical references

Meyer, Susan

Gases and their properties. Rosen Central 2011 64p il (Science made simple) lib bdg $29.25; pa $12.95

Grades: 5 6 7 8   530.4

1. Gases

ISBN 978-1-4488-1233-2 lib bdg; 1-4488-1233-X lib bdg; 978-1-4488-2243-0 pa; 1-4488-2243-2 pa

LC 2010015858

This introduction to gases and their properties includes "a lot of detailed information, making [it] useful as [a] resource . . . for science projects and reports. . . . The [book] also [includes a] brief discussion of scientists important in the field, the history of the topic, and current and future applications. . . . The straightforward, no-nonsense [narrative] and simple design make this . . . a nice package for basic science." SLJ

Includes glossary and bibliographical references

Oxlade, Chris

States of matter; [by] Chris Oxlade. rev. and updated; Heimemann Library 2007 48p il (Chemicals in action) lib bdg $31.43; pa $8.95

Grades: 6 7 8 9   530.4

1. Matter

ISBN 978-1-4329-0055-7 lib bdg; 978-1-4329-0062-5 pa

First published 2002

"Explanations are concise and clear without being oversimplified, and the arrangement is attractive and open. Colorful diagrams, drawings, and photographs appear on every page." SLJ

Includes glossary and bibliographical references

530.8   Measurement

Ball, Johnny

Why pi; how math applies to everyday life. DK Pub. 2009 93p il map $16.99

Grades: 4 5 6 7   530.8

1. Pi 2. Mathematics 3. Measurement 4. Mensuration

ISBN 978-0-7566-5164-0; 0-7566-5164-6

"Author Johnny Ball focuses on how people have used numbers to measure things through the ages, from the ways the ancient Egyptians measured the pyramids to how modern scientists measure time and space." Publisher's note

Gardner, Robert

Ace your math and measuring science project; great science fair ideas. Enslow Publishers 2009 128p il (Ace your physics science project) lib bdg $31.93

Grades: 5 6 7 8   530.8

1. Measurement 2. Science projects 3. Weights and measures 4. Science -- Experiments 5. Mensuration

6. Science projects 8. Science -- Exhibitions

ISBN 978-0-7660-3224-8 lib bdg; 0-7660-3224-8 lib bdg

LC 2008-23926

"Dozens of . . . science activities are presented with background information, step-by-step instructions, and suggestions for extending to the science fair level. . . . Color illustrations and important safety information are included." Horn Book Guide

Includes bibliographical references

531   Classical mechanics

Claybourne, Anna

Forms of energy. Raintree 2008 48p il (Sci-hi: physical science) lib bdg $22; pa $8.99

Grades: 5 6 7 8   531

1. Force and energy

ISBN 978-1-4109-3377-5 lib bdg; 1-4109-3377-6 lib bdg; 978-1-4109-3382-9 pa; 1-4109-3382-2 pa

LC 2009-3504

A "compelling read for both browsers and science buffs. . . . Information is clearly presented and flows smoothly. . . . A treasure trove of information." SLJ

Includes glossary and bibliographical references

Gut-wrenching gravity and other fatal forces; Anna Claybourne. Crabtree Publishing Company 2013 32 p. (Disgusting & dreadful science) (pbk. : alk. paper) $9.95

Grades: 4 5 6   531

1. Gravity 2. Physics 3. Force and energy

ISBN 0778709574; 9780778709503; 9780778709572

LC 2012043529

This book by Anna Claybourne is part of the Disgusting & Dreadful Science series and focuses on gravity and other physical forces. It shares facts including that "a mouse can survive a 328-foot fall, black holes have superstrong gravity that causes 'spaghettification,' and" more. Illustrations are included. (Booklist)

Includes bibliographical references and index

Energy; edited by Andrea R. Field. Britannica Educational Pub. in association with Rosen Educational Services 2012 79 p. ill. (some col.) (Introduction to physics)

Grades: 7 8 9 10   531

1. Force and energy -- Study and teaching (Middle school)

ISBN 9781615306732

LC 2011021493

"...With attractive, lively graphics, [this] will make a good supplement in libraries needing lots of science-experiment background information." Booklist

Includes bibliographical references (p. 72-75) and index

Gardner, Robert

Ace your forces and motion science project; great science fair ideas. [by] Robert Gardner and Madeline

Goodstein. Enslow Publishers 2009 128p il (Ace your physics science project) lib bdg $31.93

Grades: 5 6 7 8   **531**

1. Force and energy 2. Science projects 3. Science -- Experiments

ISBN 978-0-7660-3222-4 lib bdg; 0-7660-3222-1 lib bdg

LC 2008-49778

"Presents several science experiments and project ideas about forces and motion." Publisher's note

Includes bibliographical references

Forces and motion science fair projects; revised and expanded using the scientific method. Enslow Publishers 2010 160p il (Physics science projects using the scientific method) lib bdg $34.60

Grades: 7 8 9 10   **531**

1. Force and energy 2. Science projects 3. Science -- Experiments

ISBN 978-0-7660-3415-0 lib bdg; 0-7660-3415-1 lib bdg

LC 2008050066

First published 2004 with title: Forces and motion science fair projects using water balloons, pulleys, and other stuff

"Explains how to use the scientific method to conduct several physics experiments with forces and motion. Includes ideas for science fair projects." Publisher's note

Includes bibliographical references

Nardo, Don

Force and motion; laws of movement. by Don Nardo. Compass Point Books 2008 48p il (Exploring science) lib bdg $26.60

Grades: 7 8 9 10   **531**

1. Motion 2. Force and energy

ISBN 978-0-7565-3264-2 lib bdg; 0-7565-3264-7 lib bdg

LC 2007004604

Includes glossary and bibliographical references

O'Leary, Denyse

What are Newton's laws of motion? Crabtree Pub. Co. 2011 64p il (Shaping modern science) lib bdg $30.60; pa $10.95

Grades: 5 6 7 8   **531**

1. Motion 2. Physicists 3. Mathematicians 4. Writers on science 5. Science

ISBN 978-0-7787-7200-2 lib bdg; 0-7787-7200-4 lib bdg; 978-0-7787-7207-1 pa; 0-7787-7207-1 pa

LC 2010-52629

This book examines how Sir Isaac Newton developed three basic laws that govern the way in which objects move. It explains how Newton expanded on the work of other scientists, including Galileo and Copernicus, to make his discovery. The book also explains how Newton's laws have influenced modern science and technology in areas such as sports and transportation.

This title is "not only written and organized well, but [it is] also gorgeous in design. Full-color photographs and illustrations are set over colorful backgrounds that add depth but not distraction. [The title] includes thought-provoking quotes from famous authors and scientists and some eyebrow-raising 'Quick Facts' throughout." SLJ

Includes glossary and bibliographical references

Orr, Tamra

Motion and forces. Rosen Central 2011 64p il (Science made simple) lib bdg $29.25; pa $12.95

Grades: 5 6 7 8   **531**

1. Motion 2. Force and energy

ISBN 978-1-4488-1232-5 lib bdg; 1-4488-1232-1 lib bdg; 978-1-4488-2240-9 pa; 1-4488-2240-8 pa

LC 2010020535

This introduction to motion and forces includes "a lot of detailed information, making [it] useful as [a] resource . . . for science projects and reports. . . . The [book] also [includes a] brief discussion of scientists important in the field, the history of the topic, and current and future applications. . . . The straightforward, no-nonsense [narrative] and simple design make this . . . a nice package for basic science." SLJ

Includes glossary and bibliographical references

Phelan, Glen

Invisible force; the quest to define the laws of motion. [by] Glen Phelan. National Geographic 2006 59p il (Science quest) $17.95; lib bdg $25.90

Grades: 5 6 7 8   **531**

1. Motion 2. Gravity

ISBN 0-7922-5539-9; 0-7922-5540-2 lib bdg

LC 2005027350

This "traces the historical and scientific path to man's understanding of motion and gravity." Publisher's note

Includes glossary and bibliographical references

Pinna, Simon de

Transfer of energy; by Simon de Pinna. Gareth Stevens Pub. 2007 48p il (Gareth Stevens vital science: physical science) lib bdg $26.60; pa $11.95

Grades: 4 5 6 7   **531**

1. Force and energy

ISBN 978-0-8368-8091-5 lib bdg; 978-0-8368-8100-4 pa

LC 2006033733

This explains such terms and concepts as kinetic and potential energy, chain reactions, energy pyramid, and power grid; the uses for the varying wavelengths of the electromagnetic spectrum; the ways that plants and animals use energy; and concepts such as conduction, convection, reflection, and transmission

This is "straightforward and clear. . . . The layout is bright and colorful, with photographs and illustrations on almost every page." SLJ

Includes bibliographical references

Silverstein, Alvin

Forces and motion; [by Alvin & Virginia Silverstein & Laura Silverstein Nunn] Twenty-First Century Books 2008 112p il (Science concepts) lib bdg $31.93

Grades: 5 6 7 8 **531**

1. Motion 2. Force and energy
ISBN 978-0-8225-7514-6 lib bdg; 0-8225-7514-0
lib bdg

LC 2007-48826

"The breadth of material the authors cover in this volume is impressive. They discuss energy (kenetic and potential), forces (friction, gravity, electricity, and magnetism), simple machines (lever, wheel, pulley, ramp, and wedge), motion in fluids, and Newton's laws of motion. . . . [This offers] simple writing, many colorful pictures, and lots of examples." Sci Books Films

Includes glossary and bibliographical references

Solway, Andrew

Exploring forces and motion. Rosen Central 2008 48p il (Exploring physical science) lib bdg $26.50

Grades: 5 6 7 8 **531**

1. Motion 2. Force and energy
ISBN 978-1-4042-3747-6; 1-4042-3747-X

LC 2006036680

Includes glossary and bibliographical references

Stille, Darlene R.

★ **Waves**; energy on the move. by Darlene R. Stille. Compass Point Books 2006 48p il map (Exploring science) $25.27

Grades: 6 7 8 9 **531**

1. Waves
ISBN 0-7565-1259-X

LC 2005002477

This decribes water waves, sound waves, light waves, radio waves, and earthquake waves.

This "provides a straightforward and clear discussion of its topic. . . . Full-color photographs, illustrations, or diagrams appear on almost every page, accompanied by captions that complement the text." SLJ

Includes glossary and bibliographical references

Sullivan, Navin

Speed. Marshall Cavendish Benchmark 2007 48p il (Measure up!) lib bdg $20.90

Grades: 4 5 6 7 **531**

1. Speed 2. Measurement
ISBN 978-0-7614-2325-6 lib bdg; 0-7614-2325-7
lib bdg

"Have you ever wondered how we measure different speeds? How do we know how fast an airplane travels or how much speed a shuttle needs to travel to outer space? What does speed have to do with satellites? How does the speed of light compare with the speed of sound? Speed answers these questions and explores the history of humankind's discoveries about speed." Publisher's note

Includes glossary and bibliographical references

VanCleave, Janice Pratt, 1942-

Step-by-step science experiments in energy; by Janice VanCleave. Rosen Pub. 2013 80 p. col. ill. (Janice VanCleeve's first-place science fair projects) (library) $33.25; (paperback) $14.15

Grades: 5 6 7 8 **531**

1. Energy 2. Science -- Experiments 3. Science projects 4. Force and energy -- Experiments
ISBN 144886979X; 9781448869794; 9781448884711

LC 2012006835

This book by Janice VanCleave is part of the First-Place Science Fair Projects series. The books have an introduction to the subject—here, energy, followed by 22 simple . . . experiments. Van Cleave states the basic goal of the experiments, followed by a list of necessary materials, most of which can be found around the house or easily acquired with minimal cost. Step-by-step instructions are clearly detailed and accompanied by diagrams where needed." (School Library Journal)

Includes bibliographical references and index.

Viegas, Jennifer

★ **Kinetic** and potential energy; understanding changes within physical systems. [by] Jennifer Viegas. 1st ed.; Rosen Pub. Group 2005 48p il (Library of physics) lib bdg $25.25

Grades: 7 8 9 10 **531**

1. Dynamics 2. Force and energy
ISBN 1-4042-0333-8

LC 2004019126

"Viegas begins by explaining kinetic and potential energy and the history of their discoveries. Mechanical energy, momentum, and the laws of energy are also presented. . . . The [layout is] open and appealing and [includes] well-captioned photographs and simple diagrams." SLJ

Includes bibliographical references

532 Fluid mechanics

Meiani, Antonella

Water. Lerner Publs. 2003 40p il (Experimenting with science) lib bdg $23.93

Grades: 4 5 6 7 **532**

1. Water 2. Science -- Experiments
ISBN 0-8225-0083-3

LC 2001-50773

Describes experiments with water which answer such questions as "Why are water droplets round?" and "Why do some things, like salt, dissolve in water and other things, like fish, don't?"

This offers "straightforward, well-designed experiments. . . . Numerous clear diagrams, some photos, and occasional historical sidebars extend this material, which is notable for its substance." Horn Book Guide

Includes glossary and bibliographical references

Parker, Steve, 1952-

The **science** of water; projects with experiments with water and power. [by] Steve Parker. Heinemann Library 2005 32p il (Tabletop scientist) lib bdg $29.29; pa $7.85

Grades: 4 5 6 7 **532**

1. Water 2. Science -- Experiments
ISBN 1-4034-7282-3 lib bdg; 1-4034-7289-0 pa

LC 2005007027

This "has experiments on the water cycle, water density, water as a solvent, surface tension, capillary action, buoyancy, water power, and water propulsion. . . . The colorful illustrations, organization, and ease of use of [this title makes it an] excellent [addition]." SLJ

Includes glossary

533   Pneumatics (Gas mechanics)

Gardner, Robert

Air; green science projects for a sustainable planet. Enslow Publishers 2011 128p il (Team Green science projects) lib bdg $31.93

Grades: 6 7 8 9 10   533
1. Air 2. Air pollution 3. Science projects 4. Science -- Experiments
ISBN 978-0-7660-3646-8; 0-7660-3646-4
                                            LC 2010-1120

This book offers science experiments that explain the properties of air, how to conserve energy while heating and cooling air, and how to reduce air pollution.

"Gardner provides plenty of information, well-designed experiments, and demonstrations, and then shares brief science-fair ideas. . . . Experiments and demonstrations are presented with clear step-by-step instructions and occasional illustrations and represent a wide range of complexity." SLJ

Includes glossary and bibliographical references

Meiani, Antonella

Air. Lerner Publs. 2003 40p il (Experimenting with science) lib bdg $23.93

Grades: 4 5 6 7   533
1. Air 2. Science -- Experiments
ISBN 0-8225-0082-5
                                            LC 2001-37730

Explains the properties of air through experiments which feature such topics as what air is, how much force wind has, what shape is best for flying, and how sound travels

This offers "straightforward, well-designed experiments. . . . Numerous clear diagrams, some photos, and occasional historical sidebars extend this material, which is notable for its substance." Horn Book Guide

Includes glossary and bibliographical references

Parker, Steve, 1952-

The science of air; projects and experiments on air and flight. [by] Steve Parker. Heinemann Library 2005 32p il (Tabletop scientist) lib bdg $29.29; pa $7.85

Grades: 4 5 6 7   533
1. Air 2. Science -- Experiments
ISBN 1-4034-7280-7 lib bdg; 1-4034-7287-4 pa
                                            LC 2005006940

"The 12 experiments in [this] book have a materials list and step-by-step photo instructions. Boxed text explains the scientific ideas in each project and the processes that make it work, and offer ideas for further experimentation. The activities are followed by a history of the topic. . . . [This] title introduces air movement, air pressure, wind resistance, lift, flight, and energy from the wind. . . . The colorful illustra-

tions, organization, and ease of use [this title makes it an] excellent [addition]." SLJ

Includes glossary

534   Specific forms of energy

Gardner, Robert

★ Sound projects with a music lab you can build. Enslow Publishers 2008 128p il (Build-a-lab! science experiments) lib bdg $31.93

Grades: 6 7 8 9   534
1. Music 2. Sound 3. Science projects 4. Science -- Experiments   5. Science projects
ISBN 978-0-7660-2809-8 lib bdg; 0-7660-2809-7 lib bdg
                                            LC 2007-19458

This describes science experiments and projects about music and sound such as making a washtub bass, a two-string bottle banjo, a shoe-box guitar, or pan pipes.

"The author does an excellent job presenting a balance of open-ended questions and supporting information that provide a solid foundation for successful experimentation." Sci Books Films

Includes bibliographical references

Sound; edited by Sherman Hollar. Britannica Educational Pub. in association with Rosen Educational Services 2013 79 p. ill. (Introduction to physics) (library) $31.70

Grades: 7 8 9 10   534
1. Sound
ISBN 1615308415; 9781615308415
                                            LC 2012010563

This book on sound, edited by Sherman Hollar, is part of the "Introduction to Physics" series. It "describes how sound is produced, carried, and processed and features a chapter on acoustical engineers' applications in the life sciences, earth sciences, architecture, and the arts." (Booklist)

Includes bibliographical references and index.

535   Light and related radiation

Caes, Charles J.

★ Discovering the speed of light; by Charles J. Caes. 1st ed. Rosen Pub. 2012 112 p. ill. (chiefly col.) (Scientist's guide to physics) (library) $34.60

Grades: 5 6 7 8   535
1. Light -- Speed 2. Light -- Study and teaching -- History 3. Light -- Speed -- Measurement
ISBN 1448846994; 9781448846993
                                            LC 2010048426

This book by Charles J. Caes is part of the "Scientist's Guide to Physics" series. It "uncovers the earliest study of the speed of light, around 550 BCE in classical Greece. From classical Greece to Galileo and later Albert Einstein, this title also details the history of the discovery of light speed measurement and theories." (VOYA)

Includes bibliographical references (p. 107-108) and index.

Light; edited by Michael Anderson. Britannica Educational Pub. in association with Rosen Educational Services 2013 77 p. ill. (some col.) (Introduction to physics) (library) $31.70

Grades: 7 8 9 10   **535**

1. Light 2. Light -- Speed
ISBN 1615308407; 9781615308408

LC 2012010241

This book "teaches the reader about light's many properties. It illuminates the path between light and matter, focusing in on reflection. refraction/dispersion, and light speed." Some chapters "explain light as a wave and as a particle. This book connects the past and present theories of light" and "explains in no-nonsense terms and real life applications the hows, the whats, and the whys of light theory." (NSTA Recommends)

Includes bibliographical references (p. 74) and index.

Meiani, Antonella

Light. Lerner Publs. 2003 40p il (Experimenting with science) lib bdg $23.93

Grades: 4 5 6 7   **535**

1. Light 2. Science -- Experiments
ISBN 0-8225-0084-1

LC 2001-38947

Experiments with light explain shadows and colors, and demonstrate such concepts as reflection and refraction

This offers "straightforward, well-designed experiments. . . . Numerous clear diagrams, some photos, and occasional historical sidebars extend this material, which is notable for its substance." Horn Book Guide

Includes glossary and bibliographical references

Stille, Darlene R.

★ **Manipulating** light; reflection, refraction, and absorption. by Darlene R. Stille. Compass Point Books 2006 48p il (Exploring science) $25.27

Grades: 6 7 8 9   **535**

1. Light
ISBN 0-7565-1258-1

LC 2005003903

This "book examines how light behaves, the law of reflection, mirrors, refraction, and absorption. . . . Full-color photographs, illustrations, or diagrams appear on almost every page, accompanied by captions that complement the text." SLJ

Includes glossary and bibliographical references

536 Heat

Gardner, Robert

Easy genius science projects with temperature and heat; great experiments and ideas. by Robert Gardner and Eric Kemer. Enslow Publishers 2009 128p il (Easy genius science projects) lib bdg $31.93

Grades: 5 6 7 8   **536**

1. Heat 2. Temperature 3. Science projects 4. Science

-- Experiments
ISBN 978-0-7660-2939-2 lib bdg; 0-7660-2939-5 lib bdg

LC 2008-4675

"Presents several science experiments and science project ideas dealing with temperature and heat." Publisher's note

Includes glossary and bibliographical references

Heat; edited by Andrea R. Field. Britannica Educational Pub. 2013 76 p. ill. (some col.) (library) $31.70

Grades: 7 8 9 10   **536**

1. Heat 2. Physics
ISBN 1615308385; 9781615308385

LC 2011053232

This book looks at heat, or "the energy that is transferred from one object to another because of a difference in temperature," as well as "the related concepts of temperature, thermal energy, and thermodynamics and introduces readers to some of the great minds that furthered our understanding of this . . . area of physics." (Publisher's note)

Includes bibliographical references (p. 73) and index.

Sullivan, Navin

Temperature; [by] Navin Sullivan. Marshall Cavendish Benchmark 2007 48p il (Measure up!) lib bdg $20.90

Grades: 4 5 6 7   **536**

1. Heat 2. Temperature 3. Thermometers
ISBN 978-0-7614-2322-5 lib bdg; 0-7614-2322-2 lib bdg

LC 2006011981

This is "engaging and informative. . . . The excellent blend of photographs, charts, and diagrams complements the [text]." SLJ

Includes glossary and bibliographical references

537   Electricity and electronics

Dreier, David Louis

Electrical circuits; harnessing electricity. by David Dreier; illustrator Ashlee Schultz. Compass Point Books 2007 48p il (Exploring science: physical science) lib bdg $19.95

Grades: 6 7 8 9   **537**

1. Electricity 2. Electric circuits
ISBN 978-0-7565-3267-3 lib bdg; 0-7565-3267-1 lib bdg

LC 2007004603

"This straightforward introduction to electricity . . . covers all the bases. It begins with what electricity is, how it appears in nature, and how it has been harnessed for public use. Atoms, the concept of electric charge, and magnetism are explained clearly. . . . Dreier tries to make a complex subject more understandable by using familiar examples. . . . This helps, as does the book's clean format, illustrated with sharp, bright color photographs." Booklist

Includes glossary and bibliographical references

Electricity; edited by Michael Anderson. Britannica Educational Pub. in association with Rosen Educational Services 2012 79 p. ill. (some col.) (Introduction to physics) $31.70

Grades: 7 8 9 10   **537**

1. Electricity

ISBN 161530665X; 9781615306657

LC 2011017090

"...Features clear diagrams and is a narrow enough topic to be well covered, with chapters on circuits, magnetic fields, and generators." Booklist

Includes bibliographical references (p. 76) and index

Galiano, Dean

Electric and magnetic phenomena. Rosen Central 2011 64p il (Science made simple) lib bdg $29.25; pa $12.95

Grades: 5 6 7 8   **537**

1. Magnetism 2. Electricity

ISBN 978-1-4488-1231-8 lib bdg; 1-4488-1231-3 lib bdg; 978-1-4488-2239-3 pa; 1-4488-2239-4 pa

LC 2010014546

This introduction to electric and magnetic phenomena includes "a lot of detailed information, making [it] useful as [a] resource . . . for science projects and reports. . . . The [book] also [includes a] brief discussion of scientists important in the field, the history of the topic, and current and future applications. . . . The straightforward, no-nonsense [narrative] and simple design make this . . . a nice package for basic science." SLJ

Includes glossary and bibliographical references

Gardner, Robert

Easy genius science projects with electricity and magnetism; great experiments and ideas. Enslow Publishers 2009 128p il (Easy genius science projects) lib bdg $31.93

Grades: 5 6 7 8   **537**

1. Magnetism 2. Electricity 3. Science projects 4. Science -- Experiments

ISBN 978-0-7660-2923-1 lib bdg; 0-7660-2923-9 lib bdg

LC 2007-38470

"Science projects and experiments about electricity and magnetism." Publisher's note

Includes glossary and bibliographical references

Easy genius science projects with light; great experiments and ideas. [by] Robert Gardner. Enslow Publishers 2008 128p il (Easy genius science projects) lib bdg $31.93

Grades: 6 7 8 9   **537**

1. Light 2. Science projects 3. Science -- Experiments

ISBN 978-0-7660-2926-2; 0-7660-2926-3

LC 2007-38468

This includes science projects and experiments about such light-related topics as colors, lenses, mirages, reflections, refraction, particle theory, polarization, and after images.

"The physics involved are . . . fascinating and will grab curious readers. . . . The inviting and chatty text for each project includes a boxed list of 'things you will need,' all of them commonly available, followed by detailed step-by-step instructions with clear diagrams." Booklist

Includes glossary and bibliographical references

Electricity and magnetism science fair projects; revised and expanded using the scientific method. Enslow Publishers 2010 160p il (Physics science projects using the scientific method) lib bdg $34.60

Grades: 7 8 9 10   **537**

1. Magnetism 2. Electricity 3. Science projects 4. Science -- Experiments

ISBN 978-0-7660-3418-1 lib bdg; 0-7660-3418-6 lib bdg

First published 2004 with title: Electricity and magnetism science fair projects: using batteries, balloons, and other hair-raising stuff

"This describes experiments on such topics as static electricity, moving charges, magnets and magnetic fields, and electricity and chemistry. Includes suggestions for science projects." Publisher's note

Includes bibliographical references

Parker, Steve, 1952-

Electricity and magnetism; [by] Steve Parker. Gareth Stevens Pub. 2007 48p il (Gareth Stevens vital science: physical science) lib bdg $26.60; pa $11.95

Grades: 4 5 6 7   **537**

1. Magnetism 2. Electricity

ISBN 978-0-8368-8085-4 lib bdg; 978-0-8368-8094-6 pa

LC 2006034188

This is "straightforward and clear. . . . The layout is bright and colorful, with photographs and illustrations on almost every page." SLJ

Includes glossary and bibliographical references

Tomecek, Steve

Electromagnetism, and how it works; [by] Stephen M. Tomecek. Chelsea House 2007 72p il (Scientific American) $30

Grades: 6 7 8 9   **537**

1. Electromagnetism

ISBN 978-0-7910-9052-7; 0-7910-9052-3

LC 2007-17744

This describes the history of magnets including the discoveries of such scientists as Gilbert, Volta, Sturgeon, Edison, Westinghouse, and Tesla. It discusses inventions which depended on the understanding of magnets and electricity such as the telegraph, Morse Code, the telephone, the wireless radio, radar, the microwave, x-rays, and MRIs. The author explains how magnets work and how they can be used to create electricity.

Includes glossary and bibliographical references

Woodford, Chris

Experiments with electricity and magnetism. Gareth Stevens Pub. 2010 32p il (Cool science) lib bdg $28; pa $10.50

Grades: 4 5 6 7   **537**
1. Magnetism 2. Electricity 3. Science -- Experiments
ISBN 9781433934445 lib bdg; 1433934442 lib bdg;
9781433934452 pa; 1433934450 pa
LC 2009037141

"The book [is] written in an easy-to-understand, straightforward style with helpful real-life photographs... Students who need simple experiments or those who need more advanced projects will find [it] helpful." Library Media Connection

Includes bibliographical references

537.5   Electronics

Gifford, Clive
Cool tech; gadgets, games robots, and the digital world. written by Clive Gifford; consultant, Mike Goldsmith. DK Pub. 2011 143 p. col. ill. (hardcover) $19.99
Grades: 5 6 7   **537.5**
1. Technological innovations 2. Electronic apparatus and appliances 3. Games 4. Robots 5. Computers 6. Technology 7. Electronics 8. Computers
ISBN 0756682703; 9780756682705
LC 2011283520

This book offers "descriptions and a history of many of the prominent technological developments . . . . The topics range from coverage of notable technological breakthroughs to the individuals who made them happen. These include sections on technological products such as laptops, undersea cables, smart phones, video games, digital cameras, robots, and the Mars Rover." (SB&F: Your Guide to Science Resources for All Ages)

538   Magnetism

Meiani, Antonella
Magnetism. Lerner Publs. 2003 40p il (Experimenting with science) lib bdg $23.93
Grades: 4 5 6 7   **538**
1. Magnetism 2. Science -- Experiments
ISBN 0-8225-0085-X
LC 2001-50464

Describes a variety of experiments that explore the world of magnets and magnetism, arranged in the categories "Magnets," "Magnetic Poles," "Magnetic Force," and "Magnetism and Electricity"

This offers "straightforward, well-designed experiments. . . . Numerous clear diagrams, some photos, and occasional historical sidebars extend this material, which is notable for its substance." Horn Book Guide

Includes glossary and bibliographical references

539   Modern physics

Claybourne, Anna
Who split the atom? Arcturus Pub. 2010 46p il (Breakthroughs in science and technology) lib bdg $32.80
Grades: 5 6 7 8   **539**
1. Atoms 2. Matter 3. Atomic structure 4. Discoveries in science
ISBN 978-1-84837-683-0 lib bdg; 1-84837-683-9 lib bdg
LC 2010-11015

This book explores the ways in which scientists uncovered the atom.

The book is "divided into easy to read short chapters with large, colorful photographs and graphics on every page. . . . The added inserts provide additional information to engage readers and help them connect with the scientific details." Libr Media Connect

Includes glossary and bibliographical references

Willett, Edward
The **basics** of quantum physics; understanding the photoelectric effect and line spectra. Rosen Pub. Group 2005 48p il (Library of physics) lib bdg $25.25
Grades: 7 8 9 10   **539**
1. Quantum theory 2. Spectrum analysis
ISBN 1-4042-0334-6

"Willett introduces readers to the nature of light and of the atom. The ultraviolet catastrophe, the photoelectric effect, and line spectra are also addressed. [This title is] especially useful for reluctant readers or those new to the [topic]. The [layout is] open and appealing and [includes] well-captioned photographs and simple diagrams." SLJ

Includes bibliographical references

539.7   Atomic and nuclear physics

Campbell, Margaret Christine
★ Discovering atoms; Margaret Christine Campbell, Natalie Goldstein. 1st ed. Rosen Pub. 2012 112 p. ill. (The scientist's guide to physics) (library) $34.60
Grades: 5 6 7 8 9   **539.7**
1. Atoms 2. Atomic theory -- History 3. Atomic structure 4. Matter -- Constitution
ISBN 1448847001; 9781448847006
LC 2010048416

This book by Margaret Christine Campbell is part of the "Scientist's Guide to Physics" series. It "presents the . . . story of the atom's discovery, which is full of bizarre theories, false starts, dead ends, and . . . intellectual insight." (Publisher's Note)

"Campbell includes a . . . chronological foundation upon which the discovery of elements and the creation of the periodic table build up to the discovery of the atom, atomic rays, particles, models . . . and subatomic particles." (VOYA)

Includes bibliographical references and index.

Chaffee, Joel

Atomic and molecular structure. Rosen Central 2011 64p il (Science made simple) lib bdg $29.25; pa $12.95

Grades: 5 6 7 8   **539.7**

1. Atoms 2. Molecules

ISBN 978-1-4488-1230-1 lib bdg; 1-4488-1230-5 lib bdg; 978-1-4488-2238-6 pa; 1-4488-2238-6 pa

LC 2010015454

This introduction to atomic and molecular structure includes "a lot of detailed information, making [it] useful as [a] resource . . . for science projects and reports. . . . The [book] also [includes a] brief discussion of scientists important in the field, the history of the topic, and current and future applications. . . . The straightforward, no-nonsense [narrative] and simple design make this . . . a nice package for basic science." SLJ

Includes glossary and bibliographical references

Cregan, Elizabeth R.

The atom. Compass Point Books 2009 40p il (Mission: science) lib bdg $26.60

Grades: 4 5 6   **539.7**

1. Atoms 2. Atomic theory 3. Nuclear energy

ISBN 978-0-7565-3953-5 lib bdg; 0-7565-3953-6 lib bdg

LC 2008007724

"Cregan discusses the structure of the atom, key scientists, cathode rays and electrons, radioactivity, and atom smashers. . . . The [book has an] open [layout] and large, easy-to-read type. . . . Large eye-catching and colorful photographs and illustrations appear on every page. The [book] includes a simple activity." SLJ

Includes glossary and bibliographical references

Henderson, Harry

The Curie family; exploring radioactivity. Harry Henderson. Chelsea House 2012 117 p. (Trailblazers in science and technology) $35

Grades: 7 8 9 10 11 12   **539.7**

1. Radioactivity 2. Curie, Marie, 1867-1934 3. Curie, Pierre, 1859-1906 4. Radioactivity -- History 5. Physicists -- France -- Biography 6. Physicists -- Poland -- Biography

ISBN 1604136758; 9781604136753

LC 2011011800

This book, by Harry Henderson, is part of the "Trailblazers in Science and Technology" series. "Marie and Pierre Curie, their daughter Irène Joliot-Curie, and her husband Frédéric Joliot-Curie were one of science's most remarkable and influential families. Their painstaking research into the mysteries of radioactivity allowed scientists to reach a new understanding about the structure of atoms and opened a new field of medical treatment." (Publisher's note)

Includes bibliographical references and index

Jerome, Kate Boehm

Atomic universe; the quest to discover radioactivity. by Kate Boehm Jerome. National Geographic 2006 59p il (Science quest) $17.95; lib bdg $25.90

Grades: 5 6 7 8   **539.7**

1. Radioactivity 2. Nuclear physics

ISBN 0-7922-5543-7; 0-7922-5544-5 lib bdg

LC 2006001316

The text offers "key concepts in a pleasing and readable format that would appeal to reluctant readers." SLJ

Includes glossary and bibliographical references

Lepora, Nathan

Atoms and molecules. Marshall Cavendish Benchmark 2010 48p il (Invisible worlds) lib bdg $28.50

Grades: 4 5 6 7   **539.7**

1. Atoms 2. Molecules 3. Nanotechnology

ISBN 978-0-7614-4192-2 lib bdg; 0-7614-4192-1 lib bdg

LC 2008037237

This describes the details and characteristics of atoms and molecules that are too small for the unaided eye to see. The narrative is "clear, well written, broken down into manageable pieces, and peppered with eye-opening facts. The numerous photographs are so phenomenal that they will inspire kids to read the text . . . so that they can wrap their minds around what they see." SLJ

Includes glossary and bibliographical references

Manning, Phillip

★ Atoms, molecules, and compounds. Chelsea House 2008 137p il (Essential chemistry) $35

Grades: 7 8 9 10   **539.7**

1. Atoms 2. Matter 3. Molecules 4. Chemical reactions 5. Atoms 8. Chemical reactions 9. Matter -- Constitution

ISBN 978-0-7910-9534-8; 0-7910-9534-7

LC 2007-11403

"In relatively few pages, and with lots of colorful, clear illustrations, Manning takes us from Thompson's plum-pudding model of the atom to Rutherford's model to the quantum model, and through the discovery of atomic particles and the teasing out of atomic forces, in a very clear, compelling path. . . . The clear linkages he makes between the different types of chemical bonds and the nature of various materials will remain with the reader." Sci Books Films

Includes glossary and bibliographical references

McLean, Adam

What is atomic theory? Crabtree Pub. Co. 2011 64p il (Shaping modern science) lib bdg $30.60; pa $10.95

Grades: 5 6 7 8   **539.7**

1. Atoms 2. Chemists 3. Physicists 4. Atomic theory 5. Nuclear energy 6. Writers on science

ISBN 978-0-7787-7197-5 lib bdg; 0-7787-7197-0 lib bdg; 978-0-7787-7204-0 pa; 0-7787-7204-7 pa

This title is "not only written and organized well, but [it is] also gorgeous in design. Full-color photographs and illustrations are set over colorful backgrounds that add depth but not distraction. [The title] includes thought-provoking quotes from famous authors and scientists and some eyebrow-raising 'Quick Facts' throughout." SLJ

Includes glossary and bibliographical references

Oxlade, Chris

Atoms; [by] Chris Oxlade. rev and updated; Heinemann Library 2007 48p il (Chemicals in action) lib bdg $31.43; pa $8.99

Grades: 6 7 8 9　　　　　　　　　　　**539.7**

1. Atoms 2. Matter 3. Atomic theory
ISBN 978-1-4329-0051-9 lib bdg; 978-1-4329-0058-8 pa

First published 2002

"Explanations are concise and clear without being oversimplified, and the arrangement is attractive and open. Colorful diagrams, drawings, and photographs appear on every page." SLJ

Includes glossary and bibliographical references

540　Chemistry and allied sciences

★ **Chemistry** matters! Grolier 2007 10v set $389

Grades: 7 8 9 10　　　　　　　　　　　**540**

1. Reference books 2. Chemistry -- Encyclopedias
ISBN 0-7172-6194-8

LC 2006026209

"These volumes cover a broad range of topics. . . . Each 80 page volume could serve as a stand-alone title, introducing its subject and covering many aspects of its current study and applications." Booklist

Includes bibliographical references

Coelho, Alexa

Why Is Milk White? & 200 Other Curious Chemistry Questions. Alexa Coelho and Simon Quellen Field. Independent Pub Group 2013 288 p. ill. (paperback) $14.95

Grades: 4 5 6 7 8　　　　　　　　　　　**540**

1. Chemistry -- Miscellanea
ISBN 1613744528; 9781613744529

LC 2012040205

This juvenile chemistry book, by Alexa Coelho and Simon Quellen Field, is a "question-and-answer primer [that] provides straightforward, easy-to-understand explanations for inquisitive young scientists' questions. . . . From lifting latent fingerprints from a 'crime scene' using super glue (for smooth surfaces) or iodine (for paper) to hollowing out the zinc interior of a penny using muriatic acid . . . , this handy guide is [a] . . . resource for the budding chemist." (Publisher's note)

The **Facts** on File chemistry handbook; the Diagram Group. Facts On File 2006 272 p. ill. (hardcover) $40; (ebook) $42.00

Grades: 8 9 10 11 12　　　　　　　　　　　**540**

1. Chemistry -- Dictionaries 2. Chemistry 3. Chemistry -- Handbooks, manuals, etc
ISBN 0816058784; 9780816058785 out of print; 9781438109558 pdf

LC 2005055496

This fact book for middle-grade readers, part of the Facts on File Handbook series, looks at chemistry. Each series entry "contains, in separate sections, a dictionary of around 1500 entries; 250-400 thumbnail biographies; a multipage

chronology; and an array of field-specific charts, tables, and diagrams." (School Library Journal)

Includes bibliographical references (p. 262-264) and index

Farndon, John

Experimenting with chemistry. Marshall Cavendish Benchmark 2009 104p il (Experimenting with science) $35.64

Grades: 7 8 9 10　　　　　　　　　　　**540**

1. Chemistry 2. Science -- Experiments
ISBN 978-0-7614-3928-8; 0-7614-3928-5

LC 2008017570

"Explores and explains chemistry concepts and provides experiments to aid in understanding chemistry." Publisher's note

Gardner, Robert

Chemistry projects with a laboratory you can build. Enslow Publishers 2007 128p il (Build-a-lab! science experiments) $23.95

Grades: 6 7 8 9　　　　　　　　　　　**540**

1. Chemistry 2. Science -- Experiments 4. Science projects 5. Chemical laboratories 6. Chemistry -- Experiments
ISBN 978-0-7660-2805-0; 0-7660-2805-4

LC 2006-21071

This "is a guide to creating an at-home laboratory for conducting chemistry experiments. . . . Safety rules and ample warnings are provided. . . . The book describes 28 experiments, organized into four chapters. . . . The experiments are ongoing and would be fun activities for children who are curious about science." Sci Books Films

Includes bibliographical references

Chemistry science fair projects using inorganic stuff; revised and expanded using the scientific method. Enslow Publishers 2010 160p il (Chemistry science projects using the scientific method) lib bdg $34.60

Grades: 7 8 9 10　　　　　　　　　　　**540**

1. Chemistry 2. Science projects 3. Science -- Experiments
ISBN 978-0-7660-3413-6 lib bdg; 0-7660-3413-5 lib bdg

LC 2008046505

First published 2004 with title: Chemistry Science Fair Projects Using Acids, Bases, Metals,Salts, and Inorganic Stuff

"Colorful drawings complement the material and illustrations of chemical structures help to convey chemical processes. . . . Useful." SLJ

Includes bibliographical references

Green, Dan

Chemistry; getting a big reaction. created by Basher; written by Dan Green. Kingfisher 2010 128p il $14.99; pa $8.99

Grades: 4 5 6 7   **540**
1. Chemistry
ISBN 978-0-7534-6615-5; 0-7534-6615-5; 978-0-7534-6413-7 pa; 0-7534-6413-6 pa

This "begins with a short overview of [chemistry] and information on Antoine Lavoisier's 18th-century scientific findings. Concepts are grouped by associations: 'Basic States' (solid, liquid, etc.), 'Nuts and Bolts' (atom, ion, etc.), 'Nasty Boys' (acid, base, etc.), and more. The individual concepts are each introduced over a spread that features a computer-generated cartoon of a character representing the idea and a brief introduction to its characteristics and personality. . . . The information is presented in a chatty, first-person voice." SLJ

Hager, Thomas
  Linus Pauling and the chemistry of life. Oxford University Press 1998 142p il (Oxford portraits in science) $28
Grades: 7 8 9 10   **540**
1. Chemists 2. College teachers 3. Writers on science 4. Nobel laureates for peace 5. Nobel laureates for chemistry 6. Chemists -- United States -- Biography 7. Biochemists -- United States -- Biography 8. Social reformers -- United States -- Biography
ISBN 0-19-510853-1

LC 97-43403

Profiles the Nobel Prize-winning chemist who described the nature of chemical bonds, made important discoveries in the fields of quantum mechanics, immunology, and evolution, and used his scientific fame to help advance political causes

"Students with a strong science background will get the most out of this biography, but even young people who don't like science will be able to identify with a man whose scientific curiosity and political principles led him to try to change the world. Chronology and recommended readings." Booklist
Includes bibliographical references

Newmark, Ann
  Chemistry; written by Ann Newmark. rev ed; DK Pub. 2005 72p il (DK eyewitness books) $15.99
Grades: 4 5 6 7   **540**
1. Chemistry
ISBN 0-7566-1385-X
First published 1993

Explores the world of chemical reactions and shows the role that chemistry plays in our world.

Oxlade, Chris
  Material changes and reactions; [by] Chris Oxlade. rev. and updated; Heinemann Library 2007 48p il (Chemicals in action) lib bdg $31.43; pa $8.99
Grades: 6 7 8 9   **540**
1. Chemical reactions
ISBN 978-1-4329-0053-3 lib bdg; 978-1-4329-0053-3 pa
First published 2002

"This title explores how elements melt, boil, and freeze; how they combine with each other to make new substances;

and how chemical reactions take place every day in factories and in your home. [It also includes] several experiments that can be done at home." Publisher's note
Includes glossary and bibliographical references

Van Gorp, Lynn
  Elements. Compass Point Books 2009 40p il (Mission: science) lib bdg $26.60
Grades: 4 5 6   **540**
1. Chemical elements
ISBN 978-0-7565-3951-1 lib bdg; 0-7565-3951-X lib bdg

LC 2008007284

"Van Gorp provides an overview of matter and the elements and how the latter combine to form compounds; ionic and covalent bonds; the periodic table of the elements; reactions; and mixtures and solutions. The [book has an] open [layout] and large, easy-to-read type. . . . Large eye-catching and colorful photographs and illustrations appear on every page. . . . The [book] includes a simple activity." SLJ
Includes glossary and bibliographical references

540.7   Education, research, related topics

Gardner, Robert
  Ace your chemistry science project; great science fair ideas. [by] Robert Gardner, Salvatore Tocci, and Kenneth G. Rainis. Enslow Publishers 2009 112p il (Ace your science project) lib bdg $31.93
Grades: 5 6 7 8   **540.7**
1. Chemistry 2. Science projects 3. Science -- Experiments 4. Science projects 5. Chemistry -- Experiments
ISBN 978-0-7660-3227-9 lib bdg; 0-7660-3227-2 lib bdg

LC 2008-30800

"Presents several science projects and science project ideas about chemistry." Publisher's note
Includes bibliographical references

  Ace your science project using chemistry magic and toys; great science fair ideas. Enslow Publishers 2009 128p il (Ace your science project) lib bdg $31.93
Grades: 5 6 7 8   **540.7**
1. Toys 2. Chemistry 3. Science projects 4. Science -- Experiments
ISBN 978-0-7660-3226-2 lib bdg; 0-7660-3226-4 lib bdg

LC 2008-4685

"Dozens of . . . science activities are presented with background information, step-by-step instructions, and suggestions for extending to the science fair level. . . . Color illustrations and important safety information are included." Horn Book Guide
Includes bibliographical references

  ★ **Easy** genius science projects with chemistry; great experiments and ideas. Enslow Publishers

2009 112p il (Easy genius science projects) lib bdg $31.93

Grades: 5 6 7 8   **540.7**

1. Chemistry 2. Science projects 3. Science -- Experiments 6. Chemistry -- Experiments
ISBN 978-0-7660-2925-5 lib bdg; 0-7660-2925-5 lib bdg

LC 2007-38469

This book offers science projects and experiments about chemistry divided into the following chapters: atoms, molecules, elements, and compounds; chemical reactions; oxygen and oxidation; separating and testing substances

"Illustrations are bright and useful in explaining the techniques presented. . . . An excellent resource." Sci Books Films

Includes glossary and bibliographical references

Goodstein, Madeline

Plastics and polymers science fair projects; revised and expanded using the scientific method. Enslow Publishers 2010 160p il (Chemistry science projects using the scientific method) lib bdg $34.60

Grades: 7 8 9 10   **540.7**

1. Plastics 2. Polymers 3. Science projects 4. Science -- Experiments
ISBN 978-0-7660-3412-9 lib bdg; 0-7660-3412-7 lib bdg

LC 2008046504

"Explains how to use the scientific method to conduct several science experiments with plastics and polymers. Includes ideas for science fair projects." Publisher's note

Includes bibliographical references

541   Chemistry

Ballard, Carol

Mixtures and solutions. Raintree 2010 48p il (Sci-hi: physical science) lib bdg $22; pa $8.99

Grades: 5 6 7 8   **541**

1. Chemistry 2. Molecules
ISBN 978-1-4109-3376-8 lib bdg; 1-4109-3376-8 lib bdg; 978-1-4109-3381-2 pa; 1-4109-3381-4 pa

LC 2009-13452

A "compelling read for both browsers and science buffs. . . . Information is clearly presented and flows smoothly. . . . A treasure trove of information." SLJ

Includes glossary and bibliographical references

Manning, Phillip

Chemical bonds. Chelsea House 2009 134p il (Essential chemistry) lib bdg $35

Grades: 7 8 9 10   **541**

1. Chemistry 2. Chemical bonds 3. Science
ISBN 978-0-7910-9740-3; 0-7910-9740-4

LC 2008-1981

Examines the nature of the chemical bonds, answering questions about how they form, how they are broken, and how they help define life as we know it

Includes glossary and bibliographical references

Wolny, Philip

Chemical reactions. Rosen Central 2011 64p il (Science made simple) lib bdg $29.25; pa $12.95

Grades: 5 6 7 8   **541**

1. Chemistry 2. Chemical reactions
ISBN 978-1-4488-1235-6 lib bdg; 1-4488-1235-6 lib bdg; 978-1-4488-2242-3 pa; 1-4488-2242-4 pa

LC 2010018818

This introduction to chemical reactions includes "a lot of detailed information, making [it] useful as [a] resource . . . for science projects and reports. . . . The [book] also [includes a] brief discussion of scientists important in the field, the history of the topic, and current and future applications. . . . The straightforward, no-nonsense [narrative] and simple design make this . . . a nice package for basic science." SLJ

Includes glossary and bibliographical references

546   Inorganic chemistry

Angliss, Sarah

Gold; [by] Sarah Angliss. Benchmark Bks. 2000 32p il (The elements) lib bdg $28.50

Grades: 5 6 7 8   **546**

1. Gold
ISBN 978-0-7614-0887-1; 0-7614-0887-8

LC 98-46800

Explores the history of the precious metal gold and explains its chemistry, how it reacts, its uses, and its importance in our lives.

Includes glossary

Beatty, Richard

Boron; [by] Richard Beatty. Marshall Cavendish Benchmark 2005 32p il (The elements) lib bdg $28.50

Grades: 5 6 7 8   **546**

1. Boron
ISBN 978-0-7614-1921-1; 0-7614-1921-7

LC 2005-42159

"Included in the discussion are the uses of boron in pottery, in the nuclear industry, in living organisms, and in glassmaking. A review of the periodic table and boron's place in it, including the element's relationship to other elements, is provided." Sci Books Films

Includes glossary

Copper; [by] Richard Beatty. Benchmark Books 2001 32p il (The elements) lib bdg $28.50

Grades: 5 6 7 8   **546**

1. Copper
ISBN 978-0-7614-0945-8; 0-7614-0945-9

LC 99-54235

Explores the history of the useful metal copper and explains its chemistry, its uses, and its importance in our lives

Offers "clear, basic information, without oversimplification, in an appealing format." SLJ

Includes glossary

Manganese; [by] Richard Beatty. Benchmark Books 2005 32p il (The elements) lib bdg $28.50

Grades: 5 6 7 8 **546**

1. Manganese
ISBN 978-0-7614-1813-9; 0-7614-1813-X
LC 2004-47634

Includes glossary

"Numerous captioned color photos and sidebars augment the accurate, well-organized, but information-dense sections." Horn Book

Phosphorus; by Richard Beatty. Benchmark Books 2001 32p il (The elements) lib bdg $28.50
Grades: 5 6 7 8 **546**

1. Phosphorus
ISBN 978-0-7614-0946-5; 0-7614-0946-7
LC 99-88821

Explores the history of the nonmetallic element phosphorus and explains its chemistry, its reactions with other substances, its uses, and its importance in our lives

Offers "clear, basic information, without oversimplification, in an appealing format." SLJ

Includes glossary

Sulfur; [by] Richard Beatty. Benchmark Books 2000 32p il (The elements) lib bdg $28.50
Grades: 5 6 7 8 **546**

1. Sulphur
ISBN 978-0-7614-0948-9; 0-7614-0948-3
LC 99-86992

Explores the history of the element sulfur and explains its chemistry, its reactions with other substances, its uses, and its importance in our lives

Offers "clear, basic information, without oversimplification, in an appealing format." SLJ

Includes glossary

The **lanthanides**; [by] Richard Beatty. Marshall Cavendish Benchmark 2008 32p il (The elements) lib bdg $28.50
Grades: 5 6 7 8 **546**

1. Lanthanides
ISBN 978-0-7614-2687-5; 0-7614-2687-6
LC 2006-53053

Introduces the lanthanide elements, also known as the rare earth metals, discussing their physical and chemical properties, where they are found, and how they are used.

"Provides a comprehensive, yet easy-to-read overview. . . . The explanations are succinct and clear, without being oversimplified, and the layout is attractive. Diagrams and photographs complement the text on every page." SLJ

Includes glossary

Cobb, Allan B.
Cadmium; [by] Allan Cobb. Marshall Cavendish/Benchmark 2008 32p il (The elements) lib bdg $28.50
Grades: 5 6 7 8 **546**

1. Cadmium
ISBN 978-0-7614-2686-8; 0-7614-2686-8
LC 2006-51790

Introduces the element of cadmium, discussing its physical and chemical properties, where it is found, and how it is used.

"Provides a comprehensive, yet easy-to-read overview. . . . The explanations are succinct and clear, without being oversimplified, and the layout is attractive. Diagrams and photographs complement the text on every page." SLJ

Includes glossary

Cooper, Chris
Arsenic; [by] Chris Cooper. Marshall Cavendish Benchmark 2007 32p il (The elements) lib bdg $28.50
Grades: 5 6 7 8 **546**

1. Arsenic
ISBN 978-0-7614-2203-7; 0-7614-2203-X
LC 2006-43891

"Explanations are concise and clear without being oversimplified, and the arrangement is attractive. Diagrams, drawings, and photographs appear on every page and complement the text well." SLJ

Includes glossary

Dingle, Adrian
★ The **periodic** table; elements with style! [created by Simon Basher; written by Adrian Dingle] Kingfisher 2007 128p il pa $8.95
Grades: 4 5 6 7 **546**

1. Chemical elements 3. Periodic law
ISBN 978-0-7534-6085-6 pa; 0-7534-6085-8 pa
LC 2006022515

"After a brief introduction to Mendeleev's famous table and a spread on the chart-topping loner, hydrogen, Dingle presents the elements by group. . . . Data on featured elements includes symbol, atomic number and weight, color, standard state, classification, density, boiling and melting points, . . . a diagram of the position in the periodic table, a full-page original anime-styled icon, . . . and descriptive paragraphs that rise from informative all the way to entertaining." Bull Cent Child Books

Farndon, John
Aluminum; [by] John Farndon. Benchmark Books 2001 32p il (The elements) lib bdg $28.50
Grades: 5 6 7 8 **546**

1. Aluminum
ISBN 978-0-7614-0947-2; 0-7614-0947-5

Describes the discovery, versatility and other special characteristics, various uses, and affect on the human body of this most common metal in the world.

Includes glossary

Oxygen; [by] John Farndon. Benchmark Bks. 1999 32p il (The elements) lib bdg $28.50
Grades: 5 6 7 8 **546**

1. Oxygen
ISBN 978-0-7614-0879-6; 0-7614-0879-7
LC 97-52236

Explores the history of the chemical element oxygen and explains its chemistry, how it works in the body, and its importance in our lives.

"The captioned, full-color drawings, photographs, and diagrams clarify the text. . . . [This] will be of interest for both general reading and report writing." SLJ

Includes glossary

Furgang, Adam

The **noble** gases; helium, neon, argon, krypton, xenon, radon. Rosen Central 2010 48p il (Understanding the elements of the periodic table) lib bdg $26.50

Grades: 7 8 9 10   **546**
1. Gases 2. Periodic law 3. Chemical elements
ISBN 978-1-4358-3558-0 lib bdg; 1-4358-3558-1 lib bdg

LC 2009014409

This overview discusses "the history of each element, where it can be found, and how it is used in everyday life. . . . Charts show each element's chemical symbol, atomic number, atomic weight, melting point, and boiling point. Colorful photographs and illustrations are included on most pages. Lengthy sidebars highlight key information—some . . . present boxed information on helium versus hydrogen and on the Hindenburg disaster." SLJ

Includes bibliographical references

Goodstein, Madeline

Water science fair projects; revised and expanded using the scientific method. Enslow Publishers 2010 160p il (Chemistry science projects using the scientific method) lib bdg $34.60

Grades: 7 8 9 10   **546**
1. Water 2. Science projects 3. Science -- Experiments
ISBN 978-0-7660-3411-2 lib bdg; 0-7660-3411-9 lib bdg

LC 2008026265

First published 2004 with title: Water science fair projects using ice cubes, super soakers, and other wet stuff

"Explains how to use the scientific method to conduct several science experiments with water. Includes ideas for science fair projects." Publisher's note

Includes bibliographical references

Gray, Leon

Iodine; [by] Leon Gray. Benchmark Books 2005 32p il (The elements) lib bdg $28.50

Grades: 5 6 7 8   **546**
1. Iodine
ISBN 978-0-7614-1812-2; 0-7614-1812-1

LC 2004-47644

"After discussing the structure of the iodine atom and its place on the periodic table, Gray considers its special characteristics, the history of its discovery, and its production and uses, particularly in the medical field. . . . The color illustrations include well-designed, clearly labeled diagrams and many excellent photographs. A solid choice for science collections." Booklist

Includes glossary

Tin; [by] Leon Gray. Benchmark Books 2003 32p il (The elements) lib bdg $28.50

Grades: 5 6 7 8   **546**
1. Tin
ISBN 978-0-7614-1551-0; 0-7614-1551-3

LC 2003-52083

Examines the characteristics, sources, and uses of the element tin, as well as tin's importance in our lives

"Numerous captioned color photos and sidebars augment the accurate and well-organized but information-dense text." Horn Book Guide

Includes glossary

Zinc; [by] Leon Gray. Marshall Cavendish Benchmark 2006 32p il (The elements) lib bdg $28.50

Grades: 5 6 7 8   **546**
1. Zinc
ISBN 978-0-7614-1922-8; 0-7614-1922-5

LC 2005-42163

Discusses zinc and where it can be found, how it was discovered, its special characteristics, and their importance.

"Numerous captioned photos and sidebars augment the accurate and well-organized text." Horn Book Guide

Includes glossary

Green, Dan

The **elements**; Dan Green. Scholastic 2012 105 p. col. ill. (pbk.) $15.99

Grades: 7 8 9 10 11 12   **546**
1. Chemical elements 2. Chemical elements
ISBN 054533019X; 9780545330190

LC 2011278730

This book on the elements, part of the "Discover More" series, is "arranged in single-topic spreads grouped in five chapters based on sections of the Periodic Table." It "highlights either selected single elements or related groups. The layout includes color photos, digital diagrams and images, fact boxes, explanatory captions, and other text in a variety of sizes and weights. . . . A downloadable ebook supplement . . . extends the overall topic." (School Library Journal)

Hall, Linley Erin

The **transactinides**; rutherfordium, dubnium, seaborgium, bohrium, hassium, meitnerium, darmstadtium, roentgenium. Rosen Central 2010 48p il (Understanding the elements of the periodic table) lib bdg $26.50

Grades: 5 6 7 8   **546**
1. Periodic law 2. Chemical elements
ISBN 978-1-4358-3559-7 lib bdg; 1-4358-3559-X lib bdg

LC 2009014943

This overview discusses "the history of each element, where it can be found, and how it is used in everyday life. . . . Charts show each element's chemical symbol, atomic number, atomic weight, melting point, and boiling point. Colorful photographs and illustrations are included on most pages. Lengthy sidebars highlight key information. . . . [The book] devotes a chapter to the controversies surrounding naming its elements." SLJ

Includes bibliographical references

Hasan, Heather

Iron; by Heather Hasan. Rosen Pub. Group 2004 48p il (Understanding the elements of the periodic table) lib bdg $26.50

Grades: 5 6 7 8   **546**
  1. Iron 2. Periodic law
  ISBN 978-1-4042-0157-6; 1-4042-0157-2
                                  LC 2003-22262
  Explains the characteristics of iron, where it is found,
how it is used by humans, and its relationship to other elements found in the periodic table
  Includes bibliographical references

Jackson, Tom, 1972-
  Fluorine; [by] Tom Jackson. Benchmark Books/
Marshall Cavendish 2004 32p il (The elements) lib
bdg $28.50
  Grades: 5 6 7 8   **546**
  1. Flourine
  ISBN 978-0-7614-1549-7; 0-7614-1549-1
                                  LC 2003-43841
  Discusses the characteristics, sources, and uses
of fluorine.
  "Numerous captioned color photos and sidebars aug-
ment the accurate and well-organized but information-dense
text." Horn Book Guide
  Includes glossary

  Lithium; [by] Tom Jackson. Marshall Cavendish
Benchmark 2007 32p il (The elements) lib bdg
$28.50
  Grades: 5 6 7 8   **546**
  1. Lithium
  ISBN 978-0-7614-2199-3; 0-7614-2199-8
                                  LC 2005-55302
  Explains where lithium can be found and how it was dis-
covered, and describes its special characteristics and impor-
tance to the human body.
  "Provides a comprehensive, yet easy-to-read overview in
large, bold print. Explanations are concise and clear without
being oversimplified, and the arrangement is attractive." SLJ
  Includes glossary

  Radioactive elements; by Tom Jackson. Marshall Cavendish Benchmark 2005 32p il (The elements) lib bdg $28.50
  Grades: 5 6 7 8   **546**
  1. Radioactivity 2. Radiochemistry 3. Chemical
elements 6. Radioactive substances
  ISBN 978-0-7614-1923-5; 0-7614-1923-3
                                  LC 2005-42164
  Examines radioactive elements and discusses their discovery, their unique characteristics, their importance, and
where they are found.
  "Numerous captioned photos and sidebars augment the
accurate and well-organized text." Horn Book Guide
  Includes glossary

★ **Just** add water; science projects you can sink,
squirt, splash & sail. Children's Press 2008 32p
il (Experiment with science) lib bdg $25; pa
$7.95
  Grades: 5 6 7 8   **546**
  1. Water 2. Science -- Experiments 3. Water chemistry

4. Water -- Experiments
  ISBN 978-0-531-18545-2 lib bdg; 0-531-18545-1 lib
bdg; 978-0-531-18762-3 pa; 0-531-18762-4 pa
                                  LC 2007-21682
  "The book consists of nine hands-on activities that target physical science concepts inherent in water (e.g. density,
buoyancy, and hardness.) . . . Students . . . will likely find
the age-appropriate activities engaging and purposeful. . . .
The colorful photos augment the narrative and the science is
sound." Sci Books Films
  Includes glossary and bibliographical references

La Bella, Laura
  The **oxygen** elements; oxygen, sulfur, selenium,
tellurium, polonium. Rosen Central 2010 48p il
(Understanding the elements of the periodic table) lib
bdg $26.50
  Grades: 7 8 9 10   **546**
  1. Periodic law 2. Chemical elements
  ISBN 978-1-4358-3555-9 lib bdg; 1-4358-3555-7
lib bdg
                                  LC 2009012541
  This overview discusses "the history of each element,
where it can be found, and how it is used in everyday life.
. . . Charts show each element's chemical symbol, atomic
number, atomic weight, melting point, and boiling point.
Colorful photographs and illustrations are included on most
pages. Lengthy sidebars highlight key information. . . . [The
book] details the use of sulfur in rubber and gunpowder for
example." SLJ
  Includes bibliographical references

Lepora, Nathan
  Chromium; [by] Nathan Lepora. Marshall Cavendish Benchmark 2005 32p il (The elements) lib
bdg $28.50
  Grades: 5 6 7 8   **546**
  1. Chromium
  ISBN 978-0-7614-1920-4; 0-7614-1920-9
                                  LC 2005-42160
  Discusses chromium and where it can be found, how it
was discovered, its special characteristics, and its importance to the human body.
  "Numerous captioned photos and sidebars augment the
accurate and well-organized text." Horn Book Guide
  Includes glossary

  Molybdenum; [by] Nathan Lepora. Marshall
Cavendish Benchmark 2007 32p il (The elements)
lib bdg $28.50
  Grades: 5 6 7 8   **546**
  1. Molybdenum
  ISBN 978-0-7614-2201-3; 0-7614-2201-3
                                  LC 2005-57096
  Introduces the element of molybdenum, discussing its
physical and chemical properties, where it is found, and
what processes or objects it is used in.
  "Provides a comprehensive, yet easy-to-read overview in
large, bold print. Explanations are concise and clear without
being oversimplified, and the arrangement is attractive." SLJ
  Includes glossary

Lew, Kristi

The **15** lanthanides and the 15 actinides. Rosen Central 2010 48p il (Understanding the elements of the periodic table) lib bdg $26.50

Grades: 7 8 9 10   **546**

1. Periodic law 2. Chemical elements

ISBN 978-1-4358-3557-3; 1-4358-3557-3

LC 2009014416

This overview discusses "the history of each element, where it can be found, and how it is used in everyday life. . . . Charts show each element's chemical symbol, atomic number, atomic weight, melting point, and boiling point. Colorful photographs and illustrations are included on most pages. Lengthy sidebars highlight key information." SLJ

Includes bibliographical references

Acids and bases. Chelsea House 2008 124p il (Essential chemistry) $35

Grades: 7 8 9 10   **546**

1. Acids 2. Bases (Chemistry)

ISBN 978-0-7910-9783-0; 0-7910-9783-8

LC 2008-24015

"Annotated, colorful photographs and illustrations appear on most spreads, and boxed areas and sidebars highlight specific subjects and areas. The explanations are clear and detailed." SLJ

Includes glossary and bibliographical references

Miller, Ron

★ The **elements**. Twenty-First Century Books 2006 135p il lib bdg $28.90

Grades: 8 9 10 11 12   **546**

1. Chemical elements

ISBN 0-7613-2794-0

LC 2003-20874

Discusses the history of the periodic table of the elements, includes biographies of major figures in the field of chemistry, and provides information on each element.

"A useful overview." SLJ

Includes bibliographical references

O'Daly, Anne

Sodium; [by] Anne O'Daly. Benchmark Books 2001 32p il (The elements) lib bdg $28.50

Grades: 5 6 7 8   **546**

1. Sodium

ISBN 978-0-7614-1271-7; 0-7614-1271-9

LC 2001-25253

Discusses the characteristics, sources, and uses of sodium.

Includes glossary

Oxlade, Chris

Acids and bases; [by] Chris Oxlade. rev. and updated; Heinemann Library 2007 48p il (Chemicals in action) lib bdg $31.43; pa $8.99

Grades: 6 7 8 9   **546**

1. Acids 2. Bases (Chemistry)

ISBN 978-1-4329-0050-2 lib bdg; 978-1-4329-0057-1 pa

First published 2002

"Explanations are concise and clear without being oversimplified, and the arrangement is attractive and open. Colorful diagrams, drawings, and photographs appear on every page." SLJ

Includes glossary and bibliographical references

Elements and compounds; [by] Chris Oxlade. rev. and updated; Heinemann Library 2007 48p il (Chemicals in action) lib bdg $31.43; pa $8.99

Grades: 6 7 8 9   **546**

1. Chemical elements

ISBN 978-1-4329-0052-6 lib bdg; 978-1-4329-0059-5 pa

First published 2002

"Explanations are concise and clear without being oversimplified, and the arrangement is attractive and open. Colorful diagrams, drawings, and photographs appear on every page." SLJ

Includes glossary and bibliographical references

Metals; [by] Chris Oxlade. rev. and updated; Heinemann Library 2007 48p il (Chemicals in action) lib bdg $31.43; pa $8.99

Grades: 6 7 8 9   **546**

1. Metals

ISBN 978-1-4329-0054-0 lib bdg; 978-1-4329-0061-8 pa

First published 2002

"This title explores what metals are like, how they are mixed with each other to form alloys, and how they are used to make everything from paper clips to skyscrapers. [It also includes] several experiments that can be done at home." Publisher's note

Includes glossary and bibliographical references

Roza, Greg

The **halogen** elements; fluorine, chlorine, bromine, iodine, astatine. Rosen Central 2010 48p il (Understanding the elements of the periodic table) lib bdg $26.50

Grades: 7 8 9 10   **546**

1. Periodic law 2. Chemical elements

ISBN 978-1-4358-3556-6 lib bdg; 1-4358-3556-5 lib bdg

LC 2009012539

This overview discusses "the history of each element, where it can be found, and how it is used in everyday life. . . . Charts show each element's chemical symbol, atomic number, atomic weight, melting point, and boiling point. Colorful photographs and illustrations are included on most pages. Lengthy sidebars highlight key information." SLJ

Includes bibliographical references

Saunders, N.

Who invented the periodic table? [by] Nigel Saunders. Arcturus Pub. 2010 46p il (Breakthroughs in science and technology) lib bdg $32.80

Grades: 5 6 7 8   **546**

1. Chemists 2. Periodic law

ISBN 978-1-84837-680-9; 1-84837-680-4

LC 2010011016

"After a very brief presentation of atoms and elements, and a short, but comprehensive, view of the modern periodic table, the author presents a series of vignettes, starting with alchemy. Through these vignettes, the reader gets an appreciation of the personalities of, and challenges faced by, key contributors. . . . [This] presents an engaging story behind the story of the discovery of the periodic table." Sci Books & Films
Includes glossary

Sparrow, Giles
Iron; [by] Giles Sparrow. Benchmark Bks. 1999 32p il (The elements) lib bdg $28.50
Grades: 5 6 7 8   546
1. Iron
ISBN 978-0-7614-0880-2; 0-7614-0880-0
LC 97-48524
Discusses the origin, discovery, special characteristics, and uses of iron.
Includes glossary

Thomas, Jens
Silicon; [by] Jens Thomas. Benchmark Books 2001 32p il (The elements) lib bdg $28.50
Grades: 5 6 7 8   546
1. Silicon
ISBN 978-0-7614-1274-8; 0-7614-1274-3
LC 2001-25993
Discusses the characteristics, sources, and uses of silicon.
Includes glossary

The noble gases; [by] Jens Thomas. Benchmark Books 2002 32p il (The elements) lib bdg $28.50
Grades: 5 6 7 8   546
1. Gases
ISBN 978-0-7614-1462-9; 0-7614-1462-2
LC 2002-210
Explores the history of the noble gases and explains their chemistry, their uses, and their importance in our lives.
"The well-selected photographs and diagrams are appropriate to the text." Horn Book Guide
Includes glossary

Turrell, Kerry
Tungsten; [by] Kerry Turrell. Benchmark Books 2004 32p il (The elements) lib bdg $28.50
Grades: 5 6 7 8   546
1. Tungsten
ISBN 978-0-7614-1548-0; 0-7614-1548-3
LC 2003-52099
Examines the characteristics, sources, and uses of the element tungsten, as well as tungsten's importance in our lives.
"Numerous captioned color photos and sidebars augment the accurate and well-organized but information-dense text." Horn Book Guide
Includes glossary

Uttley, Colin
Magnesium; [by] Colin Uttley. Benchmark Bks. 2000 32p il (The elements) lib bdg $28.50

Grades: 5 6 7 8   546
1. Magnesium
ISBN 978-0-7614-0889-5; 0-7614-0889-4
LC 98-53200
Explores the history of the bright-colored metal magnesium and explains its chemistry, how it reacts, its uses, and its importance in our lives.
Includes glossary

Watt, Susan
Chlorine; [by] Susan Watt. Benchmark Books 2001 32p il (The elements) lib bdg $28.50
Grades: 5 6 7 8   546
1. Chlorine
ISBN 978-0-7614-1272-4; 0-7614-1272-7
LC 2001-25252
Discusses the characteristics, sources, and uses of chlorine.
Includes glossary

Cobalt; [by] Susan Watt. Marshall Cavendish Benchmark 2007 32p il (The elements) lib bdg $28.50
Grades: 5 6 7 8   546
1. Cobalt
ISBN 978-0-7614-2200-6; 0-7614-2200-5
LC 2005-55303
Introduces the element of cobalt, discussing its physical and chemical properties, where it is found, and what processes or objects it is used in.
"Provides a comprehensive, yet easy-to-read overview in large, bold print. Explanations are concise and clear without being oversimplified, and the arrangement is attractive." SLJ
Icludes glossary

Lead; [by] Susan Watt. Benchmark Books 2001 32p il (The elements) lib bdg $28.50
Grades: 5 6 7 8   546
1. Lead
ISBN 978-0-7614-1273-1; 0-7614-1273-5
LC 2001-35406
Explores the history of the useful metal lead and explains its chemistry, its uses, and its importance in our lives.
Includes glossary

Mercury; [by] Susan Watt. Benchmark Books 2005 32p il (The elements) lib bdg $28.50
Grades: 5 6 7 8   546
1. Mercury
ISBN 978-0-7614-1814-6; 0-7614-1814-8
LC 2004-47633
This book is part "of the 28-title The Elements series. Mercury tells the history of mercury, where it is found in nature, its place in mythology, how it is mined and refined, how it forms compounds, its uses, and its position in the periodic table." Sci Books Films
Includes glossary

Silver; [by] Susan Watt. Benchmark Books 2003 32p il (The elements) lib bdg $28.50

Grades: 5 6 7 8   **546**
  1. Silver
  ISBN 978-0-7614-1464-3; 0-7614-1464-9
                     LC 2002-6080
Explores the history of silver and explains its chemistry, its uses, and its importance in our lives.
"Explanations are succinct and clear, without being oversimplified, and supplemental information is provided in boxed sidebars. Relevant diagrams, drawings, and photographs, mainly in color, appear on every page." SLJ
  Includes glossary

Zirconium; [by] Susan Watt. Marshall Cavendish Benchmark 2008 32p il (The elements) lib bdg $28.50
Grades: 5 6 7 8   **546**
  1. Zirconium
  ISBN 978-0-7614-2688-2; 0-7614-2688-4
                   LC 2007-60885
Introduces the element of zirconium, discussing its physical and chemical properties, where it is found, and how it is used.
"Provides a comprehensive, yet easy-to-read overview. . . . The explanations are succinct and clear, without being oversimplified, and the layout is attractive." SLJ
  Includes glossary

West, Krista
  Bromine; [by] Krista West. Marshall Cavendish Benchmark 2008 32p il (The elements) lib bdg $28.50
Grades: 5 6 7 8   **546**
  1. Bromine
  ISBN 978-0-7614-2685-1; 0-7614-2685-X
                   LC 2006-51812
Introduces the element of bromine and its compounds, discussing its physical and chemical properties, where it is found, and how it is used.
"Provides a comprehensive, yet easy-to-read overview. . . . The explanations are succinct and clear, without being oversimplified, and the layout is attractive. Diagrams and photographs complement the text on every page." SLJ
  Includes glossary

Carbon chemistry. Chelsea House 2008 117p il (Essential chemistry) lib bdg $35
Grades: 7 8 9 10   **546**
  1. Carbon
  ISBN 978-0-7910-9708-3; 0-7910-9708-0
                   LC 2007-51318
Explains how carbon is integrated into all facets of life as we know it and discusses the unique properties of this essential element.
"Annotated, colorful photographs and illustrations appear on most spreads, and boxed areas and sidebars highlight specific subjects and areas. The explanations are clear and detailed." SLJ
  Includes glossary and bibliographical references

Woodford, Chris
  Potassium; [by] Chris Woodford. Benchmark Books 2002 32p il (The elements) lib bdg $28.50

Grades: 5 6 7 8   **546**
  1. Potassium
  ISBN 978-0-7614-1463-6; 0-7614-1463-0
                   LC 2002-18556
Describes the characteristics, sources, and uses of the element potassium
"Explanations are succinct and clear, without being oversimplified, and supplemental information is provided in boxed sidebars. Relevant diagrams, drawings, and photographs, mainly in color, appear on every page." SLJ
  Includes glossary

Titanium; [by] Chris Woodford. Benchmark Books 2003 32p il (The elements) lib bdg $28.50
Grades: 5 6 7 8   **546**
  1. Titanium
  ISBN 978-0-7614-1461-2; 0-7614-1461-4
                   LC 2001-8743
Discusses the characteristics, sources, and uses of the element titanium.
"The well-selected photographs and diagrams are appropriate to the text." Horn Book Guide
  Includes glossary

547   Organic chemistry

Gardner, Robert
  Organic chemistry science fair projects; revised and expanded using the scientific method. [by] Robert Gardner and Barbara Gardner Conklin. Enslow Publishers 2010 160p il (Chemistry science projects using the scientific method) lib bdg $34.60
Grades: 7 8 9 10   **547**
  1. Science projects 2. Organic chemistry 3. Science -- Experiments
  ISBN 978-0-7660-3414-3 lib bdg; 0-7660-3414-3 lib bdg
                   LC 2008050078
First published 2004 with title: Chemistry science fair projects using french fries, gumdrops, soap, and other organic stuff
"Colorful drawings complement the material and illustrations of chemical structures help to convey chemical processes. . . . Useful." SLJ
  Includes bibliographical references

549   Mineralogy

Casper, Julie Kerr
  Minerals; gifts from the Earth. Chelsea House 2007 194p il map (Natural resources) $39.50
Grades: 8 9 10 11 12   **549**
  1. Minerals 2. Mines and mineral resources
  ISBN 978-0-8160-6357-4; 0-8160-6357-5
                   LC 2006102275
Explains how minerals and formed and how they are used in technology.
  Includes bibliographical references

Chesterman, Charles W.

The **Audubon** Society field guide to North American rocks and minerals; scientific consultant, Kurt E. Lowe. Knopf 1979 850p il $19.95

Grades: 8 9 10 11 12 Adult   **549**
1. Rocks 2. Minerals
ISBN 0-394-50269-8

LC 78-54893

"Pocket guide providing color photos and descriptions of some 232 mineral species and forty types of rocks. Includes guide to mineral environments, glossary, bibliography, and indexes by name and locality." Ref Sources for Small & Medium-sized Libr. 5th edition

Pellant, Chris

Rocks and minerals; Helen Pellant, editorial consultant; photography by Harry Taylor. 2nd American ed; Dorling Kindersley 2002 256p il (Smithsonian handbooks) pa $20

Grades: 11 12 Adult   **549**
1. Rocks 2. Minerals
ISBN 0-7894-9106-0; 978-0-7894-9106-0

First published 1992 as part of the Eyewitness handbooks series

This field guide to identification of rocks and minerals includes techniques for collection and classification, and facts about physical and chemical composition and formation.

Simon and Schuster's guide to rocks and minerals; edited by Martin Prinz, George Harlow, and Joseph Peters. Simon & Schuster 1978 607p il hardcover o.p. pa $17

Grades: 8 9 10 11 12 Adult   **549**
1. Rocks 2. Minerals
ISBN 0-671-24417-5 pa

LC 78-8610

Original Italian edition, 1977

"Half of this book consists of color plates; the other half is an authoritative text which describes the elements of mineralogy and petrology. Crystal system or family, physical and chemical properties, occurrence, uses, and rarity are included for each species." Libr J

550 Earth sciences

Allaby, Michael

★ **Visual** encyclopedia of earth. National Geographic 2008 256p il map $24.95; lib bdg $32.90

Grades: 7 8 9 10   **550**
1. Reference books 2. Earth sciences -- Encyclopedias 4. Earth sciences
ISBN 978-1-4263-0366-1; 1-4263-0366-1; 978-1-4263-0367-8 lib bdg; 1-4263-0367-X lib bdg

LC 2008-301484

"This overview of the earth . . . cover[s] all aspects of earth science. . . . [This] is a feast for the eyes and an exceptional introduction to earth science. It will be a useful resource for science teachers who want to engage their students in this subject matter." Libr Media Connect

Bow, James

Earth's secrets. Marshall Cavendish Benchmark 2010 48p il (Invisible worlds) lib bdg $28.50

Grades: 4 5 6 7   **550**
1. Earth sciences
ISBN 978-0-7614-4196-0 lib bdg; 0-7614-4196-4 lib bdg

The narrative is "clear, well written, broken down into manageable pieces, and peppered with eye-opening facts. The numerous photographs are so phenomenal that they will inspire kids to read the text . . . so that they can wrap their minds around what they see." SLJ

Includes glossary and bibliographical references

Calhoun, Yael

Earth science fair projects; revised and expanded using the scientific method. Enslow Publishers 2010 160p il (Earth science projects using the scientific method) lib bdg $34.60

Grades: 7 8 9 10   **550**
1. Earth sciences 2. Science projects 3. Science -- Experiments
ISBN 978-0-7660-3425-9 lib bdg; 0-7660-3425-9 lib bdg

First published 2005 with title: Earth science fair projects using rocks, minerals, magnets, mud, and more

"This describes Earth science experiments on such topics as the geologic time, earthquakes and volcanoes, minerals and rocks, rivers, and erosion, and includes science project ideas." Publisher's note

Includes glossary and bibliographical references

Day, Trevor

DK guide to savage Earth. DK Pub. 2001 64p $15.95

Grades: 4 5 6   **550**
1. Volcanoes 2. Earthquakes 3. Natural disasters 4. Geodynamics
ISBN 0-7894-7919-2

LC 2001-275872

The author takes us on a "journey from Earth's violent beginnings to possible future destruction from such forces as asteroid strikes and other natural disasters, global warming, or a depletion of the forests and fisheries of the world. Each chapter focuses on one force of nature, discussing how and why it has shaped the Earth in the past and how it is changing the shape of the Earth in the present. . . . The text is concise, authoritative, and very interesting and easy to read." Book Rep

Includes glossary

Diagram Group

★ The **Facts** on File Earth science handbook; [by] the Diagram Group. Rev. ed.; Facts on File 2006 272p il (Facts on File science library) $35

Grades: 8 9 10 11 12   **550**
1. Earth sciences
ISBN 0-8160-5879-2

LC 2005-44692

First published 2000

This guide to earth sciences contains a dictionary with around 1400 entries, a chronology, thumbnail biographies, an A to Z list of over 150 advances in earth science, and a list of Tyler Prize winners.

Includes bibliographical references

Gardner, Robert

Earth's cycles; green science projects about the water cycle, photosynthesis, and more. Enslow Publishers 2011 112p il (Team Green science projects) lib bdg $31.93

Grades: 6 7 8 9 10   550

1. Earth sciences 2. Science projects 3. Science -- Experiments

ISBN 978-0-7660-3644-4; 0-7660-3644-8

LC 2010-25816

"Gardner provides plenty of information, well-designed experiments, and demonstrations, and then shares brief science-fair ideas. . . . Experiments and demonstrations are presented with clear step-by-step instructions and occasional illustrations and represent a wide range of complexity." SLJ

Includes glossary and bibliographical references

Gilpin, Daniel

Planet Earth; what planet are you on? created by Basher; written by Dan Gilpin. Kingfisher 2010 128p il $14.99; pa $8.99

Grades: 5 6 7 8   550

1. Earth sciences

ISBN 978-0-7534-6616-2; 0-7534-6616-3; 978-0-7534-6412-0 pa; 0-7534-6412-8 pa

LC 2010015976

Presents concepts in earth sciences using lively descriptions and cartoon illustrations personifying each concept.

"The authors blend a surprising wealth of facts into the chatty, humorous text, which is filled with analogies kids can relate to. . . . The highly approachable language, animated cast of characters, awe-inspiring facts, and conservation messages make this an appealing starting point for students seeking basic earth-science information." Booklist

Patent, Dorothy Hinshaw

★ Shaping the earth; photographs by William Muñoz. Clarion Bks. 2000 88p il maps $18

Grades: 4 5 6 7   550

1. Geology 2. Geodynamics

ISBN 0-395-85691-4

LC 99-37093

Explains the forces that have created the geological features on the Earth's surface

"This concise, attractive volume succeeds in a daunting task—to present the history of Earth in 88 pages of compelling, age-appropriate text. . . . William Muñoz's full-color photographs, well-chosen and reproduced, will draw young readers into the text. . . . A glossary and a list of further references, including Web sites, are appended." Booklist

Includes bibliographical references

Rybolt, Thomas R.

Environmental science fair projects; revised and expanded using the scientific method. [by] Thomas R. Rybolt and Robert C. Mebane. Enslow Publishers 2010 160p il (Earth science projects using the scientific method) lib bdg $34.60

Grades: 7 8 9 10   550

1. Earth sciences 2. Science projects 3. Environmental sciences 4. Science -- Experiments

ISBN 978-0-7660-3426-6 lib bdg; 0-7660-3426-7 lib bdg

First published 2005 with title: Environmental science fair projects using water, feathers, sunlight, balloons, and more

"This describes experiments on such topics as air, water, soil, pollution, and energy resources. Includes ideas for science projects." Publisher's note

Includes bibliographical references

Smithsonian Institution

Earth; editor-in-chief, James F. Luhr. Compact ed.; DK Pub. 2007 520p il map pa $24.95

Grades: 8 9 10 11 12 Adult   550

1. Earth

ISBN 978-0-7566-3332-5; 0-7566-3332-X

LC 2007282646

First published 2003

Presents an overview of the Earth, discussing its internal structure, the major features of its lands, mountains, and oceans, its climate, weather, and place in the universe.

Solway, Andrew

Understanding cycles and systems. Raintree 2008 48p il map (Sci-hi: Earth and space science) lib bdg $31.43; pa $8.99

Grades: 4 5 6 7   550

1. Earth sciences

ISBN 978-1-4109-3348-5 lib bdg; 1-4109-3348-2 lib bdg; 978-1-4109-3358-4 pa; 1-4109-3358-X pa

LC 2009-3531

"Multiple colorful sidebars and large and small diagrams and photographs will help students to grasp the fundamentals being discussed, and the easy but interesting science experiments will act as further reinforcements." SLJ

Includes glossary and bibliographical references

Woodward, John

Planet Earth; written by John Woodward; consultant Kim Bryan. DK Pub. 2009 123p il (One million things) $18.99

Grades: 5 6 7 8   550

1. Earth

ISBN 978-0-7566-5235-7; 0-7566-5235-9

"The artwork is a balanced mix of stunning photography, effective illustrations, and somewhat depth-challenged Photoshop jobs. An eye-catching catchall on the natural world, this . . . is great browsing material, packed full of well-articulated information." Booklist

550.78 Earth sciences -- Experiments

VanCleave, Janice Pratt, 1942-

Step-by-step science experiments in earth science; by Janice VanCleave. Rosen Pub. 2013 80 p. col. ill. (library) $33.25; (paperback) $14.15

Grades: 5 6 7 8 **550.78**

1. Earth sciences 2. Science -- Experiments 3. Earth sciences -- Experiments
ISBN 1448869838; 9781448869831; 9781448884674
LC 2012007944

This book by Janice VanCleave is part of the First-Place Science Fair Projects series. The books have an introduction to the subject—here, earth science, followed by 22 simple . . . experiments. Van Cleave states the basic goal of the experiments, followed by a list of necessary materials, most of which can be found around the house or easily acquired with minimal cost. Step-by-step instructions are clearly detailed and accompanied by diagrams where needed." (School Library Journal)

Includes bibliographical references (p. 78) and index.

551 Geology, hydrology, meteorology

Cobb, Allan B.

Earth chemistry. Chelsea House 2008 130p il map (Essential chemistry) $35

Grades: 7 8 9 10 **551**

1. Chemistry 2. Environmental sciences
ISBN 978-0-7910-9677-2; 0-7910-9677-7
LC 2007-51317

"Annotated, colorful photographs and illustrations appear on most spreads, and boxed areas and sidebars highlight specific subjects and areas. The explanations are clear and detailed." SLJ

Includes glossary and bibliographical references

Kelly, Erica

★ **Evolving** planet; [by] Erica Kelly & Richard Kissel. Harry N. Abrams 2008 136p il map $19.95

Grades: 5 6 7 8 **551**

1. Evolution 2. Paleontology 3. Human evolution 4. Natural history
ISBN 978-0-8109-9486-7; 0-8109-9486-0
LC 2007-36342

"Based on a exhibit at Chicago's Field Museum, this big spacious volume packs in a wealth of information about evolution over four billion years. . . . There are detailed, beautiful photographs and glorious paintings on every double-page spread and the chatty text is accessible for grade-schoolers." Booklist

Includes glossary and bibliographical references

Plate tectonics, volcanoes, and earthquakes; edited by John P. Rafferty. Britannica Educational Pub.

in association with Rosen Educational Services 2010 312p il map (Dynamic Earth) lib bdg $45

Grades: 6 7 8 9 10 **551**

1. Volcanoes 2. Earthquakes 3. Plate tectonics
ISBN 978-1-61530-106-5; 1-61530-106-2
LC 2009042303

"The 2010 earthquake in Haiti, threats to aviation from clouds of volcanic ash and aerosols, and recent changes in the Antarctic make . . . [this] a very updated resource. The process of plate tectonics and prior explanations of the dynamic nature of the earth is followed by explanations of volcanism and seismology. Charts and text describe significant volcanoes and earthquakes that have impacted humans throughout history. . . . [Recommended] for younger youth as well as high school youth since they are highly readable, with details concerning activities of interest to all ages." Voice Youth Advocates

Includes bibliographical references

551.1 Gross structure and properties of the earth

Saunders, Craig

What is the theory of plate tectonics? Crabtree Pub. Co. 2011 64p il (Shaping modern science) lib bdg $30.60; pa $10.95

Grades: 5 6 7 8 **551.1**

1. Plate tectonics 2. Geophysicists 3. Meteorologists 4. College teachers
ISBN 978-0-7787-7202-6 lib bdg; 0-7787-7202-0 lib bdg; 978-0-7787-7209-5 pa; 0-7787-7209-8 pa
LC 2010-52622

This title is "not only written and organized well, but [it is] also gorgeous in design. Full-color photographs and illustrations are set over colorful backgrounds that add depth but not distraction. [The title] includes thought-provoking quotes from famous authors and scientists and some eyebrow-raising 'Quick Facts' throughout." SLJ

Includes glossary and bibliographical references

Silverstein, Alvin

Plate tectonics; by Alvin & Virginia Silverstein & Laura Silverstein Nunn. rev. ed.; Twenty-First Century Books 2009 120p il map (Science concepts, second series) lib bdg $31.93

Grades: 6 7 8 9 **551.1**

1. Plate tectonics
ISBN 978-0-7613-3936-6; 0-7613-3936-1
LC 2007051039

First published 1998

The authors "explain the theory of plate tectonics and how moving plates can cause . . . natural disasters: earthquakes, volcanoes, and tsunamis. The authors also explore how plate tectonics are changing our planet, and how they could affect our future on Earth." Publisher's note

Includes glossary and bibliographical references

Snedden, Robert

Earth's shifting surface. Raintree 2010 48p il (Sci-hi: Earth and space science) lib bdg $31.43; pa $8.99

Grades: 4 5 6 7   **551.1**

  1. Plate tectonics

  ISBN 978-1-4109-3349-2 lib bdg; 1-4109-3349-0 lib bdg; 978-1-4109-3359-1 pa; 1-4109-3359-8 pa

                      LC 2009-3532

"Multiple colorful sidebars and large and small diagrams and photographs will help students to grasp the fundamentals being discussed, and the easy but interesting science experiments will act as further reinforcements." SLJ

Includes glossary and bibliographical references

Stille, Darlene R.

  ★ **Plate** tectonics; Earth's moving crust. Compass Point Books 2006 48p il (Exploring science) $26.60

Grades: 7 8 9 10   **551.1**

  1. Plate tectonics

  ISBN 978-0-7565-1957-5; 0-7565-1957-8

                      LC 2006-06764

This describes the shifting of the Earth's crust and its consequences.

Includes glossary and bibliographical references

Vogt, Gregory

Earth's core and mantle; heavy metal, moving rock. by Gregory L. Vogt. Twenty-First Century Books 2007 80p il map (Earth's spheres) lib bdg $29.27

Grades: 6 7 8 9   **551.1**

  ISBN 978-0-7613-2837-7 lib bdg; 0-7613-2837-8 lib bdg

                      LC 2003-23969

This "explores the makeup of the universe, the origin of the planet and its moon, and the layers under Earth's surface. . . . Each of these complex topics is made understandable by the use of colorful photographs, graphs, charts, and other illustrations. Captions include new and useful information, and the sidebars and fact pages are helpful." SLJ

Includes bibliographical references

The **lithosphere**; Earth's crust. by Gregory L. Vogt. Twenty-First Century Books 2007 80p il map (Earth's spheres) lib bdg $29.27

Grades: 6 7 8 9   **551.1**

  1. Young adult literature -- Works

  ISBN 978-0-7613-2838-4 lib bdg; 0-7613-2838-6 lib bdg

                      LC 2006-14882

This "explains the [Earth's] crust and how land is built and eroded, covering such subjects as plate tectonics, volcanoes, and geysers. Each of these complex topics is made understandable by the use of colorful photographs, graphs, charts, and other illustrations. Captions include new and useful information, and the sidebars and fact pages are helpful." SLJ

Includes bibliographical references

551.2   Volcanoes, earthquakes, thermal waters and gases

Dwyer, Helen

Earthquakes! Marshall Cavendish Benchmark 2010 32p il map (Eyewitness disaster) lib bdg $28.50

Grades: 4 5 6   **551.2**

  1. Earthquakes

  ISBN 978-1-60870-001-1; 1-60870-001-1

Provides information about earthquakes through eyewitness accounts from survivors and rescue workers.

"Bold subheadings and color captions break information into readable chunks for the younger learner. Important vocabulary is in bold print. . . . An excellent addition to your science collection." Libr Media Connect

Includes glossary and bibliographical references

Fradin, Judith Bloom

  ★ **Earthquakes**; witness to disaster. by Judy and Dennis Fradin. National Geographic 2008 48p map (Witness to disaster) $16.95; lib bdg $26.90

Grades: 4 5 6 7   **551.2**

  1. Earthquakes

  ISBN 978-1-4263-0211-4; 1-4263-0211-8; 978-1-4263-0212-1 lib bdg; 1-4263-0212-6 lib bdg

                      LC 2007044164

"The combination of good writing and excellent graphics paired with archival and personal perspectives makes this book a valuable addition." SLJ

Includes glossary and bibliographical references

Volcano! the Icelandic eruption of 2010 and other hot, smoky, fierce, and fiery mountains. [by] Judy & Dennis Fradin. National Geographic 2010 48p il map (National Geographic kids) pa $6.95

Grades: 4 5 6 7   **551.2**

  1. Volcanoes

  ISBN 978-1-4263-0815-4 pa; 1-4263-0815-9 pa

"The format includes text, quotes, and facts in sidebars, as well as photographs on each page, with a colorful layout. The photographs and maps that are shown are of good quality." Sci Books & Films

Includes glossary and bibliographical references

  ★ **Volcanoes**; by Judy and Dennis Fradin. National Geographic 2007 48p il map (Witness to disaster) $16.95; lib bdg $26.90

Grades: 4 5 6 7   **551.2**

  1. Volcanoes

  ISBN 978-0-7922-5376-1; 0-7922-5376-0; 978-0-7922-5377-8 lib bdg; 0-7922-5377-9 lib bdg

                      LC 2006-102817

This "introduces readers to these violent eruptions, using eyewitness accounts to explain the history and science involved. They begin with a report of the 1943 birth of a volcano in Paricutín, Mexico. . . . Subsequent chapters describe other celebrated volcanoes, explain their causes and types, note the benefits of these eruptions, and clarify how they are currently predicted. . . . Numerous clear, well-chosen photographs and diagrams help to convey the great power of volcanic activity and the consequences to humans. . . . This will be useful for report writers, and a fascinating pick for browsers." Booklist

Includes bibliographical references

Hague, Bradley

Alien deep; Revealing the Mysterious Living World at the Bottom of the Ocean. by Bradley Hague. National Geographic 2012 48 p. col. ill. (hardcover : alk. paper) $17.95

Grades: 4 5 6 7   **551.2**

1. Oceanography -- Research 2. Hydrothermal vent ecology 3. Natural history -- Galapagos Islands

ISBN 1426310676; 9781426310676; 9781426310683

LC 2012012939

This book by Bradley Hague "depicts adventurous and thrilling elements in oceanographic fieldwork in conjunction with a National Geographic television show." (Publisher's note)

"The book takes readers along on the 2011 exploration of vents in the Galapagos Reef area of the Pacific Ocean. . . . Future scientists will be hooked by the excitement of finding newly developing vents and the disappointment of finding older vents that once disappeared under layers of magma." (Booklist)

Includes bibliographical references and index.

Latta, Sara L.

Lava scientist; careers on the edge of volcanoes. Enslow Publishers 2009 128p il (Wild science careers) lib bdg $31.93

Grades: 5 6 7 8   **551.2**

1. Volcanoes 2. Vocational guidance

ISBN 978-0-7660-3049-7 lib bdg; 0-7660-3049-7 lib bdg

LC 2008-4679

The book's "greatest strength is in the variety of first-hand accounts and the scientists' breadth of experience. [The book has] appealing color photographs and an attractive design." SLJ

Includes glossary and bibliographical references

Levy, Matthys

Earthquakes, volcanoes, and tsunamis; projects and principles for beginning geologists. [by] Matthys Levy and Mario Salvadori. Chicago Review Press 2009 136p il pa $14.95

Grades: 5 6 7 8   **551.2**

1. Tsunamis 2. Volcanoes 3. Earthquakes

ISBN 978-1-55652-801-9 pa; 1-55652-801-9 pa

LC 2008040143

This "is an excellent introduction for young minds to the subject of earthquakes, volcanoes, and related phenomena. . . . The book is filled with projects to help young people understand the occurrence and consequences of earthquakes, volcanoes, and tsunamis." Sci Books Films

McCollum, Sean

Volcanic eruptions, earthquakes, and tsunamis. Chelsea House 2007 80p il (Scientific American) lib bdg $30

Grades: 5 6 7 8   **551.2**

1. Tsunamis 2. Volcanoes 3. Earthquakes

ISBN 978-0-7910-9047-3 lib bdg; 0-7910-9047-7 lib bdg

LC 2007017740

"Following an introduction that focuses on the formation of a volcano off the coast of Iceland in 1963 and presents the principles of seismology, geology, and the structure of the Earth, individual chapters on volcanoes, earthquakes, and tsunamis describe these phenomena, how they happen, and their characteristics. . . . The workmanlike writing is clear, with glossary terms highlighted in the text. Major events, such as Mount St. Helens, the 2004 tsunami, and the 1906 San Francisco earthquake, are used as examples, while good color diagrams and photos effectively illustrate ideas presented." SLJ

Includes bibliographical references

Nardo, Don

Volcanoes. Morgan Reynolds Pub. 2009 112p il map (Extreme threats) lib bdg $28.95

Grades: 7 8 9 10   **551.2**

1. Volcanoes

ISBN 978-1-59935-118-6; 1-59935-118-8

LC 2009-25705

This book "begins with a vivid account of the 79 CE eruption of Vesuvius, the cataclysm that buried Pompeii and Herculaneum. Later chapters explore the development of volcanology, formation and location of volcanoes, volcanic avalanches, supervolcanoes and mass extinctions, and the bleak future of humanity with regard to volcanoes. Throughout, Nardo references specific volcanoes and eruptions and brings the disasters to life by including primary source quotes from witnesses and scientists." Voice Youth Advocates

Includes glossary and bibliographical references

Person, Stephen

Devastated by a volcano! Bearport Pub. 2010 32p il map (Disaster survivors) lib bdg $25.27

Grades: 4 5 6 7   **551.2**

1. Volcanoes

ISBN 978-1-936087-50-1 lib bdg; 1-936087-50-2 lib bdg

"Captivating photos and illustrations and sidebars present interesting facts or brief anecdotes. . . . [This] should be purchased for all school and public libraries as . . . [it gives] a new perspective on the topic." Libr Media Connect

Includes glossary and bibliographical references

Prager, Ellen J.

Earthquakes and volcanoes; [by] Ellen Prager. Chelsea House Publishers 2009 118p il map (The restless Earth) lib bdg $32.95

Grades: 6 7 8 9   **551.2**

1. Volcanoes 2. Earthquakes

ISBN 978-0-7910-9705-2 lib bdg; 0-7910-9705-6 lib bdg

LC 2008-8777

"The high level of detail, perspective in world history, and solid organization provide an excellent foundation for students to throughly understand the cataclysmic events of earthquakes and tornadoes." Libr Media Connect

Includes glossary and bibliographical references

Reingold, Adam

Leveled by an earthquake! Bearport Pub. 2010 32p il map (Disaster survivors) lib bdg $25.27

Grades: 4 5 6 7   **551.2**

1. Earthquakes

ISBN 978-1-936087-53-2 lib bdg; 1-936087-53-7 lib bdg

LC 2009-36961

"Captivating photos and illustrations and sidebars present interesting facts or brief anecdotes. . . . [This] should be purchased for all school and public libraries as . . . [it gives] a new perspective on the topic." Libr Media Connect

Includes glossary and bibliographical references

Rooney, Anne

Volcanoes. New Forest Press 2010 64p il map (Cutting-edge science) lib bdg $34.25

Grades: 7 8 9 10   **551.2**

1. Volcanoes

ISBN 978-1-84898-319-9; 1-84898-319-0

This guide to volcanoes covers plate tectonics, super volcanoes, tsunamis, scientific methods for detection and prediction, case studies of real volcanoes past and present, and the effects of volcanoes on the environment.

"Chapters are well-organized and contain clear explanations. The crisp layout contains plenty of captioned photos and diagrams, as well as sidebars that feature interesting facts and suggestions for observations readers can record in their backyards." Horn Book Guide

Includes glossary and bibliographical references

Silverstein, Alvin

Earthquakes; the science behind seismic shocks and tsunamis. [by] Alvin Silverstein, Virginia Silverstein, and Laura Silverstein Nunn. Enslow Publishers 2010 48p il map (The science behind natural disasters) lib bdg $23.93

Grades: 4 5 6   **551.2**

1. Tsunamis 2. Earthquakes

ISBN 978-0-7660-2975-0 lib bdg; 0-7660-2975-1 lib bdg

LC 2008-38589

"Scientific explanations are accompanied by plentiful color diagrams that will help students to grasp causes and effects. . . . Photos . . . are effective, and are sometimes turned into helpful, lively diagrams by the addition of such features as wind-direction arrows." SLJ

Includes glossary and bibliographical references

Volcanoes; the science behind fiery eruptions. [by] Alvin Silverstein, Virginia Silverstein, and Laura Silverstein Nunn. Enslow Publishers 2010 48p il map (The science behind natural disasters) lib bdg $23.93

Grades: 4 5 6   **551.2**

1. Volcanoes

ISBN 978-0-7660-2972-9 lib bdg; 0-7660-2972-7 lib bdg

LC 2008-42866

"Scientific explanations are accompanied by plentiful color diagrams that will help students to grasp causes and effects. . . . Photos . . . are effective, and are sometimes turned into helpful, lively diagrams by the addition of such features as wind-direction arrows." SLJ

Includes glossary and bibliographical references

Stewart, Melissa

Inside Earthquakes. Sterling Publishing Co., Inc. 2011 48p il map (Inside . . .) $16.95; pa $9.95

Grades: 5 6 7 8   **551.2**

1. Earthquakes

ISBN 978-1-4027-5877-5; 978-1-4027-8163-6 pa

LC 2010046452

This book about earthquakes "explores its topic in an engaging way, and the many illustrations work well with adjacent text and captions. . . . The [book's] varied page layouts and attractive and the quality of photos, computer-generated images, original illustrations, and charts is . . . excellent. . . . [The book] looks at the geology of the Earth's crust as well as the effects of quakes on people and cities, landforms and coastlines." Booklist

Includes bibliographical references

Inside Volcanoes. Sterling Publishing Co. 2011 48p il map (Inside) $16.95; pa $9.95

Grades: 5 6 7 8   **551.2**

1. Volcanoes

ISBN 978-1-4027-5876-8; 1-4027-5876-6; 978-1-4027-8164-3 pa; 1-4027-8164-4 pa

LC 2010046451

Examines the nature of volcanoes, how they are formed, what they look like, and how they are measured, in a text with ten foldout pages.

"With pages that fold out or flip up, well-reproduced photographs of volcanoes at rest and in action, diagrams, maps, charts, timelines and short explanations, there is much to look at and to learn. . . . Appropriately for a book that is clearly designed to stimulate interest, there are solid suggestions for both books and websites for further exploration. A good starting-place for volcano explorations." Kirkus

Stille, Darlene R.

Great shakes; the science of earthquakes. Compass Point Books 2009 43p il map (Headline science) lib bdg $27.93; pa $7.95

Grades: 5 6 7 8   **551.2**

1. Earthquakes

ISBN 978-0-7565-3947-4 lib bdg; 0-7565-3947-1 lib bdg; 978-0-7565-3368-7 pa; 0-7565-3368-6 pa

LC 2008-05739

This "is an accessible, technically accurate introduction to [earthquakes]. . . . In addition to the ludic writing, this slim volume offers . . . readers comprehensive coverage of the fundamentals of earthquakes, including the effects, plate tectonics, fault systems, seismic waves, forecasting, and safer building designs. . . . The many charts and graphs enrich the volume and clarify technical issues." Sci Books Films

Includes glossary and bibliographical references

Volcans racontes aux enfants/English

★ **Volcanoes**; journey to the crater's edge. photographs by Philippe Bourseiller; adapted by Robert Burleigh; text by Helene Montardre; drawings by David Giraudon. H.N. Abrams 2003 75p il map $14.95

Grades: 4 5 6 7   **551.2**

1. Volcanoes

ISBN 0-8109-4590-8

LC 2003-971

Over thirty photographs and accompanying text reveal the facts about the world's volcanoes

"Photographer Bourseiller takes young readers to the crater's edge with truly spectacular full-color photographs. . . . The book does an excellent job of documenting the effect of volcanoes on the lives of those who live close to them, and small watercolor paintings further enliven the sense of human history." Booklist

Winchester, Simon

The **day** the world exploded; the earthshaking catastrophe at Krakatoa. adaptation by Dwight Jon Zimmerman; illustrated by Jason Chin. Collins 2008 96p il map $22.99; lib bdg $23.89

Grades: 5 6 7 8   **551.2**

1. Volcanoes

ISBN 978-0-06-123982-3; 0-06-123982-8; 978-0-06-123983-0 lib bdg; 0-06-123983-6 lib bdg

Adapted from: Krakatoa: the day the world exploded, August 27, 1883, published 2003 for adults

This presents an account of the catastrophic eruption off the coast of Java of the volcano-island of Krakatoa in 1883 and its effects

"Chin's full-color cartoon illustrations enhance the many archival and contemporary photographs, historical illustrations, and maps that accompany the text. . . . In addition to this work's educational and reference potential, it lends a human face to a natural disaster and will attract general readers as well." SLJ

Includes glossary and bibliographical references

551.3   Surface and exogenous processes and their agents

Glaciers, sea ice, and ice formation; edited by John P. Rafferty. Britannica Educational Pub. in association with Rosen Educational Services 2010 253p il map (Dynamic Earth) lib bdg $45

Grades: 6 7 8 9 10   **551.3**

1. Ice 2. Glaciers

ISBN 978-1-61530-119-5; 1-61530-119-4

LC 2010000226

This book "examines the dynamic processes of [glaciers, sea ice, and ice formation]. . . . [It] provides the reader with an understanding of basic processes, historical background,

and current phenomena. . . . [Recommended] for younger youth as well as high school youth." Voice Youth Advocates

Includes bibliographical references

Stille, Darlene R.

★ **Erosion**; how land forms, how it changes. by Darlene R. Stille. Compass Point Books 2005 48p il map (Exploring science) $25.27

Grades: 6 7 8 9   **551.3**

1. Erosion

ISBN 0-7565-0854-1

LC 2004-23077

Examines the dangers, causes, and control of erosion.

"A few maps and many clear, color photos illustrate the book." Booklist

Includes glossary and bibliographical references

551.4   Geomorphology and hydrosphere

Aleshire, Peter

Deserts. Chelsea House 2007 178p il map (The extreme Earth) $35

Grades: 8 9 10 11 12   **551.4**

1. Deserts

ISBN 978-0-8160-6434-2; 0-8160-6434-2

This describes desert locations, their plants and animals, their indigenous peoples, ecology, and history.

Mountains; foreword by Geoffrey H. Nash. Chelsea House Publishers 2008 144p il map (The extreme Earth) $35

Grades: 8 9 10 11 12   **551.4**

1. Mountains

ISBN 978-0-8160-5918-8; 0-8160-5918-7

LC 2007-20692

This describes how mountains were formed, how they have changed over the span of geologic time, and their contributions to the environment, and goes on to describe specific mountains and mountain ranges including Mount Everest, the Appalachians, the Alps, the Mid-Atlantic Ridge of North America, the Sierra Nevadas, the Andes, Mauna Kea in Hawaii, Mount Saint Helens, Mount Kilimanjaro, and Humphreys Peak, in the southwestern United States.

Includes bibliographical references

Berlatsky, Noah

Water and ice; Michael E. Mann, consulting editor. Greenhaven Press 2011 120p il map (Confronting global warming) lib bdg $37.10

Grades: 7 8 9 10 11   **551.4**

1. Ice 2. Glaciers 3. Greenhouse effect

ISBN 978-0-7377-4861-1; 0-7377-4861-3

LC 2010011348

"Presented in a scholarly design that will appeal to older readers. . . . The illustrations and pictures support the text, and the graphics and sidebars are well placed." Libr Media Connect

Includes glossary and bibliographical references

Hanson, Erik A.

Canyons; [by] Erik Hanson; foreword by Geoffrey H. Nash. Chelsea House 2007 206p il map (The extreme Earth) $35

Grades: 8 9 10 11 12   **551.4**

1. Canyons 2. Plate tectonics

ISBN 0-8160-6435-0; 978-0-8160-6435-9

LC 2006-15810

Profiles canyons around the world including the Grand Canyon, the Columbia River Gorge, Fish River Canyon, and Monterey Canyon; and describes how and when they were formed, how the landscape has changed over time, and the contribution of each to the environment.

"The story in this book may generate a longing within the reader to visit vistas and hike into canyons for an intimate view of earth history." Sci Books Films

Includes glossary and bibliographical references

Hanson, Jeanne K.

Caves; foreword by Geoffrey H. Nash. Chelsea House 2007 142p il map (The extreme Earth) $35

Grades: 8 9 10 11 12   **551.4**

1. Caves

ISBN 978-0-8160-5917-1; 0-8160-5917-9

LC 2006-11718

The describes types of caves and how they are formed, their exploration, and some specific caves including Mammoth Cave of Kentucky; the caves of Yucatan, Mexico; Lascaux Cave of southwestern France; Lubang Nasib Bagus and the Sarawak Chamber of Borneo, Malaysia; Kazumura Cave of Hawaii; Waitomo Cave of New Zealand; and Wind Cave of South Dakota.

Includes bibliographical references

Simon, Seymour

★ Mountains. Morrow Junior Bks. 1994 un il hardcover o.p. pa $6.99

Grades: 4 5 6 7   **551.4**

1. Mountains

ISBN 0-688-15477-8 pa

LC 93-11398

Introduces various mountain ranges, how they are formed and shaped, and how they affect vegetation and animals, including humans

"The striking color photographs work well with the clear text to illustrate key points and highlight the diversity among the Earth's mountain ranges." Horn Book Guide

551.46 Oceanography and submarine geology

Aleshire, Peter

Ocean ridges and trenches; foreword by Geoffrey H. Nash. Chelsea House 2007 148p il map (The extreme Earth) $35

Grades: 8 9 10 11 12   **551.46**

1. Ocean bottom 2. Marine ecology

ISBN 978-0-8160-5919-5; 0-8160-5919-5

LC 2006-32058

Provides information about the formation of ocean ridges and trenches. Includes ten examples of ridges and trenches from around the world.

Includes bibliographical references

Aronin, Miriam

Slammed by a tsunami! Bearport Pub. 2010 32p il map (Disaster survivors) lib bdg $25.27

Grades: 4 5 6 7   **551.46**

1. Tsunamis

ISBN 978-1-936087-48-8 lib bdg; 1-936087-48-0 lib bdg

LC 2009-34574

"Captivating photos and illustrations and sidebars present interesting facts or brief anecdotes. . . . [This] should be purchased for all school and public libraries as . . . [it gives] a new perspective on the topic." Libr Media Connect

Includes glossary and bibliographical references

Basher, Simon

Oceans; [making waves!] designed and created by Simon Basher; text written by Dan Green. Kingfisher 2012 128 p. ill. (paperback) $8.99; (hardcover) $14.99

Grades: 5 6 7 8   **551.46**

1. Oceanography 2. Marine ecology 3. Aquatic animals

"Following a brief introduction to oceans, the text employs an easy-to-navigate field guide like format, where facts and figures about ocean habitats, processes, and animals that live in various areas (e.g., shore, reef, deep water) face illustrations in manga style" Horn Book

"A rewarding wade, particularly for readers who think oceanography is a dry study." Booklist

Bodden, Valerie

To the ocean deep; by Valerie Bodden. Creative Education 2011 48 p. col. ill. (Great expeditions) (library) $34.25

Grades: 5 6 7 8   **551.46**

1. Ocean 2. Underwater exploration 3. Explorers -- Biography 4. Bathyscaphe -- History -- 20th century 5. Underwater exploration -- History -- 20th century

ISBN 1608180670; 9781608180677

LC 2010033416

This book by Valerie Bodden is part of the Great Expeditions series and looks at oceanic exploration expeditions. "Bodden includes brief biographies of major people involved in each expedition, interspersed with the text. There are also numerous photographs or reproductions of paintings and woodcuts from the time of the expeditions." (Library Media Connection)

Includes bibliographical references (p. 46-47) and index.

Burns, Loree Griffin

★ Tracking trash; flotsam, jetsam, and the science of ocean motion. Houghton Mifflin 2007 56p il map (Scientists in the field) $18

Grades: 5 6 7 8   **551.46**

1. Pollution 2. Ocean currents 3. Oceanographers 4.

Marine debris
ISBN 0-618-58131-6; 978-0-618-58131-3
LC 2006-11534

This book describes "Curt Ebbesmeyer's ongoing work. . . . The oceanographer has been tracing the surface currents of the seas via the movement of plastic rubbish that has escaped from broken cargo containers." (Bull Cent Child Books)

"The book profiles two oceanographers who devised experiments using computer-modeling programs of ocean surface current movement to predict the landfall of . . . drifting objects. . . . Spacious layout, exceptionally fine color photos, and handsome maps give this book an inviting look. . . . A unique and often fascinating book." Booklist

Includes glossary and bibliographical references

Carson, Rachel
The **sea** around us; [by] Rachel L. Carson; introduction by Ann H. Zwinger; afterword by Jeffrey S. Levinton. Oxford University Press 1989 xxvii, 250p hardcover o.p. pa $15.95
Grades: 8 9 10 11 12 Adult   551.46
1. Ocean
ISBN 0-19-506186-1; 0-19-506997-8 pa
LC 89-16333

First published 1951; revised edition published 1961; this is a reissue of the 1979 edition which added the introduction and afterword

Beginning with a description of how the earth acquired its oceans, the book covers such topics as how life began in the primeval sea, the hidden lands, the life discovered in the abyss by highly delicate sounding apparatus, currents and tides, the formation of volcanic islands, and mineral resources

Includes bibliographical references

Day, Trevor
Oceans; illustrations by Richard Garratt. rev ed; Facts on File 2008 318p il map (Ecosystem) $70
Grades: 8 9 10 11 12 Adult   551.46
1. Ocean 2. Oceanography 3. Marine biology
ISBN 0-8160-5932-2; 978-0-8160-5932-4
LC 2006-100769

First published 1999

This volume describes the oceans of the world with regard to their geography, geology, history, chemistry, biology, ecology, exploration, relationship to the atmosphere, economic resources, and management.

Includes glossary and bibliographical references

Desonie, Dana
Oceans; how we use the seas. Chelsea House 2007 215p il map (Our fragile planet) $35
Grades: 8 9 10 11 12   551.46
1. Ocean 2. Oceanography 3. Marine ecology
ISBN 978-0-8160-6216-4; 0-8160-6216-1
LC 2007-13560

An introduction to how life in our oceans works, and how we are threatening it with pollution and depletion of fisheries.

The author "offers a comprehensive, detailed introduction to ocean science and conservation in this amply illustrated volume." Booklist

Includes glossary and bibliographical references

Dwyer, Helen
Tsunamis! Marshall Cavendish Benchmark 2010 32p il map (Eyewitness disaster) lib bdg $28.50
Grades: 4 5 6   551.46
1. Tsunamis
ISBN 978-1-60870-005-9; 1-60870-005-4
LC 2010001801

Provides information about tsunamis through eyewitness accounts from survivors and rescue workers.

"Bold subheadings and color captions break information into readable chunks for the younger learner. Important vocabulary is in bold print. . . . An excellent addition to your science collection." Libr Media Connect

Includes glossary and bibliographical references

Fradin, Judith Bloom
★ **Tsunamis**; witness to disaster. [by] Judy & Dennis Fradin. National Geographic 2008 48p il map (Witness to disaster) $16.95; lib bdg $20.90
Grades: 4 5 6 7   551.46
1. Tsunamis
ISBN 978-0-7922-5380-8; 0-7922-5380-9; 978-0-7922-5381-5 lib bdg; 0-7922-5381-7 lib bdg
LC 2008010536

This "explores the science, history, and personal experience of tsunamis and shows kids what scientists are doing to develop early warning systems so we can survive such disasters in the future." Publisher's note

Includes glossary and bibliographical references

Kusky, Timothy M.
Tsunamis; giant waves from the sea. [by] Timothy Kusky. Facts on File 2008 134p il (The hazardous Earth) $39.50
Grades: 8 9 10 11 12   551.46
1. Tsunamis
ISBN 978-0-8160-6464-9; 0-8160-6464-4
LC 2007-23477

"This detailed study of the causes and physics of massive waves covers not only the oceanic sort but also similar phenomena, 'seiches,' that occur in closed bodies of water. . . . After analyzing tsunamis' various forms and behaviors, Kusky delivers harrowing accounts of over a dozen disasters, from those centuries past to the devastating Indian Ocean tsunami in 2004. He then closes with a discussion of early-warning systems. Occasional photos capture the devastation of which these waves are capable." Booklist

Includes bibliographical references

Lindop, Laurie
★ **Venturing** the deep sea. Twenty-First Century Books 2006 80p il map (Science on the edge) lib bdg $27.93
Grades: 5 6 7 8   551.46
1. Ocean bottom 2. Underwater exploration 4. Marine

ecology 5. Submarine topography
ISBN 0-7613-2701-0

LC 2004-29729

"The science is intriguing here. . . . The photos of undersea projects, creatures, weird cave and underwater tube formations are all intriguing." Voice Youth Advocates

Includes bibliographical references

Mallory, Kenneth

Adventure beneath the sea; living in an underwater science station. [photographs by Brian Skerry] Boyds Mills Press 2010 48p il map $18.95

Grades: 4 5 6 7   **551.46**
1. Underwater exploration
ISBN 978-1-59078-607-9; 1-59078-607-6

The author "invites readers to squeeze into Aquarius, a venerable science-station habitat resting on the sea floor at a depth of 60 feet in the Florida Keys. The readable text explains the complexities of training for a weeklong stay, the aims of the scientists on the team, and what it is like to spend 24/7 in squashed companionship in a 43' × 9' cylinder as part of a crew of seven. . . . Sidebars contain interesting information. . . . Full-color photos abound." SLJ

Includes glossary and bibliographical references

★ **Diving** to a deep-sea volcano. Houghton Mifflin Company 2006 60p il map (Scientists in the field) $17

Grades: 5 6 7 8   **551.46**
1. Ocean bottom 2. Marine biology 3. Underwater exploration 4. Deep diving 5. Oceanographic submersibles
ISBN 978-0-618-33205-2; 0-618-33205-7

LC 2005-25449

This describes the exploration by marine biologist Rich Lutz and his crew of deep sea hydrothermal vents and the creatures that survive there.

"The profile of an enthusiastic scientist injects excitement into even unassuming facts." Booklist

Includes glossary and bibliographical references

Matsen, Bradford

The **incredible** record-setting deep-sea dive of the bathysphere; [by] Brad Matsen. Enslow Pubs. 2003 48p il map (Incredible deep-sea adventures) lib bdg $18.95

Grades: 4 5 6 7   **551.46**
1. Authors 2. Inventors 3. Naturalists 4. Ocean bottom 5. Underwater exploration 6. Memoirists 7. Writers on nature 8. Writers on science 9. Hydrothermal vents
ISBN 0-7660-2188-2

LC 2002-13822

Describes the 1934 dive of a bathysphere, or "sphere of the deep," in which two explorers, William Beebe and Otis Barton, set the world depth record and saw mysterious creatures of the deep ocean

"Attractive color photos contribute to the content." SLJ
Includes glossary and bibliographical references

McMillan, Beverly

Oceans; [by] Beverly McMillan and John N. Musick. Simon & Schuster Books for Young Readers 2007 64p il map (Insiders) $16.99

Grades: 4 5 6 7   **551.46**
1. Ocean 2. Marine biology 3. Marine ecology
ISBN 978-1-4169-3859-0; 1-4169-3859-1

LC 2007-61730

This book will "assault the reader with vibrant colors and eye-popping graphics. The illustrations range in size from full-page background art to thumbnails. Even the smallest pictures are clear, with easy to distinguish details; all are either labeled or captioned. . . . You may want to purchase more than one copy." Libr Media Connect

Includes glossary

Oceans; Lauri S. Friedman, book editor. Greenhaven Press 2011 143p (Introducing issues with opposing viewpoints) $36.82

Grades: 7 8 9 10   **551.46**
1. Ocean 2. Marine pollution
ISBN 978-0-7377-5200-7; 0-7377-5200-9

LC 2011005910

This is an "excellent [resource] both for student research and for personal interest. . . . Oceans deals with dangers to the oceans and sea life, ranging from climate change, overfishing, fish farming, and ocean drilling to even noise pollution." Booklist

Includes bibliographical references

Rizzo, Johnna

Oceans; dolphins, sharks, penguins, and more!: meet 60 cool sea creatures and explore their amazing watery world. introduction by Sylvia A. Earle. National Geographic 2010 64p il $14.95; lib bdg $24.90

Grades: 4 5 6   **551.46**
1. Ocean 2. Marine animals 3. Marine biology
ISBN 978-1-4263-0686-0; 1-4263-0686-5; 978-1-4263-0724-9 lib bdg; 1-4263-0724-1 lib bdg

"A colorful olio of marine animals in eye-catching photos accompanies a cheerful conversational text. . . . Information boxes pop up all over the place as well, but it is the bright photos that steal the show. . . . This splashy volume is a nice introduction to a salty water-world." SLJ

Includes glossary

Simon, Seymour

Seymour Simon's extreme oceans; Seymour Simon. Chronicle Books 2013 60 p. col. ill. (reinforced) $17.99

Grades: 4 5 6   **551.46**
1. Ocean
ISBN 1452108331; 9781452108339

LC 2012012590

In this work of children's nonfiction, author "[Seymour] Simon examines the things that are 'most,' pertaining to oceans: the tallest sea mounts, the largest waves, the highest tides in the world, the most dangerous and largest animals, the coldest and warmest waters, the biggest storms and tsunamis, and the longest journeys, as well as a closing chapter predicting scenarios if sea levels continue to rise." (School Library Journal)

Yount, Lisa

Modern marine science; exploring the deep. Chelsea House 2006 204p il map (Milestones in discovery and invention) $35
Grades: 7 8 9 10 11 12   **551.46**
1. Marine sciences
ISBN 0-8160-5747-8
LC 2005-30562

This book "profiles 12 men and women who led the way into the oceans' deepest waters through research and new technologies. From Charles Darwin to Henry Stommel to Robert Ballard, this volume explores the lives and accomplishments of these scientific revolutionaries." Publisher's note

Includes glossary and bibliographical references

551.48   Hydrology

Burnham, Laurie

Rivers; foreword by Geoffrey H. Nash. Chelsea House 2007 176p il map (The extreme Earth) $35
Grades: 8 9 10 11 12   **551.48**
1. Rivers
ISBN 0-8160-5916-0; 978-0-8160-5916-4
LC 2006-31302

This is a "portrait of 10 of the most unusual rivers that examines what was on-site before the river, how it was formed, how and why it has changed over time, and its contributions to the environment." Publisher's note

Includes glossary and bibliographical references

Carrigan, Patricia

Waterfalls. Chelsea House 2007 146p il (The extreme Earth) $35
Grades: 8 9 10 11 12   **551.48**
1. Waterfalls
ISBN 978-0-8160-6436-6; 0-8160-6436-9

Presents an introduction to waterfalls, describing how they develop and how they are used to generate power, and providing the history and current formation of ten of the world's most famous waterfalls

Desonie, Dana

Hydrosphere; freshwater systems and pollution. Chelsea House 2008 194p il map (Our fragile planet) $35
Grades: 7 8 9 10   **551.48**
1. Water pollution 2. Water purification 3. Fresh water
ISBN 978-0-8160-6215-7; 0-8160-6215-3
LC 2007-22398

"Looks at the environmental and health effects of water pollution." Publisher's note

Includes glossary and bibliographical references

Dwyer, Helen

Floods! Marshall Cavendish Benchmark 2010 32p il map (Eyewitness Disaster) lib bdg $28.50

Grades: 4 5 6   **551.48**
1. Floods
ISBN 978-1-60870-002-8; 1-60870-002-X

Provides information about floods through eyewitness accounts from survivors and rescue workers.

"Bold subheadings and color captions break information into readable chunks for the younger learner. Important vocabulary is in bold print. . . . An excellent addition to your science collection." Libr Media Connect

Includes glossary and bibliographical references

Gardner, Robert

Water; green science projects for a sustainable planet. Enslow Publishers 2011 128p il (Team Green science projects) lib bdg $31.93
Grades: 6 7 8 9 10   **551.48**
1. Water 2. Science projects 3. Science -- Experiments
ISBN 978-0-7660-3645-1; 0-7660-3645-6
LC 2009-37902

This book offers science experiments that explain the properties of water, the water cycle, and how you can conserve water.

"Gardner provides plenty of information, well-designed experiments, and demonstrations, and then shares brief science-fair ideas. . . . Experiments and demonstrations are presented with clear step-by-step instructions and occasional illustrations and represent a wide range of complexity." SLJ

Includes glossary and bibliographical references

Hanson, Jeanne K.

Lakes; foreword, Geoffrey H. Nash. Facts on File 2007 146p il map (The extreme Earth) $35
Grades: 8 9 10 11 12   **551.48**
1. Lakes
ISBN 978-0-8160-5914-0; 0-8160-5914-4
LC 2005-34327

This describes how lakes are formed, the current environmental health of the lakes and their future prognosis, and some specific bodies of water including the Caspian Sea in the Middle East, the Aral Sea in Western Asia, Lake Superior in North America, Lake Baikal in Central Asia, and Lake Titicaca in South America.

Includes bibliographical references

551.5   Meteorology

Banqueri, Eduardo

Weather. Enchanted Lion Books 2006 33p il (Field guides) $16.95
Grades: 4 5 6 7   **551.5**
1. Weather
ISBN 1-59270-059-4
LC 2006-42864

This "book is filled with information about all aspects of weather, from why there are seasons to predicting the weather. Complementing the scientifically accurate text is an excellent mix of drawings and photographs." Sci Books and Films

Carson, Mary Kay

Weather projects for young scientists; experiments and science fair ideas. Chicago Review Press 2007 134p il $14.95

Grades: 4 5 6 7   **551.5**

1. Weather 2. Science -- Experiments 3. Science projects

ISBN 978-1-55652-629-9; 1-55652-629-6

LC 2006-16430

This "presents difficult concepts in a very concrete, basic manner." Sci Books Films

Cosgrove, Brian

Weather; written by Brian Cosgrove. rev ed; DK Publishing 2007 72p il map (DK eyewitness books) $15.99; lib bdg $19.99

Grades: 4 5 6 7   **551.5**

1. Climate 2. Weather 3. Atmosphere 4. Climatology

ISBN 978-0-7566-3006-5; 0-7566-3006-1; 978-0-7566-0737-1 lib bdg; 0-7566-0737-X lib bdg

LC 2007-281112

First published 1991 by Knopf

"Discover the world's weather—from heat waves and droughts to blizzards and floods"—Cover. Includes discussion of why the climate may change in the future.

"Accompanying the book are a poster, additional images on CD-ROM, and a useful glossary. Altogether, this book and its supplements are well crafted to motivate young learners about the importance of weather, to deepen their conceptual understanding of it, and to pique their interest in participating in its study." Sci Books Films

Includes glossary

DeLallo, Laura

Hammered by a heat wave! consultants, Daphne Thompson, Keith C. Heidorn. Bearport Pub. 2010 32p il map (Disaster survivors) lib bdg $25.27

Grades: 4 5 6 7   **551.5**

1. Meteorology

ISBN 978-1-936087-51-8 lib bdg; 1-936087-51-0 lib bdg

"Captivating photos and illustrations and sidebars present interesting facts or brief anecdotes. . . . [This] should be purchased for all school and public libraries as . . . [it gives] a new perspective on the topic." Libr Media Connect

Includes glossary and bibliographical references

Gaffney, Timothy R.

Storm scientist; careers chasing severe weather. Enslow Publishers 2009 112p il (Wild science careers) lib bdg $31.93

Grades: 5 6 7 8   **551.5**

1. Weather 2. Meteorology 3. Vocational guidance

ISBN 978-0-7660-3050-3 lib bdg; 0-7660-3050-4 lib bdg

"The day-today experiences along with the educational requirements are included in the clear, easy-to-read [text]. . . . Full-color photographs show the scientists in action." SLJ

Includes glossary and bibliographical references

Gardner, Robert

Ace your weather science project; great science fair ideas. [by] Robert Gardner and Salvatore Tocci. Enslow Publishers 2009 104p il (Ace your physics science project) lib bdg $31.93

Grades: 5 6 7 8   **551.5**

1. Weather 2. Science projects 3. Science -- Experiments

ISBN 978-0-7660-3223-1 lib bdg; 0-7660-3223-X lib bdg

LC 2008-49779

"Presents several science experiments and project ideas about weather." Publisher's note

Includes bibliographical references

Easy genius science projects with weather; great experiments and ideas. Enslow Publishers 2009 128p il (Easy genius science projects) lib bdg $31.93

Grades: 5 6 7 8   **551.5**

1. Weather 2. Science projects 3. Science -- Experiments

ISBN 978-0-7660-2924-8 lib bdg; 0-7660-2924-7 lib bdg

LC 2008-23972

"Science experiments and science project ideas about weather." Publisher's note

Includes glossary and bibliographical references

Meteorology projects with a weather station you can build; by Robert Gardner. Enslow Publishers 2008 128p il (Build-a-lab! science experiments) lib bdg $31.93

Grades: 6 7 8 9   **551.5**

1. Meteorology 2. Science projects 3. Weather forecasting 4. Science -- Experiments

ISBN 978-0-7660-2807-4 lib bdg; 0-7660-2807-0 lib bdg

LC 2007010614

This describes science experiments and projects on such topics as wind, temperature, rain, clouds, climate and other aspects of weather.

Includes bibliographical references

Streissguth, Thomas

Extreme weather; [by] Tom Streissguth; Michael E. Mann, consulting editor. Greenhaven Press/Gale, Cengage Learning 2011 116p il map (Confronting global warming) lib bdg $37.10

Grades: 7 8 9 10 11 12   **551.5**

1. Weather 2. Climate -- Environmental aspects

ISBN 978-0-7377-4859-8; 0-7377-4859-1

LC 2010-24973

"Presented in a scholarly design that will appeal to older readers. . . . The illustrations and pictures support the text, and the graphics and sidebars are well placed." Libr Media Connect

Includes glossary and bibliographical references

Vogt, Gregory
The **atmosphere**; planetary heat engine. by Gregory L. Vogt. Twenty-First Century Books 2007 80p il map (Earth spheres) lib bdg $29.27
Grades: 6 7 8 9   **551.5**
  1. Weather 2. Atmosphere
  ISBN 978-0-76132-841-4 lib bdg; 0-76132-841-6 lib bdg
                  LC 2006-07391
"The book covers a wide range of topics, including air currents, the water cycle, . . . meteorology, and climate change, and explores how they affect our daily lives. A good deal of discussion is devoted to scientists' use of satellites and other high-tech tools to study the atmosphere. Color graphs, photographs, and sidebars . . . supplement the accessible text." Booklist
Includes bibliographical references

551.51   Composition, regions, dynamics of atmosphere

Gallant, Roy A.
Atmosphere; sea of air. Benchmark Bks. 2002 79p il (Earthworks) lib bdg $19.95
Grades: 5 6 7 8   **551.51**
  1. Atmosphere 2. Meteorology
  ISBN 0-7614-1366-9
                  LC 2001-43301
Describes the atmosphere which makes life on earth possible, explores its effects on weather and climate, and examines what causes air pollution and what can be done it
"Gallant's prose is nearly conversational in its easy delivery, but his facts are always thorough and his ideas clearly explained. . . . Crisp graphs, maps, and excellent color photos illustrate [this] fine [volume]." Booklist
Includes glossary and bibliographical references

551.55   Atmospheric disturbances and formations

Aronin, Miriam
Mangled by a hurricane! consultant, James L. Franklin. Bearport Pub. 2010 32p il map (Disaster survivors) lib bdg $25.27
Grades: 4 5 6 7   **551.55**
  1. Hurricanes 2. Hurricane Katrina, 2005
  ISBN 978-1-936087-49-5 lib bdg; 1-936087-49-9 lib bdg
"Captivating photos and illustrations and sidebars present interesting facts or brief anecdotes. . . . [This] should be purchased for all school and public libraries as . . . [it gives] a new perspective on the topic." Libr Media Connect
Includes glossary and bibliographical references

Carson, Mary Kay
  ★ **Inside** hurricanes. Sterling 2010 48p il map (Inside) $16.95; pa $9.95

Grades: 5 6 7 8   **551.55**
  1. Hurricanes
  ISBN 978-1-4027-5880-5; 1-4027-5880-4; 978-1-4027-7780-6 pa; 1-4027-7780-9 pa
"This trip into the eye of the storm is enveloping in more ways than one. . . . The pages fold up, or down, or left, or right, with every turn guided by an icon familiar to anyone who lives in a storm zone: a circular blue 'Hurricane Evacuation Route' road sign. This constant motion can't help but engage. . . . The design and layout is well above par, featuring excellent cutaways of storm systems, meteorological maps, thrilling photography, and a spectacular foldout Saffir-Simpson Hurricane Scale. The text is packed with info, data, and case studies broken into digestible chunks, and boxes and sidebars . . . make this . . . very appealing." Booklist

  ★ **Inside** tornadoes. Sterling 2010 48p il map (Inside) $16.95; pa $9.95
Grades: 5 6 7 8   **551.55**
  1. Tornadoes
  ISBN 978-1-4027-5879-9; 1-4027-5879-0; 978-1-4027-7781-3 pa; 1-4027-7781-7 pa
"This visually tempting title defines and explains the storms people call twisters, gives examples of four particularly devastating ones in this country, describes tornado watchers at work, offers hands-on activity and suggests precautions for tornado safety. . . . It includes step-by-step explanatory text, striking images and helpful graphics." Kirkus
Includes glossary and bibliographical references

Ceban, Bonnie J.
Tornadoes; disaster & survival. [by] Bonnie J. Ceban. Enslow Publishers 2005 48p il map (Deadly disasters) lib bdg $23.93
Grades: 4 5 6 7   **551.55**
  1. Tornadoes
  ISBN 0-7660-2383-4
                  LC 2004-11700
This explores the causes of tornadoes, how people survive these storms, and how they are predicted
Includes glossary and bibliographical references

Challoner, Jack
Hurricane & tornado; written by Jack Challoner. rev ed.; DK Pub. 2004 72p il map (DK eyewitness books) $15.99; lib bdg $19.99
Grades: 4 5 6 7   **551.55**
  1. Storms 2. Weather 3. Natural disasters
  ISBN 0-7566-0690-X; 0-7566-0689-6 lib bdg
                  LC 2004302408
First published 2000
Describes dangerous and destructive weather conditions around the world, such as thunderstorms, tornadoes, hurricanes, lightning, hail, and drought with photographs, historical background, and legends.

Fleisher, Paul
Lightning, hurricanes, and blizzards; the science of storms. Lerner Publications 2011 48p il (Weatherwise) lib bdg $29.27

Grades: 4 5 6 7   **551.55**
1. Blizzards 2. Lightning 3. Hurricanes
ISBN 978-0-8225-7536-8; 0-8225-7536-1
         LC 2009044918

This describes how storms form, where they strike, and what makes them so powerful.

"Chapters are well-organized and contain clear explanations. The crisp layout contains plenty of captioned photos and diagrams, as well as sidebars that feature interesting facts and suggestions for observations readers can record in their backyards." Horn Book Guide

Includes glossary and bibliographical references

Fradin, Dennis Brindell

Tornado! the story behind these twisting, turning, spinning, and spiraling storms. by Judith Bloom Fradin & Dennis Brindell Fradin. National Geographic 2011 63p il map (National Geographic kids) $16.95; lib bdg $26.90

Grades: 4 5 6 7   **551.55**
1. Tornadoes
ISBN 978-1-4263-0779-9; 1-4263-0779-9; 978-1-4263-0780-5 lib bdg; 1-4263-0780-2 lib bdg
         LC 2010042813

"Two of the four chapters describe deadly twisters in the U.S., while the others discuss the science and predictability of tornadoes. Throughout, there are first-person accounts. . . . Excellent color photos make this book a magnet for browsers, while the informative text and diagrams bring meaning to the images and provide content that students will find helpful for reports." Booklist

Includes glossary and bibliographical references

Fradin, Judith Bloom

★ **Hurricanes**; by Judy and Dennis Fradin. National Geographic 2007 48p il (Witness to disaster) $16.95; lib bdg $26.90

Grades: 4 5 6 7   **551.55**
1. Hurricanes
ISBN 978-1-4262-0111-0; 1-4262-0111-7; 978-1-4262-0112-7 lib bdg; 1-4262-0112-5 lib bdg
         LC 2006-103003

This describes Hurricane Katrina, the science of hurricanes, some hurricanes of the past, and the prediction of hurricanes.

This offers "dramatic first-person quotes and an array of impressive photographs." Horn Book Guide

Includes glossary and bibliographical references

Harris, Caroline

Wild weather. Kingfisher 2005 53p il map (Kingfisher voyages) $14.95

Grades: 4 5 6 7   **551.55**
1. Storms 2. Weather
ISBN 0-7534-5931-0; 978-0-7534-5911-9

This describes weather phenomena such as monsoons, tsunamis, blizzards, tornadoes, cyclones, mirages, and El Niño.

This "book has bright and exciting pictures. . . . The organization . . . is great, and the text is easy to read." Sci Books Films

Includes glossary

Longshore, David

Encyclopedia of hurricanes, typhoons, and cyclones; New ed; Facts on File 2008 468p il map (Facts on File science library) $75

Grades: 8 9 10 11 12 Adult   **551.55**
1. Storms 2. Cyclones 3. Typhoons 4. Hurricanes 5. Reference books 6. Cyclones -- Encyclopedias 7. Typhoons -- Encyclopedias 8. Hurricanes -- Encyclopedias
ISBN 978-0-8160-6295-9; 0-8160-6295-1
         LC 2007-32336

First published 1998

This encyclopedia describes named hurricanes, typhoons and cyclones, explains meteorological terms and instruments, and includes biographical data, a chronology, and a list of hurricane safety procedures.

"This is an excellent basic reference work that belongs in all school, public, and academic libraries." Sci Books Films

Includes bibliographical references

Markovics, Joyce L.

Blitzed by a blizzard! by Joyce Markovics; consultant, Daphne Thompson. Bearport Pub. 2010 32p il map (Disaster survivors) lib bdg $25.27

Grades: 4 5 6 7   **551.55**
1. Blizzards
ISBN 978-1-936087-54-9 lib bdg; 1-936087-54-5 lib bdg
         LC 2009-36960

"Captivating photos and illustrations and sidebars present interesting facts or brief anecdotes. . . . [This] should be purchased for all school and public libraries as . . . [it gives] a new perspective on the topic." Libr Media Connect

Includes glossary and bibliographical references

Prokos, Anna

Tornadoes; by Anna Prokos. Gareth Stevens Pub. 2009 48p il map (The ultimate 10. Natural disasters) lib bdg $31

Grades: 5 6 7 8   **551.55**
1. Tornadoes
ISBN 978-0-8368-9153-9 lib bdg; 0-8368-9153-8 lib bdg
         LC 2008-18949

Tornadoes "are described, while color photos illustrate the resulting damage, conveying a significant part of the information through their captions. . . . Explanations of weather terms . . . are included; additional facts are boxed off from the text; and preparation/safety tips are appended. . . . An especially useful book." SLJ

Includes glossary and bibliographical references

Royston, Angela

Hurricanes! Marshall Cavendish Benchmark 2010 32p il map (Eyewitness disaster) lib bdg $28.50

Grades: 4 5 6   **551.55**
1. Hurricanes
ISBN 978-1-60870-003-5; 1-60870-003-8
         LC 2010001800

Provides information about hurricanes through eyewitness accounts from survivors and rescue workers.

"Bold subheadings and color captions break information into readable chunks for the younger learner. Important vocabulary is in bold print. . . . An excellent addition to your science collection." Libr Media Connect

Includes glossary and bibliographical references

Storms! Marshall Cavendish Benchmark 2010 32p il map (Eyewitness disaster) lib bdg $28.50

Grades: 4 5 6   **551.55**
1. Storms
ISBN 978-1-60870-004-2; 1-60870-004-6
LC 2009041697

Provides information about storms through eyewitness accounts from survivors and rescue workers.

"Bold subheadings and color captions break information into readable chunks for the younger learner. Important vocabulary is in bold print. . . . An excellent addition to your science collection." Libr Media Connect

Includes glossary and bibliographical references

Rudolph, Jessica
Erased by a tornado! Bearport Pub. 2010 32p il map (Disaster survivors) lib bdg $25.27

Grades: 4 5 6 7   **551.55**
1. Tornadoes
ISBN 978-1-936087-52-5 lib bdg; 1-936087-52-9 lib bdg
LC 2009-34363

"Captivating photos and illustrations and sidebars present interesting facts or brief anecdotes. . . . [This] should be purchased for all school and public libraries as . . . [it gives] a new perspective on the topic." Libr Media Connect

Includes glossary and bibliographical references

Ryback, Carol
Hurricanes; by Carol Ryback and Jayne Keedle. Gareth Stevens Pub. 2009 48p il map (The ultimate 10. Natural disasters) lib bdg $31

Grades: 5 6 7 8   **551.55**
1. Hurricanes
ISBN 978-0-8368-9152-2 lib bdg; 0-8368-9152-X lib bdg
LC 2008-24628

Hurricanes "are described, while color photos illustrate the resulting damage, conveying a significant part of the information through their captions. . . . Explanations of weather terms . . . are included; additional facts are boxed off from the text; and preparation/safety tips are appended. . . . An especially useful book." SLJ

Includes glossary and bibliographical references

Silverstein, Alvin
Hurricanes; the science behind killer storms. [by] Alvin Silverstein, Virginia Silverstein, and Laura Silverstein Nunn. Enslow Publishers 2009 48p il map (The science behind natural disasters) lib bdg $23.93

Grades: 4 5 6   **551.55**
1. Hurricanes
ISBN 978-0-7660-2971-2 lib bdg; 0-7660-2971-9 lib bdg
LC 2008-26264

"Scientific explanations are accompanied by plentiful color diagrams that will help students to grasp causes and effects. . . . Photos . . . are effective, and are sometimes turned into helpful, lively diagrams by the addition of such features as wind-direction arrows." SLJ

Includes glossary and bibliographical references

Tornadoes; the science behind terrible twisters. [by] Alvin Silverstein, Virginia Silverstein, and Laura Silverstein Nunn. Enslow Publishers 2009 48p il map (The science behind natural disasters) lib bdg $23.93

Grades: 4 5 6   **551.55**
1. Tornadoes
ISBN 978-0-7660-2976-7 lib bdg; 0-7660-2976-X lib bdg
LC 2008-29635

"Scientific explanations are accompanied by plentiful color diagrams that will help students to grasp causes and effects. . . . Photos . . . are effective, and are sometimes turned into helpful, lively diagrams by the addition of such features as wind-direction arrows." SLJ

Includes glossary and bibliographical references

Simon, Seymour
★ **Tornadoes.** Morrow Junior Bks. 1999 un il map hardcover o.p. pa $6.99

Grades: 4 5 6 7   **551.55**
1. Tornadoes
ISBN 0-688-14646-5; 0-06-443791-4 pa
LC 98-27953

Describes the location, nature, development, measurement, and destructive effects of tornadoes, as well as how to stay out of danger from them

"Incredible full-color photographs and diagrams, clearly portraying the different formations and devastating power of the windstorms, complement the text perfectly." Booklist

Stewart, Mark
Blizzards and winter storms. Gareth Stevens Pub. 2009 48p il map (The ultimate 10. Natural disasters) lib bdg $31

Grades: 5 6 7 8   **551.55**
1. Storms 2. Blizzards
ISBN 978-0-8368-9150-8 lib bdg; 0-8368-9150-3 lib bdg
LC 2008-28230

Blizzards and winter storms "are described, while color photos illustrate the resulting damage, conveying a significant part of the information through their captions. . . . An especially useful book." SLJ

Includes glossary and bibliographical references

Treaster, Joseph B.

★ **Hurricane** force; in the path of America's deadliest storms. Kingfisher 2007 128p il map $16.95

Grades: 4 5 6 7 8   **551.55**

   1. Storms 2. Hurricanes

   ISBN 978-0-7534-6086-3

                                LC 2006-22517

Describes how violent storms and hurricanes are formed and notes some of history's greatest storms to hit the U.S. such as Hurricane Katrina.

This is a "gripping photo-essay. . . . There are lots of full-color photographs that bring close the high winds and surging seas of hurricanes, the shattered homes, and pictures of people rescued or lost. The extensive back matter is an integral part of the book." Booklist

Includes bibliographical references

551.56   Atmospheric electricity and optics

Person, Stephen

   Struck by lightning! Bearport Pub. 2010 32p il map (Disaster survivors) lib bdg $25.27

Grades: 4 5 6 7   **551.56**

   1. Lightning

   ISBN 978-1-936087-47-1 lib bdg; 1-936087-47-2 lib bdg

"Introduces lightning, discussing how it is formed and where it tends to strike, and describing some of the experiences of survivors who have been hit by lightning." Publisher's note

Includes glossary and bibliographical references

Simon, Seymour

   ★ **Lightning**. Morrow Junior Bks. 1997 un il hardcover o.p. pa $6.99

Grades: 4 5 6 7   **551.56**

   1. Lightning

   ISBN 0-688-14638-4; 0-06-088435-5 pa

                                  LC 96-16962

Photographs and text explore the natural phenomenon of lightning

"The subject is exciting, the information is amazing, and the full-color photographs are riveting. . . . Simon's explanations are concise but thorough." Booklist

Stewart, Melissa

   ★ **Inside** lightning; illustrations by Cynthia Shaw. Sterling 2011 48p il (Inside . . .) $16.95

Grades: 5 6 7 8   **551.56**

   1. Lightning

   ISBN 978-1-4027-5878-2; 1-4027-5878-2

This book about lightning "explores its topic in an engaging way, and the many illustrations work well with adjacent text and captions. . . . The [book's] varied page layouts and attractive and the quality of photos, computer-generated images, original illustrations, and charts is . . . excellent. . . . Featuring a step-by-step, illustrated explanation of lightning formation as well as comments from people who have had close encounters with the phenomenon, Inside Lightning

provides a vivid and unusually informative introduction to the subject." Booklist

Includes bibliographical references

551.6   Climatology and weather

Arnold, Caroline

   El Nino; stormy weather for people and wildlife. by Caroline Arnold. Clarion Bks 1998 48 p. col. ill. (reinforced) $16.00; (paperback) $5.95

Grades: 4 5 6 7   **551.6**

   1. Climate 2. El Niño Current 3. Climatic changes

   ISBN 0395776023; 0618551107; 9780618551101

                                  LC 98004826

In this book, Caroline Arnold "explains how the warm current along the Peruvian coast can have a devastating impact on weather across the globe. Photographs of locations from California to Botswana to India document the effects on animals and plants and the increase in floods and hurricanes. Diagrams illustrate El Niño's formation, and a chart shows the recurring pattern in the past half century as well as the occurrence of its 'twin,' La Niña." (School Library Journal)

Includes bibliographical references (p. 45) and index.

Bailey, Gerry

   Changing climate. Gareth Stevens Pub. 2011 48p il map (Planet SOS) lib bdg $31.95; pa $14.05

Grades: 4 5 6   **551.6**

   1. Climate -- Environmental aspects

   ISBN 978-1-4339-4962-3 lib bdg; 1-4339-4962-8 lib bdg; 978-1-4339-4963-0 pa; 1-4339-4963-6 pa

                                  LC 2010032885

This "well-designed [book presents changing climate] . . . and how [it affects] human beings. With information about water supplies and melting ice and their impact on ecosystems, the discussion . . . of global water levels is especially enlightening. . . . The many large, colorful photos will engage readers and assist them in understanding the important concepts introduced." SLJ

Includes glossary

Baker, Stuart

   In temperate zones. Marshall Cavendish Benchmark 2009 32p il map (Climate change) lib bdg $19.95

Grades: 5 6 7 8   **551.6**

   1. Forest ecology 2. Greenhouse effect

   ISBN 978-0-7614-4441-1 lib bdg; 0-7614-4441-6 lib bdg

                                  LC 2009-5769

The book about climate change in the temperate zones "is perfectly organized for students. . . . Unique layout features serve as signposts and will help focus readers' attention. . . . [The book] features an outstanding chart of possible effects of global warming on the area in question, listing 'Possible Event', 'Predicted Result', and 'Impact' in short, bulleted statements." SLJ

Includes glossary

Christie, Peter

The **curse** of Akkad; climate upheavals that rocked human history. Annick Press 2008 144p il map $19.95; pa $11.95

Grades: 6 7 8 9   **551.6**

1. Climate 2. World history 3. Science and civilization 4. Climatic changes -- History

ISBN 978-1-55451-119-8; 1-55451-119-4; 978-1-55451-118-1 pa; 1-55451-118-6 pa

"Christie discusses the ways in which environmental conditions have shaped human history. The chapters, each discussing a different aspect of climate change, are arranged in loose chronological order. Every section opens with a fictionalized account featuring either an imagined or a real historical figure. The author then explains how climate change caused the events to occur. . . . The book is well researched. . . . The text is readable." SLJ

Includes bibliographical references

Desonie, Dana

Climate; causes and effects of climate change. Chelsea House 2008 199p il map (Our fragile planet) $35

Grades: 7 8 9 10   **551.6**

1. Greenhouse effect 2. Climate -- Environmental aspects

ISBN 978-0-8160-6214-0; 0-8160-6214-5

LC 2007-27825

"Discusses how human-related activities are contributing to the warming of the Earth's climate, describes the effects of climate change on people and the environment, and outlines measures that can be taken to help manage the problem." Publisher's note

Includes glossary and bibliographical references

Evans, Bill

It's raining fish and spiders; by Bill Evans. Forge 2012 xiv, 223 p.p col. ill. (paperback) $18.99

Grades: 5 6 7 8   **551.6**

1. Extreme weather 2. Weather forecasting 3. Weather 4. Severe storms

ISBN 0765321327; 9780765321329

LC 2011278417

This book offers "information, lists, and accounts of personal experiences involving extreme weather by meteorologist and TV personality [Bill] Evans. Included are sections on tornadoes, hurricanes, and blizzards, with a good amount of information on each and . . . photos and diagrams sprinkled throughout." (Booklist)

Includes bibliographical references (p.221-222)

Flannery, Tim F.

★ **We** are the weather makers; the history of climate change. [by] Tim Flannery; adapted by Sally M. Walker. Candlewick Press 2009 303p il map $17.99

Grades: 7 8 9 10   **551.6**

1. Greenhouse effect 2. Climate -- Environmental aspects

ISBN 978-0-7636-3656-2; 0-7636-3656-8

LC 2008-939840

An adaptation of The weather makers, published 2005 for adults by Atlantic Monthly Press

"Arguing that climate change and global warming affect us all and that we can be part of the solution, this comprehensive look at the issue includes a clear explanation of the mechanism of the carbon cycle, the role of greenhouse gases on Earth, historical instances of climate change and their causes, descriptions of effects on a variety of habitats, future scenarios and suggestions—both personal and global—about what might be done. . . . A copy belongs in every middle and high-school library." Kirkus

Includes bibliographical references

Gardner, Robert

Weather science fair projects; revised and expanded using the scientific method. Enslow Publishers 2010 160p il (Earth science projects using the scientific method) lib bdg $34.60

Grades: 7 8 9 10   **551.6**

1. Weather 2. Science projects 3. Science -- Experiments

ISBN 978-0-7660-3424-2 lib bdg; 0-7660-3424-0 lib bdg

First published 2005 with title: Weather science fair projects using sunlight, rainbows, ice cubes, and more

"Explains how to use the scientific method to conduct several science experiments about weather. Includes ideas for science fair projects." Publisher's note

Includes bibliographical references

George, Charles

Climate change research; [by] Charles George and Linda George. ReferencePoint Press 2010 96p il (Inside science) lib bdg $26.95

Grades: 7 8 9 10 11 12   **551.6**

1. Climate -- Environmental aspects

ISBN 978-1-60152-128-6; 1-60152-128-6

LC 2009-53704

"This title examines the science behind climate change research in the following chapters: What is Climate Change?; Reading Climate Change in the Earth; Temperature and Precipitation; Climate Models; and Climate Technology of the Future." Publisher's note

Includes bibliographical references

Hartman, Eve

Climate change; [by] Eve Hartman and Wendy Meshbesher. Raintree 2010 48p il map (Sci-hi: Earth and space science) lib bdg $31.43; pa $8.99

Grades: 4 5 6 7   **551.6**

1. Greenhouse effect 2. Climate -- Environmental aspects

ISBN 978-1-4109-3352-2 lib bdg; 1-4109-3352-0 lib bdg; 978-1-4109-3362-1 pa; 1-4109-3362-8 pa

LC 2009-3538

Examine the causes of climate change, and how scientists gather data about global warming. Learn about the different ways people and nations are combating climate change, and how people and animals adapt to a new climate.

"Multiple colorful sidebars and large and small diagrams and photographs will help students to grasp the fundamentals being discussed, and the easy but interesting science experiments will act as further reinforcements." SLJ

Includes glossary and bibliographical references

Johnson, Rebecca L.

Investigating climate change; scientists' search for answers in a warming world. by Rebecca L. Johnson. Twenty-First Century Books 2008 111p il map (Discovery) lib bdg $30.60

Grades: 7 8 9 10   **551.6**

1. Greenhouse effect 2. Climate -- Environmental aspects

ISBN 978-0-8225-6792-9; 0-8225-6792-X

             LC 2007-38566

This "presents contemporary scientific research into the causes of climate change. . . . Johnson . . . lays out complex scientific data and theories in an engaging, straightforward narrative that will not overwhelm readers. Complementing the text are numerous color diagrams, graphs, maps, and photographs." Booklist

Includes bibliographical references

Nardo, Don

Climate change. Morgan Reynolds Pub. 2009 112p il (Extreme threats) lib bdg $28.95

Grades: 7 8 9 10   **551.6**

1. Greenhouse effect 2. Climate -- Environmental aspects

ISBN 978-1-59935-119-3; 1-59935-119-6

             LC 2009-25704

This book about climate change has "black-and-white and color photographs on almost every page. . . . Frequent sidebars, covering as much as a spread, discuss peripheral and often unusual information. The conclusion . . . explains what scientists are doing, or what they anticipate doing, to ameliorate the threat." SLJ

Includes glossary and bibliographical references

Parker, Steve, 1952-

Climate. QEB Pub. 2010 32p il (QEB changes in . . .) lib bdg $28.50

Grades: 3 4 5 6   **551.6**

1. Climate

ISBN 978-1-59566-776-2 lib bdg; 1-59566-776-8 lib bdg

             LC 2008-56068

"The information is presented in brief paragraphs and sidebars. Suggestions for kids to help improve the planet are sprinkled throughout. . . . Students will enjoy this appealing layout and the information can spark further research on the topic[s]. . . . Either digitally or on paper, students could make fantastic presentations using a similar design." Libr Media Connect

Includes glossary

Simpson, Kathleen

★ **Extreme** weather; science tackles global warming and climate change. by Kathleen Simpson; Jonathan D.W. Kahl, consultant. National Geographic 2008 64p il map (National Geographic investigates) $17.95; lib bdg $27.90

Grades: 4 5 6 7   **551.6**

1. Greenhouse effect 2. Weather 3. Climate -- Environmental aspects 4. Global warming

ISBN 978-1-4263-0359-3; 1-4263-0359-9; 978-1-4263-0281-7 lib bdg; 1-4263-0281-9 lib bdg

This "is a well-written and engaging book. . . . Excellent descriptions of how and why these various weather patterns occur are presented. The book includes dramatic photographs and clear diagrams." Sci Books Films

Includes glossary and bibliographical references

551.609   History, geographic treatment, biography

Christie, Peter

50 climate questions; a blizzard of blistering facts. Peter Christie; illustrated by Ross Kinnaird. Annick Press 2012 117 p. ill. (50 Questions) (paperback) $14.95; (hardcover) $22.95; (ebook) $10.99

Grades: 4 5 6 7   **551.609**

1. Climate 2. Climate change 3. Climate -- History

ISBN 155451374X; 9781554513741; 9781554513758; 9781554515165

This book by Peter Christie presents a "survey of the effects of climate through history and prehistory." (Kirkus Reviews)

"Topics include global warming's effect on the Arctic . . . and how a cooling climate 2.5 million years ago forced early humans to diversify their diets. Christie also provides insight into weather events throughout history -- for example, how weather change contributed to civil unrest that spawned the French Revolution." (Publishers Weekly)

551.63   Weather forecasting and forecasts, reporting and reports

Fleisher, Paul

Doppler radar, satellites, and computer models; the science of weather forecasting. Lerner Publications 2010 48p il map (Weatherwise) lib bdg $29.27

Grades: 4 5 6   **551.63**

1. Weather forecasting

ISBN 978-0-8225-7535-1; 0-8225-7535-3

             LC 2009-44919

This describes how scientists predict the weather, the tools and instruments that help them make forecasts, and how far in advance can they make good predictions.

"Chapters are well-organized and contain clear explanations. The crisp layout contains plenty of captioned photos and diagrams, as well as sidebars that feature interesting facts and suggestions for observations readers can record in their backyards." Horn Book Guide

Includes glossary and bibliographical references

551.7 Historical geology

Gallant, Roy A.

History; journey through time. Benchmark Bks. 2002 80p il (Earthworks) lib bdg $19.95

Grades: 5 6 7 8   **551.7**

1. Evolution 2. Stratigraphic geology
ISBN 0-7614-1367-7

LC 2001-43253

An overview of the history of the Earth, the life that evolved on it, and known periods of mass extinctions, from the planet's origin to the present

Includes glossary and bibliographical references

552 Petrology

Davis, Barbara J.

Minerals, rocks, and soil. Raintree 2010 48p il map (Sci-hi: Earth and space science) lib bdg $31.43; pa $8.99

Grades: 4 5 6 7   **552**

1. Rocks 2. Minerals 3. Petrology
ISBN 978-1-4109-3347-8 lib bdg; 1-4109-3347-4 lib bdg; 978-1-4109-3357-7 pa; 1-4109-3357-1 pa

LC 2009-13459

"Multiple colorful sidebars and large and small diagrams and photographs will help students to grasp the fundamentals being discussed, and the easy but interesting science experiments will act as further reinforcements." SLJ

Includes glossary and bibliographical references

Green, Dan

Rocks and minerals; a gem of a read! by Dan Green and Simon Basher; illustrated by Simon Basher. Kingfisher 2009 128p il pa $8.99

Grades: 5 6 7 8   **552**

1. Rocks 2. Minerals
ISBN 978-0-7534-6314-7 pa; 0-7534-6314-8 pa

This "presents a portrait gallery of 56 rocks and minerals (plus four kinds of fossils) composed of smiling, round-headed, usually peanut-shaped cartoon figures wearing or bearing distinctive identifiers. . . . The entries make light-hearted but unexpectedly meaty reading." Booklist

Hynes, Margaret

Rocks & fossils; foreword by Jack Horner. Kingfisher 2006 63p il (Kingfisher knowledge) $12.95

Grades: 5 6 7 8   **552**

1. Rocks 2. Fossils
ISBN 978-0-7534-5974-4; 0-7534-5974-4

LC 2005-23897

This is a "lavishly illustrated book. . . . The well-written text is pithy and comprehensible." Voice Youth Advocates

Includes glossary and bibliographical references

Rocks and minerals; facts at your fingertips. DK Pub. 2012 156 p. col. ill., map (Pocket genius) (hardcover) $7.99

Grades: 5 6 7 8   **552**

1. Rocks 2. Minerals
ISBN 0756692857; 9780756692858

LC 2011277725

This book, part of the "Pocket Genius" encyclopedia series, "profiles nearly 200 types of rocks and minerals from volcanic rocks and granite to sparkling diamonds and explosive sulfur, and tells what they are made of, how they are formed and what they are used for." It "offers a . . . catalog-style presentation, which clearly lays out individual subcategories." (Publisher's note)

Smithsonian Institution

Extreme rocks & minerals! Q & A. Collins 2007 47p il $17.99; pa $6.99

Grades: 4 5 6   **552**

1. Rocks 2. Minerals
ISBN 978-0-06-089982-0; 0-06-089982-4; 978-0-06-089981-3 pa; 0-06-089981-6 pa

LC 2007001760

This describes types of rocks and minerals, how they are formed, and how people use them.

"It's hard to beat this title for a clear, accurate, and appealing survey. Illustrations are key to this subject, and the range of crisp photos is excellent." SLJ

Includes bibliographical references

Symes, R. F.

Rocks & minerals; written by R.F. Symes and the staff of the Natural History Museum, London; special photography by Colin Keates and Andreas Einsiedel. Revised ed. DK Pub. 2008 72 p. ill. (some col.) (hardcover: boxed; package) $29.99; (hardcover) $16.99

Grades: 5 6 7 8   **552**

1. Gems 2. Rocks 3. Geology 4. Minerals
ISBN 9780756631321 out of print; 0756637775; 9780756637774

LC 2009499083

This book is a guide to "rocks, fossils, minerals, precious metals, crystals, jewels and gemstones." Readers "see rocks that have come from outer space, stalactites as old as dinosaurs, the strange and beautiful shapes of natural crystals and priceless nuggets of gold, silver and platinum. Learn what the Earth is made of and how its rocks were formed, how early humans made the first flint tools and how diamonds and precious stones are cut, polished, and made into jewelry." (Publisher's note)

Trueit, Trudi Strain

Rocks, gems, and minerals. Watts 2003 63p il (Watts library) $24; pa $8.95

Grades: 4 5 6 7   **552**

1. Rocks 2. Minerals 3. Precious stones
ISBN 0-531-12195-X; 0-531-16241-9 pa

LC 2001-7222

This includes "attention-grabbing photography, excellent charts and diagrams, short articles with or without photographs, and vocabulary terms that appear in bold and are explained in context." Sci Books Films

Includes glossary and bibliographical references

553.7   Water

Casper, Julie Kerr

Water and atmosphere; the lifeblood of natural systems. Chelsea House 2007 207p il map (Natural resources) $39.50

Grades: 8 9 10 11 12   **553.7**
   1. Atmosphere 2. Water supply
   ISBN 978-0-8160-6359-8; 0-8160-6359-1

LC 2007-261

This covers such topics as the roles of water and atmospheric resources in exploration and trade; climate change and global warming; renewable and nonrenewable resources; surface and ground water, aquifers, and other natural water reservoirs; management and environmental issues; effects on endangered species; future issues and the importance of public education; and marine exploration.

Includes bibliographical references

Gallant, Roy A.

Water; our precious resource. Benchmark Bks. 2002 79p il map (Earthworks) lib bdg $29.93

Grades: 5 6 7 8   **553.7**
   1. Water 3. Hydrology
   ISBN 0-7614-1365-0

LC 2001-43290

An in-depth look at Earth's waters and mankind's uses of water throughout history which includes ideas about planning better use of this critical resource in the future

"Gallant's prose is nearly conversational in its easy delivery, but his facts are always thorough and his ideas clearly explained. Best of all, he raises informed points that will help readers rethink their habits and realize the complexity of the issues. . . . Crisp graphs, maps, and excellent color photos illustrate [this] fine [volume]." Booklist

Includes glossary and bibliographical references

Woodward, John

Water; written by John Woodward. DK Pub. 2009 72p il (DK eyewitness books) $16.99; lib bdg $19.99

Grades: 4 5 6 7   **553.7**
   1. Water
   ISBN 978-0-7566-4537-3; 0-7566-4537-9; 978-0-7566-4538-0 lib bdg; 0-7566-4538-7 lib bdg

Takes a look at the role of water in our bodies, our cultures, and our world.

557   Earth sciences of North America

Collier, Michael

★ **Over** the mountains; an aerial view of geology. foreword by John S. Shelton. Mikaya Press 2007 un il map (An aerial view of geology) $29.95

Grades: 8 9 10 11 12   **557**
   1. Mountains 2. Aerial photography 3. Geology -- North America 4. Geology -- United States 5. Mountains -- United States 6. Aerial photography in geology
   ISBN 1-931414-18-1; 978-1-931414-18-0

LC 2006-47151

The author "expresses his passion for geology through awe-inspiring aerial photographs that reveal how mountains were formed and modified across the eons of time. . . . The four sections of this book explore what mountains are, why some are peaked and others rounded, and why they are often strung together in ranges. . . . Collier's love for the land is contagious, and his flying field trips over the mountains are thrilling." Voice Youth Advocates

Includes bibliographical references

560   Paleontology

Bradley, Timothy J.

★ **Paleo** bugs; survival of the creepiest. written and illustrated by Timothy J. Bradley. Chronicle Books 2008 44p il $15.99

Grades: 4 5 6 7   **560**
   1. Fossils 2. Insects 3. Prehistoric animals 4. Paleontology 5. Paleoentomology 6. Arthropoda, Fossil
   ISBN 978-0-8118-6022-2; 0-8118-6022-1

LC 2007-18174

This offers an "eye-widening gallery of extinct arthropods, from the mayfly-like heptagenia to a seven-foot-long arthropleura. . . . Bradley decks out each of his painted figures in bright hues, poses them in natural settings . . . and sets them aside a human hand or body in silhouette to suggest scale. . . . Readers will . . . pore over the pictures and come away knowing more about both these extinct animals and their modern descendants." Booklist

Includes glossary and bibliographical references

Holmes, Thom

★ **Dinosaur** scientist; careers digging up the past. Enslow Publishers 2009 128p il (Wild science careers) lib bdg $31.93

Grades: 5 6 7 8   **560**
   1. Fossils 2. Vocational guidance
   ISBN 978-0-7660-3053-4 lib bdg; 0-7660-3053-9 lib bdg

LC 2008-19634

"A great read for middle school students, the book provides vocational guidance while introducing the reader to a challenging, but very exciting, career as a paleontologist." Sci Books Films

Includes glossary and bibliographical references

Larson, Peter L.

Bones rock! everything you need to know to be a paleontologist. [by] Peter Larson and Kristin Donnan. Invisible Cities Press 2004 204p il pa $19.95

Grades: 5 6 7 8   **560**
   1. Fossils 2. Paleontologists 3. Paleontology --

Vocational guidance
ISBN 1-93122-935-X

LC 2004-413

"Illustrations include high-quality color photographs and helpful diagrams and drawings. There's fascinating information here, and Larson's enthusiasm and sound advice give plenty of encouragement to young scientists." SLJ

Includes bibliographical references

Sabuda, Robert
★ **Sharks** and other sea monsters; [by] Robert Sabuda & Matthew Reinhart. Candlewick Press 2006 un il (Encyclopedia prehistorica) $27.99

Grades: 3 4 5 6 7   **560**
1. Prehistoric animals 2. Pop-up books 3. Extinct animals 4. Marine animals, Fossil
ISBN 0-7636-2229-X

LC 2005-44866

This pop-up book introduces such prehistoric creatures as giant sharks, sea scorpions, and squids

"Gatefolds and inset minibooks expand the capacity of the book's seven spreads. . . . The sheer wonder generated by the collaborators' dimensional sleight-of-hand will more than justify purchase." Booklist

Taylor, Paul D.
★ **Fossil**; written by Paul D. Taylor. rev ed; DK Pub. 2004 72p il map (DK eyewitness books) $15.99; lib bdg $19.99

Grades: 4 5 6 7   **560**
1. Fossils
ISBN 0-7566-0682-9; 0-7566-0681-0 lib bdg
First published 1990 by Knopf

This book describes different types of fossils, from algae to birds and mammals

560.973   Paleontology -- United States

Johnson, Rebecca L.
Battle of the dinosaur bones; Othniel Charles Marsh vs. Edward Drinker Cope. by Rebecca L. Johnson. Twenty-First Century Books 2013 64 p. ill., plates, charts (Scientific rivalries and scandals) (library) $33.27

Grades: 5 6 7 8   **560.973**
1. Paleontology -- History 2. Paleontologists -- United States -- Biography 3. Paleontology -- United States -- History -- 19th century
ISBN 0761354883; 9780761354888

LC 2011045648

"This entry in the Scientific Rivalries and Scandals series focuses on the bitter antagonism between two pioneering nineteenth-century paleontologists. Marsh and Cope. Their contentious rivalry to discover the largest and most unusual dinosaur fossils of the American West became know as the Bone Wars and was at the forefront of American science for decades. The moral of the story is clear, revealing how rivalry can be positive and detrimental." (Booklist)

Includes bibliographical references (p. 58 - 60) and index.

567   Fossil cold-blooded vertebrates

Holmes, Thom
The **first** vertebrates; oceans of the Paleozoic era. Chelsea House 2008 188p il (The prehistoric Earth) lib bdg $35

Grades: 7 8 9 10   **567**
1. Fossils 2. Vertebrates 4. Fishes, Fossil
ISBN 978-0-8160-5958-4; 0-8160-5958-6

LC 2007-45329

Describes the first instances of vertebrate life in the oceans of the Paleozoic Era, tracing the development of early fish from jawless species to sharks and bony fish.

This "is a comprehensive, well-written, and easily readable text. . . . The chapters are well-organized." Sci Books Films

Includes glossary and bibliographical references

567.9   Reptiles

Abramson, Andra Serlin
Inside dinosaurs; by Andra Serlin Abramson, Jason Brougham, and Carl Mehling; illustrated by Jason Brougham. Sterling Innovation 2010 48p il (Inside) $16.95; pa $9.95

Grades: 5 6 7 8   **567.9**
1. Birds 2. Fossils 3. Dinosaurs
ISBN 978-1-4027-7074-6; 1-4027-7074-X; 978-1-4027-7778-3 pa; 1-4027-7778-7 pa

LC 2010010122

"This pleasantly specific overview covers not only the dinosaurs' distinctive physical characteristics (the authors include modern birds in the group), but the work of paleontologists in both field and lab, the types and typical life cycles of what are carefully dubbed 'non-avian' dinos within each 'clade,' the mass extinction of 65,000,000 years ago . . . and how new discoveries have refined theories about wings and feathers. . . . The art mixes small color photos with soft-edged paint-and-pencil reconstructions of bones, individual live portraits and prehistoric herds in natural settings. . . . [This is an] above average series entry." Kirkus

Includes glossary and bibliographical references

Bacchin, Matteo
Giant vs. giant; Argentinosaurus and Giganotosaurus. drawings and story, Matteo Bacchin; essays, Marco Signore; translated from the Italian by Marguerite Shore. Abbeville Kids 2010 61p il (Dinosaurs) $15.95

Grades: 4 5 6 7   **567.9**
1. Fossils 2. Dinosaurs
ISBN 978-0-7892-1013-5; 0-7892-1013-4

LC 2010-21120

This "book is split into two sections: the first contains parts . . . of a serial graphic novel about dinosaur survival, complete with dramatic narrative and grisly, to-the-death battles. The second half is a higher-level traditional nonfiction text with color photographs and diagrams, focusing on the science behind the comics. The unique format is generally engaging and effective." Horn Book Guide

T. rex and the great extinction; drawings and story, Matteo Bacchin; essays, Marco Signore; translated from the Italian by Marguerite Shore. Abbeville Kids 2010 il (Dinosaurs) $15.95
Grades: 4 5 6 7   **567.9**
1. Fossils 2. Dinosaurs 3. Fossils
ISBN 9780789210142; 0789210142

     LC 2010021123
This "book is split into two sections: the first contains parts . . . of a serial graphic novel about dinosaur survival, complete with dramatic narrative and grisly, to-the-death battles. The second half is a higher-level traditional nonfiction text with color photographs and diagrams, focusing on the science behind the comics. The unique format is generally engaging and effective." Horn Book Guide

Barrett, Paul M.
★ **National** Geographic dinosaurs; illustrated by Raul Martin; introduction by Kevin Padian. National Geographic Soc. 2001 61p 192p il $29.95
Grades: 6 7 8 9   **567.9**
1. Dinosaurs 2. Dinosaurs
ISBN 0-7922-8224-8

     LC 00-45263
"Clearly distinguishing fact from theory, this book provides an exciting guide to the life and times of the dinosaurs." Sci Child
Includes glossary

Berkowitz, Jacob
★ **Jurassic** poop; what dinosaurs (and others) left behind. written by Jacob Berkowitz; illustrated by Steve Mack. Kids Can Press 2006 40p il $14.95; pa $7.95
Grades: 4 5 6 7   **567.9**
1. Feces 2. Fossils 3. Dinosaurs 4. Coprolites
ISBN 978-1-55337-860-0; 1-55337-860-1; 978-1-55337-867-9 pa; 1-55337-867-9 pa
This describes fossilized feces, or coprolites, and what we can learn from them
"Berkowitz' style is goofy and lighthearted, but there's plenty of real information. . . . The browsable format combines cartoony digital art, photographs . . . and design elements such a spiky borders and background shading." Bull Cent Child Books
Includes glossary

Bonner, Hannah
When dinos dawned, mammals got munched, and Pterosaurs took flight; a cartoon pre-history of life in the Triassic. Hannah Bonner. National Geographic Children's Books 2012 44 p. col. ill., col. maps (hardback) $25.90
Grades: 3 4 5 6 7   **567.9**
1. Dinosaurs 2. Triassic Period 3. Graphic novels 5. Paleontology -- Triassic -- Comic books, strips, etc.
ISBN 9781426308628; 9781426308635

     LC 2011029212

In this book Hannah Bonner "chronicles developments in the Triassic Period, during which life got a fresh lease on the planet in the wake of the massive Permian extinction. She tracks an explosion of biological diversity as the oceans were repopulated, lush forests grew and the dominant kinds of land animals went from clumsy-looking therapsids to sleek archosaurian dinosaurs and proto-crocodiles. Early mammals are already waiting in the wings." (Kirkus Reviews)
Includes bibliographical references and index

Collard, Sneed B.
★ **Reign** of the sea dragons; illustrated by Andrew Plant. Charlesbridge 2008 61p il $17.95; pa $8.95
Grades: 5 6 7 8 9   **567.9**
1. Marine animals 2. Prehistoric animals 3. Paleontology 4. Marine reptiles, Fossil
ISBN 978-1-58089-124-0; 978-1-58089-125-7 pa

     LC 2007-26201
"An arresting dust jacket depicting a humongous pliosaur snapping huge toothy jaws at a small, long-necked plesiosaur is an attention-grabber, but it is the informative text that brings these real sea monsters to life. Collard follows his usual pattern of careful organization, with a readable text and up-to-date information. . . . Plant has provided five full-color paintings, but it is his numerous black-and-white drawings that lend sturdy anatomical and physical information. . . . Collard's discussion on extinction theories is cogent." SLJ
Includes glossary, bibliographical references, and websites

Dingus, Lowell
★ **Dinosaur** eggs discovered! unscrambling the clues. [by] Lowell Dingus, Luis M. Chiappe [and] Rodolfo Coria. Twenty-First Century Books 2008 112p il map (Discovery!) lib bdg $30.60
Grades: 8 9 10 11 12   **567.9**
1. Eggs 2. Fossils 3. Dinosaurs 4. Dinosaurs -- Eggs
ISBN 978-0-8225-6791-2 lib bdg; 0-8225-6791-1 lib bdg

     LC 2006-102636
Recounts the discovery of a dinosaur nesting field containing a large number of eggs, describing the field work done to classify them, calculate the period of prehistory they came from, and identify the reasons why many of them never hatched.
This is "a valuable, unusually authoritative presentation for serious students of prehistoric life." Booklist
Includes glossary and bibliographical references

Dixon, Dougal
Plant-eating dinosaurs; by Dougal Dixon. North American ed. New Forest Press 2010 48 p. col. ill., col. maps (library) $28.50
Grades: 4 5 6 7   **567.9**
1. Fossils 2. Dinosaurs 3. Herbivores
ISBN 1848983336; 9781848983335

     LC 2010925201
This volume "contains detailed information about dinosaurs and other prehistoric life, covering species development in chronological order. Careful links to the fos-

sil finds that helped scientists with their explanations are found throughout. Additional text boxes cover topics from structure-function to footprints, and interpretive color illustrations and photographs further enhance the [text]." Horn Book Guide

Includes bibliographical references (p. 44-45) and index.

Prehistoric oceans. New Forest Press 2010 48p il map (Dinosaur files) lib bdg $28.50
Grades: 4 5 6 7   567.9
1. Fossils 2. Dinosaurs 3. Marine animals
ISBN 978-1-8489-8332-8; 1-8489-8332-8

This volume "contains detailed information about dinosaurs and other prehistoric life, covering species development in chronological order. Careful links to the fossil finds that helped scientists with their explanations are found throughout. Additional text boxes cover topics from structure-function to footprints, and interpretive color illustrations and photographs further enhance the [text]." Horn Book Guide

Includes glossary

Prehistoric skies. New Forest Press 2010 48p il map (Dinosaur files) lib bdg $28.50
Grades: 4 5 6 7   567.9
1. Fossils 2. Dinosaurs 3. Prehistoric animals
ISBN 978-1-8489-8331-1; 1-8489-8331-X

Discusses the physical characteristics, behavior, diet, and fossil evidence of prehistoric animals that lived in the sky.

This volume "contains detailed information about dinosaurs and other prehistoric life, covering species development in chronological order. Careful links to the fossil finds that helped scientists with their explanations are found throughout. Additional text boxes cover topics from structure-function to footprints, and interpretive color illustrations and photographs further enhance the [text]." Horn Book Guide

Includes glossary

Everhart, Michael J.
Sea monsters; prehistoric creatures of the deep. [by] Mike Everhart. National Geographic 2007 191p il map $30
Grades: 7 8 9 10   567.9
1. Fossils 2. Marine animals 3. Prehistoric animals 4. Marine animals, Fossil 5. Paleontology -- Cretaceous
ISBN 978-1-4262-0085-4; 1-4262-0085-4
LC 2007-18671

Featuring "computer-generated images and 3D film clips—with 3D glasses—field photography by National Geographic cameramen, and much more, the book interweaves dramatic scenes of the far, far distant past; up-to-the-minute scientific profiles of nearly two dozen sea monsters; and a group portrait of the eccentric Sternberg family, Kansas-bred pioneers of marine paleontology." Publisher's note

Funston, Sylvia
★ **Dino**-why? the dinosaur question and answer book. updated and rev.; Maple Tree Press 2008 64p il $22.95; pa $10.95

Grades: 4 5 6 7   567.9
1. Dinosaurs
ISBN 978-1-897349-24-3; 1-897349-24-6; 978-1-897349-25-0 pa; 1-897349-25-4 pa
LC 2007-939082

First published 1992 by Joy Street Books with title: The dinosaur question and answer book

"This book is an excellent and highly readable introduction to dinosaurs. . . . The questions are well conceived, and the answers . . . are scientifically sound and up to date. . . . The illustrations, a few of them cartoon-like, are nicely drawn and useful." Sci Books Films

Holtz, Thomas R.
★ **Dinosaurs**; the most complete, up-to-date encyclopedia for dinosaur lovers of all ages. by Dr. Thomas R. Holtz, Jr.; illustrated by Luis V. Rey. Random House 2007 427p il $34.99; lib bdg $37.99
Grades: 7 8 9 10   567.9
1. Dinosaurs
ISBN 978-0-375-82419-7; 0-375-82419-7; 978-0-375-92419-4 lib bdg; 0-375-92419-1 lib bdg
LC 2006-102491

This "covers everything from dinosaur eggs to taxonomy and cladistics to the history of paleontology, glued together with chapters on the dinosaurs themselves. . . . The illustrations range from small photos to larger sepia-toned drawings to even larger full-color paintings. . . . This eye-catching imagination grabber will be enjoyed (on different levels) by dinophiles of all ages." SLJ

Includes glossary

Kelsey, Elin
Canadian dinosaurs; Elin Kelsey. Reprint Maple Tree Press 2009 96 p. ill. (prebind) $28.95
Grades: 4 5 6   567.9
1. Fossils 2. Dinosaurs
ISBN 1442060409; 9781442060401

This book offers a "history of fossil hunting north of the border, including bio-material on dino-hunters past and present, followed by a compendium of carnivores and herbivores. . . . Illustrations, mainly in color, appear on every page. . . . The whole is rounded out with a list of dino locations, a time line, and a listing of institutions where these splendid fossils may be examined at leisure." (School Library Journal)

Lessem, Don
The **ultimate** dinopedia; the most complete dinosaur reference ever. illustrated by Franco Tempesta; with a foreword by Rodolfo Coria. National Geographic 2010 272p il map $24.95; lib bdg $34.90
Grades: 3 4 5 6   567.9
1. Dinosaurs
ISBN 978-1-4263-0164-3; 1-4263-0164-2; 978-1-4263-0165-0 lib bdg; 1-4263-0165-0 lib bdg
LC 2010-07146

In the opening chapter, Lessem "presents broad basics on [dinosaur] behavior and habitats as well as a look at major discoveries in paleontology. However, it's the later chapters, which devote two pages each to specific dinosaurs, that will hook hard-core dino lovers. . . . Tempesta's full-page illustrations appear on every spread and jump off the page, and the dynamic layout . . . is immensely appealing. . . . Lessem's comprehensive overview will satisfy the interested browser as much as the ardent dinosaur enthusiast." Booklist

Includes bibliographical references

Long, John A.

★ **Dinosaurs**; [by] John Long. Simon & Schuster Books for Young Readers 2007 64p il (Insiders) lib bdg $16.99

Grades: 4 5 6 7   **567.9**

1. Dinosaurs

ISBN 978-1-4169-3857-6 lib bdg; 1-4169-3857-5 lib bdg

LC 2007-61735

"Richly hued, crisp computer-generated art and 3D model imagery serve as a stunning and sophisticated graphic counterpoint to the educational text." Publ Wkly

Includes glossary

Feathered dinosaurs; the origin of birds. foreword by Luis M. Chiappe. Oxford University Press 2008 193p il $39.95

Grades: 7 8 9 10   **567.9**

1. Birds 2. Fossils 3. Dinosaurs

ISBN 978-0-19-537266-3; 0-19-537266-2

LC 2008-1232

A "record of feathered dinosaurs illuminates the evolutionary march from these . . . prehistoric creatures through to the first true flying birds and includes . . . text that places these feathered dinosaurs within the larger family of dinosaurs." Publisher's note

Includes bibliographical references

Malam, John

Dinosaur atlas; authors, John Malam and John Woodward; consultant Michael Benton. Dorling Kindersley 2006 96p il map $19.99

Grades: 5 6 7 8   **567.9**

1. Dinosaurs

ISBN 978-0-7566-2235-0; 0-7566-2235-2

LC 2006-285529

"The atlas is organized by continent. Each section is prefaced with a large map showing where various species are found, with a picture and a brief synopsis of each species on the facing page. . . . Each introductory map is followed by several regional maps, surveying important local fossil sites and formations. Each section provides attractive diorama snapshots for a wide range of periods and locations." Sci Books Films

Includes glossary

Manning, Phillip Lars

★ **Dinomummy**; the life, death, and discovery of Dakota, a dinosaur from Hell Creek. foreword by Tyler Lyson. Kingfisher 2007 64p il map $18.95

Grades: 4 5 6 7   **567.9**

1. Dinosaurs 2. Hadrosauridae 3. Mummified animals

ISBN 978-0-7534-6047-4; 0-7534-6047-5

LC 2007-02878

Tells about the discovery of the fossil remains of a hadrosaur in the hills of the Hell Creek Formation in North Dakota.

"The color photographs and simple text offer a detailed account of carefully unearthing the fossil and transporting it safely to the laboratory, where many tests were performed. Dinosaurs buffs and young scientists will love this book. It is a thrilling story that is part narrative, part mystery, and part science lesson." Voice Youth Advocates

McGowan, Chris

Dinosaur discovery; everything you need to be a paleontologist. illustrated by Erica Lyn Schmidt. Simon & Schuster Books for Young Readers 2011 48p il $17.99

Grades: 4 5 6 7   **567.9**

1. Fossils 2. Dinosaurs

ISBN 978-1-4169-4764-6; 1-4169-4764-7; 1416947647; 9781416947646

LC 2009044604

"In-depth facts about 13 dinosaurs are interspersed with activities that teach readers about anatomy and how paleontologists understand body structure. . . . The 27 activities and experiments illustrate the concepts presented and focus on the featured dinosaurs. By following the well-written directions as well as the picture steps, budding paleontologists will explore how a tail affects balance, discover binocular vision and learn how the two parts of a bone make them both stiff and elastic. . . . Schmidt's acrylic illustrations give life to the dinosaurs, and her scientific renderings of bones could have come straight out of an anatomy textbook. . . . A thinking, active alternative for readers who fall between adult nonfiction and all the rhyming dino fare meant for the younger set." Kirkus

Peterson, Sheryl

Pterodactyl. Creative Education 2010 48p il (Age of dinosaurs) lib bdg $34.25

Grades: 5 6 7 8   **567.9**

1. Dinosaurs

ISBN 978-1-58341-975-5 lib bdg; 1-58341-975-6 lib bdg

LC 2009025175

"Peterson nicely balances the known with conjecture. . . . The inviting design, on glossy pages, elegantly detours from the main text into details tantalizing . . .; informative . . .; and incredible. . . . The illustrations, from sharp diagrams to dramatic paintings to B-movie-worthy recreation scenes, add some nice flair to this solid entry." Booklist

Sloan, Christopher

Bizarre dinosaurs; some very strange creatures and why we think they got that way. [by] Christopher Sloan; with a foreword by James Clark and Cathy Forster. National Geographic 2008 31p il $16.95; lib bdg $25.90

Grades: 4 5 6 7   **567.9**

1. Dinosaurs

ISBN 978-1-4263-0330-2; 1-4263-0330-0; 978-1-4263-0331-9 lib bdg; 1-4263-0331-9 lib bdg

This "book should engage children of all ages who are fascinated by dinosaurs. . . . The illustrations are of uniformly high quality. . . . Each species gets two pages of text, including a full-page illustration; an inset with basic facts such as range, diet, and geological period in which it lived; a silhouette comparing their size with that of humans; and a paragraph of text." Sci Books Films

★ **How** dinosaurs took flight; the fossils, the science, what we think we know, and the mysteries yet unsolved. foreword by Dr. Xu Xing. National Geographic 2005 64p il $17.95

Grades: 5 6 7 8   **567.9**
1. Birds 2. Fossils 3. Dinosaurs 4. Birds, Fossil 5. Birds -- Origin
ISBN 0-7922-7298-6
This explains the evolutionary relationships between dinosaurs and birds, based on fossils and the latest research.
Includes glossary and bibliographical references

Supercroc and the origin of crocodiles; introduction by Paul Sereno. National Geographic Soc. 2002 55p il map $18.95

Grades: 5 6 7 8   **567.9**
1. Crocodiles 2. Fossil reptiles
ISBN 0-7922-6691-9
                     LC 2001-3976
Discusses prehistoric crocodiles, including the discovery of SuperCroc in the Sahara Desert, and the lifestyles, habitats, and conservation of modern crocodiles
"Fans of paleontology or of crocodiles will find a great deal of information clearly explained. The illustrations are up to the high National Geographic standard." Booklist
Includes glossary

Woodward, John
3-D dinosaur; by John Woodward; consultant, Darren Naish. 1st American ed. DK 2011 71 p. ill. (chiefly col.), col. maps (hardcover: interactive) $17.99

Grades: 6 7 8   **567.9**
1. Fossils 2. Dinosaurs 5. Paleontology
ISBN 0756672155; 9780756672157
                     LC 2011282389
This children's book on dinosaurs by John Woodward includes "special activating boxes that indicate the presence of digital pop outs that when held up to a webcam attached to your PC, feature . . . 3D digital animation." It explores "the anatomy, diet, and behavior of dinosaurs and how paleontologists piece together the past." (Publisher's note)
Includes bibliographical references (p. [72]) and index.

Zoehfeld, Kathleen Weidner
Dinosaur parents, dinosaur young; uncovering the mystery of dinosaur families. with full-color paintings by Paul Carrick and line drawings by Bruce Shillinglaw. Clarion Bks. 2001 58p il map $17

Grades: 4 5 6 7   **567.9**
1. Fossils 2. Dinosaurs 3. Paleontology 4. Parental behavior in animals 5. Dinosaurs -- Behavior
ISBN 0-395-91338-1
                     LC 00-43101

"High-quality, color photographs of fossils of eggs and embryos and of paleontologists at work as well as line drawings and full-color paintings add to this inviting, thought-provoking book." SLJ
Includes glossary and bibliographical references

567.912   Specific dinosaurs

Dixon, Dougal
Meat-eating dinosaurs; by Dougal Dixon. North American ed. New Forest Press 2010 47 p. col. ill., col. maps (Dinosaur files) (library) $28.50

Grades: 4 5 6 7   **567.912**
1. Fossils 2. Dinosaurs 3. Carnivorous animals
ISBN 9781848983342; 1848983344
                     LC 2010925204
This volume "contains detailed information about dinosaurs and other prehistoric life, covering species development in chronological order. Careful links to the fossil finds that helped scientists with their explanations are found throughout. Additional text boxes cover topics from structure-function to footprints, and interpretive color illustrations and photographs further enhance the [text]." Horn Book Guide
Includes bibliographical references (p. 44-45) and index.

569   Fossil mammals

Agenbroad, Larry D.
Mammoths; ice-age giants. [by] Larry D. Agenbroad and Lisa Nelson. Lerner Publs. 2002 120p il (Discovery!) lib bdg $27.93; pa $7.95

Grades: 5 6 7 8   **569**
1. Mammoths
ISBN 0-8225-2862-2 lib bdg; 0-8225-0470-7 pa
                     LC 2001-1147
"Chapters discuss what is currently known about [mammoths] . . . when and where they lived, and the discovery of remains. The authors present several theories as to why mammoths might have died out. The book is well documented, and the many photos and drawings add clarity to the text." Horn Book Guide
Includes glossary and bibliographical references

Bardoe, Cheryl
Mammoths and mastodons; titans of the Ice Age. Abrams Books for Young Readers 2010 43p il map

Grades: 4 5 6 7   **569**
1. Fossils 2. Mammoths 3. Mastodons
ISBN 0-8109-8413-X lib bdg; 978-0-8109-8413-4 lib bdg
                     LC 2009-22006
The author presents a "case study in how paleontologists examine both ancient and modern clues for insights into the diets, physical development and behavior of extinct animals. Cousins to modern elephants, mammoths and mastodons once roamed large portions of the Earth, but for reasons that are not completely understood . . . vanished relatively suddenly. Focusing particularly on . . . remnants like the 55 fos-

silized skeletons found near one sinkhole in South Dakota and 'Lyuba,' the well preserved 'prehistoric popsicle' discovered in 2007 in Siberia, the author presents both facts and educated guesses--while leaving it clear that there is much still to be learned." (Kirkus)

"This well-designed book opens with two boys finding a strange animal dead on the arctic tundra. Their father hikes four days to a village where the news can be spread; then scientists take away the frozen baby mammoth, the first example found intact, and study it intensively. The book intersperses accounts of the scientists' research and deductions with general information about mammoths and mastodons as well as imagined scenes taking place when they walked the earth. . . . A handsome introduction." Booklist

Includes glossary and bibliographical references

Turner, Alan

★ **National** Geographic prehistoric mammals; illustrated by Mauricio Antón. National Geographic 2004 192p il map $29.95; lib bdg $49.90

Grades: 5 6 7 8   **569**

1. Fossil mammals
ISBN 0-7922-7134-3; 0-7922-6997-7 lib bdg
LC 2004-1189

This describes the Age of Mammals and profiles over 100 prehistoric mammals, including time lines, fact boxes, distribution maps, photos of fossils, and illustrations

"Dramatic full-color pictures . . . and captions enhance the brief, informative text." SLJ

569.9   Homo and related genera

Aronson, Marc

★ The **skull** in the rock; how a scientist, a boy, and Google Earth opened a new window on human origins. by Marc Aronson and Lee Berger. National Geographic 2012 64 p. (hardcover : alk. paper) $18.95

Grades: 5 6 7 8 9 10   **569.9**

1. Human origins 2. Fossil hominids 3. Excavations (Archeology) 4. Paleoanthropology 5. Human beings -- Origin 6. Fossil hominids -- South Africa -- Witwatersrand Region 7. Human evolution -- South Africa -- Witwatersrand Region 8. Excavations (Archaeology) -- South Africa -- Witwatersrand Region
ISBN 1426310102; 9781426310102; 9781426310539
LC 2012012943

This book by Marc Aronson and Lee R. Berger tells the story of how "in 2008 [Berger]--with the help of his curious 9-year-old son--discovered two remarkably well preserved, two-million-year-old fossils . . . known as 'Australopithecus sediba'; a previously unknown species of ape-like creatures that may have been a direct ancestor of modern humans." (Publisher's note)

Includes bibliographical references and index.

570   Biology

Green, Dan

Extreme biology; from superbugs to clones... get to the edge of science. written and illustrated by Simon Basher. Kingfisher 2013 64 p. col. ill. (hardcover) $12.99

Grades: 4 5 6 7   **570**

1. Biology
ISBN 0753470519; 9780753470510

This book written and illustrated by Simon Basher is designed to help readers "learn about the amazing research that is revolutionizing biology, from advances in medicine to genetic engineering. [Readers will] meet the world's toughest bacterium and a biologically immortal flatworm whilst learning about epigenetics, superbugs, nanomedicine and cloning. 'Extreme Biology' is a compelling guide to developments at the very forefront of science." (Publisher's note)

McManus, Lori

Cell systems. Heinemann Library 2011 48p il (Investigating cells) lib bdg $32

Grades: 5 6 7 8   **570**

1. Cells 2. Life (Biology)
ISBN 978-1-4329-3879-6; 1-4329-3879-7
LC 2009049974

This book looks at cell systems, including the cell, tissues, organ, and organ system hierarchy.

"The abundant graphic matter—photographs, diagrams, charts and graphs—work together with the text to create visually appealing pages. . . . [This] would be very useful in any kind of formal investigation of the topic and yet attractive enough to encourage browsing. . . . [This] . . . is exceptionally well done." Libr Media Connect

Includes glossary and bibliographical references

VanCleave, Janice Pratt, 1942-

Step-by-step science experiments in biology; by Janice VanCleave. Rosen 2013 80 p. col. ill. (Janice Vancleave's first-place science fair projects) (library) $33.25; (paperback) $14.15

Grades: 5 6 7 8   **570**

1. Biology 2. Science -- Experiments 3. Biology -- Experiments
ISBN 144886982X; 9781448869824; 9781448884636
LC 2012007943

This book by Janice VanCleave presents 22 science experiments in biology for children. "Van Cleave states the basic goal of the experiments, followed by a list of necessary materials. . . . Step-by-step instructions are . . . accompanied by diagrams where needed. The results section states exactly what is expected to happen and the 'Why?' section explains in accessible terms why those specific results were achieved." (School Library Journal)

Includes bibliographical references and index.

Winston, Robert

Life as we know it; Robert Winston. 1st American ed. DK Publishing 2012 96 p. col. ill. (hardcover) $16.99

Grades: 4 5 6 **570**
1. Ecology 2. Zoology 3. Food chains (Ecology) 4. Life (Biology)
ISBN 0756691699; 9780756691691

LC 2011277462

Author Robert Winston "begins with Earth's formation billions of years ago and continues to the present day, exploring cells, the animal kingdom, ecosystems, food chains, and creatures that tolerate extreme conditions (including bacteria that thrive in volcanic pools and coffinfish that live under high pressure on the sea floor). The book's . . . design incorporates numerous photographs, sidebars, . . . digital art, and light humor, usually in the form of speech-bubble captions for the animals." (Publishers Weekly)

★ Biology matters! Grolier 2004 10v il set $389
Grades: 5 6 7 8 9 10 **570**
1. Biology 2. Reference books
ISBN 0-7172-5979-X

LC 2003-56942

"This set presents the fundamentals of the life sciences in a clear format. . . . Volumes contain between six and eight articles in 80 pages . . . introducing its subject, presenting a brief history, and covering many aspects of its current study and applications. . . . The text is large and easy to read, and the writing is straightforward. . . . This title . . . would be a useful addition for public and school libraries." Booklist

570.7   Education, research, related topics

Calhoun, Yael
Plant and animal science fair projects; revised and expanded using the scientific method. Enslow Publishers 2010 160p il (Biology science projects using the scientific method) lib bdg $34.60
Grades: 7 8 9 10 **570.7**
1. Natural history 2. Science projects 3. Science -- Experiments 4. Natural history projects
ISBN 978-0-7660-3421-1 lib bdg; 0-7660-3421-6 lib bdg

LC 2009-14805

First published 2005 with title: Plant and animal science fair projects using beetles, weeds, seeds, and more

"Explains how to use the scientific method to conduct several science experiments about plants and animals. Includes ideas for science fair projects" Publisher's note
Includes bibliographical references

570.78   Biology -- Student experiments

Latham, Donna
★ **Backyard** Biology; Investigate Habitats Outside Your Door With 25 Projects. by Donna Latham; illustrated by Beth Hetland. Nomad Press 2013 128 p. ill. (Build it yourself) (paperback) $15.95
Grades: 4 5 6 7 **570.78**
1. Biology 2. Do-it-yourself work
ISBN 1619301512; 9781619301511

This book, part of the Built It Yourself series, "incorporates 25 projects for kids to try as they explore the 'ecosystems that are outside your door.' The book's eight chapters cover biology (and microbiology), cells, and the life cycles of both plants and animals, among other topics; definitions of key terms appear throughout, as do [illustrator Beth] Hetland's cartoons and diagrams." (Publishers Weekly)

570.92   Biologists

Yount, Lisa
Craig Venter; dissecting the genome. by Lisa Yount. Chelsea House 2011 xix, 134 p.p col. ill. (Trailblazers in science and technology) (library) $35
Grades: 7 8 9 10 11 12 **570.92**
1. Human genome 2. Biologists -- United States -- Biography
ISBN 1604136626; 9781604136623

LC 2010050561

This book by Lisa Yount, part of the Trailblazers in Science and Technology series, looks at scientist Craig Venter. It "details the life and accomplishments of this trailblazing scientist, describing his early days in California and military service in Vietnam, his . . . work to map the human genome, and his other numerous scientific achievements." (Publisher's note)
Includes bibliographical references and index

571   Internal biological processes and structures

Green, Jen
Inside animals. Marshall Cavendish Benchmark 2010 48p il (Invisible worlds) $28.50
Grades: 4 5 6 7 **571**
1. Cells 2. Anatomy 3. Physiology 4. Microorganisms
ISBN 978-0-7614-4195-3; 0-7614-4195-6

LC 2008037241

This describes the animal details that are too small for the unaided eye to see, and how these microscopic systems work to keep the animal alive and healthy.

The narrative is "clear, well written, broken down into manageable pieces, and peppered with eye-opening facts. The numerous photographs are so phenomenal that they will inspire kids to read the text . . . so that they can wrap their minds around what they see." SLJ
Includes glossary and bibliographical references

571.4   Biophysics

Winner, Cherie
Cryobiology. Lerner Publications Co. 2006 48p il (Cool science) lib bdg $26.60
Grades: 4 5 6 **571.4**
1. Cryobiology
ISBN 978-0-8225-2907-1 lib bdg; 0-8225-2907-6 lib bdg

LC 2005006158

This book "discusses how different life forms survive low temperatures, e.g., hibernating animals. . . . [The book provides] clear explanations of the science and [covers] possible benefits to humans. A variety of photos and information boxes provide an eye-catching . . . layout." Horn Book Guide

Includes glossary and bibliographical references

571.6   Cell biology

Ballard, Carol

Cells and cell function. Rosen Central 2010 46p il (Living processes) lib bdg $26.50; pa $11.75

Grades: 5 6 7   **571.6**

1. Cells

ISBN 978-1-61532-342-5 lib bdg; 1-61532-342-2 lib bdg; 978-1-61532-349-4 pa; 1-61532-349-X pa

Describes what cells are and how they work.

"With colorful, quality photography, the well-organized content is divided into short chapters with bold subheadings making information easy to find. Clear and interesting writing distinguishes this . . . from older titles. The captions for pictures are used to provide identification and additional explanation for topics not included in the text." Libr Media Connect

Includes glossary and bibliographical references

Cohen, Marina

What is cell theory? Crabtree Pub. Co. 2011 64p il (Shaping modern science) lib bdg $30.60; pa $10.95

Grades: 5 6 7 8   **571.6**

1. Cells

ISBN 978-0-7787-7199-9 lib bdg; 0-7787-7199-9 lib bdg; 978-0-7787-7206-4 pa; 0-7787-7206-3 pa

LC 2010052633

This title is "not only written and organized well, but [it is] also gorgeous in design. Full-color photographs and illustrations are set over colorful backgrounds that add depth but not distraction. [The title] includes thought-provoking quotes from famous authors and scientists and some eyebrow-raising 'Quick Facts' throughout." SLJ

Includes glossary and bibliographical references

Lee, Kimberly Fekany

Cells. Compass Point Books 2009 40p il (Mission: science) lib bdg $26.60

Grades: 4 5 6   **571.6**

1. Cells

ISBN 978-0-7565-3954-2 lib bdg; 0-7565-3954-4 lib bdg

LC 2008007719

"Lee describes the difference between plant and animal cells, and their contents; diffusion; and cell storage, movement, and reproduction. . . . Large eye-catching and colorful photographs and illustrations appear on every page. . . . The [book] includes a simple activity." SLJ

Includes glossary and bibliographical references

Rainis, Kenneth G.

Cell and microbe science fair projects; revised and expanded using the scientific method. Enslow Publishers 2010 160p il (Biology science projects using the scientific method) lib bdg $34.60

Grades: 7 8 9 10   **571.6**

1. Cells 2. Biology 3. Microbiology 4. Science projects 5. Science -- Experiments

ISBN 978-0-7660-3420-4 lib bdg; 0-7660-3420-8 lib bdg

LC 2009019374

First published 2005 with title: Cell and microbe science fair projects using microscopes, mold, and more

"Explains how to use the scientific method to conduct several science experiments about cells and microbes. Includes ideas for science fair projects." Publisher's note

Includes bibliographical references

Silverstein, Alvin

Cells; by Alvin & Virginia Silverstein and Laura Silverstein Nunn. Twenty-First Century Books 2009 112p il (Science concepts, second series) lib bdg $31.93

Grades: 6 7 8 9   **571.6**

1. Cells

ISBN 978-0-7613-3934-2; 0-7613-3934-5

LC 2007051038

A presentation of the structure and function of different types of cells and of research into developing technologies such as cloning and the use of stem cells.

Includes glossary and bibliographical references

Somervill, Barbara A.

Animal cells and life processes. Heinemann Library 2011 48p il (Investigating cells) lib bdg $32

Grades: 5 6 7 8   **571.6**

1. Cells 2. Life (Biology)

ISBN 978-1-4329-3877-2; 1-4329-3877-0

LC 2009049971

Overview of animal cells and how they function.

"The abundant graphic matter—photographs, diagrams, charts and graphs—work together with the text to create visually appealing pages. . . . [This] would be very useful in any kind of formal investigation of the topic and yet attractive enough to encourage browsing. . . . [This] . . . is exceptionally well done." Libr Media Connect

Includes glossary and bibliographical references

Plant cells and life processes. Heinemann Library 2010 48p il (Investigating cells) lib bdg $32

Grades: 5 6 7 8   **571.6**

1. Cells 2. Plant physiology

ISBN 978-1-4329-3878-9; 1-4329-3878-9

LC 2009049973

This book explores the features of the plant cell and their life processes.

"The abundant graphic matter—photographs, diagrams, charts and graphs—work together with the text to create visually appealing pages. . . . [This] would be very useful in any kind of formal investigation of the topic and yet attractive enough to encourage browsing. . . . [This] . . . is exceptionally well done." Libr Media Connect

Includes glossary and bibliographical references

Stewart, Melissa

Cell biology; by Melissa Stewart. Revised ed. Twenty-First Century Books 2013 80 p. col. ill. (chiefly col.) ebook $31.95

Grades: 5 6 7 8   **571.6**
    1. Cells 2. Science -- History 3. Cytology
    ISBN 9781467703666; 1467703664
                    LC 2006028542

This book looks at cells. "From the nucleus, the cell's control center, to the tiny ribosomes, which help manufacture proteins, each part of a cell plays an essential role. This book tells the story of how biologists unlocked the secrets of cells and revolutionized the way we look at living things." (Publisher's note)

Includes bibliographical references (p. 76-77) and index

Stimola, Aubrey

Cell biology. Rosen Pubs. 2011 64p il (Science made simple) lib bdg $29.25; pa $12.95

Grades: 5 6 7 8   **571.6**
    1. Cells
    ISBN 978-1-4488-1234-9 lib bdg; 1-4488-1234-8 lib bdg; 978-1-4488-2241-6 pa; 1-4488-2241-6 pa
                    LC 2010021319

This introduction to cell biology includes "a lot of detailed information, making [it] useful as [a] resource . . . for science projects and reports. . . . The [book] also [includes a] brief discussion of scientists important in the field, the history of the topic, and current and future applications. . . . The straightforward, no-nonsense [narrative] and simple design make this . . . a nice package for basic science." SLJ

Includes glossary and bibliographical references

571.8   Reproduction, development, growth

Morgan, Sally

From sea urchins to dolly the sheep; discovering cloning. [by] Sally Morgan. Heinemann Library 2006 64p il (Chain reactions) $34.29

Grades: 6 7 8 9   **571.8**
    1. Cloning
    ISBN 1-4034-8838-X
                    LC 2006009962

This "addresses cloning, from its beginnings in the 1890s to Dolly the sheep in 2003. The [book features] clear, straightforward writing and [a] bright and open [layout] with colorful photographs and illustrations on every spread." SLJ

Includes bibliographical references

Silverstein, Virginia B.

★ **Growth** and development; by Alvin Silverstein, Virginia Silverstein, and Laura Silverstein Nunn. Twenty-First Century Books 2008 112p il (Science concepts) lib bdg $31.93

Grades: 4 5 6 7   **571.8**
    1. Growth 2. Biology
    ISBN 978-0-8225-6057-9 lib bdg; 0-8225-6057-7 lib bdg
                    LC 2006030299

This "considers the growth process, animals with and without skeletons, human and plant growth, and future trends as a result of medical technology. Clear organization, engaging anecdotes, and generally good photos and diagrams are strengths of the [volume]." Horn Book Guide

Includes glossary and bibliographical references

Spilsbury, Richard

Plant growth; [by] Richard & Louise Spilsbury. Rev. and updated.; Heinemann Library 2008 48p il (The life of plants) $27.50; pa $7.99

Grades: 5 6 7 8   **571.8**
    1. Plants -- Growth
    ISBN 978-1-4329-1500-1; 1-4329-1500-2; 978-1-4329-1507-0 pa; 1-4329-1507-X pa
                    LC 2008275394

First published 2003

Describes plant growth and development.

This book "contains many bright and colorful photographs and diagrams to support the text, boldface vocabulary terms, a series of experiments and activities to provide further investigation, a complete glossary, an index, and a list of sources for additional information. . . . [This] volume is a complete and well-rounded unit." Sci Books Films

Includes glossary and bibliographical references

571.9   Diseases

Somervill, Barbara A.

Cells and disease. Heinemann Library 2011 48p il (Investigating cells) lib bdg $32

Grades: 5 6 7 8   **571.9**
    1. Cells 2. Bacteria 3. Diseases
    ISBN 978-1-4329-3881-9; 1-4329-3881-9
                    LC 2009-49981

This book describes cells and diseases.

"The abundant graphic matter—photographs, diagrams, charts and graphs—work together with the text to create visually appealing pages. . . . [This] would be very useful in any kind of formal investigation of the topic and yet attractive enough to encourage browsing. . . . [This] . . . is exceptionally well done." Libr Media Connect

Includes glossary and bibliographical references

572   Biochemistry

Silverstein, Alvin

Photosynthesis; [by] Alvin Silverstein, Virginia Silverstein, and Laura Silverstein Nunn. rev ed.; Twenty-First Century Books 2008 79p il (Science concepts, second series) lib bdg $31.93

Grades: 6 7 8 9   **572**

1. Photosynthesis

ISBN 978-0-8225-6798-1; 0-8225-6798-9

LC 2006022566

First published 1998

"Photosynthesis explains the process; the history of discoveries leading to current understanding of photosynthesis; and related issues such as acid rain, the greenhouse effect, and the use of basic materials that are directly or indirectly dependent on photosynthesis. . . . [This book is] well researched and interesting and the format is inviting for both general-interest reading and research. . . . The high-quality, full-color photographs have informative captions." SLJ

Includes glossary and bibliographical references

Sitarski, Anita

★ **Cold** light; creatures, discoveries, and inventions that glow. Boyds Mills Press 2007 48p il $16.95

Grades: 5 6 7 8   **572**

1. Light 2. Chemists 3. Physicists 4. Bioluminescence 5. Nonfiction writers 6. Writers on science 7. Luminescence

ISBN 1-59078-468-5; 978-1-59078-468-6

"A clearly written, chatty text not only discusses the expected bioluminescent critters (think fireflies), but delves into the realms of chemiluminescence, photoluminescence, and LEDs (light-emitting diodes) as well. . . . The text lays out the historical hows and whys of cold light, its success in the natural world, and its application in medicine and domestic/industrial illumination. Clear color photos and information boxes abound." SLJ

572.8   Biochemical genetics

De la Bedoyere, Camilla

The **discovery** of DNA. World Almanac Library 2006 48p il (Milestones in modern science) $30

Grades: 6 7 8 9   **572.8**

1. DNA 2. Genetics

ISBN 0-8368-5851-4

This is an examination of the discovery of DNA, what work led to its discovery, and how that knowledge is being used today.

The text is "complete, detailed, and not difficult to follow. . . . The illustrations are adequate and plentiful, including lots of photos and diagrams." SLJ

Includes glossary and bibliographical references

Johnson, Rebecca L.

Amazing DNA; [by] Rebecca L. Johnson; illustrations by Jack Desrocher; diagrams by Jennifer E. Fairman. Millbrook Press 2008 48p il (Microquests) lib bdg $29.27

Grades: 4 5 6   **572.8**

1. DNA 2. Genetics

ISBN 978-0-8225-7139-1 lib bdg; 0-8225-7139-0 lib bdg

LC 2006-102324

This describes DNA structure, cell replication and genetic transmission.

"Johnson builds one scientific concept at a time using authentic terminology and connecting new information to familiar things. . . . Full-color microscope images, drawings, and cartoons appear in a clean, uncluttered format, combining solid science with humor." Horn Book Guide

Includes glossary and bibliographical references

Parker, Steve, 1952-

Cocci, spirilla & other bacteria. Compass Point Books 2009 48p il (Kingdom classification) lib bdg $29.32

Grades: 6 7 8 9   **572.8**

1. Bacteria 2. Microorganisms

ISBN 978-0-7565-4225-2 lib bdg; 0-7565-4225-1 lib bdg

LC 2009-7524

Discusses physical characteristics of bacteria; different types; how they move, feed, and reproduce; how people use them; how they can harm humans; and how the human body defends itself against harmful bacteria

"With its compelling facts and visuals, this is a quality choice." SLJ

Includes glossary

Rand, Casey

DNA and heredity. Heinemann Library 2011 48p il (Investigating cells) lib bdg $32

Grades: 5 6 7 8   **572.8**

1. DNA 2. Cells 3. Heredity

ISBN 978-1-4329-3880-2; 1-4329-3880-0

LC 2009049978

Learn about cells, DNA and scientists who made an impact in cell research.

"The abundant graphic matter—photographs, diagrams, charts and graphs—work together with the text to create visually appealing pages. . . . [This] would be very useful in any kind of formal investigation of the topic and yet attractive enough to encourage browsing. . . . [This] . . . is exceptionally well done." Libr Media Connect

Includes glossary and bibliographical references

Silverstein, Alvin

DNA; by Alvin Silverstein, Virginia Silverstein, Laura Silverstein Nunn. rev ed.; Twenty-First Century Books 2009 104p il (Science concepts, second series) lib bdg $31.93

Grades: 6 7 8 9   **572.8**

1. DNA 2. Genetics

ISBN 978-0-8225-8654-8; 0-8225-8654-1

LC 2007048819

First published 2002

Introduces DNA and discusses such topics as how heredity works, what can happen when the code goes wrong, and the science and technology that is being developed based on cells and DNA, including gene therapy and cloning.

Includes glossary and bibliographical references

Vaughan, Jenny

Who discovered DNA? Arcturus Pub. 2010 46p il (Breakthroughs in science and technology) lib bdg $32.80

Grades: 5 6 7 8   **572.8**
    1. DNA
    ISBN 978-1-84837-679-3; 1-84837-679-0
                      LC 2010011021

"This brief well-done book presents accurate information in an interesting way, using appropriate and appealing graphics. . . . The book not only tells us that Frederick Miesche discovered DNA in 1869, but presents many relevant discoveries before that time and, especially, after it. Applications of the discoveries are also presented, as are controversies related to the genetic knowledge of our day. . . . [This] would be useful as reference and should be available to all interested students." Sci Books & Films

Includes glossary and bibliographical references

Yount, Lisa

Rosalind Franklin; photographing biomolecules. by Lisa Yount. Chelsea House 2011 xix, 125 p.p col. ill. (Trailblazers in science and technology) (library) $35.00

Grades: 7 8 9 10 11 12   **572.8**
    1. Women scientists 2. DNA -- History 3. Molecular biologists -- Great Britain -- Biography 4. Women molecular biologists -- Great Britain -- Biography
    ISBN 160413660X; 9781604136609
                      LC 2010048229

This book by Lisa Yount is part of the Trailblazers in Science and Technology series and looks at Rosalind Franklin. "Tracing her life from her birth in Great Britain to her education at Cambridge, to her groundbreaking research [in X-ray crystallography], and to her tragic and untimely death," this book offers an "overview of the life and career of one of the most influential scientific figures of the 20th century." (Publisher's note)

Includes bibliographical references and index.

573.3   Digestive system

Deem, James M.

★ **Bodies** from the bog. Houghton Mifflin 1998 42p il hardcover o.p. pa $5.95

Grades: 4 5 6 7   **573.3**
    1. Mummies 2. Archeology 3. Prehistoric peoples 4. Bog bodies -- Europe 5. Europe -- Antiquities 6. Prehistoric peoples -- Europe 7. Human remains (Archaeology) -- Europe
    ISBN 0-395-85784-8; 0-618-35402-6 pa
                      LC 97-12010

Describes the discovery of bog bodies in northern Europe and the evidence which their remains reveal about themselves and the civilizations in which they lived

"The text is engaging and accessible, and the starkly dramatic photos are given dignity by the spacious and understated page design." Horn Book Guide

Includes bibliographical references

575   Specific parts of and physiological systems in plants

Stefoff, Rebecca

Charles Darwin and the evolution revolution. Oxford Univ. Press 1996 126p il (Oxford portraits in science) $28; pa $11.95

Grades: 7 8 9 10   **575**
    1. Evolution 2. Naturalists 3. Travel writers 4. Writers on science
    ISBN 0-19-508996-0; 0-19-512028-0 pa
                      LC 95-35802

"Extensive photos of Darwin and his family, friends, and colleagues, as well as reproductions of public notices and cartoons, are handsome additions to the nicely laid-out text. . . . It offers generally thorough, clear explanations of Darwin's scientific theories and sheds light on his personality." Booklist

Includes glossary and bibliographical references

575.6   Reproductive organs

Spilsbury, Richard

Plant reproduction; [by] Richard & Louise Spilsbury. Rev. and updated.; Heinemann Library 2008 48p il (Life of plants) $27.50; pa $7.99

Grades: 5 6 7 8   **575.6**
    1. Plants
    ISBN 978-1-4329-1501-8; 1-4329-1501-0; 978-1-4329-1508-7 pa; 1-4329-1508-8 pa
                      LC 2008275393

First published 2003

Discusses the different ways that plants reproduce, including pollination and spores.

This book "contains many bright and colorful photographs and diagrams to support the text, boldface vocabulary terms, a series of experiments and activities to provide further investigation, a complete glossary, an index, and a list of sources for additional information . . . . [This] volume is a complete and well-rounded unit." Sci Books Films

Includes glossary and bibliographical references

576   General and external biological phenomena

Gardner, Robert

Genetics and evolution science fair projects; revised and expanded using the scientific method. Enslow Publishers 2010 160p il (Biology science projects using the scientific method) lib bdg $34.60

Grades: 7 8 9 10   **576**
    1. Genetics 2. Evolution 3. Science projects 4. Science -- Experiments 5. Genetics 6. Biology projects 7. Science -- Methodology
    ISBN 978-0-7660-3422-8 lib bdg; 0-7660-3422-4 lib bdg
                      LC 2009-14803

First published 2004 with title: Genetics and evolution science fair projects using skeletons, cereal, earthworms, and more

"Explains how to use the scientific method to conduct several science experiments about genetics and evolution. Includes ideas for science fair projects" Publisher's note

Includes bibliographical references

Walker, Denise

   Inheritance and evolution. Smart Apple Media 2007 48p il (Basic biology) $34.25

Grades: 8 9 10 11 12   **576**

   1. Genetics 2. Evolution

   ISBN 978-1-58340-989-3

                      LC 2006000346

   This explains genetics, DNA, natural selection and cloning, and the process of extinction.

   This "is well written and visually appealing enough to entice a few kids who aren't normally interested in science. There's plenty of information, supported by excellent, full-color photos, charts, and graphs, as well as numerous examples that clarify facts." Booklist

576.5   Genetics

Day, Trevor

   Genetics; investigating the function of genes and the science of heredity. Trevor Day. 1st ed. Rosen Central 2013 48 p. ill. (chiefly col.) (Scientific pathways) (library) $29.25

Grades: 6 7 8 9   **576.5**

   1. Genetics 2. Scientists 3. Heredity

   ISBN 1448871999; 9781448871995

                      LC 2011047887

   This book by Trevor Day is part of the Scientific Pathways series and looks at genetics. The series authors "look at science as a process of discovery and explain how each discipline developed in different cultures over time. Significant names and important terms are printed in bold . . . . Brief biographies of thinkers, inventors, and scientists are provided along with important experiments and the conclusions that were made in relation to them." (School Library Journal)

   Includes bibliographical references and index.

Duke, Shirley Smith

   You can't wear these genes. Rourke Pub. LLC 2010 48p il (Let's explore science) $32.79

Grades: 4 5 6 7   **576.5**

   1. Genetics

   ISBN 978-1-61590-324-5; 1-61590-324-0

                      LC 2010009911

   This "offers a clear introduction to the complexities of genetics while inviting students to think about how their own DNA shaped who they are. In [this] title, well chosen boxed examples, abundant color photos, diagrams, and an appended glossary add interest and support the engaging [text]." Booklist

   Includes glossary and bibliographical references

Hand, Carol

   Introduction to genetics. Rosen Pub. 2010 80p il lib bdg $30.60

Grades: 6 7 8 9 10 11 12   **576.5**

   1. Genetics 2. Heredity

   ISBN 978-1-4358-9531-7

                      LC 2009-40364

   "The moderately technical language in the other titles discusses significant discoveries, current directions in research and•superficially•ethical and other issues. Illustrations include helpful charts, microphotos, portraits of scientists, and color photos; extensive back matter provides plenty of support for further research." SLJ

Johnson, Rebecca L.

   Genetics. Twenty-First Century Books 2005 80p il (Great ideas of science) $27.93

Grades: 5 6 7 8   **576.5**

   1. Genetics

   ISBN 0-8225-2910-6

                      LC 2004-28212

   "The history of genetics is introduced, beginning with Gregor Mendel's studies of pea-plant cross-pollination. The book skillfully explains the discovery of DNA and the emergence of modern biotechnology, including how DNA is replicated, how genes are expressed and translated as cell proteins, and how the human genome is being mapped. Thirty color photos, informational sidebars, and detailed diagrams complement the text." SLJ

   Includes bibliographical references

Morgan, Sally

   From Mendel's peas to genetic fingerprinting; discovering inheritance. Heinemann Library 2007 64p il (Chain reactions) $34.29

Grades: 6 7 8 9   **576.5**

   1. Genetics 2. Heredity

   ISBN 1-4034-8837-1; 978-1-4034-8837-4

                      LC 2006-11043

   This book "informs students about genetics and its many applications, including the Human Genome Project and genetic fingerprinting. . . . The [book features] clear, straightforward writing and [a] bright and open [layout] with colorful photographs and illustrations on every spread." SLJ

   Includes bibliographical references

Schafer, Susan

   Heredity. M.E. Sharpe 2009 96p il (Genetics: the science of life) $38.95

Grades: 6 7 8 9   **576.5**

   1. Genetics 2. Heredity

   ISBN 978-0-7656-8136-2; 0-7656-8136-6

                      LC 2008-8105

   This discusses the history of genetics, genetic dominance, hybrid animals, and the role of heredity in disease.

   "Chock-full of information. . . . The material is well organized and accessible. . . . Interest is maintained through countless fascinating examples. . . . Illustrations and color photographs enhance [the text]." SLJ

   Includes bibliographical references

Simpson, Kathleen

★ **Genetics**; from DNA to designer dogs. Sarah Tishkoff, consultant. National Geographic 2008 64p il map (National Geographic investigates) $27.90

Grades: 4 5 6 7   **576.5**

1. Genetics

ISBN 978-1-4263-0361-6; 1-4263-0361-0; 978-1-4263-0327-2 lib bdg; 1-4263-0327-0 lib bdg

This discusses topics in genetics such as the identification of an Egyptian mummy by DNA testing, the genetics of pea plants studied by Gregor Mendel, cloning, the Human Genome Project, and stem cell research.

"The content is fairly exciting and should grab the attention of its target audience. . . . The photographs throughout are of high quality. . . . An engaging look at a complex topic." Booklist

Vaughan, Jenny

Genetics. Smart Apple Media 2010 45p il (Science in the news) lib bdg $34.25

Grades: 6 7 8 9   **576.5**

1. Genetics

ISBN 978-1-59920-317-1 lib bdg; 1-59920-317-0 lib bdg

LC 2008-49275

This book about genetics "move[s] smoothly, occasionally pausing for the definition of a term. [The title] boast[s] plenty of attractive photos, and a clean layout allows the information to be easily consumed. . . . Provides the information that younger teens need." SLJ

Includes glossary

Yount, Lisa

Modern genetics; engineering life. rev ed.; Facts on File 2006 204p il map (Milestones in discovery and invention) $35

Grades: 7 8 9 10 11 12   **576.5**

1. Genetics 2. Genetic engineering 3. Genetics -- History

ISBN 0-8160-5744-3; 978-0-8160-5744-3

LC 2005-18152

First published 1997 with title: Genetics and genetic engineering

This book "profiles 14 men and women who were among the leaders in making important genetic discoveries in research and new technologies. Profiles include James Watson, Francis Crick, Herbert Boyer, Stanley N. Cohen, Michael Bishop, and Harold Varmus." Publisher's note

Includes glossary and bibliographical references

576.8   Evolution

Andryszewski, Tricia

Mass extinction; examining the current crisis. Twenty-First Century Books 2008 111p il lib bdg $30.60

Grades: 7 8 9 10 11 12   **576.8**

1. Mass extinction of species 3. Extinction (Biology)

4. Environmental degradation

ISBN 978-0-8225-7523-8; 0-8225-7523-X

LC 2007-25620

"After noting the natural causes of previous mass extinctions, this book focuses on the human element of environment destruction, especially in North America. The earnest writing is convincing and accessible. . . . Vibrant photographs, illustrations, and sidebars supplement the text." Horn Book Guide

Includes glossary and bibliographical references

Berkowitz, Jacob

Out of this world; the amazing search for an alien earth. Kids Can Press 2009 48p il $16.95; pa $8.95

Grades: 4 5 6 7   **576.8**

1. Life on other planets 3. Outer space -- Exploration

ISBN 978-1-55453-197-4; 1-55453-197-7; 978-1-55453-198-1 pa; 1-55453-198-5 pa

The author "has written a miniencyclopedic, profusely illustrated, picture book that describes, in much detail, what we all know about the universe in which we live and about the conditions that must be present on any planet in our solar system, or on an exoplanet . . . for life as we know it to exist." Sci Books Films

Bortz, Alfred B.

Astrobiology. Lerner Publications 2008 48p il map (Cool science) lib bdg $26.60

Grades: 4 5 6   **576.8**

1. Space biology 2. Life on other planets

ISBN 978-0-8225-6771-4 lib bdg; 0-8225-6771-7 lib bdg

LC 2006033268

This describes "the search for life in the universe. Astrobiologists compare life on Earth to signs of life on other planets. They test meteorites for evidence of alien bacteria. They collect soil and atmospheric samples from other planets. They study photographs taken on space missions. And they listen for signals from alien civilizations on enormous radio dishes." Publisher's note

Includes bibliographical references

Brake, Mark

Alien Hunter's Handbook; How to Look for Extra-terrestrial Life. by Mark Brake; illustrated by Colin Jack and Geriant Ford. Kingfisher 2012 111 p. (paperback) $10.99

Grades: 4 5 6 7   **576.8**

1. Extraterrestrial beings

ISBN 0753468859; 9780753468852

This book on extra-terrestrial life by Mark Brake "opens with an overview of the defining characteristics of life and some of Earth's remarkable creatures, such as the microscopic tardigrade, which can exist in the vacuum of space. Topics like the development of solar systems, the speed of evolution, and the formation of language also get attention, laying factual groundwork for suppositions about what alien life could look like." (Publishers Weekly)

Claybourne, Anna

Who discovered natural selection? Arcturus Pub. 2010 46p il (Breakthroughs in science and technology) lib bdg $32.80

Grades: 5 6 7 8   **576.8**

1. Heredity 2. Naturalists 3. Natural selection 4. Travel writers 5. Writers on science

ISBN 978-1-84837-682-3; 1-84837-682-0

LC 2010011020

"Earning high marks for clarity, organization, and visual appeal, this introduction to evolution and natural selection takes a historical approach, beginning with the philosophies of the ancients and tracing the development of evolution theory through the 19th century naturalists who set the stage for the conceptualization of natural selection. . . . Short narrative sections are interspersed with high-interest sidebars to keep the pace lively. The book ends with examples of rapid natural selection in viral strains and in antibiotic-resistant bacteria, and it raises the question of how mutually supportive behaviors evolve among social species. Colorful photographs and illustrations, each carefully chosen and placed, support the book's central theme. . . . Claybourne has made evolution theory accessible to young learners in a fresh and accurate way. This is a must buy for school libraries." Sci Books & Films

Includes glossary and bibliographical references

★ **Evolution**; Clay Farris Naff, book editor. Greenhaven Press 2005 222 p. (Exploring science and medical discoveries) lib bdg $34.95

Grades: 8 9 10 11 12   **576.8**

1. Evolution

ISBN 9780737728231

LC 2004-60590

In this anthology, "nineteen selections are arranged in roughly chronological order, beginning with ancient Greek philosophers whose ideas about nature hinted at evolutionary theories to come. . . . This solid survey provides a good overview with manageable amounts of primary-source materials that would be dauntingly difficult to comprehend in their entirety." SLJ

Includes bibliographical references

Fleisher, Paul

Evolution; by Paul Fleisher. Lerner Publications Co. 2005 80 p. ill. (chiefly col.), col. maps (library) $27.93; (ebook) $20.95

Grades: 5 6 7 8   **576.8**

1. Evolution 2. Darwin, Charles, 1809-1882

ISBN 0822521342; 9780822521341; 9781467703697

LC 2004028897

In this book, Paul Fleisher "summarizes some of the ideas about evolution before Darwin's Origin of Species. He goes on to describe the observations Darwin made while on his famous Beagle voyage. A map of the ship's course accompanies this section. . . . Objections to Darwin's theory in the 1800s and developments and discoveries in the field since then lead to a step-by-step description of how life may have come about and changed through billions of years." (School Library Journal)

Includes bibliographical references (p. 76-77) and index.

Gamlin, Linda

Evolution; written by Linda Gamlin. rev ed.; DK Pub. 2009 72p il (DK eyewitness books) $16.99

Grades: 4 5 6 7   **576.8**

1. Evolution

ISBN 978-0-7566-5028-5; 0-7566-5028-3

First published 1993

Text about and photography of experiments, animals, plants, bones, and fossils reveal the ideas and discoveries that have changed our understanding of the natural world and how life began. Includes a CD and wall chart.

Gordon, Sherri Mabry

The **evolution** debate; Darwinism vs. intelligent design. Enslow Publishers 2009 128p il (Issues in focus today) lib bdg $31.93

Grades: 7 8 9 10   **576.8**

1. Evolution 2. Intelligent design theory

ISBN 978-0-7660-2911-8 lib bdg; 0-7660-2911-5 lib bdg

LC 2008-17416

"This book is most notable for its unbiased presentation of the arguments on each side of this contentious debate." SLJ

Includes glossary and bibliographical references

Hartman, Eve

Changing life on Earth; [by] Eve Hartman and Wendy Meshbesher. Raintree 2009 48p il (Sci-hi: life science) lib bdg $31.43; pa $8.99

Grades: 5 6 7 8   **576.8**

1. Evolution

ISBN 978-1-4109-3324-9 lib bdg; 1-4109-3324-5 lib bdg; 978-1-4109-3332-4 pa; 1-4109-3332-6 pa

LC 2009003459

In this introduction to evolution "clear language, embedded definitions, and interesting examples illustrate abstract concepts through both text and well-chosen photographs. . . . [The book] provides a clear and useful explanation of the theory of evolution, with multiple sources of evidence and a discussion of how it helps scientists to predict the implications of changes to the environment. . . . [The] book also includes suggested activities to test ideas as well as a thorough glossary and a Webliography." SLJ

Includes glossary and bibliographical references

Holmes, Thom

Evolution. Chelsea House 2010 109p il (Science foundations) lib bdg $35

Grades: 7 8 9 10   **576.8**

1. Evolution

ISBN 978-1-60413-338-7; 1-60413-338-4

LC 2010015738

"A solid, competent history of the evolution of ideas and the theory of evolution itself. Indeed, the . . . book could easily be used as a basic textbook on the topic. The information-packed text begins with the very beginning: establishing the geologic time scale, via Hutton and Lyell, and going on to include Darwin's momentous work. Classification follows, and leads ultimately to adaptation and the evolution of new species." SLJ

Includes glossary and bibliographical references

Johnson, Sylvia A.

★ **Shaking** the foundation; Charles Darwin and the theory of evolution. by Sylvia A. Johnson. Twenty-First Century Books 2013 88 p. (library) $33.27

Grades: 6 7 8 9   576.8

1. Evolution 2. Evolution (Biology)
ISBN 0761354867; 9780761354864

LC 2012018075

This book offers an "overview of how [Charles] Darwin's theories of natural selection and evolution shook the foundations of religious beliefs and long-held scientific views. . . .[Sylvia A.] Johnson devotes the first half of her book to discussing the intellectual, philosophical and societal changes brought by the Enlightenment and Industrial Revolution that would make people receptive to Darwin's ideas. . . . The second half chronicles how Darwin formulated his theories." (Kirkus Reviews)

Includes bibliographical references and index

Mehling, Randi

Great extinctions of the past; by Randi Mehling. Chelsea House 2007 72p il (Scientific American) lib bdg $30

Grades: 5 6 7 8   576.8

1. Dinosaurs 2. Prehistoric animals 3. Mass extinction of species
ISBN 978-0-7910-9049-7 lib bdg; 0-7910-9049-3 lib bdg

LC 2006014851

Examines extinctions of prehistoric species including the dinosaurs, looks at the five largest extinctions ever, and explores the idea of a future mass extinction.

"The ideas in this book are . . . clearly explained. . . . [The book has] captioned color photos thoughout." SLJ

Includes glossary and bibliographical references

Newland, Sonya

Extinction! by Jim Pipe. Crabtree Publishing Company 2013 48 p. col. ill. (Crabtree chrome) (library) $30.60; (paperback) $9.95

Grades: 4 5 6   576.8

1. Extinct animals 2. End of the world 3. Mass extinction of species 4. Mass extinctions 5. Extinction (Biology)
ISBN 0778779254; 9780778779254; 9780778779346

LC 2012032046

This book by Sonya Newland "explores both the history of extinction--dating back to the mass extinction of the Ordovician period 450 million years ago and the extinction of the dinosaurs 65 million years ago--as well as the possibility of the extinction of species in existence today. . . . In addition . . . Newland considers possible scenarios that might end life on Earth: an asteroid colliding with our planet . . . or an exploding nuclear bomb that blocks out the sun." (School Library Journal)

Includes bibliographical references and index

Pringle, Laurence P.

★ **Billions** of years, amazing changes; the story of evolution. Boyds Mills Press 2011 102p il $17.95

Grades: 4 5 6 7   576.8

1. Evolution
ISBN 978-1-59078-723-6; 1-59078-723-4

"Pringle provides an accessible introduction to complex concepts such as natural selection and genetics, paired with Jenkins's characteristically elegant collages. . . . Compelling photographs of fossils and living creatures, as well as Jenkins's paper collages, augment the substantial text. The presentation should help children gain a confident grasp on the fundamentals of evolution." Publ Wkly

Scott, Elaine

★ **Mars** and the search for life. Clarion Books 2008 60p il $17

Grades: 4 5 6 7   576.8

1. Life on other planets
ISBN 978-0-618-76695-6; 0-618-76695-2

LC 2008-07243

The author discusses "the Mars Exploration Rover (MER) and tantalizing findings that suggest that conditions on the red planet may once have been hospitable to life. . . . Illustrations are arresting and clearly captioned." Bull Cent Child Books

Includes glossary and bibliographical references

Skurzynski, Gloria

★ **Are** we alone? scientists search for life in space. National Geographic Society 2004 92p il $18.95

Grades: 5 6 7 8   576.8

1. Life on other planets
ISBN 0-7922-6567-X

LC 2003-17732

The author begins with a "history of how the idea of flying saucers and extraterrestrials became part of the American consciousness. Later chapters trace specific quests . . . for signs of life beyond earth. . . . The text remains readable even while explaining intricate scientific concepts and complex . . . ideas. The vibrant full-color photos enhance the work impressively." Booklist

Includes glossary and bibliographical references

Solway, Andrew

Why is there life on Earth? Raintree 2012 48p il (Earth, space, and beyond) $32; pa $8.99

Grades: 5 6 7 8   576.8

1. Life on other planets 2. Life -- Origin
ISBN 978-1-4109-4160-2; 978-1-4109-4166-4 pa

LC 2010040160

"Delivering compact but broad summations about...life on Earth, [this] survey [is] well suited for review or reinforcement reading." SLJ

Includes glossary and bibliographical references

Turner, Pamela S.

★ **Life** on earth--and beyond; an astrobiologist's quest. Charlesbridge 2008 109p il map lib bdg $19.95; pa $11.95

Grades: 5 6 7 8   **576.8**
1. Space biology   2. Life on other planets   3. Astrophysicists   4. Exobiology
ISBN 978-1-58089-133-2 lib bdg; 1-58089-133-0 lib bdg; 978-1-58089-134-9 pa; 1-58089-134-9 pa
LC 2007-01475

"Astrobiologists look outward from the Earth seeking evidence of life elsewhere in the universe. But, as this fascinating book shows, they also travel to places on Earth where extreme conditions may be similar to those on distant worlds. Turner follows astrobiologist Chris McKay as he looks for life in apparently hostile environments. . . . Illustrated with many excellent color photos and other images." Booklist

Includes bibliographical references

Walker, Robert

What is the theory of evolution? Crabtree Pub. Co. 2011 64p il (Shaping modern science) lib bdg $30.60; pa $10.95

Grades: 5 6 7 8   **576.8**
1. Evolution   2. Naturalists   3. Travel writers   4. Writers on science
ISBN 978-0-7787-7198-2 lib bdg; 0-7787-7198-9 lib bdg; 978-0-7787-7205-7 pa; 0-7787-7205-5 pa
LC 2010052628

This title is "not only written and organized well, but [it is] also gorgeous in design. Full-color photographs and illustrations are set over colorful backgrounds that add depth but not distraction. [The title] includes thought-provoking quotes from famous authors and scientists and some eyebrow-raising 'Quick Facts' throughout." SLJ

Includes glossary and bibliographical references

Winston, Robert M. L.

★ **Evolution** revolution; [by] Robert Wilson. DK Pub. 2009 96p il $16.99

Grades: 5 6 7 8   **576.8**
1. Evolution
ISBN 978-0-7566-45243-; 0-7566-4524-7

"The first two thirds of the book are devoted to the history of thought and research on evolution, from stories of Creation, through Darwin, to genetics. The last third looks at 'Evolution in Action.' Information on the fetuses of related species rubs shoulders with variations within species and a time line of the Earth. Visually, the book snaps with colored backgrounds, cool graphics, topflight photos, and clever word balloons coming from vintage black-and-white reproductions." SLJ

577   Ecology

Ballard, Carol

Food webs. Rosen Central 2010 46p il (Living processes) lib bdg $26.50; pa $11.75

1. Food chains (Ecology)
ISBN 978-1-61532-340-1 lib bdg; 1-61532-340-6 lib bdg; 978-1-61532-351-7 pa; 1-61532-351-1 pa
LC 2009-28379

"With colorful, quality photography, the well-organized content is divided into short chapters with bold subheadings making information easy to find. Clear and interesting writing distinguishes this . . . from older titles. The captions for pictures are used to provide identification and additional explanation for topics not included in the text." Libr Media Connect

Includes glossary and bibliographical references

Ecology; the delicate balance of life on earth. edited by Sherman Hollar. Rosen Educational Services, LLC 2012 87 p. col. ill. (library) $31.70

Grades: 5 6 7 8   **577**
1. Ecology   2. Environmentalism
ISBN 1615305076; 9781615305070
LC 2010052490

This book on ecology, edited by Sherman Hollar, "explores the formation of ecological communities and examines the biological diversity that forms the backbone of life on the planet. . . . By parsing the natural world into various ecosystems and biomes" it looks at "interaction among species and between organisms and their natural habitats." (Publisher's note)

Includes bibliographical references (p. 84) and index.

Gardner, Robert

Ace your ecology and environmental science project; great science fair ideas. [by] Robert Gardner, Phyllis J. Perry, and Salvatore Tocci. Enslow Publishers 2009 128p il (Ace your science project) lib bdg $31.93

Grades: 5 6 7 8   **577**
1. Ecology   2. Science projects   3. Environmental sciences   4. Science -- Experiments
ISBN 978-0-7660-3216-3 lib bdg; 0-7660-3216-7 lib bdg
LC 2008-4683

"Dozens of . . . science activities are presented with background information, step-by-step instructions, and suggestions for extending to the science fair level. . . . Color illustrations and important safety information are included." Horn Book Guide

Includes bibliographical references

Housel, Debra J.

Ecosystems. Compass Point Books 2009 40p il map (Mission: science) lib bdg $26.60

Grades: 4 5 6   **577**
1. Ecology
ISBN 978-0-7565-4068-5 lib bdg; 0-7565-4068-2 lib bdg
LC 2008-35730

An introduction to the ways in which plants and animals interact with each other

Includes glossary

Keithley, Melanie

Eco-tracking; on the trail of habitat change. with photographs by Melanie Keithley, Jon Livingston MacLake, and the author. University of New Mexico Press 2010 85p il (Worlds of wonder) $19.95

Grades: 6 7 8 9 10   **577**

1. Ecology 2. Environmental protection

ISBN 978-0-8263-4531-8; 0-8263-4531-X

LC 2010010319

"This unique title explains how ordinary kids, with ordinary tools, can become eco-scientists in their neighborhoods. In clear prose, Shaw explains the concepts of scientific observation, data collection, and analysis. Each chapter includes explanations of basic ecology terms, the effects of different environmental forces, and how they can be observed. . . . The writing . . . moves briskly and does not get too technical. . . . The color photos are sharp and capture different kids as they work in the field. Students will find this book a super resource for starting their own habitat observations." SLJ

Includes glossary

Latham, Donna

Amazing biome projects you can build yourself; illustrated by Farah Rizvi. Nomad Press 2009 122p il map (Build it yourself) pa $15.95

Grades: 4 5 6 7   **577**

1. Ecology 2. Handicraft 3. Earth sciences 4. Science -- Experiments

ISBN 978-1-934670-40-8; 1-934670-40-5

"Although the text addresses young 'eco explorers' directly, this book will likely be used as much by teachers, parents, and organization leaders in planning group activities. Offering an overview of eight terrestrial biomes as well as the ocean, Latham crams a lot of information about climate, plants, animals, soil, and other characteristics onto every page. . . . Instructions for hands-on activities related to different biomes include craft projects such as pictographs and a cornhusk doll. Students can learn how to make a glacier, an erupting volcano, and a tornado in a bottle." SLJ

Includes glossary and bibliographical references

Ecology. Raintree 2009 48p il (Sci-hi: life science) lib bdg $31.43; pa $8.99

Grades: 5 6 7 8   **577**

1. Ecology

ISBN 978-1-4109-3328-7 lib bdg; 1-4109-3328-8 lib bdg; 978-1-4109-3336-2 pa; 1-4109-3336-9 pa

LC 2009003465

In this introduction to ecology "clear language, embedded definitions, and interesting examples illustrate abstract concepts through both text and well-chosen photographs. . . . [It] includes suggested activities to test ideas as well as a thorough glossary and a Webliography." SLJ

Includes glossary and bibliographical references

Rompella, Natalie

Ecosystems; [by] Natalie Rompella. Heinemann Library 2008 48p il (Science fair projects) $30

Grades: 5 6 7 8   **577**

1. Ecology 2. Science projects 3. Science --

Experiments

ISBN 978-1-4034-7915-0

LC 2006039543

This "describes 10 inquiry-based science projects related to life science and ecosystems. . . . Students from mid-elementary through middle school would find little difficulty following the clearly written instructions and suggestions. . . . The illustrations consist of colorful photographs and well-labeled diagrams." Sci Books Films

Includes bibliographical references

Silverstein, Alvin

Food chains; [by] Alvin Silverstein, Virginia Silverstein, and Laura Silverstein Nunn. rev ed.; Twenty-First Century Books 2008 96p il (Science concepts, second series) $31.93

Grades: 6 7 8 9   **577**

1. Food chains (Ecology)

ISBN 978-0-8225-6797-4; 0-8225-6797-0

First published 1998

Explains various components of a food chain and discusses energy flows, food webs, food pyramids, recycling in nature, and the effect of humans on food chains.

Stille, Darlene R.

Nature interrupted; the science of environmental chain reactions. Compass Point Books 2009 48p il map (Headline science) lib bdg $27.93

Grades: 5 6 7 8   **577**

1. Ecology 2. Food chains (Ecology) 3. Environmental degradation

ISBN 978-0-7565-3949-8 lib bdg; 0-7565-3949-8 lib bdg

LC 2008007282

This "reviews the importance of subtle links in the environmental chain and the far-reaching consequences of its disruption. The possible harm to the food chain caused by the use of antibacterial soap is one case study. The flow of energy from one organism to the next in the food web and the unexpected results when this relationship is disrupted are shown in examinations of monarch butterflies, zebra mussels, and algal blooms. The color illustrations and charts . . . are clear and helpful, and the text, although information rich, is not overly difficult." SLJ

Includes glossary and bibliographical references

Suzuki, David T.

★ You are the Earth; know your world so you can make it better. [by] David Suzuki and Kathy Vanderlinden; art by Wallace Edwards; diagrams by Talent Pun. rev ed; Greystone Books 2010 159p il $16.95

Grades: 4 5 6 7   **577**

1. Ecology 2. Human ecology

ISBN 978-1-55365-476-6; 1-55365-476-5

First published 1999 with title: You are the Earth: from dinosaur breath to pizza from dirt

"After devoting a chapter to each of life's necessities—air, water, soil (earth), energy (fire), love, and a spiritual connection with the universe—the authors close with a look at three social and environmental initiatives by young people;

a set of review questions (with answers); and 10 conscious-ness-raising activities, from science projects to storytelling. Sourced, briefly told versions of folktales from several traditions are interspersed throughout, and the plentiful illustrations include color diagrams, comics, and crisply reproduced photos. . . . [The authors'] eloquent plea to see ourselves and the Earth as interdependent will inspire readers to sit up, look around, and take a little less for granted." SLJ

Includes glossary

Walker, Pamela

Ecosystem science fair projects; revised and expanded using the scientific method. [by] Pam Walker and Elaine Wood. Enslow Publishers 2010 160p il (Biology science projects using the scientific method) lib bdg $34.60

Grades: 7 8 9 10   577

1. Ecology 2. Science projects 3. Science -- Experiments

ISBN 978-0-7660-3419-8 lib bdg; 0-7660-3419-4 lib bdg

LC 2009019375

First published 2005 with title: Ecosystem science fair projects using worms, leaves, crickets, and other stuff

"Explains how to use the scientific method to conduct several science experiments about ecosystems. Includes ideas for science fair projects." Publisher's note

Includes bibliographical references

Woodford, Chris

Arctic tundra and polar deserts; Revised ed. Raintree 2011 64p il map (Biomes atlases) $34

Grades: 5 6 7 8 9   577

1. Tundra ecology

ISBN 978-1-4329-4172-7; 1-4329-4172-0

LC 2010012428

Information about the animals and plants that typically make polar regions and tundra environments their homes.

"...Provides detailed information suitable for middle school research projects, and browsing potential is high due to the colorful, graphic nature." Library Media Connection

Includes bibliographical references

577.078   Ecology -- Experiments

VanCleave, Janice Pratt, 1942-

Step-by-step science experiments in ecology; by Janice VanCleave. Rosen Pub. 2013 80 p. col. ill. (Janice Vancleave's first-place science fair projects) (library) $33.25; (paperback) $14.15

Grades: 5 6 7 8   577.078

1. Ecology 2. Science -- Experiments 3. Ecology -- Experiments

ISBN 1448869803; 9781448869800; 9781448884698

This book by Janice VanCleave is part of the First-Place Science Fair Projects series. The books have an introduction to the subject—here, ecology, followed by 22 simple . . . experiments. Van Cleave states the basic goal of the experiments, followed by a list of necessary materials, most of which can be found around the house or easily acquired with

minimal cost. Step-by-step instructions are clearly detailed and accompanied by diagrams where needed." (School Library Journal)

Includes bibliographical references (p. 76-78) and index.

577.2   Specific factors affecting ecology

Simon, Seymour

★ **Wildfires**. Morrow Junior Bks. 1996 un il hardcover o.p. pa $6.99

Grades: 4 5 6 7   577.2

1. Forest fires 2. Forest ecology 3. Fire 4. Ecology

ISBN 0-688-17530-9 pa

LC 95-12653

"Exploring the place of fire in nature, Simon explains that . . . forest fires have important functions in the ecosystem. With a brilliantly clear and colorful photograph facing each page of text, the book describes the causes and the progression of the wildfires that burned areas of Yellowstone National Park in 1988, explains how the fires were beneficial in many ways. . . . Lucid writing and excellent book design." Booklist

577.3   Ecology of specific environments

Allaby, Michael

Temperate forests; illustrations by Richard Garratt. rev ed; Facts on File 2008 336p il map (Ecosystem) $70

Grades: 7 8 9 10   577.3

1. Forest ecology 2. Forests and forestry

ISBN 0-8160-5930-6; 978-0-8160-5930-0

LC 2006-28859

First published 1999

"Those who are curious about or who are studying the environment and ecosystems . . . will find this book both fascinating and enlightening." Sci Books Films

Includes glossary and bibliographical references

Burnie, David

Shrublands; David Burnie. Raintree 2011 64 p. col. ill., col. maps (Biomes atlases) (library) $34

Grades: 6 7 8   577.3

1. Biomes 2. Habitat (Ecology) 3. Shrublands 4. Shrubland ecology

ISBN 143294178X; 9781432941789

LC 2010013019

This book is from the Biomes Atlases Series and focuses on shrublands. Each book offers an introduction to a different biome. "Brief notes for 10 to 12 highlights appear on each one, commenting on the diversity of flora, fauna, and landforms that occurs. Longer overviews of climate, plants, animals, people, and future prospects for the biome alternate with the regional close-ups." (School Library Journal)

Includes bibliographical references (p. 63) and index

Greenaway, Theresa

Jungle; written by Theresa Greenaway; photographed by Geoff Dann. rev ed.; DK Pub. 2004 71p il map (DK eyewitness books) $15.99

Grades: 4 5 6 7   **577.3**

1. Rain forest ecology

ISBN 0-7566-0694-2

LC 2004558978

First published 1994

Color photographs, drawings, and brief text describe the animals, plants, and ecology of tropical forests of the world

Jackson, Kay

Rain forests; by Kay Jackson. KidHaven Press 2007 48p il (Our environment) lib bdg $23.70

Grades: 5 6 7 8   **577.3**

1. Rain forests 2. Rain forest ecology

ISBN 978-0-7377-3624-3

LC 2007006892

"Jackson defines rain forests. . . . She explains why rain forests are important, . . . the causes of rain forest destruction, and current efforts to save diverse ecosystems. The writing is clear and succinct. . . . Full-color, captioned photographs and drawings appear on nearly every page." Booklist

Includes bibliographical references

Lasky, Kathryn

The most beautiful roof in the world; exploring the rainforest canopy. photographs by Christopher G. Knight. Harcourt Brace & Co. 1997 un il hardcover o.p. pa $9

Grades: 4 5 6 7   **577.3**

1. Botanists 2. Rain forest ecology

ISBN 0-15-200893-4; 0-15-200897-7 pa

LC 95-48193

Describes the work of Meg Lowman in the rainforest canopy, an area unexplored until the last ten years and home to previously unknown species of plants and animals

"Fresh in out-look and intriguing in details, this memorable book features colorful photographs that reflect the you-are-there quality of the text." Booklist

Includes glossary

Miller-Schroeder, Patricia

Boreal forests; [by] Patricia Miller-Schroeder. Weigl Publishers 2005 32p il map (Biomes) $26; pa $7.99

Grades: 4 5 6 7   **577.3**

1. Forest ecology

ISBN 1-59036-345-0; 1-59036-351-5 pa

LC 2005005436

This discusses the ecosystem of "the northern, coniferous forests or taigas. . . . The [volume contains] succinct text and [is] full of pictures, maps, graphs, and sidebars of interesting facts." Voice Youth Advocates

Includes bibliographical references

Quinlan, Susan E.

The case of the monkeys that fell from the trees; and other mysteries in tropical nature. Boyds Mills Press 2003 171p il map $15.95

Grades: 6 7 8 9   **577.3**

1. Natural history 2. Rain forest ecology

ISBN 1-56397-902-0

LC 2002-108914

"Quinlan's book is well organized and clearly written. . . . Besides presenting some fascinating case studies in a style that conveys the thrill of the scientific chase, it also provides information on the different kinds of tropical forests and how they function." SLJ

Includes bibliographical references

Tocci, Salvatore

Life in the tropical forests. Franklin Watts 2005 63p il map (Biomes and habitats) lib bdg $25.50

Grades: 4 5 6 7   **577.3**

1. Rain forest ecology

ISBN 0-531-12364-2

LC 2004027054

Describes the animals, plants, and people that live in rainforests and the threats to their existence

Includes glossary and bibliographical references

The chaparral; life on the scrubby coast. Franklin Watts 2003 63p il map (Biomes and habitats) lib bdg $25.50; pa $8.95

Grades: 4 5 6 7   **577.3**

1. Chaparral ecology

ISBN 0-531-12303-0 lib bdg; 0-531-16671-6 pa

LC 2003-16574

A look at the plants, animals, locations, and various habitats that make up the chaparral ecosystems of the world

Vogt, Richard Carl

Rain forests. Simon & Schuster Books for Young Readers 2009 64p il (Insiders) $16.99

Grades: 4 5 6 7   **577.3**

1. Rain forests

ISBN 978-1-4169-3866-8; 1-4169-3866-4

LC 2008061111

"The layers of a rain forest are drawn with exacting detail in every imaginable shade of green, while circular inserts zoom in on flora with accompanying stats. Running down the length of the spread are markers delineating the cutoff points for each layer—emergent, canopy, and so on. The rest of the book is similarly fine, bringing animals, reptiles, and insects into the mix. . . . Some photographs join the mostly hand-illustrated affair. . . . What will grab browsers are the 3D cover and vivid drawings on thick, oversize pages, but what will keep them reading is a cumulative sense of the rain forest as a verdant universe nearly festering with life." Booklist

Warhol, Tom

Chaparral and scrub; [by] Tom Warhol. Marshall Cavendish Benchmark 2006 80p il (Earth's biomes) lib bdg $32.79

Grades: 6 7 8 9   **577.3**

1. Chaparral ecology 2. Forests and forestry

ISBN 978-0-7614-2195-5 lib bdg; 0-7614-2195-5 lib bdg

LC 2006015824

"Explores chaparral and scrub biomes and covers where they are located as well as the plants and animals that inhabit them." Publisher's note

Includes glossary and bibliographical references

Welsbacher, Anne

Protecting Earth's rain forests; by Anne Welsbacher. Lerner Publications 2009 72p il map (Saving our living Earth) lib bdg $30.60

Grades: 5 6 7 8   **577.3**

1. Rain forests 2. Environmental protection
ISBN 978-0-8225-7562-7 lib bdg; 0-8225-7562-0 lib bdg

LC 2007-38859

"Provides a thorough, interesting discussion of multiple aspects of [rain forest protection], including historical origins, the current situation, and potential solutions. . . . Photos from around the world accompany discussions. . . . Solid choice to replace outdated books." SLJ

Includes glossary and bibliographical references

577.34   Rain forest ecology

Jackson, Tom

Tropical forests; Tom Jackson. Revised ed. Raintree 2011 64 p. col. ill., col. maps (Biomes atlases) (library) $34.00

Grades: 6 7 8   **577.34**

1. Rain forests 2. Rain forest animals 3. Rain forest ecology
ISBN 1432941771; 9781432941772

LC 2010012915

This children's nonfiction book, by Tom Jackson, profiles tropical forests as part of the publisher's "Biomes Atlases" series. "Each volume opens with a colorful world map featuring the eleven biomes of the world; individual books then diverge into a specific biome. Five topics are covered in each book: climate, plants, animals, people, and future of the biome." (Publisher's note)

Includes bibliographical references (p. 63) and index.

577.4   Grassland ecology

Collard, Sneed B.

★ The **prairie** builders; reconstructing America's lost grasslands. written and photographed by Sneed B. Collard III. Houghton Mifflin Co. 2005 66p il (Scientists in the field) $17; pa $8.95

Grades: 4 5 6 7   **577.4**

1. Prairies 2. Nature conservation 3. Prairie plants 4. Prairie conservation 5. Native plants for cultivation
ISBN 978-0-618-39687-0; 0-618-39687-X; 978-0-547-01441-8 pa; 0-547-01441-4 pa

LC 2004-13201

This describes an effort to restore part of the native tall-grass prairie in the the 8,000-acre Neal Smith National Wildlife Refuge in Iowa

"The engaging text is accompanied by large, inviting color photographs. . . . An essential purchase for libraries in prairie regions and a worthwhile choice for others." SLJ

Includes bibliographical references

Hoare, Ben

Temperate grasslands; Ben Hoare. Raintree 2011 64 p. col. ill., col. maps (Biomes atlases) (library) $34.00

Grades: 6 7 8 9   **577.4**

1. Prairies 2. Grasslands 3. Prairie animals 4. Prairie ecology 5. Grassland ecology
ISBN 143294181X; 9781432941819

LC 2010013034

This book, by Ben Hoare, is part of the publisher's "Biomes Atlases" nonfiction series. "Untouched temperate grasslands can be hard to find, since the fertile soil is often converted to farmland." This book presents a profile of the wild flora and fauna which does exist in these areas. (Publisher's note)

Includes bibliographical references (p. 63) and index.

Lynch, Wayne

Rocky Mountains; text and photographs by Wayne Lynch; assisted by Aubrey Lang. NorthWord Books for Young Readers 2006 64p il map (Our wild world ecosystems) $16.95; pa $8.95

Grades: 6 7 8 9   **577.4**

1. Mountain ecology 2. Natural history -- Rocky Mountains
ISBN 1-55971-948-6; 1-55971-949-4 pa

LC 2005-38014

"Introductory chapters explain the physical science that forms mountains and their weather. Each subsequent chapter zeros in on different mountain habitats (rivers and lakes, meadows and forests, and so on), introducing facts about the animals and plants in each. The authors . . . write in vivid, clear prose that, together with the quality of the beautiful images, sets this title apart from other . . . books on the topic." Booklist

Includes bibliographical references

Martin, Patricia A. Fink

Prairies, fields, and meadows. Watts 2002 144p il map (Exploring ecosystems) lib bdg $24.50; pa $6.95

Grades: 7 8 9 10   **577.4**

1. Ecology 2. Prairie ecology 3. Grassland ecology 4. Meadow ecology
ISBN 978-0-531-11859-7; 0-531-11859-2 lib bdg; 978-0-531-16604-8 pa; 0-531-16604-X pa

LC 2001-17570

"One can glean a great deal of useful information from this text." Libr Media Connect

Includes glossary and bibliographical references

Toupin, Laurie

★ **Life** in the temperate grasslands. Franklin Watts 2005 63p il map (Biomes and habitats) lib bdg $25.50

Grades: 4 5 6 7   **577.4**
    1. Grassland ecology
    ISBN 0-531-12385-5
                                        LC 2004-13282
This describes the ecology of grasslands such as the
North American prairie, the South American pampas, the
African veldt and the European steppes
    This is "written in an accessible and interesting, conver-
sational style. The [author conveys] a good deal of information about topics such as adaptation, environmental threats,
seasonal changes, and other essentials important to report
writers and general readers." SLJ
    Includes bibliographical references

    ★ **Savannas**; life in the tropical grasslands. [by]
Laurie Peach Toupin. Franklin Watts 2005 63p il
map (Biomes and habitats) lib bdg $25.50
Grades: 4 5 6 7   **577.4**
    1. Grassland ecology
    ISBN 0-531-12386-3
                                        LC 2004-13281
This introduces "readers to the climate characteristics
as well as plants and animals of [tropical grasslands. It is]
written in an accessible and interesting, conversational style.
The authors convey a good deal of information about topics
such as adaptation, environmental threats, seasonal changes,
and other essentials important to report writers and general
readers." SLJ
    Includes bibliographical references

577.5   Ecology of miscellaneous environments

Allaby, Michael
    ★ **Deserts**; illustrations by Richard Garratt. rev
ed; Facts on File 2008 320p il map (Ecosystem)
$70
Grades: 7 8 9 10   **577.5**
    1. Deserts 2. Desert ecology
    ISBN 0-8160-5929-2; 978-0-8160-5929-4
                                        LC 2007-00477
First published 2001
    "This book is a good mix of text, excellent maps, photo-
graphs, and scientific information." Sci Books Films
    Includes glossary and bibliographical references

Banting, Erinn
    Caves; Erinn Banting. AV2 by Weigl 2012 32 p.
col. ill., col. map (Ecosystems) (hardcover) $28.55;
(paperback) $13.95
Grades: 4 5 6   **577.5**
    1. Caves 2. Cave ecology 3. Ecology
    ISBN 1616906391; 1616906456; 9781616906399;
    9781616906450
                                        LC 2010050985
This book by Erinn Banting is part of the "Biomes"
series. "Caves are unique ecosystems that are found on all
seven continents. This book explores the plants and animals
that have adapted to life in this unique environment." (Publisher's note)

"Explanations of climate and physical characteristics
are accompanied by appropriate diagrams and illustrations."
(School Library Journal)

Fridell, Ron
    Life in the desert. Franklin Watts 2005 63p il
map (Biomes and habitats) lib bdg $25.50
Grades: 4 5 6 7   **577.5**
    1. Deserts 2. Desert ecology
    ISBN 0-531-12384-7
                                        LC 2004027254
Presents an introduction to desert environments, in simple text with illustrations, providing information on its average temperature, climate, plant and animal life, and people
    Includes glossary and bibliographical references

Lynch, Wayne
    Sonoran Desert; text and photographs by Wayne
Lynch; assisted by Aubrey Lang. NorthWord Books
2009 64p il (Our wild world ecosystems) $16.95
Grades: 5 6 7 8   **577.5**
    1. Desert ecology 2. Natural history -- Sonoran Desert
    ISBN 978-1-58979-389-7; 1-58979-389-7
                                        LC 2008036635
"An in-depth look at a vibrant ecosystem. Spilling over
the Mexican border into Arizona and New Mexico, the Sonoran Desert is especially rich in varied plants, animals,
insects, and other critters that call it home. Lynch shares
his expertise and experiences in a clearly written, conversational text, lavishly illustrated with his own crisp color
photos." SLJ

Warhol, Tom
    Desert; [by] Tom Warhol. Marshall Cavendish
Benchmark 2006 80p il (Earth's biomes) lib bdg
$34.21
Grades: 6 7 8 9   **577.5**
    1. Deserts 2. Desert ecology
    ISBN 978-0-7614-2194-8 lib bdg; 0-7614-2194-7
    lib bdg
                                        LC 2006015823
"Explores desert biomes and covers where they are lo-
cated as well as the plants and animals that inhabit them."
Publisher's note
    Includes glossary and bibliographical references

    Tundra; [by] Tom Warhol. Marshall Cavendish
Benchmark 2006 80p il (Earth's biomes) lib bdg
$34.21
Grades: 6 7 8 9   **577.5**
    1. Tundra ecology
    ISBN 978-0-7614-2193-1 lib bdg; 0-7614-2193-9
    lib bdg
                                        LC 2006015822
"The clarity of the narrative and the spectacular photo-
graphs . . . make this . . . an appealing, useful addition to the
. . . school." Voice of Youth Advocates
    Includes glossary and bibliographical references

577.6   Aquatic ecology

Lynette, Rachel
   River food chains. Heinemann Library 2011
48p il map (Protecting food chains) lib bdg $32;
pa $8.99
Grades: 4 5 6 7   577.6
   1. River ecology 2. Food chains (Ecology)
   ISBN 978-1-4329-3861-1 lib bdg; 1-4329-3861-4 lib
   bdg; 978-1-4329-3868-0 pa; 1-4329-3868-1 pa
                                          LC 2009049552
   This book explores the species found in river food chains
and webs, and discusses why these food chains and webs
need to be protected.
   "Featuring colorful, glossy images and accessible
prose, this . . . offers a good introduction to the web of life
in rivers. . . . Conservation issues are highlighted throughout, with specific suggestions for youth to get involved. .
. . An informative, thought-provoking resource that conveys the fragile, interconnected web that holds ecosystems
together." Booklist
   Includes glossary and bibliographical references

Toupin, Laurie
   Freshwater habitats; life in freshwater ecosystems. F. Watts 2005 63p il map (Biomes and habitats) lib bdg $25.50; pa $8.95
Grades: 4 5 6 7   577.6
   1. Freshwater ecology
   ISBN 0-531-12305-7 lib bdg; 0-531-16675-9 pa
                                          LC 2003-16572
   A look at the plants, animals, locations, and various habitats that make up the freshwater ecosystems of the world

Warhol, Tom
   Water; [by] Tom Warhol. Marshall Cavendish
Benchmark 2006 80p il (Earth's biomes) lib bdg
$34.21
Grades: 6 7 8 9   577.6
   1. Marine ecology 2. Freshwater biology
   ISBN 978-0-7614-2192-4 lib bdg; 0-7614-2192-0
   lib bdg
                                          LC 2006011979
   "Explores water biomes and covers where they are lo-
cated as well as the plants and animals that inhabit them."
Publisher's note
   Includes glossary and bibliographical references

577.7   Marine ecology

Carson, Rachel
   The **edge** of the sea; with illustrations by Bob
Hines. Houghton Mifflin 1955 276p il hardcover
o.p. pa $14
Grades: 7 8 9 10 11 12 Adult   577.7
   1. Seashore 2. Marine biology
   ISBN 0-395-92496-0 pa
   "The seashores of the world may be divided into three
basic types: the rugged shores of rock, the sand beaches, and
the coral reefs and all their associated features. Each has its

typical community of plants and animals. The Atlantic coast
of the United States [provides] clear examples of each of
these types." Publisher's note

Cousteau, Philippe
   Make a splash! a kid's guide to protecting our
oceans, lakes, rivers & wetlands. by Cathryn Berger
Kaye; with Philippe Cousteau and EarthEcho International. Free Spirit Pub. Inc. 2013 125 p. ill. (chiefly
col.) (paperback) $13.99
Grades: 3 4 5 6   577.7
   1. Environmentalists 2. Water conservation 3. Marine
   ecology 4. Environmentalism 5. Marine pollution --
   Prevention
   ISBN 1575424177; 9781575424170
                                          LC 2012032120
   This book for elementary-age readers has "colorful photos and digital drawings [that] illustrate many aspects of water on Earth, while the text provides information and tells
stories of children in elementary schools around the world
who have translated their own environmental concerns into
action." (Booklist)

O'Neill, Michael Patrick
   Wild waters photo journal. Batfish Books 2010
106p il $29.95
Grades: 6 7 8 9 10   577.7
   1. Marine animals 2. Marine ecology
   ISBN 978-0-9728653-6-4; 0-9728653-6-5
   "This personal collection of stunning, full-color photographs highlights unique underwater habitats and the life
found in select natural communities around the world. Full
spreads provide either an overview of an ecosystem, e.g.,
Komodo National Park or Bali in Indonesia, or a signature
animal, e.g., the great white shark at Guadalupe Island,
Mexico, or a dwarf caiman in Brazil. . . . The photographs
are compelling by themselves and beautiful to browse. This
book informs readers and gives them a deeper understanding of the ever-present threats to the ecological diversity and
beauty of the planet." SLJ

Parker, Steve, 1952-
   ★ **Seashore**; written by Steve Parker. rev ed; DK
Pub. 2004 72p il (DK eyewitness books) $15.99
Grades: 4 5 6 7   577.7
   1. Seashore 2. Marine plants 3. Marine animals
   ISBN 0-7566-0721-3; 0-7566-0720-5 lib bdg
   First published 1989 by Knopf
   Brief text and photos introduce the animal inhabit-
ants of the seashore, including fish, crustaceans, snails,
and shorebirds

Pyers, Greg
   The **biodiversity** of coral reefs. Marshall Cavendish 2010 32p il map lib bdg $28.50
Grades: 4 5 6 7   577.7
   1. Coral reefs and islands
   ISBN 978-1-60870-070-7 lib bdg; 1-60870-070-4
   lib bdg
   "Discusses the variety of living things in a coral reef's
ecosystem." Publisher's note

Walker, Pamela

★ The **coral** reef; [by] Pam Walker and Elaine Wood. Facts on File 2005 140p (Life in the sea) $35

Grades: 6 7 8 9 10   **577.7**

1. Coral reefs and islands
ISBN 0-8160-5703-6

"An opening chapter gives detailed coverage of how reefs are formed. Later chapters examine the reefs' inhabitants, from essential microbes to the larger, showier fish, reptiles, and other animals. The final chapter . . . mentions environmental hazards and conservation efforts. . . . The range and depth of information . . . make this a fine addition for science collections." Booklist

577.8   Synecology and population biology

Silverstein, Alvin

★ **Symbiosis**; [by] Alvin Silverstein, Virginia Silverstein, and Laura Silverstein Nunn. rev ed.; Twenty-First Century Books 2008 96p il (Science concepts, second series) lib bdg $31.93

Grades: 6 7 8 9   **577.8**

1. Symbiosis
ISBN 978-0-8225-6799-8 lib bdg; 0-8225-6799-7 lib bdg

LC 2007003184

First published 1998

Discusses the three kinds of symbiosis—mutualism, commensalism, and parasitism—and describes examples of these relationships.

"Well researched and interesting and the format is inviting for both general-interest reading and research." SLJ [review of 1998 edition]

Includes bibliographical references

U-X-L encyclopedia of biomes; [editor] Marlene Weigel. 2nd ed.; U-X-L 2009 3v il map set $214

Grades: 7 8 9 10   **577.8**

1. Reference books 2. Ecology -- Encyclopedias
ISBN 978-1-4144-5516-7

LC 2008-14502

First published 1999

"Entries range from 35 to 45 pages and cover an overview and description, climate, elevation, soil, water bodies, vegetation, animal life, food web, plant and animal adaptations, endangered species, human effects on the biome and the effects of the environment on humans' culture and economy." Publisher's note

Includes bibliographical references

578   Natural history of organisms and related subjects

Kelsey, Elin

★ **Strange** new species; astonishing discoveries of life on earth. Maple Tree Press 2005 96p il $24.95; pa $16.95

Grades: 5 6 7 8   **578**

1. Biology 2. Scientists 3. Natural history 4. Discoveries in science
ISBN 1-897066-31-7; 1-897066-32-5 pa

"This large-format book showcases new species . . . and the scientists who have discovered them. . . . The discussion ends with information on cloning, genetically modified food, and the future of life. . . . With many excellent photos, this introductory book on new species will be an intriguing addition to classroom units on classification or biology." Booklist

Wildlife and plants; 3rd ed.; Marshall Cavendish 2007 20v il set $359.95

Grades: 4 5 6 7   **578**

1. Reference books 2. Plants -- Encyclopedias 3. Animals -- Encyclopedias
ISBN 978-0-7614-7693-1

First published 1994 with title: Wildlife and plants of the world

This set includes "more than 500 entries covering animals, plants, microorganisms, fungi, habitats, biomes, and overviews. . . . Entries provide a concise introduction followed by more detailed information including behavior, reproduction, characteristics, and survival tactics. . . . With its captivating information and photographs, students are sure to come to this easy-to-use set again and again." Booklist

578.4   Adaptation

Fullick, Ann

★ **Adaptation** and competition; [by] Ann Fullick. Heinemann Library 2006 64p il map (Life science in depth) lib bdg $34.29; pa $9.90

Grades: 6 7 8 9   **578.4**

1. Heredity 2. Adaptation (Biology)
ISBN 1-4034-7518-0 lib bdg; 1-4034-7526-1 pa

LC 2005023560

This "provides a detailed overview of how living organisms compete with one another to survive and how they adapt to climate and habitat. The style makes some complex science accessible, and the attractive book design breaks up the dense text. . . . The examples are lively." Booklist

Includes bibliographical references

Schafer, Susan

Adaptations. M.E. Sharpe 2009 96p il (Genetics: the science of life) $38.95

578.4

1. Adaptation (Biology)
ISBN 978-0-7656-8137-9; 0-7656-8137-4

LC 2008-8106

This discusses genetic adaptations in regard to defenses, feeding, and reproduction.

"Chock-full of information. . . . The material is well organized and accessible. . . . Interest is maintained through countless fascinating examples. . . . Illustrations and color photographs enhance [the text]." SLJ

Includes bibliographical references

Silverstein, Alvin

★ **Adaptation**; by Alvin Silverstein, Virginia Silverstein, and Laura Silverstein Nunn. Twenty-First Century Books 2008 112p il (Science concepts) lib bdg $31.93

Grades: 4 5 6 7   578.4
    1. Adaptation (Biology) 2. Evolution (Biology)
    ISBN 978-0-8225-3434-1 lib bdg; 0-8225-3434-7
lib bdg

                   LC 2007-02862
This "provides an accessible introduction to how living beings adapt to survive in diverse habitats. . . . The narrative gains clarity from abundant examples, colorful photos and diagrams, and fascinating sidebars." Booklist
    Includes bibliographical references

Spilsbury, Richard

Adaptation and survival. Rosen Central 2010 46p il map (Living processes) lib bdg $26.50; pa $11.75

Grades: 5 6 7   578.4
    1. Ecology 2. Adaptation (Biology)
    ISBN 978-1-61532-343-2 lib bdg; 1-61532-343-0 lib
bdg; 978-1-61532-348-7 pa; 1-61532-348-1 pa
                   LC 2009-30418
"With colorful, quality photography, the well-organized content is divided into short chapters with bold subheadings making information easy to find. Clear and interesting writing distinguishes this . . . from older titles. The captions for pictures are used to provide identification and additional explanation for topics not included in the text." Libr Media Connect
    Includes glossary and bibliographical references

578.6   Miscellaneous nontaxonomic kinds of organisms

Collard, Sneed B.

Science warriors; the battle against invasive species. written by Sneed B. Collard III. Houghton Mifflin 2008 48p il (Scientists in the field) $17

Grades: 5 6 7 8   578.6
    1. Nonindigenous pests 2. Biological invasions 4.
Scientists
    ISBN 978-0-618-75636-0; 0-618-75636-1
                   LC 2008-01867
"Collard focuses on four major invader species in the U.S.: the brown tree snake, . . . the red imported fire ant, . . . the melaleuca tree, . . . and the zebra mussel. . . . These are useful and thought-provoking case studies of a very large problem." Bull Cent Child Books
    Includes glossary and bibliographical references

Fleisher, Paul

★ **Parasites**; latching on to a free lunch. Twenty-First Century Books 2006 112p il (Discovery!) lib bdg $29.27

Grades: 7 8 9 10   578.6
    1. Parasites
    ISBN 978-0-8225-3415-0; 0-8225-3415-0
                  LC 2005-10521
This is "well organized and quite up to date. The photos . . . are plentiful, colorful, and excellent. . . . Clear, concise, and interesting." Voice Youth Advocates
    Includes bibliographical references

578.68   Rare and endangered species

Endangered species: opposing viewpoints; Viqi Wagner, book editor. Greenhaven Press 2008 230p map (Opposing viewpoints series) lib bdg $38.50; pa $26.75

Grades: 8 9 10 11 12   578.68
    1. Endangered species 2. Nature conservation
    ISBN 978-0-7377-2931-3 lib bdg; 978-0-7377-2932-0 pa
                  LC 2007-38314
This collection of articles offers varying viewpoints on extinction, preservation, property rights, and international cooperation.
    Includes bibliographical references

Pobst, Sandy

★ **Animals** on the edge; science races to save species threatened with extinction. by Sandra Pobst; Todd K. Fuller, consultant. National Geographic 2008 64p il (National Geographic investigates) $17.95; lib bdg $27.90

Grades: 4 5 6 7   578.68
    1. Endangered species 2. Wildlife conservation
    ISBN 978-1-4263-0358-6; 1-4263-0358-0; 978-1-4263-0265-7 lib bdg; 1-4263-0265-7 lib bdg
This "eye-catching [title features] full-color photographs. . . . The approach is to understand the challenges to protecting endangered animals, including global warming, destruction of habitat, tagging and tracking, poaching, captive breeding, and cloning." Voice Youth Advocates
    Includes glossary and bibliographical references

578.7   Organisms characteristic of specific kinds of environments

Conlan, Kathy

Under the ice. Kids Can Press 2002 55p il $16.95; pa $8.95

Grades: 4 5 6 7   578.7
    1. Authors 2. Marine biology 3. Marine pollution 4. Marine biologists 5. Children's authors 6. Writers on science
    ISBN 1-55337-001-5; 1-55337-060-0 pa
"The first-person text creates a feeling of immediacy. . . . Well-captioned, color photos appear throughout the book. . . . Conlan . . . offers readers an engaging account of her adventurous career in scientific field research." Booklist

Kirby, Richard R.

Ocean drifters; a secret world beneath the waves. Firefly Books 2011 192p il $29.95

Grades: 5 6 7 8 9 10 11 12 Adult   **578.7**

  1. Marine plankton

  ISBN 978-1-55407-982-7; 1-55407-982-9

                LC 2011284690

"This is a very well illustrated book of some 121 full-page color photographs of microscopic marine organisms. Each illustration is accompanied by a brief description and explanation. Phytoplankton and zooplankton are featured, but also included are picoplankton, virioplankton, and bacterioplankton, with emphasis on the role played by plankton in the carbon cycle, oxygen production, and as the base of the marine food pyramid as the primary producers. Their importance in sustaining the life of the oceans, in petroleum and natural gas resources, and in climate is also discussed." Sci Books Films

  Includes bibliographical references

Kummer, Patricia K.

The **Great** Barrier Reef; by Patricia K. Kummer. Marshall Cavendish Benchmark 2008 96p il map (Nature's wonders) lib bdg $24.95

Grades: 5 6 7 8   **578.7**

  1. Coral reefs and islands

  ISBN 978-0-7614-2852-7 lib bdg; 0-7614-2852-6 lib bdg

                LC 2007026661

"Provides comprehensive information on the geography, history, wildlife, peoples, and environmental issues of the Great Barrier Reef." Publisher's note

  Includes glossary and bibliographical references

Moore, Peter D.

Wetlands; illustrations by Richard Garratt. rev ed.; Facts on File 2008 270p il map (Ecosystem) $70

Grades: 7 8 9 10   **578.7**

  1. Wetlands

  ISBN 0-8160-5931-4; 978-0-8160-5931-7

                LC 2006-37399

First published 2000

This book "examines the diversity of wetlands in the past, present, and future, how they work, and how they can be conserved." Publisher's note

  Includes glossary and bibliographical references

Somervill, Barbara A.

Marine biologist. Cherry Lake Pub. 2009 32p il (Cool science careers) lib bdg $27.07

Grades: 3 4 5 6   **578.7**

  1. Marine biology 2. Vocational guidance

  ISBN 978-1-60279-504-4 lib bdg; 1-60279-504-5 lib bdg

                LC 2008045234

This describes the career of marine biologist, including ways to become involved in the profession, the interests and skills required, and activities for learning more

This is "highly readable. . . . Colorful photographs illustrate [the] book." SLJ

  Includes glossary and bibliographical references

Thomas, William David

Marine biologist. Gareth Stevens Pub. 2010 32p il (Cool careers: cutting edge) lib bdg $26; pa $8.95

Grades: 4 5 6   **578.7**

  1. Marine biology 2. Vocational guidance

  ISBN 978-1-4339-1957-2 lib bdg; 1-4339-1957-5 lib bdg; 978-1-4339-2156-8 pa; 1-4339-2156-1 pa

                LC 2009000239

Describes the work of a marine biologist.

This title offers "clear, solid information in a large font. . . . [This] short [book is] packed with relevant, current material." SLJ

  Includes glossary and bibliographical references

Walker, Pamela

★ The **continental** shelf; [by] Pam Walker & Elaine Wood. Facts on File 2005 142p (Life in the sea) $35

Grades: 6 7 8 9   **578.7**

  1. Marine biology 2. Continental shelf

  ISBN 0-8160-5704-4

This "title presents a comprehensive discussion of the physical aspects of the continental shelf; the variety of life beneath, on, and above the waters; and the many dangers to the health of these realms. . . . [This title has] helpful color photos and black-and-white charts and drawings. [This] important [work is] accessible to a variety of student abilities and should be considered for all collections." SLJ

  Includes bibliographical references

★ The **open** ocean; [by] Pam Walker and Elaine Wood. Facts on File 2005 132p il (Life in the sea) $35

Grades: 6 7 8 9   **578.7**

  1. Oceanography 2. Marine animals 3. Marine ecology

  ISBN 0-8160-5705-2

                LC 2004-24228

In this title "the areas beyond the continental shelf are profiled, and food chains, the diversity of life forms, and the anatomy of sea animals are discussed. . . . [This book includes] helpful color photos and black-and-white charts and drawings. [This] important [work is] accessible to a variety of student abilities and should be considered for all collections." SLJ

  Includes bibliographical references

Wallace, Marianne D.

America's forests; guide to plants and animals. Fulcrum Pub. 2009 47p il (America's ecosystems) pa $11.95

Grades: 5 6 7 8   **578.7**

  1. Forest plants 2. Forest animals 3. Forest ecology 4. Forests and forestry

  ISBN 978-1-55591-595-7 pa; 1-55591-595-7 pa

                LC 2008041005

This "is a guide to plants and animals within the context of forest communities. Marianne Wallace . . . expertly crafts this introduction to forests. . . . The book contains abundant illustrations." Sci Books Films

Includes glossary

Wechsler, Doug

Marvels in the muck; life in the salt marshes. Boyds Mills Press 2008 48p il $17.95

Grades: 4 5 6 7　　　　　　　　　　　　**578.7**

1. Salt marshes 2. Marsh ecology

ISBN 978-1-59078-588-1

LC 2007052583

"A season-by-season look at the ecology of an oft-overlooked habitat. Wechsler's lucid text introduces the insects, birds, reptiles, crustaceans, and other critters that claim this salty expanse as home. . . . Clear color photos present species mentioned in the text." SLJ

Includes glossary and bibliographical references

Winner, Cherie

Life on the edge. Lerner Publications Co. 2006 48p il (Cool science) lib bdg $26.60

Grades: 4 5 6　　　　　　　　　　　　**578.7**

1. Adaptation (Biology)

ISBN 978-0-8225-2499-1 lib bdg; 0-8225-2499-6 lib bdg

LC 2005011071

This book "introduces creatures in extreme conditions such as thermal pools, Antarctica, and the deep sea. [The book provides] clear explanations of the science and [covers] possible benefits to humans. A variety of photos and information boxes provide an eye-catching . . . layout." Horn Book Guide

Includes glossary and bibliographical references

579　Natural history of microorganisms, fungi, algae

Arato, Rona

Protists; algae, amoebas, plankton, and other protists. Crabtree Pub. Co. 2010 48p il (A class of their own) lib bdg $29.27; pa $9.95

Grades: 5 6 7 8　　　　　　　　　　　　**579**

1. Algae 2. Protists 3. Protozoa

ISBN 978-0-7787-5377-3 lib bdg; 0-7787-5377-8 lib bdg; 978-0-7787-5391-9 pa; 0-7787-5391-3 pa

LC 2009-51386

Looks at the protist kingdom, providing information and examples of species from the major phyla, as well as information about the role of protists in the food chain and in various diseases.

"Lively section headings . . . and notes on uncommon achievements, . . . lighten the substantial load of biological terminology. Illustrated with a plethora of closeup color photos and microphotos, and closing with annotated lists of recommended Web sites, . . . [this captures] the remarkable diversity of life." SLJ

Includes glossary and bibliographical references

Bardhan-Quallen, Sudipta

Kitchen science experiments; how does your mold garden grow? illustrated by Edward Miller. Sterling 2010 64p il (Mad science) $12.95

Grades: 4 5 6　　　　　　　　　　　　**579**

1. Biology 2. Microbiology 3. Science -- Experiments

ISBN 978-1-4027-2413-8; 1-4027-2413-6

LC 2010003749

"The language is as much fun as the science, including wordplay warnings . . . and the design is inviting, with colorful diagrams on each spacious, double-page spread. . . . Many students will be hooked by the fascinating revelations about the world around them." Booklist

Includes bibliographical references

Brown, Jordan

Micro mania; a really close-up look at bacteria, bedbugs & the zillions of other gross little creatures that live in, on & all around you! [by] Jordan D. Brown. Imagine! 2010 80p il $19.95

Grades: 4 5 6　　　　　　　　　　　　**579**

1. Microorganisms

ISBN 978-0-9823064-2-0; 0-9823064-2-3

"This engrossing book goes into squirm-inducing detail about the bacteria, microbes, and other assorted mini-organisms that dwell in our bodies and our homes. Each spread is well laid out with plenty of white space, large text, and colorful photos of these little critters . . . and the havoc they wreak. The writing is vivid without being breathless." SLJ

Latta, Sara L.

★ The **good,** the bad, the slimy; the secret life of microbes. [by] Sara Latta; photographs by Dennis Kunkel. Enslow Publishers 2006 128p il lib bdg $31.93

Grades: 5 6 7 8 9　　　　　　　　　　　　**579**

1. Microorganisms 2. Bacteria 3. Microbiology

ISBN 0-7660-1294-8

LC 2005-35405

"Explanations are simple and clear, and the layout is appealing, open, and colorful." SLJ

Includes glossary and bibliographical references

May, Suellen

Invasive microbes. Chelsea House 2007 112p il (Invasive species) $30

Grades: 8 9 10 11 12　　　　　　　　　　　　**579**

1. Microorganisms 2. Biological invasions

ISBN 0-7910-9131-7; 978-0-7910-9131-9

LC 2006011031

"An increase in global transportation has helped even the tiniest of organisms—microbes—find their way to new environments. . . . This . . . resource . . . [explains] the . . . impact . . . of invasive viruses, bacteria, protists, and fungi. This book evaluates scenarios for success in the escalating battle for containment." Publisher's note

Includes glossary and bibliographical references

Micro monsters. Kingfisher 2010 47p il (Kingdom) $14.99; pa $8.99

Grades: 3 4 5 6   **579**

1. Insects 2. Microorganisms

ISBN 978-0-7534-3014-9; 0-7534-3014-2; 978-0-7534-6455-7 pa; 0-7534-6455-1 pa

This book illustrates the unseen world of microscopic monsters and shows the reader how they survive and triumph. Some pages have movable flaps to show different pictures.

"Hyper-close-up photos detail all manner of stingers, stabbers, pincers, and chompers poking out from plated exoskeletons and hairy abdomens. This . . . is a great way to sneak in some basic science learning amid the din of death and destruction." Booklist

Parker, Steve, 1952-

Protozoans, algae & other protists. Compass Point Books 2009 48p il (Kingdom classification) lib bdg $29.32

Grades: 6 7 8 9   **579**

1. Algae 2. Protozoa

ISBN 978-0-7565-4224-5 lib bdg; 0-7565-4224-3 lib bdg

LC 2009-8783

Discusses the parts of protists, different types, their life cycles, and how they can be harmful to humans

"With its compelling facts and visuals, this is a quality choice." SLJ

Includes glossary

Stefoff, Rebecca

The **Moneran** kingdom; by Rebecca Stefoff. Marshall Cavendish Benchmark 2008 96p il (Family trees) $23.95

Grades: 6 7 8 9   **579**

1. Microorganisms

ISBN 978-0-7614-3076-6; 0-7614-3076-8

LC 2008-23210

"Explores the habitats, life cycles, and other characteristics of organisms in the Moneran kingdom." Publisher's note

Includes bibliographical references

Walker, Richard, 1951-

Microscopic life; [by] Richard Walker; foreword by Peter C. Doherty. Kingfisher 2004 63p il (Kingfisher knowledge) $12.95

Grades: 4 5 6 7   **579**

1. Microorganisms 2. Microbiology

ISBN 0-7534-5778-4

LC 2004-1321

"Double-page spreads introduce viruses, bacteria, 'mini animals' (e.g., Hydra and dust mites), and other microorganisms and explain how these unseen entities affect humanity in both harmful and helpful ways. The accompanying photographic enlargements . . . are fascinating." Horn Book Guide

Wearing, Judy

Fungi; mushrooms, toadstools, molds, yeasts, and other fungi. Crabtree 2010 48p il (A class of their own) lib bdg $29.27; pa $9.95

Grades: 5 6 7 8   **579**

1. Fungi

ISBN 978-0-7787-5375-9 lib bdg; 0-7787-5375-1 lib bdg; 978-0-7787-5389-6 pa; 0-7787-5389-1 pa

Features an examination of the four major groups of fungi: yeasts, toadstools, chytrids, and bread molds.

"Lively section headings . . . and notes on uncommon achievements, . . . lighten the substantial load of biological terminology. Illustrated with a plethora of closeup color photos and microphotos, and closing with annotated lists of recommended Web sites, . . . [this captures] the remarkable diversity of life." SLJ

Includes glossary and bibliographical references

Zabludoff, Marc

★ The **protoctist** kingdom. Benchmark Books 2006 95p il (Family trees) lib bdg $29.92

Grades: 5 6 7 8   **579**

1. Protoctista 2. Protista

ISBN 0-7614-1818-0

LC 2004-21821

This examines the physical traits, adaptations, diets, habitats, and life cycles of such life forms as bacteria, amoebas, slime nets, molds, algae, coccoliths, forams, and diatoms.

"Fact-filled, yet surprisingly readable. . . . [This] title contains a wide variety of excellent-quality, full-color photographs; interesting sidebars; and diagrams." SLJ

Zamosky, Lisa

Simple organisms. Compass Point Books 2009 40p il (Mission: science) lib bdg $26.60

Grades: 4 5 6   **579**

1. Microorganisms

ISBN 978-0-7565-3955-9 lib bdg; 0-7565-3955-2 lib bdg

LC 2008-7723

An introduction to microscopic organisms, including germs

Includes glossary and bibliographical references

579.3   Prokaryotes (Bacteria)

Barker, David M.

Archaea; salt-lovers, methane-makers, thermophiles, and other archaeans. by David Barker. Crabtree Pub. 2010 48p il (A class of their own) lib bdg $29.27; pa $9.95

Grades: 5 6 7 8   **579.3**

1. Bacteria

ISBN 978-0-7787-5373-5 lib bdg; 0-7787-5373-5 lib bdg; 978-0-7787-5387-2 pa; 0-7787-5387-5 pa

LC 2009-51393

Looks at the archaea domain, providing information and examples of species from the three major phyla, as well as information about why so little is known about this diverse domain.

"Lively section headings . . . and notes on uncommon achievements, . . . lighten the substantial load of biological terminology. Illustrated with a plethora of closeup color photos and microphotos, and closing with annotated lists of recommended Web sites, . . . [this captures] the remarkable diversity of life." SLJ

Includes glossary and bibliographical references

Wearing, Judy

Bacteria; staph, strep, clostridium, and other bacteria. Crabtree 2010 48p il (A class of their own) lib bdg $29.27; pa $9.95

Grades: 5 6 7 8   **579.3**
1. Bacteria
ISBN 978-0-7787-5374-2 lib bdg; 0-7787-5374-3 lib bdg; 978-0-7787-5388-9 pa; 0-7787-5388-3 pa

Examines bacteria that are found in virtually every environment-including those that are characterized by extreme heat, cold, and depth-and, of course, bacteria that are found inside our bodies.

"Lively section headings . . . and notes on uncommon achievements, . . . lighten the substantial load of biological terminology. Illustrated with a plethora of closeup color photos and microphotos, and closing with annotated lists of recommended Web sites, . . . [this captures] the remarkable diversity of life." SLJ

Includes glossary and bibliographical references

579.5   Fungi

Parker, Steve, 1952-

Molds, mushrooms & other fungi. Compass Point Books 2009 48p il (Kingdom classification) lib bdg $29.32

Grades: 6 7 8 9   **579.5**
1. Fungi 2. Mushrooms
ISBN 978-0-7565-4223-8 lib bdg; 0-7565-4223-5 lib bdg

LC 2009-10749

Discusses the parts of fungi, different types, folklore about them, where they grow, how people use them, and how they can be harmful to humans, plants, and animals

"With its compelling facts and visuals, this is a quality choice." SLJ

Includes glossary

Stefoff, Rebecca

The **fungus** kingdom. Marshall Cavendish Benchmark 2008 95p il (Family trees) lib bdg $32.79

Grades: 6 7 8 9   **579.5**
1. Fungi
ISBN 978-0-7614-2696-7; 0-7614-2696-5

LC 2007003485

"Explores the habitats, life cycles, and other characteristics of organisms in the Fungus Kingdom." Publisher's note

Includes bibliographical references

579.6   Mushrooms

Lincoff, Gary

★ The **Audubon** Society field guide to North American mushrooms; [by] Gary H. Lincoff; visual key by Carol Nehring. Knopf 1981 926p il $19.95

Grades: 7 8 9 10 11 12 Adult   **579.6**
1. Mushrooms
ISBN 0-394-51992-2

LC 81-80827

This guide to 703 species of common mushrooms provides 762 color photographs and descriptions as keys to identifying these plants.

"The author is an expert on mushroom toxins and instills responsible cautions. The photos are uncommonly beautiful." SLJ

580   Natural history of plants and animals

Ballard, Carol

Plant variation and classification. Rosen Central 2010 46p il (Living processes) lib bdg $26.50; pa $11.75

Grades: 5 6 7   **580**
1. Plants 2. Variation (Biology) 3. Biology -- Classification
ISBN 978-1-61532-345-6 lib bdg; 1-61532-345-7 lib bdg; 978-1-61532-346-3 pa; 1-61532-346-5 pa

Explains how our plant classification system works and looks at how scientists use it to identify and group plant species. The book also examines the variation between and within plants species and discusses how and why such variations have occurred.

"With colorful, quality photography, the well-organized content is divided into short chapters with bold subheadings making information easy to find. Clear and interesting writing distinguishes this . . . from older titles. The captions for pictures are used to provide identification and additional explanation for topics not included in the text." Libr Media Connect

Includes glossary and bibliographical references

Casper, Julie Kerr

Plants; life from the earth. Chelsea House 2007 194p il (Natural resources) $39.50

Grades: 8 9 10 11 12   **580**
1. Botany 2. Plants
ISBN 978-0-8160-6358-1; 0-8160-6358-3

LC 2006-28965

This "examines the many plants that exist and the role they play in biodiversity. It focuses on key preservation issues affecting plant life, and the ways everyone can become a 'backyard conservationist.'" Publisher's note

Includes bibliographical references

Gibson, J. Phil

Plant diversity; [by] J. Phil Gibson and Terri R. Gibson. Chelsea House 2006 136p il (The green world) $37.50

Grades: 7 8 9 10 11 12   **580**
1. Plants 2. Plant diversity
ISBN 0-7910-8960-6; 978-0-7910-8960-6

                   LC 2006-23234

Explores the diversity and natural history of green plants throughout the world.

This book is "lavishly illustrated with full-color photographs and illustrative diagrams . . . written in a clear but not condescending style. . . . An excellent series of sidebars presents questions and then supports the reader in reasoning to the answers. . . . [It is] well worth the investment." Libr Media Connect

Includes glossary and bibliographical references

Levine, Shar
   Plants; flowering plants, ferns, mosses, and other plants. by Shar Levine and Leslie Johnstone. Crabtree Pub. 2010 48p il (A class of their own) lib bdg $29.27; pa $9.95
Grades: 5 6 7 8   **580**
1. Plants
ISBN 978-0-7787-5376-6 lib bdg; 0-7787-5376-X lib bdg; 978-0-7787-5390-2 pa; 0-7787-5390-5 pa

                   LC 2009-51342

Describes the main groups of plants, including mosses, ferns, conifers, and flowering plants.

"Lively section headings . . . and notes on uncommon achievements, . . . lighten the substantial load of biological terminology. Illustrated with a plethora of closeup color photos and microphotos, and closing with annotated lists of recommended Web sites, . . . [this captures] the remarkable diversity of life." SLJ

Includes glossary and bibliographical references

Stefoff, Rebecca
   ★ The **flowering** plant division. Benchmark Books 2006 91p il (Family trees) $20.95
Grades: 6 7 8 9   **580**
1. Plants 2. Angiosperms
ISBN 0-7614-1817-2

This examines the physical traits, adaptations, habitats, and life cycles of flowering plants.

Includes glossary and bibliographical references

Taylor, Barbara
   Inside plants. Marshall Cavendish Benchmark 2010 48p il (Invisible worlds) lib bdg $28.50
Grades: 4 5 6 7   **580**
1. Plants
ISBN 978-0-7614-4189-2 lib bdg; 0-7614-4189-1 lib bdg

                   LC 2008037247

This describes the plant details that are too small for the unaided eye to see, and how these microscopic systems work to keep the plant alive and healthy.

The narrative is "clear, well written, broken down into manageable pieces, and peppered with eye-opening facts. The numerous photographs are so phenomenal that they will inspire kids to read the text . . . so that they can wrap their minds around what they see." SLJ

Includes glossary and bibliographical references

580.7   Education, research, related topics

Gardner, Robert
   Ace your plant science project; great science fair ideas. [by] Robert Gardner and Phyllis J. Perry. Enslow Publishers 2009 104p il (Ace your biology science project) lib bdg $31.93
Grades: 5 6 7 8   **580.7**
1. Plants 2. Science projects 3. Science -- Experiments
ISBN 978-0-7660-3221-7 lib bdg; 0-7660-3221-3 lib bdg

                   LC 2008-4687

"Presents several science experiments and project ideas using plants." Publisher's note

Includes bibliographical references

Whitehouse, Patricia
   Plants; [by] Patricia Whitehouse. Heinemann Library 2008 48p il (Science fair projects) $30
Grades: 5 6 7 8   **580.7**
1. Plants 2. Science projects 3. Science -- Experiments
ISBN 978-1-4034-7918-1

                   LC 2006039547

This guide to science fair projects about plants "is one of the better 'how-to-do-a-science-fair project' books on the market. . . . [It] guides students with initial concrete suggestions and ideas for projects, but continues to challenge students to extend their investigations. . . . The content is presented in a colorful and engaging format." Sci Books Films

Includes glossary and bibliographical references

580.75   Museum activities and services

Silvey, Anita
   The **plant** hunters; true stories of their daring adventures to the far corners of the Earth. Anita Silvey. Farrar Straus Giroux 2012 88 p. col. ill. $19.99
Grades: 6 7 8 9 10   **580.75**
1. Botanists 2. Collectors and collecting 3. Plants -- Collection and preservation 4. Plant collecting -- History 5. Plant collectors -- Biography
ISBN 0374309086; 9780374309084

                   LC 2011005161

This book "introduces European and North American plant hunters, primarily from the nineteenth and twentieth centuries. Driven by curiosity, commerce, and 'botonomania,' they sought to collect valuable plant specimens around the world. Likening Baron Alexander von Humboldt to Indiana Jones and calling the plant hunters' experiences 'amazing escapades,' [Anita] Silvey . . . recount[s] horrific experiences reported by various plant hunters." (Booklist)

"The slim, engaging narrative paints vivid portraits of these botanic adventurers. It is smoothly written, smartly paced and filled with exciting tales of risk taking and derring-do." Kirkus

581   Specific topics in natural history of plants

Munoz, William

Plants on the trail with Lewis and Clark; photographs by William Muñoz. Clarion Bks. 2003 104p il map $18

Grades: 4 5 6 7   **581**

1. Plants -- United States 2. Botany -- West (U.S.) -- History -- 19th century 3. Plant collecting -- West (U.S.) -- History -- 19th century

ISBN 0-618-06776-0

LC 2002-10383

Describes the journey of Lewis and Clark through the western United States, focusing on the plants they cataloged, their uses for food and medicine, and the plant lore of Native American people

"Good-quality, full-color photos and reproductions clearly extend the text. . . . The author's knowledge of and keen interest in her subject matter is very evident in this fascinating account." SLJ

Includes bibliographical references

581.6   Miscellaneous nontaxonomic kinds of plants

Farrell, Courtney

Plants out of place. Rourke Pub. 2010 48p il (Let's explore science) $32.79

Grades: 4 5 6 7   **581.6**

1. Plants 2. Biological invasions 3. Food chains (Ecology)

ISBN 978-1-61590-322-1; 1-61590-322-4

LC 2010009909

This "takes a lively look at invasive plants . . . and shows both the destruction that non-native plants cause and what can be done about it. . . . In [this] title, well-chosen boxed examples, abundant color photos, diagrams, and an appended glossary add interest and support the engaging [text]." Booklist

Includes glossary and bibliographical references

Young, Kim J.

Ethnobotany; series editor William G. Hopkins. Chelsea House 2006 112p il (The green world) lib bdg $37.50

Grades: 7 8 9 10   **581.6**

1. Ethnobotany 2. Economic botany 3. Human-plant relationships

ISBN 0-7910-8963-0 lib bdg

This is "a primer on plant and human relationships and interactions. . . . The reader is given insight into the importance of plants to both ancient and modern cultures and into how people's of particular cultures make use of plants." Sci Books Films

Includes glossary and bibliographical references

581.7   Plant ecology, plants characteristic of specific environments

Bodden, Valerie

Critical plant life. Creative Education 2010 48p il (Earth issues) $23.95

Grades: 7 8 9 10   **581.7**

1. Plant ecology

ISBN 978-1-58341-984-7; 1-58341-984-5

"The scientific information is up to date, well written for a lay audience, and presented in a highly engaging and visually appealing format." Sci Books Films

Includes glossary and bibliographical references

Johnson, Rebecca L.

Powerful plant cells; [by] Rebecca L. Johnson; illustrations by Jack Desrocher; diagrams by Jennifer E. Fairman. Millbrook Press 2008 48p il (Microquests) lib bdg $29.27

Grades: 5 6 7 8   **581.7**

1. Cells 2. Plants

ISBN 978-0-8225-7141-4; 0-8225-7141-2

LC 2006-36387

Explains what plant cells are, how they were discovered, their components, how they divide, different kinds, and what they do.

Includes bibliographical references

Spilsbury, Richard

Plant habitats; Richard & Louise Spilsbury. Rev. and updated; Heinemann Library 2008 48p il (Life of plants) $27.50; pa $7.99

Grades: 5 6 7 8   **581.7**

1. Plants 2. Plant ecology

ISBN 978-1-4329-1502-5; 1-4329-1502-9; 978-1-4329-1509-4 pa; 1-4329-1509-6 pa

LC 2008275392

First published 2003

Explains the different ways plants adapt to their environment in order to survive in a particular habitat.

This book "contains many bright and colorful photographs and diagrams to support the text, boldface vocabulary terms, a series of experiments and activities to provide further investigation, a complete glossary, an index, and a list of sources for additional information. . . . [This] volume is a complete and well-rounded unit." Sci Books Films

Includes glossary and bibliographical references

582.13   Plants noted for their flowers

Duncan, Wilbur Howard

Wildflowers of the eastern United States; by Wilbur H. Duncan and Marion B. Duncan. University of Georgia Press 1999 380p il $34.95; pa $24.95

Grades: 7 8 9 10 11 12 Adult   **582.13**

1. Wild flowers

ISBN 978-0-8203-2107-3; 0-8203-2107-9; 978-0-8203-2747-1 pa; 0-8203-2747-6 pa

LC 98-43314

"The eastern deciduous forest biome, . . . contains a variety of habitats supporting several thousand species of wildflowers. . . . The Duncans . . . have compiled a useful guide to more than 1,000 species. . . . A strength of the book is the photography, and although priority was given to showing diagnostic features, most photos are also very appealing visually. The 20-page introductory section includes a fine glossary and illustrations of necessary terminology." Choice

Niehaus, Theodore F.
★ A **field** guide to Pacific states wildflowers; illustrated by Charles L. Ripper. Houghton Mifflin 1976 xxxii, 432p il map (The Peterson field guide) hardcover o.p. pa $19
Grades: 7 8 9 10 11 12 Adult   **582.13**
  1. Wild flowers
  ISBN 0-395-21624-9; 0-395-91095-1 pa
                              LC 76-5873
"This offering identifies 1492 common wildflowers. . . . Common and scientific name, habitat, and recognition features are given for each plant." Libr J

Parker, Steve, 1952-
Sunflowers, magnolia trees & other flowering plants. Compass Point Books 2009 48p il (Kingdom classification) lib bdg $29.32
Grades: 6 7 8 9   **582.13**
  1. Plants 2. Flowers
  ISBN 978-0-7565-4222-1 lib bdg; 0-7565-4222-7 lib bdg
                           LC 2009-13696
Discusses the parts of flowering plants, the parts of flowers, the life cycle of flowering plants, different types that exist in different climates, how people use them, and efforts to conserve them
"With its compelling facts and visuals, this is a quality choice." SLJ
Includes glossary

Ryden, Hope
Wildflowers around the year; photographs and text by Hope Ryden. Clarion Bks. 2001 90p il $17
Grades: 5 6 7 8   **582.13**
  1. Wild flowers 2. Wild flowers -- Northeastern States 3. Wild flowers -- Northeastern States -- Identification 4. Wild flowers -- Northeastern States -- Pictorial works
  ISBN 0-395-85814-3
                           LC 00-43011
"Accompanied by exquisite, sharply focused photos. . . . Filled with interesting tidbits, Ryden's lyrical text meanders appealingly through moments of wonder, experience, explanation, and speculation." Horn Book Guide
Includes bibliographical references

Souza, D. M.
Freaky flowers. Watts 2002 63p il (Watts library) lib bdg $24.50; pa $8.95
Grades: 5 6 7 8   **582.13**
  1. Flowers
  ISBN 0-531-11981-5 lib bdg; 0-531-16221-4 pa
                          LC 2001-17573

"The book begins with a short course in botany that stresses vocabulary and processes. Subsequent chapters discuss different ways plants attract pollinators through colors, odors, and habitats. The last chapter acts as a warning that many plants are endangered because their pollinators are threatened, emphasizing the balance of nature. The outstanding full-color photos feature some of the most spectacular flowers found anywhere. Small sidebars offer interesting bits of trivia about similar plants. The text is packed with biological information and pertinent vocabulary." SLJ
Includes bibliographical references

Spellenberg, Richard
★ **National** Audubon Society field guide to North American wildflowers, western region; 2nd ed rev; Knopf 2001 862p il map $19.95
Grades: 7 8 9 10 11 12 Adult   **582.13**
  1. Wild flowers
  ISBN 0-375-40233-0
                         LC 2001-269242

First published 1979
"More than 940 . . . full-color images show the wildflowers of western North America close-up and in their natural habitats. . . . Images are grouped by flower color and shape and keyed to . . . descriptions that reflect current taxonomy." Publisher's note

Thieret, John W.
★ **National** Audubon Society field guide to North American wildflowers: eastern region; revising author, John W. Thieret; original authors, William A. Niering and Nancy C. Olmstead. Knopf 2001 879p il map (National Audubon Society field guide series) $19.95
Grades: 7 8 9 10 11 12 Adult   **582.13**
  1. Wild flowers
  ISBN 0-375-40232-2
                         LC 2001-269241
First published 1979 under the authorship of William A. Niering and Nancy C. Olmstead
"Covers the area east of the Rockies and east of the Big Bend area of Texas to the Atlantic. Color photographs together with family and species descriptions make this a most useful field guide." Sci News {review of 1979 edition}

Venning, Frank D.
Wildflowers of North America; a guide to field identification. illustrated by Manabu C. Saito. rev ed.; St. Martin's Press 2001 340p il (Golden field guides) pa $14.95
Grades: 8 9 10 11 12 Adult   **582.13**
  1. Wild flowers
  ISBN 978-1-58238-127-5; 1-58238-127-5
  First published 1984 by Golden Press
  Accurate information on size, appearance, habitat, and known ranges and full-color illustrations constitute a guide to more than fifteen hundred native and naturalized species.
  Includes bibliographical references

582.16   Trees

Brockman, C. Frank

Trees of North America; a field guide to the major native and introduced species north of Mexico. by C. Frank Brockman; illustrated by Rebecca Merrilees; revised by Jonathan P. Latimer and Karen Stray Nolting with David Challinor. rev and updated ed.; St. Martin's Press 2001 280p il map (Golden field guides) pa $14.95

Grades: 8 9 10 11 12 Adult   **582.16**
  1. Trees -- North America
  ISBN 978-1-58238-092-6 pa; 1-58238-092-9 pa
                                    LC 2001272405
First published 1968 by Golden Press
This "field guide features . . . characteristics—tree shape, bark, leaf, flower, fruit and twig—for quick identification. . . . [It includes] over 730 species in 76 families and 160 range maps." Publisher's note
Includes bibliographical references

Petrides, George A.

A **field** guide to western trees; eastern [i.e. western] United States and Canada. illustrated by Olivia Petrides. 1st ed., expanded.; Houghton Mifflin 1998 428p il map (The Peterson field guide) pa $20

Grades: 7 8 9 10 11 12 Adult   **582.16**
  1. Trees -- North America
  ISBN 978-0-395-90454-1 pa; 0-395-90454-4 pa
                                    LC 98013624
First published 1992
This "guide features detailed descriptions of 387 species, arranged in six major groups by visual similarity." Publisher's note
Includes bibliographical references

Ridsdale, Colin

Trees; [by] Colin Ridsdale, John White, Carol Usher; foreword by David Mabberley. DK 2005 360p il (Eyewitness companions) pa $25

Grades: 7 8 9 10   **582.16**
  1. Trees
  ISBN 978-0-7566-1359-4; 0-7566-1359-0
                                    LC 2005296635
"From identification and anatomy to commercial exploitation and conservation, this is [a] . . . guide to more than 500 species of trees from around the world." Publisher's note

Williams, Michael D.

Identifying trees; an all-season guide to Eastern North America. Stackpole Books 2007 406p il pa $29.95

Grades: 7 8 9   **582.16**
  1. Trees -- North America
  ISBN 978-0-8117-3360-1; 0-8117-3360-2
                                    LC 2006-10857
"Describes common locations and identifying characteristics [of trees]. . . . Covers every common tree in eastern North America." Publisher's note

583   Dicotyledons

Aaseng, Nathan

Weird meat-eating plants. Enslow Publishers 2011 48p il (Bizarre science) lib bdg $23.93

Grades: 5 6 7 8   **583**
  1. Carnivorous plants
  ISBN 978-0-7660-3672-7; 0-7660-3672-3
                                    LC 2010016602
First published 1996 with title: Meat-eating plants
This describes meat-eating plants such as butterworts, sundews, byblis, pitcher plants, cobra lilies, venus flytraps, and bladderworts.
"Aimed at reluctant readers, [this title is] sure to disgust and delight in equal measure. . . . [The title] will pique interest and get kids lining up at the reference desk looking for more. The text is complemented by illustrations and magnified photos of things that you would hope never to see." SLJ
Includes glossary and bibliographical references

Pascoe, Elaine

Carnivorous plants; text by Elaine Pascoe; photographs by Dwight Kuhn. Blackbirch Press 2005 48p il (Nature close-up) $23.70

Grades: 4 5 6 7   **583**
  1. Carnivorous plants
  ISBN 1-4103-0309-8
                                    LC 2005-276141
This describes such plants as venus flytraps, pitcher plants, cobra plants, and blatterworts, with instructions for growing and investigating them
Includes glossary and bibliographical references

584   Monocotyledons

Brown, Lauren

Grasses, an identification guide; written & illustrated by Lauren Brown. Houghton Mifflin 1979 240p il (Peterson nature library) hardcover o.p. pa $16

Grades: 7 8 11 12 Adult   **584**
  1. Grasses
  ISBN 978-0-395-27624-2; 0-395-27624-1; 978-0-395-62881-2 pa; 0-395-62881-4 pa
                                    LC 78-24545
Identifies "135 of the most common species of North American grasses, sedges, and rushes, with their economic and ecological importance." Publisher's note
Includes bibliographical references

585   Gymnosperms

Parker, Steve, 1952-

Redwoods, hemlocks & other cone-bearing plants. Compass Point Books 2010 48p il (Kingdom classification) lib bdg $29.32

Grades: 6 7 8 9   585
1. Cones 2. Redwood
ISBN 978-0-7565-4221-4 lib bdg; 0-7565-4221-9
lib bdg
LC 2009-12608
Discusses how conifers grow, their parts, the different types that grow in different climates, how people use them, and efforts to conserve them
"With its compelling facts and visuals, this is a quality choice." SLJ
Includes glossary

Stefoff, Rebecca
The **conifer** division; [by] Rebecca Stefoff. Marshall Cavendish Benchmark 2008 96p il (Family trees) $23.95
Grades: 6 7 8 9   585
1. Evergreens 2. Biology -- Classification
ISBN 978-0-7614-3077-3; 0-7614-3077-6
LC 2008-23373
"Explores the life cycles and other characteristics of plants, trees, and shrubs in the Conifer division." Publisher's note
Includes glossary and bibliographical references

587   Vascular seedless plants

Parker, Steve, 1952-
Ferns, mosses & other spore-producing plants. Compass Point Books 2010 48p il (Kingdom classification) lib bdg $29.32
Grades: 6 7 8 9   587
1. Ferns 2. Mosses
ISBN 978-0-7565-4220-7 lib bdg; 0-7565-4220-0
lib bdg
LC 2009-12060
Discusses how spore-producing plants grow and reproduce, different types, where they live, their life cycles, and how people use them
"With its compelling facts and visuals, this is a quality choice." SLJ
Includes glossary and bibliographical references

590   Animals

Amazing animals of the world 1. Grolier 2008 10v il map set $199
Grades: 6 7 8 9   590
1. Reference books 2. Animals -- Encyclopedias
ISBN 978-0-7172-6225-0 set; 0-7172-6225-1 set
LC 2007012982
This "is a 10-volume set featuring 400 animals from around the globe. Each page highlights one animal with an interesting description and full-color picture. The pictures are beautiful and visually engaging. . . . The information is concise and appealing enough for reading for personal information or for use in basic research." Sci Books Films
Includes glossary and bibliographical references

BishopRoby, Joshua
Animal kingdom. Compass Point Books 2009 40p il (Mission: science) lib bdg $26.60
Grades: 4 5 6   590
1. Animals -- Classification
ISBN 978-0-7565-4057-9 lib bdg; 0-7565-4057-7
lib bdg
LC 2008-37574
An introduction to the animal kingdom, which is made up of a variety of animals that are organized into categories based on physical attributes or ancestors
Includes glossary

Casper, Julie Kerr
Animals; creatures that roam the planet. Chelsea House Publishers 2007 179p il map (Natural resources) $39.50
Grades: 8 9 10 11 12   590
1. Animals
ISBN 978-0-8160-6353-6; 0-8160-6353-2
LC 2006030227
This describes how animals have adapted to various environments on Earth and how they have evolved, the causes of animal extinctions in the past and the present, the importance of animals to humans, and the conservation of animal resources.
Includes bibliographical references

Davies, Nicola, 1958-
Extreme animals; the toughest creatures on Earth. illustrated by Neal Layton. Candlewick Press 2006 61p il $12.99; pa $7.99
Grades: 3 4 5 6   590
1. Animals 2. Adaptation (Biology) 3. Extreme environments 4. Animals -- Adaptation 5. Children's literature -- Works -- Grades two through six
ISBN 978-0-7636-3067-6; 0-7636-3067-5; 978-0-7636-4127-6 pa; 0-7636-4127-8 pa
LC 2005-43544
"There is life everywhere on Earth . . . and much of that life thrives in conditions that humans could not endure for five minutes or less. This funny and appealing little book describes who these amazing life-forms are and how they manage to survive. Simple and inviting cartoon drawings enliven the text and convey the types of extremes in an easy-to-understand manner." SLJ
Includes glossary

The **encyclopedia** of animals; a complete visual guide. [text, Jenni Bruce . . . et al.] University of California Press 2004 608p il map $39.95
Grades: 7 8 9 10 11 12   590
1. Reference books 2. Animals -- Encyclopedias
ISBN 0-520-24406-0
LC 2004-303646
"This lavishly illustrated chronicle of Earth's biodiversity is a visual delight." Booklist

Johnson, Jinny
★ **Animal** tracks & signs. National Geographic Society 2008 192p il $24.95; lib bdg $32.90

Grades: 5 6 7 8   590
1. Animals 2. Animal tracks 3. Tracking and trailing
4. Animals -- Identification
ISBN 978-1-4263-0253-4; 1-4263-0253-3; 978-1-
4263-0254-1 lib bdg; 1-4263-0254-1 lib bdg
"This attractive book describes the tracks (paw prints,
bird claw prints, slimy trails) and signs (molted skin, food remains, scat, tree markings) that animals leave in their wake. .
. . A typical two-page layout includes a photo and short paragraph about the animal category, three or four colored boxes
containing a photo or drawing of a specific animal (serval,
bobcat), and a description of its size, geographic range, habitat, food, tracks and signs, and comments. . . . The beautiful
photos vary from action . . . to informational. . . . The language is simple and readable." Voice Youth Advocates
Includes glossary and bibliographical references

Levine, Shar
   Animals; mammals, birds, reptiles, amphibians,
fish, and other animals. by Shar Levine and Leslie
Johnstone. Crabtree Pub. 2010 48p il (A class of
their own) lib bdg $29.27; pa $9.95
Grades: 5 6 7 8   590
1. Animals -- Classification 2. Animals
ISBN 978-0-7787-5372-8 lib bdg; 0-7787-5372-7 lib
bdg; 978-0-7787-5386-5 pa; 0-7787-5386-7 pa
   Looks at the animal kingdom, providing information and
examples of species from the major phyla and classes, as well
as case histories of newly discovered endangered species.
   "Lively section headings . . . and notes on uncommon
achievements, . . . lighten the substantial load of biological terminology. Illustrated with a plethora of closeup
photos and microphotos, and closing with annotated lists of
recommended Web sites, . . . [this captures] the remarkable
diversity of life." SLJ
   Includes glossary and bibliographical references

Lewin, Ted
   ★ **Tooth** and claw; animal adventures in the
wild. HarperCollins Pubs. 2003 97p il maps
$15.99; lib bdg $16.89
Grades: 4 5 6 7   590
1. Wildlife 2. Dangerous animals
ISBN 0-688-14105-6; 0-688-14106-4 lib bdg
                                          LC 2002-4588
   Author/illustrator Ted Lewin relates fourteen of his experiences with wild animals while travelling the world, following each anecdote with facts about the featured animal
and its habitat
   "This is outstanding nature storytelling, related in a distinctive voice imbued with humor and personality; it's even
better when read aloud." Horn Book
   Includes glossary

McGhee, Karen
   ★ **Encyclopedia** of animals; [by] Karen Mc-
Ghee, George McKay. National Geographic 2007
192p il map $24.95; lib bdg $38.90
Grades: 4 5 6 7 8   590
1. Reference books 2. Animals -- Encyclopedias
ISBN 0-7922-5936-X; 0-7922-5937-8 lib bdg
                                          LC 2006299476

"This lavish, ambitious volume contains full-color illustrations of more than 1500 species. Each brief entry includes
common and scientific names and mention of an interesting
physical or behavioral trait. Range maps show where each
animal is found, and conservation data notes which species
are extinct, endangered, or vulnerable. In addition to the
realistic drawings, there are dramatic photos of animals in
their habitats." SLJ

Noyes, Deborah
   ★ **One** kingdom; our lives with animals--the human-animal bond in myth, history, science, and story.
Houghton Mifflin Company 2006 128p il $18
Grades: 7 8 9 10   590
1. Animals 2. Human-animal relationships
ISBN 0-618-49914-8
                                          LC 2005-25446
   In this "photo-essay, Noyes examines the ways that
human lives have overlapped with animals and how our
beliefs, culture, and science have been impacted throught
history by the essential but frequently paradoxical human-
animal connection. . . . Readers will find the provocative
questions Noyes raises compelling and challenging, and the
lyrical, urgent prose, along with beautiful black-and-white
photos of the animals up close, will draw serious students
and browsers alike." Booklist
   Includes bibliographical references

Silverstein, Alvin
   Dung beetles, slugs, leeches, and more; the yucky
animal book. by Alvin and Virginia Silverstein, and
Laura Silverstein Nunn; illustrated by Gerald Kelley.
Enslow Publishers 2010 48p il (Yucky science) lib
bdg $23.93
Grades: 4 5 6 7   590
1. Insects 2. Invertebrates 3. Animal behavior
ISBN 978-0-7660-3317-7 lib bdg; 0-7660-3317-1
lib bdg
                                          LC 2009012281
   "Explores 'yucky' things animals do, including slime-
producing animals, blood-ingesting animals, and more."
Publisher's note
   Includes glossary and bibliographical references

Siwanowicz, Igor
   Animals up close; zoom in on the world's most
incredible creatures. DK Pub. 2009 96p il $19.99
Grades: 4 5 6   590
1. Animals
ISBN 978-0-7566-4513-7; 0-7566-4513-1
   "An eye-catching cover will attract readers to this amazing look at some of the world's insects, fish, mammals, reptiles, amphibians, and birds. The focus is on animals small
enough to fit in a child's hand. Siwanowicz showcases each
creature with a spread containing a full-color, high-quality,
close-up photo surrounded by multiple factual asides. . . .
The book is packed with interesting material that captures
the author's fascination for small creatures." SLJ
   Includes glossary

Spilsbury, Richard

Animal variation and classification. Rosen Central 2010 46p il (Living processes) lib bdg $26.50; pa $11.75

Grades: 5 6 7 **590**

1. Variation (Biology) 2. Animals -- Classification

ISBN 978-1-61532-344-9 lib bdg; 1-61532-344-9 lib bdg; 978-1-61532-347-0 pa; 1-61532-347-3 pa

LC 2009-30564

Explains how our animal classification system works and looks at how scientists use it to identify and group animal species, explores the variation between and within animal species and discusses how and why such variations have occurred.

"With colorful, quality photography, the well-organized content is divided into short chapters with bold subheadings making information easy to find. Clear and interesting writing distinguishes this . . . from older titles. The captions for pictures are used to provide identification and additional explanation for topics not included in the text." Libr Media Connect

Includes glossary and bibliographical references

Staub, Frank J.

★ The **signs** animals leave; [by] Frank Staub. Watts 2001 63p il (Watts library) $24.50; pa $8.95

Grades: 4 5 6 **590**

1. Animal tracks 2. Animal behavior 3. Animals -- Habits and behavior

ISBN 0-531-11863-0; 0-531-16575-2 pa

LC 00-43603

This describes traces left by animals which reveal their behavior including tracks and scents

Includes bibliographical references

590.7 Education, research, related topics

Gardner, Robert

Ace your animal science project; great science fair ideas. [by] Robert Gardner . . . [et al.] Enslow Publishers 2009 128p il (Ace your biology science project) lib bdg $31.93

Grades: 5 6 7 8 **590.7**

1. Animal behavior 2. Science projects 3. Science -- Experiments

ISBN 978-0-7660-3220-0 lib bdg; 0-7660-3220-5 lib bdg

LC 2008-4234

"Dozens of . . . science activities are presented with background information, step-by-step instructions, and suggestions for extending to the science fair level. . . . Color illustrations and important safety information are included." Horn Book Guide

Includes bibliographical references

590.72 Research

Burns, Loree Griffin

Citizen scientists; be a part of scientific discovery from your own backyard. Loree Griffin Burns; photographs by Ellen Harasimowicz. H. Holt 2012 80 p. col. ill., col. maps $19.99

Grades: 3 4 5 6 7 8 **590.72**

1. Suburbs 2. Animals -- Classification 3. Research -- Citizen participation 4. Wildlife -- Geographical distribution 5. Suburban animals -- Research -- Citizen participation 6. Suburban animals -- Monitoring -- Citizen participation

ISBN 0805090622; 9780805090628; 9780805095173

LC 2011021673

AAAS/Subaru SB&F Prize for Excellence in Science Books: Hands On Science Book (2013)

In this children's book, Loree Griffin Burns "brings . . . attention to four . . . scientific projects that enlist regular people in data collection. . . . The projects include . . . the Monarch Watch butterfly tagging project, . . . the Audubon Christmas Bird Count," and a "project documenting ladybug species . . . . For each project, Burns gives detailed accounts of the procedures employed by citizen scientists." (Horn Book Magazine)

Includes bibliographical references and index

590.73 Collections and exhibits of living mammals

Zoehfeld, Kathleen Weidner

Wild lives; a history of the people & animals of the Bronx Zoo. with photographs from the Wildlife Conservation Society. Alfred A. Knopf 2006 86p il $18.95; lib bdg $20.99

Grades: 5 6 7 8 **590.73**

1. Zoos 2. Animals

ISBN 0-375-80630-X; 0-375-90630-4 lib bdg

LC 2005-18943

"Zoehfeld tells the story of the Bronx Zoo, from the preparations for its opening in 1899 to its current efforts in the areas of conservation and education. Along with information on the zoo, she discusses trends in thinking about wildlife, the ethics of removing animals from their habitats for their safety or for public display, and ongoing threats to the existence of many species. . . . The many photos, attractive layout, and use of color contribute to the visual appeal of this informative zoo story." Booklist

Includes bibliographical references

590.92 Biographies of animals

Roop, Connie

Tales of Famous Animals; Peter Roop and Connie Roop. Scholastic 2012 112 p. (reinforced) $17.99

Grades: 4 5 6 7 8 **590.92**

1. Pets 2. Animals

ISBN 0545430291; 9780545430296

This children's book, by Peter and Connie Roop, illustrated by Zachary Pullen, offers an "illustrated introduction to some of the most fascinating and admirable animals we've ever known! Everyone knows about President Obama's first dog Bo, but would you believe President Adams had a pet alligator? . . . Readers will also learn about heroic animals like Balto the sled dog and unique animals like Koko the gorilla." (Publisher's note)

591.03   Encyclopedias of animals

Spelman, Lucy

Animal encyclopedia; 2,500 animals with photos, maps, and more! National Geographic 2012 303 p. col. ill., col. maps (hardcover) $24.95; (library) $33.90

Grades: 5 6 7   **591.03**
1. Animals
ISBN 1426310226; 9781426310225; 9781426310232
LC 2012023783

This encyclopedia about animals "is separated into vertebrate and invertebrate animals and then further subdivided by phylum. Each species gets its own page with dynamic color photos of creatures in their natural habitat, while . . . information on variations within the species celebrates the diversity of animals across the globe." (Booklist)

Includes bibliographical references (p. 295) and index.

591.3   Genetics, evolution, age characteristics

Eamer, Claire

Spiked scorpions & walking whales; modern animals, ancient animals, and water. Annick Press 2009 100p il $19.95; pa $9.95

Grades: 6 7 8 9   **591.3**
1. Animals 2. Evolution
ISBN 978-1-55451-206-5; 1-55451-206-9; 978-1-55451-205-8 pa; 1-55451-205-0 pa

Describes how six different water-loving species evolved from how they appear in early fossil records to their appearance today, discussing segmented worms, platypus, and Canada geese.

"Eamer's information-packed text, often lively and conversational, can also be challenging. . . . The book features brightly colored, busy pages with sidebars, 'Fun Facts,' and small full-color photographs rimmed in bold shades. . . . Capable readers with a serious interest in animal science will find it enjoyable and even fascinating." SLJ

Super crocs & monster wings; modern animals' ancient past. [by] Claire Eamer. Annick Press 2008 93p il $19.95; pa $9.95

Grades: 4 5 6 7   **591.3**
1. Animals 2. Evolution 3. Prehistoric animals
ISBN 978-1-55451-130-3; 1-55451-130-5; 978-1-55451-129-7 pa; 1-55451-129-1 pa

"The author's conversational and often-humorous voice slides readers effortlessly through a great deal of fascinating scientific information in this title on animal evolution. After

a brief but clear introduction to geologic time and Linnaean taxonomy, six chapters compare ancient and modern dragonflies, crocodilians, camelids, sloths, glyptodonts (armadillos), and beavers. . . . Jazzy fonts; crisp photos and paintings; and tilted illustrations, titles, and captions create an up-to-the-minute feel." SLJ

591.4   Physical adaptation

Burnie, David

How animals work. Dorling Kindersley 2010 132p il $24.99

Grades: 5 6 7 8   **591.4**
1. Animals 2. Animal behavior
ISBN 978-0-7566-5897-7; 0-7566-5897-7

Describes the anatomy of many animal species and explains how their bodies work to help them survive. Covers such animals as birds, butterflies, elephants, crocodiles, and wolves, and includes color photos, illustrations, and diagrams.

"This beautifully photographed encyclopedia of animals is divided into categories that include movement, diet, senses, and animal families. . . . Diagrams showing internal organs and intimate closeups of eyes, skin, fur, and wings, should engage budding biologists." Publ Wkly

Rodriguez, Ana Maria

Secret of the puking penguins . . . and more! Enslow Publishers 2008 48p il (Animal secrets revealed!) lib bdg $23.93

Grades: 5 6 7 8   **591.4**
1. Birds 2. Reptiles
ISBN 978-0-7660-2955-2 lib bdg; 0-7660-2955-7 lib bdg

LC 2007-39490

In this title "readers learn not only why King penguin fathers regurgitate food to feed their newborn chicks, but also how chameleons grip prey with their powerful tongue, along with some unusual information about alligators, cuckoos, and peacock feathers. Each topic is covered in six to nine pages with a short Meet the Scientists section. The methodology used by each scientist or team of scientists to make the discoveries is carefully explained is a lively and accessible manner. . . . The photo illustrations . . . are of excellent quality, well placed, and helpful." Booklist

Includes glossary and bibliographical references

591.47   Protective and locomotor adaptations, color

Wilsdon, Christina

Animal defenses. Chelsea House 2009 136p il (Animal behavior) lib bdg $32.95

Grades: 6 7 8 9   **591.47**
1. Animal defenses
ISBN 978-1-60413-089-8 lib bdg; 1-60413-089-X lib bdg

LC 2008-40116

"The detailed information is well organized. . . . Color photographs appear throughout." SLJ

Includes glossary and bibliographical references

591.5   Behavior

Goldstein, Natalie

Animal hunting and feeding. Chelsea House 2009 110p il (Animal behavior) lib bdg $32.95

Grades: 6 7 8 9   591.5

1. Animals -- Food

ISBN 978-1-60413-143-7 lib bdg; 1-60413-143-8 lib bdg

LC 2008-40124

"All animals have to eat, but feeding behavior goes far beyond predators and prey. Animals have a variety of ways to find food. Some sit and wait for food to come to them. Others chase or trap their food. Other animals are scavengers and decomposers, breaking down the leftovers of other animals' meals. [This book] explains these various techniques as well as the importance of food chains and food webs." Publisher's note

Includes glossary and bibliographical references

Hile, Lori

Animal survival. Raintree 2011 56p il (Extreme survival) lib bdg $33.50

Grades: 4 5 6 7   591.5

1. Pets 2. Animals 3. Animal behavior 4. Natural disasters

ISBN 978-1-4109-3973-9; 1-4109-3973-1

LC 2010028842

This book is "fun and informative. [This] well-organized title starts with an overview [of animal survival], offers some specific examples, and includes additional facts or tips and resources. . . . [It features] dramatic archival and full-color photos on nearly every page. . . . The first chapter introduces resilient creatures that beat the odds and then follows with their journeys, animal heroes, and their work while surviving natural disasters. . . . [This is a book] that youngsters will enjoy and talk about." SLJ

Includes glossary and bibliographical references

Knapp, Ron

Bloodsucking creatures. Enslow Publishers 2011 48p il (Bizarre science) lib bdg $23.93

Grades: 5 6 7 8   591.5

1. Bloodsucking animals

ISBN 978-0-7660-3671-0; 0-7660-3671-5

LC 2010009761

First published 1996 with title: Bloodsuckers

This describes bloodsucking animals such as mosquitoes, vampire bats, and fleas.

"Aimed at reluctant readers, [this title is] sure to disgust and delight in equal measure. . . . [The title] will pique interest and get kids lining up at the reference desk looking for more. The text is complemented by illustrations and magnified photos of things that you would hope never to see." SLJ

Includes glossary and bibliographical references

Settel, Joanne

Exploding ants; amazing facts about how animals adapt. Atheneum Bks. for Young Readers 1999 40p il $16.95

Grades: 4 5 6 7   591.5

1. Animal behavior 2. Animals -- Habits and behavior

ISBN 0-689-81739-8

LC 97-35395

Describes examples of animal behavior that may strike humans as disgusting, including the "gross" ways animals find food, shelter, and safety in the natural world

"This attractive volume presents its material as wondrous science instead of sensational effect." Booklist

Includes glossary and bibliographical references

591.56   Behavior relating to life cycle

Allman, Toney

Animal life in groups. Chelsea House 2009 124p il (Animal behavior) lib bdg $32.95

Grades: 6 7 8 9   591.56

1. Animal behavior

ISBN 978-1-60413-142-0 lib bdg; 1-60413-142-X lib bdg

LC 2008-40120

This "explores the social lives of bees, meerkats, monkeys, and others, with a special emphasis on how different packs compare to one another and how living in groups benefits individual members." Publisher's note

Includes glossary and bibliographical references

Schueller, Gretel H.

Animal migration; [by] Gretel H. Schueller and Sheila K. Schueller. Chelsea House 2009 120p il (Animal behavior) lib bdg $32.95

Grades: 6 7 8 9   591.56

1. Animals -- Migration

ISBN 978-1-60413-127-7 lib bdg; 1-60413-127-6 lib bdg

LC 2008-40125

This describes "why animals are compelled to migrate, as well as the various patterns and cycles of their migrations." Publisher's note

Includes glossary and bibliographical references

Spilsbury, Richard

Life cycles. Rosen Central 2010 46p il (Life processes) lib bdg $26.50; pa $11.75

Grades: 5 6 7   591.56

1. Life cycles (Biology)

ISBN 978-1-61532-341-8 lib bdg; 1-61532-341-4 lib bdg; 978-1-61532-350-0 pa; 1-61532-350-3 pa

LC 2009-30414

"With colorful, quality photography, the well-organized content is divided into short chapters with bold subheadings making information easy to find. Clear and interesting writing distinguishes this . . . from older titles. The captions for pictures are used to provide identification and additional explanation for topics not included in the text." Libr Media Connect

Includes glossary and bibliographical references

West, Krista

Animal courtship. Chelsea House 2009 120p il (Animal behavior) lib bdg $32.95

Grades: 6 7 8 9   **591.56**

1. Animal courtship

ISBN 978-1-60413-090-4 lib bdg; 1-60413-090-3 lib bdg

LC 2008-40121

This describes "the various ways species attract mates, including by singing, dancing, glowing, and even attacking." Publisher's note

Includes glossary and bibliographical references

591.59 Communication

Sayre, April Pulley

★ **Secrets** of sound; studying the calls and songs of whales, elephants, and birds. Houghton Mifflin 2002 63p il (Scientists in the field) pbk. $7.99

Grades: 4 5 6 7   **591.59**

1. Whales 2. Birdsongs 3. Elephants 4. Animal communication 5. Bioacoustics

ISBN 9780618585465

LC 2001-51877

"The focus of this Scientists in the Field volume is scientists who study animal communication—whale songs, elephant rumbles, and nocturnal bird calls. Bioacoustics, the field encompassing their work, is a meld of biology, technology, music, and physics. . . . Christopher Clark uses underwater microphones to record whale songs. . . . Katy Payne's familiarity with the vibrations of organ music led to her discovery of the infrasound rumbles that elephants use to communicate over long distances. Bill Evans records birds at night to learn more about their migration patterns.

"This fascinating title shows the thrill of scientific discovery up close. . . . Lots of well-edited quotes from the scientists convey their contagious enthusiasm for what they do, and sharp color photos, sound charts, and activity boxes break up the text, making it even more readable." Booklist

Includes glossary and bibliographical references

Tomecek, Steve

Animal communication; [by] Stephen M. Tomecek. Chelsea House 2009 104p il (Animal behavior) lib bdg $32.95

Grades: 6 7 8 9   **591.59**

1. Animal communication

ISBN 978-1-60413-091-1 lib bdg; 1-60413-091-1 lib bdg

LC 2008-40115

This explains "the many different ways in which animals and insects express themselves and examines some of the latest scientific discoveries involving animal intelligence." Publisher's note

Includes glossary and bibliographical references

591.6 Miscellaneous nontaxonomic kinds of animals

Hammond, Paula

The **atlas** of the world's most dangerous animals; mapping nature's born killers. Marshall Cavendish 2010 224p il map lib bdg $99.93

Grades: 7 8 9 10 11 12   **591.6**

1. Dangerous animals

ISBN 978-0-7614-7870-6 lib bdg; 0-7614-7870-1 lib bdg

LC 2008-44960

First published 2004 in the United Kingdom

Explores each of the world's continents, featuring deadly species of animals.

This "beautifully illustrated . . . [book] features an appealing layout; logical organization; and plenty of full-color drawings, maps, and photographs. . . . Each entry opens with a large, colorful drawing of the creature, and a 'Key Facts' box lists basic facts at a glance. . . . Ideal for reports, but animal lovers will enjoy perusing them as well." SLJ

Singer, Marilyn

★ **Venom**. Darby Creek 2007 96p il $19.95

Grades: 5 6 7 8   **591.6**

1. Poisonous animals

ISBN 978-1-58196-043-3; 1-58196-043-3

"Singer introduces a teeming menagerie of creatures . . . that use venom for attack, defense, or, commonly, both. . . . The close-up, color photos . . . include not only views of many creepy crawlies but also such arresting scenes as wood ants spraying formic acid. . . . Browsers and dedicated young naturalists alike will enthusiastically dig their teeth into this substantial survey." Booklist

Tourville, Amanda Doering

Animal invaders. Rourke Pub. 2010 48p il (Let's explore science) $32.79

Grades: 4 5 6 7   **591.6**

1. Animals 2. Biological invasions

ISBN 978-1-61590-319-1; 1-61590-319-4

LC 2010009906

This describes non-native animal species.

Includes bibliographical references

Wilkes, Angela

Dangerous creatures; foreword by Steve Leonard. Kingfisher 2003 63p il (Kingfisher knowledge) $11.95

Grades: 5 6 7 8   **591.6**

1. Dangerous animals

ISBN 0-7534-5622-2

LC 2003-40063

Describes various kinds of dangerous animals, such as lions, piranhas, killer bees, and vampire bats

591.68 Rare and endangered animals

Hammond, Paula

The **atlas** of endangered animals; wildlife under threat around the world. Marshall Cavendish 2010 224p il map lib bdg $99.93

Grades: 7 8 9 10 11 12 **591.68**
1. Atlases 2. Reference books 3. Endangered species
ISBN 978-0-7614-7872-0; 0-7614-7872-8
LC 2008-44956

First published 2006 in the United Kingdom

This "beautifully illustrated . . . [book] features an appealing layout; logical organization; and plenty of full-color drawings, maps, and photographs. . . . Ideal for reports, but animal lovers will enjoy perusing them as well." SLJ

591.7 Animal ecology, animals characteristic of specific environments

Dawes, John

★ **Exploring** the world of aquatic life; [consultant editor, John P. Friel; authors, John Dawes and Andrew Campbell] Chelsea House Publishers 2009 6v il set $210

Grades: 5 6 7 8 **591.7**
1. Reference books 2. Marine animals -- Encyclopedias
3. Aquatic biology
ISBN 978-1-60413-255-7 set; 1-60413-255-8 set
LC 2008-30416

This set "offers an introduction to the diversity of animals that inhabit oceans, rivers, and lakes. . . . Entries are arranged alphabetically. . . . [The set includes] more than 100 articles. . . . Large photographs and illustrations appear on every two-page spread. . . . With its large typeface, clear explanations, and open layout, this set will appeal to younger students and would be a useful addition to school and public libraries." Booklist

Includes bibliographical references

The **Deep**; Claire Nouvian [editor] University of Chicago Press 2007 252p il $60

Grades: 8 9 10 11 12 Adult **591.7**
1. Marine animals 2. Marine ecology 3. Deep-sea animals 4. Deep-sea ecology 5. Marine photography
ISBN 978-0-226-59566-5; 0-226-59566-8
LC 2006-26921

"Readers will pick up science journalist Nouvian's book for its stunning, 200-plus full-page color photographs of dumbo octopi, vampire squid, frilled sharks, and hydrothermal vent worms; they will hang on to it for the well-written, extremely informative text. . . . Highly recommended for all types and sizes of libraries." Libr J

Includes bibliographical references

Johnson, Jinny

Simon & Schuster children's guide to sea creatures. Simon & Schuster Bks. for Young Readers 1998 80p il $21.95

Grades: 4 5 6 7 **591.7**
1. Marine animals
ISBN 0-689-81534-4
LC 97-8227

Describes the major groups of marine animals, including fish, birds, mammals, and crustaceans

"A beautifully illustrated guide, with a full-color drawing of each animal. . . . The book has enough information to be a useful research tool in the library. The organization, by habitat, is outstanding." Book Rep

Includes glossary

Johnson, Rebecca L.

★ **Journey** into the deep; discovering new ocean creatures. with a foreword by Sylvia A. Earle. Millbrook Press 2010 64p il lib bdg $31.93

Grades: 4 5 6 7 **591.7**
1. Ocean bottom 2. Marine animals 3. Scientific expeditions
ISBN 978-0-7613-4148-2 lib bdg; 0-7613-4148-X lib bdg
LC 2009049603

"This strikingly illustrated book takes its readers on a series of research voyages exploring the ocean from its shallow edges to unfathomable depths during the recently completed ten-year International Census of Marine Life. Clearly organized text and pictures combine to introduce newly discovered marine creatures of all kinds. . . . The excitement and challenge of discovery in tangible. Scientific photographs printed on blue-to-black background . . . illustrate animals mentioned in a nicely legible text. . . . Rich, revealing and rewarding." Kirkus

Includes glossary and bibliographical references

Miller, Sara Swan

Secret lives of burrowing beasts. Marshall Cavendish Benchmark 2010 48p il (Secret lives) lib bdg $29.93

Grades: 3 4 5 6 **591.7**
1. Burrowing animals
ISBN 978-0-7614-4221-9 lib bdg; 0-7614-4221-9 lib bdg

"The bright, sharp color photos . . . enhance, but take second fiddle to Miller's lively, well-knit [narrative]. . . . [This] volume closes with a generous selection of print and web resources." SLJ

Includes glossary

Secret lives of cave creatures. Marshall Cavendish Benchmark 2010 48p il (Secret lives) lib bdg $29.93

Grades: 3 4 5 6 **591.7**
1. Animals 2. Cave dwellers
ISBN 978-0-7614-4224-0 lib bdg; 0-7614-4224-3 lib bdg

"The bright, sharp color photos . . . enhance, but take second fiddle to Miller's lively, well-knit [narrative]. . . . [This] volume closes with a generous selection of print and web resources." SLJ

Includes glossary

Secret lives of deep-sea creatures. Marshall Cavendish Benchmark 2010 48p il (Secret lives) lib bdg $29.93

Grades: 3 4 5 6   **591.7**
1. Marine animals
ISBN 978-0-7614-4226-4 lib bdg; 0-7614-4226-X lib bdg

LC 2010000376

"The bright, sharp color photos . . . enhance, but take second fiddle to Miller's lively, well-knit [narrative]. . . . [This] volume closes with a generous selection of print and web resources." SLJ
Includes glossary

Secret lives of soil creatures. Marshall Cavendish Benchmark 2010 48p il (Secret lives) lib bdg $29.93

Grades: 3 4 5 6   **591.7**
1. Animals 2. Soil ecology
ISBN 978-0-7614-4229-5 lib bdg; 0-7614-4229-4 lib bdg

"The bright, sharp color photos . . . enhance, but take second fiddle to Miller's lively, well-knit [narrative]. . . . [This] volume closes with a generous selection of print and web resources." SLJ
Includes glossary

Turner, Pamela S.
Prowling the seas; exploring the hidden world of ocean predators. Walker & Co. 2009 39p il map $17.99; lib bdg $18.89

Grades: 4 5 6   **591.7**
1. Ocean 2. Marine animals 3. Predatory animals
ISBN 978-0-8027-9748-3; 0-8027-9748-2; 978-0-8027-9749-0 lib bdg; 0-8027-9749-0 lib bdg
"In each chapter, a clearly delineated map makes it easy to follow the animals' routes, and many clear color photos show the animals and the scientists who study them. . . . A clearly written presentation of an unusual topic." Booklist

Vogel, Carole Garbuny
Ocean wildlife. Franklin Watts 2003 95p il $29.50; pa $12.95

Grades: 5 6 7 8   **591.7**
1. Marine animals
ISBN 0-531-12324-3; 0-531-16681-3 pa

LC 2003-5302

Discusses how various underwater creatures have adapted to their environment in order to keep themselves safe from dangerous predators
This offers "magnificent, full-color photographs. . . . The clearly written narrative introduces the many creatures that have adapted to the harsh conditions of the ocean. The disastrous effects of overfishing, contamination, and pollution are briefly examined." SLJ

Webb, Sophie
Far from shore; a naturalist explores the deep ocean. written and illustrated by Sophie Webb. Houghton Mifflin Books for Children 2011 80p il $17.99

Grades: 4 5 6 7   **591.7**
1. Dolphins 2. Water birds 3. Marine animals
ISBN 978-0-618-59729-1; 0-618-59729-8

LC 2010025121

Webb "returns with another richly detailed journal of her travels as a naturalist, combining scientific information, field guide-like illustrations, and a thorough account of the day-to-day experiments of a field scientist. The setting is a four-month-long research cruise on a National Ocean and Atmospheric Administration ship to study the impact of fishing on two dolphin populations that reside in the Eastern Tropical Pacific." Horn Book
Includes glossary

Woodward, John
Creatures of the deep; written by John Woodward. Barron's Educational Series 2009 30p il (Discoverology) $18.99

Grades: 5 6 7 8   **591.7**
1. Ocean 2. Marine animals 3. Pop-up books
ISBN 978-0-7641-6232-9; 0-7641-6232-2
"Flaps, foldouts, wheels, and pop-ups spill across the pages of this colorful title. . . . Each facing page unit . . . contains an introductory paragraph and a collection of color photos, realistic illustrations, and a sampling of the aforementioned doohickeys accompanied by brief, informative captions." SLJ

591.756   Urban animals

Read, Nicholas
City critters; wildlife in the urban jungle. Nicholas Read. Orca Book Publishers 2012 134 p. (pbk.) $19.95

Grades: 6 7 8   **591.756**
1. Urban ecology 2. Birds 3. Animals 4. Mammals 5. Urban animals
ISBN 1554693942; 9781554693948

LC 2011942577

This book, by Nicholas Read, offers "a closer look [that] . . . reveals . . . we share our urban environment with a great many untamed creatures. . . . [The book] examines how and why so many wild animals choose to live in places that, on first glance at least, seem contrary to their needs. How do those . . . [animals] manage to survive in the big city? . . . And what are our responsibilities in ensuring that these animals can continue to share our city lives?" (Publisher's note)
Includes bibliographical references and index.

591.77   Marine animals

Johnson, Jinny
Coral reef life; Jinny Johnson. Smart Apple Media 2012 32 p. col. ill., col. map (Watery worlds) (library) $28.50

Grades: 4 5 6   **591.77**
1. Coral reef ecology 2. Coral reef animals
ISBN 1599205025; 9781599205021

LC 2011012947

This book by Jinny Johnson is part of the "Watery Worlds" series. "In this book, we find out how coral reefs are formed and learn why they are so important. We look at the amazing variety of fish around the reefs and discover why the reefs themselves are in danger." (Publishers note)

It "contains a map and a 'facts' page." (Library Media Connection)

Woodward, John

Ocean; an amazing window on our world. written by John Woodward; illustrations by Gary Hanna. DK Pub. 2012 59 p. col. ill. (Look closer) (hardcover) $10.99

Grades: 4 5 6 **591.77**

1. Ocean 2. Marine biology 3. Marine animals
ISBN 0756692377; 9780756692377

LC 2011277622

This book is part of DK Publishing's Look Closer series and allows readers to "explore different perspectives of . . . underwater scenes as they zoom in, zoom out, and go sideways, forward, and backward. . . . Specially commissioned computer-generated imagery" is included. (Publisher's note)

592 Specific taxonomic groups of animals

Cerullo, Mary M.

★ **Sea** soup: zooplankton; [by] Mary M. Cerullo; photography by Bill Curtsinger. Tilbury House 2001 39p il $16.95

Grades: 5 6 7 8 **592**

1. Zooplankton 2. Plankton 3. Marine zooplankton
ISBN 0-88448-219-7

LC 00-46721

This book "opens a pellucid window into the drifting world of mostly minute animals that, along with phytoplankton, form an aqueous 'soup' that nourishes a wide variety of sea creatures. . . . Curtsinger's often extraordinary color photos allow readers to envision the often microscopically small creatures delineated in the text. . . . This is a fascinating look at a watery zoo of creatures whose ecological importance is far beyond the measure of their size." SLJ

Includes glossary and bibliographical references

Meinkoth, Norman August

★ The **Audubon** Society field guide to North American seashore creatures; [by] Norman A. Meinkoth. Knopf 1981 799p il maps flexible bdg $19.95

Grades: 7 8 9 10 11 12 Adult **592**

1. Invertebrates 2. Marine biology
ISBN 0-394-51993-0

LC 81-80828

This "unique field guide covers some 850 marine invertebrate animals living in or around the shallow waters of the temperate seacoasts of the United States and Canada. Excellent color photographs are grouped at the beginning of the book, followed by text that gives, for each animal, a short description, common and scientific names, habitat, range, and comments." Malinowsky. Best Sci & Technol Ref Books for Young People

Parker, Steve, 1952-

Sponges, jellyfish & other simple animals; by Steve Parker. Compass Point Books 2006 p. cm. $29.99

Grades: 5 6 7 8 **592**

1. Sponges 2. Jellyfishes 3. Invertebrates
ISBN 0-7565-1614-5 (hard cover)

LC 2005029183

"Smoothly written, well-organized... With succinct text and colorful formats, [this] will appeal to students and browsers alike." SLJ

593 Miscellaneous marine and seashore invertebrates

Gilpin, Daniel

Starfish, urchins & other echinoderms; by Daniel Gilpin. Compass Point Books 2006 48 p. $29.99

Grades: 4 5 6 **593**

1. Starfishes 2. Sea urchins 3. Echinodermata
ISBN 0-7565-1611-0 (hard cover)

LC 2005029184

Introduces the physical characteristics, habitat, and types of echinoderms, including starfish, sea urchins, and sea cucumbers.

593.5 Coelenterates

Gray, Susan Heinrichs

Australian spotted jellyfish; [by] Susan H. Gray. Cherry Lake Pub. 2010 32p il map (Animal invaders) $27.07

Grades: 5 6 7 8 **593.5**

1. Jellyfishes 2. Biological invasions
ISBN 978-1-60279-628-7; 1-60279-628-9

LC 2009024168

This offers "an introduction to the problems caused by [the Australian spotted jellyfish], a discussion of its physical characteristics and habits, a history of how it arrived in its new habitat, and an analysis of challenges encountered by those trying to limit its spread. . . . [This] stinging jelly [was] brought by cargo ships to the Gulf of Mexico and some Atlantic coastal waters." Booklist

Includes glossary and bibliographical references

594 Mollusks and molluscoids

Arthur, Alex

Shell; written by Alex Arthur; special photography by Andreas von Einsiedel, Dave King and Colin Keates. Dk Pub 2013 72 p. (Eyewitness books) (library) $19.99

Grades: 6 7 8 **594**

1. Shells 2. Conchology
ISBN 1465409041; 9781465409041

This book is part of the DK Eyewitness Books series and focuses on shells. The titles in this series "focus on subjects that complement students' personal interests and areas of study to make learning simple and fun." Wall charts, clip art CDs, and photographs and illustrations are included. (Publisher's note)

Cerullo, Mary M.

Giant squid; searching for a sea monster. by Mary M. Cerullo with Clyde F.E. Roper. Capstone Press 2012 48 p. ill. (chiefly col.) (Smithsonian) (library) $26.86; (paperback) $8.95

Grades: 4 5 6   594
1. Giant squids
ISBN 1429680237; 9781429675413; 9781429680233
LC 2011029181

This book "recounts some of the legends and historical clues that led to the giant squid's identification in the 19th century before focusing on Dr. Clyde Roper, a renowned specialist on cephalopods. . . . The text describes how Roper gathered facts by autopsying the carcasses of giant squids and sperm whales (its chief predator), examining other squid species, etc.; it also outlines several expeditions he led in search of a live specimen." (School Library Journal)

Douglass, Jackie Leatherbury

★ Peterson first guide to shells of North America; illustrations by John Douglass. Houghton Mifflin 1989 128p il pa $5.95

Grades: 7 8 9 10 11 12 Adult   594
1. Shells
ISBN 0-395-91182-6
LC 88-32884

"Shell collectors will enjoy the basic descriptions of shell types. Douglass has included the 'most colorful, not necessarily the most common, shells.' . . . Filled with precise color drawings and concise identification information." Booklist

Gilpin, Daniel

★ Snails, shellfish & other mollusks; by Daniel Gilpin. Compass Point Books 2006 48 p. $29.99

Grades: 4 5 6   594
1. Snails. 2. Mollusks. 3. Shellfish.
ISBN 0-7565-1613-7 (hard cover)
LC 2005029182

"...Smoothly written, well-organized...With succinct texts and colorful formats, [this] will appeal to students and browsers alike." SLJ

Miller, Sara Swan

Secret lives of seashell dwellers. Marshall Cavendish Benchmark 2010 48p il (Secret lives) lib bdg $29.93

Grades: 3 4 5 6   594
1. Mollusks
ISBN 978-0-7614-4228-8 lib bdg; 0-7614-4228-6 lib bdg
LC 2010000377

"The bright, sharp color photos . . . enhance, but take second fiddle to Miller's lively, well-knit [narrative]. . . . [This] volume closes with a generous selection of print and web resources." SLJ
Includes glossary

Newquist, H. P.

Here there be monsters; the legendary kraken and the giant squid. Houghton Mifflin Harcourt 2010 73p il map $18

Grades: 4 5 6 7   594
1. Squids 2. Giant squids 3. Sea monsters
ISBN 978-0-547-07678-2; 0-547-07678-9

"This intriguing book offers a chronological account of giant squids, beginning with sailors' tales about krakens and leading up to the groundbreaking discoveries of the past few decades. . . . The many illustrations, in color when available, include photos, engravings, and maps. . . . An attractive, informative book on an underrepresented topic." Booklist

Rand, Casey

Glass squid and other spectacular squid. Raintree 2011 32p il lib bdg $29; pa $7.99

Grades: 3 4 5 6   594
1. Squids
ISBN 978-1-4109-4194-7 lib bdg; 978-1-4109-4201-2 pa
LC 2010038186

"This informative and colorful series will engage younger children to learn more about the sea and its creatures." Library Media Connection

595   Arthropods

Gilpin, Daniel

Lobsters, crabs & other crustaceans; by Daniel Gilpin. Compass Point Books 2006 48 p. $29.99

Grades: 4 5 6   595
1. Crabs 2. Lobsters 3. Crustacea
ISBN 0-7565-1612-9 (hard cover)
LC 2005029180

Introduces the physical characteristics and habitats of crustaceans, from lobsters and shrimps to sow bugs and barnacles.

595.4   Chelicerates

Heos, Bridget

Stronger Than Steel; Spider Silk DNA and the Quest for Better Bulletproof Vests, Sutures, and Parachute Rope. Bridget Heos; [illustrated by] Andy Comins. Houghton Mifflin Books for Children 2013 79 p. col. ill. (hardcover) $18.99

Grades: 5 6 7 8   595.4
1. Silk 2. Spiders 3. Inventions 4. Scientists 5. Spider webs 6. Nephila maculata 7. Spider webs -- Therapeutic use
ISBN 0547681267; 9780547681269
LC 2012010992

This children's book, by Bridget Heos, illustrated by Andy Comis, is part of the "Scientists in the Field" series. In it "readers enter Randy Lewis' lab where they come face to face with golden orb weaver spiders, and transgenic alfalfa, silkworm silk, and goats, whose milk contains the proteins to spin spider silk--and to weave a nearly indestructible fiber." (Publisher's note)

Lasky, Kathryn

Silk & venom; searching for a dangerous spider. photographs by Christopher G. Knight. Candlewick Press 2011 57p il map

Grades: 4 5 6 7   595.4

1. Spiders 2. Biologists 3. Arachnologists 4. College teachers

ISBN 0-7636-4222-3; 978-0-7636-4222-8

LC 2010-41888

"Biology professor Greta Binford studies spiders in an Oregon lab and in the field in the Dominican Republic, where she searches for L. Taino, a Caribbean relative of the venomous brown recluse that might provide clues to how and when the recluse genus arrived in North America. . . . In leisurely, literary prose, Lasky presents the ancient class of arachnids before introducing the scientist and explaining her quest. . . . On most spreads, a full-bleed photograph is opposed by substantial text and one or two smaller pictures." Kirkus

Markle, Sandra

Black widows; deadly biters. Lerner Publications 2011 48p il (Arachnid world) lib bdg $29.27

Grades: 5 6 7 8   595.4

1. Spiders

ISBN 978-0-7613-5038-5; 0-7613-5038-1

This describes how black widows are similar to and different from other arachnids. Close-up photographs and diagrams reveal details about the black widow's body both inside and out. A hands-on activity compares the black widow's web to a human hair.

Markle "presents a mix of common and less-common facts . . . and her commentary accompanies a particularly strong suite of illustrations featuring large, clear, labeled outside and inside views that display body parts. Photos go beyond the standard portraits. . . . First rate." SLJ

Includes glossary and bibliographical references

Crab spiders; phantom hunters. Sandra Markle. Lerner Pub. Company 2012 48 p. col. ill. $29.27

Grades: 4 5 6 7   595.4

1. Spiders 2. Zoology 3. Predatory animals 4. Arachnids 5. Crab spiders

ISBN 0761350454; 9780761350453

LC 2011020443

This book is part of Sandra Markle's "Arachnid World" series. "In this book, you will learn how crab spiders are similar to and different from other arachnids. Close-up photographs and diagrams reveal extraordinary details about the crab spider's body both inside and out. A hands-on activity illustrates how a crab spider can quickly ambush a flying insect. . . . Enter the . . . world of the arachnid family with award-winning science author Sandra Markle! Too often lumped together with insects, these fascinating animals have distinctive characteristics and habits that are all their own." (Publisher's note)

Includes bibliographical references

Fishing spiders; water ninjas. Sandra Markle. Lerner Publications Company 2012 48 p. col. ill. (Arachnid world) $29.27

Grades: 4 5 6 7   595.4

1. Spiders 2. Aquatic animals 3. Predatory animals 4. Zoology -- Encyclopedias 5. Arachnids 6. Dolomedes

ISBN 9780761350446

LC 2011020442

This book is part of Sandra Markle's "Arachnid World" series. "In this book, you will learn how fishing spiders are similar to and different from other arachnids. Close-up photographs and diagrams reveal extraordinary details about the fishing spider's body both inside and out. A hands-on activity shows how the fishing spider's hairy coat helps it walk on water. . . . Too often lumped together with insects, these fascinating animals have distinctive characteristics and habits that are all their own." (Publisher's note)

Includes bibliographical references

Harvestmen; secret operatives. Lerner Publications 2011 48p il (Arachnid world) lib bdg $29.27

Grades: 5 6 7 8   595.4

1. Spiders

ISBN 978-0-7613-5042-2; 0-7613-5042-X

LC 2010023491

This describes how harvestmen are similar to and different from other arachnids. Close-up photographs and diagrams reveal details about the harvestmen's bodies, both inside and out. A hands-on activity reveals how harvestmen walk on long legs using only their sense of touch to get around.

Markle "presents a mix of common and less-common facts . . . and her commentary accompanies a particularly strong suite of illustrations featuring large, clear, labeled outside and inside views that display body parts. Photos go beyond the standard portraits. . . . First rate." SLJ

Includes glossary and bibliographical references

Jumping spiders; gold-medal stalkers. by Sandra Markle. Lerner Publications 2012 48 p. col. ill.

Grades: 4 5 6 7   595.4

1. Spiders 2. Animal behavior 3. Zoology -- Encyclopedias 4. Arachnids 5. Jumping spiders

ISBN 0761350470; 9780761350477

LC 2011021598

This book is part of Sandra Markle's "Arachnid World" series. "In this book, you will learn how jumping spiders are similar to and different from other arachnids. Close-up photographs and diagrams reveal extraordinary details about the jumping spider's body both inside and out. A hands-on activity compares the reader's jumping ability with that of a jumping spider. . . . Too often lumped together with insects, these fascinating animals have distinctive characteristics and habits that are all their own." (Publisher's note)

Includes bibliographical references (p. 44-45) and index

Orb weavers; hungry spinners. Lerner Publications 2011 48p il (Arachnid world) lib bdg $29.27

Grades: 5 6 7 8   595.4

1. Spiders

ISBN 978-0-7613-5039-2; 0-7613-5039-X

LC 2010023490

This describes how orb weavers are similar to and different from other arachnids. Close-up photographs and diagrams reveal details about the spider's body both inside and out. And a hands-on activity will give you an idea of how the orb weaver can detect prey caught in its web.

Markle "presents a mix of common and less-common facts . . . and her commentary accompanies a particularly strong suite of illustrations featuring large, clear, labeled outside and inside views that display body parts. Photos go beyond the standard portraits. . . . First rate." SLJ

Includes glossary and bibliographical references

Scorpions; armed stingers. Lerner Publications 2011 48p il (Arachnid world) lib bdg $29.27
Grades: 5 6 7 8   **595.4**
1. Scorpions
ISBN 978-0-7613-5037-8; 0-7613-5037-3
LC 2010004275

This describes how scorpions are similar to and different from other arachnids. Close-up photographs and diagrams reveal details about the scorpion's body both inside and out. And a hands-on activity reveals how a scorpion's senses help it find its prey.

Markle "presents a mix of common and less-common facts . . . and her commentary accompanies a particularly strong suite of illustrations featuring large, clear, labeled outside and inside views that display body parts. Photos go beyond the standard portraits. . . . First rate." SLJ

Includes glossary and bibliographical references

Ticks; dangerous hitchhikers. Lerner Publications 2011 48p il (Arachnid world) lib bdg $29.27
Grades: 4 5 6 7   **595.4**
1. Ticks
ISBN 978-0-7613-5041-5; 0-7613-5041-1
LC 2010023484

This book about ticks offers "a clear, conversational text that will draw young people into the zoological facts with gripping, even gruesome examples that are well matched with unsparingly detailed photos. . . . The handsome design, featuring crisply magnified photos, and the approachable text from an experienced writer combine into a strong offering for both personal and classroom reading." Booklist

Includes bibliographical references

Wolf spiders; mothers on guard. Lerner Publications 2010 48p il (Arachnid world) lib bdg $29.27
Grades: 5 6 7 8   **595.4**
1. Spiders
ISBN 978-0-7613-5040-8; 0-7613-5040-3
LC 2010004273

This describes how wolf spider mothers carry their young on their backs and how wolf spiders are similar to and different from other arachnids. Close-up photographs and diagrams reveal details about the spider's body both inside and out. And a hands-on activities will let you experience how a wolf spider female keeps her eggs and young safe.

Markle "presents a mix of common and less-common facts . . . and her commentary accompanies a particularly strong suite of illustrations featuring large, clear, labeled

outside and inside views that display body parts. Photos go beyond the standard portraits. . . . First rate." SLJ

Includes glossary and bibliographical references

Markle, Sandra, 1946-
Mites; master sneaks. by Sandra Markle. Lerner Publications 2012 48 p. (Arachnid world) $29.27
Grades: 4 5 6 7   **595.4**
1. Mites 2. Animals -- Anatomy 3. Arachnids --
ISBN 9780761350460
LC 2011021462

In this book, a volume of the Arachnid World series, readers "will learn how mites are similar to and different from other arachnids. Close-up photographs, micrographs, and diagrams reveal . . . details about a mite's body both inside and out. A hands-on activity shows how quickly a few mites can multiply into hundreds." (Publisher's note)

The book "discuss[es] . . . [their] physical structure, life cycle, and characteristic behaviors. . . . In "Mites," [author Sandra] Markle discusses a variety of these . . . creatures." (Booklist)

Includes bibliographical references and index

Tarantulas; supersized predators. by Sandra Markle. Lerner Publications Company 2012 48 p. (Arachnid world) $29.27
Grades: 4 5 6 7   **595.4**
1. Tarantulas 2. Predatory animals 3. Arachnids
ISBN 9780761350439
LC 2011020437

In this book, a volume of the Arachnid World series, readers "will learn how tarantulas are similar to and different from other arachnids. Close-up photographs and diagrams reveal extraordinary details about the tarantula's body both inside and out. A hands-on activity illustrates how a tarantula grows bigger and bigger by molting." (Publisher's note)

The book "discuss[es] . . . [their] physical structure, life cycle, and characteristic behaviors. . . . "Tarantulas" looks at the lives of these large, hairy spiders and points out that they help control insect populations." (Booklist)

Includes bibliographical references and index

Wind scorpions; killer jaws. Sandra Markle. Lerner Publications 2012 48 p. (Arachnid world) (lib. bdg. : alk. paper) $30.60
Grades: 4 5 6 7   **595.4**
1. Scorpions 2. Animals -- Anatomy 3. Arachnids 4. Solpugida
ISBN 0761350489; 9780761350484
LC 2011021599

In this book, a volume of the Arachnid World series, readers "will learn how wind scorpions are similar to and very different from other arachnids. Close-up photographs and diagrams reveal extraordinary details about the wind scorpion's body both inside and out. A hands-on activity demonstrates how wind scorpions are able to pick up prey to eat it." (Publisher's note)

The book "discuss[es] . . . [their] physical structure, life cycle, and characteristic behaviors. . . . "Wind Scorpions" introduces a group of arachnids that use supersize jaws to defend themselves and to attack their prey." (Booklist)

Includes bibliographical references and index

Montgomery, Sy
★ The **tarantula** scientist. Houghton Mifflin Co. 2004 80p il map (Scientists in the field) $18; pa $7.95

Grades: 4 5 6 7   **595.4**
1. Tarantulas
ISBN 0-618-14799-3; 0-618-91577-X pa
LC 2003-20125

Describes the research that Samuel Marshall and his students are doing on tarantulas, including the largest spider on earth, the Goliath birdeating tarantula

"Enthusiasm for the subject and respect for both Marshall and his eight-legged subjects come through on every page of the clear, informative, and even occasionally humorous text. Bishop's full-color photos . . . are amazing." Booklist
Includes glossary and bibliographical references

Stefoff, Rebecca
The **arachnid** class. Marshall Cavendish Benchmark 2008 96p il (Family trees) $23.95

Grades: 6 7 8 9   **595.4**
1. Spiders
ISBN 978-0-7614-3075-9; 0-7614-3075-X
LC 2008017561

"Explores the habitats, life cycles, and other characteristics of arachnids, such as spiders, scorpions, mites, and ticks."
Includes glossary and bibliographical references

Zabludoff, Marc
★ **Spiders**; [by] Marc Zabludoff. Marshall Cavendish Benchmark 2006 112p il (Animalways) lib bdg $31.36

Grades: 7 8 9 10   **595.4**
1. Spiders
ISBN 0-7614-1747-8
LC 2004-16681

This discusses the evolution of spiders, their places in human culture, their life cycles, anatomy, and behavior

"Strong writing melds well with well-selected photos, all of which are clearly produced and of high quality. Some of the images are stunning." SLJ
Includes glossary and bibliographical references

595.7 Insects

Anderson, Margaret Jean
Bugged-out insects; [by] Margaret J. Anderson. Enslow Publishers 2011 48p il (Bizarre science) lib bdg $23.93

Grades: 4 5 6 7   **595.7**
1. Insects
ISBN 978-0-7660-3674-1; 0-7660-3674-X
LC 2010006474

First published 1996 with title: Bizarre insects

This describes insects such as cicadas, butterflies, praying mantises, walkingsticks, beetles, stinkbugs, botflies, mayflies, mosquitoes, bees, ants, and locusts.

"Aimed at reluctant readers, [this title is] sure to disgust and delight in equal measure. . . . [The title] will pique inter-est and get kids lining up at the reference desk looking for more. The text is complemented by illustrations and magnified photos of things that you would hope never to see." SLJ
Includes glossary and bibliographical references

Beccaloni, George
Biggest bugs life-size. Firefly Books 2010 84p il $19.95

Grades: 4 5 6 7   **595.7**
1. Insects
ISBN 978-1-55407-699-4; 1-55407-699-4

"This book presents 35 of the world's biggest, longest, and heaviest bugs. . . . Double-page spreads feature each bug's statistics, a map with its area of distribution, and straightforward text that explains its living conditions, eating habits, and life cycle. . . . The highlights, of course, are the numerous life-size and up-close full-color photographs of the bugs. . . . The visual appeal alone will entice even the most reluctant readers." Booklist

Dixon, Norma
Focus on flies. Fitzhenry & Whiteside 2008 32p il $18.95

Grades: 4 5 6 7   **595.7**
1. Flies
ISBN 978-1-55005-128-5; 1-55005-128-8

This "chatty, informative title, illustrated with many clear color photos and diagrams, will hook readers with its fascinating view of a fly's 'creepy cool world.' . . . The gross details will appeal to middle-grade readers, who will then go on to learn about anatomy, metamorphosis, adaptation, diversity, classification, and flies' roles in plant pollination." Booklist
Includes bibliographical references

Evans, Arthur V.
National Wildlife Federation field guide to insects and spiders & related species of North America; written by Arthur Evans; foreword by Craig Tufts. Sterling Pub. 2007 496p il map pa $19.95

Grades: 8 9 10 11 12 Adult   **595.7**
1. Insects 2. Spiders
ISBN 978-1-4027-4153-1; 1-4027-4153-7
LC 2006-19491

"This guide presents a glimpse of the incredible array of colors, shapes, and forms found within the phylum Arthropoda. . . . Over 380 pages of color photographs follow, most showing two or three different species. . . . This is a very good guide that will find a wide audience." Choice
Includes bibliographical references

Gray, Susan Heinrichs
Emerald ash borer; by Susan H. Gray. Cherry Lake Pub. 2008 32p il map (Animal invaders) lib bdg $27.07

Grades: 3 4 5 6   **595.7**
1. Emerald ash borer 2. Biological invasions
ISBN 978-1-60279-112-1 lib bdg; 1-60279-112-0 lib bdg
LC 2007-34973

This describes the Emerald ash borers' "outstanding physical and behavioral characteristics at each stage in their life cycle, diet, and natural habitat, and then [explains] how they were introduced into areas outside their natural range . . . and the nature and extent of the ecological damage they have caused, and various attempts to eradicate or at least control the animals. . . . Larvae of the emerald ash borer have infested and destroyed thousands of valuable ash trees in the Midwest. . . . Clear color photographs . . . accompany the texts on about every other page. . . . [This title is] clearly written and well organized, and [has] up-to-date information." SLJ

Includes glossary

Hamilton, Sue L.

Swarmed by bees; [by] Sue Hamilton. ABDO Pub. Co. 2010 32p il (Close encounters of the wild kind) lib bdg $27.07

Grades: 4 5 6 7   **595.7**
1. Bees 2. Animal attacks
ISBN 978-1-60453-933-2 lib bdg; 1-60453-933-X lib bdg

LC 2009-45598

Readers learn of actual human-bee encounters, information about bees, survival strategies, and attack statistics.

"Students will be drawn to the realistic full-color photographs, the realistic diagrams of the creatures' bodies, the real-life stories told by victims, and the interesting, attractive formatting that includes text, diagrams, photographs, and graphics on each page. . . . [This is] exciting and attractive in a 'gross' sort of way and will appeal particularly to boys for both leisure reading and research." Libr Media Connect

Includes glossary

Latimer, Jonathan P.

Caterpillars; [by] Jonathan P. Latimer, Karen Stray Nolting; illustrations by Amy Bartlett Wright; foreword by Virginia Marie Peterson. Houghton Mifflin 2000 48p il (Peterson field guides for young naturalists) pbk. $5.95

Grades: 4 5 6 7   **595.7**
1. Caterpillars
ISBN 9780395979457

LC 99-38944

Describes the physical characteristics, behavior, and habitat of a variety of caterpillars, arranged by the categories "Smooth," "Bumpy," "Sluglike," "Horned," "Hairy," "Bristly," and "Spiny"

Marshall, Stephen A.

Insects A to Z. Firefly 2009 32p il lib bdg $19.95; pa $7.95

Grades: 4 5 6   **595.7**
1. Insects
ISBN 978-1-55407-555-3 lib bdg; 1-55407-555-6 lib bdg; 978-1-55407-503-4 pa; 1-55407-503-3 pa

This is an illustrated dictionary of 26 insects which includes the Latin and common names of the order, family, genus and species, as well as information on geographic distribution. Fact boxes for each entry provide information detailing each insect's scientific name, diet, average size and the location at which each was photographed.

"The photography . . . is well composed and sharply focused, with a nicely varied layout from page to page. . . . The [text is] clearly written." SLJ

Milne, Lorus Johnson

★ The **Audubon** Society field guide to North American insects and spiders; [by] Lorus and Margery Milne; visual key by Susan Rayfield. Knopf 1980 989p il $19.95

Grades: 7 8 9 10 11 12 Adult   **595.7**
1. Insects 2. Spiders
ISBN 0-394-50763-0

LC 80-7620

The authors "have based their field guide on 702 excellent color photographs (75 of which are of spiders and other arachnids). In addition to some general information, the text (two thirds of the book) is made up of brief comments on each kind of arthropod pictured." Choice

Includes glossary

Pyle, Robert Michael

★ The **Audubon** Society field guide to North American butterflies; visual key by Carol Nehring and Jane Opper. Knopf 1981 916p il $19.95

Grades: 7 8 9 10 11 12 Adult   **595.7**
1. Butterflies
ISBN 0-394-51914-0

LC 80-84240

This guide "introduces more than 600 species of North American butterfly, including those native to the Hawaiian Islands. A section of brilliant color plates (more than 1,000 of them) featuring butterflies in their natural habitats, follows a general introduction and notes on text organization and use." Booklist

Rodriguez, Ana Maria

Secret of the plant-killing ants . . . and more! Enslow Publishers 2008 48p il (Animal secrets revealed!) lib bdg $23.93

Grades: 5 6 7 8   **595.7**
1. Ants 2. Insects
ISBN 978-0-7660-2953-8 lib bdg; 0-7660-2953-0 lib bdg

LC 2007039494

"Explains why ants in the Amazon rainforest kill all but one species of plant and details other strange abilities of different types of animals." Publisher's note

Includes glossary and bibliographical references

Schlaepfer, Gloria G.

Butterflies. Marshall Cavendish Benchmark 2006 112p il (Animalways) lib bdg $31.36

Grades: 6 7 8 9   **595.7**
1. Butterflies
ISBN 0-7614-1745-1

LC 2004-16682

This discusses the evolution of butterflies, their places in human culture, their life cycles, anatomy, and behavior

"Strong writing melds well with well-selected photos, all of which are clearly produced and of high quality. Some of the images are stunning." SLJ

Includes glossary and bibliographical references

Tait, Noel

Insects & spiders. Simon & Schuster Books for Young Readers 2008 64p il map (Insiders) $16.99

Grades: 5 6 7 8   595.7

1. Insects 2. Spiders

ISBN 978-1-4169-3868-2; 1-4169-3868-0

LC 2008-61110

Provides an overview of insects and spiders in a book that includes detailed three-dimensional illustrations.

"Sharp, hyper-realistic, larger-than-life drawings . . . are . . . set against a plain colored background or within a natural setting. . . . [This] title succinctly describes basic anatomy; physical and behavioral characteristics common to all [insects and spiders]." SLJ

Includes glossary

Young, Karen Romano

Bug science; 20 projects and experiments about arthropods: insects, arachnids, algae, worms, and other small creatures. illustrations by David Goldin. National Geographic 2009 80p il (Science fair winners) lib bdg $24.90; pa $12.95

Grades: 6 7 8 9   595.7

1. Insects 2. Arthropoda 3. Science projects 4. Science -- Experiments

ISBN 978-1-4263-0520-7 lib bdg; 1-4263-0520-6 lib bdg; 978-1-4263-0519-1 pa; 1-4263-0519-2 pa

LC 2009-12734

Twenty projects and experiments about arthropods: insects, arachnids, algae, worms, and other small creatures.

This book is "engaging, visually stimulating, and very student friendly. . . . Includes an introduction to the topic, suggestions for how to present the findings, and an index making the information really accessible. . . . The planning steps, guidance, and tips along the way for implementing projects are very sound." Libr Media Connect

Includes bibliographical references

Zabludoff, Marc

Beetles; by Marc Zabludoff. Marshall Cavendish Benchmark 2007 112p il (Animalways) lib bdg $34.21

Grades: 6 7 8 9   595.7

1. Beetles

ISBN 978-0-7614-2532-8

LC 2006038518

This describes the place of beetles in the animal kingdom, their evolution, anatomy, physiology, life cycle, diversity, and relationship to humans.

Includes glossary and bibliographical references

★ The **insect** class. Benchmark Books 2006 95p il (Family trees) lib bdg $29.93

Grades: 6 7 8 9   595.7

1. Insects

ISBN 0-7614-1819-9 lib bdg

LC 2004-21819

This examines physical traits, adaptations, diets, habitats, and life cycles of insects.

"Fact-filled, yet surprisingly readable. . . . [This] title contains a wide variety of excellent-quality, full-color photographs; interesting sidebars; and diagrams." SLJ

Includes glossary and bibliographical references

595.76   Beetles

Jenkins, Steve

★ The **beetle** book; Steve Jenkins. Houghton Mifflin Books for Children 2011 31 p. $16.99

Grades: 4 5 6 7   595.76

1. Beetles 2. Ecology -- Encyclopedias 3. Insects -- Encyclopedias

ISBN 9780547680842

LC 2011027129

This nonfiction natural history book presents pictures and information about an "array of beetles." Author/illustrator Steve Jenkins describes "the colors and patterns of this ubiquitous insect . . . [and] the details about the various adaptations that beetles have made over millennia in response to their environment, diet, and predators." Jenkins claims that "one out of four creatures on the planet is a beetle." (Kirkus Reviews)

595.78   Moths and butterflies

Pasternak, Carol

How to raise monarch butterflies; a step-by-step guide for kids. Carol Pasternak. Firefly Books 2012 48 p. col. ill. (bound) $19.95

Grades: 3 4 5 6 7   595.78

1. Caterpillars 2. Insects -- Care 3. Monarch butterflies 4. Monarch butterfly 5. Monarch butterfly -- Life cycles

ISBN 1770850015; 1770850023; 9781770850019; 9781770850026

LC 2012419489

This book by Carol Pasternak presents a "detailed guide to locating and hatching. . . Monarch butterflies. . . . [R]eaders will learn about the life cycle of the Monarch and how to encourage populations in their own backyards, with tips on which plants to grow, as well as the care and feeding of their pet caterpillars. 'How to Raise Monarch Butterflies' explains what threats face Monarchs and how readers can help conserve the Monarch's feeding grounds from encroachment." (Publisher's note)

Includes bibliographical references and index.

Whalley, Paul

Butterfly & moth; written by Paul Whalley. Revised ed. DK Pub. 2012 72 p. ill. (chiefly col.), col. map (Eyewitness books) (hardcover) $16.99; (library) $19.99

Grades: 4 5 6 7   **595.78**
1. Moths 2. Butterflies
ISBN 0756692989; 0756692997; 9780756692988;
9780756692995

                 LC 2012418030

This book is part of the DK Eyewitness Books series and focuses on butterflies and moths. The titles in this series "focus on subjects that complement students' personal interests and areas of study to make learning simple and fun." Wall charts, clip art CDs, and photographs and illustrations are included. (Publisher's note)

597   Cold-blooded vertebrates

Benchley, Peter

Shark life; true stories about sharks & the sea. adapted for young people by Karen Wojtyla. Delacorte 2005 193p il $15.95; lib bdg $17.99
Grades: 5 6 7 8   **597**
1. Sharks 2. Dangerous animals
ISBN 0-385-73109-4; 0-385-90135-6 lib bdg

Adapted from the title for adults, Shark trouble, published in 2003.

This "is an engaging, frequently exciting recounting of one man's fascinating adventures in the ocean." Booklist
Includes glossary

Capuzzo, Mike

Close to shore; the terrifying shark attacks of 1916. Crown 2003 140p il $16.95; lib bdg $18.99
Grades: 6 7 8 9   **597**
1. Sharks
ISBN 0-375-82231-3; 0-375-92231-8 lib bdg

                 LC 2002-29918

An adaptation of the title for adults published 2001 by Broadway Bks.

Details the first documented cases in American history of sharks attacking swimmers, which occured along the Atlantic coast of New Jersey in 1916

"This book has a rich assortment of photos and news clippings. . . . Capuzzo reconstructs events with a novelist's flair and a scientist's attention to detail, and his pacing is relentless." Booklist
Includes bibliographical references

Cerullo, Mary M.

★ The **truth** about great white sharks; written by Mary M. Cerullo; photographs by Jeffrey L. Rotman; illustrations by Michael Wertz. Chronicle Bks. 2000 48p il hardcover o.p. $14.95
Grades: 4 5 6 7   **597**
1. Sharks
ISBN 0-8118-2467-5; 0-8118-5759-X pa

                 LC 00-31506

This provides information "about shark anatomy, senses, eating habits, and their relationships with humans. . . . The book also contains unusual information such as how these fish are measured and photographed and why they are not able to survive in an aquarium. The attractive layout blends line drawings, full-color photographs, varied typefaces, and

eye-catching graphics. Rotman's pictures are clear and informative. . . . This title will be accessible to reluctant readers and is a must for most collections." SLJ
Includes bibliographical references

Gilbert, Carter Rowell

National Audubon Society field guide to fishes, North America; [by] Carter R. Gilbert, James D. Williams. rev ed, 2nd ed, fully rev; Alfred A. Knopf 2002 607p il maps pa $19.95
Grades: 7 8 9 10 11 12 Adult   **597**
1. Fishes -- North America
ISBN 0-375-41224-7

                 LC 2002-20773

First published 1983 with title: The Audubon Society field guide to North American fishes, whales, and dolphins

This guide covers over 600 freshwater and saltwater species in detail, with notes on 771 more species.

Hamilton, Sue L.

Eaten by a shark; [by] Sue Hamilton. ABDO Pub. 2010 32p il (Close encounters of the wild kind) lib bdg $22.61
Grades: 4 5 6 7   **597**
1. Sharks 2. Animal attacks
ISBN 978-1-60453-931-8 lib bdg; 1-60453-931-3 lib bdg

                 LC 2009-37230

In this volume, readers learn of actual human-wildlife encounters, creature information, survival strategies, and attack statistics.

"Students will be drawn to the realistic full-color photographs, the realistic diagrams of the creatures' bodies, the real-life stories told by victims, and the interesting, attractive formatting that includes text, diagrams, photographs, and graphics on each page. . . . [This is] exciting and attractive in a 'gross' sort of way and will appeal particularly to boys for both leisure reading and research." Libr Media Connect
Includes glossary

Miller, Sara Swan

Seahorses, pipefishes, and their kin; Sara Swan Miller. Franklin Watts 2002 47 p. col. ill. (Animals in order) (library) $26.50; (paperback) $6.95
Grades: 4 5 6   **597**
1. Marine biology 2. Marine animals 3. Gasterosteiformes
ISBN 9780531121719; 0531163792; 9780531163795

                 LC 2001003034

This book by Sara Swan Miller is part of the Animals in Order series and looks at seahorses, pipefishes, and related animals. "These colorful series entries present a wide variety of creatures that have been sorted by scientific classification into similar groupings called orders . . . . Family names, common names, genus, species, size, and/or location are given, and paragraphs describe various behaviors (food gathering, courtship, etc.)." (School Library Journal)
Includes bibliographical references (p. 46) and index.

Page, Lawrence M.
★ **Peterson** field guide to freshwater fishes of North America north of Mexico; [by] Lawrence M. Page, Brooks M. Burr; illustrations by Eugene C. Beckham III . . . [et al.]; maps by Griffin E. Sheehy. 2nd ed.; Houghton Mifflin Harcourt 2011 663p il map pa $21
Grades: 7 8 9 10 11 12 Adult   **597**
  1. Fishes -- North America
  ISBN 978-0-547-24206-4; 0-547-24206-9
                LC 2010-49219
First published 1991 with title: A field guide to freshwater fishes: North America north of Mexico
This guide to identifying different species of freshwater fish in North America includes "maps and information showing where to locate each species of fish—whether that species can be found in miles-long stretches of river or small pools that cover only dozens of square feet." Publisher's note
Includes glossary and bibliographical references

Rodriguez, Ana Maria
Secret of the suffocating slime trap . . . and more! Enslow Publishers 2008 48p il (Animal secrets revealed!) lib bdg $23.93
Grades: 5 6 7 8   **597**
  1. Fishes
  ISBN 978-0-7660-2954-5 lib bdg; 0-7660-2954-9 lib bdg
                LC 2007039493
This book offers "fascinating accounts of how scientists systematically analyzed, tested, and proved their theories or how their findings led to other, serendipitous discoveries. . . . Science experiments are thoughtfully placed to inspire exploration, and captioned, full-color photos appear throughout." SLJ
Includes glossary and bibliographical references

Stefoff, Rebecca
★ The **fish** classes; [by] Rebecca Stefoff. Marshall Cavendish Benchmark 2008 96p il (Family trees) $22.95
Grades: 6 7 8 9   **597**
  1. Fishes
  ISBN 978-0-7614-2695-0; 0-7614-2695-7
                LC 2007003483
"Skillful weaving of engaging text and superb illustrations will incite interest." Voice Youth Advocates
Includes glossary and bibliographical references

Swinney, Geoff
Fish facts; illustrated by Janeen Mason. Pelican Pub. Co. 2011 48p il $17.99
Grades: 5 6 7 8   **597**
  1. Fishes
  ISBN 978-1-58980-908-6; 1-58980-908-4
                LC 2010046220
"This comprehensive collection of facts about fish is sure to educate as well as fascinate. . . . From fish that produce light and fish that are capable of powered flight, to fish that can change sex and fish that carry their offspring in their mouths, this is chock full of both the amazing and the weird.

. . . While the rather advanced vocabulary and biology that Swinney delves into mark this as a book for older readers, younger ones can certainly enjoy both the illustrations and the occasional factoid. Mason's artwork is both painstakingly detailed and realistically colored, even down to the muting effect that water has on colors. Few books come close to this one's inclusiveness." Kirkus

Turner, Pamela S.
★ **Project** Seahorse; [photographs by Scott Tuason] Houghton Mifflin Harcourt 2010 56p il (Scientists in the field) $18
Grades: 4 5 6 7   **597**
  1. Sea horses 2. Fishing 3. Ecology -- Philippines
  ISBN 978-0-547-20713-1; 0-547-20713-1
                LC 2009-49707
"With striking images of coral-reef inhabitants, this photo-essay introduces Project Seahorse, an international effort to protect and rehabilitate the Danajon Bank, a double reef off a Philippine Island where seahorses once flourished . . . Tuason, a noted Asian marine photographer whose specialty is the Philippines, seems equally adept at photographing the land and people and the underwater world. This is another splendid demonstration of the work of Scientists in the Field." Kirkus

597.3   Selachii, Holocephali, fleshy-finned fishes

Macquitty, Miranda
Shark; written by Miranda MacQuitty. DK Pub. 2008 72 p. col. ill (Eyewitness books) (hardcover) $16.99
Grades: 4 5 6 7   **597.3**
  1. Marine biology
  ISBN 0756637783; 9780756637781
                LC 2008276031
This book is part of the DK Eyewitness Books series and focuses on sharks. The titles in this series "focus on subjects that complement students' personal interests and areas of study to make learning simple and fun." Wall charts, clip art CDs, and photographs and illustrations are included. (Publisher's note)

Mallory, Kenneth
★ **Swimming** with hammerhead sharks. Houghton Mifflin 2001 48p il (Scientists in the field) pbk. $7.99
Grades: 4 5 6 7   **597.3**
  1. Sharks 2. Hammerhead sharks 3. Hammerhead sharks -- Research
  ISBN 9780618250790
                LC 00-61401
This book follows "marine biologist Pete Klimley and an IMAX film team to seamounts off Cocos Island in the Pacific Ocean to observe and film schooling hammerhead sharks. . . . A fascinating record of research and investigation, this inviting book is larded with numerous dramatic color photos." SLJ
Includes bibliographical references

Sharks; facts at your fingertips. DK Pub. 2012 156 p. col. ill., map (Pocket genius) (hc) $7.99

Grades: 5 6 7 8   **597.3**

1. Sharks 2. Rays (Fishes)

ISBN 0756692865; 9780756692865

LC 2011277726

This book, part of the "Pocket Genius" encyclopedia series, "profiles more that 150 sharks and rays -- from the great white to the tiny dwarf lantern -- and tells what they eat, where they live and how fast they swim." It "offers a . . . catalog-style presentation, which clearly lays out individual subcategories." (Publisher's note)

Walker, Sally M.

★ **Fossil** fish found alive; discovering the coelacanth. Carolrhoda Bks. 2002 72p il map lib bdg $17.95

Grades: 5 6 7 8   **597.3**

1. Coelacanth

ISBN 1-57505-536-8

LC 2001-3815

Describes the 1938 discovery of the coelacanth, a fish previously believed to be extinct, and subsequent research about it

"Walker writes well, making this relatively unknown area of science history an exciting story of exploration and discovery. Excellent, full-color photos illustrate the text." Booklist

Includes bibliographical references

597.8 Amphibians

Beltz, Ellin

Frogs: inside their remarkable world. Firefly Books 2005 175p il $34.95

Grades: 5 6 7 8 9 10   **597.8**

1. Frogs 2. Toads

ISBN 1-55297-869-9

LC 2006-365517

The author "picture of the history of the frog, its anatomical makeup, its place in the natural world and the threats that are seriously reducing its numbers around the world." Publisher's note

Crump, Marty

★ The **mystery** of Darwin's frog; by Marty Crump; illustrated by Steve Jenkins and Edel Rodriquez. Boyds Mills Press 2013 40 p. ill. (reinforced) $16.95

Grades: 3 4 5 6 7   **597.8**

1. Frogs

ISBN 1590788648; 9781590788646

LC 2012947844

In this book, Marty Crump, a researcher who has investigated the Rhinoderma darwinii, an inch-long frog discovered by Charles Darwin in Chile in 1834, "describes the earlier investigations of this intriguing frog and records her own efforts to document how it lives in the wild. She discusses her findings and goes on to present the problems facing not only Darwin's frogs, but also frogs in general-loss of habitat,

pollution, and the assault of the lethal Bd fungus." (School Library Journal)

Gilpin, Daniel

Tree frogs, mud puppies, & other amphibians; by Daniel Gilpin. Compass Point Books 2006 48 p. col. ill. (Animal kingdom classification) (library) $29.99

Grades: 5 6 7 8   **597.8**

1. Picture books for children 2. Amphibians

ISBN 0756512492; 9780756512491

LC 2005003683

This book by Daniel Gilpin is part of the Families series and looks at tree frogs, mud puppies, and other amphibians. It "discusses the large diversity of amphibians, a typical amphibian's body, ancient amphibians, and an amphibian's skin and senses. It discusses hiding and warning, movement, prey, courtship, strange breeders, and the life-cycle." (Publisher's note)

Includes bibliographical references (p. 47) and index.

Markle, Sandra, 1946-

★ The **case** of the vanishing golden frogs. Millbrook Press 2011 48p il $29.27

Grades: 4 5 6   **597.8**

1. Frogs 2. Endangered species 3. Wildlife conservation

ISBN 0761351086; 9780761351085

LC 2010042642

"The golden frog, a Panamanian national symbol, began vanishing from its high mountain forests in the late 1990s, prompting a scientific investigation and rescue process that continues today. . . . Markle . . . describes a mission that has involved scientists from around the world." Kirkus

Includes glossary and bibliographical references

Pringle, Laurence

Frogs! strange and wonderful. Laurence Pringle; illustrated by Meryl Henderson. Boyds Mills Press 2012 30 p. col. ill (reinf. trade ed.) $16.95

Grades: 3 4 5 6   **597.8**

1. Frogs 2. Poisonous animals 3. Camouflage (Biology) 4. Amphibians

ISBN 1590783719; 9781590783719

LC 2011928834

In this book, author Laurence P. Pringle offers a "look at the similarities and differences among the many and varied species of frogs . . . The Reinwardt's flying frog glides between trees, the mantella and poison frogs come in all the colors of the rainbow and one can guess what makes the marsupial frog stand out. Camouflage, mating, development, coloring, size, locomotion, how and what they eat and how and why they make sounds are just some of the topics." (Kirkus)

Includes bibliographical references

Somervill, Barbara A.

Cane toad; by Barbara A. Somervill. Cherry Lake Pub. 2008 32p il map (Animal invaders) lib bdg $26.26

Grades: 3 4 5 6   **597.8**
1. Toads 2. Biological invasions
ISBN 978-1-60279-115-2 lib bdg; 1-60279-115-5
lib bdg

LC 2007-33510

This describes the cane toads' "outstanding physical and behavioral characteristics at each stage in their life cycle, diet, and natural habitat, and then [explains] how they were introduced into areas outside their natural range . . . and the nature and extent of the ecological damage they have caused, and various attempts to eradicate or at least control the animals. . . . The prolific cane toads, which are fast supplanting native amphibians in Australia, excrete a toxin powerful enough to kill the animals, and some humans unfortunate enough to ingest them. . . . Clear color photographs . . . accompany the [text] on about every other page. . . . [This title is] clearly written and well organized, and [has] up-to-date information." SLJ
Includes glossary

Stefoff, Rebecca
★ The **amphibian** class; [by] Rebecca Stefoff. Marshall Cavendish Benchmark 2008 96p il (Family trees) lib bdg $22.95
Grades: 6 7 8 9   **597.8**
1. Amphibians
ISBN 978-0-7614-2692-9 lib bdg; 0-7614-2692-2

LC 2007003487

This is "meticulously detailed. . . . Sharp color photographs appear on about every other page. Other illustrations consist of classification charts and anatomical diagrams. . . . [This is] well-organized and clearly written." SLJ
Includes glossary and bibliographical references

Turner, Pamela S.
★ The **frog** scientist; photographs by Andy Comins. Houghton Mifflin Books for Children 2009 58p il (Scientists in the field) lib bdg $18
Grades: 5 6 7 8   **597.8**
1. Frogs 2. Biologists 3. College teachers 4. Scientists
ISBN 978-0-618-71716-3 lib bdg; 0-618-71716-1
lib bdg

LC 2008-39770

This volume "opens with biologist Tyrone Hayes and his team collecting frogs at a pond in Wyoming. After a short chapter on Hayes' background, the discussion returns to his work: he addresses the general question of why amphibian populations world-wide are declining by studying the effects of atrizine, an agricultural pesticide, on the reproductive organs of leopard frogs from a particular pond. Well organized and clearly written. . . . Excellent color photos offer clear pictures of frogs and of this scientific team at work in the field and in the lab. . . . A vivid, realistic view of one scientist at work." Booklist
Includes glossary and bibliographical references

597.87   Bufonoidea

Solway, Andrew
Poison frogs and other amphibians; by Andrew Solway. Heinemann Library 2006 48 p. col. ill. (Adapted for success) (library) $32.00; (paperback) $8.99
Grades: 5 6 7 8 9   **597.87**
1. Frogs 2. Animal defenses 3. Amphibians 4. Dendrobatidae
ISBN 140348225X; 9781403482259; 9781403482327
out of print

LC 2006014294

This book by Andrew Solway is part of the Adapted for Success series and looks at poison frogs. "Poison Frogs are among the most poisonous animals in the world, but how have they, and other amphibians, adapted to become so successful? The series explores how some of our favorite animals are uniquely adapted to their environment. Each book . . . covers habitat, defenses, camouflage, and the way animals find food." (Publisher's note)
Includes bibliographical references and index.

597.9   Reptiles

Conant, Roger
A **field** guide to reptiles & amphibians; eastern and central North America. [by] Roger Conant and Joseph T. Collins; illustrated by Isabelle Hunt Conant and Tom R. Johnson. 3rd ed, expanded; Houghton Mifflin 1998 616p il map (Peterson field guide series) pbk $21
Grades: 7 8 9 10 11 12 Adult   **597.9**
1. Reptiles 2. Amphibians 3. Reptiles -- Canada -- Identification 4. Amphibians -- Canada -- Identification 5. Reptiles -- United States -- Identification 6. Amphibians -- United States -- Identification
ISBN 9780395904527

LC 98-13622

First published 1958 with title: A field guide to reptiles and amphibians of the United States and Canada east of the 100th meridian

This guide describes 595 species and subspecies, featuring color photos, black and white drawings, and color distribution maps of reptiles and amphibians of the region. Also includes information on transporting live reptiles and amphibians
Includes glossary and bibliographical references

Hutchinson, Mark
Reptiles. Simon & Schuster Books for Young Readers 2011 64p il (Insiders) $16.99
Grades: 4 5 6 7   **597.9**
1. Reptiles
ISBN 978-1-4424-3276-5; 1-4424-3276-4

"Arranged around the digitally rendered, sharply focused central images . . . smaller inset pictures and blocks of text systematically present distinctive physical features, typical behaviors, habitats, ranges, diets, and other information about each type of reptile. . . . This book will wow casual browsers and budding herpetologists alike." Booklist

McCarthy, Colin

Reptile; written by Colin McCarthy; [special photography, Karl Shone . . . [et al.]] Dorling Kindersley 2000 63p il (DK eyewitness books) $15.99

Grades: 4 5 6 7   597.9
   1. Reptiles
ISBN 0-7894-5786-5
First published 1991 by Knopf

Photographs and text depict the many different kinds of reptiles, their similarities and differences, habitats, and behavior

Stebbins, Robert C.

★ A **field** guide to Western reptiles and amphibians; text and illustrations by Robert C. Stebbins. 3rd ed newly rev; Houghton Mifflin 2003 533p il map (Peterson field guide series) pa $22

Grades: 7 8 9 10 11 12 Adult   597.9
   1. Reptiles 2. Amphibians 3. Reptiles -- West (U.S.) -- Identification 4. Amphibians -- West (U.S.) -- Identification 5. Reptiles -- North America -- Identification 6. Amphibians -- North America -- Identification
ISBN 0-395-98272-3

LC 2002-27561
First published 1966

This "covers all the species of reptiles and amphibians found in western North America. More than 650 full-color paintings and photographs show key details for making accurate identifications. . . . Color range maps give species' distributions. . . . [Includes] information on conservation efforts and survival status." Publisher's note

Includes bibliographical references

Zabludoff, Marc

★ The **reptile** class. Benchmark Books 2005 95p il (Family trees) lib bdg $29.92

Grades: 6 7 8 9   597.9
   1. Reptiles
ISBN 0-7614-1820-2

LC 2004-21820
This examines physical traits, adaptations, diets, habitats, and life cycles of reptiles.

"Fact-filled, yet surprisingly readable. . . . [This] title contains a wide variety of excellent-quality, full-color photos; interesting sidebars; and diagrams." SLJ

597.92   Turtles

Lockwood, Sophie

Sea turtles; by Sophie Lockwood. Child's World 2006 40p col. ill., col. maps (library) $29.93

Grades: 4 5 6   597.92
   1. Sea turtles
ISBN 1592965504; 9781592965502

LC 2005024792
"Conservation is the dominant theme of this attractive photo-essay. . . . which has beautiful full-page color photos that bring readers close to the subject. Fast-fact boxes focus on particular species, providing spot statistics on weight,

length, color, habitat, threatened or endangered status, and more." Booklist

Includes bibliographical references (p. 39) and index.

Stefoff, Rebecca

Turtles; [by] Rebecca Stefoff. Marshall Cavendish Benchmark 2007 110p il (Animalways) lib bdg $34.21

Grades: 6 7 8 9   597.92
   1. Turtles
ISBN 978-0-7614-2539-7

LC 2007013178
This describes the place of turtles in the animal kingdom, their evolution, anatomy, physiology, diversity, life cycle, and relationship to humans.

Includes glossary and bibliographical references

Stone, Lynn M.

Box turtles; written and photographed by Lynn M. Stone. Lerner Publications 2007 48p il map lib bdg $25.26

Grades: 4 5 6 7   597.92
   1. Turtles
ISBN 978-1-57505-869-6 lib bdg; 1-57505-869-3 lib bdg

LC 2006012867

597.95   Lizards

Collard III, Sneed B.

Sneed B. Collard III's most fun book ever about lizards; Sneed B. Collard III. Charlesbridge 2012 47 p. (reinforced for library use) $16.95

Grades: 3 4 5 6 7   597.95
   1. Lizards 2. Lizards as pets 3. Wildlife photography 4. Lizards -- Miscellanea
ISBN 9781580893244; 9781580893251

LC 2011000809
This book offers an "introduction to the world of lizards [which] describes their . . . variety and life in the wild and offers cautions from a long-time reptile fan for those who want to keep lizards as pets. [Author Sneed B.] Collard . . . turns his attention . . . to modern-day lizards. After presenting an exemplar, 'Joe Lizard,' a western fence lizard, he goes on to describe other well-known species, including Komodo dragons, Gila monsters, chameleons and iguanas, as well as some with unusual talents, including 'religious lizards' that can walk on water. He covers eating and being eaten, the ways saurians keep warm and reproduce, and threats to their survival. . . . [Photographs] show lizard characteristics. . . . Captions and sidebars add further information." (Kirkus)

Gish, Melissa

Komodo dragons. Creative Education 2011 48p il (Living wild) lib bdg $23.95; pa $8.99

Grades: 5 6 7 8   597.95
   1. Komodo dragon
ISBN 978-1-60818-080-6 lib bdg; 1-60818-080-8 lib bdg; 978-0-89812-672-3 pa; 0-89812-672-X pa

LC 2010028307

A look at Komodo dragons, including their habitats, physical characteristics such as their sawlike teeth, behaviors, relationships with humans, and threatened status in the world today.

"Stunning, full-page photographs create immediate visual interest. A brief narrative introduction sets the scene for the richer, more scientific information in the rest of the text." Booklist

Includes glossary and bibliographical references

Somervill, Barbara A.
Monitor lizard. Cherry Lake 2010 32p il (Animal invaders) lib bdg $27.07
Grades: 5 6 7 8   **597.95**
1. Lizards 2. Biological invasions
ISBN 978-1-60279-627-0 lib bdg; 1-60279-627-0 lib bdg
This offers "an introduction to the problems caused by [the monitor lizard], a discussion of its physical characteristics and habits, a history of how it arrived in its new habitat, and an analysis of challenges encountered by those trying to limit its spread. . . . [It] describes the threat posed by these aggressive 7-foot reptiles, sold as babies by pet vendors and now loose in Florida. . . . [This] well-focused [book is] clearly written. The uncluttered page design features at least one color photo on each page." Booklist

Includes glossary and bibliographical references

597.96   Snakes

Hamilton, Sue L.
Bitten by a rattlesnake; [by] Sue Hamilton. ABDO Pub. 2010 32p il (Close encounters of the wild kind) lib bdg $27.07
Grades: 4 5 6 7   **597.96**
1. Rattlesnakes 2. Animal attacks
ISBN 978-1-60453-930-1 lib bdg; 1-60453-930-5 lib bdg
                                                    LC 2009-45423
Readers learn of actual human-rattlesnake encounters, information about rattlesnakes, survival strategies, and attack statistics.

"Students will be drawn to the realistic full-color photographs, the realistic diagrams of the creatures' bodies, the real-life stories told by victims, and the interesting, attractive formatting that includes text, diagrams, photographs, and graphics on each page. . . . [This is] exciting and attractive in a 'gross' sort of way and will appeal particularly to boys for both leisure reading and research." Libr Media Connect

Includes glossary

Mattison, Christopher
Snake; by Chris Mattison. DK Pub. 1999 192p il hardcover o.p. pa $12.99
Grades: 7 8 9 10 11 12 Adult   **597.96**
1. Snakes
ISBN 0-7894-4660-X; 0-7566-1365-5 pa
                                                    LC 99-19957
An illustrated guide to "more than 60 types of snakes, ranging from adders to yellow anacondas. This richly for-

matted book features each snake in detailed entries with informative, readable text." Sci Child
Includes glossary

Menon, Sujatha
Discover snakes. Enslow Publishers 2008 47p il (Discover animals) lib bdg $23.93
Grades: 4 5 6 7   **597.96**
1. Snakes
ISBN 978-0-7660-3471-6 lib bdg; 0-7660-3471-2 lib bdg
                                                    LC 2008013867
First published 2005 in the United Kingdom
This "introduces readers to a variety of snakes, from pythons to boa constrictors and cobras. . . . Images and text explain about a snake's fangs, life cycle, senses, and how they fight and move. The book also discusses the different snake families and the hunting styles of each." Publisher's note
Includes glossary and bibliographical references

Montgomery, Sy
★ The **snake** scientist; photographs by Nic Bishop. Houghton Mifflin 1999 48p il map $16; pa $5.95
Grades: 4 5 6 7   **597.96**
1. Snakes 2. Snakes -- Research 3. Red-sided garter snake
ISBN 0-395-87169-7; 0-618-11119-0 pa
                                                    LC 98-6124
Discusses the work of Bob Mason and his efforts to study and protect snakes, particularly red-sided garter snakes
"The lively text communicates both the meticulous measurements required in this kind of work and the thrill of new discoveries. Large, full-color photos of the zoologist and young students at work, and lots of wriggly snakes, pull readers into the presentation." SLJ
Includes bibliographical references

Somervill, Barbara A.
Python. Cherry Lake Pub. 2010 32p il map (Animal invaders) lib bdg $27.07
Grades: 5 6 7 8   **597.96**
1. Pythons 2. Biological invasions
ISBN 978-1-60279-629-4 lib bdg; 1-60279-629-7 lib bdg
                                                    LC 2009026013
This describes "the 19-foot nocturnal snake that has infiltrated the Florida Everglades, having no natural predators above it in the food chain. . . . [This] well-focused [book is] clearly written. The uncluttered page design features at least one color photo on each spread." Booklist
Includes glossary and bibliographical references

597.98   Crocodilians

Gish, Melissa
Alligators. Creative Education 2010 46p il (Living wild) $23.95; pa $9.95

Grades: 5 6 7 8   **597.98**
1. Alligators
ISBN 978-1-58341-967-0; 1-58341-967-5; 978-0-89812-550-4 pa; 0-89812-550-2 pa

LC 2010017372

The "book lucidly discusses conservation and the animals' often tenuous relationships with humans. The layout is uniformly simple but effective, constructed with a nice balance of main text for the report writers, smaller chunks of esoterica for browsers, and . . . killer photos." Booklist

Hamilton, Sue L.

Attacked by a crocodile; [by] Sue Hamilton. ABDO Pub. 2010 32p il (Close encounters of the wild kind) lib bdg $27.07
Grades: 4 5 6 7   **597.98**
1. Crocodiles 2. Animal attacks
ISBN 978-1-60453-929-5; 1-60453-929-1

LC 2009-45514

Readers learn of actual human-crocodile encounters, information about crocodiles, survival strategies, and attack statistics.

"Students will be drawn to the realistic full-color photographs, the realistic diagrams of the creatures' bodies, the real-life stories told by victims, and the interesting, attractive formatting that includes text, diagrams, photographs, and graphics on each page. . . . [This is] exciting and attractive in a 'gross' sort of way and will appeal particularly to boys for both leisure reading and research." Libr Media Connect

Includes glossary

Simon, Seymour

★ **Crocodiles** & alligators. HarperCollins Pubs. 1999 un il hardcover o.p. pa $6.99
Grades: 4 5 6 7   **597.98**
1. Alligators 2. Crocodiles
ISBN 0-06-027473-5; 0-06-443829-5 pa

LC 98-34705

Describes the physical characteristics and behavior of various members of the family of animals known as crocodilians

"The book is filled with interesting information, and the vivid, well-composed, full-color photographs and entertaining text will draw in browsers." SLJ

Snyder, Trish

Alligator & crocodile rescue; changing the future for endangered wildlife. Firefly Books 2006 64p il (Firefly animal rescue) lib bdg $19.95; pa $9.95
Grades: 5 6 7 8   **597.98**
1. Alligators 2. Crocodiles 3. Wildlife conservation
ISBN 1-55297-920-2 lib bdg; 1-55297-919-9 pa

This "outlines the various threats to survival of [alligators and crocodiles] and introduces readers to organizations and individuals trying to save them. . . . Numerous photographs document the work of scientists, conservationists, educators, and other people around the world who are committed to wildlife preservation." SLJ

598   Birds

★ **Birds** of the world; editorial adviser, Jason A. Mobley. Marshall Cavendish Reference 2008 11v il map set $359.95
Grades: 5 6 7 8 9   **598**
1. Reference books 2. Birds -- Encyclopedias
ISBN 978-0-7614-7775-4 set; 0-7614-7775-6 set

LC 2008-62300

"This encyclopedia, designed to introduce birds in all their varieties, contributes to and encourages student research. Nearly 140 . . . articles are arranged alphbetically. . . . Articles range in length from two to eight pages and include numerous full-color photographs, diagrams, and maps. . . . Clear and concise information is provided in an appealing layout most appropriate for upper-elementary through middle-school users." Booklist

Bull, John L.

★ The **National** Audubon Society field guide to North American birds, Eastern region; [by] John Bull and John Farrand, Jr.; revised by John Farrand, Jr.; visual key by Amanda Wilson and Lori Hogan. rev ed; Knopf 1994 797p il maps pa $19.95
Grades: 7 8 9 10 11 12 Adult   **598**
1. Birds -- North America
ISBN 0-679-42852-6

LC 94-7768

First published 1977

This pictorial guide to 508 eastern species arranges birds by color and shape to simplify identification. It also includes information on bird-watching and conservation status

Includes bibliographical references

Burnie, David

Bird; written by David Burnie. rev ed.; DK Pub. 2008 72p il (DK eyewitness books) $15.99
Grades: 4 5 6 7   **598**
1. Birds
ISBN 978-0-7566-3768-2; 0-7566-3768-6

First published 1988 by Knopf

A photo essay on the world of birds examining such topics as body construction, feathers and flight, the adaptation of beaks and feet, feeding habits, courtship, nests and eggs, and bird watching.

Includes glossary

Chu, Miyoko

Birdscapes; A pop-up celebration of birdsongs in stereo sound. by Miyoko Chu, with the Cornell Lab of Ornithology; paper engineering by Gene Vosough, Renee Jablow, and Andy Baron; illustrations by Julia Hargreaves. Chronicle Books 2008 un il $60
Grades: 5 6 7 8   **598**
1. Birds 2. Pop-up books
ISBN 978-0-8118-6428-2; 0-8118-6428-6

"With marvelously detailed pop-up spreads and high-quality sound, this look at various avian ecosystems is absolutely spectacular. Double-page sections depict the environmental characteristics and native species of the following North American habitats: the Sonoran Desert; a Pacific sea-bird colony; an eastern deciduous forest; the Arctic tundra; a cypress swamp; grasslands; and the Pacific rain forest. The paper sculptures, filled with colorful and realistic renderings of flora and local birdlife, are accompanied by a soundtrack of the species' calls and songs recorded . . . from the Cornell Lab of Ornithology's Macaulay Library collection." SLJ

Gish, Melissa

★ **Eagles**. Creative Education 2010 46p il (Living wild) lib bdg $23.95; pa $9.95

Grades: 5 6 7 8   **598**

1. Eagles

ISBN 978-1-58341-968-7 lib bdg; 1-58341-968-3 lib bdg; 978-0-89812-551-1 pa; 0-89812-551-0 pa

LC 2010-17373

This "book lucidly discusses conservation and the animals' often tenuous relationship with humans. The layout is uniformly simple but effective, constructed with a nice balance of main text for the report writers, smaller chunks of esoterica for browsers, and . . . killer photos." Booklist

Hummingbirds. Creative Education 2011 46p il map (Living wild) lib bdg $23.95; pa $8.95

Grades: 5 6 7 8   **598**

1. Hummingbirds

ISBN 978-1-60818-078-3; 1-60818-078-6; 978-0-89812-670-9 pa; 0-89812-670-3 pa

LC 2010028314

A look at hummingbirds, including their habitats, physical characteristics such as their ability to hover, behaviors, relationships with humans, and admired status in the world today.

"Stunning, full-page photographs create immediate visual interest. A brief narrative introduction sets the scene for the richer, more scientific information in the rest of the text." Booklist

Includes glossary and bibliographical references

Owls. Creative Education 2011 46p il map (Living wild) lib bdg $23.95

Grades: 5 6 7 8   **598**

1. Owls

ISBN 978-1-60818-081-3; 1-60818-081-6

LC 2010028308

A look at owls, including their habitats, physical characteristics such as their large and observant eyes, behaviors, relationships with humans, and protected status in the world today.

"Stunning, full-page photographs create immediate visual interest. A brief narrative introduction sets the scene for the richer, more scientific information in the rest of the text." Booklist

Includes glossary and bibliographical references

Griggs, Jack L.

★ **All** the birds of North America; American Bird Conservancy's field guide. concept and design by Jack L. Griggs. HarperPerennial 1997 172p il maps pa $19.95

Grades: 7 8 9 10 11 12 Adult   **598**

1. Birds -- North America

ISBN 0-06-52770-6

LC 96-49679

This identification guide to North American birds uses a system based on how and where birds collect food, with icons, color bars, key numbers, and color illustrations

Hanel, Rachael

Penguins. Smart Apple Media 2009 46p il (Living wild) lib bdg $32.80

Grades: 4 5 6 7   **598**

1. Penguins

ISBN 978-1-58341-658-7 lib bdg; 1-58341-658-7 lib bdg

LC 2007008503

"The 17 species of penguins . . . fill [this] slim, informative [volume]. [The] overview is divided into several chapters . . . describing the shared and distinct physical characteristics of the various species, the location of their particular habitats, life cycle, social behavior, and the history of human awareness of and impact on these animals. Fine color photographs face pages of text with smaller views placed in colored sidebars or insets. The [book concludes] with current environmental threats and conservation efforts. . . . Handsome and appealing." SLJ

Helget, Nicole Lea

Swans; by Nicole Helget. Smart Apple Media 2009 46p il (Living wild) lib bdg $32.80

Grades: 4 5 6 7   **598**

1. Swans

ISBN 978-1-58341-659-4 lib bdg; 1-58341-659-5 lib bdg

LC 2007015242

The "7 [species] of swans fill [this] slim, informative [volume]. [The] overview is divided into several chapters . . . describing the shared and distinct physical characteristics of the various species, the location of their particular habitats, life cycle, social behavior, and the history of human awareness of and impact on these animals. Fine color photographs face pages of text with smaller views placed in colored sidebars or insets. The [book concludes] with current environmental threats and conservation efforts. . . . Handsome and appealing." SLJ

Includes bibliographical references

Hickman, Pamela M.

Birds of prey rescue; changing the future for endangered wildlife. Firefly Books 2006 64p il (Firefly animal rescue) $19.95; pa $9.95

Grades: 5 6 7   **598**

1. Birds of prey 2. Endangered species 3. Wildlife conservation

ISBN 978-1-55407-145-6; 1-55407-145-3; 978-1-55407-144-9 pa; 1-55407-144-5 pa

LC 2007271465

Provides details about birds of prey from around the world, their endangerment, and conservation programs designed to save them.

Hoose, Phillip

★ **Moonbird**; a year on the wind with the great survivor B95. Phillip Hoose. Farrar Straus Giroux 2012 148 p. col. ill. (hardcover) $21.99

Grades: 5 6 7 8   **598**

1. Endangered species 2. Birds -- Protection 3. Wildlife conservation 4. Red knot 5. Bird watching 6. Red knot -- Migration

ISBN 0374304688; 9780374304683

LC 2011035612

YALSA Award for Excellence in Nonfiction for Young Adults Finalist (2013)

Robert F. Sibert Honor Book (2013)

In this book, Phillip Hoose "explores the tragedy of extinction through a single bird species, but there is hope for survival in this story, and that hope is pinned on understanding the remarkable longevity of a single bird. . . . Hoose takes readers around the hemisphere, showing them the obstacles rufa red knots face, introducing a global team of scientists and conservationists, and offering insights about what can be done to save them before it's too late." (Kirkus Reviews)

Hoose, Phillip M.

★ The **race** to save the Lord God Bird; [by] Phillip Hoose. Farrar, Straus and Giroux 2004 196p il map $20

Grades: 7 8 9 10   **598**

1. Woodpeckers 2. Endangered species

ISBN 0-374-36173-8

Tells the story of the ivory-billed woodpecker's extinction in the United States, describing the encounters between this species and humans, and discussing what these encounters have taught us about preserving endangered creatures

"Sharp, clear, black-and-white archival photos and reproductions appear throughout. The author's passion for his subject and high standards for excellence result in readable, compelling nonfiction." SLJ

Includes glossary and bibliographical references

International Masters Publishers (Firm)

★ The **encyclopedia** of birds; edited by International Masters Publishers. Facts on File 2007 6v il set $425

Grades: 6 7 8 9 10 11 12   **598**

1. Reference books 2. Birds -- Encyclopedias

ISBN 0-8160-5904-7; 978-0-8160-5904-1

LC 2006-49526

"Each volume begins with the same general introduction, followed by a comprehensive list of the 250 species included. Entries feature several . . . closeup photographs of the bird and its home, and data on breeding, status, food, and habitat. A panel provides information on length and weight, wingspan, number of eggs, lifespan, and more. . . . Both browsers and budding ornithologists will enjoy learning about some intriguing creatures." SLJ

Includes glossary and bibliographical references

Larson, Jeanette C.

Hummingbirds; facts and folklore from the Americas. written by Jeanette Larson and Adrienne Yorinks; illustrated by Adrienne Yorinks. Charlesbridge 2011 64p il $16.95; pa $8.95

Grades: 5 6 7 8   **598**

1. Hummingbirds 2. Birds -- Folklore 3. Native Americans -- Folklore

ISBN 978-1-58089-332-9; 1-58089-332-5; 978-1-58089-333-6 pa; 1-58089-333-3 pa

LC 2010-07578

"In a narrative that flows easily between fact and lore, hummingbird behavior is thoroughly described and interwoven with the folktales it generated among Native American peoples. . . . All the stories show how ancient people answered the 'how and why' questions of the behaviors they observed, and these stories beautifully echo modern-day scientific observations. The full-color photos of quilts and embroidery by Yorinks invite readers to stop and savor each one." SLJ

Includes glossary and bibliographical references

Latimer, Jonathan P.

Backyard birds; [by] Jonathan P. Latimer, Karen Stray Nolting; illustrations by Roger Tory Peterson; foreword by Virginia Marie Peterson. Houghton Mifflin 1999 48p il (Peterson field guides for young naturalists) hardcover o.p. pa $5.95

Grades: 4 5 6 7   **598**

1. Birds

ISBN 0-395-92276-3

LC 98-35509

This is an identification guide to birds "'you are likely to see where you live.' . . . [It] includes a . . . selection of about 20 creatures . . . grouped by color. . . . Bright, full-color photographs and drawings clearly indicate distinguishing features. Useful, accessible." SLJ

Songbirds; [by] Jonathan P. Latimer, Karen Stray Nolting; illustrations by Roger Tory Peterson; foreword by Virginia Marie Peterson. Houghton Mifflin 2000 48p il (Peterson field guides for young naturalists) $15; pa $5.95

Grades: 4 5 6 7   **598**

1. Birds 2. Birdsongs

ISBN 0-395-97941-2; 0-395-97946-3 pa

LC 99-38293

Describes the physical characteristics, habitats, feeding habits, and voices of a variety of songbirds, arranged under the categories "Simple Songs," "Complex Songs," "Whistling Songs," "Warbling Songs," "Trilling Songs," "Namesayers," and "Mimics"

Laubach, Christyna M.

Raptor! a kid's guide to birds of prey; by Christyna & Rene Laubach and Charles W.G. Smith. Storey Bks. 2002 118p il maps pbk $14.95

Grades: 4 5 6 7   **598**

1. Birds of prey

ISBN 9781580174459

LC 2001-54980

This is an "overview of North American raptors. . . . After describing their characteristics and behavior, the book introduces individual species within family groups: vultures, hawks, falcons, barn owls, and true owls. . . . There is also advice on bird-watching and efforts to save endangered species. Well-designed projects . . . are followed by a glossary and extensive lists of hawk-watching sites, raptor centers, banding demonstration sites, books, videos, organizations, and Web sites related to birds in general and raptors in particular." Booklist

Miller, Sara Swan
    Woodpeckers, toucans, and their kin. Watts 2003 47p il lib bdg $25; pa $6.95
Grades: 4 5 6   **598**
    1. Toucans 2. Woodpeckers 3. Honeyguides (Birds) 4. Honeyguides 5. Piciformes
    ISBN 0-531-12243-3 lib bdg; 0-531-16661-9 pa
                      LC 2002-1732
This book makes "fascinating reading. . . . Photographs are glorious." Libr Media Connect

Peterson, Roger Tory
    Peterson field guide to birds of Eastern and Central North America; [by] Roger Tory Peterson, with contributions from Michael DiGiorgio [et al.] 6th ed; Houghton Mifflin Harcourt 2010 445p il map (Peterson field guide series) $19.95
Grades: 5 6 7 8 9 10 11 12 Adult   **598**
    1. Birds -- North America 2. Birds -- Identification
    ISBN 978-0-547-15246-2; 0-547-15246-9
                    LC 2009-37681
First published 1934 with title: A field guide to the birds
This guide to birds found east of the Rocky Mountains contains colored illustrations painted by the author, with a description of each species on the facing page. Views of young birds and seasonal variations in plumage are included.

    Peterson field guide to birds of Western North America; with contributions from Michael DiGiorgio [et al.] 4th ed; Houghton Mifflin Harcourt 2010 493p il map (Peterson field guide series) pa $19.95
Grades: 5 6 7 8 9 10 11 12 Adult   **598**
    1. Birds -- North America 2. Birds -- Western Canada 3. Birds -- Western States
    ISBN 978-0-547-15270-7; 0-547-15270-1
                    LC 2009-39158
  First published 1941 with title: A field guide to western birds
This guide illustrates over 600 species of birds on 176 color plates. In addition, over 588 range maps are included.

Peterson, Roger Tory, 1908-1996
    ★ **Peterson** field guide to birds of North America; with contributions from Michael DiGiorgio . . . [et al.] Houghton Mifflin Co. 2008 527p il map (Peterson field guide series) $26
Grades: 5 6 7 8 9 10 11 12 Adult   **598**
    1. Birds -- North America
    ISBN 0-618-96614-5; 978-0-618-96614-1
                    LC 2007-39803
First published 1934 with title: A field guide to the birds. Previously published in two separate parts as A field guide to

western birds (1990) and A field guide to the birds of eastern and central North America (2002)
  This guide to birds found in North America contains colored illustrations painted by the author, with a description of each species on the facing page. Views of young birds and seasonal variations in plumage are included. The book also includes a URL to video podcasts.
  "This field guide is of high quality and should be in millions of birders' and other nature lovers' backpacks." Sci Books Films

Robbins, Chandler S.
    Birds of North America; a guide to field identification. by Chandler S. Robbins, Bertel Bruun, and Herbert S. Zim; revised by Jonathan P. Latimer and Karen Stray Nolting and James Coe; illustrated by Arthur Singer. rev and updated; St. Martin's Press 2001 359p il maps $19.95; pa $15.95
Grades: 8 9 10 11 12 Adult   **598**
    1. Birds -- North America 2. Birds -- North America -- Identification
    ISBN 1-58238-091-0; 1-58238-090-2 pa
                    LC 2001-271739
First published 1966
This resource includes over 800 species and 600 range maps; illustrations featuring male, female, and juvenile plumage; and sonograms picturing sound for song recognition. Feeding habits, migration routes, and characteristic flight patterns as well as American Ornithologists' classifications are also provided.

Stefoff, Rebecca
    ★ The **bird** class; [by] Rebecca Stefoff. 1st ed.; Marshall Cavendish Benchmark 2008 96p il (Family trees) $22.95
Grades: 6 7 8 9   **598**
    1. Birds
    ISBN 978-0-7614-2693-6; 0-7614-2693-0
                    LC 2007007706
  "Skillful weaving of engaging text and superb illustrations will incite interest." Voice Youth Advocates
  Includes glossary and bibliographical references

Thompson, Bill
    The **young** birder's guide to birds of eastern North America; [by] Bill Thompson III; illustrations by Julie Zickefoose. Houghton Mifflin Co. 2008 256p il map (Peterson field guide series) $14.95
Grades: 3 4 5 6   **598**
    1. Birds 2. Bird watching 3. Bird watching 4. Birds -- North America
    ISBN 978-0-547-11934-2; 0-547-11934-8
                    LC 2007-43904
  This describes 200 species of birds of eastern North America, with color photos, black & white drawings, and range maps.
  Includes glossary and bibliographical references

Udvardy, Miklos D. F.
    ★ **National** Audubon Society field guide to North American birds, Western region; revised by

John Farrand, Jr.; visual key by Amanda Wilson and Lori Hogan. rev ed; Knopf 1994 822p il maps pa $19.95

Grades: 6 7 8 9 10 11 12 Adult   **598**

1. Birds -- North America

ISBN 0-679-42851-8

LC 94-7415

First published 1977

This pictorial guide to 544 western species arranges birds by color and shape to simplify identification. It also includes information on bird-watching and conservation status

Includes bibliographical references

Vogel, Carole Garbuny

The **man** who flies with birds; [by] Carole G. Vogel and Yossi Leshem. Kar-Ben Pub. 2009 64p il map lib bdg $18.95

Grades: 5 6 7 8   **598**

1. Conservationists 2. Aircraft accidents 3. Birds -- Migration 4. Birds -- Migration

ISBN 978-0-8225-7643-3 lib bdg; 0-8225-7643-0 lib bdg

LC 2008-31198

Discusses the work of the bird expert whose lifelong study of the patterns of bird migration in Israel has led to a significant reduction in the number of collisions between aircraft and bird flocks.

"The book is heavily illustrated with good-quality color photos, maps, and diagrams, many of them captioned with incredible facts about wildlife and migration. This inspiring title on a most timely topic will appeal to those who are fascinated with wildlife, Earth science, and technology." SLJ

Includes bibliographical references

Warhol, Tom

★ **Hawks**; [by] Tom Warhol. Marshall Cavendish Benchmark 2005 112p il (Animalways) lib bdg $31.36

Grades: 6 7 8 9   **598**

1. Hawks

ISBN 0-7614-1744-3

LC 2003-22138

This describes the place of hawks in human culture and history, their evolution, anatomy, habits, life cycle, and protection.

Includes glossary and bibliographical references

Owls; [by] Tom Warhol. Marshall Cavendish Benchmark 2007 111p il (Animalways) lib bdg $34.21

Grades: 6 7 8 9   **598**

1. Owls

ISBN 978-0-7614-2537-3

LC 2006019708

This describes the place of owls in the animal kingdom, owl lore and legend, owls' evolution, diversity, anatomy and behavior, life cycle, and endangered status.

This "will pique readers' curiosity, and the content will keep them hooked. Vivid color photographs and illustrations and a clear font make [this work] stand out." SLJ

Includes glossary and bibliographical references

Webb, Sophie

Looking for seabirds; journal from an Alaskan voyage. Houghton Mifflin Co. 2004 48p il $16

Grades: 4 5 6 7   **598**

1. Birds 2. Diaries 3. Birds -- Alaska 4. Sea birds -- Alaska 5. Natural history -- Alaska

ISBN 0-618-21235-3

LC 2003-12420

A journal of the author's observations and adventures while working on a research vessel counting seabirds through Alaska's Aleutian Island chain

The "immediacy of the narrative . . . and the clear and colorful watercolor-and-gouache landscapes and drawings of the birds form an appealing travelogue that is as exciting as it is informative." SLJ

Wolf, Sallie

★ The **robin** makes a laughing sound; a birder's journal. designed by Micah Bornstein. Charlesbridge 2010 43p il $11.95

Grades: 5 6 7 8   **598**

1. Birds 2. Bird watching

ISBN 978-1-58089-318-3; 1-58089-318-X

LC 2008-7248

Presents observations made through every season of the year of different birds and their behavior, from robins taking a bath, to cardinals searching for food in the snow, to an owl perched on a tree at night.

"The charming, eye-catching format includes short dated nature notes written in script, some of them on glued or taped-in torn paper pieces; other paper scraps contain short typeset poems and small, labeled watercolors. . . . Pen-and-ink sketches capture a baby house sparrow, a V-formation of geese, a downy woodpecker at a suet feeder, and more. . . . This small, instructional guide may provide the inspiration for young authors with even a bit of artistic talent to begin keeping nature journals of their own." SLJ

598.097   Birds -- North America

Alderfer, Jonathan

National Geographic kids bird guide of North America; the best birding book for kids from National Geographic's bird experts. by Jonathan Alderfer. National Geographic 2013 176 p. (paperback) $15.95; (library) $23.90

Grades: 4 5 6 7 8   **598.097**

1. Birds -- North America 2. Birds -- Identification 3. Birds -- North America -- Identification

ISBN 1426310943; 9781426310942; 9781426310959

LC 2012028615

Author "[Jonathan] Alderfer offers in-depth studies of 60 birds native to North America (plus 'mini-profiles' of another 60 specimens) in a guide for nascent birders. . . . The book is organized by region, and each bird's spread offers . . . color photographs, 'vital statistics' (including its call, diet, and habitat), maps of where it can be found, and other background." (Publishers Weekly)

Includes bibliographical references and index

598.9 Falconiformes, Caprimulgiformes, owls

Latimer, Jonathan P.

Birds of prey; [by] Jonathan P. Latimer, Karen Stray Nolting; illustrations by Roger Tory Peterson; foreword by Virginia Marie Peterson. Houghton Mifflin 1999 48p il (Peterson field guides for young naturalists) $15; pa $5.95

Grades: 4 5 6 7   **598.9**

1. Birds of prey 2. Birds of prey -- Identification
ISBN 0-395-95211-5; 0-395-92277-1 pa

LC 98-35516

This illustrated volume introduces the physical characteristics, behavior, and habitats of such birds of prey as eagles, hawks, falcons, and owls.

Sattler, Helen Roney

The **book** of North American owls; illustrated by Jean Day Zallinger. Clarion Bks. 1995 64p il maps hardcover o.p. pa $7.95

Grades: 4 5 6 7   **598.9**

1. Owls
ISBN 0-395-60524-5; 0-395-90017-4 pa

LC 91-43626

This "is a superb ornithological primer. . . . The book is lavishly illustrated." Appraisal

Includes bibliographical references

599 Mammals

★ **Exploring** mammals. Marshall Cavendish 2007 20v il map set $399.95

Grades: 5 6 7 8 9 10   **599**

1. Reference books 2. Mammals -- Encyclopedias
ISBN 978-0-76147-719-8

LC 2007060864

"About 90 animals . . . are described in these volumes. Each article includes . . . a 'Profile,' with introductory information; a discussion of anatomy, with diagrams; a discussion of habitat; descriptions of various behaviors; and a consideration of factors determining survival. Each article also has numerous boxed sections . . . as well as many color photographs and other illustrations. . . . This set has just about everything a student requires." Booklist

Includes bibliographical references

★ **Exploring** the world of mammals; [edited by Nancy Simmons, Richard Beatty, Amy Jane Beer] Chelsea House 2008 6v il map set $210

Grades: 5 6 7 8   **599**

1. Reference books 2. Mammals -- Encyclopedias
ISBN 978-0-7910-9651-2 set; 0-7910-9651-3 set

LC 2007028223

"This colorful and appealing set offers an introduction to the world of mammals. Most of entries are 2 to 4 pages in length. Sidebars offer extra details, and bright photographs and illustrations appear on every 2-page spread." Booklist

Rodriguez, Ana Maria

Secret of the singing mice . . . and more! [by] Ana Maria Rodriguez. Enslow Publishers 2008 48p il (Animal secrets revealed!) lib bdg $23.93

Grades: 5 6 7 8   **599**

1. Mammals
ISBN 978-0-7660-2956-9 lib bdg; 0-7660-2956-5 lib bdg

LC 2007-39495

This book offers "fascinating accounts of how scientists systematically analyzed, tested and proved their theories or how their findings led to other, serendipitous discoveries. . . . Science experiments are thoughtfully placed to inspire exploration, and captioned, full-color photos appear throughout." SLJ

Includes glossary and bibliographical references

Whitaker, John O.

★ **National** Audubon Society field guide to North American mammals; rev ed; Knopf 1996 937p il maps pa $19.95

Grades: 6 7 8 9 10 11 12 Adult   **599**

1. Mammals
ISBN 0-679-44631-1

LC 95-81456

First published 1980

This field guide describes 390 species of mammals of North America and includes keys for identification, range maps, information on tracks and anatomy, and 375 color photos

599.168 Extinct mammals -- Recently extinct

Mammals of the Northern Hemisphere; edited by Tim Harris. Brown Bear Books 2011 64 p. col. ill., col. maps (Facts at Your Fingertips: endangered animals) (library binding) $35.65

Grades: 7 8 9   **599.168**

1. Mammals 2. Endangered species 3. Wildlife conservation 4. Rare mammals -- Northern Hemisphere
ISBN 1936333341; 9781936333349

LC 2010053969

This book is part of the "Facts at Your Fingertips: Endangered Animals" series. "Each page has all benefits of a picture book with large, colorful photographs that accompany the encyclopedia-style text. Each new animal is accompanied by a 'data panel,' which summarizes . . . information such as location, size, habitat, population and diet. This series focuses on animals facing extinction all over the world. Factors contributing to the animal's endangered status as well as preservation techniques are also discussed." The book "talks about well-known animals like the Polar Bear and Giant Panda as well as lesser-known mammals such as the Ryukyu Flying Fox." (Children's Literature)

Includes bibliographical references (p. 63) and index.

599.2 Marsupials and monotremes

Collard, Sneed B.

★ **Pocket** babies and other amazing marsupials.
Darby Creek 2007 72p il map $18.95

Grades: 4 5 6 7   599.2
1. Marsupials
ISBN 978-1-58196-046-4; 1-58196-046-8

"This large-format book provides an attractive introduction to marsupials around the world. . . . Attractive, informative side-bars, excellent maps, and many-clear, color photos
appear throughout the book. . . . This handsomely designed
volume introduces marsupials with panache." Booklist

Includes glossary and bibliographical references

Gish, Melissa

Kangaroos. Creative Education 2010 46p il
(Living wild) $23.95; pa $9.95

Grades: 5 6 7 8   599.2
1. Kangaroos
ISBN 978-1-58341-970-0; 1-58341-970-5; 978-0-
89812-553-5 pa; 0-89812-553-7 pa

LC 2010017375

"A look at kangaroos, including their habitats, physical characteristics such as the females' pouches, behaviors,
relationships with humans, and valued status in the world
today." Publisher's note

Montgomery, Sy

★ **Quest** for the tree kangaroo; an expedition
to the cloud forest of New Guinea. text by Sy Montgomery; photographs by Nic Bishop. Houghton Mifflin 2006 79p il map (Scientists in the field) $18

Grades: 5 6 7 8   599.2
1. Zoologists 2. Tree kangaroos
ISBN 0-618-49641-6

LC 2005-34849

"The writer and photographer of this exemplary description of science field work accompanied researcher Lisa Da-
bek on an expedition high in New Guinea's mountains to
study tree kangaroos and promote the conservation of this
elusive and endangered species. . . . Montgomery . . . paces
her narrative well . . . keeping the reader engaged and concerned. . . . Bishop's photographs . . . are beautifully reproduced." Publ Wkly

Stefoff, Rebecca

★ The **marsupial** order; [by] Rebecca Stefoff.
Marshall Cavendish Benchmark 2008 96p il (Family trees) lib bdg $22.95

Grades: 6 7 8 9   599.2
1. Marsupials
ISBN 978-0-7614-2697-4 lib bdg; 0-7614-2697-3
lib bdg

LC 2007007240

This is "meticulously detailed. . . . Sharp color photographs appear on about every other page. Other illustrations
consist of classification charts and anatomical diagrams. . .
. [This is] well-organized and clearly written. . . . In addition to discussing such well-known animals as kangaroos,
koalas, and opossums, [this book] includes material on less-

familiar species 'marsupial mice,' quolls, bandicoots, and
bilbies. . . . [The book is] well-researched." SLJ

Includes glossary and bibliographical references

599.3 Miscellaneous orders of placental mammals

Lorbiecki, Marybeth

Prairie dogs; illustrations by Wayne Ford.
NorthWord Press 2004 47p il map (Our wild world
series) hardcover o.p. pa $7.95

Grades: 4 5 6   599.3
1. Prairie dogs
ISBN 978-1-55971-883-7; 1-55971-883-8; 978-1-
55971-884-4 pa; 1-55971-884-6 pa

LC 2003-59993

Discusses the physical characteristics, behavior, habitat,
and life cycle of prairie dogs

Lorbiecki "offers a thorough discussion of the rodents'
complex communication system of chirps and whistles. . . .
Clear, full-color photos provide visual appeal. . . . The text[s]
. . . [is] clearly written." SLJ

Markle, Sandra

Prairie dogs. Lerner Publications Company
2007 39p il map (Animal prey) lib bdg $25.26;
pa $7.95

Grades: 4 5 6   599.3
1. Prairie dogs
ISBN 978-0-8225-6438-6 lib bdg; 0-8225-6438-6 lib
bdg; 978-0-8225-6441-6 pa; 0-8225-6441-6 pa

LC 2006-598

Describes the behavior of prairie dogs in their native
habitat, where they are the prey of larger animals and birds
and where they must work together as a colony to create
burrows and warning systems to protect themselves and
their young

Includes glossary and bibliographical references

599.35 Rodents

Marrin, Albert

Oh, rats! the story of rats and people. illustrated
by C.B. Mordan. Dutton Children's Books 2006 48p
il $16.99

Grades: 3 4 5 6   599.35
1. Rats
ISBN 0-525-47762-4

LC 2004-24512

This is "lively and informative. . . . The nine short chapters are set in a handsome slim book with striking black-and-
white scratchboard illustrations and muted red framing on
many pages." SLJ

Includes bibliographical references

Stefoff, Rebecca

The **rodent** order; by Rebecca Stefoff. Marshall
Cavendish Benchmark 2008 96p il (Family trees)
$23.95

Grades: 6 7 8 9   **599.35**
1. Rodents
ISBN 978-0-7614-3073-5; 0-7614-3073-3
LC 2008-17555
"Explores the habitats, life cycles, and other characteristics of rodents." Publisher's note
Includes glossary and bibliographical references

599.4   Bats

Carson, Mary Kay
★ The **bat** scientists; with photographs by Tom Uhlman. Houghton Mifflin Books for Children 2010 79p il (Scientists in the field) $18
Grades: 4 5 6 7   **599.4**
1. Bats 2. Conservation biology -- Research
ISBN 978-0-547-19956-6; 0-547-19956-2
LC 2010006767
This describes "patient field work, rescue and conservation efforts to save bats. . . . Woven into particular researchers' stories is an enormous amount of information about bat biology and behavior. Uhlman's photographs are clearly identified in context and the backmatter supports further research." Kirkus
Includes glossary and bibliographical references

Gish, Melissa
Bats. Creative Paperbacks 2010 46p il (Living wild) $23.95; pa $9.95
Grades: 5 6 7 8   **599.4**
1. Bats
ISBN 978-1-58341-966-3; 1-58341-966-7; 978-0-89812-549-8 pa; 0-89812-549-9 pa
LC 2010017371
The "book lucidly discusses conservation and the animals' often tenuous relationship with humans. The layout is uniformly simple but effective, constructed with a nice balance of main text for the report writers, smaller chunks of esoterica for browsers, and . . . killer photos." Booklist

Taschek, Karen
Hanging with bats; ecobats, vampires, and movie stars. University of New Mexico Press 2008 94p il (Worlds of wonder) $16.95
Grades: 6 7 8 9   **599.4**
1. Bats
ISBN 978-0-8263-4403-8; 0-8263-4403-8
LC 2008-2076
"This book provides an all-inclusive look at the flying mammal many people do not understand well enough to appreciate. From the scientific discussion of where bats are found on the evolutionary tree to the whys and hows of building a bat house, there is little that cannot be learned from within these pages. . . . The text is written in a friendly style, with unusual words further defined or explained as needed, nicely allowing generous amounts of information to be absorbed without it feeling like work. The photographs and illustrations are fascinating, helping to lure in a reluctant reader. It should be noted that the photos of bats in action

are particularly eye-catching. . . . It is a good choice for any library." Voice Youth Advocates
Includes glossary

Williams, Kim
Stokes beginner's guide to bats; [by] Kim Williams . . . [et al.] Little, Brown, and Co. 2002 159p il map $9.99
Grades: 6 7 8 9   **599.4**
1. Bats
ISBN 978-0-316-81658-8; 0-316-81658-2
LC 2001-38112
This book about bats gives "identification and behavior information in a portable pocket-sized format." Publisher's note

599.5   Cetaceans and sea cows

Baker, Molly
The **secret** world of whales; illustrated by Molly Baker. Chronicle Books 2011 108p il $16.99
Grades: 4 5 6 7   **599.5**
1. Whales
ISBN 978-0-8118-7641-4; 0-8118-7641-1
LC 2010-27355
"In this small-format volume, Siebert creates a concise introduction to whales, addressing myths and stories, the history of the whaling industry, communication and intelligence, and encounters between whales and humans. With playful, anthropomorphic cartoons, striking photographs, and a discussion of the dangers facing whales—noise pollution from boats, potentially lethal sonar—readers should gain a vivid impression of their behavior in the wild, as well as an appreciation for their majesty." Publ Wkly

Christopherson, Sara Cohen
Top 50 reasons to care about whales and dolphins; animals in peril. Enslow Publishers 2010 103p il (Top 50 reasons to care about endangered animals) lib bdg $31.93
Grades: 4 5 6 7   **599.5**
1. Whales 2. Dolphins 3. Endangered species
ISBN 978-0-7660-3453-2 lib bdg; 0-7660-3453-4 lib bdg
LC 2008-48695
This describes whales and dolphins—their life cycles, diets, young, habitats, and reasons why they are endangered animals
"The illustrations, mostly color photographs, represent a wonderful selection of the animals and their habitats. Reluctant readers may be enticed by this . . . simply because of the great images. This . . . would make a substantial supplement to the science curriculum when studying endangered animals." Libr Media Connect
Includes glossary and bibliographical references

Gish, Melissa
Killer whales. Creative Paperbacks 2010 46p il map (Living wild) $23.95; pa $9.95

Grades: 5 6 7 8   **599.5**
1. Whales
ISBN 978-1-58341-971-7; 1-58341-971-3; 978-0-
89812-554-2 pa; 0-89812-554-5 pa

LC 2010017376

"A look at killer whales, including their habitats, physical characteristics such as their unique coloration, behaviors,
relationships with humans, and protected status in the world
today." Publisher's note

Whales. Creative Education 2011 46p il map
(Living wild) lib bdg $23.95
Grades: 5 6 7 8   **599.5**
1. Whales
ISBN 978-1-60818-084-4

LC 2010028414

A look at whales, including their habitats, physical
characteristics such as their streamlined bodies, behaviors,
relationships with humans, and threatened status in the
world today.

Includes glossary and bibliographical references

Greenberg, Dan
★ **Whales**; by Dan Greenberg. Marshall Cavendish Benchmark 2009 24 p. ill. (Benchmark rockets) (library) $24.21
Grades: 3 4 5 6 7   **599.5**
1. Marine biology 2. Whales
ISBN 0761443460; 9780761443469

LC 0024390

This book is part of the Benchmark Rockets: Animals
series and focuses on whales. Each title "tells about and illustrates the animal world. Each animal's lives and futures
are revealed in . . . dialogue with photographs and charts.
The text includes what each animal eats, how it communicates, and how it lives within a community." (Library
Media Connection)

"Describes the physical characteristics, habitat, behavior, diet, life cycle, and conservation status of whales." Publisher's note

Includes glossary

Hall, Howard
A **charm** of dolphins; the threatened life of a
flippered friend. 2nd ed.; London Town Press 2007
48p il map (Jean-Michel Cousteau presents) $8.95
Grades: 5 6 7 8   **599.5**
1. Dolphins
ISBN 978-0-9766134-8-0; 0-9766134-8-4
First published 1994 by Silver Burdett Press
Shows and describes species of dolphins around the
world, depicts dolphin characteristics and behavior, and discusses the threats that human beings pose to the animals.

This "book covers the characteristics and unique traits of
the . . . [dolphin] and includes colorful, awe-inspiring photos
and immediate first-person narratives." SLJ

Includes glossary and bibliographical references

Hodgkins, Fran
★ The **whale** scientists; solving the mystery of
whale strandings. Houghton Mifflin Co. 2007 63p
il map (Scientists in the field) $18
Grades: 5 6 7 8   **599.5**
1. Whales
ISBN 978-0-618-55673-1; 0-618-55673-7

LC 2006-34634

This describes the evolution of whales and their relationship to humans and offers various scientific theories about
their strandings.

"Hodgkins packs her text with an impressive amount of
information. . . . Well-chosen color photographs amply illustrate the well-organized discussion." SLJ

Includes glossary and bibliographical references

Leon, Vicki
A **pod** of killer whales; the mysterious life of the
intelligent orca. 2nd ed.; London Town Press 2007
48p il (Jean-Michel Cousteau presents) pa $8.95
Grades: 5 6 7 8   **599.5**
1. Whales
ISBN 978-0-9766134-7-3; 0-9766134-7-6
First published 1995 by Silver Burdett Press
Introduces killer whales, describing their social structure, eating habits, communication and hunting methods,
and threats to their way of life.

This "book covers the characteristics and unique traits
of . . . [killer whales] and includes colorful, awe-inspiring
photos and immediate first-person narratives." SLJ

Includes bibliographical references

Lockwood, Sophie
Whales; by Sophie Lockwood. Child's World
2008 40p il map (World of mammals) lib bdg
$29.93
Grades: 4 5 6   **599.5**
1. Whales
ISBN 978-1-59296-930-2 lib bdg; 1-59296-930-5
lib bdg

LC 2007020890

This book about whales presents "all the basics for reports: an introduction to the creatures' challenges, the role
humans play, physical traits and behaviors, habitats, and
struggles for survival. Every part of their life [cycle], including sexual maturity, birth, and family relationships, is explained. . . . Clear bright photographs pump up the content. .
. . The detail that Lockwood imparts is startlingly high. The
[text is] written in a dynamic and engaging style." SLJ

Includes glossary and bibliographical references

Lourie, Peter
★ **Whaling** season; a year in the life of an arctic
whale scientist. Houghton Mifflin Books for Chil-
dren 2009 80p il map (Scientists in the field) $18
Grades: 4 5 6 7   **599.5**
1. Inuit 2. Whales 3. Biologists 4. Bowhead whale 5.
Biology -- Fieldwork
ISBN 978-0-618-77709-9; 0-618-77709-1

LC 2009-18596

Profiles the work of John Craighead George, an Arctic whale scientist, as he studies the bowhead whale and works with the indigenous people of Alaska to better understand the history of the animal.

"Combining exemplary color photos and simple, vivid language, the chapters detail not only George's day-today methodology but also his motivation." Booklist

Includes glossary and bibliographical references

★ The **manatee** scientists; saving vulnerable species. Houghton Mifflin Books for Children 2011 80p il map (Scientists in the field) $18.99

Grades: 4 5 6 7   **599.5**

1. Manatees 2. Scientists 3. Marine biology 4. Endangered species 5. Wildlife conservation

ISBN 978-0-547-15254-7; 0-547-15254-X

This book highlights the work scientists are doing to protect the manatee, including John Reynolds, who does an aerial count of manatees from the Florida sky; Lucy Keith who spends a weekend rescuing manatees trapped in a dam in Senegal; and Fernando Rosas who takes the author on an Amazonian boat trip, looking for a young manatee he released back into the wild.

"The manatees photographed by Lourie and others add plenty of visual appeal. . . . A sturdy addition to a standard-setting nonfiction series." Booklist

O'Connell, Jennifer

The **eye** of the whale; a rescue story. Jennifer O'Connell. 1st hardcover ed. Tilbury House, Publishers 2012 32 p. col. ill. (hardcover) $16.95

Grades: 5 6 7 8   **599.5**

1. Whales 2. Animal rescue 3. Humpback whale -- California -- San Francisco 4. Wildlife rescue -- California -- San Francisco

ISBN 0884483355; 9780884483359

LC 2012031165

This true children's story, by Jennifer O'Connell, begins when, "near San Francisco, a distress call was radioed to shore by a local fisherman. He had discovered a humpback whale tangled in hundreds of yards of crab-trap lines. . . . A team of volunteers answered the call, and four divers risked their lives to rescue the enormous animal." (Publisher's note)

Rodriguez, Ana Maria

Secret of the sleepless whales . . . and more! by Ana Maria Rodriguez. Enslow Publishers 2008 48p il (Animal secrets revealed!) lib bdg $23.93

Grades: 5 6 7 8   **599.5**

1. Marine mammals

ISBN 978-0-7660-2957-6 lib bdg; 0-7660-2957-3 lib bdg

LC 2007039479

This book "does a thorough job of explaining the behaviors of some marine mammals and the scientific methods used to investigate them. . . . The team that worked on the specific issue is identified, and the methodology they used to answer their scientific inquiry is described in detail. . . . The full-color photos are interesting. . . . The content is solid with seamless explanations of terms, and it's fun to read." SLJ

Includes glossary and bibliographical references

Stefoff, Rebecca

Sea mammals; by Rebecca Stefoff. Marshall Cavendish Benchmark 2008 96p il (Family trees) $23.95

Grades: 6 7 8 9   **599.5**

1. Marine animals

ISBN 978-0-7614-3072-8; 0-7614-3072-5

LC 2008-11452

"Explores the habitats, life cycles, and other characteristics of sea mammals." Publisher's note

Includes glossary and bibliographical references

Swinburne, Stephen R.

Saving manatees; [by] Stephen Swinburne. Boyds Mills Press 2006 40p il map $16.95

Grades: 4 5 6 7   **599.5**

1. Manatees

ISBN 978-1-59078-319-1; 1-59078-319-0

LC 2006000523

"In each chapter, Swinburne describes a different visit to a national wildlife refuge or other area in Florida's 'manatee country,' where he consults with biologists and park rangers and joins a field trip of fourth-graders as they swim with the animals. . . . Swinburne weaves a great deal of information into his personal narrative, and his enthusiastic descriptions of his experiences with the animals are contagious and will draw children right into the subject, as will the many large color photos." Booklist

Includes bibliographical references

599.53   Dolphins and porpoises

Montgomery, Sy

Encantado; pink dolphin of the Amazon. with photographs by Dianne Taylor-Snow. Houghton Mifflin 2002 73p il $18

Grades: 4 5 6 7   **599.53**

1. Dolphins 2. River dolphins 3. Orinoco River Region (Venezuela and Colombia) 4. Boto -- Amazon River Region

ISBN 0-618-13103-5

LC 2001-39251

Introduces the world of the freshwater dolphins called Encantados, or Enchanted, by the people who live near them in the region of the Amazon and Orinoco rivers in South America

"The book contains remarkable descriptions and color photos of the Amazonian rainforest and its inhabitants." Horn Book Guide

Includes bibliographical references

599.63   Even-toed ungulates

Lockwood, Sophie

Giraffes. Child's World 2006 40p il map (World of mammals) lib bdg $29.93

Grades: 4 5 6   599.63
1. Giraffes
ISBN 978-1-59296-496-3; 1-59296-496-6
LC 2005-538

Explores the physical and behavioral characteristics of giraffes, examines their habitat and natural history, and discusses the role of humans in ensuring the continued survival of the species.

Includes glossary and bibliographical references

599.64   Bovids

Gish, Melissa
Bison. Creative Education 2011 46p il map (Living wild) $23.95
Grades: 5 6 7 8   599.64
1. Bison
ISBN 978-1-60818-077-6; 1-60818-077-8
LC 2010028305

A look at bison, including their habitats, physical characteristics such as their shaggy coats, behaviors, relationships with humans, and threatened status in the world today.

This offers "an array of interesting facts. Photography is large and beautiful—a real draw." SLJ

Includes bibliographical references

Marrin, Albert
★ **Saving** the buffalo. Scholastic Nonfiction 2006 128p il $18.99
Grades: 4 5 6 7   599.64
1. Bison 2. American bison
ISBN 0-439-71854-6
LC 2005-51827

"In characteristically robust prose, Marrin retraces the American bison's roller-coaster ride from Lord of the Great Plains to near extinction at the end of the 19th century, and slow recovery. Along with showing how the buffalo fit into the habitat's complex, interdependent ecology, he describes in vivid detail how the animals were hunted and utilized by indigenous peoples. . . . A generous array of accompanying illustrations includes crisply reproduced photos, both new and old; prints; paintings; and pictures of artifacts." SLJ

Includes glossary and bibliographical references

599.65   Deer

Gish, Melissa
Moose. Creative Education 2010 46p il map (Living wild) $23.95; pa $9.95
Grades: 5 6 7 8   599.65
1. Moose
ISBN 978-1-58341-973-1; 1-58341-973-X; 978-0-89812-556-6 pa; 0-89812-556-1 pa
LC 2010017378

"A look at moose, including their habitats, physical characteristics such as their imposing antlers, behaviors, relationships with humans, and secure status in the world today." Publisher's note

Heuer, Karsten
★ **Being** caribou; five months on foot with a caribou herd. Walker & Co. 2007 48p il map $17.95; lib bdg $18.95
Grades: 4 5 6 7   599.65
1. Caribou 2. Biologists 3. Conservationists 4. Hikers
ISBN 978-0-8027-9565-6; 0-8027-9565-X; 978-0-8027-9566-3 lib bdg; 0-8027-9566-8 lib bdg
LC 2006-27651

This is an adaptation of an adult title by the same name, published 2005 by Mountaineers Books

"The caribou calving grounds in the Arctic National Wildlife Refuge are being threatened by oil exploration. [This title] will help make kids aware of what is at stake and give them a glimpse of an extraordinary part of the world and the lengths the caribou go to traverse it. It is an important book." Quill Quire

Includes bibliographical references

Stefoff, Rebecca
Deer; [by] Rebecca Stefoff. Marshall Cavendish Benchmark 2007 108p il (Animalways) lib bdg $34.21
Grades: 6 7 8 9   599.65
1. Deer
ISBN 978-0-7614-2534-2
LC 2007016932

This describes the place of deer in the animal kingdom, their evolution, anatomy, life cycle, diversity, and relationship to humans.

This "will pique readers' curiosity, and the content will keep them hooked. Vivid color photographs and illustrations and a clear font make [this work] stand out." SLJ

Includes glossary and bibliographical references

599.66   Odd-toed ungulates

Carson, Mary Kay
★ **Emi** and the rhino scientist; [by] Mary Kay Carson; with photographs by Tom Uhlman. Houghton Mifflin Company 2007 57p il (Scientists in the field) $18
Grades: 5 6 7 8   599.66
1. Rhinoceros 2. Zoo employees 3. Animal scientists 4. Scientists 5. Sumatran rhinoceros
ISBN 978-0-618-64639-5; 0-618-64639-6
LC 2006-34517

This describes "how Terri Roth, an expert in endangered-species reproduction at the Cincinnati Zoo, helped Emi to give birth to the first Sumatran rhino born in captivity in more than 100 years. . . . The text is full of important details, and the photographs are unfailingly crisp, bright, and full of variety." SLJ

Firestone, Mary
Top 50 reasons to care about rhinos; animals in peril. Enslow Publishers 2010 103p il (Top 50 reasons to care about endangered animals) lib bdg $31.93

Grades: 4 5 6 7   **599.66**
1. Rhinoceros 2. Endangered species
ISBN 978-0-7660-3457-0 lib bdg; 0-7660-3457-7
lib bdg

LC 2008048692

This describes the different types of rhino, their life cycle, diet, young, habitat, and reasons why they are endangered animals

"The illustrations, mostly color photographs, represent a wonderful selection of the animals and their habitats. Reluctant readers may be enticed by this . . . simply because of the great images. This . . . would make a substantial supplement to the science curriculum when studying endangered animals." Libr Media Connect

Includes glossary and bibliographical references

Frydenborg, Kay

The **wild** horse scientists; written by Kay Frydenborg. Houghton Mifflin Harcourt 2013 80 p. (Scientists in the field) $18.99

Grades: 7 8 9 10   **599.66**
1. Horses 2. Scientists 3. Conservationists 4. Assateague Island National Seashore (Md. and Va.) 5. Wild horses -- Assateague Island National Seashore (Md. and Va.) 6. Wildlife conservationists -- Assateague Island National Seashore (Md. and Va.)
ISBN 0547518315; 9780547518312

LC 2011039912

This book by Kay Frydenbourg, part of the "Scientists in the Field" series, "focuses on research leading to the use of porcine zona pellucida vaccine on wild horses for reliable, reversible birth control. Frydenborg introduces her readers to several scientists involved in this work. . . . Along the way are chapters on horse ancestry and the history of wild horses in this country, as well as information about color and size and other research and researchers." (Kirkus Reviews)

Includes bibliographical references.

Gish, Melissa

Rhinoceroses. Creative Education 2011 46p il map (Living wild) lib bdg $23.95

Grades: 5 6 7 8   **599.66**
1. Rhinoceros
ISBN 978-1-60818-083-7; 1-60818-083-2

LC 2010028316

A look at rhinoceroses, including their habitats, physical characteristics such as their horned noses, behaviors, relationships with humans, and protected status in the world today.

Includes glossary and bibliographical references

Halls, Kelly Milner

Wild horses; galloping through time. [by] Kelly Milner Halls; with illustrations by Mark Hallett. Darby Creek Pub. 2008 72p il $18.95

Grades: 3 4 5 6 7   **599.66**
1. Horses
ISBN 978-1-58196-065-5; 1-58196-065-4

Introduces the horse family tree including the relatives of today's modern horse that are now extinct, as well as the species of zebras and asses that still live in the wild

"Colorful illustrations of prehistoric horses, and descriptions of differences from modern horses in terms of their size and number of toes, will intrigue readers. . . . A visual and informational blue-ribbon winner." SLJ

Includes bibliographical references

Hamilton, Garry

Rhino rescue. Firefly Books 2006 64p il map (Firefly animal rescue) $19.95; pa $9.95

Grades: 5 6 7   **599.66**
1. Rhinoceros 2. Endangered species 3. Wildlife conservation
ISBN 978-1-55297-912-9; 1-55297-912-1; 978-1-55297-910-5 pa; 1-55297-910-5 pa

LC 2006275760

Provides details about rhinoceroses from Africa and Asia, their endangerment, and conservation programs designed to save them.

Lockwood, Sophie

Zebras; by Sophie Lockwood. Child's World 2008 40p il map (World of mammals) lib bdg $29.93

Grades: 4 5 6   **599.66**
1. Zebras
ISBN 978-1-59296-931-9 lib bdg; 1-59296-931-3 lib bdg

LC 2007-21689

This book about Zebras looks "at all aspects of the mammal's life including where they live, how they live, and their unique habits. . . . Detailed and labeled color photographs enhance the information provided. Enjoyable and full of information." Libr Media Connect

Includes glossary and bibliographical references

599.67   Elephants

Downer, Ann

Elephant talk; the surprising science of elephant communication. Twenty-First Century Books 2011 112p il map lib bdg $33.26

Grades: 4 5 6   **599.67**
1. Elephants 2. Animal communication
ISBN 978-0-7613-5766-7 lib bdg; 0-7613-5766-1 lib bdg

LC 2010-24880

"The complex behavior of wild elephants is introduced in a flowing narrative accompanied by full-color photographs, diagrams and maps. Downer provides an overview of elephant evolution, places the creatures in their African and Asian contexts, and describes the lives of these intelligent social animals. Her narrative then focuses on the elephants' inticate verbal and nonverbal communication techniques. . . . The illustrations and clearly labeled diagrams and maps are well placed to amplify the text. . . . Throughout this highly readable, informative title are profiles of individuals . . . who work with these animals." SLJ

Includes glossary and bibliographical references

Firestone, Mary

Top 50 reasons to care about elephants; animals in peril. Enslow Publishers 2010 103p il (Top 50 reasons to care about endangered animals) lib bdg $31.93

Grades: 4 5 6 7   **599.67**

1. Elephants 2. Endangered species
ISBN 978-0-7660-3454-9 lib bdg; 0-7660-3454-2 lib bdg

          LC 2008-48690

This describes an elephant's ears, trunk and teeth, what they eat, their ancestors, the different kinds of elephants, and why they are on the endangered animals list

"The illustrations, mostly color photographs, represent a wonderful selection of the animals and their habitats. Reluctant readers may be enticed by this . . . simply because of the great images. This . . . would make a substantial supplement to the science curriculum when studying endangered animals." Libr Media Connect

Includes glossary and bibliographical references

Jackson, Donna M.

★ The **elephant** scientist; by Caitlin O'Connell and Donna M. Jackson; photographs by Caitlin O'Connell and Timothy Rodwell. Houghton Mifflin Books for Children 2011 70p il map $17.99

Grades: 4 5 6 7   **599.67**

1. Elephants 2. Biologists 3. Ecologists
ISBN 978-0-547-05344-8; 0-547-05344-4

          LC 2010014134

In this book, "O'Connell traveled to Africa in 1992 to observe wild animals; the trip turned into a job offer to study elephants at Etosha National Park; the text focuses on the scientists' work, findings, and problems encountered. The authors offer [a] . . . look at new discoveries about elephant communication and how this knowledge can be used to slow the animal's slump into extinction. Combined with . . . full-color photographs by the scientists, the elephants' world is brought to the forefront. Readers enter the researchers' camp to see their setup, fieldwork, and takedown in action. They will learn how elephant anatomy and hierarchy work together to aid in communication." (School Library Journal)

Redmond, Ian

Elephant; written by Ian Redmond; photographed by Dave King. Dorling Kindersley 2000 63p il (DK eyewitness books) $15.99; lib bdg $19.99

Grades: 4 5 6 7   **599.67**

1. Elephants
ISBN 0-7894-6591-4; 0-7894-6591-4 lib bdg
First published 1993 by Knopf

Discusses elephants, their physiology, behavior, evolution, relatives, uses by humans, and conservation

599.7   Carnivores

Lockwood, Sophie

Sea otters. Child's World 2006 40p il map (World of mammals) lib bdg $29.93

Grades: 4 5 6   **599.7**

1. Otters
ISBN 978-1-59296-500-7; 1-59296-500-8

          LC 2005-568

Explores the physical and behavioral characteristics of sea otters, examines their habitat and natural history, and discusses the role of humans in ensuring the continued survival of the species.

Includes glossary and bibliographical references

Skunks; by Sophie Lockwood. Child's World 2008 40p il map (World of mammals) lib bdg $29.93

Grades: 4 5 6   **599.7**

1. Skunks
ISBN 978-1-59296-929-6 lib bdg; 1-59296-929-1 lib bdg

          LC 2007022219

This book about skunks presents "all the basics for reports: an introduction to the creatures' challenges, the role humans play, physical traits and behaviors, habitats, and struggles for survival. Every part of their life [cycle], including sexual maturity, birth, and family relationships, is explained. . . . Clear bright photographs pump up the content. . . . The detail that Lockwood imparts is startlingly high. The [text is] written in a dynamic and engaging style." SLJ

Includes glossary and bibliographical references

599.74   Land carnivores

Read, Tracy C.

Exploring the world of raccoons. Firefly Books 2010 24p il (Exploring the world . . .) lib bdg $16.95; pa $6.95

Grades: 6 7 8 9   **599.74**

1. Raccoons
ISBN 978-1-55407-626-0 lib bdg; 1-55407-626-9 lib bdg; 978-1-55407-617-8 pa; 1-55407-617-X pa

This "introduces the raccoon. The discussion begins with its gradual migration, over the past 100 years, from disappearing North American forests into suburbs and cities. In illustrated two-page and four-page spreads, the book presents information on aspects of raccoon anatomy, habitat, food, seasonal cycle, care of young, and predators. Read also discusses how the raccoon's senses, particularly its 'hypersensitive paws' and the highly developed section of its cerebral cortex devoted to touch, help it survive. Color photos effectively illustrate the text. . . . The text is clearly written and informative." Booklist

Somervill, Barbara A.

Small Indian Mongoose. Cherry Lake Pub. 2010 32p il map (Animal invaders) lib bdg $27.07

Grades: 5 6 7 8   **599.74**

1. Mongooses 2. Biological invasions
ISBN 978-1-60279-630-0 lib bdg; 1-60279-630-0 lib bdg

          LC 2009028179

This offers "an introduction to the problems caused by [the Small Indian Mongoose], a discussion of its physical characteristics and habits, a history of how it arrived in its new habitat, and an analysis of challenges encountered by those trying to limit its spread. . . . [This] considers the destructive effects of these mammals on islands (including several in Hawaii), where they were initially introduced to prey on rats. . . . [This] well-focused [book is] clearly written. The uncluttered page design features at least one color photo on each spread." Booklist

Includes glossary and bibliographic references

599.75 Cat family

Alderton, David
Wild cats of the world; photographs by Bruce Tanner. Facts on File 2002 192p il map $35
Grades: 7 8 9 10   **599.75**
1. Wild cats
ISBN 0-8160-5217-4
LC 2002-34736
First published 1993
This "volume explores the development and behavior of wild cats, with chapters covering form and function, evolution, and distribution. It also examines each species in detail, providing information on distinctive features such as sight, hearing, hunting techniques, and locomotion." Publisher's note

Includes bibliographical references

Becker, John E.
★ **Wild** cats: past & present; illustrations by Mark Hallett. Darby Creek 2008 80p il $18.95
Grades: 5 6 7 8   **599.75**
1. Wild cats 2. Felidae
ISBN 978-1-58196-052-5; 1-58196-052-2
"Becker provides an informative introduction to wild cats, including an account of their ancient ancestors, an overview of the family Felidae and its subdivisions, accounts of wild cats alive in the world today, and woven throughout, discussions of the endangered status of many species. . . . Clearly written and well organized, the text is enhanced by many side-bars, maps, photos, and paintings." Booklist

Bonar, Samantha
Small wildcats. Watts 2002 63p il (Watts library) $24; pa $8.95
Grades: 4 5 6   **599.75**
1. Cats 2. Wild cats 3. Wildcat 4. Felis
ISBN 0-531-11965-3; 0-531-16632-5 pa
LC 2001-17581
In this title "the reader learns terms, including species and genus, with various species examined more closely in chapters devoted to a particular region such as Africa, Europe and Asia, and the Americas. In addition, this book also provides conservation facts and ways in which the reader can help the endangered cats of the world." Libr Media Connect

Includes glossary and bibliographical references

Firestone, Mary
Top 50 reasons to care about tigers; animals in peril. Enslow Publishers 2010 103p il (Top 50

reasons to care about endangered animals) lib bdg $31.93
Grades: 4 5 6 7   **599.75**
1. Tigers 2. Endangered species
ISBN 978-0-7660-3452-5 lib bdg; 0-7660-3452-6 lib bdg
LC 2008-48689
This describes a tiger's life, how they hunt, the purpose of its stripes, caring for young, competing with people for space, and that these animals are very close to extinction

"The illustrations, mostly color photographs, represent a wonderful selection of the animals and their habitats. Reluctant readers may be enticed by this . . . simply because of the great images. This . . . would make a substantial supplement to the science curriculum when studying endangered animals." Libr Media Connect

Includes glossary and bibliographical references

Gamble, Cyndi
Leopards; natural history & conservation. text by Cyndi Gamble; photography by Rodney Griffiths. Voyageur Press 2004 48p il map (World life library) pa $12.95
Grades: 7 8 9 10   **599.75**
1. Leopards
ISBN 0-89658-656-1
LC 2004-14316
"The text offers a comprehensive look at these endangered animals and raises awareness of various efforts to preserve their habitats and to save them from extinction. Excellent-quality photographs appear throughout. . . . An attractive and informative addition." SLJ

Inlcudes bibliographical references

Gish, Melissa
Jaguars. Creative Education 2011 46p il map (Living wild) lib bdg $23.95
Grades: 5 6 7   **599.75**
1. Jaguars
ISBN 978-1-60818-079-0; 1-60818-079-4
LC 2010028315
A look at jaguars, including their habitats, physical characteristics such as their powerful jaws, behaviors, relationships with humans, and threatened status in the world today.

This offers "an array of interesting facts. Photography is large and beautiful–a real draw." SLJ

Includes glossary and bibliographical references

Leopards. Creative Education 2010 46p il (Living wild) lib bdg $34.25; pa $8.99
Grades: 5 6 7 8   **599.75**
1. Leopards
ISBN 978-1-58341-972-4 lib bdg; 1-58341-972-1 lib bdg; 978-0-89812-555-9 pa; 0-89812-555-3 pa
LC 2010017377
"A look at leopards, including their habitats, physical characteristics such as their spotted fur, behaviors, relationships with humans, and threatened status in the world today." Publisher's note

Hamilton, Sue L.

Ambushed by a cougar; [by] Sue Hamilton. ABDO Pub. Co. 2010 32p il (Close encounters of the wild kind) lib bdg $27.07

Grades: 4 5 6 7   **599.75**

1. Pumas 2. Animal attacks

ISBN 978-1-60453-928-8 lib bdg; 1-60453-928-3 lib bdg

LC 2009-45521

Readers learn of actual human-cougar encounters, information about cougars, survival strategies, and attack statistics.

"Students will be drawn to the realistic full-color photographs, the realistic diagrams of the creatures' bodies, the real-life stories told by victims, and the interesting, attractive formatting that includes text, diagrams, photographs, and graphics on each page. . . . [This is] exciting and attractive in a 'gross' sort of way and will appeal particularly to boys for both leisure reading and research." Libr Media Connect

Includes glossary

Lockwood, Sophie

Lions; by Sophie Lockwood. Child's World 2008 40p il map (World of mammals) lib bdg $29.93

Grades: 4 5 6   **599.75**

1. Lions

ISBN 978-1-59296-933-3 lib bdg; 1-59296-933-X lib bdg

LC 2007013567

This book about lions presents "all the basics for reports: an introduction to the creatures' challenges, the role humans play, physical traits and behaviors, habitats, and struggles for survival. Every part of their life [cycle], including sexual maturity, birth, and family relationships, is explained. . . . Clear bright photographs pump up the content. . . . The detail that Lockwood imparts is startlingly high. The [text is] written in a dynamic and engaging style." SLJ

Includes glossary and bibliographical references

Montgomery, Sy

★ **Saving** the ghost of the mountain; an expedition among snow leopards in Mongolia. text by Sy Montgomery; photographs by Nic Bishop. Houghton Mifflin Books for Children 2009 48p il map (Scientists in the field) $18

Grades: 5 6 7 8   **599.75**

1. Biologists 2. Snow leopard 3. Conservationists

ISBN 978-0-618-91645-0; 0-618-91645-8

LC 2008-36762

Author Sy Montgomery and photographer Nic Bishop accompany conservationist Tom McCarthy and his team as they travel to Mongolia's Altai Mountains to gather data about snow leopard populations in an attempt to save this endangered species

"Montgomery's enthusiasm translates well to the page and will have readers cheering for the entourage as they attempt to spot a snow leopard. This slender book abounds with information. Bishop's trademark stunning photography fills out the book with breathtaking views of the extreme environs of Central Asia and warm portraits of the charming people who live there." SLJ

Stefoff, Rebecca

★ **Lions**. Marshall Cavendish Benchmark 2006 112p il map (Animalways) lib bdg $31.36

Grades: 6 7 8 9   **599.75**

1. Lions

ISBN 0-7614-1746-X

LC 2004-11466

This describes the place of lions in human history and culture, their evolution, anatomy, habits, life cycle and possible future.

Includes glossary and bibliographical references

599.756   Tiger

Montgomery, Sy

★ The **man**-eating tigers of Sundarbans; with photographs by Eleanor Briggs. Houghton Mifflin 2001 57p il map hardcover o.p. pa $6.95

Grades: 4 5 6 7   **599.756**

1. Tigers 2. Tigers -- Sundarbans (Bangladesh and India) 3. Dangerous animals -- Sundarbans (Bangladesh and India)

ISBN 0-618-07704-9; 0-618-49490-1 pa

LC 00-32031

"To draw readers into this scientific puzzle, Montgomery integrates science, storytelling, anthropology, and adventure in a unique treatment, illustrated with excellent color photos and diagrams." Horn Book Guide

Includes bibliographical references

599.77   Dog family

Halls, Kelly Milner

Wild dogs; past and present. Darby Creek Pub. 2005 64p il (World of animals) $18.95

Grades: 5 6 7 8   **599.77**

1. Wild dogs

ISBN 1-58196-027-1

This "book explains how fossils and DNA are used to show the evolutionary lines from prehistoric canids to the dogs we live with today. . . . The author presents a wealth of detail through the accessible text; the informative captions, charts, sidebars; and the simple but clear maps." SLJ

Includes bibliographical references

Imbriaco, Alison

The **red** wolf; help save this endangered species! MyReportLinks.com Books 2008 128p $33.27

Grades: 4 5 6 7   **599.77**

1. Wolves 2. Endangered species

ISBN 978-1-59845-038-5; 1-59845-038-7

LC 2006020825

This describes the red wolf "and the reasons for its decline, along with the steps being taken to reverse possible extinction. . . . The [book is a] strong research [tool] on [its] own, but the addition of vetted, linked Internet sites that are recommended throughout the text makes [it] even more valuable." Voice Youth Advocates

Includes glossary and bibliographical references

Lockwood, Sophie

Foxes. Child's World 2008 40p il map (World of mammals) lib bdg $29.93

Grades: 4 5 6   **599.77**

1. Foxes

ISBN 978-1-59296-932-6; 1-59296-932-1

LC 2007-21943

Explores the physical and behavioral characteristics of foxes.

Includes glossary and bibliographical references

McAllister, Ian

The **sea** wolves; living wild in the Great Bear Rainforest. written by Ian McAllister and Nicholas Read; photographs by Ian McAllister. Orca Book Publishers 2010 121p il $19.95

Grades: 5 6 7 8   **599.77**

1. Wolves 2. Rain forest ecology

ISBN 978-1-55469-206-4; 1-55469-206-7

The coastal wolf, a genetically distinct strain that swims and fishes, inhabits the Great Bear Rainforest on British Columbia's rugged west coast.

"This extensive, informative text is illustrated with remarkable photographs taken by McAllister, who has lived in and studied the area for years. They show the lush, old-growth forest and rocky shoreline and a variety of animals that share this habitat, but the wolves are the stars: at rest, at play, on the prowl and catching fish. . . . Fascinating and useful." Kirkus

599.78   Bears

Bortolotti, Dan

Panda rescue; changing the future for endangered wildlife. Firefly 2003 64p il map lib bdg $19.95; pa $9.95

Grades: 4 5 6 7   **599.78**

1. Giant panda 2. Wildlife conservation 3. Pandas

ISBN 1-55297-598-3 lib bdg; 1-55297-557-6 pa

This describes the panda's "natural habitat, habits, physiology, and behavior in captivity. [It also includes] a time line of conservation efforts, profiles of conservationists in the field, and forecasts of the animals' future. Throughout, the author makes clear the factors that can threaten animal populations, and discusses human attitudes toward the animals throughout history. . . . Written in accessible, lively language and nicely illustrated with exciting color photos, [this] will be useful for reports and browsing." Booklist

Firestone, Mary

Top 50 reasons to care about giant pandas; animals in peril. Enslow Publishers 2010 103p il (Top 50 reasons to care about endangered animals) lib bdg $31.93

Grades: 4 5 6 7   **599.78**

1. Giant panda 2. Endangered species

ISBN 978-0-7660-3451-8 lib bdg; 0-7660-3451-8 lib bdg

LC 2008-48953

This describes the giant panda's life cycle, habitat, young, diet, living in the wild and in captivity, and why it is endangered

"The illustrations, mostly color photographs, represent a wonderful selection of the animals and their habitats. Reluctant readers may be enticed by this . . . simply because of the great images. This . . . would make a substantial supplement to the science curriculum when studying endangered animals." Libr Media Connect

Includes glossary and bibliographical references

Gish, Melissa

Pandas. Creative Education 2011 48p il (Living wild) lib bdg $23.95; pa $8.95

Grades: 5 6 7 8   **599.78**

1. Giant panda

ISBN 978-1-60818-082-0 lib bdg; 1-60818-082-4 lib bdg; 978-1-60818-082-0 pa; 1-60818-082-4 pa

LC 2010028311

A look at pandas, including their habitats, physical characteristics such as their black-and-white fur, behaviors, relationships with humans, and threatened status in the world today.

Includes glossary and bibliographical references

Hamilton, Sue L.

Mauled by a bear; [by] Sue Hamilton. ABDO Pub. Co. 2010 32p il (Close encounters of the wild kind) lib bdg $27.07

Grades: 4 5 6 7   **599.78**

1. Bears 2. Animal attacks

ISBN 978-1-60453-932-5 lib bdg; 1-60453-932-1 lib bdg

LC 2009-35078

Readers learn of actual human-bear encounters, information about bears, survival strategies, and attack statistics.

"Students will be drawn to the realistic full-color photographs, the realistic diagrams of the creatures' bodies, the real-life stories told by victims, and the interesting, attractive formatting that includes text, diagrams, photographs, and graphics on each page. . . . [This is] exciting and attractive in a 'gross' sort of way and will appeal particularly to boys for both leisure reading and research." Libr Media Connect

Includes glossary

Hunt, Joni Phelps

A **band** of bears; the rambling life of a lovable loner. London Town Press 2007 48p il (Jean-Michel Cousteau presents) pa $8.95

Grades: 5 6 7 8   **599.78**

1. Bears

ISBN 978-0-9766134-5-9; 0-9766134-5-X

Offers an in-depth look at the survival and social skills of these creatures as they live, play, and raise their families in their natural habitats, featuring grizzlies, black bears, and polar bears.

This "book covers the characteristics and unique traits of . . . [bears] and includes colorful, awe-inspiring photos and immediate first-person narratives." SLJ

Includes bibliographical references

Lockwood, Sophie

Polar Bears. Child's World 2005 40p il (World of mammals) lib bdg $29.93

Grades: 4 5 6   **599.78**

   1. Polar bear

   ISBN 1-59296-501-6

"The first chapter of Polar Bears discusses the bond between the animal and the Inuit people, who have depended on hunting the bears for survival. Then the discussion turns to the bears themselves: their physical features, behaviors, and relatives as well as the threats to their survival." Booklist

   Includes glossary and bibliographical references

McAllister, Ian

★ **Salmon** bears; giants of the Great Bear Rainforest. [by] Ian McAllister & Nicholas Read; photographs by Ian McAllister. Orca Book Publishers 2010 89p il map pa $18.95

Grades: 5 6 7 8   **599.78**

   1. Bears 2. Salmon 3. Rain forest ecology

   ISBN 978-1-55469-205-7 pa; 1-55469-205-9 pa

"Read's conversational text and McAllister's excellent photos provide a perfect framework for this evocative look at the big bears of the Great Bear Rainforest of British Columbia, and an intriguing investigation of its ecological pattern of dependency. The authors present a round of seasons from one winter to the next, touching upon such topics as the effects of fish farms on wild salmon populations, what happens during a salmon run, and what the future may hold for the fish, the bears, and the Great Bear Rainforest itself. . . . Superbly readable, informative, and attractive." SLJ

   Includes bibliographical references

Montgomery, Sy

★ **Search** for the golden moon bear; science and adventure in the Asian tropics. Houghton Mifflin 2004 80p il $17

Grades: 5 6 7 8   **599.78**

   1. Bears

   ISBN 0-618-35650-9

                   LC 2004-5236

The author reports on an expedition into Laos and Thailand in search of a rare species of bear

"The exciting narrative is complemented by an array of full-color photos. . . . This attractive and informative offering is an intelligent reportage of science as it happens." SLJ

   Includes bibliographical references

Ovsyanikov, Nikita

Polar bears. Voyageur Press 1998 72p il maps (World life library) pa $17.95

Grades: 7 8 9 10   **599.78**

   1. Polar bear 2. Polar bear -- Russia (Federation) -- Wrangel Island

   ISBN 0-89658-358-9; 978-0-89658-358-0

                   LC 98-3431

This describes the polar bear's habits, behavior, and biology

"Approachable. . . . Written by an expert on the species. . . . Well illustrated with many excellent photos." Booklist

   Includes bibliographical references

Thomas, Keltie

Bear rescue; changing the future for endangered wildlife. Firefly Books 2006 64p il (Firefly animal rescue series) $19.95

Grades: 5 6 7 8   **599.78**

   1. Bears 2. Endangered species 3. Wildlife conservation

   ISBN 1-55297-922-9

Provides details and facts about bears from around the world, their endangerment and a range of conservation programs to save them, including profiles of individual conservationists and bear species

Ward, Paul

★ **Bears** of the world; [by] Paul Ward & Suzanne Kynaston. Facts on File 2002 191p il map $35

Grades: 6 7 8 9   **599.78**

   1. Bears

   ISBN 0-8160-5208-5

                   LC 2002034739

A revised edition of Wild bears of the world, published 1995

This "explains why bears have meant so much to humans, from early in evolutionary history to the present. It looks at how bears were depicted in ancient mythology and religion. . . . The primary focus is on introducing the living species; charting their evolutionary history; and showing how they live, what they eat, how they behave, and how they cope with their habitats." Publisher's note

   Includes bibliographical references

599.8   Primates

Barker, David

Top 50 reasons to care about great apes; animals in peril. Enslow Publishers 2010 103p il (Top 50 reasons to care about endangered animals) lib bdg $31.93

Grades: 4 5 6 7   **599.8**

   1. Apes 2. Endangered species

   ISBN 978-0-7660-3456-3 lib bdg; 0-7660-3456-9 lib bdg

                   LC 2008048691

This describes the great apes—their life cycle, habitats, young, and why these animals are endangered

"The illustrations, mostly color photographs, represent a wonderful selection of the animals and their habitats. Reluctant readers may be enticed by this . . . simply because of the great images." Libr Media Connect

   Includes glossary and bibliographical references

Bow, Patricia

Chimpanzee rescue; changing the future for endangered wildlife. Firefly Books 2004 64p il (Firefly animal rescue series) $19.95; pa $9.95

Grades: 5 6 7 8   **599.8**

   1. Chimpanzees 2. Wildlife conservation 3. Endangered species

   ISBN 1-55297-909-1; 1-55297-908-3 pa

This introduces chimpanzees, how and why they are in danger, and explains what efforts are being made to protect them.

This is "well-written. . . . Stunning, full-color photographs bring [this] species to life and depict a number of individuals in the field and laboratory working to save these animals." SLJ

Feinstein, Stephen
The **chimpanzee**; help save this endangered species! [by] Stephen Feinstein. MyReportLinks.com Books 2007 128p il (Saving endangered species) $33.27
Grades: 5 6 7 8   **599.8**
1. Chimpanzees 2. Endangered species
ISBN 978-1-59845-039-2; 1-59845-039-5
                                    LC 2006028079
"Focuses on the study of the primates, demonstrating how similar they are to humans and why they should be preserved. . . . Provide[s] an excellent tool for teaching students to do research using both books and legitimate online sources." Voice Youth Advocates
Includes glossary and bibliographical references

Gish, Melissa
Gorillas. Creative Education 2010 46p il (Living wild) $23.95; pa $9.95
Grades: 5 6 7 8   **599.8**
1. Gorillas
ISBN 978-1-58341-969-4; 1-58341-969-1; 978-0-89812-552-8 pa; 0-89812-552-9 pa
                                    LC 2010017374
This "book lucidly discusses conservation and the animals' often tenuous relationship with humans. The layout is uniformly simple but effective, constructed with a nice balance of main text for the report writers, smaller chunks of esoterica for browsers, and . . . killer photos." Booklist

Goodall, Jane
★ The **chimpanzees** I love; saving their world and ours. Scholastic Press 2001 80p il map $17.95
Grades: 4 5 6 7   **599.8**
1. Chimpanzees 2. Chimpanzees -- Behavior -- Tanzania -- Gombe Stream National Park
ISBN 0-439-21310-X
                                    LC 00-47080
"Striking an admirable balance between scientific reporting and deep affection, Goodall's . . . impassioned introduction to the creatures to whom she's dedicated her life's work may well ignite in readers a similar appreciation." Publ Wkly
Includes bibliographical references

Lockwood, Sophie
Baboons. Child's World 2006 40p il map (World of mammals) lib bdg $29.93
Grades: 4 5 6   **599.8**
1. Baboons
ISBN 978-1-59296-497-0; 1-59296-497-4
                                    LC 2005-533

Explores the physical and behavioral characteristics of baboons, examines their habitat and natural history, and discusses the role of humans in ensuring the continued survival of the species.

"Lockwood's dynamic and engaging style and intriguing insight . . . [make the] book shine. . . . Will give children solid information for reports." SLJ
Includes glossary and bibliographical references

Russon, Anne E.
Orangutans: wizards of the rainforest; rev ed.; Firefly Books 2004 240p il map pa $24.95
Grades: 8 9 10 11 12   **599.8**
1. Orangutan
ISBN 1-55297-998-9
                                    LC 2005-357221
First published 1999 in the United Kingdom
A firsthand account of the lives of orangutans including a scientific history of orangutans, a description of orangutans and their natural habitat, their behavior patterns, rehabilitation operations, the politics of orangutan rescue work, and a look at orangutans released back into the forest.
Includes bibliographical references

Sobol, Richard
Breakfast in the rainforest; a visit with mountain gorillas. with an afterword by Leonardo DiCaprio. Candlewick 2008 40p il map $18.99
Grades: 3 4 5 6   **599.8**
1. Gorillas 2. Rain forest ecology 3. Gorilla 4. Photography of animals
ISBN 978-0-7636-2281-7; 0-7636-2281-8
"Wildlife photographer Sobol recounts his travels to Uganda to observe gorillas living in the Virunga Mountains. In his personable text, he also touches on the creatures' habits, diet, and threats. Closeup photographs of the gorillas in addition to many pictures of the surrounding countryside and villagers help round out an understanding of the endangered animals' homeland." Horn Book Guide

Stefoff, Rebecca
★ The **primate** order. Benchmark Books 2005 92p il (Family trees) lib bdg $29.93
Grades: 6 7 8 9   **599.8**
1. Primates
ISBN 0-7614-1816-4
                                    LC 2004-21404
This examines physical traits, adaptations, diets, habitats, and life cycles of primates.
"Fact-filled, yet suprisingly readable. . . . [This] title contains a wide variety of excellent-quality, full-color photographs; interesting sidebars; and diagrams." SLJ

Zabludoff, Marc
Monkeys; by Marc Zabludoff. Marshall Cavendish Benchmark 2007 108p il (Animalways) lib bdg $34.21
Grades: 6 7 8 9   **599.8**
1. Monkeys
ISBN 978-0-7614-2535-9
                                    LC 2007013172

This describes the place of monkeys in the animal kingdom, their evolution, anatomy, life cycle, behavior, diversity, and relationship to humans.

This "will pique readers' curiosity, and the content will keep them hooked. Vivid color photographs and illustrations and a clear font make [this work] stand out." SLJ

Includes glossary and bibliographical references

599.9   Humans

Deem, James M.

Faces from the past; forgotten people of North America. by James M. Deem. Houghton Mifflin Harcourt 2012 154 p. $18.99

Grades: 6 7 8 9 10   **599.9**
1. Skeleton 2. Human body 3. Physical anthropology 4. North America -- Population 5. Radiocarbon dating -- North America 6. Forensic anthropology -- North America 7. Human remains (Archaeology) -- North America 8. Facial reconstruction (Anthropology) -- North America
ISBN 0547370245; 9780547370248

LC 2012006819

This book by James M. Deem looks at "nine cases in which" facial "reconstructions help interpret a specific moment in American history. . . . This title brings to life such diverse figures as paleoamerican Spirit Cave Man; 'Pearl,' a slave from eighteenth-century upstate New York; a buffalo soldier whose corpse was reassembled and given an honorable burial; [and] nine persons among the 1,271 bodies found in pauper's graves in an almshouse cemetery." (Bulletin of the Center for Children's Books)

Szpirglas, Jeff

You just can't help it! your guide to the wild and wacky world of human behavior. Josh Holinaty, illustrator. Owlkids Books 2011 64p il $22.95; pa $10.95

Grades: 4 5 6 7   **599.9**
1. Human behavior 2. Human biology
ISBN 1-926818-07-5; 1-926818-08-3 pa; 978-1-926818-07-8; 978-1-926818-08-5 pa

"How many times have you been frightened and felt the hairs on the back of your neck stand up? Or been unable to hold back a laugh? Or flinched when an object whizzed by, too close for comfort? . . . [This] book provides a cultural, historical, and sociobiological perspective on human behavior. . . . [It is an] exploration of the basic human biology that determines our reactions, social interactions, and the ways we communicate with one another." (Publisher's note)

This is a "collection of curious facts and intriguing studies about human behavior. With a breezy text supported by a lively design, the author . . . presents science in a way certain to attract middle-grade and middle-school readers. Chapters on the senses, emotions, communication, and interactions with other human beings cover a variety of topics. . . . The digital art includes bits of photographs, line drawings, the use of color and shapes to help organize the print and plenty of symbols." Kirkus

Includes index

599.9092   Physical anthropologists

Henderson, Harry, 1951-

The **Leakey** family; unearthing human ancestors. Harry Henderson. Chelsea House 2011 127 p. (Trailblazers in science and technology) (library) $35

Grades: 7 8 9 10 11 12   **599.9092**
1. Fossil hominids -- Tanzania -- Olduvai Gorge 2. Excavations (Archaeology) -- Tanzania -- Olduvai Gorge 3. Paleoanthropolgists -- Tanzania -- Olduvai Gorge -- Biography 4. Physical anthropologists -- Olduvai Gorge -- Biography
ISBN 160413674X; 9781604136746

LC 2011001972

This book, by Harry Henderson, profiles the Leakey family as part of the "Trailblazers in Science and Technology" series. "In the 20th century, the family name . . . became synonymous with paleoanthropology. . . . Louis S.B. Leakey explored East Africa and what is now Tanzania, finding skulls of human ancestors to fill in the evolutionary roadmap to modern man. Leakey worked alongside his wife, Mary, herself an experienced archaeologist and anthropologist." (Publisher's note)

Includes bibliographical references and index

599.93   Genetics, sex and age characteristics, evolution

Anderson, Dale

How do we know the nature of human origins. Rosen Pub. Group 2005 112p il (Great scientific questions and the scientists who answered them) lib bdg $31.95

Grades: 7 8 9 10   **599.93**
1. Evolution 2. Human origins 3. Fossil hominids
ISBN 978-1-4042-0077-7; 1-4042-0077-0

LC 2003-27875

Examines what is known about humankind's origins, and the scientists who have studied the topic

Anderson "enlivens the text by giving a little background information on the scientists involved. His presentation of controversies is quite well balanced [and] . . . the black-and-white photographs and charts are well chosen and well keyed to the text." SLJ

Includes bibliographical references

Boon, Kevin A.

★ The **human** genome project; what does decoding DNA mean for us? [by] Kevin Alexander Boon. Enslow Pubs. 2002 128p il (Issues in focus) lib bdg $26.60

Grades: 8 9 10 11 12   **599.93**
1. DNA 2. Genetics
ISBN 0-7660-1685-4

LC 2001-3388

Discusses genes, genetics, and the legal and ethical issues involved in mapping DNA in the human body

"Opposing viewpoints are presented and a great deal of well-documented information that could be used by debate teams is included. . . . A good update for science shelves." SLJ

Includes glossary and bibliographical references

Goldenberg, Linda

★ **Little** people and a lost world; an anthropological mystery. Twenty-First Century Books 2007 112p il (Discovery!) lib bdg $31.93

Grades: 5 6 7 8   **599.93**

1. Pygmies 2. Fossil hominids 3. Excavations (Archeology) -- Indonesia

ISBN 978-0-8225-5983-2 lib bdg; 0-8225-5983-8 lib bdg

LC 2005-33431

This is an account of the 2003 discovery of small fossil hominids on Flores Island, Indonesia

"This will add important insights to the study of early humans as well as, more broadly, how science and politics interact." Booklist

Includes bibliographical references

Holmes, Thom

Early humans; the Pleistocene & Holocene epochs. Chelsea House 2009 151p il map (The prehistoric Earth) lib bdg $35

Grades: 7 8 9 10   **599.93**

1. Evolution 2. Human origins 3. Fossil hominids 4. Human evolution 5. Pleistocene-Holocene boundary

ISBN 978-0-8160-5966-9; 0-8160-5966-7

LC 2008-38936

"The book consists of two sections. The first section describes the early hominins in Chapter 1 and the archaic species of Homo in Chapter 2. The second section reviews the origins and evolution of more modern Homo species in Chapters 3 and 4. The concluding chapter briefly discusses some contemporary topics, including the meaning of human races, the evolution of skin color, the human role in the evolution and extinction of other species, and the impact of the evolution of diseases. . . . [This] is an outstanding contribution to teaching junior high and high school students about evolution in general and human evolution in particular." Sci Books Films

Includes glossary and bibliographical references

La Pierre, Yvette

Neandertals; a prehistoric puzzle. Twenty-First Century Books 2008 112p il (Discovery!) lib bdg $30.60

Grades: 6 7 8 9   **599.93**

1. Neanderthals 2. Fossil hominids 3. Prehistoric peoples

ISBN 978-0-8225-7524-5; 0-8225-7524-8

LC 2007-22066

When the first Neanderthal skeleton was discovered nearly 150 years ago, scientists presented the race as barely developed brutes. But recent findings indicate that Neanderthals made complex tools, organized group hunts, cared for their sick and injured, and buried their dead.

"Several theories about these prehistoric humans are discussed, including evolution, creationism, linear evolution, and natural selection. This balanced presentation is a valu-

able aspect of this well–formatted and visually appealing book." Voice Youth Advocates

Includes glossary and bibliographical references

Robertshaw, Peter

★ The **early** human world; by Peter Robertshaw and Jill Rubalcaba. Oxford University Press 2005 173p il map (World in ancient times) lib bdg $32.95

Grades: 7 8 9 10   **599.93**

1. Human origins 2. Fossil hominids 3. Prehistoric peoples

ISBN 0-19-516157-2

LC 2004-9732

The author presents "information on human evolution as well as on early humanity in the New World. The text is matched with a great deal of supporting matter including time lines, maps, dramatis personae, high-quality photos, and artists' renderings." SLJ

Includes bibliographical references

Sloan, Christopher

The **human** story; our evolution from prehistoric ancestors to today. foreword by Meave Leakey and Louise Leakey; photographs by Kenneth L. Garrett; art by Kennis and Kennis. National Geographic Society 2004 80p il $21.95

Grades: 7 8 9 10   **599.93**

1. Evolution 2. Human origins 3. Human evolution

ISBN 0-7922-6325-1

LC 2003-13978

Explores the origins of humans, including how such developments as Linnaeus' classification system and recent understanding of the human genome have improved scientists' comprehension of evolution

"What many . . . readers will find most exciting is how today's cutting-edge technology helps us learn about the prehistoric connections all humans share. Great for classroom discussion." Booklist

Includes glossary and bibliographical references

Stefoff, Rebecca

★ **First** humans. Marshall Cavendish Benchmark 2009 112p il map (Humans: an evolutionary history) lib bdg $37.07

Grades: 7 8 9 10   **599.93**

1. Human origins 2. Fossil hominids

ISBN 978-0-7614-4184-7; 0-7614-4184-0

LC 2008-34330

"Stefoff provides an enlightening and entertaining history of the evolution of Homo sapiens, their ancestors, and cousins, from primitive origins to today. The clear, insightful [text is] accented by intriguing sidebars and colorful photos, maps, and graphs." SLJ

Includes glossary and bibliographical references

★ **Ice** age Neanderthals. Marshall Cavendish Benchmark 2009 112p il map (Humans: an evolutionary history) lib bdg $37.07

Grades: 7 8 9 10 **599.93**
1. Neanderthals 2. Human origins 3. Fossil hominids
ISBN 978-0-7614-4186-1; 0-7614-4186-7
LC 2008-54830
"Stefoff provides an enlightening and entertaining history of the evolution of Homo sapiens, their ancestors, and cousins, from primitive origins to today. The clear, insightful [text is] accented by intriguing sidebars and colorful photos, maps, and graphs." SLJ
Includes glossary and bibliographical references

★ **Modern** humans. Marshall Cavendish Benchmark 2009 112p il map (Humans: an evolutionary history) lib bdg $37.07
Grades: 7 8 9 10 **599.93**
1. Genetics 2. Evolution 3. Human origins 4. Fossil hominids
ISBN 978-0-7614-4187-8; 0-7614-4187-5
LC 2009-12364
"Stefoff provides an enlightening and entertaining history of the evolution of Homo sapiens, their ancestors, and cousins, from primitive origins to today. The clear, insightful [text is] accented by intriguing sidebars and colorful photos, maps, and graphs." SLJ
Includes glossary and bibliographical references

Tattersall, Ian
★ **Bones,** brains and DNA; the human genome and human evolution. by Ian Tattersall & Rob DeSalle; illustrated by Patricia J. Wynne. Bunker Hill Pub., Inc. 2007 47p il $16.95
Grades: 5 6 7 8 **599.93**
1. Genetics 2. Evolution 3. Human origins
ISBN 978-1-59373-056-7; 1-59373-056-X
LC 2006931578
The "text follows the trail of human evolution, basing its factual content on current data exhibited in the New Hall of Human Origins in New York City's American Museum of Natural History. Using the skills of anthropologists, archaeologists, and paleontologists, the authors track clues laid down in the fossil record, and, more importantly, in our DNA. . . . The very unsimple concepts are presented clearly, in an attractive format, with splashings of small photos, colorful artwork, diagrams, and maps to attract the eye and elucidate the text." SLJ

Thimmesh, Catherine
★ **Lucy** long ago; uncovering the mystery of where we came from. Houghton Mifflin Harcourt 2009 63p il $18
Grades: 4 5 6 7 **599.93**
1. Human origins 2. Fossil hominids
ISBN 978-0-547-05199-4; 0-547-05199-9
LC 2008-36761
"The 1974 discovery of the fossilized partial skeleton of a small-brained primate who apparently walked upright 3.2 million years ago in what is now Ethiopia significantly changed accepted theories about human origins. Step by step, Thimmesh presents the questions the newly discovered bones raised and how they were answered. . . . Extensive research, clear organization and writing, appropriate pacing for new ideas and intriguing graphics all contribute to this

exceptionally accessible introduction to the mystery of human origins." Kirkus

600 TECHNOLOGY

600 Technology (Applied sciences)

Macaulay, David
★ The **new** way things work; [by] David Macaulay with Neil Ardley. Houghton Mifflin 1998 400p il $35
Grades: 4 5 6 7 8 9 10 11 12 Adult **600**
1. Machinery 2. Inventions 3. Technology
ISBN 0-395-93847-3
LC 98-14224
First published 1988 with title: The way things work
Arranged in five sections this volume provides information on "the workings of hundreds of machines and devices—holograms, helicopters, airplanes, mobile phones, compact disks, hard disks, bits and bytes, cash machines. . . . . Explanations [are also given] of the scientific principles behind each machine—how gears make work easier, why jumbo jets are able to fly, how computers actually compute." Publisher's note

Piddock, Charles
Future tech; from personal robots to motorized monocycles. by Charles Piddock; Dr. James Lee, consultant. National Geographic 2009 64p il (National Geographic investigates) $17.95
Grades: 5 6 7 8 **600**
1. Technology 2. Forecasting
ISBN 978-1-4263-0468-2; 1-4263-0468-4
"This effort takes an appreciative, uncritical look at robots, transportation, bionics, nanotechnology and future life in general. It concludes with ten specific predictions for 2025. . . . Interesting color photographs appear on almost every page and entertaining text boxes with additional related information add appeal." Kirkus
Includes glossary and bibliographical references

Solway, Andrew
Inventions and investigations. Raintree 2008 48p il (Sci-hi: physical science) lib bdg $22; pa $8.99
Grades: 5 6 7 8 **600**
1. Inventors 2. Inventions
ISBN 978-1-4109-3379-9 lib bdg; 1-4109-3379-2 lib bdg; 978-1-4109-3384-3 pa; 1-4109-3384-9 pa
LC 2009-3508
This explores the scientific processes used by inventors throughout history.
A "compelling read for both browsers and science buffs. . . . Information is clearly presented and flows smoothly. . . . A treasure trove of information." SLJ
Includes glossary and bibliographical references

Woodford, Chris

★ **Cool** Stuff 2.0 and how it works; written by Chris Woodford and Jon Woodcock. DK Pub. 2007 256p il $24.99

Grades: 5 6 7 8 9 10   **600**

1. Inventions 2. Technology

ISBN 978-0-7566-3207-6; 0-7566-3207-2

LC 2007-299442

"More than 100 entries present a wide variety of topics with high child appeal, from robot cars to high-tech toilets. . . . Full but uncluttered layouts mix photos, text boxes, diagrams, and captions to highlight key elements. . . . Readers should have an easy time understanding the basics of what each item does, how it is used, and how it works. Along with up-to-date scientific information on high-interest topics, this title has very strong browsing appeal and great booktalk potential." SLJ

608   Patents

Lee, Dora

Biomimicry; Inventions inspired by nature. written by Dora Lee; illustrated by Margot Thompson. Kids Can Press 2011 40 p. $18.95

Grades: 4 5 6   **608**

1. Inventions 2. Nature study 3. Human ecology 4. Technological innovations

ISBN 9781554534678

This book explores "modern innovations [that] have sprung from observation and imitation of the natural world. In topically organized double-page spreads, [Dora] Lee describes shapes and structures, materials and designs, as well as systems for exploration, communication, rescue and delivery. . . . Three or four specific examples, each with illustrative vignettes, follow or sometimes precede the general explanation. These topics range widely and include medical marvels, new power sources, [and] biological computers and robots. . . . [The book] includes a strong ecological message: The most important natural model is the sustainable ecosystem. Through biomimicry, humans can learn to live in balance on the Earth as well." (Kirkus)

609   History, geographic treatment, biography

Bender, Lionel

Invention; written by Lionel Bender. rev ed; DK Pub. 2005 72p il (DK eyewitness books) $15.99; lib bdg $19.99

Grades: 4 5 6 7   **609**

1. Inventions

ISBN 0-7566-1076-1; 0-7566-1075-3 lib bdg

First published 1991 by Knopf

Photographs and text explore such inventions as the wheel, gears, levers, clocks, telephones, and rocket engines.

Cole, D. J.

Encyclopedia of modern everyday inventions; [by] David J. Cole, Eve Browning, and Fred E.H. Schroeder. Greenwood Press 2003 285p il $57.95

Grades: 7 8 9 10 11 12 Adult   **609**

1. Reference books 2. Inventions -- History 3. Inventions -- History -- 20th century

ISBN 0-313-31345-8

LC 2002-69620

"The analysis of each invention is thorough and lively. . . . This book . . . would make an excellent addition to any school or public library needing books on technology and inventions in the modern world." Voice Youth Advocates

Includes bibliographical references

Crowther, Robert

Robert Crowther's pop-up house of inventions; hundreds of fabulous facts about your home. Candlewick Press 2009 un il $17.99

Grades: 4 5 6 7   **609**

1. Inventions 2. Pop-up books

ISBN 978-0-7636-4253-2; 0-7636-4253-3

First published 2000 with title: Robert Crowther's amazing pop-up house of inventions

"As a beautifully engineered pop-up book, it is complex, highly visual, and inviting. . . . It is also durably manufactured. . . . The book is essentially an encyclopedic assortment of facts and anecdotes about the earliest forms of household appliances, furnishings, novelties, . . . games, clothing, and consumables such as soap, soda and candles. The author integrates history and science in a chatty, colorful, and humorous way that quickly draws readers into his subject." Sci Books Films

Diagram Group

Historical inventions on file; [by] the Diagram Group. Facts on File 1994 various paging il looseleaf $185

Grades: 6 7 8 9 10   **609**

1. Inventions -- History 2. Science -- Experiments

ISBN 0-8160-2911-3

LC 94-7098

This work contains "65 experiments re-creating famous inventions. The purpose of these re-creations is to assist students in understanding important concepts and innovations in science. Intended for grades 6-12, the work is multidisciplinary in approach, making use of history, science, mathematics, and abstract and applied thinking. . . . This will be a useful source for middle-and high-school students and teachers doing science projects and experiments." Booklist

Ferris, Julie

Ideas that changed the world; authors, Julie Ferris [et al.] DK Pub. 2010 256p il map $24.99

Grades: 6 7 8 9 10   **609**

1. Inventions -- History 2. Technology -- History

ISBN 978-0-7566-6531-9; 0-7566-6531-0

LC 2010282281

A guide to technological developments that changed the world describes each invention and explores its place in history and how it influenced civilization, discussing inventions from the wheel to computers.

"Brightly colored and packed with information, this reference volume delivers. . . . This book could be used in multiple subject areas. English classes might use it for general research or units on the decades, social studies for the major changes over time, and science due to the technological advancements." Libr Media Connect

Horne, Richard

101 things you wish you'd invented--and some you wish no one had; designed and illustrated by Richard Horne; written by Tracey Turner and Richard Horne. Walker & Co. 2008 un il pa $11.99

Grades: 6 7 8 9   **609**
1. Inventions
ISBN 978-0-80279-788-9; 0-80279-788-1
LC 2008-4990

"The authors have chosen interesting subjects and written concise and engaging histories and trivia. The quality of the book is quite impressive. With an appearance much like a field guide, this well-bound book is made with quality paper and has a very eye-catching layout." Voice Youth Advocates

Jedicke, Peter

Great inventions of the 20th century; by Peter Jedicke. Chelsea House 2007 72p il (Scientific American) $30

Grades: 5 6 7 8   **609**
1. Inventions -- History 2. Technology -- History
ISBN 978-0-7910-9048-0; 0-7910-9048-5
LC 2006014773

"The text is simple, clear, and concise. . . . [The book has] captioned color photos throughout." SLJ
Includes glossary and bibliographical references

Landau, Elaine

The **history** of everyday life. 21st Century Bks. 2005 56p il (Major inventions through history) $26.60

Grades: 5 6 7 8   **609**
1. Inventions -- History
ISBN 0-8225-3808-3

This "explores fireplaces and central heating, indoor plumbing, the washing machine, food and clothing production, and microwave ovens. . . . [It] presents information about daily living from ancient times to the present. . . . The text . . . is breezy but informative. . . . Illustrations are a mixture of period black-and-white and color photos." SLJ
Includes bibliographical references

Lee, Richard B.

Africans thought of it! amazing innovations. [by] Bathseba Opini [and] Richard B. Lee. Annick Press 2011 48p il (We thought of it) $21.95; pa $11.95

Grades: 3 4 5 6   **609**
1. Inventions
ISBN 978-1-55451-277-5; 1-55451-277-8; 978-1-55451-276-8 pa; 1-55451-276-X pa

Describes the inventions created by the peoples of Africa in hunting, agriculture, architecture, metalwork, medicine, the arts, and other fields, and how they have spread through the world and continue to fit into modern African civilization.

"Vivid photographs feature authentic objects used . . . while people engaged in activities capture an enthusiastic look at the reliance on community. Colored backgrounds

and borders present a busy, though uncluttered, dynamic portrayal of nuanced cultures. . . . Succinct definitions and compact descriptions provide a brief and interesting blend of the contemporary with the traditional." SLJ

Marshall Cavendish Corporation

★ **Inventors** and inventions. Marshall Cavendish 2008 5v il set $399.95

Grades: 6 7 8 9 10   **609**
1. Inventors 2. Reference books 3. Inventions -- History 4. Technology -- History
ISBN 978-0-7614-7761-7
LC 2007-60868

"Inventions and Inventors is designed to introduce students to an array of inventors from the past and present while encouraging 'interest in and knowledge of science' by exploring the history, development, and utility of a wide variety of inventions. This set contains 172 alphabetically arranged articles on a range of inventors as well as 21 overview articles. . . . The choice of inventors, the inclusion of more than 1,000 full-color illustrations, and the highly readable and engaging text all create a valuable reference for students and browsers alike." Booklist
Includes bibliographical references

Robinson, James

Inventions; foreword by James Dyson. Kingfisher 2006 63p il (Kingfisher knowledge) $12.95

Grades: 5 6 7 8   **609**
1. Inventions 2. Technology 3. Inventions -- History 4. Technology -- History
ISBN 978-0-7534-5973-7; 0-7534-5973-6

"A slim, colorful overview of inventions." Kirkus
Includes glossary

Rossi, Ann

★ **Bright** ideas; the age of invention in America, 1870-1910. [by] Ann Rossi. National Geographic 2005 40p il (Crossroads America) $12.95

Grades: 4 5 6   **609**
1. Inventions -- History
ISBN 0-7922-8276-0
LC 2003-19834

This describes the history of late 19th and early 20th century inventions such as the light bulb, the telegraph, the telephone, and the automobile.

This "solid [title] for report writers may even pull in a few curious browsers because of [its] plentiful, full-color photos and reproductions. The [layout is] inviting, and the [text is] clear, informative, and readable." SLJ
Includes glossary

Strapp, James

Science and technology. Sharpe Focus 2009 80p il (Inside ancient China) $31.45

Grades: 7 8 9 10   **609**
1. Science and civilization 2. Science -- China 3. Technology -- History
ISBN 978-0-7656-8169-0; 0-7656-8169-2
LC 2008-31168

"This colorful book surveys science and technology developed by the ancient Chinese. Strapp discusses early compasses and mapmaking, the building of canals, and the invention of . . . the wheelbarrow, water clocks, gunpowder, and the harness. The last chapter looks at Chinese medicine and feng shui. . . . The writing is clear and the format is inviting, with many sidebars and pictures. Illustrations include photos of artifacts and maps as well as period artwork and line-and-wash pictures." Booklist

Includes bibliographical references

Tomecek, Steve

★ **What** a great idea! inventions that changed the world. [by] Stephen M. Tomecek; illustrated by Dan Stuckenschneider. Scholastic Ref. 2003 112p il $22.99

Grades: 4 5 6 7   609

1. Inventions -- History
ISBN 0-590-68144-3

LC 2001-20937

"Tomecek puts significant inventions and discoveries in a historical context. Dividing the text into five broad time periods, he offers a series of essays on important advances that occurred in each 'age'. . . . What emerges is a sense of interconnectedness that other books often lack. . . . Full-color diagrams and illustrations are well integrated into each spread." SLJ

Includes bibliographical references

Ye, Ting-xing

The **Chinese** thought of it; amazing inventions and innovations. Annick Press 2009 48p il map (We thought of it) $19.95; pa $9.95

Grades: 5 6 7 8   609

1. Inventions -- History 2. Technology -- History
ISBN 978-1-55451-196-9; 1-55451-196-8; 978-1-55451-195-2 pa; 1-55451-195-X pa

In this survey of Chinese inventions "at least one double-page spread is devoted to each of the eleven topics: farming, working with metal, transportation and exploration, canals and bridges, weapons and warfare, paper and printing, silk, and everyday innovations. . . . The layout of the book is appealing and just right for quick reading or browsing. . . . The author's personal story about her childhood in Shanghai effectively draws the reader in." Voice Youth Advocates

Includes bibliographical references

609.2 Biography

Tucker, Tom

Brainstorm! the stories of twenty American kid inventors. with drawings by Richard Loehle. Farrar, Straus & Giroux 1995 148p il hardcover o.p. pa $6.95

Grades: 5 6 7 8   609.2

1. Inventors 2. Inventions 3. Inventors -- Biography
4. Children -- United States
ISBN 0-374-40928-5 pa

LC 94-38780

The author looks at inventions devised by children since the 18th century. Ear muffs, water skis, the popsicle, colored car wax and the electronic television are among the

products discussed. Includes a discussion of how the Patent Office works

Includes glossary and bibliographical references

610 Medicine and health

Auden, Scott

Medical mysteries; science researches conditions from bizarre to deadly. by Scott Auden; Elizabeth Brownell, consultant. National Geographic 2008 64p il (National Geographic investigates) $17.95; lib bdg $27.90

Grades: 4 5 6 7   610

1. Diseases 2. Medicine -- Research
ISBN 978-1-4263-0356-2; 1-4263-0356-4; 978-1-4263-0261-9 lib bdg; 1-4263-0261-4 lib bdg

This title features "full-color photographs that readers have come to expect from this publisher. . . . [It] focuses on diseases that are regarded as bizarre and are often deadly, including Creutzfeldt-Jakob, Progeria, and Morgellons. The approach is to examine the way in which these mysterious diseases were discovered and how they are being studied to find a cure. . . . [This book offers] explanations simple enough for middle school students but with enough content to make them a useful resource for high school students as well." Voice Youth Advocates

Includes glossary and bibliographical references

Dawson, Ian

★ **Renaissance** medicine. Enchanted Lion Books 2005 64p il (History of medicine) lib bdg $19.95

Grades: 6 7 8 9   610

1. Renaissance 2. Medicine -- History
ISBN 1-59270-038-1

This "offers a concise overview of the fascinating advancements in European medicine between 1450 and 1750. . . Dawson carefully shows how inventions such as the printing press and microscope and the work of artists such as da Vinci influenced medical knowledge. Quotes from primary sources enhance the plainspoken language, and numerous reproductions of paintings and engravings vividly evoke the realities of surgery, leech treatments, and the horrors of the plague." Booklist

Includes glossary and bibliographical references

★ **Encyclopedia** of health; 4th ed.; Marshall Cavendish 2009 18v il set $514.21

Grades: 5 6 7 8 9 10   610

1. Reference books 2. Medicine -- Encyclopedias
ISBN 978-0-7614-7845-4; 0-7614-7845-0

LC 2008033014

First published 1995 with title: The Marshall Cavendish encyclopedia of health

This reference features alphabetically arranged entries on body function; diet and nutrition; human behavior; illness, injury and disorders; and prevention and care

"Easy-to-understand language, an attractive design, and content that supports student research and interest lend value to the set." Booklist
Includes bibliographical references

Goldsmith, Connie
    Cutting-edge medicine. Lerner Publications Co. 2008 48p il (Cool science) lib bdg $26.60
Grades: 4 5 6   **610**
    1. Medicine
    ISBN 978-0-8225-6770-7 lib bdg; 0-8225-6770-9 lib bdg

      LC 2007001946
"This book explains the many amazing ways new medical techniques are helping people live longer, healthier lives." Publisher's note
Includes glossary and bibliographical references

Kelly, Kate
    Early civilizations; prehistoric times to 500 C.E. Facts on File 2010 174p il map (The history of medicine) $40
Grades: 6 7 8 9 10   **610**
    1. Ancient civilization 2. Medicine -- History
    ISBN 978-0-8160-7205-7; 0-8160-7205-1

      LC 2008-43441
"This eye-opening and information-rich [volume] . . . shows that ancient human beings were quite knowledgeable about health and well-being. This book discusses medical advances from prehistoric times through the Roman Empire. . . . Coverage is global. . . . Readers will gain a deepened appreciation of and insights into modern medicine by examining this book. Because of its inclusion of new research, it is recommended as a first purchase for most libraries." SLJ
Includes bibliographical references

Morley, David
    ★ **Healing** our world. Fitzhenry & Whiteside 2007 121p il map $18.95
Grades: 6 7 8 9   **610**
    1. War relief 2. Disaster relief 3. Medical assistance
    ISBN 978-1-55041-565-0
"Morley is a former executive director of the Canadian section of Doctors Without Borders, a humanitarian organization known throughout most of world as Medecins Sans Frontieres (MSF). With clarity and passion, he introduces the organization's history, charter, and current efforts to provide health care where it is needed most." Booklist

Rooney, Anne
    Health and medicine; the impact of science and technology. Gareth Stevens Pub. 2009 64p il (Pros and cons) lib bdg $35
Grades: 5 6 7 8   **610**
    1. Health 2. Medicine 3. Medical technology
    ISBN 978-1-4339-1988-6 lib bdg; 1-4339-1988-5 lib bdg

      LC 2008-54133
An "active layout that features color photographs, maps, graphs or charts on every spread, this . . . [book] has much to offer. . . . It conveniently outlines the range of views . .

. helping students to learn how to view both sides of [the] issue[s]." SLJ
Includes glossary and bibliographical references

Woolf, Alex, 1964-
    ★ **Death** and disease; [by] Alex Woolf. Lucent Books 2004 48p il map (Medieval realms) $29.95
Grades: 5 6 7 8   **610**
    1. Medieval civilization 2. Medicine -- History 3. Public health -- History
    ISBN 1-59018-533-1

      LC 2003-61797
"Clear, well-organized [text] along with full-color reproductions of art and artifacts and photos of period structures immerse readers in . . . medieval life and offer sufficient information for reports." SLJ
Includes glossary and bibliographical references

610.28   Auxiliary techniques and procedures; apparatus, equipment, materials

Strange, Cordelia
    Medical technicians; health-care support for the 21st century. Mason Crest Publishers 2011 64p il (New careers for the 21st century: finding your role in the global renewal) lib bdg $22.95
Grades: 7 8 9 10   **610.28**
    1. Medical personnel 2. Vocational guidance
    ISBN 978-1-4222-1817-4 lib bdg; 1-4222-1817-1 lib bdg

      LC 2010014934
"Chapters identify and emphasize specific careers-important strengths, necessary aptitudes and interests, education and training, projected earnings, closely related occupations, type of work environment, and predictions for the future of the field. . . . Color photos have a small role amid the many statistics, figures, graphs and charts that support and supplement the . . . [text]." SLJ
Includes bibliographical references

610.73   Nursing and services of allied health personnel

Glasscock, Sarah
    How nurses use math; math curriculum consultant: Rhea A. Stewart. Chelsea Clubhouse 2010 32p il (Math in the real world) lib bdg $28
Grades: 4 5 6   **610.73**
    1. Nurses 2. Mathematics 3. Vocational guidance
    ISBN 978-1-60413-607-4 lib bdg; 1-60413-607-3 lib bdg

      LC 2009-20199
This describes how nurses use math in such tasks as giving eye tests, keeping records, taking the pulse, and measuring medicine and includes relevant math problems and information about how to become a nurse
Includes glossary and bibliographical references

Strange, Cordelia

Physicians assistants & nurses; new opportunities in the 21st-century health system. Mason Crest Publishers 2011 64p il (New careers for the 21st century: finding your role in the global renewal) lib bdg $22.95

Grades: 7 8 9 10 **610.73**
1. Nurses 2. Vocational guidance
ISBN 978-1-4222-1820-4 lib bdg; 1-4222-1820-1 lib bdg

LC 2010017919

"Chapters identify and emphasize specific careers-important strengths, necessary aptitudes and interests, education and training, projected earnings, closely related occupations, type of work environment, and predictions for the future of the field. . . . Color photos have a small role amid the many statistics, figures, graphs and charts that support and supplement the . . . [text]." SLJ

Includes bibliographical references

610.9   Medicine -- History

Rooney, Anne

The **history** of medicine; Anne Rooney. Rosen Pub. Group 2013 208 p. (The history of science) (library) $42.60

Grades: 7 8 9 10 11 12 **610.9**
1. Medicine -- History 2. Medical innovations -- History
ISBN 1448872286; 9781448872282

LC 2012009971

This book, by Anne Rooney, is part of "The History of Science" series. "Organized thematically, this . . . entry . . . delves into the history of disease, diagnosis, treatment and surgery. Because of its broad scope, the book is able to make comparisons across eras, transforming . . . history into something relevant to today's teens. . . . Insets offer medical milestones, biographical sketches, and primary resources." (Booklist)

"Organized thematically, this enlightening entry into the History of Science series delves into the history of disease, diagnosis, treatment, and surgery... Rooney has crafted a highly readable tome about a dense topic." Booklist

Includes bibliographical references (p. 205) and index

611   Human anatomy, cytology, histology

Gold, Susan Dudley

Learning about the respiratory system; Susan Dudley Gold. Enslow Publishers 2013 48 p. (library) $23.93

Grades: 5 6 7 8 **611**
1. Respiratory system 2. Respiratory organs
ISBN 0766041611; 9780766041615

LC 2012011104

This book by Susan Dudley Gold is part of the Learning About the Human Body Systems series and looks at the respiratory system. She "discusses what this body system is and what organs are involved in its various processes. She

discusses the potential health problems that can affect the respiratory system, such as cancer, pneumonia, and emphysema, as well as ways to keep healthy and problem-free." (Publisher's note)

Includes bibliographical references and index.

Hall, Linley Erin

DNA and RNA. Rosen Pub. 2010 80p il lib bdg $30.60

Grades: 7 8 9 10 11 12 **611**
1. DNA 2. RNA
ISBN 978-1-4358-9532-4

LC 2009-46612

Haywood, Karen Diane

Skeletal system; [by] Karen Haywood. Marshall Cavendish Benchmark 2009 80p il (The amazing human body) lib bdg $34.21

Grades: 6 7 8 9 **611**
1. Skeleton
ISBN 978-0-7614-3056-8; 0-7614-3056-3

LC 2008-17574

"...with the liberal use of color illustrations, color sidebars, subsections labeled in bold color fonts, and patterns of chemical bonds as backgrounds, will appeal to less able and reluctant readers." Libr Media Connect

"A good choice for students beginning to research the topic." Libr Media Connect

Includes glossary and bibliographical references

Morgan, Jennifer

Cells of the nervous system; [by] Jennifer R. Morgan and Ona Bloom. Chelsea House Publishers 2006 147p il (Gray matter) lib bdg $35

Grades: 8 9 10 11 12 **611**
1. Cells 2. Nervous system
ISBN 9781438119557; 978-0-7910-8512-7; 0-7910-8512-0

LC 2005-11690

An introduction to the human brain discusses how the nervous system relates and processes information, and how its parts can be damaged and repaired.

"Valuable addition[s] to an area where little is written for high school students." Libr Media Connect

Includes bibliographical references

612   Human physiology

Basher, Simon

Human body; a book with guts! by Simon Basher and Dan Green; illustrated by Simon Basher. Kingfisher 2011 128p il $14.95; pa $8.99

Grades: 5 6 7 8 **612**
1. Human body
ISBN 978-0-7534-6628-5; 0-7534-6628-7; 978-0-7534-6501-1 pa; 0-7534-6501-9 pa

"Basher brings his signature informative irreverence and smiley little cartoon icons to the world of human biology. Not a comprehensive resource, but supplemental science reading doesn't come much more fun." Booklist

Bruhn, Aron

Inside the human body; illustrations by Joel Ito and Kathleen Kemly. Sterling 2010 48p il (Inside) $19.95; pa $9.95

Grades: 4 5 6   612

1. Human body
ISBN 978-1-4027-7091-3; 1-4027-7091-X; 978-1-4027-7779-0 pa; 1-4027-7779-5 pa

LC 2010002503

"The illustrations in [this] cool . . . [title is] enhanced by 10 large gatefolds that allow kids to dig deeper into the topics and enjoy amazing illustrations. [The] title clearly defines fact and theory, leaving puzzles for the next generation of scientists to solve. . . . [The book] touches on each of the body systems and provides a highly detailed look at a human cell." SLJ

Includes glossary and bibliographical references

Buller, Laura

Open me up; written by Laura Buller . . . [et al.]; editorial consultant: Richard Walker. Dorling Kindersley 2009 256p il $24.99

Grades: 7 8 9 10 11 12   612

1. Human body 2. Human anatomy 3. Human physiology
ISBN 978-0-7566-5532-7; 0-7566-5532-3

Provides details about the human body, from human cells and senses to brain structure and body systems.

"The juxtaposition of photographs, humor, . . . historical narratives and a variety of artwork should generate hours of gratifying discovery." Publ Wkly

Calabresi, Linda

Human body. Simon & Schuster Books for Young Readers 2008 un il (Insiders) $16.99

Grades: 4 5 6 7   612

1. Human body 2. Human physiology
ISBN 978-1-4169-3861-3; 1-4169-3861-3

LC 2007-61744

This volume "offers excellent pictures of systems, organs, and even individual cells in the human body. . . . A visually dynamic introduction to the human package." Booklist

★ The complete human body; the definitive visual guide. Alice Roberts [editor-in-chief] DK Publishing 2010 512p il $50

Grades: 8 9 10 11 12 Adult   612

1. Diseases 2. Human body 3. Human anatomy 4. Human physiology
ISBN 978-0-7566-6733-7; 0-7566-6733-X

LC 2010-282438

This incorporates "hundreds of stunning images and clearly written text. . . . The extraordinary detail of these pictures will give students an excellent understanding of the body's structure and organization." SLJ

Gardner, Robert

Ace your human biology science project; great science fair ideas. [by] Robert Gardner and Barbara Gardner Conklin. Enslow Publishers 2009 128p il (Ace your biology science project) lib bdg $31.93

Grades: 5 6 7 8   612

1. Biology 2. Science projects 3. Science -- Experiments 4. Human biology 5. Science projects
ISBN 978-0-7660-3219-4 lib bdg; 0-7660-3219-1 lib bdg

LC 2008-30799

"Dozens of . . . science activities are presented with background information, step-by-step instructions, and suggestions for extending to the science fair level. . . . Color illustrations and important safety information are included." Horn Book Guide

Includes bibliographical references

Easy genius science projects with the human body; great experiments and ideas. Enslow Publishers 2009 112p il (Easy genius science projects) lib bdg $31.93

Grades: 7 8 9 10   612

1. Human body 2. Science -- Experiments 3. Human biology 4. Biology projects
ISBN 978-0-7660-2927-9 lib bdg; 0-7660-2927-1 lib bdg

LC 2007-32315

"Both simple and complex science experiments involving the human body are included in this guide for young scientists. An introduction reviews the issues of safety and adult supervision, plus a quick review of the scientific method is included. . . . The high level vocabulary indicates that this is a book for more advanced science students. This would be a great book to put in the hands of a highly motivated student needing fresh ideas for a science fair." Libr Media Connect

Goddard, Jolyon

Inside the human body. Marshall Cavendish Benchmark 2010 48p il (Invisible worlds) lib bdg $28.50

Grades: 4 5 6 7   612

1. Human body 2. Physiology
ISBN 978-0-7614-4190-8 lib bdg; 0-7614-4190-5 lib bdg

LC 2008037254

This describes the details of the human body that are too small for the unaided eye to see, and how these microscopic systems work to keep the body alive and healthy.

The narrative is "clear, well written, broken down into manageable pieces, and peppered with eye-opening facts. The numerous photographs are so phenomenal that they will inspire kids to read the text . . . so that they can wrap their minds around what they see." SLJ

Includes glossary and bibliographical references

Macaulay, David

★ The way we work; getting to know the amazing human body. [by] David Macaulay, with Richard Walker. Houghton Mifflin 2008 336p il $35

Grades: 6 7 8 9 10   612

1. Human body 2. Human physiology
ISBN 978-0-618-23378-6; 0-618-23378-4

LC 2008-25109

Boston Globe-Horn Book Award honor book: Nonfiction (2009)

"The opening chapter introduces basic concepts of biology and chemistry at the cellular level while subsequent chapters take us through the various systems of the body. . . . [Humor] occasionally leavens the information, which, though often complex and technical, is clearly and succintly presented in double-page spreads, accompanied by an illuminating array of illustrations." Horn Book

Marshall Cavendish Reference

Human body from A to Z. Marshall Cavendish Reference 2011 480p $79.95

Grades: 6 7 8 9   **612**

1. Human anatomy
ISBN 978-0-7614-7946-8

LC 2011006783

Presents 168 entries that focus on all the elements that make up the human body, describing major body systems, physical features, and health issues.

"The writing is informal and readable, and... appropriate for upper-elementary through high-school readers." Booklist

Nagel, Rob

★ **Body** by design; from the digestive system to the skeleton. U.X.L 2000 2v set $126

Grades: 7 8 9 10   **612**

1. Physiology 2. Human anatomy 3. Human physiology
ISBN 0-7876-3897-8

LC 99-14642

"Black-and-white and color photographs are plentiful, and color is used throughout to highlight headings and sub-headings, sidebars, and other features." Booklist
Includes bibliographical references

Redd, Nancy Amanda

Body drama; real girls, real bodies, real issues, real answers. Gotham 2008 271p ebook $16.99

Grades: 6 7 8 9 10   **612**

1. Puberty 2. Human body 3. Physiology 4. Girls -- Health and hygiene
ISBN 9781101555002

Information for teenage girls about various issues pertaining to their changing physiology

"The author covers a myriad of physical as well as mental health issues, including cutting and depression. . . . It is likely to be a read-and-pass-along book not only for the helpful advice and accurate information but also for the gross-out pictures of head lice, warts, and keloid scars." Voice Youth Advocates
Includes bibliographical references

Reilly, Kathleen M.

The **human** body; 25 fantastic projects illuminate how the body works. illustrated by Shawn Braley. Nomad Press 2008 120p il $21.95; pa $15.95

Grades: 5 6 7 8   **612**

1. Human body 2. Human anatomy 3. Science projects
ISBN 978-1-934670-25-5; 1-934670-25-1; 978-1-934670-24-8 pa; 1-934670-24-3 pa

"The workings of the human body are expertly summarized in 11 tidy chapters, which include experiments that explain how the body works by creating models that either imitate or test its functions. . . . Many of the activities require adult supervision due to the materials required. . . . Simple drawings and cartoons enliven and illuminate the text. . . . The scientific explanations are superb." SLJ

Somervill, Barbara A.

★ The **human** body. Gareth Stevens Pub. 2008 48p il (Gareth Stevens vital science: life science) lib bdg $26.60; pa $11.95

Grades: 5 6 7 8   **612**

1. Human body 2. Human physiology
ISBN 978-0-8368-8441-8 lib bdg; 978-0-8368-8450-0 pa

LC 2007-16175

First published 2006 in the United Kingdom

This describes "human anatomy and physiology. . . . Factoids are scattered throughout the text in a fashion that captures the reader's attention and interest. . . . [The book offers] excellent graphics, namely photos and diagrams. The artwork complements and enhances the written content." Sci Books Films
Includes glossary and bibliographical references

Walker, Richard, 1951-

3-D human body; written by Richard Walker. DK Pub. 2011 71p il $17.99

Grades: 3 4 5 6   **612**

1. Human body
ISBN 978-0-7566-7216-4; 0-7566-7216-3

"Lively and informative spreads, along with augmented reality technology, introduce readers to the human body. . . . Readers can download software from the publisher's Web site, which can be used in combination with a webcam to make six spreads turn into animated AR pop-ups on a computer screen. Those who don't use the multimedia effect can still learn plenty from the book's detailed mix of photographs, digital graphics, and engaging captions that illuminate how intricate bodily components work together." Publ Wkly

★ **Dr.** Frankenstein's human body book; the monstrous truth about how your body works. [author, Richard Walker; artist, Nick Abadzis] DK Pub. 2008 93p il $24.99

Grades: 4 5 6 7   **612**

1. Human body 2. Human anatomy
ISBN 978-0-7566-4091-0; 0-7566-4091-1

"This anatomy book is as engrossing as any science fiction. Dr. Frankenstein, shown in a sepia photograph standing in a laboratory, gazing at a skull he holds in one hand, invites readers to join him as he creates a human being. . . . The story line is sustained with brief, pun-happy journal entries. . . . Gothic fonts and engraved illustrations and vignettes (in red and black and also hand-colored) blend with state-of-the-art images from MEG scans, gamma scans and other advanced technology. Clear explanations broken into easily assimilable captions and text blocks encourage the reader." Publ Wkly
Includes glossary

Human body; written by Richard Walker. DK Pub. 2009 72 p. ill. (chiefly col.) (DK eyewitness books) (hardcover) $16.99

Grades: 4 5 6 7   **612**
  1. Human body
  ISBN 9780756645458; 075664545X

LC 2009419529

In this book, text and illustrations present information on the parts of the body and how they work
Includes glossary and bibliographical references

Ouch! how your body makes it through a very bad day. written by Richard Walker. DK Pub. 2007 71p il $16.99

Grades: 4 5 6 7   **612**
  1. Human body
  ISBN 978-0-7566-2536-8; 0-7566-2536-X

"Tag along on a rotten day as a body copes with sneezing, getting cut, being stung by a bee, and vomiting, as well as performing more mundane actions such as urinating, tapping into its melanin supply, acting reflexively, and sweating. . . . Dramatic color graphics, both large and small, are accompanied by a multitude of informative captions. Researchers who find the information on the busy pages hard to grasp can pop in the accompanying CD-ROM and catch a ride up the esophagus on a wave of vomit. . . . Eye-catching, highly pictorial, informative, and with a megadose of ick! factor." SLJ
Includes glossary

612.1   Specific functions, systems, organs

Bjorklund, Ruth
  Circulatory system. Marshall Cavendish Benchmark 2009 80p il (The amazing human body) lib bdg $34.21

Grades: 6 7 8 9   **612.1**
  1. Cardiovascular system
  ISBN 978-0-7614-3053-7; 0-7614-3053-9

LC 2007-50436

"A good choice for students beginning to research the topic." Libr Media Connect
Includes glossary and bibliographical references

Gold, John Coopersmith
  Learning about the circulatory and lymphatic systems; by John C. Gold. Enslow Publishers 2013 48 p. (library) $23.93

Grades: 5 6 7 8   **612.1**
  1. Lymphatic system 2. Lymphatics 3. Cardiovascular system
  ISBN 0766041565; 9780766041561

LC 2012011099

This book by John Coopersmith Gold is part of the Learning About the Human Body Systems series and looks at the circulatory and lymphatic systems. "The circulatory system runs through the body carrying oxygen and nutrients to our cells and removes waste. It's driven by the never-resting heart, which pumps blood through more than 60,000 miles of arteries and veins. The lymphatic system regulates

the amount of liquid in the body among other tasks." (Publisher's note)
Includes bibliographical references and index.

Markle, Sandra
  Faulty hearts; true survival stories. Lerner Pub. 2010 48p il (Powerful medicine) lib bdg $27.93

Grades: 5 6 7 8   **612.1**
  1. Heart 2. Heart diseases 3. Cardiovascular system
  ISBN 978-0-8225-8699-9 lib bdg; 0-8225-8699-1 lib bdg

LC 2009-33980

This book "is extremely well done, with a number of great examples of survival stories. The examples exemplify different and important heart diseases, symptoms, and treatments. . . . . That the author is a former science teacher enables her to write clearly for the intended audience. The illustrations and photographs are perfect, adding to a full understanding of the diseases described." Sci Books Films
Includes glossary and bibliographical references

Newquist, Hp
  The **book** of blood; from legends and leeches to vampires and veins. HP Newquist. Houghton Mifflin Books for Children 2012 160 p. ill. (chiefly col.) (hardback) $17.99

Grades: 4 5 6   **612.1**
  1. Blood 2. Science & Nature -- Anatomy & Physiology 3. Health & Daily Living -- Diseases, Illnesses & Injuries
  ISBN 0547315848; 9780547315843

LC 2011025134

In this book, "[H.P.] Newquist . . . demystifies one of the most elemental and (literally) vital components of life as we know it. After an overview of the complex makeup of blood, Newquist dives into humankind's history with, beliefs about, and study of blood, including missteps and misconceptions along the way . . . . Newquist goes into detail to explain how blood moves through the human body and the critical role it plays in keeping us alive." (Publishers Weekly)

Simon, Seymour
  ★ The **heart**; our circulatory system. [by] Seymour Simon. rev ed.; Collins 2006 30p il hardcover o.p. pa $6.99

Grades: 4 5 6 7   **612.1**
  1. Heart 2. Cardiovascular system
  ISBN 978-0-06-087720-0; 0-06-087720-0; 978-0-06-087721-7 pa; 0-06-087721-9 pa

LC 2006-279215

First published 1996
Describes the heart, blood, and other parts of the body's circulatory system and explains how each component functions
"The text is succinct and direct, making the details understandable without losing the sense that the whole process of circulation is 'strange and wonderful.' . . . The often striking pictures include many computer-enhanced photographs as well as diagrams and highly enlarged images made possible by electron microscopes. Handsome and well-conceived in every way." Booklist [review of 1996 edition]

612.2   Respiratory system

Siy, Alexandra

★ **Sneeze!** [by] Alexandra Siy and Dennis Kunkel. Charlesbridge 2007 45p il lib bdg $16.95; pa $6.95

Grades: 4 5 6 7   612.2

1. Allergy 2. Sneezing

ISBN 978-1-57091-653-3 lib bdg; 978-1-57091-654-0 pa

LC 2005-27567

"Kunkel's big, clear, beautiful color electron micrographs on every double-page spead show everything from dust mites, mildew, and pollen to the influenza A virus." Booklist

Includes glossary and bibliographical references

612.3   Digestive system

Allman, Toney

Nutrition and disease prevention. Chelsea House 2010 191p il map (Healthy eating: a guide to nutrition) lib bdg $35

Grades: 7 8 9 10 11 12   612.3

1. Nutrition 2. Preventive medicine

ISBN 978-1-60413-777-4; 1-60413-777-0

LC 2009-41337

This "volume uses boldface type to introduce important and unknown words to the reader and explains them in an easy to understand manner so the reader can grasp the concept being discussed. . . . [For] classes needing information about the importance of good nutrition . . . [this] would be valuable." Libr Media Connect

Includes glossary and bibliographical references

Brynie, Faith Hickman

101 questions about food and digestion that have been eating at you . . . until now. 21st Cent. Bks. (Brookfield) 2002 176p il (101 questions) lib bdg $30.60

Grades: 8 9 10 11 12   612.3

1. Digestion 2. Nutrition

ISBN 0-7613-2309-0

LC 2001-52250

Questions and answers explain the human digestive system and how it uses food for nutrition

"Presenting solid research with a lively writing style, this book provides a great deal of information and sound advice on the topic." Booklist

Includes glossary and bibliographical references

Donovan, Sandra, 1967-

Hawk & Drool; gross stuff in your mouth. by Sandy Donovan; illustrated by Michael Slack. Millbrook Press 2010 48p il (Gross body science) lib bdg $29.27

Grades: 4 5 6   612.3

1. Saliva 2. Mouth -- Diseases

ISBN 978-0-8225-8966-2 lib bdg; 0-8225-8966-4 lib bdg

LC 2008-50699

Presents disgusting facts about the human mouth, how it works to aid in digestion, the organisms that live there, and ways to keep it clean and healthy

"Solid information layered between sarcastic comments and kid-friendly terminology like fart, poop, barf, and puke will keep readers engaged. . . . Labeled, captioned (and graphic) photographs, cartoon-style illustrations, and micrographs add information." SLJ

Includes glossary and bibliographical references

Rumble & spew; gross stuff in your stomach and intestines. by Sandy Donovan; illustrated by Michael Slack. Millbrook Press 2010 48p il (Gross body science) lib bdg $29.27

Grades: 4 5 6   612.3

1. Intestines

ISBN 978-0-8225-8899-3 lib bdg; 0-8225-8899-4 lib bdg

LC 2008-37713

Presents disgusting facts about the human digestive system and its functions

"Solid information layered between sarcastic comments and kid-friendly terminology like fart, poop, barf, and puke will keep readers engaged. . . . Labeled, captioned (and graphic) photographs, cartoon-style illustrations, and micrographs add information." SLJ

Includes glossary and bibliographical references

Gold, Susan Dudley

Learning about the digestive and excretory systems; by Susan Dudley Gold. Enslow Publishers 2013 48 p. (Learning about the human body systems) (library) $23.93

Grades: 5 6 7 8   612.3

1. Digestive system 2. Urinary organs 3. Digestive organs

ISBN 0766041573; 9780766041578

LC 2012011100

This book by Susan Dudley Gold is part of the Learning About the Human Body Systems series and looks at the digestive and excretory systems. She "explains why these systems are discussed together, how they work, and ways to keep healthy." Illustrations and color photographs are included. (Publisher's note)

Includes bibliographical references and index.

Hoffmann, Gretchen

Digestive system. Marshall Cavendish Benchmark 2009 80p il (The amazing human body) lib bdg $34.21

Grades: 6 7 8 9   612.3

1. Digestion

ISBN 978-0-7614-3058-2; 0-7614-3058-X

LC 2008-17573

"A good choice for students beginning to research the topic." Libr Media Connect

Includes glossary and bibliographical references

Simon, Seymour

★ **Guts**; our digestive system. [by] Seymour Simon. HarperCollins 2005 un il $16.99; lib bdg $17.89

Grades: 4 5 6 7   **612.3**

1. Digestion 2. Gastrointestinal system
ISBN 0-06-054651-4; 0-06-054652-2 lib bdg
LC 2004-14508

"Simon's specialty of drawing in readers through large, detailed, breathtaking photos and then entertaining them with facts is again in evidence. . . . The text is enhanced with detailed colored X rays, computer-generated pictures, and microscopic photos." SLJ

612.4   Hematopoietic, lymphatic, glandular, urinary systems

Kim, Melissa

Learning about the endocrine and reproductive systems; by Melissa L. Kim. Enslow Publishers 2013 48 p. (Learning about the human body systems) (library) $23.93

Grades: 5 6 7 8   **612.4**

1. Endocrine glands 2. Reproductive system 3. Generative organs
ISBN 0766041581; 9780766041585
LC 2012011101

This book by Melissa L. Kim is part of the Learning About the Human Body Systems series and looks at the endocrine and reproductive systems. "The endocrine system is essential to human life. It enables a person to grow, respond to change and stress, and helps turn food into energy. The reproductive system has one crucial task: that of making the next generation of people." (Publisher's note)

Includes bibliographical references and index.

Klosterman, Lorrie

Endocrine system. Marshall Cavendish Benchmark 2009 79p il (The amazing human body) lib bdg $34.21

Grades: 6 7 8 9   **612.4**

1. Endocrine glands
ISBN 978-0-7614-3055-1; 0-7614-3055-5
LC 2007-50444

"A good choice for students beginning to research the topic." Libr Media Connect

Includes glossary and bibliographical references

Excretory system. Marshall Cavendish Benchmark 2010 77p il (The amazing human body) lib bdg $23.95

Grades: 6 7 8 9   **612.4**

1. Feces 2. Urine 3. Excretion
ISBN 978-0-7614-4037-6 lib bdg; 0-7614-4037-2 lib bdg
LC 2008037261

"Discusses the parts that make up the human excretory system, what can go wrong, how to treat those illnesses and diseases, and how to stay healthy." Publisher's note

Includes glossary and bibliographical references

612.6   Reproduction, development, maturation

Bailey, Jacqui

Sex, puberty, and all that stuff; a guide to growing up. illustrated by Jan McCafferty. Barron's 2004 112p il pa $12.95

Grades: 5 6 7 8   **612.6**

1. Puberty 2. Adolescence 3. Sex education
ISBN 0-7641-2992-9

"A large helping of straightforward, up-to-date information peppered with humor and bright, graphic illustrations make this book one of the best texts about sex for developing adolescents." Voice Youth Advocates

Includes bibliographical references

Brynie, Faith Hickman

★ **101** questions about reproduction; or how 1 + 1. Twenty-First Century Books 2006 176p il (101 questions) lib bdg $27.90

Grades: 7 8 9   **612.6**

1. Pregnancy 2. Childbirth 3. Sex education
ISBN 0-7613-2311-2
LC 2003-16350

Uses a question-and-answer format to present information about physical, medical, and social issues surrounding human reproduction, including birth control, pregnancy, and childbirth.

"This is a splendid companion to Brynie's 101 Questions about Sex and Sexuality (21st Century Bks, 2003); together the books present informative, complementary coverage for browsers and researchers." SLJ

Includes bibliographical references

Gravelle, Karen

The **period** book; everything you don't want to ask (but need to know) by Karen Gravelle & Jennifer Gravelle; illustrations by Debbie Palen. updated ed.; Walker & Co. 2006 126p il $16.95

Grades: 4 5 6 7   **612.6**

1. Menstruation
ISBN 978-0-8027-8072-0; 0-8027-8072-5
LC 2008270981

First published 1996

Explains what happens at the onset of menstruation, discussing what to wear, going to the gynecologist, and how to handle various problems

"The cartoonlike illustrations and conversational tone make this updated edition a friendly, reassuring resource as well as a thorough one." Horn Book Guide

Holmes, Melisa

Girlology's there's something new about you; a girl's guide to growing up. [by] Melisa Holmes & Trish Hutchison. Health Communications 2010 122p il pa $12.95

Grades: 6 7 8 9   612.6
  1. Girls 2. Puberty
  ISBN 978-0-7573-1526-8; 0-7573-1526-7
                                    LC 2010021169
Written by physicians who are mothers of preteen and
teen girls, this guide explains the changes girls will be facing
as they grow up.
  "The graphics are informative without being offensive,
pictures of the friends are cute and appealing, giving a fresh
lightheartedness to the book. This is a must-have book for all
homes and libraries." Voice Youth Advocates

Jukes, Mavis
  ★ **Growing** up: it's a girl thing; straight talk
about first bras, first periods, and your changing body.
illustrations by Debbie Tilley. Knopf 1998 72p il
hardcover o.p. pa $10
Grades: 4 5 6 7   612.6
  1. Girls 2. Puberty 3. Adolescence 4. Menstruation
  5. Menarche 6. Girls -- Physiology
  ISBN 0-679-89027-0 pa
                                    LC 98-18113
This "covers body hair and shaving, perspiration and de-
odorant, and how to buy your first bra. The second half of
the book is devoted to what to expect and how to plan for
your first period. . . . The narration has an easy, comfortable
voice and imparts accurate and important information." SLJ

Katz, Anne
  Girl in the know; your inside-and-out guide to
growing up. written by Anne Katz; illustrated by
Monika Melnychuk. Kids Can Press 2010 111p il
$18.95
Grades: 4 5 6 7   612.6
  1. Puberty 2. Girls -- Health and hygiene 3. Life skills
  guides 4. Girls -- Psychology 5. Girls -- Health and
  hygiene
  ISBN 978-1-55453-303-9; 1-55453-303-1
"This reassuring title is aimed at girls who want clear
facts about puberty but who may not be ready to read in-
depth specifics of sex and birth-control. The author . . . offers
a holistic guide that covers the body changes puberty brings
as well as tips about maintaining physical and emotional
health. . . . The warm, straightforward, useful advice on a
broad range of topics . . . will captivate both middle graders and middle-schoolers, and the frequent color drawings of
stylish, diverse girls . . . reinforce the book's appeal to a wide
age group." Booklist

Madaras, Lynda
  The **what's** happening to my body? book for
boys; [by] Lynda Madaras with Area Madaras; draw-
ings by Simon Sullivan. 3rd rev ed.; Newmarket
Press 2007 xx, 233p il $24.95; pa $12.95
Grades: 4 5 6 7   612.6
  1. Puberty 2. Adolescence 3. Sex education 4. Boys
  -- Health and hygiene
  ISBN 978-1-55704-769-4; 1-55704-769-3; 978-1-
  55704-765-6 pa; 1-55704-765-0 pa
                                    LC 2007009874
  First published 1984

Discusses the changes that take place in a boy's body
during puberty, including information on the body's changing size and shape, the growth spurt, reproductive organs,
pubic hair, beards, pimples, voice changes, wet dreams, and
puberty in girls
  Includes bibliographical references

  The **what's** happening to my body? book for
girls; [by] Lynda Madaras with Area Madaras; drawings by Simon Sullivan. 3rd rev ed.; Newmarket
Press 2007 xxvi, 259p il $24.95; pa $12.95
Grades: 4 5 6 7   612.6
  1. Puberty 2. Adolescence 3. Sex education 4. Girls
  -- Health and hygiene
  ISBN 978-1-55704-768-7; 1-55704-768-5; 978-1-
  55704-764-9 pa; 1-55704-764-2 pa
                                    LC 2007009862
Discusses the changes that take place in a girl's body
during puberty, including information on the body's changing size and shape, pubic hair, breasts, reproductive organs,
the menstrual cycle, and puberty in boys
  Includes bibliographical references

Mar, Jonathan
  The **body** book for boys; by Jonathan Mar and
Grace Norwich. Scholastic 2010 128p il pa $8.99
Grades: 4 5 6   612.6
  1. Boys 2. Puberty 3. Adolescence
  ISBN 978-0-545-23751-2 pa; 0-545-23751-3 pa
"In this reassuring title aimed at boys just entering adolescence, the authors present frank information on such topics as hygiene, the changes brought on by puberty, exercise,
and dealing with girls. The tone is kept light, and the many
bright illustrations also have a fun, jokey quality." Booklist

Parker, Steve
  The **reproductive** system; by Steve Parker.
Raintree Steck-Vaughn Pubs. 1999 48 p. ill. (some
col.) (library) $27.14; (library) $32
Grades: 6 7 8 9   612.6
  1. Biology 2. Reproductive system
  ISBN 0817248064 out of print; 143293421X;
  9781432934217
                                    LC 96029685
This book for middle schoolers by Steve Parker looks
at the reproductive system. It "addresses male and female
anatomy, genes, fertility problems, contraception, STDs, and
human development from conception to adolescence." Photographs, diagrams, and illustrations are included. (School
Library Journal)
  Includes bibliographical references (p. 47) and index.

Plaisted, Caroline
  Boy talk; a survival guide to growing up. illus-
trated by Chris Dickason. QEB Pub. 2011 48p il
(Growing up) $14.99
Grades: 4 5 6 7   612.6
  1. Boys 2. Puberty
  ISBN 1-60992-085-6; 978-1-60992-085-2
                                    LC 2011009206

Discusses body changes that happen to boys during puberty, such as acne, body hair, body odor, mood swings, crushes, and more, and gives suggestions to teen boys for taking care of their hygiene and keeping good relationships.

"Using a colorful design featuring Dickason's wacky, mugging cartoon characters, this is about as appealing as a book on these topics can get, and it maintains a mildly funny, usually frank, and always healthy tone." Booklist

Rand, Casey

Human reproduction. Raintree 2009 48p il (Sci-hi: life science) lib bdg $31.43; pa $8.99
Grades: 5 6 7 8   **612.6**
1. Reproduction 2. Sex education
ISBN 978-1-4109-3327-0 lib bdg; 1-4109-3327-X lib bdg; 978-1-4109-3335-5 pa; 1-4109-3335-0 pa
LC 2009003464

In this introduction to human reproduction "clear language, embedded definitions, and interesting examples illustrate abstract concepts through both text and well-chosen photographs. . . . [It] includes suggested activities to test ideas as well as a thorough glossary and a Webliography." SLJ

Includes glossary and bibliographical references

Schwartz, John

Short; walking tall when you're not tall at all. Roaring Brook Press 2010 132p il $16.99
Grades: 4 5 6 7 8   **612.6**
1. Size 2. Growth 3. Body image 4. Prejudices 5. Human growth 6. Stature, Short
ISBN 978-1-59643-323-6; 1-59643-323-X

"In a humorous, personal voice, . . . Schwartz combines his own memories of growing up short with related discussions about physiology, statistics, popular culture, and societal prejudice, always returning to his own self-image. . . . Short kids will want every word. . . . and many readers will move on to the resource list of articles, Web sites, and scientific papers in the detailed, informal back matter." Booklist

Includes bibliographical references

Waters, Sophie

The **female** reproductive system. Rosen Central 2008 48p il (Girls' health) lib bdg $26.50
Grades: 5 6 7 8   **612.6**
1. Pregnancy 2. Birth control 3. Reproductive system
ISBN 9781435844018; 978-1-4042-1950-2; 1-4042-1950-1
LC 2006101218

Describes the parts of the female reproductive system, explains how pregnancy occurs and the steps in embryo development, and discusses various forms of birth control

"Generously interspersed with color photographs and diagrams . . . [this book will] offer girls a safe, comfortable place to get straight, honest answers about their personal health issues." Libr Media Connect

Includes glossary and bibliographical references

612.7   Musculoskeletal system, integument

Brynie, Faith Hickman

★ **101** questions about muscles to stretch your mind and flex your brain; by Faith Hickman Brynie. Twenty-First Century Books 2008 176p il (101 questions) lib bdg $30.60
Grades: 8 9 10 11 12   **612.7**
1. Muscles
ISBN 978-0-8225-6380-8; 0-8225-6380-0
LC 2006-37041

This answers such questions as "What do tendons do? What causes muscle cramps? . . . [This book] makes human physiology accessible, with questions everyone has always wondered about and up-to-date, detailed answers that discuss the complex science in chatty but never condescending style. Like the text, the clear diagrams and photographs deal with everything from basic information . . . to the more advanced." Booklist

Includes glossary and bibliographical references

Colligan, L. H.

Muscles. Marshall Cavendish Benchmark 2010 78p il (The amazing human body) lib bdg $34.21
Grades: 6 7 8 9   **612.7**
1. Muscles
ISBN 978-0-7614-4038-3 lib bdg; 0-7614-4038-0 lib bdg
LC 2008037257

Discusses human musculature, what can go wrong, how to treat those diseases and injuries, and how to stay health

Includes glossary and bibliographical references

Gold, Susan Dudley

Learning about the musculoskeletal system and the skin; Susan Dudley Gold. Enslow Publishers 2013 48 p. (Learning about the human body systems) (library) $23.93
Grades: 5 6 7 8   **612.7**
1. Musculoskeletal system 2. Skin
ISBN 076604159X; 9780766041592
LC 2012011102

This book by Susan Dudley Gold is part of the Learning About the Human Body Systems series and looks at the musculoskeletal system. "Bone and muscles join forces to move us from one place to another. The musculoskeletal system controls our breathing, allows our eyes to focus, and shapes our smiles. It enables us to talk and to eat. Our strong bones support our weight. Skin wraps our body in a tough layer of tissue that keeps moisture in and germs out." (Publisher's note)

Includes bibliographical references and index..

Hall, Margaret

Skin deep. Raintree 2007 32p il (Raintree fusion) lib bdg $28.21; pa $7.99
Grades: 5 6 7 8   **612.7**
1. Skin
ISBN 978-1-4109-2582-4 lib bdg; 1-4109-2582-X lib bdg; 978-1-4109-2611-1 pa; 1-4109-2611-7 pa
LC 2006-8771

Explains what skin is and why it is important, including protecting the body from germs, helping cool down the body when it gets too hot, and absorbing Vitamin D from sunlight.

Includes glossary and bibliographical references

Klosterman, Lorrie
Skin. Marshall Cavendish Benchmark 2009 79p il (The amazing human body) lib bdg $34.21
Grades: 6 7 8 9   **612.7**
1. Skin
ISBN 978-0-7614-3057-5; 0-7614-3057-1
LC 2008-17580
"A good choice for students beginning to research the topic." Libr Media Connect

Includes glossary and bibliographical references

Parker, Steve, 1952-
The **skeleton** and muscles; [by] Steve Parker. Raintree 2004 48p il (Our bodies) lib bdg $29.93
Grades: 5 6 7 8   **612.7**
1. Skeleton 2. Musculoskeletal system 3. Muscular system
ISBN 0-7398-6622-2
LC 2003-6594
This "takes a look at bones, muscles, and joints; how they are connected and function; and how to keep them healthy. The anatomy is accurate, and the format, with plenty of pictures, diagrams, and magnified photos, is very accessible. There are also lots of lively boxed facts." Booklist

Includes bibliographical references

612.8 Nervous system

Brynie, Faith Hickman
★ **101** questions about sleep and dreams that kept you awake nights . . . until now. Twenty-First Century Books 2006 176p il (101 questions) lib bdg $27.93
Grades: 7 8 9 10 11 12   **612.8**
1. Sleep 2. Dreams
ISBN 978-0-7613-2312-9; 0-7613-2312-0
LC 2005-17276
This book describes the physical and psychological aspects of sleep and dreams. The author "presents sometimes rather complicated scientific material in a way that is not only easily understood, but also thoroughly enjoyable." Sci Books Films

Includes bibliographical references

Gardner, Robert
Ace your science project about the senses; great science fair ideas. [by] Robert Gardner . . . [et al.] Enslow Publishers 2009 112p il (Ace your biology science project) lib bdg $31.93
Grades: 5 6 7 8   **612.8**
1. Science projects 2. Senses and sensation 3. Science -- Experiments
ISBN 978-0-7660-3217-0 lib bdg; 0-7660-3217-5 lib bdg
LC 2008-30797

"Presents several science projects and science project ideas about the senses." Publisher's note

Includes glossary and bibliographical references

Gold, Martha V.
Learning about the nervous system; by Martha V. Gold. Enslow Publishers 2013 48 p. (library) $23.93
Grades: 5 6 7 8   **612.8**
1. Nervous system
ISBN 0766041603; 9780766041608
LC 2012011103
This book by Martha V. Gold is part of the Learning About the Human Body Systems series and looks at the nervous system. "The nervous system is made up of the brain, the spinal cord and nerves. It is responsible for telling the heart to beat, the lungs to breathe, and the muscles to move. The brain—the central command center—processes everything from understanding a teacher's instructions to enjoying a piece of chocolate cake." (Publisher's note)

Includes bibliographical references and index.

Larsen, C. S.
Crust and spray; gross stuff in your eyes, ears, nose, and throat. illustrated by Michael Slack. Millbrook Press 2010 48p il (Gross body science) lib bdg $29.27
Grades: 4 5 6   **612.8**
1. Ear 2. Eye 3. Nose 4. Throat
ISBN 978-0-8225-8964-8 lib bdg; 0-8225-8964-8 lib bdg
LC 2008-33777
"Solid information layered between sarcastic comments and kid-friendly terminology like fart, poop, barf, and puke will keep readers engaged. . . . Labeled, captioned (and graphic) photographs, cartoon-style illustrations, and micrographs add information." SLJ

Includes glossary and bibliographical references

Newquist, H. P.
★ The **great** brain book; an inside look at the inside of your head. illustrations by Keith Kasnot and Eric Brace. Scholastic Reference 2005 160p il $18.95
Grades: 5 6 7 8   **612.8**
1. Brain
ISBN 0-439-45895-1
LC 2004-42955
This describes the anatomy and physiology of the brain and covers such topics as the history of brain research, neurons, learning and memory, brain diseases and mental illness, and the possible future of brain research

"With an appealing, colorful design and a flashy cover, this in-depth introduction to the human brain and its remarkable powers will attract browsers, but strong readers are its best audience. . . . The clever, kid-friendly anecdotes amid the anatomy lessons . . . enhance accessibility." Booklist

Rau, Dana Meachen

Freaking out! the science of the teenage brain. Compass Point Books 2011 64p il (Everyday science) lib bdg $33.32; pa $8.95

Grades: 7 8 9 10   **612.8**

1. Brain

ISBN 978-0-7565-4486-7 lib bdg; 0-7565-4486-6; 978-0-7565-4500-0 pa; 0-7565-4500-5 pa

LC 2010054302

This "offers a solid overview of the brain. The book begins with an explanation of what the brain does, how it looks, and its various components. It then goes on to discuss more specialized topics, such as mood changes, developmental skills, and memory. The attractive format, with easy-to-read print, features bright photographs . . . and plenty of sidebars on a variety of topics." Booklist

Includes glossary and bibliographical references

Scott, Elaine

All about sleep from A to ZZZZ; by Elaine Scott; illustrated by John O'Brien. Viking 2008 58p il $17.99

Grades: 5 6 7 8 9 10   **612.8**

1. Sleep

ISBN 978-0-670-06188-4; 0-670-06188-3

LC 2008-6074

"The book covers a range of topics, including circadian rhythms, dreams, and the functions and stages of sleep." Booklist

Simon, Seymour

★ **Eyes** and ears. HarperCollins Pubs. 2003 un il hardcover o.p. pa $6.99

Grades: 4 5 6 7   **612.8**

1. Ear 2. Eye 3. Vision 4. Hearing 5. Senses and sensation

ISBN 0-688-15303-8; 978-0-06-073302-5 pa; 0-06-073302-0 pa

LC 2002-19060

Describes the anatomy of the eye and ear, how those organs function and some ways in which they may malfunction, and how the brain is also involved in our seeing and hearing

"Simon is at his very best here. . . . The large, exquisitely reproduced photographs from a number of sources look like fiery planets, galaxies, and monster creatures. . . . The anatomy and physiology are detailed and accurate, with clear diagrams." Booklist

★ The **brain**; our nervous system. [by] Seymour Simon. rev ed.; Collins 2006 30p il $17.99; pa $6.99

Grades: 4 5 6 7   **612.8**

1. Brain 2. Nervous system

ISBN 978-0-06-087718-7; 0-06-087718-9; 978-0-06-087719-4 pa; 0-06-087719-7 pa

LC 2007-272349

First published 1997

Describes the various parts of the brain and the nervous system and how they function to enable us to think, feel, move, and remember.

Simon's "clear, concise writing style is complemented by stunning color images taken with radiological scanners, such as CAT scans, MRIs, and SEMs (scanning electron microscopes.)" SLJ [review of 1997 edition]

Includes bibliographical references

Simpson, Kathleen

The **human** brain; inside your body's control room. National Geographic 2009 64p il (National Geographic investigates) lib bdg $27.90

Grades: 5 6 7 8   **612.8**

1. Brain

ISBN 978-1-4263-0421-7 lib bdg; 1-4263-0421-8 lib bdg

"Readers will learn about . . . new brain research in this title, which includes a basic discussion of the parts of the brain, their functions, and how neurons send messages throughout the body. Information is also included about the role of the brain during sleep, dreaming, and various emotional states, as well as explanations of the various technologies available to measure brain activity. This is a well-organized, compelling introduction, sure to pique the curiosity of many children. Full-color photographs and illustrations enliven the text." SLJ

Includes bibliographical references

Wilson, M. R.

Frequently asked questions about how the teen brain works; [by] Michael R. Wilson. Rosen Pub. 2009 64p il (FAQ: teen life) lib bdg $29.25

Grades: 6 7 8 9   **612.8**

1. Brain 2. Teenagers -- Health and hygiene

ISBN 978-1-4358-5324-9 lib bdg; 1-4358-5324-5 lib bdg

LC 2008049322

Describes how the brains of adolescents differ from those of infants or adults, the structure and development of the human brain, the implications of recent discoveries for teen life and behavior, and possible future developments

"A conversational tone keeps the [book] readable, and specific topics have information relevant to teens' lives. . . . Illustrated throughout with captioned color photos." SLJ

Includes glossary and bibliographical references

Winston, Robert M. L., 1940-

What goes on in my head? how your brain works and why you do what you do. [by] Robert Winston. DK Pub. 2010 96p il $16.99

Grades: 4 5 6 7   **612.8**

1. Brain 2. Psychology

ISBN 978-0-7566-6885-3; 0-7566-6885-9

"The author presents a great deal of scientific content and supplements it with examples, anecdotes, and current findings in the field. . . . In addition, interactive brain teasers and exercises make the science come alive. . . . The book combines vibrant colors and illustrations with explanations to keep young readers engaged." Sci Books Films

613 Personal health and safety

Complementary and alternative medicine information for teens; health tips about diverse medical and wellness systems. edited by Lisa Bakewell. 2nd ed. Omnigraphics, Inc. 2013 xiii, 389 p.p (hardcover) $69
Grades: 7 8 9 10 11 12   613
1. Alternative medicine 2. Teenagers -- Health and hygiene
ISBN 0780813111; 9780780813113
                                                   LC 2012047548
This book offers information about alternative medicine for teenagers. The "volume is divided into 60 chapters, each focusing on a specific natural medicine or therapy that can be used in combination with or in place of conventional drugs to enhance health . . . . The nine parts address major categories, such as whole-medicine systems, manipulative and body-based practices, dietary and herbal remedies, and energy medicines, as well as sensory and emotional-based therapies." (School Library Journal)
Includes bibliographical references and index.

Couwenhoven, Terri
The **boys'** guide to growing up; choices & changes during puberty. Terri Couwenhoven. Woodbine House 2012 viii, 64 p.p $16.95
Grades: 6 7 8   613
1. Puberty 2. Mentally handicapped 3. Teenagers -- Sexual behavior 4. Teenage boys -- Physiology 5. Sex instruction for children with mental disabilities
ISBN 1606130897; 9781606130896
                                                   LC 2012025776
This book on puberty by Terri Couwenhoven "is geared to boys with "developmental disabilities." It explains basic information that includes body changes in growth, hair, skin, voice, and feelings. It is not a sex guide though it does not shy away from emerging sexuality." (School Library Journal)

De la Bedoyere, Camilla
Personal hygiene and sexual health. Amicus 2010 46p il (Healthy lifestyles) lib bdg $32.80
Grades: 7 8 9 10   613
1. Puberty 2. Teenagers -- Health and hygiene
ISBN 978-1-60753-087-9; 1-60753-087-2
                                                   LC 2009-47571
This book is "well-written and satisfyingly informative. . . . [The] magazine-like format includes numerous sidebars, color photos, and charts." SLJ
Includes glossary

Dicker, Katie
Diet and nutrition. Amicus 2011 45p il (Healthy lifestyles) lib bdg $32.80
Grades: 7 8 9 10   613
1. Diet 2. Nutrition 3. Physical fitness 4. Teenagers -- Health and hygiene
ISBN 978-1-60753-085-5; 1-60753-085-6
                                                   LC 2009-44219

This book is "well-written and satisfyingly informative." SLJ
Includes glossary

Dunham, Kelli
The **girl's** body book; everything you need to know for growing up you! illustrated by Laura Tallardy. Applesauce Press 2008 115p il pa $9.95
Grades: 4 5 6 7   613
1. Puberty 2. Adolescence 3. Girls -- Health and hygiene
ISBN 978-1-60433-004-5; 1-60433-004-X
"The book's tone and lively cartoon illustrations are friendly and nonthreatening. . . . A solid choice for basic information about puberty." SLJ
Includes bibliographical references

Gardner, Robert
Ace your exercise and nutrition science project: great science fair ideas; [by] Robert Gardner, Barbara Gardner Conklin, and Salvatore Tocci. Enslow Publishers 2009 128p il (Ace your biology science project) lib bdg $31.93
Grades: 5 6 7 8   613
1. Exercise 2. Nutrition 3. Science projects 4. Science -- Experiments
ISBN 978-0-7660-3218-7 lib bdg; 0-7660-3218-3 lib bdg
                                                   LC 2008-30798
"Presents several science projects and science project ideas about exercise and nutrition." Publisher's note
Includes bibliographical references

Lehman, Robert
★ **Will** puberty last my whole life? real answers to real questions from preteens about body changes, sex, and other growing-up stuff. Julie Giesy Metzger and Robert Lehman; illustrated by Cerizo. Sasquatch Books 2011 90 p. col. ill. (pbk.) $16.95
Grades: 4 5 6 7 8   613
1. Puberty 2. Questions and answers 3. Boys -- Health and hygiene 4. Girls -- Health and hygiene 5. Teenage boys -- Physiology 6. Teenage girls -- Physiology 7. Interpersonal relations in adolescence
ISBN 1570617392; 9781570617393
                                                   LC 2011038401
This book "for boys and girls between the ages of 9 and 12 has questions asked by girls in one half of the book" and "questions asked by boys are on the other side." The book contains "answers to questions pre-adolescents have about puberty, friends, feelings, sex, pimples, babies, body hair, menstruation, bras, and much more." (Amazon.com)

Libal, Autumn
★ **Can** I change the way I look? a teen's guide to the health implications of cosmetic surgery, makeovers, and beyond. Mason Crest Publishers 2005 128p il (Science of health) $24.95
Grades: 7 8 9 10   613
1. Personal grooming 2. Teenagers -- Health and

hygiene
ISBN 1-59084-843-8

LC 2004-1883

"Framing her discussion within an examination of the media influence on our culture's definition of beauty, Libal does an excellent job of discussing the risks and benefits of cosmetics, piercing and tattooing, diet, exercise, and cosmetic surgery. . . . The author also considers, in some detail, the dangers of anorexia nervosa, bulimia, and steroid use." SLJ

Includes bibliographical references

McCoy, Kathleen

The **teenage** body book; [by] Kathy McCoy and Charles Wibbelsman; illustrations by Bob Stover and Kelly Grady. Rev and updated; Hatherleigh 2008 300p il pa $17.95

Grades: 7 8 9 10 11 12   **613**
1. Adolescence 2. Sex education 3. Sex instruction for youth 4. Teenagers -- Health and hygiene
ISBN 978-1-57826-277-9

LC 2009-368424

First published 1979 by Pocket Bks. with authors' names in reverse order

A handbook for teenagers discussing nutrition, health, fitness, emotions, and sexuality, including such topics as body image, drugs, STDs, fad diets and hazards and benefits of the Internet.

"This highly informative book . . . is at the same time easily readable, nonpreachy, and comprehensive. . . . This book should be not only in the library of every middle and high school, but also in the hands of every student and in health education classes." Sci Books Films

Natterson, Cara

The **care** & keeping of you 2; the body book for older girls. Dr. Cara Natterson; illustrated by Josee Masse. American Girl 2013 96 p. (paperback) $12.99

Grades: 5 6 7 8   **613**
1. Puberty 2. Life skills -- Handbooks, manuals, etc. 3. Teenage girls -- Health and hygiene
ISBN 1609580427; 9781609580421

LC 2012045813

This book, by Cara Natterson, illustrated by Josee Masse, is a body image and physiology guide written for girls going through puberty. "This . . . advice book will guide you through the next steps of growing up. . . . This book covers new questions about periods, your growing body, peer pressure, personal care, and more." (Publisher's note)

"The friendly illustrations support the overall tone and style. . . . Its neutral, matter-of-fact approach will help show readers . . . that all the changes they may be feeling are perfectly normal." SLJ

Orr, Tamra

★ **Playing** safe, eating right; making healthy choices. ABDO Pub. 2009 112p il (Essential health: strong beautiful girls) lib bdg $22.95

Grades: 6 7 8 9   **613**
1. Health 2. Nutrition 3. Teenagers -- Health and

hygiene
ISBN 978-1-60453-103-9 lib bdg; 1-60453-103-7 lib bdg

LC 2008-17015

This features fictional narratives paired with firsthand advice from a licensed psychologist to help preteen and teen girls evaluate options and choose healthy ways of living. Topics include diet and exercise, sleep, drugs and alcohol.

"The topics are well selected, the design is attractive, and the stories features girls from a variety of cultures." Booklist

Includes glossary and bibliographical references

Pfeifer, Kate Gruenwald

★ **American** Medical Assocation boy's guide to becoming a teen. Jossey-Bass 2006 128p il pa $12.95

Grades: 4 5 6 7   **613**
1. Puberty 2. Adolescence 3. Boys -- Health and hygiene
ISBN 0-7879-8343-8

"This guide addresses puberty's changes clearly. . . . The text's approach is straightforward, accessible, and nonjudgmental, whether the topic is same-sex attraction or divorcing parents. The volume closes with an extensive resource section, including hotlines." Booklist

Includes bibliographical references

★ **American** Medical Association girl's guide to becoming a teen. Jossey-Bass 2006 128p pa $12.95

Grades: 4 5 6 7   **613**
1. Puberty 2. Adolescence 3. Girls -- Health and hygiene
ISBN 0-7879-8344-6

This "covers the physical and emotional changes that puberty brings, along with solid tips about grooming, diet, exercise, and other health issues, such as eating disorders. . . . The clear text communicates concepts clearly . . . and girls will find plenty of useful information." Booklist

Includes bibliographical references

Reber, Deborah

Chill; stress-reducing techniques for a more balanced, peaceful you. Simon Pulse 2008 196p il pa $9.99

Grades: 8 9 10 11 12   **613**
1. Stress (Psychology) 2. Girls -- Health and hygiene
ISBN 978-1-4169-5526-9 pa; 1-4169-5526-7 pa

"This book has just the right combination of smart wit, know-it-all bravado, and advice from a pseudo big sister. The pages speed by, moving from topic to topic: time management, support systems, self-help therapy, exercise, nutrition, and more. Advice is free-flowing, complete with examples, exercises, and quizzes. . . . This helpful resource will appeal to a wide variety of young women." SLJ

613.2 Dietetics

Ballard, Carol

Food for feeling healthy; [by] Carol Ballard. Heinemann Library 2006 56p il (Making healthy food choices) $32.86; pa $9.49

Grades: 7 8 9 10   **613.2**

1. Nutrition

ISBN 978-1-4034-8571-7; 1-4034-8571-2; 978-1-4034-8577-9 pa; 1-4034-8577-1 pa

LC 2006003970

"Ballard incorporates the new food pyramid into a discussion of basic nutritional requirements. She considers obesity, malnutrition, and eating disorders and comments on various factors that influence eating choices, such as advertising and peer pressure. After helping readers decipher food labels, she provides a week's worth of menus." SLJ

Includes bibliographical references

Can diets be harmful? edited by Christine Watkins. Greenhaven Press 2012 101 p. (At issue) (library) $34.45; (paperback) $25.45

Grades: 8 9 10 11 12   **613.2**

1. Diet 2. Eating habits 3. Diet in disease 4. Reducing diets -- Heath aspects

ISBN 9780737755565 lib bdg; 9780737755572 pa

LC 2011020813

This book, edited by Christine Watkins, is part of the At Issue series and looks at diets. The series "provides a wide range of opinions on individual social issues. Each volume focuses on a specific issue and offers a variety of perspectives—eyewitness accounts, governmental views, scientific analysis, newspaper and magazine accounts, and many more—to illuminate the issue." (Publisher's note)

Includes bibliographical references (p. 93-97) and index.

Currie, Stephen

Junk food. Cherry Lake Pub. 2009 32p il (Health at risk) lib bdg $27.07

Grades: 4 5 6 7 8   **613.2**

1. Nutrition

ISBN 978-1-60279-284-5 lib bdg; 1-60279-284-4 lib bdg

LC 2008017498

This describes what junk food is, why it's not good for your body, and what's being done to help us control our junk food habit.

"Great for reports or reluctant readers." Booklist

Includes bibliographical references

Dieting; Claire Kreger Boaz, book editor. Greenhaven Press 2008 117p il (Issues that concern you) lib bdg $33.70

Grades: 8 9 10 11 12   **613.2**

1. Weight loss

ISBN 978-0-7377-3644-1 lib bdg; 0-7377-3644-5 lib bdg

LC 2007-35368

This title presents various views on dieting and weight loss.

Includes bibliographical references

Doeden, Matt

Eat right! how you can make good food choices. illustrations by Jack Desrocher. Lerner Publications 2008 64p il (Health zone) lib bdg $30.60

Grades: 4 5 6 7   **613.2**

1. Nutrition

ISBN 978-0-8225-7552-8; 0-8225-7552-3

LC 2007043322

"This offers a highly readable, never preachy exploration into the benefits of providing quality fuel for your body. It opens with an anecdote of a kid who snacks on soda and chips while playing volleyball. A friend challenges him to to eat better for a week, and he comes back with more sustained energy and a fresh outlook. . . . The following chapters do a great job of detailing everything from the food pyramid and benefits of different nutrients to warnings against following the faddish, ineffective diets." Booklist

Includes bibliographical references

Edwards, Hazel

Talking about your weight; by Hazel Edwards and Goldie Alexander. Gareth Stevens 2010 32p il (Healthy living) lib bdg $26

Grades: 4 5 6 7   **613.2**

1. Obesity 2. Nutrition 3. Weight loss

ISBN 978-1-4339-3655-5; 1-4339-3655-0

"This guidebook offers a simple look at healthy lifestyle choices involving exercise and diet. It examines people's relationships with food, body shape and genetics, eating disorders, and ways to combat obesity." Publisher's note

Favor, Lesli J.

Weighing in; nutrition and weight management. Marshall Cavendish Benchmark 2007 128p il (Food and fitness) lib bdg $28

Grades: 7 8 9 10   **613.2**

1. Nutrition 2. Weight loss

ISBN 0761443673; 9780761443674

LC 2006-101930

This "offers an in-depth look at issues related to body weight. Chapters . . . discuss determining one's ideal weight; health risks associated with weight, from diabetes to anorexia; nutrition and wellness; teen dietary requirements and meal planning; and weight-loss strategies, with possible dangers highlighted. . . . Teens will find this a useful, often thought-provoking resource for personal or class research." Booklist

Includes bibliographical references

Furgang, Adam

Carbonated beverages; the incredibly disgusting story. Rosen Central 2011 48p il (Incredibly disgusting food) lib bdg $26.50; pa $11.75

Grades: 4 5 6 7   **613.2**

1. Carbonated beverages

ISBN 978-1-4488-1266-0 lib bdg; 1-4488-1266-6 lib bdg; 978-1-4488-2282-9 pa; 1-4488-2282-3 pa

LC 2010023227

This presents "straightforward information about why [carbonated beverages] are unhealthy without resorting to extreme gross-out factors. The [book contains] a breakdown of the foods' components . . . insight into how they are processed, and both short- and long-term effects of consumption. . . . Readers may or may not be disgusted, but they will definitely learn a thing or two about smart eating habits." SLJ

Includes glossary and bibliographical references

Salty and sugary snacks; the incredibly disgusting story. Rosen Central 2011 48p il (Incredibly disgusting food) lib bdg $26.50; pa $11.75

Grades: 4 5 6 7   **613.2**
1. Salt 2. Sugar 3. Nutrition 4. Snack foods
ISBN 978-1-4488-1267-7 lib bdg; 1-4488-1267-4 lib bdg; 978-1-4488-2283-6 pa; 1-4488-2283-1 pa
LC 2010025751
This book describes how salty and sugary snacks put dangerous amounts of sugar and salt into our bodies and how these unnecessary calories can have terrible effects on the body.

"Readers may or may not be disgusted, but they will definitely learn a thing or two about smart eating habits." SLJ
Includes glossary and bibliographical references

Gay, Kathlyn

The **scoop** on what to eat; what you should know about diet and nutrition. Enslow Publishers 2009 112p il (Issues in focus today) lib bdg $31.93

Grades: 7 8 9 10   **613.2**
1. Nutrition
ISBN 978-0-7660-3066-4; 0-7660-3066-0
LC 2008-40382
"Bolstered with well-integrated quotes and relevant statistics, [this book offers] an excellent starting point for students seeking [a] broad, thoroughly researched [introduction] to [diet and nutrition]. . . . Illuminating case studies, enhanced with multiple viewpoints, personalize the facts and place them in boarder context." Booklist
Includes glossary and bibliographical references

Heller, Tania

Overweight; a handbook for teens and parents. [by] Tania Heller; foreword by Mohsen Ziai. McFarland & Company 2005 180p pa $29.95

Grades: 7 8 9 10   **613.2**
1. Obesity 2. Weight loss 3. Teenagers -- Health and hygiene
ISBN 9781476603995; 0-7864-2082-0
LC 2005004360
"This work covers the causes and effects of the rise in childhood obesity while presenting . . . guidelines and recommendations for getting assessed and treated. Information is provided on healthy nutrition and physical activity for young people, tools for self-monitoring and medical conditions associated with weight gain." Publisher's note
Includes glossary and bibliographical references

Johanson, Paula

Fake foods; fried, fast, and processed: the incredibly disgusting story. Rosen Central 2011 48p il (Incredibly disgusting food) lib bdg $26.50; pa $11.75

Grades: 4 5 6 7   **613.2**
1. Nutrition 2. Natural foods 3. Convenience foods
ISBN 978-1-4488-1269-1 lib bdg; 1-4488-1269-0 lib bdg; 978-1-4488-2285-0 pa; 1-4488-2285-8 pa
LC 2010020534
This presents "straightforward information about why various junk foods are unhealthy without resorting to extreme gross-out factors. The [book contains] a breakdown of the foods' components . . . insight into how they are processed, and both short- and long-term effects of consumption. . . . Readers may or may not be disgusted, but they will definitely learn a thing or two about smart eating habits." SLJ

Includes glossary and bibliographical references

Juettner, Bonnie

Diet and disease. Lucent Books 2011 104p il (Nutrition & health) $30.85

Grades: 6 7 8 9   **613.2**
1. Nutrition 2. Preventive medicine
ISBN 978-1-4205-0269-5; 1-4205-0269-7
LC 2010035236
This "discusses the food choices that lead to the 'big four' diseases of cancer, heart disease, stroke, and type 2 diabetes and shows how good nutrition can help prevent deadly disease. . . . [This] volume is clearly written, addressing real-life concerns with solid information and perspective, and includes color photographs, notes, and [a list] of further resources." Booklist
Includes bibliographical references

Libal, Autumn

Fats, sugars, and empty calories; the fast food habit. Mason Crest Publishers 2006 104p il (Obesity: modern day epidemic) $23.95

Grades: 7 8 9 10   **613.2**
1. Health 2. Obesity 3. Nutrition
ISBN 978-1-59084-943-9; 1-59084-943-4
LC 2004-15660
Discusses the dangers of fast food.
Includes glossary and bibliographical references

Mooney, Carla

Junk food junkies. Lucent Books 2010 104p il (Nutrition & health) $30.85

Grades: 6 7 8 9   **613.2**
1. Nutrition
ISBN 978-1-4205-0271-8; 1-4205-0271-9
LC 2010016858
"A solid, detailed overview of the negative effects of a poor diet on health. Mooney livens up the dry subject matter with interesting nutrition facts, photographs, charts, tables, and anecdotes. She discusses health risks such as obesity and diabetes. The last chapter is particularly useful because it offers healthy alternatives for snacks and meals. It also explains how to read a nutrition label and tells readers what to avoid in terms of amounts of fat and calories. This book is useful for research and reports and as a teaching aid." SLJ
Includes glossary and bibliographical references

Morris, Neil

Food for sports; [by] Neil Morris. Heinemann Library 2006 56p il (Making healthy food choices) $32.86; pa $9.49

Grades: 7 8 9 10   **613.2**

1. Sports 2. Nutrition

ISBN 978-1-4034-8573-1; 1-4034-8573-9; 978-1-4034-8579-3 pa; 1-4034-8579-8 pa

LC 2006003971

This "talks about the types of foods that help athletes maximize their energy level. The information on sensible eating choices and calorie intake can help even non-athletes manage their health and weight. . . . [This is] well written. . . . There aren't many books out there that examine all aspects of food in such detail." SLJ

Includes bibliographical references

Rau, Dana Meachen

Going organic; a healthy guide to making the switch. by Dana Meachen Rau. Compass Point Books 2012 64 p. col. ill. (paperback) $8.95; (hardcover) $33.99

Grades: 6 7 8 9   **613.2**

1. Diet 2. Nutrition 3. Natural foods 4. Organic farming 5. Health

ISBN 0756545234; 0756545285; 9780756545239; 9780756545284

LC 2011040704

"[Rau] outlines the perils of factory farms and industrial food lots, both on an environmental and personal scale; distinguishes the often interrelated terms organic, sustainable, and local; offers a rundown of potentially misleading marketing terms; and even tosses in a few recipes, charts, and other helpful sidebars. Readers who find their interest piqued by this informative and concise treatment..." Booklist

Schwartz, Ellen

I'm a vegetarian; amazing facts and ideas for healthy vegetarians. illustrated by Farida Zaman. Tundra Bks. 2002 112p il pa $9.95

Grades: 6 7 8 9   **613.2**

1. Vegetarianism

ISBN 0-88776-588-2; 9781770490604

LC 2001-95376

"The author opens with an overview of the different types of vegetarians and the rationale behind their decisions, then moves into advice on handling parental concerns and sticky social situations that are sure to arise. A consideration of nutrition and how to achieve a healthy diet that provides all necessary nutrients follows, ending with a smattering of suggested menus and recipes. . . . She writes in a light, chatty tone, using a question-and-answer format, bulleted facts and lists, boxed information, and humor. Black-and-white drawings throughout add to the book's appeal." SLJ

Includes glossary and bibliographical references

Smolin, Lori A.

Nutrition and weight management; [by] Lori A. Smolin and Mary B. Grosvenor. 2nd ed.; Chelsea House 2010 184p il map (Healthy eating: a guide to nutrition) lib bdg $35

Grades: 7 8 9 10 11 12   **613.2**

1. Nutrition 2. Weight loss

ISBN 978-1-60413-803-0; 1-60413-803-3

LC 2009-41335

First published 2005

This "volume uses boldface type to introduce important and unknown words to the reader and explains them in an easy to understand manner so the reader can grasp the concept being discussed. . . . [For] classes needing information about the importance of good nutrition . . . [this] would be valuable." Libr Media Connect

Includes glossary and bibliographical references

Watson, Stephanie

Mystery meat; hot dogs, sausages, and lunch meats: the incredibly disgusting story. Rosen Pub. Group 2011 48p il (Incredibly disgusting food) lib bdg $26.50; pa $11.75

Grades: 4 5 6 7   **613.2**

1. Meat 2. Sausages 3. Nutrition 4. Frankfurters

ISBN 978-1-4488-1268-4 lib bdg; 1-4488-1268-2 lib bdg; 978-1-4488-2284-3 pa; 1-4488-2284-X pa

LC 2010013649

"The short but substantive chapters begin with a look at typical hot-dog ingredients and manufacturing practices, followed by discussions of how 'mystery meats,' including common, highly processed sandwich fillers, affect the body. A closing chapter about the components of a healthy diet widens the book into an opportunity for adults and kids to discuss general nutrition and includes useful tips on reading food labels. . . . Young readers will find plenty of browsing and report fodder in these pages." Booklist

Includes bibliographical references

Woog, Adam

Food myths and facts. Lucent Books 2011 96p il (Nutrition & health) lib bdg $30.85

Grades: 6 7 8 9   **613.2**

1. Nutrition

ISBN 978-1-4205-0270-1; 1-4205-0270-0

LC 2010035960

This "aims to clear up nutritional misinformation on topics like metabolism, sports drinks, and fad diets. . . . [This] volume is clearly written, addressing real-life concerns with solid information and perspective, and includes color photographs, notes, and [a list] of further resources." Booklist

Includes bibliographical references

Zahensky, Barbara A.

Diet fads. Rosen 2007 64p il (Danger zone: dieting and eating disorders) lib bdg $27.95

Grades: 4 5 6 7 8   **613.2**

1. Obesity 2. Weight loss

ISBN 978-1-4042-1999-1

"This clearly written overview emphasizes the impact of super-thin celebrity images on general self-esteem. . . . Zahensky considers the reasons people overeat and walks readers through practical steps to recognizing true hunger, making a weight-loss plan, and establishing good diet and exercise habits. She examines different types of fad and crash diets, pointing out their inherent dangers." SLJ

613.208   Young people

★ **Diabetes** information for teens; health tips about managing diabetes and preventing related complications, including facts about insulin, glucose control, healthy eating, physical activity, and learning to live with diabetes. edited by Karen Bellenir. Omnigraphics 2012 397 p. ill. (hardcover : alk. paper) $69.00

Grades: 7 8 9 10 11 12   **613.208**
1. Diabetes 2. Teenagers -- Health and hygiene 3. Diabetes in adolescence
ISBN 0780812182; 9780780812185
                                    LC 2011038652
This book for teenagers on the topic of diabetes, edited by Karen Bellenir, "examines the alarming trends in diabetes prevalence, and it provides information about positive steps that can be taken. The book provides facts about the different types of diabetes, its medical management, and the roles of nutrition and physical activity in averting its consequences. Suggestions are included for handling problematic situations, such as caring for diabetes at school." (Publisher's note)
Includes bibliographical references and index

★ **Diet** information for teens; health tips about nutrition fundamentals and eating plans including facts about vitamins, minerals, food additives, and weight-related concerns. edited by Zachary Klimecki and Karen Bellenir. 3rd ed. Omnigraphics, Inc. 2012 xiii, 427 p.p ill. (Teen health series) (hardcover : alk. paper) $69

Grades: 8 9 10 11 12   **613.208**
1. Diet 2. Health 3. Teenagers -- Health and hygiene 4. Teenagers -- Nutrition
ISBN 0780811569; 9780780811560
                                    LC 2011031595
This book is a "compendium of diet and nutrition" for teenagers comprising "articles on all facets of nutrition, drawn mainly from FDA documents. . . . Chapters of specialized appeal include 'Special Dietary Guidelines for Teenage Mothers' and 'Assessing School Lunches,' as well as coverage of teen snacking." (School Library Journal)
Includes bibliographical references and index

613.6   Personal safety and special topics of health

Champion, Neil
    Finding food and water. Amicus 2010 32p il (Survive alive) lib bdg $28.50

Grades: 4 5 6 7   **613.6**
1. Wilderness survival
ISBN 978-1-60753-037-4 lib bdg; 1-60753-037-6 lib bdg
                                    LC 2009030889
This offers survival tips for finding food and water in the wild, including how to know what is safe to eat or drink from land, plant, and animal sources.

This "colorful [book contains] numerous photos and illustrations that effectively break the [text] into small, readable chunks. There's lots of practical, everyday information here. . . . Brief yet gripping real-life survival stories are interspersed throughout the [book]." SLJ
Includes glossary

Finding your way. Amicus 2011 32p il (Survive alive) lib bdg $28.50

Grades: 4 5 6 7   **613.6**
1. Orienteering 2. Wilderness survival
ISBN 978-1-60753-038-1 lib bdg; 1-60753-038-4 lib bdg
                                    LC 2009030888
"With eye-catching photographs, clear explanations, a survival skills quiz, a glossary, Web sites, and 'True Survival' stories . . . this engaging text encourages readers to figure out where they are and where they want to go." Booklist
Includes glossary

In an emergency. Amicus 2010 32p il (Survive alive) lib bdg $28.50

Grades: 4 5 6 7   **613.6**
1. Survival skills
ISBN 978-1-60753-040-4; 1-60753-040-6
                                    LC 2010002517
This offers survival tips on what to do in emergency situations. Includes scenarios about fire, bad weather, accidents, injuries, extreme conditions, and more.'
This "colorful [book contains] numerous photos and illustrations that effectively break the [text] into small, readable chunks. There's lots of practical, everyday information here. . . . Brief yet gripping real-life survival stories are interspersed throughout the [book]." SLJ
Includes glossary

Making shelter. Amicus 2010 32p il (Survive alive) lib bdg $28.50

Grades: 4 5 6 7   **613.6**
1. Wilderness survival
ISBN 978-1-60753-041-1 lib bdg; 1-60753-041-4 lib bdg
                                    LC 2010001378
This offers survival tips for building shelter in the wild, including using natural means in different regions such as the desert, forest, jungle, and cold areas. Also includes information on what to bring for aid when building shelters.

Hurley, Michael
    Surviving the wilderness. Raintree 2011 56p il (Extreme survival) lib bdg $33.50

Grades: 4 5 6 7   **613.6**
1. Wilderness survival
ISBN 978-1-4109-3972-2; 1-4109-3972-3
                                    LC 2010028839
This book is "fun and informative. [This] well-organized title starts with an overview [of wilderness survival], offers some specific examples, and includes additional facts or tips and resources. . . . [It features] dramatic archival and full-color photos on nearly every page. . . . [This is a book] that youngsters will enjoy and talk about." SLJ
Includes glossary and bibliographical references

Long, Denise

Survivor kid; a practical guide to wilderness survival. Chicago Review Press 2011 222p il $12.95

Grades: 4 5 6 7   **613.6**

1. Wilderness survival

ISBN 978-1-56976-708-5; 1-56976-708-4

LC 2011004952

"Long offers lessons on how to stay healthy and out of trouble while awaiting rescue. Her matter-of-fact, no-nonsense tone will play well with young readers, and the clear writing style is appropriate to the content. The engaging guide covers everything from building shelters to avoiding pigs and javelinas. . . . The volume invites browsing as much as studying. . . . An excellent bibliography will lead young readers to a host of fascinating websites, and 150 clipart-style line drawings complement the text." Kirkus

Includes bibliographical references

Nelson, Sara Kirsten

Stay safe! how you can keep out of harm's way. by Sara Nelson; illustrated by Jack Desrocher. Lerner Publications 2008 64p il (Health zone) lib bdg $30.60

Grades: 4 5 6 7   **613.6**

1. Safety education 2. Children and strangers 3. Child sexual abuse -- Prevention

ISBN 978-0-8225-7551-1; 0-8225-7551-5

The offers safety education on such subjects as bullying in schools, inappropriate touching by family members, internet solicitations and threats in public places (such as attempted abductions).

"The format is beyond lively, with lots of color, cartoons, and an informal writing style, but it manages to present sometimes frightening material in a non-threatening and browsable way." Booklist

Includes glossary and bibliographical references

Raatma, Lucia

Safety in your neighborhood. Child's World 2005 32p il (Living well) lib bdg $25.64

Grades: 4 5 6 7   **613.6**

1. Crime prevention 2. Safety education

ISBN 1-59296-240-8

LC 2003-27214

This book teaches young readers how to keep their neighborhood a safe place and what to do if that safety is compromised.

This "clearly written [title has] an appealing layout with plenty of full-color photos and a triple-spaced text. . . . [It] provides solid tips." SLJ

Includes glossary and bibliographical references

Doeden, Matt

Safety smarts; how to manage threats, protect yourself, get help, and more. Matt Doeden. Twenty-First Century Books 2013 64 p. col. ill. (USA today teen wise guides : lifestyle choices) (library) $31.93

Grades: 8 9 10 11 12   **613.6**

1. Safety education 2. Teenagers -- Crimes against --

Prevention

ISBN 0761370226; 9780761370222

LC 2011044268

This book, by Matt Doeden, offers advice for teen safety as part of the "USA Today Teen Wise Guides: Lifestyle Choices" series. "In a perfect world, everyone would be safe all the time: in the car, at home, at school, and online. Well, . . . cars sometimes crash, burglars break into houses, kids get bullied at school, and cyberstalkers and sexual predators prowl the Internet. But that's no reason to hide in your room and worry. You can stay safe if you use some safety smarts." (Publisher's note)

Includes bibliographical references (p. 61-63) and index.

613.7   Physical fitness

Aikman, Louise

Pilates step-by-step; [by] Louise Aikman and Matthew Harvey. Rosen Central 2011 93p il (Skills in motion) lib bdg $31.95

Grades: 5 6 7 8   **613.7**

1. Pilates method

ISBN 978-1-4488-1549-4; 1-4488-1549-5

LC 2010007510

Presents a general guide to the Pilates exercise system using a sequence of stop-action images and text instructions to illustrate some of the most common movements.

Includes bibliographical references

Atha, Antony

Fitness for young people; step-by-step. [by] Antony Atha and Simon Frost. Rosen Central 2010 93p il (Skills in motion) lib bdg $31.95

Grades: 5 6 7 8   **613.7**

1. Physical fitness

ISBN 978-1-4358-3364-7; 1-4358-3364-3

LC 2009-13245

Describes how to maintain physical fitness for youth, providing exercises that are both effective and fun.

"Colorful photographs show the entire movement of each skill presented, giving new meaning to the term 'step-by-step.' Progression borders at the bottom of the pages highlight the salient points to notice in performing each skill from beginning to end." SLJ

Includes bibliographical references

Bellenir, Elizabeth

Fitness Information for Teens; Health Tips About Exercise & Active Lifestyles. edited by Elizabeth Bellenir. 3rd ed. Omnigraphics 2012 xiii, 387 p.p ill. (Teen health series) (hardcover : alk. paper) $69.00

Grades: 7 8 9 10 11 12   **613.7**

1. Physical fitness 2. Teenagers -- Health and hygiene 3. Physical fitness for youth

ISBN 9780780812673; 0780812670

LC 2012024737

This book is "earmarked to provide the tools and information needed for teens to engage in a healthier lifestyle before entering adulthood. . . . Seven main sections cover information on the human body, personal fitness plans, exercise fundamentals, team activities, sports safety, obstacles to finding fitness, and resources." (Booklist)

"In this thorough, easy-to-follow single volume, seven main sections cover information on the human body, personal fitness plans, exercise fundamentals, team activities, sports safety, obstacles to finding fitness, and resources... Highly recommended." Booklist

Includes bibliographical references and index

Birkemoe, Karen

★ **Strike** a pose; the Planet Girl guide to yoga. written by Karen Birkemoe; illustrated by Heather Collett. Kids Can Press 2007 96p il (Planet girl) spiral $12.95

Grades: 5 6 7 8   **613.7**

  1. Yoga 2. Girls -- Health and hygiene

  ISBN 978-1-55337-004-8

"This compact book offers a well-rounded overview of Hatha yoga. Using an easy conversational tone, Birkemoe relates the general practice and specific poses to reader's lives. The simple line drawings and color illustrations partner effectively with text to explain each move." SLJ

  Includes glossary

Dicker, Katie

Exercise. Amicus 2010 46p il (Healthy lifestyles) lib bdg $32.80

Grades: 7 8 9 10   **613.7**

  1. Exercise 2. Physical fitness

  ISBN 978-1-60753-086-2; 1-60753-086-4

                    LC 2009-47566

This book is "well-written and satisfyingly informative. . . . [The] magazine-like format includes numerous sidebars, color photos, and charts." SLJ

  Includes glossary

Eason, Sarah

Free running; by Paul Mason and Sarah Eason. Lerner Publications 2011 32p il (On the radar: sports) $26.60

Grades: 5 6 7 8   **613.7**

  1. Running 2. Parkour

  ISBN 076137759X; 9780761377597

                    LC 2011000467

"Free running, also known as parkour, is a combination of speed running, gymnastics, and, in some cases, sheer fearlessness. Lovers of the sport launch over walls, clear fences in a single bound, and somersault down stairwells. This . . . captures the adrenaline-fueled energy of runners, using bold graphics, bright colors, and short interviews to showcase professionals, demonstrate moves, and trace the origins of free running." Booklist

Frederick, Shane

Strength training for teen athletes; exercises to take your game to the next level. by Karen Latchana Kenney. Capstone Press 2012 48 p. col. ill. (paperback) $7.95; (library binding) $31.32

Grades: 6 7 8 9   **613.7**

  1. Athletes 2. Exercise 3. Weight lifting 4. Teenagers

-- Health and hygiene 5. Muscle strength 6. Teenage athletes -- Training of

ISBN 1429676809; 9781429680028; 1429680024; 9781429676809

                    LC 2011033561

Author Karen Latchana Kenney provides a guide for teenage athletes on how to improve their performance with strength training. "With . . . strength building exercises and tips, you'll notice a big improvement in your game. Build the power behind your baseball or softball swing, soccer kick, or swimming stroke." (Publisher's note)

Includes bibliographical references and index.

Gedatus, Gus

Exercise for weight management. LifeMatters 2001 64p il (Nutrition and fitness) lib bdg $23.93

Grades: 7 8 9 10   **613.7**

  1. Exercise 2. Physical fitness

  ISBN 9780736807067; 0-7368-0706-3

                    LC 00-34899

This offers information on physical fitness and setting up a healthy exercise plan

"This brief, well-designed title delivers informative and relevant material for the serious teen reader." Sci Books Films

  Includes glossary and bibliographical references

Jennings, Madeleine

Tai chi step-by-step; [by] Madeleine Jennings and James Drewe. Rosen Central 2011 93p il (Skills in motion) lib bdg $31.95

Grades: 5 6 7 8   **613.7**

  1. Tai chi

  ISBN 978-1-4488-1551-7; 1-4488-1551-7

                    LC 2010008411

This book introduces both basic and higher level techniques of tai chi, with step-by-step instructions, illustrated by stop-motion sequential photography.

  Includes bibliographical references

Kuskowski, Alex

Cool relaxing; healthy & fun ways to chill out! Alex Kuskowski. ABDO Pub. Co. 2012 32 p. col. ill. (Cool health and fitness) (library) $28.50

Grades: 4 5 6   **613.7**

  1. Creative activities 2. Rest 3. Relaxation

  ISBN 1617834289; 9781617834288

                    LC 2012010345

This nonfiction children's book by Alex Kuskowski presents a "hodgepodge of activities and techniques to achieve zen calm. The suggestions in this 'Cool Health and Fitness' title are all over the place--cooking, running, reading, baths, even cleaning--but that's the unspoken truth: whatever pleasantly distracts you does the trick. Eight activities are given step-by-step attention, including yoga, stretching, making a lavender pillow, and meditation." (Booklist)

Mason, Paul, 1967-

Improving endurance. PowerKids Press 2011 32p il (Training for sports) lib bdg $25.25

Grades: 5 6 7 8   **613.7**
  1. Sports 2. Exercise
  ISBN 978-1-4488-3300-9; 1-4488-3300-0
                      LC 2010024356
This offers "detailed tips on improving . . . endurance. All-around athletes will love this and so will kids who just want to work on getting fit." Booklist

Improving flexibility. PowerKids Press 2011 32p il (Training for sports) lib bdg $25.25
Grades: 5 6 7 8   **613.7**
  1. Sports 2. Exercise
  ISBN 978-1-4488-3299-6; 1-4488-3299-3
                      LC 2010024359
This offers tips on improving flexibility for sports.
  "All-around athletes will love this and so will kids who just want to work on getting fit." Booklist

Improving speed. PowerKids Press 2011 32p il (Training for sports) lib bdg $25.25
Grades: 5 6 7 8   **613.7**
  1. Speed 2. Sports 3. Exercise
  ISBN 978-1-4488-3302-3; 1-4488-3302-3
                      LC 2010024354
This offers "detailed tips on improving speed. . . . All-around athletes will love this and so will kids who just want to work on getting fit." Booklist

Improving strength & power. PowerKids Press 2011 32p il (Training for sports) lib bdg $25.25
Grades: 5 6 7 8   **613.7**
  1. Exercise 2. Physical fitness
  ISBN 978-1-4488-3301-6; 1-4488-3301-6
                      LC 2010024425
This offers tips on improving strength and power for sports.
  "All-around athletes will love this and so will kids who just want to work on getting fit." Booklist

Purperhart, Helen
  Yoga exercises for teens; developing a calmer mind and a stronger body. Hunter House Publishers 2008 160p il pa $14.95
Grades: 7 8 9 10   **613.7**
  1. Yoga 2. Physical fitness 3. Teenagers -- Health and hygiene
  ISBN 978-0-8979-3503-6; 0-8979-3503-9
                      LC 2008-24262
This book about yoga "includes the eight yoga rules for life, the five precepts, and the five yoga abstinences." Publisher's note
Includes bibliographical references

Spilling, Michael
  Yoga step-by-step; [by] Michael Spilling and Liz Lark. Rosen Central 2011 95p il (Skills in motion) lib bdg $31.95
Grades: 5 6 7 8   **613.7**
  1. Yoga
  ISBN 978-1-4488-1550-0; 1-4488-1550-9
                      LC 2010008665

Readers are introduced to basic yoga techniques through step-by-step instructions, depicted with numerous photographs.
Includes bibliographical references

Vedral, Joyce L.
  Toning for teens; the 20-minute workout that makes you look good and feel great! Warner Bks. 2002 165p il pa $15.95
Grades: 7 8 9 10   **613.7**
  1. Exercise 2. Physical fitness 3. Teenagers -- Health and hygiene
  ISBN 9780446678155; 0-446-67815-5
                      LC 2002-101020
The author offers a "workout specifically aimed at helping adolescent girls tone and firm their muscles using free weights. . . . The author emphasizes sound nutrition and exercise information. . . . The exercises are clearly described, and illustrated with photos of teens performing the routines." SLJ

613.8 Substance abuse (Drug abuse)

★ **Drug** information for teens; health tips about the physical and mental effects of substance abuse. edited by Elizabeth Magill. 3rd ed. Omnigraphics 2011 xiv, 490 p.p ill. (hardcover) $69
Grades: 7 8 9 10 11 12   **613.8**
  1. Teenagers -- Drug use 2. Teenagers -- Health and hygiene 3. Drug abuse 4. Drugs -- Physiological effect 5. Teenagers -- Drug use -- United States 6. Alcoholism -- United States -- Prevention 7. Drug abuse -- United States -- Prevention 8. Teenagers -- Alcohol use -- United States 9. Teenagers -- Health and hygiene -- United States
  ISBN 0780811542; 9780780811546
                      LC 2010048932
This book "provides updated facts about drug use, abuse, and addiction. It describes the physical and psychological effects of alcohol, marijuana, prescription drugs, inhalants, club drugs, stimulants, and many other commonly abused drugs and chemicals. It includes information about drug-related health concerns. . . . A section on substance abuse treatment describes care options and provides resources for addiction recovery." (Publisher's note)

613.81 Alcohol

★ **Alcohol** information for teens; health tips about alcohol use, abuse & dependence including facts about alcohol's effects on mental and physical health, the consequences of underage drinking & understanding alcoholic family members. edited by Karen Bellenir. 3rd ed. Omnigraphics, Inc. 2013 371 p. (hardcover) $69
Grades: 7 8 9 10 11 12   **613.81**
  1. Alcoholism 2. Teenagers -- Alcohol use 3. Drinking

of alcoholic beverages
ISBN 0780813138; 9780780813137

LC 2013000216

This book "provides updated information about the use and misuse of alcohol. It describes ways alcohol can affect mental and physical health. It discusses the special vulnerabilities of the teen brain and the changes in brain functioning that lead to dependency. A section on treatment and recovery discusses achieving and maintaining sobriety, and a section on alcohol abuse in the family addresses the special concerns of teens who live with an alcoholic relative." (Publisher's note)

Includes bibliographical references and index

613.9   Birth control, reproductive technology, sex hygiene, sexual techniques

Bell, Ruth

Changing bodies, changing lives; a book for teens on sex and relationships. [by] Ruth Bell and other co-authors of Our bodies, ourselves and Ourselves and our children, together with members of the Teen Book Project. expanded 3rd ed; Times Bks. 1998 411p il pa $24.95

Grades: 7 8 9 10 11 12   613.9

1. Sex education
ISBN 0-8129-2990-X

LC 97-29249

First published 1980

This is a "book on sex, physical and emotional health, and personal relationships. . . . Readers . . . will find emotional support as well as specific answers to most of their questions in this nonjudgmental resource." Booklist

Bringle, Jennifer

Reproductive rights; making the right choices. Rosen Pub. 2010 112p il (A young woman's guide to contemporary issues) lib bdg $31.95

Grades: 7 8 9 10   613.9

1. Pregnancy 2. Birth control 3. Teenage mothers
ISBN 978-1-4358-3542-9; 1-4358-3542-5

LC 2009-13721

"Facts are shared in a conversational tone, creating the sense of a chat with a big sister. . . . [Though] designed for personal reading and browsing, the data provided are accurate and also lend themselves to use in reports." SLJ

Includes glossary and bibliographical references

Cole, Joanna

Asking about sex & growing up; a question-and-answer book for kids. illustrated by Bill Thomas. rev ed.; Collins 2009 89p il $15.99; pa $6.99

Grades: 4 5 6   613.9

1. Sex education
ISBN 978-0-06-142987-3; 0-06-142987-2; 978-0-06-142986-6 pa; 0-06-142986-4 pa

LC 2008022710

First published 1988 by Morrow Junior Books

This book "offers straightforward information about topics such as physical changes in puberty, masturbation, birth

control, pregnancy, homosexuality, and STDs. . . . Libraries . . . should consider adding it as a source of basic information for curious preteens." SLJ

Harris, Ashley Rae

★ **Do** you love me? making healthy dating decisions. content consultant: Dr. Robyn J.A. Silverman. ABDO Pub. Company 2009 112p il (Essential health: strong beautiful girls) lib bdg $32.79

Grades: 6 7 8 9   613.9

1. Dating (Social customs) 2. Interpersonal relations 3. Sexual behavior 4. Girls -- Psychology
ISBN 978-1-60453-749-9 lib bdg; 1-60453-749-3 lib bdg

LC 2009002131

"The topics are well selected, the design is attractive, and the stories feature girls from a variety of cultures." Booklist

Harris, Robie H.

★ **It's** perfectly normal; a book about changing bodies, growing up, sex & sexual health. illustrated by Michael Emberley. 3rd ed.; Candlewick Press 2009 93p il $22.99; pa $12.99

Grades: 4 5 6 7   613.9

1. Puberty 2. Sex education
ISBN 978-0-7636-4483-3; 0-7636-4483-8; 978-0-7636-4484-0 pa; 0-7636-4484-6 pa

LC 2009008457

First published 1994

This provides information about sex, puberty, family relationships and reproduction, sexual decision-making and birth control, abortion laws, sexual abuse, sexual health, sexually transmitted diseases, and (new in this edition) internet safety.

"This caring, conscientious, and well-crafted book will be a fine library resource as well as a marvelous adjunct to the middle-school sex-education curriculum. . . . The bold color cartoon drawings are very candid. . . . Harris' text [is] as forthright as Emberley's art." Booklist [review of 1994 ed.]

★ **Sexual** health information for teens; edited by Sandra Augustyn Lawton. 2nd ed.; Omnigraphics 2008 430p il (Teen health series) $69

Grades: 7 8 9 10 11 12   613.9

1. Sex education 2. Teenagers -- Health and hygiene
ISBN 978-0-7808-1010-5; 0-7808-1010-4

LC 2007052454

First published 2003

"This offering represents the most up-to-date information available on an array of topics. . . . The range of coverage . . . is thorough and extensive. Each chapter includes a bibliographic citation, and the three back sections containing additional resources, further reading, and the index are all first-rate. The few illustrations and diagrams range in quality from good to excellent." SLJ

Includes bibliographical references

613.96 Sexual techniques

Murray, Craig
Sexpectations; Sex Stuff Straight Up. Allen & Unwin 2012 111 p. $19.95
Grades: 7 8 9 10 11 12   613.96
1. Sex education 2. Sexual hygiene 3. Teenagers -- Sexual behavior
ISBN 1741751438; 9781741751437
Includes bibliographical references.
This book, by Craig Murray and Leissa Pitts, offers a "teenage-friendly sex education and sexual health guide book, for both boys and girls, in one . . . volume. Designed to help teens make healthy, positive choices, . . . It takes teens through knowing themselves and their bodies, keeping safe, protecting themselves, thinking through pregnancy, knowing about relationships, and tapping into their personal power to make positive choices." (Publisher's note)

614 Forensic medicine; incidence of injuries, wounds, disease; public preventive medicine

Spilsbury, Richard
Bones speak! solving crimes from the past. Enslow Publishers 2009 48p il (Solve that crime!) lib bdg $23.93
Grades: 5 6 7 8   614
1. Forensic sciences 2. Forensic anthropology
ISBN 978-0-7660-3377-1 lib bdg; 0-7660-3377-5 lib bdg
LC 2008-33309
This "title boasts in-depth information, sidebars detailing events of true crime, and activities that will increase understanding. . . . Photographs are colorful, well-captioned, and related to the text." SLJ
Includes glossary and bibliographical references

Stefoff, Rebecca
Forensics and medicine. Marshall Cavendish Benchmark 2011 95p il (Forensic science investigated) $23.95
Grades: 6 7 8 9   614
1. Forensic sciences 2. Medical jurisprudence
ISBN 978-0-7614-4143-4; 0-7614-4143-3
LC 2010010526
"Numerous color photos and digital illustrations . . . add further interest." Booklist
Includes bibliographical references

Walker, Sally M.
★ Written in bone; buried lives of Jamestown and Colonial Maryland. Carolrhoda Books 2009 144p il map $22.95
Grades: 6 7 8 9 10   614
1. Anthropologists 2. Forensic sciences 3. Excavations (Archeology) -- United States 4. Forensic anthropology 5. Medical jurisprudence
ISBN 978-0-8225-7135-3; 0-8225-7135-8
LC 2007-10768

"Walker takes readers on an archaeological investigation of human and material remains from 17th- and 18th-century Jamestown and colonial Maryland, while addressing relevant topics in forensic anthropology, history, and archaeology. . . . The text succinctly explains complex forensic concepts. . . . Captioned, full-color photographs of skeletal, dental, and artifactual remains shed light on colonial life. Historical documents, illustrated maps, and anatomical drawings complement images of various specialists at work in the field. Photographs of reenactors performing period tasks . . . provide insight into the daily life of the recovered individuals." SLJ
Includes bibliographical references

614.4 Incidence of and public measures to prevent disease

Barnard, Bryn
★ Outbreak; plagues that changed history. written and illustrated by Bryn Barnard. Crown Publishers 2005 47p il maps $17.95
Grades: 5 6 7 8   614.4
1. Diseases 2. Epidemics 3. Diseases and history 4. Communicable diseases
ISBN 0-375-82986-5
LC 2005-15086
This "volume explores specific plagues that have impacted society. Barnard begins with an introduction to microbes and the positive and negative effects that they can have on humans. A history of the study of microorganisms follows. The bulk of the book then focuses on specific plagues with a chapter devoted to each, including the Black Death, smallpox, yellow fever, cholera, tuberculosis, and influenza. The final chapter discusses the modern struggle against disease. . . . The evocative paintings help to clarify the text. Browsers and report writers alike will find this to be a fascinating and informative resource." SLJ

Brownlee, Christen
Cute, furry, and deadly; diseases you can catch from your pet! [by] Christen Brownlee. Franklin Watts 2008 64p il map (24/7, science behind the scenes) lib bdg $26
Grades: 6 7 8 9 10   614.4
1. Communicable diseases 2. Pets -- Health and hygiene
ISBN 0-531-12072-4 lib bdg; 978-0-531-12072-9 lib bdg
LC 2006-21230
Hopefully, the worst thing your pet ever comes home with is bad breath. But some furry friends can carry nasty germs, and that's where zoonotic disease researchers come in and investigate and stop animal diseases before they get you!
"This series is a great pick for reluctant readers, busy teens, and anyone looking for a fun (if somewhat frightening) nonfiction read." Voice Youth Advocates
Includes glossary and bibliographical references

Epidemics: opposing viewpoints; David Haugen and Susan Musser, book editors. Greenhaven

Press 2011 273p (Opposing viewpoints series) lib bdg $39.70; pa $26.50

Grades: 8 9 10 11 12　　　**614.4**

1. Epidemics 2. Vaccination 3. Communicable diseases

ISBN 978-0-7377-5219-9; 0-7377-5219-X; 978-0-7377-5220-5 pa; 0-7377-5220-3 pa

LC 2010052249

Articles in this anthology present opposing viewpoints on the subject of epidemics.

Includes bibliographical references

Farrell, Jeanette

Invisible enemies; stories of infectious diseases. 2nd ed; Farrar, Straus & Giroux 2005 272p il $18

Grades: 7 8 9 10　　　**614.4**

1. Communicable diseases 2. Infection

ISBN 9780374336073; 0-374-33607-5

LC 2004-57668

First published 1998

The author "focuses on seven dreaded human diseases: smallpox, leprosy, plague, tuberculosis, malaria, cholera, and AIDS. Each chapter provides a description of the physical and psychological effects of the disease on its victims, early theories about its causes, and efforts made to avoid or cure it. Then the methods of research that revealed its cause and developed the means to control its spread are explained in fascinating detail. . . . If every science book for nonspecialists were written with such flair and attention to detail, science would soon become every student's favorite subject." SLJ

Includes glossary and bibliographical references

Friedlander, Mark P.

★ Outbreak; disease detectives at work. by Mark P. Friedlander Jr. [Updated and rev. ed.]; Twenty-First Century Books 2009 128p il lib bdg $31.93

Grades: 6 7 8 9　　　**614.4**

1. Diseases 2. Epidemiology

ISBN 978-0-8225-9039-2; 0-8225-9039-5

LC 2008025277

First published 2000

Describes the field of epidemiology and its history, presenting historical and modern case studies and biological explanations of some diseases and a discussion of the microbes most likely to be used by bioterrorists.

"This is a readable, intriguing overview of the destructive power of epidemics and the critical work of public health professionals." SLJ [review of 2003 edition]

Includes bibliographical references

Gleason, Carrie

Feasting bedbugs, mites, and ticks. Crabtree Pub. Co. 2010 32p il (Creepy crawlies) lib bdg $26.60; pa $8.95

Grades: 4 5 6 7　　　**614.4**

1. Mites 2. Ticks 3. Bedbugs

ISBN 978-0-7787-2500-8 lib bdg; 0-7787-2500-6 lib bdg; 978-0-7787-2507-7 pa; 0-7787-2507-3 pa

LC 2010009552

"The informational yet easy-to-read text in double-page spreads explains the classification, anatomy, life cycles,

and ideal feeding and living conditions for mites, ticks, and bedbugs as well as the differences among them. . . . Children will be most interested in the long history, myths, and lore associated with these pests as well as the eye-catching layout, with numerous color photographs. . . . [This is an] equally repulsive and fascinating book." Booklist

Includes glossary and bibliographical references

Goldsmith, Connie

★ Invisible invaders; new and dangerous infectious diseases. Twenty-First Century Books 2006 111p il (Discovery!) lib bdg $29.27

Grades: 7 8 9 10　　　**614.4**

1. Communicable diseases

ISBN 978-0-8225-3416-7; 0-8225-3416-9

LC 2005-17271

"This title is a thorough, understandable, and accessible source of current information and medical definitions, and a trail to further research." SLJ

Includes bibliographical references

Grady, Denise

★ Deadly invaders; virus outbreaks around the world, from Marburg fever to avian flu. Kingfisher 2006 128p il map $16.95

Grades: 7 8 9 10　　　**614.4**

1. Viruses 2. Marburg virus 3. Communicable diseases

ISBN 978-0-7534-5995-9; 0-7534-5995-7

LC 2006004441

The "writing is informative and compelling. . . . The layout is appealing and includes good-quality, full-color, relevant photographs on almost every spread. . . . A fast-paced, timely, and important book." SLJ

Includes bibliographical references

Miller, Debra A.

Pandemics; [by] Debra A. Miller. Lucent Books 2006 un (Hot topics) $32.45

Grades: 7 8 9 10　　　**614.4**

1. Epidemics 2. Communicable diseases

ISBN 9781420502589; 1-59018-965-5; 978-1-59018-965-8

LC 2006007057

"This comprehensive and well-organized book covers potential threats; the control and prevention of pandemics; and factors that may facilitate the outbreak and transmission of diseases, such as pollution, poverty, overpopulation, and globalization. Teens will appreciate the interesting sidebars, quotations, diagrams, and full-color photos that are integrated throughout the text and will find the annotated lists of organizations and further-reading suggestions useful." SLJ

Includes bibliographical references

Piddock, Charles

★ Outbreak; science seeks safeguards for global health. [Caryn Oryniak, consultant] National Geographic 2008 64p il (National Geographic investigates) $17.95; lib bdg $27.90

Grades: 4 5 6 7　　　**614.4**

1. Diseases 2. Epidemics 3. Medicine -- Research 4. Public health 5. Virus diseases 6. Bacterial diseases 7.

Communicable diseases
ISBN 978-1-4263-0357-9; 1-4263-0357-2; 978-1-4263-0263-3 lib bdg; 1-4263-0263-0 lib bdg

LC 2009-275290

This is an "introduction to the fight against infectious diseases, including scientists who discovered various viruses and bacteria. The text outlines how we have learned to fight nature's harmful strains and to use others to our advantage; it also provides the latest findings on bird flu and SARS, Ebola and AIDS, and highly resistant strains of tuberculosis." Publisher's note

Tilden, Thomasine E. Lewis

Help! What's eating my flesh? runaway staph and strep infections! [by] Thomasine E. Lewis Tilden. Franklin Watts 2008 64p il map (24/7, science behind the scenes) lib bdg $26

Grades: 6 7 8 9 10   **614.4**

1. Communicable diseases
ISBN 0-531-12073-2; 978-0-531-12073-6

LC 2006-5871

"A splashy tabloid-style presentation, including gross and disgusting photographs, will attract curious young teens who will be unable to resist. . . . [This] book also includes career information, resources (including Web sites and books), a historical section with key dates, and an author's note." Voice Youth Advoctaes

Includes glossary and bibliographical references

Walker, Richard, 1951-

Epidemics & plagues; foreword by Denise Grady. Kingfisher 2006 63p il (Kingfisher knowledge) hardcover o.p. $12.95

Grades: 4 5 6 7   **614.4**

1. Diseases 2. Epidemics
ISBN 978-0-7534-6035-1; 0-7534-6035-1; 978-0-7534-6161-7 pa; 0-7534-6161-7 pa

Discusses the spread of infectious diseases and their impact on human populations, from the Black Death in medieval Europe to such modern diseases as AIDS and West Nile virus, as well as efforts to stop the spread of these diseases.

Includes glossary

Willett, Edward

Disease-hunting scientist; careers hunting deadly diseases. Enslow Publishers 2009 112p il (Wild science careers) lib bdg $31.93

Grades: 5 6 7 8   **614.4**

1. Epidemiology 2. Vocational guidance
ISBN 978-0-7660-3052-7 lib bdg; 0-7660-3052-0 lib bdg

LC 2008-4674

"Full-color photographs show the scientists in action and a chart with career information including salary potentials wraps up . . . [this] book." SLJ

Includes glossary and bibliographical references

614.5 Incidence of and public measures to prevent specific diseases and kinds of diseases

Ballard, Carol

AIDS and other epidemics. Gareth Stevens Pub. 2008 48p il map (What if we do nothing?) lib bdg $31

Grades: 5 6 7 8   **614.5**

1. Epidemics 2. AIDS (Disease) 3. Communicable diseases
ISBN 978-1-4339-0085-3 lib bdg; 1-4339-0085-8 lib bdg

LC 2008029189

"Using intelligent, focused text; an open design; vivid photos; and excellent maps, [this] book demands attention." Booklist

Includes bibliographical references

Cunningham, Kevin

Flu. Morgan Reynolds Pub. 2009 176p il (Diseases in history) lib bdg $28.95

Grades: 8 9 10 11 12   **614.5**

1. Influenza
ISBN 978-1-59935-105-6; 1-59935-105-6

LC 2008-51620

"This informative title reveals the continued concerns surrounding this killer disease and the possibility of a future pandemic. The text, though somewhat scientific, will help students to better understand the history of the virus, how it has mutated and jumped from animals to humans, and new concerns regarding more dangerous forms. . . . Color and black-and-white archival photos, as well as reproduction of a three-dimensional rendering of the flu virus, enhance the text." SLJ

Includes glossary and bibliographical references

Malaria. Morgan Reynolds Pub. 2009 144p il (Diseases in history) lib bdg $28.95

Grades: 8 9 10 11 12   **614.5**

1. Malaria
ISBN 978-1-59935-103-2; 1-59935-103-X

LC 2008-51619

"Provides fascinating information about an ongoing scourge. . . . Here readers have an accessible, well presented account of the continuing struggle against a deadly disease." Voice Youth Advocates

Includes glossary and bibliographical references

Plague. Morgan Reynolds Pub. 2009 144p il (Diseases in history) lib bdg $28.95

Grades: 8 9 10 11 12   **614.5**

1. Plague
ISBN 978-1-59935-102-5; 1-59935-102-1

LC 2008-51618

"Chapters based upon plagues include one on Justinian's Plague, the Black Death, The Dreadful Pestilence, the Great Plague of London, and the current H1N1 swine flu pandemic. This detailed overview . . . will appeal to more advanced students. The research is thorough and the writing is insightful, thought provoking, and accessible." Voice Youth Advocates

Includes glossary and bibliographical references

The **bubonic** plague. ABDO Pub. Co. 2011 112p il map (Essential events) lib bdg $23.95
Grades: 7 8 9 10 11 12   **614.5**
1. Plague 2. Epidemics
ISBN 978-1-61714-762-3; 1-61714-762-1
                                          LC 2010043852
A history of the plague which caused one of the most catastrophic losses of life in history.

"The spacious . . . design is inviting, with many color illustrations and screens, and the extensive back matter includes a detailed time line, glossary, bibliography and source notes." Booklist

Includes glossary and bibliographical references

Currie, Stephen
★ The **black** death; by Stephen Currie. ReferencePoint Press, Inc. 2013 94 p. (Understanding world history series) (hardcover) $27.95
Grades: 7 8 9 10   **614.5**
1. Plague -- History 2. Black Death -- History
ISBN 1601524803; 9781601524805
                                          LC 2012021114
This book on the Black Death by Stephen Currie is part of the "Understanding World History" series. "Readers learn the surprising benefits of depopulation and how technology, medicine, and even religion changed as a result of this tragic epidemic. . . . While it briefly covers the beginnings of the plague in Asia and the many people killed there, the bulk of the book is about the impact of the disease on Europe." (School Library Journal)

Includes bibliographical references and index.

Currie-McGhee, L. K.
Sexually transmitted diseases; [by] Leanne Currie-McGhee. ReferencePoint Press 2009 104p il map (Compact research. Diseases and disorders) lib bdg $25.95
Grades: 8 9 10   **614.5**
1. Sexually transmitted diseases
ISBN 978-1-60152-045-6; 1-60152-045-X
                                          LC 2008-12554
Presents information on sexually transmitted diseases through essays, quotations, statistics, and suggestions for further research.

"Sobering, enlightening, and up-to-date, this title . . . uses an effective blend of primary sources, diagrams, and thorough text to bring the latest facts about STDs to young readers. . . . A time line and lists of key advocacy groups and further reading close this valuable resource for teens." Booklist

Includes bibliographical references

Goldsmith, Connie
Influenza: the next pandemic? Twenty-First Century Books 2007 112p il (Twenty-first century medical library) lib bdg $27.93

Grades: 6 7 8 9 10   **614.5**
1. Influenza
ISBN 978-0-7613-9457-0; 0-7613-9457-5
                                          LC 2005-23588
The author "traces the history of the flu, giving attention to past outbreaks and epidemics. She also describes flu viruses of today, explains treatments, and details health officials' concerns about bird flu. . . . Good for reports, and a worthy source to update collections." SLJ

Includes bibliographical references

Jurmain, Suzanne
★ The **secret** of the yellow death; a true story of medical sleuthing. Houghton Mifflin Books for Children 2009 104p il $19
Grades: 6 7 8 9 10   **614.5**
1. Epidemics 2. Physicians 3. Yellow fever 4. Army officers 5. Microbiologists 6. Writers on medicine 7. Medicine -- Research
ISBN 978-0-618-96581-6; 0-618-96581-5
                                          LC 2009-22499
"This medical mystery is extremely interesting, easy to read, and well illustrated with period photos." SLJ

Includes glossary and bibliographical references

Kupperberg, Paul
The **influenza** pandemic of 1918-1919. Chelsea House 2008 120p il map (Great historic disasters) $35
Grades: 7 8 9 10   **614.5**
1. Epidemics 2. Influenza
ISBN 978-0-7910-9640-6; 0-7910-9640-8
This is "well written and informative. . . . The inclusion of black-and-white and color photographs and drawings and sidebars help to make [this book] first-rate for reports and general browsing." SLJ

Murphy, Jim
★ An **American** plague; the true and terrifying story of the yellow fever epidemic of 1793. Clarion Bks. 2003 165p il map $18
Grades: 5 6 7 8   **614.5**
1. Yellow fever 2. Yellow fever -- Pennsylvania -- Philadelphia -- History -- 18th century
ISBN 0-395-77608-2
                                          LC 2002-151355
A Newbery Medal honor book, 2004

"Murphy culls from a number of historical records the story of the yellow fever epidemic that swept Philadelphia in 1793, skillfully drawing out from these sources the fear and drama of the time and making them immediate to modern readers. . . . Thoroughly documented, with an annotated source list, the work is both rigorous and inviting." Horn Book

Nardo, Don
The **Black** Death. Lucent Books 2011 96p il (World history) lib bdg $33.45

Grades: 6 7 8 9 **614.5**
1. Plague 2. Medieval civilization
ISBN 978-1-4205-0348-7; 1-4205-0348-0
LC 2010043804
This examines the 14th-century plague from such perspectives as epidemiology, the death toll, the medical response, social controls, the flagellants, the impact on economics and the population, education, agriculture, architecture, and the church.
Includes bibliographical references

Person, Stephen
Bubonic plague; the Black Death! Bearport Pub. 2010 32p il map (Nightmare plagues) lib bdg $25.27
Grades: 4 5 6 7 **614.5**
1. Plague
ISBN 978-1-936088-03-4; 1-936088-03-7
This describes what causes bubonic plague and how it affects the body.
"The writing is accessible and interspersed with interesting photographs and fact boxes. . . . [The book relies] on an honest discussion of [bubonic plague and is an] . . . effective, easily navigated [introduction]." SLJ
Includes glossary and bibliographical references

Malaria; super killer! Bearport Pub. 2011 32p il map (Nightmare plagues) lib bdg $25.27
Grades: 4 5 6 7 **614.5**
1. Malaria
ISBN 978-1-936088-07-2 lib bdg; 1-936088-07-X
lib bdg
LC 2010012018
Discover what causes malaria and how it affects the body.
"The writing is accessible and interspersed with interesting photographs and fact boxes. . . . [The book relies] on an honest discussion of [malaria and is an] . . . effective, easily navigated [introduction]." SLJ
Includes glossary and bibliographical references

Peters, Stephanie True
★ **Smallpox** in the new world. Benchmark Books 2004 69p il (Epidemic!) lib bdg $32.79
Grades: 4 5 6 7 8 **614.5**
1. Diseases 2. Smallpox 3. Smallpox -- America
ISBN 0-7614-1637-4; 9780761416371
LC 2003-2646
Describes the history of smallpox in the Americas, covering the arrival of the Spanish as carriers, its spread throughout the New World, the development of the smallpox vaccine, the elimination of the disease, and its potential use as a terrorist weapon.
Includes glossary and bibliographical references

Reingold, Adam
Smallpox; is it over? Bearport Pub. 2010 32p il map (Nightmare plagues) lib bdg $25.27
Grades: 4 5 6 7 **614.5**
1. Smallpox
ISBN 978-1-936088-02-7; 1-936088-02-9
LC 2010009371

Discover what causes smallpox and how it affects the body.
"The writing is accessible and interspersed with interesting photographs and fact boxes. . . . [The book relies] on an honest discussion of [smallpox and is an] . . . effective, easily navigated [introduction]." SLJ
Includes glossary and bibliographical references

Rudolph, Jessica
The **flu** of 1918; millions dead worldwide! Bearport Pub. 2011 32p il map (Nightmare plagues) lib bdg $25.27
Grades: 4 5 6 7 **614.5**
1. Influenza
ISBN 978-1-936088-05-8 lib bdg; 1-936088-05-3
lib bdg
LC 2010004684
Discover what caused the Influenza epidemic of 1918 and how it affected the body.
"The writing is accessible and interspersed with interesting photographs and fact boxes. . . . [The book relies] on an honest discussion of [Influenza epidemic of 1918 and is an] . . . effective, easily navigated [introduction]." SLJ
Includes glossary and bibliographical references

Slavicek, Louise Chipley
The **Black** Death. Chelsea House Publishers 2008 127p il (Great historic disasters) lib bdg $35
Grades: 6 7 8 9 10 **614.5**
1. Plague 2. Middle Ages
ISBN 978-0-7910-9649-9; 0-7910-9649-1;
9781438118154
LC 2008004887
This describes the Plague epidemic and it's effects on Europe in the Middle Ages
Includes glossary and bibliographical references

Smith, Tara C.
Ebola and Marburg viruses; 2nd ed.; Chelsea House Publishers 2011 104p il (Deadly diseases and epidemics) lib bdg $34.95
Grades: 8 9 10 11 12 **614.5**
1. Ebola virus 2. Marburg virus
ISBN 978-1-60413-252-6; 1-60413-252-3
LC 2010032999
First published 2005
This describes the outbreaks of Marburg and Ebola viruses, their characteristics and ecology, detection and treatment, developing a vaccine, and other hemorrhagic fevers.
Includes glossary and bibliographical references

Zahler, Diane
The **Black** Death. Twenty-First Century Books 2009 160p il map (Pivotal moments in history) lib bdg $38.60
Grades: 7 8 9 10 **614.5**
1. Plague 2. Middle Ages
ISBN 978-0-8225-9076-7; 0-8225-9076-X
LC 2008-26878

This book discusses the pivotal moment in history when one out of three people died and changed the course of world history, the Black Death.

"This is a well-written and well-researched volume. Full-color illustrations, a note explaining the value of primary sources, a who's who, and careful source notes make this book a valuable addition to history collections." SLJ

Includes glossary and bibliographical references

615   Pharmacology and therapeutics

Allman, Toney
  Vaccine research. ReferencePoint Press 2010 96p il (Inside science) lib bdg $26.95
Grades: 7 8 9 10   **615**
  1. Vaccination 2. Medicine -- Research
  ISBN 978-1-60152-131-6; 1-60152-131-6
                     LC 2010-20635
This book "offers the necessary information for stellar reports. Politics, debates, and ethical concerns are briefly and fairly mentioned, but the . . . [book concentrates] on consistent, documented, and well-balanced scientific coverage. The human stories sprinkled throughout will help kids identify with both scientists and patients." SLJ

Includes bibliographical references

Bjornlund, Lydia
  Oxycodone; by Lydia Bjornlund. ReferencePoint Press 2012 96 p. (Compact research series) $28.95
Grades: 7 8 9 10 11 12   **615**
  1. Narcotics 2. Analgesics 3. Drug abuse 4. Drug education 5. Drugs -- Law and legislation -- United States 6. Oxycodone 7. Oxycodone abuse
  ISBN 1601521618; 9781601521613
                     LC 2011020202
This book on oxycodone is a part of the Compact Research: Drugs series and "focus[es] on three types of information: "objective single-author narratives, opinion-based primary source quotations, and facts and statistics." What this translates to on the page is an overview of the topic and an in-depth chapter-by chapter discussion of the points raised in the overview." Lydia Bjornlund "discuss[es] . . . the health dangers of the drug and its legitimacy in medical use, government regulation of the drug, and how oxycodone abuse can be prevented." (Booklist)

Includes bibliographical references and index

Breguet, Amy
  Diet pills; by Amy E. Breguet. Chelsea House 2009 110p il (Junior drug awareness) lib bdg $30
Grades: 6 7 8 9   **615**
  1. Appetite depressants
  ISBN 978-0-7910-9750-2 lib bdg; 0-7910-9750-1 lib bdg
                     LC 2008-14068
This "explores various types of diet pills, their makers' claims, and the potential dangers associated with their use. [It also explains to readers] how to manage their weight in safe, effective ways and feel better about their bodies and themselves." Publisher's note

Includes glossary and bibliographical references

Goldsmith, Connie
  ★ **Superbugs** strike back; when antibiotics fail. Twenty-First Century Books 2007 112p il (Discovery!) lib bdg $29.27
Grades: 7 8 9 10   **615**
  1. Bacteria 2. Antibiotics 3. Drug resistance 4. Antibiotics -- Effectiveness 5. Drug resistance in microorganisms
  ISBN 978-0-8225-6607-6; 0-8225-6607-9
                     LC 2006-10726
"The emergence of 'superbugs'—antibiotic resistant bacteria—and the threat they pose to public health are examined in this detailed introduction. . . . Full-color tables, sidebars, diagrams, and good-quality photos and micrographs are interspersed throughout. The text is meticulous without being tedious." SLJ

Includes glossary and bibliographical references

Hyde, Natalie
  What is germ theory? Crabtree Pub. Co. 2011 64p il (Shaping modern science) lib bdg $30.60; pa $10.95
Grades: 5 6 7 8   **615**
  1. Chemists 2. Germ theory of disease 3. Microbiologists 4. Writers on science
  ISBN 978-0-7787-7201-9 lib bdg; 0-7787-7201-9 lib bdg; 978-0-7787-7208-8 pa; 0-7787-7208-X pa
                     LC 2010052631
This title is "not only written and organized well, but [it is] also gorgeous in design. Full-color photographs and illustrations are set over colorful backgrounds that add depth but not distraction. [The title] includes thought-provoking quotes from famous authors and scientists and some eyebrow-raising 'Quick Facts' throughout." SLJ

Includes glossary and bibliographical references

Kidd, J. S.
  ★ **Potent** natural medicines; Mother Nature's pharmacy. [by] J.S. Kidd and Renee A. Kidd. rev ed.; Chelsea House 2006 212p il (Science and society) lib bdg $35
Grades: 7 8 9 10   **615**
  1. Pharmacology 2. Medical botany
  ISBN 9781438122946; 0-8160-5607-2
                     LC 2005041741
This introduces "plants' medicinal properties, pioneers who hunted for sources of and applications for botanical treatments, and the ways phytochemical nutrients prevent disease. . . . [Also included] are chapters about recent research, including investigation into animal sources for medicine; the impact of field research on native peoples; and the federal regulation of herb and plant supplements. . . . This [is] a good choice to support research and debate projects." Booklist

Includes bibliographical references

Klosterman, Lorrie
  The **facts** about depressants; [by] Lorrie Klosterman. Marshall Cavendish Benchmark 2005 96p il (Drugs) lib bdg $42.79; pa $6.99

Grades: 7 8 9 10 **615**
1. Drug abuse 2. Tranquilizing drugs
ISBN 0-7614-1976-4 lib bdg; 0-7614-1976-4 lib bdg; 978-0-7614-3594-5 pa; 0-7614-3594-8 pa
LC 2005001729
This "useful [volume is] attractively packaged and will be of interest to report writers and general readers. [Text] and photos do an excellent job of showing how [this] group of drugs affects the body." SLJ
Includes glossary and bibliographical references

The **facts** about drugs and the body. Marshall Cavendish Benchmark 2006 143p il (Drugs) lib bdg $42.79
Grades: 7 8 9 10 11 12 **615**
1. Drugs
ISBN 978-0-7614-2675-2; 0-7614-2675-2
LC 2007-2260
This discusses the effects of various drugs on the nervous, cardiovascular, respiratory, digestive, and reproductive systems of the body.
"Klosterman has done an excellent job of demonstrating how drugs affect the body functions. The illustrations and captions enhance the information to make it more understandable." SLJ
Includes glossary and bibliographical references

Knowles, Johanna
Over-the-counter drugs. Chelsea House 2008 106p il (Junior drug awareness) lib bdg $30
Grades: 6 7 8 9 **615**
1. Drug abuse 2. Nonprescription drugs
ISBN 978-0-7910-9759-5 lib bdg; 0-7910-9759-5 lib bdg; 9781438118253
LC 2007-43665
This describes the uses and abuses of such over-the-counter drugs as cough medicines, diet pills, sleep aids, bodybuilding supplements, motion sickness medications, and caffeine
"The content is reliable and comprehensive." Horn Book Guide
Includes glossary and bibliographical references

Koellhoffer, Tara
Prozac and other antidepressants. Chelsea House 2008 120p il (Junior drug awareness) lib bdg $30
Grades: 6 7 8 9 **615**
1. Antidepressants 2. Depression (Psychology)
ISBN 978-0-7910-9747-2 lib bdg; 0-7910-9747-1 lib bdg; 9781438118260
LC 2007-43663
This "examines antidepressant therapies available today and explains how they affect the bodies and minds of people who are treated with them." Publisher's note
Includes glossary and bibliographical references

LeVert, Suzanne
The **facts** about antidepressants; [by] Suzanne LeVert. Marshall Cavendish Benchmark 2007 112p il (Drugs) lib bdg $42.79

Grades: 6 7 8 9 **615**
1. Antidepressants
ISBN 978-0-7614-2241-9 lib bdg; 0-7614-2241-2 lib bdg
LC 2006002403
This describes the benefits and risks of antidepressant drugs in the treatment of depression
Includes glossary and bibliographical references

Merino, Noel
Vaccines; Noel Merino, book editor. Greenhaven Press 2011 129p il (Introducing issues with opposing viewpoints) $35.75
Grades: 7 8 9 10 **615**
1. Vaccination
ISBN 978-0-7377-5204-5; 0-7377-5204-1
LC 2010040832
This is an "excellent [resource] both for student research and for personal interest. . . . Vaccines . . . discusses the possible connection between inoculations and autism, as well as the question of the state mandating vaccination and possible problems with giving multiple vaccines at the same time." Booklist
Includes bibliographical references

Miller, Malinda
The **pharmaceutical** industry; better medicine for the 21st century. Mason Crest Publishers 2011 64p il (New careers for the 21st century: finding your role in the global renewal) lib bdg $22.95
Grades: 7 8 9 10 **615**
1. Pharmacy 2. Drug industry 3. Vocational guidance
ISBN 978-1-4222-1819-8 lib bdg; 1-4222-1819-8 lib bdg
LC 2010020682
"Chapters identify and emphasize specific careers–important strengths, necessary aptitudes and interests, education and training, projected earnings, closely related occupations, type of work environment, and predictions for the future of the field. . . . Color photos have a small role amid the many statistics, figures, graphs and charts that support and supplement the . . . [text]." SLJ
Includes bibliographical references

Peterson, Judy Monroe
Frequently asked questions about antidepressants. Rosen Pub. 2010 64p il (FAQ: teen life) lib bdg $29.95
Grades: 7 8 9 10 **615**
1. Antidepressants 2. Depression (Psychology)
ISBN 978-1-4358-3547-4 lib bdg; 1-4358-3547-6 lib bdg
LC 2009-18962
"Defines 'antidepressants' and 'depression' in an easy-to-understand language, using words and illustrations to show the science of how these drugs work and the warning signs of different types of depression. . . . This is a good resource for teens struggling to understand what is happening to themselves or to their friends." Voice Youth Advocates
Includes glossary and bibliographical references

Rooney, Anne

   Dealing with drugs. Amicus 2010 46p il (Healthy lifestyles) lib bdg $32.80

Grades: 7 8 9 10   **615**

   1. Drugs

   ISBN 978-1-60753-084-8; 1-60753-084-8

   This book is "well-written and satisfyingly informative. . . . [The] magazine-like format includes numerous sidebars, color photos, and charts." SLJ

   Includes glossary

Winner, Cherie

   ★ **Circulating** life; blood transfusion from ancient superstition to modern medicine. Twenty-First Century Books 2007 112p il (Discovery!) $30.60

Grades: 6 7 8 9 10   **615**

   1. Blood -- Transfusion 2. Blood

   ISBN 978-0-8225-6606-9; 0-8225-6606-0

                        LC 2006-29921

   This is a study of how bloodletting was replaced by blood transfusion as a medical therapy. (Sci Books Films)

   This "compendium is both a history of the art of transfusions and a scientific discourse on the chemistry of blood. From early 'bleeding treatments' to the discovery of the circulatory system; from the earliest attempts at transfusions to Charles Drew's heroic work with plasma in World War II, Winner's clear text takes readers on an epic trip." SLJ

   Includes bibliographical references

615.7   Pharmacokinetics

Karson, Jill

   Is medical marijuana necessary? by Bonnie Szumski and Jill Karson. ReferencePoint Press, Inc. 2013 96 p. (In controversy) (hardcover) $27.95

Grades: 7 8 9 10   **615.7**

   1. Marijuana 2. Medical botany 3. Marijuana -- Therapeutic use -- United States 4. Marijuana -- Law and legislation -- United States

   ISBN 1601524587; 9781601524584

                        LC 2012011561

   This book is part of the In Controversy series and focuses on medical marijuana. "Each book explores one aspect of a debate; for instance, instead of discussing marijuana in general, the series entry focuses on medical marijuana." It notes that "most of the medical problems marijuana helps with arise later in life." (Booklist)

   Includes bibliographical references and index.

615.8   Specific therapies and kinds of therapies

Marcovitz, Hal

   Gene therapy research. ReferencePoint Press 2010 96p il (Inside science) lib bdg $26.95

Grades: 7 8 9 10 11 12   **615.8**

   1. Gene therapy 2. Medicine -- Research

   ISBN 978-1-60152-108-8; 1-60152-108-1

                        LC 2009-41686

   "Opening with an account of successful gene therapy for a rare eye disease, this introduction to the research goes on to speculate about future applications for other inherited diseases. Beginning with basic definitions of such terms as gene, human genome, and DNA, the well-organized narrative explains the impact of viruses, drugs, cloning, and stem cells on gene therapy and describes recent research." Booklist

615.9   Toxicology

Karson, Jill

   Are cell phones dangerous? by Bonnie Szumski and Jill Karson. ReferencePoint Press, Inc. 2012 96 p. col. ill. (hardcover) $27.95

Grades: 7 8 9 10   **615.9**

   1. Cellular telephones -- Health aspects 2. Cellular telephones -- Social aspects 3. Cell phones -- Health aspects

   ISBN 1601522320; 9781601522320

                        LC 2011034063

   This book on safety issues related to cell phones "begins with a brief history of this now ubiquitous technology and then analyzes the risks of cell phone usage in three main areas. It draws on numerous studies to report suspected links to cancer, a decline in male fertility, and other health-related problems as well as accidents and deaths related to texting while driving. The authors also look at such negative impacts on youth culture as addiction, bullying, and sexting." (Booklist)

   Includes bibliographical references and index.

Landau, Elaine

   Food poisoning and foodborne diseases. Twenty-First Century Books 2010 128p il (USA Today health reports: diseases and disorders) lib bdg $34.60

Grades: 7 8 9 10 11 12   **615.9**

   1. Food poisoning 2. Communicable diseases 3. Foodborne diseases

   ISBN 978-0-8225-7290-9; 0-8225-7290-7

                        LC 2009-20325

   This book "will drawn an audience with its everyday examples of food risks as well as instructions about how to buy, prepare, cook, and store food. . . . Also included are warnings about how to keep hands and kitchen surfaces clean and what to watch out for in cafeteria and fast-food outlets. . . . [The] accessible design extends the impressive educational data." Booklist

   Includes bibliographical references

616   Diseases

Calamandrei, Camilla

   ★ **Fever**. Marshall Cavendish Benchmark 2009 64p il (Health alert) $22.95

Grades: 4 5 6 7   **616**

   1. Fever

   ISBN 978-0-7614-2915-9; 0-7614-2915-8

                        LC 2007-26002

This "title features a handsome format, with well-chosen illustrations, a substantial amount of information, and some practical insights." Booklist

Includes glossary

Dendy, Leslie A.

★ **Guinea** pig scientists; bold self-experimenters in science and medicine. [by] Leslie Dendy and Mel Boring; with illustrations by C. B. Mordan. Henry Holt & Co. 2005 213p il $19.95

Grades: 5 6 7 8   **616**

1. Scientists 2. Medicine -- Research 3. Self-experimentation in medicine

ISBN 9780805073164; 0-8050-7316-7

LC 2004-52364

This is a collection of "stories of human 'guinea pigs' who have tested the limits of the human body for the sake of science. Starting with Sir Charles Blagden, M.D., and his heat experiments, the stories are chronologically ordered from the 1770s to 1989. Included are descriptions of experiments dealing with digestion, laughing gas, vaccinations, mosquitoes as vectors of yellow fever, radioactivity, [and] G-forces." (Sci Books Films) Index.

"The authors offer 10 . . . case studies of scientists from the past several centuries who became their own test subjects. . . . The accounts are lively, compelling, and not always for the squeamish. . . . The authors cogently discuss each experiment's significance in advancing our understanding of science and medicine. Illustrated with a mix of period black-and-white photos and Mordan's nineteenth-century-style portraits . . . the episodes make riveting reading." Booklist

Includes bibliographical references

Evans, Michael

The **adventures** of Medical Man; kids' illnesses and injuries explained. by Michael Evans & David Wichman; illustrated by Gareth Williams. Annick 2010 72p il $21.95; pa $12.95

Grades: 5 6 7 8   **616**

1. Diseases 2. Wounds and injuries

ISBN 978-1-55451-263-8; 1-55451-263-8; 978-1-55451-262-1 pa; 1-55451-262-X pa

"Using tangible experiences that kids can relate to, this book does a fantastic job of explaining common medical issues in an accessible way. A variety of heroic characters explain otherwise complicated and seemingly scary conditions and occurrences. Through the use of science fiction, adventure, and comics, the book covers nut allergies, concussions, broken bones, strep throat, ear infections, and asthma. . . . The extensive glossary is straightforward and user-friendly. The pumped-up graphic illustrations are extremely engaging and further bring these otherwise abstract concepts to life." SLJ

Herbst, Judith

Germ theory. Twenty-First Century Books 2008 80p il (Great ideas of science) lib bdg $27.93

Grades: 5 6 7 8   **616**

1. Germ theory of disease 2. Life -- Origin

ISBN 978-0-8225-2909-5 lib bdg; 0-8225-2909-2 lib bdg

LC 2005-08809

Discusses how the germ theory of disease came about, how it was applied to various illnesses throughout the years, and why this theory has become so important in the field of medicine

Includes glossary and bibliographical references

Marcovitz, Hal

Stem cell research. ReferencePoint Press 2011 96p il (Inside science) lib bdg $26.95

Grades: 7 8 9 10   **616**

1. Stem cell research

ISBN 978-1-60152-130-9; 1-60152-130-8

LC 2010-4128

Discusses the science behind stem cell research and the ways in which stem cells can be used in treatment of disease.

This book "offers the necessary information for stellar reports. Politics, debates, and ethical concerns are briefly and fairly mentioned, but the . . . [book concentrates] on consistent, documented, and well-balanced scientific coverage. The human stories sprinkled throughout will help kids identify with both scientists and patients." SLJ

Includes bibliographical references

Nardo, Don

Cure quest; the science of stem cell research. by Don Nardo. Compass Point Books 2009 48p il (Headline science) lib bdg $27.93; pa $7.95

Grades: 5 6 7   **616**

1. Stem cell research

ISBN 978-0-7565-3371-7 lib bdg; 0-7565-3371-6 lib bdg; 978-0-7565-3374-8 pa; 0-7565-3374-0 pa

LC 2008-5738

Explains the science behind stem cell research.

"Color photos and graphics provide visual information; a timeline is helpful to find fast facts, and the Facthound Web site provides student with additional information." Libr Media Connect

Includes glossary and bibliographical references

Skloot, Rebecca

The **immortal** life of Henrietta Lacks; by Rebecca Skloot. 1st paperback ed. Crown Publishers 2010 x, 369 p., [8] p. of plates p ill. (some col.) (hardcover) $26.00; (paperback) $16.00

Grades: 6 7 8 9   **616**

1. Cancer 2. Homemakers 3. Medical ethics 4. Human experimentation in medicine 5. African American women/Biography

ISBN 1400052173; 9781400052172; 9781400052189

LC 200931785

Here, Rebecca Skloot tells the story of Henrietta Lacks, an African American Virginia tobacco farmer who died of cervical cancer in 1951. Unbeknownst to Mrs. Lacks and her family, scientists harvested her cells to create a human cell line known as HeLa, from the first two letters of her first and last names, "that has been kept alive indefinitely, enabling discoveries in such areas as cancer research, in vitro fertilization and gene mapping." (Publisher's note)

Includes bibliographical references and index.

Stoyles, Pennie

The A-Z of health. Black Rabbit/Smart Apple 2010 6v il set $119.70

Grades: 5 6 7 8   **616**

1. Health 2. Reference books 3. Medicine -- Encyclopedias

ISBN 978-1-59920-654-7; 1-59920-654-4

"This reference set provides a simple, brief, and easy-to-read introduction to key aspects of physical and mental health, including various body processes and diseases as well as information on treatments and preventative measures. . . . The explanations are concise, clear, and easy to understand. In addition to the abundance of images, the large type and white space that is prevalent on every page will make this set accessible to a broad array of young readers." Booklist

616.02   Special topics of diseases

Green, Caroline

Stem cells. Newforest Press 2010 64p il (Cutting-edge science) lib bdg $34.25

Grades: 7 8 9 10   **616.02**

1. Stem cell research 2. Stem cells

ISBN 978-1-84898-325-0; 1-84898-325-5

This addresses the topic of stem cell research, "touching on both scientific and societal issues . . . The underlying science is addressed, as well as the current state of scientific and ethical thinking. Stock color photographs and diagrams accompany the [text]. Sidebars provide biographical information on contemporary scientists as well as highlights of their research methods and studies." Horn Book Guide

Includes glossary and bibliographical references

616.07   Pathology

Murray, Elizabeth A.

Death; corpses, cadavers, and other grave matters. Twenty-First Century Books 2010 112p il (Discovery!) lib bdg $31.93

Grades: 7 8 9 10   **616.07**

1. Death 2. Forensic sciences 3. Death (Biology) 4. Postmortem changes

ISBN 978-0-7613-3851-2; 0-7613-3851-9

LC 2009-17436

The author "has written a book that deals with the scientific aspect of life and death. Her experience as a teacher of anatomy and physiology comes through as she explains the living body, what happens when systems shut down, and how postmortem remains can give evidence to solve crimes and the mysteries of diseases. . . . First-person accounts of terminally ill patients and those working in the fields of pathology, hospice, and anatomy clarify subjects presented in the chapters. Color photographs are included throughout, some of which are potentially disturbing. The glossary and bibliography are extensive and helpful. This book provides information for those who are curious about a subject that is not easy to discuss." SLJ

Includes glossary and bibliographical references

Sherrow, Victoria

Medical imaging; [by] Victoria Sherrow. Marshall Cavendish Benchmark 2007 127p il (Great inventions) lib bdg $39.93

Grades: 7 8 9 10   **616.07**

1. Diagnostic imaging

ISBN 978-0-7614-2231-0; 0-7614-2231-5

LC 2006003229

"An examination of the origins, history, development, and societal impact of various medical-imaging devices, from X-rays to the MRI" Publisher's note

Includes glossary and bibliographical references

616.1   Specific diseases

Jones, Phill

Sickle cell disease; [by] Phill Jones. Chelsea House Pubs. 2008 143p il (Genes & disease) $35

Grades: 7 8 9 10   **616.1**

1. Sickle cell anemia

ISBN 978-0-7910-9587-4; 0-7910-9587-8

LC 2008-4959

Opens "with accounts of people who have [Sickle cell] disease . . . followed by information on history, symptoms, variations, diagnosis, treatments, and research. . . . Chapters devoted to current genetic research and therapies can become dense as they introduce complex topics but photos, diagrams and charts help to clarify the details. . . . Controversial issues . . . are introduced fairly." SLJ

Includes glossary and bibliographical references

Raabe, Michelle

Hemophilia. Chelsea House Publishers 2008 133p il (Genes & disease) lib bdg $35

Grades: 7 8 9 10   **616.1**

1. Hemophilia

ISBN 978-0-7910-9648-2 lib bdg; 0-7910-9648-3 lib bdg

LC 2008-4897

This book opens "with accounts of people who have [Hemophilia] . . . followed by information on history, symptoms, variations, diagnosis, treatments, and research. . . . Chapters devoted to current genetic research and therapies can become dense as they introduce complex topics but photos, diagrams and charts help to clarify the details. . . . Controversial issues . . . are introduced fairly." SLJ

Includes glossary and bibliographical references

Silverstein, Alvin

★ Heart disease; [by] Alvin & Virginia Silverstein & Laura Silverstein Nunn. Twenty-First Century Books 2006 112p il (Twenty-first century medical library) lib bdg $27.93

Grades: 8 9 10 11 12   **616.1**

1. Heart diseases 2. Heart -- Diseases

ISBN 0-7613-3420-3

LC 2005-04161

"The authors explain the causes, methods of prevention, and treatment of heart disease in an accessible and interesting way. Terms and procedures are clearly explained. Various chapters deal effectively with everything from how the heart works to current repairs for broken hearts to the future of cardiology." SLJ

Includes bibliographical references

616.2 Diseases of respiratory system

★ **Asthma** information for teens; health tips about managing asthma and related concerns including facts about asthma causes, triggers and symptoms, diagnosis, and treatment. edited by Kim Wohlenhaus. 2nd ed.; Omnigraphics 2010 427p il (Teen health series) $69

Grades: 7 8 9 10 11 12   **616.2**

1. Asthma

ISBN 978-0-7808-1086-0; 0-7808-1086-4

LC 2009048694

First published 2005 under the editorship of Karen Bellenir

"Provides basic consumer health information for teens about asthma causes and treatments, controlling triggers, and coping with asthma at home and school. Includes index, resource information and recommendations for further reading." Publisher's note

Includes bibliographical references

Berger, William E.

Living with asthma. Facts on File 2007 183p (Teen's guides) lib bdg $34.95

Grades: 7 8 9 10 11   **616.2**

1. Asthma

ISBN 978-0-8160-6483-0 lib bdg; 0-8160-6483-0 lib bdg; 0-8160-7560-3 pa; 9781438121055

LC 2007003664

Examines asthma and provides teens with the information they need to understand it.

"There is a great directory of referral and online resources in the appendix. Although there are no illustrations, the text is appealing, well-organized, and accessible for the teen reader." Voice Youth Advocates

Includes glossary

Bjorklund, Ruth

★ **Asthma**. Benchmark Books 2005 64p il (Health alert) $28.50

Grades: 4 5 6 7   **616.2**

1. Asthma

ISBN 0-7614-1803-2

LC 2004-5976

The author explains "the causes, physiology, treatments, and complications associated with [asthma]. The [book is] well organized. . . . The photos are colorful and . . . some are startling." SLJ

Includes bibliographical references

Giddings, Sharon

Cystic fibrosis. Chelsea House 2009 128p il (Genes & disease) lib bdg $35

Grades: 7 8 9 10   **616.2**

1. Cystic fibrosis

ISBN 978-0-7910-9694-9; 0-7910-9694-7

LC 2008-44771

"Cystic fibrosis is one of the most widespread fatal genetic diseases in the United States. . . . [This book] discusses this genetic disease, its history, current treatments, and how scientists are searching for a cure." Publisher's note

Includes glossary and bibliographical references

Goldsmith, Connie

Influenza. Twenty-First Century Books 2010 128p il (USA Today health reports: diseases and disorders) lib bdg $34.60

Grades: 7 8 9 10 11 12   **616.2**

1. Influenza

ISBN 9780761363767; 978-0-7613-5881-7; 0-7613-5881-1

LC 2010-01030

This book "talks about the science behind the highly contagious disease, how it has spread to millions, and how to prevent and treat it. . . . [The] accessible design extends the impressive educational data." Booklist

Includes bibliographical references

Hoffmann, Gretchen

★ The **flu**. Marshall Cavendish Benchmark 2007 64p il (Health alert) lib bdg $31.36

Grades: 4 5 6 7   **616.2**

1. Influenza

ISBN 978-0-7614-2208-2; 0-7614-2208-0 \

LC 2006011980

This "title features a handsome format, with well-chosen illustrations, a substantial amount of information, and some practical insights." Booklist

Includes glossary and bibliographical references

Kelly, Evelyn B.

Investigating influenza and bird flu; real facts for real lives. [by] Evelyn B. Kelly and Claire Wilson. Enslow Publishers 2010 160p il (Investigating diseases) lib bdg $34.60

Grades: 6 7 8 9 10   **616.2**

1. Influenza 2. Avian influenza

ISBN 978-0-7660-3341-2; 0-7660-3341-4

LC 2009-14802

"The authors have explained the difficult problems in a clear, readable manner with lots of added pictures. . . . [Recommended] . . . for junior and senior high school students and for the general public." Sci Books Films

Includes glossary and bibliographical references

Marcovitz, Hal

Asthma. ReferencePoint Press 2010 96p il (Compact research: diseases and disorders) lib bdg $25.95

Grades: 7 8 9 10   **616.2**

1. Asthma

ISBN 978-1-60152-104-0 lib bdg; 1-60152-104-9 lib bdg

LC 2009036844

This "title begins with an overview of [asthma], followed by chapters that define the condition, explain its causes, and discuss possible treatments. . . . The last chapter . . . is about how to live with the condition. Chapters present material in accessible language, provide report-ready, primary-source quotes from experts, and end with a Facts and Illustrations section in which information is summarized in bullet points and accompanied by colorful graphs and charts that will appeal to visual learners." SLJ

Includes bibliographical references

Parks, Peggy J., 1951-

Influenza. ReferencePoint Press 2011 96p il map (Compact research: diseases and disorders) lib bdg $26.95

Grades: 7 8 9 10 11 12   **616.2**
1. Influenza 2. Swine influenza
ISBN 978-1-60152-118-7; 1-60152-118-9
LC 2010-26063

This book about influenza "begins with a general overview followed by a focus on statistics, causes, symptoms, treatments, and prevention. [The book] discusses the virus that causes the disease; presents information on prevention through proper hygiene as well as vaccination, especially during epidemics; and warns against public apathy. . . . The readable page design features pull quotes and subtitles, with occasional photos throughout." Booklist

Includes bibliographical references

Royston, Angela

Explaining asthma. Smart Apple Media 2010 45p il (Explaining) lib bdg $34.25

Grades: 5 6 7 8   **616.2**
1. Asthma
ISBN 978-1-59920-315-7 lib bdg; 1-59920-315-4 lib bdg
LC 2008-49284

Describes what living with asthma is like, discussing symptoms, triggers, treatments, and lifestyle changes that may be necessary to prevent asthma attacks

The book provides a "basic [overview] of the health concerns related to the disease; information on diagnosis and treatment; and a discussion of the challenges or complications experienced by the affected person and their family/friends, and how to manage those problems. . . . The incorporation of quotes and personal accounts in 'Case Notes' sidebars adds to the sensitive tone found throughout [the title]." SLJ

Includes glossary

Silverstein, Alvin

★ The **asthma** update; [by] Alvin and Virginia Silverstein, and Laura Silverstein Nunn. Enslow Publishers 2006 128p il (Disease update) lib bdg $31.93

Grades: 5 6 7 8   **616.2**
1. Asthma
ISBN 0-7660-2482-2
LC 2005-18728

This describes the history, causes, diagnosis, treatment, prevention, and future of asthma

This "provides a clearly written, well-organized, and well-documented account of a disease that is increasingly prevalent among young people." Booklist

Includes glossary and bibliographical references

Smith, Terry L.

Asthma; [by] Terry L. Smith. Chelsea House 2008 128p il (Genes & disease) lib bdg $35

Grades: 7 8 9 10   **616.2**
1. Asthma
ISBN 978-0-7910-9663-5 lib bdg; 0-7910-9663-7 lib bdg
LC 2008-44774

This book opens "with accounts of people who have [asthma] . . . followed by information on history, symptoms, variations, diagnosis, treatments, and research. . . . Chapters devoted to current genetic research and therapies can become dense as they introduce complex topics but photos, diagrams and charts help to clarify the details. . . . Controversial issues . . . are introduced fairly." SLJ

Includes glossary and bibliographical references

Yancey, Diane

Tuberculosis; rev ed; Twenty-First Century Books 2008 128p il (Twenty-first century medical library) lib bdg $30.60

Grades: 8 9 10 11   **616.2**
1. Tuberculosis
ISBN 978-0-8225-9190-0 lib bdg; 0-8225-9190-1 lib bdg
LC 2007-30486

The author begins this book with a history of tuberculosis, "tracing evidence of it back to the Neolithic Age and then explores the variety of treatments used to combat it. . . . The three personal cases related are from three different socioeconomic situations. Good-quality, black-and-white photos appear throughout." SLJ [review of 2001 edition]

Includes bibliographical references

616.3   Diseases of digestive system

Allman, Toney

Obesity. Cherry Lake Pub. 2009 32p il (Health at risk) lib bdg $27.07

Grades: 4 5 6 7   **616.3**
1. Obesity
ISBN 978-1-60279-285-2 lib bdg; 1-60279-285-2 lib bdg
LC 2008017499

This describes the causes and dangers of obesity and the many efforts being made to help people control their weight.

"Great for reports or reluctant readers." Booklist

Includes bibliographical references

Bjorklund, Ruth

★ **Cystic** fibrosis. Marshall Cavendish Benchmark 2009 64p il (Health alert) $22.95

Grades: 4 5 6 7   **616.3**
  1. Cystic fibrosis
  ISBN 978-0-7614-2912-8; 0-7614-2912-3
                                        LC 2007-46674
This "title features a handsome format, with well-chosen illustrations, a substantial amount of information, and some practical insights." Booklist

Fredericks, Carrie
  Obesity. Reference Point Press 2008 104p il map (Compact research. Current issues) lib bdg $24.95
Grades: 8 9 10 11 12   **616.3**
  1. Obesity
  ISBN 978-1-60152-040-1; 1-60152-040-9
                                        LC 2007-42183
Examines the topic of obesity in a format with objective overviews, primary source quotes, illustrated facts, and statistics.
  "Both general readers and serious researchers will find something useful in this volume. It facilitates research for less-motivated students and supplies excellent information for better researchers." SLJ
  Includes bibliographical references

Goldsmith, Connie
  Hepatitis. Twenty-First Century Books 2010 128p il (USA Today health reports: diseases and disorders) lib bdg $34.60
Grades: 7 8 9 10 11 12   **616.3**
  1. Liver -- Diseases
  ISBN 978-0-8225-6787-5; 0-8225-6787-3
                                        LC 2009-20720
This "reveals that an estimated five million Americans have viral Hepatitis A, B, and C, making it a major public health problem. . . . The detailed information is combined with photos and diagrams portraying transmission, vaccines, and effective treatment. . . . [The] accessible design extends the impressive educational data." Booklist
  Includes bibliographical references

Hicks, Terry Allan
  ★ **Obesity**. Marshall Cavendish Benchmark 2009 63p il (Health alert) $22.95
Grades: 4 5 6 7   **616.3**
  1. Obesity
  ISBN 978-0-7614-2911-1; 0-7614-2911-5
                                        LC 2007-31246
This "title features a handsome format, with well-chosen illustrations, a substantial amount of information, and some practical insights." Booklist
  Includes glossary

Marcovitz, Hal
  Hepatitis. ReferencePoint Press 2009 112p il (Compact research. Diseases and disorders) lib bdg $25.95

Grades: 8 9 10 11 12   **616.3**
  1. Liver -- Diseases
  ISBN 978-1-60152-039-5 lib bdg; 1-60152-039-5 lib bdg
                                        LC 2007-38874
Presents information on hepatitis through essays, quotations, statistics, and suggestions for further research
  "The coverage is succinct . . . [and] includes colorful illustrations and figures, chronologies, related organizations, advocacy groups and sources for additional research." Libr Media Connect
  Includes bibliographical references

Obesity; Tom and Gena Metcalf, editors. Thomson / Gale 2008 136p il (Perspectives on diseases and disorders) lib bdg $34.95
Grades: 7 8 9 10   **616.3**
  1. Obesity
  ISBN 978-0-7377-3873-5; 0-7377-3873-1
                                        LC 2007-37470
"This book explains what obesity is, provides insight into its causes, and takes a serious look at why it's becoming such an epidemic. Accounts by people who have firsthand experience dealing with being overweight add value to the book." SLJ
  Includes glossary and bibliographical references

Powell, Jillian
  Explaining cystic fibrosis. Smart Apple Media 2010 45p il (Explaining) lib bdg $34.25
Grades: 5 6 7 8   **616.3**
  1. Cystic fibrosis
  ISBN 978-1-59920-312-6 lib bdg; 1-59920-312-X lib bdg
                                        LC 2008-49288
Describes the illness, including its causes, how it is diagnosed, current treatments for the illness, and how those with cystic fibrosis lead everyday lives
  The book provides a "basic [overview] of the health concerns related to the disease; information on diagnosis and treatment; and a discussion of the challenges or complications experienced by the affected person and their family/ friends, and how to manage those problems. . . . The incorporation of quotes and personal accounts in 'Case Notes' sidebars adds to the sensitive tone found throughout [the title]." SLJ
  Includes glossary and bibliographical references

616.4   Diseases of endocrine, hematopoietic, lymphatic, glandular systems; diseases of male breast

Allman, Toney
  Diabetes. Chelsea House 2008 136p il (Genes & disease) lib bdg $35
Grades: 7 8 9 10   **616.4**
  1. Diabetes
  ISBN 978-0-7910-9585-0; 0-7910-9585-1
                                        LC 2008-1195

This "well-written book . . . [discusses] diabetes, its treatments, genetic variations contributing to the disease, and the prospects for a cure. The narrative starts with the diagnosis of diabetes and follows with seven chapters." Sci Books Films

Includes glossary and bibliographical references

Ambrose, Marylou

Investigating diabetes; real facts for real lives. Enslow Publishers 2010 160p il (Investigating diseases) lib bdg $34.60

Grades: 6 7 8 9 10   **616.4**

1. Diabetes

ISBN 978-0-7660-3338-2; 0-7660-3338-4

LC 2008-30778

"The book is a comprehensive primer that can well serve patients with newly diagnosed diabetes and their families with its detailed account of diabetes, the causes of the disease, and its potential consequences." Sci Books Films

Includes glossary and bibliographical references

Brill, Marlene Targ, 1945-

Diabetes. Twenty-First Century Books 2011 128p il (USA Today health reports: diseases and disorders) lib bdg $34.60

Grades: 7 8 9 10 11 12   **616.4**

1. Diabetes

ISBN 978-0-7613-6085-8; 0-7613-6085-9

LC 2010049454

This volume explores the history of diabetes, and explains the various treatments that are available today.

"This is an important endeavor from the author [that] will be very helpful for patients and others who are looking for basic information about diabetes. The author has done a good job of helping readers understand how their bodies function and the underlying mechanism of diabetes." Sci Books Films

Includes glossary and bibliographical references

Loughrey, Anita

Explaining diabetes. Smart Apple Media 2010 45p il (Explaining) lib bdg $34.25

Grades: 5 6 7 8   **616.4**

1. Diabetes

ISBN 978-1-59920-314-0 lib bdg; 1-59920-314-6 lib bdg

LC 2008-49290

Provides an overview of Type 1 and Type 2 diabetes, discussing causes and symptoms, recommended and required lifestyle changes, how the disease is managed, and possible complications that may occur

The book provides a "basic [overview] of the health concerns related to the disease; information on diagnosis and treatment; and a discussion of the challenges or complications experienced by the affected person and their family/ friends, and how to manage those problems. . . . The incorporation of quotes and personal accounts in 'Case Notes' sidebars adds to the sensitive tone found throughout [the title]." SLJ

Includes glossary and bibliographical references

Yuwiler, Janice

Diabetes. ReferencePoint Press 2009 96p il (Compact research. Diseases and disorders) lib bdg $25.95

Grades: 7 8 9 10   **616.4**

1. Diabetes

ISBN 978-1-60152-076-0; 1-60152-076-X

LC 2009-6173

"Yuwiler discusses type 1 diabetes and its management, type 2 diabetes and its prevention, metabolic syndrome, and medical advances. . . . Subtopics are delineated by brightly colored burgundy headings; blocks of orange-colored sidebars with bright-red print and relevant color photos and illustrations appear throughout. Each chapter ends with several pages of primary-source quotes and facts and illustrations that offer greater clarity to the text." SLJ

Includes bibliographical references

616.5   Diseases of integument

Faulk, Michelle

The **case** of the flesh-eating bacteria; Annie Biotica solves skin disease crimes. by Michelle Faulk. Lake Book Manufacturing, Inc. 2013 48 p. (Body system disease investigations) (library) $23.93

Grades: 5 6 7 8   **616.5**

1. Skin -- Diseases 2. Virus diseases 3. Skin -- Infections

ISBN 0766039455; 9780766039452

LC 2011023985

This book by Michelle Faulk "from the Body System Disease Investigations series introduces Agent Annie Biotica, a 'Disease Scene Investigator' with the Major Health Crimes Unit'. This cartoon-style heroine is called in to solve a series of skin-related medical cases . . . caused by flesh-eating bacteria, pinkeye, ringworm, chicken pox, [and] measles." (Booklist)

Includes bibliographical references (p. 47) and index

Juettner, Bonnie

Acne. Lucent Books 2010 104p il (Diseases and disorders series) lib bdg $33.45

Grades: 7 8 9 10   **616.5**

1. Acne

ISBN 978-1-4205-0215-2; 1-4205-0215-8

LC 2009-33484

First published 2004

"Well-organized chapters present clear information on the causes of acne, types of self-treatment, medical and 'alternative' paths to a cure, the future of treatment, and the psychological ramifications for an affected person. . . . This title will be useful for reports and is a solid addition to health and/or disease collections." SLJ

Includes bibliographical references

Lew, Kristi

Itch & ooze; gross stuff on your skin. illustrations by Michael Slack. Millbrook Press 2010 48p il (Gross body science) lib bdg $29.27

Grades: 4 5 6   616.5
1. Skin 2. Skin -- Diseases
ISBN 978-0-8225-8963-1 lib bdg; 0-8225-8963-X
lib bdg

LC 2008-45591

Presents disgusting facts about human skin, the diseases and parasites that can cause problems with it, and how it functions to protect the body and itself.

"Solid information layered between sarcastic comments and kid-friendly terminology like fart, poop, barf, and puke will keep readers engaged. . . . Labeled, captioned (and graphic) photographs, cartoon-style illustrations, and micrographs add information." SLJ

Includes glossary and bibliographical references

Skin health information for teens; health tips about dermatological disorders and activities that affect the skin, hair, and nails. edited by Lisa Esposito. 3rd ed. Omnigraphics, Inc. 2013 424 p. (hardcover) $69.00
Grades: 7 8 9 10   616.5
1. Skin -- Care 2. Skin -- Diseases 3. Teenagers -- Health and hygiene 4. Beauty, Personal 5. Skin -- Care and hygiene
ISBN 0780813170; 9780780813175

LC 2013009908

This book "provides updated information about the skin, hair, and nails. It explains how the skin and its related structures grow and how to keep them healthy. Common ailments, including acne, eczema, impetigo, psoriasis, vitiligo, and warts are explained, and a section on skin cancer provides information about cancer risks, prevention strategies, warning signs, and treatments. The care of skin injuries, including cuts, scrapes, burns, bites, and stings, is also discussed." (Publisher's note)

Includes bibliographical references and index.

616.6 Diseases of urogenital system

The **kidneys** and the renal system; edited by Kara Rogers. Britannica Educational Pub. in association with Rosen Educational Services 2012 xvii, 174 p.p col. ill. $45.00
Grades: 7 8 9 10 11 12   616.6
1. Kidneys 2. Human anatomy 3. Urinary organs 4. Kidneys -- Diseases
ISBN 161530679X; 9781615306794

LC 2011026615

This biology reference work, edited by Kara Rogers, describes the Human waste system. "Responsible for managing the body's waste and regulating the balance of water and electrolytes, the kidneys and renal system, in a sense, make up the body's plumbing network. . . . This volume examines the various components of the renal, or urinary, system, and the consequences of dysfunction and disease." (Publisher's note)

Includes bibliographical references and index

616.7 Diseases of musculoskeletal system

Gray, Susan Heinrichs
   Living with juvenile rheumatoid arthritis. Child's World 2003 32p il (Living well) lib bdg $25.64
Grades: 4 5 6   616.7
1. Diseases 2. Arthritis 3. Rheumatoid arthritis 4. Rheumatoid arthritis in children
ISBN 1-56766-104-1

LC 2002-2870

This title "leads off with an introduction to a young person who has [juvenile rheumatoid arthritis]. Subsequent chapters explain the physiology of the illness, what causes it, and what it's like to live with it. [The concluding section looks] at possible treatments and potential cures. [The text is] clear and simple, double spaced, and punctuated by colorful exemplary photos of kids dealing with the disease." SLJ

Includes glossary and bibliographical references

Hoffmann, Gretchen
   ★ **Osteoporosis**. Marshall Cavendish Benchmark 2007 64p il (Health alert) lib bdg $21.95
Grades: 4 5 6 7   616.7
1. Osteoporosis
ISBN 978-0-7614-2702-5; 0-7614-2702-3

LC 2007008787

This describes what it is like to have osteoporosis, what it is, its history and its diagnosis and treatment

This "title features a handsome format, with well-chosen illustrations, a substantial amount of information, and some practical insights." Booklist

Includes glossary and bibliographical references

616.8 Diseases of nervous system and mental disorders

Bender, Lionel
   Explaining epilepsy. Smart Apple Media 2010 45p il (Explaining) lib bdg $34.25
Grades: 5 6 7 8   616.8
1. Epilepsy
ISBN 978-1-59920-309-6 lib bdg; 1-59920-309-X lib bdg

LC 2008-49292

Describes the nature, symptoms, and possible causes of epilepsy, gives a history of its study, and discusses its treatment

The book provides a "basic [overview] of the health concerns related to the disease; information on diagnosis and treatment; and a discussion of the challenges or complications experienced by the affected person and their family/friends, and how to manage those problems. . . . The incorporation of quotes and personal accounts in 'Case Notes' sidebars adds to the sensitive tone found throughout [the title]." SLJ

Includes glossary and bibliographical references

Bjorklund, Ruth
   ★ **Cerebral** palsy. Marshall Cavendish Benchmark 2007 64p il (Health alert) lib bdg $31.36

Grades: 4 5 6 7   **616.8**
   1. Cerebral palsy
   ISBN 978-0-7614-2209-9; 0-7614-2209-9
               LC 2006-15818
   This "title features a handsome format, with well-chosen illustrations, a substantial amount of information, and some practical insights." Booklist
   Includes glossary and bibliographical references

★ **Epilepsy**. Marshall Cavendish Benchmark 2007 63p il (Health alert) lib bdg $21.95
Grades: 4 5 6 7   **616.8**
   1. Epilepsy
   ISBN 978-0-7614-2206-8; 0-7614-2206-4
               LC 2006-15816
   This "title features a handsome format, with well-chosen illustrations, a substantial amount of information, and some practical insights." Booklist
   Includes glossary and bibliographical references

Brill, Marlene Targ
   Alzheimer's disease. Benchmark Books 2005 64p il (Health alert) $28.50
Grades: 4 5 6 7   **616.8**
   1. Alzheimer's disease
   ISBN 0-7614-1799-0
               LC 2004-6528
   The author explains "the causes, physiology, treatments, and complications associated with [Alzheimer's disease]. The [book is] well organized. . . . The photos are colorful and . . . some are startling, including the brain scans of a patient with Alzheimer's." SLJ
   Includes bibliographical references

Colligan, L. H.
   ★ **Sleep** disorders. Marshall Cavendish Benchmark 2009 64p il (Health alert) $22.95
Grades: 4 5 6 7   **616.8**
   1. Sleep disorders
   ISBN 978-0-7614-2913-5; 0-7614-2913-1
   This "title features a handsome format, with well-chosen illustrations, a substantial amount of information, and some practical insights." Booklist
   Includes glossary

Dittmer, Lori
   Parkinson's disease. Creative Education 2011 48p il (Living with disease) $23.95
Grades: 6 7 8 9   **616.8**
   1. Parkinson's disease
   ISBN 978-1-60818-076-9; 1-60818-076-X
               LC 2010030366
   A look at Parkinson's disease, examining the ways in which it develops, its symptoms and diagnosis, the effects it has on a person's daily life, and research toward finding better treatments.
   "The text is clearly written. . . . The book's design is simple and bold. . . . A brief but informative introduction to Parkinson's disease." Booklist
   Includes glossary and bibliographical references

Dougherty, Terri
   Epilepsy. Lucent Books 2010 104p il (Diseases and disorders series) lib bdg $33.45
Grades: 7 8 9 10 11 12   **616.8**
   1. Epilepsy
   ISBN 978-1-4205-0218-3; 1-4205-0218-2
               LC 2009-33344
   This "offers a thorough explanation of [epilepsy], giving a basic definition; a discussion of the causes, symptoms, and treatments; a description of living with the disease; and ideas of future treatment and diagnoses. The color photographs and sidebars help to make the information in the dense text more easily understood, and personal stories provide insight into how individuals deal with their disease. . . . Different types of seizures and the varied triggers are explained." Voice Youth Advocates
   Includes bibliographical references

Esherick, Joan
   The **journey** toward recovery; youth with brain injury. Mason Crest Publishers 2004 127p il (Youth with special needs) hardcover o.p. pa $14.95
Grades: 7 8 9 10   **616.8**
   1. Brain damaged children
   ISBN 1-59084-734-2; 1-4222-0425-1 pa
               LC 2003-18640
   Through the story of Jerome, a teenager who suffers a traumatic brain injury from a bike accident, this book discusses different "forms of brain injury; how these injuries affect people's lives; and how schools, doctors, and lawmakers are helping youth with this form of special need." Publisher's note
   Includes glossary and bibliographical references

Freedman, Jeri
   Tay-Sachs disease. Chelsea House 2009 128p il (Genes & disease) lib bdg $35
Grades: 7 8 9 10   **616.8**
   1. Medical genetics 2. Tay-Sachs disease
   ISBN 978-0-7910-9634-5; 0-7910-9634-3
               LC 2008-44770
   This book "discusses the nature of the disease, why it affects certain groups of people more often than others, how genetic screening can help detect carriers of the Tay-Sachs gene, and what options genetic testing and counseling provide for having children." Publisher's note
   Includes glossary and bibliographical references

Gay, Kathlyn
   ★ **Epilepsy**; the ultimate teen guide. [by] Kathlyn Gay and Sean McGarrahan. Scarecrow Press 2002 103p il (It happened to me) pa $12.95
Grades: 7 8 9 10 11 12   **616.8**
   1. Diseases 2. Epilepsy 3. Epilepsy in adolescence
   ISBN 978-0-8108-5835-0 pa
               LC 2002-4718
   The authors explain the various forms epilepsy takes, the history of the disease, folklore about it, and its diagnosis and treatment

"An excellent look at epilepsy and its impact on diagnosed teens, their families, friends, and communities. . . . Readable, well organized, and well documented." SLJ

Includes glossary and bibliographical references

Goldstein, Natalie

Parkinson's disease. Chelsea House 2008 128p il (Genes & disease) lib bdg $35

Grades: 7 8 9 10   616.8

   1. Parkinson's disease

   ISBN 978-0-7910-9584-3; 0-7910-9584-3

                               LC 2008-10494

This book opens "with accounts of people who have [Parkinson's] disease . . . followed by information on history, symptoms, variations, diagnosis, treatments, and research. . . . Chapters devoted to current genetic research and therapies can become dense as they introduce complex topics but photos, diagrams and charts help to clarify the details. . . . [Controversial issues] are introduced fairly." SLJ

Includes glossary and bibliographical references

Klosterman, Lorrie

★ **Meningitis**. Marshall Cavendish Benchmark 2007 64p il (Health alert) lib bdg $31.36

Grades: 4 5 6 7   616.8

   1. Meningitis

   ISBN 978-0-7614-2211-2; 0-7614-2211-0

                             LC 2006015819

This "title features a handsome format, with well-chosen illustrations, a substantial amount of information, and some practical insights." Booklist

Includes glossary and bibliographical references

Levete, Sarah

Explaining cerebral palsy. Smart Apple Media 2010 45p il (Explaining) lib bdg $34.25

Grades: 5 6 7 8   616.8

   1. Cerebral palsy

   ISBN 978-1-59920-311-9 lib bdg; 1-59920-311-1 lib bdg

                             LC 2008-49287

Describes the illness, including its causes, how it is diagnosed, current treatment methods, and how those with cerebral palsy live everyday lives

The book provides a "basic [overview] of the health concerns related to the disease; information on diagnosis and treatment; and a discussion of the challenges or complications experienced by the affected person and their family/ friends, and how to manage those problems. . . . The incorporation of quotes and personal accounts in 'Case Notes' sidebars adds to the sensitive tone found throughout [the title]." SLJ

Includes glossary and bibliographical references

Marcovitz, Hal

Meningitis. ReferencePoint Press 2009 112p il (Compact research. Diseases and disorders) lib bdg $25.95

Grades: 7 8 9 10   616.8

   1. Meningitis

   ISBN 978-1-60152-043-2 lib bdg; 1-60152-043-3 lib bdg

                             LC 2007-45213

Presents an overview of meningitis and discusses symptoms, disease contraction, social impacts, and prevention

"The coverage is succinct . . . [and] includes colorful illustrations and figures, chronologies, related organizations, advocacy groups, and sources for additional research." Libr Media Connect

Includes bibliographical references

Sleep disorders. ReferencePoint Press 2009 104p 48p il (Compact research. Diseases and disorders) lib bdg $25.95

Grades: 7 8 9 10 11 12   616.8

   1. Sleep disorders

   ISBN 978-1-60152-071-5; 1-60152-071-9

                             LC 2008-46115

"Marcovitz's coverage ranges from insomnia to potential medical conditions that can lead to death, such as sleep apnea and narcolepsy. This book is a comprehensive overview of an often misunderstood subject." SLJ

Includes bibliographical references

616.85 Miscellaneous diseases of nervous system and mental disorders

Ambrose, Marylou

Investigating eating disorders (anorexia, bulimia, and binge eating) real facts for real lives. [by] Marylou Ambrose and Veronica Deisler. Enslow Publishers 2011 160p il (Investigating diseases) lib bdg $34.60

Grades: 6 7 8 9 10   616.85

   1. Eating disorders

   ISBN 978-0-7660-3339-9; 0-7660-3339-2

                             LC 2009-6492

"This book is a well-organized, clear, succinct, and attractive presentation on anorexia, bulimia, and binge eating. In it, the authors have gathered helpful definitions, early religious history, international viewpoints, statistics, family issues, medical and psychological assessments, treatments, medications, and legislation to present information on the future outlook of, and research into, these eating disorders." Sci Books Films

Includes glossary and bibliographical references

Autism; Carrie Fredericks, book editor. Greenhaven Press 2008 168p il (Perspectives on diseases and disorders) $34.95

Grades: 7 8 9 10   616.85

   1. Autism

   ISBN 978-0-7377-3869-8

                             LC 2007-37472

"Explores the symptoms, causes and treatment of this lifelong disease that profoundly affects social functioning, language and behavior." Publisher's note

Includes glossary and bibliographical references

Baish, Vanessa

Self-image and eating disorders; by Rita Smith ... [et al.] 1st ed. Rosen Pub. 2013 48 p. col. ill. (library) $29.25

Grades: 6 7 8 9   **616.85**

1. Body image 2. Eating disorders 3. Body image in adolescence 4. Eating disorders in adolescence -- Treatment 5. Eating disorders in adolescence -- Psychological aspects

ISBN 1448868947; 9781448868940

LC 2012003030

This book on self-image and eating disorders by Rita Smith is part of the "Teen Mental Health" series. It "addresses self-esteem and negative body image. Eating disorders include anorexia nervosa, bulimia nervosa, binge eating, orthorexia nervosa, and compulsive exercise, along with related health and emotional problems. The books discuss techniques for coping and encourage teens to seek out available resources such as professional help, support groups, or school programs." (School Library Journal)

Includes bibliographical references (p. 43-46) and index.

Barbour, Scott

Post-traumatic stress disorder. ReferencePoint Press 2009 104p (Compact research: diseases and disorders) lib bdg $25.95

Grades: 7 8 9 10   **616.85**

1. Post-traumatic stress disorder

ISBN 978-1-60152-101-9 lib bdg; 1-60152-101-4 lib bdg

LC 2009033216

This "title begins with an overview of [post-traumatic stress disorder], followed by chapters that define the condition, explain its causes, and discuss possible treatments. . . . The final chapter discusses how society should help soldiers with the problem. . . . Chapters present material in accessible language, provide report-ready, primary-source quotes from experts, and end with a Facts and Illustrations section in which information is summarized in bullet points and accompanied by colorful graphs and charts that will appeal to visual learners." SLJ

Includes bibliographical references

Bingham, Jane

Eating disorders; by Jane Bingham. Gareth Stevens Pub. 2009 48p il (Emotional health issues) lib bdg $31

Grades: 6 7 8 9   **616.85**

1. Eating disorders

ISBN 978-0-8368-9200-0; 0-8368-9200-3

LC 2008-825

First published 2008 in the United Kingdom

This book about eating disorders has "clear language and explanations. . . . [It is] suitable for fact-finding missions, but the abundant graphics and case studies are likely to draw in browsers as well. Throughout, unfamiliar vocabulary is highlighted in bold and explained in context and in the glossary. . . . Fact boxes and case study sidebars add information." SLJ

Includes glossary and bibliographical references

Stress and depression; [by] Jane Bingham. Gareth Stevens 2009 48p il (Emotional health issues) lib bdg $31

Grades: 6 7 8 9   **616.85**

1. Stress (Psychology) 2. Depression (Psychology)

ISBN 978-0-8368-9203-1 lib bdg; 0-8368-9203-8 lib bdg

LC 2008-5237

First published 2008 in the United Kingdom

This book about stress and depression has "clear language and explanations. . . . [It is] suitable for fact-finding missions, but the abundant graphics and case studies are likely to draw in browsers as well. Throughout, unfamiliar vocabulary is highlighted in bold and explained in context and in the glossary. . . . Fact boxes and case study sidebars add information." SLJ

Includes glossary and bibliographical references

Bjornlund, Lydia D.

Personality disorders; by Lydia Bjornlund. ReferencePoint Press 2011 96p il (Compact research: diseases and disorders) lib bdg $26.95

Grades: 7 8 9 10   **616.85**

1. Personality disorders

ISBN 978-1-60152-139-2; 1-60152-139-1

LC 2010031384

This title provides "a systematic and focused look at [personality disorders]. . . . [It] covers 10 types, including paranoid and schizoid disorders. . . . [It explores] causes and the ways these conditions impact patients' lives and ultimately [addresses] whether sufferers can overcome them. Short sections containing primary-source quotes and bulleted facts and charts that highlight important information are appended to each chapter." SLJ

Includes bibliographical references

Brill, Marlene Targ

★ **Down** syndrome. Marshall Cavendish Benchmark 2007 64p il (Health alert) lib bdg $31.36

Grades: 4 5 6 7   **616.85**

1. Down syndrome

ISBN 978-0-7614-2207-5 lib bdg; 0-7614-2207-2 lib bdg

LC 2006-15817

This "title features a handsome format, with well-chosen illustrations, a substantial amount of information, and some practical insights." Booklist

Includes glossary and bibliographical references

Capaccio, George

★ **ADD** and ADHD. Marshall Cavendish Benchmark 2007 64p il (Health alert) lib bdg $21.95

Grades: 4 5 6 7   **616.85**

1. Attention deficit disorder

ISBN 978-0-7614-2705-6; 0-7614-2705-8

LC 2007008790

This describes what it is like to have Attention Deficit Disorder or Attention Deficit Hyperactivity Disorder, what they are, their history, and living with the disorders.

This "title features a handsome format, with well-chosen illustrations, a substantial amount of information, and some practical insights." Booklist

Includes glossary and bibliographical references

Christopherson, Sara Cohen

Living with epilepsy; by Sara Cohen Christopherson. ABDO Pub. Co. 2012 112 p. col. ill. (library) $34.22

Grades: 6 7 8   **616.85**
  1. Epilepsy
  ISBN 1617831271; 9781617831270
                                          LC 2011033155
This book "features fictional narratives paired with firsthand advice from a medical expert to help preteens and teenagers feel prepared for dealing with epilepsy during adolescence. Topics include causes, risk factors, and prevention, diagnosis, types of seizures, treatment, managing epilepsy, and dealing with social issues." (Publisher's note)

Includes bibliographical references (p. 104, 106-109) and index.

Cobain, Bev

When nothing matters anymore; a survival guide for depressed teens. edited by Elizabeth Verdick. rev and updated ed.; Free Spirit Pub. 2007 146p il pa $14.95

Grades: 7 8 9 10   **616.85**
  1. Depression (Psychology)
  ISBN 978-1-57542-235-0; 1-57542-235-2
                                          LC 2006-36325
First published 1998
This book written for teens defines depression, describes the symptoms, and explains that depression is treatable

"This practical, reassuring book should be made available to all teens." Voice Youth Advocates

Includes bibliographical references

Currie-McGhee, L. K.

Exercise addiction; by Leanne Currie-McGhee. Lucent Books 2011 96p il (Diseases & disorders) lib bdg $33.45

Grades: 7 8 9 10   **616.85**
  1. Exercise addiction
  ISBN 978-1-4205-0551-1; 1-4205-0551-3
                                          LC 2010039535
"Extremely readable, with helpful illustrations and sidebars, this book includes a definition of exercise addiction (with symptoms), describes how it may be related to other psychological disorders, profiles the types of people most at risk for developing it, discusses psychological and physiological dangers, and offers treatment options. . . . Personal stories appear throughout, and there is a helpful list of questions for readers to ask themselves. This volume is interesting enough to read even if not required for an assignment." SLJ

Includes bibliographical references

Denkmire, Heather

★ The **truth** about anxiety and depression; Heather Denkmire, principal author; John Perritano,

contributing author; Robert N. Golden, general editor, Fred L. Peterson, general editor. 2nd ed.; Facts on File 2010 199p il (Truth about series) $35

Grades: 7 8 9 10   **616.85**
  1. Anxiety 2. Depression (Psychology)
  ISBN 978-0-8160-7643-7; 0-8160-7643-X
                                          LC 2010005461
First published 2004 with title: The truth about fear and depression

Presents information on anxiety and depression, including the genetics of mood and anxiety disorders, gender and depression, types of treatments available, related disorders, and more.

Includes glossary and bibliographical references

Depression; Emma Carlson Berne, book editor. Greenhaven 2007 184p (Contemporary issues companion) $36.20; pa $24.95

Grades: 8 9 10 11 12   **616.85**
  1. Depression (Psychology)
  ISBN 978-0-7377-3645-8; 0-7377-3645-3; 978-0-7377-2451-6 pa; 0-7377-2451-X pa
                                          LC 2007-19643
First published 1999 under the editorship of Henny H. Kim

"Eighteen field specialists have each contributed an essay on topics as diverse as deep brain stimulation and alternative therapies. A chapter on antidepressants and their heavily debated effects concludes the book. Thoughtfully composed, this excellent introduction to a widely recognized condition contains an extensive bibliography and support organization contact list." Libr J

Includes bibliographical references

Donovan, Sandra, 1967-

Keep your cool! what you should know about stress. illustrations by Jack Desrocher. Lerner Publications Co. 2009 64p il (Health zone) lib bdg $30.60

Grades: 4 5 6 7   **616.85**
  1. Stress (Psychology)
  ISBN 978-0-8225-7555-9; 0-8225-7555-8
                                          LC 2007038858
This describes what causes stress and what you can do to relieve it.

"The format is beyond lively, with lots of color, cartoons, and an informal writing style, but it manages to present sometimes frightening material in a non-threatening and browsable way." Booklist

Includes glossary and bibliographical references

★ **Eating** disorders information for teens; health tips about anorexia, bulimia, binge eating, and body image disorders, including information about risk factors, prevention, diagnosis, treatment, health consequences, and other related issues. edited by Elizabeth Bellenir. 3rd ed. Omnigraphics, Inc. 2013 xiii, 380 p.p ill. (hardcover) $69

Grades: 7 8 9 10 11 12   **616.85**
  1. Eating disorders 2. Teenagers -- Health and hygiene

3. Eating disorders in adolescence
ISBN 0780812697; 9780780812697

LC 2012036612

This book "provides information about a wide range of eating and body image disorders. The volume is broken into six parts covering general information about eating disorders; specific disorders such as anorexia nervosa, bulimia nervosa, and others; the heath consequences of eating disorders; prevention, diagnosis, and treatment; healthy eating and exercise; and additional reading, research studies, and organizations." (Voice of Youth Advocates)

Includes bibliographical references and index.

Evans-Martin, Fay

Down syndrome; [by] F. Fay Evans-Martin. Chelsea House 2008 128p il (Genes & disease) lib bdg $35

Grades: 7 8 9 10   **616.85**

1. Down syndrome 2. Medical genetics
ISBN 978-0-7910-9644-4; 0-7910-9644-0

LC 2008-44773

"Down syndrome is a developmental disorder caused by the presence of an extra copy of chromosome 21. . . . [This book] explains this genetic disease, its history and characteristics, and what scientists are doing to study it." Publisher's note

Includes glossary and bibliographical references

Farrar, Amy

ADHD. Twenty-First Century Books 2010 112p il (USA Today health reports: diseases and disorders) lib bdg $34.60

Grades: 7 8 9 10 11 12   **616.85**

1. Attention deficit disorder
ISBN 978-0-7613-5455-0; 0-7613-5455-7

LC 2010-870

This book describes attention deficit-hyperactivity disorder, its causes and treatments.

This is "liberally sprinkled with relevant articles and 'snapshots' (graphs showing statistical breakdowns of the topic at hand) from the newspaper, providing a competent introduction to primary-source material." SLJ

Includes glossary and bibliographical references

Ford, Emily

★ **What** you must think of me; a firsthand account of one teenager's experience with social anxiety disorder. by Emily Ford with Michael R. Liebowitz and Linda Wasmer Andrews. Oxford University Press 2007 xxi, 152p (Annenberg Foundation Trust at Sunnylands' adolescent mental health initiative) $30; pa $9.95

Grades: 7 8 9 10 11 12   **616.85**

1. Social phobia
ISBN 978-0-19-531302-4; 0-19-531302-X; 978-0-19-531303-1 pa; 0-19-531303-8 pa

LC 2006102285

"A professor of clinical psychiatry and a woman whose life has been adversely impacted by social anxiety disorder provide a unique view of the condition and its treatment in this slim volume. . . . Readers will find helpful charts

throughout the book and an appendix loaded with further reading and contact information for advocacy groups. Thanks to its informative guide to diagnosis, suggestions for treatment and tips on dealing with the health care system, this is a must read for anyone who suffers from the disorder." Publ Wkly

Includes bibliographical references

Hallowell, Edward M.

★ **Positively** ADD; real success stories to inspire your dreams. [by] Catherine A. Corman and Edward M. Hallowell. Walker 2006 172p il $16.95; lib bdg $17.85

Grades: 8 9 10 11 12   **616.85**

1. Attention deficit disorder
ISBN 978-0-8027-8988-4; 0-8027-8988-9; 978-0-8027-8071-3 lib bdg; 0-8027-8071-7 lib bdg

LC 2005037184

This "profiles 17 adults who began dealing with attention deficit disorder in childhood. Along with political strategist [James] Carville, subjects include a Pulitzer Prize-winning photographer, a major league pitcher, and a young Rhodes scholar. . . . [This is] an encouraging, helpful book for teens with ADD as well as for their parents, teachers, and friends." Booklist

Includes bibliographical references

Hidalgo-Robert, Alberto, 1992-

Fat no more; a teenager's victory over obesity. by Alberto Hidalgo-Robert. Pinata Books 2012 184 p. $16.95

Grades: 7 8 9 10 11 12   **616.85**

1. Obesity 2. Lifestyles 3. Teenagers -- Health and hygiene 4. Weight loss -- Personal narratives 5. Weight loss 6. Teenagers -- Nutrition 7. Eating disorders in adolescence
ISBN 1558857451; 9781558857452

LC 2012003177

This book is a "weight-loss memoir. . . . [Alberto] Hidalgo-Robert . . . weighed 230 pounds at 14. The memoir opens with a lengthy indictment of not only himself for years of junk-food addiction, but also his family for being too indulgent and the pediatricians in his native El Salvador for pushing weight-loss diets. . . . "Read the following words carefully and engrave them on your brain: DIETS DO NOT WORK! Diets suck. Diets are unhealthy. . . .." What does work for him is . . . focusing less on weight loss than lifestyle changes. Aside from cutting out TV . . . those changes all seem to involve categorizing foods and limiting the intake of certain kinds. . . . Five years after starting, he's 69 pounds lighter. . . . [H]e demonstrates that the approach can lead to long-term weight loss." (Kirkus)

Hyde, Margaret Oldroyd

Stress 101; an overview for teens. by Margaret O. Hyde and Elizabeth H. Forsyth. TwentyFirst Century Books 2008 120p il (Teen overviews) lib bdg $26.60

Grades: 8 9 10 11 12   **616.85**
   1. Stress (Psychology)
ISBN 978-0-82256-788-2 lib bdg; 0-82256-788-1
lib bdg

LC 2007027631

"Beginning with a brief history of stress from the time it was first identified, Hyde and Forsyth detail its effects on a young person's brain, heart, and immune system. . . . The writing is clear and informative. Interspersed with personal vignettes, the factual information is well organized and presented in small increments." SLJ

Includes bibliographical references

It's raining cats and dogs; an autism spectrum guide to the confusing world of idioms, metaphors, and everyday expressions. Michael Barton; foreword, Delia Barton; illustrator, Michael Barton. Jessica Kingsley Publishers 2012 95 p. (alk. paper) $15.95

Grades: 3 4 5 6   **616.85**
1. Autism 2. Metaphor 3. Figures of speech 4. English language -- Idioms 5. Autistic people -- Language 6. Autism spectrum disorders -- Patients -- Language
ISBN 1849052832; 9781849052832

LC 2011039514

This book offers "insight into the mind of someone with an ASD [autism spectrum disorder]. It . . . illustrates why people with ASDs have problems understanding common phrases and idioms that others accept unquestioningly as part of everyday speech. The . . . drawings" are meant to "entertain and inspire those on the spectrum, giving them the confidence to recognise figures of speech, feel less alienated and even use idioms themselves. The drawings" are designed to "form instantly memorable references for those with ASDs to recall whenever they need to and" should "be helpful for anyone curious to understand the ASD way of thinking." (Publisher's note)

Kramer, Gerri Freid
   ★ The **truth** about eating disorders; Robert N. Golden, Fred L. Peterson general editors; Gerri Freid Kramer, principal author. 2nd ed.; Facts on File 2009 208p (Truth about series) $35

Grades: 7 8 9 10   **616.85**
1. Eating disorders
ISBN 978-0-8160-7633-8; 0-8160-7633-2

LC 2008-44036

First published 2004

This discusses anorexia, bulimia, fad diets, and laxative abuse, the causes of eating disorders, how to recognize the disorders, the portrayal of eating disorders in the media, and obesity and weight control

This title does "an excellent job of providing accurate information for teens. For reports or for self-help, [it belongs] in any library serving young adults." SLJ [review of 2004 edition]

Includes glossary and bibliographical references

Levin, Judith
   Anxiety and panic attacks; [by] Judith Levin. Rosen Pub. 2008 48p il (Teen mental health) lib bdg $19.95

Grades: 7 8 9 10   **616.85**
1. Anxiety 2. Panic disorders
ISBN 9781435848450; 978-1-4042-1797-3; 1-4042-1797-5

LC 2008-7144

This "volume offers a succinct discussion of mental disorders related to anxiety. . . . A vivid description of the causes and symptoms of panic attacks is followed up with a chapter suggesting ways to deal with these troubling events. . . . Color photos brighten this clearly written presentation." Booklist

Includes glossary and bibliographical references

Levy, Joel
   Phobiapedia; all the things we fear the most! Scholastic 2011 80p il pa $8.99

Grades: 4 5 6 7   **616.85**
1. Phobias
ISBN 978-0-545-34929-1; 0-545-34929-X

This briefly describes over 50 phobias.

"With an appealing layout, plenty of color, and enough germs, snakes, and bats to get the heart racing, this title has kid written all over it." Booklist

Lucas, Eileen
   More than the blues? understanding and dealing with depression. Enslow Publishers 2009 112p il (Issues in focus today) lib bdg $31.93

Grades: 7 8 9 10   **616.85**
1. Depression (Psychology)
ISBN 978-0-7660-3065-7 lib bdg; 0-7660-3065-2
lib bdg

LC 2008-39144

"Examines depression and mood disorders, including the causes of depression, a history of the illness, the various types of mood disorders, and treatment methods." Publisher's note

Includes glossary and bibliographical references

Marcovitz, Hal
   Phobias. ReferencePoint Press 2009 112p il (Compact research. Diseases and disorders) lib bdg $25.95

Grades: 7 8 9 10   **616.85**
1. Phobias
ISBN 978-1-60152-044-9 lib bdg; 1-60152-044-1
lib bdg

LC 2008-10894

Through overviews, primary sources, and full color illustrations this title examines phobias

"The coverage is succinct . . . [and] includes colorful illustrations and figures, chronologies, related organizations, advocacy groups, and sources for additional research." Libr Media Connect

Includes bibliographical references

Miller, Allen R.

Living with depression. Facts on File 2007 202p (Teen's guides) $34.95

Grades: 7 8 9 10   **616.85**

    1. Depression (Psychology)

    ISBN 9781438121079; 978-0-8160-6345-1; 0-8160-6345-1; 0-8160-7562-X pa

                         LC 2007-554

This "offers young adults concise information about depression and its treatments.... Chapters on treatments offer detailed information on psychotherapy, antidepressants, and self-help approaches such as diet, exercise, and stress management.... This book is a timely, useful resource." Booklist

Monaque, Mathilde

Trouble in my head; a young girl's fight with depression. translated by Lorenza Garcia. Trafalgar Square 2009 167p pa $15.95

Grades: 7 8 9 10   **616.85**

    1. Mentally ill 2. Depression (Psychology)

    ISBN 978-0-09-191723-4 pa; 0-09-191723-9 pa

"Monaque tells her own story of depression, which began at age 14. Recounting her experience from memory, the teen attempts to discern what caused the illness as well as to explain the process she went through to overcome it.... She is bright and articulate and paints a vivid picture of what depression feels like from the inside." SLJ

Mooney, Carla

Mood disorders. ReferencePoint Press 2010 96p il (Compact research: diseases and disorders) lib bdg $26.95

Grades: 8 9 10 11 12   **616.85**

    1. Depression (Psychology) 2. Manic-depressive illness

    ISBN 978-1-60152-119-4; 1-60152-119-7

                     LC 2010-5868

This book about mood disorders "begins with a general overview followed by focus on statistics, causes, symptoms, treatments, and prevention.... [The book] discusses the two main categories [of mood disorders]: unipolar (if untreated the number-one risk for suicide) and bipolar (which swings between depression and mania.)... The readable page design features pull quotes and subtitles, with occasional photos throughout." Booklist

    Includes bibliographical references

Moragne, Wendy

Depression. Twenty-First Century Books 2011 128p (USA Today health reports: diseases and disorders) lib bdg $34.60

Grades: 8 9 10 11 12   **616.85**

    1. Depression (Psychology)

    ISBN 978-0-7613-5882-4; 0-7613-5882-X

                     LC 2010034122

This book about depression will serve as "solid report fodder.... [The] volume has an introduction, a description of the condition, chapters on what it is like to live with it, and material on research and treatments. A healthy smattering of statistics and personal stories appear throughout." SLJ

    Includes bibliographical references

Parks, Peggy J.

Online addiction; by Peggy J. Parks. ReferencePoint Press, Inc. 2013 96 p. (hardcover) $27.95

Grades: 7 8 9 10 11 12   **616.85**

    1. Internet 2. Internet gambling 3. Addiction 4. Internet addiction -- Popular works

    ISBN 1601522703; 9781601522702

                     LC 2012014191

In this book about online addiction, Peggy J. Parks "addresses four basic questions: Is online addiction real? Can people get addicted to social networking? How serious of a problem is compulsive online gaming and gambling? Can people recover from online addiction? ... Parks addresses each of her four questions in separate sections of her book." (Booklist)

    Includes bibliographical references and index.

Parks, Peggy J., 1951-

Anorexia. ReferencePoint Press 2009 104p il (Compact research. Diseases and disorders) lib bdg $25.95

Grades: 7 8 9 10   **616.85**

    1. Anorexia nervosa

    ISBN 978-1-60152-042-5; 1-60152-042-5

                     LC 2008-4238

Presents information on anorexia, including its causes, its effect on health, and the possiblity of curing it, through essays, quotations, statistics, and suggestions for further research.

    "[This] quality [source] could be used in a variety of different ways–: straight reporting for speech or debate ideas, or as a springboard for further research." SLJ

    Includes bibliographical references

Anxiety disorders. ReferencePoint Press 2011 96p il (Compact research: diseases and disorders) lib bdg $26.95

Grades: 7 8 9 10   **616.85**

    1. Anxiety 2. Panic disorders 3. Obsessive-compulsive disorder

    ISBN 978-1-60152-137-8; 1-60152-137-5

                     LC 2010031813

This title provides "a systematic and focused look at [anxiety disorders].... [It] covers six main types, including panic and obsessive-compulsive disorder.... [This title is] useful for reports as well as general interest." SLJ

    Includes bibliographical references

Down syndrome. ReferencePoint Press 2009 104p il (Compact research. Diseases and disorders) $25.95

Grades: 7 8 9 10 11 12   **616.85**

    1. Down syndrome

    ISBN 978-1-60152-065-4; 1-60152-065-4

                     LC 2008-36644

"This up-to-date, excellent overview of Down syndrome addresses controversies and ethical issues associated with this genetic disorder. Parks also reports on current and potential scientific advances that may prevent it in the future and offer a better quality of life and opportunities for those born with it." SLJ

Includes bibliographical references

Obsessive-compulsive disorder. ReferencePoint Press 2010 96p il (Compact research: diseases and disorders) lib bdg $26.95

Grades: 8 9 10 11 12   **616.85**
   1. Obsessive-compulsive disorder
ISBN 978-1-60152-120-0; 1-60152-120-0
                                         LC 2010-5872

This book about obsessive-compulsive disorder is written "with objectivity and depth. . . . [It] begins with a general overview followed by a focus on statistics, treatments, and prevention. . . . [The book] shows that the irrational fears of OCD affect males and females across race and class. . . . The readable page design features pull quotes and subtitles, with occasional photos throughout." Booklist

Includes bibliographical references

Self-injury disorder. ReferencePoint Press 2011 96p il (Compact research: diseases and disorders) lib bdg $26.95

Grades: 8 9 10 11 12   **616.85**
   1. Self-mutilation
ISBN 978-1-60152-112-5; 1-60152-112-X
                                         LC 2009-50483

This book about self-injury disorder "begins with a general overview followed by a focus on statistics, causes, symptoms, treatments, and prevention. . . . [The book] states that the main cause of self-inflicted injury is to gain relief from unbearable emotional pain, and it also covers methods of treatment and prevention. The readable page design features pull quotes and subtitles, with occasional photos throughout." Booklist

Includes bibliographical references

Powell, Jillian

Self-harm and suicide; by Jillian Powell. Gareth Stevens 2009 48p il (Emotional health issues) lib bdg $31

Grades: 6 7 8 9   **616.85**
   1. Suicide 2. Self-mutilation
ISBN 978-0-8368-9202-4; 0-8368-9202-X
                                         LC 2008-4276

First published 2008 in the United Kingdom

This book about self-destructive behavior has "clear language and explanations. . . . [It is] suitable for fact-finding missions, but the abundant graphics and case studies are likely to draw in browsers as well. Throughout, unfamiliar vocabulary is highlighted in bold and explained in context and in the glossary. . . . Fact boxes and case study sidebars add information." SLJ

Includes glossary and bibliographical references

Price, Janet

Take control of Asperger's syndrome; the official strategy guide for teens with Asperger's syndrome and nonverbal learning disorder. [by] Janet Price and Jennifer Engel Fisher. Prufrock Press 2010 168p pa $16.95

Grades: 6 7 8 9 10   **616.85**
   1. Asperger's syndrome
ISBN 978-1-59363-405-6; 1-59363-405-6
                                         LC 2009-50852

"Directly addressing teens diagnosed with Asperger's Syndrome or Nonverbal Learning Disorder, two educational consultants experienced in special-needs issues lay out feasible strategies for success in school and in social interactions." Booklist

Includes bibliographical references

Quinn, Patricia O.

Attention, girls! a guide to learn all about your AD/HD. illustrated by Carl Pearce. Magination Press 2009 119p il $16.95; pa $12.95

Grades: 4 5 6 7   **616.85**
   1. Attention deficit disorder
ISBN 978-1-4338-0447-2; 1-4338-0447-6; 978-1-4338-0448-9 pa; 1-4338-0448-4 pa
                                         LC 2008054524

"Quinn has attention deficit hyperactivity disorder and is a medical doctor; she addresses the types of AD/HD; who can help; differences between girls and boys with AD/HD; making friends; talking with adults about the condition; relaxation techniques; and medication. Her aim is to give girls a variety of ways to manage their disorders. . . . The book is attractive and inviting with colorful cartoon illustrations, sidebars, and highlighted reminders." SLJ

Rodriguez, Ana Maria

Autism spectrum disorders. Twenty-First Century Books 2011 128p il (USA Today health reports: diseases and disorders) lib bdg $34.60

Grades: 8 9 10 11 12   **616.85**
   1. Autism 2. Autism spectrum disorders
ISBN 0761358838 lib bdg; 9780761358831 lib bdg
                                         LC 2010-34236

This is an account of knowledge about and research into the conditions known as autism spectrum disorders. Sci Books Films

This book about autism spectrum disorders will serve as "solid report fodder. . . . [The] volume has an introduction, a description of the condition, chapters on what it is like to live with it, and material on research and treatments. A healthy smattering of statistics and personal stories appear throughout." SLJ

Includes glossary and bibliographical references

Royston, Angela

Explaining down syndrome. Smart Apple Media 2010 45p il (Explaining) lib bdg $34.25

Grades: 5 6 7 8   **616.85**
   1. Down syndrome
ISBN 978-1-59920-308-9 lib bdg; 1-59920-308-1 lib bdg
                                         LC 2008-49291

This book about down syndrome provides a "basic [overview] of the health concerns related to the disease; information on diagnosis and treatment; and a discussion of the challenges or complications experienced by the affected person and their family/friends, and how to manage those problems. . . . The incorporation of quotes and personal accounts in 'Case Notes' sidebars adds to the sensitive tone found throughout [the title]." SLJ

Includes glossary

Scowen, Kate

My kind of sad; what it's like to be young and depressed. [by] Kate Scowen; art by Jeff Szuc. Annick Press 2006 168p il $19.95; pa $10.95

Grades: 7 8 9 10   **616.85**

1. Depression (Psychology)

ISBN 1-55037-941-0; 1-55037-940-2 pa

"The book discusses the history of depression, adolescence and depression, and treatment options. Scowen's focus is on understanding the difference between simply being sad and suffering from depression. Topics such as bipolar disorder, self-mutilation, anorexia, and suicide are also discussed. . . . Scowen's book is well-written, easy to read and use, and quite informative." Voice Youth Advocates

Includes bibliographical references

Silverstein, Alvin

★ The **ADHD** update; understanding attention-deficit/hyperactivity disorder. [by] Alvin and Virginia Silverstein and Laura Silverstein Nunn. Enslow Publishers 2008 112p il (Disease update) lib bdg $31.93

Grades: 5 6 7 8   **616.85**

1. Attention deficit disorder 2. Attention-deficit hyperactivity disorder

ISBN 978-0-7660-2800-5 lib bdg; 0-7660-2800-3 lib bdg

LC 2007-13853

This describes Attention-deficit hyperactivity disorder (ADHD) and its history, diagnosis and treatment, living with it, and its future

"This book is an excellent primer on AD/HD." Sci Books Films

Includes glossary and bibliographical references

★ The **eating** disorders update; understanding anorexia, bulimia, and binge eating. [by] Alvin and Virginia Silverstein and Laura Silverstein Nunn. Enslow Publishers 2008 128p il (Disease update) lib bdg $31.93

Grades: 5 6 7 8   **616.85**

1. Bulimia 2. Anorexia nervosa 3. Eating disorders

ISBN 978-0-7660-2802-9 lib bdg; 0-7660-2802-X lib bdg

LC 2007013985

"An introduction to the history and most up-to-date research and treatment of eating disorders." Publisher's note

Includes glossary and bibliographical references

Skotko, Brian

Fasten your seatbelt; a crash course on Down syndrome for brothers and sisters. [by] Brian G. Skotko and Susan P. Levine. Woodbine House 2009 191p il pa $18.95

Grades: 4 5 6 7   **616.85**

1. Siblings 2. Down syndrome

ISBN 978-1-890627-86-7 pa; 1-890627-86-0 pa

LC 2008049753

"Skotko and Levine address preteens and teenagers who have a sibling with Down syndrome, answering questions that have been generated through their work with this population. . . . With a wealth of information, numerous resources, and the reassurance that all siblings of people with disabilities sometimes go through periods of contradictory feelings, this is an excellent guide for young people who are trying to figure out how to negotiate an often-confusing relationship." SLJ

Includes bibliographical references

Snedden, Robert

Explaining autism. Smart Apple Media 2010 45p il (Explaining) lib bdg $34.25

Grades: 5 6 7 8   **616.85**

1. Autism 2. Asperger's syndrome

ISBN 978-1-59920-307-2 lib bdg; 1-59920-307-3 lib bdg

LC 2008-49285

Describes the illness, including its symptoms, how it affects physical and mental health, current treatments, and how people with autism live everyday lives

"The incorporation of quotes and personal accounts in 'Case Notes' sidebars adds to the sensitive tone found throughout [the title]." SLJ

Includes glossary and bibliographical references

Sonenklar, Carol

Anorexia and bulimia. Twenty-First Century Books 2010 128p il (USA Today health reports: diseases and disorders) lib bdg $34.60

Grades: 7 8 9 10 11 12   **616.85**

1. Bulimia 2. Anorexia nervosa

ISBN 978-0-8225-6786-8; 0-8225-6786-5

This describes the symptoms and treatment of anorexia and bulimia.

This book "stands out for the substantial amount of information conveyed in a lively writing style. . . . Graphs, sidebars, diagrams, and other illustrations [are] used judiciously." Booklist

Stefanski, Daniel

★ **How** to talk to an autistic kid; illustrated by Hazel Mitchell. Free Spirit 2011 43p il $12.99

Grades: 3 4 5 6   **616.85**

1. Autism

ISBN 978-1-57542-365-4; 1-57542-365-0

"Stefanski provides clear, sometimes blunt, often humorous advice for readers on how to interact with autistic classmates. An authority on this topic—he is a 14-year-old boy with autism—he begins by describing autism. . . . He describes, using a brief paragraph or two per page, some of the traits many autistic people share. . . . For each trait, he offers down-to-earth suggestions for resolving problems. . . . His insightful, matter-of-fact presentation demystifies behaviors that might confuse or disturb non-autistic classmates. Simple cartoon illustrations in black, gray and two shades of turquoise accompany the text. . . . A thought-provoking introduction to autism . . . and an essential purchase for every primary and middle-school classroom." Kirkus

Stewart, Gail

Anorexia; [by] Gail B. Stewart. Cherry Lake Pub. 2009 32p il (Health at risk) lib bdg $27.07

Grades: 4 5 6 7   **616.85**

    1. Anorexia nervosa

    ISBN 978-1-60279-281-4 lib bdg; 1-60279-281-X lib bdg

                    LC 2008017496

This explains why anorexics feel the need to keep losing weight, what can happen to them as a result of their desperate struggle to be thin, and how they can get help.

    "Great for reports or reluctant readers." Booklist

    Includes bibliographical references

Bulimia; [by] Gail B. Stewart. Cherry Lake Pub. 2009 32p il (Health at risk) lib bdg $27.07

Grades: 4 5 6 7   **616.85**

    1. Bulimia

    ISBN 978-1-60279-282-1 lib bdg; 1-60279-282-8 lib bdg

                    LC 2008-17497

This describes the health risks of bulimia and what can be done to help people fight this disease.

    "Great for reports or reluctant readers." Booklist

    Includes bibliographical references

Tompkins, Michael A.

My anxious mind; a teen's guide to managing anxiety and panic. by Michael A. Tompkins and Katherine A. Martinez; illustrated by Michael Sloan. Magination Press 2009 196p il pa $14.95

Grades: 7 8 9 10 11 12   **616.85**

    1. Anxiety 2. Panic disorders

    ISBN 978-1-4338-0450-2 pa; 1-4338-0450-6 pa

                    LC 2009011442

"Tompkins and Martinez directly address their readers: 'If you have an anxious mind,' giving teens the sense of a caring adult speaking to them. . . . Following the first chapters on definitions and how to seek help, there are several chapters with increasingly more complicated aids that teens can implement. . . . The final chapters stress the importance of proper nutrition, exercise, and sleep, and the possible need for medication. Throughout the book, first-person vignettes describe specific anxieties or phobias and how they were dealt with using the strategies outlined in the middle chapters. . . . They serve the purpose, along with the appealing line drawings, of catching readers' interest and enlivening the text." SLJ

Zucker, Bonnie

Take control of OCD; the ultimate guide for kids with OCD. Prufrock Press 2010 179p il pa $16.95

Grades: 6 7 8 9 10   **616.85**

    1. Obsessive-compulsive disorder

    ISBN 978-1-59363-429-2; 1-59363-429-3

                    LC 2010-34863

The author "addresses affected young readers directly and offers a structured set of self-help strategies for coping with diagnosed obsessive-compulsive behavior. Suggesting

that the chapters be read in order for best results, she opens with a nontechnical explanation of the disorder's genetic and neurological roots, then goes on to discuss creating written behavioral 'ladders,' using relaxation techniques effectively, building self-awareness, handling uncertainty, and managing stress." Booklist

    Includes bibliographical references

Zucker, Faye

Beating depression; teens find light at the end of the tunnel. by Faye Zucker & Joan E. Huebl. Franklin Watts 2007 112p il (Scholastic choices) lib bdg $27; pa $8.95

Grades: 6 7 8 9   **616.85**

    1. Depression (Psychology)

    ISBN 978-0-531-12462-8 lib bdg; 0-531-12462-2 lib bdg; 978-0-531-17729-7 pa; 0-531-17729-7 pa

                    LC 2006006779

Discusses the prevalence of depression among teenagers, and examines its causes and treatment options.

    Includes bibliographical references

616.86   Substance abuse (Drug abuse)

Allman, Toney

Drugs. Cherry Lake Pub. 2009 32p il (Health at risk) lib bdg $27.07

Grades: 4 5 6 7   **616.86**

    1. Drug abuse

    ISBN 978-1-60279-283-8 lib bdg; 1-60279-283-6 lib bdg

                    LC 2008017503

This describes the dangers of drug abuse, the programs that help people get off drugs, and how to avoid drug use.

    "Great for reports or reluctant readers." Booklist

    Includes bibliographical references

Esherick, Joan

Dying for acceptance; a teen's guide to drug- and alcohol-related health issues. Mason Crest Publishers 2005 128p il (The science of health) $24.95

Grades: 7 8 9 10   **616.86**

    1. Teenagers -- Drug use 2. Teenagers -- Alcohol use 3. Drugs -- Physiological effect 4. Alcohol -- Physiological effect

    ISBN 978-1-59084-847-0; 1-59084-847-0

                    LC 2004-12125

Provides teenagers with information on drug and alcohol use, discussing types of drugs, reasons for using, and the dangers of using chemical substances

No more butts; kicking the tobacco habit. Mason Crest 2009 112p il (Tobacco: the deadly drug) lib bdg $26.95

Grades: 6 7 8 9   **616.86**

    1. Smoking cessation programs

    ISBN 978-1-4222-0236-4 lib bdg; 1-4222-0236-4 lib bdg

                    LC 2008-13215

Explains how difficult smoking cessation can be and offers tips on how to quit for good.

"The writing is professional but not at a level that causes readers to struggle. The information is made relevant to the everyday reader . . . [and] . . . it would be a strong addition to the nonfiction section of any library and is appropriate for a broad age level." Voice Youth Advocates

Includes glossary and bibliographical references

Hunter, David

Born to smoke; nicotine and genetics. Mason Crest 2009 112p il (Tobacco: the deadly drug) lib bdg $26.95

Grades: 6 7 8 9   616.86

1. Smoking 2. Tobacco habit 3. Behavior genetics
ISBN 978-1-4222-0243-2; 1-4222-0243-7

LC 2008-13218

Explains how genetics may affect an individual's susceptibility to nicotine addiction, and discusses the debate over genetic predisposition to nicotine addiction versus a person's upbringing.

"The writing is professional but not at a level that causes readers to struggle. The information is made relevant to the everyday reader . . . [and] . . . it would be a strong addition to the nonfiction section of any library and is appropriate for a broad age level." Voice Youth Advocates

Includes glossary and bibliographical references

Hyde, Margaret Oldroyd

★ **Smoking** 101; an overview for teens. [by] Margaret O. Hyde, John F. Setaro. Twenty-First Century Books 2006 128p il lib bdg $26.60

Grades: 8 9 10 11 12   616.86

1. Smoking 2. Tobacco
ISBN 0-7613-2835-1

LC 2004-22757

"The message is clear, the facts are well-presented, and the tone is insightful. These authors understand the teen audience and how to reach it." SLJ

Includes bibliographical references

Miller, Heather

Smoking. Cherry Lake Pub. 2009 32p il (Health at risk) lib bdg $27.07

Grades: 4 5 6 7   616.86

1. Smoking 2. Tobacco habit
ISBN 978-1-60279-286-9 lib bdg; 1-60279-286-0 lib bdg

LC 2008017501

This describes why smoking is dangerous, how difficult it is to stop once you start, and what efforts are underway to put the brakes on this habit.

"Great for reports or reluctant readers." Booklist

Includes bibliographical references

Price, Sean

Nicotine; [by] Sean Price. Chelsea House 2008 120p il (Junior drug awareness) lib bdg $30

Grades: 6 7 8 9   616.86

1. Smoking 2. Tobacco habit
ISBN 9781438118185; 978-0-7910-9696-3 lib bdg; 0-7910-9696-3 lib bdg

LC 2007024829

This "provides the facts about tobacco use among teenagers and offers young readers the facts about one of the most prevalent and addictive drugs in the United States." Publisher's note

Includes glossary and bibliographical references

616.89   Mental disorders

Kent, Deborah

★ **Snake** pits, talking cures, & magic bullets; a history of mental illness. 21st Cent. Bks. (Brookfield) 2003 160p il lib bdg $26.90

Grades: 6 7 8 9   616.89

1. Mental illness 2. Mental illness -- History
ISBN 0-7613-2704-5

LC 2002-11208

Looks at how the mentally ill have been treated throughout history, focusing on advances made in the 19th and 20th centuries regarding mental hospitals, medications, and social acceptance

"An excellent history peppered with fascinating accounts. . . . Black-and-white archival photographs and reproductions appear throughout. . . . This is a fine treatment of a topic not heavily covered for this audience." SLJ

Includes glossary and bibliographical references

Meisel, Abigail

Investigating depression and bipolar disorder; real facts for real lives. Enslow Publishers 2010 160p il (Investigating diseases) lib bdg $34.60

Grades: 6 7 8 9 10   616.89

1. Depression (Psychology) 2. Manic-depressive illness
ISBN 978-0-7660-3340-5; 0-7660-3340-6

LC 2008-50060

"Meisel discusses the history, science, diagnosis, and treatment of depression and bipolar disorder. In addition, she shows how these illnesses affect not just the patients, but their families, peers, and friends. She explains the science behind the two conditions, their possible causes, and the varying nature of the illnesses themselves. . . . This is an excellent book for persons from high school age to adults to read and become familiar with these important illnesses." Sci Books Films

Includes glossary and bibliographical references

★ **Mental** health information for teens; health tips about mental wellness and mental illness: including facts about mental and emotional health, depression and other mood disorders, anxiety disorders, behavior disorders, self-injury . . . edited by Karen Bellenir. 3rd ed.; Omnigraphics 2010 443p (Teen health series) $62

Grades: 7 8 9 10 11 12   616.89

1. Mental health 2. Reference books 3. Adolescent

psychology 4. Teenagers -- Health and hygiene
ISBN 978-0-7808-1087-7

LC 2010-806

First published 2001

"This is an excellent resource for teens, parents, teachers, librarians, and those concerned with the mental health issues facing middle and high-schoolers today." Libr J

Includes bibliographical references

Parks, Peggy J., 1951-

Schizophrenia. ReferencePoint Press 2011 96p il (Compact research: diseases and disorders) $26.95

Grades: 7 8 9 10 11 12   **616.89**

1. Schizophrenia

ISBN 978-1-60152-140-8; 1-60152-140-5

LC 2010037253

"Fortified with contemporary individual case studies of both teens and adults [this] title . . . discusses variations of [schizophrenia], as well as the prevalence, symptoms, causes, effects, diagnoses, and treatment, drawing upon media interviews and commentary as well as clinical reports and research studies. . . . The clear design includes recent graphs and tables, color photos and diagrams, and lots of carefully documented primary-source quotes from patients, researchers, and scientists." Booklist

Includes bibliographical references

Silverstein, Alvin

★ The **depression** and bipolar disorder update; [by] Alvin and Virginia Silverstein and Laura Silverstein Nunn. Enslow Publishers 2008 128p il (Disease update) $31.93

Grades: 6 7 8 9   **616.89**

1. Depression (Psychology) 2. Manic-depressive illness

ISBN 978-0-7660-2801-2; 0-7660-2801-1

LC 2007-13854

"An introduction to the history . . . research and treatment of depression and bipolar disorder." Publisher's note

Includes bibliographical references

616.9   Other diseases

Allman, Toney

Infectious disease research; by Toney Allman. ReferencePoint Press 2012 96 p. (Inside science series) (hardback) $27.95

Grades: 6 7 8 9 10 11 12   **616.9**

1. Communicable diseases -- Encyclopedias 2. Communicable diseases

ISBN 1601521774; 9781601521774

LC 2011007745

This book, by Toney Allman, presents a research guide to infectious disease research. "Infectious diseases are responsible for untold global suffering and the loss of millions of human lives each year. This knowledge drives the research toward a fuller understanding of infectious microbial agents and the development of new treatment and prevention methods for infectious diseases." (Publisher's note)

Includes bibliographical references and index

Aronin, Miriam

Tuberculosis; the white plague! Bearport Pub. 2011 32p il map (Nightmare plagues) lib bdg $25.27

Grades: 4 5 6 7   **616.9**

1. Tuberculosis

ISBN 978-1-936088-06-5; 1-936088-06-1

LC 2010010679

Discover what causes tuberculosis and how it affects the body.

"The writing is accessible and interspersed with interesting photographs and fact boxes. . . . [The book relies] on an honest discussion of [tuberculosis and is an] . . . effective, easily navigated [introduction]." SLJ

Includes glossary and bibliographical references

Blank, Alison

Invincible microbe; tuberculosis and the never-ending search for a cure. Jim Murphy, Alison Blank. Clarion Books 2012 149 p. (hardback) $18.99

Grades: 5 6 7 8 9   **616.9**

1. Tuberculosis 2. Lungs -- Diseases 3. Communicable diseases -- Treatment 4. Microorganisms

ISBN 0618535748; 9780618535743

LC 2011025951

This book looks at tuberculosis. It "starts with archeologists finding evidence of tuberculosis in a 500,000 year old skull and continues through to the present day. Various 'cures' such as the medieval 'king's touch' . . . , bloodletting of the 19th century, twentieth century sanatoriums and modern day drug cocktails are all discussed." Also "covered is the socioeconomic side of the disease, with a discussion of how treatment often varied depending on the race and economic status of the patient." (Children's Literature)

Includes bibliographical references

Colligan, L. H.

★ **Tick**-borne illnesses. Marshall Cavendish Benchmark 2009 64p il (Health alert) $22.95

Grades: 4 5 6 7   **616.9**

1. Tick-borne diseases

ISBN 978-0-7614-2914-2; 0-7614-2914-X

LC 2007-38517

This "title features a handsome format, with well-chosen illustrations, a substantial amount of information, and some practical insights." Booklist

Includes glossary

Duke, Shirley Smith

Infections, infestations, and disease; [by] Shirley Duke. Rourke Pub. 2010 48p il (Let's explore science) $32.79

Grades: 4 5 6 7   **616.9**

1. Communicable diseases

ISBN 978-1-61590-321-4; 1-61590-321-6

LC 2010009908

Examines the dangers of infections, infestations, and diseases, describing how infections and disease are spread, and discussing treatment and prevention options, along with ways to eliminate emerging diseases before they can reach a population.

Includes bibliographical references

Emmeluth, Donald

Botulism; consulting editor, Hilary Babcock; foreword by David L. Heymann. 2nd ed.; Chelsea House 2010 144p il map (Deadly diseases and epidemics) $34.95

Grades: 7 8 9 10   **616.9**

1. Botulism

ISBN 978-1-60413-235-9; 1-60413-235-3

LC 2010-8111

First published 2005

This book contains "information on this disease, exploring its history, causes, statistics, and . . . diagnostic and treatment breakthroughs. It also includes accounts of numerous recent outbreaks." Publisher's note

Includes glossary and bibliographical references

Green, Caroline

Drug resistance. New Forest Press 2010 64p il (Cutting-edge science) lib bdg $34.25

Grades: 7 8 9 10   **616.9**

1. Drug resistance

ISBN 978-1-84898-323-6; 1-84898-323-9

This addresses the topic of drug resistance, "touching on both scientific and societal issues . . . The underlying science is addressed, as well as the current state of scientific and ethical thinking. Stock color photographs and diagrams accompany the [text]. Sidebars provide biographical information on contemporary scientists as well as highlights of their research methods and studies." Horn Book Guide

Includes glossary and bibliographical references

Hoffmann, Gretchen

★ **Chicken** pox. Marshall Cavendish Benchmark 2009 62p il (Health alert) $22.95

Grades: 4 5 6 7   **616.9**

1. Chickenpox

ISBN 978-0-7614-2916-6; 0-7614-2916-6

This "title features a handsome format, with well-chosen illustrations, a substantial amount of information, and some practical insights." Booklist

Includes glossary

Kelly, Evelyn B.

Investigating tuberculosis and superbugs; real facts for real lives. [by] Evelyn B. Kelly, Ian Wilker, and Marylou Ambrose. Enslow Publishers 2010 160p il (Investigating diseases) lib bdg $34.60

Grades: 7 8 9 10   **616.9**

1. Tuberculosis 2. Drug resistance

ISBN 978-0-7660-3343-6; 0-7660-3343-0

LC 2009-37811

This "methodically presents medical and statistical information about major kinds of tuberculosis, malaria, AIDS/ HIV, and other persistent bacterial, viral, and parasitic pandemics worldwide that are becoming ominously resistant to once-effective treatments. . . . [This is] massively documented with endnotes; supplemented by sidebar insertions, ac-

counts of specific cases, and small color photos; and rounded off with digestible lists of relevant further sources." Booklist

Includes bibliographical references

Sheen, Barbara

MRSA. Lucent Books 2010 104p il (Diseases and disorders series) $33.45

Grades: 7 8 9 10   **616.9**

1. Methicillin-Resistant Staphylococcus aureus

ISBN 978-1-4205-0144-5; 1-4205-0144-5

LC 2009-32644

This "offers a thorough explanation of [MRSA] giving a basic definition; a discussion of the causes, symptoms, and treatments; a description of living with the disease; and ideas of future treatment and diagnoses. Each volume lists source notes and organizations to contact. A glossary, index, and ideas for further reading are also included. The color photographs and sidebars help to make the information in the dense text more easily understood, and personal stories provide insight into how individuals deal with their disease." Voice Youth Advocates

Includes glossary and bibliographical references

Shmaefsky, Brian

Toxic shock syndrome; [by] Brian R. Shmaefsky; consulting editor, Hilary Babcock; foreword by David L. Heymann. 2nd ed.; Chelsea House 2010 127p il (Deadly diseases and epidemics) $34.95

Grades: 8 9 10 11 12   **616.9**

1. Toxic shock syndrome

ISBN 978-1-60413-243-4; 1-60413-243-4

LC 2010029222

First published 2003

This describes types of toxic shock syndrome, its causes, diagnosis and treatment.

Includes glossary and bibliographical references

Stress information for teens; health tips about the mental and physical consequences of stress. edited by Sandra Augustyn Lawton. 1st ed. Omnigraphics, Inc. 2008 viii, 392 p.p ill. (hardcover) $69.00

Grades: 7 8 9 10   **616.9**

1. Stress (Psychology) 2. Teenagers -- Health and hygiene 3. Stress management for teenagers

ISBN 0780810120; 9780780810129

LC 2008015151

This book, a "toolkit for coping with stress[,] discusses the causes of stress, the effects of stress on the body and mind, and managing stress while including specific problems at school and with family or peer relationships. . . . Techniques for managing stress include controlling anger, engaging in mind-body therapies, and building self-esteem." (Voice of Youth Advocates)

Includes bibliographical references and index.

616.95 Sexually transmitted diseases, zoonoses

Collins, Nicholas
Frequently asked questions about STDs; by Nicholas Collins and Samuel G. Woods. Rosen Pub. 2012 64 p. col. ill. (library) $31.95
Grades: 7 8 9 10   616.95
    1. Teenagers -- Sexual behavior 2. Sexually transmitted diseases 3. Sexually transmitted diseases -- Miscellanea
    ISBN 1448846307; 9781448846306
                                    LC 2011000303
This book by Nicholas Collins looks at STDs. "Sexually transmitted diseases are clinically explained, including how they affect the body, how to recognize symptoms of infection, and how teens can protect themselves and their partner against, not only STDs, but HIV and AIDS as well." (Voice of Youth Advocates)
    Includes bibliographical references (p. 83) and index.

Cozic, Charles P.
Herpes. ReferencePoint Press 2011 96p il (Compact research: diseases and disorders) $23.95
Grades: 7 8 9 10 11 12   616.95
    1. Herpesvirus diseases
    ISBN 978-1-60152-117-0; 1-60152-117-0
                                    LC 2010030634
Introduces herpes and discusses the symptoms, possible health effects, and treatments for the virus.
    Includes bibliographical references

Dougherty, Terri
Sexually transmitted diseases. Lucent Books 2010 96p il (Diseases and disorders series) $32.45
Grades: 7 8 9 10   616.95
    1. Sexually transmitted diseases
    ISBN 978-1-4205-0220-6
                                    LC 2009-39583
"This book discusses the most common afflictions, diseases that are usually found in combinations, medical advances, and how the outlook for STDs is complicated by new trends such as drug-resistant strains. Information is also supplied about causes, prevention, diagnosis, and treatment. . . . A number of the photos show some of the horrific physical manifestations in individuals, including infants. . . . [This book] should be considered for first purchase." SLJ
    Includes bibliographical references

Yancey, Diane
STDs. Twenty-First Century Books 2012 128p il (USA today health reports: diseases and disorders) $34.60
Grades: 7 8 9 10 11 12   616.95
    1. Sexually transmitted diseases
    ISBN 0-7613-5456-5; 978-0-7613-5456-7
                                    LC 2010036514
"Yancey writes in a straightforward manner about sexually transmitted diseases, opening with the profiles of several teens coping with an STD. . . . The causes, symptoms, and treatments of the main STDs, . . . are thoroughly covered, from the emotional side effects of genital herpes to the dangers of ordering an HIV home sample collection kit online.

. . . Students, teachers, and librarians looking to supplement health textbooks with current information will find this . . . valuable." Voice Youth Advocates
    Includes bibliographical references

616.97 Diseases of immune system

Aldridge, Susan
AIDS. New Forest Press 2010 64p il map (Cutting-edge science) lib bdg $34.25
Grades: 7 8 9 10   616.97
    1. AIDS (Disease)
    ISBN 978-1-84898-324-3; 1-84898-324-7
This addresses the topic of AIDS, "touching on both scientific and societal issues . . . The underlying science is addressed, as well as the current state of scientific and ethical thinking. Stock color photographs and diagrams accompany the [text]. Sidebars provide biographical information on contemporary scientists as well as highlights of their research methods and studies." Horn Book Guide

Ballard, Carol
Explaining food allergies. Smart Apple Media 2010 45p il (Explaining) $23.95
Grades: 5 6 7 8   616.97
    1. Food allergy
    ISBN 978-1-59920-316-4; 1-59920-316-2
                                    LC 2008049936
This "does an excellent job of discussing complex clinical science while showing what daily life is like for kids living with food allergies, from the signs and symptoms to the tests and treatments. . . . This blend of the technical and the personal will have wide appeal." Booklist

Cunningham, Kevin
HIV /AIDS. Morgan Reynolds Pub. 2009 144p il (Diseases in history) lib bdg $28.95
Grades: 8 9 10 11 12   616.97
    1. AIDS (Disease)
    ISBN 978-1-59935-104-9; 1-59935-104-8
                                    LC 2008-51616
"Explores the origin of the two types of HIV viruses and the reasons why poverty, promiscuity, and the common use of world blood supplies enable its horrible and devastatingly rapid spread. . . . This detailed overview . . . will appeal to more advanced students. The research is thorough and the writing is insightful, thought provoking, and accessible." Voice Youth Advocates
    Includes glossary and bibliographical references

Ehrlich, Paul
Living with allergies; [by] Paul M. Ehrlich, with Elizabeth Shimer Bowers. Facts On File 2009 168p (Teen's guides) $34.95; pa $14.95
Grades: 7 8 9 10 11 12   616.97
    1. Allergy
    ISBN 9781438129976; 978-0-8160-7327-6; 0-8160-7327-9; 0-8160-7742-8 pa
                                    LC 2008-34352

This "book addresses allergy triggers, preventing allergic reactions, what to expect from treatment, paying for care, and how to help yourself, friends, or family members who may have allergies." Publisher's note

Includes glossary and bibliographical references

Gordon, Sherri Mabry

★ **Peanut** butter, milk, and other deadly threats; what you should know about food allergies. Enslow Publishers 2006 112p il (Issues in focus today) $31.93

Grades: 8 9 10 11 12　　　　　　　　　616.97
　1. Food allergy
　ISBN 0-7660-2529-2

　　　　　　　　　　　　　　　　　　LC 2005-29219

Discusses what it is like to live with food allergies, how teens and their families cope with them, the causes of food allergies, and the research being done to prevent and control them

"The format is open, with plenty of white space, making the book accessible to reluctant readers. Full-color photos, helpful case studies, and a list of reputable organizations to contact for further information are included." SLJ

Includes glossary and bibliographical references

Hillstrom, Kevin

Food allergies; by Kevin Hillstrom. Lucent Books 2012 96 p. col. ill. (Nutrition and health) (hardcover) $30.95

Grades: 7 8 9 10 11 12　　　　　　　　616.97
　1. Food allergy
　ISBN 1420507206; 9781420507201

　　　　　　　　　　　　　　　　　　LC 2012002945

This book on food allergies by Kevin Hillstrom is part of the "Nutrition and Health" book series. It "discusses the rising numbers of allergic young people, the physiology of the symptoms (with a clear diagram of an anaphylactic reaction), the search for a cure, and the social stigma." Booklist

Includes bibliographical references (p. 81-84) and index.

James, Otto

AIDS. Smart Apple Media 2010 46p il (Voices) lib bdg $34.95

Grades: 7 8 9 10 11 12　　　　　　　　616.97
　1. AIDS (Disease)
　ISBN 978-1-59920-282-2; 1-59920-282-4

　　　　　　　　　　　　　　　　　　LC 2009-5417

"AIDS looks at causes, prevention, treatment, and the chances of a cure and also discusses abstinence, safe sex, the cost of AIDS drugs, and much more. . . . [The] blend of current political debate with witnesses' close-up experiences told through photos, narratives, and quotes will draw browsers, and many will go on to find out more." Booklist

Includes glossary and bibliographical references

Marsico, Katie

HIV /AIDS. ABDO Pub. Co. 2010 112p il (Essential issues) lib bdg $22.95

Grades: 7 8 9 10　　　　　　　　　　　616.97
　1. AIDS (Disease)
　ISBN 978-1-60453-955-4; 1-60453-955-0

　　　　　　　　　　　　　　　　　　LC 2009-29954

This is "well-written, providing examples that put a human face to each problem. Quotes and facts are clearly attributed, and their sources are noted in the extensive back matter. . . . Sidebars provide further information, or, more compellingly, offer stories about those touched by the topic. . . . [This] will be of great assistance to students writing reports." SLJ

Includes glossary and bibliographical references

★ **Quicksand**; HIV/AIDS in our world. by Anonymous. Candlewick Press 2009 103p $15.99

Grades: 6 7 8 9 10　　　　　　　　　　616.97
　1. AIDS (Disease)
　ISBN 978-0-7636-1589-5; 0-7636-1589-7

　　　　　　　　　　　　　　　　　　LC 2009-7761

"The anonymous author explains her motivation for writing this book by telling readers that ten years ago, when HIV/AIDS was still considered a taboo subject, her brother-in-law was diagnosed with the disease. She writes in a truthful, open manner, addressing common questions about HIV/AIDS and providing easy-to-understand and honest advice. . . . The author's personal insight is what makes this book an important addition. Topics address everything from the history of HIV/AIDS to how to protect oneself from the disease. She also provides suggestions on how to cope with hearing that a family or friend has HIV/AIDS. . . . The author's focus on how the disease affects all people, whether they have contracted HIV/AIDS or not, makes this book a must-have for all teen collections." Voice Youth Advocates

Includes glossary and bibliographical references

Sonenklar, Carol

AIDS. Twenty-First Century Books 2011 128p il (USA Today health reports: diseases and disorders) lib bdg $34.60

Grades: 8 9 10 11 12　　　　　　　　　616.97
　1. AIDS (Disease)
　ISBN 978-0-8225-8581-7 lib bdg; 0-8225-8581-2 lib bdg

　　　　　　　　　　　　　　　　　　LC 2010-37633

This book about AIDS will serve as "solid report fodder. . . . [The] volume has an introduction, a description of the condition, chapters on what it is like to live with it, and material on research and treatments. A healthy smattering of statistics and personal stories appear throughout." SLJ

Includes glossary and bibliographical references

Yount, Lisa

Luc Montagnier; identifying the AIDS virus. by Lisa Yount. Chelsea House 2011 xix, 123 p.p col. ill. (library) $35

Grades: 7 8 9 10 11 12　　　　　　　　616.97
　1. AIDS (Disease) 2. HIV (Viruses)
　ISBN 1604136618; 9781604136616

　　　　　　　　　　　　　　　　　　LC 2010047006

This book by Lisa Yount is part of the Trailblazers in Science and Technology series and looks at Luc Montagnier. It "recounts the life and career of the Nobel Prize-winning

French virologist whose contributions to the understanding of the nature of viruses led to a significant advance in cancer research and in discovering the HIV virus that causes AIDS." (Publisher's note)

Includes bibliographical references and index.

616.99 Tumors and miscellaneous communicable diseases

Cancer information for teens; edited by Lisa Bakewell and Karen Bellenir. 2nd ed.; Omnigraphics 2010 445p il (Teen health series) $69

Grades: 8 9 10 11 12   616.99

1. Cancer

ISBN 978-0-7808-1085-3; 0-7808-1085-6

LC 2009-28456

First published 2004

"Written specifically for teens or their family members who have cancer, this volume will be a helpful, authoritative resource that should lead readers to further information about it. . . . It offers information that is current, accurate, and accessible." SLJ

Includes bibliographical references

Casil, Amy Sterling

Pancreatic cancer; current and emerging trends in detection and treatment. Rosen Pub. 2009 64p il (Cancer and modern science) lib bdg $29.25

Grades: 7 8 9 10 11 12   616.99

1. Pancreas -- Cancer

ISBN 9781435856998; 978-1-4358-5008-8; 1-4358-5008-4

LC 2008-25132

This book describes pancreatic cancer and its treatment. "Clearly aimed at teens who have cancer or know someone who does, . . . [this title combines] lots of technical detail about anatomy, physiology, and pathology with a personal, interactive style. . . . With a highly readable design, including crisp color photos and anatomical diagrams, the [book] will also serve the needs of student researchers. Also features excellent, extensive back matter." Booklist

Includes glossary and bibliographical references

Freedman, Jeri

Brain cancer; current and emerging trends in detection and treatment. Rosen Pub. 2009 63p il (Cancer and modern science) lib bdg $29.25

Grades: 7 8 9 10 11 12   616.99

1. Brain -- Cancer

ISBN 9781435857025; 978-1-4358-5011-8; 1-4358-5011-4

LC 2008-22086

This book combines "lots of technical detail about anatomy, physiology, and pathology with a personal, interactive style. . . . Brain Cancer includes a section on Coping with School and Community that speaks directly to students with the disease and encourages them to stay active and involved. It also looks in detail at different types of brain

cancer, detection and diagnosis, and present and future treatments." Booklist

Includes glossary and bibliographical references

Goldsmith, Connie

Skin cancer. Twenty-First Century Books 2010 128p il (USA Today health reports: diseases and disorders) lib bdg $34.60

Grades: 7 8 9 10 11 12   616.99

1. Cancer 2. Skin -- Diseases

ISBN 978-0-7613-5469-7; 0-7613-5469-7

LC 2010-10003

This describes causes, prevention, and treatments of skin cancer.

This is "liberally sprinkled with relevant articles and 'snapshots' (graphs showing statistical breakdowns of the topic at hand) from the newspaper, providing a competent introduction to primary-source material." SLJ

Includes glossary and bibliographical references

Lew, Kristi

The **truth** about cancer; understanding and fighting a deadly disease. Enslow Publishers 2009 104p il (Issues in focus today) lib bdg $31.93

Grades: 7 8 9 10   616.99

1. Cancer

ISBN 978-0-7660-3068-8 lib bdg; 0-7660-3068-7 lib bdg

LC 2008-32026

"Examines the deadly disease cancer, including a history of the disease, diagnosis and treatment, coping with cancer, and the fight against it around the world." Publisher's note

Includes glossary and bibliographical references

Markle, Sandra

Leukemia; true survival stories. Lerner Publications 2010 48p il (Powerful medicine) lib bdg $27.93

Grades: 5 6 7 8   616.99

1. Leukemia

ISBN 978-0-8225-8700-2 lib bdg; 0-8225-8700-9 lib bdg

LC 2009-34441

This book about leukemia "will grab the attention of middle school readers. . . . The illustrations and photos are stunning with medically accurate captions. Real-life patients, whose photos are included in the text, are highlighted, with updates on their progress at the end of . . . [the] book. . . . This . . . fills the need for up-to-date books on medical topics using vocabulary that a young teenager can understand." Voice Youth Advocates

Includes glossary and bibliographical references

Parks, Peggy J., 1951-

Brain tumors. ReferencePoint Press 2011 96p il (Compact research: diseases and disorders) $26.95

Grades: 7 8 9 10 11 12   616.99

1. Brain -- Tumors

ISBN 978-1-60152-138-5; 1-60152-138-3

LC 2010040107

"Fortified with contemporary individual case studies of both teens and adults [this] title . . . discusses variations of [brain tumors], as well as the prevalence, symptoms, causes, effects, diagnoses, and treatment, drawing upon media interviews and commentary as well as clinical reports and research studies. . . . The clear design includes recent graphs and tables, color photos and diagrams, and lots of carefully documented primary-source quotes from patients, researchers, and scientists." Booklist

Includes bibliographical references

Sheen, Barbara

Prostate cancer; Barbara Sheen. Lucent Books 2008 104 p. col. ill. (hardcover) $34.95
Grades: 7 8 9 10   **616.99**
  1. Prostate gland -- Cancer 2. Cancer 3. Prostate -- Cancer
ISBN 1590185935; 9781590185933
                                                    LC 2008003808
This book is part of the Diseases & Disorders series and looks at prostate cancer. The series "offers young readers and researchers a means of understanding ailments and their ramifications. Clear, careful explanations offer insight into what these conditions are, what causes them, how people live with them, and the latest information about treatment and prevention." (Publisher's note)

Includes bibliographical references (p. 85-90, 96-97) and index.

Silver, Marc

My parent has cancer and it really sucks; Marc Silver, Maya Silver. Sourcebooks Fire 2013 272 p.
Grades: 6 7 8 9 10 11 12   **616.99**
  1. Cancer -- Psychological aspects 2. Children of cancer patients
ISBN 9781402273070
                                                    LC 2012039095
This handbook "aims to guide teens through the experience of having an ill parent. . . . Short chapters include 'Let's Talk: How to Keep Your Family Communication Lines Wide Open,' 'How Things Will Change During Cancer,' 'Dealing with Stress,' 'The Power (and the Limits) of Optimism and Faith,' 'Seeking Support,' 'Facing a Dire Prognosis,' and 'Losing a Parent to Cancer.'" (School Library Journal)

"Drawing on their experiences, the Silvers offer advice for finding solace in people who have been there and who have found ways to cope... It's admirable that the authors don't sugarcoat the realities of cancer and will speak with an honesty that teens will identify with and find comfort in." Booklist

Silverstein, Alvin

  ★ The **breast** cancer update; [by] Alvin and Virginia Silverstein and Laura Silverstein Nunn. Enslow Publishers 2008 128p il (Disease update) lib bdg $31.93
Grades: 5 6 7 8   **616.99**
  1. Breast cancer
ISBN 978-0-7660-2747-3 lib bdg; 0-7660-2747-3 lib bdg
                                                    LC 2006-32821

This offers a history of breast cancer, a definition of it, and describes its diagnosis and treatment, prevention, and future

Includes glossary and bibliographical references

Stokes, Mark

Colon cancer; current and emerging trends in detection and treatment. [by] Mark Stokes. 1st ed.; Rosen Pub. Group 2006 64p il (Cancer and modern science) lib bdg $29.25
Grades: 7 8 9 10   **616.99**
  1. Colon cancer
ISBN 1-4042-0387-7
                                                    LC 2005003626
"Photographs, diagrams, multihued headings, and spotlighted insets are plentiful. . . . [This is a] solid [overview] of the current understanding of [this condition]." SLJ

Includes bibliographical references

Prostate cancer; current and emerging trends in detection and treatment. [by] Mark Stokes. 1st ed.; Rosen Pub. Group 2006 64p il (Cancer and modern science) lib bdg $29.25
Grades: 7 8 9 10   **616.99**
  1. Prostate gland -- Cancer
ISBN 1-4042-0391-5
                                                    LC 2005003628
"Photographs, diagrams, multihued headings, and spotlighted insets are plentiful. . . . [This is a] solid [overview] of the current understanding of [this condition]." SLJ

Includes bibliographical references

Thornton, Denise

Living with cancer; the ultimate teen guide. Scarecrow Press 2011 175p il (It happened to me) $40
Grades: 7 8 9 10   **616.99**
  1. Cancer
ISBN 978-0-8108-7277-6
                                                    LC 2010044140
"Written primarily for teens surviving cancer, this guide is chock-full of advice, tips, and firsthand accounts. The views of teens with a sibling or a parent battling the disease are also presented. Honest and heart-wrenching, this title doesn't shy away from the brutal realities of the disease. . . . This is a valuable resource, reminding those affected that they are not alone." SLJ

Includes glossary and bibliographical references

617   Surgery, regional medicine, dentistry, ophthalmology, otology, audiology

Markle, Sandra

Wounded brains; true survival stories. Lerner Publications 2011 48p il (Powerful medicine) lib bdg $27.93

Grades: 5 6 7 8   **617**
1. Brain -- Wounds and injuries
ISBN 978-0-8225-8704-0 lib bdg; 0-8225-8704-1
lib bdg

     LC 2009034440

Describes several true cases of traumatic brain injury and the medical treatment that followed.

This narrative reads "like information from the Discovery Health channel, for kids: part fascinating science, part human interest story, and part 'Eew, gross!'. . . Clear, straightforward prose is supplemented by definitions and explanations of medical techniques and jargon. The numerous color photos and medical images will satisfy readers' curiosity." SLJ

Includes glossary and bibliographical references

Mullins, Matt
Surgical technologist. Cherry Lake Pub. 2010 32p il (Cool careers: career and technical education) lib bdg $27.07
Grades: 4 5 6 7   **617**
1. Surgery 2. Vocational guidance 3. Medical technologists
ISBN 978-1-60279-939-4 lib bdg; 1-60279-939-3
lib bdg

     LC 2010001437

This "provides an overview of the duties performed by these allied health professionals, requirements and training for the job, and the anticipated future of this occupation. . . . Full color, captioned photographs . . . appear on most spreads, clarifying the text. . . . This will make a useful addition to the career shelf." Booklist

Includes bibliographical references

Townsend, John
★ **Scalpels,** stitches & scars; a history of surgery. Raintree 2005 56p il (Painful history of medicine) lib bdg $32.86; pa $9.90
Grades: 6 7 8 9   **617**
1. Surgery
ISBN 1-4109-1332-5 lib bdg; 1-4109-1337-6 pa
     LC 2004-14248

A history of surgery from ancient times to the present

This is "packed with grisly facts and gory images. . . . But the science is accurate, and many readers will be intrigued by the medical drama. . . . The design, with lots of color pictures, captions, and boxes, will grab browsers, and the cover art is a thrilling story in itself." Booklist

Includes glossary and bibliographical references

Woog, Adam
The **bionic** hand. Norwood House Press 2009 48p il lib bdg $25.27
Grades: 3 4 5 6   **617**
1. Bionics 2. Artificial limbs
ISBN 978-1-59953-341-4 lib bdg; 1-59953-341-3
lib bdg

     LC 2009-15640

"Explores the development and creation of the i-LIMB which is the first commercially available bionic hand." Publisher's note

617.1   Injuries and wounds

Lew, Kristi
Clot & scab; gross stuff about your scrapes, bumps, and bruises. illustrations by Michael Slack. Millbrook Press 2010 48p il (Gross body science) lib bdg $29.27
Grades: 4 5 6   **617.1**
1. Wounds and injuries
ISBN 978-0-8225-8965-5 lib bdg; 0-8225-8965-6
lib bdg

     LC 2008-45626

"Solid information layered between sarcastic comments and kid-friendly terminology like fart, poop, barf, and puke will keep readers engaged. . . . Labeled, captioned (and graphic) photographs, cartoon-style illustrations, and micrographs add information." SLJ

Includes glossary and bibliographical references

Markle, Sandra
Bad burns; true survival stories. Lerner Publications 2010 48p il (Powerful medicine) lib bdg $27.93
Grades: 5 6 7 8   **617.1**
1. Burns and scalds
ISBN 978-0-8225-8702-6 lib bdg; 0-8225-8702-5
lib bdg

     LC 2009034439

Explores how advancements in medicine and technology have helped victims of severe skin burns, and includes real-life stories of burn survivors and tips on burn prevention and treatment.

This narrative reads "like information from the Discovery Health channel, for kids: part fascinating science, part human interest story, and part 'Eew, gross!'. . . Clear, straightforward prose is supplemented by definitions and explanations of medical techniques and jargon. The numerous color photos and medical images will satisfy readers' curiosity." SLJ

Includes glossary and bibliographical references

Shattered bones; true survival stories. Lerner Publications 2010 48p il (Powerful medicine) lib bdg $27.93
Grades: 5 6 7 8   **617.1**
1. Bones 2. Fractures
ISBN 978-0-8225-8703-3 lib bdg; 0-8225-8703-3
lib bdg

     LC 2009034442

Offers true stories of people who suffered broken bones, along with information on the skeleton, its structure and function, and the treatments doctors use for injuries.

This narrative reads "like information from the Discovery Health channel, for kids: part fascinating science, part human interest story, and part 'Eew, gross!'. . . Clear, straightforward prose is supplemented by definitions and explanations of medical techniques and jargon. The numerous color photos and medical images will satisfy readers' curiosity." SLJ

Includes glossary and bibliographical references

Nagle, Jeanne

Frequently asked questions about Wii and video game injuries and fitness. Rosen Pub. 2009 64p il (FAQ: teen life) lib bdg $29.25

Grades: 6 7 8 9   **617.1**

1. Exercise 2. Video games 3. Physical fitness 4. Wounds and injuries
ISBN 978-1-4358-5329-4 lib bdg; 1-4358-5329-6 lib bdg

LC 2009001046

"While conversational, [this volume is] surprisingly helpful—and even emotive. . . . [This book] will delight anyone who has given themselves carpal tunnel playing Wii sports. Nagle's conclusion is that 'exergames' at the very least reinforce healthy behavior." Booklist

Includes glossary and bibliographical references

★ **Sports** injuries information for teens; health tips about acute, traumatic, and chronic injuries in adolescent athletes. edited by Zachary Klimecki and Elizabeth Bellenir. 3rd ed. Omnigraphics, Inc. 2012 xiii, 401 p.p (hardcover) $69

Grades: 7 8 9 10 11 12   **617.1**

1. Athletes -- Wounds and injuries 2. Teenagers -- Health and hygiene 3. Sports injuries 4. Wounds and injuries 5. Teenagers -- Wounds and injuries -- Prevention
ISBN 0780812654; 9780780812659

LC 2012018884

This book offers teens a "guide to being a healthy athlete. It includes guidelines for participating safely in sports and avoiding injury. It also discusses how to deal with injuries when they do occur. It explains diagnostic and treatment procedures and discusses issues related to rehabilitation, including suggestions for making decisions about returning to play. The book concludes with directories of resources for more information about sports-related injuries and fitness." (Publisher's note)

Includes bibliographical references and index.

617.4   Surgery by systems and regions

Yount, Lisa

Alfred Blalock, Helen Taussig, and Vivien Thomas; mending children's hearts. by Lisa Yount. Chelsea House 2012 xviii, 127 p.p col. ill. (Trailblazers in science and technology) (library) $35

Grades: 7 8 9 10 11 12   **617.4**

1. Heart -- Surgery 2. Surgeons 3. Pediatric cardiology -- History 4. Heart surgeons -- United States -- Biography
ISBN 1604136588; 9781604136586

LC 2010035656

This book, part of the Trailblazers in Science and Technology series, focuses on medical professionals Alfred Blalock, Helen Taussig, and Vivien Thomas. The book "recounts the lives and careers of three medical pioneers—a white male surgeon (Blalock), a white female cardiologist (Taussig), and an African-American male laboratory technician (Thomas)—

who combined their skills in 1944 to create a groundbreaking operation" for pediatric cardiology. (Publisher's note)

Includes bibliographical references and index.

617.5   Regional medicine

Ear, nose, and throat; edited by Kara Rogers. Britannica Educational Pub. in association with Rosen Educational Services 2012 xvii, 186 p.p col. ill. $45.00

Grades: 7 8 9 10 11 12   **617.5**

1. Ear 2. Nose 3. Throat 4. Otolaryngology -- Popular works
ISBN 1615306579; 9781615306572

LC 2011013432

Editor Kara Rogers presents a book on otolaryngology. "The interconnectedness of the ear, nose, and throat is evident when you consider how the smell . . . can affect your perception of their taste, or how a runny nose and scratchy throat can lead to an ear infection. In addition to enabling sensory perception, the ear, nose, and throat perform a number of vital functions in the human body. This incisive volume examines the structure of each in turn and in concert with the other, also exploring the diseases and disorders that sometimes afflict them." (Publisher's note)

Includes bibliographical references (p. 170-171) and index

617.7   Ophthalmology

Bender, Lionel

Explaining blindness. Smart Apple Media 2010 45p il (Explaining) lib bdg $34.25

Grades: 5 6 7 8   **617.7**

1. Blind
ISBN 978-1-59920-310-2 lib bdg; 1-59920-310-3 lib bdg

LC 2008-49286

Describes blindness, including its possible causes, the different types of visual impairment, current treatments and cures, and how blind and visually impaired people live everyday lives

"The incorporation of quotes and personal accounts in 'Case Notes' sidebars adds to the sensitive tone found throughout [the title]." SLJ

Includes glossary

Markle, Sandra

Lost sight; true survival stories. Lerner Publications 2010 48p il (Powerful medicine) lib bdg $27.93

Grades: 5 6 7 8   **617.7**

1. Eye 2. Blind 3. Vision
ISBN 978-0-8225-8701-9 lib bdg; 0-8225-8701-7 lib bdg

LC 2009-34443

This book about vision loss "will grab the attention of middle school readers. . . . The illustrations and photos are stunning with medically accurate captions. Real-life pa-

tients, whose photos are included in the text, are highlighted, with updates on their progress at the end of . . . [the] book."
Voice Youth Advocates

Includes glossary and bibliographical references

617.8 Otology and audiology

Levete, Sarah

Explaining deafness. Smart Apple Media 2010 45p il (Explaining) lib bdg $34.25

Grades: 5 6 7 8   **617.8**

1. Deafness

ISBN 978-1-59920-313-3 lib bdg; 1-59920-313-8 lib bdg

LC 2008-49289

Discusses the history, diagnosis, and treatment of deafness, including ways to cope with living with the condition

"The incorporation of quotes and personal accounts in 'Case Notes' sidebars adds to the sensitive tone found throughout [the title]." SLJ

Includes glossary, bibliographical references and filmography

617.9 Operative surgery and special fields of surgery

Campbell, Andrew

Cosmetic surgery. Smart Apple Media 2010 44p il (Science in the news) lib bdg $34.25

Grades: 6 7 8 9   **617.9**

1. Plastic surgery

ISBN 978-1-59920-322-5 lib bdg; 1-59920-322-7 lib bdg

LC 2008-49274

This book about cosmetic surgery "move[s] smoothly, occasionally pausing for the definition of a term. [The title] boast[s] plenty of attractive photos, and a clean layout allows the information to be easily consumed. . . . Provides the information that younger teens need." SLJ

Includes glossary

Organ transplants. Smart Apple Media 2010 45p il (Science in the news) lib bdg $34.25

Grades: 6 7 8 9   **617.9**

1. Transplantation of organs, tissues, etc.

ISBN 978-1-59920-321-8 lib bdg; 1-59920-321-9 lib bdg

LC 2008-41436

"Discusses current practices of organ transplants, developments in science that make transplants possible, and the history of organ transplants as well as issues surrounding organ shortage and organ selling." Publisher's note

Includes glossary

Jango-Cohen, Judith

Bionics; [by] Judith Jango-Cohen. Lerner Publications Co. 2007 48p il (Cool science) lib bdg $26.60

Grades: 4 5 6 7   **617.9**

1. Bionics 2. Artificial organs

ISBN 978-0-8225-5937-5 lib bdg; 0-8225-5937-4 lib bdg

LC 2005032221

This "introduction to the field of bionics is divided into four chapters: 'Replacing Parts,' 'Fixing Malfunctions,' 'Assisting the Senses,' and 'Facing the Future.' Jango-Cohen uses a number of personal stories and references to pop culture to engage readers. . . . The explanations are clearly written and easily understood. Colorful photographs and illustrations are featured throughout the text." SLJ

Includes bibliographical references

Schwartz, Tina P.

Organ transplants; a survival guide for the entire family: the ultimate teen guide. Scarecrow Press 2005 243p il (It happened to me) $36.50

Grades: 7 8 9 10   **617.9**

1. Transplantation of organs, tissues, etc.

ISBN 0-8108-4924-0

LC 2004-21563

"The 13 chapters, written in a question-and-answer format, detail the steps involved from diagnosis and being placed on a waiting list to pre and post-surgery. . . .The well-written text is complemented by a comprehensive section of suggestions for additional information. . . . Texts with this breadth of coverage are rare." SLJ

Includes bibliographical references

618.1 Gynecology and obstetrics

Fullick, Ann

Test tube babies; in-vitro fertilization. Ann Fullick. Rev. and updated Heinemann Library 2002 64 p. col. ill. (Science at the edge) (library) $34.29 (USD); (library) $35

Grades: 7 8 9 10   **618.1**

1. Fertilization in vitro 2. Reproductive technology 3. Infertility 4. Reproduction 5. Test tube babies

ISBN 1432924532; 1588107035 out of print; 9781432924539

LC 2001006080

This book by Ann Fullick is part of the Science at the Edge series and looks at in vitro fertilization. It "begins with a discussion of the causes of infertility, the biology of reproduction, and the development of a human embryo from conception to birth. The choice between the use of infertility drugs or in-vitro fertilization is mentioned." An "explanation of in-vitro fertilization follows, with some . . . illustrations, taking readers stepwise through the process." (NSTA Recommends)

Includes bibliographical references (p. 63) and index.

Vaughan, Jenny

Making new life. Smart Apple Media 2010 45p il (Science in the news) lib bdg $34.25

Grades: 6 7 8 9   **618.1**
   1. Reproductive technology
ISBN 978-1-59920-318-8 lib bdg; 1-59920-318-9
lib bdg

LC 2008-49276

This book about reproductive technologies "move[s] smoothly, occasionally pausing for the definition of a term. [The title] boast[s] plenty of attractive photos, and a clean layout allows the information to be easily consumed. . . . Provides the information that younger teens need." SLJ
   Includes glossary

Waters, Sophie
   Seeing the gynecologist. Rosen Pub. Group 2007 47p il (Girls' health) $19.95
Grades: 7 8 9 10 11 12   **618.1**
   1. Girls -- Health and hygiene 2. Women -- Health and hygiene
ISBN 978-1-4042-1948-9; 1-4042-1948-X

LC 2007-1633

"Introductory chapters include a brief introduction to the physiology of women's reproduction and menstruation, but the majority of the book covers the specifics of a gynecological visit, from choosing a doctor and insurance concerns to what happens during a pelvic exam. . . . The accessible text is informative and supportive." Booklist
   Includes bibliographical references

Winkler, Kathleen
   ★ **High**-tech babies; the debate over assisted reproductive technology. [by] Kathleen Winkler. Enslow Publishers 2006 58p il (Issues in focus today) lib bdg $31.93
Grades: 7 8 9 10 11 12   **618.1**
   1. Infertility 2. Medical ethics 3. Fertilization in vitro
ISBN 0-7660-2528-4

LC 2005-34656

This discusses infertility and how it is diagnosed, assisted reproductive technologies such as intrauterine insemination (IUI) and in vitro fertilization (IVF), and the ethics of those technologies.
   Includes glossary and bibliographical references

★ **Pregnancy** information for teens; health tips about teen pregnancy and teen parenting. edited by Elizabeth Magill. 2nd ed. Omnigraphics 2012 xiii, 396 p.p ill. (hardcover) $69.00
Grades: 7 8 9 10   **618.1**
   1. Teenage pregnancy 2. Teenagers -- Health and hygiene 3. Teenage parents
ISBN 0780812204; 9780780812208

LC 2011042323

This book uses "articles reprinted with permission from sources such as the March of Dimes and The National Campaign to Prevent Teen Pregnancy." This "second edition gives updated information on unplanned pregnancies. While part one features aspects of the phenomenon as a social issue, the rest of the book provides health tips and options for teens who are pregnant." (School Library Journal)
   Includes bibliographical references and index.

618.92   Pediatrics

★ **Allergy** information for teens; health tips about allergic reactions to food, pollen, mold, and other substances, including facts about diagnosing, treating, and preventing allergic responses and complications. edited by Karen Bellenir. 2nd ed. Omnigraphics, Inc. 2013 xiii, 388 p.p ill. (hardcover) $69
Grades: 8 9 10 11 12   **618.92**
   1. Allergy -- Encyclopedias 2. Teenagers -- Health and hygiene 3. Allergy 4. Food allergy 5. Insect allergy 6. Allergy in children
ISBN 0780812883; 9780780812888

LC 2012038514

This book is a "51-chapter resource for reliable information about the many kinds of allergic reactions, triggers, symptoms, tests, treatments, and management strategies. Each chapter presents topics in short sections, using a handy question-and-answer format interwoven with many diagrams and sidebars. The volume concludes with lists of 19 additional titles, 10 cookbooks, and 24 articles, many with 2005 publication dates." (School Library Journal)
   Includes bibliographical references and index.

Chesner, Jonathan
   ADHD in HD; brains gone wild. by Jonathan Chesner. Free Spirit Pub. 2012 145 p. ill. (some col.) (pbk.) $14.99
Grades: 6 7 8 9   **618.92**
   1. Attention deficit disorder 2. Abnormal psychology 3. Anxiety in adolescence 4. Teenagers -- Family relationships 5. Attention-deficit disorder in adolescence
ISBN 1575423863; 9781575423869; 9781575426716

LC 2011047036

This book, by actor Jonathan Chesner, "is a kinetic collection of frank personal stories of failure and success, hilarious anecdotes, wild ideas, and point-blank advice that will resonate with teens and young adults. . . . The book addresses the four main characteristics of ADHD: hyperactivity, impulsivity, inattention, and indecisiveness. It provides positive advice about school, family life, social life, dating, careers, medicine, and how to be like Mr. T." (Publisher's note)
   "With much practical advice (for example, taking "baby steps" when trying to establish eating habits), this packs in plenty of valuable content—and is pretty enjoyable, too." Booklist

Currie-McGhee, Leanne K.
   Childhood obesity; by Leanne K. Currie-McGhee. Lucent Books 2012 104 p. ill. (some col.) (Nutrition and health) (hardcover) $30.95
Grades: 7 8 9 10 11 12   **618.92**
   1. Obesity in children
ISBN 1420507230; 9781420507232

LC 2012002939

This book by Leanne K. Currie-McGhee, part of the "Nutrition & Health" series, "explores global issue of childhood obesity. Causes of and proposed solutions to this public health issue are explored, and the findings of current studies are detailed. The text features comments from scientists and researchers, but also includes first-hand accounts from children and teens who have struggled with obesity." (Publisher's note)

Includes bibliographical references (p. 90-93) and index.

Grossberg, Blythe

★ **Asperger's** rules! how to make sense of school and friends. by Blythe Grossberg. Magination Press 2012 127 p. col. ill. (paperback) $9.95; (hardcover) $14.95

Grades: 5 6 7 8   **618.92**
  1. Life skills 2. Social skills 3. Asperger's syndrome 4. Autism in children 5. Autistic children -- Education 6. Asperger's syndrome -- Social aspects
ISBN 1433811286; 9781433811272; 9781433811289
                                                          LC 2011053483

This book by Blythe Grossberg presents a "guide for readers with Asperger's, covering feelings and emotions, teachers, asking for help, and dealing with bullies. Quizzes let readers reflect on their own approaches to situations like interacting with kids at school, and Grossberg also includes tips on how to interpret social situations. . . . Flowcharts illustrate how various conversations might progress, and other sections focus on dressing properly and eating healthful meals." (Publishers Weekly)

Reeve, Elizabeth

The **survival** guide for kids with autism spectrum disorders (and their parents) by Elizabeth Verdick & Elizabeth Reeve; illustrated by Nick Kobyluch. Free Spirit Pub. 2012 234 p. col. ill. (pbk.) $16.99

Grades: 5 6 7 8 Adult   **618.92**
  1. Autism 2. Children with autism 3. Parents of autistic children 4. Autistic children -- Family relationships
ISBN 1575423855; 9781575423852; 9781575426747
                                                          LC 2011046520

This book "offers kids with autism spectrum disorders (ASDs) their own comprehensive resource for both understanding their condition and finding tools to cope with the challenges they face every day . . . with an emphasis on helping children gain new self-understanding and self-acceptance. Meant to be read with a parent, the book addresses questions . . . and provides strategies for communicating, making and keeping friends, and succeeding in school." (Publisher's note)

"This volume could become a treasured resource for families looking for help in successfully working through some of the problems faced by higher-functioning children with ASD." SLJ

618.927 Pediatric musculoskeletal diseases

Skrypuch, Marsha Forchuk

One Step at a Time; A Vietnamese Child Finds Her Way. by Marsha Forchuk Skrypuch. Pajama Press 2013 vii, 93 p.p (hardcover) $17.95

Grades: 6 7 8   **618.927**
  1. Orphans 2. Poliomyelitis
ISBN 1927485010; 9781927485019

In this true story, Marsha Forchuk Skrypuch "continues the story of Tuyet, an eight-year-old Vietnamese refugee and polio survivor with a damaged leg, whose rescue she narrated in 'Last Airlift: A Vietnamese Orphan's Rescue from War.' Adopted by an unconditionally loving and supportive Canadian family, unable to understand or express much in English, Tuyet begins a difficult journey through surgeries and arduous physical therapy to repair her leg." (Publishers Weekly)

620 Engineering and allied operations

Johnson, Rebecca L.

Nanotechnology. Lerner Publications 2006 48p il (Cool science) lib bdg $25.26

Grades: 4 5 6   **620**
  1. Nanotechnology
ISBN 978-0-8225-2111-2 lib bdg; 0-8225-2111-3 lib bdg
                                                          LC 2005008791

"From clear sunscreen to space elevators, nanotechnology promises big changes in our daily lives. . . . Pointing to recent advances in sports equipment, stain resistant fabrics and moving parts for dolls that are but harbingers of revolutionary new developments in science, medicine and the whole approach to manufacturing things. In a final chapter, 'Nanobots and Beyond,' [the author] considers the potential—and . . . the dangers—of submicroscopic self-replicating machines." Kirkus

Includes glossary and bibliographical references

620.1 Engineering mechanics and materials

Finkelstein, Norman H.

Plastics; [by] Norman H. Finkelstein. Marshall Cavendish Benchmark 2007 144p il (Great inventions) lib bdg $27.95

Grades: 7 8 9 10   **620.1**
  1. Plastics
ISBN 978-0-7614-2600-4
                                                          LC 2006020909

"An examination of the origin, history, development, and societal impact of the development of plastics." Publisher's note

Includes glossary and bibliographical references

Kassinger, Ruth

Glass; from Cinderella's slippers to fiber optics. [by] Ruth G. Kassinger. Twenty-First Century Bks. 2003 80p il lib bdg $25.90

Grades: 7 8 9 10   **620.1**
  1. Glass
ISBN 0-7613-2109-8
                                                          LC 2002-5329

Describes the physical composition and characteristics of glass, and presents glassmaking techniques and the various uses made of glass throughout history

This "will catch the interest of a wide variety of readers. The color photographs are clear, interesting, and self-explanatory." Libr Media Connect

Includes bibliographical references

Knapp, Brian J.
  Materials science. Grolier 2003 9v il set $319
  Grades: 7 8 9 10   **620.1**
    1. Air 2. Wood 3. Glass 4. Paint 5. Paper 6. Water
    7. Fibers 8. Metals 9. Ceramics 10. Plastics 11.
    Adhesives 12. Materials 13. Dyes and dyeing 14.
    Reference books 15. Materials science
    ISBN 0-7172-5697-9

                                            LC 2002-44537
Presents the main scientific properties of materials and how they are determined, as well as how substances can be manipulated or modified to produce a wide array of materials with an equally wide array of applications

"The volumes are generously enhanced with photographs and appropriate illustrative figures. . . . The written presentations are all brief, but clear and understandable for anyone who has had a general science background." Sci Books Films

Morris, Neil
  Glass. Amicus 2010 48p il (Materials that matter) lib bdg $28.50
  Grades: 4 5 6 7   **620.1**
    1. Glass
    ISBN 978-1-60753-065-7 lib bdg; 1-60753-065-1
    lib bdg

                                            LC 2009029796
"The clean layout includes photographs and occasional charts, graphs, and technical illustrations against a range of pastel backgrounds. Inset boxes provide further detail, interesting extras, and recycling information. . . . [This book offers] easily accessible background information for report writers." SLJ

Includes glossary and bibliographical references

  Metals. Amicus 2010 48p il (Materials that matter) lib bdg $28.50
  Grades: 4 5 6 7   **620.1**
    1. Metals
    ISBN 978-1-60753-066-4 lib bdg; 1-60753-066-X
    lib bdg

                                            LC 2009029797
"The clean layout includes photographs and occasional charts, graphs, and technical illustrations against a range of pastel backgrounds. Inset boxes provide further detail, interesting extras, and recycling information. . . . [This book offers] easily accessible background information for report writers." SLJ

Includes glossary and bibliographical references

Ward, David J.
  Materials science; by D. J. Ward. Lerner Publications 2009 47p il (Cool science) lib bdg $26.60

Grades: 4 5 6   **620.1**
    1. Materials
    ISBN 978-0-8225-7588-7 lib bdg; 0-8225-7588-4
    lib bdg

                                            LC 2007042176
This describes how scientists study the microscopic parts of materials such as plastic, glass, or stainless steel, how they learn how each part makes something hard or soft, strong or weak, or good or bad at carrying heat, and how they use that knowledge to create supermaterials to help make better sports equipment, tinier computer chips, and more.

Includes glossary and bibliographical references

621   Applied physics

Silverstein, Alvin
  Energy; [by] Alvin Silverstein, Virginia Silverstein, Laura Silverstein Nunn. rev ed.; Twenty-First Century Books 2008 128p il (Science concepts, second series) lib bdg $31.93
  Grades: 6 7 8 9   **621**
    1. Energy resources
    ISBN 978-0-8225-8655-5 lib bdg; 0-8225-8655-X
    lib bdg

                                            LC 2007049535
First published 1998
Discusses the sources and uses of different types of energy, both natural and manmade, including electrical, magnetic, light, heat, sound, and nuclear energy

Includes glossary and bibliographical references

Sobey, Ed
  Electric motor experiments. Enslow Publishers 2011 128p il (Cool science projects with technology) lib bdg $31.93
  Grades: 6 7 8 9   **621**
    1. Electric motors 2. Science -- Experiments
    ISBN 978-0-7660-3306-1; 0-7660-3306-6
This explains how motors work and includes experiments in how to build and use a motor.

Includes glossary and bibliographical references

621.1   Fluid-power technologies

Collier, James Lincoln
  ★ The **steam** engine. Marshall Cavendish Benchmark 2006 112p il (Great inventions) lib bdg $37.07
  Grades: 7 8 9 10   **621.1**
    1. Steam engines
    ISBN 0-7614-1880-6
This is a history of the steam engine and its influence on American history and culture.

This is presented "thoughfully yet conversationally. . . . [It] will reward steady reading." Horn Book Guide

Includes glossary and bibliographical references

O'Neal, Claire

How to use waste energy to heat and light your home. Mitchell Lane Publishers 2009 47p il (Tell your parents) lib bdg $21.50

Grades: 4 5 6 7   **621.1**
   1. Recycling 2. Waste products as fuel
   ISBN 978-1-58415-765-6 lib bdg; 1-58415-765-8 lib bdg

LC 2009-4483

Explores how to reduce the amount of trash produced and stored by reusing items and recycling materials, and describes how these efforts can help protect the environment

This title "offers numerous facts and statistics, all of which are cited. . . . Chapters cover present-day issues and . . . are interspersed with full-color photographs and short 'Did You Know' trivia boxes. . . . Back matter includes detailed resource lists and 'Try This!' experiments." SLJ

Includes glossary and bibliographical references

621.3092   Electrical engineers

Yount, Lisa

Nikola Tesla; harnessing electricity. by Lisa Yount. Chelsea House 2012 xviii, 128 p.p col. ill. (Trailblazers in science and technology) (library) $35

Grades: 7 8 9 10 11 12   **621.3092**
   1. Electricity 2. Tesla, Nikola, 1856-1943 3. Inventors -- United States -- Biography 4. Electrical engineers -- United States -- Biography
   ISBN 1604136707; 9781604136708

LC 2010052627

This book by Lisa Yount is part of the Trailblazers in Science and Technology series and looks at Nikola Tesla. He "saw his fortunes reverse as many times." He "drew the attention of businessman George Westinghouse with his alternating current (AC), a method of delivering electricity more efficiently and over greater distances than Edison's direct current (DC). With Westinghouse's support, Tesla's method soon became dominant in the industry." (Publisher's note)

Includes bibliographical references and index.

621.31   Generation, modification, storage, transmission of electric power

Lew, Kristi

Goodbye, gasoline; the science of fuel cells. Compass Point Books 2009 48p il (Headline science) lib bdg $27.93

Grades: 5 6 7 8   **621.31**
   1. Fuel cells
   ISBN 978-0-7565-3521-6 lib bdg; 0-7565-3521-2 lib bdg

LC 2008011729

This "clearly examines the history and technology of hydrogen fuel cells, including the various types such as proton exchange membrane and alkaline cells. An excellent description of how the technology works gives readers an understanding of both the successes and problems relating

to these promising energy sources. . . . The color illustrations and charts . . . are clear and helpful, and the text, although information rich, is not overly difficult." SLJ

O'Neal, Claire

How to use wind power to light and heat your home. Mitchell Lane Publishers 2009 47p il map (Tell your parents) lib bdg $21.50

Grades: 4 5 6 7   **621.31**
   1. Wind power 2. Renewable energy resources
   ISBN 978-1-58415-762-5 lib bdg; 1-58415-762-3 lib bdg

LC 2009-4530

Introduces wind power, including the history of harnessing the wind for work, how modern wind power generates electricity, and how to install a turbine to a home

This book "offers numerous facts and statistics, all of which are cited. . . . Chapters cover present-day issues and . . . are interspersed with full-color photographs and short 'Did You Know' trivia boxes. . . . Back matter includes detailed resource lists and 'Try This!' experiments." SLJ

Includes glossary and bibliographical references

621.32   Lighting

Collier, James Lincoln

★ Electricity and the light bulb; [by] James Lincoln Collier. Marshall Cavendish Benchmark 2006 112p il (Great inventions) lib bdg $37.07

Grades: 7 8 9 10   **621.32**
   1. Electric power 2. Electric lighting
   ISBN 0-7614-1878-4

LC 2004-21623

This is a history of electric power and the invention of the light bulb and their influence on American history and culture.

This is presented "thoughfully yet conversationally. . . . [It] will reward steady reading." Horn Book Guide

Includes glossary and bibliographical references

Sonneborn, Liz

The electric light; Thomas Edison's illuminating invention. Chelsea House 2007 120p il (Milestones in American history) lib bdg $35

Grades: 7 8 9 10   **621.32**
   1. Inventors 2. Electric lighting
   ISBN 978-0-7910-9350-4 lib bdg; 0-7910-9350-6 lib bdg

LC 2006-34432

This "accessible [volume captures] the hard work, perseverance, and natural talent of Edison. . . . The [text explores] the [man's life] along with providing information about the genesis and development of [electric light]. Many photographs, reproductions, and sidebars contribute to a clean design and help clarify topics." Horn Book Guide

Includes bibliographical references

621.381   Electronics

Electronics;   edited by Sherman Hollar.   Britannica
Educational Pub. in association with Rosen Educational Services   2012   80 p.   (Introduction to
physics) (library binding) $31.70
Grades: 7 8 9 10 11 12   **621.381**
1. Electronics 2. Electronics
ISBN 9781615306640; 1615306641

LC 2011017100

This book, edited by Sherman Hollar, is part of the Introduction to Physics series. It "examines various components,
such as electron tubes and semiconductors, that have been
essential to electronics over the years, as well as the history
of the field in general and its applications in everyday life."
(Publisher's note)

Includes bibliographical references and index

621.383   Specific communications systems

Coe, Lewis

The **telegraph**; a history of Morse's invention
and its predecessors in the United States. McFarland
& Co. 1993 184p il hardcover o.p. pa $29.95
Grades: 7 8 9 10   **621.383**
1. Artists 2. Painters 3. Inventors 4. Telegraph
ISBN 0-7864-1808-7 pa

LC 92-53597

This study of the development of the telegraph includes brief biographical sketches of Samuel Morse and
other inventors

Includes bibliographical references

621.384   Radio and radar

Firestone, Mary

Wireless technology. Lerner Publications 2009
48p il (Cool science) lib bdg $27.93
Grades: 4 5 6   **621.384**
1. Wireless communication systems
ISBN 978-0-8225-7590-0 lib bdg; 0-8225-7590-6
lib bdg

LC 2007041102

This describes "how cutting-edge science helps people
communicate better, live healthier, and have more fun!"
Publisher's note

Includes glossary and bibliographical references

Kling, Andrew A.

Cell phones. Lucent Books 2010 112p il (Technology 360) $33.45
Grades: 8 9 10 11 12   **621.384**
1. Cellular telephones
ISBN 978-1-4205-0164-3; 1-4205-0164-X

LC 2009-6249

This book explores "the early development and advances of [cell phone] technology, its impact on society
both positive and negative, and the importance it plays in
our lives. . . . The history . . . progresses from the telegraph

to the invention of the telephone, the merging of radio and
telephone, and the implementation of computers to replace
humans, eventually leading to wireless phones. Issues in regard to texting, the addition of cameras, video capabilities,
disposal, safety, multimedia, and numerous other advances
are addressed. . . . numerous color photos, diagrams, 'Bits
& Bytes' boxes as well as many other additional text boxes
create appeal and provide beneficial informative and complementary material to aid in understanding the technical
details of the [text]." SLJ

Includes glossary and bibliographical references

Sequeira, Michele

Cell phone science; what happens when you call
and why. [by] Michele Sequeira, Michael Westphal.
University of New Mexico Press 2010 174p il (Barbara Guth worlds of wonder science series for young
readers) $24.95
Grades: 6 7 8 9   **621.384**
1. Cellular telephones 2. Wireless communication
systems
ISBN 978-0-8263-4968-2; 0-8263-4968-4

LC 2010028600

"The book sets out to help readers understand the complex science behind . . . [cell phones]. . . . The book features
clear explanations, easy-to-read text, and colorful photographs and illustrations on almost every page. Boxed areas
and information in the margins supplement the text. Students
interested in learning the story of the science behind their
cell phone will be well rewarded with this title." SLJ

Includes glossary and bibliographical references

621.385   Telephony

Kummer, Patricia K.

The **telephone**. Franklin Watts 2006 80p il (Inventions that shaped the world) lib bdg $30.50
Grades: 6 7 8 9   **621.385**
1. Telephone
ISBN 978-0-531-12407-9 lib bdg; 0-531-12407-X
lib bdg

LC 2005-9958

"Describes the evolution of communication from smoke
signals to e-mail, focusing on the invention of the telephone
by Alexander Graham Bell in 1876, and explains how this
technology changed America's economy and environment."
Publisher's note

Includes bibliographical references

Spilsbury, Richard

The **telephone**; [by] Richard and Louise Spilsbury. Heinemann Library 2011 32p il (Tales of
invention) lib bdg $29; pa $7.99
Grades: 4 5 6 7   **621.385**
1. Telephone 2. Cellular telephones
ISBN 978-1-4329-3826-0 lib bdg; 1-4329-3826-6 lib
bdg; 978-1-4329-3833-8 pa; 1-4329-3833-9 pa

LC 2009049027

"Beginning with the first telegraph, the book discusses
how sound travels, how speech is transmitted by wire, and

how Alexander Graham Bell's first telephones worked. Then the text quickly traces later technological developments, from transatlantic cables to early cell phones to the small, light, versatile models available today. . . . The many photographs and other illustrations include excellent labeled diagrams." Booklist

Includes bibliographical references

Stefoff, Rebecca

★ The **telephone**; by Rebecca Stefoff. Marshall Cavendish Benchmark 2006 127p il (Great inventions) lib bdg $37.07

Grades: 7 8 9 10   **621.385**
    1. Telephone
    ISBN 0-7614-1879-2
                               LC 2004-22108

This is a history of the telephone, from Alexander Graham Bell to today's cell phones.

This is presented "thoughtfully yet conversationally. . . . [It] will reward steady reading." Horn Book Guide

Includes glossary and bibliographical references

621.388   Television

Grabowski, John

Television. Lucent Books 2011 112p il (Technology 360) $33.45

Grades: 7 8 9 10   **621.388**
    1. Television
    ISBN 978-1-4205-0169-8; 1-4205-0169-0
                               LC 2010033525

This book offers "clean design with clear explanations of sometimes-complicated scientific subjects. . . . This brings the information [about television] up to date with flat screens and 3-D. . . . A strong [title] for report writers and students with a serious interest in technology and its inventions." Booklist

Includes bibliographical references

Otfinoski, Steven

Television; [by] Steven Otfinoski. 1st ed.; Marshall Cavendish Benchmark 2007 111p il (Great inventions) lib bdg $42.79

Grades: 7 8 9 10   **621.388**
    1. Television
    ISBN 978-0-7614-2228-0 lib bdg; 0-7614-2228-5 lib bdg
                               LC 2005026787

"An examination of the origin, history, development, and societal impact of television." Publisher's note

Includes glossary and bibliographical references

621.39   Computer engineering

Blumenthal, Karen

Steve Jobs; the man who thought different : a biography. by Karen Blumenthal. Feiwel and Friends 2012 310 p. ill., ports. $9.99

Grades: 7 8 9 10   **621.39**
    1. Businesspeople -- United States -- Biography 2. Computer industry -- United States -- History 3. Computer engineers -- United States -- Biography
    ISBN 125001445X; 125001557X; 9781250014450; 9781250015570
                               LC 2012376637

YALSA Award for Excellence in Nonfiction for Young Adults Finalist (2013)

This book is a biography of technology executive Steve Jobs. "[Karen] Blumenthal weaves her portrait on the thematic frame used by Jobs himself in his autobiographical 2005 Stanford commencement address." She chronicles "his adoption as an infant through his 'phone phreaking' days to a spectacular rise and just as meteoric fall from corporate grace in the 1980s. Following a decade of diminished fortunes and largely self-inflicted complications in personal relationships, he returned to Apple." (Kirkus)

Includes bibliographical references (p. [278]-283) and index

621.4   Prime movers and heat engineering

Woelfle, Gretchen

The **wind** at work; an activity guide to windmills. Gretchen Woelfle. 2nd ed. Chicago Review Press 2013 vii, 145 p.p ill. (paperback) $16.95

Grades: 4 5 6   **621.4**
    1. Windmills 2. Wind power 3. Science -- Experiments
    ISBN 1613741006; 9781613741009
                               LC 2012046319

This introduction to windmills "discusses their history and function through modern times. . . . About one-third of the book is devoted to activities illustrating the properties of wind and the jobs performed by windmills. . . . The concluding chapters focus on windmills as a source of energy and suggest how to chart household energy use." (Booklist)

"The historical information is excellent, and includes Persian windmills of 1000 years ago, Dutch windmills of the 17th century, and modern wind turbines. Amusing anecdotes and intriguing facts are woven into the text, keeping it lively. . . . Black-and-white historical prints, photographs, and diagrams appear throughout." SLJ

Includes bibliographical references (pages 133-135) and index

621.43   Internal-combustion engines

Miller, Ron

Rockets. Lerner 2008 112p il (Space innovations) lib bdg $31.93

Grades: 7 8 9 10   **621.43**
    1. Rocketry 2. Rockets (Aeronautics)
    ISBN 978-0-8225-7153-7; 0-8225-7153-6
                               LC 2006-21220

The author "describes the history of rocket science, beginning in ancient China, where saltpeter, sulfur, and charcoal were first combined to create gunpowder. . . . The stories of the development of rockets through time are complemented by short biographies of important scientists such as

Robert Goddard, stories of young model rocket makers, and sidebars explaining the science that makes rockets work. . . . It is a good choice for high school libraries, as well as for boys who are interested in science and nonfiction." Voice Youth Advocates

Includes bibliographical references

Otfinoski, Steven

Rockets; [by] Steven Otfinoski. Marshall Cavendish Benchmark 2007 111p il (Great inventions) lib bdg $42.79

Grades: 7 8 9 10   **621.43**
1. Rocketry 2. Rockets (Aeronautics)
ISBN 978-0-7614-2232-7 lib bdg; 0-7614-2232-3 lib bdg

LC 2005034205

"An examination of the origins, history, development, and impact of rockets and rocketry science." Publisher's note

Includes glossary and bibliographical references

621.46   Electric and related motors

Gabrielson, Curt

Kinetic contraptions; build a hovercraft, airboat, and more with a hobby motor. Chicago Review Press 2010 176p il pa $16.95

Grades: 7 8 9 10   **621.46**
1. Airplanes -- Models 2. Motorboats -- Models 3. Automobiles -- Models
ISBN 978-1-55652-957-3; 1-55652-957-0

LC 2009-25695

The author "describes projects intended to foster in students a passion for electrical experimentation as they construct more than 20 motor-powered devices. With sections dedicated to creating machines that run on land, water, and air, as well as spinning machines (such as a snow globe) and bizarre machines (such as a bubble maker), the book has projects designed to appeal to everyone." Education Digest

621.47   Solar-energy engineering

Bearce, Stephanie

How to harness solar power for your home. Mitchell Lane Publishers 2009 47p il map (Tell your parents) lib bdg $21.50

Grades: 4 5 6 7   **621.47**
1. Solar energy
ISBN 978-1-58415-761-8 lib bdg; 1-58415-761-5 lib bdg

LC 2009-4529

This title about solar power "offers numerous facts and statistics, all of which are cited. . . . Chapters cover present-day issues and . . . are interspersed with full-color photographs and short 'Did You Know' trivia boxes. . . . Back matter includes detailed resource lists and 'Try This!' experiments." SLJ

Includes glossary and bibliographical references

Walker, Niki

Harnessing power from the sun; [by] Niki Walker. Crabtree Pub. Co. 2007 32p il map (Energy revolution) lib bdg $23.93; pa $8.95

Grades: 5 6 7 8   **621.47**
1. Solar energy
ISBN 978-0-7787-2912-9 lib bdg; 0-7787-2912-5 lib bdg; 978-0-7787-2926-6 pa; 0-7787-2926-5 pa

LC 2006014368

This describes various ways of gathering and distributing solar energy, and includes a brief history of solar power, and tips on energy conservation

"Vivid color photographs with informative captions extend the [text], showing diverse people and applications." SLJ

Includes glossary

621.48   Nuclear engineering

Kidd, J. S.

★ Nuclear power; the study of quarks and sparks. [by] J.S. Kidd and Renee A. Kidd. rev ed.; Chelsea House 2006 208p il (Science and society) $35

Grades: 7 8 9 10   **621.48**
1. Nuclear energy
ISBN 978-0-8160-5606-4; 0-8160-5606-4

LC 2005-52872

First published 1999 with title: Quarks and sparks: the story of nuclear power

Examines the people, events, and motivations leading up to modern-day discoveries and advances in nuclear physics

"Extensive scientific explanations are kept manageable, thanks to consistent references to their historical context; and descriptions of the nuclear race during the Second World War are especially riveting." Booklist [review of 1999 edition]

Includes bibliographical references

Mahaffey, James A.

Fusion; James A. Mahaffey. Facts on File 2012 x, 142 p.p (ebook) $45.00; (hardcover) $45.00

Grades: 7 8 9 10 11 12   **621.48**
1. Sun 2. Nuclear fusion 3. Big bang theory 4. Nuclear reactors 5. Fusion -- Popular works
ISBN 9781438138435; 0816076537; 9780816076536

LC 2011012505

This book, by author James A. Mahaffey, "deliver[s] complex information including background on the theories, applications, devices, and future of fusion. [Topics include] . . . hydrogen fusion in the Sun . . . the big bang nucleosynthesis . . . [and] the International Tokamak Experimental Reactor and the Demonstration Power Plant." (School Library Journal)

Includes bibliographical references and index.

Oxlade, Chris

Nuclear power. Smart Apple Media 2010 44p il map (Science in the news) lib bdg $34.25

Grades: 6 7 8 9 **621.48**
1. Nuclear energy 2. Nuclear engineering
ISBN 978-1-59920-320-1 lib bdg; 1-59920-320-0
lib bdg

LC 2008-49277

This book about nuclear power "move[s] smoothly, occasionally pausing for the definition of a term. [The title] boast[s] plenty of attractive photos, and a clean layout allows the information to be easily consumed. . . . Provides the information that younger teens need." SLJ

Includes glossary

621.5 Pneumatic, vacuum, low-temperature technologies

Pringle, Laurence
Ice! the amazing history of the ice business. Laurence Pringle. Calkins Creek 2012 74 p. $17.95
Grades: 4 5 6 7 8 **621.5**
1. Ice 2. Refrigeration 3. Food -- Preservation
ISBN 159078801X; 9781590788011

LC 2012937320

This book looks at "iceboxes, icehouses, icemen, and . . . more about the history of the harvesting, storage, and delivery of ice." Author Laurence Pringle "briefly covers early food preservation . . . before delving into the rise of the ice industry in the early 1800s, and, in particular, the harvesting of the frozen stuff at pristine Rockland Lake in New York." (School Library Journal)

Includes bibliographical references and index.

621.9 Tools

Tomecek, Steve
Tools and machines; by Stephen M. Tomecek. Chelsea House Publishers 2010 182p il (Experimenting with everyday science) $35
Grades: 5 6 7 8 **621.9**
1. Tools 2. Machinery 3. Science -- Experiments
ISBN 978-1-60413-171-0; 1-60413-171-3

LC 2009-22332

This "offers 25 easy-to-perform activities that illuminate scientific principles. . . . [This] discusses levers, pulleys, and meters and explains how people use them in their daily lives. . . . Following each experiment are additional comments on the science behind the experiment and link to the one that follows. Photographs, simple diagrams and illustrations, and sample data tables appear throughout, and the [layout is] clear and colorful." SLJ

Includes bibliographical references

623.4 Ordnance

Boos, Ben
Swords; an artist's devotion. written & illustrated by Ben Boos. Candlewick Press 2008 82p il $24.99; pa $12.99

Grades: 6 7 8 9 **623.4**
1. Swords
ISBN 978-0-7636-3148-2; 0-7636-3148-5; 978-0-7636-5098-8 pa

LC 2007-52333

"This absorbing, large-format collection of sketches, paintings, and historical notes on sword craft is not called an artist's devotion for nothing. Boos's treatment of his subject is reverential and his artwork is outstanding, combining meticulous attention to detail and a designer's sense for layout. The spare text provides just enough information but generally allows the illustrations to speak for themselves." SLJ

Includes bibliographical references

Collier, James Lincoln
★ Gunpowder and weaponry. Benchmark Bks. 2004 124p il (Great inventions) lib bdg $37.07
Grades: 6 7 8 9 **623.4**
1. Firearms 2. Gunpowder 3. Military art and science 4. Weapons -- History 5. Firearms -- History 6. Ordnance -- History 7. Gunpowder -- History 8. Military art and science -- History
ISBN 0-7614-1540-8

LC 2002-156289

This is a history of warfare and weaponry with emphasis on the significance of the invention of gunpowder

Includes bibliographical references

Diagram Group
The new weapons of the world encyclopedia; an international encyclopedia from 5000 B.C. to the 21st century. [by] the Diagram Group. rev ed.; St Martin's Press 2007 368p il pa $24.95
Grades: 8 9 10 11 12 Adult **623.4**
1. Reference books 2. Weapons -- History
ISBN 978-0-312-36832-6 pa; 0-312-36832-1 pa

First published 1980 with title: Weapons: an international encyclopedia from 5000 B.C. to 2000 A.D

This "guide covers the entire history of weapons, from the earliest, most primitive instruments up to remarkable advances in modern defense and warfare. . . . Includes weapons used in Kosovo, Afghanistan, Iraq and the Israel-Lebanon conflict. . . . [This book is] illustrated, with hundreds of color diagrams, charts [and] photographs." Publisher's note

Includes bibliographical references

Gurstelle, William
The art of the catapult; build Greek ballistae, Roman onagers, English trebuchets, and more ancient artillery. Chicago Review Press 2004 172p il map $16.95
Grades: 5 6 7 8 **623.4**
1. Catapult
ISBN 1-55652-526-5

"This collection of 10 working catapult projects offers a fascinating look at world history, military strategy, and physics, related with an engaging yet lighthearted touch. . . . Instructions are clear, with full materials lists, helpful diagrams, and no skipped steps. . . . There's excellent booktalk potential here, and lively reading even for those who never get around to constructing a catapult." SLJ

Includes bibliographical references

Sheinkin, Steve

★ **Bomb**; the race to build and steal the world's most dangerous weapon. Steve Sheinkin. Roaring Brook Press 2012 266 p. ill. (hc) $19.99

Grades: 5 6 7 8 9 10 11 12 Adult   **623.4**

1. Nuclear warfare 2. Nuclear weapons 3. World War, 1914-1918 -- Chemical warfare 4. Atomic bomb -- History 5. Operation Freshman, 1942 6. Atomic bomb -- Germany -- History 7. World War, 1939-1945 -- Secret service -- Soviet Union 8. World War, 1939-1945 -- Secret service -- Great Britain 9. World War, 1939-1945 -- Commando operations -- Norway -- Vemork

ISBN 1596434872; 9781596434875

LC 2011044096

Robert F. Sibert Informational Book Medal (2013)

YALSA Award for Excellence in Nonfiction for Young Adults (2013)

John Newbery Honor Book (2013)

Author Steve Sheinkin's "story unfolds in three parts, covering American attempts to build the [atomic] bomb, how the Soviets tried to steal American designs and how the Americans tried to keep the Germans from building a bomb. It was the eve of World War II, and the fate of the world was at stake . . . all along the way spies in the United States were feeding sensitive information to the KGB." (Kirkus Reviews)

Includes bibliographical references (p. [243]-259) and index

Trueit, Trudi Strain

Gunpowder. Franklin Watts 2005 80p il (Inventions that shaped the world) $30.50

Grades: 6 7 8 9   **623.4**

1. Gunpowder

ISBN 978-0-531-12371-3; 0-531-12371-5

LC 2004030437

Describes the invention of gunpowder, the impact it has had on modern culture, and patterns of change that resulted from its use

Includes bibliographical references

623.7 Communications, vehicles, sanitation, related topics

101 great tanks; edited by Robert Jackson. Rosen Pub. 2010 112p il (The 101 greatest weapons of all times) lib bdg $31.95

Grades: 7 8 9 10   **623.7**

1. Military tanks

ISBN 978-1-4358-3595-5 lib bdg; 1-4358-3595-6 lib bdg

LC 2009-32880

Presents photographs and detailed information about 101 great tanks, from the very first British tank to ultramodern armored fighting vehicles.

Describes "why and when the type of vehicle was created, its advantages and disadvantages, when and where it served, countries that may have purchased or license-built it, and when it was removed from service. . . . Contains a detailed two-dimensional color drawing and black-and-white or color photo of the featured vehicle. . . . Back matter in-

cludes a listing of memorials and museums and an excellent further-reading list. A first purchase where the subject is popular." SLJ

Includes glossary

Mooney, Carla

Pilotless planes. Norwood House Press 2010 48p il (A great idea) lib bdg $25.27

Grades: 3 4 5 6   **623.7**

1. Drone aircraft 2. Military aeronautics

ISBN 978-1-59953-381-0 lib bdg; 1-59953-381-2 lib bdg

LC 2010008500

This "discusses the development and use of unmanned aerial vehicles, also called UAVs or drones, such as the Predator planes currently used by the U.S. Air Force. Looking beyond military uses, the last chapter also considers future public safety, environmental, and commercial applications. . . . Presenting specific, current information, [this book] will appeal to young people intrigued by inventions." Booklist

Includes glossary and bibliographical references

623.74 Vehicles

101 great bombers; Robert Jackson, editor. Rosen Pub. 2010 112p il (The 101 greatest weapons of all times) lib bdg $31.95

Grades: 7 8 9 10   **623.74**

1. Bombers

ISBN 978-1-4358-3594-8 lib bdg; 1-4358-3594-8 lib bdg

LC 2009-32090

Presents photographs and detailed information about 101 great bombers, from the early twentieth-century biplanes to ultramodern stealth bombers.

Describes "why and when the type of vehicle was created, its advantages and disadvantages, when and where it served, countries that may have purchased or license-built it, and when it was removed from service. . . . Contains a detailed two-dimensional color drawing and black-and-white or color photo of the featured vehicle. . . . Back matter includes a listing of memorials and museums and an excellent further-reading list. A first purchase where the subject is popular." SLJ

Includes glossary

101 great fighters; edited by Robert Jackson. Rosen Pub. 2010 112p il (The 101 greatest weapons of all times) lib bdg $31.95

Grades: 7 8 9 10   **623.74**

1. Fighter planes

ISBN 978-1-4358-3597-9 lib bdg; 1-4358-3597-2 lib bdg

LC 2009-32122

Presents photographs and detailed information about 101 great fighter planes, from the early twentieth-century biplanes to ultramodern jet fighters.

Describes "why and when the type of vehicle was created, its advantages and disadvantages, when and where it served, countries that may have purchased or license-built it, and when it was removed from service. . . . Contains a detailed two-dimensional color drawing and black-and-white or color photo of the featured vehicle. . . . Back matter includes a listing of memorials and museums and an excellent further-reading list. A first purchase where the subject is popular." SLJ

Includes glossary

623.82 Nautical craft

101 great warships; Robert Jackson, editor. Rosen Pub. 2010 112p il (The 101 greatest weapons of all times) lib bdg $31.95

Grades: 7 8 9 10   **623.82**

1. Warships

ISBN 978-1-4358-3596-2 lib bdg; 1-4358-3596-4 lib bdg

LC 2009-32929

Presents photographs and detailed information about 101 great warship, from the early twentieth-century battleships to ultramodern aircraft carriers.

Describes "why and when the type of vehicle was created, its advantages and disadvantages, when and where it served, countries that may have purchased or license-built it, and when it was removed from service. . . . Contains a detailed two-dimensional color drawing and black-and-white or color photo of the featured vehicle. . . . Back matter includes a listing of memorials and museums and an excellent further-reading list. A first purchase where the subject is popular." SLJ

Includes glossary

Stefoff, Rebecca

Submarines; [by] Rebecca Stefoff. Marshall Cavendish Benchmark 2006 127p il (Great inventions) lib bdg $39.93

Grades: 7 8 9 10   **623.82**

1. Submarines

ISBN 978-0-7614-2229-7 lib bdg; 0-7614-2229-3 lib bdg

LC 2005033984

"An examination of the origin, history, development, and impact of the submarine and related underwater exploration and transport technology." Publisher's note

Includes glossary and bibliographical references

623.89 Navigation

Morrison, Taylor

The **coast** mappers. Houghton Mifflin Co. 2004 45p il map $16

Grades: 5 6 7 8   **623.89**

1. Maps 2. Surveying 3. Astronomers 4. Geographers 5. Cartographers 6. College teachers 7. Cartography

ISBN 0-618-25408-0

LC 2003-13534

Chronicles the difficulties encountered by George Davidson and others as they attempted to create nautical charts to complete the U.S. Coast Survey of the West Coast in the mid-nineteenth century

"Cartographic methods are clearly explained through both the carefully researched text and the precise illustrations. . . . The artwork clarifies the text, depicts the breathtaking beauty of the coastline, and adds a sense of adventure." SLJ

Includes glossary and bibliographical references

Williams, Linda D.

Navigational aids; [by] Linda Williams. Marshall Cavendish Benchmark 2007 128p il (Great inventions) lib bdg $27.95

Grades: 6 7 8 9   **623.89**

1. Navigation 2. Aids to navigation

ISBN 978-0-7614-2599-1

LC 2006028959

"An examination of the origins, history, development, and impact of the various navigational aids humans have used through the centuries." Publisher's note

Includes glossary and bibliographical references

Young, Karen Romano

Across the wide ocean; the why, how, and where of navigation for humans and animals at sea. Greenwillow Books 2007 78p il $18.99; lib bdg $19.89

Grades: 4 5 6 7   **623.89**

1. Ocean 2. Navigation 3. Marine animals 4. Animal navigation

ISBN 978-0-06-009086-9; 0-06-009086-3; 978-0-06-009087-6 lib bdg; 0-06-009087-1 lib bdg

LC 2005-46146

"Readers follow such disparate entities as a loggerhead sea turtle, a nuclear submarine, and a sailboat crew seeking scientific sightings of North Atlantic right whales as Young explores the concept of navigation. . . . Larded with photos, diagrams, and maps. . . . Deceptively simple in appearance, the informative text can push some intense mental activity." SLJ

624 Civil engineering

Aaseng, Nathan

Construction: building the impossible. Oliver Press (Minneapolis) 2000 144p il (Innovators) $21.95

Grades: 6 7 8 9   **624**

1. Building 2. Generals 3. Pyramids 4. Inventors 5. Architects 6. Physicians 7. Panama Canal 8. Civil engineering 9. Hoover Dam (Ariz. and Nev.) 10. Civil engineers 11. Bridge engineers 12. Mechanical engineers 13. Structural engineers 14. Civil engineering -- History 15. Civil engineers -- Biography

ISBN 1-88150-859-5

LC 98-51815

Profiles eight builders and their famous construction projects, including Imhotep and the Step Pyramid, Alexandre Eiffel and the Eiffel Tower, and William Lamb and the Empire State Building

"The prose is clear and engaging, with a layperson's approach to technical information. Sidebars feature related anecdotes, fun facts, and word definitions. Historical photos, drawings, and diagrams are fascinating and well chosen." Booklist

Includes glossary and bibliographical references

Caney, Steven

★ **Steven** Caney's ultimate building book. Running Press 2006 596p il $29.95

Grades: 4 5 6 7 8   **624**

1. Building 2. Civil engineering

ISBN 0-7624-0409-4

"Caney examines 'building' in its broadest sense, encompassing everything from skyscrapers and bridges to bird feeders and peanut-shell 'bricks.' Opening sections investigate the history and techniques of construction, with clearly written explanations supported by black-and-white photographs and diagrams. . . . The author reinforces important concepts of design in a way that is fascinating and effective." SLJ

Levy, Matthys

Engineering the city; how infrastructure works: projects and principles for beginners. [by] Matthys Levy and Richard Panchyk. Chicago Review Press 2000 129p pa $14.95

Grades: 6 7 8 9   **624**

1. Civil engineering 2. Municipal engineering

ISBN 1-55652-419-6

LC 00-31774

"Combining a study of urban infrastructure with the history of human development, the authors examine the topics of water, transportation, waste and garbage disposal, and pollution. A wide variety of projects include scientific experiments and extension activities. . . . Containing scientific and historical information, this book will serve as a springboard for cross-curricular projects in history and science, with connections to math and language arts." Book Rep

Includes glossary and bibliographical references

Macaulay, David

★ **Underground**. Houghton Mifflin 1976 109p il hardcover o.p. pa $9.95

Grades: 5 6 7 8 9   **624**

1. Subways 2. Building 3. Sewerage 4. Electric lines 5. Public utilities 6. Civil engineering

ISBN 0-395-24739-X; 0-395-34065-9 pa

"Introduced by a visual index—a bird's eye view of a busy, hypothetical intersection with colored indicators marking the specific locations analyzed in subsequent pages—detailed illustrations are combined with a clear, precise narrative to make the subject comprehensible and fascinating." Horn Book

Includes glossary

Reeves, Diane Lindsey

Career ideas for teens in architecture and construction; [by] Diane Lindsey Reeves with Gail Karlitz and Don Rauf. Ferguson 2005 170p il (Career ideas for teens) $40

Grades: 7 8 9 10   **624**

1. Building 2. Engineering 3. Architecture 4.

Vocational guidance

ISBN 0-8160-5289-1

LC 2004-20030

The careers described in this book include architect, carpenter, electrician, interior designer, and urban planner

Sullivan, George

★ **Built** to last; building America's amazing bridges, dams, tunnels, and skyscrapers. Scholastic Nonfiction 2005 128p il map $18.99

Grades: 5 6 7 8   **624**

1. Civil engineering 2. Civil engineering -- United States

ISBN 0-439-51737-0

LC 2004-60996

This is a "survey of American building—from the Erie Canal to Boston's current 'Big Dig.' Chronological chapters describe the historical forces that helped drive each project as well as the specific technological feats linked to each pioneering structure. . . . The wide selection of captivating illustrations includes archival photos and engravings, architectural drawings, and color photos. . . . Sullivan's skillful integration of social and economic history distinguishes this clear, well-designed title." Booklist

Fantastic feats and failures; by the editors of YES magazine. Kids Can Press 2004 52p il hardcover o.p. pa $7.95

Grades: 4 5 6 7   **624**

1. Civil engineering 2. Structural design 3. Structural failures

ISBN 1-55337-633-1; 1-55337-634-X pa

This "book spotlights 20 notable highs and lows in engineering. The 'feats' celebrated include the Sydney Opera House, the Brooklyn Bridge, and Canadarm (a huge, Canadian-built robotic arm used for repairs in space). Among the 'failures' are the space shuttle Challenger, the Tacoma Narrows Bridge, and the Chernobyl nuclear power plant. . . . Well organized and engagingly written. . . . Excellent photos . . . illustrate the places and events discussed, while colorful drawings visually represent concepts." Booklist

624.1 Structural engineering and underground construction

Graham, Ian

Tremendous tunnels. Amicus 2010 32p il (Superstructures) lib bdg $28.50

Grades: 5 6 7 8   **624.1**

1. Tunnels

ISBN 978-1-60753-134-0; 1-60753-134-8

LC 2009030865

"The vivid illustrations often help clarify points made in the text. . . . [This] colorful, informative [book offers] intriguing glimpses of notable engineering feats." Booklist

Includes glossary and bibliographical references

624.2 Bridges

Graham, Ian

Fabulous bridges. Amicus 2010 32p il (Super-structures) lib bdg $28.50

Grades: 5 6 7 8 **624.2**
   1. Bridges
   ISBN 978-1-60753-132-6; 1-60753-132-1
                    LC 2009030864

"The vivid illustrations often help clarify points made in the text. . . . [This] colorful, informative [book offers] intriguing glimpses of notable engineering feats." Booklist
   Includes glossary and bibliographical references

Prentzas, G. S.

The **Brooklyn** Bridge. Chelsea House Publishers 2009 120p il (Building America: then and now) lib bdg $35

Grades: 6 7 8 9 **624.2**
   1. Bridges
   ISBN 978-1-60413-073-7 lib bdg; 1-60413-073-3 lib bdg
                    LC 2008-25543

This describes the construction and impact of the Brooklyn Bridge
   Includes glossary and bibliographical references

627 Hydraulic engineering

Aldridge, Rebecca

The **Hoover** Dam. Chelsea House 2009 119p il (Building America: then and now) lib bdg $35

Grades: 6 7 8 9 **627**
   1. Dams 2. Hoover Dam (Ariz. and Nev.)
   ISBN 978-1-60413-069-0 lib bdg; 1-60413-069-5 lib bdg
                    LC 2008-25545

This describes the history and impact of Hoover Dam
"Photos, maps, and informative sidebars supplement the densely detailed writing. American history buffs will find [this volume] useful for doing research." Horn Book Guide
   Includes bibliographical references

Mann, Elizabeth

Hoover Dam; with illustrations by Alan Witschonke. Mikaya Press 2001 44p il (Wonders of the world) $19.95; pa $9.95

Grades: 4 5 6 7 **627**
   1. Hoover Dam (Ariz. and Nev.) 2. Hoover Dam (Ariz. and Nev.) -- History
   ISBN 978-1-931414-02-9; 1-931414-02-5; 978-1-931414-13-5 pa; 1-931414-13-0 pa
                    LC 2001-34520

Describes the engineering, construction, and social and historical contexts of the Hoover Dam
"A wonderfully readable, well-organized book filled with fascinating detail." SLJ

628 Sanitary engineering

Harmon, Dan

Jobs in environmental cleanup and emergency hazmat response; [by] Daniel E. Harmon. Rosen Pub. 2010 80p il (Green careers) lib bdg $30.60

Grades: 7 8 9 **628**
   1. Hazardous wastes 2. Vocational guidance 3. Environmental sciences
   ISBN 978-1-4358-3570-2; 1-4358-3570-0
                    LC 2009-14946

"Written in clear, concise language, . . . [this] features color pictures and boxes with supplementary information. Chapters and sections are broken into reasonable lengths suitable for reluctant readers, but interesting enough for advanced students." Libr Media Connect
   Includes glossary and bibliographical references

Horn, Geoffrey

Environmental engineer; by Geoffrey M. Horn. Gareth Stevens Pub. 2010 32p il (Cool careers: cutting edge) lib bdg $26; pa $8.95

Grades: 4 5 6 **628**
   1. Vocational guidance 2. Sanitary engineering 3. Environmental protection
   ISBN 978-1-4339-1956-5 lib bdg; 1-4339-1956-7 lib bdg; 978-1-4339-2155-1 pa; 1-4339-2155-3 pa
                    LC 2009004746

This introduction to environmental engineering careers offers "clear, solid information in a large font. . . . [This] short [book is] packed with relevant, current material." SLJ
   Includes glossary and bibliographical references

628.4 Waste technology, public toilets, street cleaning

Gardner, Robert

Recycle; green science projects for a sustainable planet. Enslow Publishers 2011 128p il (Team Green science projects) lib bdg $31.93

Grades: 6 7 8 9 10 **628.4**
   1. Recycling 2. Science projects 3. Science -- Experiments
   ISBN 978-0-7660-3648-2; 0-7660-3648-0
                    LC 2009-37903

This describes science projects about recycling, including experiments and information about plastics, solid waste and decomposition, composting, aluminum, and paper.

"Gardner provides plenty of information, well-designed experiments, and demonstrations, and then shares brief science-fair ideas. . . . Experiments and demonstrations are presented with clear step-by-step instructions and occasional illustrations and represent a wide range of complexity." SLJ
   Includes glossary and bibliographical references

629   Other branches of engineering

Richie, Jason

Space flight; crossing the last frontier. Oliver Press (Minneapolis) 2002 144p il (Innovators) lib bdg $21.95

Grades: 5 6 7 8   **629**

1. Physicists 2. Scientists 3. Space flight 4. Aerospace engineers 5. NASA officials 6. Electrical engineers 7. Aeronautical engineers 8. Space flight -- History 9. Aerospace industry executives 10. Manned space flight -- History 11. Aerospace engineers -- Biography

ISBN 1-881508-77-3

LC 2001-36507

Profiles seven engineers and scientists who made space flight possible, including Robert Goddard, Sergei Korolev, and Wernher von Braun

"The biographies are readable, entertaining, and informative." SLJ

Includes glossary and bibliographical references

629.1   Aerospace engineering

Hickam, Homer H.

★ **Rocket** boys; a memoir. [by] Homer H. Hickam, Jr. Delacorte Press 1998 368p $25.95; pa $14

Grades: 7 8 9 10 11 12 Adult   **629.1**

1. Authors 2. Novelists 3. Aerospace engineers 4. Memoirists 5. Authors, American 6. Writers on science 7. Aerospace engineers -- United States -- Biography

ISBN 0-385-33320-X; 0-385-33321-8 pa

LC 98-19304

"Even if Hickam stretched the strict truth to metamorphose his memories into Stand By Me-like material for Hollywood . . . the embellishing only converts what is a good story into an absorbing, rapidly readable one that is unsentimental but artful about adolescence, high school, and family life." Booklist

629.13   Aeronautics

Carson, Mary Kay

★ The **Wright** Brothers for kids; how they invented the airplane: 21 activities exploring the science and history of flight. illustrations by Laura D'Argo. Chicago Review Press 2003 146p il pa $14.95

Grades: 4 5 6 7   **629.13**

1. Inventors 2. Aeronautics 3. Aeronautics -- History 4. Science -- Experiments 5. Aircraft industry executives

ISBN 1-55652-477-3

LC 2002-155449

This account of the Wright brothers' invention of the airplane, explains the forces of flight-lift, thrust, gravity, and drag and includes such activities as making a Chinese flying top, building a kite, bird watching, making a paper glider and a rubber-band-powered flyer

"A treasure trove of activities awaits readers of this wonderfully executed survey of the Wright brothers and their invention. The narrative flows easily and is complemented by numerous photographs that give a sense of history and this event. . . . This is a valuable resource for student reports and projects, and for classroom units." SLJ

Includes glossary and bibliographical references

Finkelstein, Norman H.

Three across; the great transatlantic air race of 1927. [by] Norman H. Finkelstein. Calkins Creek 2008 134p il $17.95

Grades: 5 6 7 8   **629.13**

1. Admirals 2. Generals 3. Explorers 4. Air pilots 5. Memoirists 6. Travel writers 7. Air force officers 8. Aeronautics -- History 9. Metal industry executives 10. Aircraft industry executives

ISBN 978-1-59078-462-4; 1-59078-462-6

LC 2007-18345

"Framing the story in way that should enthrall any aviation fan, Finklestein traces the rise of aviation from Kitty Hawk to the 1927 Orteig Prize, a $25,000 award for the first person to fly nonstop across the Atlantic. This book focuses on the first three flights to pull it off: the Spirit of St. Louis, piloted by Charles Lindbergh; the Columbia, led by ambitious shyster Charles A. Levine; and the America, boasting Arctic explorer Richard E. Byrd at the controls." Booklist

Includes bibliographical references

★ **Flight** and motion; the history and science of flying. M.E. Sharpe 2008 5v il set $325

Grades: 6 7 8 9 10   **629.13**

1. Reference books 2. Flight -- Encyclopedias 3. Aeronautics -- Encyclopedias

ISBN 978-0-7656-8100-3 set; 0-7656-8100-5 set

LC 2007030815

"Report writers as well as those simply interested in browsing will find much to hold their interest in this set, which provides comprehensive coverage of the history of aviation, including spaceflight, as well as the science and technology on which it depends." Booklist

Includes bibliographical references

Giblin, James

★ **Charles** A. Lindbergh; a human hero. [by] James Cross Giblin. Clarion Bks. 1997 212p il $22

Grades: 6 7 8 9   **629.13**

1. Generals 2. Air pilots 3. Memoirists 4. Air force officers

ISBN 0-395-63389-3

LC 96-9501

A biography of the pilot whose life was full of controversy and tragedy, but also fulfilling achievements

"This sympathetic and informed account (beautifully illustrated with contemporary photographs) is an excellent introduction to Lindbergh and also to the early years of the celebrity society in which we live now." N Y Times Book Rev

Includes bibliographical references

Hardesty, Von

Epic flights. Kingfisher 2011 64p il (Epic adventure) $19.99

Grades: 5 6 7 8   **629.13**
1. Aeronautics -- History
ISBN 978-0-7534-6669-8; 0-7534-6669-4
       LC 2011041637
This describes Charles Lindbergh's transatlantic flight; the Breitling Orbiter 3 which set a record for non-stop around the world flight by balloon; the Apollo 11 flight to the moon; Amy Johnson's solo flight from England to Australia in a small bi-plane; and the Voyager, which set a record by flying non-stop around the world without refueling.

"The graphics will grab readers in [this] exciting, extra-large-size [title] . . . packed with high-quality color photos on every double-page spread. Just as gripping are the narratives, captions, and technical details of exploration, adventure, and survival." Booklist
Includes glossary

Hense, Mary
How fighter pilots use math; math curriculum consultant: Rhea A. Stewart. Chelsea Clubhouse 2010 32p il (Math in the real world) lib bdg $28
Grades: 4 5 6   **629.13**
1. Air pilots 2. Aeronautics 3. Mathematics 4. Vocational guidance
ISBN 978-1-60413-605-0 lib bdg; 1-60413-605-7 lib bdg
       LC 2009-20242
This describes how fighter pilots use math to judge speed, attain altitude, and maintain safety, and includes relevant math problems and information about how to become a fighter pilot
Includes glossary and bibliographical references

629.130   Biography of flight

Brown, Jeremy K.
Amelia Earhart; by Jeremy K. Brown. Chelsea House 2011 132p ill. (hardcover : acid-free paper) $35.00
Grades: 6 7 8 9   **629.130**
1. Women air pilots 2. Air pilots -- United States -- Biography 3. Women air pilots -- United States -- Biography 4. Cross-country flying -- History -- 20th century 5. Flights around the world -- History -- 20th century
ISBN 9781604139105
       LC 2011000037
This book chronicles the life of female aviator Amelia Earhart. "From her . . . beginnings in a small Kansas town to her . . . solo flight across the Atlantic, Earhart defied expectations and rose to become the most famous female pilot of all time. Despite the restrictions placed on women of her era, she broke through barriers and refused to allow society to label her. As a result, she made history through her daring flights all over the world. In 1937, she disappeared without a trace while on a solo flight around the world." (Kids' Catalog Web)
Includes bibliographical references (p. 124-125) and index

629.133   Aircraft types

Faber, Harold
★ The **airplane**; [by] Harold Faber. Marshall Cavendish Benchmark 2006 128p il (Great inventions) lib bdg $37.07
Grades: 7 8 9 10   **629.133**
1. Airplanes 2. Aeronautics -- History
ISBN 0-7614-1876-8
       LC 2004-22107
This is history of aviation and its influence on American history and culture.

This is presented "thoughtfully yet conversationally. . . . [It] will reward steady reading." Horn Book Guide
Includes glossary and bibliographical references

Greger, Margaret
Kites for everyone; how to make and fly them. diagrams by Del Greger. 3rd ed.; Dover Publications 2006 121p il pa $9.95
Grades: 7 8 9 10 11 12 Adult   **629.133**
1. Kites
ISBN 978-0-4864-5295-1 pa; 0-4864-5295-6 pa
       LC 2006048453
First published 1984 by Richland, WA
This is a "guide with . . . illustrated instructions for creating more than 50 . . . airborne objects—everything from simple bag kites to Vietnamese, Snake, Dutch, Dragon, Bullet, Delta, and Flowform flyers." Publisher's note
Includes bibliographical references

Nahum, Andrew
Flying machine; written by Andrew Nahum. rev ed; DK Pub. 2004 72p il (DK eyewitness books) $15.99; lib bdg $19.99
Grades: 4 5 6 7   **629.133**
1. Aeronautics -- History
ISBN 0-7566-0680-2; 0-7566-0679-9 lib bdg
First published 1990 by Knopf
A photo essay tracing the history and development of aircraft from hot-air balloons to jetliners. Includes information on the principles of flight and the inner workings of various flying machines.

Oxlade, Chris
Airplanes; uncovering technology. Firefly Books 2006 52p il $16.95
Grades: 4 5 6 7   **629.133**
1. Airplanes
ISBN 1-55407-134-8
This offers "appealing visuals and plenty of well-chosen facts." SLJ

629.2   Motor land vehicles, cycles

Mara, Wil
From locusts to...automobile anti-collision systems; by Wil Mara. Cherry Lake Pub. 2012 32 p.

col. ill. (Innovations from nature) (library) $28.50; (e-book) $28.50; (paperback) $14.21

Grades: 4 5 6 7   **629.2**

1. Automobiles -- Collision avoidance systems 2. Locusts 3. Biomimicry

ISBN 1610805011; 9781610805018; 9781610805889; 9781610806756

LC 2012011856

"This . . . entry in the '21st Century Skills Innovation Library: Innovations from Nature' series explores how automobile manufacturers and scientists are trying to develop . . . collision avoidance systems based on the instincts of the humble locust, which has the ability to avoid oncoming objects while in a swarm. . . . [Wil] Mara describes the science of biomimicry, or 'the practice of copying nature--plants and animals--to build or improve something.'" (Booklist)

Includes bibliographical references (p. 31) and index.

Smith, Miranda

Speed machines; and other record-breaking vehicles. Kingfisher 2009 63p il (Kingfisher knowledge) $12.95

Grades: 5 6 7 8   **629.2**

1. Speed 2. Vehicles

ISBN 978-0-7534-6287-4; 0-7534-6287-7

"This well-organized, full-color book is packed with facts, photos, and history. It covers all aspects in history dealing with humankind's quest for speed, including land, water and air. . . . There are short blocks of main text and sidebars or blurbs to add additional information. Besides the usual suspects in books that cover this topic—cars, motorcycles, and planes—this book includes boats, gliders, hot air balloons, trains, and windsurfing among other speed machines. . . . It is an essential purchase, especially where books about racing, cars, planes, trucks, motorcycles, etc. are popular." Voice Youth Advocates

629.22   Types of vehicles

Balmer, Alden J.

Doc Fizzix mousetrap racers; the complete builder's manual. [by] Alden J. Balmer; [illustrations by Mike Harnisch] Fox Chapel 2008 142p il pa $14.95

Grades: 6 7 8 9   **629.22**

1. Physics 2. Automobiles -- Models

ISBN 978-1-56523-359-1; 1-56523-359-X

"Building a mousetrap-powered model racer is more complex than it first appears, and Balmer uses this project as a springboard for teaching principles of physics such as energy, forces, torque, friction, and traction. . . . The author's enthusiasm for the topic and for teaching are apparent throughout, and his focus on safety is consistent. The thorough instructions are complemented by clear, captioned, full-color photos and line drawings and diagrams that illustrate each step of the construction process." SLJ

Mackay, Jenny

Electric cars. Lucent Books 2011 104p il (Technology 360) $33.45

Grades: 7 8 9 10   **629.22**

1. Electric automobiles

ISBN 978-1-4205-0612-9; 1-4205-0612-9

LC 2011016597

This book describes the technology of electric cars.

Includes bibliographical references

629.222   Gasoline-powered, oil-powered, man-powered vehicles

Bearce, Stephanie

All about electric and hybrid cars; and who's driving them. Mitchell Lane Publishers 2009 47p il (Tell your parents) lib bdg $21.50

Grades: 4 5 6 7   **629.222**

1. Electric automobiles

ISBN 978-1-58415-763-2 lib bdg; 1-58415-763-1 lib bdg

LC 2009004528

This describes how hybrid and electric cars work and new inventions in the automotive industry, including vehicles powered by hydrogen and solar powered cars

Includes bibliographical references

Collier, James Lincoln

★ The **automobile**; by James Lincoln Collier. Marshall Cavendish Benchmark 2005 112p il (Great inventions) lib bdg $37.07

Grades: 7 8 9 10   **629.222**

1. Automobiles

ISBN 0-7614-1877-6

LC 2004-22109

This is a history of the automobile and its affects on American culture.

This is presented "thoughtfully yet conversationally. . . . [It] will reward steady reading." Horn Book Guide

Includes glossary and bibliographical references

Harmon, Dan

First car smarts; by Daniel E. Harmon. Rosen Pub. 2010 64p il (Get smart with your money) lib bdg $29.95; pa $12.95

Grades: 7 8 9 10 11 12   **629.222**

1. Automobiles

ISBN 978-1-4358-5269-3 lib bdg; 1-4358-5269-9 lib bdg; 978-1-4358-5544-1 pa; 1-4358-5544-2 pa

This is a guide to buying your first car and the costs of car ownership including maintanence and insurance.

This offers "practical information and advice. . . . The writing is accessible. . . . The [book is] heavily illustrated with large, clear, up-to-date photographs of teens." SLJ

Includes glossary and bibliographical references

Williams, Brian

Who invented the automobile? Arcturus Pub. 2010 46p il (Breakthroughs in science and technology) lib bdg $32.80

Grades: 5 6 7 8   **629.222**
1. Engines 2. Automobiles
ISBN 978-1-84837-681-6; 1-84837-681-2
LC 2010011019
Examines the history of the automobile.

This book is "divided into easy to read short chapters with large, colorful photographs and graphics on every page. . . . The added inserts provide additional information to engage readers and help them connect with the scientific details." Libr Media Connect

Woods, Bob
Hottest muscle cars; by Bob Woods. Enslow Publishers 2008 48p il (Wild wheels!) lib bdg $23.93; pa $7.95
Grades: 4 5 6 7   **629.222**
1. Automobiles
ISBN 978-0-7660-2872-2 lib bdg; 0-7660-2872-0 lib bdg; 978-0-7660-3611-6 pa; 0-7660-3611-1 pa
LC 2007007423
This focuses on "the beginning of America's love for muscle cars, and see why they are still loved today." Publisher's note
Includes glossary and bibliographical references

Hottest sports cars; by Bob Woods. Enslow Publishers 2008 48p il (Wild wheels!) lib bdg $23.93; pa $7.95
Grades: 4 5 6 7   **629.222**
1. Automobiles
ISBN 978-0-7660-2873-9 lib bdg; 0-7660-2873-9 lib bdg; 978-0-7660-3609-3 pa; 0-7660-3909-X pa
LC 2007007428
This focuses on "some of the world's most famous sports cars; how they began, and where they are going in the future." Publisher's note
Includes glossary and bibliographical references

629.227   Cycles

Haduch, Bill
★ **Go** fly a bike! the ultimate book about bicycle fun, freedom & science. illustrated by Chris Murphy. Dutton Children's Books 2004 83p il $16.99
Grades: 4 5 6 7   **629.227**
1. Cycling 2. Bicycles
ISBN 0-525-47024-7
Gives the history, science, types of cycles, safety and the basics and maintenance of bicycles

"Halftone cartoonlike illustrations are scattered throughout, and a funny fact or joke appears in an inset on most pages. . . . This is a versatile, fact-packed book that can work for both research and recreational reading." Booklist

Smedman, Lisa
From boneshakers to choppers; the rip-roaring history of motorcycles. Annick Press 2007 120p il $24.95; pa $14.95

Grades: 5 6 7 8   **629.227**
1. Motorcycles 2. Motorcycles -- History
ISBN 978-1-55451-016-0; 1-55451-016-3; 978-1-55451-015-3 pa; 1-55451-015-5 pa
"Smedman defines 'motorcycles' broadly enough to include everything from Harleys to Vespas, and even bicycles, in this lively, wide-ranging history. . . . Illustrated with a generous array of action photos, historical shots, and period advertisements." Booklist
Includes bibliographical references

Woods, Bob
Hottest motorcycles; by Bob Woods. Enslow Publishers 2008 48p il (Wild wheels!) lib bdg $23.93; pa $7.95
Grades: 4 5 6 7   **629.227**
1. Motorcycles
ISBN 978-0-7660-2874-6 lib bdg; 0-7660-2874-7 lib bdg; 978-0-7660-3608-6 pa; 0-7660-3608-1 pa
LC 2007007425
This focuses on "the motorcycle's beginning, the chopper phenomenon, and motorcycle racing." Publisher's note
Includes bibliographical references

629.28   Tests, driving, maintenance, repair

Miller, Malinda
Modern mechanics; maintaining tomorrow's green vehicles. Mason Crest Publishers 2011 64p il (New careers for the 21st century: finding your role in the global renewal) lib bdg $22.95
Grades: 7 8 9 10   **629.28**
1. Machinery 2. Mechanics (Persons) 3. Vocational guidance
ISBN 978-1-4222-1818-1 lib bdg; 1-4222-1818-X lib bdg
LC 2010016870
"Chapters identify and emphasize specific careers-important strengths, necessary aptitudes and interests, education and training, projected earnings, closely related occupations, type of work environment, and predictions for the future of the field. . . . Color photos have a small role amid the many statistics, figures, graphs and charts that support and supplement the . . . [text]." SLJ
Includes bibliographical references

629.4   Astronautics

Benoit, Peter
The **space** race; by Peter Benoit. Children's Press 2012 64 p. ill. (some col.) (library) $30.00; (paperback) $8.95
Grades: 4 5 6   **629.4**
1. Astronautics -- United States 2. Space flight 3. Astronautics -- Soviet Union -- History 4. Astronautics -- United States -- History 5. Space race -- History 6. Space flight -- History
ISBN 0531281655; 9780531230657; 9780531281659
LC 2011031454

This book by Peter Benoit is part of the "Cornerstones of Freedom" series. It "attempts to provide an historical overview of the race between the United States and Soviet Union to explore space. . . . The book ends with a map . . . a . . . list of influential individuals, a timeline, and a glossary." (Children's Literature)

Includes bibliographical references (p. 60-61) and index.

Bortz, Alfred B.

Seven wonders of space technology; by Fred Bortz. Twenty-First Century Books 2011 80p il (Seven wonders) lib bdg $33.26; ebook $24.95

Grades: 5 6 7 8   629.4

1. Astronautics 2. Space vehicles 3. Outer space -- Exploration

ISBN 978-0-7613-5453-6 lib bdg; 0-7613-5453-0 lib bdg; 9780761372806

LC 2010-23996

"Highlights some of astronomy's greatest technical advancements, from land observatories to spinning satellites to moon bases. . . . [This] volume makes basic concepts clear in lively, energetic language that, along with the mesmerizing color photos and artists' renderings of space, will easily captivate a young audience, while up-to-date examples, including discoveries made in the last five years, will only increase the sense of immediacy and excitement." Booklist

Includes glossary and bibliographical references

Carlisle, Rodney P.

Exploring space; rev ed.; Chelsea House 2010 120p il (Discovery and exploration) lib bdg $35

Grades: 7 8 9 10   629.4

1. Astronautics

ISBN 978-1-60413-188-8; 1-60413-188-8

LC 2009-25585

First published 2005 by Facts on File

This describes the history of space exploration, from early astronomers to first steps into space by Germans, Soviets, and Americans, space flight to the Moon, space stations, space shuttles, unmanned space exploration, the Hubble space telescope, radio telescopes, and possible future explorations

Includes glossary and bibliographical references

Chaikin, Andrew

★ **Space**; a history of space exploration in photographs. [by] Andrew Chaikin; foreword by James A. Lovell. Firefly Books 2004 249p il pa $24.95

Grades: 6 7 8 9   629.4

1. Outer space -- Exploration

ISBN 1-55297-987-3

First published 2002 in the United Kingdom

"This book is proof that scientific photos not only can educate but also can be admired for their beauty. Text explains the intriguing photos and helps introduce each chapter." Voice Youth Advocates

Crompton, Samuel

Sputnik /Explorer 1; the race to conquer space. [by] Samuel Willard Crompton. Chelsea House 2007

106p il (Milestones in American history) lib bdg $35

Grades: 7 8 9 10   629.4

1. Astronautics 2. Space flight

ISBN 0-7910-9357-3 lib bdg; 978-0-7910-9357-3 lib bdg

LC 2006034127

"This book begins in 1957 with Russia's successful launch of the first artificial sattelite. With the Cold War as a backdrop, the text goes on to describe the space race between the United States and Russia. . . . Many photographs, quotations, and sidebars detail the roles played by key figures." Horn Book Guide

Includes bibliographical references

Harris, Joseph

Space exploration; impact of science and technology. Gareth Stevens Pub. 2010 64p il map (Pros and cons) lib bdg $35

Grades: 5 6 7 8   629.4

1. Astronautics

ISBN 978-1-4339-1989-3 lib bdg; 1-4339-1989-3 lib bdg

LC 2009-12436

An "active layout that features color photographs, maps, graphs or charts on every spread, this . . . [book] has much to offer. . . . It conveniently outlines the range of views . . . helping students to learn how to view both sides of [the] issue[s]." SLJ

Includes glossary and bibliographical references

Jedicke, Peter

Great moments in space exploration. Chelsea House 2007 72p il (Scientific American) $30

Grades: 5 6 7 8   629.4

1. Astronautics 2. Astronautics -- History 3. Outer space -- Exploration

ISBN 978-0-7910-9046-6; 0-7910-9046-9

LC 2006-14774

This "introduction to the history of space exploration is well illustrated with numerous photos, many from NASA. The history is well told, with the achievements of the Soviet Union, in particular, covered quite nicely." Sci Books Films

Includes glossary and bibliographical references

Miller, Ron

Space exploration. Twenty-First Century Books 2008 112p il (Space innovations) lib bdg $31.93

Grades: 4 5 6 7   629.4

1. Astronautics

ISBN 978-0-8225-7155-1; 0-8225-7155-2

LC 2007002863

"Busy pages include text, photographs, sidebars, and diagrams. . . . The information . . . is accurate and focused." Horn Book Guide

Includes glossary and bibliographical references

Nagel, Rob

Space exploration, Almanac; [by] Rob Nagel; Sarah Hermsen, project editor. U.X.L, Thomson Gale

2005 2v il (Space exploration reference library) set $115

Grades: 7 8 9 10 **629.4**
1. Astronautics
ISBN 0-7876-9209-3

LC 2004-15823

Presenting key developments, discussion ranges from ancient views of a sun-centered universe to current understanding of planetary motion and gravity

Includes bibliographical references

Saari, Peggy

Space exploration, Primary sources; [by] Peggy Saari. U.X.L, Thomson Gale 2005 203p il (Space exploration reference library) $63

Grades: 7 8 9 10 **629.4**
1. Astronautics
ISBN 0-7876-9213-1

LC 2004-15879

This volume contains excerpts from 17 documents and speeches, beginning with a chapter from a Jules Verne book and ending with remarks made in early 2004 by George W. Bush on a new vision for space exploration. Each selection is introduced with material on the context, key points, and information on the author

Includes glossary and bibliographical references

Skurzynski, Gloria

★ **This** is rocket science; true stories of the risk-taking scientists who figure out ways to explore beyond Earth. National Geographic 2010 80p il $18.95; lib bdg $28.90

Grades: 5 6 7 8 **629.4**
1. Rocketry 2. Aeronautics 3. Aerospace engineers
ISBN 978-1-4263-0597-9; 1-4263-0597-4; 978-1-4263-0598-6 lib bdg; 1-4263-0598-2 lib bdg

LC 2009-20386

"This concise book provides a historical, as well as contemporary, introduction to the field of aeronautical engineering with a decidedly human interest perspective. . . . This text will be a great introduction to many of the significant contributors to the field of rocket science." Sci Books Films

Includes glossary and bibliographical references

Stott, Carole

Space exploration; written by Carole Stott; photographed by Steve Gorton. Dorling Kindersley 2009 71p il (DK eyewitness books) $16.99

Grades: 4 5 6 7 **629.4**
1. Astronautics
ISBN 978-0-7566-5828-1; 0-7566-5828-4
First published 1997 by Knopf

Describes rockets, exploratory vehicles, and other technological aspects of space exploration, satellites, space stations, and the life and work of astronauts.

629.43 Unmanned space flight

Kerrod, Robin

★ **Space** probes; [by] Robin Kerrod. World Almanac Library 2005 48p il (History of space exploration) hardcover o.p. lib bdg $30

Grades: 5 6 7 8 **629.43**
1. Space probes
ISBN 0-8368-5708-9 lib bdg; 0-8368-5715-1 pa

LC 2004-48207

Discusses how technology has changed the way we look at the celestial bodies of our Solar System, and examines how the space probes have helped discover black holes, star clusters, and nebulae

This "is profusely illustrated with sharply reproduced space photos and artists' conceptions. . . . [This] makes an important addition for any collection supporting avid young scientists or strong science curricula." SLJ

Includes bibliographical references

Miller, Ron

Robot explorers. Twenty-First Century Books 2007 112p il (Space innovations) lib bdg $31.93

Grades: 4 5 6 **629.43**
1. Robots 2. Space probes
ISBN 978-0-8225-7152-0 lib bdg; 0-8225-7152-8 lib bdg

LC 2007002864

This describes how robots are used for space exploration

Includes bibliographical references

Siy, Alexandra

★ **Cars** on Mars; roving the red planet. Charlesbridge 2009 57p il $18.95

Grades: 5 6 7 8 **629.43**
1. Space vehicles 2. Roving vehicles (Astronautics)
ISBN 978-1-57091-462-1; 1-57091-462-1

LC 2008-40751

Presents an introduction to the Mars Exploration Rovers (MERS), 'Spirit' and 'Opportunity,' with photographs of the Mars landscape taken over a five-year period as the rovers searched for water on the red planet

"This title will sweep readers up in an exploratory mission that has come closer than any other so far to finding sure signs of extraterrestrial life." SLJ

Includes glossary and bibliographical references

629.44 Auxiliary spacecraft

Cole, Michael D.

The **Columbia** space shuttle disaster; from first liftoff to tragic final flight. Enslow Pubs. 2003 48p il (Countdown to space) lib bdg $18.95

Grades: 4 5 6 **629.44**
1. Space vehicle accidents
ISBN 0-7660-2295-1

LC 2003-4823

First published 1995 with title: Columbia

Details the first flight of the space shuttle Columbia, as well as its tragic final flight

"The account offers a lot of information, helping to make sense of a highly complicated subject. . . . The color and b&w photographs complement the story." Libr Media Connect

Includes glossary and bibliographical references

Holden, Henry M.

The **coolest** job in the universe; working aboard the International Space Station. Henry M. Holden. Enslow 2013 48 p. American space missions, astronauts, exploration, and discovery) (hbk.) $23.93

Grades: 4 5 6 7 8   **629.44**

1. Space flight 2. Space sciences 3. Manned space flight 4. Space sciences -- Research
ISBN 0766040747; 9780766040748

LC 2012002222

This book, by Henry M. Holden, is part of the "American Space Missions: Astronauts, Exploration, and Discovery" series. In it the daily life of astronauts working on the International Space Station is explored. This book "focuses on the construction of the ISS, what life is like onboard, and the importance of the research projects conducted. . . . Throughout, the courage, dedication, and sacrifice of the astronauts are emphasized." (School Library Journal)

Includes bibliographical references (p. 43-45, 47) and index

Kerrod, Robin

Space shuttles; [by] Robin Kerrod. World Almanac Library 2005 48p il (History of space exploration) hardcover o.p. lib bdg $30

Grades: 5 6 7 8   **629.44**

1. Space shuttles
ISBN 0-8368-5709-7 lib bdg; 0-8368-5716-X pa

LC 2004-49217

Explores the successes of the shuttle program, including the daring recovery and repair of satellites by space-walking astronauts, and examines the human and technological costs of its tragic failures, such as the losses the Challenger and Columbia

This "is profusely illustrated with sharply reproduced space photos and artists' conceptions. . . . [This] makes an important addition for any collection supporting avid young scientists or strong science curricula." SLJ

Includes bibliographical references

Space stations; [by] Robin Kerrod. World Almanac Library 2005 48p il (History of space exploration) hardcover o.p. lib bdg $30

Grades: 5 6 7 8   **629.44**

1. Space stations
ISBN 0-8368-5710-0 lib bdg; 0-8368-5717-8 pa

LC 2004-49071

Explores the history of space homes such as the Soviet's Salyut 1, Mir, the United States's Skylab, and the International Space Station, a truly international venture between several countries and scheduled for completion in 2008

This "is profusely illustrated with sharply reproduced space photos and artists' conceptions. . . . [This] makes an important addition for any collection supporting avid young scientists or strong science curricula." SLJ

Includes bibliographical references

Miller, Ron

Satellites; by Ron Miller. Twenty-First Century Books 2007 112p il (Space innovations) lib bdg $31.93

Grades: 7 8 9 10   **629.44**

1. Artificial satellites
ISBN 978-0-8225-7154-4

LC 2007001075

This "begins with the science of Newton, the history of rockets, and the vivid imaginations of nineteenth-century science-fiction writers. It traces the historical development of man-made satellites from Sputnik 1 to the Earth orbiters currently transmitting everything from Earth-based communications signals to images of the universe. . . . Illustrations include many small color photos and some paintings, diagrams, satellite images, and black-and-white photos. . . . Miller synthesizes his evident research into a well-organized discussion." Booklist

Includes bibliographical references

629.45   Manned space flight

Bodden, Valerie

Man walks on the Moon. Creative Education 2009 48p il map (Days of change) $32.80

Grades: 5 6 7 8   **629.45**

1. Space flight to the moon
ISBN 978-1-58341-735-5; 1-58341-735-4

LC 2008009166

"With elegant design and mature prose, the Days of Change series is an ideal starting point for all manner of school projects. . . . The very first page of Man Walks on the Moon questions whether or not the feat was worth the resources, before reveling in the tech-heavy details of spaceflight and offering up some telling photos." Booklist

Includes bibliographical references

To the moon; by Valerie Bodden. Creative Education 2011 48 p. col. ill. (Great expeditions) (paperback) $12.00; (hardcover) $34.25

Grades: 5 6 7 8   **629.45**

1. Apollo project 2. Space flight to the moon -- History 3. Space flight to the moon -- History
ISBN 1608180689; 9780898126662; 9781608180684

LC 2010033549

This book by Valerie Bodden on the 1969 moon landing is part of the "Great Expeditions" series. "This factual account is . . . accompanied with both black and white and color photographs. Profiles of four of the astronauts, reproductions of some of their significant journal entries, and inset boxes of supplemental information aid in understanding. Includes a table of contents, a timeline, end notes, a bibliography, and an index." (Children's Literature)

Includes bibliographical references (p. 46-47) and index.

Chaikin, Andrew

★ **Mission** control, this is Apollo; the story of the first voyages to the moon. [by] Andrew Chaikin, with Victoria Kohl; [with paintings by] Alan Bean. Penguin Group 2009 114p il $23.99

Grades: 5 6 7 8 9   **629.45**

1. Astronautics 2. Space flight to the moon 3. Project Apollo 4. Astronautics -- History
ISBN 978-0-670-01156-8; 0-670-01156-8

LC 2009000833

"Based on interviews with 28 astronauts, this history of the Apollo program masterfully describes the missions and personalizes them with astronauts' own words. Chaikin starts with a brief overview of its origins and of the Mercury and Gemini missions. He then highlights the significance of each manned Apollo mission in chronological chapters, with full-page sidebars on such topics as food, TV coverage, space sickness and going to the bathroom in space. The handsome design has many photographs, diagrams of the rockets and modules and more than 30 well-reproduced paintings by Apollo 12 astronaut Bean." Kirkus

Includes bibliographical references

Collins, Michael

Flying to the moon; an astronaut's story. 2nd ed, with a preface & a revised final chapter; Farrar, Straus & Giroux 1994 162p il pa $6.95

Grades: 5 6 7 8   **629.45**

1. Astronauts 2. Space flight to the moon
ISBN 0-374-42356-3

LC 93-42001

First published 1976 with title: Flying to the moon, and other strange places

The author recounts his early days as an Air Force test pilot, his NASA training and his experiences aboard Gemini 10 and the Apollo 11 mission to the moon. Collins also advocates continued exploration of the universe

"A well told tale, which includes a lot of easily explained science." BAYA Book Rev

Dell, Pamela

Man on the moon; how a photograph made anything seem possible. Compass Point Books 2011 64p il (Captured history) lib bdg $33.99

Grades: 6 7 8 9   **629.45**

1. Astronauts 2. Documentary photography 3. Space flight to the moon 4. Air force officers
ISBN 978-0-7565-4396-9; 0-7565-4396-7

LC 2010038577

This book about the iconic photograph of Neil Armstrong walking on the moon, taken by fellow astronaut Buzz Aldrin, places the photo "in historical context, profiles the photographer, describes the conditions under which it was taken, and analyzes both its immediate and its continuing impact. The [text includes] ample background information and details and [is] enhanced by large photos and sidebars." SLJ

Includes glossary and bibliographical references

Dyer, Alan

Mission to the moon. Simon & Schuster Books for Young Readers 2009 80p il $19.99

Grades: 5 6 7 8   **629.45**

1. Space flight to the moon 2. Project Apollo
ISBN 978-1-4169-7935-7; 1-4169-7935-2

LC 2008-61118

"Sporting a highly visual encyclopedic format, this informative book features 200 photographs documenting early

research into mankind's history with the moon, early space exploration and the space race, and the Apollo missions. Detailed cross-sections of modules, space suits and other equipment offer a sound technological overview, while information on the phases, structure and surface of the moon provides added insight. . . . A DVD and poster are included." Publ Wkly

Dyson, Marianne J.

Home on the moon; living on a space frontier. National Geographic Soc. 2003 64p il $18.95

Grades: 4 5 6 7   **629.45**

1. Moon
ISBN 0-7922-7193-9

LC 2002-5280

Considers the moon as a frontier that has been only partially explored, looking at its history, geography, and weather, as well as what people would require to live and work there. Includes activities

"Clear writing, vivid images, interesting details, and quotes from astronauts and scientists make this a lively, fact-filled introduction." Booklist

Includes glossary and bibliographical references

Godwin, Robert

Project Apollo; exploring the Moon. Apogee Books 2006 49p il (Pocket space guide) pa $9.95

Grades: 7 8 9 10 11 12   **629.45**

1. Space flight to the moon 2. Project Apollo
ISBN 978-1-894959-37-7 pa; 1-894959-37-X pa

LC 2007-5457

"Facts and images for Apollo missions 12 through 17 are covered in this concise guide to the program's essentials—mission objectives, dates, flight plans, astronauts, space suits, and vehicles—for collectors, educators, space enthusiasts, and those just discovering the history of the space program." Publisher's note

Goodman, Susan

Ultimate field trip 5; blasting off to Space Academy. by Susan E. Goodman; photographs by Michael J. Doolittle. Atheneum Bks. for Young Readers 2001 41p il hardcover o.p. $17

Grades: 4 5 6 7   **629.45**

1. Astronauts 2. Space flight 3. School field trips 4. Astronauts -- Training of -- United States 5. Space flight training facilities -- United States
ISBN 0-689-83044-0; 0-689-84863-3 pa

LC 00-38082

"This book follows student trainees through a weeklong session at the U.S. Space Academy in Huntsville, AL, as they are exposed to what it takes to become an astronaut and to the inner workings of the entire space program. . . . Varied-colored pages, replete with outstanding full-color, captioned photos, are artistically appealing as well as informative." SLJ

Includes glossary and bibliographical references

Green, Carl R.

Spacewalk; the astounding Gemini 4 mission. Carl R. Green. Enslow Publishers 2013 48 p. $23.93

Grades: 4 5 6 7 8   629.45

1. Gemini project 2. Outer space 3. Space flight

ISBN 0766040755; 9780766040755

LC 2011030869

This children's book, by Carl R. Green, "explores the astounding GEMINI 4 mission. . . . Pilot Ed White could see Hawaii, California, Texas, and Florida . . . while walking in space! . . . The first American spacewalk was a monumental achievement, and it helped push the space program toward its ultimate goal of landing men on the Moon." (Publisher's note)

Includes bibliographical references and index

Hartman, Eve

Mission to Mars; [by] Eve Hartman and Wendy Meshbesher. Raintree 2010 56p il (Science missions) lib bdg $33.50; pa $9.49

Grades: 5 6 7 8   629.45

1. Space flight to Mars

ISBN 9781-1-4109-3821-3 lib bdg; 1-4109-3821-2 lib bdg; 978-1-4109-3996-8 pa; 1-4109-3996-0 pa

LC 2009-53209

"Excellent black-and-white and color photos throughout are matched perfectly to the texts and well captioned. Good choices for reports and debates." SLJ

Includes glossary and bibliographical references

Hense, Mary

How astronauts use math; math curriculum consultant: Rhea A. Stewart. Chelsea Clubhouse 2010 32p il (Math in the real world) lib bdg $28

Grades: 4 5 6   629.45

1. Astronauts 2. Mathematics 3. Astronautics 4. Vocational guidance

ISBN 978-1-60413-610-4 lib bdg; 1-60413-610-3 lib bdg

LC 2009-23926

This describes how astronauts use math for such tasks as calculating distance, speed, and velocity, and includes relevant math problems and information about how to become an astronaut

Includes glossary and bibliographical references

Holden, Henry M.

Danger in space; surviving the Apollo 13 disaster. Henry M. Holden. Enslow Publishers 2013 48 p. $23.93

Grades: 4 5 6 7 8   629.45

1. Apollo project 2. Apollo 13 (Spacecraft) 3. Space vehicle accidents -- United States

ISBN 0766040720; 9780766040724

LC 2011037734

This children's picture book tells the story of the U.S. National Aerospace and Space Administration's Apollo 13 mission. "Soaring through space at twenty-five thousand miles per hour, Apollo 13 was on course for the Moon. Suddenly, the three astronauts aboard the spacecraft heard a loud bang. A strong vibration rumbled through the crew cabin. There had been an explosion in the oxygen tank! More than two hundred thousand miles from Earth, Apollo 13 was in grave danger." (Publisher's note)

Includes bibliographical references and index

Kuhn, Betsy

★ The **race** for space; the United States and Soviet Union compete for the new frontier. Lerner 2006 112p il (People's history) lib bdg $31.93

Grades: 6 7 8 9   629.45

1. Astronautics

ISBN 978-0-8225-5984-9 lib bdg; 0-8225-5984-6 lib bdg

"Kuhn has seamlessly woven the history into a compelling story." Booklist

Includes bibliographical references

Ottaviani, Jim

T-Minus: the race to the moon; [illustrated by] Zander Cannon, Kevin Cannon. Aladdin 2009 124p il $21.99; pa $12.99

Grades: 4 5 6 7 8 9 10 11 12 Adult   629.45

1. Graphic novels 2. Apollo project -- Graphic novels 3. Gemini project -- Graphic novels 4. Space race 5. Astronautics 6. Space flight to the moon -- Graphic novels

ISBN 978-1-4169-8682-9; 1-4169-8682-0; 978-1-4169-4960-2 pa; 1-4169-4960-7 pa

LC 2009-920999

Ottaviani, Zander Cannon, and Kevin Cannon show what happened when the U.S. and the U.S.S.R. started the space race in the 1950s, and how it progressed to the NASA Apollo 11 mission which landed two men on the moon in July of 1969.

"Organized as a countdown, making the outcome seem inevitable, the frequent, prominent sidebars list a type of rocket, the duration of its flight, and whether the mission was a success or a failure. There are more than 30 attempts chronicled, and the shift between Soviet and U.S. successes creates an interesting balance in the narrative. . . . Ottaviani is particular with facts and eager to inspire readers with regard to the scientific process." SLJ

Platt, Richard

★ **Moon** landing; a pop-up celebration of Apollo 11. by Richard Platt; paper engineering by David Hawcock. Candlewick Press 2008 un il $29.99

Grades: 4 5 6 7   629.45

1. Space flight to the moon 2. Pop-up books

ISBN 978-0-7636-4046-0; 0-7636-4046-8

"This is a handsome, carefully engineered compendium. The text begins with the so-called space race between the United States and the Soviet Union in the 1950s and '60s and then offers brief descriptions of the 17 flights that made up the Apollo program. Here the emphasis is on the famous landing of the Eagle on the Moon in July 1969. The pop-ups and foldout pages on sturdy, shiny paper demonstrate the mechanical aspects of the spacecraft and offer a bold sense of both the rocketry and the trip. Small photographs and drawings surround the larger views." SLJ

Ross, Stewart

Moon: science, history, and mystery. Scholastic 2009 128p il lib bdg $18.99

Grades: 4 5 6   **629.45**
  1. Astronautics   2. Space flight to the moon
  ISBN 978-0-545-12732-5 lib bdg; 0-545-12732-7
  lib bdg
"Jam-packed with information, this colorful oversize volume chronicles the race to land a person on the Moon. Alternating chapters describe Moon mythologies and superstitions, the history of astronomical study, and the efforts involved in launching a lunar expedition. . . . The photographs pop with color and action. . . . The invaluable contribution of Muslim scientists is included. . . . [The book's] multicultural history will expand any collection." SLJ
  Includes glossary

Saari, Peggy
  Space exploration, Biographies; [by] Peggy Saar; Lawrence W. Baker, Sarah Hermsen, and Deborah J. Baker, project editors. U.X.L, Thomson Gale 2005 219p il (Space exploration reference library) $63
Grades: 7 8 9 10   **629.45**
  1. Astronauts
  ISBN 0-7876-9212-3
                  LC 2004-15822
This volume profiles 25 astronauts, scientists, theorists, and writers involved in space exploration, including Sally Ride, Yuri A. Gagarin, Neil Armstrong, John H. Glenn, Jr., Ellen Ochoa, Hermann Oberth and others
  Includes bibliographical references

Solway, Andrew
  Can we travel to the stars? space flight and space exploration. Heinemann Library 2006 48p il (Stargazers guides) lib bdg $31.43; pa $8.99
Grades: 4 5 6   **629.45**
  1. Astronautics   2. Space flight   3. Interplanetary voyages
  ISBN 978-1-4034-7711-8 lib bdg; 1-4034-7711-6 lib bdg; 978-1-4034-7718-7 pa; 1-4034-7718-3 pa
                  LC 2005-29086
Realistically explores the possibility of mankind ever achieving the goal of traveling to the planets and to other stars
  This book "is clearly written and engaging . . . with just the right level of information and explanation." Horn Book Guide
  Includes glossary and bibliographical references

Stone, Tanya Lee
  ★ **Almost** astronauts; 13 women who dared to dream. Candlewick Press 2008 133p il $24.99; pa $17.99
Grades: 5 6 7 8 9 10   **629.45**
  1. Women astronauts   2. Sex discrimination   3. Sex discrimination against women
  ISBN 0-7636-3611-8; 0-7636-4502-8 pa; 978-0-7636-3611-1; 978-0-7636-4502-1 pa
                  LC 2008-17487
Boston Globe-Horn Book Award honor book: Nonfiction (2009)
  "In 1960, thirteen American women passed the physical exams required to become astronauts as surely as any of the men already involved in NASA's early space flight endeavors, but they were disqualified solely because of their gender. This book is their story. . . . Any girl with an interest in space flight or the history of women's rights will enjoy this account and applaud these courageous pioneers." Voice Youth Advocates
  Includes bibliographical references

Thimmesh, Catherine
  ★ **Team** moon; how 400,000 people landed Apollo 11 on the moon. Houghton Mifflin Company 2006 80p il $19.95
Grades: 5 6 7 8   **629.45**
  1. Space flight to the moon
  ISBN 0-618-50757-4
                  LC 2005-10755
"Thimmesh retraces the course of the space mission that landed an actual man, on the actual Moon. It's an oft-told tale, but the author tells it from the point of view not of astronauts or general observers, but of some of the 17,000 behind-the-scenes workers at Kennedy Space Center, the 7500 Grumman employees who built the lunar module, the 500 designers and seamstresses who actually constructed the space suits, and other low-profile contributors who made the historic flight possible. . . . This dramatic account will mesmerize even readers already familiar with the event. . . . This stirring, authoritative tribute to the collective effort . . . belongs in every collection." SLJ
  Includes glossary and bibliographical references

629.46   Engineering of unmanned spacecraft

Johnson, Rebecca L.
  Satellites. Lerner Publications Co. 2006 48p il (Cool science) lib bdg $25.26
Grades: 4 5 6   **629.46**
  1. Artificial satellites
  ISBN 978-0-8225-2908-8 lib bdg; 0-8225-2908-4 lib bdg
                  LC 2004-30298
This book has "an attractive, colorful layout that will appeal to readers. Each spread includes captioned, color photographs and/or illustrations; text boxes; and, often, a 'fun fact.' . . . [This] title explains what a satellite is and discusses many aspects of satellites, including how they pertain to television broadcasts, weather forecasting, and locating black holes. Numerous amazing facts are included to pique readers' interest." SLJ
  Includes bibliographical references

629.8   Automatic control engineering

Chaffee, Joel
  How to build a prize-winning robot. Rosen Central 2011 48p il (Robotics) lib bdg $26.50; pa $11.75

Grades: 5 6 7 8   **629.8**
1. Robots
ISBN 978-1-4488-1238-7 lib bdg; 1-4488-1238-0 lib
bdg; 978-1-4488-2252-2 pa; 1-4488-2252-1 pa
LC 2010025748
"Kids who are fascinated with robots will want [this
title] available." SLJ
Includes glossary and bibliographical references

Domaine, Helena
Robotics. Lerner Publications 2005 48p il
(Cool science) lib bdg $25.26
Grades: 4 5 6   **629.8**
1. Robots 2. Robotics
ISBN 0-8225-2112-1
LC 2004-13938
This has "an attractive, colorful layout that will appeal
to readers. Each spread includes captioned, color photo-
graphs and/or illustrations; text boxes; and, often, a fun fact.
. . . The content is sound and should be accessible to most
students." SLJ

Freedman, Jeri
Robots through history. Rosen Central 2011 48p
il (Robotics) lib bdg $26.50; pa $11.75
Grades: 5 6 7 8   **629.8**
1. Robots
ISBN 978-1-4488-1236-3 lib bdg; 1-4488-1236-4 lib
bdg; 978-1-4488-2250-8 pa; 1-4488-2250-5 pa
LC 2010024139
"Kids who are fascinated with robots will want [this
title] available." SLJ
Includes glossary and bibliographical references

Graham, Ian
Robot technology. Smart Apple Media 2012
46p il (New technology) $35.65
Grades: 4 5 6 7   **629.8**
1. Robots
ISBN 1-599-20533-5; 978-1-599-20533-5
LC 2010044240
Describes current robotics technology, including the applications of robots in space, in the military, in industry, and
around the house. Discusses the pros and cons of creating
fully autonomous robots.
This "offers a fine overview for reports, and its attractive design may also entice middle-grade readers to learn
more." Booklist

Henderson, Harry
Modern robotics; building versatile machines.
Chelsea House 2006 xx, 188p il (Milestones in
discovery and invention) $35
Grades: 7 8 9 10 11 12   **629.8**
1. Robots
ISBN 0-8160-5745-1
LC 2005-31805
This book presents "biographies of the men and women
who were and are the leaders in bringing about this change
through research and new technologies." Publisher's note
Includes glossary and bibliographical references

Mackay, Jenny
Robots. Lucent Books 2010 104p il (Technology 360) $32.45
Grades: 8 9 10 11 12   **629.8**
1. Robots
ISBN 978-1-4205-0168-1; 1-4205-0168-2
LC 2009045634
This book explores "the early development and advances of [robotics], its impact on society both positive and
negative, and the importance it plays in our lives. . . . [It]
describes the technical aspects of movement, artificial intelligence, and robots of the future. . . . Numerous color photos,
diagrams, 'Bits & Bytes' boxes as well as many other additional text boxes create appeal and provide beneficial informative and complementary material to aid in understanding
the technical details of the [text]." SLJ
Includes glossary and bibliographical references

Payment, Simone
Robotics careers; preparing for the future. Rosen
Central 2011 48p il (Robotics) lib bdg $26.50; pa
$11.75
Grades: 5 6 7 8   **629.8**
1. Robots 2. Vocational guidance
ISBN 978-1-4488-1239-4 lib bdg; 1-4488-1239-9 lib
bdg; 978-1-4488-2253-9 pa; 1-4488-2253-X pa
LC 2010024134
"Kids who are fascinated with robots will want [this
title] available." SLJ
Includes glossary and bibliographical references

Shea, Therese
The **robotics** club; teaming up to build robots.
Rosen Central 2011 48p il (Robotics) lib bdg
$26.50; pa $11.75
Grades: 5 6 7 8   **629.8**
1. Clubs 2. Robots
ISBN 978-1-4488-1237-0 lib bdg; 1-4488-1237-2 lib
bdg; 978-1-4488-2251-5 pa; 1-4488-2251-3 pa
This title "will provide students with the information
necessary to form a club and compete at making and using
robots. Kids who are fascinated with robots will want [this
title] available." SLJ

Sobey, Ed
Robot experiments. Enslow Publishers 2011
128p il (Cool science projects with technology) lib
bdg $31.93
Grades: 6 7 8 9   **629.8**
1. Robots 2. Science projects 3. Science -- Experiments
ISBN 978-0-7660-3303-0; 0-7660-3303-1
LC 2009037897
While this book "includes some suggestions for science-
fair projects and a few experiments throughout, it also provides a detailed description of each component and step-by-
step instruction for building a robot. This highly complicated
process is explained using understandable terms and in a
well-organized manner and includes information as detailed
as computer-programming codes." SLJ
Includes glossary and bibliographical references

Stefoff, Rebecca

Robots. Marshall Cavendish Benchmark 2007 144p il (Great inventions) lib bdg $27.95

Grades: 6 7 8 9   629.8
  1. Robots
  ISBN 978-0-7614-2601-1

This is a history of robots in the imagination, from ancient myths to motion pictures, and in reality, including toy robots and robots in medicine, manufacturing, the military, science, and space exploration

Includes glossary and bibliographical references

VanVoorst, Jennifer

Rise of the thinking machines; the science of robots. Compass Point Books 2009 48p il (Headline science) lib bdg $27.93; pa $7.95

Grades: 5 6 7   629.8
  1. Robots
  ISBN 978-0-7565-3377-9 lib bdg; 0-7565-3377-5 lib bdg; 978-0-7565-3518-6 pa; 0-7565-3518-2 pa
                                                      LC 2008-05732

"Describes various types of robots and their functions, discusses technological advancements in the field of robotics, and considers the ethical issues surrounding autonomous robots." Publisher's note

Includes glossary and bibliographical references

Woog, Adam

SCRATCHbot. Norwood House Press 2010 48p il (A great idea) lib bdg $25.27

Grades: 3 4 5 6   629.8
  1. Robots
  ISBN 978-1-59953-380-3 lib bdg; 1-59953-380-4 lib bdg
                                                      LC 2010008502

"Woog introduces a small, rolling robot with prominent whiskers, used to mimic a rodent's ability to sense its surroundings through touch. Discussions include how inventors are inspired by nature and how this appealing robot might be useful. Presenting specific, current information, [this book] will appeal to young people intrigued by inventions." Booklist

Includes glossary and bibliographical references

630   Agriculture and related technologies

Apte, Sunita

Eating green. Bearport Pub. 2009 32p il map (Going green) lib bdg $25.27

Grades: 4 5 6 7   630
  1. Natural foods 2. Sustainable agriculture
  ISBN 978-1-59716-965-3 lib bdg; 1-59716-965-X lib bdg
                                                      LC 2009-19183

"Color photographs (most full page) and a few diagrams accompany the informative text. . . . Overall, the [book] . . . is user-friendly and covers topics that are not easily found elsewhere." SLJ

Includes glossary and bibliographical references

Bailey, Gerry

Farming for the future. Gareth Stevens Pub. 2011 48p il (Planet SOS) lib bdg $31.95; pa $14.05

Grades: 4 5 6   630
  1. Agriculture 2. Food supply
  ISBN 978-1-4339-4966-1 lib bdg; 1-4339-4966-0 lib bdg; 978-1-4339-4967-8 pa; 1-4339-4967-9 pa
                                                      LC 2010032887

This well-designed book presents farming methods "and how they affect human beings. . . . [It] includes a chapter on new types of farms and foods. . . . The many large, colorful photos will engage readers and assist them in understanding the important concepts introduced." SLJ

Includes glossary

Casper, Julie Kerr

Agriculture; the food we grow and animals we raise. Chelsea House 2007 210p il (Natural resources) $39.50

Grades: 8 9 10 11 12   630
  1. Agriculture
  ISBN 978-0-8160-6352-9; 0-8160-6352-4
                                                      LC 2006027454

This "explores why managing the land, water, and soil is a balancing act and why recycling, reducing, and reusing are concepts that affect everyone—now and in the future." Publisher's note

Includes bibliographical references

Hopkins, William G.

Plant biotechnology. Chelsea House 2006 143p il (The green world) lib bdg $37.50

Grades: 7 8 9 10   630
  1. Plants 2. Biotechnology 3. Food -- Biotechnology 4. Plant biotechnology
  ISBN 0-7910-8964-9

"This is a highly accurate, very well written book about both the history of and current innovations in, plant biotechnology. The illustrative pictures are clear and attractive." Sci Books Films

Includes bibliographical references

Johanson, Paula

Jobs in sustainable agriculture. Rosen Pub. 2010 80p il (Green careers) lib bdg $30.60

Grades: 7 8 9 10   630
  1. Vocational guidance 2. Sustainable agriculture
  ISBN 978-1-4358-3568-9 lib bdg; 1-4358-3568-9 lib bdg
                                                      LC 2009014426

In this book "only one chapter is devoted to farm-based employment; work in a slaughterhouse, a recycling plant, in transportation, and in restaurant management are given equal space. Careers in research or legislative work are also considered. . . . [This] slim [title is] well organized and [contains] informatively captioned color photos." SLJ

Includes glossary and bibliographical references

Parker, Steve, 1952-

Food and farming. QEB Pub. 2010 32p il (QEB changes in . . .) lib bdg $28.50

Grades: 3 4 5 6   **630**
   1. Farms 2. Agriculture 3. Food supply
ISBN 978-1-59566-775-5 lib bdg; 1-59566-775-X
lib bdg

LC 2008-56069

"The information is presented in brief paragraphs and sidebars. Suggestions for kids to help improve the planet are sprinkled throughout. . . . Students will enjoy this appealing layout and the information can spark further research on the topic. . . . Either digitally or on paper, students could make fantastic presentations using a similar design." Libr Media Connect

   Includes glossary

Rosen, Michael J.
   ★ **Our** farm; four seasons with five kids on one family's farm. written and photographed by Michael J. Rosen. Darby Creek Pub. 2008 144p il $18.95
Grades: 4 5 6 7 8   **630**
   1. Family life 2. Farm life -- United States 3. Farms
ISBN 978-1-58196-067-9; 1-58196-067-0

A journal of one year on the Bennett farm in central Ohio. Shows how one family, with the help of relatives and friends, creates a life and livelihood on a 150-acre farm.

"This engaging book is an unsentimental, appreciative look into the world of one farm family." SLJ

Rothman, Julia
   Farm anatomy; the curious parts & pieces of country life. Julia Rothman. Storey Pub. 2011 223 p. col. ill., col. maps $16.95
Grades: 7 8 9 10 11 12   **630**
   1. Barns 2. Farms 3. Farm life 4. Farm produce 5. Domestic animals 6. Farm life -- Miscellanea 7. Farm life -- Pictorial works
ISBN 1603429816; 9781603429818

LC 2012360929

This book explains the "difference between a weanling and a yearling, or a farrow and a barrow . . . [in this] guide to the curious parts and pieces of rural living. Dissecting everything from tractors and pigs to fences, hay bales, crop rotation patterns, and farm tools, [Julia] Rothman gives a . . . tour of the quirky details of country life. From the shapes of squash varieties to the parts of a goat; from how a barn is constructed to what makes up a beehive, every corner of the barnyard is uncovered and celebrated." (Publisher's note)

   Includes bibliographical references (p. 220-222).

630.9 Agriculture -- History

Richardson, Gillian
   10 plants that shook the world; Gillian Richardson; illustrated by Kim Rosen. Annick Press 2013 132 p. (hardcover) $24.95
Grades: 4 5 6 7 8   **630.9**
   1. Plants 2. Agriculture -- History
ISBN 1554514452; 9781554514458

This book, by Gillian Richardson, illustrated by Kim Rosen, profiles ten plants with significant histories. It describes how "countries went to war to control trade centers for pepper . . . , a grass called papyrus became the first effective tool for sharing knowledge through writing . . . , Europeans in the 1600s cut down rainforests to grow sugar, contributing to soil erosion . . . [and] dependence on the potato caused one of the greatest tragedies in history." (Publisher's note)

"With bold, lively caricatures from Rosen throughout, it's an intriguing and well-designed study of the ways plants have helped start wars, cure diseases, and advance technology." Pub Wkly

631.4 Soil science

Gardner, Robert
   Soil; green science projects for a sustainable planet. Enslow Publishers 2011 128p il (Team Green science projects) lib bdg $31.93
Grades: 6 7 8 9 10   **631.4**
   1. Soils 2. Science projects 3. Science -- Experiments
ISBN 978-0-7660-3647-5; 0-7660-3647-2

This book offers science experiments that explain the properties of soil, erosion, and methods to conserve soil.

"Gardner provides plenty of information, well-designed experiments, and demonstrations, and then shares brief science-fair ideas. . . . Experiments and demonstrations are presented with clear step-by-step instructions and occasional illustrations and represent a wide range of complexity." SLJ

   Includes glossary and bibliographical references

633.1 Cereals

Sobol, Richard
   The **life** of rice; from seedling to supper. Candlewick Press 2010 36p il map (Traveling photographer) $17.99
Grades: 3 4 5 6   **633.1**
   1. Rice
ISBN 978-0-7636-3252-6; 0-7636-3252-X

LC 2009-15138

"Turning his lens to the rice fields of Thailand, Sobol begins this affectionate account with a description of the Royal Plowing Ceremony that kicks off the planting season and continues through cultivation and into the harvest. Brief explanations of the growing stages of rice are accompanied by beautiful color photographs of the fields in their various phases. . . . Sobol offers an interesting look at a country and its people, and their relationship to the land. The writing is accessible and lively, providing a unique, specific look at one of the world's most important staples." SLJ

633.5 Fiber crops

Meltzer, Milton
   ★ The **cotton** gin. Benchmark Bks. 2003 123p il (Great inventions) lib bdg $25.95

Grades: 6 7 8 9   **633.5**
1. Cotton 2. Cotton gins and ginning
ISBN 0-7614-1537-8

LC 2002-15308

The author describes the invention of the cotton gin and its effects on history including "the influence of mechanized cotton processing on the growth of slavery in the United States and the increase in textile mills. . . . The author expertly describes a setting that is ripe for invention. Powerful photographs . . . historical artwork, and personal narratives make the times real and relevant to readers." SLJ

Includes bibliographical references

634.9   Forestry

Colson, Mary
Forest furnace; wildfires. Raintree 2004 48p il (Turbulent planet) lib bdg $22; pa $8.99
Grades: 6 7 8 9   **634.9**
1. Fires 2. Wildfires 3. Forest fires
ISBN 978-1-410-90588-8; 1-410-90588-8; 978-1-410-91026-4 pa; 1-410-91026-1 pa

LC 2003-8295

Presents information on forest fires, giving specific examples from around the world

Includes bibliographical references

Morris, Neil
Wood. Amicus 2011 48p il map (Materials that matter) lib bdg $28.50
Grades: 4 5 6 7   **634.9**
1. Wood
ISBN 978-1-60753-070-1 lib bdg; 1-60753-070-8 lib bdg

LC 2010001621

"The clean layout includes photographs and occasional charts, graphs, and technical illustrations against a range of pastel backgrounds. Inset boxes provide further detail, interesting extras, and recycling information. . . . [This book offers] easily accessible background information for report writers." SLJ

Includes glossary and bibliographical references

Morrison, Taylor
Wildfire. Houghton Mifflin Co. 2006 48p il $17
Grades: 4 5 6   **634.9**
1. Wildfires 2. Forest fires
ISBN 978-0-618-50900-3; 0-618-50900-3

LC 2005-30483

This is an "overview of the people involved in fighting wildfires and the techniques and equipment they use. Detailed paintings aid in explaining how firefighters work and in describing the natural conditions that lead to initial fires and more dangerous developments. . . . The pages are packed with visual and textual information." SLJ

Includes glossary and bibliographical references

Silverstein, Alvin
Wildfires; the science behind raging infernos. [by] Alvin and Virginia Silverstein and Laura Silver-

stein Nunn. Enslow Publishers 2010 48p il map (The science behind natural disasters) lib bdg $23.93
Grades: 4 5 6   **634.9**
1. Wildfires
ISBN 978-0-7660-2973-6 lib bdg; 0-7660-2973-5 lib bdg

LC 2008-48025

"Scientific explanations are accompanied by plentiful color diagrams that will help students to grasp causes and effects. . . . Photos . . . are effective, and are sometimes turned into helpful, lively diagrams by the addition of such features as wind-direction arrows." SLJ

Includes glossary and bibliographical references

Trammel, Howard K.
Wildfires; by Howard K. Trammel. Children's Press 2009 48 p. col. ill. (A true book) (library) $29
Grades: 4 5 6   **634.9**
1. Wildfires 2. Natural disasters
ISBN 0531168875; 9780531168875

LC 2008014796

This book by Howard K. Trammel is part of the True Books: Earth Science series and looks at wildfires. The series answers questions such as "what makes the earth quake, rivers flood, and volcanoes blow their tops? How do natural forces become natural disasters?" (Publisher's note)

635   Garden crops (Horticulture)

Cohen, Whitney
The **book** of gardening projects for kids; 101 ways to get kids outside, dirty, and having fun. Whitney Cohen and John Fisher. 1st ed. Timber Press 2012 264 p. col. ill. $29.95
Grades: Adult Professional   **635**
1. Gardening 2. Gardens -- Guidebooks 3. Gardens -- Activity Projects 4. Gardening for children
ISBN 1604693738; 9781604692457

LC 2011036778

In this book, "Whitney Cohen and John Fisher draw on years of experience in the Life Lab Garden Classroom and gardening with their own children to teach parents how to integrate the garden into their family life, no matter its scope or scale. The book features . . . gardening advice, including how to design a play-friendly garden, ideas for fun-filled theme gardens, and how to cook and preserve the garden's bounty. 101 . . . garden activities are also featured." (Publisher's note)

Morris, Karyn
★ The **Kids** Can Press jumbo book of gardening; written by Karyn Morris; illustrated by Jane Kurisu. Kids Can Press 2000 240p il pa $14.95
Grades: 4 5 6 7   **635**
1. Gardening
ISBN 1-55074-690-1

"Sections cover general information; fruit, vegetable, and flower gardens; noninvasive native plants; gardens that attract wildlife; and group projects. Projects range from a few annuals in a container and thickets designed with native wildlife in mind to community gardens. Directions are clear, with plenty of diagrams and illustrations." Booklist

635.9   Flowers and ornamental plants

Rice, Barry A.

Growing carnivorous plants; [by] Barry A. Rice. Timber 2006 224p il $39.95

Grades: 7 8 9   635.9

1. Carnivorous plants

ISBN 978-0-8819-2807-5; 0-8819-2807-0

LC 2007295063

A "guide to identifying and cultivating [carnivorous plants]. . . . This book will help readers select the best plants to grow on a windowsill, in a terrarium or greenhouse. Information on how to feed carnivorous plants [is included]." Publisher's note

Includes bibliographical references

636   Animal husbandry

Keenan, Sheila

★ **Animals** in the house; a history of pets and people. Scholastic Nonfiction 2007 112p il $17.99

Grades: 4 5 6   636

1. Pets

ISBN 978-0-439-69286-1; 0-439-69286-5

"Keenan provides an overview of pets and their people. Beginning with statistics about pet ownership, the text goes on to describe how animals and humans came together . . . and discusses how this relationship has changed and deepened. . . . Eye-catchingly designed, the format uses Photoshop to best advantage, providing interesting graphics, popping borders, and plenty of pictures featuring adorable animals." Booklist

Includes bibliographical references

Martin, Claudia

Farming. Marshall Cavendish Benchmark 2010 64p il (Working animals) $28.50

Grades: 4 5 6 7   636

1. Agriculture 2. Domestic animals

ISBN 978-1-60870-162-9; 1-60870-162-X

LC 2010006895

"Attractively designed and packed with information. . . . The composition of each page is attractively set up with well-selected and reproduced stock and historical photos." SLJ

McAlpine, Margaret

Working with animals. Gareth Stevens Pub. 2005 64p il (My future career) lib bdg $24

Grades: 6 7 8 9   636

1. Animals 2. Vocational guidance

ISBN 0-8368-4240-5

LC 2004-45229

This describes seven occupations related to animals, such as animal groomer and zookeeper, including the re-

sponsibilities, qualifications, and best personality type for each one

"The writing is clear and interesting, and the [book is] visually well organized." SLJ

Includes bibliographical references

Montgomery, Sy

Temple Grandin; how the girl who loved cows embraced autism and changed the world. by Sy Montgomery. Houghton Mifflin Harcourt 2012 147 p. col. ill. $17.99

Grades: 4 5 6 7 8   636

1. Autism 2. Cattle 3. Women scientists -- Biography 4. Animal welfare -- United States 5. Livestock -- Housing -- United States 6. Livestock -- Handling -- United States 7. Autistic people -- United States -- Biography 8. Animal scientists -- United States -- Biography 9. Animal specialists -- United States -- Biography 10. Women animal specialists -- United States -- Biography

ISBN 0547443153; 9780547443157

LC 2011039911

AAAS/Subaru SB&F Prize for Excellence in Science Books: Middle Grade Science Book (2013)

This book by Sy Montgomery presents a biography of autistic animal scientist Temple Grandin. Sy Montgomery argues that "though one never outgrows autism, it doesn't condemn those who have it to unproductive lives, and an appendix, 'Temple's Advice for Kids on the Spectrum,' provides first-hand wisdom. Photos and diagrams depict Grandin's work as well as documenting her early life and career." (Kirkus Reviews)

Includes bibliographical references and index.

Steele, Christy

Cattle ranching in the American West; by Christy Steele. World Almanac Library 2005 48p il map (America's westward expansion) lib bdg $30; pa $11.95

Grades: 5 6 7 8   636

1. Cattle 2. Ranch life

ISBN 0-8368-5787-9 lib bdg; 0-8368-5794-1 pa

LC 2004-56769

This volume describing Western cattle ranching is "richly illustrated with historical photographs, illustrations, maps, and quotes from primary sources presented in sidebars." SLJ

Includes bibliographical references

636.088   Animals for specific purposes

Grayson, Robert

Transportation. Marshall Cavendish Benchmark 2010 64p il (Working animals) $28.50

Grades: 4 5 6 7   636.088

1. Pack animals (Transportation)

ISBN 978-1-60870-167-4; 1-60870-167-0

LC 2010006899

"Describes animals that people all over the world use to transport people and goods, such as elephants, horses, yaks, water buffalo, and dogs." Publisher's note

Includes glossary and bibliographical references

Halls, Kelly Milner

Saving the Baghdad Zoo; a true story of hope and heroes. by Kelly Milner Halls, with William Sumner. Greenwillow Books 2010 64p il map $17.99

Grades: 4 5 6 7   **636.088**
1. Zoos 2. Wildlife conservation 3. Army officers 4. Iraq War, 2003-
ISBN 978-0-06-177202-3; 0-06-177202-X

LC 2008-52820

"This eye-opening tale of compassion and cooperation chronicles the mission of an international team of military personnel, zoo staffers, veterinarians, and relief workers to rescue neglected animals in Baghdad. . . . Sobering and uplifting photographs—many taken by Sumner—underscore both the direness of the situation and the spirit of hope that drove the project." Publ Wkly

Includes bibliographical references

Kent, Deborah

Animal helpers for the disabled. Watts 2003 63p il (Watts library) hardcover o.p. $25.50

Grades: 4 5 6 7   **636.088**
1. Dogs 2. Guide dogs 3. Working animals 4. Animals and the handicapped 5. Animals -- Training 6. Animals -- Therapeutic use 7. Animals as aids for people with disabilities
ISBN 0-531-12017-1; 0-531-16663-5 pa

LC 2002-8885

Explores the history of guide dogs, service animals, and assistance dogs, and discusses the process of training them to help people who have physical disabilities

This is an "informative, often inspirational and thought-provoking [book]." Booklist

Includes bibliographical references

Laidlaw, Rob

Wild animals in captivity; [by] Rob Laidlaw. Fitzhenry & Whiteside 2008 48p il $19.95

Grades: 5 6 7 8   **636.088**
1. Zoos 2. Animal welfare
ISBN 978-1-55455-025-8; 1-55455-025-4

"A passionate, well-written, and well-researched argument against the practices of most zoos around the world. . . . Describes the damage done when animals are unnaturally confined and moved to inhospitable climates, and compares the wild and captive lives of polar bears, orcas, elephants, and great apes—the four species most harmed by captivity. . . . The issues raised in this important and powerful book will resonate with young and old." SLJ

Markle, Sandra

Animal heroes; true rescue stories. by Sandra Markle. Millbrook Press 2009 64p il lib bdg $29.27

Grades: 4 5 6 7   **636.088**
1. Pets 2. Animals 3. Rescue work
ISBN 978-0-8225-7884-0 lib bdg; 0-8225-7884-0 lib bdg

LC 2007-50435

"Nine stories, based on interviews with the grateful survivors, describe how brave animals rescued people in catastrophic circumstances. Each edgy retelling reveals details that only the participants could know, including sounds, smells, sights, and the knowledge that at any moment they could die, deepening the tension. Mixed in are Markle's broad and perfectly attuned insights about animal behavior." SLJ

Includes glossary and bibliographical references

636.089   Veterinary medicine

Jackson, Donna M.

★ **ER** vets; life in an animal emergency room. Houghton Mifflin 2005 88p il $17

Grades: 5 6 7 8   **636.089**
1. Veterinary medicine 2. Young adult literature -- Works 3. Veterinarians 4. Veterinary emergencies
ISBN 0-618-43663-4

"With plentiful, excellent-quality photographs, this highly visual book offers a behind-the-scenes look at an emergency animal hospital in Colorado. . . . A section on grief counseling for families with critically ill pets and a spread on how to put together a pet first-aid kit are included. Well-researched and well-written, ER Vets is an engaging book on a hot topic." SLJ

636.1   Horses

Bowers, Nathan

4-H guide to training horses. Voyageur Press 2009 176p il $18.99

Grades: 5 6 7 8   **636.1**
1. Horses -- Training
ISBN 978-0-7603-3627-4; 0-7603-3627-X

LC 2009015299

This provides "sound and comprehensive information. [The book] covers basic training techniques and riding skills such as mounting, saddling, reining, stopping and starting, and posture among other topics. The training techniques offer insight into equine behavior based on their history as prey animals. The authors also emphasize that horse owners' success will be determined by how much effort they are willing to expend on their relationship with their animals. The many color photographs clearly depict the methods and activities that are taking place, and the accompanying images further clarify what is happening and its significance." SLJ

Includes glossary

Clutton-Brock, Juliet

Horse; written by Juliet Clutton-Brock. DK Pub. 2008 72p il (DK eyewitness books) $15.99

Grades: 4 5 6 7   **636.1**
1. Horses
ISBN 978-0-7566-3775-0; 0-7566-3775-9
LC 2008276033
First published 2003 in the United Kingdom
Examines the anatomy, history, and breeds of horses, and discusses the different ways horses have been used throughout history

Crosby, Jeff

Harness horses, bucking broncos & pit ponies; a history of horse breeds. written and illustrated by Jeff Crosby and Shelley Ann Jackson. Tundra Books 2011 69p il map $21.99
Grades: 4 5 6 7   **636.1**
1. Horses
ISBN 978-0-88776-986-3; 0-88776-986-1
"After a brief introduction, the animals are grouped by the roles they have played in relation to people: 'Rapid Transit,' 'Military Advantage,' 'Horsepower,' 'Equine Entertainment,' and 'Feral Horses.' The concise and interesting information on each of the 43 breeds is accompanied by an illustration of the type as well as one of the horse in action and often includes a small map showing its origins. The excellent painterly pictures clearly capture the unique life of each horse." SLJ
Includes bibliographical references

Ransford, Sandy

★ The **Kingfisher** illustrated horse & pony encyclopedia; written by Sandy Ransford; photographed by Bob Langrish. Kingfisher 2004 224p il $24.95
Grades: 4 5 6 7   **636.1**
1. Horses 2. Horsemanship
ISBN 0-7534-5781-4
LC 2003-27293
"The first part of the book covers the life cycle, domestication, and types of horses and ponies. . . . The second part deals with how to care for these animals and discusses horsemanship from taking riding lessons to training and driving a horse. . . . Filled with appealing photos of young people interacting with their four-legged friends, this title is an extremely useful addition to any collection." SLJ

Wilsdon, Christina

For horse-crazy girls only; everything you want to know about horses. illustrated by Alecia Underhill. Feiwel and Friends 2010 150p il $14.99
Grades: 4 5 6 7   **636.1**
1. Horses
ISBN 978-0-312-60323-6; 0-312-60323-1
LC 2010015677
"Filled with quizzes, trivia, top 10 lists, and information about equine behavior, history, sports, and more, this guidebook aims straight at the hearts of horse-loving tweens. . . . The book runs the gamut from how to pick a horse's name to horses in popular culture, the evolution of the species, and horse-related events nationwide. The many sidebars, tidbits, and anecdotes encourage casual browsing-horse lovers will be in heaven." Publ Wkly

636.2   Cattle and related animals

Freedman, Russell

★ **In** the days of the vaqueros; America's first true cowboys. Clarion Bks. 2001 70p il $18; pa $9.99
Grades: 4 5 6 7   **636.2**
1. Cowhands 2. Ranch life 3. Mexican Americans 4. Southwest, New -- History 5. Ranch life -- Southwest, New -- History 6. Southwest, New -- Social life and customs 7. Frontier and pioneer life -- Southwest, New 8. Mexican American cowboys -- Southwest, New -- History
ISBN 0-395-96788-0; 978-0-395-96788-1; 978-0-547-13365-2 pa; 0-547-13365-0 pa
LC 2001-17357
The author "tells the story with depth, clarity, and a vigor that conveys the thrilling excitement of the work and the macho swagger of the culture. . . . The book's design is beautiful, with spacious type on thick paper, and the dazzling illustrations—prints, paintings, and photos on almost every page." Booklist
Includes glossary and bibliographical references

636.5   Chickens and other kinds of domestic birds

Kindschi, Tara

4-H guide to raising chickens. Voyageur Press 2010 176p il pa $18.99
Grades: 5 6 7 8   **636.5**
1. Chickens
ISBN 978-0-7603-3628-1 pa; 0-7603-3628-8 pa
LC 2009015300
"This title has everything one ever wanted to know about chickens but didn't know enough to ask. Eight chapters divide the text into broad topics such as getting started, choosing a breed, housing equipment, and exhibiting chickens. . . . Line drawings and charts give additional information, and the excellent color photography is profuse." SLJ
Includes glossary and bibliographical references

636.7   Dogs

American Kennel Club

★ The **Complete** dog book for kids; official publication of the American Kennel Club. Howell Book House 1996 274p il maps hardcover o.p. pa $22.95
Grades: 4 5 6 7   **636.7**
1. Dogs
ISBN 0-87605-458-0; 0-87605-460-2 pa
LC 96-29228
This "begins with a general section that advises readers on buying a dog, responsibilities, rewards, and how to match a dog with one's situation. . . . More than 100 dogs are profiled, with information on history, appearance, health, and 'fun facts.' Crisp color photographs accompany each article.

. . . A final section gives good advice about nutrition and health issues." Booklist

The **complete** dog book; American Kennel Club. 20th ed.; Ballantine Books 2006 xxi, 858p il $35

Grades: 7 8 9 10 11 12 Adult   **636.7**

   1. Dogs

   ISBN 0-345-47626-3; 978-0-345-47626-5

                          LC 2005-48263

   First published 1935. Periodically revised

   "The official guide to 124 AKC registered breeds and their history, appearance, selection, training, care and feeding, and first aid. Some color plates." N Y Public Libr. Ref Books for Child Collect. 2d edition

Bial, Raymond

   Rescuing Rover; saving America's dogs. Houghton Mifflin 2011 80p il

Grades: 4 5 6 7   **636.7**

   1. Dogs 2. Animal welfare

   ISBN 0-547-34125-3; 978-0-547-34125-5

                          LC 2010025123

   "This accessible, amply illustrated title offers and informative introduction to canine-rescue endeavors. After recounting his own moving story of adopting a rescue dog, Bial provides a history of human-dog relationships. . . . Bial also explores rescue organizations, such as the ASPCA. . . . Bial frankly discusses the abuse many dogs experience . . . as well as euthanasia. . . . Historical and contemporary photos; extensive book lists . . .; websites; and detailed index complete this well-presented resource." Booklist

   Includes bibliographical references

Biniok, Janice

   The **miniature** schnauzer. Eldorado Ink 2010 112p il (Our best friends) lib bdg $34.95

Grades: 4 5 6 7   **636.7**

   1. Dogs

   ISBN 978-1-932904-61-1 lib bdg; 1-932904-61-1 lib bdg

   "The Our Best Friends series continues to be an ideal resource for those kids (or even adults) looking for a cradle-to-grave primer on responsible pet ownership. . . . These [books] offer far more than the customary cursory enticements and warnings usually aimed at first-time animal caregivers, with in-depth information on health issues and extensive explanations of the various types of species. . . . This is required (if sobering) reading for the serious pet owner." Booklist

   Includes bibliographical references

   The **rottweiler**. Eldorado Ink 2010 112p il (Our best friends) lib bdg $34.95

Grades: 4 5 6 7   **636.7**

   1. Dogs

   ISBN 978-1-932904-64-2 lib bdg; 1-932904-64-6 lib bdg

   "The Our Best Friends series continues to be an ideal resource for those kids (or even adults) looking for a cradle-to-grave primer on responsible pet ownership. . . . These [books] offer far more than the customary cursory enticements and warnings usually aimed at first-time animal

caregivers, with in-depth information on health issues and extensive explanations of the various types of species. . . . This is required (if sobering) reading for the serious pet owner." Booklist

   Includes bibliographical references

Bolan, Sandra

   Caring for your mutt; [by] Sandra Bolan. Eldorado Ink 2008 128p (Our best friends) lib bdg $25.95

Grades: 4 5 6 7   **636.7**

   1. Dogs

   ISBN 978-1-932904-20-8; 1-932904-20-4

                          LC 2007051607

   "Although Bolan's excellent advice on selection, training, and care applies to nearly all canines, she makes it plain that mixed breeds can be a 'challenging guessing game' when it comes to predicting size, temperment, and overall health. All the expected information is here, clearly presented and quite thorough." Booklist

   Includes bibliographical references

Gewirtz, Elaine Waldorf

   Fetch this book. Eldorado Ink 2010 112p il (Our best friends) lib bdg $34.95

Grades: 4 5 6 7   **636.7**

   1. Dogs -- Training

   ISBN 978-1-932904-60-4 lib bdg; 1-932904-60-3 lib bdg

   This "is a dog-training manual, with pet-care advice only in reference to training. [This] well-written [book provides] examples to support [its] points and solid online and text resources and feature [a] clean, uncluttered [layout]. . . . There is plenty of practical information that motivated readers can glean from [this title]." SLJ

   Includes bibliographical references

   The **bulldog**. Eldorado Ink 2010 112p il (Our best friends) lib bdg $34.95

Grades: 4 5 6 7   **636.7**

   1. Dogs

   ISBN 978-1-932904-58-1 lib bdg; 1-932904-58-1 lib bdg

   "The Our Best Friends series continues to be an ideal resource for those kids (or even adults) looking for a cradle-to-grave primer on responsible pet ownership. These [books] offer far more than the customary cursory enticements and warnings usually aimed at first-time animal caregivers, with in-depth information on health issues and extensive explanations of the various types of species. . . . This is required (if sobering) reading for the serious pet owner." Booklist

   Includes bibliographical references

Gorrell, Gena K.

   Working like a dog; the story of working dogs through history. Tundra 2003 156p il pa $16.95

Grades: 4 5 6 7   **636.7**

   1. Working dogs

   ISBN 0-88776-589-0

   "Gorrell begins by tracing the evolution of 'household canids' from the wild into the civilized world. Other chapters delve into the many ways in which these animals have been viewed throughout history, what makes particular breeds right for certain jobs, dogs at war, famous pooches, etc. . . . The well-captioned, black-and-white photographs and reproductions add greatly to a narrative that's packed with intriguing details." SLJ

Includes bibliographical references

Houston, Dick

Bulu, African wonder dog. Random House 2010 323p il $15.99; lib bdg $18.99

Grades: 5 6 7 8   **636.7**

1. Dogs 2. Wildlife conservation

ISBN 978-0-375-84723-3; 0-375-84723-5; 978-0-375-94720-9 lib bdg; 0-375-94720-5 lib bdg

LC 2009015804

"In the Nyanja language, bulu means 'wild dog,' and that's what Steve and Anna Tolan named the beloved little Jack Russell mix they adopted. Disregarding warnings about the dangers of raising a dog in the bush, the Tolans moved from England to rural Zambia to fulfill their lifelong dream of setting up an animal rescue and conservation center. . . . Bulu's energy, high spirits, and loyalty to his masters make the book read like a praise song to dogs. Houston's account is an animal-lover's delight, complete with the action-adventure of surviving the bush, fighting poachers, and spreading a message of conservation." Booklist

Laidlaw, Rob

No shelter here; Making the world a kinder place for dogs. Rob Laidlaw. Pajama Press 2012 63 p.

Grades: 3 4 5 6 7 8   **636.7**

1. Dogs 2. Animal rights 3. Animal welfare

ISBN 0986949558; 9780986949555

This book provides an "informative and visually varied introduction to problems affecting dogs worldwide. In a short, colorful volume with sidebars and photographs on nearly every page, professional dog advocate [Rob] Laidlaw . . . presents facts about how dogs live, provides an overview of the cruelty dogs face at the hands of humans and offers profiles of young activists who are working to better dogs' lives. . . . A list of animal welfare websites points interested readers toward further information." (Kirkus)

Includes bibliographical references and index.

Mehus-Roe, Kristin

Dogs for kids! everything you need to know about dogs. by Kristin Mehus-Roe. BowTie Press 2007 384p il pa $14.95

Grades: 4 5 6 7   **636.7**

1. Dogs

ISBN 978-1-931993-83-8 pa; 1-931993-83-1 pa

LC 2006035434

"If you are looking for a book about canines that is entertaining as well as immensely informative, this is it. In a lively, conversational tone, Mehus-Roe offers a vast amount of material, from the history of dogs to vacationing with a pet, and provides practical and upbeat explanations, ideas, offbeat tidbits, and pertinent details." SLJ

Includes bibliographical references

Morn, September B.

The **pug.** Eldorado Ink 2010 112p il (Our best friends) lib bdg $34.95

Grades: 4 5 6 7   **636.7**

1. Dogs

ISBN 978-1-932904-63-5 lib bdg; 1-932904-63-8 lib bdg

"The Our Best Friends series continues to be an ideal resource for those kids (or even adults) looking for a cradle-to-grave primer on responsible pet ownership. . . . These [books] offer far more than the customary cursory enticements and warnings usually aimed at first-time animal caregivers, with in-depth information on health issues and extensive explanations of the various types of species. . . . This is required (if sobering) reading for the serious pet owner." Booklist

Includes bibliographical references

Rogers, Tammie

4-H guide to dog training and dog tricks. Voyageur Press 2009 176p il pa $18.99

Grades: 5 6 7 8 9 10   **636.7**

1. Dogs -- Training

ISBN 978-0-7603-3629-8; 0-7603-3629-6

LC 2009-17040

"This is not simply a how-to-train book; it is also a guide to cultivating a respectful relationship with your dog. The excellent information is comprehensive, and it is presented in a clear and detailed style. The author covers different training methods, discussing the tools needed from food to collar selection. Using this manual, dog owners can move through the basics (sit, down, etc.) to obedience competition and fun tricks and activities." SLJ

Includes bibliographical references

Schweitzer, Karen

The **beagle.** Eldorado Ink 2010 112p il (Our best friends) lib bdg $34.95

Grades: 4 5 6 7   **636.7**

1. Dogs

ISBN 978-1-932904-57-4 lib bdg; 1-932904-57-3 lib bdg

"The Our Best Friends series continues to be an ideal resource for those kids (or even adults) looking for a cradle-to-grave primer on responsible pet ownership. . . . These [books] offer far more than the customary cursory enticements and warnings usually aimed at first-time animal caregivers, with in-depth information on health issues and extensive explanations of the various types of species. . . . This is required (if sobering) reading for the serious pet owner." Booklist

Includes bibliographical references

The **dachshund.** Eldorado Ink 2010 112p il (Our best friends) lib bdg $34.95

Grades: 4 5 6 7   **636.7**

1. Dogs

ISBN 978-1-932904-59-8 lib bdg; 1-932904-59-X lib bdg

"The Our Best Friends series continues to be an ideal resource for those kids (or even adults) looking for a cradle-to-grave primer on responsible pet ownership. . . . These [books] offer far more than the customary cursory entice-ments and warnings usually aimed at first-time animal caregivers, with in-depth information on health issues and extensive explanations of the various types of species. . . . This is required (if sobering) reading for the serious pet owner." Booklist

Includes bibliographical references

Whitehead, Sarah

How to speak dog. Scholastic Reference 2008 96p il pa $6.99

Grades: 4 5 6 7 8   **636.7**

1. Dogs

ISBN 978-0-545-02078-7 pa; 0-545-02078-6 pa

Explains how to read a dog's body language and vocal-izations and presents step-by-step instructions for training, housebreaking, teaching tricks, and playing several types of games.

This is "well-organized and interesting. . . . Whitehead discusses, and clearly shows in good-quality, full-color pho-tographs, various canine emotions." SLJ

636.8   Cats

Bidner, Jenni

Is my cat a tiger? how your cat compares to its wild cousins. Lark Books 2006 64p il $9.95

Grades: 3 4 5 6   **636.8**

1. Cats 2. Wild cats

ISBN 1-57990-815-2

LC 2006023356

"This book shows how domestic cats compare with their wild cousins. Specifically, it addresses what domestic behav-ior reveals about wild roots. . . . The color photographs are fantastic. . . . This is a fascinating volume." SLJ

Biniok, Janice

Mixed breed cats. Eldorado Ink 2010 112p il (Our best friends) lib bdg $34.95

Grades: 4 5 6 7   **636.8**

1. Cats

ISBN 978-1-932904-62-8 lib bdg; 1-932904-62-X lib bdg

This "is a cradle-to-grave overview of a cat's life. . . . [This] well-written [book provides] examples to support [its] points and solid online and text resources and feature [a] clean, uncluttered [layout]. . . . There is plenty of practi-cal information that motivated readers can glean from [this title]. [It] debunks some presumptions about domesticated felines, commenting that the 'finicky eater' tag is unwarrant-ed, and that cats are easier to train than people think." SLJ

Includes bibliographical references

Edney, A. T. B.

ASPCA complete cat care manual; [by] Andrew Edney; foreword by Roger Caras. Dorling Kinders-ley 1992 192p il hardcover o.p. pa $14.95

Grades: 8 9 10 11 12 Adult   **636.8**

1. Cats

ISBN 1-56458-064-4; 0-7566-1742-1 pa

LC 92-52783

"Cat care is made easy through step-by-step photographs that illustrate grooming, handling, detecting illness, first aid, and other concerns. Difficult-to-explain procedures, such as how to administer medication or transport an injured cat, are clearly understandable." Libr J

Includes bibliographical references

Myron, Vicki

Dewey the library cat; a true story. [by] Vicki Myron with Bret Witter. Little, Brown 2010 214p $16.99

Grades: 4 5 6 7 8   **636.8**

1. Cats 2. Libraries

ISBN 978-0-316-06871-0; 0-316-06871-3

Adapted from: Dewey: the small town library cat who touched the world, published 2008 by Grand Central Pub-lisher for adults

"From the opening chapter, when librarian Vicki Myron finds a fragile, freezing kitten in the book return, children will be hooked on her heartwarming story about Dewey Re-admore Books. . . . Anecdotes such as Dewey's fascination with rubber bands, his bizarre behavior during a bat inva-sion, and his finicky eating habits are ideal booktalk mate-rial. So are descriptions of Dewey's tender, intuitive inter-actions with people of all ages and backgrounds." Booklist

Stefoff, Rebecca

Cats. Benchmark Bks. 2004 112p il (Animal-ways) $34.21

Grades: 6 7 8 9   **636.8**

1. Cats

ISBN 0-7614-1577-7

LC 2002-155247

This introduction to cat biology, life cycle, behavior, and relationship to people offers "a strong combination of text and illustration." SLJ

Includes bibliographical references

Whitehead, Sarah

How to speak cat. Scholastic 2009 96p il pa $6.99

Grades: 4 5 6 7 8   **636.8**

1. Cats

ISBN 978-0-545-02079-4 pa; 0-545-02079-4 pa

"This pet-care book focuses on developing a relationship with a pet. The author states that the communication process is a two-way street, and she describes how readers can trans-late a cat's body language and vocalizations. . . . the bright color photographs of children with their cats on every page will appeal greatly to readers. This is a fun book that offers a good understanding of its audience and subject." SLJ

636.9   Other mammals

McNicholas, June

Rats. Heinemann Lib. 2003 48p il (Keeping unusual pets) $24.22

Grades: 4 5 6 7   **636.9**
1. Rats
ISBN 1-4034-0283-3

LC 2002-3164

Describes how to select a pet rat, what to feed it, and when to take it to the vet, as well as how to keep a pet scrapbook

"A valuable, accessible resource." Booklist

Includes bibliographical references

Sullivant, Holly J.

Hamsters. ElDorado Ink 2009 il (Our best friends) $26.95

Grades: 7 8 9 10 11 12   **636.9**
1. Hamsters
ISBN 978-1-93290430-7

LC 2008040365

This is a guide to caring for a pet hamster.

"An ideal resource for those kids (or even adults) looking for a cradle-to-grave primer on responsible pet ownership. . . . Well formatted and broken up with vivid photographs and fascinating 'Fast Facts.'" Booklist

636.935   Rodents

Boruchowitz, David E.

Sugar gliders; David E. Boruchowitz; [editor, Thomas Mazorlig] T.F.H. 2012 111 p. (Animal planet. Pet care library) (pbk. : alk. paper) $10.95

Grades: 4 5 6 7   **636.935**
1. Sugar glider 2. Sugar gliders as pets
ISBN 0793837111; 9780793837113

LC 2011049947

This book on sugar gliders by David E. Boruchowitz is part of the "Animal Planet Pet Care Library" series. "According to Boruchowitz, they make excellent house pets due to their affinity for cuddling in tiny places. . . . Every aspect of ownership is covered, from basic dietary requirements to grooming and socialization." (Booklist)

Includes bibliographical references and index

638   Insect culture

Buchmann, Stephen

Honey bees; letters from the hive. Delacorte Press 2010 212p il $16.99; lib bdg $19.99

Grades: 7 8 9 10   **638**
1. Bees 2. Honey
ISBN 978-0-385-73770-8; 0-385-73770-X; 978-0-385-90683-8 lib bdg; 0-385-90683-8 lib bdg

LC 2010-6093

Based on the adult book, Letters from the hive: an intimate history of bees, honey, and humankind published by Delacorte Press in 2005

"This sweeping survey engagingly discusses bee biology and behavior and examines humanity's relationship with bees, from prehistoric times to the present, through their significant roles in art, religion, literature and medicine. Buchmann, a beekeeper and entomologist, also offers a great deal of information about honey. . . . The text is illustrated with black-and-white photographs and documented with source notes." Kirkus

Burns, L. G.

★ The **hive** detectives; chronicle of a honey bee catastrophe. with photographs by Ellen Harasimowicz. Houghton Mifflin Books for Children 2010 66p il (Scientists in the field) $18

Grades: 5 6 7 8 9 10   **638**
1. Beekeeping 2. Honeybee 3. Bee culture
ISBN 978-0-547-15231-8; 0-547-15231-0

LC 2009-45249

"Not long after beekeepers encountered a devastating new problem in their hives in 2006, a team of bee scientists began working to discover the causes of colony collapse disorder (CCD), now attributed to a combination of factors possibly including pesticides, nutrition, mites and viruses. . . . Mock notebook pages break up the narrative with biographies of the individual scientists, information about who and what can be found inside the hive and the features of bee bodies. An appendix adds varied fascinating facts about bees—again using the format of an illustrated research journal. Harasimowicz's clear, beautifully reproduced photographs support and extend the text." Kirkus

Includes glossary and bibliographical references

Harkins, Susan Sales

Design your own butterfly garden; by Susan Sales Harkins and William H. Harkins. Mitchell Lane Publishers 2008 48p il (Gardening for kids) lib bdg $29.95

Grades: 3 4 5 6   **638**
1. Butterfly gardens
ISBN 978-1-58415-638-3 lib bdg; 1-58415-638-4 lib bdg

LC 2008-2245

Introduces the principles of butterfly gardening, discussing how to plan the garden, what flowers to plant there, and how to maintain it in all seasons

"All the tasks delineated are well within the scope of children's abilities, and the items needed to complete them are not hard to find. . . . [The book has] excellent full-color photography and include[s] charts and diagrams to assist in the completion of the projects." SLJ

Includes bibliographical references

639.2   Commercial fishing, whaling, sealing

Foster, Mark

★ **Whale** port; a history of Tuckanucket. written by Mark Foster; illustrated by Gerald Foster. Houghton Mifflin Company 2007 64p il $18

Grades: 4 5 6 7   **639.2**
1. Whaling 2. Whaling -- New England 3. City and

town life -- New England -- History
ISBN 978-0-618-54722-7; 0-618-54722-3

LC 2006018772

This describes the history of whaling in New England through the fictional village of Tuckanucket and Zachariah Taber, his family and neighbors.

The village is "depicted in precisely detailed ink and crayon pictures. . . . The Fosters . . . have elegantly synthesized a tremendous amount of information into a beguiling format." Horn Book

McKissack, Patricia C.

★ **Black** hands, white sails; the story of African-American whalers. [by] Patricia C. McKissack & Fredrick L. McKissack. Scholastic Press 1999 xxiv, 152p il $17.95

Grades: 5 6 7 8   **639.2**

1. Whaling 2. Abolitionists 3. African Americans
ISBN 0-590-48313-7

LC 99-11439

A Coretta Scott King honor book for text, 2000

A history of African-American whalers between 1730 and 1880, describing their contributions to the whaling industry and their role in the abolitionist movement

"A well-researched and detailed book." SLJ

Includes bibliographical references

Sandler, Martin W.

Trapped in ice! an amazing true whaling adventure. Scholastic Nonfiction 2006 168p il $16.99

Grades: 5 6 7 8   **639.2**

1. Whaling 2. Whaling -- Arctic regions
ISBN 0-439-74363-X

LC 2005-42644

"In 1871, people aboard 32 whaling ships discovered just how dangerous Arctic waters could be after they ignored warnings of an early winter. As conditions worsened, the ships were trapped by ice, forcing the 1,219 people to abandon the vessels or die. Sandler's account of this true story is both informative and absorbing. . . . Well-chosen illustrations and side notes on such topics as life aboard ship and women at sea extend readers' understanding." Booklist

Includes glossary and bibliographical references

Somervill, Barbara A.

Commercial fisher. Cherry Lake Pub. 2011 32p il (Cool careers) lib bdg $27.07

Grades: 4 5 6 7   **639.2**

1. Commercial fishing 2. Vocational guidance
ISBN 978-1-60279-986-8; 1-60279-986-5

LC 2010029123

This book begins "with a personal story of a teen and then [segues] into the occupation [of commercial fisher]. . . . [It covers] the necessary training and skills for the job (and options for obtaining them), a typical day, salary expectations, and well-known professionals in the field. The [text is] accessible and clearly written. . . . The [volume has] a generous number of clear color photographs that depict people at work." SLJ

Includes glossary and bibliographical references

639.3   Culture of cold-blooded vertebrates

Bartlett, Richard D.

Aquatic turtles; sliders, cooters, painted, and map turtles. [by] R.D. Bartlett, Patricia Bartlett. Barron's Educational Series 2003 46p il (Reptile keeper's guides) pa $7.99

Grades: 6 7 8 9   **639.3**

1. Turtles
ISBN 978-0-7641-2278-1 pa; 0-7641-2278-9 pa

LC 2002-26264

"This guide offers . . . advice on the maintenance and care of [aquatic turtles]. . . . Readers . . . get advice on selecting a good specimen, determining sex, and providing proper housing, feeding, and health care." Publisher's note

Geckos; everything about housing, health, nutrition, and breeding. [by] R.D. Bartlett and Patricia P. Bartlett. Barron's 2006 95p il (A Complete pet owner's manual) pa $8.99

Grades: 6 7 8 9   **639.3**

1. Geckos
ISBN 978-0-7641-2855-4 pa; 0-7641-2855-8 pa

LC 2005-50024

First published 1995

"Advice on purchasing geckos, as well as feeding, breeding, and health care." Publisher's note

Includes glossary and bibliograpical references

Turtles and tortoises; everything about selection, care, nutrition, housing, and behavior. [by] R.D. Bartlett and Patricia P. Bartlett; with full-color photographs; illustrations by Michele Earl-Bridges. Barron's 2006 111p il (A complete pet owner's manual) pa $8.99

Grades: 6 7 8 9   **639.3**

1. Turtles
ISBN 978-0-7641-3400-5; 0-7641-3400-0

LC 2006-40101

"Information on both land and water species, with specifics on determining sex, life expectancy, housing, feeding, and health care." Publisher's note

Includes bibliographical references

Coates, Jennifer

Lizards. ElDorado Ink 2008 112p il (Our best friends) $26.95

Grades: 7 8 9 10 11 12   **639.3**

1. Lizards
ISBN 978-1-93290-431-4

LC 2008033060

This is a guide to caring for lizards as pets.

"An ideal resource for those kids (or even adults) looking for a cradle-to-grave primer on responsible pet ownership. . . . Well formatted and broken up with vivid photographs and fascinating 'Fast Facts.'" Booklist

639.34   Fish culture in aquariums

Indiviglio, Frank

The **everything** aquarium book; all you need to build the aquarium of your dreams. Adams Media 2007 287p il (Everything series) pa $14.95

Grades: 7 8 9 10   **639.34**
1. Aquariums
ISBN 978-1-59337-715-1; 1-59337-715-0
LC 2006-28187

This book about aquariums includes information about "proper fish selection, marine plants and understanding fish behavior." Publisher's note
Includes bibliographical references

Mills, Dick

Aquarium fish. DK 2004 72p il (101 essential tips) pa $5

Grades: 7 8 9 10 11 12 Adult   **639.34**
1. Fishes 2. Aquariums
ISBN 0-7566-0611-X; 978-0-7566-0611-4
LC 2004-303366

Reprint of paperback printed by DK Pub. in 1996

This book offers advice on choosing fish for aquariums, aquarium equipment, decoration, feeding, and health care, and describes various species of tropical, coldwater, freshwater, and marine fishes.

"Accurate, clear, and concise writing is enhanced with wonderful color photographs on each page." Voice Youth Advocates [review of 1996 edition]

Wood, Kathleen

The **101** best tropical fishes; how to choose & keep hardy, brilliant, fascinating species that will thrive in your home aquarium. by Kathleen Wood; with Mary E. Sweeney and Scott W. Michael. T.F.H. Publications 2007 192p il (Adventurous aquarist guide) $18.95

Grades: 6 7 8 9   **639.34**
1. Aquariums 2. Tropical fish
ISBN 978-1-8900-8793-7; 1-8900-8793-9
LC 2008-28294

"Presents 101 full-page species accounts of fishes that not only have high survival rates in captivity but also are appealing in appearance and behave well in community tanks. Also included are 33 species to avoid—fishes that most commonly wreak havoc in home aquariums because of their size or aggressiveness, or that tend to perish in the hands of inexperienced aquarists." Publisher's note
Includes bibliographical references

639.9   Conservation of biological resources

George, Jean Craighead

A **tarantula** in my purse; and 172 other wild pets. written and illustrated by Jean Craighead George. HarperCollins Pubs. 1996 134p il hardcover o.p. pa $5.99

Grades: 4 5 6   **639.9**
1. Pets 2. Artists 3. Authors 4. Naturalists 5. Illustrators 6. Women authors 7. Wildlife conservation
ISBN 0-06-023626-4; 0-06-446201-3 pa
LC 95-54151

"Brief, engaging stories about the many wild animals that lived in and around the author's home over the years are filled with humor, affection, and just enough drama." Horn Book

"Told in a casual and thoroughly engaging manner, the stories will enchant all animal lovers and even those who aren't." SLJ

Montgomery, Sy

★ **Kakapo** rescue; saving the world's strangest parrot. text by Sy Montgomery; photographs by Nic Bishop. Houghton Mifflin 2010 73p il map (Scientists in the field) $18

Grades: 4 5 6 7   **639.9**
1. Parrots 2. Endangered species 3. Wildlife conservation 4. Kakapo
ISBN 978-0-618-49417-0; 0-618-49417-0
LC 2009-45250

Awarded the Robert F. Sibert Medal, 2011

Montgomery and Bishop head "to a remote island off the southern tip of New Zealand, where they join a local government-sponsored research team that is working to save the Kakapo parrot from extinction. . . . Montgomery's delight in her subject is contagious, and throughout her enthusiastic text, she nimbly blends scientific and historical facts with immediate, sensory descriptions of fieldwork. Young readers will be fascinated. . . . Bishop's photos of the creatures and their habitat are stunning." Booklist

640   Home and family management

Walsh, Peter

It's all too much, so get it together; with illustrations by John Hendrix. Simon & Schuster BFYR 2009 278p il pa $12.99

Grades: 7 8 9 10   **640**
1. House cleaning 2. Storage in the home
ISBN 978-1-4169-9549-4 pa; 1-4169-9549-8 pa

This book suggests ways for teens to get rid of clutter and lead more organized, less stressful lives.

This is "is fun and light in tone. . . . For teens who are as overwhelmed by their lives as they are by their stuff, the quizzes and fictional scenarios will be right on point and may help them approach what they own and why in a new way. In addition to the suggestions for managing clutter (physical and mental), Walsh also offers tips for clutter-free friendships, jobs, studying, and even family fights." Voice Youth Advocates

641.3 Food

Chapman, Garry

Coffee; by Garry Chapman and Gary Hodges. Black Rabbit 2010 32p il (World commodities) lib bdg $28.50

Grades: 5 6 7 8 **641.3**

1. Coffee

ISBN 978-1-59920-584-7 lib bdg; 1-59920-584-X lib bdg

"The first part of the book discusses how coffee beans are grown, treated, prepared, and enjoyed around the world. . . . The second section offers an opportunity to use the commodity of coffee to understand such economics concepts as supply and demand or futures trading. . . . Finally, the book spins through a look at fair trade practices; political, environmental, and social issues surrounding coffee trade; and the sustainability and outlook of the global coffee industry. In all, the book gleans a pretty impressive and diverse array of accessible information from such a small bean." Booklist

Includes glossary

Jango-Cohen, Judith

The **history** of food; [by] Judith Jango-Cohen. Twenty-First Century Books 2006 56p il (Major inventions through history) lib bdg $26.60

Grades: 5 6 7 8 **641.3**

1. Food -- History

ISBN 0-8225-2484-8

LC 2004-23022

This history of food "discusses canning, pasteurization, refrigeration, supermarkets, and genetically modified foods. . . . The text . . . is breezy but informative; unfamiliar terms are defined. Illustrations are a mixture of period black-and-white and color photos." SLJ

Includes bibliographical references

Llewellyn, Claire

Cooking with fruits and vegetables; by Claire Llewellyn with recipes by Clare O'Shea. Rosen Central 2011 48p il (Cooking healthy) lib bdg $27.95

Grades: 5 6 7 8 **641.3**

1. Fruit 2. Cooking 3. Vegetables

ISBN 978-1-4488-4844-7; 1-4488-4844-X

LC 2010039333

This book pairs "facts about [fruits and vegetables], including where it is eaten, with eye-catching photos. . . . Each course (section) has an overview of the vegetable group . . . followed by recipes from all over the world. They vary in difficulty. . . . The cooking directions are clear and straightforward. . . . [The book is] profusely illustrated with full-color photos. Students who are learning to cook will appreciate [this] excellently organized [read]." SLJ

Includes bibliographical references

Menzel, Peter

★ What the world eats; photographed by Peter Menzel; written by Faith D'Aluisio. Tricycle Press 2008 160p il map $22.99

Grades: 4 5 6 7 8 **641.3**

1. Diet 2. Eating customs 3. Food -- Pictorial works

4. Food habits

ISBN 978-1-58246-246-2; 1-58246-246-1

LC 2007-41439

An adaptation of Hungry Planet, published 2005 by Ten Speed Press for adults

"Stunning color photographs of mealtimes and daily activities illustrate the warm, informative, anecdotal narratives. . . . This is a fascinating, sobering, and instructive look at daily life around the world." Booklist

Includes bibliographical references

Miller, Debra A.

Organic foods; by Debra A. Miller. Thomson/Gale 2008 111p il (Hot topics) lib bdg $32.45

Grades: 6 7 8 9 **641.3**

1. Natural foods 2. Natural foods industry

ISBN 978-1-59018-994-8 lib bdg; 1-59018-994-9 lib bdg

LC 2007-35909

"This title about organic foods gives a concise but thorough overview of a complex issue. . . . Sidebars, study questions, ample photos, and comprehensive chapter notes complete this on-target resource." Booklist

Includes bibliographical references

Miller, Jeanne

Food science. Lerner Publications 2009 48p il (Cool science) lib bdg $27.93

Grades: 4 5 6 **641.3**

1. Food

ISBN 978-0-8225-7589-4 lib bdg; 0-8225-7589-2 lib bdg

This describes how food scientists "explore how cooking changes food, create dishes that surprise the senses, and help farmers grow food in healthier ways." Publisher's note

Includes glossary and bibliographical references

Organic food and farming; Lauri S. Friedman, book editor. Greenhaven Press 2009 138p il (Introducing issues with opposing viewpoints) $34.70

Grades: 6 7 8 9 10 **641.3**

1. Natural foods 2. Organic farming

ISBN 978-0-7377-4483-5; 0-7377-4483-9

LC 2009-36912

"This title first examines the difference between organic and conventional food in terms of human health. The articles have been successfully edited for brevity and clarity. Whether organic farming can improve the world is discussed in the second . . . section of the book. . . . The bulk of the final section discusses the future of organic food and looks at the debate within the organic community on the direction of sustainable agriculture and the label organic. . . . With its colorful graphs and photographs nicely breaking up the text, this . . . book will provide a starting point for assignments." SLJ

Includes bibliographical references

Reilly, Kathleen M.

Food; 25 amazing projects investigate the history and science of what we eat. illustrated by Farah Rizvi. Nomad Press 2010 124p il (Build it yourself) pa $15.95

Grades: 4 5 6   641.3
    1. Food
    ISBN 978-1-934670-59-0; 1-934670-59-6

"This broad overview of food touches on its history and future, production and packaging, social and cultural practices, and health and safety concerns. . . . The information presented and questions posed on food packaging, mega-farming, locally grown vs. commercially grown foods, free-range grazing, and healthy food choices make this a particularly up-to-date survey. . . . Every chapter concludes with two to three hands-on activities that range from cooking to science and art projects. . . . This soup-to-nuts look at the business and consumption of food will make a good addition to most collections." SLJ

Includes glossary and bibliographical references

Thornhill, Jan

    Who wants pizza? the kids' guide to the history, science & culture of food. Maple Tree Press 2010 64p il $22.95; pa $10.95

Grades: 4 5 6   641.3
    1. Food 2. Agriculture
    ISBN 978-1-897349-96-0; 1-897349-96-3; 978-1-897349-97-7 pa; 1-897349-97-1 pa

This discusses "where food comes from and if there's enough to go around. Amid color photographs and sidebars, Thornhill writes concisely about hunter-gatherers, agriculture, processed foods, globalization, and poverty, among numerous other topics, providing a straightforward and balanced overview of the modern food industry, and the choices readers have when it comes to their own meals." Publ Wkly

641.5   Cooking

Arroyo, Sheri L.

    How chefs use math; math curriculum consultant, Rhea A. Stewart. Chelsea Clubhouse 2010 32p il (Math in the real world) lib bdg $28

Grades: 4 5 6   641.5
    1. Cooks 2. Cooking 3. Mathematics 4. Vocational guidance
    ISBN 978-1-60413-608-1 lib bdg; 1-60413-608-1 lib bdg

                            LC 2009-14180

This describes how chefs use math for such tasks as measuring ingredients, watching temperatures, buying food, setting menu prices, and managing restaurant and catering businesses, and includes relevant math problems and information about how to become a chef

Includes glossary and bibliographical references

Batmanglij, Najmieh

    Happy Nowruz; cooking with children to celebrate the Persian New Year. [by] Najmieh Batmanglij. Mage Publishers 2008 119p il $40

Grades: 4 5 6 7 8   641.5
    1. New Year 2. Eating customs 3. Middle Eastern cooking 4. Iran -- Social life and customs
    ISBN 1-933823-16-X; 978-1-933823-16-4

                            LC 2007-036047

"Combining a cookbook format with straightforward, informational text, this amply illustrated title offers a detailed introduction to the history and customs surrounding Nowruz, the Persian New Year. . . . The covered spiral binding allows pages to remain open while cooking, and the uncluttered, attractive format, featuring color photos of kids in the kitchen and whimsical illustrations, will attract interested browsers." Booklist

Behnke, Alison

    Cooking the Central American way; [by] Alison M. Behnke, in consultation with Griselda Aracely Chacon and Kristina Anderson. Lerner Publications Co. 2005 72p il (Easy menu ethnic cookbooks) lib bdg $25.26

Grades: 5 6 7 8   641.5
    1. Central American cooking
    ISBN 978-0-8225-1236-3; 0-8225-1236-X

                            LC 2004-11870

An introduction to the cooking of Central America.

Includes glossary

    Cooking the Mediterranean way; culturally authentic foods, including low-fat and vegetarian recipes. Alison M. Behnke, in consultation with Anna and Lazaros Christoforides. Lerner Publications 2005 72p il map (Easy menu ethnic cookbooks) lib bdg $25.26

Grades: 5 6 7 8   641.5
    1. Mediterranean cooking
    ISBN 0-8225-1237-8; 978-0-8225-1237-0

                            LC 2004-11054

An introduction to Mediterranean cooking and food habits, featuring traditional recipes and including information on the history, geography, customs, and people of this region of the world.

Includes glossary

    Cooking the Middle Eastern way; culturally authentic foods including low-fat and vegetarian recipes. Alison Behnke in consultation with Vartkes Ehramjian. Lerner Publications Co. 2005 72p il map (Easy menu ethnic cookbooks) lib bdg $25.26

Grades: 5 6 7 8   641.5
    1. Middle Eastern cooking
    ISBN 978-0-8225-1238-7; 0-8225-1238-6

                            LC 2004-19658

"This volume begins with an introduction to the history and varied cultures of the Middle East, followed by lists of cooking tips, utensils, terminology, and regional ingredients as well as a discussion of healthy, low-fat choices. . . . This is a well-designed, attractive source of recipes for Middle Eastern fare." Booklist

Includes glossary

Bloomfield, Jill

    Jewish holidays cookbook; by Jill Colella Bloomfield; Janet Ozur Bass, consultant; photography by Angela Coppola. DK Pub. 2008 128p il spiral bdg $19.99

Grades: 4 5 6 7   641.5
  1. Jewish cooking 2. Jewish holidays
  ISBN 978-0-7566-4089-7 spiral bdg; 0-7566-4089-X
  spiral bdg
"More than 40 recipes are included for celebrations
from Shabbat to Lag B'Omer. Several introductions explain
cooking tools, kitchen safety, and the general principles of
keeping kosher, and brief background information is given
for each holiday. Simple step-by-step instructions make the
recipes easy. . . . Beautiful color photographs, both full page
and spot, whet the appetite." SLJ

Carle, Megan
  Teens cook; how to make what you want to eat.
[by] Megan and Jill Carle with Judi Carle. Ten Speed
Press 2004 146p il pa $19.95
Grades: 7 8 9 10   641.5
  1. Cooking
  ISBN 1-58008-584-9
This cookbook features "recipes for a variety of dishes including chocolate chip scones, potato skins, broccoli
cheese soup, steak fajitas, baked macaroni and cheese, and
toffee bars. Because Megan is a vegetarian, there are several
vegetarian recipes or vegetarian substitutes. . . . Attractive,
engaging, and told from a teen perspective, this cookbook
will make an excellent addition to any nonfiction collection." Voice Youth Advocates

Cornell, Kari A.
  Cooking the Indonesian way; [by] Kari A. Cornell and Merry Anwar. Lerner Publications Company
2004 72p il (Easy menu ethnic cookbooks) lib bdg
$25.26
Grades: 5 6 7 8   641.5
  1. Indonesian cooking
  ISBN 978-0-8225-4127-1; 0-8225-4127-0
                                          LC 2003-11205
Introduces the land, people, and regional cooking of Indonesia and includes recipes for such dishes as pork sate,
corn fritters, and chicken in coconut cream sauce.
  Includes glossary

  Cooking the southern African way; by Kari Cornell in consultaiton with Peter Thomas. Lerner Publications Co. 2005 72p il map (Easy menu ethnic
cookbooks) lib bdg $25.26
Grades: 5 6 7 8   641.5
  1. South African cooking
  ISBN 978-0-8225-1239-4; 0-8225-1239-4
                                          LC 2004-11869
Introduces the history, land, and food of South Africa
and includes recipes.
  Includes glossary

D'Amico, Joan
  ★ The **coming** to America cookbook; delicious
recipes and fascinating stories from America's many
cultures. [by] Joan D'Amico, Karen Eich Drummond. Wiley 2005 180p il pa $14.95

Grades: 5 6 7 8   641.5
  1. Cooking
  ISBN 0-471-48335-4
                                          LC 2004-14947
The authors "provide information about American immigrants from 18 nations as well as recipes representing each
group. . . . Accompanied by line drawings of ethnic families
choosing, preparing, and eating food, . . . chapters discuss
each country's climate, history, major waves of emigration, and traditional foods. Typically, three recipes follow.
. . . Teachers and students looking for recipes from American immigrant cultures will make good use of this handy
resource." Booklist

Ejaz, Khadija
  Recipe and craft guide to India. Mitchell Lane
Publishers 2010 63p il map (World crafts and reci-
pes) lib bdg $33.95
Grades: 4 5 6 7 8   641.5
  1. Handicraft 2. Indic cooking
  ISBN 978-1-58415-938-4 lib bdg; 1-58415-938-3
  lib bdg
                                          LC 2010008950
Provides recipes for several popular Indian dishes and
includes instructions on creating colorful and traditional
Indian crafts.
  This provides "plenty of ideas for adding tasty
treats and impressive visual aids to cultural reports or
presentations." SLJ
  Includes glossary and bibliographical references

Gold, Rozanne
  ★ **Eat** fresh food; awesome recipes for teen
chefs. by Rozanne Gold and her all-star team; photographs by Phil Mansfield. Bloomsbury Children's
Books 2009 160p il $21.99; pa $17.99
Grades: 6 7 8 9 10   641.5
  1. Cooking
  ISBN 978-1-59990-282-1; 1-59990-282-6; 978-1-
  59990-445-0 pa; 1-59990-445-4 pa
                                          LC 2008-42443
"This joyful recipe book features fresh, healthful ingredients and encourages ambitious young chefs to collaborate
on such mature dishes as Grape-and-Pignoli Breakfast Cake,
Crunchy Wasabi-Lime Salmon with red cabbage and sugar
snaps and orange-ginger sweet potato puree. . . . A prime
pick for adventurous eaters and a potential catalyst for those
in a junk food rut." Publ Wkly

Gregory, Josh
  Chef. Cherry Lake Pub. 2011 32p il (Cool careers) lib bdg $27.07
Grades: 4 5 6 7   641.5
  1. Cooks 2. Cooking 3. Vocational guidance
  ISBN 978-1-60279-985-1; 1-60279-985-7
                                          LC 2010029085
This book begins "with a personal story of a teen and
then [segues] into the occupation [of chef]. . . . [It covers]
the necessary training and skills for the job (and options for
obtaining them), a typical day, salary expectations, and well-
known professionals in the field. The [text is] accessible and

clearly written. . . . The [volume has] a generous number of clear color photographs that depict people at work." SLJ

Includes glossary and bibliographical references

Hargittai, Magdolna

Cooking the Hungarian way; by Magdolna Hargittai. rev and expanded; Lerner Publications Co 2003 72p il map (Easy menu ethnic cookbooks) lib bdg $25.26

Grades: 5 6 7 8   641.5

1. Hungarian cooking

ISBN 978-0-8225-4132-5; 0-8225-4132-7

LC 2001-6612

First published 1986

An overview of Hungarian cookery, including information about the country's geography, history, holidays, and festivals. Features simple recipes, menu planning, and information about low-fat cooking and vegetarian options

Includes glossary and bibliographical references

How to cook; delicious dishes perfect for teen cooks. DK Pub. 2011 127p il $17.99

Grades: 7 8 9 10   641.5

1. Cooking

ISBN 978-0-7566-7214-0; 0-7566-7214-7

"This attractive book has dozens of recipes with an international flair. Some spreads feature a single dish, like lamb tagine, while others focus on several recipes using a single ingredient or technique. Experimentation is encouraged, and developing confidence is an unstated but obvious goal. This book is not for beginners, but teens with a bit of experience will enjoy trying the many tasty-sounding recipes for everything from jambalaya to macaroons. Vegetarian options are included throughout. Bright color photos show the finished dishes, and the pages are embellished with simple drawings showing processes and ingredients." SLJ

Includes glossary

Hughes, Helga

Cooking the Austrian way; [by] Helga Hughes. rev and expanded ed; Lerner Publications 2004 72p il map (Easy menu ethnic cookbooks) lib bdg $25.26

Grades: 5 6 7 8   641.5

1. Austrian cooking

ISBN 978-0-8225-4102-8; 0-8225-4102-5

LC 2002-152146

First published 1990

An introduction to the cooking of Austria including such traditional recipes as Wiener schnitzel, potato noodles, and Sacher cake. Also includes information on the geography, customs, and people of this European country

"Updated to include low-fat and vegetarian options. . . . Color photos and definitions of cooking terms and unusual ingredients will aid novice cooks." Horn Book Guide

Includes glossary

Jacob, Jeanne

The **world** cookbook for students; [by] Jeanne Jacob, Michael Ashkenazi. Greenwood Press 2007 5v il map set $225

Grades: 7 8 9 10 11 12   641.5

1. Cooking 2. Eating customs

ISBN 0-313-33454-4; 978-0-313-33454-2

LC 2006-26184

"The volumes are organized alphabetically by country or group name. Each entry includes a brief introduction to the land and people and their cuisine and then an overview of the foodstuffs, typical dishes, and styles of eating in simple bulleted lists. Approximately 5 recipes are provided per country/ethnic group of typical dishes and holiday fare, for a total of 1,198." Publisher's note

Includes bibliographical references

LaRoche, Amelia

Recipe and craft guide to France. Mitchell Lane Publishers 2010 63p il map (World crafts and recipes) lib bdg $33.95

Grades: 4 5 6 7 8   641.5

1. Handicraft 2. French cooking

ISBN 978-1-58415-936-0 lib bdg; 1-58415-936-7 lib bdg

LC 2010008949

Provides recipes for several popular French dishes and includes instructions on creating crafts using household items.

This provides "plenty of ideas for adding tasty treats and impressive visual aids to cultural reports or presentations." SLJ

Includes glossary and bibliographical references

Lagasse, Emeril

★ **Emeril's** there's a chef in my world! recipes that take you places. illustrated by Charles Yuen; photographs of Emeril Lagasse and children by Quentin Bacon. HarperCollins Publishers 2006 210p il $22.99

Grades: 5 6 7 8   641.5

1. Cooking 2. Cookery, International

ISBN 978-0-06-073926-3; 0-06-073926-6

LC 2005-15133

"The famous chef introduces dishes from around the world, dividing the recipes into familiar food categories—sweets, snacks, sandwiches, entrees, etc. . . . The recipes, from latkes to egg-drop soup, are good choices for open-minded eaters. . . . Many children will enjoy the mix of maps, flags, cartoon drawings, and color photos . . . and the cultural facts woven into each recipe." Booklist

Lee, Frances

Fun with Chinese cooking. PowerKids Press 2009 32p il (Let's get cooking!) lib bdg $18.95; pa $11.75

Grades: 4 5 6 7   641.5

1. Chinese cooking

ISBN 978-1-4358-3453-8 lib bdg; 1-4358-3453-4 lib bdg; 978-1-4358-3475-0 pa; 1-4358-3475-5 pa

LC 2009010337

This includes recipes for such Chinese dishes as spring rolls and braised mushrooms, and highlights the history and dishes that surround the Chinese New Year.

"The photography is exceptional, with children engaged in the cooking process. . . . Children, and the adults who assist them, will spend hours together mastering the techniques." SLJ

Locricchio, Matthew

The **2nd** international cookbook for kids; photographs by Jack McConnell. Marshall Cavendish 2008 176p il $18.99

Grades: 5 6 7 8   **641.5**
1. Cooking
ISBN 978-0-7614-5513-4

LC 2008003178

The recipes are "presented in a challenging yet teen-friendly step-by-step sequence. The book is best for patient chefs with kitchen experience and adventurous appetites. Informative sidebars provide facts about the recipes and cultures." Horn Book Guide

Teen cuisine; illustrated by Janet Hamlin; photographs by James Peterson. Marshall Cavendish Children 2010 207p il $22.95

Grades: 6 7 8 9 10   **641.5**
1. Cooking
ISBN 978-0-7614-5715-2; 0-7614-5715-1

LC 2009-46847

"This contemporary collection of recipes will appeal to teen cooks and would make a great gift or an excellent addition to a library's cookbook collection." Voice Youth Advocates

The **international** cookbook for kids; by Matthew Locricchio; photographs by Jack McConnell. Reprint Marshall Cavendish 2012 175p il $12.99

Grades: 5 6 7 8   **641.5**
1. Cooking 2. Cookery, International
ISBN 9780761463139

LC 2004-5894

This includes "60 classic recipes from Italy, France, China, and Mexico, . . . chef's tips discussing ingredients, nutrition, and technique, safety section discussing basic kitchen precautions, cooking terms and definitions." Publisher's note

Mattern, Joanne

Recipe and craft guide to China. Mitchell Lane Publishers 2010 63p il map (World crafts and recipes) lib bdg $33.95

Grades: 4 5 6 7 8   **641.5**
1. Handicraft 2. Chinese cooking
ISBN 978-1-58415-937-7 lib bdg; 1-58415-937-5 lib bdg

LC 2010009242

Provides recipes for several popular Chinese dishes and includes instructions on creating crafts using household items.

This provides "plenty of ideas for adding tasty treats and impressive visual aids to cultural reports or presentations." SLJ

Includes glossary and bibliographical references

Mofford, Juliet Haines

Recipe and craft guide to Japan. Mitchell Lane Publishers 2010 63p il map (World crafts and recipes) lib bdg $33.95

Grades: 4 5 6 7 8   **641.5**
1. Handicraft 2. Japanese cooking
ISBN 978-1-58415-933-9 lib bdg; 1-58415-933-2 lib bdg

LC 2010008951

Provides recipes for several popular Japanese dishes and includes instructions on creating traditional Japanese crafts using household items.

This provides "plenty of ideas for adding tasty treats and impressive visual aids to cultural reports or presentations." SLJ

Includes glossary and bibliographical references

Recipe and craft guide to the Caribbean. Mitchell Lane Publishers 2010 64p il map (World crafts and recipes) lib bdg $33.95

Grades: 4 5 6 7 8   **641.5**
1. Handicraft 2. Caribbean cooking
ISBN 978-1-58415-935-3 lib bdg; 1-58415-935-9 lib bdg

LC 2010009240

Provides recipes for several popular Caribbean dishes and includes instructions on creating traditional Caribbean crafts using household items.

This provides "plenty of ideas for adding tasty treats and impressive visual aids to cultural reports or presentations." SLJ

Includes glossary and bibliographical references

Paul, Anthea

★ **Girlosophy**: real girls eat. Allen & Unwin 2006 199p pa $19.95

Grades: 8 9 10 11 12   **641.5**
1. Cooking 2. Girls -- Health and hygiene
ISBN 1-74114-142-7

"Paul has created a gloriously photographed and superbly art-directed text." SLJ

Rau, Dana Meachen

Teen guide to breakfast on the go. Compass Point Books 2011 64p il (Teen cookbooks) lib bdg $33.99

Grades: 6 7 8 9   **641.5**
1. Cooking 2. Breakfasts
ISBN 978-0-7565-4407-2; 0-7565-4407-6

LC 2010038580

Information and recipes help readers create quick, healthy, and tasty breakfasts.

An overview "about produce, packaged foods, organics, and kitchen and food safety [sets] the tone for the rest of the content, which encourages kids to hit the kitchen and helps them to make good nutritional choices. . . . Suggestions for vegetarian options, prep time, and substitute ingredients pop up periodically. . . . [The] full-page color photographs make even a simple rice cake topped with cheese and a few apple slices look delectable." SLJ

Includes glossary and bibliographical references

Teen guide to creative, delightful dinners. Compass Point Books 2011 64p il (Teen cookbooks) lib bdg $33.99

Grades: 6 7 8 9   **641.5**

    1. Dining 2. Cooking

    ISBN 978-0-7565-4408-9; 0-7565-4408-4

                LC 2010040682

Information and recipes help readers create quick, healthy, and tasty dinners.

An overview "about produce, packaged foods, organics, and kitchen and food safety [sets] the tone for the rest of the content, which encourages kids to hit the kitchen and helps them to make good nutritional choices. . . . Suggestions for vegetarian options, prep time, and substitute ingredients pop up periodically. . . . [The] full-page color photographs make even a simple rice cake topped with cheese and a few apple slices look delectable." SLJ

Includes glossary and bibliographical references

Teen guide to fast, delicious lunches. Compass Point Books 2011 64p il (Teen cookbooks) lib bdg $33.99

Grades: 6 7 8 9   **641.5**

    1. Cooking 2. Luncheons

    ISBN 978-0-7565-4405-8; 0-7565-4405-X

                LC 2010040680

Information and recipes help readers create quick, healthy, and tasty lunches.

An overview "about produce, packaged foods, organics, and kitchen and food safety [sets] the tone for the rest of the content, which encourages kids to hit the kitchen and helps them to make good nutritional choices. . . . Suggestions for vegetarian options, prep time, and substitute ingredients pop up periodically. . . . [The] full-page color photographs make even a simple rice cake topped with cheese and a few apple slices look delectable." SLJ

Includes glossary and bibliographical references

Teen guide to quick, healthy snacks. Compass Point Books 2011 64p il (Teen cookbooks) lib bdg $33.99

Grades: 6 7 8 9   **641.5**

    1. Cooking 2. Snack foods

    ISBN 978-0-7565-4406-5; 0-7565-4406-8

                LC 2010040681

Information and recipes help readers create quick, healthy, and tasty snacks.

An overview "about produce, packaged foods, organics, and kitchen and food safety [sets] the tone for the rest of the content, which encourages kids to hit the kitchen and helps them to make good nutritional choices. . . . Suggestions for vegetarian options, prep time, and substitute ingredients pop up periodically. . . . [The] full-page color photographs make even a simple rice cake topped with cheese and a few apple slices look delectable." SLJ

Reusser, Kayleen

Recipe and craft guide to Indonesia. Mitchell Lane Publishers 2010 64p il map (World crafts and recipes) lib bdg $33.95

Grades: 4 5 6 7 8   **641.5**

    1. Handicraft 2. Indonesian cooking

    ISBN 978-1-58415-934-6 lib bdg; 1-58415-934-0 lib bdg

                LC 2010009243

Provides recipes for several popular Indonesian dishes and includes instructions on creating crafts using household items.

This provides "plenty of ideas for adding tasty treats and impressive visual aids to cultural reports or presentations." SLJ

Includes glossary and bibliographical references

Sheen, Barbara

Foods of Chile. KidHaven Press 2011 64p il map (A taste of culture) $28.75

Grades: 4 5 6   **641.5**

    1. Chilean cooking

    ISBN 978-0-7377-5421-6; 0-7377-5421-4

                LC 2010035995

"Demonstrating that a nation's cuisine springs from its geography, history, and traditions, [this volume explores Chile's background], the availability of fresh ingredients, and recipes that followed. . . . Culturally specific foods are described alongside some accompanying recipes and photos of people enjoying the dishes." Horn Book Guide

Includes glossary and bibliographical references

Foods of Cuba. KidHaven Press 2011 64p il map (A taste of culture) $28.75

Grades: 4 5 6   **641.5**

    1. Cuban cooking

    ISBN 978-0-7377-5113-0; 0-7377-5113-4

                LC 2010030795

"Demonstrating that a nation's cuisine springs from its geography, history, and traditions, [this volume explores Cuba's background], the availability of fresh ingredients, and recipes that followed. . . . Culturally specific foods are described alongside some accompanying recipes and photos of people enjoying the dishes." Horn Book Guide

Includes glossary and bibliographical references

Foods of Egypt. KidHaven Press 2010 64p il map (A taste of culture) $28.75

Grades: 4 5 6   **641.5**

    1. Egyptian cooking

    ISBN 978-0-7377-4843-7; 0-7377-4843-5

                LC 2009038461

"Sheen explores how different native dishes and types of local celebrations emerge from [Egypt's] culture and surroundings. [An] introductory [map] with a [key] to areas of food production illuminate the country's cuisine by identifying geographical landforms and climate. Traditions and tastes are described in accessible detail; key recipes are included and unfamiliar foods are pictured." Horn Book Guide

Includes glossary and bibliographical references

Foods of Ireland. KidHaven Press 2011 64p il map (A taste of culture) $28.75

Grades: 4 5 6   **641.5**
  1. Irish cooking
  ISBN 978-0-7377-5114-7; 0-7377-5114-2
                                                    LC 2010018791

"Sheen explores how different native dishes and types of local celebrations emerge from [Ireland's] culture and surroundings. [An] introductory [map] with a [key] to areas of food production illuminate the country's cuisine by identifying geographical landforms and climate. Traditions and tastes are described in accessible detail; key recipes are included and unfamiliar foods are pictured." Horn Book Guide
  Includes glossary and bibliographical references

Foods of Kenya. KidHaven Press 2010 64p il map (A taste of culture) $28.75

Grades: 4 5 6   **641.5**
  1. African cooking 2. Kenyan cooking
  ISBN 978-0-7377-4813-0; 0-7377-4813-3
                                                    LC 2009048378

"Sheen explores how different native dishes and types of local celebrations emerge from [Kenya's] culture and surroundings. [An] introductory [map] with a [key] to areas of food production illuminate the country's cuisine by identifying geographical landforms and climate. Traditions and tastes are described in accessible detail; key recipes are included and unfamiliar foods are pictured." Horn Book Guide
  Includes glossary and bibliographical references

Foods of Korea. KidHaven Press 2011 64p il map (A taste of culture) $26.75

Grades: 4 5 6   **641.5**
  1. Korean cooking
  ISBN 978-0-7377-5115-4; 0-7377-5115-0
                                                    LC 2010018789

"Demonstrating that a nation's cuisine springs from its geography, history, and traditions, [this volume explores Korea's background], the availability of fresh ingredients, and recipes that followed. . . . Culturally specific foods are described alongside some accompanying recipes and photos of people enjoying the dishes." Horn Book Guide
  Includes glossary and bibliographical references

Foods of Peru. KidHaven Press 2011 64p il map (A taste of culture) $28.75

Grades: 4 5 6   **641.5**
  1. Peruvian cooking
  ISBN 978-0-7377-5346-2; 0-7377-5346-3
                                                    LC 2010032959

"Demonstrating that a nation's cuisine springs from its geography, history, and traditions, [this volume explores Peru's background], the availability of fresh ingredients, and recipes that followed. . . . Culturally specific foods are described alongside some accompanying recipes and photos of people enjoying the dishes." Horn Book Guide
  Includes glossary and bibliographical references

Smart, Denise

The **cookbook** for girls; written by Denise Smart; photography by Howard Shooter. DK Pub. 2009 128p il $17.99

Grades: 4 5 6   **641.5**
  1. Cooking
  ISBN 978-0-7566-4500-7; 0-7566-4500-X

"The photos alone make this attractive cookbook worth the price of admission. . . . Most of these dishes will appeal to adventurous eaters and their foodie parents." SLJ

Stern, Sam

Real food, real fast; [by] Sam Stern & Susan Stern. Candlewick Press 2008 128p il $16.99

Grades: 6 7 8 9   **641.5**
  1. Cooking
  ISBN 978-0-7636-3533-6; 0-7636-3533-2
                                                    LC 2007025635

"This book is full of time-management advice, recipes, and tips for combining dishes. Cross-references enable novices to put together full meals, and the index encourages browsing by ingredient or type of recipe. . . . Each recipe includes serving sizes, variations to adapt the recipes to one's own taste, pictures of the author and friends, and often pictures of the finished product. The directions are easy. . . . A teen-friendly guide to healthy eating, featuring foods that are fast and easy to make." SLJ

Sam Stern's get cooking. Candlewick Press 2009 144p $17.99

Grades: 6 7 8 9   **641.5**
  1. Cooking
  ISBN 978-0-7636-3926-6; 0-7636-3926-5

British teenage cook Sam Stern presents over 100 new recipes based on his own favorite ingredient, chocolate, and the favorite ingredients of seven of his friends.

"Stern does an excellent job of introducing teens to the kitchen. . . . Every page boasts bright colors and pictures with large print and a user-friendly ingredients list in sidebar format. The recipes run from very easy to a bit challenging, but the step-by-step directions will help even the most challenged cook find a way around the kitchen." Voice Youth Advocates

Traugh, Susan M.

Vegetarianism. Lucent Books 2011 96p il (Nutrition & health) lib bdg $30.85

Grades: 6 7 8 9   **641.5**
  1. Vegetarianism
  ISBN 978-1-4205-0272-5; 1-4205-0272-7
                                                    LC 2010014015

This "explains the different types of vegetarians, from ovo-lacto to vegan, touches briefly on the lifestyle's difficulties, and depicts in an overall positive way why it is a healthy choice. [This] volume is clearly written, addressing real-life concerns with solid information and perspective, and includes color photographs, notes, and [a list] of further resources." Booklist
  Includes bibliographical references

Webb, Lois Sinaiko

Holidays of the world cookbook for students; [by] Lois Sinaiko Webb and Lindsay Grace Roten. updated and rev.; Greenwood 2011 442p il map $95; pa $32.95

Grades: 5 6 7 8 9 10   **641.5**
1. Cooking 2. Holidays
ISBN 978-0-313-38393-9; 0-313-38393-6; 978-0-313-39790-5 pa; 0-313-39790-2 pa; 978-0-313-38394-6 ebook

LC 2011-8458

First published 1995 by Oryx Press

"The recipes appear with each country entry, and the countries are arranged in alphabetical order within each region: Africa, Asia and the South Pacific, the Caribbean, Europe, Latin America, the Middle East, and North America." Publisher's note

The **multicultural** cookbook for students; [by] Lois Sinaiko Webb and Lindsay Grace Roten. Updated & rev.; Greenwood Press 2009 354p map $85
Grades: 7 8 9 10   **641.5**
1. Cooking
ISBN 978-0-313-37558-3; 0-313-37558-5

LC 2009-26718

First published 1993 under the authorship of Carole Lisa Albyn

"This highly informative cookbook includes not only recipes, but also information on the country, its food staples, and ethnic and cultural divisions. Recipes are divided into seven sections according to geography: Africa, Asia and South Pacific, The Caribbean, Europe, Latin America, The Middle East, and North America. . . . Recipes are then divided by country with a description of the country concentrating on culinary information. A minimum of two recipes per country are also annotated with information about the ingredients or why the dish was important to the area. . . . This book is a great resource for cultural research even if the actual recipes will not be prepared. There is a comprehensive index by recipe name, country, and ingredients." Libr Media Connect

Includes glossary and bibliographical references

641.509   History, geographic treatment, biography

Abrams, Dennis
Julia Child, chef; by Dennis Abrams. Chelsea House 2011 134 p. ill. (some col.) $35.00
Grades: 6 7 8 9   **641.509**
1. Cooks 2. Women -- United States -- Biography 3. Cooks -- United States -- Biography
ISBN 9781604139129

LC 2011000039

'This book offers a biography of chef "Julia Child . . . [who] started a cooking revolution when she burst onto television screens in the 1960s. Before long, Americans inspired by her example began cooking French food at home in droves and truly appreciating the pleasure that preparing good food can provide. Yet Child did not grow up knowing how to cook or even with an interest in fine cuisine. Her story is one of an American woman's quest to find herself, to find her passion, and then to find a way to share that passion with the world. It is the story of how Julia McWilliams of

Pasadena, California, transformed herself into Julia Child, 'The French Chef.'" (Publisher's note)

Includes bibliographical references and index

641.59   Cooking characteristic of specific geographic environments, ethnic cooking

D'Amico, Joan
The **United** States cookbook; fabulous foods and fascinating facts from all 50 states. [by] Joan D'Amico and Karen Eich Drummond; illustrations by Jeff Cline and Tina Cash-Walsh. Wiley 2000 186p il pa $12.95
Grades: 5 6 7 8   **641.59**
1. Cooking 2. Cookery, American 3. Cookery -- United States
ISBN 0-471-35839-8

LC 99-39548

Provides information about the fifty states along with a recipe native to each of them, such as Boston baked beans from Massachusetts, crab cakes from Maryland, Key lime pie from Florida, corn dogs from Iowa, and taco soup from New Mexico

"There are helpful sections on the use of equipment; cooking skills, such as cutting, measuring, and mixing, and safety rules." SLJ

641.598   Cooking -- South America

Locricchio, Matthew
The **cooking** of Brazil; Matthew Locricchio; with photos by Jack McConnell. 2nd ed. Marshall Cavendish Benchmark 2012 96 p. ill. (library) $35.64; (ebook) $35.64
Grades: 7 8 9 10 11 12   **641.598**
1. Cookbooks 2. Brazilian cooking 3. Cooking 4. Food -- Brazil 5. Cooking, Brazilian
ISBN 1608705498; 9781608705498; 9781608707379

LC 2011004948

This book, by Matthew Locricchio, "invites . . . readers to the kitchen to experience the satisfaction of preparing authentic [Brazilian] recipes." The book "opens with a . . . look at the . . . country and their culinary traditions and contributions to international cuisine. This cultural introduction is followed with an overview of kitchen safety, food handling, and common sense nutrition, then on to a wide variety of recipes that range from soups and salads to main entrees and desserts." (Publisher's note)

Includes bibliographical references and index.

641.6   Cooking specific materials

Llewellyn, Claire
Cooking with meat and fish; [by] Claire Llewellyn, Clare O'Shea. Rosen Central 2011 48p il map (Cooking healthy) lib bdg $27.95

Grades: 5 6 7 8   **641.6**
1. Meat 2. Cooking 3. Seafood
ISBN 978-1-4488-4845-4; 1-4488-4845-8
LC 2010039337

A description of each type of meat and fish, how to cook them in a healthy manner, and recipe examples of each.

This book pairs "facts about [meat and fish], including where it is eaten, with eye-catching photos. . . . Each course (section) has an overview of the . . . [meat] followed by recipes from all over the world. They vary in difficulty. . . . The cooking directions are clear and straightforward. . . . [The book is] profusely illustrated with full-color photos. Students who are learning to cook will appreciate [this] excellently organized [read]." SLJ

Includes glossary and bibliographical references

641.8   Cooking specific kinds of dishes and preparing beverages

Carle, Megan
Teens cook dessert; [by] Megan and Jill Carle, with Judi Carle. Ten Speed Press 2006 158p pa $19.95
Grades: 6 7 8 9 10   **641.8**
1. Cooking 2. Desserts
ISBN 978-1-58008-752-0; 1-58008-752-3
LC 2005-24343

The authors "start out with the all-around favorites, like classic chocolate chip cookies. There are holiday recipes for Halloween dirt pie, complete with cookie tombstones and gummy worms that seem to crawl out of the chocolate 'earth.' The final chapter has fancy foods like vanilla soufflt with chocolate sauce or fresh raspberry napoleons. . . . Not only do the recipes sound delicious, they look delicious in glossy color pictures. . . . The instructions are easy to understand." Voice Youth Advocates

Love, Ann
Sweet! the delicious story of candy. [by] Ann Love & Jane Drake; illustrated by Claudia Dávila. Tundra Books 2007 64p il map $19.95
Grades: 4 5 6 7   **641.8**
1. Candy
ISBN 978-0-88776-752-4

"This history of things sweet and sugary is a yummy feast. The prose is chatty and inviting. Color cartoon illustrations show multiethnic people in the process of making or enjoying everything from honey to ice cream to cotton candy (called candy floss here) to jelly beans and chocolate." SLJ

646.2   Sewing and related operations

Plumley, Amie Petronis
Sewing school; 21 sewing projects kids will love to make. [by] Amie Petronis Plumley & Andria Lisle; photography by Justin Fox Burks. Storey Pub. 2010 143p il $16.95

Grades: 3 4 5 6   **646.2**
1. Sewing
ISBN 978-1-60342-578-0; 1-60342-578-0
LC 2010022154

"This large-format book offers appealing projects illustrated with color photos of step-by-step directions as well as kids engaged in sewing and showing off work. The opening 12 lessons begin with topics such as threading a needle, knotting the thread, and making a basic running stitch. After covering basic knowledge and skills, the presentation moves on to instructions for fun easy projects." Booklist

646.4   Clothing and accessories construction

Torres, Laura
Rock your wardrobe. QEB Pub. 2010 32p il (Rock your . . .) lib bdg $28.50
Grades: 4 5 6   **646.4**
1. Fashion 2. Handicraft 3. Clothing and dress
ISBN 978-1-59566-937-7; 1-59566-937-X
LC 2010010671

This book "gives kids easy step-by-step ways to . . . fashion clothes with simple, easily found scraps and a little glue and paint. Colorful photographs show youngsters crafting appealing T-shirts . . . etc., some of which are created from recycled found items. All are projects they can complete by themselves." Horn Book Guide

Zent, Sheila
Sew teen; make your own cool clothes. Sterling 2006 160p il pa $17.95
Grades: 7 8 9 10   **646.4**
1. Sewing 2. Clothing and dress
ISBN 1-931543-90-9

"Zent presents 21 projects and accessory designs that will appeal to budding seamstresses and novice stitchers alike, although teens should know the basics of using a sewing machine or have assistance. . . . The step-by-step instructions include drawn renderings to assist with the construction and full-color photographs of teen models wearing each garment or accessory." SLJ

646.7   Management of personal and family life

Bergamotto, Lori
Skin; the bare facts. Zest Books 2009 97p il pa $18.95
Grades: 6 7 8 9 10   **646.7**
1. Skin -- Care 2. Teenagers -- Health and hygiene
ISBN 978-0-9800732-5-6; 0-9800732-5-1

Presents an overview on skin types, methods for treating common problems, and tips for skin care and makeup application.

"There's something for every girl here, whether she's just had her first breakout or needs a refresher on which sunscreen to use and when to reapply." SLJ

Buchholz, Rachel

How to survive anything; shark attack, quicksand, embarrassing parents, pop quizzes, and other perilous situations. illustrations by Chris Philpot. National Geographic 2011 176p il (National geographic kids) pa $12.95

Grades: 5 6 7 8   **646.7**

   1. Life skills 2. Survival skills

   ISBN 978-1-4263-0774-4; 1-4263-0774-8

                           LC 2010028045

"Buchholz doles out hilarious and handy advice for suffering though both natural and manmade catastrophes. Part survival guide and part self-help book, it provides honest, tongue-in-cheek answers to questions teens may be reluctant to ask out loud, in addition to imparting disaster preparedness strategies. It's a clever, winning combination. Superb full-color digital illustrations and photographs and a lively, conversational tone will catch and keep readers' attention, and the list-heavy layout is fun to read and easy to understand." SLJ

Ehrman, M. K.

★ **Taking** a stand; being a leader & helping others. ABDO Pub. Co. 2009 112p il (Essential health: strong beautiful girls) lib bdg $22.95

Grades: 6 7 8 9   **646.7**

   1. Leadership 2. Life skills 3. Attitude (Psychology)

   ISBN 978-1-60453-105-3 lib bdg; 1-60453-105-3 lib bdg

                           LC 2008-15211

This features fictional narratives paired with firsthand advice from a licensed psychologist to help preteen and teen girls evaluate success and build leadership skills. Topics include the challenges of competition, and taking on too much.

"The topics are well selected, the design is attractive, and the stories feature girls from a variety of cultures." Booklist

Includes glossary and bibliographical references

Fornay, Alfred

Born beautiful; the African American teenager's complete beauty guide. John Wiley & Sons 2002 166p il pa $14.95

Grades: 8 9 10 11 12   **646.7**

   1. Personal grooming 2. Personal appearance 3. Teenagers -- Health and hygiene 4. African American women -- Health and hygiene

   ISBN 0-471-40275-3

                           LC 2002-18131

This book on beauty and grooming for African American teenage girls includes information on makeup, hairstyles, nail and skin care, diet, and clothing.

Harris, Ashley Rae

★ **Is** this really my family? relating to your relatives. ABDO Pub. Co. 2009 112p il (Essential health: strong, beautiful girls) lib bdg $22.95

Grades: 6 7 8 9   **646.7**

   1. Family 2. Parent-child relationship

   ISBN 978-1-60453-101-5 lib bdg; 1-60453-101-0 lib bdg

                           LC 2008-12105

Presents character narratives and discussion questions to help teenage girls develop positive ways to build healthy relationships with members of their immediate family.

"The topics are well selected, the design is attractive, and the stories feature girls from a variety of cultures." Booklist

Includes glossary and bibliographical references

Heos, Bridget

A **career** as a hairstylist. Rosen 2010 80p il (Essential careers) lib bdg $30.60

Grades: 7 8 9 10 11 12   **646.7**

   1. Hairstylists 2. Vocational guidance

   ISBN 978-1-4358-9474-7 lib bdg; 1-4358-9474-X lib bdg

This title "is so informative it could be subtitled 'Everything You Want to Know about Becoming a Hair Stylist.' . . . After the basics, Heos discusses the nitty-gritty of finding a job, keeping it, and running one's own business. The history of hair-cutting careers follows, and there are even ethical discussions. . . . A must for career shelves." Booklist

Jeffrie, Sally

The **girls'** book of glamour; a guide to being a goddess. 1st American ed.; Scholastic, Inc. 2009 126p il $9.99

Grades: 6 7 8 9 10   **646.7**

   1. Girls 2. Etiquette 3. Life skills

   ISBN 978-0-545-08537-3; 0-545-08537-3

                           LC 2008-17119

First published 2008 in the United Kingdom

This is "focused on lifestyle, health, and beauty. Each entry has simple instructions accompanied by entertaining illustrations. This upbeat and amusing style guide adopts a hip tone for the tween and young-teen set. . . . Jeffrie's snappy writing and Ryan's great line drawings and stylish design make [this] an easy, breezy read." SLJ

Morgenstern, Julie

★ **Organizing** from the inside out for teens; the foolproof system for organizing your room, your time, and your life. [by] Julie Morgenstern and Jessi Morgenstern-Colón; illustrations by Janet Pedersen. Holt & Co. 2002 238p il pa $15

Grades: 7 8 9 10   **646.7**

   1. Life skills 2. Orderliness 3. Time management 4. Teenagers -- Life skills guides

   ISBN 0-8050-6470-2

                           LC 2002-68552

The authors "offer practical advice to teenagers who want to get organized. After considering what might be holding them back and the three steps to success (analyze, strategize, attack), the discussion shifts to the two major areas of concern: managing space and managing time. . . . Useful advice in an accessible paperback format." Booklist

Rosenwald, Laurie

★ **All** the wrong people have self esteem; an inappropriate book for young ladies (or, frankly, anybody else) Bloomsbury Children's Books 2008 un il $16.99

Grades: 6 7 8 9 **646.7**
1. Life skills 2. Teenage girls -- Life skills guides
ISBN 978-1-59990-240-1; 1-59990-240-0
LC 2008-14386

Rosenwald "tackles political correctness, the follies of prevailing wisdom and her favorite peeves using all the tools in her arsenal: her spread-size collages feature fonts on sterioids, magazine cut-outs, photos and cartoons paired with witty diatribes confessions. . . . Funny, fresh and impossible not to read cover to cover." Publ Wkly

Buchanan, Andrea J.
The **daring** book for girls; Andrea Buchanan, Miriam Peskowitz; illustrated by Alexis Seabrook. 1st ed. Collins 2007 viii, 279 p.p ill. (some col.), col. map (hardcover) $26.95
Grades: 4 5 6 7 8 9 **646.7**
1. Girls 2. Amusements 3. Recreation 4. Curiosities and wonders 5. Girls in literature 6. Girls -- Life skills guides
ISBN 0061472573; 9780061472572
LC 2007031986

This book is "filled with interesting activities to try and important facts [girls] may not know, but are sure to keep them busy for hours. The authors cover everything from making a lemon-powered clock to the history of writing and cursive, from how to paddle a canoe to the Periodic Table of the Elements." (School Library Journal)

Includes bibliographical references (p. 274-276).

649   Child rearing; home care of people with disabilities and illnesses

Buckley, Annie
Be a better babysitter; by Annie Buckley. Child's World 2007 32p il (Girls rock!) lib bdg $24.21
Grades: 5 6 7 8 **649**
1. Babysitting
ISBN 1-59296-740-X
LC 2006001639

This "describes what babysitting entails, examines pros and cons, discusses safety issues, offers tips for doing a good job, and suggests saving as much as half of any money earned. . . . [This] realistic [title is] well written and [provides] excellent information." SLJ

Includes bibliographical references

Chasse, Jill D.
The **babysitter's** survival guide; fun games, cool crafts, and how to be the best babysitter in town. illustrated by Jessica Secheret. Sterling Pub. Co. 2010 107p il $12.95
Grades: 5 6 7 8 **649**
1. Babysitting
ISBN 978-1-4027-4654-3; 1-4027-4654-7
LC 2009-2538

"This useful, up-to-date handbook offers plenty of practical advice with a wise emphasis on safety, which makes it a good choice for new sitters as well as those with experience. Chassé starts with information on starting a business, includ-

ing references, advertising, and interviewing. Child development is a main focus; suggested activities and tips on interaction with children at different developmental stages will be appreciated by sitters and parents alike. . . . Occasional two-color cartoons feature diverse children and sitters." SLJ

Includes bibliographical references

Crissey, Pat
Personal hygiene? What's that got to do with me? Jessica Kingsley 2005 94p il pa $19.95
Grades: 5 6 7 **649**
1. Autism 2. Hygiene 3. Asperger's syndrome
ISBN 978-1-8431-0796-5; 1-8431-0796-1
LC 2004-24966

Explains the importance of personal hygiene to children with autism and asperger's syndrome.

649.1   Child rearing

Bondy, Halley
Don't sit on the baby; the ultimate guide to sane, skilled, and safe babysitting. Halley Bondy. Zest Books 2012 127 p. (pbk.) $12.99
Grades: 7 8 9 10 11 12 **649.1**
1. Child care 2. Babysitting 3. Infants -- Care
ISBN 0982732236; 9780982732236
LC 2011942757

This book is a "how to guide [that] covers everything . . . that a teen might need to know to become a babysitter. The first section covers topics such as . . . what to expect from kids ages newborn to ten. Section two covers essential skills such as feeding, dressing, playing, bathing, bedtime, and keeping kids healthy. The final section includes tips on how to get a job, how to interview, how much to charge, and even how to quit a job." (Children's Literature)

Includes web resources and index.

650.1   Personal success in business

Fischer, James
Earning money; jobs. Mason Crest Publishers 2011 64p il (Junior library of money) $22.95
Grades: 6 7 8 9 **650.1**
1. Work 2. Employment 3. Job hunting
ISBN 978-1-4222-1763-4; 1-4222-1763-9
LC 2010-28156

"Teens learn why working is important and how to find the right job, including what steps to take in preparation and what is expected of them once they have a job. . . . This . . . is stunning, with vivid color illustrations on every page. Each subtopic is covered in a two-page spread that features bold graphics and bright colors. This succinct and visually appealing coverage is sure to fit the attention span of students." Voice Youth Advocates

Includes glossary and bibliographical references

Harmon, Dan

First job smarts; by Daniel E. Harmon. Rosen Pub. 2010 64p il (Get smart with your money) lib bdg $29.95; pa $12.95

Grades: 7 8 9 10 11 12   **650.1**
1. Personal finance 2. Part-time employment 3. Teenagers -- Employment
ISBN 978-1-4358-5268-6 lib bdg; 1-4358-5268-0 lib bdg; 978-1-4358-5542-7 pa; 1-4358-5542-6 pa
        LC 2008-42892

This offers information on topics such as income tax and saving and investing.

This offers "practical information and advice. The writing is accessible. . . . [The book is] heavily illustrated with large, clear, up-to-date photographs of teens." SLJ

Includes glossary and bibliographical references

652   Processes of written communication

Bell-Rehwoldt, Sheri

Speaking secret codes. Capstone Press 2010 32p il (Edge books: making and breaking codes) lib bdg $26.65

Grades: 4 5 6 7   **652**
1. Ciphers 2. Cryptography
ISBN 978-1-4296-4569-0 lib bdg; 1-4296-4569-5 lib bdg
        LC 2010004163

"Spoken codes in history, including the Underground Railroad and POWs during the Vietnam War, are introduced by using various examples of word substitutions. Educators will appreciate the concise information provided by codes that have shaped world history. . . . Historical photographs, highlighted vocabulary words and definitions, and do-it-yourself suggestions will keep readers interested." SLJ

Includes glossary and bibliographical references

Blackwood, Gary L.

Mysterious messages; a history of codes and ciphers. [by] Gary Blackwood; designed and illustrated by Jason Henry. Dutton Children's Books 2009 170p il $16.99

Grades: 5 6 7 8   **652**
1. Ciphers 2. Cryptography
ISBN 978-0-525-47960-4; 0-525-47960-0
        LC 2008-48970

"This well-written history of cryptography begins with a pottery-glaze formula encrypted in cuneiform on a clay tablet (1500 BCE) and traces the uses of secret messages in statecraft, espionage, warfare, crime, literature, and business up to the present. Along the way, Blackwood . . . discusses the historical development of coding and encryption and tells many good stories of messages ciphered and deciphered. . . . The many sidebars and illustrations, including photos, reproductions of artworks and artifacts, and the pictures demonstrating the codes themselves, contribute to the book's approachable look." Booklist

Gregory, Jillian

Breaking secret codes. Capstone Press 2010 32p il (Edge books: making and breaking codes) lib bdg $26.65

Grades: 4 5 6 7   **652**
1. Ciphers 2. Cryptography
ISBN 978-1-4296-4568-3 lib bdg; 1-4296-4568-7 lib bdg
        LC 2010004162

"Educators will appreciate the concise information provided by codes that have shaped world history. Sample cryptographs are scattered throughout the pages, along with other noteworthy facts. Historical photographs, highlighted vocabulary words and definitions, and do-it-yourself suggestions will keep readers interested." SLJ

Includes glossary and bibliographical references

Making secret codes. Capstone Press 2010 32p il (Edge books: making and breaking codes) lib bdg $26.65

Grades: 4 5 6 7   **652**
1. Ciphers 2. Cryptography
ISBN 978-1-4296-4567-6 lib bdg; 1-4296-4567-9 lib bdg
        LC 2010004161

"Educators will appreciate the concise information provided by codes that have shaped world history. Sample cryptographs are scattered throughout the pages, along with other noteworthy facts. Historical photographs, highlighted vocabulary words and definitions, and do-it-yourself suggestions will keep readers interested." SLJ

Includes glossary and bibliographical references

Mitchell, Susan K.

Spy codes and ciphers. Enslow Publishers 2011 48p il (The secret world of spies) lib bdg $23.93

Grades: 4 5 6   **652**
1. Spies 2. Ciphers 3. Espionage 4. Cryptography
ISBN 978-0-7660-3709-0
        LC 2010006176

Discusses different methods of secret communications used by spies, such as Morse code, the Enigma machine, the Najavo language, and digital steganography, and includes career information.

Includes glossary and bibliographical references

Pincock, Stephen

★ **Codebreaker**; the history of codes and ciphers, from the ancient pharaohs to quantum cryptography. 1st U.S. ed; Walker 2006 176p il $19.95

Grades: 6 7 8 9   **652**
1. Ciphers 2. Cryptography
ISBN 978-0-8027-1547-0; 0-8027-1547-8
        LC 2007310362

"Pincock's fascinating book reveals to the reader that codes and ciphers have been used by pharaohs, queens, generals, politicians, and lovers for at least 4,000 years. . . . Beautifully written, entertaining but never shallow, and replete with fascinating insights into the arcane world of cryptography, Codebreaker is that rare work—a nonfiction title that is as appealing as a fast-paced thriller. It should

be an essential purchase for libraries serving young adults."
Voice Youth Advocates

Includes bibliographical references

658   General management

Andrews, David

Business without borders; globalization. Heinemann Library 2010 56p il map (The global marketplace) lib bdg $33.50

Grades: 6 7 8 9   658

1. Globalization 2. International trade
ISBN 978-1-4329-3933-5 lib bdg; 1-4329-3933-5
lib bdg

LC 2010004097

This title covers "a wealth of material in concise paragraphs with pertinent subheadings. . . . [It has] clearly written, accessible content. It touches on currency, global trade,
and purchasing power, and stresses that globalization is 'a
process that is still going on today.'" SLJ

Includes glossary and bibliographical references

Bochner, Arthur Berg

The **new** totally awesome business book for kids
(and their parents) with twenty super businesses you
can start right now! [by] Arthur Bochner & Rose
Bochner; foreword by Andriane G. Berg. rev and updated 3rd ed.; Newmarket Press 2007 188p il pa
$9.95

Grades: 4 5 6 7   658

1. Small business 2. Money-making projects for
children
ISBN 978-1-55704-757-1 pa; 1-55704-757-X pa

LC 2007002637

First published 1995 with title: The totally awesome
business book for kids

A comprehensive look at the basic financial and management aspects of moneymaking businesses for children

"This book can certainly be thought provoking for young
people with an entrepreneurial spirit. . . . The illustrations
are lively and engaging, and the text non-threatening." Voice
Youth Advocates

Includes bibliographical references

658.1   Organization and financial management

Bielagus, Peter G.

Quick cash for teens; be your own boss and make
big bucks. Sterling Pub. 2009 249p pa $12.95

Grades: 7 8 9 10 11 12   658.1

1. Small business 2. Entrepreneurship 3. Money-
making projects for children
ISBN 978-1-4027-6038-9; 1-4027-6038-8

LC 2008-42793

"Young entrepreneurs wanting to own and operate their
own businesses will find this practical, introductory guide an
excellent source of advice. . . . Bielagus' conversational style
and the frequent insertion of anecdotes from successful teen
entrepreneurs make the text accessible." Booklist

658.8   Management of marketing

Weinick, Suzanne

Increasing your tweets, likes, and ratings; marketing your digital business. Suzanne Weinick. 1st
ed. Rosen Pub. 2013 64 p. col. ill. (Digital entrepreneurship in the age of apps, the web, and mobile
devices) (library) $31.95; (paperback) $12.95

Grades: 8 9 10 11 12   658.8

1. Marketing 2. Social media 3. Internet marketing 4.
Electronic commerce -- Marketing
ISBN 1448869285; 9781448869282; 9781448869763;
9781448869770

LC 2012006836

This "entry in the . . . Digital Entrepreneurship in the
Age of Apps, the Web, and Mobile Devices series . . . focuses on marketing minutiae, including giving your app a
savvy name, choosing a useful Twitter image, monitoring
your Facebook page, vlogging, and knowing your SEO
[search engine optimization] from your PPC [pay per click]
and CPM [cost per impression]." (Booklist)

Includes bibliographical references (p. 57-62) and index.

659.1   Advertising

Beker, Jeanne

Strutting it! the grit behind the glamour. Tundra
Books 2011 78p il pa $17.95

Grades: 6 7 8 9   659.1

1. Fashion models 2. Vocational guidance 3. Modeling
ISBN 978-1-77049-224-0 pa; 1-77049-224-0 pa

"Beker—for 25 years a host of Canada's Fashion Television—distills the essence of her many years of experience as
a model-watcher into this slim but engaging combination of
advice, history and truth-telling. Each chapter showcases a
different aspect of a model's career development. . . . Bless-
edly responsible and sane, a worthy title for any career collection for teens and a must for aspiring models." Kirkus

660.6   Biotechnology

Biotechnology: changing life through science; [by]
K. Lee Lerner and Brenda Wilmoth Lerner, editors. Thomson/Gale 2007 3v il set $196

Grades: 8 9 10 11 12   660.6

1. Biotechnology 2. Reference books
ISBN 978-1-4144-0151-5

"This set introduces students to the science of biotechnology, the issues pertaining to biotechnology, and how the
issues impact society. . . . The clean layout features more
than 150 color photographs as well as many diagrams and
boxed areas. . . . The articles contain more than enough information to meet the needs of younger students as well as
general readers." Booklist

Aldridge, Susan

Cloning. New Forest Press 2010 64p il (Cutting-edge science) $34.25

Grades: 7 8 9 10   660.6
1. Cloning
ISBN 978-1-84898-326-7; 1-84898-326-3

"Beginning with a description of cell division and cloning in nature, [this book] continues with the differences between cloning plants and more complex animals. . . . In a
balanced treatment of the topic, Aldridge explains both the
ethical debate surrounding stem cell research and human
cloning and the possibilities of stem cell therapy to treat de-
generative diseases. . . . The presentation is effective, with
an attractive and colorful layout featuring photographs of
various cells, chromosomes, and actual cloned animals. . . .
Equally enticing and informational." Booklist

George, Charles

Biotech research; by Charles and Linda George.
ReferencePoint Press 2012 96 p. (Inside science)
(hardback) $27.95
Grades: 6 7 8 9 10 11 12   660.6
1. Discoveries in science 2. Biotechnology
ISBN 1601521766; 9781601521767

LC 2011007744

This juvenile academic book, by Charles George and
Linda George, presents an overview of bio-technological
research in the 21st century. "Biotech research has expanded
exponentially since the mapping of the Human Genome.
This knowledge drives the research toward finding genetic
causes and cures for thousands of human conditions and diseases, and toward enhancing agricultural products, improving industrial processes, and toward environmental reclamation and conservation." (Publisher's note)

Includes bibliographical references and index

664   Food technology

Aronson, Marc

★ **Sugar** changed the world; a story of magic,
spice, slavery, freedom, and science. by Marc Aronson and Marina Budhos. Clarion Books 2010 166p
il map $20.00
Grades: 7 8 9 10 11 12   664
1. Slavery 2. World history 3. Sugar -- History 5.
Sugar trade
ISBN 0618574921; 9780618574926

LC 2009033579

The book discusses the history of sweet substances.
"Sugar was the substance that drove the bloody slave trade
and caused the loss of countless lives but it also planted the
seeds of revolution that led to freedom in the American colonies, Haiti, and France." (Publisher's note)

"From 1600 to the 1800s, sugar drove the economies
of Europe, the Americas, Asia and Africa and did more 'to
reshape the world than any ruler, empire, or war had ever
done.' Millions of people were taken from Africa and enslaved to work the sugar plantations throughout the Caribbean, worked to death to supply the demand for sugar in
Europe. . . . Maps, photographs and archival illustrations,
all with captions that are informative in their own right,
richly complement the text, and superb documentation and

an essay addressed to teachers round out the fascinating
volume." Kirkus

Includes bibliographical references

Gardner, Robert

Ace your food science project; great science fair
ideas. [by] Robert Gardner, Salvatore Tocci, and
Thomas R. Rybolt. Enslow Publishers 2009 128p il
(Ace your science project) lib bdg $31.93
Grades: 5 6 7 8   664
1. Food 2. Science projects 3. Science -- Experiments
ISBN 978-0-7660-3228-6 lib bdg; 0-7660-3228-0
lib bdg

LC 2008-49780

"Presents several science experiments and project ideas
using food." Publisher's note

Includes bibliographical references

665   Technology of industrial oils, fats, waxes, gases

Walker, Niki

Hydrogen; running on water. [by] Niki Walker.
Crabtree Pub. 2007 32p il (Energy revolution) lib
bdg $25.20; pa $8.95
Grades: 5 6 7 8   665
1. Hydrogen as fuel
ISBN 978-0-7787-2915-0 lib bdg; 0-7787-2915-X lib
bdg; 978-0-7787-2929-7 pa; 0-7787-2929-X pa

LC 2006014369

This describes various sources of hydrogen power, including natural gas, gasified coal, fuel from water, and biomass gas, and how it is stored and distributed, and offers
energy conservation tips.

Includes glossary

668.4   Plastics

Morris, Neil

Plastics. Amicus 2010 48p il (Materials that
matter) lib bdg $28.50
Grades: 4 5 6 7   668.4
1. Plastics
ISBN 978-1-60753-068-8 lib bdg; 1-60753-068-6
lib bdg

LC 2009051435

"The clean layout includes photographs and occasional
charts, graphs, and technical illustrations against a range of
pastel backgrounds. Inset boxes provide further detail, interesting extras, and recycling information. . . . [This book
offers] easily accessible background information for report
writers." SLJ

Includes glossary and bibliographical references

670 Manufacturing

Slavin, Bill

Transformed; how everyday things are made. written by Bill Slavin with Jim Slavin; illustrated by Bill Slavin. Kids Can Press 2005 160p il $24.95

Grades: 4 5 6 7 **670**

1. Manufactures
ISBN 1-55337-179-8

This describes the manufacture of such items "as baseballs, plastic dinosaurs, toothpaste, cereal, paper, and bricks. Each two-page spread covers the making of one of the 69 items in numbered paragraphs. The pictures are the best part—clear watercolor and ink images, made all the more engaging by folks in overalls directing the action." Booklist

Includes glossary and bibliographical references

676 Pulp and paper technology

Morris, Neil

Paper. Amicus 2010 48p il (Materials that matter) lib bdg $28.50

Grades: 4 5 6 7 **676**

1. Paper
ISBN 978-1-60753-067-1 lib bdg; 1-60753-067-8 lib bdg

LC 2009051436

"The clean layout includes photographs and occasional charts, graphs, and technical illustrations against a range of pastel backgrounds. Inset boxes provide further detail, interesting extras, and recycling information. . . . [This book offers] easily accessible background information for report writers." SLJ

Includes glossary and bibliographical references

677 Textiles

Morris, Neil

Textiles. Amicus 2010 48p il (Materials that matter) lib bdg $28.50

Grades: 4 5 6 7 **677**

1. Fabrics
ISBN 978-1-60753-069-5 lib bdg; 1-60753-069-4 lib bdg

LC 2009051434

"The clean layout includes photographs and occasional charts, graphs, and technical illustrations against a range of pastel backgrounds. Inset boxes provide further detail, interesting extras, and recycling information. . . . [This book offers] easily accessible background information for report writers." SLJ

Includes glossary and bibliographical references

681.1 Instruments for measuring time, counting and calculating machines and instruments

Collier, James Lincoln

★ Clocks. Benchmark Bks. 2004 126p il (Great inventions) lib bdg $37.08

Grades: 6 7 8 9 **681.1**

1. Time 2. Clocks and watches 3. Time measurements 4. Clocks and watches -- History
ISBN 0-7614-1538-6

LC 2002-156288

This describes the history and significance of clocks and other time-keeping devices from prehistoric times to the present

Includes bibliographical references

682 Small forge work (Blacksmithing)

Weitzman, David

★ Skywalkers; Mohawk ironworkers build the city. Roaring Brook Press/Flash Point 2010 124p il $19.99

Grades: 8 9 10 11 12 Adult **682**

1. Bridges 2. Building 3. Skyscrapers 4. Mohawk Indians 5. Steel construction 6. Mohawk Indians 7. Construction workers 8. Skyscrapers -- History
ISBN 1-59643-162-8; 978-1-59643-162-1

Weitzman relates the history of Mohawks from Kahnawàke, Québec, known for their ability to navigate heights, who worked on the construction of bridges and tall buildings in Canada and New York City.

"Stunning photographs complement Weitzman's comprehensive research and clear text in this memorable tribute to Mohawk ironworkers. . . . Weitzman wisely intersperses passages of construction history and technical technique with numerous personal stories. . . . Plentiful black and white archival photographs . . . are chilling or breathtaking. Throughout, Weitzman's admiration and respect for the Mohawk people shine through." Voice Youth Advocates

Includes glossary and bibliographical references

685 Leather and fur goods, and related products

Blaxland, Wendy

Sneakers. Marshall Cavendish Benchmark 2009 32p il (How are they made?) $19.95

Grades: 4 5 6 **685**

1. Sneakers
ISBN 978-0-7614-3810-6; 0-7614-3810-6

LC 2008026211

This is an "introduction to athletic shoes and the global trade involved in their manufacture and marketing. . . . A typical page offers a paragraph or more of informative text as well as a color photo and, perhaps, a small sidebar." Booklist

688.7   Recreational equipment

Fridell, Ron

Sports technology. Lerner Publications 2009 48p il (Cool science) lib bdg $27.93

Grades: 4 5 6   **688.7**

1. Sports 2. Technology

ISBN 978-0-8225-7587-0 lib bdg; 0-8225-7587-6 lib bdg

LC 2007050905

This describes "how science helps athletes stay safer, perform better, and have more fun." Publisher's notes

Includes glossary and bibliographical references

Oxlade, Chris

Gadgets and games; Chris Oxlade. Capstone Heinemann Library 2013 56 p. col. ill. (Design and engineering for STEM) (library) $33.50; (paperback) $9.49

Grades: 5 6 7   **688.7**

1. Electronics 2. Industrial design 3. Product life cycle 4. Toys -- Design and construction 5. Household appliances -- Design and construction 6. Electronic apparatus and appliances -- Design and construction

ISBN 1432970364; 9781432970314; 9781432970369

LC 2012013468

This book, part of the Design and Engineering for STEM series, looks at electronic devices and mobile games. It looks at the life cycle of these items, or "the stages from their design, manufacture, and sale to their use, maintenance, and disposal." Topics include "prototyping, the sourcing of components, the production process, the decisions made by designers and engineers, and recycling." (Publisher's note)

Includes bibliographical references (p. 54) and index.

Ross, Stewart

Sports technology. Smart Apple Media 2011 46p il (New technology) $35.65

Grades: 4 5 6 7   **688.7**

1. Sports

ISBN 1-599-20534-3; 978-1-599-20534-2

LC 2010044241

Describes the technological advances in the sports industry, including the technology used to create better equipment, sports wear, judging tools, and playing surfaces.

This "offers a fine overview for reports, and its attractive design may also entice middle-grade readers to learn more." Booklist

Stone, Tanya Lee

★ The **good,** the bad, and the Barbie; a doll's history and her impact on us. Viking 2010 130p il $19.99

Grades: 6 7 8 9 10   **688.7**

1. Barbie dolls 2. Toy industry executives

ISBN 978-0-670-01187-2; 0-670-01187-8

LC 2010-7507

"Stone tantalizes with her brief and intriguing survey of Barbie. She begins with the history of Mattel, started by self-made businesswoman Ruth Handler in the 1940s, and

moves onto materialism, body image, portrayals of ethnicity, nudity, taboo and art." Kirkus

Includes bibliographical references

Wulffson, Don L.

Toys! amazing stories behind some great inventions. [by] Don Wulffson; with illustrations by Laurie Keller. Holt & Co. 2000 137p il $16.95

Grades: 4 5 6 7   **688.7**

1. Toys 2. Inventions 3. Toys -- History 4. Inventions -- History

ISBN 0-8050-6196-7

LC 99-58440

Describes the creation of a variety of toys and games, from seesaws to Silly Putty and toy soldiers to Trivial Pursuit

"Each of the 25 chapters is illustrated with small, humorous drawings and discusses a particular toy or game's origin and development. The book ends with a bibliography and a list of Web sites. Good, readable fare for browsing or light research." Booklist

Includes bibliographical references

690   Construction of buildings

Byers, Ann

Jobs as green builders and planners. Rosen Pub. 2010 80p il (Green careers) lib bdg $30.60

Grades: 5 6 7 8   **690**

1. Building 2. Vocational guidance 3. Environmental science

ISBN 978-1-4358-3566-5 lib bdg; 1-4358-3566-2 lib bdg

LC 2009015517

This "well-conceived [introduction focuses] on various jobs in [building and construction planning], the education and experience required, and expected earnings. The [book is] well organized, making it easy to gain an overview of the major aspects of the work. . . . [This book] will make [a] good [addition] to career collections. Photographs from the field and website and contact information for professional organizations add value." SLJ

Includes glossary and bibliographical references

Macaulay, David

★ **Unbuilding**. Houghton Mifflin 1980 78p il $18; pa $9.95

Grades: 4 5 6 7 8 9   **690**

1. Building 2. Skyscrapers

ISBN 0-395-29457-6; 0-395-45425-5 pa

LC 80-15491

This fictional account of the dismantling and removal of the Empire State Building describes the structure of a skyscraper and explains how such an edifice would be demolished

"Save for the fact that one particularly stunning double-page spread is marred by tight binding, the book is a joy: accurate, informative, handsome, and eminently readable." Bull Cent Child Books

Miller, Malinda

Green construction; creating energy-efficient, low-impact buildings. Mason Crest Publishers 2010 64p il (New careers for the 21st century: finding your role in the global renewal) lib bdg $22.95

Grades: 7 8 9 10 **690**
1. Vocational guidance 2. Sustainable architecture
ISBN 978-1-4222-1815-0 lib bdg; 1-4222-1815-5 lib bdg

LC 2010010013

"Chapters identify and emphasize specific careers—important strengths, necessary aptitudes and interests, education and training, projected earnings, closely related occupations, type of work environment, and predictions for the future of the field. . . . Color photos have a small role amid the many statistics, figures, graphs and charts that support and supplement the . . . [text]." SLJ

Includes bibliographical references

Somervill, Barbara A.

Green general contractor. Cherry Lake Pub. 2011 32p il (Cool careers) lib bdg $27.07

Grades: 4 5 6 7 **690**
1. Building 2. Vocational guidance 3. Sustainable architecture
ISBN 978-1-60279-987-5; 1-60279-987-3

LC 2010029535

This book begins "with a personal story of a teen and then [segues] into the occupation [of general contractor]. . . . [It covers] the necessary training and skills for the job (and options for obtaining them), a typical day, salary expectations, and well-known professionals in the field. The [text is] accessible and clearly written. . . . The [volume has] a generous number of clear color photographs that depict people at work." SLJ

Includes glossary and bibliographical references

Woolf, Alex

Buildings; by Alex Woolf. Heinemann Library 2013 56 p. ill. (chiefly col.) (library) $33.50; (paperback) $9.49

Grades: 6 7 8 9 **690**
1. Building 2. Architecture
ISBN 1432970291; 9781432970291; 9781432970345

LC 2012013465

This book by Alex Woolf examines the life cycle of a building, covering "the stages from its design, construction, and opening to its use, maintenance, and demolition and disposal at the end of its useful life. This book explains what happens during these stages, such as planning, the sourcing of materials, the construction process, the decisions made by designers and engineers, and refurbishing and recycling." (Publisher's note)

Includes bibliographical references (page 55) and index.

696 Utilities

Gregory, Josh

Plumber. Cherry Lake Pub. 2011 32p il (Cool careers) lib bdg $27.07

Grades: 4 5 6 7 **696**
1. Plumbing 2. Vocational guidance
ISBN 978-1-60279-984-4; 1-60279-984-9

LC 2010029538

This book begins "with a personal story of a teen and then [segues] into the occupation [of plumber]. . . . [It covers] the necessary training and skills for the job (and options for obtaining them), a typical day, salary expectations, and wellknown professionals in the field. The [text is] accessible and clearly written. . . . The [volume has] a generous number of clear color photographs that depict people at work." SLJ

Includes glossary and bibliographical references

700 ARTS

700 The arts

Johnson, Dolores

★ The **Harlem** Renaissance; by Dolores Johnson with Virginia Schomp. Marshall Cavendish Benchmark 2008 80p il (Drama of African-American history) lib bdg $23.95

Grades: 5 6 7 8 **700**
1. Harlem Renaissance 2. African American arts
ISBN 978-0-7614-2641-7

LC 2007034691

This is an account of the flowering of African American art, literature, music, and political commentary of the 1920s and 1930s centered in the Harlem section of New York City.

Includes glossary and bibliographical references

Makosz, Rory

Latino arts and their influence on the United States; songs, dreams, and dances. Mason Crest Publishers 2005 112p il (Hispanic heritage) $22.95

Grades: 7 8 9 10 **700**
1. Latin American art 2. Arts -- United States
ISBN 1-59084-938-8

LC 2004022968

This "book begins with a general discussion of the ways in which cultures express themselves through their arts. It goes on to discuss the arts of Latin American cultures and their growing prominence in the United States, with emphasis on dance and music. Writing, painting, theater arts, and holidays are also included. . . . [This is] an excellent resource both for students researching Latino arts for reports and for general readers." SLJ

Includes bibliographical references

Nardo, Don

Arts and literature in ancient Mesopotamia. Lucent Books 2008 104p il map (Lucent library of historical eras) $32.45

Grades: 6 7 8 9 **700**
1. Arts -- Iraq
ISBN 978-1-4205-0099-8; 1-4205-0099-6

LC 2008-22045

Introduces the cultural activities of ancient Mesopotamia, discussing art, language, metalwork, sculpture, cuneiform writing, mapmaking, epic poetry, and sacred literature.

This is "ideal for research projects. . . . [The author] provides diverse annotated suggestions (including Web sites) for further study." SLJ

Includes bibliographical references

Robson, David

The **Black** arts movement. Lucent Books 2009 104p il (Lucent Library of Black History) $32.45

Grades: 7 8 9 10   **700**

1. African American arts 2. Arts -- United States
ISBN 978-1-4205-0053-0; 1-4205-0053-8

LC 2008016446

This focuses on African American literature, music, and art.

This is "highly accessible and [provides] cultural context to help readers understand [the] topic. . . . [The] book includes captioned color and black-and-white photographs and reproductions on every spread. Well-organized and clearly written." SLJ

Includes bibliographical references

700.9 History, geographic treatment, biography of the arts

Flatt, Lizann

Arts and culture in the early Islamic world; Lizann Flatt. Crabtree Pub. Company 2012 48 p. col. ill., col. map (Life in the early Islamic world) (reinforced library binding : alk. paper) $30.60

Grades: 5 6 7   **700.9**

1. Islamic art 2. Islamic civilization
ISBN 0778721671; 9780778721673; 9780778721741; 9781427195609; 9781427198372

LC 2012000074

This book by Lizann Flatt is part of the "Life in the Early Islamic World" series. It "introduces the important roles that many of the arts, but especially calligraphy, architecture, and the decorative arts, have had in Islamic culture, in which art is meant to be 'useful as well as beautiful.'" (Booklist)

"The main texts are supplemented with blue boxes of information, subsections, and many high-quality reproductions, maps, and paintings." (School Library Journal)

701 Philosophy and theory of fine and decorative arts

Dickins, Rosie

The **Usborne** art treasury; pictures, paintings, and projects. [by] Rosie Dickins; designed by Nicola Butler. Usborne 2007 94p il $19.99

Grades: 4 5 6 7   **701**

1. Painting 2. Art appreciation
ISBN 978-0-7945-1452-5

"Each project in this colorful, attractive compendium of art projects begins with a particular work of art. . . . Throughout the book, the excellent presentation of the proj-

ects makes them seem not only possible to complete but also worth doing. Illustrated step-by-step, the instructions are clearly written and practical." Booklist

Hensley, Laura

Art for all; what is public art? Raintree 2010 32p il (Culture in action) $29

Grades: 5 6 7 8   **701**

1. Art
ISBN 978-1-4109-3923-4; 1-4109-3923-5

LC 2009051126

This "briefly surveys public art, from murals and graffiti to obelisks and religious statues. . . . A world map shows the locations of 16 public artworks mentioned in the text. . . . The quality of the illustrations is fine. . . . Given the book's broad scope and few pages, it accomplishes a good deal. Three activities, a time line, a glossary, and a brief bibliography round out this attractive presentation." Booklist

Includes glossary and bibliographical references

Sousa, Jean

★ **Faces,** places and inner spaces; a guide to looking at art. [by] Jean Sousa. Abrams Books for Young Readers 2006 48p il $18.95

Grades: 5 6 7 8   **701**

1. Art appreciation 2. Art -- Themes, motives
ISBN 978-0-8109-5966-8; 0-8109-5966-6

LC 2005-21053

"This introduction to art is an offshoot of an ongoing exhibit of the same name at the Art Institute of Chicago. . . . An assortment of artworks from the museum's collection is arranged into the three broad categories listed in the title, and with accessible, expert observations, Sousa pulls readers straight into the images. . . . This offers an unpretentious, dynamic approach to art education." Booklist

Includes glossary

Tomecek, Steve

Art & architecture; by Stephen M. Tomecek. Chelsea House Publishers 2010 174p il (Experimenting with everyday science) $35

Grades: 4 5 6 7   **701**

1. Architecture 2. Art and science 3. Science -- Experiments 4. Art -- Study and teaching
ISBN 978-1-60413-168-0; 1-60413-168-3

LC 2009030195

"This fun and informative book features 25 simple experiments using common household items and foods such as blueberries, colored cellophane, food coloring, Magic Markers, miniature marshmallows, and wooden toothpicks to demonstrate principles and inspire creative thought about the intersection of science with the visual and mechanical arts. The six chapters include activities that illuminate certain scientific aspects of each respective subject. . . . Accessible for independent reading by children with a scientific bent or curiosity about how the world works, these experiments would also be useful for scout projects or science clubs." SLJ

Includes bibliographical references

702.8 Auxiliary techniques and procedures; apparatus, equipment, materials

Luxbacher, Irene

★ The **jumbo** book of art; written and illustrated by Irene Luxbacher. Kids Can Press 2003 208p il pa $14.95

Grades: 4 5 6 7   **702.8**

1. Color 2. Drawing 3. Painting 4. Sculpture 5. Art -- Study and teaching
ISBN 1-55074-762-2

"Each of the four chapters is devoted to instructing readers in the basics of one technique—drawing, creating with color, sculpture, and mixed-media projects, respectively—and then inspires those readers to let loose and have fun making something beautiful. . . . The book features clear layouts, well-written definitions of terms, full-color illustrations, and more than 90 projects. . . . This practical, lively, and smart package is a must-have for every art and elementary school classroom, and a welcome addition to most library collections." SLJ

Includes glossary

703 Dictionaries, encyclopedias, concordances of fine and decorative arts

★ **Encyclopedia** of art for young people. Chelsea House 2008 8v il set $280

Grades: 6 7 8 9 10   **703**

1. Reference books 2. Art -- History 3. Art -- Encyclopedias
ISBN 978-0-7910-9477-8; 0-7910-9477-4

                 LC 2007-31020

This "survey of world art offers . . . illustrated chapters covering the major schools, styles, and specific regions, with sidebars that earmark specific artists, works of art, movements, and techniques, or note 'Connections' (historical and cultural)." SLJ

Includes glossary and bibliographical references

704 Special topics in fine and decorative arts

Barber, Nicola

★ **Islamic** empires; [by] Nicola Barber. Raintree 2005 48p il map (History in art) $31.43

Grades: 4 5 6 7   **704**

1. Islam 2. Islamic art
ISBN 1-4109-0522-5

                 LC 2004-7527

This is an introduction to the art, culture, and history of Islamic empires.

This book has "a depth of content that is unusual in art-history books for this age group. . . . [It] is amply illustrated with full-color photographs and reproductions. . . . Well-written, informative." SLJ

Includes bibliographical references

Bolden, Tonya

★ **Wake** up our souls; a celebration of Black American artists. Published in association with Smithsonian American Art Museum. Harry N. Abrams 2004 128p il $24.95

Grades: 6 7 8 9 10   **704**

1. African American art 2. African American artists
ISBN 0-8109-4527-4

Presents a history of African American visual arts and artists from the days of slavery to the present

"Bolden's writing is rich and lyrical. She smoothly incorporates the historical context, explaining pivotal events and relevant artistic movements clearly and succinctly." SLJ

January, Brendan

★ **Native** American art & culture; [by] Brendan January. Raintree 2005 56p il map (World art & culture) lib bdg $23; pa $9.99

Grades: 5 6 7 8   **704**

1. Native Americans 2. Native American art
ISBN 978-1-4109-1108-7 lib bdg; 1-4109-1108-X lib bdg; 978-1-4109-2118-5 pa; 1-4109-2118-2 pa

                 LC 2004-8072

"January investigates the many art forms of the Native American tribes. . . . Chapters are dedicated to pottery, textiles, carving, and painting as well as body art, architecture, ceremonies, songs, and dances. . . . Numerous color photographs of both ancient and modern artwork are included on each spread, and they are exceptional. . . . This fresh look at Native American culture through its artwork will be a welcome alternative for reports and classroom discussion, and the popularity of the subject matter and appealing design will attract readers outside the classroom environment." SLJ

Includes bibliographical references

Raczka, Bob

Before they were famous; how seven artists got their start. Millbrook Press 2010 32p il (Art adventures) $25.26

Grades: 4 5 6 7   **704**

1. Artists 2. Creative ability
ISBN 978-0-7613-6077-3; 0-7613-6077-8

                 LC 2009049596

"Short biographies written in conversational, jargon-free text introduce seven great artists, as young beginners and then as creators of famous works. From Dürer and Michelangelo to Picasso and Dali, the featured artists are presented chronologically on uncluttered, open spreads that include beautiful full-page reproductions. . . . Great preparation for a gallery visit, this will appeal to older readers, too, for its exciting, never-condescending talk about the pictures and the artists who created them." Booklist

704.9 Iconography

Bingham, Jane

Society & class; [by] Jane Bingham. Raintree 2006 56p il map (Through artists' eyes) lib bdg $32.86

Grades: 4 5 6 7   **704.9**
1. Society in art 2. Art appreciation 3. Social classes in art
ISBN 1-4109-2237-5
LC 2005025028

This "succinctly looks at how artists have depicted the lives of farmers, hunters, rulers, slaves, soldiers, and merchants throughout history. Social change such as the French and American Revolutions inspired artists, while the rise of Communism and Fascism had a chilling effect on art. . . . The full-color reproductions are well chosen and of good quality. The information is brief, but it provides a well-thought-out overview of these artistic interpretations." SLJ
Includes bibliographical references

Stieff, Barbara
Earth, sea, sun, and sky; art in nature. translated from German by Cynthia Hall; illustrated by Michael Schmölzl. Prestel 2011 88p il lib bdg $14.95
Grades: 6 7 8 9   **704.9**
1. Art 2. Nature 3. Aesthetics
ISBN 978-3-7913-7048-4; 3-7913-7048-0

"A conversational writing style combines with many color photographs and drawings to convey information about art inspired by nature. In the beginning, Stieff describes the historical development of gardens and how they are an art form. She moves on to provide many examples of how art is found on land, in water, and in the air. The photographs, which range in size, further illuminate the text. Throughout the work, references are made to activities detailed in the final section. These projects, which include making daisy soup, learning some water games, forming seed balls, and creating pictures in water, encourage readers to look at or create art." SLJ

709   History, geographic treatment, biography

Ayres, Charlie
Lives of the great artists. Thames & Hudson 2008 96p il $19.95
Grades: 5 6 7 8   **709**
1. Artists 2. Art -- History
ISBN 978-0-500-23853-0; 0-500-23853-7
LC 2008-91000

Presents illustrated and age-appropriate imaginary tours of the studios of famous artists from Leonardo da Vinci and Michelangelo to Monet and van Gogh, in an anecdotal reference that is complemented by reproductions of famous works and introductory portraits

This is "brightly written and augmented with activities, Web resources, and fun facts. . . . The works of art chosen to represent each artist are heavy on the drama and detail, resulting in high kid appeal and interesting captions. . . . The layout is clean and clear." SLJ

Bingham, Jane
★ **African** art & culture. Raintree 2004 56p il map (World art & culture) hardcover o.p. pa $9.99

Grades: 6 7 8 9 10   **709**
1. African art 2. Art, African
ISBN 978-0-7398-6606-1 lib bdg; 0-7398-6606-0 lib bdg; 978-1-4109-2105-5 pa; 1-4109-2105-0 pa
LC 2003-1955

This describes a variety of art forms of the African continent and their roles in their respective cultures.

This book is "stunningly illustrated. . . . Every page includes interesting and vivid color photographs of the different art forms and of artists at work. [This title is] well worth purchasing for the illustrations alone." SLJ
Includes glossary and bibliographical references

★ **Indian** art & culture. Raintree 2004 56p il map (World art & culture) hardcover o.p. pa $9.99
Grades: 6 7 8 9 10   **709**
1. Indic arts 2. Arts, Indic
ISBN 978-0-7398-6607-8 lib bdg; 0-7398-6607-9 lib bdg; 978-1-4109-2106-2 pa; 1-4109-2106-9 pa
LC 2003-1956

This offers a history of the arts of India, including architecture, wall painting and decoration, stone and wood carving, painting, textiles, ceramics, music, dance, theater and film, and writing, and explains their roles in Indian culture.

"Every page includes interesting and vivid color photographs of the different art forms and of artists at work. [This title is] well worth purchasing for the illustrations alone." SLJ
Includes glossary and bibliographical references

Children's book of art; an introduction to the world's most amazing paintings and sculptures. DK Pub. 2009 139p il $24.99
Grades: 4 5 6 7   **709**
1. Art appreciation 2. Art -- History
ISBN 978-0-7566-5511-2; 0-7566-5511-0

"From prehistoric to modern times, this expertly designed survey delivers a wealth of information. Much more than a mere time line, the focus shifts from artist to movement to medium with fluidity. Gallery pages examine how particular subjects are depicted in art from a variety of cultures and time periods. Hundreds of color reproductions are sure to hold readers' interest. . . . The vast amount of information presented is neither overwhelming nor superficial." SLJ

Finger, Brad
13 American artists children should know. Prestel 2010 46p il $14.95
Grades: 4 5 6   **709**
1. American art 2. Art appreciation 3. Artists -- United States
ISBN 978-3-7913-7036-1; 3-7913-7036-7

"Beginning with Winslow Homer and ending with Andy Warhol and Jasper Johns, this picture-book overview introduces 13 well-known American artists. On each double-page spread, short biographies combine with richly reproduced images of the artists' famous works. . . . Finger . . . writes with clarity and enthusiasm." Booklist
Includes glossary

Khanduri, Kamini

★ **Japanese** art & culture. Raintree 2004 56p il map (World art & culture) lib bdg $33.50

Grades: 6 7 8 9 10   **709**

1. Japanese arts

ISBN 978-0-7398-6609-2; 0-7398-6609-5

LC 2003-1957

This offers a history of the arts of Japan including painting, woodblock prints, sculpture, metalwork, pottery, lacquerware, architecture, gardens, calligraphy, and theater, and explains their places in Japanese culture.

Includes glossary and bibliographical references

Lewis, Elizabeth

★ **Mexican** art & culture. Raintree 2004 56p il map (World art & culture) lib bdg $33.50

Grades: 6 7 8 9 10   **709**

1. Mexican art 2. Arts, Mexican

ISBN 978-0-7398-6610-8; 0-7398-6610-9

LC 2003-1958

This offers a history of the arts of Mexico including architecture, carvings and sculpture, pottery and ceramics, masks, lacquering, textiles and clothing, jewelry, painting, music and musical instruments, fiestas and festivals, death and burial customs, and toys, and explains their roles in Mexican culture.

The text is "straightforward and concise, but it's the excellent selection of high-quality color photos that really stand out." Booklist

Includes glossary and bibliographical references

Mason, Antony

A **history** of Western art; from prehistory to the 20th century. edited by John T. Spike. Abrams Books for Young Readers 2007 128p il $22.50

Grades: 7 8 9 10   **709**

1. Art -- History

ISBN 978-0-8109-9421-8; 0-8109-9421-6

LC 2007-10291

This is a survey of "Western art's 50,000-year history. . . . With a few exceptions, each spread focuses on a different time period or movement, spotlighting representative work, from prehistoric cave paintings and ancient artifacts to contemporary new media. . . . A short narrative paragraph accompanies beautifully reproduced color images, extensive captions, and text boxes. . . . This overview gives students a strong visual introduction to Western art." Booklist

Raczka, Bob

★ **Name** that style; all about isms in art. by Bob Raczka. Millbrook Press 2008 32p il (Art adventures) lib bdg $25.26; pa $9.95

Grades: 5 6 7 8   **709**

1. Art -- History

ISBN 978-0-8225-7586-3 lib bdg; 0-8225-7586-8 lib bdg; 978-1-58013-824-6 pa; 1-58013-824-1 pa

LC 2008000312

"Beginning with naturalism and ending with photorealism, with many stops along the way, this compact overview documents the shifts, both in terms of technique as well as subject matter, that differentiate each style from its prede-

cessors. Each 'ism' gets a two-page spread, with a beautifully reproduced example. . . . This is . . . indispensible for any middle-grade classrooms introducing art history." Booklist

Sayre, Henry M.

★ **Cave** paintings to Picasso; the inside scoop on 50 art masterpieces. by Henry Sayre. Chronicle Books 2004 93p il $22.95

Grades: 5 6 7 8   **709**

1. Art -- History

ISBN 0-8118-3767-X

LC 2002-15583

Introduces fifty celebrated works of art, including King Tut's sarcophagus and Andy Warhol's paintings of Campbell's soup cans, with historical and interpretive information for each piece

"The author's breezy style captures interest early on. . . . Many of the world's cultures are represented and a variety of techniques are explained. . . . A dazzling and accessible introduction to art history." SLJ

Includes glossary

Schumann, Bettina

13 women artists children should know; [by] Bettina Schumann; [translated from German by Jane Michael] Prestel 2009 46p il $14.95

Grades: 5 6 7 8   **709**

1. Women artists 2. Art appreciation

ISBN 978-3-7913-4333-4; 3-7913-4333-5

This is profiles women artists such as Sofonisba Anguissola, Maria Sybilla Merian, Mary Cassatt, Georgia O'Keeffe, Frida Kahlo, Louise Bourgeois, and Cindy Sherma

This "large-format, brightly colored [survey proves a] solid, even inspiring [introduction] to the art world. . . . Leading questions encourage budding artists to use the featured subjects and artworks as inspiration." Horn Book Guide

Includes glossary

Wenzel, Angela

13 artists children should know; [translation by Jane Michael] Prestel 2010 46p il $14.95

Grades: 4 5 6   **709**

1. Artists 2. Art appreciation 3. Art -- History

ISBN 978-3-7913-4173-6; 3-7913-4173-1

This profiles 13 artists such as Leonardo da Vinci, Vincent Van Gogh, Vermeer, and Henri Matisse

This "large-format, brightly colored [survey provides a] solid, even inspiring [introduction] to the art world. . . . Leading questions encourage budding artists to use the featured subjects and artworks as inspiration." Horn Book Guide

Includes glossary

709.02   6th-15th centuries, 500-1499

Spilsbury, Richard

The **Renaissance**. Heinemann Library 2009 48p il (Art on the wall) lib bdg $32.86

Grades: 5 6 7 8 9 10   **709.02**
1. Renaissance 2. Art -- 15th and 16th centuries
ISBN 978-1-4329-1372-4; 1-4329-1372-7
LC 2008020357
This "discusses how a revival of interest in the classical
world inspired a new approach to art, describes the developments that took place in art during the Renaissance period,
and examines how Renaissance artists created lifelike paintings and sculptures." Publisher's note
Includes glossary and bibliographical references

709.03   Modern period, 1500-

Gunderson, Jessica
  Impressionism; by Jessica Gunderson. Creative
Education 2008 48p il (Movements in art) lib bdg
$32.80
Grades: 6 7 8 9   **709.03**
1. Impressionism (Art)
ISBN 978-1-58341-611-2 lib bdg; 1-58341-611-0
lib bdg
LC 2007008493
This "discusses the leading Impressionist artists, their
subjects, and their techniques. Quality reproductions of
many paintings and occasional sepia photos of the paint-
ers and their settings illustrate the detailed, informative
overview." Booklist
Includes glossary and bibliographical references

  Realism; by Jessica Gunderson. 1st ed.; Creative
Education 2009 48p il (Movements in art) lib bdg
$32.80
Grades: 6 7 8 9   **709.03**
1. Realism in art
ISBN 978-1-58341-612-9 lib bdg; 1-58341-612-9
lib bdg
LC 2007008494
"Gunderson describes how art trends, politics, and inventions informed the work that was produced during [the
Realism] movement.... [The] book provides an overview of
the movement and its key players in continuous prose that is
broken up by an occasional highlighted section of text. The
color photographs, illustrations, and reproductions, many of
them full page, are relevant and of high quality.... The
[text delivers a] well-rounded [account] that students will
find accessible." SLJ
Includes glossary and bibliographical references

  Romanticism; [by] Jessica Gunderson. Creative
Education 2009 48p il (Movements in art) lib bdg
$32.80
Grades: 6 7 8 9   **709.03**
1. Romanticism in art
ISBN 978-1-58341-613-6; 1-58341-613-7
LC 2007008495
"Gunderson describes how art trends, politics, and in-
ventions informed the work that was produced during [the
Romantic] movement.... [The] book provides an overview
of the movement and its key players in continuous prose that
is broken up by an occasional highlighted section of text.

The color photographs, illustrations, and reproductions,
many of them full page, are relevant and of high quality...
. The [text delivers a] well-rounded [account] that students
will find accessible." SLJ
Includes glossary and bibliographical references

709.04   20th century, 1900-1999

Claybourne, Anna
  Surrealism. Heinemann Library 2009 48p il
(Art on the wall) lib bdg $32.86
Grades: 5 6 7 8 9 10   **709.04**
1. Surrealism 2. Modern art
ISBN 978-1-4329-1367-0; 1-4329-1367-0
LC 2008020316
This title succeeds "in presenting a bird's-eye view of
[Surrealism] without oversimplification. Information on
individual artists is included in the broader context of the
movement. Visually exciting, with plenty of color, [the lay-
out is] hip and should appeal to the target audience." SLJ
Includes glossary and bibliographical references

Demilly, Christian
  Pop art; [translated from the French by Rosie
Jackson] Prestel 2007 31p il $14.95
Grades: 8 9 10 11 12   **709.04**
1. Pop art
ISBN 978-3-7913-3894-1; 3-7913-3894-3
"An excellent introduction to this artistic movement.
Demilly traces its beginnings to the work of early-20th-cen-
tury French and German artists such as Marcel Duchamp,
Kurt Schwitters, and Fernand Léger. He then shows how
Pop Art grew to comment particularly on American society,
both in its glamour and its excesses. Each clear, one-page
explanation of the various aspects of Pop Art is set opposite
a one-half or full-page, high-quality color reproduction of a
famous work." SLJ

Spilsbury, Richard
  Abstract expressionism. Heinemann Library
2009 48p il (Art on the wall) lib bdg $32.86
Grades: 5 6 7 8 9 10   **709.04**
1. American art 2. Abstract expressionism
ISBN 978-1-4329-1370-0 lib bdg; 1-4329-1370-0
lib bdg
LC 2008020361
This title succeeds "in presenting a bird's-eye view of
[Abstract expressionism] without oversimplification. Information on individual artists is included in the broader
context of the movement. Visually exciting, with plenty
of color, [the layout is] hip and should appeal to the target
audience." SLJ
Includes glossary and bibliographical references

  Pop art. Heinemann Library 2009 48p il (Art
on the wall) lib bdg $23

Grades: 5 6 7 8 9 10   **709.04**
1. Pop art
ISBN 978-1-4329-1368-7 lib bdg; 1-4329-1368-9
lib bdg
LC 2008020358
This describes how Pop art began, some of the movement's artists, and the influence of Pop art

This title succeeds "in presenting a bird's-eye view of [Pop art] without oversimplification. Information on individual artists is included in the broader context of the movement. Visually exciting, with plenty of color, [the layout is] hip and should appeal to the target audience." SLJ

Includes glossary and bibliographical references

Yancey, Diane
Art deco. Lucent Books 2010 112p il (Eye on art) $33.45
Grades: 7 8 9 10   **709.04**
1. Art deco
ISBN 978-1-4205-0340-1; 1-4205-0340-5
LC 2010032961
"Presents an in-depth look at the art deco movement and its lasting legacy. . . . [It provides] a great deal of information, so middle school readers may not read them cover to cover; however, ample cover photos and quotes from artists will make this . . . appealing to students interested in art." Voice Youth Advocates

Includes glossary and bibliographical references

709.2   Biography

Amado, Elisa
High riders, saints and death cars; a life saved by art. as told to Elisa Amado; photos by John T. Denne. Groundwood Books/House of Anansi Press 2011 55p il $24.95
Grades: 9 10 11 12   **709.2**
1. Motorcycles 2. Art and religion 3. American folk art 4. Hispanic American artists -- Biography 5. Sculptors -- United States -- Biography 6. Artists 7. Sculptors 8. Artists -- United States 9. Hispanic Americans -- Biography
ISBN 0888998546; 9780888998545
In "New Mexican folk artist [Nicholas] Herrera's autobiography (told to and written by [Elisa] Amado) . . . even Herrera's mother wasn't sure he would survive his wild and self-destructive teenage years during the 1960s. . . . Herrera does make it--barely. After emerging from a coma following an alcohol-related car accident, Herrera devotes his life to creating art, following in the footsteps of his great-uncle, a 'santero' who created statues of saints. Herrera's folk art sculptures are all his own, however, blending religious iconography with imagery from contemporary Hispanic and biker culture, as well as social and political commentary (the . . . The Three Kings shows the Holy Family fleeing Herod on an eight-cylinder 'trike' motorcycle)." (Publishers Weekly)

"The subtitle of New Mexican folk artist Herrera's autobiography (told to and written by Amado) isn't hyperbole: even Herrera's mother wasn't sure he would survive his wild and self-destructive teenage years during the 1960s. . . . After emerging from a coma following an alcohol-related car accident, Herrera devotes his life to creating art. . . . Herrera's folk art sculptures . . . [blend] religious iconography with imagery from contemporary Hispanic and biker culture, as well as social and political commentary. . . . Never minimizing the gravity of Herrera's struggles, the book makes clear the concrete impact that art can have." Publ Wkly

Bernier-Grand, Carmen T.
Pablo Picasso; I the king, yo el rey. by Carmen T. Bernier-Grand; illustrated by David Diaz. 1st ed. Marshall Cavendish 2012 64 p. ill. (hardcover) $19.99
Grades: 5 6 7   **709.2**
1. Art -- History
ISBN 0761461779; 9780761461777
LC 2011032177
This biography of painter Pablo Picasso is written "in free-verse style. . . . The artist's strong will and drive are demonstrated in his decision to wander Madrid with sketchbook in lieu of attending art school; by his insistent attempts to develop his own style (e.g., his Blue Period; his fascination with masklike faces; his creation of Cubism); by his move to Paris; and his insatiable desire for women." (School Library Journal)

Spence, David
Michelangelo; written by David Spence; editor, Guy Croton. North American ed. New Forest Press 2010 48 p. col. ill. (Great artists and their world) (library) $32.80
Grades: 6 7 8 9   **709.2**
1. Artists 2. Painters 3. Sculptors 4. Architects 5. Artists, Italian 6. Art, Renaissance -- Italy 7. Art -- 15th and 16th centuries
ISBN 1848983093; 9781848983090
"Offers biographical information [of Michelangelo Buonarroti] . . . interspersed with art history and criticism in an eye-catching format. . . . [Includes] a long introductory paragraph and four-to-six images with explanatory notes. . . . Spence . . . does a good job of explaining why art that might seem ordinary today was revolutionary at the time of its creation." SLJ

Includes bibliographical references and index.

709.3   Specific continents, countries, localities

Langley, Andrew
★ **Ancient** Greece. Raintree 2005 48p il (History in art) lib bdg $31.43; pa $8.99
Grades: 4 5 6 7   **709.3**
1. Greek art
ISBN 978-1-4109-0517-8 lib bdg; 1-4109-0517-9 lib bdg; 978-1-4109-2035-5 pa; 1-4109-2035-6 pa
LC 2004-7523
The author shows "how art provides primary-source information about everyday and family life, beliefs and religion, and philosophy and mythology in . . . ancient [Greece]. . . . The [book follows] a well-organized format that makes the history accessible for reports, but the [author takes the

book] beyond a reports-only status. Captions for the two or three illustrations per spread are clear." SLJ

Includes glossary and bibliographical references

711 Area planning (Civic art)

Macaulay, David

★ **City**: a story of Roman planning and construction. Houghton Mifflin 1974 112p il $18; pa $10.99

Grades: 4 5 6 7 8 9 10   **711**
    1. Civil engineering 2. Roman architecture 3. City planning -- Rome
    ISBN 0-395-19492-X; 0-395-34922-2 pa

LC 74-4280

"By following the inception, construction, and development of an imaginary Roman city, the account traces the evolution of Verbonia from the selection of its site under religious auspices in 26 B.C. to its completion in 100 A.D." Horn Book

Includes glossary

720 Architecture

Barker, Geoff P.

Incredible skyscrapers. Amicus 2011 32p il (Superstructures) lib bdg $28.50

Grades: 5 6 7 8   **720**
    1. Skyscrapers
    ISBN 978-1-6075-3133-3; 1-6075-3133-X

LC 2009044044

"The vivid illustrations often help clarify points made in the text. . . . [This] colorful, informative [book offers] intriguing glimpses of notable engineering feats." Booklist

Includes bibliographical references

Farrell, Courtney

Build it green. Rourke Pub. LLC 2010 48p il (Let's explore science) lib bdg $32.79

Grades: 4 5 6 7   **720**
    1. Sustainable architecture
    ISBN 978-1-61590-320-7 lib bdg; 1-61590-320-8 lib bdg

LC 2010009907

This "introduces concepts of eco-friendly architecture with specific examples, from abode houses to Earthships, while it talks about the large impact that small home energy-saving adjustments, such as water-conserving toilets, can make. . . . In [this] title, well-chosen boxed examples, abundant color photos, diagrams, and an appended glossary add interest and support the engaging [text]." Booklist

Includes glossary and bibliographical references

Hosack, Karen

Buildings; [by] Karen Hosack. Raintree 2009 32p il map (What is art?) lib bdg $27.50

Grades: 5 6 7 8   **720**
    1. Buildings 2. Architecture
    ISBN 978-1-4109-3165-8 lib bdg; 1-4109-3165-X lib bdg

LC 2008-9700

This "features public spaces and private residences created from a variety of materials. Every page includes a paragraph about the structure with glossary terms in bold type. . . . [Title is] consistent in quality of design and content." SLJ

Includes glossary and bibliographical references

Laroche, Giles

What's inside; fascinating structures around the world. Houghton Mifflin Books for Children 2009 un il $17

Grades: 4 5 6 7   **720**
    1. Architecture 2. Historic buildings
    ISBN 978-0-618-86247-4; 0-618-86247-1

LC 2008-33832

"This beautiful book presents interior and exterior views of 14 extraordinary structures, from King Tut's tomb and the Temple of Kukulcan to the Sydney Opera House and the Georgia Aquarium. . . . The text is good, the organization is clever, but it's the art here that is truly masterful. The illustrations are made from layers and layers of cut and painted paper." SLJ

Macaulay, David

★ **Building** big. Houghton Mifflin 2000 192p il $30; pa $12.95

Grades: 5 6 7 8 9 10   **720**
    1. Dams 2. Bridges 3. Tunnels 4. Engineering 5. Skyscrapers 6. Architecture
    ISBN 0-395-96331-1; 0-618-46527-8 pa

LC 00-28116

"Macaulay combines his detailed yet vaguely whimsical illustrations with simple, straightforward prose that breaks down complex architectural and engineering accomplishments into easily digestible tidbits that don't insult the intelligence of the reader of any age." N Y Times Book Rev

Includes glossary

Oxlade, Chris

Skyscrapers; uncovering technology. Firefly Books 2006 52p il $16.95

Grades: 4 5 6 7   **720**
    1. Skyscrapers
    ISBN 1-55407-136-4

"This tour of big buildings flits around the world and through history with a kaleidoscopic mix of small, finely detailed artrists' renditions and five-sentence-or-less text munchies. . . . It also features four mylar overlays that offer an inside look at a few towering structures. . . . Blending eye-catching visuals with specific facts and comparisons, this quick survey will please both browsers and assignment-driven readers." Booklist

Paxmann, Christine

From mud huts to skyscrapers; architecture for children. by Christine Paxmann; illustrated by Anne

Ibelings. Prestel Pub. Random House 2012 64 p. ill. (hardcover) $19.95

Grades: 4 5 6   **720**
    1. Architecture
    ISBN 3791371134; 9783791371139
                   LC 2012939038

This book "takes readers on a journey through time, exploring well-known structures such as the pyramids, Hagia Sophia, Versailles, and the Guggenheim Museum. Each spread is dedicated to a single building; in addition to a detailed illustration of the structure, it also includes information about the architect, the architectural style, and/or definitions of particular details." (School Library Journal)

Roeder, Annette

13 buildings children should know; [translator, Jane Michael] Prestel 2009 46p il $14.95

Grades: 5 6 7 8   **720**
    1. Architecture
    ISBN 978-3-7913-4171-2; 3-7913-4171-5

"The famous buildings featured in this pictorial collection include Notre Dame cathedral in Paris, Neuschwanstein Castle in Germany, New York City's Guggenheim Museum and the Beijing National Stadium (built for the 2008 Olympics), each pictured in color photographs, cross-sections and/or ground plans, with time lines tracing the buildings' developments and changes over time. . . . A sound introduction to some impressive structures." Publ Wkly

Stern, Steven L.

Building greenscrapers; consultant, Frank Robbins. Bearport Pub. 2009 32p il (Going green) lib bdg $25.27

Grades: 4 5 6 7   **720**
    1. Skyscrapers 2. Sustainable architecture
    ISBN 978-1-59716-962-2 lib bdg; 1-59716-962-5 lib bdg
                   LC 2009-12494

"Color photographs (most full page) and a few diagrams accompany the informative text. . . . Overall, the [book] . . . is user-friendly and covers topics that are not easily found elsewhere." SLJ

Includes glossary and bibliographical references

720.9   History, geographic treatment, biography

Clements, Gillian

A **picture** history of great buildings. Frances Lincoln Children's 2007 61p il map $19.95

Grades: 7 8 9 10   **720.9**
    1. Buildings 2. Architecture -- History
    ISBN 978-1-84507-488-3; 1-84507-488-2

An illustrated history of over 9,000 years of great buildings around the world from the tombs of ancient Egypt to the modern skyscrapers of today.

This is "an excellent resource, jam-packed with information for anyone interested in a basic study of architecture throughout the ages." Libr Media Connect

Includes glossary

725   Specific types of structures

Graham, Ian

Amazing stadiums. Amicus 2010 32p il (Superstructures) lib bdg $28.50

Grades: 5 6 7 8   **725**
    1. Stadiums
    ISBN 978-1-6075-3131-9; 1-6075-3131-3
                   LC 2009044043

"The vivid illustrations often help clarify points made in the text. . . . [This] colorful, informative [book offers] intriguing glimpses of notable engineering feats." Booklist

Includes glossary and bibliographical references

726   Buildings for religious and related purposes

DuTemple, Lesley A.

The **Pantheon**. Lerner Publs. 2003 72p il (Great building feats) lib bdg $27.93

Grades: 5 6 7 8   **726**
    1. Temples 2. Roman architecture
    ISBN 0-8225-0376-X
                   LC 2001-05694

Describes the building of the Pantheon, discussing the role of the Roman emperor Hadrian and the significance of the Pantheon in the fields of history and architecture

This offers a "clear and straightforward text. . . . There are numerous color photographs, clear diagrams, and architectural drawings of the building and its interior." SLJ

Includes bibliographical references

The **Taj** Mahal. Lerner Publs. 2003 88p il (Great building feats) lib bdg $27.93

Grades: 5 6 7 8   **726**
    1. Taj Mahal (Agra, India) 2. Architecture, Mogul -- India -- Agra 3. Agra (India) -- Buildings, structures, etc
    ISBN 0-8225-4694-9
                   LC 2002-151380

Recounts the history of the creation of the Taj Mahal, built as a tomb and memorial for the wife of the Mughal emperor Shah Jahan

The text is "enriched with interesting sidebars, diagrams that clarify the description of the building techniques, and many color photographs and reproductions." SLJ

Includes bibliographical references

Macaulay, David

★ **Mosque**. Houghton Mifflin 2003 96p il $18

Grades: 4 5 6 7 8 9 10   **726**
    1. Mosques 2. Mosques -- Design and construction
    ISBN 0-618-24034-9
                   LC 2003-177

"Once again Macaulay uses clear words and exemplary drawings to explore a majestic structure's design and construction. . . . In his respectful, straightforward explanation of the mosque's design, Macaulay offers an unusual, inspiring perspective into Islamic society." Booklist

Includes glossary

★ **Pyramid**. Houghton Mifflin 1975 80p il
$20; pa $9.95
Grades: 4 5 6 7 8 9 10   **726**
    1. Pyramids
    ISBN 0-395-21407-6; 0-395-32121-2 pa
                   LC 75-9964
The construction of a pyramid in 25th century B.C.
Egypt is described. "Information about selection of the site,
drawing of the plans, calculating compass directions, clear-
ing and leveling the ground, and quarrying and hauling the
tremendous blocks of granite and limestone is conveyed as
much by pictures as by text." Horn Book
    Includes glossary

Mann, Elizabeth
    The **Parthenon**; illustrations by Yuan Lee. Mi-
kaya Press 2006 47p il (Wonders of the world)
$22.95
Grades: 4 5 6 7   **726**
    ISBN 1-931414-15-7
This "volume introduces the history of ancient Athens
culminating in the building of the Parthenon. . . . [The text
is] well-researched and clearly written. . . . The color illustrations include an excellent map of Greece, photos of artifacts and sculptures, and many clearly deliniated, large-scale
paintings." Booklist

726.6   Cathedrals

Macaulay, David
    Building the book Cathedral. Houghton Mifflin
1999 112p il $29.95
Grades: 4 5 6 7 8 9   **726.6**
    1. Cathedrals 2. Gothic architecture 3. Architecture,
Gothic
    ISBN 0-395-92147-3
                   LC 99-17975
"On its twenty-fifth anniversary, the author recounts the
origins of his first book and suggests revisions he'd make
in light of what he's learned. . . . Most of the original Cathedral: the story of it's construction is reproduced in this
oversized celebratory volume, along with lots of preliminary
sketches, new commentary, and revised, or newly deployed,
art. . . . Touches of informal humor further enliven a book
that's already mesmerizing for both its original content and
its insights into this author-illustrator's incisive, ebulliently
creative mind." Horn Book

728.8   Large and elaborate private dwellings

Humphrey, Paul
    Building a castle; by Paul Humphrey. Arcturus
Pub. 2012 32 p. col. ill. (library) $28.50
Grades: 4 5 6   **728.8**
    1. Castles -- Design and construction 2. Castles --
Europe -- Design and construction
    ISBN 1848585594; 9781848585591
                   LC 2011051450

This book by Paul Humphrey "takes readers on a journey from the very beginnings of castles as fortresses to the
lavish tourist destinations of today." The text, along with
"contextual photographs, staged reenactments, and detailed
diagrams offers . . . [an] overview of how an architectural
structure reveals the culture, class system, and daily life of
the Middle Ages. Castles from the Czech Republic, Scotland, England, Turkey, and Holland are highlighted." (Children's Literature)

729   Design and decoration of structures and accessories

Macaulay, David
    ★ **Built** to last. Houghton Mifflin Harcourt
2010 272p il $24.99
Grades: 4 5 6 7 8 9 10   **729**
    1. Castles 2. Cathedrals 3. Architecture 4. Mosques
5. Mosques -- Design and construction 6. Architecture,
Medieval
    ISBN 978-0-547-34240-5; 0-547-34240-3
"Significantly updating the Caldecott Honor-winning
Castle (1977) and Cathedral (1973) with new text and full-
color illustrations, this hefty volume combines them with a
very lightly revised Mosque (2003) for a three-in-one architectural spree. No mere colorization of the black-and-white
originals of the first two books, . . . the all-new, often breathtaking images have been drawn by hand and then digitally
colored to harmonize, beautifully with the look of Mosque. .
. . Take a moment to mourn the originals, then celebrate this
entirely worthy revision." Kirkus

731   Sculpture

Wenzel, Angela
    13 sculptures children should know. Prestel 2010
45p il $14.95
Grades: 4 5 6   **731**
    1. Sculpture 2. Art appreciation
    ISBN 978-3-7913-7010-1; 3-7913-7010-3
This "large-format, brightly colored [survey provides a]
well-oranized [introduction] to the . . . world [of sculpture].
[It] highlights a variety of works from antiquity to modern
times. . . . Leading questions encourage budding artists to
use the featured subjects and artworks as inspiration." Horn
Book Guide
    Includes glossary

736   Other plastic arts

Boursin, Didier
    ★ **Easy** origami. Firefly 2005 64p il $19.95;
pa $9.95
Grades: 4 5 6 7   **736**
    1. Origami 2. Paper crafts
    ISBN 1-55297-928-8; 1-55297-939-3 pa

This guide provides step-by-step instructions for 24 origami projects, ranked as very easy, easy, and detailed, and the book includes tips for best results

"Paper-folding novices in particular may be drawn to this collection by its unusually clean design and bright, inviting colors." SLJ

Henry, Sally

Paper folding; [by] Sally Henry. PowerKids Press 2009 32p il (Make your own crafts) lib bdg $25.25

Grades: 3 4 5 6   **736**

1. Origami 2. Paper crafts

ISBN 978-1-4358-2507-9 lib bdg; 1-4358-2507-1 lib bdg

LC 2008-4524

"After describing different kinds of paper, Henry explains the difference between a fold, a crease, and a burnished fold, and then lists all the other supplies besides paper (glue, rubber cement) that should be on hand. The rest of the book devotes two-page spreads to each project. . . . The ideas are fantastic. . . . This will keep plenty of hands and minds busy." Booklist

Includes glossary

Krier, Ann Kristen

Totally cool origami animals. Sterling Pub. 2007 96p il $19.95

Grades: 4 5 6   **736**

1. Origami

ISBN 978-1-4027-2448-0; 1-4027-2448-9

LC 2006029593

"Each of these twenty-eight origami animal projects is accompanied by clear step-by-step instructions and photos. Projects are conveniently labeled 'beginner,' 'intermediate,' or 'advanced.' . . . The projects . . . are typically well explained. Paper-folders of all abilities should be able to tackle these projects with success." Horn Book Guide

Nguyen, Duy

Monster origami. Sterling Pub. 2007 96p il pa $9.95

Grades: 5 6 7 8   **736**

1. Origami 2. Monsters

ISBN 978-1-4027-4014-5 pa; 1-4027-4014-X pa

LC 2007003244

This "volume offers step-by-step instructions for using paper to create 'creatures of horror from books and movies.' . . . Nguyen begins with an overview of basic folds, each demonstrated in clear illustrations. . . . Nguyen shows, in easy-to-follow diagrams, how to use the folds in intricate combinations to create an array of familiar, frightening characters, ranging from Count Dracula to Godzilla's foe, King Ghidora. A final spread shows color photographs of the finished projects." Booklist

Origami birds. Sterling Pub. 2006 96p il $19.95

Grades: 5 6 7 8   **736**

1. Origami 2. Birds in art

ISBN 978-1-4027-1932-5; 1-4027-1932-9

LC 2005037669

This offers instructions for creating origami representations of 19 species of birds including cardinals, cockatoos, falcons, flying ducks, parakeets, and penguins

"The instructions are direct and thorough. . . . Spare line drawings show each step of construction, and color photos spotlight the finished project against a background photo of the bird's natural habitat." Booklist

Zombigami; paper folding for the living dead. Sterling 2011 96p il pa $9.95

Grades: 5 6 7 8   **736**

1. Origami 2. Zombies

ISBN 978-1-4027-8646-4; 1-4027-8646-8

"Featuring both a detachable photo gallery of folded ghouls placed in atmospheric settings and a package of origami paper in suitably ominous colors and patterns, this collection of 13 undead figures may not survive intact for long but offers experienced paper folders hours of creepy fun. Nguyen opens with a tutorial of creases and folding symbology then . . . goes on to show how each figure is folded with plenty of carefully drawn and clearly labeled step diagrams. Nonetheless, most of these models are challenging projects." SLJ

Stern, Joel

Jewish holiday origami; photographs by David Greenfield. Dover Publications 2006 64p il pa $5.95

Grades: 8 9 10 11 12 Adult   **736**

1. Origami 2. Jewish holidays

ISBN 0-486-45076-7; 978-0-486-45076-6

LC 2005-56934

This book contains a "year's worth of holiday projects—from Chanukah dreidels and a menorah with candles, to Passover pyramids and an image of the Red Sea parting." Publisher's note

Temko, Florence

Origami holiday decorations for Christmas, Hanukkah, and Kwanzaa. Tuttle Pub. 2003 63p il pa $8.95

Grades: 5 6 7 8   **736**

1. Origami 2. Holiday decorations

ISBN 0-8048-3477-6 pa; 978-0-8048-3477-3 pa

LC 2002075060

"Among the 25 original projects are a Holiday Calendar, Jewish Star, Kwanzaa Bowl, and Santa Claus Table Decoration." Publisher's note

738.5 Mosaics

Harris, Nathaniel

Mosaics. PowerKids Press 2009 30p il (Stories in art) lib bdg $25.25

Grades: 4 5 6 7   **738.5**

1. Mosaics

ISBN 978-1-4042-4438-2; 1-4042-4438-7

LC 2007052714

"After introducing the ancient roots of mosaic art in many cultures, this colorfully illustrated book discusses the methods used in making mosaics. Each of the next six double-page spreads presents a single, narrative mosaic. . . . Four mosaic craft ideas follow, with detailed instructions and photos of key construction steps as well as finished products. . . . [Illustrated with] fine color photos. . . . This book nicely combines art appreciation with hands-on learning." Booklist

739.27 Jewelry

Macfarlane, Katherine

The **jeweler's** art; by Katherine Nell Macfarlane. Lucent Books 2007 112p il (Eye on art) lib bdg $32.45

Grades: 7 8 9 10 11 12   **739.27**
1. Jewelry
ISBN 978-1-59018-984-9

LC 2007-7804

A look at jewelry through the ages.

This "title is thoroughly researched and fully referenced, and contains quotations from artists and art historians. The writing is generally clear and fluid. . . . Many of the pages have good-quality photos of artwork and artists." SLJ

Includes bibliographical references

741.2 Techniques, procedures, apparatus, equipment, materials

Ames, Lee J.

Drawing with Lee Ames; from the bestselling, award-winning creator of the Draw 50 series, a proven step-by-step guide to the fundamentals of drawing for all ages. Doubleday 1990 262p il pa $21

Grades: 6 7 8 9   **741.2**
1. Drawing
ISBN 0-385-23701-4

LC 90-31436

The author "offers a compendium of samples for beginning artists. Ames explains his approach to beginning art instruction as a form of mimicry, where students copy samples in order to get a feel for the process of drawing. . . . This is definitely for the beginning student who possesses very little to no drawing experience. . . . Ames's approach offers a good base from which students can then move on to more in-depth instruction." Voice Youth Advocates

Includes bibliographical references

McMillan, Sue

How to improve at drawing. Crabtree Pub. Co. 2010 48p il (How to improve at) lib bdg $29.27; pa $9.95

Grades: 7 8 9 10   **741.2**
1. Drawing -- Technique
ISBN 978-0-7787-3576-2 lib bdg; 0-7787-3576-1 lib bdg; 978-0-7787-3598-4 pa; 0-7787-3598-2 pa

"McMillan begins [this] book with a spread each on the history of drawing, equipment, perspective, color and textures, and composition. . . . [The] book has step-by-step instructions for a variety of attractive projects. The . . . book has, for each project, a series of four to six pre-liminary sketches that show the progression from first line to complete outline, but it is left to the artist to add the final shading." SLJ

Includes glossary

Scott, Damion

★ **How** to draw hip-hop; [by] Damion Scott and Kris Ex. Watson-Guptill 2006 144p il pa $19.95

Grades: 7 8 9 10   **741.2**
1. Drawing 2. Hip-hop 3. Drawing -- Technique
ISBN 0-8230-1446-0

LC 2005-29156

"This book combines the bold and energetic lines of graffiti art with the bright colors of cel-shaded video games and an obvious Japanese manga influence. . . . [It discusses] genre-specific concepts like wild style lettering [and] hip-hop clothing. . . . There is no other book of this kind on the market, making it a necessary and relevant purchase." SLJ

Temple, Kathryn

★ **Drawing**; the only drawing book you'll ever need to be the artist you've always wanted to be. [by] Kathryn Temple. Lark Books 2005 112p il (Art for kids) $17.95

Grades: 5 6 7 8   **741.2**
1. Drawing
ISBN 1-57990-587-0

LC 2004-17909

This "introduction to essential drawing techniques builds from the starting points of lines and simple shapes. . . . Eight concise chapters explore seeing with artist's eyes, line drawing, light and shadow, proportion and scale, perspective, drawing faces, drawing bodies, and using imagination. The succinct text reads smoothly and is written in a clear, understandable style. Sample sketches and crisp, color photographs extend the text." SLJ

Drawing in color. Lark Books 2009 112p il (Art for kids) $17.95

Grades: 5 6 7 8   **741.2**
1. Color 2. Drawing
ISBN 978-1-57990-821-8; 1-57990-821-7

LC 2008050618

"This heavily illustrated guide encourages budding artists to learn some basic skills and decide what works for them. Before jumping into project ideas, Temple explains some drawing tools and the basics of color theory. She provides clear, step-by-step instructions while reminding children that there is no right or wrong way to draw. Then, in nine chapters that each cover a particular technique or type of subject. . . . Projects use a variety of mediums, including colored pencils, markers, and oil pastels. The balance of detailed text and color images is visually appealing. Children will enjoy honing their observation skills as they practice using color in new ways." SLJ

741.5 Cartoons, graphic novels, caricatures, comics

Abadzis, Nick

★ **Laika**. First Second Books 2007 205p il

Grades: 5 6 7 8 9 10 11 12 Adult   **741.5**

1. Graphic novels 2. Space flight -- Graphic novels 3. Soviet Union -- History -- 1953-1991 -- Graphic novels

ISBN 1-59643-101-6; 978-1-59643-101-0

LC 2006-51907

This graphic novel tells the story of Laika, the dog sent into space aboard Sputnik II.

"Although the tightly packed and vividly inked panels of Abadzis's art tell an impressively complex tale . . . Laika's palpable spirit is what readers will remember." Publ Wkly

Akira, Shouko

Monkey High!: vol. 1; story and art by Shouko Akira; [translation and adaptation, Mai Ihara] Viz Media 2008 il pa $8.99

Grades: 7 8 9 10 11 12   **741.5**

1. Anime 2. Graphic novels 3. Romance -- Graphic novels 4. High school students -- Graphic novels

ISBN 978-1-4215-1518-2 pa; 1-4215-1518-0 pa

"Haruna sees the students in her new school . . . as acting ike monkeys. . . . She wants to keep to herself, but because she's beautiful, the boys start vying for her attention and the girls are getting jealous. . . . The artwork is lively and bright. . . . Readers who get caught up in the couple's first fight, first hand-holding, and first kiss will wait breathlessly for the other volumes in this series." SLJ

Ames, Lee J.

Draw 50 animal 'toons; [by] Lee J. Ames and Bob Singer. Doubleday 2000 un il (Draw 50) hardcover o.p. pa $8.95

Grades: 4 5 6 7   **741.5**

1. Animals in art 2. Cartooning -- Technique

ISBN 978-0-385-49142-6; 0-385-49142-5; 978-0-767-90544-2 pa; 0-767-90544-X pa

LC 00020750

"Step-by-step method shows how to draw cartoon animals, including dogs, mice, and a skateboarding crocodile." Publisher's note

Anderson, Eric A.

PX! Book one: a girl and her panda; written by Eric A. Anderson and Manny Trembley; illustrated by Manny Trembley. Image Comics 2007 un il $16.99

Grades: 6 7 8 9 10 11 12 Adult   **741.5**

1. Graphic novels 2. Humorous graphic novels 3. Adventure graphic novels 4. Science fiction graphic novels

ISBN 978-1-58240-820-0; 1-58240-820-3

A young girl named Dahlia and her trusty (robot) panda sidekick set off on a journey around the world to save her missing scientist father, who has been kidnapped by Pollo, an evil goat mastermind who wants to take over the world (and yes, people keep telling him his name means chicken" in Spanish). Along the way, Dahlia meets Weatherby Ian Poppington III, a Victorian English secret agent also known as Double Aught Seven," and Wikkity Jones, a rollerskating swordsman who talks like a hillbilly and stands ready to fight ninja any time. The absurd humor is punctuated by moments of intense violent action, especially in the side story about fighting zombies. This book collects the webcomic.

Appignanesi, Richard

As you like it; by William Shakespeare; illustrated by Chie Kutsuwada; adapted by Richard Appignanesi. Amulet Books 2009 207p (Manga Shakespeare) pa $10.95

Grades: 7 8 9 10   **741.5**

1. Poets 2. Authors 3. Dramatists 4. Graphic novels

ISBN 978-0-8109-8351-9; 0-8109-8351-6

LC 2008-45920

Banished to the Forest of Arden, Rosalind, disguised as a boy, reunites with true love Orlando.

"While maintaining considerable Shakespearian language, the plot is staged in a thoroughly manga manner, with Japanese settings, hairstyles, and posturing readily recognizable to the contemporary teen manga fan. . . . This is an excellent choice not only as curriculum support but also for manga readers." Booklist

Hamlet; [Richard Appignanesi, text adaptor]; illustrated by Emma Vieceli. Harry N. Abrams/Amulet Books 2007 195p (Manga Shakespeare) pa $9.95

Grades: 8 9 10 11 12 Adult   **741.5**

1. Poets 2. Authors 3. Dramatists 4. Graphic novels

ISBN 978-0-8109-9324-2; 0-8109-9324-4

Shakespeare's classic play of murder and revenge is here adapted into a manga-style graphic novel. It's now set in 2107, after global climate change has devastated the Earth. Appignanesi uses the text of the play and abridges it to fit the pages, while Vieceli's art vigorously carries the story along. The book includes a summary of the plot and a brief biography of Shakespeare.

Romeo and Juliet; by William Shakespeare; adapted by Richard Appignanesi; illustrated by Sonia Leong. Amulet Books 2007 195p (Manga Shakespeare) pa $9.95

Grades: 8 9 10 11 12   **741.5**

1. Poets 2. Authors 3. Dramatists 4. Graphic novels

ISBN 978-0-8109-9325-9; 0-8109-9325-2

LC 2006-100362

First published in the United Kingdom

Shakespeare's classic play of star-crossed young lovers gets the manga treatment. The book is set in modern Tokyo with rival yakuza gangs and uses somewhat abridged text from the play for the dialogue.

"Although the richness of the language may be lost, the script keeps the spirit of the story intact, hitting all the major speeches." Booklist

A midsummer night's dream; illustrated by Kate Brown. Abrams 2008 207p (Manga Shakespeare) pa $9.95

Grades: 7 8 9 10   **741.5**

1. Poets 2. Authors 3. Dramatists 4. Graphic novels

ISBN 978-0-8109-9475-1; 0-8109-9475-5

Shakespeare's comedy of romance, Faerie, and she-nanigans in the forest is adapted into a manga-style graphic novel. Hermia is in love with Lysander, while Demetrius is in love with Hermia, and Helen loves Demetrius. When mischievous fairy Puck decides to have some fun with the powerful love potion he has fetched for Fairy King Oberon, chaos reigns. While the human foursome needs to sort itself out, Oberon seeks revenge against his wife, Queen Titania, by having Puck use the love potion on her so she falls in love with the first creature she sees—who happens to be a yokel to whom Puck gave a donkey's head. The text takes dialog from the original play. The book includes a plot summary and a brief biography of Shakespeare.

The **tempest**; illustrated by Paul Duffield; [adaptor, Richard Appignanesi] Abrams 2008 207p il (Manga Shakespeare) pa $9.95

Grades: 7 8 9 10   **741.5**
    1. Poets 2. Authors 3. Dramatists 4. Graphic novels
    ISBN 978-0-8109-9476-8

Prospero and his daughter Miranda have lived on an isolated island for twelve years, after he had been deposed from his rule as Duke of Naples and cast out to sea to die. A powerful magician, Prospero has caused the survivors of a shipwreck to land on his island, in order to get his revenge, for these survivors are his enemies. Problems arise when Miranda falls in love with Ferdinand, the monster Caliban tries to use the survivors to kill Prospero, and Ariel the sprite is trying to set things right while still obeying Prospero. The book includes a plot summary and a brief biography of Shakespeare

"This adaptation would be useful both as an introduction to the play and as a companion piece for classroom study of it, using images to illuminate the Bard's eloquent poetry." SLJ

Arai, Kiyoko

Beauty Pop, Vol. 1; story and art by Kiyoko Arai. Viz Media/Shojo Beat 2006 194p il pa $8.99

Grades: 7 8 9 10 11 12   **741.5**
    1. Manga 2. Shojo manga 3. Graphic novels 4. Hair -- Graphic novels
    ISBN 978-1-4215-0575-6

At Kiri Koshiba's high school, three popular upper classmen do occasional "Scissors Projects," working makeovers on specially selected girls. Narumi Shogo, who cuts hair, wants to become the best beautician in Japan and has won every youth competition - except one, years ago, that a younger girl won. When girls who aren't already pretty ask Narumi for a makeover, he tells them they're too ugly. Kiri helps two of the girls, working a stylist's magic that makes the girls glow; she's not interested in competition, even though her family owns a salon. Narumi wants to know who dares to be the upstart and challenge him, and he sets up the school's cultural festival to be a haircutting duel. Will Kiri even bother to compete?

Other titles in this series are:
Beauty pop, Vol. 2 (2006) (978-1-4215-0576-6)
Beauty pop, Vol. 3 (2007) (978-1-4215-1009-5)
Beauty pop, Vol. 4 (2007) (978-1-4215-1010-1)
Beauty pop, Vol. 5 (2007) (978-1-4215-1011-8)
Beauty pop, Vol. 6 (2007) (978-1-4215-1323-2)
Beauty pop, Vol. 7 (2008) (978-1-4215-1784-1)

Beauty pop. Vol. 8 (2008) (978-1-4215-2310-1)
Beauty pop. Vol. 9 (2008) (978-1-4215-2310-1)
Beauty pop. Vol. 10 (2009) (978-1-4215-2594-5)

Aristophane

The **Zabime** sisters; translation & afterword by Matt Madden; lettering by Nicholas Breutzman. First Second 2010 80p il pa $16.99

Grades: 7 8 9 10   **741.5**
    1. Graphic novels 2. Sisters -- Graphic novels
    ISBN 978-1-59643-638-1; 1-59643-638-7

LC 2010-33986

On the first day of summer vacation, teenaged sisters M'Rose, Elle, and Celina step out into the tropical heat of their island home of Guadaloupe and encounter boys, schoolyard fights, petty thievery, and even illicit alcohol.

"The text is coupled with expressive images that offer glimpses into the personality of each character and allow the story to slowly unfold. The interplay among the siblings and each girl's singular response to events allow readers to establish a personal connection with each sister. The artist's dry brush technique and controlled use of line, mastery of light and shadow, interesting and unusual framing, and expressive facial close-ups are compelling." SLJ

Arni, Samhita

★ **Sita's** Ramayana; Moyna Chitrakar, illustrator. Groundwood Books 2011 il $24.95

Grades: 5 6 7 8   **741.5**
    1. Graphic novels 2. Hindu mythology -- Graphic novels
    ISBN 978-1-55498-145-8; 1-55498-145-X

"The Ramayana is the story of the exiled prince Rama and his beautiful wife, Sita. When she is kidnapped by a love-struck demon king, her husband's efforts to rescue her result in a war that eventually involves not only demons and mortals, but also gods, monsters, and even animals. . . . Here, a Patua scroll painter has adapted it as a fast-paced, brilliantly bold graphic novel. All of the suspense, treachery, sorcery, and pathos of this epic is depicted in homemade natural dyes layered onto paper in energetic lines, rhythmic patterns, and fields of hot, bright colors. . . . This book would be a must-purchase based on the strength of its dramatic story and arresting art, enhanced by superior design and high-quality production. Brilliant and fresh." SLJ

Atangan, Patrick

The **yellow** jar; two tales from Japanese tradition. NBM 2003 48p il (Songs of our ancestors) $12.92

Grades: 5 6 7 8 9 10 11 12   **741.5**
    1. Graphic novels 2. Folklore -- Japan -- Graphic novels
    ISBN 1-56163-331-3

LC 2002-32132

"To render two magical Japanese legends, one about a fisherman who discovers a fair maiden in a big pot, the other about a monk whose fastidiously kept garden is invaded by two chrysanthemums, Atangan charmingly adopts the sharp outlines, boldly juxtaposed color fields, and striking compositions of eighteenth-century Japanese woodblock prints." Booklist

Other titles in this series are:

Silk tapestry and other Chinese folktales (2004)
Tree of love (2005)

Avery, Ben

The **hedge** knight; [by] George R. R. Martin; Ben Avery, adapter; Mike S. Miller, artist. Marvel Enterprises 2006 160p il $19.95; bookstore ed $19.95

Grades: 9 10 11 12 Adult   **741.5**
1. Graphic novels 2. Fantasy graphic novels 3. Knights and knighthood -- Graphic novels
ISBN 978-0-7851-2577-8; 978-0-7851-2578-5

"Hulking young Dunk is the squire of an elderly warrior. When Dunk's master dies, he rides on to the next tournament in hopes of winning recognition for his knightly prowess. He acquires a squire of his own, a bald little boy who calls himself Egg, and gives himself the more elegant title of Duncan the Tall. . . . This heroic fantasy tale reinvigorates the tired category of sword and sorcery fiction by emphasizing the human angle." Publ Wkly

Baker, Kyle

How to draw stupid and other essentials of cartooning. Watson-Guptill 2008 110p il pa $16.95

Grades: 8 9 10 11 12 Adult   **741.5**
1. Cartooning -- Technique 2. Graphic novels -- Drawing
ISBN 978-0-8230-0143-9

LC 2008-922161

"Baker, an award-winning cartoonist and graphic-novel illustrator, gives aspiring cartoonists irreverent advice about how to succeed in their chosen field. He offers instruction in basic drawing techniques such as choosing the right tools and discusses the importance of learning to draw shapes, exaggerating, and using references. But the author's most inspiring advice focuses on how to succeed as a cartoonist." SLJ

Bannister

The **Master** of Shadows; art by Bannister; story by Nykko; [colors by Jaffre; translation by Carol Klio Burrell] Graphic Universe 2009 46p il (The Elsewhere chronicles) lib bdg $27.93; pa $6.95

Grades: 4 5 6 7   **741.5**
1. Graphic novels 2. Horror graphic novels
ISBN 978-0-7613-4461-2 lib bdg; 0-7613-4461-6 lib bdg; 978-0-7613-4744-6 pa; 0-7613-4744-5 pa

LC 2008-39444

After discovering that Grandpa Gabe has sealed the passageways between worlds, Max, Rebecca, Theo, and Noah must confront the Master of Shadows himself to find another way home.

"This other world is . . . tantalizingly imagined and gorgeously rendered." Booklist

Bannister (Person)

The **Shadow** Spies; art by Bannister; story by Nykko; [colors by Jaffre; translation by Carol Klio Burrell] Graphic Universe 2009 46p il (The Elsewhere chronicles) lib bdg $27.93; pa $6.95

Grades: 4 5 6 7   **741.5**
1. Graphic novels 2. Horror graphic novels
ISBN 978-0-7613-4460-5; 0-7613-4460-8; 978-0-7613-3964-9 pa; 0-7613-3964-7 pa

LC 2008-39443

Rebecca, Max, Theo, and Noah continue their journey through the other world in search of a way home, pursued by the Shadow Spies and the mysterious Master of Shadows. "The action sequences are clear and suspenseful." SLJ

The **shadow** door; art by Bannister; story by Nykko; [colors by Jaffre; translation by Carol Klio Burrell] Graphic Universe 2009 46p il (The Elsewhere chronicles) lib bdg $27.93; pa $6.95

Grades: 4 5 6 7   **741.5**
1. Graphic novels 2. Horror graphic novels
ISBN 978-0-7613-4459-9 lib bdg; 0-7613-4459-4 lib bdg; 978-0-7613-3963-2 pa; 0-7613-3963-9 pa

LC 2008-39442

Four friends discover a movie projector that opens a passageway into a world threatened by creatures of shadow, where their only weapon is light

"This is an undeniably attractive offering, as the artwork, with deep darks and effervescent lights splayed across large, glossy pages, is strikingly rendered. . . . [This] should have no problem gaining an appreciative readership." Booklist

Other titles in this series are:
Shadow spies (2009)
Master of shadows (2009)

Beagle, Peter S.

The **last** unicorn; original story by Peter S. Beagle; adaptation by Peter B. Gillis; art by Renae De Liz. IDW 2011 167p il rpt $16.00; $24.99

Grades: 6 7 8 9 10   **741.5**
1. Graphic novels 2. Unicorns -- Fiction
ISBN 9780451450524 rpt; 978-1-60010-851-8; 1-60010-851-2

Presents a graphic novel adaptation of the famous novel, in which a unicorn, alone in an enchanted wood, discovers she might be the last of her kind and sets out on a journey to find others like her.

"A beloved story is now a graphic novel in this excellent adaptation. . . . Much of the original novel's lyrical language has been included, and readers will be eager to find out if the unicorn will give up her quest for love, or if any of Schmendrick's spells will ever turn out right. . . . The illustrations are graceful and detailed, and inked in warm, glowing colors. This is a worthy successor to the classic novel and film." SLJ

Beatty, Scott

Superman; the ultimate guide to the Man of Steel. written by Scott Beatty. rev ed.; DK 2006 144p il $24.99

Grades: 7 8 9 10   **741.5**
1. Comic books, strips, etc.
ISBN 978-0-7566-2067-7; 0-7566-2067-8

LC 2005035040

First published 2002

Surveys the nature and history of the hero Superman, discussing his birth, career, secrets, equipment, and enemies

Beechen, Adam

Justice League Unlimited: the ties that bind; written by Adam Beechen and Paul Storrie; illustrated by Carlo Barberi, Rick Burchett and others. DC Comics 2008 un il (Justice league unlimited) $12.99

Grades: 3 4 5 6 7 8 9   **741.5**

1. Graphic novels 2. Superhero graphic novels 3. Justice League (Fictional characters)

ISBN 978-1-4012-1691-7; 1-4012-1691-9

This version of the Justice League was created for the Cartoon Network animated series and features such superheroes as Superman, Batman, Wonder Woman, Green Lantern, the Flash, Hawkgirl, J'onn Jonnz the Martian Manhunter, Power Girl, Green Arrow, and others. The stories collected in this volume include a clash of misunderstanding with Uncle Sam and the Freedom Fighters, a jaunt backwards in time, getting involved in a lovers' spat between super villains whose fight could destroy a city, and more. The book includes superhero vs supervillain fighting action with no bloodshed.

Another title in this series is:

Justice league unlimited. Heroes (2009)

Bendis, Brian Michael

Takio, vol. 1. Marvel Icon 2011 un il $9.95

Grades: 5 6 7 8   **741.5**

1. Graphic novels 2. Superhero graphic novels 3. Sisters -- Graphic novels

ISBN 978-0-7851-5326-9; 0-7851-5326-8

"This entertaining graphic novel features a crunchy and kinetic art style, quick pacing, realistic dialogue, and enough action to appeal to most middle-school readers." Booklist

Benjamin, P

Hulk: misunderstood monster; Writer, Paul Benjamin; illustrated by David Nakayama and Juan Santacruz. Marvel 2007 v1 il (Marvel adventures Hulk) $6.99

Grades: 5 6 7 8 9   **741.5**

1. Graphic novels 2. Superhero graphic novels 3. The Hulk (Fictional character)

ISBN 978-0-7851-2642-3; 0-7851-2642-2

Caught in the explosion of a gamma bomb, brilliant scientist Bruce Banner was transformed into a hulking beast. With no control over the transformations, Banner lives on the run, helping those less fortunate than he, hoping to one day find a cure to rid himself of the rampaging Hulk.

Other titles in this series are:

Hulk: defenders (2007)

Hulk: strongest one there is (2008)

Hulk: tales to astonish (2008)

Bertozzi, Nick

★ **Lewis** & Clark. First Second 2011 136p il pa $16.99

Grades: 5 6 7 8   **741.5**

1. Explorers 2. Graphic novels 3. Territorial governors

ISBN 978-1-59643-450-9 pa; 1-59643-450-3 pa

LC 2010-36255

Presents, in graphic novel format, the adventures of explorers Lewis and Clark during their journey from St. Louis to the Pacific Ocean.

Bertozzi "brings new life to the epic westward journey of explorers Lewis and Clark in this graphic novel perfect for history buffs. . . . Lewis's . . . deteriorating mental state throughout the expedition and particularly on the return trip is eloquently drawn, with Bertozzi managing to combine both history lesson and character study in strong, gripping drawings." SLJ

Black, Holly

The **Good** Neighbors; book one: Kin. Graphix 2008 117p (The Good Neighbors) $16.99

Grades: 7 8 9 10 11 12   **741.5**

1. Graphic novels 2. Fantasy graphic novels 3. Fairies -- Graphic novels

ISBN 978-0-439-85562-4; 0-439-85562-4

LC 2007-49008

Sixteen-year-old Rue has grown up in a world much like ours, except that the human world and the world of faerie have co-existed, as good neighbors, for a long time. When Rue's mother disappears and her professor father becomes the main suspect in the murder of a young woman, Rue's life turns strange. As she digs for information to figure out what is happening in her life, Rue discovers that her mother is a faerie and has returned to that realm because of a broken promise.

"This sophisticated tale is well served by Naifeh's stylish, angular illustrations." SLJ

Other titles in this series are:

Kith (2009)

Kind (2010)

Bohl, Al

Guide to cartooning. Pelican 1997 176p il hardcover o.p. pa $14.95

Grades: 8 9 10 11   **741.5**

1. Drawing 2. Cartooning 3. Cartoons and caricatures

ISBN 1-56554-367-X; 1-56554-177-4 pa

LC 96-44340

This guide to the art of cartooning includes "history, the fundamentals of the craft, and discussions of various modes, including political panels, strips, greeting cards, comic books, and animation.

This "is so chockablock with information that any teen interested in cartooning will come away with a multitude of tips and tricks." Booklist

Includes bibliographical references

Bouchard, Hervé

Harvey; how I became invisible. [by] Hervé Bouchard and Janice Nadeau; translated by Helen Mixter. Groundwood Books/House of Anansi Press 2010 un il $19.95

Grades: 5 6 7 8   **741.5**

1. Graphic novels 2. Death -- Fiction 3. Fathers -- Fiction 4. Bereavement -- Fiction 5. Family life -- Fiction

ISBN 978-1-55498-075-8; 1-55498-075-5

Original French edition 2009

"This open-ended book is deserving of discussion, difficult though it may be." Booklist

Bowers, Rick

Superman versus the Ku Klux Klan; the true story of how the iconic superhero battled the men of hate. by Rick Bowers. National Geographic 2012 160 p.

Grades: 7 8 9 10 11 12   **741.5**

1. Superman (Fictional character) 2. Comic books, strips, etc. -- History and criticism 3. United States -- Social life and customs -- History 4. Comic books, strips, etc. -- Social aspects

ISBN 1426309155; 1426309163; 9781426309151; 9781426309168

LC 2011024660

This book by Richard Bowers relates how "In 1946 . . . the powers behind the Superman franchise decided to use the superhero (in his radio incarnation) to take on a growing concern: the reemergence of the Ku Klux Klan . . . [Rick] Bowers begins with the story of Superman's creators, two Jewish kids who grew up in Cleveland. In alternating sections, he also follows the evolution of the Klan, from its beginnings after the Civil War to its renaissance . . . in the 1920s and beyond. A dual biography of both the hero and the hate group, this book also chronicles the early years of comics . . . and discusses how both Superman and the Klan came with values they wanted to impress upon young people." (Booklist)

Includes bibliographical references and index.

Bronte, Charlotte

Jane Eyre; the graphic novel. [by] Charlotte Bronte; original script by Amy Corzine. Lucent 2010 160p il (Classic graphic novel collection) $32.45

Grades: 7 8 9 10   **741.5**

1. Graphic novels 2. Orphans -- Graphic novels

ISBN 978-1-4205-0375-3; 1-4205-0375-8

LC 2010924004

In graphic novel format, presents an adaptation of Brontë's story about an orphaned young English woman who accepts employment as a governess at Thornfield Hall, a country estate owned by the mysterious and remote Mr. Rochester.

"The entire [story is] told through speech balloons. . . . This format offers readers an experience closer to a theatrical performance than a prose condensation of the plot. . . . Excellent graphics bring the [story] to life and set the mood. Lush art in jewel tones heightens interest. [The title is] replete with support materials beginning with an illustrated cast of characters and an introduction or plot summary and concluding with back matter." SLJ

Brooks, Terry

Dark wraith of Shannara; [by] Terry Brooks; illustrated by Edwin David; adapted by Robert Place Napton. Ballantine Books 2008 199p il pa $13.95

Grades: 6 7 8 9   **741.5**

1. Graphic novels 2. Fantasy graphic novels

ISBN 978-0-345-49462-7 pa; 0-345-49462-8 pa

LC 2008000466

"The first graphic novel based on Brooks' popular, long-running Shannara series features an original story plotted by Brooks himself. . . . The Elven Jair embarks on a journey to keep the location of a powerful magic castle secret from a murderous cult, the Mwellrets. . . . It is . . . a solid, straightforward, highly accessible, action-heavy adventure with black-and-white art that hovers between classic comic and manga style." Booklist

Brosgol, Vera

★ **Anya's** ghost. First Second 2011 221p il $19.99; pa $15.99

Grades: 6 7 8 9 10   **741.5**

1. Graphic novels 2. Ghosts -- Graphic novels 3. School stories -- Graphic novels

ISBN 978-1-59643-713-5; 1-59643-713-8; 978-1-59643-552-0 pa; 1-59643-552-6 pa

LC 2010036251

"A deliciously creepy page-turning gem from first-time writer and illustrator Brosgol. . . . A moodily atmospheric spectrum of grays washes over the clean, tidy panels, setting a distinct stage before the first words appear. . . . In addition to the supernatural elements, Brosgol interweaves some savvy insights about the illusion of perfection and outward appearance. . . . A book sure to haunt its reader long after the last page is turned—exquisitely eerie." Kirkus

Brubaker, Jason

ReMIND. Coffee Table Comics 2011 il $24.95

Grades: 7 8 9 10   **741.5**

1. Fantasy graphic novels 2. Cats -- Graphic novels

ISBN 978-0-9831149-0-1; 0-9831149-0-0

"Sonia and her cat live in the quiet coastal town of Cripple Peaks, which is most famous for being the home of the 'lizard man,' a legendary creature that her father claimed to have seen in 1974. . . . One day Victuals disappears, and as the days pass Sonia loses hope for his return. Then a week later the feline suddenly comes back, but with two alarming changes: there are stitches in his head, and now he can talk. Brubaker's artwork will definitely pull readers into this unusual story and keep them there. The illustrations are colorful and expressive, combining cartoon line drawings with jewel-toned paintings. . . . [This] is sure to capture readers' imaginations and keep them turning the pages." SLJ

Caldwell, Ben

Fantasy! cartooning; [by] Ben Caldwell. Sterling Pub. Co. 2005 95p il pa $9.95

Grades: 5 6 7 8   **741.5**

1. Drawing 2. Fantasy in art 3. Cartoons and comics 4. Cartooning -- Technique

ISBN 1-4027-1612-5

LC 2005041676

Caldwell's "drawing style is . . . a blend of modern Disney (Hercules, Mulan), Don Bluth (Dragon's Lair), and the Cartoon Network (Powderpuff Girls, Samurai Jack, Star Wars: Clone Wars). . . . Caldwell shows original thinking, and his technique is exciting, modern, and unique." SLJ

Campbell, Ross

★ **Shadoweyes**; written and illustrated by Ross Campbell. SLG Publishing 2010 un il pa $14.95

Grades: 8 9 10 11 12   **741.5**
1. Graphic novels 2. Superhero graphic novels 3. Science fiction graphic novels 4. Crime -- Graphic novels
ISBN 978-1-59362-189-6; 1-59362-189-2

"Most convincing is the sharp dialogue, which speaks with such familiar rhythms and sentiment that teens will swear it came out of their own mouths. The art, too, balances a sleek manga technique, credible future looks and grunge fashions, the grotesquerie of zombie flesh, and inventive page composition." Booklist

Card, Orson Scott
Laddertop. Tor 2011 un il pa $10.99
Grades: 6 7 8 9 10   **741.5**
1. Graphic novels 2. Science fiction graphic novels
ISBN 978-0-7653-2460-3; 0-7653-2460-1

"Preteens Robbi and Azure are best friends, though the girls couldn't be more opposite: Robbi is a sensitive dreamer, while Azure is a driven go-getter with a short temper. Azure's biggest dream is to be picked for Laddertop. This is a program of the Givers, aliens who claim to help conserve Earth's resources by building power-providing space stations 36,000 feet above the Earth; these are reached by giant ladders. . . . The main characters in this volume are largely female, strong and intelligent, a wonderful departure from male-dominated extraterrestrial offerings. Ibardolaza's muscular art blends manga and Western aesthetics." Kirkus

Carey, Mike
★ **Re**-Gifters; written by Mike Carey; art by Sonny Liew and Marc Hempel. DC Comics/Minx 2007 148p il pa $9.99
Grades: 7 8 9 10 11 12   **741.5**
1. Graphic novels 2. Romance graphic novels 3. Martial arts -- Graphic novels 4. School stories -- Graphic novels 5. High school students -- Graphic novels
ISBN 978-1-4012-0371-9 pa; 1-4109-0371-X pa

"Jen Dik Seong, or Dixie, is having trouble getting her ki focused. Normally an outstanding hapkido student, she finds that her crush on classmate Adam is affecting her ability to fight. This is not good, as the national competition is fast approaching, and her parents expect her to do well. . . . Dixie makes a series of poor choices. She decides to spend the entry fee . . . on an elaborate birthday present for Adam. . . . This is a terrific read that features complex characters dealing with internal and external conflicts that make them believable and endearing. Lively black-and-white illustrations bring action and emotion to the story." SLJ

Carroll, Lewis, 1832-1898
Through the looking-glass; by Lewis Carroll; adapted by Kyle Baker. Papercutz 2008 un il (Classics illustrated) $9.95
Grades: 3 4 5 6 7 8 9   **741.5**
1. Authors 2. Novelists 3. Graphic novels 4. Mathematicians 5. Fantasy graphic novels 6. Children's authors 7. Writers on science
ISBN 978-1-59707-115-4; 1-59707-115-3

This is Carroll's sequel to Alice's Adventures in Wonderland. This time, Alice climbs through the looking-glass in

her house and finds herself in a land with talking flowers and insects, Tweedledee and Tweedledum (who recite "The Walrus and the Carpenter"), the White Queen who needs help pinning her shawl straight, Humpty Dumpty, the Red Queen, and more. The Eisner Award-winning Baker uses a different style from his usual cartoony look here, more reminiscent of Tenniel's classic illustrations of Carroll's books.

Castellucci, Cecil
Janes in love; by Cecil Castellucci and Jim Rugg; with lettering by Rob Clark Jr. and gray tones by Jasen Lex. DC Comics/Minx 2008 176p il (Plain Janes) pa $9.99
Grades: 7 8 9 10 11 12   **741.5**
1. Graphic novels 2. Romance graphic novels 3. Art -- Graphic novels 4. Friendship -- Graphic novels 5. School stories -- Graphic novels 6. High school students -- Graphic novels
ISBN 978-1-4012-1387-9 pa; 1-4012-1387-1 pa

"Castellucci deftly deals with a number of serious issues, including anxiety and depression, mortality, body image, gay relationships, and community activism. Fortunately, they never weigh down the narrative: this is a sweet, quirky story with some uplifting (though never pedantic) messages. Rugg's clean, crisp illustrations are the perfect accompaniment." SLJ

★ The **Plain** Janes; [illustrated by] Jim Rugg. DC Comics/Minx 2007 un il pa $9.99
Grades: 7 8 9 10 11 12   **741.5**
1. Graphic novels 2. Art -- Graphic novels 3. Friendship -- Graphic novels 4. School stories -- Graphic novels 6. High school students -- Graphic novels
ISBN 978-1-4012-1115-8

After a bomb attack in Metro City, Jane's parents move to suburban Kent Waters, where Jane feels lost. Then she meets three other Janes at the "reject" table in the high school lunch room, and she convinces them to help her form their own secret club: P.L.A.I.N.—People Loving Art in Neighborhoods. However, their "art attacks" cause the authorities to think that P.L.A.I.N. is a terrorist group.

"The art, inspired by Dan Clowes' work, is absolutely engaging. Packaged like manga this is a fresh, exciting use of the graphic-novel format." Booklist

Another title about the Janes is:
Janes in love (2008)

Christmas classics; edited by Tom Pomplun. Eureka 2010 144p il (Graphic classics) $17.95
Grades: 7 8 9 10 11 12   **741.5**
1. Graphic novels 2. Christmas -- Fiction
ISBN 978-0-9825630-1-4; 0-9825630-1-9

This is a collection of graphic adaptations of Christmas classics including Charles Dickens' "A Christmas Carol," an early F. Scott Fitzgerald tale, an O. Henry western, a fairy tale by Willa Cather, and a Christmas horror story by Fitz-James O'Brien, a seasonal Sherlock Holmes adventure by Arthur Conan Doyle, Clement C. Moore's classic poem "A Visit from St. Nicholas," and a letter from Santa Claus to Mark Twain's daughter.

"The variety of art styles and solid selection choices make this . . . essential for collections that include holiday books for teens and adults." Booklist

Chwast, Seymour

★ The **odyssey**; [Homer]; adapted by Seymour Chwast. 1st U.S. ed. Bloomsbury 2012 128 p. ill. (All-action classics) (hardcover) $20.00

Grades: Adult   **741.5**
  1. Epic literature 2. Adventure graphic novels 3. Odysseus (Greek mythology) 4. Graphic novels
  ISBN 9781608194865
                 LC 2012010047

In this graphic retelling of Homer's "The Odyssey," "Odysseus faces storm and shipwreck, a terrifying man-eating Cyclops, the alluring but deadly Sirens, and the fury of the sea-god Poseidon as he makes his ten-year journey home from the Trojan War. While Odysseus struggles to make it home, his wife, Penelope, fights a different kind of battle as her palace is invaded by forceful, greedy men who tell her that Odysseus is dead and she must choose a new husband." (Publisher's note)

This graphic novel adaptation of Homer's classic epic is "a crackling adventure that also penetrates the recessess of the human heart. . . . Caldwell's art has the force and vibrant life of a Samurai Jack cartoon." Booklist

Colfer, Eoin

Artemis Fowl: the graphic novel; adapted by Eoin Colfer and Andrew Donkin; art by Giovanni Rigano; color by Paolo Lammana. Hyperion Books for Children 2007 un il $18.99; pa $9.99

Grades: 4 5 6 7 8 9   **741.5**
  1. Graphic novels 2. Fantasy graphic novels 3. Adventure graphic novels
  ISBN 978-0-7868-4881-2; 0-7868-4881-2; 978-0-7868-4882-9 pa; 0-7868-4882-0 pa

Twelve-year-old genius and criminal mastermind Artemis Fowl runs his missing father's crime empire and gets his hands on a book that will give him access to the underground fairy world. This graphic novel adaptation gives the book a European look and color palette

"Excellent use of color and shading gives the panels a tremendous sense of light with enchanting effect. Characters are expressively brought to life with fun, exaggerated style." SLJ

Collar, Orpheus

★ The **Red** Pyramid. Hyperion 2012 192 p. (Kane chronicles) (hardback) $21.99

Grades: 4 5 6 7   **741.5**
  1. Occult fiction 2. Fantasy fiction 3. Siblings -- Fiction 4. Secret societies -- Fiction 5. Gods and goddesses -- Fiction 6. Voyages and travels -- Fiction 7. Graphic novels
  ISBN 1423150686; 9781423150688

This is the first installment of the Kane chronicles. "Since their mother's death, Carter and Sadie have become near strangers. While Sadie has lived with her grandparents in London, her brother has traveled the world with their father, the brilliant Egyptologist, Dr. Julius Kane. . . . [Dr. Kane] unleashes the Egyptian god Set, who banished him

to oblivion and forces the children to flee for their lives." (Publisher's note)

"The first-person narrative shifts between Carter and Sadie, giving the novel an intriguing dual perspective made more complex by their biracial heritage and the tension between the siblings. . . . This fantasy adventure delivers . . . . young protagonists with previously unsuspected magical powers, a riveting story marked by headlong adventure, a complex background rooted in ancient mythology, and wry, witty twenty-first-century narration." Booklist

Crilley, Mark

Miki Falls, Book One: Spring. HarperCollins/HarperTeen 2007 176p il pa $7.99

Grades: 7 8 9 10 11 12   **741.5**
  1. Graphic novels 2. Friendship -- Graphic novels 3. School stories -- Graphic novels 4. High school students -- Graphic novels
  ISBN 978-0-06-084616-9

"Crilley uses mystery to drive the narrative and creates characters that the reader will care about. The black-and-white, manga-style art is beautiful." Voice Youth Advocates

  Other titles in this series are:
  Miki Falls, Book Two: Summer
  Miki Falls, Book Three: Autumn
  Miki Falls, Book Four: Winter

Dahl, Michael

Alien snow; illustrated by Roberta Pares. Stone Arch Books 2011 un il (Good vs evil) lib bdg $22.65

Grades: 4 5 6 7   **741.5**
  1. Graphic novels 2. Good and evil -- Fiction 3. Extraterrestrial beings -- Fiction
  ISBN 978-1-4342-2090-5; 1-4342-2090-7
                 LC 2010004111

"When young Noah Urbain walks into an antique shop, he unknowinly walks into a trap. . . . In this story, told from two perspectives ('evil' and 'good'), the storekeeper traps Noah in a snow globe. . . . The ultralow word count . . . and suspenseful action of this title . . . will help lure in reluctant readers." Booklist

Dawson, Willow

Lila & Ecco's do-it-yourself comics club. Kids Can Press 2010 112p il $16.95

Grades: 4 5 6 7   **741.5**
  1. Graphic novels 2. Cartoons and caricatures
  ISBN 978-1-55453-438-8; 1-55453-438-0

Twelve-year-olds Lila and Ecco are obsessed with comics. Every summer, they dress up as their favorite characters to attend the local comic book convention. This year, after they stumble into a workshop of comics creators, Lila and Ecco come to an exciting realization they can make their very own comic books!.

"Is it a story of two friends creating a comic, or a step-by-step guide to making comics? Why, it's both, actually. And what's most surprising is not that the guide is so comprehensive and easy to follow but that the framing story not only couches the lessons in comfortable language but is also diverting in its own right. . . . Dawson's savvy, sassy black-

and-white art gives the static idea of instructions some pep, and the information is quite complete." Booklist

Deas, Mike

Dalen & Gole; scandal in Port Angus. Orca Book Publishers 2011 123p il pa $9.95

Grades: 4 5 6 7   **741.5**

1. Graphic novels 2. Science fiction graphic novels 3. Extraterrestrial beings -- Graphic novels

ISBN 978-1-55469-800-4; 1-55469-800-6

Dalen and Gole, refugees on Earth from the distant planet of Budap, must solve the mystery of diminishing fish stocks and save their home planet from an evil plot.

Deas "provides solid graphics, pacing, dialogue, and humor. . . . A fun mystery-adventure that's just right for young space cases." Booklist

Dezago, Todd

Spider-man: Spidey strikes back Vol. 1 digest. Marvel Comics 2005 96p il pa $5.99

Grades: 4 5 6 7 8 9   **741.5**

1. Graphic novels 2. Superhero graphic novels 3. Spider-Man (Fictional character) 4. Superheroes (Fictional characters) -- Fiction

ISBN 0-7851-1632-X

Tired of saving the day and getting no respect, Spider-Man considers taking a break from his superhero duties, which leaves the city wide open for the likes of the Sandman and the Enforcers. Will Spidey let it all go to pot, or will he step up to the plate and take one for the team? This volume collects Marvel Age Spider-Man issues 17-20. Previous volumes were published under the series title Marvel Age Spider-Man. The Marvel Age titles are being collected and published in the digest size, similar to manga, and at an affordable price. The Marvel Age series are aimed at younger audiences than the other superhero titles from Marvel.

Dixon, Chuck

Hobbit: an illustrated edition of the fantasy classic; [by] J. R. R. Tolkien; Chuck Dixon, adapter; David Wenzel, illustrator. Del Rey Books 2001 133p il pa $15.95

Grades: 5 6 7 8   **741.5**

1. Graphic novels

ISBN 0-345-44560-0

The tale of how dwarfs came to ask the hobbit Bilbo Baggins to leave his comfortable home in the Shire to travel with them on their quest to recover their gold from the evil dragon Smaug is adapted to comic book form, with lush, colorful illustrations by David Wenzel. All the adventures recounted in Tolkien's novel are here, retold in a format for all ages to enjoy

Dunn, Joeming W.

The **phantom** of the opera; adapted by Joeming Dunn; illustrated by Rod Espinosa. Magic Wagon/Graphic Planet 2009 32p il $27.07

Grades: 3 4 5 6 7   **741.5**

1. Authors 2. Novelists 3. Graphic novels 4. Horror graphic novels 5. Mystery writers 6. Opera -- Graphic

novels

ISBN 978-1-6027-0679-8; 1-6027-0679-4

LC 2009-8606

Born with a hideous appearance, Erik has a glorious voice but must hide his face with a mask. After living for a time in Persia, he returns to France, where he builds a warren of tunnels and passageways under and throughout a new opera house in Paris. There, the young opera singer Christine achieves success because the unseen Angel of Music had trained her; the Angel is Erik. He loves Christine and wishes for her to remain with him always, but she fears he is mad and loves the wealthy Raoul. This graphic novel adaptation provides an easy-reading introduction to Gaston Leroux's famous novel, which was also the basis for the long-running stage musical, Phantom, written by Andrew Lloyd Webber. Back matter includes a brief biography of Leroux, a list of Leroux's other novels, and a short glossary.

Emerson, Sharon

Zebrafish; written by Sharon Emerson; drawn by Renee Kurilla. Atheneum Books for Young Readers 2010 119p il $16.99

Grades: 4 5 6 7   **741.5**

1. Graphic novels 2. Rock music -- Graphic novels

ISBN 978-1-4169-9525-8; 1-4169-9525-0

LC 2009-41683

When their rock band becomes popular, five middle schoolers use their new fame to generate awareness (and donations) for an important cause.

Fairfield, Lesley

★ **Tyranny**. Tundra Books 2009 114p il pa $10.95

Grades: 8 9 10 11 12   **741.5**

1. Graphic novels 2. Eating disorders -- Graphic novels

ISBN 978-0-88776-903-0; 0-88776-903-9

"This is one of the most moving and important graphic novels to come along in years. Many stories have been written about teens who try to change what they see in the mirror through anorexia and bulimia, but this one features a girl who is driven by her own personal demon. That demon is called Tyranny, and it is represented by an angry and chaotic swirl of lines that form the shape of a person. . . . Fairfield treats this important subject with intelligence and empathy. . . . The simple yet powerful black-and-white drawings do wonders in bringing the book's message to its readers." SLJ

Fajardo, Alexis E.

Kid Beowulf and the blood-bound oath. Bowler Hat 2008 il pa $14.95

Grades: 6 7 8 9   **741.5**

1. Graphic novels 2. Monsters -- Graphic novels

ISBN 978-0-9801419-1-7 pa; 0-9801419-1-5 pa

"In the standard Beowulf story, the character appears as a full-fledged hero, with little concept of how he actually became one. Fajardo tells the backstory, using a blend of humor and soap-opera plot twists. . . . The cartoon-style illustrations are lively and contain lots of visual humor." SLJ

Farr, James

EV: vol. 1. Tokyopop 2008 il pa $9.99

Grades: 6 7 8 9   **741.5**
1. Graphic novels 2. Science fiction -- Graphic novels
ISBN 978-1-4278-0714-4 pa; 1-4278-0714-0 pa

"Evie's father, Dr. Richard Wymond . . . is locked in a nearly five-year struggle to devise an advanced superhuman to send as a delegate into space. . . . Dr. Wymond has created the ZETTA serum, which . . . creates nanoscopic machines that interact with the body on an atomic level. . . . With five hours to go before the emissaries return to retrieve the delegate, Dr. Wymond learns that all of the candidates have been assassinated, and he must inject himself with the serum and travel into space. . . . Evie and her mother are slammed by a diesel truck, leaving Evie on the brink of death. . . . Dr. Wymond injects his daughter with the serum, and . . . she is saved from death, but with side effects. . . . As Evie is both brainy and beautiful, both male and female readers should enjoy this highly readable graphic novel." SLJ

Fisch, Sholly
Super friends: for justice! y. Sholly Fisch writer; Dario Brizuela ... [et. al] artists. DC Comics 2009 un il $12.99
Grades: 5 6 7 8 9   **741.5**
1. Graphic novels 2. Superhero graphic novels 3. Batman (Fictional character) 4. Superman (Fictional character) 5. Wonder Woman (Fictional character)
ISBN 978-1-4012-2156-0; 1-4012-2156-4

"This volume features the JLA facing off with some of their biggest foes including the power-stealing android Amazo and the super-ape known as Gorilla Grodd." Publisher's note

Flight explorer; edited by Kazu Kibuishi. Villard 2008 112p il pa $10
Grades: 4 5 6 7   **741.5**
1. Graphic novels 2. Fantasy graphic novels 3. Humorous graphic novels 4. Adventure graphic novels 5. Science fiction graphic novels
ISBN 978-0-345-50313-8 pa; 0-345-50313-9 pa

This anthology includes stories that Kibuishi kept from Flight Volume 4 because they had all-ages appeal, as well as stories submitted especially for this volume. Kibuishi's own Copper and his talking dog cross a deep canyon by leaping onto mushrooms, only to discover the vegetation is intelligent. Kean Soo's Jellaby and his human friends frolic in the snow. Missile Mouse by Jake Parker defends a village on another planet, only to discover his coming was prophesied (this story includes two uses of the word "crap"). The other stories will appeal to younger readers, while some of the humor will also appeal to older readers. Other than the one bad word in "Missile Mouse" (noted above), there shouldn't be any other content that would keep this book out of most elementary and middle schools.

"Every story has a layout that promotes an acute sense of pacing and showcases the crisp, defined, full-color art." SLJ

★ **Fractured** fables; edited by Jim Valentino and Kristen K. Simon; book design by Jim Valentino; cover illustration by Michael and Laura Allred from a sketch by Jim Valentino; cover design and

graphics by Tim Daniel. Image Comics 2010 159p il $29.99
Grades: 6 7 8 9   **741.5**
1. Graphic novels 2. Literature -- Collections
ISBN 978-1-60706-269-1; 1-60706-269-0
LC 2010014838

Presents, in comic book format, thirty familiar fairy tales, songs, fables, and stories as retold by such acclaimed authors and illustrators as Ben Templesmith, Jim Di Bartolo, Scott Morse, and May Ann Licudine.

"This is a great adaptation highly worth reading or just browsing the artwork and illustrations." Voice Youth Advocates

Foley, Ryan
Stolen hearts; the love of Eros and Psyche. illustrated by Sankha Banerjee. Campfire 2011 84p il (Campfire mythology) pa $11.99
Grades: 6 7 8 9   **741.5**
1. Graphic novels 2. Love -- Graphic novels 3. Greek mythology -- Graphic novels
ISBN 978-93-80028-48-4; 93-80028-48-2

Aphrodite, the Greek goddess of beauty, has grown jealous of a young girl named Psyche. The goddess decides to dispatch her mischievous son Eros, the god of love, to perform a nasty trick. When the trick goes awry, Eros finds himself falling in love with Psyche.

"Foley retells one of the most famous love stories of all time, and it is certainly beautiful to behold. Banerjee's lovely, jewel-toned paintings will keep readers' eyes glued to the page. . . . This is a good adaptation of an old story, and one that will entice today's readers." SLJ

Ford, Christopher
Stickman Odyssey; an epic doodle. Philomel Books 2011 200p il $12.99
Grades: 5 6 7 8   **741.5**
1. Graphic novels 2. Humorous graphic novels 3. Adventure graphic novels 4. Greek mythology -- Graphic novels 5. Graphic novels
ISBN 978-0-399-25426-0; 0-399-25426-9
LC 2010-36900

In this humorous take on the Odyssey, Zozimos, banished from his country by his evil stepmother, has many adventures as he prepares to return home to reclaim the throne that is rightfully his.

"The black-and-white illustrations are occasionally simple to the point of hilarity. . . . There is subtlety and depth here, however, and the contrast between the intentionally plain characters and their seemingly larger-than-life (but ultimately universal) quests . . . makes the final product both the promised Greek epic tale and an examination of the ways in which modern humans are isolated and lost. . . . Ford balances allegory and madcap quest so perfectly that the book inspires reflection even while it is clearly a quick-reading, ridiculous, often gross adventure." Bull Cent Child Books

Friesen, Ray
Cupcakes of doom! Don't Eat Any Bugs Productions 2008 98p il pa $12.95
Grades: 3 4 5 6 7 8   **741.5**
1. Graphic novels 2. Humorous graphic novels 3.

Adventure graphic novels 4. Pirates -- Graphic novels
ISBN 978-0-9802314-1-0 pa; 0-9802314-1-8 pa

The Pirate band led by Captain Scurvybeard must do battle with the Vikings to decide the fate of the kingdom called Pellmellia. With a decidedly shifty fellow named Flambe testing them to see if they deserve to be pirates, Yoho Joseph, Peglegless Pete (he's just a kid), Lester the parrot, Pete's sister Jamie, and the rest of the crew must find the long lost recipe for the Cupcakes of Doom, or the Deliciously-Evil Viking Pie will take over as the people's favorite baked good. The book is full of silly humor, wacky characters (including identical twin sea serpents and a Viking penguin), and a lot of action without violence or bad language. The book is suitable for younger readers, but adults will enjoy the silliness and catch more of the jokes

Geary, Rick

Great expectations; adapted by Rick Geary. rev ed; Papercutz 2008 56p il (Classics illustrated) $9.95

Grades: 4 5 6 7 8 9   **741.5**
1. Authors 2. Novelists 3. Graphic novels 4. Orphans -- Graphic novels
ISBN 978-1-59707-097-3; 1-59707-097-1

After harsh early years, Pip, an orphan growing up in Victorian England, is given the means to become a gentleman by an unknown benefactor and learns that outward appearances can be deceiving. Presented in comic book format.

"This pleasant graphic interpretation can serve as an introduction to Dickens for younger readers and perhaps eventually steer them to the wider world of the source material and beyond." Publ Wkly

The **invisible** man; by H.G. Wells; adapted by Rick Geary. NBM/Papercutz 2008 un il (Classics illustrated) $9.95

Grades: 5 6 7 8 9 10 11 12   **741.5**
1. Authors 2. Novelists 3. Historians 4. Graphic novels 5. Mystery graphic novels 6. Science fiction graphic novels 7. Writers on science 8. Writers on politics 9. Science fiction writers
ISBN 978-1-59707-106-2; 1-59707-106-4

A stranger comes to the small town of Iping, his face covered in bandages and dark lensed spectacles. After a few months, the townspeople learn that this mysterious man is invisible and responsible for recent crimes. After he escapes from Iping, he ends up in the house of Kemp, who had studied at University College with him. The man's name is Griffin, he was a scientist who became obsessed with finding the secret of invisibility and who would stop at nothing, including stealing money from his own father to fund his experiments. And he will stop at nothing including murder to remain free. The book includes a couple of panels showing partial nudity.

Giarrano, Vince

★ **Comics** crash course; [by] Vincent Giarrano. Impact Books 2004 127p il pa $19.99

Grades: 5 6 7 8   **741.5**
1. Drawing 2. Cartoons and comics 3. Cartoons and

caricatures
ISBN 1-58180-533-0

LC 2004-43969

This is a guide to creating comic book stories and characters.

This offers "plenty of great art advice, striking imagery, and just enough edginess to satisfy most aspiring comic-book artists.... An excellent introduction to comic drawing, composition, and graphic storytelling." SLJ

Glass, Bryan J. L.

The **mice** templar, volume one: the prophecy; created by Bryan J.L. Glass & Michael Avon Oeming. Image Comics 2008 256p il $29.99

Grades: 6 7 8 9 10 11 12 Adult   **741.5**
1. Graphic novels 2. Fantasy graphic novels 3. Adventure graphic novels 4. Mice -- Graphic novels
ISBN 978-1-58240-871-2; 1-58240-871-8

In a land populated by animals, the Mice Templar used to protect the people of the mouse kingdom, but a civil war destroyed them; the king now employs rat soldiers, and they prey upon the mouse villages. Young Karic still idolizes the Mice Templar, but everything he knows and believes is shattered when his village is raided by rats, burned, and his family captured as slaves. He survives, saved by a mysterious mouse named Pilot, who says he was once a Templar and offers to train Karic. The salmon in the river say that Karic is the one prophesied to restore the Templar, but can he truly be the one? The book includes considerable battle violence.

"Equal parts Norse myth, Arthurian legend, and Mrs. Frisby and the Rats of N.I.M.H., The Mice Templar series re-imagines the warrior animal tale with just enough of its own spin to make it well worth adding to the collection." Voice Youth Advocates

Gorman, Michele

★ **Getting** graphic! using graphic novels to promote literacy with preteens and teens. with a foreword by Jeff Smith. Linworth Pub. 2003 100p il pa $36.95

Grades: Adult Professional   **741.5**
1. Graphic novels 2. Graphic novels -- Administration 3. Graphic novels -- History and criticism
ISBN 1-58683-089-9

LC 2003-13199

"A must-have first resource for school and public libraries that are considering adding graphic novels to their collections but are unsure how to proceed." Booklist

Includes bibliographical references

Grant, Alan

Robert Louis Stevenson's Kidnapped; adaptation by Alan Grant; illustrator, Cam Kennedy. Tundra Books 2007 un il pa $11.95

Grades: 6 7 8 9 10   **741.5**
1. Poets 2. Authors 3. Novelists 4. Graphic novels 5. Adventure graphic novels 6. Essayists 7. Travel writers 8. Short story writers
ISBN 978-0-88776-843-9 pa; 0-88776-843-1 pa

LC 2007921350

Kidnapped is set in 1751, during the time of the Jacobite rebellion — a tumultuous and tragic period in Scottish history. When David Balfour sets out to find his uncle, he never dreamed that he would be kidnapped — but saved from a life of slavery — and thrown from one escapade to another in the company of the fugitive, masterful swordsman Alan Breck Stewart.

"This is an engaging adaptation, aided by Kennedy's vibrant illustrations in a palette dominated by blues, greens, and sepia tones. The action scenes are exciting." SLJ

Robert Louis Stevenson's Strange case of Dr. Jekyll and Mr. Hyde; adapted by Alan Grant; illustrated by Cam Kennedy; colored and lettered by Jamie Grant. Tundra Books 2008 40p il pa $11.95

Grades: 6 7 8 9 10   **741.5**
1. Poets 2. Authors 3. Novelists 4. Graphic novels 5. Horror graphic novels 6. Essayists 7. Travel writers 8. Short story writers
ISBN 978-0-88776-882-8 pa; 0-88776-882-2 pa

"Stevenson's classic tale takes on a new format in a vivid graphic novel. This mysterious story of the struggle between good and evil is one that has been popular since its publication and continues to hold its appeal. Much about this adaptation honors the original version of the story—the language of the period remains true, and the drawings of 1880s London and the furnishings and fashion within it are realistic as well." Voice Youth Advocates

★ **Graphic** novels and comic books; edited by Kat Kan. The H.W. Wilson Co. 2010 195p il (Reference shelf) pa $35

Grades: Adult Professional   **741.5**
1. Graphic novels 2. Comic books, strips, etc. 3. Graphic novels -- History and criticism 4. Comic books, strips, etc. -- History and criticism
ISBN 978-0-8242-1100-4; 0-8242-1100-6
      LC 2010-34209

"This collection of articles from scholarly journals, newspapers, and blogs gives a well-rounded overview of graphic novels, as well as a strong argument for their place in schools and libraries. The first section chronicles the growing mainstream acceptance of graphic novels in the United States. . . . Susequent sections look at these books as complex works of literature, as education and literacy aids, and as significant additions to library collections, with advice for librarians on how to purchase, catalog, file, and promote them. In the final section, readers hear from writers and artists . . . who clearly convey the joy they get from this medium. This is both an entertaining and highly practical read." SLJ

Includes bibliographical references

Grayson, Devin
Uglies; Shay's story. created by Scott Westerfeld; written by Scott Westerfeld and Devin Grayson; illustrations by Steven Cummings. Del Rey 2012 160 p. chiefly ill. (prebind) $22.10; (paperback) $10.99

Grades: 7 8 9 10   **741.5**
1. Dystopian graphic novels 2. Conformity -- Graphic novels 3. Plastic surgery -- Graphic novels 4. Graphic Novels 5. Science fiction 6. Friiendship -- Fiction 7.

Beauty, Personal -- Fiction
ISBN 9780606264754; 0345527224; 9780345527226
      LC 2012374898

This young adult graphic novel retells the story of author Scott Westerfeld's dystopia "Uglies" from "the point of view of recurring frenemy Shay." It is "set in a . . . future time when discord is suppressed through ruthlessly enforced conformity and obligatory plastic surgery at age 16. . . . Shay yearns for freedom. An encounter with the flawed and alluring David, a covert envoy from the Smoke, a secret community of nonconformists, may offer Shay the escape she craves." (Publishers Weekly)

Gulledge, Laura Lee
Page by Paige. Amulet Books 2011 un il $18.95; pa $9.95

Grades: 7 8 9 10 11 12   **741.5**
1. Graphic novels 2. Humorous graphic novels 3. Artists -- Graphic novels 4. Friendship -- Graphic novels
ISBN 0-8109-9721-5; 0-8109-9722-3 pa; 978-0-8109-9721-9; 978-0-8109-9722-6 pa

Teenage Paige Turner (blame her writer parents) moves to New York City from Virginia, and she finds the big city rather overwhelming. She decides to buy a sketchbook and sort out her thoughts and feelings in drawings. Soon she does make some friends, and she explores more of the city, but as she begins to feel happier, she clashes with her parents. All of this goes into her sketchbook journal, which she starts to show to her new friends—Jules, Longo, and Gabe. The book is organized by Paige's "rules," which she uses to try to change herself, such as "Rule #2: Draw what you know. If you feel it or see it . . . DRAW IT!"

"Gulledge's b&w illustrations are simple but well-suited to their subject matter; the work as a whole is a good-natured, optimistic portrait of a young woman evolving toward adulthood." Publ Wkly

Hale, Dean
★ **Rapunzel's** revenge; [by] Shannon and Dean Hale; illustrated by Nathan Hale. Bloomsbury 2008 144p il map $18.99; pa $14.99

Grades: 5 6 7 8   **741.5**
1. Graphic novels 2. Fantasy graphic novels 3. Humorous graphic novels 4. Fairy tales -- Graphic novels
ISBN 1-59990-070-X; 1-59990-288-5 pa; 978-1-59990-070-4; 978-1-59990-288-3 pa
      LC 2007-37670

In this graphic novel, Rapunzel escapes "from the enchanted tree where Mother Gothel imprisoned her. Rapunzel sets off alone through the ghost towns and Badlands of Gothel's Reach. She is determined to find Gothel's Villa and teach Mother Gothel a long-overdue lesson for her years of treachery and lies, and help her real mother get out of the mine camps where Mother Gothel has kept her enslaved." (Publisher's note) "Grades four to seven." (Bull Cent Child Books)

"The dialogue is witty, the story is an enticing departure from the original, and the illustrations are magically fun and expressive." SLJ

Another title about these characters is:

Calamity Jack (2009)

Hale, Shannon

Calamity Jack; [by] Shannon Hale, Dean Hale, and Nathan Hale. Bloomsbury 2010 144p il $19.99; pa $14.99

Grades: 5 6 7 8   **741.5**

1. Graphic novels 2. Fairy tales -- Graphic novels

ISBN 978-1-59990-076-6; 1-59900-076-9; 978-1-59990-373-6 pa; 1-59990-373-3 pa

LC 2008-41332

In this graphic novel interpretation of "Jack and the beanstalk," Jack is a born schemer who climbs a magical beanstalk in the hope of exacting justice from a mean giant and gaining a fortune for his widowed mother, aided by some friends.

"The urban setting suits this retelling of the familiar beanstalk tale; Nathan Hale's art gives it a steampunk twist, and the addition of fairy-tale creatures like giants and pixies is natural and convincing." Booklist

Hart, Christopher

Drawing the new adventure cartoons; cool spies, evil guys and action heroes. Sixth & Spring Books 2008 126p il pa $19.95

Grades: 4 5 6 7   **741.5**

1. Drawing 2. Cartoons and caricatures

ISBN 978-1-933027-60-9 pa; 1-933027-60-6 pa

"This fun guide works best for those with some previous figure-drawing experience. . . . Sections on 'Drawing the Head,' 'Drawing the Teen Action Body,' and 'Using Body Language to Convey Emotion' offer detailed and, for the most part, step-by-step instructions. Subsequent sections . . . provide examples of unique and zany aspects of adventure-style characters. . . . Throughout the book, Hart also includes useful tip boxes, often demonstrating how not to draw a character. These suggestions are invaluable, providing insight into creating kinetic and expressive cartoons." SLJ

How to draw comic book bad guys and gals. Watson-Guptill 1998 64p il pa $10.95

Grades: 6 7 8 9 10 11 12   **741.5**

1. Drawing 2. Cartoons and caricatures 3. Comic books, strips, etc. 4. Comic strip characters 5. Cartooning -- Technique 6. Comic books, strips, etc -- Technique

ISBN 0-8230-2372-9

LC 98-6411

This guide to drawing comic book villains covers such topics as head tilts, facial expressions, hands and muscle groups, the body in action, using light and shadow, composition, and storytelling

"Not for beginners, but for those who already have some knowledge of drawing and ability. . . . Boldly colored illustrations combined with the line drawings add to the professional look of the book." Voice Youth Advocates

Manga for the beginner; everything you need to start drawing right away! Watson-Guptill Publications 2008 192p il $21.95

Grades: 5 6 7 8 9 10   **741.5**

1. Manga -- Drawing 2. Graphic novels -- Drawing

ISBN 978-0-8230-3083-5; 0-8230-3083-0

LC 2007-40490

"Hart's latest drawing book . . . contains detailed and easy-to-follow instructions for drawing types of shojo manga (aimed at girls) and shonen manga (aimed at boys). . . . He describes in concise language and through clear illustrations how to use lettering, lighting effects, and other techniques to achieve a certain mood to advance a plot. . . . Anyone even slightly interested in drawing manga will find it appealing." Voice Youth Advocates

Manga mania romance; drawing shojo girls and bishie boys. [by] Chris Hart. Chris Hart Books 2008 147p il pa $19.95

Grades: 6 7 8 9 10   **741.5**

1. Drawing 2. Manga -- Drawing 3. Cartooning -- Technique

ISBN 978-1-933027-43-2; 1-933027-43-6

LC 2007-907250

"This crisply illustrated work aims to give aspiring cartoonists the basics of drawing. . . . A wonderful introduction to the shojo style. A great first choice for creating a cartooning/drawing collection." SLJ

Mecha mania; how to draw the battling robots, cool spaceships, and military vehicles of Japanese comics. Watson-Guptill 2002 128p il pa $19.95

Grades: 5 6 7 8   **741.5**

1. Robots 2. Drawing 3. Cartoons and comics 4. Cartoons and caricatures 5. Drawing -- Technique 6. Comic books, strips, etc -- Japan -- Technique

ISBN 0-8230-3056-3

LC 2002-6402

"Hart offers budding cartoonists a mix of basic instructions and savvy technical advice for creating a wide variety of generic giant robots, robotlike craft, cyborgs of both sexes, and bad-guy types . . . then posing them for maximum visual effect. . . . His 'can-do!' tone and cogent instructions, as well as the gallery of chiseled, heavily armed, hypercomplicated machines, will make this volume appealing to both casual browsers and serious young artists." SLJ

Helfand, Lewis

Conquering Everest; the lives of Edmund Hillary and Tenzing Norgay. illustrated by Amit Tayal. Kalyani Navyug Media 2011 91p il (Campfire Graphic Novels Series) pa $12.99

Grades: 5 6 7 8   **741.5**

1. Mountaineering 2. Mountaineers 3. Nonfiction writers

ISBN 978-93-80741-24-6; 93-80741-24-3

LC 2011321480

"The exploits of two young men mad for climbing mountains are retold in graphic panels. . . . Tayal captures their likeness in flurries of small but visually varied cartoon scenes, often placing figures in front of reworked photos of forbidding ice fields and peaks. Helfand fills the dialogue-heavy narrative with specific biographical details amd exciting accounts of some of the great triumphs and tragedies of Himalayan mountaineering. . . . A vivid double character portrait, enhanced by equally sharp glimpses of climbing techniques, strategies and hazards." Kirkus

Kim; [by] Rudyard Kipling; [adapted by Lewis Helfand; illustrated by Rakesh Kumar] Kalyani Navyug Media 2011 68p il pa $9.99
Grades: 6 7 8 9   741.5
  1. Graphic novels 2. Adventure graphic novels
ISBN 978-8-1907326-3-5; 8-1907326-3-3
                           LC 2010319053
"Rudyard Kipling's adventure novel is luminiously visualized in this adaptation. The story line remains true to the original and follows Kim as he departs from his boyhood home with a Buddhist lama and embarks on adventures as a boy spy. Kumar's watercolor scenes and expressions lend authentic views of Kim's moods as well as his surroundings." Booklist

Henry V; the graphic novel. [by] William Shakespeare; script by John McDonald; adapted by Brigit Viney. Lucent 2010 160p il (Classic graphic novel collection) $32.45
Grades: 7 8 9 10   741.5
  1. Poets 2. Authors 3. Dramatists 4. Graphic novels
ISBN 978-1-4205-0371-5; 1-4205-0371-5
                           LC 2010924003
In this graphic novel retelling of Shakespeare's Henry V, "the entire [story is] told through speech balloons. . . . This format offers readers an experience closer to a theatrical performance than a prose condensation of the plot. . . . Excellent graphics bring the [story] to life and set the mood. Lush art in jewel tones heightens interest. . . . [The title is] replete with support materials beginning with an illustrated cast of characters and an introduction or plot summary and concluding with back matter." SLJ

Heuvel, Eric
  ★ A **family** secret; [English translation, Lorraine T. Miller] Farrar, Straus and Giroux 2009 62p il pa $9.99; $18.99
Grades: 7 8 9 10 11 12   741.5
  1. Graphic novels 2. Jews -- Graphic novels 3. Grandmothers -- Graphic novels 5. Holocaust, 1933-1945 -- Graphic novels
ISBN 0-374-32271-6; 978-0-374-42265-3 pa; 0-374-42265-6 pa; 978-0-374-32271-7
                           LC 2009-13943
Original Dutch edition, 2003
While searching his Dutch grandmother's attic for yard sale items, Jeroen finds a scrapbook which leads Gran to tell of her experiences as a girl living in Amsterdam during the Holocaust, when her father was a Nazi sympathizer and Esther, her Jewish best friend, disappeared
  This is a "moving graphic novel. . . . The art is in ink and watercolor, with very clear, highly detailed panels. . . . [A] gripping story." Booklist

Hicks, Faith Erin
  Friends with boys. First Second 2012 224p $15.99

Grades: 5 6 7   741.5
  1. Ghost stories 2. Graphic novels 3. Teenagers -- Fiction
ISBN 9781596435568
                           LC 2011030470
In this graphic novel, "[the] youngest of four siblings and the only girl, Maggie is both excited and worried about starting high school after being home-schooled her whole life. . . . As Maggie makes friends with a perky indie girl named Lucy and her mysterious brother, Alistair, she broods over the loss of her mother, who recently left the family without much of an explanation, and tries to figure out what the ghost wants from her." (Bulletin of the Center for Children's Books)

The **war** at Ellsmere. Slave Labor Graphics 2008 156p il pa $12.95
Grades: 6 7 8 9 10 11   741.5
  1. Graphic novels 2. Humorous graphic novels 3. Friendship -- Graphic novels 4. School stories -- Graphic novels
ISBN 1-59362-140-X; 978-1-59362-140-7
Juniper is the newest scholarship student at the prestigious Ellsmere Academy; she wanted to attend there in order to increase her chances of getting into a good medical school. She's on scholarship because her mom has had to raise her alone since her father died when she was young. Jun makes one friend at Ellsmere, Cassie, who calls herself the cliche of the poor little rich girl. Wealthy Emily calls Cassie "Orphan" because her parents ignore her, and chooses to call Jun "Project," as in Headmistress Ms. Bishop's latest project. Emily is also determined to get rid of Jun, especially when Jun encourages Cassie to work harder and even win the extra credit essay contest. Now it's war, or as Jun puts it, "It's like Upstairs Downstairs meets Lord of the Flies. In plaid skirts. And sweater vests." There's one incident when Jun punches Emily in the face.
  "Hicks gives readers enough tension and quirky turns to satisfy and pleasantly surprise." Booklist

Hinds, Gareth
  ★ **Beowulf**; adapted and illustrated by Gareth Hinds. Candlewick Press 2007 un il $21.99; pa $9.99
Grades: 8 9 10 11 12 Adult   741.5
  1. Graphic novels 2. Adventure graphic novels 3. Monsters -- Graphic novels
ISBN 978-0-7636-3022-5; 0-7636-3022-5; 978-0-7636-3023-2 pa; 0-7636-3023-3 pa
                           LC 2006-49023
Graphic novel adaptation of the Old English epic poem, Beowulf
  "For fantasy fans both young and old, this makes an ideal introduction to a story without which the entire fantasy genre would look very different; many scenes may be too intense for very young readers." Publ Wkly

  ★ **King** Lear; a play by William Shakespeare; adapted and illustrated by Gareth Hinds. Candlewick Press 2009 123p il $22.99; pa $11.99

Grades: 7 8 9 10 11 12   741.5
1. Poets 2. Authors 3. Dramatists 4. Graphic novels
ISBN 978-0-7636-4343-0; 0-7636-4343-2; 978-0-7636-4344-7 pa; 0-7636-4344-0 pa

A reissue of the title first published 2007 by Thecomic.com

This graphic novel adaptation of Shakespeare's King Lear is "an excellent rendition of one the bard's great tragedies. Using splash pages that open up the settings, washes of otherworldly colors, grotesquely expressive faces . . . and figural work . . . Hinds occasionally attains a visual poetry." Booklist

★ The **Odyssey**. Candlewick Press 2010 248p il $24.99; pa $14.99
Grades: 7 8 9 10 11 12   741.5
1. Poets 2. Authors 3. Graphic novels 5. Greek mythology -- Graphic novels 6. Mythology, Greek
ISBN 978-0-7636-4266-2; 0-7636-4266-5; 978-0-7636-4268-6 pa; 0-7636-4268-1 pa

This is "the most lavish retelling of Homer yet. . . . Hinds lets the epic story take its time, with a slow build and pages that aren't afraid to alternate packed dialogue with titanic action. The sumptuous art, produced with grain, texture, and hue, evokes a time long past while detailing every line and drop of sweat on Odysseus' face and conveying the sheer grandeur of seeing a god rise out of the ocean." Booklist

The **merchant** of Venice; a play. by William Shakespeare; adapted and illustrated by Gareth Hinds. Candlewick Press 2008 68p il $21.99; pa $11.99
Grades: 8 9 10 11 12 Adult   741.5
1. Poets 2. Authors 3. Dramatists 4. Graphic novels 5. Drama
ISBN 978-0-7636-3024-9; 978-0-7636-3025-6 pa
LC 2007-938349

Hinds uses a sketchy art style and blue and gray tones to illustrate his graphic adaptation of Shakespeare's controversial play. He sets the play in modern Venice and uses more modern language, including prose, at the beginning of the play and then gradually returns to Shakespeare's original language for the courtroom scenes. The play tells the story of a debt owed to a Jewish merchant of Venice, of a strong-willed young woman who is determined to choose her own husband, and of the quest to save a young man from the fate of having a pound of flesh cut from him.

"Fans of the play will find this an intriguing adaptation." Publ Wkly

Hitch, Bryan

Bryan Hitch's Ultimate Comics Studio. Impact 2010 128p il pa $24.99
Grades: 7 8 9 10   741.5
1. Comic books, strips, etc.
ISBN 978-1-6006-1327-2; 1-6006-1327-6

"Well-known illustrator of Marvel classics such as Fantastic Four and Captain America, Hitch has a passion for comics and comic art that is evident in this well-designed volume. The book is a skillful blend of text, photos of the artist at work, annotated sketches, and finished illustrations. . . Filled with sound advice, the book is useful to both comic

artists and those desiring a deeper understanding of comic art." SLJ

Hoena, B. A.

Perseus and Medusa; by Blake A. Hoena; illustrated by Daniel Perez. Stone Arch Books 2009 72p il (Graphic revolve) lib bdg $23.93; pa $6.95
Grades: 4 5 6 7 8 9   741.5
1. Graphic novels 2. Monsters -- Graphic novels 3. Greek mythology -- Graphic novels
ISBN 978-1-4342-1170-5 lib bdg; 1-4342-1170-3 lib bdg; 978-1-4342-1394-5 pa; 1-4342-1386-2 pa
LC 2008-32065

Perseus is the son of Danae, daughter of the King of Argos, and of Zeus; due to a prophecy that Perseus would cause his death, the King puts his daughter and grandson into a wooden chest and has it cast out to sea. A fisherman rescues them, and Perseus grows up unaware of his royal lineage. King Polydectes wants Danae for himself and sends Perseus on what should be an impossible task that will kill him he wants Perseus to bring him the head of Medusa, whose gaze turns anyone into stone. Perseus enjoys the guidance and advice of gods and goddesses to accomplish his task

This title has a "solid awareness of how to balance visual depiction and expository captions, evident right from the striking prologue. While the artwork is cartoony and the dialogue deliberately casual and modern, the style doesn't prevent the artist from providing heroic vistas, or the author from slipping in a couple of humorous moments, and the action is sufficiently thrilling." SLJ

Horowitz, Anthony

Point blank: the graphic novel; by Anthony Horowitz and Antony Johnston; illustrated by Kanako Damerum and Yuzuru Takasaki. Philomel Books 2008 un il (Alex Rider) pa $14.99
Grades: 5 6 7 8 9 10   741.5
1. Graphic novels 2. Adventure graphic novels 3. Spies -- Graphic novels
ISBN 978-0-399-25026-2 pa; 0-399-25026-3 pa

"Rapid-fire action, appealing manga-style artwork, and a heavy reliance on the James Bond formula drive this second graphic adaptation of Horowitz's . . . Alex Rider books. . . . Rider, a 14-year-old British spy, is sent to a mysterious Swiss boarding school to investigate the nefarious plot of its headmaster." Booklist

Stormbreaker: the graphic novel; [by] Anthony Horowitz; adapted Antony Johnston; illustrated by Kanako Damerum & Yusuru Takasaki. Philomel Books 2006 un il (Alex Rider) pa $14.99
Grades: 5 6 7 8   741.5
1. Graphic novels 2. Spies -- Graphic novels
ISBN 0-399-24633-9

In this graphic novel version on Horowitz's novel, fourteen-year-old Alex Rider is coerced into continuing his uncle's dangerous work for Britain's intelligence agency, MI6.

"If it's possible, this is even more rapidly paced than the novel. Alex remains an appealing hero here, and the idea of a heroic teen up against insidious adults continues to be an extremely powerful draw for readers." Booklist

Hosler, Jay

Clan Apis. Active Synapse 2000 158p il pa
$15

Grades: 4 5 6 7 8 9 10 11 12   741.5

1. Graphic novels 2. Bees -- Graphic novels 3. Science
-- Graphic novels

ISBN 0-9677255-0-X

"Opening with a creation myth . . . and working through
the biological, sociological, and ecological changes affecting the life of Nyuki the bee, the text is a combination of
authoritative science; appealing, detailed black-and-white
drawings; and dialogue replete with humor, pubescent angst,
political sloganeering, and more. Nyuki's colony undertakes migration to a new hive, is beset by a woodpecker,
and hibernates through a winter that yields to a revitalizing
spring." Booklist

Hotta, Yumi

Hikaru No Go, Volume 1; [by] Yumi Hotta and
Takeshi Obata. Viz Media, LLC 2004 192p il pa
$7.95

Grades: 5 6 7 8 9 10 11 12   741.5

1. Manga 2. Shonen manga 3. Graphic novels 4.
Board games -- Graphic novels

ISBN 1-59116-222-X

Sixth-grader Hikaru Shindo is not interested in intellectual pursuits, but by a twist of fate, the spirit of Fujiwara
no Sai, the ghost of an ancient Go master, manages to bond
with Hikaru. Now, suddenly, Hikaru can play Go, a complex
board game of strategy, better than almost anyone under 18
and most adults, too. Akira, who has been raised by his Go
master father, needs to know more about the upstart Hikaru,
who beats him and yet seems so casual about the game. This
is the first volume of an ongoing series.

Hunter, Erin

Warriors: Tiger & Sasha #1: into the woods; created by Erin Hunter; written by Dan Jolley; art by
Don Hudson. HarperCollins/Tokyopop 2008 108p
il $6.99

Grades: 3 4 5 6 7 8 9   741.5

1. Graphic novels 2. Adventure graphic novels 3. Cats
-- Graphic novels

ISBN 978-0-06-154792-8; 0-06-154792-1

Sasha was a loved, pampered kittypet, but when one of
the housefolk dies and the other moves away, they leave
her behind. She had always explored the woods at night,
but now she has to survive on her own. Then she meets Tigerstar, leader of ShadowClan, and they spend a lot of time
together as he teaches her how to improve her hunting. He
even offers her membership in the clan, but he has secrets,
and when Sasha discovers one of them, she has to decide if
she can trust him. There are scenes of cats hunting prey such
as mice and squirrels, and fighting with foxes.

Followed by: Warriors, Tigerstar & Sasha #2, Escape
from the Forest (2009)

The lost warrior; created by Erin Hunter; written by Dan Jolley; art by James L. Barry. Tokyopop/
HarperCollins Publishers 2007 96p il (Warriors)
$6.99

Grades: 4 5 6 7 8 9   741.5

1. Graphic novels 2. Adventure graphic novels 3. Cats
-- Graphic novels

ISBN 978-0-06-124020-1; 0-06-124020-6

LC 2006-30426

Thunderclan warrior Greystripe helps clan members escape when the twolegs destroy their forest home and capture
many of them, but he himself gets captured. Now he's a
kittypet and desperate to return home to his clan. He meets
Millie, another kittypet who wants to learn how to become a
warrior, but can Greystripe find his way out of the twolegs'
land?

Other titles in this series are:
Warrior's refuge (2008)
Warrior's return (2008)
The rise of the scourge (2008)

Ichiro; written & illustrated by Ryan Inzana. Houghton Mifflin/Houghton Mifflin Harcourt 2012 288
p.

Grades: 7 8 9 10   741.5

1. Fantasy graphic novels 2. Supernatural graphic
novels 3. Japan -- History -- Graphic novels 4. Folklore
-- Japan -- Graphic novels 5. Japanese Americans
-- Graphic novels 6. Graphic novels 7. Monsters --
Fiction 8. Grandfathers -- Fiction 9. Supernatural --
Fiction 10. Gods and goddesses -- Fiction 11. Japanese
Americans -- Fiction 12. Fantasy comic books, strips,
etc. 13. Monsters -- Comic books, strips, etc. 14.
Grandfathers -- Comic books, strips, etc. 15. Japanese
Americans -- Comic books, strips, etc.

ISBN 0547252692; 9780547252698

LC 2011277558

This graphic novel depicts the story of Ichiro, "a young
American teen, son of a Japanese immigrant and an American soldier killed in combat, [who] goes to Japan with his
mother on an extended visit and begins to grapple with
sophisticated cultural complexities. . . . After his mother
and Japanese grandfather tell him stories of Japanese history and folklore, Ichiro has a fantastical adventure involving the Japanese myth of the shape-shifting tanuki spirit."
(Kirkus Reviews)

Igarashi, Daisuke

★ Children of the sea, vol. 1. Viz Media/Viz
Signature 2009 320p il pa $14.99

Grades: 7 8 9 10 11 12   741.5

1. Manga 2. Graphic novels 3. Fantasy graphic novels
4. Mystery graphic novels 5. Adventure graphic novels
6. Ocean -- Graphic novels

ISBN 978-1-4215-2914-1; 1-4215-2914-9

"Igarashi's storytelling is quiet, thoughtful, and thought
provoking, but it is his drawings that make this manga so
amazing. Extremely detailed settings turn panels into mini-
masterpieces." Booklist

Irwin, Jane

Vogelein; clockwork faerie. [by] Jane Irwin with
Jeff Berndt; foreword by Jennifer M. Contino. Fiery
Studios 2003 167p il pa $12.95

Grades: 6 7 8 9 10 11 12   741.5

1. Graphic novels 2. Fantasy graphic novels 3. Fairies

-- Graphic novels
ISBN 0-9743110-06

This is a "graphic novel about Vogelein, a beautiful mechanical fairy created in the seventeenth century. Although she is immortal, she must be wound every 36 hours. After her old friend and caretaker dies, she must find someone new to take care of her. . . . This modern fable is a rare treasure that weaves fanciful imagination into themes of individuality, diversity, and independence. The art is beautifully shaded black and white, and it carries the narrative impeccably." Booklist

Ita, Sam

★ The **Odyssey**; a pop-up book. Sterling 2011 il $26.95

Grades: 4 5 6 7   741.5
1. Graphic novels 2. Adventure graphic novels 3. Pop-up books
ISBN 978-1-4027-5867-6; 1-4027-5867-7

"A highlight-reel version of Odysseus' journey home, framed as a graphic novel and plastered with fantastically dramatic pop-ups and other special effects. Opening with Penelope working on a tapestry that transforms into an entirely different scene with the drop of a step-flap, the tale plunges on into the many escapes of Odysseus and his crew. . . . Ita . . . tells the tale in balloons of colloquial dialogue. . . . Even newbies will be riveted by this nonstop, high-energy retelling. Homer himself would be agog." Kirkus

Jablonski, Carla

Defiance; written by Carla Jablonski; art by Leland Purvis; color by Hilary Sycamore. First Second 2011 126p il (Resistance) $16.99

Grades: 7 8 9 10 11 12   741.5
1. Graphic novels 2. World War, 1939-1945 -- Fiction 3. World War, 1939-1945 -- Underground movements -- Fiction
ISBN 978-1-59643-292-5; 1-59643-292-6
LC 2010036253

In 1943, as the German occupation of France continues, the Tessier siblings increase their involvement in the Resistance while staying out of the way of the Millice, the Vichy military police. Includes facts about Charles De Gaulle and his support of resistance movements.

"The graphic novel format effectively portrays the layers of story and emotion, words and visual elements working in tandem to bring a complicated story to life. . . . As in the first volume, historical notes at the beginning and end are essential for placing the story in the larger context of World War II." Horn Book

Resistance, book 1; art by Leland Purvis; color by Hilary Sycamore. First Second Books 2010 121p il (Resistance) pa $16.99

Grades: 6 7 8 9 10 11 12   741.5
1. Graphic novels 2. Adventure graphic novels 3. World War, 1939-1945 -- Jews -- Rescue -- Graphic novels 4. World War, 1939-1945 -- Underground movements -- Graphic novels
ISBN 978-1-59643-291-8; 1-59643-291-8

Paul and his younger sister Marie live in a small village in Vichy France during World War II. Thus far, the war hasn't really touched them, but now Nazi soldiers come, and Paul's friend, Henri, and his parents are Jews and therefore in danger. When Paul and Marie try to protect Henri, their secret leaks out to members of the Resistance. Although they are young, they soon become recruits in the Resistance. Paul's incessant sketching in his book turns out to be a valuable talent, but he and Marie, and then their older sister, Sylvie, don't quite realize just how dangerous things can get. The cover is very striking, with Paul aiming a slingshot at a Nazi soldier. The Author's Note at the end of the book talks about history, the Resistance, and why the events in France during World War II should not be depicted as black and white, heroic Resistance versus villainous Vichy.

Jacques, Brian

Redwall: the graphic novel; by Brian Jacques; illustrated by Bret Blevins; adapted by Stuart Moore; lettering by Richard Starkings. Philomel Books 2007 143p il pa $12.99

Grades: 4 5 6 7 8 9   741.5
1. Graphic novels 2. Fantasy graphic novels 3. Adventure graphic novels 4. Mice -- Graphic novels
ISBN 978-0-399-24481-0; 0-399-24481-6

When Cluny the rat's army attacks Redwall Abbey, young Matthias the mouse follows in the footsteps of the long-ago hero Martin the Warrior to defend his home

"The story is a page-turner, and the detailed black-and-white drawings capture both the passion and the pathos." SLJ

Jaffe, Michele

Bad kitty volume 1: catnipped. HarperCollins/Tokyopop 2008 176p il $9.99

Grades: 7 8 9 10 11 12   741.5
1. Graphic novels 2. Mystery graphic novels 3. Humorous graphic novels
ISBN 978-0-06-135162-4; 0-06-135162-8

Teenage aspiring detective Jasmine Callihan just wants to hang out with her boyfriend, rock star Jack, but while they're at the mall, trouble strikes. First, Jas finds a schoolmate's purse, then there's a jewelry store heist and the cops arrest the store owner whom she believes is innocent, then she says exactly the wrong thing to Jack, and her cousin Alyson with her Evil Hench Twin Veronique decided to join the investigation along with Jas and her best friends Roxy, Polly, and Tom. This global manga is an original story using the same characters as Jaffe's prose teen novels Bad Kitty and Kitty Kitty.

"Catnipped will be especially appreciated by fans of Jaffe's novels, but it is not necessary to have read them to enjoy this rollicking, fast-paced, and funny mystery." SLJ

Jolley, Dan

My boyfriend bites; illustrated by Alitha E. Martinez. Graphic Universe 2011 126p il (My boyfriend is a monster) lib bdg $29.27; pa $9.95; e-book $21.95

Grades: 7 8 9 10 11 12   741.5
1. Graphic novels 2. Horror graphic novels 3. Vampires

-- Graphic novels
ISBN 978-0-7613-5599-1 lib bdg; 0-7613-5599-5 lib bdg; 978-0-7613-7078-9 pa; 0-7613-7078-1 pa; 978-0-7613-7187-8 e-book

LC 2010028723

Seventeen-year-old New Mexico high school senior Vanessa Shingle learns that she destined to be a monster-hunter like her Van Helsing ancestor, and that the gorgeous janitor she is dating, Jean-Paul, is there to help although he, himself, is a vampire.

"Hip, steamy fun." Kirkus

Wrapped up in you; by Dan Jolley; illustrated by Natalie Nourigat. Graphic Universe 2012 127 p. (lib. bdg.) $29.27

Grades: 6 7 8 9 10 11 12   741.5

1. Horror graphic novels 2. Mummies -- Graphic novels 3. Supernatural graphic novels 4. Love stories -- Graphic novels 5. Graphic novels 6. Horror stories 7. Mummies -- Fiction 8. Witches -- Fiction
ISBN 0761368566; 9780761368564

LC 2011044655

This graphic novel, by Dan Jolley, illustrated by Natalie Nourigat, is book 6 in the "My Boyfriend Is a Monster" series. "Prince Pachacutec--or 'Chuck'--is a man with a past. He died tragically five hundred years ago, but that's all ancient history as far as Staci is concerned. He is everything she could want. . . . But the witches aren't willing to live and let live. Will Staci fight for Chuck? Or do the witches have a point when they say reanimated corpses make bad boyfriends?" (Publisher's note)

Kibuishi, Kazu

★ **Amulet,** book one: The Stonekeeper. Graphix 2008 185p $21.99; pa $9.99

Grades: 3 4 5 6 7 8   741.5

1. Graphic novels 2. Fantasy graphic novels 3. Mystery graphic novels 4. Adventure graphic novels
ISBN 978-0-439-84680-6; 0-439-84680-3; 978-0-439-84681-3 pa; 0-439-84681-1 pa

After a family tragedy, Emily, Navin, and their mother move to an ancestral home to start a new life. When their mother is kidnapped by a tentacled creature, Em and Navin have to figure out how to set things straight and save their mother's life.

"Filled with excitement, monsters, robots, and mysteries, this fantasy adventure will appeal to many readers." SLJ
Other titles in this series are:
Amulet: The Stonekeeper's curse (2009)
Amulet: The Cloud Searchers (2010)
Amulet: The Last Council (2011)

Copper. Graphix/Scholastic 2010 94p il $21.99; pa $12.99

Grades: 5 6 7 8   741.5

1. Graphic novels 2. Adventure graphic novels 3. Science fiction graphic novels 4. Dogs -- Graphic novels
ISBN 978-0-545-09892-2; 0-545-09892-0; 978-0-545-09893-9 pa; 0-545-09893-9 pa

A collection of graphic novel adventures about a boy named Copper and his dog, Fred, including "navigating

a dangerous forest of giant mushrooms, [and] surviving a crash landing in a homemade airplane—that run from lyrical to the downright apocalyptic. Illustrated in a deceptively simple style, its solemn tenor and deep strangeness . . . will likely inspire heavy investment from those who prefer a somewhat off-kilter read." Booklist

Kim, Derek Kirk

★ **Good** as Lily; written by Derek Kirk Kim; illustrated by Jesse Hamm; lettering by Jared K. Fletcher. DC Comics/Minx 2007 un il pa $9.99

Grades: 7 8 9 10 11 12   741.5

1. Graphic novels 2. Fantasy graphic novels 3. Humorous graphic novels
ISBN 978-1-4012-1381-7

"On her eighteenth birthday, Korean American Grace suddenly finds herself surrounded by three very corporeal essences of herself: as a small child, as a 30-year-old woman, and as 'a cranky old fart.' Each of these incarnations is at an emotional precipice, which teenage Grace helps resolve, allowing the other self to quietly disappear. . . . Kim's pacing and plotting are excellent, and Hamm's black, white, and gray artwork is lively, witty, and full of appropriate comedy and melodrama." Booklist

Kim, Susan

★ **City** of spies; [by] Susan Kim [and] Laurence Klavan; illustrated by Pascal Dizin. First Second 2010 172p il pa $17

Grades: 4 5 6 7   741.5

1. Graphic novels 2. Adventure graphic novels 3. Spies -- Graphic novels 5. Graphic novels 6. World War, 1939-1945 -- Graphic novels
ISBN 1-59643-262-4 pa; 978-1-59643-262-8 pa

This graphic novel, set in New York City during World War II, tells the story of Kim and Klavan, who are hunting for Nazi spies. "Grades seven to ten." (Bull Cent Child Books)

"With her mother gone and a father who has better things to do than be bothered raising a daughter, Evelyn is sent to live with her unconventional Aunt Lia in the bohemian art world of 1942 New York City. . . . Evelyn spends much of her time in the company of imaginary superheroes, fouling up the plans of Nazi spies. Before long she finds an unlikely friend in the building superintendent's son, Tony. Together, they . . . stumble upon an actual Nazi plot. With stupefying precision, Dizin's art channels Hergé's Tintin in tone, palette, and with the remarkable expressiveness of the clean, flexible figures. . . . With villains and danger that just border on the genuinely scary, the tale is filled not only with a thrilling sense of excitement but also with a child's longing for a grown-up to believe in." Booklist

Kitoh, Mohiro

Bokurano: Ours. Viz Media 2010 198p il pa $12.99

Grades: 6 7 8 9   741.5

1. Science fiction graphic novels 2. Robots -- Graphic novels
ISBN 978-1-4215-3361-2 pa; 1-4215-3361-8 pa

"After wandering into a cave by the sea, 15 kids meet Kokopelli, who invites them to play a video game that involves piloting a giant robot. They are asked to sign a contract, not knowing the deadly repercussions or that they will have to protect the planet. The cockpit consists of designated, floating chairs for each one while at the controls of the robot designed to defeat alien invaders. . . . Sound effects and large frames help create action and edginess on the pages. This story will intrigue readers." SLJ

Klimowski, Andrzej

Dr. Jekyll and Mr. Hyde; a graphic novel. illustrated and adapted by Andrzej Klimowski and Danusia Schejbal. Sterling 2009 122p il (Illustrated classics) pa $14.95

Grades: 6 7 8 9   741.5
1. Poets 2. Authors 3. Novelists 4. Graphic novels 5. Horror graphic novels 6. Essayists 7. Travel writers 8. Short story writers
ISBN 978-1-4114-1595-9 pa; 1-4114-1595-7 pa

"Klimowski captures a . . . formal air with a literal but still quick-moving adaptation, and Schejbal's grainy art displays a Richard Sala-like sense of both grit and unease. . . . Overall, this will have the most appeal for readers with an eye for the moody and strange." Booklist

Konomi, Takeshi

The **Prince** of Tennis, Vol. 1. Viz Media, LLC 2004 192p il pa $7.95

Grades: 6 7 8 9 10   741.5
1. Manga 2. Shonen manga 3. Graphic novels 4. Tennis -- Fiction 5. Tennis -- Graphic novels
ISBN 1-59116-435-4

"Ryoma is a former U.S. junior tennis champion who attends a Japanese academy, where his skill and natural talent make him nearly unbeatable. The younger students are inspired by him, but he's ruffling the feathers of the older tennis team members. Then the journalists appear, trying to discover the next champion, adding to the pressure. There's lots of tennis action, dramatically illustrated, and the characters, already pretty boys, are made even more attractive with their intensity." Publ Wkly

Kovac, Tommy

Wonderland; written by Tommy Kovac; illustrated by Sonny Liew. Disney Press 2008 159p il $19.99

Grades: 4 5 6 7 8   741.5
1. Graphic novels 2. Fantasy graphic novels
ISBN 978-1-4231-0451-3; 1-4231-0451-X

First published as single-issue comics by SLG Publishing

"Ever wonder what happened in Wonderland after Alice left? Follow the quirky tale of Mary Ann, the meticulous and dutiful housekeeper for the White Rabbit, as she continues the tale. Her boss is now wanted for treason by the Queen of Hearts for allowing the Alice Monster to enter the kingdom–off with his head! On the run and fearing for their lives, Mary Ann and White Rabbit encounter the meddlesome Cheshire Cat, the ever-contentious troublemaker, sending the White Rabbit straight into the clutches of the queen and poor Mary Ann tumbling into the Treacle Well. . . . This is a terrific look at a great classic. The energetic, action-packed illustrations complement the story in Disney-cartoon style, making for a great read for all ages" SLJ

Kreisberg, Andrew

Green Arrow and Black Canary: five stages; [by] Andrew Kreisberg, J.T. Krul, writers; Mike Norton, Renato Guedes, Diogenes Neves, pencillers; Bill Sienkiewicz . . . [et al.], inkers. DC Comics 2010 un pa $17.99

Grades: 7 8 9 10   741.5
1. Graphic novels 2. Superhero graphic novels 3. Green Arrow (Fictional character) 4. Black Canary (Fictional character)
ISBN 978-1-4012-2898-9; 1-4012-2898-4

"Oliver Queen, a spoiled rich playboy who eventually becomes the heroic Green Arrow, has recently married his longtime girlfriend Dinah Lance, the Black Canary. The emerald archer's latest adventure pits him against the murderous Cupid, a female soldier twisted to darkness during an experimental drug trial. . . . The gritty, urban artwork includes muted colors that add to the militaristic and ultimately sadistic feel of the antagonist Cupid, whose origin story is revealed in this volume. Perfect for readers looking to break into superhero comics." SLJ

Krensky, Stephen

Comic book century; the history of American comic books. Twenty-First Century Books 2007 112p il lib bdg $30.60

Grades: 5 6 7 8 9 10   741.5
1. Cartoons and caricatures 2. Comic books, strips, etc. 3. Cartoons and comics
ISBN 978-0-8225-6654-0; 0-8225-6654-0
LC 2006-20795

Provides a history of comic books in America during the twentieth century, showing how it has influenced and been influenced by American culture. Includes an epilogue about comics in the early twenty-first century

"Frequent full-color comic-book representations and black-and-white photographs, . . . flashy sidebars, and a striking blue background combine well with the accessible text, making this . . . visually appealing as well as highly entertaining." Bull Cent Child Books

Includes bibliographical references

Kurilla, Renee

Peter H. Reynolds and FableVision present Zebrafish. Atheneum 2010 il $16.99

Grades: 6 7 8 9   741.5
1. Graphic novels
ISBN 978-1-4169-9525-8

L'Engle, Madeleine, 1918-2007

A **wrinkle** in time; the graphic novel. Madeleine L'Engle; adapted and illustrated by Hope Larson. Farrar Straus Giroux 2012 392 p. $19.99

Grades: 4 5 6 7   741.5
1. Time travel -- Fiction 2. Space and time -- Fiction 3. United States -- Politics and government -- Graphic novels 4. Graphic novels 5. Science fiction
ISBN 0374386153; 9780374386153
LC 2010044120

Author Madeleine L'Engle presents an illustrated version of her "allegorical fantasy in which a group of young people are guided through the universe by Mrs. Who, Mrs. Which and Mrs. What -- women who possess supernatural powers. They traverse fictitious regions, meet and face evil and demonstrate courage at the right moment. Religious allusions are secondary to the philosophical struggle designed to yield the meaning of life and one's place on earth." (Kirkus Reviews)

Lagos, Alexander

The **sons** of liberty; created and written by Alexander Lagos and Joseph Lagos; art by Steve Walker; color by Oren Kramek; letters by Chris Dickey. Random House 2010 un il $18.99; lib bdg $21.99; pa $12.99

Grades: 6 7 8 9 10 11 12   **741.5**
1. Graphic novels 2. Adventure graphic novels 3. Superhero graphic novels 4. African Americans -- Graphic novels 5. Graphic novels
ISBN 978-0-375-85670-9; 0-375-85670-6; 978-0-375-95667-6 lib bdg; 0-375-95667-6 lib bdg; 978-0-375-85667-9 pa; 0-375-85667-9 pa

In the mid-eighteenth century American colonies, Graham and Brody work as slaves on a tobacco plantation not far from Philadelphia. When they run away after injuring the plantation owner's son for threatening another slave, they seek Benjamin Lay, an eccentric abolitionist who might give them shelter. Instead, William Franklin, son of Benjamin Franklin, finds them and conducts unknown experiments on them.

"History offers few villains as vile as slaveholders, but this graphic novel is far from being a simple revenge thriller. The use of historical figures and well-researched (but embellished) history, and a willingness to flesh out characters and set up situations to pay off in future installments, makes for an uncommonly complex, literate, and satisfying adventure." Booklist

The **sons** of liberty 2; death and taxes. created and written by Alexander Lagos and Joseph Lagos; art by Steve Walker; color by Oren Kramek; letters by Chris Dickey. Random House Children's Books 2011 un il $18.99; pa $12.99

Grades: 6 7 8 9 10 11 12   **741.5**
1. Authors 2. Diplomats 3. Inventors 4. Statesmen 5. Scientists 6. Graphic novels 7. Adventure graphic novels 8. Superhero graphic novels 9. Writers on science 10. Members of Congress 11. African Americans -- Graphic novels
ISBN 978-0-375-85671-6; 978-0-375-85668-6 pa

"Graham and Brody, escaped slaves gifted with superpowers, remain at the center of this continuing pre–Revolutionary War saga of political intrigue and reimagined history. As Benjamin Franklin seeks to stop the stamp tax from falling on the colonies and enemies attack his good name, Graham attempts to arrange an escape back to Africa along with his love, the slave girl Isabel. . . . The embellishments, literate dialogue, and several historical truths—effectively counterpointed with glossy contemporary art—keep things fun and suspenseful." Booklist

Langridge, Roger

★ **Thor,** the mighty avenger, v.1. Marvel 2011 un il pa $14.99

Grades: 8 9 10 11 12   **741.5**
1. Graphic novels 2. Greek mythology -- Graphic novels
ISBN 978-0-7851-4121-1; 0-7851-4121-9

"Readers meet the mysterious blond-haired God of Thunder with no memory when historian Jane Foster watches him get tossed out of a Norse exhibition one day. After the gallant fellow helps her out and she takes him in, an utterly charming romance ensues. . . . Langridge deserves top marks for taking a character whose story possibilities might seem limited and imbuing him with a fresh and highly entertaining life. . . . Samnee's art grounds the vigorous superhero action with expressive faces, subtle lighting tones, and an individual style that makes the drama sing." Booklist

Larson, Hope

Chiggers; [by] Hope Larson; lettered by Jason Azzopardi. Atheneum Books for Young Readers 2008 170p il $17.99; pa $9.99

Grades: 5 6 7 8 9   **741.5**
1. Graphic novels 2. Camps -- Fiction 3. Friendship -- Graphic novels
ISBN 978-1-4169-3584-1; 978-1-4169-3587-2 pa
         LC 2008-09557

When Abby returns to the same summer camp she always goes to, she is dismayed to find that her old friends have changed, and the only person who wants to be her friend is the strange new girl, Shasta.

"Chiggers provides a ticket to summer fun. Larson delicately handles both the usual middle-school angst and the additional pressures that come with being somewhat different. . . . The content is perfect for upper elementary and middle school students." SLJ

★ **Mercury**. Atheneum Books for Young Readers 2010 234p il $19.99; pa $9.99

Grades: 8 9 10 11 12   **741.5**
1. Graphic novels 2. Supernatural graphic novels
ISBN 978-1-4169-3585-8; 1-4169-3585-1; 978-1-4169-3588-9 pa; 1-4169-3588-6 pa
         LC 2009-903638

Tara is forced to move in with her cousins after her house burns down. She faces a difficult adjustment while her mother is away trying to earn money. Interwoven with this story is that of Tara's ancestors, who in 1859 were convinced by a mysterious stranger to put all their money into searching their property for gold.

"The storytelling, both in words and pictures, brilliantly offers details from Canadian history and modern life. The dialogue varies from funny to poignant. An excellent graphic novel." SLJ

Lat

★ **Kampung** boy. First Second 2006 141p il pa $16.95

Grades: 7 8 9 10 11 12 Adult   **741.5**
1. Muslims 2. Family life 3. Graphic novels 4. Muslims -- Graphic novels 5. Family life -- Graphic

novels
ISBN 1-59643-121-0

LC 2005-34135

First published 1979 in Malaysia with title: Lat, the kampung boy

"Malaysian cartoonist Lat uses the graphic novel format to share the story of his childhood in a small village, or kampung. From his birth and adventures as a toddler to the enlargement of his world as he attends classes in the village, makes friends, and, finally, departs for a prestigious city boarding school, this autobiography is warm, authentic, and wholly engaging." Booklist

★ **Town** boy. First Second Books 2007 191p il pa $16.95

Grades: 7 8 9 10 11 12 Adult   **741.5**
1. Graphic novels 2. Humorous graphic novels 3. Bildungsromans -- Graphic novels
ISBN 978-1-59643-331-1; 1-59643-331-0

LC 2006-102857

In this sequel to Kampung Boy, it's the late 1960s and Mat is now a teenager attending a boarding school in the town of Ipoh, far from his kampung. He discovers bustling streets, hip music, heady literature, budding romance, and through it all his growing passion for art.

Lee, Tony

Excalibur; the legend of King Arthur, a graphic novel. written by Tony Lee; illustrated, colored, and lettered by Sam Hart. Candlewick Press 2011 un il

Grades: 7 8 9 10   **741.5**
1. Graphic novels 2. Fantasy graphic novels 3. Kings 4. Middle Ages -- Graphic novels 5. Kings and rulers -- Graphic novels 6. Knights and knighthood -- Graphic novels 7. Merlin (Legendary character) -- Graphic novels
ISBN 0-7636-4643-1 pa; 0-7636-4644-X; 978-0-7636-4643-1 pa; 978-0-7636-4644-8

LC 2010-39163

Retells, in graphic novel form, the tale of Arthur Pendragon who, raised in obscurity, draws a legendary sword from a stone and begins the life he was born to lead, guided by the elusive wizard Merlin.

The author is "a master of graphic-novel adaptations. Teaming up with illustrator and colorist Hart, . . . Lee negotiates the terrain of medieval legend with finesse, rendering it easily accessible for a new generation of readers." Kirkus

★ **Outlaw**: the legend of Robin Hood; a graphic novel. written by Tony Lee; illustrated by Sam Hart; colored by Artur Fujita. Candlewick Press 2009 un il $21.99; pa $11.99

Grades: 7 8 9 10 11 12   **741.5**
1. Graphic novels 2. Adventure graphic novels 3. Robin Hood (Fictional character)
ISBN 978-0-7636-4399-7; 0-7636-4399-8; 978-0-7636-4400-0 pa; 0-7636-4400-5 pa

LC 2008-943331

In this retelling of the Robin Hood legend, it's the year 1192, and Robin of Loxley has returned home from the Crusades after receiving news of his father's death. The Sheriff of Nottingham and Sir Guy of Gisburn govern Nottingham

at the pleasure of Prince John. When Gisburn treacherously stabs Robin in a murder attempt, Robin escapes to Sherwood Forest, where the outlaws befriend him. With the help of such men as Little John and Friar Tuck, he organizes the outlaws and they start hurting Prince John where it matters-- in his moneybags.

"Lee's excellent rendition of the famed selfless hero goes hand-in-hand with Hart's expressive illustrations, featuring lots of closeups and dramatic lighting and a beautiful jewel-toned palette. Teens will get caught up in this exciting page-turner." SLJ

Li, Nana

Twelfth night; adapted by Richard Appignanesi; illustrated by Nana Li. Amulet Books 2011 207p il (Manga Shakespeare) pa $10.95

Grades: 7 8 9 10   **741.5**
1. Poets 2. Authors 3. Dramatists 4. Graphic novels
ISBN 978-0-8109-9718-9; 0-8109-9718-5

LC 2010024429

Retells, in comic book format, Shakespeare's comedy about Viola who, upon finding herself shipwrecked, pretends to be a servant but finds herself falling in love with Duke Orsino.

"Since plays are written to be performed, to be seen, a manga adaptation is a very satisfying way to enjoy Shakespeare. . . . Fans of the Bard should be delighted to experience his works through comics, while manga fans can be exposed to Shakespeare in a familiar way." Voice Youth Advocates

Liu, Na

★ **Little** White Duck; a childhood in China. by Andrés Vera Martínez and Na Liu; illustrated by Andrés Vera Martínez. Graphic Universe 2012 96 p. col. ill. (lib. bdg. : alk. paper) $29.27; (pbk.) $9.95

Grades: 4 5 6   **741.5**
1. China -- History -- 1976- 2. Biographical graphic novels 3. Graphic novels 4. China -- History -- 1976-2002 -- Comic books, strips, etc
ISBN 0761365877; 9780761365877; 9780761381150; 0761381155

LC 2011005347

This graphic novel provides a "glimpse into Chinese girlhood during the 1970s and '80s. It begins with the 3-year-old narrator trying to understand the death of Chairman Mao. "From there, her life unfolds in short sketches. . . . She explains about the four pests that plague China . . . and her stomach-turning school assignment to catch rats and deliver the severed tails to her teacher . . . [as well as] the origins of Chinese New Year, her favorite holiday." (Kirkus Reviews)

"This picturesque treasure introduces Chinese culture through a personal perspective that is both delightful and thought-provoking." SLJ

Lutes, Jason

★ **Houdini**: the handcuff king. Hyperion Books for Children/Jump at the Sun 2007 90p il (Center for Cartoon Studies presents) $16.99; pa $9.99

Grades: 4 5 6 7 8 9 10   **741.5**
1. Magicians 2. Graphic novels 3. Biographical graphic novels 4. Nonfiction writers 5. Magicians --

Graphic novels

ISBN 978-0-7868-3902-5; 978-0-7868-3903-2 pa

On May 1, 1908, magician Harry Houdini performed one of his famous handcuff escapes, this time in handcuffs and leg irons, while jumping off the Cambridge Bridge in Massachusetts into the frigid Boston River. This graphic novel takes the reader through Houdini's day, from 5:00 a.m. as he makes his preparations, makes a practice jump, coaches his wife Bess on how she's to help him, and then makes the jump.

This is a "fascinating graphic novel. . . . The format will instantly draw a lot of attention from readers and then hold on to it. Lutes and Bertozzi use grayscale comic panels to share their story about the life of Harry Houdini in a unique way. . . . The book resembles a hybrid between fiction and nonfiction, and the ingenious choice of format will appeal to a broad age range of readers." Voice Youth Advocates

Lyga, Barry

Mangaman. Houghton Mifflin 2011 il $18.99

Grades: 7 8 9 10   **741.5**

   1. Graphic novels 2. School stories

   ISBN 978-0-547-42315-9; 0-547-42315-2

                                LC 2011403000

"A daring piece of graphic-novel meta-fiction. . . . In complement to Lyga's clever meta tone is Doran's highly stylized black-and-white art, seamlessly melding both the Western and Japanese comics aesthetics." Kirkus

Wolverine: worst day ever; by Barry Lyga; artist, Todd Nauck. Marvel Publishing 2009 184p il $14.99

Grades: 5 6 7 8 9   **741.5**

   1. Graphic novels 2. Humorous graphic novels 3. Superhero graphic novels 4. Wolverine (Fictional character)

   ISBN 978-0-7851-3757-3; 0-7851-3757-2

Teenager Eric Mattias has just recently discovered he has mutant powers. Very sucky mutant powers: suddenly no one notices him even when he's in the same room. He's not invisible, but he might as well be, and people don't even notice him when he speaks. Eric decides to follow Wolverine around and see if he can't pick up a few pointers about living a loner-type life, as the adamantium-clawed mutant tends to do. Only when they end up in a remote forested area does Eric realize he may not have made the smartest move, because someone else has come, someone who is as strong as Wolverine, and maybe meaner: Sabretooth.

"It's a coming-of-age tale with bursts of action that's sure to appeal to its large, built-in audience." Booklist

MacHale, D. J.

Pendragon book one: the merchant of death graphic novel; adapted and illustrated by Carla Speed McNeil. Aladdin Paperbacks 2008 172p il $9.99

Grades: 5 6 7 8 9 10   **741.5**

   1. Graphic novels 2. Fantasy graphic novels 3. Adventure graphic novels

   ISBN 978-1-4169-5080-6; 1-4169-5080-X

                                LC 2007-937920

Fourteen-year-old Bobby Pendragon has had a good life with a loving family, friends, and sports, but it all changes the night his Uncle Press takes him into New York City, to a deserted subway station that contains a gate that leads them to another world. On Denduron, a peaceful tribe called the Milago face annihilation from the Bedowan, and Uncle Press expects Bobby to help him stop it. Press is what he calls a Traveler, and he says Bobby is one, too, and they have a job to do. Bobby is able to write journals and send them home to his best friends Mark and Courtney. Meanwhile, he needs to learn so much, can he do it in time to help—and stay alive?

"This graphic-format adaptation streamlines the already fast-moving experience, providing satisfying interpretations of favorite characters and situations." Booklist

Macdonald, Fiona

Journey to the Center of the Earth; by Jules Verne; Fiona Macdonald, adapter; illustrated by Penko Gelev. Barron's Educational Series, Inc. 2007 48p il (Graphic classics) $15.99; pa $8.99

Grades: 3 4 5 6 7 8   **741.5**

   1. Authors 2. Novelists 3. Graphic novels 4. Adventure graphic novels 5. Children's authors 6. Science fiction writers

   ISBN 978-0-7641-5982-4; 978-0-7641-3495-1 pa

In Hamburg, Germany in 1863, eccentric Professor Otto Lidenbrock acquires a book by the sixteenth-century alchemist, Arne Saknussemm; the book includes a parchment page written in coded runes, and Lidenbrock's nephew Axel helps him decode it. To Axel's horror, the message tells of a way to get to the Center of the Earth, and Lidenbrock drags him along on the adventure.

The "story progresses in short two-page episodes, helped along by a few sentences of narration under each frame. Detailed illustrations in muted colors work with . . . the dim underground setting. . . . Dramatic, action-filled scenes and highly expressive faces catch readers eyes and pull them into the [story]." SLJ

Kidnapped; by Robert Louis Stevenson; Fiona Macdonald, adapter; illustrated by Penko Gelev. Barron's Educational Series, Inc. 2007 48p il (Graphic classics) $15.99; pa $8.99

Grades: 3 4 5 6 7 8   **741.5**

   1. Poets 2. Authors 3. Novelists 4. Graphic novels 5. Adventure graphic novels 6. Essayists 7. Travel writers 8. Short story writers

   ISBN 978-0-7641-5980-0; 978-0-7641-3494-4 pa

Orphaned David Balfour goes to his uncle, who first tries to kill him and then tricks him into going onboard a ship that leaves Scotland with David aboard. David befriends a passenger, Alan Breck, then learns he's a Jacobite in exile. They survive a shipwreck, witness a murder, and become fugitives on the run back in Scotland.

The "story progresses in short two-page episodes, helped along by a few sentences of narration under each frame. Detailed illustrations in muted colors work with the stormy, furtive story. . . . Dramatic, action-filled scenes and highly expressive faces catch readers eyes and pull them into the [story]." SLJ

Macherot, R.

Sibyl-Anne vs. Ratticus; translated from the French by Kim Thompson. Fantagraphics 2011 64p il $16.99

Grades: 5 6 7 8   741.5

1. Graphic novels 2. Mice -- Graphic novels
ISBN 978-1-60699-452-8; 1-60699-452-2

"This collection of comics, originally published in Spirou magazine in 1966 and 1967, contains several stories in which the mouse Sibyl-Anne and her friends fight back the greedy villain Ratticus. This is the first time that American audiences will be able to appreciate this story arc from the golden age of Franco-Belgian comics. . . . [The stories] are lighthearted and sometimes surreal adventures that use an artistic style reminiscent of classic comics such as Blondie or Pogo. The colors are bright and the creatures are adorable. . . . An enjoyable read for kids, teens, and even adults." SLJ

Manning, Matthew K.

Ali Baba and the forty thieves; retold by Matthew K. Manning; illustrated by Ricardo Osnaya. Stone Arch Books 2010 63p il lib bdg $26.65; pa $6.95

Grades: 4 5 6   741.5

1. Graphic novels 2. Folklore -- Graphic novels
ISBN 978-1-4342-1988-6 lib bdg; 1-4342-1988-7 lib bdg; 978-1-4342-2776-8 pa; 1-4342-2776-6 pa
LC 2010020144

"Ali Baba is a poor man who stumbles upon a hidden cave where a band of thieves hides its loot, opening the cave with the phrase open sesame and closing it with close sesame. When he brings some of the treasure home, his greedy brother, Kasim, finds out and forces Ali Baba to tell him everything; but the thieves discover Kasim in their cave and kill him. When they hunt after Ali Baba, it takes the courage and cunning of the servant girl Marjana to save Ali Baba and his family. Osnaya's stylish art and Manning's story combine to make a dynamic comic book." Booklist

Wolverine; inside the world of the living weapon. written by Matthew K. Manning. DK 2009 199p il $24.95

Grades: 6 7 8 9   741.5

1. Wolverine (Fictional character)
ISBN 978-0-7566-4547-2; 0-7566-4547-6
LC 2009284799

Presents a chiefly illustrated a look at Wolverine's history, a summation of Logan's rather extensive past, and his alternate futures.

"Decades of information merge seamlessly in a beautifully illustrated package. Practically every nook and cranny of the character's history gets attention, from a long line of love interests to his mortal enemies. . . . The book is no doubt of greatest interest to diehard fans, if readers have ever opened an issue of X-Men, even with vague interest, chances are there is something here for them. If not, odds are good that the book will do a good job of convincing one to do so. Even those who remain steadfast in their dislike for comic books will find something of value here." Voice Youth Advocates

McAdoo, David

★ Red moon. Cossack Comics 2010 un il $19.99

Grades: 7 8 9 10   741.5

1. Graphic novels 2. Fantasy graphic novels 3. Dogs -- Graphic novels 4. Crows -- Graphic novels
ISBN 978-0-615-35324-1; 0-615-35324-X

"This graphic novel is told entirely from the point of view of a small dog. After Mox runs away from his family, he starts having visions of an ominous red moon heralding destruction and runs afoul of a pack of crows determined to bring a new world order where birds, not humans, reign supreme. . . . The . . . characters are carefully constructed, with clear, ringing voices that will linger in readers' minds. McAdoo's highly detailed style . . . adds gripping tension to every panel. . . . [An] action-packed, beautifully illustrated tale." Booklist

McCann, Jim

★ Return of the Dapper Men; written by Jim McCann; art by Janet Lee; lettered by Dave Lanphear; edited by Stephen Christy. Archaia Comics 2010 un il $24.95

Grades: 4 5 6 7 8   741.5

1. Graphic novels 2. Science fiction graphic novels 3. Robots -- Graphic novels
ISBN 978-1-932386-90-5; 1-932386-90-4

"In the dreamy land of Anorev, children, all under age 11, live underground among intricate gear-work mechanisms, while elegant robots live in abandoned houses aboveground. . . . All are perpetually stuck in the same day, and time has, essentially, ceased to mean anything—until 314 Dapper Men rain from the sky and set in motion the impetus for change. . . . Where this book truly stands out is how well the story works in concert with Lee's stunning artwork, which employs an art nouveau sheen. . . . A true dazzler that speaks on multiple levels for both child and adult readers and one that gets richer with each read." Booklist

Mechner, Jordan

Solomon's thieves; artwork by LeUyen Pham & Alex Puvilland. First Second 2010 139p il pa $12.99

Grades: 6 7 8 9 10   741.5

1. Graphic novels 2. Middle Ages -- Graphic novels 3. Knights and knighthood -- Graphic novels
ISBN 978-1-59643-391-5; 1-59643-391-4
LC 2010-282641

Life as a Templar Knight returning from the Crusades is dull—bread, beans, and lots and lots of walking. But after Martin stumbles upon his lost love (now married—to someone else), things begin to get more interesting very quickly. There's a vast conspiracy afoot to destroy the Templar Order and steal their treasure. Soon, Martin finds himself one of the only Templars out of prison—and out for revenge!

"Pham and Puvilland . . . are again in top form, balancing grainy, hatched textures and clean spaces to lend a weighty historical feel as a vibrant sense of kineticism brings the action sequences to life." Booklist

Includes bibliographical references

The **merchant** of Venice; adapted by Richard Appignanesi; illustrated by Faye Yong. Amulet Books 2011 207p il (Manga Shakespeare) pa $10.95
Grades: 7 8 9 10   **741.5**
1. Poets 2. Authors 3. Dramatists 4. Graphic novels
ISBN 978-0-8109-9717-2; 0-8109-9717-7
LC 2010021938

In sixteenth-century Venice, when a merchant must default on a large loan from an abused Jewish moneylender for a friend with romantic ambitions, the bitterly vengeful creditor demands a gruesome payment instead. Presented in comic book format.

"Since plays are written to be performed, to be seen, a manga adaptation is a very satisfying way to enjoy Shakespeare. . . . Fans of the Bard should be delighted to experience his works through comics, while manga fans can be exposed to Shakespeare in a familiar way." Voice Youth Advocates

Medley, Linda
★ **Castle** waiting. Fantagraphics 2006 456p il $29.95
Grades: 5 6 7 8 9 10 11 12   **741.5**
1. Fairy tales 2. Graphic novels 3. Fantasy graphic novels 4. Fairy tales -- Graphic novels
ISBN 1-56097-747-7

All of Medley's previously self-published comics are collected here in one volume for the first time. The titular castle was the home of Sleeping Beauty, whose story is retold from the viewpoint of the flibbertigibbet ladies in waiting. After the flighty princess awakens with the kiss of a handsome but not too bright prince, the castle becomes a sanctuary for various misfits. Readers will find references to many fairy tales, folk tales, and nursery rhymes in Medley's book, and her clean, clear black-and-white art reflects the works of classic illustrators such as Arthur Rackham.

Momo no Tane
Shugo chara! Peach-Pit; translated by June Kato; adapted by David Walsh; lettered by North Market Street Graphics. Del Rey/Ballantine Books 2007 v1-v6 il v1 $10.95; v2 $10.95; v3 $10.95; v4 $10.95; v5 $10.95; v6 $10.95
Grades: 5 6 7 8 9   **741.5**
1. Graphic novels
ISBN 978-0-345-49745-1 v1; 978-0-345-49927-1 v2; 978-0-345-50146-2 v3; 978-0-345-50522--4 v4; 978-0-345-50804-1 v5; 978-0-345-51032-7 v6
LC 2007296632

"Readers should revel in the lightly romantic and comedic plot and delight in the adorably stylized characters, from brooding mysterious cat-eared boys to small, sweet doll-like girls. Fans of CLAMP's Cardcaptor Sakura (Tokyopop) will enjoy these adventures of another plucky fourth grader uncovering magical secrets and learning of her wondrous fantasy world. Sheer bubblegum fun." SLJ

Mouly, Francoise
★ The **TOON** treasury of classic children's comics; selected and edited by Art Spiegelman and Françoise Mouly; introduction by Jon Scieszka. Abrams ComicArts 2009 350p il $40

Grades: 3 4 5 6   **741.5**
1. Comic books, strips, etc.
ISBN 978-0-8109-5730-5; 0-8109-5730-2
LC 2009009830

"These stories are terrifically funny, joltingly exuberant, bafflingly bizarre, and best of all, compiled into one hearty, hefty, handsome volume." Booklist

Nagatomo, Haruno
Draw your own Manga; beyond the basics. translated by Françoise White. Kodansha International 2005 111p il pa $19.95
Grades: 7 8 9 10 11 12   **741.5**
1. Drawing 2. Manga -- Drawing 3. Graphic novels -- Drawing
ISBN 4-7700-2304-9; 978-4-7700-2304-9

"This advanced manual looks at how to enhance manga with a range of special effects as well as how to use various types of color ink, markers, and airbrushes to reach more creative levels. Supplemented by an interview with the immensely popular Japanese sports manga artist Shinji Mizushima, this book is recommended for any cartoon or animation library." Libr J

Nakajo, Hisaya
Sugar Princess volume 1: skating to win; story & art by Hisaya Nakajo. Viz Media/Shojo Beat 2008 184p il $8.99
Grades: 7 8 9 10 11 12   **741.5**
1. Manga 2. Shojo manga 3. Graphic novels 4. Romance graphic novels 5. Ice skating -- Graphic novels
ISBN 978-1-4215-1930-2; 1-4215-1930-5
Orginal Japanese edition, 2005

Maya Kurinoko takes her little brother to the local ice-skating rink with free tickets, but he won't skate unless she does a jump just like they saw on television the night before. So, she attempts a double axel, and lands it. Skating coach Eishi Todo sees her make the jump and scouts her as an ice skater. He wants famous skater Shun Kano (who attends Maya's high school she's in junior high) to coach and then partner with her, but Shun doesn't want it. However, Maya loves ice skating and realizes it may be the one thing she can be good at doing, and she's willing to persevere.

Neri, Greg
★ **Yummy**; the last days of a Southside Shorty. by G. Neri; illustrated by Randy DuBurke. Lee & Low Books 2010 94p il pa $16.95
Grades: 8 9 10 11 12   **741.5**
1. Children 2. Graphic novels 3. Biographical graphic novels 4. Gang members 5. Murder victims 6. Gangs -- Graphic novels 7. Violence -- Graphic novels 8. African Americans -- Graphic novels
ISBN 978-1-58430-267-4 pa; 1-58430-267-4 pa
LC 2006-17771
Coretta Scott King Author Award honor book, 2011

"Neri's straightforward, unadorned prose is the perfect complement to DuBurke's stark black-and-white inks; great slabs of shadow and masterfully rendered faces breathe real, tragic life into the players." Publ Wkly

Nobleman, Marc Tyler

★ **Boys** of Steel; The Creators of Superman. Random House Childrens Books 2013 40 p. (library) $19.99; (paperback) $7.99

Grades: 4 5 6 7   741.5

1. Superman (Fictional character) 2. Superhero comic books, strips, etc.

ISBN 9780375938023; 0449810631; 9780449810637

This book by Marc Tyler Nobleman and illustrated by Ross MacDonald "tells how writer Jerry Siegel and artist Joe Shuster, two misfit teens in Depression-era Cleveland who were more like Clark Kent than his alter ego, created this superhero [Superman] and published his adventures in comic-book format." (Publishers Weekly)

O'Connor, George

Athena; grey-eyed goddess. First Second 2010 76p il (Olympians) $16.99; pa $9.99

Grades: 5 6 7 8   741.5

1. Graphic novels 2. Classical mythology 3. Athena (Greek deity)

ISBN 978-1-59643-649-7; 1-59643-649-2; 978-1-59643-432-5 pa; 1-59643-432-5 pa

"O'Connor's drawings, full of energetic diagonals and expressive faces, are nicely balanced by spare settings and minimalistic backgrounds. A sophisticated color palette, full of midtones and subtle contrasts, and panel layouts that vary from page to page further distinguish the art. The author's affection for his subject is evident in a chatty note. Profiles of major characters, notes, and discussion questions appear in addition to the usual back matter. An exceptional graphic novel." SLJ

Includes bibliographical references

Hera: the goddess and her glory. First Second 2011 76p il (Olympians) pa $9.99

Grades: 5 6 7 8   741.5

1. Graphic novels 2. Hera (Greek deity) 3. Classical mythology

ISBN 978-1-59643-433-2; 1-59643-433-3

"O'Connor picks a few telling episodes from the goddess' legacy for a more nuanced tale of Zeus' long-suffering, acid-tongued queen. Central to this reclamation project are the 10 labors she indirectly visits upon Heracles. . . . With dedication to the source material, even at its thorniest, and fantastic artwork, O'Connors top-notch Olympians series continues to drive home the point that not only were these gods and goddesses the world's first superheroes but their labyrinthine web of weak-willed failings, spiteful jealousies, and titanic retaliations made for the world's foremost, must-see soap opera." Booklist

★ **Zeus**; king of the gods. Roaring Brook Press 2010 76p il (Olympians) $16.99; pa $9.99

Grades: 5 6 7 8   741.5

1. Graphic novels 2. Zeus (Greek deity) 3. Classical mythology

ISBN 978-1-59643-431-8; 1-59643-625-5; 978-1-59643-432-5 pa; 1-59643-431-7 pa

Retells in graphic novel format stories from Greek mythology about the exploits of the young Zeus and how he rallied an army and overthrew his father, Kronos, to become king of the gods

"It's [the] balance between respect for myth and adherence to comic-book form that works so wonderfully well here." Bull Cent Child Books

O'Donnell, Liam

Media meltdown: a graphic guide adventure; written by Liam O'Donnell; illustrated by Mike Deas. Orca Book Publishers 2009 un il pa $9.95

Grades: 6 7 8 9 10   741.5

1. Graphic novels 2. Mystery graphic novels 3. Media literacy -- Graphic novels

ISBN 978-1-55469-065-7 pa; 1-55469-065-X pa
                                          LC 2009-927573

Pema and Bounce find a new housing development going up in the middle of what used to be their favorite biking trail, and then they learn that the developer is trying to force Jagroop's farmer father to sell his land. Pema's older sister Nima has been working as an intern at the local TV station, and she tries to help the teens put together a news story about what's happening. Then they learn that the developer buys a lot of advertising on the station, and he gets the station owner to pressure the producer to kill their story. They need to get their story out, but since traditional media won't help them, they turn to alternate media on the internet and a little guerilla newscasting by Nima to stop the developer and preserve their land.

This "is an excellent choice for developing media literacy. . . . The design and layout are colorful and fast paced. The text is well written and paired with useful imagery." SLJ

Ottaviani, Jim

Levitation: physics and psychology in the service of deception; [by] Jim Ottaviani and Janine Johnston; lettering by Tom Orzechowski. G. T. Labs 2007 71p il pa $12.95

Grades: 6 7 8 9 10 11 12 Adult   741.5

1. Graphic novels 2. Magic tricks -- Graphic novels

ISBN 978-0-9788037-0-4

This book tells the story of how John Neville Maskelyne developed the stage magic trick of levitation, of the American Harry Kellar, who acquired the trick through devious means, of the old school engineer Guy Jarrett, who perfected the magicians' tricks, and of stage performer Howard Thurston, who inherited the levitation trick from Kellar and ruined it. Or did he? The book includes notes and reprints of old posters and other information on the magicians.

Includes bibliographical references

Parker, Jeff

The **avengers**: heroes assembled; artist, Manuel Garcia. Marvel 2006 v1 il (Marvel adventures: the avengers) pa $6.99

Grades: 5 6 7 8 9   741.5

1. Graphic novels 2. Superhero graphic novels

ISBN 978-0-7851-2306-4; 0-7851-2306-7

Presents adventures in which various superheroes, including Captain America, Storm, Wolverine, and Spider-Man battle numerous foes. Publisher's note

Other titles in the series about the Avengers are:

The avengers v2: mischief (2007)

The avengers v3: bizarre adventures (2007)

The avengers v4: dream team (2007)

The avengers v5: some assembling required (2008)

The avengers v6: mighty marvels (2008)

The avengers v7: weirder and wilder (2008)

The avengers v8: the new recruits (2009)

Pearson, Luke

Hilda and the Midnight Giant; Luke Pearson. Consortium Book Sales & Dist 2012 40p chiefly col. ill. $24

Grades: 4 5 6 7 8   741.5

1. Occult fiction 2. Girls -- Fiction 3. Forests and forestry -- Fiction

ISBN 1907704256; 9781907704253

In this book, the "protagonist finds her world turned upside down as she faces the prospect of leaving her snow-capped birthplace for the hum of the megalopolis, where her mother (an architect) has been offered a prestigious job. During Hilda's daily one-and-a-half hour trek to school she looks for ways to stall her mother's decision. She conspires with the beings of the mystical Blue Forest to delay the inevitable. Will they help or hinder her? More importantly, who is this mysterious Midnight Giant? This is the first part of the Hildafolk series, a series that follows Hilda on her many adventures and travels through the magical fjords and enchanted mountains of her birthplace as she unravels the mysteries of the supernatural world that surrounds her." (Amazon.com)

Petersen, David

★ **Mouse** Guard: Fall 1152. Archaia Studios Press 2007 un il $24.95

Grades: 5 6 7 8   741.5

1. Graphic novels 2. Fantasy graphic novels 3. Mice -- Graphic novels

ISBN 978-1-932386-57-8; 1-932386-57-2

In a medieval world populated by animals, mice have their own civilization but live in constant peril from predators. They live in hidden towns protected by the Guard, who also escort travelers between towns. Three young members of the Guard, Lieam, Saxon, and Kenzie, go in search of a missing grain merchant. They find him dead in the belly of a snake who tried to eat them; but they also find evidence that the dead merchant is a traitor. Now they need to find out to whom he was betraying the Guard and why. While this story features animals and is suitable for most readers who can handle some fighting action, there's nothing cute or Disney-esque in the art. Characters die, this is a serious story, but readers who have read Bone or the Harry Potter series can handle the action in this book. This is the first in a series.

Another title in this series is:

Mouse Guard: Winter 1152 (2009)

Mouse Guard: Winter 1152; story & art by David Petersen. Archaia Studios Press 2009 un il $24.95

Grades: 5 6 7 8   741.5

1. Graphic novels 2. Fantasy graphic novels 3. Mice -- Graphic novels

ISBN 978-1-932386-74-5; 1-932386-74-2

"Picking up where Fall 1152 . . . left off, Winter 1152 follows the darkening adventures of the brave troops of the Mouse Guard as they battle the elements, predators, and even other mice in order to secure their way of life. The

high-quality artwork found in the first volume carries over into this one. The narrative . . . is fast paced and compelling. . . . Combining a tale of action, romance, comedy, and tragedy with the graphic-novel format results in a topnotch work with wide appeal." SLJ

Petrucha, Stefan

Beowulf; story by Stefan Petrucha; artwork by Kody Chamberlain. 1st Harper Trophy ed.; Harper-Trophy 2007 un il $8.99

Grades: 6 7 8 9 11 12 Adult   741.5

1. Graphic novels 2. Adventure graphic novels 3. Monsters -- Graphic novels

ISBN 978-0-06-134390-2

LC 2007003923

For a dozen years, the monster Grendel has haunted the Danish kingdom ruled over by Hrothgar. Word of the monster spreads far and wide, and from across the sea comes the warrior Beowulf to battle the monster and free the Danes from Grendel's reign of terror.

"In this stunning graphic novel, Beowulf comes to life for young readers. . . . The illustrations are detailed and energetic and convey the sinister nature of the evil Beowulf encounters." SLJ

Phelan, Matt

★ **Around** the world. Candlewick Press 2011 240p il $24.99

Grades: 4 5 6 7   741.5

1. Graphic novels 2. Voyages and travels

ISBN 978-0-7636-3619-7; 0-7636-3619-3

LC 2010043153

"Phelan presents three true stories of around-the-world adventures inspired by Jules Verne's Around the World in Eighty Days that, even though they were undertaken in the late 1800s, would be hardly less arduous today. Thomas Stevens, Joshua Slocum, and Nellie Bly saw the world from the seat of a bicycle, aboard a 36-foot sloop, and via trains and ships, respectively. The small, specific pleasures of Phelan's work . . . are showcased in panels laid out in horizontal bands, reinforcing the linear, ever-onward nature of each narrative. The use of limited color palettes enhances the artist's characteristic delicate, expressive pen-and-ink drawings without overpowering them, allowing each traveler's character to be the dominant story element. . . . Design elements such as borders and frames lend a jaunty festivity to a graphic novel that will appeal to aficionados of the form and any reader in search of engrossing true journeys." SLJ

★ The **storm** in the barn. Candlewick Press 2009 201p il $24.99; pa $14.99

Grades: 4 5 6 7 8 9   741.5

1. Graphic novels 2. Adventure graphic novels 3. Kansas -- Graphic novels 4. Monsters -- Graphic novels 5. Dust storms -- Graphic novels

ISBN 978-0-7636-3618-0; 0-7636-3618-5; 978-0-7636-5290-6 pa; 0-7636-5290-3 pa

In Kansas of 1937, the land has been in the grip of the Dust Bowl for four years, and eleven-year-old Jack Carter has seen his family worn down by it. But the day Jack outruns a dust storm all the way home from town, he glimpses something odd in the abandoned Talbot barn, and he tries to find the courage to go into the barn and confront what is there.

"Children can read this as a work of historical fiction, a piece of folklore, a scary story, a graphic novel, or all four. Written with simple, direct language, it's an almost wordless book: the illustrations' shadowy grays and blurry lines eloquently depict the haze of the dust. A complex but accessible and fascinating book." SLJ

Poe, Edgar Allan

The **raven** and other poems; illustrated by Gahan Wilson. Papercutz 2009 56p il (Classics illustrated) $9.95

Grades: 5 6 7 8 9 10 11 12   741.5
1. Poets 2. Authors 3. Graphic novels 4. Essayists 5. Short story writers 6. American poetry -- Graphic novels
ISBN 978-1-59707-140-6; 1-59707-140-4
Cartoonist Gahan Wilson brings his moody, macabre drawing style to illustrate poems by Edgar Allan Poe. This book includes "The Raven," "Annabel Lee," "The Sleeper," "Eldorado," "Lines on Ale," "The City in the Sea," "Alone," "The Haunted Palace," and "The Conqueror Worm." This book was first published in 1990 by First Publishing in partnership with Berkley Publishing Group.

Powell, Martin

The **seven** voyages of Sinbad; retold by Martin Powell; illustrated by Ferran [Daniel Perez] Stone Arch Books 2010 63p il lib bdg $26.65; pa $6.95
Grades: 4 5 6   741.5
1. Graphic novels 2. Folklore -- Graphic novels
ISBN 978-1-4342-1987-9 lib bdg; 1-4342-1987-9 lib bdg; 978-1-4342-2775-1 pa; 1-4342-2775-8 pa
LC 2010020159
Sinbad the sailor "recounts his miraculous travels to a beggar before giving him the riches to set out on his own adventures. . . . The artwork is as comics-inspired as it gets—all dramatic poses and forced perspective. [This] may succeed in introducing . . . Sinbad to new readers." SLJ

Pyle, Kevin C.

Katman. Henry Holt and Co. 2009 un il pa $12.99
Grades: 7 8 9 10 11 12   741.5
1. Graphic novels 2. Cats -- Graphic novels 3. Friendship -- Graphic novels
ISBN 978-0-8050-8285-2; 0-8050-8285-9
LC 2008-937398
Kit is a bored sixteen-year-old with nothing to do one summer when he starts feeding stray cats. He loves it when cool, artistic Jess helps him out, even though he has to endure constant taunting by her disaffected metalhead friends. They make fun of him for being like the local cat lady, but Kit doesn't care—especially after Jess draws him an anime-style avatar named Katman.

"Beautifully simple and straightforward." Voice Youth Advocates

Rafter, Dan

Atlas; illustrated by Adam Ellis . . . [et al.] Bluewater Comics 2010 un il pa $9.99

Grades: 5 6 7 8   741.5
1. Graphic novels 2. Superhero graphic novels
ISBN 978-1-61623-931-2; 1-61623-931-X
"Atlas is a typical square-jawed superhero; in fact, he's pretty angular and blocky all over. His other primary characteristics are that he's always hungry and that he's kind of a dim bulb. As the story begins, his long-suffering partner, Wonder Boy, has to drag him away from yet another Chicago-style hot dog to fight some villains who are threatening the city. . . . The artwork is well suited to this witty story. The images are eye-catching and filled with life and humor." SLJ

Raven, Nicky

Bram Stoker's Dracula; adapted by Nicky Raven; illustrated by Anne Yvonne Gilbert. Candlewick Press 2010 96p il $19.99
Grades: 7 8 9 10   741.5
1. Authors 2. Novelists 3. Graphic novels 4. Horror graphic novels 5. Short story writers 6. Vampires -- Graphic novels
ISBN 978-0-7636-4793-3; 0-7636-4793-4
LC 2009-22116
A modern, illustrated retelling of the Bram Stoker classic, in which young Jonathan Harker first meets and then must destroy the vampire, Count Dracula, in order to save those closest to him.

Raven "successfully abridges a vaunted classic. . . . Raven does a great job fleshing out characters that even in Stoker's original felt bloodless. . . . Gilbert's gothic drawings, the crosshatches of which often conceal layers of spooky elements, are a perfect fit for the somber tone." Booklist

Reed, Gary

Mary Shelley's Frankenstein: the graphic novel. Puffin Graphics 2005 176p il pa $9.99
Grades: 5 6 7 8 9 10 11 12   741.5
1. Authors 2. Novelists 3. Graphic novels 4. Horror graphic novels
ISBN 0-14-240407-1
Scientist Victor Frankenstein decided to create a man, only to create something he deemed a monster.

"Reed concentrates on the emotional anguish of the story, ably capturing the rage, the hurt, and the guilt of both monster and creator. Irving . . . creates a hazy, suitably murky black-and-white backdrop, never exploiting the violence inherent in the monster's quest for vengeance." Booklist

Reed, M. K.

Americus. First Second 2011 215p il pa $14.99
Grades: 8 9 10 11 12   741.5
1. Graphic novels 2. Libraries -- Fiction 3. Censorship -- Fiction 4. Books and reading -- Fiction 5. Christian fundamentalism -- Fiction
ISBN 978-1-59643-601-5; 1-59643-601-8
LC 2010051586
"The clever mix of fantasy and realistic fiction, thoughtful pacing, authentic dialogue, and expressive art perfectly captures the angst of a nerdy teen who is at first ostracized but then finds his niche as he finds his voice." Booklist

Renier, Aaron

★ The **Unsinkable** Walker Bean; written and illustrated by Aaron Renier; colored by Alec Long-streth. First Second 2010 191p il pa $13.99

Grades: 5 6 7 8   **741.5**

1. Graphic novels 2. Adventure graphic novels
ISBN 978-1-59643-453-0 pa; 1-59643-453-8 pa

The story "centers around a cursed skull stolen from the lair of two deep-sea crustacean witches. Like all who look upon the skull, Walker's beloved grandpa falls deathly ill when he finds it, and the boy sets out to return the skull from whence it came. . . . The generous page size lets [the] reader dive into Renier's quavery and painstakingly detailed cartooning, and he really shows off his stuff with a bounty of full-splash dazzlers. . . . Exciting, deep, funny, and scary, with tremendous villains and valor galore." Booklist

Robbins, Trina

Go girl!. Vol. 1, The time team; story, Trina Robbins, art , Anne Timmons. Dark Horse Comics 2004 95p il pa $5.95

Grades: 3 4 5 6 7 8   **741.5**

1. Graphic novels 2. Adventure graphic novels 3. Superhero graphic novels 4. Go Girl (Fictional character) -- Graphic novels
ISBN 1-59307-230-9

"Robbins, who has made a name for herself as a feminist in the comics world, creates a story about three stereotypical high school girls—the dismissive cheerleader, the misunderstood brain, and the daughter of a 1970s-era superheroine—who become stranded in prehistory. The girls are quick-witted, the dinosaurs are cartoony, and a late appearance by Vikings offers readers a taste of what Nordic women might have been like in a confrontation. This isn't high concept, but it's definitely good, clean fun." Booklist

The **drained** brains caper; [by] Trina Robbins and Tyler Page. Lerner Publishing Group/Graphic Universe 2010 64p il (Chicagoland Detective Agency) lib bdg $27.97; pa $6.95

Grades: 4 5 6 7   **741.5**

1. Graphic novels 2. Mystery graphic novels 3. Humorous graphic novels 4. Brainwashing -- Fiction 5. Schools -- Graphic novels 6. Japanese Americans -- Graphic novels
ISBN 978-0-7613-4601-2 lib bdg; 0-7613-4601-5 lib bdg; 978-0-7613-5635-6 pa; 0-7613-5635-5 pa
LC 2009-32620

Required to attend summer school after moving to Chicagoland, thirteen-year-old manga-love Megan Yamamura needs help from twelve-year-old computer genius Raf Hernandez to escape the maniacal principal's mind control experiment.

This tells "an entertaining story. . . . Page's black-and-white cartooning has a loose manga slant, with peppy goofiness popping out from stippled screen tones." Booklist

Another title in this series is:
The Maltese mummy (2011)

Roche, Art

Comic strips; create your own comic strips from start to finish. Lark 2007 112p il (Art for kids) $17.95

Grades: 4 5 6 7   **741.5**

1. Drawing 2. Cartoons and caricatures 3. Cartooning -- Technique 4. Comic books, strips, etc.
ISBN 978-1-57990-788-4; 1-57990-788-1

Explains the process of drawing comic strips and makes suggestions for developing a style all one's own

"The bright, dynamic layout includes full-color illustrations. The writing is clear and concise so that after completing the book, readers will feel confident to branch out on their own." SLJ

Rocks, Misako

Detective Jermain, volume 1; story and art by Misako Rocks. Henry Holt and Company 2008 152p il $9.95

Grades: 6 7 8 9 10   **741.5**

1. Graphic novels 2. Mystery graphic novels
ISBN 978-0-8050-8155-8; 0-8050-8155-0
LC 2007-938579

Seventeen-year-old Jermain wants to be a detective, just like her father was before he was murdered. In her senior year of high school, she finds a mystery: a student and a teacher are killed in an automobile accident, and they were both behaving very strangely in school that day. Jermain enlists the help of her two best friends, Travis and Andy, to help her find out what is going on at school that would cost the lives of their friends.

"The author/artist is adept at portraying emotions, and employs a variety of visual effects that pull readers into the story. The b&w artwork is crisp and effectively propels the action. This is an auspicious start to a series that should prove popular with its intended audience." Libr Media Connect

Roman, Dave

Astronaut Academy: Zero gravity. First Second Books 2011 185p il $16.99; pa $9.99

Grades: 4 5 6 7 8 9 10   **741.5**

1. Graphic novels 2. Humorous graphic novels 3. Science fiction graphic novels 4. School life -- Graphic novels
ISBN 978-1-59643-756-2; 1-59643-756-2; 978-1-59643-20-6 pa; 1-59643-620-4 pa
LC 2010-941434

Hakata Soy has been the leader of a futuristic superhero team, but he has given that up and just wants to be a normal student at Astronaut Academy, a school on a space station, where students take such courses as anti-gravity gymnastics and fire-throwing. Other students include Doug Hiro, who always wears his space helmet, rich girl Maribelle Mellonbelly, Miyumi San (Maribelle's rival), and egotistical Billy Lee. Hakata Soy has some trouble adjusting to school life, and things get much worse when the villainous Gotcha Birds steal a robotic twin to Hakata Soy and reprogram it to kill him. The comics originally appeared as web comics, then as mini comics that Roman took to various comic cons; this is the first trade book collection of the stories. Middle grade students, boys and girls, will enjoy this book, which is full of humor and action with little actual violence.

"Students like the introspective Hakata Soy, the space-gymnastics-obsessed Doug Hiro, and the snooty rich girl Mirabelle Mellonbelly meet up at Astronaut Academy, a middle school where the zany mixes with the postmodern. . . . Silliness is high on the agenda, aided by minimal, cartoonish art that plays on manga tropes but also manages to build character into the simple lines of a face. . . . This is one for readers looking for more involved and complex comedy than a cursory glance at the images might lead one to expect." Booklist

Rosinsky, Natalie M.

Graphic content! the culture of comic books. Compass Point Books 2010 64p il (Pop culture revolutions) lib bdg $31.99

Grades: 5 6 7 8 9 10   **741.5**

   1. Comic books, strips, etc. -- History and criticism

   ISBN 978-0-7565-4241-2 lib bdg; 0-7565-4241-3 lib bdg

Traces the origins of comic books and discusses the emergence of superheroes, censorship issues, their depiction of increased social diversity, and their impact on society

"This slim and splashily designed book . . . does an admirable job of keeping things succinct yet thorough. . . . [The author] maintains a nice international scope throughout. . . . This is a super resource to have on hand to give a broader context of the medium and its fascinating history." Booklist

Write your own graphic novel. Compass Point Books 2009 64p il (Write your own) lib bdg $33.26

Grades: 5 6 7 8 9 10 11 12   **741.5**

   1. Graphic novels -- Authorship

   ISBN 978-0-7565-3856-9 lib bdg; 0-7565-3856-4 lib bdg

                       LC 2008-6506

This book offers tips, advice, end encouragement to readers who might want to try their hand at writing their own comics and graphic novels. Rosinsky uses many examples from Stone Arch and Capstone Press books along with many others, and the "case study" side bars provide glimpses into the work of such graphic novelists as Marjane Satrapi, Art Spiegelman, and Craig Thompson. The back matter includes a list of suggested graphic novels that are suitable for teen readers

"Students wishing to explore the graphic-novel format will benefit from clear explanations of how to portray heroes and villains, use dramatic dialogue, and create a story map. Excerpts from several popular graphic novels are included." SLJ

Russell, P. Craig

  ★ **Coraline**; based on the novel by Neil Gaiman; adapted and illustrated by P. Craig Russell; colorist, Lovern Kindzierski; letterer, Todd Klein. HarperCollins 2008 186p il $18.99; lib bdg $19.89

Grades: 4 5 6 7   **741.5**

   1. Authors 2. Novelists 3. Graphic novels 4. Horror graphic novels 5. Comic book writers 6. Short story writers 7. Science fiction writers

   ISBN 978-0-06-082543-0; 978-0-06-082544-7 lib bdg

                      LC 2007-930658

"An adaptation of Gaiman's 2002 novel Coraline, . . . a tale of childhood nightmares. As in the original story, Coraline wanders around her new house and discovers a door leading into a mirror place, where she finds her button-eyed 'other mother,' who is determined to secure Coraline's love one way or another. This version is a virtuoso adaptation. . . . A master of fantastical landscapes, Russell sharpens the realism of his imagery, perserving the humanity of the characters and heightening the horror." Booklist

Sakura, Kenichi

Dragon drive. Vol. 1, D-break; story & art by Ken-ichi Sakura. Viz Media/Shonen Jump 2007 195p il $7.99

Grades: 6 7 8 9 10   **741.5**

   1. Manga 2. Shonen manga 3. Graphic novels 4. Video games -- Graphic novels

   ISBN 978-1-4215-1187-0; 1-4215-1187-8

Reiji Ozora knows that he's no good at anything, people keep telling him that. Then best friend Maiko takes him to a secret center where people play a virtual reality game, Dragon Drive. Reiji signs up and finds that, despite the fact that his virtual dragon, Chibi, is small and weak, together they have more power than meets the eye. While they play the game, they're in a world called Rikyu, where everything feels all too real; can Reiji, Chibi, and their friends be in real danger?

Other titles in the Dragon Drive series are:

Dragon drive. Vol. 2: another world (2007)
Dragon drive. Vol. 3: believe (2007)
Dragon drive. Vol. 4: hero (2007)
Dragon drive. Vol. 5: mission (2007)
Dragon drive. Vol. 6: hope (2008)
Dragon drive. Vol. 7: decisive battle (2008)
Dragon drive. Vol. 8: excitement (2008)
Dragon drive. Vol. 9: reshuffle (2008)
Dragon drive. Vol. 10: departure (2008)
Dragon drive. Vol. 11: trust (2008)
Dragon drive. Vol. 12: promise (2009)
Dragon drive. Vol. 13: reunion (2009)
Dragon drive. Vol. 14: wait (2009)

Sala, Richard

Cat burglar black. First Second 2009 126p il pa $16.99

Grades: 5 6 7 8 9 10   **741.5**

   1. Graphic novels 2. Mystery graphic novels 3. Orphans -- Graphic novels 4. Comic books, strips, etc.

   ISBN 978-1-59643-144-7; 1-59643-144-X

K.'s aunt, who works at the Bellsong Academy for Girls, has invited K. to attend the school. But as soon as she arrives, K. notices some strange goings-on: her aunt has suddenly taken ill; there are only three other students and no regular classes; and a statue speaks to K. when no one else is around.

"The story is structured like a lighthearted cross between a fable and a horror film, but only ever teetering on the edge of horror without depicting it. This could have resulted in a mishmash, but Sala elegantly dances through the creepy and the sweet." SLJ

Sanderson, Peter

X-men: the ultimate guide; [by] Peter Sanderson. Updated ed.; Dorling Kindersley Pub. 2006 192p il $24.99

Grades: 7 8 9 10   741.5

1. Comic books, strips, etc.

ISBN 978-0-7566-2005-9; 0-7566-2005-8

LC 2005-33592

First published 2003 with title: Ultimate X-men

This is an "overview of the history of the X-Men comics, detailing the stories and characters that have appeared on their pages." Publisher's note

Schreiber, Ellen

Vampire kisses: blood relatives. Katherine Tegen Books 2007 96p il pa $7.99

Grades: 7 8 9 10   741.5

1. Vampires -- Graphic novels

ISBN 978-0-06-134081-9 pa; 0-06-134081-2 pa

LC 2007-03677

"Raven is a cute Goth girl who just happens to have a vampire for a boyfriend. . . . [The] over-the-top romanticism . . . will be devoured . . . by teens who like their horror more sweet than scary. . . . The stylized artwork is an excellent match for this vampire-lite romance." SLJ

Schweizer, Chris

Crogan's march. Oni Press 2009 212p il $14.95

Grades: 8 9 10 11 12 Adult   741.5

1. Graphic novels 2. Adventure graphic novels 3. Imperialism -- Graphic novels

ISBN 978-1-934964-24-8

When brothers Eric and Cory squabble at the dinner table, their father tells them the story of Peter Crogan, one of their ancestors, who fought in the French Foreign Legion in 1912. Crogan's five-year term of service is one month from completion when he's asked to stay and become an officer. His unit is stationed in North Africa, where the French hold territory and depend on the French Foreign Legion to police the territory, putting down the rebellious attacks of the Tuaregs. He finds himself torn between the heroic Captain Poitelet (who tends to be the sole survivor of various battles) and the grizzled sergeant who actually cares about the people the Legion polices. When Crogan's unit escorts a caravan that endures an attack by Tuaregs, the captain's reckless actions endanger everyone, and Crogan must find help. Schweizer's story includes the kind of violence military actions cause, but very little in the way of bad language. Some may wince at the heavily French-accented English of some of the characters ("zee Daughters of France send zem out to all of zee units," etc.). This action-packed historical fiction graphic novel will appeal to teens, but adults who remember such novels as Beau Geste by Percival Christopher Wren (and the movies, of course) will also enjoy reading Schweizer's tale.

Serling, Rod

The Twilight Zone: the after hours; adaptation by Mark Kneece; illustrated by Rebekah Isaacs. Walker & Company 2008 un il $16.99; pa $9.99

Grades: 5 6 7 8 9 10   741.5

1. Graphic novels 2. Supernatural graphic novels

ISBN 978-0-8027-9716-2; 978-0-8027-9717-9 pa

LC 2008-4310

Marsha White visits a department store to buy an advertised gold thimble, is taken by elevator to a floor with empty display cases except for one, which has the thimble, and she deals with an odd saleswoman who knows her name. When Marsha is in the elevator, she discovers the thimble is defective and tries to complain, but the manager insists there is no eighteenth floor, the store has no elevator, and the store has never carried gold thimbles. As she begins to leave, Marsha faints at the sight of a mannequin that looks exactly like the strange saleswoman, and she's put into a back room to recover. When she wakes up, the store has been closed and she's locked in. This is an actual episode of the old Twilight Zone television show.

"Kneece's adaptation is quick and enjoyable and introduces a classic TV series to a new generation of readers. Isaacs's illustrations are clean, distinct and cinematic in scope, employing an interesting variety of angles." Kirkus

The Twilight Zone: walking distance; adaptation from Rod Serling's original script by Mark Kneece; illustrated by Dove McHargue. Walker & Company 2008 un il $16.99; pa $9.99

Grades: 5 6 7 8 9 10   741.5

1. Graphic novels 2. Supernatural graphic novels

ISBN 978-0-8027-9714-8; 978-0-8027-9715-5 pa

LC 2008-4273

Thirty-nine-year-old businessman Martin Sloan's car blows a tire as he's driving, and he realizes he is within walking distance of his hometown. Leaving his car to be repaired, he decides to walk there. However, when he reaches town, he has also gone back in time. Can he find his boyhood self and give his younger self advice? Or will everyone think he's just crazy? This is an actual episode of the old Twilight Zone television show.

The story is "exceptionally well told and . . . [is] brilliantly adapted to a new medium." SLJ

Sfar, Joann

Dungeon Vol. 1: Duck Heart; [by] Joann Sfar & Lewis Trondheim. NBM 2003 96p il pa $14.95

Grades: 7 8 9 10 11 12   741.5

1. Graphic novels 2. Fantasy graphic novels 3. Humorous graphic novels

ISBN 1-56163-401-8

"As a result of some unfortunate accidents, Herbert, usually a lowly messenger in the great Dungeon, is called upon to defend it from all manner of beasties. In his endeavors to become a warrior, he is helped by his friend Marvin the vegetarian dragon and by the Dungeon Keeper. Although there's a solid dose of cartoon-style violence and gore, teens will appreciate Herbert's pseudo-slacker attitude, which turns him into an accidental hero time and time again." Booklist

Other titles in this series are:

Dungeon, the early years: the night shirt (2005)

Zenith: the barbarian princess (2005)

★ The little prince; adapted from the book by Antoine de Saint-Exupéry; translated by Sarah Ardizzone; colour by Brigitte Findakly. Houghton Mifflin Harcourt 2010 110p il $19.99

Grades: 5 6 7 8 9   **741.5**

1. Authors 2. Novelists 3. Air pilots 4. Graphic novels 5. Fantasy graphic novels 6. Essayists 7. Children's authors 8. Air pilots -- Graphic novels 9 Extraterrestrial beings -- Graphic novels

ISBN 978-0-547-33802-6; 0-547-33802-3

"On the surface, this is a straight graphic-novel retelling of the narrator pilot getting stranded in the desert, where he meets a curious little boy who claims to be from a wee planet very far away. . . . The ultimately tricky task is to honor the source but not sound like an adaptation (otherwise, why not just read the original?) and Sfar nails it on both counts. . . . Everything is handled with both reverence and ingenuity." Booklist

Shakespeare, William, 1564-1616

Macbeth; the graphic novel. [by] William Shakespeare; script by John McDonald; adapted by Brigit Viney. Lucent Books 2010 144p il (Classic graphic novel collection) $34.10

Grades: 7 8 9 10   **741.5**

1. Poets 2. Authors 3. Dramatists 4. Graphic novels

ISBN 978-1-4205-0373-9; 1-4205-0373-1

First published 2008 in the United Kingdom

In graphic novel format, presents an adaptation of Shakespeare's classic tale about a man who kills his king after hearing the prophesies of three witches.

"The entire [story is] told through speech balloons. . . . This format offers readers an experience closer to a theatrical performance than a prose condensation of the plot. . . . Excellent graphics bring the [story] to life and set the mood. Lush art in jewel tones heightens interest. . . . Macbeth . . . includes a wealth of additional resources such as a main-character summary, family tree, link map of characters, and listing of famous quotations." SLJ

Includes glossary

Shelley, Mary Wollstonecraft

Frankenstein; illustrated by Marion Mousse. Papercutz 2009 144p 144p il (Classics illustrated) $17.95; pa $13.95

Grades: 6 7 8 9   **741.5**

1. Graphic novels 2. Monsters -- Graphic novels

ISBN 978-1-597071-30-7; 1-597071-30-7; 978-1-597071-31-4 pa; 1-597071-31-5 pa

"In this graphic novel adaptation of the classic story, Dr. Victor Frankenstein tries to create life, but instead creates a monster, one who vows revenge on the scientist for creating and abandoning him." Publisher's note

Shiga, Jason

★ **Meanwhile**. Abrams/Amulet 2010 un il $15.95

Grades: 4 5 6 7 8 9   **741.5**

1. Graphic novels 2. Science fiction graphic novels

ISBN 978-0-8109-8423-3; 0-8109-8423-7

LC 2009-39844

"In this graphic novel mind boggler . . . readers play the role of little Jimmy and on the first page make the seemingly innocuous decision of ordering a vanilla or chocolate ice-cream cone. Tubes connect panels in all directions and veer off into tabs to other pages, creating a head-spinningly tangled web of story. . . . The crux is that Jimmy stumbles into the lab of an affable mad scientist and is allowed to tinker with three inventions: a mind reader, a time machine, and the Killitron, which obliterates all life on earth aside from the user's. . . . It's maddening and challenging, all right, but that's precisely what makes it so crazy fun." Booklist

Siddell, Thomas

★ **Gunnerkrigg** Court: orientation; [by] Tom Siddell. Archaia Studios Press 2009 296p il $26.95

Grades: 6 7 8 9 10 11 12   **741.5**

1. Graphic novels 2. Fantasy graphic novels

ISBN 978-1-932386-34-9; 1-932386-34-3

"The first 14 chapters of Siddell's popular webcomic are collected here in an alluring hardcover. The premise, best described as science-fantasy, involves a young girl named Antimony plopped into a strange boarding-school/industrial-complex which . . . she knows nothing about. Discrete chapters . . . all feature varying levels of jaw-dropping peculiarity, devilish bursts of humor, and sublime creativity that lurk at the ends of the school's corridors. The darkly hued artwork is deceptively simplistic and displays a flair for the crucial details of setting and atmosphere." Booklist

Gunnerkrigg Court: research. Archia Studios 2010 251p il $26.95

Grades: 6 7 8 9 10 11 12   **741.5**

1. Graphic novels 2. Fantasy graphic novels

ISBN 978-1-932386-77-6; 1-932386-77-7

"Collecting year two of Siddell's widely acclaimed science-fantasy webcomic, this graphic novel follows Antimony Carver and her pal, Kat, as they uncover more delectable oddities in their industrial complex/boarding school." Booklist

Sizer, Paul

Little White Mouse collection 1; Dream of the ghost. Café Digital Comics 2004 144p ill. $14.95

Grades: 7 8 9 10   **741.5**

1. Graphic novels

ISBN 9781888429077

In a future universe, sixteen-year-old Loo is shipwrecked on a remote, automated mining satellite when the space liner on which she and her sister were traveling was destroyed. Considered an intruder by the satellite's computer, she must survive, build a robot body for her dead sister's preserved memory, and find a way home before the satellite's life support system shuts down. Creator Sizer is now self-publishing this series of four volumes and selling it at his website, www.paulsizer.com.

Slate, Barbara

You can do a graphic novel. Alpha Books 2010 187p il pa $19.95

Grades: 7 8 9 10   **741.5**

1. Graphic novels -- Authorship

ISBN 978-1-59257-955-6; 1-59257-955-8

LC 2009-930703

"This is a practical book for those who aspire to create their own graphic novels. Slate . . . is fair handed with the advice she gives to writers as well as artists. . . . The instructions and illustrations are easy to follow, and the format is colorful and eye-catching." SLJ

Smith, Jeff

Bone: Rose; with illustrations by Charles Vess. Scholastic Graphix 2009 138p il $21.99; pa $10.99

Grades: 4 5 6 7 8   **741.5**

1. Graphic novels 2. Fantasy graphic novels 3. Adventure graphic novels

ISBN 978-0-545-13542-9; 0-545-13542-7; 978-0-545-13543-6 pa; 0-545-13543-5 pa

"When a terrifying dragon attacks the small towns of the Northern Valley, a young Princess Rose (known later as Gran'ma Ben) must defeat it. The beast is actually the ancient evil, the Lord of the Locusts, and while Rose faces danger with honor, her elder sister, Princess Briar, follows a more sinister path." Publisher's note

Bone: out from Boneville. Scholastic Graphix 2005 144p il $18.95; pa $9.99

Grades: 4 5 6 7 8 9 10 11 12   **741.5**

1. Graphic novels 2. Fantasy graphic novels 3. Adventure graphic novels

ISBN 0-439-70623-8; 0-439-70640-8 pa

"The story follows three cousins who have been thrown out of their town for cheating the citizens. Shortly thereafter, they are separated. Each Bone stumbles into a mysterious valley full of odd creatures that reveal strange happenings. The story is well paced with smooth transitions. It is dark, witty, mysterious, and exciting. The full-color art reflects that of classic comic books." SLJ

Other titles in this series are:

Bone: the great cow race (vol. 2)

Bone: eyes of the storm (vol. 3)

Bone: the dragonslayer (vol. 4)

Bone: Rock Jaw Master the Eastern Border (vol. 5)

Bone: old man's cave (vol. 6)

Bone: ghost circles (vol. 7)

Bone: treasure hunters (vol. 8)

Bone: crown of horns (vol. 9)

Bone: rose (vol. 10)

Bone: tall tales (vol. 11)

Soo, Kean

Jellaby: monster in the city. Hyperion Books 2009 172p il pa $9.99

Grades: 4 5 6 7 8 9   **741.5**

1. Graphic novels 2. Fantasy graphic novels 3. Monsters -- Graphic novels 4. Friendship -- Graphic novels

ISBN 978-1-4231-0565-7 pa; 1-4231-0565-6 pa

Beginning right where the first book ended, Portia, Jason, and Jellaby continue on their way to Toronto, walking after Portia panicked and they got off the train. They're searching for a way home for Jellaby, and they think a door somewhere in Exhibition Place, where the Canadian National Exhibition is taking place, holds a clue. Portia feels torn between wanting to help her friend yet not wanting to say goodbye forever, and her ambivalence causes a rift between her and

Jason. When she doesn't want to trust a masked magician who seems to know too much about them and Jellaby, Portia leaves Jason. They all end up in the Automotive Building, where the masked man leads Jason and Jellaby down below the building, while Portia seems to find her long lost father. But is he really her father, and just what is waiting for Jason and Jellaby under the Automotive Building? Soo again uses a mostly purple color palette.

Stephens, Jay

Heroes! draw your own superheroes, gadget geeks & other do-gooders. [by] Jay Stephens. Lark Books 2007 64p il $12.95; pa $5.95

Grades: 4 5 6 7   **741.5**

1. Drawing 2. Superheroes 3. Cartoons and caricatures

ISBN 978-1-57990-934-5; 1-57990-934-5; 978-1-60059-179-2 pa; 1-60059-179-5 pa

LC 2006101661

"Stephens shows just how to draw [superheroes]. . . . Stephens does a good job organizing his material, beginning with a bit of history, then moving quickly to hero heads, . . . and on to masks, disguises, physical features, power effects, and action moves. The brightly colored illustrations offer plenty of how-to info and lots of great heroes, male and female, to use as models." Booklist

Monsters! draw your own mutants, freaks & creeps. [by] Jay Stephens. Lark Books 2007 64p il $12.95; pa $5.95

Grades: 4 5 6 7   **741.5**

1. Drawing 2. Monsters in art 3. Cartoons and caricatures

ISBN 978-1-57990-935-2; 1-57990-935-3; 978-1-60059-178-5 pa; 1-60059-178-7 pa

LC 2006036104

This offers instruction in drawing such cartoon monsters as Dockula, the aquatic nibbler; Skeeterman, the campground creep; and Spook Ook, the attic thumper

Robots! draw your own androids, cyborgs & fighting bots. [by] Jay Stephens. Lark Books 2007 64p il $12.95

Grades: 4 5 6 7   **741.5**

1. Drawing 2. Robots in art 3. Cartoons and caricatures

ISBN 978-1-57990-937-6; 1-57990-937-X

LC 2007027637

"With simple detailed instructions, an inviting text, and entertaining cartoon scenarios, . . . Stephens explains, step by step, how to draw a variety of robots." Booklist

Stolarz, Laurie Faria

Black is for beginnings; adaptation by Barbara Randall Kesel; artwork by Janina Gørrissen. Llewellyn Publications/Flux 2009 160p il pa $9.95

Grades: 8 9 10 11 12   **741.5**

1. Graphic novels 2. Romance graphic novels 3. Supernatural graphic novels 4. Dreams -- Graphic novels

ISBN 978-0-7387-1438-7; 0-7387-1438-0

When Stacey, a college student and hereditary witch, again begins to have disturbing dreams about her former boyfriend and a little girl who was murdered years earlier, she knows that the dreams are trying to tell her something important, but she does not know what

"The story's weirdo flashes of humor make the darkness bearable, as do the everyday settings of a pizza parlor and dorm room. A unique and somewhat unhinged blend of realism and fantasy." Booklist

Storrie, Paul D.

★ **Beowulf**; monster slayer: a British legend. story by Paul D. Storrie; pencils and inks by Ron Randall. Lerner Publishing Group/Graphic Universe 2008 48p il (Graphic myths and legends) lib bdg $26.60

Grades: 4 5 6 7   **741.5**
1. Graphic novels 2. Monsters -- Graphic novels
ISBN 978-0-8225-6757-8 lib bdg; 0-8225-6757-1 lib bdg

LC 2006-39094

An adaptation of the epic poem in which the hero Beowulf slays the monster Grendel

This "reads like ancient poetry. . . . The action and character design are strong and clear, with solid, comfortable storytelling that is strongly helped by capable color artwork." SLJ

Made for each other; or I made my prom date of Hunkenstein or love in stitches or our love's aliiiiive!! illustrated by Eldon Cowgur. Graphic Universe 2011 127p il (My boyfriend is a monster) lib bdg $29.27; pa $9.95

Grades: 7 8 9 10   **741.5**
1. Graphic novels 2. Romance graphic novels 3. Monsters -- Graphic novels
ISBN 978-0-7613-5601-1 lib bdg; 0-7613-5601-0 lib bdg; 978-0-7613-7077-2 pa; 0-7613-7077-3 pa

LC 2010028722

"Maria falls for the new guy in school, Tom, and he likes her, too. The problem is that the recent mysterious rash of deaths in their town might have something to do with his strange family. Will Maria be able to save the guy she loves, or will monstrous history repeat itself? . . . The black-and-white art brings the wilds of both high school and Alaska to life . . . The romance and scares are real, but light, and make for a thoroughly enjoyable read." Booklist

Stroud, Jonathan

The **Amulet** of Samarkand; a Bartimaeus graphic novel. adapted by Jonathan Stroud and Andrew Donkin; art by Lee Sullivan; color by Nicolas Chapuis; lettering by Chris Dickey. Disney/Hyperion Books 2010 un il $19.99

Grades: 7 8 9 10   **741.5**
1. Magic -- Graphic novels
ISBN 978-1-4231-1146-7; 1-4231-1146-X

LC 2010-35513

Nathaniel, a magician's apprentice, summons up the djinni Bartimaeus and instructs him to steal the Amulet of Samarkand from the powerful magician Simon Lovelace.

"The artwork is lively, atmospheric, and exciting. . . .The depth of Stroud's alternate London, some complex political machinations, and the large cast of human and demon characters are all well realized here." Booklist

★ **Stuck** in the middle; seventeen comics from an unpleasant age. edited by Ariel Schrag. Viking 2007 210p il $18.99

Grades: 7 8 9 10   **741.5**
1. Graphic novels 2. Young adult literature -- Works
ISBN 978-0-670-06221-8

LC 2006-52581

This graphic novel collects seventeen short stories about the perils of middle school, each by independent comics creators, including editor Schrag, her younger sister Tania Schrag, Aaron Renier, Daniel Clowes, Gabrielle Bell, and others.

"Highly recommended for junior high graphic novel collections on up; but please keep in mind that this graphic novel does contain some strong material, including obscenities . . . and sexual material." Kliatt

Sturm, James

★ **Satchel** Paige; striking out Jim Crow. by James Sturm & Rich Tommaso; with an introduction by Gerald Early. Jump at the Sun 2007 89p il $16.99; pa $9.99

Grades: 6 7 8 9 10 11 12   **741.5**
1. Graphic novels 2. Baseball players 3. Baseball -- Graphic novels
ISBN 0-7868-3900-7; 0-7868-3901-5 pa

LC 2007-61362

This graphic novel is "about fictional Emmet Wilson, a black farmer whose moment of glory as a player in the Negro Leagues came when he scored a run off the great pitcher, Satchel Paige. . . . This visually powerful, suspenseful, even profound story makes an excellent choice for readers interested in baseball or in the history of race relations." Booklist

The Superhero book; the ultimate encyclopedia of comic-book icons and Hollywood heroes. edited by Gina Misiroglu with David A. Roach. Visible Ink Press 2004 xxi, 725p il $63.00

Grades: 7 8 9 10   **741.5**
1. Superheroes 2. Motion pictures 3. Cartoons and comics 4. Cartoons and caricatures 5. Superheroes (Fictional characters)
ISBN 0-7808-0772-3

LC 2004019059

This reference book on superheroes "focus[es] on character origins, key historical episodes, powers, weaknesses, archfoes, and romantic distractions. . . . The book's introduction to superhero history includes political and comics-publishing frameworks and a . . . definition of the term 'superhero' itself. . . . Also included are entries covering major players, stories, and history in specific categories, such as 'Alternative superheroes,' 'Multiculturalism,' [and] 'Robot heroes'." (Booklist)

This is an "encyclopedic reference work that profiles superheroes from all companies and in all media. . . . Its 300 full entries provide information on more than 1,000 mythic overachievers, covering . . . comic book, movie, television, and novel superheroes." Publisher's note

Tamaki, Mariko

★ **Emiko** superstar; written by Mariko Tamaki; illustrated by Steve Rolston. DC Comics/Minx 2008 149p il pa $9.99

Grades: 7 8 9 10 11 12   **741.5**

1. Graphic novels 2. Performance art -- Graphic novels 3. Racially mixed people -- Graphic novels

ISBN 978-1-4012-1536-1

"Emiko, a half-Japanese, half-Caucasian Canadian, is a self-described geek facing a summer of babysitting and isolation. Things change when she stumbles upon an underground performing art scene inspired by Andy Warhol's Factory. She eventually takes to the stage . . . and achieves minor celebrity. Soon, though, Emiko must face the troubling complexities in the lives of her new friends and the consequences of her own questionable actions. . . . Rolston's playful, vibrant b&w illustrations bring the characters to life." Publ Wkly

Skim; words by Mariko Tamaki; drawings by Jillian Tamaki. Groundwood Books 2008 144p il $18.95

Grades: 7 8 9 10 11 12   **741.5**

1. Graphic novels 2. Humorous graphic novels 3. Friendship -- Graphic novels 4. School stories -- Graphic novels

ISBN 978-0-88899-753-1; 0-88899-753-1

Skim is Kimberly Keiko Cameron, a not-slim half-Japanese would-be Wiccan goth who attends a private school. When classmate Katie Matthews' ex-boyfriend commits suicide, concerned guidance counselors descend upon the school because so many of the student body goes into mourning overdrive. The popular clique starts a new club, Girls Celebrate Life, and make Katie their project, especially after she falls off her roof and breaks both arms. Kim and her best friend Lisa observe all this, but counselors target Kim for her goth tendencies and are convinced she'll become suicidal any moment. All she is, is in love with her English teacher, Ms. Archer, who seems to reciprocate and then leaves the school. As Lisa starts to get sucked into the GLC, Kim and Katie tentatively begin a new friendship. There is only one rather chaste kiss between Kim and Ms. Archer. Artist Jillian Tamaki draws Kim to look like a classical Heian period Japanese woman.

Tan, Shaun

★ The **arrival**. Arthur A. Levine Books 2007 un il $19.99

Grades: 6 7 8 9 10   **741.5**

1. Graphic novels 2. Stories without words 3. Immigrants -- Graphic novels

ISBN 0-439-89529-4

LC 2006-21706

Boston Globe-Horn Book Award special citation (2008)

In this wordless graphic novel, a man leaves his homeland and sets off for a new country, where he must build a new life for himself and his family.

"Young readers will be fascinated by the strange new world the artist creates. . . . They will linger over the details in the beautiful sepia pictures and will likely pick up the book to pore over it again and again." SLJ

Telgemeier, Raina

Drama; Raina Telgemeier; with color by Gurihiru. 1st ed. Graphix 2012 233 p. chiefly ill. $23.99

Grades: 3 4 5 6 7   **741.5**

1. Graphic novels 2. School stories 3. Middle schools -- Fiction 4. Schools -- Fiction 5. Theater -- Fiction 6. Interpersonal relations -- Fiction

ISBN 0545326982; 0545326990; 9780545326988; 9780545326995

LC 2011040748

Stonewall Honor Book (2013)

Author Raina Telgemeier's book focuses on a middle school drama production. "Callie loves theater . . . [S]he's the set designer for the stage crew, and this year she's determined to create a set worthy of Broadway on a middle-school budget. But how can she, when she doesn't know much about carpentry, ticket sales are down, and the crew members are having trouble working together?" (Publisher's note)

Includes bibliographical references

TenNapel, Doug

Ghostopolis; created, written, and drawn by Doug TenNapel. Graphix 2010 266 p. il pa $12.99; $24.99

Grades: 7 8 9 10   **741.5**

1. Graphic novels 2. Ghosts -- Graphic novels 3. Young adult literature -- Works 4. Graphic novels

ISBN 9780545210287; 9780545210270; 0545210275

LC 20090942984

This graphic novel, a "Kirkus Reviews" Best Children's Books of 2010 title, tells the story of an "agent for the Supernatural Immigration Task Force, . . . Frank Gallows[, whose] . . . job [is] to catch ghosts on Earth and send them back to the afterlife. However, during one particularly tricky deportation, he accidentally zaps a young—living—boy. Garth Hale suddenly finds himself surrounded by mummies and goblins in a crumbling, ghastly city, with a skeleton horse and his long-departed grandfather as his only friends. Gallows comes crashing into the afterlife, as well, on a daring rescue mission. As this bumbling team tries to find a way home, they end up face to face with the evil ruler of Ghostopolis, who doesn't look too kindly upon mortals in his city." (Kirkus)

TenNapel mixes emotional epiphanies with humor in a way that will appeal to a broad audience. Characters experience personal growth and learn lessons about themselves throughout the course of this book. . . . TenNapel's colorful illustrations are filled with energy and life, and they use shade and silhouettes to great advantage." SLJ

TenNapel, Douglas R.

Flink. Image Comics 2007 122p il $13.99

Grades: 6 7 8 9 10 11 12 Adult   **741.5**

1. Graphic novels 2. Adventure graphic novels 3. Sasquatch -- Graphic novels

ISBN 978-1-58240-891-0; 1-58240-891-2

Conrad is flying with his father on his first hunting trip when the plane crashes in the wilderness. When Conrad comes to after the crash, he's completely alone, with only the clothes on his back, a handheld game player, and a pocketknife his father had just given him. When he wakes up from a sleep, he finds a deerskin wrapped around him and follows a trail of berries; a Bigfoot named Flink has saved him. Now they have to deal with a rabid she-bear that injures Flink; he needs his brother's medicine to heal, but the Bigfoot community hates humans who hunt them. How can Flink convince them that Conrad is harmless? The book includes some violence and one scene where Conrad pees on a tree.

Tommysaurus Rex. Image Comics 2005 110p il pa $11.95

Grades: 5 6 7 8 9 10 11 12   **741.5**

1. Graphic novels 2. Dinosaurs -- Graphic novels
ISBN 1-58240-395-3

When Ely loses his dog, Tommy, in a car accident, his parents send him to Grandpa Joe's farm for the summer. He discovers a live, 40-foot Tyrannosaurus Rex in a cave on the farm, and soon the boy and his pet dinosaur cause a big ruckus in town. Ely promises to train the dinosaur he names Tommysaurus, but not if the town's bully, Randy, has his way.

Toriyama, Akira

Cowa! story and art by Akira Toriyama; translation & English adaptation Alexander O. Smith, et. al. Viz Media/Shonen Jump 2008 208p il $7.99

Grades: 5 6 7 8 9 10 11 12   **741.5**

1. Manga 2. Graphic novels 3. Humorous graphic novels 4. Monsters -- Graphic novels
ISBN 978-1-4215-1805-3; 1-4215-1805-8
Original Japanese edition, 1997

Mischievous Paifu is half-vampire and half-werekoala, and he's usually getting into lots of trouble with his best buddy, Jose the ghost. When the Monster Flu sweeps through town, the doctor says that without medicine, everyone will die. The only person who makes the medicine is the witch who lives hundreds of miles away, and all the adults except for the doctor are ill. Paifu and Jose team up with grumpy ex-sumo wrestler Maruyama to make the journey; will they make it before they get sick? The book includes some potty humor (Jose farts a lot) and lots of fighting scenes (Toriyama created Dragon Ball Z).

Torres, J.

Lola: a ghost story; [by] J. Torres & [illustrated by] Elbert Or. Oni Press 2009 102p il $14.95

Grades: 4 5 6 7 8   **741.5**

1. Graphic novels 2. Ghosts -- Graphic novels 3. Family life -- Graphic novels
ISBN 978-1-934964-33-0; 1-934964-33-6

"Lola ('grandmother' in Tagalog) has just died, and Jesse is reluctant to visit her home in the Philippines. He was afraid of her because she was rumored to have magical abilities, and because he thinks she tried to drown him when he was a baby. Jesse listens to family members tell stories about her as he tries to adjust to their strange mix of superstitions and religion. . . . Jesse is an unusually nuanced character. . . . When he sees something extraordinary, it's unclear if he is dreaming, hallucinating, or if he has inherited his grandmother's abilities. Torres's gradual revelation of details will keep readers hanging until they learn the truth. Or's artwork uses sepia tones and smooth lines, and features characters

with cute button eyes. But the sweet images can quickly turn horrific when Jesse has his visions. " SLJ

Trondheim, Lewis

Tiny Tyrant; by Lewis Trondheim; translated from the French by Alexis Siegel; illustrated by Fabrice Parme. First Second Books 2007 124p il $12.95

Grades: 4 5 6 7 8 9 10 11 12 Adult   **741.5**

1. Graphic novels 2. Humorous graphic novels
ISBN 978-1-59643-094-5

LC 2006021479

"Tiny child-king Ethelbert is spoiled and difficult, expecting to have his every whim fulfilled-or else. . . . In the end, though, he becomes a hero. The dynamic cartoons are filled with details and riddled with humor; most pages have between six and eight small pictures. . . . This title will have wide appeal. It's young and accessible enough for elementary-grade kids, but teens will also be charmed by the rascally king." SLJ

Tsang, Evonne

I love him to pieces; or my date is dead weight or he only loves me for my brains. illustrated by Janina G["o]rrissen. Graphic Universe 2011 123p il (My boyfriend is a monster) lib bdg $29.27; pa $9.95

Grades: 6 7 8 9 10 11 12   **741.5**

1. Graphic novels 2. Horror graphic novels 3. Romance graphic novels 4. Humorous graphic novels 5. Zombies -- Graphic novels
ISBN 978-0-7613-6004-9 lib bdg; 0-7613-6004-2 lib bdg; 978-0-7613-7079-6 pa; 0-7613-7079-X pa

LC 2010-30774

Dicey Bell, star of her high school baseball team in St. Petersburg, Florida, falls for Jack Chen, the star of the science program, and she wangles her way into partnering with Jack on a school project. They work together well, like each other a lot, and things look good for a romance, when a weird infection hits the city. The infection attacks the brain and turns the infected people into human flesh-craving monsters. Dicey and Jack try to get to safety, but find themselves surrounded by zombie-like monsters. This story combines romance with zombie fighting in a story that works like a lighter version of The Walking Dead; the extra subtitles on the title page indicate the humor: "My Date is Dead Weight, or He Only Loves Me For My Brains." Gorrissen's black and white art makes the teens look like teens, and the zombies look yucky and scary without being too icky for most teen readers. This is the first volume in a series of standalone stories, each taking on a different kind of monster.

Van Meter, Jen

Hopeless Savages; greatest hits, 2000-2010. Oni 2010 391p pa $19.99

Grades: 7 8 9 10   **741.5**

1. Graphic novels
ISBN 978-1-934964-48-4; 1-934964-48-4

Follows the Hopeless Savages, the first family of punk, as they navigate through kidnapping plots, first love, and international intrigue.

"The characters are richly developed; the plots in each chapter are engaging and fast moving, and the stylized black-and-white illustrations will keep readers engaged and begging for more. . . . This collection of stories can serve as an appealing entree into the world of graphic novels." Voice Youth Advocates

Vansant, Wayne

The **red** badge of courage; [by] Stephen Crane; Wayne Vansant, adapter. Puffin Graphics 2005 176p il pa $9.99

Grades: 5 6 7 8 9 10 11 12   741.5

1. Authors 2. Novelists 3. Graphic novels
ISBN 0-14-240410-1

"Artist Vansant captures Fleming's uncertainty and fear quite well, sometimes through effectively understated facial expressions." Publ Wkly

Venditti, Robert

★ The **lightning** thief: the graphic novel; by Rick Riordan; adapted by Robert Venditti; art by Attila Futaki; color by Jose Villarrubia; layouts by Orpheus Collar; lettering by Chris Dickey. Disney/Hyperion Books 2010 un il (Percy Jackson and the Olympians) $19.99; pa $9.99

Grades: 5 6 7 8   741.5

1. Graphic novels 2. Greek mythology -- Graphic novels
ISBN 978-1-4231-1696-7; 1-4231-1696-8; 978-1-4231-1710-0 pa; 1-4231-1710-7 pa

LC 2010035512

After learning that he is the son of a mortal woman and Poseidon, god of the sea, twelve-year-old Percy is sent to a summer camp for demigods like himself, and joins his new friends on a quest to prevent a war between the gods.

This graphic novel adaptation of Rick Riordan's novel "succeeds in spectacular fashion. . . . The book retains the excellent pacing of the original and gives a face to Riordan's vision of the mythological made modern. Futaki's artwork is exemplary but what leaves such a lasting impression is Villarrubia's coloring, which reveals both subtlety and spectacle when needed." Publ Wkly

Viney, Brigit

Frankenstein; [by] Mary Shelley; [adapted and illustrated by Brigit Viney] Lucent 2010 144p il (Classic comics) $32.45

Grades: 6 7 8 9   741.5

1. Graphic novels 2. Horror graphic novels
ISBN 978-1-4205-0374-6; 1-4205-0374-X

"Much of the power of Viney's adaptation of Mary Shelley's horror classic lies within the artwork. Action sequences jump off the page, while portraits of each character provide nuance and depth to the text. . . . This . . . wins points for a masterful rendition that adds much value to the original." Kirkus

Vollmar, Rob

★ The **castaways**; illustrated by Pablo G. Callejo. NBM/ComicsLit 2007 64p il pa $17.95

Grades: 6 7 8 9 10 11 12   741.5

1. Graphic novels 2. Tramps -- Fiction 3. Runaway children -- Fiction 4. Great Depression, 1929-1939 --

Fiction
ISBN 978-1-56163-492-7

An expanded and newly illustrated edition of the title first published 2002 by Absence of Ink Comic Press

"Afraid that he's just a burden on his family, 13-year-old Tucker Freeman lets himself be driven away from home and jumps on a freight train heading west. His inexperience makes him vulnerable to all the angry, desperate people looking for any way they can survive during America's economic collapse, but fortunately he's taken under the wing of Elijah Hopkins, an elderly colored man who introduces him to the cooperative hobo subculture. . . . Vollmer's script, based on family reminiscences, rings true; his dialogue has the vocabulary and the rhythms of real people talking. . . . Callejo's art creates a solid setting in which Tucker's experience can reveal squalor or grace." Publ Wkly

Walker, Landry Q.

The **super** scary monster show, featuring Little Gloomy; written by Landry Walker; drawn by Eric Jones; tones by Rikki Simons. Amaze Ink/SLG Publishing 2008 un il $9.95

Grades: 3 4 5 6 7 8 9   741.5

1. Graphic novels 2. Horror graphic novels 3. Humorous graphic novels
ISBN 978-1-59362-103-2; 1-59362-103-5

This book collects the three issues (so far) of The Super Scary Monster Show comics. Little Gloomy, her friends, and her enemies, live in the world called Frightsylvania. Gloomy deals with an alien who crashlands in her backyard and wants to take over the world (she has plenty of "pet" monsters in her house who take care of her problem). Carl the squid lies to his parents about taking over the world and enslaving all its creatures, then they come for a visit. . . . Gloomy buys a golden scorpion as a gift for her friend the Mummy, but it turns out to be cursed, and everyone around her suffers accidents. The witch Evey has come up with a new spell to torment Gloomy, but it hits werewolf buddy Larry instead and shrinks him. There are plenty more stories, all written with tongue-in-cheek humor and just a touch of horror for younger readers. Gloomy does not suffer fools gladly, so the invading alien gets eaten (off page), and other inimical creatures suffer similar fates, so this book shouldn't be given to younger readers who are sensitive and don't like any violence. There is little in the way of any gore or overt violence, except for poor Frank, whose body parts often come apart.

Watson, Andi

Princess at midnight. Image Comics 2008 un il $5.99

Grades: 4 5 6 7 8 9 10   741.5

1. Graphic novels 2. Fantasy graphic novels 3. War -- Graphic novels 4. Princesses -- Graphic novels
ISBN 978-1-58240-928-3; 1-58240-928-5

Holly Crescent and her twin brother Henry lead sheltered lives as home-schooled children by day; their parents don't want any harm to come to their children after they were born prematurely and their early lives were so worrisome. At night, however, Holly becomes Princess of Castle Waxing, where life is good until the Horrible Horde takes over one of her favorite picnic spots. All too soon, her nights are spent in warfare against the Horde, and her days in reading books on war strategy. And when she wins, she's not satisfied with winning, she must pursue more warfare against the Horde, even as her dragon Chancellor warns her of overspending and the consequences of war on her people.

Weing, Drew

★ **Set** to sea. Fantagraphics 2010 un il $16.99

Grades: 8 9 10 11 12   **741.5**

1. Graphic novels 2. Poets -- Graphic novels 3. Sea stories -- Graphic novels 4. Seafaring life -- Graphic novels

ISBN 978-1-60699-368-2; 1-60699-368-2

The author "has produced a beautiful gem here, with minimal dialogue, one jolting battle scene, and each small page owned by a single panel filled with art whose figures have a comfortable roundness dredged up from the cartoon landscapes of our childhood unconscious, even as the intensely crosshatched shadings suggest the darkness that sometimes traces the edges of our lives. . . . [This book] is playful, atmospheric, dark, wistful, and wise." Booklist

Weinstein, Lauren

★ **Girl** stories; by Lauren R. Weinstein. Henry Holt 2006 237p il pa $16.95

Grades: 7 8 9 10 11 12 Adult   **741.5**

1. Graphic novels 2. Humorous graphic novels 3. Girls -- Graphic novels 4. Friendship -- Graphic novels

ISBN 978-0-8050-7863-3; 0-8050-7863-0

LC 2005-46205

"Smart, creative Lauren sheds her geeky rep in high school in Weinstein's collection of comic strips, which have to intimacy of a teen's diary. The color-washed sketches have an edgy quality." Booklist

White, Tracy

How I made it to eighteen; a mostly true story. Roaring Brook 2010 151p il $16.99

Grades: 8 9 10 11 12   **741.5**

1. Graphic novels 2. Autobiographical graphic novels 3. Mental illness -- Graphic novels

ISBN 978-1-59643-454-7; 1-59643-454-6

"White's story of a 17-year-old girl's ordeals with depression, addiction, and body image issues is all the more powerful because of its basis in truth. The story follows Stacy Black, whose nervous breakdown leads to her decision to check into the Golden Meadows Hospital for mental health. . . . White's very simple hand-drawn, b&w artistic style enhances the personal touch of the work, creating the effect of an illustrated diary. While text-heavy, the narration is clear-eyed and affecting." Publ Wkly

Wilson, Tom

Ziggy goes for broke; a cartoon collection. Andrews McMeel Publisher 2010 128p il pa $12.99

Grades: 7 8 9 10   **741.5**

1. Graphic novels

ISBN 978-0-7407-9153-6; 0-7407-9153-2

LC 2010481277

"Ziggy brings to life both the simplicities and complexities of daily life. His struggles with lost luggage, insurance, finances, dating, and customer service are sure to hit home

with many adults. Teens will find humor in his interactions with his pets and the pigeons in the park. Ziggy's experiences can evoke a contemplative mood or an inspiring and uplifting change of heart. The humor in the one-liners goes hand-in-hand with Wilson's simple yet effective rendering of the little bald man who rarely wears pants." SLJ

Wood, Don

★ **Into** the volcano; a graphic novel. Blue Sky Press 2008 174p il map $18.99

Grades: 2 3 4 5 6 7 8   **741.5**

1. Graphic novels 2. Adventure graphic novels 3. Brothers -- Graphic novels

ISBN 978-0-439-72671-9; 0-439-72671-9

LC 2007-51084

While their parents are away doing research, brothers Duffy and Sumo Pugg go with their cousin, Mister Come-and-Go, to Kokalaha Island, where they meet Aunt Lulu and become trapped in an erupting volcano.

"The visual format combined with nonstop action will keep reluctant readers and adventure fans turning pages to the very end." Voice Youth Advocates

Yakin, Boaz

Marathon; by Boaz Yakin; [illustrations by Joe Infurnari] First Second 2012 186 p. $16.99

Grades: 6 7 8 9   **741.5**

1. Adventure graphic novels 2. Greece -- History -- Graphic novels 3. Marathon, Battle of, 490 B.C. -- Graphic novels 4. Graphic novels

ISBN 9781596436800; 1596436808

LC 2011030472

This book is a graphical "account of the battle of Marathon" in which "Hippias, former king of Athens, is on his way back with a huge army of Persians to reclaim the throne and crush Athenian democracy. . . . Eucles, Athens' best runner, is charged to race the 153 miles to Sparta in hopes of finding an ally, . . . [returning] with the dismaying news that the Spartans will not be coming in time. He joins the savage fight and then runs 26 more miles over rugged mountains to Athens . . . warning of an impending surprise attack by sea." (Kirkus Reviews)

Yang, Gene

★ **American** born Chinese; color by Lark Pien. First Second 2006 233p il pa $16.95

Grades: 7 8 9 10 11 12   **741.5**

1. Graphic novels 2. Chinese Americans -- Graphic novels

ISBN 978-1-59643-152-2; 1-59643-152-0

LC 2005-58105

Michael L. Printz Award, 2007

In three interconnected stories, the reader meets the Monkey King, who wants to be more than he is, Jin Wang, a Chinese American middle school student who desperately wants to fit in at his new school, and Caucasian-looking Danny, who unaccountably has an extremely stereotypically Chinese cousin, Chin-Kee, whose visit causes great embarrassment.

"True to its origin as a Web comic, this story's clear, concise lines and expert coloring are deceptively simple yet expressive. Even when Yang slips in an occasional Chinese ideogram or myth, the sentiments he's depicting need no translation. Yang accomplishes the remarkable feat of practicing what he preaches with this book: accept who you are and you'll already have reached out to others." Publ Wkly

Yolen, Jane

Foiled; written by Jane Yolen; artwork by Mike Cavallaro. First Second 2010 160p il pa $15.99
Grades: 7 8 9 10 **741.5**
    1. Graphic novels 2. Fantasy graphic novels 3. Fencing -- Graphic novels
    ISBN 978-1-59643-279-6; 1-59643-279-9
"Besting competitors twice her age in tournaments, and keeping a strict routine of fencing practice, homework, and role-playing games, Aliera is a loner and likes it that way—until she becomes lab partners with the cutest boy in school. . . . Turns out her new ruby-handled foil is the key to his interest in her, and to the yet-unseen magical dimension she must keep in balance. . . . [Yolen] has created a strong, conflicted, and relatable girl hero. . . . Cavallaro's artwork suits Aliera's monochrome existence, but burst into life when she finally sees (in color!) the faerie beasties cheering her on." Booklist

Zornow, Jeff

The **legend** of Sleepy Hollow; adapted and illustrated by Jeff Zornow; based upon the works of Washington Irving. Magic Wagon 2007 un il (Graphic horror) $18.95
Grades: 5 6 7 8 9 10 11 12 **741.5**
    ISBN 978-1-60270-060-4; 1-60270-060-5
                  LC 2007-9615
This "is an entertaining and faithful, if much adapted version of Irving's classic story. Zornow's illustrations are the highlight of the work, successfully bringing the characters of the story to life." Booklist

741.6 Graphic design, illustration, commercial art

★ Artist to artist; 23 major illustrators talk to children about their art. Philomel Books 2007 105p il $30
Grades: 4 5 6 7 **741.6**
    1. Illustrators 2. Illustration of books
    ISBN 978-0-399-24600-5
"This anthology celebrates and elucidates contemporary picture-book art. . . . Ashley Bryan, Quentin Blake, Leo Lionni, Alice Provensen, and Gennady Spirin are among the contributors, whose comments are formatted as signed letters illustrated with childhood photographs. . . . Each artist includes glorious self-portraits and a gatefold page that reveals a marvelous array of sketches, color mixes, and studio scenes. All readers will find something that piques curiosity or provides insight." Booklist

Ellabbad, Mohieddine

The **illustrator's** notebook; [translated from the Arabic by Sarah Quinn] Groundwood Books/House of Anansi Press 2006 30p il $16.95

Grades: 5 6 7 8 **741.6**
    1. Artists 2. Illustrators 3. Illustration of books
    ISBN 0-88899-700-0
"Part children's book, part autobiography, part design treatise, this hard-to-categorize Egyptian import is full of wonders from start to finish. Ellabbad uses excerpts from his notebooks to discuss ways of seeing art from an artist's perspective and as someone from an Arabic culture. Printed like the Egyptian edition—read right to left—the pages are magnificently and surprisingly illustrated, juxtaposing Arabic script (English translations appear in the margins), watercolor paintings, pasted-in photos and pictures from comic books, and all manner of characters from Eastern and Western cultures." SLJ

Flath, Camden

Media in the 21st century; artists, animators, and graphic designers. Mason Crest Publishers 2010 64p il (New careers for the 21st century: finding your role in the global renewal) lib bdg $22.95; pa $9.95
Grades: 7 8 9 10 **741.6**
    1. Artists 2. Vocational guidance
    ISBN 978-1-4222-1816-7 lib bdg; 1-4222-1816-3 lib bdg; 978-1-4222-2037-5 pa; 1-4222-2037-0 pa
                  LC 2010014935
"Chapters identify and emphasize specific careers—important strengths, necessary aptitudes and interests, education and training, projected earnings, closely related occupations, type of work environment, and predictions for the future of the field. . . . Color photos have a small role amid the many statistics, figures, graphs and charts that support and supplement the . . . [text]." SLJ
Includes bibliographical references

Neuburger, Emily K.

A **Caldecott** celebration; seven artists and their paths to the Caldecott medal. rev ed.; Walker & Co. 2008 55p il $19.95; lib bdg $20.85
Grades: Adult Professional **741.6**
    1. Illustrators 2. Caldecott Medal 3. Illustration of books
    ISBN 978-0-8027-9703-2; 0-8027-9703-2; 978-0-8027-9704-9 lib bdg; 0-8027-9704-0 lib bdg
                  LC 2007-23132
First published 1998
Profiles seven Caldecott award winning books and their authors, including Robert McCloskey's "Make Way for Ducklings," Marcia Brown's "Cinderella," Maurice Sendak's "Where the Wild Things Are," William Steig's "Sylvester and the Magic Pebble," Chris Van Allsburg's "Jumanji," David Wiesner's "Tuesday," and Mordicai Gerstein's "The Man Who Walked Between the Towers"
"The value of this volume is that Marcus makes these exceptional author/illustrators, and the processes by which they created their award-winning picture books, accessible to children and to adults who value children's literature." SLJ

Tan, Shaun

★ The **bird** king; an artist's notebook. Shaun Tan. Arthur A. Levine Books 2013 128 p. (hardcover: alk. paper) $19.99

Grades: 3 4 5 6 7   741.6
    1. Artists' notebooks
    ISBN 0545465133; 9780545465137

LC 2012016625

This book by author and illustrator Shaun Tan "is a collection of sketches, random jottings, preliminary designs for book, film and theatre projects, sketchbook pages and drawings from life. Each of these represent some aspect of a working process, whereby stories generally evolve from visual research and free-wheeling doodles. They are also 'unfinished' pieces created in a single sitting, not originally intended for publication." (Publisher's note)

741.9   Collections of drawings

Volavkova, Hana

    --I never saw another butterfly-- children's drawings and poems from Terezin concentration camp, 1942-1944. edited by Hana Volavková; foreword by Chaim Potok; afterword by Vaclav Havel. expanded 2nd ed; Schocken Bks. 1993 xxii, 106p il hardcover o.p. pa $17.50
Grades: 4 5 6 7   741.9
    1. Child artists 2. Children's writings 3. Holocaust, 1933-1945
    ISBN 0-8052-1015-6 pa

LC 92-50477

Original Czech edition, 1959; first American edition published 1964 by McGraw-Hill

"Of the 15,000 children who passed through Terezin before going to Auschwitz, only 100 lived. This book is a collection of poems and drawings by some of them. . . . This touching book adds another facet to library collections on the Holocaust." SLJ

742   Perspective in drawing

DuBosque, Doug

    ★ Draw 3-D; a step-by-step guide to perspective drawing. Peel Productions 1999 63p il pa $8.99
Grades: 6 7 8 9 10   742
    1. Drawing 2. Perspective
    ISBN 0-939217-14-7

LC 98-42174

"Using easy-to-follow, step-by-step sketches, DuBosque introduces readers to the techniques of three-dimensional drawing. Beginning with such elementary concepts as depth, he progresses logically through shading, reflections, and multiple vanishing points. The supportive tone encourages novices to keep trying and not become discouraged." SLJ

743   Drawing and drawings by subject

Ames, Lee J., 1921-

    [Draw 50 series] Doubleday 1974-2003 21v pa each $8.95
Grades: 4 5 6 7   743
    1. Drawing

Each volume presents step-by-step instructions for drawing a variety of animals, people, or objects
    Available titles are:
    Draw 50 aliens
    Draw 50 animals
    Draw 50 athletes
    Draw 50 baby animals
    Draw 50 beasties and yugglies and turnover uglies and things that go bump in the night
    Draw 50 birds
    Draw 50 boats, ships, trucks & trains
    Draw 50 buildings and other structures
    Draw 50 cats
    Draw 50 dinosaurs and other prehistoric animals
    Draw 50 dogs
    Draw 50 endangered animals
    Draw 50 famous faces
    Draw 50 flowers, trees, and other plants
    Draw 50 holiday decorations
    Draw 50 horses
    Draw 50 monsters, creeps, superheroes, demons, dragons, nerds, dirts, ghouls, giants, vampires, zombies, and other curiosa
    Draw 50 people

Bergin, Mark

    How to draw pets. PowerKids Press 2011 32p il (How to draw) lib bdg $25.25; pa $11.75
Grades: 4 5 6 7   743
    1. Animals in art 2. Drawing -- Technique
    ISBN 978-1-4488-4511-8 lib bdg; 978-1-4488-4517-0 pa

LC 2010049184

"The cover features sketches of a cat, dog, and rabbit, allowing children to see both structure as well as finished product. Inside, the book starts by showing pictures of animals drawn with different materials such as pencils, ink, charcoals, and pastels, and explains what each medium accomplishes. Next comes an introduction to perspective and looks at different parts of animals. The familiar circle method then gets kids drawing pets from head to tails. . . . The amount of information throughout is just right: thorough but not overwhelming." Booklist
    Includes glossary

Butkus, Mike

    How to draw zombies; discover the secrets to drawing, painting, and illustrating the undead. by Mike Butkus and Merrie Destefano. Walter Foster 2011 128p il map $48.95
Grades: 8 9 10 11 12   743
    1. Zombies 2. Monsters in art 3. Drawing -- Technique
    ISBN 978-1-936309-63-4; 1-936309-63-7

LC 2010052983

"For young artists fascinated by the living dead, this sophisticated drawing book gives step-by-step instructions for creating a variety of unexpected characters. . . . Most of the drawings are done in pencil, but acrylic paints are also occasionally featured. An added bonus is the instructions for giving a final digital touch to the drawings on the computer.

. . . Extra bits of zombie lore are added. Fans of the truly terrifying will appreciate the fact that the featured pictures attain a high level of creepiness. . . . Those looking for a zombie drawing book with added bite will find hours of fun with this one." Booklist

Eggleton, Bob

Dragons' domain; the ultimate dragon painting workshop. foreword by John A. Davis. Impact 2010 127p il pa $22.99

Grades: 7 8 9 10   743

1. Drawing 2. Dragons in art
ISBN 978-1-60061-457-6; 1-60061-457-4

"Here is a book for those dragon lovers who are bored with beginner drawing books. Eggleton starts with a thorough discussion of materials and some basic drawing and painting techniques. Then he spends an entire page on each of several key dragon body parts, such as feet, wings, frills, and tails. After some insightful discussion of finding inspiration and references from nature and fantasy pop culture, the artist demonstrates how to create a handful of different types of dragons. . . . The book is full of Eggleton's own work in progressive stages of completion, photographed in color and attractively placed on backgrounds with fantasy-themed borders." SLJ

Hodges, Jared

Draw furries; how to create anthropomorphic and fantasy animals. by Jared Hodges and Lindsay Cibos. IMPACT Books 2009 127p il pa $22.99

Grades: 7 8 9 10   743

1. Animals in art 2. Fantasy in art 3. Drawing -- Technique
ISBN 978-1-60061-417-0 pa; 1-60061-417-5 pa
LC 2009019609

"Hodges and Cibos have created a thorough guide. Describing creatures in terms of a sliding scale from human to animal, they begin with some tips on basic anatomy and style. . . . The instruction is grouped by the kind of animal portrayed. . . . Full-color spreads throughout show what can be achieved with practice, and the book concludes with chapters on color and perspective." SLJ

Masiello, Ralph

Ralph Masiello's ancient Egypt drawing book. Charlesbridge 2008 un $16.95; pa $7.95

Grades: 4 5 6 7   743

1. Drawing
ISBN 978-1-57091-533-8; 978-1-57091-534-5 pa
LC 2007027023

"Masiello starts by showing readers how to draw the Great Pyramid of Khafre using simple shapes and lines. His easy-to-follow instructions gradually build in complexity, as he moves to ancient symbols, then Egyptian gods, Queen Nefertiti, and King Tutankhamen. The finished pictures are colored with mixed media. Concise paragraphs tell more about each subject, including historical context." Horn Book Guide

Includes bibliographical references

Miller, Steve

Dinosaurs: how to draw thunder lizards and other prehistoric beasts; [by] Steve Miller. Watson-Guptill Publications 2008 144p il pa $19.95

Grades: 8 9 10 11 12 Adult   743

1. Drawing 2. Dinosaurs in art
ISBN 978-0-8230-9919-1 pa; 0-8230-9919-9 pa
LC 2008531195

First published 2005 with title: Thunder lizards; how to draw fantastic dinosaurs

This offers instruction in drawing dinosaurs based on scientific research and includes examples of the work of such artists as Arthur Adams, Bryan Baugh, Brett Booth, Scott Harman, Gregory S. Paul, and Bernie Wrightson

Includes bibliographical references

Peffer, Jessica

DragonArt; how to draw fantastic dragons and fantasy creatures. Impact Books 2005 127p il pa $19.99

Grades: 5 6 7 8   743

1. Dragons 2. Drawing 3. Mythical animals
ISBN 1-58180-657-4
LC 2005013013

This is a guide to drawing dragons and other mythical beasts such as griffins, guardian gargoyles, and deadly basilisks.

"This book has great writing and superb illustrations and manages to do everything right from the front cover to the index." SLJ

745   Decorative arts

Govenar, Alan B.

★ **Extraordinary** ordinary people; five American masters of traditional arts. Candlewick Press 2006 85p il $22.99

Grades: 6 7 8 9   745

1. Folk art 2. Handicraft 3. Folk artists
ISBN 0-7636-2047-5
LC 2005-44864

"The featured artists all live in the United States but come from a variety of cultural backgrounds. The art forms they practice include singing with the Bejing Opera, boat building, waxflower making, weaving, and performing at Mardi Gras. Govenar's interviews with them not only explore their art, but also their history. . . . High-quality color and black-and-white photographs appear throughout." SLJ

Includes bibliographical references

Major, John S.

★ **Caravan** to America; living arts of the Silk Road. [by] John S. Major and Betty J. Belanus. Cricket Bks. 2002 130p il map hardcover o.p. pa $15.95

Grades: 4 5 6 7   745

1. Arts 2. Cookbook writers 3. Cooking teachers
ISBN 0-8126-2666-4; 0-8126-2677-X pa
LC 2002-5477

Profiles eight artists and artisans now living in America who are originally from the "Silk Road," an ancient network of caravan trails through which trade goods, ideas, and arts pass between Asia and the Mediterranean

"Full of colorful and informative archival and contemporary photographs and drawings. . . . Each person's story is told in an interesting manner, and information about their specialty and its history is woven throughout the text. . . . Not only is the work informative, but it is handsome as well." SLJ

Includes glossary and bibliographical references

Panchyk, Richard

American folk art for kids; with 21 activities. Chicago Review Press 2004 118p il $16.95

Grades: 4 5 6 7   **745**

1. Handicraft 2. American folk art 3. Folk art -- United States

ISBN 1-55652-499-4

LC 2004-4879

"Panchyk begins with a general introduction to folk art, and then explicates the main categories of these traditional crafts. He covers a variety of decorative arts, including painting, fabric work, woodworking, and found objects. Each chapter contains several related projects ranging from reverse painting on glass to quilting, stenciling, and tin-can sculpture. . . . Many quality, full-color photos are included." SLJ

Includes bibliographical references

Tejubehan (Singer)

★ **Drawing** from the City; Teju Behan. Pgw 2012 28 p. $35.95

Grades: 3 4 5 6 7 8   **745**

1. India 2. Artists 3. Poverty

ISBN 9380340176; 9789380340173

This "autobiographical art book recounts self-taught artist Teju Behan's journey from an impoverished childhood in rural India, through her family's efforts to improve their lot in a tent city in Mumbai, and into her adulthood, when she lived as a singer and artist with her husband. . . . Hand-screen-printed illustrations comprised of intricate linework and patterns of dots underscore elements of the text." (Kirkus)

745.2   Industrial art and design

Arato, Rona

Design it! the ordinary things we use every day and the not-so-ordinary ways they came to be. illustrations by Claudia Newell. Tundra Books 2010 71p il pa $20.95

Grades: 4 5 6 7   **745.2**

1. Industrial design 2. Inventors 3. Inventions 4. Design, Industrial

ISBN 978-0-88776-846-0 pa; 0-88776-846-6 pa

"This book opens with an explanation of what industrial designers do and with whom they work to make better products. Brief chapters then cover such topics as home, communications, lighting, and toy design and include a good-design checklist that takes function, usability, ergonomics, aesthet-

ics, and greenness into consideration. The language is chatty and inviting, and the pages are full of cartoon illustrations and text superimposed on colorful geometric backgrounds. Sidebars offer a wealth of further information." SLJ

Welsbacher, Anne

Earth-friendly design; by Anne Welsbacher. Lerner Publications Company 2009 72p il (Saving our living Earth) lib bdg $30.60

Grades: 5 6 7 8   **745.2**

1. Industrial design 2. Environmental protection

ISBN 978-0-8225-7564-1 lib bdg; 0-8225-7564-7 lib bdg

LC 2007-35925

"Provides a thorough, interesting discussion of multiple aspects of [Earth-friendly design], including historical origins, the current situation, and potential solutions. . . . Photos from around the world accompany discussions. . . . [This is a] solid choice to replace outdated books." SLJ

Includes glossary and bibliographical references

745.5   Handicrafts

Bell-Rehwoldt, Sheri

The **kids'** guide to building cool stuff; by Sheri Bell-Rehwoldt. Capstone Press 2009 32p il (Kids' guides) lib bdg $23.99

Grades: 4 5 6 7   **745.5**

1. Amusements 2. Handicraft 3. Science -- Experiments

ISBN 978-1-4296-2276-9 lib bdg; 1-4296-2276-8 lib bdg

LC 2008-29687

This provides instructions for building such items as a kite, a balloon rocket, a paper boat, a milk carton bird feeder, and a plastic plate hovercraft

Includes glossary and bibliographical references

Cano-Murillo, Kathy

The **crafty** diva's lifestyle makeover; awesome ideas to spice up your life. by Kathy Cano Murillo; illustrated by Carrie Wheeler; photography by John Samora. Watson-Guptill Publications 2005 144p il pa $12.95

Grades: 5 6 7 8   **745.5**

1. Handicraft

ISBN 0-8230-1008-2

"Chapters include Redo Your Room, Wake Up Your Workout, and Get a Passion for Fashion. Complete with media references, each chapter includes three crafts with instructions, a difficulty meter for each one, and a list of needed supplies. A picture of the finished item, more ideas, and illustrations of supplies and the more difficult steps are included. The result is [a] fun, imaginative book." SLJ

Check, Laura

Create your own candles; 30 easy-to-make designs. illustrations by Norma Jean Martin-Jourdenais. Williamson Books 2004 62p il (Quick starts for kids!) pa $8.95

Grades: 5 6 7 8   **745.5**
1. Candles 2. Candlemaking
ISBN 1-88559-352-X

LC 2004-40870

"Check begins this useful resource with 'Ten Hot Safety Tips.' . . . Next, she lists and describes basic equipment. . . . The projects range from simple beeswax candles to molded candles, hand-dipped candles, and gel candles." SLJ

Crafty activities; over 50 fun and easy things to make. by Judy Balchin . . . [et al.] Search 2007 un il pa $19.95
Grades: 4 5 6 7   **745.5**
1. Handicraft
ISBN 978-1-84448-250-4 pa; 1-84448-250-2 pa

"The book is divided into six chapters—mosaics, printing, lettering, papier-mâché, handmade cards, and origami—with projects ranging from simple leaf prints to an elaborate necklace made from dried pasta. . . . The photos of smiling kids showing off their creations, the attractive, spacious page design, and, above all the ingenious projects will attract kids—as well as teachers." Booklist

Dobson, Jolie
The **duct** tape book; 25 Projects to Make With Duct Tape. Firefly Books Ltd 2012 144 p. (paperback) $14.95
Grades: 7 8 9 10 11 12   **745.5**
1. Duct tape 2. Handicraft
ISBN 1770850988; 9781770850989

This book by Jolie Dobson on crafting with duct tape "contains 25 . . . projects" with "instructions and color photographs." The projects include a "bike pannier . . . vest . . . purse . . . piggy bank . . . wallet . . . bow ties . . . picture frames . . . knapsack . . . skirt and chaps . . . [and] tissue box." (Publisher's note)

Fox, Tom
Snowball launchers, giant-pumpkin growers, and other cool contraptions; [by] Tom Fox. Sterling Pub. 2006 127p il pa $9.95
Grades: 4 5 6 7   **745.5**
1. Handicraft
ISBN 978-0-8069-5515-5 pa; 0-8069-5515-5 pa

LC 2005032781

"The 20 projects in this collection range from a simple 'Heartbeat Monitor' to a fairly complex 'Moth-Bot,' a wheeled vehicle that moves toward light with the flick of a switch. Most have strong kid appeal. . . . Instructions are written in an engaging, conversational tone, with background information about concepts such as gravity and electricity woven into the text." SLJ

Haab, Sherri
Dangles and bangles; 25 funky accessories to make and wear. by Sherri Haab and Michelle Haab; with illustrations by Barbara Pollak. Watson-Guptill Publications 2005 96p il pa $9.95
Grades: 5 6 7 8   **745.5**
1. Jewelry 2. Handicraft
ISBN 0-8230-0064-8

This describes "jewelry hardware, . . . tools, glues and adhesives, and . . . craft supplies, as well as ideas about where to purchase these materials. A spread on basic techniques explains how to work with cord and elastic, glue, rings/pins, etc. The projects . . . range from necklaces to key chains to hair accessories. . . . The mix of colorful photographs, full-page paintings of stylishly dressed youngsters, and varied typefaces makes for an attractive layout. Packed full of wonderful ideas, this irresistible title will be popular with young crafters as well as with adults who plan craft programs." SLJ

Martin, Laura C.
Nature's art box; from t-shirts to twig baskets: 65 cool projects for crafty kids to make with natural materials you can find anywhere. written by Laura C. Martin; with drawings by David Cain. Storey Bks. 2003 215p il hardcover o.p. pa $16.95
Grades: 4 5 6 7   **745.5**
1. Handicraft 2. Nature craft 3. Found objects (Art)
ISBN 1-58017-503-1; 1-58017-490-6 pa

LC 2002-154374

"Each chapter includes information about historical and ethnic uses for the natural substances. Activities are rated by level of difficulty; all have easy-to-follow instructions. Projects range from baskets, picture frames, wreaths, necklaces, and gift wrap to body paint, amulet bags, and painted stones. . . . The projects display a respect for nature and art, and a simple, subtle beauty." SLJ

Includes bibliographical references

O'Donnell, Rosie
Rosie O'Donnell's crafty U; 100 easy projects the whole family can enjoy all year long. Simon & Schuster 2008 206p il $21.95
Grades: 3 4 5 6   **745.5**
1. Handicraft
ISBN 978-1-4165-5341-0; 1-4165-5341-X

LC 2007031249

"Projects include bunny piñatas for spring, tie-dye T-shirts for summer, creepy costumes for Halloween, very merry garlands for the holidays, Valentine's Day bouquets, and much more. Packed with practical advice, step-by-step instructions, and . . . full-color illustrations." Publisher's note

Includes bibliographical references

Ross, Kathy
Earth-friendly crafts; clever ways to reuse everyday items. [by] Kathy Ross; illustrated by Celine Malepart. Millbrook Press 2009 48p il lib bdg $26.60
Grades: 3 4 5 6   **745.5**
1. Recycling 2. Handicraft
ISBN 978-0-8225-9099-6 lib bdg; 0-8225-9099-9 lib bdg

LC 2008025481

"This clear, colorful title offers a selection of environmentally focused projects that encourage kids to reduce, reuse, and recycle. Both practical and eye-catching, the projects, from pencil cups to decorative pins, rely on everyday discarded items that many kids will find around their homes.

. . . [The crafts] are presented in line drawings that demonstrate the construction step by step along with color photos of the finished product." Booklist

Torres, Laura

Best friends forever! 199 crafts to make and share. Workman Pub. 2004 148p il pa $13.95

Grades: 5 6 7 8　　　　　　　　　　　**745.5**
  1. Handicraft
  ISBN 0-7611-3274-0

                         LC 2004-45635

"These projects are organized into seven categories: 'Photo Fun,' 'Cool Notes,' 'Gifts to Make Together,' 'Home and School,' 'Fashions,' 'Fun and Games,' and 'Jewelry.' . . . Using clear language, detailed directions, and bright color photos of the finished products, Torres has pulled together a wealth of craft ideas." SLJ

Rock your school stuff. QEB Pub. 2010 32p il (Rock your . . .) lib bdg $28.50

Grades: 4 5 6　　　　　　　　　　　**745.5**
  1. Handicraft 2. Schools -- Equipment and supplies
  ISBN 978-1-59566-936-0; 1-59566-936-1

                       LC 2010010670

This book "gives kids easy step-by-step ways to . . . personalize school supplies. . . . Colorful photographs show youngsters crafting [such items as beaded pens, recycled paperclip bookmarks, backpack zipper pulls] . . . some of which are created from recycled found items. All are projects they can complete by themselves." Horn Book Guide

Warwick, Ellen

Everywear; written by Ellen Warwick; illustrated by Bernice Lum. Kids Can Press 2008 80p il (Planet girl) $14.95

Grades: 5 6 7 8　　　　　　　　　　　**745.5**
  1. Handicraft 2. Dress accessories 3. Jewelry making
  4. Dress accessories
  ISBN 978-1-55337-799-3; 1-55337-799-0

"After several opening pages that introduce supplies, . . . very basic stitching skills, and terminology, girls turn to the . . . issue of hair: woven-ribbon bands, jazzed-up chopsticks; fabric-flower-bedecked combs; reversible ponytail wraps. Next come body adornments . . . followed by stuff to stow it in, of clutched, dangled, and toted varieties. Each project features a list of supplies, . . . clearly numbered steps with cartoon-styled illustrations . . . and full-color photograph of the finished item. . . . [This has] genuine sleepover appeal." Bull Cent Child Books

Wolf, Laurie Goldrich

Recyclo-gami; 40 crafts to make your friends green with envy! Running Press Teens 2010 112p il $14.95

Grades: 4 5 6 7　　　　　　　　　　　**745.5**
  1. Recycling 2. Handicraft
  ISBN 978-0-7624-4052-8; 0-7624-4052-X

"Wolf's fun, resourceful projects offer straightforward ways to reuse common materials to make accessories, jewelry, household decorations, games, and gifts. Leftover tissue or wrapping paper can be used to create decoupage plates; old crayons are melted and baked into molds to make

multicolored crayons; and unused CDs and DVDs are transformed into funky, freeform bowls when melted in the oven. . . . The ease of most of the activities should inspire readers to see the recycling bin as a potential treasure trove." Publ Wkly

Wolfe, Brian

Extreme face painting; 50 friendly & fiendish demos. [by] Brian and Nick Wolfe. IMPACT Books 2010 127p il pa $24.99

Grades: 6 7 8 9 10 11 12 Adult　　　　　**745.5**
  1. Face painting
  ISBN 978-1-4403-0270-1; 1-4403-0270-7

                       LC 2010-17861

"This is a guide for experienced artists ready to take their craft to the next level. . . . These instructions show how to use shading and highlights to shape a variety of frightening and whimsical forms. The authors open the book with basic information about materials, colors, and techniques. Then they demonstrate different projects. . . . Each entry has a full-page color photograph of the final product and smaller photos of each step in the painting process. Clearly written instructions appear below each photo. . . . Some of the fiendish visages are quite frightening. The book comes with an informative DVD where the authors demonstrate two of the face paintings from the book. . . . This is a great resource." SLJ

745.54　Papers

Diehn, Gwen

★ **Making** books that fly, fold, wrap, hide, pop up, twist, and turn; books for kids to make. Lark Bks. 1998 96p il hardcover o.p. pa $12.95

Grades: 4 5 6 7　　　　　　　　　　　**745.54**
  1. Handicraft 2. Paper crafts
  ISBN 1-57990-023-2; 978-1-57990-326-8 pa;
  1-57990-326-6 pa

                       LC 97-41037

Presents instructions for making various kinds of books including those that carry messages across space and time as well as those that save words, ideas, and pictures

"Clear directions and diagrams and attractive full-color photographs of completed projects will make it easy for readers to duplicate 18 different folded, wrapped, and pop-up books." Booklist

Includes glossary

Latno, Mark

The **paper** boomerang book; build them, throw them, and get them to return every time. Chicago Review Press 2010 245p il pa $12.95

Grades: 5 6 7 8　　　　　　　　　　　**745.54**
  1. Boomerangs 2. Paper crafts
  ISBN 978-1-56976-282-0 pa; 1-56976-282-1 pa

                       LC 2010007251

"In a unique . . . guide Latno . . . [explains] how to make, fine-tune, and decorate a type of paper boomerang that can be constructed with commonly available materials and thrown with (relative) safety indoors. The instructions and simply drawn diagrams are embedded in a history of boomerangs and throwing sticks, a challenging technical discussion of the physics of boomerangs and gyroscopes, and very detailed descriptions of the characteristics of railroad board (Latno's preferred paper) and alternatives, plus art-and-craft materials that can be used to dress up finished models." SLJ

Includes glossary and bibliographical references

Torres, Laura

Rock your party. QEB Pub. 2010 32p il (Rock your . . .) lib bdg $28.50

Grades: 4 5 6   **745.54**

1. Parties 2. Handicraft 3. Paper crafts

ISBN 978-1-59566-935-3; 1-59566-935-3

LC 2010010668

This book "gives kids easy step-by-step ways to make decorations for their . . . parties. . . . Colorful photographs show youngsters crafting appealing . . . party hats, etc. some of which are created from recycled found items. All are projects they can complete by themselves." Horn Book Guide

745.58   Beads, found and other objects

Boonyadhistarn, Thiranut

Beading; bracelets, barrettes, and beyond. by Thiranut Boonyadhistarn. Capstone Press 2007 32p il (Snap books) $25.26

Grades: 4 5 6 7   **745.58**

1. Beadwork

ISBN 978-0-7368-6472-5; 0-7368-6472-5

LC 2006004102

This describes how to create such bead crafts as safety-pin bracelets and bag charms.

"Girls will appreciate these ideas for recreating fashion trends and for achieving the artistic effects that they want. . . . Page layouts are lively and attractive. The projects use easily obtainable materials, and the directions are simple and well numbered." SLJ

Includes bibliographical references

745.592   Toys, models, miniatures, related objects

Aranzi Aronzo Inc.

Cute dolls; by Aranzi Aronzo! Vertical Inc. 2007 79p il (Let's make cute stuff) pa $14.95

Grades: 6 7 8 9 10   **745.592**

1. Dolls 2. Handicraft

ISBN 978-1-932234-78-7 pa; 1-932234-78-0 pa

Original Japanese edition 2002

"Familiarity with Japan's Aranzi Aronzo brand . . . won't be necessary to muster an audience for this doll-making book. The felt-trimmed, jersey-cloth, self-consciously cute 'mascots' will be an instant draw for manga-loving teens. . . . Those who attempt one of the 21 rag dolls, for which a sewing machine is recommended, will find the techniques well explained, as well as supported by and entertainingly extended by photographs and small cartoon representations of the doll characters." Booklist

Castleforte, Brian

Papertoy monsters; 50 cool papertoys you can make yourself! Workman Pub. Co. 2010 233p il pa $16.95

Grades: 4 5 6 7   **745.592**

1. Paper crafts 2. Monsters in art

ISBN 978-0-7611-5882-0 pa; 0-7611-5882-0 pa

"Twenty-five 'papertoy' artists contribute 50 original monster designs made of colorful cardstock that can be punched out and glued together to form three dimensional cartoon characters, each with its own quirky backstory. The menagerie includes the tentacled OctoPup, who devours small boats; Yucky Chuck, a serrated-toothed 'mutant lunchbox monster'; and Lester Rottenbottom, a teacher-turned-mad-scientist. The designers' enthusiasm for their subjects should inspire readers to invent their own monsters on the blank templates provided." Publ Wkly

Harbo, Christopher L.

Paper airplanes: Captain, level 4. Capstone Press 2010 32p il (Edge books. Paper airplanes) lib bdg $26.65

Grades: 3 4 5 6   **745.592**

1. Paper crafts 2. Airplanes -- Models

ISBN 978-1-4296-4744-1 lib bdg; 1-4296-4744-2 lib bdg

LC 2010001003

This "includes a list of basic materials and an overview of folding instructions and techniques. . . . Along with hints on how to hold the plane for take-off to maximize strengths are suggestions on conducting friendly competitions with the finished products. Sure to keep readers busy for hours." SLJ

Includes bibliographical references

Paper airplanes: Copilot, level 2. Capstone Press 2010 32p il (Edge books. Paper airplanes) lib bdg $26.65

Grades: 3 4 5 6   **745.592**

1. Paper crafts 2. Airplanes -- Models

ISBN 978-1-4296-4742-7 lib bdg; 1-4296-4742-6 lib bdg

LC 2010001004

This "includes a list of basic materials and an overview of folding instructions and techniques. . . . Along with hints on how to hold the plane for takeoff to maximize strengths are suggestions on conducting friendly competitions with the finished products. Sure to keep readers busy for hours." SLJ

Includes bibliographical references

Paper airplanes: Flight school, level 1. Capstone Press 2010 32p il (Edge books. Paper airplanes) lib bdg $26.65

Grades: 3 4 5 6   **745.592**

1. Paper crafts 2. Airplanes -- Models

ISBN 978-1-4296-4741-0 lib bdg; 1-4296-4741-8 lib bdg

LC 2010001005

This "includes a list of basic materials and an overview of folding instructions and techniques. . . . Along with hints on how to hold the plane for takeoff to maximize strengths are suggestions on conducting friendly competitions with the finished products. Sure to keep readers busy for hours." SLJ

Includes bibliographical references

Paper airplanes: Pilot, level 3. Capstone Press 2010 32p il (Edge books. Paper airplanes) lib bdg $26.65

Grades: 3 4 5 6   745.592

1. Paper crafts 2. Airplanes -- Models
ISBN 978-1-4296-4743-4 lib bdg; 1-4296-4743-4 lib bdg

LC 2010001006

This "includes a list of basic materials and an overview of folding instructions and techniques. . . . Along with hints on how to hold the plane for takeoff to maximize strengths are suggestions on conducting friendly competitions with the finished products. Sure to keep readers busy for hours." SLJ

Includes bibliographical references

The **kids'** guide to paper airplanes. Capstone Press 2009 32p il (Kids' guides) $23.93

Grades: 4 5 6 7   745.592

1. Paper crafts 2. Airplanes -- Models
ISBN 978-1-4296-2274-5; 1-4296-2274-1

LC 2008029688

"Using colorful, vivid, and clear step-by-step illustrations, Harbo demonstrates how to construct everything from the classic Dart to the circular Space Ring to the 18-step Silent Huntress." Booklist

Includes glossary and bibliographical references

Mercer, Bobby

The **flying** machine book; build and launch 35 rockets, gliders, helicopters, boomerangs, and more. Bobby Mercer. Chicago Review Press 2012 ix, 197 p.p ill. (pbk.) $14.95

Grades: 4 5 6   745.592

1. Flight 2. Aeronautics 3. Airplanes -- Models 4. Models and modelmaking 5. Paper airplanes 6. Flying-machines -- Models
ISBN 9781613740866

LC 2011041174

This book provides "step-by-step instructions for 35 aerodynamic projects . . . Physics teacher [Bobby] Mercer . . . here provides . . . directions for building a variety of flying machines including rockets, gliders, helicopters, boomerangs and assorted launchers. An opening chapter called 'Flight School' introduces the Bernoulli principle and four forces: lift, thrust, drag and weight. . . . Each subsequent chapter begins with more flight school, repeating the relevant principles and applying them to the different forms of flying machines described. Many of the constructions use similar techniques and most are not difficult. The models are made of common materials: card stock and old folders, drinking straws, rubber bands and duct tape." (Kirkus Reviews)

Rigsby, Mike

Amazing rubber band cars; easy-to-build wind-up racers, models, and toys. [by] Mike Rigsby. Chicago Review Press 2007 121p il lib bdg $12.95

Grades: 4 5 6 7   745.592

1. Toys 2. Handicraft 3. Automobiles -- Models
ISBN 978-1-55652-736-4 lib bdg; 1-55652-736-5 lib bdg

LC 2007013969

This offers instructions for making toy and model cars "using mostly cardboard, glue, pencils, rubber bands, and a few other easily obtainable materials. . . . Readers will learn about corrugated and flat cardboard, and how to use glue and work with templates. Excellent instructions are accompanied by black-and-white photos every step of the way. . . . These projects are fun to construct, and inquisitive minds will be fascinated by the moving cars." SLJ

Thomson, Ruth

Toys and models; photography by Neil Thomson. Sea-to-Sea Publications 2010 32p il (World of design) lib bdg $28.50

Grades: 4 5 6 7   745.592

1. Toys 2. Handicraft 3. Models and modelmaking
ISBN 978-1-59771-209-5 lib bdg; 1-59771-209-4 lib bdg

LC 2008-43868

This "volume presents examples of crafts made around the world, then offers six simple items inspired by these goods that children can make (mostly using recycled materials). The directions allow for easy replication, while information about the crafts provides a window into world cultures. . . . The colorful close-up photographs provide . . . interesting details." Horn Book Guide

Includes glossary and bibliographical references

745.593   Useful objects

Hennessy, Alena

Alter this! radical ideas for transforming books into art. Lark Books 2007 96p il $14.95

Grades: 8 9 10 11 12   745.593

1. Books 2. Handicraft
ISBN 1-57990-948-5

LC 2006-34669

"Hennessy offers 39 ways in which books can be scribbed in, sliced up, and otherwise transformed into vehicles for creative expression. Diverse objects, contributed by numerous artists, are shown in sharp, color photos." Booklist

Includes bibliographical references

Ransom, Candice F.

Scrapbooking just for you! how to make fun, personal, save-them-forever keepsakes. [by] Candice Ransom. Sterling Pub. 2010 120p il $14.95

Grades: 4 5 6 7   745.593

1. Scrapbooks
ISBN 978-1-4027-4096-1; 1-4027-4096-4

LC 2008038982

"Ransom's well-organized introduction showcases her enthusiasm for scrapbooking and also includes material for more experienced crafters. . . . High-quality color photos that are a good match with the directions make the pages pop, and directions are clear." SLJ

745.594 Decorative objects

Trusty, Brad
The **kids'** guide to balloon twisting; by Brad and Cindy Trusty. Capstone Press 2011 32p il (Kids' guides) lib bdg $26.65
Grades: 4 5 6 7   **745.594**
1. Balloons 2. Handicraft
ISBN 978-1-4296-5444-9; 1-4296-5444-9
LC 2010036470
Gives kids step-by-step instructions about how to twist balloon animals and other shapes.
"Rare is the kid not dazzled by the squeaking, twisting balloon maestros out there, and this brightly illustrated, step-by-step guide makes it easy—well, easy-ish." Booklist
Includes bibliographical references

745.6 Calligraphy, heraldic design, illumination

Winters, Eleanor
1 2 3 calligraphy! letters and projects for beginners and beyond. Sterling Pub. Co. 2006 128p il $14.95
Grades: 4 5 6 7   **745.6**
1. Calligraphy
ISBN 1-4027-1839-X; 978-1-4027-1839-7
LC 2005022071
"Twenty well-written, easy-to-follow explanatory chapters are filled with plenty of practical exercises. Chapters are grouped into three parts with the first reviewing calligraphy basics, vocabulary, and types of writing instruments. The second part teaches italic, swing gothic, and modern gothic alphabets. Finally, creative projects such as stationery, envelopes, signs, and 'calligrams' are described." SLJ

★ **Calligraphy** for kids. Sterling Pub. Co. 2004 128p il $14.95
Grades: 6 7 8 9   **745.6**
1. Calligraphy
ISBN 1-4027-0664-2
LC 2003-23438
This "guide to calligraphy begins with a survey of materials, a glossary, and suggestions on posture and pen and paper positions. Succinct chapters showing how to create a variety of alphabets follow. Winters . . . folds fascinating history into her expert instructions. Her clean layouts showcase beautifully rendered examples and practical exercises." Booklist

746 Textile arts

Torres, Laura
Rock your room. QEB Pub. 2010 32p il (Rock your . . .) $28.50
Grades: 4 5 6   **746**
1. Handicraft 2. Interior design
ISBN 978-1-59566-938-4; 1-59566-938-8
This book "gives kids easy step-by-step ways to make decorations for their rooms . . . . Colorful photographs show youngsters crafting appealing . . . . wall decorations, . . . etc., some of which are created from recycled found items. All are projects they can complete by themselves." Horn Book Guide

Warwick, Ellen
Injeanuity; written by Ellen Warwick; illustrated by Bernice Lum. Kids Can Press 2006 80p il (Planet girl) spiral bdg $12.95
Grades: 5 6 7 8   **746**
1. Sewing 2. Handicraft 3. Denim 4. Textile crafts 5. Jeans (Clothing)
ISBN 978-1-55337-681-1 spiral bdg; 1-55337-681-1 spiral bdg
"Warwick combines a love of denim with some simple crafts that will have readers thinking and feeling like fashion designers. . . . [The book] includes 17 projects from re-wearable jeans to purses and wallets to bolsters and footstools to halters and skirts and more. All include clear, easy-to-follow instructions and informative illustrations." SLJ

746.41 Weaving, braiding, matting unaltered vegetable fibers

Swett, Sarah
Kids weaving; [by] Sarah Swett; photographs by Chris Hartlove; illustrations by Lena Corwin. Stewart, Tabori & Chang 2005 128p il $19.95
Grades: 4 5 6 7   **746.41**
1. Weaving
ISBN 1-58479-467-4
LC 2005000650
"Swett introduces this craft with a simple weaving of a checkerboard note card—a task requiring two pieces of paper and a pair of scissors. After mastering the technique with several different small projects, she explains how to weave a hideout out of sticks and vines in the yard. She demonstrates techniques on a cardboard loom and progresses to skills for weaving on a pipe loom. These projects show the whimsical and the practical, the useful and the decorative aspects of the art. Hartlove's excellent-quality, full-color photos depict children enjoying the craft in many different settings. . . . In addition, the helpful step-by-step drawings clearly depict the processes and techniques." SLJ
Includes bibliographical references

746.43 Knitting, crocheting, tatting

Bradberry, Sarah
★ **Kids** knit! simple steps to nifty projects. [by] Sarah Bradberry. Sterling Pub. Co. 2004 96p il hardcover o.p. pa $9.95
Grades: 5 6 7 8   **746.43**
1. Knitting
ISBN 0-8069-7733-7; 978-1-4027-4057-2 pa; 1-4027-4057-3 pa
LC 2004-19375
Presents basic knitting techniques and instructions for making a backpack, pillow, doll, and other simple projects

This "book works equally well for beginners and experienced knitters. . . . Besides the requisite information on knitting and purling, there are invaluable tips about finishing garments, fixing mistakes, and adding embellishments. The projects have been chosen with an eye toward simplicity, yet they have real appeal." Booklist

Davis, Jane

★ Crochet; fantastic jewelry, hats, purses, pillows & more. Lark Books 2005 112p il (Kids' crafts) $19.95; pa $9.95

Grades: 5 6 7 8   **746.43**

1. Crocheting

ISBN 978-1-57990-477-7; 1-57990-477-7; 978-1-60059-138-9 pa; 1-60059-138-8 pa

LC 2004-13288

This describes basic crochet techniques and includes instructions for 50 projects

"The book is a pleasure to look at. . . . Photographs are large and crisp. . . . Davis clearly knows what kids like. . . . Both visual and text explanations are very clear. . . . This is a must for your craft shelves." Booklist

Haden, Christen

Creepy cute crochet; zombies, ninjas, robots, and more! Quirk Books 2008 96p il $14.95

Grades: 7 8 9 10 11 12 Adult   **746.43**

1. Toys 2. Crocheting

ISBN 978-1-5947-4232-3; 1-5947-4232-4

"Japanese-inspired amigurumi (literal translation: 'knitted stuffed toy') is one of the latest crafting crazes, and Haden's first book puts a unique spin on amigurumi by focusing on the creepy side of crocheted creatures. . . . There are . . . crocheted ninjas, a Grim Reaper, Day of the Dead figures, and vampires, all lovingly rendered. Although some beginner information is provided, a basic knowledge of crochet stitches and techniques is assumed." Libr J

Ogawa, Narumi

Mr. Funky's super crochet wonderful. North Light Books 2007 111p il pa $16.99

Grades: 7 8 9 10   **746.43**

1. Crocheting

ISBN 978-1-5818-0966-4; 1-5818-0966-2

LC 2006038689

This book "features 30 projects including stuffed animals (amirgurumi) and wearable accessories such as scarves, hats, crochet flowers, headbands, a water bottle carrier, fun kids stuff and more." Publisher's note

Okey, Shannon

★ Knitgrrl; learn to knit with 15 fun and funky projects. photography by Shannon Fagan, Christine Okey, and Tamas Jakab; illustrations by Kathleen Jacques. Watson-Guptill 2005 96p il pa $9.95

Grades: 7 8 9 10   **746.43**

1. Knitting

ISBN 0-8230-2618-3

This offers instructions for basic knitting techniques and for such projects as scarves, hats, leg warmers, mittens, and bags.

"A lively, teen-friendly book with all the basics, plenty of additional information, and appealing color photos and illustrations." SLJ

Rimoli, Ana Paula

Amigurumi world; seriously cute crochet. Martingale & Co. 2008 80p il $18.95

Grades: 7 8 9 10 11 12 Adult   **746.43**

1. Toys 2. Crocheting

ISBN 978-1-5647-7847-5; 1-5647-7847-9

LC 2007041240

This offers instructions for crocheting toy animals such as baby monkeys, bears, owls, hedgehogs, and elephants.

Snow, Tamie

Tiny yarn animals; amigurumi friends to make and enjoy. Home 2008 61p il $12.95

Grades: 8 9 10 11 12 Adult   **746.43**

1. Toys 2. Crocheting

ISBN 978-1-55788-530-2; 1-55788-530-3

LC 2008-013935

This is a "book of crocheted animal patterns. The 20 toys in the collection range from the expected (pig, lamb, and mouse) to the quirky (beaver, lemur, and hedgehog) and they are all cheery, colorful, and cute. A beginners' tutorial provides full-color photographic illustrations of basic crochet stitches, and the directions are clear enough for first-time crocheters to understand." Libr J

Turner, Sharon

Find your style and knit it too; by Sharon Turner. Wiley 2007 165p il pa $14.99

Grades: 6 7 8 9   **746.43**

1. Knitting

ISBN 978-0-470-13987-5 pa; 0-470-13987-0 pa

LC 2007028419

This is a "full-service knit book for teens and pre-teens. . . . The book works on every level. Beginning with knitting basics, Turner explains everything from choosing materials to fundamental how-tos . . . to fixing mistakes. . . . [This offers] easy-to-follow patterns, each illustrated by a crisp color photograph." Booklist

Werker, Kim P.

★ Get hooked; simple steps to crochet cool stuff. by Kim Werker; photography by Angela Fama and Pamela Bethel; illustrations by Cynthia Frenette. Watson-Guptill Pub. 2006 96p il $11.95

Grades: 6 7 8 9 10   **746.43**

1. Crocheting

ISBN 0-8230-5092-0

This "offers 15 patterns that will appeal to those new to crochet. Most of the projects are simple belts, scarves, pillows, and tiny bags. . . . Crotchet basics are shown primarily in helpful color photographs . . . and the book touches on subjects that such books sometimes miss: yarn weight, edging, and custom fitting. The pop-art graphics are very cool." Booklist

Includes bibliographical references

★ **Get** hooked again; simple steps to crochet more cool stuff. by Kim Werker; photography by Angela Fama and Pamela Bethel; illustrations by Cynthia Frenette. Watson-Guptill Pub. 2007 96p il pa $11.95

Grades: 6 7 8 9 10   **746.43**

1. Crocheting

ISBN 0-8230-5110-2 pa; 978-0-8230-5110-6 pa

This book about crocheting offers "lots of solid information; clear, crisp photographs; and . . . appealing projects. . . . The book covers crochet basics in a conversational tone that will keep readers engaged. The easy-to-follow text and the excellent photos do a great job of helping kids handle the crochet hook." Booklist

Includes bibliographical references

746.9   Other textile products

Bertoletti, John C.

How fashion designers use math; math curriculum consultant: Rhea A. Stewart. Chelsea Clubhouse 2010 32p il (Math in the real world) lib bdg $28

Grades: 4 5 6   **746.9**

1. Mathematics 2. Fashion design 3. Fashion -- Vocational guidance

ISBN 978-1-60413-606-7 lib bdg; 1-60413-606-5 lib bdg

LC 2009-22683

This describes how designers use math to measure, create, and produce their fashions, and includes problems to solve and information about how to become a fashion designer

"Color photos of designers in action combine with diagrams that further clarify the easily digestible text." Booklist

Includes glossary and bibliographical references

★ The **teen** vogue handbook; an insider's guide to careers in fashion. Razorbill 2009 276p il pa $24.95

Grades: 7 8 9 10 11 12   **746.9**

1. Clothing industry 2. Fashion -- Vocational guidance 3. Fashion merchandising

ISBN 978-1-59514-261-0; 1-59514-261-4

LC 2009-10626

"Any teen interested in a career in fashion should read this handbook. It is filled with advice from top designers, photographers, models, stylists, makeup artists, writers, and their interns and assistants. They share how they got started and give tips to those interested in a fashion career. This book looks and reads like a magazine on glossy pages filled with photographs and sidebars, but the interviews give pertinent information on every aspect of work in fashion." Voice Youth Advocates

Includes bibliographical references

747   Interior decoration

Weaver, Janice

★ **It's** your room; a decorating guide for real kids. [by] Janice Weaver and Frieda Wishinsky; illustrated by Claudia Dávila. Tundra Books 2006 63p il pa $14.95

Grades: 5 6 7 8   **747**

1. Interior design

ISBN 0-88776-711-7

"Budding interior designers and readers who want to personalize their rooms will appreciate this title. It is filled with step-by-step guidelines for creating a budget, selecting paint colors and fabrics, organizing closets and desks, laying everything out, and adding finishing touches. The illustrations will be a hit with first-time decorators just starting to develop their own color sense." SLJ

748.2   Blown, cast, decorated, fashioned, molded, pressed glass

Emert, Phyllis Raybin

Art in glass. Lucent Books 2007 112p il map (Eye on art) $32.45

Grades: 7 8 9 10 11 12   **748.2**

1. Glassware

ISBN 978-1-59018-983-2; 1-59018-983-3

LC 2007-10118

This is an introduction to the history of glassmaking, including its ancient origins, Roman glass, Middle Eastern and Venetian glass, European and American glass, and contemporary glass.

This "title is thoroughly researched and fully referenced, and contains quotations from artists and art historians. The writing is generally clear and fluid. . . . Many of the pages have good-quality photos of artwork and artists." SLJ

Includes bibliographical references

750   Painting and paintings

D'Harcourt, Claire

★ **Masterpieces** up close; by Claire d'Harcourt. Chronicle Books 2006 63p il $22.95

Grades: 4 5 6 7   **750**

1. Painting 2. Art appreciation 3. Painting -- Appreciation 4. Painting -- Themes, motives

ISBN 0-8118-5403-5

LC 2004-16341

"From Giotto to Warhol, d'Harcourt selects some of the most famous icons of Western art for a closer look. . . . The format of this oversize volume [consists of] boldly colored spreads featuring a central, large image surrounded by smaller details from it. Interesting tidbits and questions accompany each small picture, inviting viewers to wonder, think, and question what they see. . . . The last pages include lift-the-flap copies of the paintings and biographical sketches of the artists. A visually striking volume for browsers and art education." SLJ

Raczka, Bob

Unlikely pairs; fun with famous works of art. [by] Bob Raczka. Millbrook Press 2006 31p il lib bdg $23.93; pa $9.95

Grades: 4 5 6 7   **750**

1. Painting 2. Art appreciation
ISBN 0-7613-2936-6 lib bdg; 0-7613-2378-3 pa

LC 2003-14078

Invites the reader to discover fourteen funny stories produced by pairing twenty-eight paintings from different eras and styles

"Raczka deserves an A+ for cleverness. . . . Rodin's The Thinker is juxtaposed with Klee's modernistic painting of a chessboard so that the statue looks as if it is contemplating the next move. Siméon-Chardin's picture of a boy blowing soap bubbles seems to be creating Kandinsky's Several Circles. Each selection takes up a page and is reproduced in crisp color. . . . This book is an amusing way to introduce children to famous works of art." SLJ

Wenzel, Angela

13 paintings children should know. Prestel 2009 46p il $14.95

Grades: 5 6 7 8   **750**

1. Painting 2. Art appreciation
ISBN 978-3-7913-4323-5; 3-7913-4323-8

This "large-format, brightly colored [survey provides a] solid, even inspiring [introduction] to the art world. . . . Leading questions encourage budding artists to use the featured subjects and artworks as inspiration." Horn Book Guide

Includes glossary

750.1   Philosophy and theory

Richardson, Joy

Looking at pictures; an introduction to art for young people. with illustrations by Charlotte Voake. rev ed.; Abrams Books for Young Readers 2009 80p il $21.95

Grades: 4 5 6 7   **750.1**

1. Painting 2. Art appreciation
ISBN 978-0-8109-8288-8; 0-8109-8288-9

LC 2008055684

First published 1997

This "exploration of thirteenth- to twentieth-century European paintings examines the subject matter and techniques used and also delves into how the pieces were restored. Other topics covered are pigments, the use of light and perspective, the depiction of special events and daily life, and painting people and nature. Occasional well-placed illustrations supplement the numerous color reproductions." Horn Book Guide

Includes bibliographical references

751.4   Techniques and procedures

Peot, Margaret

★ **Inkblot**; drip, splat, and squish your way to creativity. Boyds Mills Press 2011 56p il $19.95

Grades: 4 5 6 7   **751.4**

1. Ink painting 2. Art -- Technique 3. Painting -- Technique
ISBN 1-59078-720-X; 978-1-59078-720-5

LC 22010-929541

This describes how to make inkblots and use them in art and as inspiration for writing and other forms of creativity.

"Peot's own entrancing inkblots . . . plus a few guest blots, illustrate every step, showing how the pure blot becomes a final artwork. . . . Readers get clear directions and lively encouragement." Kirkus

Includes bibliographical references

Self, Caroline

Chinese brush painting; [by] Caroline Self and Susan Self. 1st ed.; Tuttle 2007 64p il $16.95

Grades: 7 8 9 10 11 12   **751.4**

1. Calligraphy 2. Ink painting 3. Chinese painting
ISBN 978-0-8048-3877-1; 0-8048-3877-1

LC 2006037838

This "introduces readers to the art of Chinese calligraphy and brush painting. The text is fluid and graceful . . . and the authors wrap succinct accounts of Chinese history and lore around their clear, step-by-step, illustrated instructions." Booklist

Includes bibliographical references

751.7   Specific forms

Bingham, Jane

Graffiti. Raintree 2009 32p il (Culture in action) $28.21; pa $7.99

Grades: 5 6 7 8   **751.7**

1. Graffiti 2. Mural painting and decoration
ISBN 978-1-4109-3401-7; 1-4109-3401-2; 978-1-4109-3418-5 pa; 1-4109-3418-7 pa

LC 2008054323

"According to the time line in the . . . book, graffiti can be traced back to 60,000 BCE and paintings on cave walls. A note on the contents page states that it is illegal to draw on other people's property without permission. The different types of graffiti described are interesting, and some of the artwork is beautiful. A section on problems talks about ugly tags (short nicknames), the expense of cleanup, and how some cities have legal graffiti walls. . . . Well organized and with bright, colorful photography, [this] introductory [title gives] readers good basic knowledge." SLJ

Includes glossary and bibliographical references

Harris, Nathaniel

Wall paintings. PowerKids Press 2009 30p il (Stories in art) lib bdg $25.25

Grades: 4 5 6 7   **751.7**

1. Mural painting and decoration
ISBN 978-1-4042-4440-5 lib bdg; 1-4042-4440-9 lib bdg

LC 2007-52739

"This title explains the concept of wall paintings and how they were executed by using well-known examples. . . . Pages are well-designed with a paragraph about the painting and a section which gives some background information. . . . This is a useful addition to the art shelves." Libr Media Connect

Includes glossary and bibliographical references

Uschan, Michael V., 1948-

Graffiti. Lucent Books 2010 112p il (Eye on art) $33.45

Grades: 7 8 9 10   **751.7**
  1. Graffiti
  ISBN 978-1-4205-0324-1; 1-4205-0324-3
                                            LC 2010028699

Looks at the history of painted graffiti and explores the work of early artists as well as current ones.

This provides "a great deal of information, so middle school readers may not read them cover to cover; however, ample color photos and quotes from artists will make this . . . appealing to students interested in art." Voice Youth Advocates

Includes glossary and bibliographical references

---

758 Nature, architectural subjects and cityscapes, other specific subjects

Lanza, Barbara

Enchanting elves; paint elven worlds and fantasy characters. IMPACT Books 2009 128p il pa $22.99

Grades: 7 8 9 10   **758**
  1. Fantasy in art 2. Watercolor painting -- Technique
  ISBN 978-1-60061-307-4; 1-60061-307-1
                                            LC 2009014745

"Lanza includes watercolors of elves and similar creatures such as sprites, gnomes, and dwarves. Materials and basic skills are explained before moving on to chapters that explore faces, figures, and settings. This approach makes the projects accessible to artists who may not have worked with watercolor before. . . . Useful coloring instructions specify brush and color choices." SLJ

---

759 History, geographic treatment, biography

Barter, James

A **Renaissance** painter's studio; by James E. Barter. Lucent Bks. 2003 112p il (Working life) lib bdg $21.96

Grades: 6 7 8 9   **759**
  1. Renaissance 2. Artists, Italian 3. Italian painting 4. Painting, Renaissance 5. Art -- 15th and 16th centuries 6. Renaissance -- Italy -- Florence 7. Artists -- Social conditions -- History 8. Artists' studios -- Italy -- Florence -- History 9. Artists' studios -- Europe -- History 10. Painters -- Europe -- Social conditions -- History
  ISBN 1-59018-178-6
                                            LC 2002-7892

Describes the arduous training and difficult day-to-day working lives of painters in Florence during the Renaissance and discusses how their changing approach to the

art they created elevated their standing and influence in Florentine society

"Barter gives readers a fascinating glimpse . . . into the lives and work of the artists of Florence." SLJ

Includes bibliographical references

Serres, Alain

★ **And** Picasso painted Guernica; written and designed by Alain Serres; translated by Rosalind Price. Allen & Unwin Children's 2010 51p il $24.99

Grades: 5 6 7 8   **759**
  1. Artists 2. Painters 3. War in art
  ISBN 978-1-74175-994-5; 1-74175-994-3
  Original French edition, 2007

"Serres explains the mechanics of cubism . . . , tells the story of the horrifying German bombing of the civilians of Guernica and Picasso's reaction to it . . . , and finishes by tracing the rest of Picasso's career as he paints 'all the beauty of the world and its monstrous face as well.' The oversize pages are packed with period photographs and color reproductions of Picasso's sketches and paintings, each captioned in detail, with a double gatefold of Guernica at the center. . . . A passionate and intelligent tribute to the transformative power of art." Publ Wkly

---

759.03 1400-1599

D'Elia, Una Roman

Painting in the Renaissance; [by] Una D'Elia. Crabtree Pub. Co. 2009 32p il pa $8.95; lib bdg $26.60

Grades: 6 7 8 9   **759.03**
  1. Art -- 15th and 16th centuries
  ISBN 978-0-7787-4612-6; 978-0-7787-4592-1
                                            LC 2008-52600

"–Ideal introductions to concepts, people, and events of the Renaissance... succinct and thorough." SLJ

759.05 1800-1899

Bingham, Jane

Impressionism. Heinemann Library 2008 48p il (Art on the wall) lib bdg $32.86

Grades: 5 6 7 8 9 10   **759.05**
  1. French painting 2. Impressionism (Art)
  ISBN 978-1-4329-1371-7; 1-4329-1371-9
                                            LC 2008020468

This title succeeds "in presenting a bird's-eye view of [Impressionism] without oversimplification. Information on individual artists is included in the broader context of the movement. Visually exciting, with plenty of color, [the layout is] hip and should appeal to the target audience." SLJ

Includes glossary and bibliographical references

Post-Impressionism. Heinemann Library 2009 48p il (Art on the wall) lib bdg $32.86

Grades: 5 6 7 8 9 10   759.05
1. French painting 2. Postimpressionism (Art)
ISBN 978-1-4329-1369-4; 1-4329-1369-7
LC 2008020464
This book "discusses how Post-Impresssionism developed, examines the distinctive styles of individual Post-Impressionist artists, and looks at how the Post-Impressionists used colour, shape, and composition." Publisher's note
Includes glossary and bibliographical references

Sabbeth, Carol
★ **Monet** and the impressionists for kids; their lives and ideas, 21 activities. Chicago Review Press 2002 140p il pa $17.95
Grades: 5 6 7 8   759.05
1. Art appreciation 2. Impressionism (Art) 3. Art, French -- 19th century 4. Impressionist artists -- France -- Biography
ISBN 1-55652-397-1
LC 2001-47191
Discusses the nineteenth-century French art movement known as Impressionism, focusing on the works of Monet, Renoir, Degas, Cassatt, Cezanne, Gauguin, and Seurat
"A beautifully designed introduction to Impressionism. . . . Sabbeth also includes 21 appealing extension activities such as recipes, crafts, games, and writing suggestions. Quality color reproductions on glossy pages, and varied, attractive layouts add to the book." SLJ
Includes glossary and bibliographical references

Van Gogh and the Post-Impressionists for kids; their lives and ideas, 21 activities. Chicago Review Press 2011 160p il $17.95
Grades: 4 5 6 7   759.05
1. Artists 2. Painters 3. Art appreciation 4. Postimpressionism (Art)
ISBN 1-56976-275-9; 978-1-56976-275-2
LC 2010053908
"The bulk of this wonderfully thorough study of Post-Impressionist artists focuses on van Gogh, with smaller sections devoted to Paul Gauguin, Henri de Toulouse-Lautrec, Paul Signac, and Emile Bernard. The highly engaging text follows the artists' lives with crisp writing and vivid detail, delving into their family backgrounds and relationships, and doesn't sugarcoat dark and gritty incidents such as van Gogh's self-inflicted ear amputation. Information is well organized. . . . Full-color reproductions of paintings discussed in the text add visual interest, and educational sidebars expound on topics mentioned in the main narrative. . . . With its creative, hands-on ideas for teaching art technique and history, this book is an excellent resource for students and teachers." SLJ
Includes glossary and bibliographical references

759.06   1900-1999

Barsony, Piotr
The **stories** of the Mona Lisa; an imaginary museum tale about the history of modern art. Piotr Barsony; translated from the French by Joanna Oseman.

Skyhorse Publishing 2012 55 p. (hardcover: alk. paper) $19.95
Grades: 5 6 7 8   759.06
1. Art -- History 2. Mona Lisa (Painting) 3. Art movements 4. Painting, Modern
ISBN 1620872285; 9781620872284
LC 2012015603
"As [this book by Pietr Barsony] begins, a little girl asks: 'Dad, will you tell me a story?' The story her painter father tells is a history of art with the Mona Lisa as its central character. . . . He takes daughter and readers both on a journey of discovery through an imaginary museum. . . . Each painting is of only the Mona Lisa. . . . They are his own responses to and interpretations of Leonardo's masterpiece as filtered through the vision of other artists and movements." (Kirkus Reviews)

759.13   United States

Duggleby, John
★ **Story** painter: the life of Jacob Lawrence. Chronicle Bks. 1998 55p il $16.95
Grades: 4 5 6 7   759.13
1. Artists 2. Painters 3. Illustrators 4. African American artists 5. African American painters -- Biography 6. African Americans in art
ISBN 0-8118-2082-3
LC 98-4513
This is a biography of the twentieth-century African American painter. Bibliography. "Grades four to eight." (SLJ)
"Lawrence's expressionistic, stark paintings, in excellent full-page color reproduction . . . nicely complement Duggleby's measured account of a materially poor but culturally rich childhood and Lawrence's subsequent struggles and successes." Publ Wkly
Includes bibliographical references

Gherman, Beverly
Norman Rockwell; storyteller with a brush. Atheneum Bks. for Young Readers 2000 57p il $19.95
Grades: 4 5 6 7   759.13
1. Artists 2. Painters 3. Illustrators 4. Artists -- United States 5. Painters -- United States -- Biography
ISBN 0-689-82001-1
LC 98-36546
Describes the life and work of the popular American artist who depicted both traditional and contemporary subjects, including children, family scenes, astronauts, and the poor
"The format of the biography is appealing and attractive. The pages are replete with color reproductions of Rockwell's paintings as well as photographs of the man and his family. The text is well researched and authentic; the writing style is free-flowing and the words capture the naturalness of Rockwell's paintings." SLJ
Includes bibliographical references

Lawrence, Jacob
The **great** migration; an American story. paintings by Jacob Lawrence; with a poem in appreciation

by Walter Dean Myers. HarperCollins Pubs. 1993
un il hardcover o.p. pa $8.99

Grades: 4 5 6 7   **759.13**
    1. African Americans in art
    ISBN 0-06-023037-1; 0-06-443428-1 pa
                   LC 93-16788

"Lawrence is a storyteller with words as well as pictures: his captions and his own 1992 introduction to this book are the best commentary on his work." Booklist

759.2   European painting

Wenzel, Angela
   13 art mysteries children should know. Prestel 2011 45p il $14.95

Grades: 4 5 6   **759.2**
    1. Art 2. Artists 3. Painting
    ISBN 978-3-7913-7044-6; 379-1-37044-8

Presents information about thirteen mysteries from the art world, including questions about the Mona Lisa, van Gogh, and the street artist Banksy.

"Excellent-quality reproductions appear throughout. This is definitely a different approach for introducing young people to various aspects of art history. . . . The illustrations are well chosen to support these succinct inquiries into some perplexing puzzlements from the world of art." SLJ

759.9494   Swiss painting

Vry, Silke
   Paul Klee for children; Silke Vry; [translation, Jane Michael] Prestel 2011 95 p. $14.95

Grades: 4 5 6   **759.9494**
    1. Art -- Technique 2. Art appreciation
    ISBN 3791370774; 9783791370774
                LC 2011937220

This book, by Silke Vry, is about the art work of Paul Klee. "Paul Klee's playful paintings are a natural introduction for children to the world of creativity and art. . . . The German artist was fascinated by children's drawings, and incorporated their energy and simplicity into his own work. This . . . introduction to Klee's paintings focuses on the artist's love of color and symbols, his lighthearted technique, and his belief that music and painting were inextricably linked." (Publisher's note)

759.972   Mexican painting

Rubin, Susan Goldman
   ★ **Diego** Rivera; an artist for the people. by Susan Goldman Rubin. Abrams Books for Young Readers 2013 56 p. (reinforced) $21.95

Grades: 5 6 7 8   **759.972**
    1. Mural painting and decoration 2. Painters -- Mexico -- Biography
    ISBN 0810984113; 9780810984110
                LC 2012010022

This book, by Susan Goldman Rubin, "offers young readers . . . insight into the life and artwork of the famous Mexican painter and muralist [Diego Rivera]. The book follows Rivera's career, looking at his influences and tracing the evolution of his style. His work often called attention to the culture and struggles of the Mexican working class. . . . The book contains a list of museums where you can see Rivera's art, a historical note, a glossary, and a bibliography." (Publisher's note)

Includes bibliographical references and index

761   Printmaking

Boonyadhistarn, Thiranut
   Stamping art; imprint your designs. by Thiranut Boonyadhistarn. Capstone Press 2007 31p il $25.26

Grades: 4 5 6 7   **761**
    1. Handicraft 2. Rubber stamp printing
    ISBN 978-0-7368-6477-0; 0-7368-6477-6
                LC 2006004077

This "describes how to make stamps from common household objects, create 'embossed' cards, make a 'stained glass' lampshade, and more." SLJ

Includes bibliographical references

769.56   Postage stamps and related devices

Postal Service guide to U.S. stamps. U.S. Postal Service il

Grades: 8 9 10 11 12 Adult   **769.56**
    1. Postage stamps 2. Reference books 3. Postage stamps -- Catalogs

First published 1974 with title: United States stamps and stories. Revised annually

Contains reproductions and histories of U.S. postage stamps

770   Photography, computer art, cinematography, videography

Finger, Brad
   13 photos children should know. Prestel 2011 45p il lib bdg $14.95

Grades: 4 5 6   **770**
    1. Modern history 2. Documentary photography
    ISBN 978-3-7913-7047-7; 3-7913-7047-2

Examines the history behind thirteen popular photographs, including the moon landing, the fall of the Berlin Wall, and the wedding of Prince Charles and Princess Diana.

Kallen, Stuart A.
   Photography. Lucent Books 2007 112p il (Eye on art) $32.45

Grades: 7 8 9 10 11 12   **770**
    1. Photography -- History
    ISBN 978-1-59018-986-3
                LC 2007015978

"This volume surveys the history of photography, from the ancient camera obscura to the digital camera. . . . This title offers a clear overview of an art form that many teens both practice and appreciate." Booklist

Includes bibliographical references

770.9   History, geographical treatment, biography

Sandler, Martin W.

★ **America** through the lens; photographers who changed the nation. Henry Holt and Co. 2005 182p il $19.95

Grades: 6 7 8 9   770.9

1. Photography 2. Photographers
ISBN 0-8050-7367-1

"The photographs are stunning." SLJ

Includes bibliographical references

771   Techniques, procedures, apparatus, equipment, materials

Stefoff, Rebecca

The **camera**; [by] Rebecca Stefoff. Marshall Cavendish Benchmark 2007 143p il (Great inventions) lib bdg $27.95

Grades: 6 7 8 9   771

1. Photography -- History
ISBN 978-0-7614-2596-0

                   LC 2007002897

"An exploration of the origin, development, and societal impact of the camera." Publisher's note

Includes glossary and bibliographical references

775   Digital photography

Johnson, Daniel

4-H guide to digital photography. Voyageur Press 2009 176p $18.99

Grades: 5 6 7 8   775

1. Digital photography
ISBN 978-0-7603-3652-6; 0-7603-3652-0

                   LC 2009014679

This guide to digital photography offers "sound and comprehensive information. . . . [It] features numerous excellent photos that support the text. It explores types of digital cameras, how to take good photos, the complexities of lighting, managing images . . . and the importance of just enjoying this activity. Types of photography such as landscape and macro are explained. The author does an excellent job of discussing the importance of both technological details and artistic creativity." SLJ

Includes glossary

Rabbat, Suzy

Using digital images. Cherry Lake Pub. 2010 32p il (Super smart information strategies) lib bdg $27.07

Grades: 3 4 5 6   775

1. Digital photography
ISBN 978-1-60279-954-7 lib bdg; 1-60279-954-7 lib bdg

                   LC 2010018941

"The information on deciding between file formats and resolutions in Using Digital Images will be tremendously helpful, and some beginner techniques on taking and editing effective photos are a nice bonus." Booklist

Includes bibliographical references

778.5   Cinematography and videography

Green, Julie

Shooting video to make learning fun. Cherry Lake Pub. 2010 32p il (Super smart information strategies) lib bdg $27.07

Grades: 3 4 5 6   778.5

1. Digital video recording 2. Motion pictures -- Production and direction
ISBN 978-1-60279-955-4 lib bdg; 1-60279-955-5 lib bdg

                   LC 2010002022

"This books helps students learn how to harness the power of video to inform and entertain. Includes background information and practical hands on activities." Publisher's note

Includes bibliographical references

Miller, Ron

★ **Special** effects; an introduction to movie magic. [by] Ron Miller. Twenty-first Century Books 2006 128p il lib bdg $26.60

Grades: 7 8 9 10   778.5

1. Cinematography
ISBN 978-0-7613-2918-3 lib bdg; 0-7613-2918-8 lib bdg

                   LC 2005013123

"An excellent mix of photographs, including stills of special-effects triumphs ranging from the original King Kong to The Matrix and closeups of experts at work, will easily pull browsers and researchers alike to this comprehensive title." Booklist

Includes bibliographical references

779   Photographic images

Delannoy, Isabelle

★ **Our** living Earth; a story of people, ecology, and preservation. by Isabelle Delannoy; photographs by Yann Arthus-Bertrand. Harry N. Abrams 2008 157p il $24.95

Grades: 5 6 7 8   **779**
1. Human geography 2. Aerial photography
ISBN 978-0-8109-7132-5; 0-8109-7132-1
LC 2008010324

"Wrapped around Arthus-Bertrand's magnificent aerial photographs from around the world, Delannoy's text is organized thematically, covering fresh water, biodiversity, oceans, land, cities, people, food, and climate. . . . Readers will find surprising information and images to ponder. Almost every page supports the overarching theme that social justice and environmental protection are inextricably related. . . . This volume raises awareness, and the striking images, astonishing statistics, and brief explanations will stimulate readers to investigate further and possibly to take action." SLJ

780   Music

Bourne, Joyce

The **concise** Oxford dictionary of music; [by] Michael Kennedy and Joyce Bourne Kennedy. 5th ed.; Oxford University Press 2007 839p il (Oxford paperback reference) pa $17.99
Grades: 8 9 10 11 12 Adult   **780**
1. Reference books 2. Music -- Dictionaries 3. Musicians -- Dictionaries
ISBN 978-0-19-920383-3 pa; 0-19-920383-0 pa
LC 2007008461

First published 1952 as a condensation of the Oxford companion to music

This music "dictionary includes over 14,000 entries on terms from 'allegro' to 'zingaro,' and on works from 'Aida' to 'Tosca,' as well as instruments and their history, composers, librettists, musicians, singers, and orchestras. It also [includes] comprehensive works lists for major composers." Publisher's note

McAlpine, Margaret

Working in music and dance; [by] Margaret McAlpine. Gareth Stevens Pub. 2006 54p il (My future career) lib bdg $26
Grades: 6 7 8 9   **780**
1. Dance 2. Music 3. Vocational guidance
ISBN 0-8368-4777-6
LC 2005042522

This is "well organized, full of beautiful photography, and [presents] honest snapshots of the featured professions. . . . Attractive, informative, and interesting." SLJ
Includes bibliographical references

Nathan, Amy

Meet the musicians; from prodigy (or not) to pro. Henry Holt and Co. 2006 168p il $17.95
Grades: 5 6 7 8   **780**
1. Music 2. Musicians
ISBN 978-0-8050-7743-8; 0-8050-7743-X
LC 2005026508

The author "interviewed 13 of the New York Philharmonic's members, representing 11 different instruments, and spun their articulate comments into brief, readable pro-files, supplemented by various sidebars—among them, an invaluable feature outlining pros and cons of individual instruments. . . . The practical advice mixed with inspirational words strikes just the right note for children at many different stages in their musical education." Booklist
Includes bibliographical references

780.89   Ethnic and national groups

Tsoukanelis, Erika Alexia

The **Latin** music scene; the stars, the fans, the music. Enslow Publishers 2009 48p il (The music scene) lib bdg $23.93
Grades: 6 7 8 9   **780.89**
1. Music -- Latin America
ISBN 978-0-7660-3399-3 lib bdg; 0-7660-3399-6 lib bdg
LC 2008-48013

This describes the music, stars, clothes, contracts, and world of Latin music
Includes glossary and bibliographical references

780.9   History, geographic treatment, biography

Children's book of music; an introduction to the world's most amazing music and its creators. DK Publishing 2010 142p il $24.99
Grades: 3 4 5 6   **780.9**
1. Music -- History and criticism
ISBN 978-0-7566-6734-4; 0-7566-6734-8
LC 2010564872

"Concise summaries and eye-catching photography are combined in this chronological look at music 'from the first hum' to digital recording and reactable electronic instruments. The book explores the nature of music, its origins, and varied sounds. The organization creates a useful resource for research as well as for casual browsing. . . . While the information is succinct, there is enough depth for basic information and unusual facts. . . . Thirty-five musical highlights are included on the CD . . . each tagged by an icon and explanation within the book, provide teaching and listening aids. A solid resource for any library." SLJ
Includes glossary

Solway, Andrew

Africa; [by] Andrew Solway. Heinemann Library 2008 48p il (World of music) lib bdg $22
Grades: 5 6 7 8   **780.9**
1. African music
ISBN 978-1-4034-9891-5 lib bdg; 1-4034-9891-1 lib bdg
LC 2006100578

This introduction to African music discusses "instruments, dance, and vocal styles. The photographs presented are wonderfully colorful in quality and narrative. Topics covered include history, famous players, current styles, pop-culture, politics, world-wide connections." Libr Media Connect
Includes glossary and bibliographical references

Latin America and the Caribbean; [by] Andrew Solway. Heinemann Library 2008 48p il (World of music) lib bdg $22

Grades: 5 6 7 8   **780.9**

    1. Music -- Latin America 2. Music -- Caribbean region
ISBN 978-1-4034-9889-2 lib bdg; 1-4034-9889-X lib bdg

                               LC 2006100579

This introduction to music of Latin America and the Caribbean discusses "instruments, dance, and vocal styles. The photographs presented are wonderfully colorful in quality and narrative. Topics covered include history, famous players, current styles, pop-culture, politics, and world-wide connections." Libr Media Connect

    Includes glossary and bibliographical references

Underwood, Deborah

Australia, Hawaii, and the Pacific; [by] Deborah Underwood. Heinemann Library 2008 48p il (World of music) lib bdg $22

Grades: 5 6 7 8   **780.9**

    1. Music -- Hawaii 2. Music -- Oceania 3. Music -- Australia
ISBN 978-1-4034-9894-6 lib bdg; 1-4034-9894-6 lib bdg

                               LC 2006100576

This introduction to the music of Australia, Hawaii, and the Pacific discusses "instruments, dance, and vocal styles. The photographs presented are wonderfully colorful in quality and narrative. Topics covered include history, famous players, current styles, pop-culture, politics, and world-wide connections." Libr Media Connect

    Includes glossary and bibliographical references

780.92   Biography

Behnke, Alison Marie

Death of a dreamer; the assassination of John Lennon. Alison Marie Behnke. Twenty-First Century Books 2012 96 p.

Grades: 5 6 7 8   **780.92**

    1. Assassination 2. Rock musicians -- Political activity 3. Rock musicians -- England -- Biography 4. Rock musicians 5. Murder -- New York (State) -- New York 6. Murderers -- New York (State) -- Biography
ISBN 0822590360; 9780822590361

                               LC 2010005550

In this young adult book, "[t]win narratives converge in New York City on December 8, 1980, when John Lennon was murdered by Mark David Chapman. [Alison Marie] Behnke calls the murder an assassination, and by the general definition of the word—to murder (a usually prominent person) by sudden or secret attack, often for political reasons"--the murder of John Lennon might qualify. Lennon was political by the end of his life, writing "Give Peace a Chance," which became the anthem of the peace movement, but he was hardly a revolutionary, as Behnke terms him. Chapman was not especially political, and he didn't really seem to know why he attacked Lennon; it was certainly not from

any well-thought-out political motives, as the author herself describes." (Kirkus)

    Includes bibliographical references (p. 92), discography (p. 93), filmography (p. 93), and index

Cartlidge, Cherese

Jennifer Hudson; by Cherese Cartlidge. Lucent Books 2011 96 p. ill. (hardcover) $33.95

Grades: 6 7 8 9   **780.92**

    1. Actresses 2. African American singers 3. Singers -- United States -- Biography 4. Motion picture actors and actresses -- United States -- Biography
ISBN 1420506072; 9781420506075

                               LC 2011006366

This book offers a biography of actress Jennifer Hudson by author Cherese Cartlidge. It is part of the "People in the News" series, which "profiles the lives and careers of some of today's most prominent newsmakers. Whether covering contributions and achievements or notorious deeds, books in this series examine why these well-known individuals garnered public attention." (Publisher's note)

    Includes bibliographical references

Earls, Irene

Young musicians in world history. Greenwood Press 2002 139p il $44.95

Grades: 8 9 10 11 12   **780.92**

    1. Musicians
ISBN 0-313-31442-X

                               LC 2001-40559

Profiles thirteen musicians who achieved high honors and fame before the age of twenty-five, representing many different time periods and musical styles

    "A useful introduction to some of the musical giants of the last four centuries." SLJ

    Includes glossary and bibliographical references

Roberts, Russell, 1953-

  ★ **Scott** Joplin; by Russell Roberts. Mitchell Lane Publishers 2012 47 p. ill. (chiefly col.) (library) $29.95

Grades: 6 7 8 9   **780.92**

    1. Jazz music 2. Composers -- United States -- Biography
ISBN 1612282733; 9781612282732

                               LC 2012008633

    This book by Russ Roberts is part of the American Jazz series and looks at musician Scott Joplin. Within each entry, "information about the subjects' childhoods and preparation for their musical careers is included, as are the positive and negative aspects of their adult lives. Their contributions to the world of jazz are . . . explored." (School Library Journal)

    Includes bibliographical references (pages 44-45), chronology (pages 40-41) and index.

780.94   Music of Europe

Allen, Patrick

Europe; [by] Patrick Allen. Heinemann Library 2008 48p il (World of music) lib bdg $22

Grades: 5 6 7 8   **780.94**
1. Music -- Europe
ISBN 978-1-4034-9890-8 lib bdg; 1-4034-9890-3 lib bdg
LC 2006100580

This introduction to European music discusses "instruments, dance, and vocal styles. The photographs presented are wonderfully colorful in quality and narrative. Topics covered include history, famous players, current styles, pop-culture, politics, and world-wide connections." Libr Media Connect

Includes glossary and bibliographical references

781.2   Elements of music

Tomecek, Steve
Music; [by] Stephen M. Tomecek. Chelsea House 2010 165p il (Experimenting with everyday science) $35
Grades: 5 6 7 8   **781.2**
1. Musical instruments 2. Science -- Experiments 3. Music -- Acoustics and physics
ISBN 978-1-60413-169-7; 1-60413-169-1
LC 2009-22333

This "offers 25 easy-to-perform activities that illuminate scientific principles. . . . Topics . . . include the history of music, various instruments, and how scientific principles explain the creation of sounds. . . . Following each experiment are additional comments on the science behind the experiment and link to the one that follows. Photographs, simple diagrams and illustrations, and sample data tables appear throughout, and the [layout is] clear and colorful." SLJ

Includes bibliographical references

781.49   Recording of music

Miles, Liz
Making a recording. Raintree 2009 32p il (Culture in action) $28.21; pa $7.99
Grades: 5 6 7 8   **781.49**
1. Sound recordings 2. Music industry -- Vocational guidance
ISBN 978-1-4109-3392-8; 1-4109-3392-X; 978-1-4109-3409-3 pa; 1-4109-3409-8 pa
LC 2009000416

This "is a must-read for any aspiring musician. A brief history is followed by a discussion of modern techniques, and technical terms are explained in simple language. Fun activities include designing a label. . . . Well organized and with bright, colorful photography, [this] introductory [title gives] readers good basic knowledge." SLJ

Includes glossary and bibliographical references

781.6   Traditions of music

Kallen, Stuart A.
The **history** of classical music. Lucent Bks. 2002 112p il (Music library) $28.70

Grades: 6 7 8 9   **781.6**
1. Music -- History and criticism
ISBN 978-1-59018-123-2; 1-59018-123-9
LC 2002-3815

This follows classical music "from Medieval times into the present, closing with a description of avant-garde composer John Cage's 4'33"—4 minutes and 33 seconds of silence. . . . [The volume is] greatly enhanced by fascinating excerpts from primary material, including articles, letters, and diaries, often in the words of the composer or musician. . . . Students reading for reports or for personal interest will find much useful information." Booklist

Includes bibliographical references

781.62   Folk music

Handyside, Chris
★ **Folk**. Heinemann Library 2006 48p il (A history of American music) lib bdg $31.43
Grades: 5 6 7 8   **781.62**
1. Folk music
ISBN 1-4034-8150-4

This history of folk music is an "excellent, clear [introduction]. . . . [It] starts with the post-Civil War era, when folklorists gathered slave songs. It describes the music's commercial success beginning with early recordings of the Carter family and Jimmie Rodgers in the 1920s and continuing with Leadbelly, Woody Guthrie, Pete Seeger, and the many musicians who became popular during the folk revival of the late 50s and early 60s. . . . It concludes with sections on folk rock, punk rock, and the future of folk music." SLJ

Includes bibliographical references

781.642   Country music

Bertholf, Bret
★ **Long** gone lonesome history of country music; by Bret Bertholf. Little, Brown 2007 un il $18.99
Grades: 4 5 6   **781.642**
1. Country music
ISBN 978-0-316-52393-6; 0-316-52393-3
LC 2005016036

"This tongue-in-cheek overview features a folksy narrative of how and why country music developed in the barns and back roads of rural America. The text . . . covers instruments, early recordings, yodeling, . . . the Great Depression, gospel, movie cowboys, a 'paper-doll' spoof of singers' costumes, hillbilly jazz, World War II, . . . and much more. While poking fun at itself . . . the book offers a vast amount of historical fact amid a multitude of caricatures of country stars. . . . The ever-changing backgrounds and fonts with colored-pencil and crayon illustrations carry an amazing variation of detail." SLJ

Kallen, Stuart A.
The **history** of country music. Lucent Bks. 2002 112p il (Music library) $28.70

Grades: 6 7 8 9   781.642
　　1. Country music
　　ISBN 1-59018-124-7
　　　　　　　　　　　　　　　　　　LC 2002-664
　　A history of country music which discusses its roots, influences, and various types including bluegrass, honky tonk, cowboy music, western swing, and rockabilly
　　Includes bibliographical references

781.643   Blues

Handyside, Chris
　　★ **Blues**; [by] Christopher Handyside. Heinemann Library 2006 48p il (A history of American music) lib bdg $31.43
Grades: 5 6 7 8   781.643
　　1. Blues music
　　ISBN 1-4034-8148-2
　　　　　　　　　　　　　　　　　LC 2005019280
　　"This book charts the development of this uniquely American Music form from the 1600s through to the present. It also shows how social, economic, and regional factors have all helped to shape the blues over time and, in turn, how this music has gone on to influence other genres." Publisher's note
　　Includes glossary and bibliographical references

781.644   Soul

Handyside, Chris
　　★ **Soul** and R&B; [by] Christopher Handyside. Heinemann Library 2006 48p il (A history of American music) lib bdg $31.43
Grades: 5 6 7 8   781.644
　　1. Soul music 2. Rhythm and blues music
　　ISBN 1-4034-8153-9
　　　　　　　　　　　　　　　　　LC 2005019324
　　"This book charts the development of this uniquely American music form from the 1800s through to the present. It also shows how social, economic, and regional factors have all helped to shape soul and R&B over time and, in turn, how this music has gone on to influence other genres." Publisher's note
　　Includes glossary and bibliographical references

Mendelson, Aaron A
　　★ **American** R & B; Gospel grooves, funky drummers, and soul power. Aaron Mendelson. Twenty-First Century Books 2013 64 p. (lib. bdg.: alk. paper) $30.60
Grades: 7 8 9 10 11 12   781.644
　　1. Blues music 2. American songs 3. African American music 4. Soul music -- History and criticism 5. Rhythm and blues music -- History and criticism
　　ISBN 0761345019; 9780761345015
　　　　　　　　　　　　　　　　　LC 2011045636
　　Author Aaron Mendelson's book focuses on R&B music. "Rhythm and blues music evolved from all sorts of sounds: swinging jazz, gritty blues, and African American

spiritual songs. The music's smooth mix of styles made it unique, and its passionate performers made it a sensation. Ever since Ray Charles hit the charts in the 1950s, R & B fans have held it down on dance floors. And R & B singers have belted out messages of love and calls for social change." (Publisher's note)
　　Includes bibliographical references and index.

781.646   Reggae

Neely, Daniel T.
　　The **reggae** scene; the stars, the fans, the music. [by] Peter Manuel and Daniel T. Neely. Enslow Publishers 2009 48p il (The music scene) lib bdg $23.93
Grades: 6 7 8 9   781.646
　　1. Reggae music
　　ISBN 978-0-7660-3400-6 lib bdg; 0-7660-3400-3 lib bdg
　　　　　　　　　　　　　　　　　LC 2008-48014
　　This describes the music, stars, clothes, contracts, and world of reggae music
　　This "is clearly written, well organized, and copiously illustrated with full-color photographs of noted performers." SLJ
　　Includes glossary and bibliographical references

781.65   Jazz

Handyside, Chris
　　★ **Jazz**; [by] Christopher Handyside. Heinemann Library 2006 48p il (A history of American music) lib bdg $31.43
Grades: 5 6 7 8   781.65
　　1. Jazz music
　　ISBN 1-4034-8149-0
　　　　　　　　　　　　　　　　　LC 2005019305
　　"This book charts the development of this uniquely American Music form from the 1600s through to the present. It also shows how social, economic, and regional factors have all helped to shape Jazz over time and, in turn, how this music has gone on to influence other genres." Publisher's note
　　Includes glossary and bibliographical references

Kallen, Stuart A.
　　The **history** of jazz. Lucent Bks. 2003 112p il (Music library) lib bdg $21.96
Grades: 6 7 8 9   781.65
　　1. Jazz music 2. Jazz -- History and criticism
　　ISBN 1-59018-125-5
　　　　　　　　　　　　　　　　　LC 2002-2220
　　This follows jazz music's "evolution from its African roots through contemporary forms. [The volume is] greatly enhanced by fascinating excerpts from primary material, including articles, letters, and diaries, often in the words of the composer or musician. . . . Students reading

for reports or for personal interest will find much useful information." Booklist

Includes bibliographical references

Marsalis, Wynton

★ **Jazz** A-B-Z; [by] Wynton Marsalis and Paul Rogers; with biographical sketches by Phil Schaap. Candlewick Press 2005 un il $24.99

Grades: 5 6 7 8 9 10   **781.65**

1. Jazz music 2. Jazz musicians 3. Alphabet
ISBN 978-0-7636-3434-6

LC 2005-48448

This is an illustrated alphabetically arranged introduction to jazz musicians.

This is a "witty, stunningly designed alphabet catalog. . . . The biographical sketches and notes on poetic forms by Phil Schaap are concise and genuinely informative. . . . Rogers's pastiche full-page portraits, his use of expressive typography and the smaller vignettes he sprinkles throughout are bound to heighten any reader's appreciation of both the musicians and the music. . . . [Marsalis offers] clever . . . poems, wordplays, odes and limericks." N Y Times Book Rev

781.65092   Jazz musicians

Mattern, Joanne

★ **Benny** Goodman; by Joanne Mattern. Mitchell Lane Publishers 2013 47 p. ill. (some col.) (library) $29.95

Grades: 6 7 8 9   **781.65092**

1. Jazz musicians 2. Clarinetists -- United States -- Biography 3. Jazz musicians -- United States -- Biography
ISBN 1612282695; 9781612282695

LC 2012008483

This book by Joanne Mattern is part of the American Jazz series and looks at musician Benny Goodman. Within each entry, "information about the subjects' childhoods and preparation for their musical careers is included, as are the positive and negative aspects of their adult lives. Their contributions to the world of jazz are . . . explored." (School Library Journal)

Includes bibliographical references (p. 44-45) and index.

Orr, Tamra

★ **Louis** Armstrong; by Tamra Orr. Mitchell Lane Publishers 2012 47 p. ill. (chiefly col.) (library) $29.95

Grades: 6 7 8 9   **781.65092**

1. Jazz musicians -- United States -- Biography
ISBN 1612282644; 9781612282640

LC 2012008631

Includes bibliographical references (pages 44-45) and index.

781.66   Rock (Rock 'n' roll)

Aberback, Brian

Black Sabbath; pioneers of heavy metal. Enslow Publishers 2010 112p il (Rebels of rock) lib bdg $31.93

Grades: 6 7 8 9 10   **781.66**

1. Rock musicians
ISBN 978-0-7660-3379-5 lib bdg; 0-7660-3379-1 lib bdg

LC 2009012295

"Refreshingly levelheaded and loaded with sourced quotes, [this is] that rare middle-grade biography . . . that is able to trace a band's history, revel in its rock awesomeness, and be blunt about such things as drug abuse, all the while keeping things at an age-appropriate keel. . . . Packed with pics, it's all here." Booklist

Includes bibliographical references

Bowe, Brian J.

The **Ramones**; American Punk Rock Band. Enslow Publishers 2010 128p il (Rebels of rock) lib bdg $31.93

Grades: 6 7 8 9 10   **781.66**

1. Rock musicians
ISBN 978-0-7660-3233-0; 0-7660-3233-7

LC 2008040362

"Avid fans of rock music will find [this title] appealing, entertaining, and enlightening. [The] book begins with a brief introduction to the band through an account of a major musical event. Subsequent chapters include short biographies of the various band members. . . . Direct quotes add life to the well-written and lively [narrative]. . . . Descriptions and analyses of the music and albums offer insight into the impact [the] band had on today's rock music." SLJ

Includes bibliographical references

Burlingame, Jeff

Aerosmith; hard rock superstars. Enslow Publishers 2010 112p il (Rebels of rock) lib bdg $31.93

Grades: 6 7 8 9 10   **781.66**

1. Rock musicians
ISBN 978-0-7660-3236-1; 0-7660-3236-1

LC 2009006469

"Avid fans of rock music will find [this title] appealing, entertaining, and enlightening. [The] book begins with a brief introduction to the band through an account of a major musical event. Subsequent chapters include short biographies of the various band members. . . . Direct quotes add life to the well-written and lively [narrative]. . . . Descriptions and analyses of the music and albums offer insight into the impact [the] band had on today's rock music." SLJ

Includes bibliographical references

Gaines, Ann

The **hip**-hop scene; the stars, the fans, the music. [by] Ann Graham Gaines and Reggie Majors. Enslow Publishers 2009 48p il (The music scene) lib bdg $23.93

Grades: 6 7 8 9   **781.66**
  1. Rap music
  ISBN 978-0-7660-3396-2 lib bdg; 0-7660-3396-1
  lib bdg

                  LC 2008048010

This is about the music, stars, clothes, contracts, and world of hip-hop music

This "is clearly written, well organized, and copiously illustrated with full-color photographs of noted performers." SLJ

Includes glossary and bibliographical references

George-Warren, Holly

  Shake, rattle, & roll; the founders of rock & roll. words by Holly George-Warren; pictures by Laura Levine. Houghton Mifflin 2001 un il hardcover o.p. pa $5.95

Grades: 3 4 5 6   **781.66**
  1. Musicians 2. Rock music 3. Rock musicians -- Biography
  ISBN 0-618-05540-1; 0-618-43229-9 pa

                  LC 00-33480

"A wonderfully entertaining browsing book that will also fill a gap in most music collections." SLJ

Goodmark, Robyn

  Girls rock; how to get your group together and make some noise. [by] Robyn Goodmark; illustrated by Adrienne Yan. Billboard Books 2008 178p il pa $13.95

Grades: 6 7 8 9 10   **781.66**
  1. Rock music 2. Bands (Music) 3. Women musicians
  ISBN 978-0-8230-9948-1; 0-8230-9948-2

                  LC 2008007386

This "shows the ins, outs, and good and bad things that come with starting a band and making it successful. . . . The conversational tone and quizzes throughout give the presentation the feel of a teen magazine. . . . Clever cartoon illustrations appear throughout. . . . Not only does this book provide the technical assistance newbie musicians might need, but it also provides advice on choosing a band name and more emotional topics like how to find creative inspiration. This is a wonderful guide for any girl who wants to start a band." SLJ

Guillain, Charlotte

  Punk; music, fashion, attitude! Raintree 2011 32p il (Culture in action) lib bdg $29

Grades: 5 6 7 8   **781.66**
  1. Punk rock music
  ISBN 978-1-4109-3916-6; 1-4109-3916-2

                  LC 2009052585

"Guillain delves into the history of punk and follows its influence on modern art, fashion, and politics. . . . [This volume is] quick, interesting, up-to-date . . . with plenty of supportive, captioned, full-color photographs. [It] also [provides] related project suggestions." SLJ

Includes glossary and bibliographical references

Handyside, Chris

  ★ **Rock**. Heinemann Library 2006 48p il (A history of American music) lib bdg $31.43

Grades: 5 6 7 8   **781.66**
  1. Rock music
  ISBN 1-4034-8150-4

This history of rock music is an "excellent, clear [introduction]. . . . [It] opens with the mid-1950s advent of rock n roll and continues with surf music, girl groups, the British invasion, psychedelic rock, heavy metal, punk, and grunge. Featured musicians range from Elvis Presley to Kurt Cobain." SLJ

Includes bibliographical references

Kallen, Stuart A.

  The **history** of rock and roll. Lucent Bks. 2003 128p il (Music library) lib bdg $21.96

Grades: 6 7 8 9   **781.66**
  1. Rock music 2. Rock music -- History and criticism
  ISBN 1-59018-126-3

                  LC 2002-3923

"Kallen traces the history of rock and roll from its early 1950s beginnings through its most significant developments to date." Publisher's note

Includes bibliographical references

Kenney, Karen Latchana

  Cool hip-hop music; create & appreciate what makes music great! [by] Karen Latchana Kenney. ABDO Pub. 2008 32p il (Cool music) lib bdg $24.21

Grades: 4 5 6 7   **781.66**
  1. Hip-hop
  ISBN 978-1-59928-971-7 lib bdg; 1-59928-971-7
  lib bdg

                  LC 2007-40585

Introduces the reader to hip-hop music and includes activities that immerse children in musical tradition.

This book "supplies a wealth of fascinating information to those who are new to the field. Reluctant readers will be attracted to these interesting reads." Libr Media Connect

  Cool rock music; create & appreciate what makes music great! [by] Karen Latchana Kenney. ABDO Pub. 2008 32p il (Cool music) lib bdg $24.21

Grades: 4 5 6 7   **781.66**
  1. Rock music
  ISBN 978-1-59928-974-8 lib bdg; 1-59928-974-1
  lib bdg

                  LC 2007-38169

Introduces readers to rock music and includes activities that will immerse children in musical traditions.

This book "supplies a wealth of fascinating information to those who are new to the field. Reluctant readers will be attracted to [this] interesting [read]." Libr Media Connect

Mead, Wendy

  The **alternative** rock scene; the stars, the fans, the music. [by] Wendy S. Mead. Enslow Publishers 2009 48p il (The music scene) lib bdg $23.93

Grades: 6 7 8 9   781.66
1. Rock music
ISBN 978-0-7660-3401-3 lib bdg; 0-7660-3401-1
lib bdg
LC 2008-48015

This describes the music, stars, clothes, contracts, and world of alternative rock music

This "is clearly written, well organized, and copiously illustrated with full-color photographs of noted performers." SLJ

Includes glossary and bibliographical references

Moore, Sarah W.
The **rap** scene; the stars, the fans, the music. Enslow Publishers 2009 48p il (The music scene) lib bdg $23.95
Grades: 6 7 8 9   781.66
1. Rap music
ISBN 978-0-7660-3397-9 lib bdg; 0-7660-3397-X
lib bdg
LC 2008048011

This is about the music, stars, clothes, contracts, and world of rap music

Includes glossary and bibliographical references

Nichols, Travis
★ **Punk** rock etiquette; the ultimate how-to guide for punk, underground, DIY, and indie bands. Roaring Brook Press 2008 128p il pa $10.95
Grades: 7 8 9 10 11 12   781.66
1. Punk rock music 2. Rock music 3. Music industry -- Vocational guidance
ISBN 978-1-59643-415-8; 1-59643-415-5
LC 2008-11706

"Lively, knowledgeable, witty, and wise, this title offers a sound foundation in the social economics of indie rock. . . . From how to put together a band that functions rather than fights, to designing and creating appealing merchandise and running a successful tour, this heavily illustrated guide covers every aspect of how to be a bona fide DIY rock star for the twenty-first century." Voice Youth Advocates

Roberts, Jeremy
The **Beatles**; music revolutionaries. Twenty-First Century Books 2011 112p il (USA Today lifeline biographies) lib bdg $33.26
Grades: 6 7 8 9 10   781.66
1. Singers 2. Guitarists 3. Rock musicians 4. Drummers 5. Songwriters
ISBN 978-0-7613-6421-4; 0-7613-6421-8
LC 2010031041

This "takes readers on an accessible tour of the band's rollicking run from Liverpool's underground scene to its nearly decade-long perch atop the charts. Written in a straightforward, reportorial style, . . . the book offers a fine dissection of the Beatle phenomenon. . . . As easy on the eyes as it is fun to read." Booklist

Includes discography, filmography, and bibliographical references

Sanna, Ellyn
Hip-hop: a short history; [by] Rosa Waters. Mason Crest Publishers 2007 64p il (Hip-hop) lib bdg $22.95; pa $7.95
Grades: 4 5 6 7   781.66
1. Hip-hop 2. Rap music
ISBN 1-4222-0109-0 lib bdg; 978-1-4222-0109-1 lib bdg; 1-4222-0261-5 pa; 978-1-4222-0261-6 pa
LC 2006004320

"The book begins with a visually eye-popping time line, then moves quickly through the roots of hip-hop—through slavery, the civil rights movement, and the black church. Musical influences included gospel, blues, jazz, funk, and rock. . . . A wide-awake design, full-color photos, and a winning writing style put a positive spin on this musical phenomenon." Booklist

Includes glossary and bibliographical references

Tanner, Mike
Flat-out rock; ten great bands of the '60s. Annick Press 2006 158p $24.95; pa $12.95
Grades: 7 8 9 10   781.66
1. Rock music
ISBN 1-55451-036-8; 1-55451-035-X pa

"Ten of the great bands in the forefront of the music scene from 1964 to 1974 are highlighted here. Tanner offers a description of how each group came together and how its distinctive style developed. The discussion includes the social and political history of the period and shows how the musicians were impacted by broader events. . . . The narrative style will hold readers' attention. . . . This book would be a helpful resource." SLJ

Witmer, Scott
Bookings & gigs. ABDO 2009 32p il (Rock band) lib bdg $27.07
Grades: 6 7 8 9   781.66
1. Rock music 2. Music industry -- Vocational guidance
ISBN 978-1-60453-689-8 lib bdg; 1-60453-689-6 lib bdg
LC 2009-6606

This offers advice to rock bands on how to find places to perform

"Copious examples and photos of bands drawn from a wide chronological and stylistic range ensure that every reader, from metalheads (Metallica) to Linkin Park fans will find something of interest here." SLJ

Includes glossary

History of rock bands. ABDO 2010 32p il (Rock band) lib bdg $27.07
Grades: 6 7 8 9   781.66
1. Rock music -- History and criticism
ISBN 978-1-60453-692-8 lib bdg; 1-60453-692-6 lib bdg
LC 2009-6609

This is a history of rock music

"Copious examples and photos of bands drawn from a wide chronological and stylistic range ensure that every reader, from metalheads (Metallica) to Linkin Park fans will find something of interest here." SLJ

Includes glossary

Managing your band. ABDO 2010 32p il (Rock band) lib bdg $27.07

Grades: 6 7 8 9   **781.66**

1. Rock music 2. Music industry -- Vocational guidance
ISBN 978-1-60453-693-5 lib bdg; 1-60453-693-4 lib bdg

LC 2009-6610

This offers information and advice about managing a rock music band

"Copious examples and photos of bands drawn from a wide chronological and stylistic range ensure that every reader, from metalheads (Metallica) to Linkin Park fans will find something of interest here." SLJ

Includes glossary

Recording. ABDO 2010 32p il (Rock band) lib bdg $27.07

Grades: 6 7 8 9   **781.66**

1. Rock music 2. Sound recordings 3. Music industry -- Vocational guidance
ISBN 978-1-60453-694-2 lib bdg; 1-60453-694-2 lib bdg

LC 2009-6611

This offers information and advice on recording for rock bands

"Copious examples and photos of bands drawn from a wide chronological and stylistic range ensure that every reader, from metalheads (Metallica) to Linkin Park fans will find something of interest here." SLJ

Includes glossary

The **Rolling** Stone encyclopedia of rock & roll; edited by Holly George-Warren and Patricia Romanowski; consulting editor, Jon Pareles. rev and updated for the 21st century; Fireside 2001 1114p il $27

Grades: 7 8 9 10 11 12 Adult   **781.66**

1. Reference books 2. Rock music -- Encyclopedias
ISBN 0-7432-0120-5

LC 2001-40285

"The scope is excellent: few works can compete in terms of blanket coverage of the major rock'n'roll players." Libr J

Includes discographies

The **show**. ABDO 2010 32p il (Rock band) lib bdg $27.07

Grades: 6 7 8 9   **781.66**

1. Rock music 2. Music industry -- Vocational guidance
ISBN 978-1-60453-695-9 lib bdg; 1-60453-695-0 lib bdg

LC 2009-6612

This offers information and advice about performing for rock bands

"Copious examples and photos of bands drawn from a wide chronological and stylistic range ensure that every

reader, from metalheads (Metallica) to Linkin Park fans will find something of interest here." SLJ

Includes glossary

782.1   Vocal forms

Siberell, Anne

★ **Bravo!** brava! a night at the opera; behind the scenes with composers, cast, and crew. introduction by Frederica von Stade. Oxford Univ. Press 2001 64p il $19.95

Grades: 4 5 6 7   **782.1**

1. Opera 2. Questions and answers
ISBN 0-19-513966-6

LC 2001-21206

"An excellent resource for reports, this unusual book has an exceptional range of topics for younger students and is an essential purchase for upper elementary and middle school music programs." SLJ

Includes glossary and bibliographical references

782.25   Small-scale vocal forms

Cooper, Michael L.

★ **Slave** spirituals and the Jubilee Singers. Clarion Bks. 2001 86p il music $16

Grades: 7 8 9 10   **782.25**

1. Spirituals (Songs) 2. African American music 3. African Americans -- Music 4. Spirituals (Songs) -- History and criticism
ISBN 0-395-97829-7

LC 00-65854

"The first half of this book traces the development of spirituals from African musical traditions and discusses the place of religion in the lives of the slaves. The second half focuses on Fisk University's Jubilee Singers. . . . Illustrated with many archival prints and photographs, the book includes extensive annotated source notes and the words and music to seven of the spirituals popularized by the Jubilee Singers." SLJ

Includes bibliographical references

Giovanni, Nikki

★ **On** my journey now; looking at African-American history through the spirituals. [by] Nikki Giovanni; foreword by Arthur C. Jones. 1st ed.; Candlewick Press 2007 116p $18.99; pa $8.99

Grades: 7 8 9 10   **782.25**

1. Spirituals (Songs) 2. African Americans -- History
ISBN 978-0-7636-2885-7; 0-7636-2885-9; 978-0-7636-4380-5 pa; 0-7636-4380-7 pa

LC 2006051695

"Personal and passionate, Giovanni's short narrative talks about the sacred songs first sung by slaves, tracing how the people in bondage created the great spirituals to tell their stories, and what the songs still mean to us today." Booklist

782.42   Songs

Crossingham, John

★ **Learn** to speak music; a guide to creating, performing, and promoting your songs. written by John Crossingham; illustrated by Jeff Kulak. Owl-Kids 2009 96p il $27.95; pa $17.95

Grades: 6 7 8 9   **782.42**
> 1. Songwriters and songwriting 2. Music industry -- Vocational guidance 3. Popular music -- Writing and publishing
> ISBN 978-1-897349-64-9; 1-897349-64-5; 978-1-897349-65-6 pa; 1-897349-65-3 pa

This is an "incredibly readable book. Crossingham uses a comfortable, conversational tone with a sensibility that will appeal to teens and preteens alike. . . . The exceptional graphic design and illustrations . . . enhance and broaden the musical themes addressed with humor, wit, and style." SLJ

★ **National** anthems of the world; edited by Michael Jamieson Bristow. 11th ed.; Weidenfeld & Nicolson 2006 629p $90

Grades: 5 6 7 8 9 10 11 12 Adult   **782.42**
> 1. National songs
> ISBN 0-304-36826-1

First published 1943 in the United Kingdom with title: National anthems of the United Nations and France

This volume contains national anthems of about 198 nations, including melody and accompaniment. Words are presented in the native language with transliteration provided where necessary. English translations follow. Brief historical notes on the adoption of each anthem are included

"An essential reference resource for all libraries." Libr J

Silverman, Jerry

Songs and stories of the Civil War. 21st Cent. Bks. (Brookfield) 2002 96p il lib bdg $30.60

Grades: 5 6 7 8   **782.42**
> 1. Music -- United States -- 19th century -- History and criticism
> ISBN 0-7613-2305-8

LC 2001-35795

Provides a history of the music and lyrics of a dozen Civil War songs, describing the circumstances under which they were created and performed

"Black-and-white reproductions of period photos, engravings, paintings, and drawings illustrate the text. A good resource offering an interesting sidelight on the times." Booklist

Includes discography and bibliographical references

Stotts, Stuart

★ **We** shall overcome; a song that changed the world. by Stuart Stotts; foreword by Pete Seeger; with illustrations by Terrance Cummings. Clarion Books 2009 72p il $18

Grades: 5 6 7 8   **782.42**
> 1. African Americans -- Civil rights -- Songs
> ISBN 978-0-547-18210-0; 0-547-18210-4

LC 2009022578

"This smart, effective telling has few missteps. From the informative black-and-white photographs to the solid back matter to the CD sung by Pete Seeger, it is a complete package." Booklist

Witmer, Scott

Songwriting. ABDO 2010 32p il (Rock band) lib bdg $27.07

Grades: 6 7 8 9   **782.42**
> 1. Rock music 2. Vocational guidance 3. Songwriters and songwriting
> ISBN 978-1-60453-696-6 lib bdg; 1-60453-696-9 lib bdg

LC 2009-6613

This offers advice on songwriting for rock bands

"Copious examples and photos of bands drawn from a wide chronological and stylistic range ensure that every reader, from metalheads (Metallica) to Linkin Park fans will find something of interest here." SLJ

Includes glossary

Yolen, Jane

★ **Apple** for the teacher; thirty songs for singing while you work. collected and introduced by Jane Yolen; music arranged by Adam Stemple; art edited by Eileen Michaelis Smiles. Harry N. Abrams 2005 117p il $24.95

Grades: 4 5 6 7   **782.42**
> 1. Songs 2. Work -- Songs
> ISBN 0-8109-4825-7

LC 2004-24404

"Yolen has brought together a collection of 30 work songs . . . which represent a wide variety of occupations. . . . She introduces each job, explaining unusual vocabulary and references in the songs. . . . The artwork . . . is elegant. Ranging from sculpture to paintings to needlework, each selection of Americana has been carefully matched to the occupation, beautifully reproduced on high-quality paper, and meticulously identified." Booklist

783   Music for single voices

Fishkin, Rebecca Love

Singing; a practical guide to pursuing the art. Compass Point Books 2010 48p il (Performing arts) lib bdg $28.65

Grades: 5 6 7 8   **783**
> 1. Singing 2. Vocational guidance
> ISBN 978-0-7565-4362-4 lib bdg; 0-7565-4362-2 lib bdg

LC 2010012607

This guide on a singing career includes tips on education, technique, and more.

"Meant for students contemplating a career in the field . . . [this book goes] beyond basic introductions and into more detail about what it takes to make it as a professional. . . . [The author maintains] . . . a frank, realistic tone, stressing the importance of hard work and dedication. Great [resource] . . . for those wanting to make their passions more than just a hobby." SLJ

Includes glossary and bibliographical references

Landau, Elaine

Is singing for you? Lerner Publications 2011 40p il (Ready to make music) lib bdg $27.93

Grades: 4 5 6 7   783
1. Singing
ISBN 978-0-7613-5427-7 lib bdg; 0-7613-5427-1 lib bdg

LC 2009052350

Helps readers explore the art of singing. This book covers the basics, including tips for getting started and info on vocal technique.

"Landau covers all the bases so that prospective musicians have the information they need. . . . Kids thinking about taking up an instrument will find . . . [this book] helpful in their decision-making process." SLJ

Includes glossary and bibliographical references

784.19   Instruments

Baines, Anthony

The Oxford companion to musical instruments; written and edited by Anthony Baines. Oxford University Press 1992 404p il $85

Grades: 8 9 10 11 12 Adult   784.19
1. Reference books 2. Musical instruments -- Dictionaries
ISBN 0-19-311334-1

LC 92-8635

Based on The New Oxford companion to music (1983)

This volume presents alphabetically arranged entries for musical instruments. "The individual entries cover specific instruments and families thereof (e.g., Wind Instruments) as well as their representation in different countries (e.g., Africa) and time periods (e.g., Baroque). . . . Playing techniques, a brief history, and a list of the major repertory are [discussed]." Booklist

Helsby, Genevieve

★ Those amazing musical instruments; [by] Genevieve Helsby; with Marin Alsop as your guide. Sourcebooks Jabberwocky 2007 176p il $19.95

Grades: 4 5 6 7 8 9   784.19
1. Musical instruments
ISBN 978-1-4022-0825-6; 1-4022-0825-1

LC 2007013821

This is "a guide to instruments commonly found in an orchestra. . . . Utilizing large print; ample, colorful illustrations; and an open format, the book is logically organized into chapters about each of the musical instrument families, including keyboards, the voice, and modern electronic instruments. Throughout, readers are prompted to listen to the accompanying CD-ROM, which features more than 100 musical samples. Information is clearly presented, and the author's enthusiasm for her subject is contagious." SLJ

Kallen, Stuart A.

The instruments of music. Lucent Bks. 2003 112p il (Music library) lib bdg $27.45

Grades: 6 7 8 9   784.19
1. Musical instruments
ISBN 1-59018-127-1

LC 2001-6609

This volume "includes history, cultural background, and the place of individual instruments in music from classical orchestra to rock and roll." Publisher's note

Includes bibliographical references

VanHecke, Susan

★ Raggin', jazzin', rockin' a history of American musical instrument makers. Boyds Mills Press 2011 136p il $17.95

Grades: 5 6 7 8 9   784.19
1. Musical instruments 2. Manufacturing executives 3. Musical instrument makers
ISBN 1-59078-574-6; 978-1-59078-574-4

LC 2010-04877

This is a history of American musical instrument making, including the stories of the Zildjian family's cymbals, Steinway's pianos, Charles Gerard Conn's brass instruments, C. F. Martin's guitars, William F. Ludwig's drums, Hammond keyboards, Fender electric guitars, and Moog synthesizers.

"Musicians and music lovers look no further. [This] is a book for everyone. . . . This is an interesting book." Voice of Youth Advocates

Includes bibliographical references

784.192   Techniques and procedures for instruments themselves

Pagliaro, Michael

The musical instrument desk reference; a guide to how band and orchestral instruments work. Michael J. Pagliaro. Scarecrow Press 2012 189 p. (cloth: alk. paper) $65

Grades: Adult Professional   784.192
1. Musical instruments 2. Wind instruments -- Construction 3. Bowed stringed instruments -- Construction
ISBN 0810882701; 9780810882706; 9780810882713

LC 2012007244

This book "begins with an 'easy-reference quick start' section on woodwinds, followed by more in-depth chapters on the flute, clarinet, saxophone, oboe, and the bassoon. For the brass instruments, there are fingering charts, an expanded in-depth study chapter, and a chapter on functioning. Nonfretted string instruments . . . are also given a chapter on producing sound and an expanded in-depth study chapter. The final chapter consists of an overview of percussion instruments." Booklist

784.2   Full orchestra (Symphony orchestra)

Ganeri, Anita

★ The **young** person's guide to the orchestra; Benjamin Britten's composition on CD narrated by Ben Kingsley. book written by Anita Ganeri. Harcourt Brace & Co. 1996 56p il $25

Grades: 4 5 6 7   784.2
    1. Orchestra 2. Music appreciation 3. Musical instruments
    ISBN 0-15-201304-0
                       LC 95-41478

"Accompanying this book on orchestral music is a CD featuring Britten's A Young Person's Guide to the Orchestra . . . as well as Dukas' The Sorcerer's Apprentice. The book begins with an overview of the orchestra and then centers around groups of instruments, explaining a bit of their history and their sound's distinctive quality. . . . The book also introduces eight famous composers, world music, Benjamin Britten, and the background of The YoungPerson's Guide to the Orchestra. . . . Handsome and useful." Booklist
    Includes glossary

784.4   Light orchestra

Bolden, Tonya

Take-off! American all-girl bands during WW II. Alfred A. Knopf 2007 76p il $18.99; lib bdg $21.99

Grades: 6 7 8 9   784.4
    1. Jazz musicians 2. Women musicians 3. Big bands 4. Women jazz musicians
    ISBN 978-0-375-82797-6; 0-375-82797-8; 978-0-375-92797-3 lib bdg; 0-375-92797-2 lib bdg
                       LC 2006-24523

"To appreciate this book, readers need at least a nodding acquaintance with swing music. The accompanying CD will help, and Bolden's introduction, which features opinions from Benny Goodman, Ella Fitzgerald, and others, gets things off to a good start. Then, using fascinating archival material . . . she goes on to discuss pioneering female jazz bands. . . . Bolden [uses] a fresh style of writing, as bouncy as the music." Booklist
    Includes glossary and bibliographical references

785   Ensembles with only one instrument per part

Marx, Trish

Steel drumming at the Apollo; the road to Super Top Dog. by Trish Marx; photographs by Ellen B. Senisi. Lee & Low Books 2007 56p il $22

Grades: 4 5 6 7   785
    1. Musicians 2. Bands (Music) 3. Steel drum (Musical instrument)
    ISBN 978-1-60060-124-8; 1-60060-124-3
                     LC 2007008947

"Marx traces the band's progress through the tiers of competition in clear evocative prose depicting the visceral experience of performing as well as the hard work of practice and composition. Senisi's color photographs enliven every page." SLJ

786   Specific instruments and their music

Witmer, Scott

Drums, keyboards, and other instruments. ABDO 2009 32p il (Rock band) lib bdg $27.07

Grades: 6 7 8 9   786
    1. Drums 2. Rock music 3. Musical instruments 4. Keyboards (Electronics)
    ISBN 978-1-60453-690-4 lib bdg; 1-60453-690-X lib bdg
                     LC 2009-6607

This offers information for rock bands about keyboards, drums, and other instruments
    "Copious examples and photos of bands drawn from a wide chronological and stylistic range ensure that every reader, from metalheads (Metallica) to Linkin Park fans will find something of interest here." SLJ
    Includes glossary

786.2   Keyboard instruments

Batten, Jack

Oscar Peterson; the man and his jazz. Jack Batten. Tundra Books of Northern New York 2012 165 p. (hardcover) $19.95

Grades: 6 7 8   786.2
    1. Jazz music -- History and criticism
    ISBN 1770492690; 9781770492691
                   LC 2011940582

This children's book, by Jack Batten, is a biography of the Jazz pianist Oscar Peterson. "Oscar Peterson released over 200 recordings, won seven Grammy Awards, received the Order of Canada and is considered to have been one of the greatest jazz pianists of all time. This new biography . . . is the story of a black kid from a Montreal ghetto who reached acclaim in the great music halls of the world." (Publisher's note)

Reich, Susanna

★ **Clara** Schumann; piano virtuoso. Clarion Bks. 1999 118p il $18; pa $9.95

Grades: 5 6 7 8   786.2
    1. Pianists 2. Women composers 3. Pianists -- Germany -- Biography
    ISBN 0-395-89119-1; 0-618-55160-3 pa
                   LC 98-24510

Describes the life of the German pianist and composer who made her professional debut at age nine and who devoted her life to music and to her family
    "This thoroughly researched book draws on primary sources, both Clara's own diaries and her voluminous correspondence with her husband. . . . Reich's lucid, quietly passionate biography is liberally illustrated with photographs and reproductions." Horn Book Guide

786.7   Electronic instruments (Electrophones)

Cohn, Jessica

The **electronic** music scene; the stars, the fans, the music. Enslow Publishers 2009 48p il (The music scene) lib bdg $23.93

Grades: 6 7 8 9   **786.7**

1. Electronic music
ISBN 978-0-7660-3398-6 lib bdg; 0-7660-3398-8 lib bdg

LC 2008-48012

This describes the music, stars, clothes, contracts, and world of electronic music

Includes glossary and bibliographical references

786.9   Drums and devices used for percussive effects

Landau, Elaine

Are the drums for you? Lerner Publications 2011 40p il (Ready to make music) lib bdg $27.93

Grades: 4 5 6 7   **786.9**

1. Drums 2. Percussion instruments
ISBN 978-0-7613-5426-0 lib bdg; 0-7613-5426-3 lib bdg

LC 2009-48971

Hear what professional drummers like about their instrument, and learn what skills a good drummer needs.

"Landau covers all the bases so that prospective musicians have the information they need. . . . Kids thinking about taking up an instrument will find . . . [this book] helpful in their decision-making process." SLJ

Includes glossary and bibliographical references

787   Stringed instruments (Chordophones)

Ganeri, Anita

Stringed instruments. Smart Apple Media 2011 32p il (How the world makes music) lib bdg $28.50

Grades: 4 5 6   **787**

1. Stringed instruments
ISBN 978-1-599-20480-2

LC 2010042418

Describes various stringed instruments from around the world including familiar instruments such as the guitar and violin, along with other traditional instruments such as the Japanese Koto and Indian lutes.

787.2   Violins

Landau, Elaine

Is the violin for you? Lerner Publications 2011 40p il (Ready to make music) lib bdg $27.93

Grades: 4 5 6 7   **787.2**

1. Violins
ISBN 978-0-7613-5423-9 lib bdg; 0-7613-5423-9 lib bdg

LC 2009045609

Hear what professional violinists like about their instrument, and learn what skills a good violinist needs.

"Landau covers all the bases so that prospective musicians have the information they need. . . . Kids thinking about taking up an instrument will find . . . [this book] helpful in their decision-making process." SLJ

Includes glossary and bibliographical references

787.8   Plectral lute family

Ellis, Rex M.

With a banjo on my knee; a musical journey from slavery to freedom. Watts 2001 160p il lib bdg $28

Grades: 7 8 9 10   **787.8**

1. Banjo 2. Banjos 3. African American music 4. Banjoists 5. Afro-Americans 6. Afro-American musicians -- Biography 7. Banjoists -- United States -- Biography
ISBN 0-531-11747-2 lib bdg; 978-0-531-11747-7 lib bdg

LC 00-33035

This is a "well-written, attractive work, which unveils a segment of social history both powerful and far reaching." Booklist

Includes   glossary,   discography   and bibliographical references

787.87   Guitars

Landau, Elaine

Is the guitar for you? Lerner Publications 2011 40p il (Ready to make music) lib bdg $27.93

Grades: 4 5 6 7   **787.87**

1. Guitars
ISBN 978-0-7613-5424-6 lib bdg; 0-7613-5424-7 lib bdg

LC 2009-48750

Hear what professional guitarists like about their instrument, and learn what skills a good guitarist needs.

"Landau covers all the bases so that prospective musicians have the information they need. . . . Kids thinking about taking up an instrument will find . . . [this book] helpful in their decision-making process." SLJ

Includes glossary and bibliographical references

Witmer, Scott

Guitars & bass. ABDO 2010 32p il (Rock band) lib bdg $27.07

Grades: 6 7 8 9   **787.87**

1. Guitars 2. Rock music
ISBN 978-1-60453-691-1 lib bdg; 1-60453-691-8 lib bdg

LC 2009-6608

This offers information about guitars and basses for rock bands

"Copious examples and photos of bands drawn from a wide chronological and stylistic range ensure that every reader, from metalheads (Metallica) to Linkin Park fans will find something of interest here." SLJ

Includes glossary

788   Wind instruments (Aerophones)

Landau, Elaine

Is the flute for you? Lerner Publications 2011 40p il (Ready to make music) lib bdg $27.93

Grades: 4 5 6 7   **788**

1. Flutes

ISBN 978-0-7613-5420-8 lib bdg; 0-7613-5420-4 lib bdg

LC 2009048970

Hear what professional flutists like about their instrument, and learn what skills a good flutist needs.

"Landau covers all the bases so that prospective musicians have the information they need. . . . Kids thinking about taking up an instrument will find . . . [this book] helpful in their decision-making process." SLJ

Includes glossary and bibliographical references

Is the trumpet for you? Lerner Publications 2011 40p il (Ready to make music) lib bdg $27.93

Grades: 4 5 6 7   **788**

1. Trumpet

ISBN 978-0-7613-5422-2 lib bdg; 0-7613-5422-0 lib bdg

LC 2009048280

Hear what professional trumpeters like about their instrument, and learn what skills a good trumpeter needs.

"Landau covers all the bases so that prospective musicians have the information they need. . . . Kids thinking about taking up an instrument will find . . . [this book] helpful in their decision-making process." SLJ

Includes glossary and bibliographical references

788.7   Saxophones

Golio, Gary

Spirit seeker; John Coltrane's musical journey. by Gary Golio; paintings by Rudy Gutierrez. Clarion Books 2012 48 p. (hardcover) $17.99

Grades: 3 4 5 6 7   **788.7**

1. Music and religion 2. Creation (Literary, artistic, etc.) 3. Saxophonists -- United States -- Biography 4. Jazz musicians -- United States -- Biography

ISBN 0547239947; 9780547239941

LC 2011045948

Includes bibliographical references and discography.

This book, by Gary Golio, illustrated by Rudy Gutierrez, explores the musical career of Jazz saxophonist John Coltrane. "Growing up, John was a seeker. He wondered about spirit, and the meaning of life. And whether music could be a key to unlocking those mysteries. . . . This is the story of a shy, curious boy from a deeply religious family who grew up to find solace and inspiration in his own unique approach to both spirituality and music." (Publisher's note)

Rice, Earle

★ **Charlie** Parker; by Earle Rice Jr. Mitchell Lane Publishers 2012 47 p. ill. (library) $29.95

Grades: 6 7 8 9   **788.7**

1. Jazz musicians -- Biography 2. African American musicians -- Biography 3. Jazz musicians -- United States -- Biography

ISBN 1612282660; 9781612282664

LC 2012008628

This biography of musician Charlie Parker, part of the American Jazz series, presents an "account of Parker's drug-abuse-shortened life and stellar career--along with a . . . technical, specific analysis of his musical education and innovations." It includes "period photos of 'Bird' and his bandmates, plus a time line, a discography, and . . . sets of print and web resources for children and adults alike." Booklist

Includes discography, bibliographical references

788.9   Brass instruments (Lip-reed instruments)

Boone, Mary

★ **Dizzy** Gillespie; by Mary Boone. Mitchell Lane Publishers 2013 47 p. ill. (some col.) (library) $29.95

Grades: 6 7 8 9   **788.9**

1. Jazz musicians -- Biography 2. Gillespie, Dizzy, 1917-1993 3. Bop (Music) -- History and criticism 4. Jazz musicians -- United States -- Biography

ISBN 9781612282725

LC 2012008630

This book by Mary Boone, part of the "American Jazz" series, presents a "biography of Jazz great Dizzy Gillespie written for intermediate through middle school age readers. . . . Gillespie owed much of his success to an elementary school teacher who worked to harness his energy and anger by recruiting him for the school band. . . . In the 1940s, the trumpet virtuoso and respected improviser teamed up with musician Charlie Parker to lay the foundations for bebop." (Publisher's note)

Includes discography, bibliographical references

Lynette, Rachel

Miles Davis; legendary jazz musician. by Rachel Lynette. KidHaven Press 2010 48 p. ill. (some col.) (hardcover) $29.95

Grades: 5 6 7 8   **788.9**

1. Jazz music 2. Jazz musicians -- United States -- Biography

ISBN 0737750340; 9780737750348

LC 2009045056

This biography of Miles Davis by Rachel Lynette is part of the Innovators series. Lynette "pinpoints the many works in which Davis pushed musical boundaries." She "refrains from mentioning the album Bitches Brew by name, instead offering . . . 'Davis and his band made an album that sold more than . . . any other jazz record ever.'" Booklist

Includes bibliographical references

Orr, Tamra

★ **Miles** Davis; by Tamra Orr. Mitchell Lane Publishers 2012 47 p. ill. (library) $29.95

Grades: 6 7 8 9   **788.9**

    1. Jazz musicians -- United States

    ISBN 1612282652; 9781612282657

                            LC 2012008632

This book by Tamra Orr is part of the American Jazz series and looks at Miles Davis. "Known to jazz lovers around the world as the Prince of Darkness, Miles Davis lived a roller-coaster life of highs and lows. . . . You can follow his lows of grappling with the power of drug and alcohol addiction and racial prejudice to his highs of achieving world fame and appreciation, plus becoming a husband, father, and grandfather." (Publisher's note)

    Includes discography, bibliographical references

790   Recreational and performing arts

Glenn, Joshua

Unbored; the essential field guide to serious fun. [compiled by] Joshua Glenn & Elizabeth Foy Larsen; design by Tony Leone. Bloomsbury USA 2012 352 p. (hardback) $25

Grades: 5 6 7   **790**

    1. Amusements 2. GAMES -- General 3. CRAFTS & HOBBIES -- General 4. Games 5. SPORTS & RECREATION -- General 6. REFERENCE -- Handbooks & Manuals 7. Handicraft 8. Recreation 9. FAMILY & RELATIONSHIPS -- Activities 10. Activity Books 11. Curiosities & Wonders 12. FAMILY & RELATIONSHIPS -- Parenting -- Child Rearing

    ISBN 1608196410; 9781608196418

                            LC 2012012368

This activity book by Elizabeth Foy Larsen and Joshua Glen, illustrated by Heather Kasunick and Mister Reusch, "provides kids with information to round out their world view and inspire them to learn more. From how-tos on using the library or writing your representative to a graphic history of video games, the book isn't shy about teaching. Yet the bulk of the 350-page mega-resource presents hands-on activities." (Publisher's note)

790.1   General kinds of recreational activities

Ball, Jacqueline A.

Traveling green. Bearport Pub. 2009 32p il (Going green) lib bdg $25.27

Grades: 4 5 6 7   **790.1**

    1. Travel -- Environmental aspects

    ISBN 978-1-59716-964-6 lib bdg; 1-59716-964-1 lib bdg

                           LC 2009-19836

"Color photographs (most full page) and a few diagrams accompany the informative text[s]. . . . Overall, the [book] . . . is user-friendly and covers topics that are not easily found elsewhere." SLJ

    Includes glossary and bibliographical references

Bell-Rehwoldt, Sheri

The **kids'** guide to classic games. Capstone Press 2009 32p il (Kids' guides) lib bdg $23.99

Grades: 4 5 6 7   **790.1**

    1. Games

    ISBN 978-1-4296-2273-8 lib bdg; 1-4296-2273-3 lib bdg

                            LC 2008-29686

This provides instructions and rules for indoor and outdoor games such as ping-pong soccer, ringer, paper football, spiderweb, tug-of-war, and pipeline

    Includes glossary and bibliographical references

Danks, Fiona

Run wild! outdoor games and adventures. [by] Fiona Danks and [phototgraphy by] Jo Schofield. Frances Lincoln 2011 159p il pa $24.95

Grades: 5 6 7 8   **790.1**

    1. Games 2. Parties 3. Handicraft 4. Nature study 5. Outdoor life 6. Storytelling

    ISBN 978-0-7112-3172-6; 0-7112-3172-9

"This large-format book introduces a cornucopia of ideas for outdoor activities, along with mesmerizing color photos of children and teens creatively enjoying themselves in fields, woods, backyards, and at rivers and beaches. . . . From skimming stones to making leaf masks to whittling walking sticks to following treasure trails, here's an enticing array of ideas for outdoor fun and wilderness discovery." Booklist

Ferrer, J. J.

The **art** of stone skipping and other fun old-time games; stoopball, jacks, string games, coin flipping, line baseball, jump rope, and more. by J.J. Ferrer; illustrated by Todd Dakins. Charlesbridge Pub., Inc. 2012 192 p. (paperback) $14.95

Grades: K 1 2 3 4 5 6 7 8 9 10 11 12 Adult   **790.1**

    1. Games

    ISBN 1936140748; 9781936140749

                            LC 2012015052

This book, by J. J. Ferrer, offers a "collection of timeless games that guarantees kids a good time- by themselves, with a group of friends, or with family. Includes ball games . . . , card games . . . , sack races, and old favorites such as Duck, Duck, Goose and Red Rover. There is also a chapter for car games. Simple instructions explain the rules, how many people can play, the object of the game, and what you need." (Publisher's note)

    Includes bibliographical references and index.

Hines-Stephens, Sarah

Show off; how to do absolutely everything one step at a time. [by] Sarah Hines Stephens and Bethany Mann. Candlewick Press 2009 224p il $18.99

Grades: 5 6 7 8   **790.1**

    1. Amusements 2. Handicraft 3. Recreation

    ISBN 978-0-7636-4599-1; 0-7636-4599-0

                            LC 2009015847

"This lively illustrated activity book delivers concise instructions for a variety of indoor and outdoor activities. Projects include crafts, pranks and magic tricks; ideas for nature exploration; and other purely entertaining feats. . . .

The instructions are heavy on graphics and light on detail, making for an eye-catching but potentially frustrating experience. But readers should enjoy the irreverence and variety." Publ Wkly

Rowell, Victoria

Tag, toss & run; 40 classic lawn games. Paul Tukey & Victoria Rowell. Storey Pub. 2012 207 p. (pbk.: alk. paper) $14.95

Grades: Adult Professional **790.1**
    1. Games 2. Outdoor recreation 3. Outdoor games
    ISBN 1603425608; 9781603425605

                            LC 2011049410

This book on "family lawn games" presents a "guide to 40 time-tested favorites -- from classics like capture the flag, croquet, badminton, and bocce to the lesser-known Cherokee marbles, cornhole, and Kubb. The authors offer a quick overview of the basic structure of each game, as well as strategies for playing and tips for creating fun variations." (Publisher's note)

Includes bibliographical references

791   Public performances

Lusted, Marcia Amidon

Entertainment. ABDO Pub. Company 2011 112p il (Inside the industry) $23.95

Grades: 5 6 7 8 **791**
    1. Performing arts -- Vocational guidance
    ISBN 978-1-61714-799-9; 1-61714-799-0

                            LC 2010041255

This "well-designed [book describes] a variety of careers in [entertainment]. Because [it helps] readers assess if these positions are suitable for their personality types and backgrounds, the [title is a] good [choice] for career exploration and self-discovery. [It is] also useful for research and reports. . . . Sidebars and full-color photos appear throughout." SLJ

Includes bibliographical references

791.43   Motion pictures

Baker, Frank W.

Coming distractions; questioning movies. by Frank W. Baker. Fact Finders 2007 32p (Media literacy) lib bdg $22.60; pa $7.95

Grades: 4 5 6 7 **791.43**
    1. Motion pictures
    ISBN 978-0-7368-6766-5 lib bdg; 0-7368-6766-X lib bdg; 978-0-7368-7862-3 pa; 0-7368-7862-9 pa

                            LC 2006021441

This is a "solid title. . . . The book's punchy headlines, sound-bite-style text, and bold design will help hold readers' attention." Booklist

Includes bibliographical references

Bliss, John

Art that moves; animation around the world. Raintree 2011 32p il (Culture in action) lib bdg $29

Grades: 5 6 7 8 **791.43**
    1. Animated films
    ISBN 978-1-4109-3922-7; 1-4109-3922-7

                            LC 2009051125

This "is a good choice for children interested in animated movies. Bliss looks at techniques from the early beginnings to modern times and mentions recent film releases such as Cars (2006) and Where the Wild Things Are (2010). . . . [This volume is] quick, interesting, up-to-date . . . with plenty of supportive, captioned, full-color photographs. [It] also [provides] related project suggestions." SLJ

Includes bibliographical references

Cohn, Jessica

Animator. Gareth Stevens Pub. 2010 32p il (Cool careers: cutting edge) lib bdg $26; pa $8.95

Grades: 4 5 6 **791.43**
    1. Vocational guidance 2. Animation (Cinematography)
    ISBN 978-1-4339-1953-4 lib bdg; 1-4339-1953-2 lib bdg; 978-1-4339-2152-0 pa; 1-4339-2152-9 pa

                            LC 2009002006

Describes the work of an animator.

This title offers "clear, solid information in a large font. . . . [This] short [book is] packed with relevant, current material." SLJ

Includes glossary and bibliographical references

Finch, Christopher

The **art** of Walt Disney; from Mickey Mouse to the Magic Kingdoms. rev and expanded ed; Harry N. Abrams 2004 504p il $60

Grades: 7 8 9 10 **791.43**
    1. Animators 2. Motion picture producers 3. Motion picture executives
    ISBN 0-8109-4964-4

                            LC 2004-10016

First published 1973

This is the "story of Walt Disney and the company he built, from Mickey Mouse to animated feature films to theme parks. The text is illustrated with more than 800 illustrations." Publisher's note

Indovino, Shaina Carmel

Dracula and beyond; famous vampires & werewolves in literature and film. Mason Crest Publishers 2011 63p il (The making of a monster: vampires & werewolves) lib bdg $22.95; pa $9.95

Grades: 7 8 9 10 **791.43**
    1. Vampires 2. Werewolves 3. Vampires in literature 4. Horror fiction -- History and criticism
    ISBN 978-1-4222-1803-7 lib bdg; 1-4222-1803-1 lib bdg; 978-1-4222-1956-0 pa; 1-4222-1956-9 pa

                            LC 2010020684

Explores portrayals of vampires and werewolves in literature and movies.

"The writing is engaging and accessible, and peppered easily with teen vernacular. . . . Large, clear photographs and period and contemporary drawings appear on every other page or so. . . . First-rate entertainment." SLJ

Includes glossary and bibliographical references

Kinney, Jeff

The **wimpy** kid movie diary; how Greg Heffley went Hollywood. Amulet Books 2010 199p il $14.95

Grades: 4 5 6 7   **791.43**

    1. Motion pictures -- Production and direction
    ISBN 978-0-8109-9616-8; 0-8109-9616-2
                   LC 2010001859

"Diary of a Wimpy Kid was made into a movie in 2010. The process is here chronicled, through text, photos, and illustrations. Many details are included, from the way the actors were chosen to how the moldy cheese was filmed. The process is explained clearly and will be interesting to new and seasoned Kid fans and future filmmakers alike." Horn Book Guide

Lace, William W.

Blacks in film; by William W. Lace. Lucent Books 2008 104p il (Lucent library of Black history) $32.45

Grades: 7 8 9 10   **791.43**

    1. African Americans in motion pictures
    ISBN 978-1-4205-0084-4; 1-4205-0084-8
                   LC 2008018289

"This volume on black actors in American cinema begins with the 'Toms' found in early silent films and goes all the way up to . . . Oscar winners Jamie Foxx and Morgan Freeman. . . . [The book includes] high quality film stills and boxed sections." Booklist

Includes bibliographical references

O'Brien, Lisa

Lights, camera, action! making movies and TV from the inside out. [by] Lisa O'Brien; illustrated by Stephen MacEachern. 2nd ed.; Maple Tree Press 2007 64p il $21.95; pa $12.95

Grades: 4 5 6 7   **791.43**

    1. Acting 2. Motion pictures -- Production and direction
    ISBN 978-1-897066-88-1; 1-897066-88-0; 978-1-897066-89-8 pa; 1-897066-89-9 pa
    First published 1998 by Firefly Books

This book "follows Johnny, a young aspiring actor, as he auditions for and gets a part in a new movie called The Mists of Time. Author Lisa O'Brien examines the development and production of movies from early concept through final production. Along the way, readers get a guided tour of the world of acting, from finding an agent, through to 'acting' an audition, to handling the media." Publisher's note

Reynolds, David West

Star Wars: the complete visual dictionary; written by David West Reynolds (episodes I, II and IV-VI) and James Luceno (episode III); updates and new material by Ryder Windham; special fabrications by Robert E. Barnes . . . [et. al.]; new photography by Alex Ivanov. 1st American ed.; DK Pub. 2006 270p il $40

Grades: 6 7 8 9 10 11 12 Adult   **791.43**

    1. Star Wars films
    ISBN 0-7566-2238-7; 978-0-7566-2238-1
                   LC 2006298949

Material in this book was originally published in various DK Pub. publications, 1998-2005

"Star Wars Complete Visual Dictionary brings together all four . . . titles from The Visual Dictionary series (Episode I-III and the Trilogy) in one volume. . . . This book is [a] comprehensive visual guide to every character, weapon, starship, droid, creature and alien in the Star Wars universe." Publisher's note

Seba, Jaime

Gay characters in theatre, movies, and television: new roles, new attitudes; by Jaime A. Seba. Mason Crest Publishers 2011 64p il (Gallup's guide to modern gay, lesbian, and transgender lifestyle) lib bdg $22.95; pa $9.95

Grades: 8 9 10 11 12   **791.43**

    1. Gay men 2. Lesbians 3. Homosexuality in literature 4. Homosexuality on television 5. Homosexuality in motion pictures
    ISBN 978-1-4222-2012-2 lib bdg; 1-4222-2012-5 lib bdg; 978-1-4222-2013-9 pa; 1-4222-2013-3 pa
                   LC 2010017051

"This slender, accessible overview uses numerous examples, past and present, to show how the depiction of gay, lesbian, bisexual, and transgender (GLBT) characters in the entertainment industry affects popular culture and has helped push growing acceptance into the mainstream. . . . The book features an open, inviting format, and portraits, reproduced posters, and short profiles of GLTB stars . . . add to the title's browsability." Booklist

Includes bibliographical references

Woog, Adam

Vampires in the movies. ReferencePoint Press, Inc. 2010 80p il (The vampire library) $26.95

Grades: 7 8 9 10   **791.43**

    1. Vampires 2. Motion pictures -- History and criticism
    ISBN 978-1-60152-135-4; 1-60152-135-9
                   LC 2010017982

Examines different ways vampires have been presented throughout history in films, from the early-twentieth century for Lugosi films to the present-day mania for Twilight and other modern takes.

"Energetic and suprisingly educational, this lively [book] seizes upon a zietgeist topic and takes it as far as possible." Booklist

Includes bibliographical references

791.5   Puppetry and toy theaters

Kennedy, John E.

   ★ **Puppet** planet. North Light Books 2006 79p il $16.99

Grades: 4 5 6 7   **791.5**

    1. Puppets and puppet plays
    ISBN 978-1-58180-794-3; 1-58180-794-5
                   LC 2005033711

This book offers twelve "puppet projects, each using a variety of techniques, [and] features 'action panels' so readers can see how each puppet comes to life. [It also] Includes staging ideas to play up each project's uniqueness." Publisher's note

791.8 Animal performances

Collard III, Sneed B.

The **world** famous Miles City Bucking Horse Sale. Bucking Horse Books 2010 64p il $18
Grades: 5 6 7 8 **791.8**
1. Horses 2. Rodeos
ISBN 978-0-9844460-0-1

"Collard takes readers inside the Miles City [Montana] Bucking Horse Sale, a four-day event that draws visitors from across the country. Started in 1951 as a sale of wild horses, it's evolved into a jamboree of music, rodeo, food, contests, and a parade. . . . Plenty of action-filled color photographs break up the narrative. . . . Handsomely designed, . . . this is a fascinating look at a fresh topic."

"Collard takes readers inside the Miles City [Montana] Bucking Horse Sale, a four-day event that draws visitors from across the country. Started in 1951 as a sale of wild horses, it's evolved into a jamboree of music, rodeo, food, contests, and a parade. . . . Plenty of action-filled color photographs break up the narrative. . . . Handsomely designed, . . . this is a fascinating look at a fresh topic." Booklist

Includes glossary

Grayson, Robert

Performers. Marshall Cavendish Benchmark 2010 64p il (Working animals) lib bdg $28.50
Grades: 4 5 6 7 **791.8**
1. Animals in entertainment
ISBN 978-1-60870-165-0 lib bdg; 1-60870-165-4 lib bdg

LC 2010006893

"Describes the role of animals in movies, sporting events, and various competitions." Publisher's note

Includes glossary and bibliographical references

Laidlaw, Rob

On parade; the hidden world of animals in entertainment. Fitzhenry & Whiteside 2010 55p il $19.95
Grades: 4 5 6 **791.8**
1. Zoos 2. Circus 3. Animal welfare 4. Animals in entertainment
ISBN 978-1-55455-143-9; 1-55455-143-9

This book examines animals at the zoo and circus, animals working in movies and television, violence in the world of performing animals and offers ways to improve conditions and prevent animal abuse.

The author's "clearly argued text; crisp, captioned color photos; and appended list of organizations make this an important source for animal advocates." Booklist

792 Stage presentations

Becker, Helaine

Funny business; clowning around, practical jokes, cool comedy, cartooning, and more . . . illustrated by Claudia Dávila. Maple Tree 2005 160p il $21.95; pa $9.95
Grades: 5 6 7 8 **792**
1. Clowns 2. Cartooning 3. Wit and humor 4. Cartoons and comics
ISBN 1-897066-40-6; 1-897066-41-4 pa

"Becker offers funny facts, an informative diagram showing what goes on in the body when you laugh, brief discussions of different types of humor (situation comedy, parody, farce, riddles, puns), a How Funny Are You? quiz, tips and timing for standup routines, body lingo, props, six improvisation games, clowning material, and more. For kids who want to learn how to juggle, tell jokes, or use sight-gag items, it's all here. Cartooning is explained as well." SLJ

Belli, Mary Lou

Acting for young actors; the ultimate teen guide. [by] Mary Lou Belli & Dinah Lenney. Back Stage Books 2006 205p il pa $16.96
Grades: 7 8 9 10 11 12 **792**
1. Acting
ISBN 978-0-8230-4947-9 pa; 0-8230-4947-7 pa

LC 2006007265

"Belli and Lenney, an Emmy-winning director of Girlfriends and a Yale-educated ER actress offer stagestruck teens trunks-full of sound advice packaged with a conversational tone and grounded experience. . . . The authors offer a series of questions for character analysis; suggested readings and viewings abound. . . . The handbook succeeds at communicating clearly without talking down to readers; engaging prose makes it an ideal text for classes and teens who want commonsense career prep and insight." Voice Youth Advocates

Includes bibliographical references

Kenney, Karen Latchana

Cool costumes; how to stage your very own show. ABDO Pub. Company 2010 32p il (Cool performances) lib bdg $17.95
Grades: 4 5 6 **792**
1. Costume 2. Theater
ISBN 978-1-60453-714-7 lib bdg; 1-60453-714-0 lib bdg

LC 2009-1751

Includes step-by-step instructions on how to create royalty robes, animal ears, baseball T-Shirts and more

"Simple language, colorful page design, and detailed step-by-step photos invite children to gather some easily available household items, apply paint and some imagination, and put on a play—or just play." SLJ

Includes glossary and webliography

Cool makeup; how to stage your very own show. ABDO Pub. Company 2010 32p il (Cool performances) lib bdg $17.95

Grades: 4 5 6   792

1. Theatrical makeup

ISBN 978-1-60453-715-4 lib bdg; 1-60453-715-9 lib bdg

LC 2009-1752

Offers instructions and step-by-step pictures to reveal how theatrical makeup can create the illusion of facial hair, bruises and wounds, animals, skeletons, or old age.

"Simple language, colorful page design, and detailed step-by-step photos invite children to gather some easily available household items, apply paint and some imagination, and put on a play—or just play." SLJ

Includes glossary and webliography

Cool productions; how to stage your very own show. ABDO Pub. Co. 2010 32p il (Cool performances) lib bdg $17.95

Grades: 4 5 6   792

1. Theater -- Production and direction

ISBN 978-1-60453-716-1 lib bdg; 1-60453-716-7 lib bdg

LC 2009-405

Includes step-by-step instructions on how to make flyers, tickets, programs and more

"Simple language, colorful page design, and detailed step-by-step photos invite children to gather some easily available household items, apply paint and some imagination, and put on a play—or just play." SLJ

Includes glossary

Cool scripts & acting; how to stage your very own show. ABDO Pub. Company 2010 32p il (Cool performances) lib bdg $17.95

Grades: 4 5 6   792

1. Acting 2. Drama -- Technique 3. Theater -- Production and direction

ISBN 978-1-60453-717-8 lib bdg; 1-60453-717-5 lib bdg

LC 2009-406

Includes step-by-step instructions on how to write a script, use stage directions, play acting games and more

"Simple language, colorful page design, and detailed step-by-step photos invite children to gather some easily available household items, apply paint and some imagination, and put on a play—or just play." SLJ

Includes glossary

Cool sets & props; how to stage your very own show. ABDO Pub. Company 2010 32p il (Cool performances) lib bdg $17.95

Grades: 4 5 6   792

1. Theaters -- Stage setting and scenery

ISBN 978-1-60453-718-5 lib bdg; 1-60453-718-3 lib bdg

LC 2009-408

"This volume focuses on the primarily cardboard and paper objects that motivated youngsters can turn into backdrops, set pieces, and props. Photo examples set the bar high (though many are achievable). It's fairly challenging stuff, but the information is metered out so ef-ficiently that patience, not artistic ability, will be the key to success." Booklist

Includes glossary and webliography

Cool special effects; how to stage your very own show. ABDO Pub. Company 2010 32p il (Cool performances) lib bdg $17.95

Grades: 4 5 6   792

1. Stage lighting 2. Theaters -- Stage setting and scenery

ISBN 978-1-60453-719-2 lib bdg; 1-60453-719-1 lib bdg

LC 2009-1753

Offers instructions on creating special effects for a theatrical production, including information on different light effects, keeping a prompt book, and recording your own sound effects

"Simple language, colorful page design, and detailed step-by-step photos invite children to gather some easily available household items, apply paint and some imagination, and put on a play—or just play." SLJ

Includes glossary and webliography

Lamedman, Debbie

The **ultimate** audition book for teens; 111 one-minute monologues. Smith & Kraus (Young actor series)

Grades: 7 8 9 10 11 12   792

1. Acting 2. Monologues 3. Auditions 4. Acting -- Auditions

A series of collections of 111 original monologues, all about one minute long, to be used by male and female teenage actors in auditions.

"Some suggestive sexual situations described here will not be acceptable in some classrooms. Drama teachers may, however, welcome some of this material for beginning acting students." Book Rep [review of volume one]

Millennium monologs; 95 contemporary characterizations for young actors. edited by Gerald Lee Ratliff. Meriwether 2002 261p pa $15.95

Grades: 8 9 10 11 12   792

1. Acting 2. Monologues 3. American drama -- Collections

ISBN 1-56608-082-7

LC 2002-13009

An anthology of monologues by contemporary writers, divided into four categories: "Hope and Longing," "Spirit and Soul," "Fun and Fantasy," and "Doubt and Despair." Includes audition techniques

"This fine collection of American monologues is notable for its diversity as well as for the high quality of the material." Booklist

Rogers, Barb

Costumes, accessories, props, and stage illusions made easy. Meriwether Pub. 2005 205p il pa $19.95

Grades: 8 9 10 11 12 **792**
1. Costume 2. Theater -- Production and direction
ISBN 978-1-56608-103-0; 1-56608-103-3

LC 2005-4359

This book details ways to make theater "costumes with simple tools such as scissors, glue guns, and paint. In addition, there are chapters on how to make hats, gloves, armor, and animal heads, as well as other props and accessories from rummage-sale finds and a little imagination. . . . This is a useful volume for schools and community theaters with little or no budgets for costumes and props." SLJ

Includes bibliographical references

Schumacher, Thomas L.
How does the show go on? an introduction to the theater. by Thomas Schumacher with Jeff Kurtti. 2nd ed; Disney 2008 128p il $22.95
Grades: 4 5 6 7 **792**
1. Theater
ISBN 978-1-4231-2031-5; 1-4231-2031-0
"Filled with lavish color photos of Disney theater productions, this eye-catching volume has clever chapter titles, beginning with 'Overture,' which tells about 'styles of theaters' and 'kinds of shows.' In 'Act One' and 'Act Two,' aspects of the front and back of the house are discussed, including the marquee, the box office, props, special effects, and so on. Interspersed throughout the facts and photos are 'Stage Notes,' where bits of trivia are doled out." SLJ

Skog, Jason
Acting; a practical guide to pursuing the art. Compass Point Books 2010 48p il (Performing arts) lib bdg $28.65
Grades: 5 6 7 8 **792**
1. Acting 2. Vocational guidance
ISBN 978-0-7565-4364-8 lib bdg; 0-7565-4364-9 lib bdg

LC 2010012604

A guide for those interested in a career in acting, and includes tips on education, technique, and more.
"Meant for students contemplating a career in the field . . . [this book goes] beyond basic introductions and into more detail about what it takes to make it as a professional. . . . [The author maintains] . . . a frank, realistic tone, stressing the importance of hard work and dedication. Great [resource] . . . for those wanting to make their passions more than just a hobby." SLJ

Includes glossary and bibliographical references

Underwood, Deborah
Staging a play. Raintree 2009 32p il (Culture in action) $28.21; pa $7.99
Grades: 5 6 7 8 **792**
1. Theater -- Production and direction
ISBN 978-1-4109-3396-6; 1-4109-3396-2; 978-1-4109-3413-0 pa; 1-4109-3413-6 pa

LC 2009000417

This "discusses the various professionals involved in a production, such as actors, costume designers, prop masters, and stage handlers. Well organized and with bright, colorful

photography, [this] introductory [title gives] readers good basic knowledge." SLJ

Includes glossary and bibliographical references

792.09 History, geographic treatment, biography

Aliki
★ **William** Shakespeare & the Globe; written & illustrated by Aliki. HarperCollins Pubs. 1999 48p il hardcover o.p. pa $6.99
Grades: 4 5 6 7 8 9 **792.09**
1. Poets 2. Authors 3. Dramatists 4. Theaters -- England -- London -- Reconstruction 5. Theater -- England -- London -- History -- 16th century
ISBN 0-06-027820-X; 0-06-443722-1 pa

LC 98-7903

"A logically organized and engaging text, plenty of detailed illustrations with informative captions, and a clean design provide a fine introduction to both bard and theater." Horn Book Guide

Currie, Stephen
An **actor** on the Elizabethan stage. Lucent Bks. 2003 96p il maps (Working life) $27.45
Grades: 6 7 8 9 **792.09**
1. Theater -- History 2. Theater -- England -- History -- 16th century
ISBN 1-59018-174-3

LC 2002-9460

Discusses various aspects of theatrical life, including staging and performance, financing, types of acting troupes, and social and economic influences
This is "well written and the [author draws on quotes] from many primary sources." Libr Media Connect

Includes bibliographical references

792.6 Musical plays

Amendola, Dana
★ A **day** at the New Amsterdam Theatre; photos by Gino Domenico; written by Dana Amendola. Disney Editions 2004 125p il $24.95
Grades: 4 5 6 7 **792.6**
1. Theater
ISBN 0-7868-5438-3
"This title covers a day in the life of Disney's The Lion King, the long-running Broadway musical. . . . A clock in a corner of each spread guides readers through the day as box-office personnel, makeup designers, dancers, actors, cleaning staff, and others do their jobs. Each spread includes several full-color photos that are often gritty, sometimes glamorous. . . . This unique volume provides an honest, realistic, eye-opening look at the behind-the-scenes work that goes into the running of a Broadway show." SLJ

Bezdecheck, Bethany
Directing. Rosen Pub. 2009 64p il (High school musicals) lib bdg $21.95

Grades: 7 8 9 10   **792.6**
    1. Musicals -- Production and direction
ISBN 978-1-4358-5259-4 lib bdg; 1-4358-5259-1
lib bdg
      LC 2008041598
"Bezdecheck lays out the process of directing a musical
production, from play selection to auditions to dress rehearsals. . . . There's some good, practical advice here." Booklist
    Includes bibliographical references

Michael, Ted
    So you wanna be a superstar? the ultimate au-
dition guide. by Ted Michael; with contributions by
Nic Cory & Mara Jill Herman; introduction by Lea
Salonga; edited by Lisa Cheng. RP Kids 2012 151
(paperback) $10.95; (ebook) $10.95
Grades: 4 5 6 7 8   **792.6**
    1. Auditions 2. Voice culture
ISBN 0762446102; 9780762446100; 9780762447015
pdf
      LC 2012932845
    This book by Ted Michael presents a guide for "hopeful
musical theater, show choir, a cappella, and glee club singers" with advice designed to help readers "train [their] vocal
cords, pick the right audition material, and become comfortable with the spotlight. Interactive quizzes . . . and words
of advice from industry professionals" are also included.
(Publisher's note)

792.8   Ballet and modern dance

Augustyn, Frank
    ★ **Footnotes**; dancing the world's best-loved
ballets. [by] Frank Augustyn and Shelley Tanaka.
Millbrook Press 2001 94p il $17.95
Grades: 5 6 7 8   **792.8**
    1. Ballet
ISBN 0-7613-1646-9
      LC 00-50075
"Fine photographs, most in color, add enormously to the
book's appeal. A well-crafted, readable volume." Booklist

Freedman, Russell
    ★ **Martha** Graham, a dancer's life. Clarion Bks.
1998 175p il $18
Grades: 7 8 9 10   **792.8**
    1. Dancers 2. Modern dance 3. Choreographers 4.
Dance teachers 5. Women dancers -- United States
-- Biography 6. Choreographers -- United States --
Biography
ISBN 0-395-74655-8
      LC 97-15832
    A photo-biography of the American dancer, teacher, and
choreographer who was born in Pittsburgh in 1895 and who
became a leading figure in the world of modern dance
    "A showstopping biography that captures its dynamic
subject's personality, vision, and artistry." SLJ
    Includes bibliographical references

Kupesic, Rajka
    The **white** ballets. Tundra Books 2011 40p il
$19.95
Grades: 4 5 6 7   **792.8**
    1. Ballet -- Stories, plots, etc.
ISBN 978-0-88776-923-8; 0-88776-923-3
    This retells the stories of Swan Lake, Giselle, and La
Bayadère and includes information and comments on the
three ballets.
    "The tales are well told, and the author, a former balle-
rina, provides information on the history of the ballet. Each
painting in gold leaf and oil represents a scene from one of
the ballets. The richly colored illustrations are very stylized
with graceful figures dressed in flowing, romantic costumes,
and Kupesic elaborates on the details, symbols, and characters in her artwork. . . . For ballet enthusiasts this is a unique
look at these classics." SLJ

Lee, Laura
    A **child's** introduction to ballet; the stories, mu-
sic and magic of classical dance. [by] Laura Lee; illustrated by Meredith Hamilton. Black Dog & Leventhal Publishers 2007 96p il $19.95
Grades: 4 5 6 7 8   **792.8**
    1. Ballet
ISBN 978-1-57912-699-5; 1-57912-699-5
      LC 2006048867
    "This lively and attractive volume delves into the his-
tory of ballet from its beginnings in Italy through the 20th
century. . . . Detailed and well-written descriptions of 25 of
the most famous and influential ballets are provided along
with colorful illustrations of scenes. A CD presents excerpts
from them and the author poses some questions and gives
some insights to think about as one listens to the music." SLJ

Marsico, Katie
    Choreographer. Cherry Lake Pub. 2011 32p il
(Cool arts careers) lib bdg $18.95
Grades: 4 5 6 7   **792.8**
    1. Dance 2. Choreographers 3. Vocational guidance
ISBN 978-1-61080-136-2; 1-61080-136-9
      LC 2011001170
    "Illustrated with color photos of the famous, the young,
and the fabulously festooned, this is a sturdy presentation
of facts and case studies that will bring the process of professional choreography home to those students considering
such a competitive and demanding career." Booklist
    Includes bibliographical references

Schorer, Suki
    Put your best foot forward; a young dancer's
guide to life. by Suki Schorer and the School of
American Ballet; illustrations by Donna Ingemanson.
Workman Publishing 2005 96p il pa $9.95
Grades: 4 5 6 7   **792.8**
    1. Ballet
ISBN 978-0-7611-3795-5 pa; 0-7611-3795-5 pa
      LC 2005051428
    "The words of counsel proffered by the author, who
was a principal dancer for the New York City Ballet and is
a teacher at the School of American Ballet, are engaging,

imaginative, and right on target. . . . Practical tips such as essentials that need to be in your bag and behavioral advice such as being grateful for criticism are nicely woven into the book. The photographs, mainly of female dancers, are clear and colorful. These words of wisdom will keep dancers on their toes and stretching their minds and hearts." SLJ

Solway, Andrew

Modern dance; [by] Andrew Solway. Heinemann Library 2009 48p il (Dance) lib bdg $31.43

Grades: 4 5 6 7 8   **792.8**

    1. Modern dance

    ISBN 978-1-4329-1376-2 lib bdg; 1-4329-1376-X lib bdg

                    LC 2008-14295

This book "is enhanced by eye-catching photography that shows costumes, famous dancers, technique and people dancing. . . . [Those] thinking about dance as a career will find this . . . helpful. . . . [This] is a definite must have." Libr Media Connect

Includes glossary and bibliographical references

792.802   Specific aspects of ballet and modern dance

Bernstein, Richard

A **girl** named Faithful Plum; Richard Bernstein. Alfred A. Knopf Books for Young Readers 2011 270p. ill. $15.99; lib bdg $18.99

Grades: 7 8 9 10 11 12   **792.802**

    1. Dancers 2. Arts -- China 3. Dance directors

    ISBN 978-0-375-86960-0; 0-375-86960-3; 978-0-375-96960-7 lib bdg; 0-375-96960-8 lib bdg

                    LC 2010048722

"In 1978, an 11-year-old girl fights poverty and prejudice with gutsy perseverance and talent to fulfill her dream of studying at the Beijing Dance Academy. . . . Faithful Plum, or Zhongmei, lives in a remote area of China near Siberia. . . . She loves to dance, though, and upon hearing that the Academy is holding national auditions she sets her mind on going. . . . After a horrific three-day journey by trains and buses, Zhongmei comes through the difficult audition only to face an extreme daily regimen of exercise and instruction, an appallingly rigid dormitory supervisor and a ballet teacher scarred by the Cultural Revolution. . . . The conversations ring true, albeit 'imagined,' and events have been compressed to keep the pace flowing. A fascinating and memorable account of a life and times difficult to imagine today." Kirkus

792.9   Stage productions

Cox, Carole

Shakespeare kids; performing his plays, speaking his words. Libraries Unlimited 2010 xx, 126p il pa $30

Grades: Adult Professional   **792.9**

    1. Poets 2. Authors 3. Dramatists 4. Theater --

Production and direction

    ISBN 978-1-59158-838-2 pa; 1-59158-838-3 pa

                    LC 2009041731

This is a "a practical guide for performing Shakespeare's plays, albeit in condensed form, without changing his poetic dialogue. . . . Cox gears her work to teachers of students in grades 3-8, librarians, or adults leading recreational programs, providing precise, detailed instructions on all facets of youth-oriented Shakespearean play production. . . . The text is clear and concise . . . Black-and-white photos capture specific moments that illustrate the performers' enthusiasm." SLJ

Includes bibliographical references

793.3   Social, folk, national dancing

Ancona, George

★ **Ole!** Flamenco. Lee & Low 2010 un il map $19.95

Grades: 5 6 7 8   **793.3**

    1. Flamenco

    ISBN 978-1-60060-361-7; 1-60060-361-0

                    LC 2010-22272

Ancona tells "the story of flamenco, an art form that's more than dancing and has been around for hundreds of years. He begins with a short introduction that chronicles his visit to Spain. . . . He then returns readers to Santa Fe, New Mexico, where a group of young people are learning flamenco. A helpful map traces the art form's roots, while the text explains both the history of the Gypsies and flamenco. Full-color photographs capture the excitement and dazzle. . . . All aspects of flamenco are explored, including movements, facial expressions, and sound effects." Booklist

Includes glossary and bibliographical references

Fishkin, Rebecca Love

Dance; a practical guide to pursuing the art. content adviser, Hannah Seidel and Chris Ferris and dancers; reading adviser, Alexa L. Sandmann. Compass Point Books 2011 48p il (Performing arts) lib bdg $28.65

Grades: 5 6 7 8   **793.3**

    1. Dance 2. Vocational guidance

    ISBN 978-0-7565-4363-1 lib bdg; 0-7565-4363-0 lib bdg

                    LC 2010012605

This guide about a career in dance includes tips on education, technique, and more.

"Meant for students contemplating a career in the field . . . [this book goes] beyond basic introductions and into more detail about what it takes to make it as a professional. . . . [The author maintains] . . . a frank, realistic tone, stressing the importance of hard work and dedication. Great [resource] . . . for those wanting to make their passions more than just a hobby." SLJ

Includes glossary and bibliographical references

Garofoli, Wendy

Hip-hop dancing. Capstone Press 2011 4v il lib bdg ea $30.65

Grades: 4 5 6   793.3
1. Dance 2. Hip-hop
ISBN 978-1-4296-5484-5 v1; 1-4296-5484-5 v1;
978-1-4296-5485-2 v2; 1-4296-5485-6 v2; 978-1-
4296-5486-9 v3; 1-4296-5486-9 v3; 978-1-4296-
5487-6 v4; 1-4296-5487-2 v4
LC 2010030394
Provides instructions for joining or starting a hip-hop
dance crew, and includes information about real-life crews.
"These volumes cover the basic moves as well as more
detailed movements often seen on television programs.
. . . Everything about the set is jazzy and current. Sentences are short and direct, with a small-sized font detailing step-by-step instructions and fact boxes extending the
information." Booklist
Includes bibliographical references

Haney, Johannah
Capoeira. Marshall Cavendish Benchmark 2011
47p il (Martial arts in action) $29.93
Grades: 4 5 6 7   793.3
1. Capoeira (Dance)
ISBN 978-0-7614-4932-4; 978-1-6087-0362-3 e-book
LC 2010013829
This describes the history, equipment, and technique
of capoeira.
This treats "martial arts with the dignity that serious
enthusiasts bring to the sport. . . . Illustrations include not
only photos of modern gear and from films but also historical images." Booklist

Smith, Karen Lynn
Popular dance; from ballroom to hip-hop. consulting editor, Elizabeth A. Hanley; foreword by
Jacques D'Amboisse. Chelsea House Publishers
2010 165p il (World of dance) lib bdg $35
Grades: 6 7 8 9   793.3
1. Dance
ISBN 978-1-60413-484-1; 1-60413-484-4
LC 2009053491
"Students who want a deeper and more comprehensive
understanding of the origins and present status of various
styles [of popular dance] will find this volume useful. It takes
readers from the saltarello and galliard of the Renaissance to
present-day hip-hop and zumba. . . . It has an encyclopedic
approach as it identifies and defines the dances and touches
on their cultural influences. . . . This volume would be a
valuable resource for research and casual browsing." SLJ
Includes glossary and bibliographical references

793.73 Puzzles and puzzle games

Moscovich, Ivan
Big book of brain games; 1000 playthinks of art,
mathematics & science. by Ivan Moscovich; foreword by Ian Stewart; illustrated by Tim Robinson.
Workman Pub. 2006 420p il pa $22.95

Grades: 7 8 9 10   793.73
1. Scientific recreations
ISBN 0-7611-3466-2 pa; 978-0-7611-3466-4 pa
LC 2006299017
First published 2001 with title: 1000 playthinks: puzzles,
paradoxes, illusions & games
This is a "collection of 1,000 challenges, puzzles, riddles, illusions. . . . Twelve basic categories include Geometry, Patterns, Numbers, Logic and Probability, and Perception. [A] key at the top of each game ranks its difficulty on a
scale of 1 to 10, while indices in the back cross-reference the
puzzles." Publisher's note
Includes bibliographical references

793.74 Mathematical games and recreations

Ball, Johnny
Go figure! DK Pub. 2005 96p il map $15.99
Grades: 4 5 6 7   793.74
1. Mathematics 2. Mathematical recreations
ISBN 0-7566-1374-4
A collection of math activities that include brainteasers,
magic tricks, and mind-reading games
"A dynamic book. . . . Blocks of color, diagrams, and
photo collages contribute to the exciting layout. . . . A fun
romp for number and puzzle lovers." SLJ

793.8 Magic and related activities

Jennings, Madeleine
Magic step-by-step; [by] Madeleine Jennings
and Colin Francome. Rosen Central 2010 89p il
(Skills in motion) lib bdg $31.95
Grades: 5 6 7 8   793.8
1. Magic tricks
ISBN 978-1-4358-3363-0; 1-4358-3363-5
LC 2009-13221
Presents step-by-step instructions on performing magic
tricks, including card tricks, rope tricks, and sleight of hand.
"Colorful photographs show the entire movement of
each skill presented, giving new meaning to the term 'step-
by-step.' Progression borders at the bottom of the pages
highlight the salient points to notice in performing each skill
from beginning to end." SLJ
Includes bibliographical references

793.8092 Magicians (Performers)

Jarrow, Gail
★ The **amazing** Harry Kellar; great American
magician. Gail G. Jarrow. Calkins Creek 2012 96
p. col. ill. $17.95
Grades: 3 4 5 6 7 8   793.8092
1. Magicians 2. Optical illusions
ISBN 1590788656; 9781590788653
LC 2011940465
This book is a biography of Harry Keller (later Kellar),
"the first dean of the Society of American Magicians, a man

[magician Harry] Houdini regarded as a mentor. . . . Few secrets of the illusions are revealed here, but [Gail] Jarrow makes it clear that it was Kellar's art that made them seem like real magic." The book also includes "[d]ozens of . . . Kellar posters" and a "timeline, bibliography, [and] annotated sources." (Kirkus)

794.1   Chess

Basman, Michael

Chess for kids; written by Michael Basman. Dorling Kindersley 2001 45p il $12.99; pa $6.99
Grades: 4 5 6 7   **794.1**
  1. Chess 2. Chess for children
  ISBN 0-7894-6540-X; 0-7566-1807-X pa
                                         LC 00-59018
This guide to chess explains the rudiments of the game, techniques and winning strategies
  "A solid introduction for novices and good for skilled players wanting to develop their strategies and find out about chess clubs and tournaments." Booklist

King, Daniel

  ★ **Chess**; from first moves to checkmate. New ed.; Kingfisher 2010 64p il pa $8.99
Grades: 5 6 7 8 9 10 11 12   **794.1**
  1. Chess
  ISBN 978-0-7534-1930-4
  First published 2000
Introduces the rules and strategies of chess, as well as its history and some of the great players and matches.

794.8   Electronic games

Egan, Jill

  How video game designers use math; math curriculum consultant: Rhea A. Stewart. Chelsea Clubhouse 2010 32p il (Math in the real world) lib bdg $28
Grades: 4 5 6   **794.8**
  1. Mathematics 2. Video games 3. Computer games 4. Computer animation 5. Vocational guidance
  ISBN 978-1-60413-603-6 lib bdg; 1-60413-603-0 lib bdg
                                         LC 2009-24173
This describes how video game designers use math to create and produce their games and includes relevant math problems and information about how to become a video game designer
  Includes glossary and bibliographical references

Gerardi, David

  Careers in the computer game industry; [by] Dave Gerardi and Peter Suciu. Rosen Pub. Group 2005 144p il (Careers in the new economy) lib bdg $31.95

Grades: 6 7 8 9   **794.8**
  1. Computer games 2. Vocational guidance
  ISBN 1-4042-0252-8
                                         LC 2004-11258
"This is a realistic view of getting into the industry and the nonglamorous side of the business. The history of computer games and anecdotes of those currently working in the field will entertain and inform. Some of the topics included are: The Role of Game Testers, Computer Game Designers, Programmers, Graphic Artists and Animators, and The Future of Gaming. Qualifications and career growth are discussed." SLJ
  Includes bibliographical references

Jozefowicz, Chris

  Video game developer. Gareth Stevens Pub. 2010 32p il (Cool careers: cutting edge) lib bdg $26; pa $8.95
Grades: 4 5 6   **794.8**
  1. Video games 2. Computer games 3. Vocational guidance
  ISBN 978-1-4339-1958-9 lib bdg; 1-4339-1958-3 lib bdg; 978-1-4339-2157-5 pa; 1-4339-2157-X pa
                                         LC 2008053549
This introduction to video game developer careers offers "clear, solid information in a large font. . . . [This] short [book is] packed with relevant, current material." SLJ
  Includes glossary and bibliographical references

Oxlade, Chris

  Gaming technology. Smart Apple Media 2011 46p il (New technology) lib bdg $34.25
Grades: 4 5 6 7   **794.8**
  1. Video games 2. Computer games
  ISBN 9781599205311
                                         LC 2010044239
Describes the technology used for creating and playing video games. Includes information on how different platforms work and the direction video game technology may be going.
  This "offers a fine overview for reports, and its attractive design may also entice middle-grade readers to learn more." Booklist
  Includes glossary and bibliographical references

Parks, Peggy J., 1951-

  Video games. ReferencePoint Press 2008 104p il map (Compact research. Current issues) $25.95
Grades: 8 9 10 11 12   **794.8**
  1. Video games
  ISBN 978-1-60152-053-1; 1-60152-053-0
                                         LC 2007-49886
This "book opens with descriptions of the growing popularity of video games and the regulation and legislation of content and sales; ratings; connections with violent crime; and health effects, including addiction. An overview provides further background and context to these issues, and . . . chapters follow addressing related questions and providing other related material." SLJ
  Includes bibliographical references

Rauf, Don

Computer game designer; [by] Don Rauf and Monique Vescia. Ferguson 2007 un il (Virtual apprentice) lib bdg $29.95; pa $9.95

Grades: 6 7 8 9   **794.8**

   1. Computer games 2. Vocational guidance

   ISBN 978-0-8160-6754-1 lib bdg; 0-8160-6754-6 lib bdg; 0-8160-7550-6 pa; 978-0-8160-7550-8 pa

                LC 2006036565

"This in-depth introduction to the field of computer-game design offers specific practical advice. . . . Following a basic history of computer games and information about game types and rating levels, chapters, which are illustrated with many color photos, profile contemporary professionals and delve into current trends and the day-to-day work of game creators." Booklist

796   Athletic and outdoor sports and games

2009 ESPN sports almanac; Gerry Brown, Michael Morrison, editors. ESPN Books 2008 975p il pa $12.99

Grades: 8 9 10 11 12   **796**

   1. Sports 2. Reference books

   ISBN 978-0-345-51172-0

Annual. First published 2004 as a continuation of ESPN information please sports almanac

"The almanac examines in detail baseball, college football, professional football, college basketball, professional basketball, other college sports, and hockey. The editors touch upon many other less conventional sports, such as archery, dog sledding, gymnastics, auto racing, boxing, and so on. Each section looks at statistics of the game and offers an essay highlighting an important event of the past year. Related topics cover ballparks and arenas, halls of fame and awards, who's who, and business." Recomm Ref Books in Paperback. 3d edition

Sports illustrated 2011 almanac; by the editors of Sports illustrated. Time Home Entertainment 2010 559p il pa $14.99

Grades: 7 8 9 10 11 12 Adult   **796**

   1. Sports 2. Reference books

   ISBN 978-1-60320-863-5

Annual. First published 1991 with title: Sports illustrated . . . sports almanac

"Provides team and individual records and highlights for all major sports. . . . A brief essay opens the section on each sport, followed by page upon page of records, both current and retrospective. Interspersed throughout . . . are black-and-white and color photographs and notable quotations by sports figures." Am Ref Books Annu, 1993

Berman, Len

The **greatest** moments in sports. Sourcebooks 2009 136p il $16.99

Grades: 5 6 7 8   **796**

   1. Sports

   ISBN 978-1-4022-2099-9; 1-4022-2099-5

                LC 2009023686

"Forty years as a sportscaster gives Berman plenty of experience to choose the 25 greatest sports moments. His writing is lively, humorous, and informative—just right to sustain kids' (or adults') interest. Quality photos throughout are another plus. . . . An audio CD that includes many of the moments as they were broadcast live is part of the package." SLJ

Includes bibliographical references

The **greatest** moments in sports; upsets and underdogs. Len Berman. Sourcebooks Jabberwocky 2012 iv, 124 p.p ill. (hardcover) $19.99

Grades: 5 6 7 8   **796**

   1. Sports upsets -- History

   ISBN 140227226X; 9781402272264

In this sports book, "[Len] Berman offers his take on 25 of the most unexpected victories. . . . Youngsters learn about Billy Mills's surprise win of Olympic Gold for the 10,000 meter run in 1964, and Mexico's Little League World Series win of 1957. Text boxes . . . [present] biographical information and quick glimpses into the records of the 'champions' versus the 'underdogs.' The accompanying CD offers additional insight from Berman on 10 of the upsets." (School Library Journal)

Blumenthal, Karen

★ **Let** me play; the story of Title IX, the law that changed the future of girls in America. Atheneum Books for Young Readers 2005 152p il $19.95

Grades: 6 7 8 9 10   **796**

   1. Women athletes 2. Sex discrimination

   ISBN 0-689-85957-0

                LC 2004-1450

Title IX legislation assured "that 'no one could be closed out of any educational program or activity receiving federal money simply because of sex.' After explaining the genesis of the legislation, . . . Blumenthal discusses how evolving guidelines and interpretations brought girls' school athletic programs into its purview. Bull Cent Child Books

"The author looks at American women's evolving rights by focusing on the history and future of Title IX, which bans sex discrimination in U.S. education. . . . The images are . . . gripping, and relevant political cartoons and fact boxes add further interest. Few books cover the last few decades of American women's history with such clarity and detail." Booklist

Includes bibliographical references

Diagram Group

Sports rules on file; [by] the Diagram Group. Facts on File 2000 various paging (Facts on File reference library) loose leaf $185

Grades: Adult Professional   **796**

   1. Sports 2. Sports -- United States -- Rules 3. School sports -- United States -- Rules 4. College sports -- United States -- Rules

   ISBN 0-8160-4117-2

                LC 00-37137

"The coverage of each activity includes a synopsis; a competition overview; some historical background; playing field or arena diagrams; information on dress and equipment; play and scoring regulations; officials' duties; and discussion and line drawings that focus on skills, plays, and the basic rules. All of the major sports played at the U.S. high school and college level are covered. . . . An effective, easy-to-use reference tool." SLJ

Gifford, Clive
  Sports. Amicus 2010 46p il (Healthy lifestyles) lib bdg $32.80
Grades: 7 8 9 10   796
  1. Sports 2. Physical fitness
  ISBN 978-1-60753-088-6; 1-60753-088-0
                              LC 2009-47567
  This book is "well-written and satisfyingly informative. . . . [The] magazine-like format includes numerous sidebars, color photos, and charts." SLJ
  Includes glossary and bibliographical references

Hile, Lori
  Surviving extreme sports. Raintree 2011 56p il (Extreme survival) lib bdg $33.50
Grades: 4 5 6 7   796
  1. Extreme sports 2. Wilderness survival
  ISBN 978-1-4109-3968-5; 1-4109-3968-5
                              LC 2010028689
  This book is "fun and informative. [This] well-organized title starts with an overview [of extreme sports], offers some specific examples, and includes additional facts or tips and resources. . . . [It features] dramatic archival and full-color photos on nearly every page. . . . [This is a book] that youngsters will enjoy and talk about." SLJ
  Includes glossary and bibliographical references

Howell, Brian
  Sports. ABDO Pub. Co. 2011 112p il (Inside the industry) lib bdg $23.95
Grades: 5 6 7 8   796
  1. Sports -- Vocational guidance
  ISBN 978-1-61714-804-0; 1-61714-804-0
                              LC 2010042558
  This " well-designed [book describes] a variety of careers in [sports]. Because [it helps] readers assess if these positions are suitable for their personality types and backgrounds, the [title is a] good [choice] for career exploration and self-discovery. [It is] also useful for research and reports. . . . Sidebars and full-color photos appear throughout." SLJ
  Includes bibliographical references

Ralston, Birgitta
  Snow play; how to make forts & slides & winter campfires plus the coolest Loch Ness monster and 23 other brrrilliant [i.e. brilliant] project in the snow. Artisan 2010 111p il $14.95
Grades: 4 5 6 7 8 9 10 11 12 Adult   796
  1. Snow 2. Outdoor recreation
  ISBN 978-1-57965-405-4; 1-57965-405-3
  "Opening with explanations of different types of snow and the various tools needed to work with it, this how-to book describes more than two dozen projects, most of which will require adult help and supervision. . . . Ratings of difficulty, the number of people and tools needed, the type of snow required, and the time frame are included with each

project. Short snow-related facts appear throughout. . . . A brief listing of worldwide snow festivals, snow hotels and igloos, and an ice museum completes the package. While kids can certainly use this book to inspire ideas for winter fun, adults will find it equally useful, especially for generating ideas for family projects." SLJ

Rand, Casey
  Graphing sports. Heinemann Library 2009 32p il (Real world data) $28.21; pa $7.99
Grades: 5 6 7 8   796
  1. Graphic methods 2. Sports -- Statistics
  ISBN 978-1-4329-2621-2; 1-4329-2621-7; 978-1-4329-2630-4 pa; 1-4329-2630-6 pa
                              LC 2009001189
  This explains sports related concepts through charts and graphs.
  "The writing is spot-on for the audience. Most importantly, the statistics used are well chosen and instantly understandable, and the text clearly explains how each type of graph can be used to best display different types of data." SLJ
  Includes glossary and bibliographical references

Strother, Scott
  The adventurous book of outdoor games; classic fun for daring boys and girls. [by] Scott Strother. Sourcebooks 2008 293p il pa $14.99
Grades: 4 5 6 7 Adult Professional   796
  1. Games
  ISBN 978-1-4022-1443-1 pa; 1-4022-1443-X pa
  This book "outlines more than 100 games, each at different activity levels set by the amount of physical exertion required. . . . Each game discusses the number of players, ages, time allotted, and type of playing field, followed by a brief description of equipment, startup, object of the game, and how to play. . . . The easy-to-read, easy-to-follow format will provide hours of imaginative play for all of those who are willing to try. An excellent resource for parents, teachers, and activity directors and even for children themselves." SLJ

796.1   Miscellaneous games

Birmingham, Maria
  Weird zone; sports. Maria Birmingham. Owlkids Books Inc. 2013 128 p. (Weird zone) $22.95
Grades: 4 5 6 7   796.1
  1. Sports
  ISBN 1926973607; 9781926973609
                              LC 2012948714
  This book on unusual sports by Maria Birmingham is part of the "Weird Zone" book series. It includes such sports as "rolling down a hill in a plastic ball (aka 'zorbing') . . . professional-grade pillow fighting . . . lawn-mower racing . . . [and] extreme ironing. . . . Each sport gets a two-page spread." Kirkus

Sobey, Ed
  Radio-controlled car experiments. Enslow Publishers 2011 128p il (Cool science projects with technology) lib bdg $31.93

Grades: 6 7 8 9   **796.1**
1. Science projects 2. Automobiles -- Models 3. Science -- Experiments
ISBN 978-0-7660-3304-7; 0-7660-3304-X

This explains how and why radio-controlled cars work, and offers experiments.

This book "is bursting with fast-paced experiments that have easy-to-follow instructions and are sure to interest young car enthusiasts." SLJ

Includes glossary and bibliographical references

796.2   Activities and games requiring equipment

Bell-Rehwoldt, Sheri
The **kids'** guide to jumping rope. Capstone Press 2011 32p il (Kids' guides) lib bdg $26.65
Grades: 4 5 6 7   **796.2**
1. Rope skipping
ISBN 978-1-4296-5443-2; 1-4296-5443-0
                 LC 2010035018

Describes the sport of jumping rope, including how-to information on jumps and tricks.

This includes "plentiful photos of giddy girls (and a few guys) madly skipping rope. . . . This makes jumping rope look like the best time in the world." Booklist

Includes bibliographical references

796.22   Skateboarding

Fitzpatrick, Jim
Skateboarding. Cherry Lake Pub. 2009 32p il (Innovation in sports) lib bdg $27.07
Grades: 4 5 6 7   **796.22**
1. Skateboarding
ISBN 978-1-60279-259-3 lib bdg; 1-60279-259-3 lib bdg
                 LC 2008007548

This describes skateboarding history, equipment, safety, and health benefits

This "stands out by emphasizing monumental shifts and advances in the events themselves. . . . Concise and occasionally revelatory." Booklist

Includes glossary and bibliographical references

Powell, Ben
Skateboarding skills; the rider's guide. Firefly Books 2008 128p il pa $16.95
Grades: 7 8 9 10 11 12 Adult   **796.22**
1. Skateboarding
ISBN 978-1-55407-360-3; 1-55407-360-X
                 LC 2008-275044

The author "offers a colorful and useful manual for mastering numerous skateboard tricks. Intended for riders of all ages, the book presents step-by-step breakdowns of skills illustrated with photographs of children around age 12; each step of a trick features a picture and a written description." Libr J

Stock, Charlotte
Skateboarding step-by-step; [by] Charlotte Stock and Ben Powell. Rosen Central 2010 91p il (Skills in motion) lib bdg $31.95
Grades: 5 6 7 8   **796.22**
1. Skateboarding
ISBN 978-1-4358-3365-4; 1-4358-3365-1
                 LC 2009-11414

Presents instructions on skateboarding from learning to skateboard to executing jumps, flips, and tricks.

"Colorful photographs show the entire movement of each skill presented, giving new meaning to the term 'step-by-step.' Progression borders at the bottom of the pages highlight the salient points to notice in performing each skill from beginning to end." SLJ

Includes bibliographical references

796.3   Ball games

Chetwynd, Josh
The **secret** history of balls; Josh Chetwynd; Illustrations by Emily Stackhouse. Perigee Trade 2011 xiv, 221p ill.
Grades: 7 8 9 10 11 12 Adult   **796.3**
1. Ball games 2. Sporting goods 3. Sports -- History
ISBN 9780399536748
                 LC 2010054221

This book "mines the stories and lore of sports and recreation to offer insight into 60 balls - whether they're hollow, solid, full of air, or stuffed with twine or made of leather, metal, rubber, plastic, or polyurethane - that give us joy on playing fields and in every arena from backyards to stadiums around the globe." (Publishers' note)

796.323   Basketball

Burns, Brian
Basketball step-by-step; [by] Brian Burns and Mark Dunning. Rosen Central 2010 95p il (Skills in motion) lib bdg $31.95
Grades: 5 6 7 8   **796.323**
1. Basketball
ISBN 978-1-4358-3360-9; 1-4358-3360-0
                 LC 2009-14417

An introduction to the skills needed to play basketball uses a sequence of stop-action images and text instructions to illustrate such offensive and defensive moves as inside pivot and shoot, blocking out, and overhead pass.

"Colorful photographs show the entire movement of each skill presented, giving new meaning to the term 'step-by-step.' Progression borders at the bottom of the pages highlight the salient points to notice in performing each skill from beginning to end." SLJ

Includes bibliographical references

Doeden, Matt
The **greatest** basketball records; by Matt Doeden. Capstone Press 2009 32p il (Sports records) lib bdg $17.95

Grades: 4 5 6 7 8   **796.323**
1. Basketball
ISBN 978-1-4296-2006-2 lib bdg; 1-4296-2006-4
lib bdg

LC 2008-2033

This "has enough historical insight and trivia to remain appealing over time. . . . Brief, lively sentences sum up individual feats and set them in context. . . . [This] should appeal to a wide audience." SLJ

Includes glossary and bibliographical references

Gifford, Clive

Basketball; [by] Clive Gifford. PowerKids Press 2009 32p il (Personal best) lib bdg $25.25

Grades: 4 5 6 7 8   **796.323**
1. Basketball
ISBN 978-1-4042-4444-3 lib bdg; 1-4042-4444-1
lib bdg

LC 2007-42989

This guide to basketball "offers well-organized and easy-to-follow instructions, focusing on rules, clothing, specific skills, and competitions. . . . Informative, readable." SLJ

Includes bibliographical references

Labrecque, Ellen

Basketball; by Ellen Labrecque. Cherry Lake Pub. 2009 32p il (Innovation in sports) lib bdg $27.07

Grades: 4 5 6 7   **796.323**
1. Basketball
ISBN 978-1-60279-256-2 lib bdg; 1-60279-256-9
lib bdg

LC 2008002044

This describes basketball history, rules, equipment, training, and great players

This "stands out by emphasizing monumental shifts and advances in the events themselves. . . . Concise and occasionally revelatory." Booklist

Includes glossary and bibliographical references

Robinson, Tom

Basketball. Norwood House Press 2010 64p il (Girls play to win) lib bdg $26.60

Grades: 4 5 6 7   **796.323**
1. Basketball
ISBN 978-1-59953-388-9; 1-59953-388-X

LC 2010009814

Covers the history, rules, fundamentals and significant personalities of the sport of women's basketball. Topics include: techniques, strategies, competitive events, and equipment.

"With an easy design and format, the [text is] highly accessible to even the most reluctant readers and [provides] great exposure and insight into the world of female professional sports." Horn Book Guide

Includes glossary and bibliographical references

Slade, Suzanne

Basketball; how it works. Capstone Press 2010 48p il (Science of sports) lib bdg $29.32; pa $7.95

Grades: 4 5 6 7   **796.323**
1. Basketball
ISBN 978-1-4296-4021-3 lib bdg; 1-4296-4021-9 lib bdg; 978-1-4296-4873-8 pa; 1-4296-4873-2 pa

The book's "photograph-heavy design works to engage its audience, while the easy-to-read [text explains] the science." Horn Book Guide

Includes glossary

Stewart, Mark

Swish; the quest for basketball's perfect shot. by Mark Stewart and Mike Kennedy. Millbrook Press 2009 64p il lib bdg $25.26

Grades: 5 6 7 8   **796.323**
1. Basketball
ISBN 978-0-8225-8752-1 lib bdg; 0-8225-8752-1
lib bdg

LC 2008-24958

"The wide pages offer plenty of room for well-spaced text, sidebars, and illustrations. Each page has at least one picture, with mostly color photos, and the many action shots make the book more exciting. With information on women's and men's basketball at both collegiate and professional levels, this is a nice addition to sports collections." Booklist

Includes bibliographical references

Thomas, Keltie

★ **How** basketball works. Maple Tree Press 2005 64p il hardcover o.p. $16.95

Grades: 5 6 7 8   **796.323**
1. Basketball
ISBN 1-89706-618-X; 1-89706-619-8 pa

This guide to basketball offers information about the game's origins, history, and equipment as well as positions, training, skills, stats, & rules of the game. It also offers tips and fascinating factoids.

"The writing style is razzle-dazzle energetic. . . . The layout features numerous sidebars and brightly colored photos and digital drawings. Even longtime fans will learn something from this engaging, enthusiastic book." Booklist

Thornley, Stew

Kevin Garnett; champion basketball star. by Stew Thornley. Enslow Publishers 2013 48 p. col. ill. (library) $23.93

Grades: 4 5 6 7   **796.323**
1. Basketball players -- United States -- Biography
ISBN 0766040283; 9780766040281

LC 2011031517

This book by Stew Thornley is a children's picture book biography of professional basketball player Kevin Garnett. In his "career, Garnett has won MVP trophies and other individual awards, but his NBA championship ring is most important to him. The team has always come first for KG." (Publisher's note)

Includes bibliographical references

Kobe Bryant; champion basketball star. by Stew Thornley. Enslow Publishers 2013 48 p. col. ill. (library) $23.93

Grades: 4 5 6 7   **796.323**
   1. Bryant, Kobe, 1978- 2. Basketball players -- United States -- Biography
   ISBN 0766040291; 9780766040298

                           LC 2011038174

This picture book by Stew Thornley is a biography of professional basketball player Kobe Bryant. "He can swish shots from long range or drive to the basket for a vicious dunk. Bryant once scored 81 points in a single game! He can also dish it to his teammates and play lockdown defense. . . . The Los Angeles Lakers superstar has won five NBA titles since coming out of high school, and he has earned many individual awards." (Publisher's note)

  Tim Duncan; champion basketball star. by Stew Thornley. Enslow Publishers 2013 48 p. col. ill. (Sports Star Champions) (library) $23.93
Grades: 4 5 6 7   **796.323**
   1. Basketball players -- United States -- Biography
   ISBN 0766040305; 9780766040304

                           LC 2011050440

This book by Stew Thornley is part of the Sports Star Champions series and looks at basketball player Tim Duncan. The texts "focus on the athletes' professional careers, with very little information about their personal lives. . . . Each book ends with career statistics, the player's address, and a brief list for further reading."
Includes bibliographical references

Yancey, Diane
  Basketball. Lucent Books 2011 112p il (Science behind sports) lib bdg $33.45
Grades: 5 6 7 8   **796.323**
   1. Basketball
   ISBN 978-1-4205-0293-0; 1-4205-0293-X

                           LC 2010035239

This "explores the scientific principles such as momentum, gravity, friction, and aerodynamics, plus many more, behind [basketball]. . . . [The author discusses the sport's] origins, history, and changes, . . . the biomechanics and physiology of playing, related health and medical concerns, and the causes and treatment of sports-related injuries. Additional information tells how exercise, diet and nutrition, warming up, and training relate to peak performance and enjoyment of the sport. . . . [The book] has features on possible side effects of anabolic steroid use; how MRIs work; and how various improvements to the courts, basketballs, shoes, and uniforms have affected the game. The action photography . . . is fantastic. . . . [A must-have] for sports fans, athletes, science students, and even anyone considering a career in sports-related medicine, coaching, or other connected fields." SLJ
Includes glossary and bibliographical references

796.325   Volleyball

Crisfield, Deborah
  Winning volleyball for girls; [by] Deborah W. Crisfield, John Monteleone; foreword by Maria Nolan. 3rd ed.; Chelsea House 2009 189p il (Winning sports for girls) lib bdg $44.95; pa $11.96

Grades: 7 8 9 10 11 12   **796.325**
   1. Volleyball
   ISBN 978-0-8160-7720-5 lib bdg; 0-8160-7720-7 lib bdg; 978-0-8160-7721-2 pa; 0-8160-7721-5 pa

                           LC 2009-5733

First published 1995 by Facts on File
This includes a brief history of volleyball followed by descriptions of the rules, court and equipment, training, techniques such as the spike, the serve, the block, and the pass, offensive and defensive play, putting a team together, and game strategies.
Includes glossary and bibliographical references

McDougall, Chros
  Volleyball. Norwood House Press 2010 64p il (Girls play to win) lib bdg $26.60
Grades: 4 5 6 7   **796.325**
   1. Volleyball
   ISBN 978-1-59953-392-6; 1-59953-392-8

                           LC 2010009810

Covers the history, rules, fundamentals and significant personalities of the sport of women's volleyball. Topics include: techniques, strategies, competitive events, and equipment.
"With an easy design and format, the [text is] highly accessible to even the most reluctant readers and [provides] great exposure and insight into the world of female professional sports." Horn Book Guide
Includes glossary and bibliographical references

796.332   American football

Buckley, James
  The **Child's** World encyclopedia of the NFL; by James Buckley, Jr. . . . [et al.] Child's World 2007 4v il
Grades: 3 4 5 6 7   **796.332**
   1. Reference books 2. Football -- Encyclopedias
   ISBN 978-1-59296-922-7 v1; 978-1-59296-923-4 v2; 978-1-59296-924-1 v3; 978-1-59296-925-8 v4

                           LC 2007005662

This encyclopedia of the National Football League is "full of color photos; significant names, terms, and events; and plenty of popular football figures. The authors are all experienced sportswriters and editors." Booklist

  Ultimate guide to football; by James Buckley, Jr. Franklin Watts 2010 160p il $30; pa $7.99
Grades: 4 5 6 7   **796.332**
   1. Football
   ISBN 978-0-531-20752-9; 0-531-20752-8; 978-0-531-21023-9 pa; 0-531-21023-5 pa

                           LC 2009011003

This guide to football covers "historical highlights and delectable ephemera . . . with spreads covering each NFL team interspersed among chatty tales. . . . The highlighter-green color scheme matches the loud, vibrant layout and heightens the contrasting black-and-white player photos, while sporadic cartoons add some pep to the presentation." Booklist
Includes bibliographical references

Dougherty, Terri

The **greatest** football records; by Terri Dougherty. Capstone Press 2009 32p il (Sports records) lib bdg $17.95

Grades: 4 5 6 7 8   **796.332**

    1. Football

    ISBN 978-1-4296-2007-9 lib bdg; 1-4296-2007-2 lib bdg

                     LC 2008-2035

This "has enough historical insight and trivia to remain appealing over time. . . . Brief, lively sentences sum up individual feats and set them in context. . . . [This] should appeal to a wide audience." SLJ

Includes glossary and bibliographical references

Frederick, Shane

Football; the math of the game. Capstone Press 2011 il (Sports math) lib bdg $30.65; pa $7.95

Grades: 6 7 8 9   **796.332**

    1. Football 2. Mathematics

    ISBN 978-1-4296-6567-4 lib bdg; 1-4296-6567-X lib bdg; 978-1-4296-7319-8 pa; 1-4296-7319-2 pa

                     LC 2011007864

Presents the mathematical concepts involved with the sport of football.

This offers a "dazzling layout, which includes countless vivid photographs and overlays of facts and figures. . . . This takes its concept and runs all the way to the end zone with it—dense and heavy, but undoubtedly impressive." Booklist

Includes bibliographical references

Gigliotti, Jim

Football. Cherry Lake Pub. 2009 32p il (Innovation in sports) lib bdg $27.07

Grades: 4 5 6 7   **796.332**

    1. Football

    ISBN 978-1-60279-257-9 lib bdg; 1-60279-257-7 lib bdg

                     LC 2008002305

This describes football history, rules, equipment, training and strategy, and innovators

This "stands out by emphasizing monumental shifts and advances in the events themselves. . . . Concise and occasionally revelatory." Booklist

Includes glossary and bibliographical references

Gilbert, Sara

The **story** of the NFL. Creative Education 2011 un il (Built for success) $23.95

Grades: 6 7 8 9   **796.332**

    1. Football

    ISBN 978-1-60818-063-9; 1-60818-063-8

                     LC 2010031224

A look at the origins, leaders, growth, and management of the NFL, the professional football league that was formed in 1920 and today governs 32 teams throughout the United States.

This book is "written in a lively style, yet with a minimum of fuss. . . . The slim, gleaming format, well-chosen photos, and the effort to explore what makes a company successful today [makes this title] unique." Booklist

Includes bibliographical references

Madden, John

John Madden's heroes of football; the story of America's game. with Bill Gutman. Dutton Childrens Book 2006 80p il $18.99

Grades: 5 6 7 8   **796.332**

    1. Football

    ISBN 0-525-47698-9

                     LC 2005036019

"This title traces the evolution of professional football from its humble beginnings as an Ivy League-college pastime in the 19th century to one of the most popular spectator sports in the United States. . . . This clear, well-organized account is appropriate for report writers and is a solid choice for libraries needing to update their sports-history collections." SLJ

Includes glossary and bibliographical references

Rappoport, Ken

Peyton Manning; champion football star. by Ken Rappoport. Enslow Publishers 2013 48 p. col. ill. (Sports Star Champions) (library) $23.93

Grades: 4 5 6 7   **796.332**

    1. Quarterbacks (Football) 2. Football players -- United States -- Biography 3. Quarterbacks (Football) -- United States -- Biography

    ISBN 0766040275; 9780766040274

                     LC 2011052759

This book is part of the Sports Star Champion series and looks at quarterback Peyton Manning. The "texts focus on the athletes' professional careers, with very little information about their personal lives. Occasional sidebars add additional interest, and each book ends with career statistics, the player's address, and a brief list for further reading."

Includes bibliographical references

Stewart, Mark

Touchdown; the power and precision of football's perfect play. by Mark Stewart and Mike Kennedy. Millbrook Press 2009 64p il lib bdg $27.93

Grades: 5 6 7 8   **796.332**

    1. Football

    ISBN 978-0-8225-8751-4 lib bdg; 0-8225-8751-3 lib bdg

                     LC 2008044295

"This attractive book opens with an intriguing history of American football. . . . Next, 10 double-page spreads feature 'Ten Unforgettable Touchdowns' in both professional and collegiate games from 1913 to 2006. After a chapter on 'touchdown makers,' spotlighting outstanding players . . . comes a short section on notable touchdown bloopers and another on trick plays and the element of surprise. . . . Photos, period prints, and reproductions of trading cards illustrate the text while adding color to the pages. . . . This nicely designed book provides plenty of on-the-field drama as well as pertinent information in a smoothly written overview of the touchdown." Booklist

796.334   Soccer (Association football)

Bazemore, Suzanne

Soccer: how it works. Capstone Press 2010 48p il (Science of sports) lib bdg $29.32; pa $7.95

Grades: 4 5 6 7   **796.334**

1. Soccer

ISBN 978-1-4296-4025-1 lib bdg; 1-4296-4025-1 lib bdg; 978-1-4296-4876-9 pa; 1-4296-4876-7 pa

The book's "photography-heavy design works to engage its audience, while the easy-to-read [text explains] the science." Horn Book Guide

Includes glossary

Crisfield, Deborah

Winning soccer for girls; [by] Deborah W. Crisfield; foreword by Bill Hawkey and Patrick Murphy. 3rd ed.; Chelsea House 2010 164p il (Winning sports for girls) lib bdg $39.50; pa $14.95

Grades: 7 8 9 10   **796.334**

1. Soccer

ISBN 978-0-8160-7714-4 lib bdg; 0-8160-7714-2 lib bdg; 978-0-8160-7715-1 pa; 0-8160-7715-0 pa

LC 2008-50595

First published 1996 by Facts on File

This soccer guidebook contains "material on developing agility, power, and strength and improving ball control and handling. The history and rules of the game are also examined, and a glossary lists soccer terms." Publisher's note

Includes glossary and bibliographical references

Gifford, Clive

The **Kingfisher** soccer encyclopedia. Kingfisher 2010 144p il $19.99

Grades: 5 6 7 8   **796.334**

1. Reference books 2. Soccer -- Encyclopedias

ISBN 978-0-7534-6397-0; 0-7534-6397-0

First published 2006

"Gifford does an excellent job of covering most aspects of the game from its history of a hundred-plus years to its current rules and tactics, teams, competitions, and famous players. Each section is clearly identified and provides additional information about the game. . . . Students involved in the sport or interested in specific teams or players will appreciate this book." Voice Youth Advocates

Includes glossary and bibliographical references

Soccer; Clive Gifford. 1st ed. PowerKids Press 2009 32 p. col. ill. (Personal best) (library) $26.50

Grades: 4 5 6 7 8   **796.334**

1. Soccer

ISBN 9781404244412; 1404244417

LC 2007042997

This guide to soccer "offers well-organized and easy-to-follow instructions, focusing on rules, clothing, specific skills, and competitions. . . . Informative, readable." SLJ

Hornby, Hugh

Soccer; written by Hugh Hornby; photographed by Andy Crawford. DK Pub. 2008 70p il (DK eyewitness books) $15.99

Grades: 4 5 6 7   **796.334**

1. Soccer

ISBN 978-0-7566-3779-8; 0-7566-3779-1

LC 2008276290

First published 2000

Examines all aspects of the game of soccer: its history, rules, techniques, tactics, equipment, playing fields, competitive play, and more.

Jennings, Madeleine

Soccer step-by-step; [by] Madeleine Jennings and Ian Howe. Rosen Central 2010 95p il (Skills in motion) lib bdg $31.95

Grades: 5 6 7 8   **796.334**

1. Soccer

ISBN 978-1-4358-3362-3; 1-4358-3362-7

LC 2009-12538

Presents instructions on the basic movements of soccer, including passing, shooting, and goalkeeping.

"Colorful photographs show the entire movement of each skill presented, giving new meaning to the term 'step-by-step.' Progression borders at the bottom of the pages highlight the salient points to notice in performing each skill from beginning to end." SLJ

Includes bibliographical references

Kassouf, Jeff

Soccer. Norwood House Press 2011 64p il (Girls play to win) lib bdg $26.60

Grades: 4 5 6 7   **796.334**

1. Soccer

ISBN 978-1-59953-464-0; 1-59953-464-9

LC 2011011037

Covers the history, rules, fundamentals, and significant personalities of the sport of women's soccer. Topics include: techniques, strategies, competitive events, and equipment.

Includes glossary and bibliographical references

Kelley, K. C.

Soccer. Cherry Lake Pub. 2008 32p il (Innovation in sports) lib bdg $27.07

Grades: 4 5 6 7   **796.334**

1. Soccer

ISBN 978-1-60279-261-6 lib bdg; 1-60279-261-5 lib bdg

LC 2008006749

This describes soccer history, rules, styles of play, equipment, and innovators

This "stands out by emphasizing monumental shifts and advances in the events themselves. . . . Concise and occasionally revelatory." Booklist

Includes glossary and bibliographical references

St. John, Warren

Outcasts united; the story of a refugee soccer team that changed a town. Warren St. John. Delacorte Press 2012 226 p. $16.99

Grades: 6 7 8   **796.334**

1. Refugees 2. Soccer teams 3. Soccer coaches 4. Refugees -- Africa 5. Refugee children -- Georgia -- Clarkston 6. Soccer coaches -- Georgia -- Clarkston

-- Biography
ISBN 0385741944; 9780375988806; 9780375990335; 9780385741941

LC 2012001412

This book by Warren St. John "is the story of a refugee soccer team, a remarkable woman coach and a small southern town turned upside down by the process of refugee resettlement. It's a tale about resilience, the power of one person to make a difference and the daunting challenge of creating community in a place where people seem to have little in common." (Publisher's note)

Stewart, Mark

★ Goal!: the fire and fury of soccer's greatest moment; [by] Mark Stewart and Mike Kennedy. Millbrook Press 2010 64p il lib bdg $27.93

Grades: 5 6 7 8 **796.334**

1. Soccer
ISBN 978-0-8225-8754-5 lib bdg; 0-8225-8754-8 lib bdg

LC 2009014098

"This well-written book explores the nuances of scoring in the world's most popular sport. A quick history of the game lays the groundwork with details that may be new to even hard-core fans. The second chapter jumps right into the good stuff with descriptions of 10 of the most famous goals. . . . Also included is a rundown of the best male and female scorers from the early twentieth century to the present and weird anomalies and amusing anecdotes from soccer lore." Booklist

796.34   Racket games

Smolka, Bo

Lacrosse. Norwood House Press 2011 64p il (Girls play to win) lib bdg $26.60

Grades: 4 5 6 7 **796.34**

1. Lacrosse
ISBN 978-1-59953-463-3; 1-59953-463-0

LC 2011011050

Covers the history, rules, fundamentals, and significant personalities of the sport of women's lacrosse. Topics include: techniques, strategies, competitive events, and equipment.

Includes glossary and bibliographical references

Swissler, Becky

Winning lacrosse for girls; foreword by Katie Bergstrom. 2nd ed.; Chelsea House 2010 212p il (Winning sports for girls) lib bdg $44.95; pa $14.95

Grades: 7 8 9 10 **796.34**

1. Lacrosse
ISBN 978-0-8160-7712-0 lib bdg; 0-8160-7712-6 lib bdg; 978-0-8160-7713-7 pa; 0-8160-7713-4 pa

LC 2008-51346

First published 2004 by Facts on File

This lacrosse guidebook "teaches the game's basic skills, strategies, and drills and how to master them. Chapters cover the history of the game, the basics of stick handling, the rules of play, passing and receiving, offense and defense, key

strategies, skills and tactics, conditioning, and . . . more." Publisher's note

Includes bibliographical references

796.342   Tennis (Lawn tennis)

Gifford, Clive

Tennis; [by] Clive Gifford. Sea-to-Sea Publications 2009 30p il (Know your sport) lib bdg $27.10

Grades: 5 6 7 8 **796.342**

1. Tennis
ISBN 978-1-59771-153-1 lib bdg; 1-59771-153-5 lib bdg

LC 2008-7322

"Describes the equipment, courts, training, moves, and competitions of tennis. Includes step-by-step descriptions of moves." Publisher's note

Includes glossary

796.352   Golf

Gifford, Clive

Golf: from tee to green; the essential guide for young golfers. Sea-to-Sea Publications 2010 64p il (Know your sport) $16.99

Grades: 5 6 7 8 **796.352**

1. Golf
ISBN 978-1-59771-217-0; 1-59771-217-5

LC 2008045861

Presents an instructional guide to the sport of golf, with information on different aspects of play and the equipment used.

"This book will be welcomed by young golf enthusiasts, whether they're beginners or experienced players. . . . A useful and attractive guide." Horn Book Guide

Includes bibliographical references

Kelley, K. C.

Golf. Cherry Lake Pub. 2009 32p il (Innovation in sports) lib bdg $27.07

Grades: 4 5 6 7 **796.352**

1. Golf
ISBN 978-1-60279-262-3 lib bdg; 1-60279-262-3 lib bdg

LC 2008002045

This describes golf history, rules, balls, and club technology, and innovators

This "stands out by emphasizing monumental shifts and advances in the events themselves. . . . Concise and occasionally revelatory." Booklist

Includes bibliographical references

796.357   Baseball

Adamson, Thomas K.

Baseball; the math of the game. Capstone Sports 2012 48p il (Sports math) lib bdg $30.65

Grades: 6 7 8 9   796.357
  1. Baseball 2. Mathematics
  ISBN 978-1-4296-6569-8

                                    LC 2011004483
"Overall these books will appeal to serious sports fans who want to learn more about the numbers of the game." SLJ

Includes bibliographical references

Bertoletti, John C.
  How baseball managers use math; math curriculum consultant: Rhea A. Stewart. Chelsea Clubhouse 2010 32p il (Math in the real world) lib bdg $28

Grades: 4 5 6   796.357
  1. Baseball 2. Mathematics 3. Vocational guidance
  ISBN 978-1-60413-604-3 lib bdg; 1-60413-604-9 lib bdg

                                    LC 2009-16265
"The layout for [this] slim [title] is bright and colorful with a photograph and a 'You Do the Math' problem to solve and large, easy-to-read text on every spread. An answer key is included in the back matter, along with a page detailing the career choices and the educational requirements. . . . [It] includes such topics as how managers rely on player statistics to make decisions and why the pitch count is important to monitor. [This title] would be useful to supplement lessons on mathematics. [It] will also appeal to students wanting to learn more about math as it relates to specific careers." SLJ

Includes glossary and bibliographical references

Buckley, James
  Ultimate guide to baseball. Shoreline Pub. 2010 160p il $30; pa $7.99

Grades: 4 5 6 7   796.357
  1. Baseball
  ISBN 978-0-531-20750-5; 0-531-20750-1; 978-0-531-21021-5 pa; 0-531-21021-9 pa

                                    LC 2009043684
"This is a wide-ranging, brisk overview of the game. Sections briefly skim baseball history, hitting, pitching, defense and baserunning, and the World Series. Each major league team is introduced in a thumbnail sketch. . . . Other topics include baseball slang and nicknames, the 11 ways to get on base, and the author's choices for the best defensive players of all time. . . . Buckley writes with a lightly humorous touch that should appeal to fans and browsers." SLJ

Includes bibliographical references

Child's World (Firm)
  The **Child's** World encyclopedia of baseball; by James Buckley, Jr. . . . [et al.] Child's World 2009 5v il set $247.75

Grades: 4 5 6 7 8   796.357
  1. Baseball -- Encyclopedias
  ISBN 978-1-60253-175-8 set; 1-60253-175-7 set

                                    LC 2008039461
In this baseball encyclopedia, the authors "definitely convey an enthusiasm for their subject." Booklist

Dreier, David
  Baseball; how it works. Capstone Press 2010 48p il (Science of sports) lib bdg $29.32; pa $7.95

Grades: 4 5 6 7   796.357
  1. Baseball
  ISBN 978-1-4296-4020-6 lib bdg; 1-4296-4020-0 lib bdg; 978-1-4296-4872-1 pa; 1-4296-4872-4 pa

"The well-designed layout, featuring glossy color visuals, is stimulating, and the concepts are further reinforced in brief definitions that appear at the bottom of many pages and in an appended glossary. . . . The clever approach will help draw interest and build understanding." Booklist

Includes glossary

Frager, Ray
  Baltimore Orioles. ABDO Pub. Co. 2011 48p il (Inside MLB) $31.35

Grades: 4 5 6   796.357
  1. Baseball
  ISBN 978-1-61714-036-5; 1-61714-036-8

                                    LC 2010036557
"Written by [a] professional [sportswriter], peppered with well-chosen quotations and illustrated with photos on every page turn, this [book about the Baltimore Orioles] will interest die-hard baseball fans and is likely to engage reluctant readers." Horn Book Guide

Includes glossary and bibliographical references

Freedman, Lew
  Boston Red Sox. ABDO Pub. Co. 2011 48p il (Inside MLB) $31.35

Grades: 4 5 6   796.357
  1. Baseball
  ISBN 9781617140372; 1617140376

                                    LC 2010036554
"Written by [a] professional [sportswriter], peppered with well-chosen quotations and illustrated with photos on every page turn, this [book about the Boston Red Sox] will interest diehard baseball fans and is likely to engage reluctant readers." Horn Book Guide

Includes glossary and bibliographical references

Gitlin, Marty
  Softball. Norwood House Press 2011 64p il (Girls play to win) lib bdg $26.60

Grades: 4 5 6 7   796.357
  1. Softball
  ISBN 978-1-59953-465-7; 1-59953-465-7

                                    LC 2011011051
Covers the history, rules, fundamentals, and significant personalities of the sport of women's softball. Topics include: techniques, strategies, competitive events, and equipment.

Includes glossary and bibliographical references

Gola, Mark
  Winning softball for girls; foreword by Gretchen Cammiso. 2nd ed.; Chelsea House 2009 220p il (Winning sports for girls) pa $14.95; lib bdg $44.95

Grades: 7 8 9 10   **796.357**
   1. Softball
   ISBN 0-8160-7716-9 lib bdg; 978-0-8160-7717-5 pa;
   0-8160-7717-7 pa; 978-0-8160-7716-8 lib bdg
                           LC 2008-54453
First published 2002 by Facts on File
"Gola covers the history, rules of the game, and necessary equipment as well as tips for hitting, pitching, and base running. The fundamentals of defense and offense are covered, along with a number of drills in each area. In addition, the author details the various positions and gives advice on conditioning. . . . This title could prove useful in balancing baseball-laden collections." SLJ
  Includes bibliographical references

Jennings, Madeleine
  Baseball step-by-step; [by] Madeleine Jennings, Alan Smith, and Alan Bloomfield. Rosen Central 2009 95p il (Skills in motion) lib bdg $31.95
Grades: 5 6 7 8   **796.357**
   1. Baseball
   ISBN 978-1-4358-3361-6; 1-4358-3361-9
                           LC 2009-13246
An introduction to the skills needed to play baseball uses a sequence of stop-action images and text instructions to illustrate the moves needed to pitch, catch, field, hit, and run bases.
"Colorful photographs show the entire movement of each skill presented, giving new meaning to the term 'step-by-step.' Progression borders at the bottom of the pages highlight the salient points to notice in performing each skill from beginning to end." SLJ
  Includes bibliographical references

Lipsyte, Robert
  Heroes of baseball; the men who made it America's favorite game. [by] Robert Lipsyte. Atheneum Books for Young Readers 2006 92p il $19.95
Grades: 4 5 6 7   **796.357**
   1. Baseball -- Biography 2. Baseball players
   ISBN 0-689-86741-7; 978-0-689-86741-5
                           LC 2005010841
"Using as a focus some of baseball's greats—Big Al Spalding, Babe Ruth, Mickey Mantle, Jackie Robinson, Curt Flood . . .—Lipsyte offers a strong history of the game and its place in American culture. . . . Although much of this material, including the pictures, might be familiar to young readers already absorbed in the game, it is nicely laid out and colorfully formatted. Lipsyte has a clear, vivid style." Booklist
  Includes glossary and bibliographical references

Rappoport, Ken
  Alex Rodriguez; champion baseball star. by Ken Rappoport. Enslow Publishers 2013 48 p. col. ill. (Sports star champions) (library) $23.93
Grades: 4 5 6 7   **796.357**
   1. Baseball players -- Biography 2. Baseball players -- United States -- Biography
   ISBN 0766040267; 9780766040267
                           LC 2011043754

"Of the forty-three glossy story pages in the book, fifteen describe . . . [baseball player Alex Rodriguez's] career from 2004 forward. A Career Statistics Chart follows his performance through 2011. Color photos include A-Rod's early baseball career through 2011. Many of his impressive stats are discussed, including being the only major league player to hit thirty home runs and drive in one hundred runs in thirteen consecutive seasons." (Children's Literature)

  Derek Jeter; champion baseball star. by Ken Rappoport. Enslow Publishers 2013 48 p. col. ill. (Sports star champions) (library) $23.93
Grades: 4 5 6 7   **796.357**
   1. Baseball players -- Biography 2. Baseball players -- United States -- Biography
   ISBN 0766040259; 9780766040250
                           LC 2011033514
This book by Ken Rappoport, part of the Sports Star Champions series, presents a biography of "New York Yankees shortstop" Derek Jeter, who "has led the Yankees to five World Series titles and has won several individual awards." (Publisher's note)
The "book ends with career statistics, the player's address, and a brief list for further reading." (School Library Journal)

Teitelbaum, Michael
  Baseball; by Michael Teitelbaum. Cherry Lake Pub. 2009 32p il (Innovation in sports) lib bdg $18.95
Grades: 5 6 7 8   **796.357**
   1. Baseball
   ISBN 978-1-60279-255-5 lib bdg; 1-60279-255-0 lib bdg
                           LC 2008-2310
This title "traces the many leaps forward in the history of baseball. [It] chronicles innovations that changed the game. . . . Nice-sized color photographs and sidebars . . . accompany the concise and easy-to-follow text." Booklist
  Includes glossary and bibliographical references

Thorn, John
  First pitch; how baseball began. Beach Ball Books 2011 40p il pa $14.99
Grades: 4 5 6 7   **796.357**
   1. Baseball -- History
   ISBN 978-1-936310-04-3; 1-936310-04-X
"Packed with vintage images and photographs, this history of baseball takes readers from the origins of the sport to the present day. . . . Thorn . . . writes clearly and eloquently. . . . Fans who think they know baseball may discover they have much to learn." Publ Wkly

Wong, Stephen
  Baseball treasures; by Stephen Wong; photographs by Susan Einstein. Collins 2007 58p il $16.99; lib bdg $17.89

Grades: 5 6 7 8   **796.357**
1. Baseball -- History 2. Baseball -- Collectibles
ISBN 978-0-06-114464-6; 0-06-114464-9; 978-0-06-114473-8 lib bdg; 0-06-114473-8 lib bdg
LC 2006036069

This describes collectibles connected with the history of baseball, including balls, gloves and bats, jerseys, baseball cards, World Series memorabilia, and trophies.

This is "a well-designed, well-illustrated book for kids. . . . The text manages to impart the essential information without becoming bogged down in too much detail." Booklist

796.4   Weight lifting, track and field, gymnastics

Bobrick, Benson
A **passion** for victory: the story of the Olympics in ancient and early modern times; the story of the Olympics in ancient and early modern times. Benson Bobrick. Alfred A. Knopf 2012 xvi, 143 p.p ill. (hardback) $19.99
Grades: 4 5 6 7   **796.4**
1. Olympic games 2. Sports tournaments 3. Olympics
ISBN 9780375868696; 9780375968693
LC 2011016036

The book offers an "account of the Olympic Games and their place in history. . . . [Athletes] Milo of Croton, Jim Thorpe, Johnny Weissmuller and Jesse Owens are given their due here. The photo-essay format conveys their stories . . . as well as the glory, shenanigans and pettiness of the Olympics throughout history. Almost every full-page spread includes at least one photograph, and the text . . . addresses the cultural context of the games." Kirkus

Includes bibliographical references.

Schwartz, Heather E.
Gymnastics. Lucent Books 2011 96p il (Science behind sports) lib bdg $33.45
Grades: 5 6 7 8   **796.4**
1. Gymnastics
ISBN 978-1-4205-0277-0; 1-4205-0277-8
LC 2010033544

This "explores the scientific principles such as momentum, gravity, friction, and aerodynamics, plus many more, behind [gymnastics]. . . . [The author discusses the sport's] origins, history, and changes, . . . the biomechanics and physiology of playing, related health and medical concerns, and the causes and treatment of sports-related injuries. [This volume is] jam-packed full of information. [A must-have] for sports fans, athletes, science students, and even anyone considering a career in sports-related medicine, coaching, or other connected fields." SLJ

Includes glossary and bibliographical references

796.42   Track and field

Cantor, George
Usain Bolt; by George Cantor. Lucent Books 2011 96 p. col. ill. (People in the News) $33.95

Grades: 6 7 8 9   **796.42**
1. Sprinters 2. Olympic athletes 3. Track and field athletes -- Jamaica -- Biography
ISBN 1420503413; 9781420503418
LC 2011006980

This book offers a biography of Olympic sprinter Usain Bolt, a Jamaican athlete who set several world records, by author George Cantor. It is part of the "People in the News" series, which "profiles the lives and careers of some of today's most prominent newsmakers. Whether covering contributions and achievements or notorious deeds, books in this series examine why these well-known individuals garnered public attention." (Publisher's note)

Includes bibliographical references and index

Gifford, Clive
Track and field; [by] Clive Gifford. PowerKids Press 2009 32p il (Personal best) lib bdg $25.25
Grades: 4 5 6 7 8   **796.42**
1. Track athletics
ISBN 978-1-4042-4442-9 lib bdg; 1-4042-4442-5 lib bdg
LC 2007-42984

This guide to track and field "offers well-organized and easy-to-follow instructions, focusing on rules, clothing, specific skills, and competitions. . . . Informative, readable." SLJ

Includes bibliographical references

Track athletics; [by] Clive Gifford. Sea-to-Sea Publications 2009 30p il (Know your sport) lib bdg $27.10
Grades: 5 6 7 8   **796.42**
1. Track athletics
ISBN 978-1-59771-154-8 lib bdg; 1-59771-154-3 lib bdg
LC 2008-7323

"Describes the equipment, training, moves, and running events of track competitions. Includes step-by-step descriptions of moves." Publisher's note

Includes glossary

Housewright, Ed
Winning track and field for girls; foreword by Jason-Lamont Jackson. 2nd ed.; Chelsea House 2009 194p il (Winning sports for girls) lib bdg $44.95; pa $11.96
Grades: 7 8 9 10 11 12   **796.42**
1. Track athletics
ISBN 978-0-8160-7718-2 lib bdg; 0-8160-7718-5 lib bdg; 978-0-8160-7719-9 pa; 0-8160-7719-3 pa
LC 2009-9019

First published 2004 by Facts on File

This includes a brief history of women's track, followed by topics including sprints, hurdles, middle and long distances, relays, jumping events, throwing events, the heptathlon, cross-country, and the triathlon, mental preparations and nutrition, stetches and weight lifting.

Includes bibliographical references

McDougall, Chros
Track & field. Norwood House Press 2011 64p il (Girls play to win) lib bdg $26.60
Grades: 4 5 6 7   **796.42**
   1. Track athletics
   ISBN 978-1-59953-467-1; 1-59953-467-3
                       LC 2011011053
Covers the history, rules, fundamentals, and significant personalities of the sport of women's track and field. Topics include: techniques, strategies, competitive events, and equipment.
   Includes glossary and bibliographical references

796.440   Biography

Burford, Michelle
Grace, gold and glory; my leap of faith: the Gabrielle Douglas story. by Gabrielle Douglas; with Michelle Burford. Zondervan 2012 222 p. ill. (hardcover) $24.99
Grades: 4 5 6 7 8   **796.440**
   1. Gymnastics 2. Olympic athletes 3. Women gymnasts -- United States -- Biography 4. Women Olympic athletes -- United States -- Biography
   ISBN 0310740614; 9780310740612
                       LC 2012042389
This book is a "first-person account of 2012 Olympic gold medalist [Gabrielle] Douglas's life from birth to the Olympics written in collaboration with [Michelle] Burford. . . . Douglas mentions the lows—her family lived in their van for months when she was an infant—and bullying, but never dwells on them. . . . Supported by her mother and siblings, and by her strong faith in God, she sees herself as capable of achieving greatness 'because God has equipped me with all I need to succeed.'" (Publishers Weekly)

796.48   Olympic games

Butterfield, Moira
Events. Sea-to-Sea Publications 2011 32p il (The Olympics) lib bdg $19.95
Grades: 4 5 6 7   **796.48**
   1. Olympic games
   ISBN 978-1-5977-1321-4; 1-5977-1321-X
                       LC 2011006465
This describes events of the Olympics.
   Includes glossary and bibliographical references

History. Sea-to-Sea Publications 2011 32p il (The Olympics) lib bdg $28.50
Grades: 4 5 6 7   **796.48**
   1. Olympic games
   ISBN 978-1-5977-1319-1; 1-5977-1319-8
                       LC 2011006470
This is a history of the Olympics.
   Includes glossary and bibliographical references

Scandals. Sea-to-Sea Publications 2011 32p il (The Olympics) lib bdg $28.50

Grades: 4 5 6 7   **796.48**
   1. Olympic games 2. Sports -- Corrupt practices
   ISBN 978-1-5977-1320-7; 1-5977-1320-1
                       LC 2011006473
"The book is divided into chapters that cover such topics as bribes, doping, and political problems. Along with famous events, such as the tragedy at the Munich Olympics, in which Israeli athletes were murdered, and the Marion Jones running scandal, in which she was stripped of her medals, there are other shocking and suprising moments. . . . This . . . volume, full of historical and contemporary photos, gives readers a lot to think about." Booklist

Farrell, Courtney
Terror at the Munich Olympics. ABDO 2010 112p il map (Essential events) $22.95
Grades: 6 7 8 9   **796.48**
   1. Terrorism 2. Olympic games, 1972 (Munich, Ger.)
   ISBN 978-1-60453-945-5; 1-60453-945-3
                       LC 2009-30426
This offers "vivid detail as well as historical and political context. . . . Farrell starts with the Munich Olympics but quickly backtracks to offer an explanation of the conflicts in the Middle East surrounding the creation of the State of Israel, and the rise of terrorism in response to these conflicts. The kidnapping and murder of the Israeli athletes is then described, along with the apparent bungling of rescue efforts. The book concludes with chapters on the response to the killings by Israel, as well as attempts at brokering peace in the region among the various countries in conflict. . . . [This title has] pertinent sidebars with primary source material. Archival photos add to the dramatic [narrative]." SLJ
   Includes bibliographical references

Hotchkiss, Ron
The matchless six; the story of Canada's first women's Olympic team. Tundra Books 2006 194p il pa $16.95
Grades: 7 8 9 10   **796.48**
   1. Olympic games 2. Women athletes 3. Track athletics 4. Women athletes -- Canada 5. Olympic Games (9th: 1928: Amsterdam, Netherlands)
   ISBN 0-88776-738-9; 978-0-88776-738-8
"Hotchkiss provides detailed information on the six Canadian athletes who won the track-and-field event in 1928, the first Olympics that included women. The personalities and accomplishments of Jane Bell, Myrtle Cook, Bobbie Rosenfeld, Ethel Smith, Ethel Catherwood, and Jean Thompson are highlighted with biographical information. . . . Accuracy is supported by quotes from newspapers, sports writers, coaches, and managers. . . . Anyone interested in the history of the Olympics, the history of women in the Games, or of track and field will find the book worth reading." SLJ

Macy, Sue
  ★ Swifter, higher, stronger; a photographic history of the Summer Olympics. by Sue Macy; foreword by Bob Costas. updated for the 2008 Summer Olympics; National Geographic 2008 96p il $18.95; lib bdg $27.90

Grades: 4 5 6 7   **796.48**
1. Olympic games
ISBN 978-1-4263-0290-9; 1-4263-0290-8; 978-1-4263-0302-9 lib bdg; 1-4263-0302-5 lib bdg
First published 2004

A detailed look at the history of the Olympic Games, from their origins in Ancient Greece, through their rebirth in nineteenth century France, to the present, highlighting the contributions of individuals to the Games' success and popularity.

"While other books on the topic go into more depth on specific sports, athletes, or historical events, none are as enthusiastically broad or as enjoyable to read as this one. And, it's superbly illustrated with colorful, well-chosen, and enticing photographs." SLJ [review of 2004 ed.]

Includes bibliographical references

796.5   Outdoor life

George, Jean Craighead
★ **Pocket** guide to the outdoors; [by] Jean Craighead George; with Twig C. George . . . [et al.] Dutton Children's Books 2009 138p il pa $9.99
Grades: 5 6 7 8   **796.5**
1. Camping 2. Outdoor life 3. Wilderness survival 4. Outdoor recreation
ISBN 978-0-525-42163-4 pa; 0-525-42163-7 pa

"This survival guide is the book to read before a wilderness adventure. In short, clearly written chapters, it provides practical tips about ways to enjoy nature and includes information about building shelters, starting fires, making a fishing line and cleaning a fish, outdoor cooking, identifying animal tracks and edible and poisonous plants, and the basics of orienteering. Safety is always considered. Drawings and clearly labeled sketches help with identification." SLJ

Includes bibliographical references

Paulsen, Gary
★ **Woodsong**. Bradbury Press 1990 132p map hardcover o.p. pa $6.99
Grades: 7 8 9 10   **796.5**
1. Authors 2. Outdoor life 3. Sled dog racing 4. Sled dog racers 5. Children's authors 6. Short story writers 7. Young adult authors 8. Dogs 9. Sledding -- Personal narratives
ISBN 0-02-770221-9; 1-4169-3939-3 pa
LC 89-70835
ALA YALSA Margaret A. Edwards Award (1997)

For the author and his family, life in northern Minnesota is a wild experience involving wolves, deer, and the sled dogs that make their way of life possible. Includes an account of Paulsen's first Iditarod, a dogsled race across Alaska

"The book is packed with vignettes that range among various shades of terror and lyrical beauty." Voice Youth Advocates

Schofield, Jo
Make it wild; 101 things to make and do outdoors. [by] Jo Schofield and Fiona Danks. Frances Lincoln 2010 159p il pa $24.95

Grades: 4 5 6 7 8   **796.5**
1. Nature craft 2. Outdoor life
ISBN 978-0-7112-2885-6; 0-7112-2885-X

"Using the raw materials nature has to offer, the authors offer clear, concise instructions on how to create ephemeral art, outdoor toys, jewelry, sculptures, and dozens of other things using materials like clay, ice, leaves, sand, and wood. The instructions offer good guidance but also encourage children to use their own creativity and imagination to craft the final product. The projects range in level of difficulty and, depending on the age of the child, can be done individually or in collaboration with siblings, peers, or parents. The authors include safety instructions and recommendations for further resources on outdoor creative exercises. The activities will teach problem solving and commonsense, useful skills; instill a deeper appreciation of nature; and encourage creativity and ingenuity. An excellent choice for any library collection." Booklist

796.51   Walking

Hart, John
Walking softly in the wilderness; the Sierra Club guide to backpacking. 4th ed, complete rev and updated; Sierra Club Books 2005 508p il map (Sierra Club outdoor adventure guide) pa $16.95
Grades: 8 9 10 11 12 Adult   **796.51**
1. Backpacking 2. Wilderness areas
ISBN 1-57805-123-1
LC 2004-56554
First published 1977

This guide for both the novice and experienced hiker reflects the environmental concerns of the Sierra Club. Among topics covered are: clothing and equipment; making and breaking camp; problem animals and plants; hiking and camping with kids. Listings of conservation and wilderness travel organizations, map and equipment sources, land management agencies, and Internet contacts are appended.

Includes bibliographical references

796.52   Walking and exploring by kind of terrain

Bodden, Valerie
To the top of Mount Everest; by Valerie Bodden. 1st ed. Creative Education 2012 48 p. ill. (some col.) (Great Expeditions) (paperback) $12.00; (library) $34.25
Grades: 5 6 7 8   **796.52**
1. Exploration 2. Mount Everest (China and Nepal) 3. Mountaineering -- Everest, Mount (China and Nepal) -- History 4. Mountaineers -- Everest, Mount (China and Nepal) -- Biography
ISBN 1608180700; 9780898126686; 9781608180707
LC 2010033553

This book by Valerie Bodden is part of the Great Expeditions series and looks at expeditions to the top of Mount Everest. "Bodden includes brief biographies of major people involved in each expedition, interspersed with the text. There are also numerous photographs or reproductions of paintings and woodcuts from the time of the expeditions." (Library Media Connection)

Includes bibliographical references and index.

Brennan, Kristine

Sir Edmund Hillary, modern day explorer. Chelsea House 2001 63p il (Explorers of new worlds) hardcover o.p. lib bdg $21.85

Grades: 4 5 6 7   **796.52**

1. Mountaineering 2. Mountaineers 3. Nonfiction writers 4. Mountaineers -- New Zealand -- Biography

ISBN 0-7910-5953-7 lib bdg; 0-7910-6163-9 pa

LC 00-43077

A biography of the New Zealander who, with his Sherpa climbing partner Tenzing Norgay, first reached the Summit of Mount Everest in 1953

"Accessible and well organized. . . . Fresh, appealing, and well written." SLJ

Includes glossary and bibliographical references

Cleare, John

Epic climbs. Kingfisher 2011 64p il (Epic adventure) $19.95

Grades: 5 6 7 8   **796.52**

1. Mountaineering

ISBN 978-0-7534-6573-8; 0-7534-6573-6

"Cleare gives the history of five of the most famous and dangerous mountains to climb: Eiger, K2, Everest, McKinley, and Matterhorn. Each section has a short, easy-to-read summary that gives the history of climbers who have conquered these peaks. Full-color photos include the view from the top and historical and contemporary climbing equipment." SLJ

Skreslet, Laurie

To the top of Everest; [by] Laurie Skreslet with Elizabeth MacLeod. Kids Can Press 2001 56p il hardcover o.p. pa $9.95

Grades: 4 5 6 7   **796.52**

1. Mountaineering

ISBN 1-55074-721-5; 1-55074-814-9 pa

This is an account of Skreslet's "1982 trek up Everest when he became one of the first Canadians to make it to the top. Skreslet takes readers through every exciting, excruciating element of the climb. Beautiful color photographs abound." Booklist

Includes glossary

Wurdinger, Scott D.

Rock climbing; [by] Scott Wurdinger and Leslie Rapparlie. Creative Education 2007 48p il (Adventure sports) $31.35

Grades: 6 7 8 9   **796.52**

1. Mountaineering

ISBN 978-1-58341-394-4; 1-58341-394-4

LC 2005051785

This outlines "the history, gear, safety equipment, and competitions for [rock climbing]. . . . Large, full-color glossy photos . . . include action shots, closeup views of equipment and techniques, and pictures of exotic landscapes." SLJ

Includes bibliographical references

796.54 Camping

Champion, Neil

Fire and cooking. Amicus 2010 32p il (Survive alive) lib bdg $19.95

Grades: 4 5 6 7   **796.54**

1. Fires 2. Camping 3. Wilderness survival

ISBN 978-1-60753-039-8 lib bdg; 1-60753-039-2 lib bdg

LC 2010001626

This offers survival tips for building a fire and cooking in the wild, including information on different kinds of fires. Also discusses how to know what to cook and utensils to use.

This "colorful [book contains] numerous photos and illustrations that effectively break the [text] into small, readable chucks. There's lots of practical, everyday information here. . . . Brief yet gripping real-life survival stories are interspersed throughout the [book]." SLJ

796.6 Cycling and related activities

Macy, Sue

★ **Wheels** of change; how women rode the bicycle to freedom (with a few flat tires along the way) National Geographic 2011 96p il map $18.95; lib bdg $27.90

Grades: 4 5 6 7 8   **796.6**

1. Cycling 2. Bicycles 3. Gender role 4. Women athletes 5. Sex role 6. Feminism 7. Women -- United States -- History 8. Cycling for women

ISBN 978-1-4263-0761-4; 1-4263-0761-6; 978-1-4263-0762-1 lib bdg; 1-4263-0762-4 lib bdg

LC 2010-27141

This is an "engaging look at the emancipating impact that bikes had on late-nineteenth-century U.S. women. The eye-catching chapters, filled with archival images . . . zero in on the profound ways that bicycles subverted traditional notions of femininity. . . . Macy seamlessly weaves together research, direct quotes . . . and historical overviews that put the facts into context, while sidebars expand on related topics. . . . A strong, high-interest choice for both classroom and personal reading." Booklist

Includes bibliographical references

Robinson, Laura

★ **Cyclist** bikelist; a book for every rider. illustrated by Ramón K. Pérez. Tundra Books 2010 55p il pa $17.95

Grades: 4 5 6 7   **796.6**

1. Cycling 2. Bicycles

ISBN 978-0-88776-784-5; 0-88776-784-2

The author "covers a broad range of topics, from choosing and caring for a bike to differences in tires, how gear ratios work, and even proper dress and nutrition. She also provides a quick overview of the bicycle's history and inspiring sketches of several renowned racers. . . . Supplemented by photos of different types of bikes, Pérez's bright, cartoon-style pictures add both humor and . . . sharply drawn details. A first-rate guide." Booklist

796.72   Automobile racing

Arroyo, Sheri L.

How race car drivers use math; math curriculum consultant: Rhea A. Stewart. Chelsea Clubhouse 2010 32p il (Math in the real world) lib bdg $28

Grades: 4 5 6   **796.72**

1. Mathematics 2. Automobile racing 3. Vocational guidance

ISBN 978-1-60413-609-8 lib bdg; 1-60413-609-X lib bdg

LC 2009-21476

"The layout for [this slim [title] is bright and colorful with a photograph and a 'You Do the Math' problem to solve and large, easy-to-read text on every spread. An answer key is included in the back matter, along with a page detailing the career choices and the educational requirements. . . . In [this title], readers learn about qualifying times, track designs, and tracking fuel. . . . [This title] would be useful to supplement lessons on mathematics. [It] will also appeal to students wanting to learn more about math as it relates to specific careers." SLJ

Includes glossary and bibliographical references

Blackwood, Gary L.

The **Great** Race; the amazing round-the-world auto race of 1908. [by] Gary Blackwood. Abrams Books for Young Readers 2008 141p il $19.95

Grades: 6 7 8 9   **796.72**

1. Automobile racing 2. Voyages around the world 3. Automobile racing -- History

ISBN 978-0-8109-9489-8; 0-8109-9489-5

LC 2007-22414

"In 1908, several car manufacturers sponsored a global race that was routed across America, then across Siberia and Europe, ending in Paris. . . . Blackwood presents an extremely well-researched and detailed account of this large-scale publicity stunt. . . . There's enough sheer adventure here, carried out by some eccentric characters, to attract almost every reader. Helping things along are the photographs from the event. . . . A fascinating account." Booklist

Eagen, Rachel

NASCAR; written by Rachel Eagen. Crabtree Pub. Co. 2007 32p il (Automania!) lib bdg $25.20; pa $8.95

Grades: 4 5 6   **796.72**

1. Automobile racing

ISBN 978-0-7787-3007-1 lib bdg; 0-7787-3007-7 lib bdg; 978-0-7787-3029-3 pa; 0-7787-3029-8 pa

LC 2006012406

"Eagen has done an excellent job explaining the National Association of Stock Car Automobile Racing—the history, the modification of the cars, the drivers, and the competitions—while conveying a sense of the magnitude of the sport's current fan base. Her lucid, interesting text gets a lift from plenty of high-energy photos." Booklist

Kelley, K. C.

Hottest NASCAR machines; by K. C. Kelley. Enslow Publishers 2008 48p il (Wild wheels!) lib bdg $23.93

Grades: 4 5 6 7   **796.72**

1. Automobile racing

ISBN 978-0-7660-2869-2 lib bdg; 0-7660-2869-0 lib bdg

LC 2007007426

"Experience the thrill of a NASCAR race, and learn about the cars, personalities, and races associated with this sport." Publisher's note

Includes glossary and bibliographical references

Morganelli, Adrianna

Formula One. Crabtree Pub. 2007 32p il (Automania!) lib bdg $25.20; pa $8.95

Grades: 4 5 6   **796.72**

1. Automobile racing

ISBN 978-0-7787-3009-5 lib bdg; 0-7787-3009-3 lib bdg; 978-0-7787-3031-6 pa; 0-7787-3031-X pa

LC 2006-14362

This book "traces the history of Grand Prix racing, the development of the cars and their equipment, qualifying and racing, the tracks, safety measures, racing teams, and dominant drivers, with a sidebar on women in F1 racing. . . . Morganelli's writing is . . . organized and . . . readable. . . . [This] book is an attractive introduction." SLJ

Includes glossary

Pimm, Nancy Roe

The **Daytona** 500; the thrill and thunder of the great American race. Milbrook Press 2011 64p il (Spectacular sports) lib bdg $29.27

Grades: 5 6 7 8   **796.72**

1. Automobile racing

ISBN 978-0-7613-6677-5; 0-7613-6677-6

LC 2010027263

"Pimm, who worked in the pit box during her husband Ed Pimm's NASCAR racing days, offers an informative introduction to the Daytona 500. Beginning in 1903 . . . this traces the event's history and discusses the cars, drivers, strategies, and memorable moments. Colorful photos illustrate the clear text, while the many sidebars spotlight related facts." Booklist

Includes bibliographical references

796.8   Combat sports

Bjorklund, Ruth

Aikido. Marshall Cavendish Benchmark 2011 47p il (Martial arts in action) $29.93

Grades: 4 5 6 7   **796.8**

1. Aikido

ISBN 978-0-7614-4931-7; 978-1-6087-0361-6 e-book

LC 2010013820

This describes the history, equipment, and technique of aikido.

This treats "martial arts with the dignity that serious enthusiasts bring to the sport. . . . Illustrations include not only photos of modern gear and from films but also historical images." Booklist

Ellis, Carol

Judo and jujitsu. Marshall Cavendish Benchmark 2011 47p il (Martial arts in action) $29.93
Grades: 4 5 6 7   **796.8**
 1. Judo 2. Jiu-jitsu
 ISBN 978-0-7614-4933-1; 978-1-6087-0363-0 e-book
                                    LC 2010013821

This describes the history, equipment, and technique of judo and jujitsu.

This treats "martial arts with the dignity that serious enthusiasts bring to the sport. . . . Illustrations include not only photos of modern gear and from films but also historical images." Booklist

Kendo. Marshall Cavendish Benchmark 2010 47p il (Martial arts in action) $29.93
Grades: 4 5 6 7   **796.8**
 1. Kendo
 ISBN 978-0-7614-4935-5; 0-7614-4935-3
                                    LC 2010013827

This book about kendo offers "an introduction, a brief history, and expectations for students who begin taking classes. . . . [This title is] outstanding, using an approachable voice without fictionalizing and presenting the history of [kendo] in a way that makes it feel relevant." SLJ

Includes glossary and bibliographical references

Wrestling. Marshall Cavendish Benchmark 2010 47p il (Martial arts in action) $29.93
Grades: 4 5 6 7   **796.8**
 1. Wrestling
 ISBN 978-0-7614-4941-6; 0-7614-4941-8
                                    LC 2010013819

This book about wrestling offers "an introduction, a brief history, and expectations for students who begin taking classes. . . . [This title is] outstanding, using an approachable voice without fictionalizing and presenting the history of [wrestling] in a way that makes it feel relevant." SLJ

Includes glossary and bibliographical references

Haney-Withrow, Anna

Tae kwon do. Marshall Cavendish Benchmark 2011 47p il (Martial arts in action) $29.93
Grades: 4 5 6 7   **796.8**
 1. Tae kwon do
 ISBN 978-0-7614-4940-9; 978-1-6087-0368-5 e-book
                                    LC 2010013828

This describes the history, equipment, and technique of tae kwon do.

This treats "martial arts with the dignity that serious enthusiasts bring to the sport. . . . Illustrations include not only photos of modern gear and from films but also historical images." Booklist

Inman, Roy

The **judo** handbook; [by] Roy Inman. North American ed.; Rosen Pub. 2008 256p il (Martial arts) lib bdg $39.95

Grades: 7 8 9 10 11 12   **796.8**
 1. Judo
 ISBN 978-1-4042-1393-7; 1-4042-1393-7
                                    LC 2007-37742

This features "step-by-step descriptions of various moves, accompanied by detailed, full-color photographs. [This] volume offers a background on the history of the art and its use as a sport as well as a system for self-defense. [The] handbook features a concise description of the judo fundamentals, then begins describing the techniques: throwing techniques, combination and counter-techniques, ground techniques, and combination and counter-techniques against them. The book makes good use of the Japanese terms used in judo study, integrating their meanings seamlessly into the text." SLJ

Includes bibliographical references

Mack, Gail

Kickboxing. Marshall Cavendish Benchmark 2011 47p il lib bdg $29.93
Grades: 4 5 6 7   **796.8**
 1. Kickboxing
 ISBN 978-0-7614-4936-2; 978-1-6087-0366-1 e-book
                                    LC 2010014798

This describes the history, equipment, and technique of kickboxing.

This treats "martial arts with the dignity that serious enthusiasts bring to the sport. . . . Illustrations include not only photos of modern gear and from films but also historical images." Booklist

Mason, Paul, 1967-

Boxing. Sea-to-Sea Publications 2011 32p il (Combat sports) lib bdg $28.50
Grades: 4 5 6   **796.8**
 1. Boxing
 ISBN 978-1-59771-273-6; 1-59771-273-6

"...[Provides] an inviting look for students who are learning about techniques and for examining records and statistics... Use to refresh an older collection." SLJ

Includes glossary and bibliographical references

Pawlett, Mark

The **tae** kwon do handbook; [by] Mark and Ray Pawlett. Rosen Pub. 2008 256p il (Martial arts) lib bdg $39.95
Grades: 7 8 9 10 11 12   **796.8**
 1. Tae kwon do
 ISBN 978-1-4042-1396-8; 1-4042-1396-1
                                    LC 2007-31559

This features "step-by-step descriptions of various moves, accompanied by detailed, full-color photographs. [The] volume offers a background on the history of the art and its use as a sport as well as a system for self-defense. . . . [The book] spends about 150 pages on techniques, and also covers dietary recommendations, a history of Korea, a description of the I Ching, and other concepts. . . . It [includes] an excellent section on strength training . . . and the text devoted to basic fundamentals of the sport, such as stances and stepping, gives those building blocks appropriate importance." SLJ

Includes bibliographical references

Pawlett, Raymond

The **karate** handbook; [by] Ray Pawlett. Rosen Pub. Group 2008 256p il (Martial arts) $39.95

Grades: 7 8 9 10 11 12   **796.8**
1. Karate
ISBN 978-1-4042-1394-4; 1-4042-1394-5
                                LC 2007-32795

This "offers a thorough introduction to karate that covers both the underlying philosophy and the physical practice. A thoughtful, sophisticated history opens the book and discusses karate's roots in Zen Buddhism, the styles of karate, and dojo etiquette. Later spreads feature lucid, step-by-step instructions." Booklist

Includes bibliographical references

Ritschel, John

The **kickboxing** handbook; [by] John Ritschel. Rosen Pub. 2008 256p il (Martial arts) lib bdg $39.95

Grades: 7 8 9 10 11 12   **796.8**
1. Martial arts
ISBN 978-1-4042-1395-1; 1-4042-1395-3
                                LC 2007-37746

"This volume features step-by-step descriptions of various moves and strength-building exercises, accompanied by detailed, full-color photographs. . . . [This book] does emphasize safety, showing the correct way to punch in order to avoid injuring one's hand and displaying clear photographs on striking areas of the foot in order to perform kicks properly." SLJ

Whiting, Jim

Blood and guts; the basics of mixed martial arts. Capstone Press 2010 48p il (Velocity. the world of mixed martial arts) lib bdg $27.99

Grades: 5 6 7 8   **796.8**
1. Martial arts
ISBN 978-1-4296-3428-1 lib bdg; 1-4296-3428-6 lib bdg
                                LC 2009-7346

"Whiting provides information in fact boxes and in short bursts of text. Dramatic camera angles show sweating, bloody kickboxers, and cagefighters from just outside the ring. . . . The author also discusses how politics has entered into the viewing of competitions on network and pay-per-view television. Fans of the sport will be mesmerized." SLJ

Includes glossary and bibliographical references

Inside the cage; the greatest fights of mixed martial arts. Capstone Press 2010 48p il (Velocity. the world of mixed martial arts) lib bdg $27.99

Grades: 5 6 7 8   **796.8**
1. Martial arts
ISBN 978-1-4296-3426-7 lib bdg; 1-4296-3426-X lib bdg
                                LC 2009-7344

"Whiting provides information in fact boxes and in short bursts of text. Dramatic camera angles show sweating, bloody kickboxers, and cagefighters from just outside the ring. . . . The author also discusses how politics has entered

into the viewing of competitions on network and pay-per-view television. Fans of the sport will be mesmerized." SLJ

Includes glossary and bibliographical references

Striking, grappling, and ground fighting; the skills behind mixed martial arts. Capstone Press 2010 48p il (Velocity. the world of mixed martial arts) lib bdg $27.99

Grades: 5 6 7 8   **796.8**
1. Martial arts
ISBN 978-1-4296-3425-0 lib bdg; 1-4296-3425-1 lib bdg
                                LC 2009-7337

"Whiting provides information in fact boxes and in short bursts of text. Dramatic camera angles show sweating, bloody kickboxers, and cagefighters from just outside the ring. . . . The author also discusses how politics has entered into the viewing of competitions on network and pay-per-view television. Fans of the sport will be mesmerized." SLJ

Includes glossary and bibliographical references

A **new** generation of warriors; the history of mixed martial arts. Capstone Press 2010 48p il (Velocity. The world of mixed martial arts) lib bdg $27.99

Grades: 5 6 7 8   **796.8**
1. Martial arts
ISBN 978-1-4296-3427-4 lib bdg; 1-4296-3427-8 lib bdg
                                LC 2009-7339

"Whiting provides information in fact boxes and in short bursts of text. Dramatic camera angles show sweating, bloody kickboxers, and cagefighters from just outside the ring. . . . The author also discusses how politics has entered into the viewing of competitions on network and pay-per-view television. Fans of the sport will be mesmerized." SLJ

Includes glossary and bibliographical references

796.815   Oriental martial arts forms

Mason, Paul, 1967-

Judo; [by] Paul Mason. Sea-to-Sea Publications 2009 30 p. col. ill. (Know your sport) (library) $27.10

Grades: 5 6 7 8   **796.815**
1. Judo
ISBN 978-1-59771-151-7; 1-59771-151-9
                                LC 2008007318

"Describes the equipment, training, moves, and competitions of judo. Includes step-by-step descriptions of moves." Publisher's note

Includes index.

796.91   Ice skating

McDougall, Chros

Figure skating. Norwood House Press 2010 64p il (Girls play to win) lib bdg $26.60

Grades: 4 5 6 7   **796.91**
1. Ice skating
ISBN 978-1-59953-389-6; 1-59953-389-8
LC 2010009809
"This begins with a look back at the origin of [figure skating] and the traces the young women who played a role in skating from the olden days to today. The first of six chapters describes skating basics . . . and then the progression of stars begins. . . . Color photos, sidebars, and boxed explanations break up the text. . . . A nicely compact history." Booklist
Includes glossary and bibliographical references

Uschan, Michael V., 1948-
Apolo Anton Ohno; by Michael V. Uschan. Lucent Books 2011 104 p. (People in the News) (hbk.) $33.95
Grades: 7 8 9 10   **796.91**
1. Speed skating 2. Olympic athletes 3. Speed skaters -- United States 4. Speed skaters -- United States -- Biography
ISBN 142050603X; 9781420506037
LC 2011003418
This book offers a biography of Olympic speed skater Apolo Anton Ohno, an athlete who has won eight Olympic medals as of 2012, by author Michael V. Uschan. It is part of the "People in the News" series, which "profiles the lives and careers of some of today's most prominent newsmakers. Whether covering contributions and achievements or notorious deeds, books in this series examine why these well-known individuals garnered public attention." (Publisher's note)
Includes bibliographical references and index.

796.93   Skiing and snowboarding

Kenney, Karen Latchana
Skiing & snowboarding. Norwood House Press 2010 64p il (Girls play to win) lib bdg $26.60
Grades: 4 5 6 7   **796.93**
1. Skiing 2. Snowboarding
ISBN 978-1-59953-391-9; 1-59953-391-X
LC 2010009808
Covers the history, rules, fundamentals and significant personalities of the sports of women's skiing and snowboarding. Topics include: techniques, strategies, competitive events, and equipment.
"With an easy design and format, the [text is] highly accessible to even the most reluctant readers and [provides] great exposure and insight into the world of female professional sports." Horn Book Guide
Includes glossary and bibliographical references

Schwartz, Heather E.
Snowboarding. Lucent Books 2011 104p il (Science behind sports) $33.45
Grades: 5 6 7 8   **796.93**
1. Snowboarding
ISBN 978-1-4205-0322-7; 1-4205-0322-7
LC 2010033274
This "explores the scientific principles such as momentum, gravity, friction, and aerodynamics, plus many more,

behind [snowbarding]. . . . [The author discusses the sport's] origins, history, and changes, . . . the biomechanics and physiology of playing, related health and medical concerns, and the causes and treatment of sports-related injuries. Additional information tells how exercise, diet and nutrition, warming up, and training relate to peak performance and enjoyment of the sport. . . . The action photography . . . is fantastic. . . . [This volume is] jam-packed full of information. [A must-have] for sports fans, athletes, science students, and even anyone considering a career in sports-related medicine, coaching, or other connected fields." SLJ
Includes glossary and bibliographical references

796.94   Snowmobiling

Woods, Bob
Snowmobile racers. Enslow Publishers 2010 48p il (Kid racers) lib bdg $23.93
Grades: 5 6 7 8   **796.94**
1. Snowmobiles
ISBN 978-0-7660-3487-7 lib bdg; 0-7660-3487-9 lib bdg
LC 2009020784
This describes snowmobiles and races for kids, discussing which snowmobiles qualify, how they are built and raced, who the best drivers are, what to look for in a snowmobile, safety, good sportsmanship, and how racing activities can be a good part of family life.
"The easily digestible text gets more visual weight on the page, but there are plenty of captioned color photos depicting different sorts of races as well as recreational snowmobiling." Booklist
Includes glossary and bibliographical references

796.962   Ice hockey

Adams, Carly
Queens of the ice; they were fast, they were fierce, they were teenage girls. Lorimer 2011 131p il (Record books) $16.95; pa $9.95
Grades: 5 6 7 8   **796.962**
1. Hockey 2. Women athletes
ISBN 978-1-55277-721-3; 1-55277-721-9; 978-1-55277-720-6 pa; 1-55277-720-0 pa
"Filled with exciting action, this . . . title . . . showcases the history of the Preston Rivulettes, a Canadian hockey team of teenage girls who played together for 10 seasons, from 1931 until 1940, without losing a game and at a time when many believed that girls could not play the sport and needed chaperones. . . . Adams deepens the story with the historical background of the Great Depression and the team's struggle to find money. Occasional achival photos and boxed inserts add to the clear, readable account." Booklist

Johnstone, Robb
Hockey; rev ed.; Weigl Publishers 2009 24p il (In the zone) $24.45; pa $8.95

Grades: 4 5 6 7 **796.962**
1. Hockey
ISBN 978-1-6059-6130-9; 1-6059-6130-2; 978-1-
6059-6131-6 pa; 1-6059-6131-0 pa
LC 2009005607
First published 2001
"Colorful, informative. . . . For those just showing an interest in the bone-crushing sport, [this is] an excellent place
to get their bearings. Using short, mostly two-page chapters,
Johnstone explains the genesis of the sport, the gear needed,
the rules, the positions, and the leagues, before concluding
with biographies of eight legendary NHL players." Booklist

McKinley, Michael
Ice time; the story of hockey. Tundra Books
2006 80p il $18.95
Grades: 5 6 7 8 **796.962**
1. Hockey 2. Hockey -- Canada
ISBN 978-0-88776-762-3; 0-88776-762-1
"This straightforward history of hockey emphasizes the
professional game and Canadian players. . . . Hockey enthusiasts will find this a welcome arrival." Booklist

McMahon, Dave
Hockey. Norwood House Press 2010 64p il
(Girls play to win) lib bdg $26.60
Grades: 4 5 6 7 **796.962**
1. Hockey
ISBN 978-1-59953-390-2; 1-59953-390-1
LC 2010009811
Covers the history, rules, fundamentals and significant
personalities of the sport of women's hockey. Topics include:
techniques, strategies, competitive events, and equipment.
"With an easy design and format, the [text is] highly ac-
cessible to even the most reluctant readers and [provides]
great exposure and insight into the world of female profes-
sional sports." Horn Book Guide
Includes glossary and bibliographical references

Sharp, Anne Wallace
Ice hockey. Lucent Books 2011 112p il map
(Science behind sports) lib bdg $33.45
Grades: 5 6 7 8 **796.962**
1. Hockey
ISBN 978-1-4205-0281-7; 1-4205-0281-6
LC 2010025670
This book about ice hockey highlights "performance;
chapter headings include topics such as 'Training and Nutri-
tion,' 'High-Tech Equipment,' and 'Injuries and Treatments.'
Physics, biology, and psychology concepts related to the
[sport] are . . . wrapped into technical discussions of moves
and techniques. Many photographs of pros and novices in
action add interest." Horn Book Guide
Includes glossary and bibliographical references

Stewart, Mark
Score! the action and artistry of hockey's magnif-
icent moment. Millbrook Press 2010 64p il $29.27
Grades: 5 6 7 8 **796.962**
1. Hockey
ISBN 978-0-8225-8753-8; 0-8225-8753-X

"Stewart and Kennedy take readers on a chatty, photo-
studded tour of the art of scoring in the rink. This interme-
diate-level hockey book definitely isn't for beginners. . . .
What savvy readers will get, however, is a bounty of information on the game's defining goals, goal scorers, and goal-
scoring techniques. . . . This makes a worthy addition to any
sports shelf." Booklist

796.98   Winter Olympic games

Macy, Sue
★ **Freeze** frame; a photographic history of the
Winter Olympics. National Geographic 2006 96p il
map $18.95
Grades: 5 6 7 8 9 10 **796.98**
1. Olympic games 2. Winter sports
ISBN 0-7922-7887-9; 978-0-7922-7887-0
Highlights in the history of the Winter Olympics from
their inception in 1924 to today, including profiles of the
Olympic athletes and information on the lesser-known win-
ter sports. Also includes an Olympic almanac with informa-
tion about each Olympiad.
This book "has spectacular photographs and clear, cap-
tivating prose." SLJ
Includes bibliographical references

797.1   Aquatic sports

Storey, Rita
Sailing. Sea-to-Sea Publications 2011 30p il
(Know your sport) lib bdg $28.50
Grades: 4 5 6 **797.1**
1. Sailing
ISBN 978-1-59771-286-6
LC 2010003439
This "volume provides an introduction to the equipment,
techniques, and safety measures for [sailing]. . . . Instruc-
tive photographs help illustrate such concepts as [tacking a
sailboat], . . . while engaging stock images capture the ex-
citement on the water. The [volume concludes] with racing
information, profiling top racers, rules, and tactics." Horn
Book Guide
Includes glossary

Thorpe, Yvonne
Canoeing and kayaking. Sea-to-Sea Publications
2011 30p il (Know your sport) $28.50
Grades: 4 5 6 **797.1**
1. Canoes and canoeing 2. Kayaks and kayaking
ISBN 9781597712859
LC 2010003438
This "volume provides an introduction to the equipment,
techniques, and safety measures for [canoeing and kayak-
ing]. . . . Instructive photographs help illustrate such concepts as . . . paddling a kayak, while engaging stock images
capture the excitement on the water. The [volume concludes]
with racing information, profiling top racers, rules, and tactics." Horn Book Guide
Includes glossary

Wurdinger, Scott D.

Kayaking; by Scott Wurdinger and Leslie Rap-parlie. Creative Education 2006 48p il (Adventure sports) $21.95

Grades: 5 6 7 8   **797.1**

1. Kayaks and kayaking
ISBN 978-1-58341-397-5

LC 2005051057

"Strong, full-page color photographs illustrate this overview of kayaking. . . . Tracing the use of kayaks back thousands of years, the authors touch on the history of the boats before moving on to contemporary usage for sports and recreation. . . . The exciting views . . . will instantly draw browsers and serious readers alike." Booklist

Includes bibliographical references

797.2 Swimming and diving

Arroyo, Sheri L.

How deep sea divers use math; math curriculum consultant: Rhea A. Stewart. Chelsea Clubhouse 2010 32p il (Math in the real world) lib bdg $28

Grades: 4 5 6   **797.2**

1. Mathematics 2. Scuba diving 3. Vocational guidance
ISBN 978-1-60413-611-1 lib bdg; 1-60413-611-1 lib bdg

LC 2009-18413

"The layout for [this] slim [title] is bright and colorful with a photograph and a 'You Do the Math' problem to solve and large, easy-to-read text on every spread. An answer key is included in the back matter, along with a page detailing the career choices and the educational requirements. . . . [It] discusses how divers use math to determine how much air they will need in their tanks and use grids to map underwater shipwrecks. The mathematical topics covered include measurement, estimation, data analysis, and problem solving. . . . [This title] would be useful to supplement lessons on mathematics. [It] will also appeal to students wanting to learn more about math as it relates to specific careers." SLJ

Includes glossary and bibliographical references

Gifford, Clive

Swimming; [by] Clive Gifford. PowerKids Press 2009 32p il (Personal best) lib bdg $25.25

Grades: 4 5 6 7 8   **797.2**

1. Swimming
ISBN 978-1-4042-4443-6 lib bdg; 1-4042-4443-3 lib bdg

LC 2007-43003

This guide to swimming "offers well-organized and easy-to-follow instructions, focusing on rules, clothing, specific skills, and competitions. . . . Informative, readable." SLJ

Hoblin, Paul

Swimming & diving. Norwood House Press 2011 64p il (Girls play to win) lib bdg $26.60

Grades: 4 5 6 7   **797.2**

1. Diving 2. Swimming
ISBN 978-1-59953-466-4; 1-59953-466-5

LC 2011011038

Covers the history, rules, fundamentals, and significant personalities of the sport of women's swimming and diving. Topics include: techniques, strategies, competitive events, and equipment.

Includes glossary and bibliographical references

Timblin, Stephen

Swimming. Cherry Lake Pub. 2009 32p il (Innovation in sports) lib bdg $27.07

Grades: 4 5 6 7   **797.2**

1. Swimming
ISBN 978-1-60279-258-6 lib bdg; 1-60279-258-5 lib bdg

LC 2008002046

This describes swimming history, rules, equipment, training, and swimming stars

This "stands out by emphasizing monumental shifts and advances in the events themselves. . . . Concise and occasionally revelatory." Booklist

Includes glossary and bibliographical references

797.5 Air sports

Blair, Margaret Whitman

The roaring 20; the first cross-country air race for women. National Geographic 2006 128p il map $21.95

Grades: 6 7 8 9   **797.5**

1. Airplane racing 2. Women air pilots
ISBN 0-7922-5389-2

LC 2005-05472

"This book offers a detailed look at the first 'Powder Puff Derby' run in the summer of 1929. . . . Starting in Santa Monica, California, and ending in Cleveland, Ohio, the women flew over deserts and mountains. . . . It was an all-star event with racers including Amelia Earhart, 'Pancho' Barnes, and Louise Thaden. . . . The photos of flyers, landscapes, and memorabilia bring the story to life. This book is a welcome addition." Voice Youth Advocates

Includes bibliographical references

798.4 Horse racing

Scanlan, Lawrence

The big red horse; the story of Secretariat and the loyal groom who loved him. with photos by Raymond Woolfe. Harper Trophy 2011 166p il pa $7.99

Grades: 4 5 6 7   **798.4**

1. Horse racing 2. Stablehands
ISBN 978-0-06-202669-9; 0-06-202669-0

"This biography of the legendary racehorse provides many intimate details about his daily life and incredible prowess. . . . His good looks and tremendous athletic ability enabled him to win the Triple Crown at a record-breaking pace and the hearts of the American people. Scanlan focuses on the special relationship between Secretariat and his groom, Eddie Sweat. . . . Black-and-white photos are scattered throughout. . . . This solid book will have special appeal for horse lovers." SLJ

Tate, Nikki

Behind the scenes: the racehorse. Fitzhenry & Whiteside 2008 72p il $22.95; pa $18.95

Grades: 5 6 7 8   **798.4**

1. Horse racing 2. Racetracks (Horse racing)

ISBN 978-1-55455-018-0; 1-55455-018-1; 978-1-55455-032-6 pa; 1-55455-032-7 pa

"A short history of horse racing opens this attractive and informative book. Tate discusses the breeding, training, and care of the horses but devotes plenty of space to the people who are involved in the sport. . . . The many color photos . . . are quite clear and well matched to the text." Booklist

799.2   Hunting

Peterson, Judy Monroe

Big game hunting. Rosen Central 2011 64p il map (Hunting: pursuing wild game!)) lib bdg $29.25; pa $12.95

Grades: 5 6 7 8   **799.2**

1. Hunting

ISBN 978-1-4488-1240-0 lib bdg; 1-4488-1240-2 lib bdg; 978-1-4488-2270-6 pa; 1-4488-2270-X pa

LC 2010006859

In this introduction to big game hunting "Peterson displays an impressive grasp of the pastime by throwing in almost everything: types of guns and bows, safety laws, licenses, land access, animal behavior, clothing, methods of hunting, and preparing harvested meat. . . . [The book] is jam-packed with info. . . . A green-heavy design, bright photoss of hunters . . . and prey, and above average back matter close out this solid entry." Booklist

Includes bibliographical references

Wolny, Philip

Waterfowl. Rosen Central 2011 64p il (Hunting: pursuing wild game!) lib bdg $29.25; pa $12.95

Grades: 4 5 6 7   **799.2**

1. Hunting 2. Water birds

ISBN 978-1-4488-1243-1 lib bdg; 1-4488-1243-7 lib bdg; 978-1-4488-2273-7 pa; 1-4488-2273-4 pa

LC 2010017396

This guide to waterfowl hunting covers what to wear and pack, shooting strategies, the construction of duck blinds, gun safety, hunting permits and licenses, and other laws relating to hunting limits, seasons, and private and public property.

Includes bibliographical references

800   LITERATURE, RHETORIC & CRITICISM

803   Dictionaries, encyclopedias, concordances

Benet's reader's encyclopedia; edited by Bruce F. Murphy. 5th ed.; Collins 2008 1210p $60

Grades: 8 9 10 11 12 Adult   **803**

1. Reference books 2. Literature -- Dictionaries

ISBN 978-0-06-089016-2

LC 2008-31430

First published 1948 under the editorship of William Rose Benet

This encyclopedia contains over 10,000 entries and covers world literature from early times to the present. Includes entries on authors, literary movements, principal characters, plot synopses, terms, awards, myths and legends, etc.

This is "an edifying staple for any literary library." Libr J

Dictionary of phrase and fable

Brewer's dictionary of phrase & fable; edited by Camilla Rockwood. 18th ed.; Brewer's 2009 xxv, 1460p il $49.95

Grades: 5 6 7 8 9 10 11 12 Adult   **803**

1. Allusions 2. Reference books 3. Mythology -- Dictionaries 4. Literature -- Dictionaries 5. English language -- Terms and phrases

ISBN 978-0-550-10411-3

LC 2009-379960

First published 1870 under the editorship of Ebenezer Cobham Brewer

"Over 15,000 brief entries give the meanings and origins of a broad range of terms, expressions, and names of real, fictitious and mythical characters from world history, science, the arts and literature." N Y Public Libr. Ref Books for Child Collect. 2d edition

808   Rhetoric and collections of literary texts from more than two literatures

Bauer, Marion Dane

A **writer's** story; from life to fiction. Clarion Bks. 1995 134p $14.95; pa $6.95

Grades: 7 8 9 10   **808**

1. Authors 2. Women authors 3. Authors, American 4. Children's authors 5. Authorship

ISBN 0-395-72094-X; 0-395-75053-9 pa

LC 94-48800

"Drawing on her own experiences, the novelist examines the origins of inspiration and the subconscious drives that compel authors to write. She points out that many components of fiction—characters, settings, plot details—need not be autobiographical, yet the text does suggest that a story's meaning is directly linked to the unique experiences of its creator. . . . Bauer provides invaluable information for both writers and readers of fiction." Publ Wkly

Cornwall, Phyllis

Put it all together. Cherry Lake Pub. 2010 32p il (Super smart information strategies) lib bdg $27.97

Grades: 3 4 5 6 **808**

1. Report writing

ISBN 978-1-60279-643-0 lib bdg; 1-60279-643-2 lib bdg

LC 2009027806

"The appealing layout includes manageable paragraphs, a variety of engaging illustrations, and examples that clearly guide readers through each topic. In [this book], strategies include gathering resources, organizing information, and ways of presenting discoveries." SLJ

Includes glossary and bibliographical references

Dunn, Jessica

★ A **teen's** guide to getting published; publishing for profit, recognition, and academic success. [by] Jessica Dunn & Danielle Dunn. 2nd ed.; Prufrock Press 2006 249p pa $14.95

Grades: 7 8 9 10 11 12 **808**

1. Authorship 2. Publishers and publishing

ISBN 1-59363-182-0

LC 2006005109

First published 1997

"In addition to standard advice on publishers and agents, the authors give practical suggestions for finding a writing environment that is accessible to teens, such as school publication staffs and local newspaper internships. . . . Annotated appendixes list Web sites, books, journals, and contests. Also provided is information on mentors, writing camps, and courses catering to young authors, and a valuable list of mainstream publishers who have expressed openness to submissions from teens. This compact, sensible book discusses all kinds of writing." SLJ

Flath, Camden

Freelance and technical writers; words for sale. Mason Crest Publishers 2010 64p il (New careers for the 21st century: finding your role in the global renewal) $22.95

Grades: 7 8 9 10 **808**

1. Authorship 2. Technical writing 3. Vocational guidance

ISBN 1-4222-1814-7; 978-1-4222-1814-3

LC 2010011419

"Each chapter divides information between general freelance writing and technical writing, with the latter painted as the way of the future. . . . Flath carefully details the highs and lows of self-employment, keeping readers abreast of freelancers' special concerns, including taxes, time management, networking, and health insurance. He also highlights which personality types might enjoy writing projects. . . . Overall, the information is helpful for anxious students concerned about job prospects." Booklist

Fletcher, Ralph

How to write your life story; [by] Ralph Fletcher. Collins 2007 102p $15.99; pa $5.99

Grades: 5 6 7 8 **808**

1. Authorship 2. Autobiography -- Authorship

ISBN 978-0-06-050770-1; 978-0-06-050769-5 pa

LC 2007010990

A guide to help write an autobiography

"Fletcher gives readers and educators many practical and supportive tips. . . . Interspersed within the text are interviews with Jack Gantos, Kathi Appelt, and Jerry Spinelli, along with passages from the author's own memoir." SLJ

How writers work; finding a process that works for you. HarperTrophy 2000 114p pa $4.99

Grades: 4 5 6 7 **808**

1. Authorship 2. Creative writing

ISBN 0-380-79702-X

LC 00-27573

Focuses on the skills and techniques necessary for good writing, with excerpts from established writers and samples of young people's work as examples

"The book makes youngsters feel good about their writing without making light of the work involved. . . . This is a useful resource." SLJ

Includes bibliographical references

Gaines, Ann

★ **Don't** steal copyrighted stuff! avoiding plagiarism and illegal internet downloading. [by] Ann Graham Gaines. Enslow Publishers 2008 192p il (Prime) $38.60

Grades: 7 8 9 10 **808**

1. Copyright 2. Plagiarism 3. Bibliographical citations

ISBN 978-0-7660-2861-6; 0-7660-2861-5

LC 2007-8370

"The first three chapters explain just what plagiarism is, the types of plagiarism, and what copyright and fair use are. Two chapters explain how to find sources, take notes properly, and construct a project or paper using proper citations in MLA format. . . . Every student should be required to read this. . . . Librarians and teachers who are looking for explanations of copyright and plagiarism and illustrative examples will find this book to be a good resource." Libr Media Connect

Includes bibliographical references

Gilbert, Sara

Write your own article; newspaper, magazine, online. by Sara Gilbert. Compass Point Books 2009 64p il (Write your own) lib bdg $33.26; pa $5.95

Grades: 6 7 8 9 **808**

1. Authorship 2. Journalism

ISBN 978-0-7565-3855-2 lib bdg; 0-7565-3855-6 lib bdg; 978-0-7565-3945-0 pa; 0-7565-3945-5 pa

LC 2008-13342

"There is much useful information provided. . . . [The book has] full-color photos, graphics, and tinted text boxes on nearly every page. [This is a solid selection] for aspiring writers." SLJ

Includes glossary and bibliographical references

Harper, Elizabeth

Your name in print; a teen's guide to publishing for fun, profit, and academic success. [by] Elizabeth Harper and Timothy Harper. St. Martin's Griffin 2005 186p pa $13.95

Grades: 7 8 9 10   **808**

1. Authorship 2. Publishers and publishing 3. Authorship -- Handbooks, manuals, etc.

ISBN 0-312-33759-0

LC 2004-24675

The authors "offer chapters and features on a variety of subjects: writing outlets (such as local papers and blogs); article topics; workspaces; book publishing and agents; tips from pros; sample columns; [and] 'glances' at current teen writers. . . . This book will be a useful addition for most libraries." Voice Youth Advocates

Includes bibliographical references

Janeczko, Paul B.

★ **Writing** winning reports and essays. Scholastic Reference 2003 224p (Scholastic guides) lib bdg $16.95; pa $7.95

Grades: 5 6 7 8   **808**

1. Authorship 2. Report writing 3. Essay -- Authorship 4. English language -- Composition and exercises

ISBN 0-439-28717-0 lib bdg; 0-439-28718-9 pa

LC 2002-30543

Provides strategies for writing successful research reports and essays, including social studies reports, book reports, persuasive essays, personal essays, and descriptive essays

"A solid and useful resource." SLJ

Mack, James

Journals and blogging; [by] Jim Mack. Raintree 2009 32p il (Culture in action) $28.21; pa $7.99

Grades: 5 6 7 8   **808**

1. Diaries 2. Weblogs

ISBN 978-1-4109-3406-2; 1-4109-3406-3; 978-1-4109-3423-9 pa; 1-4109-3423-3 pa

LC 2009000490

This "encourages readers to write as a way to express their feelings. It describes different types of journals and blogs. A page on Internet safety and the danger of downloading material encourages adult supervision. . . . Well organized and with bright, colorful photography, [this] introductory [title gives] readers good basic knowledge." SLJ

Includes glossary and bibliographical references

Miles, Liz

Writing a screenplay. Raintree 2009 32p il (Culture in action) $28.21; pa $7.99

Grades: 5 6 7 8   **808**

1. Drama -- Technique

ISBN 978-1-4109-3407-9; 1-4109-3407-1; 978-1-4109-3424-6 pa; 1-4109-3424-1 pa

This covers writing for "film and television. Plot, location, characters, dialogue, and mood are a few of the components discussed. . . . Well organized and with bright, colorful photography, [this] introductory [title gives] readers good basic knowledge." SLJ

Includes glossary and bibliographical references

Nobleman, Marc Tyler

★ **Extraordinary** e-mails, letters, and resumes; by Marc Tyler Nobleman. Watts 2005 128p il (F. W. Prep) $30.50

Grades: 7 8 9 10   **808**

1. Letter writing 2. Resumes (Employment) 3. Electronic mail systems

ISBN 0-531-16759-3

This "builds a resume step-by-step, shows examples of different types of business letters, and addresses basic and not-so-basic netiquette. . . . [It is] laid out clearly and attractively, using bulleted lists, sample writings, and tables comparing examples of outstanding versus dull writing. The language is easy to follow, and the graphics and coloring enhances the books' readability." Voice Youth Advocates

Nuwer, Hank

To the young writer; nine writers talk about their craft. Watts 2002 111p il lib bdg $23

       808

1. Authorship 2. Authors, American 3. Authorship -- Vocational guidance 4. Authors, American -- 20th century -- Biography

ISBN 0-531-11591-7

LC 2001-24895

Nine writers, including a Hollywood screenwriter, a novelist, and a sportswriter, talk about their craft

"A concise, practical, and accessible guide. . . . A range of topics is discussed including the thrill of reporting, editing, storytelling, and writing for student publications, different audiences, and from personal experience. Also included are tips for aspiring writers. . . . This inspiring book offers a number of options for those considering the field." SLJ

Includes bibliographical references

Rosinsky, Natalie M.

Write your own biography; by Natalie M. Rosinsky. Compass Point Books 2008 64p il (Write your own) lib bdg $31.93

Grades: 5 6 7 8   **808**

1. Biography -- Authorship

ISBN 978-0-7565-3366-3 lib bdg; 0-7565-3366-X lib bdg

LC 2007011471

"Rosinsky adroitly leads readers through the challenging process of researching and writing a biography. Chapters include helpful suggestions, excerpts from published works, and writing exercises. Full-color photos, charts, and graphics break up the text." SLJ

Includes glossary and bibliographical references

Sendak, Maurice, 1928-2012

★ **My** brother's book; Maurice Sendak; [edited by] Michael di Capua. HarperCollins 2013 32 p. (hardcover bdg.) $18.95

Grades: 4 5 6 7 8   **808**

1. Poetry 2. Poetry -- Collections

ISBN 0062234897; 9780062234896

LC 2012942549

In this book, "with influences from Shakespeare and William Blake, [Maurice] Sendak pays homage to his late brother, Jack, whom he credited for his passion for writing and drawing. Pairing Sendak's . . . poetry with his . . . artwork, . . . Sendak's tribute to his brother is an expression of both grief and love. . . . Pulitzer Prize--winning literary critic and Shakespearean scholar Stephen Greenblatt contributes a[n] . . . introduction." (Publisher's note)

Tadjo, Veronique

★ **Talking** drums; a selection of poems from Africa south of the Sahara. edited and illustrated by Véronique Tadjo. Bloomsbury Children's Books 2003 96p il map $15.95

Grades: 5 6 7 8   **808**

1. African poetry 2. African poetry (English) 3. African poetry -- Collections 4. African poetry -- Translations into English
ISBN 1-58234-813-8

LC 2003-52173

A collection of traditional and twentieth-century poems from sub-Saharan Africa, written in or translated into English, that expresses the spirit and history of this region

"The contemporary and the traditional are both well represented in this lively anthology. . . . Illustrated with small, black-and-white folk-art drawings, the collection ranges widely, including poems of love, sorrow, and pride. . . . This [is a] fine resource for social studies and literature classes, which will also be great for reading aloud." Booklist

Includes glossary

★ **Welcome** to Bordertown; new stories and poems of the Borderlands. edited by Holly Black and Ellen Kushner; introduction by Terri Windling. Random House 2011 517p $19.99; lib bdg $22.99; e-book $19.99

Grades: 7 8 9 10   **808**

1. Short stories 2. Fantasy fiction 3. Poetry -- Collections 4. Supernatural -- Fiction
ISBN 978-0-375-86705-7; 0-375-86705-8; 978-0-375-96705-4 lib bdg; 0-375-96705-2 lib bdg; 978-0-375-89745-0 e-book

LC 2010-35558

This collection of short stories and poems focuses on Bordertown, "a city on the border between our human world and the elfin realm. Runaway teens come from both sides of the border to find adventure, to find themselves. Elves play in rock bands and race down the street on spell-powered motorbikes. Human kids recreate themselves in the squats and clubs and artists' studios of Soho." (Publisher's note)

"This is punk-rock, DIY fantasy, full of harsh reality and incandescent magic . . . Many of the stories echo with loss and discomfort; standouts include 'Crossings' by Janni Lee Simner, a chilling look at the difference between dreams and reality, and 'A Tangle of Green Men,' Charles De Lint's heartbreaking examination of love, loss and life. Poems and songs (from Patricia A. McKillip, Neil Gaiman and Jane Yolen, among others) balance the fiction. . . . A masterful anthology." Kirkus

Where we are, what we see; the best young artists and writers in America: a Push anthology. edited

by David Levithan. PUSH/Scholastic 2005 220p il pa $7.99

Grades: 7 8 9 10   **808**

1. Teenagers' writings 2. American literature -- Collections
ISBN 0-439-73646-3

LC 2005-296492

The "young writers and artists in this anthology have been selected from the winners of the Scholastic Art & Writing Awards program. The offerings range from an intense recollection, 'What Cancer Meant,' to a whimsical dictionary of words that don't exist but should. . . . This collection is a real boon for budding writers and artists, who will feel the encouragement and see the possibility of publication." Booklist

Writing and publishing; the librarian's handbook. edited by Carol Smallwood. American Library Association 2010 189p (ALA guides for the busy librarian) pa $65

Grades: Adult Professional   **808**

1. Authorship 2. Library science
ISBN 978-0-8389-0996-6; 0-8389-0996-5

LC 2009-25047

"This important writer's guide is readable from cover to cover or by bits and pieces and is a helpful and handy read for every librarian." Libr Media Connect

Includes bibliographical references

808.02   Authorship techniques, plagiarism, editorial techniques

Myers, Walter Dean, 1937-

Just write; here's how. Walter Dean Myers. 1st ed. Collins 2012 161 p. (lib. bdg.) $17.99; (trade paperback) $7.99

Grades: 7 8 9   **808.02**

1. Authorship 2. Fiction -- Technique 3. Creative writing 4. Authorship -- Miscellanea
ISBN 0062203894; 9780062203892; 9780062203908

LC 2012931468

In this book, "[t]he third National Ambassador for Young People's Literature offers a how-to guide for young writing enthusiasts. . . . [Walter Dean] Myers tells about his own life and how he became a writer before moving on to the craft itself, offering advice on structuring fiction using a six-box outline and nonfiction with a four-box outline. Excerpts from his own notebooks and commentaries on his work with teen writer Ross Workman" are also presented. Kirkus

808.1   Rhetoric in specific literary forms

Fandel, Jennifer

Puns, allusions, and other word secrets; [by] Jennifer Fandel. Creative Education 2005 48p il (Understanding poetry) $21.95

Grades: 7 8 9 10   **808.1**
   1. Poetics
   ISBN 1-58341-341-3
                        LC 2004058229
This "deals with the importance of choosing the right word, the opportunity to create new words or strange combinations, point of view, and hidden meanings. An excellent choice of poems . . . enhances the discussion of these aspects of poetry. The text asks readers questions about their impressions and reactions to the various verses." SLJ
   Includes bibliographical references

   Rhyme, meter, and other word music; [by] Jennifer Fandel. Creative Education 2005 48p il (Understanding poetry) $21.95
Grades: 7 8 9 10   **808.1**
   1. Poetics
   ISBN 1-58341-342-1
                        LC 2004058230
This "title offers clear explanations and examples of perfect, slant, and internal rhymes. The various forms a poem can take, including haiku, limerick, and sonnet, are also described. . . . The selections will increase young peoples understanding and appreciation of this word music." SLJ
   Includes bibliographical references

Fletcher, Ralph
   Poetry matters; writing a poem from the inside out. HarperCollins Pubs. 2002 142p hardcover o.p. pa $4.99
Grades: 4 5 6 7   **808.1**
   1. Poetry 2. Poetics 3. Creative writing 4. Poetry -- Authorship
   ISBN 0-06-623599-5 lib bdg; 0-380-79703-8 pa
                        LC 2001-24640
"Chapters deal with images; creating 'music,' or sounds and rhythms; how to generate ideas for poems; the construction of the words on the page; and more. Tips on fine-tuning are also given. . . . Major poetic forms are defined, including haiku, ode, and free verse, and there is a section on ways to share your work. Interspersed are Fletcher's personal insights and interviews with three poets—Kristine O'Connell George, Janet S. Wong, and J. Patrick Lewis. . . . Since this thought-provoking book covers more of the internal, less-tangible aspects of poetry, it may be more suited for readers who have some experience with the genre." SLJ
   Includes bibliographical references

Prelutsky, Jack
   ★ **Pizza,** pigs, and poetry; how to write a poem. Greenwillow Books 2008 191p il $16.99; pa $5.99
Grades: 4 5 6   **808.1**
   1. Poets 2. Authors 3. Poetics 4. Singers 5. Translators 6. Children's authors 7. Poetry -- By individual authors 8. Poetry -- Authorship
   ISBN 978-0-06-143449-5; 0-06-143449-3; 978-0-06-143448-8 pa; 0-06-143448-5 pa
                        LC 2007-36738
"Along with easy-to-follow tips for creating verse, haiku, and concrete poetry, the reigning Children's Poet Laureate offers insights into his own thought processes, . . . glimpses of his childhood, and personal anecdotes. . . . Pre-

lutsky tucks in more than a dozen examples of his own work, plus 10 two-and-part-of-a-third line 'poem starts.'" Booklist

   Seeing the blue between; advice and inspiration for young poets. compiled by Paul B. Janeczko. Candlewick Press 2002 132p $18.99; pa $7.99
Grades: 7 8 9 10   **808.1**
   1. Poetics 2. Poetry -- Authorship 3. Young adult poetry, American 4. American poetry -- Collections 5. American poetry -- 20th century
   ISBN 0-7636-0881-5; 0-7636-2909-X pa
                        LC 2001-25882
"The letters are personal, friendly, and supportive. . . . A valuable addition to public and school libraries, with the potential for much classroom and personal use." SLJ

Wolf, Allan
   Immersed in verse; an informative, slightly irreverent & totally tremendous guide to living the poet's life. [by] Allan Wolf; illustrated by Tuesday Mourning. Lark Books 2006 112p il $14.95
Grades: 5 6 7 8   **808.1**
   1. Poetics
   ISBN 1-57990-628-1
                        LC 2005024825
Contains advice, ideas, writing activities, and encouragement from a working poet for aspiring poets. Includes poems by a variety of poets from the unknown to the famous, including Langston Hughes, E.E. Cummings, Eve Merriam, and more
   "This how-to guide—chock-full of examples—is sure to inspire and nurture young poets. The information is intensive without being overwhelming, wise without being didactic. Wolf's love of language is evident throughout." SLJ
   Includes glossary and bibliographical references

808.2   Rhetoric of drama

Elish, Dan
   Screenplays. Marshall Cavendish 2011 95p il (Craft of writing) $34.21
Grades: 7 8 9 10   **808.2**
   1. Motion picture plays -- Technique
   ISBN 1-6087-0501-3; 978-1-6087-0501-6
This "deftly explores the essentials of the form and function of storytelling for a visual medium. Beginning with an extensive history of filmmaking . . . young writers get a glimpse of the evolution of the writer's role. . . . Snippets of scripts and full-page film stills used to illustrate various stages of writing reinforce the thrilling idea that your work could come to life onscreen. . . . Writing exercises and a further-reading section are included." Booklist
   Includes bibliographical references

Lawrence, Colton
   Big fat paycheck; a young person's guide to writing for the movies. Bantam Bks. 2004 269p il hardcover o.p. $11.99
Grades: 7 8 9 10   **808.2**
   1. Motion picture plays -- Technique 2. Motion picture

authorship
ISBN 0-553-13122-2; 0-553-13122-2 pa
"A lively, compelling, and concisely concrete guide for creative kids with big-screen dreams." SLJ

808.3 Rhetoric of fiction

Bodden, Valerie
Creating the character; dialogue and characterization. [by] Valerie Bodden. Creative Education 2009 48p il (The art of creative prose) lib bdg $22.95
Grades: 6 7 8 9   808.3
1. Authorship 2. Creative writing 3. Characters and characteristics in literature 4. Fiction -- Technique
ISBN 978-1-58341-622-8 lib bdg; 1-58341-622-6
lib bdg
LC 2007-19611
"Young authors learn the importance of showing, rather than telling, when developing a character, as well as creating well-developed protagonists and antagonists, memorable minor characters, and natural-sounding dialogue. . . . Young writers who pick [this] up . . . will find valuable guidance." SLJ
Includes glossary and bibliographical references

Painting the picture; imagery and description. by Valerie Bodden. Creative Education 2009 48p il (The art of creative prose) lib bdg $22.95
Grades: 6 7 8 9   808.3
1. Authorship 2. Creative writing 3. Fiction -- Technique
ISBN 978-1-58341-623-5 lib bdg; 1-58341-623-4
lib bdg
LC 2007-18964
"Highlights the use of images that appeal to the senses, word choice, and figurative language. . . . Concludes with several suggested exercises. . . . Young writers who pick [this] up . . . will find valuable guidance." SLJ
Includes glossary and bibliographical references

Setting the style; wording and tone. [by] Valerie Bodden. Creative Education 2009 48p il (The art of creative prose) lib bdg $22.95
Grades: 6 7 8 9   808.3
1. Authorship 2. Creative writing 3. Fiction -- Technique
ISBN 978-1-58341-625-9 lib bdg; 1-58341-625-0
lib bdg
LC 2007-19609
"Encourages authors to find their own voice, explaining the difference between literary and direct styles and detailing the importance of rhythm, tone, and atmosphere in fiction writing. . . . Young writers who pick [this] up . . . will find valuable guidance." SLJ
Includes glossary and bibliographical references

Telling the tale; narration and point of view. [by] Valerie Bodden. Creative Education 2009 48p il (The art of creative prose) lib bdg $22.95

Grades: 6 7 8 9   808.3
1. Authorship 2. Creative writing 3. Fiction -- Technique
ISBN 978-1-58341-624-2 lib bdg; 1-58341-624-2
lib bdg
LC 2007-4198
"Covers the choice of a narrator and viewpoint, including multiple and unreliable narrators. . . . Young writers who pick [this] up . . . will find valuable guidance." SLJ
Includes glossary and bibliographical references

Farrell, Tish
Write your own fantasy story; by Tish Farrell. Compass Point Books 2006 64p il $31.93; pa $6.95
Grades: 4 5 6 7   808.3
1. Creative writing 2. Fantasy fiction -- Authorship
ISBN 0-7565-1639-0; 0-7565-1814-8 pa
LC 2005033654
"Full-color photographs, movie stills, and fun graphics enliven the [presentation]. . . . It's hard to think of a better way to hook emerging writers up with good advice about honing their skills." SLJ
Includes bibliographical references

Write your own mystery story; by Tish Farrell. Compass Point Books 2006 64p il $31.93; pa $6.95
Grades: 4 5 6 7   808.3
1. Creative writing 2. Mystery fiction -- Authorship
ISBN 0-7565-1641-2; 0-7565-1816-4 pa
LC 2005030730
"Full-color photographs, movie stills, and fun graphics enliven the [presentation]. . . . It's hard to think of a better way to hook emerging writers up with good advice about honing their skills." SLJ
Includes bibliographical references

Write your own science fiction story; by Tish Farrell. Compass Point Books 2006 64p il $31.93; pa $6.95
Grades: 4 5 6 7   808.3
1. Creative writing 2. Science fiction -- Authorship
ISBN 0-7565-1643-9; 0-7565-1818-0 pa
LC 2005030732
"Full-color photographs, movie stills, and fun graphics enliven the [presentation]. . . . It's hard to think of a better way to hook emerging writers up with good advice about honing their skills." SLJ
Includes bibliographical references

Hanley, Victoria
★ **Seize** the story; a handbook for teens who like to write. [by] Victoria Hanley. Cottonwood Press 2008 213p il pa $15.95
Grades: 7 8 9 10   808.3
1. Authorship 2. Creative writing 3. Fiction -- Technique
ISBN 978-1-877673-81-8 pa; 1-877673-81-1 pa
A guide to fiction writing for teenagers with advice on approaching the young-adult market, and discusses dialogue, plot, and other related topics; and presents interviews

with established authors such as T. A. Barron, Joan Bauer, and Chris Crutcher.

"Hanley uses examples from familiar novels and authors such as 'Harry Potter' and Stephenie Meyer's Twilight . . . to illustrate elements of writing. . . . This book is an excellent resource for creative writing classes as well as individuals." SLJ

Includes bibliographical references

Levine, Gail Carson

★ **Writing** magic; creating stories that fly. Collins 2006 167p $16.99; pa $5.99

Grades: 5 6 7 8   **808.3**

1. Authorship 2. Creative writing 3. Fiction -- Technique 5. Fiction -- Authorship

ISBN 978-0-06-051961-2; 0-06-051969-4; 978-0-06-051960-5 pa; 0-06-051960-6 pa

LC 2006-00481

"Levine, best known for Ella Enchanted (1997), offers middle-graders ideas about making their own writing take flight. . . . Among the topics she covers are shaping character, beginnings and endings, revising, and finding ideas. . . . Each chapter concludes with writing exercises. . . . A terrific item to have on hand for writing groups or for individual young writers who want to improve." Booklist

Litwin, Laura Baskes

Write horror fiction in 5 simple steps; Laura Baskes Litwin. Enslow Publishers 2013 48 p $23.93

Grades: 4 5 6   **808.3**

1. Horror fiction -- Authorship 2. Horror tales -- Technique 3. Horror tales -- Authorship

ISBN 076603836X; 9780766038363

LC 2010038776

This book by Laura Baskes Litwin, part of the Creative Writing in 5 Simple Steps series, "shows aspiring writers how to write a terrifying tale of horror. . . . A good horror story is like a good ride at an amusement park. Feeling scared without having to face real danger is exhilarating. The story builds with tantalizing ideas. The reader inches out on the coaster track, knowing the precarious drop is seconds away." (Publisher's note)

Includes bibliographical references and filmography

Mazer, Anne

★ **Spilling** ink; a young writer's handbook. by Anne Mazer and Ellen Potter; illustrated by Matt Phelan. Flash Point 2010 275p il $17.99; pa $9.99

Grades: 5 6 7 8   **808.3**

1. Authorship 2. Creative writing 3. Fiction -- Technique 4. Fiction -- Authorship

ISBN 978-1-59643-514-8; 1-59643-514-3; 978-1-59643-628-2 pa; 1-59643-628-X pa

"Two fine writers put their heads together and come up with an equally fine guide to their craft for beginners. . . . Mazer speaks to beginnings . . . while Potter tackles endings; and both have diverting things to say about everything that happens in between, whether it's the narrative voice or (eek) writer's block. [They are] always agreeable, practical, and commonsensical in their approach. . . . Their text is enlivened with sidebar features, personal anecdotes, and suggestions to readers for exercising their new skills. . . . Such

devices, along with the authors' unfailing good humor, will go a long way to convincing their audience that writing can actually be fun! A notion that is nicely underscored by Phelan's engaging and always appealing illustrations." Booklist

Mlynowski, Sarah

See Jane write; a girl's guide to writing chick lit. by Sarah Mlynowski and Farrin Jacobs. Quirk Books 2006 191p il pa $14.95

Grades: 8 9 10 11 12   **808.3**

1. Authorship 2. Creative writing 3. Publishers and publishing 4. Fiction -- Technique

ISBN 1-59474-115-8

"Fun, inspiring, and organized in a clear and encouraging style, this book covers topics from what chick lit is to how to create believable characters, develop a plot, and set a tone. The authors discuss seeing a project through to the finish and getting it published. The writing style is quirky and the advice is sound." SLJ

Otfinoski, Steven

★ **Extraordinary** short story writing; by Steven Otfinoski. Franklin Watts 2005 128p il (F.W. prep) lib bdg $30.50; pa $9.95

Grades: 5 6 7 8   **808.3**

1. Authorship 2. Short story 3. Creative writing 4. Fiction -- Technique

ISBN 0-531-16760-7 lib bdg; 0-531-17578-2 pa

LC 2005006650

"In this excellent resource, specific ways to write different types of stories, project ideas, and resources are presented in such a way as to make short story assignments enjoyable. Readers are given many tips and practice activities in chapters that progress from gathering ideas to the final revision. Each section includes quotes from wellknown authors such as Edgar Allan Poe, Richard Peck, and Louis Sachar." SLJ

Includes bibliographical references

Rosinsky, Natalie M.

Write your own fairy tale; by Natalie M. Rosinsky. Compass Point Books 2008 64p il (Write your own) lib bdg $33.26; pa $6.95

Grades: 5 6 7 8   **808.3**

1. Creative writing 2. Fairy tales -- Authorship

ISBN 978-0-7565-3369-4 lib bdg; 0-7565-3369-4 lib bdg; 978-0-7565-3370-0 pa; 0-7565-3370-8 pa

LC 2007015720

This offers suggestions on how to write fairy tales, discussing settings, characters, viewpoint, plots, and style

Includes glossary and bibliographical references

Write your own myth; by Natalie M. Rosinsky. Compass Point Books 2008 64p il (Write your own) lib bdg $33.26; pa $6.95

Grades: 5 6 7 8   **808.3**

1. Creative writing 2. Authorship -- Myths

ISBN 978-0-7565-3372-4 lib bdg; 0-7565-3372-4 lib bdg; 978-0-7565-3373-1 pa; 0-7565-3373-2 pa

LC 2007011472

This offers suggestions for writing myths, discussing setting, characters, viewpoint, plots and style

Includes bibliographical references

Write your own tall tale; by Natalie M. Rosinsky. Compass Point Books 2008 64p il (Write your own) pa $6.95; lib bdg $33.26

Grades: 5 6 7 8 **808.3**

1. Creative writing 2. Tall tales -- Authorship
ISBN 978-0-7565-3376-2 pa; 0-7565-3376-7 pa; 978-0-7565-3375-5 lib bdg; 0-7565-3375-9 lib bdg
LC 2007012462

This offers suggestions for writing tall tales, discussing settings, characters, viewpoint, plots, and style

Includes glossary and bibliographical references

808.4 Rhetoric of essays

Orr, Tamra

★ **Extraordinary** essays. Franklin Watts 2005 128p il (F. W. Prep) $31; pa $9.95

Grades: 7 8 9 10 **808.4**

1. Essay 2. Authorship
ISBN 0-531-16761-5; 0-531-17576-6 pa

"This concise, appealingly designed writing guide offers practical advice to students on how to successfully complete essay assignments. Topics covered include choosing a topic, brainstorming, researching, crafting and defending a thesis statement, and revising." Booklist

Includes bibliographical references

808.5 Rhetoric of speech

Ryan, Margaret

★ **Extraordinary** oral presentations. Franklin Watts 2005 128p il (F. W. Prep) $31; pa $9.95

Grades: 7 8 9 10 **808.5**

1. Public speaking
ISBN 0-531-16758-5; 0-531-17577-4 pa

This offers advice on preparing oral presentations

This book provides "good, practical ideas for students." SLJ

Includes bibliographical references

808.8 Collections of literary texts from more than two literatures

Beware! R.L. Stine picks his favorite scary stories. HarperCollins Pubs. 2002 214p il $16.99; pa $5.99

Grades: 4 5 6 7 **808.8**

1. Horror fiction 2. Horror tales, English 3. Horror tales, American 4. Literature -- Collections 5. Children's stories, English 6. Children's stories, American
ISBN 0-06-623842-0; 0-06-055547-5 pa
LC 2002-18938

Stine "brings together 19 brief stories, folktales, poems, and cartoons from the likes of Ray Bradbury, William

Sleator, Robert W. Service . . . Gahan Wilson, and Alvin Schwartz. . . . There's something in this diverse literary buffet for every taste—including enough genuine eeriness to make it a discomfiting choice for under-the-covers reading." Booklist

Classic horse stories; compiled by Christina Rossetti Darling and Blue Lantern Studio. Chronicle Books 2010 144p $19.99

Grades: 4 5 6 **808.8**

1. Horses 2. Literature -- Collections
ISBN 978-0-8118-6569-2; 0-8118-6569-X
LC 2010008550

"This compilation of stories, poems, and artwork celebrates the relationship between horses and their devotees. Darling pulls from a wide range of familiar, beloved material: excerpts from Steinbeck's The Red Pony, Farley's The Black Stallion, and Lewis's The Horse and His Boy join poetry from Shakespeare, Farjeon, and Stevenson. Varied paintings and illustrations from throughout the 20th century underscore the point that the book offers something for all tastes." Publ Wkly

Classic western stories; the most beloved stories. compiled by Cooper Edens. Chronicle Books 2009 140p il $19.99

Grades: 5 6 7 8 **808.8**

1. American literature -- Collections
ISBN 978-0-8118-6325-4
LC 2008009819

Stories, folktales, and poems with a western setting, including stories of Paul Bunyan, Pecos Bill, Indian legends, and tales of Lewis and Clark, among others.

"Colorful, often full-page, exquisitely produced illustrations by artists such as Frederic Remington, N. C. Wyeth, and Winslow Homer bring the words to life. Overall a visual delight, this stunning book is an excellent addition to art and literature collections." SLJ

The **Coyote** Road; trickster tales. edited by Ellen Datlow and Terri Windling; introduction by Terri Windling; decorations by Charles Vess. Viking Childrens Books 2007 523p il $19.99; pa $10.99

Grades: 7 8 9 10 11 12 **808.8**

1. Short stories 2. Literature -- Collections
ISBN 978-0-670-06194-5; 0-670-06194-8; 978-0-14-241300-5 pa; 0-14-241300-3 pa
LC 2007-12414

A collection of stories and poems about tricksters in all parts of the world by a variety of authors.

"This excellent collection is bound to find an audience among experienced readers of the genre but is attractive to less-able readers, as well, for the short, punchy stories and an always-engaging trickster character." SLJ

First kiss (then tell) [edited by] Cylin Busby. Bloomsbury Children's Books 2008 212p il $15.95; pa $8.95

Grades: 7 8 9 10   **808.8**

1. Kissing 2. Literature -- Collections

ISBN 978-1-59990-199-2; 978-1-59990-241-8 pa

LC 2007-42365

Twenty-five best-selling young adult authors share stories about their first kiss. Includes quotations, facts, advice, and illustrations.

This is an "entertaining collection. . . . These authors treat their own stories with the same freshness and respect with which they approach their YA novels. . . . Some stories are poems, one is a play, and a few are in comic form. . . . This is a good collection for browsing." Booklist

Flake, Sharon G.

You don't even know me; stories and poems about boys. Hyperion/Jump at the Sun 2010 195p $16.99

Grades: 7 8 9 10   **808.8**

1. Short stories 2. Children's poetry 3. Boys -- Poetry 4. Boys -- Fiction 5. African Americans -- Poetry 6. African Americans -- Fiction 7. African American children

ISBN 978-1-4231-0014-0; 1-4231-0014-X

"This memorable collection of short stories and poems offers a glimpse into the urban lives of several African American boys. . . . Flake offers a vivid, unforgettable collection. . . . The voices ring true. . . . The stories and poetry are quite thought provoking." Voice Youth Advocates

Hip deep; opinions, essays, and vision from American teenagers. edited by Abe Louise Young. Next Generation Press 2006 164p pa $12.95 **808.8**

1. Teenagers' writings 2. American literature -- Collections

ISBN 0-9762706-2-5

"This collection of essays and poems by teens should inspire even the most reluctant writer to press on. By writing about their feelings on subjects ranging from frustration and anger to determination and renewal, these young people expose themselves from the inside out and launch themselves onto new paths." Voice Youth Advocates

I can't keep my own secrets; six-word memoirs by teens famous & obscure: from Smith magazine. edited by Rachel Fershleiser and Larry Smith. HarperTeen 2009 184p il pa $8.99

Grades: 7 8 9 10   **808.8**

1. Autobiographies 2. Teenagers' writings 3. Teenagers

ISBN 978-0-06-172684-2; 0-06-172684-2

LC 2009-14584

"The ruminations span from the haunting . . . to the funny . . . to the inspirational. . . . A razor focus is put on issues that hit youths the hardest. . . . It has just the right proportion of humor and heartbreak." Booklist

Jocelyn, Marthe

Scribbling women; true tales from astonishing lives. Tundra Books 2011 197p il $19.95

Grades: 6 7 8 9 10   **808.8**

1. Literature -- Biography 2. Literature -- Women authors 3. Women authors -- Biography

ISBN 978-0-88776-952-8; 0-88776-952-7

Profiles women authors who have defied something that would have held others back, from societal convention to oppression, including Nellie Bly, Daisy Ashford, and Dang Thuy Tram.

"Liberally using each writer's own words, Jocelyn's lyrical prose takes us deep into their lives, but mostly into their spirits and courageous souls. Young readers can share the obstacles, joys, and/or sorrows each women faced," Kirkus

Includes bibliographical references

★ **Leaving** home: stories; selected by Hazel Rochman and Darlene Z. McCampbell. HarperCollins Pubs. 1997 231p hardcover o.p. pa $11.99

Grades: 6 7 8 9 10   **808.8**

1. Short stories 2. Youth -- Fiction

ISBN 0-06-440706-3

LC 96-28979

An international anthology that reflects the thoughts and feelings of young people as they make their way into the world. Authors represented include Amy Tan, Sandra Cisneros, Tim Wynne-Jones, and Toni Morrison

"The editors have varied the tones, the music, the voices, and the meanings of the pieces, which provide both humorous and heartbreaking stories of the meaning of adolescence." ALAN

Read all about it! great read-aloud stories, poems, and newspaper pieces for preteens and teens. edited by Jim Trelease. Penguin Bks. 1993 489p il pa $13.95

Grades: 8 9 10 11 12   **808.8**

1. Authors 2. Young adult literature 3. Literature -- Collections

ISBN 0-14-014655-5

LC 93-21781

This is a collection of 52 selections of fiction, poetry, and nonfiction from newspapers, magazines, and books by such authors as Cynthia Rylant, Jerry Spinelli, Howard Pyle, Rudyard Kipling, Robert W. Service, Maya Angelou, Moss Hart, Pete Hamill, and Leon Garfield. Includes biographical information about the authors

Spinelli, Eileen

Today I will; a year of quotes, notes, and promises to myself. [by] Eileen & Jerry Spinelli; illustrated by Julia Rothman. Alfred A. Knopf 2009 un il $15.99; lib bdg $18.99

Grades: 5 6 7 8   **808.8**

1. Quotations 2. Conduct of life 3. American literature -- Collections

ISBN 978-0-375-84057-9; 0-375-84057-5; 978-0-375-96230-1 lib bdg; 0-375-96230-1 lib bdg

LC 2008047869

"The Spinellis turn their skills to inspiring readers with quotes and promises for every day of the year. There is a single-page entry for each day, and each one begins with a quote from children's literature. . . . Each quote is followed by an explanatory note. Each note is then summarized into a short promise on which readers can reflect. . . . The book covers a vast array of topics and themes, from serious to silly, and is inspiring and helpful." SLJ

808.81 Collections in specific forms

The **Body** eclectic; an anthology of poems. edited by Patrice Vecchione. Holt & Co. 2002 192p $16.95

Grades: 7 8 9 10   **808.81**
1. Children's poetry 2. Body, Human -- Poetry 3. Poetry -- Collections
ISBN 0-8050-6935-6
        LC 2001-51900
This collection of poetry focuses on the human body and its parts, including works by poets such as Gary Soto, Shel Silverstein, Paul Laurence Dunbar, Pablo Neruda, Walt Whitman and Shakespeare

"Excellent notes at the back introduce each writer and suggest more books to read. A great collection to show teens that literature is about their intimate selves and their connections with people everywhere." Booklist

Includes bibliographical references

★ **Crush**: love poems. Word of Mouth Books/KA Productions 2007 72p pa $10

Grades: 8 9 10 11 12   **808.81**
1. Love poetry 2. Poetry -- Collections
ISBN 978-1-88801-840-0
"Alexander offers a cosmopolitan menu of tanka, haiku, long titles that lead into short first lines, verbal formulas that lead to sung discoveries, French phrases, prose poems, and poems written in Spanglish. The book is divided into three sections with various speakers, and a fourth section that includes poems by Sherman Alexie, Pablo Neruda, Nikki Giovanni, and the title poem, 'Crush' by Naomi Shihab Nye. . . . This well-crafted anthology will capture the interest of teens." SLJ

★ **I** feel a little jumpy around you; a book of her poems & his poems collected in pairs. [by] Naomi Shihab Nye and Paul B. Janeczko. Simon & Schuster Bks. for Young Readers 1996 256p hardcover o.p. pa $10

Grades: 7 8 9 10   **808.81**
1. Poetry -- Collections 2. Men 3. Women 4. Children's poetry -- Collections
ISBN 0-689-81341-4
        LC 95-44904
A collection of poems, by male and female authors, presented in pairings that offer insight into how men and women look at the world, both separately and together

"Though the gender counterpoint really plays little part in the juxtaposition, the pairings are piquant and provide a manageable way to start talking about a very large collection of poetry. An engaging marginal dialogue, taken from Nye's and Janeczko's collaborative fax correspondence, appears alongside the appendix and permits a revealing peek behind the scences. Highly readable notes from contributors are included, as is an index of poems and a gender-segregated index of poets." Bull Cent Child Books

I wouldn't thank you for a valentine; poems for young feminists. edited by Carol Ann Duffy; illustrated by Trisha Rafferty. Holt & Co. 1993 104p il hardcover o.p. pa $6.95

Grades: 6 7 8 9 10 11 12   **808.81**
1. Feminism -- Poetry 2. Poetry -- Collections 3. Children's poetry -- Collections
ISBN 0-8050-5545-2
        LC 93-3172
First published 1992 in the United Kingdom
A collection of poems by women from different cultures and backgrounds, portraying the varied facets of the female experience from childhood to old age

"The anthology draws on poets from many cultures and includes well-known poets, such as Nikki Giovani, Sharon Olds, and Mary Oliver, as well as several new voices. . . . These poems open up the range of love and family." Booklist

★ **It's** a woman's world; a century of women's voices in poetry. edited by Neil Philip. Dutton Children's Bks. 2000 93p il $17.99

Grades: 7 8 9 10   **808.81**
1. Women 2. Poetry 3. Women poets 4. Poetry -- Collections 5. Children's poetry -- Women authors
ISBN 0-525-46328-3
        LC 99-88363
An anthology of poetry by twentieth-century women from around the world including, Sylvia Plath, Nigar Hanim, Sonia Sanchez, and Nellie Wong

"Beautifully reproduced black-and-white photos introduce each section. Overall, this book is dense, challenging, and provocative." SLJ

Light-gathering poems; edited by Liz Rosenberg. Holt & Co. 2000 146p $15.95

Grades: 7 8 9 10   **808.81**
1. Young adult poetry 2. Poetry -- Collections
ISBN 0-8050-6223-8
        LC 99-49231
"Poems were chosen for their ability to 'gather light,' some representing beauty, some joy, some fascinating imagery, and some the illusive light at the end of a dark tunnel. . . . Notable writers such as Robert Frost, Walt Whitman, Langston Hughes, Edna St. Vincent Millay, Emily Dickinson, and Allen Ginsberg share the spotlight with contemporaries such as Gary Soto, Kate Schmitt, Mary Oliver, Steven Dauer, and Henry M. Seiden." Voice Youth Advocates

Includes bibliographical references

The **Oxford** book of story poems; [compiled by] Michael Harrison and Christopher Stuart-Clark. Oxford University Press 2006 175p il pa $18.95

Grades: 5 6 7 8   **808.81**
1. Poetry -- Collections
ISBN 978-0-19-276344-0 pa; 0-19-276344-X pa
        LC 2007282711
First published 1990
This anthology contains "narrative verse by British and American poets, from traditional ballads such as 'Sir Patrick Spens' to contemporary poems such as Judith Nicholls' 'Storytime.' . . . The poets include Carroll, Keats, de la Mare, Kennedy, Lear, Lindsay, Longfellow, Noyes, Poe, Southey,

and Tolkien. . . . A handy collection of story poems for reading aloud or alone." Booklist [review of 1990 edition]

The **Oxford** book of war poetry; chosen and edited by Jon Stallworthy. Oxford University Press 2008 xxxi, 358 p.p (paperback) $19.95
Grades: 8 9 10 11 12 Adult   **808.81**
1. War poetry 2. Poetry -- Collections
ISBN 0199554536; 9780199554539

LC 8319303

This book is a collection of war poetry, arranged chronologically by conflict. The "250 poems in John Stallworthy's . . . anthology span centuries of human experience of war, from David's 'Lament for Saul and Jonathan,' and Homer's 'Iliad,' to the finest poems of the First and Second World Wars, and beyond." (Publisher's note)
Includes bibliographical references and indexes.

★ **Poetry** speaks: who I am; poems of discovery, inspiration, independence, and everything else. Sourcebooks Jabberwocky 2010 136p $19.99
Grades: 5 6 7 8 9 10   **808.81**
1. Poetry -- Collections
ISBN 978-1-4022-1074-7; 1-4022-1074-4

This collection "aims at middle-grade readers with more than 100 strikingly diverse poems by writers including Poe, Frost, Nikki Giovanni, and Sandra Cisneros. The works are slotted together in mindful thematic order, beside occasional spot art. . . . Pairing a contemporary poem like Toi Derricotte's 'Fears of the Eighth Grade' alongside Keats's 'When I Have Fears That I May Cease to Be,' results in a refreshing lack of literary hierarchy that enables disparate works to build and reflect upon one another. An accompanying CD features recordings of 44 of the poems. . . . A sound and rewarding introduction to the joys of poetry." Publ Wkly

Revenge and forgiveness; an anthology of poems. edited by Patrice Vecchione. Henry Holt 2004 148p $16.95
Grades: 7 8 9 10   **808.81**
1. Poetry 2. Revenge 3. Forgiveness 4. Children's poetry 5. Poetry -- Collections 6. Poetry -- Translations into English 7. Children's poetry -- Translations into English
ISBN 0-8050-7376-0

LC 2003-56631

A collection of nearly sixty poems dealing with revenge and forgiveness, plus suggested readings about each contributing poet
"For students who are of a philosophical bent and for teachers of poetry, this book of poems about love, hate, and war will be a useful resource." Libr Media Connect
Includes bibliographical references

★ **River** of words; young poets and artists on the nature of things. edited by Pamela Michael; introduced by Robert Hass. Milkweed Editions 2008 298p il hardcover o.p. pa $18
Grades: 4 5 6 7 8 9   **808.81**
1. Nature poetry 2. Children's art 3. Children's

writings 4. Teenagers' writings 5. Poetry -- Collections
ISBN 978-1-57131-685-1; 1-57131-685-X; 978-1-57131-680-6 pa; 1-57131-680-9 pa
"In 1995 Michael and Hass . . . cofounded the River of Words project, designed to connect students' art and poetry education to the natural world immediately around them. . . . The poems and pictures in this handsomely designed volume have been culled from yearly contests. . . . The works are startling, many of them dislocating and highly complex." Publ Wkly

★ **Side** by side; new poetry inspired by art from around our world. collected by Jan Greenberg. Abrams Books for Young Readers 2008 88p il $19.95
Grades: 8 9 10 11 12   **808.81**
1. Art -- Poetry 2. Poetry -- Collections
ISBN 978-0-8109-9471-3; 0-8109-9471-2

LC 2007-11973

This is an "anthology of accomplished poems inspired by artworks. . . . [Greenberg brings] together the work of poets and artists from around the globe. . . . The poems are grouped loosely into categories, defined in Greenberg's inspirational introduction. . . . Each spread features a poem in its original language, the English translation, and an artwork, usually from the same country or culture as the poem. With a few exceptions, the reproductions of the art, which ranges from ancient to contemporary work, are sharp and clear, and the moving, often startling poems invite readers to savor the words and then look closely at each image." Booklist

Step lightly; poems for the journey. collected by Nancy Willard. Harcourt Brace & Co. 1998 99p hardcover o.p. pa $12
Grades: 7 8 9 10   **808.81**
1. Poetry -- Collections
ISBN 0-15-202052-7

LC 98-5228

A collection of poems celebrating the ordinary in an unordinary way, by such authors as Emily Dickinson, Theodore Roethke, and D. H. Lawrence
"Willard weaves an anthology in which readers can find happiness, insight, inspiration, and wisdom." SLJ

★ **War** and the pity of war; edited by Neil Philip; illustrated by Michael McCurdy. Clarion Bks. 1998 96p il $20
Grades: 5 6 7 8 9 10   **808.81**
1. War poetry 2. Children's poetry 3. Poetry -- Collections
ISBN 0-395-84982-9

LC 97-32897

"The selections, covering conflicts from ancient Persia to modern-day Bosnia, are by a wide variety of poets, from the well known (Tennyson, Whitman, Sandburg, Auden), to the obscure (Anakreon from ancient Greece and 11th-century Chinese poet Bunno). . . . The stark and simple scratchboard drawings are reminiscent of the Ernie Pyle illustrations from World War II and are as memorable as the best propaganda." SLJ

★ **What** have you lost? poems. selected by Naomi Shihab Nye; photographs by Michael Nye. Greenwillow Bks. 1999 206p hardcover o.p. pa $9.99

Grades: 7 8 9 10 **808.81**

1. Loss (Psychology) 2. Young adult poetry 3. Poetry -- Collections 4. Loss (Psychology) -- Poetry
ISBN 0-380-73307-2

LC 98-26674

In her "introduction, the anthologist-poet considers loss—its certainty, scope, and effect, and its ability to give rise to art. The topic is thoroughly explored by the one hundred and forty poets whose work is collected here in twenty-two unlabeled, thematically arranged sections. . . . The poets are all contemporary, with a dozen or so hailing from outside the United States." Horn Book

★ A **foot** in the mouth; poems to speak, sing, and shout. [edited by Paul B. Janeczko; illustrated by Chris Raschka] Candlewick Press 2009 64p il $17.99

Grades: 4 5 6 7 **808.81**

1. Children's poetry 2. Poetry -- Collections
ISBN 978-0-7636-0663-3; 0-7636-0663-4

LC 2008-935581

"The poems in Janeczko and Raschka's collection . . . are not complacent, although plenty are funny and some are familiar. . . . Punchy collages flutter across airy white pages in loose visual arrangements; torn scraps of origami paper layer with fluid lines in tart color. Janeczko introduces the collection with the idea that 'Poetry is sound,' a pleasure to vocalize and memorize. . . . Readers will be emboldened to join in the 'song.'" Publ Wkly

The **tree** that time built; a celebration of nature, science, and imagination. selected by Mary Ann Hoberman and Linda Winston; [illustrations by Barbara Fortin] Sourcebooks Jabberwocky 2009 209p il $19.99

Grades: 5 6 7 8 **808.81**

1. Nature poetry 2. Science -- Poetry 3. Poetry -- Collections
ISBN 978-1-4022-2517-8; 1-4022-2517-2

LC 2009032608

An anthology of more than 100 poems celebrating the wonders of the natural world and encouraging environmental awareness. Includes an audio CD that comprises readings of 44 of the poems, many performed by the poets themselves.

"Classic works by Walt Whitman, Emily Dickinson, Christina Rossetti, and the like, and selections from contemporary poets are included. . . . This handsome collection is especially appropriate for classroom use and instruction. . . . From the playful to the profound, the poems invite reflection and inspire further investigation." SLJ

Includes glossary and bibliographical references

808.82   Collections of drama

Actor's choice; monologues for teens. edited by Erin Detrick. Playscripts 2008 131p pa $14.95

Grades: 6 7 8 9 10 **808.82**

1. Acting 2. Monologues 3. Drama -- Collections
ISBN 978-0-9709046-6-9; 0-9709046-6-5

LC 2007-50166

"This volume of highly entertaining monologues is gleaned from one-act and full-length plays published by Playscripts, Inc. . . . This is an excellent volume to help students prepare for competitions as well as to use in drama, speech, or English classes." SLJ

The **Book** of monologues for aspiring actors; [edited by] Marsh Cassady. NTC Pub. Group 1995 212p il pa $23.96

Grades: 7 8 9 10 **808.82**

1. Acting 2. Monologues 3. Drama -- Collections
ISBN 0-8442-5771-0

LC 94-66239

"The selections range from the classical Greeks to Sam Shepard and Oscar Wilde; they give YA's the opportunity to develop characters of like ages in many different settings. Several questions to probe the actors' imaginations appear at the end of each monologue." SLJ

Great monologues for young actors; Craig Slaight, Jack Sharrar, editors. Smith & Kraus 1992 3v v1 pa $11.95; v2-v3 pa ea $14.95

Grades: 8 9 10 11 12 **808.82**

1. Acting 2. Monologues 3. Children's plays 4. Drama -- Collections
ISBN 1-880399-03-2 v1; 0-57525-106-X v2; 1-57525-408-1 v3

These volumes provide an introduction and acting notes for monologues for men and women drawn from contemporary and classic works

★ **Great** scenes for young actors from the stage; Craig Slaight, Jack Sharrar, editors. Smith & Kraus 1991 256p 2v v1 pa $11.95; v2 pa $14.95

Grades: 7 8 9 10 **808.82**

1. Acting 2. Drama -- Collections
ISBN 0-9622722-6-4 v1; 1-57525-107-8 v2

Contains scenes from classic and contemporary plays. The selections, graded according to ability level, include a range of roles for men, women, and groups. Includes a brief synopsis of each play along with special notes

New audition scenes and monologs from contemporary playwrights; the best new cuttings from around the world. edited by Roger Ellis. Meriwether Pub. 2005 177p pa $15.95

Grades: 6 7 8 9 **808.82**

1. Acting 2. Monologues 3. Drama -- Collections
ISBN 1-56608-105-X

"This work presents a wide variety of scenes selected especially for performers aged 12 to 24. . . . Introductions to each scene are informative and were reviewed and approved with some reshaping by the authors. . . . A good choice for students who seek new ideas for drama, forensic, and writing classes." SLJ

Surface, Mary Hall

★ **More** short scenes and monologues for middle school students; inspired by literature, social studies, and real life. by Mary Hall Surface. 1st ed.; Smith and Kraus 2007 207p (Young actors series) pa $11.95

Grades: 6 7 8 9   808.82
1. Acting 2. Monologues 3. Drama -- Collections
ISBN 978-1-57525-560-6 pa; 1-57525-560-X pa
LC 2007281299

A collection of original scenes and monologues written especially for middle-school actors

"This volume stands out for its distinct voices, multicultural characters, and engaging scenes. The book is well organized. . . . This excellent book would be useful in a variety of classrooms including speech/communication, drama, English, and social studies." SLJ

Includes bibliographical references

★ **Short** scenes and monologues for middle school actors. Smith & Kraus 1999 183p (Young actors series) pa $11.95

Grades: 6 7 8 9   808.82
1. Acting 2. Monologues 3. Drama -- Collections 4. Dialogues
ISBN 1-57525-179-5
LC 99-52457

A collection of original scenes and monologues written especially for middle-school actors

"A welcome find for young actors in search of material for auditions." SLJ

Includes bibliographical references

808.83   Collections of fiction

Hague, Michael

The **Book** of dragons; selected and illustrated by Michael Hague. Morrow 1995 146p il hardcover o.p. pa $10.99

Grades: 5 6 7 8   808.83
1. Short stories 2. Fantasy fiction 3. Dragons 4. Folklore 5. Short stories -- Collections
ISBN 0-688-10879-2; 0-06-075968-2 pa
LC 94-42958

This collection comprises an anonymous poem, "The Dragon of Wantley," and sixteen literary fairy tales and retellings of folktales and legends about dragons. The tales include "Kenneth Grahame's 'Reluctant Dragon,' Kan Pao's 'Li Chi Slays the Serpent,' J.R.R. Tolkien's 'Bilbo Baggins and Smaug,' the Grimms' 'Devil and His Grandmother,' and William H.H. Kingston's 'St. George and the Dragon.'" (Booklist) "Grades three to six." (SLJ)

"Excerpts from classic novels such as J. R. R. Tolkien's The Hobbit, C. S. Lewis's Voyage of the Dawn Treader, and short stories such as Kenneth Grahame's 'The Reluctant Dragon' are included. In addition, there are folktales from China, Italy, and Germany. Most of the heroes are men, but occasionally children are the only ones who can outsmart the dragon. . . . Hague's beautiful full-page watercolors reflect the different moods of the stories and the temperaments of the dragons depicted." SLJ

808.85   Collections of speeches

Lend me your ears; great speeches in history. selected and introduced by William Safire. Updated and expanded; W.W. Norton 2004 1157p $39.95

Grades: 8 9 10 11 12 Adult   808.85
1. Speeches
ISBN 978-0-393-05931-1; 0-393-05931-6
LC 2004-13625

First published 1992

This "is a good addition for those . . . in need of modern speeches. With an excellent index." Libr J

808.88   Collections of miscellaneous writings

Alcorn, Stephen

A **gift** of days; the greatest words to live by. Atheneum Books for Young Readers 2009 115p il $21.99

Grades: 5 6 7 8   808.88
1. Quotations 2. Celebrities
ISBN 978-1-4169-6776-7; 1-4169-6776-1
LC 2007-48766

"Beautifully designed and imaginatively conceptualized, this volume presents 366 days and 366 quotations from famous people, tagged to the days they were born. Alcorn lays this out on each double-page spread with a stunning polychrome-relief block-print bordered with pattern on one leaf and, facing, a week of birthdays and quotes. These images are often brilliantly inventive. . . . Librarians, educators and historically minded kids will take much pleasure from looking up birthdays to see the associated wisdom from women and men across the ages." Kirkus

Bartlett's familiar quotations; a collection of passages, phrases, and proverbs traced to their sources in ancient and modern literature. by John Bartlett; Geoffrey O'Brien, general editor. 18th ed. Little, Brown, and Co. 2012 lxi, 1438 p.p (hardcover) $50.00

Grades: 8 9 10 11 12 Adult   808.88
1. Quotations 2. Quotations, English
ISBN 0316017590; 9780316017596
LC 2012019870

This book, in its 18th edition, presents a collection of quotations "from the times of ancient Egyptians to the present day." (Publisher's note)

It "includes 2500 new quotes and more than 800 newcomers, from Julia Child to David Foster Wallace. Quotes have been culled to bring in more foreigners and women and more material from fiction and poetry." (Library Journal)

809   History, description, critical appraisal of more than two literatures

Bookmarked; teen essays on life and literature from Tolkien to Twilight. edited by Ann Camacho. Free Spirit Pub. 2012 215 p. $15.99
Grades: 6 7 8   **809**
1. Essays 2. Literature -- History and criticism 3. Life in literature 4. Literature and morals 5. Literature -- Appreciation 6. Teenagers -- Books and reading
ISBN 1575423960; 9781575423968
LC 2011043942
Edited by Ann Camacho, the book offers 50 essays in which "young people from a wide range of backgrounds reflect on how words from literature connect with and influence their lives, goals, and personal philosophies. Essays explore character building topics including suffering the death of a parent, facing a life-threatening illness, letting go of perfectionism, making friends, reaching goals, and grappling with questions of identity." (Publisher's note)

Campbell, Kimberly
    Less is more; teaching literature with short texts, grades 6-12. [by] Kimberly Hill Campbell. Stenhouse Publishers 2007 222p il pa $18.50
Grades: Adult Professional   **809**
1. Literature -- Study and teaching
ISBN 978-1-57110-710-7; 1-57110-710-X
LC 2007019310
"Campbell's book makes a very good case for teaching with short texts. Through chapters on short stories, essays, memoirs, poetry, picture books, and graphic novels, she shows how all aspects of literature can be taught using a variety of short pieces. She suggests structures for the classroom and strategies for eliciting both written and oral responses to these texts. She ties reading short texts to ways of looking at student writing in similar genres. . . . This book will be valuable for beginning and veteran teachers because of the lists of short texts." Voice Youth Advocates
    Includes bibliographical references

Campbell, Patricia J.
    Campbell's scoop; reflections on young adult literature. [by] Patty Campbell. Scarecrow Press 2010 245p (Scarecrow studies in young adult literature) $40
Grades: Adult Professional   **809**
1. Teenagers -- Books and reading 2. Young adult literature -- History and criticism
ISBN 978-0-8108-7293-6; 0-8108-7293-5
LC 2009-45563
"This resource represents the accumulated wisdom of a veteran librarian, author, speaker, critic, and pioneer of young adult services. Selected from several sources over many years, these essays and articles present a broad collection of critical writing. The articles are grouped into categories that include 'How We Got Here,' 'Trends and Tendencies,' 'Defining YA,' and 'Censorship Near and Far.' . . . Campbell's Scoop is a solidly useful professional title that weighs in on a diversity of topics. Unlike professional books that discuss and recommend specific YA titles, Campbell's Scoop is timeless. The information will not become dated

and the breadth of the articles makes the collection relevant to a wide audience." Voice Youth Advocates
    Includes bibliographical references

Hirschmann, Kris
    Vampires in literature. ReferencePoint Press 2010 80p il (The vampire library) lib bdg $26.95
Grades: 7 8 9 10   **809**
1. Vampires in literature
ISBN 978-1-60152-134-7; 1-60152-134-0
LC 2010010104
Examines different ways vampires have been presented in literature from the first vampire novel in 1819 to the present-day.
    "Energetic and surprisingly educational, this lively [book] seizes upon a zietgeist and takes it as far as possible." Booklist

Krull, Kathleen
    ★ **Lives** of the writers; comedies, tragedies (and what the neighbors thought) written by Kathleen Krull; illustrated by Kathryn Hewitt. 1st ed. Harcourt Brace & Co. 1994 96 p. col. ill. (reinforced) $21
Grades: 4 5 6 7   **809**
1. Poets 2. Authors 3. Humorists 4. Novelists 5. Dramatists 6. Historians 7. Journalists
ISBN 0152480099; 9780152480097
LC 93032436
This volume presents biographical sketches of writers. Arranged "in chronological order by date of birth, the selection of writers begins with Murasaki Shikibu, the first-century Japanese author of 'The Tale of Genji' . . . and concludes with Isaac Bashevis Singer, the Jewish American storyteller who died in 1991." (Horn Book Magazine)
    This offers "views of twenty writers . . . from various countries and historical periods. Included are William Shakespeare, Edgar Allan Poe, Mark Twain, Zora Neale Hurston, Isaac Bashevis Singer, and many others." Publisher's note
    Includes bibliographical references (p. 96) and index.

Sutton, Roger
    A **family** of readers; the book lover's guide to children's and young adult literature. [by] Roger Sutton and Martha V. Parravano; foreword by Gregory Maguire. Candlewick Press 2010 350p il $22; pa $14.99
Grades: Adult Professional   **809**
1. Children -- Books and reading 2. Teenagers -- Books and reading 3. Children's literature -- History and criticism
ISBN 978-0-7636-3280-9; 0-7636-3280-5; 978-0-7636-5755-0 pa; 0-7636-5755-7 pa
"This collection of essays from editors, reviewers, and authors emanates enthusiasm for books and reading. . . . Each section begins with an overview, followed by a selection of essays. The first chapter addresses the very smallest book lovers, and the last tackles the needs of young adults. Each chapter is followed by an annotated list of books. A complete bibliography and biographical sketches of the contributors

are included in the end. . . . It should be required reading for every youth services librarian." Voice Youth Advocates

809.1   Literature in specific forms other than miscellaneous writings

Bodden, Valerie

Concrete poetry. Creative Education 2010 32p il (Poetry basics) $28.50

Grades: 5 6 7 8   **809.1**
   1. Poetry -- History and criticism
   ISBN 978-1-58341-775-1; 1-58341-775-3
                        LC 2008009156

This book describes concrete poetry's "history, characteristics, and variations. Many examples are provided as well as ideas for how children can write their own pieces. The information is accessible, and the writing is sufficiently lively to engage readers. The well-designed pages feature a variety of art reproductions from different literary eras and some photographs." Horn Book Guide

Includes glossary and bibliographical references

Haiku. Creative Education 2010 32p il (Poetry basics) $19.95

Grades: 5 6 7 8   **809.1**
   1. Haiku
   ISBN 978-1-58341-776-8; 1-58341-776-1
                       LC 2008-9158

Presents history and examples of the Japanese form of poetry called haiku.

"The information is accessible, and the writing is sufficiently lively to engage readers. The well-designed pages feature a variety of art reproductions from different literary eras and some photographs." Horn Book Guide

Includes glossary and bibliographical references

Limericks. Creative Education 2010 32p il (Poetry basics) $19.95

Grades: 5 6 7 8   **809.1**
   1. Limericks
   ISBN 978-1-58341-777-5; 1-58341-777-X
                       LC 2008-9159

This describes limericks' "history, characteristics, and variations. Many examples are provided as well as ideas for how children can write their own pieces. The information is accessible, and the writing is sufficiently lively to engage readers. The well-designed pages feature a variety of art reproductions from different literary eras and some photographs." Horn Book Guide

Includes glossary and bibliographical references

810   Literatures of specific languages and language families

33 things every girl should know; stories, songs, poems, and smart talk by 33 extraordinary women.

edited by Tonya Bolden. Crown 1998 159p il hardcover o.p. pa $13

Grades: 7 8 9 10   **810**
   1. Girls 2. American literature -- Collections
   ISBN 0-517-70936-8
                       LC 97-29431

A mix of short stories, essays, a comic strip, a speech, an interview, poems, and more which offer insights and advice for girls

"Astute, compassionate, sometimes witty, sometimes painfully honest, the pieces are highly readable, entertaining, and educational." Booklist

911: the book of help; edited by Michael Cart; with Marianne Carus and Marc Aronson. Cricket Bks. 2002 178p $17.95; pa $9.95

Grades: 8 9 10 11 12   **810**
   1. Terrorism 2. September 11 terrorist attacks, 2001 3. American literature -- Collections
   ISBN 0-8126-2659-1; 0-8126-2676-1 pa
                       LC 2002-4707

A collection of essays, poems, and short fiction, created in response to the terrorist attacks of September 11, 2001. Contributors include Katherine Paterson, Joan Bauer, Walter Dean Myers, Nikki Giovanni, Arnold Adoff, and Russell Freedman

This "stands out for its rich prose, its unusual reporting, its search for context, its reminder of wonders." NY Times Book Rev

Amend, Allison

Hispanic-American writers. Chelsea House 2010 128p il (Multicultural voices) $35

Grades: 7 8 9 10 11 12   **810**
   1. Latino authors 2. Hispanic American authors 3. American literature -- Hispanic American authors -- History and criticism
   ISBN 978-1-60413-312-7; 1-60413-312-0
                       LC 2009-46535

Profiles notable Hispanic Americans and their work in the field of literature, including Sandra Cisneros, Julia Alvarez, and Junot Diaz.

"This volume opens with a succinct yet thorough introduction to the historical and cultural context of eight authors. The overview explains the origins and uses of the terms Chicano, Hispanic, and Latino and sketches the histories of the nations where most Hispanic-Americans have their roots. Amend also identifies common themes in Hispanic-American literature such as language and family; however, she also notes each community's unique concerns. . . . Amend also suggests books by other Latino writers for further reading." SLJ

Includes bibliographical references

Aronson, Marc

Beyond the pale; new essays for a new era. Scarecrow Press 2003 145p (Scarecrow studies in young adult literature) $37.50

Grades: Adult Professional   **810**
   1. Books and reading 2. Teenagers -- Books and reading 3. Young adults -- Books and reading 4. Young

adult literature -- History and criticism
ISBN 0-8108-4638-1; 978-0-8108-4638-8

LC 2002-151299

"Teachers, librarians, and students of children's and young adult literature will appreciate the breadth and clarity of this book, as well as the impressive bibliographies of fantasy and of professional reading on it." SLJ

Includes bibliographical references

Crowe, Chris

More than a game; sports literature for young adults. [by] Chris Crowe. Scarecrow Press 2004 171p (Scarecrow studies in young adult literature) $45

Grades: Adult Professional **810**
1. Sports in literature 2. Young adult literature -- History and criticism
ISBN 0-8108-4900-3; 978-0-8108-4900-6

LC 2003-13561

"Readable and fascinating. . . . Categorizing and listing every sports-related book with teen appeal is an impossible feat, but the appendixes earn a medal for their impressive range. If only all professional reading could be so brainy and muscular." Voice Youth Advocates

Includes bibliographical references

Dude! stories and stuff for boys. edited by Sandy Asher and David Harrison. Dutton Childrens Books 2006 258p il $17.99

Grades: 4 5 6 7 **810**
1. Boys 2. American literature -- Collections
ISBN 0-525-47684-9

LC 2005025060

"These 18 original stories, plays, and poems by prize-winning writers range from entertaining to challenging and offer an array of characters and experiences. In Bill C. Davis' intimate, thought-provoking 'Family Meeting,' a boy whose stepbrother committed suicide discovers the value of life. Jamie Adoff's 'Twelve' is a rap poem about experiencing violence but still retaining hope. Jose Cruz Gonzalez's play Watermelon Kisses is an amusing, credible portrayal of brotherly love and squabbles. The selections, which include many well-written gems, will resonate with and also amuse middle-grade boys." Booklist

★ **Girls** got game; sports stories and poems. edited by Sue Macy. Holt & Co. 2001 152p $17.95

Grades: 6 7 8 9 **810**
1. Sports 2. Women athletes 3. Sports -- Literary collections 4. American literature -- Collections 5. Women athletes -- Literary collections
ISBN 0-8050-6568-7

LC 00-47297

A collection of short stories and poems written by and about young women in sports

"The lineup of authors includes heavy hitters such as Virginia Euwer Wolff and Jacqueline Woodson as well as some lesser-known talents. . . . This earnest and high-minded anthology can be dipped into or devoured in one sitting; however it is read, it should empower girls and guide them along their paths toward becoming strong, independent women." SLJ

★ **Growing** up Latino; memoirs and stories. edited with an introduction by Harold Augenbraum and Ilan Stavans; foreword by Ilan Stavans. Houghton Mifflin 1993 xxix, 344p hardcover o.p. pa $15

Grades: 6 7 8 9 10 **810**
1. Short stories 2. Latinos (U.S.) 3. Culture conflict 4. Hispanic Americans 5. Hispanic Americans -- Fiction 6. Hispanic Americans -- Biography 7. American literature -- Collections 8. American literature -- Hispanic American authors 9. American literature -- Hispanic American authors -- Collections
ISBN 0-395-66124-2

LC 92-32624

A collection of short stories and excerpts from novels and memoirs written by twenty-five Latino authors. Among the contributors are Julia Alvarez, Oscar Hijuelos, Denise Chávez, Rolando Hinojosa, and Sandra Cisneros.

Includes bibliographical references

★ **Guys** write for Guys Read; edited by Jon Scieszka. Viking 2005 272p il $16.99; pa $11.99

Grades: 6 7 8 9 10 **810**
1. American literature -- Collections
ISBN 0-670-06007-0; 0-670-01144-4 pa

LC 2004-28984

This is a collection of short stories, essays, columns, cartoons, anecdotes, and artwork by such writers and illustrators as Brian Jacques, Jerry Spinelli, Chris Crutcher, Mo Willems, Chris Van Allsburg, Matt Groening, and Neil Gaiman, selected by voters at the Guys Read web site.

This is "a diverse and fast-paced anthology . . . that deserves a permanent place in any collection . . . . There's something undeniably grand about this collective celebration of the intellectual life of the common boy." SLJ

Hill, Laban Carrick

★ **Harlem** stomp! a cultural history of the Harlem Renaissance. Little, Brown 2004 151p il hardcover o.p. pa $12.99

Grades: 7 8 9 10 **810**
1. Harlem Renaissance 2. African American arts 3. African Americans -- Intellectual life 4. African American arts -- History -- 20th century 5. African Americans -- Intellectual life -- 20th century 6. Harlem (New York, N.Y.) -- Intellectual life -- 20th century
ISBN 0-316-81411-3; 0-316-03424-X pa

LC 2002-73067

"The vibrancy, energy, and color of the Harlem Renaissance come to life in this gem of a book packed with poetry, prose, song lyrics, art, and photography created by some of the period's most influential figures. . . . Informative and highly entertaining, it deserves to be shelved in any library." Voice Youth Advocates

Includes bibliographical references

Hillstrom, Kevin

The **Harlem** Renaissance. Omnigraphics 2008 228p il map (Defining moments) $49

Grades: 7 8 9 10   810
1. Harlem Renaissance 2. African American arts
ISBN 978-0-7808-1027-3; 0-7808-1027-9

LC 2007-51132

"This an insightful, highly accessible subject primer for general collections." Libr J

Includes glossary and bibliographical references

Otfinoski, Steven

Native American writers. Chelsea House 2010 126p il (Multicultural voices) $35

Grades: 8 9 10 11 12   810
1. American literature -- Native American authors 2. Native American literature -- History and criticism
ISBN 978-1-60413-314-1; 1-60413-314-7

LC 2009-41334

"This title introduces 10 major Native American poets and writers, such as N. Scott Momaday, Louise Erdrich, James Welch, and Sherman Alexie. An overview preceding the author entries explains the impact of white settlers on the culture of Native Americans, as well as the utilization of Native American storytelling and traditions in their literature and development of their writings. . . . The easily accessible information and fascinating details of the lives and writings of these authors make this a useful resource for both informative reading and research." SLJ

Includes bibliographical references

Sidman, Joyce

The **world** according to dog; poems and teen voices. with photographs by Doug Mindell. Houghton Mifflin 2003 71p il hardcover o.p. pa $7.95

Grades: 8 9 10 11 12   810
1. Dogs 2. Teenagers' writings 3. American literature -- Collections
ISBN 0-618-17497-4; 0-618-28381-1 pa

LC 2002-476

A collection of poems about dogs is accompanied by essays by young people about the dogs in their lives

"The teen essays are heartfelt and honest. . . . Sidman's poetic form is succinct, evoking images, memories, and even smells. . . . Readers of all ages who appreciate their canine companions will thoroughly enjoy this slim book." Voice Youth Advocates

Things I have to tell you; poems and writing by teen-age girls. edited by Betsy Franco; photographs by Nina Nickles. Candlewick Press 2001 63p il hardcover o.p. pa $8.99

Grades: 7 8 9 10   810
1. Girls 2. Teenagers' writings 3. Secrets 4. Youths' writings 5. American literature -- Collections 6. Teenage girls -- Literary collections
ISBN 0-7636-0905-6; 0-7636-1035-6 pa

LC 99-46884

A collection of poems, stories, and essays written by girls twelve to eighteen years of age and revealing the secrets which enabled them to overcome the challenges they faced

Wachale! poetry and prose on growing up Latino in America; edited by Ilan Stavans. Cricket Publs. 2001 146p $16.95

Grades: 5 6 7 8   810
1. Latinos (U.S.) 2. Hispanic Americans 3. Bilingual books -- English-Spanish 4. American literature -- Hispanic American authors -- Collections
ISBN 0-8126-4750-5

LC 2001-47189

A bilingual collection of poems, stories, and other writings which celebrates diversity among Latinos.

"This collection would make a fine classroom text, great for reading aloud and for stimulating students from everywhere to write about their roots and celebrate their shifting places across borders." Booklist

Includes glossary and bibliographical references

Walking on earth and touching the sky; poetry and prose by Lakota youth at Red Cloud Indian School. edited by Timothy P. McLaughlin; illustrations by S.D. Nelson; with a foreword by Joseph M. Marshall III. Abrams Books for Young Readers 2012 80 p. $19.95

Grades: 6 7 8   810
1. Children's writings 2. Native American children 3. Poor children -- United States 4. Indian children's writings 5. American literature -- Indian authors 6. Teton Indians -- Literary collections
ISBN 1419701797; 9781419701795

LC 2011036454

This book is an "anthology of work by children in grades five through eight." Poet "and teacher [Timothy P.] McLaughlin, after gradually connecting with his students at Red Cloud Indian School, provided them with creative-writing prompts that yielded sometimes-magical outcomes." The students, living in "the second-poorest county in the country," wrote on themes like the :Natural World" and "Family, Youth, and Dreams." (Kirkus)

Wilkin, Binnie Tate

African and African American images in Newbery Award winning titles; progress in portrayals. Scarecrow Press 2009 195p pa $40

Grades: Adult Professional   810
1. Newbery Medal 2. African Americans in literature 3. Children's literature -- History and criticism
ISBN 978-0-8108-6959-2 pa; 0-8108-6959-4 pa

LC 2009017726

"The author has exhaustively examined all books that have won the Newbery Medal and been cited as honor books since the award's creation in 1922. Her purpose is to evaluate the representation of Africans and African Americans, and to describe how these groups are portrayed in each title's historical context. . . . Books with the most positive images are awarded three pluses, while books with marginal African-American characters are indicated with an 'M.' . . . An essential volume for scholars, teachers, and librarians." SLJ

Includes bibliographical references

WritersCorps

City of one; young writers speak to the world. from WritersCorps; foreword by Isabel Allende; edited by Collete DeDonato. Aunt Lute Books 2004 239p pa $10.95

Grades: 7 8 9 10   **810**

1. Teenagers' writings 2. Youth -- Poetry 3. Immigrants -- Poetry 4. American poetry -- 21st century 5. Children of immigrants -- Poetry 6. Youths' writings, American -- Washington (D.C.) 7. Immigrants' writings, American -- Washington (D.C.) 8. Youths' writings, American -- California -- San Francisco 9. Youths' writings, American -- New York (State) -- New York 10. Immigrants' writings, American -- California -- San Francisco 11. Immigrants' writings, American -- New York (State) -- New York

ISBN 1-87996-069-9

LC 2004-45089

"This anthology celebrates the 10th anniversary of WritersCorps workshops, which bring creative-writing instruction to low-income kids from public schools, youth detention centers, halfway houses, and afterschool programs. More than 150 young people ranging in age from 9 to 23 write about their lives and the state of the world. . . . Poems about family, freedom, inner peace, self-identity, and the writing process round out this remarkable anthology." SLJ

You hear me? poems and writing by teenage boys. edited by Betsy Franco. Candlewick Press 2000 107p hardcover o.p. pa $6.99

Grades: 7 8 9 10   **810**

1. Boys 2. Adolescence 3. Teenagers' writings 4. Youths' writings 5. American literature -- Collections 6. Adolescence -- Literary collections

ISBN 0-7636-1158-1; 0-7636-1159-X pa

LC 99-57129

"The voices range from painfully honest to playfully ironic, but all are controlled and powerful as they speak to subjects that teen readers will be familiar with." Voice Youth Advocates

810.9 American literature (English)--history and criticism

Student's encyclopedia of great American writers; edited by Patricia Gantt and Robert Evan. 1st ed. Facts On File, Inc. 2009 2576p 5 v. $425

Grades: 8 9 10 11 12   **810.9**

1. Authors, American -- Encyclopedias 2. American literature -- Encyclopedias 3. American literature -- Encyclopedias 4. Authors, American -- Biography -- Encyclopedias

ISBN 9780816060870, 0816060878

"More than 180 writers currently studied are profiled in this set. Arranged chronologically, the volumes begin with colonists . . . . Subsequent volumes feature both canonical figures identified with America's literary movements and lesser-known writers gaining public and scholarly interest." (School Library Journal)

Includes bibliographical references and index

811 American poetry

Adoff, Jaime

The **song** shoots out of my mouth; illustrated by Martin French. Dutton Children's Bks. 2002 48p il $17.99

Grades: 7 8 9   **811**

1. Music -- Poetry 2. Children's poetry, American 3. Poetry -- By individual authors

ISBN 0-525-46949-4

LC 2002-284232

This is a "collection of 24 poems. Though free in form and diverse in mood and tone, all are about music, from Hip Hop to classical and from reggae to gospel. Another common element is the energy underscoring Adoff's language, which invites readers to move to the rhythm of the words. . . . All shine with the poet's obvious love of music and musicians." Booklist

Includes glossary and discography

African American Poetry; edited by Arnold Rampersad and Marcellus Blount; illustrated by Karen Barbour. Sterling Pub Co Inc. 2013 48 $14.95

Grades: 3 4 5 6 7   **811**

1. American poetry -- Asian American authors

ISBN 1402716893; 9781402716898

This book of poetry by African American authors"introduces 27 poets from the days of Phillis Wheatley to well-established poets writing in the 21st century. A four-page introduction outlines historical periods and influences. Presented chronologically, the entries begin with a paragraph describing the poet's life and work. Paul Laurence Dunbar, Countee Cullen, Langston Hughes, Lucille Clifton, Maya Angelou, and others are joined by George Moses Horton . . .and others."

Alexander, Elizabeth

Miss Crandall's School for Young Ladies and Little Misses of Color; poems. by Elizabeth Alexander and Marilyn Nelson; pictures by Floyd Cooper. Wordsong 2007 47p il $17.95

Grades: 7 8 9 10   **811**

1. Teachers 2. Abolitionists 3. Children's poetry 4. Schools -- Poetry 5. African Americans -- Poetry 6. Poetry -- By individual authors

ISBN 978-1-59078-456-3; 1-59078-456-1

LC 2006-38985

"Twenty-four sonnets tell the story of Prudence Crandall and her efforts to educate young African-American women in Canterbury, CT, 1833-1834. . . . The sonnet format is challenging but compelling. . . . There are empty spaces in the pictures just as the language of the poetry leaves openness for readers' interpretation. A heartfelt, unusual presentation." SLJ

★ **America** at war; poems. selected by Lee Bennett Hopkins; illlustrated by Stephen Alcorn. Margaret K. McElderry Books 2008 84p il $21.99

Grades: 5 6 7 8   **811**

1. War poetry 2. Children's poetry 3. War poetry,

American 4. American poetry -- Collections
ISBN 978-1-4169-1832-5; 1-4169-1832-9

LC 2006-08723

"This handsome anthology, expressing Americans' varied experience during wartime, is a fine selection of poems accessible to children. . . . The poems will touch readers with their sharp poignancy and undeniable power. Throughout the well-designed book, the expressive watercolor artwork enhances the poetry." Booklist

Angelou, Maya

★ **Maya** Angelou; edited by Edwin Graves Wilson; illustrated by Jerome Lagarrigue. Sterling Pub. 2007 48 p. col. ill. (Poetry for young people) (hardcover) $14.95

Grades: 4 5 6 7 **811**

1. African American women 2. Poets, American 3. African Americans -- Poetry 4. Poetry -- By individual authors
ISBN 9781402720239; 1402720238

LC 2006013803

"Wilson's introduction . . . addresses how Angelou's life has informed her imagination. . . . Twenty-five poems show her concern with the African-American experience. . . . Dignity, pride, and resiliancy are at this collection's core. . . . Footnotes offer definitions of colloquialisms and difficult words. Lagarrigue's painterly artwork uses golds, greens, and violets to capture the luminescent quality of the poems. . . . This [is a] distinguished work." SLJ

Appelt, Kathi

Poems from homeroom; a writer's place to start. Holt & Co. 2002 114p hardcover o.p. pa $14.95

Grades: 7 8 9 10 **811**

1. Poetics 2. Teenagers 3. American poetry 4. Teenagers -- Poetry 5. Poetry -- Authorship 6. Young adult poetry, American 7. High school students -- Poetry 8. Poetry -- By individual authors
ISBN 0-8050-6978-X; 0-8050-7596-8 pa

LC 2002-67886

A collection of poems about the experiences of young people and a section with information about how each poem was written to enable readers to create their own original poems

Appelt's "poems are at times sensual, dramatic, or violent, and always rhythmic. They are fascinating, smooth, and 'with it.'" SLJ

Includes bibliographical references

Atkins, Jeannine

★ **Borrowed** names; poems about Laura Ingalls Wilder, Madam C. J. Walker, Marie Curie, and their daughters. Henry Holt & Co. 2010 209p il $16.99

Grades: 6 7 8 9 10 **811**

1. Authors 2. Chemists 3. Novelists 4. Physicists 5. Entrepreneurs 6. Philanthropists 7. Children's poetry 8. Cosmeticians 9. Western writers 10. College teachers 11. Children's authors 12. Nonfiction writers 13. Patrons of the arts 14. Young adult authors 15. Nobel laureates for physics 16. Cosmetics industry executives 17. Nobel laureates for chemistry 18. Poetry -- By individual authors 19. Mother-daughter relationship -- Poetry
ISBN 978-0-8050-8934-9; 0-8050-8934-9

LC 2009-23446

"In 1867, three women who achieved great success were born: writer Laura Ingalls Wilder, entrepreneur Madam C. J. Walker, and scientist Marie Curie. All three had complicated relationships with their daughters, relationships that Atkins explores in this unusual volume of poetry. . . . In vivid scenes written with keen insight and subtle imagery, the poems offer a strong sense of each daughter's personality as well as the tensions and ties they shared with their notable mothers." Booklist

Bernier-Grand, Carmen

★ **Frida**; viva la vida = long live life. by Carmen T. Bernier-Grand. Marshall Cavendish Children 2007 64 p. ill. $14.24

Grades: 8 9 10 11 12 **811**

1. Artists 2. Painters 3. Poetry -- By individual authors 4. Painters -- Mexico -- Biography
ISBN 9780761453369

LC 2006014479

In this book, "Frida Kahlo, a native of Mexico, is described . . . in biographical poems accompanied by her own artwork. Both text and images reveal the anguish and joy of her two marriages to muralist Diego Rivera, her life-long suffering from a crippling bus accident, and her thirst for life, even as she tasted death. . . . Back matter includes excerpts from Frida's diary and letters, a prose biography, a chronology of the artist's life, a glossary of Spanish words, sources, and notes." (Publisher's note)

"Bernier-Grand introduces a famous life with lyrical free-verse poems. Nearly every double-page spread pairs a well-reproduced painting by Frida Kahlo with an original poem that defines turning points in the artist's life. Bernier-Grand's words expertly extend the autobiographical imagery so evident in the art." Booklist

Includes bibliographical references (p. 61).

Bernier-Grand, Carmen T.

★ **Diego**; bigger than life. illustrated by David Diaz. Marshall Cavendish Children 2009 64p il $18.99

Grades: 8 9 10 11 12 **811**

1. Artists 2. Painters 3. Children's poetry 4. Poetry -- By individual authors 6. Art -- History
ISBN 978-0-7614-5383-3; 0-7614-5383-0

LC 2007-13761

ALA ALSC Belpre Illustrator Medal Honor Book (2010)
ALA ALSC Belpre Author Medal Honor Book (2010)

This is a "well written and beautifully illustrated volume. . . . Almost all written in first-person from the artist's point of view, the poems convey information succinctly within a context of colorful narrative and clearly expressed emotion. . . . Apart from four reproductions of Rivera's paintings and one photo of the artist, the illustrations are mixed-media pictures by Diaz. Depicting Rivera and his world, these iconic images glow with warmth, light, and color." Booklist

Includes bibliographical references

Borus, Audrey

A **student's** guide to Emily Dickinson. Enslow Publishers 2005 152p il (Understanding literature) $27.93

Grades: 7 8 9 10 **811**

1. Poets 2. Authors

ISBN 0-7660-2285-4

LC 2004-18098

"A short discussion of Dickinson's life and times is followed by a chapter on how to read and analyze her poems, which would be particularly useful for students reading her work for the first time. Subsequent chapters focus on particular themes in the poems such as death and eternity, truth, faith and reality, the natural world, and the influence of the Civil War." SLJ

Includes bibliographical references

Bulion, Leslie

At the sea floor cafe; odd ocean critter poems. written by Leslie Bulion; illustrated by Leslie Evans. Peachtree Publishers 2011 45p il $14.95

Grades: 5 6 7 8 **811**

1. Marine animals -- Poetry 2. Poetry -- By individual authors

ISBN 978-1-56145-565-2; 1-56145-565-2

LC 2010026691

"Using complex poetry forms and cleverly constructed lines, Bulion plays tribute to sea creatures. . . . Evans's spare, well-placed hand-colored linoleum block prints hold their own without overwhelming the text." Horn Book Guide

Burleigh, Robert

★ **Hoops**; illustrated by Stephen T. Johnson. Harcourt Brace & Co. 1997 un il hardcover o.p. pa $6

Grades: 6 7 8 9 **811**

1. Children's poetry 2. Basketball -- Poetry 3. Poetry -- By individual authors 4. Basketball

ISBN 0-15-201450-0; 0-15-216380-8 pa

LC 96-18440

Illustrations and poetic text describe the movement and feel of the game of basketball

"Burleigh's staccato text is well matched by Johnson's dynamic pastels. Muted colors and a strong sense of motion as bodies leap and lift, pounce and poke, aptly complement the words." SLJ

★ **Cool** salsa; bilingual poems on growing up Latino in the United States. edited by Lori M. Carlson; introduction by Oscar Hijuelos. Holt & Co. 1994 xx, 123p il hardcover o.p. pa $6.99

Grades: 5 6 7 8 9 10 **811**

1. Bilingual books -- English-Spanish 2. American poetry -- Hispanic American authors -- Collections

ISBN 0-8050-3135-9; 978-0-449-70436-3 pa; 0-449-70436-X pa

LC 93-45798

"This collection presents poems by 29 Mexican-American, Cuban-American, Puerto Rican, and other Central and South American poets, including Sandra Cisneros, Luis J. Rodriguez, Pat Mora, Gary Soto, Ana Castillo, Oscar Hijue-los, Ed J. Vega, Judith Ortiz-Cofer, and other Latino writers both contemporary and historical. Brief biographical notes on the authors are provided. All the poems deal with experiences of teenagers." Book Rep

Crisler, Curtis L.

★ **Tough** boy sonatas; illustrations by Floyd Cooper. Wordsong 2007 86p il $19.95

Grades: 8 9 10 11 12 **811**

1. Children's poetry 2. African Americans -- Poetry 3. City and town life -- Poetry 4. Poetry -- By individual authors

ISBN 978-1-932425-77-2; 1-932425-77-2

LC 2006-11836

"Crisler presents a collection of potent, hard-hitting poems about growing up in Gary, Indiana. Written mostly in voices of young African American males, the poems evoke the grit and ash of crumbling, burned-out streets as well as the realities of hardscrabble life. . . . Written with skillful manipulation of sound, rhythm, and form, the poems are filled with sophisticated imagery and graphic words . . . and Cooper's illustrations extend . . . the poems' impact. Created in sooty black and gray, the powerful drawings are mostly portraits of anguished young men." Booklist

Dickinson, Emily, 1830-1886

My letter to the world and other poems; with illustrations by Isabelle Arsenault. KCP Poetry 2008 un il (Visions in poetry) $17.95; pa $9.95

Grades: 7 8 9 10 11 12 **811**

1. Poets 2. Authors 3. Children's poetry 4. Poetry -- By individual authors

ISBN 1-55453-103-9; 1-55453-339-2 pa; 978-1-55453-103-5; 978-1-55453-339-8 pa

This is an illustrated edition of seven Emily Dickinson poems. "Age ten and up." (N Y Times Book Rev)

"The long final biographical note about the introvert and recluse who gloried in being 'Nobody' will take readers back to the poetry, which speaks as a 'letter to the world,' as will the clear analysis of the mixed-media illustrations, in which Arsenault links the poet's repeated images of isolation with her intense connections to nature. . . . Dickinson's exploration of the difference between loneliness and rich solitude will resonate with teens." Booklist

Engle, Margarita

The **poet** slave of Cuba: a biography of Juan Francisco Manzano; art by Sean Qualls. Henry Holt 2006 183p il $16.95

Grades: 7 8 9 10 **811**

1. Poets 2. Slaves 3. Authors

ISBN 0-8050-7706-5; 978-0-8050-7706-3

LC 2005-46200

Awarded the Pura Belpré Author Award, 2008

"This is a book that should be read by young and old, black and white, Anglo and Latino." SLJ

★ The **surrender** tree; poems of Cuba's struggle for freedom. Henry Holt and Co. 2008 169p $17.95

Grades: 7 8 9 10 11 12   **811**
1. Novels in verse 2. Children's poetry
ISBN 978-0-8050-8674-4; 0-8050-8674-9

     LC 2007-27591

Pura Belpre Author Award, 2009

A Newbery Medal honor book, 2009

This "book is written in clear, short lines of stirring free verse. . . . [The author] draws on her own Cuban American roots . . . to describe those who fought in the nineteenth-century Cuban struggle for independence. At the center is Rosa, a traditional healer, who nurses runaway slaves and deserters in caves and other secret hideaways. . . . Many readers will be caught by the compelling narrative voices and want to pursue the historical accounts in Engle's bibliography." Booklist

Fields, Terri

After the death of Anna Gonzales. Holt & Co. 2002 100p $16.95

Grades: 7 8 9 10   **811**
1. Schools 2. High schools 3. American poetry 4. Suicide -- Poetry 5. Teenagers -- Poetry 6. Suicide victims -- Poetry 7. Young adult poetry, American 8. High school students -- Poetry 9. Poetry -- By individual authors 10. Teenagers -- Suicidal behavior -- Poetry
ISBN 0-8050-7127-X

     LC 2002-24074

Poems written in the voices of forty-seven people, including students, teachers, and other school staff, record the aftermath of a high school student's suicide and the preoccupations of teen life

"A short book, easily read, which should generate serious thought and discussion." BAYA Book Rev

Fleischman, Paul

★ **Big** talk; poems for four voices. illustrated by Beppe Giacobbe. Candlewick Press 2000 44p il $17.99; pa $7.99

Grades: 4 5 6 7   **811**
1. Children's poetry, American 2. Poetry -- By individual authors
ISBN 0-7636-0636-7; 0-7636-3805-6 pa

     LC 99-46882

A collection of poems to be read aloud by four people, with color-coded text to indicate which lines are read by which readers

"Each poem is more demanding, and more rewarding, than the last. Giacobbe highlights the humor in strips of vignettes that run along the bottom of the page. This is 'toe-tapping, tongue-flapping fun.'" Horn Book Guide

★ **I** am phoenix: poems for two voices; illustrated by Ken Nutt. Harper & Row 1985 51p il hardcover o.p. pa $5.99

Grades: 4 5 6 7   **811**
1. Children's poetry 2. Birds -- Poetry 3. Poetry -- By individual authors
ISBN 0-06-446092-4 pa

     LC 85-42615

A collection of poems about birds to be read aloud by two voices

"Devotés of the almost lost art of choral reading should be among the first to appreciate this collection. . . . Printed in script form, the selections . . . have a cadenced pace and dignified flow; their combination of imaginative imagery and realistic detail is echoed by the combination of stylized fantasy and representational drawings in the black and white pictures, all soft line and strong nuance." Bull Cent Child Books

★ **Joyful** noise: poems for two voices; illustrated by Eric Beddows. Harper & Row 1988 44p il $15.99; lib bdg $16.89; pa $5.99

Grades: 4 5 6 7   **811**
1. Insects -- Poetry 2. Poetry -- By individual authors
ISBN 0-06-021852-5; 0-06-021853-3 lib bdg; 0-06-446093-2 pa

     LC 87-45280

Awarded the Newbery Medal, 1989

"There are fourteen poems in the handsomely designed volume, with stylish endpapers and wonderfully interpretive black-and-white illustrations. Each selection is a gem, polished perfection." Horn Book

Forbes, Robert L.

Beast Friends Forever; by Robert L. Forbes; illustrated by Ronald Searle. Penguin Group USA 2013 80 p. (hardcover) $19.95

Grades: 4 5 6 7   **811**
1. Animal courtship 2. Animals -- Poetry
ISBN 1590208080; 9781590208083

In this book of children's poetry by Robert Forbes, "animal courtship is infused with quirky human characteristics and some sneaky social commentary. Readers meet Lancelot the Ocelot, doing time for 'his romance turned to tragedy, ending in a crime.' And Babette the Skunk, having studied with 'Parisian perfumers,' has fashioned a new scent, 'packaged in black and called "In-d-scent,"/It's sure to enflame any white-striped gent.'" (School Library Journal)

Forler, Nan

Winterberries and apple blossoms; reflections and flavors of a Mennonite year. paintings by Peter Etril Snyder. Tundra Books 2011 39p il $22.95

Grades: 4 5 6 7   **811**
1. Cooking 2. Months -- Poetry 3. Mennonites -- Poetry 4. Poetry -- By individual authors
ISBN 978-1-77049-254-7; 1-77049-254-2

With a poem for every month of the year, young Naomi introduces us to her family and hosts a journey through the seasonal rhythms of her rural Mennonite community. Includes a recipe for each month of the year.

This includes "12 evocative poems. . . . Snyder . . . contributes smudgy, sunlit acrylic scenes that convey a close-knit family that works, plays, and prays together. Along with Forler's graceful verse, and recipes for every season, it all adds up to a warm portrait of a community seldom found in the spotlight." Publ Wkly

Frost, Robert

★ **Robert** Frost; edited by Gary D. Schmidt; illustrated by Henri Sorensen. Sterling 1994 48p il (Poetry for young people) $14.95; pa $6.95

Grades: 4 5 6 7   **811**

1. Children's poetry 2. Poetry -- By individual authors
ISBN 0-8069-0633-2; 1-4027-5475-2 pa

LC 94-11161

This volume "contains a three-page overview of the poet's life, 29 poems selected and arranged around the seasons of the year, brief and apt commentaries on each, and a useful index of titles and subject matter. The realistic watercolor illustrations capture the delicate beauty of a New England spring and the glory of fall while still suggesting the around-the-corner chill of winter, a disquiet echoing throughout much of Frost's poetry." SLJ

George, Kristine O'Connell

★ **Swimming** upstream; middle school poems. illustrated by Debbie Tilley. Clarion Bks. 2002 79p il $14

Grades: 5 6 7 8   **811**

1. Schools -- Poetry 2. Girls -- poetry 3. Children's poetry, American 4. Poetry -- By individual authors 5. Middle schools -- poetry 6. Middle school students -- poetry
ISBN 0-618-15250-4

LC 2002-2746

A collection of poems capture the feelings and experiences of a girl in middle school

"Students will relate to this voice 'navigating upstream,' while they try to find their own place in the middle-school wilderness." SLJ

Giovanni, Nikki

Ego-tripping and other poems for young people; illustrations by George Ford; foreword by Virginia Hamilton. 2nd ed; Hill Bks. 1993 52p il hardcover o.p. pa $10.95

Grades: 5 6 7 8   **811**

1. Children's poetry 2. African Americans -- Poetry 3. Poetry -- By individual authors
ISBN 1-55652-189-8; 1-55652-188-X pa

LC 93-29578

First published 1974

Giovanni has added 10 new poems to her earlier "collection of 23 poems for young people. Ford's illustrations in sepia shades are bold and full of character and dreaming. As Virginia Hamilton says in her foreword, Giovanni's voice is personal and warm, she 'celebrates ordinary folks' and writes of struggle and liberation. She's upbeat and celebratory without minimizing hard times." Booklist

Grandits, John

★ **Blue** lipstick; concrete poems. Clarion Books 2007 un il $15; pa $5.95

Grades: 5 6 7 8 9 10   **811**

1. Children's poetry 2. Poetry -- By individual authors

3. Teenagers
ISBN 978-0-618-56860-4; 0-618-56860-3; 978-0-618-85132-4 pa; 0-618-85132-1 pa

LC 2006-23332

"This selection introduces readers to Jessie, who impulsively purchases blue lipstick, but later, regretfully decides to give it 'the kiss-off.' Jessie is big sister to Robert, who was featured in Grandits's Technically, It's Not My Fault (Clarion, 2004). As he did in that terrific collection, the author uses artful arrangements of text on the page, along with 54 different typefaces, to bring his images and ideas to life. . . . This irreverent, witty collection should resonate with a wide audience." SLJ

★ **Technically,** it's not my fault; concrete poems. by John Grandits. Clarion Books 2004 un il $15; pa $5.95

Grades: 5 6 7 8   **811**

1. Children's poetry 2. Poetry -- By individual authors
ISBN 0-618-42833-X; 0-618-50361-7 pa

LC 2004-231

A collection of concrete poems on such topics as roller coasters, linguini, basketball, and sisters

"Grandits combines technical brilliance and goofy good humor to provide an accessible, fun-filled collection of poems, dramatically brought to life through a brilliant book design." SLJ

Grimes, Nikki

At Jerusalem's gate; poems of Easter. with woodcuts by David Frampton. Eerdmans Books for Young Readers 2005 un il $20

Grades: 5 6 7 8   **811**

1. Children's poetry 2. American poetry 3. Easter -- Poetry 4. Poetry -- By individual authors
ISBN 0-8028-5183-5

LC 2003-1089

"Twenty-two poems trace the events celebrated by Christians as Easter Week, from Jesus' entry into Jerusalem through his appearance to disciples after the Resurrection. . . . Grades five to eight." Bull Cent Child Books

"Each poem is preceded by a brief synopsis of the event, often accompanied by the author's own musings and queries, which prompt readers to think and ask questions of their own. . . . Bold, handsome woodcuts reinforce the powerful drama depicted in poetry. An outstanding effort." SLJ

A **dime** a dozen; pictures by Angelo. Dial Bks. for Young Readers 1998 54p il $17.99

Grades: 5 6 7 8   **811**

1. American poetry 2. African Americans 3. African Americans -- Poetry 4. Children's poetry, American 5. Poetry -- By individual authors 6. African Americans -- poetry
ISBN 0-8037-2227-3

LC 97-5798

A collection of poems about an African-American girl growing up in New York

"Free-flowing and very accessible, the poetry may inspire readers to distill their own life experiences into precise, imaginative words and phrases." Booklist

Grover, Lorie Ann

Loose threads. Margaret K. McElderry Bks. 2002 296p $16.95

811

1. Grandmothers 2. American poetry 3. Mothers and daughters 4. Breast cancer -- Poetry 5. Death -- poetry 6. Cancer -- poetry 7. Children's poetry, American 8. Grandmothers -- poetry 9. Poetry -- By individual authors 10. Junior high schools -- poetry 11. Breast -- Cancer -- Patients -- poetry

ISBN 0-689-84419-0

LC 2001-44724

A series of poems describes how seventh-grader Kay Garber faces her grandmother's battle with breast cancer while living with her mother and great-grandmother and dealing with everyday junior high school concerns

"The poetic, spare language, written in Kay's self-possessed, first-person voice, is refreshingly frank about the disease. . . . Grover's book balances vivid emotional scenes with plenty of space between the words." Booklist

Includes bibliographical references

Harley, Avis

★ **African** acrostics; a word in edgeways. poems by Avis Harley; photographs by Deborah Noyes. Candlewick Press 2009 un il $17.99; pa $6.99

Grades: 4 5 6 7

811

1. Acrostics 2. Children's poetry 3. Animals -- Africa 4. Animals -- Poetry 5. Poetry -- By individual authors ISBN 978-0-7636-3621-0; 0-7636-3621-5; 978-0-7636-5818-2 pa

LC 2008017916

This volume depicts "such wild animals as giraffes, zebras, and lions, in poems written to contain acrostics, in which beginning or ending letters from the poetry lines can be used to spell other words." (Publisher's note)

"Harley has written 18 poems, each one featuring a different animal. All are written as acrostics, with most of them based on the first letter of each line, but several with more unusual patterns. . . . Much of Harley's poetry consists of carefully crafted descriptive word imagery that is right on target. . . . Most of the full-page, full-color photos of the animals are perfect companions to the facing selections." SLJ

Haskins-Bookser, Laura

The **softer** side of hip-hop; poetic reflections on love, family, and relationships. by Laura Haskins-Bookser; illustrated by Jami Moffett. Morning Glory Press 2008 il pa $9.95

Grades: 8 9 10 11 12

811

1. Teenage mothers -- Poetry 2. Poetry -- By individual authors ISBN 978-1-932538-83-0 pa; 1-932538-83-6 pa

"Haskins-Bookser brings her hip-hop sensibility to a genre—poetry—that is really at the heart and soul of both hip-hop and rap. She voices the hopes, fears, and joys of a single teen mother. . . . Her poems are at once cautionary, but are tales of hope and transcendence as well. Each poem is heartfelt and well crafted. This is a lovely treasure, enhanced by Moffett's beautifully executed drawings and quotes from teen mothers." SLJ

★ **Heart** to heart; new poems inspired by twentieth-century American art. edited by Jan Greenberg. Abrams 2001 80p il map $19.95

Grades: 5 6 7 8 9 10

811

1. American art 2. Art, American 3. Art -- 20th century 4. Art, Modern -- 20th century 5. American poetry -- Collections

ISBN 0-8109-4386-7

LC 99-462335

Michael L. Printz Award honor book, 2002

A compilation of poems by Americans writing about American art in the twentieth century, including such writers as Nancy Willard, Jane Yolen, and X. J. Kennedy.

"From a tight diamante and pantoum to lyrical free verse, the range of poetic styles will speak to a wide age group. . . . Concluding with biographical notes on each poet and artist, this rich resource is an obvious choice for teachers, and the exciting interplay between art and the written word will encourage many readers to return again and again to the book." Booklist

Hemphill, Stephanie

Your own, Sylvia; a verse portrait of Sylvia Plath. Alfred A. Knopf 2007 261p $15.99; lib bdg $18.99

Grades: 8 9 10 11 12

811

1. Poets 2. Authors 3. Novelists 4. Children's poetry 5. Poetry -- By individual authors ISBN 978-0-375-83799-9; 978-0-375-93799-6 lib bdg

LC 2006-07253

Michael L. Printz Award honor book, 2008

The author interprets the people, events, influences and art that made up the brief life of Sylvia Plath.

"Hemphill's verse, like Plath's, is completely compelling: every word, every line, worth reading." Horn Book

Includes bibliographical references

Herrera, Juan Felipe

★ **Laughing** out loud, I fly; poems in English and Spanish. drawings by Karen Barbour. HarperCollins Pubs. 1998 un il $15.99

Grades: 6 7 8 9

811

1. Mexican Americans -- Poetry 2. Poetry -- By individual authors 3. Bilingual books -- English-Spanish

ISBN 0-06-027604-5

LC 96-45476

A collection of poems in Spanish and English about childhood, place, and identity

"Barbour's black-and-white drawings accompany each poem, delicately underlining its images but allowing the strong sensuality of the words to seep into readers' minds." SLJ

Holbrook, Sara

More than friends; poems from him and her. [by] Sara Holbrook and Allan Wolf. Wordsong 2008 64p il $16.95

Grades: 6 7 8 9 10

811

1. Love poetry 2. Children's poetry 3. Poetry -- By

individual authors
ISBN 978-1-59078-587-4; 1-59078-587-8

LC 2007-50282

"In these parallel poems, a boy and a girl describe their progression from friendship to romance. . . . The simple language expresses strong feelings in a variety of poetic forms. . . . Small black-and-white photos never get in the way of the words, which tell the edgy truth of romance in all its joy and confusion." Booklist

Hopkins, Lee Bennett

Been to yesterdays: poems of a life; illustrations by Charlene Rendeiro. Wordsong 1995 64p il $15.95; pa $9.95

Grades: 4 5 6 7 **811**
1. Children's poetry 2. Poetry -- By individual authors
ISBN 1-56397-467-3; 1-56397-808-3 pa

LC 94-73320

"Hopkins distills the experience of his middle-grade years into 28 poems of poignant clarity. . . . Good reading and an excellent, unconventional choice for teachers doing units on poetry and autobiography." Booklist

Hovey, Kate

★ **Ancient** voices; written by Kate Hovey; with illustrations by Murray Kimber. Margaret McElderry Books 2004 un il $18.95

Grades: 6 7 8 9 **811**
1. Children's poetry 2. Classical mythology -- Poetry 3. Poetry -- By individual authors
ISBN 0-689-83342-3

LC 00-28359

Twenty-three poems give voice to a variety of goddesses, gods, and mortals from Greek and Roman mythology

"These lyrical poems and dramatic picture-book-size illustrations humanize the Greek myths with flashes of contemporary realism. . . . The poetry here is both intense and accessible, with unobtrusive rhyme that adds to the music of the lines." Booklist

Hughes, Langston

★ **Langston** Hughes; edited by Arnold Rampersad & David Roessel; illustrations by Benny Andrews. Sterling Pub. 2006 48p il (Poetry for young people) $14.95

Grades: 5 6 7 8 **811**
1. African Americans -- Poetry 2. Poetry -- By individual authors
ISBN 1-4027-1845-4; 978-1-4027-1845-8

LC 2005025369

A brief profile of African American poet Langston Hughes accompanies some of his better known poems for children.

"This charming collection of 26 poems is vibrantly illustrated with depictions of African Americans in varied settings. . . . This will be a welcome introduction to Hughes's poetry for elementary students, and it includes sufficient detail to make it useful and enjoyable for older students." SLJ

★ The **dream** keeper and other poems; including seven additional poems. [by] Langston Hughes;

illustrated by Brian Pinkney. 75th anniversary ed.; Alfred A. Knopf 2007 83p il $16.99

Grades: 4 5 6 7 **811**
1. African Americans -- Poetry 2. Poetry -- By individual authors
ISBN 978-0-679-84421-1

First published 1932; this is a reissue of the 1994 edition

A collection of sixty-six poems, selected by the author for young readers, including lyrical poems, songs, and blues, many exploring the black experience

"Black-and-white scratchboard illustrations in Pinkney's signature style express the emotion and beat of the poetry. . . . The poems are . . . colloquial and direct yet mysterious and complex." Booklist

★ **I** am the darker brother; an anthology of modern poems by African Americans. edited and with an afterword by Arnold Adoff; drawings by Benny Andrews; introduction by Rudine Sims Bishop; foreword by Nikki Giovanni. rev ed; Simon & Schuster Bks. for Young Readers 1997 208p il hardcover o.p. pa $5.99

Grades: 6 7 8 9 10 **811**
1. Children's poetry -- Collections 2. American poetry -- African American authors -- Collections 3. American poetry -- African American authors
ISBN 0-689-81241-8; 0-689-80869-0 pa

LC 97-144181

First published 1968

This anthology presents "the African-American experience through poetry that speaks for itself. . . . Because of the historical context of many of the poems, the book will be much in demand during Black History Month, but it should be used and treasured as part of the larger canon of literature to be enjoyed by all Americans at all times of the year. An indispensable addition to library collections." SLJ

★ **I,** too, sing America; three centuries of African American poetry. [selected and annotated by] Catherine Clinton; illustrated by Stephen Alcorn. Houghton Mifflin 1998 128p il $21

Grades: 6 7 8 9 **811**
1. African Americans -- Poetry 2. American poetry -- Afro-American authors 3. American poetry -- African American authors -- Collections
ISBN 0-395-89599-5

LC 97-46137

"For each poet, Clinton provides a biography and a brief, insightful commentary on the poem(s) she has chosen, including a discussion of political as well as literary connections. Alcorn's dramatic, full-page, full-color illustrations opposite each poem evoke the quiltlike patterns and rhythmic figures of folk art." Booklist

The **Invisible** ladder; an anthology of contemporary American poems for young readers with the poets' own photos and commentary. edited by Liz Rosenberg. Holt & Co. 1996 210p il $21.95

Grades: 7 8 9 10 **811**
1. Poets, American 2. American poetry -- Collections

3. Children's poetry -- Collections
ISBN 0-8050-3836-1

LC 96-12361

Features such poets as Robert Bly, Allen Ginsberg, Nikki Giovanni, and Galway Kinnell by including photos, selections of their work, and comments on their poetry

Rosenberg "introduces many exciting new adult voices to young people. Some of the poets' commentaries are sophisticated, some are pretentious; but most are immediate and extraordinarily moving, nearly as powerful as the poetry they lead into." Booklist

Janeczko, Paul B.

Worlds afire. Candlewick Press 2004 92p hardcover o.p. pa $6.99

811

1. Circus 2. Poetry 3. American poetry 4. Fire -- Poetry 5. Fires -- Fiction 6. Circus -- Fiction 7. Children's poetry, American 9. Fires -- Connecticut -- Hartford
ISBN 0-7636-2235-4; 0-7636-3400-X pa

LC 2003-55337

"Janeczko never sensationalizes the horror, but the combination of a thrilling circus and true catastrophe will grab middle-schoolers, especially for readers' theater." Booklist

Janeczko, Paul B., 1945-

Requiem; poems of the Terezin ghetto. Candlewick Press 2011 112p $16.99

Grades: 7 8 9 10 **811**

1. Children's poetry 2. Holocaust, 1933-1945 -- Poetry 3. Poetry -- By individual authors
ISBN 978-0-7636-4727-8; 0-7636-4727-6

LC 2010-38882

"Janeczko reflects on Terezin through thirty-five compact free-verse poems, most written in the voice of named (and numbered) inhabitants and guards, almost all fictional, of the camp. . . . The verses are spare and accessible, filled with crushing historical weight; the first-person approach will make the entries particularly compelling as readers theater or readalouds." Bull Cent Child Books

Johnston, Tony

Voice from afar; poems of peace. by Tony Johnston; paintings by Susan Guevara. Holiday House 2008 32p il $16.95

Grades: 5 6 7 8 **811**

1. War poetry 2. Poetry -- By individual authors
ISBN 978-0-8234-2012-4; 0-8234-2012-4

LC 2007031434

"Johnston offers thoughtful responses to war's senseless violence. Her free-verse word pictures call to mind scenes of terrible devastation. . . . Yet Johnston finds cause for hope amid the grimness. . . . Johnston adds her own voice, the sympathetic observer from afar, sending prayers for peace. Guevara's paintings, crafted with acrylic and oil paint with collage on textured canvas, feature subdued, neutral colors and haunting images." SLJ

Katz, Bobbi

Trailblazers; poems of exploration. by Bobbi Katz; illustrations by Carin Berger. Greenwillow Books 2007 208p il $18.99; lib bdg $19.89

Grades: 5 6 7 8 **811**

1. Explorers -- Poetry 2. Poetry -- By individual authors
ISBN 978-0-688-16533-8; 0-688-16533-8; 978-0-688-16534-5 lib bdg; 0-688-16534-6 lib bdg

LC 2006016696

This is a collection of poems about "the lives of more than 120 explorers, from ancient times to the present. . . . Katz challenges readers to consider not only the courage of these individuals, but also to broaden their horizons in terms of the definition of exploration and the motivations behind it. . . . All the selections encourage reading aloud, especially the poems for two voices. The few black-and-white illustrations scattered throughout are small and iconic." SLJ

Includes bibliographical references

★ **A kick** in the head; selected by Paul B. Janeczko; illustrated by Chris Raschka. Candlewick Press 2005 61p il $17.99; pa $9.99

Grades: 4 5 6 7 **811**

1. Children's poetry 2. Poetry -- Collections 3. American poetry -- Collections
ISBN 978-0-7636-0662-6; 0-7636-0662-6; 978-0-7636-4132-0 pa; 0-7636-4132-4 pa

LC 2004-48508

"Raschka's high-spirited, spare torn-paper-and-paint collages ingeniously broaden the poems' wide-ranging emotional tones. . . . Clear, very brief explanations of poetic forms . . . accompany each entry; a fine introduction and appended notes offer further information. . . . This is the introduction that will ignite enthusiasm." Booklist

Kirk, Connie Ann

A **student's** guide to Robert Frost. Enslow Pubs. 2006 160p il (Understanding literature) $27.93

Grades: 7 8 9 10 **811**

1. Poets 2. Authors
ISBN 0-7660-2434-2

LC 2005-13392

In this book, "the career of this literary giant is examined. . . . Poems are put into historical and biographical context, with special emphasis placed on curriculum-related works, including 'Stopping by Woods on a Snowy Evening,' 'The Road Not Taken,' 'The Gift Outright,' and 'Fire and Ice.'" Publisher's note

Lawson, JonArno

Black stars in a white night sky; [by] JonArno Lawson; illustrated by Sherwin Tjia. Wordsong 2008 118p il $16.95

Grades: 4 5 6 7 **811**

1. Humorous poetry 2. Poetry -- By individual authors
ISBN 978-1-59078-521-8

LC 2007018927

First published 2006 in Canada

"This uproarious collection blends slapstick, puns, parodies, and sheer absurdity with lots of wry ideas. . . . Tjia's surreal art, in black-and-white silhouettes, is as rhythmic and absurd as the verse, which is perfect for reading aloud." Booklist

Think again; written by JonArno Lawson; illustrated by Julie Morstad. Kids Can Press 2010 62p il $16.95

Grades: 6 7 8 9   **811**

1. Children's poetry 2. Poetry -- By individual authors 3. Interpersonal relations -- Poetry

ISBN 978-1-55453-423-4; 1-55453-423-2

"More than 40 introspective poems and accompanying illustrations explore the complexity of close relationships. . . . Ever playful, the poet's pithy quatrains distill relational truths to their essence. . . . The illustrator's spare grayscale drawings . . . effectively amplify the tension they masterfully depict. An entirely rewarding combination." Kirkus

Levy, Debbie

★ The **year** of goodbyes; a true story of friendship, family and farewells. Disney-Hyperion Books 2010 136p il $16.99

Grades: 5 6 7 8   **811**

1. Jews -- Poetry 2. Holocaust, 1933-1945 -- Poetry 3. Poetry -- By individual authors

ISBN 978-1-4231-2901-1; 1-4231-2901-6

LC 2009-18671

"Artfully weaving together her mother's poesiealbum (autograph/poetry album), diary, and her own verse, Levy crafts a poignant portrait of her Jewish mother's life in 1938 Nazi Germany that crackles with adolescent vitality." Publ Wkly

Lewis, J. Patrick

★ **Black** cat bone; [by] J. Patrick Lewis; illustrations by Gary Kelley. Creative Editions 2006 48p il $19.95

Grades: 6 7 8 9 10   **811**

1. Singers 2. Guitarists 3. Blues musicians 4. Songwriters 5. Blues music -- Poetry 6. Poetry -- By individual authors 7. African American musicians -- Poetry

ISBN 978-1-56846-194-6

LC 2005-52298

"Robert Johnson, the celebrated blues musician, is said to have sold his soul to the devil for his skills on the guitar. . . . Lewis's verse echoes Johnson's music. . . . A single line of text parades ghostlike across the bottom of each page, explaining the aspect of the man's life that the poem sings of, and becoming a cumulative mini-bio in itself. A couple of Johnson's own lyrics appear with the sequence of Lewis's poems where they add to the narrative tension. Kelley's mixed-media illustrations in blues and browns add to the mood and enliven the layout." SLJ

Countdown to summer; a poems for every day of the school year. illustrations by Ethan Long. Little, Brown and Co. 2009 un il $15.99

Grades: 4 5 6   **811**

1. Schools -- Poetry 2. Poetry -- By individual authors

ISBN 978-0-316-02089-3; 0-316-02089-3

LC 2008016772

"180 poems are here gathered to be enjoyed on a vitamin-like one-a-day basis. . . . Some verses are long, some short, some thought-provoking, some laugh-provoking. Long's penciled spot art provides an agreeable visual accompaniment." Kirkus

★ **Monumental** verses. National Geographic 2005 31p il $16.95; lib bdg $25.90

Grades: 5 6 7 8   **811**

1. Monuments -- Poetry 2. Poetry -- By individual authors

ISBN 0-7922-7135-1; 0-7922-7139-4 lib bdg

"Lewis offers 14 poems celebrating monumental structures. From the remnants of civilizations at Stonehenge, Easter Island, and Machu Picchu to the more modern achievements of the Taj Mahal, the Eiffel Tower, and the Statue of Liberty, the subjects are varied and the accompanying photos are striking." Booklist

★ **Self**-portrait with seven fingers; the life of Marc Chagall in verse. [by] J. Patrick Lewis &Jane Yolen. Creative Editions 2011 38p il $18.99

Grades: 5 6 7 8   **811**

1. Artists 2. Painters 3. Jews -- Poetry 4. Artists -- Poetry 5. Jews -- Biography

ISBN 978-1-56846-211-0; 1-56846-211-5

LC 2009034767

"Lewis and Yolen pair 14 poems about Marc Chagall (1887–1985) with reproductions of more than a dozen of his paintings (as well as vintage photographs) in this moving account of the artist's Jewish upbringing in what is now Belarus, . . . his ascent in the art world, and his loves and losses, including arrest by the Nazis while living in Paris. . . . The duo's emphatic and empathetic verse is put into context by informative biographical sidebars that appear beneath each poem. A study in resilience, dedication, and wide-ranging talent." Publ Wkly

Includes bibliographical references

★ The **brothers'** war; Civil War voices in verse. including photographs by Civil War photographers. National Geographic 2007 31p il $17.95; lib bdg $20.90

Grades: 5 6 7 8 9 10   **811**

1. Children's poetry 2. Poetry -- By individual authors

ISBN 978-1-4263-0036-3; 978-1-4263-0037-0 lib bdg

LC 2006-103275

"This heartrending collection of original poems paired with photographs by Civil War photographers makes real what statistics about war cannot—that the casualties of any war have human faces. Lewis . . . writes poignantly and lyrically. . . . An elegant design of gold, silver and black handsomely frames the text and photographs." Publ Wkly

The **house**; illustrated by Roberto Innocenti. Creative Editions 2009 un il $19.95

Grades: 4 5 6 7   **811**

1. Houses -- Poetry 2. Poetry -- By individual authors

ISBN 978-1-56846-201-1; 1-56846-201-8

"The walls in a stone farmhouse literally talk in this first-person narrative that deals with the ravages of time and their effects on the structure and its inhabitants. After a brief history, the house (constructed in 1656, 'a plague year') fast forwards to the dawn of the 20th century, when children discover its ruins. The quatrains, one to a spread, alternate between an AABB and ABBA rhyme scheme, thus avoiding singsong predictability. . . . Children will pore over Innocenti's marvelously detailed spreads, composed in an oversize, vertical format and set in an Italian hill town. . . . In the subset of books dealing intelligently with the effects of time on a single location, this is a provocative choice." SLJ

★ **Lives**: poems about famous Americans; selected by Lee Bennett Hopkins; illustrated by Leslie Staub. HarperCollins Pubs. 1999 31p il $15.99
Grades: 4 5 6 7   **811**
1. American poetry -- Collections
ISBN 0-06-027767-X; 0-06-027768-8 lib bdg
LC 98-29851

A collection of poetic portraits of sixteen famous Americans from Paul Revere to Neil Armstrong, by such authors as Jane Yolen, Nikki Grimes, and X. J. Kennedy

"Hopkins's eloquent introduction praises the power of poetry. Concluding 'Notes on the Lives' give readers useful biographical information. Full-page portraits feature Staub's distinctive, flat, primitive style, and their backgrounds have details particular to the subject. . . . A winning combination of poems and illustrations." SLJ

Longfellow, Henry Wadsworth
★ **Henry** Wadsworth Longfellow; edited by Frances Schoonmaker; illustrated by Chad Wallace. Sterling 1998 48p il (Poetry for young people) $14.95
Grades: 4 5 6 7   **811**
1. Children's poetry, American 2. Poetry -- By individual authors
ISBN 0-8069-9417-7
LC 98-14833

A collection of 27 poems, "among them, 'The Village Blacksmith,' 'The Wreck of the Hesperus.' 'The Children's Hour,' 'Paul Revere's Ride,' and 'Hiawatha's Childhood' from 'The Song of Hiawatha.' A several-page introduction to Longfellow's life also includes some of the stories behind the poems." Booklist

Hiawatha and Megissogwon; illustrated by Jeffrey Thompson; afterword by Joseph Bruchac. National Geographic Soc. 2001 un il $16.95
Grades: 5 6 7 8   **811**
1. Indians of North America 2. Native Americans -- Poetry 3. Children's poetry, American 4. Poetry -- By individual authors
ISBN 0-7922-6676-5
LC 00-12719

"Readers who persevere through the no-longer-familiar poem will be rewarded for their efforts by Hiawatha's exciting adventures, ferocious battles, and victorious homecoming. The text has been capably illustrated in a complex process utilizing original drawings, black-and-white scratchboard, and a computer program for color." SLJ

Maddox, Marjorie
Rules of the game; baseball poems. illustrated by John Sandford. Wordsong 2009 32p il $16.95
Grades: 5 6 7 8   **811**
1. Children's poetry 2. Baseball -- Poetry 3. Poetry -- By individual authors
ISBN 978-1-59078-603-1; 1-59078-603-3
LC 2008-19018

"Sports fans will find themselves nodding in recognition of Maddox's sophisticated grasp of the game's intricacies, while language mavens will appreciate her joyous wordplay and dead-on command of poetic devices. . . . Sandford's charcoal pencil drawings, backed by sepia-toned pages . . . impart a classy timelessness to the book that's a nice match to its subject." Booklist

Meltzer, Milton
★ **Walt** Whitman; a biography. 21st Cent. Bks. (Brookfield) 2002 160p il lib bdg $31.90
Grades: 7 8 9 10   **811**
1. Poets 2. Authors 3. Essayists 4. Poets, American 5. Poets, American -- 19th century -- Biography
ISBN 0-7613-2272-8
LC 2001-27798

"The book honestly explores Whitman's character and actions, including his racial prejudice and his tendency to write anonymous (and effective) praises of his own writing. Ultimately, this has a definite edge and relevance that gives it more resonance than blander overviews of the poet. . . . Photographs of Whitman and his family, images of his work, and reproductions of period illustrations . . . liven up the formatting." Bull Cent Child Books
Includes bibliographical references

Mora, Pat
Dizzy in your eyes; poems about love. Alfred A. Knopf 2010 165p il $15.99; lib bdg $18.99
Grades: 7 8 9 10   **811**
1. Love poetry 2. Children's poetry 3. Poetry -- By individual authors
ISBN 978-0-375-84375-4; 0-375-84375-2; 978-0-375-94565-6 lib bdg; 0-375-94565-2 lib bdg
LC 2009-04300

"From family and school to dating and being dumped, the subjects in these 50 poems cover teens' experiences of love in many voices and situations. . . . Mora writes in free verse, as well as a variety of classic poetic forms—including haiku, clerihew, sonnet, cinquain, and blank verse—and for each form, there is an unobtrusive explanatory note on the facing page. The tight structures intensify the strong feelings in the poems, which teens will enjoy reading on their own or hearing aloud in the classroom." Booklist

★ **My** America; a poetry atlas of the United States. selected by Lee Bennett Hopkins; illustrated by Stephen Alcorn. Simon & Schuster Bks. for Young Readers 2000 83p il $21.95
Grades: 4 5 6 7   **811**
1. Children's poetry, American 2. American poetry -- Collections 3. United States -- poetry
ISBN 0-689-81247-7
LC 98-47402

A collection of poems evocative of seven geographical regions of the United States, including the Northeast, Southeast, Great Lakes, Plains, Mountain, Southwest, and Pacific Coast States.

"Some poems are purposive, but the best . . . capture places and people in all their diversity. Stephen Alcorn's handsome, multi-textured pictures . . . avoid literal interpretation and capture the sweep of the land and the rhythm of the words." Booklist

My black me; a beginning book of black poetry. edited by Arnold Adoff. [rev ed.]; Dutton Children's Bks. 1994 83p hardcover o.p. pa $6.99

Grades: 5 6 7 8   **811**

1. African Americans -- Poetry 2. American poetry -- African American authors -- Collections

ISBN 0-525-45216-8; 0-14-037443-4 pa

First published 1974

A compilation of poems reflecting thoughts on being black by such authors as Langston Hughes, Lucille Clifton, Nikki Giovanni, and Imamu Amiri Baraka

Myers, Walter Dean, 1937-

★ **Harlem**; a poem. pictures by Christopher Myers. Scholastic 1997 un il $16.95

Grades: 5 6 7 8 9 10   **811**

1. African Americans -- Poetry 2. Poetry -- By individual authors

ISBN 0-590-54340-7

LC 96-8108

A Caldecott Medal honor book, 1998

A poem celebrating the people, sights, and sounds of Harlem

"Myers's paean to Harlem sings, dances, and swaggers across the pages, conveying the myriad sounds on the streets. . . . Christopher Myers's collages add an edge to his father's words, vividly bringing to life the sights and scenes of Lenox Avenue." Horn Book Guide

Here in Harlem; poems in many voices. written by Walter Dean Myers. Holiday House 2004 88p il $16.95

Grades: 7 8 9 10   **811**

1. Children's poetry 2. African Americans -- Poetry 3. Poetry -- By individual authors

ISBN 0-8234-1853-7

LC 2003-67605

"In each poem here, a resident of Harlem speaks in a distinctive voice, offering a story, a thought, a reflection, or a memory. The poetic forms are varied and well chosen. . . . Expressive period photos from Myers' collection accompany the text of this handsome book." Booklist

National Council of Teachers of English

A **Jar** of tiny stars: poems by NCTE award-winning poets; Bernice E. Cullinan, editor; illustrations by Andi MacLeod; portraits by Marc Nadel. Wordsong 1996 94p il $17.95

Grades: 4 5 6 7   **811**

1. American poetry -- Collections

ISBN 1-56397-087-2

LC 93-60466

"Each poet who has won the NCTE Poetry Award—David McCord, Aileen Fisher, Karla Kuskin, Myra Cohn Livingston, Eve Merriam, John Ciardi, Lilian Moore, Arnold Adoff, Valerie Worth, and Barbara Esbensen—is pictured at the beginning of a section that includes several representative poems and a significant quote. The portraits are watercolor renditions from photographs, with cheerful pen-and-ink sketches accompanying the verse; all are in black and white." Bull Cent Child Books

Nelson, Marilyn

Carver, a life in poems. Front St. 2001 103p il $16.95

Grades: 7 8 9 10   **811**

1. Botanists 2. American poetry 3. Agriculturists -- Poetry 4. Poetry -- By individual authors 5. African American agriculturists -- Poetry

ISBN 1-88691-053-7

LC 00-63624

A Newbery Medal honor book, 2002

"A series of fifty-nine poems portrays George Washington Carver as a private, scholarly man of great personal faith and social purpose. Nelson fills in the trajectory of Carver's life with details of the cultural and political contexts that shaped him even as he shaped history. As individual works, each poem stands as a finely wrought whole of . . . high caliber." Horn Book Guide

★ **Fortune's** bones; the manumission requiem. Front Street 2004 32p il $16.95

Grades: 7 8 9 10   **811**

1. Children's poetry 2. Slavery -- Poetry 3. African Americans -- Poetry 4. Poetry -- By individual authors

ISBN 1-932425-12-8

LC 2004-46917

"This requiem honors a slave who died in Connecticut in 1798. His owner, a doctor, dissected his body, boiling down his bones to preserve them for anatomy studies. The skeleton . . . hung in a local museum until 1970. . . . The museum . . . uncovered the skeleton's provenance, created a new exhibit, and led to the commissioning of these six poems. The selections . . . arc from grief to triumph. . . . The facts inform the verse and open up a full appreciation of its rich imagery and rhythmic, lyrical language." SLJ

Includes bibliographical references

★ **Sweethearts** of rhythm; the story of the greatest all-girl swing band in the world. written by Marilyn Nelson; illustrated by Jerry Pinkney. Dial Books 2009 un il $21.99

Grades: 4 5 6 7   **811**

1. Women musicians 2. Jazz music -- Poetry 3. Jazz 4. Poetry -- By individual authors

ISBN 978-0-8037-3187-5; 0-8037-3187-6

LC 2008-46255

"On all fronts, a resonant performance." Publ Wkly

★ The **freedom** business; including a narrative of the life & adventures of Venture, a native of Africa. Wordsong 2008 72p il $18.95

Grades: 8 9 10 11 12   **811**

1. Slaves 2. Farmers 3. Children's poetry 4. Fishermen 5. Memoirists 6. Slavery -- Poetry 7. African Americans -- Poetry 8. Slavery -- United States

ISBN 978-1-932425-57-4; 1-932425-57-8

LC 2008-04437

"Venture Smith, born Broteer Furro in Guinea, was captured and enslaved at the age of six and brought to America in 1738. . . . His narrative, published in 1798, appears continuously on the left-hand page of each spread; Nelson's luminous poems appear on the right. Both are thrown into relief by Dancy's mixed-media artwork, which includes images of birds, ropes, chains and blood to heighten the visceral emotions of both texts. . . . Tragic, important, breathtaking." Kirkus

★ A **wreath** for Emmett Till; illustrated by Philippe Lardy. Houghton Mifflin 2005 un il $17

Grades: 8 9 10 11 12   **811**

1. Children 2. Murder victims 3. Lynching -- Poetry 4. African Americans -- Poetry 5. Poetry -- By individual authors

ISBN 0-618-39752-3

LC 2004-9205

Michael L. Printz Award honor book, 2006

This is a "poetry collection about Till's brutal, racially motivated murder. The poems form a heroic crown of sonnets—a sequence in which the last line of one poem becomes the first line of the next. . . . The rigid form distills the words' overwhelming emotion into potent, heart-stopping lines that speak from changing perspectives. . . . When matched with Lardy's gripping, spare, symbolic paintings of tree trunks, blood-red roots, and wreaths of thorns, these poems are a powerful achievement that teens and adults will want to discuss together." Booklist

Nye, Naomi Shihab

★ **19** varieties of gazelle; poems of the Middle East. Greenwillow Bks. 2002 142p $16.95; pa $6.99

Grades: 7 8 9 10   **811**

1. Poetry -- By individual authors

ISBN 0-06-009765-5; 0-06-050404-8 pa

LC 2002-771

In this "volume, Nye collects her poems about growing up as an Arab American (her ancestry is Palestinian), including previously published poems and newly written pieces. This rich and varied volume offers insights into the experience of childhood in two very different worlds. . . . This volume will fill a need for classroom use, for young people seeking a more personal understanding of the Middle East, and for readers seeking a connection with their own Middle Eastern background." Bull Cent Child Books

★ **Honeybee**; poems & short prose. Greenwillow Books 2008 164p $16.99; lib bdg $17.89

Grades: 8 9 10 11 12   **811**

1. Children's poetry 2. Poetry -- By individual authors

ISBN 978-0-06-085390-7; 0-06-085390-5; 978-0-06-085391-4 lib bdg; 0-06-085391-3 lib bdg

LC 2007-36742

This poetry "anthology is a rallying cry, a call for us to rediscover such beelike traits as interconnectedness, strong community, and honest communication. . . . Teens at the very start of their questioning years will recognize their own angst in Nye's sense of irony, their idealistic optimism in her simple wonder." SLJ

Salting the ocean; 100 poems by young poets. selected by Naomi Shihab Nye; pictures by Ashley Bryan. Greenwillow Bks. 2000 111p il $16.99

Grades: 4 5 6 7   **811**

1. Children's writings 2. Children's poetry, American 3. American poetry -- Collections

ISBN 0-688-16193-6

LC 99-30590

"While working within various school systems during the 1970s, Nye collected and saved these poems written by students in grades 1-12. . . . The collection is divided into four sections, each of which has approximately 25 poems. . . . In 'The Self and the Inner World,' the young poets express their thoughts about growing up, how they feel about their bodies . . . and make observations about people and events that surround them. 'Where We Live' looks at the trees, birds, sounds, and other aspects of the community in which the children live. 'Anybody's Family' includes poems about ethnicity, members of the students' households, and their feelings toward family members. In 'The Wide Imagination,' the poets . . . write about such topics as mirrors, history, time, words, and love." (SLJ)

"These poems are divided into four topics: The Self and the Inner World, Where We Live, Anybody's Family, and the Wide Imagination." Horn Book Guide

Includes bibliographical references

A **maze** me; poems for girls. pictures by Terre Maher. 1st ed; Greenwillow Books 2005 118p il $16.99; lib bdg $17.89

Grades: 7 8 9 10   **811**

1. Children's poetry 2. Girls -- Poetry 3. Poetry -- By individual authors

ISBN 0-06-058189-1; 0-06-058190-5 lib bdg

LC 2004-3283

These "poems draw from Nye's observations about nature, home, school, and neighborhood to make connections to a girl's inner world. . . . Most poems . . . speak with a powerful immediacy. . . . A wide age range will respond to these deeply felt poems about everyday experiences." Booklist

The **Oxford** book of American poetry; chosen and edited by David Lehman; associate editor, John Brehm. Oxford University Press 2006 lvii, 1132p $35

Grades: 8 9 10 11 12 Adult   **811**

1. American poetry 2. Poetry -- Collections 3. American poetry -- Collections

ISBN 0-19-516251-X; 978-0-19-516251-6

LC 2005-36590

First published 1950 with title: The Oxford book of American verse

"The book is not only a sound historical survey, but also gives the reader a powerful taste of poetry's impact upon the wider world." Economist

Includes bibliographical references

The **Oxford** book of children's verse in America; edited by Donald Hall. Oxford University Press 1985 xxxviii, 319p $39.95; pa $19.95
Grades: 5 6 7 8 9 10 11 12 Adult **811**
1. American poetry -- Collections 2. Children's poetry -- Collections
ISBN 0-19-503539-9; 0-19-506761-4 pa
LC 84-20755
"A fine and carefully winnowed collection of American poetry is gathered in a book that will interest students of children's literature and young people who simply enjoy browsing." Horn Book

The **Pain** tree, and other teenage angst-ridden poetry; collected and illustrated by Esther Pearl Watson and Mark Todd. Houghton Mifflin 2000 62p il hardcover o.p. pa $6.95
Grades: 7 8 9 10 **811**
1. Teenagers' writings 2. American poetry -- Collections
ISBN 0-618-01588-2; 0-618-04758-1 pa
LC 99-48905
"Readers will be struck by the brutal honesty of this collection. . . . Watson and Todd have managed to compile a collection that will strike a chord with teen readers." Voice Youth Advocates

★ The **Place** my words are looking for; what poets say about and through their work. selected by Paul B. Janeczko. Bradbury Press 1990 150p il $17.95
Grades: 4 5 6 7 **811**
1. Poetics 2. American poetry -- Collections 3. Children's poetry -- Collections 4. American poets
ISBN 0-02-747671-5
LC 89-39331
"More than forty contemporary poets are included: Eve Merriam, X. J. Kennedy, Felice Holman, Gary Soto, Mark Vinz, Karla Kuskin, and John Updike, among others. Their contributions vary widely in theme and mood and style, though the preponderance of the pieces are written in modern idiom and unrhymed meter. The accompanying comments frequently are as insightful and eloquent as the poems themselves." Horn Book

Poe, Edgar Allan
The **raven**; with illustrations by Ryan Price. KCP Poetry 2006 un il (Visions in poetry) $17.95
Grades: 7 8 9 10 **811**
1. Poetry 2. Poetry -- By individual authors
ISBN 978-1-55337-473-2; 1-55337-473-8
"In this small, handsome volume, Price's grim, sepia-tone stylized pictures, decorated with feathery, black cross-hatching, do a great job of evoking the brooding guilt, terror, grief, and love in Poe's famous poem." Booklist

★ A **Poem** of her own; voices of American women yesterday and today. edited by Catherine Clinton; illustrated by Stephen Alcorn. Abrams 2003 79p il $17.95
Grades: 6 7 8 9 **811**
1. Women 2. American poetry 3. Women -- United States 4. Children's poetry, American -- Women authors 5. American poetry -- Women authors -- Collections
ISBN 0-8109-4240-2
LC 2002-12851
Presents a collection of more than twenty poems by American women published between 1678 and 2001. Includes poems by Phillis Wheatley, Gertrude Stein, Lucille Clifton, Sandra Cisneros, and Naomi Shihab Nye
"The intelligent selection is matched by the fresh, open design, highlighted by Alcorn's exciting paintings, executed in light-fast casein paint." Booklist

Poetry from the masters: the pioneers; edited by Wade Hudson; illustrated by Stephan J. Hudson. Just Us Books 2003 88p il pa $9.95
Grades: 7 8 9 10 **811**
1. African American authors 2. American poetry -- African American authors -- Collections
ISBN 0-940975-96-3
This book "focuses on a particular group of black poets, 'trailblazers' who forged a path by overcoming 'almost impossible obstacles.' Hudson puts these writers in perspective and provides a social and literary context. Eleven poets are profiled, starting with Phillis Wheatley and ending with Gwendolyn Brooks. . . . Each writer is introduced with a brief biographical sketch that highlights his or her literary significance and contributions, followed by the full text of two or more poems. . . . This is an excellent resource for students seeking research materials or just looking for wonderful examples of poetry to read." SLJ
Includes bibliographical references

★ A **Poke** in the I; [selected by] Paul Janeczko; illustrated by Chris Raschka. Candlewick Press 2001 35p il hardcover o.p. pa $7.99
Grades: 4 5 6 7 8 9 10 **811**
1. American poetry 2. Concrete poetry, American 3. Children's poetry, American 4. American poetry -- Collections
ISBN 0-7636-0661-8; 0-7636-2376-8 pa
LC 00-33675
"Thirty concrete poems of all shapes and sizes are carefully laid on large white spreads, extended by Raschka's quirky watercolor and paper-collage illustrations. . . . Beautiful and playful, this title should find use in storytimes, in the classroom, and just for pleasure anywhere." SLJ

★ The **Random** House book of poetry for children; selected and introduced by Jack Prelutsky; illustrated by Arnold Lobel. Random House 1983 248p il $19.95; lib bdg $21.99
Grades: 3 4 5 6 **811**
1. English poetry -- Collections 2. American poetry --

Collections 3. Children's poetry -- Collections
ISBN 0-394-85010-6; 0-394-95010-0 lib bdg

LC 83-2990

In this anthology emphasis "is placed on humor and light verse; but serious and thoughtful poems are also included. . . . Approximately two thirds of the selections were written within the past forty years—the splendid contributions of such writers as John Ciardi, Aileen Fisher, Dennis Lee, Myra Cohn Livingston, David McCord, Eve Merriam, and Lilian Moore. [There are] . . . samplings of earlier poets from Shakespeare and Blake to Emily Dickinson and Walter de la Mare." Horn Book

Reef, Catherine

Walt Whitman. Clarion Bks. 1995 148p il hardcover o.p. pa $7.95

Grades: 7 8 9 10   **811**

1. Poets 2. Authors 3. Essayists 4. Poets, American
ISBN 0-395-68705-5; 0-618-24616-9 pa

LC 94-7405

"This is not a biography for pleasure reading, but it could be a source for those interested in historical events of 19th century America. It also would be a good resource for students doing a critique of Whitman's work for an American literature course." Book Rep

Includes bibliographical references

★ **Reflections** on a gift of watermelon pickle--and other modern verse; [compiled by] Stephen Dunning, Edward Lueders, Hugh Smith. Lothrop, Lee & Shepard Bks. 1967 139p il $19.99

Grades: 6 7 8 9 10   **811**

1. American poetry -- Collections
ISBN 0-688-41231-9

First published 1966 by Scott, Foresman in a text edition
"Although some of the [114] selections are by recognized modern writers, many are by minor or unknown poets, and few will be familiar to the reader. Nearly all are fresh in approach and contemporary in expression. . . . Striking photographs complementing or illuminating many of the poems enhance the attractiveness of the volume." Booklist

Rylant, Cynthia

Something permanent; photographs by Walker Evans; poetry by Cynthia Rylant. Harcourt Brace & Co. 1994 61p il $18

Grades: 7 8 9 10   **811**

1. Children's poetry 2. Poetry -- By individual authors 3. Depressions 4. Documentary photography
ISBN 0-15-277090-9

LC 93-3861

"For students in junior high and high school, the juxtaposition of Evans' photos and Rylant's poems will demonstrate how emotions can be rooted in objects and how, to dig them out, you need to use strong, sturdy words." Booklist

Service, Robert W.

★ The **cremation** of Sam McGee; by Robert W. Service; paintings by Ted Harrison; introduction by Pierre Berton. 20th anniversary ed.; Kids Can Press 2006 un il $17.95

Grades: 4 5 6 7   **811**

1. Poetry -- By individual authors
ISBN 978-1-55453-092-2; 1-55453-092-X

Text first published 1907. This is a reissue of the edition first published 1986 in Canada and 1987 in the United States by Greenwillow Bks.

This poem "has gripped readers and listeners for decades. . . . [The illustrator] obviously appreciates the humor inherent in the text. . . . As Pierre Berton observes in his introduction, [Harrison's] 'style is unique: part Oriental, part native American, part Ted Harrison.'" Horn Book

Shange, Ntozake

★ **Freedom's** a-callin' me; poems by Ntozake Shange; paintings by Rod Brown. Amisatd/Collins 2012 il $16.99

Grades: 4 5 6 7   **811**

1. Slavery -- Poetry 2. African Americans -- Poetry 3. Underground railroad -- Poetry
ISBN 978-0-06-133741-3; 0-06-133741-2

LC 2010050515

The author and illustrator present "a series of poems and paintings that express the hope and frustration of enslaved people trying to navigate the Underground Railroad. Using dialect to convey a Southern cadence, Shange's poems communicate powerful emotions. . . . These poems are a cry from the heart. . . . The expressive, impressionistic paintings capture attention with their bold strokes and vivid coloring." SLJ

★ **We** troubled the waters; poems by Ntozake Shange; paintings by Rod Brown. Amisatd/Collins 2009 un il $16.99; lib bdg $17.89

Grades: 4 5 6 7 8 9 10   **811**

1. Poetry -- By individual authors 2. African Americans -- Civil rights -- Poetry
ISBN 978-0-06-133735-2; 0-06-133735-8; 978-0-06-133737-6 lib bdg; 0-06-133737-4 lib bdg

LC 2008025360

"Each spread pairs a poem with blurred, expressive acrylic paintings, and the pages feature both well-known civil rights leaders and ordinary people who endured oppression. . . . The messages are haunting. . . . The colloquial lines, indelible images, and comparisons between then and now will keep readers talking." Booklist

Shields, Carol Diggory

English, fresh squeezed! 40 thirst-for-knowledge-quenching poems. by Carol Diggory Shields; illustrations by Tony Ross. Handprint Books 2004 80p il $14.95

Grades: 4 5 6 7   **811**

1. English language -- Poetry 2. Poetry -- By individual authors
ISBN 1-59354-053-1

LC 2004-53905

"Shields presents humorous poems both celebrating and bemoaning parts of speech, grammatical rules, and other annoyances of English class. Her rhyming verse is generally snappy and pointed. . . . Ross's spot illustrations in black and white with a blue tone add visual amusement without overwhelming." SLJ

★ **Shimmy** shimmy shimmy like my sister Kate; looking at the Harlem Renaissance through poems. [edited by] Nikki Giovanni. Holt & Co. 1995 186p $17.95

Grades: 8 9 10 11 12   **811**

1. Harlem Renaissance 2. Children's poetry -- Collections 3. Harlem Renaissance 4. American poetry -- African American authors -- Collections 5. American poetry -- History and criticism 6. American poetry -- African American authors
ISBN 0-8050-3494-3

LC 95-38617

This anthology includes poems by such authors as Paul Laurence Dunbar, Langston Hughes, Countee Cullen, Gwendolyn Brooks, and Amiri Baraka. Commentary and a discussion of the development of African American arts known as the Harlem Renaissance is provided by editor Giovanni
Includes bibliographical references

Silverstein, Shel
★ **Every** thing on it; poems and drawings by Shel Silverstein. Harper 2011 194p il $19.99; lib bdg $20.89

Grades: 3 4 5 6   **811**

1. Humorous poetry 2. Nonsense verses 3. Poetry -- By individual authors
ISBN 978-0-06-199816-4; 0-06-199816-8; 978-0-06-199817-1 lib bdg; 0-06-199817-6 lib bdg

The second original book to be published since Silverstein's passing in 1999, this poetry collection includes more than one hundred and thirty never-before-seen poems and drawings completed by the cherished American artist and selected by his family from his archives.

"Silverstein's inspired word play and impish sense of humor are in abundant evidence. His signature line drawings accompany many of the poems and complete the jokes of some. . . . Adults who grew up with Uncle Shelby will find themselves wiping their eyes by the time they get to the end of this collection; children new to the master will find themselves hooked." Kirkus

Falling up; poems and drawings by Shel Silverstein. HarperCollins Pubs. 1996 171p il $17.99; lib bdg $18.89

Grades: 3 4 5 6   **811**

1. Humorous poetry 2. Nonsense verses 3. Children's poetry 4. Poetry -- By individual authors
ISBN 0-06-024802-5; 0-06-024803-3 lib bdg

LC 96-75736

This "collection includes more than 150 poems. . . . As always, Silverstein has a direct line to what kids like, and he gives them poems celebrating the gross, the scary, the absurd, and the comical. The drawings are much more than decoration. They often extend a poem's meaning and, in many cases, add some great comedy." Booklist

★ **Where** the sidewalk ends; the poems & drawings of Shel Silverstein. 30th anniversary special ed; HarperCollins 2004 183p il $17.99; lib bdg $18.89

Grades: 3 4 5 6 7 8 9 10   **811**

1. Humorous poetry 2. Nonsense verses 3. Poetry --

By individual authors
ISBN 0-06-057234-5; 0-06-058653-2 lib bdg

LC 2004-269335

First published 1974

"There are skillful, sometimes grotesque line drawings with each of the 127 poems, which run in length from a few lines to a couple of pages. The poems are tender, funny, sentimental, philosophical, and ridiculous in turn, and they're for all ages." Sat Rev

★ A **light** in the attic; Special edition; Harper 2009 185p il $18.99

Grades: 3 4 5 6   **811**

1. Humorous poetry 2. Nonsense verses 3. Poetry -- By individual authors
ISBN 978-0-06-190585-8; 0-06-190585-2

First published 1981

This collection of more than one hundred poems "will delight lovers of Silverstein's raucous, rollicking verse and his often tender, whimsical, philosophical advice. . . . The poems are tuned in to kids' most hidden feelings, dark wishes and enjoyment of the silly. . . . The witty line drawings are a full half of the treat of this wholly satisfying anthology by the modern successor to Edward Lear and Hilaire Belloc." SLJ [review of 1981 edition]

Singer, Marilyn
★ **Central** heating; poems about fire and warmth. illustrated by Meilo So. Alfred A. Knopf 2005 41p il $15.95; lib bdg $17.99

Grades: 4 5 6 7   **811**

1. Fire -- Poetry 2. Heat -- Poetry 3. Poetry -- By individual authors
ISBN 0-375-82912-1; 0-375-92912-6 lib bdg

LC 2004-4274

"The complicated nature of fire is explored in Singer's energetic short poems and So's deceptively simple single-color illustrations. . . . This title . . . belongs on library shelves everywhere." SLJ

Smith, Charles R., 1969-
★ **Hoop** queens; poems. Candlewick Press 2003 35p il hardcover o.p. pa $5.99

Grades: 4 5 6 7   **811**

1. Basketball -- Poetry 2. Women athletes -- Poetry 3. Poetry -- By individual authors
ISBN 0-7636-1422-X; 0-7636-3561-8 pa

LC 2002-41111

A collection of twelve poems that celebrate contemporary women basketball stars, including Yolanda Griffith, Chamique Holdsclaw, and Natalie Williams

"Action photos of the athletes are pasted large on colorful, dynamic backgrounds that barely hold the motion-filled poems to the page. Notes about each player and poem communicate the joy Smith finds both in watching the game and writing poetry. Pure pleasure for basketball fans and inspiration for kids who doubted poetry was alive." SLJ

Smith, Hope Anita
★ **Mother** poems; words and pictures by Hope Anita Smith. Henry Holt and Co. 2009 72p il $16.95

Grades: 4 5 6 7   **811**
1. Death -- Poetry 2. Mothers -- Poetry 3. Bereavement -- Poetry 4. African Americans -- Poetry 5. Poetry -- By individual authors
ISBN 978-0-8050-8231-9; 0-8050-8231-X
LC 2008-18342

"Smith writes about an African American child's grief at the sudden death of her mother. . . . Like the poetry, Smith's simple, torn-paper collages in a folk-art style show the close embraces and vignettes without overwhelming the words." Booklist

Soto, Gary

Canto familiar; [illustrated by Annika Nelson] Harcourt Brace & Co. 1995 79p il $18; pa $5.95
Grades: 4 5 6   **811**
1. Children's poetry 2. Mexican Americans -- Poetry 3. Poetry -- By individual authors
ISBN 978-0-15-200067-7; 0-15-200067-4; 978-0-15-205885-2 pa; 0-15-205885-0 pa
LC 94-24218

"This collection of simple free verse captures common childhood moments at home, at school, and in the street. Many of the experiences are Mexican American . . . and occasional Spanish words are part of the easy, colloquial, short lines. . . . The occasional full-page, richly colored woodcuts by Annika Nelson capture the child's imaginative take on ordinary things." Booklist

★ **Neighborhood** odes; illustrated by David Diaz. Harcourt Brace Jovanovich 1992 68p il hardcover o.p. pa $5.95
Grades: 4 5 6   **811**
1. Children's poetry 2. Hispanic Americans -- Poetry 3. Poetry -- By individual authors
ISBN 0-15-256879-4; 0-15-205364-6 pa
LC 91-20710

"Twenty-one poems, all odes, celebrate life in a Hispanic neighborhood. Other than the small details of daily life—peoples' names or the foods they eat—these poems could be about any neighborhood. With humor, sensitivity, and insight, Soto explores the lives of children. . . . David Diaz's contemporary black-and-white illustrations, which often resemble cut paper, effortlessly capture the varied moods—happiness, fear, longing, shame, and greed—of this remarkable collection. With a glossary of thirty Spanish words and phrases." Horn Book

Partly cloudy; poems of love and longing. Harcourt 2009 100p $16
Grades: 7 8 9 10   **811**
1. Love poetry 2. Children's poetry 3. Poetry -- By individual authors
ISBN 978-0-15-206301-6; 0-15-206301-3
LC 2008-22267

Poet Gary Soto captures the voices of young people as they venture toward their first kiss, brood over bruised hearts, and feel the thrill of first love.

"Soto's new book of verse about adolescent love is remarkable. . . . The language of the poems is spare but evocative, with not one word wasted. . . . Teens will find these poems very engaging and will relate to how the emotion of love is expressed in everyday moments." Voice Youth Advocates

★ A **fire** in my hands; poems by Gary Soto. rev and expanded ed.; Harcourt 2006 74p $16
Grades: 6 7 8 9   **811**
1. Mexican Americans -- Poetry 2. Poetry -- By individual authors
ISBN 0-15-205564-9
LC 2005024610

First published 1991 by Scholastic

"Half the poems are new to this expanded edition of a collection first published 15 years ago, including some great ones from Soto's adult books that speak about feeling stuck at home and growing up poor, Catholic, and Mexican American. Soto's chatty introduction about writing poetry that celebrates small, common things will appeal to both readers and writers, as will the informal questions and answers at the back of the book and the brief autobiographical notes Soto includes with each poem." Booklist

A **natural** man. Chronicle Bks. 2000 71p pa $13.95
Grades: 7 8 9 10   **811**
1. Mexican Americans -- Poetry 2. Poetry -- By individual authors
ISBN 0-8118-2518-3
LC 99-18353

"This poetry anthology offers a photographic glimpse into the lives of California's Chicanos. But although the titles and use of Spanish words create a very particular setting, the characters, stories, and truths of these selections have a universal resonance." SLJ

★ **Soul** looks back in wonder; [illustrated by] Tom Feelings. Dial Bks. 1993 un il hardcover o.p. pa $7.99
Grades: 4 5 6 7   **811**
1. African Americans -- Poetry 2. Children's poetry -- Collections 3. American poetry -- Collections 4. American poetry -- African American authors -- Collections 5. American poetry -- African American authors
ISBN 0-8037-1001-1; 0-14-056501-9 pa
LC 93-824

Coretta Scott King Award for illustration

Artwork and poems by such writers as Maya Angelou, Langston Hughes, and Askia Toure portray the creativity, strength, and beauty of their African American heritage

"This thoughtful collection of poetry is unique. . . . Feelings selected sketches done while he was in West Africa, South America, and at home in America. The original drawings were enhanced with colored pencils, colored papers, stencil cut-outs, and other techniques to give a collage effect. Marbled textures bring vibrancy to the work." Horn Book

Spires, Elizabeth

★ **I** heard God talking to me; William Edmondson and his stone carvings. Farrar, Straus and Giroux 2009 56p il $17.95
Grades: 8 9 10 11 12 Adult   **811**
1. Artists 2. Sculptors 3. Religious poetry 4.

Children's poetry 5. Artists -- Poetry 6. Sculpture -- Poetry 7. African Americans -- Poetry 8. Poetry -- By individual authors
ISBN 978-0-374-33528-1; 0-374-33528-1
LC 2008-02343
"Moved by a religious vision at age 57, Nashville janitor William Edmondson began carving tombstones and whimsical figures out of stone in 1931 and went on to attract the attention of international collectors, eventually becoming the first African American artist to have a solo show at the Museum of Modern Art in New York. This handsome picture-book-sized poetry collection pairs full-page, black-and-white photos of Edmondson and his works with poems inspired by the images. . . . Supported by an appended prose biography, these playful, thought-provoking poems introduce a fascinating artist." Booklist

Tell the world; teen poems from WritersCorps. HarperTeen 2008 116p $16.99; pa $8.99
Grades: 7 8 9 10 11 12 **811**
1. Children's poetry 2. Teenagers' writings 3. American poetry -- Collections
ISBN 978-0-06-134505-0; 0-06-134505-9; 978-0-06-134504-3 pa; 0-06-134504-0 pa
LC 2007-49577
"This worthy collection of brief poems offers an array of teen voices. . . . An essay by WritersCorps teacher Michelle Matz adds a vivid picture of her students and their lives. This fine collection should inspire creativity and resonate with teens who find their own hopes, fears, and dreams eloquently voiced in the works of these young poets." SLJ

Testa, Maria
Becoming Joe DiMaggio; with illustrations by Scott Hunt. Candlewick Press 2002 51p il hardcover o.p. pa $5.99
Grades: 4 5 6 7 **811**
1. Grandfathers 2. American poetry 3. Italian Americans 4. Grandfathers -- Poetry 5. Children's poetry, American 6. Italian Americans -- Poetry 7. Poetry -- By individual authors
ISBN 0-7636-1537-4; 0-7636-2444-6 pa
LC 2001-25886
"Growing up in New York City during the 1940s and 1950s, Joseph Paul, an Italian boy, finds solace from a difficult life by listening to baseball games with his beloved grandfather. This powerful story, told in 24 poems, describes their relationship and their love of listening to another Italian, Joe DiMaggio, achieve success. . . . The beauty and the charm of the poetry—its concise language, its flow and descriptive power—add to the intensity of the experiences described. Hunt's charcoal-and-pastel spot illustrations are scattered throughout." SLJ

Something about America. Candlewick Press 2005 84p $14.99
Grades: 6 7 8 9 **811**
1. Immigrants -- Poetry 2. Burns and scalds -- Poetry 3. Serbian Americans -- Poetry 4. Poetry -- By individual authors
ISBN 0-7636-2528-0
LC 2005-47064

"Testa's distilled poetry never seems forced, and her stirring words enhance a sense of the characters' experiences and emotions. . . . Based on an actual incident, this is an excellent choice for readers' theater and classroom discussion." Booklist

Thayer, Ernest Lawrence
Casey at the bat; written by Ernest L. Thayer; with illustrations by Joe Morse. Kids Can Press 2006 un il (Visions in poetry) $16.95
Grades: 5 6 7 8 **811**
1. Baseball -- Poetry 2. Poetry -- By individual authors
ISBN 1-55337-827-X; 978-1-55337-827-3
"Morse updates Thayer's baseball classic to a modern, urban setting with a multiracial cast filling the familiar roles. As tall buildings loom above them, metallic fences confine the players who seem pensive and watchful. The figures are strikingly rendered in oils and acrylics, their features sharply limned in thick black lines and smudges of neutral color." SLJ

★ **Time** you let me in; 25 poets under 25. selected by Naomi Shihab Nye. Greenwillow Books 2010 236p $16.99; lib bdg $17.89
Grades: 8 9 10 11 12 **811**
1. Children's poetry 2. Poetry -- Collections 3. American poetry -- Collections
ISBN 978-0-06-189637-8; 0-06-189637-3; 978-0-06-189638-5 lib bdg; 0-06-189638-1 lib bdg
LC 2009-19387
"This lively collection by young contemporary writers is rooted in the strong, emotional particulars of family, friendship, childhood memories, school, dislocation, war, and more. . . . Teens will connect with the passionate, unmoderated feelings that are given clarity and shape in each poem." Booklist
Includes bibliographical references

Wayland, April Halprin
Girl coming in for a landing; a novel in poems. illustrations by Elaine Clayton. Knopf 2002 134p il $14.95; lib bdg $16.99; pa $5.50
Grades: 7 8 9 10 **811**
1. School stories 2. Novels in verse 3. Schools -- Poetry 4. Children's poetry, American 5. Teenage girls -- poetry 6. High school students -- poetry
ISBN 0-375-80158-8; 0-375-90158-2 lib bdg; 0-440-41903-4 pa
LC 2001-38107
A collection of over 100 poems recounting the ups and downs of one adolescent girl's school year
"Wayland's spare lines and unpretentious words get right to the heart of situations and emotions, and the familiarity and candor in the speaker's voice—warm and authentic—will invite teens to value the small moments in their own experiences and put them into verse." Booklist

Weatherford, Carole Boston
Remember the bridge; poems of a people. designed by Semador Megged. Philomel Bks. 2002 53p il $17.99

Grades: 5 6 7 8   **811**

1. African Americans -- Poetry 2. Children's poetry, American 3. Poetry -- By individual authors 4. African Americans -- poetry
ISBN 0-399-23726-7

LC 2001-36161

"The author evokes imagined and actual individual experiences of the people . . . in the historical black-and-white photos, drawings, and etchings. . . . This celebratory, visually striking book will be appreciated in most collections." SLJ

Whipple, Laura

If the shoe fits; voices from Cinderella. illustrations by Laura Beingessner. Margaret K. McElderry Bks. 2002 67p il $17.95

Grades: 5 6 7 8   **811**

1. American poetry 2. Fairy tales -- Poetry 3. Characters in literature 4. Children's poetry, American 5. Poetry -- By individual authors 6. Cinderella (Legendary character) -- poetry
ISBN 0-689-84070-5

LC 2001-30778

In this version of the fairy tale "the characters tell the story in blank verses. . . . The story unfolds just as it always does, but the multiple points of view—from Cinderella's to the prince's to the rat's to the queen's—enlarge and enrich the familiar tale to win a more sophisticated audience. . . . Paintings by Beingessner achieve just the right mixture of sorrow, beauty, and humor." Booklist

Whisper and shout; poems to memorize. edited by Patrice Vecchione. Cricket Bks. 2002 120p $16.95

Grades: 4 5 6 7   **811**

1. English poetry 2. American poetry 3. Children's poetry, English 4. Children's poetry, American 5. American poetry -- Collections
ISBN 0-8126-2656-7

LC 2002-591

A collection of poems on different subjects and in different styles, that lend themselves to memorization. Among the poets represented are Jack Prelutsky, Edward Lear, Ogden Nash, T. S. Eliot, Edna St. Vincent Millay, Christina Rossetti, and Lewis Carroll

"With a lengthy, enthusiastic introduction and a generous final section of resources and biographies, this anthology will get as much use in the classroom as with individual readers." Booklist

Includes bibliographical references

Whitman, Walt

★ **Walt** Whitman; edited by Jonathan Levin; illustrated by Jim Burke. Sterling 1997 48p il (Poetry for young people) $14.95; pa $6.95

Grades: 5 6 7 8 9   **811**

1. Children's poetry, American 2. Poetry -- By individual authors
ISBN 0-8069-9530-0; 1-4027-5477-9 pa

LC 97-433

An illustrated collection of twenty-six poems and excerpts from longer poems by the renowned nineteenth-century poet

"An outstanding introduction to Whitman's life and work. . . . This superb volume can be used to teach literature or to show a variety of poetic devices and style." SLJ

Wicked poems; edited by Roger McGough; illustrated by Neal Layton. Bloomsbury Children's Books 2004 208p il $15

Grades: 4 5 6 7   **811**

1. Poetry -- Collections 2. Good and evil -- Poetry 3. American poetry -- Collections
ISBN 1-58234-854-5

LC 2002-38551

"The 134 poems in this . . . collection focus on people exhibiting various degrees of wickedness. The book includes works from well-known poets . . . and children's authors such as Shel Silverstein, Eve Merriam, Myra Cohn Livingston, and Jack Prelutsky. . . . Childlike, black-and-white cartoons are laugh-out-loud funny. . . . A perfect choice for reading aloud as well as independent browsing." SLJ

Williams, William Carlos

William Carlos Williams; edited by Christopher MacGowan; illustrated by Robert Crockett. Sterling Pub. Co. 2004 48p il (Poetry for young people) $14.95

Grades: 7 8 9 10   **811**

1. Poetry -- By individual authors
ISBN 1-4027-0006-7

LC 2003-6885

A collection of thirty poems with illustrations and brief introductory remarks

"The introduction and commentary that MacGowan . . . provides not only fills in biographical details but expertly illuminates the craft and sensibility behind these 31 deceptively simple imagist poems . . . Despite its simple language and clear imagery, Williams' poetry is not widely available to young readers. This gathering should help to remedy that." Booklist

Words with wings; a treasury of African-American poetry and art. selected by Belinda Rochelle. HarperCollins Pubs. 2001 un il lib bdg $18.99

Grades: 4 5 6 7   **811**

1. American poetry 2. African Americans in art 3. Afro-Americans 4. Afro-Americans in art 5. African Americans -- Poetry 6. Afro-Americans poetry 7. Children's poetry, American -- Afro-American authors 8. American poetry -- African American authors -- Collections
ISBN 0-688-16415-3

LC 00-26864

Pairs twenty works of art by African-American artists such as Horace Pippin and Jacob Lawrence with twenty poems by African-American poets such as Langston Hughes, Countee Cullen, and Lucille Clifton

"Most of the combinations are stunning. . . . Short biographical paragraphs on each poet and artist round out this moving presentation." SLJ

Worth, Valerie

Pug and other animal poems; Valerie Worth; pictures by Steve Jenkins. Margaret Ferguson Books, Farrar Straus Giroux 2012 40 p. $16.99

Grades: 2 3 4 5   **811**

1. Animals -- Poetry 2. Children's poetry 3. Children's poetry, American

ISBN 0374350248; 9780374350246

LC 2010034300

This juvenile poetry collection, by Valerie Worth, illustrated by Steve Jenkins, "examines a wide range of animal behavior, from the fleetingness of a fly sipping spilled milk to the constant steely presence of a powerful bull; the greedy meal of a street rat to a cat's quiet gift of a dead mouse on the doorstep." (Publisher's note)

WritersCorps

Paint me like I am; teen poems from WritersCorps. HarperTempest 2003 128p hardcover o.p. pa $6.99

Grades: 7 8 9 10   **811**

1. Teenagers' writings 2. American poetry -- Collections

ISBN 0-06-029288-1; 0-06-447264-7 pa

LC 2002-5942

"The teen voices in these poems, collected from the WritersCorps youth program, are LOUD—raging, defiant, giddy, lusty, and hopeful. Grouped into arbitrary categories, the poems explore identity, creative expressions, family, neighborhood, drugs, and relationships. . . . A foreword from Nikki Giovanni rounds out this moving collection, which also includes a few thoughtful writing exercises." Booklist

Yolen, Jane

The **Emily** sonnets; the life of Emily Dickinson. by Jane Yolen; illustrations by Gary Kelley. 1st ed. Creative Editions 2012 40 p. col. ill. (reinforced) $19.99

Grades: 5 6 7   **811**

1. Dickinson, Emily, 1830-1886 -- Poetry

ISBN 1568462158; 9781568462158

LC 2011040841

This book by Jane Yolen presents 15 sonnets about poet Emily Dickinson. "The selections are constructed in various voices. . . . In the first five pieces, Emily speaks of the family's brick house, her close relationship with her sister Vinnie, her schooling, her variance with her family's religious beliefs, and the companionship of her dog. . . . The other speakers . . . tell of her always dressing in white, her life as a recluse, and her work." (School Library Journal)

★ **Sacred** places; illustrated by David Shannon. Harcourt Brace & Co. 1996 38p il $16

Grades: 4 5 6 7   **811**

1. Religious poetry 2. Children's poetry 3. Shrines 4. Poetry -- By individual authors 5. Historic sites

ISBN 0-15-269953-8

LC 92-30323

"The hazy moodiness of Shannon's paintings capture the mystery Yolen explores in her text, while his dense figures and literal interpretations of a passage from each poem draw Yolen's mystical flights back down to solid ground. Append-

ed notes offer historical information on each sacred place." Bull Cent Child Books

Young, Ed

Beyond the great mountains; a visual poem about China. Chronicle Books 2005 32p il $17.95

Grades: 4 5 6 7   **811**

1. Poetry -- By individual authors

ISBN 0-8118-4343-2

"The book is comprised of 14 lines, each of which is accompanied by its own double-page illustration, done in cut and torn-paper collage. Young also provides the ancient characters for the images he presents. . . . Designed to be read vertically, each page is flipped up to reveal the accompanying illustration. In this way, the entire book becomes a piece of art, a visual treat of sublime colors and textures that joins with text and characters to describe the vastness and beauty of China." SLJ

812   American drama in English

Acting out; six one-act plays!: six Newbery stars! edited by Justin Chanda; featuring the playwrights, Avi . . . [et. al.] Atheneum Books for Young Readers 2008 175p il $16.99

Grades: 5 6 7 8 9   **812**

1. One act plays 2. American drama -- Collections

ISBN 978-1-4169-3848-4; 1-4169-3848-6

Contains six original one-act plays by Newbery Award-winning children's authors, including Sharon Creech, Susan Cooper, Avi, Patricia Maclachlan, Katherine Paterson, and Richard Peck

"Each play was inspired by a theater-improv game in which the authors started with the selection of a single word. The pieces all include the following words: 'dollop,' 'hoodwink,' 'Justin,' 'knuckleball,' 'panhandle,' and 'raven.'. . . An engaging choice for literature and acting classes as well as general reading." SLJ

Includes bibliographical references

Black, Ann N.

Readers theatre for middle school boys; investigating the strange and mysterious. illustrated by Cody Rust. Teachers Idea Press 2008 190p il (Readers theatre) pa $30

Grades: Adult Professional   **812**

1. Readers' theater 2. Drama -- Collections 3. Children's reading -- Projects 4. Plays for library presentation

ISBN 978-1-59158-535-0 pa; 1-59158-535-X pa

LC 2007034923

"This book provides solid offerings of Readers Theater scripts for educators working with middle school boys. Selections include adaptations of such creepy classics as 'The Legend of Sleepy Hollow,' 'The Masque of the Red Death,' . . . and 'The Monkey's Paw.' The scripts have a new, fresh feel, and contain plenty of elements to capture and maintain adolescent males' attention." Libr Media Connect

Includes bibliographical references

Children's Theatre Company (Minneapolis, Minn.)

Fierce & true; plays for teen audiences. Peter & Elissa Adams, editors; The Children's Theatre Company. University of Minnesota Press 2010 219p il pa $17.95

Grades: 7 8 9 10 11 12   812

1. Drama -- Collections

ISBN 978-0-8166-7311-7; 0-8166-7311-X

The Children's Theatre Company "located in Minneapolis, wanted to broaden its audience, so it commissioned four playwrights to create works with young people (ages 12-18) specifically in mind. The results are the full-length plays in this anthology. . . . 'Anon(ymous)' is a contemporary retelling of Homer's Odyssey, set in a dirty North American city, and 'Five Fingers of Funk' is a mature musical celebrating the roots of hip-hop while dealing with issues of poverty and drugs. In 'The Lost Boys of Sudan,' three Dinka refugees flee the horrors of war and begin a harrowing yet humorous journey that takes them to Fargo, ND. And 'Prom' is played out as a frenetic battle between students and chaperones. Each of these selections has a distinctive voice, honoring adolescents as both actor and audience capable of understanding and engaging in today's complex issues." SLJ

Dunkleberger, Amy

A student's guide to Arthur Miller. Enslow Publs. 2005 160p il (Understanding literature) lib bdg $27.93

Grades: 7 8 9 10   812

1. Authors 2. Dramatists 3. Screenwriters

ISBN 0-7660-2432-6

This discusses the life of Arthur Miller and his works All My Sons, Death of a Salesman, The Crucible, A View From the Bridge, After the Fall, Incident at Vichy, and The Price

"Engaging and informative. . . . The very accessible format and the solid information make [this book] useful to students, and the engaging style should interest casual readers." SLJ

Includes glossary and bibliographical references

Hermann, Spring

A student's guide to Eugene O'Neill. Enslow Publishers 2009 176p il (Understanding literature) lib bdg $27.93

Grades: 7 8 9 10   812

1. Authors 2. Dramatists 3. Nobel laureates for literature

ISBN 978-0-7660-2886-9; 0-7660-2886-0

LC 2008-14599

"An introduction to the work of Eugene O'Neill for . . . students, which includes relevant biographical background on the author, explanations of various literary devices and techniques, and literary criticism for the novice reader." Publisher's note

Includes glossary and bibliographical references

Levine, Karen

★ Hana's suitcase on stage; original story by Karen Levine; play by Emil Sher. Second Story 2007

171p il (Holocaust remembrance book for young readers) pa $18.95

Grades: 5 6 7 8   812

1. Children's plays 2. Holocaust victims 3. Holocaust, 1933-1945 -- Drama

ISBN 978-1-89718-705-0 pa; 1-89718-705-X pa

"Set in the Tokyo Holocaust Center, the two-act play opens with the woman and two of her student helpers questioning and searching for answers to the suitcase's history. . . . Act II blends characters of Ishioka and her students with Hana and her family, each group individually recounting their stories in alternating voices. As with the original book, this title succeeds in recreating a striking representation of one child's tragic and beautiful life in a terrifying world of hate and prejudice. This volume will serve as one of the most effective teaching models for Holocaust curriculums available. Photographs and facsimiles of Nazi documents are included." SLJ

Loos, Pamela

A reader's guide to Lorraine Hansberry's A raisin in the sun. Enslow Publishers 2008 128p il (Multicultural literature) lib bdg $31.93

Grades: 7 8 9 10   812

1. Authors 2. Dramatists 3. African Americans in literature 4. Essayists 5. Newspaper editors 6. Nonfiction writers 7. American drama -- History and criticism

ISBN 978-0-7660-2830-2; 0-7660-2830-5

LC 2006-17900

"A Raisin in the Sun has become part of the literary canon and is required reading for many students. This guide is intended to help them better appreciate the social milieu out of which this play emerged . . . making this volume a fine resource." SLJ

Includes bibliographical references

Soto, Gary

★ Novio boy; a play. Harcourt 2006 78p pa $5.95

Grades: 7 8 9 10   812

1. Mexican Americans -- Drama 2. Dating (Social customs) -- Drama

ISBN 978-0-15-205863-0; 0-15-205863-X

LC 2007-271308

First published 1997

Rudy anxiously prepares for and then goes out on a first date with an attractive girl who is older than he is.

Stuyvesant High School (New York, N.Y.)

With their eyes; September 11th: the view from a high school at ground zero. edited by Annie Thoms; created by Taresh Batra [et. al.]; photos by Ethan Moses. HarperTempest 2002 228p il hardcover o.p. pa $6.99

Grades: 7 8 9 10   812

1. Teenagers' writings 2. American drama -- Collections 3. September 11 terrorist attacks, 2001 -- Drama

ISBN 0-06-051806-5; 0-06-051718-2 pa

LC 2002-4552

"The speakers reveal their emotions with painful honesty. . . . The book is an obvious choice for reader's theater and for use across the curriculum; its deeply affecting contents will also make compelling personal-interest reading." Booklist

Theatre for young audiences; 20 great plays for children. edited by Coleman A. Jennings; foreword by Maurice Sendak. St. Martin's Press 1998 604p il $35; pa $19.95

812

1. Drama -- Collections 2. Plays -- Collections 3. Children's plays, American
ISBN 0-312-18194-9; 0-312-33714-0 pa

LC 97-36542

A collection of plays, many of which are based on favorite children's tales, including such titles as: "Charlotte's Web," "Really Rosie," "Wiley and the Hairy Man," "Wise Men of Chelm," and "The Crane Wife"

"Highly recommended for school and public libraries and anyone interested in a substantial collection of plays for children." Booklist

813   American fiction in English

Anderson, William T.

Laura Ingalls Wilder; a biography. by William Anderson. HarperCollins Pubs. 1992 240p il hardcover o.p. pa $6.99

Grades: 4 5 6 7

813

1. Authors 2. Novelists 3. Women authors 4. Frontier and pioneer life 5. Western writers 6. Authors, American 7. Children's authors 8. Young adult authors
ISBN 0-06-020113-4; 0-06-088552-1 pa

LC 91-33805

A biography of the writer whose pioneer life on the American prairie became the basis for her "Little House" books

"A readable biography that is easily accessible to middle grade children who are likely to read the Little House books. Particularly interesting are the sections that fill in the gaps in Wilder's stories." Booklist

Blasingame, James B.

Gary Paulsen. Greenwood Press 2007 164p (Teen reads: student companions to young adult literature) $45

Grades: 7 8 9 10 11 12

813

1. Authors 2. Sled dog racers 3. Children's authors 4. Short story writers 5. Young adult authors
ISBN 978-0-313-33532-7; 0-313-33532-X

LC 2007-21446

"This volume examines a sample of . . . books by Paulsen. A biographical chapter demonstrates how Paulsen's life experiences, notably the Iditarod, have influenced his writing. Each book is analyzed for plot, characterization, setting, and themes." Publisher's note

Includes bibliographical references

Bodart, Joni Richards

They suck, they bite, they eat, they kill; the psychological meaning of supernatural monsters in young adult fiction. Joni Richards Bodart. Scarecrow Press 2012 xxxi, 268 p.p (Scarecrow studies in young adult literature) $45

Grades: Adult Professional

813

1. Folklore in literature 2. Monsters in literature 3. Supernatural in literature 4. Literature -- Psychological aspects 5. Young adult literature -- History and criticism
ISBN 9780810882270

LC 2011029544

This book examines the "rise of paranormal young adult fiction" and "focuses on popular contemporary titles lightly contextualized in a historical frame. . . . The book is divided into four sections: 'Vampires: The Aristocratic Monster'; 'Shapeshifters: The Transforming Monster'; 'Zombies: The Reanimated, Resurrected Monster'; and 'Angels, Unicorns, Demons: The Unexpectedly Deadly Monsters.' Each section opens with an overview of the literary and, when applicable, folkloric history of each supernatural being." (School Libr J) "Chapters focusing on individual authors follow . . . . [T]he chapters serve both as a tour through each invented universe and as a study of the author's relationship to the books, drawn mostly through existing interviews." (Booklist)

Includes bibliographical references

Byars, Betsy Cromer

The **moon** and I. Beech Tree Bks. 1996 96p il pa $5.99

Grades: 4 5 6 7

813

1. Authors 2. Women authors 3. Authors, American 4. Children's authors 5. Young adult authors
ISBN 0-688-13704-0

LC 95-53100

First published 1991 by Messner

A "personal narrative that gives readers some info about snakes, a fair amount of insight into how writers do what they do, and the unmistakable impression that autobiographies are great entertainment. Byars's genuine, humorous outlook on life shines through on every page." SLJ

Cammarano, Rita

Betsy Byars. Chelsea House 2002 106p il (Who wrote that?) lib bdg $30

Grades: 4 5 6 7

813

1. Authors 2. Women authors 3. Authors, American 4. Children's authors 5. Young adult authors 6. Children's stories -- Authorship 7. Authors, American -- 20th century -- Biography
ISBN 0-7910-6720-3

LC 2001-8337

Describes the personal life and successful writing career of the Newbery Award-winning author, whose memorable characters include Bingo Brown, Herculeah Jones, and the Golly sisters

"An excellent resource for author studies and creative writing classes." Book Rep

Includes bibliographical references

Carroll, Pamela S.

Sharon Creech; [by] Pamela Sissi Carroll. Greenwood Press 2007 195p (Teen reads: student companions to young adult literature) lib bdg $45

Grades: 7 8 9 10 11 12   **813**
1. Authors 2. Novelists 3. Authors, American 4. Children's authors 5. Young adult authors 6. Young adult literature -- History and criticism
ISBN 978-0-313-33598-3 lib bdg; 0-313-33598-2 lib bdg

LC 2007-21470

This focuses on Sharon Creech's "work as a teacher and shows how she uses the practice of journal-keeping to create an emotional experience for both character and reader. Of special interest are the chapters on Creech's life and those that discuss Absolutely Normal Chaos, Bloomability, and The Wanderer." Voice Youth Advocates
Includes bibliographical references

Cart, Michael

The **heart** has its reasons; young adult literature with gay/lesbian/queer content, 1969-2004. [by] Michael Cart [and] Christine A. Jenkins. Scarecrow Press 2006 207p (Scarecrow studies in young adult literature) $42
Grades: Adult Professional   **813**
1. Homosexuality in literature 2. Young adult fiction, American 3. Teenagers -- Books and reading 4. Young adult literature -- History and criticism
ISBN 0-8108-5071-0

LC 2005-31320

"Both a comprehensive overview and a lively, detailed discussion of individual landmark books, this highly readable title . . . discusses 35 years of YA books with gay, lesbian, bisexual, transgender, and queer/questioning (GLBTQ) content. . . . With fully annotated bibliographies, including a chronological list, this is a valuable YA and adult resource, sure to be in great demand for personal reference and group discussion." Booklist
Includes bibliographical references

Cook, Judy

Natural writer: a story about Marjorie Kinnan Rawlings; by Judy Cook and Laura Lee Smith; illustrated by Laurie Harden. Carolrhoda Bks. 2001 64p il (Creative minds biography) lib bdg $21.27
Grades: 4 5 6   **813**
1. Authors 2. Novelists 3. Women authors 4. Frontier and pioneer life 5. Authors, American 6. Children's authors 7. Short story writers 8. Frontier and pioneer life -- Florida 9. Women pioneers -- Florida -- Biography 10. Authors, American -- 20th century -- Biography
ISBN 1-57505-468-X

LC 00-9657

"This biography begins with Rawling's childhood in the early 1900s and shows her development as a writer through her death. . . . This easy-to-read biography has an attractive cover and a full-page charcoal illustration in each chapter." SLJ
Includes bibliographical references

Crayton, Lisa A.

A **student's** guide to Toni Morrison. Enslow Publs. 2006 160p il (Understanding literature) lib bdg $27.93

Grades: 7 8 9 10   **813**
1. Authors 2. Novelists 3. Dramatists 4. Essayists 5. College teachers 6. Literary critics 7. Nobel laureates for literature
ISBN 0-7660-2436-9

LC 2005-19069

"Each work is placed in historical and biographical context, with special emphasis placed on curriculum-related material, including The Bluest Eye, Song of Solomon, and Beloved, along with several other noteworthy works." Publisher's note
Includes glossary and bibliographical references

Dean, Tanya

Theodor Geisel. Chelsea House 2002 112p il (Who wrote that?) $22.95
Grades: 4 5 6 7   **813**
1. Artists 2. Authors 3. Humorists 4. Illustrators 5. Authors, American 6. Children's authors 7. Children's literature -- Authorship 8. Illustrators -- United States -- Biography 9. Authors, American -- 20th century -- Biography
ISBN 0-7910-6724-6

LC 2002-166

Describes the life and career of the author and illustrator known as Dr. Seuss who created such popular children's picture books as The cat in the hat, How the Grinch stole Christmas, and Horton hears a Who
"Well organized and clearly written." Booklist
Includes bibliographical references

Diorio, Mary Ann L.

A **student's** guide to Herman Melville. Enslow Publs. 2006 160p il (Understanding literature) lib bdg $27.93
Grades: 7 8 9 10   **813**
1. Authors 2. Novelists
ISBN 0-7660-2435-0

LC 2005-10159

"Each work is placed in historical and biographical context, with special emphasis placed on curriculum-related works, including his masterpiece, Moby Dick, along with Billy Budd, several of his short stories, including 'Bartleby the Scrivener,' and several of his poetic works." Publisher's note
Includes glossary and bibliographical references

A **student's** guide to Mark Twain; [by] Mary Ann L. Diorio. Enslow Publishers 2007 160p il (Understanding literature) $27.93
Grades: 7 8 9 10   **813**
1. Authors 2. Humorists 3. Novelists 4. Essayists 5. Satirists 6. Memoirists 7. Travel writers 8. Short story writers
ISBN 978-0-7660-2438-0; 0-7660-2438-5

LC 2006005888

"After a brief account of the writer's life, Diorio discusses 11 of his major works in chronological order, starting with 'The Jumping Frog' and ending with The Tragedy of Pudd'nhead Wilson. For each highlighted selection, she gives a bare-bones plot summary and a brief discussion of major themes, characters, and literary devices. . . . The book is nicely formatted, with readable font on uncluttered pages. There are a few black-and-white photographs of Twain and some relevant reproductions." SLJ

Includes bibliographical references

Don, Katherine

Real courage; the story of Harper Lee. by Katherine Don. Morgan Reynolds Pub. 2013 128 p. ill. (some col.) $28.95

Grades: 7 8 9 10   813

1. Women -- Biography 2. American authors -- Biography 3. Authors, American -- 20th century -- Biography

ISBN 9781599353487; 9781599353494

LC 2012016871

This book examines author Nelle Harper Lee and "the publication and film adaptation of her novel 'To Kill a Mockingbird.'" The book looks at "the turbulent 1960's civil rights movement and how Lee's book, which spoke of racial injustice, struck a nerve with the public. Lee grew up in a small Mississippi town that experienced segregation, which she later used as the fictional setting for 'Mockingbird.' The biography describes Lee's rise to fame and the legacy she left." (Voice of Youth Advocates)

"Students and teachers looking for a solid, accessible biography will find this to be a fine choice as the writing is straightforward and engaging." SLJ

Includes bibliographical references and index

Fleischman, Sid

★ The **abracadabra** kid; a writer's life. Greenwillow Bks. 1996 198p il hardcover o.p. $16.99

Grades: 5 6 7 8   813

1. Authors 2. Magicians 3. Magazine editors 4. Authors, American 5. Children's authors 6. Young adult authors

ISBN 0-688-14859-X; 0-688-15855-2 pa

LC 95-47382

This autobiography, "turns real life into a story complete with cliffhangers. And it's a classic boy's story, from card tricks and traveling magic shows to World War II naval experiences and screen-writing gigs for John Wayne movies. En route, we learn how Fleischman learned the craft of writing." Bull Cent Child Books

Includes bibliographical references

Fradin, Dennis Brindell

★ **Zora!** the life of Zora Neal Hurston. Judith Bloom Fradin and Dennis Brindell Fradin. Clarion Books 2012 xi, 180 p.p ill. $17.99

Grades: 5 6 7 8   813

1. African American authors -- Biography 2. African American women -- Biography 3. Folklorists -- United States -- Biography 4. Authors, American -- 20th century -- Biography

ISBN 0547006950; 9780547006956

LC 2011025949

This book by Dennis Brindell Fradin and Judith Bloom Fradin presents a "biography of . . . African-American author . . . [Zora Neale] Hurston. . . . Beginning with a . . . scene of the 59-year-old Hurston, already a well-known author, working as a white family's domestic helper because she needed a paycheck, the Fradins . . . establish the complexities of Zora's inner and external worlds, before offering highlights of her life in chronological order." (Publishers Weekly)

Includes bibliographical references and index.

Fritz, Jean

★ **Harriet** Beecher Stowe and the Beecher preachers. Putnam 1994 144p il $15.99; pa $5.99

Grades: 5 6 7 8   813

1. Authors 2. Novelists 3. Abolitionists 4. Women authors 5. Authors, American 6. Children's authors 7. Nonfiction writers 8. Short story writers

ISBN 0-399-22666-4; 0-698-11660-7 pa

LC 93-6408

This is a biography of the abolitionist author of "Uncle Tom's Cabin" with an emphasis on the influence of her preacher father and her family on her life and work.

"Written with vivacity and insight, this readable and engrossing biography is an important contribution to women's history as well as to the history of American letters." Horn Book

Includes bibliographical references

Gallo, Donald R.

Richard Peck; the past is paramount. [by] Donald R. Gallo, Wendy J. Glenn. Scarecrow Press 2009 208p (Scarecrow studies in young adult literature) $35

Grades: 7 8 9 10 Adult Professional   813

1. Authors 2. Novelists 3. Children's authors 4. Young adult authors

ISBN 978-0-8108-5848-0; 0-8108-5848-7

LC 2008036524

"Gallo and Wendy J. Glenn recount the highlights of Peck's life, focusing on his world travels, his accomplishments as a teacher and his renowned writing career. Gallo and Glenn examine Peck's 30 novels, as well as his short stories and children's books, poems, essays and other nonfiction." Publisher's note

Includes bibliographical references

Gantos, Jack

★ **Hole** in my life. Farrar, Straus & Giroux 2002 199p il $16; pa $8

Grades: 7 8 9 10   813

1. Authors 2. College teachers 3. Authors, American 4. Children's authors 5. Ex-convicts -- United States -- Biography 6. Authors, American -- 20th century -- Biography

ISBN 0-374-39988-3; 0-374-43089-6 pa

LC 2001-40957

Michael L. Printz Award honor book, 2003

The author relates how, as a young adult, he became a drug user and smuggler, was arrested, did time in prison, and eventually got out and went to college, all the while hoping to become a writer

"Gantos' spare narrative style and straightforward revelation of the truth have, together, a cumulative power that will capture not only a reader's attention but also empathy and imagination." Booklist

The **girl** who was on fire; your favorite authors on Suzanne Collins' Hunger games trilogy. edited by Leah Wilson. BenBella Books 2011 211p pa $12.95

Grades: Adult Professional   **813**

1. Authors 2. Novelists 3. Fantasy writers 4. Young adult authors

ISBN 978-1-935618-04-1; 1-935618-04-0

LC 2011007180

"Fans of the trilogy will undoubtedly enjoy exploring elements of the series through the eyes of the author's contemporaries, each with a different expertise. The selections address the deeper social and political issues as well as the development of multilayered characters through witty and sometimes raw essays that ask readers to look deeper. . . . Essays explore . . . subjects from within Katniss's world of Panem with humor, irreverence, and social understanding. This thought-provoking text will be especially useful for educators or librarians utilizing the multidiscplinary themes in this trilogy with their students." SLJ

Includes bibliographical references

Glenn, Wendy J.

Sarah Dessen; from burritos to box office. [by] Wendy J. Glenn. Scarecrow Press 2005 147p (Scarecrow studies in young adult literature) $45

Grades: 7 8 9 10 Adult Professional   **813**

1. Authors 2. Novelists 3. Young adult authors

ISBN 0-8108-5325-6; 978-0-8108-5325-6

LC 2004016058

This offers literary criticism of the works of Sarah Dessen, author of such young adult novels as The Truth About Forever, and Lock and Key

"Glenn's book is an excellent example of the kind of meaning-making exploration that students can examine in a work of literature written for adolescents. . . . Informative and lively." Voice Youth Advocates

Includes bibliographical references

Hamilton, Virginia

★ **Virginia** Hamilton: speeches, essays, and conversations; edited by Arnold Adoff & Kacy Cook. Blue Sky Press 2010 368p $29.99

Grades: 8 9 10 11 12 Adult Professional   **813**

1. Authorship 2. Children's literature -- History and criticism

ISBN 978-0-439-27193-6; 0-439-27193-2

LC 2009031676

"A groundbreaking writer of children's fiction, folktales, biography, and picture books, Hamilton won every major award, and much of this book is made up of her acceptance speeches, including those for the Newbery, Hans Christian Andersen, and Coretta Scott King awards, as well as her Arbuthnot and Zena Sutherland lectures. Aimed at a general audience, the book employs a tone both scholarly and informal, as Hamilton talks about her career as a woman and a black writer in America and about the form and content of her work in general and with particular titles. . . . Many speeches include introductions by children's literature scholars and editors, who add perspective on Hamilton's lasting influence, while family members fill in biographical details. A must for YAs who love her books, this will also appeal to librarians, teachers, and children's literature students." Booklist

Includes bibliographical references

Hickam, Homer H.

The **Coalwood** way; by Homer H. Hickam, Jr. Delacorte Press 2000 318p hardcover o.p. pa $6.99

Grades: 7 8 9 10 11 12 Adult   **813**

1. Authors 2. Novelists 3. Aerospace engineers 4. Memoirists 5. Authors, American 6. Writers on science 7. Novelists, American -- 20th century -- Biography 8. Aerospace engineers -- United States -- Biography

ISBN 0-440-23716-5

LC 00-35884

This sequel to Rocket boys "continues the author's life story with his senior year in high school, 1959, in the declining West Virginia mining town of Coalwood. The rocket club, featured in the last book, is pushed to the periphery, and the focus shifts to Hickam's teenage problems, which include his parents, girls, and a sadness whose cause he cannot divine." Booklist

Hinds, Maurene J.

A **reader's** guide to Richard Wright's Black boy. Enslow Publishers 2010 128p il (Multicultural literature) lib bdg $31.93

Grades: 6 7 8 9   **813**

1. Authors 2. Novelists 3. Dramatists 4. Essayists 5. Nonfiction writers 6. Short story writers 7. American literature -- African American authors

ISBN 978-0-7660-3165-4 lib bdg; 0-7660-3165-9 lib bdg

LC 2008-36473

"An introduction to Richard Wright's novel Black Boy . . . which includes relevant biographical background on the author, explanations of various literary devices and techniques, and literary criticism for the novice reader." Publisher's note

Includes glossary and bibliographical references

Hinton, KaaVonia

Angela Johnson; poetic prose. [by] KaaVonia Hinton. Scarecrow Press 2006 107p (Scarecrow studies in young adult literature) $35

Grades: 7 8 9 10 Adult Professional   **813**

1. Poets 2. Authors 3. Novelists 4. Children's authors 5. Short story writers 6. Young adult authors

ISBN 978-0-8108-5092-7; 0-8108-5092-3

LC 2006001893

The examines the life and works of Angela Johnson, author of such novels as Toning the Sweep and A Cool Moonlight

"This book is a well-researched biography suitable for reports or even thoughtful fans. Certainly teachers seeking to use Johnson's books in their classes should find the literary criticism very useful." Voice Youth Advocates

Includes bibliographical references

Sharon M. Draper; embracing literacy. [by] KaaVonia Hinton. Scarecrow Press 2009 131p (Scarecrow studies in young adult literature) $35

Grades: 7 8 9 10 Adult Professional **813**

1. Authors 2. Teachers 3. Novelists 4. Children's authors 5. Young adult authors
ISBN 978-0-8108-5985-2; 0-8108-5985-8

LC 2008036695

"Author KaaVonia Hinton reveals how Draper became an exceptional teacher and writer, and how she uses her writing to urge young people to embrace literacy. Hinton also explores how Draper has made a lasting contribution to the field of young adult literature. This book-length study examines both her life and work." Publisher's note

Includes bibliographical references

Hirschmann, Kris

Frankenstein. ReferencePoint Press 2011 80p il (Monsters and mythical creatures) $27.95

Grades: 6 7 8 9 **813**

1. Authors 2. Novelists 3. Monsters in literature
ISBN 978-1-60152-180-4; 1-60152-180-4

LC 2011002145

This is "an ideal starting point for young researchers interested in the weird, mysterious, and paranormal. Using fleet, descriptive prose to communicate the impressively researched (and sourced) information, [this] medium-length [work manages] to rope in just about everything, from folklore to history to pop culture. The bulk of Frankenstein focuses upon Mary Shelley's masterpiece, not just the infamous contest for which it was written but also the reception and critical analysis, both then and now. . . . The illustrations are fine and varied, the sidebars always illuminating, and the back matter robust." Booklist

Includes bibliographical references

Hogan, Walter

★ **Humor** in young adult literature; a time to laugh. Scarecrow Press 2005 223p (Scarecrow studies in young adult literature) $40

Grades: Adult Professional **813**

1. Teenagers -- Books and reading 2. Wit and humor -- History and criticism
ISBN 0-8108-5072-9

LC 2004-18903

"As a reader's advisory tool, this book is invaluable, paving the way for many laughter-filled hours to come." Voice Youth Advocates

Includes bibliographical references

Jones, Jen

A **reader's** guide to Gary Soto's Taking sides. Enslow Publishers 2010 127p il (Multicultural literature) lib bdg $31.93

Grades: 8 9 10 11 12 **813**

1. Poets 2. Authors 3. Novelists 4. Hispanic Americans in literature 5. Essayists 6. College teachers 7. Children's authors 8. Young adult authors
ISBN 978-0-7660-3168-5 lib bdg; 0-7660-3168-3 lib bdg

LC 2008-38587

An introduction to Gary Soto's novel Taking sides for high school students, which includes biographical background on the author, explanations of various literary devices and techniques, and literary criticism for the novice reader.

Includes glossary and bibliographical references

Juster, Norton

The **annotated** Phantom tollbooth; by Norton Juster; illustrations by Jules Feiffer; introduction and notes by Leonard Marcus. Alfred A. Knopf 2011 284p il $29.99; lib bdg $32.22

Grades: Adult Professional **813**

1. Authors 2. Architects 3. Children's authors
ISBN 978-0-375-85715-7; 0-375-85715-X; 978-0-375-95715-4 lib bdg; 0-375-95715-4 lib bdg

LC 2011013174

"Still ferrying dazzled readers to Dictionopolis and beyond 50 years after his first appearance, young Milo is accompanied this time through by encyclopedic commentary from our generation's leading (and most readable) expert on the history of children's literature and publishing. . . . Leonard opens with typically lucid and well-organized pictures of both Juster's and Feiffer's formative years and later careers, interwoven with accounts of the book's conception, publication and critical response. In notes running alongside the ensuing facsimile, he puts on an intellectual show. . . . he delivers notes on topics as diverse as the etymological origins of "BALDERDASH!" and mimetic architecture to textual parallels with the Wizard of Oz and echoes of Winsor McKay and George Grosz in the art. Family photos, scrawled notes and images of handwritten and typescript manuscript pages further gloss a work that never ages nor fails to astonish." Kirkus

Kramer, Barbara

Toni Morrison; a biography of a nobel prize-winning writer. by Barbara Kramer. Enslow Publishers 2012 104 p. (library) $26.60

Grades: 7 8 9 10 **813**

1. Morrison, Toni 2. African American novelists -- Biography 3. Novelists, American -- 20th century -- Biography
ISBN 0766039897; 9780766039896

LC 2011024344

In this biography of African American author Toni Morrison, "Barbara Kramer explores the life and career of this talented writer. From her childhood in Loraine, Ohio, to her creative expressions of African-American culture, Morrison has always remembered her past. She has taught at several universities, as well as being the author of novels, short stories essays, and a play." (Publisher's note)

Includes bibliographical references

Lazo, Caroline Evensen

F. Scott Fitzgerald; voice of the Jazz Age. {by} Caroline Lazo. Lerner Publs. 2003 128p il (Lerner long biographies) lib bdg $25.26

813

1. Authors 2. Novelists 3. Screenwriters 4. Authors, American 5. Short story writers 6. Authors, American -- 20th century -- Biography
ISBN 0-8225-0074-4

LC 2001-7210

"This well-documented book offers a fascinating glimpse into the acclaimed author's early years, unremarkable academic record, extravagant lifestyle, and work." SLJ

Includes bibliographical references

Litwin, Laura Baskes

A **reader's** guide to Zora Neale Hurston's Their eyes were watching god. Enslow Publishers 2010 128p il (Multicultural literature) lib bdg $31.93

Grades: 8 9 10 11 12   **813**

1. Authors 2. Novelists 3. Dramatists 4. African Americans in literature 5. Memoirists 6. Folklorists 7. Short story writers

ISBN 978-0-7660-3164-7; 0-7660-3164-0

LC 2008-38524

An introduction to Zora Neale Hurston's novel Their eyes were watching God for high school students, which includes biographical background on the author, explanations of various literary devices and techniques, and literary criticism for the novice reader.

Includes glossary and bibliographical references

Loos, Pamela

A **reader's** guide to Amy Tan's The joy luck club. Enslow Publishers 2008 112p il (Multicultural literature) $31.93

Grades: 6 7 8 9   **813**

1. Authors 2. Novelists 3. Mother-daughter relationships in literature 4. Essayists 5. Children's authors 6. Short story writers 7. Literature -- Women authors 8. American literature -- Asian American authors

ISBN 978-0-7660-2832-6; 0-7660-2832-1

LC 2006102440

The book is "an excellent resource for the student wanting to do more in depth research. . . . [The] photos . . . chosen are of good quality. . . . The [volume is] well organized, clearly written, and simple to understand." Voice Youth Advocates

Includes bibliographical references

Lowry, Lois

★ **Looking** back; a book of memories. Houghton Mifflin 1998 181p il $17

Grades: 5 6 7 8   **813**

1. Authors 2. Novelists 3. Women authors 4. Authors, American 5. Young adult authors 6. Authors, American -- 20th century -- Biography

ISBN 0-395-89543-X

LC 98-11376

Using family photographs and quotes from her books, the author provides glimpses into her life

"A compelling and inspirational portrait of the author emerges from these vivid snapshots of life's joyful, sad and surprising moments." Publ Wkly

Lukes, Bonnie L.

Soldier's courage: the story of Stephen Crane. Morgan Reynolds 2002 144p il lib bdg $21.95

Grades: 7 8 9 10   **813**

1. Authors 2. Novelists 3. Authors, American

ISBN 1-88384-694-3

LC 2002-5095

"Lukes's gift for storytelling and her stirring prose result in a thoroughly readable and informative volume." SLJ

Includes bibliographical references

Marler, Myrna Dee

Walter Dean Myers. Greenwood Press 2008 198p (Teen reads: student companions to young adult literature) $45

Grades: 8 9 10 11 12 Adult Professional   **813**

1. Poets 2. Authors 3. Novelists 4. Editors 5. Children's authors 6. Young adult authors 7. Children's literature -- Authors and illustrators

ISBN 978-0-313-33628-7; 0-313-33628-8

LC 2008010070

"Marler analyzes the life and works of the accomplished author. The first two chapters are devoted to a brief biography and the historical and cultural influences on Myers's writing. The remainder of the volume looks at his books, including comparisons of plots and characters as well as thematic development within each novel." SLJ

Includes bibliographical references

McArthur, Debra

A **student's** guide to Edgar Allan Poe. Enslow Publishers 2006 160p il por (Understanding literature) lib bdg $27.93

Grades: 7 8 9 10   **813**

1. Poets 2. Authors 3. Essayists 4. Short story writers

ISBN 0-7660-2437-7

LC 2005024273

This examines the life and career of Edgar Allan Poe, discussing such works as The Raven, The Fall of the House of Usher, and The Tell-Tale Heart.

Includes glossary and bibliographical references

A **student's** guide to William Faulkner; [by] Debra A. McArthur. Enslow Publishers 2009 160p il (Understanding literature) lib bdg $27.93

Grades: 7 8 9 10   **813**

1. Authors 2. Novelists 3. Screenwriters 4. Short story writers 5. Nobel laureates for literature

ISBN 978-0-7660-2885-2; 0-7660-2885-2

LC 2008-3010

"An introduction to the work of William Faulkner for . . . students, which includes relevant biographical background on the author, explanations of various literary devices and techniques, and literary criticism for the novice reader." Publisher's note

Includes glossary and bibliographical references

McClellan, Marilyn

Madeleine L'Engle; banned, challenged, and censored. Enslow Publishers 2008 160p il (Authors of banned books) $25.95

Grades: 8 9 10 11 12   **813**

1. Authors 2. Novelists 3. Censorship 4. Essayists 5. Memoirists 6. Mystery writers 7. Children's authors 8.

Books -- Censorship 9. Short story writers 10. Writers on religion 11. Young adult authors 12. Science fiction writers

ISBN 978-0-7660-2708-4; 0-7660-2708-2

LC 2007015134

This "uses the attacks on one classic yet frequently challenged book, L'Engle's 1963 Newbery Medal winner, A Wrinkle in Time, to draw teens into a dynamic discussion of general censorship history and issues. McClellan describes the objections, frequently Christian fundamentalists citing the book's 'satanic content,' and counters them with comments from the other side. . . . Readers will also find a succinct biography of L'Engle. . . . occasional photos, a chapter of literary analysis, and summaries of both Wrinkle and L'Engle's Many Waters (1986)." Booklist

Includes bibliographical references

Myers, Walter Dean, 1937-

★ **Bad** boy; a memoir. HarperCollins Pubs. 2001 214p $15.95; pa $6.99

Grades: 7 8 9 10   **813**

1. Poets 2. Authors 3. Novelists 4. African American authors 5. Editors 6. Authors, American 7. Children's authors 8. Young adult authors 9. Children's stories -- Authorship 10. African American authors -- Biography 11. Authors, American -- 20th century -- Biography

ISBN 0-06-029523-6; 0-06-447288-4 pa

LC 00-52978

This "is a story full of funny anecdotes, lofty ideals, and tender moments." SLJ

Napoli, Donna Jo

Zel. Dutton Children's Bks. 1996 227p hardcover o.p. pa $5.99

Grades: 7 8 9 10   **813**

1. Fairy tales 2. Mother-daughter relationship -- Fiction

ISBN 0-525-45612-0; 0-14-130116-3 pa

LC 96-15135

Based on the fairy tale Rapunzel, the story is told in alternating chapters from the point of view of Zel, her mother, and the prince, and delves into the psychological motivations of the characters

"This version, with its Faustian overtones, will challenge readers to think about this old story on a deeper level. It begs for discussion in literature classes." SLJ

Nilsen, Alleen Pace

Names and naming in young adult literature; [by] Alleen Pace Nilsen, Don L. F. Nilsen. Scarecrow Press 2007 173p (Scarecrow studies in young adult literature) $45

Grades: Adult Professional   **813**

1. Personal names in literature 2. Characters and characteristics in literature 3. Young adult literature -- History and criticism

ISBN 978-0-8108-5808-4; 0-8108-5808-8

LC 2007-11281

This "book consists of an introduction about the role of names in young adult literature, eight essay chapters, a bibliography, and an index. . . . The authors do a good job in

writing engaging content. . . . School, public, and academic libraries will find this title an asset." Booklist

Includes bibliographical references

Paulsen, Gary

★ **Guts**; the true stories behind Hatchet and the Brian books. Delacorte Press 2001 148p hardcover o.p. pa $5.50

Grades: 6 7 8 9   **813**

1. Authors 2. Hunting 3. Wilderness survival 4. Sled dog racers 5. Authors, American 6. Children's authors 7. Short story writers 8. Young adult authors 9. Children's stories -- Authorship 10. Authors, American -- 20th century -- Biography

ISBN 0385326505; 0440407125

LC 00-34061

The author relates incidents in his life and how they inspired parts of his books about the character, Brian Robeson

"Readers squeamish about hunting or the death of animals will find many of the stories disturbing . . . but those who embrace the sport or have enjoyed the novels will see in Paulsen a responsible role model—a man who respects life and death as equal partners." Booklist

★ **How** Angel Peterson got his name; and other outrageous tales about extreme sports. Wendy Lamb Bks. 2003 111p hardcover o.p. pa $5.99

Grades: 5 6 7 8   **813**

1. Authors 2. Sled dog racers 3. Authors, American 4. Children's authors 5. Short story writers 6. Young adult authors 7. Authors, American -- 20th century -- Biography

ISBN 0-385-72949-9; 0-385-90090-2 lib bdg; 978-0-440-22935-3 pa; 0-440-22935-9 pa

LC 2002-7668

Author Gary Paulsen relates tales from his youth in a small town in northwestern Minnesota in the late 1940s and early 1950s, such as skiing behind a souped-up car and imitating daredevil Evel Knievel

"Writing with humor and sensitivity, Paulsen shows boys moving into adolescence believing they can do anything. . . . None of them dies (amazingly), and even if Paulsen exaggerates the teensiest bit, his tales are side-splittingly funny and more than a little frightening." Booklist

★ **My** life in dog years; with drawings by Ruth Wright Paulsen. Delacorte Press 1998 137p il $15.95; pa $6.50

Grades: 4 5 6 7   **813**

1. Dogs 2. Authors 3. Sled dog racers 4. Authors, American 5. Children's authors 6. Short story writers 7. Young adult authors 8. Dogs -- United States -- Anecdotes 9. Dog owners -- United States -- Biography 10. Authors, American -- 20th century -- Biography

ISBN 0-385-32570-3; 0-440-41471-7 pa

LC 97-40254

The author describes some of the dogs that have had special places in his life, including his first dog, Snowball, in the Philippines; Dirk, who protected him from bullies; and Cookie, who saved his life

"Paulsen differentiates his canine friends beautifully, as only a keen observer and lover of dogs can. At the same time, he presents an intimate glimpse of himself, a lonely child of alcoholic parents, who drew strength and solace from his four-legged companions and a love of the great outdoors. Poignant but never saccharine, honest, and open." Booklist

Peet, Bill

★ **Bill** Peet: an autobiography. Houghton Mifflin 1989 190p il hardcover o.p. pa $15

Grades: 4 5 6 7   **813**

1. Artists 2. Authors 3. Illustrators 4. Authors, American 5. Children's authors

ISBN 0-395-50932-7; 0-395-68982-1 pa

LC 88-37067

A Caldecott Medal honor book, 1990

"Every page of this oversized book is illustrated with Peet's unmistakable black-and-white drawings of himself and the people, places, and events described in the text. Familiar characters from his books and movies appear often." SLJ

Pingelton, Timothy J.

A **student's** guide to Ernest Hemingway. Enslow Publishers 2005 160p il map (Understanding literature) lib bdg $27.93

Grades: 7 8 9 10   **813**

1. Poets 2. Authors 3. Novelists 4. Short story writers 5. Nobel laureates for literature

ISBN 0-7660-2431-8

This discusses Hemingway's life and his novels In Our Time, The Sun Also Rises, A Farewell to Arms, and The Old Man and the Sea

"Engaging and informative. . . . The very accessible format and the solid information make [this book] useful to students, and the engaging style should interest casual readers." SLJ

Includes glossary and bibliographical references

Reef, Catherine

★ **John** Steinbeck. Clarion Bks. 1996 163p il $17.95; pa $8.95

Grades: 7 8 9 10   **813**

1. Authors 2. Novelists 3. Screenwriters 4. Authors, American 5. Nobel laureates for literature

ISBN 0-395-71278-5; 0-618-43244-2 pa

LC 95-11500

"The book traces Steinbeck's life from his childhood in California, to his burgeoning writing career and his passion for social justice, to his worldwide recognition. Reef does an excellent job of synthesizing Steinbeck's work, his private life, and his politics and philosophy." Bull Cent Child Books

Includes bibliographical references

Reid, Suzanne Elizabeth

Virginia Euwer Wolff; capturing the music of young voices. [by] Suzanne Elizabeth Reid. Scarecrow Press 2003 137p il (Scarecrow studies in young adult literature) $49

Grades: 8 9 10 11 12 Adult Professional   **813**

1. Authors 2. Children's authors 3. Young adult authors

ISBN 978-0-8108-4858-0; 0-8108-4858-9

LC 2003-10897

"In five short chapters, Reid provides an intriguing exploration of this popular author's personal life along with an in-depth summary and analysis of five of her young adult novels." Voice Youth Advocates

Includes bibliographical references

Ross-Stroud, Catherine

Janet McDonald; the original project girl. [by] Catherine Ross-Stroud. Scarecrow Press 2009 137p il (Scarecrow studies in young adult literature) $35

Grades: 7 8 9 10 Adult Professional   **813**

1. Authors 2. Lawyers 3. Novelists 4. Young adult authors

ISBN 978-0-8108-5802-2; 0-8108-5802-9

LC 2008030712

This "is a bio-critical study of McDonald and her work as it relates to the contributions she has made to the genre of teen fiction." Publisher's note

Includes bibliographical references

Schroeder, Heather Lee

A **reader's** guide to Marjane Satrapi's Persepolis. Enslow Publishers 2010 152p il map (Multicultural literature) lib bdg $34.60

Grades: 8 9 10 11 12   **813**

1. Artists 2. Authors 3. Novelists 4. Cartoonists 5. Memoirists

ISBN 978-0-7660-3166-1; 0-7660-3166-7

LC 2008-51820

An introduction to Marjane Satrapi's graphic novel Persepolis for high school students, which includes biographical background on the author, explanations of various literary devices and techniques, and literary criticism for the novice reader.

Includes glossary and bibliographical references

Spinelli, Jerry

★ **Knots** in my yo-yo string; the autobiography of a kid. Knopf 1998 148p il hardcover o.p. pa $10.95

Grades: 4 5 6 7   **813**

1. Authors 2. Magazine editors 3. Authors, American 4. Children's authors

ISBN 0-679-98791-6; 0-679-88791-1 pa

LC 97-30827

This Italian-American Newbery Medalist presents a humorous account of his childhood and youth in Norristown, Pennsylvania

"There is an 'everyboy' universality to Spinelli's experiences, but his keen powers of observation and recall turn the story into a richly rewarding personal history." Horn Book Guide

Stefoff, Rebecca

Jack London; an American original. Oxford Univ. Press 2002 127p il maps (Oxford portraits) lib bdg $28

Grades: 7 8 9 10   **813**

1. Authors 2. Novelists 3. Authors, American 4. Short story writers 5. Authors, American -- 20th century --

Biography
ISBN 0-19-512223-2

LC 2001-53087

"This volume does an excellent job of illuminating London's extraordinary life and career. The narrative is exciting and accessible. . . . The text is supplemented by interesting and informative illustrations, and includes excerpts from primary-source material." SLJ
Includes bibliographical references

Stover, Lois T.
Jacqueline Woodson; the real thing. [by] Lois Thomas Stover. Scarecrow Press 2003 189p (Scarecrow studies in young adult literature) $49
Grades: 8 9 10 11 12 Adult Professional   **813**
   1. Authors 2. Novelists 3. African Americans in literature 4. College teachers 5. Children's authors 6. Young adult authors 7. Young adult fiction, American -- History and criticism 8. Women and literature -- United States -- History -- 20th century
   ISBN 978-0-8108-4857-3; 0-8108-4857-0

LC 2003-9881

"Students who are interested in learning more about this particular author will find plenty of information that will illuminate second and deeper readings of her works. Teachers searching for ways to help make connections among the books will find Stover's work of great value." Voice Youth Advocates
Includes bibliographical references

Tighe, Mary Ann
  Sharon Creech; the words we choose to say. Scarecrow Press 2006 123p (Scarecrow studies in young adult literature) $35
Grades: 7 8 9 10   **813**
   1. Authors 2. Novelists 3. Children's authors 4. Young adult authors
   ISBN 978-0-8108-5086-6; 0-8108-5086-9

LC 2005037615

"Tighe bills her resource as a 'biocritical volume' on Sharon Creech, beginning with a chronology of her life before continuing with a more complete look, as well as the influence of her life experiences on her writing. . . . Tighe does an admirable and complete job of examining Creech's body of work." Voice Youth Advocates
Includes bibliographical references

Tyson, Edith S.
  Orson Scott Card; writer of the terrible choice. Scarecrow Press 2003 xxv, 187p (Scarecrow studies in young adult literature) $40
Grades: 8 9 10 11 12 Adult Professional   **813**
   1. Authors 2. Novelists 3. Editors 4. Fantasy writers 5. Short story writers 6. Science fiction writers 7. Youth -- Books and reading -- United States 8. Young adult fiction, American -- History and criticism
   ISBN 0-8108-4790-6

LC 2003-5730

"Tyson begins her book with a . . . preface gleaned from Card's own explanation of the purpose of his writing, followed by a light biographical skimming of his life and development as a writer. The best features of the book are Tyson's excellent analyses of Card's books. Each book is summarized . . . and then enriched with different perspectives on the meaning, or some relevant background information, or something that Card himself wrote about that particular book. The sequence and interrelatedness of his books are also well documented. This book is a must-have for both professional and circulating collections." Voice Youth Advocates
Includes bibliographical references

★ The **wand** in the word; conversations with writers of fantasy. compiled and edited by Leonard S. Marcus. Candlewick Press 2006 202p il $19.99
Grades: 6 7 8 9   **813**
   1. Authors, English 2. Authors, American 3. Fantasy fiction -- History and criticism 4. Authors -- Interviews
   ISBN 0-7636-2625-2

LC 2005-46913

"Marcus presents interviews with 13 fantasy luminaries, including Lloyd Alexander, Susan Cooper, Nancy Farmer, Brian Jacques, Garth Nix, Tamora Pierce, and Philip Pullman. The writers' distinct personalities and career paths emerge, as do intriguing similarities. . . . Each profile includes a black-and-white author's photo, a reading list, and a bit of ephemera, often a handwritten manuscript page. . . . [This is] a rich resource that will be consulted as frequently by children's literature professionals as by genre fans themselves." Booklist

Yolen, Jane
  Passager. Harcourt Brace & Co. 1996 76p (Young Merlin trilogy) $16
Grades: 4 5 6 7   **813**
   1. Fantasy fiction 2. Merlin (Legendary character) -- Fiction
   ISBN 0-15-200391-6

LC 94-27101

A foundling rediscovers his identity through the help of the falconer who adopts him
A "stark, poignant, and absorbing tale. . . . This 'skinny' book will entice reluctant readers, but its rich language and poetic phrasing make it compelling and challenging." SLJ
Other titles in the Young Merlin trilogy are:
Hobby (1996)
Merlin (1997)

814 American essays in English

Kirk, Andrew
  Understanding Thoreau's Civil disobedience. Rosen Pub. 2010 128p il (Words that changed the world) lib bdg $31.95
Grades: 7 8 9 10   **814**
   1. Authors 2. Naturalists 3. Resistance to government 4. Essayists 5. Pacifists 6. Writers on nature 7. Nonfiction writers
   ISBN 978-1-4488-1671-2; 1-4488-1671-8

LC 2010-10221

First published 2004 by Barrons with title: Civil disobedience

This considers Thoreau's Civil Disobedience, including its "'Context and Creator,' 'Immediate Impact,' 'Legacy,' and 'Aftermath.' . . . [Exploring] the historical context of transcendentalism and resistance to big government. . . . [The] author provides a balance of deep context, expressive writing, and pertinent information." SLJ

Includes glossary and bibliographical references

Red; the next generation of American writers--teen-age girls--on what fires up their lives today. edited by Amy Goldwasser. Hudson Street Press 2007 267p $21.95

Grades: 8 9 10 11 12 Adult   814

1. Girls 2. Essays 3. Teenagers' writings

ISBN 978-1-59463-040-8; 1-59463-040-2

LC 2007027247

"The authors are complicated and real, with interests and concerns of immense scope. . . . It will be a surefire hit for girls." Voice Youth Advocates

815   American speeches in English

★   American Heritage book of great American speeches for young people; edited by Suzanne McIntire. Wiley 2001 292p il pa $14.95

Grades: 7 8 9 10   815

1. American speeches 2. Speeches, addresses, etc 3. Speeches, addresses, etc., American

ISBN 0-471-38942-0

LC 00-43749

This is a "compendium of more than 100 speeches that span nearly 400 years of American history, from Powhatan (1609) to Senator Charles Robb (2000). Prominent orators include Patrick Henry, Thomas Jefferson, John Kennedy, Richard Nixon, Martin Luther King, Jr., and Malcolm X. . . . The speeches inform readers and provide examples of how the spoken word has affected Americans throughout our past." SLJ

★   U-X-L Asian American voices; edited by Debo-rah Gillan Straub. 2nd ed; U.X.L 2004 xxv, 315p il $58

Grades: 7 8 9 10 11 12   815

1. Asian Americans 2. American speeches

ISBN 0-7876-7600-4

LC 2003-110048

First published 1997 with title: Asian American voices

This "reference presents full or excerpted speeches, ser-mons, orations, poems, testimony and other notable spoken words of Asian Americans. Each entry is accompanied by an introduction and boxes explaining terms and events to which the speech refers. The volume is illustrated with photographs and drawings." Publisher's note

817   American humor and satire in English

Cleary, Brian P.

The **laugh** stand; adventures in humor. by Brian P. Cleary; illustrated by J.P. Sandy. Millbrook Press 2008 48p il lib bdg $16.95

Grades: 4 5 6   817

1. Word games 2. Wit and humor

ISBN 978-0-8225-7849-9

LC 2007021889

Cleary "promotes fun with words in 13 small sections that toy with puns, anagrams, daffynitions, Tom Swift-ies, and more. . . . Sandy's ideally matched cartoons are a google-eyed cast that includes humans, animals, food items with faces, and societal icons. This team marries humor with sublime learning." SLJ

Includes bibliographical references

818   American miscellaneous writings in English

Hargrave, John

Sir John Hargrave's mischief maker's manual; by Sir John Hargrave. Grosset & Dunlap 2009 270p il $15.99

Grades: 7 8 9 10   818

1. Practical jokes

ISBN 978-0-448-44982-1; 0-448-44982-X

LC 2008-34518

Presents a definitive guide to pulling off such perfect pranks as making crank calls and freezing worms inside ice cubes, divided into five specific sections.

"Pranks include making a 'Screaming Cabinet' (using the device from musical greeting cards), creating the 'World's Largest Butt Photo' and faking an alien landing. What's most appealing, however, is the emphasis on being clever, cre-ative and funny while making mischief." Publ Wkly

Mark Twain; Todd Howard, book editor. Green-haven Press 2002 190p il (People who made history) lib bdg $34.95; pa $23.70

818

1. Authors 2. Humorists 3. Novelists 4. Essayists 5. Satirists 6. Memoirists 7. Travel writers 8. Authors, American 9. Short story writers 10. Authors, American -- 19th century -- Biography 11. Humorists, American -- 19th century -- Biography

ISBN 0-7377-0897-2 lib bdg; 0-7377-0896-4 pa

LC 2001-28923

A collection of essays about the American author and humorist with primary source documents

Includes bibliographical references

McCurdy, Michael

Walden then & now; an alphabetical tour of Henry Thoreau's pond. Charlesbridge 2010 un il lib bdg $16.95

Grades: 4 5 6 7   818

1. Authors 2. Alphabet 3. Naturalists 4. Essayists 5. Pacifists 6. Writers on nature 7. Nonfiction writers 8.

Natural history -- Massachusetts

ISBN 978-1-58089-253-7 lib bdg; 1-58089-253-1 lib bdg

LC 2009-26645

"Elegiac woodcarvings evoke the setting of Henry Thoreau's Walden Pond as the text weaves past and present in this lengthy alphabet poem. On each spread, consecutive letters face one another, making a couplet of the lines. A dark, but not somber, woodcarving illustrates each letter, and an explanatory paragraph expands upon the information in the verse. . . . The book ends with entries from Thoreau's diary and McCurdy's inspiration and starting point for this book. Purchase as an introduction to Thoreau and for poetry shelves." SLJ

Paulsen, Gary

★ **Caught** by the sea; my life on boats. Delacorte Press 2001 103p maps $15.95; pa $5.50

Grades: 5 6 7 8 **818**

1. Authors 2. Ocean travel 3. Boats and boating 4. Sled dog racers 5. Authors, American 6. Children's authors 7. Short story writers 8. Young adult authors 9. Authors, American -- 20th century -- Biography

ISBN 0-385-32645-9; 0-440-40716-8 pa

LC 2001-17336

"Paulsen traces his life at sea, from buying his first sailboat to getting lost in the Pacific to encountering sharks. . . . His sometimes comic, sometimes near-fatal sea-going errors make for absorbing, captivating reading." Booklist

821   English poetry

Blake, William

William Blake; edited by John Maynard; illustrated by Alessandra Cimatoribus. Sterling Pub. 2006 48p il (Poetry for young people) $14.95

Grades: 5 6 7 8 **821**

1. Children's poetry, English. 2. Poetry -- By individual authors

ISBN 978-0-8069-3647-5; 0-8069-3647-9

LC 2006013858

"The book begins with a heroic attempt to explain some of [Blake's] themes and philosophy in a four-page introduction. Maynard speaks of the poet with insight, eloquence, and obvious admiration. . . . He prefaces each poem with explanatory comments that are also thought-provoking and illuminating. . . . The artwork is well matched to the tone of the poems. Cimatoribus's illustrations are at the same time childlike and surreal." SLJ

Carroll, Lewis, 1832-1898

★ **Jabberwocky**; the classic poem from Lewis Carroll's Through the looking glass, and what Alice found there. reimagined and illustrated by Chistopher Myers. 1st ed. Jump at the Sun/Hyperion Books for Children 2007 1 v. (unpaged) col. ill. $15.99

Grades: 4 5 6 7 **821**

1. Nonsense verses 2. Children's poetry 3. Poetry --

By individual authors

ISBN 978-1-4231-0372-1; 1-4231-0372-6

LC 2007018337

This reinterpretation of Lewis Carroll's poem about the Jabberwock uses a basketball court as setting. "Ages five to nine." N Y Times Book Rev

"Myers cleverly translates Carroll's nonsense poem into a contemporary tale through sports imagery. . . . The spectacular paintings have silhouetted figures on vibrant backgrounds. . . . The jaunty text is in capital letters in an extra-large black font, with some words highlighted in color." SLJ

Classic poetry; an illustrated collection. selected by Michael Rosen; pictures by Paul Howard. Candlewick Press 1998 160p il $21.99; pa $12.99

Grades: 7 8 9 10 **821**

1. Poetry -- Collections

ISBN 978-1-56402-890-7; 1-56402-890-9; 978-0-7636-4210-5 pa; 0-7636-4210-X pa

LC 98-18282

A collection of favorite poems by such writers as William Shakespeare, Emily Dickinson, Edward Lear, Walt Whitman, and Langston Hughes, with portraits of the poets, brief biographical background, and illustrations

"This handsome edition introduces major poets through works accessible to young people. Each section begins with a portrait of the author and a short summary of his or her life, followed by one or two poems or parts of poems. Each spread includes at least one illustration evocative of the tone of the poetry as well as the times of the poet. . . . Illustrator Paul Howard's gifts are not diminished by the smaller size of some pictures, for some of his best work here is in miniature. . . . Few anthologies for this age group include such a fine selection of works from beyond the childhood classics, introduce the poets so vividly, or provide such a rich collection of haunting illustrations." Booklist

Cohen, Barbara

★ **Canterbury** tales; [by] Geoffrey Chaucer; selected, translated, and adapted by Barbara Cohen; illustrated by Trina Schart Hyman. Lothrop, Lee & Shepard Bks. 1988 87p il $24.99

Grades: 4 5 6 7 **821**

1. Poets 2. Authors 3. Middle Ages 4. Poetry -- By individual authors

ISBN 0-688-06201-6

LC 86-21045

"Cohen's evident love and respect for Chaucer's writing keep her close to the text. Her writing retains the flavor of the times and the spirit of Chaucer's words while her prose retelling, enriched by Hyman's lively full-color paintings, enhances the book's appeal to young people. . . . An excellent introduction to The Canterbury Tales for young readers." Booklist

Coleridge, Samuel Taylor

Samuel Taylor Coleridge; edited by James Engell; illustrated by Harvey Chan. Sterling 2003 48p il (Poetry for young people) $14.95

Grades: 7 8 9 10 **821**

1. English poetry 2. Children's poetry, English 3.

Poetry -- By individual authors
ISBN 0-8069-6951-2

LC 2003-6549

Introduces the life of author Samuel Taylor Coleridge and presents a sample of his poetry, including complete works and excerpts, with a brief, explanatory introduction to each

"Chan's enchanting paintings embellish the text and do a nice job of capturing the mood of the poetry without dominating it. . . . A useful purchase for any collection." SLJ

The **Kingfisher** book of funny poems; selected by Roger McGough; illustrated by Caroline Holden. Kingfisher (NY) 2002 256p il $18.95

Grades: 4 5 6 7   **821**

1. English poetry 2. American poetry 3. Humorous poetry 4. Humorous poetry, English 5. Humorous poetry, American 6. Children's poetry, English 7. Children's poetry, American 8. English poetry -- Collections 9. American poetry -- Collections
ISBN 0-7534-5480-7

LC 2001-38942

A collection of over 200 poems, limericks, and verses from such authors as Emily Dickinson, Lewis Carroll, and Shel Silverstein

"This collection is chock-full of wacky, witty, and whimsical poems that will hook readers from the first stanza to the last. . . . What really brings out the humor are the equally zany black-and-white drawings that appear on almost every page." SLJ

Kipling, Rudyard, 1865-1936

If; a father's advice to his son. [by] Rudyard Kipling; photographs by Charles R. Smith. Atheneum Books for Young Readers 2007 un il $14.99

Grades: 4 5 6   **821**

1. Poetry -- By individual authors
ISBN 978-0-689-87799-5; 0-689-87799-4

LC 2006005312

"Kipling's powerful poem comes to life for a contemporary audience in atmospheric photographs that use the metaphor of sports. A lovely shot of a boy heading a soccer ball accompanies the opening couplet: 'If you can keep your head/when all about you/are losing theirs/and blaming it on you.' The mood and actions in most of the illustrations clearly invoke the verse." SLJ

Lear, Edward

The **owl** and the pussycat; illustrations by Stephane Jorisch. KCP Poetry 2007 un il (Visions in poetry) $16.95; pa $9.95

Grades: 5 6 7 8   **821**

1. Nonsense verses 2. Cats -- Poetry 3. Owls -- Poetry 4. Poetry -- By individual authors
ISBN 978-1-55337-828-0; 1-55337-828-8; 978-1-55453-232-2 pa; 1-55453-232-9 pa

"This striking entry in an aptly named series envisions a darker subtext to Lear's well-known poem. Jorisch consulted Lear's own drawings when preparing his winsome watercolor and ink illustrations, noting the melancholy quality of the title characters. The light verse is transformed by the artist's vision into a mismatched couple seeking a place

of acceptance. . . . For older readers, this book shows true artistic vision and a great example of the power of personal interpretation and inspiration." SLJ

Love and longing; a collection of classic poetry and prose. introduced by Jacqueline Wilson; edited by Kate Agnew. Totem 2011 128p pa $9.95

Grades: 8 9 10 11 12   **821**

1. Love poetry 2. English poetry -- Collections
ISBN 978-1-840-46523-5; 1-840-46523-9

First published 2004 in the United Kingdom

This collection "features love poems and prose excerpts by writers including Sappho, Shakespeare, Milton, the Brontës, and Wordsworth. Works are loosely arranged according to chapter headings drawn from particular poems. . . . creating an engaging interchange of images and ideas. . . . This is a resonant sampling of both standards and lesser-known gems." Publ Wkly

Noyes, Alfred

The **highwayman**; [by] Alfred Noyes; with illustrations by Murray Kimber. Kids Can Press 2005 un il (Visions in poetry) $17.95

Grades: 7 8 9 10   **821**

1. Thieves -- Poetry 2. Poetry -- By individual authors
ISBN 978-1-55337-425-1; 1-55337-425-8

"Painting in an art deco style and film noir palette, Kimber casts a motorcycle-riding rebel as the highwayman; a curvaceous glamour girl as Bess; and tommy-gun toting cops as the soldiers who intrude upon the lovers' tryst. . . . The dramatic artwork plays up the elements teens will find most rewarding—particularly the protagonists' defiance of authority and the unblushingly melodramatic conclusion." Booklist

Tennyson, Alfred Tennyson

The **Lady** of Shalott; illustrated by Geneviève Côté. Kids Can Press 2005 un il (Visions in poetry) $16.95

Grades: 7 8 9 10   **821**

1. Arthurian romances 2. Poetry -- By individual authors
ISBN 978-1-55337-874-7; 1-55337-874-1

"The pictures in this small book bring an early-twentieth-century urban setting to Tennyson's classic Arthurian poem, written in 1842, about a young woman imprisoned in a tower, endlessly weaving what she sees in the mirror, until she dares to break free and look outside. . . . Cote's quiet line-and-watercolor and pastel artwork opens up the story, preserving the romance and mystery without filling in too much." Booklist

Williams, Marcia

★ **Chaucer's** Canterbury Tales; retold and illustrated by Marcia Williams. Candlewick Press 2007 45p il $16.99

Grades: 4 5 6 7   **821**

1. Poets 2. Authors 3. Middle Ages 4. Poetry -- By individual authors
ISBN 978-0-7636-3197-0; 0-7636-3197-3

A retelling in comic strip form of Geoffrey Chaucer's famous work in which a group of pilgrims in fourteenth-century England tell each other stories as they travel on a pilgrimage to the cathedral at Canterbury

"Chaucer's pilgrims come to life in the energetic retelling of nine tales. . . . The watercolor-and-ink cartoon-art displayed in a comic-book format is a perfect match for the raucous and sometimes-raw humor." SLJ

Wordsworth, William

William Wordsworth; edited by Alan Liu; illustrated by James Muir. Sterling 2003 48p il (Poetry for young people) $14.95

Grades: 7 8 9 10   **821**
1. English poetry 2. Children's poetry, English 3. Poetry -- By individual authors
ISBN 0-8069-8277-2

LC 2003-6163

An illustrated collection of nineteen popular poems by William Wordsworth, who was the poet laureate of England in the mid-nineteenth century. Includes an introduction to the poet's life and work

The editor has "chosen well, bringing together about 20 of [the] great poet's most accessible, compelling poems. . . . The full color paintings on each page are beautiful." Booklist

822   English drama

Christie, Agatha

The **mousetrap** and other plays. New American Library 2000 742p hardcover o.p. pa $7.99

Grades: 7 8 9 10 11 12 Adult   **822**
1. English drama -- Collections
ISBN 0-451-20118-3; 0-451-20114-0 pa

LC 00-64727

First published 1978 by Dodd, Mead

"The noted mystery writer composed adaptations of seven novels and stories into arresting plays as well as creating one original theater piece ('Verdict'). . . . All are as delightful to read for pleasure as Christie's mystery novels, especially since some that earlier appeared in the latter form have been intriguingly altered." Booklist

822.3   Drama of Elizabethan period, 1558-1625

Coville, Bruce

William Shakespeare's A midsummer night's dream. Dial Bks. 1996 un $17.95; pa $7.99

Grades: 5 6 7 8 9   **822.3**
1. Poets 2. Authors 3. Audiobooks 4. Dramatists
ISBN 0-8037-1784-9; 0-14-250168-9 pa

LC 94-12600

A simplified prose retelling of Shakespeare's play about the strange events that take place in a forest inhabited by fairies who magically transform the romantic fate of two young couples.

"Coville introduces the story and also conveys something of the poetry and drama. Nolan's framed graphite and watercolor paintings express the dreaminess and absurdity of the play, and the pictures have a theatrical flair." Booklist

William Shakespeare's Romeo and Juliet; retold by Bruce Coville; pictures by Dennis Nolan. Dial Bks. 1999 un il $16.99

Grades: 5 6 7 8 9   **822.3**
1. Poets 2. Authors 3. Dramatists 4. Verona (Italy) -- fiction 5. Romeo (Fictitious character) -- fiction 6. Juliet (Fictitious character) -- fiction
ISBN 0-8037-2462-4

LC 98-36178

A simplified prose retelling of Shakespeare's play about two young people who defy their warring families' prejudices and dare to fall in love

"Coville's treatment is generally faithful to the original and is nicely enhanced by Dennis Nolan's lushly romantic illustrations. . . . This is an accessible and enticing introduction to one of Shakespeare's most popular works." Booklist

Garfield, Leon

Shakespeare stories [I]-II; illustrated by Michael Foreman. Houghton Mifflin 1991 2v il hardcover o.p. v1 pa $19.95; v2 pa $17

Grades: 7 8 9 10 11 12   **822.3**
1. Poets 2. Authors 3. Dramatists
ISBN 0-395-56397-6 v1; 0-395-86140-3 v1 pa; 0-395-70893-1 v2; 0-395-89109-4 v2 pa
Original volume first published 1985 by Schocken Bks.

In these volumes Garfield has rewritten twenty-one of Shakespeare's plays in narrative form, retaining much of the original language

Krueger, Susan Heidi

The **tempest**; [by] Susan H. Krueger; introduction by Joseph Sobran. Marshall Cavendish Benchmark 2009 127p il (Shakespeare explained) lib bdg $29.93

Grades: 7 8 9 10 11 12   **822.3**
1. Poets 2. Authors 3. Dramatists
ISBN 978-0-7614-3423-8; 0-7614-3423-2

LC 2009-2587

This book offers an "engaging [introduction] to the Bard's work. . . . Krueger's lively, opinionated, and knowledgeable analysis of the complex play . . . will easily draw students into further discussion." Booklist

Includes glossary and bibliographical references

McDermott, Kristen

William Shakespeare; his life and times. [by] Kristen McDermott, and Ari Berk; including extracts from the works of William Shakespeare. Candlewick Press 2010 un il $19.99

Grades: 6 7 8 9   **822.3**
1. Poets 2. Authors 3. Dramatists
ISBN 978-0-7636-4794-0; 0-7636-4794-2

"This fictionalized amalgamation of original and secondary source materials is presented with panache. . . . The authors succinctly sum up Shakespeare's life and works with the help of snippets from his plays. Contemporaneous images and literary excerpts, in addition to pop-ups, foldouts, and removable letters, help set the scene for readers." Horn Book Guide

McKeown, Adam

Julius Caesar; a retelling by Adam McKeown; illustrated by Janet Hamlin. Sterling Pub. Co. 2008 80p il (Young reader's Shakespeare) $14.95

Grades: 6 7 8 9   **822.3**
1. Poets 2. Authors 3. Statesmen 4. Dramatists 5. Historians
ISBN 978-1-4027-3579-0; 1-4027-3579-0
LC 2007030733

"This handsomely illustrated retelling . . . stays true both to the rousing action of [Shakespeare's] play and to the characters' inner conflicts. McKeown's clear, stimulating introduction raises the complex moral issues. . . . Hamlin's dramatic, full-color art . . . ably captures the personal torment as well as the dynamics of the battlefield." Booklist

Mussari, Mark

Othello; [by] Mark Mussari; introduction by Joseph Sobran. Marshall Cavendish Benchmark 2009 111p il (Shakespeare explained) lib bdg $29.95

Grades: 7 8 9 10 11 12   **822.3**
1. Poets 2. Authors 3. Dramatists
ISBN 978-0-7614-3422-1; 0-7614-3422-4
LC 2008-37506

"A literary analysis of the play Othello. Includes information on the history and culture of Elizabethan England." Publisher's note

Includes glossary and bibliographical references

Nettleton, Pamela Hill

William Shakespeare; playwright and poet. by Pamela Hill Nettleton. Compass Point Books 2005 112p il map (Signature lives) lib bdg $30.60

Grades: 5 6 7 8   **822.3**
1. Poets 2. Authors 3. Dramatists
ISBN 0-7565-0816-9
LC 2004-23081

Profiles the life and work of William Shakespeare

"This biography is one of the best available for younger students. Nettleton supplements what little is actually known about the bard's life with detailed and accurate information about everyday life in England during the period, the theater, and publishing practices of the time. The text is enhanced by full-color illustrations and black-and-white reproductions." SLJ

Includes bibliographical references

Packer, Tina

★ Tales from Shakespeare; retold by Tina Packer; illustrated by Gail de Marcken . . . [et al.] Scholastic Press 2004 192p il $24.95

Grades: 5 6 7 8   **822.3**
1. Poets 2. Authors 3. Dramatists
ISBN 0-439-32107-7
LC 2003-42710

Tina Packer retells ten of Shakespeare's plays. The stories are illustrated by various artists: Macbeth by Barry Moser, The Tempest by Mark Teague, Othello by Kadir Nelson,

Twelfth Night by Chesley McLaren, Romeo and Juliet by David Shannon, Much Ado About Nothing by Mary Grand-Pre, King Lear by Leo and Diane Dillon, As You Like It by Barbara McClintock, A Midsummer Night's Dream by Gail De Marcken, and Hamlet by P.J. Lynch

This is "a treasure trove of well-told tales. In these adaptations, Packer captures the essence of the playwright's words and ideas, placing them in concise and clearly told stories. . . . Each illustrator sets the appropriate tone for and conveys the mood of the tale, and the breadth of artistic interpretations gives the book appeal to a wide audience." SLJ

Raum, Elizabeth

Twenty-first-century Shakespeare. Raintree 2011 32p il (Culture in action) lib bdg $29

Grades: 5 6 7 8   **822.3**
1. Poets 2. Authors 3. Dramatists 4. Dramatists, English 5. Authors, English
ISBN 978-1-4109-3920-3; 1-4109-3920-0
LC 2009050693

This "discusses modern adaptations of the Bard's classic works; teachers may find this a useful resource to help students see how Shakespeare remains a part of today's culture. [This volume is] quick, interesting, up-to-date . . . with plenty of supportive, captioned, full-color photographs. [It] also [provides] related project suggestions." SLJ

Includes glossary and bibliographical references

Shakespeare, William, 1564-1616

One hundred and eleven Shakespeare monologues; the ultimate audition book for teens. edited by Lisa Bansavage and L. E. McCullough; introduction by Jill K. Swanson. Smith & Kraus 2003 176p (Young actors series) pa $11.95

Grades: 7 8 9 10 11 12   **822.3**
1. Acting 2. Monologues
ISBN 1-57525-356-9

"These monologues are divided into three sections: those for female actors, male actors, or either. They are further subdivided into comedies, histories, and tragedies. . . . The genius of this book is in the introduction, which offers a wealth of information for teens who have never encountered Shakespeare." SLJ

Sobran, Joseph

A midsummer night's dream; Joseph Sobran. Marshall Cavendish Benchmark 2008 111p. ill. (some col.) lib bdg $29.95

Grades: 7 8 9 10 11 12   **822.3**
1. Poets 2. Authors 3. Dramatists
ISBN 978-0-7614-3030-8; 0-7614-3030-X
LC 2008007079

"A literary analysis of the play A Midsummer Night's Dream. Includes information on the history and culture of Elizabethan England." Publisher's note

"[This book] provides practical information, skillfully presented, making the complexities of Shakespearean theater accessible to present-day students. [The] author's contagious enthusiasm and attractive presentation make [it] imminently useful for high school and public libraries."

Includes glossary and bibliographical references

Stanley, Diane

★ **Bard** of Avon: the story of William Shakespeare; by Diane Stanley and Peter Vennema; illustrated by Diane Stanley. Morrow Junior Bks. 1992 un il hardcover o.p. pa $6.99

Grades: 4 5 6 7   **822.3**

1. Poets 2. Authors 3. Dramatists

ISBN 0-688-09108-3; 0-688-09109-1 lib bdg; 0-688-16294-0 pa

LC 90-46564

A brief biography of the world's most famous playwright, using only historically correct information

"A remarkably rounded picture of Shakespeare's life and the period in which he lived is presented . . . together with a thoughtful attempt to relate circumstances in his personal life to the content of his plays. . . . The text is splendidly supported by the illustrations, which are stylized, yet recognizable, and present a clear view of life in the late sixteenth century. A discerning, knowledgeable biography, rising far above the ordinary." Horn Book

Includes bibliographical references

823   English fiction

Beahm, George W.

Discovering The golden compass; a guide to Philip Pullman's Dark Materials. [by] George Beahm; art by Tim Kirk. Hampton Roads Pub. Co. 2007 xxiv, 206p il $16.95

Grades: 7 8 9 10 11 12   **823**

1. Authors 2. Novelists 3. Fantasy writers 4. Young adult authors

ISBN 978-1-57174-506-4

LC 2007020694

"This accessible guide to the author and His Dark Materials trilogy is the perfect passport to Pullman's imaginative universe. Fans will appreciate the information provided about the author and his world in all formats: books, . . . plays, audiobooks, and the upcoming movie. . . . Fascinating and well-written." Voice Youth Advocates

Includes bibliographical references

Colbert, David

The **magical** worlds of Harry Potter; David Colbert. Updated and complete ed. Berkley Books 2008 xi, 209 p.p ill. (paperback) $14.00

Grades: 5 6 7 8   **823**

1. Authors 2. Novelists 3. Fantasy writers 4. Children's authors 5. Young adult authors 6. Fantasy fiction -- History and criticism

ISBN 0425223183; 9780425223185

LC 2008274096

First published 2001 in the United Kingdom; first United States edition 2002

Explores the sources and meanings of aspects of the literary world of Harry Potter within myths, legends, and history.

"Long after the enthusiasm for Harry and friends has abated, this small volume will serve as a resource to answer questions that may result from reading other stories in the genre." SLJ [review of 2002 edition]

Includes bibliographical references (p. 317-318) and index.

Cooling, Wendy

D is for Dahl; a gloriumptious A-Z guide to the world of Roald Dahl. illustrations by Quentin Blake; compiled by Wendy Cooling. Viking 2005 149p il hardcover o.p. pa $5.99

Grades: 4 5 6 7   **823**

1. Authors 2. Authors, English 3. Children's authors 4. Short story writers

ISBN 0-670-06023-2; 0-14-240934-0 pa

This is an alphabetically arranged collection of facts about the life and work of the popular author of children's books

"This dictionary-of-sorts is entertaining, insightful, and of particular interest to Dahl's fans. . . . The writing is clear, wicked, and fun. An occasional black-and-white photograph complements Blake's illustrations." SLJ

Gribbin, Mary

The **science** of Philip Pullman's His Dark Materials; [by] Mary and John Gribbon; with an introduction by Philip Pullman. Knopf 2005 203p il $15.95; lib bdg $17.99; pa $5.99

Grades: 6 7 8 9   **823**

1. Authors 2. Science 3. Novelists 4. Fantasy writers 5. Young adult authors 6. Science

ISBN 0-375-83144-4; 0-375-93144-9 lib bdg; 0-375-83146-0 pa

LC 2004-57731

"The Gribbins show how concepts are the real magic of Pullman's trilogy. Each chapter begins with a quote drawn from the books, which leads to an elegantly written explanation of the science. . . . The authors do an amazing job teasing an introduction to string theory from Will's 'subtle knife.' . . . Naturally, fans of the series will be the best audience, but the book offers much to readers simply interested in the advanced sciences, who then may be led back to His Dark Materials." Booklist

Jones, Diana Wynne, 1934-2011

Reflections; on the magic of writing. by Diana Wynne Jones. Greenwillow Books 2012 368 p. (hardback) $24.99

Grades: 7 8 9 10 11 12   **823**

1. Fantasy fiction -- Authorship 2. Children's stories -- Authorship 3. BIOGRAPHY & AUTOBIOGRAPHY -- Women 4. BIOGRAPHY & AUTOBIOGRAPHY -- Literary 5. BIOGRAPHY & AUTOBIOGRAPHY -- Personal Memoirs

ISBN 0062219898; 9780062219893

LC 2012018080

This book, by Diana Wynne Jones, was arranged "after being informed that she had terminal cancer in 2010." It "pull[s] together" a "group of essays, lectures, and articles . . . about writing fantasy for children. . . . The selected pieces are thematically arranged, beginning with . . . a contemplative piece about watching children at play that sets the stage for her subsequent arguments regarding the importance of imagination and creativity." (Bulletin of the Center for Children's Books)

Includes bibliographical references and index

Latham, Don

David Almond; memory and magic. Scarecrow Press 2006 151p (Scarecrow studies in young adult literature) $40

Grades: 7 8 9 10 11 12 Adult Professional   **823**

1. Authors 2. Fantasy 3. Novelists 4. Short story writers 5. Young adult authors 6. Children's literature -- Authors and illustrators

ISBN 978-0-8108-5500-7; 0-8108-5500-3

LC 2006002300

This "explores the writings of the critically acclaimed YA author best known for Skellig . . . and Kit's Wilderness. . . . After a brief biography and thematic overview, Latham addresses Almond's published works one by one. . . . Weaving his explorations almost as seamlessly as Almond wove the original stories, Latham clearly illustrates the novels' inherent depth and teachability." Voice Youth Advocates

Includes bibliographical references

Nardo, Don

Understanding Frankenstein. Lucent Bks. 2003 128p il (Understanding great literature) lib bdg $27.45

Grades: 7 8 9 10   **823**

1. Authors 2. Novelists 3. Frankenstein (Fictitious character)

ISBN 1-59018-147-6

LC 2002-12560

Discusses Mary Shelley's sources of ideas for the compelling plot, well-developed characters, and universal themes of "Frankenstein" which have led to its enduring popularity.

"The text is easy to understand. A solid introduction for middle school students." SLJ

Includes bibliographical references

Pascal, Janet B.

Arthur Conan Doyle; beyond Baker Street. Oxford Univ. Press 1999 158p il (Oxford portraits) $28

Grades: 7 8 9 10   **823**

1. Authors 2. Novelists 3. Authors, Scottish 4. Mystery writers 5. Holmes, Sherlock (Fictitious character) 6. Physicians -- Great Britain -- Biography 7. Detective and mystery stories -- Authorship 8. Spiritualists -- Great Britain -- Biography 9. Authors, Scottish -- 19th century -- Biography

ISBN 0-19-512262-3

LC 99-36643

"Pascal does a fine job of conveying the era in which her object lived." SLJ

Includes bibliographical references

Reef, Catherine

★ The **Bronte** sisters; the brief lives of Charlotte, Emily and Anne. by Catherine Reef. Clarion Books 2012 240 p. ill. (hardcover) $18.99

Grades: 7 8 9 10   **823**

1. Bronte family 2. Women authors -- Biography 3. Women authors, English -- Biography 4. Sisters -- England -- Yorkshire -- Biography 5. Authors, English -- 19th century -- Biography

ISBN 0547579667; 9780547579665

LC 2011043559

"This collective biography of the Brontë family fills in . . . detail of their personal and public lives: what they wrote, their family stories as a minister's unmarried daughters, how they published under men's names, and how their groundbreaking novels were received at a time when women were expected to 'stay home and be quiet.'" (Booklist)

"A solid and captivating look at these remarkable pioneers of modern fiction." Kirkus

Includes bibliographical references (p. 212-217) and index.

Shea, George

A **reader's** guide to Chinua Achebe's Things fall apart; [by] George Shea. Enslow Publishers 2008 128p il (Multicultural literature) lib bdg $31.93

Grades: 7 8 9 10   **823**

1. Poets 2. Authors 3. Novelists 4. Essayists 5. Short story writers

ISBN 978-0-7660-2831-9 lib bdg; 0-7660-2831-3 lib bdg

LC 2006038486

"Shea explores why many consider the book to be the greatest African novel ever written. . . . Extensive back matter includes a chronology, glossary, chapter notes, and a bibliography of books and Web sites." Booklist

Includes glossary and bibliographical references

Squires, Claire

Philip Pullman, master storyteller; a guide to the worlds of His Dark Materials. Continuum 2006 214p $60; pa $14.95

Grades: 8 9 10 11 12   **823**

1. Authors 2. Novelists 3. Fantasy writers 4. Young adult authors

ISBN 978-0-8264-2764-9; 0-8264-2764-2; 978-0-8264-1716-9 pa; 0-8264-1716-7 pa

LC 2006019766

A comprehensive study of Philip Pullman, with focus on the contexts, sources, influences and controversies of the his Dark Materials trilogy.

"Squires does not shy away from the controversy that Pullman's themes have stirred up. . . . [This is an] accessible study." SLJ

Includes bibliographical references

Wells-Cole, Catherine

Charles Dickens; England's most captivating storyteller. written by Catherine Wells-Cole; including extracts from the works of Charles Dickens. 1st U.S. ed. Candlewick/Templar Books 2011 28 p. ill., maps (some col.) (Historical notebook) (hardcover) $19.99

Grades: 7 8 9 10 11 12 **823**
1. Authors 2. Novelists 3. Authors, English
ISBN 0763655678; 9780763655679

LC 2011013677

This book by Catherine Wells-Cole "provides a . . . glimpse into the life" of author Charles Dickens. "Like a scrapbook, the book includes excerpts from Dickens' personal letters, illustrations from his original books, family photos, and other images from the Victorian age. . . . Double-page spreads focus on Dickens' childhood, family life, and fame. Other spreads focus on topics that influenced his writing, including schools, prisons, and workhouses." (Library Media Connection)

"In this scrapbook homage to Dickens, each page teems with images and reproductions, from letters to book excerpts to maps, all pertaining to a different area of Dickens's life and work. The topics range widely, skimming the surface of both the esteemed author's life and the subjects that interested him most. . . . The gorgeous, high-quality reproductions make a strong visual impact, and while the flaps, folds, and envelopes make readers work to uncover information, most will be quickly drawn into the hunt for more treasured tidbits about Dickens and his time." SLJ

828 English miscellaneous writings

Jones, Diana Wynne
★ The **tough** guide to Fantasyland; rev and updated ed.; Firebird 2006 234p pa $9.99
Grades: 8 9 10 11 12 **828**
1. Fantasy fiction
ISBN 0-14-240722-4

LC 2006041153

First published 1996

This "book contains alphabetical entries for people, places, and events in a fantasy world and information on how travelers can best find their way to the epic final battle. Icons conveniently identify lodging, food, and other necessary elements that travelers will need in their journey. . . . This brilliantly written satire perfectly celebrates and skewers the clichés of the fantasy genre." Voice Youth Advocates

Means, A. L.
A **student's** guide to George Orwell. Enslow Pubs. 2005 176p il (Understanding literature) lib bdg $27.93
Grades: 7 8 9 10 **828**
1. Authors 2. Novelists 3. Essayists
ISBN 0-7660-2433-4
An introduction to the life and work of the author of 1984, Animal Farm and other works
Includes glossary and bibliographical references

Neimark, Anne E.
Myth maker: J.R.R. Tolkien; illustrated by Brad Weinman. Harcourt Brace & Co. 1996 118p il rpt $12.99

828
1. Authors 2. Novelists 3. Linguists 4. Philologists 5. Fantasy writers 6. Authors, English 7. Children's

authors
ISBN 0-15-298847-5; 9780547997346 rpt

LC 96-4196

Follows the life and work of the renowned fantasy writer, creator of hobbits and Middle Earth and "The Lord of the Rings."

843 French fiction

Schoell, William
Remarkable journeys: the story of Jules Verne. Morgan Reynolds 2002 112p il (World writers) lib bdg $21.95

843
1. Authors 2. Novelists 3. Authors, French 4. Children's authors 5. Science fiction writers 6. Authors, French -- 19th century -- Biography
ISBN 1-88384-692-7

LC 2002-2016

A biography of the nineteenth-century Frenchman whose childhood love of literature, science, and adventure, along with his vivid imagination, led him to become a highly successful science fiction author

"Thanks to Schoell's smooth, crisp writing, this fascinating, approachable biography, which lends insight into Verne's eccentric characters and relatives, proves nearly as exciting as the writer's best stories." Booklist
Includes bibliographical references

860 Literatures of Spanish, Portuguese, Galician languages

★ The **Tree** is older than you are; a bilingual gathering of poems & stories from Mexico with paintings by Mexican artists. selected by Naomi Shihab Nye. Simon & Schuster Bks. for Young Readers 1995 111p il hardcover o.p. pa $13.95
Grades: 7 8 9 10 **860**
1. Mexican literature -- Collections 2. Bilingual books -- English-Spanish
ISBN 0-689-82097-8; 0-689-82087-9 pa

LC 95-1565

"This bilingual anthology of poems, stories, and paintings by Mexican writers and artists brims over with a sense of wonder and playful exuberance, its themes as varied and inventive as a child's imagination." Voice Youth Advocates

883 Classical Greek epic poetry and fiction

Homer
The **Iliad**; translated by Robert Fagles; introduction and notes by Bernard Knox. Viking 1990 683p $40; pa $15.95
Grades: 8 9 10 11 12 Adult **883**
1. Trojan War 2. Poetry -- By individual authors
ISBN 978-0-670-83510-2; 978-0-14-027536-0 pa

LC 89-70695

Homer's epic of the Trojan War.

"Fagles gives us a stark and terrible poem, an Iliad about, as its first word announces, rage. He conveys, far better than either Lattimore or Fitzgerald, the psychological experience of combat and war." Classical World

Landmann, Bimba

★ The **fate** of Achilles. Getty 2011 36p il $19.95

Grades: 4 5 6 7   **883**

  1. Poets 2. Authors

  ISBN 978-1-60606-085-8; 1-60606-085-6

"Landmann (The Incredible Voyage of Ulysses) continues her retelling of Homer's epics with this haunting version of the Iliad. Ghostly, Giacometti-style figures accompany the story of Achilles's life, from his baptism in the river Styx . . . to his departure for Troy, . . . the death of his dearest friend, . . . and his reconciliation with the father of the enemy he has slain. . . . Readers with the patience to sit through saga-length narratives will be fascinated by her prose, which moves easily through the sprawling epic without feeling ponderous or hurried. These kinds of retellings are few and far between, and hers are magic." Publ Wkly

The **incredible** voyage of Ulysses; text and illustrations by Bimba Landmann. Getty Publications 2010 un il $19.95

Grades: 4 5 6 7   **883**

  1. Poets 2. Authors

  ISBN 978-1-60606-012-4; 1-60606-012-0

"With narrative restraint and illustrative power, Landmann's . . . retelling of Homer's Odyssey follows Ulysses as he battles frightening creatures and endures the treachery of the gods while sailing home to Ithaca. . . . The paintings, worked with swift, bold strokes, combine the solemn stiffness of Greek statuary with the prophetic sweep of William Blake's imaginings." Publ Wkly

Lister, Robin

The **odyssey**; retold by Robin Lister; illustrated by Alan Baker. reformatted ed.; Kingfisher 2004 175p il (Kingfisher epics) pa $7.95

Grades: 5 6 7 8   **883**

  1. Poets 2. Authors 3. Odysseus (Greek mythology)

  ISBN 0-7534-5723-7

  First published 1988

A retelling of Homer's epic poem that describes the wanderings of Odysseus after the fall of Troy.

Odyssey

The **Odyssey**; translated by Robert Fagles; introduction and notes by Bernard Knox. Viking 1996 541p $35; pa $16

Grades: 8 9 10 11 12 Adult   **883**

  1. Poetry -- By individual authors

  ISBN 978-0-670-82162-4; 978-0-14-026886-7 pa

            LC 96-17280

This is a verse translation of Homer's epic poem

"Fagles' Odyssey is the one to put into the hands of younger, first-time readers, not least because of its paucity of notes, which, though sometimes frustrating, is a sign that translation has been used to do the work of explanation. Altogether, an outstanding piece of work." Booklist

  Includes bibliographical references

Osborne, Mary Pope

Return to Ithaca; with artwork by Troy Howell. Hyperion Books for Children 2004 105p (Mary Pope Osborne's Tales from the Odyssey) $9.99

Grades: 4 5 6 7   **883**

  1. Poets 2. Authors 3. Odysseus (Greek mythology)

  4. Mythology, Greek

  ISBN 0-7868-0774-1

            LC 2003-60355

Retells part of Homer's Odyssey in which Odysseus, with the help of the goddess Athena, plans to get revenge on those who have plagued his wife and son during his absence

The **gray**-eyed goddess; with artwork by Troy Howell. Hyperion Bks. for Children 2003 120p il (Mary Pope Osborne's Tales from the Odyssey) hardcover o.p. pa $4.99

Grades: 4 5 6 7   **883**

  1. Poets 2. Authors 3. Odysseus (Greek mythology)

  ISBN 0-7868-0773-3; 0-7868-0931-0 pa

Retells a part of the Odyssey in which Odysseus' wife, Penelope, and their son, Telemachus, are desperately warding off the men who want to marry her. Then a visit from a mysterious stranger gives Telemachus the courage to confront the suitors, and to search for his long-lost father

The **land** of the dead; illustrated by Troy Howell. Hyperion Bks. for Children 2002 105p il (Mary Pope Osborne's Tales from the Odyssey) $9.99; pa $4.99

Grades: 4 5 6 7   **883**

  1. Poets 2. Authors 3. Odysseus (Greek mythology)

  ISBN 0-7868-0771-7; 0-7868-0929-9 pa

            LC 2002-69078

A retelling of part of the Odyssey in which Odysseus and his fleet continue their journey and encounter giant cannibals, a beautiful witch, and the Land of the Dead

"Osborne's simple, engaging narrative will surely capture interest as it presents a great hero in bold, yet human, dimensions." Booklist

The **one**-eyed giant; with artwork by Troy Howell. Hyperion Bks. for Children 2002 105p il (Mary Pope Osborne's Tales from the Odyssey) hardcover o.p. pa $4.99

Grades: 4 5 6 7   **883**

  1. Poets 2. Authors 3. Odysseus (Greek mythology)

  ISBN 0-7868-0770-9; 0-7868-0928-0 pa

            LC 2002-68539

Retells a part of the Odyssey in which King Odysseus fights the cyclops

"In brief chapters and concise sentences, Osborne pares down . . . [this adventure] into easily absorbed, swiftly paced episodes." Publ Wkly

895.1   Chinese literature

Liu Siyu
★ A **thousand** peaks; poems from China. [by] Siyu Liu and Orel Protopopescu; illustrated by Siyu Liu. Pacific View Press 2002 52p il $19.95

Grades: 5 6 7 8 9 10   **895.1**
1. Chinese poetry 2. Bilingual books -- English-Chinese
ISBN 1-88189-624-2

LC 2001-34008

A collection of thirty-five poems spanning nineteen centuries, representing both famous and lesser-known poets, including both the Chinese text and a literal translation.

This "is an anthology of considerable fascination and broad utility. . . . The layout is neat, tidily fitting each poem's material on a single page and adding a line drawing featuring a relevant Chinese character. The wealth of material here provides a more stimulating entree to Chinese history than any dry textbook." Bull Cent Child Books

Includes bibliographical references

897   Literatures of North American native languages

★ **Dancing** teepees: poems of American Indian youth; selected by Virginia Driving Hawk Sneve, with art by Stephen Gammell. Holiday House 1989 32p il $17.95; pa $8.95

Grades: 4 5 6   **897**
1. Native Americans -- Poetry
ISBN 0-8234-0724-1; 0-8234-0879-5 pa

LC 88-11075

An illustrated collection of poems from the oral tradition of Native Americans

This is an "eclectic collection, drawn from a variety of tribal traditions. Printed on heavy paper, the book is illustrated with a catalogue of marvelously rendered designs and motifs, ranging from those of the Northwest Coast to the intricate beadwork patterns of the Great Lakes and the zigzag geometric borders of Southwestern pottery." N Y Times Book Rev

900   HISTORY

901   Philosophy and theory of history

Beller, Susan Provost
★ The **history** puzzle; how we know what we know about the past. [by] Susan Provost Beller. Twenty-First Century Books 2006 128p il lib bdg $26.60

Grades: 7 8 9 10   **901**
1. History -- Philosophy
ISBN 978-0-7613-2877-3; 0-7613-2877-7

LC 2005017745

"Beller looks at more than 20 historical sites or archaeological excavations . . . in order to present the varying interpretations of history and how they have been colored by tradition, socioeconomic factors, and religious beliefs. . . . . Frequent, well-placed sepia-toned photographs and period reproductions serve to enhance the text, and the source notes, further reading, and list of Web sites give students an ample list of resources for further study." SLJ

Includes bibliographical references

902   Miscellany of history

Hughes, Susan
Case closed? nine mysteries unlocked by modern science. written by Susan Hughes; illustrated by Michael Wandelmaier. Kids Can Press 2010 88p il map $17.95

Grades: 6 7 8 9   **902**
1. Archeology 2. Technological innovations 3. History -- Miscellanea
ISBN 978-1-55453-362-6; 1-55453-362-7

Examines how developments in modern science, such as DNA analysis and spectroscopy, have helped to re-open archaeological mysteries about ancient cities, Egypt's first female pharaoh, a missing expedition to find the Northwest Passage, and more.

"The writing is clear and engaging. The full-color illustrations are a mix of photographs, maps, and flat, animation-style art." SLJ

Includes glossary

904   Collected accounts of events

Beyer, Rick
The **greatest** stories never told; 100 tales from history to astonish, bewilder, & stupefy. HarperResource 2003 214p il $17.95

Grades: 7 8 9 10   **904**
1. History -- Miscellanea
ISBN 0-06-001401-6

LC 2004-296419

"Beginning with the year 46 B.C. and ending in 1990, Beyer presents a chronological account of one hundred unknown, partially known, and familar tales about an array of people and events that have shaped the world. . . . They range from the mundane to the fantastic. . . . Extensive research went into the production of this charming work. Primary documents in the form of letters, laws, illustrations, and photographs bring to life these unique and incredible anecdotes." Voice Youth Advocates

Includes bibliographical references

Blackwood, Gary L.
Enigmatic events. Marshall Cavendish Benchmark 2005 72p il (Unsolved history) lib bdg $29.93

Grades: 4 5 6 7   **904**
1. Disasters 2. Curiosities and wonders 3. History -- Miscellanea
ISBN 0-7614-1889-X

LC 2004-23755

Explores several events that have baffled scientists and historians for years, such as the demise of the dinosaurs, the "lost colony" of Roanoke, the sinking of the Main, and the Hindenberg disaster

This collection of "tidbits about lingering mysteries of the past . . . [offers] more substance than most. . . . [This offers] a full-page illustration opening each chapter; reproductions, many in color; and a generously spaced format." SLJ

Includes glossary and bibliographical references

Guiberson, Brenda Z.

★ **Disasters**; natural and man-made catastrophes through the centuries. Henry Holt and Company 2010 228p il $18.99

Grades: 5 6 7 8 9   **904**

1. Disasters 2. Natural disasters
ISBN 978-0-8050-8170-1; 0-8050-8170-4

LC 2009018908

"The subtitle provides an accurate outline of the contents of this lively treatment of disasters from smallpox to Hurricane Katrina. In each chapter, Guiberson outlines the sources of the disaster, the results, and means of obviating the problems that caused these tragedies. For example, the chapter on the Great Chicago Fire begins with the construction of the city over unstable marshland. . . . This kind of exhaustive background serves to create an understanding of the contributory issues and demonstrates possible preventive steps. Guiberson's compellingly written exegesis is equally good in the other nine chapters. Well-placed, black-and-white reproductions and photos extend the text. A perfect example of solid historical research coupled with engaging writing." SLJ

Includes bibliographical references

Meissner, David

Call of the Klondike; a true gold rush adventure. by David Meissner and Kim Richardson. Calkins Creek 2013 168 p. (reinforced) $16.95

Grades: 6 7 8   **904**

1. Alaska -- Gold discoveries 2. Klondike River valley (Yukon) -- Gold discoveries
ISBN 1590788230; 9781590788233

LC 2013931060

Here, the authors share the experience of two 20-something Yale graduates from 1897, Stanley Pearce and Marshall Bond, who participated in the Klondike gold rush. Their letters are offered along with "diary entries, telegrams and Pearce's articles for the Denver Republican." The book also incorporates "pull-out quotes, maps, posters, documents and many . . . captioned photographs, including one of Jack London, who camped near Pearce and Bond's cabin." Kirkus

909   World history

Adams, Simon

★ The **Kingfisher** atlas of world history; a pictorial guide to the world's people and events, 10,000 BCE-present. Kingfisher 2010 181p il map $24.99

Grades: 4 5 6 7   **909**

1. World history 2. Historical geography
ISBN 978-0-7534-6388-8; 0-7534-6388-1

"This colorful and fact-packed book is not only informative but well organized. Sections cover 'The Ancient World,' 'The Medieval World,' 'Exploration and Empire,' and 'The Modern World,' and each section contains 15 or 16 thematic maps presented in chronological order. . . . It is very useful and entertaining as well as data-filled." Booklist

Badcott, Nicholas

Pocket timeline of Islamic civilizations. Interlink 2009 32p il $13.95

Grades: 7 8 9 10   **909**

1. Reference books 2. Islamic civilization -- Chronology
ISBN 978-1-56656-758-9; 1-56656-758-0

"Badcott takes readers on a colorful and captivating tour of Islamic civilizations from the 7th to the 20th century. He discusses the rise and fall of dynasties, along with their achievements and contributions in art, medicine, architecture, commerce, and science. . . . The writing style is easy to read. . . . Attractive color photographs of buildings, pottery, jewelry, art, and inventions help maintain readers' interest throughout." SLJ

Includes bibliographical references

Eamer, Claire

Traitors' Gate and other doorways to the past. Annick Press 2008 154p il $24.95; pa $12.95

Grades: 6 7 8 9   **909**

1. Doorways 2. World history
ISBN 978-1-55451-145-7; 1-55451-145-3; 978-1-55451-144-0 pa; 1-55451-144-5 pa

"Eamer uses the concrete image of doorways to introduce famous (and not-so-famous) structures. She begins with perhaps the most amazing one, located in Petra, Jordan. Al-Khazner is hidden in a sandstone cliff. . . . Among the other structures discussed are Cape Coast Castle in Ghana, through whose doorway Africans were led to slave ships; the six doors of the Kremlin's Holy Antechamber; . . . and Spruce Tree House, an ancient cliff house in Colorado. . . . The many photographs are nicely reproduced, and Eamer's text is always solid and sometimes soars." Booklist

Includes bibliographical references

Hinds, Kathryn, 1962-

★ The **city**; by Kathryn Hinds. Marshall Cavendish Benchmark 2008 96 p. col. ill., maps (library) $8.66

Grades: 6 7 8 9 10   **909**

1. Middle Ages 2. City and town life 3. Medieval civilization
ISBN 076143089X; 9780761430896

LC 2008019432

"A social history of the Islamic world from the eighth through the mid-thirteenth century, with a focus on life in the cities" Publisher's note

Includes bibliographical references and index.

★ The **countryside**; by Kathryn Hinds. Marshall Cavendish Benchmark 2008 95 p. col. ill. (library) $8.66

Grades: 6 7 8 9 10   **909**

1. Deserts 2. Middle Ages 3. Country life 4. Medieval

civilization
ISBN 0761430911; 9780761430919

LC 2008019266

"Presents a social history of the Islamic world from the eighth through the mid-thirteenth century, with a focus on life in the desert and countryside." Publisher's note

Includes bibliographical references

Moore, Christopher, 1957-

From then to now; a short history of the world. illustrated by Andrej Krystoforski. Tundra Books 2011 188p il map $25.95

Grades: 7 8 9 10 **909**

1. World history 2. Civilization -- History
ISBN 978-0-88776-540-7; 0-88776-540-8

"Capably told and uniquely illustrated, From Then to Now explains how imaginative human cultures have produced an intellectually and socially dynamic world. The work follows the course of human history from hunter-gatherer beginnings, through expansion and contact, to a modern, tightly interconnected global world. Along the way, Moore tackles how humanity, through agricultural and industrial innovations, has shaped and been shaped by environmental obstacles. Full-color spot art appears occasionally, and color sidebars provide information on a number of subjects. . . . This exceptional history of humanity is a breath of fresh air." SLJ

Morris, Neil

Beyond Europe; [by] Neil Morris and John Malam. Zak Books 2009 48p il map (History of the world) lib bdg $34.25

Grades: 7 8 9 10 **909**

1. Middle Ages 2. Medieval civilization
ISBN 978-88-6098-151-6 lib bdg; 88-6098-151-4 lib bdg

LC 2008-8406

The "effectiveness lies in the combination of lush illustrations, well-chosen, captioned photographs of contemporary artifacts, and . . . [a] reasoned, concise [narrative]. Succinct time lines border most pages, and . . . the proper amount of white space, and clear dark print maintain organization and clarity. A superior choice." SLJ

Includes glossary

Smith, Tom

Discovery of the Americas, 1492-1800; rev ed.; Chelsea House 2010 134p il map (Discovery and exploration) lib bdg $35

Grades: 7 8 9 10 11 **909**

1. Explorers
ISBN 978-1-60413-195-6; 1-60413-195-0

LC 2009-22330

First published 2005

"The chapters are well-illustrated with color and black and white historic photos, illustrations and maps. Chapter layout is clearly organized with helpful subtitles; sidebars develop related themes in eye-catching colors." Libr Media Connect

Includes glossary and bibliographical references

Technology in world history; W. Bernard Carlson, editor. Oxford University Press 2005 7v il maps set $299

Grades: 7 8 9 10 **909**

1. Reference books 2. Technology and civilization
ISBN 0-19-521820-5; 978-0-19-521820-6

LC 2003-55300

"Seeking to explore how people have used technology to shape societies, Carlson and 10 other scholars examine the distinctive development and effects of technology in 18 cultures—defined either geographically (Pacific Peoples, Sub-Saharan Africa) or by historical period (Stone Age, The World Since 1970)." SLJ

Includes bibliographical references

909.07   General historical periods

Currie, Stephen

The **Medieval** crusades; by Stephen Currie. Lucent Books 2009 96 p. ill. (chiefly col.), col. map (library) $34.95

Grades: 6 7 8 9 **909.07**

1. Middle Ages 2. Crusades 3. Civilization, Medieval
ISBN 1420500627; 9781420500622

LC 2008046532

This book by Stephen Currie is part of the World History series and looks at the medieval crusades. It "begins with an explanation of early Christendom and Islam and the schisms that existed within each religion. . . . The focus of the book falls on the long-term effects of the Crusades, creating European awareness of other countries and cultures that led to increased commerce and trade, which in turn led to the Age of Exploration and the Renaissance." (Voice of Youth Advocates)

Includes bibliographical references and index.

Hinds, Kathryn, 1962-

★ The **palace**; [by] Kathryn Hinds. Marshall Cavendish Benchmark 2008 96p il map (Life in the Medieval Muslim world) lib bdg $23.95

Grades: 6 7 8 9 10 **909.07**

1. Middle Ages 2. Medieval civilization 3. Elite (Social sciences)
ISBN 978-0-7614-3088-9 lib bdg; 0-7614-3088-1 lib bdg

LC 2008010734

"Richly illustrated with art reproductions, maps, photos, and ornate Islamic border designs, [this] . . . will entice visual learners." Libr Media Connect

Includes glossary and bibliographical references

Knight, Judson

Middle ages: almanac; edited by Judy Galens. U.X.L 2001 lxv, 226p il map (Middle Ages reference library) $60

Grades: 8 9 10 11 12 **909.07**

1. Middle Ages 2. World history 3. Reference books 4. Medieval civilization
ISBN 0-7876-4856-6

LC 00-59442

This reference's 19 chapters review world history from the fall of the Roman Empire in 500 A.D. to the beginning of the Renaissance in 1500 A.D.

"The volume's strength is its broad coverage; it includes material on India, Southeast Asia, China, Japan, the Americas, and Africa as well as Europe and the Middle East, making it unique among other books for this age group." SLJ

Includes bibliographical references

Middle ages: primary sources; [compiled by] Judson Knight; Judy Galens, editor. U.X.L 2000 xxxiv, 161p il (Middle Ages reference library) $60
Grades: 8 9 10 11 12   **909.07**
1. Middle Ages 2. Middle Ages -- History -- Sources
ISBN 0-7876-4860-4

LC 00-59441

This volume contains "19 full or excerpted documents written during this period, including the work of celebrated writers such as St. Augustine, Marco Polo, and Dante as well as less familiar individuals such as Anna Comnena and Lo Kuan-chung. Each selection is placed in its historical context and followed by a section entitled 'What happened next'.... Unfamiliar words or terms are defined in sidebars. Each entry has a box profiling the author of the documents and at least two illustrations." Booklist

Includes bibliographical references

909.08   Modern history, 1450/1500-

Huff, Toby E.
★ An **age** of science and revolutions, 1600-1800; [by] Toby Huff. Oxford University Press 2005 173p il map (Medieval & early modern world) lib bdg $32.95
Grades: 7 8 9 10   **909.08**
1. World history -- 17th century 2. World history -- 18th century
ISBN 0-19-517724-X

LC 2004-21612

This volume "looks at 200 years of world history.... [It includes] overview chapters on China, India, and the Middle East . . . [and] discusses the Enlightenment in Europe in some depth. . . . [This is a] useful book, which may spark discussion about current controversies about connections between science and religion." Booklist

Includes bibliographical references

Wiesner, Merry E.
★ An **age** of voyages, 1350-1600; [by] Merry E. Wiesner-Hanks. Oxford University Press 2005 189p il map (Medieval & early modern world) $32.95
Grades: 7 8 9 10   **909.08**
1. Middle Ages 2. World history -- 16th century
ISBN 0-19-517672-3; 978-0-19-517672-8

LC 2004021178

"In accessible language supported by prolific illustrations and primary sources, [this volume describes an era] that transformed the world." SLJ

Includes bibliographical references

909.8   -1800

Winkler, Allan M.
The **Cold** War; a history in documents. by Allan M. Winkler. 2nd ed. Oxford University Press 2011 ix, 160 p.p ill., maps (Pages from History) (paperback) $34.95; (hardcover) $42.95
Grades: 8 9 10 11 12   **909.8**
1. Cold War 2. United States -- Foreign relations -- Soviet Union 3. Cold War -- Sources 4. World politics -- 1945-1989 -- Sources
ISBN 0199765995; 9780199765980; 9780199765997

LC 2010049111

This book by Allan M. Winkler is part of the Pages from History series and "traces the evolution of the Cold War.... By addressing the key issues of the Cold War via documents, the author provides a . . . look into a time that set the table for the modern era. Topics such as nuclear proliferation, McCarthyism, censorship, the Vietnam War and the Civil Rights Movement are all" addressed. (Children's Literature)

Includes bibliographical references and index.

909.82   20th century, 1900-1999

Bodden, Valerie
The **Cold** War; by Valerie Bodden. Creative Education 2007 48p il (Days of change) lib bdg $31.35
Grades: 6 7 8 9   **909.82**
1. Cold war 2. World politics -- 1945-1991
ISBN 978-1-58341-546-7 lib bdg; 1-58341-546-7 lib bdg

LC 2006019825

This is a "cogent [overview] of [The Cold War]. . . . Carefully selected photographs help to explicate the text, and quotes from those involved in and affected by events— from world leaders to ordinary citizens—add compelling detail and immediacy." Horn Book Guide

Includes bibliographical references

Grant, R. G.
The **Cold** War. Arcturus Pub. 2011 46p il (Secret history) lib bdg $32.80
     909.82
1. Cold war
ISBN 978-1-84837-696-0; 1-84837-696-0

LC 2010011765

This book explores the secrets of the Cold War. The superpowers never fought openly on a battlefield. Instead, they attacked one another by underhand means-spying, propaganda, secret operations, and guerrilla wars.

"The title of the Secret History series will grab readers, even reluctant ones, and they won't be disappointed by the intriguing info regarding codes and code breakers, spies, terrorists, and double agents, with profiles of heroes and traitors on all sides. . . . The readable design, with clear type on thick, high-quality paper, includes lots of sidebars, photos, screens, and quotes." Booklist

Includes bibliographical references

Harrison, Paul

Why did the Cold War happen? Gareth Stevens Pub. 2011 48p il map (Moments in history) lib bdg $31.95; pa $14.05

Grades: 6 7 8 9   **909.82**

  1. Cold war 2. World politics -- 1945-1991
  ISBN 978-1-4339-4166-5 lib bdg; 1-4339-4166-X lib bdg; 978-1-4339-4167-2 pa; 1-4339-4167-8 pa
                  LC 2010012456

"Examines the events that served as . . . [precursors to the Cold War]. . . . Brightly colored pullout boxes highlight important turning points, the perspective of the everyday man, and further information on why specific events occurred. Numerous photographs help readers visualize concepts more fully. . . . Students should be able to easily use this resource." Libr Media Connect

Includes glossary and bibliographical references

Kaufman, Michael T.

★ **1968**. Roaring Brook Press 2009 148p il $22.95

Grades: 7 8 9 10 11 12   **909.82**

  1. Journalists 2. World history -- 20th century 3. Nineteen sixties 4. Nineteen sixty-eight, A.D.
  ISBN 978-1-59643-428-8; 1-59643-428-7
                  LC 2008-15471

Kaufman "expertly draws young readers into the worldwide events of a single, watershed year: 1968. . . . Each chapter focuses on a different hot spot around the globe, beginning with the Tet Offensive and the Vietnam War and moving through uprisings in New York, Paris, Prague, Chicago, and Mexico City, as well as the assassinations of Martin Luther King Jr. and Robert F. Kennedy. . . . The images, drawn from the [New York] Times archives, are riveting and will easily draw young people into the fascinating, often horrifying events." Booklist

909.83   21st century, 2000-2099

Lace, William W.

The **Indian** Ocean tsunami of 2004. Chelsea House 2008 127p il map (Great historic disasters) $35

Grades: 7 8 9 10   **909.83**

  1. Indian Ocean earthquake and tsunami, 2004
  ISBN 978-0-7910-9642-0; 0-7910-9642-4
                  LC 2007-36950

"The author explains in detail the seismic activities that caused the 2004 Indian Ocean tsunami, as well as the lack of systems in place to quickly notify those in danger. Also included are many well-captioned photos . . . and short but interesting personal stories of both survivors and victims." Horn Book Guide

Includes glossary and bibliographical references

Stewart, Gail

Catastrophe in southern Asia; the Tsunami of 2004. by Gail B. Stewart. Lucent Books 2005 112p il map (Lucent overview series) $28.70

Grades: 7 8 9 10   **909.83**

  1. Indian Ocean earthquake and tsunami, 2004
  ISBN 1-59018-831-4
                  LC 2005006036

The focuses on "the December 2004 Indian Ocean disaster. . . . Stewart includes accounts of the event itself and images of destruction, following up with the causes of tsunamis, inadequate warning systems, dealing with the casualties, continuing risks for survivors, response efforts, and rebuilding of the stricken areas. The book's real strength comes in its level of detail, as the author goes well beyond the obvious in exploring issues. . . . Compelling writing is enhanced with clear, informative, and often dramatic black-and-white photos." SLJ

Includes bibliographical references

Torres, John Albert

Disaster in the Indian Ocean, Tsunami 2004; [by] John A. Torres. Mitchell Lane 2005 48p il map (Monumental milestones) lib bdg $19.95

Grades: 5 6 7 8   **909.83**

  1. Indian Ocean earthquake and tsunami, 2004
  ISBN 1-58415-344-X

This "emerges from the author's personal trip to Indonesia after the December 26, 2004, catastrophe. . . . Primary-source accounts, many taken from Torres' own interviews, chillingly recreate the tsunami's initial strike, its chaotic aftermath, and the challenges of recovery." Booklist

Includes bibliographical references

910   Geography and travel

Belmont, Helen

★ **Looking** at aerial photographs; [by] Helen Belmont. Smart Apple Media 2008 46p il map (Geography skills) $22.95

Grades: 6 7 8 9   **910**

  1. Geography 2. Aerial photography
  ISBN 978-1-59920-048-4; 1-59920-048-1
                  LC 2006036139

"The text is easy to follow. . . . The examples given in the text that involve places are almost always accompanied by excellent photographs. . . . Maps, block diagrams, tables, and graphs are clearly presented and easy to interpret." Sci Books Films

Includes glossary and bibliographical references

Dumont-Le Cornec, Elisabeth

Wonders of the world; natural and man-made majesties. by Elisabeth Dumont-Le Cornec; illustrated by Laureen Topalian and Kristel Riethmuller. Abrams Books for Young Readers 2007 151p il $24.95

Grades: 6 7 8 9   **910**

  1. Antiquities 2. Civilization 3. Historic sites 4. Natural monuments 5. Curiosities and wonders
  ISBN 978-0-8109-9417-1; 0-8109-9417-8
                  LC 2007016198

This "volume features 71 natural and man-made wonders selected from sites on the UNESCO World Heritage list. . . . This visually stunning book presents each selected site on a double-page spread. Most of the spread is devoted to an excellent color photo reproduced on heavy, glossy paper and accompanied by several paragraphs of explanatory text, good captions, and a small washed drawing. . . . A rich visual experience." Booklist

Elliott, Lynne

Exploration in the Renaissance; [by] Lynne Elliott. Crabtree 2009 32p il pa $8.95; lib bdg $26.60

Grades: 6 7 8 9   **910**

1. Renaissance 2. Discoveries in geography -- European
ISBN 978-0-7787-4613-3 pa; 978-0-7787-4593-8 lib bdg

LC 2008-52601

"Ideal introductions to concepts, people, and events of the Renaissance... succinct and thorough." SLJ

Goodman, Joan E.

A long and uncertain journey: the 27,000 mile voyage of Vasco da Gama; by Joan Elizabeth Goodman; illustrated by Tom McNeely. Mikaya Press 2001 47p il map (Great explorers book) $22.95

Grades: 4 5 6 7   **910**

1. Explorers 2. Explorers -- Portugal -- Biography 3. Discoveries in geography -- Portuguese
ISBN 0-9650493-7-X

LC 00-63795

"McNeely's full-page illustrations, which vibrate with life and action, lighten the format, and quotations from the diary of an anonymous sailor on the voyage add fascinating detail and vivid description. . . . A good resource for reports, but the book is also intelligently written and exciting." Booklist

Gritzner, Charles F.

The tropics. Chelsea House 2007 128p il map (Geography of extreme environments) $30

Grades: 6 7 8 9   **910**

1. Tropics
ISBN 0-7910-9233-X

LC 2006019747

This geography of tropical lands describes their populations, weather and climate, and their plants and animals.
Includes bibliographical references

Wojtanik, Andrew, 1989-

The National Geographic Bee ultimate fact book; countries A to Z. Andrew Wojtanik. National Geographic 2012 384 p. maps (pbk.) $21.90; (reinforced library binding) $21.90

Grades: 5 6 7 8 9 10   **910**

1. Atlases 2. Nations 3. Geography 4. Geography -- Encyclopedias
ISBN 1426309473; 1426309635; 9781426309472; 9781426309632

LC 2011282873

This book "provides statistical information for the world's 195 countries at a glance. The book starts off with a world map and full-page continental maps. Individual entries for countries are listed alphabetically. . . . A glossary explains terms that may be unfamiliar to students . . . . Each country entry includes a map with longitude and latitude and basic facts: continent, size, population, and capital." (Voice of Youth Advocates)

Includes bibliographical references (p. 382)

910.2   Miscellany

Ching, Jacqueline

Jobs in green travel and tourism. Rosen Pub. 2010 80p il (Green careers) lib bdg $30.60

Grades: 5 6 7 8   **910.2**

1. Tourist trade 2. Vocational guidance 3. Environmental movement 4. Environmental protection 5. Travel -- Environmental aspects
ISBN 978-1-4358-3571-9 lib bdg; 1-4358-3571-9 lib bdg

LC 2009016587

This "well-conceived [introduction focuses] on various jobs in [travel and tourism], the education and experience required, and expected earnings. The [book is] well organized, making it easy to gain an overview of the major aspects of the work. . . . [This book] will make [a] good [addition] to career collections. Photographs from the field and website and contact information for professional organizations add value." SLJ

Includes glossary and bibliographical references

Hillstrom, Laurie Collier

Global positioning systems. Lucent Books 2011 96p il map (Technology 360) lib bdg $33.45

Grades: 7 8 9 10   **910.2**

1. Global Positioning System
ISBN 978-1-4205-0325-8; 1-4205-0325-1

LC 2010030623

This offers "clean design with clear explanations of sometimes-complicated scientific subjects. . . . Global Positioning Systems discusses how GPS was developed, from its origins in the military to everyday life uses, such as tracking pets. . . . . A strong [title] for report writers and students with a serious interest in technology and its inventions." Booklist

Includes bibliographical references

910.3   Dictionaries, encyclopedias, concordances, gazetteers

Gifford, Clive

The Kingfisher geography encyclopedia; 2nd ed., rev. and updated ed.; Kingfisher 2011 487p il map $34.99

Grades: 4 5 6 7   **910.3**

1. Reference books 2. Geography -- Encyclopedias
ISBN 978-0-7534-6575-2; 0-7534-6575-2

Statistics, text, and color maps reveal the physical geography, peoples, politics, governments, languages, religions, and currencies of each nation of the world.

"The geographical descriptions are well written and include striking photos. The text is large and easy to read.

. . . It is a great book to keep around the library for students to browse and dream about their next journey." Voice Youth Advocates

★ **Junior** worldmark encyclopedia of the nations; Timothy L. Gall, Susan Bevan Gall, and Derek M. Gleason, editors. 6th ed; Gale, Cengage Learning 2012 3200 p. 10v col. ill. (set: alk. paper) $677
Grades: 5 6 7 8 **910.3**
1. Geography -- Encyclopedias 2. World history -- Encyclopedias 3. Political science -- Encyclopedias 4. History -- Encyclopedias
ISBN 1414463138; 9781414463131; 9781414463148; 9781414463155; 9781414463162; 9781414463179; 9781414463186; 9781414463193; 9781414463209; 9781414463216; 9781414463223; 9781414463230; 9781414490861
LC 2011050016
First published 1996
This book series, edited by Timothy L. Gall, Susan Bevan Gall, and Derek M. Gleason, is a juvenile national encyclopedia. "Each volume . . . starts with a table of contents for the specific volume and a guide to country articles. Each country profile, organized alphabetically, begins with . . . capital, flag, anthem, monetary unit, weights and measures. . . . Thirty-five color-coded subheadings and their corresponding numbers, as well as geographical profiles, complete each section." (Booklist)
"This new edition contains 196 countries of the world and the Palestinian Territories. Color maps... photos, and charts enhance the overall attractiveness of this updated set... This well-written encyclopedia would be a valuable resource for elementary, middle-school, and public libraries." Booklist
Includes bibliographical references and index

910.4 Accounts of travel and facilities for travelers

Anderson, Harry S.
Exploring the polar regions; rev ed.; Chelsea House 2010 116p il map (Discovery and exploration) lib bdg $35
Grades: 7 8 9 10 **910.4**
ISBN 978-1-60413-190-1; 1-60413-190-X
LC 2009-22863
First published 2004 by Facts on File
Covers exploration and discovery of the Arctic and Antarctic regions.
"The chapters are well-illustrated with color and black and white historic photos, illustrations and maps. Chapter layout is clearly organized with helpful subtitles; sidebars develop related themes in eye-catching colors. . . . [This book] attractively and effectively surveys an important . . . area in world studies." Libr Media Connect
Includes glossary and bibliographical references

Aronson, Marc
★ The **world** made new; why the Age of Exploration happened & how it changed the world. [by]

Marc Aronson & John W. Glenn. National Geographic 2007 64p il map $17.95; lib bdg $27.90
Grades: 4 5 6 7 **910.4**
1. Explorers 2. Exploration
ISBN 978-0-7922-6454-5; 978-0-7922-6978-6 lib bdg
LC 2006022091
"This highly pictorial, readable overview provides significant depth of coverage. . . . The illustrations, most in full color, make ample and appropriate use of period prints as well as contemporary illustrations and photographs. The result is a visual feast that fleshes out the . . . remarkably evenhanded narrative." SLJ
Includes glossary and bibliographical references

Baker, Julie
The **great** whaleship disaster of 1871; [by] Julie Baker. Morgan Reynolds Pub. 2007 144p $27.95
Grades: 6 7 8 9 **910.4**
1. Whaling 2. Survival after airplane accidents, shipwrecks, etc.
ISBN 978-1-59935-043-1; 1-59935-043-2
LC 2007002807
"A compelling tale of survival. In 1871, at the peak of whale hunting, a fleet of 32 ships was trapped in Arctic ice, and the 1200 men, women, and children onboard faced a long winter with limited supplies. . . . Readers are given a picture of the hazards of whaling and the endurance required in the best of conditions. In the final chapters, the events leading up to the disaster are described. . . . The account is presented in an easy-to-follow, attractive format with concise chapters and ample diagrams, full-color reproductions, illustrations, and maps." SLJ
Includes bibliographical references

Bristow, David
★ **Sky** sailors; true stories of the balloon era. [by] David L. Bristow. Farrar Straus Giroux 2010 134p il $18.99
Grades: 4 5 6 7 **910.4**
1. Balloons 2. Balloonists
ISBN 978-0-374-37014-5; 0-374-37014-1
LC 2009037285
"This lively look at escapades of daring men—and a surprising number of women—who risked their lives flying in balloons will appeal to adventure, history and science buffs—and perhaps steampunk fans as well. Each of the nine chapters, which are chronologically arranged, focuses on an exciting story, starting with the first confirmed human balloon flight in 1783 . . . and ending with Dolly Shepherd, a young British woman in the early 1900s who parachuted out of balloons, hanging onto a trapeze. . . . Useful captions accompany many full-color illustrations of artwork and photographs." Kirkus
Includes bibliographical references

Burlingame, Jeff
The **Titanic** tragedy. Marshall Cavendish Benchmark 2011 111p il (Perspectives on) lib bdg $33.93

Grades: 8 9 10 11 12   **910.4**
1. Shipwrecks
ISBN 978-1-60870-450-7 lib bdg; 1-60870-450-5 lib bdg; 978-1-60870-722-5 ebook

LC 2010041560

This tltle offers "excellent, thorough, and accurate information for reports or for general reading. [It] examines safety issues in the shipping industry in relation to the importance of profit, the historical background of the Gilded Age, the effects of privilege on the survivors of the disaster, the economic impact on those less well off, and the way the disaster affected future regulation of the shipping industry." SLJ

Includes bibliographical references

Cerullo, Mary M.
Shipwrecks; exploring sunken cities beneath the sea. [by] Mary M. Cerullo. Dutton Children's Books 2009 64p il $18.99
Grades: 5 6 7 8   **910.4**
1. Shipwrecks   2. Underwater archaeology   3. Underwater exploration
ISBN 978-0-525-47968-0; 0-525-47968-6

LC 2008-48967

This focuses "on two wrecks: the Henrietta Marie, sunk in 1700 near the Florida Keys, and the Portland, sunk in 1898 off the coast of Massachusetts. The book makes the convincing case that these wrecks are important not only for historical reasons but also for the underwater ecosystems their structures now host. . . . This delivers both education and shivers." Booklist

Clifford, Barry
Real pirates; the untold story of the Whydah from slave ship to pirate ship. by Barry Clifford and Kenneth J. Kinkor with Sharon Simpson; photography by Kenneth Garrett. National Geographic 2008 175p il map $16.95
Grades: 4 5 6 7   **910.4**
1. Pirates 2. Archeology 3. Shipwrecks 4. Slave trade
ISBN 978-1-4263-0279-4; 1-4263-0279-7

LC 2008299778

"Clifford, an underwater archaeological explorer, used research and the artifacts recovered from the Whydah to tell the story of its life as a slave galley and pirate ship. In the process, he dispels many myths about buccaneers. . . . Photographs of artifacts . . . and the recovery crew at work combine with large visually appealing paintings of dramatic battle, storm, and courtroom scenes. . . . The book is a fascinating blend of history, ocean-diving recovery, and archaeology, and demonstrates archaeology in action and the role artifacts play in informing us about the past." SLJ

Includes bibliographical references

Denenberg, Barry
★ **Titanic** sinks! Viking 2011 72p il $19.99
Grades: 5 6 7 8   **910.4**
1. Shipwrecks
ISBN 0670012432; 9780670012435

LC 2011012040

This is a "gripping recounting of the Titanic's doomed maiden voyage, chronicled in the tabloid-style pages of a

fictional magazine. . . . Melding fact and fiction, the book compiles dramatic headlines, articles that range from news bulletins about the building of the ship to a chatty tour of its lavish interior, and an array of stunning period photographs." Publ Wkly

Gilkerson, William
A **thousand** years of pirates. Tundra Books 2009 96p il map $32.95
Grades: 6 7 8 9 10   **910.4**
1. Pirates
ISBN 978-0-88776-924-5; 0-88776-924-1

"Pirates are given scholarly scrutiny in this handsome and invigorating overview. Short but dense chapters introduce the major factions, characters, and incidents that connect the scattered history of seagoing bandits. . . . Gilkerson's grasp of the politics surrounding each nation's pirates . . . is most impressive." Booklist

Includes bibliographical references

Hagglund, Betty
Epic treks. Kingfisher 2011 64p il (Epic adventure) $19.99
Grades: 5 6 7 8   **910.4**
1. Explorers 2. Voyages and travels
ISBN 978-0-7534-6668-1; 0-7534-6668-6

LC 2011041638

"The graphics will grab readers in [this] exciting, extra-large-size [title] . . . packed with high-quality color photos on every double-page spread. Just as gripping are the narratives, captions, and technical details of exploration, adventure, and survival. . . . Epic Treks covers Lewis and Clark, Livingston and Stanley, Burk and Wells, and Amundsen and Scott, each journey an exciting adventure filled with details about what they endured and what they found, as well as their failures and shortcomings." Booklist

Includes glossary

Hanel, Rachael
Pirates; [by] Rachael Hanel. Creative Education 2008 48p il map (Fearsome fighters) $31.35
Grades: 4 5 6   **910.4**
1. Pirates
ISBN 978-1-58341-537-5; 1-58341-537-8

LC 2006021844

"This book explores 'the golden age of piracy' from the sixteenth through the nineteenth centuries. Hanel discusses battles, types of ships and weapons, and attire and behavior. Vignettes of well-known male and female pirates are included. Archival reproductions and sidebars provide additional information." Horn Book Guide

Includes glossary and bibliographical references

Hopkinson, Deborah
★ **Titanic**; voices from the disaster. by Deborah Hopkinson. Scholastic Press 2012 289 p. $17.99
Grades: 5 6 7 8   **910.4**
1. Titanic (Steamship) 2. Shipwrecks
ISBN 0545116740; 9780545116749

LC 2011006695

YALSA Award for Excellence in Nonfiction for Young Adults Finalist (2013)

Robert F. Sibert Honor Book (2013)

In this book about the sinking of the Titanic, author Deborah "Hopkinson begins with a description of the ship . . . and introduces some of the passengers who embarked on its maiden voyage. The narrative shifts . . . to the disaster itself with a litany of things gone wrong. . . . [M]emoirs . . . are interlaced throughout the text, as survivors testified . . . on the relative chaos or calm, heroism or cowardice, of passengers and crew." (Bulletin of the Center for Children's Books)

Includes bibliographical references

Lawlor, Laurie

Magnificent voyage; an American adventurer on Captain James Cook's final expedition. Holiday House 2002 236p il maps $22.95

Grades: 7 8 9 10   910.4

1. Explorers 2. Naval officers 3. Travel writers 4. Oceania -- Discovery and exploration 5. Travelers -- United States -- Biography

ISBN 0-8234-1575-9

LC 2002-17148

Based on the writings of John Ledyard, an American cook on the ship Resolution, tells of explorer James Cook's final voyage in search of the Northwest Passage, discovery of the Hawaiian Islands, and murder

"The author's detailed picture of the voyage, and of Ledyard's relatively brief career, makes engrossing, if gloomy, reading." Booklist

Includes glossary and bibliographical references

Marschall, Ken

Inside the Titanic; illustrated by Ken Marschall; text by Hugh Brewster. Little, Brown 1997 32p il $19.95

Grades: 4 5 6 7   910.4

1. Shipwrecks

ISBN 0-316-55716-1

LC 97-382

"Color cutaway paintings of the Titanic in this oversize book allow readers to view every deck as they follow two 12-year-old boys exploring the vessel, and to see how the liner struck the iceberg and sank." Booklist

Includes glossary and bibliographical references

McPherson, Stephanie Sammartino

★ **Iceberg** right ahead! the tragedy of the Titanic. Twenty-First Century Books 2011 112p il $33.26

Grades: 4 5 6 7 8   910.4

1. Shipwrecks

ISBN 9780761367567

LC 2011002352

"With innumerable books, movies, documentaries, novels, and biographies all telling versions of the Titanic story, it would seem that there is little more to learn, yet by providing more details and some of the most up-to-date research, McPherson's compelling, thoughtful narrative proves otherwise. . . . The layout includes plenty of period photographs, diagrams, artwork, and sidebars with interesting tangential tidbits, making for a thorough resource. . . . A comprehensive, well-written, thoroughly researched title." SLJ

Includes bibliographical references

Morris, Neil

Voyages of discovery. Zak Books 2009 48p il map (History of the world) lib bdg $34.25

Grades: 7 8 9 10   910.4

1. Explorers 2. Exploration

ISBN 978-88-6098-154-7 lib bdg; 88-6098-154-9 lib bdg

LC 2008-8409

The "effectiveness lies in the combination of lush illustrations, well-chosen, captioned photographs of contemporary artifacts, and . . . [a] reasoned, concise [narrative]. Succinct time lines border most pages, and . . . the proper amount of white space, and clear dark print maintain organization and clarity. A superior choice." SLJ

Includes glossary

Mundy, Robyn

Epic voyages. Kingfisher 2011 64p il (Epic adventure) $19.99

Grades: 5 6 7 8   910.4

1. Explorers

ISBN 978-0-7534-6574-5; 0-7534-6574-4

"The graphics will grab readers in [this] exciting, extra-large-size [title] . . . packed with high-quality color photos on every double-page spread. Just as gripping are the narratives, captions, and technical details of exploration, adventure, and survival. . . . [This] book covers Magellan, Cook, Shackleton, Heyedahl and also Chichester, who, in 1966, sailed alone around the world." Booklist

Nardo, Don

Polar explorations; by Don Nardo. Lucent Books 2011 104 p. ill., col. maps, photographs (library) $34.95

Grades: 6 7 8 9   910.4

1. Polar regions -- Exploration 2. Exploration 3. Explorers -- Polar regions -- Biography

ISBN 142050360X; 9781420503609

LC 2010039667

This book by Don Nardo is part of the World History series and looks at polar explorations. The series "examines the eras, events, civilizations, and movements that have shaped human history, providing readers with insight into the past and its many legacies. Vivid writing, full-color photographs and extensive use of fully cited primary and secondary source quotations provide a sense of immediacy." (Publisher's note)

Includes bibliographical references and (p. 95-97) index.

Philbrick, Nathaniel

★ **Revenge** of the whale; the true story of the whaleship Essex. Putnam 2002 164p il maps $16.99; pa $7.99

Grades: 7 8 9 10   910.4

1. Whaling 2. Shipwrecks 3. Shipwrecks -- Pacific Ocean

ISBN 0-399-23795-X; 0-14-240068-8 pa

LC 2002-667

Recounts the 1820 sinking of the whaleship "Essex" by an enraged sperm whale and how the crew of young men survived against impossible odds. Based on the author's adult book "In the heart of the sea"

"The story of the Essex crew is a compelling saga of desperation and survival that will appeal to young people. The grisly details of cannibalism necessary to the telling of the story may provoke shivers but should not give anyone nightmares." SLJ

Includes bibliographical references

Rose, Jamaica

The **book** of pirates; a guide to plundering, pillaging, and other pursuits. [by] Jamaica Rose & Michael MacLeod. Gibbs Smith 2010 224p il map $12.99

Grades: 6 7 8 9 10   **910.4**
  1. Pirates
  ISBN 978-1-4236-0670-3; 1-4236-0670-1
                                         LC 2010009086

"This delightful book, written partly in pirate dialect, is full of creative activities, interspersed with plenty of fascinating historical facts. . . . The introduction defines piracy. The opening chapter is a true-or-false account of some of the many well-known myths about pirates. . . . The authors discuss the origins and history of these rogues, the lives of famous pirates (including females), rules and codes and behavior, and present-day piracy. Those planning to attend an event as a pirate can follow the instructions for proper attire, along with diagrams and directions for makeup and the construction of a foam cutlass. . . . Jokes, games, songs, and a recipe for making cannonballs (from peanut butter) add to the fun." SLJ

Includes glossary

Ross, Stewart

★ **Into** the unknown; how great explorers found their way by land, sea, and air. Candlewick Press 2011 un il map $19.99

Grades: 4 5 6 7   **910.4**
  1. Explorers 2. Discoveries in geography
  ISBN 978-0-7636-4948-7; 0-7636-4948-1
                                         LC 2010038720

"Biesty's trademark amusing, informatively detailed illustrations are a highlight of this entertaining examination of several voyages of exploration. . . . Chapters cover an impressive range of exploration. In addition to the usual suspects, they include a 340 B.C.E. Greek voyage to the Arctic Circle; Chinese Admiral Zheng He to India; [and] David Livingston and Mary Kingsley into the African interior. . . . Each chapter includes a fold-out section of illustrations with a map of the journey and a cross-section of the method of transportation. . . . An altogether agreeable package for armchair explorers." Kirkus

Vail, Martha

Exploring the Pacific; [by] Martha Vail; John S. Bowman and Maurice Isserman, general editors. rev ed.; Chelsea House 2010 120p il map (Discovery and exploration) $35

Grades: 7 8 9 10   **910.4**
  1. Explorers
  ISBN 978-1-60413-197-0; 1-60413-197-7
                                         LC 2009-22106

First published 2005 by Facts on File

"The chapters are well-illustrated with color and black and white historic photos, illustrations, and maps. Chapter layout is clearly organized with helpful subtitles; sidebars develop related themes in catching colors." Libr Media Connect

Includes glossary and bibliographical references

Weatherly, Myra

Women of the sea; ten pirate stories. Morgan Reynolds 2006 160p il map lib bdg $26.95

Grades: 7 8 9 10   **910.4**
  1. Women pirates
  ISBN 1-931798-80-X

A revised edition of Women pirates: eight stories of adventure (1998)

This is a collective biography of such women pirates as Lady Killigrew, Lai Choi San, and Maria Cobham

Includes glossary and bibliographical references

White, Pamela

Exploration in the world of the Middle Ages, 500-1500; Pamela White, John S. Bowman, and Maurice Isserman, general editors. Rev. ed.; Chelsea House 2010 132p il map (Discovery and exploration) $35

Grades: 7 8 9 10   **910.4**
  1. Explorers 2. Exploration 3. Middle Ages
  ISBN 978-1-60413-193-2; 1-60413-193-4
                                         LC 2009-30202

First published 2005 by Facts On File

This describes world exploration in the Middle Ages by pilgrims and missionaries, the Vikings, Muslim travelers, Europeans seeking Asia, Marco Polo, and Portuguese sailors, and describes Medieval legends of mythical monsters and lands

Includes glossary and bibliographical references

910.92   Geographers, travelers, explorers regardless of country of origin

Fritz, Jean

Around the world in a hundred years; from Henry the Navigator to Magellan. illustrated by Anthony Bacon Venti. Putnam 1994 128p il map hardcover o.p. pa $8.99

Grades: 4 5 6 7   **910.92**
  1. Princes 2. Explorers 3. Colonial administrators 4. Exploration
  ISBN 0-399-22527-7; 0-698-11638-0 pa
                                         LC 92-27042

"Fritz examines the voyages of ten explorers, acknowledging that their contributions, though deserving of recognition, were dearly bought. Opening and closing chapters summarize the fourteenth-century world view and indicate later expansion of geographic understanding. As always, Fritz tempers scholarship with humor in this brief volume—illustrated with drawings in pencil—which reads like an adventure story." Horn Book Guide

Includes bibliographical references

911   Historical geography

Chrisp, Peter
   Atlas of ancient worlds; author, Peter Chrisp; consultant, Philip Parker. DK Pub. 2009 96p il map $21.99
Grades: 4 5 6 7 8   911
   1. Reference books 2. Historical atlases 3. Ancient civilization
   ISBN 978-0-7566-4512-0; 0-7566-4512-3
   This atlas consists "of maps and illustrations accompanied by extensive captions outlining the cultures of many civilizations. Each section begins with a map of a continent and a table of contents detailing which peoples will be discussed in it. Each civilization is covered in a chapter spread that includes a small map of the extent of each empire and many photos, pictures, and captioned drawings. . . . The accompanying clip art CD contains images of many of the artifacts as well as of the maps found in the book. . . . This atlas offers a wonderful introduction to [ancient civilizations] as well as solid geography basics." SLJ
   Includes glossary

Leacock, Elspeth
   Places in time; a new atlas of American history. [by] Elspeth Leacock and Susan Buckley; illustrations by Randy Jones. Houghton Mifflin 2001 48p il $15; pa $6.95
Grades: 4 5 6 7   911
   1. Reference books 2. Children's atlases 3. United States -- Historical geography 4. United States -- History -- Miscellanea
   ISBN 0-395-97958-7; 0-618-3113-0 pa
                                        LC 00-59741
   This book presents "20 sites in American history at the moment of their historical significance, beginning in 1200 (Cahokia) and ending in 1953. Places and times include New Plymouth—1627, Charlestown—1739, Saratoga—1777, Philadelphia—1787, Abilene—1871, and Chicago—1893. The detailed cutaway views of homes, forts, and mills are impressive enough to keep readers looking again and again. These fascinating slices of life stir the imagination and lead to questions and further research." SLJ
   Includes bibliographical references

Todras, Ellen H.
   Explorers, trappers, and pioneers; by Ellen H. Todras. Kingfisher 2012 32 p. ill. (All About America) (paperback) $9.99
Grades: 4 5 6   911
   1. America -- Exploration 2. Frontier and pioneer life -- United States
   ISBN 0753465159; 9780753465158
   This book by Ellen H. Todras is part of the "All About America" series. It "begins with the Vikings landing in Newfoundland 1,000 years ago and concludes with the Oklahoma Land Rush in 1889." It "offers 13 highly illustrated double-page spreads that present topics using a few paragraphs of information, related text boxes, and several color illustrations and five or more captioned illustrations." (Booklist)

912   Graphic representations of surface of earth and of extraterrestrial worlds

Facts on File, Inc.
   Maps on file. Facts on File 2v maps
Grades: Adult Professional   912
   1. Atlases 2. Reference books
   First published 1981. Frequently revised
   A collection of approximately 500 black-and-white maps covering countries, every U.S. state, Canadian provinces, oceans, and continents

Hollingum, Ben
   Maps and mapping the world; [Ben Hollingum, editor] Gareth Stevens Pub. 2010 48p il map (Understanding maps of our world) lib bdg $31; pa $14.95
Grades: 6 7 8 9   912
   1. Maps
   ISBN 978-1-4339-3498-8 lib bdg; 1-4339-3498-1 lib bdg; 978-1-4339-3501-5 pa; 1-4339-3501-5 pa
                                        LC 2009-37275
   "These fascinating books open with an identical whirlwind time line of cartographic history, beginning with a map of the world as 15th-century Europeans knew it and ending with the first photos of Earth taken from space...Related events and topics also spring up... The books' further-reading lists, which include print and Web materials, are particularly extensive. Wonderful resources." SLJ
   Includes glossary and bibliographical references

   Travel maps; [Ben Hollingum, editor] Gareth Stevens Pub. 2010 48p il map (Understanding maps of our world) lib bdg $31; pa $14.95
Grades: 6 7 8 9   912
   1. Maps
   ISBN 978-1-4339-3506-0 lib bdg; 1-4339-3506-6 lib bdg; 978-1-4339-3507-7 pa; 1-4339-3507-4 pa
                                        LC 2009-37277
   "These fascinating books open with an identical whirlwind time line of cartographic history...descriptions of cartographic challenges, old and new, result in a lot of valuable extras–. Wonderful resources." SLJ
   Includes glossary and bibliographical references

★   **National** Geographic United States atlas for young explorers; 3rd ed.; National Geographic 2008 175p il map $24.95
Grades: 4 5 6 7   912
   1. Atlases 2. Reference books
   ISBN 978-1-4263-0255-8; 1-4263-0255-X
   First published 1999
   This atlas offers maps of each of the states in the United States, divided into five geographical regions, plus U.S. territories. Each state map indicates physical features such as mountains and rivers, national forests, cities, major interstate roads, and industries, and is accompanied by color photos and facts about the state. An introductory section describes how to use the companion web site for more information, maps of the United States biomes, climates, natural hazards, political states, population, ethnic diversity, and energy use.

★ **National** Geographic atlas of the world; 9th ed.; National Geographic Society 2010 153p il $175
Grades: 5 6 7 8 9 10   **912**
1. Atlases 2. Reference books
ISBN 978-1-4262-0634-4
First published 1963
"The National Geographic Society presents more than 80 large-format color maps grouped by continent portraying the world with detailed, digitally painted terrain modeling. Each continent is introduced by satellite, political, and physical maps. Political maps for regions and specific countries follow." Libr J

National Geographic student atlas of the world; 3rd ed; National Geographic 2009 143p il map pa $12.95
Grades: 6 7 8 9   **912**
1. Atlases 2. Reference books 3. Children's atlases 4. Physical geography
ISBN 978-1-4263-0446-0 pa; 1-4263-0446-3 pa; 978-1-4263-0458-3 lib bdg; 1-4263-0458-7 lib bdg; 978-1-4263-0445-3; 1-4263-0445-5
LC 2009-583028
First published 2001
This offers information "about maps and how to read them. Then [it describes] the world's physical and human systems, including Earth's geologic history, natural vegetation, and world cultures. A . . . view from space introduces each continent, and full-page, full-color maps represent its physical and political makeup, its climate and precipitation, and its population and predominant economies. A . . . photo essay highlights an issue relevant to each continent, such as the European Union, or deforestation in the Amazon." Publisher's note

★ **Oxford** Atlas of the world; [cartography by Philip's] 19th ed. Oxford University Press 2012 448 p. il map (hardcover) $89.95
Grades: 7 8 9 10 11 12 Adult   **912**
1. Atlases 2. Earth -- Maps 3. Physical geography 4. Reference books
ISBN 0199937826; 9780199937820
LC 20100594813
First published 1992. Frequently revised. Variant title: Atlas of the world
This world atlas offers "new census information, dozens of city maps . . . satellite images of Earth, and a geographical glossary." It " provides details on such topics as climate, the greenhouse effect, employment and industry, standards of living, agriculture, population and migration, and global conflicts." (Publisher's note)
"...[U]pdated annually, this large-format resource continues to earn pride of place on the atlas case's top shelf for its combination of currency and eye-widening graphics. The physical, political, and country and regional maps that make up the volume's core are works of art-brilliantly designed for easy comprehension, rendered in bright colors and sharp detail... Atlases are among the quickest reference sources to age, so for classroom or library collections in which students search in vain...this makes a first-rate replacement." SLJ

Oxford new concise world atlas; [cartography by Philip's; text, Keith Lye]. 3rd ed; Oxford University Press 2010 1 atlas (224 p.) col. ill., col. maps $39.95
Grades: 6 7 8 9 10 11 12 Adult   **912**
1. Atlases 2. Reference books
ISBN 0195393295; 9780195393293
LC 2009292676
Containing over 100 pages of the most up-to-date topographic and political maps, the New Concise World Atlas also features a unique overview of the planet's human and natural processes in photographs, accessible text, and thematic maps. (Publisher's note)
"This update of the 2006 edition contains 128 pages of full-color, computer-generated maps by Philip's, a division of Octopus Publishing, with detailed and dramatic terrain modeling... This condensed and abridged version of the premium Oxford Atlas of the World offers all libraries outstanding value in an up-to-date, medium-sized atlas for an amazingly low price."

Panchyk, Richard
Charting the world; geography and maps from cave paintings to GPS with 21 activities. by Richard Panchyk. Chicago Review Press 2011 xi, 132 p.p ill., maps (some col.) (paperback) $18.95
Grades: 7 8 9 10   **912**
1. Maps 2. Cartography -- Maps 3. Cartography 4. Map reading 5. Maps -- History
ISBN 1569763445; 9781569763445
LC 2011019317
Author "[Richard] Panchyk's book helps explain why maps are exciting, how they expand our world, and have done so for generations. . . . Maps document the lay of the land, the placement of cities, and the height of mountains, among many other things. Panchyk walks us through these mapmaking skills, offering activities along the way. . . .Panchyk also provides sidebars about such notable explorers as Amerigo Vespucci, for whom America was named." (Children's Literature)
Includes bibliographical references

Ross, Val
The **road** to there; mapmakers and their stories. Tundra Books 2003 146p il map $22.95; pa $15.95
Grades: 6 7 8 9   **912**
1. Maps 2. Cartographers 3. Cartography -- History
ISBN 0-88776-621-8; 0-88776-933-0 pa
"Ross presents an intriguing look at several mapmakers and the way that their work reflected not only physical boundaries, but also important aspects of their lives and the times in which they lived. . . . The tone of the text is chatty, sometimes humorous, and never dry. . . . Filled with details and insights and written with a storyteller's touch, this book will simultaneously inform and fascinate readers." SLJ

Student atlas; Dorling Kindersley, Inc. 6th ed. DK Pub. 2013 176 p. ill. (hardcover) $14.99
Grades: 5 6 7 8   **912**
1. Atlases 2. Geography
ISBN 0756663199; 9780756663193

This book from DK Publishing is part of the Student Atlas series. It is a "single-volume guide to the nations of the world. [It's] fully revised and updated, and packed with clear, detailed maps highlighting landscape, industry, land use, population, climate and environmental issues." (Publisher's note)

Taylor, Barbara
★ **Looking** at maps; [by] Barbara Taylor. Smart Apple Media 2008 46p il map (Geography skills) $22.95

Grades: 6 7 8 9   **912**
1. Maps
ISBN 1-59920-050-3; 978-1-59920-050-7
     LC 2006100224

"The text is easy to follow. . . . The examples given in the text that involve places are almost always accompanied by excellent photographs. . . . Maps, block diagrams, tables, and graphs are clearly presented and easy to interpret." Sci Books Films

Includes glossary and bibliographical references

916   Geography of and travel in Africa

Bodden, Valerie
To the heart of Africa; by Valerie Bodden. Creative Education 2011 48 p. col. ill. (Great Expeditions) (library) $34.25

Grades: 5 6 7 8   **916**
1. Africa -- Exploration 2. Exploration and discovery 3. Explorers -- Scotland -- Biography 4. Explorers -- Africa, Southern -- Biography 5. Missionaries, Medical -- Africa, Southern -- Biography
ISBN 1608180662; 9781608180660
     LC 2010033414

This book by Valerie Bodden is part of the Great Expeditions series and looks at expeditions into Africa. "Bodden includes brief biographies of major people involved in each expedition, interspersed with the text. There are also numerous photographs or reproductions of paintings and woodcuts from the time of the expeditions." (Library Media Connection)

Includes bibliographical references (p. 46-47) and index.

917   Geography of and travel in North America

Butts, Edward
Shipwrecks, monsters, and mysteries of the Great Lakes; [by] Ed Butts. Tundra Books 2010 80p il pa $14.95

Grades: 4 5 6 7   **917**
1. Shipwrecks 2. Sea monsters 3. Shipwrecks -- Great Lakes
ISBN 978-1-77049-206-6 pa; 1-77049-206-2 pa

"In 1679, a French ship called the Griffon left Green Bay on Lake Michigan, bound for Niagara with a cargo of furs. Neither the Griffon nor the five-man crew was ever seen again. . . . Its disappearance was probably the result of the first shipwreck on a Great Lake. Since then, more than six thousand vessels, large and small, have met tragic ends. . . . Shoals and reefs, uncharted rocks, and sandbars could snare a ship or rip open a hull. Unpredictable winds could capsize a vessel at any moment. . . . The wreckage of ships and the bones of the people who sail them litter the bottoms of the five lakes: Ontario, Erie, Huron, Michigan, and Superior. Ed Butts has gathered stories and lake lore in this [volume]." (Publisher's note)

Includes bibliographical references

Clark, William
Off the map; the journals of Lewis and Clark. edited by Peter and Connie Roop; illustrations by Tim Tanner. Walker & Co. 1993 40p il hardcover o.p. pa $8.95

Grades: 5 6 7 8   **917**
1. Explorers 2. Territorial governors
ISBN 0-8027-7546-2
     LC 92-18340

A compilation of entries and excerpts from the journals of William Clark and Meriwether Lewis, describing their historic expedition

"The full-color illustrations, mainly in warm earth tones, give the pages an attractive look, but the most vivid pictures come from the journals themselves. . . . This vivid source material would be a welcome part of any classroom study of the subject." Booklist

Hirschfelder, Arlene B.
Photo odyssey: Solomon Carvalho's remarkable Western adventure, 1853-54. Clarion Bks. 2000 118p il $18

Grades: 6 7 8 9   **917**
1. Artists 2. Painters 3. Photographers 4. Jews -- West (U.S.) -- Biography 5. Explorers -- West (U.S.) -- Biography 6. West (U.S.) -- Discovery and exploration 7. Photographers -- West (U.S.) -- Biography
ISBN 0-395-89123-X
     LC 99-42201

Describes the life of Carvalho, a Jewish photographer who accompanied John Charles Fremont on his last expedition to the West

"Through the author's historically accurate, vivid descriptions of the various stages of this journey, the reader gains incredible insight into the rigors endured by those who explored the vastness of our country during the 19th century." Book Rep

Includes bibliographical references

Patent, Dorothy Hinshaw
Animals on the trail with Lewis and Clark; photographs by William Muñoz. Clarion Bks. 2002 118p il map $18

Grades: 4 5 6 7   **917**
1. Animals -- United States 2. West (U.S.) -- Description and travel 3. Animals -- West (U.S.) -- History -- 19th century
ISBN 0-395-91415-9
     LC 2001-42200

Retraces the Lewis and Clark journey and blends their observations of previously unknown animals with modern information about those same animals

"The spacious page layouts, beautiful illustrations, and well-written text help ensure that this historically significant story will be read and enjoyed." Booklist

Includes bibliographical references

917.804 West (U.S.)--travel

Bodden, Valerie

Through the American West; by Valerie Bodden. Creative Education 2011 48 p. col. ill. (Great Expeditions) (library) $34.25

Grades: 5 6 7 8   **917.804**

1. Lewis and Clark Expedition (1804-1806)
ISBN 1608180654; 9781608180653

LC 2010033413

This book by Valerie Bodden is part of the "Great Expeditions" series. It describes an expedition "led by William Clark and Meriwether Lewis to explore the wilderness to the west and look for an all water route to the Pacific Ocean. They were aided by Sacagawea, a Shoshone Indian. The adventures and hardships of the arduous three-year journey include both the achievements and the disappointments encountered along the way". (Children's Literature)

Includes bibliographical references

Stille, Darlene R., 1942-

The **journals** of Lewis and Clark; by Darlene R. Stille. Heinemann Library 2012 48 p. ill. (some col.), col. map (Documenting U.S. History) (library) $32; (paperback) $8.99

Grades: 4 5 6   **917.804**

1. United States -- History -- Sources 2. Explorers -- West (U.S.) -- Diaries
ISBN 1432967541; 9781432967543; 9781432967635

LC 2011037783

This book on the journals of Meriwether Lewis and William Clark by Darlene R. Stille is part of the "Documenting U.S. History" series. It answers such questions as "What writing materials did Lewis and Clark take on their expedition? What types of plants and animals did Lewis and Clark describe in their journals? [and] where can the journals be seen and read today?" (Publisher's note)

Includes bibliographical references and index

919.89 Antarctica -- geography

Armstrong, Jennifer

★ **Shipwreck** at the bottom of the world; the extraordinary true story of Shackleton and the Endurance. Crown 1998 134p il maps pbk $12.95

Grades: 7 8 9 10 11 12   **919.89**

1. Explorers
ISBN 0-517-80014-4; 9780375810497

LC 97-52063

This book describes the events of the 1914 Shackleton Antarctic expedition when, after being trapped in a frozen sea for nine months, their ship, Endurance, was finally crushed, forcing Shackleton and his men to make a very long

and perilous journey across ice and stormy seas to reach inhabited land. Booklist

A book that will capture the attention and imagination of any reader." SLJ

Includes bibliographical references and index

Bodden, Valerie

To the South Pole; by Valerie Bodden. Creative Education 2011 48 p. col. ill. (Great Expeditions) (library) $34.25

Grades: 5 6 7 8   **919.89**

1. South Pole -- Exploration 2. Amundsen, Roald, 1872-1928 3. Explorers -- Norway -- Biography
ISBN 1608180697; 9781608180691

LC 2010033552

This book by Valerie Bodden, part of the "Great Expeditions" series, presents "a history of Roald Amundsen's . . . 1911 trip to the South Pole, detailing the challenges encountered, the individuals involved, the discoveries made, and how the expedition left its mark upon the world." (Publisher's note) . Major historical milestones and details about the search for the southernmost tip of the world are related in" addition to "profiles of four of the major explorers." (Children's Literature)

Includes bibliographical references

92 Biography

Aaron, Hank, 1934-

Stanton, Tom. **Hank** Aaron and the home run that changed America. William Morrow 2004 249p il hardcover o.p. pa $13.95

Grades: 7 8 9 10   **92**

1. Baseball players 2. African American athletes 3. Home runs (Baseball) 4. Baseball -- Biography 5. Racism in sports -- United States 6. Baseball players -- United States -- Biography
ISBN 0-06-057976-5; 0-06-072290-8 pa

LC 2004-46092

"Stanton deftly balances the story of Aaron's professional career, his personal life, and the changes in baseball between the years of Jackie Robinson and today's megastars, such as Ken Griffey, Jr. and Barry Bonds. . . . This book is a must for young adult collections." Voice Youth Advocates

Includes bibliographical references

Abbott, Berenice, 1898-1991

★ Sullivan, George. **Berenice** Abbott, photographer; an independent vision. Clarion Books 2006 170p il $20

Grades: 7 8 9 10   **92**

1. Photographers 2. Women photographers
ISBN 978-0-618-44026-9; 0-618-44026-7

LC 2005-30736

A biography of Berenice Abbott, who was a pioneer in the field of professional photography and is particularly acclaimed for her photographs of the streets and buildings of New York City before they were replaced by skyscrapers during a building boom in the 1920s and early 1930s.

"Sullivan brings together an enormous amount of information about Abbott and presents it in a clear, thoughtful manner. . . . Large, clear reproductions of Abbott's photos appear throughout the book." Booklist

Includes bibliographical references

Abu al-Qasim al-Zah-rawi d. 1013?

Ramen, Fred. **Albucasis** (Abu al-Qasim al-Zah-rawi) renowned Muslim surgeon of the Tenth Century. [by] Fred Ramen. Rosen Pub. Group 2006 112p il map (Great Muslim philosophers and scientists of the Middle Ages) lib bdg $33.25

Grades: 5 6 7 8   **92**
    1. Arabs 2. Surgeons 3. Physicians 4. Medieval civilization 5. Writers on medicine
    ISBN 1-4042-0510-1

                    LC 2005015786

"Acknowledging the skimpy historical record on his subject, Ramen fleshes out this profile of an influential Spanish physician with sweeping histories of ancient Mediterranean civilizations, early medicine, the rise of Islam, and the rise and fall of Muslim culture in Spain. Readers will come away impressed by the surgeon's contributions to medicine, which ranged from an encyclopedic surgical text to the invention of the forceps to the pioneering use of sutures. The information is buttressed by color photos of architectural remains and manuscript pages." Booklist

Includes glossary and bibliographical references

Adams, Ansel, 1902-1984

West, Krista. **Ansel** Adams. Chelsea House 2011 124p il map (Conservation heroes) lib bdg $35

Grades: 6 7 8 9   **92**
    1. Photographers
    ISBN 978-1-60413-946-4; 1-60413-946-3

                    LC 2010030591

This is a biography of the American photographer and environmentalist, best known for his black-and-white photographs of the American West,

"Captivating, richly informative. . . . The scope of [this book] is comprehensive. . . . [The book is] engaging as [it is] educational and will be ideal for research and reports." SLJ

Includes glossary and bibliographical references

Adams, John, 1735-1826

Adams, John. **John** Adams the writer; a treasury of letters, diaries, and public documents. compiled and edited by Carolyn P. Yoder. 1st ed.; Calkins Creek 2007 144p il $16.95

Grades: 8 9 10 11 12   **92**
    1. Presidents 2. Vice-presidents 3. Presidents -- United States
    ISBN 978-1-59078-247-7; 1-59078-247-X

                    LC 2006101748

"Yoder's succinct introductions provide ample context for each selection, and the diverse writings give a sense of the man's intelligence, resolve, and dedication to the ideals that created America. . . . Numerous black-and-white illustrations and a list of historic sites round out the title. . . . Those who seek an easily digestible overview of the second

president's life and times will find this book both informative and appealing." SLJ

Includes bibliographical references

Addams, Jane, 1860-1935

★ Caravantes, Peggy. **Waging** peace; the story of Jane Addams. [by] Peggy Caravantes. rev ed; Morgan Reynolds Publishing 2004 144p il lib bdg $23.95

Grades: 5 6 7 8   **92**
    1. Authors 2. Philanthropists 3. Essayists 4. Pacifists 5. Social welfare leaders 6. Nobel laureates for peace
    ISBN 1-93179-840-0

                    LC 2004-8357

This is a "biography of the social reformer, humanitarian, and winner of the 1931 Nobel Peace Prize. . . . Archival black-and-white photos . . . grace the book. This is a solid addition to women's history collections." SLJ

Includes bibliographical references

Fradin, Judith Bloom. **Jane** Addams; champion of democracy. by Judith Bloom Fradin and Dennis Brindell Fradin. Clarion Books 2006 216p il $21

Grades: 7 8 9 10   **92**
    1. Authors 2. Philanthropists 3. Essayists 4. Pacifists 5. Social welfare leaders 6. Nobel laureates for peace
    ISBN 0-618-50436-1

A biography of the social activist, pacifist, author, founder of Hull House in Chicago, and winner of the Nobel Peace Prize.

"A fascinating and rich life is related in strong, unfussy prose." Booklist

Includes bibliographical references

Aguirre, Hank, 1932-1994

Copley, Bob. The **tall** Mexican: the life of Hank Aguirre, all-star pitcher, businessman, humanitarian; with a foreword by Jose F. Niño. Piñata Bks. 1998 159p il hardcover o.p. pa $9.95

Grades: 7 8 9 10   **92**
    1. Businessmen 2. Businesspeople 3. Baseball players 4. Automobile executives 5. Baseball -- Biography
    ISBN 1-55885-294-8

                    LC 98-3185

A biography of the All-Star major-league pitcher whose commitment to his Hispanic heritage led him to found Mexican Industries to help provide economic opportunities to the inner-city Detroit community

"Myriad reminiscences from friends, family, employees, colleagues, and fellow athletes provide readers with the sense of true admiration felt for the subject." SLJ

Albright, Madeleine Korbel, 1937-

Madeleine Albright. Chelsea House 1999 134p il (Women of achievement) lib bdg $23.95; pa $9.95

                                92
    1. Cabinet officers 2. Women politicians 3. College teachers 4. Political scientists 5. Secretaries of state 6. United Nations officials 7. Cabinet officers -- United States -- Biography 8. Women cabinet officers -- United

States -- Biography
ISBN 0-7910-4708-3 lib bdg; 0-7910-4709-1 pa
LC 98-14110

Focuses on the accomplishments of the former United States ambassador to the United Nations who became the first woman to serve as Secretary of State

"Good for assignments year-round, and especially valuable for women's history month." SLJ

Includes bibliographical references

Alcott, Louisa May, 1832-1888

Meigs, Cornelia Lynde. **Invincible** Louisa; the story of the author of Little Women. with a new introduction by the author. Little, Brown 1968 195p il hardcover o.p. pa $6.95

92

1. Authors 2. Novelists 3. Women authors 4. Authors, American 5. Young adult authors
ISBN 0-316-56594-6 pa
First published 1933
Awarded the Newbery Medal, 1934

This biography "is to be praised still for its straightforward account of a life of struggle and success. . . . If you want to know about Louisa's external life, and trace there the events which gave rise to the internal urges and passions that produced 'Little Women,' this book will serve well." N Y Times Book Rev

Silverthorne, Elizabeth. **Louisa** May Alcott; foreword by Kyle Zimmer. 2nd ed; Chelsea House 2011 117p il (Who wrote that?) lib bdg $35
Grades: 6 7 8 9   92
1. Authors 2. Novelists 3. Women authors 4. Authors, American 5. Young adult authors
ISBN 978-1-60413-760-6; 1-60413-760-6
First published 2002

"Silverthorne covers Alcott's life from her birth in 1832 to her death in 1888, with information about her writing life and major titles. The author creates a clear picture of the period and of a determined, diligent, and loyal woman who was shocked at the popularity of her most famous work." SLJ [review of 2002 edition]

Includes bibliographical references

Alexander, the Great, 356-323 B.C.

★ Adams, Simon. **Alexander**; the boy soldier who conquered the world. National Geographic 2005 64p il map (World history biographies) $17.95; lib bdg $27.90
Grades: 4 5 6 7   92
1. Ancient civilization 2. Kings
ISBN 0-7922-3660-2; 0-7922-3661-0 lib bdg

This describes the life and times of Alexander the Great.

This is a "handsomely designed [book]. . . . illustrated with maps and many color photographs of art and sculpture that give substance to [the era]. . . . Adams does not downplay Alexander's brutality or all-consuming ambition and includes examples of both." SLJ

Includes bibliographical references

Behnke, Alison. The **conquests** of Alexander the Great; by Alison Behnke. Twenty-First Century Books 2008 159p il map (Pivotal moments in history) lib bdg $38.60
Grades: 6 7 8 9   92
1. Kings and rulers 2. Kings
ISBN 978-0-8225-5920-7 lib bdg; 0-8225-5920-X lib bdg
LC 2006-11824

Presents a profile of the young military leader and king of ancient Macedonia, who conquered most of the known world of his era, before his untimely death at the age of thirty-three.

This is a "very thorough account. . . . Behnke gives enough background information about Greece and the world in which Alexander was raised to bring him to life for readers. . . . Helpful maps of the route through the Middle East and Asia and interesting sidebars and illustrations of Alexander and his contemporaries appear throughout." SLJ

Includes bibliographical references

Demi. **Alexander** the Great; written and illustrated by Demi. Marshall Cavendish 2010 59p il $19.99
Grades: 4 5 6 7   92
1. Kings and rulers 2. Kings
ISBN 978-0-7614-5700-8; 0-7614-5700-3

"Demi's meticulous, expansive story highlights the achievements of Alexander the Great, who conquered much of the known world (to the Greeks) in only 12 years. . . . Illustrated with Demi's customary skill, . . . Alexander's conflicts and victories will delight young history lovers with their daring." Publ Wkly

Alhazen, 965-1039

Steffens, Bradley. **Ibn** al-Haytham; first scientist. Morgan Reynolds Pub. 2007 128p il (Profiles in science) lib bdg $27.95
Grades: 7 8 9 10   92
1. Physicists 2. Scientists 3. Mathematicians
ISBN 978-1-59935-024-0; 1-59935-024-6
LC 2006-23970

The author "has organized what is known of his subject's life and work into a coherent narrative. . . . Like the history of mathematics, the history of science is incomplete without an acknowledgment of early scholars in the Middle East. This clearly written introduction to al-Haytham, his society, and his contributions does that." Booklist

Includes bibliographical references

Ali, Muhammad, 1942-

Micklos, John. **Muhammad** Ali; I am the greatest. [by] John Micklos, Jr. Enslow Publishers 2010 160p il (American rebels) lib bdg $34.60
Grades: 6 7 8 9 10   92
1. African American athletes 2. Boxers (Persons) 3. Boxing -- Biography
ISBN 978-0-7660-3381-8; 0-7660-3381-3
LC 2009-17593

"This biography of the three-time heavyweight world champion, Vietnam War protester, and Nobel Peace Prize nominee includes useful context-setting background; Micklos's play-by-play descriptions of Ali's bouts provide just enough detail for boxing fans." Horn Book Guide

Includes bibliographical references

Myers, Walter Dean, 1937- The **greatest**: Muhammad Ali. Scholastic 2001 172p il hardcover o.p. pa $4.99

Grades: 7 8 9 10   92

1. African American athletes 2. Boxers (Persons) 3. Boxing -- Biography

ISBN 0-590-54342-3; 0-590-54343-1 pa

In this biography Myers combines "reportage of Ali's major fights (especially against Sonny Liston, Joe Frazier, and George Foreman) with his own reflections about the sport's destructiveness and about Ali's unpopular views." Horn Book

Owens, Tom. **Muhammad** Ali; boxing champ & role model. by Thomas S. Owens. ABDO Pub. Co. 2011 112p il (Legendary athletes) lib bdg $34.22

Grades: 6 7 8 9   92

1. African American athletes 2. Boxers (Persons) 3. Boxing -- Biography

ISBN 978-1-61714-752-4; 1-61714-752-4

LC 2010046233

This biography of boxing champion Muhammed Ali "goes beyond merely discussing [his] accomplishments. . . . [It] also [explores] the social and political [influence he] had on society as a whole. In addition, [it introduces] historical events in the context of [his life]. . . . This . . . is teeming with information and is a must-purchase for sports fans and readers interested in social activism." SLJ

Includes glossary and bibliographical references

★ Smith, Charles R., 1969- **Twelve** rounds to glory: the story of Muhammad Ali; illustrated by Bryan Collier. Candlewick Press 2007 80p il $19.99

Grades: 5 6 7 8   92

1. African American athletes 2. Boxers (Persons) 3. Boxing -- Biography

ISBN 978-0-7636-1692-2; 0-7636-1692-3

LC 2007-25998

"Rap-style cadences perfectly capture the drama that has always surrounded the boxer's life. . . . Collier's compelling watercolor collages with their brown overtones beautifully portray Ali's determination and strength." SLJ

Ali, Rubina

Ali, Rubina. **Slumgirl** dreaming; Rubina's journey to the stars. [by] Rubina Ali in collaboration with Anne Berthod and Divya Dugar. Delacorte Press 2009 187p il pa $9.99

Grades: 5 6 7 8   92

1. Actors 2. Children

ISBN 978-0-385-73908-5 pa; 0-385-73908-7 pa

LC 2009029305

The young actress describes her life growing up in the slums of Mumbai, her experiences on the set of the film "Slumdog Millionaire," and how her life has changed as a result of her role in the film

"The writing here has a journalistic feel. It is not poetic or especially nuanced. But in a sea of cookie-cutter biography series, this book stands out. It has heart, and is aimed at an age group that will identify with Ali in essential ways." SLJ

Allende, Isabel

Axelrod-Contrada, Joan. **Isabel** Allende. Marshall Cavendish Benchmark 2010 159p il (Today's writers and their works) $42.79

Grades: 8 9 10 11 12   92

1. Authors 2. Novelists 3. Dramatists 4. Journalists 5. Women authors 6. Authors, Chilean 7. Children's authors

ISBN 978-0-7614-4116-8; 0-7614-4116-6

This biography of Isabel Allende places the author in the context of her times and discusses her work.

This book provides "excellent information for reports. . . . [The text is] organized well, lending [itself] to be read in [its] entirety or used as needed for research, and [includes] full-color photos and illustrations." SLJ

Includes bibliographical references

McNeese, Tim. **Isabel** Allende. Chelsea House 2006 112p il (Great Hispanic heritage) lib bdg $30

Grades: 6 7 8 9   92

1. Authors 2. Novelists 3. Dramatists 4. Journalists 5. Women authors 6. Authors, Chilean 7. Children's authors

ISBN 0-7910-8836-7

LC 2006008379

A biography of the Chilean-American novelist

Includes bibliographical references

Alonso, Alicia

★ Bernier-Grand, Carmen T. **Alicia** Alonso; prima ballerina. illustrated by Raúl Colón. Marshall Cavendish Children's 2011 64p il $19.99

Grades: 4 5 6 7   92

1. Cubans 2. Ballet dancers 3. Choreographers 4. Dance directors

ISBN 978-0-7614-5562-2; 0-7614-5562-0

LC 2010018269

"An informative, beautifully illustrated introduction to the world-renowned dancer. Alonso's focused life and illustrious career are made even more remarkable by the fact that she lost her peripheral vision at age 19 and had to learn to visualize both the stage set and the dance itself in order to execute spins and lifts, and to choreograph ballets. Each one is presented as a titled one-page piece in abbreviated poetic prose; many face full-page textured paintings rendered in Colón's distinctive mix of watercolor, colored, and lithograph pencils." SLJ

Includes bibliographical references

Alvarez, Julia, 1950-

Aykroyd, Clarissa. **Julia** Alvarez; novelist and poet. by Clarissa Aykroyd. Lucent Books 2008 104p il (The twentieth century's most influential Hispanics) $32.45

Grades: 7 8 9 10   **92**
1. Poets 2. Authors 3. Novelists 4. Women authors 5. Hispanic American women 6. Essayists 7. Poets, American 8. College teachers 9. Children's authors
ISBN 978-1-4205-0022-6; 1-4205-0022-8
           LC 2007025974
"This introduction to author Alvarez gives a comprehensive look at the Dominican American writer's life and literary career. The lively writing . . . is supported by numerous quotes from Alvarez and details . . . that will pique kids' interest." Booklist
Includes bibliographical references

Andersen, Hans Christian, 1805-1875
★ Varmer, Hjordis. **Hans** Christian Andersen; his fairy tale life. illustrated by Lilian Brogger; translated by Tiina Nunnally. Groundwood Books 2005 111p il $19.95
Grades: 5 6 7 8   **92**
1. Authors 2. Novelists 3. Dramatists 4. Authors, Danish 5. Children's authors 6. Short story writers 7. Young adult literature -- Works 8. Biography, Individual
ISBN 0-88899-690-X
"Most of this book describes Andersen's childhood and belated schooling, showing his poverty and the grief he experienced over the death of his beloved father, as well as several horrifying events such as being forced by a teacher to witness the beheading of three young people. . . . The biography is divided into 11 chapters, set up as if they were stories. . . . The writing flows smoothly, with many details provided to help students picture the places and events. Brøgger's haunting, mixed-media illustrations add to the somber and at times surreal feeling of the text." SLJ

Anderson, Laurie Halse, 1961-
Glenn, Wendy J. **Laurie** Halse Anderson; speaking in tongues. Scarecrow Press 2010 169p (Scarecrow studies in young adult literature) $40
Grades: 8 9 10 11 12   **92**
1. Authors 2. Novelists 3. Women authors 4. Authors, American 5. Young adult authors
ISBN 978-0-8108-7281-3
           LC 2009-30545
"This book is a comprehensive look at the life, work, and thoughts of Laurie Halse Anderson. . . . Any teen with a research paper on Laurie Halse Anderson who is lucky enough to have access to this title will walk away with a high mark." Voice Youth Advocates
Includes bibliographical references

Anderson, Marian, 1897-1993
★ Freedman, Russell. The **voice** that challenged a nation; Marian Anderson and the struggle for equal rights. Clarion Books 2004 114p il $18
Grades: 5 6 7 8   **92**
1. African American women 2. African American singers 3. Opera singers 4. African Americans -- Civil rights 5. African American women -- Biography 6. African American singers -- Biography 7. Contraltos -- United States -- Biography
ISBN 0-618-15976-2
           LC 2003-19558

A Newbery Medal honor book, 2005
In the mid-1930s, Marian Anderson was a famed vocalist who had been applauded by European royalty and welcomed at the White House. But, because of her race, she was denied the right to sing at Constitution Hall in Washington, D.C. This is the story of her resulting involvement in the civil rights movement of the time.
"In his signature prose, plain yet eloquent, Freedman tells Anderson's triumphant story, with numerous black-and-white photos and prints that convey her personal struggle, professional artistry, and landmark civil rights role." Booklist
Includes bibliographical references

Jones, Victoria Garrett. **Marian** Anderson; a voice uplifted. [by] Victoria Garrett Jones. Sterling Pub. 2007 124p il (Sterling biographies) $12.95
Grades: 6 7 8 9   **92**
1. African American singers 2. Opera singers 3. African American women -- Biography
ISBN 978-1-4027-4239-2; 1-4027-4239-8
           LC 2007019268
"Filled with archival photographs and quotes, this stirring biography of Anderson gives a concise, yet thorough introduction to the famous contralto's life." Booklist
Includes bibligraphical references

Andrews, Roy Chapman, 1884-1960
★ Bausum, Ann. **Dragon** bones and dinosaur eggs: a photobiography of Roy Chapman Andrews. National Geographic Soc. 2000 64p il map $17.95
Grades: 5 6 7 8   **92**
1. Fossils 2. Dinosaurs 3. Explorers 4. Zoologists 5. Naturalists 6. Travel writers 7. Writers on nature 8. Writers on science 9. Museum administrators
ISBN 0-7922-7123-8
           LC 99-38363
A biography of the great explorer-adventurer, who discovered huge finds of dinosaur bones in Mongolia, pioneered modern paleontology field research, and became the director of the American Museum of Natural History
"Bausum's account reads smoothly, and a layout dense with captioned sepia photographs and quotes from Andrews provides plenty of oases for readers as they follow him through the desert." Bull Cent Child Books
Includes bibliographical references

Anthony, Susan B., 1820-1906
Colman, Penny. **Elizabeth** Cady Stanton and Susan B. Anthony; a friendship that changed the world. Henry Holt and Company 2011 256p il $18.99
Grades: 7 8 9 10   **92**
1. Feminism 2. Suffragists 3. Women -- Suffrage
ISBN 978-0-8050-8293-7; 0-8050-8293-X
           LC 2010-39762
"Elizabeth Cady Stanton, a married mother of four boys at the time they met, and Susan B. Anthony, an unmarried schoolteacher, formed a friendship that lasted until Elizabeth's death more than 50 years later. Their tireless work, including advocacy, speeches, organizing and writing, placed them at the center of tumultuous events in the middle of the 19th century. . . . This [is a] lively, very readable narrative.

. . . This thoughtful portrayal to two complex women is . . . enhanced by comprehensive backmatter, making this an invaluable addition to the literature of suffrage." Kirkus

Includes bibliographical references

Todd, Anne M. **Susan** B. Anthony; activist. Chelsea House Publishers 2009 128p il (Women of achievement) $30

Grades: 6 7 8 9   92

1. Feminism 2. Suffragists 3. Abolitionists

ISBN 978-1-60413-087-4; 1-60413-087-3

LC 2008034641

A biography of the women's rights activist.

The book is "well written; sidebars supplement the [narrative] with interesting facts." Horn Book Guide

Includes bibliographical references

Appleseed, Johnny, 1774-1845

Worth, Richard. **Johnny** Appleseed; select good seeds and plant them in good ground. Enslow Publishers 2010 128p il map (Americans: the spirit of a nation) $23.95

Grades: 4 5 6 7   92

1. Apples 2. Frontier and pioneer life 3. Pioneers 4. Fruit growers

ISBN 978-0-7660-3352-8; 0-7660-3352-X

LC 2008048701

"This nicely illustrated and sourced [biography] . . . includes full-page sidebars." Booklist

Includes glossary and bibliographical references

Archimedes, ca. 287-212 B.C.

Hightower, Paul. The **greatest** mathematician; Archimedes and his eureka! moment. Enslow Publishers 2010 128p il (Great minds of ancient science and math) lib bdg $31.93

Grades: 5 6 7 8   92

1. Mathematicians 2. Writers on science

ISBN 978-0-7660-3408-2 lib bdg; 0-7660-3408-9 lib bdg

LC 2008051818

This biography is a "solid [choice], as . . . [it provides] a good overview of the cultural and political landscape of the times, as well as pictures." SLJ

Includes glossary and bibliographical references

Aristotle, 384-322 B.C.

Gow, Mary. The **great** thinker: Aristotle and the foundations of science. Enslow Publishers 2010 128p il (Great minds of ancient science and math) lib bdg $31.93

Grades: 6 7 8 9   92

1. Philosophy 2. Scientists 3. Philosophers 4. Writers on science

ISBN 978-0-7660-3121-0; 0-7660-3121-7

LC 2009023813

"Presents a biography of the fourth-century B.C.E. Greek philosopher and scientist Aristotle, whose writings on logic, metaphysics, ethics, politics, and literary criticism influenced Western thought for hundreds of years. . . . [This] colorful, attractive book includes simple, straightforward

text with nice illustrations and appendixes of suggested activities, a supplemental chronology, chapter notes, and glossary." Voice Youth Advocates

Includes glossary and bibliographical references

Katz Cooper, Sharon. **Aristotle**; philosopher, teacher, and scientist. Compass Point Books 2006 112p il (Signature lives) $31.93

Grades: 6 7 8 9   92

1. Philosophers 2. Writers on science

ISBN 978-0-7565-1873-8; 0-7565-1873-3

LC 2006005403

A biography of the Greek philosopher

Includes glossary and bibliographical references

Katz Cooper, Sharon. **Aristotle**; philosopher, teacher, and scientist. Compass Point Books 2006 112p il (Signature lives) $31.93

Grades: 6 7 8 9   92

1. Philosophers 2. Writers on science

ISBN 978-0-7565-1873-8; 0-7565-1873-3

LC 2006005403

Includes glossary and bibliographical references

Armstrong, John Barclay, 1850-1913

Alter, Judy. **John** Barclay Armstrong; Texas Ranger. by Judy Alter. Bright Sky Press 2007 59p il $14.95

Grades: 4 5 6 7   92

1. Sheriffs 2. Texas Rangers

ISBN 978-1-931721-86-8

"Born in 1850 and raised in Tennessee, Armstrong went west to seek his fortune. At 25, he joined the Texas Rangers and soon came to embody the legendary qualities of these remarkable lawmen. He is an interesting character, and the author aptly tells his tale. The archival black-and-white photos add authenticity and help bring the man to life." SLJ

Armstrong, Louis, 1900-1971

Partridge, Kenneth. **Louis** Armstrong; musician. Chelsea House 2011 110p il (Black Americans of achievement) lib bdg $35

Grades: 6 7 8 9   92

1. Singers 2. Jazz musicians 3. African American musicians 4. Band leaders 5. Trumpet players

ISBN 978-1-60413-833-7; 1-60413-833-5

This "is a sweet, touching biography that looks at the extraordinary life of a musical genius. The writing is clear and engaging, with a light, humorous touch. . . . Readers are treated to an overview of a unique personality." SLJ

Includes bibliographical references

Arnold, Benedict, 1741-1801

Fritz, Jean. **Traitor**: the case of Benedict Arnold. Putnam 1981 191p il hardcover o.p. pa $5.99

Grades: 5 6 7 8   92

1. Spies 2. Generals 3. Army officers

ISBN 0-399-20834-8; 0-698-11553-8 pa

LC 81-10584

"The writing is smooth, the material carefully organized and used in the best of biographical style—that is, Arnold is presented accurately and the reader is left to judge the strength and weaknesses of his character rather than being told by the author." Bull Cent Child Books

Includes bibliographical references

★ Murphy, Jim. The **real** Benedict Arnold. Clarion Books 2007 264p il map $20

Grades: 7 8 9 10   **92**

1. Spies 2. Generals 3. Army officers
ISBN 978-0-395-77609-4; 0-395-77609-0

LC 2007-5700

"Using Arnold's surviving military journals and political documents, Murphy carefully contrasts popular myth with historical fact. . . . As far as possible, he meticulously traces Arnold's life, revealing a complex man who was actually as much admired as he was loathed." Booklist

Includes bibliographical references

★ Sheinkin, Steve. The **notorious** Benedict Arnold; a true story of adventure, heroism, & treachery. Steve Sheinkin. Roaring Brook Press 2010 337p. ill. $19.99

Grades: 7 8 9 10   **92**

1. Spies 2. Generals 3. American Loyalists 4. Army officers
ISBN 1-59643-486-4; 978-1-59643-486-8

LC 201034797

Boston Globe-Horn Book Awards: Nonfiction (2012)
YALSA Award for Excellence in Nonfiction for Young Adults (2012)

This is a biography of the Continental Army officer who won battles for the Americans during the Revolutionary War but felt ill-used and unappreciated by the Continental Congress. He obtained command of the fort at West Point, New York, and plotted to surrender it to the British. After the plot was exposed in September 1780, he was commissioned into the British Army. (Horn Book)

"Sheinkin sees Arnold as America's 'original action hero' and succeeds in writing a brilliant, fast-paced biography that reads like an adventure novel. . . . The author's obvious mastery of his material, lively prose and abundant use of eyewitness accounts make this one of the most exciting biographies young readers will find." Kirkus

Includes bibliographical references

Ashe, Arthur, 1943-1993

McDougall, Chros. **Arthur** Ashe; tennis great and civil rights leader. ABDO Pub. Co. 2011 112p il (Legendary athletes) lib bdg $34.22

Grades: 6 7 8 9   **92**

1. African American athletes 2. Tennis players 3. Nonfiction writers 4. Tennis -- Biography
ISBN 978-1-61714-753-1; 1-61714-753-2

LC 2010046583

This biography of tennis champion Arthur Ashe "goes beyond merely discussing [his] accomplishments. . . . [It] also [explores] the social and political [influence he] had on society as a whole. In addition, [it introduces] historical events in the context of [his life]. . . . This . . . is teeming with information and is a must-purchase for sports fans and readers interested in social activism." SLJ

Includes glossary and bibliographical references

Asimov, Isaac, 1920-1992

Hoppa, Jocelyn. **Isaac** Asimov; science fiction trailblazer. [by] Jocelyn Hoppa. Enslow Publishers 2009 104p il (Authors teens love) lib bdg $31.93

Grades: 6 7 8 9   **92**

1. Authors 2. Novelists 3. Biochemists 4. Authors, American 5. Children's authors 6. Writers on science 7. Short story writers 8. Young adult authors 9. Science fiction writers
ISBN 978-0-7660-2961-3; 0-7660-2961-1

LC 2008-12299

"A biography of Russian-American science-fiction author Isaac Asimov." Publisher's note

Includes bibliographical references

Attila, King of the Huns, d. 453

★ Price, Sean. **Attila** the Hun; leader of the barbarian hordes. [by] Sean Stewart Price. Franklin Watts 2009 128p il (A wicked history) $30; pa $5.95

Grades: 6 7 8 9   **92**

1. Huns 2. Kings and rulers 3. Tribal leaders
ISBN 978-0-531-21801-3; 0-531-21801-5; 978-0-531-20737-6 pa; 0-531-20737-4 pa

LC 2008040520

"In fascinating detail, the book not only introduces Attila, but gives the backstory on what made the rise of the Huns possible. The exciting yet concise writing brings readers close to the battlefield, but the fighting and intrigue are neatly set against the sweep of history." Booklist

Includes bibliographical references

Audubon, John James, 1785-1851

Sherman, Pat. **John** James Audubon. Chelsea House 2010 152p il map (Conservation heroes) lib bdg $35

Grades: 6 7 8 9 10   **92**

1. Artists 2. Painters 3. Naturalists 4. Ornithologists 5. Writers on science 6. Birds -- United States 7. Artists -- United States
ISBN 978-1-60413-953-2; 1-60413-953-6

LC 2010026480

A biography of the French American ornithologist and artist famous for his paintings and study of American birds.

"Captivating, richly informative. . . . The scope of [this book] is comprehensive. . . . [The book is] engaging as [it is] educational and will be ideal for research and reports." SLJ

Includes glossary and bibliographical references

Aung San Suu Kyi

Rose, Simon. **Aung** San Suu Kyi. 2011 24p il (Remarkable people) $27.13; pa $12.95

Grades: 4 5 6 7   **92**

1. Political prisoners 2. Women political activists 3. Dissenters 4. Political leaders 5. Nonfiction writers 6. Human rights activists 7. Nobel laureates for peace
ISBN 978-1-61690-833-1; 1-61690-833-5; 978-1-61690-834-8 pa; 1-61690-834-3 pa

LC 2011011584

This looks at Aung San Suu Kyi's "life, accomplishments, and challenges while including a page of quotes, an annotated list of contemporaries and influences, starter suggestions for writing a paper, and a time line and glossary. [The book] looks into the Nobel Peace Prize– winning Myanmar activist, whose struggle for democracy has landed her under house arrest multiple times." Booklist

Austen, Jane, 1775-1817

Locke, Juliane Poirier. **England's** Jane; the story of Jane Austen. [by] Juliane Locke. Morgan Reynolds Pub. 2006 144p il lib bdg $26.95

Grades: 7 8 9 10   92
1. Authors 2. Novelists 3. Women authors 4. Authors, English
ISBN 978-1-931798-82-2 lib bdg; 1-931798-82-6 (lib. bdg.)
LC 2005026279

"Drawing on letters, biographical works, archival pictures, and Austens novels, Locke offers a readable biography for students who cant manage a larger work. The language is uncomplicated and the topics are aimed at helping readers better understand Pride and Prejudice, Emma, and Austen's other writings." SLJ
Includes bibliographical references

★ Reef, Catherine. **Jane** Austen; a life revealed. Clarion Books 2011 192p il $18.99

Grades: 6 7 8 9 10   92
1. Authors 2. Novelists 3. Women authors 4. Novelists, English
ISBN 0-547-37021-0; 978-0-547-37021-7
LC 2011008146

Reef "combines firsthand accounts of Austen written by relatives and friends, historical information about Britain in the late 1700s, the basic facts of Austen's life that are readily known, and Austen's own novels and surviving letters, presented in a chronological format. . . . Reef's account also focuses on Austen's large family and many friends, highlighting the connections between Austen's novels and her life. . . . For devout Janeites it's fascinating to see all this information combined, and for others it's a worthwhile introduction to a masterful writer's life." Horn Book
Includes bibliographical references

Babbage, Charles, 1791-1871

Charles Babbage and the engines of perfection; [by] Bruce Collier and James MacLachlan. Oxford Univ. Press 1998 123p il (Oxford portraits in science) $28

Grades: 7 8 9 10   92
1. Mathematicians 2. Writers on science 3. Computers -- History 4. Mathematicians -- Great Britain -- Biography
ISBN 0-19-508997-9
LC 98-17054

Traces the life and work of the man whose nineteenth century inventions led to the development of the computer
"This is a fascinating portrait of Charles Babbage. . . . Generous b&w illustrations enliven the work." Book Rep
Includes bibliographical references

Baker, Ella, 1903-1986

Bohannon, Lisa Frederiksen. **Freedom** cannot rest; Ella Baker and the civil rights movement. [by] Lisa Frederiksen Bohannon. 1st ed; Morgan Reynolds Pub. 2005 176p il map (Portraits of Black Americans) lib bdg $26.95

Grades: 7 8 9 10   92
1. Essayists 2. Political leaders 3. Civil rights activists 4. African Americans -- Civil rights
ISBN 978-1-931798-71-6; 1-931798-71-0
LC 2005007156

"Baker was a major player in the Civil Rights movement of the 1960s. She was the principal organizer of SNCC, the Student Nonviolent Coordinating Committee. . . . Bohannon . . . makes good use of vintage photographs, artwork, and text boxes that further explain historical events. . . . Her biography might be a good place to start to get a good overview of Baker's life and the times in which she lived." SLJ
Includes bibliographical references

Banks, Tyra

Todd, Anne M. **Tyra** Banks; model and talk show host. Chelsea House 2009 120p il (Women of achievement) $30

Grades: 6 7 8 9   92
1. Actors 2. Fashion models 3. Television personalities 4. Talk show hosts 5. Models (Persons) 6. African American women -- Biography
ISBN 978-1-60413-462-9; 1-60413-462-3
LC 2009-9915

A biography of the African American fashion model, TV talk show host, and businesswoman.
Includes bibliographical references

Barakat, Ibtisam

★ Barakat, Ibtisam. **Tasting** the sky; a Palestinian childhood. Farrar, Straus & Giroux 2007 176p $16

Grades: 6 7 8 9 10   92
1. Poets 2. Authors 3. Palestinian Arabs 4. Israel-Arab conflicts 5. Memoirists 6. College teachers 7. Young adult authors 8. Arab-Israeli conflict -- 1967-1973
ISBN 0-374-35733-1; 978-0-374-35733-7
LC 2006-41265

"In 1981 the author, then in high school, boarded a bus bound for Ramallah. The bus was detained by Israeli soldiers at a checkpoint on the West Bank, and she was taken to a detention center before being released. The episode triggers sometimes heart-wrenching memories of herself as a young child, at the start of the 1967 Six Days' War, as Israeli soldiers conducted raids, their planes bombed her home, and she fled with her family across the border to Jordan. . . . What makes the memoir so compelling is the immediacy of the child's viewpoint, which depicts both conflict and daily life without exploitation or sentimentality." Booklist

Barnum, P. T. (Phineas Taylor), 1810-1891

★ Fleming, Candace. The **great** and only Barnum; the tremendous, stupendous life of showman

P.T. Barnum. illustrated by Ray Fenwick. Schwartz & Wade Books 2009 151p il $18.99; lib bdg $21.99
Grades: 5 6 7 8   **92**
1. Circus 2. Circus executives
ISBN 978-0-375-84197-2; 0-375-84197-0; 978-0-375-94597-7 lib bdg; 0-375-94597-0 lib bdg
LC 2008-45847
"In this sweeping yet cohesive biography, Fleming so finely tunes Barnum's legendary ballyhoo that you can practically hear the hucksterism and smell the sawdust. . . . The material is inherently juicy, but credit Fleming's vivacious prose, bountiful period illustrations, and copious source notes for fashioning a full picture on one of the forebearers of modern celebrity." Booklist
Includes bibliographical references

Barton, Clara, 1821-1912
Hamen, Susan E. **Clara** Barton; Civil War hero & American Red Cross founder. ABDO Pub. 2010 112p il map (Military heroes) lib bdg $22.95
Grades: 7 8 9   **92**
1. Nurses 2. Red Cross officials 3. Social welfare leaders
ISBN 978-1-60453-960-8; 1-60453-960-7
LC 2009-32363
"The rush of literary adrenalin will hook readers immediately and keep them enthralled until the end. . . . Given the dynamic topic [and] . . . appealing layout . . . [this is] likely to attract reluctant readers. In addition, sources are plentiful and well documented." SLJ
Includes glossary and bibliographical references

Krensky, Stephen. **Clara** Barton. DK Pub. 2011 128p il (DK biography) $14.99; pa $5.99
Grades: 5 6 7 8   **92**
1. Nurses 2. Red Cross officials 3. Social welfare leaders
ISBN 978-0-7566-7279-9; 0-7566-7279-1; 978-0-7566-7278-2 pa; 0-7566-7278-3 pa
Describes the life and accomplishments of Clara Barton, a teacher who organized efforts to bring nursing care to wounded soldiers during the Civil War and who went on to become the founder of the American Red Cross.
"Barton is placed in historical context, and key concepts, such as the causes of the Civil War, the struggle for women's suffrage, and the importance of the Geneva Convention, are explained. Compact in form, the text is complemented by full-color and archival photographs and reproductions on every spread. . . . An excellent resource for reports that will also appeal to fans of biography." SLJ
Includes bibliographical references

Somervill, Barbara A. **Clara** Barton; founder of the American Red Cross. Compass Point Books 2007 112p il lib bdg $23.95
Grades: 5 6 7 8   **92**
1. Nurses 2. Red Cross officials 3. Social welfare leaders
ISBN 978-0-7565-1888-2 lib bdg; 0-7565-1888-1 lib bdg
LC 2006027071

"With an open design, clear type, and period prints and photos on every double-page spread, this highly readable biography . . . does a great job of setting Barton's personal story within the history of her time." Booklist
Includes bibliographical references

Bates, Daisy
★ **Fight** on!: Mary Church Terrell's battle for integration; [by] Dennis Brindell Fradin & Judith Bloom Fradin. Clarion Bks. 2003 181p il $17
Grades: 6 7 8 9   **92**
1. Travelers 2. African American women 3. Feminists 4. Memoirists 5. Nonfiction writers 6. Civil rights activists 7. African Americans -- Civil rights 8. African American women -- Biography
ISBN 0-618-13349-6
LC 2002-151356
Profiles the first black Washington D.C. Board of Education member, who helped to found the NAACP and organized pickets and boycotts that led to the 1953 Supreme Court decision to integrate D.C. area restaurants
"In this carefully researched, fascinating biography, the life of the feisty, courageous, and determined woman . . . vividly unfolds." SLJ
Includes bibliographical references

Beethoven, Ludwig van, 1770-1827
Bauer, Helen. **Beethoven** for kids; his life and music with 21 activities. Chicago Review Press 2011 129p il pa $16.95
Grades: 4 5 6 7   **92**
1. Composers 2. Composers, Austrian
ISBN 1-56976-711-4; 978-1-56976-711-5
LC 2011018131
"This introduction to the towering classical composer sets the story of his life and work in the context of the revolutionary events of early-19th-century Europe. . . . The author's own extensive musical experience contributes to the breadth of this title. Sidebars and historical prints add further information about musical forms and instruments, historical events and people mentioned. . . . This will be particularly useful for parents and classroom teachers hoping to make the study of great music more interesting." Kirkus
Includes bibliographical references

Martin, Russell. The **mysteries** of Beethoven's hair; [by Russell Martin and Lydia Nibley] Charlesbridge 2009 120p il lib bdg $15.95
Grades: 5 6 7 8   **92**
1. Composers
ISBN 978-1-57091-714-1 lib bdg; 1-57091-714-0 lib bdg
LC 2008-07257
"Based on Martin's adult book Beethoven's Hair: An Extraordinary Historical Odyssey and Scientific Mystery Solved (Broadway, 2000), this reworking for a young audience presents an intriguing interdisciplinary story. Martin and Nibley trace the labyrinthine journey of a lock of Beethoven's hair encased in a glass and wooden locket from the 18th century to the present. . . . This is a most unusual, thoroughly researched detective story written in a clearly accessible and lively tone. Black-and-white photos and re-

productions appear throughout. . . . It is . . . an incredibly readable and absorbing selection that demonstrates the multidimensional nature of true scholarship." SLJ

Viegas, Jennifer. **Beethoven's** world; [by] Jennifer Viegas. Rosen Pub. Group 2008 64p il (Music throughout history) lib bdg $29.25

Grades: 5 6 7 8   92

    1. Composers

    ISBN 1-4042-0724-4 lib bdg; 978-1-4042-0724-0 lib bdg

                           LC 2005028917

This "book begins with an introduction briefly addressing social issues of the day, historical background, or other significant information. . . . Successive chapters discuss the [man's] early [life], family background, social status, personality characteristics, musical training and education, obstacles or challenges, and influences. A chapter . . . focuses on the musician's well-known compositions, describing through lively and colorful language some of the musical elements employed . . . The format and layout are appealing and uncluttered." SLJ

Includes glossary and bibliographical references

Bell, Alexander Graham, 1847-1922

Carson, Mary Kay. **Alexander** Graham Bell; giving voice to the world. [by] Mary Kay Carson. Sterling 2007 124p il (Sterling biographies) lib bdg $12.95; pa $5.95

Grades: 6 7 8 9   92

    1. Inventors   2. Teachers of the deaf   3. Telecommunications executives

    ISBN 978-1-4027-4951-3 lib bdg; 1-4027-4951-1 lib bdg; 1-4027-3230-9 pa; 978-1-4027-3230-0 pa

                           LC 2007003502

"Carson introduces Bell's life, giving readers an excellent picture of why this man became so famous. . . . [The book provides] clear, concise information in an easy-to-follow format with captioned photographs and illustrations on most pages." SLJ

Includes glossary and bibliographical references

Bell, Cool Papa, 1903-1991

McCormack, Shaun. **Cool** Papa Bell. Rosen Pub. Group 2002 112p il (Baseball Hall of Famers of the Negro leagues) lib bdg $29.25

Grades: 5 6 7 8   92

    1. Baseball players   2. African American athletes   3. Baseball -- Biography

    ISBN 0-8239-3474-8

                           LC 2001-3121

This is a biography of the African American who played in the Negro Leagues and was elected to the Baseball Hall of Fame in 1974

This "title presents an unvarnished picture of the racism in this country and how it impacted amateur and professional baseball from 1868 onward. . . . The layout . . . is attractive, the style . . . is engaging, and the b&w photographs enhance the narrative." Book Rep

Includes glossary and bibliographical references

Berlin, Irving, 1888-1989

Furstinger, Nancy. **Say** it with music; the story of Irving Berlin. Morgan Reynolds 2003 128p il (Masters of music) lib bdg $21.95

Grades: 6 7 8 9   92

    1. Composers   2. Lyricists   3. Centenarians   4. Composers -- United States

    ISBN 1-931798-12-5

                           LC 2003-6039

A biography of the Russian immigrant who came to America as a boy and became one of the most successful composers of popular songs, including "White Christmas" and "God Bless America"

"Written in a lively style, the text is clearly documented with source notes, and well-placed, black-and-white photographs appear throughout." SLJ

Includes bibliographical references

Bernstein, Leonard, 1918-1990

★ Rubin, Susan Goldman. **Music** was IT: young Leonard Bernstein. Charlesbridge 2011 178p il lib bdg $19.95

Grades: 5 6 7 8   92

    1. Composers   2. Conductors (Music)   3. Jews -- Biography

    ISBN 1-58089-344-9 lib bdg; 978-1-58089-344-2 lib bdg; 978-1-60734-276-2 e-book

                           LC 2010-07584

"An impeccably researched and told biography of Leonard Bernstein's musical apprenticeship, from toddlerhood to his conducting debut with the New York Philharmonic at age 25. . . . Drawn from interviews, family memoirs and other print resources, quotations are well-integrated and assiduously attributed. Photos, concert programs, early doodles and letters, excerpts from musical scores and other primary documentation enhance the text. Excellent bookmaking— from type to trim size—complements a remarkable celebration of a uniquely American musical genius." Kirkus

Bezos, Jeffrey, 1964-

Jeff Bezos; business genius of Amazon.com. Enslow Pubs. 2003 48p il (Internet biographies) lib bdg $18.95

Grades: 6 7 8 9   92

    1. Entrepreneurs   2. Retail executives   3. Internet executives   4. Booksellers and bookselling -- United States -- Biography

    ISBN 0-7660-1972-1

                           LC 2002-153174

Explores the life and career of the creator of the online bookstore Amazon.com, discussing his early interest in computers, business philosophy, and plans for the future

"Brief but thorough. . . . Jeff Bezos is written in approachable, descriptive language. . . . The accompanying photographs are not to be missed." Booklist

Includes bibliographical references

Robinson, Tom. **Jeff** Bezos; Amazon.com architect. ABDO Pub. Co. 2010 112p il (Publishing pioneers) $22.95

Grades: 5 6 7 8   **92**
1. Businessmen 2. Internet marketing 3. Booksellers and bookselling 4. Retail executives 5. Internet executives
ISBN 978-1-60453-759-8; 1-60453-759-0
LC 2009015989
In this biography of Amazon.com executive Jeff Bezos "the research is solid and there are extensive source notes. . . . With marbled borders and an array of photographs, maps, diagrams, and document reproductions, [this book has] an engaging and pleasing design. " SLJ
Includes glossary and bibliographical references

Scally, Robert. **Jeff** Bezos; founder of Amazon and the Kindle. by Robert D. Scally. Morgan Reynolds Pub. 2011 112p il (Business leaders) $28.95
Grades: 7 8 9 10 11 12   **92**
1. Businessmen 2. Retail executives 3. Internet executives
ISBN 978-1-59935-178-0; 1-59935-178-1; 978-1-59935-214-5 e-book
LC 2011015611
This biography of Jeff Bezos, founder of Amazon and Kindle, "will grab YAs. . . . The design is browsable, with clear type and lots of color screens and informal photos of young people at work." Booklist
Includes bibliographical references

Bhutto, Benazir
Naden, Corinne J. **Benazir** Bhutto. Marshall Cavendish Benchmark 2010 96p il (Leading women) $39.93
Grades: 5 6 7 8   **92**
1. Prime ministers 2. Women politicians 3. Political leaders
ISBN 978-0-7614-4952-2; 0-7614-4952-3
In this biography "readers learn about Bhutto's student years at Radcliffe College and her rise to prime minister of Pakistan, the first woman to lead a Muslim state. . . . The [woman's life is] revealed within the political and historical context of [her] times and [includes] quotes from autobiographical material. . . . Color and black-and-white photos are included. . . . The compact size, chronological organization, and accessible writing [style makes this biography a] good [resource] for reports." SLJ
Includes bibliographical references

★ Price, Sean. **Benazir** Bhutto. Heinemann Library 2009 112p il map (Front-page lives) $38.93
Grades: 6 7 8 9 10   **92**
1. Prime ministers 2. Political leaders 3. Women -- Pakistan 4. Prime ministers -- Pakistan
ISBN 978-1-43293-222-0; 1-43293-222-5
LC 2009018315
"This volume, on the assassinated leader of Pakistan, is particularly well done, thanks to Price's clear and compelling text. . . . The many color photographs are particularly crisp and colorful, and the sidebars briefly but effectively deal with important topics." Booklist
Includes bibliographical references

Biden, Joseph R.
Young, Jeff C. **Joe** Biden. Morgan Reynolds Pub. 2009 112p il (Political profiles) lib bdg $28.95
Grades: 6 7 8 9   **92**
1. Vice-presidents 2. Senators 3. Presidential candidates 4. Vice-presidents -- United States
ISBN 978-159935-131-5 lib bdg; 1-59935-131-5 lib bdg
LC 2009028467
A biography of Vice-President Joseph Biden
This biography is "solid, evenhanded, and wonderfully helpful. . . . Unusually well-chosen photos, fine notes, and [a list] of further sources add to the usefulness and appeal of this [book]." Booklist
Includes bibliographical references

Bieber, Justin, 1994-
Bieber, Justin. **Justin** Bieber: first step 2 forever; my story. HarperCollins Children's Books 2010 236p il $21.99
Grades: 4 5 6 7   **92**
1. Singers 2. Pop musicians
ISBN 978-0-06-203974-3; 0-06-203974-1
"Bieber, the platinum-selling singer/songwriter . . . debuts with an account of his 16-year-old life that's cheeky yet entirely in line with his safe and wholesome image. . . . The book covers his upbringing in Ontario, his early introduction to music, YouTube stardom, his love of pranks, and the stratospheric success he now enjoys—all interspersed with lyrics, tweets, and numerous full-bleed photographs of Bieber." Publ Wkly

Yasuda, Anita. **Justin** Bieber. 2011 24p il (Remarkable people) lib bdg $27.13; pa $12.95
Grades: 4 5 6 7   **92**
1. Singers 2. Pop musicians
ISBN 978-1-61690-667-2 lib bdg; 1-61690-667-7 lib bdg; 978-1-61690-672-6 pa; 1-61690-672-3 pa
LC 2010051002
This looks at Justin Bieber's "life, accomplishments, and challenges while including a page of quotes, an annotated list of contemporaries and influences, starter suggestions for writing a paper, and a time line and glossary. . . . [This book] tracks the music sensation from 12-year-old YouTube phenom to the kind of celebrity who's earned such numbing fun facts as 'Justin has a dog named Sam.'" Booklist

Binstock, Melissa
Binstock, Melissa. **Nourishment**; feeding my starving soul when my mind and body betrayed me. Health Communications 2011 276p pa $14.95
Grades: 7 8 9 10   **92**
1. Students 2. Mentally ill 3. Tourette syndrome 4. Learning disabilities 5. Attention deficit disorder 6. Obsessive-compulsive disorder 7. Memoirists 8. Anorexia nervosa -- Personal narratives
ISBN 978-0-7573-1542-8 pa; 0-7573-1542-9 pa; 978-0-7573-9193-4 ebook; 0-7573-9193-1 ebook
LC 2010039690
"This unforgettable memoir chronicles the torment and challenges that plague the author. She is diagnosed with var-

ious psychological and neurological disorders by the young age of eleven years. . . . Melissa becomes acquainted with a new-type of therapy through her equestrian accomplishments. Soon however, . . . Melissa's fragile system, sends Melissa into a serious bout of mental illness and anorexia nervosa. . . . Once inside this facility, Melissa generously allows readers to eavesdrop into the day-to-day world of those who suffer from this plight. . . . This is a great read for teenagers who suffer from mental illness, peer acceptance issues, and eating disorders." Voice Youth Advocates

Black Elk, 1863-1950

★ Nelson, S. D. **Black** Elk's vision; a Lakota story. Abrams Books for Young Readers 2010 47p il $19.95

Grades: 5 6 7 8   **92**

1. Shamans 2. Oglala Indians 3. Indian leaders 4. Native Americans -- Biography

ISBN 978-0-8109-8399-1; 0-8109-8399-0

LC 2009-9392

"This handsomely designed, large-format book tells the story of Black Elk (1863-1950), a Lakota man who saw many changes come to his people. . . . Often quoting from Black Elk Speaks (1932), Nelson makes vivid the painful ways life changed for the Lakotain in the 1800s. . . . Colorful, imaginative artwork, created using pencils and acrylic paints, is interspersed with nineteenth-century photos, underscoring that this dramatic account reflects the experiences of a man who witnessed history." Booklist

Blake, William, 1757-1827

Bedard, Michael. **William** Blake; the gates of paradise. Tundra Books 2006 192p il $28.99

Grades: 8 9 10 11 12   **92**

1. Poets 2. Artists 3. Authors 4. Engravers 5. Illustrators 6. Poets, English 7. Authors, English

ISBN 978-0-88776-763-0; 0-88776-763-X

"Bedard provides a satisfying biography of English artist, poet and visionary William Blake. . . . Illustrated with drawings, paintings, engravings, and photos of sites and artifacts, the book is handsomely produced. . . . Bedard writes with precision, simplicity, and grace." Booklist

Includes bibliographical references

Bloomberg, Michael

Shichtman, Sandra H. **Michael** Bloomberg. Morgan Reynolds Pub. 2011 112p il (Political profiles) $28.95

Grades: 6 7 8 9   **92**

1. Mayors 2. Businesspeople 3. Financial executives 4. News agency executives 5. Broadcasting executives

ISBN 978-1-59935-135-3; 1-59935-135-8

LC 2009054286

"This solid biography of Michael Bloomberg spends a good deal of space on his early life. . . . His ambition and willingness to work hard were factors in his early business success at Salomon Brothers. . . . The second half of the book covers Bloomberg's political career. . . . His personal life is deftly handled with pictures of both his daughters and his significant other. The book features an engaging design highlighted by plenty of bright, well-captioned color photo-

graphs. . . . Although mostly for report writers, even browsers might find this biography worth their while." Booklist

Includes bibliographical references

Bly, Nellie, 1864-1922

★ Macy, Sue. **Bylines**: a photobiography of Nellie Bly; foreword by Linda Ellerbee. National Geographic 2009 64p il map $19.95; lib bdg $28.90

Grades: 5 6 7 8   **92**

1. Authors 2. Journalists 3. Women journalists 4. Nonfiction writers

ISBN 978-1-4263-0513-9; 1-4263-0513-3; 978-1-4263-0514-6 lib bdg; 1-4263-0514-1 lib bdg

LC 2008-52329

"This detailed biography of the trailblazing 19th-century journalist incorporates photographs of Bly and her subjects. The extensive text explores the details of a life spent seeking justice. . . . A thorough introduction to the life of a fascinating figure." Publ Wkly

Bohr, Niels

Spangenburg, Ray. **Niels** Bohr; atomic theorist. [by] Ray Spangenburg and Diane Kit Moser. Rev ed; Chelsea House 2008 141p il (Makers of modern science) $35.00

Grades: 7 8 9 10 11 12   **92**

1. Physicists 2. Scientists 3. Nobel laureates for physics

ISBN 978-0-8160-6178-5; 0-8160-6178-5

LC 2008-1196

"Spangenburg and Moser delve into Bohr's background and present him as a loving, talkative, and inquisitive person who liked soccer. He was also concerned about the consequences of his work with nuclear weapons and was involved in many humanitarian efforts... New content includes informational sidebars and a discussion of string theory." SLJ

Includes bibliographical references

Bolívar, Simón, 1783-1830

Reis, Ronald A. **Simon** Bolivar. Chelsea House 2010 120p il (The great Hispanic heritage) $30

Grades: 6 7 8 9   **92**

1. Generals 2. Statesmen 3. Revolutionaries

ISBN 978-1-60413-731-6; 1-60413-731-2

LC 2010-9485

This "offers a balanced view of El Liberator, who shed his privileged youth in a wealthy Creole Venezuelan family and became a military strategist determined to create independent Latin American states. . . . A selection of well-chosen images, a chronology, chapter notes, and [a] suggested reading [list] round out [this] engaging [title] in a sure-to-be popular [book] for reports and personal interest." Booklist

Includes bibliographical references

Borges, Jorge Luis, 1899-1986

McNeese, Tim. **Jorge** Luis Borges; [by] Tim McNeese. Chelsea House 2008 119p il (The great Hispanic heritage) $30

Grades: 6 7 8 9   **92**

1. Poets 2. Authors 3. Novelists 4. Authors, Argentine 5. Essayists 6. Translators 7. Literary critics 8. Short

story writers
ISBN 978-0-7910-9665-9; 0-7910-9665-3

LC 2007032008

This biography provides a "substantive [portrait], including background information and historical context, of . . . beloved writer Borges. . . . The well-documented [text] effectively [combines] anecdotes, quotations, and historical details. Many photographs and sidebars are also included." Horn Book Guide

Includes bibliographical references

Bourgeois, Louise, 1911-2010

★ Greenberg, Jan. **Runaway** girl: the artist Louise Bourgeois; [by] Jan Greenberg and Sandra Jordan. Abrams 2003 80p il $19.95

Grades: 7 8 9 10   92

1. Artists 2. Sculptors 3. Women artists 4. Artists -- United States
ISBN 0-8109-4237-2

LC 2002-11922

Introduces the life of renowned modern artist Louise Bourgeois, who is known primarily for her sculptures

"In clear, elegant prose, bolstered with numerous quotes from the artist, the authors seamlessly juxtapose stories of Bourgeois' life with relevant artworks. . . . Beautifully reproduced photographs, printed on well-designed pages, offer an excellent mix of the artist's personal life and her art." Booklist

Includes bibliographical references

Boyle, Robert, 1627-1691

Baxter, Roberta. **Skeptical** chemist; the story of Robert Boyle. Morgan Reynolds Pub. 2006 128p il (Profiles in science) lib bdg $27.95

Grades: 7 8 9 10   92

1. Chemists 2. Physicists 3. Scientists 4. Nonfiction writers 5. Writers on science
ISBN 978-1-59935-025-7; 1-59935-025-4

LC 2006-23969

The author makes a "case for Boyle's significance as a key figure in the field of scientific experimentation as well as his contributions to modern chemistry and physics. Well organized and clearly written, her book offers a good view of changes in science and society at this pivotal time and presents a well-rounded view of Boyle, whose interests extended beyond scientific inquiry and discussion." Booklist

Includes bibliographical references

Bradbury, Ray, 1920-

Bankston, John. **Ray** Bradbury; foreword by Kyle Zimmer. Chelsea House 2011 140p il (Who wrote that?) $35

Grades: 6 7 8 9 10   92

1. Authors 2. Novelists 3. Screenwriters 4. Authors, American 5. Children's authors 6. Short story writers 7. Science fiction writers
ISBN 1-60413-778-9; 978-1-60413-778-1

This discusses the life and work of author Ray Bradbury.

Includes bibliographical references

Brahe, Tycho, 1546-1601

Boerst, William J. **Tycho** Brahe; mapping the heavens. Morgan Reynolds 2003 144p il maps (Renaissance scientists) lib bdg $23.95

Grades: 7 8 9 10   92

1. Poets 2. Authors 3. Astronomers 4. Astronomers -- Denmark -- Biography
ISBN 1-88384-697-8

LC 2002-153640

Presents the life and work of the famous sixteenth-century Danish astronomer

"Boerst provides a clearly written account of Brahe's education, background, personality, and career. Full-color illustrations, including many reproductions of period portraits and other artwork, appear throughout the book." Booklist

Includes bibliographical references

Nardo, Don. **Tycho** Brahe; pioneer of astronomy. by Don Nardo. Compass Point Books 2008 112p il (Signature lives) lib bdg $23.95

Grades: 6 7 8 9   92

1. Poets 2. Authors 3. Astronomers
ISBN 978-0-7565-3309-0 lib bdg; 0-7565-3309-0 lib bdg

LC 2007004608

A biography of the sixteenth-century Danish astronomer Tycho Brahe.

"Nardo brings his lively, informative approach to this stanout biography." Booklist

Includes bibliographical references

Braille, Louis, 1809-1852

★ Freedman, Russell. **Out** of darkness: the story of Louis Braille; illustrated by Kate Kiesler. Clarion Bks. 1997 81p il $16.95; pa $7.95

Grades: 4 5 6 7   92

1. Blind 2. Inventors 3. Teachers of the blind 4. Blind -- Books and reading
ISBN 0-395-77516-7; 0-395-96888-7 pa

LC 95-52353

"Without melodrama, Freedman tells the momentous story in quiet chapters in his best plain style, making the facts immediate and personal. . . . A diagram explains how the Braille alphabet works, and Kate Kessler's full-page shaded pencil illustrations are part of the understated poignant drama." Booklist

Brave Bird, Mary

Brave Bird, Mary. **Lakota** woman; by Mary Crow Dog and Richard Erdoes. 1st HarperPerennial ed; HarperPerennial 1991 263p il rpt $14.95

Grades: 8 9 10 11 12 Adult   92

1. Dakota Indians 2. Political activists 3. Memoirists 4. Indian leaders 5. Native Americans -- Biography
ISBN 0-06-097389-7; 9780802145420 rpt

LC 90-55980

First published 1990 by Grove Weidenfeld

"Born in 1955 and raised in poverty on the Rosebud Reservation, Mary Crow Dog escaped an oppressive Catholic boarding school but fell into a marginal life of urban shoplifting and barhopping. A 1971 encounter with AIM (the

American Indian Movement), participation in the 1972 Trail of Broken Treaties march on Washington, and giving birth to her first child while under fire at the 1973 siege of Wounded Knee radicalized her." Libr J

Breckinridge, Mary, 1881-1965

★ Wells, Rosemary. **Mary** on horseback; three mountain stories. pictures by Peter McCarty. Dial Bks. for Young Readers 1998 53p il $16.99; pa $4.99

Grades: 4 5 6 7   **92**

1. Nurses 2. Midwives 3. Nurses -- Kentucky 4. Medical care -- Kentucky -- History
ISBN 0-670-88923-7; 0-14-130815-X pa

LC 97-43409

Tells the stories of three families who were helped by the work of Mary Breckinridge, the first nurse to go into the Appalachian Mountains and give medical care to the isolated inhabitants. Includes an afterword with facts about Breckinridge and the Frontier Nursing Service she founded

"These beautifully written stories will remain with the reader long after the book is closed." Booklist

Bridgman, Laura Dewey, 1829-1889

Alexander, Sally Hobart. **She** touched the world: Laura Bridgman, deaf-blind pioneer; by Sally Hobart Alexander and Robert Alexander. Clarion Books 2008 100p il $18

Grades: 5 6 7 8   **92**

1. Deaf 2. Blind 3. Students 4. Physicians 5. Philanthropists 6. Humanitarians 7. Teachers of the blind
ISBN 978-0-618-85299-4; 0-618-85299-9

"At the age of three, in 1832, Laura Bridgman contracted scarlet fever and lost her sight, her hearing, her sense of smell, and much of her sense of taste. Her family sent her to Dr. Samuel [Gridley] Howe at the New England Institute for the Education of the Blind, and by the age of 10, Laura was world-famous for her accomplishments. . . . Alexander . . . presents a well-written and thoroughly researched biography of this remarkable woman, with numerous black-and-white photos." Booklist

Includes bibliographical references

Brin, Sergey

Sapet, Kerrily. **Google** founders: Larry Page and Sergey Brin. Morgan Reynolds Pub. 2011 112p il (Business leaders) $28.95

Grades: 7 8 9 10 11 12   **92**

1. Businesspeople 2. Web search engines 3. Computer scientists 4. Internet executives 5. Information technology executives
ISBN 978-1-59935-177-3; 1-59935-177-3; 978-1-59935-213-8 e-book

LC 2011014665

This biography of Google founders Larry Page and Sergey Bring "will grab YAs. . . . The design is browsable, with clear type and lots of color screens and informal photos of young people at work." Booklist

Includes bibliographical references

Brown, Jeremy K.

Amelia Earhart. Chelsea House 2011 132p il lib bdg $35

Grades: 6 7 8   **92**

1. Air pilots 2. Missing persons 3. Women air pilots 4. Memoirists
ISBN 978-1-60413-910-5; 1-60413-910-2

This "supplies an evenhanded account of Earhart's personal life, her challenges as a woman in aviation, and her many achievements in flight. . . . Solid fare for the biography collection." Booklist

Brown, John, 1800-1859

★ Hendrix, John. **John** Brown; his fight for freedom. written and illustrated by John Hendrix. Abrams Books for Young Readers 2009 39p il $18.95

Grades: 4 5 6 7   **92**

1. Abolitionists 2. Slavery -- United States 3. Slavery -- History
ISBN 978-0-8109-3798-7; 0-8109-3798-0

LC 2008-45969

The author "traces how John Brown went from conducting slaves along the Underground Railroad to espousing violent insurrection as a means to end slavery. . . . Reinforcing Brown as a larger-than-life folk hero, the pictures are exhilarating. . . . By embracing Brown's complexity, especially in the well-argued afterword, Hendrix sows acres of fertile ground for discussion." Booklist

Sterngass, Jon. **John** Brown. Chelsea House 2009 144p il (Leaders of the Civil War era) lib bdg $30

Grades: 7 8 9 10   **92**

1. Abolitionists
ISBN 978-1-60413-305-9; 1-60413-305-8

LC 2008-44622

This is a biography of the abolitionist, John Brown.

This is an "even-keeled and well-written account of the man's life and times. . . . Sterngass displays a sharp awareness that what makes the man so controversial is also what makes him so fascinating. . . . [This book] should add depth to Civil War studies." Booklist

Includes glossary and bibliographical references

Bruchac, Joseph, 1942-

★ Bruchac, Joseph. **Bowman's** store; a journey to myself. 1st Lee & Low ed; Lee & Low Books 2001 315p il pa $9.95

Grades: 7 8 9 10   **92**

1. Poets 2. Authors 3. Abnaki Indians 4. Storytellers 5. College teachers 6. Magazine editors 7. Authors, American 8. Children's authors 9. Nonfiction writers 10. Native Americans -- Biography
ISBN 1-58430-027-2; 978-1-58430-027-4

LC 2001-16435

A reissue of the title first published 1997 by Dial Books

"Each episode is constructed with a true storyteller's attention to language and plot development. Students of modern Native American cultures will find plenty of food for thought." Booklist

Buchanan, James, 1791-1868

Burgan, Michael. **James** Buchanan. Marshall Cavendish Benchmark 2011 112p il (Presidents and their times) lib bdg $23.95

Grades: 5 6 7 8   92

1. Presidents 2. Senators 3. Members of Congress 4. Secretaries of state 5. Presidents -- United States
ISBN 978-0-7614-4810-5; 0-7614-4810-1

LC 2009025933

This offers information on President James Buchanan and places him within his historical and cultural context. Also explored are the formative events of his times and how he responded.

"The abundant sidebars provide a good deal of background information that will be helpful to students. . . . Attractive . . . as well as useful." Booklist

Includes glossary and bibliographical references

Buffett, Warren E.

Johnson, Anne Janette. **Warren** Buffett; [by] Anne Janette Johnson. Morgan Reynolds Pub. 2008 128p il (Business leaders) $28.95

Grades: 7 8 9 10   92

1. Capitalists and financiers 2. Financiers
ISBN 978-1-59935-080-6; 1-59935-080-7

LC 2007045963

"This book answers many questions about the unassuming billionaire from Omaha. Buffett's life . . . is detailed on both personal and professional levels. . . . Anecdotes make the book accessible and demystify the sometimes-confusing world of stocks and investments. . . . A fair number of color photos is included." SLJ

Includes bibliographical references

Burns, Anthony, 1834-1862

★ Hamilton, Virginia. **Anthony** Burns: the defeat and triumph of a fugitive slave. Knopf 1988 193p hardcover o.p. pa $5.50

Grades: 5 6 7 8   92

1. Slaves 2. Slavery -- United States 3. African Americans -- Biography
ISBN 0-679-83997-6 pa

LC 87-38063

A biography of the slave who escaped to Boston in 1854, was arrested at the instigation of his owner, and whose trial caused a furor between abolitionists and those determined to enforce the Fugitive Slave Act

"This book does exactly what good biography for children ought to do: takes readers directly into the life of the subject and makes them feel what it was like to be that person in those times." Horn Book

Includes bibliographical references

Burr, Aaron, 1756-1836

★ St. George, Judith. The **duel**: the parallel lives of Alexander Hamilton and Aaron Burr. Viking 2009 97p il $16.99

Grades: 6 7 8 9 10   92

1. Statesmen 2. Vice-presidents 3. Secretaries of the treasury 4. Politicians -- United States 5. Burr-Hamilton Duel, Weehawken, N.J., 1804
ISBN 978-0-670-01124-7; 0-670-01124-X

LC 2009-5660

"After a prologue following the steps of Alexander Hamilton and Aaron Burr on the morning of their famous duel, St. George backtracks to trace the 'parallel lives' mentioned in the subtitle. . . . Well researched and organized, the book offers insights into the personalities, lives, and times of Burr and Hamilton." Booklist

Burton, Richard Francis Sir, 1821-1890

Young, Serinity. **Richard** Francis Burton; explorer, scholar, spy. [by] Serinity Young. Marshall Cavendish Benchmark 2006 80p il map (Great explorations) lib bdg $32.79

Grades: 5 6 7 8   92

1. Explorers 2. Travel writers 3. Asian studies specialists 4. Middle Eastern studies specialists
ISBN 978-0-7614-2222-8 lib bdg; 0-7614-2222-6 lib bdg

LC 2005027932

A biography of the 19th century English explorer of Asia and Africa

Includes bibliographical references

Busby, Cylin, 1970-

★ Busby, Cylin. The **year** we disappeared; a father-daughter memoir. [by] Cylin Busby & John Busby. Bloomsbury 2008 329p $16.99

Grades: 8 9 10 11 12   92

1. Police 2. Authors 3. Violence 4. Father-daughter relationship 5. Magazine editors 6. Children's authors
ISBN 978-1-59990-141-1; 1-59990-141-2

LC 2008017215

"No one with even a marginal interest in true crime writing should miss this page-turner, by turns shocking and almost unbearably sad. In 1979, in an underworld-style hit, a gunman shot John Busby, a policeman in Cape Cod; a fluke saved John's life, but he was permanently disfigured and disabled, and the family placed under 24-hour protection. Eventually the family went into hiding in Tennessee, but arguably their 'disappearance' takes place long before they move—as John and his daughter, Cylin, alternately narrate, readers can see how the shooting erased the family's sense of themselves. . . . Where John's chapters provide the grim facts, it is Cylin's authentically childlike perspective that, in revealing the cost to her innocence, renders the tragic experience most searingly." Publ Wkly

Includes bibliographical references

Busby, John, 1942-

★ Busby, Cylin. The **year** we disappeared; a father-daughter memoir. [by] Cylin Busby & John Busby. Bloomsbury 2008 329p $16.99

Grades: 8 9 10 11 12   92

1. Police 2. Authors 3. Violence 4. Father-daughter relationship 5. Magazine editors 6. Children's authors
ISBN 978-1-59990-141-1; 1-59990-141-2

LC 2008017215

"No one with even a marginal interest in true crime writing should miss this page-turner, by turns shocking and almost unbearably sad. In 1979, in an underworld-style hit, a gunman shot John Busby, a policeman in Cape Cod; a fluke saved John's life, but he was permanently disfigured and disabled, and the family placed under 24-hour protection. Eventually the family went into hiding in Tennessee, but arguably their 'disappearance' takes place long before they move—as John and his daughter, Cylin, alternately narrate, readers can see how the shooting erased the family's sense of themselves. . . . Where John's chapters provide the grim facts, it is Cylin's authentically childlike perspective that, in revealing the cost to her innocence, renders the tragic experience most searingly." Publ Wkly

Includes bibliographical references

Caesar, Julius, 100-44 B.C.

Galford, Ellen. **Julius** Caesar; the boy who conquered an empire. [by] Ellen Galford. National Geographic 2007 64p il map (World history biographies) $17.95; lib bdg $27.90

Grades: 5 6 7 8   92

1. Statesmen 2. Historians 3. Emperors -- Rome
ISBN 978-1-4263-0064-6; 978-1-4263-0065-3 lib bdg
LC 2006020777

A biography of the Roman emperor

This "visually appealing [title is] packed with excellent photographs and reproductions, interesting sidebars, and [has] a time line running along the bottom of every page. . . . [This book is] useful, well-written." SLJ

Includes glossary and bibliographical references

Calcines, Eduardo F., 1955-

★ Calcines, Eduardo F. **Leaving** Glorytown; one boy's struggle under Castro. Farrar, Straus & Giroux 2009 221p il $17.95

Grades: 7 8 9 10   92

1. Businesspeople 2. Cuban refugees 3. Memoirists
ISBN 978-0-374-34394-1; 0-374-34394-2
LC 2008-7506

"Calcines's spirited memoir captures the political tension, economic hardship, family stress, and personal anxiety of growing up during the early years of the Castro regime in Cuba. . . . The author shares startling, clear memories about his life in the Glorytown barrio of Cienfuegos. . . . Calcines writes about Cuba with immediacy, nostalgia, and passion. This personal account will acquaint readers with the oppressive and ironic effects of communism." SLJ

Callwood, June, 1924-2007

Dublin, Anne. **June** Callwood; a life of action. Second Story Press 2007 140p il pa $14.95

Grades: 7 8 9 10 11 12   92

1. Canadians 2. Journalists 3. Social action 4. Women journalists 5. Feminists 6. Social activists
ISBN 978-1-89718-714-2

"This biography of the Canadian journalist and social activist chronicles Callwood's long life with loving care and places her activism within the cultural and historical context of pre and postwar Canada. . . . This is a well-told life story, with many black-and-white photographs that infuse the subject with personality." SLJ

Canaletto, 1697-1768

Rice, Earle. **Canaletto**; by Earle Rice Jr. Mitchell Lane Publishers 2007 48p il (Art profiles for kids) lib bdg $29.95

Grades: 7 8 9 10   92

1. Artists 2. Painters 3. Artists, Italian
ISBN 978-1-58415-561-4 lib bdg; 1-58415-561-2 lib bdg
LC 2007023412

This offers "well-documented information for teens doing reports. [The] volume covers the painter's childhood, training, travels, influences, and historical context. The chronological chapters build a survey of the [artist's] oeuvres, including the style and subject matter of [his] works and past and present critical reaction." SLJ

Includes glossary and bibliographical references

Carnegie, Andrew, 1835-1919

Edge, Laura Bufano. **Andrew** Carnegie; industrial philanthropist. [by] Laura B. Edge. Lerner Publications Co. 2004 128p il (Lerner biography) lib bdg $27.93

Grades: 6 7 8 9   92

1. Businessmen 2. Steel industry 3. Philanthropists 4. Capitalists and financiers 5. Metal industry executives 6. Industrialists -- United States -- Biography 7. Philanthropists -- United States -- Biography
ISBN 0-8225-4965-4
LC 2002-152936

Chronicles the rags-to-riches tale of a Scottish immigrant who used most of the millions he earned as a steel tycoon to set up a fund for the advancement of science, education, and peace.

"Children will come away with a good sense of a man driven by contradictory impulses." Booklist

Includes bibliographical references

Carr, Emily, 1871-1945

★ Debon, Nicolas. **Four** pictures by Emily Carr. Douglas & McIntyre 2003 un il $15.95

Grades: 4 5 6 7   92

1. Artists 2. Painters 3. Women artists 4. Artists, Canadian 5. Diarists 6. Memoirists
ISBN 0-88899-532-6

"Debon has distilled four periods in the Canadian artist's life (1871-1945) into enticing vignettes that illuminate her passions, determination, health problems, relationships with fellow Group of Seven artists, and, most of all, her dramatic progression as a painter. . . . Engaging artwork and brisk storytelling make this a consideration for most libraries." SLJ

Carroll, Lewis, 1832-1898

Carpenter, Angelica Shirley. **Lewis** Carroll; through the looking glass. Lerner Publs. 2003 128p il map (Lerner biography) lib bdg $27.93

Grades: 7 8 9 10   92

1. Authors 2. Novelists 3. Mathematicians 4. Authors, English 5. Children's authors 6. Writers on science 7. Children's stories -- Authorship 8. Authors, English --

19th century -- Biography
ISBN 0-8225-0073-6

LC 2002-3266

A biography of the mathematician, teacher, photographer, and author who wrote "Alice in Wonderland"

"An accessible, well-documented portrait." SLJ

Includes bibliographical references

Rubin, C. M. The **real** Alice in Wonderland; a role model for the ages. [by] C.M. Rubin with Gabriella Rose Rubin. AuthorHouse 2010 134p il $29.95

Grades: 7 8 9 10   **92**

1. Authors 2. Children 3. Novelists 4. Mathematicians 5. Characters and characteristics in literature 6. Children's authors 7. Writers on science

ISBN 978-1-4490-8131-7; 1-4490-8131-2

LC 2010-901865

"Readers will follow this title down the rabbit hole to discover the world of the real Alice who inspired Lewis Carroll's Alice in Wonderland. The book moves seamlessly through the life of Alice Pleasance Liddell. . . . This offering paints a full picture of Alice, not only as a child who has captivated literature but also as a woman who was truly ahead of her time. This is a purchase that will do well with a range of people and should be offered as a standard accompaniment to Alice in Wonderland. The illustrations and pictures will make it quite popular in a public library." Voice Youth Advocates

Includes bibliographical references

Carson, Rachel, 1907-1964

Piddock, Charles. **Rachel** Carson; a voice for the natural world. Gareth Stevens Pub. 2009 112p il map (Life portraits) lib bdg $34

Grades: 7 8 9 10   **92**

1. Authors 2. Biologists 3. Conservationists 4. Women scientists 5. Environmentalists 6. College teachers 7. Marine biologists 8. Writers on nature 9. Writers on science

ISBN 978-1-4339-0058-7 lib bdg; 1-4339-0058-0 lib bdg

LC 2008-31544

"Readers learn not only about . . . [Carson's] successful writing career but also about the sacrifices she made for her family and the injustices she sometimes suffered, both as a woman scientist and as someone who fought against chemical companies long before today's environmental movement. . . . Many photos, images, and sidebars . . . inform without being didactic and educate without preaching." Voice Youth Advocates

Includes glossary and bibliographical references

Scherer, Glenn. **Who** on earth is Rachel Carson? mother of the environmental movement. [by] Glenn Scherer and Marty Fletcher. Enslow Publishers 2009 112p il (Scientists saving the earth) lib bdg $31.93

Grades: 5 6 7 8   **92**

1. Authors 2. Biologists 3. Conservationists 4. Women scientists 5. Environmentalists 6. College teachers 7. Marine biologists 8. Writers on nature 9.

Writers on science
ISBN 978-1-59845-116-0 lib bdg; 1-59845-116-2 lib bdg

LC 2008028498

"The writing is clear and informative. . . . Color photographs are relevant and of good quality." SLJ

Includes bibliographical references

Cartier, Jacques, 1491-1557

Woog, Adam. **Jacques** Cartier. Chelsea House 2009 109p il map (Great explorers) lib bdg $30

Grades: 6 7 8 9   **92**

1. Explorers

ISBN 978-1-60413-430-8 lib bdg; 1-60413-430-5 lib bdg

LC 2009-16267

Biography of the explorer Jacques Cartier

"The information . . . is presented in such a way as to attract and maintain readers' interest. . . . With a full complement of maps, photographs (where available), illustrations, time lines, and document reproductions, a full story is told. Well-written and thoroughly researched, this . . . will make a solid addition." SLJ

Includes glossary and bibliographical references

Carver, George Washington, 1864?-1943

Abrams, Dennis. **George** Washington Carver; scientist and educator. [by] Dennis Abrams. Chelsea House 2008 119p il (Black Americans of achievement) $30

Grades: 6 7 8 9   **92**

1. Botanists 2. Scientists 3. African Americans -- Biography

ISBN 978-0-7910-9717-5; 0-7910-9717-X

LC 2007035677

This biography details the African American scientist's "rise from adversity to . . . recognition. The [book goes] beyond the typical personal information to provide some social history relevant to the subject's time. Captioned photographs and boxed inserts enhance the conversational [text]." Horn Book Guide

Includes bibliographical references

Harness, Cheryl. The **groundbreaking,** chance-taking life of George Washington Carver and science & invention in America; by Cheryl Harness. National Geographic 2008 143p il map (Cherly Harness histories) $16.95; lib bdg $25.90

Grades: 4 5 6 7   **92**

1. Botanists 2. Scientists 3. African Americans -- Biography

ISBN 978-1-4263-0196-4; 1-4263-0196-0; 978-1-4263-0197-1 lib bdg; 1-4263-0197-9 lib bdg

LC 2007029316

"Harness presents Carver as a man who, regardless of constant hardship and racial prejudice, persevered to become a beloved teacher and devoted scientist. . . . The author raises challenging questions throughout. . . . The lively prose style conveys his sense of passion and adventure about the man and his intellectual pursuits, and the simple black-and-white drawings add a further sense of drama." SLJ

Includes bibliographical references

★ MacLeod, Elizabeth. **George** Washington Carver; an innovative life. written by Elizabeth MacLeod. Kids Can Press 2007 32p il $14.95

Grades: 4 5 6 7   92

1. Botanists 2. Scientists 3. African Americans -- Biography

ISBN 978-1-55337-906-5; 1-55337-906-3

"MacLeod chronicles Carver's life from childhood to the end of his career, and the recognition he received posthumously. Each spread has a page of text with a quote from Carver in the margin and a page filled with many graphics in black and white and color, including photographs, illustrations, and reproductions of artifacts, all with captions. . . . With the richness of detail presented, even reluctant readers will find something of interest about this exceptional individual." SLJ

Cash, Johnny

Willett, Edward. **Johnny** Cash; the man in black. Enslow Publishers 2010 160p il (American rebels) lib bdg $34.60

Grades: 6 7 8 9   92

1. Singers 2. Country music 3. Country musicians 4. Songwriters

ISBN 978-0-7660-3386-3 lib bdg; 0-7660-3386-4 lib bdg

LC 2009017346

This "fascinating, well-organized [portrait of the country music singer] . . . opens with the infamous 1968 live-album recording at California's Folsom State Prison. . . . Skillfully chosen photos, chapter notes, and [a] suggested-reading [list completes this] well-researched, wholly engaging [introduction]." Booklist

Includes bibliographical references

Cather, Willa, 1873-1947

Meltzer, Milton. **Willa** Cather; a biography. Twenty-First Century Books 2008 160p il (Literary greats) $33.26

Grades: 7 8 9 10 11 12   92

1. Authors 2. Novelists 3. Women authors 4. Western writers 5. Authors, American 6. Short story writers

ISBN 978-0-8225-7604-4; 0-8225-7604-X

LC 2007-25629

A biography of the author of such novels as O Pioneers! and My Antonia.

"With signature clarity, Meltzer's . . . biography . . . sets his detailed discussion of Cather's life and work against the larger backdrop of her times. . . . The book's handsome, inviting design includes photos on almost every spread." Booklist

Includes bibliographical references

Catherine II, the Great, Empress of Russia, 1729-

1796

★ Vincent, Zu. **Catherine** the Great; Empress of Russia. Franklin Watts 2009 128p il map (A wicked history) $30; pa $5.95

Grades: 6 7 8 9   92

1. Empresses

ISBN 978-0-531-21802-0 lib bdg; 0-531-21802-3 lib bdg; 978-0-531-20738-3 pa; 0-531-20738-2 pa

LC 2008041543

"Catherine the Great might be . . . known as a cruel dictator with lots of lovers, but author Vincent shows how the Empress of Russia actually took on her position (well, after she had her husband murdered) with some good intentions. . . . Young readers will find the manipulation of Catherine's early days particularly interesting." Booklist

Includes bibliographical references

Catherine, Duchess of Cambridge, 1982-

Doeden, Matt. **Prince** William & Kate; a royal romance. Lerner Publications 2011 48p il lib bdg $26.60

Grades: 5 6 7 8   92

1. Princes 2. Princesses

ISBN 978-0-7613-8029-0; 0-7613-8029-9

LC 2011003413

"This short and sweet volume accents what down-to-earth and normal newlyweds Prince William and Kate Middleton are really like. After a brief recap of the couple's engagement interview, the book goes on to profile the pair individually and then as a duo. . . . This is an upbeat, readable narrative about a handsome, appealing couple. The color photographs are well chosen." Booklist

Includes glossary and bibliographical references

Catlin, George, 1796-1872

★ Reich, Susanna. **Painting** the wild frontier: the art and adventures of George Catlin. Clarion Books 2008 160p il map $21

Grades: 7 8 9 10 11 12   92

1. Artists 2. Painters 3. West (U.S.) in art 4. Native Americans in art 5. Artists -- United States 6. Indians in art

ISBN 978-0-618-71470-4; 0-618-71470-7

LC 2007-38847

This is a "biography of nineteenth-century painter George Catlin, famous for his portraits of Native American life. . . . A great introduction to Catlin's work as well as an excellent title to use in social studies, history, and art classes." Booklist

Includes bibliographical references

Worth, Richard. **George** Catlin; painter of Indian life. Sharpe Focus 2009 80p il (Show me America) $32.95

Grades: 6 7 8 9   92

1. Artists 2. Painters 3. Artists -- United States

ISBN 978-0-7656-8152-2; 0-7656-8152-8

LC 2007040694

"This is an attractive book with an engaging text that relates the remarkable story of an early American artist who is best remembered for his lifelike depictions of Native

Americans. The book incorporates outstanding full-color reproductions of his sketches and paintings, with explanations of their context." SLJ

Includes bibliographical references

Cavell, Edith, 1865-1915

Batten, Jack. **Silent** in an evil time: the brave war of Edith Cavell. Tundra Books 2007 135p il pa $16.95

Grades: 7 8 9 10   92

1. Nurses 2. World War, 1914-1918 3. World War, 1914-1918 -- Belgium

ISBN 978-0-88776-737-1

A biography of the British nurse who was executed by the Germans for sheltering British and French soldiers in Brussels during World War I

"This exceptional biography reads like an adventure novel. . . . The historical facts are well explained and Cavell is placed clearly in context." SLJ

Chaplin, Charlie, 1889-1977

★ Fleischman, Sid. **Sir** Charlie; Chaplin, the funniest man in the world. Greenwillow Books 2010 268p il $19.99; lib bdg $20.89

Grades: 5 6 7 8 9   92

1. Actors 2. Comedians 3. Motion pictures 4. Motion picture directors 5. Motion picture producers

ISBN 0-06-189640-3; 0-06-189641-1 lib bdg; 978-0-06-189640-8; 978-0-06-189641-5 lib bdg

LC 2009019689

This is a biography of the actor and director who starred in such films as City Lights (1931), Modern Times (1940), The Great Dictator (1947) and Limelight (1952). Chronology. Bibliography. Index. "Grades six to ten." (Bull Cent Child Books)

"This lively and engaging account of a poor Cockney boy who became the world's greatest silent-movie comedian is a must for biography collections. . . . Brief, easily digestible chapters, an extensive time line, and plenty of photos make the book's well-researched content accessible and appealing." SLJ

Charles, Ray

Duggleby, John. **Uh** huh!: the story of Ray Charles. Morgan Reynolds Pub. 2005 160p il $26.95

Grades: 7 8 9 10   92

1. Blind 2. Singers 3. Pianists 4. Blues musicians 5. African American singers

ISBN 1-931798-65-6

LC 2005-1287

The author "traces Charles' long career and displays a sensitivity to the events surrounding his life (including his bitter battles with heroin and alcohol addiction), as well as a genuine understanding of his music and the breadth of his musical influence. Sidebars on 'race' music, Braille, the Grammys, soul, and rock and roll enrich the narrative." Booklist

Includes bibliographical references

★ Woog, Adam. **Ray** Charles and the birth of soul; [by] Adam Woog. Lucent Books 2006 112p il (Lucent library of Black history) lib bdg $28.70

Grades: 7 8 9 10   92

1. Blind 2. Singers 3. Pianists 4. Soul music 5. Blues musicians 6. African American singers

ISBN 1-59018-844-6

LC 2005022586

"Woog does an excellent job of describing Charles's rare talent and the trajectory of his long and legendary career. . . . The text is clearly written and well organized. Black-and-white photographs illustrate and inform." SLJ

Includes bibliographical references

Chavez, Cesar, 1927-1993

Haugen, Brenda. **Cesar** Chavez; crusader for social change. by Brenda Haugen. Compass Point Books 2008 112p il map $35.32

Grades: 6 7 8 9   92

1. Agricultural laborers 2. Labor leaders 3. Mexican Americans -- Biography. 4. Mexican American migrant agricultural laborers. 5. Labor leaders -- United States -- Biography 6. Mexican American migrant agricultural laborers -- Biography

ISBN 978-0-7565-3321-2 (lib bdg); 0-7565-3321-X (lib bdg)

LC 2007003939

Profiles the Mexican American who helped create a union to protect the rights of migrant agricultural laborers. (Publisher's note)

"Provides solid basic information... attractively packaged with many photos, interesting sidebars, and reader-friendly text arrangement." VOYA

Includes bibliographical references

Stavans, Ilan, 1961- **Cesar** Chavez; a photographic essay. Cinco Puntos Press 2010 91p il pa $13.95

Grades: 7 8 9 10   92

1. Agricultural laborers 2. Migrant agricultural laborers 3. Labor leaders 4. Mexican Americans -- Biography

ISBN 1-933693-22-3; 978-1-933693-22-4

LC 2009044179

"Chavez secured better working conditions for thousands with his 1970 victory for the United Farm Workers Union by bargaining with the table-grape growers. This photo-biography covers the high points of his career, including ample and pointed quotes by him and touching on his global recognition and interactions with activist Fred Ross Jr., Dolores Huerta, Pope Paul VI, and Senator Robert F. Kennedy. The full-page black-and-white photos give a sense of the man at various ages, of the migrant workers' lives, and of being on the road demonstrating and striking. The book also includes a comprehensive time line. It is an excellent introduction to social activism from the 1950s through the 1980s." SLJ

Child, Julia

Abrams, Dennis. **Julia** Child. Chelsea House 2011 134p il (Women of achievement) lib bdg $35

Grades: 6 7 8 9   92
1. Cooks 2. Television personalities 3. Cookbook writers
ISBN 978-1-60413-912-9; 1-60413-912-9
'This book offers a biography of chef "Julia Child . . . [who] started a cooking revolution when she burst onto television screens in the 1960s. Before long, Americans inspired by her example began cooking French food at home in droves and truly appreciating the pleasure that preparing good food can provide. Yet Child did not grow up knowing how to cook or even with an interest in fine cuisine. Her story is one of an American woman's quest to find herself, to find her passion, and then to find a way to share that passion with the world. It is the story of how Julia McWilliams of Pasadena, California, transformed herself into Julia Child, 'The French Chef.'" (Publisher's note)
This "provides an engaging introduction to the chef as a privileged but the individualistic woman who took some time to find her way in life but eventually shared her passion for French cooking with the world. . . . Solid fare for the biography collection." Booklist
Includes bibliographical references

Chisholm, Shirley, 1924-2005
Raatma, Lucia. **Shirley** Chisholm. Marshall Cavendish Benchmark 2010 96p il (Leading women) $39.93
Grades: 4 5 6 7   92
1. Women politicians 2. Members of Congress 3. Presidential candidates 4. African American women -- Biography
ISBN 978-0-7614-4953-9; 0-7614-4953-1
"The arresting portrait on the cover will guide readers right into this well-written [biography of] . . . the first African American woman to enter Congress. . . . Raatma vividly explains what was happening in the country at the time and uses those events effectively as a backdrop. The many photos, both black and white and color, are good choices for the well-designed book." Booklist
Includes bibliographical references

Cho, Margaret, 1968-
Tiger, Caroline. **Margaret** Cho. Chelsea House 2007 111p bibl il (Asian Americans of achievement) lib bdg $30
Grades: 7 8 9 10   92
1. Comedians 2. Korean Americans -- Biography
ISBN 0-7910-9275-5; 978-0-7910-9275-0
                                          LC 2006028385
This is "a lively introduction to the comedian, from her rebellious childhood and teen years to her current successes. . . . The frequent quotes from Cho's funny insightful material will guide readers to seek out her performances." Booklist
Includes glossary and bibliographical references

Choo, Jimmy, 1961-
Sapet, Kerrily. **Jimmy** Choo. Morgan Reynolds Pub. 2010 112p il (Profiles in fashion) $28.95
Grades: 7 8 9 10   92
1. Shoemakers 2. Fashion designers 3. Shoe designers
ISBN 978-1-59935-151-3; 1-59935-151-X
                                          LC 2010018813

"Malaysian-born Choo has shod some of the most famous feet in the world. . . . Sapet provides insider details about Choo's remarkable career. . . . Explanations of shoe-biz terms, as well as Asian concepts such as feng shui, enliven the text, and the eye-catching design includes many color photos of both the shoes and their celebrity fans. . . . This [is an] engrossing introduction to both an exemplary designer and to the fashion business." Booklist
Includes bibliographical references

Chopin, Frédéric, 1810-1849
Malaspina, Ann. **Chopin's** world; [by] Ann Malaspina. Rosen Pub. Group 2008 64p il (Music throughout history) lib bdg $29.25
Grades: 5 6 7 8   92
1. Pianists 2. Composers 3. Classical musicians
ISBN 978-1-4042-0723-3 lib bdg; 1-4042-0723-6 lib bdg
                                          LC 2005031281
This "book begins with an introduction briefly addressing social issues of the day, historical background, or other significant information. . . . Successive chapters discuss the [man's] early [life], family background, social status, personality characteristics, musical training and education, obstacles or challenges, and influences. A chapter . . . focuses on the musician's well-known compositions, describing through lively and colorful language some of the musical elements employed. . . . The format and layout are appealing and uncluttered." SLJ
Includes glossary and bibliographical references

Christo, Jeanne-Claude, 1935-2009
★ Greenberg, Jan. **Christo** & Jeanne-Claude; through the Gates and beyond. [by] Jan Greenberg and Sandra Jordan. Roaring Brook Press 2008 50p il $19.95
Grades: 6 7 8 9   92
1. Artists 2. Artists -- Biography 3. Art
ISBN 978-1-59643-071-6; 1-59643-071-0
                                          LC 2007-19951
"In 2005, the dull gray of a New York City winter was interrupted when two indominable artists, Christo and his partner, Jeanne-Claude, brought Central Park brilliantly to life with their outdoor work The Gates. . . . This book, chronicling both The Gates as well as the artists' other projects, is as thoughtful, eye-opening, and meticulous as the work it celebrates." Booklist
Includes bibliographical references

Cisneros, Sandra
Warrick, Karen Clemens. **Sandra** Cisneros; inspiring Latina author. Enslow Publishers 2009 128p il (Latino biography library) $31.93
Grades: 6 7 8 9   92
1. Poets 2. Authors 3. Novelists 4. Women authors 5. Mexican American authors 6. Essayists 7. Authors, American 8. Short story writers
ISBN 978-0-7660-3162-3; 0-7660-3162-4
                                          LC 2008041798
Discusses the life of Latina author Sandra Cisneros, including her childhood in Chicago, her path to becoming an accomplished author, and her work in the Latino community.

"Warrick brings originality to Cisnero's story by explaining how the facts of the novelist's life provide a foundation for her advocacy on behalf of others. . . . The text is well documented. . . . This straightforward, thorough biography is a solid addition to most collections." SLJ

Includes bibliographical references

Clark, William, 1770-1838

Crompton, Samuel. **Lewis** and Clark; [by] Samuel Willard Crompton. Chelsea House 2009 116p il map (Great explorers) lib bdg $30

Grades: 6 7 8 9   92

1. Explorers 2. Territorial governors
ISBN 978-1-60413-418-6 lib bdg; 1-60413-418-6 lib bdg

LC 2009-8687

Biography of the explorers Lewis and Clark

"The information . . . is presented in such a way as to attract and maintain readers' interest. . . . With a full complement of maps, photographs (where available), illustrations, time lines, and document reproductions, a full story is told. Well-written and throughly researched, this . . . will make a solid addition." SLJ

Includes glossary and bibliographical references

Cleary, Beverly

Cleary, Beverly. A **girl** from Yamhill: a memoir. Morrow 1988 279p il hardcover o.p. pa $12.99

Grades: 6 7 8 9   92

1. Authors 2. Women authors 3. Authors, American 4. Children's authors
ISBN 0-688-07800-1; 0-380-72740-4 pa

LC 87-31554

Follows the popular children's author from her childhood years in Oregon through high school and into young adulthood, highlighting her family life and her growing interest in writing

"The author sees her child self with the same clarity and objectivity as she has seen her fictional characters, and her reminiscences have a resultant integrity and candor." Bull Cent Child Books

Clemente, Roberto, 1934-1972

Freedman, Lew. **Roberto** Clemente; baseball star & humanitarian. ABDO Pub. Co. 2011 112p il (Legendary athletes) lib bdg $34.22

Grades: 6 7 8 9   92

1. Baseball players 2. Baseball -- Biography 3. Puerto Ricans -- Biography
ISBN 978-1-61714-754-8; 1-61714-754-0

LC 2010041161

This biography of baseball star Roberto Clemente "goes beyond merely discussing [his] accomplishments. . . . [It] also [explores] the social and political [influence he] had on society as a whole. In addition, [it introduces] historical events in the context of [his life]. . . . This . . . is teeming with information and is a must-purchase for sports fans and readers interested in social activism." SLJ

Includes glossary and bibliographical references

Marquez, Heron. **Roberto** Clemente; baseball's humanitarian hero. by Herón Márquez. Carolrhoda

Books 2005 112p il (Trailblazer biography) lib bdg $27.93

Grades: 4 5 6 7   92

1. Baseball players 2. Baseball -- Biography 3. Puerto Ricans -- Biography
ISBN 1-57505-767-0

LC 2004-2319

"This excellent biography is well organized and enlivened with interesting details and anecdotes. . . . Balancing facts with insightful perspective, this is a readable, well-rounded portrait." SLJ

Includes bibliographical references

Cleopatra, Queen of Egypt, d. 30 B.C.

Blackaby, Susan. **Cleopatra**; Egypt's last and greatest queen. Sterling Pub. 2009 124p il (Sterling biographies) $12.95; pa $5.95

Grades: 5 6 7 8   92

1. Queens
ISBN 978-1-4027-6540-7; 1-4027-6540-1; 978-1-4027-5710-5 pa; 1-4027-5710-7 pa

LC 2008030146

"Villainess or goddess, a great queen or a selfish and overly ambitious woman—readers get to decide. They will be drawn into this biography by a description of a legendary magnificent banquet given by Mark Antony for Cleopatra. The lively narrative maintains interest from her birth in 69 BCE to her death in 31 BCE. . . . Sidebars, color photographs, and reproductions appear throughout. . . . This book leaves readers fascinated and eager to learn more about her time in history." SLJ

Includes glossary and bibliographical references

Morgan, Julian. **Cleopatra**; ruling in the shadow of Rome. Rosen Pub. Group 2003 112p il (Leaders of ancient Egypt) lib bdg $31.95

Grades: 5 6 7 8   92

1. Queens
ISBN 0-8239-3591-4

LC 2002-1214

"This title focuses on Cleopatra VII and her volatile relationship with Rome. A brief history of the Ptolemies and their rule in Egypt provides readers with essential background information. Vivid descriptions of Cleopatra's relationships with Julius Caesar and Mark Antony include possible motives for the alliances she formed. Clear discussions of the intricate politics, fragile unions, and the possibility of foreign invasions and internal rebellion are also provided. . . . Full-color photographs of the art, architecture, and artifacts of this time period enhance understanding." SLJ

Includes bibliographical references

Sapet, Kerrily. **Cleopatra**; ruler of Egypt. [by] Kerrily Sapet. Morgan Reynolds Pub. 2007 176p il map (World leaders) lib bdg $27.95

Grades: 8 9 10 11 12   92

1. Queens
ISBN 978-1-59935-035-6 lib bdg; 1-59935-035-1 lib bdg

LC 2006033381

"This biography of the legendary but somewhat mysterious Cleopatra provides a balanced account of her life and legacy. . . . The text is strongest in its descriptions of Egyptian culture and religion, the role of women, and life in the Nile Valley. . . . Numerous color reproductions and illustrations brighten the text." SLJ

Includes bibliographical references

Shecter, Vicky Alvear. **Cleopatra** rules! the amazing life of the original teen queen. Boyds Mills Press 2010 128p il map $17.95

Grades: 5 6 7 8   **92**
  1. Queens
  ISBN 1590787188; 9781590787182
                         LC 2009-26737

This is a biography of "Cleopatra VII, the last pharaoh of Egypt." (Publisher's note)

"This attractive book presents Cleopatra's story through an unusual text, informative sidebars, and excellent color illustrations. . . . Calling attention to the writing as much as its story, the text includes puns, informal language, and contemporary metaphors. . . . Shecter's solid research is evident." Booklist

Includes glossary and bibliographical references

Clinton, Hillary Rodham, 1947-
Abrams, Dennis. **Hillary** Rodham Clinton; politician. Chelsea House Publishers 2009 144p il (Women of achievement) lib bdg $30

Grades: 6 7 8 9   **92**
  1. Lawyers 2. Women politicians 3. Senators 4. Secretaries of state 5. Spouses of presidents 6. Presidential candidates 7. Presidents' spouses -- United States
  ISBN 978-1-60413-077-5; 1-60413-077-6
                         LC 2008-34639

A biography of the Secretary of State, former presidential candidate, and former First Lady.

Includes bibliographical references

Blashfield, Jean F. **Hillary** Clinton. Marshall Cavendish Benchmark 2010 112p il (Leading women) $39.93

Grades: 4 5 6 7   **92**
  1. Lawyers 2. Women politicians 3. Senators 4. Secretaries of state 5. Spouses of presidents 6. Presidential candidates 7. Presidents' spouses -- United States
  ISBN 978-0-7614-4954-6; 0-7614-4954-X

A biography of the Secretary of State and former Senator, presidential candidate, and First Lady.

Includes bibliographical references

Tracy, Kathleen. The **Clinton** view; the historic fight for the 2008 Democratic presidential nomination. Mitchell Lane Publishers 2009 48p il (Monumental milestones) lib bdg $29.95

Grades: 6 7 8 9   **92**
  1. Lawyers 2. Women politicians 3. Senators 4. Secretaries of state 5. Spouses of presidents 6. Presidential candidates 7. Presidents' spouses -- United

States 8. Presidents -- United States -- Election -- 2008
  ISBN 978-1-58415-731-1; 1-58415-731-3
                         LC 2008053545

This looks at the 2008 presidential campaign from the point of view of candidate Hillary Clinton

This "begins with the Iowa caucus, the effect the loss had on front-runner Clinton, and how her win in New Hampshire made her the second Clinton 'comeback kid.' Then, the book goes back to Clinton's early years, her academic successes, and her tenures as First Lady and senator. Tracy captures some of the excitement of the campaign. . . . The design is lively and colorful, and the photos will draw readers." Booklist

Includes bibliographical references

Cobain, Kurt, 1967-1994
Burlingame, Jeff. **Kurt** Cobain; oh well, whatever, nevermind. Enslow Publishers 2006 160p il (American rebels) lib bdg $27.93

Grades: 6 7 8 9   **92**
  1. Singers 2. Guitarists 3. Rock musicians
  ISBN 0-7660-2426-1
                         LC 2006001742

A biography of the Rock musician belonging to the group Nirvana

This "is an unusually intimate account of the rock legend. A resident of Cobain's hometown, Burlingame supports his well-researched portrait with personal interviews with Cobain's family, friends, and other local acquaintances." Booklist

Includes glossary and bibliographical references

Collins, Michael, 1930-
Schyffert, Bea Uusma. The **man** who went to the far side of the moon: the story of Apollo 11 astronaut Michael Collins. Chronicle 2003 77p il $14.95

Grades: 5 6 7 8   **92**
  1. Astronauts 2. Space flight 3. Aerospace consultants 4. Museum administrators
  ISBN 0-8118-4007-7

A biography of the astronaut, Michael Collins, who circled the moon in the Apollo 12 space capsule while his colleagues Neil Armstrong and Buzz Aldrin landed the lunar module and walked on the moon.

"This excellent book—illustrated scrapbook-style with a cleverly presented mix of photographs, illustrations, and charts—communicates the excitement of space travel." Booklist

Columbus, Christopher
Feinstein, Stephen. **Columbus**; opening up the new world. Enslow Publishers 2009 112p il (Great explorers of the world) lib bdg $31.93

Grades: 6 7 8 9   **92**
  1. Explorers
  ISBN 978-1-59845-101-6 lib bdg; 1-59845-101-4 lib bdg
                         LC 2008-38633

This "balances the explorer's achievements with his inhumane treatment of Indians. The last chapter offers an unusually good summary of how the world changed as different cultures encountered the others' foods, products, diseases, and social ideologies." Booklist

Includes glossary and bibliographical references

Colvin, Claudette

★ Hoose, Phillip. **Claudette** Colvin; twice toward justice. by Phillip Hoose. Melanie Kroupa Books 2009 133p il $19.95

Grades: 6 7 8 9 10   92

1. Civil rights activists 2. African Americans -- Civil rights 3. African American women -- Biography 4. Civil rights movements 5. African Americans -- Civil rights -- History

ISBN 978-0-374-31322-7; 0-374-31322-9

LC 2008-05435

ALA ALSC Newbery Medal Honor Book (2010)

"Teenager Claudette Colvin's significant contribution to the struggle for equal accommodation is presented in this biography that smoothly weaves excerpts from Hoose's extensive interviews with Colvin and his own supplementary commentary. . . . [Readers learn] why her arrest for refusing to give up her bus seat to a white passenger never became the crucial incident to spark the Montgomery Bus Boycott. . . . Plenty of black-and-white photographs and well-deployed sidebars enhance the text." Bull Cent Child Books

Includes bibliographical references

Cone, Claribel, 1864-1929

★ Fillion, Susan. **Miss** Etta and Dr. Claribel; Bringing Matisse to America. David R. Godine 2011 83p il $18.95

Grades: 4 5 6 7   92

1. Artists 2. Painters 3. Physicians 4. Art collectors 5. Art -- Collectors and collecting

ISBN 978-1-56792-434-3; 1-56792-434-4

LC 2010048937

"An affectionate, lively examination of the reciprocal relationship between a great artist and two great art lovers. Etta and Claribel Cone, unmarried sisters from a wealthy Baltimore family . . . [were] discerning collectors of modern art, particularly that of Henri Matisse. . . . Their account is lavishly illustrated in full color by reproductions from the Cone Collection at the Baltimore Museum of Art and Matisse-inflected paintings by the author, who drew extensively on the Cone archive that is also housed at the museum. . . . This appealing work stands as both a portrait of two unconventional women and a celebration of the possibilties of arts patronage." Kirkus

Cone, Etta, 1870-1949

★ Fillion, Susan. **Miss** Etta and Dr. Claribel; Bringing Matisse to America. David R. Godine 2011 83p il $18.95

Grades: 4 5 6 7   92

1. Artists 2. Painters 3. Physicians 4. Art collectors 5. Art -- Collectors and collecting

ISBN 978-1-56792-434-3; 1-56792-434-4

LC 2010048937

"An affectionate, lively examination of the reciprocal relationship between a great artist and two great art lovers. Etta and Claribel Cone, unmarried sisters from a wealthy Baltimore family . . . [were] discerning collectors of mod-

ern art, particularly that of Henri Matisse. . . . Their account is lavishly illustrated in full color by reproductions from the Cone Collection at the Baltimore Museum of Art and Matisse-inflected paintings by the author, who drew extensively on the Cone archive that is also housed at the museum. . . . This appealing work stands as both a portrait of two unconventional women and a celebration of the possibilties of arts patronage." Kirkus

Cook, James, 1728-1779

Feinstein, Stephen. **Captain** Cook; great explorer of the Pacific. Enslow 2010 112p il (Great explorers of the world) lib bdg $31.93

Grades: 6 7 8 9   92

1. Explorers 2. Voyages around the world 3. Naval officers 4. Travel writers

ISBN 978-1-59845-102-3; 1-59845-102-2

LC 2009006503

Examines the life of Captain James Cook, a British explorer and scientist, including his early life, his many Pacific voyages, and his death and legacy

This "provides a harrowing and enlightening account of Cook's discoveries. . . . Cook is portrayed as an intelligent and thoughtful man who regretted some of these negative impacts. Each volume is well organized, with text that is easy to read. . . . This . . . would serve as a useful resource for middle and elementary school students and may inspire them to read further." Voice Youth Advocates

Includes glossary and bibliographical references

Lace, William W. **Captain** James Cook. Chelsea House Publishers 2009 112p il (Great explorers) lib bdg $30

Grades: 6 7 8 9   92

1. Explorers 2. Voyages around the world 3. Naval officers 4. Travel writers

ISBN 978-1-60413-416-2 lib bdg; 1-60413-416-X lib bdg

LC 2009-9891

Biography of the explorer Captain James Cook.

"The information . . . is presented in such a way as to attract and maintain readers' interest. . . . With a full complement of maps, photographs (where available), illustrations, time lines, and document reproductions, a full story is told. Well-written and thoroughly researched, this . . . will make a solid addition." SLJ

Includes glossary and bibliographical references

Copernicus, Nicolaus, 1473-1543

Andronik, Catherine M. **Copernicus**; founder of modern astronomy. rev ed; Enslow Publishers 2009 128p il (Great minds of science) lib bdg $31.93

Grades: 5 6 7 8   92

1. Astronomers

ISBN 978-0-7660-3013-8 lib bdg; 0-7660-3013-X lib bdg

LC 2008-23940

First published 2002

"A highly readable book that presents a good balance between the biographical information needed to understand Copernicus as a man and the scientific explanations necessary to understand his work. . . . Good-quality, black-and-white reproductions, illustrations, and photographs add interest to the clearly written text." SLJ [review of 2002 edition]

Includes glossary and bibliographical references

Sakolsky, Josh. **Copernicus** and modern astronomy. Rosen Pub. Group 2005 64p il (Primary sources of revolutionary scientific discoveries and theories) $29.25

Grades: 6 7 8 9   92

1. Astronomy 2. Astronomers

ISBN 1-4042-0305-2; 978-1-4042-0305-1

LC 2004011296

An introduction to the life and work of the pioneering astronomer who proved that the earth revolved around the sun

Includes bibliographical references

Cormier, Robert

Beckman, Wendy Hart. **Robert** Cormier; banned, challenged, and censored. Enslow Publishers 2008 160p bibl il por (Authors of banned books) lib bdg $34.60

Grades: 6 7 8 9 10   92

1. Authors 2. Novelists 3. Censorship 4. Authors, American 5. Young adult authors

ISBN 978-0-7660-2691-9; 0-7660-2691-4

LC 2007-28003

"Cormier is generally cited as one of the finest and most challenged writers for teens. This combination of biography and literary criticism explains his appeal to readers as well as the most common objections to his works from parents and school districts. A history of other censorship, including several recent court cases involving the First Amendment, and a biographical sketch of Cormier precede the discussion of The Chocolate War (1974), I Am the Cheese (1977), and After the First Death (1979, all Knopf). . . . A helpful overview of the works of a major YA author." SLJ

Includes glossary and bibliographical references

Cortés, Hernán, 1485-1547

Wagner, Heather Lehr. **Hernan** Cortes. Chelsea House 2009 119p il map (Great explorers) lib bdg $30

Grades: 6 7 8 9   92

1. Explorers 2. Colonial administrators

ISBN 978-1-60413-424-7 lib bdg; 1-60413-424-0 lib bdg

LC 2009-14165

Biography of the explorer Hernan Cortes

"The information . . . is presented in such a way as to attract and maintain readers' interest. . . . With a full complement of maps, photographs (where available), illustrations, time lines, and document reproductions, a full story is told. Well-written and thoroughly researched, this . . . will make a solid addition." SLJ

Includes glossary and bibliographical references

Corwin, Jeff

Corwin, Jeff. **Jeff** Corwin: a wild life; the authorized biography. Penguin Group 2009 100p il pa $6.99

Grades: 4 5 6 7   92

1. Biologists 2. Naturalists 3. Conservationists 4. Television personalities

ISBN 978-0-14-241403-3 pa; 0-14-241403-4 pa

LC 2009008092

"The host of Animal Planet . . . and other popular TV programs blends his exciting adventure in the wild with his passionate call for conservation. . . . An insert of beautifully reproduced color photos from his global travels show him with a giraffe in Kenya, a moose in Alaska, and more. . . . The adventures are thrilling, and the messages are urgent." Booklist

Cosgrove, Miranda, 1993-

Yasuda, Anita. **Miranda** Cosgrove. Weigl 2011 24p il (Remarkable people) $27.13; pa $12.95

Grades: 4 5 6 7   92

1. Actors 2. Singers

ISBN 978-1-6169-0668-9; 1-6169-0668-5; 978-1-6169-0673-3 pa; 1-6169-0673-1 pa

LC 2010051144

A biography of actress and singer Miranda Cosgrove

Cousteau, Jacques Yves, 1910-1997

Knowles, Johanna. **Jacques** Cousteau. Chelsea House 2011 117p il (Conservation heroes) lib bdg $35

Grades: 6 7 8 9 10   92

1. Ocean 2. Authors 3. Scientists 4. Skin diving 5. Divers 6. Naval officers 7. Oceanographers 8. Nonfiction writers

ISBN 978-1-60413-947-1; 1-60413-947-1

LC 2010030584

A biography of the French undersea explorer and conservationist.

"Captivating, richly informative. . . . The scope of [this book] is comprehensive. . . . [The book is] engaging as [it is] educational and will be ideal for research and reports." SLJ

Includes glossary and bibliographical references

Olmstead, Kathleen A. **Jacques** Cousteau; a life under the sea. [by] Kathleen Olmstead. Sterling Pub. Co. 2008 124p il (Sterling biographies) pa $5.99

Grades: 7 8 9 10   92

1. Ocean 2. Authors 3. Scientists 4. Oceanography 5. Divers 6. Naval officers 7. Oceanographers 8. Nonfiction writers

ISBN 978-1-4027-4440-2; 1-4027-4440-4

LC 2007048195

"Most of the text . . . is concerned with Cousteau's evolving inventions for breathing and exploring underwater. Olmstead describes how his films and television specials opened a new world to viewers, and how he became a leading advocate for the oceans. She also makes mention of Cousteau's secret second family and his dispute with his son Jean-Michel over using the family name for an ecotourist resort. . . . [This] attractively formatted [title has] black-and-white and full-color photographs or reproductions as well as sidebars. [A] solid [addition] to biography shelves." SLJ

Includes glossary and bibliographical references

Coville, Bruce

Marcovitz, Hal. **Bruce** Coville. Chelsea House 2006 124p bibl il por (Who wrote that?) $30

Grades: 6 7 8 9   **92**

1. Authors 2. Authors, American 3. Children's authors 4. Children's literature -- Authors and illustrators
ISBN 0-7910-8656-9

LC 2005008182

A biography of the popular author of children's and young adult fantasy and science fiction books.
Includes bibliographical references

Crandall, Prudence, 1803-1890

★ Jurmain, Suzanne. The **forbidden** schoolhouse; the true and dramatic story of Prudence Crandall and her students. Houghton Mifflin 2005 150p il $18

Grades: 5 6 7 8   **92**

1. Teachers 2. Educators 3. Abolitionists 4. African Americans -- Education
ISBN 0-618-47302-5

This is the story of Prudence Crandall, who, in 1831, opened a school for African American girls in Canterbury, Connecticut.

"A compelling, highly readable book. . . . Writing with a sense of drama that propels readers forward . . . Jurmain makes painfully clear what Crandall and her students faced. . . . Including a number of sepia-toned and color photographs as well as historical engravings, the book's look will draw in readers." Booklist
Includes bibliographical references

Creech, Sharon

Baptiste, Tracey. **Sharon** Creech; foreword by Kyle Zimmer. Chelsea House 2011 118p il (Who wrote that?) lib bdg $35

Grades: 6 7 8 9   **92**

1. Authors 2. Novelists 3. Women authors 4. Authors, American 5. Children's authors 6. Young adult authors
ISBN 978-1-60413-774-3; 1-60413-774-6

LC 2010030595

A biography of the author of Walk Two Moons and Absolutely Normal Chaos.
Includes bibliographical references

Cromwell, Oliver, 1599-1658

Aronson, Marc. **John** Winthrop, Oliver Cromwell, and the Land of Promise. Clarion Books 2004 205p il map $20

Grades: 7 8 9 10   **92**

1. Clergy 2. Puritans 3. Heads of state 4. Revolutionaries 5. Government officials 6. Colonial administrators 7. Puritans -- Massachusetts -- Biography 8. Governors -- Massachusetts -- Biography 9. Massachusetts -- History -- Colonial period, ca. 1600-1775
ISBN 0-618-18177-6

LC 2003-16418

"The accessible text is accompanied by excerpts from primary source documents and vivid illustrations. The author's passion for the period comes across in his writing.

Aronson provides an excellent source for historical and biographical data." Voice Youth Advocates
Includes bibliographical references

Crutcher, Chris, 1946-

★ Crutcher, Chris. **King** of the mild frontier: an ill-advised autobiography. Greenwillow Bks. 2003 260p il $16.99; pa $6.99

Grades: 8 9 10 11 12   **92**

1. Authors 2. Novelists 3. Authors, American 4. Young adult authors
ISBN 0-06-050249-5; 0-06-050251-7 pa

LC 2002-11224

Chris Crutcher, author of young adult novels such as "Ironman" and "Whale Talk," as well as short stories, tells of growing up in Cascade, Idaho, and becoming a writer

"Like his novels, Crutcher's autobiography is full of heartbreak, poignancy, and hilarity. . . . This honest, insightful, revealing autobiography is a joy to read." Booklist

Sommers, Michael A. **Chris** Crutcher; Michael A. Sommers. 1st ed; Rosen Pub. Group 2005 112p il (Library of author biographies) lib bdg $26.50

Grades: 5 6 7 8   **92**

1. Authors 2. Novelists 3. Authors, American 4. Young adult authors
ISBN 1-4042-0325-7

LC 2004-13100

"Sommers describes Crutcher as an author who writes from his experience as a teacher, therapist, and writer. . . . Selections of book reviews of [his] work are included. . . . [This is] well-written." SLJ
Includes bibliographical references

Cruz, Celia, 1929-2003

Cartlidge, Cherese. **Celia** Cruz. Chelsea House Publishers 2010 112p il (The great Hispanic heritage) lib bdg $30

Grades: 6 7 8 9   **92**

1. Singers 2. Salsa musicians
ISBN 978-1-60413-771-2; 1-60413-771-1

LC 2010007809

This "delves frankly into the Cuban-born singer-songwriter's life, including her blatant rejection of Fidel Castro and her subsequent immigration to the U.S., where President Clinton eventually honored her with a Presidential Medal. . . . A selection of well-chosen images, a chronology, chapter notes, and [a] suggested reading [list] round out [this] engaging and sure-to-be-popular [book] for reports and personal interest." Booklist

Cummings, E. E. (Edward Estlin), 1894-1962

Reef, Catherine. **E.** E. Cummings. Clarion Books 2006 149p il $21

Grades: 7 8 9 10 11 12   **92**

1. Poets 2. Authors 3. Poets, American
ISBN 978-0-618-56849-9; 0-618-56849-2

LC 2006-10453

This "is an engaging look behind the typography at one of the twentieth century's most familiar poets." Bull Cent Child Books

Includes bibliographical references

Curie, Marie, 1867-1934

Borzendowski, Janice. **Marie** Curie; mother of modern physics. Sterling Pub 2009 124p il map (Sterling biographies) $12.95; pa $5.95

Grades: 7 8 9 10   **92**
  1. Chemists 2. Physicists 3. Women scientists 4. Nobel laureates for physics
  ISBN 978-1-4027-6543-8; 1-4027-6543-6; 978-1-4027-5318-3 pa; 1-4027-5318-7 pa
                    LC 2008-30701
"This interesting, informative biography of the scientist and Nobel Prize winner explores both Curie's personal and professional life. It includes numerous archival and modern photos and reproductions. . . . The book is far more thorough and satisfying than most biographies of Curie for teens." SLJ

Includes bibliographical references

Cregan, Elizabeth R. **Marie** Curie; pioneering physicist. Compass Point Books 2009 40p il map (Mission: Science) lib bdg $26.60

Grades: 4 5 6   **92**
  1. Chemists 2. Physicists 3. Women scientists 4. Nobel laureates for physics
  ISBN 978-0-7565-3960-3
This biography of the discoverer of radium "does a good job of connecting the scientist's work to our lives today. . . . [The] book has a variety of graphics including diagrams, photos, and reproductions of paintings and sketches. [This volume is] a definite plus for a school library or the juvenile collection in a public library." Libr Media Connect

Koestler-Grack, Rachel A. **Marie** Curie; scientist. Chelsea House 2009 136p bibl il por (Women of achievement) $30

Grades: 6 7 8 9   **92**
  1. Chemists 2. Physicists 3. Women scientists 4. Nobel laureates for physics
  ISBN 978-1-60413-086-7; 1-60413-086-5
                    LC 2008034999
A biography of the scientist who, with her husband, Pierre Curie, discovered the phenomenon of radioactivity.

The book is "well written; sidebars supplement the [narrative] with interesting facts." Horn Book Guide

Includes bibliographical references

★ Krull, Kathleen. **Marie** Curie; [illustrations by] Boris Kulikov. Viking 2007 128p il (Giants of science) $15.99

Grades: 5 6 7 8   **92**
  1. Chemists 2. Physicists 3. Women scientists 4. Nobel laureates for physics 5. Science -- History
  ISBN 978-0-670-05894-5; 0-670-05894-7
                    LC 2007-24251
"The compelling and conversational narrative (ably assisted by Kulikov's black-and-white drawings) portrays a brilliant . . . woman with plenty of idiosyncrasies, and the

story of her discovery of radium . . . is as engaging as any of her personal dramas and challenges." Horn Book

MacLeod, Elizabeth. **Marie** Curie; a brilliant life. written by Elizabeth MacLeod. Kids Can Press 2004 32p il $14.95; pa $6.95

Grades: 5 6 7 8   **92**
  1. Chemists 2. Physicists 3. Women scientists 4. Nobel laureates for physics 5. Young adult literature -- Works 6. Biography, Individual
  ISBN 1-55337-570-X; 1-55337-571-8 pa
"The drive and self-sacrifice that enabled Marie Curie to win two Nobel Prizes and become the most acclaimed female scientist to date are explored in this accessible biography, which covers Curie's personal and professional lives. Illustrated with well-chosen archival photos." Horn Book Guide

★ McClafferty, Carla Killough. **Something** out of nothing; Marie Curie and radium. Farrar, Straus & Giroux 2006 134p il $18

Grades: 5 6 7 8 9 10   **92**
  1. Chemists 2. Physicists 3. Women scientists 4. Nobel laureates for physics
  ISBN 0-374-38036-8; 0374380368
                    LC 2004056414
This "biography examines Curie's life and work as a groundbreaking scientist and as an independent woman. . . . The groundbreaking science is as thrilling as the personal story. . . . The spacious design makes the text easy to read, and occasional photos . . . bring the story closer." Booklist

Yannuzzi, Della A. **New** elements; the story of Marie Curie. [by] Della Yannuzzi. Morgan Reynolds Pub. 2006 144p il (Profiles in science) lib bdg $27.95

Grades: 7 8 9 10   **92**
  1. Chemists 2. Physicists 3. Women scientists 4. Nobel laureates for physics
  ISBN 978-1-59935-023-3; 1-59935-023-8
                    LC 2006-18887
This is a biography "of the first woman to win a Nobel Prize in science. . . . Readers will come away with a strong portrait of the heralded scientist's life and times (the historical context is nicely integrated), and serious researchers will turn to the bibliography's sturdy selection of titles." Booklist

Includes bibliographical references

Cézanne, Paul, 1839-1906

Burleigh, Robert. **Paul** Cezanne; a painter's journey. H.N. Abrams 2006 31p il $17.95

Grades: 4 5 6 7   **92**
  1. Artists 2. Painters 3. Artists, French
  ISBN 0-8109-5784-1
                    LC 2005011779
"Burleigh offers brief insights into Cézanne's personal life, such as his relationship with his father, who did not support his sons interest in art. However, the emphasis is on interpreting some individual paintings and understanding the artist's various styles, including the impact of the Impressionists and his evolution to a freer and simpler manner

of expression in his later years. . . . The high-quality reproductions demonstrate Burleigh's points. . . . A solid, lively introduction." SLJ

Spence, David. **Cezanne**. New Forest Press 2010 48p il (Great artists and their world) lib bdg $32.80
Grades: 6 7 8 9   92
    1. Artists 2. Painters 3. Artists, French
    ISBN 978-1-84898-315-1; 1-84898-315-8
"Offers biographical information [of Paul Cezanne] . . . interspersed with art history and criticism in an eye-catching format. . . . [Includes] a long introductory paragraph and four-to-six images with explanatory notes. . . . Spence . . . does a good job of explaining why art that might seem ordinary today was revolutionary at the time of its creation." SLJ
    Includes glossary

Dahl, Roald

★ Dahl, Roald. **Boy**: tales of childhood. Farrar, Straus & Giroux 1984 160p il hardcover o.p. rpt $6.99
Grades: 6 7 8 9   92
    1. Authors 2. Authors, English 3. Children's authors 4. Short story writers
    ISBN 0-14-130305-0; 9780142413814 rpt
                                                    LC 84-48462
"In these memoirs, Dahl reminisces about growing up in a large Norwegian family living in Wales during the 1920s and 1930s. The text is illustrated with sketches, old photographs and excerpts of letters he wrote as a boy." SLJ

Dahl, Roald. **More** about Boy; Roald Dahl's tales from childhood. Farrar, Straus, and Giroux 2009 229p il $16.99
Grades: 5 6 7 8   92
    1. Authors 2. Authors, English 3. Children's authors 4. Short story writers
    ISBN 978-0-374-35055-0; 0-374-35055-8
                                                    LC 2009016118
First published 2008 in the United Kingdom
"Containing the entire text and artwork from Dahl's 1984 autobiography Boy, this reworked and expanded version also incorporates previously unpublished materials from the Roald Dahl Museum and Story Centre in England, as well as excerpts that have appeared in earlier books. . . . Dahl's revealing writing, open and full of wicked humor, is certain to endear the beloved writer . . . to a new generation." Publ Wkly

Dalai Lama XIV, 1935-

Kimmel, Elizabeth Cody. **Boy** on the lion throne; the childhood of the 14th Dalai Lama. with a foreword by His Holiness the Dalai Lama. Roaring Brook Press 2009 146p il map $18.95
Grades: 4 5 6 7   92
    1. Buddhism 2. Buddhist leaders 3. Political leaders 4. Nobel laureates for peace
    ISBN 978-1-59643-394-6; 1-59643-394-9
Follows the childhood of Lhamo Thondup, who was identified at the age of two as the fourteenth reincarnation of

the Dalai Lama, describing the humble life he was born into and how his life changed after he was recognized
"Kimmel is reverent without being adulatory, and her explanation of the Dalai Lama's relationship with Maoist China is presented in simple, clear language. This is a strange and fascinating story told in an engaging style, and young readers will find lots to keep them turning the pages." Bull Cent Child Books
    Includes bibliographical references

Dalí, Salvador, 1904-1989

McNeese, Tim. **Salvador** Dali; [by] Tim McNeese. Chelsea House Publishers 2006 122p il (Great Hispanic heritage) lib bdg $30
Grades: 7 8 9 10   92
    1. Artists 2. Painters 3. Artists, Spanish
    ISBN 0-7910-8837-5
                                                    LC 2005025998
A biography of the 20th century surrealist painter.
"McNeese does a wonderful job of describing [this man's life] and, more importantly, the times in which [he] lived. . . . [The book is] expertly researched." SLJ
    Includes bibliographical references

Dandridge, Dorothy

Herringshaw, DeAnn. **Dorothy** Dandridge; singer & actress. ABDO Pub. Co. 2011 112p il (Essential lives) $23.95
Grades: 6 7 8 9 10   92
    1. Actors 2. Singers 3. African American actors
    ISBN 978-1-61714-779-1; 1-61714-779-6
                                                    LC 2010042150
"This volume profiles the life of . . . actress Dorothy Dandridge . . . Dandridge's life reads much like a screenplay. . . . Students will be captivated by Dandridge's guts and by the naked hypocrisy of the racisim that she faced even as a movie star." Booklist
    Includes bibliographical references

Dante Alighieri, 1265-1321

Davenport, John. **Dante**; poet, author, and proud Florentine. [by] John Davenport. Chelsea House 2006 140p il (Makers of the Middle Ages and Renaissance) lib bdg $30
Grades: 6 7 8 9   92
    1. Poets 2. Authors 3. Authors, Italian
    ISBN 0-7910-8634-8
                                                    LC 2005007492
This biography of the Italian Renaissance author of The Divine Comedy describes his "childhood and background as well as his influences, career, and writing. The colorful illustrations, many from illuminated manuscripts, short chapters, simple vocabulary, and large print present an attractive format. Sidebars and captions contain additional information." SLJ
    Includes bibliographical references

Darwin, Charles, 1809-1882

Ashby, Ruth. **Young** Charles Darwin and the voyage of the Beagle; written by Ruth Ashby. Peachtree 2009 116p il map $12.95

Grades: 4 5 6   **92**
1. Evolution 2. Naturalists 3. Travel writers 4. Writers on science 5. Natural history
ISBN 978-1-56145-478-5; 1-56145-478-8
LC 2008-36747
"Beginning with the letter inviting him to sail aboard the Beagle, this traditional biography relates Darwin's life with an emphasis on the trip that led him to forge his theory about natural selection. Ashby makes good use of Darwin's own writing, sprinkling quotes throughout the text, which allow his adventures and opinions to come to life. . . . This biography will work well for book reports . . . providing accurate and readable information about the scientist and his journey." Booklist
Includes bibliographical references

★ Eldredge, Niles. **Charles** Darwin and the mystery of mysteries; by Niles Eldredge and Susan Pearson. Rb Flash Point 2010 135p il map lib bdg $19.99
Grades: 7 8 9 10   **92**
1. Naturalists 2. Travel writers 3. Writers on science
ISBN 978-1-59643-374-8; 1-59643-374-4
Follows Charles Darwin on his journey aboard the HMS Beagle and presents the thinking that led him to the theory of evolution and the writing of The origin of the species. Includes historical photographs and passages from Darwin's personal diary.
"Numerous quotations from Darwin's works and correspondence bring his voice to readers. . . . Eldredge and Pearson have done a fine job of summarizing both Darwin's life and work." SLJ

Gibbons, Alan. **Charles** Darwin; illustrated by Leo Brown. Kingfisher 2008 63p il $16.95
Grades: 3 4 5 6   **92**
1. Evolution 2. Naturalists 3. Travel writers 4. Writers on science
ISBN 978-0-7534-6251-5; 0-7534-6251-6
LC 2007-48365
"Large, brightly colored line-and-wash pictures appear throughout the diary section, along with smaller photos of period artifacts. Illustrated mainly with drawings and photos, the last third of the book offers straightforward discussions of topics such as the ship, the route of the voyage, life at sea, Darwin's later life and work, and other notable nineteenth-century scientists." Booklist
Includes glossary

★ Heiligman, Deborah. **Charles** and Emma; the Darwins' leap of faith. Henry Holt and Company 2009 268p il $18.95
Grades: 7 8 9 10 11 12   **92**
1. Naturalists 2. Travel writers 3. Writers on science 4. Spouses of prominent persons 5. Evolution (Biology)
ISBN 978-0-8050-8721-5; 0-8050-8721-4
LC 2008-26091
ALA YALSA Printz Award Honor Book (2010)
ALA Excellence in Nonfiction Award (2010)
"This rewarding biography of Charles Darwin investigates his marriage to his cousin Emma Wedgwood. . . . Embracing the paradoxes in her subjects' personalities, the author unfolds a sympathetic and illuminating account, bolstered by quotations from their personal writings as well as significant research into the historical context." Publ Wkly
Includes bibliographical references

★ Krull, Kathleen. **Charles** Darwin; illustrated by Boris Kulikov. Viking 2010 144p il (Giants of science) $15.99
Grades: 5 6 7 8   **92**
1. Evolution 2. Naturalists 3. Travel writers 4. Writers on science
ISBN 978-0-670-06335-2; 0-670-06335-5
LC 2010-07315
"Krull once again offers an illuminating, humanizing portrait of a famous scientist. . . . Krull . . . writes in easily paced, lively, conversational prose, knitting together interesting facts, anecdotes, and historical overviews into a fascinating whole. She offers clear definitions of not only Darwin's theories but also how his discoveries built on previous scientists' work. . . . Kulikov's whimsical ink drawings and well-culled list of resources round out this strong entry in the series." Booklist

Leone, Bruno. **Origin**; the story of Charles Darwin. by Bruno Leone. Morgan Reynolds Pub. 2009 160p il (Profiles in science) $28.95
Grades: 6 7 8 9   **92**
1. Evolution 2. Naturalists 3. Travel writers 4. Writers on science
ISBN 978-1-59935-110-0; 1-59935-110-2
LC 2008047204
This "focuses primarily on Darwin's scientific achievements. . . . Leone offers a vivid portrait of Darwin as an avid naturalist, keen and patient observer, cautious scientist, and master of synthesizing and articulating his theories and observations. . . . The book is illustrated throughout with photographs, diagrams, and drawings." Booklist
Includes bibliographical references

Schanzer, Rosalyn. **What** Darwin saw; the journey that changed the world. National Geographic 2009 47p il map $17.95; lib bdg $26.90
Grades: 3 4 5 6   **92**
1. Evolution 2. Naturalists 3. Travel writers 4. Writers on science 5. Natural history
ISBN 978-1-4263-0396-8; 1-4263-0396-3; 978-1-4263-0397-5 lib bdg; 1-4263-0397-1 lib bdg
LC 2008-39809
"Schanzer uses Darwin's own words, taken from his journals, books, and letters, in the speech balloons of her graphic depiction of the voyage of the Beagle. This is not a full biography, but begins with Darwin's acceptance of the offer to sail on the expedition and ends with the presentation of his theory of evolution in 1860. Bright, watercolor cartoons accurately portray landscapes and specimens while also creating a vivid sense of adventure." SLJ
Includes bibligraphical references

Darwin, Emma Wedgwood, 1808-1896
★ Heiligman, Deborah. **Charles** and Emma; the Darwins' leap of faith. Henry Holt and Company 2009 268p il $18.95

Grades: 7 8 9 10 11 12   **92**

1. Naturalists 2. Travel writers 3. Writers on science 4. Spouses of prominent persons 5. Evolution (Biology)
ISBN 978-0-8050-8721-5; 0-8050-8721-4

LC 2008-26091

ALA YALSA Printz Award Honor Book (2010)
ALA Excellence in Nonfiction Award (2010)

"This rewarding biography of Charles Darwin investigates his marriage to his cousin Emma Wedgwood. . . . Embracing the paradoxes in her subjects' personalities, the author unfolds a sympathetic and illuminating account, bolstered by quotations from their personal writings as well as significant research into the historical context." Publ Wkly

Includes bibliographical references

Davis, Benjamin O., Jr.

★ Earl, Sari. **Benjamin** O. Davis, Jr. Air Force general & Tuskegee Airmen leader. ABDO Pub. Co. 2010 111p il map (Military heroes) lib bdg $22.95
Grades: 7 8 9   **92**

1. Generals 2. Air force officers
ISBN 978-1-60453-961-5; 1-60453-961-5

LC 2009-32339

Biography of Benjamin O. Davis Jr.

"The rush of literary adrenalin will hook readers immediately and keep them enthralled until the end. . . . Given the dynamic topic [and] . . . appealing layout . . . [this is] likely to attract reluctant readers. In addition, sources are plentiful and well documented." SLJ

Includes glossary and bibliographical references

De Paola, Tomie, 1934-

De Paola, Tomie. **Christmas** remembered; [by] Tomie dePaola. G. P. Putnam's Sons 2006 86p il $19.99; pa $9.99
Grades: 5 6 7 8   **92**

1. Artists 2. Authors 3. Painters 4. Christmas 5. Illustrators 6. Authors, American 7. Children's authors
ISBN 0-399-24622-3; 0-14-241481-6 pa

LC 2005032658

The children's author and artist shares his love of Christmas in 15 memories, which span six decades

"Brightening the pages are illustrations in varied styles and media, from an intriguing portrait of dePaola's Italian grandmother to decorative paper collages to iconic paintings of great stillness and beauty. . . . Written with dialogue and humor as well as reflection." Booklist

De la Renta, Oscar

Darraj, Susan Muaddi. **Oscar** de la Renta. Chelsea House 2010 116p il (The great Hispanic heritage) lib bdg $30
Grades: 6 7 8 9   **92**

1. Fashion designers
ISBN 978-1-60413-733-0; 1-60413-733-9

LC 2010009488

This "presents a warm, almost fawning account of the wildly successful fashion designer, who maintains a home in and close ties to his native Dominican Republic. . . . A selection of well-chosen images, a chronology, chapter notes, and [a] suggested reading [list] round out [this] engaging

[title] in a sure-to-be-popular [book] for reports and personal interest." Booklist

Includes bibliographical references

DeGeneres, Ellen

Paprocki, Sherry Beck. **Ellen** Degeneres; entertainer. Sherry Beck Paprocki. Chelsea House Publishers 2009 136p il (Women of achievement) $30
Grades: 6 7 8 9   **92**

1. Actors 2. Comedians 3. Entertainers 4. Television personalities 5. Talk show hosts
ISBN 978-1-60413-082-9; 1-60413-082-2

LC 2008034638

A biography of comedian, actress, and TV talk show host Ellen Degeneres.

Includes bibliographical references

Degas, Edgar, 1834-1917

Spence, David. **Degas**. New Forest Press 2010 48p il (Great artists and their world) lib bdg $32.80
Grades: 6 7 8 9   **92**

1. Artists 2. Painters 3. Artists, French
ISBN 978-1-84898-318-2; 1-84898-318-2

"Offers biographical information [of Edgar Degas] . . . interspersed with art history and criticism in an eye-catching format. . . . [Includes] a long introductory paragraph and four-to-six images with explanatory notes. . . . Spence . . . does a good job of explaining why art that might seem ordinary today was revolutionary at the time of its creation." SLJ

Includes glossary

Democritus

Macfarlane, Katherine. The **father** of the atom; Democritus and the nature of matter. Enslow Publishers 2010 112p il map (Great minds of ancient science and math) lib bdg $31.93
Grades: 5 6 7 8   **92**

1. Atoms 2. Matter 3. Mathematics 4. Philosophers 5. Writers on science
ISBN 978-0-7660-3410-5 lib bdg; 0-7660-3410-0 lib bdg

LC 2008-46265

This biography is a "solid [choice], as . . . [it provides] a good overview of the cultural and political landscape of the times, as well as pictures." SLJ

Includes glossary and bibliographical references

Diana, Princess of Wales, 1961-1997

Paprocki, Sherry Beck. **Diana,** Princess of Wales; humanitarian. Chelsea House 2009 136p il (Women of achievement) $30
Grades: 6 7 8 9   **92**

1. Princesses
ISBN 978-1-60413-463-6; 1-60413-463-1

LC 2009008690

A biography of Lady Diana Spencer who became Princess of Wales when she married Prince Charles in 1981, and who became known as The People's Princess for her charitable works.

Includes bibliographical references

Dickens, Charles, 1812-1870

Caravantes, Peggy. **Best** of times: the story of Charles Dickens. Morgan Reynolds Pub. 2005 160p il (World writers) $26.95

Grades: 7 8 9 10   **92**

1. Authors 2. Novelists 3. Authors, English

ISBN 1-931798-68-0

LC 2005-8405

"Beginning with Dickens' childhood trauma (his father was put in debtors' prison, and Charles, 12, had to work in a blacking factory), this highly readable [book] . . . relates the extraordinary writer's stories to his life and times. . . . [It includes] many interesting quotes, color prints, and photos." Booklist

Includes bibliographical references

★ Rosen, Michael, 1946- **Dickens**; his work and his world. illustrated by Robert Ingpen. Candlewick Press 2005 95p il $19.99

Grades: 5 6 7 8   **92**

1. Authors 2. Novelists 3. Authors, English

ISBN 0-7636-2752-6

LC 2004-61847

"The art adds to the richness of a volume designed and written with care." Booklist

★ Warren, Andrea. **Charles** Dickens and the street children of London. Houghton Mifflin Books for Children/Houghton Mifflin Harcourt 2011 144p il $18.99

Grades: 6 7 8 9 10   **92**

1. Authors 2. Novelists 3. Children in literature 4. Authors, English 5. Poor -- Great Britain

ISBN 978-0-547-39574-6; 0-547-39574-4

LC 2011003450

"This absorbing book introduces Dickens within the context of his times. . . . Chapters about his life and his novels alternate with related chapters describing the plight of the poor (especially children) in Victorian England (especially London). . . . Glimpses of his world are offered in reproductions of illustrations from Dickens' novels as well as period portraits and photos of people and places that appear throughout the book. . . . Warren writes in a clear, direct, vivid manner that brings it all to life." Booklist

Dickinson, Emily, 1830-1886

★ Meltzer, Milton. **Emily** Dickinson; a biography. Twenty-first Century Books 2006 128p il (American literary greats) lib bdg $31.93

Grades: 7 8 9 10   **92**

1. Poets 2. Authors 3. Women poets 4. Poets, American

ISBN 0-7613-2949-8; 978-0-7613-2949-7

LC 2003-22978

Examines the life of the reclusive nineteenth-century Massachusetts poet whose posthumously published poetry brought her the public attention she had carefully avoided during her lifetime.

"This introduction to an important American literary figure is notable for its clear and succinct writing. . . . Excerpts from her letters and poems appear throughout. A worthwhile

book for students who might have difficulty with more scholarly works." SLJ

Includes bibliographical references

Dorsey, Jack

Smith, Chris. **Twitter**; Jack Dorsey, Biz Stone and Evan Williams. [by] Chris Smith and Marci McGrath. Morgan Reynolds Pub. 2011 112p il (Business leaders) $28.95

Grades: 7 8 9 10 11 12   **92**

1. Online social networks 2. Internet executives 3. Computer programmers 4. Computer software executives

ISBN 978-1-59935-179-7; 1-59935-179-X; 978-1-59935-216-9 e-book

LC 2011024699

This biography of the founders of Twitter "will grab YAs. . . . The design is browsable, with clear type and lots of color screens and informal photos of young people at work." Booklist

Includes bibliographical references

Douglass, Frederick, 1817?-1895

★ Adler, David A. **Frederick** Douglass; a noble life. Holiday House 2010 138p il $18.95

Grades: 7 8 9 10   **92**

1. Slaves 2. Authors 3. Abolitionists 4. Memoirists 5. African Americans -- Biography 6. Slavery -- History

ISBN 978-0-8234-2056-8; 0-8234-2056-6

LC 2009-29970

A biography of Frederick Douglass, who was born into slavery in 1818 and raised on a Maryland plantation under brutal conditions and who grew up to become a famous orator, journalist, author, and adviser to U.S. presidents.

This is "a thoroughly researched, lucidly written biography. . . . Adler does an excellent job of exploring the atrocities and dehumanizing indignities . . . visited on those who lived in slavery." Booklist

Includes bibliographical references

Esty, Amos. **Unbound** and unbroken: the story of Frederick Douglass. Morgan Reynolds Pub. 2010 143p il map (Civil rights leaders) lib bdg $28.95

Grades: 7 8 9 10   **92**

1. Slaves 2. Authors 3. Abolitionists 4. Memoirists 5. African Americans -- Biography

ISBN 978-1-59935-136-0; 1-59935-136-6

LC 2009-54287

Traces the life and historical impact of the noted abolitionist, detailing his birth into slavery and harsh upbringing, his subsequent escape, and his emergence as a leader.

"Multiple biographies have been written about Douglass; however, few capture the depth of his intellect as an orator and writer. Through interwoven quotes from his autobiography, speeches, and pictures, this story also serves as prime research material. Douglass's ingenious case for the Constitution and fifth of July speech make the biography accessible from cover to cover." Voice Youth Advocates

Includes bibliographical references

Schuman, Michael. **Frederick** Douglass; truth is of no color. [by] Michael A. Schuman. Enslow

Publishers 2009 128p il map (Americans: the spirit of a nation) lib bdg $31.93

Grades: 6 7 8 9   **92**

1. Slaves 2. Authors 3. Abolitionists 4. Memoirists 5. African Americans -- Biography

ISBN 978-0-7660-3025-1 lib bdg; 0-7660-3025-3 lib bdg

LC 2008-29634

This "is an engaging introduction to famous abolitionist. Well-sourced excerpts, including many passages from Douglass' own writings, and vivid description enliven the text. . . . The visuals ably support the writing, with a strong mix of engravings, maps, and photos." Booklist

Includes glossary and bibliographical references

Drake, Francis Sir, 1540?-1596

Lace, William W. **Sir** Francis Drake. Chelsea House 2009 112p il map (Great explorers) lib bdg $30

Grades: 6 7 8 9   **92**

1. Admirals 2. Explorers 3. Voyages around the world

ISBN 978-1-60413-417-9 lib bdg; 1-60413-417-8 lib bdg

LC 2009-15017

Biography of the explorer Sir Francis Drake

"The information . . . is presented in such a way as to attract and maintain readers' interest. . . . With a full complement of maps, photographs (where available), illustrations, time lines, and document reproductions, a full story is told. Well-written and thoroughly researched, this . . . will make a solid addition." SLJ

Includes glossary and bibliographical references

Du Bois, W. E. B. (William Edward Burghardt), 1868-1963

Bolden, Tonya. **W.E.B.** Du Bois; a twentieth-century life. Viking Children's Books 2008 224p il (Up close) $16.99

Grades: 7 8 9 10   **92**

1. Authors 2. Novelists 3. Historians 4. Editors 5. Essayists 6. Sociologists 7. Nonfiction writers 8. Civil rights activists 9. African Americans -- Biography 10. African Americans -- Civil rights

ISBN 978-0-670-06302-4; 0-670-06302-9

LC 2007-52380

"The author covers her subject's life, which spanned 95 years, from Reconstruction to the modern Civil Rights Movement. . . . This balanced, lively account records his many contributions as a teacher, speaker, Civil Rights activist, sociologist, writer, and cofounder of several organizations, including the NAACP, as well as his failings." SLJ

Includes bibliographical references

Hinman, Bonnie. A **stranger** in my own house; the story of W.E.B. Du Bois. Morgan Reynolds Pub. 2005 176p il map $26.95

Grades: 7 8 9 10   **92**

1. Authors 2. Novelists 3. Historians 4. Editors 5. Essayists 6. Sociologists 7. Nonfiction writers 8. Civil rights activists 9. African Americans -- Biography 10.

African Americans -- Civil rights

ISBN 1-931798-45-1

LC 2004-26460

"The long, complex life of this scholar and controversial civil rights leader is examined in this . . . biography. Hinman offers insights into the background, beliefs, and conflicts that shaped and defined Du Bois. . . . The engaging, informative, balanced text is enhanced with documentary photographs and illustrations." SLJ

Includes bibliographical references

Whiting, Jim. **W.E.B.** Du Bois; civil rights activist, author, historian. Mason Crest Publishers 2010 64p il (Transcending race in America: biographies of biracial achievers) $22.95; pa $9.95

Grades: 5 6 7 8   **92**

1. Authors 2. Novelists 3. Historians 4. Editors 5. Essayists 6. Sociologists 7. Nonfiction writers 8. Civil rights activists 9. African Americans -- Biography 10. African Americans -- Civil rights

ISBN 978-1-4222-1618-7; 1-4222-1618-7; 978-1-4222-1632-3 pa; 1-4222-1632-2 pa

LC 2009022049

"The author openly discusses Du Bois' political and ideological struggles, which concluded with his move to Ghana and admittance into the Communist Party. . . . The book . . . provides solid information about Du Bois." Booklist

Includes glossary and bibliographical references

Duncan, Lois, 1934-

Campbell, Kimberly Edwina. **Lois** Duncan; author of I know what you did last summer. [by] Kimberly Campbell. Enslow Publishers 2009 104p bibl il por (Authors teens love) lib bdg $31.93

Grades: 6 7 8 9   **92**

1. Authors 2. Novelists 3. Women authors 4. Authors, American 5. Young adult authors

ISBN 978-0-7660-2963-7 lib bdg; 0-7660-2963-8 lib bdg

LC 2008013874

This discusses the life and work of author Lois Duncan

Includes glossary and bibliographical references

Dvořák, Antonín, 1841-1904

Horowitz, Joseph. **Dvorak** in America; in search of the New World. Cricket Bks. 2003 158p il $17.95

Grades: 7 8 9 10   **92**

1. Composers

ISBN 0-8126-2681-8

LC 2002-151456

An account of Antonin Dvorak's 1890s stay in America, where he took the essences of Indian drums, slave spirituals, and other musical forms and created from them a distinctly new music

"A welcome addition to music and biography collections." SLJ

Includes bibliographical references

Délano, Poli, 1936-

Delano, Poli. **When** I was a boy Neruda called me Policarpo; illustrated by Manuel Monroy. Groundwood Books/House of Anansi Press 2006 84p il $15.95

Grades: 5 6 7 8   92

1. Poets 2. Authors 3. Diplomats 4. Novelists 5. Poets, Chilean 6. Memoirists 7. Short story writers 8. Nobel laureates for peace 9. Nobel laureates for literature

ISBN 0-88899-726-4

In this book, the author "offers seven vignettes, interspersed with six of Neruda's . . . poems and biographical information, to give middle-grade readers a sense of what it was like to grow up in the constant presence of a kindly, though spoiled and eccentric, celebrity. . . ." (MultiCult Rev)

"Based on the author's childhood remembrances of when he and his diplomat parents lived with Tío Pablo [Neruda] in Mexico, these seven chapters reveal both the genius and the eccentricities of the Nobel Prize-winning Chilean poet. . . . The chapters are short, well written, and filled with interesting details that will open up a new and exotic world. . . . Monroy's pen-and-sepia-toned drawings are . . . at times humorous, at times dramatic, but always enticing." SLJ

Earhart, Amelia, 1898-1937

★ Fleming, Candace. **Amelia** lost: the life and disappearance of Amelia Earhart. Schwartz & Wade Books 2011 118p il map

Grades: 4 5 6 7   92

1. Air pilots 2. Missing persons 3. Women air pilots 4. Memoirists

ISBN 0-375-84198-9; 0-375-94598-9 lib bdg; 978-0-375-84198-9; 978-0-375-94598-4 lib bdg

LC 2010-05279

Fleming "offers a fresh look at this famous aviatrix. Employing dual narratives—straightforward biographical chapters alternating with a chilling recounting of Earhart's final flight and the search that followed—Fleming seeks to uncover the 'history of the hype,' pointing out numerous examples in which Earhart took an active role in mythologizing her own life. . . . Frequent sidebars, well-chosen maps, archival documents, and photos further clarify textual references without disturbing the overall narrative flow." Booklist

★ Micklos, John. **Unsolved**: what really happened to Amelia Earhart? [by] John Micklos, Jr. Enslow Publishers 2006 144p bibl il map por lib bdg $31.93

Grades: 5 6 7 8   92

1. Air pilots 2. Missing persons 3. Women air pilots 4. Memoirists

ISBN 0-7660-2365-6

LC 2005020875

"Micklos discusses the pilot's childhood, including what made her tick and what made her fly. However, the book's real focus is on the events of her fateful round-the-world adventure. . . . There are several theories about what happened to her and her copilot, Fred Noonan, on July 2, 1937. . . . As the plane and remains have never been found and identified, no one really knows. Fully half of this book is devoted to the famous flight and the possible explanations for what

occurred. Chock-full of photos . . . Unsolved captures the imagination." SLJ

Includes glossary and bibliographical references

Tanaka, Shelley. **Amelia** Earhart; the legend of the lost aviator. by Shelley Tanaka; illustrated by David Craig. Abrams Books for Young Readers 2008 48p il map $18.95

Grades: 3 4 5 6   92

1. Air pilots 2. Missing persons 3. Women air pilots 4. Memoirists 5. Astronautics -- History

ISBN 978-0-8109-7095-3; 0-8109-7095-3

LC 2007-39749

NCTE Orbis Pictus Award (2009)

This is an account of the life of aviator Amelia Earhart from her childhood up to the time she disappeared on a flight in 1937.

"This title is notable . . . for its smooth, powerful storytelling, ample gallery of well-chosen photographs, and nicely placed sidebar information on such topics as flight delays, navigation, and around-the-world flight records." Bull Cent Child Books

Includes bibliographical references

Earle, Sylvia A., 1935-

Reichard, Susan E. **Who** on earth is Sylvia Earle? undersea explorer of the ocean. Enslow Publishers 2009 112p il (Scientists saving the earth) lib bdg $31.93

Grades: 5 6 7 8   92

1. Botanists 2. Marine biology 3. Women scientists 4. Underwater exploration 5. Divers 6. Marine biologists

ISBN 978-1-59845-118-4 lib bdg; 1-59845-118-9 lib bdg

LC 2008032014

"The writing is clear and informative. . . . Color photographs are relevant and of good quality." SLJ

Includes glossary and bibliographical references

Edison, Thomas A. (Thomas Alva), 1847-1931

Baxter, Roberta. **Illuminated** progress; the story of Thomas Edison. [by] Roberta Baxter. Morgan Reynolds Pub. 2009 144p il (Profiles in science) lib bdg $27.95

Grades: 6 7 8 9   92

1. Inventors

ISBN 978-1-59935-085-1 lib bdg; 1-59935-085-8 lib bdg

LC 2008007411

This title "offers a concise, informative overview of the inventor who ushered in the world the Age of Electricity. . . . This well-documented biography is illustrated throughout with photographs." Booklist

Includes bibliographical references

★ Carlson, Laurie M. **Thomas** Edison for kids; his life and ideas: 21 activities. [by] Laurie Carlson. Chicago Review Press 2006 147p il $14.95

Grades: 5 6 7 8   **92**
  1. Inventors 2. Science -- Experiments
ISBN 1-55652-584-2
           LC 2005025659
"Part biography, part science activity book, this resource will appeal to casual researchers and novice inventors. It contains a wealth of full-page primary source archival photographs, sidebars, and short biographical profiles of Edison's contemporaries, in addition to short and straightforward experiments." Voice Youth Advocates
Includes bibliographical references

Woodside, Martin. **Thomas** A. Edison; the man who lit up the world. [by] Martin Woodside. Sterling 2007 124p (Sterling biographies) lib bdg $12.95; pa $5.95
Grades: 5 6 7 8   **92**
  1. Inventors
ISBN 978-1-4027-4955-1 lib bdg; 1-4027-4955-4 lib bdg; 978-1-4027-3229-4 pa; 1-4027-3229-5 pa
           LC 2007003509
"Woodside presents the life, struggles, failures, and successes of a man whose motto was 'the most important way to succeed is always to try one more time.' [The book provides] clear, concise information in an easy-to-read format with captioned photographs and illustrations on most pages." SLJ
Includes glossary and bibliographical references

Einstein, Albert, 1879-1955

★ Delano, Marfe Ferguson. **Genius**; a photobiography of Albert Einstein. National Geographic 2005 64p il $17.95; lib bdg $27.90; pa $7.95
Grades: 5 6 7 8   **92**
  1. Physicists 2. Nobel laureates for physics
ISBN 0-7922-9544-7; 0-7922-9545-5 lib bdg; 1-4263-0294-0 pa
           LC 2004-15001
A biography of the German American physicist.
This "combines a solid text with a particularly attractive format. . . . Delano offers just enough information about Einstein's theories to give a sense of his work. . . . Oversize and filled with well-selected photographs, the book is very handsome." Booklist

★ Krull, Kathleen. **Albert** Einstein; illustrated by Boris Kulikov. Viking 2009 141p il (Giants of science) $15.99
Grades: 5 6 7 8   **92**
  1. Physicists 2. Nobel laureates for physics 3. Physics 4. Science -- History
ISBN 978-0-670-06332-1; 0-670-06332-0
           LC 2009-16037
"Krull delivers a splendidly humane biography of that gold standard of brilliance, Albert Einstein. . . . Drawing extensively on Einstein's writings, she presents a fully rounded portrait of a man whose genius combined with a bad temper and arrogance, to the detriment of his own professional advancement, not to mention his relationships with women and his children. Using concrete examples, the author brings such mind-bending notions as his General Theory of Relativity within the grasp of child readers." Kirkus

Eisenhower, Dwight D. (Dwight David), 1890-1969

Mara, Wil. **Dwight** Eisenhower. Marshall Cavendish Benchmark 2011 112p il (Presidents and their times) lib bdg $34.21
Grades: 5 6 7 8   **92**
  1. Generals 2. Presidents 3. College presidents 4. Presidents -- United States
ISBN 978-0-7614-4812-9; 0-7614-4812-8
           LC 2009033042
"The size makes it ideal for that one-hundred page biography assignment; the readability makes the titles accessible to reluctant readers in high school; the succinct, well-presented information makes the volumes fitting for initial research at both the middle and high school level." Voice Youth Advocates
Includes glossary and bibliographical references

Eisner, Will, 1917-2005

Greenberger, Robert. **Will** Eisner; [by] Robert Greenberger. Rosen Pub. Group 2005 112p il (Library of graphic novelists) lib bdg $31.95
Grades: 6 7 8 9   **92**
  1. Authors 2. Cartoonists 3. Cartoons and comics 4. Cartoons and caricatures 5. Comic book writers 6. Publishing executives
ISBN 1-4042-0286-2
           LC 2004-16656
This "book focuses on the artist's work rather than on his life. It sketches in major events, . . . but dwells heavily on the characters he created and his influence on the graphic-novel format. This is a well-organized and easy-to-read volume." SLJ
Includes bibliographical references

Eleanor, of Aquitaine, Queen, consort of Henry II, King of England, 1122?-1204

★ Kramer, Ann. **Eleanor** of Aquitaine; the queen who rode off to battle. National Geographic 2006 64p il map (World history biographies) $17.95; lib bdg $27.90
Grades: 5 6 7 8   **92**
  1. Queens
ISBN 0-7922-5895-9; 0-7922-5896-7 lib bdg
An illustrated biography of the medieval queen who traveled to the Crusades with her first husband King Louis VII of France and later married King Henry II of England.
Includes glossary and bibliographical references

Elizabeth I, Queen of England, 1533-1603

★ Adams, Simon. **Elizabeth** I; the outcast who became England's queen. [by] Simon Adams. National Geographic 2005 64p il map (World history biographies) $17.95; lib bdg $27.90
Grades: 4 5 6 7   **92**
  1. Queens
ISBN 0-7922-3649-1; 0-7922-3654-8 lib bdg
           LC 2005001359
An illustrated introduction to the life and times of the 16th century queen of England

"Accomplishments and hardships are clearly explained with supporting quotes and facts. . . . Beautifully illustrated and visually appealing." SLJ

Includes glossary and bibliographical references

Stanley, Diane. **Good** Queen Bess: the story of Elizabeth I of England; by Diane Stanley and Peter Vennema; illustrated by Diane Stanley. HarperCollins Pubs. 2001 un il $16.99

Grades: 4 5 6 7   **92**

1. Queens 2. Queens -- Great Britain -- Biography

ISBN 0-688-17961-4

LC 00-47267

A reissue of the title first published 1990 by Four Winds Press

Follows the life of the strong-willed queen who ruled England in the time of Shakespeare and the defeat of the Spanish Armada

"The handsome illustrations . . . are worthy of their subject. Although the format suggests a picture-book audience, this biography needs to be introduced to older readers who have the background to appreciate and understand this woman who dominated and named an age." SLJ

Includes bibliographical references

Weatherly, Myra. **Elizabeth** I; Queen of Tudor England. by Myra Weatherly. Compass Point Books 2006 112p il (Signature lives) $30

Grades: 6 7 8 9   **92**

1. Queens

ISBN 0-7565-0988-2

LC 2005002790

"This engaging biography brings the monarch's complicated and fascinating life to light. . . . The text is clearly written and highly readable." SLJ

Includes bibliographical references

Ellington, Duke, 1899-1974

Stein, Stephanie. **Duke** Ellington; his life in jazz with 21 activities. [by] Stephanie Stein Crease. Chicago Review Press 2009 148p il (For kids) pa $16.95

Grades: 5 6 7 8   **92**

1. Composers 2. Jazz musicians 3. Band leaders

ISBN 978-1-55652-724-1; 1-55652-724-1

LC 2008-23742

"This large-format book combines an illustrated biography of Duke Ellington with activities designed to offer insights into Ellington s era and his music. An informative account in an attractive...format." Booklist

Includes bibliographical references, discography, and filmography

Stein, Stephanie. **Duke** Ellington; his life in jazz with 21 activities. [by] Stephanie Stein Crease. Chicago Review Press 2009 148p il $16.95

Grades: 4 5 6 7 8   **92**

1. Composers 2. Jazz musicians 3. African American musicians 4. Band leaders

ISBN 978-1-55652-724-1; 1-55652-724-1

LC 2008023742

"This biography begins with a brief discussion of the lives of Ellington's parents and his childhood introduction to music and instruments. As each chapter introduces separate highlights of the man's life and musical growth, sidebar articles emphasize historical milestones in music . . . and the impact of individuals or events on his life. The book also features 21 interactive activities, each of which is positioned to provide a greater understanding of an instrument, performance, or music theory in jazz style. . . . Illustrations include performance photographs and portraits of notable names from the Big Band era." SLJ

Emerson, Ralph Waldo, 1803-1882

Caravantes, Peggy. **Self**-reliance: the story of Ralph Waldo Emerson. Morgan Reynolds Pub. 2010 143p il map (World writers) lib bdg $28.95

Grades: 7 8 9 10   **92**

1. Poets 2. Authors 3. Philosophers 4. Essayists 5. Authors, American

ISBN 978-1-59935-124-7; 1-59935-124-2

LC 2010-8143

Presents the life and career of the eighteenth century New England essayist, poet, and lecturer who advocated a philosophy of self-reliance and individualism and was an important figure in the American Transcendental Movement.

This volume treats "young adult readers with respect and . . . [works] to ease them into scholarly research and writing in an engaging manner." Voice Youth Advocates

Includes bibliographical references

Eratosthenes, 3rd cent. B.C.

Gow, Mary. **Measuring** the Earth; Eratosthenes and his celestial geometry. Enslow 2010 128p il (Great minds of ancient science and math) lib bdg $31.93

Grades: 5 6 7 8   **92**

1. Astronomers 2. Mathematicians 3. Geographers 4. Writers on science 5. Geometry

ISBN 978-0-7660-3120-3 lib bdg; 0-7660-3120-9 lib bdg

LC 2008-38523

This biography is a "solid [choice], as . . . [it provides] a good overview of the cultural and political landscape of the times, as well as pictures." SLJ

Includes glossary and bibliographical references

Euclid

Hightower, Paul. The **father** of geometry: Euclid and his 3D world. Enslow Publishers 2010 112p il (Great minds of ancient science and math) lib bdg $31.93

Grades: 6 7 8 9   **92**

1. Geometry 2. Mathematicians 3. Writers on science

ISBN 978-0-7660-3409-9 lib bdg; 0-7660-3409-7 lib bdg

LC 2009-23814

"Describes the life of another fourth-century B.C.E. man who would ultimately become known as the 'father of geometry.' He was not famous like the philosophers of his time, but his book The Elements totally revised what was known of mathematics at the time. . . . Includes simple, straightforward text with nice illustrations and appendixes of suggested activities, a supplemental chronology, chapter notes, and glossary." Voice Youth Advocates

Includes glossary and bibliographical references

Fermi, Enrico, 1901-1954

Cooper, Dan. **Enrico** Fermi and the revolutions in modern physics. Oxford Univ. Press 1999 117p il (Oxford portraits in science) lib bdg $28

Grades: 7 8 9 10   92

1. Physicists 2. College teachers 3. Nobel laureates for physics

ISBN 0-19-511762-X

LC 98-34471

A biography of the Nobel Prize-winning physicist whose work led to the discovery of nuclear fission, the basis of nuclear power and the atom bomb

"This book will be useful for reports. . . . The extensive list for further reading includes biographies of Fermi, books on both scientific and political aspects of the atomic-bomb project, and information on tours of laboratories involved in nuclear research today." SLJ

Ferrera, America, 1984-

Abrams, Dennis. **America** Ferrera. Chelsea House Publishers 2010 107p il (The great Hispanic heritage) lib bdg $30

Grades: 6 7 8 9   92

1. Actors

ISBN 978-1-60413-967-9; 1-60413-967-6

LC 2010009481

A biography of the actress best known for her roles in television's Ugly Betty and in films such as Real Women Have Curves and The Sisterhood of the Traveling Pants.

Fey, Tina, 1970-

Friedman, Lauri S. **Tina** Fey. Lucent Books 2010 96p il (People in the news) $33.45

Grades: 7 8 9 10   92

1. Actors 2. Comedians 3. Screenwriters 4. Television scriptwriters

ISBN 978-1-4205-0238-1; 1-4205-0238-7

LC 2009039362

A biography of writer, producer and Saturday Night Live funnygirl Tina Fey.

"With color photos of the actress at work throughout, this . . . does an excellent job of contexualizing Fey's comedy in the stream of current events. . . . This offers plenty of insight and inspiration for budding comedians, actors, and writers as well as researchers." Booklist

Includes bibliographical references

Feynman, Richard Phillips, 1918-1988

★ Henderson, Harry. **Richard** Feynman; quarks, bombs, and bongos. Chelsea House 2010 138p il (Makers of modern science) $35

Grades: 7 8 9 10   92

1. Authors 2. Physicists 3. Writers on science 4. Nobel laureates for physics

ISBN 978-0-8160-6176-1; 0-8160-6176-9

A biography of physicist Richard Feyman.

"The mark of a good biography is when it makes people you may never have heard of, in fields you might not be interested in, fascinating. [This book] does this with [a] well-chosen [subject], engaging writing, plenty of sidebars that take the text in new directions, and perhaps most importantly, the determination to present a fully-rounded person, not just a scientist." Booklist

LeVine, Harry. The **great** explainer; the story of Richard Feynman. by Harry LeVine, III. Morgan Reynolds Pub. 2009 144p il $28.95

Grades: 6 7 8 9   92

1. Authors 2. Physicists 3. Writers on science 4. Nobel laureates for physics

ISBN 978-1-59935-113-1; 1-59935-113-7

LC 2009006677

"Feynman was a particularly fascinating fellow who was involved in everything from building the atomic bomb at Los Alamos to constructing the first computers to figuring out why the Space Shuttle Challenger crashed. Children who might have trouble with the specifics of physics will be drawn in by Feynman's personal story. . . . Throughout there is a very personal feel, and when the science becomes difficult to understand, readers will still want to learn more about Feynman and his restless, sometimes chaotic search for knowledge." Booklist

Includes bibliographical references

Filipovic, Zlata

Filipovic, Zlata. **Zlata's** diary; a child's life in Sarajevo. with an introduction by Janine Di Giovanni; translated with notes by Christina Pribichevich-Zoric. Penguin Books 2006 195p il pa $13

Grades: 6 7 8 9   92

1. Children 2. Diarists

ISBN 0-14-303687-4

A reissue with a new preface of the title first published 1994 by Viking

"Filipovic's diary personalizes the tragedy in war-torn Sarajevo." Booklist

Fillmore, Millard, 1800-1874

Gottfried, Ted. **Millard** Fillmore; by Ted Gottfried. Marshall Cavendish Benchmark 2007 96p il (Presidents and their times) lib bdg $22.95

Grades: 5 6 7 8   92

1. Presidents 2. Vice-presidents 3. Members of Congress 4. Presidents -- United States

ISBN 978-0-7614-2431-4

LC 2006019707

"Primary-source materials and quotes, helpful insets, and carefully selected . . . reproductions bring history to life and help make [this] clearly written [biography] highly readable." SLJ

Includes glossary and bibliographical references

Fitzgerald, Ella

★ Stone, Tanya Lee. **Ella** Fitzgerald. Viking 2008 203p il (Up close) $16.99

Grades: 7 8 9 10   92

1. Singers 2. African American singers 3. Pop

musicians 4. African American women -- Biography
ISBN 978-0-670-06149-5; 0-670-06149-2

LC 2007-23117

This is a "strong biography [of the African American singer]. . . . Stone's smooth, straightforward narrative draws from authoritative sources. . . . The abundant quotes from Fitzgerald and her musician peers greatly develop the narrative." Booklist

Includes bibliographical references

Fleischman, Sid, 1920-2010

Freedman, Jeri. **Sid** Fleischman; [by] Jeri Freedman. Rosen Pub. Group 2004 112p (Library of author biographies) lib bdg $31.95

Grades: 5 6 7 8   **92**

1. Authors 2. Magicians 3. Authorship 4. Magazine editors 5. Authors, American 6. Children's authors 7. Young adult authors 8. Children's stories -- Authorship 9. Authors, American -- 20th century -- Biography
ISBN 0-8239-4019-5

LC 2003-5203

Discusses the life and work of this popular author, including his writing process and methods, inspirations, a critical discussion of his books, biographical timeline, and awards

"Libraries looking to expand their biography section will be well served by [this] informative [title]." SLJ

Includes bibliographical references

Ford, Henry, 1863-1947

Mitchell, Don. **Driven**; a photobiography of Henry Ford. foreword by Lee Iacocca. National Geographic 2010 64p il map $18.95; lib bdg $27.90

Grades: 5 6 7 8   **92**

1. Businessmen 2. Philanthropists 3. Automobile industry 4. Automobile executives 5. Automobiles
ISBN 978-1-4263-0155-1; 1-4263-0155-3; 978-1-4263-0156-8 lib bdg; 1-4263-0156-1 lib bdg

LC 2009-07136

"Mitchell introduces readers to the founder of the auto company. . . . Thoughts, feelings, and quotes abound, and they are well sourced. . . . The writing is clear, and the organization is chronological. . . . Driven combines fine photography and an inviting text to depict Ford's life and his impact on the world." SLJ

Includes bibliographical references

Fossey, Dian

Kushner, Jill Menkes. **Who** on earth is Dian Fossey? defender of the mountain gorillas. Enslow Publishers 2009 112p il (Scientists saving the earth) lib bdg $31.93

Grades: 5 6 7 8   **92**

1. Authors 2. Gorillas 3. Women scientists 4. Murder victims 5. Primatologists 6. Writers on science
ISBN 1-59845-117-0 lib bdg; 978-1-59845-117-7 lib bdg

LC 2008029376

"The book is filled with factual information, yet is written in a manner that makes both Fossey and her gorillas come to life for the reader." Sci Books Films

Includes glossary and bibliographical references

Fox, Paula

Daniel, Susanna. **Paula** Fox; [by] Susanna Daniel. 1st ed; Rosen Central 2004 112p il (Library of author biographies) lib bdg $26.50

Grades: 7 8 9 10   **92**

1. Authors 2. Novelists 3. Women authors 4. Authors, American 5. Children's authors 6. Young adult authors
ISBN 0-8239-4525-1

LC 2003-9176

Discusses the life and work of this award-winning author, including her writing process and methods, inspirations, a critical discussion of her books, biographical timeline, and awards.

Includes bibliographical references

France, Diane L.

★ Hopping, Lorraine Jean. **Bone** detective; the story of forensic anthropologist Diane France. Franklin Watts 2005 118p il (Women's adventures in science) lib bdg $31.50

Grades: 7 8 9 10   **92**

1. Anthropologists 2. Women scientists 3. Forensic anthropology 4. Forensic scientists 5. Forensic sciences
ISBN 0-531-16776-3

LC 2005-0784

This "introduces the life and work of a contemporary forensic anthropologist, from her rural childhood to her work identifying the victims of the 9/11 tragedies. . . . The extensive detail gives readers a vivid sense of the daily work of a 'bone detective,' and clear explanations of the science will intrigue and inspire readers." Booklist

Includes glossary and bibliographical references

Frank, Anne, 1929-1945

★ Metselaar, Menno. **Anne** Frank: her life in words and pictures; from the archives of The Anne Frank House. [by] Menno Metselaar and Ruud van der Rol; translated by Arnold J. Pomerans. Roaring Brook Press 2009 215p il map pa $12.99

Grades: 5 6 7 8   **92**

1. Children 2. Diarists 3. Holocaust victims 4. Jews -- Netherlands 5. Holocaust, 1933-1945 6. World War, 1939-1945 -- Jews
ISBN 978-1-59643-546-9; 1-59643-546-1; 978-1-59643-547-6 pa; 1-59643-547-X pa

First published 2004 in the Netherlands with title: The story of Anne Frank

Boston Globe-Horn Book Award honor book: Nonfiction (2010)

"Beginning with a single photograph of the cover of Anne Frank's diary and the quote, 'One of my nicest presents,' this small, beautifully formatted book is accessible, compelling, and richly pictorial. . . . The book immediately immerses readers in the girl's life via a series of family photographs, many previously unpublished. Divided chronologically, the accompanying text is enhanced by diary entries, resulting in a historically succinct yet descriptive presentation. . . . Even for those collections where Anne Frank is well represented, this is a moving and valuable book." SLJ

Franklin, Benjamin, 1706-1790

★ Dash, Joan. A **dangerous** engine; Benjamin Franklin, from scientist to diplomat. pictures by Dusan Petricic. Frances Foster Books 2006 246p il $17

Grades: 7 8 9 10   92

1. Authors 2. Diplomats 3. Inventors 4. Statesmen 5. Scientists 6. Writers on science 7. Members of Congress

ISBN 0-374-30669-9

LC 2004-63204

"Franklin's long, productive, and interesting life is vividly recounted in a lively manner. Familiar aspects are covered, from his days as a printer in Philadelphia to his diplomatic service and his role in the development of the fledgling United States democracy. What may be new to some readers is Franklin's dedication to, and life-long love of, science and invention. . . . Witty pen-and-ink illustrations appear throughout." SLJ

★ Fleming, Candace. **Ben** Franklin's almanac; being a true account of the good gentleman's life. Atheneum Bks. for Young Readers 2003 120p il $19.95

Grades: 5 6 7 8   92

1. Authors 2. Diplomats 3. Inventors 4. Statesmen 5. Scientists 6. Writers on science 7. Members of Congress 8. Statesmen -- United States

ISBN 0-689-83549-3

LC 2002-6136

Brings together eighteenth century etchings, artifacts, and quotations to create the effect of a scrapbook of the life of Benjamin Franklin

"An authoritative work of depth, humor, and interest, presenting Franklin in all his complexity, ranging from the heroic to the vulgar, the saintly to the callous." SLJ

Miller, Brandon Marie. **Benjamin** Franklin, American genius; his life and ideas, with 21 activities. Chicago Review Press 2009 125p il pa $16.95

Grades: 4 5 6 7   92

1. Authors 2. Diplomats 3. Inventors 4. Statesmen 5. Scientists 6. Writers on science 7. Members of Congress

ISBN 978-1-55652-757-9 pa; 1-55652-757-8 pa

LC 2009012456

"Miller does an excellent job of presenting a synopsis of Franklin's life in a highly readable manner. . . . Imbedded in each chapter are asides that further elaborate on Franklin's life and times and activities that coordinate with the text or the historical facts presented. The directions are easy to follow and enhance the overall presentation, especially in terms of classroom connections. Illustrations accompany each project and reproductions of primary documents, renderings, and paintings provide added value." SLJ

Includes glossary and bibliographical references

Franklin, Rosalind, 1920-1958

Polcovar, Jane. **Rosalind** Franklin and the structure of life. Morgan Reynolds 2006 144p il lib bdg $26.95

Grades: 7 8 9 10   92

1. DNA 2. Chemists 3. Biologists 4. Women scientists 5. Geochemists

ISBN 978-1-59935-022-6; 1-59935-022-X

LC 2006-16864

A biography of the scientist whose unpublished research led to the discovery of the structure of DNA

"Polcovar writes a rattling good story on two fronts: a woman becoming a scientist in an age when that was still unusual and the complex dynamics of personalities in a field sometimes thought of as impersonal." Booklist

Includes bibliographical references

Friedman, Cory

Patterson, James. **Med** head; my knock-down, drag-out, drugged-up battle with my brain. as told by James Patterson & Hal Friedman. Little Brown & Co. 2010 302p il pa $8.99

Grades: 6 7 8 9 10   92

1. Mentally ill 2. Tourette syndrome 3. Obsessive-compulsive disorder

ISBN 978-0-316-076173 pa; 0-316-07617-1 pa

The story of Cory Friedman and his family's decades-long struggle to determine the cause of Cory's neurological disease.

"Based on detailed notes on medications, physician appointments, and school visits, this is a page-turning examination of what could have been a wasted, despairing life. . . . While nonfiction resources can provide the facts on mental disorders, this excellent biography puts them into a context that promotes compassion. " Voice Youth Advocates

Friedman, Milton, 1912-2006

Crain, Cynthia D. **Milton** Friedman; by Cynthia D. Crain and Dwight R. Lee. Morgan Reynolds Pub. 2009 144p il (Profiles in economics) lib bdg $28.95

Grades: 8 9 10 11 12   92

1. Economists 2. College teachers 3. Nobel laureates for economic sciences

ISBN 978-1-59935-108-7 lib bdg; 1-59935-108-0 lib bdg

LC 2009-169

Biography of the economist Milton Friedman

"Relationships, education, early influences, and family life are all described . . . [and] economic theory is closely tied to cultural and political events. . . . The writing is straightforward, the . . . [author] assume[s] a certain level of knowledge about world events." SLJ

Includes bibliographical references

Fritz, Jean

★ Fritz, Jean. **Homesick**: my own story; illustrated with drawings by Margot Tomes and photographs. Putnam 1982 163p il $16.99; pa $5.99

Grades: 5 6 7 8   92

1. Authors 2. Women authors 3. Children's authors

ISBN 0-399-20933-6; 0-698-11782-4 pa

LC 82-7646

A Newbery Medal honor book, 1983

"The descriptions of places and the times are vivid in a book that brings to the reader, with sharp clarity and candor, the yearnings and fears and ambivalent loyalties of a young girl." Bull Cent Child Books

Frost, Robert, 1874-1963

★ Caravantes, Peggy. **Deep** woods; the story of Robert Frost. Morgan Reynolds 2006 176p il (World writers) lib bdg $27.95

Grades: 7 8 9 10   92

1. Poets 2. Authors 3. Poets, American
ISBN 978-1-931798-92-1; 1-931798-92-3
LC 2005037514

This "introduces poet Robert Frost. . . . Though focused on the man, Caravantes' presentation includes a few short selections from Frost's verse and, in sidebars, a bit of information about poetic forms. . . . Well organized and clearly written, the book offers a very readable account of Frost's often troubled life as an individual, a family man, a poet, and a public figure." Booklist

Includes bibliographical references

Wooten, Sara McIntosh. **Robert** Frost; the life of America's poet. Enslow Publishers 2006 128p (People to know today) lib bdg $31.93

Grades: 6 7 8 9   92

1. Poets 2. Authors 3. Poets, American
ISBN 0-7660-2627-2 lib bdg; 978-0-7660-2627-8 lib bdg
LC 2005034882

"In this insightful biography, Wooten recounts Frost's difficult life from his childhood with an abusive, alcoholic father, through his many financial challenges as he tried to establish a career, to his constant struggle with shyness and depression. . . . Her book is thoroughly researched." SLJ

Includes bibliographical references

Fry, Varian, 1907-1967

★ McClafferty, Carla Killough. **In** defiance of Hitler; the secret mission of Varian Fry. Farrar, Straus & Giroux 2008 196p il $19.95

Grades: 7 8 9 10 11 12   92

1. Journalists 2. Editors 3. Classicists 4. Humanitarians 5. Holocaust, 1933-1945 6. World War, 1939-1945 -- France 7. World War, 1939-1945 -- Jews -- Rescue 8. Holocaust, Jewish (1939-1945) -- France
ISBN 978-0-374-38204-9; 0-374-38204-2
LC 2007-33271

"This stirring account of a young New York City journalist who secretly helped more than 2,000 refugees escape Nazi-occupied France blends exciting adventure with the grim history. . . . The author begins with a brief overview of Hitler's rise and the threat to the Jews, and then draws heavily on Fry's autobiography and his letters home." Booklist

Fulton, Robert, 1765-1815

Herweck, Don. **Robert** Fulton; engineer of the steamboat. Compass Point Books 2009 40p il (Mission: Science) lib bdg $26.60

Grades: 4 5 6 7   92

1. Engineers 2. Inventors 3. Steamboats
ISBN 978-0-7565-3961-0 lib bdg; 0-7565-3961-7 lib bdg
LC 2008007728

Covers the life and accomplishments of American inventor and mechanic, Robert Fulton, who is best known for building the first successful steamboat

Pierce, Morris A. **Robert** Fulton and the development of the steamboat. PowerPlus Books 2003 112p il map (Library of American lives and times) lib bdg $31.95

Grades: 4 5 6 7   92

1. Engineers 2. Inventors 3. Steamboats
ISBN 0-8239-5737-3
LC 2001-5541

"The life and times of this complex and creative man are captured in this attractive presentation replete with maps and full-color reproductions of building sketches and period paintings." SLJ

Includes glossary and bibliographical references

Gaines, Ernest J., 1933-

Abrams, Dennis. **Ernest** J. Gaines. Chelsea House 2010 120p il (Who wrote that?) lib bdg $30

Grades: 6 7 8 9   92

1. Authors 2. Novelists 3. African American authors 4. Authors, American 5. Children's authors 6. Short story writers
ISBN 978-1-60413-683-8; 1-60413-683-9
LC 2009022340

This discusses the life and work of author Ernest J. Gaines.

Includes bibliographical references

Galen, ca. 129-ca. 200

Yount, Lisa. The **father** of anatomy; Galen and his dissections. Enslow Publishers 2010 128p il (Great minds of ancient science and math) lib bdg $31.93

Grades: 6 7 8 9   92

1. Physicians 2. Human anatomy 3. Writers on medicine
ISBN 978-0-7660-3380-1; 0-7660-3380-5
LC 2008-29633

"A biography of ancient Greek physician Galen, whose dissections of animals led to discoveries about human anatomy. He was the authority on medical knowledge in the Western world for more than fifteen hundred years." Publisher's note

Includes glossary and bibliographical references

Galilei, Galileo, 1564-1642

Hightower, Paul. **Galileo**; astronomer and physicist. rev ed; Enslow Publishers 2008 128p il (Great minds of science) lib bdg $31.93

Grades: 5 6 7 8   92
1. Astronomers 2. Writers on science
ISBN 978-0-7660-3008-4 lib bdg; 0-7660-3008-3
lib bdg
LC 2007020302
First published 1997
"A biography of the seventeenth-century Italian astrono-
mer and physicist Galileo and includes related activities for
readers." Publisher's note
Includes glossary and bibliographical references

★ Panchyk, Richard. **Galileo** for kids; his life
and ideas: 25 activities. foreword by Buzz Aldrin.
Chicago Review Press 2005 166p il map pa $16.95
Grades: 5 6 7 8   92
1. Astronomers 2. Writers on science
ISBN 1-55652-566-4
LC 2004-22936
A biography of the Renaissance scientist and his times
with related activities
"Clear . . . writing places Galileo squarely within the
historical context of the turbulent Italian Renaissance. . . .
Panchyk's title is a good choice for those interested in inte-
grating history and science curriculums." SLJ
Includes bibliographical references

★ Steele, Philip. **Galileo**; the genius who faced
the Inquisition. National Geographic 2005 64p il
(World history biographies) $17.95; lib bdg $27.90
Grades: 4 5 6 7   92
1. Astronomers 2. Writers on science
ISBN 0-7922-3656-4; 0-7922-3657-2 lib bdg
LC 2005-01357
An illustrated introduction to the 16th century astrono-
mer and his times
"Accomplments and hardships are clearly explained
with supporting quotes and facts. . . . Beautifully illustrated
and visually appealing." SLJ

Gama, Vasco da, 1469-1524
★ Calvert, Patricia. **Vasco** da Gama; so strong a
spirit. [by] Patricia Calvert. Benchmark Books 2005
96p il map (Great explorations) lib bdg $29.93
Grades: 5 6 7 8   92
1. Explorers 2. Explorers -- Portugal -- Biography 3.
Discoveries in geography -- Portuguese
ISBN 0-7614-1611-0
LC 2003-22946
Recounts the voyages undertaken by fifteenth-century
Portuguese explorer Vasco da Gama to strengthen his na-
tion's power by establishing a sea trade route to India.
Includes bibliographical references

Gandhi, Mahatma, 1869-1948
De Lambilly, Elisabeth. **Gandhi**; his life, his
struggles, his words. written by Elisabeth de Lam-
billy; illustrated by Severine Cordier; [translated by
Robert Brent] Enchanted Lion Books 2010 67p il
(Great spiritual leaders of modern times)
Grades: 6 7 8 9   92
1. Authors 2. Pacifism 3. Journalists 4. Nonviolence

5. Resistance to government 6. Essayists 7. Pacifists
8. Memoirists 9. Political leaders 10. Statesmen --
India 11. Writers on politics
ISBN 1-59270-094-2; 978-1-59270-094-3
LC 2010025235
Original French edition, 2007
"The historical facts are as compelling as the biographi-
cal story, and the message of nonviolence will spark intense
debate about political action, then and now." Booklist
Includes bibliographical references

Ebine, Kazuki. **Gandhi**: a manga biography.
Penguin 2011 192p il pa $15
Grades: 7 8 9 10   92
1. Manga 2. Authors 3. Journalists 4. Graphic novels
5. Essayists 6. Pacifists 7. Memoirists 8. Political
leaders 9. Statesmen -- India 10. Writers on politics
ISBN 978-0-14-312024-7; 0-14-312024-7
"Ebine's nicely drawn manga biography is a clear and
concise introduction to Gandhi's life. The biography not
only touches upon Gandhi's major accomplishements . . .
but also humanizes Gandhi by showing his struggles with
insecurity as a young man. . . . This title is a great addition
to social studies curricula, and it will have special appeal to
budding young activists and idealists." Booklist

Sawyer, Kem Knapp. **Mohandas** Gandhi. Morgan Reynolds Pub. 2011 144p il (Champion of freedom) lib bdg $28.95
Grades: 6 7 8 9 10   92
1. Authors 2. Journalists 3. Essayists 4. Pacifists 5.
Memoirists 6. Political leaders 7. Statesmen -- India
8. Writers on politics
ISBN 978-1-59935-166-7; 1-59935-166-8
LC 2010047904
This title "starts with an overview of the British Raj at
the time of Mohandas Gandhi's birth and what life was like
for those living under it. The thorough biography then goes
on to trace the key events, philosophical influences, and personal relationships that shaped the life of a man who spread
the doctrine of nonviolence. Interesting anecdotes, explanations of Indian culture, and an engaging, well-organized narrative make this a solid resource." Booklist
Includes bibliographical references

★ Wilkinson, Philip. **Gandhi**; the young protester who founded a nation. National Geographic
2005 64p il (World history biographies) $17.95;
lib bdg $27.90
Grades: 4 5 6 7   92
1. Authors 2. Journalists 3. Passive resistance 4.
Essayists 5. Pacifists 6. Memoirists 7. Political
leaders 8. Writers on politics
ISBN 0-7922-3647-5; 0-7922-3648-3 lib bdg
"Double-page spreads describe phases in Gandhi's life,
from childhood to his tragic death, detailed in Wilkinson's
straightforward, succinct language and in anecdotes, which
will capture young people's attention and also humanize the
great leader." Booklist
Includes glossary and bibliographical references

García Márquez, Gabriel, 1928-

Darraj, Susan Muaddi. **Gabriel** Garcia Marquez. Chelsea House 2006 112p il (Great Hispanic heritage) lib bdg $30

Grades: 6 7 8 9   92

1. Authors 2. Novelists 3. Journalists 4. Authors, Colombian 5. Short story writers 6. Nobel laureates for literature
ISBN 0-7910-8839-1

LC 2006010615

A biography of the Colombian novelist who won the Nobel Prize for Literature in 1982

"A great deal of biographical information and some historical context is imparted in [this volume]. . . . Scattered throughout are many photographs and helpful boxed historical asides." Horn Book Guide

Includes bibliographical references

Garrison, William Lloyd, 1805-1879

Esty, Amos. The **liberator**: the story of William Lloyd Garrison. Morgan Reynolds Pub. 2010 144p il (Civil rights leaders) lib bdg $28.95

Grades: 7 8 9 10   92

1. Abolitionists 2. Newspaper editors 3. Slavery -- United States
ISBN 978-1-59935-137-7; 1-59935-137-4

LC 2009-54290

This biography of abolitionist William Lloyd Garrison "will hook readers with discussions of the larger political issues as well as [Garrison's] personal struggles. . . . The design . . . is readable, with spacious type and many kinds of illustrations, including color and sepia photos, paintings, and reproductions of famous documents." Booklist

Includes bibliographical references

Garvey, Marcus, 1887-1940

Kallen, Stuart A. **Marcus** Garvey and the Back to Africa Movement. Lucent Books 2006 112p il map (Lucent library of Black history) $32.45

Grades: 7 8 9 10   92

1. Writers on politics 2. Civil rights activists 3. African Americans -- Civil rights
ISBN 1-59018-838-1

LC 2005027286

"Kallen seeks . . . to discuss and expand on [Garvey's] contributions to Black Nationalism, and to place his particular movement within the context of his times. Here, Garvey emerges as a man who anticipated those later movements that centered on black pride and black power. In an exceptionally evenhanded manner, the author also shows Garvey to have been naive, unrealistic, and lacking in management skills. A superb speechmaker, a charismatic leader, and an excellent propagandist, he seemed ill prepared to deal with the powerful enemies he made. . . . Kallen describes this all in clear, well-written prose. Archival photographs are placed throughout to good advantage." SLJ

Includes bibliographical references

Gates, Bill, 1955-

★ Aronson, Marc. **Bill** Gates; a twentieth-century life. Penguin Group 2008 192p il (Up close) $16.99

Grades: 7 8 9 10   92

1. Businesspeople 2. Computer software industry 3. Computer software executives
ISBN 978-0-670-06348-2; 0-670-06348-7

LC 2008-15552

This is a biography of the businessman who co-founded Microsoft.

"Well researched, thought-provoking, and up-to-date, this biography . . . offers insights into Gates' character as well as an engaging account of his life." Booklist

Isaacs, Sally Senzell. **Bill** and Melinda Gates; [by] Sally Isaacs. Heinemann Library 2010 112p il (Front-page lives) $38.93

Grades: 6 7 8 9 10   92

1. Businesspeople 2. Philanthropists 3. Computer industry 4. Foundation officials 5. Computer software executives 6. Spouses of prominent persons
ISBN 978-1-4329-3220-6; 1-4329-3220-9

LC 2009-18180

A biography of Microsoft founder and billionaire Bill Gates his wife, Melinda who, through the Bill and Melinda Gates Foundation, have helped people around the world by donating billions of dollars to solve global health problems and other issues.

"The subjects' lives are presented with depth and breadth and in such a way as to make clear how their actions impacted the world and why they are or were so important. . . . The writing is accessible and engaging, with color and black-and-white photographs." SLJ

Includes glossary and bibliographical references

Lesinski, Jeanne M. **Bill** Gates; entrepreneur and philanthropist. rev ed; Twenty-First Century Books 2009 112p il (Lifeline biographies) lib bdg $33.26

Grades: 6 7 8 9   92

1. Businesspeople 2. Computer software industry 3. Computer software executives
ISBN 978-1-58013-570-2; 1-58013-570-6

LC 2008008565

A revised edition of the title first published 2000

This biography "boasts lively, credible writing and a compelling layout. Particularly interesting are the reprints of USA Today articles found throughout, which flesh out the [narrative] in a unique and appealing manner. . . . Full-color and black-and-white photos appear on almost every spread." SLJ

Includes bibliographical references

Gates, Melinda French

Isaacs, Sally Senzell. **Bill** and Melinda Gates; [by] Sally Isaacs. Heinemann Library 2010 112p il (Front-page lives) $38.93

Grades: 6 7 8 9 10   92

1. Businesspeople 2. Philanthropists 3. Computer industry 4. Foundation officials 5. Computer software

executives 6. Spouses of prominent persons
ISBN 978-1-4329-3220-6; 1-4329-3220-9

LC 2009-18180

A biography of Microsoft founder and billionaire Bill
Gates and his wife, Melinda who, through the Bill and
Melinda Gates Foundation, have helped people around the
world by donating billions of dollars to solve global health
problems and other issues.

"The subjects' lives are presented with depth and breadth
and in such a way as to make clear how their actions impacted the world and why they are or were so important. .
. . The writing is accessible and engaging, with color and
black-and-white photographs." SLJ

Includes glossary and bibliographical references

Gauguin, Paul, 1848-1903

Spence, David. **Gauguin**. New Forest Press
2010 48p il map (Great artists and their world) lib
bdg $32.80

Grades: 6 7 8 9   92

1. Artists 2. Painters 3. Artists, French
ISBN 978-1-84898-316-8; 1-84898-316-6

"Offers biographical information [of Paul Gauguin] . . .
interspersed with art history and criticism in an eye-catching
format. . . . [Includes] a long introductory paragraph and
four-to-six images with explanatory notes. . . . Spence . . .
does a good job of explaining why art that might seem ordinary today was revolutionary at the time of its creation." SLJ

Includes glossary

Gehrig, Lou, 1903-1941

Buckley, James. **Lou** Gehrig; Iron Horse of baseball. Sterling 2010 124p il (Sterling biographies)
pa $5.95

Grades: 6 7 8 9   92

1. Baseball players 2. Baseball -- Biography
ISBN 978-1-4027-7151-4 pa; 1-4027-7151-7 pa

This biography of Lou Gehrig is "studded with quotes
and illustrated with photos. . . . Lou Gehrig is today inextricably linked with ALS, the progressive nerve disease that
ended his baseball career and ultimately his life, but he is
also remembered as the Iron Horse of baseball, the legendary slugger who played a phenomenal 2,130 consecutive
games for the Yankees. Written in a straightforward, journalistic style, [this biography presents a] very readable [ac-
count] of the [life] of [an athlete] who made [his mark] on
American culture." Booklist

Includes glossary and bibliographical references

Gehry, Frank

Bodden, Valerie. **Frank** Gehry. Creative Education 2009 48p il (Xtraordinary artists) lib bdg
$32.80

Grades: 4 5 6 7   92

1. Architects
ISBN 978-1-58341-662-4 lib bdg; 1-58341-662-5
lib bdg

LC 2007004201

This is a biography of architect Frank Gehry

This offers an "interesting [layout]; big, high-quality
reproductions and photographs on heavy paper; insightful
quotes from diverse sources; and . . . an excerpt from an

essay about [Gehry] at the end of the book. Readers get a
strong sense of [the] artist's personality along with an excellent survey of his work." SLJ

Includes bibliographical references

Genghis Khan, 1162-1227

★ Demi. **Genghis** Khan. Marshall Cavendish
Children 2009 un il $19.99

Grades: 4 5 6 7   92

1. Mongols 2. Kings and rulers 3. Kings
ISBN 978-0-7614-5547-9; 0-7614-5547-7

LC 2008006001

A reissue of Chingis Khan, published 1991 by Henry
Holt & Co.

A biography of the Mongol leader and military-strategist
who, at the height of his power, was supreme master of the
largest empire ever created in the lifetime of one man.

"Demi has managed to portray a fierce conqueror as a
sympathetic character who follows a strict code that places
loyalty, obedience, and discipline above all else. . . . The
artist achieves a clever grandeur with the liberal use of iridescent gold and detailed scenes that spill out of their gilded
borders and nearly off the pages. . . . This handsome biography is a feast for the eyes from cover to cover." Booklist

Geronimo, Apache Chief, 1829-1909

Sullivan, George. **Geronimo**; Apache renegade.
Sterling 2010 124p il map (Sterling biographies)
lib bdg $12.95; pa $5.95

Grades: 7 8 9 10   92

1. Apache Indians 2. Indian chiefs 3. Native Americans
-- Biography
ISBN 978-1-4027-6843-9 lib bdg; 1-4027-6843-5 lib
bdg; 978-1-4027-6279-6 pa; 1-4027-6279-8 pa

LC 2009-24135

"Geronmino describes how the Apache leader was
feared and hated as he led violent clashes with whites, pursuing bloody vengeance for the massacre of his family and
all that his people had lost, an identity far from the roman-
ticized image that glorified him. . . . [The] spacious design
is highly scannable, with color background screens, photos,
maps, and historic prints throughout." Booklist

Includes glossary and bibliographical references

Gibson, Josh, 1911-1947

Twemlow, Nick. **Josh** Gibson. Rosen Pub.
Group 2002 112p il (Baseball Hall of Famers of the
Negro leagues) lib bdg $29.25

Grades: 5 6 7 8   92

1. Baseball players 2. African American athletes 3.
Baseball -- Biography 4. African American baseball
players -- Biography 5. Baseball players -- United
States -- Biography
ISBN 0-8239-3475-6

LC 2001-4143

Presents a biography of the powerful home run hitter and
chronicles the history of African American participation in
organized baseball, the formation of the Negro leagues, and
racial politics in America

Includes glossary and bibliographical references

Giff, Patricia Reilly

Giff, Patricia Reilly. **Don't** tell the girls; a family memoir. by Patricia Reilly Giff. Holiday House 2005 131p il $16.95

Grades: 4 5 6 7   **92**

1. Authors 2. Teachers 3. Women authors 4. Authors, American 5. Children's authors

ISBN 0-8234-1813-8

LC 2004-47452

"Giff reflects on her childhood and her family, going back through several generations. Spotlighting her two grandmothers, she lovingly relates remembered conversations and incidents involving the one she knew well before turning to the other grandmother, whom she never met. . . . This little book has much to offer thoughtful children. . . . With . . . sharply reproduced family photos and documents, this handsome book's small format reflects its intimate, conversational style." Booklist

Ginsberg, Blaze

Ginsberg, Blaze. **Episodes**; my life as I see it. Roaring Brook Press 2009 274p $16.99

Grades: 6 7 8 9 10   **92**

1. Autism 2. Teenagers' writings 3. Memoirists

ISBN 978-1-59643-461-5; 1-59643-461-9

"The high-functioning spectrum-disorder child portrayed in his mother Debra's Raising Blaze (2002) steps up to offer his own views of high school and after. He structures his memoir . . . as thumbnail summaries of concurrent or successive TV series. . . . He writes in a distant but often humorous voice about feelings, fixations, and the seemingly aimless way people move in and out of his life. . . . This book provides memorable insight into the author's distinctive mind and spirit." Booklist

Glenn, John, 1921-

Mitchell, Don. **Liftoff**; a photobiography of John Glenn. National Geographic Society 2006 64p il $17.95; lib bdg $27.90

Grades: 5 6 7 8   **92**

1. Astronauts 2. Senators 3. Statesmen -- United States

ISBN 0-7922-5899-1; 0-7922-5900-9 lib bdg

LC 2005-30916

This is a biography of the American astronaut, pilot, and U.S. Senator from Ohio.

This is "well-written and well-illustrated." Sci Books Films

Includes bibliographical references

Goeppert-Mayer, Maria, 1906-1972

Ferry, Joseph. **Maria** Goeppert Mayer; [by] Joseph P. Ferry. Chelsea House 2003 110p il (Women in science) lib bdg $22.95

Grades: 7 8 9 10   **92**

1. Physicists 2. Women scientists 3. College teachers 4. Nobel laureates for physics 5. Physicists -- United States -- Biography 6. Women scientists -- United States -- Biography

ISBN 0-7910-7247-9

LC 2002-15580

A biography of Maria Goeppert-Mayer, a physicist who contributed to the development of the atomic bomb and who, in 1963, was cowinner of the Nobel Prize in Physics for her work on the nuclear shell model theory

This is "well written and well organized." SLJ

Includes bibliographical references

Gogh, Vincent van, 1853-1890

Bassil, Andrea. **Vincent** van Gogh; by Andrea Bassil. new ed.; World Almanac Library 2004 48p il (Lives of the artists) lib bdg $31; pa $14.05

Grades: 4 5 6 7   **92**

1. Artists 2. Painters 3. Artists, Dutch 4. Painters -- Netherlands -- Biography

ISBN 0-8368-5602-3 lib bdg; 0-8368-5607-4 pa

LC 2003-67236

Original Italian edition 2003

This is a biography of the Dutch painter

This is "concise and straightforward, and there's no sensationalizing: Van Gogh's famous ear injury is only mentioned in a brief, matter-of-fact note. The interesting mix of photos and art is the biggest attraction." Booklist

Bodden, Valerie. **Vincent** van Gogh. Creative Education 2009 48p il (Xtraordinary artists) lib bdg $32.80

Grades: 4 5 6 7   **92**

1. Artists 2. Painters 3. Artists, Dutch

ISBN 978-1-58341-663-1 lib bdg; 1-58341-663-3 lib bdg

LC 2007002118

This biography of the artist offers an "interesting [layout]; big, high-quality reproductions and photographs on heavy paper; insightful quotes from diverse sources; and meaty selections of the artist's own writing . . . at the end of the book. Readers get a strong sense of [the] artist's personality along with an excellent survey of his work." SLJ

Includes bibliographical references

Crispino, Enrica. **Van** Gogh; illustrated by Simone Boni . . . [et. al.]; [English translation, Susan Ashley] Oliver Press 2008 64p il (Art masters) $27.95

Grades: 6 7 8 9 10   **92**

1. Artists 2. Painters 3. Artists, Dutch

ISBN 978-1-934545-05-8; 1-934545-05-8

"Using generous, colorful, and cleanly designed two-page spreads, Crispino situates Van Gogh among other artists within certain time periods and locations, portraying his work and life as a counterpoint to various traditions and trends. Most topics are centered by an original drawing that is surrounded by photographs, paintings, artifacts, and descriptions. . . . Consider this volume the equivalent of an unusually insightful museum tour guide." Booklist

Whiting, Jim. **Vincent** Van Gogh; by Jim Whiting. Mitchell Lane 2007 48p il (Art profiles for kids) lib bdg $29.95

Grades: 7 8 9 10   **92**
1. Artists 2. Painters 3. Artists, Dutch
ISBN 978-1-58415-564-5 lib bdg; 1-58415-564-7
lib bdg
LC 2007000662

This offers "well-documented information for teens doing reports. [The] volume covers the painter's childhood, training, travels, influences, and historical context. The chronological chapters build a survey of the [artist's] oeuvres, including the style and subject matter of [his] works and past and present critical reaction." SLJ

Includes glossary and bibliographical references

Goh, Chan Hon, 1969-

Goh, Chan Hon. **Beyond** the dance; a ballerina's life. [by] Chan Hon Goh with Cary Fagan. Tundra Bks. 2002 151p lib bdg $15.95
Grades: 6 7 8 9   **92**
1. Ballet 2. Authors 3. Ballet dancers 4. Children's authors
ISBN 0-88776-596-3
LC 2002-101724

This "autobiography introduces a prima ballerina with the National Ballet of Canada. Goh was born in Beijing but raised in Vancouver by her dancer parents. She discusses the events in her homeland that led her family to emigrate, their adjustment to life in Vancouver, and her parents' struggles to build the Goh Ballet Company. . . . The book is lavishly illustrated with black-and-white photographs, and balletomanes will enjoy poring over every detail." SLJ

Goodall, Jane, 1934-

Bardhan-Quallen, Sudipta. **Jane** Goodall; a twentieth-century life. Penguin Group 2008 218p (Up close) $16.99
Grades: 7 8 9 10   **92**
1. Women scientists 2. Primatologists 3. Writers on nature 4. Nonfiction writers
ISBN 978-0-670-06263-8; 0-670-06263-4
LC 2007-38206

"This profile of the renowned primatologist highlights her independent spirit and deep love of animals as well as the significant roles Goodall's long-lived mother, Vanne, and the scientist Louis B. Leakey . . . played in shaping her character and career. . . . Readers will be inspired by this account." Booklist

Jane Goodall. Chelsea House 2003 116p il (Women in science) lib bdg $22.95
Grades: 7 8 9 10   **92**
1. Chimpanzees 2. Women scientists 3. Primatologists 4. Writers on nature 5. Nonfiction writers 6. Primatologists -- England -- Biography
ISBN 0-7910-6905-2
LC 2002-15591

A biography of the zoologist, discussing her personal life as well as her work with chimpanzees at the Gombe Stream Reserve in Tanzania

"The writing is clear and engaging, enhanced by well-captioned, color photographs." SLJ

Includes bibliographical references

Welty, Tara. **Jane** Goodall. Chelsea House 2011 124p il (Conservation heroes) lib bdg $35
Grades: 6 7 8 9   **92**
1. Chimpanzees 2. Women scientists 3. Primatologists 4. Writers on nature 5. Nonfiction writers
ISBN 978-1-60413-952-5; 1-60413-952-8
LC 2010030583

This is a biography of primatologist and conservationist Jane Goodall, who studied the chimpanzees of Tanzania.

"Captivating, richly informative. . . . The scope of [this book] is comprehensive. . . . [The book is] engaging as [it is] educational and will be ideal for research and reports." SLJ

Includes glossary and bibliographical references

Gore, Al, 1948-

Baptiste, Tracey. **Al** Gore. Chelsea House 2011 119p il (Conservation heroes) lib bdg $35
Grades: 6 7 8 9   **92**
1. Vice-presidents 2. Conservationists 3. Environmentalists 4. Senators 5. Members of Congress 6. Presidential candidates 7. Nobel laureates for peace 8. Vice-presidents -- United States
ISBN 978-1-60413-949-5; 1-60413-949-8
LC 2010030592

A biography of the environmentalist and former vice-president.

"Captivating, richly informative. . . . The scope of [this book] is comprehensive. . . . [The book is] engaging as [it is] educational and will be ideal for research and reports." SLJ

Includes glossary and bibliographical references

Greenberg, Hank, 1911-1986

Sommer, Shelley. **Hammerin'** Hank Greenberg; baseball pioneer. Calkins Creek 2011 135p il $17.95
Grades: 5 6 7 8   **92**
1. Baseball players 2. Jews -- Biography 3. Baseball -- Biography
ISBN 1-59078-452-9; 978-1-59078-452-5

"Greenberg grew up in an Orthodox Jewish family in New York and went on to be a Hall-of-Fame first baseman and left fielder, playing most of his career with the Detroit Tigers in the 1930s and 1940s. . . . Sommer presents a fast-moving, straightforward biography. . . . Numerous black-and-white photos enhance the text. . . . An excellent choice for kids who enjoy delving into baseball history." Booklist

Greene, Nathanael, 1742-1786

Mierka, Gregg A. **Nathanael** Greene; the general who saved the Revolution. [by] Gregg A. Mierka. OTTN Pub. 2007 88p il map (Forgotten heroes of the American Revolution) $23.95; pa $12.95
Grades: 5 6 7 8   **92**
1. Generals 2. Society of Friends
ISBN 978-1-59556-012-4; 1-59556-012-2; 978-1-59556-017-9 pa; 1-59556-017-3 pa
LC 2006021044

"This lively profile combines an engrossing account of the Revolutionary War with healthy measures of images and passages drawn from primary—and sometimes previously unpublished—sources." Booklist

Includes bibliographical references

Grimberg, Tina

Grimberg, Tina. **Out** of line; growing up Soviet. Tundra Books 2007 117p il $22.95

Grades: 7 8 9 10   92

1. Rabbis 2. Memoirists 3. Jews -- Russia 4. Jews -- Biography 5. Children's authors 6. Jews -- Soviet Union

ISBN 978-0-88776-803-3; 0-88776-803-2

"In this warm memoir, Grimberg recalls her childhood in Kiev during the '60s and '70s. She shares the difficulties of Soviet life and explains how members of her family coped with challenges such as shortages. . . . Interwoven with her own experience of growing up in a Jewish family are the stories of her maternal and paternal grandparents. . . . The book is an exemplar of clear, graceful writing and fine storytelling skills." SLJ

Gross, Elly Berkovits, 1929-

Gross, Elly Berkovits. **Elly**; my true story of the Holocaust. [by] Elly Berkovits Gross. Scholastic Press 2009 125p il $14.99

Grades: 4 5 6 7   92

1. Poets 2. Authors 3. Holocaust survivors 4. Memoirists 5. Jews -- Romania 6. Holocaust, 1933-1945 -- Personal narratives

ISBN 978-0-545-07494-0; 0-545-07494-0

Relates how the author was torn from her happy home and sent to Birkenau by the Nazis, describing how she worked long hours and fought for survival before being set free at the end of the war and beginning a new life in America.

"As a powerful reminder of man's capacity for inhumanity, this memoir is essential reading." Booklist

Guevara, Ernesto, 1928-1967

Abrams, Dennis. **Ernesto** Che Guevara. Chelsea House Publishers 2010 128p il (The great Hispanic heritage) lib bdg $30

Grades: 6 7 8 9   92

1. Guerrillas 2. Physicians 3. Revolutionaries

ISBN 978-1-60413-732-3; 1-60413-732-0

This "begins with Guevara's childhood as the son of Argentinean aristocrats and gives a balanced portrait of the controversial figure, from his famous worldwide revolutionary efforts to his assassination at the age of 39. . . . A selection of well-chosen images, a chronology, chapter notes, and [a] suggested reading [list] round out [this] engaging [title] in a sure-to-be popular [book] for reports and personal interest." Booklist

Includes bibliographical references

★ Miller, Calvin Craig. **Che** Guevara; in search of revolution. Morgan Reynolds Pub. 2006 192p il map (World leaders) lib bdg $27.95

Grades: 7 8 9 10   92

1. Guerrillas 2. Physicians 3. Revolutionaries

ISBN 978-1-931798-93-8; 1-931798-93-1

LC 2006-5975

This biography of the guerilla leader is "woven into . . . [an] account of the global politics of his day, including his role in the Cuban revolution and the showdown with the U.S. The design is appealing, with clear type, occasional photos, and maps, and teens will be drawn to the account of the young leader who made a difference in spite of an inglorious defeat." Booklist

Includes bibliographical references

Gunther, John, 1929-1947

Gunther, John. **Death** be not proud; a memoir. Harper & Row 1949 261p il hardcover o.p. pa $13.95

Grades: 7 8 9 10   92

1. Sick 2. Cancer 3. Brain -- Tumors

ISBN 0-06-123097-9

A memoir of John Gunther's seventeen-year-old son, who died after a series of operations for a brain tumor. Not only a tribute to a remarkable boy but an account of a brave fight against disease

Guthrie, Woody, 1912-1967

★ Partridge, Elizabeth. **This** land was made for you and me; the life and songs of Woody Guthrie. Viking 2002 217p il $21.99

Grades: 7 8 9 10   92

1. Singers 2. Folk musicians 3. Memoirists 4. Songwriters 5. Folk singers -- United States -- Biography

ISBN 0-670-03535-1

LC 2001-46770

A biography of Woody Guthrie, a singer who wrote over 3,000 folk songs and ballads as he traveled around the United States, including "This Land is Your Land" and "So Long It's Been Good to Know Yuh"

This "presents an unflinchingly accurate portrait of a rambling and unpredictable man. . . . In addition to a panoply of archival photographs, which add realism to this engrossing story of a life, the book includes carefully selected quotes from songs, acquaintances, and documents to punctuate the story with authenticating detail without detracting from the momentum of the narrative." Bull Cent Child Books

Includes bibliographical references

Halley, Edmond, 1656-1742

Fox, Mary Virginia. **Scheduling** the heavens; the story of Edmond Halley. [by] Mary Virginia Fox. Morgan Reynolds Pub. 2007 128p il map por (Profiles in science) lib bdg $27.95

Grades: 6 7 8 9   92

1. Astronomers

ISBN 978-1-59935-021-9 lib bdg; 1-59935-021-1 lib bdg

LC 2006031269

"Though best known for calculating the orbit and predicting the return on a regular schedule of the eponymous comet, the brilliant scientist Halley excelled in many other fields besides astronomy. . . . Fox conveys Halley's life and times, and his lasting contributions to science, in vivid detail. The informative text is supported with maps and portraits." Includes bibliographical references

Halvorsen, Gail

★ Tunnell, Michael. **Candy** bomber; the story of the Berlin airlift's chocolate pilot. Charlesbridge 2010 110p il $18.95 pa $9.95

Grades: 4 5 6 7   92

1. Air pilots 2. Air force officers

ISBN 1-58089-336-8; 1-58089-337-6 pa; 978-1-58089-336-7; 978-1-58089-337-4 pa

This book takes place "[i]n 1948, after World War II, [in] Berlin, . . . [where Michael] Tunnell tells us that pilot Gail Halvorsen spent a night in the city, noticing kids behind a fence watching the planes land. He offered sticks of Doublemint gum to two of the kids, who passed them around so their pals could get a whiff. . . . Soon people all over began sending candy-and-handkerchief parachutes to Halvorsen and other pilots to drop over Berlin." (School Library Journal)

"Curious about the city into which he ferried goods during the Berlin Airlift in 1948, pilot Gail Halvorsen stayed over to visit, met some children, and offered to drop candy and gum when he next flew over. This simple idea grew into a massive project with reverberations today. Tunnell tell this appealing story . . . , clearly and chronologically, weaving just enough background for twenty-first century readers and illustrating almost every page with black-and-white photographs, many from Halvorsen's own collection." Booklist

Includes bibliographical references

Hamilton, Alexander, 1757-1804

★ Fritz, Jean. **Alexander** Hamilton; the outsider. illustrations by Ian Schoenherr. G.P. Putnam's Sons 2011 144p il $16.99

Grades: 5 6 7 8   92

1. Statesmen 2. Statesmen -- United States 3. Secretaries of the treasury

ISBN 039925546X; 9780399255465

LC 2010006008

Fritz "provides a brisk, well-written account introducing Founding Father Alexander Hamilton as an outsider to America. . . . Fast moving and engaging, this straightforward biography acknowledges Hamilton's flaws while portraying him as an intelligent, energetic man who rose to the challenge of his times. . . . In addition to the black-and-white reproductions of period paintings and prints that illustrate the text, Schoenherr's striking, engraving-like images of Hamilton as scholar, soldier, aide-decamp, statesman, and duelist introduce each section." Booklist

Includes bibliographical references

★ St. George, Judith. The **duel**: the parallel lives of Alexander Hamilton and Aaron Burr. Viking 2009 97p il $16.99

Grades: 6 7 8 9 10   92

1. Statesmen 2. Vice-presidents 3. Secretaries of the treasury 4. Politicians -- United States 5. Burr-Hamilton Duel, Weehawken, N.J., 1804

ISBN 978-0-670-01124-7; 0-670-01124-X

LC 2009-5660

"After a prologue following the steps of Alexander Hamilton and Aaron Burr on the morning of their famous duel, St. George backtracks to trace the 'parallel lives' mentioned in the subtitle. . . . Well researched and organized, the book offers insights into the personalities, lives, and times of Burr and Hamilton." Booklist

Hammel, Heidi B.

★ Bortz, Alfred B. **Beyond** Jupiter; the story of planetary astronomer Heidi Hammel. [by] Fred Bortz. Franklin Watts 2005 110p il (Women's adventures in science) lib bdg $31.50

Grades: 7 8 9 10   92

1. Astronomers 2. Women astronomers 3. College teachers

ISBN 0-531-16775-5

LC 2005-0778

This is a biography of the American astronomer Heidi Hammel

The author "has captured some of the engaging qualities of Heidi Hammel's personality through extensive work with her and with the cooperation of her friends and family." Sci Books Films

Includes glossary and bibliographical references

Handel, George Frideric, 1685-1759

Getzinger, Donna. **George** Frideric Handel and music for voices; [by] Donna Getzinger and Daniel Felsenfeld. Morgan Reynolds Pub. 2004 144p il (Classical composers) lib bdg $28.95

Grades: 7 8 9 10   92

1. Composers 2. Composers -- Biography

ISBN 1-931798-23-0

LC 2003-26729

"Handel's importance in the field of music is described in this carefully researched and highly detailed biography. The authors explain how the composer's focus on music began at an early age and how he managed to pursue his interests despite his father's belief that music was not an acceptable profession. A social history of the time underscores the details of Handel's career. Black-and-white and full-color reproductions appear throughout." SLJ

Includes bibliographical references

Lee, Lavina. **Handel's** world; [by] Lavina Lee. Rosen Pub. Group 2008 64p il (Music throughout history) lib bdg $29.25

Grades: 5 6 7 8   92

1. Composers

ISBN 978-1-4042-0726-4 lib bdg; 1-4042-0726-0 lib bdg

LC 2005030127

This "book begins with an introduction briefly addressing social issues of the day, historical background, or other significant information. . . . Successive chapters discuss the [man's] early [life], family background, social status, personality characteristics, musical training and education, obstacles or challenges, and influences. A chapter . . . focuses on the musician's well-known compositions, describing through lively and colorful language some of the musical elements employed." SLJ

Includes glossary and bibliographical references

Hannibal, 247-183 B.C.

Mills, Cliff. **Hannibal**; [by] Cliff Mills. Chelsea House 2008 120p bibl il map (Ancient world leaders) lib bdg $30
Grades: 6 7 8 9   92
  1. Generals
ISBN 978-0-7910-9580-5 lib bdg; 0-7910-9580-0 lib bdg

                    LC 2007-50493

"Mills's informative biography starts with Hannibal preparing to attack the Romans and then goes back in time to explain the founding of Carthage and the history of its conflict with Rome, mainly focusing on the Second Punic War and the subject's journey and battles during that time. . . . Frequent inserts add extra information . . . without distracting readers from the narrative. Colorful reproductions are also interspersed throughout. . . . [This offers] clear, descriptive writing." SLJ

Includes bibliographical references

Hargreaves, Alice Pleasance Liddell, 1852-1934

Rubin, C. M. The **real** Alice in Wonderland; a role model for the ages. [by] C.M. Rubin with Gabriella Rose Rubin. AuthorHouse 2010 134p il $29.95
Grades: 7 8 9 10   92
  1. Authors 2. Children 3. Novelists 4. Mathematicians 5. Characters and characteristics in literature 6. Children's authors 7. Writers on science
ISBN 978-1-4490-8131-7; 1-4490-8131-2

                    LC 2010-901865

"Readers will follow this title down the rabbit hole to discover the world of the real Alice who inspired Lewis Carroll's Alice in Wonderland. The book moves seamlessly through the life of Alice Pleasance Liddell. . . . This offering paints a full picture of Alice, not only as a child who has captivated literature but also as a woman who was truly ahead of her time. This is a purchase that will do well with a range of people and should be offered as a standard accompaniment to Alice in Wonderland. The illustrations and pictures will make it quite popular in a public library." Voice Youth Advocates

Includes bibliographical references

Harvey, William, 1578-1657

Yount, Lisa. **William** Harvey; discoverer of how blood circulates. [by] Lisa Yount. rev ed.; Enslow Publishers 2008 128p il map (Great minds of science) lib bdg $31.93
Grades: 5 6 7 8   92
  1. Biologists 2. Physicians 3. Physiologists 4. Writers on science 5. Writers on medicine 6. Blood -- Circulation
ISBN 978-0-7660-3010-7 lib bdg; 0-7660-3010-5 lib bdg

                    LC 2007020301

First published 1994

"A biography of the seventeenth-century English physician William Harvey and includes related activities for readers." Publisher's note

Includes glossary and bibliographical references

Hatshepsut, Queen of Egypt

Dell, Pamela. **Hatshepsut**; Egypt's first female pharaoh. Compass Point Books 2009 112p il map (Signature lives) lib bdg $34.60
Grades: 6 7 8 9   92
  1. Queens 2. Kings and rulers
ISBN 978-0-7565-3835-4 lib bdg; 0-7565-3835-1 lib bdg

                    LC 2008005721

This biography of the Egypt's first female pharaoh offers "details about the history and daily life of Egypt's New Kingdom era. . . . It also discusses . . . topics concerning women, such as giving birth and the role of female royalty. The book expects some sophistication from its readers. . . . [The text is] accompanied by high-quality photographs of artifacts, maps, and floor plans. [The] book's detailed time line, comparing events in Egypt to those throughout the world, is helpful for placing the lives of the pharaohs in context." SLJ

Includes glossary and bibliographical references

★ Galford, Ellen. **Hatshepsut**; the princess who became king. National Geographic 2005 64p il map (World history biographies) $17.95; lib bdg $27.90
Grades: 4 5 6 7   92
  1. Queens 2. Kings and rulers
ISBN 0-7922-3645-9; 0-7922-3646-7 lib bdg

This "presents the life of Queen Hatshepsut, who ruled Egypt as pharaoh during the New Kingdom, around 3500 years ago. Illustrated with clear, color photos of artifacts and sites as well as colorful maps, the text discusses aspects of Egyptian life such as education and religion in Hatshepsut's life. . . . With a clearly written text and many handsome photos, this provides an accessible introduction to Hatshepsut and her times." Booklist

Hautzig, Esther, 1930-2009

Hautzig, Esther. The **endless** steppe: growing up in Siberia; by Esther Hautzig. Crowell 1968 243p hardcover o.p. pa $5.99
                            92
  1. Authors 2. Translators 3. Children's authors 4. World War, 1939-1945 -- Personal narratives
ISBN 0-06-447027-X pa

"This is a magnificent book. Amazingly free of bitterness and hate, it radiates the optimism, the resilience of the human spirit as typified in its vital young author." Book World

Hawking, Stephen W., 1942-

★ Bankston, John. **Stephen** Hawking; breaking the boundaries of time and space. [by] John Bankston. Enslow Publishers 2005 128p il (Great minds of science) $26.60
Grades: 5 6 7 8   92
  1. Physicists 2. Handicapped 3. Physically handicapped 4. College teachers 5. Writers on science
ISBN 0-7660-2281-1

                    LC 2004-9193

This biography of the English physicist, who suffers from amyotrophic lateral sclerosis, includes explanations of his theories and experiments

"This excellent book features large font size and double spacing that makes it easy for any one to read. . . . The activities part of the book is outstanding." Sci Books Films

Includes glossary and bibliographical references

Hawthorne, Nathaniel, 1804-1864

Meltzer, Milton. **Nathaniel** Hawthorne; a biography. Twenty-First Century Books 2007 160p il (American literary greats) lib bdg $31.93

Grades: 7 8 9 10   92

1. Authors 2. Novelists 3. Authors, American 4. Short story writers

ISBN 978-0-7613-3459-0 lib bdg; 0-7613-3459-9 lib bdg

LC 2005000018

"The legendary novelist's life is portrayed as being as dramatic as the plotlines of his novels, and readers will be captivated by the detailed accounts of the family tragedies that made up his childhood and the financial and literary vicissitudes of his adult life. Meltzer provides sufficient background about New England at the time as well as accounts of the historical events that were shaping the country." SLJ

Includes bibliographical references

Hemingway, Ernest, 1899-1961

★ Reef, Catherine. **Ernest** Hemingway; a writer's life. Clarion Books 2009 183p il $20

Grades: 8 9 10 11 12   92

1. Poets 2. Authors 3. Novelists 4. Authors, American 5. Short story writers 6. Nobel laureates for literature

ISBN 978-0-618-98705-4; 0-618-98705-3

LC 2008-32885

"Reef creates a memorable portrait of the writer and his times, and even readers too young for most of Hemingway's oeuvre will enjoy armchair traveling to the bullfights in Spain, fishing expeditions to the Dry Tortugas and the Marquesas Keys, big-game hunting on the Serengeti and covering the Spanish Civil War. Along the way, they will gain a sense of the writer and his times and will even pick up some writing tips." Kirkus

Includes bibliographical references

Whiting, Jim. **Ernest** Hemingway. Mitchell Lane 2005 48p il (Classic storytellers) lib bdg $19.95

Grades: 7 8 9 10   92

1. Poets 2. Authors 3. Novelists 4. Authors, American 5. Short story writers 6. Nobel laureates for literature

ISBN 1-58415-376-8

A biography of the American author.

"A brief, accessible introduction to this classic writer. Whiting balances the extremes in Hemingway's life, from his literary successes to his risky stunts, drinking, and bullying. . . . The book's design is attractive, with good use of color and photos." SLJ

Hendrix, Jimi

Gelfand, Dale Evva. **Jimi** Hendrix; musician. [by] Dale Evva Gelfand. Legacy ed; Chelsea House 2006 120p il (Black Americans of achievement) lib bdg $30

Grades: 6 7 8 9   92

1. Singers 2. Guitarists 3. Rock musicians 4. African American musicians

ISBN 0-7910-9214-3

LC 2006004574

A biography of the rock musician

This book goes "beyond the typical personal information to provide some social history relevant to the subject's time. Captioned photographs and boxed inserts enhance the conversational [text]." Horn Book Guide

Includes bibliographical references

Willett, Edward. **Jimi** Hendrix; kiss the sky. Enslow Publishers 2006 160p bibl por (American rebels) lib bdg $27.93

Grades: 7 8 9 10   92

1. Singers 2. Guitarists 3. Rock musicians 4. African American musicians

ISBN 0-7660-2449-0

LC 2005033751

"This biography introduces electric-guitar virtuouso Jimi Hendrix. . . . [This is a] good, basic introduction to Hendrix's life and the reasons for his enduring fame." Booklist

Includes bibliographical references

Henry, John William, 1847?-ca. 1875

★ Nelson, Scott Reynolds. **Ain't** nothing but a man; my quest to find the real John Henry. [by] Scott Reynolds Nelson with Marc Aronson. National Geographic 2008 64p il $18.95; lib bdg $27.90

Grades: 4 5 6 7 8   92

1. John Henry (Legendary character) 2. Railroad workers 3. Railroads -- History 4. African Americans -- Biography

ISBN 978-1-4263-0000-4; 1-4263-0000-X; 978-1-4263-0001-1 lib bdg; 1-4263-0001-8 lib bdg

LC 2007-12446

This describes the author's research to find the real man who inspired the songs and legends about the African American steel-driving hero.

"The layout is attractive, with a sepia and beige background for the text and sepia-toned photographs. . . . This is an excellent example of how much detective work is needed for original research." SLJ

Includes bibliographical references

Henry, O., 1862-1910

Caravantes, Peggy. **Writing** is my business; the story of O. Henry. Morgan Reynolds Pub. 2006 160p il map (World writers) lib bdg $27.95

Grades: 7 8 9 10   92

1. Authors 2. Authors, American 3. Short story writers

ISBN 978-1-59935-031-8; 1-59935-031-9

LC 2006-16126

This is a biography of the short story writer

"This title grabs readers' attention and never lets go." SLJ

Includes bibliographical references

Henson, Matthew Alexander, 1866-1955

★ Johnson, Dolores. **Onward**; a photobiography of African-American polar explorer Matthew Henson. National Geographic 2006 64p il $17.95

Grades: 5 6 7 8   **92**

1. Explorers 2. African Americans -- Biography
ISBN 0-7922-7914-X

LC 2005-05837

"The quest to be the first to reach the North Pole is an exciting adventure story, and Henson got there first, as part of the ninth expedition led by Robert Peary in 1909. But Henson was African American, labeled as Peary's 'Negro manservant,' and he did not get full recognition until 2001. This . . . focuses on the physical details of the dangerous Arctic journeys . . . the repeated failures and the teamwork, as well as Henson's skills, stamina, and essential role in forging relationships with the Inuit. . . . The book design is beautiful: thick paper, spacious type, and stirring photos that capture the icy storms as well as the people involved in the history." Booklist

Olmstead, Kathleen A. **Matthew** Henson; the quest for the North Pole. [by] Kathleen Olmstead. Sterling Pub. Co. 2008 124p il (Sterling biographies) pa $5.95

Grades: 7 8 9 10   **92**

1. Explorers 2. African Americans -- Biography
ISBN 978-1-4027-4441-9 pa; 1-4027-4441-2 pa

LC 2007048106

"Henson's own contradictory and partially fabricated writing about his effort to reach the North Pole with Robert Peary presented some challenges to the biographer, but she gamely sorts out the most likely version of the story, letting readers know what is unsubstantiated and what is corroborated fact. . . . [This] attractively formatted [title has] black-and-white and full-color photographs or reproductions as well as sidebars. [A] solid [addition] to biography shelves." SLJ

Includes glossary and bibliographical references

Hillary, Edmund Sir

Crompton, Samuel. **Sir** Edmund Hillary; [by] Samuel Willard Crompton. Chelsea House 2009 112p il map (Great explorers) lib bdg $30

Grades: 6 7 8 9 10 11 12   **92**

1. Mountaineering 2. Mountaineers 3. Nonfiction writers
ISBN 978-1-60413-420-9 lib bdg; 1-60413-420-8 lib bdg

LC 2009-8688

Biography of the explorer Sir Edmund Hillary

"The information . . . is presented in such a way as to attract and maintain readers' interest. . . . With a full complement of maps, photographs (where available), illustrations, time lines, and document reproductions, a full story is told. Well-written and throughly researched, this . . . will make a solid addition." SLJ

Includes glossary and bibliographical references

★ Elish, Dan. **Edmund** Hillary; first to the top. [by] Dan Elish. Marshall Cavendish Bench-

mark 2007 80p il map (Great explorations) lib bdg $32.79

Grades: 5 6 7 8   **92**

1. Mountaineering 2. Mountaineers 3. Nonfiction writers
ISBN 978-0-7614-2224-2 lib bdg; 0-7614-2224-2 lib bdg

LC 2005027929

This "appealing [title features] readable [text], solid research, and variety of color illustrations." SLJ

Includes bibliographical references

Hines, Gregory

Abrams, Dennis. **Gregory** Hines; entertainer. [by] Dennis Abrams. Legacy ed; Chelsea House 2008 98p il (Black Americans of achievement) lib bdg $30

Grades: 6 7 8 9   **92**

1. Actors 2. Dancers 3. African American actors
ISBN 978-0-7910-9718-2 lib bdg; 0-7910-9718-8 lib bdg

LC 2007045506

This biography details the African American actor's "rise from adversity to . . . recognition. The [book goes] beyond the typical personal information to provide some social history relevant to the subject's time. Captioned photographs and boxed inserts enhance the conversational [text]." Horn Book Guide

Includes bibliographical references

Hinton, S. E.

★ Kjelle, Marylou Morano. **S.E.** Hinton; author of The outsiders. Enslow Publishers 2007 112p bibl il por (Authors teens love) lib bdg $31.93

Grades: 6 7 8 9   **92**

1. Authors 2. Novelists 3. Women authors 4. Authors, American 5. Children's authors 6. Young adult authors
ISBN 978-0-7660-2720-6 lib bdg; 0-7660-2720-1 lib bdg

LC 2006036820

"This well-written and informative biography weaves facts about Hinton's life with analyses of and reflections on her novels." SLJ

Includes glossary and bibliographical references

Hippocrates

Gow, Mary. The **greatest** doctor of ancient times: Hippocrates and his oath. Enslow Publishers 2009 128p il map (Great minds of ancient science and math) lib bdg $31.93

Grades: 5 6 7 8   **92**

1. Physicians 2. Medicine -- History 3. Writers on medicine
ISBN 978-0-7660-3118-0 lib bdg; 0-7660-3118-7 lib bdg

LC 2008029630

"This interesting take on medicine concludes with several activities. . . . Photographs on sepia-colored pages are a good match for the subject." Booklist

Includes glossary and bibliographical references

Hitler, Adolf, 1889-1945

Rice, Earle. **Adolf** Hitler and Nazi Germany. Morgan Reynolds 2005 176p il map lib bdg $28.95

Grades: 7 8 9 10   92

1. Dictators 2. Heads of state 3. National socialism 4. Nazi leaders

ISBN 978-1-931798-78-5; 1-931798-78-8

LC 2005-17825

"Clear, concise writing coupled with impressive illustrations that include black-and-white and color photos of cityscapes and individuals make this book a useful resource." SLJ

Hodgman, Ann

Hodgman, Ann. **How** to die of embarrassment every day. Henry Holt and Co. 2011 208p il $16.99

Grades: 5 6 7 8   92

1. Authors 2. Women authors 3. Cookbook writers 4. Authors, American 5. Children's authors

ISBN 978-0-8050-8705-5; 0-8050-8705-2

LC 2010-49004

Hodgman offers a "chatty personal narrative . . . focusing on her childhood years and her tendency to land herself into humiliating situations. . . . The generous supply of spot art and relevant images from Hodgman's childhood adds to the browsibility. . . . There's . . . plenty of humor . . . but more importantly there's a tacit message about the survivability of embarrassment and the fact that we all, even seemingly perfect and polished adults, spend our lives goofing up." Bull Cent Child Books

Hopper, Edward, 1882-1967

★ Rubin, Susan Goldman. **Edward** Hopper; painter of light and shadow. Abrams Books for Young Readers 2007 47p il $18.95

Grades: 5 6 7 8   92

1. Artists 2. Painters 3. Artists -- United States

ISBN 978-0-8109-9347-1; 0-8109-9347-3

LC 2006-31978

"On every page of this beautifully designed biography, readers will find a reproduction of Hopper's work, matched to clear, eloquent commentary. . . . Readers . . . will come back to read about the man and look at his art again and again." Booklist

Includes bibliographical references

Horowitz, Anthony, 1955-

Abrams, Dennis. **Anthony** Horowitz; [by] Dennis Abrams; foreword by Kyle Zimmer. Chelsea House Publishers 2006 123p il map (Who wrote that?) lib bdg $30

Grades: 6 7 8 9   92

1. Authors 2. Novelists 3. Authors, English 4. Short story writers 5. Young adult authors

ISBN 0-7910-8968-1

LC 2005030090

A biography of the author of the popular Alex Rider series

"Even teens who don't know Horowitz's books will enjoy reading this frank account that describes how his unhappy childhood . . . influenced his books. . . . Just as compelling are Horowitz's perspectives on what makes good horror and spy fiction." Booklist

Includes bibliographical references

Houdini, Harry, 1874-1926

Biskup, Agnieszka. **Houdini**; the life of the great escape artist. illustrated by Pat Kinsella. Capstone Press 2011 32p il (Graphic library: American graphic) lib bdg $29.32; pa $7.95

Grades: 4 5 6 7   92

1. Magicians 2. Biographical graphic novels 3. Nonfiction writers

ISBN 978-1-4296-5474-6 lib bdg; 1-4296-5474-0 lib bdg; 978-1-4296-6268-0 pa; 1-4296-6268-9 pa

LC 2010024848

In graphic novel format, explores the life of Harry Houdini and describes some of his most daring escapes.

"The illustrations are eye-catching and the narration is presented simply, yet compellingly. . . . Fact-filled, entertaining, and accessible." SLJ

Includes bibliographical references

Carlson, Laurie M. **Harry** Houdini for kids; his life and adventures with 21 magic tricks and illusions. Chicago Review Press 2009 136p il pa $16.95

Grades: 4 5 6 7   92

1. Magicians 2. Magic tricks 3. Nonfiction writers

ISBN 978-1-55652-782-1 pa; 1-55652-782-9 pa

LC 2008021404

"Reluctant readers (as well as budding troublemakers) will flock to this biography/handbook hybrid about one of the most famous magicians who ever lived. Even for those familiar with Houdini's fascinating story, Carlson's snappy writing gives it new life. . . . Nearly every page is enlivened with period photographs, boxed sections containing biographies and definitions, and, most important, 21 magic tricks that will have readers breaking out their deck of cards and practicing their sleight of hand." Booklist

★ Fleischman, Sid. **Escape!** the story of the great Houdini. Greenwillow Books 2006 210p il $18.99; lib bdg $19.89

Grades: 5 6 7 8   92

1. Magicians 2. Nonfiction writers

ISBN 978-0-06-085094-4; 0-06-085094-9; 978-0-06-085095-1 lib bdg; 0-06-0850957-1 lib bdg

LC 2005052631

"Fleischman looks at Houdini's life through his own eyes, as a fellow magician. . . . Fleischman's tone is lively and he develops a relationship with readers by revealing just enough truth behind Houdini's razzle-dazzle to keep the legend alive. . . . Engaging and fascinating." SLJ

Includes bibliographical references

Houston, Samuel, 1793-1863

Bodden, Valerie. **Samuel** Houston; Army leader & historic politician. ABDO Pub. Co. 2010 112p il map (Military heroes) lib bdg $22.95

Grades: 7 8 9   92

1. Governors 2. Statesmen 3. Senators 4. Army

officers 5. Politicians -- United States
ISBN 978-1-60453-962-2; 1-60453-962-3

LC 2009-32373

Biography of Samuel Houston.

"The rush of literary adrenalin will hook readers immediately and keep them enthralled until the end. . . . Given the dynamic topic [and] . . . appealing layout . . . [this is] likely to attract reluctant readers. In addition, sources are plentiful and well documented." SLJ

Includes glossary and bibliographical references

Howe, Samuel Gridley, 1801-1876

Alexander, Sally Hobart. **She** touched the world: Laura Bridgman, deaf-blind pioneer; by Sally Hobart Alexander and Robert Alexander. Clarion Books 2008 100p il $18

Grades: 5 6 7 8   92

1. Deaf 2. Blind 3. Students 4. Physicians 5. Philanthropists 6. Humanitarians 7. Teachers of the blind
ISBN 978-0-618-85299-4; 0-618-85299-9

"At the age of three, in 1832, Laura Bridgman contracted scarlet fever and lost her sight, her hearing, her sense of smell, and much of her sense of taste. Her family sent her to Dr. Samuel [Gridley] Howe at the New England Institute for the Education of the Blind, and by the age of 10, Laura was world-famous for her accomplishments. . . . Alexander . . . presents a well-written and thoroughly researched biography of this remarkable woman, with numerous black-and-white photos." Booklist

Includes bibliographical references

Hubble, Edwin Powell, 1889-1953

Datnow, Claire L. **Edwin** Hubble; discoverer of galaxies. rev ed; Enslow Publishers 2007 128p il (Great minds of science) lib bdg $31.93

Grades: 5 6 7 8   92

1. Astronomers
ISBN 978-0-7660-2791-6 lib bdg; 0-7660-2791-0 lib bdg

LC 2006-20111

First published 1997

Traces the life and work of the man whose study of galaxies led to a new understanding of the universe

Includes glossary and bibliographical references

Hudson, Henry, d. 1611

★ Otfinoski, Steven. **Henry** Hudson; in search of the Northwest Passage. [by] Steven Otfinoski. Marshall Cavendish Benchmark 2006 80p il map (Great explorations) lib bdg $32.79

Grades: 5 6 7 8   92

1. Explorers
ISBN 978-0-7614-2225-9 lib bdg; 0-7614-2225-0 lib bdg

"An examination of the life and accomplishments of the famed explorer who lent his name to several geographic locations in North America" Publisher's note

Includes bibliographical references

★ Weaver, Janice. **Hudson**; written by Janice Weaver; illustrated by David Craig. Tundra Books 2010 47p il map $22.95

Grades: 3 4 5 6   92

1. Explorers
ISBN 978-0-88776-814-9; 0-88776-814-8

This is a biography of the explorer. "The grandson of a trader, Hudson sailed under both British and Dutch flags, looking for a northern route to China. Although none of his voyages led to the discovery of a northwest passage, he did explore what is now Hudson's Bay and what is now New York City." (Publisher's note)

"This dramatic picture-book biography about Henry Hudson, who discovered neither the new land nor the passage to Asia he sought, makes the explorer's lack of success a gripping read. . . . Weaver is clear about what is fact and what is supposition, and the tumultuous early-seventeenth-century history is meticulously documented. . . . Craig's glowing period portraits, landscapes, and watercolors of the ship in dangerous seas intensify the drama, and archival prints and maps add interest." Booklist

Includes bibliographical references

Young, Jeff C. **Henry** Hudson; discoverer of the Hudson River. Enslow Publishers 2009 112p il map (Great explorers of the world) lib bdg $31.93

Grades: 6 7 8 9   92

1. Explorers
ISBN 978-1-59845-123-8 lib bdg; 1-59845-123-5 lib bdg

LC 2008-30752

"Examines the life of explorer Henry Hudson, including his quest for the elusive Northeast passage, his discovery of the Hudson River, and his mysterious death." Publisher's note

Includes glossary and bibliographical references

Hunter, Clementine, 1886?-1988

Whitehead, Kathy. **Art** from her heart: folk artist Clementine Hunter; [illustrated by] Shane Evans. G.P. Putnam's Sons 2008 un il $16.99

Grades: 4 5 6 7   92

1. Artists 2. Folk art 3. Painters 4. Women artists 5. African American artists 6. Centenarians
ISBN 978-0-399-24219-9; 0-399-24219-8

LC 2006-34458

"Whitehead's lyrical text speaks of Hunter's perseverance and talent as well as of the simplicity, love of nature, and caring of friends and family that informed her work. Evans bolsters Whitehead's words with bold mixed-media illustrations that portray Hunter in hard times and in good." SLJ

Hurston, Zora Neale, 1891-1960

★ Litwin, Laura Baskes. **Zora** Neale Hurston; I have been in sorrow's kitchen. Enslow Publishers 2007 128p il (African-American biography library) lib bdg $23.95

Grades: 7 8 9 10   92

1. Authors 2. Novelists 3. Dramatists 4. Women authors 5. African American authors 6. Memoirists 7.

Folklorists 8. Short story writers
ISBN 978-0-7660-2536-5 lib bdg; 0-7660-2536-5
lib bdg

LC 2005034881

Litwin "offers an engaging portrait of legendary author and folklorist Zora Neale Hurston. . . . Well-paced . . . chapters follow Hurston through her remarkable career. . . . Generously sprinkled with excerpts from Hurston's own works and illustrated with numerous black-and-white portraits of Hurston and her prominent friends and collaborators." Booklist
Includes bibliographical references

★ Lyons, Mary E. **Sorrow's** kitchen; the life and folklore of Zora Neale Hurston. 1st Collier Books ed; Collier Books 1993 144p il (Great achievers) pa $7.99

Grades: 7 8 9 10   92

1. Authors 2. Novelists 3. Dramatists 4. Women authors 5. African American authors 6. Memoirists 7. Folklorists 8. Short story writers
ISBN 0-02-044445-1

LC 92-30600

First published 1990 by Scribner
This biography details "Hurston's migration from Florida to Baltimore, Washington, D.C., and finally Harlem as well as her travels through the West Indies to collect folklore. The text contains eleven excerpts from Hurston's books. . . . Lyons has created a prime example of biography—fascinating, enlightening, stimulating, and satisfying." Horn Book
Includes bibliographical references

Sapet, Kerrily. **Rhythm** and folklore; the story of Zora Neale Hurston. Morgan Reynolds Pub. 2008 160p il lib bdg $27.95

Grades: 7 8 9 10 11 12   92

1. Authors 2. Novelists 3. Dramatists 4. Women authors 5. African American authors 6. Memoirists 7. Folklorists 8. Short story writers
ISBN 978-1-59935-067-7; 1-59935-067-X

LC 2008-844

A biography of the African American author and folklorist
"With lots of personal quotes, this lively biography stays true to Hurston's defiant, independent spirit. . . . Sapet give a strong sense of the times, including the Harlem Renaissance. . . . With lots of full-page photos, this biography will encourage teens to read and discuss Hurston's work." Booklist
Includes bibliographical references

Hutchinson, Anne Marbury, 1591-1643

Stille, Darlene R. **Anne** Hutchinson; Puritan protester. by Darlene R. Stille. Compass Point Books 2006 112p il map (Signature lives) lib bdg $31.93

Grades: 6 7 8 9   92

1. Puritans 2. Colonists 3. Dissenters 4. Religious leaders
ISBN 978-07565-1577-5 lib bdg; 0-7565-1577-7
lib bdg

LC 2005025093

A biography of Anne Hutchinson, who was put on trial in colonial Massachusetts for challenging Puritan beliefs

This is an "excellent biography. . . . Stille neither glorifies nor condemns her but rather reveals her strength of character in the context of her historical era, enhancing the interesting, accessible narrative with numerous full-color illustrations." Booklist
Includes bibliographical references

Inouye, Daniel K.

Slavicek, Louise Chipley. **Daniel** Inouye. Chelsea House 2007 128p bibl il por (Asian Americans of achievement) lib bdg $30

Grades: 6 7 8 9   92

1. Lawyers 2. Senators 3. State legislators 4. District attorneys 5. Members of Congress 6. Statesmen -- United States 7. Asian Americans -- Biography
ISBN 978-0-7910-9271-2 lib bdg; 0-7910-9271-2
lib bdg

LC 2006026062

A biography of the Senator from Hawaii
This is "well-researched . . . attractive . . . solid." SLJ
Includes glossary and bibliographical references

IraqiGirl

IraqiGirl. **IraqiGirl**; diary of a teenage girl in Iraq. Haymarket 2009 205p pa $13

Grades: 6 7 8 9 10   92

1. Weblogs 2. Bloggers 3. Iraq War, 2003- -- Personal narratives
ISBN 978-1-931859-73-8; 1-931859-73-6

"In 2004 in Mosul (the third largest city in Iraq), a 15-year-old girl started a blog detailing her life in the midst of the Iraq War. Her journal encompasses the day-to-day trauma the American invasion has caused her city, her family and friends. . . . [The author's] authentically teenage voice, emotional struggles and concerns make her story all the more resonant." Publ Wkly

Irwin, Bindi, 1998-

Breguet, Amy. **Steve** and Bindi Irwin. Chelsea House 2011 140p il map (Conservation heroes) lib bdg $35

Grades: 6 7 8 9   92

1. Conservationists 2. Wildlife conservation 3. Television personalities 4. Zoo directors 5. Herpetologists 6. Children of prominent persons
ISBN 978-1-60413-957-0; 1-60413-957-9

A biography of Steve Irwin, Australian star of The Crocodile Hunter, who died in 2006, and his daughter, Bindi.
"Captivating, richly informative. . . . The scope of [this book] is comprehensive. . . . [The book is] engaging as [it is] educational and will be ideal for research and reports." SLJ

Irwin, Steve, 1962-2006

Breguet, Amy. **Steve** and Bindi Irwin. Chelsea House 2011 140p il map (Conservation heroes) lib bdg $35

Grades: 6 7 8 9   92

1. Conservationists 2. Wildlife conservation 3. Television personalities 4. Zoo directors 5. Herpetologists 6. Children of prominent persons
ISBN 978-1-60413-957-0; 1-60413-957-9

A biography of Steve Irwin, Australian star of The Crocodile Hunter, who died in 2006, and his daughter, Bindi.

"Captivating, richly informative. . . . The scope of [this book] is comprehensive. . . . [The book is] engaging as [it is] educational and will be ideal for research and reports." SLJ

Jackson, Michael, 1958-2009

Pratt, Mary. **Michael** Jackson; king of pop. ABDO Pub. Co. 2010 112p il (Lives cut short) lib bdg $32.79

Grades: 5 6 7 8   **92**

1. Singers 2. Rock musicians 3. African American musicians 4. Songwriters 5. Pop musicians
ISBN 978-1-60453-788-8 lib bdg; 1-60453-788-4 lib bdg

This discusses Michael Jackson's "early life, providing details that give insight into later success and troubles and maintaining a laudatory tone that focuses on the individual's artistic achievements and hard work to achieve fame. Details [such as] explaining . . . that young Michael Jackson never got to play with his peers . . . are bound to resonate with readers. Numerous photos and sidebars appear throughout. [A] worthwhile [resource] for reports as well as popular reading." SLJ

Includes glossary and bibliographical references

Jackson, Robert Houghwout, 1892-1954

Jarrow, Gail. **Robert** H. Jackson; New Deal lawyer, Supreme Court Justice, Nuremberg prosecutor. Calkins Creek 2008 128p il $18.95

Grades: 7 8 9 10   **92**

1. Judges 2. Lawyers 3. Nuremberg Trial of Major German War Criminals, 1945-1946 4. Attorneys general 5. Government officials 6. Supreme Court justices
ISBN 978-1-59078-511-9

LC 2007-18858

"Framed by Jackson's famous speech as chief American prosecutor at the 1945 international Nuremberg trial of Nazi war criminals, this detailed biography sets his law career within the history and politics of his time and raises essential issues of human rights." Booklist

Includes bibliographical references

Jacobs, Jane, 1916-2006

Lang, Glenna. **Genius** of common sense; Jane Jacobs and the story of The death and life of great American cities. [by] Glenna Lang & Marjory Wunsch. David R. Godine 2009 127p il map $17.95

Grades: 7 8 9 10 11 12   **92**

1. Authors 2. City planning 3. Urban sociology 4. Urban planners 5. Nonfiction writers
ISBN 978-1-56792-384-1; 1-56792-384-4

LC 2009-08304

"This is the story of a remarkable woman, brought up during the Depression and with no college education, who single-handedly changed the way America viewed its cities. . . . At 18, she moved to New York to pursue her career as a writer and fell in love with the city. It was there that she had her infamous battles with Robert Moses over urban renewal and did the research for her most famous book, The Death and Life of Great American Cities. Black-and-white photographs, maps, and political cartoons and other repro-

ductions appear on most pages. . . . Lang and Wunsch are to be commended for introducing a fascinating female role model." SLJ

Includes bibliographical references

Jacobs, Marc, 1963-

Branscomb, Leslie Wolf. **Marc** Jacobs. Morgan Reynolds Pub. 2011 112p il (Profiles in fashion) $28.95

Grades: 7 8 9 10   **92**

1. Fashion designers
ISBN 978-1-59935-153-7; 1-59935-153-6

LC 2010022226

This biography of Marc Jacobs describes "the personal [life] and economic details of the multimillion-dollar business of [this] high-profile [designer]. [It discusses] the designer's cultural background, childhood, family, work history and education. The . . . [author describes] the early influences that inspired the [designer] to pursue this career and [provides] details of the philosophy [the] designer uses to make [his] clothing unique. . . . The writing is clear and well organized. Color photos are included and give readers a feel for the time period and the types of clothing and accessories the [designer] created." Voice Youth Advocates

Includes bibliographical references

Jalal al-Din Rumi Maulana, 1207-1273

★ Demi. **Rumi**; whirling dervish. written and illustrated by Demi. Marshall Cavendish Children 2009 31p il $19.99

Grades: 4 5 6 7   **92**

1. Poets 2. Persian poetry
ISBN 978-0-7614-5527-1; 0-7614-5527-2

LC 2008012920

"Demi presents this picture-book introduction to the thirteenth-century mystical poet. . . . Demi condenses her famous subject's life into a brief but substantive text. . . . She adds frequent excerpts from Rumi's poems and writings. . . . In an introductory note, Demi cites Turkish miniatures as her inspiration for the small-scale, elaborately patterned pictures, rendered in Turkish and Chinese inks with gold overlay. . . . The gilded, celebratory pictures create shimmering beauty from the smallest details." Booklist

James, LeBron

Yasuda, Anita. **Lebron** James. 2011 24p il (Remarkable people) $27.13; pa $12.95

Grades: 4 5 6 7   **92**

1. Basketball players 2. Basketball -- Biography
ISBN 978-1-6169-0669-6; 1-6169-0669-3; 978-1-6169-0674-0 pa; 1-6169-0674-X pa

LC 2010051003

This looks at Lebron James' "life, accomplishments, and challenges while including a page of quotes, an annotated list of contemporaries and influences, starter suggestions for writing a paper, and a time line and glossary. . . . [This book] follows basketball's 'King James' from his early life with a single teen mother to his splashy entry into the NBA at age 19." Booklist

Jefferson, Thomas, 1743-1826

Miller, Brandon Marie. **Thomas** Jefferson for kids; his life and times, with 21 activities. Chicago Review Press 2011 ix, 132p il $16.95

Grades: 4 5 6 7   92

    1. Architects 2. Presidents 3. Vice-presidents 4. Essayists 5. Presidents -- United States

    ISBN 978-1-56976-348-3; 1-56976-348-8

                    LC 2011019318

"Miller offers a thorough and methodical overview of Jefferson's life and political career. . . . The presentation is expecially forthright about Jefferson's ownership of slaves and his fathering of children with Sally Hemmings. . . . The volume offers the chance to delve into Jefferson's life and be inspired by the range of his interests." Kirkus

    Includes bibliographical references

Jemison, Mae C.

Jemison, Mae C. **Find** where the wind goes; moments from my life. [by] Mae Jemison. Scholastic Press 2001 196p il hardcover o.p. $16.95

Grades: 5 6 7 8   92

    1. Astronauts 2. Physicians 3. African American women 4. African American women -- Biography 5. African American women astronauts -- Biography

    ISBN 0-439-13195-2; 0-439-13196-0 pa

                    LC 00-41008

"Mae Jemsion, doctor, scientist, astronaut, and professor, here tells of the formative incidents of her life. . . . The author discusses her youth—her days in the South, her family's move to Chicago's South Side, school experiences, and growing up—as well as her later life and her place in the space program." (Bull Cent Child Books)

"Dr. Jemison, the first woman of color to travel in space, shares her life story in this autobiographical selection." Book Rep

Jobs, Steven, 1955-2011

Goldsworthy, Steve. **Steve** Jobs. Weigl 2011 24p il (Remarkable people) $27.13; pa $12.95 92

    1. Entrepreneurs 2. Businesspeople 3. Computer industry 4. Computer scientists 5. Computer industry executives 6. Electronics industry executives

    ISBN 978-1-6169-0670-2; 1-6169-0670-7; 978-1-6169-0675-7 pa; 1-6169-0675-8 pa

                    LC 2010050999

This looks at Steve Jobs' "life, accomplishments, and challenges while including a page of quotes, an annotated list of contemporaries and influences, starter suggestions for writing a paper, and a time line and glossary. . . . [This book] kicks off as current as possible with a picture of the bearded Apple CEO displaying an iPad, before getting into the ups (he became a multimillionaire in just two years) and downs (his struggle with cancer)." Booklist

Steve Jobs; genius by design. by Jason Quinn; illustrated by Amit Tayal. Random House Inc 2012 104 p. $12.99

Grades: 7 8 9 10 11 12 Adult   92

    1. Computer industry 2. Biographical graphic novels

    ISBN 9380028768; 9789380028767

This graphic novel, by Jason Quinn, illustrated by Amit Tayal, presents a biography of the 20th-century technology entrepreneur and Apple Inc. founder Steve Jobs. "Steve Jobs and his inventions changed the world we live in." The book ranges "from his birth and his adoption, through the advent of the computer age and on into the digital age. Forced out of the company he created, his indomitable vision allowed him to change the world of computers, movies, music and telecommunications." (Publisher's note)

Johansson, Scarlett, 1984-

Schuman, Michael. **Scarlet** Johansson; hollywood superstar. [by] Michael A. Schuman. Enslow Publishers 2011 112p il (People to know today) lib bdg $31.93

Grades: 6 7 8 9   92

    1. Twins 2. Actors

    ISBN 978-0-7660-3556-0; 0-7660-3556-5

This "title is an enjoyable introduction to Johansson that avoids a gossipy, tabloid tone. After general background on family and childhood, . . . the chapters detail Johansson's progress from stage to screen. . . . Her experiences afford an interesting glimpse into Hollywood and the film industry." Booklist

John Paul II, Pope, 1920-2005

Renehan, Edward J. **Pope** John Paul II; [by] Edward J. Renehan, Jr. Chelsea House 2007 109p il (Modern world leaders) lib bdg $30

Grades: 7 8 9 10 11 12   92

    1. Popes

    ISBN 978-0-7910-9227-9 lib bdg; 0-7910-9227-5 lib bdg

                    LC 2006-10612

This "biography follows the arch of the pontiff's life in the context of world politics." Publisher's note

    Includes bibliographical references

Johnson, Earvin, 1959-

Roselius, J Chris. **Magic** Johnson; basketball star and entrepreneur. ABDO Pub. Co. 2011 112p il (Legendary athletes) lib bdg $34.22

Grades: 6 7 8 9   92

    1. African American athletes 2. Basketball coaches 3. Basketball players 4. Real estate developers 5. Basketball -- Biography

    ISBN 978-1-61714-756-2; 1-61714-756-7

                    LC 2010046696

This biography of basketball star Magic Johnson "goes beyond merely discussing [his] accomplishments. . . . [It] also [explores] the social and political [influence he] had on society as a whole. In addition, [it introduces] historical events in the context of [his life]. . . . This . . . is teeming with information and is a must-purchase for sports fans and readers interested in social activism." SLJ

    Includes glossary and bibliographical references

Johnson, Lyndon B. (Lyndon Baines), 1908-1973

Gold, Susan Dudley. **Lyndon** B. Johnson. Marshall Cavendish Benchmark 2009 112p il (Presidents and their times) lib bdg $34.21

Grades: 5 6 7 8   92

1. Presidents 2. Vice-presidents 3. Senators 4. Members of Congress 5. Presidents -- United States
ISBN 978-0-7614-2837-4 lib bdg; 0-7614-2837-2 lib bdg

LC 2007038518

A biography of the thirty-sixth president of the United States discusses his personal life, education, and political career and covers the formative events of his time

Includes glossary and bibliographical references

Johnson, Mamie, 1935-

★ Green, Michelle Y. A **strong** right arm: the story of Mamie Peanut Johnson; introduction by Mamie Johnson. Dial Bks. for Young Readers 2002 111p il $15.99; pa $5.99

Grades: 4 5 6 7   92

1. Women 2. Women athletes 3. Baseball players 4. African Americans 5. African American athletes 6. Collectibles dealers 7. Baseball -- Biography 8. African American baseball players -- Biography 9. Baseball players -- United States -- Biography 10. Women baseball players -- United States -- Biography
ISBN 0-8037-2661-9; 0-14-240072-6 pa

LC 2001-28616

"Johnson was a pitcher with the Negro Leagues' Indianapolis Clowns from 1953 to 1955. In the introduction, Johnson speaks directly and movingly to the reader about her meeting with author Green, who then lets the famous ballplayer tell her own story in a lively first-person narrative. Johnson's ebullient personality and determination fairly leap off the page." Booklist

Includes bibliographical references

Jolie, Angelina

Abrams, Dennis. **Angelina** Jolie; actress and activist. Chelsea House 2011 146p il (Women of achievement) $35

Grades: 6 7 8 9   92

1. Actors
ISBN 978-1-60413-909-9; 1-60413-909-9

This "focuses on the superstar's troubled youth, her award-winning performances as an actress, and her work on behalf of refugees around the world. Abrams is frank in discussing Jolie's fascination, in her younger years, with knives, cutting, and blood. . . . Solid fare for the biography collection." Booklist

Jones, John Paul, 1747-1792

Brager, Bruce L., 1949- **John** Paul Jones; America's sailor. Morgan Reynolds Pub. 2006 160p il map lib bdg $26.95

Grades: 7 8 9 10   92

1. Admirals 2. Naval officers
ISBN 978-1-931798-84-6; 1-931798-84-2

LC 2005-30443

The author "begins with Jones's Scottish childhood, where he developed a bitter resentment of the British class system. He then traces the man's career as a commercial seaman, privateer, naval commander, and soldier of fortune. . . . This often-unflattering portrait of Jones will require readers who can place his good and bad traits in perspective and

judge his place in history, making it a good choice for mature students." SLJ

Includes bibliographical references

Cooper, Michael L. **Hero** of the high seas; John Paul Jones and the American Revolution. National Geographic 2006 128p il map $21.95; lib bdg $32.90

Grades: 5 6 7 8   92

1. Admirals 2. Naval officers
ISBN 0-7922-5547-X; 0-7922-5548-8 lib bdg

LC 2005-36256

"Cooper charts his subject's life from a scandal-ridden Scottish captain on a trading ship to a man of self-invention who came to the American colonies to start a new life and became a naval hero. Jones is presented as a loyal captain, an arrogant leader, a determined sailor, and a flagrant social climber. The narrative style will appeal to reluctant readers, for it reads like a chronicle of thrilling naval adventures. . . . The text is clear and understandable." SLJ

Includes bibliographical references

Joseph, Nez Percé Chief, 1840-1904

Biskup, Agnieszka. **Thunder** rolling down the mountain; the story of Chief Joseph and the Nez Perce. illustrated by Rusty Zimmerman. Capstone Press 2011 32p il (Graphic library: American graphic) lib bdg $29.32; pa $7.95

Grades: 4 5 6 7   92

1. Biographical graphic novels 2. Indian chiefs 3. Nez Percé Indians
ISBN 978-1-4296-5472-2 lib bdg; 1-4296-5472-4 lib bdg; 978-1-4296-6270-3 pa; 1-4296-6270-0 pa

LC 2010027914

In graphic novel format, explores the battles and hardships faced by Chief Joseph and the Nez Perce when they were forced to leave their homelands.

"The illustrations are eye-catching and the narration is presented simply, yet compellingly. . . . Fact-filled, entertaining, and accessible." SLJ

Includes bibliographical references

Hopping, Lorraine Jean. **Chief** Joseph; the voice for peace. Sterling 2010 124p il map (Sterling biographies) lib bdg $12.95

Grades: 7 8 9 10   92

1. Indian chiefs 2. Nez Percé Indians 3. Native Americans -- Biography
ISBN 978-1-4027-6842-2; 1-4027-6842-7

LC 2009-24132

This biography is "packed with fast action and detailed analysis. . . . Hopping tells of Joseph's painful decision to leave his land to save Nez Percé lives, choosing peace because he knew they could not win against the U.S. . . . [The] spacious design is highly scannable, with color background screens, photos, maps, and historic prints throughout." Booklist

Includes glossary and bibliographical references

Julian, Percy L., 1899-1975

Stille, Darlene R. **Percy** Lavon Julian; pioneering chemist. Compass Point Books 2009 112p il map (Signature lives) lib bdg $34.65

Grades: 6 7 8 9 10   92

1. Chemists 2. Pharmaceutical executives
ISBN 978-0-7565-4089-0; 0-7565-4089-5

LC 2008-38462

Details the life of chemist Percy Lavon Julian and his accomplishments

The "inviting page design features photos and boxed screens on each spread, and . . . includes a detailed bibliography, source notes, time line and glossary." Booklist

Includes glossary and bibliographical references

Juárez, Benito, 1806-1872

Stein, R. Conrad. **Benito** Juarez and the French intervention; [by] R. Conrad Stein. Morgan Reynolds Pub. 2008 160p il map (The story of Mexico) lib bdg $27.95

Grades: 6 7 8 9   92

1. Presidents
ISBN 978-1-59935-052-3 lib bdg; 1-59935-052-1 lib bdg

LC 2007016005

The book provides "detailed information in a readable format, and [a] lively writing style. . . . Colorful reproductions and photographs help to maintain interest. [This] title tells the story of Juárez, a Zapotec Indian, and his rise to political leadership. Born into poverty in 1806, he became Mexico's first Indian president, presiding over a country in turmoil." SLJ

Includes glossary and bibliographical references

Kahlo, Frida, 1907-1954

Hillstrom, Laurie. **Frida** Kahlo; painter. by Laurie Collier Hillstrom. Lucent Books 2008 104p il (The twentieth century's most influential Hispanics) lib bdg $32.45

Grades: 6 7 8 9 10   92

1. Artists 2. Painters 3. Women artists 4. Artists, Mexican
ISBN 978-1-4205-0019-6 lib bdg; 1-4205-0019-8 lib bdg

LC 2007-32106

"Kahlo's life . . . is chronicled as are the influences of her marriage to Rivera and her physical pain on on her art. . . . The layout draws the eye with colorful chapter headings and highlighted quotes." Lib Media Connect

Includes bibliographical references

Keat, Nawuth, 1964-

Keat, Nawuth. **Alive** in the killing fields; surviving the Khmer Rouge genocide. by Nawuth Keat with Martha E. Kendall. National Geographic 2009 127p il map $15.95; lib bdg $23.90

Grades: 7 8 9 10 11   92

1. Authors 2. Cambodian refugees 3. Political refugees

4. Young adult authors
ISBN 978-1-4263-0515-3; 1-4263-0515-X; 978-1-4263-0516-0 lib bdg; 1-4263-0516-8 lib bdg

LC 2008-39805

"Told with stark simplicity, Nawuth's narrative is memorable yet accessible to young readers." Voice Youth Advocates

Includes bibliographical references

Keckley, Elizabeth, ca. 1818-1907

Jones, Lynda. **Mrs.** Lincoln's dressmaker: the unlikely friendship of Elizabeth Keckley and Mary Todd Lincoln; by Lynda D. Jones. National Geographic 2009 80p il $18.95; lib bdg $27.90

Grades: 5 6 7 8   92

1. Memoirists 2. Dressmakers 3. Spouses of presidents 4. Slavery -- United States 5. African American women -- Biography 6. Presidents' spouses -- United States
ISBN 978-1-4263-0377-7; 1-4263-0377-7; 978-1-4263-0378-4 lib bdg; 1-4263-0378-5 lib bdg

LC 2008-29314

"Readers may be familiar with the ups and downs of Lincoln's life, but details of Keckley's story . . . will give them new insights into the life of a slave, in this case, one who was educated and had a profession." Booklist

Includes bibliographical references

Keller, Helen, 1880-1968

Delano, Marfe Ferguson. **Helen's** eyes; a photobiography of Annie Sullivan, Helen Keller's teacher. [foreword by Keller Johnson Thompson] National Geographic 2008 63p il map $17.95; lib bdg $27.90

Grades: 4 5 6 7   92

1. Deaf 2. Blind 3. Authors 4. Teachers 5. Memoirists 6. Humanitarians 7. Teachers of the deaf 8. Inspirational writers 9. Teachers of the blind 10. Social welfare leaders
ISBN 978-1-4263-02-9-1; 1-4263-0209-6; 978-1-4263-0210-7 lib bdg; 1-4263-0210-X lib bdg

"There are many biographies of Helen Keller and Annie Sullivan, but this one is very nicely done. . . . The book is honest in its portrayals, especially of Sullivan. . . . What makes this oversize book so appealing is the clean design, with large typeface. The many fascinating photographs are sometimes placed over historical documents." Booklist

Includes bibliographical references

★ Keller, Helen. The **story** of my life; edited and with a preface by James Berger. The restored ed.; Modern Library 2003 xlvi, 343p il hardcover o.p. pa $9.95

Grades: 8 9 10 11 12 Adult   92

1. Deaf 2. Blind 3. Authors 4. Memoirists 5. Humanitarians 6. Inspirational writers 7. Social welfare leaders 8. Deaf women -- United States -- Biography 9. Blind women -- United States -- Biography 10. People with disabilities -- Education -- United States
ISBN 0-679-64287-0; 0-8129-6886-7 pa

LC 2002-40971

First published 1903

This biography of the inspirational Keller contains accounts of her home life and her relationship with her devoted teacher Anne Sullivan.

Includes bibliographical references

Lawlor, Laurie. **Helen** Keller: rebellious spirit. Holiday House 2001 168p il $22.95

Grades: 5 6 7 8   **92**
1. Deaf 2. Blind 3. Authors 4. Memoirists 5. Humanitarians 6. Inspirational writers 7. Social welfare leaders

ISBN 0-8234-1588-0
LC 00-36950

A "biography of the most famous deaf and blind person in history. Drawing on social and scientific studies of deafness and blindness as well as on American history texts, Lawlor puts Keller's experiences in context. . . . At the same time, readers get a strong feel for Keller's personality and for the personalities of Annie Sullivan, Alexander Graham Bell, and other major figures in her life. Aided by numerous well-chosen photographs and excerpts from Keller's writings." Horn Book

Includes bibliographical references

MacLeod, Elizabeth. **Helen** Keller; a determined life. written by Elizabeth MacLeod. Kids Can Press 2004 32p il (Snapshots: Images of People and Places in History) $14.95; pa $6.95

Grades: 4 5 6   **92**
1. Deaf 2. Blind 3. Authors 4. Memoirists 5. Humanitarians 6. Inspirational writers 7. Social welfare leaders

ISBN 1-55337-508-4; 1-55337-509-2 pa

An illustrated biography of the woman renowned for overcoming her handicaps of being blind and deaf

"This biography tells Keller's story in a readable, sometimes fictionalized narrative and busy, colorful page layouts. On each spread, the main text appears on the left, while the opposite page consists of a visually appealing collage of black-and-white, full-color, and tinted photos and interesting tidbits set against a pastel background." SLJ

Sullivan, George. **Helen** Keller; her life in pictures. foreword by Keller Johnson Thompson. Scholastic Nonfiction 2007 80p il $17.99

Grades: 4 5 6 7   **92**
1. Deaf 2. Blind 3. Authors 4. Memoirists 5. Humanitarians 6. Inspirational writers 7. Social welfare leaders

ISBN 0-439-91815-4; 978-0-439-91815-2
LC 2006-51401

"Accompanied by brief, simply phrased commentary from Sullivan, this suite of photos portrays Keller from early childhood into her 80s. . . . This profile will serve equally well as an introduction, or as supplementary reading for confirmed admirers." Booklist

Includes bibliographical references

Kennedy, Edward Moore, 1932-2009

Sapet, Kerrily. **Ted** Kennedy. Morgan Reynolds Pub. 2009 144p il (Political profiles) lib bdg $28.95

Grades: 6 7 8 9 10   **92**
1. Senators 2. Siblings of presidents 3. Presidential candidates 4. Statesmen -- United States

ISBN 978-1-59935-089-9; 1-59935-089-0
LC 2008-34943

This offers "a detailed examination of the senator's life and career. . . . This is a meaty offering that is especially good at setting Kennedy's story against the events of his time. . . . Black-and-white and color photos are well chosen." Booklist

Includes bibliographical references

Kennedy, John F. (John Fitzgerald), 1917-1963

★ Heiligman, Deborah. **High** hopes; a photobiography of John F. Kennedy. National Geographic 2003 63p il map $17.95

Grades: 4 5 6 7   **92**
1. Presidents 2. Senators 3. Members of Congress 4. Presidents -- United States 5. Presidents -- United States -- Biography 6. Presidents -- United States -- Pictorial works

ISBN 0-7922-6141-0
LC 2003-7819

Photographs and text trace the life of President John F. Kennedy.

The text "successfully captures the spirit that makes Kennedy an enduring figure in our history. . . . This well-designed book features large, well-chosen, black-and-white photographs." SLJ

Includes bibliographical references

Sandler, Martin W. **Kennedy** through the lens; how photography and television revealed and shaped an extraordinary leader. Walker & Co. 2011 96p il

Grades: 6 7 8 9 10   **92**
1. Presidents 2. Senators 3. Members of Congress 4. Presidents -- United States

ISBN 0802721605; 0802721613; 9780802721600; 9780802721617
LC 2010-11103

This book describes how John F. Kennedy used the medium of television and advances in photography to mold his image and further his political agenda. (Bull Cent Child Books)

"Sandler offers a fascinating photo-essay examining how images shaped public perceptions of John F. Kennedy. . . . The book begins with an overview of Kennedy's life and the role photography and television played in his career. Subsequent spreads are chronological, covering Kennedy's life from childhood through assassination. . . . Kennedy's life and administration were documented with a groundbreaking intimacy the public had never known before, making this an accessible, insightful perspective on one of America's most famous presidents." Kirkus

Kennedy, Robert F., 1925-1968

Aronson, Marc. **Robert** F. Kennedy; a twentieth-century life. Viking 2007 204p il (Up close) $15.99

Grades: 8 9 10 11 12   **92**
1. Senators 2. Attorneys general 3. Siblings of presidents 4. Presidential candidates 5. Politicians --

United States
ISBN 978-0-670-06066-5; 0-670-06066-6
LC 2006-102150

Explores Robert F. Kennedy's life from his childhood to his adult years as Attorney General, New York state senator, and candidate for the presidency of the United States.

"Aronson draws on a wide variety of sources and is very honest in examining his subject as a complete human being, warts and all. . . . This text stands as an unbiased and illuminating resource." SLJ

Includes bibliographical references

Kepler, Johannes, 1571-1630

Hasan, Heather. **Kepler** and the laws of planetary motion. Rosen Pub. Group 2005 64p il (Primary sources of revolutionary scientific discoveries and theories) lib bdg $29.25

Grades: 6 7 8 9   92
1. Astronomers 2. Mathematicians
ISBN 1-40420-308-7
LC 2004007794

"Using primary sources, this book illustrates the timeline of Kepler's discovery of planetary motion. . . . Also included are Kepler's notes and manuscripts as well as reproductions of some of the tools he used." Publisher's note

Includes bibliographical references

Keynes, John Maynard, 1883-1946

Crain, Cynthia D. **John** Maynard Keynes; by Cynthia D. Crain and Dwight R. Lee. Morgan Reynolds Pub. 2009 144p il (Profiles in economics) lib bdg $28.95

Grades: 8 9 10 11 12   92
1. Economists 2. Nonfiction writers 3. Patrons of the arts
ISBN 978-1-59935-109-4 lib bdg; 1-59935-109-9 lib bdg
LC 2009-168

Biography of the economist John Maynard Keynes

"Relationships, education, early influences, and family life are all described . . . [and] economic theory is closely tied to cultural and political events. . . . The writing is straightforward, the . . . [author] assume[s] a certain level of knowledge about world events." SLJ

Includes bibliographical references

★ Kidder, Tracy. **Mountains** beyond mountains; the quest of Dr. Paul Farmer, a man who would cure the world. by Tracy Kidder; adapted for young people by Michael French. Delacorte Press 2013 288 p. hardcover o.p. (hardcover trade) $16.99

Grades: 7 8 9 10 11 12 Adult   92
1. Physicians 2. Access to health care 3. Human rights 4. Right to health 5. Poor -- Medical care 6. Physicians -- Biography 7. Missionaries, Medical -- Biography
ISBN 0385743181; 9780307980885; 9780375990991; 9780385743181
LC 2012024905

This book is a study of Paul Farmer, an American doctor who opened a healthcare center for the poor in Haiti. "By Farmer's decree, no patient can be turned away. But medi-

cal aid alone is not enough. He also emphasizes the need to eliminate problems that contribute to illness: dirty water, inadequate nutrition, poor sanitation, illiteracy. . . . Encouraged by the success of his clinic, Farmer wants to replicate it as 'a laboratory for the world.'" (Christian Science Monitor)

This is a "portrait of Paul Farmer (MacArthur 'genius' grant, 1993), a driven, dedicated, rigidly idealistic doctor who commutes between Harvard and Haiti, where he works . . . to relieve the suffering of some of the poorest people on earth." N Y Times Book Rev

Includes bibliographical references

King, Billie Jean

Gitlin, Marty. **Billie** Jean King; tennis star and social activist. ABDO Pub. Co. 2011 112p il (Legendary athletes) lib bdg $34.22

Grades: 6 7 8 9   92
1. Women athletes 2. Sportscasters 3. Tennis players 4. Tennis -- Biography
ISBN 978-1-61714-757-9; 1-61714-757-5
LC 2010046584

This biography of tennis champion Billie Jean King "goes beyond merely discussing [her] accomplishments. . . . [It] also [explores] the social and political [influence she] had on society as a whole. In addition, [it introduces] historical events in the context of [her life]. . . . This . . . is teeming with information and is a must-purchase for sports fans and readers interested in social activism." SLJ

Includes glossary and bibliographical references

King, Coretta Scott, 1927-2006

Gelfand, Dale Evva. **Coretta** Scott King; civil rights activist. Legacy ed; Chelsea House 2006 137p il (Black Americans of achievement) lib bdg $30

Grades: 7 8 9 10   92
1. Singers 2. Civil rights activists 3. African Americans -- Civil rights
ISBN 0-7910-9522-3
LC 2006022651

First published 1997 under the authorship of Lisa Renee Rhodes

A biography of the civil rights activist and widow of Martin Luther King

Includes bibliographical references

King, Martin Luther, Jr., 1929-1968

★ Bolden, Tonya. **M.L.K.** journey of a King. photography editor, Bob Adelman. Abrams Books for Young Readers 2006 128p il $19.95

Grades: 7 8 9 10   92
1. Clergy 2. Nonfiction writers 3. Civil rights activists 4. Nobel laureates for peace 5. African Americans -- Biography 6. African Americans -- Civil rights 8. Civil rights movements
ISBN 978-0-8109-5476-2; 0-8109-5476-1
LC 2006-13332

"Do libraries need another biography of King? Yes, if it's as good as this one, which will reach a wide audience. . . . Stirring, beautifully reproduced, well-captioned photos . . . accompany the text." Booklist

King, Stephen, 1947-

Stefoff, Rebecca, 1951- **Stephen** King. Marshall Cavendish Benchmark 2010 175p il (Today's writers and their works) $42.79

Grades: 8 9 10 11 12   **92**

1. Authors 2. Novelists 3. Authors, American 4. Short story writers 5. Science fiction writers

ISBN 0-7614-4122-0; 978-0-7614-4122-9

This biography of Stephen King places the author in the context of his times and discusses his work.

This book provides "excellent information for reports." SLJ

Includes bibliographical references

Whitelaw, Nancy. **Dark** dreams; the story of Stephen King. Morgan Reynolds 2005 128p il map (World writers) $26.95

Grades: 7 8 9 10   **92**

1. Authors 2. Novelists 3. Authors, American 4. Short story writers 5. Science fiction writers 6. Horror fiction -- Authorship

ISBN 1-931798-77-X

LC 2005-20112

"This well-documented look at King's life introduces the man who has become a legend for reinventing and legitimizing horror. Whitelaw has put together a seamless synthesis of interviews, biographies, and King's own writing, pared down for younger readers and illustrated with plenty of full-color photographs." Booklist

Koehl, Mimi, 1948-

Parks, Deborah. **Nature's** machines; the story of biomechanist Mimi Koehl. by Deborah Amel Parks. Joseph Henry Press 2005 118p il (Women's adventures in science) lib bdg $31; pa $9.95

Grades: 7 8 9 10   **92**

1. Biologists 2. Women scientists 3. Human engineering 4. Bioengineers 5. College teachers

ISBN 0-531-16780-1 lib bdg; 0-309-09559-X pa

LC 2005-10201

Mimi Koehl "wanted to know more about sea anemones, particularly how they survive the turbulent surf on rocky beaches. Her inquiries and experiments led to discoveries in a new field, biomechanics, in which scientists examine how form determines movement and function in the animal kingdom. . . . This [book] should spark the curiosity of any reader." Voice Youth Advocates

Includes bibliographical references

Kor, Eva Mozes, 1935-

Kor, Eva Mozes. **Surviving** the Angel of Death; the story of a Mengele twin in Auschwitz. [by] Eva Mozes Kor and Lisa Rojany Buccieri. Tanglewood Pub. 2009 141p il map $14.95

Grades: 7 8 9 10   **92**

1. Twins 2. Holocaust survivors 3. Jews -- Hungary 4. Jews -- Persecutions 5. Holocaust, 1933-1945 -- Personal narratives

ISBN 978-1-933718-28-6; 1-933718-28-5

LC 2009-9494

"Born in 1934, Eva and her identical twin, Miriam, were loved and doted over. They lived a comfortable and happy life on their family's farm in Transylvania until the summer of 1940, when their family was herded onto a train with the other Jews in their town and transported to Auschwitz supposedly for their 'protection.' . . . They soon joined a large group of other twins who were under the care of Dr. Josef Mengele, otherwise known as the Angel of Death. . . . Eva's story will have the reader hooked until the very end. . . . This book is an essential purchase for libraries with a Holocaust collection, but it would also be a valuable addition to any library with young impressionable readers." Voice Youth Advocates

Kwan, Michelle

Koestler-Grack, Rachel A. **Michelle** Kwan. Chelsea House 2007 127p (Asian Americans of achievement) lib bdg $30

Grades: 7 8 9 10   **92**

1. Ice skaters 2. Olympic athletes 3. Ice skating -- Biography 4. Asian Americans -- Biography

ISBN 0-7910-9273-9 lib bdg; 978-0-7910-9273-6 lib bdg

LC 2006026069

Profiles the life and career of figure skating champion Michelle Kwan.

"With clear, full-color photos and lots of detail about training and competition, this lively biography . . . will grab fans." Booklist

Includes bibliographical references

La Salle, Robert Cavelier, sieur de, 1643-1687

Aretha, David. **La** Salle; French explorer of the Mississippi. Enslow Publishers 2009 112p il map (Great explorers of the world) lib bdg $31.93

Grades: 6 7 8 9   **92**

1. Explorers

ISBN 978-1-59845-098-9 lib bdg; 1-59845-098-0 lib bdg

LC 2008-25054

"Aretha gives a convincing portrayal of the explorer as a reserved, resilient, and determined man, while offering a readable account of his travels from France to Canada, down the Mississippi to the Gulf of Mexico." Booklist

Includes glossary and bibliographical references

Crompton, Samuel. **Robert** de La Salle; [by] Samuel Willard Crompton. Chelsea House 2009 110p il map (Great explorers) lib bdg $30

Grades: 6 7 8 9   **92**

1. Explorers

ISBN 978-1-60413-419-3 lib bdg; 1-60413-419-4 lib bdg

LC 2009014166

Bipgraphy of the explorer Robert de La Salle

"The information . . . is presented in such a way as to attract and maintain readers' interest. . . . With a full complement of maps, photographs (where available), illustrations, time lines, and document reproductions, a full story is told.

Well-written and throughly researched, this . . . will make a solid addition." SLJ

Includes glossary and bibliographical references

Goodman, Joan E. **Despite** all obstacles: La Salle and the conquest of the Mississippi; by Joan Elizabeth Goodman; illustrated by Tom McNeely. Mikaya Press 2001 47p il map (Great explorers book) $19.95

Grades: 4 5 6 7   92

1. Explorers 2. Explorers -- France -- Biography 3. Canada -- History -- To 1763 (New France) 4. Explorers -- Mississippi River -- Biography 5. Mississippi River Valley -- History -- To 1803 6. Mississippi River -- Discovery and exploration -- French 7. Mississippi River Valley -- Discovery and exploration -- French

ISBN 1-931414-01-7

LC 2001-31732

A biography of the man who explored the St. Lawrence, Ohio, Illinois, and Mississippi rivers, and who claimed America's heartland for King Louis XIV and France

"Vivid color illustrations and Goodman's exciting writing style will attract both researchers and pleasure readers." Voice Youth Advocates

Lafayette, Marie Joseph Paul Yves Roch Gilbert du Motier, marquis de, 1757-1834

★ Freedman, Russell. **Lafayette** and the American Revolution. Holiday House 2010 88p il $24.95

Grades: 6 7 8 9   92

1. Generals 2. Statesmen

ISBN 978-0-8234-2182-4; 0-8234-2182-1

LC 2009052342

A Robert F. Sibert Medal honor book, 2011

A biography of the French general who fought Cornwallis' troops at Yorktown in the American Revolution.

"In this solidly researched and smoothly written biography, Freeman creates a vivid portrait of Lafayette. . . . Handsomely designed with a spacious format and good use of color, the book includes many clearly reproduced paintings and prints." Booklist

Includes bibliographical references

Lang, Lang, 1982-

★ Lang, Lang. **Lang** Lang; playing with flying keys. by Lang Lang with Michael French; introduction by Daniel Barenboim. Delacorte Press 2008 215p il $16.99; lib bdg $19.99

Grades: 7 8 9 10   92

1. Pianists 2. Classical musicians

ISBN 978-0-385-73578-0; 0-385-73578-2; 978-0-385-90564-0 lib bdg; 0-385-90564-5 lib bdg

LC 2007-51597

"Although he is only 26, Chinese-born Lang is recognized as one of the world's most accomplished classical pianists. This smoothly paced, often rivetingly candid autobiography . . . follows the musician through his first encounters with the keyboard and grueling training to his triumphant debut concerts with the Chicago Symphony." Booklist

Lauren, Ralph

Mattern, Joanne. **Ralph** Lauren. Chelsea House 2011 101p il (Famous fashion designers) lib bdg $35

Grades: 6 7 8 9 10   92

1. Fashion designers

ISBN 978-1-60413-978-5; 1-60413-978-1

LC 2010036192

This is a biography of fashion designer Ralph Lauren. Includes glossary and bibliographical references

Lavoisier, Antoine Laurent, 1743-1794

Van Gorp, Lynn. **Antoine** Lavoisier; and his impact on modern chemistry. Compass Point Books 2009 40p il (Mission: Science) lib bdg $26.60

Grades: 4 5 6 7   92

1. Chemists 2. Scientists

ISBN 978-0-7565-3959-7 lib bdg; 0-7565-3959-5 lib bdg

LC 2008007283

Profiles the life and career of the Frenchman who is considered the founder of chemistry

"Color photographs, reproductions, diagrams, and maps are liberally sprinkled throughout [this] attractive [book]. Numerous sidebars offer tangential information." SLJ

Layson, Annelex Hofstra

Layson, Annelex Hofstra. **Lost** childhood; my life in a Japanese prison camp during World War II. [by] Annelex Hofstra Layson; with Herman Viola. National Geographic 2008 111p il $15.95; lib bdg $23.90

Grades: 5 6 7 8 9   92

1. Prisoners of war 2. Memoirists 3. World War, 1939-1945 -- Personal narratives 4. World War, 1939-1945 -- Prisoners and prisons 5. World War, 1939-1945 -- Children 6. World War, 1939-1945 -- Indonesia -- Prisoners and prisons, Japanese

ISBN 978-1-4263-0321-0; 1-4263-0321-1; 978-1-4263-0322-7 lib bdg; 1-4263-0322-X lib bdg

LC 2008-11671

In a shockingly honest narrative, a former prisoner-of-war tells how her family, along with ten thousand other Dutch residents living in the Dutch East Indies were shipped off to interment camps where food rationing, terrible sanitary conditions, and an uncertain future were the norms for more than three years

The author's narrative is warm and enthralling. . . . Layson's voice captivates and engages. Libr Media Connect

Includes bibliographical references

Le Guin, Ursula K., 1929-

Brown, Jeremy K. **Ursula** K. Le Guin; foreword by Kyle Zimmer. Chelsea House Publishers 2010 128p il (Who wrote that?) lib bdg $35

Grades: 6 7 8 9 10   92

1. Authors 2. Novelists 3. Women authors 4. Fantasy writers 5. College teachers 6. Authors, American 7. Children's authors 8. Short story writers 9. Science

fiction writers

ISBN 978-1-60413-724-8; 1-60413-724-X

LC 2010006600

"Le Guin's work raises questions about identity and morality, and Brown explores her treatment of these themes in a way that readers, whether they're reading for pleasure or for reports, will appreciate. . . . This title does a fine job of conveying both the story of an author's long career and the vision that fuels it." SLJ

Includes bibliographical references

Ledger, Heath, 1979-2008

Watson, Stephanie. **Heath** Ledger; talented actor. ABDO Pub. Company 2010 112p il (Lives cut short) lib bdg $32.79

Grades: 5 6 7 8   92

1. Actors

ISBN 978-1-60453-789-5 lib bdg; 1-60453-789-2 lib bdg

LC 2009034353

This discusses Heath Ledger's "early life, providing details that give insight into later success and troubles and maintaining a laudatory tone that focuses on the individual's artistic achievements and hard work to achieve fame. Details [such as] explaining that Jack Nicholson warned Heath Ledger about the Joker role . . . are bound to resonate with readers. Numerous photos and sidebars appear throughout. [A] worthwhile [resource] for reports as well as popular reading." SLJ

Includes bibliographical references

Lee, Harper, 1926-

★ Madden, Kerry. **Harper** Lee; a twentieth-century life. Viking Children's Books 2009 223p il map (Up close) $16.99

Grades: 7 8 9 10   92

1. Authors 2. Novelists 3. Women authors 4. Essayists 5. Authors, American 6. Short story writers

ISBN 978-0-670-01095-0; 0-670-01095-2

LC 2008-53911

"A narrative both well paced and richly detailed . . . this biography will appeal to fans of the novel and to newcomers. . . . Extensive source notes and an excellent bibliography round out this superb biography." Kirkus

Includes bibliographical references

Shields, Charles J. **I** am Scout: the biography of Harper Lee. Henry Holt & Co. 2008 245p il $18.95

Grades: 7 8 9 10   92

1. Authors 2. Novelists 3. Women authors 4. Essayists 5. Authors, American 6. Short story writers

ISBN 978-0-8050-8334-7; 0-8050-8334-0

LC 2007-27572

A biography of the author of To Kill a Mockingbird

Shields "offers a fascinating look at the unconventional Lee, which captures his elusive subject and her lifelong friend, Truman Capote. . . . Shields' formidable research . . . will impress any student who has ever written a term paper." Booklist

Includes bibliographical references

Lee, Robert E. (Robert Edward), 1807-1870

Robertson, James I. **Robert** E. Lee; Virginian soldier, American citizen. [by] James I. Robertson, Jr. Atheneum Books for Young Readers 2005 159p il maps $21.95

Grades: 7 8 9 10   92

1. Generals 2. College presidents

ISBN 0-689-85731-4

LC 2003-22108

This portrait of the Confederate general "puts particular emphasis on his life during the Civil War years but provides plenty of information on his youth, his early military career, and his postwar years. . . . Useful for reports and interesting in its own right, this well-researched biography will be a solid addition to library collections." Booklist

Includes bibliographical references

Leeuwenhoek, Antoni van, 1632-1723

Yount, Lisa. **Antoni** van Leeuwenhoek; first to see microscopic life. [by] Lisa Yount. rev ed.; Enslow Publishers 2008 128p il map (Great minds of science) lib bdg $31.93

Grades: 5 6 7 8   92

1. Biologists 2. Microscopes 3. Microscopists

ISBN 978-0-7660-3012-1 lib bdg; 0-7660-3012-1 lib bdg

LC 2007020300

First published 1996

This biography of seventeenth-century Dutch scientist Antoni van Leeuwenhoek includes related activities

Includes glossary and bibliographical references

Leif Eriksson, fl. 1000

DeFries, Cheryl L. **Leif** Eriksson; Viking explorer of the New World. Enslow Publishers 2010 112p il map (Great explorers of the world) lib bdg $31.93

Grades: 6 7 8 9   92

1. Vikings 2. Explorers

ISBN 978-1-59845-126-9; 1-59845-126-X

This "provides some interesting stories from the Vikings' family history. Readers will be intrigued by the folklore and legends. The mystery behind [Ericksson's] discovery of America is explored briefly, as well as his impact on navigation, law, and culture. Photographs of Viking artifacts bring provide an interesting glimpse into the past. . . . This . . . would serve as a useful resource for middle and elementary school students and may inspire them to read further." Voice Youth Advocates

Includes glossary and bibliographical references

Lennon, John, 1940-1980

Anderson, Jennifer Joline. **John** Lennon; legendary musician & Beatle. ABDO 2010 112p il (Lives cut short) lib bdg $32.79

Grades: 5 6 7 8   92

1. Singers 2. Rock musicians 3. Songwriters

ISBN 978-1-60453-790-1 lib bdg; 1-60453-790-6 lib bdg

LC 2009034354

This discusses the John Lennon's "early life, providing details that give insight into later success and troubles and maintaining a laudatory tone that focuses on the individual's artistic achievements and hard work to achieve fame. Details [such as] explaining that . . . John Lennon had no musical training . . . are bound to resonate with readers. Numerous photos and sidebars appear throughout. [A] worthwhile [resource] for reports as well as popular reading." SLJ

Includes glossary and bibliographical references

Burlingame, Jeff. **John** Lennon; Imagine. Enslow Publishers 2010 160p il (American rebels) lib bdg $34.60

Grades: 6 7 8 9   **92**
1. Singers 2. Rock musicians 3. Songwriters
ISBN 978-0-7660-3675-8 lib bdg; 0-7660-3675-8 lib bdg

LC 2009040045

A biography of the rock musician and peace-activist John Lennon.

"This attractive biography includes sidebars, wide margins, large type, and many photographs throughout. Burlingame maintains readers' interest." SLJ

Includes bibliographical references

★ Partridge, Elizabeth. **John** Lennon; all I want is the truth. a photographic biography by Elizabeth Partridge. Viking 2005 232p il $24.99

Grades: 8 9 10 11 12   **92**
1. Singers 2. Rock musicians 3. Songwriters
ISBN 0-670-05954-4

LC 2005-11850

Michael L. Printz Award honor book, 2006

"This handsome book will be eagerly received by both Beatles fans, who are legion, and their elders, who will enjoy reliving the glory days of the Fab Four and exploring the inner workings of a creative talent." SLJ

Includes bibliographical references

★ Rappaport, Doreen. **John's** secret dreams; the life of John Lennon. written by Doreen Rappaport; illustrated by Bryan Collier. Hyperion Books for Children 2004 un il $16.99

Grades: 4 5 6 7   **92**
1. Singers 2. Rock musicians 3. Songwriters
ISBN 0-7868-0817-9

LC 2003-57116

"Using a combination of simple prose, song lyrics, and illustration, this heartfelt picture-book biography traces Lennon's life from his childhood to his death. Striking in both its simplicity and complexity, it captures this enigmatic singer, artist, songwriter, and folk hero in a way that will move and fascinate those too young to remember the man but are surrounded by his music and myth." SLJ

Leonard, Buck, 1907-1997

Payment, Simone. **Buck** Leonard. Rosen Pub. Group 2002 112p il (Baseball Hall of Famers of the Negro leagues) lib bdg $29.25

Grades: 5 6 7 8   **92**
1. Baseball players 2. African American athletes 3. Baseball -- Biography 4. Negro leagues -- History 5. African American baseball players -- Biography 6.

Baseball players -- United States -- Biography
ISBN 0-8239-3473-X

LC 2001-3151

A biography of first-baseman who played in the Negro Leagues and was inducted into the Baseball Hall of Fame in 1972

This "title presents an unvarnished picture of the racism in this country and how it impacted amateur and professional baseball from 1868 onward. . . . The layout . . . is attractive, the style . . . is engaging." Book Rep

Includes glossary and bibliographical references

Leonardo, da Vinci, 1452-1519

Anderson, Maxine. **Amazing** Leonardo da Vinci inventions you can build yourself. Nomad Press 2006 122p il map (Learn some hands-on history) pa $14.95

Grades: 5 6 7 8   **92**
1. Artists 2. Painters 3. Handicraft 4. Inventions 5. Scientists 6. Renaissance 7. Artists, Italian 8. Writers on science
ISBN 0-9749344-2-9

"Anderson has combined biography with doable activities that mirror ideas found in Leonardo's notebooks. Using common household objects (duct tape, foil, cereal boxes, paper-towel tubes, etc.), readers can make a parachute, hydrometer, invisible ink, walk-on-water shoes, etc. Anderson introduces each project with an explanation of why Leonardo came up with the idea and whether he created just the sketch or the sketch and the object. Detailed steps and illustrations provide clarity." SLJ

★ Krull, Kathleen. **Leonardo** da Vinci; illustrated by Boris Kulikov. Viking 2005 128p il (Giants of science) $15.99

Grades: 5 6 7 8   **92**
1. Artists 2. Painters 3. Scientists 4. Renaissance 5. Artists, Italian 6. Writers on science
ISBN 0-670-05920-X

This is a "biography of Leonardo da Vinci that highlights his scientific approach to understanding the physical world. The first half of the book describes Leonardo's apprenticeship and his work as an artist in Milan. The second half relates events in his later life, emphasizing his observation and investigation of the human body and nature. . . . Six excellent ink drawings illustrate this attractive volume. A very readable, vivid portrait set against the backdrop of remarkable times." Booklist

Includes bibliographical references

Phillips, John. **Leonardo** da Vinci; the genius who defined the Renaissance. National Geographic 2006 64p bibl il (World history biographies) $17.95; lib bdg $27.90; pa $6.95

Grades: 5 6 7 8   **92**
1. Artists 2. Painters 3. Scientists 4. Renaissance 5. Artists, Italian 6. Writers on science
ISBN 978-0-7922-5385-3; 0-7922-5385-X; 978-0-7922-5386-0 lib bdg; 0-7922-5386-8 lib bdg; 978-1-4263-0248-0 pa; 1-4263-0249-7 pa

Examines the life of Renaissance genius Leonardo da Vinci, discussing his inquiries and accomplishments in art and various fields of science

Includes bibliographical references

Levine, Gail Carson, 1947-

Abrams, Dennis. **Gail** Carson Levine; [by] Dennis Abrams; foreword by Kyle Zimmer. Chelsea House 2007 120p bibl il por (Who wrote that?) $30 Grades: 6 7 8 9   92

1. Authors 2. Women authors 3. Authors, American 4. Children's authors

ISBN 978-0-7910-8970-5; 0-7910-8970-3

LC 2007019449

This biography examines the "writer's life, including the inspiration behind some of [her] works. [The] volume includes photographs and quotations from interviews, as well as descriptions of main characters and annotated lists of books and awards. Useful for aspiring authors as well as book report writers." Horn Book Guide

Includes bibliographical references

Lewis, C. S. (Clive Staples), 1898-1963

Hamilton, Janet. **C.** S. Lewis; twentieth century pilgrim. Morgan Reynolds Pub. 2010 128p il (World writers) lib bdg $28.95 Grades: 7 8 9 10   92

1. Authors 2. Novelists 3. Theologians 4. Essayists 5. Satirists 6. Authors, English 7. Literary critics 8. Children's authors

ISBN 978-1-59935-112-4; 1-59935-112-9

LC 2009-7134

In this biography of the British author, "Lewis' childhood is well-documented, as is his love of literature as an escape from the real world. Hamilton clearly shows the importance religion played in Lewis's life. The impact that war, and the resulting loss of the imaginative worlds he could find in literature, and his struggle with religious belief are tied directly to his writing." Voice Youth Advocates

Includes bibliographical references

Lewis, John, 1940-

Sapet, Kerrily. **John** Lewis. Morgan Reynolds Pub. 2009 128p il (Political profiles) lib bdg $28.95 Grades: 6 7 8 9   92

1. Members of Congress 2. Civil rights activists 3. African Americans -- Civil rights

ISBN 978-1-59935-130-8 lib bdg; 1-59935-130-7 lib bdg

LC 2009027748

A biography of African American civil rights activist John Lewis

This is "solid, evenhanded, and wonderfully helpful. . . . Particularly interesting is the section of the book that describes Lewis' congressional race against fellow civil rights activist Julian Bond. . . . Unusually well-chosen photos, fine notes, and [a list] of further sources add to the usefulness and appeal of this [book]." Booklist

Includes bibliographical references

Lewis, Meriwether, 1774-1809

Crompton, Samuel. **Lewis** and Clark; [by] Samuel Willard Crompton. Chelsea House 2009 116p il map (Great explorers) lib bdg $30 92

1. Explorers 2. Territorial governors

ISBN 978-1-60413-418-6 lib bdg; 1-60413-418-6 lib bdg

LC 2009-8687

Biography of the explorers Lewis and Clark

"The information . . . is presented in such a way as to attract and maintain readers' interest. . . . With a full complement of maps, photographs (where available), illustrations, time lines, and document reproductions, a full story is told. Well-written and throughly researched, this . . . will make a solid addition." SLJ

Includes glossary and bibliographical references

Li Cunxin

Li Cunxin. **Mao's** last dancer; [by] Li Cunxin. Young readers' ed.; Walker & Co. 2008 290p il map $16.99 Grades: 6 7 8 9   92

1. Defectors 2. Ballet dancers 3. Securities brokers

ISBN 978-0-8027-9779-7; 0-8027-9779-2

LC 2008-6104

An adaptation of the title published 2003 by Putnam for adults

Chosen from millions of children to serve in Mao's cultural revolution by studying at the Beijing Dance Academy, Li knew ballet would be his family's best opportunity to escape the bitter poverty in his rural China home. From one hardship to another, Li persevered, never forgetting the family he left behind.

"Cunxin's tale is a wonderfully crafted coming-of-age story. . . . He paints a clear picture of harsh realities of life in communist China but does so without being overly negative. . . . Photographs provide readers with a glimpse of varying aspects of Cunxin's life, a short note on the history of China, and a time line of China in the twentieth century." Voice Youth Advocates

Li, Moying, 1954-

★ Moying Li. **Snow** falling in spring; coming of age in China during the cultural revolution. Farrar, Straus and Giroux 2008 176p $16 Grades: 7 8 9 10 11 12   92

1. Memoirists 2. Financial consultants

ISBN 978-0-374-39922-1; 0-374-39922-0

LC 2006-38356

"This memoir . . . offers a highly personal look at China's Cultural Revolution. The author is four years old when Mao initiates the Great Leap Forward in 1958. . . . Li effectively builds the climate of fear that accompanies the rise of the Red Guard, while accounts of her headmaster's suicide and the pulping of her father's book collection give a harrowing, closeup view of the persecution. Sketches about her grandparents root the narrative within a broader context of Chinese traditions as well as her own family's values." Publ Wkly

Lichtenstein, Roy, 1923-1997

★ Rubin, Susan Goldman. **Whaam!**: the art & life of Roy Lichtenstein. Abrams 2008 47p il $18.95

Grades: 4 5 6 7   92

1. Artists 2. Pop art 3. Painters 4. Sculptors 5. Printmakers 6. Artists -- United States

ISBN 978-0-8109-9492-8; 0-8109-9492-5

LC 2007-42048

"Rubin presents an overview of a modern master with clear writing and an abundance of his eye-popping works, all framed on pages that mirror the artist's signature use of primary colors and Benday dots." Booklist

Lin, Maya Ying

Lashnits, Tom. **Maya** Lin; [by] Tom Lashnits. Chelsea House 2007 128p il (Asian Americans of achievement) lib bdg $30

Grades: 7 8 9 10   92

1. Artists 2. Sculptors 3. Architects 4. Women architects 5. Vietnam Veterans Memorial (Washington, D.C.) 6. Asian Americans -- Biography

ISBN 978-0-7910-9268-2 lib bdg; 0-7910-9268-2 lib bdg

LC 2006026064

A biography of the architect who designed the Vietnam Veterans' Memorial in Washington D.C.

This is "well-researched . . . attractive . . . solid." SLJ

Includes glossary and bibliographical references

Lincoln, Abraham, 1809-1865

Aronson, Billy. **Abraham** Lincoln. Marshall Cavendish Benchmark 2009 112p il (Presidents and their times) lib bdg $23.95

Grades: 5 6 7 8   92

1. Lawyers 2. Presidents 3. State legislators 4. Members of Congress 5. Presidents -- United States

ISBN 978-0-7614-2839-8 lib bdg; 0-7614-2839-9 lib bdg

LC 2007019190

This provides "information on President Abraham Lincoln and places him within his historical and cultural context. Also explored are the formative events of his times and how he responded." Publisher's note

Includes glossary and bibliographical references

★ Denenberg, Barry. **Lincoln** shot! a president's life remembered. chief writer, Barry Denenberg; artist, Christopher Bing. Feiwel and Friends 2008 40p il $24.95

Grades: 5 6 7 8   92

1. Lawyers 2. Presidents 3. State legislators 4. Members of Congress 5. Presidents -- United States

ISBN 978-0-312-37013-8; 0-312-37013-X

LC 2007-48851

"The concept is that this is a commemorative edition of 'The National News' published one year after Lincoln's death . . . Also included is an engaging, readable yet detailed account of Lincoln's life. . . . [This book] is an example of how high-quality bookmaking can turn a history lesson into an authentic experience." Booklist

★ Fleming, Candace. The **Lincolns**; a scrapbook look at Abraham and Mary. Schwartz & Wade Books 2008 177p il map $24.99; lib bdg $28.99

Grades: 7 8 9 10 11 12   92

1. Lawyers 2. Presidents 3. State legislators 4. Members of Congress 5. Spouses of presidents 6. Presidents -- United States 7. Presidents' spouses -- United States

ISBN 978-0-375-83618-3; 0-375-83618-7; 978-0-375-93618-0 lib bdg; 0-375-93618-1 lib bdg

LC 2007-44113

Boston Globe-Horn Book Award: Nonfiction (2009)

Fleming twines "accounts of two lives—Abraham and Mary Todd Lincoln—into one fascinating whole. On spreads that combine well-chosen visuals with blocks of headlined text, Fleming gives a full, birth-to-death view of the 'inextricably bound' Lincolns." Booklist

★ Freedman, Russell. **Lincoln**: a photobiography. Clarion Bks. 1987 149p il $18; pa $7.95

Grades: 5 6 7 8 9 10   92

1. Lawyers 2. Presidents 3. State legislators 4. Members of Congress 5. Presidents -- United States

ISBN 0-89919-380-3; 0-395-51848-2 pa

LC 86-33379

Awarded the Newbery Medal, 1988

This is "a balanced work, elegantly designed and enhanced by dozens of period photographs and drawings, some familiar, some refreshingly unfamiliar." Publ Wkly

Includes bibliographical references

Giblin, James. **Good** brother, bad brother; the story of Edwin Booth and John Wilkes Booth. Clarion Books 2005 244p il $22

Grades: 5 6 7 8   92

1. Actors 2. Lawyers 3. Brothers 4. Presidents 5. Murderers 6. State legislators 7. Members of Congress

ISBN 0-618-09642-6

LC 2004-21260

This is a dual biography of John Wilkes Booth, who assassinated Abraham Lincoln, and his brother, Edwin, an actor.

Giblin "frames the intertwined tale of two brothers with accounts of their families, friends, the Civil War, and nineteenth-century theater. . . . Alcoholism and depression afflicted the family, but Giblin is brilliant at showing that darkness was only one part of a life. . . . Giblin's book will engross readers until the very last footnote." Booklist

Includes bibliographical references

★ Holzer, Harold. **Father** Abraham; Lincoln and his sons. Calkins Creek 2011 231p il $17.95

Grades: 6 7 8 9   92

1. Lawyers 2. Presidents 3. Pioneers 4. State legislators 5. Members of Congress 6. Presidents -- United States

ISBN 1590783034; 9781590783030

This biography "looks at the lives of Abraham Lincoln and his family, including the relationship between the president and his sons." (Publisher's note)

"This profile of 'the clan that might have become America's royal family but instead became America's cursed family' offers both a wagonload of fascinating period photos and a case study in domestic tragedy and dysfunction. . . . If the author sometimes hobbles his narrative with fussy details, he also tucks in such intimate touches as samples of homely verse from both parents and children and finishes off with quick looks at all of the direct descendants." Kirkus

Lincoln, Abraham. **Abraham** Lincoln the writer; a treasury of his greatest speeches and letters. compiled and edited by Harold Holzer. Boyds Mills Press 2000 106p il lib bdg $15.95

Grades: 7 8 9 10   92
  1. Lawyers 2. Presidents 3. State legislators 4. Members of Congress 5. Presidents -- United States 6. Presidents -- United States -- Biography 7. Illinois -- Politics and government -- To 1865 -- Sources 8. United States -- Politics and government -- 1815-1861 -- Sources 9. United States -- Politics and government -- 1861-1865 -- Sources
  ISBN 1-56397-772-9
                                        LC 99-66551
"Lincoln's writings include personal letters, notes on the law, excerpts from speeches, debates, and inaugural addresses, letters to parents of fallen soldiers, and telegrams to his family. Reproductions of period photos, portraits, and documents illustrate the text effectively. . . . Highly interesting and a fine resource for students seeking quotations or for those wanting to meet Lincoln through his own words." Booklist

★ Sandler, Martin W. **Lincoln** through the lens; how photography revealed and shaped an extraordinary life. Walker Pub. Co. 2008 97p il $19.99; lib bdg $20.89

Grades: 6 7 8 9 10   92
  1. Lawyers 2. Presidents 3. State legislators 4. Members of Congress 5. Photography -- History 6. Presidents -- United States
  ISBN 978-0-8027-9666-0; 0-8027-9666-4; 978-0-8027-9667-7 lib bdg; 0-8027-9667-2 lib bdg
                                        LC 2008-0219
"When Lincoln became president, photography was new and he joined the 'very first generation of human beings ever to be photographed.' . . . This extraordinary book is a tribute to the way contemporary and future generations came to view Lincoln. . . . Part biography, part history of of the Civil War, the book touches on many interesting topics. . . . Every step of the way there are fascinating photographs. . . . Although it's the pictures that provide the 'wow factor,' Sandler's perceptive words have their own elegance." Booklist

★ Swanson, James L. **Chasing** Lincoln's killer; the search for John Wilkes Booth. Scholastic Press 2009 194p il map $16.99

Grades: 7 8 9 10   92
  1. Actors 2. Lawyers 3. Presidents 4. Murderers 5.

State legislators 6. Members of Congress
  ISBN 978-0-439-90354-7; 0-439-90354-8
                                        LC 2008-17994
"This volume is an adaptation of Swanson's Manhunt: The 12-Day Chase for Lincoln's Killer (HarperCollins, 2006). Divided into 14 chapters and an epilogue, the sentences are shorter and chapters are condensed from the original but the rich details and suspense are ever present. . . . Excellent black-and-white illustrations complement the text. . . . Readers will be engrossed by the almost hour-by-hour search and by the many people who encountered the killer as he tried to escape. It is a tale of intrigue and an engrossing mystery." SLJ

Waldman, Neil. **Voyages**; reminiscences of young Abe Lincoln. Calkins Creek 2009 32p $16.95

Grades: 4 5 6 7   92
  1. Lawyers 2. Presidents 3. State legislators 4. Members of Congress 5. Slavery -- United States 6. Presidents -- United States
  ISBN 978-1-59078-471-6
                                        LC 2008024022
This "volume integrates some of Lincoln's own words with an imagined narrative based on documented accounts of river voyages he took between the ages of 18 and 22. . . . The two narratives blend fairly smoothly, and the book offers both a quick read and extensive opportunities for study and discussion. . . . The nostalgic design, featuring a distressed sepia-toned appearance and the author's own illustrations, further adds to the book's appeal." Booklist
  Includes bibliographical references

★ Zeller, Bob. **Lincoln** in 3-D; by Bob Zeller and John Richter. Chronicle Books 2010 223p il $35

Grades: 6 7 8 9   92
  1. Lawyers 2. Presidents 3. Three dimensional photography 4. State legislators 5. Members of Congress
  ISBN 978-0-8118-7231-7; 0-8118-7231-9
                                        LC 2010013792
"This visually striking volume is built around 185 stereoscopic photographs from the Civil War era. Glasses included in the back give the full three-dimensional effect. . . . The introduction offers fascinating background on stereoscopic pictures, followed by a narrative text tracing Lincoln's life and the stages of the war. All of the photos include informative captions that give context even for images not mentioned in the text. . . . The striking images make this a powerful visual depiction of Lincoln and his times." SLJ
  Includes bibliographical references

Lincoln, Mary Todd, 1818-1882

Jones, Lynda. **Mrs.** Lincoln's dressmaker: the unlikely friendship of Elizabeth Keckley and Mary Todd Lincoln; by Lynda D. Jones. National Geographic 2009 80p il $18.95; lib bdg $27.90

Grades: 5 6 7 8   92
  1. Memoirists 2. Dressmakers 3. Spouses of presidents 4. Slavery -- United States 5. African American women

-- Biography 7. Presidents' spouses -- United States
ISBN 978-1-4263-0377-7; 1-4263-0377-7; 978-1-
4263-0378-4 lib bdg; 1-4263-0378-5 lib bdg

LC 2008-29314

"Readers may be familiar with the ups and downs of Lincoln's life, but details of Keckley's story . . . will give them new insights into the life of a slave, in this case, one who was educated and had a profession." Booklist

Includes bibliographical references

Lindbergh, Anne Morrow, 1906-2001

Gherman, Beverly. **Anne** Morrow Lindbergh; between the sea and the stars. [by] Beverly Gherman. Twenty-first Century Books 2008 160p (Lerner biography) lib bdg $27.93

Grades: 6 7 8 9   92

1. Poets 2. Authors 3. Generals 4. Novelists 5. Air pilots 6. Women air pilots 7. Diarists 8. Essayists 9. Memoirists 10. Air force officers 11. Spouses of prominent persons
ISBN 978-0-8225-5970-2 lib bdg; 0-8225-5970-6 lib bdg

LC 2005022498

Explores the life and career of Anne Morrow Lindbergh, including her marriage to Charles Lindbergh, flying experiences, and success as an author.

"Clearly written and illustrated with frequent, clear black-and-white photos, the book is strongest in demonstrating Gherman's thorough understanding of Anne's emotional core. . . . A solid resource for reports as well as a fascinating portrait for biography fans." Booklist

Includes bibliographical references

Lindbergh, Charles, 1902-1974

Gherman, Beverly. **Anne** Morrow Lindbergh; between the sea and the stars. [by] Beverly Gherman. Twenty-first Century Books 2008 160p (Lerner biography) lib bdg $27.93

Grades: 6 7 8 9   92

1. Poets 2. Authors 3. Generals 4. Novelists 5. Air pilots 6. Women air pilots 7. Diarists 8. Essayists 9. Memoirists 10. Air force officers 11. Spouses of prominent persons
ISBN 978-0-8225-5970-2 lib bdg; 0-8225-5970-6 lib bdg

LC 2005022498

Explores the life and career of Anne Morrow Lindbergh, including her marriage to Charles Lindbergh, flying experiences, and success as an author.

"Clearly written and illustrated with frequent, clear black-and-white photos, the book is strongest in demonstrating Gherman's thorough understanding of Anne's emotional core. . . . A solid resource for reports as well as a fascinating portrait for biography fans." Booklist

Includes bibliographical references

Linné, Carl von, 1707-1778

Anderson, Margaret Jean. **Carl** Linnaeus; father of classification. [by] Margaret J. Anderson. rev ed; Enslow Publishers 2009 128p il (Great minds of science) lib bdg $31.93

Grades: 5 6 7 8 9   92

1. Botanists 2. Naturalists 3. Writers on science
ISBN 978-0-7660-3009-1 lib bdg; 0-7660-3009-1 lib bdg

LC 2008-23941

First published 1997

"Budding scientists will surely draw inspiration from this biography of Linnaeus. . . . Anderson creates a dramatic narrative fully capable of keeping readers enthralled." Kirkus

Includes glossary and bibliographical references

Lockwood, Belva Ann, 1830-1917

Norgren, Jill. **Belva** Lockwood; equal rights pioneer. by Jill Norgren. Twenty-First Century Books 2009 112p il (Trailblazer biography) lib bdg $31.93

Grades: 6 7 8 9   92

1. Lawyers 2. Suffragists 3. Women lawyers 4. Women's rights 5. Lecturers 6. Presidential candidates
ISBN 978-0-8225-9068-2 lib bdg; 0-8225-9068-9 lib bdg

LC 2007-50265

First published 2007 by New York University Press with title: Belva Lockwood: the woman who would be president

"Through a clear and engaging text, this biography shows how Lockwood, a relatively unknown historical figure, was an inspiring pioneer of the equal-rights movement." SLJ

Includes bibliographical references

Louis, Joe, 1914-1981

Sullivan, George. **Knockout!**: a photobiography of boxer Joe Louis. National Geographic 2008 64p il $17.95; lib bdg $27.90

Grades: 6 7 8 9   92

1. Soldiers 2. African American athletes 3. Boxers (Persons) 4. Boxing -- Biography
ISBN 978-1-4263-0328-9; 1-4263-0328-9; 978-1-4263-0329-6 lib bdg; 1-4263-0329-7 lib bdg

LC 2008-25036

"This oversize biography of Joe Louis is just the thing for getting the blood of reluctant readers and sports fans pumping. Using copious period photographs . . . and full-color reproductions of fight posters and memoriblia, Sullivan relays in straightforward language the rags-to-riches saga of the 'Brown Bomber,' and sets the story against the rampant racism of 1920s America. . . . Sullivan's fight recaps are clear and vivid." Booklist

Includes bibliographical references

Love, Nat, 1854-1921

Bloom, Barbara Lee. **Nat** Love. Chelsea House 2010 102p il (Legends of the Wild West) lib bdg $35

Grades: 6 7 8 9   92

1. Cowhands 2. Cowboys 3. Porters 4. African Americans -- Biography
ISBN 978-1-60413-599-2; 1-60413-599-9

A biography of Nat Love, who was born in a log cabin in Tennessee in 1854 as the slave of Robert Love and who, in 1869, four years after the slaves had been freed, moved out West to find work as a cowhand.

Bloom "does a fine job chronicling [Love's] exploits as a black cowboy and beyond. . . . Weaving historical context throughout in related sidebars and lengthy captions, the book features black-and-white and color photos, paintings, and other illustrations." Booklist

Includes glossary and bibliographical references

Lowry, Lois

Albert, Lisa Rondinelli. **Lois** Lowry; the giver of stories and memories. Enslow Publishers 2008 128p il (Authors teens love) lib bdg $31.93

Grades: 5 6 7 8   92
1. Authors 2. Novelists 3. Women authors 4. Authors, American 5. Young adult authors 6. Children's literature -- Authors and illustrators
ISBN 978-0-7660-2722-0 lib bdg; 0-7660-2722-8 lib bdg

LC 2006034045

A biography of the author of the Anastasia Krupnik series, as well as the Newbery Medal winning novels The giver and Number the Stars
Includes bibliographical references

Bankston, John. **Lois** Lowry; [by] John Bankston. Chelsea House 2009 127p il (Who wrote that?) lib bdg $30

Grades: 6 7 8 9   92
1. Authors 2. Novelists 3. Women authors 4. Authors, American 5. Young adult authors 6. Children's literature -- Authors and illustrators
ISBN 978-1-6041-3335-6 lib bdg; 1-6041-3335-X lib bdg

LC 2008035039

This examines the life and work of the popular author for children and young adults
Includes bibliographical references

Lugovskaia, Nina, 1918-1993

Lugovskaia, Nina. **I** want to live; the diary of a young girl in Stalin's Russia. translated by Andrew Bromfield. Houghton Mifflin 2006 280p il $17.99

Grades: 7 8 9 10 11 12   92
1. Artists 2. Painters 3. Persecution 4. Diarists
ISBN 978-0-618-60575-0; 0-618-60575-4
Original Russian edition, 2003

Reveals the life of a teenage girl in Stalin's Russia, where fear of arrest was a fact of daily life.

"Lugovskaya's diary, which was found in the NKVD archives, stands as a compelling historical artifact and Nina's story gives a moving—if relentlessly melancholy—personal account of life in Communist Russia." Publ Wkly
Includes bibliographical references

Lyons, Maritcha Rémond, 1848-1929

★ Bolden, Tonya. **Maritcha**; a nineteenth-century American girl. Abrams 2005 47p il $17.95

Grades: 4 5 6 7 8 9 10   92
1. Teachers 2. African American women 3. Civic leaders 4. African American women -- Biography 5. African Americans -- New York (N.Y.)
ISBN 0-8109-5045-6

LC 2004-05849

"The high quality of writing and the excellent documentation make this a first choice for all collections." SLJ

Ma, Yo-Yo, 1955-

Worth, Richard. **Yo**-Yo Ma. Chelsea House 2006 119p il (Asian Americans of achievement) lib bdg $30

Grades: 7 8 9 10   92
1. Chinese Americans 2. Cellists 3. Violoncellists 4. Classical musicians
ISBN 978-0-7910-9270-5 lib bdg; 0-7910-9270-4 lib bdg

LC 2006026335

A biography of the cellist
This is "well-researched . . . attractive . . . solid." SLJ
Includes glossary and bibliographical references

MacMillan, Donald, 1874-1970

Cowan, Mary Morton. **Captain** Mac: the life of Donald Baxter MacMillan, Arctic explorer. Calkins Creek 2010 208p il $17.95

Grades: 6 7 8 9   92
1. Explorers
ISBN 978-1-59078-709-0; 1-59078-709-9

LC 2009-36113

"This biography, written with obvious respect and admiration, covers the life and achievements of the Arctic explorer. . . . The author skillfully weaves primary-source quotes with short, action-oriented sentences. . . . This engaging biography is also a solid overview of an era of exploration that still captivates adventurous youths." SLJ
Includes bibliographical references

Madison, James, 1751-1836

Elish, Dan. **James** Madison; [by] Dan Elish. Marshall Cavendish Benchmark 2007 96p il (Presidents and their times) lib bdg $22.95

Grades: 5 6 7 8   92
1. Presidents 2. Members of Congress 3. Secretaries of state 4. Presidents -- United States
ISBN 978-0-7614-2432-1

LC 2006036856

A biography of the fourth president of the United States.
"Primary-source materials and quotes, helpful insets, and carefully selected . . . reproductions bring history to life and help make [this] clearly written [biography] highly readable." SLJ
Includes glossary and bibliographical references

Magellan, Ferdinand, 1480?-1521

Aretha, David. **Magellan**; first to circle the globe. Enslow Publishers 2009 112p il map (Great explorers of the world) lib bdg $31.93

Grades: 6 7 8 9   92
1. Explorers
ISBN 978-1-59845-097-2 lib bdg; 1-59845-097-2 lib bdg

LC 2008-13550

This "biography of Magellan reads like an adventure, detailing his life, while intriguing the reader with the danger and adversity surrounding his career. . . . Antique and current maps punctuate the text together with modern photographs and historic illustrations. The monumental implications of Magellan's life and voyage make this true adventure a winner." Libr Media Connect

Includes glosaary and bibliographical references

Koestler-Grack, Rachel A. **Ferdinand** Magellan. Chelsea House 2009 112p il map (Great explorers) lib bdg $30

Grades: 6 7 8 9   92

1. Explorers 2. Voyages around the world
ISBN 978-1-60413-422-3 lib bdg; 1-60413-422-4 lib bdg

LC 2009011587

Biography of the explorer Ferdinand Magellan

"The information . . . is presented in such a way as to attract and maintain readers' interest. . . . With a full complement of maps, photographs (where available), illustrations, time lines, and document reproductions, a full story is told. Well-written and throughly researched, this . . . will make a solid addition." SLJ

Includes glossary and bibliographical references

Malcolm X, 1925-1965

Burlingame, Jeff. **Malcolm** X. Enslow Publishers 2010 160p il lib bdg $34.60

Grades: 6 7 8 9   92

1. Black Muslims 2. Black Muslim leaders 3. Civil rights activists 4. African Americans -- Biography 5. African Americans -- Civil rights
ISBN 978-0-7660-3384-9; 0-7660-3384-8

LC 2009017597

In this biography the life of Malcolm X is "effectively explored to provide an understanding of [the] man's ideals, values, and perspectives on society as well as his reactions to pivotal events. . . . [The book] highlights the development of the human-rights activist's philosophy by exploring the impact of several childhood tragedies, causing him to question authority and to encourage others to do so as well. . . . [This title is] clear and concise and [includes] many images and descriptions of important events and people that [Malcolm X] interacted with and [was] impacted by." SLJ

Gunderson, Jessica. **X**: the biography of Malcolm X; illustrated by Seitu Hayden. Graphic Library 2011 32p il (Graphic library: American graphic) lib bdg $29.32; pa $7.95

Grades: 4 5 6 7   92

1. Black Muslims 2. Biographical graphic novels 3. Black Muslim leaders 4. Civil rights activists 5. African Americans -- Biography
ISBN 978-1-4296-5471-5 lib bdg; 1-4296-5471-6 lib bdg; 978-1-4296-6267-3 pa; 1-4296-6267-0 pa

LC 2010037029

In graphic novel format, explores the life and death of Malcolm X.

"The illustrations are eye-catching and the narration is presented simply, yet compellingly. . . . Fact-filled, entertaining, and accessible." SLJ

Includes glossary and bibliographical references

★ Sharp, Anne Wallace. **Malcolm** X and Black pride. Lucent Books 2010 104p il (Lucent library of black history) $32.45

Grades: 6 7 8 9   92

1. Black Muslims 2. Black Muslim leaders 3. Civil rights activists 4. African Americans -- Biography 5. African Americans -- Civil rights
ISBN 978-1-4205-0123-0; 1-4205-0123-2

LC 2009038463

This book takes "a frank, balanced, and compelling look at the man who was born Malcolm Little and whose furious insistence on equality for African Americans continues to both inspire and provoke controversy. . . . Supported by well-selected photos, extensive chapter notes, and further-reading suggestions, this is a strong choice for student research." Booklist

Includes bibliographical references

Mandela, Nelson

Catel, Patrick. **Nelson** Mandela. Heinemann Library 2010 112p il map (Front-page lives) $38.93

Grades: 6 7 8 9 10   92

1. Presidents 2. Political prisoners 3. Political leaders 4. Human rights activists 5. Nobel laureates for peace
ISBN 978-1-4329-3219-0; 1-4329-3219-5

LC 2009-18178

The life of South African President Nelson Mandela is "presented with depth and breadth. . . . The writing is accessible and engaging, with color and black-and-white photographs and . . . color maps complementing the text." SLJ

Includes glossary and bibliographical references

Keller, Bill. **Tree** shaker; the story of Nelson Mandela. Kingfisher 2008 128p il $17.95

Grades: 8 9 10 11 12   92

1. Presidents 2. Political prisoners 3. Political leaders 4. Human rights activists 5. Nobel laureates for peace
ISBN 978-0-7534-5992-8; 0-7534-5992-2

LC 2007-03559

The author "offers a balanced, thoughtful account of Mandela's political activism and accomplishments and his pivotal role in South Africa's modern history. . . . [The book is] packed with dramatic photos, swathes of paint, handprints and images of the African continent." Publ Wkly

Includes bibliographical references

★ Kramer, Ann. **Mandela**; the rebel who led his nation to freedom. National Geographic 2005 63p il (World history biographies) $17.95; lib bdg $27.90

Grades: 4 5 6 7   92

1. Presidents 2. Political prisoners 3. Political leaders 4. Human rights activists 5. Nobel laureates for peace
ISBN 0-7922-3658-0; 0-7922-3659-9 lib bdg

"This biography introduces readers not only to Mandela, but also to the political turmoil that affected South Africa for over a century. It begins with his birth, and covers his school years, his political ventures, imprisonment, release, presidency, Nobel Peace Prize, and retirement. Full-color photographs appear throughout and a time line runs along the bottom of each spread. . . . the book is well worth purchasing." SLJ

Includes glossary and bibliographical references

Manet, Édouard, 1832-1883

Spence, David. **Manet**. New Forest Press 2010 48p il (Great artists and their world) lib bdg $32.80

Grades: 6 7 8 9   **92**

1. Artists 2. Painters 3. Artists, French

ISBN 978-1-84898-313-7; 1-84898-313-1

"Offers biographical information [of Edouard Manet] . . . interspersed with art history and criticism in an eye-catching format. . . . [Includes] a long introductory paragraph and four-to-six images with explanatory notes. . . . Spence . . . does a good job of explaining why art that might seem ordinary today was revolutionary at the time of its creation." SLJ

Includes glossary

Mankiller, Wilma

Sonneborn, Liz. **Wilma** Mankiller. Marshall Cavendish Benchmark 2010 112p il (Leading women) $39.93

Grades: 5 6 7 8   **92**

1. Cherokee Indians 2. Indian chiefs

ISBN 978-0-7614-4959-1; 0-7614-4959-0

LC 2009029399

"The story of Mankiller's lifelong work for the Cherokee Nation and her role as its first female principal chief will absorb readers. The [woman's life is] revealed within the political and historical context of [her] times and [includes] quotes from autobiographical material. . . . Color and black-and-white photos are included. . . . The compact size, chronological organization, and accessible writing [style makes this biography a] good [resource] for reports." SLJ

Mao Zedong, 1893-1976

Heuston, Kimberley Burton. **Mao** Zedong; [by] Kimberley Heuston. Franklin Watts 2010 128p il map (Wicked history) lib bdg $30

Grades: 5 6 7 8   **92**

1. Heads of state 2. Communist leaders 3. Political leaders

ISBN 978-0-531-20756-7; 0-531-20756-0

LC 2009034157

"...short enough not to intimidate yet long enough to impart the enormity of the tyrant's atrocities. Opening with a description of Zedong's ruthlessness as an early revolutionary, Heuston follows him through the 82 years of his life, describing his devastating impact on China. Black-and-white photos, maps of Uganda and of China, time lines of the men's lives, and labeled webs showing their allies and enemies... make the books accessible." SLJ

Includes glossary and bibliographical references

Naden, Corinne J. **Mao** Zedong and the Chinese Revolution. Morgan Reynolds Pub. 2009 144p il map (World leaders) lib bdg $28.95

Grades: 7 8 9 10 11 12   **92**

1. Heads of state 2. Communist leaders 3. Political leaders

ISBN 978-1-59935-100-1; 1-59935-100-5

LC 2008-27829

This "discusses Chariman Mao Zedong's rise to power and his crucial role in national and international history. . . . Naden's analysis of the significant role of young people will draw YA readers for reports and for personal interest. The readable design, with clear type and lots of historic color photos as well as screens and detailed maps, includes spacious back matter." Booklist

Includes bibliographical references

Slavicek, Louise Chipley. **Mao** Zedong. Chelsea House 2004 116p il (Great military leaders of the 20th century) lib bdg $23.95

Grades: 6 7 8 9   **92**

1. Heads of state 2. Communist leaders 3. Political leaders 4. China -- History -- 1949-1976

ISBN 0-7910-7407-2

LC 2003-6929

A biography of Chinese leader Mao Zedong, discussing the battles that helped shape him and reasons behind his popularity among his countrymen

"Slavicek blends personal, philosophical, and historical information to trace Mao's journey to power. Clear accounts of the communist movement, the Long March, and the eventual battle with the Nationalists and Japanese are included." SLJ

Includes bibliographical references

Marconi, Guglielmo, 1874-1937

Zannos, Susan. **Guglielmo** Marconi and the story of radio waves. Mitchell Lane Publishers 2004 48p il (Uncharted, unexplored and unexplained) lib bdg $29.95

Grades: 6 7 8 9   **92**

1. Inventors 2. Telegraph 3. Radio -- History 4. Electrical engineers 5. Nobel laureates for physics

ISBN 978-1-58415-265-1 lib bdg; 1-58415-265-6 lib bdg

LC 2003-24133

Tells the story of Guglielmo Marconi and his invention of the wireless telegraph

Includes bibliographical references

Marley, Bob

★ Medina, Tony. **I** and I; Bob Marley. illustrated by Jesse Joshua Watson. Lee & Low Books 2009 un il $19.95

Grades: 4 5 6   **92**

1. Singers 2. Reggae musicians

ISBN 978-1-60060-257-3; 1-60060-257-6

LC 2008-33485

"In the words and rhythms of Jamaican patois, Medina's lyrical, direct lines make the most sense when read in tandem with the extensive appended notes. . . . Like the words, Watson's beautifully expressive acrylic paintings evoke a strong sense of Marley's remarkable life and his Caribbean homeland." Booklist

Includes bibliographical references

Miller, Calvin Craig. **Reggae** poet: the story of Bob Marley. Morgan Reynolds Pub. 2007 128p il $27.95

Grades: 7 8 9 10   **92**

1. Singers 2. Musicians 3. Reggae music 4. Reggae

musicians
ISBN 978-1-59935-071-4; 1-59935-071-8

LC 2007-27476

In this biography of the Jamaican musician "Miller does a fine job showing the effect the music and the politics had on each other. He also skillfully weaves in the complicated topic of the Rastaferian religion and the part ganja (marijuana) plays in it, and he doesn't hesitate when explaining Marley's complicated romantic life. The . . . photos are well chosen." Booklist

Includes bibliographical references

Paprocki, Sherry Beck. **Bob** Marley; musician. [by] Sherry Beck Paprocki. legacy ed.; Chelsea House 2006 111p il (Black Americans of achievement) lib bdg $30

Grades: 6 7 8 9   **92**

1. Singers 2. Musicians 3. Reggae music 4. Reggae musicians
ISBN 0-7910-9213-5

LC 2006004578

A biography of the Jamaican reggae musician.

The book goes "beyond the typical personal information to provide some social history revelant to the subject's time. Captioned photographs and boxed inserts enhance the conversational [text]." Horn Book Guide

Includes bibliographical references

Marquette, Jacques, 1637-1675

Harkins, Susan Sales. The **life** and times of Father Jacques Marquette; by Susan Sales Harkins and William H. Harkins. Mitchell Lane Publishers 2008 48p il (Profiles in American history) lib bdg $29.95

Grades: 6 7 8 9   **92**

1. Priests 2. Explorers 3. Missionaries
ISBN 978-1-58415-528-7; 1-58415-528-0

LC 2007000793

This is a biography of Father Jacques Marquette who, with his companion explorer Louis Jolliet, hoped to discover the Northwest Passage across North America in 1673.

This biography offers "a wealth of concise and well-organized information. . . . [The] book is fair and balanced and includes viewpoints from those who opposed or disagreed with [the subject's] accomplishments. The design is crisp and colorful without overwhelming the words on the page." SLJ

Includes bibliographical references

Marshall, Thurgood, 1908-1993

Crowe, Chris. **Thurgood** Marshall; a twentieth-century life. Viking 2008 248p il (Up close) $16.99

Grades: 6 7 8 9 10   **92**

1. Judges 2. Lawyers 3. Solicitors general 4. Civil rights activists 5. Supreme Court justices 6. African Americans -- Biography
ISBN 978-0-670-06228-7; 0-670-06228-6

LC 2007-042794

"This is a captivating portrait of a heroic champion of justice that also offers great insight into the most pivotal moments of the Civil Rights Movement." Kirkus

Marx, Karl, 1818-1883

Rossig, Wolfgang. **Karl** Marx. Morgan Reynolds 2009 112p il (Profiles in economics) lib bdg $28.95

Grades: 8 9 10   **92**

1. Philosophers 2. Writers on politics 3. Political and social philosophers
ISBN 978-1-59935-132-2; 1-59935-132-3

LC 2009-29563

"This book presents the life of Karl Marx and places his social and economic theories within the useful context of his youth in a prosperous German family. . . . [The author] provides a well-researched account of Marx's life and his work." Booklist

Includes bibliographical references

Matisse, Henri

★ Fillion, Susan. **Miss** Etta and Dr. Claribel; Bringing Matisse to America. David R. Godine 2011 83p il $18.95

Grades: 4 5 6 7   **92**

1. Artists 2. Painters 3. Physicians 4. Art collectors 5. Art -- Collectors and collecting
ISBN 978-1-56792-434-3; 1-56792-434-4

LC 2010048937

"An affectionate, lively examination of the reciprocal relationship between a great artist and two great art lovers. Etta and Claribel Cone, unmarried sisters from a wealthy Baltimore family . . . [were] discerning collectors of modern art, particularly that of Henri Matisse. . . . Their account is lavishly illustrated in full color by reproductions from the Cone Collection at the Baltimore Museum of Art and Matisse-inflected paintings by the author, who drew extensively on the Cone archive that is also housed at the museum. . . . This appealing work stands as both a portrait of two unconventional women and a celebration of the possibilties of arts patronage." Kirkus

Welton, Jude. **Henri** Matisse. Watts 2002 46p il (Artists in their time) $22; pa $6.95

Grades: 5 6 7 8   **92**

1. Artists 2. Painters 3. Artists, French 4. Artists -- France -- Biography
ISBN 0-531-12228-X; 0-531-16621-X pa

LC 2002-69106

Discusses the life and career of this French artist, describing and giving examples of his work

This offers a "clear and lively [text]. . . . Captioned, full-color and black-and-white photographs and art reproductions are liberally scattered throughout." SLJ

Mawson, Douglas Sir, 1882-1958

Bredeson, Carmen. **After** the last dog died; the true-life, hair-raising adventure of Douglas Mawson and his 1912 Antarctic Expedition. National Geographic 2003 63p il map $18.95

Grades: 5 6 7 8   **92**

1. Explorers 2. Geologists 3. Mountaineers 4. Antarctica
ISBN 0-7922-6140-2

LC 2003-0756

Describes the life and career of the Australian explorer, Sir Douglas Mawson, focusing on his 1912 scientific expedition to Antarctica

"Bredson's compelling story of courage and survival draws heavily on quotes from Mawson and other primary source documents; there are also charts, maps, and many photographs." Booklist

McCain, John S., 1936-

Robinson, Tom. **John** McCain; POW & statesman. ABDO Pub. 2010 112p il map (Military heroes) lib bdg $22.95

Grades: 7 8 9   92

1. Prisoners of war 2. Senators 3. Members of Congress 4. Presidential candidates 5. Politicians -- United States

ISBN 978-1-60453-963-9; 1-60453-963-1

LC 2009-32369

"The rush of literary adrenalin will hook readers immediately and keep them enthralled until the end. . . . Given the dynamic topic [and] . . . appealing layout . . . [this is] likely to attract reluctant readers. In addition, sources are plentiful and well documented." SLJ

Includes glossary and bibliographical references

McCarthy, Joseph, 1908-1957

★ Giblin, James Cross, 1933- The **rise** and fall of Senator Joe McCarthy; [by] James Cross Giblin. Clarion Books 2009 294p il $22.00

Grades: 8 9 10 11 12   92

1. Anticommunist movements 2. Senators

ISBN 0-618-61058-8; 978-0-618-61058-7

LC 2009015005

Giblin examines the life of Joseph Mccarthy, the junior senator from Wisconsin. The book "discusses the Cold War tensions that shaped his beliefs and the unconstitutional methods he used to further his ends." (Publisher's note)

"YAs will see the contemporary parallels in this biography of the anti-Communist crusader who rose to power over 50 years ago. . . . Giblin's title, formatted with an open, photo-filled design and written in easy, direct style, makes no superficial connections, and the afterword, 'Another McCarthy?' will prompt discussion about the accusations of terrorism in the aftermath of 9/11. Just as memorable is the scathing commentary from famous journalist Edward Murrow about the differences between dissent and disloyalty." Booklist

Includes bibliographical references

McCartney, Stella

Aldridge, Rebecca. **Stella** McCartney. Chelsea House 2011 112p il (Famous fashion designers) lib bdg $35

Grades: 6 7 8 9 10   92

1. Fashion designers

ISBN 978-1-60413-982-2; 1-60413-982-X

LC 2010033972

A biography of fashion designer Stella McCartney.

"Biography collections in need of a bit of sprucing up should find [this title] helpful." SLJ

Includes glossary and bibliographical references

McClintock, Barbara

Cullen, J. Heather. **Barbara** McClintock, geneticist. Chelsea House 2003 122p il (Women in science) lib bdg $22.95

Grades: 7 8 9 10   92

1. Genetics 2. Women scientists 3. Geneticists 4. Nobel laureates for physiology or medicine 5. Women geneticists -- United States -- Biography

ISBN 0-7910-7248-7

LC 2002-15549

Presents the life and career of the geneticist who in 1983 was awarded the Nobel Prize for her study of maize cells

This is "well written and well organized." SLJ

Includes bibliographical references

Spangenburg, Ray. **Barbara** McClintock; pioneering geneticist. by Ray Spangenburg and Diane Kit Moser. Chelsea House 2008 xxi, 136p il (Makers of modern science) $29.95

Grades: 8 9 10 11 12   92

1. Genetics 2. Women scientists 3. Geneticists 4. Nobel laureates for physiology or medicine

ISBN 978-0-8160-6172-3; 0-8160-6172-6

LC 2006032356

A biography of the Nobel Prize winning geneticist.

Includes glossary and bibliographical references

Mead, Margaret, 1901-1978

Margaret Mead; coming of age in America. [by] Joan Mark. Oxford Univ. Press 1998 110p il (Oxford portraits in science) $28

Grades: 7 8 9 10   92

1. Anthropologists 2. Curators 3. Writers on science 4. Ethnology -- Melanesia 5. Women anthropologists -- United States -- Biography

ISBN 0-19-511679-8

LC 98-18604

An "account of the life and works of the influential, pioneering anthropologist. . . . Mark does a fine job of abstracting Mead's research and published works and showing why they were both critically acclaimed and criticized. The reader-friendly prose is peppered with fascinating anecdotes and photos. Mead herself is presented as a complex, intriguing figure, with fascinating, often contradictory, public and private lives." Booklist

Includes bibliographical references

Meir, Golda, 1898-1978

Blashfield, Jean F. **Golda** Meir. Marshall Cavendish Benchmark 2010 112p il (Leading women) $39.93

Grades: 5 6 7 8   92

1. Diplomats 2. Prime ministers 3. Women politicians 4. Cabinet members 5. Jews -- Biography

ISBN 978-0-7614-4960-7; 0-7614-4960-4

"Meir survived pogroms in Russia as a child and became prime minister of Israel. . . . The [woman's life is] revealed within the political and historical context of [her] times and [includes] quotes from autobiographical material. . . . Color and black-and-white photos are included. . . . The compact size, chronological organization, and accessible writing [style makes this biography a] good [resource] for reports." SLJ

Includes bibliographical references

Meltzer, Milton, 1915-2009

★ Meltzer, Milton. **Milton** Meltzer; writing matters. Franklin Watts 2004 160p il lib bdg $29

Grades: 7 8 9 10   **92**

1. Authors 2. Historians 3. Biographers 4. Authors, American 5. Children's authors 6. Nonfiction writers

ISBN 0-531-12257-3

LC 2004-2947

"The author includes clear, interesting explanations about the American historical and economic events that influenced his life. While this book is a pleasure to read for general interest, it would also supplement units on American history." SLJ

Includes bibliographical references

Menchú, Rigoberta

Kallen, Stuart A. **Rigoberta** Menchu, Indian rights activist; by Stuart A. Kallen. Lucent Books 2007 104p il (The 20th century's most influential Hispanics) $31.20

Grades: 6 7 8 9   **92**

1. Mayas 2. Memoirists 3. Indian leaders 4. Human rights activists 5. Nobel laureates for peace 6. Native Americans -- Civil rights

ISBN 1-59018-975-2

LC 2006025690

Presents the life and accomplishments of the human rights activist who won the Noble Peace Prize in 1992 for her work to stop the oppression of her people, the Mayas of Guatemala.

This is a "stirring biography. . . . The selection of photos and captions enhance the text." SLJ

Includes bibliographical references

Mendel, Gregor, 1822-1884

Van Gorp, Lynn. **Gregor** Mendel; genetics pioneer. science contributor, Sally Ride Science. Compass Point Books 2008 40p il (Mission: Science) lib bdg $26.60

Grades: 4 5 6   **92**

1. Genetics 2. Scientists 3. Geneticists 4. Genetics -- History

ISBN 978-0-7565-3963-4 lib bdg; 0-7565-3963-3 lib bdg

LC 2008-07725

A biography of scientist Gregor Mendel, with an introduction to the principles of genetics

This "will entice students to become excited about an assignment or just satisfy their own curiosity. . . . The text . . . does a good job of connecting the scientist's work to our lives today. . . . [The] book has a variety of graphics including diagrams, [and] photos." Libr Media Connect

Mendes, Chico

Murphy, Alexa Gordon. **Chico** Mendes. Chelsea House 2011 126p il (Conservation heroes) lib bdg $35

Grades: 6 7 8 9   **92**

1. Rubber 2. Rain forests 3. Conservationists 4. Social activists

ISBN 978-1-60413-951-8; 1-60413-951-X

LC 2010030590

A biography of the Brazilian rubber tapper, trade union leader and environmentalist who fought to preserve the Amazon rainforest

"Captivating, richly informative. . . . The scope of [this book] is comprehensive. . . . [The book is] engaging as [it is] educational and will be ideal for research and reports." SLJ

Includes glossary and bibliographical references

Mercator, Gerardus, 1512-1594

Heinrichs, Ann. **Gerardus** Mercator; father of modern mapmaking. by Ann Heinrichs. Compass Point Books 2008 112p il map (Signature lives) lib bdg $31.93

Grades: 6 7 8 9   **92**

1. Maps 2. Cartographers

ISBN 978-0-7565-3312-0 lib bdg; 0-7565-3312-0 lib bdg

LC 2007004902

A biography of the sixteenth-century geographer who created a world map in 1569 which introduced a new way of showing the spherical earth on a flat sheet of paper.

"Clear explanations of scientific thought and fact are presented in conversational tones and illuminated by easily grasped examples. . . . [The book includes] sidebars, maps, and well-captioned illustrations." SLJ

Includes glossary and bibliographical references

Mexia, Ynes, 1870-1938

Anema, Durlynn. **Ynes** Mexia, botanist and adventurer; [by] Durlynn Anema. 1st ed; Morgan Reynolds Pub. 2005 144p il (Women adventurers) lib bdg $26.95

Grades: 6 7 8 9   **92**

1. Botanists 2. Explorers 3. Women scientists 4. Mexican Americans -- Biography

ISBN 1-931798-67-2; 978-1-931798-67-9

LC 2005010694

A biography of the botanist who traveled on expeditions throughout South America and Mexico during the 1920s and collected over 500 new plant species.

"An interesting and colorful look at a Mexican-American scientist. The easy-to-read narrative draws on the woman's correspondences." SLJ

Includes bibliographical references

Meyer, Stephenie, 1973-

★ Krohn, Katherine E. **Stephenie** Meyer; dreaming of Twilight. Twenty-First Century Books 2010 112p il (USA Today: lifeline biographies) lib bdg $33.26

Grades: 7 8 9 10 11 12   **92**

1. Authors 2. Novelists 3. Women authors 4. Authors, American

ISBN 978-0-7613-5220-4; 0-7613-5220-1

LC 2010-1425

This book, which profiles "the author of the Twilight series, will certainly attract readers. The fascinating story of where Meyer's initial idea came from (a dream) will intrigue, while the twists and turns it took to get the first book published should be edifying. In a nice bit of balance, the book gives Meyer's critics a voice too." Booklist

Michelangelo Buonarroti, 1475-1564

Spence, David. **Michelangelo**; [written by David Spence]; editor Guy Croton. North American ed.; New Forest Press 2010 48p il map (Great artists & their world) lib bdg $32.80

Grades: 6 7 8 9   92

1. Artists 2. Painters 3. Sculptors 4. Architects 5. Artists, Italian 6. Art -- 15th and 16th centuries

ISBN 978-1-84898-309-0; 1-84898-309-3

LC 2010925210

Explores the world, art, and life of the great Italian artist. Includes glossary and bibliographical references

★ Stanley, Diane. **Michelangelo**. HarperCollins Pubs. 2000 un il $18.99; pa $6.99

Grades: 4 5 6 7   92

1. Artists 2. Painters 3. Sculptors 4. Architects 5. Renaissance 6. Artists, Italian

ISBN 0-688-15085-3; 0-06-052113-9 pa

A biography of the Renaissance sculptor, painter, architect, and poet, well known for his work on the Sistine Chapel in Rome's St. Peter's Cathedral

This is "as readable as it is useful. . . . Integrating Michelangelo's art with Stanley's watercolor, gouache, and colored-pencil figures and settings has the desired effect: readers will be dazzled with the master's ability, while at the same time pulled into his daily life and struggles." SLJ

Includes bibliographical references

Milk, Harvey

Aretha, David. **No** compromise: the story of Harvey Milk. Morgan Reynolds 2010 128p il (Civil rights leaders) lib bdg $28.95

Grades: 7 8 9 10 11 12   92

1. Gay rights activists 2. Gay men -- Civil rights 3. Local government officials

ISBN 1-59935-129-3; 978-1-59935-129-2

LC 2009-25708

This is a biography of the gay-rights activist and San Francisco politician who was killed in 1973.

This is written "with simple and engaging prose. . . . Full-color and black-and-white photos are interspersed thoughout, giving a sense of the time period." SLJ

Miller, Arthur, 1915-2005

Andersen, Richard. **Arthur** Miller. Marshall Cavendish Benchmark 2005 144p il (Writers and their works) lib bdg $25.95

Grades: 7 8 9 10   92

1. Authors 2. Dramatists 3. Screenwriters 4. Authors, American

ISBN 0-7614-1946-2

This "attractive, well-organized [book fills] a gap in literary criticism for intermediate readers. Heavily illustrated

with color and black-and-white photographs, [it] will appeal to students who might be intimidated by longer or more scholarly titles." SLJ

Mitchell, Maria, 1818-1889

Anderson, Dale. **Maria** Mitchell, astronomer. Chelsea House 2003 110p il (Women in science) $22.95

Grades: 7 8 9 10   92

1. Astronomers 2. Women astronomers 3. College teachers 4. Astronomers -- United States -- Biography

ISBN 0-7910-7249-5

LC 2002-13738

Profiles a Vassar professor who was one of the most famous astronomers in the United States at the end of the nineteenth century and whose central message to her students was never cease to wonder

"Color prints or photographs with brief descriptions are interspersed throughout and add considerably to the [text]." Libr Media Connect

Includes bibliographical references

Gormley, Beatrice. **Maria** Mitchell; the soul of an astronomer. [by] Beatrice Gormley. Eerdmans Books for Young Readers 2004 137p il pa $12

Grades: 7 8 9 10   92

1. Astronomers 2. Women astronomers 3. College teachers

ISBN 978-0-8028-5264-9 pa; 0-8028-5264-5 pa

First published 1995

A biography of the first female science professor at Vassar College and the first American woman astronomer

"With a smoothly flowing and lively style, this biography introduces readers to the 19th-century astronomer. Well-chosen, primary-source quotations and quality black-and-white photos add authenticity to the text, and contribute greatly to the author's objective and comprehensive description of Mitchell's accomplishments." SLJ [review of 1995 edition]

Includes bibliographical references

Mizrahi, Isaac

Petrillo, Lisa. **Isaac** Mizrahi. Morgan Reynolds Pub. 2011 111p il $28.95

Grades: 7 8 9 10   92

1. Fashion designers 2. Television personalities 3. Talk show hosts

ISBN 978-1-59935-152-0; 1-59935-152-8

LC 2010018312

This biography of Isaac Mizrahi discusses "the designer's cultural background, childhood, family, work history and education. The [author describes] the early influences that inspired the [designer] to pursue this career and [provides] details of the philosophy [the] designer uses to make [his] clothing unique. . . . The writing is clear and well organized. Color photos are included and give readers a feel for the time period and the types of clothing and accessories the [designer] created." Voice Youth Advocates

Includes bibliographical references

Mohapatra, Jyotirmayee, 1978-

Woog, Adam. **Jyotirmayee** Mohapatra; by Adam Woog. KidHaven Press 2006 48p il $24.95

Grades: 4 5 6 7   **92**

1. Social action 2. Feminists 3. Women -- India 4. Children's rights advocates

ISBN 0-7377-3611-9

LC 2006009121

"Mohapatra grew up in a rural village in India and became a leader in the fight for the rights of girls and women. . . . The power of one individual to inspire others to action is clearly expressed in this well-written profile. Full-color photos and a map enhance the presentation." SLJ

Includes bibliographical references

Molnar, Haya Leah

Molnar, Haya Leah. **Under** a red sky; memoir of a childhood in Communist Romania. Farrar Straus Giroux 2010 302p il $17.99

Grades: 6 7 8 9 10   **92**

1. Copywriters 2. Jews -- Romania 3. Advertising executives

ISBN 978-0-374-31840-6; 0-374-31840-9

LC 2008055562

"Molnar began life as Eva Zimmerman . . . in Bucharest, Romania. . . . It came as a huge shock to Molnar when she learned in 1958 that her entire family had applied to emigrate to Israel and that she was Jewish. . . . As Eva pieces together her family's history, a vivid story emerges, ranging from funny, tender moments of family life to the horrific revelations of the Romanian holocaust. . . . Black-and-white family photos illustrate this poignant, memorable offering." Booklist

Monet, Claude, 1840-1926

Kallen, Stuart A. **Claude** Monet. Lucent Books 2009 112p il (Eye on art) lib bdg $32.45

Grades: 7 8 9 10   **92**

1. Artists 2. Painters 3. Artists, French 4. Impressionism (Art)

ISBN 978-1-4205-0074-5; 1-4205-0074-0

LC 2008-20640

An introduction to the life and career of the artist Claude Monet, and how he painted his way into history.

"This biography paints a clear picture of the artist's life, work, and legacy. . . . The accompanying color reproductions of the artworks and black-and-white photographs of Monet contribute to the book's clean and attractive design. . . . This work stands out as a balanced description of the man's legacy and an enjoyable read." SLJ

Includes glossary and bibliographical references

Spence, David. **Monet**. New Forest Press 2010 48p il (Great artists and their world) lib bdg $32.80

Grades: 6 7 8 9   **92**

1. Artists 2. Painters 3. Artists, French

ISBN 978-1-848983-12-0; 1-848983-12-3

"This slender title offers a thorough introduction to Oscar Claude Monet, who, before helping to found the French Impressionist movement, was known for his sharp-eyed, witty caricature drawings. . . . The spreads cover a wide range of topics, all presented in short paragraphs and long

captions that accompany the multiple, mostly well-reproduced artwork and archival photos on every page." Booklist

Monroe, James, 1758-1831

Naden, Corinne J. **James** Monroe; [by] Corinne J. Naden and Rose Blue. Marshall Cavendish Benchmark 2009 96p il map (Presidents and their times) lib bdg $34.21

Grades: 5 6 7 8   **92**

1. Presidents 2. Secretaries of state 3. Presidents -- United States

ISBN 978-0-7614-2838-1 lib bdg; 0-7614-2838-0 lib bdg

LC 2007-29480

"Provides comprehensive information on President James Monroe and places him within his historical and cultural context. Also explored are the formative events of his times and how he responded." Publisher's note

Includes glossary and bibliographical references

Mora, Pat

Marcovitz, Hal. **Pat** Mora; [by] Hal Marcovitz; forward by Kyle Zimmer. Chelsea House 2008 134p il (Who wrote that?) $30

Grades: 6 7 8 9   **92**

1. Poets 2. Authors 3. Women authors 4. Mexican American authors 5. Essayists 6. Poets, American 7. College teachers 8. Children's authors 9. Young adult authors 10. Museum administrators 11. College administrators 12. Mexican Americans -- Biography

ISBN 978-0-7910-9528-7; 0-7910-9528-2

LC 2007019452

This biography examines the "writer's life, including the inspiration behind some of [her] works. [The] volume includes photographs and quotations from interviews, as well as descriptions of main characters and annotated lists of books and awards. Useful for aspiring authors as well as book report writers." Horn Book Guide

Includes bibliographical references

Mowat, Farley

Mowat, Farley. **Born** naked. Houghton Mifflin 1994 256p il maps hardcover o.p. pa $13

Grades: 7 8 9 10   **92**

1. Authors 2. Historians 3. Naturalists 4. Authors, Canadian 5. Ethnologists 6. Children's authors 7. Nonfiction writers

ISBN 0-395-73528-9

LC 93-23702

First published 1993 in Canada

"There are no dull pages here; every man, woman, child, and animal mentioned even casually makes an impression. . . . Highly recommended to all those who like good writing." Libr J

Mozart, Wolfgang Amadeus, 1756-1791

Riggs, Kate. **Wolfgang** Amadeus Mozart. Creative Education 2009 48p il (Xtraordinary artists) lib bdg $32.80

Grades: 4 5 6 7   **92**
1. Composers
ISBN 978-1-58341-664-8 lib bdg; 1-58341-664-1
lib bdg

LC 2007008963

This biography of the composer offers an "interesting [layout]; big, high-quality reproductions and photographs on heavy paper; insightful quotes from diverse sources; and meaty selections of the artist's own writing . . . at the end of the book. Readers get a strong sense of [Mozart's] personality along with an excellent survey of his work." SLJ

Includes bibliographical references

Weeks, Marcus. **Mozart**; the boy who changed the world with his music. [by] Marcus Weeks. National Geographic 2007 64p il map (World history biographies) $17.95; lib bdg $27.90
Grades: 5 6 7 8   **92**
1. Composers
ISBN 978-1-4263-0002-8; 1-4263-0002-6; 978-1-4263-0003-5 lib bdg; 1-4263-0003-4 lib bdg

LC 2006020783

An introduction to the life and music of the composer and musician Mozart.

This "visually appealing [title is] packed with excellent photographs and reproductions, interesting sidebars, and have a time line running along the bottom of every page. . . . [The book is] useful, well-written." SLJ

Includes bibliographical references

Mozes, Miriam, 1935-1993
Kor, Eva Mozes. **Surviving** the Angel of Death; the story of a Mengele twin in Auschwitz. [by] Eva Mozes Kor and Lisa Rojany Buccieri. Tanglewood Pub. 2009 141p il map $14.95
Grades: 7 8 9 10   **92**
1. Twins 2. Holocaust survivors 3. Jews -- Hungary 4. Jews -- Persecutions 5. Holocaust, 1933-1945 -- Personal narratives
ISBN 978-1-933718-28-6; 1-933718-28-5

LC 2009-9494

"Born in 1934, Eva and her identical twin, Miriam, were loved and doted over. They lived a comfortable and happy life on their family's farm in Transylvania until the summer of 1940, when their family was herded onto a train with the other Jews in their town and transported to Auschwitz supposedly for their 'protection.' . . . They soon joined a large group of other twins who were under the care of Dr. Josef Mengele, otherwise known as the Angel of Death. . . . Eva's story will have the reader hooked until the very end. . . . This book is an essential purchase for libraries with a Holocaust collection, but it would also be a valuable addition to any library with young impressionable readers." Voice Youth Advocates

Muir, John, 1838-1914
Goldstein, Natalie. **John** Muir. Chelsea House 2011 139p il (Conservation heroes) lib bdg $35
Grades: 6 7 8 9   **92**
1. Authors 2. Naturalists 3. Conservationists 4.

Nature conservation 5. Writers on nature
ISBN 978-1-60413-945-7; 1-60413-945-5

LC 2010030582

This is a biography of naturalist John Muir, who founded the Sierra Club and helped save forest areas in the American West.

"Captivating, richly informative. . . . The scope of [this book] is comprehensive. . . . [The book is] engaging as [it is] educational and will be ideal for research and reports." SLJ

Includes glossary and bibliographical references

Naden, Corinne J. **John** Muir; saving the wilderness. [by] Corinne J. Naden and Rose Blue. Millbrook Press 1992 48p il (Gateway biography) hardcover o.p. pa $9.95
Grades: 4 5 6 7   **92**
1. Authors 2. Naturalists 3. Nature conservation 4. Writers on nature
ISBN 1-56294-797-4 pa

LC 91-18106

This book profiles the life and times of naturalist John Muir

"Attractively designed with clear framed text and lots of photographs. . . . Kids will be intrigued by Muir's work for conservation, especially his role in founding the national parks." Booklist

Includes bibliographical references

Munch, Edvard, 1863-1944
Whiting, Jim. **Edvard** Munch; by Jim Whiting. Mitchell Lane 2009 48p il (Art profiles for kids) lib bdg $20.95
Grades: 7 8 9 10   **92**
1. Artists 2. Painters 3. Artists, Norwegian
ISBN 978-1-58415-712-0; 1-58415-712-7

LC 2008-2250

"The profile of Munch explains how the artist attempted to convey his deep feelings of anxiety in his paintings. . . . [Goes] beyond basic facts, providing historical context and significance of the art and the artist. . . . Provide[s] plenty of information for reports in a reader-friendly format." SLJ

Includes glossary and bibliographical references

Murakami, Haruki, 1949-
Mussari, Mark. **Haruki** Murakami. Marshall Cavendish Benchmark 2010 127p il (Today's writers and their works) lib bdg $42.79
Grades: 8 9 10 11 12   **92**
1. Authors 2. Novelists 3. Authors, Japanese 4. Nonfiction writers 5. Short story writers
ISBN 978-0-7614-4124-3; 0-7614-4124-7

This biography of Haruki Murakami places the author in the context of his times and discusses his work.

Includes bibliographical references

Myers, Walter Dean, 1937-
Sickels, Amy. **Walter** Dean Myers; [by] Amy Sickels. Chelsea House 2008 128p il (Who wrote that?) $30
Grades: 6 7 8 9   **92**
1. Poets 2. Authors 3. Novelists 4. African American

authors 5. Editors 6. Authors, American 7. Children's authors 8. Young adult authors
ISBN 978-0-7910-9524-9; 0-7910-9524-X

LC 2007045507

This biography examines the "writer's life, including the inspiration behind some if [his] works. [The] volume includes photographs and quotations from interviews, as well as descriptions of main characters and annotated lists of books and awards. Useful for aspiring authors as well as book report writers." Horn Book Guide

Includes bibliographical references

Nakahama, Manjiro, 1827-1898

★ Blumberg, Rhoda. **Shipwrecked!**: the true adventures of a Japanese boy. HarperCollins Pubs. 2000 80p il map hardcover o.p. pa $7.99
Grades: 5 6 7 8   **92**
1. Survival after airplane accidents, shipwrecks, etc. 2. Interpreters 3. Japanese -- United States 4. Shipwreck victims -- Japan
ISBN 0-688-17484-1; 0-688-17485-X pa

LC 99-86664

In 1841, rescued by an American whaler after a terrible shipwreck leaves him and his four companions castaways on a remote island, fourteen-year-old Manjiro learns new laws and customs as he becomes the first Japanese person to set foot in the United States

"Exemplary in both her research and writing, Blumberg hooks readers with anecdotes that astonish without sensationalizing, and she uses language that's elegant and challenging, yet always clear. Particularly notable is the well-chosen reproductions of original artwork." Booklist

Includes bibliographical references

Napoleon I, Emperor of the French, 1769-1821

Burleigh, Robert. **Napoleon**; the story of the little corporal. Abrams Books for Young Readers 2007 43p il map $18.95
Grades: 4 5 6 7   **92**
1. Emperors
ISBN 978-0-8109-1378-3; 0-8109-1378-X

LC 2006-23610

"Burleigh's straightforward style and clear focus make accessible this account of the rapid rise and fall of the skilled military leader and emperor of France. The period artwork, accompanied by helpful captions, enhances the cleanly designed presentation." Horn Book Guide

Nefertiti, Queen, consort of Akhenaton, King of Egypt, 14th cent. B.C.

Lange, Brenda. **Nefertiti**. Chelsea House Publishers 2009 108p il (Ancient world leaders) lib bdg $30
Grades: 6 7 8 9   **92**
1. Queens
ISBN 978-0-7910-9581-2 lib bdg; 0-7910-9581-9 lib bdg

LC 2008004869

This biography of Nefertiti "deals less with the specifics of the [ancient Egyptian queen] and more with [her world] and times, including religious and political issues. The [author uses] speculation, derived from both tradition and

scholarship, as to who [this] ancient [leader] may have been and how [she] might have governed." SLJ

Includes bibliographical references

Neruda, Pablo, 1904-1973

Delano, Poli. **When** I was a boy Neruda called me Policarpo; illustrated by Manuel Monroy. Groundwood Books/House of Anansi Press 2006 84p il $15.95
Grades: 5 6 7 8   **92**
1. Poets 2. Authors 3. Diplomats 4. Novelists 5. Poets, Chilean 6. Memoirists 7. Short story writers 8. Nobel laureates for peace 9. Nobel laureates for literature
ISBN 0-88899-726-4

In this book, the author "offers seven vignettes, interspersed with six of Neruda's . . . poems and biographical information, to give middle-grade readers a sense of what it was like to grow up in the constant presence of a kindly, though spoiled and eccentric, celebrity. . . . Grades four to six." (MultiCult Rev)

"Based on the author's childhood remembrances of when he and his diplomat parents lived with Tío Pablo [Neruda] in Mexico, these seven chapters reveal both the genius and the eccentricities of the Nobel Prize-winning Chilean poet. . . . The chapters are short, well written, and filled with interesting details that will open up a new and exotic world. . . . Monroy's pen-and-sepia-toned drawings are . . . at times humorous, at times dramatic, but always enticing." SLJ

Newton, Isaac Sir, 1642-1727

Boerst, William J. **Isaac** Newton; organizing the universe. Morgan Reynolds Pub. 2004 144p il (Renaissance scientists) lib bdg $23.95
Grades: 7 8 9 10   **92**
1. Physicists 2. Scientists 3. Mathematicians 4. Writers on science 5. Physicists -- Great Britain -- Biography
ISBN 1-931798-01-X

LC 2003-14571

"Boerst describes Newton's life from his premature birth through an isolated adulthood dominated by study and experimentation to his death at the age of 84. The author deftly explores his subject's accomplishments in relation to the scientific community and notable historical events of the time and includes information concerning his religious views. . . . This well-written book makes an excellent choice for teens exploring scientists or just looking for a good biography." SLJ

Includes bibliographical references

Hollihan, Kerrie Logan. **Isaac** Newton and physics for kids; his life and ideas with 21 activities. Chicago Review Press 2009 131p il map pa $16.95
Grades: 4 5 6 7   **92**
1. Physicists 2. Scientists 3. Mathematicians 4. Writers on science
ISBN 978-1-55652-778-4 pa; 1-55652-778-0 pa

LC 2008048635

"Hollihan introduces readers to the scientific brilliance, as well as the social isolation, of this giant figure, blending a readable narrative with an attractive format that incorporates maps, diagrams, historical photographs, and physics activities." Booklist

Includes bibliographical references

★ Krull, Kathleen. **Isaac** Newton; illustrated by Boris Kulikov. Viking 2006 126p il (Giants of science) $15.99

Grades: 5 6 7 8   **92**
1. Physicists 2. Scientists 3. Mathematicians 4. Writers on science
ISBN 0-670-05921-8

LC 2005017741

This "profiles Sir Isaac Newton, the secretive, obsessive, and brilliant English scientist who invented calculus, built the first reflecting telescope, developed the modern scientific method, and discerned many of our laws of physics and optics. . . . The lively, conversational style will appeal to readers. . . . Kulikov's humorous pen-and-ink drawings complement the lighthearted text of this fascinating introduction." Booklist

Steele, Philip. **Isaac** Newton; the scientist who changed everything. [by] Philip Steele. National Geographic Society 2007 64p il map (World history biographies) $17.95; lib bdg $27.90

Grades: 4 5 6 7   **92**
1. Physicists 2. Scientists 3. Mathematicians 4. Writers on science
ISBN 978-1-4263-0114-8; 978-1-4263-0115-5 lib bdg
LC 2006020772

"The cradle-to-grave text includes vivid descriptions of Newton's youth. . . . The dynamic format is a draw; numerous mostly archival images . . . and a time-line border add interest and cultural context on each spacious page." Booklist

Includes bibliographical references

Nezahualcóyotl, King of Texcoco, 1402-1472

★ Serrano, Francisco. The **poet** king of Tezcoco; a great leader of Ancient Mexico. illustrated by Pablo Serrano; biography translated and adapted by Trudy Balch; poetry translated by Jo Anne Engelbert. Groundwood Books/House of Anansi Press 2007 35p il $18.95

Grades: 4 5 6 7   **92**
1. Aztecs 2. Kings
ISBN 978-0-88899-787-6; 0-88899-787-6

"In the fifteenth century, the land where Mexico City now sprawls was a vast, green kingdom called Tezcoco. This . . . introduces one of Tezcoco's greatest rulers, a Toltec royal named Nezahualcoyotl. . . . The folk-art inspired illustrations echo the area's artistic traditions with beautiful patterning and symbolic imagery and flat , simplified characters reminiscent of hieroglyphics. Groundbreaking in its coverage of exciting history, this book offers details that are rarely presented to young people." Booklist

Nixon, Richard M. (Richard Milhous), 1913-1994

★ Aronson, Billy. **Richard** M. Nixon; [by] Billy Aronson. Marshall Cavendish Benchmark 2007 96p il (Presidents and their times) lib bdg $22.95

Grades: 5 6 7 8   **92**
1. Presidents 2. Vice-presidents 3. Senators 4. Nonfiction writers 5. Members of Congress 6. Presidents -- United States
ISBN 978-0-7614-2428-4

LC 2006013839

Aronson "is able to paint a picture so full that readers will come away feeling that they know the man and understand at least some of the forces that shaped him. . . . The narrative moves chronologically, marching through the war years, Nixon's tenure in Congress and as vice-president, his presidential loss to JFK, his successful efforts to remake himself as a politician, and his years as president. . . . The typeface is clear, the photographs are well chosen." Booklist

Includes glossary and bibliographical references

Barron, Rachel. **Richard** Nixon; American politician. rev ed.; Morgan Reynolds 2004 128p il (Notable Americans) lib bdg $24.95

Grades: 7 8 9 10   **92**
1. Presidents 2. Vice-presidents 3. Senators 4. Nonfiction writers 5. Members of Congress 6. Presidents -- United States
ISBN 1-93179-830-3 lib bdg; 978-1-93179-830-3 lib bdg
LC 2003-27425

First published 1998

"A comprehensive portrait of the statesman's political career and personal life. . . . Barron is objective about her subject, giving him credit for his considerable successes and holding him responsible for his failures." SLJ [review of 1998 edition]

Includes bibliographical references

Noguchi, Isamu, 1904-1988

Tiger, Caroline. **Isamu** Noguchi. Chelsea House 2007 112p il (Asian Americans of achievement) lib bdg $30

Grades: 6 7 8 9   **92**
1. Artists 2. Sculptors 3. Industrial designers 4. Japanese Americans -- Biography
ISBN 0-7910-9276-3 lib bdg; 978-0-7910-9276-7 lib bdg
LC 2006026230

A biography of the artist, born in 1904 to an American mother and a Japanese poet father, who created sculpture, furniture, stage sets, and public gardens.

"This engaging account of the prolific and diverse artist will add depth to any biography collection." SLJ

Includes bibliographical references

Nuñez Cabeza de Vaca, Alvar, 16th cent.

Childress, Diana. **Barefoot** conquistador; Cabeza de Vaca and the struggle for Native American rights. Twenty-First Century Books 2008 160p il map lib bdg $30.60

Grades: 7 8 9 10   **92**
1. Explorers 2. Historians 3. Travel writers 4. Government officials 5. Colonial administrators
ISBN 978-0-8225-7517-7; 0-8225-7517-5

LC 2007-22059

"This clearly written biography introduces a 16th-century Spanish explorer who made two expeditions to North and South America and eventually became a champion for Native Americans. . . . Childress's well-researched, lively text will fascinate readers. . . . The pages are sprinkled with period illustrations and maps." SLJ

Includes bibliographical references

Lourie, Peter. **On** the Texas trail of Cabeza de Vaca; 1st ed.; Boyds Mills Press 2008 48p il map $17.95

Grades: 4 5 6 7   92

1. Explorers 2. Historians 3. Travel writers 4. Government officials 5. Colonial administrators

ISBN 978-1-59078-492-1; 1-59078-492-8

LC 2007049180

"In 1527, Governor Pánfilo de Narváez sailed westward from Spain to explore the land that stretched between present-day Florida and Mexico, colonizing and conquering. With him, as his treasurer and sheriff, was Cabeza de Vaca. . . . He [returned] with a wealth of information, codified in La Relación , his account of his experience. Then, 475 years later, Lourie set out to follow Cabeza de Vaca's trail through Texas. . . . This well-researched, beautifully composed book is the result. Using primary sources and period reproductions as well as the author's experiences and contemporary pictures, it highlights historical information within the context of current circumstances. Beautifully placed photos, reproductions, maps, and sidebars enhance the fluid text." SLJ

Includes bibliographical references

Nye, Naomi Shihab, 1952-

Nye, Naomi Shihab. **I'll** ask you three times, are you ok? tales of driving and being driven. Greenwillow Books 2007 242p $15.99; lib bdg $16.89

Grades: 7 8 9 10 11 12   92

1. Poets 2. Authors 3. Voyages and travels 4. Editors 5. Essayists 6. Children's authors

ISBN 978-0-06-085392-1; 978-0-06-085393-8 lib bdg

LC 2006-36548

The author "writes about sudden intimate connections with strangers, especially taxi drivers, who often yield glimpses of family and exile that can sometimes change us. . . . The prose is chatty, fast, and unpretentious, and teens will enjoy the driving stuff and the idea of her kissing in the backseat, and they'll feel her sense of control when she is behind the wheel herself." Booklist

O'Connor, Sandra Day

Abrams, Dennis. **Sandra** Day O'Connor; U.S. Supreme Court Justice. Chelsea House 2009 136p il (Women of achievement) $30

Grades: 6 7 8 9   92

1. Judges 2. Supreme Court justices

ISBN 978-1-60413-337-0; 1-60413-337-6

LC 2008055367

A biography of the first woman U. S. Supreme Court Justice.

Includes bibliographical references

O'Dell, Scott, 1898-1989

Marcovitz, Hal. **Scott** O'Dell; [by] Hal Marcovitz; foreword by Kyle Zimmer. Chelsea House 2008 128p il (Who wrote that?) lib bdg $30

Grades: 6 7 8 9   92

1. Authors 2. Novelists 3. Authors, American 4. Children's authors 5. Nonfiction writers 6. Short story writers 7. Young adult authors

ISBN 978-0-7910-9526-3 lib bdg; 0-7910-9526-6 lib bdg

LC 2007019577

This biography examines the "writer's life, including the inspiration behind some of [his] works. [The] volume includes photographs and quotations from interviews, as well as descriptions of main characters and annotated lists of books and awards. Useful for aspiring authors as well as book report writers." Horn Book Guide

Includes bibliographical references

O'Keeffe, Georgia, 1887-1986

Rubin, Susan Goldman. **Wideness** and wonder: the life and art of Georgia O'Keeffe. Chronicle Books 2011 117p il $16.99

Grades: 6 7 8 9   92

1. Artists 2. Painters 3. Women artists 4. Artists -- United States

ISBN 0-8118-6983-0; 978-0-8118-6983-6

LC 2010008256

This is a biography of the American artist and a study of her work.

Rubin "here looks at the life and work of Georgia O'Keeffe. Nicely illustrated with family photos, portrait photos by Stieglitz, and many reproductions of the artist's drawings and paintings, the book builds a convincing portrayal of O'Keeffe from her student days to her ultimate recognition as an important American artist. The book's design is striking." Booklist

Includes bibliographical references

Oakley, Annie, 1860-1926

Koestler-Grack, Rachel A. **Annie** Oakley. Chelsea House 2010 102p bibl il por (Legends of the wild west) lib bdg $30

Grades: 6 7 8 9   92

1. Entertainers 2. Marksmen

ISBN 978-1-60413-594-7; 1-60413-594-8

LC 2009041338

"[A] fluid, straightforward writing style is a series mainstay that makes the figures and the era come alive. The sepia-toned illustrations, most of which are period photographs, corroborate the texts effectively. This is top-notch nonfiction." SLJ

Includes glossary and bibliographical references

Wills, Charles A. **Annie** Oakley: a photographic story of a life; [by] Chuck Wills. DK Pub. 2007 128p il (DK biography) $14.99

Grades: 4 5 6 7   92

1. Entertainers 2. Marksmen

ISBN 978-0-7566-2986-1

A biography of the sharp-shooter in Buffalo Bill's Wild West Show, from her humble Quaker heritage, her childhood filled with poverty and abuse, to her rise to international fame.

"This highly readable book has a rich layout of photographs and illustrations on every spread." SLJ

Obama, Barack, 1961-

Abramson, Jill. **Obama**; the historic journey. Young reader's ed.; Callaway 2009 94p il map $24.95

Grades: 5 6 7 8   92

1. Lawyers 2. Presidents 3. Racially mixed people 4. Senators 5. State legislators 6. Nobel laureates for peace 7. Presidents -- United States 8. African Americans -- Biography

ISBN 978-0-670-01208-4; 0-670-01208-4

LC 2009-5051

"This scaled down, teen-friendly version of The New York Times's adult biography is geared for middle school students. Containing many of the same photos, it provides a brief overview of the President's life, information that has been revealed over the election year and during his administration. . . . Its allure is in the many photographs with captions, sidebars, speech quotes, and charts. The book is nicely organized. The writing is direct and simple, explaining things such as convention delegates. . . . The book should entice young readers to explore his life further." Voice Youth Advocates

Burgan, Michael. **Barack** Obama. Heinemann Library 2010 112p il (Front-page lives) $38.93

Grades: 6 7 8 9 10   92

1. Lawyers 2. Presidents 3. Racially mixed people 4. Senators 5. State legislators 6. Nobel laureates for peace 7. Presidents -- United States 8. African Americans -- Biography

ISBN 978-1-4329-3218-3; 1-4329-3218-7

LC 2009-18176

President Obama's life is "presented with depth and breadth. . . . The writing is accessible and engaging, with color and black-and-white photographs." SLJ

Includes glossary and bibliographical references

Gibson, Karen Bush. The **Obama** view; the historic fight for the 2008 Democratic presidential nomination. Mitchell Lane Publishers 2009 il (Monumental milestones) lib bdg $20.95

Grades: 6 7 8 9   92

1. Lawyers 2. Presidents 3. Racially mixed people 4. Senators 5. State legislators 6. Nobel laureates for peace 7. African Americans -- Biography 8. Presidents -- United States -- Election -- 2008

ISBN 978-1-5841-5732-8; 1-5841-5732-1

LC 2008053464

This book is "clearly and crisply written. Starting with Obama's career in Illinois politics, the book then details his unlikely journey to the presidency, starting with his childhood in Hawaii and Indonesia. The final chapter deals with the presidential election and doesn't shy away from such issues as the way race was an election subtext. . . .

The design is lively and colorful, and the photos will draw readers." Booklist

Includes bibliographical references

Krensky, Stephen. **Barack** Obama. DK Pub. 2010 128p il map (DK biography) $14.99; pa $5.99

Grades: 6 7 8 9   92

1. Lawyers 2. Presidents 3. Racially mixed people 4. Senators 5. State legislators 6. Nobel laureates for peace 7. Presidents -- United States 8. African Americans -- Biography

ISBN 978-0-7566-5804-5; 0-7566-5804-7; 978-0-7566-5805-2 pa; 0-7566-5805-5 pa

LC 2010277785

Presents the life of Barack Obama, including his childhood in the United States and abroad, careers as a community organizer and lawyer, and his election as the forty-four president.

"Krensky excels at providing context not only for Obama's election, but also for his unlikely rise to prominence. . . . DK's powerful photographic format and the usual blurbs and sidebars work well at keeping this age group's interest." SLJ

Includes bibliographical references

Obama, Barack. **Dreams** from my father; a story of race and inheritance. Crown Publishers 2007 442p $25.95

Grades: 7 8 9 10 11 12 Adult   92

1. Lawyers 2. Presidents 3. Racially mixed people 4. Senators 5. State legislators 6. Nobel laureates for peace 7. Presidents -- United States 8. African Americans -- Biography

ISBN 978-0-307-38341-9

LC 2007-271892

First published 1995 by Times Books

This is the autobiography of the Illinois senator who would later become the 44th president of the United States.

The author "offers an account of his life's journey that reflects brilliantly on the power of race consciousness in America. . . . Obama writes well; his account is sensitive, probing, and compelling." Choice [review of 1995 edition]

Thomas, Garen Eileen. **Yes** we can: a biography of Barack Obama. Feiwel and Friends 2009 236p il map pa $6.99

Grades: 6 7 8 9   92

1. Lawyers 2. Presidents 3. Racially mixed people 4. Senators 5. State legislators 6. Nobel laureates for peace 7. Presidents -- United States 8. African Americans -- Biography

ISBN 978-0-312-58639-3 pa; 0-312-58639-6 pa

"The updated edition of this bestselling biography of Barack Obama covers his life from birth through the 2008 Presidential election. . . . [This] is a nice, fast introduction to the nation's current president for those who want more than an encyclopedia article and less then the autobiographical volumes and speeches." Voice Youth Advocates

Includes bibliographical references

Obama, Michelle

Brophy, David. **Michelle** Obama; meet the First Lady. by David Bergen Brophy. HarperCollins 2009 114p il $16.99; pa $6.99

Grades: 5 6 7 8   92

1. Lawyers 2. Spouses of presidents 3. Hospital administrators 4. African American women -- Biography 5. Presidents' spouses -- United States
ISBN 978-0-06-177991-6; 0-06-177991-1; 978-0-06-177990-9 pa; 0-06-177990-3 pa

A brief biography of Michelle Obama, wife of President Barack Obama

"The author . . . mixes personal data with information about the political process that brought the Obamas to the White House. . . . This biography is a must-have for all school libraries." Voice Youth Advocates

Includes glossary

Colbert, David. **Michelle** Obama; an American story. Houghton Mifflin Harcourt 2009 151p il $16

Grades: 5 6 7 8   92

1. Lawyers 2. Spouses of presidents 3. Hospital administrators 4. African American women -- Biography 5. Presidents' spouses -- United States
ISBN 978-0-547-24941-4; 0-547-24941-1

This biography delves into "the subject of The First Lady's family roots. . . . It offers a strong sense of who Obama was as a child, her solid upbringing, and her adult choices, all bolstered with numerous quotes from Obama and those who know her best. . . . Two sections of color photos and appended source notes for direct quotes complete this timely, highly readable biography." Booklist

Uschan, Michael V., 1948- **Michelle** Obama. Lucent Books 2010 112p il (People in the news) $32.45

Grades: 8 9 10 11 12   92

1. Lawyers 2. Spouses of presidents 3. Hospital administrators 4. African American women -- Biography 5. Presidents' spouses -- United States
ISBN 978-1-4205-0209-1; 1-4205-0209-3

LC 2009036557

"This biography is enjoyable reading for those writing reports and for those who simply want to learn more about the First Lady. As well as covering her life with Barack Obama and in the White House, Uschan discusses her family life, education, and early career and includes sidebars on such topics as her experience as a black student at mostly white Ivy League schools. Quotes from interviews with Obama reveal her intelligence, humor, and down-to-earth sensibility." SLJ

Includes bibliographical references

Ocampo, Adriana C., 1955-

Hopping, Lorraine Jean. **Space** rocks; the story of planetary geologist Adriana Ocampo. Franklin Watts 2005 118p il (Women's adventures in science) $9.95

Grades: 7 8 9 10   92

1. Geologists 2. Women scientists
ISBN 0-531-16783-6

LC 2005006644

"Adriana Ocampo grew up in Argentina. . . . When her father moved the family to the United States. . . . her enthusiasm for satellite design and interest in geology eventually led to a job [with NASA]. First helping to design a Mars rover, she then got involved in the search for a crater created by a massive asteroid collision that evidently caused mass extinctions in the age of dinosaurs. She now examines photos of distant planets taken by 'flyby' space probes and [plans] new geological expeditions." Voice Youth Advocates

Includes bibliographical references

Ochoa, Ellen, 1958-

Schraff, Anne E. **Ellen** Ochoa; astronaut and inventor. [by] Anne Schraff. Enslow Publishers 2010 128p il (Latino biography library) lib bdg $31.93

Grades: 6 7 8 9   92

1. Inventors 2. Astronauts 3. Women inventors 4. Women astronauts 5. NASA officials 6. Hispanic Americans -- Biography
ISBN 978-0-7660-3163-0; 0-7660-3163-2

LC 2008-40349

"Explores the life of Ellen Ochoa, including her childhood in California, her rise through the ranks in NASA, several space shuttle missions, and becoming the first Latino woman in space." Publisher's note

Includes bibliographical references

Ohno, Apolo, 1982-

Aldridge, Rebecca. **Apolo** Anton Ohno. Chelsea House 2009 120p il (Asian Americans of achievement) lib bdg $30

Grades: 7 8 9 10   92

1. Ice skaters 2. Olympic athletes 3. Ice skating -- Biography
ISBN 978-1-60413-565-7; 1-60413-565-4

LC 2009-9918

A biography of Olympic champion speed skater Apolo Anton Ohno.

"Nineteen color photos show Ohno's competitions. . . . The quality of research and in-depth coverage broadens [the book's] usefulness." SLJ

Includes glossary and bibliographical references

Owens, Jesse, 1913-1980

Burlingame, Jeff. **Jesse** Owens; I always loved running. Enslow Publishers 2011 128p il (African-American biography library) lib bdg $31.93

Grades: 6 7 8 9   92

1. Track athletics 2. African American athletes 3. Olympic athletes 4. Runners (Athletes)
ISBN 978-0-7660-3497-6; 0-7660-3497-6

LC 2010015697

"This book opens with Jesse Owens' celebrated victory in the 1936 Olympics in Berlin, when he triumphed in the 100-meter dash and Hitler refused to congratulate him. In a more nuanced historical account than many books offer, Burlingame looks at different interpretations of the day's events and comments on how Owens' own account changed over time.... After the dramatic opening chapter, the book offers a chronological account of Owens' life.... On every page, color brightens the headings, backgrounds, bordered photos, sidebars, and boxed quotes." Booklist

Includes bibliographical references

Gigliotti, Jim. **Jesse** Owens; gold medal hero. Sterling 2010 124p il $12.95; pa $5.95

Grades: 6 7 8 9   **92**

1. Track athletics 2. African American athletes 3. Olympic athletes 4. Runners (Athletes)

ISBN 978-1-4027-7149-1; 1-4027-7149-5; 978-1-4027-6361-8 pa; 1-4027-6361-1 pa

LC 2009024221

A biography of African-American runner Jesse Owens, whose success in the 1936 Berlin Olympic games was a victory for equality and an affront to Nazi leader Adolf Hitler's view of Aryan supremacy.

"Opinionated yet informative, ... [this blends] anecdotes, quotations, and facts to create [an] engaging [portrait].... Photographs and sidebars are incorporated into [a] reader-friendly [design]." Horn Book Guide

Includes glossary and bibliographical references

McDougall, Chros. **Jesse** Owens; trailblazing sprinter. ABDO Pub. Co. 2011 112p il (Legendary athletes) lib bdg $34.22

Grades: 6 7 8 9   **92**

1. Track athletics 2. African American athletes 3. Olympic athletes 4. Runners (Athletes)

ISBN 978-1-61714-758-6; 1-61714-758-3

LC 2010046697

This biography of track star Jesse Owens "goes beyond merely discussing [his] accomplishments.... [It] also [explores] the social and political [influence he] had on society as a whole. In addition, [it introduces] historical events in the context of [his life].... This ... is teeming with information and is a must-purchase for sports fans and readers interested in social activism." SLJ

Includes glossary and bibliographical references

Page, Larry

Sapet, Kerrily. **Google** founders: Larry Page and Sergey Brin. Morgan Reynolds Pub. 2011 112p il (Business leaders) $28.95

Grades: 7 8 9 10 11 12   **92**

1. Businesspeople 2. Web search engines 3. Computer scientists 4. Internet executives 5. Information technology executives

ISBN 978-1-59935-177-3; 1-59935-177-3; 978-1-59935-213-8 e-book

LC 2011014665

This biography of Google founders Larry Page and Sergey Bring "will grab YAs.... The design is browsable, with clear type and lots of color screens and informal photos of young people at work." Booklist

Includes bibliographical references

Palin, Sarah, 1964-

Petrillo, Lisa. **Sarah** Palin. Morgan Reynolds 2009 112p il (Political profiles) lib bdg $28.95

Grades: 6 7 8 9   **92**

1. Mayors 2. Governors 3. Women politicians

ISBN 978-1-59935-133-9 lib bdg; 1-59935-133-1 lib bdg

LC 2009040834

A biography of the former governor of Alaska, and former vice-presidential candidate

This is "solid, evenhanded, and wonderfully helpful. ... Unusually well-chosen photos, fine notes, and [a list] of further sources add to the usefulness and appeal of this [book]." Booklist

Paolini, Christopher

Bankston, John. **Christopher** Paolini; foreword by Kyle Zimmer. Chelsea House Publishers 2010 132p il (Who wrote that?) lib bdg $35

Grades: 6 7 8 9 10   **92**

1. Authors 2. Novelists 3. Fantasy writers 4. Authors, American 5. Young adult authors

ISBN 978-1-60413-727-9; 1-60413-727-4

LC 2010001366

This discusses the life and work of author Christopher Paolini.

Includes bibliographical references

Parks, Rosa, 1913-2005

Tracy, Kathleen. The **life** and times of Rosa Parks. Mitchell Lane Publishers 2009 48p il (Profiles in American history) lib bdg $29.95

Grades: 6 7 8 9   **92**

1. Civil rights activists 2. African Americans -- Civil rights 3. African American women -- Biography

ISBN 978-1-58415-666-6 lib bdg; 1-58415-666-X lib bdg

LC 2008020927

This a biography of the American American seamstress who refused to give up her seat on a Montgomery, Albama, city bus to a white passenger, which led to challenging the constitutionality of Montgomery's bus segregation laws

This offers "a wealth of concise and well-organized information.... [The] book is fair and balanced and includes viewpoints from those who opposed or disagreed with [Parks'] accomplishments. The design is crisp and colorful without overwhelming the words on the page." SLJ

Includes glossary and bibliographical references

Pasteur, Louis, 1822-1895

Robbins, Louise E. **Louis** Pasteur; and the hidden world of microbes. Oxford Univ. Press 2001 140p il (Oxford portraits in science) lib bdg $28

Grades: 7 8 9 10   **92**

1. Chemists 2. Scientists 3. Microbiologists 4. Writers on science

ISBN 0-19-512227-5

LC 2001-31405

This provides a "view of one of microbiology's best-known scientists, from his childhood in France as a tanner's son to his death 73 years later. The inviting format is easy to read and includes many well-captioned, black and white photographs.... The chronology will be especially helpful for reports. This is a valuable research tool for any library." SLJ

Includes glossary and bibliographical references

Zamosky, Lisa. **Louis** Pasteur; founder of microbiology. Compass Point Books 2009 40p il map (Mission: Science) lib bdg $26.60

Grades: 4 5 6   **92**
1. Chemists 2. Scientists 3. Microbiologists 4. Writers on science

ISBN 978-0-7565-3962-7

LC 2008007726

This biography of the father of microbiology "does a good job of connecting the scientist's work to our lives today. . . . [The] book has a variety of graphics including diagrams, photos, and reproductions of paintings and sketches. [This volume is] a definite plus for a school library or the juvenile collection in a public library." Libr Media Connect

Includes glossary and bibliographical references

Paterson, Katherine

Bankston, John. **Katherine** Paterson. Chelsea House 2010 128p il (Who wrote that?) lib bdg $30

Grades: 6 7 8 9   **92**
1. Authors 2. Novelists 3. Women authors 4. Authors, American 5. Young adult authors

ISBN 978-1-60413-499-5; 1-60413-499-2

LC 2009022345

This discusses the life and work of author Katherine Paterson.

Includes bibliographical references

McGinty, Alice B. **Katherine** Paterson; [by] Alice B. McGinty. 1st ed; Rosen Publishing Group 2005 112p il (Library of author biographies) lib bdg $26.50

Grades: 5 6 7 8   **92**
1. Authors 2. Novelists 3. Women authors 4. Young adult authors

ISBN 1-4042-0328-1

LC 2004-11420

This biography of the Newbery award-winning author "explains that Paterson's experiences growing up as the daughter of missionaries shaped her commitment to reflect the realistic feelings of children in her literature. . . . [This is] well-written." SLJ

Includes bibliographical references

Patrick, Danica, 1982-

★ Sirvaitis, Karen. **Danica** Patrick; racing's trailblazer. Twenty-First Century Books 2010 112p il (USA Today: lifeline biographies) lib bdg $33.26

Grades: 7 8 9 10 11 12   **92**
1. Women athletes 2. Automobile racing 3. Automobile racing drivers

ISBN 978-0-7613-5222-8; 0-7613-5222-8

LC 2009-45846

This biography is "both informative and eye-catching. . . . Even young readers with little interest in car racing will be caught up in the story behind Danica Patrick. . . . This involving story does more than recount the high times. Team-

mates are killed, loyalties switch, and personal criticism is a fact of life in the limelight." Booklist

Patton, George S. (George Smith), 1885-1945

Gitlin, Marty. **George** S. Patton; World War II general & military innovator. ABDO Pub. Co. 2010 112p il (Military heroes) lib bdg $22.95

Grades: 7 8 9 10   **92**
1. Generals 2. Army officers 3. World War, 1939-1945 -- Campaigns

ISBN 978-1-60453-964-6; 1-60453-964-X

LC 2009032371

This volume "offers a solid introduction to the controversial World War II commander, chronicling Patton's life from his childhood through his untimely death from injuries suffered in an automobile accident. . . . Quoting primary sources, Gitlin effectively portrays Patton as an aggressive, ambitious, courageous, often reckless, and occasionally visionary military commander. The volume is illustrated throughout with black-and-white photographs." Booklist

Includes bibliographical references

Pavlov, Ivan Petrovich, 1849-1936

Saunders, Barbara R. **Ivan** Pavlov; exploring the mysteries of behavior. Enslow Publishers 2006 112p il (Great minds of science) lib bdg $31.93

Grades: 5 6 7 8   **92**
1. Scientists 2. Behaviorism 3. Physiologists 4. Writers on medicine 5. Nobel laureates for physiology or medicine

ISBN 0-7660-2506-3

LC 2005031648

This is a biography of Russian scientist Ivan Pavlov, best known for his experiments with dogs, which were key to the development of behaviorism, and who won the 1904 Nobel Prize for his research on digestion

"The accessible [text has] an inviting, open format and [offers] many anecdotes. . . . Good-quality photos and illustrations complement the [narrative]." SLJ

Includes glossary and bibliographical references

Peary, Marie Ahnighito, 1893-1978

Kirkpatrick, Katherine A. **Snow** baby; the Arctic childhood of Admiral Robert E. Peary's daring daughter. [by] Katherine Kirkpatrick. Holiday House 2007 50p il map $16.95

Grades: 5 6 7 8   **92**
1. Admirals 2. Explorers 3. Children of prominent persons

ISBN 978-0-8234-1973-9; 0-8234-1973-8

LC 2006-02016

"Born north of the Arctic Circle in 1893, Marie Ahnighito Peary published her own version of her youth in 1934 (The Snowbaby's Own Story), on which this book is based. Kirkpatrick's engaging text captures the girl's adventurous spirit and the opportunities that her father's life as an explorer presented, as well as her love of the North and her Inuit friends." SLJ

Peary, Robert Edwin, 1856-1920

Kirkpatrick, Katherine A. **Snow** baby; the Arctic childhood of Admiral Robert E. Peary's daring daughter. [by] Katherine Kirkpatrick. Holiday House 2007 50p il map $16.95

Grades: 5 6 7 8　　　　　　　　　　　　　　92

1. Admirals 2. Explorers 3. Children of prominent persons

ISBN 978-0-8234-1973-9; 0-8234-1973-8

LC 2006-02016

"Born north of the Arctic Circle in 1893, Marie Ahnighito Peary published her own version of her youth in 1934 (The Snowbaby's Own Story), on which this book is based. Kirkpatrick's engaging text captures the girl's adventurous spirit and the opportunities that her father's life as an explorer presented, as well as her love of the North and her Inuit friends." SLJ

Peck, Richard, 1934-

Campbell, Kimberly. **Richard** Peck; a spellbinding storyteller. Enslow Publishers 2008 112p (Authors teens love) lib bdg $31.93

Grades: 6 7 8 9　　　　　　　　　　　　　　92

1. Authors 2. Novelists 3. Authors, American 4. Children's authors 5. Young adult authors 6. Children's literature -- Authors and illustrators

ISBN 978-0-7660-2723-7 lib bdg; 0-7660-2723-6 lib bdg

LC 2006034069

A biography of the 2001 Newbery-winning book, A Year Down Yonder

Includes bibliographical references

Sickels, Amy. **Richard** Peck. Chelsea House 2009 124p il (Who wrote that?) lib bdg $30

Grades: 6 7 8 9　　　　　　　　　　　　　　92

1. Authors 2. Novelists 3. Authors, American 4. Children's authors 5. Young adult authors

ISBN 978-0-7910-9530-0 lib bdg; 0-7910-9530-4 lib bdg

LC 2008-35035

A biography of the author of such young adult novels as Are You in the House Alone? and A Long Way from Chicago.

Includes bibliographical references

Pei, I. M., 1917-

★ Rubalcaba, Jill. **I.M.** Pei; architect of time, place, and purpose. Marshall Cavendish 2011 92p il map $23.99; ebook $23.99

Grades: 6 7 8 9 10 11 12　　　　　　　　　　92

1. Architects 2. Chinese Americans

ISBN 978-0-7614-5973-6; 0-7614-5973-1; 978-0-7614-6081-7 ebook; 0-7614-6081-0 ebook

LC 2011001910

"An exquisite package, much like one of Pei's buildings." Kirkus

Includes bibliographical references

Slavicek, Louise Chipley. **I.M.** Pei. Chelsea House 2009 120p bibl il por (Asian Americans of achievement) lib bdg $30

Grades: 6 7 8 9　　　　　　　　　　　　　　92

1. Architects 2. Chinese Americans

ISBN 978-1-60413-567-1; 1-60413-567-0

LC 2009014609

"A fascinating look at the world-renowned architect. . . . Slavecek deftly covers Pei's life, including his childhood and political events that were going on in China at the time. . . . The narrative is easy to read, the sidebars are informative, and the chronology and glossary are very helpful. A solid choice for most libraries." SLJ

Includes glossary and bibliographical references

Pelosi, Nancy, 1940-

Marcovitz, Hal. **Nancy** Pelosi; politician. Chelsea House Publishers 2009 144p il (Women of achievement) lib bdg $30

Grades: 7 8 9 10　　　　　　　　　　　　　92

1. Women politicians 2. Members of Congress 3. Speakers of the House

ISBN 978-1-60413-075-1 lib bdg; 1-60413-075-X lib bdg

LC 2008-34674

This is a biography of the first woman to serve as speaker of the U.S. House of Representatives

Includes bibliographical references

Pelé, 1940-

Buckley, James. **Pele**. DK Pub. 2007 128p il (DK biography) $14.99; pa $4.99

Grades: 6 7 8 9　　　　　　　　　　　　　　92

1. Soccer players 2. Soccer -- Biography

ISBN 978-0-7566-2996-0; 978-0-7566-2987-8 pa

This "introduces Edson Arantes do Nascimento, know to the world as soccer legend Pelé. The chapters stretch from Pelé's Brazilian youth . . . through is astonishing career and his current retirement. . . . Buckley grounds his enthusiasm with well-integrated facts and quotes. . . . Crisply reproduced photographs appear on every page." Booklist

Includes bibliographical references

Perkins, Frances, 1882-1965

Keller, Emily. **Frances** Perkins; first woman cabinet member. Morgan Reynolds Pub. 2006 160p il lib bdg $27.95

Grades: 8 9 10 11 12　　　　　　　　　　　92

1. Cabinet officers 2. Women politicians 3. College teachers 4. Secretaries of labor 5. State government officials

ISBN 978-1-931798-91-4 lib bdg; 1-931798-91-5 lib bdg

LC 2006023971

"This clearly written title highlights the groundbreaking accomplishments of the woman who served under Franklin D. Roosevelt as the U.S. Secretary of Labor. . . . The narrative is well researched and includes numerous quotes that are cited in a source notes section. Good-quality photographs depict many of the individuals mentioned in the text and illustrate the historical period." SLJ

Includes bibliographical references

Perón, Eva, 1919-1952

Favor, Lesli J. **Eva** Peron. Marshall Cavendish Benchmark 2010 112p il (Leading women) $39.93

Grades: 5 6 7 8 **92**

1. Women politicians 2. Spouses of presidents

ISBN 978-0-7614-4962-1; 0-7614-4962-0

A biography of the influential and admired First Lady of Argentina.

Includes bibliographical references

Picasso, Pablo, 1881-1973

Kallen, Stuart A. **Pablo** Picasso. Lucent Books 2009 104p il (Eye on art) lib bdg $32.45

Grades: 7 8 9 10 **92**

1. Cubism 2. Artists 3. Painters 4. Artists, French

ISBN 978-1-4205-0045-5; 1-4205-0045-7

LC 2008-13338

"Kallen tackles the complicated man that was Pablo Picasso and gives readers a look at both his genius and his eccentricities. . . . Visually, this is supported by the many photos of Picasso's art that appear throughout. Excellent sidebars offer solid information on such topics as communism or the influence of the Impressionists. This is just the kind of book that engages enough to become a gateway." Booklist

Includes bibliographical references

Spence, David. **Picasso**. New Forest Press 2010 48p il (Great artists and their world) lib bdg $32.80

Grades: 6 7 8 9 **92**

1. Cubism 2. Artists 3. Painters 4. Artists, French

ISBN 978-1-848983-14-4; 1-848983-14-X

"Offers biographical information [of Pablo Picasso] . . . interspersed with art history and criticism in an eye-catching format. . . . [Includes] a long introductory paragraph and four-to-six images with explanatory notes. . . . Spence . . . does a good job of explaining why art that might seem ordinary today was revolutionary at the time of its creation." SLJ

Includes glossary

Pierce, Tamora, 1954-

Dailey, Donna. **Tamora** Pierce; foreword by Kyle Zimmer. Chelsea House Publishers 2006 146p bibl il por (Who wrote that?) lib bdg $30

Grades: 6 7 8 9 **92**

1. Authors 2. Novelists 3. Women authors 4. Fantasy writers 5. College teachers 6. Authors, American 7. Children's authors

ISBN 978-0-7910-8795-4 lib bdg; 0-7910-8795-6 lib bdg

LC 2005025041

This biography, which examines the "writer's personal life and writing career, [is] ideal for fans. . . . The synopses of most popular books, and lists of works, well-known characters, and major awards may help report writers." Horn Book Guide

Includes bibliographical references

Planck, Max, 1858-1947

Weir, Jane. **Max** Planck; revolutionary physicist. Compass Point Books 2009 40p il (Mission: science) lib bdg $26.60

Grades: 4 5 6 **92**

1. Physicists 2. Nobel laureates for physics

ISBN 978-0-7565-4073-9 lib bdg; 0-7565-4073-9 lib bdg

LC 2008-37622

Biography of the physicist Max Planck

Includes glossary and bibliographical references

Pocahontas, d. 1617

Jones, Victoria Garrett. **Pocahontas**; a life in two worlds. Sterling 2010 124p il map (Sterling biographies) lib bdg $12.95; pa $9.95

Grades: 7 8 9 10 **92**

1. Princesses 2. Powhatan Indians 3. Indian leaders 4. Native Americans -- Biography

ISBN 978-1-4027-6844-6 lib bdg; 1-4027-6844-3 lib bdg; 978-1-4027-5158-5 pa; 1-4027-5158-3 pa

LC 2009-24136

A biography of the daughter of Chief Powhatan and her friendship with the colonists of the Jamestown settlement.

Includes glossary and bibliographical references

Poe, Edgar Allan, 1809-1849

Lange, Karen E. **Nevermore**; a photobiography of Edgar Allan Poe. National Geographic 2009 64p il $19.95; lib bdg $28.90

Grades: 6 7 8 9 **92**

1. Poets 2. Authors 3. Essayists 4. Authors, American 5. Short story writers

ISBN 978-1-4263-0398-2; 1-4263-0398-X; 978-1-4263-0399-9 lib bdg; 1-4263-0399-8 lib bdg

LC 2008-39833

In text and photographs, this volume depicts the life of the poet and short story writer.

"The drama of Poe's tortured life unfolds in accessible prose. Textual information is interspersed with photos, artistic interpretations, and revealing quotations presented in script. . . . This volume offers a fairly complete and thoroughly readable description of Poe's life and his importance to literature." SLJ

Includes bibliographical references

★ Meltzer, Milton. **Edgar** Allan Poe; a biography. Twenty-First Century Books 2003 144p $31.90

Grades: 7 8 9 10 **92**

1. Poets 2. Authors 3. Essayists 4. Authors, American 5. Short story writers 6. Authors, American -- 19th century -- Biography

ISBN 0-7613-2910-2

LC 2002-155802

"More than most other biographers for young people, Meltzer places his subject within the framework of his society. Readers will come away not only with greater knowledge of Poe's life and accomplishments but also a clearer picture of American life in the first half of the nineteenth century." Booklist

Includes bibliographical references

Polo, Marco, 1254-1323?

Childress, Diana. **Marco** Polo's journey to China; [by] Diana Childress. Twenty-First Century

Books 2008 160p (Pivotal moments in history) lib bdg $38.60

Grades: 7 8 9 10 11 12   **92**
1. Travelers 2. Voyages and travels 3. Travel writers
ISBN 978-0-8225-5903-0 lib bdg; 0-8225-5903-X lib bdg

LC 2005024003

This details the travels of the medieval explorer through Asia.

"Sure to satisfy history buffs, [the book] not only [relates] facts about the . . . [topic] but also [delves] into the events leading up to [the journey] as well as exploring [its] effects throughout history. Numerous sidebars, illustrations, maps, and art reproductions provide additional information." Horn Book Guide

Includes glossary and bibliographical references

Demi. **Marco** Polo; written and illustrated by Demi. Marshall Cavendish 2008 un il map $19.99

Grades: 4 5 6 7   **92**
1. Explorers 2. Travelers 3. Voyages and travels 4. Travel writers
ISBN 978-0-7614-5433-5; 0-7614-5433-0

"This elegant, scholarly picture-book biography brings the explorer's fantastic journey to life. . . . Demi weaves her subject's own accounts into a seamless tale of wonder. . . . The delicately rendered illustrations, painted with Chinese inks and gold overlays . . . capture the exotic beauty of 13th-century China." SLJ

Feinstein, Stephen. **Marco** Polo; amazing adventures in China. Enslow Publishers 2009 112p il (Great explorers of the world) lib bdg $31.93

Grades: 6 7 8 9   **92**
1. Explorers 2. Travelers 3. Voyages and travels 4. Travel writers
ISBN 978-1-59845-103-0 lib bdg; 1-59845-103-0 lib bdg

LC 2008-40344

"Examines the life of Italian explorer Marco Polo, including a childhood in Venice, his travels in China and the Mongol empire, his service to Kublai Khan, and his imprisonment in Genoa." Publisher's note

Includes glossary and bibliographical references

McCarty, Nick. **Marco** Polo; the boy who traveled the medieval world. National Geographic 2006 64p il map (World history biographies) $17.95; lib bdg $27.90

Grades: 5 6 7 8   **92**
1. Explorers 2. Travelers 3. Voyages and travels 4. Travel writers
ISBN 0-7922-5893-2; 0-7922-5894-0 lib bdg

A biography of the Italian explorer who became famous for his travels in Asia

Includes glossary and bibliographical references

Twist, Clint. **Marco** Polo; history's great adventurer. Candlewick Press 2011 un il (Historical notebooks) $19.99

Grades: 5 6 7 8   **92**
1. Explorers 2. Travelers 3. Voyages and travels 4. Travel writers
ISBN 978-0-7636-5286-9; 0-7636-5286-5

LC 2010040131

First published 2010 in the United Kingdom with title: Marco Polo; geographer of distant lands

"In this sumptuous scrapbook, excerpts from Marco Polo's own account of his travels are paired with beautiful maps, drawings, and illustrations. . . . This volume is well suited to browsing, and many readers will want to spend time poring over the many details." SLJ

Powell, Colin L., 1937-
Shichtman, Sandra H. **Colin** Powell; Have a vision. Be demanding. [by] Sandra H. Shichtman. Enslow 2005 128p il lib bdg $31.93

Grades: 5 6 7 8   **92**
1. Generals 2. Secretaries of state 3. Statesmen -- United States 4. African Americans -- Biography
ISBN 0-7660-2464-4

LC 2004-16799

This is "clearly written. . . . The captioned color photos add to the visual appeal." SLJ

Vander Hook, Sue. **Colin** Powell; general & statesman. ABDO Pub. Co. 2010 112p il (Military heroes) lib bdg $22.95

Grades: 7 8 9 10   **92**
1. Generals 2. Statesmen 3. Secretaries of state 4. African Americans -- Biography
ISBN 978-1-60453-965-3; 1-60453-965-8

LC 2009032364

This biography of Colin Powell covers Powell's service in the Vietnam War, his role as a White House fellow, a four-star general, and commander-in-chief of Forces Command and Powell's service to the U.S. presidents as the chairman of the Joint Chiefs of Staff and the secretary of state.

"The rush of literary adrenalin will hook readers immediately and keep them enthralled until the end. . . . Given the dynamic topic . . . [and] appealing layout [this book is] likely to appeal to reluctant readers. In addition, sources are plentiful and well-documented, making the [title] suitable for research projects." SLJ

Includes bibliographical references

Presley, Elvis, 1935-1977
Collins, Terry. **Elvis**; a graphic novel. illustrated by Michele Melcher. Capstone Press 2011 32p il (Graphic library: American graphic) lib bdg $29.32; pa $7.95

Grades: 4 5 6 7   **92**
1. Actors 2. Singers 3. Rock musicians 4. Biographical graphic novels
ISBN 978-1-4296-5476-0 lib bdg; 1-4296-5476-7 lib bdg; 978-1-4296-6266-6 pa; 1-4296-6266-2 pa

LC 2010024847

In graphic novel format, explores the life of Elvis Presley and describes his return to stardom through his '68 Comeback Special.

"The illustrations are eye-catching and the narration is presented simply, yet compellingly. . . . Fact-filled, entertaining, and accessible." SLJ

Includes glossary and bibliographical references

Hampton, Wilborn. **Elvis** Presley; a twentieth century life. Viking 2007 197p il (Up close) $15.99 Grades: 7 8 9 10　　　　　　　　　　　　92

1. Actors 2. Singers 3. Rock musicians

ISBN 978-0-670-06166-2

LC 2006029074

A biography of the legendary "King of rock and roll."

The author's "enthusiasm and passion for his subject are evident throughout this appealing biography, yet he remains objective about the performer's virtues as well as his tragic flaws. The striking cover photograph complements the lively and accessible text that delves not only into Elvis's life but also his impact on music and American culture." SLJ

Micklos, John. **Elvis** Presley; I want to entertain people. [by] John Micklos, Jr. Enslow Publishers 2010 160p il (American rebels) lib bdg $34.60 Grades: 6 7 8 9　　　　　　　　　　　　92

1. Actors 2. Singers 3. Rock musicians

ISBN 978-0-7660-3382-5 lib bdg; 0-7660-3382-1 lib bdg

LC 2009017595

The first chapter of this "fascinating, well-organized [portrait of the the rock musician] . . . describes the King's 1956 Ed Sullivan Show appearance, which was watched by a screaming audience of 60 million home viewers. . . . Skillfully chosen photos, chapter notes, and [a] suggested-reading [list completes this] well-researched, wholly engaging [introduction]." Booklist

Includes bibliographical references

Priestley, Joseph, 1733-1804

Conley, Kate A. **Joseph** Priestley and the discovery of oxygen. Mitchell Lane 2006 48p il (Uncharted, unexplored, and unexplained) $19.95 Grades: 6 7 8 9　　　　　　　　　　　　92

1. Clergy 2. Oxygen 3. Chemists 4. Writers on science

ISBN 1-58415-367-9

"This introductory title follows the scientist from his childhood in Fieldhead, England, to his death in Northumberland, PA. . . . Color photographs and illustrations are featured throughout. The attractive, open layout makes this title especially appealing to reluctant readers." SLJ

Puente, Tito, 1923-2000

McNeese, Tim. **Tito** Puente; [by] Tim McNeese. Chelsea House 2008 118p il (The great Hispanic heritage) lib bdg $30 Grades: 6 7 8 9　　　　　　　　　　　　92

1. Composers 2. Musicians 3. Band leaders 4. Percussionists 5. Music arrangers 6. Puerto Ricans -- Biography

ISBN 978-0-7910-9666-6 lib bdg; 0-7910-9666-1 lib bdg

LC 2007031984

This biography provides a "substantive [portrait], including background information and historical context of . . . charismatic band leader Puente. . . . The well-documented [text] effectively [combines] anecdotes, quotations, and historical details. Many photographs and sidebars are also included." Horn Book Guide

Includes bibliographical references

Pujols, Albert, 1980-

Needham, Tom. **Albert** Pujols; MVP on and off the field. Enslow Publishers 2007 128p (Sports stars with heart) lib bdg $23.95 Grades: 4 5 6 7　　　　　　　　　　　　92

1. Baseball players 2. Baseball -- Biography

ISBN 978-0-7660-2866-1 lib bdg; 0-7660-2866-6 lib bdg

LC 2006031843

"Baseball fans know Pujols from his outstanding record: Rookie of the Year, a National League MVP, a team leader helping the St. Louis Cardinals win the World Series in 2006. However, with its combination of sharp writing, eye-catching design, and well-chosen photos, this . . . is so pleasing that even those who don't follow baseball will enjoy learning about Pujols." Booklist

Includes bibliographical references

Pullman, Philip, 1946-

Speaker-Yuan, Margaret. **Philip** Pullman. Chelsea House 2006 118p il (Who wrote that?) lib bdg $30 Grades: 6 7 8 9　　　　　　　　　　　　92

1. Authors 2. Fantasy 3. Novelists 4. Fantasy writers 5. Authors, English 6. Young adult authors 7. Children's literature -- Authors and illustrators

ISBN 0-7910-8658-5

LC 2005-8184

This "draws upon an impressive array of sources—particularly Pullman's own writings—to present the groundbreaking author's life and work. . . . What may thrill readers most . . . are the insights into the writing process." Booklist

Includes bibliographical references

Putin, Vladimir

Shields, Charles J. **Vladimir** Putin; 2nd ed.; Chelsea House 2007 120p il (Modern world leaders) lib bdg $30 Grades: 7 8 9 10　　　　　　　　　　　　92

1. Presidents 2. Prime ministers

ISBN 0-7910-9215-1

LC 2006013657

First published 2003

A biography of the Russian president.

Includes bibliographical references

Ramirez, Manny, 1972-

Friedman, Ian C. **Manny** Ramirez. Chelsea House Publishers 2010 111p il (The great Hispanic heritage) lib bdg $30

Grades: 6 7 8 9   92

1. Baseball players 2. Baseball -- Biography
ISBN 978-1-60413-730-9; 1-60413-730-4

LC 2010007813

A biography of the baseball player.
Includes bibliographical references

Ramses II, King of Egypt

Fitzgerald, Stephanie J. **Ramses** II; Egyptian
pharaoh, warrior, and builder. Compass Point Books
2009 112p il map (Signature lives) lib bdg $34.60

Grades: 6 7 8 9   92

1. Kings and rulers 2. Kings
ISBN 978-0-7565-3836-1 lib bdg; 0-7565-3836-X
lib bdg

LC 2008005726

This biography of the pharaoh Ramses II offers "details
about the history and daily life of Egypt's New Kingdom
era. . . . [The texts is] accompanied by high-quality photographs of artifacts, maps, and floor plans. [The] book's detailed time line, comparing events in Egypt to those throughout the world, is helpful for placing the lives of the pharaohs
in context." SLJ
Includes glossary and bibliographical references

Randolph, Asa Philip, 1889-1979

Miller, Calvin Craig. **A.** Philip Randolph and the
African American labor movement. Morgan Reynolds 2005 160p il (Portraits of Black Americans)
$24.95

Grades: 8 9 10 11 12   92

1. Labor unions 2. Labor leaders 3. Civil rights
activists 4. African Americans -- Biography 5. African
Americans -- Civil rights
ISBN 1-931798-50-8

LC 2004-23706

A biography of the African American leader
"Miller lucidly traces Randolph's spectacular career
while presenting a case study in the effective use of hard-
nosed rhetoric and nonviolent tactics to achieve breakthroughs in the fight against segregation. Profusely illustrated with photographs, sometimes in color, and capped by
resource lists." Booklist
Includes bibliographical references

Rasputin, Grigori Efimovich, 1871-1916

Goldberg, Enid A. **Grigory** Rasputin; holy man
or mad monk? [by] Enid A. Goldberg & Norman Itz-
kowitz. Scholastic 2008 128p il map (Wicked history) lib bdg $30

Grades: 6 7 8 9   92

1. Monks 2. Courtiers
ISBN 978-0-531-12594-6 lib bdg; 0-531-12594-7
lib bdg

LC 2007001692

"This engaging, thought-provoking book provides a
chronological account of Rasputin's life as well as the historical background necessary to understand it in context.
Was Rasputin a holy man, or was he simply a philander-
ing charlatan who rose to power because of his unique relationship with Tsar Nicholas and Tsarina Alexandra? . . .

Captioned, black-and-white period photographs enhance the
text. Recommended for both curricular pursuits and pleasure
reading." SLJ
Includes glossary and bibliographical references

Ray, Rachael

★ Abrams, Dennis. **Rachael** Ray; food entrepreneur. Chelsea House Publishers 2009 128p bibl
il por (Women of achievement) lib bdg $30

Grades: 6 7 8 9   92

1. Cooks 2. Television personalities 3. Talk show
hosts 4. Cookbook writers
ISBN 978-1-60413-078-2 lib bdg; 1-60413-078-4
lib bdg

LC 2008034642

"Rachael Ray will be familiar to kids for her talk show
and other television appearances, and that will draw them
in. But once there, they'll respond to the story of Ray. . . .
As a cook who never went to culinary school, Ray knows
that her career is an unlikely one. Abrams does a particularly good job of capturing that unpredictability as well as
Ray's uniquely exuberant personality. . . . Enjoyable and
useful." Booklist
Includes bibliographical references

Reagan, Ronald, 1911-2004

Burgan, Michael. **Ronald** Reagan; a photographic story of a life. DK Pub. 2011 128p il (DK
biography) $14.99; pa $5.99

Grades: 5 6 7 8   92

1. Actors 2. Governors 3. Presidents 4. Presidents
-- United States
ISBN 978-0-7566-7075-7; 0-7566-7075-6; 978-0-
7566-7074-0 pa; 0-7566-7074-8 pa

"Burgan's survey covers the basic facts in a positive but
not propagandistic introduction. . . . Featuring small but clear
photos or boxed commentary on every page and capped with
a substantial . . . multimedia resource list, this compact volume . . . gives readers a broad picture of his achievements
and a sense of his compelling personal style." Booklist
Includes bibliographical references

Marsico, Katie. **Ronald** Reagan. Marshall Cavendish Benchmark 2011 112p il (Presidents and
their times) lib bdg $23.95

Grades: 5 6 7 8   92

1. Actors 2. Governors 3. Presidents 4. Presidents
-- United States
ISBN 978-0-7614-4814-3; 0-7614-4814-4

LC 2009044590

This offers information on President Ronald Reagan
and places him within his historical and cultural context.
Also explored are the formative events of his times and how
he responded.
"The abundant sidebars provide a good deal of background information that will be helpful to students. . . . Attractive . . . as well as useful." Booklist
Includes glossary and bibliographical references

Sutherland, James. **Ronald** Reagan; a twentieth century life. Penguin Group 2008 252p il (Up close) $16.99

Grades: 6 7 8 9 10   **92**

1. Actors 2. Governors 3. Presidents 4. Presidents -- United States

ISBN 978-0-670-06345-1; 0-670-06345-2

LC 2008-21328

"Both a character portrait and an account of Ronald Reagan's life and career(s), this profile sheds as much light on his goals and outlook as it does on his accomplishments. . . . This entry in the valuable Up Close series is a thought-provoking alternative to the plethora of routine assignment titles." Booklist

Reiss, Johanna

Reiss, Johanna. The **journey** back. Crowell 1976 212p hardcover o.p. pa $17.95

Grades: 5 6 7 8 9 10   **92**

1. Authors 2. Holocaust survivors 3. Children's authors 4. Jews -- Netherlands

ISBN 978-0-690-01252-1; 978-0-59543-050-5 pa

"The journey is the return home in the spring of 1945 for thirteen-year-old Annie and her older sister Sini. . . . The background of the early years is recapitulated. . . . The book offers an intensely provocative story, recalling many personal crises and tests of human nature cruelly beset by the dangers and deprivations of war." Horn Book

★ Reiss, Johanna. The **upstairs** room. Crowell 1972 273p hardcover o.p. pa $5.99

Grades: 5 6 7 8 9 10   **92**

1. Authors 2. Holocaust survivors 3. Children's authors 4. Jews -- Netherlands 5. World War, 1939-1945 -- Jews 6. Holocaust, 1933-1945 -- Personal narratives

ISBN 0-690-85127-8; 0-06-440370-X pa

A Newbery Medal honor book, 1973

"In a vital, moving account the author recalls her experiences as a Jewish child hiding from the Germans occupying her native Holland during World War II. . . . Ten-year-old Annie and her twenty-year-old sister Sini, . . . are taken in by a Dutch farmer, his wife, and mother who hide the girls in an upstairs room of the farm house. Written from the perspective of a child the story affords a child's-eye-view of the war." Booklist

Rembrandt Harmenszoon van Rijn, 1606-1669

Roberts, Russell. **Rembrandt**; [by] Russell Roberts. Mitchell Lane 2009 48p il (Art profiles for kids) lib bdg $20.95

Grades: 7 8 9 10   **92**

1. Artists 2. Etchers 3. Painters 4. Artists, Dutch 5. Drafters

ISBN 978-1-58415-710-6 lib bdg; 1-58415-710-0 lib bdg

LC 2008-2241

"Tracks the artist's rise to fame and the bitter years and bankruptcy that followed. . . . [Goes] beyond basic facts, providing historical context and significance of the art and the artist. . . . Provide[s] plenty of information for reports in a reader-friendly format." SLJ

Includes glossary and bibliographical references

Renoir, Auguste, 1841-1919

Somervill, Barbara A. **Pierre**-Auguste Renoir; [by] Barbara Somervill. Mitchell Lane 2007 48p il (Art profiles for kids) lib bdg $29.95

Grades: 5 6 7 8   **92**

1. Artists 2. Painters 3. Artists, French

ISBN 978-1-58415-566-9 lib bdg; 1-58415-566-3 lib bdg

LC 2007000661

Profiles the famous French artist best known for his portraits and his paintings such as "The Luncheon of the Boating Party" that depict people enjoying themselves

"The glossy pages allow for good reproductions of paintings as well as a few photos. . . . Back matter includes a glossary, chronology, chapter notes for quotes, lists of books and Internet sites, and a Timeline in History . . . offers a concise, readable account of the artist's life." Booklist

Includes glossary and bibliographical references

Spence, David. **Renoir**. New Forest Press 2010 48p il (Great artists and their world) lib bdg $32.80

Grades: 6 7 8 9   **92**

1. Artists 2. Painters 3. Artists, French 4. Impressionism (Art)

ISBN 978-1-848983-15-5; 1-848983-17-4

"Offers biographical information [of Auguste Renoir] . . . interspersed with art history and criticism in an eye-catching format. . . . [Includes] a long introductory paragraph and four-to-six images with explanatory notes. . . . Spence . . . does a good job of explaining why art that might seem ordinary today was revolutionary at the time of its creation." SLJ

Includes glossary

Revere, Paul, 1735-1818

★ Giblin, James. The **many** rides of Paul Revere; by James Cross Giblin. Scholastic Press 2007 85p il map $17.99

Grades: 4 5 6 7   **92**

1. Artisans 2. Metalworkers 3. Revolutionaries

ISBN 978-0-439-57290-3; 0-439-57290-8

LC 2006-38369

"This well-organized biography presents a lucid account of Revere's childhood, his limited education, his training in his father's workshop, his brief military career, and his adult life as a silversmith, family man, and Revolutionary War leader. . . . Giblin presents salient facts and intriguing details to create a well-rounded and credible image of the man. Among the many illustrations are period portraits, narrative paintings, engravings, drawings, and maps as well as photos of significant sites and artifacts." Booklist

Includes bibliographical references

Rhodes-Courter, Ashley Marie

Rhodes-Courter, Ashley Marie. **Three** little words; a memoir. Atheneum Books for Young Readers 2008 304p il $17.99; pa $9.99

Grades: 8 9 10 11 12 Adult   **92**

1. Foster children 2. Adopted children 3. Foster home

care 4. Memoirists 5. Child benefactors
ISBN 978-1-4169-4806-3; 1-4169-4806-6; 978-1-4169-4807-0 pa; 1-4169-4807-4 pa

LC 2007-21629

"This memoir lends a powerful voice to thousands of 'boomerang kids' who repeatedly wind up back in foster care." SLJ

Rice, Condoleezza, 1954-

Hubbard-Brown, Janet. **Condoleezza** Rice; stateswoman. Chelsea House Publishers 2008 113p il (Black Americans of achievement) lib bdg $30
Grades: 6 7 8 9   **92**
1. Women politicians 2. College teachers 3. Government officials 4. Political scientists 5. Secretaries of state 6. Presidential advisers 7. College administrators 8. African American women -- Biography
ISBN 978-0-7910-9715-1; 0-7910-9715-3

LC 2007035678

This biography details the African American stateswoman's "rise from adversity to . . . recognition. The [book goes] beyond the typical personal information to provide some social history relevant to the subject's time. Captioned photographs and boxed inserts enhance the conversational [text]." Horn Book Guide
Includes bibliographical references

Rivera, Diego, 1886-1957

Hillstrom, Kevin. **Diego** Rivera; muralist. by Kevin Hillstrom. Lucent Books 2008 104p il (The twentieth century's most influential Hispanics) lib bdg $32.45
Grades: 6 7 8 9 10   **92**
1. Artists 2. Painters 3. Artists, Mexican
ISBN 978-1-4205-0018-9 lib bdg; 1-4205-0018-X lib bdg

LC 2007-32104

"Rivera's life, beginnning with his childhood, is placed in the context of the artistic, political, and economic influences on family and his career. . . . The layout draws the eye with colorful headings and highlighted quotes." Libr Media Connect
Includes bibliographical references

Rizal, José, 1861-1896

Arruda, Suzanne Middendorf. **Freedom's** martyr; the story of Jose Rizal, national hero of the Phillipines. [by] Suzanne Middendorf Arruda. Avisson Press 2003 106p il (Avisson young adult series) pa $19.95
Grades: 7 8 9 10   **92**
1. Authors 2. Novelists 3. Physicians 4. Revolutionaries 5. Political leaders 6. Revolutionaries -- Philippines -- Biography
ISBN 1-88810-555-0

LC 2003-45320

"Born in the Philippines on June 19, 1861, Rizal was executed by the Spanish for treason on December 30, 1896. . . . Rizal wanted representation for native peoples in the Spanish government and wrote three novels and several poems detailing their plight. . . . This well-written, readable biography will prove useful for reports and background information on the history of the Philippines." SLJ
Includes bibliographical references

Robeson, Paul, 1898-1976

Slavicek, Louise Chipley. **Paul** Robeson; entertainer and activist. Chelsea House 2011 112p il (Black Americans of achievement) lib bdg $35
Grades: 6 7 8 9 10   **92**
1. Actors 2. Singers 3. Football players 4. African American actors 5. African American singers 6. Civil rights activists 7. African Americans -- Biography
ISBN 978-1-60413-843-6; 1-60413-843-2

This biography of the African American singer, actor, and activist "chronicles Robeson's struggles to overcome racial prejudice, leading to his staunch support of communism—a stand that caused him to lose favor in Hollywood and contributed to his eventual reclusion. Slavicek delves deeply into Robeson's story, giving readers a strong sense of the challenges Robeson faced, as well as the complex, courageous individual behind the legend. Archival black-and-white photos further lend a sense of intimacy, while 'did you know' sidebars expand on related topics." Booklist
Includes bibliographical references

Robinson, Jackie, 1919-1972

★ Robinson, Sharon. **Promises** to keep: how Jackie Robinson changed America. Scholastic 2004 64p il $16.95
Grades: 4 5 6 7   **92**
1. Baseball players 2. African American athletes 3. Army officers 4. Baseball -- Biography
ISBN 0-439-42592-1

LC 2003-42709

"Robinson's daughter, Sharon, describes her father's youth, his rise to become major-league baseball's first African American player, and his involvement in the civil rights movement. . . . Her private view of her father's accomplishments, placed within the context of American sports and social history, makes for absorbing reading. An excellent selection of family and team photographs and other materials . . . illustrate this fine tribute." Booklist

Wukovits, John F. **Jackie** Robinson and the integration of baseball; [by] John F. Wukovits. Lucent Books 2007 104p il (Lucent library of Black history) $28.70
Grades: 7 8 9 10   **92**
1. Baseball players 2. African American athletes 3. Army officers 4. Baseball -- Biography
ISBN 1-59018-913-2; 978-1-59018-913-9

LC 2006010831

"Wukovits does a credible job of adding historical perspective to a straightforward account of Robinson's life and accomplishments. He sets the stage by focusing on baseball's history of racial exclusion, and on the discrimination faced by the athlete and his family. He covers Robinson's military career and his brief stint in the Negro Leagues before he signed with the Brooklyn Dodgers. Robinson's triumphant career in the major leagues and his later life are detailed as well. This is a well-researched and concise account." SLJ
Includes bibliographical references

Roosevelt, Eleanor, 1884-1962

★ Fleming, Candace. **Our** Eleanor; a scrapbook look at Eleanor Roosevelt's remarkable life. Atheneum Books for Young Readers 2005 176p il $19.95

Grades: 5 6 7 8   **92**

1. Diplomats 2. Columnists 3. Humanitarians 4. Social activists 5. Spouses of presidents 6. United Nations officials 7. Presidents' spouses -- United States
ISBN 0-689-86544-9

LC 2004-22825

Told in scrapbook style, this biography looks behind the politics to present First Lady Eleanor Roosevelt in her many roles: wife and mother, United Nations delegate, popular columnist, civil rights crusader, and champion of the underprivileged.

"Each of the seven chapters leads readers through the subject's busy life with short sections of text filled with well-documented first-person accounts and direct quotes. . . . Not a spread goes by without incredible archival photographs or reproductions, newspaper and magazine clippings, handwritten letters, and diary entries. . . . They all provide relevant and fascinating insight." SLJ

MacLeod, Elizabeth. **Eleanor** Roosevelt; an inspiring life. written by Elizabeth MacLeod. Kids Can Press 2006 32p il (Snapshots) $14.95; pa $6.95

Grades: 4 5 6   **92**

1. Diplomats 2. Columnists 3. Humanitarians 4. Social activists 5. Spouses of presidents 6. United Nations officials 7. Presidents' spouses -- United States
ISBN 978-1-55337-778-8; 1-55337-778-8; 978-1-55337-811-2 pa; 1-55337-811-3 pa

"Fourteen short chapters take readers from Roosevelt's privileged but sad childhood through her marriage, political and family life, and post-FDR humanitarian work. . . . The period photographs . . . [are] plentiful and engrossing. . . . This attractive title will appeal to browsers and report writers." SLJ

Roosevelt, Franklin D. (Franklin Delano), 1882-1945

Panchyk, Richard. **Franklin** Delano Roosevelt for kids; his life and times with 21 activities. [by] Richard Panchyk. Chicago Review Press 2007 147p il pa $14.95

Grades: 4 5 6 7   **92**

1. Governors 2. Presidents 3. Handicapped 4. Philatelists 5. Presidents -- United States
ISBN 978-1-55652-657-2 pa; 1-55652-657-1 pa

LC 2007003484

"There are many interesting photos . . . and they are all sufficiently captioned. . . . Information about the Roosevelts [is] presented in a lively, engaging manner." SLJ

Includes bibliographical references

Roosevelt, Theodore, 1858-1919

★ Cooper, Michael L. **Theodore** Roosevelt; a twentieth-century life. Viking 2009 208p il (Up close) $16.99

Grades: 7 8 9 10   **92**

1. Governors 2. Presidents 3. Vice-presidents 4. Nobel laureates for peace 5. Presidents -- United States
ISBN 978-0-670-01134-6; 0-670-01134-7

LC 2010-279534

"This biography presents an evenhanded account of the life and presidency of Theodore Roosevelt. . . . This clearly written biography includes many anecdotes and well-chosen quotes that help bring Roosevelt to life. . . . Cooper offers a solid portrayal of this noteworthy American president." Booklist

Includes bibliographical references

Elish, Dan. **Theodore** Roosevelt; by Dan Elish. Marshall Cavendish Benchmark 2008 96p il (Presidents and their times) lib bdg $22.95

Grades: 5 6 7 8   **92**

1. Governors 2. Presidents 3. Vice-presidents 4. Nobel laureates for peace 5. Presidents -- United States
ISBN 978-0-7614-2429-1

LC 2006012987

A biography of the president

"Primary-source materials and quotes, helpful insets, and carefully selected photographs and/or reproductions bring history to life and help make [this] clearly written [biography] highly readable." SLJ

Includes glossary and bibliographical references

Fitzpatrick, Brad. **Theodore** Roosevelt. Chelsea House 2011 142p il (Conservation heroes) lib bdg $35

Grades: 6 7 8 9 10   **92**

1. Governors 2. Presidents 3. Vice-presidents 4. Nobel laureates for peace 5. Presidents -- United States
ISBN 978-1-60413-948-8; 1-60413-948-X

LC 2010026475

A biography of President Theodore Roosevelt which concentrates on his contributions to environmental conservation.

"Captivating, richly informative. . . . The scope of [this book] is comprehensive. . . . [The book is] engaging as [it is] educational and will be ideal for research and reports." SLJ

Includes glossary and bibliographical references

★ Fritz, Jean. **Bully** for you, Teddy Roosevelt! illustrations by Mike Wimmer. Putnam 1991 127p il hardcover o.p. pa $5.99

Grades: 5 6 7 8   **92**

1. Governors 2. Presidents 3. Vice-presidents 4. Nobel laureates for peace 5. Presidents -- United States
ISBN 0-399-21769-X; 0-698-11609-7 pa

LC 90-8142

Follows the life of the twenty-sixth president, discussing his conservation work, hunting expeditions, family life, and political career

"Jean Fritz gives a rounded picture of her subject and deftly blends the story of a person and a picture of an era." Bull Cent Child Books

Includes bibliographical references

Harness, Cheryl. The **remarkable,** rough-riding life of Theodore Roosevelt and the rise of empire America; painstakingly written and illustrated by

Cheryl Harness. National Geographic 2007 144p il map $16.95; lib bdg $25.90

Grades: 4 5 6 7   92

    1. Governors 2. Presidents 3. Vice-presidents 4. Nobel laureates for peace 5. Presidents -- United States
ISBN 978-1-4263-0008-0; 1-4263-0008-5; 978-1-4263-0009-7 lib bdg; 1-4263-0009-3 lib bdg
                LC 2006029039

"Animated writing and intricate black-and-white illustrations drive this biography of the ever-enthusiastic twenty-sixth president of the United States. An extensive running timeline at the bottom of the pages emphasizes the dramatic changes that occurred during Roosevelt's life. The book is jam-packed with information." Horn Book Guide
    Includes bibliographical references

Hollihan, Kerrie Logan. **Theodore** Roosevelt for kids; his life and times + 21 activities. Chicago Review Press 2010 133p il pa $16.95

Grades: 5 6 7 8   92

    1. Governors 2. Handicraft 3. Presidents 4. Vice-presidents 5. Nobel laureates for peace 6. Presidents -- United States
ISBN 978-1-55652-955-9 pa; 1-55652-955-4 pa

"What stands out in this volume is the writing, which presents history as an engaging and informative story. . . . The projects are interesting and accessible. . . . Both useful and entertaining, this is a worthy addition to most collections." SLJ

Rowling, J. K.

Peterson-Hilleque, Victoria. **J.K.** Rowling, extraordinary author. ABDO Pub. Company 2010 112p il (Essential lives) $32.79

Grades: 5 6 7 8   92

    1. Authors 2. Novelists 3. Women authors 4. Fantasy writers 5. Authors, English 6. Children's authors 7. Young adult authors
ISBN 978-1-61613-517-1; 1-61613-517-4
                LC 2010000503

This biography of author J. K. Rowling "toggles between the subject's personal and professional life. . . . [The book] offers sidebar . . . definitions of particular characters or events in the 'Harry Potter' series. The writing is accessible, the format is open, and full-color photos appear throughout." SLJ
    Includes glossary and bibliographical references

Sickels, Amy. **Mythmaker**: the story of J.K. Rowling; foreword by Kyle Zimmer. 2nd ed; Chelsea House Pubs. 2008 136p bibl il por (Who wrote that?) lib bdg $30

Grades: 5 6 7 8   92

    1. Authors 2. Fantasy 3. Novelists 4. Women authors 5. Fantasy writers 6. Authors, English 7. Children's authors 8. Harry Potter books 9. Young adult authors 10. Children's literature -- Authors and illustrators
ISBN 978-0-7910-9632-1 lib bdg; 0-7910-9632-7 lib bdg
                LC 2008001202

A revised edition of Mythmaker by Charles J. Shields published 2002
    "Useful for report writers and aspiring authors." Horn Book Guide
    Includes bibliographical references

Rudolph, Wilma, 1940-1994

Anderson, Jennifer Joline. **Wilma** Rudolph; track and field inspiration. ABDO Pub. Co. 2011 112p il (Legendary athletes) lib bdg $34.22

Grades: 6 7 8 9   92

    1. Women athletes 2. Track athletics 3. Olympic athletes 4. Runners (Athletes)
ISBN 978-1-61714-759-3; 1-61714-759-1
              LC 2010046698

This biography of track star Wilma Rudolph "goes beyond merely discussing [her] accomplishments. . . . [It] also [explores] the social and political [influence she] had on society as a whole. In addition, [it introduces] historical events in the context of [her life]. . . . This . . . is teeming with information and is a must-purchase for sports fans and readers interested in social activism." SLJ
    Includes glossary and bibliographical references

Runyon, Brent

Runyon, Brent. The **burn** journals. Alfred A. Knopf 2004 373p hardcover o.p. pa $13.95

Grades: 7 8 9 10   92

    1. Authors 2. Suicide 3. Burns and scalds 4. Essayists 5. Memoirists 6. Teenage boys -- Virginia -- Biography 7. Teenage boys -- Suicidal behavior -- Virginia -- Case studies
ISBN 0-375-82621-1; 1-4000-9642-1 pa
              LC 2004-5643

"One February day in 1991, Runyon came home from eighth grade . . . and set himself on fire. . . . The dialogue between Runyon and his nurses, parents, and especially his hapless psychotherapists is natural and believable, and his inner dialogue is flip, often funny, and sometimes raw. . . . The authentically adolescent voice of the journals will engage even those reluctant to read such a dark story." SLJ

Rustin, Bayard, 1910-1987

★ Brimner, Larry Dane. **We** are one: the story of Bayard Rustin. Calkins Creek 2007 48p il $17.95

Grades: 5 6 7 8   92

    1. Civil rights activists 2. African Americans -- Biography 3. African Americans -- Civil rights
ISBN 1-59078-498-7

"Brimner sets Rustin's personal story against the history of segregation in his time and focuses on his leadership role . . . in the struggle for civil rights. On each page, the clearly written, informal text is accompanied by eloquently captioned archival photos." Booklist
    Includes bibliographical references

★ Miller, Calvin Craig. **No** easy answers; Bayard Rustin and the civil rights movement. Morgan Reynolds Pub. 2005 160p il lib bdg $24.95

Grades: 7 8 9 10   92

    1. Civil rights activists 2. African Americans --

Biography 3. African Americans -- Civil rights
ISBN 1-931798-43-5

LC 2004-18518

"Miller combines the life story of a great social activist with the history of the struggle for civil rights in the U.S. The politics are exciting, with details of the radical campaigns in the 1940s and 1950s, Rustin's impassioned call for nonviolent protest, and his role in organizing both the Montgomery Bus Boycott and the 1963 March on Washington." Booklist
Includes bibliographical references

Ruth, Babe, 1895-1948

Hampton, Wilborn. **Babe** Ruth; a twentieth-century life. Viking 2009 203p il (Up close) $16.99
Grades: 6 7 8 9 10   92
1. Baseball players 2. Baseball -- Biography 3. Baseball -- History
ISBN 978-0-670-06305-5; 0-670-06305-3

LC 2008-21550

"Hampton announces early in this biography of Babe Ruth that his emphasis is on separating fact from legend, and he is not afraid to dig up some of the more tawdry aspects of the slugger's life. . . . The focus here is on Ruth's sad early life and his career as a pitcher with the Boston Red Sox. Throughout, an attempt is made to give some sense of the grace, power, and skill of Ruth on the field. . . . [This title,] illustrated with a nice selection of photos, has the advantage of telling the complete, unvarnished story in a snappy, concise style." Booklist
Includes bibliographical references

Yomtov, Nelson. The **Bambino**: the story of Babe Ruth's legendary 1927 season; illustrated by Tim Foley. Capstone Press 2011 32p il (Graphic library: American graphic) lib bdg $29.32; pa $7.95
Grades: 4 5 6 7   92
1. Baseball players 2. Biographical graphic novels 3. Baseball -- Biography
ISBN 978-1-4296-5473-9 lib bdg; 1-4296-5473-2 lib bdg; 978-1-4296-6265-9 pa; 1-4296-6265-4 pa

LC 2010024764

In graphic novel format, follows Babe Ruth through the 1927 season and describes his attempt to break his own home run record.
"The illustrations are eye-catching and the narration is presented simply, yet compellingly. . . . Fact-filled, entertaining, and accessible." SLJ
Includes glossary and bibliographical references

Sís, Peter, 1949-

★ Sís, Peter, 1949- The **wall**; growing up behind the Iron Curtain. Farrar, Straus and Giroux 2007 un il $18
Grades: 4 5 6 7 8 9 10   92
1. Artists 2. Authors 3. Cold war 4. Animators 5. Illustrators 6. Set designers 7. Children's authors
ISBN 978-0-374-34701-7; 0-374-34701-8

LC 2006-49149

Boston Globe-Horn Book Award: Nonfiction (2008)
"The author pairs his remarkable artistry with journal entries, historical context and period photography to create a powerful account of his childhood in Cold War-era Prague." Publ Wkly

Sacagawea, b. 1786

Berne, Emma Carlson. **Sacagawea**; crossing the continent with Lewis & Clark. Sterling 2010 124p il map (Sterling biographies) lib bdg $12.95; pa $5.95
Grades: 7 8 9 10   92
1. Shoshone Indians 2. Interpreters 3. Guides (Persons) 4. Native Americans -- Biography
ISBN 978-1-4027-6845-3 lib bdg; 1-4027-6845-1 lib bdg; 978-1-4027-5738-9 pa; 1-4027-5738-7 pa

LC 2009-24139

"Contrary to myth, Sacagawea explains that the Shoshone teen was not a princess, her relationship with Clark was platonic, and she was a peace symbol rather than a guide until they finally reached the Shoshone tribe. . . . [The] spacious design is highly scannable, with color background screens, photos, maps, and historic prints throughout." Booklist
Includes glossary and bibliographical references

Crosby, Michael T. **Sacagawea**; Shoshone explorer. OTTN Pub. 2008 144p il map (Shapers of America) lib bdg $25.95
Grades: 6 7 8 9 10   92
1. Shoshoni Indians 2. Interpreters 3. Guides (Persons) 4. Native Americans -- Biography
ISBN 978-1-59556-026-1 lib bdg; 1-59556-026-2 lib bdg

LC 2007-24698

"This attractive title introduces the young Shoshone woman who accompanied the Lewis and Clark Expedition. . . . Full of clear maps, historical paintings, reproductions of period documents (including journals), and color photographs of landmarks along the route, this is a visually attractive package. . . . Detailed endnotes show the depth of the author's research, and the suggested reading includes books for both younger and older students and Internet sources." SLJ
Includes glossary and bibliographical references

Saint-Georges, Joseph Boulogne, chevalier de, 1745-1799

Brewster, Hugh. The **other** Mozart; the life of the famous Chevalier de Saint George. [by] Hugh Brewster; illustrated by Eric Velasquez. Abrams Books for Young Readers 2007 48p il $18.95
Grades: 4 5 6 7   92
1. Nobility 2. Composers 3. Violinists 4. Racially mixed people
ISBN 978-0-8109-5720-6; 0-8109-5720-5

LC 2006-07488

"Born to a white plantation owner and a black slave in eighteenth-century Guadeloupe, Joseph Bologne grew up to become the Chevalier de Saint-George, one of France's most accomplished composers. In this picture-book biography for middle-graders, Brewster introduces his subject's fascinating life. . . . Archival images and Velasquez's arresting full-page portraits will captivate many young readers." Booklist

Salisbury, Graham, 1944-

★ Gill, David Macinnis. **Graham** Salisbury; island boy. David Macinnis Gill. Scarecrow Press 2005 109p (Scarecrow studies in young adult literature) $35

Grades: 7 8 9 10   **92**
1. Authors 2. Novelists 3. Authors, American 4. Children's authors 5. Short story writers
ISBN 0-8108-5338-8
LC 2004031042
"Part literary analysis and part biography, this is a well-balanced look at an unusual talent, a writer who has an eye for the frailties of life and the rites of adolescence. Gill discusses how growing up in Hawaii in the '50s influenced Salisbury's writing and does a fine job of showing the complexity of his work." SLJ
Includes bibliographical references

Salk, Jonas, 1914-1995

Sherrow, Victoria. **Jonas** Salk; beyond the microscope. 2nd rev ed; Chelsea House 2008 146p il (Makers of modern science) $35

Grades: 7 8 9 10   **92**
1. Physicians 2. Scientists 3. Poliomyelitis vaccine 4. Microbiologists 5. Writers on medicine
ISBN 978-0-8160-6180-8; 0-8160-6180-7
LC 2006-33429
First published 1993 by Facts on File
This biography of Jonas Salk "describes this respected immunologist's medical research and his lifelong efforts to promote scientific and human progress on a global scale." Publisher's note
Includes glossary and bibliographical references

Santa Anna, Antonio López de, 1794?-1876

Lange, Brenda. **Antonio** Lopez de Santa Anna. Chelsea House Publishers 2010 102p il map (The great Hispanic heritage) lib bdg $30

Grades: 6 7 8 9   **92**
1. Generals 2. Presidents
ISBN 978-1-60413-734-7; 1-60413-734-7
LC 2010007515
A biography the Mexican general and president who is well-known for his part in the Battle of the Alamo during the U.S. Mexican War.
Includes bibliographical references

Santana, Carlos, 1947-

Slavicek, Louise Chipley. **Carlos** Santana. Chelsea House Publishers 2006 120p il (Great Hispanic heritage) lib bdg $30

Grades: 6 7 8 9   **92**
1. Guitarists 2. Rock musicians 3. Band leaders 4. Mexican Americans -- Biography
ISBN 978-0-7910-8844-9 lib bdg; 0-7910-8844-8 lib bdg
LC 2005026000
This biography of rock musician Santana is filled "with excellent details—music and familial [history sheds] light on the man's roots and focus strongly on his humanitarian efforts. . . . Color photos and sidebars add interest, and quotes from magazines, newspapers, and interviews are meticulously cited in the endnotes." SLJ
Includes bibliographical references

Sarkozy, Nicolas, 1955-

Abrams, Dennis. **Nicolas** Sarkozy. Chelsea House 2009 136p il (Modern world leaders) lib bdg $30

Grades: 6 7 8 9   **92**
1. Mayors 2. Lawyers 3. Presidents 4. Cabinet members 5. Members of Parliament
ISBN 978-1-60413-081-2 lib bdg; 1-60413-081-4 lib bdg
LC 2008-26567
"Abrams deftly explores both the personal and public spheres of this 'most untraditional politician.' . . . Probing, evenhanded." Booklist
Includes bibliographical references

Schaller, George B.

★ Turner, Pamela S. A **life** in the wild; George Schaller's struggle to save the last great beasts. Farrar, Straus and Giroux 2008 103p il map $21.95

Grades: 5 6 7 8   **92**
1. Zoologists 2. Wildlife conservation 3. Nonfiction writers 4. Animal behavior
ISBN 978-0-374-34578-5; 0-374-34578-3
LC 2007-42844
"The author interviewed Schaller and had access to his photos, which allowed her to capture beautifully the spirit of Schaller's work. The book is organized chronologically, and each chapter covers a geographic area and the principal animals that Schaller studied there. . . . Animal lovers and conservation-minded students will enjoy this excellent introduction to Schaller and his ideals." Voice Youth Advocates
Includes bibliographical references

Schliemann, Heinrich, 1822-1890

★ Schlitz, Laura Amy. The **hero** Schliemann; the dreamer who dug for Troy. illustrated by Robert Byrd. Candlewick Press 2006 72p il $12.23

Grades: 4 5 6   **92**
1. Archeologists 2. Excavations (Archeology) 3. Excavations (Archaeology) -- Turkey -- Troy (Extinct city)
ISBN 0-7636-2283-4
LC 2005046916
This is a biography of the archaeologist who rediscovered ancient Troy. (Horn Book)
"In this slim biography, Schlitz introduces Heinrich Schliemann, a nineteenth-century 'storyteller, archaeologist, and crook,' who led a search for the lost cities of Homer's epic poems." Booklist

Schloss, Eva

Schloss, Eva. **Eva's** story; a survivor's tale by the stepsister of Anne Frank. [by] Eva Schloss with Evelyn Julia Kent. W.B. Eerdmans Pub. Co. 2010 226p il map pa $14.99

Grades: 7 8 9 10   **92**
1. Jewish refugees 2. Holocaust survivors 3. Jews

-- Netherlands 4. Holocaust, 1933-1945 -- Personal narratives
ISBN 978-0-8028-6495-6; 0-8028-6495-3

LC 2009-51022

Schulke, Flip

Schulke, Flip. **Witness** to our times; my life as a photojournalist. [by] Flip Schulke; in association with Matt Schudel. Cricket Books 2003 112p il $19.95

Grades: 8 9 10 11 12   **92**

1. Photographers 2. Documentary photography 3. Photojournalists 4. Documentary photography -- United States 5. News photographers -- United States -- Biography
ISBN 0-8126-2682-6

LC 2002-151457

An autobiography of a man whose documentary photographs in American magazines helped to shape public opinion on such issues as the civil rights movement and the space race

"Photojournalist Schulke shot some of the most important photographs of the twentieth century, and the passion, concentration, and sensitivity that characterize his photos come across as powerfully in his prose. . . . His black-and-white photos make up most of the book, and they express such strong emotion that readers will feel the depth of his passion even on pages without a word of text." Booklist

Includes bibliographical references

Schulz, Charles M.

★ Gherman, Beverly. **Sparky**: the life and art of Charles Schulz. Chronicle Books 2010 125p il $16.99

Grades: 5 6 7 8   **92**

1. Cartoonists
ISBN 978-0-8118-6790-0; 0-8118-6790-0

A look at the life and influences of Charles Schulz, creator of the beloved comic strip Peanuts.

"Gherman's clear and direct prose is just right for portraying the life of the famous cartoonist for young readers. The splashy, bright design, with multicolored pages and several of Schulz's cartoons included, makes this a cheery read that may well introduce the Peanuts comic strip to a new generation, who likely know Charlie Brown mostly through the holiday TV specials. An informative yet lighthearted look at the life of an American icon." Kirkus

Schumann, Clara, 1819-1896

Shichtman, Sandra H. The **joy** of creation; the story of Clara Schumann. by Sandra Shichtman and Dorothy Indenbaum. Morgan Reynolds 2011 159p il (Classical composers) lib bdg $28.95

Grades: 6 7 8 9 10   **92**

1. Pianists 2. Composers
ISBN 978-1-59935-123-0; 1-59935-123-4

LC 2009054289

This title "provides a detailed account of the acclaimed nineteenth-century German pianist and composer Clara Schumann. . . . Adundant quotes, many from Schumann's diary, add intimacy to the straightforward, sometimes dense narrative, which also provides historical context and background to her notable life and legacy. The attractively designed volume intersperses color and black-and-white illustrations." Booklist

Includes bibliographical references

Schutz, Samantha, 1978-

Schutz, Samantha. **I** don't want to be crazy; a memoir of anxiety disorder. PUSH Books 2006 280p $16.99

Grades: 8 9 10 11 12   **92**

1. Anxiety 2. Panic disorders 3. Editors 4. Memoirists
ISBN 0-439-80518-X

LC 2005028964

"In this moving memoir, Schutz details her struggle with anxiety disorder. . . . Written in verse, this memoir successfully conveys what it is like to suffer from panic attacks." Voice Youth Advocates

Scieszka, Jon, 1954-

Scieszka, Jon. **Knucklehead**; tall tales and mostly true stories of growing up Scieszka. Viking 2008 106p il $16.99; pa $12.99

Grades: 4 5 6 7   **92**

1. Authors 2. Authors, American 3. Children's authors
ISBN 978-0-670-01106-3; 0-670-01106-1; 978-0-670-01138-4 pa; 0-670-01138-X pa

LC 2008-16870

"Scieszka . . . has written an autobiography about boys, for boys and anyone else interested in baseball, fire and peeing on stuff. . . . The text is divided into two- to three-page nonsequential chapters and peppered with scrapbook snapshots and comic-book-ad reproductions. . . . By themselves, the chapters entertain with abrupt, vulgar fun. Taken together, they offer a look at the makings of one very funny author." Booklist

Selkirk, Alexander, 1676-1721

Kraske, Robert. **Marooned**; the strange but true adventures of Alexander Selkirk, the real Robinson Crusoe. illustrated by Robert Andrew Parker. Clarion Books 2005 120p il map $15

Grades: 5 6 7 8   **92**

1. Sailors 2. Survival after airplane accidents, shipwrecks, etc.
ISBN 0-618-56843-3

LC 2004-28769

"In 1704, English sailing master Alexander Selkirk was marooned on Juan Fernandez, an isolated Pacific island. . . . In 1709, two English ships rescued him, hired him as a second mate, and later captured a Spanish treasure ship. . . . Kraske offers a well-focused look at life in several quite different settings during the early eighteenth century as well as an absorbing telling of Selkirk's story." Booklist

Includes glossary and bibliographical references

Seuss, Dr.

Anderson, Tanya. **Dr.** Seuss (Theodor Geisel) foreword by Kyle Zimmer. 2nd ed; Chelsea House 2011 128p il (Who wrote that?) lib bdg $35

Grades: 6 7 8 9   **92**

1. Artists 2. Authors 3. Humorists 4. Illustrators 5.

Authors, American 6. Children's authors
ISBN 978-1-60413-750-7; 1-60413-750-9

LC 2010030589

This discusses the life and work of author Theodor Geisel, known as Dr. Seuss.
Includes bibliographical references

Severance, John B.

★ **Winston** Churchill; soldier, statesman, artist. Clarion Bks. 1996 144p il map $17.95

Grades: 5 6 7 8　　　　　　　　　　　　　　　92

1. Statesmen 2. Historians 3. Prime ministers 4. Memoirists 5. Cabinet members 6. Members of Parliament 7. Nobel laureates for literature 9. Prime ministers -- Great Britain
ISBN 0-395-69853-7

LC 94-25129

"This fair, balanced, and duly appreciative biography is handsomely produced and illustrated with a fine collection of photographs." Horn Book Guide
Includes bibliographical references

Sewall, May Wright, 1844-1920

Boomhower, Ray E. **Fighting** for equality; a life of May Wright Sewall. [by] Ray E. Boomhower. Indiana Historical Society Press 2007 160p il $17.95

Grades: 4 5 6　　　　　　　　　　　　　　　92

1. Feminism 2. Educators 3. Reformers 4. Suffragists 5. Lecturers 6. Pacifists
ISBN 978-0-87195-253-0; 0-87195-253-X

LC 2007008517

"This accessible volume tells of the life and work of suffragist and educator [May] Wright Sewall. . . . Archival black-and-white photos enhance the text." Horn Book Guide
Includes bibliographical references

Shackleton, Ernest Henry Sir, 1874-1922

Johnson, Rebecca L. **Ernest** Shackleton; gripped by the Antarctic. Carolrhoda Bks. 2003 112p il map (Trailblazer biography) lib bdg $25.26

Grades: 6 7 8 9　　　　　　　　　　　　　　92

1. Explorers 2. Explorers -- Great Britain -- Biography
ISBN 0-87614-920-4

LC 2002-6816

A biography of Sir Ernest Shackleton, the daring, charismatic Antarctic explorer who fell short of his goal of crossing Antarctica, but accomplished a far greater feat by bringing every member of his crew back alive
"The writing is lively and clear and the story is compelling. A useful title for reports and recreational reading." SLJ
Includes bibliographical references

Koestler-Grack, Rachel A. **Sir** Ernest Shackleton; [by] Linda Davis. Chelsea House 2009 143p il (Great explorers) lib bdg $30

Grades: 6 7 8 9　　　　　　　　　　　　　　92

1. Explorers
ISBN 978-1-60413-421-6 lib bdg; 1-60413-421-6 lib bdg

LC 2009-14164

Biography of Sir Ernest Shackleton

"The information . . . is presented in such a way as to attract and maintain readers' interest. . . . With a full complement of maps, photographs (where available), illustrations, time lines, and document reproductions, a full story is told. Well-written and throughly researched, this . . . will make a solid addition." SLJ
Includes glossary and bibliographical references

Shakur, Tupac

★ Golus, Carrie. **Tupac** Shakur; hip-hop idol. Twenty-First Century Books 2010 112p il (USA Today: lifeline biographies) lib bdg $33.26

Grades: 7 8 9 10 11 12　　　　　　　　　　　92

1. Poets 2. Actors 3. Rap music 4. African American musicians 5. Rap musicians
ISBN 978-0-7613-5473-4; 0-7613-5473-5

LC 2009-38127

"The story told in Tupac Shakur will be inspirational for some and a cautionary tale for others. Born into poverty, Shakur became one of hip-hop's biggest stars. But even as he climbed up the ladder of success, drugs and violence were always there to pull him back down." Booklist
Includes bibliographical references

Harris, Ashley Rae. **Tupac** Shakur; multi-platinum rapper. ABDO Pub. Co. 2010 112p il (Lives cut short) lib bdg $32.79

Grades: 5 6 7 8　　　　　　　　　　　　　　92

1. Poets 2. Actors 3. Hip-hop 4. Rap music 5. African American musicians 6. Rap musicians
ISBN 978-1-60453-791-8; 1-60453-791-4

This discusses Tupac Shakur's early life, "providing details that give insight into later success and troubles and maintaining a laudatory tone that focuses on the individual's artistic achievements and hard work to achieve fame. Details [such as] explaining . . . that Tupac Shakur was a standout student in high school are bound to resonate with readers. Numerous photos and sidebars appear throughout. [A] worthwhile [resource] for reports as well as popular reading." SLJ

Sheba, Queen of

Lucks, Naomi. **Queen** of Sheba. Chelsea House Publishers 2009 112p il (Ancient world leaders) lib bdg $30

Grades: 6 7 8 9　　　　　　　　　　　　　　92

1. Queens 2. Biblical characters
ISBN 978-0-7910-9579-9 lib bdg; 0-7910-9579-9 lib bdg

LC 2008004872

This biography of the Queen of Sheba "references various oral traditions from Europe, the Middle East, and Ethiopia to reveal aspects of the woman's personality. Classical paintings and full-color photographs of sculptures, landscapes, and archaeological finds complement the text. . . . The [text is] easily digestible and appropriate for the intended age group." SLJ
Includes glossary and bibliographical references

Shelley, Mary Wollstonecraft, 1797-1851

Wells, Catherine. **Strange** creatures: the story of Mary Shelley. Morgan Reynolds 2009 160p il (World writers) $28.95

Grades: 7 8 9 10   **92**

1. Authors 2. Novelists 3. Women authors 4. Authors, English

ISBN 978-1-59935-092-9; 1-59935-092-0

LC 2008039042

"This engaging biography limns [Mary Shelley's] unconventional life, focusing on her love affair (and later marriage) with poet Percy Bysshe Shelley, the writing of Frankenstein when she was still a teenager, and the novel's infamy and lasting influence. Period illustrations and photographs appear throughout." Horn Book Guide

Includes bibliographical references

Shivack, Nadia

Shivack, Nadia. **Inside** out; portrait of an eating disorder. written and illustrated by Nadia Shivack. Atheneum Books for Young Readers 2007 un il $17.99

Grades: 6 7 8 9   **92**

1. Graphic novels 2. Memoirists 3. Bulimia -- Graphic novels

ISBN 0-689-85216-9; 978-0-689-85216-9

LC 2004016096

"In this heartfelt, honest memoir, the author uses a graphic novel format to reveal her anguished, ongoing struggle with bulimia. . . . Though intensely personal and—perhaps of necessity—repetitious, this harrowing chronicle may well provide support and solace to teens facing a similar crisis." Publ Wkly

Siegal, Aranka

Siegal, Aranka. **Memories** of Babi; stories. Farrar, Straus & Giroux 2008 116p $16

Grades: 4 5 6 7   **92**

1. Authors 2. Farm life 3. Grandmothers 4. Holocaust survivors 5. Jews -- Biography 6. Children's authors 7. Short stories -- By individual authors

ISBN 978-0-374-39978-8; 0-374-39978-6

LC 2007007002

Siegal's "Upon the Head of the Goat (1981) is about her childhood in Hungary as Hitler comes to power. In this follow-up, written in nine wry sketches, she remembers the years before that—especially her close relationship with her Jewish grandmother, who lived on a small farm just across the Hungarian border in Ukraine." Booklist

★ Siegal, Aranka. **Upon** the head of the goat: a childhood in Hungary, 1939-1944. Farrar, Straus & Giroux 1981 213p hardcover o.p. pa $5.95

Grades: 6 7 8 9   **92**

1. Authors 2. Holocaust survivors 3. Jews -- Hungary 4. Children's authors 5. World War, 1939-1945 -- Jews 6. Holocaust, 1933-1945 -- Personal narratives

ISBN 0-374-38059-7; 0-374-48079-6 pa

LC 81-12642

A Newbery Medal honor book, 1982

"The story is familiar . . . but a few pages into Aranka Siegal's fine memoir . . . you feel the power and interest of her particular experience and remember that this story cannot be told too often." Newsweek

Silverstein, Shel

Baughan, Michael Gray. **Shel** Silverstein; [by] Michael Gray Baughan. Chelsea House 2008 120p il (Who wrote that?) lib bdg $30

Grades: 6 7 8 9   **92**

1. Poets 2. Authors 3. Singers 4. Cartoonists 5. Songwriters 6. Authors, American 7. Children's authors

ISBN 978-0-7910-9676-5 lib bdg; 0-7910-9676-9 lib bdg

LC 2007045336

This biography of the popular author of Where the Sidewalk Ends examines the writer's "life, including the inspiration behind some of [his] works. [The] volume includes photographs and quotations from interviews, as well as descriptions of main characters and annotations lists of books and awards. Useful for aspiring authors as well as book report writers." Horn Book Guide

Includes bibliographical references

Simmons, Russell, 1957-

Baughan, Brian. **Russell** Simmons; [by] Brian Baughan. Morgan Reynolds 2009 112p il (Business leaders) lib bdg $27.95

Grades: 6 7 8 9   **92**

1. Record producers 2. Broadcasting executives 3. Motion picture executives 4. Recording industry executives

ISBN 978-1-59935-075-2 lib bdg; 1-59935-075-0 lib bdg

LC 2007-37797

"Baughan describes Simmons's childhood in Queens, NY, his college days as a rap promoter, his teen years when he was involved with drugs, his early efforts as a music producer, business collaborations, and media empire. . . . Contain[s] full-color photos that add visual appeal, sidebars about related topics, and helpful time lines." SLJ

Includes bibliographical references

Lommel, Cookie. **Russell** Simmons. Chelsea House 2007 104p il (Hip-hop stars) lib bdg $30

Grades: 7 8 9 10   **92**

1. Record producers 2. Broadcasting executives 3. Motion picture executives 4. Recording industry executives

ISBN 978-0-7910-9467-9 lib bdg; 0-7910-9467-7 lib bdg

LC 2007001463

This "weaves a concise history of hip-hop music and culture into a solid biography of one of its originators, Def Jam Records founder Russell Simmons. . . . [This is an] inspiring title that's sure to find wide circulation among hip-hop fans." Booklist

Includes glossary and bibliographical references

Sitting Bull, Dakota Chief, 1831-1890

Stanley, George Edward. **Sitting** Bull; great Sioux hero. Sterling 2010 124p il map (Sterling biographies) lib bdg $12.95

Grades: 7 8 9 10   92

1. Dakota Indians 2. Indian chiefs 3. Native Americans -- Biography

ISBN 978-1-4027-6846-0 lib bdg; 1-4027-6846-X lib bdg

LC 2009-24141

This is a biography of the Sioux Indian chief.

Includes glossary and bibliographical references

Smith, Adam, 1723-1790

Crain, Cynthia D. **Adam** Smith; by Cynthia D. Crain and Dwight R. Lee. Morgan Reynolds Pub. 2009 160p il map (Profiles in economics) lib bdg $28.95

Grades: 8 9 10 11 12   92

1. Economists 2. Nonfiction writers

ISBN 978-1-59935-107-0 lib bdg; 1-59935-107-2 lib bdg

LC 2009-138

Biography of the economist Adam Smith

"Relationships, education, early influences, and family life are all described . . . [and] economic theory is closely tied to cultural and political events. . . . The writing is straightforward, the . . . [author] assume[s] a certain level of knowledge about world events." SLJ

Includes bibliographical references

Snicket, Lemony, 1970-

Abrams, Dennis. **Lemony** Snicket (Daniel Handler) foreword by Kyle Zimmer. Chelsea House Publishers 2010 117p il (Who wrote that?) lib bdg $35

Grades: 6 7 8 9 10   92

1. Authors 2. Novelists 3. Authors, American 4. Children's authors

ISBN 978-1-60413-726-2; 1-60413-726-6

LC 2010006599

A biography of the author of the A Series of Unfortunate Events series.

"Abrams delivers a witty account of his subject. . . . He presents a substantive look at Snicket/Handler, including synopses of and reactions to his adult books, his major influences, and musical interests. Abundant secondary-source quotes, full-color photos and film stills, and a chapter devoted to the series that made him famous will appeal to many readers. This lively biography will not disappoint." SLJ

Includes bibliographical references

Snyder, Grace, 1882-1982

Warren, Andrea. **Pioneer** girl; a true story of growing up on the prairie. with a new afterword by the author. University of Nebraska Press 2009 104p il map pa $14.95

Grades: 5 6 7 8   92

1. Frontier and pioneer life 2. Quiltmakers 3. Centenarians

ISBN 978-0-8032-2526-8 pa; 0-8032-2526-1 pa

LC 2009-20883

First published 1998 by Morrow Junior Books

Biography of Nebraska homesteader, Grace McCance Snyder

"This new edition offers an afterword that includes information about black homesteaders, Native Americans, and the specific tasks of women, especially quilting. . . . Although it is written for younger readers than a teen audience, readability and intense subject matter should make the book popular with those readers." Voice Youth Advocates

Includes bibliographical references

Soto, Gary

Abrams, Dennis. **Gary** Soto; foreword by Kyle Zimmer. Chelsea House Pubs. 2008 120p il (Who wrote that?) $30

Grades: 5 6 7 8   92

1. Poets 2. Authors 3. Novelists 4. Mexican American authors 5. Essayists 6. College teachers 7. Authors, American 8. Children's authors 9. Young adult authors 10. Mexican Americans -- Biography 11. Children's literature -- Authors and illustrators

ISBN 978-0-7910-9529-4; 0-7910-9529-0

LC 2007045509

A biography of the popular Mexican American author for children and young adults.

Includes bibliographical references

Soto, Hernando de, ca. 1500-1542

Young, Jeff C. **Hernando** de Soto; Spanish conquistador in the Americas. Enslow Publishers 2009 112p il (Great explorers of the world) lib bdg $31.93

Grades: 6 7 8 9   92

1. Explorers 2. Colonial administrators

ISBN 978-1-59845-104-7 lib bdg; 1-59845-104-9 lib bdg

LC 2008-30753

"Discusses the life of Spanish explorer Hernando de Soto, including his travels in the Americas, the claim of Florida for Spain, and his eventual discovery of the Mississippi River." Publisher's note

Includes glossary and bibliographical references

Sotomayor, Sonia, 1954-

Gitlin, Marty. **Sonia** Sotomayor; Supreme Court justice. by Martin Gitlin. ABDO Pub. Co. 2011 112p il (Essential lives) $32.79

Grades: 5 6 7 8   92

1. Judges 2. Women judges 3. District attorneys 4. Supreme Court justices 5. Hispanic Americans -- Biography

ISBN 978-1-61613-518-8; 1-61613-518-2

LC 2010000499

This biography of Supreme Court Justice Sonia Sotomayor "toggles between the subject's personal and professional life; [it] offers sidebar explanations of legal issues. . . . The writing is accessible, the format is open, and full-color photos appear throughout." SLJ

Includes glossary and bibliographical references

McElroy, Lisa Tucker. **Sonia** Sotomayor; first Hispanic U.S. Supreme Court justice. Lerner Publications 2010 48p il lib bdg $26.60

Grades: 5 6 7 8   92

1. Judges 2. Women judges 3. District attorneys 4. Supreme Court justices 5. Hispanic Americans -- Biography

ISBN 978-0-7613-5861-9 lib bdg; 0-7613-5861-7 lib bdg

LC 2009037703

"Well organized and straightforward, this biography is appealing with its bright photographs and bold, easy-to-read font. Starting with Sotomayor's childhood in the Bronx, the author covers the justice's life and career up to her nomination to the Supreme Court. . . . An informative, interesting, and, most of all, inspiring read." SLJ

Includes bibliographical references

Spade, Kate

Freistadt, Margo. **Kate** Spade. Morgan Reynolds Pub. 2011 112p il (Profiles in fashion) $28.95

Grades: 7 8 9 10   92

1. Fashion designers

ISBN 978-1-59935-154-4; 1-59935-154-4

LC 2010022227

A biography of Kate Spade, designer of handbags, luggage, stationery, shoes, eyeglasses, homewares and other products.

Includes bibliographical references

Standish, Myles, 1584?-1656

Harness, Cheryl. The **adventurous** life of Myles Standish; and the amazing-but-true survival story of Plymouth Colony. painstakingly written and illustrated by Cheryl Harness. National Geographic 2006 144p il map (Cheryl Harness history) $16.95; lib bdg $25.90

Grades: 4 5 6 7   92

1. Pilgrims (New England colonists) 2. Colonists 3. Pilgrim fathers 4. Colonial leaders

ISBN 978-0-7922-5918-3; 0-7922-5918-1; 978-0-7922-5919-0 lib bdg; 0-7922-5919-X lib bdg

"Harness chronicles the history of the Plymouth Pilgrims from their troubles in England to their first years in North America, with the focus on Standish. Separating documented history from speculation, the narrative explains religious movements, introduces key figures, and gives a balanced account of Pilgrim-Indian relationships. . . . The tone is casual. . . . A reader-friendly approach to history." Booklist

Includes bibliographical references

Stanton, Elizabeth Cady, 1815-1902

Colman, Penny. **Elizabeth** Cady Stanton and Susan B. Anthony; a friendship that changed the world. Henry Holt and Company 2011 256p il $18.99

Grades: 7 8 9 10   92

1. Feminism 2. Suffragists 3. Women -- Suffrage

ISBN 978-0-8050-8293-7; 0-8050-8293-X

LC 2010-39762

"Elizabeth Cady Stanton, a married mother of four boys at the time they met, and Susan B. Anthony, an unmarried schoolteacher, formed a friendship that lasted until Elizabeth's death more than 50 years later. Their tireless work, including advocacy, speeches, organizing and writing, placed them at the center of tumultuous events in the middle of the 19th century. . . . This [is a] lively, very readable narrative. . . . This thoughtful portrayal to two complex women is . . . enhanced by comprehensive backmatter, making this an invaluable addition to the literature of suffrage." Kirkus

Includes bibliographical references

Elizabeth Cady Stanton; the right is ours. by Sigerman, Harriet. Oxford Univ. Press 2001 143p il (Oxford portraits) $28

Grades: 7 8 9 10   92

1. Feminism 2. Suffragists 3. Women -- Suffrage 4. Feminists -- United States 5. Women's rights -- United States -- History

ISBN 0-19-511969-X

LC 2001-31404

A biography of one of the first leaders of the women's rights movement, whose work led to women's right to vote

"This inspiring biography . . . is both interestingly written and easy to follow. . . . Black-and-white photographs and original documents add greatly to the appeal of this resource." SLJ

Includes bibliographical references

Steiner, Matt

Warren, Andrea. **Escape** from Saigon; how a Vietnam War orphan became an American boy. Farrar, Straus and Giroux 2004 110p il map hardcover o.p. pa $9.95

Grades: 6 7 8 9 10   92

1. Refugees 2. Physicians 3. Interracial adoption 4. Vietnamese Americans 5. Racially mixed people 6. Vietnam War, 1961-1975

ISBN 978-0-374-32224-3; 0-374-32224-4; 978-0-374-40023-1 pa; 0-374-40023-7 pa

LC 2003-60672

Chronicles the experiences of Matt Steiner, an orphaned Amerasian boy, from his birth and early childhood in Saigon through his departure from Vietnam in the 1975 Operation Babylift and his subsequent life as the adopted son of an American family in Ohio.

"The child-at-war story and the facts about the Operation Babylift rescue are tense and exciting. Just as gripping is the boy's personal conflict." Booklist

Steller, Georg Wilhelm, 1700-1746

Arnold, Ann. **Sea** cows, shamans, and scurvy: Alaska's first naturalist: Georg Wilhelm Steller. Farrar, Straus & Giroux 2008 227p il map $21

Grades: 6 7 8 9   92

1. Explorers 2. Naturalists 3. Natural history

ISBN 978-0-374-39947-4; 0-374-39947-6

LC 2006037400

"This is a detailed and lavishly illustrated biography of Georg Wilhelm Steller (1707-1746), Alaska's first naturalist. . . . He is the only scientist ever to describe, dissect, and eat the flightless spectacled cormorant. Species bear his name, including Steller's albatross, eider, jay, sculpin, sea cow, sea eagle, and sea lion. Arnold's exciting, harrowing account is personalized by excerpts from Steller's journal." KLIATT

Includes bibliographical references

Stine, R. L., 1943-

Marcovitz, Hal. **R.L.** Stine; foreword by Kyle Zimmer. Chelsea House Publishers 2006 134p il (Who wrote that?) lib bdg $30

Grades: 6 7 8 9   **92**
1. Authors 2. Horror fiction 3. Magazine editors 4. Authors, American 5. Children's authors 6. Children's literature -- Authors and illustrators
ISBN 0-7910-8659-3

LC 2005008186

A biography of the popular author of Goosebumps and other children's horror stories.

Includes bibliographical references

Stone, Biz

Smith, Chris. **Twitter**; Jack Dorsey, Biz Stone and Evan Williams. [by] Chris Smith and Marci Mc-Grath. Morgan Reynolds Pub. 2011 112p il (Business leaders) $28.95

Grades: 7 8 9 10 11 12   **92**
1. Online social networks 2. Internet executives 3. Computer programmers 4. Computer software executives
ISBN 978-1-59935-179-7; 1-59935-179-X; 978-1-59935-216-9 e-book

LC 2011024699

This biography of the founders of Twitter "will grab YAs. . . . The design is browsable, with clear type and lots of color screens and informal photos of young people at work." Booklist

Includes bibliographical references

Sui, Anna

Darraj, Susan Muaddi. **Anna** Sui. Chelsea House Publishers 2009 120p il (Asian Americans of achievement) $30

Grades: 7 8 9 10   **92**
1. Fashion designers
ISBN 978-1-60413-570-1; 1-60413-570-0

LC 2009-14608

"Anna Sui is known for her youthful 'baby doll' designs and extravagant combinations inspired by the hippie and rock-'n'-roll fashions of the '60s and early '70s. Readers learn about the setbacks and hard work required to become successful. . . . The quality of research and in-depth coverage broadens [the book's] usefulness. . . . [This book is] inspiring." SLJ

Includes glossary and bibliographical references

Sullivan, Anne, 1866-1936

Delano, Marfe Ferguson. **Helen's** eyes; a photobiography of Annie Sullivan, Helen Keller's teacher. [foreword by Keller Johnson Thompson] National Geographic 2008 63p il map $17.95; lib bdg $27.90

Grades: 4 5 6 7   **92**
1. Deaf 2. Blind 3. Authors 4. Teachers 5.

Memoirists 6. Humanitarians 7. Teachers of the deaf 8. Inspirational writers 9. Teachers of the blind 10. Social welfare leaders
ISBN 978-1-4263-02-9-1; 1-4263-0209-6; 978-1-4263-0210-7 lib bdg; 1-4263-0210-X lib bdg

"There are many biographies of Helen Keller and Annie Sullivan, but this one is very nicely done. . . . The book is honest in its portrayals, especially of Sullivan. . . . What makes this oversize book so appealing is the clean design, with large typeface. The many fascinating photographs are sometimes placed over historical documents." Booklist

Includes bibliographical references

Tan, Amy

Mussari, Mark. **Amy** Tan. Marshall Cavendish Benchmark 2010 125p il (Today's writers and their works) lib bdg $42.79

Grades: 8 9 10 11 12   **92**
1. Authors 2. Novelists 3. Women authors 4. Essayists 5. Authors, American 6. Children's authors 7. Short story writers 8. Chinese Americans -- Biography
ISBN 978-0-7614-4127-4; 0-7614-4127-1

This biography of Amy Tan places the author in the context of her times and discusses her work.

Includes bibliographical references

O'Keefe, Sherry. **From** China to America; the story of Amy Tan. Morgan Reynolds Pub. 2011 112p il lib bdg $28.95

Grades: 7 8 9 10   **92**
1. Authors 2. Novelists 3. Women authors 4. Essayists 5. Authors, American 6. Children's authors 7. Short story writers 8. Chinese Americans -- Biography
ISBN 978-1-59935-138-4; 1-59935-138-2

LC 2010-7594

"Born in California, the daughter of Chinese immigrants, Tan grew up as an American on the outside and Chinese on the inside. . . . Growing up, Tan faced the loss of her brother and father and the morbid outlook of her mother. Their tumultuous relationship led her to write stories about mother-and-daughter conflict, which later became the basis for The Joy Luck Club. This book gives readers a brief overview of the novelist's life and a greater understanding of the inspiration behind her novels." SLJ

Includes bibliographical references

Taylor, Major, 1878-1932

Brill, Marlene Targ. **Marshall** Major Taylor; world champion bicyclist, 1899-1901. by Marlene Targ Brill. Twenty-First Century Books 2008 112p il (Trailblazer biography) lib bdg $31.93

Grades: 5 6 7 8   **92**
1. Bicycle racing 2. African American athletes 3. Cyclists
ISBN 978-0-8225-6610-6 lib bdg; 0-8225-6610-9 lib bdg

LC 2006003883

"Marshall Taylor, an African American bicyclist who, despite facing prejudice in racing and in life, achieved world renown at the turn of the last century. . . . Brill's accessible, personable prose vividly relates Taylor's experiences." Booklist

Includes bibliographical references

Tecumseh, Shawnee Chief, 1768-1813

Zimmerman, Dwight Jon. **Tecumseh**; shooting star of the Shawnee. Sterling 2010 124p il map (Sterling biographies) lib bdg $12.95

Grades: 7 8 9 10   92

1. Shawnee Indians 2. Indian chiefs 3. Native Americans -- Biography

ISBN 978-1-4027-6847-7; 1-4027-6847-8

LC 2009-24142

"Lots of detailed physical battles dominate Tecumseh, with a strong focus on the Shawnee's brutal displacement by white settlers and the Indians caught up in the tensions between the U.S. and Great Britain. . . . [The] spacious design is highly scannable, with color background screens, photos, maps, and historic prints throughout." Booklist

Includes glossary and bibliographical references

Teresa, Mother, 1910-1997

Slavicek, Louise Chipley. **Mother** Teresa; caring for the world's poor. Chelsea House 2007 113p bibl il por (Modern peacemakers) lib bdg $30

Grades: 7 8 9 10   92

1. Nuns 2. Missionaries 3. Nobel laureates for peace

ISBN 0-7910-9433-2 lib bdg; 978-0-7910-9433-4 lib bdg

LC 2006028383

A biography of the nun who won the Nobel Peace Prize for her work with the poor of India

This "book is well organized and well written, and reads like a story. It is balanced in that it points out the critics of Mother Teresa's selection for the Nobel Peace Prize . . . as well as her admirers." SLJ

Includes bibliographical references

Tesla, Nikola, 1856-1943

Burgan, Michael. **Nikola** Tesla; physicist, inventor, electrical engineer. Compass Point Books 2009 112p il map (Signature lives) lib bdg $34.65

Grades: 6 7 8 9 10   92

1. Inventors 2. Electrical engineers

ISBN 978-0-7565-4086-9; 0-7565-4086-0

LC 2008-35725

A biography of Nikola Tesla, physicist, inventor, and electrical engineer

The "inviting page design features photos and boxed screens on each spread, and . . . includes a detailed bibliography, source notes, time line and glossary." Booklist

Includes glossary and bibliographical references

Thoreau, Henry David, 1817-1862

★ Meltzer, Milton. **Henry** David Thoreau; a biography. Twenty-First Century Books 2007 160p il lib bdg $31.93

Grades: 7 8 9 10 11 12   92

1. Authors 2. Naturalists 3. Essayists 4. Pacifists 5. Authors, American 6. Writers on nature 7. Nonfiction

writers

ISBN 978-0-8225-5893-4 lib bdg; 0-8225-5893-9 lib bdg

LC 2006013747

In this biography "readers see Thoreau through a variety of lenses—brother, friend, pencil maker, abolitionist, naturalist, and transcendentalist—to name only a few. Meltzer's clear and succinct writing style is punctuated with well-chosen and good-quality photographs and reproductions. . . . A first-rate choice for any student seeking a well-organized introduction to the life of the author and philosopher." SLJ

Includes bibliographical references

Thorpe, Jim, 1888-1953

Bruchac, Joseph. **Jim** Thorpe; original All-American. Dial Books/Walden Media 2006 277p il $16.99

Grades: 6 7 8 9   92

1. Athletes 2. Decathletes 3. Pentathletes 4. Olympic athletes 5. Native Americans -- Biography

ISBN 0-8037-3118-3

LC 2005-32173

A biography of Native American athlete Jim Thorpe, focusing on his early athletic career.

"Bruchac relates the story in first person as if the reader is listening to Thorpe tell about his early life. . . . This conceit is extremely effective, and combined with Bruchac's excellently written first-person reminiscences of key football plays and Olympic competition, will make the book appeal to reluctant readers who might otherwise not read biographies." Voice Youth Advocates

Includes bibliographical references

Labrecque, Ellen. **Jim** Thorpe; an athlete for the ages. Sterling 2010 124p il (Sterling biographies) $12.95

Grades: 7 8 9 10   92

1. Athletes 2. Decathletes 3. Pentathletes 4. Olympic athletes 5. Native Americans -- Biography

ISBN 978-1-4027-7150-7; 1-4027-7150-9

This biography of Native American athlete Jim Thorpe is "studded with quotes and illustrated with photos. . . . [It] details his taking of Olympic gold in the 1912 decathlon and pentathlon events, though he was forced to return the medals the following year amid charges of professionalism, a matter resolved in his favor 70 years later. Written in a straightforward, journalistic style, [this biography presents a] very readable [account] of the [life] of [an athlete] who made [his mark] on American culture." Booklist

Schuman, Michael. **Jim** Thorpe; There's no such thing as 'can't' [by] Michael A. Schuman. Enslow Publishers 2009 128p il map (Americans: the spirit of a nation) lib bdg $31.93

Grades: 6 7 8 9   92

1. Athletes 2. Decathletes 3. Pentathletes 4. Olympic athletes 5. Native Americans -- Biography

ISBN 978-0-7660-3021-3 lib bdg; 0-7660-3021-0 lib bdg

LC 2008-21486

This "describes the Native American baseball player's birth in the Indian Territory of Oklahoma, his education at the repressive Indian schools, and his groundbreaking career as one of the most well-rounded and talented athletes of the 20th century." SLJ

Includes glossary and bibliographical references

Tillage, Leon, 1936-

★ Tillage, Leon. **Leon's** story; [by] Leon Walter Tillage; collage art by Susan L. Roth. Farrar, Straus & Giroux 1997 107p il hardcover o.p. pa $6.95

Grades: 4 5 6 7 8 9 10   92

1. African Americans -- Biography

ISBN 0-374-34379-9; 0-374-44330-0 pa

LC 96-43544

The son of a North Carolina sharecropper recalls the hard times faced by his family and other African Americans in the first half of the twentieth century and the changes that the civil rights movement helped bring about

The author's "voice is direct, the words are simple. There is no rhetoric, no commentary, no bitterness. . . . This quiet drama will move readers of all ages . . . and may encourage them to record their own family stories." Booklist

Tolkien, J. R. R. (John Ronald Reuel), 1892-1973

Willett, Edward. **J.R.R.** Tolkien; master of imaginary worlds. Enslow Publishers 2004 128p il (Authors teens love) lib bdg $26.60

Grades: 6 7 8 9   92

1. Authors 2. Novelists 3. Linguists 4. Philologists 5. Fantasy writers 6. Authors, English 7. Children's authors

ISBN 0-7660-2246-3

LC 2003-15657

Examines the personal life and literary career of the author of the Lord of the Rings trilogy

This "clearly goes a step beyond the typical series book, offering a more perceptive and more detailed, satisfying portrayal of its subject. . . . [The] volume includes a great deal of back matter: a time line, a list of selected works, a glossary, detailed chapter notes, and lists of recommended books and Internet sites." Booklist

Includes bibliographical references

Tom Thumb, 1838-1883

★ Sullivan, George. **Tom** Thumb; the remarkable true story of a man in miniature. Clarion Books 2010 200p il $20

Grades: 6 7 8 9   92

1. Circus 2. Dwarfs 3. Little people 4. Circus performers

ISBN 0-547-18203-1; 978-0-547-18203-2

LC 2009-52910

This is a biography of the circus performer who was part of the P.T. Barnum troupe.

"Insets on dwarfism appear early in the text, elucidating Tom Thumb's condition for readers without seriously interrupting to genial flow of the narration. Generous leading and a large stock of photographs and period reproductions will entice readers who shy away from longer works of nonfiction." Bull Cent Child Books

Toussaint Louverture, 1743?-1803

★ Rockwell, Anne F. **Open** the door to liberty!: a biography of Toussaint L'Ouverture; illustrated by R. Gregory Christie. Houghton Mifflin Books for Children 2009 64p il $18

Grades: 5 6 7 8   92

1. Generals 2. Revolutionaries 3. Blacks -- Biography 4. Slavery -- West Indies

ISBN 978-0-618-60570-5; 0-618-60570-3

LC 2007-25746

"In this eye-opening biography, Rockwell makes a strong case that Toussaint L'Ouverture is one of the most overlooked heroes of the eighteenth century. A freed slave of the French colony of St. Domingue (what we now know as Haiti), L'Ouverture was 48 when he was so inspired by his people's uprising against the French that he joined them and, through his oratory and strategical skills, became their leader. In 1793, he led history's first triumphant slave rebellion, but the resulting freedom would not last long. . . . Evocative paintings in primary colors help tell the story." Booklist

Includes bibliographical references

Truth, Sojourner, d. 1883

Butler, Mary G. **Sojourner** Truth; from slave to activist for freedom. PowerPlus Bks. 2003 112p il map (Library of American lives and times) lib bdg $31.95

Grades: 5 6 7 8   92

1. Feminism 2. Abolitionists 3. African American women 4. Memoirists 5. African American women -- Biography

ISBN 0-8239-5736-5

LC 2001-6169

A biography of the former slave who became an abolitionist and advocate for women's rights

"The text is well documented, and the numerous illustrations, photos, and reproductions, both in color and in black and white, are authoritative and informative." SLJ

Includes glossary and bibliographical references

Sojourner Truth; speaking up for freedom. by Geoffrey Michael Horn. Crabtree Pub. Co. 2010 64 p. ill. (some col.) (pbk. : alk. paper) $10.95

Grades: 4 5 6 7 8   92

1. Abolitionists -- United States -- Biography 2. African American women -- Biography 3. African American abolitionists -- Biography 4. Social reformers -- United States -- Biography

ISBN 0778748405; 9780778748243; 9780778748403

LC 2009022428

This children's picture book by Geoffrey M. Horn in the Voices for Freedom: Abolitionist Views series looks at abolitionist Sojourner Truth. It "relates and details Truth's life and times, from her often-brutal treatment as a slave, named Isabella at birth, to her freedom, religious influences, and self-determination . . . and path to outspoken, sometimes provocative, and influential traveling speaker on a mission to raise awareness of and support for abolitionism." (Booklist)

"Combining accessible, lively prose and abundant visuals, this title . . . offers an engaging, informative introduction to the early advocate for the rights of African Americans and women." Booklist

Tubman, Harriet, 1820?-1913

★ Allen, Thomas B. **Harriet** Tubman, secret agent; how daring slaves and free Blacks spied for the Union during the Civil War. featuring illustrations by Carla Bauer. National Geographic Society 2006 191p il map $16.95; lib bdg $25.90

Grades: 6 7 8 9   **92**

1. Abolitionists 2. Underground railroad 3. African American women 4. Slavery -- United States 5. African American women -- Biography

ISBN 0-7922-7889-5; 0-7922-7890-9 lib bdg

LC 2005030927

"Allen brings readers much more than the usual biography of the brave rescuer on the Underground Railroad. This small, packed volume tells of Harriet Tubman's astonishing roles as spy, secret agent, and military leader, and it combines her personal story with a history of the abolitionist movement and the Civil War, focusing on how ex-slaves and free blacks served the Union cause. . . . The dense history is illustrated with numerous archival images, maps, and woodcuts, and the documentation is meticulous." Booklist

Includes bibliographical references

Sawyer, Kem Knapp. **Harriet** Tubman. DK Publishing 2010 128p il (DK biography) pa $5.99

Grades: 6 7 8 9   **92**

1. Abolitionists 2. Underground railroad 3. Slavery -- United States 4. African American women -- Biography

ISBN 978-0-7566-5806-9; 0-7566-5806-3

An illustrated exploration of the life of Harriet Tubman that covers her childhood, experiences as a slave, escape to freedom, work on the Underground Railroad, antislavery activism, and other topics.

"Meticulous about what is known and what is 'not confirmed,' the simple prose is eloquent in describing how Tubman started as a passenger on the Underground Railroad and went on to become one of its most famous conductors. . . . Highly readable, the series design, with highly legible type on thick paper, includes color photographs and prints on every spread." Booklist

Includes bibliographical references

Turing, Alan Mathison, 1912-1954

Corrigan, Jim. **Alan** Turing. Morgan Reynolds Pub. 2008 112p il (Profiles in mathematics) lib bdg $27.95

Grades: 7 8 9 10   **92**

1. Mathematicians

ISBN 978-1-59935-064-6; 1-59935-064-5

LC 2007-11704

"Corrigan's descriptions of English mathematician Turing as sporting 'ragged, wrinkled clothes' and few social graces will fit many readers' mental image of a numbers genius. But other aspects of this portrait push against stereotypes. . . . Throughout, candid mentions of Turing's homosexuality help readers contextualize the scandal he endured after running afoul of the era's discriminatory legislation. Equal sensitivity distinguishes Corringan's handling of Turing's death, officially (but not decisively) a suicide." Booklist

Includes bibliographical references

★ Henderson, Harry. **Alan** Turing; computing genius and wartime code breaker. Chelsea House 2011 133p il (Makers of modern science) $35

Grades: 7 8 9 10   **92**

1. Mathematicians 2. Artificial intelligence 3. Computers -- History

ISBN 978-0-8160-6175-4; 0-8160-6175-0

LC 2010-15798

A biography of code breaker and computer pioneer Alan Turing.

"The mark of a good biography is when it makes people you may never have heard of, in fields you might not be interested in, fascinating. [This book] does this with [a] well-chosen [subject], engaging writing, plenty of sidebars that take the text in new directions, and perhaps most importantly, the determination to present a fully-rounded person, not just a scientist." Booklist

Includes bibliographical references

Tutankhamen, King of Egypt

★ Demi. **Tutankhamun**; written and illustrated by Demi. Marshall Cavendish Children 2009 un il map $19.99

Grades: 4 5 6 7   **92**

1. Kings and rulers 2. Kings

ISBN 978-0-7614-5558-5; 0-7614-5558-2

LC 2008029313

"The unmistakable designs and opulent glitter of ancient Egyptian art gleam on every page of Demi's picture-book introduction to Tutankhamun. Beginning with King Tut's great-grandfather, Demi presents the broad historical context surrounding the young monarch's reign. . . . Demi's language, organized into brief but pithy paragraphs, is clear. . . . It's the beautiful illustrations that will attract and hold a young audience most, and as usual, Demi incorporates artistic motifs and materials appropriate to her subject." Booklist

Twain, Mark, 1835-1910

Caravantes, Peggy. A **great** and sublime fool; the story of Mark Twain. Morgan Reynolds Pub. 2009 176p il map (World writers) lib bdg $28.95

Grades: 7 8 9 10   **92**

1. Authors 2. Humorists 3. Novelists 4. Essayists 5. Satirists 6. Memoirists 7. Travel writers 8. Authors, American 9. Short story writers

ISBN 978-1-599-35088-2; 1-599-35088-2

LC 2008-34139

This "offers a workmanlike but readable account of one of America's first great writers. . . . A nice selection of photographs and artwork complement the narrative. . . . Detailed source notes and an in-depth time line round out this even and reliable . . . biography." Booklist

Includes bibliographical references

★ Fleischman, Sid. The **trouble** begins at 8; a life of Mark Twain in the wild, wild West. Greenwillow Books 2008 224p il $18.99; lib bdg $19.89

Grades: 5 6 7 8   **92**

1. Authors 2. Humorists 3. Novelists 4. Essayists 5. Satirists 6. Memoirists 7. Travel writers 8. Authors,

American 9. Short story writers
ISBN 0-06-134431-1; 0-06-134432-X lib bdg; 978-0-06-134431-2; 978-0-06-134432-9 lib bdg

LC 2007-37891

This biography of Mark Twain focuses on his travels. "Fleischman writes a charming biography of Samuel Clemens before he became Mark Twain, the great American novelist. . . . Written with a sense of humor and wit that honors Twain, this book is sprinkled with famous Twain quotes, excerpts of his writing, and pictures of Twain and other primary documents from the era Clemens spent both on the Mississippi River and in the West." Voice Youth Advocates

Includes bibliographical references

Houle, Michelle M. **Mark** Twain; banned, challenged, and censored. Enslow Publishers 2008 160p il (Authors of banned books) lib bdg $34.60
Grades: 8 9 10 11 12   92
1. Authors 2. Humorists 3. Novelists 4. Censorship 5. Essayists 6. Satirists 7. Memoirists 8. Travel writers 9. Authors, American 10. Short story writers
ISBN 978-0-7660-2689-6 lib bdg; 0-7660-2689-2 lib bdg

LC 2007-22362

"This book combines biography, criticism, and an exploration of the role of censorship in literature and education. . . . Houle offers a brief history of censorship in literature in order to place Twain's case in context, and a history of the challenges and defenses of the author's work from his contemporaries and modern critics. Illustrations include color photographs of related modern scenes (such as one that shows book burning), reproductions of artwork from early editions of Twain's works, and period cartoons and photographs." SLJ

Includes glossary and bibliographical references

Sonneborn, Liz. **Mark** Twain; foreword by Kyle Zimmer. Chelsea House Publishers 2010 125p il (Who wrote that?) lib bdg $35
Grades: 6 7 8 9 10   92
1. Authors 2. Humorists 3. Novelists 4. Essayists 5. Satirists 6. Memoirists 7. Travel writers 8. Authors, American 9. Short story writers
ISBN 978-1-60413-728-6; 1-60413-728-2

LC 2010006601

This biography of Mark Twain "begins with the writer's memorable visit to his Missouri hometown in 1902, then tracks back to his early days and his well-known transformation from Sam Clemens to Mark Twain. Sonneborn deals with her material well, hitting all the highlights and keeping the narrative moving along. Good use of details adds interest. . . . A solid purchase." SLJ

Includes bibliographical references

Valentino
Reis, Ronald A. **Valentino**. Chelsea House 2011 119p il (Famous fashion designers) lib bdg $35
Grades: 6 7 8 9 10   92
1. Fashion designers
ISBN 978-1-60413-983-9; 1-60413-983-8

LC 2010034101

This is a biography of fashion designer Valentino. Includes glossary and bibliographical references

Vedder, Amy
Ebersole, Rene. **Gorilla** mountain; the story of wildlife biologist, Amy Vedder. [by] Rene Ebersole. F. Watts 2005 118p il (Women's adventures in science) lib bdg $31
Grades: 7 8 9 10   92
1. Gorillas 2. Conservationists 3. Women scientists
ISBN 0-531-16779-8

LC 2005-00823

A biography of wildlife biologist Amy Vedder
This is "interesting, substantive, and eminently readable." SLJ

Includes bibliographical references

Versace, Gianni, 1946-1997
Davis, Daniel K. **Versace**. Chelsea House 2011 116p il (Famous fashion designers) lib bdg $35
Grades: 6 7 8 9 10   92
1. Fashion designers
ISBN 978-1-60413-980-8; 1-60413-980-3

LC 2010034103

This is a biography of fashion designer Gianni Versace. "Biography collections in need of a bit of sprucing up should find [this title] helpful." SLJ

Includes glossary and bibliographical references

Vincent, Erin
Vincent, Erin. **Grief** girl; my true story. Delacorte Press 2007 306p $15.99; lib bdg $18.99
Grades: 8 9 10 11 12   92
1. Authors 2. Bereavement 3. Memoirists
ISBN 978-0-385-73353-3; 0-385-73353-4; 978-0-385-90368-4 lib bdg; 0-385-90368-5 lib bdg

LC 2006-11650

"In 1983, Vincent, then 14, lost both her parents in a road accident. In this poignant memoir, she chronicles her rocky journey through adolescence as she, her 17-year-old sister, Tracy, and their brother, Trent, learn to cope on their own." Booklist

Wagué Diakité, Baba
Wague Diakite, Baba. A **gift** from childhood; memories of an African boyhood. Groundwood Books 2010 134p il $18.95
Grades: 5 6 7 8   92
1. Artists 2. Authors 3. Illustrators 4. Children's authors
ISBN 978-0-88899-931-3; 0-88899-931-3

"Diakite's . . . illustrated memoir focuses on his childhood in a small Malian village. . . . Interspersed with Diakite's recounting of his youth . . . are stories about his grandfather's brokering peaceful relations with the French, a blacksmith who stymies Death, and others. . . . Diakite's precise language and vibrant illustrations, created on earthenware tiles, form an engrossing story of community life. Studded with Malian proverbs, metaphors, and morals . . . it's a memoir alive with far more voices than just that of the author." Publ Wkly

Waldman, Neil, 1947-

★ Waldman, Neil. **Out** of the shadows; an artist's journey. Boyds Mills Press 2006 144p il $21.95

Grades: 5 6 7 8   92

1. Artists 2. Authors 3. Illustrators 4. Jews -- Biography 5. Children's authors 6. Artists -- United States

ISBN 1-59078-411-1

Neil Waldman reveals how his passion for art emerged in the kitchen of his family's apartment, where he discovered the work of Vincent Van Gogh and the ability to use illustration as a means to escape the sadness that plagued his home.

"Young artists, as well as readers who wonder about the person behind the pictures they have seen, will appreciate every element of this book: well-constructed story, visual richness, and uncompromising honesty." Booklist

Walker, C. J., Madame, 1867-1919

Bundles, A'Lelia P. **Madam** C.J. Walker; entrepreneur. [by] A'Lelia Bundles. Legacy ed; Chelsea House Publishers 2008 103p (Black Americans of achievement) lib bdg $30

Grades: 6 7 8 9   92

1. Philanthropists 2. African American businesspeople 3. Cosmeticians 4. Cosmetics industry executives 5. African American women -- Biography

ISBN 978-1-60413-072-0 lib bdg; 1-60413-072-5 lib bdg

LC 2008008429

First published 1991

A biography of the African American businesswoman whose invention of facial creams and other cosmetics led to great financial success

The book goes "beyond the typical personal information to provide some social history relevant to the subject's time. Captioned photographs and boxed inserts enhance the conversational [text]." Horn Book Guide

Includes bibliographical references

Walker, Maggie Lena, 1867-1934

Ransom, Candice F. **Maggie** L. Walker; pioneering banker and community leader. Twenty-First Century Books 2009 112p il (Trailblazer biographies) lib bdg $31.93

Grades: 6 7 8 9   92

1. African American businesspeople 2. Bankers 3. African American women -- Biography

ISBN 978-0-8225-6611-3 lib bdg; 0-8225-6611-7 lib bdg

LC 2007-42906

Retells the life and career of Maggie L. Walker, who founded the St. Luke Penny Savings Bank, the first bank established specifically for African Americans.

"The text is thoroughly researched and well organized... . Good-quality archival photographs add interest and clarity. A solid selection for report writers." SLJ

Includes bibliographical references

Walker, Mary Edwards, 1832-1919

Goldsmith, Bonnie Zucker. **Dr.** Mary Edwards Walker; Civil War surgeon & medal of honor recipient. [by] Bonnie Z. Goldsmith. ABDO Pub. 2010 112p il (Military heroes) lib bdg $22.65

Grades: 7 8 9   92

1. Physicians 2. Suffragists 3. Women physicians 4. Feminists

ISBN 978-1-60453-966-0; 1-60453-966-6

LC 2009-32367

Biography of suffragist and physician, Dr. Mary Edwards Walker.

"The rush of literary adrenalin will hook readers immediately and keep them enthralled until the end. . . . Given the dynamic topic [and] . . . appealing layout . . . [this is] likely to attract reluctant readers. In addition, sources are plentiful and well documented." SLJ

Includes glossary and bibliographical references

Wallenberg, Raoul

★ Borden, Louise, 1949- **His** name was Raoul Wallenberg. Houghton Mifflin 2012 135p il $18.99

Grades: 7 8 9 10 11 12   92

1. Diplomats 2. Missing persons 3. Political prisoners 4. Humanitarians 5. Holocaust, 1933-1945 6. World War, 1939-1945 -- Jews -- Rescue

ISBN 0-618-50755-8; 978-0-618-50755-9

This book offers a "biography . . . of Raoul Wallenberg, a Swedish businessman who dedicated the latter part of his life to helping Hungarian Jews escape from Budapest at the end of the Second World War. . . . Wallenberg's business dealings in Hungary made him an ideal candidate when the American-based War Refugee Board came to Sweden seeking someone for a mission to Hungary, to provide assistance to Jews who were being deported to Auschwitz by the trainload. Upon arrival in Budapest, Wallenberg invented the 'schutzpasse' system, wherein falsified documents connected Hungarian Jews to neutral Sweden and subsequently saved the lives of thousands." (Bulletin of the Center for Children's Books)

"Based on Borden's years of intensive personal research, including interviews and archival sources, this account written in rapid-reading free verse . . . is presented in a spacious, accessible format that includes lots of historic and personal photos, documents, and profiles of victims and heroes. Borden skillfully places the biographical story in historical context. . . . This is an important addition to the Holocaust curriculum." Booklist

Walton, Sam

Blumenthal, Karen. **Mr.** Sam; how Sam Walton built Wal-Mart and became America's richest man. Penguin Group 2011 183p il $17.99

Grades: 5 6 7 8   92

1. Businessmen 2. Discount stores 3. Retail executives

ISBN 978-0-670-01177-3; 0-670-01177-0

LC 2010049520

"This spectacular success story tracks Walton's rise from lower-middle-class origins to, by the mid-1980s, the top of the 'America's Richest' list. . . . Written in a fluid, journalistic style and enhanced by photos, boxed-out 'Sam stories,' charts tracking changes in Americans' spending habits, and a lavish source list, this account of the man who created what is today the world's largest company makes compelling reading." Booklist

Wang, Vera

Krohn, Katherine E. **Vera** Wang; enduring style. by Katherine Krohn. Twenty-First Century Books 2009 112p il (Lifeline biographies) lib bdg $33.26
Grades: 6 7 8 9   **92**
  1. Fashion designers 2. Magazine editors
  ISBN 978-1-58013-572-6 lib bdg; 1-58013-572-2 lib bdg

                          LC 2008009198
This biography "boasts lively, credible writing and a compelling layout. Particularly interesting are the reprints of USA Today articles found throughout, which flesh out the [narrative] in a unique and appealing manner. . . . Full-color and black-and-white photos appear on almost every spread." SLJ
Includes bibliographical references

Petrillo, Lisa. **Vera** Wang. Morgan Reynolds 2010 112p il (Profiles in fashion) $28.95
Grades: 7 8 9 10   **92**
  1. Fashion designers 2. Magazine editors
  ISBN 978-159935-150-6; 1-59935-150-1
This discusses the fashion "designer's cultural background, childhood, family, work history and education. . . . The writing is clear and well organized. Color photos are included and give readers a feel for the time period and the types of clothing and accessories the [designer] created." Voice Youth Advocates

Todd, Anne M. **Vera** Wang; [by] Anne M. Todd. Chelsea House 2007 120p bibl il por (Asian Americans of achievement) lib bdg $30
Grades: 7 8 9 10   **92**
  1. Fashion designers 2. Magazine editors
  ISBN 978-0-7910-9272-9 lib bdg; 0-7910-9272-0 lib bdg

                          LC 2006028386
A biography of the fashion designer
This is "well-researched . . . attractive . . . solid." SLJ

Warhol, Andy, 1928?-1987

★ Greenberg, Jan. **Andy** Warhol; prince of pop. [by] Jan Greenberg & Sandra Jordan. Delacorte Press 2004 193p il hardcover o.p. pa $6.99
Grades: 7 8 9 10   **92**
  1. Artists 2. Pop art 3. Artists -- United States 4. Motion picture directors
  ISBN 0-385-73056-X; 0-385-73275-9 pa

                          LC 2003-24102
A biography of the 20th century American artist famous for his Pop art images of Campbell's soup cans and Marilyn Monroe.
"Greenberg and Jordan offer a riveting biography that humanizes their controversial subject without making judgments or sensationalizing." Booklist
Includes glossary and bibliographical references

★ Rubin, Susan Goldman. **Andy** Warhol; pop art painter. H.N. Abrams 2006 48p il $18.95
Grades: 4 5 6 7   **92**
  1. Artists 2. Pop art 3. Artists -- United States 4. Motion picture directors
  ISBN 0-8109-5477-X

                          LC 2005-13238
"Andy Warhol was a colorful figure who revolutionized how the world looks at art. Rubin's coherent and interesting narrative is filled with quotes by the artist and people who knew him. . . . Excellent-quality black-and-white and full-color photographs of Warhol and his family and reproductions of his paintings and those of others who influenced him appear throughout." SLJ

Willett, Edward. **Andy** Warhol; everyone will be famous for 15 minutes. Enslow Publishers 2010 160p il (American rebels) lib bdg $34.60
Grades: 6 7 8 9   **92**
  1. Artists 2. Pop art 3. Artists -- United States 4. Motion picture directors
  ISBN 978-0-7660-3385-6 lib bdg; 0-7660-3385-6 lib bdg

                          LC 2009017596
This "fascinating, well organized [portrait] . . . starts with the 1962 L.A. art exhibition at which the artist first presented his iconic paintings of Campbell Soup cans that kicked off the pop-art movement into high gear. . . . Skillfully chosen photos, chapter notes, and [a] suggested-reading [list completes this] well-researched, wholly engaging [introduction]." Booklist
Includes bibliographical references

Warren, Earl, 1891-1974

Branscomb, Leslie Wolf. **Earl** Warren. Morgan Reynolds Pub. 2011 112p il (Supreme Court justices) lib bdg $28.95
Grades: 7 8 9 10   **92**
  1. Judges 2. Governors 3. Supreme Court justices
  ISBN 978-1-59935158-2; 1-59935158-7

                          LC 2010020403
This "offers a balanced look at the life and career of Earl Warren. . . . He was appointed chief justice of the U.S. Supreme Court in 1953. Branscomb includes Warren's mistakes but portrays him as a fair-minded man who led the court ably through a series of controversial and significant decisions. . . . Well-chosen boxed quotes and period photos appear throughout the book, with color used sparingly but effectively. This well-researched and clearly written volume offers a good introduction to Warren." Booklist
Includes bibliographical references

Washington, Booker T., 1856-1915

★ Washington, Booker T. **Up** from slavery; edited with an introduction and notes by William L. Andrews. Oxford University Press 2008 xxvii, 196p (Oxford world's classics) pa $9.95
Grades: 7 8 9 10 11 12 Adult   **92**
  1. Slaves 2. Authors 3. Educators 4. African American educators 5. Memoirists 6. Nonfiction writers 7. Civil

rights activists 8. African Americans -- Biography
ISBN 978-0-19-955239-9

LC 2008-279129

First published 1901

"The classic autobiography of the man who, though born in slavery, educated himself and went on to found Tuskegee Institute." N Y Public Libr

Includes bibliographical references

Washington, George, 1732-1799

★ Adler, David A. **George** Washington; an illustrated biography. by David A. Adler. Holiday House 2004 274p il map $24.95

Grades: 5 6 7 8   **92**

1. Generals 2. Presidents 3. Presidents -- United States
ISBN 0-8234-1838-3

LC 2003-67606

This "look at America's premier founding father literally spans his lifetime and attempts to focus . . . on how Washington's early character formation impacted his decisions as a military officer and later as president. . . . The illustrations are largely engravings from the late 19th century. . . . The writing style is accessible without ever falling prey to oversimplification." SLJ

Allen, Thomas B. **George** Washington, spymaster; how America outspied the British and won the Revolutionary War. featuring illustrations by Cheryl Harness. National Geographic 2004 184p il $16.95

Grades: 6 7 8 9   **92**

1. Generals 2. Presidents
ISBN 0-7922-5126-1

LC 2003-6019

Dolan, Edward F. **George** Washington; [by] Edward F. Dolan. Marshall Cavendish Benchmark 2008 96p il (Presidents and their times) lib bdg $32.79

Grades: 5 6 7 8   **92**

1. Generals 2. Presidents 3. Presidents -- United States
ISBN 978-0-7614-2427-7 lib bdg; 0-7614-2427-X lib bdg

LC 2006037802

This biography of the first president of the United States "is illustrated with color photos and contains boxed descriptions of key historical events, artwork, and political concepts experienced during the time period. . . . This . . . will be of great use both for biographical research and for enriching the curriculum." Libr Media Connect

Includes glossary and bibliographical references

Earl, Sari. **George** Washington; revolutionary leader & founding father. by Sari K. Earl. ABDO Pub. 2010 112p il map (Military heroes) lib bdg $22.95

Grades: 7 8 9   **92**

1. Generals 2. Presidents 3. Presidents -- United States
ISBN 978-1-60453-967-7; 1-60453-967-4

LC 2009-32372

"The rush of literary adrenalin will hook readers immediately and keep them enthralled until the end. . . . Given the dynamic topic [and] . . . appealing layout . . . [this is] likely to attract reluctant readers. In addition, sources are plentiful and well documented." SLJ

Includes glossary and bibliographical references

★ McClafferty, Carla Killough. The **many** faces of George Washington; remaking a presidential icon. Carolrhoda Books 2011 120p il lib bdg $20.95

Grades: 6 7 8 9   **92**

1. Generals 2. Presidents 3. Presidents -- United States
ISBN 978-0-7613-5608-0; 0-7613-5608-8

LC 2010-28178

"With the goal of boosting interest in George Washington, in 2005 Mount Vernon commissioned three life-size reproductions of him at ages 19, 45 and 57. Enthusiastic prose and informative photographs convey in considerable detail the work on this project by a variety of experts, including sculptors, archaeologists, historians, dentists, painters, taxidermists and more. . . . Quotations from Washington and his contemporaries add a personal note, while reproductions of portraits, statues and artifacts supply visual interest. Color photographs show some of the steps in the reconstruction." Kirkus

Includes bibliographical references

Miller, Brandon Marie. **George** Washington for kids; his life and times with 21 activities. [by] Brandon Marie Miller. Chicago Review Press 2007 130p il pa $14.95

Grades: 4 5 6 7   **92**

1. Generals 2. Presidents 3. Presidents -- United States
ISBN 1-55652-655-5 pa; 978-1-55652-655-8 pa

This book covers Washington's life and includes 21 hands-on projects based on his experiences and the times in which he lived.

This is "accessible and absorbing . . . clearly written and informative. . . . Primary quotes are interposed throughout, and illustrations, photographs, and visual aids are plentiful and well placed." SLJ

Mooney, Carla. **George** Washington; 25 great projects you can build yourself. illustrated by Samuel Carbaugh. Nomad 2011 121p il (Build it yourself) $21.95; pa $15.95

Grades: 4 5 6 7   **92**

1. Generals 2. Handicraft 3. Presidents 4. Presidents -- United States
ISBN 978-1-934670-64-4; 1-934670-64-2; 978-1-934670-63-7 pa pa; 1-934670-63-4 pa

"The life of George Washington lends itself remarkably well to a variety of kid-friendly crafts that don't require old-fashioned materials or 18th-century skills. . . . The projects separate biographical chapters that are thorough and clear. . . . Sidebars with vocabulary words, quotes, interesting facts about the man and his time, and 'What if?' questions regarding pivotal moments in Washington's life add to the text. These sidebars, as well as amusing cartoon illustrations, make the subject light and approachable." SLJ

Includes glossary and bibliographical references

Weber, EdNah New Rider

Weber, EdNah New Rider. **Rattlesnake** Mesa; stories from a native American childhood. by EdNah New Rider Weber; photographs by Richela Renkun. Lee & Low Books 2004 132p il $18.95

Grades: 4 5 6 7   **92**

1. Native Americans 2. Artisans 3. Memoirists 4. Storytellers 5. Native Americans -- Biography
ISBN 1-58430-231-3

LC 2004-2385

"Weber describes her experiences with warmth and affection in this unusually compelling memoir. Striking black-and-white photos . . . add to the book's appeal." Horn Book Guide

Wells, H. G. (Herbert George), 1866-1946

Abrams, Dennis. **H.G.** Wells; foreword by Kyle Zimmer. Chelsea House 2011 128p il (Who wrote that?) lib bdg $35

Grades: 6 7 8 9 10   **92**

1. Authors 2. Novelists 3. Historians 4. Authors, English 5. Writers on science 6. Writers on politics 7. Science fiction writers
ISBN 978-1-60413-770-5; 1-60413-770-3

LC 2010030588

This discusses the life and work of author H. G. Wells.
Includes bibliographical references

Wells-Barnett, Ida B., 1862-1931

Hinman, Bonnie. **Eternal** vigilance: the story of Ida B. Wells-Barnett. Morgan Reynolds Pub. 2010 128p il (Civil rights leaders) $28.95

Grades: 7 8 9 10   **92**

1. Authors 2. Lynching 3. Journalists 4. Women journalists 5. African American educators 6. Essayists 7. Nonfiction writers 8. Newspaper executives 9. Civil rights activists 10. African Americans -- Civil rights 11. African American women -- Biography 12. African Americans -- Social conditions
ISBN 978-1-59935-111-7; 1-59935-111-0

LC 2010-8144

"Hinman tells of Wells-Barnett's tireless efforts as an antilynching crusader and civil rights advocate. . . . Hinman paints an engaging portrait of the activist who was instrumental in the formation of the NAACP. Each stage of Wells-Barnett's life is placed in historical context, providing students with a better understanding of the world in which she lived. Well-chosen black-and-white photographs and other period materials are included throughout the text." SLJ
Includes bibliographical references

Schraff, Anne E. **Ida** B. Wells-Barnett; strike a blow against a glaring evil; [by] Anne Schraff. Enslow Publishers 2008 128p il map (African-American biography library) lib bdg $23.95

Grades: 6 7 8 9 10   **92**

1. Authors 2. Journalists 3. Essayists 4. Nonfiction writers 5. Newspaper executives 6. Civil rights activists 7. African Americans -- Civil rights 8. African

American women -- Biography
ISBN 978-0-7660-2704-6 lib bdg; 0-7660-2704-X lib bdg

LC 2007016051

"Short chapters, succinct text, frequent sidebars, and numerous period photographs keep the narrative from becoming overwhelming. . . . This will . . . aid report writers." Booklist
Includes bibliographical references

Wharton, Edith, 1862-1937

★ Wooldridge, Connie Nordhielm. The **brave** escape of Edith Wharton; a biography. Clarion Books 2010 184p il $20

Grades: 7 8 9 10   **92**

1. Authors 2. Novelists 3. Women authors 4. Authors, American 5. Nonfiction writers 6. Short story writers
ISBN 978-0-547-23630-8; 0-547-23630-1

LC 2009-33574

"In this thoroughly researched, humanizing biography, Wooldridge writes with lively specifics about both the author and her time. . . . Frequent, well-woven quotes from Wharton's family and friends contribute to a strong sense of an energetic, groundbreaking, and ferociously intelligent writer, but it's the many quotes in Wharton's own voice that leave the most indelible impact." Booklist

Whitfield, Simon, 1975-

Whitfield, Simon. **Simon** says gold: Simon Whitfield's pursuit of athletic excellence; by Simon Whitfield with Cleve Dheensaw. Orca Publishers 2009 118p il pa $14

Grades: 5 6 7 8   **92**

1. Athletes 2. Track athletics 3. Triathletes
ISBN 978-1-55469-141-8 pa; 1-55469-141-9 pa

"In 2000, Whitfield won a gold medal in the inaugural triathlon race held in the Sydney Summer Olympics. . . . He tells his story with candor, and he sheds light on the dark side of early success and the pressures athletes face. Sidebars offer more information on the sport of triathlon, and scrapbook-style color photographs enliven the tale." SLJ

Whitman, Narcissa Prentiss, 1808-1847

Harness, Cheryl. The **tragic** tale of Narcissa Whitman and a faithful history of the Oregon Trail; written and illustrated by Cheryl Harness. National Geographic Society 2006 144p il map (Cheryl Harness history) $16.95; lib bdg $25.90

Grades: 4 5 6 7   **92**

1. Frontier and pioneer life 2. Overland journeys to the Pacific 3. Pioneers 4. Missionaries
ISBN 0-7922-5920-3; 0-7922-7890-9 lib bdg

LC 2005-30930

This "introduces a nineteenth-century pioneer and missionary. . . . [She and her husband Marcus Whitman] journeyed along the Oregon Trail to the Waiilatpu Mission, where they ministered to the Cayuse. . . . Harness' chatty, conversational style makes the pair accessible to modern readers, and frequent quotes from Narcissa's diaries and letters and a time line help to frame the story in light of world and national events. Harness' black-line illustrations . . . help to break up the text for younger readers." Booklist

Includes bibliographical references

Whitman, Walt, 1819-1892

Kerley, Barbara. **Walt** Whitman; words for America. illustrated by Brian Selznick. Scholastic Press 2004 un il $16.95

Grades: 4 5 6 7   92

1. Poets 2. Authors 3. Essayists 4. Poets, American
ISBN 0-439-35791-8

LC 2003-20085

A biography of the American poet whose compassion led him to nurse soldiers during the Civil War, to give voice to the nation's grief at Lincoln's assassination, and to capture the true American spirit in verse

"Delightfully old-fashioned in design, [the book's] oversized pages are replete with graceful illustrations and snippets of poetry. The brilliantly inventive paintings add vibrant testimonial to the nuanced text." SLJ

Wiesel, Elie, 1928-

Koestler-Grack, Rachel A. **Elie** Wiesel; witness for humanity. by Rachel Koestler-Grack. Gareth Stevens Pub. 2009 112p il map (Life portraits) lib bdg $34

Grades: 7 8 9 10   92

1. Authors 2. Novelists 3. Journalists 4. Holocaust survivors 5. Jews -- Romania 6. Holocaust, 1933-1945 7. Human rights activists 8. Nobel laureates for peace
ISBN 978-1-4339-0054-9 lib bdg; 1-4339-0054-8 lib bdg

LC 2008-31630

"Recounts the struggles . . . [Wiesel] experienced as a Holocaust survivor and as someone who still works to end all violence against humanity. . . . Many photos, images, and sidebars, as well as the expected back matter contribute . . . without being didactic and educate without preaching." Voice Youth Advocates

Includes glossary and bibliographical references

Wiesenthal, Simon

★ Rubin, Susan Goldman. The **Anne** Frank Case: Simon Wiesenthal's search for the truth; illustrated by Bill Farnsworth. Holiday House 2009 40p il $18.95

Grades: 4 5 6 7   92

1. Authors 2. Children 3. Architects 4. Holocaust survivors 5. Diarists 6. Essayists 7. Memoirists 8. Nazi hunters 9. Jewish leaders 10. Holocaust victims 11. Jews -- Biography 12. Holocaust, 1933-1945
ISBN 978-0-8234-2109-1; 0-8234-2109-0

LC 2007-28396

"Even those who have heard of Wiesenthal will be thrilled by this account. . . . Farnsworth's stirring full-page oil paintings are filled with emotion." Booklist

Includes glossary and bibliographical references

Wilder, Laura Ingalls, 1867-1957

Berne, Emma Carlson. **Laura** Ingalls Wilder; by Emma Carlson Berne. ABDO Pub. 2008 112p il map $22.95

Grades: 4 5 6 7   92

1. Authors 2. Novelists 3. Women authors 4. Frontier and pioneer life 5. Western writers 6. Authors, American 7. Children's authors 8. Young adult authors
ISBN 978-1-59928-843-7; 1-59928-843-5

LC 2007012513

"Beginning in 1929 with the events that led up to the publication of Little House in the Big Woods , this readable biography further amplifies Wilder's life and correlates it with her books. . . . This volume is packed with relevant material, a time line, archival photographs, quotes from primary sources, and an official Web site." SLJ

Includes glossary and bibliographical references

Sickels, Amy. **Laura** Ingalls Wilder; [by] Amy Sickels. Chelsea House 2007 125p il (Who wrote that?) lib bdg $30

Grades: 6 7 8 9   92

1. Authors 2. Novelists 3. Women authors 4. Frontier and pioneer life 5. Western writers 6. Authors, American 7. Children's authors 8. Young adult authors
ISBN 978-0-7910-9525-6 lib bdg; 0-7910-9525-8 lib bdg

LC 2007019615

This biography examines the "writer's life, including the inspiration behind some of [her] works. [The] volume includes photographs and quotations from interviews, as well as descriptions of main characters and annotated lists of books and awards. Useful for aspiring writers as well as book report writers." Horn Book Guide

Includes bibliographical references

Wilder, Laura Ingalls. A **Little** House traveler; writings from Laura Ingalls Wilder's journeys across America. by Laura Ingalls Wilder. HarperCollins 2006 344p il $16.99; pa $7.99

Grades: 5 6 7 8   92

1. Authors 2. Novelists 3. Women authors 4. Western writers 5. Authors, American 6. Children's authors 7. Young adult authors
ISBN 978-0-06-072491-7; 0-06-072491-9; 978-0-06-072492-4 pa; 0-06-072492-7 pa

LC 2005014975

"This volume combines three Wilder travel diaries: On the Way Home, recounting the 1894 trip from South Dakota to Missouri, with husband Almanzo and daughter Rose; West from Home, featuring letters written by Laura to Almanzo during her 1915 solo visit to Rose in San Francisco; and The Road Back, highlighting Laura's previously unpublished record of a 1931 trip with Almanzo to De Smet, South Dakota, and the Black Hills. . . . This offers an amazing look at a beloved author, as well as a fascinating account of travel before interstate highways and air-conditioning." Booklist

William, Prince, Duke of Cambridge, 1982-

Doeden, Matt. **Prince** William & Kate; a royal romance. Lerner Publications 2011 48p il lib bdg $26.60

Grades: 5 6 7 8   92

1. Princes 2. Princesses
ISBN 978-0-7613-8029-0; 0-7613-8029-9

LC 2011003413

"This short and sweet volume accents what down-to-earth and normal newlyweds Prince William and Kate Middleton are really like. After a brief recap of the couple's engagement interview, the book goes on to profile the pair individually and then as a duo.... This is an upbeat, readable narrative about a handsome, appealing couple. The color photographs are well chosen." Booklist

Includes glossary and bibliographical references

Williams, Evan

Smith, Chris. **Twitter**; Jack Dorsey, Biz Stone and Evan Williams. [by] Chris Smith and Marci Mc-Grath. Morgan Reynolds Pub. 2011 112p il (Business leaders) $28.95

Grades: 7 8 9 10 11 12   92

1. Online social networks 2. Internet executives 3. Computer programmers 4. Computer software executives
ISBN 978-1-59935-179-7; 1-59935-179-X; 978-1-59935-216-9 e-book

LC 2011024699

This biography of the founders of Twitter "will grab YAs.... The design is browsable, with clear type and lots of color screens and informal photos of young people at work." Booklist

Includes bibliographical references

Williams, Lindsey, 1987-

Houle, Michelle E. **Lindsey** Williams; gardening for impoverished families. [by] Michelle Houle. KidHaven Press 2008 48p il (Young heroes) lib bdg $27.45

Grades: 4 5 6 7   92

1. Gardening 2. Food relief 3. Social action 4. Gardeners 5. Humanitarians
ISBN 978-0-7377-3867-4 lib bdg; 0-7377-3867-7 lib bdg

LC 2007022923

This "introduces 20-year-old Lindsey Williams, who has won numerous awards, including the International Eco-Hero Award, for her groundbreaking work with agriculture and hunger issues.... Williams has developed growing techniques that produce more food using fewer natural resources.... The straightforward text, with many quotes from Williams, will draw children into the science and environmental issues." Booklist

Includes glossary and bibliographical references

Williams, Serena, 1981-

Williams, Venus. **Venus** & Serena; serving from the hip, ten rules for living, loving, and winning. [by] Venus and Serena Williams with Hilary Beard. Houghton Mifflin 2005 133p il pa $14

Grades: 7 8 9 10   92

1. Tennis 2. Women athletes 3. African American athletes 4. Tennis players 5. Tennis -- Biography
ISBN 0-618-57653-3

LC 2004-13204

"The sisters and tennis players . . . give teens advice on everyday living, showing them how to aim high and reach their goals. The 10 rules for success include building a 'dream team' (people who support your goals), doing well in school, learning self-respect, valuing friendships, taking care of yourself emotionally and physically, obtaining financial security, and overcoming setbacks. The final chapter discusses the virtues of volunteerism and charity. . . . Never preachy and always practical, this is a welcome addition to most collections." SLJ

Williams, Venus, 1980-

Williams, Venus. **Venus** & Serena; serving from the hip, ten rules for living, loving, and winning. [by] Venus and Serena Williams with Hilary Beard. Houghton Mifflin 2005 133p il pa $14

Grades: 7 8 9 10   92

1. Tennis 2. Women athletes 3. African American athletes 4. Tennis players 5. Tennis -- Biography
ISBN 0-618-57653-3

LC 2004-13204

"The sisters and tennis players . . . give teens advice on everyday living, showing them how to aim high and reach their goals. The 10 rules for success include building a 'dream team' (people who support your goals), doing well in school, learning self-respect, valuing friendships, taking care of yourself emotionally and physically, obtaining financial security, and overcoming setbacks. The final chapter discusses the virtues of volunteerism and charity. . . . Never preachy and always practical, this is a welcome addition to most collections." SLJ

Wilson, Jacqueline

Bankston, John. **Jacqueline** Wilson. Chelsea House 2011 128p il (Who wrote that?) lib bdg $35

Grades: 6 7 8 9 10   92

1. Authors 2. Novelists 3. Women authors 4. Authors, American 5. Young adult authors
ISBN 978-1-60413-773-6; 1-60413-773-8

LC 2010047679

"Wilson knew from an early age that writing was her calling. Growing up in a turbulent home and dropping out of school at 16 pushed her to start writing for Jackie, a magazine for teenage girls. This well-written biography includes a quick-paced, fact-filled synopsis of her life." SLJ

Includes bibliographical references

Wilson, Woodrow, 1856-1924

Lukes, Bonnie L. **Woodrow** Wilson and the Progressive Era. Morgan Reynolds 2005 192p il lib bdg $26.95

Grades: 7 8 9 10   92

1. Governors 2. Presidents 3. College presidents 4. Nobel laureates for peace 5. Presidents -- United States
ISBN 978-1-93179-879-2; 1-93179-879-6

LC 2005-15999

"This well-documented, chronological account begins with Wilson's birth in 1856, describes his varied careers, and continues through his death in 1924. . . . The author describes the intense political conflicts of the time, mostly concerning Americas involvement in World War I and then in the League of Nations. Lukes's approach is balanced. . . . Good-quality, full-color and black-and-white photos and reproductions appear throughout." SLJ

Includes bibliographical references

Marsico, Katie. **Woodrow** Wilson. Marshall Cavendish Benchmark 2011 112p il (Presidents and their times) $23.95

Grades: 5 6 7 8   **92**
1. Governors 2. Presidents 3. College presidents 4. Nobel laureates for peace 5. Presidents -- United States
ISBN 978-0-7614-4815-0; 0-7614-4815-2

LC 2009041116

This offers information on President Woodrow Wilson and places him within his historical and cultural context. Also explored are the formative events of his times and how he responded.

"The abundant sidebars provide a good deal of background information that will be helpful to students. . . . Attractive . . . as well as useful." Booklist

Includes glossary and bibliographical references

Winfrey, Oprah

★ Cooper, Ilene. **Oprah** Winfrey. Viking 2007 204p il (Up close) $15.99

Grades: 7 8 9 10   **92**
1. Philanthropists 2. African American actors 3. Television personalities 4. Talk show hosts 5. Television producers 6. African American women -- Biography
ISBN 978-0-670-06162-4

LC 2006-9805

"Cooper discusses her subject's early traumatic and dramatic experiences. She shows how a poor, abused, bright child from Mississippi overcame her past, becoming perhaps the most influential woman in America. Much of the book focuses on Winfrey's work and philanthropy. . . . This well-documented, easy-to-read biography is a good resource for reports." SLJ

Krohn, Katherine E. **Oprah** Winfrey; global media leader. by Katherine Krohn. rev ed; Twenty-First Century Books 2009 112p il (Lifeline biographies) lib bdg $33.26

Grades: 6 7 8 9   **92**
1. Philanthropists 2. African American actors 3. Television personalities 4. Talk show hosts 5. Television producers 6. African American women -- Biography
ISBN 978-1-58013-571-9 lib bdg; 1-58013-571-4 lib bdg

LC 2008016951

First published 2002 by Lerner Publications

This biography "boasts lively, credible writing and a compelling layout. Particularly interesting are the reprints of USA Today articles found throughout, which flesh out the [narrative] in a unique and appealing manner. . . . Full-

color and black-and-white photos appear on almost every spread." SLJ

Includes bibliographical references

Winthrop, John, 1588-1649

Aronson, Marc. **John** Winthrop, Oliver Cromwell, and the Land of Promise. Clarion Books 2004 205p il map $20

Grades: 7 8 9 10   **92**
1. Clergy 2. Puritans 3. Heads of state 4. Revolutionaries 5. Government officials 6. Colonial administrators 7. Puritans -- Massachusetts -- Biography 8. Governors -- Massachusetts -- Biography 9. Massachusetts -- History -- Colonial period, ca. 1600-1775
ISBN 0-618-18177-6

LC 2003-16418

"The accessible text is accompanied by excerpts from primary source documents and vivid illustrations. The author's passion for the period comes across in his writing. Aronson provides an excellent source for historical and biographical data." Voice Youth Advocates

Includes bibliographical references

Woodhull, Victoria C., 1838-1927

Havelin, Kate. **Victoria** Woodhull. Twenty-First Century Books 2007 112p (Trailblazer biography) lib bdg $30.60

Grades: 7 8 9 10   **92**
1. Feminism 2. Suffragists 3. Feminists 4. Presidential candidates
ISBN 978-0-8225-5986-3 lib bdg; 0-8225-5986-2 lib bdg

LC 2005022824

A biography of the nineteenth century feminist who became the first woman to run for president of the U.S.

"A well-researched, well-organized biography. . . . [Woodhull's] fascinating and full life is expertly detailed in this narrative." SLJ

Includes bibliographical references

Woods, Tiger, 1975-

Roberts, Jeremy. **Tiger** Woods; golf's master. by Jeremy Roberts. Twenty-First Century Books 2009 112p il (Lifeline biographies) lib bdg $33.26

Grades: 6 7 8 9   **92**
1. Golf 2. Golfers
ISBN 978-1-58013-569-6 lib bdg; 1-58013-569-2 lib bdg

LC 2008-3098

"There are a number of biographies about the world's best golfer, but this one is particularly good. Not only does it chronicle the life of Woods but it offers a solid look at family influences, various tournaments, and personal relationships. . . . Color photographs are well chosen." Booklist

Includes bibliographical references

Woodson, Jacqueline

Hinton, KaaVonia. **Jacqueline** Woodson; by KaaVonia Hinton. Mitchell Lane Publishers 2008 48p il (Classic storytellers) lib bdg $29.95

Grades: 5 6 7 8 **92**
1. Authors 2. Novelists 3. Women authors 4. African American authors 5. College teachers 6. Children's authors 7. Young adult authors
ISBN 978-1-58415-533-1 lib bdg; 1-58415-533-7 lib bdg

LC 2007-669

"This biography details the life of a popular African-American author. It covers her childhood, the challenges she faced growing up during the height of the Civil Rights Movement, what inspired her to begin to write, and her many literary successes. The book is filled with photos of the writer at various stages of her life and the covers of some of her books. Young people should find inspiration in Woodson's story." SLJ

Includes glossary and bibliographical references

Wright, Orville, 1871-1948

★ Collins, Mary. **Airborne**: a photobiography of Wilbur and Orville Wright. National Geographic Soc. 2003 63p il maps $18.95
Grades: 4 5 6 7 **92**
1. Inventors 2. Aeronautics -- History 3. Aircraft industry executives
ISBN 0-7922-6957-8

LC 2002-5279

Examines the lives of the Wright brothers and discusses their experiments and triumphs in the field of flight

"The well-chosen photos give readers a feel for Kitty Hawk—windy, sandy, solitary. This is an exceptionally well-informed picture of the Wright brothers and what their 100-year-old achievement really meant." SLJ

Crompton, Samuel. The **Wright** brothers; first in flight. [by] Samuel Willard Crompton. Chelsea House 2007 110p il (Milestones in American history) lib bdg $35
Grades: 7 8 9 10 **92**
1. Inventors 2. Aeronautics -- History 3. Aircraft industry executives
ISBN 978-0-7910-9356-6 lib bdg; 0-7910-9356-5

LC 2006034131

Describes the careers and achievements of the Wright Brothers, who are credited with the invention of the airplane in 1903.

An "interesting and factual account of the Wright brothers. . . . [This book has] well-reproduced archival photos and drawings with explanatory captions . . . [and an] open layout and lively [text]." SLJ

Includes bibliographical references

★ Freedman, Russell. The **Wright** brothers: how they invented the airplane; with original photographs by Wilbur and Orville Wright. Holiday House 1991 129p il hardcover o.p. pa $14.95
Grades: 5 6 7 8 9 10 **92**
1. Inventors 2. Aeronautics -- History 3. Aircraft industry executives
ISBN 0-8234-0875-2; 0-8234-1082-X pa

LC 90-48440

A Newbery Medal honor book, 1992

In this "combination of photography and text, Freedman reveals the frustrating, exciting, and ultimately successful journey of these two brothers from their bicycle shop in Dayton, Ohio, to their Kitty Hawk flights and beyond. . . . An essential purchase for younger YAs." Voice Youth Advocates

Includes bibliographical references

Wright, Richard, 1908-1960

Hart, Joyce. **Native** son: the story of Richard Wright. Morgan Reynolds 2002 128p il (World writers) lib bdg $21.95
Grades: 7 8 9 10 **92**
1. Authors 2. Novelists 3. Dramatists 4. African American authors 5. Essayists 6. Authors, American 7. Nonfiction writers 8. Short story writers
ISBN 1-931798-06-0

LC 2002-13686

"The writing is accessible and flows smoothly." SLJ
Includes bibliographical references

Levy, Debbie. **Richard** Wright. Twenty-First Century Books 2008 160p (Literary greats) $33.26
Grades: 7 8 9 10 11 12 **92**
1. Authors 2. Novelists 3. Dramatists 4. African American authors 5. Essayists 6. Nonfiction writers 7. Short story writers
ISBN 978-0-8225-6793-6

LC 2006-101189

A biography of the African American author of Native Son and Black Boy

This "absorbing biography . . . does a fine job of placing Wright's personal life in the context of black history. . . . Cleanly designed and featuring a small photo on every double-page spread." Booklist

Includes bibliographical references

Wright, Wilbur, 1867-1912

★ Collins, Mary. **Airborne**: a photobiography of Wilbur and Orville Wright. National Geographic Soc. 2003 63p il maps $18.95
Grades: 4 5 6 7 **92**
1. Inventors 2. Aeronautics -- History 3. Aircraft industry executives
ISBN 0-7922-6957-8

LC 2002-5279

Examines the lives of the Wright brothers and discusses their experiments and triumphs in the field of flight

"The well-chosen photos give readers a feel for Kitty Hawk—windy, sandy, solitary. This is an exceptionally well-informed picture of the Wright brothers and what their 100-year-old achievement really meant." SLJ

Crompton, Samuel. The **Wright** brothers; first in flight. [by] Samuel Willard Crompton. Chelsea House 2007 110p il (Milestones in American history) lib bdg $35
Grades: 7 8 9 10 **92**
1. Inventors 2. Aeronautics -- History 3. Aircraft industry executives
ISBN 978-0-7910-9356-6 lib bdg; 0-7910-9356-5

LC 2006034131

Describes the careers and achievements of the Wright Brothers, who are credited with the invention of the airplane in 1903.

An "interesting and factual account of the Wright brothers. . . . [This book has] well-reproduced archival photos and drawings with explanatory captions . . . [and an] open layout and lively [text]." SLJ

Includes bibliographical references

★ Freedman, Russell. The **Wright** brothers: how they invented the airplane; with original photographs by Wilbur and Orville Wright. Holiday House 1991 129p il hardcover o.p. pa $14.95

Grades: 5 6 7 8 9 10   92
1. Inventors 2. Aeronautics -- History 3. Aircraft industry executives
ISBN 0-8234-0875-2; 0-8234-1082-X pa
LC 90-48440
A Newbery Medal honor book, 1992

In this "combination of photography and text, Freedman reveals the frustrating, exciting, and ultimately successful journey of these two brothers from their bicycle shop in Dayton, Ohio, to their Kitty Hawk flights and beyond. . . . An essential purchase for younger YAs." Voice Youth Advocates

Includes bibliographical references

Yep, Laurence

Marcovitz, Hal. **Laurence** Yep; [by] Hal Marcovitz. Chelsea House 2008 136p il (Who wrote that?) $30

Grades: 6 7 8 9   92
1. Authors 2. Novelists 3. College teachers 4. Authors, American 5. Children's authors 6. Young adult authors 7. Chinese Americans -- Biography
ISBN 978-0-7910-9527-0; 0-7910-9527-4
LC 2007045508

This biography of the Chinese American author examines the "writer's life, including the inspiration behind some of [his] works. [The] volume includes photographs and quotations from interviews, as well as descriptions of main characters and annotated lists of books and awards. Useful for aspiring authors as well as book report writers." Horn Book Guide

Includes bibliographical references

Yolen, Jane

Carpan, Carolyn. **Jane** Yolen; [by] Carolyn Carpan. Chelsea House 2006 128p il (Who wrote that?) lib bdg $30

Grades: 6 7 8 9   92
1. Authors 2. Novelists 3. Women authors 4. Editors 5. Fantasy writers 6. Authors, American 7. Children's authors 8. Science fiction writers
ISBN 978-0-7910-8660-5 lib bdg; 0-7910-8660-7 lib bdg
LC 2005007828

This describes the life and work of author Jane Yolen
"The photographs that illustrate the text show places from the author's life or period photos. . . . The extensive quotes from Yolen share her feelings as she wrote full time and published more than 250 books while raising a family. . . . [The book includes] extensive notes, a chronology, works

by the author listed by publication date, major awards, and most wellknown characters." Voice Youth Advocates

Includes bibliographical references

Zaharias, Babe Didrikson, 1911-1956

Lobby, Mackenzie. **Babe** Didrikson Zaharias; groundbreaking all-around athlete. ABDO Pub. Co. 2011 112p il (Legendary athletes) lib bdg $34.22

Grades: 6 7 8 9   92
1. Women athletes 2. Golfers 3. Hurdlers 4. High jumpers 5. Javelin throwers 6. Olympic athletes
ISBN 978-1-61714-755-5; 1-61714-755-9
LC 2010041158

This biography of athlete Babe Didrikson Zaharias "goes beyond merely discussing [her] accomplishments. . . . [It] also [explores] the social and political [influence she] had on society as a whole. In addition, [it introduces] historical events in the context of [her life]. . . . This . . . is teeming with information and is a must-purchase for sports fans and readers interested in social activism." SLJ

Includes glossary and bibliographical references

Van Natta, Don, 1964- **Wonder** girl; the magnificent sporting life of Babe Didrikson Zaharias. Little, Brown and Co. 2011 403p il $27.99

Grades: 5 6 7 8   92
1. Women athletes 2. Golfers 3. Hurdlers 4. High jumpers 5. Javelin throwers 6. Olympic athletes
ISBN 978-0-316-05699-1; 0-316-05699-5
LC 2010041794

Describes the life and times of LPGA founder Babe Didrikson, the Texas woman who achieved All-American status in basketball, won gold medals in track and field in the 1932 Olympics, and became the first woman to play against men in a PGA tournament.

This is an "engaging biography. . . . Van Natta marvelously narrates the forgotten life of the 'greatest all-around athlete of all time,' a story that every American sport fan should relish." Publ Wkly

Includes bibliographical references

Zapata, Emiliano, 1879-1919

Stein, R. Conrad. **Emiliano** Zapata and the Mexican Revolution. Morgan Reynolds Pub. 2011 144p il map (The story of Mexico) $28.95

Grades: 6 7 8 9   92
1. Generals 2. Revolutionaries
ISBN 978-1-5993-5163-6; 1-5993-5163-3
LC 2010041616

This traces the life and impact of Zapata and his revolutionary movement on the history of Mexico.

"Stein organizes and clearly presents a great deal of information. . . . The . . . format features a chronological text supplemented with useful sidebars and brightened with color illustrations, including many photos, artifacts, and period artworks." Booklist

Includes bibliographical references

Zenatti, Valérie, 1970-

Zenatti, Valerie. **When** I was a soldier; a memoir. translated by Adriana Hunter. Bloomsbury Children's Books 2005 235p $16.95

Grades: 7 8 9 10   92

1. Authors 2. Soldiers 3. Novelists 4. Women soldiers 5. Memoirists 6. Translators 7. Children's authors

ISBN 1-58234-978-9

A "fast, wry, present-tense memoir. . . . Readers on all sides of the war-peace continuum, here and there, will find much to talk about." Booklist

Zindel, Paul

Daniel, Susanna. **Paul** Zindel. Rosen Publishing Group 2004 112p il (Library of author biographies) lib bdg $26.50

Grades: 5 6 7 8   92

1. Authors 2. Novelists 3. Dramatists 4. Authors, American 5. Children's authors

ISBN 0-8239-4524-3

Discusses the life and work of this popular author, including his writing process and methods, inspirations, a critical discussion of his books, biographical timeline, and awards.

Includes bibliographical references

Zuckerberg, Mark

Hasday, Judy L. **Facebook** and Mark Zuckerberg. Morgan Reynolds Pub. 2011 112p il (Business leaders) $28.95

Grades: 7 8 9 10 11 12   92

1. Businessmen 2. Online social networks 3. Internet executives

ISBN 978-1-59935-176-6; 1-59935-176-5; 978-1-59935-215-2 e-book

LC 2011023210

This biography of Mark Zuckerberg and how he started Facebook "will grab YAs. . . . The design is browsable, with clear type and lots of color screens and informal photos of young people at work." Booklist

Includes bibliographical references

Woog, Adam. **Mark** Zuckerberg, Facebook creator. KidHaven Press 2009 48p il map (Innovators) $28.25

Grades: 4 5 6 7   92

1. Businesspeople 2. Internet executives

ISBN 978-0-7377-4566-5; 0-7377-4566-5

LC 2009013458

"This brisk, readable [biography the creator of Facebook] . . . presents an appealing picture of the shy, lonely future billionaire . . . This is fascinating and relevant stuff." Booklist

Includes bibliographical references

920   Biography, genealogy, insignia

Aaseng, Nathan

Business builders in sweets and treats; [by] Nathan Aaseng. Oliver Press 2005 160p il (Business builders) $24.95

Grades: 5 6 7 8   920

1. Food industry 2. Businesspeople

ISBN 1-881508-84-6

LC 2003-64984

This is a "study of Hershey and chocolate, Wrigley and chewing gum, Ben and Jerry and ice cream, and others who make things we love to eat. . . . A few well-chosen sidebars document sweets that don't get a whole chapter. Excellent sources and citations, boxed facts, a lively style, and sometimes mouthwatering pictures finish the package." Booklist

Includes bibliographical references

Almanac of Famous People; A Comprehensive Reference Guide to More Than 40,000 Famous and Infamous Newsmakers from Biblical Times to the Present. edited by Kristin Mallegg. 10th ed. Gale / Cengage Learning 2011 2887 p. (hardcover) $280

Grades: 7 8 9 10 11 12 Adult   920

1. Celebrities -- Encyclopedias

ISBN 1414445482; 9781414445489

This reference book offers "biographical information on more than 30,000 famous individuals and groups." Entries provide the "subject's best-known name, complete name, nickname, [and] name of group," "dates and places of birth and death," and "nationality and occupation. Most entries include citations to sources that provide additional biographical information." (Publisher's note)

Armstrong, Mabel

Women astronomers; reaching for the stars. Stone Pine Press 2008 179p il (Discovering women in science series) pa $16.95

Grades: 7 8 9 10   920

1. Women astronomers

ISBN 978-0-972892-95-7 pa; 0-972892-95-8 pa

LC 2007-22318

This introduces 21 women astronomers, from ancient times to the present.

"A worthy addition to science collections, this well-documented collective biography not only fills gaps in existing books on astronomers, but also offers engaging accounts of the women's careers as well as unusually clear explanations of what they achieved and why each discovery was important." Booklist

Includes bibliographical references

Bausum, Ann

★ **Our** country's first ladies; [by] Ann Bausum; with a foreword by First Lady Laura Bush. National Geographic 2007 127p il $19.95; lib bdg $28.90

Grades: 5 6 7 8   920

1. Presidents' spouses -- United States

ISBN 978-1-4263-0006-6; 978-1-4263-0007-3 lib bdg

LC 2006021284

"A well-researched, thoughtfully written, attractive account. Fact boxes provide basic information such as birth and death dates, marriage dates, and children's names; a 'Did You Know' section shares interesting personal tidbits. Periodic time lines help to place the women's lives within the broader events of history. There is enough information here for simple reports. Interesting facts and anecdotes will hold readers' attention. . . . An excellent layout and clear, colorful photographs and reproductions will further entice readers." SLJ

Includes bibliographical references

Beccia, Carlyn

The **raucous** royals; test your royal wits: crack codes, solve mysteries, and deduce which royal rumors are true. Houghton Mifflin 2008 64p il $17

Grades: 4 5 6 7   **920**

1. Nobility 2. Historiography 3. Kings and rulers 4. Nobility -- Biography 5. Kings and rulers -- Biography
ISBN 978-0-618-89130-6; 0-618-89130-7

                           LC 2008-298419

"Thirteen beliefs about rulers receive an acerbic and irreverent interrogation in this blend of royal-watching and skeptical investigation. The royal rumors, arranged chronologically, start with the real story behind Prince Dracula and Richard III's murderous ways, stopping en route at Napoleon's short stature and Marie Antoinette's 'let them eat cake' utterance, and finish up with Catherine the Great's death and King George's madness. . . . The energy and gleefully gossipy nature makes this a fine companion for Krull's Lives of . . . series, while its verve particularly recommends it as an entrée into historiography and critical thinking." Bull Cent Child Books

Includes bibliographical references

Benjamin, Michelle

Nobel's women of peace; by Michelle Benjamin and Maggie Mooney. Second Story Press 2008 146p il (Women's Hall of fame) pa $10.95

Grades: 6 7 8 9   **920**

1. Nobel Prizes 2. Women -- Biography
ISBN 978-1-897187-38-8; 1-897187-38-6 pa

Profiles the twelve female recipients of the Nobel Peace Prize since its creation, including how they became activists for peace and their accomplishments before and after winning the prestigious award.

"Substantive enough to support basic reports, the profiles include many women who are rarely featured in books for youth. . . . The international stories of individuals dedicating their lives to humanitarian efforts will inspire young activists, who will want to move on to the extensive list of appended resources." Booklist

Includes bibliographical references

Benson, Sonia

Korean War: biographies; [by] Sonia G. Benson; Gerda-Ann Raffaelle, editor. U.X.L 2002 xxx, 268p il pa $60

Grades: 7 8 9 10   **920**

1. Korean War, 1950-1953 -- Biography
ISBN 0-7876-5692-5

                           LC 2001-44241

Presents biographies of twenty-six men and women who participated in or were affected by the Korean War, including politicians, military leaders, journalists, and nurses

"An excellent starting point for researching the . . . people of the Korean War." Booklist

Includes bibliographical references

Bolden, Tonya

Portraits of African-American heroes; paintings by Ansel Pitcairn. Dutton Children's Books 2003 88p il $18.99; pa $11.99

Grades: 4 5 6 7   **920**

1. African Americans -- Biography
ISBN 0-525-47043-3; 0-14-240473-X pa

                           LC 2002-75911

"Each profile lists expected biographical information, but offers even more by way of keen insights into a subject's personality based on interviews and information drawn from personal memoirs. . . . Pitcairn's beautifully rendered sepia-toned portraits make each subject jump from the page, beckoning children to come ever closer and learn." Booklist

Bragg, Georgia

★ **How** they croaked; the awful ends of the awfully famous. Walker & Co. 2011 178p il $17.99; lib bdg $18.89

Grades: 5 6 7 8   **920**

1. Death 2. Biography 3. Celebrities -- Death
ISBN 978-0-8027-9817-6; 0-8027-9817-9; 978-0-8027-9818-3 lib bdg; 0-8027-9818-7 lib bdg

                           LC 2010-08659

"Bragg chronicles with ghoulish glee the chronic or fatal maladies that afflicted 19 historical figures. Nonsqueamish readers will by entranced by her riveting descriptions. . . . The author tucks quick notes on at least marginally relevant topics, such as leeching, scurvy, presidential assassins, and mummy eyes . . . between the chapters. . . . O'Malley's cartoon portraits and spot art add just the right notes of humor to keep the contents from becoming too gross." Booklist

Butts, Edward

She dared; true stories of heroines, scoundrels, and renegades. [by] Ed Butts; illustrated by Heather Collins. Tundra Bks. 2005 121p il pa $8.95

Grades: 6 7 8 9 10   **920**

1. Women -- Biography
ISBN 0-88776-718-4

This "details the lives of some of Canada's most famous and infamous women. The stories showcase explorers, spies, criminals, and pioneers in a variety of career fields. Organized chronologically from the 16th to the mid-20th century, this 12-chapter offering is historically sound and well researched." SLJ

Castro, Ivan A.

★ **100** hispanics you should know. Libraries Unlimited 2007 303p bibl il $55

Grades: 6 7 8 9   **920**

1. Hispanic Americans -- Biography
ISBN 1-59158-327-6

"This eye-opening and valuable reference is one of the few biographical compilations for young people that address the achievements of Spanish-speaking individuals across the world and throughout history, especially in the sciences, arts, politics, and military. The alphabetically arranged entries begin with key information about the individuals, such as birthplaces, birth and death dates, career highlights, and b&w portraits; then continue with important contributions; and end with bibliographies." Libr Media Connect

Chemistry, Earth, and space sciences; edited by Derek Hall. Brown Bear Books 2010 64p il (Facts at your fingertips) lib bdg $35.65

Grades: 8 9 10 11   **920**
1. Chemists 2. Scientists 3. Astronomers 4. Space sciences 5. Science -- History 6. Chemistry -- History
ISBN 978-1-933834-47-4 lib bdg; 1-933834-47-1 lib bdg

              LC 2009-13342

Profiles the lives and work of nine scientists and chemists who have made significant contributions to modern science, including Nicolaus Copernicus, Antoine Lavoisier, Dmitri Mendeleev, and Stephen Hawking

This provides "explanations about important discoveries, related work, and social and political influences that impacted the subjects' work. . . . The approximately six-to-eight page entries include important dates, photographs, diagrams, and sidebars on relevant scientists. The writing is often highly technical and some knowledge of the basics is assumed." SLJ

Includes glossary and bibliographical references

Chin-Lee, Cynthia
   ★ **Amelia** to Zora; twenty-six women who changed the world. illustrated by Megan Halsey and Sean Addy. Charlesbridge 2005 32p il $15.95

Grades: 4 5 6 7   **920**
1. Women -- Biography
ISBN 1-57091-522-9

"The illustrations are done in a remarkable mix of media. . . . The text portions are short . . . but they are enticing. By choosing her subjects from every culture, the author introduces children to the scope of the struggles and achievements of women from many times and many places." Booklist

Cotter, Charis
   Born to write; the remarkable lives of six famous authors. Annick Press 2009 167p il $24.95; pa $14.95

Grades: 5 6 7 8   **920**
1. Authors
ISBN 978-1-55451-192-1; 1-55451-192-5; 978-1-55451-191-4 pa; 1-55451-191-7 pa

A collective biography of authors Lucy Maud Montgomery, Christopher Paul Curtis, C. S. Lewis, E.B. White, Madeleine L'Engle, and Philip Pullman

"Younger readers will find the presentation of the book appealing, with many colorful photographs and illustrations; however, more mature readers will gain the most enjoyment as they discover the backgrounds and inspirations of some of

their favorite writers. . . . An excellent resource for reports and pleasure reading." SLJ

   Kids who rule; the remarkable lives of five child monarchs. Annick Press 2007 120p il map $24.95; pa $14.95

Grades: 5 6 7 8   **920**
1. Queens 2. Emperors 3. Kings and rulers 4. Kings 5. Buddhist leaders 6. Political leaders 7. Nobel laureates for peace 8. Queens -- Biography 10. Children -- Biography 11. Kings and rulers -- Biography
ISBN 978-1-55451-062-7; 1-55451-062-7; 978-1-55451-061-0 pa; 1-55451-061-9 pa

This "book discusses five people who became monarchs as children: Tutankhamen of Egypt, Mary Queen of Scots, Queen Christina of Sweden, China's Emperor Puyi, and the fourteenth Dalai Lama. . . . The illustrations, many in color, include portrait paintings, engravings, and maps as well as photos of people, places, and artifacts. . . . This appealing collective biography presents five unusual children whose stories are well worth reading." Booklist

D'Agnese, Joseph
   Signing their rights away; the fame and misfortune of the men who signed the United States Constitution. by Denise Kiernan & Joseph D'Agnese. Quirk Books 2011 254p il $19.95

Grades: 8 9 10 11 12 Adult   **920**
1. Statesmen -- United States 2. Presidents -- United States
ISBN 978-1-59474-520-1

Presents the lives, deaths, and scandals involving the thirty-nine signers of the United States Constitution, including Benjamin Franklin, Alexander Hamilton, and James McHenry.

"For readers of American history, this is both educational and entertaining." Booklist

Includes bibliographical references

Drucker, Malka
   Portraits of Jewish American heroes; by Malka Drucker; illustrated by Elizabeth Rosen. Dutton Children's Books 2008 96p il $22.99

Grades: 4 5 6   **920**
1. Jews -- United States -- Biography
ISBN 978-0-525-47771-6; 0-525-47771-3

              LC 2007-028481

"From Albert Einstein and Bella Abzug to Ruth Bader Ginsburg, Hank Greenberg, and Steven Spielberg, this invitingly illustrated collective biography celebrates 20 Jewish American heroes in all their diversity. . . . The nicely designed volume includes full-page portraits of the subjects in various media. . . . Drucker's eloquent, chatty style opens up big issues about Judaism as a source of idealism and for a just, compassionate society." Booklist

Includes bibliographical references

Dublin, Anne
   Dynamic women dancers. Second Story Press 2009 128p il (The women's hall of fame) pa $10.95

Grades: 6 7 8 9   920
1. Dancers
ISBN 978-1-897187-56-2 pa; 1-897187-56-4 pa
"Profiles ten dancers, each from different countries and
backgrounds. Most of the dancers performed ballet or modern dance, but a flamenco dancer and a South Indian classical dancer are also included. Entries are brief, detailing their
backgrounds, studies, and the challenges each woman faced.
. . . Black-and-white pictures help break up the text, and a
few inset boxes offer supplemental quotes or information. . .
. Present[s] information well, and the lives profiled are both
interesting and inspirational." Voice Youth Advocates
Includes glossary and bibliographical references

Fortey, Jacqueline
   Great scientists; written by Jacqueline Fortey.
DK Pub. 2007 72p il map (DK eyewitness books)
$15.99
Grades: 5 6 7 8   920
1. Scientists 2. Science
ISBN 978-0-7566-2974-8; 0-7566-2974-8
                 LC 2007-298205
This introduces readers to the great scientists and their
discoveries from ancient history to modern times.
   "An accompanying CD provides clip art taken from the
book; this art can prove invaluable to both teachers and stu-
dents. . . . A very fine book for elementary and middle school
students and those who teach them." Sci Books and Films

Fradin, Dennis B.
   ★ The **founders**; the 39 stories behind the U.S.
Constitution. [by] Dennis Brindell Fradin; illustrated
by Michael McCurdy. Walker & Co. 2005 162p il
map $22.95; lib bdg $23.95
Grades: 4 5 6 7   920
1. Statesmen -- United States
ISBN 0-8027-8972-2; 0-8027-8973-0 lib bdg
"The makers of the U.S. Constitution are profiled in
two or three pages each, in sections introduced by a brief
note about their home states. McCurdy's black-and-white
scratchboard illustrations are properly stately and engaging.
Readers will find great nuggets of fact." Booklist
   Includes bibliographical references

   ★ **Funny** business; conversations with writers of
comedy. compiled and edited by Leonard S. Mar-
cus. Candlewick Press 2009 214p il $21.99
Grades: 5 6 7 8 9 10   920
1. Authors 2. Authorship 3. Wit and humor 4.
Authors, American -- Biography
ISBN 978-0-7636-3254-0; 0-7636-3254-6
This book comprises interviews with writers of humor-
ous books for young people: Judy Blume, Beverly Cleary,
Sharon Creech, Christopher Paul Curtis, Anne Fine, Daniel
Handler, Carl Hiaasen, Norton Juster, Dick King-Smith, Hil-
ary McKay, Daniel Pinkwater, Louis Sachar, and Jon Sci-
eszka. (Horn Book)
   "In 12 entertaining interviews . . . Marcus's compilation
explores the childhoods, writing processes and senses of
humor of well-known writers for children, including Judy
Blume, Beverly Cleary, Daniel Handler, Norton Juster and
Jon Scieszka. Marcus's evident knowledge of his subjects'

writing makes for some intriguing questions and answers.
. . . Photographs, manuscript pages and even e-mail chains
between the writers and their editors add fascinating tidbits."
Publ Wkly

Gifford, Clive
   10 inventors who changed the world; written by
Clive Gifford; illustrated by David Cousens. Kingfisher 2009 63p il $14.99
Grades: 4 5 6 7   920
1. Inventors 2. Inventions
ISBN 978-0-7534-6259-1; 0-7534-6259-1
"The innovative efforts of nine men and one woman are
presented here. Some of the names will be familiar (Galileo, Franklin, Edison, Curie) while others will prove less so
(Isambard Kindgom Brunel, Glenn Curtiss, Sergei Korolev).
Starting in ancient times with Archimedes, the chronology
ends in modern times with Korolev, a Soviet-era rocket designer. Each section offers a succinct yet thorough biography
of the inventors. Striking graphic-novel-style art is a visual
aid to draw readers into each setting and era." SLJ

   10 kings & queens who changed the world; written by Clive Gifford; illustrated by David Cousens.
Kingfisher 2009 63p il map $14.99
Grades: 4 5 6 7   920
1. Kings and rulers
ISBN 978-0-7534-6252-2; 0-7534-6252-4
"Cousens' bright graphic novel-style artwork is the grabber here; he uses theatrical angles to portray each historical
figure as a chiseled or beautiful adventurer. . . . The writing is clear, packed with information, and presented in agile
paragraphs that twist around the scenes of war, plotting, and
murder." Booklist

Gourse, Leslie
   Sophisticated ladies; the great women of jazz.
illustrated by Martin French. Dutton Children's
Books/Penguin Young Readers Group 2007 64p il
$19.99
Grades: 7 8 9 10 11 12   920
1. Singers 2. Jazz music 3. Women -- Biography 4.
Women jazz singers
ISBN 978-0-525-47198-1; 0-525-47198-7
                 LC 2006-14852
"This lively collective biography of 14 singers begins in
the 1920s with Bessie Smith and Ethel Waters and moves
on through current performers Cassandra Wilson and Diana
Krall. A vibrant, full-page portrait opens each chapter, de-
picting the performer with bold vitality, in a style suggestive
of a theater poster." SLJ
   Includes discography and bibliographical references

Graham, Amy
   Astonishing ancient world scientists; 8 great
brains. MyReportLinks.com Books 2010 128p il
(Great scientists and famous inventors) $33.27
Grades: 6 7 8 9   920
1. Scientists 2. Mathematicians 3. Science -- History
4. Mathematics -- History 5. Science, Ancient 6.

Mathematics, Ancient
ISBN 978-1-59845-079-8; 1-59845-079-4

LC 2008-53925

This is a collective biography of ancient scientists and mathematicians: Pythagoras, Hippocrates, Aristotle, Archimedes, Galen, Ptolemy, Zhang Heng, and al-Khwarizmi.

"An interesting and sometimes amusing book. . . . The illustrations are captivating and will appeal to students, as will some of the anecdotes about scientists." Sci Books Films

Includes glossary and bibliographical references

Greathouse, Lisa E.

Skygazers; from Hypatia to Faber. Compass Point Books 2009 40p il (Mission: science) lib bdg $26.60

Grades: 4 5 6   **920**

1. Stars 2. Astronomy 3. Astronomers
ISBN 978-0-7565-4075-3 lib bdg; 0-7565-4075-5
lib bdg

LC 2008-35734

Brief lives of outstanding astronomers through the ages, beginning with the first notable woman astronomer, Hypatia of Alexandria

Includes glossary and bibliographical references

Haskins, James

African American religious leaders; [by] Jim Haskins and Kathleen Benson. Wiley 2008 162p il (Black stars) lib bdg $24.95

Grades: 6 7 8 9 10 11 12 Adult   **920**

1. African Americans -- Religion 2. African Americans -- Biography
ISBN 978-0-471-73632-5; 0-471-73632-5

LC 2007-27347

"It's great to have all these figures between two covers, and even a sampling of the entries captures the importance of religion, and its leaders, in African American life." Booklist

Includes bibliographical references

Hodgkins, Fran

Champions of the ocean; illustrations by Cris Arbo. Dawn Publications 2009 144p il (Earth heroes) pa $11.95

Grades: 5 6 7 8   **920**

1. Scientists 2. Oceanography 3. Environmentalists 4. Oceanographers
ISBN 978-1-58469-119-8 pa; 1-58469-119-0 pa

LC 2009-17926

This is a collective biography of oceanographers William Beebe, Archie Carr, Jacques-Yves Cousteau, Margaret Wentworth Owings, Eugenie Clark, Roger Payne, Sylvia Earle, and Tierney Thys.

This is illustrated with "black-and-white photographs and illustrations. [The book] provides young readers with fascinating facts and insights. . . . This volume is an excellent introduction to the biography genre, as well as a terrific research book." Sci Books Films

Includes bibliographical references

Housel, Debra J.

Ecologists; from Woodward to Miranda. Compass Point Books 2009 40p il (Mission: science) lib bdg $26.60

Grades: 4 5 6   **920**

1. Ecology 2. Environmentalists
ISBN 978-0-7565-4076-0 lib bdg; 0-7565-4076-3
lib bdg

LC 2008-35733

Profiles ecologists John Woodward, Aldo Leopold, Rachel Carson, Ruth Patrick, Eugene Odum, Lan Lubchenco, and Neo Martinez

Includes glossary and bibliographical references

Inspiring African-American inventors; 9 extraordinary lives. Enslow Publishers 2009 128p il (Great scientists and famous inventors) lib bdg $33.27

Grades: 5 6 7   **920**

1. African American inventors
ISBN 978-1-59845-080-4 lib bdg; 1-59845-080-8
lib bdg

LC 2007-22937

"This collective biography . . . profiles nine African American inventors: Lewis Howard Latimer, Jan E. Matziliger, Granville T. Woods, George Washington Carver, Madam C. J. Walker, Garrett A. Morgan, Percy Lavon Julian, Patricia Era Bath, and Lonnie G. Johnson. . . . Clearly written and logically organized, this volume provides a useful guide to the subject." Booklist

Includes glossary and bibliographical references

Jankowski, Connie

Astronomers; from Copernicus to Crisp. Compass Point Books 2009 40p il (Mission: science) lib bdg $26.60

Grades: 4 5 6   **920**

1. Astronomers
ISBN 978-0-7565-3965-8 lib bdg; 0-7565-3965-X
lib bdg

LC 2008-8325

Explores the lives and discoveries of noted astronomers from the fifteenth to the twenty-first century.

Includes glossary and bibliographical references

Kane, Joseph Nathan

★ **Facts** about the presidents; a compilation of biographical and historical information. Joseph Nathan Kane, Janet Podell [editors] 8th ed; Wilson, H.W. 2009 720p $150

Grades: 8 9 10 11 12 Adult   **920**

1. Reference books 2. Presidents -- United States
ISBN 9780824210878

LC 2008056016

First published 1959

The main part of this work provides an individual chapter on each President, from Washington through Barack Obama, presenting such information as family, education, election, Vice President, main events and accomplishments of his administration, and First Lady. Part two contains tables and lists presenting comparative data on all the Presidents

Kennedy, John F.

Profiles in courage. HarperCollins Pubs. 2003 xxii, 245p $19.95; pa $13.95

Grades: 7 8 9 10 11 12 Adult　　　　　**920**

1. Judges 2. Courage 3. Lawyers 4. Governors 5. Statesmen 6. Presidents 7. Senators 8. Army officers 9. Political leaders 10. State legislators 11. Members of Congress 12. Newspaper executives 13. Secretaries of state 14. Territorial governors 15. Supreme Court justices 16. Presidential candidates 17. Secretaries of the interior 18. Politicians -- United States 19. Legislators -- United States -- Biography

ISBN 0-06-053062-6; 0-06-085493-6 pa

LC 2003-40676

A reissue of the title first published 1956

This series of profiles of Americans who took courageous stands at crucial moments in public life includes John Quincy Adams, Daniel Webster, Thomas Hart Benton, Sam Houston, Edmund G. Ross, Lucius Q. C. Lamar, George Norris, Robert A. Taft and others.

Includes bibliographical references

Kennedy, Kerry

Speak truth to power; human rights defenders who are changing our world. photographs by Eddie Adams; edited by Nan Richardson. Crown 2000 256p il hardcover o.p. pa $34.95

Grades: 7 8 9 10　　　　　**920**

1. Human rights

ISBN 0-8129-3062-2; 1-88416-733-0 pa

LC 00-34557

This book "is composed of fifty three-page interviews with people who have made strides in the global fight to ensure basic human rights for everyone. . . . The Dalai Lama, Desmond Tutu, and Elie Wiesel are included, but most subjects are everyday people who have survived imprisonment, death threats, and torture to bring about change. . . . Their reports are sad but inspiring. . . . The haunting photographs and stories are gripping." Voice Youth Advocates

Kiernan, Denise

★ **Signing** our lives away; the fame and misfortune of the men who signed the Declaration of Independence. by Denise Kiernan & Joseph D'Agnese. Quirk 2009 255p $19.95

Grades: 5 6 7 8　　　　　**920**

1. Statesmen -- United States

ISBN 978-1-59474-330-6; 1-59474-330-4

"Kiernan and D'Agnese present readers with astonishing individual portraits of all the signers [of the Declaration of Independence] in an attempt both to dispel some of the mythology surrounding the document as well as to establish a place in the historical discourse for those men not named Jefferson, Hancock, Franklin, or Adams. The marvelously arranged work lends itself to either straightforward reading or skipping around. . . . An entertaining and effective narrative of about three to five pages per individual is presented." SLJ

Includes bibliographical references

Kimmel, Elizabeth Cody

Ladies first; 40 daring American women who were second to none. [by] Elizabeth Cody Kimmel; foreword by Stacy Allison. National Geographic 2006 192p il $18.95

Grades: 5 6 7 8　　　　　**920**

1. Women -- Biography

ISBN 0-7922-5393-0

LC 2005005113

This offers "introductions to forty of America's most brilliant and courageous women. Each essay is three pages in length and includes a fourth full-page portrait of the woman being introduced. . . . The women chosen achieved greatness in a wide range of endeavors, from athletics to the arts to politics. . . . Students will find these excellent essays useful as an introduction to the women portrayed and as a good jumping off point for further research." Voice Youth Advocates

Includes bibliographical references

The **look**-it-up book of explorers. Random House 2004 128p il map hardcover o.p. pa $19.99

Grades: 5 6 7 8　　　　　**920**

1. Explorers 2. Exploration

ISBN 0-375-92478-7; 0-375-82478-2 pa

"Beginning with Leif Ericksson and his trip to Greenland and the Americas to Robert Ballard's 1985 expedition to search for the Titanic , the chronologically arranged spreads give readers a better understanding of how the world was explored. . . . Informative black-and-white photos and reproductions appear throughout. . . . This is an excellent quick resource that will appeal to researchers and general readers alike." SLJ

Krull, Kathleen

★ **Lives** of extraordinary women; rulers, rebels (and what the neighbors thought) written by Kathleen Krull; illustrated by Kathryn Hewitt. Harcourt 2000 95p il $21

Grades: 4 5 6 7　　　　　**920**

1. Queens 2. Saints 3. Diplomats 4. Empresses 5. Explorers 6. Travelers 7. Suffragists 8. Abolitionists 9. Prime ministers 10. Women in politics 11. Regents 12. Feminists 13. Pacifists 14. Columnists 15. Dissenters 16. Memoirists 17. Humanitarians 18. Indian chiefs 19. Archaeologists 20. Indian leaders 21. Cabinet members 22. Social activists 23. Political leaders 24. Nonfiction writers 25. Women -- Biography 26. Members of Congress 27. Spouses of presidents 28. Human rights activists 29. United Nations officials 30. Nobel laureates for peace 31. Women in politics -- Biography 32. Women heads of state -- Biography

ISBN 0-15-200807-1

LC 99-6840

"Each entry offers a tightly written biography, often filled with delicious anecdote. . . . Each biographical essay is accompanied by one of Hewitt's full-page, full-color caricatures. Both artful and witty, the illustrations provide perfect accompaniments to the often breezy and accessible text." N Y Times Book Rev

Includes bibliographical references

★ **Lives** of the presidents; fame, shame (and what the neighbors thought) written by Kathleen Krull; illustrated by Kathryn Hewitt. updated ed.; Harcourt Children's Books 2011 104p il $21

Grades: 4 5 6 7   920

1. Presidents -- United States

ISBN 978-0-547-49809-6; 0-547-49809-8

First published 1998

"This new edition is sure to be even more popular than the original title (Harcourt, 1998) as it includes Presidents George W. Bush and Barack Obama, who are given the same cheeky-but-respectful treatment as their predecessors. . . . [Krull] provides further information on ex-Presidential activity since 1998, such as Jimmy Carter's Nobel Prize, Ronald Reagan's passing, and the Clintons' post-White House work. All other entries and art are virtually unaltered. Guaranteed to inject some levity into the ubiquitous presidential biography assignment, the 2011 Lives of the Presidents is a must-have for elementary schools and public libraries." SLJ

Includes bibliographical references

Langley, Wanda

Women of the wind; early women aviators. [by] Wanda Langley. Morgan Reynolds Pub. 2006 160p il map lib bdg $26.95

Grades: 6 7 8 9   920

1. Women air pilots

ISBN 978-1-931798-81-5; 1-931798-81-8

LC 2005022951

"This collective biography celebrates the accomplishments of nine American women who pioneered in the field of aviation: Harriet Quimby, Katherine Stinson, Ruth Law, Bessie Coleman, Amelia Earhart, Ruth Nichols, Louise Thaden, Anne Morrow Lindbergh, and Jacqueline Cochran. . . . Well reproduced and often in color, the illustrations include a great many photos, as well as maps and period advertisements. . . . Langley . . . offers information, anecdotes, and inspiring stories." Booklist

Includes bibliographical references

Life sciences; edited by Derek Hall. Brown Bear Books 2010 64p il (Facts at your fingertips) lib bdg $35.65

Grades: 8 9 10 11   920

1. Scientists 2. Life sciences

ISBN 978-1-933834-45-0 lib bdg; 1-933834-45-5 lib bdg

LC 2009-13343

Profiles the lives and work of famous life scientists, including Charles Darwin, Louis Pasteur, and Alexander Fleming

This provides "explanations about important discoveries, related work, and social and political influences that impacted the subjects' work. . . . The approximately six-to-eight page entries include important dates, photographs, diagrams, and sidebars on relevant scientists. The writing is often highly technical and some knowledge of the basics is assumed." SLJ

Includes glossary and bibliographical references

Malnor, Bruce

Champions of the wilderness; by Bruce and Carol L. Malnor; illustrated by Anisa Claire Hovemann. Dawn Publications 2009 143p il (Earth heroes) pa $11.95

Grades: 5 6 7 8   920

1. Environmentalists

ISBN 978-1-58469-116-7 pa; 1-58469-116-6 pa

LC 2008-53670

"This is a short gem of a book that includes short biographies of eight 'heroes' who have championed the preservation and/or conservation of wilderness areas around the world over the past two centuries. Henry David Thoreau, John Muir, Teddy Roosevelt, Aldo Leopold, Richard St. Barbe Baker, Mardy Murie, David Suzuki, and Wangari Maathai are the heroes in question. The storytelling is fluent and engaging." Sci Books Films

Includes bibliographical references

Malnor, Carol

Champions of wild animals; by Carol L. and Bruce Malnor; illustrations by Anisa Claire Hovemann. Dawn Publications 2010 144p il (Earth heroes) pa $11.95

Grades: 5 6 7 8   920

1. Naturalists 2. Endangered species 3. Wildlife conservation 4. Wildlife conservationists

ISBN 978-1-58469-123-5 pa; 1-58469-123-9 pa

LC 2010-16030

This describes "the youth and careers of eight of the world's greatest environmentalists who championed the protection of wildlife, including William Hornaday (saved the bison from extinction), Ding Darling (A Duck's Best Friend), Rachel Carson (author of Silent Spring), Roger Tory Peterson (Inventor of the Modern Field Guide), R.D. Lawrence (Storyteller for Wolves), E.O. Wilson (Lord of the Ants), Jane Goodall (Champion for Chimps), and Ian and Saba Douglas-Hamilton (Saving the Elephants)." Publisher's note

Includes bibliographical references

Mattern, Joanne

Mystics and psychics. Morgan Reynolds Pub. 2011 128p il (World religions and beliefs) $28.95

Grades: 6 7 8 9   920

1. Mysticism 2. Extrasensory perception

ISBN 978-1-59935-148-3; 1-59935-148-X

LC 2010008690

"Mattern offers an evenhanded look at some of the most famous (and controversial) of those with otherworldly powers. The mystics are Hildegard of Bingen, a twelfth-century German anchoress, and Padre Pio, and Italian monk who died in 1968. . . . Others profiled include Nostradamus; Edgar Cayce . . . Jeanne Dixon . . . and Peter Hurkos. . . . The profiles are interspersed with comments from skeptics and other reasons for visions. . . . Good illustrations and excellent back matter extend the well-written text." Booklist

Includes bibliographical references

Maydell, Natalie

★ **Extraordinary** women from the Muslim world. Global Content Publishing 2008 117p il map $16.95

Grades: 5 6 7 8   **920**

1. Muslim women 2. Women -- Biography
ISBN 978-0-97999-010-6; 0-97999-010-6

This "is an illustrative introduction to 13 Muslim women in history who have lived extraordinary lives and influenced their communities in a positive way, often overcoming extreme hardship and inaccurate stereotypes that have been placed on the role of women in Islam." Publisher's note

Nathan, Amy

Meet the dancers; from ballet, broadway, and beyond. Henry Holt 2008 231p il $18.95

Grades: 5 6 7 8   **920**

1. Dance 2. Dancers 3. Ballet dancers
ISBN 978-0-8050-8071-1; 0-8050-8071-6

LC 2007-27589

"This collective biography reveals the paths that 16 diverse dancers followed to become professionals and to join prestigious companies. . . . The tone of the text is conversational. . . . The pictures dramatically capture how talented these performers are. Anyone, whether considering a career in dance or not, will be inspired and educated by these up-close-and-personal accounts." SLJ

Open the unusual door; true life stories of challenge, adventure, and success by black Americans. edited and with an introduction by Barbara Summers. Graphia 2005 206p pa $7.99

Grades: 7 8 9 10   **920**

1. African Americans -- Biography
ISBN 0-618-58531-1

"A wonderful cross section of excerpts from published autobiographies. The 16 stories tell of challenges met and opportunities recognized and realized. Colin Powell's recollection of his introduction to the military life at City College in New York City stands alongside Russell Simmons's retelling of the turning point in his life when, at 16 years of age, he shot at and missed a fellow drug dealer. . . . This little gem of a book should be a first purchase for public and school libraries." SLJ

Orgill, Roxane

★ **Shout,** sister, shout! the girl singers who shaped a century. Margaret K. McElderry Bks. 2001 148p il hardcover o.p. pa $12.95

Grades: 6 7 8 9   **920**

1. Actors 2. Singers 3. Popular music 4. Folk musicians 5. Jazz musicians 6. Blues musicians 7. Songwriters 8. Pop musicians 9. Children's authors 10. Women -- Biography
ISBN 0-689-81991-9; 978-1-4169-6391-2 pa; 1-4169-6391-X pa

LC 99-54374

"The lives of ten 'girl singers,' representing different genres of popular music, from vaudeville to blues to jazz to country, are arranged by decade. Profiles of Sophie Tucker, Ma Rainey, Bessie Smith, Ethel Merman, Judy Garland,

Anita O'Day, Joan Baez, Bette Midler, Madonna, and Lucinda Williams are included." Voice Youth Advocates

Includes discography and bibliographical references

Ottaviani, Jim

★ **Dignifying** science; stories about women scientists. written by Jim Ottaviani and illustrated by Donna Barr . . . [et al.] 3rd ed; G.T. Labs 2009 142p il pa $16.95

Grades: 6 7 8 9 10 11 12   **920**

1. Graphic novels 2. Biographical graphic novels 3. Women scientists -- Graphic novels
ISBN 978-0-9788037-3-5; 0-9788037-3-5

First published 1999

Ottaviani provides biographical sketches of women scientists such as Lise Meitner, Rosalind Franklin, Barbara McClintock, and Hedy Lamarr (yes, the actress was also an inventor); all the stories are illustrated by women comics artists, including Lea Hernandez, Linda Medley, Anne Timmons, and others.

★ **Philosophy**, invention, and engineering; edited by Derek Hall. Brown Bear Books 2009 64p il (Facts at your fingertips) lib bdg $35.65

Grades: 8 9 10 11 12   **920**

1. Inventors 2. Inventions 3. Scientists 4. Philosophers
ISBN 978-1-93383-448-1 lib bdg; 1-93383-448-X lib bdg

LC 2009013344

"The book provides a multitude of facts—and fairly deep content—about Aristotle, James Watt, Charles Babbage and Ada Lovelace, Turing, and Jonas Salk. . . . Rich in synthesized information, this book encompasses a wealth of knowledge and gives a clear overall picture of the world at the time of each scientist's life." Booklist

Physical sciences; edited by Derek Hall. Brown Bear Books 2010 64p il (Facts at your fingertips) lib bdg $35.65

Grades: 8 9 10 11   **920**

1. Chemists 2. Physicists 3. Scientists
ISBN 978-1-933834-46-7; 1-933834-46-3

LC 2009-13345

Profiles the lives and work of people who have made significant contributions in physical sciences, including Isaac Newton, Marie and Pierre Curie, Albert Einstein and Richard Feynman.

This provides "explanations about important discoveries, related work, and social and political influences that impacted the subjects' work. . . . The approximately six-to-eight page entries include important dates, photographs, diagrams, and sidebars on relevant scientists. The writing is often highly technical and some knowledge of the basics is assumed." SLJ

Includes glossary and bibliographical references

Pinkney, Andrea Davis

★ **Let** it shine; stories of Black women freedom fighters. illustrated by Stephen Alcorn. Harcourt 2000 107p il $20

Grades: 4 5 6 7   920
1. Slaves 2. Authors 3. Midwives 4. Educators
5. Journalists 6. Abolitionists 7. Philanthropists 8.
African American women 9. Essayists 10. Memoirists
11. Political leaders 12. Nonfiction writers 13.
Members of Congress 14. Newspaper executives 15.
Presidential advisers 16. Civil rights activists 17.
Organization officials 18. Political party leaders 19.
Presidential candidates 20. African Americans -- Civil
rights 21. African American women -- Biography 22.
African Americans -- Civil rights -- History 23. African
American women civil rights workers -- Biography
ISBN 0-15-201005-X

LC 99-42806

This "collective biography tells of 10 extraordinary
black women. From Sojourner Truth to Shirley Chisholm,
this is also a view of African American history through individual lives. . . . Stephen Alcorn's allegorical oil portraits are
dramatic and beautiful. . . . The immediacy of the text and
the spacious design of the large volume make this a natural
for reading aloud." Booklist
Includes bibliographical references

Pouy, Jean-Bernard

The **big** book of dummies, rebels and other ge-
niuses; [by] Jean-Bernard Pouy & Serge Bloch; Anne
Blanchard. 1st American ed.; Enchanted Lion Books
2008 123p il $19.95
Grades: 6 7 8 9   920
1. Celebrities 2. Reference books 3. Biography --
Dictionaries
ISBN 978-1-59270-103-2; 1-59270-103-5

LC 2008-12278

Original French edition, 2006
"Pouy offers a wide variety of biographical sketches of
famous names . . . from Charlie Chaplin to Louis Armstrong
and Albert Einstein. The author nicely makes sure to include
little-known details. . . . [This book] will sell itself." Voice
Youth Advocates
Includes bibliographical references

Reed, Jennifer

The **Saudi** royal family; [by] Jennifer Bond
Reed. Chelsea House Publishers 2007 120p il
(Modern world leaders) lib bdg $30
Grades: 6 7 8 9 10   920
ISBN 978-0-7910-9218-7; 0-7910-9218-6

LC 2006-10613

First published 2003 by Chelsea House in the series: Major world leaders
This book "deciphers the nuances of Islamic law, an integral part of the Arabian peninsula's history. Tumultuous and
violent times are recorded, and democratic-like changes are
chronicled as well. The result is as neutral and evenhanded
an approach as a Westerner can use to describe this succession of Arab leaders." Libr Media Connect
Includes bibliographical references

Rosenberg, Aaron

The **Civil** War; one event, six people. Scholastic
2011 160p il map (Profiles) $14.99

Grades: 5 6 7 8   920
1. Nurses 2. Slaves 3. Authors 4. Lawyers 5. Generals
6. Presidents 7. Abolitionists 8. Photographers 9.
Memoirists 10. Police officials 11. State legislators 12.
College presidents 13. Members of Congress 14. Red
Cross officials 15. Social welfare leaders
ISBN 978-0-545-28926-9; 0-545-28926-2
"This collective biography . . . introduces Abraham Lincoln, Frederick Douglass, Clara Barton, George McClellan,
Robert E. Lee, and Matthew Brady. Single paragraph summaries of each subject's historical relevance are followed
by resumes of their lives that focus on how each affected
and was affected by the Civil War and that point out connections between them all. . . . Archival photographs are
instuctive." Booklist
Includes bibliographical references

Simoni, Suzanne

Fantastic women filmmakers. Second Story
Press 2008 122p il (Women's hall of fame) pa
$10.95
Grades: 7 8 9 10   920
1. Women in the motion picture industry 2. Motion
picture producers and directors -- Biography
ISBN 978-1-897187-36-4 pa; 1-897187-36-X pa
"Includes profiles of earlier filmmakers such as Nell
Shipman and Ida Lupiano as well as contemporary directors
like Deepa Mehta, Patricia Rozema, and Mira Nair. The author includes filmmakers who found varied and unique ways
to navigate the industry. . . . The profiles . . . are revealing,
inspiring, and insightful." Voice Youth Advocates
Includes glossary and bibliographical references

Spitz, Bob

Yeah! yeah! yeah! the Beatles, Beatlemania,
and the music that changed the world. Little, Brown
2007 234p il $18.99
Grades: 7 8 9 10   920
1. Singers 2. Guitarists 3. Rock musicians 4.
Drummers 5. Songwriters
ISBN 978-0-316-11555-1; 0-316-11555-X

LC 2006-39575

Based on the author's title for adults: The Beatles (2005)
This is "packed with all the fun and fabulousness that
were the Beatles. The book begins at the church festival
where John and Paul met as teens, and ends with Paul's formal declaration to leave the group. . . . [This is] comprehensive, sensitive to its subjects, and told with a flow that
carries readers along. Many smartly chosen black-and-white
photographs help re-create the times." Booklist

Stout, Glenn

Yes she can! women's sports pioneers. Houghton
Mifflin Harcourt 2011 117p il (Good sports) pa
$5.99
Grades: 4 5 6 7   920
1. Women athletes
ISBN 978-0-547-41725-7; 0-547-41725-X
"In chapters devoted to swimmer Trudy Ederle, runners
Louise Stokes and Tidye Pickett, jockey Julie Krone, and
Indy car driver Danica Patrick, Stout covers each woman's
hard work, setbacks, and triumphs without minimizing the

challenges and disappointments along the way. . . . Accessible and inspirational." Publ Wkly

Sullivan, Otha Richard

African American millionaires. John Wiley & Sons 2004 158p il (Black stars) $24.95

Grades: 6 7 8 9   920

1. African Americans -- Biography
ISBN 0-471-46928-9

LC 2004-14694

This profiles 25 African American millionaires

"Sullivan offers an exemplary compilation of a relatively unexplored subject area. . . . The book is well organized, highly readable, and inspiring." SLJ

Includes bibliographical references

Tate, Eleanora E.

★ African American musicians; Jim Haskins, general editor. Wiley 2000 70p il (Black stars) $24.95

Grades: 6 7 8 9   920

1. African American musicians 2. Afro-American musicians
ISBN 0-471-25356-1

LC 99-51360

"Many genres and skills are represented from spirituals, gospel, ragtime, blues, jazz, and soul. Scott Joplin, Marian Anderson, Duke Ellington, and Aretha Franklin are here as well as Michael Jackson and a few lesser-known individuals. Each entry includes a black-and-white photo or reproduction and sidebars on pertinent topics." SLJ

Includes bibliographical references

Thimmesh, Catherine

★ Girls think of everything; illustrated by Melissa Sweet. Houghton Mifflin 2000 57p $16; pa $6.95

Grades: 5 6 7 8   920

1. Women 2. Admirals 3. Chemists 4. Students 5. Inventors 6. Inventions 7. Physicists 8. Women inventors 9. Computer scientists 10. Home economists 11. Clothing industry executives 12. Office supply industry executives 13. Inventions -- United States -- History 14. Women inventors -- United States -- Biography
ISBN 0-395-93744-2; 0-618-19563-7 pa

LC 99-36270

"Ten women and two girls are given a few pages each. Included are Mary Anderson, who invented the windshield wiper (after she was told it wouldn't work); Ruth Wakefield, who, by throwing chunks of chocolate in her cookie batter, gave Toll House cookies to the world; and young Becky Schroeder, who invented Glo-paper because she wanted to write in the dark. The text is written in a fresh, breezy manner, but it is the artwork that is really outstanding." Booklist

Walters, Eric

When elephants fight; written by Eric Walters and Adrian Bradbury. Orca Book Publishers 2008 89p il $19.95

Grades: 7 8 9 10   920

1. Children and war
ISBN 978-1-55143-900-6; 1-55143-900-X

"The authors detail the lives of children growing up in . . . [war torn nations]. They provide rich, detailed histories of each nation, and explain the current conflicts which have led to the destruction of families and normal childhood. . . . This would be an excellent supplemental text for a high school geography or world civilization program." Libr Media Connect

Winter, Jonah

Peaceful heroes; illustrated by Sean Addy. Arthur A. Levine Books 2009 56p il $17.99

Grades: 4 5 6 7   920

1. Peace 2. Heroes and heroines
ISBN 978-0-439-62307-0; 0-439-62307-3

LC 2008-48311

"Starting off with Jesus, Gandhi, King, and Sojourner Truth, this collective biography goes on to profile many less well-known peace activists across the world. . . . The detailed portraits never deny the horrifying realities that the peace-seeking leaders are fighting against. With the chatty interactive text, there are handsome full-page pictures of each activist, rendered in oil, acrylic, and collage in shades of red and brown." Booklist

Ying, Chris

109 forgotten American heroes; created by Chris Ying and Brian McMullen. DK Publishing 2009 175p il $19.99

Grades: 6 7 8   920

1. Heroes and heroines
ISBN 978-0-7566-5405-4; 0-7566-5405-X

Photographs, graphics, and text bring to life the contributions, inventions, wisdom, savvy, and courage of 109 American originals, including Frank Epperson, the inventor of the popsicle, cereal creator John Harvey Kellogg, and Shamu, the killer whale who began her stay at the San Diego Sea World in 1965.

"Reading this book is a rip-roaring, entertaining experience with a lot of American history woven through its pages. Some articles might inspire further research and report topics." Voice Youth Advocates

Yolen, Jane

Sea queens; women pirates around the world. illustrated by Christine Joy Pratt. Charlesbridge 2008 103p il $18.95

Grades: 4 5 6 7   920

1. Women pirates 2. Women -- Biography
ISBN 978-1-58089-131-8; 1-58089-131-4

LC 2007026983

This offers "12 portraits of sword-swinging, seafaring women throughout history, from Artemisia, in 500 B.C.E. Persia, to Madame Ching, an early nineteenth-century Chinese woman and named here as 'the most successful pirate in the world.' . . . The scratchboard illustrations work well as portraits. . . . The book is filled with fascinating, dramatically told stories and sidebars." Booklist

Includes bibliographical references

Young, Jeff C.

Brilliant African-American scientists; 9 exceptional lives. MyReportLinks.com Books 2009 128p il (Great scientists and famous inventors) lib bdg $33.27

Grades: 5 6 7 8   920

1. Scientists 2. African Americans -- Biography
ISBN 978-1-59845-083-5 lib bdg; 1-59845-083-2 lib bdg

LC 2008053924

"Each chapter provides a graphic time line of the milestones in each of the scientists' lives and relates details on their early life, education, research and accomplishments. Several disciplines and science-related careers are highlighted. . . . Each of the chapters contains an inset that provides a link to a website for information on the scientist. A listing of Internet sites and brief descriptions of them are included, as are a glossary, chapter notes, and suggestions for further reading." Sci Books Films

Includes glossary and bibliographical references

920.003 Dictionaries, encyclopedias, concordances of biography as a discipline

Rich, Mari

World authors, 2000-2005; editors, Jennifer Curry, David Ramm, Mari Rich, Albert Rolls. Wilson, H. W. 2007 800p il (Authors series) $170

Grades: 11 12 Adult   920.003

1. Authors 2. Literature 3. Reference books 4. Authors -- Dictionaries 5. Literature -- Bio-bibliography 6. Literature -- History and criticism
ISBN 978-0-8242-1077-9

This book "covers some 300 novelists, poets, dramatists, essayists, scientists, biographers, and other authors whose books [were] published 2000 through 2005." Publisher's note

Riley, Sam G.

African Americans in the media today; an encyclopedia. [by] Sam G. Riley. Greenwood Press 2007 581p 2v set$175

Grades: 7 8 9 10 11 12   920.003

1. Mass media 2. Reference books 3. African Americans in television broadcasting 4. African Americans -- Biography 5. Celebrities -- United States -- Biography 6. African Americans -- Biography -- Dictionaries
ISBN 978-0-313-33679-9; 0-313-33679-2 set; 978-0-313-33680-5 v1; 0-313-33680-6 v1; 978-0-313-33681-2 v2; 0-313-33681-4 v2

LC 2007008192

"This concise, alphabetically arranged work describes hundreds of people . . . in various fields of communications. It includes, for example, reporters, anchormen and women, talk-show hosts, and television producers. . . . Each of the mostly one to two-page entries includes biographical information, . . . work experience, awards, and, in some cases, includes anecdotes or articles by or about the individual. .

. . A worthwhile resource for biography or communications projects." SLJ

Includes bibliographical references

Rockman, Connie C.

Tenth book of junior authors and illustrators; edited by Connie C. Rockman. Wilson, H.W. 2008 803p il (Junior authors & illustrators series) hardcover o.p. $120

Grades: Adult Professional   920.003

1. Reference books 2. Authors -- Dictionaries 3. Illustrators -- Dictionaries 4. Children's literature -- Bio-bibliography 5. Children's literature -- History and criticism 6. Young adult literature -- History and criticism 7. Children's literature -- Authors and illustrators
ISBN 978-0-8242-1066-3; 0-8242-1066-2

LC 2008043312

This volume covers some 200 authors and illustrators of books for children and young adults including David Almond, Blue Balliett, Terry Pratchett, and Laura Vaccaro Seeger. For 17 authors and artists whose careers include significant new works and honors since their profile in earlier editions of the series, newly written entries are featured

"Standard resource for libraries serving young readers and students studying children's and young adult literature." Booklist

Includes bibliographical references

Sonneborn, Liz

★ **A to Z of American Indian women**; rev ed; Facts on File 2007 320p il map (Facts on File library of American history) $60

Grades: 8 9 10 11 12   920.003

1. Reference books 2. Indian women -- North America 3. Native American women -- Dictionaries
ISBN 978-0-8160-6694-0

LC 2007-8162

First published 1998 with title: A to Z of Native American women

"This resource is of exceptionally high quality." SLJ

Includes bibliographical references

Yount, Lisa

A to Z of women in science and math; rev ed; Facts on File 2007 368p il (Facts on File library of world history) $60

Grades: 8 9 10 11 12   920.003

1. Reference books 2. Women scientists 3. Women in science 4. Women scientists -- Dictionaries 5. Women mathematicians -- Dictionaries
ISBN 978-0-8160-6695-7; 0-8160-6695-7

LC 2007-23966

First published 1999

"More than 195 alphabetically arranged articles detail the lives of women from antiquity through modern day, including well-known scientists and mathematicians and less well-documented individuals. . . . The usefulness of this resource lies not only in the balanced group of profiles that have been assembled, providing a valuable tool for teachers and curriculum developers, but also in the readable and engaging entries themselves." Booklist

Includes bibliographical references

American Indian biographies; edited by Carole Barrett, Harvey Markowitz, project editor, R. Kent Rasmussen. rev ed.; Salem Press 2005 623p il map (Magill's choice) $62

Grades: 8 9 10 11 12 Adult   **920.003**

1. Reference books 2. Indian women 3. Indians of North America 4. Native Americans -- Biography 5. Indians of North America -- Kings and rulers

ISBN 1-58765-233-1; 978-1-58765-233-2

LC 2004-28872

First published 1999; some essays originally appeared in Dictionary of world biography, Great lives from history: the Renaissance & early modern era, 1454-1600 (2005), and American ethnic writers (2000)

"The book contains essays on religious, social, and political leaders; warriors; and reformers from the past as well as modern activists, writers, artists, entertainers, scientists, and athletes. . . . A great bargain and an asset in any library that supports an American history curriculum." Booklist

Includes bibliographical references

★ **Great** athletes; edited by The Editors of Salem Press; special consultant Rafer Johnson. Salem Press 2010 13v il set $1,020

Grades: 7 8 9 10 11 12   **920.003**

1. Reference books 2. Athletes -- Dictionaries

ISBN 978-1-58765-473-2; 1-58765-473-3

LC 2009-21905

"This massive undertaking totals 1,470 entries covering athletes in baseball, basketball, boxing, football, golf, auto racing, soccer, tennis, and Olympic sports. Additionally, well-known athletes in other, less recognized sports—such as cycling, skateboarding, stunt riding, martial-arts and chess—are included. . . . Overall, this is a well-put-together and wide-ranging set." Booklist

Includes bibliographical references

Lifelines in world history; general editor, Mounir A. Farah. Sharpe Reference 2009 4v il map set $299

Grades: 6 7 8 9 10 11 12   **920.003**

1. World history 2. Reference books 3. Civilization -- History 4. Biography -- Dictionaries

ISBN 978-0-7656-8125-6; 0-7656-8125-0

LC 2008-16288

"This set provides profiles of influential world leaders. Each volume contains 15 to 20 sketches that include basic biographical information, an overview of the subject's achievements, and analysis of the 'interplay' between the person and the 'political, economic, and social circumstances' in which he or she lived. . . . Entries range in length from five to eight pages and offer well-captioned color reproductions, photos, and maps. . . . This attractive set provides well-illustrated, objective information in a global context." SLJ

Includes bibliographical references

Something about the author; facts and pictures about authors and illustrators of books for young people. Gale Res. il

Grades: Adult Professional   **920.003**

1. Reference books 2. Authors -- Dictionaries 3. Illustrators -- Dictionaries 4. Children's literature -- Bio-bibliography

First published 1971. Frequency varies

"This important series gives comprehensive coverage of the individuals who write and illustrate books for children. Each new volume adds about 100 profiles. Entries include career and personal data, a bibliography of the author's works, information on works in progress and references to further information." Safford. Guide to Ref Materials for Sch Libr Media Cent. 5th edition

Something about the author: autobiography series. Gale Res. il

Grades: Adult Professional   **920.003**

1. Reference books 2. Authors -- Dictionaries 3. Illustrators -- Dictionaries 4. Children's literature -- Bio-bibliography

First published 1986

An "ongoing series in which juvenile authors discuss their lives, careers, and published works. Each volume contains essays by 20 established writers or illustrators (e.g., Evaline Ness, Nonny Hogrogian, Betsy Byars, Jean Fritz) who represent all types of literature, preschool to young adult. . . . Some articles focus on biographical information, while others emphasize the writing career. Most, however, address young readers and provide family background, discuss the writing experience, and cite some factors that influenced it. Illustrations include portraits of the authors as children and more recent action pictures and portraits. There are cumulative indexes by authors, important published works, and geographical locations mentioned in the essays." Safford. Guide to Ref Books for Sch Libr Media Cent. 5th edition

920.02   General collections of biography

Donovan, Sandy

Lethal leaders and military madmen; by Sandy Donovan. Lerner Publications Company 2013 32 p. col. ill. (library) $26.60

Grades: 5 6 7 8   **920.02**

1. Kings and rulers 2. Dictators 3. Dictatorship 4. Military government

ISBN 1467706094; 9781467706094

LC 2012018444

This book by Sandy Donovan is part of the Shockzone Villains series and looks at political and military leaders. "Some of history's most ruthless leaders are headed your way. Some of these rulers schemed their way to the top. Others just conquered everything around them." (Publisher's note)

920.03 General collections of biography by specific continents, countries, localities

Baker, Rosalie F.

Ancient Egyptians; people of the pyramids. [by] Rosalie F. and Charles F. Baker. Oxford Univ. Press 2001 189p il maps (Oxford profiles) $50

Grades: 7 8 9 10 **920.03**

1. Egypt -- History -- To 332 B.C -- Biography
ISBN 0-19-512221-6

LC 2001-21209

"Divided into five periods from the Old Kingdom, about 2686 B.C., to the declining New Kingdom, about 245 B.C., this book profiles some 30 Egyptian leaders, devoting a three- to seven-page chapter to each one. . . . The entries are well written and researched. . . . A useful addition for report writers and subject enthusiasts." SLJ

Includes glossary and bibliographical references

920.72 Women

Branzei, Sylvia

Adventurers; Sylvia Branzei; illustrated by Melissa Sweet. Running Press 2011 96 p. ill., maps (ebook) $10.95; (paperback) $10.95

Grades: 3 4 5 6 7 **920.72**

1. Women 2. Adventure and adventurers 3. Women -- Biography 4. Women adventurers -- Biography 5. Adventure and adventurers -- Biography
ISBN 9780762443857; 0762436964; 9780762436965

LC 2009923889

This book "provides 6- to 8-page biographical sketches of 12 women who are 'the stuff of legends.' Each one is identified with a character trait, e.g. balloonist Sophie Blanchard is 'Intrepid' and Margaret Bourke-White is 'Relentless,' although most of the adjectives could apply to every subject, as [Sylvia] Branzei makes plain." Among those included are Amelia Earhart, Nellie Bly, Susan Butcher, and Kit Deslauriers. (School Library Journal)

Cowgirls; by Sylvia Branzei; illustratrated by Melissa Sweet. Running Press Kids 2011 96 p. ill. (some col.), map (paperback) $10.95

Grades: 3 4 5 6 7 **920.72**

1. Cowgirls 2. Ranch life -- West (U.S.) 3. Cowgirls -- West (U.S.) -- History 4. Cowgirls -- West (U.S.) -- Biography
ISBN 0762436956; 9780762436958

LC 2009923890

This book "profiles 12 sketches of working cowgirls and rodeo riders from the 19th century through the present day. The term 'cowgirl' also covers other Western types: stagecoach driver Mary Fields is here, along with outlaw Sally Skull and 'Little Sure-Shot' Annie Oakley. 'Lady cowboy poet' Georgie Sicking will probably be new to most readers; one of her poems is included." (School Library Journal)

Includes bibliographical references (p. 92-96)

León, Vicki

★ **Outrageous** women of the Middle Ages; by Vicki Leon. Wiley 1998 ix, 118 p.p ill., maps hardcover o.p. (paperback) $14.95; (prebind) $23.95

Grades: 4 5 6 7 8 **920.72**

1. Middle Ages 2. Women -- History 3. Women -- Biography 4. Women -- History -- Middle Ages, 500-1500 5. Civilization, Medieval 6. Biography -- Middle Ages, 500-1500
ISBN 9780471170044; 9781435280090

LC 97030307

In this book, Vicki Leon looks at women of the Middle Ages. She "tells of a Viking killed by a severed head, a queen who knew the meaning of congregating frogs, and much more. The stories and sidebars provide a detailed picture of the times. . . . The women profiled lived in the 6th through 14th centuries in Europe, Asia, and Africa. Their spheres included everything from astronomy to warfare. They were nomads and empresses." (School Library Journal)

Includes bibliographical references (p. 115-117).

McCann, Michelle Roehm

Girls who rocked the world; heroines from Sacagawea to Natalie Portman. Michelle Roehm McCann and Amelie Welden. Simon & Schuster 2012 p. cm. (hardcover: alk. paper) $18.99

Grades: 5 6 7 8 **920.72**

1. Feminism 2. Women -- History 3. Women -- Biography 4. Girls -- Biography 5. Heros -- Biography 6. Women heros -- Biography
ISBN 9781582703022; 9781582703619

LC 2011050502

Author Michelle Roehm McCann presents "examples of strong, independent female role models, all of whom first impacted the world as teenagers or younger." The book "spans a variety of achievements, interests, and backgrounds, from Harriet Tubman and Coco Chanel to S.E. Hinton and Maya Lin--each with her own incredible story of how she created life-changing opportunities for herself and the world." (Publisher's note)

Includes bibliographical references and index.

921 Philosophers and psychologists

Wyborny, Sheila

Kim Jong Il; by Sheila Wyborny. Lucent Books 2009 104 p. ill. (some col.), map (People in the News) (library) $35.95

Grades: 6 7 8 9 **921**

1. Heads of state 2. Communist leaders
ISBN 9781420500912; 1420500910

LC 2008049567

This book by Sheila Wyborny is part of the People in the News series and focuses on late North Korean leader Kim Jong Il. The series "profiles the lives and careers of some of today's most prominent newsmakers. Whether covering contributions and achievements or notorious deeds, books in this series examine why these well-known people garner public attention." (Publisher's note)

Includes bibliographical references (p. 90-91) and index.

929   Genealogy, names, insignia

Ollhoff, Jim

Beginning genealogy; expert tips to help you trace your own ancestors. ABDO Pub. Co. 2011 32p il (Your family tree) $18.95

Grades: 4 5 6 7   929

1. Research 2. Genealogy

ISBN 978-1-61613-460-0; 1-61613-460-7

LC 2009050812

This is "great . . . for kids interested in genealogy. . . . [It does] a wonderful job of presenting the fundamentals of genealogical research in a clear and exciting manner. . . . Understanding and properly using primary documents is stressed throughout. . . . [An] attractive, spacious [layout]; full-color, sharp images; clearly labeled diagrams; and scattered maps add information and appeal." SLJ

Includes glossary

Collecting primary records. ABDO Pub. Co. 2011 32p il (Your family tree) $18.95

Grades: 4 5 6 7   929

1. Research 2. Genealogy

ISBN 978-1-61613-461-7; 1-61613-461-5

LC 2009050811

This describes how to collect primary records for geneological research.

This is "great . . . for kids interested in genealogy. . . . [It does] a wonderful job of presenting the fundamentals of genealogical research in a clear and exciting manner. . . . Understanding and properly using primary documents is stressed throughout. . . . [An] attractive, spacious [layout]; full-color, sharp images; clearly labeled diagrams; and scattered maps add information and appeal." SLJ

Includes glossary

DNA; window to the past: how science can help untangle your family roots. ABDO Pub. Co. 2011 32p il map (Your family tree) $18.95

Grades: 4 5 6 7   929

1. Genetics 2. Genealogy

ISBN 978-1-61613-462-4; 1-61613-462-3

LC 2009050808

This explains how DNA is used in geneology.

This is "great . . . for kids interested in genealogy. . . . [It does] a wonderful job of presenting the fundamentals of genealogical research in a clear and exciting manner. . . . Understanding and properly using primary documents is stressed throughout. . . . [An] attractive, spacious [layout]; full-color, sharp images; clearly labeled diagrams; and scattered maps add information and appeal." SLJ

Includes glossary

Filling the family tree. ABDO Pub. Co. 2011 32p il (Your family tree) lib bdg $18.95

Grades: 4 5 6 7   929

1. Research 2. Genealogy

ISBN 978-1-61613-464-8; 1-61613-464-X

LC 2009050806

This is "great . . . for kids interested in genealogy. . . . [It does] a wonderful job of presenting the fundamentals of genealogical research in a clear and exciting manner. . . .

. Understanding and properly using primary documents is stressed throughout. . . . [An] attractive, spacious [layout]; full-color, sharp images; clearly labeled diagrams; and scattered maps add information and appeal." SLJ

Using your research; how to check your facts and use your information. ABDO Pub. Co. 2011 32p il (Your family tree) lib bdg $18.95

Grades: 4 5 6 7   929

1. Research 2. Genealogy

ISBN 978-1-61613-465-5; 1-61613-465-8

LC 2009050805

Presents a brief guide on how to check facts and use other information in genealogical research.

This is "great . . . for kids interested in genealogy. . . . [It does] a wonderful job of presenting the fundamentals of genealogical research in a clear and exciting manner. . . . Understanding and properly using primary documents is stressed throughout. . . . [An] attractive, spacious [layout]; full-color, sharp images; clearly labeled diagrams; and scattered maps add information and appeal." SLJ

Includes glossary

929.9   Forms of insignia and identification

Bateman, Teresa

Red, white, blue, and Uncle who? the stories behind some of America's patriotic symbols. illustrated by John O'Brien. Holiday House 2001 64p il $16.95; pa $6.95

Grades: 4 5 6 7   929.9

1. National emblems 2. Emblems, National 3. National monuments 4. Emblems, National -- United States

ISBN 0-8234-1285-7; 0-8234-1784-0 pa

LC 00-57258

This "volume presents 17 'patriotic symbols,' an umbrella term that encompasses everything from the flag to Uncle Sam, from Mount Rushmore to the Korean War Memorial. Bateman finds plenty of interesting information to share about each symbol or site, and browsers will be entertained by the many stories of origination, construction, and history." Booklist

Includes bibliographical references

Jackson, Donna M.

The **name** game; a look behind the labels. illustrated by Ted Stearn. Viking 2009 64p il $16.99

Grades: 4 5 6 7 8   929.9

1. Names

ISBN 978-0-670-01197-1; 0-670-01197-5

LC 2008-37705

"All kinds of entertaining and random facts are found in this quirky book. Tips for naming pets and companies are given, in a chapter each, along with hints for remembering people's names, explanations of conventions in other countries, and the system of choosing hurricane monikers. Sports, people, and geographic locations all have different sections. Black-and-white cartoons add a bit of humor. Students will navigate this book with ease." SLJ

Shearer, Benjamin F.

State names, seals, flags, and symbols; a historical guide. [by] Benjamin F. Shearer and Barbara S. Shearer. 3rd ed, rev and expanded; Greenwood Press 2001 495p il $73.95

Grades: 8 9 10 11 12 Adult   **929.9**

1. Reference books 2. Seals (Numismatics) 3. Flags -- United States 4. Geographic names -- United States

ISBN 0-313-31534-5

LC 2001-23525

First published 1987

"Chapters on mottoes, flowers, trees, birds, songs, holidays, and license plates are just a sampling of what is covered, and the format is such that the concisely written material can be found as expeditiously as possible. Even though the book is touted predominantly as a reference tool, the information provided makes fascinating and enlightening reading." Libr J [review of 1994 edition]

Includes bibliographical references

930   History of specific continents, countries, localities; extraterrestrial worlds

Adams, Simon

The **Kingfisher** atlas of the ancient world; illustrated by Katherine Baxter. Kingfisher 2006 44p il $15.95

Grades: 4 5 6 7   **930**

1. Reference books 2. Ancient civilization 3. Historical geography

ISBN 978-0-7534-5914-0; 0-7534-5914-0

"Featuring seventeen . . . hand-illustrated maps and . . . with . . . information about ancient civilizations and peoples, this is [a] . . . pictorial guide to what the world was like between 10,000 B.C. and A.D. 1000. Each . . . map shows the major sites from a particular civilization or group of civilizations. . . . Feature spreads use photographs of cultural and architectural artifacts, as well as additional information, to focus in greater depth on the key cultures of Egypt, Greece, and Rome." Publisher's note

Morris, Neil

Prehistory. Zak Books 2009 48p il map (History of the world) lib bdg $34.25

Grades: 7 8 9 10   **930**

1. History 2. Prehistoric peoples

ISBN 978-88-6098-156-1 lib bdg; 88-6098-156-5 lib bdg

LC 2008-8399

The "effectiveness lies in the combination of lush illustrations, well-chosen, captioned photographs of contemporary artifacts, and . . . [a] reasoned, concise [narrative]. Succinct time lines border most pages, . . . the proper amount of white space, and clear dark print maintain organization and clarity. A superior choice." SLJ

Includes glossary

The **world** in ancient times; primary sources and reference volume. Ronald Mellor & Amanda Poda-

ny, general editors. Oxford University Press 2005 188p il map (World in ancient times) $32.95

Grades: 7 8 9 10   **930**

1. Ancient history 2. Reference books 3. Ancient civilization

ISBN 978-0-19-522220-3; 0-19-522220-2

LC 2004026578

"An excellent introduction to the use of primary resources in historical research. The 76 selections include poems, letters, inscriptions, and other contemporary accounts from antiquity as well as more modern descriptions and excerpts. Materials from Asia, Europe, and the Americas are highlighted." SLJ

Includes bibliograghical references

930.1   Archaeology

Barber, Nicola

Lost cities; by Nicola Barber. Capstone Raintree 2013 48 p. col. ill. (Treasure Hunters) (hardcover) $29.33; (paperback) $8.99

Grades: 5 6 7 8   **930.1**

1. Extinct cities 2. Legends 3. Civilization, Ancient 4. Archaeology -- History

ISBN 1410949524; 1410949591; 9781410949523; 9781410949592

LC 2012012891

This book by Nicola Barber is part of the Treasure Hunters series and looks at lost cities. This entry "examines the search for lost cities and the important artefacts within them that can offer us an extraordinary window on to the past. . . . Cities covered in the book include Pompeii, Troy, the desert city of Ubar, and the Inca city of Machu Picchu." (Publisher's note)

Includes bibliographical references

Tomb explorers; by Nicola Barber. Capstone Raintree 2013 48 p. ill. (mostly col.) (Treasure Hunters) $29.33; (paperback) $8.99

Grades: 5 6 7 8   **930.1**

1. Tombs 2. Antiquities 3. Archaeology 4. Treasure troves 5. Civilization, Ancient 6. Archaeology -- History

ISBN 1410949559; 9781410949554; 9781410949622

LC 2012012894

This book by Nicola Barber "examines the hunt for and discovery of ancient tombs, and the valuable treasures they hold. . . . Part of the Treasure Hunters series, 'Tomb Explorers' offers a crosscurricular mix of science & technology and history & civilizations. . . . Tombs covered in the book include that of Tutankhamun, the Sumerian royal tombs of Ur, the Terracotta Army of ancient China, and the Mayan tombs of Palanque in the Mexican Rainforest, and the Oseberg ship burial." (Publisher's note)

Includes bibliographical references

Compoint, Stephane

Buried treasures; uncovering secrets of the past. Abrams Books for Young Readers 2011 72p il $19.95

Grades: 5 6 7 8   **930.1**
1. Archeology 2. Antiquities 3. Ancient civilization
ISBN 978-0-8109-9781-3; 0-8109-9781-9

LC 2010021626

"Showcasing the work of a specialist in archaeological photography, this loosely themed album offers a broad range of eye candy for fans of ancient artifacts, fossils, remote natural locales, and rare animals. . . . Confined to captions and a few introductory paragraphs, the text supplies useful background. . . . The photos are . . . dramatically lit, sharply reproduced, and tellingly angled. . . . Casual browsers will consider this book a real find." Booklist

Croy, Anita
Exploring the past. Marshall Cavendish Benchmark 2010 48p il (Invisible worlds) $28.50
Grades: 4 5 6 7   **930.1**
1. Fossils 2. Archeology 3. Human origins 4. Prehistoric peoples 5. Ancient civilization
ISBN 978-0-7614-4194-6; 0-7614-4194-8
The narrative is "clear, well written, broken down into manageable pieces, and peppered with eye-opening facts. The numerous photographs are so phenomenal that they will inspire kids to read the text . . . so that they can wrap their minds around what they see." SLJ
Includes glossary and bibliographical references

Getz, David
Frozen man; illustrated by Peter McCarty. Holt & Co. 1994 68p il maps hardcover o.p. pa $10.99
Grades: 5 6 7 8   **930.1**
1. Mummies 2. Archeology 3. Prehistoric peoples 4. Italy -- Antiquities
ISBN 0-8050-3261-4; 0-8050-4645-3 pa

LC 94-9109

"This is an account of the mummified stone-age corpse who was found in Austria in 1991. . . . Getz's generally well-organized information and smooth exposition makes the effort to understand the Iceman, as this book calls him, into an intriguing detective story. This could well stimulate the interest of kids who didn't think they liked science or archeology. Black-and-white drawings include useful maps and diagrams." Bull Cent Child Books
Includes glossary and bibliographical references

Hunter, Nick
Ancient treasures; by Nick Hunter; edited by Laura Knowles ... [et al.]; illustrated by Martin Bustamante. Raintree 2013 48 p. col. ill., col. maps (Treasure hunters) (hardcover) $29.33; (paperback) $8.99
Grades: 5 6 7 8   **930.1**
1. Archaeology 2. Buried treasure 3. Ancient civilization 4. Treasure troves 5. Civilization, Ancient 6. Archaeology -- History
ISBN 1410949508; 9781410949509; 9781410949578

LC 2012012757

"Part of the Treasure Hunters series, 'Ancient Treasures' offers a crosscurricular mix of science & technology and history. . . .Treasures covered in the book include the Roman Hoxne Hoard, the Anglo-Saxon Staffordshire Hoard, the extraordinary discoveries of the Rosetta Stone and Dead Sea Scrolls, and the South American treasures of Lake Guatavita. The book also looks at the motives for these searches, and the importance of responsible archaeology." (Publisher's note)
Includes bibliographical references (p. 46-47) and index.

Matthews, Rupert
Ancient mysteries. QEB Pub. 2011 32p il (Unexplained) lib bdg $28.50
Grades: 4 5 6 7   **930.1**
1. Legends 2. Ancient civilization 3. Curiosities and wonders
ISBN 978-1-59566-854-7; 1-59566-854-3

LC 2010014189

This discusses mysteries in the ancient world.
"This well-written and thoughtfully designed [book] features [an] engrossing [topic]. . . . Though the pages are profusely illustrated with large, well-reproduced photographs and drawings, the layout is not cluttered. This [book] just might inspire kids to seek out more in-depth materials." SLJ

Rubalcaba, Jill
Every bone tells a story; hominid discoveries, deductions, and debates. [by] Jill Rubalcaba and Peter Robertshaw. Charlesbridge 2010 185p il map lib bdg $18.95
Grades: 8 9 10 11 12   **930.1**
1. Archeology 2. Fossil hominids 3. Prehistoric peoples 4. Excavations (Archeology) 5. Human remains (Archaeology)
ISBN 978-1-58089-164-6; 1-58089-164-0

LC 2008-26961

"Archaeology and paleontology are the exciting focus in this accessible account of four hominins who lived long before recorded history. . . . The informal style never oversimplifies the engaging science and technology, and the authors raise as many questions as they answer in the detailed chapters." Booklist

931   Specific places

Ball, Jacqueline A.
★ **Ancient** China; archaeology unlocks the secrets of China's past. by Jacqueline Ball and Richard Levey, Robert Murowchick, consultant. National Geographic 2006 64p il (National Geographic investigates) hardcover o.p. lib bdg $27.90; $17.95
Grades: 5 6 7 8   **931**
1. China -- Civilization 2. China -- Antiquities
ISBN 9780792278566 lib bdg; 9780792277835
"This volume spotlights archaeological finds from Ancient China. . . . While the discussions of archaeology will hold readers' interest, the accompanying illustrations steal the show." Booklist

Kleeman, Terry F.
The **ancient** Chinese world; [by] Terry Kleeman & Tracy Barrett. Oxford University Press 2005 174p il map (World in ancient times) $32.95

Grades: 7 8 9 10   **931**
1. China -- History
ISBN 0-19-517102-0
LC 2004-14408

"Readers seriously interested in history, in archaeology—or in China—will be well served by this engrossing book." SLJ

Includes bibliographical references

O'Connor, Jane

★ The **emperor's** silent army; terracotta warriors of Ancient China. Viking 2002 48p il $17.99

Grades: 4 5 6 7   **931**
1. Emperors 2. Shaanxi Sheng (China) -- Antiquities 3. Terra-cotta sculpture, Chinese -- Qin-Han dynasties, 221 B.C.-220 A.D
ISBN 0-670-03512-2
LC 2001-46900

Describes the archaeological discovery of thousands of life-sized terracotta warrior statues in northern China in 1974, and discusses the emperor who had them created and placed near his tomb

"This intriguing book is enhanced by beautiful illustrations—pictures of stone engravings, colorful paintings, drawings, and maps—while numerous photographs show the clay soldiers from different perspectives. . . . The author's writing style is entertaining, yet informative." Book Rep

Includes bibliographical references

Rosinsky, Natalie M.

Ancient China; by Natalie M. Rosinsky. Compass Point Books 2013 48 p. col. ill., col. maps (Exploring the ancient world) (library) $28.65; (paperback) $8.95

Grades: 6 7 8   **931**
1. China -- History 2. Ancient civilization
ISBN 0756545684; 9780756545680; 9780756545789
LC 2012001965

This book is part of the Exploring the Ancient World series and focuses on Ancient China. Topics include "advancements in science and knowledge, the arts, social structures, religious practices, and the causes for the civilization's eventual demise." This entry "covers the dynasties beginning with Xia and ending with Qing. . . . Each title includes maps, a table listing periods or rulers, and well-chosen photographs and art reproductions." (School Library Journal)

Includes bibliographical references (p. 46-47) and index.

Shaughnessy, Edward L.

Exploring the life, myth, and art of ancient China. Rosen 2009 144p il map (Civilizations of the world) lib bdg $29.95

Grades: 7 8 9 10 11 12   **931**
1. Chinese mythology 2. Arts -- China
ISBN 978-1-4358-5617-2; 1-4358-5617-1
LC 2009-10290

This is an introduction to ancient Chinese civilization

"This beautifully illustrated and well-written [title] . . . is perfect for those assignments where students must look at the culture of a civilization. Artwork and pictures blend seamlessly with the information and the reader is taken on a journey of discovery. Myths are used as the story of how

the people view themselves, blended with the discussion of the reality of life. Everyday life is tied to the belief systems and is explained in light of those beliefs. The pictures are beautifully done and there is almost as much information in the captions as there is in the text." Libr Media Connect

Includes glossary and bibliographical references

Shuter, Jane

Ancient China; [by] Jane Shuter. Raintree 2007 64p il map (Time travel guide) lib bdg $34.29; pa $9.99

Grades: 6 7 8 9   **931**
1. China -- Civilization
ISBN 978-1-4109-2729-3 lib bdg; 1-4109-2729-6 lib bdg; 978-1-4109-2736-1 pa; 1-4109-2736-9 pa
LC 2006033868

This describes life in Ancient China in the form of a travel guide.

Includes glossary and bibliographical references

932   Egypt to 640

Ancient Egypt; edited by Sherman Hollar. Britannica Educational Pub. in association with Rosen Educational Services 2011 87p il map (Ancient civilizations) lib bdg $31.70

Grades: 5 6 7 8   **932**
1. Egypt -- History 2. Egypt -- Civilization
ISBN 978-1-61530-523-0; 1-61530-523-8
LC 2011004714

This book provides "enough information about the development, way of life, accomplishments, and decline of [Ancient Egypt] without overwhelming readers. Maps; full-color illustrations and photographs, many full page; and sidebars provide additional focus. . . . The use of the Nile and its influence on the development of this civilization is emphasized. . . . The building of the great pyramids and the art of mummification are also mentioned. A detailed discussion of the everyday lives of the rich and the poor provide valuable insight." SLJ

Includes glossary and bibliographical references

Berger, Melvin

★ **Mummies** of the pharaohs; exploring the Valley of the Kings. [by] Melvin Berger & Gilda Berger. National Geographic Soc. 2001 64p il $17.95

Grades: 4 5 6 7   **932**
1. Mummies 2. Mummies -- Egypt 3. Pharaohs -- History
ISBN 0-7922-7223-4
LC 00-55411

This offers "stunning photographs and clear, compelling text. . . . A fascinating historical resource that kids will read straight through for pleasure and also find useful for report writing." Booklist

Fletcher, Joann

Exploring the life, myth, and art of ancient Egypt. Rosen Pub. 2009 144p il map (Civilizations of the world) $29.95

Grades: 7 8 9 10 11 12 **932**
1. Egypt -- Antiquities 2. Egypt -- Civilization
ISBN 978-1-4358-5616-5; 1-4358-5616-3
LC 2009-8792

"This attractively designed and handsomely illustrated book offers a rich and informative introduction to ancient Egyptian culture. Abundantly illustrated with beautifully rendered color representations of architecture, works of art, and other artifacts, the book offers insight into the beliefs and rituals, economy, and social organization of ancient Egyptian civilization." Booklist

Includes glossary and bibliographical references

George, Charles, 1949-
★ The **pyramids** of Giza; by Charles and Linda George. ReferencePoint Press 2012 80 p. (Ancient Egyptian Wonders) (hardcover) $28.95
Grades: 8 9 10 11 12 **932**
1. Pyramids 2. Egypt -- Antiquities 3. Pyramids of Giza (Egypt)
ISBN 1601522584; 9781601522580
LC 2012000282

This book by Charles George is part of the Ancient Egyptian Wonders series and looks at the pyramids of Giza. "Three of the grandest of all the pyramids built by the pharaohs of Egypt still stand on the Giza Plateau. These monuments serve as reminders of their builders but also of the glory and grandeur that was ancient Egypt." (Publisher's note)

Includes bibliographical references and index.

Grant, Neil
Ancient Egypt and Greece. Zak Books 2009 48p il map (History of the world) lib bdg $34.25
Grades: 7 8 9 10 **932**
1. Greece -- Civilization 2. Egypt -- Civilization
ISBN 978-88-6098-158-5 lib bdg; 88-6098-158-1 lib bdg
LC 2008-8401

The "effectiveness lies in the combination of lush illustrations, well-chosen, captioned photographs of contemporary artifacts, and [a] reasoned, concise [narrative]. . . . A superior choice." SLJ

Includes glossary

Kerrigan, Michael
Egyptians. Marshall Cavendish Benchmark 2010 64p il (Ancients in their own words) $32.79
Grades: 5 6 7 8 **932**
1. Egypt -- Civilization
ISBN 978-1-60870-064-6; 1-60870-064-X

Features "Numerous photographs provide visual interest, with text describing the images to give details and background. Translations of the writings offer primary sources to accompany the secondary material presented. . . . The text is interesting enough to read cover to cover while the table of contents' descriptive chapter titles and the comprehensive index enable the . . . [book] to be used for specific research." Libr Media Connect

Includes bibliographical references

Lace, William
★ **King** Tut's curse; by William W. Lace. ReferencePoint Press 2012 80 p. ill. (Ancient Egyptian wonders series.) (hardcover) $27.95
Grades: 8 9 10 11 12 **932**
1. Egypt -- Antiquities 2. Tutankhamen, King of Egypt -- Tombs 3. Excavations (Archaeology) -- Egypt -- Valley of the Kings
ISBN 1601522509; 9781601522504
LC 2011048987

This "explores Egyptian history, mummy making, the discovery and opening of the tomb of Tutankhamen in 1922, and the events that happened after that. Much of the book is based on archaeologist Howard Carter's diaries and letters, and on period newspaper articles. The color photographs in [this attractive [book] are excellent, and the readable [text is] interesting." SLJ

★ **Mummification** and death rituals of ancient Egypt; by William W. Lace. ReferencePoint Press, Inc. 2013 80 p. (Ancient Egyptian Wonders) $27.95
Grades: 8 9 10 11 12 **932**
1. Egypt -- Antiquities 2. Ancient civilization 3. Mummies -- Egypt 4. Funeral rites and ceremonies -- Egypt -- History
ISBN 1601522541; 9781601522542
LC 2012011481

This book is part of the Ancient Egyptian Wonders series and focuses on mummification and death rituals of ancient Egypt. "Each book contains a timeline, important facts highlighted in sidebars, and websites." Each book "includes quotes from experts and ancient texts." (Library Media Connection)

Includes bibliographical references and index.

Netzley, Patricia D.
The **Greenhaven** encyclopedia of ancient Egypt. Greenhaven Press 2003 336p (Greenhaven encyclopedia of) $74.95
Grades: 8 9 10 11 12 **932**
1. Reference books 2. Egypt -- Antiquities -- Encyclopedias
ISBN 0-7377-1150-7
LC 2002-6965

"Alphabetical entries range from prehistory to the time of Greco-Roman domination and are generally between a paragraph and a page in length. Coverage includes individual pharaohs, places, practices, trades, beliefs, artwork, and aspects of daily and family life with entries such as 'furniture,' 'children,' and 'entertaining guests.' Important individuals such as archaeologist Howard Carter are also included." SLJ

Includes bibliographical references

The **new** cultural atlas of Egypt; edited by Leon Gray. Marshall Cavendish References 2010 192p il map lib bdg $99.93
Grades: 7 8 9 10 **932**
1. Atlases 2. Egypt -- Civilization 3. Egypt -- History 4. Egypt -- Antiquities
ISBN 978-0-7614-7877-5; 0-7614-7877-9

This title offers "students a wealth of information on all aspects of [Ancient Egyptian civilization]. . . . Packed with well-chosen, pertinent photos and artwork that add stunning detail to the study of [this culture] . . . [this book stands] out with excellent maps inserted within lucid, relevant text." SLJ

Includes glossary and bibliographical references

Rubalcaba, Jill

★ **Ancient** Egypt; archaeology unlocks the secrets of Egypt's past. by Jill Rubalcaba. National Geographic 2007 64p il map (National Geographic investigates) $17.95; lib bdg $27.90

Grades: 5 6 7 8   932

1. Excavations (Archeology) -- Egypt
ISBN 0-7922-7784-8; 978-0-7922-7784-2; 0-7922-7857-7 lib bdg; 978-0-7922-7857-3 lib bdg
LC 2006032111

This describes how archeologists have learned about Ancient Egypt.

This offers "the beautiful photography and illustrations characteristic of the National Geographic Society, [a] well-written [text] and sidebars, and information on recent archaeological finds." SLJ

Includes bibliographical references

Smith, Miranda

Ancient Egypt. Kingfisher 2010 48p (Navigators) $12.99

Grades: 4 5 6 7   932

1. Egypt -- Civilization
ISBN 978-0-7534-6429-8; 0-7534-6429-2

"Ancient Egypt opens with prominent pharaohs and continues with life at home, within a palace, and amidst the construction of a pyramid. Although it includes such typical subjects as religion, mummification, and tomb raiders, it also comprises female rulers, taxes, and extensive trading expeditions... a good first stop in the research process." Booklist

Stanley, Diane

★ **Cleopatra**; [by] Diane Stanley, Peter Vennema; illustrated by Diane Stanley. Morrow Junior Bks. 1994 un il map hardcover o.p. pa $7.99

Grades: 4 5 6 7   932

1. Queens
ISBN 0-688-10413-4; 0-688-10414-2 lib bdg; 0-688-15480-8 pa
LC 93-27032

This is a biography of the ancient Egyptian queen

"Lucid writing combines with carefully selected anecdotes, often attributed to the Greek historian Plutarch to create an engaging narrative. . . . Stanley's stunning, full-color gouache artwork is arresting in its large, well-composed images executed in flat Greek style." SLJ

Includes bibliographical references

Weitzman, David L.

★ **Pharaoh's** boat; written and illustrated by David Weitzman. Houghton Mifflin Harcourt 2009 un il map $17

Grades: 4 5 6 7   932

1. Ships 2. Kings 3. Ships, Ancient -- Egypt
ISBN 978-0-547-05341-7; 0-547-05341-X
LC 2008036081

"Weitzman recounts the construction of a boat made for the Pharaoh Cheops and discusses its rediscovery and restoration in the 20th century. He weaves the history, texts, mythology, and customs of ancient Egypt into an effective narrative. . . . The volume's stylized illustrations are inspired by the two-dimensional depictions from ancient Egyptian art. The paintings' earth tones, accentuated by bright greens and blues, are both appropriate for the subject matter and pleasing to the eye." SLJ

932.01   Egypt--Early history to 332 B.C.

Kallen, Stuart A.

★ **Pharaohs** of Egypt; by Stuart A Kallen. ReferencePoint Press, Inc. 2013 80 p. (Ancient Egyptian wonders series) (hardcover) $27.95

Grades: 8 9 10 11 12   932.01

1. Pharaohs -- Egypt 2. Egypt -- Civilization 3. Pharaohs -- History
ISBN 1601522568; 9781601522566
LC 2012000360

This book is part of the Ancient Egyptian Wonders series and looks at the pharaohs of Egypt. The series provides an "overview of ancient Egyptian civilization. . . . Each book contains a timeline, important facts highlighted in sidebars, and websites." Photographs and artwork are included. (Library Media Connection)

Includes bibliographical references and index

Whiting, Jim

★ **Life** along the ancient Nile; by Jim Whiting. ReferencePoint Press, Inc. 2013 80 p. (Ancient Egyptian wonders series.) (hardcover) $27.95

Grades: 8 9 10 11 12   932.01

1. Egypt -- History 2. Ancient civilization
ISBN 1601522525; 9781601522528
LC 2012000358

This book is part of the Ancient Egyptian Wonders series and focuses on life along the ancient Nile. It offers "coverage of marriage, fashion, medicine, and social classes" as well as dental procedures and wild parties. "Each book contains a timeline, important facts highlighted in sidebars, and websites." (Library Media Connection)

Includes bibliographical references and index.

935   Mesopotamia to 637 and Iranian Plateau to 637

Ancient Mesopotamia; edited by Anita Dalal. Brown Bear Books 2010 64p il map (Facts at your fingertips) lib bdg $35.65

Grades: 6 7 8 9   **935**

1. Iraq -- Civilization

ISBN 978-1-933834-57-3 lib bdg; 1-933834-57-9 lib bdg

LC 2009-16804

Presents the history of ancient Mesopotamia, describing the succession of civilizations that existed there and the agriculture, trade, religion, art, writing, and warfare practices of each one

This begins "with an introduction accompanied by a striking full-page photo, followed by a two-page time line, and a two-paged spread for each topic. This format makes information easily accessible. Beautiful color photos of ancient ruins, drawings, maps, diagrams, and re-creations create appeal and enhance the information. . . . Whether for recreational browsing or serious research, this . . . will certainly prove useful for students." Libr Media Connect

Includes glossary and bibliographical references

Gruber, Beth

★ **Ancient** Iraq; archaeology unlocks the secrets of Iraq's past. by Beth Gruber; Tony Wilkinson, consultant. National Geographic 2007 64p il map (National Geographic investigates) $17.95; lib bdg $27.90

Grades: 5 6 7 8   **935**

1. Excavations (Archeology) -- Iraq 2. Iraq -- Antiquities 3. Iraq -- Civilization

ISBN 978-0-7922-5382-2; 978-0-7922-5383-9 lib bdg

LC 2006032109

This explores the "world of ancient Iraq, in the region once known as Mesopotamia, the cradle of civilization. Join scientists as they study the Citadel in northern Iraq; explore the ancient city of Nineveh; and see how ancient treasures help scientists reassemble the mosaic-like puzzle of Iraq's past." Publisher's note

Includes bibliographical references

Kerrigan, Michael

Mesopotamians. Marshall Cavendish Benchmark 2010 64p il (Ancients in their own words) lib bdg $32.79

Grades: 5 6 7 8   **935**

1. Iraq -- Civilization

ISBN 978-1-60870-066-0; 1-60870-066-6

"Numerous photographs provide visual interest, with text describing the images to give details and background. Translations of the writings offer primary sources to accompany the secondary material presented. . . . The text is interesting enough to read cover to cover while the table of contents' descriptive chapter titles and the comprehensive index enable the . . . [book] to be used for specific research." Libr Media Connect

Includes bibliographical references

Morris, Neil

Mesopotamia and the Bible lands. Zak Books 2009 48p il map (History of the world) lib bdg $34.25

Grades: 7 8 9 10   **935**

1. Iraq -- History 2. Middle East -- History

ISBN 978-88-6098-157-8 lib bdg; 88-6098-157-3 lib bdg

LC 2008-8400

The "effectiveness lies in the combination of lush illustrations, well-chosen, captioned photographs of contemporary artifacts, and . . . [a] reasoned, concise [narrative]. Succinct time lines border most pages, and . . . the proper amount of white space, and clear dark print maintain organization and clarity. A superior choice." SLJ

Includes glossary

Schomp, Virginia

The **ancient** Mesopotamians; [by] Virginia Schomp. Marshall Cavendish Benchmark 2008 94p il map (Myths of the world) lib bdg $23.95

Grades: 6 7 8 9   **935**

1. Iraq -- Civilization

ISBN 978-0-7614-3095-7 lib bdg; 0-7614-3095-4 lib bdg

LC 2008007052

"A retelling of several major ancient Mesopotamian myths, with background information describing the history, geography, belief systems, and customs of Mesopotamia" Publisher's note

Includes glossary and bibliographical references

936   Europe north and west of Italian Peninsula to ca. 499

Aronson, Marc

★ **If** stones could speak; unlocking the secrets of Stonehenge. by Marc Aronson; with Mike Parker Pearson and the Riverside Project. National Geographic 2010 64p il map $17.95; lib bdg $26.90

Grades: 4 5 6 7   **936**

1. Archeology 2. Archaeologists 3. College teachers 4. Excavations (Archeology) -- England 5. Excavations (Archaeology) 6. Stonehenge (England)

ISBN 978-1-4263-0599-3; 1-4263-0599-0; 978-1-4263-0600-6 lib bdg; 1-4263-0600-8 lib bdg

"Aronson investigates the work of archaeologist Mike Parker Pearson and his controversial theory that Stonehenge is but one end of a memorial ritual pathway that would have had an equivalent wood structure at the other end. . . . Time lines, resource lists, and photos of researchers at work add even more value to this informative, thought-provoking study. A uniquely perceptive look at how real science works." Booklist

Includes bibliographical references

Green, Jen

★ **Ancient** Celts; archaeology unlocks the secrets of the Celts' past. by Jen Green; Bettina Arnold, consultant. National Geographic 2008 64p il map

(National Geographic investigates) $17.95; lib bdg $27.90

Grades: 4 5 6 7   **936**
1. Celts 2. Celtic civilization 3. Excavations (Archeology) -- Europe
ISBN 978-1-4263-0225-1; 1-4263-0225-8; 978-1-4263-0226-8 lib bdg; 1-4263-0226-6 lib bdg
LC 2007047836
This describes ancient Celtic civilization and how archeologists have found out about it.
"With excellent-quality photographs and a well-written text, this is a thorough presentation of the most up-to-date knowledge about this ancient European culture." SLJ
Includes glossary and bibliographical references

Hinds, Kathryn, 1962-
Ancient Celts. Marshall Cavendish Benchmark 2009 79p il map (Barbarians!) lib bdg $35.64

Grades: 6 7 8 9   **936**
1. Celts
ISBN 978-0-7614-4062-8 lib bdg; 0-7614-4062-3 lib bdg
LC 2008-35976
This book has "wonderful photographs of contemporaneous and more recent artwork and sculpture, which bring the . . . [Ancient Celts] to life for the modern reader." Voice Youth Advocates
Includes glossary and bibliographical references

Early Germans. Marshall Cavendish Benchmark 2009 80p il (Barbarians!) lib bdg $35.64

Grades: 6 7 8 9   **936**
1. Germanic peoples
ISBN 978-0-7614-4064-2 lib bdg; 0-7614-4064-X lib bdg
LC 2008055789
"This . . . devotes excellent coverage and exposure to the emergence, development, and legacy of [the early Germans]." Libr Media Connect
Includes glossary and bibliographical references

Goths. Marshall Cavendish Benchmark 2009 80p il (Barbarians!) lib bdg $35.64

Grades: 6 7 8 9   **936**
1. Goths
ISBN 978-07614-4065-9 lib bdg; 0-7614-4065-8 lib bdg
LC 2009014114
This has "wonderful photographs of contemporaneous and more recent artwork and sculpture, which bring the . . . [Goths] to life for the modern reader." Voice Youth Advocates
Includes glossary and bibliographical references

Huns. Marshall Cavendish Benchmark 2009 80p il (Barbarians!) lib bdg $35.64

Grades: 6 7 8 9   **936**
1. Huns 2. Nomads 3. Tribal leaders
ISBN 978-0-7614-4066-6 lib bdg; 0-7614-4066-6 lib bdg
LC 2008054828

"This . . . devotes excellent coverage and exposure to the emergence, development, and legacy of [the Huns]." Libr Media Connect
Includes glossary and bibliographical references

Millard, Anne
A **street** through time; written by Anne Millard; illustrated by Steve Noon. Revised ed. DK Pub. 2012 32p col il $17.99

Grades: 4 5 6 7   **936**
1. Cities and towns
ISBN 0-7894-3426-1
LC 98-3226
Traces the development of one street from the Stone Age to the present day, from dirt track to the rebuilding of inns as wine bars, showing how people lived and what they did all day
"The time-line construct is a useful demonstration for children, and the busy vistas would make a fine spring-board for encouraging students to create scenes of local history." Horn Book Guide
Includes glossary

937   Italian Peninsula to 476 and adjacent territories to 476

Allan, Tony
Exploring the life, myth, and art of ancient Rome; Tony Allan. Rosen Pub. 2012 144 p. (lib. bdg.) $39.95

Grades: 7 8 9 10 11   **937**
1. Roman art 2. Roman mythology 3. Rome -- History 4. Rome -- Civilization 5. Art, Roman 6. Mythology, Roman
ISBN 9781448848317
LC 2011009799
This book on Ancient Rome "offers an informative overview of . . . political and social history as well as its art, architecture, and mythology, all bolstered with plenty of . . . details and narratives. . . . [T]he illustrations include artworks, documents, and handsome maps as well as photos of significant sites and artifacts. . . . Besides showing how the great city rose to domination, 'Ancient Rome' looks at how it changed and was changed by the civilizations it housed." (Booklist)
Includes bibliographical references and index

The **Roman** world. Zak Books 2009 48p il map (History of the world) lib bdg $34.25

Grades: 7 8 9 10   **937**
1. Ancient civilization 2. Rome -- Civilization 3. Rome -- History
ISBN 978-88-6098-159-2 lib bdg; 88-6098-159-X lib bdg
LC 2008-8402
The "effectiveness lies in the combination of lush illustrations, well-chosen, captioned photographs of contemporary artifacts, and [a] reasoned, concise [narrative]. Succinct time lines border most pages, and [a] . . . clear dark print maintain organization and clarity. A superior choice." SLJ
Includes glossary

Ancient Rome; edited by Michael Anderson. Britannica Educational Pub. in association with Rosen Educational Services 2011 88p il map (Ancient civilizations) lib bdg $31.70

Grades: 5 6 7 8   937

1. Rome -- Civilization 2. Rome -- History
ISBN 978-1-61530-522-3; 1-61530-522-X

LC 2011004749

This book provides "enough information about the development, way of life, accomplishments, and decline of [Ancient Rome] without overwhelming readers. Maps; full-color illustrations and photographs, many full page; and sidebars provide additional focus. . . . [The book] discusses the military expertise of Caesar and Pompey and the winning of the Punic Wars that led to world domination. The Romans' genius in engineering is highlighted." SLJ

Includes glossary and bibliographical references

Beller, Susan Provost

Roman legions on the march; soldiering in the ancient Roman Army. by Susan Provost Beller. Twenty-First Century Books 2008 112p il map (Soldiers on the battlefront) lib bdg $33.26

Grades: 5 6 7 8   937

1. Soldiers -- Rome 2. Rome -- Civilization
ISBN 978-0-8225-6781-3

LC 2006037829

"The format is inviting with a variety of fonts at the beginning of each chapter, quotations, and a multitude of illustrations. . . . The text is clear and to the point, and chapters are divided into short topics." SLJ

Includes bibliographical references

Bingham, Jane

How people lived in ancient Rome. PowerKids Press 2009 30p il map (How people lived) lib bdg $25.25; pa $10.60

Grades: 4 5 6 7   937

1. Rome -- Social life and customs
ISBN 978-1-4042-4432-0 lib bdg; 1-4042-4432-8 lib bdg; 978-1-4358-2622-9 pa; 1-4358-2622-1 pa

LC 2007-40221

Describes everyday life among the ancient Romans, covering family life, marriage, leisure, education, clothing, food and drink, warfare, religion, and funerals

"Clear, readable narrative is supplemented by large color and b&w reproductions of Roman art and artifacts. . . . It will hold the attention of both readers and reasearchers, and is a good choice for collections that serve elementary and younger middle level students." Libr Media Connect

Includes bibliographical references

Deckker, Zilah

★ **Ancient** Rome; archaeology unlocks the secrets of Rome's past. by Zilah Deckker; Robert Lindley Vann, Consultant. National Geographic 2007 64p il map (National Geographic investigates) $17.95; lib bdg $27.90

Grades: 4 5 6 7   937

1. Archeology 2. Rome -- Civilization 3. Rome --

Antiquities
ISBN 978-1-4263-0128-5; 978-1-4263-0129-2 lib bdg

LC 2007024795

This describes what archeologists have learned about Ancient Rome

Includes glossary and bibliographical references

Deem, James M.

★ **Bodies** from the ash. Houghton Mifflin 2005 50p il $16

Grades: 4 5 6 7   937

1. Pompeii (Extinct city)
ISBN 0-618-47308-4

LC 2004-26553

"On August 24, 79 C.E., the long-silent Mt. Vesuvius erupted, and volcanic ash rained down on the 20,000 residents of Pompeii. This photo-essay explains what happened when the volcano exploded—and how the results of this disaster were discovered hundreds of years later. . . . [This offers an] enormous amount of information. . . . But the jewels here are the numerous . . . photographs, especially those featuring the plaster casts and skeletons of people in their death throes. . . . Excellent for browsers as well as researchers." Booklist

Hanel, Rachael

Gladiators. Creative Education 2008 48p il (Fearsome fighters) lib bdg $31.35

Grades: 4 5 6   937

1. Gladiators 2. Rome -- Civilization
ISBN 978-1-58341-535-1 lib bdg; 1-58341-535-1 lib bdg

LC 2006021842

This "recounts the brutality and cruelty of fighting for sport celebrated during Roman times. . . . [The book does] an adequate job of covering fighting techniques, weapons, and history. Photographs and archival reproductions enhance the [presentation]; sidebars provide additional information." Horn Book Guide

Includes glossary and bibliographical references

Hinds, Kathryn, 1962-

★ **Everyday** life in the Roman Empire. Marshall Cavendish Benchmark 2010 320p il lib bdg $42.79

Grades: 7 8 9 10   937

1. Holy Roman Empire 2. Rome -- History
ISBN 978-0-7614-4484-8; 0-7614-4484-X

LC 2009-5913

A compilation of four titles in the Everyday Life in the Roman Empire series, published 2004: The city; The countryside; The Patricians; Religion

This book combines "clear, bold text with vivid reproductions of period paintings, frescoes, and sculptures, making for [a] stunning [presentation]." SLJ

Includes glossary and bibliographical references

★ The **countryside**; by Kathryn Hinds. Benchmark Books 2005 72 p. col. ill. (library) $8.66

Grades: 6 7 8 9   937

1. Country life 2. Rome -- Civilization
ISBN 0761416560; 9780761416562

LC 2004009496

This examines country life during the Roman Empire, describing the economy, homes, labor, roles of men and women, childhood, and holidays.

Includes bibliographical references (p. 65-67) and index.

James, Simon

Ancient Rome; written by Simon James. rev ed.; DK Pub. 2008 72p il map (DK eyewitness books) $15.99

Grades: 4 5 6 7   **937**

1. Rome -- Antiquities 2. Rome -- Civilization

ISBN 978-0-7566-3766-8; 0-7566-3766-X

LC 2008-276034

First published 1990 by Knopf

A photo essay documenting ancient Rome and the people who lived there as revealed through the many artifacts they left behind, including shields, swords, tools, toys, cosmetics, and jewelry

Includes glossary

Kerrigan, Michael

Romans. Marshall Cavendish Benchmark 2010 64p il (Ancients in their own words) lib bdg $32.79

Grades: 5 6 7 8   **937**

1. Rome -- Civilization

ISBN 978-1-60870-067-7; 1-60870-067-4

"Numerous photographs provide visual interest, with text describing the images to give details and background. Translations of the writings offer primary sources to accompany the secondary material presented. . . . The text is interesting enough to read cover to cover while the table of contents' descriptive chapter titles and the comprehensive index enable the . . . [book] to be used for specific research." Libr Media Connect

Includes bibliographical references

Lassieur, Allison

★ The **ancient** Romans; written by Allison Lassieur. Franklin Watts 2004 112p il map (People of the ancient world) lib bdg $30.50; pa $9.95

Grades: 5 6 7 8   **937**

1. Rome -- Civilization

ISBN 0-531-12338-3 lib bdg; 0-531-16742-9 pa

LC 2004-1955

"This attractive, thorough, and comprehensible book . . . offers a stellar introduction to life in ancient Rome." Booklist

Includes bibliographical references

Mann, Elizabeth

The **Roman** Colosseum; with illustrations by Michael Racz. Mikaya Press 1998 45p il (Wonders of the world) $19.95

Grades: 4 5 6   **937**

1. Amphitheaters -- Rome 2. Rome (Italy) -- Antiquities 3. Rome (Italy) -- Buildings, structures, etc

ISBN 0-9650493-3-7

LC 98-20060

Describes the building of the Colosseum in ancient Rome, and tells how it was used

This offers "a clear, well-written text and full-color drawings and paintings." SLJ

Includes glossary

Markel, Rita J.

The **fall** of the Roman Empire; by Rita J. Markel. Twenty-First Century Books 2008 160p il map (Pivotal moments in history) lib bdg $38.60

Grades: 7 8 9 10 11 12   **937**

1. Rome -- History 2. Rome -- Civilization

ISBN 978-0-8225-5919-1 lib bdg; 0-8225-5919-6 lib bdg

LC 2006100918

This offers a brief history of the rise of the Roman Empire and explores the factors that contributed to its decline.

"Sure to satisfy history buffs. . . . Numerous sidebars, illustrations, maps, and art reproductions provide additional information." Horn Book Guide

Includes glossary and bibliographical references

Mellor, Ronald

The **ancient** Roman world; [by] Ronald J. Mellor & Marni McGee. Oxford University Press 2004 190p il map (World in ancient times) $32.95

Grades: 7 8 9 10   **937**

1. Rome -- History -- Kings, 753-510 B.C 2. Rome -- History -- Republic, 510-30 B.C 3. Rome -- History -- Empire, 30 B.C.-284 A.D 4. Rome -- Civilization

ISBN 0-19-515380-4

LC 2003-17799

Introduces the history, culture, and people of ancient Rome and examines its many contributions to the development of Western society.

This volume is "somewhat more inclusive than many other works for this audience. What makes this book accessible is the lively writing. . . . The numerous illustrations include full-color photographs and reproductions of sites, artifacts, period artwork, and an occasional movie still. " SLJ

Includes bibliographical references

Moser, Barry

Ashen sky; the letters of Pliny the Younger on the eruption of Vesuvius. illustrated by Barry Moser; written and translated by Benedicte Gilman. The J. Paul Getty Museum 2007 39p il map $19.95

Grades: 7 8 9 10 11 12 Adult   **937**

1. Pompeii (Extinct city)

ISBN 978-0-89236-900-3; 0-89236-900-0

LC 2007-2781

This is a "handsome volume. Using an advanced vocabulary and sophisticated sentence structure, the text sets the event in historical context and gives brief biographical information about the elder and younger Pliny and Tacitus. . . . Moser's engravings reflect the darkness described in the text as day was turned to night by clouds of ash." SLJ

Includes bibliographical references

Nardo, Don

Classical civilization; by Don Nardo. Morgan Reynolds Pub. 2011 128 p. col. ill., maps (library) $28.95

Grades: 6 7 8 9   **937**
1. Rome -- History 2. Rome -- Civilization
ISBN 1599351749; 9781599351742

LC 2011005672

This book by Don Nardo on ancient Rome is part of the World history series. "Nardo provides a framework of history, then discusses aspects of the culture with far-reaching effects, such as its government, laws, architecture, roads, and language. The section called 'The First Urban Civilization' reveals surprising similarities between ancient Roman cities and their modern counterparts." (Booklist)

Includes bibliographical references (p. 120-121) and index.

Words of the ancient Romans; primary sources. Don Nardo, editor. Lucent Books 2003 128p il (The Lucent library of historical eras, Ancient Rome) $27.45
Grades: 6 7 8 9   **937**
1. Rome -- History -- Sources
ISBN 1-59018-318-5

LC 2003-1645

"Excerpts from historians such as Plutarch, Livy, and Suetonius, as well as the satires of Juvenal and poetry of Ovid, are included in this history of ancient Rome as told through the words of those who lived at the time. Various chapters cover the founding of the city, Julius Caesar's life, the reign of Augustus, home and family life, entertainment, leisure, and religion. . . . Each chapter . . . [begins] with an introduction that helps to put the subject in perspective for modern readers." SLJ

Park, Louise
The **Roman** gladiators; by Louise Park and Timothy Love. Marshall Cavendish Benchmark 2009 32p il (Ancient and medieval people) $19.95
Grades: 4 5 6   **937**
1. Gladiators 2. Rome -- Social life and customs 3. Rome -- History
ISBN 978-0-7614-4443-5; 0-7614-4443-2

This title has "a simple and elegant design with the proper balance of quality writing and quantity of information. . . . Handy time lines, well-chosen photos of ruins and artifacts, quality illustrations, inset 'Quick Facts,' and 'What You Should Know About' features will grab reluctant readers and captivate even those with short attention spans." SLJ

Includes glossary

Sonneborn, Liz
Pompeii; by Liz Sonneborn. Twenty-First Century Books 2008 80p il map (Unearthing ancient worlds) lib bdg $30.60
Grades: 5 6 7 8   **937**
1. Excavations (Archeology) -- Italy 2. Pompeii (Extinct city)
ISBN 978-0-8225-7505-4 lib bdg; 0-8225-7505-1 lib bdg

LC 2007022058

This describes the excavation of the Roman city buried in lava and ash when the volcano Mount Vesuvius erupted in A.D. 79.

This "clearly written [title is] illustrated with large photographs and period artwork, and the pages are broken up with text boxes featuring quotes and interesting anecdotes." SLJ

Includes glossary and bibliographical references

938   Greece to 323

Ancient Greece; edited by Anita Croy. Brown Bear Books 2010 64p il map (Facts at your fingertips) lib bdg $35.65
Grades: 6 7 8 9   **938**
1. Greece -- Civilization
ISBN 978-1-933834-55-9 lib bdg; 1-933834-55-2 lib bdg

LC 2009-16803

Presents an introduction to ancient Greece, discussing its history, wars, system of government, everyday life, religion, and architecture

This begins "with an introduction accompanied by a striking full-page photo, followed by a two-page time line, and a two-paged spread for each topic. This format makes information easily accessible. Beautiful color photos of ancient ruins, drawings, maps, diagrams, and re-creations create appeal and enhance the information. . . . Whether for recreational browsing or serious research, this . . . will certainly prove useful for students." Libr Media Connect

Includes glossary and bibliographical references

Kerrigan, Michael
Greeks. Marshall Cavendish Benchmark 2010 64p il (Ancients in their own words) lib bdg $32.79
Grades: 5 6 7 8   **938**
1. Greece -- Civilization
ISBN 978-1-60870-065-3; 1-60870-065-8

"Numerous photographs provide visual interest, with text describing the images to give details and background. Translations of the writings offer primary sources to accompany the secondary material presented. . . . The text is interesting enough to read cover to cover while the table of contents' descriptive chapter titles and the comprehensive index enable the . . . [book] to be used for specific research." Libr Media Connect

Includes bibliographical references

Marcovitz, Hal
★ **Ancient** Greece; by Hal Marcovitz. ReferencePoint Press 2012 96 p. (Understanding world history) (hardcover) $27.95
Grades: 7 8 9 10   **938**
1. Greece -- History 2. Greece -- Civilization
ISBN 9781601522849; 1601522843

LC 2011048991

This book on ancient Greece by Hal Marcovitz is part of "Understanding World History, a series that surveys the political, social, and cultural trends of major periods and events in world history."(Publisher's note)

It "combines mythology, history, and politics and provides an enlightening perspective on the treatment of women in the cultures of Athens and Sparta." (Booklist)

Includes bibliographical references and index.

McGee, Marni

★ **Ancient** Greece; archaeology unlocks the secrets of Greece's past. by Marni McGee; Michael Shanks, consultant. National Geographic 2007 64p il map (National Geographic investigates) $17.95; lib bdg $27.90

Grades: 5 6 7 8   **938**

1. Excavations (Archeology) -- Greece 2. Greece -- Antiquities 3. Greece -- Civilization
ISBN 978-0-7922-7826-9; 0-7922-7826-7; 978-0-7922-7872-6 lib bdg; 0-7922-7872-0 lib bdg
LC 2006032108

This describes how archeologists have found out about Ancient Greek civilization

This offers "the beautiful photography and illustrations characteristic of the National Geographic Society, [a] well-written [text] and sidebars, and information on recent archaeological finds." SLJ

Includes bibliographical references

Nardo, Don

Classical civilization; by Don Nardo. Morgan Reynolds Pub. 2011 112 p. ill. (some col.), col. map (library) $28.95

Grades: 6 7 8 9   **938**

1. Greece -- History 2. Greece -- Civilization
ISBN 1599351730; 9781599351735
LC 2011000235

This book by Don Nardo on ancient Greece is part of the World History series. It "encompasses not only political history but also influential developments in political thinking, philosophy, science, literature, architecture, sports, and the military. The section on the Olympics debunks the notion that early Olympic athletes were amateurs without financial backing." (Booklist)

Includes bibliographical references and index.

The **new** cultural atlas of the Greek world; edited by Tim Cooke. Marshall Cavendish Reference 2010 192p il map lib bdg $99.93

Grades: 7 8 9 10   **938**

1. Atlases 2. Greece -- Antiquities 3. Greece -- Civilization 4. Greece -- History
ISBN 978-0-7614-7878-2; 0-7614-7878-7

This offers "students a wealth of information on all aspects of . . . ancient [Greek civilization]. . . . Packed with well-chosen, pertinent photos and artwork that add stunning detail to the study of [this culture] . . . [this book stands] out with excellent maps inserted within lucid, relevant text." SLJ

Includes glossary and bibliographical references

Park, Louise

The **Spartan** hoplites; by Louise Park and Timothy Love. Marshall Cavendish Benchmark 2009 32p il map (Ancient and medieval people) $19.95

Grades: 4 5 6   **938**

1. Soldiers 2. Athens (Greece) -- History 3. Sparta (Extinct city)
ISBN 978-0-7614-4449-7; 0-7614-4449-1
LC 2008-55779

This title has "a simple and elegant design with the proper balance of quality writing and quantity of information. . . . Handy time lines, well-chosen photos of ruins and artifacts, quality illustrations, inset 'Quick Facts', and 'What You Should Know About' features will grab reluctant readers and captivate even those with short attention spans." SLJ

Includes glossary

Powell, Anton

Ancient Greece; 3rd ed.; Chelsea House 2007 96p il map (Cultural atlas for young people) $35

Grades: 5 6 7 8   **938**

1. Greece -- Civilization
ISBN 978-0-8160-6821-0; 0-8160-6821-6
First published 1989

Maps, charts, illustrations, and text trace the history and culture of ancient Greece.

"Filled with excellent captioned, color maps, photographs, and illustrations of primary source materials. There are sidebars, gazetteers, and timelines of events in politics, war, art, technology, etc." Libr Media Connect

Includes glossary and bibliographical references

Roberts, Jennifer Tolbert

The **ancient** Greek world. Oxford University Press 2004 190p il map $32.95

Grades: 7 8 9 10   **938**

1. Greece -- Civilization
ISBN 0-19-515696-X

Introduces the history, culture, and people of ancient Greece and examines its many contributions to the development of Western society

"A thoroughly researched political and cultural history. . . . Extensive quotes from primary sources, attractive page layouts, numerous good-quality color photographs of ruins and artifacts, plus the infusion of humor make for a palatable, solid resource for any collection. " SLJ

Stafford, Emma J.

Exploring the life, myth, and art of ancient Greece; Emma J. Stafford. Rosen Pub. 2012 144 p. $42.60

Grades: 7 8 9 10 11   **938**

1. Greek art 2. Greek mythology 3. Greece -- Religion 4. Greece -- Civilization 5. Greece -- History -- 0-323
ISBN 9781448848300
LC 2011009898

This book on Ancient Greece "offers an informative overview of . . . political and social history as well as its art, architecture, and mythology, all bolstered with plenty of . . . details and narratives. . . . [T]he illustrations include artworks, documents, and handsome maps as well as photos of significant sites and artifacts. 'Ancient Greece' traces the development of Greek society and its expression through mythology and the arts." (Booklist)

The book "put[s] the art . . . in context, explaining how a society's religious beliefs, legends, and cultural traditions manifest themselves through images and iconography. The . . . layout features full-color photographs of architecture, sculpture, and painting on every page, accompanied by informative captions." (School Libr J)

Includes bibliographical references (p. 137) and index

Steele, Phillip

Ancient Greece; by Philip Steele. Kingfisher 2011 48 p. ill. (hardcover) $12.99

Grades: 4 5 6 7   **938**

1. Greece -- History 2. Greece -- Civilization

ISBN 0753465795; 9780753465790

In this "look at ancient Greece," author Philip Steele "offers young readers insight into the origins of all things Greek. Two page spreads cover Minoan civilization, the rise of the Mycenaean, war with Troy, the establishment of city-states, and the spread of the Hellenistic empire in a somewhat chronological order. Digital illustrations merge with historical artifacts, maps, works of art, and photographs." (Children's Literature)

Villing, Alexandra

The ancient Greeks; their lives and their world. J. Paul Getty Museum 2010 80p il $17.95

Grades: 7 8 9 10   **938**

1. Greece -- Civilization

ISBN 978-0-89236-985-0; 0-89236-985-X

"This volume provides a colorful overview of life in ancient Greece. Each chapter covers a different topic and, though short, contains lots of information. Numerous photographs of art and artifacts, along with accompanying captions, illustrate the bygone culture." Horn Book Guide

939   Other parts of ancient world

Cline, Eric H.

★ Digging for Troy; from Homer to Hisarlik. [by] Jill Rubalcaba and Eric H. Cline; with illustrations by Sarah S. Brannen. Charlesbridge 2011 74p il map $17.95; pa $9.95

Grades: 5 6 7 8   **939**

1. Trojan War 2. Excavations (Archaeology) -- Turkey 3. Archaeologists 4. Civilization, Mycenaean 5. Excavations (Archaeology) -- Turkey -- Troy (Extinct city)

ISBN 978-1-58089-326-8; 1-58089-326-0; 978-1-58089-327-5 pa; 1-58089-327-9 pa

LC 2010-07586

"Rubalcaba teams up with a noted archaeologist to make sense of the complicated, controversial, contradictory history and remains of the Turkish site called Hisarlik, better known as Troy. . . . The book begins with a brief but exciting retelling of the Trojan War . . . and goes on to profile Heinrich Schliemann. . . . After Schliemann, generations of archaeologists have excavated Hisarlik: along with the history of the excavations, readers are given an overview of technological developments in the field. . . . Source notes and an impressive bibliography attest to meticulous research and guide readers to journal articles, books, and online museum exhibits. Elegant illustrations mimicking Greek red-figure pottery are lovely and appropriate. Extraordinarily readable, gracefully laid out, and speckled with lines from The Iliad, this book will inspire young people interested in solving the mysteries of the past." SLJ

Includes bibliographical references

Hinds, Kathryn, 1962-

Scythians and Sarmatians. Marshall Cavendish Benchmark 2009 80p il map (Barbarians!) lib bdg $35.64

Grades: 6 7 8 9   **939**

1. Horses 2. Nomads 3. Scythians 4. Sarmatians

ISBN 978-0-7614-4072-7 lib bdg; 0-7614-4072-0 lib bdg

LC 2009016496

"This . . . devotes excellent coverage and exposure to the emergence, development, and legacy of [the Scythians and Sarmatians]." Libr Media Connect

Includes glossary and bibliographical references

Podany, Amanda H.

The ancient Near Eastern world; [by] Amanda H. Podany & Marni McGee. Oxford University Press 2005 174p il map (World in ancient times) $32.95

Grades: 7 8 9 10   **939**

1. Middle East -- Civilization 2. Middle East -- Antiquities

ISBN 0-19-516159-9

LC 2004-13622

This "traces the history of the Fertile Crescent until Alexander the Great's conquest in 330 B.C.E. . . . The text is matched with a great deal of supporting matter including time lines, maps, dramatis personae, high-quality photos, and artists' renderings. [This] fine [volume is a] worthy [addition] to most libraries." SLJ

Includes bibliographical references

Sherrow, Victoria

Ancient Africa; archaeology unlocks the secrets of Africa's past. by Victoria Sherrow; James Denbow, consultant. National Geographic Society 2007 64p il map (National Geographic investigates) $17.95

Grades: 4 5 6 7   **939**

1. Africa -- Antiquities 2. Africa -- Civilization

ISBN 978-0-7922-5384-6; 0-7922-5384-1

LC 2007277594

This describes archeological discoveries about ancient peoples of Africa including the Dogon people of Mali, the ancient city of Jenne-jeno, and the Kushite temples at Jebel Barkal.

Includes bibliographical references

940   History of specific continents, countries, localities in modern world; extraterrestrial worlds

Feed the children first; Irish memories of the Great Hunger. edited by Mary E. Lyons. Atheneum Bks. for Young Readers 2002 43p il pbk. $22.99

Grades: 5 6 7 8   **940**

1. Famines

ISBN 9781442482920

LC 00-49606

Lyons "compiles quotations from Irish citizens on the devastating effects of the potato famine that ravaged Ireland between 1845 and 1852." Publ Wkly
Includes bibliographical references

940.1   History of Europe-- Early history to 1453

Corbishley, Mike

The **Middle** Ages; 3rd ed.; Chelsea House 2007 96p il map (Cultural atlas for young people) $35
Grades: 5 6 7 8   **940.1**
1. Middle Ages 2. Medieval civilization
ISBN 978-0-8160-6825-8; 0-8160-6825-9
First published 1989
Maps, charts, illustrations, and text explore the history and culture of the Middle Ages.
"The maps are excellent, precise, clear, and easy to read and understand, and the illustrations, particularly those of works of art, are wonderful. . . . This attractive volume provides an intriguing cross-cultural look at the medieval world. An excellent addition." SLJ
Includes glossary and bibliographical references

Durman, Laura

Castle life; by Laura Durman. Arcturus Pub. 2013 32 p. col. ill. (library) $28.50
Grades: 4 5 6   **940.1**
1. Castles 2. Medieval civilization 3. Civilization, Medieval
ISBN 1848585608; 9781848585607
LC 2011051440
In this book, author "[Laura] Durman presents young readers with a . . . view of what life was really like for everyday people in the Middle Ages. Bound by the strict societal system known as feudalism, peasants, knights, and nobles shared space . . . in castles. Readers take a room by room tour, learning how castles functioned both day-to-day, when under siege, and at times of feasting and banqueting." (Children's Literature)

Knights; by Laura Durman. Arcturus Pub. 2012 32 p. col. ill. (Knights and castles) (library) $28.50
Grades: 4 5 6   **940.1**
1. Knights and knighthood 3. Civilization, Medieval
ISBN 1848585616; 9781848585614
LC 2011051452
This book by Laura Durman is part of the Knights and Castles series and looks at knights. The "books cover a wide range of topics such as weapons, castle construction, food, religion, and the structure and hierarchy of society." Full-color photographs and illustrations are included. (School Library Journal)
Includes bibliographical references (p. 31) and index.

Helget, Nicole

Barbarians; Nicole Helget. Creative Education 2012 48 p. (alk. paper) $35.65
Grades: 5 6 7 8   **940.1**
1. Huns 2. Nomads 3. Vikings 4. Teutonic peoples 5. Classical civilization 6. Middle Ages 7. Migrations

of nations
ISBN 1608181820; 9781608181827
LC 2011035798
This book by Nicole Lea Helget "focuses on the transient, adaptable Gelts, Franks, Goths, Huns, and Vikings, collectively known as 'barbarians,' and their differing warring skills against the Greek and Roman Empires." (Booklist)
"Viewed as threats by the Romans in particular, the barbarian people were often co-opted or conquered and then integrated into the Empire. Eventually, as the Roman Empire waned, the pressure of nomadic barbarians proved too much to withstand and Rome fell." (Children's Literature)
Includes bibliographical references and index

Hinds, Kathryn, 1962-

★ **Everyday** life in medieval Europe. Marshall Cavendish Benchmark 2009 285p il lib bdg $42.79
Grades: 6 7 8 9   **940.1**
1. Middle Ages 2. Medieval civilization 3. Europe -- Social conditions 4. Europe -- Economic conditions 5. Europe -- Social life and customs
ISBN 978-0-7614-3927-1; 0-7614-3927-7
LC 2008012748
"Fluid, approachable, beautifully illustrated, and fascinatingly detailed." Booklist
Includes glossary and bibliographical references

Langley, Andrew

Medieval life; written by Andrew Langley; photographed by Geoff Brightling. rev ed; DK Pub. 2011 72p il (DK eyewitness books) lib bdg $19.99
Grades: 4 5 6 7   **940.1**
1. Medieval civilization
ISBN 9780756682828 lib bdg
First published 1996 by Knopf
An illustrated look at various aspects of life in medieval Europe, covering everyday life, religion, royalty, and more.

Malam, John

Early medieval times. Zak Books 2009 48p il map (History of the world) lib bdg $34.25
Grades: 7 8 9 10   **940.1**
1. Middle Ages 2. Medieval civilization
ISBN 978-88-6098-150-9 lib bdg; 88-6098-150-6 lib bdg
LC 2008-8405
The "effectiveness lies in the combination of lush illustrations, well-chosen, captioned photographs of contemporary artifacts, and . . . [a] reasoned, concise [narrative]. Succinct time lines border most pages, and . . . the proper amount of white space, and clear dark print maintain organization and clarity. A superior choice." SLJ
Includes glossary

Morris, Neil

Late medieval Europe. Zak Books 2009 48p il map (History of the world) lib bdg $34.25

Grades: 7 8 9 10   **940.1**
1. Middle Ages 2. Medieval civilization
ISBN 978-88-6098-152-3 lib bdg; 88-6098-152-2
lib bdg
                                    LC 2008-8407
The "effectiveness lies in the combination of lush illustrations, well-chosen, captioned photographs of contemporary artifacts, and . . . [a] reasoned, concise [narrative].
Succinct time lines border most pages, and . . . the proper
amount of white space, and clear dark print maintain organization and clarity. A superior choice." SLJ
Includes glossary

Nardo, Don
   Medieval Europe; by Don Nardo. 1st ed. Morgan Reynolds Pub. 2011 128 p. col. ill., maps
(World History) (library) $28.95
Grades: 6 7 8 9   **940.1**
1. Middle Ages 2. Great Britain -- History -- 1066-
1485, Medieval period 3. Civilization, Medieval
ISBN 1599351722; 9781599351728
                                    LC 2010054477
This book by Don Nardo, part of the World History series, focuses on Medieval Europe. Medieval Europe "was
the bridge that led from the ancient world to the modern
one." Topics include the Roman Catholic Church, the stone
castles built by kings and nobles, the Crusades, and the Renaissance. (Publisher's note)
Includes bibliographical references   (p. 120-121)
and index.

Park, Louise
   The **medieval** knights; by Louise Park and Timothy Love. Marshall Cavendish Benchmark 2009
32p il map (Ancient and medieval people) $19.95
Grades: 4 5 6   **940.1**
1. Medieval civilization 2. Knights and knighthood
ISBN 978-0-7614-4444-2; 0-7614-4444-0
                                    LC 2008-55777
This title has "a simple and elegant design with the
proper balance of quality writing and quantity of information. . . . Handy time lines, well-chosen photos of ruins and
artifacts, quality illustrations, inset 'Quick Facts', and 'What
You Should Know About' features will grab reluctant readers and captivate even those with short attention spans." SLJ
Includes glossary

Schlitz, Laura Amy
   ★ **Good** masters! Sweet ladies! voices from a
medieval village. [by] Laura Amy Schlitz; illustrated
by Robert Byrd. Candlewick Press 2007 85p il
$19.99; pa $9.99
Grades: 5 6 7 8   **940.1**
1. Monologues 2. Children's plays 3. Middle Ages
-- Drama
ISBN 978-0-7636-1578-9; 0-7636-1578-1; 978-0-
7636-4332-4 pa; 0-7636-4332-7 pa
Awarded the Newbery Medal, 2008
A collection of short one-person plays featuring characters, between ten and fifteen years old, who live in or near a
thirteenth-century English manor

"Designed for performance and excellent for use in interdisciplinary history classrooms, the book offers students
an incredibly approachable format for learning about the
Middle Ages that makes the period both realistic and relevant. . . . Byrd's illustrations evoke the era and give dramatists ideas for appropriate costuming and props." SLJ

940.2   History of Europe-- 1453-

Claybourne, Anna
   The **Renaissance**; [by] Anna Claybourne. Raintree 2008 64p il map (Time travel guide) lib bdg
$34.29; pa $9.99
Grades: 6 7 8 9   **940.2**
1. Renaissance
ISBN 978-1-4109-2910-5 lib bdg; 978-1-4109-2916-
7 pa
                                    LC 2007006027
This describes life in 15th and 16th century Europe in the
form of travel guide.
The book "is chock-full of color photographs and reproductions, maps, sidebars, and age-appropriate humor. . . .
The [author has] done a commendable job of writing [text]
that [measures] up to the rich visual layout." SLJ
Includes bibliographical references

Currie, Stephen
   ★ The **Renaissance**; by Stephen Currie. ReferencePoint Press, Inc. 2012 96 p. (hardcover) $27.95
Grades: 7 8 9 10   **940.2**
1. Renaissance
ISBN 1601521898; 9781601521897
                                    LC 2011048993
This book by Stephen Currie is part of the "Understanding World History" series. It "opens with an . . . overview
of the circumstances that came together to inspire a Renaissance." (School Library Journal)
It profiles "artists and philosophers . . . along with scientists like [Isaac] Newton. Also discussed is the tension
between religion and humanism." (Booklist)
Includes bibliographical references and index.

Elliott, Lynne
   The **Renaissance** in Europe; [by] Lynne Elliott.
Crabtree Pub. Co. 2009 32p il lib bdg $26.60; pa
$8.95
Grades: 6 7 8 9   **940.2**
1. Renaissance
ISBN 978-0-7787-4591-4 lib bdg; 0-7787-4591-0 lib
bdg; 978-0-7787-4611-9 pa; 0-7787-4611-9 pa
                                    LC 2008-52410
"Ideal introductions to concepts, people, and events of
the Renaissance... succinct and thorough. "SLJ

Encyclopedia of women in the Renaissance; Italy,
France, and England. Diana Robin, Anne R. Lars-
en, Carole Levin, editors. ABC-CLIO 2007 xx,
459p il $95
Grades: 7 8 9 10 11 12   **940.2**
1. Renaissance 2. Women -- Europe 3. Women --

History
ISBN 1-85109-772-4; 978-1-85109-772-2

LC 2006038854

"This work covers how women of the [Renaissance] lived; how they were treated and viewed; and literary, artistic musical, social, political, scientific, and religious contributions they made. Most of the roughly 150 entries are biographies. . . . Each of the alphabetically arranged essays is about one-half to two pages long, and is signed, concise, and well written. . . . An excellent addition." SLJ

Includes bibliographical references

Grant, Neil

Renaissance Europe. Zak Books 2009 48p il map (History of the world) lib bdg $34.25
Grades: 7 8 9 10   **940.2**
1. Renaissance 2. Medieval civilization
ISBN 978-88-6098-153-0 lib bdg; 88-6098-153-0 lib bdg

LC 2008-8408

The "effectiveness lies in the combination of lush illustrations, well-chosen, captioned photographs of contemporary artifacts, and . . . [a] reasoned, concise [narrative]. Succinct time lines border most pages, and . . . clear dark print maintain organization and clarity. A superior choice." SLJ

Includes glossary

Hinds, Kathryn, 1962-

★ **Everyday** life in the Renaissance. Marshall Cavendish Benchmark 2010 327p il lib bdg $42.79
Grades: 7 8 9 10   **940.2**
1. Renaissance
ISBN 978-0-7614-4483-1; 0-7614-4483-1

LC 2008-54829

A compilation of four titles in the Everyday Life in the Renaissance series, published 2004: The church; The city; The countryside; The court

This book combines "clear, bold text with vivid reproductions of period paintings, frescoes, and sculptures, making for [a] stunning [presentation]." SLJ

Includes glossary and bibliographical references

Malam, John

The **birth** of modern nations. Zak Books 2009 48p il map (History of the world) lib bdg $34.25
Grades: 7 8 9 10   **940.2**
ISBN 978-88-6098-155-4 lib bdg; 88-6098-155-7 lib bdg

LC 2008-8570

The "effectiveness lies in the combination of lush illustrations, well-chosen, captioned photographs of contemporary artifacts, and . . . [a] reasoned, concise [narrative]. Succinct time lines border most pages, and . . . the proper amount of white space, and clear dark print maintain organization and clarity. A superior choice." SLJ

Includes glossary

940.3   World War I, 1914-1918

Adams, Simon

World War I; written by Simon Adams; photographed by Andy Crawford. rev ed.; DK Pub. 2007 72p il (DK eyewitness books) $15.99
Grades: 4 5 6 7   **940.3**
1. World War, 1914-1918
ISBN 978-0-7566-3007-2; 0-7566-3007-X

LC 2007279476

First published 2001

This look at World War I examines life in the trenches and the devastation of Europe by the Great War

Barber, Nicola

World War I; by Nicola Barber. Heinemann Library 2012 80 p. ill. (some col.), col. maps (library) $36.50; (paperback) $10.99
Grades: 6 7 8 9   **940.3**
1. World War, 1914-1918
ISBN 1432960105; 9781432960018; 9781432960100

LC 2011015931

In this book on World War I, part of the "Living Through" series, "[Nicola] Barber explains the European political powder keg of the late 1800s and the turn of the last century before telling of the assassination of Archduke Franz Ferdinand." (VOYA)

Includes bibliographical references (p. 76-78) and index.

Batten, Jack

The **war** to end all wars; the story of World War I. Tundra Books 2009 154p il $22.95
Grades: 7 8 9 10 11 12   **940.3**
1. World War, 1914-1918
ISBN 978-0-88776-879-8; 0-88776-879-2

"More than six million soldiers perished in World War I . . . and this beautifully designed, highly readable photo-essay combines a few of their personal stories with the larger picture of politics and military strategies on all sides. . . . Young people with a particular interest in the war will be enthralled." Booklist

Bausum, Ann

★ **Unraveling** freedom; the battle for democracy on the home front during World War I. National Geographic 2010 88p il $19.95; lib bdg $28.90
Grades: 7 8 9 10   **940.3**
1. Governors 2. Presidents 3. Civil rights 4. German Americans 5. College presidents 6. Nobel laureates for peace 7. World War, 1914-1918 -- United States
ISBN 978-1-4263-0702-7; 1-4263-0702-0; 978-1-4263-0703-4 lib bdg; 1-4263-0703-9 lib bdg

LC 2010-10631

"Bausum describes the events that would eventually lead the U.S. into the European conflict that ultimately led to World War I. She then turns her attention to describing the destruction of civil liberties by President Wilson, Congress, and those in control of political power during the country's campaign to 'make the world safe for democracy.' . . . Black-and-white archival photos and political cartoons are arranged in an artistic manner with informative captions.

Appropriate quotations by various people of the time are displayed in elegant fonts. Make this unique and timely offering a definite first purchase." SLJ

Includes bibliographical references

Carlisle, Rodney P.

World War I. Facts on File 2006 454p il map (Eyewitness history) $75

Grades: 8 9 10 11 12   **940.3**

1. World War, 1914-1918 2. World War, 1914-1918 -- Personal narratives

ISBN 0-8160-6061-4; 978-0-8160-6061-0

LC 2005-27236

First published 1992 under the authorship of Joe H. Kirchberger with title: The First World War

This book "provides hundreds of firsthand accounts—from diary entries, letters, speeches, and newspaper accounts—that focus on different warfare issues and on the social and cultural impacts of the war on Europe and the United States. . . . This volume also includes critical documents related to this topic, as well as capsule biographies of key figures, narrative sections, eyewitness testimonies, 102 black-and-white photographs, maps and graphs, a bibliography, notes, a glossary, chronologies, appendixes, and an index." Publisher's note

Includes bibliographical references

Coetzee, Marilyn Shevin

★ World War I; a history in documents. [by] Marilyn Shevin-Coetzee and Frans Coetzee. 2nd ed; Oxford University Press 2011 182p il (Pages from history) $39.95; pa $24.95

Grades: 7 8 9 10   **940.3**

1. World War, 1914-1918 -- Sources

ISBN 978-0-19-973151-0; 978-0-19-973152-7 pa

LC 2009049519

First published 2002 with authors' names in reverse order

Offering an "account of the war as more than a purely military phenomenon, . . . [this book] also addresses its profound social, cultural, and economic implications. Authors Marilyn Shevin-Coetzee and Frans Coetzee use editorials, memoirs, newspaper articles, poems, and letters to recreate the many facets of the war." Publisher's note

Includes bibliographical references

Freedman, Russell

★ The war to end all wars; World War I. Clarion Books 2010 176p il map $22

Grades: 6 7 8 9 10   **940.3**

1. World War, 1914-1918

ISBN 978-0-547-02686-2; 0-547-02686-2

LC 2009-28971

"In his signature lucid style, Freedman offers a photo-essay that examines World War I, the first global war in which modern weapons inflicted mass slaughter and an estimated 20 million people were killed. Interwoven into the big picture of the war's causes and consequences are unforgettable vignettes of German and Allied soldiers, drawn from reports, letters, and diaries, and the personal details are heartbreaking." Booklist

Grant, R. G.

Why did World War I happen? Gareth Stevens Pub. 2011 48p il map (Moments in history) lib bdg $31.95; pa $14.05

Grades: 6 7 8 9   **940.3**

1. World War, 1914-1918

ISBN 978-1-4339-4181-8 lib bdg; 1-4339-4181-3 lib bdg; 978-1-4339-4182-5 pa; 1-4339-4182-1 pa

LC 2010012459

"Examines the events that served as . . . [precursors to World War I]. . . . Brightly colored pull-out boxes highlight important turning points, the perspective of the everyday man, and further information on why specific events occurred. Numerous photographs help readers visualize concepts more fully. . . . Students should be able to easily use this resource." Libr Media Connect

Includes glossary and bibliographical references

Swain, Gwenyth

World War I; an interactive history adventure. by Gwenyth Swain; consultant: Timothy Solie. Capstone Press 2012 112 p. ill. (some col.) (library) $31.32; (paperback) $6.95

Grades: 3 4 5 6   **940.3**

1. World War, 1914-1918

ISBN 1429679972; 9781429660204; 9781429679978

LC 2011033624

This book by Gwenyth Swain is part of the You Choose series. "At the bottom of many pages, you are asked to make a decision about what to do or where to go. Subsequent decisions take you to the adventure's end, at which point readers may choose to go back and begin again and find out where an alternate path might have led. . . . [In] Belgium . . . student nurses must decide whether to stay at their hospital or flee. Later, a British teen has to choose whether to enlist or wait." (Booklist)

Includes bibliographical references (p. 111) and index.

940.4   Military history of World War I

Beller, Susan Provost

The doughboys over there; soldiering in World War I. by Susan Provost Beller. Twenty-First Century Books 2008 112p il map (Soldiers on the battlefront) lib bdg $33.26

Grades: 5 6 7 8   **940.4**

1. World War, 1914-1918 2. Soldiers -- United States

ISBN 978-0-8225-6295-5 lib bdg; 0-8225-6295-2 lib bdg

LC 2006026249

The is an account of the U.S. soldiers who fought in Europe in the First World War.

"The format is inviting with a variety of fonts at the beginning of each chapter, quotations, and a multitude of illustrations. . . . The text is clear and to the point, and chapters are divided into short topics." SLJ

Includes bibliographical references

Murphy, Jim

★ **Truce**; the day the soldiers stopped fighting. Scholastic Press 2009 116p il map $19.99

Grades: 5 6 7 8   **940.4**

1. World War, 1914-1918 2 Christmas Truce, 1914 4. World War, 1914-1918 -- Armistices 5. World War, 1914-1918 -- Campaigns -- Western Front

ISBN 978-0-545-13049-3; 0-545-13049-2

LC 2008-40500

"By December 1918, the western front of World War I featured two parallel trenches stretching from the North Sea to the Alps. . . . On Christmas Day, an informal peace broke out in many locations along the front. . . . Murphy's excellent telling of this unusual war story begins with an account of the events that led to WWI and follows the shift in the soldiers' mind-sets. . . . Printed in tones of sepia, the illustrations in this handsome volume include many period photos as well as paintings and maps. . . . Well organized and clearly written, this presentation vividly portrays the context and events of the Christmas Truce." Booklist

Includes bibliographical references

Oxlade, Chris

World War I. Arcturus Pub. 2011 46p il (Secret history) lib bdg $32.80

Grades: 7 8 9 10   **940.4**

1. World War, 1914-1918

ISBN 978-1-84837-700-4; 1-84837-700-2

LC 2010011012

This book explores the secrets of World War I. As in all wars, each side needed to keep secrets from the enemy. At the same time, they tried to discover the enemy's secrets, using spies and code-breakers.

"The title of the Secret History series will grab readers, even reluctant ones, and they won't be disappointed by the intriguing info regarding codes and code breakers, spies, terrorists, and double agents, with profiles of heroes and traitors on all sides. . . . The readable design, with clear type on thick, high-quality paper, includes lots of sidebars, photos, screens, and quotes." Booklist

Includes bibliographical references

940.53   World War II, 1939-1945

Adams, Simon

World War II; written by Simon Adams; photographed by Andy Crawford. rev ed.; DK Pub. 2007 72p il (DK eyewitness books) $16.99

Grades: 4 5 6 7   **940.53**

1. World War, 1939-1945

ISBN 978-0-7566-3008-9; 0-7566-3008-8

LC 2008273315

First published 2000

Provides a concise history of World War II including information about the Holocaust, the code-breaking Enigma, and the deadly V2 rocket

Alma, Ann

Brave deeds; how one family saved many from the Nazis. Groundwood Books 2008 95p il map $17.95

Grades: 4 5 6 7   **940.53**

1. Holocaust, 1933-1945 2. World War, 1939-1945 -- Netherlands 3. World War, 1939-1945 -- Jews -- Rescue

ISBN 978-0-88899-791-3; 0-88899-791-4

This recounts "how the Braal family, living in Holland near the end of World War II, set up a hideout on the island of Voorne and rescued many from the Nazis. . . . What will excite kids are the facts, full explained in a long historical note, accompanied by a map, and the many archival black-and-white photos." Booklist

Includes glossary

Altman, Linda Jacobs

Escape--teens on the run; primary sources from the Holocaust. Holocaust research by Margaret Shannon. Enslow Publishers 2010 128p il map (True stories of teens in the Holocaust) lib bdg $31.93

Grades: 7 8 9 10 11 12   **940.53**

1. Holocaust, 1933-1945 2. World War, 1939-1945 -- Children 3. World War, 1939-1945 -- Refugees

ISBN 978-0-7660-3270-5 lib bdg; 0-7660-3270-1 lib bdg

LC 2009021378

Discusses children and teens on the run during the Holocaust in Europe, including the different ways young people escaped the Nazis, places of refuge in Europe, and hiding and resistance.

The "book provides historical background, but the narratives rest upon the recollections, making the material immediate and horrifyingly real." SLJ

Includes glossary and bibliographical references

Hidden teens, hidden lives; primary sources from the Holocaust. Enslow Publishers 2010 128p il (True stories of teens in the Holocaust) lib bdg $31.93

Grades: 8 9 10 11 12   **940.53**

1. Holocaust survivors 2. Holocaust, 1933-1945 3. World War, 1939-1945 -- Children 4. World War, 1939-1945 -- Personal narratives

ISBN 978-0-7660-3271-2; 0-7660-3271-X

LC 2009-6504

"Explores the lives of children and teens who went into hiding during the Holocaust; looks at various places used as hiding spots, such as barns and attics, and different ways to hide, like assuming false identities, and how these were used as a tool to survive." Publisher's note

Includes bibliographical references

Shattered youth in Nazi Germany; primary sources from the Holocaust. Holocaust research by Margaret Shannon. Enslow Publishers 2010 128p il map (True stories of teens in the Holocaust) lib bdg $31.93

Grades: 8 9 10 11 12   **940.53**
1. National socialism 2. Holocaust, 1933-1945
ISBN 978-0-7660-3268-2 lib bdg; 0-7660-3268-X
lib bdg

LC 2008048002

Examines the lives of children and teens living in Germany before and during the Holocaust, including the rise of Nazism, growing persecution of Jews, and the Hitler Youth

The "book provides historical background, but the narratives rest upon the recollections, making the material immediate and horrifyingly real." SLJ

Includes glossary and bibliographical references

The **Warsaw** Ghetto Uprising; striking a blow against the Nazis. Enslow 2011 128p il map (The Holocaust through primary sources) lib bdg $31.93
Grades: 7 8 9 10 11 12   **940.53**
1. Jews -- Poland 2. Holocaust, 1933-1945
ISBN 978-0-7660-3320-7; 0-7660-3320-1

LC 2010021596

Examines the Warsaw ghetto uprising, including the roots of the resistance in the Warsaw ghetto, stories from the participants in the uprising, how the battle ended, and how the small group of fighters became heroes during the Holocaust

Includes glossary and bibliographical references

Ambrose, Stephen E.
★ The **good** fight; how World War II was won. Atheneum Bks. for Young Readers 2001 96p il maps $19.95
Grades: 5 6 7 8   **940.53**
1. World War, 1939-1945 2. World War, 1939-1945 -- United States
ISBN 0-689-84361-5

LC 00-49600

"An excellent balance between the big picture and the humanizing details, well supported by fact boxes, tinted photographs, and battlefield maps that are both simple and clear. . . . Ambrose's style is authoritative and warm." Booklist

Includes glossary and bibliographical references

Bitton-Jackson, Livia
★ **I** have lived a thousand years; growing up in the Holocaust. by Livia E. Bitton-Jackson. Simon & Schuster Bks. for Young Readers 1997 224p hardcover o.p. pa $5.99
Grades: 7 8 9 10   **940.53**
1. Holocaust survivors 2. Hebraists 3. Memoirists 4. Jews -- Hungary 5. College teachers 6. Holocaust, 1933-1945 -- Personal narratives
ISBN 0-689-81022-9; 0-689-82395-9 pa

LC 96-19971

Based on the author's book for adults, Elli: coming of age in the Holocaust (1980)

"This is a memorable addition to the searing accounts of Holocaust survivors." Horn Book

Includes glossary

My bridges of hope; searching for life and love after Auschwitz. Simon & Schuster Bks. for Young Readers 1999 258p hardcover o.p. pa $4.99
Grades: 7 8 9 10   **940.53**
1. Holocaust survivors 2. Hebraists 3. Memoirists 4. College teachers 5. Jewish teenagers -- Slovakia -- Biography 6. Holocaust survivors -- Slovakia -- Biography
ISBN 0-689-84898-6 pa

LC 98-8046

In 1945, after surviving a harrowing year in Auschwitz, fourteen-year-old Elli returns, along with her mother and brother, to the family home, now part of Slovakia, where they try to find a way to rebuild their shattered lives

The author's "story is utterly involving, and adds an important chapter to the ongoing attempt to understand the Holocaust and its consequences." Publ Wkly

Includes glossary

Byers, Ann
Courageous teen resisters; primary sources from the Holocaust. Holocaust research by Margaret Shannon. Enslow Publishers 2010 128p il map (True stories of teens in the Holocaust) lib bdg $31.93
Grades: 8 9 10 11 12   **940.53**
1. Holocaust, 1933-1945 2. Jews -- Persecutions 3. World War, 1939-1945 -- Jews 4. World War, 1939-1945 -- Children 5. Holocaust, 1933-1945 -- Personal narratives
ISBN 978-0-7660-3269-9; 0-7660-3269-8

LC 2009-1374

This is an "interesting and revealing collection of personal accounts. . . . Lively writing, which connects paragraphs, brings the events and actions alive with each personal account flowing smoothly. Black and white photos provide an even more personal connection to the teens and the horrific events." Libr Media Connect

Includes glossary and bibliographical references

Rescuing the Danish Jews; a heroic story from the Holocaust. Enslow Publishers 2011 128p il map (The Holocaust through primary sources) lib bdg $31.95
Grades: 7 8 9 10 11 12   **940.53**
1. Holocaust, 1933-1945 2. Jews -- Persecutions 3. World War, 1939-1945 -- Jews -- Rescue
ISBN 978-0-7660-3321-4; 0-7660-3321-X

LC 2009053595

Examines the rescue of the Danish Jews during World War II, including background on Denmark and the Holocaust, firsthand accounts from the many people involved, and how thousands of Jews were saved from the Nazis.

Includes glossary and bibliographical references

Saving children from the Holocaust; the Kindertransport. Enslow Publishers 2011 128p il (The Holocaust through primary sources) lib bdg $31.93
Grades: 7 8 9 10 11 12   **940.53**
1. Holocaust, 1933-1945 2. World War, 1939-1945 --

Jews -- Rescue
ISBN 978-0-7660-3323-8; 0-7660-3323-6
LC 2010014215
Discusses the Kindertransport, including the people who organized the operation, how the transports worked, the children's lives who escaped on a transport, and how ten thousand children were saved from the Holocaust.
Includes glossary and bibliographical references

Trapped--youth in the Nazi ghettos; primary sources from the Holocaust. Holocaust research by Margaret Shannon. Enslow Publishers 2010 128p il (True stories of teens in the Holocaust) lib bdg $31.95
Grades: 8 9 10 11 12   **940.53**
1. Holocaust, 1933-1945 2. World War, 1939-1945 -- Children 3. World War, 1939-1945 -- Personal narratives
ISBN 978-0-7660-3272-9; 0-7660-3272-8
LC 2009013475
Examines the lives of Jewish children and teens in the ghettos during the Holocaust, including the formation of the ghettos, the miserable conditions, hard labor, and the deportations to camps.
The "book provides historical background, but the narratives rest upon the recollections, making the material immediate and horrifyingly real." SLJ
Includes glossary and bibliographical references

Youth destroyed--the Nazi camps; primary sources from the Holocaust. Holocaust research by Margaret Shannon. Enslow Publishers 2010 128p il map (True stories of teens in the Holocaust) lib bdg $31.93
Grades: 7 8 9 10 11 12   **940.53**
1. Concentration camps 2. Holocaust, 1933-1945
ISBN 978-0-7660-3273-6; 0-7660-3273-6
Discusses the experiences of children and teens in concentration camps during the Holocaust, including the first camps in Germany, the forced labor camps, the six death camps, and the aftermath
The "book provides historical background, but the narratives rest upon the recollections, making the material immediate and horrifyingly real." SLJ
Includes glossary and bibliographical references

Callery, Sean
★ **World** War II; Visual history of the world's darkest days. by Sean Callery. 1st ed. Scholastic 2013 105 p. ill. (some col.), col. maps (paperback) $15.99
Grades: 5 6 7 8   **940.53**
1. Military history 2. World War, 1939-1945
ISBN 0545479754; 9780545479752
LC 2012285678
This book presents "World War II in a nutshell. The text is divided into five chapters: 'The Path to War,' 'Europe & the Atlantic War,' the Pacific theater, Africa & the Middle East, and the end of the war. Each section is divided into several two-page topics. The title page of each chapter asks three questions that are answered in the text. It is followed

by a two-page time line with boxed information and vintage photos." (School Library Journal)

Davenport, John
The **internment** of Japanese Americans during World War II; detention of American citizens. [by] John C. Davenport. Chelsea House Publishers 2010 122p il (Milestones in American history) lib bdg $35
Grades: 6 7 8 9 10   **940.53**
1. Japanese Americans -- Evacuation and relocation, 1942-1945
ISBN 978-1-60413-681-4; 1-60413-681-2
LC 2009-29613
The "chapters outline the impact of the bombing [of Pearl Harbor], the history of Japanese immigrants and citizens in the United States, Executive Order 9066 (permitting evacuation and internment of Japanese citizens on the West coast), Japanese American participation in the armed forces, reparations, and the legacy left by the internment. . . . A sound reference and research work." SLJ
Includes bibliographical references

DeSaix, Debbi Durland
Hidden on the mountain; stories of children sheltered from the Nazis in Le Chambon. [by] Deborah Durland DeSaix [and] Karen Gray Ruelle. Holiday House 2007 275p il map $24.95
Grades: 7 8 9 10   **940.53**
1. Holocaust, 1933-1945 2. Holocaust, Jewish (1939-1945) 3. World War, 1939-1945 -- France 4. World War, 1939-1945 -- Jews -- Rescue 5. World War, 1939-1945 -- Underground movements -- France 8. Jewish children in the Holocaust -- France -- Le Chambon-sur-Lignon
ISBN 978-0-8234-1928-9; 0-8234-1928-2
LC 2006-02033
This is the "story of the thousands of children who were sheltered in the tiny mountainous French village of Le Chambon-sur-Lignon during the Holocaust. The first chapters provide readers with an introduction to World War II, the Vichy government, and the region in southern France of La Montange Protestante. Subsequent chapters contain first-person accounts by individuals who, as children, were hidden on the mountain, along with black-and-white photographs and an epilogue detailing their lives after the war. . . . The book is an invaluable resource for Holocaust educators, and many of the children's narratives would read beautifully out loud." SLJ
Includes glossary and bibliographical references

Deem, James M.
Auschwitz; voices from the death camp. Enslow Publishers 2011 128p il map (The Holocaust through primary sources) lib bdg $31.93
Grades: 7 8 9 10 11 12   **940.53**
1. Holocaust, 1933-1945 2. Jews -- Persecutions
ISBN 978-0-7660-3322-1; 0-7660-3322-8
LC 2010003064
Examines Auschwitz, a death camp during the Holocaust, including its construction and daily workings, true

accounts from prisoners of the camp and Nazi perpetrators, and how more than 1 million people were murdered there.

Includes glossary and bibliographical references

Kristallnacht; the Nazi terror that began the Holocaust. Enslow Publishers 2011 128p il (The Holocaust through primary sources) lib bdg $31.93
Grades: 7 8 9 10 11 12   **940.53**
1. Kristallnacht, 1938 2. Jews -- Germany 3. Holocaust, 1933-1945 4. Jews -- Persecutions
ISBN 978-0-7660-3324-5; 0-7660-3324-4
LC 2010015696
Discusses Kristallnacht, a four-day pogrom instigated by the Nazis against Germany's Jews, including stories from the victims, witnesses and perpetrators of the attack, and how it marked the beginning of the Holocaust.

"Personal testimony is a powerful way to tell history. . . . These accounts . . . are tightly edited, drawing on the memories of victims, perpetrators, and witnesses. . . . Each chapter blends an individual's testimony with historical background and commentary as well as photos of the witness and of the brutal events." Booklist

Includes glossary and bibliographical references

Downing, David
★ The **origins** of the Holocaust; [by] David Downing. World Almanac Library 2006 48p il map (World Almanac Library of the Holocaust) lib bdg $30
Grades: 7 8 9 10   **940.53**
1. Antisemitism 2. Holocaust, 1933-1945
ISBN 0-8368-5943-X
LC 2005042114
This "adds essential background history to the many accounts of the Nazi genocide. Downing goes back nearly 2,000 years to show the roots of antiSemitism and the long persecution of the Jews. . . . The clear overview connects that history with the rise of the Nazi Party and Hitler's vision of the Aryan master race. . . . The book design is spacious, with many photos, clear maps, and boxed insets." Booklist

Includes glossary and bibliographical references

Finkelstein, Norman H.
Remember not to forget; a memory of the Holocaust. [by] Norman H. Finkelstein; illustrated by Lois and Lars Hokanson. Jewish Publication Society 2004 31p il pa $9.95
Grades: 4 5 6 7   **940.53**
1. Jews -- History 2. Holocaust, 1933-1945
ISBN 0-82760-770-9
LC 2004556462
A reissue of the title first published 1985 by Watts
"This spare, starkly illustrated book explains what the Holocaust was and how it is remembered on Yom Hashoa, Holocaust Remembrance Day. The explanation reaches back to the explusion of the Jews from Jerusalem in A.D. 70 and describes how Jews . . . became targets of anti-Semitism, which culminated in the systematic murder of six million by the Nazis in World War II. The tone is straightforward and matter-of-fact. Black-and-white woodcuts accompany the text with somber scenes reflective of the narrative." Booklist [review of 1985 edition]

Fishkin, Rebecca Love
Heroes of the Holocaust. Compass Point Books 2011 64p il (The holocaust) lib bdg $33.32; pa $8.95
Grades: 6 7 8 9   **940.53**
1. Holocaust, 1933-1945 2. World War, 1939-1945 -- Jews -- Rescue 3. World War, 1939-1945 -- Underground movements
ISBN 978-0-7565-4391-4 lib bdg; 0-7565-4391-6 lib bdg; 978-0-7565-4443-0 pa; 0-7565-4443-2 pa
LC 2010026492
This book tells the stories of those who defied and resisted the Nazis. Some helped one person or family, some saved dozens, and others organized efforts that helped thousands.

This volume "succeeds in outlining a horrific chapter in history without oversimplifying. . . . [This] book features multiple quotes from survivors about their wartime experiences, providing voices with which young people can identify." SLJ

Includes glossary and bibliographical references

Fitzgerald, Stephanie
Children of the Holocaust. Compass Point Books 2011 64p il (The holocaust) lib bdg $33.32; pa $8.95
Grades: 6 7 8 9   **940.53**
1. Holocaust survivors 2. Holocaust, 1933-1945 3. World War, 1939-1945 -- Children
ISBN 978-0-7565-4390-7 lib bdg; 0-7565-4390-8 lib bdg; 978-0-7565-4442-3 pa; 0-7565-4442-4 pa
LC 2010019975
At the start of World War II, there were about 1.6 million Jewish children living in Europe. Fewer than one in 10 of those children survived German leader Adolf Hitlers reign of terror. More than 100,000 Jewish children did survive, however through a combination of strength, cleverness, the help of others, and, more often than not, simple good luck. Children of the Holocaust tells the stories of these young people.

This volume "succeeds in outlining a horrific chapter in history without oversimplifying. . . . [This] book features multiple quotes from survivors about their wartime experiences, providing voices with which young people can identify." SLJ

Includes glossary and bibliographical references

Fitzgerald, Stephanie J.
Kristallnacht, the night of broken glass; igniting the Nazi War against Jews. by Stephanie Fitzgerald. Compass Point Books 2008 96p il map (Snapshots in history) lib bdg $33.26
Grades: 6 7 8 9   **940.53**
1. Kristallnacht, 1938 2. Jews -- Germany 3. Holocaust, 1933-1945
ISBN 978-0-7565-3489-9; 0-7565-3489-5
LC 2007-32701
"Opening with an overview of November 9, 1938, Kristallnacht goes on to provide background on anti-Semitism, the rise of the Nazis, . . . the impact of Herschel Grynszpan's shooting of Ernst vom Rath . . . and its aftermath. . . . Abundant archival photographs (some full color), quotes from eyewitnesses, and accessible maps enhance chapter

content. An excellent time line and information on related historic sites further enrich the [work]." SLJ

Includes bibliographical references

Fox, Anne L.

Ten thousand children; true stories told by children who escaped the Holocaust on the Kindertransport. by Anne L. Fox and Eva Abraham-Podietz. Behrman House 1998 128p il pa $11.75

Grades: 5 6 7 8   **940.53**

1. Jewish refugees 2. World War, 1939-1945 3. Jews -- Germany 4. Refugees -- Great Britain 5. Holocaust, 1933-1945 -- Personal narratives 6. Jewish children -- Germany -- Biography 7. Jews -- Germany -- History -- 1933-1945 8. Jewish children -- Great Britain -- Biography 9. Refugees, Jewish -- Great Britain -- Biography

ISBN 0-87441-648-5

LC 98-33600

Tells the true stories of children who escaped Nazi Germany on the Kindertransport, a rescue mission led by concerned British to save Jewish children from the Holocaust

"The design is like an open scrapbook, with different size typefaces, snapshots, news photos, and marginal notes; and the combination of the general overview with personal memories will bring readers, from middle grades through adult, close to the experience." Booklist

Frank, Anne

The **diary** of a young girl: the definitive edition; edited by Otto H. Frank and Mirjam Pressler; translated by Susan Massotty. Doubleday 1995 340p $29.95; pa $6.99

Grades: 6 7 8 9   **940.53**

1. Children 2. Diarists 3. Holocaust victims 4. Jews -- Netherlands 5. Holocaust, 1933-1945 6. World War, 1939-1945 -- Jews

ISBN 0-385-47378-8; 0-553-57712-3 pa

LC 94-41379

"This new translation of Frank's famous diary includes material about her emerging sexuality and her relationship with her mother that was originally excised by Frank's father, the only family member to survive the Holocaust." Libr J

Friedman, Ina R.

★ The **other** victims; first-person stories of non-Jews persecuted by the Nazis. Houghton Mifflin 1990 214p hardcover o.p. pa $6.95

Grades: 6 7 8 9   **940.53**

1. Holocaust survivors 2. Holocaust, 1933-1945 -- Personal narratives 3. World War, 1939-1945 -- Atrocities

ISBN 0-395-74515-2 pa

LC 89-27036

Personal narratives of Christians, Gypsies, deaf people, homosexuals, and blacks who suffered at the hands of the Nazis before and during World War II.

"Well organized and edited, the tales are harrowing, though they all end happily, often with escape or immigration to America and highly successful careers. Friedman points out that these were the lucky ones, and her book

serves as a much-needed reminder that the Nazi nightmare extended far beyond Europe's Jewish population." Bull Cent Child Books

Includes bibliographical references

Heinrichs, Ann

The **Japanese** American internment; innocence, guilt, and wartime justice. Marshall Cavendish Benchmark 2010 112p il (Perspectives on) $39.93

Grades: 7 8 9 10   **940.53**

1. Japanese Americans -- Evacuation and relocation, 1942-1945

ISBN 978-0-7614-4983-6; 0-7614-4983-3

"A solid resource for school reports, this straightforward account includes an overview of the events that led up to the signing of Executive Order 9066, which authorized the relocation of Japanese Americans; details about life in the internment camps; and an examination of the long-term ramifications for the Japanese-American community. Information is accompanied by photographs and illustrations in color and black-and-white. A balanced view of the internment is presented." SLJ

Hillman, Laura

I will plant you a lilac tree; a memoir of a Schindler's list survivor. Atheneum Books for Young Readers 2005 243p il map $16.95

Grades: 7 8 9 10   **940.53**

1. Jews -- Germany 2. Holocaust, 1933-1945 -- Personal narratives

ISBN 0-689-86980-0

LC 2004-10534

"In 1942 Berlin, Hannelore, 16, bravely volunteers to be deported with her mother and two younger brothers to Poland. . . . They are soon separated, and during the next three years Hannelore is moved through eight concentration camps. In clipped, first-person narrative, she remembers the worst. . . . She tells it as she endured it, quietly relaying the facts without sensationalism or sentimentality." Booklist

Hodge, Deborah

Rescuing the children; the story of the kindertransport. Deborah Hodge. Tundra Books of Northern New York 2012 60 p. (hardcover) $17.95

Grades: 4 5 6   **940.53**

1. Holocaust, 1939-1945 2. Jewish children in the Holocaust 3. World War, 1939-1945 -- Children 4. World War, 1939-1945 -- Refugees 5. Child refugees -- Great Britain -- History

ISBN 1770492569; 9781770492561

LC 2011938776

This children's book, by Deborah Hodge, "tells the story of how ten thousand Jewish children were rescued out of Nazi Europe just before the outbreak of World War 2. They were saved by the Kindertransport--a rescue mission that transported the children (or Kinder) from Nazi-ruled countries to safety in Britain. The book includes real-life accounts of the children and is illustrated with archival photographs . . . and original art by the Kinder commemorating their rescue." (Publisher's note)

Hoffman, Betty N.

Liberation; stories of survival from the Holocaust. Enslow Publishers 2011 128p il map (The Holocaust through primary sources) lib bdg $31.93
Grades: 7 8 9 10 11 12   **940.53**
1. Immigrants 2. Jewish refugees 3. Holocaust survivors 4. Jews -- Europe 5. Holocaust, 1933-1945 6. World War, 1939-1945 -- Europe 7. World War, 1939-1945 -- Refugees
ISBN 978-0-7660-3319-1; 0-7660-3319-8
LC 2010007234
Discusses the liberation of Europe and the aftermath of the Holocaust, including the displaced persons camps, primary source accounts from Holocaust survivors, and how those survivors started new lives in new countries
Includes glossary and bibliographical references

Houston, Jeanne Wakatsuki

★ **Farewell** to Manzanar; a true story of Japanese American experience during and after the World War II internment. [by] Jeanne Wakatsuki Houston and James D. Houston. Houghton Mifflin 2002 188p $15
Grades: 7 8 9 10   **940.53**
1. Authors 2. Journalists 3. Essayists 4. Memoirists 5. Japanese Americans -- Biography 6. World War, 1939-1945 -- United States 7. World War, 1939-1945 -- Concentration camps -- California 8. Japanese Americans -- Evacuation and relocation, 1942-1945
ISBN 0-618-21620-0
LC 2002-727748
A reissue with a new afterword of the title first published 1973
"The author tells of the three years she and her family spent at Manzanar, a Japanese internment camp. . . . The last part of the book deals with her postwar adolescence and reentry into American life." Libr J

Isserman, Maurice

★ **World** War II; John S. Bowman, general editor. rev ed; Chelsea House 2010 256p il map (America at war) lib bdg $45
Grades: 8 9 10 11 12   **940.53**
1. World War, 1939-1945 -- United States
ISBN 978-0-8160-8185-1; 0-8160-8185-9
LC 2009-52541
First published 1991
This book describes and interprets the role of the United States in World War II.
Includes glossary and bibliographical references

Kacer, Kathy

Hiding Edith; a true story. Second Story 2006 120p (Holocaust remembrance book for young readers) pa $10.95
Grades: 4 5 6 7   **940.53**
1. Holocaust survivors 2. Jews -- France 3. Holocaust, 1933-1945
ISBN 1-897187-06-8
"Kacer recounts some extraordinary history: in Moissac, France, under Nazi occupation, a French Jewish couple hid

100 Jewish refugee children—with the support of the townspeople. Kacer, who based her account on interviews, tells the story of one child, Edith Schwalb. Captioned black-and-white photos on almost every page show Edith at home in Vienna before the war, then in Belgium, and then, separated from her parents, living with the rescuers." Booklist

We Are Their Voice; Young People Respond to the Holocaust. created and edited by Kathy Kacer with Karen Krasny ... [et al.] Orca Book Pub 2012 232 p. ill. (paperback) $16.95
Grades: 7 8 9 10 11 12   **940.53**
1. Children's writings 2. Holocaust, 1939-1945
ISBN 1926920775; 9781926920771
"This volume is a compilation of present-day students' responses to the Holocaust. It includes imagined diary entries, reflections on archival photographs, artwork by students, letters to relevant figures such as Anne Frank, and, finally, the retelling of stories told by Holocaust survivors. These original student works are organized by topic, such as Hope." (School Library Journal)

Kent, Deborah

The **tragic** history of the Japanese-American internment camps; [by] Deborah Kent. Enslow Pub. 2007 128p il (From many cultures, one history) lib bdg $31.93
Grades: 6 7 8 9   **940.53**
1. World War, 1939-1945 -- United States 2. Japanese Americans -- Evacuation and relocation, 1942-1945
ISBN 978-0-7660-2797-8 lib bdg; 0-7660-2797-X lib bdg
LC 2007015125
This "will provide clear, easy-to-understand facts with critical analysis and will be useful for reports." Libr Media Connect
Includes glossary and bibliographical references

Langley, Andrew

World War II; by Andrew Langley. Heinemann Library 2012 80 p. ill. (some col.), col. maps (library) $36.50; (paperback) $10.99
Grades: 6 7 8 9   **940.53**
1. World War, 1939-1945
ISBN 1432960024; 9781432960025; 9781432960117
LC 2011016056
This book by Andrew Langley is part of the Living Through series and looks at World War II. It answers questions including "why was World War II so devastating, and how had the world become so divided into armed camps? How did the war affect people on both sides of the conflict, and why are its consequences still felt today?" (Publisher's note)
Includes bibliographical references (p. 76-78) and index.

Laskier, Rutka

Rutka's notebook; a voice from the Holocaust. Time Books 2008 90p il map $19.95
Grades: 7 8 9 10 11 12   **940.53**
1. Jews -- Poland 2. Holocaust, 1933-1945 -- Personal

narratives

ISBN 978-1-60320-019-6; 1-60320-019-3

"Rutka Laskier was a Jewish teenager in Poland during World War II. For a few short months, before being deported to a concentration camp, she kept a diary describing her experiences. It was kept safe by a non-Jewish friend for 60 years following the war, and was finally published in Poland and Israel. This is the first U.S. edition. The diary itself is a combination of wartime horrors, social gossip, and teen angst. Photos and editorial notes clarify the situations that Laskier describes. . . . A must-have for Holocaust collections, and a solid purchase for general YA collections." SLJ

Lee, Carol Ann

Anne Frank and the children of the Holocaust. Viking 2006 242p il map $16.99

Grades: 6 7 8 9 10   940.53

1. Children 2. Diarists 3. Holocaust victims 4. Holocaust, 1933-1945 5. Holocaust, Jewish (1939-1945)

ISBN 0-670-06107-7

"This book will still serve as an excellent overview in the classroom and for personal reading." Booklist

Includes bibliographical references

Levine, Karen

Hana's suitcase; a true story. Whitman, A. 2003 111p il lib bdg $15.95

Grades: 4 5 6 7   940.53

1. Holocaust victims 2. Holocaust, 1933-1945 3. Nové Město nad Metuji (Czech Republic) -- Biography 4. Holocaust, Jewish (1939-1945) -- Czech Republic -- Nové Město nad Metuji -- Biography 5. Jewish children in the Holocaust -- Czech Republic -- Nové Město nad Metuji -- Biography

ISBN 0-8075-3148-0

LC 2002-27439

First published 2002 in Canada

A biography of a Czech girl who died in the Holocaust, told in alternating chapters with an account of how the curator of a Japanese Holocaust center learned about her life after Hana's suitcase was sent to her

"The account, based on a radio documentary Levine did in Canada . . . is part history, part suspenseful mystery, and always anguished family drama, with an incredible climactic revelation." Booklist

Meltzer, Milton

★ **Never** to forget: the Jews of the Holocaust. Harper & Row 1976 217p maps hardcover o.p. pa $9.99

Grades: 6 7 8 9   940.53

1. Holocaust, 1933-1945

ISBN 0-06-446118-1 pa

"The mass murder of six million Jews by the Nazis during World War II is the subject of this compelling history. Interweaving background information, chilling statistics, individual accounts and newspaper reports, it provides an excellent introduction to its subject." Interracial Books Child Bull

Includes bibliographical references

★ **Rescue**: the story of how Gentiles saved Jews in the Holocaust. Harper & Row 1988 168p maps hardcover o.p. pa $9.99

Grades: 6 7 8 9   940.53

1. Holocaust, 1933-1945 2. World War, 1939-1945 -- Jews -- Rescue

ISBN 0-06-024210-8; 0-06-446117-3 pa

LC 87-47816

A recounting drawn from historic source material of the many individual acts of heroism performed by righteous gentiles who sought to thwart the extermination of the Jews during the Holocaust

"This is an excellent portrayal of a difficult topic. Meltzer manages to both explain without accusing, and to laud without glorifying. . . . The discussion of the complicated relations between countries are clear, but not simplistic. An impressive aspect of this book is its lack of didacticism." Voice Youth Advocates

Includes bibliographical references

Mullenbach, Cheryl

★ **Double** victory; how African American women broke race and gender barriers to help win World War II. Cheryl Mullenbach. Chicago Review Press 2012 272 p. (hardcover) $19.95

Grades: 7 8 9 10 11 12   940.53

1. World War, 1939-1945 -- Women 2. African American women -- Biography 3. United States -- Race relations -- History 4. African Americans -- Employment 5. African Americans -- Civil rights 6. World War, 1939-1945 -- African Americans 7. World War, 1939-1945 -- Women -- United States 8. African American women -- History -- 20th century 9. African American women -- Employment -- History -- 20th century 10. African American women -- Civil rights -- History -- 20th century

ISBN 1569768080; 9781569768082

LC 2012021343

This book, by Cheryl Mullenbach, is part of the "Women of Action" series. "African American women . . . did extraordinary things to help their country during World War II. In these pages young readers meet a range of remarkable women: war workers, political activists, military women, volunteers, and entertainers. . . . But many others fought discrimination at home and abroad in order to contribute to the war effort." (Publisher's note)

Includes bibliographical references and index

Müller, Melissa

Anne Frank; the biography. by Melissa Muller; translated by Rita and Robert Kimber. 2nd U.S. ed. Metropolitan Books/Henry Holt and Company 2013 480 p. (hardcover) $35

Grades: 7 8 9 10 11 12 Adult   940.53

1. Children 2. Jewish children in the Holocaust -- Biography 3. Jews -- Netherlands -- Amsterdam -- Biography 4. Holocaust, Jewish (1939-1945) -- Netherlands -- Amsterdam -- Biography

ISBN 0805087311; 9780805087314

LC 2013000297

This biography of Anne Frank "was originally published in 1998, but this expanded edition takes into account diary entries that had previously been redacted by Anne's father [Otto], as well as recently discovered letters from Otto to relatives in the United States and unpublished documents provided to [Melissa] Müller during interviews with those who knew Anne and her family." (Publishers Weekly)

"Müller includes a family tree; a family history; and considerable insight into the character, personality, and quality of life of Anne's parents, relatives, and friends. Interviews with many of these surviving people give a clearer idea of the situation and Anne's reactions to it." SLJ

Nolan, Cathal J.

The **concise** encyclopedia of World War II. Greenwood Press 2010 2v set $195

Grades: 7 8 9 10 11 12 Adult   **940.53**

1. World War, 1939-1945 -- Encyclopedias
ISBN 978-0-313-33050-6 set; 0-313-33050-6 set; 978-0-313-36527-0 set: ebook; 0-313-36527-X set: ebook

LC 2009036965

"This rigorous A-Z set will be valuable for defining vocabulary such as 'friendly fire' or 'leaflet bombing,' and identifying people, places, tactics, and campaigns. Included are numerous Russian, Japanese, and German terms. . . . Entries vary in length, from mere definitions to 17 pages (on Adolf Hitler), and are often followed up with 'see' or 'see-also' references and additional reading suggestions. . . . A first stop for researchers." SLJ

Includes bibliographical references

Opdyke, Irene Gut

In my hands; memories of a Holocaust rescuer. [by] Irene Gut Opdyke with Jennifer Armstrong. Knopf 1999 276p il hardcover o.p. pa $12

Grades: 7 8 9 10   **940.53**

1. Nurses 2. Domestics 3. Humanitarians 4. World War, 1939-1945 -- Poland 5. World War, 1939-1945 -- Jews -- Rescue 6. Holocaust, 1933-1945 -- Personal narratives 7. World War, 1939-1945 -- Personal narratives 8. Holocaust, Jewish (1939-1945) -- Poland 9. World War, 1939-1945 -- Jews -- Rescue -- Poland 10. World War, 1939-1945 -- Personal narratives, Polish 11. Righteous Gentiles in the Holocaust -- Poland -- Biography
ISBN 0-679-89181-1; 0-385-72032-7 pa

LC 98-54095

Recounts the experiences of the author who, as a young Polish girl, hid and saved Jews during the Holocaust

"No matter how many Holocaust stories one has read, this one is a must, for its impact is so powerful. . . . Opdyke's remarkable story is simply told, with clarity and feeling." SLJ

Oppenheim, Joanne

★ **Dear** Miss Breed; true stories of the Japanese American incarceration during World War II and a librarian who made a difference. foreword by Elizabeth Kikuchi Yamada; afterword by Snowden Becker. Scholastic 2006 287p il $22.99

Grades: 7 8 9 10   **940.53**

1. Librarians 2. World War, 1939-1945 -- United States 4. Japanese Americans -- Evacuation and relocation,

1942-1945
ISBN 0-439-56992-3; 978-0-439-56992-7

LC 2004-59009

This "account focuses on Clara Breed, a children's librarian at the San Diego Public Library, and the Japanese-American children she served prior to World War II and whom she continued to serve after their families were sent to an Arizona internment camp. . . . Illustrated with numerous photographs . . . and incorporating copious letters and documents, the book is . . . compelling." Horn Book

Includes bibliographical references

Perl, Lila

Four perfect pebbles; a Holocaust story. by Lila Perl and Marion Blumenthal Lazan. Greenwillow Bks. 1996 130p il $16.99; pa $5.99

Grades: 6 7 8 9   **940.53**

1. Holocaust survivors 2. Jews -- Germany 3. Holocaust, 1933-1945 -- Personal narratives
ISBN 0-688-14294-X; 0-380-73188-6 pa

LC 95-9752

"This book warrants attention both for the uncommon experiences it records and for the fullness of that record. . . . Quotes from Lazan's 87-year-old mother are invaluable— her memories of the family's experiences afford Marion's story a precision and wholeness rarely available to child survivors." Publ Wkly

Includes bibliographical references

Rappaport, Doreen, 1939-

★ **Beyond** courage; the untold story of Jewish resistance during the Holocaust. by Doreen Rappaport. 1st ed. Candlewick Press 2012 228 p. ill., maps (hardcover) $22.99

Grades: 6 7 8 9 10 11 12   **940.53**

1. Jews -- History 2. Resistance to government 3. Holocaust, Jewish (1939-1945) 4. Righteous Gentiles in the Holocaust 5. World War, 1939-1945 -- Jews -- Rescue 6. World War, 1939-1945 -- Jewish resistance
ISBN 0763629766; 9780763629762

LC 2011048116

In this book, Doreen Rappaport offers "more than 20 stories of Jewish resistance to the Holocaust, some never before told. From all corners of Nazi-occupied Europe, these harrowing accounts . . . pay tribute to the brave thousands who defied their oppressors in ways large and small. In one, 12-year-old Mordechai Shlayan . . . blows up a hotel where German officers are dining. In another, 22-year-old Marianne Cohn is caught smuggling children into Switzerland." (Publishers Weekly)

Includes bibliographical references (p. 209-221) and index.

Robbins, Trina

Lily Renée, escape artist; illustrated by Anne Timmons and Mo Oh. Graphic Universe 2011 96p. chiefly col. ill. $7.95

Grades: 4 5 6 7 8   **940.53**

1. Artists 2. Illustrators 3. Graphic novels 4. Jews -- Biography 5. Holocaust, 1933-1945 -- Graphic novels
ISBN 978-0-7613-6010-0; 0-7613-6010-7

LC 2011001084

Presents the story of Lily Renée Wilheim, the Jewish girl who escaped from the Nazis through the Kindertransport operation, leaving her parents behind and traveling alone to England, later becoming a comic book artist in New York.

"This comic-book biography of a Jewish girl's life under the Nazi jackboot and then as a refugee is low key and that much more profound for it. The panels are brightly lit, and the narrative is crisp, both of which serve to chillingly amplify the everyday banality of evil. . . . A fitting tribute." Kirkus

Rol, Ruud van der

★ **Anne** Frank, beyond the diary; a photographic remembrance. by Ruud van der Rol and Rian Verhoeven; in association with the Anne Frank House; translated by Tony Langham and Plym Peters; with an introduction by Anna Quindlen. Viking 1993 113p il map hardcover o.p. pa $10.99

Grades: 5 6 7 8   940.53
1. Children 2. Diarists 3. Holocaust victims 4. Jews -- Netherlands 5. Holocaust, 1933-1945 6. World War, 1939-1945 -- Jews
ISBN 0-670-84932-4; 0-14-036926-0 pa
LC 92-41528

Original Dutch edition, 1992

Photographs, illustrations, and maps accompany historical essays, diary excerpts, and interviews, providing an insight to Anne Frank and the massive upheaval which tore apart her world

"Readers will become absorbed in the richness of the detail and careful explanation which revisit and expand the familiar, well-loved story." Horn Book

Samuels, Charlie

Home front; by Charlie Samuels. Brown Bear Books 2012 48 p $35.65

Grades: 5 6 7 8   940.53
1. Military history 2. World War, 1939-1945 3. World War, 1939-1945 -- Social aspects 4. World War, 1939-1945 -- Economic aspects
ISBN 1936333228; 9781936333226
LC 2011007054

This book by Charlie Samuels is part of the World War II Sourcebook series and focuses on the home front. "Each page is illustrated. Little-known facts and, sometimes, direct narratives are presented with the information given to the reader. . . . Each book has the same timeline of World War II, maps of both the European and Pacific theaters, interesting biographical snapshots of people involved, and a list of websites that students may use to further explore World War II." (Library Media Connection)

Life under occupation; by Charlie Samuels. Brown Bear Books 2011 48 p. ill. (chiefly col.), col. maps (World War II sourcebook) (library) $35.65

Grades: 5 6 7 8   940.53
1. World War, 1939-1945 2. World War, 1939-1945 -- Occupied territories 3. World War, 1939-1945 -- Europe 4. World War, 1939-1945 -- Atrocities 5. World War, 1939-1945 -- Pacific Area
ISBN 1936333260; 9781936333264
LC 2011007055

This book by Charlie Samuels, part of the World War II Sourcebook series, and focuses on life under occupation. "Each page is illustrated. Little-known facts and, sometimes, direct narratives are presented with the information given to the reader. . . . Each book has the same timeline of World War II, maps of both the European and Pacific theaters, . . . biographical snapshots of people involved, and a list of websites." (Library Media Connection)

Includes bibliographical references and index.

Sanders, Ronald

Storming the tulips; by Ronald Sanders; translated and revised by Hannie J. Voyles. StoneBrook 2011 164p il map pa $14.00

Grades: 7 8 9 10   940.53
1. World War, 1939-1945 -- Netherlands 2. Holocaust, 1933-1945 -- Personal narratives 3. World War, 1939-1945 -- Underground movements
ISBN 978-0-9830800-0-8; 0-9830800-0-3

"The tragic story of the Netherlands under Nazi occupation resounds dramatically through the words of 20 survivors from the first Montessori school in Amsterdam. Contemporaries of Anne Frank, they were interviewed by Ronald Sanders, now a teacher at the school. Though the book focuses on this small group, it presents a well-documented history of the country during World War II. In addition to the essays, descriptions of unusual heroes from the Resistance help to round out the picture." SLJ

Sandler, Martin W.

Imprisoned; the betrayal of japanese americans during world war II. by Martin W. Sandler. Walker Books For Young Readers 2013 176 p. (hardcover) $22.99; (library) $23.89

Grades: 6 7 8 9 10   940.53
1. World War, 1939-1945 2. Japanese Americans -- Evacuation and relocation, 1942-1945 3. World War, 1939-1945 -- Japanese Americans 4. Japanese Americans -- History -- 20th century
ISBN 0802722776; 0802722784; 9780802722775; 9780802722782
LC 2012032295

This book offers a "survey of Executive Order 9066 and its aftermath. The order authorized the U.S. military to relocate over 100,000 Japanese-Americans--many were U.S. citizens--from their homes in Washington, Oregon and California to detention camps. . . . A few government officials did object to the order, questioning its constitutionality." (Kirkus Reviews)

Schroeder, Peter W.

Six million paper clips; the making of a children's Holocaust memorial. [by] Peter W. Schroeder & Dagmar Schroeder-Hildebrand. Kar-Ben Publishing 2004 64p il lib bdg $17.95; pa $7.95

Grades: 5 6 7 8   940.53
1. Holocaust, 1933-1945 -- Study and teaching
ISBN 1-58013-169-7 lib bdg; 1-58013-176-X pa
LC 2004-19598

"With clear and concise language, color photographs, and an attractive layout, this book tells [an] inspiring and touching story." SLJ

Sender, Ruth Minsky

The **cage**. Macmillan 1986 245p hardcover o.p.
pa $5.99

Grades: 7 8 9 10   **940.53**

1. Jews -- Poland 2. Holocaust, 1933-1945 -- Personal narratives

ISBN 0-02-781830-6; 0-689-81321-X pa

LC 86-8562

This "Holocaust memoir presents a series of brief scenes from 1939, when the author was 12 and Hitler invaded Poland, through the Russian liberation of the Mitelsteine labor camp in 1945. . . . Older students with previous knowledge of the subject will find Sender's narrative moving and thought provoking." SLJ

Senker, Cath

Why did World War II happen? Gareth Stevens Pub. 2011 48p il map (Moments in history) lib bdg $31.95; pa $14.05

Grades: 6 7 8 9   **940.53**

1. World War, 1939-1945

ISBN 978-1-4339-4184-9 lib bdg; 1-4339-4184-8 lib bdg; 978-1-4339-4185-6 pa; 1-4339-4185-6 pa

LC 2010015834

"Examines the events that served as . . . [precursors to World War II]. . . . Brightly colored pull-out boxes highlight important turning points, the perspective of the everyday man, and further information on why specific events occurred. Numerous photographs help readers visualize concepts more fully. . . . Students should be able to easily use this resource." Libr Media Connect

Includes glossary and bibliographical references

Sheehan, Sean

Auschwitz. Arcturus Pub. 2011 46p il map (A place in history) lib bdg $34.25

Grades: 7 8 9 10   **940.53**

1. Holocaust, 1933-1945

ISBN 978-1-84837-672-4; 1-84837-672-3

LC 2010014147

This book begins with the Auschwitz concentration camp as a landmark and broadens "outward, describing the political and economic situations that led up to notable events there. The approach works beautifully. Quotes from participants are a highlight of the [book], and all the maps and photos are clear and informative. [This] will be [a] useful [supplement] to history classes, but [is] accessible enough to appeal as extracurricular material for students already interested in the [topic]." SLJ

Includes glossary and bibliographical references

Why did the Holocaust happen? Gareth Stevens 2010 48p il map (Moments in history) lib bdg $31.95; pa $14.05

Grades: 6 7 8 9   **940.53**

1. Holocaust, 1933-1945

ISBN 978-1-4339-4172-6 lib bdg; 1-4339-4172-4; 978-1-4339-4173-3 pa; 1-4339-4173-2 pa

LC 2010015833

This "explains the before, during, and after of [the Holocaust] in a clear, unbiased manner. . . . Sidebars include

meticulously cited eyewitness quotes or extra insight on particularly important events. Even more information is contained in the maps, period photographs, and well-placed captions that grace every page." SLJ

Includes glossary and bibliographical references

Skog, Jason

The **legacy** of the Holocaust. Compass Point Books 2011 64p il (The holocaust) lib bdg $33.32; pa $8.95

Grades: 6 7 8 9   **940.53**

1. Holocaust, 1933-1945

ISBN 978-0-7565-4393-8 lib bdg; 0-7565-4393-2 lib bdg; 978-0-7565-4444-7 pa; 0-7565-4444-0 pa

LC 2010026494

This discusses the lasting impact of the Holocaust, including its effects on people and families and entire cities and countries, and its influence on popular culture, art, music, and international law.

This volume "succeeds in outlining a horrific chapter in history without oversimplifying. . . . [This] book features multiple quotes from survivors about their wartime experiences, providing voices with which young people can identify." SLJ

Includes glossary and bibliographical references

Spiegelman, Art

★ **Maus**; a survivor's tale. Pantheon Bks. 1996 2v in 1 il $35

Grades: 7 8 9 10 11 12 Adult   **940.53**

1. Graphic novels 2. Biographical graphic novels 3. Holocaust, 1933-1945 -- Graphic novels 4. Holocaust, 1933-1945 -- Comic books, strips, etc.

ISBN 0-679-40641-7

LC 96-32796

A combined edition of Maus (1986) and Maus II (1991)

Awards: 1992 Pulitzer Prize Special Award; Eisner Award for Best Graphic Album: Reprint for Maus II; Harvey Award for Best Graphic Album of Previously Published Work (for Maus II); 1993 Los Angeles Times Book Prize for Fiction (for Maus II)

In this work "Spiegelman takes the comic book to a new level of seriousness, portraying Jews as mice and Nazis as cats. Depicting himself being told about the Holocaust by his Polish survivor father, Spiegelman not only explores the concentration-camp experience, but also the guilt, love, and anger between father and son." Rochman. Against borders

Stille, Darlene R.

Architects of the Holocaust. Compass Point Books 2010 64p il (The holocaust) lib bdg $33.32; pa $8.95

Grades: 6 7 8 9   **940.53**

1. Holocaust, 1933-1945

ISBN 978-0-7565-4392-1 lib bdg; 0-7565-4392-4 lib bdg; 978-0-7565-4441-6 pa; 0-7565-4441-6 pa

LC 2010026493

While this book "covers the rise of Hitler and spends some time discussing others who organized the atrocities, its latter half discusses concentration and extermination camps and the Nuremberg trials. . . . [This volume] succeeds in outlining a horrific chapter in history without oversimplifying. .

.. [This] book features multiple quotes from survivors about their wartime experiences, providing voices with which young people can identify." SLJ

Includes glossary and bibliographical references

Taylor, Peter Lane

★ The **secret** of Priest's Grotto; a Holocaust survival story. [by] Peter Lane Taylor with Christos Nicola. Kar-Ben Pub. 2007 64p il map lib bdg $10.95; pa $8.95

Grades: 5 6 7 8 9 10 11 12   **940.53**

1. Caves 2. Jews -- Ukraine 3. Holocaust, 1933-1945 4. Jews -- Ukraine 5. Holocaust survivors

ISBN 978-1-58013-260-2 lib bdg; 1-58013-260-X lib bdg; 978-1-58013-261-9 pa; 1-58013-261-8 pa

LC 2006-21709

"This volume relays the tale of 38 Ukrainian Jews who sought refuge in a local cave to escape the invading Nazis in fall of 1942 and remained there for 344 days. . . . At once sobering and uplifting, this is an astounding story of survival, powerfully told." Publ Wkly

Thomson, Ruth

★ **Terezin**; voices from the Holocaust. Candlewick Press 2011 64p il $18.99

Grades: 5 6 7 8   **940.53**

1. Jews -- Czechoslovakia 2. Holocaust, 1933-1945 -- Personal narratives 3. Holocaust, Jewish (1939-1945)

ISBN 0-7636-4963-5; 978-0-7636-4963-0

LC 2010-39164

"Two years after the Nazi invasion of Czechoslovakia, the small fortress village of Terezin was converted into a Jewish ghetto, and over the next four years, ten of thousands of Jews were transported there while in transit to death camps in the east. The history of Terezin is fascinating: the camp housed many noted artists. . . . Much of the art created at Terezin survived the Holocaust, and a generous sampling is included in this volume. Thomson opts to tell the story of Terezin almost entirely in the voices of those who lived there. . . . This is an accessible, carefully researched work that effectively uses primary-source material to make the experience of the Jews of Terezin come alive for today's students." Bull Cent Child Books

Includes glossary and bibliographical references

Warren, Andrea

Surviving Hitler; a boy in the Nazi death camps. HarperCollins Pubs. 2001 146p il hardcover o.p. pa $6.99

Grades: 5 6 7 8   **940.53**

1. Holocaust, 1933-1945 2. Gdynia (Poland) -- Biography 3. Jewish children in the Holocaust -- Biography 4. Holocaust, Jewish (1939-1945) -- Poland -- Gdynia -- Personal narratives

ISBN 0-688-17497-3; 0-06-029218-0 lib bdg; 0-06-000767-2 pa

LC 00-38899

"Simply told, Warren's powerful story blends the personal testimony of Holocaust survivor Jack Mandelbaum with the history of his time, documented by stirring photos from the archives of the U.S. Holocaust Memorial Museum.

. . . An excellent introduction for readers who don't know much about the history." Booklist

Includes bibliographical references

940.54   Military history of World War II

Allen, Thomas B.

★ **Remember** Pearl Harbor; American and Japanese survivors tell their stories. foreword by Robert D. Ballard. National Geographic Soc. 2001 57p il maps $17.95

Grades: 5 6 7 8   **940.54**

1. Pearl Harbor (Oahu, Hawaii), Attack on, 1941 2. Pearl Harbor (Hawaii), Attack on, 1941 3. World War, 1939-1945 -- Personal narratives

ISBN 0-7922-6690-0

LC 2001-796

Personal accounts of the Japanese attack on Pearl Harbor, with background information.

"Eyewitness testimony of Japanese and American men and women from various backgrounds enriches this balanced treatment of World War II. . . . The first-person voices along with dozens of black-and-white photos and several full-color maps make this a draw for both browsers and World War II buffs." Booklist

Includes bibliographical references

Allport, Alan

The **Battle** of Britain; by Alan Allport. Chelsea House 2012 128 p. (Milestones in modern world history) (hardcover) $35

Grades: 7 8 9 10 11 12   **940.54**

1. Britain, Battle of, 1940 2. World War, 1939-1945 -- Aerial operations 3. World War, 1939-1945 -- Great Britain 4. Britain, Battle of, Great Britain, 1940

ISBN 160413920X; 9781604139204

LC 2011023053

This book, part of the Milestones in Modern World History series, "describes the air campaign waged by the Luftwaffe (German air force) against England's Royal Air Force during WWII. It starts with a look at [Adolph] Hitler's rise to power and continues with such pivotal conflicts as the Blitz. The author also notes how important the burgeoning radar technology of the time aided England's defense." (Booklist)

Includes bibliographical references and index

The **attack** on Pearl Harbor; David Haugen and Susan Musser, book editors. Greenhaven Press 2011 204p il map (Perspectives on modern world history) lib bdg $39.70

Grades: 8 9 10 11 12   **940.54**

1. Pearl Harbor (Oahu, Hawaii), Attack on, 1941

ISBN 978-0-7377-5004-1; 0-7377-5004-9

LC 2010033590

In "discussing the events of December 7, 1941. . . [this] well-organized [volume presents] a wealth of clearly written analyses from a rich variety of viewpoints. With the inclusion of historical background, firsthand experiences, and discussions of particular points of controversy, [it helps] to familiarize readers with the [attack on Pearl Harbor] and [serves] as [an exercise] in the development of analytical thinking skills." SLJ

Includes bibliographical references

Atwood, Kathryn

Women heroes of World War II; 26 stories of espionage, sabotage, resistance, and rescue. Chicago Review Press 2011 266p il map $19.95

Grades: 7 8 9 10   940.54

1. World War, 1939-1945 -- Women 2. World War, 1939-1945 -- Underground movements

ISBN 978-1-55652-961-0; 1-55652-961-9

LC 2010-41830

"The 26 women profiled in this collective biography served on the front lines and behind enemy lines in Europe as correspondents, couriers, propagandists, Resistance fighters, saboteurs and spies. . . . Atwood's admiration and enthusiasm for her subjects is apparent in these engaging profiles, and readers will likely be inspired to investigate these fascinating women further." Kirkus

Includes glossary and bibliographical references

Bradley, James

Flags of our fathers; heroes of Iwo Jima. [by] James Bradley with Ron Powers; adapted for young people by Michael French. Delacorte Press 2001 211p il $15.95; pa $8.95

Grades: 7 8 9 10   940.54

1. Iwo Jima, Battle of, 1945 2. Photojournalists 3. Photographs -- History -- 20th century 4. Iwo Jima, Battle of, Japan, 1945 -- Pictorial works

ISBN 0-385-72932-4; 0-385-73064-0 pa

LC 00-50914

"A journalistic, accessible adaptation of the earlier book for adult readers, this account by a survivor's son centers on [Rosenthal's] famous photo of six Marines raising a U.S. flag on Iwo Jima. The accurate, engaging text provides the men's pre-war backgrounds, their war service to that time, what they actually did on the island and afterward, and the consequences of the famous photo." Horn Book Guide

Includes bibliographical references

Burgan, Michael

Hiroshima; birth of the nuclear age. Marshall Cavendish Benchmark 2009 128p il (Perspectives on) lib bdg $27.95

Grades: 8 9 10 11 12   940.54

1. Atomic bomb

ISBN 978-0-7614-4023-9; 0-7614-4023-2

LC 2008-29249

This provides information on the Manhattan Project, the bombing of Hiroshima, and its legacy.

"Utilizing an unbiased and chronological narrative, [the author delves] deeply into the [topic], providing an overall representation as well as a substantial degree of insight. . . . The potency of [this title] lies in the excellent arrangement of numerous well-chosen sidebars and photos, and fluent, concise prose." SLJ

Includes bibliographical references

Raising the flag; how a photograph gave a nation hope in wartime. Compass Point Books 2011 64p il (Captured history) lib bdg $33.99; pa $8.95

Grades: 6 7 8 9   940.54

1. World War, 1939-1945 2. Documentary photography 3. Iwo Jima, Battle of, 1945 4. Photojournalists

ISBN 978-0-7565-4395-2; 0-7565-4395-9; 978-0-7565-4449-2 pa; 0-7565-4449-1 pa

LC 2010038572

This book about the iconic Joe Rosenthal photograph of American soldiers raising the flag at Iwo Jima places the photo "in historical context, profiles the photographer, describes the conditions under which it was taken, and analyzes both its immediate and its continuing impact. The [text includes] ample background information and details and [is] enhanced by large photos and sidebars." SLJ

Includes glossary and bibliographical references

Chrisp, Peter

World War II: fighting for freedom; the story of the conflict that changed the world 1939-1945. Scholastic 2010 63p il map $12.99

Grades: 4 5 6 7   940.54

1. World War, 1939-1945

ISBN 978-0-545-24984-3; 0-545-24984-8

Provides information and facts on events leading up to the war, important battles and campaigns, political and military leaders, and life on the home fronts.

"Fascinating photographs dominate each spread, but there are also maps, quotations, diagrams, and interesting text box features. . . . This book provides a solid overview of World War II, but it is the visual aspect that makes it stand out." Libr Media Connect

Includes glossary

De Capua, Sarah

The **Tuskegee** airmen; by Sarah E. De Capua. Child's World 2009 32p il map (Journey to freedom) lib bdg $28.50

Grades: 4 5 6   940.54

1. African American pilots 2. World War, 1939-1945 -- Aerial operations

ISBN 978-1-60253-138-3 lib bdg; 1-60253-138-2 lib bdg

LC 2008031939

Tuskegee "Airmen celebrates the pilots' extraordinary achievements by placing them within the context of their time, when segregation was common. . . . Personal accounts, historical photographs of training, news stories about the men's fighting ability, and records of successful missions help to explain the squadron's determination not only to fly but also to prove its proficiency and bravery. . . . The [book is] concise and direct, yet the writing remains sophisticated. Vibrant personal stories accompanied by striking photographs of historical figures and artifacts provide a sense of the subjects' hopes and dreams." SLJ

Includes glossary and bibliographical references

DeMallie, H. R.

Behind enemy lines; a young pilot's story. [by] Howard R. DeMallie. Updated ed; Sterling Pub. 2007 178p il map $12.95; pa $6.95

Grades: 6 7 8 9   **940.54**
1. Air pilots 2. Army officers 3. Air force officers 4. World War, 1939-1945 -- Personal narratives
ISBN 978-1-4027-4517-1; 1-4027-4517-6; 978-1-4027-4137-1 pa; 1-4027-4137-5 pa
                                    LC 2006032134

First published 2000 by Dry Bones Press with title: Beyond the dikes

"The story follows the 22-year-old American Air Force officer who was forced to bail out of his B-17 in 1944, highlighting his hiding out in the Netherlands, imprisonment in a German POW camp, and liberation by Russian soldiers. There are vivid recollections of hunger, loneliness, and uncertainty. . . . This a a good choice for nonfiction enthusiasts." SLJ

Dougherty, Steve

Pearl Harbor; the U.S. enters World War II. Franklin Watts 2010 64p il map (24/7 goes to war) lib bdg $27; pa $7.95

Grades: 6 7 8 9   **940.54**
1. Pearl Harbor (Oahu, Hawaii), Attack on, 1941 2. World War, 1939-1945 -- Causes
ISBN 978-0-531-25525-4 lib bdg; 0-531-25525-5 lib bdg; 978-0-531-25450-9 pa; 0-531-25450-X pa
                                    LC 2009-20143

Describes the Japanese surprise attack on the United States naval base at Pearl Harbor, which resulted in the deaths of more than 2,000 American officers and servicemen and an immediate declaration of war on Japan.

This "will appeal to these readers, because . . . [it tells] a story while presenting the facts. . . . The first chapter gives the historic details concerning the war up to the particular battle, with the story of the battle told from a first-person perspective. A mixture of news photos and photos taken by the men involved appear throughout the book." Libr Media Connect

Includes glossary and bibliographical references

Drez, Ronald J.

★ **Remember** D-day; the plan, the invasion, survivor stories. National Geographic Books 2004 61p il map $17.95; lib bdg $27.90

Grades: 5 6 7 8   **940.54**
1. Operation Overlord 2. World War, 1939-1945 -- Campaigns -- France 3. World War, 1939-1945 -- Germany 4. World War, 1939-1945 -- Campaigns -- France -- Normandy
ISBN 0-7922-6666-8; 0-7922-6965-9 lib bdg
                                    LC 2003-17733

Discusses the events and personalities involved in the momentous Allied invasion of France on June 6, 1944

"This well-organized, clearly written account provides a solid overview for readers unfamiliar with the subject. A first-rate purchase." SLJ

Includes bibliographical references

Grant, R. G.

Why did Hiroshima happen? Gareth Stevens Pub. 2010 48p il map (Moments in history) lib bdg $31.95; pa $14.05

Grades: 6 7 8 9   **940.54**
1. Atomic bomb 2. World War, 1939-1945 -- Japan 3. World War, 1939-1945 -- United States 4. Hiroshima (Japan) -- Bombardment, 1945
ISBN 978-1-4339-4163-4 lib bdg; 1-4339-4163-5 lib bdg; 978-1-4339-4164-1 pa; 1-4339-4164-3 pa
                                    LC 2010012464

This "explains the before, during, and after of [the bombing of Hiroshima]. . . . Sidebars include meticulously cited eyewitness quotes or extra insight on particularly important events. Even more information is contained in the maps, period photographs, and well-placed captions that grace every page." SLJ

Includes glossary and bibliographical references

Hama, Larry

★ The **battle** of Iwo Jima; guerilla warfare in the Pacific. by Larry Hama; illustrated by Anthony Williams. Rosen Pub. 2007 48p il map (Graphic battles of World War II) lib bdg $29.25

Grades: 5 6 7 8 9   **940.54**
1. Graphic novels 2. World War, 1939-1945 -- Graphic novels 3. Iwo Jima, Battle of, 1945 -- Graphic novels
ISBN 978-1-4042-0781-3 lib bdg; 1-4042-0781-3 lib bdg
                                    LC 2006007645

"Using a graphic novel to introduce the battle for Iwo Jima makes it very accessible. Before the graphic-novel section of the book begins, Hama provides a short, informative background piece describing the run-up to World War II, the significance of the Japanese war machine, and the importance of the tiny island of Iwo Jima. Then the graphic novel, illustrated by Williams in camouflage colors, does a terrific job of examining the ups and downs of the battle as well as the horror of so many losses—on both sides." Booklist

Includes bibliographical references

Hillstrom, Laurie

The **attack** on Pearl Harbor; [by] Laurie Collier Hillstrom. Omnigraphics 2009 237p il (Defining moments) $49

Grades: 7 8 9 10 11 12   **940.54**
1. Reference books 2. Pearl Harbor (Oahu, Hawaii), Attack on, 1941 3. Pearl Harbor (Hawaii), Attack on, 1941
ISBN 978-0-7808-1069-3; 0-7808-1069-4
                                    LC 2009-4236

"This book is divided into three well-organized sections. Part one provides a narrative overview detailing the events leading up to the attack, the attack itself, and the aftermath, including the U.S. victory in the Pacific as well as the occupation and reconstruction of Japan after World War II. Part two is composed of eight two to three-page biographies of the important figures such as Yamamoto, Roosevelt, and Doris Miller, the first African-American to receive the Navy Cross. A final section of primary documents from the Japanese attack plan to Truman's announcement of the end of the war provides insight into the war in the Pacific. . . . This work is a must-have for reports and assignments." SLJ

Includes glossary and bibliographical references

Holm, Tom

Code talkers and warriors; Native Americans and World War II. Chelsea House 2007 168p il map (Landmark events in Native American history) $35

Grades: 7 8 9 10   940.54

1. World War, 1939-1945 -- Native Americans

ISBN 978-0-7910-9340-5; 0-7910-9340-9

LC 2006102263

"In this title about Native Americans in World War II, Holm . . . expands considerably on his specific topic to highlight significant miliary roles played by Native Americans in conflicts dating back to the sixteenth century. . . . [This is] outstanding. . . . [A] valuable resource." Booklist

Includes bibliographical references

Kuhn, Betsy

Angels of mercy; the Army nurses of World War II. Atheneum Bks. for Young Readers 1999 114p il map $18

Grades: 5 6 7 8   940.54

1. Women in the armed forces 2. World War, 1939-1945 -- Women 3. World War, 1939-1945 -- Medical care -- United States

ISBN 0-689-82044-5

LC 98-36610

Relates the experiences of World War II Army nurses, who brought medical skills, courage, and cheer to hospitals throughout Europe, North Africa, and the Pacific

"Excellent reproductions, maps and a time line accompany the clear, well-written text." SLJ

Includes bibliographical references

Lawton, Clive

★ **Hiroshima**; the story of the first atom bomb. [by] Clive A. Lawton. Candlewick Press 2004 48p il map $18.99

Grades: 5 6 7 8   940.54

1. Atomic bomb 2. World War, 1939-1945 -- Japan 2. Hiroshima (Japan) -- Bombardment, 1945

ISBN 0-7636-2271-0

LC 2004-45166

"Engaging text and powerful photographs are intricately woven together to make a long-lasting impact on readers." Libr Media Connect

Miller, Terry

D-Day; the Allies strike back during World War II. Franklin Watts 2009 64p il map (24/7 goes to war) lib bdg $27; pa $7.95

Grades: 4 5 6   940.54

1. World War, 1939-1945 -- Campaigns -- France

ISBN 978-0-531-25527-8 lib bdg; 0-531-25527-1 lib bdg; 978-0-531-25452-3 pa; 0-531-25452-6 pa

LC 2009016544

The author has "done a remarkable job of discussing and describing [the World War II D-Day invasion] in a limited number of pages. . . . The [book provides a] solid [introduc-

tion], followed by three chapters, one of which is based on the personal experiences of a named soldier, and the other two covering broader historical details and strategies of the battle. . . . Excellent maps and plenty of paintings and vintage photos enhance the [text]." SLJ

Includes bibliographical references

Moore, Kate

★ The **Battle** of Britain. Osprey 2010 200p il map $29.95

Grades: 7 8 9 10   940.54

1. Britain, Battle of, 1940 2. World War, 1939-1945 -- Great Britain

ISBN 978-1-84603-474-9; 1-84603-474-4

"In the summer and autumn of 1940, Britain faced an unparalleled challenge. Forced to beat a quick retreat from Dunkirk with the German Luftwaffe in hot pursuit, the British dug in for what was to be one of the most remarkable feats in the history of human endurance. In this spectacular oversize volume, Moore recounts with notable lucidity and depth the events and characters from both the British and German home fronts during this critical moment in world history and offers an excellent analysis of prewar preparations by both sides. The most outstanding feature of the work is without a doubt the stunning visuals. The book is packed with a fantastic range of archival photos, maps, and war posters." SLJ

Nathan, Amy

Yankee doodle gals; women pilots of World War II. foreword by Eileen Collins. National Geographic Soc. 2001 86p il maps $21

Grades: 6 7 8 9   940.54

1. Women air pilots 2. World War, 1939-1945 -- Aerial operations

ISBN 0-7922-8216-7

LC 2001-560

This describes the Women's Air Force Service Pilots of World War II

"There's plenty of action to involve readers, and the women's perseverance in the face of obstacles is inspiring. Wonderful black-and-white photos extend the text." Booklist

Includes bibliographical references

Nelson, Pete

Left for dead; a young man's search for justice for the USS Indianapolis. [by] Peter Nelson; with a preface by Hunter Scott. Delacorte Press 2002 xx, 201p il hardcover o.p. pa $8.95

Grades: 7 8 9 10   940.54

1. Children 2. Students 3. Naval officers 4. World War, 1939-1945 -- Naval operations 5. Trials (Naval offenses) -- United States 6. World War, 1939-1945 -- Naval operations, American

ISBN 0-385-72959-6; 0-385-73091-8 pa

LC 2001-53774

Recalls the sinking of the U.S.S. Indianapolis at the end of World War II, the navy cover-up and unfair court martial of the ship's captain, and how a young boy helped the survivors set the record straight fifty-five years later.

"Written in simple chronological order, it tells a powerful story." Book Rep

Includes bibliographical references

Ross, Stewart

Hiroshima. Arcturus Pub. 2011 46p il map (A place in history) lib bdg $34.25

Grades: 7 8 9 10　　　　　　　　　　　**940.54**

1. Atomic bomb 2. Hiroshima (Japan) -- Bombardment, 1945

ISBN 978-1-84837-674-8; 1-84837-674-X

LC 2010014149

This describes the city of Hiroshima and broadens "outward, describing the political and economic situations that led up to notable events there. The approach works beautifully. Quotes from participants are a highlight of the [book], and all the maps and photos are clear and informative. [This] will be [a] useful [supplement] to history classes, but [is] accessible enough to appeal as extracurricular material for students already interested in the [topic]." SLJ

Includes glossary and bibliographical references

Pearl Harbor; [by] Stewart Ross and Joe Woodward. Arcturus Pub. 2010 46p il map (A place in history) lib bdg $34.25

Grades: 7 8 9 10　　　　　　　　　　　**940.54**

1. World War, 1939-1945 2. Pearl Harbor (Oahu, Hawaii), Attack on, 1941

ISBN 978-1-84837-676-2; 1-84837-676-6

LC 2010017108

This book describes Pearl Harbor and broadens "outward, describing the political and economic situations that led up to notable events there. The approach works beautifully. Quotes from participants are a highlight of the [book], and all the maps and photos are clear and informative. [This] will be [a] useful [supplement] to history classes, but [is] accessible enough to appeal as extracurricular material for students already interested in the [topic]." SLJ

Includes glossary and bibliographical references

Samuels, Charlie

Propaganda; by Charlie Samuels. Brown Bear Books 2011 48 p. ill. (chiefly col.), col. maps (library) $35.65

Grades: 5 6 7 8　　　　　　　　　　　**940.54**

1. World War, 1939-1945 -- Propaganda 2. World War, 1939-1945

ISBN 1936333236; 9781936333233

LC 2011010241

This book by Charlie Samuels on propaganda is part of the World War II Sourcebook series. "Each page is illustrated. Little-known facts and, sometimes, direct narratives are presented with the information given to the reader. . . . Each book has the same timeline of World War II, maps of both the European and Pacific theaters, interesting biographical snapshots of people involved, and a list of websites that students may use to further explore World War II." (Library Media Connection)

Includes bibliographical references and index.

Soldiers; [Charlie Samuels] Brown Bear Books 2011 48 p. ill. (some col.), maps (col.) (World War II sourcebook) $35.65

Grades: 5 6 7 8　　　　　　　　　　　**940.54**

1. Soldiers 2. World War, 1939-1945 3. Soldiers -- History -- 20th century

ISBN 1936333244; 9781936333240

LC 2011007057

This book by Charlie Samuels, part of the World War II Sourcebook series, "Describes the life of a soldier in World War II, from recruitment efforts around the world, to the daily life during the fighting." (Publisher's note)

Includes bibliographical references (p. 47) and index

Spying and security; by Charlie Samuels. Brown Bear Books 2012 48 p. ill. (some col.) (World War II Sourcebook) $35.65

Grades: 5 6 7 8　　　　　　　　　　　**940.54**

1. Police -- History -- 20th century 2. World War, 1939-1945 -- Secret service 3. Spies -- History -- 20th century 4. Espionage -- History -- 20th century 5. World War, 1939-1945 -- Cryptography

ISBN 1936333252; 9781936333257

LC 2011007058

This book by Charlie Samuels, part of the World War II Sourcebook, provides a history of spying and security for young readers. It "Describes the role spies and police played around the world during World War II, from controlling riots to gathering intelligence from the enemy." (Publisher's note)

Seiple, Samantha

Ghosts in the fog; the untold story of Alaska's WWII invasion. Scholastic 2011 221p il map $16.99

Grades: 5 6 7 8　　　　　　　　　　　**940.54**

1. World War, 1939-1945 -- Campaigns

ISBN 978-0-545-29654-0; 0-545-29654-4

LC 2011027821

"A little-known story from World War II shows the unique role played by a small group of military personal and native civilians in a remote region of the county. The role of Alaska in World War II following the attack on Pearl Harbor is not often told. . . . The story illuminates the cultural differences between the American and Japanese cultures at that time as well as the reluctance of the U.S. government to treat the native Alaskans as full citizens. The narrative is full of details, and . . . the text is supported by many photographs of those involved. Maps, including a strategic military map, increase the level of specificity." Kirkus

Includes bibliographical references

Stone, Tanya Lee

★ **Courage** has no color, the true story of the Triple Nickles; America's first black paratroopers. Tanya Lee Stone. Candlewick Press 2013 160 p. $24.99

Grades: 5 6 7 8　　　　　　　　　　　**940.54**

1. Parachute troops 2. World War, 1939-1945 3. African American soldiers

ISBN 0763651176; 9780763651176

LC 2012942315

This book tells the "untold story of the 555th Parachute Infantry Battalion, America's first black paratroopers." Enlisted black men "faced the tyranny of racial discrimination on the homefront. . . . When 1st Sgt. Walter Morris, whose men served as guards at The Parachute School at Fort Benning, saw white soldiers training to be paratroopers, he knew his men would have to train and act like them to be treated like soldiers." (Kirkus Reviews)

Torres, John Albert

The **Battle** of Midway; by John A. Torres. Mitchell Lane Publishers 2011 48p il map (Technologies and strategies in battle) lib bdg $29.95

Grades: 6 7 8 9   940.54

1. Midway, Battle of, 1942 2. World War, 1939-1945 -- Campaigns

ISBN 978-1-61228-078-3; 1-61228-078-1

LC 2011002746

This "is an in-depth account of the 1942 Battle of Midway, detailing how it was fought by sea and air by the U.S. and Japan. . . . This useful research source packs a wealth of information into its straightforward narrative. This colorful layout intersperses abundant visuals, including maps and archival photos as well as sidebars." Booklist

Includes glossary and bibliographical references

Townsend, John

World War II. Arcturus Pub. 2011 46p il (Secret history) lib bdg $32.80

Grades: 7 8 9 10   940.54

1. World War, 1939-1945

ISBN 978-1-84837-701-1; 1-84837-701-0

LC 2010012017

This book explores the secrets of World War II. Throughout the war, both sides made great efforts to uncover enemy plans and keep their own secrets hidden. They engaged in secret operations, plots, and missions, always attempting to wrongfoot the enemy or take them by surprise.

"The title of the Secret History series will grab readers, even reluctant ones, and they won't be disappointed by the intriguing info regarding codes and code breakers, spies, terrorists, and double agents, with profiles of heroes and traitors on all sides. . . . The readable design, with clear type on thick, high-quality paper, includes lots of sidebars, photos, screens, and quotes." Booklist

Includes bibliographical references

Williams, Brian

The **Normandy** beaches. Arcturus Pub. 2011 46p il map (A place in history) lib bdg $34.25

Grades: 7 8 9 10   940.54

1. Normandy (France), Attack on, 1944 2. World War, 1939-1945 -- Campaigns -- France

ISBN 978-1-84837-675-5; 1-84837-675-8

LC 2010014194

This book begins with describing the Normandy beaches and broadens "outward, describing the political and economic situations that led up to notable events there. The approach works beautifully. Quotes from participants are a highlight of the [book], and all the maps and photos are clear and informative. [This] will be [a] useful [supplement] to history classes, but [is] accessible enough to appeal as ex-

tracurricular material for students already interested in the [topic]." SLJ

Includes glossary and bibliographical references

Wukovits, John F., 1944-

The **bombing** of Pearl Harbor; by John F. Wukovits. Lucent Books 2011 112 p. ill. (some col.), photographs (library) $34.95

Grades: 6 7 8 9   940.54

1. World War, 1939-1945 -- Causes 2. Pearl Harbor (Oahu, Hawaii), Attack on, 1941 3. Pearl Harbor (Hawaii), Attack on, 1941

ISBN 1420503308; 9781420503302

LC 2010035993

This book by John Wukovits is part of the World History series and looks at the bombing of Pearl Harbor. Each book in the series offers an "overview of an important historical event or period. The series is designed both to acquaint readers with the basics of history and to make them aware that their lives and their own historical era are an intimate part of the ongoing human saga." (Publisher's note)

Includes bibliographical references (p. 97-100) and index.

Zaloga, Steven J.

The **most** daring raid of World War II; D-Day--Pointe-du-Hoc. Rosen Pub. 2011 64p il map (The most daring raids in history) lib bdg $29.25

Grades: 7 8 9 10   940.54

1. Normandy (France), Attack on, 1944 2. World War, 1939-1945 -- Campaigns -- France

ISBN 978-1-4488-1867-9; 1-4488-1867-2

LC 2010030631

This describes the U.S. Army Rangers' attack on the German gun battery on Pointe-du-Hoc in Normandy on D-day in 1944.

This book is "packed with facts, covering the details of the action, the people involved, and the tools used, in engaging prose. The authors cite their sources thoroughly. . . . Diagrams, photos, . . . and maps make the action easy to follow and provide visual context for the raids. . . . This . . . is sure to find a large readership." SLJ

Includes glossary and bibliographical references

941   British Isles

Dillon, Patrick

The **story** of Britain from the Norman Conquest to the European Union; illustrated by P.J. Lynch. Candlewick Press 2011 341p il map $21.99

Grades: 5 6 7 8   941

1. Great Britain -- History

ISBN 978-0-7636-5122-0; 0-7636-5122-2

LC 2010038883

"This well-written, thoughtfully illustrated volume [is] an indispensible tool for European history buffs." Horn Book Guide

Indovino, Shaina C.

United Kingdom; by Rae Simons and Shaina C. Indovino. Mason Crest Publishers 2012 64 p. col. ill., col. maps (library) $22.95

Grades: 5 6 7 8   **941**
  1. Great Britain
  ISBN 1422222616; 9781422222614; 9781422222928
                      LC 2010051852

This book on the United Kingdom by Rae Simons and Shaina Carmel Indovino "covers Modern Issues, History and Government, The Economy, People and Culture, and Looking to the Future. . . Identical information on "The Formation of the European Union" appears in every book" in the series. (Library Media Connection)

Includes bibliographical references (p. 60) and index.

941.081   Reign of Victoria, 1837-1901

Schomp, Virginia

Victoria and her court. Marshall Cavendish Benchmark 2010 80p il (Life in Victorian England) lib bdg $34.21

Grades: 6 7 8 9   **941.081**
  1. Queens 2. Courts and courtiers
  ISBN 978-1-60870-028-8 lib bdg; 1-60870-028-3 lib bdg

A social history of Victorian England, focusing on the upper echelons of society during the reign of Queen Victoria (1837-1901)

This "is clearly written, thorough, and informative. The visually rich layout includes photographs and paintings from the time period, full-page illustrations, and attention-grabbing sidebars. Most appealing are the primary source quotations, which are plentiful and relevant.." Libr Media Connect

Includes glossary and bibliographical references

941.1   Scotland

Waldron, Melanie

Scotland; by Melanie Waldron. Heinemann Library 2012 48 p. col. ill., col. maps (library) $32.65; (paperback) $8.99

Grades: 6 7 8 9   **941.1**
  1. Culture 2. Scotland
  ISBN 1432952161; 9781432952167; 9781432952419
                      LC 2010044776

This book by Melanie Waldron is part of the Countries Around the World series and looks at Scotland. This entry "offers complete coverage of this . . . country, including sections on history, geography, wildlife, infrastructure and government, and culture. It also includes a detailed fact file, maps and charts, and a traceable flag." (Publisher's note)

Includes bibliographical references (p. 44) and index.

941.5   Ireland

McQuinn, Colm

★ Ireland; [by] Anna and Colm McQuinn; Elizabeth Malcolm and John McDonagh, consultants. National Geographic 2008 64p il map (Countries of the world) lib bdg $27.90

Grades: 4 5 6 7   **941.5**
  1. Ireland
  ISBN 978-1-4263-0299-2 lib bdg; 1-4263-0299-1 lib bdg

This describes the geography, nature, history, people and culture, government, and economy of Ireland.

Includes glossary and bibliographical references

941.508   Ireland-- 1800-

Bartoletti, Susan Campbell

★ Black potatoes; the story of the great Irish famine, 1845-1850. Houghton Mifflin 2001 184p il hardcover o.p. pa $9.95

Grades: 7 8 9 10   **941.508**
  1. Famines 2. Ireland -- History -- Famine, 1845-1852
  ISBN 0-618-00271-5; 0-618-54883-1 pa
                      LC 2001-24156

Bartoletti discusses "the potato blight, its . . . causes, and the societal attitudes and political legacies that exacerbated the famine.

"The bibliography (also narrative) provides some of the most fascinating historical reading in the book. Overall, a useful addition to collections, for both personal and research uses." SLJ

Includes bibliographical references

Fradin, Dennis Brindell

The Irish potato famine; by Dennis Fradin. Marshall Cavendish Benchmark 2012 32 p. (library) $34.21

Grades: 5 6 7 8   **941.508**
  1. Famines 2. Ireland -- History -- Famine, 1845-1852 3. Escapes -- Ireland -- History -- 19th century 4. Disaster victims -- Ireland -- History -- 19th century
  ISBN 1608704734; 9781608704736
                      LC 2010018788

This book, part of the Great Escapes series, focuses on the Irish Potato Famine. "Each book begins with an introduction to an individual who escaped, followed by the history of the precipitating events, the escape itself, and a follow-up on what happened after the escape. Each title includes a timeline, notes, and additional information on the topic." (Library Media Connection)

Includes bibliographical references and index.

942   England and Wales

Banting, Erinn

England; by Erinn Banting; edited by Sarah Cairns; illustrated by Jeff Crosby, Dianne Eastman, and David Wysotski. Revised ed. Crabtree Pub. Co.

2012 32 p. ill. (some col.) (library) $26.60; (paperback) $8.95; (ebook) $26.60

Grades: 4 5 6   **942**

1. Culture 2. England

ISBN 0778798283; 9780778798286; 9780778798316; 9781427180056 pdf

LC 2012013776

This book by Erinn Banting is part of the Lands, Peoples and Cultures Series and looks at the culture of England. The books offer information about "folktales, sports, and history." Also included are "a table of contents, short glossary (words highlighted in test) and index." (Catholic Library World)

Includes index

Blashfield, Jean F.

England; by Jean F. Blashfield. Children's Press 2013 144 p. ill. (some col.), col. maps (library) $40.00

Grades: 4 5 6 7   **942**

1. England

ISBN 9780531275429

LC 2012000503

This book by Jean F. Blashfield, part of the "Enchantment of the World" series, "describes the geography, history, economy, language, religions, culture, people, plants, and animals of England." (Publisher's note)

It includes "topics as recent as the 2012 Olympics and 2012 Grammy winners, as well as the latest royal wedding." (Children's Literature)

Includes bibliographical references (p. 134-135) and index.

942.02   Norman period, 1066-1154

Hamilton, Janice

The **Norman** conquest of England; by Janice Hamilton. Twenty-First Century Books 2008 un il map (Pivotal moments in history) lib bdg $38.60

Grades: 7 8 9 10   **942.02**

1. Normans 2. Kings

ISBN 978-0-8225-5902-3

LC 2006102629

This is an account of the invasion and conquest of England by the Normans in 1066 and its consequences.

This is "clearly written and interesting enough for browsers as well as report writers. Maps, full-color and black-and-white photos, and reproductions of manuscripts contribute to the attractive format and make the subject matter come alive." SLJ

Includes glossary and bibliographical references

942.03   Period of House of Plantagenet, 1154-1399

Brooks, Polly Schoyer

Queen Eleanor, Independent Spirit of the Medieval World; A Biography of Eleanor of Aquitaine.

1st ed. Houghton Mifflin 1999 vii, 183 p.p ill. (paperback) $8.95

Grades: 7 8 9   **942.03**

1. Queens

ISBN 0395981395; 9780395981399

LC 82048776

This is a biography of Eleanor of Aquitaine, the twelfth-century queen, first of France, then of England, who was the wife of Henry II and mother of several notable sons, including Richard the Lionhearted. "Born in 1122, Eleanor refused to be confined by the traditional gender roles of her time. She became well educated, gaining political and governing know-how from her father, William X, duke of Aquitaine." (Publisher's note)

Includes bibliography (p. 171-172) and index.

Levy, Debbie

The **signing** of the Magna Carta. Twenty-First Century Books 2008 160p il map (Pivotal moments in history) lib bdg $38.60

Grades: 7 8 9 10 11 12   **942.03**

1. Magna Carta 2. Great Britain -- History -- 1154-1399, Plantagenets

ISBN 978-0-8225-5917-7 lib bdg; 0-8225-5917-X lib bdg

LC 2005-20971

This "research source explains the intent of the treaty of 1215 that became the Magna Carta, the factors that produced it, as well as its evolution, historical significance, and relevance today. . . . The clear explanation of the 'Great Charter's' historical context accompanied by informative inserts and beautiful, relevant illustrations make this a book to dip into as well as to read through." Voice Youth Advocates

Includes glossary and bibliographical references

942.05   Period of House of Tudor, 1485-1603

Aronson, Marc

★ **Sir** Walter Ralegh and the quest for El Dorado. Clarion Bks. 2000 222p il map $20

Grades: 7 8 9 10   **942.05**

1. Poets 2. Authors 3. Explorers 4. Historians 5. Courtiers 6. Travel writers 7. Guiana -- Discovery and exploration 8. Explorers -- Great Britain -- Biography 9. Great Britain -- Court and courtiers -- Biography

ISBN 0-395-84827-X

LC 99-43096

"Incorporating critical examinations of period art and poetry as well as standard historical documentary evidence and pausing frequently to review and explicitly support its thesis, this title is at once lively, accessible, and challenging. Period illustrations, an index, and fastidiously annotated endnotes and bibliography are included." Bull Cent Child Books

Includes bibliographical references

Hollihan, Kerrie Logan

Elizabeth I--the people's queen; her life and times: 21 activities. Chicago Review Press 2011 129p il pa $16.95

Grades: 4 5 6 7 8   **942.05**
1. Queens 2. Great Britain -- History -- 1485-1603, Tudors
ISBN 978-1-56976-349-0; 1-56976-349-6
    LC 2010047647
This is an interactive biography of Queen Elizabeth I.
"The writing is clear and suited to readers with no previous knowledge of the topic. The activities vary in difficulty, from reading The Faerie Queen, to creating a family coat of arms, to growing a knot garden. The book is well illustrated with black-and-white reproductions of portraits, engravings, and paintings depicting major events in the Tudors' lives. . . . This well-organized book succeeds at being interesting and scholarly at the same time." SLJ
Includes bibliographical references

Kallen, Stuart A.
★ **Elizabethan** England; by Stuart A. Kallen. ReferencePoint Press 2013 96 p. (Understanding world history series) (hardcover) $27.95
Grades: 7 8 9 10   **942.05**
1. Great Britain -- History -- 1558-1603, Elizabeth
ISBN 1601524846; 9781601524843
    LC 2012026174
This book, part of the Understanding World History series, looks at Elizabethan England. It "relates Queen Elizabeth I's advance to power and considers the hardships of life in London, the rise of the arts during the Renaissance, and Elizabeth's role as 'pirate queen,' endorsing privateering, slave trading, and the defeat of the Spanish Armanda." (Booklist)
Includes bibliographical references and index

942.9   Wales

Hestler, Anna
Wales; [by] Anna Hestler and Jo-Ann Spilling. 2nd ed.; Marshall Cavendish Benchmark 2011 144p il map (Cultures of the world) lib bdg $42.79
Grades: 5 6 7 8   **942.9**
1. Wales
ISBN 978-1-6087-0457-6; 1-6087-0457-2
    LC 2010030339
First published 2001
Provides information on the geography, history, wildlife, governmental structure, economy, cultural diversity, peoples, religion, and culture of Wales.
"Plentiful color photographs accompany substantial amounts of information." Booklist
Includes glossary and bibliographical references

943   Germany and neighboring central European countries

Burgan, Michael
The **Berlin** airlift; by Michael Burgan. Compass Point Books 2007 48 p. ill. (some col.) (We the people) (paperback) $7.95; (library) $27.99

Grades: 4 5 6 7   **943**
1. Berlin (Germany) -- History -- Blockade, 1948-1949
ISBN 9780756520366; 0756520363; 075652024X; 9780756520243
    LC 2006006766
Examines the joint effort of the United States and Great Britain who flew in around the clock to deliver supplies to Berlin during the Soviet blockade of 1948-49.
"The writing is clear and concise and the vocabulary is age-appropriate. [This] title contains excellent contemporary photographs." SLJ
Includes bibliographical references (p. 46-47) and index.

Indovino, Shaina C.
Germany; by Ida Walker and Shaina C. Indovino. Mason Crest Publishers 2013 64 p. ill. (some col.), col. maps (library) $22.95
Grades: 5 6 7 8   **943**
1. Germany 2. Germany -- Politics and government
ISBN 1422222438; 9781422222430
    LC 2010051291
This book on Germany by Ida Walker and Shaina Carmel Indovino is part of the "Major European Nations" series, which "stresses the modern relationships, goals, and problems of the European Union. . . . Chapters begin with 'Modern Issues' and a brief summary of the country's history and government, followed by chapters on economy, people and culture, and 'Looking to the Future.' In addition, there is a time line and a few suggestions for finding out more." (School Library Journal)

Rooney, Anne
The **Berlin** Wall. Arcturus Pub. 2011 46p il (A place in history) lib bdg $34.25
Grades: 7 8 9 10   **943**
1. Cold war 2. Berlin Wall (1961-1989) 3. Germany -- History -- 1945-1990
ISBN 978-1-84837-673-1; 1-84837-673-1
    LC 2010014193
This book begins with The Berlin Wall as a landmark and broadens "outward, describing the political and economic situations that led up to notable events there. The approach works beautifully. Quotes from participants are a highlight of the [book], and all the maps and photos are clear and informative. [This] will be [a] useful [supplement] to history classes, but [is] accessible enough to appeal as extracurricular material for students already interested in the [topic]." SLJ
Includes glossary and bibliographical references

Russell, Henry
★ **Germany**; [by] Henry Russell; Benedict Kork and Antje Schlottmann, consultants. National Geographic 2007 64p il map (Countries of the world) lib bdg $27.90
Grades: 4 5 6 7   **943**
1. Germany
ISBN 978-1-4263-0059-2
    LC 2007024677
Describes the geography, nature, history, people and culture, government and economy of Germany.

This "appealing [title has] wonderful photographs and maps. . . . The [book offers] reliable sources for country research, and the interesting and current material holds browsing potential as well." SLJ

Includes glossary and bibliographical references

943.085   Period of Weimar Republic, 1918-1933

Freeman, Charles

Why did the rise of the Nazis happen? Gareth Stevens Pub. 2011 48p il map (Moments in history) lib bdg $31.75; pa $14.05

Grades: 6 7 8 9   943.085

1. Heads of state 2. National socialism 3. Nazi leaders
ISBN 978-1-4339-4175-7 lib bdg; 1-4339-4175-9 lib bdg; 978-1-4339-4176-4 pa; 1-4339-4176-7 pa

LC 2010017229

"Examines the events that served as . . . [precursors to the rise of the Nazis]. . . . Brightly colored pullout boxes highlight important turning points, the perspective of the everyday man, and further information on why specific events occurred. Numerous photographs help readers visualize concepts more fully. . . . Students should be able to easily use this resource." Libr Media Connect

Includes glossary and bibliographical references

943.086   Period of Third Reich, 1933-1945

Bartoletti, Susan Campbell

★ Hitler Youth; growing up in Hitler's shadow. Scholastic Nonfiction 2005 176p il map $19.95

Grades: 7 8 9 10   943.086

1. National socialism 2. Holocaust, 1933-1945
ISBN 0-439-35379-3

LC 2004-51040

A Newbery Medal honor book, 2006

"Bartoletti draws on oral histories, diaries, letters, and her own extensive interviews with Holocaust survivors, Hitler Youth, resisters, and bystanders to tell the history from the viewpoints of people who were there. . . . The stirring photos tell more of the story. . . . The extensive back matter is a part of the gripping narrative." Booklist

Includes bibliographical references

Living in Nazi Germany; Elaine Halleck, book editor. Greenhaven Press 2004 158p il map (Exploring cultural history) $29.95; pa $21.20

Grades: 7 8 9 10   943.086

1. National socialism 2. Germany -- Politics and government -- 1933-1945
ISBN 0-7377-1731-9; 0-7377-1732-7 pa

LC 2003-57961

This includes "eyewitness accounts from victims of Hitler's brutality as well as from those who found places in the Nazi machine. . . . Most of the accounts are from less well known sources, and many are compelling. Excerpts from a few familiar volumes, such as Albert Speer's memoirs and the wartime diaries of Joseph Goebbels, also ap-

pear. . . . An effective, insightful look at aspects of the Nazi system." Booklist

Includes bibliographical references

Shuter, Jane

Resistance to the Nazis. Heinemann Lib. 2003 56p il map (Holocaust) lib bdg $28.50; pa $8.95

Grades: 7 8 9 10   943.086

1. Holocaust, 1933-1945 2. World War, 1939-1945 -- Underground movements 3. Anti-Nazi movement -- Europe 4. Holocaust, Jewish (1939-1945)
ISBN 1-4034-0814-9 lib bdg; 1-4034-3206-6 pa

LC 2002-6853

This is "an excellent blend of overview and personal stories." SLJ

Includes glossary and bibliographical references

943.6   Austria and Liechtenstein

Indovino, Shaina C.

Austria; by Jeanine Sanna and Shaina C. Indovino. Mason Crest Publishers 2012 64 p. col. ill., col. maps (library) $22.95

Grades: 5 6 7 8   943.6

1. Austria -- History 2. Austria
ISBN 1422222322; 9781422222324

LC 2010051075

This book, part of the Major European Union Nations series, focuses on Austria. In "addition to history, the book details government, economy, culture, and prospects for the future. There is a glossary and an index and a nice chronology in the back of the book as well as a brief bibliography and a list of photo credits." Children's Literature

Includes bibliographical references (p. 57) and index.

943.7   Czech Republic and Slovakia

Sioras, Efstathia

Czech Republic; [by] Efstathia Sioras and Michael Spilling. Marshall Cavendish Benchmark 2010 144p il map (Cultures of the world) lib bdg $42.79

Grades: 5 6 7 8   943.7

1. Czech Republic
ISBN 978-0-7614-4476-3 lib bdg; 0-7614-4476-9 lib bdg

LC 2009003185

This describes the geography, history, wildlife, governmental structure, economy, cultural diversity, peoples, religion, and culture of the Czech Republic

Includes glossary and bibliographical references

943.710   Period of Republic, 1993-

Docalavich, Heather

Czech Republic; by Heather Docalavich and Shaina C. Indovino. Mason Crest Publishers 2013

64 p. col. ill. col. maps (library) $344.25; (library) $22.95; (ebook) $28.95

Grades: 5 6 7 8   **943.710**

  1. Czech Republic 2. European Union
  ISBN 1422222373; 9781422222317 set;
  9781422222379; 9781422222683; 9781422292648

             LC 2010051083

This book by Heather Docalavich is part of the Major European Union Nations series and focuses on the Czech Republic. "The Czech Republic is one of the newest countries in the world. It's also new to the EU—it joined in 2004. People have lived in what we now call the Czech Republic for thousands of years, however. This land has a long history and is moving forward while dealing with challenges like the recent global recession." (Publisher's note)

Includes bibliographical references (p. 57-58, 63) and index.

943.8 Poland

Deckker, Zilah

  ★ **Poland**; [by] Zilah Deckker; Richard Butterwick and Iwona Sagan, consultants. National Geographic 2008 64p il map (Countries of the world) lib bdg $27.90

Grades: 4 5 6 7   **943.8**

  1. Poland
  ISBN 978-1-4263-0201-5

             LC 2007047823

This describes the geography, nature, history, people and culture, government, and economy of Poland.

Includes glossary and bibliographical references

Docalavich, Heather

  Poland; by Healther Docalavich and Shaina C. Indovino. Mason Crest Publishers 2013 64 p. col. ill., col. maps (library) $22.95

Grades: 5 6 7 8   **943.8**

  1. Poland 2. European Union
  ISBN 1422222543; 9781422222546

             LC 2010051465

This book by Heather Docalavich and Shaina C. Indovino is part of the Major European Union Nations series and looks at Poland. "It joined the EU in 2004 . . . . For long time, Poland has been home to scientific thinkers, artists, and musicians. Today, it is one of the countries that have weathered the global recession the best, proving this nation's strength." (Publisher's note)

Includes bibliographical references

Kadziolka, Jan

  Poland; [by] Jan Kadziolka, Tadeusz Wojciechowski. Oliver Press 2011 48p il map (Looking at Europe) lib bdg $24.95

Grades: 7 8 9 10   **943.8**

  1. Poland
  ISBN 978-1-881508-89-2; 1-881508-89-7

             LC 2009035350

This describes Poland today, its history, cities, transportation, culture, education, economy, cuisine, tourism, and natural environment.

This will "best suit students with good vocabularies and some knowledge of European history. . . . [It is] clearly written and well organized. . . . [It includes] many clear photos as well as colorful sidebars. . . . Attractive, informative." Booklist

Includes glossary and bibliographical references

943.9 Hungary

Lang, Stephan

  Hungary. Oliver Press 2011 48p il map (Looking at Europe) lib bdg $24.95

Grades: 7 8 9 10   **943.9**

  1. Hungary
  ISBN 978-1-881508-88-5; 1-881508-88-9

             LC 2009033276

This describes Hungary today, its history, cities, transportation, culture, education, economy, cuisine, tourism, and natural environment.

This will "best suit students with good vocabularies and some knowledge of European history. . . . [It is] clearly written and well organized. . . . [It includes] many clear photos as well as colorful sidebars. . . . Attractive, informative." Booklist

Includes glossary and bibliographical references

944 France and Monaco

Indovino, Shaina C.

  France; by Jeanine Sanna and Shaina C. Indovino. Mason Crest Publishers 2013 64 p. col. ill., col. maps (hardcover) $22.95

Grades: 5 6 7 8   **944**

  1. France
  ISBN 142222242X; 9781422222423

             LC 2010051290

This book about France "covers Modern Issues, History and Government, The Economy, People and Culture, and Looking to the Future." Lib Med Con

Includes bibliographical references

King, David C.

  ★ **Monaco**; [by] David C. King. Marshall Cavendish Benchmark 2008 144p il map (Cultures of the world) lib bdg $42.79

Grades: 5 6 7 8   **944**

  1. Monaco
  ISBN 978-0-7614-2567-0

             LC 2006030238

This describes the geography, history, government, economy, environment, people, and culture of Monaco

Includes glossary and bibliographical references

Sonneborn, Liz

  France; by Liz Sonneborn. Children's Press 2013 144 p. ill., maps (library) $40

Grades: 5 6 7 8   **944**
1. France
ISBN 0531256006; 9780531256008

LC 2012047113

This book by Liz Sonneborn is part of the Enchantment of the World series and looks at France. It covers "history, government, geography, natural resources, economics, the arts, and culture. . . . Maps, charts, sidebars highlighting items of interest, a time line, and a 'Fast Facts' section add to the presentation."

Includes bibliographical references (page 134) and index

944.04   France since 1789

Riggs, Kate
The **French** Revolution. Creative Education 2009 48p il map (Days of change) lib bdg $32.80
Grades: 5 6 7 8   **944.04**
1. France -- History -- 1789-1799, Revolution
ISBN 978-1-58341-734-8 lib bdg; 1-58341-734-6 lib bdg

LC 2008009728

"With elegant design and mature prose, the Days of Change series is an ideal starting point for all manner of school projects. . . . The political pressures at the center of The French Revolution are difficult to dramatize, but Riggs carefully lays out the factions and civil disobedience that led to the Declaration of the Rights of Man and of The Citizen—and then the emperor's reign that overthrew everything." Booklist

Includes bibliographical references

945   Italy, San Marino, Vatican City, Malta

Indovino, Shaina C.
Italy; by Ademola O. Sadik and Shaina C. Indovino. Mason Crest Publishers 2013 64 p. ill. (col. ill.), maps (library) $22.95
Grades: 5 6 7 8   **945**
1. Women in the workplace 2. Italy
ISBN 1422222489; 9781422222485

LC 2010051333

This book by Ademola O. Sadek and Shaina C. Indovino is part of the Major European Nations series and looks at Italy. "Chapters begin with "Modem Issues" and a brief summary of the country's history and government, followed by chapters on economy, people and culture, and 'Looking to the Future.'" The texts "liken Italy's treatment of the "Roma" (Gypsies) to the U.S. treatment of the American Indian; the social standing of Italy's women is examined." (School Library Journal)

945.8   Sicily and adjacent islands

Sheehan, Sean
Malta; by Sean Sheehan and Yong Jui Lin. 2nd ed. Marshall Cavendish Benchmark 2010 144 p. col. ill. (library) $47.07

Grades: 5 6 7 8   **945.8**
1. Malta 2. Culture
ISBN 1608700240; 9781608700240

LC 2010000733

This book by Sean Sheehan is part of the Cultures of the World series and looks at Malta. The books in the series provide "broad overviews of each country's culture, geography, and history. The . . . texts discuss government, economy, people, lifestyles, religion, language, arts and leisure, festivals, and food." (School Library Journal)

Includes bibliographical references (p. 142) and index.

946   Spain, Andorra, Gibraltar, Portugal

Augustin, Byron
Andorra; by Byron D. Augustin. Marshall Cavendish Benchmark 2009 144p il map (Cultures of the world) lib bdg $42.79
Grades: 5 6 7 8   **946**
1. Andorra
ISBN 978-0-7614-3122-0 lib bdg; 0-7614-3122-5 lib bdg

LC 2007040356

"Provides comprehensive information on the geography, history, governmental structure, economy, cultural diversity, peoples, religion, and culture of Andorra." Publisher's note

Includes glossary and bibliographical references

Croy, Anita
Spain. National Geographic 2010 64p il map (Countries of the world) lib bdg $27.90
Grades: 4 5 6 7   **946**
1. Spain
ISBN 978-1-4263-0633-4 lib bdg; 1-4263-0633-4 lib bdg

This describes the geography, nature, history, people and culture, government and economy of Spain

"The information is substantial but not overwhelming. The [text is] clear, and the discussion points are well chosen. . . . [The text is] complemented with stunning photographs." SLJ

Includes glossary and bibliographical references

Hanks, Reuel R.
Spain; by Zoran Pavlovic and Reuel Hanks. Chelsea House 2006 104 p. col. ill., col. maps (library) $35.00; (hardcover) $35
Grades: 5 6 7 8   **946**
1. Spain 2. European Union
ISBN 9780791066973 out of print; 1617530476; 9781617530470

LC 2006002218

This book by Zoran Pavlovic is part of the Modem World Nations series and looks at Spain. "Although Spain is now part of a unified Europe, . . . it is also a land divided by a combination of its own history, ethnicity, and geography." This entry "offers readers a wealth of information about this nation, touching on a variety of topics such as Spanish geography, history, political evolution, and ethnic issues." (Publisher's note)

Includes bibliographical references (p. 96) and index.

Indovino, Shaina C.
Spain; by Rae Simons and Shaina C. Indovino. Mason Crest Publishers 2013 64 p. col. ill., col. maps (library) $22.95
Grades: 5 6 7 8   **946**
  1. Spain 2. European Union
  ISBN 9781422222904; 1422222594; 9781422222591
             LC 2010051847

This book by Rae Simons is part of the Major European Union Nations series and looks at Spain. "Spain has it all: beaches, modern cities, soaring architecture, mountains, and more. It has been a member of the EU since 1986. From the ancient Celts to the Moors to the Christian kings and queens, many people have influenced Spain. It has recently taken a step back in the current financial crisis, but this proud nation is slowly getting back on its feet." (Publisher's note)

946.9   Portugal

Deckker, Zilah
  ★ **Portugal**. National Geographic 2009 64p il map (Countries of the world) lib bdg $27.90
Grades: 4 5 6 7   **946.9**
  1. Portugal
  ISBN 978-1-4263-0390-6 lib bdg; 1-4263-0390-4 lib bdg
             LC 2009275584

This describes the geography, nature, history, people and culture, government and economy of Portugal
  Includes glossary and bibliographical references

Etingoff, Kim
  Portugal; by Kim Etingoff and Shaina C. Indovino. Mason Crest Publishers 2013 64 p. col. ill. (library) $22.95
Grades: 5 6 7 8   **946.9**
  1. Portugal 2. European Union
  ISBN 1422222551; 9781422222553
             LC 2010051466

This book by Kim Etingoff and Shaina C. Indovino is part of the Major European Union Nations series and looks at Portugal. "Long ago, Portugal was one of the world's most powerful countries, as it explored and conquered places far from home. Today, it is a nation that has had some economic and social struggles, but also some triumphs. It joined the EU in 1986." (Publisher's note)

947   Russia and neighboring east European countries

Gottfried, Ted
  The **road** to Communism; illustrated by Melanie Reim. 21st Cent. Bks. (Brookfield) 2002 144p il lib bdg $28.90

Grades: 8 9 10 11 12   **947**
  1. Soviet Union -- History -- 1917-1921, Revolution
  ISBN 0-7613-2557-3
             LC 2001-52252

Chronicles the Czarist Russian Empire in the 1800s, the birth of Bolshevism, events leading to the Russian Revolution of 1917, and the development of new political structures in its aftermath

"Gottfried writes with clarity and distance even as he narrates the dramatic details of the political conflict and the emotion of the 'dream that failed.'" Booklist
  Includes glossary and bibliographical references

Yomtov, Nel
  Russia; by Nel Yomtov. Children's Press 2012 144 p. col. ill., col. maps (library) $40
Grades: 5 6 7 8   **947**
  1. Russia (Federation)
  ISBN 0531275450; 9780531275450
             LC 2012000520

This children's book, by Nel Yomtov, describes the geography and culture of Russia as part of the "Enchantment of the World" series. The book includes "colourful photos . . . [with] views of foreign cities and landscapes," facts and statistics on "interesting people, places, and events" in Russian history, and "delicious, easy recipes [to] give readers the opportunity to experience foreign cuisine firsthand." (Publisher's note)
  Includes bibliographical references

947.084   Russia -- 1917-1991

Gay, Kathlyn
  The **aftermath** of the Russian Revolution. Twenty-First Century Books 2009 160p il (Aftermath of history) lib bdg $38.60
Grades: 8 9 10 11 12   **947.084**
  1. Soviet Union -- History
  ISBN 978-0-8225-9092-7; 0-8225-9092-1
             LC 2008-25276

This book "begins with an overview of the Czar's Russia and the political machinations that brought about revolution. The disputes between different revolutionary groups led to the eventual triumph of the Bolsheviks and the reigns of Lenin and Stalin. Stalin's brutality in particular receives a lot of attention. The final chapters cover the transition to a more open society, the fall of the Soviet Union, and the age of Putin." SLJ
  Includes glossary and bibliographical references

The **Rise** of the Soviet Union; Tom Streissguth, book editor. Greenhaven Press 2002 256p (Turning points in world history) hardcover o.p. pa $23.70
Grades: 7 8 9 10   **947.084**
1. Soviet Union -- History
  ISBN 0-7377-0929-4; 0-7377-0928-6 pa
             LC 2001-40866

A collection of essays concerning the social, economic and political issues in the history of the Soviet Union
  Includes bibliographical references

947.085 Russia -- 1953-1991

Langley, Andrew
The **collapse** of the Soviet Union; the end of
an empire. Compass Point Books 2006 96p il map
(Snapshots in history) lib bdg $31.93
Grades: 7 8 9 10   **947.085**
   1. Soviet Union -- History
   ISBN 978-0-7565-2009-0; 0-7565-2009-6
                                   LC 2006003003
   This "describes leaders, their plans, and their ultimate
downfalls, from the removal of Tsar Nicholas II to the prob-
lems of present-day Russia. [This book is] great for research
. . . brief but comprehensive." SLJ
   Includes glossary and bibliographical references

947.5 Caucasus

Dhilawala, Sakina
   ★ **Armenia**; [by] Sakina Dhilawala. 2nd ed.;
Marshall Cavendish Benchmark 2008 144p il map
(Cultures of the world) lib bdg $39.93
Grades: 5 6 7 8   **947.5**
   ISBN 978-0-7614-2029-3
                                   LC 2007014890
   First published 1997
   "Provides comprehensive information on the geography,
history, wildlife, governmental structure, economy, cultural
diversity, peoples, religion, and culture of Armenia." Pub-
lisher's note
   Includes glossary and bibliographical references

947.7 Ukraine

Bassis, Volodymyr
   ★ **Ukraine**; [by] Volodymyr Bassis & Sakina
Dhilawala. 2nd ed.; Marshall Cavendish Benchmark
2008 144p il map (Cultures of the world) lib bdg
$42.79
Grades: 5 6 7 8   **947.7**
   ISBN 978-0-7614-2090-3
                                   LC 2007019179
   First published 1997
   "Provides comprehensive information on the geography,
history, wildlife, governmental structure, economy, cultural
diversity, peoples, religion, and culture of Ukraine." Pub-
lisher's note
   Includes glossary and bibliographical references

Cooper, Catherine W.
   Ukraine; [by] Catherine W. Cooper; with ad-
ditional text by Zoran Pavlovic. 2nd ed.; Chelsea
House 2006 120p il map (Modern world nations)
lib bdg $30
Grades: 7 8 9 10   **947.7**
   ISBN 0-7910-9207-0
                                   LC 2006015643
   First published 2003

This describes the geography, history, people, and culture of Ukraine.
   Includes bibliographical references

947.93 Lithuania

Kagda, Sakina
   ★ **Lithuania**; [by] Sakina Kagda & Zawiah Ab-
dul Latif. 2nd ed.; Marshall Cavendish Benchmark
2008 144p il map (Cultures of the world) lib bdg
$42.79
Grades: 5 6 7 8   **947.93**
   ISBN 978-0-7614-2087-3
                                   LC 2007016290
   First published 1997
   "Provides comprehensive information on the geography,
history, wildlife, governmental structure, economy, cultural
diversity, peoples, religion, and culture of Lithuania." Pub-
lisher's note
   Includes glossary and bibliographical references

947.98 Estonia

Spilling, Michael
   Estonia; 2nd ed.; Marshall Cavendish Bench-
mark 2010 142p il map (Cultures of the world) lib
bdg $42.79
Grades: 5 6 7 8   **947.98**
   ISBN 978-0-7614-4846-4 lib bdg; 0-7614-4846-2
   lib bdg
                                   LC 2009021201
   First published 1999
   This describes the geography, history, wildlife, govern-
mental structure, economy, cultural diversity, peoples, reli-
gion, and culture of Estonia
   Includes glossary and bibliographical references

948 Scandinavia

Allan, Tony
   Exploring the life, myth, and art of the Vikings;
Tony Allan. Rosen Pub. 2012 144 p. (Civilizations
of the world) $42.60
Grades: 7 8 9 10 11   **948**
   1. Vikings 2. Viking art 3. Norse mythology 4. Viking
civilization 5. Art, Viking 6. Mythology, Norse 7.
Civilization, Viking
   ISBN 9781448848331
                                   LC 2011008856
   This book on the Vikings "offers an informative overview of . . . political and social history as well as its art,
architecture, and mythology, all bolstered with plenty of . .
. details and narratives. . . . [T]he illustrations include artworks, documents, and handsome maps as well as photos of
significant sites and artifacts. . . . 'Vikings' explores heritage
that the Norse people shared and their history as traders,
raiders, and settlers in other lands." (Booklist)

The book "put[s] the art . . . in context, explaining how a society's religious beliefs, legends, and cultural traditions manifest themselves through images and iconography. The . . . layout features full-color photographs of architecture, sculpture, and painting on every page, accompanied by informative captions." (School Libr J)

Includes bibliographical references (p. 136-137) and index

Hinds, Kathryn, 1962-

Vikings; masters of the sea. Marshall Cavendish Benchmark 2009 79p il (Barbarians!) lib bdg $24.95

Grades: 6 7 8 9   **948**

1. Vikings

ISBN 978-0-7614-4074-1 lib bdg; 0-7614-4074-7 lib bdg

LC 2008039052

"This . . . devotes excellent coverage and exposure to the emergence, development, and legacy of [the Vikings]." Libr Media Connect

Includes glossary and bibliographical references

Nardo, Don

The **Vikings**. Lucent Books 2010 112p il (World history) lib bdg $33.45

Grades: 6 7 8 9   **948**

1. Vikings

ISBN 978-1-4205-0316-6; 1-4205-0316-2

LC 2010010500

This is an introduction to Viking civilization.

This "shines as it provides a contemporaneous writing as well as work by scholars that offer plenty of drama—and lots of facts too. . . . [It also] provides a solid time line, plenty of photographs, sourced quotes, and a list of books and websites for further investigation. Excellent for reports and research." Booklist

Includes bibliographical references

Park, Louise

The **Scandinavian** Vikings; by Louise Park and Timothy Love. Marshall Cavendish Benchmark 2009 32p il map (Ancient and medieval people) $19.95

Grades: 4 5 6   **948**

1. Vikings

ISBN 978-0-7614-4445-9; 0-7614-4445-9

This title has "a simple and elegant design with the proper balance of quality writing and quantity of information. . . . Handy time lines, well-chosen photos of ruins and artifacts, quality illustrations, inset 'Quick Facts', and 'What You Should Know About' features will grab reluctant readers and captivate even those with short attention spans." SLJ

Includes glossary

948.5   Sweden

Docalavich, Heather

Sweden; by Heather Docalavich and Shaina C. Indovino. Mason Crest Publishers 2013 64 p. col. ill., col. maps (library) $22.95

Grades: 5 6 7 8   **948.5**

1. Sweden 2. European Union

ISBN 1422222608; 9781422222607; 9781422222911

LC 2010051848

This book by Heather Docalavich is part of the Major European Union Nations series and looks at Sweden. "A member of the EU since 1995, Sweden is one of the most stable and [peaceful] countries in the world. It takes caring for its people and the environment very seriously." The 2008-2009 financial crisis is discussed. (Publisher's note)

Includes bibliographical references (p. 57-58) and index

Phillips, Charles

★ **Sweden**; [by] Charles Phillips; Susan C. Brantly and Eric Clark consultants. National Geographic 2009 64p il map (Countries of the world) lib bdg $27.90

Grades: 4 5 6 7   **948.5**

ISBN 978-1-4263-0389-0 lib bdg; 1-4263-0389-0 lib bdg

LC 2009275585

This describes the geography, nature, history, people & culture, and government & economy of Sweden

Includes glossary and bibliographical references

948.9   Denmark and Finland

Docalavich, Heather

Denmark; by Heather Docalavich and Shaina C. Indovino. Mason Crest Publishers 2013 64 p. col. ill., col. maps (hardcover) $22.95

Grades: 5 6 7 8   **948.9**

1. Denmark 2. European Union

ISBN 1422222381; 9781422222386

LC 2010051090

This book by Heather Docalavich and Shaina Carmel Indovino is part of the Major European Union Nations series and focuses on Denmark. "Denmark is a peaceful northern country that joined the EU in 1973. From the Vikings to the modern day, Denmark has a long [history]. Today, Denmark is a very environmentally conscious nation with a lot going on. It also must figure out how to deal with issues of immigration and the global recession as it looks to the future." (Publisher's note)

Includes bibliographical references

948.97   Finland

Skog, Jason

Teens in Finland. Compass Point Books 2008 96p il map (Global connections) lib bdg $31.93

Grades: 7 8 9 10   **948.97**
1. Teenagers 2. Finland
ISBN 978-0-7565-3405-9 lib bdg; 0-7565-3405-4
lib bdg
                                    LC 2007032691
Uncovers the challenges, pastimes, customs and culture
of teens in Finland
"Information is solid, giving readers an informed and
realistic view of life in that country. A historical timeline
is included, and suggestions for other nonfiction and fiction
titles for further reading." Youth Voice Advocate
Includes glossary and bibliographical references

Tan, Chung Lee
★ **Finland**; [by] Tan Chung Lee. 2nd ed.; Mar-
shall Cavendish Benchmark 2007 144p il map (Cul-
tures of the world) lib bdg $39.93
Grades: 5 6 7 8   **948.97**
ISBN 978-0-7614-2073-6 lib bdg; 0-7614-2073-8
lib bdg
                                    LC 2006015897
First published 1996
This provides "information on the geography, history,
governmental structure, economy, cultural diversity, peo-
ples, religion, and culture of Finland." Publisher's note
Includes glossary and bibliographical references

949.12   Iceland

Somervill, Barbara A.
Iceland; by Barbara A. Somervill. Children's
Press 2013 144 p. ill., maps (library) $40
Grades: 5 6 7 8   **949.12**
1. Iceland 2. Icelandic language
ISBN 0531256022; 9780531256022
                                    LC 2012047117
This book by Barbara A. Somervill is part of the Enchantment of the World series and looks at Iceland. A discussion is offered of "how this land near the Arctic Circle came
to be. . . . Maps and illustrations show the variety in the terrain and the areas of major geological activity. . . . Chapters
[are] devoted to history, the economy, the government and
the flora and fauna." (Children's Literature)
Includes bibliographical references (page 134) and index.

949.2   Netherlands

Docalavich, Heather
The **Netherlands**; by Heather Docalavich and
Shaina Carmel Indovino. Mason Crest Publishers
2013 64 p. col. ill. (series hardcover) $344.25; (li-
brary) $22.95; (ebook) $28.95
Grades: 5 6 7 8   **949.2**
1. Netherlands
ISBN 9781422222317; 9781422222539;
9781422222843; 9781422292716
                                    LC 2010051464
This book on the Netherlands by Heather Docalvich
and Shaina Carmel Indovino is part of the "Major European

Union Nations" series. It presents an "overview of some of
the successes and challenges that the Netherlands has faced
and continues to face." Topics include "history, one on government, the economy, people and culture, and . . . global
climate change." (Children's Literature)
Includes bibliographical references (p. 57-58, 63)
and index.

949.304   Belgium and Luxembourg-- 1909-

Indovino, Shaina C.
Belgium; by Ida Walker and Shaina C. Indovino.
Mason Crest Publishers 2012 64 p. col. ill., col.
maps (library) $22.95
Grades: 5 6 7 8   **949.304**
1. Belgium
ISBN 1422222330; 9781422222331
                                    LC 2010051078
This book, "part of the 'Modern World Nations' series, is
an . . . introduction to the kingdom of Belgium. For middle
school and high school readers, the chapters are descriptive
of the physical features, the history, people, government, and
economy. There is a chapter about the future of the nation
as well as a description of life in the country today." (Children's Literature)
Includes bibliographical references and index.

949.35   Luxembourg

Sheehan, Patricia
★ **Luxembourg**; by Patricia Sheehan & Sakina
Dhilawala. 2nd ed.; Marshall Cavendish Benchmark
2008 144p il map (Cultures of the world) lib bdg
$42.79
Grades: 5 6 7 8   **949.35**
ISBN 978-0-7614-2088-0
                                    LC 2007014891
First published 1997
Discusses the geography, history, government, economy,
and customs of the smallest of the Benelux countries
Includes glossary and bibliographical references

949.5   Greece

Etingoff, Kim
Greece; by Kim Etingoff and Shaina C. Indovino.
Mason Crest Publishers 2013 64 p. ill. (library)
$22.95
Grades: 5 6 7 8   **949.5**
1. Greece 2. European Union
ISBN 1422222446; 9781422222447; 9781422222751
                                    LC 2010051304
This book by Kim Etingoff and Shaina C. Indovino is
part of the Major European Union Nations series and looks
at Greece. The series "stresses the modern relationships,
goals, and problems of the European Union. . . . Chapters
begin with 'Modem Issues' and a brief summary of the
country's history and government, followed by chapters on

economy, people and culture, and 'Looking to the Future.'"
(School Library Journal)

Feldman, Ruth Tenzer
The **fall** of Constantinople. Twenty-First Century Books 2008 160p il map (Pivotal moments in history) lib bdg $38.60
Grades: 7 8 9 10   **949.5**
1. Byzantine Empire 2. Istanbul (Turkey) -- History -- Siege, 1453
ISBN 978-0-8225-5918-4 lib bdg; 0-8225-5918-8 lib bdg

LC 2006037501

"This volume examines the fall of Constantinople, marking the end of the Middle Ages. Sure to satisfy history buffs, the book not only relates military facts but also delves into the events leading up to Constantinople's defeat as well as exploring its effects throughout history. Numerous sidebars, illustrations, maps, and art reproductions provide additional information." Horn Book Guide
Includes glossary and bibliographical references

Green, Jen
★ **Greece**; [by] Greg Anderson and Kostas Vlassopoulos, consultants. National Geographic 2009 64p il map (Countries of the world) lib bdg $27.90
Grades: 4 5 6 7   **949.5**
ISBN 978-1-4263-0470-5 lib bdg; 1-4263-0470-6 lib bdg
This describes the geography, nature, history, people and culture, government and economy of Greece
Includes glossary and bibliographical references

Heinrichs, Ann
Greece; by Ann Heinrichs. Children's Press 2012 144 p. col. ill., col. maps (library) $40
Grades: 5 6 7 8   **949.5**
1. Greece -- History 2. Greece -- Civilization
ISBN 0531275434; 9780531275436

LC 2012000519

This book, part of the Enchantment of the World series, focuses on Greece. The books in the series each feature 10 "chapters, several maps, a fast-facts section, and a few references to other sources, including a referral to a Scholastic website . . . . The chapters cover geography, natural environment, history, politics, people and culture." (School Library Journal)
Includes bibliographical references and index.

Vanvoorst, Jennifer Fretland
The **Byzantine** Empire; by Jenny Fretland VanVoorst. Compass Point Books 2013 48 p. ill. (chiefly col.), col. map (library) $28.65; (paperback) $8.95
Grades: 6 7 8   **949.5**
1. Byzantine Empire -- Civilization
ISBN 075654565X; 0756545862; 9780756545659; 9780756545864

LC 2012001994

This children's nonfiction book, by Jennifer Fretland VanVoorst, profiles the Byzantine Empire as part of the "Ex-

ploring the Ancient World" series. "The Byzantine Empire, which thrived from 395 to 1453, was a fascinating place. Its people thought of themselves as Romans, spoke Greek, and hailed from all across Europe and Asia. . . . It was a Christian empire that preserved and developed Europe's intellectual heritage at a time when western Europe was in decline." (Publisher's note)
Includes bibliographical references (p. 46-47) and index.

949.65   Albania

Knowlton, MaryLee
★ **Albania**; by MaryLee Knowlton. Marshall Cavendish Benchmark 2005 144p il map (Cultures of the world) lib bdg $42.79
Grades: 5 6 7 8   **949.65**
ISBN 0-7614-1852-0

LC 2004-22236

An overview of the history, culture, peoples, religion, government, and geography of Albania
Includes glossary and bibliographical references

949.7   Serbia, Croatia, Slovenia, Bosnia and Hercegovina, Montenegro, Macedonia

Cooper, Robert
Croatia; [by] Robert Cooper and Michael Spilling. 2nd ed; Marshall Cavendish Benchmark 2011 144p il map (Cultures of the world) lib bdg $42.79
Grades: 5 6 7 8   **949.7**
ISBN 978-1-6087-0215-2; 1-6087-0215-4

LC 2010019626

First published 2001
Provides information on the geography, history, wildlife, governmental structure, economy, cultural diversity, peoples, religion, and culture of Croatia.
"Plentiful color photographs accompany substantial amounts of information." SLJ
Includes glossary and bibliographical references

Halilbegovich, Nadja
My childhood under fire; a Sarajevo diary. Kids Can Press 2006 120p il $14.95
Grades: 5 6 7 8   **949.7**
1. Yugoslav War, 1991-1995 2. Diarists 3. Pacifists
ISBN 1-55337-797-4
"In 1992, when the bombing started in Sarajevo, Halilbegovich, 12, kept a diary of her terrifying daily life under siege. Her terse vignettes replay the horror of her comfortable home torn apart." Booklist

Knowlton, MaryLee
★ **Macedonia**; by MaryLee Knowlton. Benchmark Books 2005 144p il map (Cultures of the world) lib bdg $42.79
Grades: 5 6 7 8   **949.7**
ISBN 0-7614-1854-7

LC 2004-22735

Describes the geography, history, government, economy, people, and culture of Macedonia

Includes glossary and bibliographical references

949.8   Romania

Bos, Jan-Willem

   Romania. Oliver Press 2011 48p il map (Looking at Europe) lib bdg $24.95

Grades: 7 8 9 10   **949.8**

   ISBN 978-1-881508-86-1; 1-881508-86-2

                     LC 2009034604

   This describes Romania today, its history, cities, transportation, culture, education, economy, cuisine, tourism, and natural environment.

   This will "best suit students with good vocabularies and some knowledge of European history. . . . [It is] clearly written and well organized. . . . [It includes] many clear photos as well as colorful sidebars. . . . Attractive, informative." Booklist

   Includes glossary and bibliographical references

949.9   Bulgaria

Prazdny, Bronja

   Bulgaria. Oliver Press 2011 48p il map (Looking at Europe) lib bdg $24.95

Grades: 7 8 9 10   **949.9**

   ISBN 978-1-881508-85-4; 1-881508-85-4

                     LC 2009032670

   This describes Bulgaria today, its history, cities, transportation, culture, education, economy, cuisine, tourism, and natural environment.

   This will "best suit students with good vocabularies and some knowledge of European history. . . . [It is] clearly written and well organized. . . . [It includes] many clear photos as well as colorful sidebars. . . . Attractive, informative." Booklist

   Includes glossary and bibliographical references

950   History of Asia

Campbell, Rusty

   Atlas of Asia; [by] Rusty Campbell, Malcolm Porter, and Keith Lye. Rosen Central 2010 il map lib bdg $26.50; pa $11.75

Grades: 4 5 6 7   **950**

   1. Asia

   ISBN 978-1-4358-8455-7 lib bdg; 1-4358-8455-8 lib bdg; 978-1-4358-9112-8 pa; 1-4358-9112-0 pa

   "Most of the spreads cover a region or one of the continent's bigger countries and provide large, clear maps and columns of almanac data surrounded by short chapters on famous people, animals, industries, cities, sports, and more, all accompanied by color illustrations or photographs and informative sidebars... with guidance [children] will encounter some absorbing and informative material." SLJ

Galloway, Priscilla

   ★ **Adventures** on the ancient Silk Road; [by] Priscilla Galloway with Dawn Hunter. Annick Press 2009 164p il $24.95; pa $14.95

Grades: 6 7 8 9   **950**

   1. Explorers 2. Travelers 3. Voyages and travels 4. Kings 5. Buddhist monks 6. Travel writers

   ISBN 978-1-55451-198-3; 1-55451-198-4; 978-1-55451-197-6 pa; 1-55451-197-6 pa

   "The monk Xuanzang, the conqueror Genghis Khan, and the merchant Marco Polo each traveled the Silk Road, years apart. Their journeys, by different routes and for different motives, are gripping historical narratives, sensitively and excitingly fictionalized here, in language that is lively and descriptive, clear but not oversimplified. Vibrant reproductions of art and photos of artifacts leap off every colorful page." SLJ

Helget, Nicole

   Mongols; Nicole Helget. Creative Education 2013 48 p. (Fearsome fighters) (alk. paper) $35.65

Grades: 5 6 7 8   **950**

   1. Mongols 2. Asia -- History 3. Military art and science -- History 4. Mongols -- History 5. Mongols -- Warfare 6. Military art and science -- Mongolia -- History -- To 1500

   ISBN 1608181847; 9781608181841

                     LC 2011035800

   Author Nicole Helget presents a book on the history of the people of Mongolia, their influence on world culture, and their impact on society. The book presents a "look at the Mongols, including how they built the most widespread empire in history, their lifestyle, their weapons, and how they remain a part of today's culture through books and film." (Publisher's note)

   Includes bibliographical references (p. 48) and index

Morris, Neil

   Asian civilizations. Zak Books 2009 48p il map (History of the world) lib bdg $34.25

Grades: 7 8 9 10   **950**

   1. Ancient civilization 2. Asia -- History 3. Asia -- Civilization

   ISBN 978-88-6098-160-8 lib bdg; 88-6098-160-3 lib bdg

                     LC 2008-8403

   The "effectiveness lies in the combination of lush illustrations, well-chosen, captioned photographs of contemporary artifacts, and . . . [a] reasoned, concise [narrative]. Succinct time lines border most pages, and . . . the proper amount of white space, and clear dark print maintain organization and clarity. A superior choice." SLJ

   Includes glossary

Nardo, Don

   Genghis Khan and the Mongol Empire. Lucent Books 2011 96p il map (World history) $33.45

Grades: 5 6 7 8 9   **950**

   1. Mongols

   ISBN 978-1-4205-0326-5; 1-4205-0326-X

                     LC 2010032960

"Using new scholarship, Nardo paints a more nuanced and sophisticated picture of a man who united several nomadic clans and then went on to found history's largest empire. Starting with his early childhood and ending with the death of his grandson, Kublai Khan, the book focuses on Genghis Khan's empire building and leadership, including his code of laws and justice. The book features several color photographs of present-day Mongolia period reenactments, as well as artistic representations from the era. . . . Nardo includes quotations from several scholars while still keeping the book engaging and accessible for a wide variety of readers." SLJ

Includes glossary and bibliographical references

Woods, Michael

Seven wonders of Ancient Asia; by Michael Woods and Mary B. Woods. Twenty-First Century Books 2008 80p il map (Seven wonders) lib bdg $33.26

Grades: 6 7 8 9   **950**
1. Asian architecture 2. Asia -- History
ISBN 978-0-8225-7569-6 lib bdg; 0-8225-7569-8 lib bdg
                                        LC 2007-40824

"This handsome volume presents seven notable 'wonders' of ancient Asia: the Great Wall of China, Mahabodhi Temple in India, Angkor Wat in Cambodia, Todaiji Temple in Japan, Pha That Luang in Laos, Borobudur Temple on Java in Indonesia, and the Banaue Rice Terraces of the Philippines. . . . With good writing and a nice design, this book offers a fine introduction to some historically significant places." Booklist

Includes glossary and bibliographical references

951   China and adjacent areas

Langley, Andrew

Cultural Revolution; years of chaos in China. by Andrew Langley. Compass Point Books 2008 96p il map (Snapshots in history) lib bdg $33.26

Grades: 6 7 8 9   **951**
1. China -- History -- 1949-1976
ISBN 978-0-7565-3483-7 lib bdg; 0-7565-3483-6 lib bdg
                                        LC 2007032699

This book "provides more than just a 'snapshot' of China's violent Cultural Revolution . . . The inviting layout has a photo and boxed data on almost every double-page spread, and the main account is buoyed by extensive back matter, including chapter notes for quotations." Booklist

Includes bibliographical references

Levy, Patricia

★ **Tibet**; [by] Patricia Levy & Don Bosco. 2nd ed.; Marshall Cavendish Benchmark 2007 144p il map (Cultures of the world) lib bdg $42.79

Grades: 5 6 7 8   **951**
ISBN 978-0-7614-2076-7 lib bdg; 0-7614-2076-2 lib bdg
                                        LC 2006015826

First published 1996

This provides "information on the geography, history, wildlife, governmental structure, economy, diversity, peoples, religion, and culture of Tibet." Publisher's note

Includes glossary and bibliographical references

Mara, Wil

People's Republic of China; by Wil Mara. Children's Press 2012 144 p. ill., maps (library) $40

Grades: 5 6 7 8   **951**
1. China -- Economic conditions 2. China
ISBN 053125352X; 9780531253526
                                        LC 2011011308

This book, part of the Enchantment of the World, offers an "introduction to China. The book covers geography, climate, history, language, different ethnic groups, religion, government structure, and the arts. Frequent text boxes and large, bright photographs add extra information and deeper context. There is a heavy focus on the Chinese economy and recent strides made in human rights." (School Library Journal)

Includes bibliographical references and index.

Marx, Trish

Elephants and golden thrones; inside China's Forbidden City. written by Trish Marx; photographs and photograph selection by Ellen B. Senisi; foreword by Li Ji. Abrams Books for Young Readers 2008 48p il $18.95

Grades: 4 5 6 7   **951**
1. Forbidden City (Beijing, China) 2. China
ISBN 978-0-8109-9485-0; 0-8109-9485-2
                                        LC 2007-022413

Introduces Beijing's Forbidden City, recounting some of the most famous incidents from its past, and describing its rooms, their function, and some of the daily rituals of palace life.

The author "brings the Forbidden City to life by telling stories about six different royal inhabitants from Zhengde, 'one of the worst emperors in Chinese history,' to Puyi, who became a pawn of the invading Japanese. . . . Beautiful drawings and photographs, some provided by the Palace Museum and some taken for this book, lend color and provide additional information. Of particular note are the photos of the interiors of buildings, a number of which are not regularly open to the public." Booklist

Includes bibliographical references

Pelleschi, Andrea

China. ABDO 2012 144p. il (Countries of the world) lib bdg $35.64

Grades: 6 7 8 9   **951**
ISBN 978-1-61783-107-2
                                        LC 2011019959

" Chapters then cover all the expected details for report-writers... Vivid photographs and useful maps in an eye-pleasing design enliven the presentation." Horn Book

Includes glossary and bibliographical references

Sis, Peter

★ **Tibet**; through the red box. Farrar, Straus & Giroux 1998 un il maps $25

Grades: 4 5 6 7   **951**

1. Tibet (China)

ISBN 0-374-37552-6

LC 97-50175

A Caldecott Medal honor book, 1999

"When Sis opens the red lacquered box that has sat on his father's table for decades, he finds the diary his father kept when he was lost in Tibet in the mid-1950s. The text replicates the diary's spidery handwriting, while the illustrations depict elaborate mazes and mandalas, along with dreamlike spreads that are filled with fragmented details of the father's and son's lives. . . . Impeccably designed and beautifully made, the book has a dreamlike quality that will keep readers of many ages coming back to find more in its pages." Booklist

Ting, Renee

Chinese history stories; edited by Renee Ting; translated from Chinese by Qian Jifang. Shens Books 2009 2v il ea $19.95

Grades: 6 7 8 9   **951**

1. China -- History

ISBN 978-1-885008-37-4 v1; 1-885008-37-6 v1; 978-1885008-38-1 v2; 1-885008-38-4 v2

LC 2009027288

"These first two entries in a planned series of 12 volumes offer gripping introductions to China's cultural narratives. From the initial two-page condensation of 3000 years of history to the suggestions to 'Learn More' after (often more useful to read before), the well-told stories and the attractively varied illustrations are riveting. . . . Multiple illustrators provide changing art styles and historical allusions, but all are detailed, lively, and colorful." SLJ

951.04   Period of Republic, 1912-1949

Gay, Kathlyn

The **aftermath** of the Chinese nationalist revolution. Twenty-First Century Books 2008 160p il (Aftermath of history) lib bdg $38.60

Grades: 7 8 9 10   **951.04**

1. China -- History -- 1912-1949

ISBN 978-0-8225-7601-3; 0-8225-7601-5

LC 2007-15082

This book "offers a lucid account of the civil turmoil that began in China with the successful revolution led by Dr. Sun Yat-sen in 1911, and culminated in the establishment of the People's Republic in 1949." Booklist

Includes bibliographical references

951.05   Period of People's Republic, 1949-

The **diary** of Ma Yan; the struggles and hopes of a Chinese schoolgirl. edited and introduced by Pierre Haski; translated from the French by Lisa

Appignanesi. HarperCollins 2005 166p $15.99; lib bdg $16.89

Grades: 5 6 7 8   **951.05**

1. Students 2. Diarists

ISBN 0-06-076496-1; 0-06-076497-X lib bdg

LC 2004-16136

Original French edition, 2002

This book, edited by Pierre Haski offers "Ma Yan's . . . diary chronicles her struggle to escape hardship and bring prosperity to her family through her persistent, sometimes desperate, attempts to continue her schooling." The book discusses her efforts to continue schooling despite the hunger and poverty she endures in rural China. (Publisher's note)

"In 2001, while a French journalist was visiting remote Ningxia province in northwest China, a Muslim woman wearing the white headscarf of the Hui people thrust the diaries of her daughter into his hands. The three small notebooks described the girl's struggle to get an education despite extreme poverty. . . . The girl's feelings for her mother were powerful and complex, and she alternated between overwhelming love and rage at the injustices she suffered." SLJ

Jiang, Ji-li

★ **Red** scarf girl; a memoir of the Cultural Revolution. foreword by David Henry Hwang. HarperCollins Pubs. 1997 285p $16.99; pa $6.99

Grades: 6 7 8 9 10   **951.05**

1. Authors 2. Businesspeople 3. Communism -- China

ISBN 0-06-027585-5; 0-06-446208-0 pa

LC 97-5089

"This is an autobiographical account of growing up during Mao's Cultural Revolution in China in 1966. . . . Jiang describes in terrifying detail the ordeals of her family and those like them, including unauthorized search and seizure, persecution, arrest and torture, hunger, and public humiliation. . . . Her voice is that of an intelligent, confused adolescent, and her focus on the effects of the revolution on herself, her family, and her friends provides an emotional focal point for the book, and will allow even those with limited knowledge of Chinese history to access the text." Bull Cent Child Books

Slavicek, Louise Chipley

The **Chinese** Cultural Revolution. Chelsea House Publishers 2010 128p il (Milestones in modern world history) lib bdg $35

Grades: 8 9 10 11 12   **951.05**

1. China -- History -- 1949-1976

ISBN 978-1-60413-278-6; 1-60413-278-7

LC 2008-54885

"From the cover photo onward, young people are front and center in [this book,] . . . which focuses on the Red Guards who heard the anti-establishment call of their leader, Mao Zedong, in 1966. This political upheaval led to the deaths of up to four million Chinese over 10 years." Booklist

Includes bibliographical references

The **Tiananmen** Square protests of 1989; Jeff Hay, editor. Greenhaven Press 2010 177p il map

(Perspectives on modern world history) lib bdg $39.70

Grades: 7 8 9 10   951.05
1. Tiananmen Square Incident, Beijing (China), 1989
ISBN 978-0-7377-4796-6; 0-7377-4796-X

LC 2009041850

Offers basic historical information about the Tiananmen Square protests of 1989 , examining the controversies surrounding this event and providing first-person narratives from people who lived through or were impacted by it.

"The book has numerous full-color photographs, sidebars to enhance the text, and illustrations. This is a highly readable book and would be a good addition to the library's world history collection." Libr Media Connect

Includes glossary and bibliographical references

Uschan, Michael V., 1948-
China since World War II; by Michael V. Uschan. Lucent Books 2008 104 p. ill. (some col.), col. map (library) $34.95

Grades: 6 7 8 9   951.05
1. China -- History -- 1949-
ISBN 142050097X; 9781420500974

LC 2008014727

This book by Michael V. Uschan looks at the history of China since World War II. "Mao [Zedong] naturally dominates, the focus of five chapters. . . . One of the remaining two chapters is devoted to Deng Xiaoping, and the other to the Chinese economy. . . . There is no mention of the environmental consequences of China's prosperity, the human costs of the disappearance of social security . . . or the widespread corruption reflected in such recent events as collapsing schools." (School Library Journal)

Includes bibliographical references and index.

Yu Chun
Little Green; growing up during the Chinese Cultural Revolution. [by] Chun Yu. Simon & Schuster Books for Young Readers 2005 112p il $15.95

Grades: 6 7 8 9   951.05
1. Poets 2. Authors 3. Chemists 4. Memoirists 5. Short story writers
ISBN 0-689-86943-6

LC 2003-27433

"Chun Yu was born in China in 1966, the year the Great Cultural Revolution began, and in spare poetry she remembers the first 10 years of her life. True to a child's bewildered viewpoint and augmented by occasional, small black-and-white family photos, Yu gets across the grief at home and the school indoctrination." Booklist

951.25   Hong Kong

Kagda, Falaq
★ **Hong** Kong; [by] Falaq Kagda & Magdalene Koh. 2nd ed.; Marshall Cavendish Benchmark 2008 144p il map (Cultures of the world) lib bdg $42.79

Grades: 5 6 7 8   951.25
ISBN 978-0-7614-3034-6 lib bdg; 0-7614-3034-2 lib bdg

LC 2007048285

First published 1998

Surveys the geography, history, government, economy, and culture of Hong Kong

Includes glossary and bibliographical references

951.7   Mongolia

Pang, Guek-Cheng, 1950-
Mongolia; Pang Guek Cheng. Marshall Cavendish Benchmark 2010 144 p. col. ill., col. maps (Cultures of the world) (library) $42.79

Grades: 5 6 7 8   951.7
ISBN 9780761448495; 0761448497

LC 2009022643

This describes the geography, history, wildlife, governmental structure, economy, cultural diversity, peoples, religion, and culture of Mongolia

Includes bibliographical references and index.

951.9   Korea

Bowler, Ann Martin
All about Korea; stories, songs, crafts, and more. illustrated by Soosoonam Barg. Periplus Editions 2011 64p il $16.95

Grades: 3 4 5 6   951.9
1. Korea
ISBN 978-0-8048-4012-5; 0-8048-4012-1 (hardcover)

LC 2010040845

Introduces Korea, describing its history, culture, everyday life, food, sports, and holidays, as well as providing examples of Korean poems, songs, handicrafts, writing, legends, and folkore.

Reece, Richard
The **Korean** War. ABDO Pub. 2011 112p il map (Essential events) lib bdg $23.95

Grades: 7 8 9 10 11 12   951.9
1. Korean War, 1950-1953
ISBN 978-1-61714-766-1; 1-61714-766-4

LC 2010044661

This describes the Korean War and discusses the political and social issues pertaining to it.

Includes glossary and bibliographical references

Santella, Andrew
The **Korean** War; by Andrew Santella. Compass Point Books 2007 48p il map (We the people) lib bdg $25.26; pa $8.95

Grades: 4 5 6 7   951.9
1. Korean War, 1950-1953
ISBN 978-0-7565-2027-4 lib bdg; 0-7565-2027-4 lib bdg; 978-0-7565-2039-7 pa; 0-7565-2039-8 pa

LC 2006006767

This "begins by explaining how North and South Korea became divided; the involvement of the United Nations and the United States; conflict between President Harry Truman and General Douglas MacArthur; eventual peace talks; and the division still occurring today. Accessible and straightforward, this book is an excellent one for the intended audience." SLJ

Includes bibliographical references

Senker, Cath

★ **North** Korea and South Korea; by Cath Senker. 1st ed. Rosen Pub. 2013 48 p. col. ill. (library) $29.25

Grades: 6 7 8   **951.9**
   1. Korea (North) 2. Korea (South)
   ISBN 1448860296; 9781448860296

LC 2012010617

This book by Cath Senker is part of the Our World Divided series and looks at North Korea and South Korea. "Each of these volumes begins with a recent news event pertaining to the featured conflict and then looks back at the origin and milestones of the discord. . . . 'Viewpoints' sidebars are . . . supplementary features. They showcase quotations about a specific matter from individuals on opposing sides." (School Library Journal)

Includes bibliographical references (p. 46) and index.

951.93   North Korea (People's Democratic Republic of Korea)

Kummer, Patricia K.

North Korea; by Patricia K. Kummer. Children's Press 2008 144p il map (Enchantment of the world, second series) lib bdg $38

Grades: 5 6 7 8 9   **951.93**
   ISBN 978-0-531-18485-1 lib bdg; 0-531-18485-4 lib bdg

LC 2007025693

In this introduction to North Korea "geography is the focus, but Kummer also discusses ancient and recent history, . . . the economy, religion, sports, education, and more. Without discounting the rich culture, the book doesn't shy away from more sensitive issues. . . . The open design will draw readers, with clear type on thick, high-quality paper; numerous maps and color photos and spacious back matter are also included." Booklist

Includes bibliographical references

952   Japan

Blumberg, Rhoda

★ **Commodore** Perry in the land of the Shogun. Lothrop, Lee & Shepard Bks. 1985 144p il map $21.99; pa $8.99

Grades: 5 6 7 8   **952**
   1. Naval officers 2. Japan -- Foreign relations -- United States 3. United States -- Foreign relations -- Japan
   ISBN 0-688-03723-2; 0-06-008625-4 pa

LC 84-21800

A Newbery Medal honor book, 1986

This "is a well-written story of Matthew Perry's expedition to open Japan to American trade and whaling ports. The account is sensitive to the extreme cultural differences that both the Japanese and Americans had to overcome. Especially good are the chapters and paragraphs explaining Japanese feudal society and culture. The text is marvelously complemented by the illustrations, almost all reproductions of contemporary Japanese art." SLJ

Includes bibliographical references

Moore, Willamarie

All about Japan; stories, songs, crafts, and more. illustrated by Kazumi Wilds. Tuttle Pub. 2011 63p il $16.95

Grades: 3 4 5 6   **952**
   1. Japan
   ISBN 978-4-8053-1077-9; 4-8053-1077-4

LC 2010040843

"In this treasure-trove of information, two children, one a Tokyo urbanite and the other from a rural village, introduce readers to their country and its culture, including geography, language, traditional arts, costume, etiquette, sports, and festivals. The dual narrators' conversational descriptions of their homes and daily routines will engage young readers while highlighting the differences between the Westernized big-city existence and the traditional way of life in Japan's countryside, deftly demonstrating the rich variety of lifestyles within this island nation. The scope of this book is remarkably comprehensive, covering almost anything a child would want to know." SLJ

Niz, Xavier

Samurai; a guide to the feudal knights. by Xavier W. Niz. Capstone Press 2012 48p il map (History's greatest warriors) lib bdg $30.65

Grades: 6 7 8   **952**
   1. Samurai
   ISBN 978-1-4296-6601-5 lib bdg; 1-4296-6601-3 lib bdg

LC 2011004956

"...Focuses [more] on relaying facts about the four groups of exceptional fighters than on a narrative... [and has] extensive modern cultural references to which students will relate." SLJ

Includes bibliographical references

Somervill, Barbara A.

Japan; by Barbara A. Somervill. Children's Press 2012 144 p. ill., maps (library) $40

Grades: 5 6 7 8   **952**
   1. Japan 2. Japan -- Social life and customs
   ISBN 0531253546; 9780531253540

LC 2011009503

This book is part of the Enchantment of the World series and focuses on Japan. "Topics such as climate, wildlife, history, government, pop culture, and the arts are all addressed, providing a . . . look at Japan's past and present. With content revised considerably from previous editions, this book goes beyond facts and statistics to give readers an intimate glimpse at typical Japanese youth through fictionalized anecdotes detailing moments in their daily lives." (School Library Journal)

Includes bibliographical references and index.

Turnbull, Stephen R.

The **most** daring raid of the samurai. Rosen Pub. 2011 64p il map (The most daring raids in history) lib bdg $29.25

Grades: 7 8 9 10 **952**

1. Samurai

ISBN 978-1-4488-1872-3; 1-4488-1872-9

LC 2010030843

First published 2009 in the United Kingdom with title: The samurai capture a king

In 1609, the Samurai from the Shimazu clan of Satsuma took control of the independent kingdom of Ryukyu. This audacious military campaign brought an end to centuries of warfare between the Shimazu clan and the king of Ryukyu.

This book is "packed with facts, covering the details of the action, the people involved, and the tools used, in engaging prose. The authors cite their sources thoroughly. . . . Diagrams, . . . and maps make the action easy to follow and provide visual context for the raids. . . . This . . . is sure to find a large readership." SLJ

Includes glossary and bibliographical references

953   Arabian Peninsula and adjacent areas

King, David C.

★ The **United** Arab Emirates; [by] David C. King. 2nd ed; Marshall Cavendish Benchmark 2008 144p il map (Cultures of the world) lib bdg $42.79

Grades: 5 6 7 8 **953**

ISBN 978-0-7614-2565-6

LC 2006030237

This describes the geography, history, government, economy, environment, people, and culture of the United Arab Emirates.

Includes glossary and bibliographical references

953.3   Yemen

Hestler, Anna

Yemen; by Anna Hestler and Jo-Ann Spilling. 2nd ed.; Marshall Cavendish Benchmark 2010 144p il map (Cultures of the world) lib bdg $42.79

Grades: 5 6 7 8 **953.3**

ISBN 978-0-7614-4850-1 lib bdg; 0-7614-4850-0 lib bdg

LC 2009021200

First published 1999

This describes the geography, history, wildlife, governmental structure, economy, cultural diversity, peoples, religion, and culture of Yemen

Includes glossary and bibliographical references

O'Neal, Claire

We visit Yemen; by Claire O'Neal. Mitchell Lane Publishers 2012 63 p. ill. (chiefly col.), col. maps (library) $33.95; (ebook) $33.95

Grades: 4 5 6 7 8 **953.3**

1. Yemen -- Description and travel

ISBN 1584159618; 1612281060; 9781584159612; 9781612281063

LC 2011016773

This book on Yemen by Claire O'Neal is part of the "Your Land and My Land: The Middle East" series, which "provides an . . . introduction to the history and geography of several Middle Eastern and Southeast Asian countries from a tourist's perspective." Also included are a "recipe and a . . . craft project representing the country." (Booklist)

Includes bibliographical references and index.

953.53

Ejaz, Khadija

We visit Oman; by Khadija Ejaz. Mitchell Lane Publishers 2012 63 p. col. ill., col. maps (library) $33.95; (ebook) $33.95

Grades: 4 5 6 7 8 **953.53**

1. Oman -- Description and travel

ISBN 1584159626; 1612281044; 9781584159629; 9781612281049

LC 2011000724

This book on Oman by Khadija Ejaz is part of the "Your Land and My Land: The Middle East" series, which "provides an . . . introduction to the history and geography of several Middle Eastern and Southeast Asian countries from a tourist's perspective." Also included are a "recipe and a . . . craft project representing the country." (Booklist)

Includes bibliographical references (p. 59-61) and index.

953.6   Persian Gulf States

Cooper, Robert

Bahrain; [by] Robert Cooper and Jo-Ann Spilling. 2nd ed.; Marshall Cavendish Benchmark 2011 144p il map (Cultures of the world) lib bdg $42.79

Grades: 5 6 7 8 **953.6**

ISBN 978-1-6087-0213-8; 1-6087-0213-8

LC 2010019621

First published 2000

Provides information on the geography, history, wildlife, governmental structure, economy, cultural diversity, peoples, religion, and culture of Bahrain.

Includes glossary and bibliographical references

Orr, Tamra

★ Qatar; [by] Tamra Orr. Marshall Cavendish Benchmark 2008 144p il map (Cultures of the world) lib bdg $42.79

Grades: 5 6 7 8 **953.6**

ISBN 978-0-7614-2566-3; 0-7614-2566-7

LC 2006033626

This describes the geography, history, government, economy, environment, people, and culture of Qatar

Includes glossary and bibliographical references

953.67 Kuwait

O'Shea, Maria

Kuwait; by Maria O'Shea and Michael Spilling. 2nd ed.; Marshall Cavendish Benchmark 2010 144p il map (Cultures of the world) lib bdg $42.79

Grades: 5 6 7 8   953.67

ISBN 978-0-7614-4479-4 lib bdg; 0-7614-4479-3 lib bdg

LC 2009007069

First published 1999

Provides information on the geography, history, wildlife, governmental structure, economy, cultural diversity, peoples, religion, and culture of Kuwait

Includes glossary and bibliographical references

Tracy, Kathleen

We visit Kuwait; by Kathleen Tracy. Mitchell Lane Publishers 2012 63 p. ill. (chiefly col.), col. maps (Your land and my land. The Middle East) (library bound) $33.95; (ebook) $33.95

Grades: 4 5 6 7 8   953.67

1. Kuwait -- Description and travel
ISBN 1584159588; 1612281001; 9781584159582; 9781612281001

LC 2011002756

This book on Kuwait by Kathleen Tracy is part of the "Your Land and My Land: The Middle East" series, which "provides an . . . introduction to the history and geography of several Middle Eastern and Southeast Asian countries from a tourist's perspective." Also included are a "recipe and a . . . craft project representing the country." (Booklist)

Includes bibliographical references (p. 58-61) and index.

953.8 Saudi Arabia

Tracy, Kathleen

We visit Saudi Arabia; by Kathleen Tracy. Mitchell Lane Publishers 2011 63 p. col. ill., map (library) $33.95

Grades: 4 5 6 7 8   953.8

1. Persian Gulf region 2. Saudi Arabia
ISBN 1584159634; 9781584159636

LC 2011000728

This book by Kathleen Tracy is part of the Social Studies series and looks at Saudi Arabia. "One of the most socially conservative countries on earth, Saudi Arabia is defined by Islam and ancient traditions. At the same time, its vast oil fields have helped build glistening, modern cities filled with world-class restaurants and designer shops." (Publisher's note)

Includes bibliographical references and index.

954 India and neighboring south Asian countries

Arnold, Caroline

★ Taj Mahal; by Caroline Arnold and Madeleine Comora; illustrated by Rahul Bhushan. Carolrhoda Books 2007 un il lib bdg $17.95

Grades: 4 5 6 7   954

1. Emperors 2. Mogul Empire 3. Taj Mahal (Agra, India)
ISBN 978-0-7613-2609-0 lib bdg; 0-7613-2609-X lib bdg

LC 2001006685

Recounts the love story behind the building of the Taj Mahal in India, discussing how it was constructed and providing information on Indian culture.

"The small, detailed paintings are . . . set on beautifully constructed pages resembling those of illuminated manuscripts. . . . The book is sumptuous in appearance and presents a bit of history not often told for children." SLJ

Mann, Elizabeth

★ Taj Mahal; a story of love and empire. by Elizabeth Mann; with illustrations by Alan Witschonke. Mikaya 2008 47p il (Wonders of the world) $22.95

Grades: 4 5 6 7   954

1. Mogul Empire 2. Taj Mahal (Agra, India)
ISBN 1-931414-20-3; 978-1-931414-20-3

LC 2008060054

This is a "dramatic retelling of the construction of the Taj Mahal. Mann begins with two pages of prose that relay the commonly told legend, but then proceeds to explode that legend with descriptive writing, colorful illustrations, ancient paintings, maps, and photographs." Booklist

Includes bibliographical references

Ram-Prasad, Chakravarthi

Exploring the life, myth, and art of India. Rosen 2009 144p il map (Civilizations of the world) lib bdg $29.95

Grades: 7 8 9 10 11 12   954

1. Indic mythology 2. Indic art
ISBN 978-1-4358-5615-8; 1-4358-5615-5

LC 2009-9274

This describes the civilization, mythology and art of ancient India

"This beautifully illustrated and well-written [title] . . . is perfect for those assignments where students must look at the culture of a civilization. Artwork and pictures blend seamlessly with the information and the reader is taken on a journey of discovery. Myths are used as the story of how the people view themselves, blended with the discussion of the reality of life. Everyday life is tied to the belief systems and is explained in light of those beliefs. The pictures are beautifully done and there is almost as much information in the captions as there is in the text." Libr Media Connect

Includes glossary and bibliographical references

954.9 Other jurisdictions

NgCheong-Lum, Roseline
Maldives; 2nd ed.; Marshall Cavendish Benchmark 2011 144p il map (Cultures of the world) lib bdg $42.79
Grades: 5 6 7 8   954.9
ISBN 978-1-6087-0217-6; 1-6087-0217-0
LC 2010019746
First published 2001
Provides information on the geography, history, wildlife, governmental structure, economy, cultural diversity, peoples, religion, and culture of Maldives.
Includes glossary and bibliographical references

Taylor-Butler, Christine
Sacred mountain; Everest. Lee & Low Books 2009 48p il $19.95
Grades: 5 6 7 8   954.9
1. Sherpa (Nepalese people) 2. Mountaineering -- Mount Everest (China and Nepal) 3. Mount Everest (China and Nepal)
ISBN 978-1-60060-255-9; 1-60060-255-X
LC 2008-30423
"The informative text is amply illustrated with well-chosen black-and-white and color photographs." SLJ
Includes glossary

Yackley-Franken, Nicki
Teens in Nepal; by Nicki Yackley-Franken. Compass Point Books 2008 96p map (Global connections) lib bdg $31.93
Grades: 7 8 9 10   954.9
1. Teenagers 2. Nepal
ISBN 978-0-7565-3411-0 lib bdg; 0-7565-3411-9 lib bdg
LC 2007-32693
Uncovers the challenges, pastimes, customs and cultures of teens in Nepal.
"Information is solid, giving readers an informed and realistic view of life in that country. A historical time line is included, and suggestions for other nonfiction and fiction titles for further reading." Voice Youth Advocates
Includes glossary and bibliographical references

954.91 Pakistan

Hinman, Bonnie
We visit Pakistan; by Bonnie Hinman. Mitchell Lane Publishers 2012 63 p. ill. (chiefly col.), col. maps (Your land and my land. The Middle East) (library) $33.95
Grades: 4 5 6 7 8   954.91
1. Pakistan
ISBN 158415960X; 9781584159605
LC 2011030763
This book on Pakistan by Bonnie Hinman is part of the "Your Land and My Land: The Middle East" series, which "provides an . . . introduction to the history and geography of several Middle Eastern and Southeast Asian countries

from a tourist's perspective." Topics such as "terrorism and al-Qaeda" are covered along with "descriptions of the country's history and attractions." Also included are a "recipe and a . . . craft project representing the country." (Booklist)
Includes bibliographical references (p. 59-61) and index.

Morgan, Sally
Focus on Pakistan; [by] Sally Morgan. World Almanac Library 2007 64p il map (World in focus) lib bdg $33.27; pa $11.95
Grades: 6 7 8 9   954.91
1. Pakistan
ISBN 978-0-8368-6752-7 lib bdg; 978-0-8368-6759-6 pa
LC 2007022011
This describes the history, landscape and climate, population and settlements, government and politics, energy and resources, economy and income, global connections, transportation and communications, education and health, culture and religion, leisure and tourism, environment and conservation, and future challenges of Pakistan.
"Attractive color photographs, graphs, and charts illustrate [this] volume. . . . [This book presents] current, accurate information in a way that is not too dry or overwhelming for the intended age group." SLJ
Includes glossary and bibliographical references

Sonneborn, Liz
Pakistan; by Liz Sonneborn. Children's Press 2013 144 p. ill. (mostly col.), col. maps. (Enchantment of the world, second series) (library) $40
Grades: 5 6 7 8   954.91
1. Pakistan 2. Pakistan -- Description and travel
ISBN 0531275442; 9780531275443
LC 2012000505
This book, by Liz Sonneborn, is part of the "Enchantment of the World" series. In it the author provides information and photographs showcasing the people, places and events surrounding the South Asian country of Pakistan. Contents include photographs of Pakistani cities and landscapes, statistics describing the nation's features, and traditional Pakistani recipes.
Includes bibliographical references and index

954.92 Bangladesh

Phillips, Douglas A.
Bangladesh; [by] Douglas A. Phillips and Charles F. Gritzner. Chelsea House 2007 107p il map (Modern world nations) lib bdg $30
Grades: 7 8 9 10   954.92
ISBN 0-7910-9251-8 lib bdg; 978-0-7910-9251-4 lib bdg
LC 2006032006
Describes the geography, history, people, culture, economy, and government of Bangladesh
Includes bibliographical references

955   Iran

DiPrimio, Pete

We visit Iran; by Pete DiPrimio. Mitchell Lane Publishers 2012 63 p. col. ill., maps (library) $33.95
Grades: 4 5 6 7 8   955
  1. Iran -- History 2. Iran
  ISBN 1584159545; 9781584159544
                           LC 2011016765

This book by Pete DiPrimio looks at Iran. "It is a Middle Eastern country with European (not Arabian) founders. It was the home of one of the ancient world's greatest empires, the Persian Empire. Its many ancient ruins include the palace complex of Persepolis, which was so big it took 150 years to finish. While the nation develops nuclear technology, its government—called an Islamic Republic—dictates people's lives, from the clothing they wear to the news they hear." (Publisher's note)

Includes bibliographical references

Seidman, David

Teens in Iran; by David Seidman. Compass Point Books 2008 96p il map (Global connections) lib bdg $31.93
Grades: 7 8 9 10   955
  1. Youth -- Iran
  ISBN 978-0-7565-3300-7 lib bdg; 0-7565-3300-7 lib bdg
                           LC 2007-5411

Explores the daily lives and customs of Iranian teenagers, discussing holidays, education, religion, employment, and culture.

"The information is solid, giving readers an informed and realistic view of life in that country. A historical time line is included, and suggestions for other nonfiction and fiction titles for further reading. Readers are directed to a Web site, where Internet links and a list of additional nonfiction titles are provided." Voice Youth Advocates

Shapera, Paul M.

Iran's religious leaders. Rosen Pub. 2009 80p il (Understanding Iran) lib bdg $22.95
Grades: 6 7 8 9   955
  1. Islam 2. Religion and politics 3. Iran -- Politics and government
  ISBN 978-1-4358-5283-9 lib bdg; 1-4358-5283-4 lib bdg
                           LC 2008047709

"The book begins with an introduction to Islam, including differences between the Sunni and Shi'a branches. There's also a history lesson. . . . The book [describes] . . . religious leaders and how the Iranian government is organized. . . . [The book offers] an accessible format and a layout filled with many interesting color photographs. . . . An extremely helpful book for report writers, this also works for anyone who wants to understand how and why Iran functions the way it does." Booklist

Includes glossary and bibliographical references

Wagner, Heather Lehr

The Iranian Revolution. Chelsea House 2010 111p il (Milestones in modern world history) lib bdg $35
Grades: 7 8 9 10 11 12   955
  1. Iran -- History -- 1941-1979
  ISBN 978-1-60413-490-2; 1-60413-490-9
                           LC 2009-22336

"Chapters cover the origin of the Pahlavi dynasty, [Ayatollah] Khomeini's early life and how he came to symbolize opposition to the shah's regime, and the shah's aggressive campaigns of reform and Westernization. . . . A solid addition to the series." SLJ

Includes bibliographical references

955.06   Iran-- 2005-

Steele, Philip

★ Iran and the West; by Philip Steele. 1st ed. Rosen Pub. 2013 48 p. col. ill. (library) $29.25
Grades: 6 7 8   955.06
  1. Iran -- Foreign relations 2. Iran
  ISBN 1448860318; 9781448860319
                           LC 2012010613

In this book, readers "explore the long history and culture of Iran—the rise of the Ayatollah, the election of current president Mahmoud Ahmadinejad, diplomatic relations with countries in Europe and the United States, and the importance of Iran in the global economy." Photographs, illustrations, maps, and further reading are included. (Publisher's note)

Includes bibliographical references (p. 46) and index.

956   Middle East (Near East)

Abbott, David

Conflict in the Middle East. Arcturus Pub. 2011 46p il (Secret history) lib bdg $32.80
Grades: 7 8 9 10   956
  1. Spies 2. Espionage 3. Israel-Arab conflicts
  ISBN 978-1-8483-7697-7; 1-8483-7697-9
                           LC 2010011001

This book explores the secrets of the Arab-Israeli conflict. Both sides in this war have made use of spies, surveillance, special operations, and secret weapons. Even the peace talks have their own secret history.

"The title of the Secret History series will grab readers, even reluctant ones, and they won't be disappointed by the intriguing info regarding codes and code breakers, spies, terrorists, and double agents, with profiles of heroes and traitors on all sides. . . . The readable design, with clear type on thick, high-quality paper, includes lots of sidebars, photos, screens, and quotes." Booklist

Includes bibliographical references

Crompton, Samuel

The Third Crusade; Richard the Lionhearted vs. Saladin. [by] Samuel Willard Crompton. Chelsea

House 2003 114p il map (Great battles through the ages) $22.95

Grades: 7 8 9 10 **956**

1. Crusades 2. Kings 3. Sultans 4. Islamic leaders
ISBN 0-7910-7437-4

LC 2003-4593

"In 1187 King Richard I sought control of the Holy Land. This text details the Third Crusade in which the king of England lead an army of Christians to sieze the Holy Land from the Muslims." Publisher's note

Includes bibliographical references

Gritzner, Jeffrey A.

North Africa and the Middle East; [by] Jeffrey A. Gritzner and Charles F. Gritzner. Chelsea House 2006 120p il map (Modern world cultures) lib bdg $30

Grades: 7 8 9 10 **956**

1. North Africa 2. Middle East
ISBN 0-7910-8145-1

LC 2006011649

Describes the history, culture, peoples, and physical geography of North Africa and the Middle East.

Includes bibliographical references

January, Brendan

The **Arab** Conquests of the Middle East. Twenty First Century Books 2009 160p il (Pivotal moments in history) $38.60

Grades: 8 9 10 11 12 **956**

1. Islam -- History
ISBN 978-0-8225-8744-6; 0-8225-8744-0

"One hundred years after the death of Muhammad, Muslim armies had conquered most of North Africa, the Middle East, and parts of Spain and were fighting as far north as modern France. This attractively illustrated history begins with Muhammad's life and revelations and covers the early period of the Muslim community first as it struggled to survive and then as it gradually assumed dominance over the Arabian peninsula.... A section on primary-source research will intrigue historically minded readers, and a who's who and lists of further reading make this volume highly useful for reports." SLJ

Includes bibliographical references

Kort, Michael

The **handbook** of the Middle East; by Michael G. Kort. rev ed.; Twenty-First Century Books 2008 320p il map lib bdg $39.95

Grades: 8 9 10 11 12 **956**

1. Middle East
ISBN 978-0-8225-7143-8; 0-8225-7143-9

LC 2006-34917

First published 2002

Examines the past, present, and future of all the countries in the Middle East, discussing their history and culture

Includes bibliographical references

The **Middle** East: opposing viewpoints; David M. Haugen, Susan Musser and Kacy Lovelace, book editors. Greenhaven Press 2009 261p il map

(Opposing viewpoints series) lib bdg $38.50; pa $26.75

Grades: 8 9 10 11 12 **956**

1. Middle East -- Politics and government United States -- Foreign relations -- Middle East 3. Middle East -- Foreign relations -- United States
ISBN 978-0-7377-4532-0 lib bdg; 0-7377-4532-0 lib bdg; 978-0-7377-4533-7 pa; 0-7377-4533-9 pa

LC 2008-55848

The articles in this anthology cover such topics as U.S. relations with Middle Eastern nations, the Israeli/Palestinian conflict, whether Iran is a threat to the United States, and counterterrorism efforts in Middle Eastern nations.

Includes bibliographical references

956.04 Middle East-- 1945-1980

Hampton, Wilborn

★ **War** in the Middle East; a reporter's story. Candlewick Press 2007 112p il map $19.99

Grades: 6 7 8 9 10 11 12 **956.04**

1. Israel-Arab War, 1973
ISBN 978-0-7636-2493-4; 0-7636-2493-4

LC 2006-51694

"Recalling experiences as a reporter assigned to cover the 1970 Jordanian civil conflict dubbed Black September, and the Yom Kippur War that began in October 1973, Hampton not only presents a clear summary of the issues that provoked each outbreak of violence but also provides both personal slant and a sense of immediacy to his account of events." Booklist

Includes bibliographical references

Senker, Cath

The **Arab**-Israeli conflict; [by] Cath Senker. new ed.; Arcturus Pub. 2008 48p il map (Timelines) lib bdg $32.80

Grades: 5 6 7 8 **956.04**

1. Israel-Arab conflicts
ISBN 978-1-84193-725-0 lib bdg; 1-84193-725-8 lib bdg

LC 2007-7547

First published 2005 by Smart Apple Media

This describes current conditions in Israel and the occupied territories and includes a history of major events and political developments.

"A complex situation is clearly explained.... [This is] well-illustrated.... Throughout, the tone is nonjudgmental." SLJ [review of 2005 edition]

Includes bibliographical references

Woolf, Alex

The **Arab**-Israeli War since 1948; by Alex Woolf. 1st ed. Heinemann Library 2011 80 p. ill. (some col.), col. maps (library) $36.50; (paperback) $10.99

Grades: 6 7 8 9 **956.04**

1. Israel-Arab conflicts 2. Arab-Israeli conflict
ISBN 1432959956; 9781432959951; 9781432960049

LC 2011015920

"In this volume of the illustrated 'Living Through' series, readers are given a . . . summary of the critical events that shaped what we now think of as the Arab-Israeli Wars. . . . Readers will encounter some of the individuals, causes, and ongoing contradictions that make this international issue so seemingly unsolvable." Children's Literature

Includes bibliographical references

956.1   Turkey

LaRoche, Amelia

We visit Turkey; by Amelia LaRoche. Mitchell Lane Publishers 2012 63 p. ill. (chiefly col.), col. maps (library) $33.95

Grades: 4 5 6 7 8   **956.1**
    1. Turkey -- Description and travel
    ISBN 1584159561; 9781584159568
                         LC 2011030765

This book on Turkey by Amelia Laroche is part of the "Your Land and My Land: The Middle East" series, which "provides an . . . introduction to the history and geography of several Middle Eastern and Southeast Asian countries from a tourist's perspective." It "similarly mentions but does not dwell upon the rise of Islam and the hijab controversy." Also included are a "recipe and a . . . craft project representing the country." Booklist

Includes bibliographical references (p, 59-61) and index.

Lace, William W.

★ The **unholy** crusade; the ransacking of medieval Constantinople. [by] William W. Lace. Lucent Books 2007 104p il map (Lucent library of historical eras, Middle Ages) lib bdg $32.45

Grades: 6 7 8 9   **956.1**
    1. Crusades 2. Middle Ages
    ISBN 978-1-59018-846-0 lib bdg; 1-59018-846-2 lib bdg
                         LC 2006002572

"Lace gives equal attention to the events leading up to the destruction of Constantinople and traces the planning and plotting of the Crusades. . . . [The book has] numerous color reproductions. Clear, concise writing makes [it] highly readable, while the scholarship makes [it a] valuable [resource]." SLJ

Includes bibliographical references

Shields, Sarah D.

★ **Turkey**; [by] Sarah Shields. National Geographic 2009 64p il map (Countries of the world) lib bdg $27.90

Grades: 4 5 6 7   **956.1**
    ISBN 978-1-4263-0387-6 lib bdg; 1-4263-0387-4 lib bdg
                         LC 2009275583

This describes the geography, nature, history, people and culture, government and economy of Turkey

Includes glossary and bibliographical references

956.7   Iraq

Adams, Simon

The **Iraq** War. Arcturus Pub. 2011 46p il map (Secret history) lib bdg $32.80

Grades: 7 8 9 10   **956.7**
    1. Iraq War, 2003-2011 2. Iraq War, 2003-
    ISBN 978-1-84837-698-4; 1-84837-698-7
                         LC 2010011764

This examines the Iraq War, including "from propaganda and intelligence to technology and sacrifice. . . . Archival photographs combine with a busy but well-organized design to present an engaging perspective. . . . Both reluctant readers and history buffs in need of a fresh approach to events will appreciate this [book]." Horn Book Guide

Includes bibliographical references

Ellis, Deborah

★ **Children** of war; voices of Iraqi refugees. Groundwood Books 2009 128p il $15.95; pa $9.95

Grades: 7 8 9 10 11 12   **956.7**
    1. Refugees 2. Children and war 3. Iraq War, 2003-2011 4. Iraq War, 2003- 5. Children and war
    ISBN 978-0-88899-907-8; 0-88899-907-0; 978-0-88899-908-5 pa; 0-88899-908-9 pa

Ellis "interviews child refugees from Iraq, now living in Jordan, and a few who have made it to Canada. . . . Accompanying each of the . . . interviews with young people is a brief introduction and a photo. . . . What is haunting are their graphic recent memories of what they witnessed. . . . An important, current title that will have lasting significance." Booklist

Includes glossary

Mason, Paul, 1967-

The **Iraq** War. Arcturus Pub. 2011 48p il map (Secret history) lib bdg $32.80

Grades: 7 8 9 10   **956.7**
    1. Iraq War, 2003-2011 2. Iraq War, 2003-
    ISBN 978-1-84837-639-7; 1-84837-639-1
                         LC 2009051266

"The title of the Secret History series will grab readers, even reluctant ones, and they won't be disappointed by the intriguing info regarding codes and code breakers, spies, terrorists, and double agents, with profiles of heroes and traitors on all sides. . . . The readable design, with clear type on thick, high-quality paper, includes lots of sidebars, photos, screens, and quotes." Booklist

Includes bibliographical references

O'Neal, Claire

We visit Iraq; by Claire O'Neal. Mitchell Lane Publishers 2012 63 p. ill. (chiefly col.), col. maps (library bound) $33.95

Grades: 4 5 6 7 8   **956.7**
    1. Persian Gulf region 2. Iraq
    ISBN 1584159553; 9781584159551
                         LC 2011016771

This book by Claire O'Neal is part of the Social Studies series and looks at Iraq. "Iraq's Tigris and Euphrates rivers turned this Middle Eastern desert into the world's first farmland. Over six millenia, Iraq's civilizations have laid foundations for the rest of the world. They built great stone ziggurats and soaring mosques. They invented the wheel, the calendar, and the written word. With their riches, they also attracted war." (Publisher's note)

Includes bibliographical references (p. 59-61) and index.

Samuels, Charlie

★ **Iraq**; [by] Charlie Samuels; Sarah Shields and Shakir Mustafa, consultants. National Geographic 2007 64p il map (Countries of the world) lib bdg $27.90

Grades: 4 5 6 7   **956.7**
  ISBN 978-1-4263-0061-5
                                        LC 2007024675
This describes the geography, nature, history, people and culture, government and economy of Iraq.

Includes glossary and bibliographical references

Smithson, Ryan

Ghosts of war; my tour of duty. HarperTeen 2009 321p il $16.99; lib bdg $17.89

Grades: 8 9 10 11 12   **956.7**
  1. Soldiers 2. Soldiers -- United States 3. Iraq War, 2003- -- Personal narratives
  ISBN 978-0-06-166468-7; 0-06-166468-5; 978-0-06-166470-0 lib bdg; 0-06-166470-7 lib bdg
                                        LC 2008-35420
"Ryan Smithson was a typical 16-year-old high-school student until 9/11. . . . Smithson enlisted in the Army Reserve the following year and, a year into the Iraq war, was deployed to an Army engineer unit as a heavy-equipment operator. His poignant, often harrowing account, especially vivid in sensory details, chronicles his experiences in basic training and in Iraq. . . . This memoir is a remarkable, deeply penetrating read that will compel teens to reflect on their own thoughts about duty, patriotism and sacrifice." Kirkus

Includes glossary and bibliographical references

Wilkes, Sybella

Out of Iraq; refugees' stories in words, paintings and music. Evans 2010 70p il map $17.99

Grades: 4 5 6 7   **956.7**
  1. Refugees 2. Iraq
  ISBN 978-0-237-53930-6; 0-237-53930-6
"Provides an concise overview of events before and during the invasion, interspersed with first-person narratives of Iraqi refugees, gathered while Wilkes worked with the United Nations Refugee Agency in Syria. . . . Moving photographs and artwork, quotations from political figures, and accessible language form a harrowing window into lives rarely paid witness." Publ Wkly

Zeinert, Karen

The **brave** women of the Gulf Wars; Operation Desert Storm and Operation Iraqi Freedom. [by] Karen Zeinert & Mary Miller. 21st Century Bks. 2006 112p il $30.60

Grades: 7 8 9 10   **956.7**
  1. Iraq War, 2003 2. Women in the armed forces 3. Persian Gulf War, 1991 -- Women
  ISBN 0-7613-2705-3

"Zeinert and Miller reinforce the argument that women do, indeed, belong in the U.S. military by highlighting their contributions in Operations Desert Storm (Kuwait) and Iraqi Freedom. . . . The narrative paints a picture of consistent courage under fire and, one terse mention of the abuses at Abu Ghraib Prison aside, of professional conduct. The authors extend their purview with a chapter on women journalists in the campaigns, and while thoroughly villainizing Saddam Hussein, they also indicate that the official justifications for the war in Iraq turned out to be weak at best. A utilitarian but cogent assessment of the topic, well supported by notes and sources." Booklist

Includes bibliographical references

956.704   Iraq-- 1979-

Bingham, Jane

The **Gulf** wars with Iraq; by Jane Bingham. Heinemann Library 2012 80 p. ill., maps (library) $36.50; (paperback) $10.99

Grades: 6 7 8 9   **956.704**
  1. Iraq War, 2003-2011 2. Persian Gulf War, 1991
  ISBN 1432959972; 9781432959975; 9781432960063
                                        LC 2011015922
This book by Jane Bingham is part of the Living Through series and looks at the U.S. Gulf Wars with Iraq. Here, "Bingham takes her readers back through the twists and turns of fact and fiction that are part and parcel of these connected conflicts." Topics include "the falsification of intelligence linked to Saddam Hussein's weapons program, the ruthless nature of the Iraqi dictator and his family, and the human cost of these two wars." (Children's Literature)

Includes bibliographical references (p. 77-78) and index.

956.91   Syria

Gelfand, Dale Evva

Syria; by Dale Evva Gelfand. ABDO Pub. Co. 2013 144 p. (library) $35.64

Grades: 8 9 10 11 12   **956.91**
  1. Syria
  ISBN 1617836397; 9781617836398
                                        LC 2012946084
This book by Dale Ewa Gelfant is part of the Countries of the World series and looks at Syria. It "introduces Syria's history, geography, culture, climate, government, economy, and other significant features. Sidebars, maps, fact pages, a glossary, a timeline, historic images and full-color photos" are included. (Publisher's note)

956.92   Lebanon

Sheehan, Sean

Lebanon; [by] Sean Sheehan & Zawiah Abdul Latif. 2nd ed.; Marshall Cavendish Benchmark 2008 144p il map (Cultures of the world) lib bdg $42.79

Grades: 5 6 7 8   **956.92**

    ISBN 978-0-7614-2081-1 lib bdg; 0-7614-2081-9 lib bdg

                    LC 2006101735

    First published 1997

    "Provides comprehensive information on the geography, history, wildlife, governmental structure, economy, cultural diversity, peoples, religion, and culture of Lebanon." Publisher's note

    Includes bibliographical references

956.93   Cyprus

Spilling, Michael

    Cyprus; [by] Michael Spilling and Jo-Ann Spilling. 2nd ed.; Marshall Cavendish Benchmark 2010 144p il map (Cultures of the world) lib bdg $42.79

Grades: 5 6 7 8   **956.93**

    ISBN 978-0-7614-4855-6 lib bdg; 0-7614-4855-1 lib bdg

                    LC 2009045689

    First published 2000

    This offers information on the geography, history, wildlife, governmental structure, economy, cultural diversity, peoples, religion, and culture of Cyprus

    Includes glossary and bibliographical references

956.94   Palestine; Israel

Ellis, Deborah

    ★ Three wishes; Palestinian and Israeli children speak. Groundwood Bks. 2004 110p il map hardcover o.p. pa $9.99

Grades: 5 6 7 8   **956.94**

    1. Palestinian Arabs 2. Israel-Arab conflicts

    ISBN 0-88899-608-X; 0-88899-645-4 pa

    "An excellent presentation of a confusing historic struggle, told within a palpable, perceptive and empathetic format." SLJ

    Includes bibliographical references

Frank, Mitch

    Understanding the Holy Land; answering questions about the Israeli-Palestinian Conflict. Viking 2005 152p il map (paperback) $8.99

Grades: 6 7 8 9 10   **956.94**

    1. Israel-Arab conflicts 2. Arab-Israeli conflict

    ISBN 0670060437; 9780670060436

                    LC 2004014973

    The author "tackles the complex subject of the Israeli-Palestinian conflict, making it comprehensible, if not any less horrific. . . . He uses a simple yet wonderfully effective technique to present the information: questions and answers. . . . Evenhanded and honest." Booklist

    Includes bibliographical references

Israel: opposing viewpoints; Myra Immell, book editor. Greenhaven Press 2011 193p map (Opposing viewpoints series) $41.70; pa $28.90

Grades: 8 9 10 11 12   **956.94**

    1. Israel-Arab conflicts

    ISBN 978-0-7377-4974-8; 0-7377-4974-1; 978-0-7377-4975-5 pa; 0-7377-4975-X pa

                    LC 2010022999

    Articles in this anthology discuss Israel's right to exist, key issues in the conflict between Israel and Palestine, and what U.S. policy should be regarding Israel.

    Includes bibliographical references

Owings, Lisa

    Israel; by Lisa Owings. ABDO Pub. Co. 2013 144 p. (library) $35.64

Grades: 8 9 10 11 12   **956.94**

    1. Israel

    ISBN 1617836303; 9781617836305

                    LC 2012946075

    This book by Lisa Owings is part of the Countries of the World series and looks at Israel. It "introduces Israel's history, geography, culture, climate, government, economy, and other significant features. Sidebars, maps, fact pages, a glossary, a timeline, historic images and full-color photos, and well-placed graphs and charts" are included. (Publisher's note)

Saul, Laya

    We visit Israel; by Laya Saul. Mitchell Lane Publishers 2012 63 p. ill., maps (library) $33.95

Grades: 4 5 6 7 8   **956.94**

    1. Israel -- Description and travel

    ISBN 158415957X; 9781584159575

                    LC 2011024706

    This book on Israel by Laya Saul is part of the "Your Land and My Land: The Middle East" series, which "provides an . . . introduction to the history and geography of several Middle Eastern and Southeast Asian countries from a tourist's perspective. . . . 'We Visit Israel' is clearly written from a Jewish Israeli perspective, but Saul makes sure to mention areas of conflict and controversy." Also included are a "recipe and a . . . craft project representing the country." (Booklist)

    Includes bibliographical references (p. 60-61) and index.

Wingate, Katherine

    The Intifadas; by Katherine Wingate. Rosen Pub. Group 2004 64p il map (War and conflict in the Middle East) lib bdg $26.50

Grades: 5 6 7 8   **956.95**

    1. Israel-Arab conflicts

    ISBN 0-8239-4546-4

                    LC 2003-12562

    "Wingate focuses on how the Palestinians lost their land and how the Palestinians in occupied territories retaliated. . . . Wingate sees hope in the peace organizations that work with young people. The series design is spacious, with clear type, lots of well-captioned news photos, up-to-date statistics, maps, and occasional boxed profiles of important leaders. . . . There's a lot to spark discussion." Booklist

    Includes glossary and bibliographical references

Young, Emma

★ Israel; [by] Emma Young; Zvi Ben-Dor Benite, George Kanazi, and Aviva Halamish, consultants. National Geographic 2008 64p il map (Countries of the world) lib bdg $27.90

Grades: 4 5 6 7   **956.94**

ISBN 978-1-4263-0258-9 lib bdg; 1-4263-0258-4 lib bdg

This describes the geography, nature, history, people and culture, government, and economy of Israel.

Includes glossary and bibliographical references

Zeigler, Donald J.

Israel; [by] Donald J. Zeigler. 2nd ed.; Chelsea House 2007 120p il map (Modern world nations) lib bdg $30

Grades: 7 8 9 10   **956.94**

ISBN 0-7910-9210-0

LC 2006014242

First published 2002

Describes the geography, history, people and culture, politics, and economy of Israel

Includes bibliographical references

956.95   Jordan and West Bank

958.1   Afghanistan

Ali, Sharifah Enayat

★ Afghanistan; by Sharifah Enayat Ali. 2nd ed.; Marshall Cavendish Benchmark 2006 144p il map (Cultures of the world) lib bdg $42.79

Grades: 5 6 7 8   **958.1**

ISBN 978-0-7614-2064-4 lib bdg; 0-7614-2064-9 lib bdg

LC 2005034789

First published 1995

This is "well organized, informative, and entertaining. . . . Excellent-quality full-color photographs and reproductions show the people, landforms, buildings, and everyday activities of [Afghanistan]." SLJ [review of 1995 edtion]

Includes glossary and bibliographical references

Behnke, Alison

Afghanistan in pictures; rev and expanded; Lerner Publs. 2003 80p il map (Visual geography series) lib bdg $31.93

Grades: 5 6 7 8   **958.1**

1. Afghanistan

ISBN 0-8225-4683-3

LC 2002-13613

An introduction to the geography, history, government, people, and economy of this landlocked country with a long history of warfare and conquest

Includes glossary and bibliographical references

Bjorklund, Ruth

Afghanistan; by Ruth Bjorklund. Children's Press 2012 144 p. col. ill., col. maps (library) $40

Grades: 5 6 7 8   **958.1**

1. Afghanistan 2. Afghanistan -- Description and travel

ISBN 0531253503; 9780531253502

LC 2011013627

This book by Ruth Bjorklund is part of the Enchantment of the World series and looks at Afghanistan. In each book, "colourful photos provide . . . views of foreign cities and landscapes," "sidebars highlight especially interesting people, places, and events," and "recipes give readers the opportunity to experience foreign cuisine firsthand." (Publisher's note)

Includes bibliographical references (p. 134-135) and index.

Hunter, Dawn

Beyond bullets; a photo journal of Afghanistan. by Rafal Gerszak, with Dawn Hunter; photographs by Rafal Gerszak. Annick Press 2011 127p il $19.95

Grades: 7 8 9 10 11 12   **958.1**

1. Photographers 2. Photojournalism 3. Afghan War, 2001- 4. Afghanistan

ISBN 978-1-55451-293-5; 1-55451-293-X

"Photographer Rafal Gerszak spent a year embedded with the American military in Afghanistan, where he used his camera to document everyday life in the wartorn country. While there, he developed a deep affection for the land and its people, and he later returned on his own. Framed by journal entries that relate his experiences on two levels—as a foreigner looking for a deeper connection to a country that has stirred him and as a journalist looking for another side to the story—Beyond Bullets addresses the volatile situation in Afghanistan." (Publisher's note)

"Author/photographer Gerszak first went to Afghanistan to spend a year embedded with an American military unit documenting house searches, disputes with village elders and the aftermath of battles. He returned as an unaffiliated photographer without a military escort, determined to document civilian life. This 'photo journal' features images from both trips to Afghanistan, accompanied by diary-like accounts of his travels. Gerszak's frank and descriptive observations effectively convey the ugliness, monotony and tragedy of war." Kirkus

Lusted, Marcia Amidon

The capture and killing of Osama bin Laden. ABDO Pub. Co. 2012 112p il (Essential events) lib bdg $23.95

Grades: 6 7 8   **958.1**

1. Terrorism 2. Terrorists

ISBN 978-1-61783-180-5; 1-61783-180-8

LC 2011025479

"Lusted explores Osama bin Laden's early life and the influences leading to his radicalization...The hunt for and eventual killing of bin Laden are not sensationalized." Horn Book

Includes glossary and bibliographical references

Steele, Philip

★ **Afghanistan**; from war to peace? by Philip Steele. 1st ed. Rosen Central 2012 48 p. col. ill., col. maps (library) $29.25

Grades: 6 7 8   **958.1**

1. Afghanistan -- History 2. Afghanistan -- Foreign relations 3. Afghanistan -- Politics and government

ISBN 9781448860302

LC 2012010616

This book by Philip Steele " examine[s] the history of Afghanistan, including its wars with the British Empire through its present-day occupation by American and NATO forces. Issues explored include the rise of the Taliban, the 9/11 attacks and the subsequent U.S. military ouster of the Taliban, the war of insurgency, and the plan for military withdrawal." (Publisher's note)

Includes bibliographical references and index.

Whitehead, Kim

Afghanistan; Revised ed. Mason Crest 2009 112 p. il map (Major Muslim Nations) lib bdg $25.95

Grades: 7 8 9 10   **958.1**

1. Islam

ISBN 9781422214039

This examines the ways Islam has influenced the culture and politics of Afghanistan, including how the Taliban came to power.

This "presents a cogent overview of [Afghanistan]. Excellent-quality photos and reproductions appear throughout." SLJ

Includes bibliographical references

Whitfield, Susan

★ **Afghanistan**; [by] Susan Whitfield; Thomas Barfield and Maliha Zulfacar, consultants. National Geographic 2008 64p il map (Countries of the world) lib bdg $27.90

Grades: 4 5 6 7   **958.1**

ISBN 978-1-4263-0256-5 lib bdg; 1-4263-0256-8 lib bdg

This describes the geography, nature, history, people and culture, government, and economy of Afghanistan.

Includes glossary and bibliographical references

958.4   Turkestan

King, David C.

Kyrgyzstan; [by] David C. King. Marshall Cavendish Benchmark 2005 144p il map (Cultures of the world) lib bdg $42.79

Grades: 5 6 7 8   **958.4**

ISBN 0-7614-2013-4

LC 2005001314

Describes the geography, history, government, economy, people, and culture of Kyrgyzstan

Includes glossary and bibliographical references

Pang, Guek-Cheng, 1950-

Kazakhstan; 2nd ed.; Marshall Cavendish Benchmark 2011 144p il map (Cultures of the world) lib bdg $42.79

Grades: 5 6 7 8   **958.4**

ISBN 978-1-6087-0455-2; 1-6087-0455-6

First published 2001

This offers information on the geography, history, wildlife, governmental structure, economy, cultural diversity, peoples, religion, and culture of Kazakhstan.

958.5   Turkmenistan

Knowlton, MaryLee

Turkmenistan; [by] MaryLee Knowlton. Marshall Cavendish Benchmark 2006 144p il map (Cultures of the world) lib bdg $42.79

Grades: 5 6 7 8   **958.5**

ISBN 0-7614-2014-2

LC 2005006455

Describes the geography, history, government, economy, people, and culture of Turkmenistan

Includes glossary and bibliographical references

958.6   Tajikistan

Abazov, Rafis

Tajikistan; [by] Rafis Abazov. Marshall Cavendish Benchmark 2006 144p il map (Cultures of the world) lib bdg $42.79

Grades: 5 6 7 8   **958.6**

ISBN 0-7614-2012-6

LC 2005001166

Describes the geography, history, government, economy, people, and culture of the former Soviet republic of Tajikistan

Includes glossary and bibliographical references

959   Southeast Asia

Phillips, Douglas A.

Southeast Asia; series consulting editor Charles F. Gritzner. Chelsea House Publishers 2006 129p (Modern world cultures) lib bdg $30

Grades: 7 8 9 10   **959**

ISBN 0-7910-8149-4

This describes the geography, history, people and cultures, politics, economics, and possible future of Southeast Asia.

This "accessible [title is] generously illustrated with colorful photos, maps, and clear charts, graphs, and other statistical data. . . . Phillips does an excellent job of organizing each topic by providing clear and outlined information. The research is well done, and information and statistics are up to date." SLJ

959.105   Myanmar-- 1948-

O'Keefe, Sherry

Champion of freedom; Aung San Suu Kyi. Sherry O'Keefe. Morgan Reynolds Pub. 2011 160 p. ill. (some col.), col. maps $28.95

Grades: 7 8 9 10 11 12   **959.105**
  1. Myanmar 2. Political activists 3. Democracy -- Burma 4. Women Nobel Prize winners -- Burma -- Biography 5. Women political activists -- Burma -- Biography 6. Women political prisoners -- Burma -- Biography
  ISBN 1599351684; 9781599351681; 9781599353142
                                          LC 2011035740
Author Sherry O'Keefe tells the story of politician Aung San Suu Kyi. "Knowing that the military regime will not allow her to return if she leaves, the Nobel Peace Prize laureate has remained in Burma, enduring extreme isolation, the threat of death, and personal pain and sacrifice, including the chance to see her dying husband one last time. . . . [Suu Kyi] remains as determined as ever to see Burma emerge from its isolation and join the family of democratic nations in the world." (Publisher's note)
Includes bibliographical references and index.

959.3   Thailand

Phillips, Douglas A.

Thailand. Chelsea House 2007 108p il map (Modern world nations) lib bdg $30

Grades: 7 8 9 10   **959.3**
  ISBN 978-0-7910-9250-7 lib bdg; 0-7910-9250-X lib bdg
                                          LC 2006032009
Describes the geography, history, people, culture, economy, and government of Thailand
Includes bibliographical references

959.4   Laos

Dalal, A. Kamala

  ★ **Laos**; [by] A. Kamala Dalal. National Geographic 2009 64p il (Countries of the world) lib bdg $27.90

Grades: 4 5 6 7   **959.4**
  ISBN 978-1-4263-0388-3 lib bdg; 1-4263-0388-2 lib bdg
This describes the geography, nature, history, people and culture, and govenment and economy of Laos
Includes glossary and bibliographical references

959.5   Malaysia, Brunei, Singapore

Foo Yuk Yee

  Malaysia; by Heidi Munan, Foo Yuk Yee, and Jo-Ann Spilling. 3rd ed. Marshall Cavendish Benchmark 2012 144 p. col. ill., col. maps (library) $47.07

Grades: 5 6 7 8   **959.5**
  1. Culture 2. Malaysia
  ISBN 1608707857; 9781608707850
                                          LC 2011004468
This book by Heidi Munan is part of the Cultures of the World series and looks at Malaysia. The "geography, history, economy and culture are all covered . . . . An entire chapter is devoted to the festivals, which are many because of the ethnic diversity of Malaysia. This is also made apparent in the section about food and manners, as the Muslims do not eat pork and the Hindus and Sikhs cannot eat beef, making it necessary to prepare various dishes for parties." Children's Literature
Includes bibliographical references

959.57   Singapore

Layton, Leslie

  Singapore; by Lesley Layton, Pang Guek Cheng,and Jo-Ann Spilling. 3rd ed. Marshall Cavendish Benchmark 2012 144 p. (library) $47.07

Grades: 5 6 7 8   **959.57**
  1. Singapore
  ISBN 1608707873; 9781608707874
                                          LC 2011004479
This book is part of the Cultures of the World series and looks at Singapore. "Singapore is a small but mighty nation. Thanks to its strategic position and the energy of its people—the Malays, and migrant Chinese, Indians, and Eurasians—it is now the world's number one airport and sea port, a regional financial center, a telecommunications hub, and a favored tourist destination." (Publisher's note)
Includes bibliographical references

959.604   Cambodia-- 1949-

Sonneborn, Liz

  The **Khmer** Rouge; by Liz Sonneborn. Marshall Cavendish Benchmark 2012 80 p. ill. (some col.), col. map (library) $34.21; (ebook) $34.21

Grades: 5 6 7 8   **959.604**
  1. Dith Pran, 1942-2008 2. Genocide -- Cambodia 3. Cambodia -- History -- 1975- 4. Political atrocities -- Cambodia 5. Journalists -- Cambodia -- Biography 6. Political refugees -- Cambodia -- Biography
  ISBN 1608704742; 9781608704743; 9781608706952 pdf
                                          LC 2011005595
This book "tells the story of Dith Pran, a Cambodian journalist and translator who provided support to Sydney Schanberg, a New York Times correspondent. . . . Sadly, when Schanberg evacuated, Pran was forced to remain behind where he fell into captivity. Over a three year period Dith Pran survived horrendous conditions but ultimately escaped and fled to Thailand. There, in a refugee camp, Pran was rescued by Schanberg and relocated to the United States." Children's Literature
Includes bibliographical references

959.7   Vietnam

Green, Jen
★ **Vietnam**; [by] Jen Green. National Geographic 2008 64p il map (Countries of the world) lib bdg $27.90
Grades: 4 5 6 7   959.7
   ISBN 978-1-4263-0202-2
                                    LC 2007047832
   This describes the geography, nature, history, people and culture, government, and economy of Vietnam.
   Includes glossary and bibliographical references

959.704   Vietnam-- 1945-

Caputo, Philip
★ **10,000** days of thunder; a history of the Vietnam War. [by] Philip Caputo. 1st ed; Atheneum Books for Young Readers 2005 128p il $22.95
Grades: 6 7 8 9   959.704
   1. Vietnam War, 1961-1975 2. Vietnamese Conflict, 1961-1975
   ISBN 0-689-86231-8
                                    LC 2004-15468
   In this history of the Vietnam War "Caputo has produced what is at once an overview and a sensitive, resonant picture of the war as seen and experienced by American soldiers, the Viet Cong, North Vietnamese guerrillas, and the citizens of both South Vietnam and the United States. . . . Caputo's prose is clear and direct, and the award-winning photos . . . add an immediacy that sets this title apart from more conventional treatments." SLJ
   Includes glossary and bibliographical references

DiConsiglio, John
   Vietnam; the bloodbath at Hamburger Hill. Franklin Watts 2010 64p il map (24/7: goes to war) lib bdg $27; pa $7.95
Grades: 6 7 8 9   959.704
   1. Hamburger Hill, Battle of, Vietnam, 1969
   ISBN 978-0-531-25526-1 lib bdg; 0-531-25526-3 lib bdg; 978-0-531-25451-6 pa; 0-531-25451-8 pa
                                    LC 2009-14912
   Describes the eight-day battle in May 1969 where American forces struggled to capture a tiny piece of the Vietnam countryside, considered a watershed turning point in the Vietnam War
   This "will appeal to these readers, because . . . [it tells] a story while presenting the facts. . . . The first chapter gives the historic details concerning the war up to the particular battle, with the story of the battle told from a first-person perspective. A mixture of news photos and photos taken by the men involved appear throughout the book." Libr Media Connect
   Includes glossary and bibliographical references

Gifford, Clive
   Why did the Vietnam War happen? Gareth Stevens 2011 48p il map (Moments in history) lib bdg $31.95; pa $14.05

Grades: 6 7 8 9   959.704
   1. Vietnam War, 1961-1975
   ISBN 978-1-4339-4178-8 lib bdg; 1-4339-4178-3 lib bdg; 978-1-4339-4179-5 pa; 1-4339-4179-1 pa
                                    LC 2010015835
   This book looks at the causes of the Vietnam War and surrounding controversies.
   "Brightly colored pull-out boxes highlight important turning points, the perspective of the everyday man, and further information on why specific events occurred. Numerous photographs help readers visualize concepts more fully. . . . Students should be able to easily use this resource." Libr Media Connect
   Includes glossary and bibliographical references

Gitlin, Marty
   U.S. involvement in Vietnam; by Martin Gitlin; content consultant Clarence R. Wyatt. ABDO Pub. Co. 2010 112p il map (Essential events) lib bdg $32.79
Grades: 6 7 8 9   959.704
   1. Vietnam War, 1961-1975
   ISBN 978-1-60453-949-3; 1-60453-949-6
                                    LC 2009-31071
   This title examines an important historic event, the U.S. involvement in Vietnam. Readers will learn about the events leading up to this, including Communist North Vietnam taking military action over South Vietnam, the United States sending aid to South Vietnam.
   "The writing is accessible and is richer than a lot of history writing, allowing the reader to become engaged in the text as a story, and the layout provides enought white space to allow lower level readers to feel confident." Libr Media Connect
   Includes glossary and bibliographical references

Senker, Cath
   The **Vietnam** War; by Cath Senker. Heinemann Library 2012 80 p. ill. (some col.), col. maps (Living through) (library) $36.50; (paperback) $10.99
Grades: 6 7 8 9   959.704
   1. Vietnam War, 1961-1975
   ISBN 1432960008; 9781432960001; 9781432960094
                                    LC 2011015928
   In this book on the Vietnam War, part of the "Living Through" series, author "[Cath] Senker begins her story with the French colonization of Southeast Asia and ends it with an analysis of why the war ended the way it did. In between, Senker takes her readers back to a time in American history when policies went awry and the nation imposed terrible destruction on foreign lands and its own people." (Children's Literature)
   Includes bibliographical references (p. 76-77) and index

Skrypuch, Marsha Forchuk
   Last airlift; a Vietnamese orphan's rescue from war. Marsha Forchuk Skrypuch. Pajama Press 2012 120 p. $17.95
Grades: 3 4 5 6   959.704
   1. Orphans 2. Aeronautics -- Flights 3. International adoption 4. Evacuation of civilians -- Vietnam 5.

Vietnam War, 1961-1975 -- Children
ISBN 098694954X; 9780986949548

This book "tells the story of the last Canadian airlift [from Vietnam] through the memories of one child, Son Thi Anh Tuyet. Nearly 8 years old, the sad-eyed girl . . . had lived nearly all her life in a Catholic orphanage." When "she and a number of the institution babies were taken away, placed on an airplane and flown to a new world. . . . she assumed that John and Dorothy Morris had chosen her to help with their three children; instead, she had acquired a family." (Kirkus Reviews)

Young, Marilyn Blatt

The **Vietnam** War: a history in documents; [by] Marilyn B. Young, John J. Fitzgerald, A. Tom Grunfeld. Oxford Univ. Press 2002 175p il maps (Pages from history) lib bdg $32.95; pa $19.95
Grades: 7 8 9 10   **959.704**
1. Vietnam War, 1961-1975 2. Vietnamese Conflict, 1961-1975 -- History -- Sources
ISBN 0-19-512278-X lib bdg; 0-19-516635-3 pa
LC 2001-52338

"The documents are skillfully tied together by brief text that gives good background information. . . . The book is well balanced in showing both sides. . . . Good-quality, black-and-white photos and illustrations are plentiful and informative." SLJ

Includes glossary and bibliographical references

959.8   Indonesia and East Timor

Cooper, Robert

Indonesia; by Gouri Mirpuri and Robert Cooper. 3rd ed. Marshall Cavendish Benchmark 2012 144 p. ill., maps (library) $47.07
Grades: 5 6 7 8   **959.8**
1. Indonesia -- History 2. Indonesia
ISBN 1608707830; 9781608707836
LC 200128607

First published 1990

This "nonfiction book in the 'Cultures of the World' series presents a . . . story of the physical, social and historical characteristics of Indonesia. . . . Throughout the book, also, there are textboxes that add . . . information to the subject matter and include . . . drawings of native musical instruments, weapons, foods and other" things. (Children's Literature)

"The pictures are lush, with captions in tiny print offering much additional information. The text is written smoothly and readably, and it contains a substantial amount of information." Booklist

Includes bibliographical references and index.

959.9   Philippines

Skog, Jason

Teens in the Philippines; by Jason Skog. Compass Point Books 2009 96p il map (Global connections) lib bdg $33.26

Grades: 6 7 8 9   **959.9**
1. Teenagers 2. Philippines
ISBN 978-0-7565-3853-8 lib bdg; 0-7565-3853-X lib bdg
LC 2008-6504

Uncovers the challenges, pastimes, customs and culture of teens in the Philippines

This book is "concise and highly readable. . . . Clear, colorful photos and sidebars on a range of topics provide further context. . . . [This title] will enrich young adult collections." SLJ

Includes glossary and bibliographical references

960   History of Africa

Africa: an encyclopedia for students; John Middleton, editor. Scribner 2002 4v il maps set $395
Grades: 7 8 9 10   **960**
1. Reference books 2. Africa -- Encyclopedias
ISBN 0-684-80650-9
LC 2001-49348

A comprehensive look at the continent of Africa and the countries that comprise it, including peoples and cultures, the land and its history, art and architecture, and daily life

Africa: opposing viewpoints; David M. Haugen, book editor. Gale/Cengage Learning 2008 219p (Opposing viewpoints series) lib bdg $39.70; pa $27.50
Grades: 8 9 10 11 12   **960**
1. Africa -- Politics and government 2. Africa -- Social conditions 3. Africa -- Economic conditions
ISBN 978-0-7377-3988-6 lib bdg; 978-0-7377-3989-3 pa
LC 2008-811

Articles in this anthology discuss important issues facing Africa today, foreign aid and free trade, the status of democracy and human rights in Africa, and ways the United States and other western nations can help Africa.

Includes bibliographical references

Bowden, Rob, 1973-

★ **African** culture; [by] Rob Bowden and Rosie Wilson. Heinemann Library 2009 48p il map (Africa focus) $30; pa $8.99
Grades: 4 5 6   **960**
1. Africa -- Civilization 2. Africa -- Social life and customs
ISBN 978-1-4329-2440-9; 1-4329-2440-0; 978-1-4329-2445-4 pa; 1-4329-2445-1 pa
LC 2008-48310

This book "presents a clear and timely overview of the diverse and complex continent. The full-color photographs are of exceptional quality. [The] book also includes interesting fact boxes, sidebars, maps, and a time line. [It] focuses on traditions and how they are relevant for today. Highlights include family and daily life; religion, beliefs, and customs; and the performing and visual arts." SLJ

Includes bibliographical references

★ **Ancient** Africa; [by] Rob Bowden and Rosie Wilson. Heinemann Library 2008 48p il map (Africa focus) $30; pa $8.99

Grades: 4 5 6   **960**
1. Africa -- History
ISBN 978-1-4329-2439-3; 1-4329-2439-7; 978-1-4329-2444-7 pa; 1-4329-2444-3 pa
LC 2008-48306

This book "presents a clear and timely overview of the diverse and complex continent. The full-color photographs are of exceptional quality. [The] book also includes interesting fact boxes, sidebars, maps, and a time line. . . . [It] begins with the origin of humankind and continues through the beginning of the slave trade in Europe and America. Early civilizations such as Egypt, ancient Ghana, the Mali Empire, Great Zimbabwe, and Kongo are represented. Invasions and explorations are discussed, as is slavery and colonialism." SLJ
Includes bibliographical references

★ **Changing** Africa; [by] Rob Bowden and Rosie Wilson. Heinemann Library 2009 48p il map (Africa focus) $30; pa $8.99

Grades: 4 5 6   **960**
1. Africa -- Social conditions 2. Africa -- Economic conditions
ISBN 978-1-4329-2437-9; 1-4329-2437-0; 978-1-4329-2442-3 pa; 1-4329-2442-7 pa
LC 2008-48277

This book "presents a clear and timely overview of the diverse and complex continent. The full-color photographs are of exceptional quality. [The] book also includes interesting fact boxes, sidebars, maps, and a time line. . . . [It] presents recent positive and negative changes. The rise of poverty and slums is explored, as is the lowered life expectancy due to the spread of malaria and HIV/AIDS. Positive changes include the freedom that voting has brought." SLJ
Includes bibliographical references

★ **Modern** Africa; [by] Rosie Wilson and Rob Bowden. Heinemann Library 2009 48p il map (Africa focus) $30; pa $8.99

Grades: 4 5 6   **960**
1. Africa
ISBN 978-1-4329-2438-6; 1-4329-2438-9; 978-1-4329-2443-0 pa; 1-4329-2443-5 pa

This book "presents a clear and timely overview of the diverse and complex continent. The full-color photographs are of exceptional quality. [The] book also includes interesting fact boxes, sidebars, maps, and a time line. . . . [It] chronicles the history of colonial Africa to independence, and the changes that have arisen and continue to manifest themselves. Topics include apartheid and recent and ongoing violence in Rwanda, Darfur, and the Congo. While corrupt leaders continue to hamper Africa's attempts at advancement, the exportation of oil as well as aid from missionaries and international organizations are presented as hopes for the future." SLJ

Diagram Group
African history on file; rev ed; Facts on File 2003 various paging il maps loose-leaf $185

Grades: Adult Professional   **960**
1. Africa -- History
ISBN 0-8160-5139-9
LC 2002-192848

First published 1994
More than 500 "reproducible maps, charts, timelines, and drawings visually detail the broad range of human experience in Africa, from prehistory to the present." Publisher's note
Includes bibliographical references

Habeeb, William Mark
Africa; Facts and Figures. by William Mark Habeeb. Mason Crest Publishers 2012 87 p. ill. (chiefly col.), col. map (library) $22.95

Grades: 7 8 9 10   **960**
1. Africa -- History 2. Africa -- Social conditions 3. Africa -- Politics and government 4. Africa
ISBN 1422221768; 9781422221761
LC 2010048000

This book is "[t]he first of a new series, 'Continent in the Balance: Africa,' . . . introduces the continent in all its geographical and cultural diversity. . . . [H]istorian [William Mark] Habeeb discusses the huge contemporary problems in many countries, including poverty and AIDS, and examines how colonialism carved up the continent with arbitrary borders that have resulted in devastating ethnic and religious conflicts that exist even today." Booklist

This is an "excellent, detailed overview. . . . The attractive, open design, with clear type, beautiful photos, maps, and lots of extras in lists and insets, manages to pack in an extraordinary amount of information." Booklist
Includes bibliographical references

Mooney, Carla
Amazing Africa; projects you can build yourself. illustrated by Megan Stearns. Nomad Press 2010 122p il (Build it yourself) pa $15.95

Grades: 4 5 6 7   **960**
1. Handicraft 2. Africa
ISBN 978-1-934670-41-5; 1-934670-41-3

"Casual and informative, this large, attractive, browsable paperback . . . offers a view of contemporary African life that reaches far beyond the usual scenery-and-wildlife tourists' perspective. Blending history, culture, and tradition with politics and life in both cities and rural areas, the chapters begin with a look at natural wonders and dangerous wildlife that will grab readers, then move on to historical discussions of humankind's birthplace and early civilizations. . . . The open design includes sketches on every page. . . . The craft projects [include making] your own Maasai beaded necklace, kente cloth, woven basket, galimoto doll, and . . . more." Booklist

Murray, Jocelyn
Africa; updated by Brian A. Stewart. 3rd ed.; Chelsea House 2007 96p il map (Cultural atlas for young people) $35

Grades: 5 6 7 8   **960**
ISBN 978-0-8160-6826-5; 0-8160-6826-7
First published 1990

Presents information on the history and various regions and cultures of Africa.

Includes glossary and bibliographical references

Nardo, Don

The **European** colonization of Africa. Morgan Reynolds 2010 112p il (World history) lib bdg $28.95

Grades: 7 8 9 10 11 12   960

1. Colonies -- Africa

ISBN 978-1-59935-142-1 lib bdg; 1-59935-142-0 lib bdg

"Drawing on some of the best scholarship, this compelling account of Europeans' colonization of Africa begins with Greco-Roman and early medieval times. Then, with the horiffic facts of the slave trade, Nardo goes on to discuss the greed and brutality of the mad 'scramble' for African land by those who saw themselves as chosen people of God. . . . With period illustrations, the design . . . is clear and open, and the excellent back matter . . . will spark further research." Booklist

Includes bibliographical references (p. 98-106)

Peoples and cultures of Africa; edited by Peter Mitchell. Chelsea House 2006 6v il map set $234

Grades: 5 6 7 8   960

1. Reference books 2. Ethnology -- Africa

ISBN 0-8160-6260-9 set; 978-0-8160-6261-4 v1; 978-0-8160-6262-1 v2; 978-0-8160-6263-8 v3; 978-0-8160-6264-5 v4; 978-0-8160-6265-2 v5; 978-0-8160-6266-9 v6

LC 2006040011

"This attractive and informative set provides well-written, well-researched introductory information about African geography and culture. Each of the first five volumes covers a region within the continent . . . and opens with introductory information on that area's physical features, biomes, religions, languages, and cultures, and includes an extensive time line. It is followed by color-coded, alphabetically arranged entries examining the region's tribal and ethnic groups; art, sculpture, and textiles; performing arts and literature; and religion and individual cultures in further detail. . . . The final volume is devoted to single-page geographic and economic profiles of Africa's nations. . . . This quality set will give report writers a solid introduction to the diversity of Africa." SLJ

Includes bibliographical references

961.1   Tunisia

Brown, Roslind Varghese

Tunisia; [by] Roslind Varghese Brown & Michael Spilling. 2nd ed.; Marshall Cavendish Benchmark 2008 144p il map (Cultures of the world) lib bdg $42.79

Grades: 5 6 7 8   961.1

ISBN 978-0-7614-3037-7 lib bdg; 0-7614-3037-7 lib bdg

LC 2007050798

First published 1998

"Provides comprehensive information on the geography, history, wildlife, governmental structure, economy, cultural diversity, peoples, religion, and culture of Tunisia." Publisher note

Includes glossary and bibliographical references

962   Egypt, Sudan, South Sudan

Heinrichs, Ann

The **Nile**. Marshall Cavendish Benchmark 2008 96p il map (Nature's wonders) lib bdg $24.95

Grades: 5 6 7 8   962

1. Nile River 2. Nile River valley

ISBN 978-0-7614-2854-1

LC 2007019187

"It's tough to make a river interesting, but this . . . does an admirable job of it. . . . Crisp, full-color photos and original artwork decorate nearly every page. . . . [This is a] well-thought-out natural history." Booklist

Includes glossary and bibliographical references

Zuehlke, Jeffrey

Egypt in pictures. Lerner Publs. 2003 80p il map (Visual geography series) lib bdg $31.93

Grades: 5 6 7 8   962

1. Egypt

ISBN 0-8225-0367-0

LC 2001-6613

Discusses the physical features, history, government, people, culture, and economy of Egypt

Includes bibliographical references

962.4   Sudan and South Sudan

Brownlie, Ali

Sudan in our world; by Ali Brownlie Bojang. Smart Apple Media 2010 32p il (Countries in our world) lib bdg $28.50

Grades: 5 6 7 8   962.4

1. Sudan

ISBN 978-1-59920-434-5 lib bdg; 1-59920-434-7 lib bdg

LC 2009052421

"Issues such as Civil War, fighting in Darfur, the government, and millions of displaced refugees continue to cripple the country and impede its advancement. While Sudan is rich in resources, its future remains uncertain. [This title] will appeal to children interested in learning more about Africa and those needing factual information for reports." SLJ

Includes glossary and bibliographical references

The **crisis** in Darfur; Jeff Hay, book editor. Greenhaven Press 2011 165p il map (Perspectives on modern world history) $39.70

Grades: 8 9 10 11 12   962.4

1. Sudan -- History -- Darfur conflict, 2003-

ISBN 978-0-7377-5257-1; 0-7377-5257-2

LC 2010033168

In discussing "the continuing human tragedy in Darfur, [this] well-organized [volume presents] a wealth of clearly written analyses from a rich variety of viewpoints. With the inclusion of historical background, firsthand experiences, and discussions of particular points of controversy, [it helps] to familiarize readers with the [topic] . . . and [serves] as [an exercise] in the development of analytical thinking skills." SLJ

Includes bibliographical references

Dau, John Bul

Lost boy, lost girl; escaping civil war in Sudan. by John Bul Dau and Martha Arual Akech; with Michael Sweeney and K. M. Kostyal. National Geographic 2010 159p il map $15.95; lib bdg $23.90

Grades: 7 8 9 10   962.4

1. Refugees 2. Students 3. Memoirists

ISBN 978-1-4263-0708-9; 1-4263-0708-X; 978-1-4263-0709-6 lib bdg; 1-4263-0709-8 lib bdg

LC 2010-17960

"The tragic story of Sudan's Lost Boys and Lost [Girls] is told in simple language by two survivors. . . . In 1987, when Dau was 13 and Akech was 6, war came to their village. Both traveled hundreds of miles to a UN refugee camp in Ethiopia. After a few years of safety, the refugees were forced to move again. . . . Teens who know little about Sudan and its problems will be drawn into this moving, inspiration story." SLJ

Levy, Patricia

Sudan; [by] Patricia Levy and Zawiah Abdul Latif. 2nd ed.; Marshall Cavendish Benchmark 2008 144p il map (Cultures of the world) lib bdg $42.79

Grades: 5 6 7 8   962.4

ISBN 978-0-7614-2083-5 lib bdg; 0-7614-2083-5 lib bdg

LC 2006101725

Describes the geography, history, government, economy, people, lifestyle, religion, language, arts, leisure, festivals, and food of Sudan

Includes bibliographical references

Steele, Philip

★ **Sudan,** Darfur and the nomadic conflicts; by Philip Steele. 1st ed. Rosen Pub. 2013 48 p. col. ill. (library) $29.25

Grades: 6 7 8   962.4

1. Current events 2. Sudan -- History -- Darfur conflict, 2003-

ISBN 1448860288; 9781448860289

LC 2012010639

This book by Philip Steele is part of the Our World Divided series and looks at Sudan, Darfur, and the nomadic conflicts. "Each of these volumes begins with a recent news event pertaining to the featured conflict and then looks back at the origin and milestones of the discord. . . . 'Viewpoints' sidebars . . . showcase quotations about a specific matter from individuals on opposing sides." (School Library Journal)

Includes bibliographical references (p. 46) and index.

Xavier, John

★ **Darfur**; African genocide. [by] John Xavier. 1st ed.; Rosen Pub. Group 2008 64p il map (In the news) $29.95

Grades: 6 7 8 9   962.4

1. Genocide 2. Sudan -- History -- Darfur conflict, 2003-

ISBN 978-1-4042-1912-0; 1-4042-1912-9

LC 2007002909

An overview of the crisis in Darfur, its history and why it matters.

"Informative reflection of today's headlines. . . . In-depth exploration of the crisis in Darfur, the history of the conflict, and why it matters to the rest of the world. . . . The glossaries and Web sites at the end of each are most helpful." Voice Youth Advocates

Includes glossary and bibliographical references

963   Ethiopia and Eritrea

Gish, Steven

★ **Ethiopia**; [by] Steven Gish & Winnie Thay & Zawiah Abdul Latif. 2nd ed.; Marshall Cavendish Benchmark 2007 144p il map (Cultures of the world) lib bdg $42.79

Grades: 5 6 7 8   963

ISBN 978-0-7614-2025-5 lib bdg; 0-7614-2025-8 lib bdg

LC 2006020819

First published 1996

This provides "information on the geography, history, governmental structure, economy, cultural diversity, peoples, religion, and culture of Ethiopia." Publisher's note

Includes glossary and bibliographical references

963.5   Eritrea

NgCheong-Lum, Roseline

Eritrea; 2nd ed.; Marshall Cavendish Benchmark 2011 144p il map (Cultures of the world) lib bdg $42.79

Grades: 5 6 7 8   963.5

ISBN 978-1-6087-0454-5; 1-6087-0454-8

LC 2010035973

First published 2001

Provides information on the geography, history, wildlife, governmental structure, economy, cultural diversity, peoples, religion, and culture of Eritea.

"Plentiful color photographs accompany substantial amounts of information." SLJ

Includes glossary and bibliographical references

964 Morocco, Ceuta, Melilla, Western Sahara, Canary Islands

Seward, Pat

Morocco; [by] Pat Seward & Orin Hargraves. 2nd ed.; Marshall Cavendish Benchmark 2006 144p il map (Cultures of the world) lib bdg $42.79

Grades: 5 6 7 8   **964**

ISBN 0-7614-2051-7

LC 2005020782

First published 1995

Describes the geography, history, government, economy, people, and culture of Morocco

Includes glossary and bibliographical references

965 Algeria

Kagda, Falaq

Algeria; [by] Falaq Kagda & Zawiah Abdul Latif. 2nd ed.; Marshall Cavendish Benchmark 2008 144p il map (Cultures of the world) lib bdg $42.79

Grades: 5 6 7 8   **965**

ISBN 978-0-7614-2085-9 lib bdg; 0-7614-2085-1 lib bdg

LC 2007014888

First published 1997

"Provides comprehensive information on the geography, history, wildlife, governmental structure, economy, cultural diversity, peoples, religion, and culture of Algeria." Publisher's note

Includes glossary and bibliographical references

Wagner, Heather Lehr

The Algerian war; by Heather Lehr Wagner. Chelsea House 2012 120 p. (Milestones in modern world history) (hardcover) $35

Grades: 7 8 9 10 11 12   **965**

1. France -- Foreign relations -- Algeria 2. Algeria -- History -- 1954-1962, Revolution 3. National liberation movements -- Algeria
ISBN 1604139234; 9781604139235

LC 2011023060

This book, part of the Milestones in Modern World History series, "opens with a triumphant France celebrating its freedom at the end of WWII while citizens of its colony, Algeria, were denied their own equality and freedom. Following an overview of Algerian possession, the text outlines French injustices toward Algeria, most notably discrimination of its Muslim population and the rise of revolution." (Booklist)

Includes bibliographical references

966 West Africa and offshore islands

Haywood, John

West African kingdoms; [by] John Haywood. Raintree 2008 64p il map (Time travel guide) lib bdg $34.29; pa $9.99

Grades: 6 7 8 9   **966**

1. Mali -- History 2. Songhai Empire 3. West Africa 4. Ghana Empire
ISBN 978-1-4109-2912-9 lib bdg; 978-1-4109-2918-1 pa

LC 2007006053

This describes life in West Africa between 1200 and 1600 AD, including the kingdoms of Mali, Songhai, and Benin, in the form of a travel guide.

Includes glossary and bibliographical references

Heinrichs, Ann

The Sahara; [by] Ann Heinrichs. Marshall Cavendish Benchmark 2009 96p il map (Nature's wonders) lib bdg $24.95

Grades: 5 6 7 8   **966**

1. Sahara Desert
ISBN 978-0-7614-2855-8 lib bdg; 0-7614-2855-0 lib bdg

LC 2007-20326

This book is "full of interesting information and feature[s] a format that enables students to quickly find specific information." Voice Youth Advocates

Includes glossary and bibliographical references

966.1 Mauritania

Blauer, Ettagale

Mauritania; [by] Ettagale Blauer & Jason Lauré. Marshall Cavendish Benchmark 2009 144p il map (Cultures of the world) lib bdg $42.79

Grades: 5 6 7 8   **966.1**

ISBN 978-0-7614-3116-9

This describes the geography, history, government, economy, environment, people, and culture of Mauritania

966.2 Mali, Burkina Faso, Niger

Blauer, Ettagale

Mali; [by] Ettagale Blauer & Jason Lauré. 2nd ed.; Marshall Cavendish Benchmark 2008 144p il map (Cultures of the world) lib bdg $42.79

Grades: 5 6 7 8   **966.2**

ISBN 978-0-7614-2568-7

First published 1997

This describes the geography, history, government, economy, environment, people, and culture of Mali

Includes glossary and bibliographical references

McKissack, Patricia C.

The royal kingdoms of Ghana, Mali, and Songhay; life in medieval Africa. [by] Patricia and Fredrick McKissack. Holt & Co. 1993 142p il maps hardcover o.p. pa $12.99

Grades: 5 6 7 8   **966.2**
1. Mali -- History 2. Ghana Empire 3.
Songhai Empire
ISBN 0-8050-4259-8 pa

LC 93-4838

Examines the civilizations of the Western Sudan which flourished from 700 to 1700 A.D., acquiring such vast wealth that they became centers of trade and culture for a continent

"The McKissacks are careful to distinguish what is known from what is surmised; they draw on the oral tradition, eyewitness accounts, and contemporary scholarship; and chapter source notes discuss various conflicting views of events." Booklist
Includes bibliographical references

966.3   Senegal

Berg, Elizabeth
   Senegal; by Elizabeth L. Berg and Ruth Lau. 2nd ed.; Marshall Cavendish Benchmark 2009 144p il map (Cultures of the world) lib bdg $42.79
Grades: 5 6 7 8   **966.3**
   ISBN 978-0-7614-4481-7 lib bdg; 0-7614-4481-5 lib bdg

LC 2009007067

First published 1999
Describes the geography, history, wildlife, governmental structure, economy, cultural diversity, peoples, religion, and culture of Senegal
Includes glossary and bibliographical references

Mulroy, Tanya
   Senegal; [by] Tanya Mulroy. Mason Crest Publishers 2008 79p il map (Africa: continent in the balance) lib bdg $21.95
Grades: 5 6 7 8   **966.3**
   ISBN 978-1-4222-0091-9 lib bdg; 1-4222-0091-4 lib bdg

LC 2006-17341

This book is "clear and concise, and the authors' easy-to-read texts impart a good deal of up-to-date information. . . . Chapters . . . cover the . . . country's history; politics and government; economy; and people, including discussions of family life, education, ethnic groups, health care, sports, and the arts, with the focus being on the largest cities." SLJ
Includes glossary and bibliographical references

966.4   Sierra Leone

Fowler, Will
   Counterterrorism in West Africa; the most dangerous SAS assault. Rosen Pub. 2011 64p il map (The most daring raids in history) lib bdg $29.25
Grades: 7 8 9 10   **966.4**
   1. Rescue work 2. Sierra Leone -- History -- Civil War, 1991- 3. Great Britain -- Army -- Special Air Service Regiment
ISBN 978-1-4488-1871-6; 1-4488-1871-0

LC 2010029621

This book offers a scene-by-scene account of the SAS (Special Air Service) and Operation Barras in Sierra Leone in 2000.

This book is "packed with facts, covering the details of the action, the people involved, and the tools used, in engaging prose. The authors cite their sources thoroughly. . . . Diagrams, photos, . . . and maps make the action easy to follow and provide visual context for the raids. . . . This . . . is sure to find a large readership." SLJ
Includes glossary and bibliographical references

Hasday, Judy L.
   Sierra Leone; [by] Judy Hasday. Mason Crest Publishers 2008 79p il map (Africa: continent in the balance) lib bdg $21.95
Grades: 5 6 7 8   **966.4**
   ISBN 978-1-4222-0092-6; 1-4222-0092-2

LC 2006-17342

This book features the country's "history; politics and government; economy; and people, including discussions of family life, education, ethnic groups, health care, sports, and the arts, with the focus being on the largest cities. . . . Interspersed throughout are numerous color and some black-and-white photographs, with descriptive captions, as well as 'Quick Facts' regarding geography, the economy, and the people. . . . The information is presented in an engaging manner." SLJ
Includes glossary and bibliographical references

LeVert, Suzanne
   ★ Sierra Leone; [by] Suzanne LeVert. Marshall Cavendish Benchmark 2007 144p il map (Cultures of the world) lib bdg $42.79
Grades: 5 6 7 8   **966.4**
   ISBN 978-0-7614-2334-8 lib bdg; 0-7614-2334-6 lib bdg

LC 2005035964

This provides "information on the geography, history, governmental structure, economy, cultural diversity, peoples, religion, and culture of Sierra Leone." Publisher's note
Includes glossary and bibliographical references

966.62   Liberia

Reef, Catherine
   ★ **This** our dark country; the American settlers of Liberia. Clarion Bks. 2002 136p il maps $17
Grades: 7 8 9 10   **966.62**
   1. Liberia -- History 2. Slavery -- United States 3. African Americans -- History 4. African Americans -- Colonization -- Liberia
ISBN 0-618-14785-3

LC 2002-3966

Explores the history of the colony, later the independent nation of Liberia, which was established on the west coast of Africa in 1822 as a haven for free African Americans

"This photo-essay is a grim, disturbing history of Liberia. . . . Reef tells it in clear, plain style, always showing the connections between the two homelands. The handsome, very spacious design . . . makes the hard facts accessible. . . . A must for history collections." Booklist

Includes bibliographical references

966.68 Cote d'Ivoire (Ivory Coast)

Sheehan, Patricia

Cote d'Ivoire; [by] Patricia Sheehan and Jacqueline Ong. 2nd ed.; Marshall Cavendish Benchmark 2010 144p il map (Cultures of the world) lib bdg $42.79

Grades: 5 6 7 8   966.68

ISBN 978-0-7614-4854-9 lib bdg; 0-7614-4854-3 lib bdg

LC 2009045688

First published 2000

This offers information on the geography, history, wildlife, governmental structure, economy, cultural diversity, peoples, religion, and culture of Cote d'Ivoire

Includes glossary and bibliographical references

966.7 Ghana

Levy, Patricia

Ghana; [by] Patricia Levy and Winnie Wong. 2nd ed.; Marshall Cavendish Benchmark 2010 144p il map (Cultures of the world) lib bdg $42.79

Grades: 5 6 7 8   966.7

ISBN 978-0-7614-4847-1 lib bdg; 0-7614-4847-0 lib bdg

First published 1999

Introduces the geography, history, government, economy, culture, and people of Ghana

Includes glossary and bibliographical references

Weatherly, Myra

Teens in Ghana. Compass Point Books 2008 96p il map (Global connections) lib bdg $33.26

Grades: 7 8 9 10   966.7

1. Teenagers 2. Ghana

ISBN 978-0-7565-3417-2; 0-7565-3417-8

LC 2007-33086

Uncovers the challenges, pastimes, customs and culture of teens in Ghana

"Color photographs of native teens enliven the text and help reinforce the connection between reader and subject matter. . . . Religion is discussed, as well as technology, government, and social roles and expectations. . . . [This] would be a wonderful addition to any library." Voice Youth Advocates

Includes bibliographical references

966.9 Nigeria

Giles, Bridget

★ Nigeria; [by] Bridget Giles. National Geographic 2007 64p il map (Countries of the world) lib bdg $27.90

Grades: 4 5 6 7   966.9

ISBN 978-1-4263-0124-7

LC 2007024729

This describes the geography, nature, history, people and culture, government, and economy of Nigeria

"What helps [this book] stand out from the pack is [its] high-quality, rich photography. . . . The photos provide as much information as the [text]. . . . The writing is straightforward and solid." SLJ

Includes glossary and bibliographical references

Walker, Ida

Nigeria. Mason Crest Publishers 2005 79p il map (Africa: continent in the balance) lib bdg $21.95

Grades: 7 8 9 10   966.9

ISBN 1-59084-811-X

LC 2004-7100

An introduction to the geography, history, government, economy, people, and customs of Nigeria

The information in this book is "is well organized and presented in a clear, logical manner. . . . The bright, attractive photographs are well matched to the [text]." SLJ

Includes glossary and bibliographical references

967 Central Africa and offshore islands

Oppong, Joseph R.

Africa South of the Sahara; series consulting editor Charles F. Gritzner. Chelsea House Publishers 2006 124p il map (Modern world cultures) lib bdg $30

Grades: 6 7 8 9 10   967

1. Sub-Saharan Africa

ISBN 0-7910-8146-X

This describes the physical and historical geography, population and settlement, cultures, politics, and economy of sub-Saharan Africa.

This "accessible [title is] generously illustrated with colorful photos, maps, and clear charts, graphs, and other statistical data." SLJ

967.11 Cameroon

Sheehan, Sean

Cameroon; [by] Sean Sheehan and Josie Elias. 2nd ed.; Marshall Cavendish Benchmark 2011 144p il map (Cultures of the world) lib bdg $42.79

Grades: 5 6 7 8   967.11

ISBN 978-1-6087-0214-5; 1-6087-0214-6

LC 2010019623

First published 2001

Provides information on the geography, history, wildlife, governmental structure, economy, cultural diversity, peoples, religion, and culture of Cameroon.

Includes glossary and bibliographical references

967.3   Angola

Sheehan, Sean

   Angola; [by] Sean Sheehan and Jui Lin Yong. 2nd ed.; Marshall Cavendish Benchmark 2010 144p il map (Cultures of the world) lib bdg $42.79

Grades: 5 6 7 8   **967.3**

   1. Angola

   ISBN 978-0-7614-4845-7 lib bdg; 0-7614-4845-4 lib bdg

                         LC 2009021203

   "Provides comprehensive information on the geography, history, wildlife, governmental structure, economy, cultural diversity, peoples, religion, and culture of Angola." Publisher's note

   Includes glossary and bibliographical references

967.43   Chad

Kneib, Martha

   Chad; [by] Martha Kneib. Marshall Cavendish Benchmark 2007 144p il map (Cultures of the world) lib bdg $42.79

Grades: 5 6 7 8   **967.43**

   ISBN 978-0-7614-2327-0 lib bdg; 0-7614-2327-3 lib bdg

                         LC 2005027079

   This provides "information on the geography, history, governmental structure, economy, cultural diversity, peoples, religion, and culture of Chad." Publisher's note

   Includes glossary and bibliographical references

967.51   Democratic Republic of the Congo

Heale, Jay

   Democratic Republic of the Congo; by Jay Heale and Yong Jui Lin. 2nd ed.; Marshall Cavendish Benchmark 2009 144p il map (Cultures of the world) lib bdg $42.79

Grades: 5 6 7 8   **967.51**

   ISBN 978-0-7614-4478-7 lib bdg; 0-7614-4478-5 lib bdg

                         LC 2009003195

   First published 1999

   Describes the geography, history, government, economy, people, lifestyle, religion, languages, arts, leisure, festivals, and food of The Democratic Republic of the Congo

   Includes glossary and bibliographical references

967.571   Rwanda

King, David C.

   Rwanda; [by] David C. King. Marshall Cavendish Benchmark 2007 144p il map (Cultures of the world) lib bdg $42.79

Grades: 5 6 7 8   **967.571**

   ISBN 978-0-7614-2333-1 lib bdg; 0-7614-2333-8 lib bdg

                         LC 2005031817

   This provides "information on the geography, history, governmental structure, economy, cultural diversity, peoples, religion, and culture of Rwanda." Publisher's note

   Includes glossary and bibliographical references

Koopmans, Andy

   Rwanda. Mason Crest Publishers 2005 87p il map (Africa: continent in the balance) lib bdg $21.95

Grades: 7 8 9 10   **967.571**

   ISBN 1-59084-812-8

                         LC 2004-4826

   This is an introduction to the geography, history, government, economy, people, and customs of Rwanda

   The information in this book is "is well organized and presented in a clear, logical manner. . . . The bright, attractive photographs are well matched to the [text]." SLJ

   Includes glossary and bibliographical references

Nardo, Don

   The **Rwandan** genocide; by Don Nardo. Lucent Books 2011 104 p. ill. (hardcover) $34.95

Grades: 6 7 8 9   **967.571**

   1. Genocide 2. Ethnic relations 3. Rwanda -- History 4. Genocide -- Rwanda -- History -- 20th century 5. Ethnic conflict -- Rwanda -- History -- 20th century

   ISBN 142050567X; 9781420505672

                         LC 2010039533

   This book by Don Nardo is part of the World History series and looks at the Rwandan Genocide. The series "examines the eras, events, civilizations, and movements that have shaped human history, providing readers with insight into the past and its many legacies." Photographs, timelines, sidebars, and annotated bibliographies are included. (Publisher's note)

   Includes bibliographical references and index.

967.61   Uganda

Barlas, Robert

   Uganda; [by] Robert Barlas and Yong Jui Lin. 2nd ed.; Marshall Cavendish Benchmark 2010 144p il map (Cultures of the world) lib bdg $42.79

Grades: 5 6 7 8   **967.61**

   ISBN 978-0-7614-4859-4 lib bdg; 0-7614-4859-4 lib bdg

                         LC 2009046002

   First published 2000

This offers information on the geography, history, wild-life, governmental structure, economy, cultural diversity, peoples, religion, and culture of Uganda

Includes glossary and bibliographical references

Dunstan, Simon

Entebbe; the most daring raid of Israel's special forces. Rosen Pub. 2011 64p il map (The most daring raids in history) lib bdg $29.25

Grades: 7 8 9 10   967.61

1. Israel -- History

ISBN 978-1-4488-1868-6; 1-4488-1868-0

LC 2010029622

The Israeli Forces operation at Entebbe was one of the most daring counter-terrorist assaults of all time. This book explores this important piece of history with narration and illustrations and diagrams.

This book is "packed with facts, covering the details of the action, the people involved, and the tools used, in engaging prose. The authors cite their sources thoroughly. . . . Diagrams, photos (where available), and maps make the action easy to follow and provide visual context for the raids. . . . This . . . is sure to find a large readership." SLJ

Includes glossary and bibliographical references

967.62   Kenya

Bowden, Rob, 1973-

Kenya; Rob Bowden. Facts on File 2003 61 p. ill., map (Countries of the world) (hardcover) $30

Grades: 7 8 9 10   967.62

ISBN 9780816053841; 0816053847

This covers Kenya's "physical geography, resources, ethnic populations, tourism, and commerce. . . . It includes a detailed overview of the tensions between commercial development in an impoverished nation and the need to protect natural resources and wildlife. . . . [This title offers] a wealth of nearly up-to-date information and a realistic introduction to [its subject]. . . . [It also features] good-quality color photos of urban and rural homes and buildings and traditional and western lifestyles." Booklist

Includes bibliographical references

Broberg, Catherine

Kenya in pictures; rev and expanded; Lerner Publs. 2003 80p il map (Visual geography series) lib bdg $31.93

Grades: 5 6 7 8   967.62

1. Kenya

ISBN 0-8225-1957-7

LC 2001-3829

First published 1988 under the authorship of Joel Reuben

A brief overview of Kenya's land, history, government, people, and culture

The book is "visually appealing with photos and sidebars that complement the text." Libr Media Connect

Includes bibliographical references

Lekuton, Joseph

★ Facing the lion; growing up Maasai on the African savanna. by Joseph Lekuton with Herman Viola. National Geographic Soc. 2003 127p il map $15.95

Grades: 7 8 9 10 11 12   967.62

1. Authors 2. Teachers 3. Masai (African people) 4. Memoirists

ISBN 0-7922-5125-3

LC 2003-750

A member of the Masai people describes his life as he grew up in a northern Kenya village, travelled to America to attend college, and became an elementary school teacher in Virginia

"Lekuton's story touches a universal chord, and shows readers the beauty of another culture from the inside. Simple and direct enough for reluctant readers, and written in a conversational and occasionally wryly humorous style, this book will be enjoyed by a wide range of readers." SLJ

967.73   Somalia

Hassig, Susan M.

Somalia; by Susan M. Hassig & Zawiah Abdul Latif. 2nd ed.; Marshall Cavendish Benchmark 2008 144p il map (Cultures of the world) lib bdg $42.79

Grades: 5 6 7 8   967.73

ISBN 978-0-7614-2082-8 lib bdg; 0-7614-2082-7 lib bdg

LC 2006102270

First published 1997

"Provides comprehensive information on the geography, history, wildlife, governmental structure, economy, cultural diversity, peoples, religion, and culture of Somalia." Publisher's note

Includes glossary and bibliographical references

967.8   Tanzania

Heale, Jay

Tanzania; by Jay Heale & Winnie Wong. 2nd ed.; Marshall Cavendish Benchmark 2009 144p il map (Cultures of the world) lib bdg $42.79

Grades: 5 6 7 8   967.8

ISBN 978-0-7614-3417-7 lib bdg; 0-7614-3417-8 lib bdg

LC 2008028802

First published 1998

"Provides comprehensive information on the geography, history, wildlife, governmental structure, economy, cultural diversity, peoples, religion, and culture of Tanzania." Publisher's note

Includes glossary and bibliographical references

MacDonald, Joan Vos

Tanzania; [by] Joan Vos MacDonald. Mason Crest Publishers 2005 85p il map (Africa: continent in the balance) $21.95

Grades: 7 8 9 10   **967.8**
ISBN 1-59084-813-6

LC 2004-7103

Describes the history, geography, and culture of Tanzania
"The information in [this book] is well organized and presented in a clear, logical manner. . . . [It is illustrated with] bright, attractive photographs." SLJ

Includes glossary and bibliographical references

967.9   Mozambique

King, David C.
  Mozambique; [by] David C. King. Marshall Cavendish Benchmark 2007 144p il map (Cultures of the world) lib bdg $42.79
Grades: 5 6 7 8   **967.9**
ISBN 978-0-7614-2331-7 lib bdg; 0-7614-2331-1 lib bdg

LC 2006002302

This provides "information on the geography, history, wildlife, governmental structure, economy, cultural diversity, peoples, religion, and culture of Mozambique." Publisher's note

Includes glossary and bibliographical references

Mulroy, Tanya
  Mozambique; [by] Tanya Mulroy. Mason Crest Publishers 2008 87p il map (Africa: continent in the balance) lib bdg $21.95
Grades: 5 6 7 8   **967.9**
ISBN 978-1-4222-0090-2 lib bdg; 1-4222-0090-6 lib bdg

LC 2006-17340

This book is "clear and concise, and the . . . easy-to-read texts impart a good deal of up-to-date information. . . . Chapters . . . cover the . . . country's history; politics and government; economy; and people, including discussions of family life, education, ethnic groups, health care, sports, and the arts, with the focus being on the largest cities." SLJ

Includes glossary and bibliographical references

968   Republic of South Africa and neighboring southern African countries

Coster, Patience
  The **struggle** against apartheid. Arcturus Pub. 2010 48p il (Timelines) lib bdg $34.25
Grades: 7 8 9 10   **968**
  1. Apartheid 2. South Africa -- History 3. South Africa -- Race relations
ISBN 978-1-84837-640-3; 1-84837-640-5

LC 2009051269

Discusses events in South Africa that lead up to and followed the end of apartheid, beginning with the peace treaty of Vereeniging and continuing through the election of Jacob Zuma.

"Background information about major figures is appended. The many images are relevant and well-placed." Horn Book Guide

Includes glossary and bibliographical references

Downing, David
  ★ **Apartheid** in South Africa; [by] David Downing. Heinemann Library 2004 56p il (Witness to history) $31.36
Grades: 7 8 9 10   **968**
  1. Apartheid 2. South Africa -- Race relations
ISBN 1-4034-4870-1; 9780431170619

LC 2003-18235

Examines the historical forces that led to the development of the system of apartheid, what life was like under the system for both blacks and whites, and the efforts that caused the end of this system
"This dense volume is an excellent narrative overview of the apartheid struggle, drawing extensively on primary sources that provide depth, detail, drama, and authenticity." Booklist

Mace, Virginia
  ★ **South** Africa; [by] Virginia Mace; Kate Rowntree and Vukile Khumalo, consultants. National Geographic 2008 64p il map (Countries of the world) lib bdg $27.90
Grades: 4 5 6 7   **968**
ISBN 978-1-4263-0203-9

LC 2007047835

This describes the geography, nature, history, people and culture, government, and economy of South Africa.
"Through its numerous maps and standout photographs, this book provides a general overview of South Africa that will satisfy the basic needs of upper-elementary research paper writers." Horn Book Guide

Includes glossary and bibliographical references

Seidman, David
  Teens in South Africa; by David Seidman. Compass Point Books 2009 96p il map (Global connections) lib bdg $33.26
Grades: 6 7 8 9   **968**
  1. Teenagers 2. South Africa
ISBN 978-0-7565-3854-5 lib bdg; 0-7565-3854-8 lib bdg

LC 2008-9480

Uncovers the challenges, pastimes, customs and culture of teens in South Africa
This book is "concise and highly readable. . . . Clear, colorful photos and sidebars on a range of topics provide further context. . . . [This title] will enrich young adult collections." SLJ

Inlcudes glossary and bibliographical references

Weltig, Matthew Scott
  The **aftermath** of the Anglo-Zulu war; by Matthew S. Weltig. Twenty-First Century Books 2008 160p il (Aftermath of history) lib bdg $38.60

Grades: 6 7 8 9 10   **968**
1. Zulu War, 1879 2. Zulu (African people)
ISBN 978-0-8225-7599-3; 0-8225-7599-X
LC 2007-50826
"The well–written text provides a detailed account of the devastation and ruin brought to Zululand by the British government and by Boer settlers, replete with text boxes that provide clarification and further explanation of what are often complex and confusing issues and events. Illustrations consist of both period photographs and paintings of the fierce fighting. Reckless bravery, treachery, cruelty, betrayal, and greed are all here, resulting in an absorbing, but tragic story." SLJ
Includes glossary and bibliographical references

968.06   Period as Republic, 1961-

Beecroft, Simon
The **release** of Nelson Mandela; by Simon Beecroft. World Almanac Library 2004 48p il (Days that changed the world) lib bdg $30; pa $11.95
Grades: 5 6 7 8   **968.06**
1. Apartheid 2. Presidents 3. Political prisoners 4. Political leaders 5. Human rights activists 6. Nobel laureates for peace 7. Presidents -- South Africa -- Biography
ISBN 0-8368-5571-X lib bdg; 0-8368-5578-7 pa
LC 2003-65807
First published 2003 in the United Kingdom with title: The freeing of Nelson Mandela
A biography of the black South African leader who became a civil rights activist, political prisoner, and president of South Africa, told in the context of the history of his country
This does "a fine job of combining a closeup view of an earth-shattering event with what led up to the drama and a sense of the event's impact on the future. . . . The . . . design is ideal for browsing." Booklist
Includes bibliographical references

Brownlie, Ali
South Africa in our world; [by] Ali Brownlie Bojang. Smart Apple Media 2010 32p il (Countries in our world) lib bdg $28.50
Grades: 5 6 7 8   **968.06**
1. South Africa
ISBN 978-1-59920-444-4 lib bdg; 1-59920-444-4 lib bdg
LC 2009043163
This "contains relevant information presented in a visually appealing layout. Large colorful photographs inform readers about the past, present, and future of the country. . . . The book gives an honest view of apartheid, poverty, and government conflicts. At the same time, it is hopeful about recent changes, such as the hosting of the World Cup and the growing economy." SLJ
Includes glossary and bibliographical references

Sonneborn, Liz
★ The **end** of apartheid in South Africa. Chelsea House Publishers 2010 120p il (Milestones in modern world history) lib bdg $35
Grades: 8 9 10 11 12   **968.06**
1. Apartheid 2. Anti-apartheid movement
ISBN 978-1-60413-409-4; 1-60413-409-7
LC 2008-54805
This is "an excellent in-depth overview, one of the best on the subject, with chapters on the early history before the establishment of the apartheid regime and with profiles of many important leaders (not just Nelson Mandela), as well as clear discussion of present-day politics, the role of the Truth and Reconciliation Commission, and the ongoing inequality. Never simplistic, it is an outstanding overview for teens new to the subject; for those who know something of the history, it fills in the big picture with depth and detail about both leaders and ordinary people, what has changed, and how much still needs to be done." Booklist
Includes bibliographical references

968.83   Botswana

Wittmann, Kelly
Botswana; [by] Kelly Wittmann. Mason Crest Publishers 2008 79p il map (Africa: continent in the balance) lib bdg $21.95
Grades: 5 6 7 8   **968.83**
ISBN 978-1-4222-0087-2 lib bdg; 1-4222-0087-6 lib bdg
LC 2006-17333
This book features the country's "history; politics and government; economy; and people, including discussions of family life, education, ethnic groups, health care, sports, and the arts, with the focus being on the largest cities. . . . Interspersed throughout are numerous color and some black-and-white photographs, with descriptive captions, as well as 'Quick Facts' regarding geography, the economy, and the people. . . . The information is presented in an engaging manner." SLJ
Includes glossary and bibliographical references

968.91   Zimbabwe

Arnold, James R.
Robert Mugabe's Zimbabwe; by James R. Arnold and Roberta Wiener. Twenty-First Century Books 2008 160p (Dictatorships) lib bdg $38.60
Grades: 7 8 9 10   **968.91**
1. Presidents 2. Prime ministers 3. Zimbabwe
ISBN 978-0-8225-7283-1
LC 2006-100765
This history of Zimbabwe under the dictatorship of Robert Mugabe gives "students a glimpse into the repression and daily struggle for survival under [this] brutal [government]." SLJ
Includes glossary and bibliographical references

Hall, Martin

Great Zimbabwe; [by] Martin Hall and Rebecca Stefoff. 1st ed.; Oxford University Press 2006 47p il map (Digging for the past) $23

Grades: 7 8 9 10   **968.91**
1. Archeology 2. Shona (African people) 3. Zimbabwe
ISBN 978-0-19-515773-4; 0-19-515773-7
LC 2005014607

This "explores a ruined fourteenth-century stone city in Zimbabwe and covers controversies over its origin, its artifacts, and theories about its former inhabitants. The well-written text will spur readers' curiosity, while archival and modern photos, ancient maps, and European explorers' notes add a fascinating variety to the book's visual presentation." Horn Book Guide

Includes glossary and bibliographical references

968.94   Zambia

Holmes, Timothy

Zambia; by Timothy Holmes & Winnie Wong. rev ed.; Marshall Cavendish Benchmark 2008 144p il map (Cultures of the world) lib bdg $42.79

Grades: 5 6 7 8   **968.94**
ISBN 978-0-7614-3039-1 lib bdg; 0-7614-3039-3 lib bdg
LC 2007050794

First published 1998

Describes the geography, history, government, economy, people, lifestyle, religion, language, arts, leisure, festivals, and food of Zambia

Includes glossary and bibliographical references

969.1   Madagascar

Heale, Jay

Madagascar; [by] Jay Heale & Zawiah Abdul Latif. 2nd ed.; Marshall Cavendish Benchmark 2008 144p il map (Cultures of the world) lib bdg $42.79

Grades: 5 6 7 8   **969.1**
ISBN 978-0-7614-3036-0 lib bdg; 0-7614-3036-9 lib bdg
LC 2007048288

First published 1998

"Provides comprehensive information on the geography, history, wildlife, governmental structure, economy, cultural diversity, peoples, religion, and culture of Madagascar." Publisher's note

Includes glossary and bibliographical references

970   History of North America

Bial, Raymond

The **Crow**. Marshall Cavendish Benchmark 2006 124p il map (Lifeways) lib bdg $38.50

Grades: 5 6 7 8   **970**
1. Crow Indians 2. Native Americans
ISBN 978-0-7614-1901-3; 0-7614-1901-2
LC 2004-22235

Discusses the history, culture, beliefs, changing ways, and notable people of the Crow.

Includes glossary and bibliographical references

Desaulniers, Kristi L.

Northern America; [by] Kristi L. Desaulniers and Charles F. Gritzner. Chelsea House 2006 128p il map (Modern world cultures) lib bdg $30

Grades: 7 8 9 10   **970**
1. North America
ISBN 0-7910-8141-9
LC 2005031766

This describes the geography, history, culture, population, politics, economy, regions, and possible future of The United States and Canada.

Includes bibliographical references

970.004   North American native peoples

Bial, Raymond

The **Apache**. Benchmark Books 2001 128p il map (Lifeways) lib bdg $38.50

Grades: 5 6 7 8   **970.004**
1. Apache Indians 2. Native Americans 3. Indians of North America -- New Mexico
ISBN 978-0-7614-0939-7; 0-7614-0939-4
LC 99-44717

Discusses the history, culture, beliefs, changing ways, and notable people of the Apache.

"Crisp, clear photos in full color and black and white, some taken by the author and some archival, as well as original art, appear on almost every other page. . . . It's the comprehensive content, the attractive presentation, and the varied and well-chosen illustrations that make [this book] . . . worthy of consideration." SLJ

Includes glossary and bibliographical references

The **Huron**. Benchmark Bks. 2001 128p il (Lifeways) lib bdg $38.50

Grades: 5 6 7 8   **970.004**
1. Huron Indians 2. Native Americans 3. Wyandot Indians 4. Indians of North America 5. Wyandot Indians -- History 6. Wyandot Indians -- Social life and customs
ISBN 978-0-7614-0940-3; 0-7614-0940-8
LC 99-49261

Discusses the history, culture, social structure, beliefs, and customs of the Huron people, also known as the Wyandot.

Includes glossary and bibliographical references

Lifeways [series] Benchmark Books 1999 28v il map Each group set of four volumes $136.86

Grades: 5 6 7 8 **970.004**
1. Native Americans
ISBN 0-614-0800-2 Group 1; 0-7614-0860-6 Group
2; 0-7614-0936-X Group 3; 0-7614-1208-5 Group
4; 0-7614-1412-6 Group 5; 0-7614-1680-3 Group 6;
0-7614-1900-4 Group 7
"It's the comprehensive content, the attractive presentation, and the varied and well-chosen illustrations that make these books worthy of consideration." SLJ

The **Long** Walk; the story of Navajo captivity. Benchmark Bks. 2003 94p il map (Great journeys) lib bdg $31.36
Grades: 5 6 7 8 **970.004**
1. Navajo Indians 2. Scouts 3. Pioneers 4. Indian chiefs 5. Navajo Long Walk, 1863-1867
ISBN 0-7614-1322-7
LC 2001-43969
"The book is illustrated with informative black-and-white photographs and reproductions." SLJ
Includes bibliographical references

The **Shoshone**. Benchmark Bks. 2001 128p il (Lifeways) lib bdg $38.50
Grades: 5 6 7 8 **970.004**
1. Shoshoni Indians 2. Indians of North America 3. Shoshoni Indians -- History 4. Shoshoni Indians -- Social life and customs
ISBN 978-0-7614-1211-3; 0-7614-1211-5
LC 2001-18496
This examines the origins, villages and camps, lifeways, beliefs, history, language, and social conditions of The Shoshone Indians
Includes glossary and bibliographical references

Bjornlund, Lydia D.
The **Trail** of Tears; the relocation of the Cherokee Nation. Lucent Books 2010 104p il map (American history) lib bdg $33.45
Grades: 5 6 7 8 **970.004**
1. Cherokee Indians 2. Native Americans -- Relocation
ISBN 978-1-4205-0211-4; 1-4205-0211-5
LC 2010001549
Describes the Federal government's seizure of Cherokee lands in Georgia and the forced migration of the Cherokee Nation to Oklahoma along the route that came to be known as the Trail of Tears.
This is "well written and [includes] primary sources, photographs, reproductions, and maps." SLJ
Includes bibliographical references

Brown, Dee Alexander
★ **Bury** my heart at Wounded Knee; an Indian history of the American West. [by] Dee Brown. Thirtieth anniversary ed; Holt & Co. 2001 487p il hardcover o.p. pa $16
Grades: 8 9 10 11 12 Adult **970.004**
1. Generals 2. Indian chiefs 3. Civil engineers 4. Government officials 5. Native Americans -- Wars 6. Native Americans -- West (U.S.) 7. Indians of North America -- Wars -- West (U.S.) 8. Indians of North

America -- West (U.S.) -- History
ISBN 0-8050-6634-9; 0-8050-6669-1 pa
LC 00-40958
First published 1970
This is an account of the experience of the American Indian during the white man's expansion westward.
Includes bibliographical references

Connolly, Sean
The **Americas** and the Pacific. Zak Books 2009 48p il map (History of the world) lib bdg $34.25
Grades: 4 5 6 7 8 **970.004**
1. Maoris 2. Aboriginal Australians 3. Native Americans -- History
ISBN 978-88-60981-61-5 lib bdg; 88-60981-61-1 lib bdg
LC 2008008404
"Artists' renderings show groups of people engaged in representative activities, but it's the reproductions of artifacts . . . that will pull readers and browsers most. . . . [This is an] engaging overview." Booklist
Includes bibliographical references

Denetdale, Jennifer
The **Long** Walk; the forced Navajo exile. [by] Jennifer Denetdale. Chelsea House 2007 143p il map (Landmark events in Native American history) lib bdg $30
Grades: 7 8 9 10 **970.004**
1. Navajo Indians
ISBN 978-0-7910-9344-3 lib bdg; 0-7910-9344-1 lib bdg
LC 2007021723
"In 1863, the Diné (Navajo) faced transformations to their way of life with the Americans' determination to first subjugate and then remove them to a reservation. . . . This book exposes the series of events that facilitated the Navajo's removal from their homeland, their experiences during the Long Walk, their time at the Bosque Redondo reservation, their return home, and the ways in which they remember the Long Walk and the Bosque Redondo." Publisher's note
Includes bibliographical references

Dolan, Edward F.
The **American** Indian wars; [by] Edward F. Dolan. Millbrook Press 2003 112p il map lib bdg $29.90
Grades: 5 6 7 8 **970.004**
1. Native Americans -- Wars 2. Indians of North America -- Wars
ISBN 0-7613-1968-9
LC 2002-153012
Examines the battles and treaties between native peoples and early European settlers of what was to become the United States, as conflicts arose primarily over land, but also over food and other issues
"Period drawings, paintings, and photographs effectively illustrate a text packed with history." Booklist
Includes bibliographical references

Edwards, Judith

The **history** of the American Indians and the reservation; [by] Judith Edwards. Enslow Publishers 2008 128p il map (From many cultures, one history) lib bdg $31.93

Grades: 6 7 8 9　　　　　　　　　　　**970.004**

1. Native Americans -- History

ISBN 978-0-7660-2798-5 lib bdg; 0-7660-2798-8 lib bdg

LC 2007028275

"Explores the difficult changes American Indians were forced to make, including moving off their land, adapting to like on reservations, and how those reservations have changed since their creation." Publisher's note

Includes glossary and bibliographical references

Ehrlich, Amy

★ **Wounded** Knee: an Indian history of the American West; adapted for young readers by Amy Ehrlich from Dee Brown's Bury my heart at Wounded Knee. Holt & Co. 1974 202p il maps hardcover o.p. pa $13.95

Grades: 6 7 8 9　　　　　　　　　　　**970.004**

1. Generals 2. Ghost dance 3. Apache Indians 4. Dakota Indians 5. Navajo Indians 6. Arapaho Indians 7. Cheyenne Indians 8. Sand Creek, Battle of, 1864 9. Indian chiefs 10. Civil engineers 11. Government officials 12. Native Americans -- Wars 13. Native Americans -- West (U.S.)

ISBN 0-8050-2700-9 pa

This book traces the plight of the Navaho, Apache, Cheyenne and Sioux Indians in their struggles against the white man in the West between 1860 and 1890. It recounts battles and their causes, participants, and consequences during this era

"Some chapters [of the original] have been deleted, others condensed, and in some instances sentence structure and language have been simplified. The editing is good, and this version is interesting, readable, and smooth." SLJ

Includes bibliographical references

Elish, Dan

★ The **Trail** of Tears; the story of the Cherokee removal. Benchmark Books 2002 96p il map (Great journeys) lib bdg $32.79

Grades: 5 6 7 8　　　　　　　　　　　**970.004**

1. Cherokee Indians 2. Native Americans -- Relocation

ISBN 0-7614-1228-X

LC 00-52902

This "is particularly moving. Elish does a fine job introducing the Cherokee nation. . . . Filled with crisp, well-selected photographs and historical illustrations." Booklist

Includes bibliographical references

Encyclopedia of Native American wars and warfare; general editors, William B. Kessel, Robert Wooster. Facts on File 2005 398p il map $75; pa $21.95

Grades: 7 8 9 10　　　　　　　　　　　**970.004**

1. Reference books 2. Indians of North America -- Wars 3. Indians of North America -- Warfare 4. Native

Americans -- Wars -- Encyclopedias

ISBN 0-8160-3337-4; 0-8160-6430-X pa

LC 00-56200

"This encyclopedia offers readers a wide range of information about Native American history in North America after 1492." Choice

Includes bibliographical references

Freedman, Russell

★ **Indian** chiefs. Holiday House 1987 151p il $24.95; pa $14.95

Grades: 6 7 8 9 10　　　　　　　　　　　**970.004**

1. Kiowa Indians 2. Dakota Indians 3. Oglala Indians 4. Comanche Indians 5. Shoshone Indians 6. Shoshoni Indians 7. Centenarians 8. Indian chiefs 9. Nez Percé Indians 10. Native Americans -- Biography 11. Indians of North America -- Biography

ISBN 0-8234-0625-3; 0-8234-0971-6 pa

LC 86-46198

This "book chronicles the lives of six renowned Indian chiefs, each of whom served as a leader during a critical period in his tribe's history. . . . The text relates information about the lives of each chief and aspects of Indian/white relationships that illuminate his actions. Interesting vignettes and quotations are well integrated into the narrative as are dramatic accounts of battles. While the tone of the text is nonjudgmental, an underlying sympathy for the Indians' situation is apparent." Horn Book

Includes bibliographical references

Gibson, Karen Bush

Native American history for kids; with 21 activities. Chicago Review Press 2010 127p il pa $16.95

Grades: 6 7 8 9 10　　　　　　　　　　　**970.004**

1. Native Americans

ISBN 978-1-56976-280-6 pa; 1-56976-280-5 pa

LC 2010005695

"This gripping, highly readable overview will draw teens and even some adults into the history of Native Americans, from early times and the arrival of European settlers up to the present. The examples of racism are horrifying. . . . Also horrifying are the accounts of forced assimilation." Booklist

Includes glossary and bibliographical references

Gitlin, Marty

Wounded Knee Massacre. Greenwood 2011 xxiii, 185p il (Landmarks of the American mosaic) $35; e-book $35

Grades: 7 8 9 10　　　　　　　　　　　**970.004**

1. Wounded Knee Creek, Battle of, 1890 2. Native Americans -- West (U.S.)

ISBN 978-1-59884-409-2; 1-59884-409-1; 978-1-59884-410-8 e-book; 1-59884-410-5 e-book

LC 2010035200

"This concise, chronologically arranged text places the massacre in context by concisely examining the 'seeds of conflict' into the late 1860s; the fallout from Little Big Horn; the reemergence of the Ghost Dance; and, ultimately, the worst slaughter of Native men, women, and children in American history. . . . Substantial back matter includes lucid biographies of key figures and 13 primary documents." SLJ

Includes glossary and bibliographical references

Goble, Paul

★ **All** our relatives; traditional Native American thoughts about nature. compiled and illustrated by Paul Goble. World Wisdom 2005 un il $15.95

Grades: 5 6 7 8 **970.004**

1. Native Americans 2. Philosophy of nature
ISBN 0-941532-77-1; 978-0-941532-77-8

LC 2005004285

"The pages of this book are chock-full of quotations, songs, and brief stories that exemplify Native American attitudes toward nature. . . . Black Elk, Standing Bear, Brave Buffalo, and others observe the importance of various animals and the sacred qualities of all living things. . . . The spaces between text blocks are filled with Goble's familiar illustrations based on traditional Native American designs and colors." SLJ

Includes bibliographical references

Jastrzembski, Joseph C.

The **Apache** wars; the final resistance. Chelsea House Publishers 2007 133p il map (Landmark events in Native American history) lib bdg $35

Grades: 7 8 9 10 **970.004**

1. Apache Indians
ISBN 978-0-7910-9343-6; 0-7910-9343-3

LC 2007-990

This account features "lively writing and direct quotes, and [is] enhanced by many color and black-and-white photos, drawings, and illustrations." SLJ

Includes bibliographical references

Keoke, Emory Dean

★ **American** Indian contributions to the world; [by] Emory Dean Keoke and Kay Marie Porterfield. Facts on File 2005 5v il map set$175

Grades: 7 8 9 10 **970.004**

1. Native Americans
ISBN 0-8160-5392-8

This set "focuses on the many significant contributions that members of North, Central, and South American tribes have made to both United States and world culture. . . . The appendixes are well organized. . . . This set would be an excellent addition to any school media center's collection." Voice Youth Advocates

Includes glossary and bibliographical references

King, David C.

First people; an illustrated history of American Indians. DK Pub. 2008 192p il map $19.99

Grades: 5 6 7 8 **970.004**

1. Native Americans
ISBN 978-0-7566-4092-7; 0-7566-4092-X

"This rich pictorial work serves as an entertaining, informative, and visually appealing introduction to American Indian culture and history. Each of the seven chapters covers a different time period in chronological order. . . . The glossy photographs, colorful drawings, and easily accessible paragraphs . . . make for an easy-to-use overall package." SLJ

McNeese, Tim

The **fascinating** history of American Indians; the age before Columbus. Enslow Publishers 2009 128p il map (America's living history) lib bdg $31.93

Grades: 5 6 7 8 **970.004**

1. Native Americans
ISBN 978-0-7660-2938-5 lib bdg; 0-7660-2938-7 lib bdg

"This thorough discussion of Native American life prior to Columbus's arrival combines theories of archaeologists, anthropologists, historians, and scientists to provide an engaging portrayal of the daily experiences of regional tribes. Based mostly on archaeological discoveries, the accessible text is supported by archival photographs, maps, and sidebars." Horn Book Guide

Includes glossary and bibliographical references

Media Projects Incorporated

Student almanac of Native American history; Media Projects, Inc. Greenwood Press 2003 2v il map (Middle school reference) set$80

Grades: 6 7 8 9 **970.004**

1. Reference books 2. Native Americans -- History 3. Indians of North America -- History
ISBN 0-313-32599-5

LC 2002-35215

Presents an overview of the history of Native Americans from before European contact up to the present day, including historical documents, legislation, statistics, court cases, and timelines

"This attractive almanac provides information on topics of interest to users in middle school and up. . . . [This] will be a welcome addition to school and public libraries where there is a need for additional information about Native Americans." Booklist

Includes bibliographical references

Murdoch, David Hamilton

North American Indian; written by David Murdoch; chief consultant, Stanley A. Freed; photographed by Lynton Gardiner. rev ed; DK Pubs. 2005 72p il (DK eyewitness books) $16.99; lib bdg $19.99

Grades: 4 5 6 7 **970.004**

1. Native Americans
ISBN 0-7566-1081-8; 0-7566-1082-6 lib bdg

First published 1995 by Knopf

This is a guide to the civilizations of North American Indians including full-color photographs of artifacts and descriptions ceremonies and customs.

National Museum of the American Indian (U.S.)

Do all Indians live in tipis? questions and answers. from the National Museum of the American Indian; foreword by Rick West; introduction by Wilma Mankiller. Collins, in association with the National Museum of the American Indian, Smithsonian Institution 2007 239p il pa $14.95

Grades: 8 9 10 11 12　　　　　　　**970.004**
　1. Native Americans
　ISBN 978-0-06-115301-3;　0-06-115301-X
　　　　　　　　　　　　　LC 2007-60874
"This highly accessible and informative book aims to dispel some of the major myths and stereotypes still surrounding Native people in the United States and Canada. . . . The straightforward questions were compiled from actual phone calls, emails, letters, and in-person visits to the George Gustav Heye Center in New York, a major branch of the National Museum of the American Indian. The Native American writers who answered them did so concisely with hints of humor and an abundance of research and experience. . . . This is a topnotch resource for both people just learning about Native American cultures and those who think they know the facts." SLJ

Philip, Neil
　★ The **great** circle; a history of the First Nations. foreword by Dennis Hastings. Clarion Books 2006 153p il map $25
Grades: 7 8 9 10 11 12 Adult　　　**970.004**
　1. Native Americans　2. Indians of North America --
　History
　ISBN 978-0-618-15941-3;　0-618-15941-X
　　　　　　　　　　　　　LC 2005032743
"Philip takes on a huge challenge here: to present a unified narrative that explains the complex and confrontational relationships between Native Americans and white settlers. . . . He pulls it off, however, thanks to solid research, an engaging writing style, and a talent for making individual stories serve the whole. . . . Top marks, too, for the volume's photographs and historical renderings, which so intensely illustrate the pages." Booklist
　Includes bibliographical references

Schomp, Virginia
　The **Native** Americans; [by] Virginia Schomp. Marshall Cavendish Benchmark 2007 96p il map (Myths of the world) lib bdg $34.21
Grades: 6 7 8 9　　　　　　　　**970.004**
　1. Native Americans
　ISBN 978-0-7614-2550-2 lib bdg;　0-7614-2550-0
　lib bdg
　　　　　　　　　　　　　LC 2007013511
"With [its] beautiful illustrations, high-quality production, and focus on source material, the [book] should whet the interest of readers." SLJ
　Includes glossary and bibliographical references

Terry, Michael Bad Hand
　Daily life in a Plains Indian village, 1868. Clarion Bks. 1999 48p il map hardcover o.p. pa $9.95
Grades: 4 5 6 7　　　　　　　　**970.004**
　1. Native Americans -- Great Plains　2. Indians of North America -- Great Plains　3. Indians of North America -- Great Plains -- History　4. Indians of North America -- Material culture -- Great Plains　5. Indians of North America -- Great Plains -- Social life and customs
　ISBN 0-395-94542-9;　0-395-97499-2　pa
　　　　　　　　　　　　　LC 98-32382

Depicts the historical background, social organization, and daily life of a Plains Indian village in 1868, presenting interiors, landscapes, clothing, and everyday objects
　"The author presents short paragraphs of fascinating information accompanied by visuals that explain even more than the text." SLJ
　Includes glossary

Vander Hook, Sue
　Trail of Tears. ABDO Pub. 2010 112p il map (Essential events) lib bdg $32.79
Grades: 6 7 8 9　　　　　　　　**970.004**
　1. Cherokee Indians　2. Native Americans -- Relocation
　ISBN 978-1-60453-946-2;　1-60453-946-1
　　　　　　　　　　　　　LC 2009-31066
This title examines an important historic event, the Trail of Tears. Readers will learn the background of European settlement in Native American lands, relations between the groups, and how this led to the Trail of Tears.
　"The writing is accessible and is richer than a lot of history writing, allowing the reader to become engaged in the text as a story, and the layout provides enough white space to allow lower level readers to feel confident." Libr Media Connect
　Includes glossary and bibliographical references

Waldman, Carl
　Encyclopedia of Native American tribes; 3rd rev ed; Facts on File 2006 xxiv, 360p il map (Facts on File library of American history) $75; pa $21.95
Grades: 6 7 8 9 10 11 12 Adult　　　**970.004**
　1. Reference books　2. Indians of North America　3. Native Americans -- Encyclopedias
　ISBN 978-0-8160-6273-7;　0-8160-6273-0;　978-0-8160-6274-4 pa;　0-8160-6274-9 pa
　　　　　　　　　　　　　LC 2006-12529
First published 1988
　"This well-written and easily accessible encyclopedia of a good starting point for research on Native American tribes." Libr Media Connect
　Includes bibliographical references

Yue, Charlotte
　★ The **wigwam** and the longhouse; [by] Charlotte and David Yue. Houghton Mifflin 2000 118p il $15
Grades: 4 5 6 7　　　　　　　　**970.004**
　1. Woodland Indians
　ISBN 0-395-84169-0
　　　　　　　　　　　　　LC 98-28971
Describes the history, customs, religion, government, homes, and present-day status of the various native peoples that inhabited the eastern woodlands since before the coming of the Europeans
　Includes bibliographical references

Zimmerman, Dwight Jon
　Saga of the Sioux; an adaptation of Dee Brown's Bury My Heart at Wounded Knee. [adapted] by Dwight Jon Zimmerman. Henry Holt and Company 2011 208p il map $18.99

Grades: 5 6 7 8 **970.004**
1. Dakota Indians 2. Native Americans -- Wars
ISBN 978-0-8050-9364-3; 0-8050-9364-8
LC 2011004792

"Dwight Jon Zimmerman has created a masterful adaptation of Dee Brown's Bury My Heart at Wounded Knee, presenting late nineteenth century history from a Native American viewpoint. While Brown's book traces the fates of several Native American tribes in the western United States, Zimmerman's adaptation focuses solely on the Sioux. . . . Historical figures central to the narrative, both Native American and white, are portrayed as real people, rather than caricatures. Rather than simply describing what happened, the book looks at why it happened. Individuals' motivations, strengths, and flaws are all explored in relation to how historical events unfolded. The book includes numerous photographs, illustrations, and maps that aid understanding and create visual appeal. . . . This is a must-have addition to any United States history collection serving teens." Voice Youth Advocates

Includes glossary and bibliographical references

Zimmerman, Larry J.
Exploring the life, myth, and art of Native Americans. Rosen Pub. 2009 144p il map (Civilizations of the world) lib bdg $29.95
Grades: 7 8 9 10 11 12 **970.004**
1. Native Americans -- Art 2. Native Americans -- Religion
ISBN 978-1-4358-5614-1; 1-4358-5614-7
LC 2009-9268

This book describes the cultures, myths, and art of Native Americans.

"This beautifully illustrated and well-written [title] . . . is perfect for those assignments where students must look at the culture of a civilization. Artwork and pictures blend seamlessly with the information and the reader is taken on a journey of discovery. Myths are used as the story of how the people view themselves, blended with the discussion of the reality of life. Everyday life is tied to the belief systems and is explained in light of those beliefs. The pictures are beautifully done and there is almost as much information in the captions as there is in the text." Libr Media Connect

Includes glossary and bibliographical references

970.01 Historical periods

Berne, Emma Carlson
Christopher Columbus; the voyage that changed the world. by Emma Carlson Berne. Sterling Pub. Co. 2008 124 p. ill. (some col.) (paperback) $5.95; (hardcover) $12.95
Grades: 4 5 6 7 **970.01**
1. Exploration 2. Columbus, Christopher, 1451-1506 3. Explorers -- Spain -- Biography 4. Explorers -- America -- Biography
ISBN 1402744072; 1402760566; 9781402744075; 9781402760563
LC 2007048197

This book by Emma Carlson Berne, part of the Sterling Biographies series, looks at explorer Christopher Columbus, who "made the voyage that, for better and worse, changed history. Born in the bustling port city of Genoa, Italy, Columbus fell in love with the sea, and spent his youth learning all he could about steering and navigating a ship. Dreaming of wealth and fame, he believed he could find a new route to the Indies by sailing westward." (Publisher's note)

Includes bibliographical references (p. 119-120) and index.

Demi, 1942-
Columbus; by Demi. Marshall Cavendish 2012 64 p. ill. (hardcover) $19.99
Grades: 3 4 5 6 **970.01**
1. America -- Exploration 2. Columbus, Christopher, 1451-1506 3. Explorers -- Spain -- Biography 4. Explorers -- America -- Biography
ISBN 0761461671; 9780761461678
LC 2011036019

This book on Christopher Columbus was written and illustrated by the children's book author Demi. "From his childhood in Italy to his death in Spain, this biography presents a detailed view of the explorer's life. . . .Columbus's faults and accomplishments are both presented, acknowledging that his drive to explore furthered Europeans' knowledge of other lands, but that his mistreatment of Native peoples devastated their lives and culture." (School Library Journal)

Edwards, Judith
Henry Hudson and his voyages of exploration in world history. Enslow Pubs. 2002 128p il maps (In world history) lib bdg $26.60
Grades: 7 8 9 10 **970.01**
1. Explorers 2. Explorers -- America -- Biography 3. Explorers -- Great Britain -- Biography
ISBN 0-7660-1885-7
LC 2001-4119

Examines the life and career of Henry Hudson, tracing his voyages in the Arctic and North America and his discovery of the Hudson River and other bodies of water during his unsuccessful search for a Northwest Passage to Asia

Includes bibliographical references and index

Freedman, Russell
★ **Who** was first? discovering the Americas. Clarion Books 2007 88p il map $19
Grades: 6 7 8 9 **970.01**
1. Explorers
ISBN 978-0-618-66391-0
LC 2006-102485

This "looks at various ideas about the discovery of the Americas. . . . Beyond the very readable presentation of facts and theories, the book's main accomplishment is in showing that history is . . . an evolving process of logically interpreted evidence continually questioned, disputed, and revised. . . . The illustrations, many in color, include many excellent maps as well as reproductions of period drawings, paintings, engravings, and photos. . . . A well-researched, intelligent account." Booklist

Includes bibliographical references

Gaines, Ann

Hernando de Soto and the Spanish search for gold in world history; {by} Ann Graham Gaines. Enslow Pubs. 2002 112p il maps (In world history) lib bdg $26.60

Grades: 7 8 9 10   **970.01**

1. Explorers 2. Colonial administrators 3. Explorers -- Spain -- Biography 4. Explorers -- America -- Biography 5. America -- Discovery and exploration -- Spanish 6. Southern States -- Discovery and exploration -- Spanish 7. Mississippi River -- Discovery and exploration -- Spanish

ISBN 0-7660-1821-0

LC 2001-1975

In this book "about the explorer's life and adventures, Gaines also gives substantial attention to the culture and history of the various Native American groups that the Spaniard encountered on his travels. . . . This detailed book should provide much information for reports." SLJ

Includes bibliographical references

Gunderson, Jessica

Conquistadors; by Jessica Gunderson. Creative Education 2011 48 p. (alk. paper) $35.65

Grades: 5 6 7 8   **970.01**

1. United States -- History 2. Soldiers 3. Military art and science -- History 4. Soldiers -- Spain -- History

ISBN 1608181839; 9781608181834

LC 2011035799

Author Jessica Gunderson's book "covers the beginnings of the people, weaponry, war tactics, and famous leaders, and examines the current perception of the group in popular culture in an appealing, detailed, and evenhanded manner. Historical reproductions, primary documents, photographs, maps, and film stills appear throughout" the "explorations of history." (Publisher's note)

Includes bibliographical references and index

Harrison, David L.

Mammoth bones and broken stones; the mystery of North America's first people. with illustrations by Richard Hilliard and archaeological photographs. Boyds Mills Press 2010 48p il map $18.95

Grades: 4 5 6 7   **970.01**

1. Prehistoric peoples

ISBN 978-1-59078-561-4; 1-59078-561-4

LC 2009020247

"How and when the Western Hemisphere . . . came to be populated continues to be both mysterious and controversial for scientists. . . . Harrison does a good job setting the issue in context. He describes the earliest efforts to identify the original inhabitants of the continents, exploring the Clovis culture. . . . After clearly explaining how scholars decided that they were the first, he then lists the arguments against this hypothesis. . . . The narrative is aided by both photographs and original illustrations that imagine scenes from both the distant past and the field experiences." Kirkus

Includes glossary and bibliographical references

Hernandez, Roger E.

Early explorations: the 1500s. Marshall Cavendish Benchmark 2009 79p il map (Hispanic America) lib bdg $34.21

Grades: 4 5 6 7   **970.01**

1. Explorers 2. Southwestern States -- History

ISBN 978-0-7614-2937-1 lib bdg; 0-7614-2937-9 lib bdg

"Provides comprehensive information on the history of Spanish exploration in the United States." Publisher's note

Includes glossary and bibliographical references

Huey, Lois Miner

American archaeology uncovers the Vikings. Marshall Cavendish Benchmark 2009 64p il map (American archaeology) lib bdg $21.95

Grades: 4 5 6 7   **970.01**

1. Vikings -- North America 2. Excavations (Archeology) -- Canada 3. Excavations (Archeology) -- United States

ISBN 978-0-7614-4270-7 lib bdg; 0-7614-4270-7 lib bdg

LC 2008050266

This describes how archeologists have learned about the Vikings in America.

This is "both intriguing and engaging for young readers. . . . A welcomed addition to classroom and school libraries." Libr Media Connect

Includes glossary and bibliographical references

Mann, Charles C.

★ **Before** Columbus; the Americas of 1491. Atheneum Books for Young Readers 2009 117p il map $24.99

Grades: 5 6 7 8 9 10   **970.01**

1. Native Americans -- Origin 2. Native Americans -- History

ISBN 978-1-4169-4900-8; 1-4169-4900-3

LC 2009007691

Adapted from 1491, published 2006 by Knopf for adults

"Mann paints a superb picture of pre-Columbian America. In the process, he overturns the misconceived image of Natives as simple, widely scattered savages with minimal impact on their surroundings. Well-chosen, vividly colored graphics and photographs of mummies, pyramids, artifacts, and landscapes as well as the author's skillful storytelling will command the attention of even the most reluctant readers." SLJ

Includes glossary and bibliographical references

Mooney, Carla

Explorers of the New World; discover the golden age of exploration; with 22 projects. illustrated by Tom Casteel. Nomad 2011 120p il map (Build it yourself) pa $15.95

      970.01

1. Explorers

ISBN 978-1-936313-44-0; 1-936313-44-8

Provides twenty-two step-by-step projects to help readers learn about the explorers that discovered America and their voyages.

"This informative, entertaining activity book takes readers on a fascinating voyage of their own. . . . Each chapter concludes with 'Make Your Own' activities that bring life to the history with instructions for the construction of a logbook, clay activities, recipes, games, etc. Some may require the assistance of an adult but are not complicated or time consuming." SLJ

Includes glossary and bibliographical references

Owsley, Douglas W.

★ **Their** skeletons speak; Kennewick man and the Paleoamerican world. by Sally M. Walker and Douglas W. Owsley. Carolrhoda Books 2012 136 p. (lib. bdg.: alk. paper) $22.95

Grades: 8 9 10 11 12   **970.01**
1. Kennewick Man 2. Paleo-Indians 3. Human remains (Archaeology) 4. Paleo-Indians -- Washington (State) -- Origin 5. Human remains (Archaeology) -- Washington (State) 6. Paleo-Indians -- Anthropometry -- Washington (State) 7. Indians of North America -- Washington (State) -- Antiquities
ISBN 0761374574; 9780761374572
LC 2011051329
This book by Sally M. Walker and Douglas W. Owsley presents a "detailed study of the discovery and forensic evaluation of the skeleton dubbed 'Kennewick Man.' . . . From his accidental discovery in 1996 through multiple examinations by scientists with ever-improving forensic tools . . . an actual human being emerges from a time long gone, speaking to us through his bones. . . . A final facial reconstruction leaves readers face-to-face with a real person." (School Library Journal)
Includes bibliographical references and index.

Peterson, Cris

Birchbark brigade; a fur trade history. Calkins Creek 2009 135p il $18.95

Grades: 7 8 9 10   **970.01**
1. Fur trade 2. Frontier and pioneer life 3. Native Americans -- History
ISBN 978-1-59078-426-6; 1-59078-426-X
LC 2008055109
"Peterson first provides a history of the military, political and economic development of the [fur] trade and then gives readers a snapshot of the lives of the Indians and voyageurs who did the actual work. She relies on a wealth of primary-source material, from archival illustrations to quotes from players both large and small. . . . The author's enthusiasm for her subject will communicate itself to readers, even those who never dreamed they'd be interested, making this the best kind of discovery." Kirkus
Includes bibliographical references

Wulffson, Don L.

Before Columbus; early voyages to the Americas. by Don Wulffson. Twenty-First Century Books 2008 128p il map lib bdg $30.60

Grades: 6 7 8 9   **970.01**
1. Explorers
ISBN 978-0-8225-5978-8 lib bdg; 0-8225-5978-1 lib bdg
LC 2005-24487

"This engaging presentation of early exploration of the Americas offers both fact and speculation on who, when, and why voyagers came; how they traveled; and what evidence they left behind. . . . Citing legends and sagas, oral and written histories, and archaeological discoveries, Wulffson presents an intriguing array of possibilities. . . . The stories and unanswered questions about pre-Columbian voyagers will capture the imaginations of many readers, offer fascinating glimpses of different cultural groups, [and] stimulate further research." SLJ

Includes bibliographical references

971   Canada

Baker, Stuart

In the Arctic. Marshall Cavendish Benchmark 2010 32p il map (Climate change) lib bdg $19.95

Grades: 5 6 7 8   **971**
1. Greenhouse effect
ISBN 978-0-7614-4437-4 lib bdg; 0-7614-4437-8 lib bdg
LC 2009-5767
The book about climate change in the Arctic "is perfectly organized for students. . . . Unique layout features serve as signposts and will help focus readers' attention. . . . [The book] features an outstanding chart of possible effects of global warming on the area in question, listing 'Possible Event,' 'Predicted Result,' and 'Impact' in short, bulleted statements." SLJ
Includes glossary

Bial, Raymond

The **Cree**. Marshall Cavendish Benchmark 2005 128p il map (Lifeways) lib bdg $38.50

Grades: 5 6 7 8   **971**
1. Cree Indians 2. Native Americans
ISBN 978-0-7614-1902-0; 0-7614-1902-0
LC 2004-22394
Discusses the history, culture, beliefs, changing ways, and notable people of the Cree.
This books "is as attractive as it is useful. . . . The clean design includes plenty of white space and eye-catching photographs, maps, and prints." Horn Book Guide
Includes glossary and bibliographical references

Ferry, Steven

Ontario. Lucent Books 2003 112p il map (Exploring Canada) $29.95

Grades: 6 7 8 9   **971**
ISBN 978-1-59018-050-1; 1-59018-050-X
LC 2002-14351
Examines the history, geography, climate, industries, people, and culture of what is by far the most populous of Canada's provinces
Includes bibliographical references

Quebec. Lucent Books 2003 112p il map (Exploring Canada) $29.95

Grades: 6 7 8 9   **971**
ISBN 978-1-59018-051-8; 1-59018-051-8
LC 2002-4111
Examines the history, geography, climate, industries, people, culture, and ongoing separatist struggle of Canada's largest province
Includes bibliographical references

Yukon Territory; by Steven Ferry, Blake Harris, and Liz Szynkowski. Lucent Books 2003 112p il map (Exploring Canada) $29.95
Grades: 6 7 8 9   **971**
ISBN 978-1-59018-053-2; 1-59018-053-4
LC 2002-4110
Examines the history, geography, climate, industries, people, and culture of Canada's most remote and untamed region.
Includes bibliographical references

★ **Junior** Worldmark encyclopedia of the Canadian provinces; [Timothy L. Gall and Susan Bevan Gall, editors] 5th ed.; U.X.L 2007 294p il map $70
Grades: 5 6 7 8 9 10   **971**
1. Reference books 2. Canada
ISBN 978-1-4144-1060-9; 1-4144-1060-3
LC 2007003908
First published 1997
"Arranged by 40 . . . subheadings . . . this . . . resource provides . . . information on all of Canada's provinces and territories. [It includes] details on Canada's arts, climate, government, health, languages, notable persons, ethnic groups and . . . more." Publisher's note
Includes bibliographical references

Laws, Gordon D.
Alberta; by Gordon D. Laws and Lauren M. Laws. Lucent Books 2003 112p il map (Exploring Canada) $29.95
Grades: 6 7 8 9   **971**
ISBN 978-1-59018-045-7; 1-59018-045-3
LC 2002-9880
Explains the history, geography, climate, industry, people, and culture of Canada's princess province, having been named after the daughter of Queen Victoria.
Includes bibliographical references

Manitoba; by Gordon D. Laws and Lauren M. Laws. Lucent Books 2003 112p il map (Exploring Canada) $29.95
Grades: 6 7 8 9   **971**
ISBN 978-1-59018-047-1; 1-59018-047-X
LC 2002-14364
Examines the history, geography, climate, industries, people, and culture of one of the most diverse of Canada's provinces
Includes bibliographical references

The **Northwest** Territories; by Gordon Laws and Lauren M. Laws. Lucent Books 2004 112p il map (Exploring Canada) $29.95

Grades: 6 7 8 9   **971**
ISBN 978-1-59018-049-5; 1-59018-049-6
LC 2002-156055
Examines the history, geography, climate, industries, people, and culture of Canada's Northwest Territories
Includes bibliographical references

Mayell, Mark
Newfoundland. Lucent Books 2003 112p il map (Exploring Canada) $29.95
Grades: 6 7 8 9   **971**
ISBN 978-1-59018-048-8; 1-59018-048-8
LC 2003-2060
Examines the history, geography, climate, industries, people, and culture of Canada's Newfoundland
Includes bibliographical references

Saskatchewan. Lucent Books 2003 128p il map (Exploring Canada) $29.95
Grades: 6 7 8 9   **971**
ISBN 978-1-59018-052-5; 1-59018-052-6
LC 2003-43346
Examines the history, geography, climate, industries, people, and culture of the central province known as Canada's breadbasket
Includes bibliographical references

Palana, Brett J.
British Columbia. Lucent Books 2003 112p il map (Exploring Canada) $29.95
Grades: 6 7 8 9   **971**
ISBN 978-1-59018-046-4; 1-59018-046-1
LC 2002-4112
Examines the history, geography, climate, industries, people, and culture of Canada's westernmost province
Includes bibliographical references

Shea, Kitty
Teens in Canada. Compass Point Books 2008 96p il map (Global connections) lib bdg $31.93
Grades: 7 8 9 10   **971**
1. Teenagers 2. Canada
ISBN 978-0-7565-3303-8 lib bdg; 0-7565-3303-1 lib bdg
LC 2007-4899
Explores the culture and customs of Canadian teenagers
"Information is solid, giving readers an informed and realistic view of life in that country." Voice Youth Advocates
Includes glossary and bibliographical references

Sonneborn, Liz
Canada; by Liz Sonneborn. Children's Press 2012 144 p. col. ill.. col. maps (library) $40
Grades: 5 6 7 8   **971**
1. Canada 2. Canada -- Social life and customs
ISBN 0531253511; 9780531253519
LC 2011011970
This book by Liz Sonneborn is part of the Enchantment of the World series and looks at Canada. The introduction focuses on Canadian Terry Fox. Sonneborn "covers geography, natural resources, environment, history, govern-

ment, diversity, religions, culture, and everyday life. She includes details like 'poutine' (fries, cheese curds, and gravy) and 'Timmies' (a coffee and doughnut chain)." (School Library Journal)

Includes bibliographical references (p. 134) and index.

Walker, Sally M.

★ **Blizzard** of glass; the Halifax explosion of 1917. Henry Holt 2011 xii, 145p il $18.99

Grades: 5 6 7 8   **971**

1. World War, 1914-1918 -- Naval operations
ISBN 978-0-8050-8945-5; 0-8050-8945-4

LC 2011005914

"The text reads smoothly with unfamiliar words defined in the text. Illustrations consist of two full-page maps and numerous black-and-white photos. The final chapter revisits the featured families and their descendants, thus tying up the loose ends. . . . This tragic, but well-told story belongs in most collections." SLJ

Includes bibliographical references

Wallace, Mary

Inuksuk journey; an artist at the top of the world. Maple Tree Press 2008 64p il $24.95

Grades: 5 6 7 8   **971**

1. Inuit
ISBN 978-1-897349-26-7; 1-897349-26-2

"Nunavut, an Arctic territory in northern Canada, is a cold, open space where inuksuk, piles of stone in the shape of a person used to 'mark a family home, welcome guests, guide travelers, and ensure safe passage,' are commonly found. Wallace has developed a passion for these ancient messengers, and here she presents a journal of her week-long trek to Inuksugassait, a place where countless numbers of the stone markers stand. . . . Wallace includes personal photos, sketches, and comments that give readers an intimate portrait of life in this place. Over a dozen vibrant oil paintings depicting scenes from her journey are scattered throughout. . . . Readers will be fascinated by this firsthand account of true adventure." SLJ

Weaver, Janice

Mirror with a memory; a nation's story in photographs. Tundra Books 2007 159p il $29.95

Grades: 6 7 8 9   **971**

1. Canada -- History
ISBN 0-88776-747-8; 978-0-88776-747-0

"Defining moments in Canadian history are thematically presented in this photography collection. . . . In the conversational commentary that accompanies each image, Weaver provides historical context. Thought-provoking media literacy issues are also raised. . . . A great visual retrospective of a nation's people, places, and events." SLJ

Williams, Brian

★ **Canada**; [by] Brian Williams; Tom Carter and Ben Cecil, consultants. National Geographic 2007 64p il map (Countries of the world) lib bdg $27.90; pa $12.95

Grades: 4 5 6 7   **971**

ISBN 978-1-4263-0025-7 lib bdg; 978-1-4263-0573-3 pa

LC 2007296572

A basic overview of the history, geography, climate and culture of Canada

This "clear, succinct [overview] will support assignments without overwhelming casual readers. . . . A good selection of recent, high-quality color photographs gives the [book] visual appeal." SLJ

Includes glossary and bibliographical references

971.01   Early history to 1763

Worth, Richard

New France, 1534-1763; featuring the region that now includes all or parts of Michigan, Minnesota, Wisconsin, Illinois, Indiana, Ohio, Pennsylvania, Vermont, Maine, and Canada from Manitoba to Newfoundland. by Richard Worth. National Geographic Society 2007 109p il map (Voices from colonial America) $21.95; lib bdg $32.90

Grades: 5 6 7 8   **971.01**

1. Mississippi River valley -- History 2. Canada -- History
ISBN 978-1-4263-0147-6; 1-4263-0147-2; 978-1-4263-0148-3 lib bdg; 1-4263-0148-0 lib bdg

LC 2007-29544

"Worth presents the history of the vast French colony known as New France. Clearly written, the book is studded with quotes from people living in the colony and illustrated with colorful paintings, prints, and maps from a variety of periods. . . . This nicely designed introduction to a historically significant area fills a gap in many colonial history series and library collections." Booklist

Includes bibliographical references

971.1

Hyde, Natalie

Cryptic Canada; unsolved mysteries from coast to coast. Natalie Hyde. Owlkids Books Inc. 2012 48 p. $16.95

Grades: 4 5 6   **971.1**

1. Canada -- History 2. Unsolved mysteries
ISBN 1926973380; 9781926973388

LC 2011944600

This book by Natalie Hyde explores seven of Canada's "unsolved mysteries . . . beginning with the ongoing hunt in Nova Scotia for the legendary treasure of Captain Kidd and his crew, moving to the discovery of the mummified Franklin Expedition in Nunavut by modern-day scientists, and ending with an exploration of the Great Lakes Triangle phenomenon. . . . Each chapter . . . ends with an interview with an expert in the field." (Publisher's note)

971.5   Atlantic Provinces

Laws, Gordon D.

The **Maritime** Provinces; by Gordon D. Laws and Lauren M. Laws. Lucent Books 2004 112p il map (Exploring Canada) $29.95

Grades: 6 7 8 9   **971.5**

1. Canada 2. Maritime Provinces

ISBN 978-1-59018-335-9; 1-59018-335-5

LC 2003-5440

Examines the history, geography, climate, industries, people, and culture of Canada's Maritime Provinces

Includes bibliographical references

972   Mexico, Central America, West Indies, Bermuda

Ancient Aztec and Maya; edited by Anita Croy. Brown Bear Books 2010 64p il map (Facts at your fingertips) lib bdg $35.65

Grades: 6 7 8 9   **972**

1. Mayas 2. Aztecs

ISBN 978-1-933834-58-0 lib bdg; 1-933834-58-7 lib bdg

LC 2009-17295

Examines the leading Indian civilizations of Latin America and native North Americans, discussing their history, culture, food and shelter, government and trade, and geographical information

This begins "with an introduction accompanied by a striking full-page photo, followed by a two-page time line, and a two-paged spread for each topic. This format makes information easily accessible. Beautiful color photos of ancient ruins, drawings, maps, diagrams, and re-creations create appeal and enhance the information. . . . Whether for recreational browsing or serious research, this . . . will certainly prove useful for students." Libr Media Connect

Includes glossary and bibliographical references

Bingham, Jane

The **Aztec** empire; [by] Jane Bingham. Raintree 2007 64p il map (Time travel guide) lib bdg $34.29; pa $9.99

Grades: 6 7 8 9   **972**

1. Aztecs

ISBN 978-1-4109-2730-9 lib bdg; 1-4109-2730-X lib bdg; 978-1-4109-2737-8 pa; 1-4109-2737-7 pa

LC 2006033875

A description of life in the Aztec empire written in the form of a travel guide.

Includes glossary and bibliographical references

Cooke, Tim

★ **Ancient** Aztec; archaeology unlocks the secrets of Mexico's past. National Geographic 2007 64p il map (National Geographic investigates) $17.95; lib bdg $27.90

Grades: 4 5 6 7   **972**

1. Aztecs 2. Excavations (Archeology) -- Mexico

ISBN 978-1-4263-0072-1; 1-4263-0072-7; 978-1-4263-0073-8 lib bdg; 1-4263-0073-5 lib bdg

LC 2007024813

This describes ancient Aztec origins, technology, major archeological sites, civilization, and connections to the present

"Pithy and appealing. . . . Aerial photos, time [line], informative sidebars, an interview with an archaeologist, and excellent maps augment rigorously supported [text] that [asks] and [answers] interesting questions." SLJ

George, Charles

Maya civilization; [by] Charles and Linda George. Lucent Books 2010 96p il (World history) lib bdg $33.45

Grades: 6 7 8 9   **972**

1. Mayas

ISBN 978-1-4205-0240-4; 1-4205-0240-9

LC 2009053266

This is an introduction to Mayan civilization, including research which explains some of its mysteries.

This "shines as it provides a contemporaneous writing as well as work by scholars that offer plenty of drama—and lots of facts too. . . . [It also] provides a solid time line, plenty of photographs, sourced quotes, and a list of books and websites for further investigation. Excellent for reports and research." Booklist

Includes bibliographical references

Gruber, Beth

★ **Mexico**; [by] Beth Gruber; Gary S. Elbow and Jorge Zamora, consultants. National Geographic 2007 64p il map (Countries of the world) lib bdg $27.90; pa $12.95

Grades: 4 5 6 7   **972**

ISBN 0-7922-7669-8 lib bdg; 1-4263-0566-4 pa

LC 2004026452

"This volume introduces Mexico's geography, history, wildlife, culture, and government. The many excellent color photos and maps are a striking feature of the series. . . . This will be a useful addition to many libraries." Booklist

Includes glossary and bibliographical references

Harris, Nathaniel

★ **Ancient** Maya; archaeology unlocks the secrets to the Maya's past. by Nathaniel Harris; Elizabeth Graham, consultant. National Geographic 2008 64p il map (National Geographic investigates) $17.95; lib bdg $27.90

Grades: 4 5 6 7   **972**

1. Mayas 2. Excavations (Archeology) -- Mexico

ISBN 978-1-4263-0227-5; 1-4263-0227-4; 978-1-4263-0228-2 lib bdg; 1-4263-0228-2 lib bdg

LC 2007047837

This describes ancient Mayan civilization and how archeologists found out about it.

Includes glossary and bibliographical references

★ **Junior** Worldmark encyclopedia of the Mexican states; [Timothy L. Gall and Susan Bevan Gall, editors] 2nd ed.; U.X.L,Thomson/Gale 2007 423p il map $70

Grades: 5 6 7 8 9 10   972

1. Reference books

ISBN 978-1-4144-1112-5

LC 2007003906

First published 2004

"Arranged by 28 . . . subheadings . . . Junior Worldmark Encyclopedia of the Mexican States provides . . . information on each of Mexico's 31 states. Topics covered include climate, plants and animals, population and ethnic groups, religions, transportation, history, state and local governments, political parties, judicial system, economy, education, arts, media, tourism, sports, famous people and . . . more." Publisher's note

Includes bibliographical references

Kent, Deborah

Mexico; by Deborah Kent. Children's Press 2012 144 p. cil. ill., photographs (library) $40

Grades: 5 6 7 8   972

1. Mexico 2. Culture

ISBN 0531253554; 9780531253557

LC 2011010812

This book by Deborah Kent is part of the Enchantment of the World series and looks at Mexico. The books in the series offer 10 "chapters, several maps, a fast-facts section, and a few references to other sources, including a referral to a Scholastic website (new). The chapters cover geography, natural environment, history, politics, people and culture." (School Library Journal)

Includes bibliographical references and index.

Kops, Deborah

Palenque; by Deborah Kops. Twenty-First Century Books 2008 80p il (Unearthing ancient worlds) lib bdg $30.60

Grades: 5 6 7 8   972

1. Mayas 2. Excavations (Archeology) -- Mexico

ISBN 978-0-8225-7504-7 lib bdg; 0-8225-7504-3 lib bdg

LC 2007021323

This describes the discovery of the ancient Mayan site of Palenque in 1840 by John Stephens and Frederick Catherwood, and the mid-20th century excavations of the site by Alberto Ruz Lhuillier, who discovered the tomb of the Mayan king Pakal, who died in 683 A.D., inside a pyramid

This "clearly written [title is] illustrated with large photographs and period artwork, and the pages are broken up with text boxes featuring quotes and interesting anecdotes." SLJ

Includes glossary and bibliographical references

Lourie, Peter

★ **Hidden** world of the Aztec. Boyds Mills Press 2006 48p il map $17.95

Grades: 4 5 6 7   972

1. Aztecs 2. Excavations (Archeology) -- Mexico

ISBN 978-1-59078-069-5; 1-59078-069-8

The author takes a "look at the Aztecs from the perspective of archaeological digs at the Great Temple in modern-day Mexico City and at the Pyramid of the Moon in Teotihuacan. . . . The writing style is clear, informative, and interesting." SLJ

Includes glossary and bibliographical references

Nardo, Don

Aztec civilization. Lucent Books 2010 104p il map (World history) lib bdg $33.45

Grades: 6 7 8 9   972

1. Aztecs

ISBN 978-1-4205-0242-8; 1-4205-0242-5

LC 2009040802

This is an introduction to Aztec civilization, including its rise and fall and the role of women.

This "shines as it provides a contemporaneous writing as well as work by scholars that offer plenty of drama—and lots of facts too. . . . [It also] provides a solid time line, plenty of photographs, sourced quotes, and a list of books and websites for further investigation. Excellent for reports and research." Booklist

Includes bibliographical references

Schomp, Virginia

The **Aztecs**; [by] Virginia Schomp. Marshall Cavendish Benchmark 2009 96p il map (Myths of the world) lib bdg $23.95

Grades: 6 7 8 9   972

1. Aztecs

ISBN 978-0-7614-3096-4 lib bdg; 0-7614-3096-2 lib bdg

LC 2008007082

"A retelling of several key Aztec myths, with background information describing the history, geography, belief systems, and customs of the Aztecs." Publisher's note

Includes glossary and bibliographical references

Stein, R. Conrad, 1937-

Ancient Mexico. Morgan Reynolds Pub. 2011 144p il map (The story of Mexico) $28.95

Grades: 6 7 8 9   972

1. Native Americans -- Mexico

ISBN 1-59935-161-7; 978-1-59935-161-2

LC 2010041379

"Stein organizes and clearly presents a great deal of information. . . . The . . . format features a chonological text supplemented with useful sidebars and brightened with color illustrations, including many photos, artifacts, and period artworks. . . . [The book] provides a historical survey of Mexico's early inhabitants, from the arrival of Paleo-Indians through civilizations such as the Olmecs, the Maya, and Toltecs, and the Aztecs." Booklist

Includes bibliographical references

Cortes and the Spanish Conquest; [by] R. Conrad Stein. 1st ed.; Morgan Reynolds Pub. 2008 160p il map (The story of Mexico) lib bdg $27.95

Grades: 6 7 8 9 10   **972**
1. Aztecs 2. Explorers 3. Colonial administrators
ISBN 978-1-59935-053-0 lib bdg; 1-59935-053-X
lib bdg
                                    LC 2007016004
This "identifies the 'encounter' between the Spanish and
Aztecs as one that 'would put the human character itself on
trial.' The author provides a look at both societies, tracing
the Aztecs' rise to power and the Spaniards' interest in exploration. The Spanish conquest of the Aztecs, led by Hernando Cortés, is related in great depth, and the book ends
with a discussion of its legacy. [An] excellent [introduction]
to Mexican history." SLJ
Includes bibliographical references

The **Mexican** Revolution. Morgan Reynolds
Pub. 2008 160p il map (The story of Mexico) lib
bdg $27.95
Grades: 6 7 8 9 10   **972**
1. Mexico -- History
ISBN 978-1-59935-051-6; 1-59935-051-3
                                    LC 2007-22136
"Opening with Porfirio Díaz's presidency (beginning in
1876), [this book] explains how Indian land was expropriat-
ed and allotted to rich hacienda owners, describes resistance
movements led by Emiliano Zapata and Pancho Villa, and
details 10 years of political upheaval and violent uprisings
(1910-1920), ending with Alvaro Obregó's election as president of Mexico. . . . [The book has] a lively narrative style.
. . . Pertinent illustrations, including photographs, historical
paintings, and maps are sprinkled throughout. . . . Well-written and well-researched." SLJ
Includes bibliographical references

The **Mexican** War of Independence; [by] R.
Conrad Stein. Morgan Reynolds Pub. 2008 144p il
map (The story of Mexico) lib bdg $27.95
Grades: 6 7 8 9 10   **972**
1. Mexico -- History
ISBN 978-1-59935-054-7 lib bdg; 1-59935-054-8
lib bdg
                                    LC 2007022137
This "covers the years between 1521, when Hernando
Cortés completed his conquest of the Aztec empire, and
1855, when Antonio Lopez Santa Anna was overthrown. The
book provides excellent background information about three
centuries of Spain's rule over Mexico. . . . [The book has] a
lively narrative style. . . . Pertinent illustrations, including
photographs, historical paintings, and maps are sprinkled
throughout. . . . Well-written and well-researched." SLJ
Includes bibliographical references

972.08   Mexico since 1867

Stein, R. Conrad
Modern Mexico. Morgan Reynolds Pub. 2011
144p il map (The story of Mexico) $28.95

Grades: 6 7 8 9   **972.08**
1. Mexico -- History 2. Mexico -- Politics
and government
ISBN 978-1-5993-5162-9; 1-5993-5162-5
                                    LC 2010053630
"Stein organizes and clearly presents a great deal of
information. . . . The . . . format features a chronological
text supplemented with useful sidebars and brightened
with color illustrations, including many photos, artifacts,
and period artworks. . . . [The book] looks at events in
Mexico since 1920, focusing primarily on presidential administrations, economic problems, political unrest, and
emigration." Booklist
Includes bibliographical references

972.81   Guatemala

Croy, Anita
★ **Guatemala**. National Geographic 2009 64p
il map (Countries of the world) lib bdg $27.90
Grades: 4 5 6 7   **972.81**
ISBN 978-1-4263-0471-2 lib bdg; 1-4263-0471-4
lib bdg
This describes the geography, nature, history, people and
culture, government and economy of Guatemala
Includes glossary and bibliographical references

Laughton, Timothy
Exploring the life, myth, and art of the Maya;
Timothy Laughton. Rosen Pub. 2012 144 p. (Civilizations of the world)
Grades: 7 8 9 10 11   **972.81**
1. Mayan art 2. Mayas -- History 3. Mayas -- Folklore
4. Mayas -- Social life and customs 5. Maya art
ISBN 9781448848324
                                    LC 2011009790
This book on the Maya "offers an informative overview of . . . political and social history as well as its art,
architecture, and mythology, all bolstered with plenty of . .
. details and narratives. . . . [T]he illustrations include artworks, documents, and handsome maps as well as photos
of significant sites and artifacts. . . . In "Maya," [Timothy]
Laughton shows how archaeology and scholarship have
shifted accepted views on this culture over the last century."
(Booklist)
The book "put[s] the art . . . in context, explaining how
a society's religious beliefs, legends, and cultural traditions
manifest themselves through images and iconography. The
. . . layout features full-color photographs of architecture,
sculpture, and painting on every page, accompanied by informative captions." (School Libr J)
Includes bibliographical references (p. 138) and index

Mann, Elizabeth
Tikal; the center of the Maya world. with illustrations by Tom McNeely. Mikaya Press 2002 47p
il map (Wonders of the world) $19.95

Grades: 4 5 6 7　　　　　　　　　972.81
　1. Mayas -- Antiquities
　ISBN 1-931414-05-X

LC 2002-29599

A history of the Maya Indians in the city of Tikal, founded in 800 B.C.

"Mann's narrative flows smoothly, and frequent, full-color illustrations . . . help to clarify the details mentioned in the text." Booklist

Includes glossary

Ollhoff, Jim

Mayan and Aztec mythology; by Jim Ollhoff. ABDO Publishing Company 2011 32p. ill. (The world of mythology) lib bdg $27.07

Grades: 5 6 7 8　　　　　　　　972.81
　1. Mythology 2. Mayas -- Folklore 3. Aztecs -- Folklore 4. Mayas -- Religion 5. Aztecs -- Religion
　ISBN 978-1-61714-724-1; 1-61714-724-9;
　9781617147241

LC 2010042976

This describes the history of myths of the Maya and Aztecs, their meaning, and their gods and goddesses including Itzamna, Xolotl, the Aztec feathered serpent god Quetzalcoatl, and the Mayan rain god Chac.

"Ollhoff writes in a clear and engaging fashion, presenting complex issues in a way that will be easy for youngsters to grasp. . . . The photographs and reproductions of art tie directly to the [text]." SLJ

Vanvoorst, Jennifer Fretland

The **ancient** Maya; by Jenny Fretland VanVoorst. Compass Point Books 2013 48 p. col. ill. (library) $28.65; (paperback) $8.95

Grades: 4 5 6 7 8　　　　　　　972.81
　1. Mayas 2. Civilization, Ancient 3. Mayas -- Social life and customs
　ISBN 0756545641; 0756545846; 9780756545642;
　9780756545840

LC 2012001966

This children's nonfiction book, by Jennifer Fretland VanVoorst, profiles the Mayan civilization as part of the "Exploring the Ancient World" series. "The civilization of the . . . Maya reached its peak about 2,000 years ago. The Maya held a complex religious view of the world. In an effort to maintain order by pleasing their many gods, they built imposing stone temples, developed a written language, and played a ball game with life-or-death consequences." (Publisher's note)

Includes bibliographical references (p. 46) and index.

972.82　Belize

Jermyn, Leslie

Belize; [by] Leslie Jermyn and Yong Jui Lin. 2nd ed.; Marshall Cavendish Benchmark 2012 144p il map (Cultures of the world) lib bdg $42.79

Grades: 5 6 7 8　　　　　　　　972.82
　ISBN 978-1-60870-452-1; 1-60870-452-1

LC 2010035966

Provides information on the geography, history, wildlife, governmental structure, economy, cultural diversity, peoples, religion, and culture of Belize.

"The concise writing offers enough material for report writers without overwhelming them. Numerous full-color and black-and-white photos of interest, a clean layout, and use of pastels to highlight headings and sidebars contribute to the attractiveness of . . . [this presentation]." SLJ

Includes glossary and bibliographical references

972.83　Honduras

Kras, Sara Louise

Honduras; by Sara Louise Kras. Children's Press 2006 144p il map (Enchantment of the world, second series) lib bdg $37

Grades: 5 6 7 8　　　　　　　　972.83
　ISBN 978-0-516-24871-4 lib bdg; 0-516-24871-5
　lib bdg

LC 2005024240

Describes the geography, history, culture, religion, and people of Honduras

Includes bibliographical references

McGaffey, Leta

Honduras; [by] Leta McGaffey and Michael Spilling. 2nd ed.; Marshall Cavendish Benchmark 2010 144p il map (Cultures of the world) lib bdg $42.79

Grades: 5 6 7 8　　　　　　　　972.83
　ISBN 978-0-7614-4848-8 lib bdg; 0-7614-4848-9
　lib bdg

LC 2009022642

First published 1999

"Provides comprehensive information on the geography, history, wildlife, governmental structure, economy, cultural diversity, peoples, religion, and culture of Honduras." Publisher's note

Includes glossary and bibliographical references

Shields, Charles J.

Honduras. Mason Crest Pubs. 2003 63p il map (Discovering Central America) lib bdg $19.95

Grades: 4 5 6 7　　　　　　　　972.83
　ISBN 1-59084-096-8

LC 2002-9089

This describes the history, geography, and culture of Honduras

This is "jam-packed with useful information. . . . [It contains] straightforward writing, clearly titled chapters, high quality color, and well-captioned photographs and graphics." Libr Media Connect

Includes glossary and bibliographical references

972.84   El Salvador

Foley, Erin
El Salvador; [by] Erin Foley, Rafiz Hapipi. 2nd ed.; Benchmark Bks. 2005 144p il map (Cultures of the world) lib bdg $42.79
Grades: 5 6 7 8   **972.84**
ISBN 0-7614-1967-5
LC 2005009360
First published 1994
This describes the geography, history, government, economy, environment, people, lifestyle, religion, language, arts, leisure, festivals, and food of El Salvador
Includes glossary and bibliographical references

972.85   Nicaragua

Kallen, Stuart A.
The **aftermath** of the Sandinista Revolution. Twenty-First Century Books 2009 160p il (Aftermath of history) lib bdg $38.60
Grades: 8 9 10 11 12   **972.85**
1. Nicaragua -- Politics and government
ISBN 978-0-8225-9091-0; 0-8225-9091-3
LC 2008-25356
"The 1979 overthrow of the corrupt Nicaraguan government by the Marxist Sandinistas brought change to one of the poorest countries in the Americas and instilled in the U.S. new fears about the spread of Communism. . . . Kallen offers a good overview of one of the Latin American theaters of the Cold War." SLJ
Includes glossary and bibliographical references

Kott, Jennifer
Nicaragua; [by] Jennifer Kott, Kristi Streiffert. 2nd ed.; Benchmark Bks. 2005 144p il map (Cultures of the world) lib bdg $42.79
Grades: 5 6 7 8   **972.85**
ISBN 0-7614-1969-1
LC 2005009240
First published 1994
An illustrated overview of the geography, economy, history, government, politics, and culture of Nicaragua
Includes glossary and bibliographical references

972.86   Costa Rica

Foley, Erin
Costa Rica; [by] Erin Foley and Barbara Cooke. 2nd ed.; Marshall Cavendish Benchmark 2008 144p il map (Cultures of the world) lib bdg $42.79
Grades: 5 6 7 8   **972.86**
ISBN 978-0-7614-2079-8 lib bdg; 0-7614-2079-7 lib bdg
LC 2006101736
First published 1997
This offers "information on the geography, history, wildlife, governmental structure, economy, cultural diversity, peoples, religion, and culture of Costa Rica." Publisher's note
Includes glossary and bibliographical references

972.87   Panama

DuTemple, Lesley A.
The **Panama** Canal. Lerner Publs. 2003 96p il maps (Great building feats) lib bdg $27.93
Grades: 6 7 8 9   **972.87**
1. Panama Canal
ISBN 0-8225-0079-5
LC 2001-4656
A history of the building of the Panama Canal, with emphasis on the difficulties of digging a canal where some engineers said it could not be done
"The text is peppered with quotes from letters, speeches, and diaries of those involved in the project. . . . Sidebars present interesting asides. . . . A fascinating and well-documented blend of history and engineering." SLJ
Includes bibliographical references

Hassig, Susan M.
★ **Panama**; [by] Susan Hassig & Lynette Quek. 2nd ed.; Marshall Cavendish Benchmark 2007 144p il map (Cultures of the world) lib bdg $42.79
Grades: 5 6 7 8   **972.87**
ISBN 978-0-7614-2028-6 lib bdg; 0-7614-2028-2 lib bdg
LC 2006020824
First published 1996
This provides "information on the geography, history, wildlife, governmental structure, economy, cultural diversity, peoples, religion, and culture of Panama." Publisher's note
Includes glossary and bibliographical references

Vander Hook, Sue
Building the Panama Canal. ABDO Pub. Co. 2010 112p il map (Essential events) lib bdg $32.79
Grades: 6 7 8 9   **972.87**
1. Panama Canal
ISBN 978-1-60453-942-4; 1-60453-942-9
LC 2009-30373
Readers will learn about the historic quests to find a pathway between the Atlantic and Pacific oceans, France's pursuit in building a canal, and the United States' first trials in building the Panama Canal.
"The writing is accessible and is richer than a lot of history writing, allowing the reader to become engaged in the text as a story, and the layout provides enough white space to allow lower level readers to feel confident." Libr Media Connect
Includes glossary and bibliographical references

972.9   West Indies (Antilles) and Bermuda

Kras, Sara Louise

Antigua and Barbuda; [by] Sara Louise Kras. Marshall Cavendish Benchmark 2008 144p il map (Cultures of the world) lib bdg $42.79

Grades: 5 6 7 8   **972.9**
   ISBN 978-0-7614-2570-0
                          LC 2006031537

This describes the geography, history, government, economy, environment, people, and culture of Antigua and Barbuda

Includes glossary and bibliographical references

972.91   Cuba

★ **Castro's** Cuba; Charles W. Carey Jr., book editor. Greenhaven Press 2004 205p il (History firsthand) $37.95; pa $23.70

Grades: 8 9 10 11 12   **972.91**
   1. Presidents 2. Communist leaders 3. Socialism -- Cuba 4. Cuba -- Economic conditions -- 1959-
   ISBN 0-7377-1654-1; 0-7377-1655-X pa
                          LC 2003-47286

"Through the use of interviews, articles, and first-person narratives, this book focuses on the significance of the 1959 revolution and its aftermath. An extensive introduction explaining events precipitating the rise of Fidel Castro, the revolution, and the current situation in Cuba provides readers with a necessary overview to understand the succeeding chapters." SLJ

Includes bibliographical references

Donovan, Sandra, 1967-

Teens in Cuba; by Sandy Donovan. Compass Point Books 2009 96p il (Global connections) lib bdg $33.26

Grades: 6 7 8 9   **972.91**
   1. Teenagers 2. Cuba
   ISBN 978-0-7565-3851-4 lib bdg; 0-7565-3851-3 lib bdg
                          LC 2008-6284

Uncovers the challenges, pastimes, customs and culture of teens in Cuba

This book is "concise and highly readable. . . . Clear, colorful photos and sidebars on a range of topics provide further context. . . . [This title] will enrich young adult collections." SLJ

Includes glossary and bibliographic references

Sheehan, Sean

Cuba; [by] Sean Sheehan, Leslie Jermyn. 2nd ed.; Benchmark Bks. 2005 144p il map (Cultures of the world) lib bdg $42.79

Grades: 5 6 7 8   **972.91**
   ISBN 0-7614-1965-9
                          LC 2005009362

First published 1994

This describes the geography, history, government, economy, population, lifestyle, religion, language, arts, leisure, festivals, and food of Cuba

Includes glossary and bibliographical references

Stein, R. Conrad

Cuban Missile Crisis; in the shadow of nuclear war. Enslow Publishers 2009 128p il map (America's living history) lib bdg $31.93

Grades: 5 6 7 8   **972.91**
   1. Cuban Missile Crisis, 1962
   ISBN 978-0-7660-2905-7 lib bdg; 0-7660-2905-0 lib bdg
                          LC 2008-4703

"This engaging account provides a thorough discussion of events. . . . Archival photographs, maps, sidebars, and many primary sources effectively depict key figures, political posturing, and the nation's anxiety." Horn Book Guide

Includes glossary and bibliographical references

Tracy, Kathleen

We visit Cuba. Mitchell Lane Publishers 2010 63p il (Your land and my land) lib bdg $33.95

Grades: 4 5 6 7   **972.91**
   1. Cuba
   ISBN 978-1-58415-890-5 lib bdg; 1-58415-890-5 lib bdg
                          LC 2010006558

"With an inviting format that includes bright color photos on every spread, this title . . . offers an appealing overview of Cuba's history, geography, culture and lifestyle, politics, economics, and more. . . . A good starting point for research as well as for personal interest." Booklist

Includes glossary and bibliographical references

Wright, David K.

Cuba; by David K. Wright. Children's Press 2009 144p il map (Enchantment of the world, second series) lib bdg $38

Grades: 5 6 7 8   **972.91**
   ISBN 978-0-531-12096-5 lib bdg; 0-531-12096-1 lib bdg
                          LC 2008008423

This describes the geography, history, culture, people, and government of Cuba

Includes bibliographical references

972.910   Cuba-- 1899-

Marsico, Katie

Fidel Castro; Cuban president & revolutionary. by Katie Marsico. ABDO Pub. Co. 2009 112 p. ill. (some col.) (library) $34.22

Grades: 6 7 8   **972.910**
   1. Cuba 2. Heads of state 3. Heads of state -- Cuba -- Biography 4. Revolutionaries -- Cuba -- Biography
   ISBN 1604535229; 9781604535228
                          LC 2008033493

This book by Katie Marsico is part of the Essential Lives series and looks at Cuban dictator Fidel Castro. This entry "focuses as much on Cuban history and its relationship with the U.S. as it does on its former leader; details about Castro's family life, for example, often appear in sidebars." (Booklist)

Includes bibliographical references and index.

972.92   Jamaica and Cayman Islands

Green, Jen

★ **Jamaica**; [by] Jen Green; David J. Howard and Joel Frater, consultants. National Geographic 2008 64p il map (Countries of the world) lib bdg $27.90

Grades: 4 5 6 7   **972.92**

ISBN 978-1-4263-0300-5 lib bdg; 1-4263-0300-9 lib bdg

This describes the geography, nature, history, people and culture, government, and economy of Jamaica.

Includes glossary and bibligraphical references

Sheehan, Sean

Jamaica; [by] Sean Sheehan & Angela Black. 2nd ed; Benchmark Books 2004 144p il map (Cultures of the world) lib bdg $42.79

Grades: 5 6 7 8   **972.92**

ISBN 0-7614-1785-0

                            LC 2004-7676

First published 1996

Introduces the geography, history, religion, government, economy, and culture of Jamaica

"An informative book with captivating pictures, a visually attractive layout, and flowing text. . . . A well-balanced and interesting look at one country's culture." SLJ

Includes glossary and bibliographical references

972.93   Dominican Republic

Foley, Erin

★ **Dominican** Republic; [by] Erin Foley & Leslie Jermyn. 2nd ed; Marshall Cavendish Benchmark 2005 144p (Cultures of the world) lib bdg $42.79

Grades: 5 6 7 8   **972.93**

ISBN 0-7614-1966-7

First published 1995

"The material is well organized in easily readable sections, accurately illustrated with well-placed, full-color photographs on every page." SLJ

Rogers Seavey, Lura

Dominican Republic; by Lura Rogers and Barbara Radcliffe Rogers. Children's Press 2009 144p il map (Enchantment of the world, second series) lib bdg $37

Grades: 5 6 7 8   **972.93**

ISBN 978-0-531-12097-2 lib bdg; 0-531-12097-X lib bdg

                            LC 2008000087

Describes the geography, history, culture, religion, and people of the Caribbean island nation of the Dominican Republic

Includes bibliographical references

972.94   Haiti

Aronin, Miriam

Earthquake in Haiti. Bearport Pub. 2011 32p il map (Code red) lib bdg $25.27

Grades: 4 5 6 7   **972.94**

1. Earthquakes

ISBN 978-1-936088-66-9; 1-936088-66-5

                            LC 2010011126

Describes the devastating earthquake that occurred in Haiti on January 12, 2010.

"The text is written from the points of view of some of the people involved, including primary source direct quotes. Some of the pictures are necessarily graphic, which adds to the authenticity. . . . This title will be used for browsing as well as for reports." Libr Media Connect

Includes glossary and bibliographical references

Cheong-Lum, Roseline Ng

★ **Haiti**; [by] Roseline Ng Cheong-Lum & Leslie Jermyn. 2nd ed; Marshall Cavendish Benchmark 2005 144p il map (Cultures of the world) lib bdg $42.79

Grades: 5 6 7 8   **972.94**

ISBN 0-7614-1968-3

First published 1995

Describes the geography, history, government, economy, culture, peoples, and religion of Haiti

Includes glossary and bibliographical references

Yomtov, Nel

Haiti; by Nel Yomtov. Children's Press 2012 144 p. col. ill. (library) $40

Grades: 5 6 7 8   **972.94**

1. Haiti

ISBN 0531253538; 9780531253533

                            LC 2011010048

This book is part of the Enchantment of the World series and focuses on Haiti. This series presents "factual information against a backdrop of brightly colored pictures and maps. . . . Each book provides a timeline, Fast Facts, and embassies." The books also include "brief chapters that follow real people in their daily lives." (Library Media Connection)

Includes bibliographical references and index.

972.95   Puerto Rico

Lopez, Jose Javier

Puerto Rico; [by] José Javier López. Chelsea House Pub. 2006 108p il map (Modern world nations) lib bdg $30

Grades: 7 8 9 10   **972.95**

ISBN 0-7910-8798-0

                            LC 2005028216

Describes the geography, history, people and culture, politics, and economy of Puerto Rico

Includes bibliographical references

Schwabacher, Martin

Puerto Rico; by Martin Schwabacher and Steve Otfinoski. 2nd ed.; Marshall Cavendish Benchmark 2010 144p il map (Celebrate the states) $42.79

Grades: 5 6 7 8   **972.95**

ISBN 978-0-7614-4734-4; 0-7614-4734-2

LC 2009007066

First published 2001

This offers information on the geography, history, wildlife, governmental structure, economy, cultural diversity, peoples, religion, and landmarks of Puerto Rico.

Includes bibliographical references

Stille, Darlene R.

Puerto Rico. Children's Press 2009 144p il map (America the beautiful, third series) lib bdg $39

Grades: 4 5 6 7   **972.95**

ISBN 978-0-531-18589-6; 0-531-18589-3

LC 2008000819

An introduction to the land, history, and people of Puerto Rico.

Includes glossary and bibliographical references

Worth, Richard

Puerto Rico in American history. Enslow Publishers 2008 128p il map (From many cultures, one history) lib bdg $23.95

Grades: 6 7 8 9 10   **972.95**

1. Puerto Rico

ISBN 978-0-7660-2836-4; 0-7660-2836-4

LC 2006-37087

This is a "book about the ties between Puerto Rico and the U.S. . . . Worth's overview will help to acclimate readers new to the island's history. . . . Writing in short, plain sentences, the author touches upon the commonwealth's ongoing struggle with poverty, migration, and language and the current conflicts about statehood and independence. The book's clean design is inviting, with lots of color-screened boxes, full-color photos, archival artwork, and maps." Booklist

Includes glossary and bibliographical references

972.96   Bahama Islands

Hintz, Martin

The **Bahamas**; by Martin Hintz. Children's Press 2013 144 p. col. ill., col. maps (Enchantment of the world. Second series) (library) $40

Grades: 5 6 7 8   **972.96**

1. Bahamas 2. Bahamas -- Description and travel

ISBN 0531275418; 9780531275412

LC 2012000513

This book, by Martin Hintz, is part of the "Enchantment of the World" series. In it the author provides information and photographs showcasing the people, places and events surrounding the Caribbean island chain of the Bahamas.

Contents include photographs of Bahaman cities and landscapes, statistics describing the islands' features, and traditional Bahaman recipes.

Includes bibliographical references and index

972.98   Windward and other southern islands

Elias, Marie Louise

Barbados; [by] Marie Louise Elias and Josie Elias. 2nd ed.; Marshall Cavendish Benchmark 2010 144p il map (Cultures of the world) lib bdg $42.79

Grades: 5 6 7 8   **972.98**

ISBN 978-0-7614-4853-2 lib bdg; 0-7614-4853-5 lib bdg

LC 2009044592

First published 2000

This offers information on the geography, history, wildlife, governmental structure, economy, cultural diversity, peoples, religion, and culture of Barbados

Includes glossary and bibliographical references

Orr, Tamra

Saint Lucia; [by] Tamra Orr. 2nd ed.; Marshall Cavendish Benchmark 2008 144p il map (Cultures of the world) lib bdg $42.79

Grades: 5 6 7 8   **972.98**

ISBN 978-0-7614-2569-4

First published 1997

This describes the geography, history, government, economy, environment, people, and culture of Saint Lucia

Includes glossary and bibliographical references

Pang, Guek-Cheng, 1950-

Grenada; 2nd ed.; Marshall Cavendish Benchmark 2011 144p il map (Cultures of the world) lib bdg $42.79

Grades: 5 6 7 8   **972.98**

ISBN 978-1-6087-0216-9; 1-6087-0216-2

LC 2010019807

First published 2001

Provides information on the geography, history, wildlife, governmental structure, economy, cultural diversity, peoples, religion, and culture of Grenada.

Includes glossary and bibliographical references

972.983   Trinidad and Tobago

Sheehan, Sean

Trinidad & Tobago. Benchmark Bks. 2001 128p il maps (Cultures of the world) lib bdg $37.07

Grades: 5 6 7 8   **972.983**

ISBN 0-7614-1194-1

LC 00-47457

"The exuberance of the many different ethnic groups shines out of the photographs." Horn Book Guide

Includes glossary and bibliographical references

973   United States

Addasi, Maha

A **kid's** guide to Arab American history; more than 50 activities. by Yvonne Wakim Dennis and Maha Addasi. 1st ed. Chicago Review Press 2013 xx, 204 p.p ill. (paperback) $16.95

Grades: 4 5 6 7   **973**
    1. Arab Americans -- History   2. Arab Americans -- Social life and customs   3. Arab Americans -- History -- Study and teaching -- Activity programs
    ISBN 1613740174; 9781613740170

           LC 2012035758

This book by Yvonne Wakim Dennis and Maha Addasi "provides a contemporary as well as historical look at the people and experiences that have shaped Arab American culture. Each chapter focuses on a different group of Arab Americans including those of Lebanese, Syrian, Palestinian, Jordanian, Egyptian, Iraqi, and Yemeni descent and features more than 50 fun activities that highlight their distinct arts, games, clothing, and food." (Publisher's note)

Africa to America; from the Middle Passage through the 1930s. edited by Jeff Wallenfeldt, Manager, Geography and History. Britannica Educational Pub. 2010 268 p. (library binding) $45.00

Grades: 6 7 8   **973**
    1. Slavery   2. Human rights   3. Harlem Renaissance   4. African Americans -- History   5. African Americans -- Biography   6. African Americans -- Intellectual life
    ISBN 1615301267; 9781615301263

           LC 2009054299

Editor Jeff Wallenfeldt offers a history of African Americans. "At the expense of basic human rights, dignity, and decency, Africans were torn from their native countries and first brought to the United State as slaves. Yet even in the face of injustice and hardship they have endured since then, African Americans have been bolstered by the sacrifices, leadership, and determination of courageous individuals . . . [Wallenfeldt captures] the history of African Americans . . . from origins on the African continent to the end of the Harlem Renaissance." (Barnes & Noble)

Includes bibliographical references and index

America the Beautiful, third series. Children's Press 2007 52v il map lib bdg set $851.20

Grades: 4 5 6 7   **973**
    ISBN 978-0-531-20407-8 lib bdg; 0-531-20407-3 lib bdg

Replaces America the Beautiful, second series, published 1998-2001; Original series published 1987-1992

This series describes the geography, history, people, economy, and government of each state

"Most students should be able to satisfy their information needs with these polished new editions, and the copious extras and lively presentation will help keep them interested too." Booklist

American history on file; [by] George Ochoa and Melinda Corey, editors. Facts on File 2002 un 2v il set$297

Grades: Adult Professional   **973**
    ISBN 0-8160-4661-1

           LC 2002-1673

This includes maps, timelines, illustrations and text divided into ten eras of United States history, which may be reproduced for classroom use

Includes bibliographical references

Armstrong, Jennifer

★ The **American** story; 100 true tales from American history. illustrated by Roger Roth. Alfred A. Knopf 2006 358p il map $34.95; lib bdg $39.99

Grades: 4 5 6 7   **973**
    1. United States -- History
    ISBN 0-375-81256-3; 0-375-91256-8 lib bdg

           LC 2005-34822

"This large, fully illustrated compendium features 100 stories, familiar and lesser known, drawn from America's past and arranged in chronological order. . . . Thanks to writing that is consistently good and sometimes excellent, the tales will certainly hold readers' attention, and brightening nearly every page are lively drawings enhanced by watercolor washes." Booklist

Includes bibliographical references

Benson, Sonia

★ **UXL** encyclopedia of U.S. history; [by] Sonia Benson, Daniel E. Brannen Jr., and Rebecca Valentine; Lawrence W. Baker and Sarah Hermsen, project editors. U.X.L 2008 8v il map set$485

Grades: 6 7 8 9 10 11 12   **973**
    1. Reference books
    ISBN 978-1-4144-3043-0

           LC 2008022347

"This set offers more than 700 entries addressing various cultural, political, economic, and social events, trends, movements, and developments that shaped American history. . . . Black-and-white illustrations, reproductions, archival photographs, maps, sidebars, and inserts accompany the text. . . . Most school and public library collections that serve students in grades 6 through 12 will want to have this recommended resource." Booklist

Includes bibliographical references

Bockenhauer, Mark H.

Our fifty states; by Mark H. Bockenhauer and Stephen F. Cunha; foreword by former president Jimmy Carter. National Geographic Society 2004 239p il map $25.95; lib bdg $45.90

Grades: 4 5 6 7   **973**
    1. Reference books
    ISBN 0-7922-6402-9; 0-7922-6992-6 lib bdg

           LC 2004-1190

This "book is organized by regions: the Northeast, Southeast, Midwest, Southwest, and West, with a map of each region and a short history. Four pages are devoted to each state and include basic facts and a map. The full-color photographs are outstanding. Reproductions of archival illustrations depict four important events from each state's history. The final sections offer a paragraph about each of the territories and a page of facts and figures about the United States." SLJ

Includes bibliographical references

Brownstone, David M.

The **young** nation: America 1787-1861; [by] David M. Brownstone, Irene M. Franck. Grolier Educ. 2002 10v il maps set$339

Grades: 5 6 7 8   **973**
1. United States -- History
ISBN 0-7172-5645-6

LC 2002-20047

This "set covers American history during the period beginning with the Constitution and ending with the Civil War. . . . A handsome layout and many excellent pictures, most in full color, give the books an inviting look. The illustrations include many period paintings and engravings as well as maps, documents, and photos of historic sites and reenactments of events." Booklist

Includes bibliographical references

Buckley, Susan

★ **Journeys** for freedom; a new look at America's story. [by] Susan Buckley and Elspeth Leacock; illustrations by Rodica Prato. Houghton Mifflin Co. 2006 48p il map $17

Grades: 4 5 6 7   **973**
1. United States -- History
ISBN 978-0-618-22323-7; 0-618-22323-1

LC 2004000974

This "history focuses on 20 individuals' quest for freedom across U.S. history. Some . . . will be familiar, but most will not. The stories, both varied and fascinating, often go beyond the personal. . . . Running along the bottom of each double-page spread is a pictorial map keyed to the text. . . . The authors make excellent use of primary sources. . . . As powerful as it is useful." Booklist

Kids make history; a new look at America's story. [by] Susan Buckley and Elspeth Leacock; Illustrations by Randy Jones. Houghton Mifflin 2006 48p il $17

Grades: 4 5 6 7   **973**
1. United States -- History
ISBN 978-0-618-22329-9; 0-618-22329-0

LC 2005036309

"This book introduces 20 children in extraordinary times, starting in 1607 with Pocahontas and ending in 2001 with 9/11 as experienced by high school senior Jukay Hsu. Laura Ingalls Wilder; John Rankin, Jr.; and Susie Baker, a young slave celebrating her independence in 1863, are among those included. The text and the highly detailed watercolor illustrations are married with numbers in small red boxes keyed to both elements for clarification. . . . A good browsing choice for children interested in American history." SLJ

Cooper, Ilene

★ **Jack**; the early years of John F. Kennedy. by Ilene Cooper. 1st ed. Penguin Group USA 2013 168 p. ill. (paperback) $12.99

Grades: 5 6 7 8 9 10 11 12   **973**
1. Catholics 2. Presidents 3. Presidents -- United States
ISBN 0147510317; 9780147510310

LC 2002075912

This book by Ilene Cooper offers a "portrait of [John F.] Kennedy's "youth and the forces that shaped it. . . . Readers discover what it was like for Jack to grow up under the paradoxical influences of privilege and prejudice. His father's wealth . . . couldn't remove the perceived taint of the family's Irish Catholic heritage . . . . To compensate, Joseph and Rose Kennedy pushed their children to excel at everything they did," leading to rivalry between Jack and his brother Joe. Horn Book Magazine

"Intelligent design and numerous fabulous, well-placed, and well-captioned black-and-white photographs enrich Cooper's clear prose. . . . This sensitive, well-researched biography will enhance any collection." Voice Youth Advocates

Includes bibliographical references

Croy, Elden

United States. National Geographic 2010 64p il map (Countries of the world) lib bdg $27.90

Grades: 4 5 6 7   **973**
ISBN 978-1-4263-0632-7 lib bdg; 1-4263-0632-6 lib bdg

This describes the geography, nature, history, people and culture, government and economy of the United States.

"The information is substantial but not overwhelming. The [text is] clear, and the discussion points are well chosen. . . . [The text is] complemented with stunning photographs." SLJ

★ **Exploring** American history: from colonial times to 1877; editors, Tom Lansford, Thomas E. Woods, Jr. Marshall Cavendish Reference 2008 11v il map set$359.95

Grades: 6 7 8 9   **973**
1. Reference books
ISBN 978-0-7614-7746-4; 0-7614-7746-2

LC 2007060896

"This set contains 219 signed articles on the nearly 250 years of American life. . . . The articles have a uniform format and are color coded to indicate broad subject areas—culture, government, laws, people, or places. . . . The articles present a solid overview of current research as well as a rich array of information. . . . The set is thoughtfully arranged, easy to use, and accessible for a wide range of students." Booklist

Includes bibliographical references

Hoose, Phillip M.

★ **We** were there, too! young people in U.S. history. [by] Phillip Hoose. Farrar, Straus & Giroux 2001 264p il $28

Grades: 5 6 7 8   **973**
1. Youth 2. Children 3. Youth -- United States --

Biography -- Anecdotes 4. Children -- United States
-- Biography -- Anecdotes
ISBN 0-374-38252-2

LC 99-89052

Biographies of dozens of young people who made a mark
in American history, including explorers, planters, spies,
cowpunchers, sweatshop workers, and civil rights workers

"A treasure chest of history come to life, this is an inspired collection. . . . Because the book is packed with historical documents, evocatively illustrated . . . and full of
eyewitness quotations, it should prove valuable to young
historians and researchers." SLJ

Includes bibliographical references

Johnston, Robert D.

★ The **making** of America; the history of the
United States from 1492 to the present. Robert D.
Johnston; with a foreword by Douglas Brinkley.
Revised ed. National Geographic 2010 240 p. ill.
(chiefly col.), col. maps (hardcover) $29.95; (li-
brary) $38.90

Grades: 5 6 7 8   973

1. United States -- History
ISBN 9781426306631; 1426306636; 9781426306655;
1426306652

LC 2011401219

First published 2002

Includes bibliographical references (p. 226-234)
and index.

"This energetically written and profusely illustrated history remains one of the top-drawer single-volume accounts
of the founding and growth of the U.S. for middle grade students. The previous edition ended with 9/11; here, into the
same page count, Johnston fits Hurricane Katrina, the wars
in Iraq and Afghanistan, Barack Obama's election, and other
major events." Booklist

★ **Junior** Worldmark encyclopedia of the states;
[Timothy L. Gall and Susan Bevan Gall, editors]
5th ed.; Thomson Gale 2007 4v il map set $235

Grades: 5 6 7 8 9 10   973

1. Reference books
ISBN 978-1-4144-1106-4 set; 1-4144-1106-5 set

LC 2007003910

First published 1996

This reference "includes facts and details on every state
in the U.S., including the District of Columbia and U.S. de-
pendencies. Entries cover the geography, history, politics,
economy and other facts about each state. Alphabetically
arranged entries feature . . . subheadings for each state. . . .
An index of people, places and subjects [is included]." Publisher's note

Includes bibliographical references

King, David C.

★ **Children's** encyclopedia of American history.
DK Pub. 2003 304p il map $29.99

Grades: 5 6 7 8   973

1. Reference books
ISBN 0-7894-8330-0

LC 2002-73388

Full-color maps, photographs, and paintings illustrate a
comprehensive reference guide to American history

"A visually enticing and textually fascinating
survey." SLJ

Lake, Matthew

Weird U.S. a freaky field trip through the 50
states. [by] Matt Lake and Randy Fairbanks. Sterling
Pub. 2011 128p il $14.95

Grades: 6 7 8 9   973

1. Curiosities and wonders 2. Folklore -- United States
ISBN 978-1-4027-5462-3; 1-4027-5462-0

LC 2010027019

"Imagine the kitsch of a field trip to the world's largest ball of twine and multiple it by about a thousand and
you'll begin to appreciate the imaginative and colorful romp
through the United States' weirdest roadside attractions.
Each site . . . is described in detail with full-color photographs. . . . Sure to be a hit with students that pore over the
Guiness Book of World Records and Ripley's Believe It or
Not!." Booklist

Leacock, Elspeth

Journeys in time; a new atlas of American history. [by] Elspeth Leacock and Susan Buckley; illustrations by Rodica Prato. Houghton Mifflin 2001
48p il maps $15; pa $6.95

Grades: 4 5 6 7   973

1. United States -- History
ISBN 0-395-97956-0; 0-618-31114-9 pa

LC 00-40803

Each double-page spread of this book "takes an individual who was part of a historic movement (such as the
Underground Railroad or immigration) and gives a brief narrative outlining his or her circumstances. Added to the text
are sequential numbers that indicate major events in each
of the twenty journeys. A double-page location map traces
the routes each took, using illustrative vignettes marked with
corresponding numbers that reference the text." Horn Book

Our country's founders; a book of advice for young
people. edited with commentary by William J.
Bennett. Simon & Schuster 1998 314p il hardcover o.p. pa $16.95

Grades: 7 8 9 10   973

1. Social ethics
ISBN 0-689-82106-9; 0-689-84469-7 pa

LC 98-6592

A book of advice from our nation's founders on how to
be a good citizen and a worthy member of civil society

Bennett "draws on a wide variety of primary, secondary,
and tertiary sources, ranging from the love letters of John
and Abigail Adams to Mason Weems' apocryphal tale of
George Washington and the cherry tree. Few young adults
are likely to pick this up on their own, but teachers will find
it a valuable resource." Booklist

Includes bibliographical references

Panchyk, Richard

★ The **keys** to American history; understanding our most important historic documents. Chicago Review Press 2009 241p il map $24.95; pa $19.95

Grades: 7 8 9 10 11 12   973

ISBN 978-1-55652-716-6; 1-55652-716-0; 978-1-55652-804-0 pa; 1-55652-804-3 pa

"This impressive collection is a valuable resource for gaining a greater appreciation for and understanding of our nation's dynamic history." SLJ

Includes bibliographical references

Pinkney, Andrea Davis

Hand in hand; ten Black men who changed America. by Andrea Davis Pinkney; paintings by Brian Pinkney. Disney/Jump at the Sun 2012 243 p. $19.99

Grades: 4 5 6 7   973

1. United States -- History 2. African Americans -- Biography 3. African American men -- Biography 4. Social change -- United States -- History

ISBN 1423142578; 9781423142577

LC 2011051348

Coretta Scott King Author Book Award (2013)

Boston Globe-Horn Book Honor: Nonfiction (2013).

In this book, Andrea Davis Pinkney profiles "ten influential black men--including Frederick Douglass, W.E.B. Du Bois, Thurgood Marshall, Jackie Robinson, and Martin Luther King Jr." She presents "descriptions of each man's influence on civil rights, culture, art, or politics. . . . An examination of Barack Obama's life and presidential election carries readers into the present day, placing the achievements of those who came before him into perspective." (Publishers Weekly)

Includes bibliographical references and index.

Rubel, David

★ **Scholastic** encyclopedia of the presidents and their times; by David Rubel. Scholastic 1994 vii, 216 p.p ill. (some col.), col. maps (hardcover) $24.99

Grades: 5 6 7 8   973

1. Presidents -- United States -- Encyclopedias 2. United States -- History

ISBN 0545499852; 9780545499859

LC 93011810

This book is an encyclopedia of the U.S. presidency. It "begins each president's entry with a list including birth and death dates, party, vice president, and nickname, and then describes key elements of each man's presidency. Short sidebars discuss famous people and events of the time." (Cobblestone Magazine)

An "examination of the political and personal lives of U.S. Presidents that begins with George Washington and ends halfway through Bill Clinton's current term in office." SLJ

Selzer, Adam

The **smart** aleck's guide to American history. Delacorte Press 2009 326p il lib bdg $15.99; pa $12.95

Grades: 7 8 9 10 11 12   973

1. United States -- History

ISBN 978-0-385-90613-5 lib bdg; 0-385-90613-7 lib bdg; 978-0-385-73650-3 pa; 0-385-73650-9 pa

LC 2009-03897

"This irreverent guide to American history takes readers from the earliest days of settlement to the presidency of Barack Obama. . . . The flippant tone, mock quiz and essay questions and silly categories of information . . . are sure to appeal to the surliest of . . . students. Numerous sidebars, reproductions of paintings, engravings and photographs and even a recipe for making mustard gas keep the text from becoming dull, and students may find that they have learned a lot of history along the way." Kirkus

Yorinks, Adrienne

Quilt of states; quilts by Adrienne Yorinks; written by Adrienne Yorinks and 50 librarians from across the nation; librarian contributions compiled and edited by Jeanette Larson. National Geographic 2005 122p il $19.95

Grades: 5 6 7 8   973

1. United States -- History

ISBN 0-7922-7285-4

LC 2004-17796

"The United States is stitched together chronologically in this stunning book that features a quilted spread for each state. Yorinks enlisted a librarian from each state to contribute a short entry to point up a few significant facts that add to the tapestry of the emerging nation. . . . The quilted representations are not only artistically intricate and beautiful, but also informative. A handsome book to linger over and learn from." SLJ

973.09 Presidents

Bausum, Ann

★ **Our** Country's Presidents; All You Need to Know About the Presidents, From George Washington to Barack Obama. by Ann Bausum; foreword by President Barack Obama. 4th ed. National Geographic 2013 223 p. ill., maps (hardcover) $24.95

Grades: 5 6 7 8   973.09

1. Presidents -- United States -- Encyclopedias 2. Presidents -- United States

ISBN 1426310897; 9781426310898

LC 2009290293

First published 2001

This book by Ann Bausum looks at U.S. presidents. The text shares "facts about the men's personal lives, humorous incidents, political backgrounds, records, struggles, battles, successes, what they are most famous for, events that occurred during their administrations, and memorable quotes."

"This exceedingly attractive offering is . . . chock-full of information, presented . . . in such an inviting manner that children will enjoy paging through, even if there's no school report looming. . . . Full of interesting tidbits as well as solid information." Booklist

Includes bibliographical references

★ The **presidency** A to Z; Gerhard Peters, editor; John T. Woolley, editor. 5th ed. CQ Press 2012 xix, 715 p.p ill. (hardcover) $125

Grades: 8 9 10 11 12 Adult   **973.09**

1. Presidents -- United States -- Biography 2. Presidents -- United States -- Encyclopedias
ISBN 1608719081; 9781608719082

LC 2012023290

This book, by Gerhard Peters, presents a dictionary of the U.S. presidency. The book is a "tool for understanding the presidency, both historically and today and for appraising how it and the executive branch have responded to the challenges facing the nation. It provides readers with quick information and in-depth background on the presidency through a comprehensive encyclopedia of over 300 easy-to-read entries." (Publisher's note)

"At over 700 pages and also available online, this core title. . . provid[es] a comprehensive encyclopedic treatment of the U.S. presidency. . . . A recommended purchase for all libraries and a required one for those with earlier editions, which it supplants." LJ

Includes bibliographical references (p. 684-690) and index.

Rhatigan, Joe

White House kids; the perks, pleasures, problems, and pratfalls of the Presidents' children. Joe Rhatigan; with illustrations by Jay Shin. Charlesbridge Pub. 2012 96 p. ill. (chiefly col.) $14.95

Grades: 5 6 7 8   **973.09**

1. Presidents -- United States -- Family 2. Presidents -- United States -- Children 3. Children of presidents -- United States 4. Children of presidents -- United States -- Biography
ISBN 1936140802; 9781936140800

LC 2011045090

This book presents "an overview of the young occupants of the White House . . . [and] details the perks and downfalls of being a president's child. Information on pets, favorite games and activities . . . and education of presidential offspring is . . . presented. [Joe] Rhatigan explores the press's and the public's fascination with the children . . . as well as the scrutiny and negative press endured by Amy Carter and Chelsea Clinton." (School Library Journal)

"An inviting collection of insightful, interesting and often wacky and weird facts and stories about U.S. presidents and their families." Kirkus

Includes bibliographical references and index

973.1   Early history to 1607

Hernandez, Roger E.

New Spain: 1600-1760s. Marshall Cavendish Benchmark 2009 79p il map (Hispanic America) lib bdg $34.21

Grades: 4 5 6 7   **973.1**

1. Spaniards -- United States 2. Southwestern States -- History
ISBN 978-0-7614-2936-4 lib bdg; 0-7614-2936-0 lib bdg

"Provides comprehensive information on the history of Spanish exploration in the United States." Publisher's note
Includes glossary and bibliographical references

Stefoff, Rebecca

Exploration and settlement. M.E. Sharpe 2008 95p il map (Colonial life) $37.95

Grades: 6 7 8 9 10 11 12   **973.1**

1. Explorers 2. Frontier and pioneer life
ISBN 978-0-7656-8108-9

LC 2007-3960

This "presents a solid and highly readable overview of the theories regarding the peopling of America. Stefoff skillfully interweaves world events that led up to the European exploration race of the 15th and 16th centuries and shares illuminating biographies of the key explorers of the period. . . . The author's conversational tone and generous use of full-color reproductions, maps, and sidebars will engage readers." SLJ

Includes glossary and bibliographical references

973.2   Colonial period, 1607-1775

Cooper, Michael L.

Jamestown, 1607. Holiday House 2007 98p il $18.95

Grades: 6 7 8 9   **973.2**

ISBN 978-0-8234-1948-7; 0-8234-1948-7

LC 2006-02018

This " book presents a history of Jamestown from late 1606, when the Discovery, the Susan Constant, and the Godspeed set sail from London to Virginia, to 1609, when John Smith's injuries forced his return to England. Based largely on the writings of those present, notably Smith, the book offers a very readable, detailed account of the settlers' exploration, deprivation, starvation, illness, and political infighting as well as their relations with Native Americans. . . . Large black-and-white reproductions of period paintings, engravings, drawings, maps, and documents illustrate the book." Booklist

Includes bibliographical references

Doherty, Kieran

To conquer is to live: the life of Captain John Smith of Jamestown. 21st Cent. Bks. (Brookfield) 2001 144p il lib bdg $23.90

Grades: 6 7 8 9   **973.2**

1. Colonists 2. Travel writers 3. Jamestown (Va.) -- Biography 4. Jamestown (Va.) -- History -- 17th century 5. Colonists -- Virginia -- Jamestown -- Biography 6. Virginia -- History -- Colonial period, ca. 1600-1775
ISBN 0-7613-1820-8

LC 00-44309

A biography of the English soldier and adventurer who helped establish the colony of Jamestown, Virginia

A "well-written, appealing biography. . . . This book reads much like a swashbuckling adventure and most likely will inspire further interest in the man." SLJ

Includes bibliographical references

Gray, Edward G.

Colonial America; a history in documents. 2nd ed.; Oxford University Press 2011 211p il map (Pages from history) $39.95; pa $24.95

Grades: 7 8 9 10   **973.2**

1. United States -- History -- 1600-1775, Colonial period

ISBN 978-0-19-976594-2; 978-0-19-976595-9 pa

LC 2010038458

First published 2003

This collection of primary sources examines "the lives of the colonists through their own words—in diaries, letters, sermons, newspaper columns, and poems." Publisher's note

Includes bibliographical references

Huey, Lois Miner

American archaeology uncovers the earliest English colonies. Marshall Cavendish Benchmark 2009 64p il map (American archaeology) lib bdg $31.36

Grades: 4 5 6 7   **973.2**

1. Excavations (Archeology) -- United States

ISBN 978-0-7614-4264-6 lib bdg; 0-7614-4264-2 lib bdg

LC 2008050259

This describes how archeologists have learned about the history of early English colonists in America at Jamestown, Popham Colony, and Roanoke

"Huey enthusiastically brings . . . [this era] to life through artifacts and field research. . . . [The volume begins with an] introduction that defines 'historical archaeology' and explains its value in terms simple enough for lower-elementary readers to comprehend, yet detailed enough for older children to enjoy, an approach followed in the remaining chapters. . . . Huey's focus on American history, which is broken down into small, manageable chunks, is sure to entice budding historians." SLJ

Includes glossary and bibliographical references

Mandell, Daniel R.

King Philip's war; the conflict over New England. Chelsea House 2007 144p il map (Landmark events in Native American history) lib bdg $35

Grades: 7 8 9 10   **973.2**

1. Wampanoag Indians 2. King Philip's War, 1675-1676

ISBN 978-0-7910-9346-7; 0-7910-9346-8

LC 2006-102258

This account features "lively writing and direct quotes, and [is] enhanced by many color and black-and-white photos, drawings, and illustrations." SLJ

Includes bibliographical references

McNeese, Tim

Colonial America, 1543-1763. Chelsea House 2010 136p il map (Discovering U.S. history) $35

Grades: 5 6 7 8   **973.2**

1. United States -- History -- 1600-1775, Colonial period

ISBN 978-1-60413-349-3; 1-60413-349-X

LC 2008055170

This history of Colonial America "begins with a chapter on 'Rivals for North America' and ends with 'The Fight for the Ohio Country.' . . . [The] book has an excellent chronology; rich sidebars; and numerous well-captioned illustrations, maps, and photos that enhance the texts. [This book provides a] satisfying [introduction] to American history for students." SLJ

Includes glossary and bibliographical references

Nardo, Don

Daily life in colonial America. Lucent Books 2010 96p il (Lucent library of historical eras) $32.45

Grades: 6 7 8 9   **973.2**

1. United States -- History -- 1600-1775, Colonial period

ISBN 978-1-4205-0264-0; 1-4205-0264-6

LC 2009045636

Presents an introduction to life in colonial America, discussing family and home life, occupations, education, recreation, medicine, and laws.

Includes bibliographical references

Government and social class in colonial America. Lucent Books 2010 96p il map (Lucent library of historical eras) lib bdg $32.45

Grades: 6 7 8 9   **973.2**

1. Social classes

ISBN 978-1-4205-0265-7; 1-4205-0265-4

LC 2009043640

"The detailed text is interspersed with sidebars of primary and secondary quotations and historical color illustrations that add both substance and visual interest. With its long paragraphs and dutiful citations, this is a fairly advanced take on the topic." Booklist

Includes bibliographical references

The **establishment** of the thirteen colonies. Lucent Books 2010 96p il (Lucent library of historical eras) lib bdg $32.45

Grades: 6 7 8 9   **973.2**

1. United States -- History -- 1600-1775, Colonial period

ISBN 978-1-4205-0267-1 lib bdg; 1-4205-0267-0 lib bdg

In this history of the establishment of the thirteen colonies in North America, "the detailed text is interspersed with sidebars of primary and secondary quotations and historical color illustrations that add both substance and visual interest. With its long paragraphs and dutiful citations, this is a fairy advanced take on the topic." Booklist

Includes bibliographical references

Pederson, Charles E.

The **French** & Indian War. ABDO Pub. Co. 2010 112p il map (Essential events) lib bdg $32.79

Grades: 6 7 8 9   **973.2**

ISBN 978-1-60453-943-1; 1-60453-943-7

LC 2009-30425

This title examines an important historic event, the French & Indian War. Readers will learn the background of French and British settlement on Native American land and how conflict developed as a result.

"The writing is accessible and is richer than a lot of history writing, allowing the reader to become engaged in the text as a story, and the layout provides enough white space to allow lower level readers to feel confident." Libr Media Connect

Includes glossary and bibliographical references

Philbrick, Nathaniel

★ The **Mayflower** and the Pilgrims' New World. G.P. Putnam's Sons 2008 338p il map $19.99

Grades: 7 8 9 10 11 12   **973.2**
    1. Farmers 2. Historians 3. Native Americans 4. Pilgrims (New England colonists) 5. Colonists 6. Carpenters 7. Army officers 8. Pilgrim fathers 9. Pilgrims (New Plymouth Colony) 10. Indians of North America -- Wars
    ISBN 978-0-399-24795-8; 0-399-24795-5
                                        LC 2007-30669
An adaptation of Mayflower: a story of community, courage, and war, published 2006 by Viking for adults

"This volume highlights both the Pilgrims' determination to find and settle a home where they could worship freely and the perilous journey that it took to make that happen. In accessible prose, the author shatters the American myth of the landing at Plymouth Rock and the first Thanksgiving... . The various maps, reproductions of historical documents, photographs of significant locations, and illustrations all come together with the text to help separate fact from legend and create a realistic, readable portrayal of the Pilgrims and their first 50 years in America." SLJ

Includes bibliographical references

Saari, Peggy

Colonial America: almanac. U.X.L 2000 2v (Colonial America reference library) set $110

Grades: 8 9 10 11 12   **973.2**
    1. Almanacs 2. Reference books 3. Almanacs, American
    ISBN 0-7876-3763-7
                                        LC 99-39081
Examines the colonial period in America, discussing both the Native American culture before the arrival of Europeans and the exploration and settlement of different parts of the New World.

Includes bibliographical references

Colonial America: primary sources; Julie Carnagie, editor. U.X.L 1999 297p il (Colonial America reference library) $67

Grades: 8 9 10 11 12   **973.2**
    1. United States -- History -- 1600-1775, Colonial period
    ISBN 0-7876-3766-1
                                        LC 99-34460
Presents the historical events and social issues of colonial America through twenty-four primary documents, including diary entries, poems, and personal narratives

"Each chapter adds helpful material before and after the excerpt to explain its importance. Illustrations and sidebars are used in this volume also, and difficult words are defined." Booklist

Stanley, George Edward

★ The **European** settlement of North America (1492-1763) by George E. Stanley. World Almanac Library 2005 48p il (Primary source history of the United States) lib bdg $31; pa $14.05

Grades: 5 6 7 8   **973.2**
    1. Frontier and pioneer life
    ISBN 0-8368-5824-7 lib bdg; 0-8368-5833-6 pa
"Stanley includes the efforts of Columbus to gain the support of the Spanish royals, a lithograph of Columbus and Queen Isabella, and primary-source material containing the permission for exploration. The motivation of other early explorers and their financial supporters is treated in a similar manner. Coverage of Native Americans includes text from the Constitution of the Iroquois Confederation, c. 1500, used by Benjamin Franklin during the creation of the United States Constitution. . . . Well-organized, highly attractive." SLJ

Includes bibliographical references

★ The **New** Republic (1763-1815) by George E. Stanley. World Almanac Library 2005 48p il (Primary source history of the United States) lib bdg $31; pa $14.05

Grades: 5 6 7 8   **973.2**
    ISBN 0-8368-5825-5 lib bdg; 0-8368-5834-4 pa
"The series of events that lead to the American Revolution is explained, helping readers to understand the connections of events inherent in historical study. Stanley's analysis of the constitutional debates of the Federalists and Anti-Federalists is exceptionally clear. Well-organized, highly attractive." SLJ

Includes bibliographical references

Stefoff, Rebecca

★ **American** voices from Colonial life. Benchmark Bks. 2003 119p (American voices from--) lib bdg $32.79

Grades: 6 7 8 9   **973.2**
    1. United States -- History -- 1600-1775, Colonial period
    ISBN 0-7614-1205-0
                                        LC 2002-3223
Presents the history of the British colonies in North America, beginning with the Jamestown settlement, through excerpts from letters, pamphlets, journal entries, and other documents of the time

Includes glossary and bibliographical references

Cities and towns. M.E. Sharpe 2008 95p il map (Colonial life) $37.95

Grades: 5 6 7 8 9 10 11 12   **973.2**
    1. Cities and towns
    ISBN 978-0-7656-8109-6
                                        LC 2007-7843
This provides "an informative look into how the forts and fishing camps of the early Colonial period became the cities and towns of the 17th and 18th centuries, and what life was like in these developing communities. The author's

conversational tone and generous use of full-color reproductions, maps, and sidebars will engage readers." SLJ

Includes glossary and bibliographical references

Voices from colonial America [series] National Geographic 2005 18v il map

Grades: 5 6 7 8   **973.2**

Each volume in this series describes the colonial history of a state illustrated with historical maps and reprints of period artwork, and includes excerpts from first-person accounts.

"Presented in clear, succinct text . . . this resource, containing a great deal of information, will be a welcome addition to history classes and a great source for report writers." Booklist [review of New Jersey volume]

Includes bibliographical references

973.3   Periods of Revolution and Confederation, 1775-1789

Adler, David A.

★ **B.** Franklin, printer. Holiday House 2001 126p il lib bdg $19.95

Grades: 4 5 6 7   **973.3**

1. Authors 2. Diplomats 3. Inventors 4. Statesmen 5. Scientists 6. Writers on science 7. Members of Congress 8. Statesmen -- United States 9. Printers -- United States -- Biography 10. Inventors -- United States -- Biography 11. Statesmen -- United States -- Biography 12. Scientists -- United States -- Biography
ISBN 0-8234-1675-5

LC 2001-24535

This "surveys Benjamin Franklin's life as a printer, a scientist, an inventor, a writer, and a statesman. . . . Throughout the book, details, anecdotes, and quotations bring the man's portrait into clearer focus, while period illustrations . . . help readers envision the background of his times." Booklist

Includes bibliographical references

Allen, Thomas B.

George Washington, spymaster; how America outspied the British and won the Revolutionary War. featuring illustrations by Cheryl Harness. National Geographic 2004 184 p ill., maps (hardcover) $16.95

Grades: 6 7 8 9   **973.3**

1. Spies 2. Generals 3. Presidents 4. Presidents -- United States
ISBN 0792251261

LC 2003006019

This biography of Revolutionary War general and first President of the United States, George Washington, focuses on his use of spies to gather intelligence that helped the colonies win the war. "Grades six to ten." (Bull Cent Child Books)

"Allen presents the facts with a gleeful edge, clearly enjoying his subject and writing with vigor. . . . Set in an antique typeface, [the book] is well illustrated with black-and-white reproductions of archival art and Harness's charming pen-and-ink sketches." SLJ

Includes glossary and bibliographical references

★ **Remember** Valley Forge; patriots, Tories, and Redcoats tell their stories. [by] Thomas B. Allen. National Geographic 2007 61p il map $17.95; lib bdg $27.90

Grades: 5 6 7 8   **973.3**

1. Generals 2. Presidents
ISBN 978-1-4263-0149-0; 978-1-4263-0150-6 lib bdg

LC 2007024821

The author "recounts here the activities of Washington and his soldiers during the winter of 1777-8, spent regrouping at Valley Forge, Pennsylvania. . . . Allen's strength is his attention to military details and strategies, but his account is clearly presented and succinctly written as well. . . . Illustrated with reproductions of period artwork, drawings, maps, and a few contemporary photographs." Booklist

American Revolution: primary sources; [compiled by] Linda Schmittroth; Lawrence W. Baker and Stacy A. McConnell, editors. U.X.L 2000 xxxiii, 264p il lib bdg $60

Grades: 8 9 10 11 12   **973.3**

ISBN 0-7876-3790-4

LC 99-46940

This volume "presents 32 excerpted documents, beginning with the 1765 Stamp Act and ending with Washington's farewell address to the Continental Army in 1783. Each entry has helpful material to give the context for the document. The adjoining margins contain definitions of terms that may be unfamiliar. . . . [This volume] is attractive and easy to use." Booklist

Includes bibliographical references

The **American** revolutionaries: a history in their own words, 1750-1800; edited by Milton Meltzer. Crowell 1987 210p il hardcover o.p. pa $8.99

Grades: 6 7 8 9   **973.3**

1. United States -- History -- 1775-1783, Revolution
ISBN 0-06-446145-9 pa

LC 86-47846

"Meltzer has assembled a collage of eyewitness accounts, speech and diary excerpts, letters, and other documents for a chronological account of the half century that included the American Revolution. . . . The voices of women who accompanied the troops and of blacks who fought with the army are both represented." Bull Cent Child Books

Aronson, Marc

★ The **real** revolution; the global story of American independence. Clarion Books 2005 238p il map lib bdg $21

Grades: 7 8 9 10   **973.3**

1. World history
ISBN 0-618-18179-2

LC 2005-1088

In this "volume, Aronson investigates the origins of the American Revolution and discovers some startling global connections. The colonies' quest for independence is tied to such seemingly unrelated incidents as Robert Clive's triumph over the French in India in 1750 and John Wilkes's accusations against the king in his newspaper, The North Briton, in the 1760s. . . . This outstanding work is highly compelling reading and belongs in every library." SLJ

Includes bibliographical references

Bigelow, Barbara Carlisle

American Revolution: almanac; [by] Barbara Bigelow and Linda Schmittroth; Stacy A. McConnell, editor. U.X.L 2000 xxxiii, 188, xxxv-xlip il map lib bdg $60

Grades: 5 6 7 8   **973.3**

1. Almanacs 2. Reference books 3. Almanacs, American

ISBN 0-7876-3795-5

LC 99-46939

Provides in-depth background and interpretation of the American Revolution, with short biographies of people relevant to the topics discussed in each chapter

"Illustrations, sidebars, a time line, glossary, and activity ideas enhance the value of the volume." Booklist

Includes bibliographical references

Blair, Margaret Whitman

Liberty or death; the surprising story of runaway slaves who sided with the British during the American Revolution. National Geographic 2010 64p il map lib bdg $27.90

Grades: 5 6 7 8   **973.3**

1. African American soldiers 2. Slavery -- United States 3. Freedmen 4. Fugitive slaves 5. African American loyalists 6. African Americans -- History

ISBN 978-1-4263-0590-0 lib bdg; 1-4263-0590-7 lib bdg

LC 2009-26853

"Blair provides a well-researched account of slaves in Virginia who, beginning in 1775, fled to the British. . . . Though told in a matter-of-fact tone, the story is often heart-wrenching. . . . Colorful reproductions of period paintings, prints, and documents illustrate the clearly written text. . . . A fine and singular addition to American history collections." Booklist

Includes bibliographical references

Bobrick, Benson

Fight for freedom; the American Revolutionary War. Atheneum Books for Young Readers 2004 96p il map $22.95

Grades: 5 6 7 8   **973.3**

1. United States -- History -- 1775-1783, Revolution

ISBN 0-689-86422-1

LC 2003-25548

"This large-format volume profiles significant individuals and discusses the progress of the Revolutionary War. . . . Printed in color, most of the illustrations are period paintings and prints. . . . Students will find the book a well-organized and clearly written introduction to the war." Booklist

Includes glossary and bibliographical references

Driver, Stephanie Schwartz

Understanding the Declaration of Independence. Rosen Pub. 2010 128p il (Words that changed the world) lib bdg $31.95

Grades: 7 8 9 10   **973.3**

1. Architects 2. Presidents 3. Vice-presidents 4. Essayists

ISBN 978-1-4488-1669-9; 1-4488-1669-6

LC 2010-10371

This surveys The Declaration of Independence, considering the "document's 'Context and Creator,' 'Immediate Impact,' 'Legacy,' and 'Aftermath.' . . . Exploring the colonial crisis leading to America's formal separation from the British Empire, . . . [the] author provides a balance of deep context, expressive writing, and pertinent information. Scattered throughout the [text] are a good number of well-captioned, color illustrations and photos. [This book is a] valuable [resource] for teachers and students doing research projects across the curriculum." SLJ

Includes glossary and bibliographical references

Fleming, Thomas J.

★ **Everybody's** revolution; a new look at the people who won America's freedom. [by] Thomas Fleming. Scholastic Nonfiction 2006 96p il $19.99

Grades: 4 5 6 7   **973.3**

1. United States -- History -- 1775-1783, Revolution

ISBN 0-439-63404-0

LC 2005051814

A history of the American Revolution, focusing on the roles played by women, young people, and various ethnic groups.

"With an open layout and clean typeface, this clearly written title is attractive and inviting. . . . Fleming's sound offering is an excellent starting point for discussions of the implications of the Revolutionary War in terms of freedom for all people." SLJ

Includes glossary and bibliographical references

Fradin, Dennis B.

★ The **signers**; the fifty-six stories behind the Declaration of Independence. [by] Dennis Brindell Fradin; illustrations by Michael McCurdy. Walker & Co. 2002 164p il map $22.95; lib bdg $23.85

Grades: 4 5 6 7   **973.3**

1. Statesmen -- United States 2. Statesmen -- United States -- Biography

ISBN 0-8027-8849-1; 0-8027-8850-5 lib bdg

LC 2002-66364

Profiles each of the fifty-six men who signed the Declaration of Independence, giving historical information about the colonies they represented. Includes the text of the Declaration and its history

"Fradin gives brief, fascinating glimpses into the people who have been overlooked as well as those with whom readers might be familiar. . . . An excellent resource for report writing." SLJ

Includes bibliographical references

Freedman, Russell

★ **Washington** at Valley Forge. Holiday House 2008 100p il map $24.95

Grades: 5 6 7 8 9   **973.3**

1. Generals 2. Presidents

ISBN 978-0-8234-2069-8; 0-8234-2069-8

LC 2007-52467

NCTE Orbis Pictus Award honor book (2009)

"With his usual clarity of focus and keen eye for telling quotations, Freedman documents how Washington struggled to maintain morale despite hunger, near-nakedness, and freezing conditions. . . . Throughout, high-quality reproductions depict Washington among the men, and with the numerous other influential people who played crucial roles." Booklist

Freedman, Russell, 1929-

★ **Give** me liberty! the story of the Declaration of Independence. Holiday House 2000 90p il $24.95; pa $14.95

Grades: 5 6 7 8 9 10   **973.3**

1. United States -- History -- 1775-1783, Revolution

ISBN 0-8234-1448-5; 0-8234-1753-0 pa

LC 99-57513

This book describes the events leading up to the Declaration of Independence as well as the personalities and politics behind its framing. Chronology. Annotated bibliography. Index. "Grades five to eight." (Bull Cent Child Books)

"Handsomely designed with a generous and thoughtful selection of period art, the book is dramatic and inspiring." Horn Book

Includes bibliographical references

The **Founding** of America; Leora Maltz, book editor. Greenhaven Press 2002 236p il (Great speeches in history series) lib bdg $34.95; pa $23.70

Grades: 8 9 10 11 12 Adult   **973.3**

1. American speeches 2. Speeches, addresses, etc., American 3. Freedom of speech -- United States -- History -- Sources 4. Liberty -- Political aspects -- United States -- History -- Sources

ISBN 0-7377-0871-9 lib bdg; 0-7377-0870-0 pa

LC 2001-40736

This collection of American speeches from the late 18th and early 19th centuries includes an introductory essay, introductions to each speech and an appendix of biographical sketches

Includes bibliographical references

Hughes, Christopher

★ The **Constitutional** Convention; by Chris Hughes. Blackbirch Press 2005 48p il map (People at the center of) $23.70

Grades: 5 6 7 8   **973.3**

ISBN 1-56711-918-2

LC 2004-17601

This profiles men who participated in the United States Constitutional Convention such as George Washington, Benjamin Franklin, James Madison, and Alexander Hamilton

"Maps, photos, drawings, and a two-page artistic rendition of the event add to the appeal of [this title]. Great for reports and as supplemental teaching [material]." SLJ

Includes bibliographical references

Irvin, Benjamin

Samuel Adams; son of liberty, father of revolution. [by] Benjamin H. Irvin. Oxford University Press 2002 176p il (Oxford portraits) $28

Grades: 7 8 9 10   **973.3**

1. Statesmen 2. Members of Congress 3. Writers on politics 4. Politicians -- United States -- Biography

ISBN 0-19-513225-4

LC 2002-4283

Examines the life of Samuel Adams, a hero of the American Revolution who is credited by some with having fired the first shot at Lexington Green, the "shot heard 'round the world"

"Irvin's account of events is exciting and written in a compelling narrative style. He presents an unbiased assessment of Adams's actions and character." SLJ

Includes bibliographical references

Kostyal, K. M.

1776; a new look at revolutionary Williamsburg. by K.M. Kostyal with the Colonial Williamsburg Foundation; photographs by Lori Epstein. National Geographic 2009 48p il $17.95; lib bdg $27.90

Grades: 4 5 6   **973.3**

1. United States -- History -- 1775-1783, Revolution

ISBN 978-1-4263-0517-7; 1-4263-0517-6; 978-1-4263-0518-4 lib bdg; 1-4263-0518-4 lib bdg

LC 2009-18002

"Clear, distinctive photos add visual appeal to this short history of the American Revolution, written from the point of view of those living in Williamsburg, Virginia's capital in 1776. Kostyal blends political and social history into a readable account of the period, bolstered by informative sidebars, a chronology, and a closing note about the restoration of colonial Williamsburg. . . . The increasing inclusion of nonwhite colonists in the illustrations as well as the text is a welcome trend." Booklist

Includes bibliographical references

McNeese, Tim

Revolutionary America, 1764-1789; consulting editor, Richard Jensen. Chelsea House 2010 128p il map (Discovering U.S. history) $35

Grades: 5 6 7 8   **973.3**

1. United States -- History -- 1775-1783, Revolution

ISBN 978-1-60413-350-9; 1-60413-350-3

LC 2008-55179

"The information is accurate and easy to understand. Pictures are well placed, and primary sources are included. . . . The maps are well done and there are sidebars with additional information. . . . [This would be good] to have on hand for reports as it is well laid out and easy to use." Libr Media Connect

Includes glossary and bibliographical references

Murphy, Jim

★ The **crossing**; how George Washington saved the American Revolution. Scholastic Press 2010 96p il map $21.99

Grades: 5 6 7 8   **973.3**

1. Generals 2. Presidents 3. Trenton (N.J.), Battle of, 1776

ISBN 978-0-439-69186-4; 0-439-69186-9

LC 2009-11561

Murphy "again digs into the well of history, this time emerging with a well-researched, absorbing account of the early battles of the Revolutionary War with General George Washington at their center. Enhanced by numerous sepia maps of troop movements, prints, paintings, and portraits of prominent figures, the blow-by-blow narrative begins with the shots fired at Lexington and Concord in 1775 and continues until the tide-turning battles at Trenton and Princeton in early 1777." Publ Wkly

Includes bibliographical references

A **young** patriot; the American Revolution as experienced by one boy. Clarion Bks. 1996 101p il maps $16; pa $7.95

Grades: 5 6 7 8   **973.3**

1. Soldiers 2. United States -- History -- 1775-1783, Revolution -- Campaigns

ISBN 0-395-60523-7; 0-395-90019-0 pa

LC 93-38789

"Using Joseph Plumb Martin's first person account of his participation in the Revolutionary War as primary source material, Murphy intertwines this story of one teenager's life as a soldier with broader information about the Revolution, to put Martin's story in context. The handsome, informative, and fascinating look at American history is illustrated with many period reproductions." Horn Book Guide

Includes bibliographical references

Nardo, Don

The **Civil** War. Lucent Bks. 2003 109p il maps (History of weapons and warfare) $27.45

Grades: 7 8 9 10   **973.3**

1. Military art and science 2. Military weapons -- United States -- History -- 19th century

ISBN 1-59018-068-2

LC 2002-11032

Discusses the weapons of American Civil War soldiers and different means of warfare used during that conflict.

Includes glossary and bibliographical references

Nash, Gary B.

Landmarks of the American Revolution. Oxford University Press 2003 158p il map (American landmarks) lib bdg $30

Grades: 6 7 8 9   **973.3**

1. Historic sites 2. Historic sites -- United States

ISBN 0-19-512849-4

LC 2002-14152

"Written with the idea that historic sites can be considered primary sources, this book skillfully demonstrates the 'power of places.' Traditional documents, such as excerpts from letters, broadsides, and maps, as well as well-placed

quotes, are incorporated into the text. The places include churches, halls, homes, and battlefields, covering the many facets of the Revolution: political, religious, and actual battles. . . . This well-organized book includes clear, full-color photographs or reproductions and a small inset map for each site." SLJ

Includes bibliographical references

Otfinoski, Steven

The **new** republic: 1760-1840s. Marshall Cavendish Benchmark 2009 79p il map (Hispanic America) lib bdg $23.95

Grades: 4 5 6 7   **973.3**

1. Latinos (U.S.) 2. Hispanic Americans 3. Spaniards -- United States

ISBN 978-0-7614-2938-8 lib bdg; 0-7614-2938-7 lib bdg

LC 2007-45958

"Provides comprehensive information on the history of the Spanish exploring the United States." Publisher's note

Includes glossary and bibliographical references

Renehan, Edward J.

The **Treaty** of Paris; the precursor to a new nation. [by] Edward J. Renehan, Jr. Chelsea House 2007 121p il map (Milestones in American history) lib bdg $35

Grades: 7 8 9 10   **973.3**

ISBN 0-7910-9352-2 lib bdg; 978-0-7910-9352-8 lib bdg

LC 2006034129

This describes the treaty signed in Paris in 1782 in which Benjamin Franklin, John Adams, and John Jay worked to bring about British recognition of American independence and a cessation to hostilities.

The book has "well-reproduced archival photos and drawings with explanatory captions. . . . [and an] open layout and lively [text]." SLJ

Includes bibliographical references

Sanders, Nancy I.

America's black founders; revolutionary heroes & early leaders with 21 activities. Chicago Review Press 2010 150p il $16.95

Grades: 4 5 6 7   **973.3**

1. African Americans -- History

ISBN 978-1-55652-811-8; 1-55652-811-6

"This activity-based guide reveals how African Americans played crucial roles in helping the United States gain its independence. Sanders includes well-known figures such as Phillis Wheatley, Crispus Attucks, and James Forten in her narrative, but also enriches traditional accounts of the period by explaining the contributions of lesser-known patriots. . . . Most of the activities help make this period real to young people. . . . Sanders makes excellent use of primary sources." SLJ

Schanzer, Rosalyn

★ **George** vs. George; the American Revolution as seen from both sides. National Geographic 2004 60p il maps $16.95

Grades: 3 4 5 6   973.3

1. Generals 2. Presidents 3. Kings
ISBN 0-7922-7349-4

LC 2003-20843

This book explores how the characters and lives of King George III of England and George Washington affected he progress and outcome of the American Revolution. Bibliography. Index. "Grades four to six." Bull Cent Child Books

"A carefully researched, evenhanded narrative with well-crafted, vibrant, watercolor illustrations. . . . This is a lovely book, showing historical inquiry at its best." SLJ

Includes bibliographical references

Stewart, Gail

Life of a soldier in Washington's army; by Gail B. Stewart. Lucent Bks. 2003 112p il map (American war library, American Revolution) lib bdg $21.96

Grades: 7 8 9 10   973.3

1. Soldiers -- United States 2. Soldiers -- United States -- Social conditions -- 18th century
ISBN 1-59018-215-4

LC 2002-6602

Discusses the training, organization, diversity, fighting and survival skills, daily routine, diseases, fears, and morale of the first army of the United States

This volume is "thorough, but not overwhelming." SLJ

Includes bibliographical references

973.3092 United States--1775-1789--biography

Freedman, Russell, 1929-

Becoming Ben Franklin; how a candle-maker's son helped light the flame of liberty. Russell Freedman. 1st ed. Holiday House 2013 86 p. col. ill. (hardcover) $24.95

Grades: 5 6 7 8   973.3092

1. Franklin, Benjamin, 1706-1790 2. Founding Fathers of the United States 3. Printers -- United States -- Biography 4. Inventors -- United States -- Biography 5. Statesmen -- United States -- Biography 6. Scientists -- United States -- Biography
ISBN 0823423743; 9780823423743

LC 2012002971

This book is a biography of Ben Franklin. Russell Freedman "chose episodes that reflect how the young man, disgruntled with being his brother's apprentice, made a life for himself . . . . By describing the obstacles Franklin overcame in establishing his print shop in Philadelphia, Freedman delineates a . . . path between his subject's early ambition and his ease with people to his success in business and then to his later roles as a diplomat, revolutionary, and public servant." (School Library Journal)

Includes bibliographical references (p. 78-82) and index.

973.4 Constitutional period, 1789-1809

Bober, Natalie

Abigail Adams; witness to a revolution. {by} Natalie S. Bober. Atheneum Bks. for Young Readers 1995 248p il maps hardcover o.p. pa $9.99

Grades: 7 8 9 10   973.4

1. Parents of presidents 2. Spouses of presidents 3. Presidents' spouses -- United States
ISBN 0-689-31760-3; 0-689-81916-1 pa

LC 94-19259

"By interweaving excerpts from Adams's correspondence into a coherent biography, Bober creates a vibrant, three-dimensional portrait of a fascinating person whose comments on women's place have reverberated throughout history. This scholarly, thoroughly documented study will appeal to more mature readers, but it is more formidable in appearance than in presentation. Black-and-white reproductions are included." Horn Book Guide

Includes bibliographical references

Corrick, James A.

The **Louisiana** Purchase. Lucent Bks. 2001 108p il maps (World history series) lib bdg $27.45

Grades: 7 8 9 10   973.4

1. Louisiana Purchase
ISBN 1-56006-637-7

LC 00-9156

Examines the Louisiana Purchase, discussing the negotiation of the treaty with France, the formation of Louisiana, taking possession of the land, and the exploration, growth, and settlement of the territory

This overview is "well-written . . . [and] thought-provoking." SLJ

Includes bibliographical references

Lanier, Shannon

Jefferson's children; the story of one American family. by Shannon Lanier and Jane Feldman; with photographs by Jane Feldman; and an introduction by Lucian K. Truscott IV. Random House 2000 144p il hardcover o.p. pa $16.95

Grades: 7 8 9 10   973.4

1. Slaves 2. Architects 3. Presidents 4. Vice-presidents 5. Racially mixed people 6. Essayists 7. Mistresses 8. African Americans -- Biography 9. African Americans -- Genealogy 10. African Americans -- Interviews 11. Racially mixed people -- United States -- Genealogy 12. Racially mixed people -- United States -- Interviews
ISBN 0-375-80597-4; 0-375-82168-6 pa

LC 00-44551

This is an "anthology of personal meditations by a variety of Jefferson's living descendants. Edited by Shannon Lanier, a descendant through Sally's son Madison Hemings's line, the portraits that emerge are as generous and jumbled as America itself. The statements range from hostile to conciliatory to indifferent to eloquent." NY Times Book Rev

Includes bibliographical references

McNeese, Tim

Early national America, 1790-1850. Chelsea House 2010 136p il map (Discovering U.S. history) $35

Grades: 5 6 7 8　　　　　　　　**973.4**
1. United States -- History -- 1783-1865
ISBN 978-1-60413-351-6; 1-60413-351-1

LC 2009003679

McNeese "discusses the people, politics, economic conditions, and foreign affairs of [the U.S. from 1790 to 1850], objectively explaining how the attitudes, perceptions, and expectations of the American people and their leaders shaped the development of the country. . . . Color period art and photos, maps, and cutaway drawings supplement the [text]." SLJ

Includes glossary and bibliographical references

Severance, John B.

Thomas Jefferson; architect of democracy. Clarion Bks. 1998 192p il map $18

Grades: 7 8 9 10　　　　　　　**973.4**
1. Architects 2. Presidents 3. Vice-presidents 4. Essayists 5. Presidents -- United States 6. Presidents -- United States -- Biography 7. United States -- Politics and government -- 1783-1809
ISBN 0-395-84513-0

LC 97-31010

Explores the life of the third president, from his childhood in Virginia, through his involvement in the Revolutionary War, to his years in office

"In this respectful, literate, and handsomely illustrated biography, Severance focuses equally on Jefferson's remarkable accomplishments and the beliefs behind them." Booklist

Includes bibliographical references

Stefoff, Rebecca

★ **American** voices from the new republic, 1783-1830. Benchmark Books 2004 xxiii, 116p (American voices from--) lib bdg $34.21

Grades: 6 7 8 9 10　　　　　　**973.4**
1. United States -- History -- 1783-1865
ISBN 0-7614-1695-1

LC 2004-11391

Describes, through excerpts from diaries, speeches, newspaper articles, and other documents of the time, United States history from 1783 to 1830. Includes review questions.

Whitelaw, Nancy

★ **Thomas** Jefferson; philosopher and president. Morgan Reynolds 2002 144p il $21.95

Grades: 7 8 9 10　　　　　　　**973.4**
1. Architects 2. Presidents 3. Vice-presidents 4. Essayists 5. Presidents -- United States 6. Presidents -- United States -- Biography
ISBN 1-88384-681-1

LC 2001-44960

An account of Jefferson's life highlighting his many accomplishments as governor, architect, gardener, inventor, and president

"A clear, crisp biography. . . . A solid and practical book for reports." SLJ

Includes bibliographical references

973.5　1809-1845

Bowes, John P.

Black Hawk and the War of 1832; removal in the north. [by] John P. Bowes. Chelsea House 2007 131p bibl il map (Landmark events in Native American history) lib bdg $35

Grades: 6 7 8 9　　　　　　　**973.5**
1. Sauk Indians 2. Black Hawk War, 1832 3. Indian chiefs 4. Native Americans -- Biography
ISBN 978-0-7910-9342-9 lib bdg; 0-7910-9342-5 lib bdg

LC 2007004927

This "provides a clear overview of early American expansion in the Northwest Territory, from the 1780s through the 1930s, detailing government actions and policies of Indian Removal and how they specifically affected the Sauks and Mesquakies, now known as the Sac and Fox tribes. . . . The battles that ensued (both intertribal and against the U.S. forces) are described, as are the policies created during this period. . . . Attractive color paintings, maps, and photographs appear throughout." SLJ

Includes bibliographical references

Macleod, D. Peter

Four Wars of 1812; One War, Four Perspectives. by D. Peter MacLeod. Pgw 2012 95 p. ill. (paperback) $19.95

Grades: 6 7 8　　　　　　　　**973.5**
1. War of 1812
ISBN 1771000503; 9781771000505

This book on the war of 1812 "examine[s] the viewpoints, goals, and outcomes for its four major participants: Britain, Canada, the United States, and Native American nations. . . , Its four chapters, each focused on one combatant, are made up of spreads that feature either a color photo of period artifacts and weapons or reproductions of artwork . . . on one side and a[n] . . . essay that describes how it illustrates a . . . perspective about the war on the other." (School Library Journal)

Stewart, Mark

The **Indian** Removal Act; forced relocation. Compass Point Books 2007 96p il map (Snapshots in history) $23.95

Grades: 6 7 8 9　　　　　　　**973.5**
1. Cherokee Indians 2. Native Americans -- Relocation
ISBN 978-0-7565-2452-4; 0-7565-2452-0

LC 2006027084

Profiles the "Trail of Tears," the forced removal of five Southeastern Native American tribes to land west of the Mississippi River during the winter of 1838 and 1839.

"The book organizes a good deal of historical information into a cogent presentation. . . . Illustrations, many in color, include photos and maps as well as period engravings, portraits, and documents." Booklist

Includes glossary and bibliographical references

Warrick, Karen Clemens

The **War** of 1812; We have met the enemy and they are ours. Enslow Pubs. 2002 128p il maps (American war series) lib bdg $26.60

Grades: 6 7 8 9   **973.5**

  1. War of 1812
  ISBN 0-7660-1854-7

LC 2001-4120

Traces the history of the War of 1812, examining the maritime and boundary issues that caused it and highlighting the roles of famous personalities, including Oliver Hazard Perry, Andrew Jackson, and Dolley Madison

"With a text that is less dry than many history books, this title will earn its keep as a circulating resource for assignments. . . . [This book has] numerous black-and-white illustrations, a time line, solid footnotes, and chapters that begin with relevant quotes." SLJ

Includes bibliographical references

973.6   1845-1861

Carey, Charles W.

The **Mexican** War; Mr. Polk's war. [by] Charles W. Carey, Jr. Enslow Pubs. 2002 128p il (American war series) lib bdg $26.60

Grades: 6 7 8 9   **973.6**

  1. Mexican War, 1846-1848
  ISBN 0-7660-1853-9

LC 2001-817

This "account of the 1846-1848 war addresses the origins, strategies, battles, and people involved in the conflict. The ramifications of the war for each country are discussed in separate chapters. . . . [This volume has] numerous black-and-white illustrations, a time line, solid footnotes, and chapters that begin with relevant quotes." SLJ

Includes bibliographical references

DiConsiglio, John

The **Mexican**-American War; by John DiConsiglio. Heinemann Library 2012 80 p. ill. (some col.), col. maps (library) $36.50; (paperback) $10.99

Grades: 6 7 8 9   **973.6**

  1. Mexican War, 1846-1848
  ISBN 1432959980; 9781432959982; 9781432960070

LC 2011016817

This book on the Mexican-American War by John DiConsiglio is part of the "Living Through" series. It "provid[e]s . . . an overview of the causes, events, and leading personalities that shaped this 19th century conflict" as well as "snapshots of the daily life of soldiers and civilians. . . . Issues linked to the legitimacy of the American invasion of Mexico, the dictatorial leadership of Mexican commanders, and the shifting course of military fortunes all are presented." Children's Literature

Includes bibliographical references (p. 76-77) and index.

Stein, R. Conrad

The **Mexican**-American War. Morgan Reynolds Pub. 2011 144p il map (The story of Mexico) $28.95

Grades: 6 7 8 9   **973.6**

  1. Mexican War, 1846-1848
  ISBN 978-1-5993-5160-5; 1-5993-5160-9

LC 2010041378

"Stein organizes and clearly presents a great deal of information. . . . The . . . format features a chronological text supplemented with useful sidebars and brightened with color illustrations, including many photos, artifacts, and period artworks. . . . [The book] explains the war's causes, its progress, and it aftermath in both countries." Booklist

Includes bibliographical references

973.7   Administration of Abraham Lincoln, 1861-1865

Adler, David A., 1947-

Harriet Tubman and the Underground Railroad; by David A. Adler. Holiday House 2013 140 p. ill. (hardcover) $18.95

Grades: 5 6 7 8   **973.7**

  1. Underground Railroad 2. African American women -- Biography 3. Slaves -- United States -- Biography
  ISBN 0823423654; 9780823423651

LC 2012006582

This book, by David A. Adler, gives a biography of the ex-slave Harriet Tubman. "She escaped from her owners in Maryland on the Underground Railroad in 1849 and then fearlessly returned . . . to help guide . . . others to freedom as the most famous conductor of the Underground Railroad. . . . During and after the war, she helped hundreds of freed slaves begin new lives, and she later founded a home for elderly former slaves and became active in the women's suffrage movement." (Publisher's note)

Includes bibliographical references

Allen, Thomas B.

★ **Mr.** Lincoln's high-tech war; how the North used the telegraph, railroads, surveillance balloons, ironclads, high-powered weapons, and more to win the Civil War. [by] Thomas B. Allen & Roger MacBride Allen. National Geographic Society 2009 144p il $18.95; lib bdg $25.90

Grades: 5 6 7 8 9 10   **973.7**

  1. Lawyers 2. Presidents 3. State legislators 4. Members of Congress 5. Technology -- History 6. Technology -- United States -- History
  ISBN 978-1-4263-0379-1; 1-4263-0379-3; 978-1-4263-0380-7 lib bdg; 1-4263-0380-7 lib bdg

LC 2008-24546

"Well researched and clearly written, the book discusses the course of the Civil War in terms of new technology, from the ironclad and the submarine to the rapid-fire, repeating rifle and the use of railroads to carry troops and supplies. . . . The many illustrations include captioned black-and-white reproductions of period prints, paintings, and photos as well as clearly labeled drawings. . . . [Readers] will gain a fascinating perspective on why the war progressed as it did and how it was ultimately won." Booklist

Includes bibliographical references

Anderson, Maxine

Great Civil War projects you can build yourself. Nomad Press 2005 140p il $14.95

Grades: 7 8 9 10   **973.7**

1. Handicraft 2. Inventions

ISBN 0-9749344-1-0

From uniforms and submarines to potato cannons and regimental flags, this interactive book explores the history and inventions of the Civil War by providing building projects and activities.

"Besides the drawings that accompany these projects, other illustrations include many period photographs and engravings. . . . Useful for Civil War reenactments as well as school projects." Booklist

Includes glossary and bibliographical references

Armstrong, Jennifer

Photo by Brady; a picture of the Civil War. Atheneum Books For Young Readers 2005 160p il $18.95

Grades: 6 7 8 9 10   **973.7**

1. Photographers 2. Photography -- History

ISBN 0-689-85785-3

LC 2004-8967

"Armstrong chronicles the Civil War from Lincoln's election to his death with both a storylike narrative of events and a photo-essay. . . . This book is also a look at early photographic techniques and offers a description of [Mathew] Brady's rare collection. . . . When readers remember that the pictures are more than 100 years old, they should recognize their exquisiteness, grandeur, and genius." SLJ

Includes bibliographical references

Barney, William L.

The **Civil** War and Reconstruction; a student companion. Oxford Univ. Press 2001 368p il maps (Oxford student companions to American history) $60

Grades: 7 8 9 10   **973.7**

1. Reconstruction (1865-1876) 2. Reconstruction (U.S. history, 1865-1877) -- Encyclopedias

ISBN 0-19-511559-7

LC 00-57444

"The book is encyclopedic in format, with many useful access points, and bibliographic information is located both at the ends of the articles and in several appendixes that suggest books, historic sites and addresses, and Web sites." Voice Youth Advocates

Includes bibliographical references (p. 358-359) and index

Beller, Susan Provost

Billy Yank and Johnny Reb; soldiering in the Civil War. Twenty-First Century Books 2008 112p il map (Soldiers on the battlefront) lib bdg $33.26

Grades: 5 6 7 8   **973.7**

1. Soldiers -- United States

ISBN 978-0-8225-6803-2 lib bdg; 0-8225-6803-9 lib bdg

LC 2006010240

First published 2000

Describes military life for the average soldier in the Civil War, including camp life, diseases, and conditions for the wounded and prisoners of war. Includes excerpts from first-person accounts, letters, and diaries

The author "presents a good deal of solid information in an interesting manner. . . . Good black-and-white reproductions, mainly of photographs from the 1860s, appear throughout the book." Booklist [review of 2000 ed]

Includes bibliographical references

Benoit, Peter

The **surrender** at Appomattox; by Peter Benoit. Children's Press 2012 64 p. chiefly col. ill., col. map (library) $30.00; (paperback) $8.95

Grades: 4 5 6   **973.7**

1. Appomattox Campaign, 1865 2. United States -- History -- 1861-1865, Civil War -- Peace

ISBN 0531250415; 9780531250419; 9780531265666

LC 2011011967

This book by Peter Benoit, part of the "Cornerstones of Freedom" series, describes the events leading up to the end of the U.S. Civil War. It "sketches the events of the Battle of the Wilderness and the capture of Richmond as well as the meeting between [Ulysses S.] Grant and [Robert E.] Lee on April 9, 1865." (School Library Journal)

Includes bibliographical references (p. 61) and index.

Bobrick, Benson

The **Battle** of Nashville; General George H. Thomas & the most decisive battle of the Civil War. Alfred A. Knopf 2010 132p il map $19.99; lib bdg $22.99

Grades: 7 8 9 10   **973.7**

1. Nashville (Tenn.), Battle of, 1864

ISBN 978-0-375-84887-2; 0-375-84887-8; 978-0-375-94887-9 lib bdg; 0-375-94887-2 lib bdg

"Background, strategies, and key individuals involved in the 1864 battle of Nashville come to life in this engaging piece of history. Starting on the eve of the fighting, the narrative then shifts back to examine the complex series of events leading to that moment, outlining the causes of the Civil War, key developments, and major figures. . . . Battle scenes are vivid, capturing the chaos and emotion involved, and military strategies, such as the innovative use of cavalry, are explained clearly. Plentiful illustrations from the period, including many portraits and several dramatic two-page paintings, help bring the period to life." SLJ

Includes bibliographical references

Bolden, Tonya

★ **Cause**: Reconstruction America, 1863-1877. Knopf 2005 138p il $19.95; lib bdg $21.99

Grades: 7 8 9 10   **973.7**

1. Reconstruction (1865-1876)

ISBN 0-375-82795-1; 0-375-92795-6 lib bdg

"This examination of America during Reconstruction covers Lincoln's Proclamation of Amnesty and Reconstruction, the Civil Rights Act of 1866, the troubles of freed slaves, the expansion of the nation and the plight of Native Americans, the 15th Amendment, and the women's suffrage movement. While this is well-documented nonfiction, Bolden writes in the voice of a storyteller. The excellent graphics include archival photos, political cartoons, and primary resources." SLJ

Emancipation Proclamation; Lincoln and the dawn of liberty. Tonya Bolden. Abrams Books for Young Readers 2012 128 p. (alk. paper) $24.95
Grades: 6 7 8 9   **973.7**
1. Slaves -- Emancipation 2. Emancipation Proclamation 3. United States -- History -- 1861-1865, Civil War 4. Slaves -- Emancipation -- United States
ISBN 1419703900; 9781419703904
LC 2012000845
This book offers a "depiction of the issues and tensions surrounding abolition and the development of [Abraham] Lincoln's responses to them as the United States plunged into the Civil War. . . . The author tracks rising tides of both rhetoric and violence, as well as the evolution of President Abraham Lincoln's determined efforts to forge a policy that would serve military, political and moral necessities alike." (Kirkus Reviews)
Includes bibliographical references and index

Burgan, Michael
North over South; final victory in the Civil War. Compass Point Books 2011 64p il map (The Civil War) lib bdg $33.32; pa $6.95
Grades: 5 6 7 8   **973.7**
1. United States -- History -- 1861-1865, Civil War
ISBN 978-0-7565-4369-3 lib bdg; 0-7565-4369-X lib bdg; 978-0-7565-4413-3 pa; 0-7565-4413-0 pa
LC 2010001018
Recounts the end of the Civil War with insight into the key victories at Gettysburg and Vicksburg.
The layout is "clean and attractive, with a large font and reproductions of period illustrations and photos. . . . This . . . will help students understand the era's most important issues and events. A quality choice for reports." SLJ
Includes glossary and bibliographical references

Carlisle, Rodney P.
Civil War and Reconstruction. Facts on File 2008 452p il map (Eyewitness history) $75
Grades: 7 8 9 10   **973.7**
1. Reconstruction (1865-1876)
ISBN 978-0-8160-6347-5
LC 2006-35425
First published 1991 under the authorship of Joe H. Kirchberger
"This illustrated chronology of the Civil War contains over 100 black-and-white photographs (mostly from the Library of Congress Prints and Photographs Division), 16 maps, and biographies of 50 key figures in the era. Each period-based chapter offers a narrative that delves into deeper issues of the causation of war; a chronicle of events, detailed to the week; and eyewitness testimony, includ-

ing diaries, journals, correspondence, editorials, and news accounts." Choice
Includes bibliographical references

The **Civil** War; James Tackach, book editor. Greenhaven Press 2004 186 p. ill. (Turning points) (library) $42.15
Grades: 7 8 9 10   **973.7**
1. United States -- History -- 1861-1865, Civil War
ISBN 0737711140; 9780737711141
LC 2003064297
"Comprised of 17 essays, this book is divided into four chapters: 'A Nation Divides: The Causes of the Civil War,' 'Early Battlefield Victories and the Prospect of European Intervention Fuel the South's Hope for Independence,' 'The North Gains the Advantage,' and 'A Changed Nation.' Many of the most respected Civil War historians . . . are excerpted. . . . Outstanding features of the book are discussion questions and the appendix of documents that are sure to inspire additional research and assist classroom teachers." SLJ
Includes bibliographical references (p. 179-181) and index.

A **Civil** War scrapbook; I was there too! History Colorado. Fulcrum Pub. 2012 64 p. ill. (some col.), maps (paperback) $14.95
Grades: 4 5 6 7 8   **973.7**
1. United States -- History -- 1861-1865, Civil War
ISBN 1555916686; 9781555916688
LC 2011042043
This book is "a multicultural Civil War history for children. The book . . . feature[es] chronological information" and "focus[es] on the different types of people and their place in the war. This . . . book emphasizes the roles of the children, women, minorities, and even pets that became mascots in the war." Also included are "historical photographs, drawings, maps, games, and primary quotes from children." (Publisher's Note)
Includes bibliographical references (p. 62-63) and index.

★ The **Civil** War: a visual history. DK Pub. 2011 360p il map $40
Grades: 5 6 7 8   **973.7**
1. United States -- History -- 1861-1865, Civil War -- Pictorial works
ISBN 978-0-7566-7185-3; 0-7566-7185-X
"A stunning, large-format pictorial history. The seven chapters are arranged chronologically, beginning with an overview of slavery in the United States, 1815 to 1860, and ending with a survey of the legacies of the conflict during the period 1865 to 1877. . . . Chapter introductions are followed by illustrated time lines and by short topical divisions that include biographies, maps, original documents or eyewitness accounts, illustrations, historical photographs, artifacts, and reproductions of paintings. Page layouts and the use of color are superb, and sidebars abound, adding to this extraordinary book." SLJ

Cloud Tapper, Suzanne
The **abolition** of slavery; fighting for a free America. [by] Suzanne Cloud Tapper. Enslow Pub-

lishers 2006 128p il (The American saga) lib bdg
$31.93

Grades: 7 8 9 10   **973.7**
1. Abolitionists 2. Slavery -- United States
ISBN 0-7660-2605-1

LC 2006001739

"The book begins with descriptions of two murders. .
. . The killings point to the indiscriminate hatred of both
slave and anti-slaver. Following the account of the murders,
the author describes the dilemma of slavery that faced the
Founding Fathers, then moves through the decades to discuss the growing political, ethical, and religious opposition
to the institution, and ends with the Civil War. . . . The author
makes great use of direct quotes from those who lived the
events, newspaper accounts, and excerpts from court proceedings. Black-and-white and color archival photographs
and illustrations depict slave life. Clearly written and well
researched, this logically organized book is an excellent purchase for most libraries." SLJ
Includes glossary and bibliographical references

DeFord, Deborah H.
African Americans during the Civil War; [by]
Deborah H. DeFord. Chelsea House 2006 112p il
map (Slavery in the Americas) $35

Grades: 6 7 8 9   **973.7**
1. African American soldiers 2. African Americans --
History
ISBN 0-8160-6138-6

LC 2005021497

This "covers not only African Americans but also the
forces that created the 'U.S. Colored Troops' and the spread
of rights during and after the war. . . . Clearly written, accessible, and well organized, [this] volume is illustrated with
black-and-white drawings, period photographs, and explanatory text boxes." SLJ
Includes bibliographical references

Golay, Michael
Civil War; rev ed.; Chelsea House 2011 266p il
map (America at war) lib bdg $45

Grades: 8 9 10 11 12   **973.7**
1. United States -- History -- 1861-1865, Civil War
ISBN 978-0-8160-8190-5 lib bdg; 0-8160-8190-5
lib bdg
First published 1992
An account of the Civil War, discussing political back-
ground, military strategy, and battles.
Includes glossary and bibliographical references

Gourley, Catherine
The **horrors** of Andersonville; life and death inside a Civil War prison. Twenty-First Century Books
2010 193p il lib bdg $38.60

Grades: 8 9 10 11 12   **973.7**
1. War criminals 2. Prisoners of war 3. Army officers
ISBN 978-0-7613-4212-0; 0-7613-4212-5

LC 2008-46595

"This well-researched book describes the notorious Confederate prison camp known as Andersonville, where more
than 45,000 Union soldiers lived in deplorable conditions
and some 13,000 died, beginning in 1864. . . . Illustrated

with many captioned photos and prints and enlivened with
quotes from firsthand accounts, this book provides a balanced, informative introduction to Andersonville." Booklist
Includes bibliographical references

Gregory, Josh
Gettysburg; by Josh Gregory. Children's Press
2012 64 p. chiefly col. ill. (library) $30.00; (paper-
back) $8.95

Grades: 4 5 6   **973.7**
1. Gettysburg (Pa.), Battle of, 1863 2. Gettysburg,
Battle of, Gettysburg, Pa., 1863
ISBN 0531250342; 9780531250341; 9780531265598

LC 2011010751

In this book on the 1863 Battle of Gettysburg, "[Josh]
Gregory takes his readers back to the precursor events that
set the stage for this meeting engagement pitting General
[Robert E.] Lee's Army of Northern Virginia against General
[George] Meade's oft times defeated Union Army of the Po-
tomac. In the end the efforts of Lee's seemingly indomitable
veterans were not enough to overcome the forces of fate and
tactics." (Children's Literature)
Includes bibliographical references (p. 61) and index.

Hernandez, Roger E.
The **Civil** War, 1840s-1890s. Marshall Cavendish Benchmark 2008 80p il map (Hispanic America) lib bdg $34.21

Grades: 4 5 6 7   **973.7**
1. Latinos (U.S.) 2. Hispanic Americans
ISBN 978-0-7614-2939-5 lib bdg; 0-7614-2939-5
lib bdg

LC 2007049525

Discusses Hispanic participation during the Civil War
Includes glossary and bibliographical references

Hillstrom, Kevin
American Civil War: almanac; [by] Kevin Hill-
strom and Laurie Collier Hillstrom; Lawrence W.
Baker, editor. U.X.L 2000 xlvi, 251, xlvii-lxip il
$60

Grades: 8 9 10 11 12   **973.7**
1. Almanacs 2. Reference books 3. Almanacs,
American 4. United States -- History -- Civil War,
1861-1865 -- Miscellanea
ISBN 0-7876-3823-4

LC 99-46918

Describes and interprets the era of the Civil War, its
events, and topics with viewpoints, definitions, report topics, chronologies, sidebars, and indexes
"Added features such as 'Words to Know' and 'People
to Know' sidebars in each chapter and research and activity
ideas help make the volume a good jumping-off point for
research on Civil War-era events." Booklist
Includes bibliographical references

American Civil War: biographies; [by] Kevin
Hillstrom and Laurie Collier Hillstrom; Lawrence W.
Baker, editor. U.X.L 2000 2v il (American Civil
War reference library) set $110

Grades: 8 9 10 11 12   973.7
   1. United States -- History -- 1861-1865, Civil War
ISBN 0-7876-3820-X

                       LC 99-46920
This set "chronicles the lives of 60 famous and lesser-known men and women, including abolitionists, spies, commanders, and writers." SLJ
Includes bibliographical references

American Civil War: primary sources; [by] Kevin Hillstrom and Laurie Collier Hillstrom; Lawrence W. Baker, editor. U.X.L 2000 xxxi, 176, xxxiii-xliiip il $60
Grades: 8 9 10 11 12   973.7
   1. United States -- History -- 1861-1865, Civil War -- Sources
ISBN 0-7876-3824-2

                       LC 99-46919
This volume "offers 14 full or excerpted speeches and written works. Each entry provides context, telling students what to keep in mind while reading the sources, as well as 'what happened next.' The speeches and writings come from Frederick Douglass, Abraham Lincoln, William Tecumseh Sherman, and Harriet Beecher Stowe, among others." Booklist

Experiencing the American Civil War; [by] Kevin Hillstrom and Laurie Collier Hillstrom; Lawrence W. Baker, editor. U.X.L 2002 2v il maps lib bdg set$105
Grades: 8 9 10 11 12   973.7
   1. Reference books
ISBN 0-7876-5585-6
"Although most useful as a supplementary source for classroom study, this reference tool has sufficient visual and textual appeal to arouse browers' curiosity about the materials discussed." SLJ
Includes bibliographical references

Holzer, Harold
The **president** is shot! the assassination of Abraham Lincoln. Boyds Mills Press 2004 181p il $17.95
Grades: 5 6 7 8   973.7
   1. Lawyers 2. Presidents 3. State legislators 4. Members of Congress
ISBN 1-56397-985-3
"A page-turner of a text, a fascinating array of photos and archival illustrations, and an event that changed the course of history: all these elements combine in this strong, highly readable book." Booklist
Includes bibliographical references

Howse, Jennifer
The **Civil** War. Weigl Publishers 2009 48p il map (African American history) lib bdg $29.05; pa $10.95
Grades: 6 7 8 9   973.7
   1. African American soldiers 2. African Americans --

History
ISBN 978-1-59036-876-3 lib bdg; 1-59036-876-2 lib bdg; 978-1-59036-877-0 pa; 1-59036-877-0 pa

                       LC 2008-42478
"Howse creates a broad picture of the foundations leading to war, Afican Americans' role during the war, and finally the aftermath of the war, touching upon the civil rights movement. . . . This . . . is fabulous for students interested in or researching history. Glossy pictures, quick facts, technology links, and sidebars of information interrupt the text, giving readers interesting and important information without overwhelming them." Voice Youth Advocates
Includes glossary and bibliographical references

Huey, Lois Miner
American archaeology uncovers the Underground Railroad. Marshall Cavendish Benchmark 2009 64p il map (American archaeology) lib bdg $21.95
Grades: 4 5 6 7   973.7
   1. Abolitionists 2. Underground railroad 3. Slavery -- United States 4. Excavations (Archeology) -- United States
ISBN 978-0-7614-4267-7 lib bdg; 0-7614-4267-7 lib bdg

                       LC 2009003168
This describes how archeologists have learned about the history of the Underground Railroad.
This is "both intriguing and engaging for young readers. . . . A welcomed addition to classroom and school libraries." Libr Media Connect
Includes glossary and bibliographical references

Hughes, Chris
The **Battle** of Antietam. Blackbirch Press 2001 32p il maps (Civil War) $22.45
Grades: 6 7 8 9   973.7
   1. Antietam (Md.), Battle of, 1862 2. Antietam, Battle of, Md., 1862
ISBN 1-56711-551-9

                       LC 01-1572
Describes the 1862 battle in Maryland
This offers "a readable text that makes judicious use of quotes from participants. . . . Supplemental information about notable figures, locations, and incidents is included in sidebars, while historical reproductions and occasional photographs add further accessibility." Horn Book Guide
Includes glossary and bibliographical references

Isaacs, Sally Senzell
The **Civil** War; Sally Senzell Isaacs. Kingfisher 2011 32 p. ill., map (hardcover) $19.89
Grades: 3 4 5 6   973.7
   1. United States -- History -- 1861-1865, Civil War
ISBN 0753466937; 9780753466933

                       LC 2011049248
This book is part of the "All About America" series which "covers the most important periods in the history of a burgeoning nation, from Colonists and Independence to The Civil War, and from Cowboys and the Wild West to the early inhabitants, the Native Americans." In this volume, readers learn about the American Civil War. (Publisher's note)

Jarrow, Gail

Lincoln's flying spies; Thaddeus Lowe and the Civil War Balloon Corp. Calkins Creek 2010 109p il $18.95

Grades: 7 8 9 10　　　　**973.7**

　1. Spies 2. Balloons 3. Inventors
　ISBN 978-1-59078-719-9; 1-59078-719-6

"This well-researched volume introduces American aeronaut and showman Thaddeus Lowe, who convinced President Lincoln that hydrogen-filled balloons, rising high above the countryside, could provide Union generals with useful information about the position, strength, and movements of Confederate troops and artillery. . . . The text offers a detailed account of [Lowe's] contribution to the Union war effort. Many period photos, prints, and drawings illustrate the book in black and white. . . . Jarrow provides a solid introduction to an intriguing aspect of Civil War history." Booklist

Includes bibliographical references

Johnson, Jennifer

Gettysburg; the bloodiest battle of the Civil War. Franklin Watts 2009 64p il map (24/7 goes to war) lib bdg $27; pa $7.95

Grades: 4 5 6　　　　**973.7**

　1. Gettysburg (Pa.), Battle of, 1863
　ISBN 978-0-531-25528-5 lib bdg; 0-531-25528-X lib bdg; 978-0-531-25453-0 pa; 0-531-25453-4 pa
　　　　　　　　　　　LC 2009016545

The author has done "a remarkable job of discussing and describing [the Civil War Battle of Gettysburg] in a limited number of pages. . . . The [book provides a] solid [introduction], followed by three chapters, one of which is based on the personal experiences of a named soldier, and the other two covering broader historical details and strategies of the battle. . . . Excellent maps and plenty of paintings and vintage photos enhance the [text]." SLJ

Includes bibliographical references

Jordan, Anne Devereaux

　★ The **Civil** War; by Anne Devereaux Jordan; with Virginia Schomp. Marshall Cavendish Benchmark 2007 72p il (Drama of African-American history) lib bdg $34.21

Grades: 5 6 7 8　　　　**973.7**

　1. African Americans -- History
　ISBN 978-0-7614-2179-5 lib bdg; 0-7614-2179-3 lib bdg
　　　　　　　　　　　LC 2006012472

Describes the role of African Americans during the Civil War (1861-1865)

Includes glossary and bibliographical references

Landau, Elaine

　★ **Fleeing** to freedom on the Underground Railroad; the courageous slaves, agents, and conductors. Twenty-First Century Books 2006 88p il map (People's history) lib bdg $26.60

Grades: 5 6 7 8　　　　**973.7**

　1. Abolitionists 2. Underground railroad 3. Slavery

-- United States
　ISBN 978-0-8225-3490-7 lib bdg; 0-8225-3490-8 lib bdg
　　　　　　　　　　　LC 2005020358

"Landau discusses the history of slavery in the United States, slave life, the Underground Railroad, and the leaders, both black and white, of antislavery organizations. Three chapters outline specifics of slaves' escapes. . . . An outstanding feature of this book is the use of primary sources and quotes from former slaves, contemporary newspaper accounts, and reminiscences of escaped slaves. . . . Excellent historical photographs and illustrations enhance the text." SLJ

Includes bibliographical references

Matthews, Tom L.

Grierson's raid; a daring cavalry strike through the heart of the Confederacy. [by] Tom Lalicki; original maps by David Cain. Farrar, Straus and Giroux 2004 200p il map $18

Grades: 7 8 9 10　　　　**973.7**

　1. Grierson's Cavalry Raid, 1863
　ISBN 0-374-32787-4
　　　　　　　　　　　LC 2003-49253

Describes Colonel Benjamin H. Grierson's sixteen-day raid through central Mississippi in the spring of 1863, which distracted Confederate attention while Union troops moved on Vicksburg

"The use of firsthand accounts brings the events vividly to life in a way that makes the book read more like an adventure story than a history text. . . . Accessibly written and scrupulously researched." Booklist

Includes glossary and bibliographical references

McNeese, Tim

Civil War battles. Chelsea House Publishers 2009 140p il (Civil War: a nation divided) lib bdg $35

Grades: 6 7 8 9　　　　**973.7**

　1. United States -- History -- 1861-1865, Civil War -- Campaigns
　ISBN 978-1-60413-034-8 lib bdg; 1-60413-034-2 lib bdg
　　　　　　　　　　　LC 2008-26561

This describes battles of the Civil War

Includes glossary and bibliographical references

The **Civil** War era, 1851-1865; consulting editor, Richard Jensen. Chelsea House 2010 144p il map (Discovering U.S. history) $35

Grades: 5 6 7 8　　　　**973.7**

　1. United States -- History -- 1861-1865, Civil War
　ISBN 978-1-60413-352-3; 1-60413-352-X
　　　　　　　　　　　LC 2009-3660

"The information is accurate and easy to understand. Pictures are well placed, and primary sources are included. . . . The maps are well done and there are sidebars with additional information. . . . [This would be good] to have on hand for reports as it is well laid out and easy to use." Libr Media Connect

Includes glossary and bibliographical references

Civil War leaders. Chelsea House Publishers 2009 144p il (Civil War: a nation divided) lib bdg $35

Grades: 6 7 8 9   **973.7**

1. United States -- History -- 1861-1865, Civil War -- Biography

ISBN 978-1-60413-033-1 lib bdg; 1-60413-033-4 lib bdg

LC 2009-655

This "features Abraham Lincoln, Jefferson Davis, Robert E. Lee, Ulysses S. Grant, Thomas 'Stonewall' Jackson, and Frederick Douglass. A short biography is followed by a brief description of the individual's part in the Civil War. . . . [The book includes] many black-and-white and color photographs and reproductions. . . . [This] well-organized [volume is a] first-rate [introduction] for students beginning their study of the era, or for those who want a basic review." SLJ

Includes glossary and bibliographical references

The **abolitionist** movement; ending slavery. Chelsea House 2007 142p il (Reform movements in American history) lib bdg $30

Grades: 8 9 10 11 12   **973.7**

1. Abolitionists 2. Slavery -- United States

ISBN 978-0-7910-9502-7; 0-7910-9502-9

LC 2007-14766

"Complex, detailed, and yet very readable, this title . . . discusses the struggles and differences within the antislavery movement as well as the fight for emancipation and its crucial role in the Civil War. . . . The book offers a sound exploration of the topic." Booklist

Includes bibliographical references

McPherson, James M.

Fields of fury; the American Civil War. Atheneum Bks. for Young Readers 2002 96p il map $22.95

Grades: 5 6 7 8   **973.7**

ISBN 0-689-84833-1

LC 2001-46048

Examines the events and effects of the American Civil War

"McPherson writes with authority, offering a broad overview as well as many details and anecdotes that give his account a human dimension. . . . The many fine illustrations include period photographs, paintings, prints, some excellent maps." Booklist

Includes glossary and bibliographical references

Mountjoy, Shane

Causes of the Civil War; the differences between the North and South. Chelsea House Publishers 2009 136p il (Civil War: a nation divided) lib bdg $35

Grades: 6 7 8 9   **973.7**

1. United States -- History -- 1861-1865, Civil War -- Causes

ISBN 978-1-60413-036-2 lib bdg; 1-60413-036-9 lib bdg

LC 2008-30242

Examines the sectional rivalries that surfaced in the early 19th century and intensified in the decades leading up to the war

This "is especially well written. Its eight chapters outline the economic, social, and political causes of the war. There are careful explanations of the importance of slavery to southern states, nullification and states' rights, the controversy of slavery expanding to western territories, and the impact of Lincoln's election to the presidency in 1860. [The book includes] many black-and-white and color photographs and reproductions." SLJ

Includes glossary and bibliographical references

Technology and the Civil War. Chelsea House Publishers 2009 136p il (Civil War: a nation divided) lib bdg $35

Grades: 6 7 8 9   **973.7**

1. Technology -- History

ISBN 978-1-60413-037-9 lib bdg; 1-60413-037-7 lib bdg

LC 2008-26563

This "describes advancements sparked by the Civil War: the creation of new ships and weaponry, the use of the railroad to move troops and supplies, and of the telegraph to speed dispersal of information, and improvements in medicine and photography. The book also outlines how many of the inventions and innovations of the period laid the foundation for America's economic growth in the following decades. . . . Sidebars, quotes from primary sources, color and black-and-white illustrations, and historical photographs are scattered throughout [this] clearly written, well-organized [text]." SLJ

Includes glossary and bibliographical references

Murphy, Jim

★ The **boys'** war; Confederate and Union soldiers talk about the Civil War. Clarion Bks. 1990 110p il hardcover o.p. pa $8.95

Grades: 5 6 7 8 9 10   **973.7**

1. United States -- History -- 1861-1865, Civil War

ISBN 0-89919-893-7; 0-395-66412-8 pa

LC 89-23959

This book includes diary entries, personal letters, and archival photographs to describe the experiences of boys, sixteen years old or younger, who fought in the Civil War.

"An excellent selection of more than 45 sepia-toned contemporary photographs augment the text of this informative, moving work." SLJ

Includes bibliographical references

★ The **long** road to Gettysburg. Clarion Bks. 1992 116p il maps $17; pa $7.95

Grades: 5 6 7 8 9 10   **973.7**

1. Gettysburg (Pa.), Battle of, 1863

ISBN 0-395-55965-0; 0-618-05157-0 pa

LC 90-21881

Describes the events of the Battle of Gettysburg in 1863 as seen through the eyes of two actual participants, nineteen-year-old Confederate lieutenant John Dooley and seventeen-year-old Union soldier Thomas Galway. Also discusses Lincoln's famous speech delivered at the dedication of the National Cemetery at Gettysburg

The author "uses all of his fine skills as an information writer—clarity of detail, conciseness, understanding of his age group, and ability to find the drama appealing to readers—to frame a well-crafted account of a single battle in the war." Horn Book

Includes bibliographical references

★ A **savage** thunder; Antietam and the bloody road to freedom. Margaret K. McElderry Books 2009 103p il map $17.99

Grades: 5 6 7 8 9   973.7

1. Generals 2. Governors 3. Antietam (Md.), Battle of, 1862 4. College presidents 5. Presidential candidates
ISBN 978-0-689-87633-2; 0-689-87633-5

LC 2008-32738

"Murphy provides readers with a lucid and compelling narrative, drawn mainly from firsthand accounts. . . . Replete with excellent-quality archival photos, reproductions, and maps, this is an outstanding account of a battle." SLJ

Includes bibliographical references

Nardo, Don

Bull Run to Gettysburg; early battles of the Civil War. Compass Point Books 2011 64p il map (The Civil War) lib bdg $33.32; pa $6.95

Grades: 5 6 7 8   973.7

1. United States -- History -- 1861-1865, Civil War -- Campaigns
ISBN 978-0-7565-4368-6 lib bdg; 0-7565-4368-1 lib bdg; 978-0-7565-4411-9 pa; 0-7565-4411-4 pa

LC 2010001017

Reviews the early battles of the Civil War from the attack on Fort Sumter and the battle of the ironclads to Bull Run and Gettysburg.

The layout is "clean and attractive, with a large font and reproductions of period illustrations and photos. . . . This . . . will help students understand the era's most important issues and events. A quality choice for reports." SLJ

Includes glossary and bibliographical references

A **nation** divided; the long road to the Civil War. Compass Point Books 2010 64p il map (The Civil War) lib bdg $33.32

Grades: 5 6 7 8   973.7

1. United States -- History -- 1861-1865, Civil War -- Causes
ISBN 978-0-7565-4367-9 lib bdg; 0-7565-4367-3 lib bdg

LC 2010001016

Recounts events leading up to the Civil War and provides insight into the economic, cultural, and educational differences of the Northerners and Southerners.

The layout is "clean and attractive, with a large font and reproductions of period illustrations and photos. . . . This . . . will help students understand the era's most important issues and events. A quality choice for reports." SLJ

Includes glossary and bibliographical references

Netzley, Patricia D.

Civil War. Greenhaven Press 2004 336p il (Greenhaven encyclopedia of) lib bdg $74.95

Grades: 8 9 10 11 12   973.7

1. Reference books
ISBN 0-7377-0438-1

LC 2003-11808

An alphabetical presentation of definitions and descriptions of terms, people, and events of the Civil War

"Basic, accurate information about many aspects of the war. . . . The well-written, objective entries are cross-referenced. . . . Netzley's solid volume will be helpful to students needing introductory research material." SLJ

Includes bibliographical references

Osborne, Linda Barrett

★ **Traveling** the freedom road; from slavery and the Civil War through Reconstruction. Abrams Books for Young Readers 2009 128p il map $24.95

Grades: 6 7 8 9 10   973.7

1. Reconstruction (1865-1876) 2. Slavery -- United States 3. African Americans -- History
ISBN 978-0-8109-8338-0; 0-8109-8338-9

LC 2008-22298

"This fascinating, well-designed volume offers an essential introduction to the experiences of African Americans between 1800 and 1877. . . . Osborne moves from . . . personal stories to broader historical milestones, and in highly accessible language, she provides basic background even as she challenges readers with philosophical questions. . . . This fluid exchange between political events and intimate, human stories creates a highly absorbing whole." Booklist

Porterfield, Jason

The **Lincoln**-Douglas senatorial debates of 1858; a primary source investigation. [by] Jason Porterfield. 1st ed; Rosen Central Primary Sources 2005 64p il map (Great historic debates and speeches) lib bdg $29.25

Grades: 5 6 7 8   973.7

1. Lawyers 2. Presidents 3. Senators 4. Political leaders 5. State legislators 6. Members of Congress 7. Presidential candidates
ISBN 1-4042-0153-X

LC 2003-25408

Discusses the debates between Lincoln and Douglas and how they influenced political campaigns throughout history.

This "readable [text provides a] balanced [overview]. Primary-source materials include archival maps, photos, reproductions, letters, and speeches that are examined in context." SLJ

Includes bibliographical references

Raatma, Lucia

The **Underground** Railroad; by Lucia Raatma. Children's Press 2011 64 p. col. ill. (library) $30.00; (paperback) $8.95

Grades: 4 5 6   973.7

1. Fugitive slaves 2. Underground Railroad 3. Fugitive slaves -- United States -- History -- 19th century 4. Antislavery movements -- United States -- History -- 19th century
ISBN 0531250431; 9780531250433; 9780531265680

LC 2011009493

This book by Lucia Raatma is part of the Cornerstones of Freedom series and looks at the Underground Railroad. The entry "explains how the system worked, the journey, and important people who guided slaves such as Harriet Tubman and Levi and Catherine White Coffin of Indiana, who helped about 2,000 slaves reach freedom."

Includes bibliographical references

Rees, Bob

The **Civil** War; by Bob Rees. Heinemann Library 2012 80 p. ill. (some col.), col. maps (library) $36.50; (paperback) $10.99

Grades: 6 7 8 9   **973.7**

   1. United States -- History -- 1861-1865, Civil War
   ISBN 1432959964; 9781432959968; 9781432960056
                       LC 2011018258

This book by Bob Rees is part of the Living Through . . . series and looks at the U.S. Civil War. The "set summarizes events in major conflicts using brief first-person accounts, sidebars, short biographies, color and archival photos, maps, and other graphics." The authors include "views from multiple perspectives." (School Library Journal)

Includes bibliographical references (p. 76) and index.

Reis, Ronald A.

African Americans and the Civil War. Chelsea House Publishers 2009 134p il (The Civil War: a nation divided) lib bdg $35

Grades: 6 7 8 9   **973.7**

   1. African American soldiers 2. Slavery -- United States
   ISBN 978-1-60413-038-6 lib bdg; 1-60413-038-5
   lib bdg

                       LC 2008-25665

This describes the roles African Americans played in the Civil War

Includes glossary and bibliographical references

Rottman, Gordon L.

The **most** daring raid of the Civil War; the great locomotive chase. Rosen Pub. 2011 64p il map (The most daring raids in history) lib bdg $29.25

Grades: 7 8 9 10   **973.7**

   1. Chattanooga, Battle of, 1863
   ISBN 978-1-4488-1870-9; 1-4488-1870-2
                       LC 2010030195

In a daring attempt to cut off the supply lines of Confederate forces, Union soldiers planned to steal a train and disable the line as they traveled to Chattanooga, TN. One man's daring pursuit led to their ultimate failure. This book tells the story of how the raid was planned, and how it ultimately fell apart.

This book is "packed with facts, covering the details of the action, the people involved, and the tools used, in engaging prose. The authors cite their sources thoroughly. . . . Diagrams, . . . and maps make the action easy to follow and provide visual context for the raids. . . . This . . . is sure to find a large readership." SLJ

Includes glossary and bibliographical references

Seidman, Rachel Filene

The **Civil** war: a history in documents. Oxford University Press 2001 206p il map (Pages from history) lib bdg $39.95

Grades: 8 9 10 11 12   **973.7**

   1. United States -- History -- 1861-1865, Civil War
   -- Sources
   ISBN 978-0-19-511558-1; 0-19-511558-9
                       LC 00-37523

"Seidman's documents bookend the Civil War with the territorial expansion that preceded the conflict and with the Reconstruction that followed it. In this structure the documents, under the guidance of Seidman's linking narrative, all make a powerful impression of immediacy about ordinary people's experience of, and condemnation or defense of, slavery." Booklist

Includes bibliographical references

Silvey, Anita

★ **I'll** pass for your comrade; women soldiers in the Civil War. Clarion Books 2008 115p il map $17

Grades: 6 7 8 9   **973.7**

   1. Women soldiers 2. Women soldiers -- United States
   ISBN 978-0-618-57491-9; 0-618-57491-3
                       LC 2008018053

This "spotlights Union and Confederate women who fought on the battlefields. . . . Period photos, prints, drawings, and documents are among the many illustrations. . . . Well researched and clearly written, this attractive book illuminates an aspect of the Civil War that is often overlooked." Booklist

Includes bibliographical references

Slavicek, Louise Chipley

Women and the Civil War. Chelsea House Publishers 2009 128p il (The Civil War: a nation divided) lib bdg $35

Grades: 6 7 8 9   **973.7**

   1. Women -- United States -- History
   ISBN 978-1-60413-040-9 lib bdg; 1-60413-040-7
   lib bdg

                       LC 2008-26562

"After a historical overview, six chapters . . . present information on female roles during the [Civil] war. . . . Women worked as nurses and caregivers and organized aid and relief societies. . . . Hundreds disguised themselves as men to fight and others worked as spies and saboteurs. They were forced to oversee and run family farms and plantations or to find employment in factories or government offices. A chapter on African-American women reviews how the war impacted their lives and mentions significant figures such as Harriet Tubman. Sidebars, quotes from primary sources, color and black-and-white illustrations, and historical photographs are scattered throughout [this] clearly written, well-organized [text]." SLJ

Includes glossary and bibliographical references

Stein, R. Conrad

Escaping slavery on the Underground Railroad; [by] R. Conrad Stein. Enslow Publishers 2008 128p il (From many cultures, one history) lib bdg $31.93

Grades: 6 7 8 9   973.7
1. Abolitionists 2. Underground railroad 3. Slavery -- United States
ISBN 978-0-7660-2799-2 lib bdg; 0-7660-2799-6 lib bdg

LC 2007015124

This is an account of American slavery, the Abolitionist movement, and escapes from slavery on the The Underground Railroad.

This "will provide clear, easy-to-understand facts with critical analysis and will be useful for reports." Libr Media Connect

Includes glossary and bibliographical references

Sullivan, George
The **Civil** War at sea. 21st Cent. Bks. (Brookfield) 2001 80p il lib bdg $27.90
Grades: 8 9 10 11 12   973.7
1. United States -- History -- 1861-1865, Civil War -- Naval operations
ISBN 0-7613-1553-5

LC 00-41805

"The illustrations and reproductions included here and the lively text will appeal to every Civil War buff, and will be an excellent source of information for reports." SLJ

Includes bibliographical references

Swanson, James L.
★ **Bloody** times; the funeral of Abraham Lincoln and the manhunt for Jefferson Davis. Collins 2011 196p il $16.99
Grades: 6 7 8 9   973.7
1. Lawyers 2. Statesmen 3. Presidents 4. Senators 5. Political leaders 6. State legislators 7. Secretaries of war 8. Members of Congress
ISBN 978-0-06-156089-7; 0-06-156089-8

LC 2010045611

An adaptation for young people of Bloody Crimes, published 2010 by William Morrow for adults

This tells "the story of Lincoln's assassination, detailing the funeral and the return of the body for burial in Springfield, IL. Juxtaposed with this compelling drama is that of Jefferson Davis, president of the Confederate States of America, as he learned of Lee's surrender and traveled across the South trying to keep the Confederacy alive while being pursued by Federal forces bent on his arrest. . . . Lincoln's body was placed aboard a train that retraced the route taken by Lincoln as he traveled to the capital as president-elect. Readers will be fascinated by the details needed to plan this trip and the people involved. . . . Just as riveting is Davis's fruitless effort to avoid arrest. . . . A brilliant book that is sure to be hit with history aficionados." SLJ

Includes glossary and bibliographical references

Trudeau, Noah Andre
Like men of war; black troops in the Civil War, 1862-1865. Little, Brown 1998 xxii, 548p il maps hardcover o.p. pa $18
Grades: 7 8 9 10   973.7
1. African American soldiers
ISBN 0-316-85325-9; 0-316-85344-5 pa

LC 97-15380

A "study of the battlefield experiences of black Union regiments. Some 60 maps help the reader make sense of famous engagements (Fort Wagner and the Crater) and notorious incidents (Fort Pillow) in which black soldiers fought, as well as scores of lesser-known clashes. Rich archival research is integrated into a lively narrative that places the raising and deployment of black regiments in broader contexts. This book will become a basic source of information on the subject." Libr J

Includes bibliographical references

Uschan, Michael V., 1948-
The **cavalry** during the Civil War. Lucent Bks. 2003 112p il maps (Working life) $27.45
Grades: 6 7 8 9   973.7
1. Soldiers -- United States
ISBN 1-59018-175-1

LC 2002-11840

This examines the life of cavalry soldiers during the civil war

This is "well written and the authors draw on and quote from many primary sources." Libr Media Connect

Includes bibliographical references

Wagner, Heather Lehr
Spies in the Civil War. Chelsea House Publishers 2009 112p il (The Civil War: a nation divided) lib bdg $35
Grades: 6 7 8 9   973.7
1. Spies
ISBN 978-1-60413-039-3 lib bdg; 1-60413-039-3 lib bdg

LC 2008-26568

This describes the work of Civil War spies Allan Pinkerton, Elizabeth Van Lew, Belle Boyd, and Rose O'Neal Greenhow and others

Includes glossary and bibliographical references

Walker, Sally M.
Secrets of a Civil War submarine; solving the mysteries of the H.L. Hunley. Carolrhoda Books 2005 112p il lib bdg $17.95
Grades: 7 8 9 10   973.7
1. Shipwrecks 2. Submarines 3. Underwater exploration
ISBN 1-57505-830-8

LC 2004-19646

This discusses "the Confederate submarine H. L. Hunley. . . . Walker begins with the history of the Hunley's design and construction as well as its place in Civil War and naval history. She really hits her stride, though, in explaining the complex techniques and loving care used in raising the craft, recovering its contents, and even reconstructing models of the crewmembers' bodies. . . . Thoroughly researched, nicely designed, and well illustrated with clear, color photos." Booklist

Includes glossary and bibliographical references

Warren, Andrea

★ **Under** siege! three children at the Civil War battle for Vicksburg. Melanie Kroupa Books 2009 166p il map $21.95

Grades: 7 8 9 10   **973.7**
1. Children -- United States -- History
ISBN 978-0-374-31255-8; 0-374-31255-9

LC 2008-1136

"Warren creates a compelling account of the 1863 siege at Vicksburg that follows three young people from December 1862 through the aftermath of the surrender on July 4, 1863. . . . The author uses primary sources throughout, including scores of quotes, many attributed to the children themselves, period photographs, maps, and paintings. . . . The back matter is extensive, including an annotated list of recommended Civil War books, a longer bibliography of sources, and extensive endnotes and illustration credits." Voice Youth Advocates

Includes bibliographical references and index

Watkins, Samuel R.

The **diary** of Sam Watkins, a confederate soldier; edited by Ruth Ashby; illustrations by Laszlo Kubinyi. Benchmark Bks. 2004 95p il (In my own words) lib bdg $18.95

Grades: 5 6 7 8   **973.7**
1. Soldiers 2. Soldiers -- Tennessee -- Biography
ISBN 0-7614-1646-3

LC 2003-1478

Excerpts from the diary of a Confederate soldier from Tennessee, describing the battles he fought in during the Civil War

This offers "an engaging history lesson." Horn Book Guide

Includes bibliographical references

Weapons, tactics, and strategy; edited by Tim Cooke. Brown Bear Books 2011 112p il (Curriculum connections: Civil War) lib bdg $39.95

Grades: 7 8 9 10   **973.7**
1. Reference books 2. Military art and science
ISBN 978-1-936333-46-2; 1-936333-46-5

LC 2011005412

In an alphabetical almanac format, describes the weapons used, tactics invented, and strategies employed by both sides during the U.S. Civil War.

"Well researched and clearly written, the chapters offer informative discussions supported by sidebars, page references to related content in other chapters, and definitions of terms in the margins. . . . The many small illustrations include period photos as well as prints, drawings, and paintings. A useful addition to library collections." Booklist

Weber, Jennifer L.

Summer's bloodiest days; the Battle of Gettysburg as told from all sides. foreword by James M. McPherson. National Geographic 2010 61p il map $17.95; lib bdg $27.90

Grades: 5 6 7 8   **973.7**
1. Gettysburg (Pa.), Battle of, 1863
ISBN 978-1-4263-0706-5; 1-4263-0706-3; 978-1-4263-0707-2 lib bdg; 1-4263-0707-1 lib bdg

"This colorful book tells of the Battle of Gettysburg, a dramatic event that becomes even more compelling because the text is laced with pertinent quotes from those who were there. Weber's vivid, pithy writing packs a great deal of information and many anecdotes into a relatively short account. . . . Many battle maps, short, informative sidebars, and the use of modern realistic paintings and photos of artifacts as well as period photographs . . . illustrate the book." Booklist

Includes bibliographical references

Williams, Carla

The **Underground** Railroad. Child's World 2009 32p il (Journey to freedom) lib bdg $28.50

Grades: 4 5 6   **973.7**
1. Underground railroad 2. Slavery -- United States
ISBN 978-1-60253-139-0 lib bdg; 1-60253-139-0 lib bdg

LC 2008031946

"Underground Railroad describes how this secret system worked and introduces key figures. Williams discusses relevant laws and amendments as well as the advent and conclusion of the Civil War. The facts, presented through stories, historical news accounts, and biographical sketches of Harriet Tubman and Levi Weeks, capture the desperation of the enslaved as well as the abolitionists' commitment to them. The [book is] concise and direct, yet the writing remains sophisticated. Vibrant personal stories accompanied by striking photographs of historical figures and artifacts provide a sense of the subjects' hopes and dreams." SLJ

Includes glossary and bibliographical references

Woog, Adam

The **Emancipation** Proclamation; ending slavery in America. Chelsea House Publishers 2009 117p il (Milestones in American history) lib bdg $35

Grades: 6 7 8 9   **973.7**
1. Lawyers 2. Presidents 3. State legislators 4. Members of Congress 5. Slavery -- United States
ISBN 978-1-60413-307-3 lib bdg; 1-60413-307-4 lib bdg

LC 2008030742

This explores Lincoln's proclamation which ended slavery during the Civil War

This offers "short, clearly written chapters. . . . [It is] amply illustrated with black-and-white and color photographs and reproductions and supported with biographical sketches and excerpts from primary documents." Horn Book Guide

Includes bibliographical references

973.709 Biography

Freedman, Russell

★ **Abraham** Lincoln and Frederick Douglass; the story behind an American friendship. by Russell

Freedman. Houghton Mifflin Harcourt 2012 119 p. $18.99

Grades: 4 5 6 7 8   **973.709**
1. Friendship 2. Abolitionists -- United States 3. United States -- History -- 1861-1865, Civil War -- Biography 4. Friendship -- United States 5. Presidents -- United States -- Biography 6. African American abolitionists -- Biography
ISBN 9780547385624

                      LC 2011025953

This book tells the story of Abraham Lincoln, "the 16th president, . . . [along] with his friend and ally, abolitionist Frederick Douglass. The story opens with Douglass anxiously waiting to meet Lincoln for the first time to air grievances about the treatment of African-American soldiers during the Civil War. . . . Subsequent chapters detail the leaders' often parallel biographies. Both were self-made and shared a passion for reading, rising from poverty to prominence." (Publishers Weekly)

Includes bibliographical references (p. [108]-109) and index

Sheinkin, Steve
  Lincoln's Grave Robbers. Scholastic 2013 224 p. $16.99

Grades: 5 6 7 8   **973.709**
1. Grave robbing 2. Counterfeits and counterfeiting
ISBN 0545405726; 9780545405720

This book is an "account of the attempted heist of Abraham Lincoln's body in 1876." Steve Sheinkin first "delv[es] into the history of counterfeiting. . . . James Kennally, leader of one of the largest counterfeiting rings in the Midwest, masterminded the plot to steal the late president's body from the Lincoln Monument," intending "to ransom the purloined corpse" and extort "the government for a tidy sum of money and the freedom of his jailed, top-notch engraver." (Publishers Weekly)

973.8   Reconstruction period, 1865-1901

Cline-Ransome, Lesa
  Words set me free; the story of young Frederick Douglass. Lesa Cline-Ransome; illustrated by James E. Ransome. Simon & Schuster Books for Young Readers 2012 32 p. $17.99

Grades: 6 7 8   **973.8**
1. Abolitionists 2. Slaves -- Emancipation 3. African Americans -- Biography 4. Slaves -- United States -- Biography 5. Abolitionists -- United States -- Biography 6. African American abolitionists -- Biography 7. Antislavery movements -- United States -- History -- 19th century
ISBN 9781416959038

                      LC 2011013323

In this book, the historical character Frederick Douglass "relates his early years, from first vague memories of his mother . . . through his childhood, with his service leased to the Auld family of Baltimore; to his first attempt to make an escape from Talbot County, Maryland. The narration is . . . focused on the way learning to read both inspired and enabled young Frederick to plan for a life of freedom in the North . . . This chapter in Douglass' story concludes with his forgery of a pass, written 'in a firm and steady hand,' which would allow him to 'walk right out of Talbot County and into freedom up north.'" (Bulletin of the Center for Children's Books)

Includes bibliographical references and index

Collier, Christopher
  ★ The **United** States enters the world stage: from the Alaska Purchase through World War I, 1867-1919; [by] Christopher Collier, James Lincoln Collier. Benchmark Bks. (Tarrytown) 2001 94p il map (Drama of American history) lib bdg $31.36

Grades: 6 7 8 9   **973.8**
1. World War, 1914-1918 2. Spanish-American War, 1898
ISBN 0-7614-1053-8

                      LC 00-29483

This discusses topics in United States history and politics including Westward expansion, imperialism, the Spanish-American War, the Panama Canal, and World War I

Includes bibliographical references

Custer's last stand; Thomas Streissguth, book editor. Greenhaven Press 2003 142p il maps (At issue in history) lib bdg $21.96; pa $14.96

Grades: 7 8 9 10   **973.8**
1. Generals 2. Little Bighorn, Battle of the, 1876 3. Army officers 4. Little Bighorn, Battle of the, Mont., 1876
ISBN 0-7377-1358-5 lib bdg; 0-7377-1359-3 pa

                      LC 2002-27875

"Using primary and secondary sources, this volume examines the controversial history of the Battle at the Little Bighorn in June, 1876. . . . Each of the 11 entries is preceded by a summary of the author's main points and conclusions. This excellent volume helps students understand the 'what' and 'why' of history." SLJ

Includes bibliographical references

Fitzgerald, Stephanie
  Reconstruction; rebuilding America after the Civil War. Compass Point Books 2011 64p il map (The Civil War) lib bdg $33.32; pa $6.95

Grades: 5 6 7 8   **973.8**
1. Reconstruction (1865-1876)
ISBN 978-0-7565-4370-9 lib bdg; 0-7565-4370-3 lib bdg; 978-0-7565-4414-0 pa; 0-7565-4414-9 pa

                      LC 2010001019

Recounts the history of the Reconstruction, as the United States government and people worked to recover from the effects of the Civil War.

The layout is "clean and attractive, with a large font and reproductions of period illustrations and photos. . . . This . . . will help students understand the era's most important issues and events. A quality choice for reports." SLJ

Includes glossary and bibliographical references

The **Gilded** Age: a history in documents; [compiled by] Janette Thomas Greenwood. Oxford Univ.

Press 2000 191p il map (Pages from history) $39.95; pa $24.95

Grades: 7 8 9 10   **973.8**

ISBN 978-0-19-510523-0; 0-19-510523-0; 978-0-19-516638-5 pa; 0-19-516638-8 pa

LC 99-98194

Uses a wide variety of documents to show how Americans dealt with an age of extremes from 1887 to 1900, including rapid industrialization, unemployment, unprecedented wealth, and immigration

Hillstrom, Kevin

American Indian removal and the trail to Wounded Knee; [by] Kevin Hillstrom and Laurie Collier Hillstrom. Omnigraphics 2010 250p il (Defining moments) lib bdg $55

Grades: 8 9 10 11 12   **973.8**

1. Wounded Knee Creek, Battle of, 1890 2. Native Americans -- Relocation 3. Native Americans -- Great Plains

ISBN 978-0-7808-1129-4; 0-7808-1129-1

LC 2010-4676

"This well-written volume effectively explores a topic of intense historical debate. Fascinating sidebars add significantly to the text." SLJ

Includes glossary and bibliographical references

McNeese, Tim

The **Gilded** Age and Progressivism, 1891-1913; Tim McNeese; consulting editor, Richard Jensen. Chelsea House 2010 136 p. ill. (some col.) (Discovering U.S. history) (library) $35.00

Grades: 5 6 7 8   **973.8**

1. Progressivism (United States politics) 2. -- History -- 19th century 3. Progressivism (United States politics) -- History -- 19th century 4. Progressivism (United States politics) -- History -- 20th century

ISBN 1604133554; 9781604133554

LC 2009015012

McNeese "discusses the people, politics, economic conditions, and foreign affairs of [the U.S. from 1891 to 1913], objectively explaining how the attitudes, perceptions, and expectations of the American people and their leaders shaped the development of the country. . . . Color period art and photos, maps, and cutaway drawings supplement the [text]." SLJ

Includes bibliographical references and index.

Reconstruction; life after the Civil War. Chelsea House Publishers 2009 140p il (The Civil War: a nation divided) lib bdg $35

Grades: 6 7 8 9   **973.8**

1. Reconstruction (1865-1876)

ISBN 978-1-60413-035-5 lib bdg; 1-60413-035-0 lib bdg

LC 2008-26564

"Reconstruction examines one of the most controversial eras in U.S. history. During Reconstruction, the nation sought to reestablish itself in the aftermath of the Civil War, to overcome regional politics, and to redefine the political,

social, and economic realities of the nation's four million black citizens." Publisher's note

Includes glossary and bibliographical references

Ruggiero, Adriane

★ **American** voices from Reconstruction. Marshall Cavendish Benchmark 2006 103p il (American voices from--) lib bdg $37.07

Grades: 6 7 8 9 10 11 12   **973.8**

1. Reconstruction (1865-1876)

ISBN 978-0-7614-2168-9 lib bdg; 0-7614-2168-8 lib bdg

LC 2005-24949

This "does an excellent job of bringing history close. . . . The spacious design . . . is very approachable, and the combination of voices and commentary will readers think critically." Booklist

Includes glossary and bibliographical references

Sanders, Nancy I.

Frederick Douglass for kids; his life and times with 21 activities. Nancy I. Sanders. Chicago Review Press 2012 ix, 145 p.p ill. (paperback) $16.95; (ebook) $11.99; (prebind) $25.95

Grades: 5 6 7   **973.8**

1. Biography 2. Slavery -- History 3. African Americans -- Biography 4. Abolitionists -- United States -- Biography 5. African American abolitionists -- Biography 6. Antislavery movements -- United States -- Study and teaching -- Activity programs 7. Antislavery movements -- United States -- History -- 19th century

ISBN 1569767173; 9781569767177; 9781613743560; 9781451774788

LC 2011050092

Author Nancy I. Sanders presents information on Frederick Douglass. "Born on a plantation, he later escaped slavery and helped others to freedom via the Underground Railroad. In time he became a bestselling author, an outspoken newspaper editor, a brilliant orator, a tireless abolitionist, and a brave civil rights leader. He was famous on both sides of the Atlantic in the years leading up to the Civil War, and when war broke out, Abraham Lincoln invited him to the White House for counsel and advice." (Publisher's note)

Includes bibliographical references (p. 136-137) and index.

Stroud, Bettye

★ The **Reconstruction** era; by Bettye M. Stroud with Virginia Schomp. Marshall Cavendish Benchmark 2007 70p il (Drama of African-American history) lib bdg $34.21

Grades: 5 6 7 8   **973.8**

1. Reconstruction (1865-1876) 2. African Americans -- History

ISBN 978-0-7614-2181-8 lib bdg; 0-7614-2181-5 lib bdg

LC 2006012149

"Traces the history of Reconstruction, from the end of the Civil War in 1865 to 1877, when federal troops were removed from the South." Publisher's note

Includes glossary and bibliographical references

Telgen, Diane

The **Gilded** Age; Diane Telgen. Omnigraphics 2012 xvi, 252 p.p ill. (hardcover: alk. paper) $16.99

Grades: 7 8 9 10 11 12   **973.8**

1. United States -- History -- 1865-1898 2. United States -- History -- 1865-1921 -- Sources 3. United States -- History -- 1865-1921 4. United States -- Politics and government -- 1865-1933 -- Sources

ISBN 0780812387; 9780780812383

LC 2011048642

This book by Diane Telgen "surveys America's rapid economic, social, demographic, and political changes from the end of the Civil War to the dawn of the twentieth century. . . . The volume also explains how various hallmarks of this era -- including rapid industrialization and urbanization, the economic divide between rich and poor, political corruption and reform, and social and religious activism -- laid the groundwork for the United States we live in today." (Publisher's note)

Includes bibliographical references (p. 237-242) and index

Walker, Paul Robert

★ **Remember** Little Bighorn; Indians, soldiers, and scouts tell their stories. [by] Paul Robert Walker; [foreword by John A. Doerner] National Geographic Society 2006 61p il map $17.95; lib bdg $27.90

Grades: 5 6 7 8   **973.8**

1. Little Bighorn, Battle of the, 1876

ISBN 0-7922-5521-6; 0-7922-5522-4 lib bdg

LC 2005030929

This "volume gives an almost blow-by-blow account of the famous battle that came to be known as Custer's Last Stand. Walker concentrates on the battle itself, fought on the Great Plains in 1876, and the book includes diagrams of each side's tactics. . . . Walker's exhaustive research . . . [brings] together the conflicting viewpoints of the whites and the Lakota Sioux, Cheyenne, and Arapaho fighters, documenting everything in source notes. The handsome book design, with thick paper, clear type, maps, stirring photos, and archival images, will attract readers to the battle story and then start them thinking about lasting historical issues." Booklist

Includes bibliographical references

Worth, Richard

African Americans during Reconstruction; [by] Richard Worth. Chelsea House 2006 112p il map (Slavery in the Americas) $35

Grades: 6 7 8 9   **973.8**

1. Reconstruction (1865-1876) 2. African Americans -- Civil rights

ISBN 0-81606-139-4

LC 2005015720

Tells the history of African Americans from the end of the Civil War through the nation's reconstruction.

Includes bibliographical references

"There's plenty to absorb and much to capture the imagination. . . . Greenwood presents the history as a seamless tapestry sewn by the people who lived it." Booklist

Includes bibliographical references

973.9 United States -- History -- 1898-1919

Brill, Marlene Targ

America in the 1900s. Twenty-First Century Books 2010 144p il (The decades of twentieth-century America) lib bdg $38.60

Grades: 7 8 9 10   **973.9**

ISBN 978-0-8225-3436-5 lib bdg; 0-8225-3436-3 lib bdg

LC 2007-40983

This is an overview of the 1900's

"The text is clear but not condescending, with unfamiliar terms defined in parentheses. Frequent, mostly black-and-white photographs punctuate pages with clear print and lots of white space. Time lines recap major events, while 'To Learn More' suggests not only books but also Web sites and films. . . . A worthwhile addition." Voice Youth Advocates

Includes bibliographical references

Sandler, Martin W.

★ The **Dust** Bowl through the lens; how photography revealed and helped remedy a national disaster. Walker & Co. 2008 96p il map $15.99; lib bdg $20.89

Grades: 5 6 7 8   **973.9**

1. Dust storms 2. Documentary photography 3. Dust Bowl Era, 1931-1939

ISBN 978-0-8027-9547-2; 0-8027-9547-1; 978-0-8027-9548-9 lib bdg; 0-8027-9548-X lib bdg

LC 2008-55979

"This excellent photo-essay traces the history of the Dust Bowl from its causes to its resolution. In tandem, Sandler treats the role of the budding field of photojournalism. Forty-four spreads feature a page of clear, direct text with a large, well-reproduced image, many of which are set on color pages. . . . Seldom has the connection between the arts and the general quality of life been made so clear. The text deals equally with those who fled the decimated Bread Basket for California and those who waited out the devastation and dust. Throughout, the use of primary sources is superb, with quotations from affected citizens, the photojournalists themselves, political and entertainment figures, and writers, giving a multifaceted picture of a seminal time in United States history." SLJ

973.91 1901-1953

Allen, Michael Geoffrey

Calvin Coolidge. Enslow 2002 112p il (United States presidents) $20.95

Grades: 7 8 9 10   **973.91**

1. Governors 2. Presidents 3. Vice-presidents 4. Presidents -- United States 5. Presidents -- United States -- Biography

ISBN 0-7660-1703-6

LC 2001-4206

The author highlights President Coolidge's childhood, family influences, education, career, and journey to the White House. {The author does} an impressive job of emphasizing the strength of character of {the} president while still providing a balanced history of {his} influence on U.S. history. Booklist

Includes bibliographical references

Bingham, Jane

The **Great** Depression; the Jazz Age, Prohibition, and the Great Depression, 1921-1937. Chelsea House 2011 64p il (A cultural history of women in America) $35

Grades: 5 6 7 8   973.91

1. Great Depression, 1929-1939 2. Women -- United States 3. Women -- United States -- History

ISBN 978-1-60413-933-4; 1-60413-933-1

LC 2010044889

An "eye-catching [layout] with good use of color, photographs, and informative sidebars, many of which use primary-source quotations, are the highlights of [this] appealing [volume]. . . . After a succinct overview of contemporary events, the chapters describe women's lives at home, at work, in education, in politics, in the arts, and their role in the general culture. . . . [This book] surveys an era after women won the right to vote and when the nation's economic crash placed new hardships on families." SLJ

Includes glossary and bibliographical references

Brill, Marlene Targ

America in the 1910s; by Marlee Richards. Twenty-First Century Books 2010 144p il (The decades of twentieth-century America) lib bdg $38.60

Grades: 7 8 9 10   973.91

1. United States -- History -- 1898-1919

ISBN 978-0-8225-3437-2 lib bdg; 0-8225-3437-1 lib bdg

LC 2007-42905

Presents the social, political, economical, and technological changes in the United States during the nineteen tens, including World War I, the Prohibition era, and the birth of the skyscraper.

The text is "enlivened with quotes and excerpts from primary sources, period photos, and two sets of sidebars. 'Profiles' provides biographical sketches of important people and 'Turning Points' explains the significance of important events. . . . A solid choice for readers and researchers." SLJ

Includes bibliographical references and filmography

Burg, David F.

The **Great** Depression; updated ed; Facts on File 2005 xx, 444p il (Eyewitness history) $75

Grades: 8 9 10 11 12   973.91

1. Great Depression, 1929-1939 2. Depressions -- 1929

ISBN 0-8160-5709-5; 978-0-8160-5709-2

LC 2004-29126

First published 1996

"The book is divided into seven chapters, each covering a specific timeframe beginning with causative events preceding the crisis (1919-1928) and ending with the emerging Second World War (1939-1941.) Each chapter opens with a narrative summary and analysis of the period, followed by a chronological listing of significant events and then by primary-source contemporary quotations from pri-

vate citizens, politicians, radio broadcasts, and more." Voice Youth Advocates

Includes bibliographical references

Collier, Christopher

★ **Progressivism,** the Great Depression, and the New Deal, 1901 to 1941; by Christopher Collier, James Lincoln Collier. Benchmark Bks. (Tarrytown) 2001 95p il map (Drama of American history) lib bdg $31.36

Grades: 6 7 8 9   973.91

1. New Deal, 1933-1939 2. Great Depression, 1929-1939 3. Progressivism (United States politics) 4. Depressions -- 1929 5. Depressions -- 1929 -- United States 6. Progressivism (United States politics) -- History -- 20th century

ISBN 0-7614-1054-6

LC 00-29481

This "follows events and movements during the first four decades of the twentieth century, including the growing involvement of government in reforming business practices, the impact of the Great Depression, and the social policies of Franklin D. Roosevelt's New Deal. . . . Illustrations, many in color, include period photographs and engravings as well as maps and charts. . . . Highly readable and informative." Booklist

Includes bibliographical references

Corrigan, Jim

The **1900s** decade in photos; a decade of discovery. Enslow Publishers 2010 64p il (Amazing decades in photos) lib bdg $27.93

Grades: 4 5 6 7   973.91

1. United States -- History -- 1898-1919

ISBN 978-0-7660-3129-6 lib bdg; 0-7660-3129-2 lib bdg

LC 2008042900

This highlights the important world, national, and cultural developments of the 1900s.

This is illustrated with "large, well-chosen black-and-white and color photos. . . . Captions provide specific information about the photos and supplement, rather than repeat, information in the [narrative]. Attractive and readable, this . . . will be popular with browsers and beginning researchers." SLJ

Includes glossary and bibliographical references

The **1910s** decade in photos; a decade that shook the world. Enslow Publishers 2010 64p il (Amazing decades in photos) lib bdg $27.93

Grades: 4 5 6 7   973.91

1. United States -- History -- 20th century

ISBN 978-0-7660-3130-2 lib bdg; 0-7660-3130-6 lib bdg

LC 2008042902

This highlights the important world, national, and cultural developments of the decade 1910-1919, including the sinking of the Titanic, the establishment of the Boy Scouts and Girl Scouts, immigration, income tax, Hollywood feature films, World War I, the Lusitania sinking, and more.

Includes glossary and bibliographical references

The **1920s** decade in photos; the Roaring Twenties. Enslow Publishers 2010 64p il (Amazing decades in photos) lib bdg $27.93

Grades: 4 5 6 7   **973.91**

1. United States -- History -- 20th century

ISBN 978-0-7660-3131-9 lib bdg; 0-7660-3131-4 lib bdg

LC 2008042903

This highlights the important world, national, and cultural developments of the decade 1920-1929, including Prohibition, jazz music, women's suffrage, the rise of Mussolini, flappers fashions, the KKK, U.S. Presidents Harding and Coolidge, the Teapot Dome Scandal, the rise of the Nazi Party, and more.

Includes glossary and bibliographical references

Davis, Barbara J.

The **Teapot** Dome Scandal; corruption rocks 1920s America. by Barbara J. Davis. Compass Point Books 2008 96p il map (Snapshots in history) lib bdg $31.93

Grades: 6 7 8 9   **973.91**

1. Teapot Dome Scandal, 1921-1924

ISBN 978-0-7565-3336-6 lib bdg; 0-7565-3336-8 lib bdg

LC 2007004920

"Describes the signature scandal of the 1920s, through which political appointees and personal friends of President Warren G. Harding used their positions to solicit bribes from powerful oil companies in return for rich Western oil leases. . . . [This] volume includes a minimal glossary, a helpful time line, and suggestions for further reading." Voice Youth Advocates

Includes glossary

Howes, Kelly King

The **roaring** twenties almanac and primary sources; [by] Kelly King Howes; Julie L. Carnagie, project editor. U.X.L 2006 liv, 286p il (The roaring twenties reference library) $60

Grades: 7 8 9 10   **973.91**

1. United States -- History -- 1919-1933

ISBN 1-4144-0212-0

LC 2005007800

This volume begins with a timeline placing the 1920s in historical context. Illustrated entries highlight such topics as politics, economics, technological advances, women's changing roles, creationism vs. evolution, anti-immigrationism, Prohibition, and writers such as Sinclair Lewis, and Langston Hughes

Includes bibliographical references

Kraft, Betsy Harvey

Theodore Roosevelt; champion of the American spirit. Clarion Bks. 2003 180p il $19

Grades: 5 6 7 8   **973.91**

1. Governors 2. Presidents 3. Vice-presidents 4. Nobel laureates for peace 5. Presidents -- United States

ISBN 0-618-14264-9

LC 2002-152825

A biography of the energetic New Yorker who became the twenty-sixth president of the United States and who once exclaimed "No one has ever enjoyed life more than I have"

"Interwoven with the well-told story of Roosevelt's public activities is Kraft's vivid portrayal of his personal life, laced with anecdotes and quotations (mainly from letters) that help bring the famous figure to life. The spacious layout and the many black-and-white reproductions of photos, drawings, and prints add to the book's appeal." Booklist

Includes bibliographical references

Lindop, Edmund

America in the 1920s; by Edmund Lindop and Margaret J. Goldstein. Twenty-First Century Books 2010 144p il (The decades of twentieth-century America) lib bdg $38.60

Grades: 7 8 9 10   **973.91**

1. United States -- History -- 1919-1933

ISBN 978-0-7613-2831-5 lib bdg; 0-7613-2831-9 lib bdg

LC 2009-703

Outlines life in the United States in the 1920s, including Prohibition, the stock market crash, and advances in technology and entertainment such as the first radios and first talking movies

The text is "enlivened with quotes and excerpts from primary sources, period photos, and two sets of sidebars. 'Profiles' provides biographical sketches of important people and 'Turning Points' explains the significance of important events. . . . A solid choice for readers and researchers." SLJ

Includes bibliographical references

McElvaine, Robert S., 1947-

★ The **Depression** and New Deal; a history in documents. Oxford Univ. Press 2000 192p il (Pages from history) hardcover o.p. pa $19.95

Grades: 7 8 9 10   **973.91**

1. Great Depression, 1929-1939 2. New Deal, 1933-1939 -- Sources 3. Depressions -- 1929 -- United States -- Sources

ISBN 0-19-510493-5; 0-19-516636-1 pa

LC 99-36644

"A vast assortment of diary entries, newspaper articles, campaign memos and speeches, political cartoons, songs, poetry, art, advertisements, photographs, and personal letters provide students with a political, economic, and social picture of this nation during the Depression. . . . [This] provides a balanced, inclusive picture of the period through the senses of the people who lived it." SLJ

Includes bibliographical references

Stanley, George Edward

An **emerging** world power (1900-1929) [by] George E. Stanley. World Almanac Library 2005 48p il (Primary source history of the United States) lib bdg $30

Grades: 5 6 7 8   **973.91**

1. United States -- History -- 1919-1933 2. United States -- Politics and government -- 1919-1933

ISBN 0-8368-5828-X

LC 2004-61501

The author describes United States politics and foreign relations in the 1920s.

"Stanley explains and connects events utilizing clear language and a blending of text, images, and primary accounts. . . . Well-organized, highly attractive." SLJ

Includes bibliographical references

973.917 Administration of Franklin Delano Roosevelt, 1933-1945

Bolden, Tonya

★ **FDR's** alphabet soup; New Deal America, 1932-1939. Alfred A. Knopf 2010 136p il $19.99; lib bdg $22.99

Grades: 5 6 7 8   **973.917**

1. Governors 2. Presidents 3. Handicapped 4. New Deal, 1933-1939 5. Philatelists

ISBN 978-0-375-85214-5; 0-375-85214-X; 978-0-375-95214-2 lib bdg; 0-375-95214-4 lib bdg

LC 2009-10362

"Retracing the course of New Deal intiatives from the newly elected Roosevelt's 'famous First Hundred Days of action! action! action!' to his creation of the powerful Executive Office of the President in 1939, [Bolden] presents a coherent account of how FDR and his adminstration successfully (mostly) battled political, ideological, and legal challenges to create a sweeping recovery agenda. . . . Generally illustrated with period photos . . . this lively look back both invites and equips readers to ponder the pros and cons of 'gumptious government' in any era." Booklist

Includes glossary and bibliographical references

Cooper, Michael L.

★ **Dust** to eat; drought and depression in the 1930's. Clarion Books 2004 81p il map hardcover o.p. $15

Grades: 4 5 6 7   **973.917**

1. Droughts 2. Migrant labor 3. Great Depression, 1929-1939 4. Depressions -- 1929 5. Droughts -- Great Plains -- History -- 20th century 6. Dust storms -- Great Plains -- History -- 20th century

ISBN 0-618-15449-3

LC 2003-17807

This book begins "with the 1929 stock market crash that ushered in the Great Depression and {continues} with the severe drought in the Midwest, known as the Dust Bowl." (Publisher's note)

This includes "lots of stunning black-and-white archival photos and a clear, spacious text that draws on eloquent eyewitness reports—including comments from John Steinbeck and Woody Guthrie. . . . This is an excellent historical account." Booklist

Includes bibliographical references

Corrigan, Jim

The **1930s** decade in photos; Depression and hope. Enslow Publishers 2010 64p il (Amazing decades in photos) lib bdg $27.93

Grades: 4 5 6 7   **973.917**

1. Great Depression, 1929-1939

ISBN 978-0-7660-3132-6 lib bdg; 0-7660-3132-2 lib bdg

LC 2008042904

This highlights the important world, national, and cultural developments of the decade 1930-1939, including the Great Depression, the Lindbergh kidnapping, the administration of FDR, the New Deal, jazz and swing music, the rise of Nazism, the repeal of Prohibition and more.

Includes glossary and bibliographical references

The **1940s** decade in photos; a world at war. Enslow Publishers 2010 64p il (Amazing decades in photos) lib bdg $27.93

Grades: 4 5 6 7   **973.917**

1. World War, 1939-1945

ISBN 978-0-7660-3133-3 lib bdg; 0-7660-3133-0 lib bdg

LC 2008042910

This covers the important world, national, and cultural developments of the decade 1940-1949, focusing on World War I.

This is illustrated with "large, well-chosen black-and-white and color photos. . . . Captions provide specific information about the photos and supplement, rather than repeat, information in the [narrative]. Attractive and readable, this . . . will be popular with browsers and beginning researchers." SLJ

Includes glossary and bibliographical references

Freedman, Russell

★ **Eleanor** Roosevelt; a life of discovery. Clarion Bks. 1993 198p il hardcover o.p. pa $11.95

Grades: 5 6 7 8 9 10   **973.917**

1. Diplomats 2. Columnists 3. Humanitarians 4. Social activists 5. Spouses of presidents 6. United Nations officials 7. Presidents' spouses -- United States

ISBN 0-89919-862-7; 0-395-84520-3 pa

LC 92-25024

A Newbery Medal honor book, 1994

"This impeccably researched, highly readable study of one of this country's greatest First Ladies is nonfiction at its best. . . . Approximately 140 well-chosen black-and-white photos amplify the text." Publ Wkly

Includes bibliographical references

★ **Franklin** Delano Roosevelt. Clarion Bks. 1990 200p il hardcover o.p. pa $9.95

Grades: 5 6 7 8 9 10   **973.917**

1. Governors 2. Presidents 3. Handicapped 4. Philatelists 5. Presidents -- United States

ISBN 0-89919-379-X; 0-395-62978-0 pa

LC 89-34986

"The carefully researched, highly readable text and extremely effective coordination of black-and-white photographs chronicle Roosevelt's priviledged youth, his early influences, and his maturation. . . . Even students with little or no background in American history will find this an intriguing and inspirational human portrait." SLJ

Includes bibliographical references

Lindop, Edmund

America in the 1930s; [by] Edmund Lindop and Margaret J. Goldstein. Twenty-First Century Books 2010 144p il (The decades of twentieth-century America) lib bdg $38.60

Grades: 7 8 9 10   **973.917**

    1. New Deal, 1933-1939

    ISBN 978-0-7613-2832-2 lib bdg; 0-7613-2832-7 lib bdg

                  LC 2007-42902

The text is "enlivened with quotes and excerpts from primary sources, period photos, and two sets of sidebars. 'Profiles' provides biographical sketches of important people and 'Turning Points' explains the significance of important events. . . . A solid choice for readers and researchers." SLJ

Includes bibliographical references and filmography

America in the 1940s; by Edmund Lindop and Margaret J. Goldstein. Twenty-First Century Books 2010 144p il (The decades of twentieth-century America) lib bdg $38.60

Grades: 7 8 9 10   **973.917**

    1. United States -- History -- 1933-1945

    ISBN 978-0-7613-2945-9 lib bdg; 0-7613-2945-5 lib bdg

                  LC 2007-42904

Discusses the political, economic, social, cultural, and technology landscape of the United States in the fifth decade of the 20th century

The text is "enlivened with quotes and excerpts from primary sources, period photos, and two sets of sidebars. 'Profiles' provides biographical sketches of important people and 'Turning Points' explains the significance of important events. . . . A solid choice for readers and researchers." SLJ

Includes bibliographical references

McNeese, Tim

The Great Depression, 1929-1940; consulting editor Richard Jensen. Chelsea House 2010 136p il map (Discovering U.S. history) $35

Grades: 5 6 7 8   **973.917**

    1. Economic conditions 2. Great Depression, 1929-1939

    ISBN 978-1-60413-357-8; 1-60413-357-0

                  LC 2009-22090

"The information is accurate and easy to understand. Pictures are well placed, and primary sources are included. . . . The maps are well done and there are sidebars with additional information. . . . [This would be good] to have on hand for reports as it is well laid out and easy to use." Libr Media Connect

Includes glossary and bibliographical references

Nardo, Don

★ Migrant mother; how a photograph defined the Great Depression. Compass Point Books 2011 64p il (Captured history) lib bdg $33.99

Grades: 6 7 8 9   **973.917**

    1. Photographers 2. Documentary photography 3.

Great Depression, 1929-1939

ISBN 978-0-7565-4397-6; 0-7565-4397-5

                  LC 2010038578

This describes the significance of the iconic Dorothea Lange photograph of a migrant mother during the Great Depression and places it "in historical context, profiles the photographer, describes the conditions under which it was taken, and analyzes both its immediate and continuing impact. The [text includes] ample background information and details and [is] enhanced by large photos and sidebars." SLJ

Includes glossary and bibliographical references

Ruggiero, Adriane

★ American voices from The Great Depression. Benchmark Books 2004 xxi, 116p il (American voices from--) lib bdg $32.21

Grades: 6 7 8 9   **973.917**

    1. Great Depression, 1929-1939 2. Depressions -- 1929 -- United States -- Sources

    ISBN 0-7614-1696-X

                  LC 2004-865

Presents the history of the Great Depression through excerpts from letters, newspaper articles, speeches, and songs dating from the period. Includes review questions.

This "excellent [resource stands] out . . . because [it deals] strictly with primary sources, [contains] topnotch illustrations, and [enables] students to grasp the concepts without being overwhelmed." SLJ

Includes glossary and bibliographical references

973.92   1953-2001

Brill, Marlene Targ

America in the 1970s. Lerner 2009 144p il (The decades of twentieth-century America) lib bdg $38.60

Grades: 7 8 9 10   **973.92**

    1. United States -- History -- 1961-1974 2. United States -- Social conditions

    ISBN 978-0-8225-3438-9; 0-8225-3438-X

                  LC 2007-38570

This is "a tightly constructed, smoothly phrased overview of the tumultuous 1970s. . . . The serviceable text is bolstered by skillful connections between events and movements, well-chosen representative quotes . . . and occasional snappy headlines . . . while sidebars profiling individuals and historical turning points . . . and a well-edited selection of photos add more interest." Booklist

America in the 1990s. Twenty-First Century Books 2010 144p il (The decades of twentieth-century America) lib bdg $38.60

Grades: 7 8 9 10   **973.92**

    1. United States -- History -- 1989-

    ISBN 978-0-8225-7603-7 lib bdg; 0-8225-7603-1 lib bdg

                  LC 2009-11628

Presents the social, political, economical, and technological changes in the United States during the 1990's

The text is "enlivened with quotes and excerpts from primary sources, period photos, and two sets of sidebars. 'Profiles' provides biographical sketches of important people and 'Turning Points' explains the significance of important events. . . . A solid choice for readers and researchers." SLJ

Includes bibliographical references and filmography

Campbell, Geoffrey A.

The **home** front. Lucent Bks. 2003 112p il map (American war library, Cold War) $27.45

Grades: 7 8 9 10   **973.92**

1. Cold war 2. Cold War -- Social aspects -- United States

ISBN 1-59018-213-8

LC 2002-663

Examines how the Cold War period in America, lasting roughly fifty years following World War II, was a contradictory time of prosperity and optimism coupled with concerns over Soviet espionage infiltrating American institutions and fear of nuclear apocalypse

Includes bibliographical references

Collier, Christopher

★ The **changing** face of American society: 1945-2000; [by] Christopher Collier, James Lincoln Collier. Benchmark Bks. 2002 94p il (Drama of American history) lib bdg $31.36

Grades: 6 7 8 9   **973.92**

1. United States -- History -- 1945-

ISBN 0-7614-1319-7

LC 2001-25963

This outlines American social conditions from 1945 to 2000, including greater prosperity, the movements for African American civil rights and women's rights, the 1960s counterculture, the Vietnam War, scientific advancements and social changes

"Illustrations are plentiful, uniformly well chosen, and include photographs, paintings, posters, and in some titles, maps. . . . [This title is] easy to read and informative." Book Rep

Includes bibliographical references

★ The **middle** road: American politics, 1945-2000; [by] Christopher Collier, James Lincoln Collier. Benchmark Bks. 2002 95p il maps (Drama of American history) lib bdg $31.36

Grades: 6 7 8 9   **973.92**

1. United States -- Politics and government -- 1945-

ISBN 0-7614-1318-9

LC 2001-25615

This outlines the course of American politics from the end of World War II, through McCarthyism, the 1960s, President Nixon and the Watergate scandal, and Presidents Carter, Reagan, Bush, and Clinton

"Illustrations are plentiful, uniformly well chosen, and include photographs, paintings, posters, and in some titles, maps. . . . [This title is] easy to read and informative." Book Rep

Includes bibliographical references

Corrigan, Jim

The **1990s** decade in photos; the rise of technology. Enslow Publishers 2010 64p il (Amazing decades in photos) lib bdg $27.93

Grades: 4 5 6 7   **973.92**

1. World history -- 20th century

ISBN 978-0-7660-3138-8 lib bdg; 0-7660-3138-1 lib bdg

LC 2008054648

This highlights the important world, national, and cultural developments of the decade 1990-1999, including Operation Desert Storm in 1991, race riots in Los Angeles, the election of President Clinton, the 1993 bombing of the World Trade Center, the Human Genome Project, the end of Apartheid, massacres in Bosnia and Rwanda, the Oklahoma City bombing, the O.J. Simpson murder trial, the Columbine High School shootings, and more

Includes glossary and bibliographical references

Lindop, Edmund

America in the 1950s; by Edmund Lindop; with Sarah Decapua. Twenty-First Century Books 2010 144p il (The decades of twentieth-century America) lib bdg $38.60

Grades: 7 8 9 10   **973.92**

1. United States -- History -- 1953-1961

ISBN 978-0-8225-7642-6 lib bdg; 0-8225-7642-2 lib bdg

LC 2008-40127

Presents the social, political, economical, and technological changes in the United States during the 1950s, including school integration, the Cold War, and the popularization of rock and roll

The text is "enlivened with quotes and excerpts from primary sources, period photos, and two sets of sidebars. 'Profiles' provides biographical sketches of important people and 'Turning Points' explains the significance of important events. . . . A solid choice for readers and researchers." SLJ

Includes bibliographical references and filmography

The **McCarthy** hearings; Jesse G. Cunningham, book editor; Laura K. Egendorf, assistant book editor. Greenhaven Press 2003 144p (At issue in history) lib bdg $21.96; pa $14.96

Grades: 7 8 9 10   **973.921**

1. Senators 2. Army-McCarthy Controversy, 1954

ISBN 0-7377-1346-1 lib bdg; 0-7377-1347-X pa

LC 2002-69323

"Because of the evenhanded presentation, the title makes a strong and lasting impression. The writings are well chosen." SLJ

Includes bibliographical references

McNeese, Tim

Modern America, 1964-present; consulting editor, Richard Jensen. Chelsea House 2010 144p il map (Discovering U.S. history) $35

Grades: 5 6 7 8   **973.92**
    1. United States -- History -- 1961-1974 2. United
States -- History -- 1974-1989 3. United States -- History -- 1989-
    ISBN 978-1-60413-361-5; 1-60413-361-9
    "Through a good balance of social and political topics, McNeese capably covers a diverse range of subjects in [this] volume. . . . Modern America discusses civil rights, terrorism, and Barack Obama's first year as president. [The] book has an excellent chronology; rich sidebars; and numerous well-captioned illustrations, maps, and photos that enhance the [text]. [This book provides a] satisfying [introduction] to American history for students." SLJ
    Includes glossary and bibliographical references

973.921   Administration of Dwight David Eisenhower, 1953-1961

Corrigan, Jim
    The **1950s** decade in photos; the American decade. Enslow Publishers 2010 64p il (Amazing decades in photos) lib bdg $27.93
Grades: 4 5 6 7   **973.921**
    1. United States -- History -- 1945-1953 2. United States -- History -- 1953-1961
    ISBN 978-0-7660-3134-0 lib bdg; 0-7660-3134-9 lib bdg
                   LC 2008042994
    This highlights the important world, national, and cultural developments of the decade 1950-1959, including the Korean War, McCarthyism, the Baby Boom generation, the execution of the Rosenbergs, the Beat Generation, the polio epidemic and vaccine, the Montgomery Bus Boycott, the Suez Crisis, the beginning of rock music, the launching of Sputnik, and the Cuban Revolution
    Includes glossary and bibliographical references

Fitzgerald, Brian
    McCarthyism; the red scare. Compass Point Books 2007 96p il map (Snapshots in history) lib bdg $31.93
Grades: 7 8 9 10   **973.921**
    1. Cold war 2. Senators 3. Communism -- United States
    ISBN 978-0-7565-2007-6 lib bdg; 0-7565-2007-X lib bdg
                   LC 2006003005
    This "vividly portrays the fear of Communism in the U.S., beginning after the Russian Revolution. This book shows, in clear language, how McCarthy spread paranoia throughout the country and ruined many lives and careers." SLJ
    Includes glossary and bibliographical references

Young, Jeff C.
    Dwight D. Eisenhower; soldier and president. Morgan Reynolds 2002 128p il (Notable Americans) lib bdg $21.95
Grades: 7 8 9 10   **973.921**
    1. Generals 2. Presidents 3. College presidents 4.

Presidents -- United States 5. Generals -- United States -- Biography 6. Presidents -- United States -- Biography
    ISBN 1-88384-676-5
                   LC 2001-30822
    A biography of the World War II commander general who became the thirty-fourth President of the United States
    "Young reveals Ike's story with a flair that makes both the man's questionable and admirable traits interesting. . . . There is enough drama here to make the story of the thirty-fourth president a surprisingly dynamic tale." Booklist
    Includes bibliographical references

973.922   Administration of John Fitzgerald Kennedy, 1961-1963

O'Reilly, Bill, 1949-
    Kennedy's last days; the assassination that defined a generation. by Bill O'Reilly. 1st ed. Henry Holt and Co. 2013 336 p. (hardcover) $19.99
Grades: 6 7 8 9   **973.922**
    1. Assassination
    ISBN 080509802X; 9780805098020
                   LC 2013009026
    This book by Bill O'Reilly "chronicles John F. Kennedy's course from PT-109 through a challenging presidency and positively harps on Lee Harvey Oswald's determined but doomed quest to become a 'great man.' . . . News photos or snapshots on nearly every page provide views of the Kennedy and Oswald families over time, as well as important figures, places and major world events." Kirkus Reviews
    Includes bibliographical references

Stockland, Patricia M.
    The **assassination** of John F. Kennedy; by Patricia M. Stockland. ABDO Pub. Co. 2008 112 p. ill. (some col.), map (library) $34.22
Grades: 7 8 9 10   **973.922**
    1. Kennedy, John F. (John Fitzgerald), 1917-1963 -- Assassination
    ISBN 1599288486; 9781599288482
                   LC 2007011999
    This book by Patricia Stockland is part of the Essential Events series and looks at the assassination of former U.S. President John F. (Fitzgerald) Kennedy. The series "explores historic happenings around the globe and how those events have sculpted societies, the sciences, and politics." (Publisher's note)
    Includes bibliographical references (p. 102) and index.

973.923   Administration of Lyndon Baines Johnson, 1963-1969

Corrigan, Jim
    The **1960s** decade in photos; love, freedom, and flower power. Enslow Publishers 2010 64p il (Amazing decades in photos) lib bdg $27.93

Grades: 4 5 6 7   **973.923**
ISBN 978-0-7660-3135-7 lib bdg; 0-7660-3135-7
lib bdg

LC 2008042996

This highlights the important world, national, and cultural developments of the decade 1960-1969, including the U-2 spy plane, the election and assassination of JFK, the beginnings of manned space exploration, the Bay of Pigs invasion, the Vietnam War, the Cuban Missile Crisis, the British invasion in rock music, the Civil Rights movement, the Six-Day War in the Middle East, the assassinations of RFK and Martin Luther King, and Hippie culture

Includes glossary and bibliographical references

Lindop, Edmund
America in the 1960s; [by] Edmund Lindop; with Margaret J. Goldstein. Twenty-First Century Books 2009 144p il (Decades of twentieth century America) lib bdg $38.60

Grades: 7 8 9 10   **973.923**
1. United States -- History -- 1961-1974
ISBN 978-0-7613-3453-8 lib bdg; 0-7613-3453-X
lib bdg

LC 2007-38028

Presents the social, political, economic, and technological changes in the United States during the nineteen sixties, including the civil rights movement, the popularization of rock music, and the expedition to the Moon

The text is "enlivened with quotes and excerpts from primary sources, period photos, and two sets of sidebars. 'Profiles' provides biographical sketches of important people and 'Turning Points' explains the significance of important events. . . . A solid choice for readers and researchers." SLJ

Includes bibliographical references and filmography

973.924   Administration of Richard Milhous Nixon, 1969-1974

Corrigan, Jim
The **1970s** decade in photos; protest and change. Enslow Publishers 2010 64p il (Amazing decades in photos) lib bdg $27.93

Grades: 4 5 6 7   **973.924**
1. United States -- History -- 1961-1974 2. United States -- History -- 1974-1989
ISBN 978-0-7660-3136-4 lib bdg; 0-7660-3136-5
lib bdg

LC 2008042998

This highlights the important world, national, and cultural developments of the decade 1970-1979, including protests against the Vietnam War, terrorist airplane hijackings, the thawing of the Cold War, the deaths of rock musicians Jimi Hendrix, Janice Joplin, and Jim Morrison, the attack at the Munich Olympics, Watergate and the resignation of President Nixon, Three Mile Island, and more.

Includes glossary and bibliographical references

973.927   Administration of Ronald Reagan, 1981-1989

Brill, Marlene Targ
America in the 1980s. Twenty-First Century Books 2009 144p il (The decades of twentieth-century America) lib bdg $38.60

Grades: 7 8 9 10   **973.927**
1. Actors 2. Governors 3. Presidents
ISBN 978-0-8225-7602-0 lib bdg; 0-8225-7602-3
lib bdg

LC 2008-50116

Presents the social, political, economical, and technological changes in the United States during the 1980's

The text is "enlivened with quotes and excerpts from primary sources, period photos, and two sets of sidebars. 'Profiles' provides biographical sketches of important people and 'Turning Points' explains the significance of important events. . . . A solid choice for readers and researchers." SLJ

Includes bibliographical references

Corrigan, Jim
The **1980s** decade in photos; the triumph of democracy. Enslow Publishers 2010 64p il (Amazing decades in photos) lib bdg $27.93

Grades: 4 5 6 7   **973.927**
1. World history -- 20th century
ISBN 978-0-7660-3137-1 lib bdg; 0-7660-3137-3
lib bdg

LC 2008052627

This highlights the important world, national, and cultural developments of the decade 1980-1989, including the 1980 Winter Olympics, the presidency of Ronald Reagan, the Iran hostage crisis, the Space Shuttle, MTV, the War on Drugs, AIDS, the rise of the computer, fashion, the Chernobyl nuclear disaster, the Iran-Contra Affair, the massacre in Tiananmen Square, the fall of the Berlin Wall, and the U.S. invasion of Panama

Includes glossary and bibliographical references

973.93   -2001

Corrigan, Jim
The **2000s** decade in photos; a new millennium. Enslow Publishers 2010 64p il (Amazing decades in photos) lib bdg $27.93

Grades: 4 5 6 7   **973.93**
1. World history -- 21st century
ISBN 978-0-7660-3139-5 lib bdg; 0-7660-3139-X
lib bdg

LC 2008054644

This highlights the important world, national, and cultural developments of the first decade of the 21st century, including the disputed presidential election of 2000, the attacks of September 11, 2001, the Iraq War, digital technology and gadgets, the drop in stock market prices of internet companies, steroid use in sports, the Space Shuttle disaster of 2003, the tsunami of 2004, Hurricane Katrina, the massacre at Virginia Tech, the energy crisis, and the 2008 presidential election

Includes glossary and bibliographical references

Sutherland, James

The **ten**-year century; explaining the first decade of the new millennium. Viking 2010 152p il $18.99

Grades: 7 8 9 10   **973.93**

1. Modern history

ISBN 978-0-670-01223-7; 0-670-01223-8

LC 2010007314

"This overview of the first 10 years of the new millennium focuses on significant developments that have shaped life in the United States today. . . . The lucid, balanced narration results in a nuanced representation of a rapidly changing era." Publ Wkly

Includes bibliographical references

973.931   Administration of George W. Bush, 2001-2009

Abbott, David

The **Twin** Towers. Arcturus Pub. 2011 46p il (A place in history) lib bdg $34.25

Grades: 7 8 9 10   **973.931**

1. Terrorism 2. September 11 terrorist attacks, 2001 3. World Trade Center terrorist attack, 2001

ISBN 978-1-84837-677-9; 1-84837-677-4

LC 2010014195

"A recap of American Airlines Flight 11 just before it struck the north tower of the World Trade Center opens this thorough coverage of the events leading up to the attack and its affect on the nation. Following a look at the Twin Towers, this . . . title focuses on the motivation behind the terrorist attacks by addressing the rise of Islam, anti-Americanism, and al-Qaeda. . . . Additional quotes from Osama bin Laden and individuals affected by the attacks; related facts . . .; and attention-getting photos . . . make this a solid choice for U.S. studies." Booklist

Includes bibliographical references

Benoit, Peter

September 11 we will never forget; by Peter Benoit. Children's Press 2012 64 p. col. ill., col. map Cornerstones of freedom) (library) $30.00; (paperback) $8.95

Grades: 4 5 6 7   **973.931**

1. September 11 terrorist attacks, 2001 2. Terrorism -- United States

ISBN 0531250407; 9780531250402; 9780531265659

LC 2011009586

This book presents an "overview of the events of September 11, 2001 and the impact the day continues to have on present day life. . . . Boxed text adds information about international reaction, and the life of Osama Bin Laden, and other topics throughout the book. . . . .The immediate emergency responses at each site are described as well as government actions such as immediate grounding of planes . . . and military initiatives in the Middle East." (Children's Literature)

Includes bibliographical references (p. 61) and index.

Burgan, Michael

George W. Bush; Michael Burgan. Marshall Cavendish Benchmark 2012 112 p. $34.21

Grades: 5 6 7 8   **973.931**

1. Terrorism 2. Presidents -- United States 3. Presidents -- United States -- Biography

ISBN 1608701840; 9781608701841

LC 2010014801

This book "in the 'Presidents and Their Times' series provides . . . information about George W. Bush and how he handled critical situations (e.g., domestic spying vis-a-vis telephone records to highlight the difficulty battling terrorism and the effect of Bush's response to Hurricane Katrina). . . . Personal information is also provided about his early years, including his marriage to Laura, entry into politics, relationships with other family members, a decision to stop drinking, and his choice to become a Christian fundamentalist." Also included are "color and older black and white photos" and back matter such as "a timeline, chapter notes with complete citations, a glossary, books and websites for additional information, bibliography (books, articles, media), and index." Children's Literature

Includes bibliographical references

Frank, Mitch

Understanding September 11th; answering questions about the attacks on America. Viking 2002 136p il maps $16.99; pa $8.99

Grades: 7 8 9 10   **973.931**

1. Islam 2. Terrorism 3. Terrorists 4. September 11 terrorist attacks, 2001 5. Terrorism -- United States

ISBN 0-670-03582-3; 0-670-03587-4 pa

LC 2002-1725

Explains the historical and religious issues that sparked terrorists to attack America on September 11, 2001, including information on Islam, Osama bin Laden, and the Middle East

This is written "in remarkably simple, accessible language. . . . Direct, unflinching, intelligent, and humane, this is an invaluable resource." Booklist

Includes glossary and bibliographical references

Hillstrom, Kevin

The **September** 11 terrorist attacks; by Kevin Hillstrom. Omnigraphics 2012 xv, 268 p.p (Defining moments) (hardcover: alk. paper) $55

Grades: 8 9 10 11 12   **973.931**

1. September 11 terrorist attacks, 2001 2. Qaida (Organization) 3. Terrorism -- United States

ISBN 0780812409; 9780780812406

LC 2011050673

This teen nonfiction reference book, by Kevin Hillstrom, is part of the "Defining Moments" series. It "opens with a lengthy overview that traces the origins and evolution of radical Islam, the birth and growth of Al Qaeda and its early attacks on the West, the events of September 11th, and the lasting . . . effects of the attack. The next section provides brief biographical sketches of eight terrorists and American . . . officials." (School Library Journal)

Includes bibliographical references and index

Wachtel, Alan

★ **September** 11; a primary source history. Gareth Stevens Pub. 2009 48p il (In their own words) lib bdg $27

Grades: 5 6 7 8   **973.931**

1. Terrorism 2. September 11 terrorist attacks, 2001
ISBN 978-1-4339-0048-8; 1-4339-0048-3

LC 2008045132

"The horror of September 11 feels very immediate, and uses both quotes from those who lived through it and stills from the attacks. The book does a fine job of chronicling the events, up to and including the controversies surrounding the New York memorial. The use of transcripts of phone conversations that took place aboard the doomed planes gives the book's beginning an almost 'you are there' effect. Later chapters feature such diverse sources as text from the Patriot Act and lyrics from Neil Young's song 'Let's Roll' to amplify the mood of the country." Booklist

Includes bibliographical references

Williams, Brian

The **war** on terror. Arcturus Pub. 2011 46p il (Secret history) lib bdg $32.80

Grades: 7 8 9 10   **973.931**

1. Terrorism 2. September 11 terrorist attacks, 2001 3. War on terrorism
ISBN 978-1-84837-699-1; 1-84837-699-5

LC 2010011013

This book explores the secrets of the War on Terror. It began with the terrorist attacks of 9/11, but the War on Terror is mostly fought in secret. Its fighters are spies, analysts, moles, and informers. Its weapons are phone taps, satellites, and killer drones.

"The title of the Secret History series will grab readers, even reluctant ones, and they won't be disappointed by the intriguing info regarding codes and code breakers, spies, terrorists, and double agents, with profiles of heroes and traitors on all sides. . . . The readable design, with clear type on thick, high-quality paper, includes lots of sidebars, photos, screens, and quotes." Booklist

Includes bibliographical references

973.932 Administration of Barack Obama, 2009-

Zeiger, Jennifer

Barack Obama; by Jennifer Zeiger. Children's Press 2012 64 p. ill. (chiefly col.), col. map (library binding) $30.00; (paperback) $8.95

Grades: 4 5 6   **973.932**

1. Presidents -- United States -- Biography 2. Racially mixed people -- United States -- Biography
ISBN 0531230503; 0531281507; 9780531230503; 9780531281505

LC 2011031124

This book presents a "nonfiction account of President [Barack]Obama's life for middle school students. . . . The book includes many color photographs of the President as a young boy and young adult. It gives the details of his life in Indonesia and Hawaii and traces his career up to the 2012 reelection campaign. His education is a focus of the biography and there is ample discussion of his educational career and

how it has helped to shape him into the man he is today." Children's Literature

Includes bibliographical references (p. 61) and index.

974   Specific states of United States

Bial, Raymond

The **Delaware**. Marshall Cavendish Benchmark 2005 127p il map (Lifeways) lib bdg $38.50

Grades: 5 6 7 8   **974**

1. Delaware Indians 2. Native Americans
ISBN 978-0-7614-1904-4; 0-7614-1904-7

LC 2004-3088

Discusses the history, culture, beliefs, changing ways, and notable people of the Delaware.

Includes glossary and bibliographical references

Johnson, Claudia D.

Daily life in colonial New England; [by] Claudia Durst Johnson. Greenwood Press 2002 xxvii, 215p (Daily life through history) $49.95

Grades: 7 8 9 10   **974**

1. New England -- History
ISBN 0-313-31458-6

LC 00-61721

This description of colonial life in New England covers such topics as the clergy and the church, crime and punishment, government and law, labor, shelter and attire, food and health, marriage and sex, arts and amusements, and Native Americans and Africans in New England

"In this excellent volume, Johnson draws a remarkably clear and complete picture of the day-to-day existence of the first European settlers in New England." Voice Youth Advocates

Includes bibliographical references

Rylant, Cynthia

★ **Appalachia**; the voices of sleeping birds. illustrated by Barry Moser. Harcourt Brace Jovanovich 1991 21p il $17; pa $6

Grades: 4 5 6 7   **974**

1. Appalachian region
ISBN 0-15-201605-8; 0-15-201893-X pa

LC 90-36798

"Taking her subtitle from a passage by James Agee, the author conveys with a marvelous economy of words the essence of the very special part of America where she was raised. A poetic text projects emotion as well as information. . . . Moser's watercolors capture the scene perfectly. . . . The book is a treasure—simply a beautiful combination of text and art." Horn Book

974.1   Maine

Dornfeld, Margaret

Maine; by Margaret Dornfeld and Joyce Hart. 2nd ed.; Marshall Cavendish Benchmark 2010 144p il map (Celebrate the states) lib bdg $42.79

Grades: 5 6 7 8   **974.1**
    ISBN 978-0-7614-4726-9; 0-7614-4726-1
                                            LC 2009002583
This offers information on the geography, history, wildlife, governmental structure, economy, cultural diversity,
peoples, religion, and landmarks of Maine.
    Includes bibliographical references

Heinrichs, Ann
    Maine; by Ann Heinrichs. Children's Press 2008
144p il map (America the beautiful, third series) lib
bdg $38
Grades: 4 5 6 7   **974.1**
    ISBN 978-0-531-18575-9; 0-531-18575-3
                                            LC 2007-302
Describes the history, geography, ecology, people, economy, cities, and sights of the state of Maine.
    Includes glossary and bibliographical references

974.2   New Hampshire

Auden, Scott
    New Hampshire, 1603-1776; [by] Scott Auden;
with Alan Taylor, consultant. National Geographic
Society 2007 109p il map (Voices from colonial
America) $21.95; lib bdg $32.90
Grades: 5 6 7 8   **974.2**
    ISBN 978-1-4263-0034-9; 1-4263-0034-4; 978-1-
    4263-0035-6 lib bdg; 1-4263-0035-2 lib bdg
                                            LC 2006-36055
Provides a look at the long and changing colonial history
of the state of New Hampshire through a review of its borders, founding fathers, motto, and more, complete with archival images, period maps, and various first-person accounts.
    Offers " thorough, well-documented information about
the struggles and successes of early non-native settlers [in
New Hampshire]. . . . Many reproductions of period illustrations (both color and sepia) and some photos of archival
documents and maps enhance the text." Horn Book Guide
    Includes bibliographical references

Kent, Deborah
    New Hampshire. Children's Press 2010 144p il
map (America the beautiful, third series) lib bdg $39
Grades: 4 5 6 7   **974.2**
    ISBN 978-0-531-18501-8; 0-531-18501-X
                                            LC 2008048940
Takes readers on a tour of New Hampshire, describing
the state's history, culture, land, economy, government, and
sights, and including unique facts, color maps and photos,
the state song, suggested activities, lists of famous people,
cultural institutions, and annual events, and other resources.
    Includes glossary and bibliographical references

Otfinoski, Steven
    New Hampshire; [by] Steve Otfinoski. 2nd ed.;
Marshall Cavendish Benchmark 2008 144p il map
(Celebrate the states) lib bdg $39.93

Grades: 4 5 6 7   **974.2**
    ISBN 978-0-7614-2718-6; 0-7614-2718-X
                                            LC 2007-9944
    First published 1999
"Provides comprehensive information on the geography,
history, wildlife, governmental structure, economy, cultural
diversity, peoples, religion, and landmarks of New Hampshire." Publisher's note
    Includes bibliographical references

974.3   Vermont

Heinrichs, Ann
    Vermont. Children's Press 2010 144p il map
(America the beautiful, third series) lib bdg $39
Grades: 4 5 6 7   **974.3**
    ISBN 978-0-531-18506-3; 0-531-18506-0
                                            LC 2008007241
Presents an introduction to the geography, natural re-
sources, history, economy, important sites, daily life, and
people of Vermont.
    Includes glossary and bibliographical references

974.4   Massachusetts

Doherty, Kieran
    William Bradford; rock of Plymouth. 21st Cent.
Bks. (Brookfield) 1999 192p il lib bdg $24.90
Grades: 6 7 8 9   **974.4**
    1. Historians 2. Pilgrims (New England colonists) 3.
    Colonists 4. Pilgrim fathers 5. Plymouth (Mass.) --
    Biography 6. Governors -- Massachusetts -- Biography
    7. Pilgrims (New Plymouth Colony) -- Biography 8.
    Massachusetts -- History -- New Plymouth, 1620-1691
    ISBN 0-7613-1304-4
                                            LC 99-10631
A biography of one of the founders of the Plymouth Colony in Massachusetts and a history of the Pilgrims' difficult
times during their early years in the New World
    Includes bibliographical references

Edwards, Judith
    The **Plymouth** Colony and the Pilgrim adventure
in American history. Enslow Pubs. 2003 128p il
map (In American history) lib bdg $26.60
Grades: 7 8 9 10   **974.4**
    1. Pilgrims (New England colonists) 2. Pilgrims (New
    Plymouth Colony)
    ISBN 0-7660-1989-6
                                            LC 2002-12809
Traces the dangers and adventures surrounding the history of the Pilgrim settlement at Plymouth, Massachusetts,
highlighting the roles played by William Brewster, Miles
Standish, and other individuals
    Includes bibliographical references

Erickson, Paul
    Daily life in the Pilgrim colony, 1636. Clarion
Bks. 2001 48p il map $20; pa $9.95

Grades: 4 5 6 7 **974.4**

1. Pilgrims (New England colonists) 2. Pilgrims (New Plymouth Colony) 3. Pilgrims (New Plymouth Colony) -- Social life and customs
ISBN 0-618-05846-X; 0-395-98841-1 pa
LC 2001-17203

This "describes the day-to-day activities of the Prentiss family, owners of a small farm just outside the colony of Plymouth. Full-color photographs, maps, line drawings, and detailed illustrations accompany engaging present-tense text to provide insight into Pilgrim society as a whole, and into the lives of specific family members as well." Book Rep

LeVert, Suzanne

Massachusetts; by Suzanne LeVert and Tamra B. Orr. 2nd ed.; Marshall Cavendish Benchmark 2009 144p il map (Celebrate the states) lib bdg $42.79
Grades: 4 5 6 7 **974.4**
ISBN 978-0-7614-3005-6; 0-7614-3005-9
First published 2000
"Provides comprehensive information on the geography, history, wildlife, governmental structure, economy, cultural diversity, peoples, religion, and landmarks of Massachusetts." Publisher's note
Includes glossary and bibliographical references

Trueit, Trudi Strain

Massachusetts; by Trudi Strain Trueit. Children's Press 2008 144p il map (America the beautiful, third series) lib bdg $38
Grades: 4 5 6 7 **974.4**
ISBN 978-0-531-18561-2; 0-531-18561-3
LC 2006-39235
Describes the history, geography, ecology, people, economy, cities, and sights of the state of Massachusetts.
Includes glossary and bibliographical references

974.5 Rhode Island

Burgan, Michael

Rhode Island. Children's Press 2009 144p il map (America the beautiful, third series) $39
Grades: 4 5 6 7 **974.5**
1. Connecticut -- History -- 1600-1775, Colonial period
ISBN 978-0-531-18590-2; 0-531-18590-7
LC 2007037178
Presents an introduction to the geography, natural resources, history, economy, important sites, daily life, and people of Rhode Island.
Includes glossary and bibliographical references

Klein, Ted

Rhode Island; by Ted Klein. 2nd ed.; Marshall Cavendish Benchmark 2008 144p il map (Celebrate the states) lib bdg $39.93
Grades: 4 5 6 7 **974.5**
ISBN 978-0-7614-2560-1; 0-7614-2560-8
LC 2006-36490
First published 1999

"Provides comprehensive information on the geography, history, wildlife, governmental structure, economy, cultural diversity, peoples, religion, and landmarks of Rhode Island." Publisher's note
Includes bibliographical references

974.6 Connecticut

Burgan, Michael

Connecticut, 1614-1776. National Geographic Society 2007 109p il map (Voices from colonial America) $21.95; lib bdg $32.90
Grades: 5 6 7 8 **974.6**
ISBN 978-1-4263-0068-4; 1-4263-0068-9; 978-1-4263-0069-1 lib bdg; 1-4263-0069-7 lib bdg
LC 2007-3123
A history of Connecticut from its beginning as an English colony to 1788 when it became the fifth state.
Offers " thorough, well-documented information about the struggles and successes of early colonial settlers and settlements. . . . Many reproductions of period illustrations and some photographs of period documents and maps with relevant captions are included." Horn Book Guide
Includes bibliographical references

Kent, Zachary

Connecticut; by Zachary Kent. Children's Press 2008 144p il map (America the beautiful, third series) lib bdg $38
Grades: 4 5 6 7 **974.6**
ISBN 978-0-531-18571-1; 0-531-18571-0
LC 2007-2328
Describes the history, geography, ecology, people, economy, cities, and sights of the state of Connecticut.
Includes glossary and bibliographical references

974.7 New York

Bial, Raymond

★ **Tenement**; immigrant life on the Lower East Side. Houghton Mifflin 2002 48p il $16
Grades: 4 5 6 7 **974.7**
1. Poor 2. Immigrants -- United States 3. Tenement-houses 4. Immigrants -- New York (N.Y.) -- History
ISBN 0-618-13849-8
LC 2002-00407
Presents a view of New York City's tenements during the peak years of foreign immigration, discussing living conditions, laws pertaining to tenements, and the occupations of their residents
"The writing is particularly clear and sharp. Calling upon and quoting the writing of reformer Jacob Riis (and featuring his compelling photographs), Bial explains simply, yet engagingly, what tenement life was like. . . . Along with Riis' photographs, Bial provides some of his own, taken at the Lower East Side Tenement Museum in New York City." Booklist
Includes bibliographical references

Burgan, Michael

New York, 1609-1776; [by] Michael Burgan; with Timothy J. Shannon, consultant. National Geographic Society 2006 109p il map (Voices from colonial America) $21.95; lib bdg $32.90

Grades: 5 6 7 8   **974.7**

1. New York (State) -- History
ISBN 978-0-7922-6390-6; 0-7922-6390-1; 978-0-7922-6860-4 lib bdg; 0-7922-6860-1 lib bdg
LC 2005-22033

Presents a brief history of colonial New York, from 1609 to 1776, and contains illustrations, historical maps, and first-person accounts from explorers, Native Americans, and colonists on early settlements.

Includes bibliographical references

Getzinger, Donna

★ The **Triangle** Shirtwaist Factory fire. Morgan Reynolds Pub. 2008 128p il map (American workers) $27.95

Grades: 7 8 9 10   **974.7**

1. Labor -- Law and legislation
ISBN 978-1-59935-099-8; 1-59935-099-8
LC 2008-4077

"Beginning with a brief account of the disaster, a description of the popular shirtwaist and the fabric used to make the blouse, the women who lost their lives, and the impact of the lack of communication among the workers, the first chapter is sure to hook readers. Successive chapters look more closely at New York City's growth, the varied immigrant population at that time, overcrowded factory conditions, the failure to enforce building regulations, and the many sweatshops developed from the desire of contractors to make money. . . . Archival photos and diagrams with captions add to the meaning of this devastating and important event in the history of labor." SLJ

Includes bibliographical references

Hansen, Joyce

★ **Breaking** ground, breaking silence; the story of New York's African burial ground. by Joyce Hansen and Gary McGowan. Holt & Co. 1998 130p il maps $19.95

Grades: 8 9 10 11 12 Adult   **974.7**

1. Cemeteries 2. Excavations (Archeology) 3. African Americans -- History
ISBN 0-8050-5012-4
LC 97-19105

Describes the discovery and study of the African burial site found in Manhattan in 1991, while excavating for a new building, and what it reveals about the lives of black people in Colonial times

"This book is well written and attractively designed, and readers should have access to it in social studies classrooms as well as in libraries. It will generate lots of class discussion and writing projects." Voice Youth Advocates

Houle, Michelle M.

Triangle Shirtwaist Factory fire; flames of labor reform. Enslow Pubs. 2002 48p il (American disasters) lib bdg $23.93

Grades: 4 5 6 7   **974.7**

1. Factories 2. Clothing industry 3. Labor laws and legislation -- New York (State) -- New York -- History -- 20th century 4. Clothing factories -- New York (State) -- New York -- Safety measures -- History -- 20th century
ISBN 0-7660-1785-0
LC 2001-7667

Discusses the 1911 fire that killed 146 New York garment factory workers, the conditions that led up to it, and some of the legislation that came about to prevent the occurrence of similar disasters

"The short chapters are enlivened with period photographs, including a horrific view of the bodies of women who had leaped to their deaths to escape the flames. Although the text is easy to read, the horror is not sugarcoated." SLJ

Includes bibliographical references

Huey, Lois Miner

American archaeology uncovers the Dutch colonies. Marshall Cavendish Benchmark 2009 64p il map (American archaeology) lib bdg $21.95

Grades: 4 5 6 7   **974.7**

1. Dutch Americans 2. Excavations (Archeology) -- United States
ISBN 978-0-7614-4263-9 lib bdg; 0-7614-4263-4 lib bdg
LC 2008050187

This describes how archeologists have learned about the history of Dutch settlers in America

"The text is quite chatty in this attractive title. . . . An inviting design with clear type includes several paintings of the period by a modern artist as well as maps and photos of excavation sites." Booklist

Includes glossary and bibliographical references

Mann, Elizabeth

Statue of Liberty; a tale of two countries. with illustrations by Alan Witschonke. Mikaya Press 2011 47p il map (Wonders of the world) $22.95

Grades: 4 5 6 7   **974.7**

1. Artists 2. Authors 3. Lawyers 4. Sculptors 5. National monuments 6. Children's authors 7. Fairy tale writers 8. Members of Parliament
ISBN 978-1-931414-43-2; 1-931414-43-2

"The story of how Lady Liberty was conceived, constructed and bestowed makes a compelling tale. Pointing to the disparate long-term outcomes of the American and French revolutions to explain why the U.S. system of government became so admired in France, Mann takes the statue from Edouard Laboulaye's pie-in-the-sky proposal at a dinner party in 1865 to the massive opening ceremonies in 1886. . . . Witschonke supplements an array of period photos and prints with full-page or larger painted reconstructions of Bartholdi's studio and workshop, of the statue's piecemeal creation and finally of the Lady herself, properly copper colored as she initially was, presiding of New York's crowded harbor. As she still does." Kirkus

Includes bibliographical references

Marrin, Albert

★ **Flesh** & blood so cheap; the Triangle fire and its legacy. Alfred A. Knopf 2011 182p il map $19.99; lib bdg $22.99

Grades: 5 6 7 8   **974.7**

1. Fires 2. Italian Americans 3. Jews -- United States 4. Labor -- United States 5. Industrial safety

ISBN 978-0-375-86889-4; 0-375-86889-5; 978-0-375-96889-1 lib bdg; 0-375-96889-X lib bdg

LC 2010-21533

"Published to coincide with the centennial anniversary of the 1911 fire that erupted in the Triangle Shirtwaist Factory, this powerful chronicle examines the circumstances surrounding the disaster, which resulted in the deaths of 146 workers, mostly young Italian and Jewish women. . . . B&W photographs and illustrations reveal immigrant families' impoverished living environments, while testimonials describe the 'humiliating' work rules and unsafe conditions of factories like Triangle. . . . A concluding description of a Bangladeshi garment factory fire in 2010 offers contemporary parallels. Marrin's message that protecting human dignity is our shared responsibility is vitally resonant." Publ Wkly

Includes bibliographical references

Marsico, Katie

The **Triangle** Shirtwaist Factory fire; its legacy of labor rights. Marshall Cavendish Benchmark 2010 112p il (Perspectives on) lib bdg $27.95

Grades: 7 8 9 10   **974.7**

1. Fires

ISBN 978-0-7614-4027-7; 0-7614-4027-5

LC 2008-23267

"This well-written title examines many of the details preceding the 1911 disaster, the conditions that caused it, and the impact the incident continues to have on labor and businesses today. Historical accounts of the event, told through numerous direct quotes and shown in black-and-white photos of sweatshops and descriptions of tenement living conditions, reveal that poor labor laws and factory regulations were to blame. . . . Color photos and full-page sidebars provide additional information." SLJ

Includes bibliographical references

Murphy, Jim

★ The **giant** and how he humbugged America; by Jim Murphy. Scholastic Press 2012 112 p. (hardcover: alk. paper) $19.99

Grades: 5 6 7 8   **974.7**

1. Relics 2. Sculpture 3. Impostors and imposture 4. Cardiff giant 5. Forgery of antiquities -- New York (State) -- Cardiff

ISBN 0439691842; 9780439691840

LC 2011036798

In this book, "[Jim] Murphy traces the checkered career of the 'Cardiff Giant,' a 10-foot-long stone figure unearthed in 1869 in an upstate New York farmyard. The giant was a national sensation until its unmasking as a hoax a few months later. Almost from the outset, both educated and popular opinion was divided over whether the figure was a fossilized human or a carving, an ancient relic or a modern

'humbug.' Murphy shows how the controversy itself fueled the giant's notoriety." Booklist

Includes bibliographical references and index

Pellowski, Michael

The **terrorist** trial of the 1993 bombing of the World Trade Center; a headline court case. Enslow Pubs. 2003 112p il (Headline court cases) lib bdg $26.60

Grades: 6 7 8 9   **974.7**

1. Trials 2. Terrorism 3. World Trade Center Bombing, New York, N.Y., 1993 4. Trials (Terrorism) 5. Trials (Conspiracy) 6. Terrorism -- New York (State) -- New York 7. World Trade Center Bombing, New York, N.Y., 1993 8. Trials (Terrorism) -- United States -- New York (State) -- New York

ISBN 0-7660-2045-2

LC 2002-156033

Examines the trials of Mahmoud Abouhalima, Ramzi Yousef, Mohammad Salameh, Sheik Omar Abdel-Rahman, and others for their roles in the 1993 bombing of the World Trade Center

"A well-balanced look at the events leading up to, during, and after the 1993 bombing. . . . The text is clear and succinct." SLJ

Includes glossary and bibliographical references

Platt, Richard

New York City; an illustrated history of the Big Apple. illustrated by Manuela Cappon. Kingfisher 2010 45p il map (Through time) $16.99

Grades: 4 5 6 7   **974.7**

1. New York (N.Y.) -- History

ISBN 978-0-7534-6416-8; 0-7534-6416-0

This is a history of New York City from its Native American origins to the present.

"In this magnificently illustrated work, historical happenings and intriguing offshoots are showcased like stars on Broadway. . . . A wealth of information in an engaging format." Booklist

Schomp, Virginia

New York; [by] Virginia Schomp. 2nd ed.; Benchmark Books 2006 144p il map (Celebrate the states) lib bdg $39.93

Grades: 4 5 6 7   **974.7**

ISBN 978-0-7614-1738-5; 0-7614-1738-9

LC 2004-853

First published 1997

This book about New York covers "standard facts: geography, history, government, economy, landmarks, and regions. . . . [It is] attractively illustrated with clear maps, charts, and pie graphs. Photos and reproductions of original documents add to overall effectiveness. . . . Excellent additions for reports or general interest." SLJ

Includes bibliographical references

Slavicek, Louise Chipley

New York City's Central Park. Chelsea House Publishers 2009 120p il (Building America, then and now) lib bdg $35

Grades: 6 7 8 9   **974.7**
   1. Central Park (New York, N.Y.)
   ISBN 978-1-60413-044-7 lib bdg; 1-60413-044-X
lib bdg
                         LC 2008-25548
   This describes the history and impact of New York City's
Central Park
   "Photos, maps, and informative sidebars supplement the
densely detailed writing. American history buffs will find
[this volume] useful for doing research." Horn Book Guide
   Includes glossary and bibliographical references

Somervill, Barbara A.
   New York; by Barbara A. Somervill. Children's
Press 2008 144p il map (America the beautiful,
third series) lib bdg $38
Grades: 4 5 6 7   **974.7**
   ISBN 978-0-531-18565-0; 0-531-18565-6
                         LC 2006101742
   Describes the history, geography, ecology, famous peo-
ple, economy, cities, and sights of the state of New York.
   Includes glossary and bibliographical references

Talbott, Hudson
   ★ **River** of dreams; the story of the Hudson
River. G. P. Putnam's Sons 2009 un il map $17.99
Grades: 4 5 6 7   **974.7**
   1. Hudson River (N.Y. and N.J.)
   ISBN 978-0-399-24521-3; 0-399-24521-9
   Talbott offers a "compelling blend of political and natu-
ral history in this beautifully illustrated celebration of the
Hudson River. Combining delicate watercolor-and-pencil
illustrations with accessible text, the spreads move briskly
through the Hudson's River's history." Booklist

974.8   Pennsylvania

Koestler-Grack, Rachel A.
   The **Johnstown** flood of 1889. Chelsea House
2008 101p il (Great historic disasters) lib bdg $35
Grades: 6 7 8 9   **974.8**
   1. Floods
   ISBN 978-0-7910-9763-2 lib bdg; 0-7910-9763-3
lib bdg
                         LC 2008-4894
   This is a history of the flood of May 31, 1889 in
Johnstown Pennsylvania
   "Combining first-hand accounts, photographs, and other
primary sources with a detailed and lively text, [this] fact-
packed [resource offers] much to both report writers and history buffs." Horn Book Guide
   Includes glossary and bibliographical references

Peters, Stephen
   Pennsylvania; by Stephen Peters and Joyce Hart.
2nd ed.; Marshall Cavendish Benchmark 2009 144p
il map (Celebrate the states) lib bdg $42.79
Grades: 4 5 6 7   **974.8**
   ISBN 978-0-7614-3403-0; 0-7614-3403-8
                         LC 2008-8032

   First published 2000
   "Provides comprehensive information on the geography,
history, wildlife, governmental structure, economy, cultural
diversity, peoples, religion, and landmarks of Pennsylvania." Publisher's note
   Includes bibliographical references

Somervill, Barbara A.
   Pennsylvania. Children's Press 2009 144p il
map (America the beautiful, third series) lib bdg $39
Grades: 4 5 6 7   **974.8**
   ISBN 978-0-531-18588-9; 0-531-18588-5
                         LC 2007031121
   Presents an introduction to the geography, natural re-
sources, history, economy, important sites, daily life, and
people of Pennsylvania.
   Includes glossary and bibliographical references

974.9   New Jersey

Doak, Robin S.
   New Jersey 1609-1776; y. [by] Robin Doak with
Brendan McConville. National Geographic 2005
109p il map (Voices from colonial America) $21.95;
lib bdg $32.90
Grades: 5 6 7 8   **974.9**
   1. New Jersey -- History
   ISBN 978-0-7922-6385-2; 0-7922-6385-5; 978-0-
7922-6680-8 lib bdg; 0-7922-6680-3 lib bdg
                         LC 2004-26242
   "This book gives detailed descriptions of family life
and working in a Colonial village and the fight for independence. It also includes information about the Native people,
early settlers, and first developments. . . . Paintings, maps,
woodcuts, portraits, and reproductions accompany the well-
written text. . . . An excellent resource." SLJ
   Includes bibliographical references

Kent, Deborah
   New Jersey; by Deborah Kent. Children's Press
2008 144p il map (America the beautiful, third se-
ries) lib bdg $38
Grades: 4 5 6 7   **974.9**
   ISBN 978-0-531-18564-3; 0-531-18564-8
                         LC 2006100058
   Describes the history, geography, ecology, people, econ-
omy, cities, and sights of the state of New Jersey.
   Includes glossary and bibliographical references

Moragne, Wendy
   New Jersey; by Wendy Moragne and Tamra B.
Orr. 2nd ed.; Marshall Cavendish Benchmark 2009
144p il map (Celebrate the states) lib bdg $39.93
Grades: 4 5 6 7   **974.9**
   ISBN 978-0-7614-3006-3; 0-7614-3006-7
                         LC 2007-38642
   First published 2000
   "Provides comprehensive information on the geography,
history, wildlife, governmental structure, economy, cultural

diversity, peoples, religion, and landmarks of New Jersey."
Publisher's note

Includes bibliographical references

975.1 Delaware

Price, Karen

Delaware, 1638-1776; [by] Karen Hossell, with Karin Wulf, consultant. National Geographic Society 2006 109p il map (Voices from colonial America) $21.95; lib bdg $32.90

Grades: 5 6 7 8   **975.1**

1. Delaware -- History

ISBN 978-0-7922-6408-8; 0-7922-6408-8; 978-0-7922-6864-2 lib bdg; 0-7922-6864-4 lib bdg

LC 2006-13444

"Discusses the Native American massacre of the first European settlers in the Delaware region, and follows the events that helped the area develop into a thriving colony as it changed from Swedish to Dutch to British control." Publisher's note

Includes bibliographical references

Schuman, Michael

Delaware; by Michael Schuman and Marlee Richards. 2nd ed.; Marshall Cavendish Benchmark 2009 144p il map (Celebrate the states) lib bdg $42.79

Grades: 4 5 6 7   **975.1**

ISBN 978-0-7614-3399-6; 0-7614-3399-6

LC 2008-5369

First published 2000

"Provides comprehensive information on the geography, history, wildlife, governmental structure, economy, cultural diversity, peoples, religion, and landmarks of Delaware." Publisher's note

Includes bibliographical references

975.2 Maryland

Blashfield, Jean F.

Maryland; by Jean F. Blashfield. Children's Press 2008 144p il map (America the beautiful, third series) lib bdg $38

Grades: 5 6 7 8   **975.2**

ISBN 978-0-531-18576-6; 0-531-18576-1

LC 2007-12699

Describes the history, geography, ecology, people, economy, cities, and sights of the state of Maryland.

Includes glossary and bibliographical references

Doak, Robin S.

Maryland, 1634-1776. National Geographic 2007 105p il map (Voices from colonial America) $21.95; lib bdg $32.90

Grades: 5 6 7 8   **975.2**

1. Maryland -- History

ISBN 978-1-4263-0143-8; 1-4263-0143-x; 978-1-4263-0144-5 lib bdg; 1-4263-0144-8 lib bdg

LC 2007-27886

Offers "thorough, well-documented information about the struggles and successes of early colonial settlers and settlements. . . . Many reproductions of period illustrations and some photographs of period documents and maps with relevant captions are included." Horn Book Guide

Includes bibliographical references

Moore, Wes

Discovering Wes Moore; Wes Moore. Delacorte Press 2012 160 p. (hardcover) $15.99

Grades: 7 8 9 10 11 12   **975.2**

1. Family life 2. Blacks -- Biography 3. Youth 4. African American men -- Biography 5. Soldiers -- United States -- Biography 6. Criminals -- Maryland -- Baltimore -- Biography 7. African Americans -- Maryland -- Baltimore -- Social conditions -- 20th century 8. African Americans -- Bronx (New York, N.Y.) -- Social conditions -- 20th century

ISBN 0385741677; 9780375986703; 9780375990182; 9780385741675

LC 2011049135

Author Wes Moore describes his experiences growing up. "After receiving poor grades and falling in with a bad crowd, his family pooled their limited finances to send him to Valley Forge Military Academy, where he found positive role models and became a Corps commander and star athlete. After earning an undergraduate degree, Wes attended Oxford as a Rhodes Scholar. When the author read about the conviction of another Wes Moore for armed robbery and killing a police officer, he wanted to find out how two youths . . . could take such divergent paths." (Kirkus)

Pietrzyk, Leslie

Maryland; by Leslie Rauth and Martha Kneib. 2nd ed.; Marshall Cavendish Benchmark 2008 144p il map (Celebrate the states) lib bdg $39.93

Grades: 4 5 6 7   **975.2**

ISBN 978-0-7614-3004-9; 0-7614-3004-0

LC 2007-29497

First published 2000

"Provides comprehensive information on the geography, history, wildlife, governmental structure, economy, cultural diversity, peoples, religion, and landmarks of Maryland." Publisher's note

Includes bibliographical references

975.3 District of Columbia (Washington)

Elish, Dan

Washington, D.C. by Dan Elish. 2nd ed.; Marshall Cavendish Benchmark 2007 144p il map (Celebrate the states) lib bdg $39.93

Grades: 4 5 6 7   **975.3**

ISBN 978-0-7614-2352-2; 0-7614-2352-4

LC 2006-13838

First published 1998

"Provides comprehensive information on the geography, history, wildlife, governmental structure, economy, cultural diversity, peoples, religion, and landmarks of Washington, D.C." Publisher's note

Includes bibliographical references

Kent, Deborah

Washington, D.C. Children's Press 2010 144p il map (America the beautiful, third series) lib bdg $39

Grades: 4 5 6 7   **975.3**

ISBN 978-0-531-18593-3; 0-531-18593-1

LC 2008019546

Discusses the geography, history, people, government, economy, and recreation of Washington, D.C.

Includes glossary and bibliographical references

★ **Our** White House; looking in, looking out. created by The National Children's Book and Literacy Alliance; introduction by David McCullough. Candlewick Press 2008 241p il $29.99

Grades: 5 6 7 8   **975.3**

1. Short stories -- Collections 2. Presidents -- United States -- Family

ISBN 0-7636-2067-X; 978-0-7636-2067-7

This is a collection of essays, personal accounts, historical fiction, and poetry devoted to the history of the White House.

"The White House is the focus of this handsome, large-format compendium of writings, both factual and fictional, and illustrations. . . . Poems and essays, stories and memoirs—all combine to create a mosaic of impressions of the house's residents and visitors and of the important events that occurred there. . . . The often-spectacular, beautifully reproduced on glossy paper, is particularly striking." Booklist

975.4   West Virginia

Hoffman, Nancy

West Virginia; [by] Nancy Hoffman and Joyce Hart. 2nd ed.; Marshall Cavendish Benchmark 2007 144p il map (Celebrate the states) lib bdg $39.93

Grades: 4 5 6 7   **975.4**

ISBN 978-0-7614-2562-5; 0-7614-2562-4

LC 2006-29393

First published 1999

Relates the history and describes the geographic features, places of interest, government, industry, environmental concerns, and life of the people of West Virginia.

Includes bibliographical references

975.5   Virginia

Kent, Deborah

Virginia. Children's Press 2008 144p il map (America the beautiful, third series) lib bdg $39

Grades: 4 5 6 7   **975.5**

ISBN 978-0-531-18581-0; 0-531-18581-8

LC 2007028463

Presents an introduction to the geography, natural resources, history, economy, important sites, daily life, and people of Virginia.

Includes glossary and bibliographical references

Pobst, Sandy

Virginia, 1607-1776; [by] Sandy Pobst with Kevin D. Roberts, consultant. National Geographic Society 2005 109p il map (Voices from colonial America) $21.95; lib bdg $32.90

Grades: 5 6 7 8   **975.5**

1. Virginia -- History

ISBN 978-0-7922-6388-3; 0-7922-6388-X; 978-0-7922-6771-3 lib bdg; 0-7922-6771-0 lib bdg

LC 2005-8885

"This title discusses the colony's founding, life on the Tidewater plantations, the struggles to survive, and the desire for independence. Full of period maps; portraits; photographs; and first-person accounts from masters and slaves, explorers, Native Americans, servants, and other residents, this is narrative nonfiction at its best. . . . An excellent resource." SLJ

Includes bibliographical references

975.6   North Carolina

Cannavale, Matthew C.

North Carolina, 1524-1776; by Matthew C. Cannavale; with Patrick Griffith, consultant. National Geographic Society 2007 109p il map (Voices from colonial America) $21.95; lib bdg $32.90

Grades: 5 6 7 8   **975.6**

1. North Carolina -- History

ISBN 978-1-4263-0032-5; 1-4263-0032-8; 978-1-4263-0033-2 lib bdg; 1-4263-0033-6 lib bdg

LC 2006-36004

A history of colonial North Carolina.

Includes bibliographical references

Heinrichs, Ann

North Carolina. Children's Press 2009 144p il map (America the beautiful, third series) lib bdg $39

Grades: 4 5 6 7   **975.6**

ISBN 978-0-531-18566-7; 0-531-18566-4

LC 2007039773

Presents an introduction to the geography, natural resources, history, economy, important sites, daily life, and people of North Carolina.

Includes glossary and bibliographical references

Miller, Lee

Roanoke; the mystery of the Lost Colony. Scholastic Nonfiction 2007 112p il map $18.99

Grades: 4 5 6 7   **975.6**

1. Roanoke Island (N.C.) -- History

ISBN 0-439-71266-1; 978-0-439-71266-8

LC 2005-51820

"Miller, author of Roanoke: solving the mystery of the Lost Colony (2001), here reprises for a young audience her historical theory that a certain man sabotaged the expedition eventually known as the Lost Colony. . . . Miller does an exceptional job of preseneting the Native American culture and viewpoint. . . . This handsomely designed book features one or two illustrations on each spread, many in color, including reproductions or period drawings, paintings, and maps, as well as modern photos of sites and wildlife." Booklist
Includes bibliographical references

Reed, Jennifer
   Cape Hatteras National Seashore; adventure, explore, discover. [by] Jennifer Reed. MyReportLinks.com Books 2008 128p il map (America's national parks) lib bdg $33.27
Grades: 5 6 7 8   **975.6**
   1. Cape Hatteras National Seashore (N.C.) 2. National parks and reserves -- United States
   ISBN 978-1-59845-086-6 lib bdg; 1-59845-086-7 lib bdg
                                              LC 2006102321
   This "informative, well-written book contains a physical description of the park; a summary of its history including the Native peoples of the area; activities such as hiking trails, campsites, and visitor centers; information about the park's plants, animals, and weather; full-color photographs; and numerous approved links available through the publisher's Web page. . . . Thorough, useful, and appealing, this . . . is a great update for collections." SLJ
   Includes glossary and bibliographical references

Shirley, David
   North Carolina; by David Shirley and Joyce Hart. 2nd ed.; Marshall Cavendish Benchmark 2010 144p il map (Celebrate the states) lib bdg $43.79
Grades: 5 6 7 8   **975.6**
   ISBN 978-0-7614-4729-0; 0-7614-4729-6
                                              LC 2009007139
   First published 2001
   This offers information on the geography, history, wildlife, governmental structure, economy, cultural diversity, peoples, religion, and landmarks of North Carolina.
   Includes bibliographical references

975.7   South Carolina

Doak, Robin S.
   South Carolina, 1540-1776; by Robin Doak with Robert Olwell. National Geographic Society 2007 109p il map (Voices from colonial America) $21.95; lib bdg $32.90
Grades: 5 6 7 8   **975.7**
   1. South Carolina -- History
   ISBN 978-1-4263-0066-0; 1-4263-0066-2; 978-1-4263-0067-7 lib bdg; 1-4263-0067-0 lib bdg
                                              LC 2007-3120
   A history of South Carolina from its beginning as an English colony to 1788 when it became the eighth state.

Offers "thorough, well-documented information about the struggles and successes of early colonial settlers and settlements. . . . Many reproductions of period illustrations and some photographs of period documents and maps with relevant captions are included" Horn Book Guide
Includes bibliographical references

Hoffman, Nancy
   South Carolina; by Nancy Hoffman and Joyce Hart. 2nd ed.; Marshall Cavendish Benchmark 2010 144p il map (Celebrate the states) lib bdg $42.79
Grades: 5 6 7 8   **975.7**
   ISBN 978-0-7614-4034-5; 0-7614-4034-8
                                              LC 2008038266
   First published 2001
   This offers information on the geography, history, wildlife, governmental structure, economy, cultural diversity, peoples, religion, and landmarks of South Carolina.
   Includes bibliographical references

Somervill, Barbara A.
   South Carolina. Children's Press 2009 144p il map (America the beautiful, third series) lib bdg $39
Grades: 4 5 6 7   **975.7**
   ISBN 978-0-531-18591-9; 0-531-18591-5
                                              LC 2007031030
   Presents an introduction to the geography, natural resources, history, economy, important sites, daily life, and people of South Carolina.
   Includes glossary and bibliographical references

975.8   Georgia

Doak, Robin S.
   Georgia, 1521-1776. National Geographic Society 2006 109p il map (Voices from colonial America) $21.95; lib bdg $32.90
Grades: 5 6 7 8   **975.8**
   1. Georgia -- History
   ISBN 978-0-7922-6389-0; 0-7922-6389-8; 978-0-7922-6858-1 lib bdg; 0-7922-6858-X lib bdg
                                              LC 2005-22141
   Provides a history of Georgia from the arrival of European explorers in the sixteenth century to its becoming a state in 1788.
   Includes bibliographical references

Otfinoski, Steven
   Georgia; 2nd ed.; Marshall Cavendish Benchmark 2010 144p il map (Celebrate the states) lib bdg $42.79
Grades: 5 6 7 8   **975.8**
   ISBN 978-0-7614-4031-4; 0-7614-4031-3
                                              LC 2008041711
   First published 2001
   This offers information on the geography, history, wildlife, governmental structure, economy, cultural diversity, peoples, religion, and landmarks of Georgia.
   Includes bibliographical references

Prentzas, G. S.

Georgia; by G.S. Prentzas. Children's Press 2008 144p il map (America the beautiful, third series) lib bdg $38

Grades: 4 5 6 7   **975.8**

ISBN 978-0-531-18572-8; 0-531-18572-9

LC 2007-8256

Describes the history, geography, ecology, people, economy, cities, and sights of the state of Georgia.

Includes glossary and bibliographical references

975.9   Florida

Cannavale, Matthew C.

Florida, 1513-1821; [by] Matthew C. Cannavale with Robert Olwell, consultant. National Geographic 2006 109p il map (Voices from colonial America) $21.95; lib bdg $32.90

Grades: 5 6 7 8   **975.9**

1. Florida -- History

ISBN 978-0-7922-6409-5; 0-7922-6409-6; 978-0-7922-6866-6 lib bdg; 0-7922-6866-0 lib bdg

LC 2006-20505

Offers "thorough, well-documented information about the struggles and successes of early nonnative settlers [in Florida]. . . . Many reproductions of period illustrations (both color and sepia) and some photos of archival documents and maps enhance the text." Horn Book Guide

Includes bibliographical references

Hart, Joyce

Florida; [by] Perry Chang and Joyce Hart. 2nd ed.; Marshall Cavendish Benchmark 2007 144p il map (Celebrate the states) lib bdg $39.93

Grades: 4 5 6 7   **975.9**

ISBN 978-0-7614-2348-5; 0-7614-2348-6

LC 2006-8174

First published 1998

"Provides comprehensive information on the geography, history, wildlife, governmental structure, economy, cultural diversity, peoples, religion, and landmarks of Florida." Publisher's note

Includes bibliographical references

Jankowski, Susan

Everglades National Park; adventure, explore, discover. [by] Susan Jankowski. MyReportLinks. com Books 2009 128p il map (America's national parks) lib bdg $33.27

Grades: 5 6 7 8   **975.9**

1. Everglades National Park (Fla.) 2. National parks and reserves -- United States

ISBN 978-1-59845-091-0 lib bdg; 1-59845-091-3 lib bdg

LC 2007-38262

This "informative, well-written book contains a physical description of the park; a summary of its history including the Native peoples of the area; activities such as hiking trails, campsites, and visitor centers; information about the park's plants, animals, and weather; full-color photographs;

and numerous approved links available through the publisher's Web page. . . . Thorough, useful, and appealing, this . . . is a great update for collections." SLJ

Includes glossary and bibliographical references

Orr, Tamra

Florida; by Tamra B. Orr. Children's Press 2008 144p il map (America the beautiful, third series) lib bdg $38

Grades: 4 5 6 7   **975.9**

ISBN 0-531-18558-3; 978-0-531-18558-2

LC 2006100102

Describes the history, geography, ecology, people, economy, cities, and sights of the state of Florida.

Includes glossary and bibliographical references

Turner, Glennette Tilley

★ **Fort** Mose; and the story of the man who built the first free black settlement in Colonial America. Abrams Books for Young Readers 2010 42p il map $18.95

Grades: 5 6 7 8   **975.9**

1. Army officers 2. Slavery -- United States 3. African Americans -- History 4. Fugitive slaves

ISBN 978-0-8109-4056-7; 0-8109-4056-6

LC 2009-52205

"In the 18th century, some Africans escaped slavery in England's southern colonies to find freedom in the Spanish colony of Florida. As a leader of St. Augustine's community, African-born Francisco Menendez helped establish Fort Mose, the first free black community on North American soil. Turner does an excellent job of explaining how the residents of Fort Mose probably blended African, English, and Spanish traditions to create a unique—and uniquely American—culture." SLJ

Includes glossary and bibliographical references

975.900   Seminole Indians

Sanford, William R.

Seminole chief Osceola; by William R. Sanford. Enslow Publishers 2013 48 p. (library) $21.26

Grades: 6 7 8 9   **975.900**

1. Native Americans -- United States 2. Seminole Indians -- Kings and rulers -- Biography

ISBN 0766041174; 9780766041172

LC 2011050996

This book is part of the Native American Chiefs and Warriors series and looks at Seminole Chief Osceola. "Osceola led his people, the Seminoles, in one of the longest struggles of the Indian Wars. In a game of hide and seek in the Florida wetlands, the Seminoles struck deadly blows to the U.S. Army. Osceoloa was never defeated, but was finally double-crossed and captured." (Publisher's note)

Includes bibliographical references and index.

976.1   Alabama

Parks, Rosa

★ **Rosa** Parks: my story; by Rosa Parks with Jim Haskins. Dial Bks. 1992 192p il $17.99; pa $6.99
Grades: 5 6 7 8   **976.1**
  1. African American women 2. Civil rights activists 3. African Americans -- Civil rights 4. African American women -- Biography
  ISBN 0-8037-0673-1; 0-14-130120-1 pa
                                                    LC 89-1124
  Rosa Parks describes her early life and experiences with race discrimination, and her participation in the Montgomery bus boycott and the civil rights movement
  "A remarkable story, a record of quiet bravery and modesty, a document of social significance, a taut drama told with candor." Bull Cent Child Books

Shirley, David

  Alabama; by David Shirley and Joyce Hart. 2nd ed.; Marshall Cavendish Benchmark 2009 144p il map (Celebrate the states) lib bdg $39.93
Grades: 4 5 6 7   **976.1**
  ISBN 978-0-7614-3397-2; 0-7614-3397-X
                                                 LC 2008-4601
  First published 2000
  "Provides comprehensive information on the geography, history, wildlife, governmental structure, economy, cultural diversity, peoples, religion, and landmarks of Alabama." Publisher's note
  Includes bibliographical references

Somervill, Barbara A.

  Alabama; by Barbara A. Somervill. Children's Press 2008 144p il map (America the beautiful, third series) lib bdg $38
Grades: 4 5 6 7   **976.1**
  ISBN 978-0-531-18556-8; 0-531-18556-7
                                                LC 2006-37697
  Describes the history, geography, ecology, people, economy, cities, and sights of the state of Alabama.
  Includes glossary and bibliographical references

976.2   Mississippi

Dell, Pamela

  Mississippi. Children's Press 2008 144p il map (America the beautiful, third series) lib bdg $39
Grades: 4 5 6 7   **976.2**
  ISBN 978-0-531-18563-6; 0-531-18563-X
                                               LC 2006101965
  Presents an introduction to the geography, natural resources, history, economy, important sites, daily life, and people of Mississippi.
  Includes glossary and bibliographical references

Ribeiro, Myra

  The **assassination** of Medgar Evers. Rosen Pub. Group 2002 64p il (Library of political assassinations) $26.50

Grades: 5 6 7 8   **976.2**
  1. Civil rights activists 2. African Americans -- Civil rights 3. African American civil rights workers -- Mississippi -- Jackson -- Biography
  ISBN 0-8239-3544-2
                                                 LC 2001-2389
  The author "does a good job of introducing the inspiring leader and the cause he fought for." Booklist
  Includes glossary and bibliographical references

Shirley, David

  Mississippi; [by] David Shirley and Patricia K. Kummer. Marshall Cavendish Benchmark 2008 144p il map (Celebrate the states) lib bdg $39.93
Grades: 4 5 6 7   **976.2**
  ISBN 978-0-7614-2717-9; 0-7614-2717-1
                                                 LC 2007-7868
  First published 1999
  "Provides comprehensive information on the geography, history, wildlife, governmental structure, economy, cultural diversity, peoples, religion, and landmarks of Mississippi." Publisher's note
  Includes bibliographical references

976.3   Louisiana

Lassieur, Allison

  Louisiana; by Allison Lassieur. Children's Press 2008 144p il map (America the beautiful, third series) lib bdg $38
Grades: 4 5 6 7   **976.3**
  ISBN 978-0-531-18560-5; 0-531-18560-5
                                                  LC 2007-300
  Describes the history, geography, ecology, people, economy, cities, and sights of the state of Louisiana.
  Includes glossary and bibliographical references

Worth, Richard

  Louisiana, 1682-1803. National Geographic Society 2005 109p il map (Voices from colonial America) $21.95; lib bdg $32.90
Grades: 5 6 7 8   **976.3**
  ISBN 978-0-7922-6544-3; 0-7922-6544-0; 978-0-7922-6850-5 lib bdg; 0-7922-6850-4 lib bdg
                                                LC 2005-16225
  This "history of Louisiana begins in 1682 when Sieur de La Salle claimed the region for France. After that time, the region was governed under several different flags, including France, Spain, and Great Britain. . . . Thomas Jefferson purchased the land for the United States in 1803." Publisher's note
  Includes bibliographical references

976.4   Texas

Chemerka, William R.

  Juan Seguin; Tejano leader. William R. Chemerka; illustrations by Don Collins. Bright Sky Press 2012 64 p. ill. $16.95

Grades: 3 4 5 6   **976.4**
1. Texas -- History 2. Political activists 3. Soldiers --
Texas -- Biography 4. Politicians -- Texas -- Biography
ISBN 1933979798; 9781933979793
LC 2011052720

This book is a biography of Texan Juan Seguin by William R. Chemerka. Despite "having been forced to flee to Mexico and die in obscurity, Tejano Juan Seguin is recognised as a Texas hero. From his family's early support of settlers such as Stephen F. Austin to his years in the Texas Senate and as mayor of Bexar, this biography celebrates the life of Juan Seguin and his . . . efforts in securing Texas' independence." (WorldCat)

Green, Carl R.
Sam Houston; courageous Texas hero. by William R. Sanford and Carl R. Green. Enslow Publishers 2013 48 p. ill., map (library) $21.26; (paperback) $7.95
Grades: 5 6 7 8   **976.4**
1. Governors -- Texas -- Biography 2. Legislators --
United States -- Biography
ISBN 0766040097; 9780766040090; 9781464400926
LC 2011051265

This book, part of the Courageous Heroes of the American West series, looks at Sam Houston. "One of the founders of Texas, Sam Houston served the state as governor and senator—but he is most remembered as an American hero" for defeating the Mexican army. "Surprising the Mexican troops with their bold attack, . . . the fiery Texans rallied to an overwhelming victory, claiming their independence." (Publisher's note)

Includes bibliographical references (p. 47) and index.

Haley, James L.
Stephen F. Austin and the founding of Texas. PowerPlus Bks. 2003 112p il map (Library of American lives and times) lib bdg $31.95 **976.4**
1. Pioneers 2. Frontier and pioneer life -- Texas
ISBN 0-8239-5738-1
LC 2001-4955

Surveys the life of Stephen Austin, an American pioneer, who later became one of the founders of Texas

"Clear and engaging.... The good-quality illustrations are almost all reproductions of period paintings, maps, and documents." SLJ

Includes glossary and bibliographical references

Levy, Janey
The **Alamo**; a primary source history of the legendary Texas mission. Rosen Central Primary Source 2003 64p il maps (Primary sources in American history) lib bdg $29.25
Grades: 7 8 9 10   **976.4**
ISBN 0-8239-3681-3
LC 2002-2368

A collection of primary source materials highlights the story behind the Alamo and its place in the history of San Antonio, Texas

This "will be extremely effective when introducing students to primary source material." Libr Media Connect

Includes bibliographical references

McNeese, Tim
The **Alamo**. Chelsea House 2003 136p il map (Sieges that changed the world) lib bdg $22.95
Grades: 5 6 7 8   **976.4**
ISBN 0-7910-7101-4
LC 2002-12914

Describes the historical background, events, and aftermath of the 1836 attack on the Alamo, in which Jim Bowie and Davy Crockett were among the many Texans killed or captured by Santa Ana's troops

The author presents "an excellent overview of Texas history in the first half of the book and details the two-week siege in the second. . . . A well-written, well-researched chronicle." SLJ

Includes bibliographical references

Newton, Michael
★ The **Texas** Rangers. Chelsea House Publishers 2011 128p il (Law enforcement agencies) lib bdg $35
Grades: 6 7 8 9   **976.4**
1. Law enforcement
ISBN 978-1-60413-626-5; 1-60413-626-X

"Solidly and comprehensively researched. . . . In The Texas Rangers, a group that has long excited the country's imagination gets a full treatment, including its appearances on screen. An attractive design, plenty of photos, and solid back matter complete [the] package. Extremely useful for students and appealing for browsers." Booklist

Includes bibliographical references

Somervill, Barbara A.
Texas. Children's Press 2009 144p il map (America the beautiful, third series) lib bdg $39
Grades: 4 5 6 7   **976.4**
ISBN 978-0-531-18580-3; 0-531-18580-X
LC 2007017787

Presents an introduction to the geography, natural resources, history, economy, important sites, daily life, and people of Texas.

Includes glossary and bibliographical references

Teitelbaum, Michael
Texas, 1527-1836. National Geographic Society 2005 109p il map (Voices from colonial America) $21.95; lib bdg $32.90
Grades: 5 6 7 8   **976.4**
ISBN 978-0-7922-6387-6; 0-7922-6387-1; 978-0-7922-6682-2 lib bdg; 0-7922-6682-X lib bdg
LC 2005-11450

"Presents the history of Texas, including life in Spanish Texas, the arrival of American settlers, and The Texas Republic and statehood." Publisher's note

Includes bibliographical references

Wade, Mary Dodson
Henrietta King, la patrona; by Mary Dodson Wade; illustrated by Bill Farnsworth. Bright Sky Press 2012 23 p $16.95
Grades: 4 5 6 7   **976.4**
1. Women ranchers -- Biography 2. Women

philanthropists -- Biography 3. King Ranch (Tex.) 4. Ranchers -- Texas -- Biography 5. Women ranchers -- Texas -- Biography 6. Philanthropists -- Texas -- Biography 7. Women philanthropists -- Texas -- Biography
ISBN 1933979631; 9781933979632

LC 2011052721

This book by Mary Dodson Wade "examines the . . . life of one of Texas's foremost frontier women and philanthropists, Henrietta Maria Morse Chamberlain King. . . . Henrietta accompanied her missionary father on his travels and later settled with her husband Richard King in the untamed frontiers of the south Texas gulf coast. . . . Under her stewardship, the family ranch went from . . . $500,000 in debt at her husband's death to a debt-free enterprise of more than one million acres." (Publisher's note)

Walker, Paul Robert

Remember the Alamo; Texians, Tejanos, and Mexicans tell their stories. by Paul Robert Walker. National Geographic 2007 61p il map $17.95; lib bdg $27.90

Grades: 5 6 7 8   976.4

1. Texas -- History 2. Alamo (San Antonio, Tex.)
ISBN 978-1-4263-0010-3; 978-1-4263-0011-0 lib bdg
LC 2006034497

"Opening with clear context about why tensions between Texas residents and the Mexican government were brought to a head, the book then chronicles events directly leading to the siege of the Alamo and its immediate aftermath, following up with an epilogue on the decisive battle of San Jacinto 10 months later. Bringing the history to life is a healthy selection of dramatic, modern paintings along with plenty of archival drawings, maps, and old photos." Booklist
Includes bibliographical references

Warrick, Karen Clemens

Alamo; victory or death on the Texas frontier. Enslow Publishers 2008 128p il map (America's living history) lib bdg $31.93

Grades: 5 6 7 8   976.4

1. Texas -- History 2. Alamo (San Antonio, Tex.)
ISBN 978-0-7660-2937-8; 0-7660-2937-9
LC 2007038458

"Archival photographs, reproductions, maps, and sidebars combine with vivid [text] to provide [a] comprehensive [introduction] to [the siege and battle of the Alamo]. . . . [This] engaging [volume] vividly [brings its] time [period] to life." Horn Book Guide
Includes glossary and bibliographical references

Worth, Richard

The **Texas** war of independence: the 1800s; by Richard Worth. Marshall Cavendish Benchmark 2009 79p il map (Hispanic America) lib bdg $23.95

Grades: 6 7 8 9   976.4

1. Mexican Americans 2. Mexican War, 1846-1848
ISBN 978-0-7614-2934-0
LC 2007029478

This "provides a solid overview of these pivotal events in Hispanic American history. Illustrated throughout with maps and archival images." Booklist
Includes glossary and bibliographical references

976.6   Oklahoma

Baldwin, Guy

Oklahoma; by Guy Baldwin and Joyce Hart. 2nd ed.; Marshall Cavendish Benchmark 2009 144p il map (Celebrate the states) lib bdg $42.79

Grades: 5 6 7 8   976.6

ISBN 978-0-7614-4032-1; 0-7614-4032-1
LC 2008044261

First published 2001

This offers information on the geography, history, wildlife, governmental structure, economy, cultural diversity, peoples, religion, and landmarks of Oklahoma.
Includes bibliographical references

Orr, Tamra

Oklahoma; by Tamra B. Orr. Children's Press 2008 144p il map (America the beautiful, third series) lib bdg $38

Grades: 4 5 6 7   976.6

ISBN 978-0-531-18567-4; 0-531-18567-2
LC 2007-4774

Describes the history, geography, ecology, people, economy, cities and sights of the state of Oklahoma.
Includes glossary and bibliographical references

976.7   Arkansas

Altman, Linda Jacobs

Arkansas; [by] Linda Jacobs Altman, Ettagale Blauer, and Jason Laure. 2nd ed.; Marshall Cavendish Benchmark 2009 144p il map (Celebrate the states) lib bdg $42.79

Grades: 4 5 6 7   976.7

ISBN 978-0-7614-3001-8; 0-7614-3001-6
First published 2000

"Provides comprehensive information on the geography, history, wildlife, governmental structure, economy, cultural diversity, peoples, religion, and landmarks of Arkansas." Publisher's note
Includes bibliographical references

976.8   Tennessee

Barrett, Tracy

Tennessee; by Tracy Barrett. 2nd ed.; Marshall Cavendish Benchmark 2006 144p il map (Celebrate the states) lib bdg $39.93

Grades: 4 5 6 7   976.8

ISBN 978-0-7614-2151-1; 0-7614-2151-3
LC 2005-24055

First published 1998

"Provides comprehensive information on the geography, history, wildlife, governmental structure, economy, cultural diversity, peoples, religion, and landmarks of Tennessee." Publisher's note

Includes bibliographical references

Graham, Amy

Great Smoky Mountains National Park; adventure, explore, discover. [by] Amy Graham. MyReportLinks.com Books 2009 128p il map (America's national parks) lib bdg $33.27

Grades: 5 6 7 8   **976.8**

   1. Great Smoky Mountains National Park (N.C. and Tenn.) 2. National parks and reserves -- United States ISBN 978-1-59845-093-4 lib bdg; 1-59845-093-X lib bdg

                 LC 2007-13456

This "informative, well-written book contains a physical description of the park; a summary of its history including the Native peoples of the area; activities such as hiking trails, campsites, and visitor centers; information about the park's plants, animals, and weather; full-color photographs; and numerous approved links available through the publisher's Web page. . . . Thorough, useful, and appealing, this . . . is a great update for collections." SLJ

Includes glossary and bibliographical references

Green, Carl R.

Davy Crockett; courageous hero of the Alamo. by William R. Sanford and Carl R. Green. Rev. ed. Enslow Publishers 2013 48 p. col. ill., map (library) $21.26; (paperback) $7.95

Grades: 5 6 7 8   **976.8**

   1. Alamo (San Antonio, Tex.) -- History -- Siege, 1836 2. Pioneers -- Tennessee -- Biography 3. Legislators -- United States -- Biography ISBN 0766040054; 9780766040052; 9781464400865

                 LC 2011037749

This book by William Sanford is part of the Courageous Heroes of the American West series and focuses on Davy Crockett. "The courageous Texans chose to defend the fort in San Antonio against more than two thousands Mexican soldiers. . . . Although his brave deeds at the Alamo made him legendary, Crockett had already gained fame as a hunter, soldier, and U.S. Congressman." (Publisher's note)

Includes bibliographical references.

Somervill, Barbara A.

Tennessee. Children's Press/Scholastic 2010 144p il map (America the beautiful, third series) lib bdg $39

                       976.8

   ISBN 978-0-531-18504-9; 0-531-18504-4

                 LC 2008000505

Presents an introduction to the geography, natural resources, history, economy, important sites, daily life, and people of Tennessee.

Includes glossary and bibliographical references

976.9   Kentucky

Barrett, Tracy

Kentucky; [by] Tracy Barrett. 2nd ed.; Marshall Cavendish Benchmark 2008 144p il map (Celebrate the states) lib bdg $39.93

Grades: 4 5 6 7   **976.9**

   ISBN 978-0-7614-2715-5; 0-7614-2715-5

                 LC 2007-6388

   First published 1999

"Provides comprehensive information on the geography, history, wildlife, governmental structure, economy, cultural diversity, peoples, religion, and landmarks of Kentucky." Publisher's note

Includes bibliographical references

Green, Carl R.

Daniel Boone; courageous frontiersman. by William R. Sanford and Carl R. Green. Enslow Publishers 2013 48 p. col. ill., map (library) $21.26; (paperback) $7.95

Grades: 5 6 7 8   **976.9**

   1. Frontier and pioneer life -- United States 2. Pioneers -- Kentucky -- Biography 3. Frontier and pioneer life -- Kentucky ISBN 076604002X; 9780766040021; 9781464400858; 9781464509926; 9781464609923

                 LC 2011037736

This book by William Sanford is part of the Courageous Heroes of the American West series and focuses on Daniel Boone. "Through the untamed wilderness, Daniel Boone marched forward. He was leading a group of workers to carve out the Wilderness Road. Over hills, through dense forests, along stony paths, and fending off American Indian attacks, Boone never quit. He opened the way for thousands of settlers to move west, establishing the settlement of Boonesborough in 1775." (Publisher's note)

Includes bibliographical references (p. 47) and index.

Santella, Andrew

Kentucky; by Andrew Santella. Children's Press 2008 144p il map (America the beautiful, third series) lib bdg $38

Grades: 4 5 6 7   **976.9**

   ISBN 978-0-531-18574-2; 0-531-18574-5

                 LC 2007-4803

Describes the history, geography, ecology, people, economy, cities, and sights of the state of Kentucky.

Includes glossary and bibliographical references

977   North central United States

Kummer, Patricia K.

The **Great** Lakes; [by] Patricia K. Kummer. Marshall Cavendish Benchmark 2008 96p il map (Nature's wonders) lib bdg $35.64

Grades: 5 6 7 8   **977**

   ISBN 978-0-7614-2853-4 lib bdg; 0-7614-2853-4 lib bdg

                 LC 2007019728

"Provides comprehensive information on the geography, history, wildlife, peoples, and environmental issues of the Great Lakes." Publisher's note

Includes glossary and bibliographical references

977.1   Ohio

Sherrow, Victoria

Ohio; [by] Victoria Sherrow. 2nd. ed.; Marshall Cavendish Benchmark 2008 144p il map (Celebrate the states) lib bdg $39.93

Grades: 4 5 6 7   **977.1**

ISBN 978-0-7614-2558-8; 0-7614-2558-6

LC 2006-34103

First published 1999

"Provides comprehensive information on the geography, history, wildlife, governmental structure, economy, cultural diversity, peoples, religion, and landmarks of Ohio." Publisher's note

Includes bibliographical references

Stille, Darlene R.

Ohio. Children's Press 2009 144p il map (America the beautiful, third series) lib bdg $39

Grades: 4 5 6 7   **977.1**

ISBN 978-0-531-18579-7; 0-531-18579-6

LC 2007037177

Presents an introduction to the geography, natural resources, history, economy, important sites, daily life, and people of Ohio.

Includes glossary and bibliographical references

977.2   Indiana

Stille, Darlene R.

Indiana. Children's Press 2009 144p il map (America the beautiful, third series) lib bdg $39

Grades: 4 5 6 7   **977.2**

ISBN 978-0-531-18582-7; 0-531-18582-6

LC 2007043670

Presents an introduction to the geography, natural resources, history, economy, important sites, daily life, and people of Indiana.

Includes glossary and bibliographical references

977.3   Illinois

Burgan, Michael

Illinois; by Michael Burgan. Children's Press 2008 144p il map (America the beautiful, third series) lib bdg $38

Grades: 4 5 6 7   **977.3**

ISBN 978-0-531-18559-9; 0-531-18559-1

LC 2006-36020

Describes the history, geography, ecology, people, economy, cities, and sights of the state of Illinois.

Includes glossary and bibliographical references

Hurd, Owen

Chicago history for kids; triumphs and tragedies of the Windy city, includes 21 activities. [by] Owen Hurd. Chicago Review Press 2007 182p il map $14.95

Grades: 5 6 7 8   **977.3**

1. Chicago (Ill.) -- History

ISBN 978-1-55652-654-1; 1-55652-654-7

LC 2006031807

"This attractive overview begins with geography and moves to the colorful stories that characterize the city. Hurd tapped local experts and collections, using primary and secondary sources and the responses of young readers to craft this engaging resource. . . . Excellent-quality photos, maps, illustrations, or boxed facts appear on every page." SLJ

Includes bibliographical references

Morrison, Joan Wehlen

Home front girl; a diary of love, literature, and growing up in wartime America. Joan Wehlen Morrison; edited by Susan Signe Morrison. Chicago Review Press 2012 272 p $19.95

Grades: 7 8 9 10 11 12   **977.3**

1. History -- Sources 2. World War, 1939-1945 -- United States 3. Schoolgirls -- Illinois -- Chicago -- Diaries

ISBN 1613744579; 9781613744574

LC 2012027068

This book is a "collection of journal entries, poems, clippings, and sketches by the late [Joan Wehlen] Morrison, edited by her daughter, span[ing] the tumultuous years between 1937 and 1943, which took Morrison from age 14 to 20, and took the world from the Great Depression into WWII. . . . Morrison details her school day concerns and studies, exploring the city, her crushes on boys, attending the University of Chicago, and her thoughts on religion, books, films, and more." (Publishers Weekly)

Murphy, Jim

★ The **great** fire. Scholastic 1995 144p il maps $16.95; pa $12.99

Grades: 5 6 7 8 9 10   **977.3**

1. Fires -- Chicago (Ill.)

ISBN 0-590-47267-4; 0-439-20307-4 pa

LC 94-9963

Newbery honor book, 1996

"Firsthand descriptions by persons who lived through the 1871 Chicago fire are woven into a gripping account of this famous disaster. Murphy also examines the origins of the fire, the errors of judgment that delayed the effective response, the organizational problems of the city's firefighters, and the postfire efforts to rebuild the city. Newspaper lithographs and a few historical photographs convey the magnitude of human suffering and confusion." Horn Book Guide

Includes bibliographical references

977.4 Michigan

Bial, Raymond
The **Menominee**. Marshall Cavendish Benchmark 2006 127p il map (Lifeways) lib bdg $38.50
Grades: 5 6 7 8   **977.4**
1. Native Americans 2. Menominee Indians
ISBN 978-0-7614-1903-7; 0-7614-1903-9
LC 2004-22392
Discusses the history, culture, beliefs, changing ways, and notable people of the Menominee.
Includes glossary and bibliographical references

Brill, Marlene Targ
Michigan; by Marlene Targ Brill. 2d ed.; Marshall Cavendish Benchmark 2007 144p il map (Celebrate the states) lib bdg $39.93
Grades: 4 5 6 7   **977.4**
ISBN 978-0-7614-2351-5; 0-7614-2351-6
LC 2006-8181
First published 1998
"Provides comprehensive information on the geography, history, wildlife, governmental structure, economy, cultural diversity, peoples, religion, and landmarks of Michigan." Publisher's note
Includes bibliographical references

Raatma, Lucia
Michigan; by Lucia Raatma. Children's Press 2008 144p il map (America the beautiful, third series) lib bdg $38
Grades: 4 5 6 7   **977.4**
ISBN 978-0-531-18562-9; 0-531-18562-1
LC 2006100708
Describes the history, geography, ecology, people, economy, cities, and sights of the state of Michigan.
Includes glossary, filmography and bibliographical references

977.5 Wisconsin

Blashfield, Jean F.
Wisconsin; by Jean F. Blashfield. Children's Press 2008 144p il map (America the beautiful, third series) lib bdg $38
Grades: 4 5 6 7   **977.5**
ISBN 978-0-531-18568-1; 0-531-18568-0
LC 2006102490
Describes the history, geography, ecology, famous people, economy, cities and sights of the state of Wisconsin.
Includes glossary and bibliographical references

977.6 Minnesota

Schwabacher, Martin
Minnesota; [by] Martin Schwabacher and Patricia K. Kummer. 2nd ed.; Marshall Cavendish Benchmark 2008 144p il map (Celebrate the states) lib bdg $39.93
Grades: 4 5 6 7   **977.6**
ISBN 978-0-7614-2716-2; 0-7614-2716-3
LC 2007-2895
First published 1999
"Provides comprehensive information on the geography, history, wildlife, governmental structure, economy, cultural diversity, peoples, religion, and landmarks of Minnesota." Publisher's note
Includes bibliographical references

977.7 Iowa

Blashfield, Jean F.
Iowa. Children's Press 2010 144p il map (America the beautiful, third series) lib bdg $39
Grades: 4 5 6 7   **977.7**
ISBN 978-0-531-18599-5; 0-531-18599-0
LC 2008004841
Presents an introduction to the geography, natural resources, history, economy, important sites, daily life, and people of Iowa.
Includes glossary and bibliographical references

Morrice, Polly Alison
Iowa; by Polly Morrice and Joyce Hart. 2nd ed.; Marshall Cavendish Benchmark 2007 144p il map (Celebrate the states) lib bdg $39.93
Grades: 4 5 6 7   **977.7**
ISBN 978-0-7614-2350-8; 0-7614-2350-8
LC 2006-13620
First published 1998
"Provides comprehensive information on the geography, history, wildlife, governmental structure, economy, cultural diversity, peoples, religion, and landmarks of Iowa." Publisher's note
Includes bibliographical references

977.8 Missouri

Bennett, Michelle
Missouri; by Michelle Bennett and Joyce Hart. 2nd ed.; Marshall Cavendish Benchmark 2010 144p il map (Celebrate the states) lib bdg $42.79 **977.8**
ISBN 978-0-7614-4727-6; 0-7614-4727-X
LC 2009005754
First published 2001
This offers information on the geography, history, wildlife, governmental structure, economy, cultural diversity, peoples, religion, and landmarks of Missouri.
Includes bibliographical references

Blashfield, Jean F.
Missouri. Children's Press 2009 144p il map (America the beautiful, third series) lib bdg $39
Grades: 4 5 6 7   **977.8**
ISBN 978-0-531-18585-8; 0-531-18585-0
LC 2007035320

Presents an introduction to the geography, natural resources, history, economy, important sites, daily life, and people of Missouri.

Includes glossary and bibliographical references

978   Western United States

The **American** frontier; James D. Torr, book editor. Greenhaven Press 2002 240p il (Turning points in world history) lib bdg $34.95; pa $23.70

Grades: 7 8 9 10   978

1. Frontier and pioneer life -- West (U.S.) 2. Frontier and pioneer life -- United States 3. Frontier and pioneer life -- Western States

ISBN 0-7377-0786-0 lib bdg; 0-7377-0785-2 pa

LC 2001-33514

This is a collection of essays about the American frontier, with an introduction and summaries

Includes bibliographical references

★ The **Old** West: history and heritage. Marshall Cavendish Reference 2009 11v il map set$359.95

Grades: 6 7 8 9   978

1. Reference books

ISBN 978-0-7614-7829-4; 0-7614-7829-9

LC 2008062302

In this set "each volume contains about 100 pages with 18 to 21 signed articles that vary in length from 3 to 10 pages and are arranged in an easy-to-use alphabetical sequence. The overall style is lively and enticing. The scope of the 193 articles includes the Canadian West and the Mexican territory and deals with the time period from 1787 to 1912. . . . The set is thoughtfully arranged and can be used by a wide range of students. The articles are interesting and enlightening." Booklist

Includes glossary and bibliographical references

Collier, Christopher

★ **Indians,** cowboys, and farmers and the battle for the Great Plains, 1865-1910; [by] Christopher Collier, James Lincoln Collier. Benchmark Bks. (Tarrytown) 2001 95p il map (Drama of American history) lib bdg $31.36

Grades: 6 7 8 9   978

1. Farmers 2. Cowhands 3. Railroads 4. Native Americans -- Great Plains 5. Frontier and pioneer life -- West (U.S.) 6. Great Plains -- Social life and customs 7. Indians of North America -- Wars -- Great Plains 8. Frontier and pioneer life -- Great Plains -- History 9. Indians of North America -- Land tenure -- Great Plains

ISBN 0-7614-1052-X

LC 00-21103

Discusses the settling of the area between the Missouri River and the Rocky Mountains and the conflicting interests of the different groups involved—the Indians, cowboys, farmers, sheepherders, and railroad barons

Includes bibliographical references

Croy, Anita

★ **Ancient** Pueblo; archaeology unlocks the secrets of America's past. by Anita Croy; J. Jefferson Reid, consultant. National Geographic 2007 64p il map (National Geographic investigates) $17.95; lib bdg $27.90

Grades: 4 5 6 7   978

1. Archeology 2. Pueblo Indians 3. Southwestern States -- Antiquities

ISBN 978-1-4263-0130-8; 978-1-4263-0131-5 lib bdg

LC 2007024800

This describes the prehistoric sites of the American Southwest, and what archeologists have learned from them about the lives of ancient Pueblo peoples.

Includes glossary and bibliographical references

Freedman, Russell

★ The **life** and death of Crazy Horse; drawings by Amos Bad Heart Bull. Holiday House 1996 166p il maps $22.95

Grades: 5 6 7 8 9 10   978

1. Oglala Indians 2. Indian chiefs 3. Native Americans -- Biography

ISBN 0-8234-1219-9

LC 95-33303

A biography of the Oglala Indian leader who relentlessly resisted the white man's attempt to take over Indian lands.

This is "a compelling biography that is based on primary source documents and illustrated with pictographs by a Sioux band historian." Voice Youth Advocates

Includes bibliographical references

George-Warren, Holly

The **cowgirl** way; hats off to America's women of the West. Houghton Mifflin Books for Children 2010 112p il $18

Grades: 4 5 6 7   978

1. Cowhands 2. Women -- West (U.S.) 3. Cowgirls -- Western States 4. Women -- United States -- History

ISBN 978-0-618-73738-3; 0-618-73738-3

"With ample dynamic photos and lively quotes throughout, George-Warren presents a thoroughly absorbing overview of the history of cowgirls up to the present. . . . Famous figures such as Belle Starr, Calamity Jane, and Annie Oakley are discussed in brief, but the real delights here are the anecdotes on lesser-known figures such as Lucille Mulhall, the first woman to be dubbed a cowgirl in print. . . . The introduction of women as rodeo and trick riders and their contributions to the sports in the 1920s and '30s are covered in fascinating detail, as are the film and singing sensations of the 1940s and '50s." SLJ

Green, Carl R.

Buffalo Bill Cody; courageous wild west showman. by William R. Sanford and Carl R. Green. Enslow Publishers 2013 48 p. ill., map (library) $21.26; (paperback) $7.95

Grades: 5 6 7 8   978

1. Buffalo Bill's Wild West Show 2. Frontier and pioneer life -- West (U.S.) 3. Pioneers -- West (U.S.) --

Biography 4. Entertainers -- United States -- Biography
ISBN 0766040070; 9780766040076; 9781464400902
LC 2011031052

This book by William Sanford and Carl R. Green is part of the "Courageious Heroes of the American West" series. It presents a biography of Buffalo Bill Cody, who "had many jobs--Pony Express rider, scout, soldier, buffalo hunter. But he was most famous for entertaining audiences with his Wild West show. Many Americans and others around the world could not travel to see the real Wild West, so Buffalo Bill Brought it to them." (Publisher's note)

Includes bibliographical references (p. 47) and index.

Calamity Jane; courageous wild west woman. by William R. Sanford and Carl R. Green. Enslow Publishers 2013 48 p. ill., map (library) $21.26; (paperback) $7.95

Grades: 5 6 7 8   **978**

1. Cowgirls 2. Pioneers -- West (U.S.) -- Biography 3. Women pioneers -- West (U.S.) -- Biography
ISBN 0766040100; 9780766040106; 9781464400933
LC 2011033840

This book by William Sanford is part of the Courageous Heroes of the American West series and focuses on Calamity Jane. "The truth and myth are difficult to separate in the wild life of Calamity Jane. An independent spirit, she never stayed in one place for long. She worked as a gold prospector, bullwhacker, nurse, and had many other jobs, Calamity Jane refused to conform to the typical roles of a nineteenth-century woman." (Publisher's note)

Includes bibliographical references (p. 47) and index.

Zebulon Pike; courageous Rocky Mountain explorer. by William R. Sanford and Carl R. Green. Enslow Publishers 2013 48 p. ill. (library) $21.26; (paperback) $7.95

Grades: 5 6 7 8   **978**

1. Exploration 2. Explorers -- West (U.S.) -- Biography
ISBN 1464400954; 9780766040120; 9781464400957
LC 2011051629

This book by William R. Sanford is part of the Courageous Heroes of the American West series and looks at Zebulon Pike. "After the United States purchased the Louisiana Territory in 1803, the young nation needed brave pioneers to explore this vast uncharted land. Zebulon Pike . . . led an expedition across rolling prairies before arriving at the towering mountains" and being the first to explore the southern Rocky Mountains. (Publisher's note)

Includes bibliographical references (p. 47) and index.

Huey, Lois Miner

American archaeology uncovers the westward movement. Marshall Cavendish Benchmark 2009 64p il map (American archaeology) lib bdg $21.95

Grades: 4 5 6 7   **978**

1. Historical geography 2. Frontier and pioneer life -- West (U.S.) 3. Excavations (Archeology) -- United States
ISBN 978-0-7614-4265-3 lib bdg; 0-7614-4265-0 lib bdg
LC 2009003167

This describes how archeologists have learned about the history of the American West.

"The visually pleasing . . . [book is] replete with maps, paintings, and photographs, all appropriately placed and thoughtfully captioned. . . . Huey's focus on American history, which is broken down into small, manageable chunks, is sure to entice budding historians." SLJ

Includes glossary and bibliographical references

Marrin, Albert

★ **Years** of dust; the story of the Dust Bowl. Dutton Children's Books 2009 128p il map $22.99

Grades: 6 7 8 9 10   **978**

1. Droughts 2. Dust storms 3. Great Depression, 1929-1939 4. Depressions -- 1929 5. Dust Bowl Era, 1931-1939 6. Droughts -- Great Plains -- History -- 20th century 7. Dust storms -- Great Plains -- History -- 20th century
ISBN 978-0-525-42077-4; 0-525-42077-0
LC 2008-13898

"The engaging narrative includes quotes from a variety of primary sources, and it is abundantly illustrated throughout with photographs and other archival material, making this a reader-friendly, insightful work of history." Kirkus

Includes glossary and bibliographical references

McKissack, Fredrick, 1939-2013

★ **Best** shot in the West; the adventures of Nat Love. by Patricia C. McKissack and Fredrick L. McKissack, Jr.; illustrated by Randy DuBurke. Chronicle Books 2012 129 p. $19.99

Grades: 7 8 9   **978**

1. Cowhands -- Graphic novels 2. Railroads -- United States 3. West (U.S.) -- History -- Graphic novels 4. African Americans -- Biography -- Graphic novels 5. Cartoons and comics 6. Cowboys -- West (U.S.) -- Cartoons and comics 7. African American cowboys -- West (U.S.) -- Cartoons and comics 8. African Americans -- West (U.S.) -- Biography -- Cartoons and comics 9. Cowboys -- West (U.S.) -- Biography -- Comic books, strips, etc. 10. African American cowboys -- West (U.S.) -- Biography -- Comic books, strips, etc.
ISBN 0811857492; 9780811857499
LC 2007021419

In this graphic novel, "Nat Love's cattle-driving days are long over and America is a much tamer place when the black cowboy, now a Pullman porter, runs into 'Bugler,' a man he knew back in the day. Bugler's son is a publisher . . . of . . . stories from the Wild West, and Love is persuaded to contribute his memoirs. From this . . . story, . . . [Patricia C. and Frederick L.] McKissack . . . segue into Love's adventures, based on his autobiography." (Bulletin of the Center for Children's Books)

Miller, Brandon Marie

Women of the frontier; 16 tales of trailblazing homesteaders, entrepreneurs, and rabble-rousers. Brandon Marie Miller. Chicago Review Press 2013 256 p. (hardcover) $19.95

Grades: 7 8 9 10 11 12   **978**

1. Women -- United States 2. Frontier and pioneer life

-- United States 3. Women pioneers -- West (U.S.) -- History -- Biography
ISBN 1883052971; 9781883052973

LC 2012035756

This book, part of the Women of Action series, is a collection of "tales of women's trials and triumphs during the years of settlement in the [U.S.] West. . . . [The section] 'Many a Weary Mile' describes the trip west by wagon; 'Oh Give Me a Home' explores early pioneering experiences. 'A Woman Can Work,' 'And Now the Fun Begins' and 'Great Expectations for the Future' all examine the careers of women who stepped out of typical female roles of the era." (Kirkus)

Includes bibliographical references and index

Olson, Tod

How to get rich on a Texas cattle drive; afterword by Marc Aronson; illustrations by Scott Allred & Gregory Proch. National Geographic 2010 47p il map $18.95

Grades: 4 5 6 7   **978**

1. Cowhands 2. Frontier and pioneer life -- West (U.S.)
ISBN 978-1-4263-0524-5; 1-4263-0524-9

"This book provides one of the better true-to-life insider accounts of what happens on a cattle drive: why the cattle are being driven, where they're being driven to and from, and the multitude of daily chores and unforeseen obstacles along the way. Period photos and artwork, as well as original drawings, make for a lively design, and an ongoing ledger keeps track of the main character's mostly modest finances." Booklist

★ **How** to get rich on the Oregon Trail; my adventures among cows, crooks & heroes on the road to fame and fortune. [illustrations by Scott Allred & Gregory Proch; afterword by Marc Anonson] National Geographic 2009 47p il (How to get rich) $18.95; lib bdg $27.90

Grades: 4 5 6 7   **978**

1. Oregon Trail 2. Frontier and pioneer life 3. Overland journeys to the Pacific
ISBN 978-1-4263-0412-5; 1-4263-0412-9; 978-1-4263-0413-2 lib bdg; 1-4263-0413-7 lib bdg

"The action follows young Will Reed and his family as they set off from Illinois to find their fortune along the 2,000-mile Oregon Trail. . . . Informing Will's impish sketches and wry journal entries is a wealth of information about life along the trail. . . . An ongoing ledger calculates the family's balance as it fluctuates from $10.70 to $3,021.70, but it's clear that this journey is more about survival than riches. The illustrations, historical anecdotes, and run-ins with everyone from the Mormons to escaped slaves to Abraham Lincoln form a perfect blend of history and humbuggery." Booklist

Patent, Dorothy Hinshaw

The **horse** and the Plains indians; a powerful partnership. Dorothy Hinshaw Patent; photographs by William Munoz. Clarion Books 2012 xiii, 98 p.p ill. (chiefly col.) $17.99

Grades: 4 5 6 7 8   **978**

1. Horses 2. Domestic animals 3. Native Americans

-- Great Plains 4. Horses -- Great Plains -- History 5. Human-animal relationships -- Great Plains -- History 6. Indians of North America -- Domestic animals -- Great Plains
ISBN 9780547125510

LC 2011025954

This book explores the relationship between Plains Indians and horses. The "Plains Indians and the horse were not always inseparable. Once, Native Americans used dogs to help carry their goods, and even after the Spaniards introduced the horse to the Americas," the Spanish hoarded the valuable animals. But "soon horses escaped from Spanish settlements, and Native Americans quickly learned how valuable the horse could be as a hunting mount, beast of burden, and military steed." (Publisher's note)

Includes bibliographical references (p. [94]) and index

Pendergast, Tom

Westward expansion: almanac; [by] Tom Pendergast and Sara Pendergast; Christine Slovey, editor. U.X.L 2000 xlvi, 254p il (Westward expansion reference library) $60

Grades: 8 9 10 11 12   **978**

1. Reference books 2. Frontier and pioneer life -- West (U.S.)
ISBN 0-7876-4862-0

LC 00-36375

This almanac "documents the chronological events that created a romantic national mythology around the pioneers who blazed trails through the wilderness." Publisher's note

Includes bibliographical references

Westward expansion: primary sources; [by] Tom Pendergast and Sara Pendergast; Christine Slovey, editor. U.X.L 2001 xxix, 260p (Westward expansion reference library) $60

Grades: 7 8 9 10   **978**

1. West (U.S.) -- History 2. United States -- Territorial expansion
ISBN 0-7876-4864-7

LC 00-107861

This volume provides "full text or excerpts from diaries, books, letters and many other documents." Publisher's note

Includes bibliographical references

Reis, Ronald A.

The **Dust** Bowl. Chelsea House Publishers 2008 128p il (Great historic disasters) lib bdg $35

Grades: 6 7 8 9   **978**

1. Droughts 2. Dust storms
ISBN 978-0-7910-9737-3 lib bdg; 0-7910-9737-4 lib bdg

LC 2008004952

This describes the conditions that led up to the disastrous dust storms of the 1930s in the American Great Plains, and their consequences

The book covers its topic "thoroughly and [includes] high-quality photographs and occasional sidebars. . . . Reis includes solid research and numerous points of view." SLJ

Includes glossary and bibliographical references

Schlissel, Lillian

Black frontiers; a history of African American heroes in the Old West. Simon & Schuster Bks. for Young Readers 1995 80p il hardcover o.p. pa $7.99
Grades: 5 6 7 8   **978**
    1. African Americans -- History 2. Frontier and pioneer life -- West (U.S.) 3. African Americans -- West (U.S.)
    ISBN 0-689-80285-4; 0-689-83315-6 pa
        LC 92-120
Focuses on the experiences of blacks as mountain men, soldiers, homesteaders, and scouts on the frontiers of the American West
"Good-quality period photos and black-and-white reproductions appear on nearly every page, adding human interest and realism to the text. An excellent addition to black history or westward movement units." Booklist
Includes bibliographical references

Sheinkin, Steve

Which way to the wild West? everything your schoolbooks didn't tell you about America's westward expansion. illustrated by Tim Robinson. Roaring Brook Press 2009 260p il map $19.95
Grades: 5 6 7 8   **978**
    1. Frontier and pioneer life -- West (U.S.)
    ISBN 978-1-59643-321-2; 1-59643-321-3
Presents the greatest adventures of America's Westward expansion, from the Louisiana Purchase and the gold rush to the Indian wars and life of the cowboy, as well as the everyday happenings that defined living on the frontier
"An engaging storyteller, the author uses humor and little-known anecdotes to make such subjects as Manifest Destiny, the Mexican-American War, the Gold Rush and Custer's Last Stand entertaining for readers. His chatty, informal style . . . will appeal to young readers turned off to history by stale textbooks. Robinson's cartoons complement the text. . . . An accessible and engaging historical overview." Kirkus
Includes bibliographical references

Stefoff, Rebecca

★ **American** voices from the Wild West. Marshall Cavendish Benchmark 2007 111p (American voices from--) lib bdg $37.07
Grades: 6 7 8 9   **978**
    1. West (U.S.) -- History
    ISBN 978-0-7614-2170-2 lib bdg; 0-7614-2170-X lib bdg
        LC 2005028192
"Presents the history of the Wild West through a variety of primary source images and documents, such as diary entries, newspaper accounts, public speeches, popular literature, and personal letters." Publisher's note
Includes glossary and bibliographical references

★ **American** voices from the opening of the West. Benchmark Bks. 2002 105p (American voices from--) lib bdg $32.79

Grades: 6 7 8 9   **978**
    1. Frontier and pioneer life -- West (U.S.)
    ISBN 0-7614-1201-8
        LC 2001-8681
Presents the history of the westward expansion of the United States in the eighteenth and nineteenth centuries through excerpts from letters, newspaper articles, journal entries, and laws of the time
Includes glossary and bibliographical references

Tunis, Edwin

★ **Frontier** living; written and illustrated by Edwin Tunis. Lyons Press 2000 165p il map pa $18.95
Grades: 5 6 7 8 9 10   **978**
    1. Frontier and pioneer life -- West (U.S.)
    ISBN 1-58574-137-X
        LC 00-710694
First published 1961 by World Publishing Company
This volume "portrays the manners and customs of the frontiersman and his family from the beginning of the westward movement through the 19th century in . . . text and more than 200 drawings." Wis Libr Bull

Vivian, R. Gwinn

Chaco Canyon; [by] R. Gwinn Vivian and Margaret Anderson. Oxford University Press 2002 47p il maps (Digging for the past) $19.95
Grades: 5 6 7 8   **978**
    1. Archeology 2. Pueblo Indians 3. Cliff dwellers and cliff dwellings 4. Cliff-dwellings -- New Mexico -- Chaco Canyon 5. Pueblo Indians -- New Mexico -- Chaco Canyon -- Antiquities
    ISBN 0-19-514280-2
        LC 2001-54855
Relates the nineteenth-century discovery of cliff dwellings in the Chaco Canyon of northwest New Mexico, the excavations of the ancient ruins, and what the artifacts reveal about the civilization of the ancient Pueblo Indians
This "brings young readers up close to the field of archaeology. . . . Sharp color photos show the sites, artifacts, and the scientists at work." Booklist
Includes glossary and bibliographical references

978.00497 American native peoples--Great Plains

Green, Carl R.

Sacagawea; courageous American Indian guide. by William R. Sanford and Carl R. Green. Enslow Publishers 2013 48 p. ill., map (library) $21.26
Grades: 5 6 7 8   **978.00497**
    1. Native Americans -- United States 2. Shoshoni women -- Biography 3. Shoshoni Indians -- Biography
    ISBN 0766040062; 9780766040069
        LC 2011048291
This book, part of the Courageous Heroes of the American West series, looks at Sacagawea. "Throughout Lewis and Clark's journey in the uncharted American West, this young America Indian woman proved to be an invaluable member

of the expedition. Sacagawea served as translator and guide, all while caring for her infant son." (Publisher's note)

Includes bibliographical references (p. 47) and index.

Langley, Andrew

The **Plains** Indian wars 1864-1890; by Andrew Langley. Heinemann Library 2012 80 p. ill. (some col.), col. maps (hardcover) $36.50; (paperback) $10.99

Grades: 6 7 8 9   **978.00497**
1. United States -- Military history 2. Native Americans -- Wars 3. Indians of North America -- Wars -- 1866-1895 4. Indians of North America -- Wars -- Great Plains 5. Indians of North America -- Great Plains -- History -- 19th century -- Chronology
ISBN 1432959999; 9781432959999; 9781432960087
     LC 2011015925

This book by Andrew Langley is part of the Living Through series and focuses on the Plains Indian Wars. "The Plains Indian Wars were not like most other wars. There were few large battles, and they took place across a huge but sparsely populated region over several decades. . . . The Living Through series relates the overall chronology of major wars and shows their impact on everyday lives." (Publisher's note)

Includes bibliographical references (p. 76-78) and index.

Sanford, William R.

Comanche Chief Quanah Parker; by William R. Sanford. Enslow Publishers 2013 48 p. ill., map (library) $21.26

Grades: 6 7 8 9   **978.00497**
1. Parker, Quanah, 1845?-1911 2. Comanche Indians -- History 3. Comanche Indians -- Wars 4. Comanche Indians -- Kings and rulers -- Biography
ISBN 076604095X; 9780766040953
     LC 2011048762

This book by William R. Sanford is part of the Native American Chiefs and Warriors series. It "tells how Quanah, the last Comanche chief, at first drew controversy for surrendering to the U.S. government and agreeing to live on a reservation. He later earned praise for effectively bridging both cultures." Booklist

Includes bibliographical references

Oglala Lakota Chief Red Cloud; by William R. Sanford. Enslow Publishers 2013 48 p. (library) $21.26

Grades: 6 7 8 9   **978.00497**
1. Oglala Indians -- Wars 2. Oglala Indians -- Kings and rulers -- Biography
ISBN 0766040968; 9780766040960
     LC 2011048760

This book is part of the Native American Chiefs and Warriors series and looks at Oglala Lakota Chief Red Cloud. Each title "focuses on the U.S. government's infringement upon Native American land and how these leaders responded." This entry "recounts Red Cloud's fight to prevent whites from traveling along the Bozeman and Oregon Trails, his

meeting with President Ulysses Grant, and his band's forced move to a reservation." (Booklist)

Includes bibliographical references and index.

Oglala Sioux Chief Crazy Horse; by William R. Sanford. Enslow Publishers 2013 48 p. (library) $21.26

Grades: 6 7 8 9   **978.00497**
1. Little Bighorn, Battle of the, Mont., 1876 2. Oglala Indians -- Kings and rulers -- Biography
ISBN 0766040941; 9780766040946
     LC 2011048758

This book is part of the Native American Chiefs and Warriors series and looks at Oglala Sioux Chief Crazy Horse. Each title "focuses on the U.S. government's infringement upon Native American land and how these leaders responded." This entry "describes Crazy Horse's success as a chief and warrior, particularly during the Battle of the Little Bighorn, and the resulting jealousy among other Sioux leaders that led to his contentious death." (Booklist)

Includes bibliographical references (p. 46) and index.

978.1   Kansas

Bjorklund, Ruth

Kansas; by Ruth Bjorklund and Trudi Strain Trueit. 2nd ed.; Marshall Cavendish Benchmark 2009 144p il map (Celebrate the states) lib bdg $42.79

Grades: 4 5 6 7   **978.1**
ISBN 978-0-7614-3400-9; 0-7614-3400-3
     LC 2008-5537

"Provides comprehensive information on the geography, history, wildlife, governmental structure, economy, cultural diversity, peoples, religion, and landmarks of Kansas." Publisher's note

Includes bibliographical references

Cannarella, Deborah

Kansas. Children's Press 2009 144p il map (America the beautiful, third series) lib bdg $39

Grades: 4 5 6 7   **978.1**
ISBN 978-0-531-18583-4; 0-531-18583-4
     LC 2007028461

Presents an introduction to the geography, natural resources, history, economy, important sites, daily life, and people of Kansas.

Includes glossary and bibliographical references

McArthur, Debra

The **Kansas**-Nebraska Act and Bleeding Kansas in American history. Enslow Pubs. 2003 128p il map (In American history) lib bdg $26.60

Grades: 6 7 8 9   **978.1**
1. Abolitionists 2. Slavery -- United States 3. Missouri compromise 4. Kansas-Nebraska bill
ISBN 0-7660-1988-8
     LC 2002-152064

Describes the violent period of Kansas Territory history, prior to statehood and the Civil War, when abolitionists and pro-slavery factions openly murdered in defense of their cause

Includes bibliographical references

978.2   Nebraska

Bjorklund, Ruth

    Nebraska; [by] Ruth Bjorklund and Marlee Richards. 2nd ed.; Marshall Cavendish Benchmark 2010 144p il map (Celebrate the states) $42.79

Grades: 5 6 7 8   **978.2**

    ISBN 978-0-7614-4732-0; 0-7614-4732-6

    "Every school library should purchase this." Voice Youth Advocates

Heinrichs, Ann

    Nebraska; by Ann Heinrichs. Children's Press 2008 144p il map (America the beautiful, third series) lib bdg $38

Grades: 4 5 6 7   **978.2**

    ISBN 978-0-531-18577-3; 0-531-18577-X

                      LC 2007-6720

    Describes the history, geography, ecology, people, economy, cities, and sights of the state of Nebraska.

    Includes glossary and bibliographical references

978.3   South Dakota

Burgan, Michael

    South Dakota. Children's Press 2010 144p il map (America the beautiful, third series) lib bdg $39

Grades: 4 5 6 7   **978.3**

    ISBN 978-0-531-18503-2; 0-531-18503-6

                     LC 2008002299

    Takes readers on a tour of South Dakota, describing the state's history, culture, land, economy, government, and sights, and including unique facts, color maps and photos, the state song, suggested activities, lists of famous people, cultural institutions, and annual events, and other resources.

    Includes glossary and bibliographical references

978.4   North Dakota

McDaniel, Melissa

    North Dakota; by Melissa McDaniel and Sara Louise Kras. 2nd ed.; Marshall Cavendish Benchmark 2010 144p il map (Celebrate the states) lib bdg $42.79

Grades: 5 6 7 8   **978.4**

    ISBN 978-0-7614-4733-7; 0-7614-4733-4

                     LC 2009002584

    First published 2001

    This offers information on the geography, history, wildlife, governmental structure, economy, cultural diversity, peoples, religion, and landmarks of North Dakota.

    Includes bibliographical references

Stille, Darlene R.

    North Dakota. Children's Press 2010 144p il map (America the beautiful, third series) lib bdg $39

Grades: 4 5 6 7   **978.4**

    ISBN 978-0-531-18502-5; 0-531-18502-8

                     LC 2008011282

    Presents an introduction to the geography, natural resources, history, economy, important sites, daily life, and people of North Dakota.

    Includes glossary and bibliographical references

978.6   Montana

Bennett, Clayton

    Montana; by Clayton Bennett and Wendy Mead. 2nd ed.; Marshall Cavendish Benchmark 2010 144p il map (Celebrate the states) $42.79

Grades: 5 6 7 8   **978.6**

    ISBN 978-0-7614-4731-3; 0-7614-4731-8

                     LC 2009007939

    First published 2001

    This offers information on the geography, history, wildlife, governmental structure, economy, cultural diversity, peoples, religion, and landmarks of Montana.

    Includes bibliographical references

Stein, R. Conrad

    Montana. Children's Press 2010 144p il map (America the beautiful, third series) lib bdg $39

Grades: 4 5 6 7   **978.6**

    ISBN 978-0-531-18500-1; 0-531-18500-1

                     LC 2008000823

    Takes readers on a tour of Montana, describing the state's history, culture, land, economy, government, and sights, and including unique facts, color maps and photos, the state song, suggested activities, lists of famous people, cultural institutions, and annual events, and other resources.

    Includes glossary and bibliographical references

978.7   Wyoming

Baldwin, Guy

    Wyoming; [by] Guy Baldwin and Joyce Hart. 2nd ed.; Marshall Cavendish Benchmark 2008 144p il map (Celebrate the states) lib bdg $39.93

Grades: 4 5 6 7   **978.7**

    ISBN 978-0-7614-2563-2; 0-7614-2563-2

                     LC 2007-19560

    First publsihed 1999

    "Provides comprehensive information on the geography, history, wildlife, governmental structure, economy, cultural diversity, peoples, religion, and landmarks of Wyoming." Publisher's note

    Includes bibliographical references

Prentzas, G. S.

    Wyoming. Children's Press 2010 144p il map (America the beautiful, third series) lib bdg $39

Grades: 4 5 6 7   **978.7**
ISBN 978-0-531-18508-7; 0-531-18508-7
LC 2008016789
Takes readers on a tour of Wyoming, describing the state's history, culture, land, economy, government, and sights, and including unique facts, color maps and photos, the state song, suggested activities, lists of famous people, cultural institutions, and annual events, and other resources.
Includes glossary and bibliographical references

978.8   Colorado

Somervill, Barbara A.
Colorado; by Barbara A. Somervill. Children's Press 2008 144p il map (America the beautiful, third series) lib bdg $38
Grades: 4 5 6 7   **978.8**
ISBN 978-0-531-18570-4; 0-531-18570-2
LC 2007-301
Describes the history, geography, ecology, people, economy, cities, and sights of the state of Colorado.
Includes glossary and bibliographical references

978.9   New Mexico

Burgan, Michael
New Mexico. Children's Press 2008 144p il map (America the beautiful, third series) lib bdg $39
Grades: 4 5 6 7   **978.9**
ISBN 978-0-531-18578-0; 0-531-18578-8
LC 2007007728
Presents an introduction to the geography, natural resources, history, economy, important sites, daily life, and people of New Mexico.
Includes glossary and bibliographical references

979.1   Arizona

Hernandez, Daniel
They call me a hero; a memoir of my youth. Daniel Hernandez and Susan Goldman Rubin. Simon & Schuster Books for Young Readers 2013 240 p. (hardcover) $17.99
Grades: 7 8 9 10 11 12   **979.1**
1. Courage 2. Interns -- United States -- Biography 3. Heroes -- Arizona -- Tucson -- Biography 4. Sexual minorities -- Civil rights -- Arizona -- Tucson 5. Courage -- Arizona -- Tucson -- History -- 21st century
ISBN 1442462280; 9781442462281; 9781442462380
LC 2012019829
This book, by Daniel Hernandez, with Susan Gldman Rubin, is a memoir about heroism. "Daniel Hernandez was . . . working as an intern for U.S. Representative Gabrielle Giffords. On January 8, 2011, . . . Giffords was shot. Daniel Hernandez's quick thinking saved Giffords's life. . . . But while that may have been his most well-known moment in the spotlight, Daniel Hernandez, Jr. . . . [had] already accomplished much in his young life, and is working to achieve much more." (Publisher's note)

McDaniel, Melissa
Arizona; by Melissa McDaniel and Wendy Mead. 2nd ed.; Marshall Cavendish Benchmark 2009 144p il map (Celebrate the states) lib bdg $39.93
Grades: 4 5 6 7   **979.1**
ISBN 978-0-7614-3398-9; 0-7614-3398-8
LC 2008-6212
First published 2000
"Provides comprehensive information on the geography, history, wildlife, governmental structure, economy, cultural diversity, peoples, religion, and landmarks of Arizona." Publisher's note
Includes bibliographical references

Somervill, Barbara A.
Arizona; by Barbara A. Somervill. Children's Press 2008 144p il map (America the beautiful, third series) lib bdg $38
Grades: 4 5 6 7   **979.1**
ISBN 978-0-531-18595-7; 0-531-18595-8
LC 2007-37923
Presents an introduction to the geography, natural resources, history, economy, important sites, daily life, and people of Arizona.
"This title in the America the Beautiful series is also a fun read, with a chatty style, open design, and color photos, maps, screens, and charts on just about every spread." Booklist
Includes glossary and bibliographical references

979.2   Utah

Kent, Deborah
Utah. Children's Press 2009 144p il map (America the beautiful, third series) $39
Grades: 4 5 6 7   **979.2**
ISBN 978-0-531-18592-6; 0-531-18592-3
LC 2007051225
Presents an introduction to the geography, natural resources, history, economy, important sites, daily life, and people of Utah.
Includes glossary and bibliographical references

Stefoff, Rebecca
Utah; by Rebecca Stefoff and Wendy Mead. 2nd ed.; Marshall Cavendish Benchmark 2010 144p il map (Celebrate the states) lib bdg $42.79
Grades: 5 6 7 8   **979.2**
ISBN 978-0-7614-4035-2; 0-7614-4035-6
LC 2008040026
This offers information on the geography, history, wildlife, governmental structure, economy, cultural diversity, peoples, religion, and landmarks of Utah.
Includes bibliographical references

979.3   Nevada

Heinrichs, Ann

   Nevada;   by Ann Heinrichs. Children's Press 2008 144p il map (America the beautiful, third series) lib bdg $38

Grades: 4 5 6 7   **979.3**

   ISBN 978-0-531-18586-5; 0-531-18586-9

                        LC 2006-39526

   Describes the history, geography, ecology, people, economy, cities, and sights of the state of Nevada.

   Includes glossary and bibliographical references

Stefoff, Rebecca

   Nevada;   2nd ed.; Marshall Cavendish Benchmark 2010 144p il map (Celebrate the states) lib bdg $42.79

Grades: 5 6 7 8   **979.3**

   ISBN 978-0-7614-4728-3; 0-7614-4728-8

                        LC 2009007137

   This offers information on the geography, history, wildlife, governmental structure, economy, cultural diversity, peoples, religion, and landmarks of Nevada.

   Includes bibliographical references

979.4   California

Calabro, Marian

   ★ The **perilous** journey of the Donner Party. Clarion Bks. 1999 192p il maps $20

Grades: 5 6 7 8   **979.4**

   1. Donner party 2. Overland journeys to the Pacific 3. Survival 4. Donner Party 4. Frontier and pioneer life -- West (U.S.) 7. Pioneer children -- West (U.S.) -- History -- 19th century

   ISBN 0-395-86610-3

                        LC 98-29610

   Uses materials from letters and diaries written by survivors of the Donner Party to relate the experiences of that ill-fated group as they endured horrific circumstances on their way to California in 1846-47

   "Calabro's offering is a fine addition to the Donner Party canon and particularly well suited to its young audience, for whom the story of hardship and survival will be nothing short of riveting. . . . From the haunting cover with its lonely campfire to the recounting of a survivors' reunion, this is a page-turner." Booklist

   Includes bibliographical references

Doak, Robin S.

   California, 1542-1850; by Robin Doak; Andres Resendez, consultant. National Geographic Society 2006 109p map il (Voices from colonial America) $21.95; lib bdg $32.90

Grades: 5 6 7 8   **979.4**

   1. California -- History

   ISBN 978-0-7922-6391-3; 0-7922-6391-X; 978-0-7922-6861-1 lib bdg; 0-7922-6861-X lib bdg

                        LC 2005-30920

   "Traces California's history from its origins as a sparsely populated outpost of the Spanish empire in the sixteenth century to the frenzied westward migration of the 1850s." Publisher's note

   Includes bibliograhical references

McNeese, Tim

   The **Donner** Party; a doomed journey. [by] Tim McNeese. Chelsea House 2009 146p il (Milestones in American history) lib bdg $35

Grades: 6 7 8 9 10   **979.4**

   1. Donner party 2. Overland journeys to the Pacific 3. Frontier and pioneer life -- California 4. Frontier and pioneer life -- West (U.S.)

   ISBN 978-1-60413-025-6 lib bdg; 1-60413-025-3 lib bdg

                        LC 2008-29652

   "McNeese presents a thoroughly researched, clearly written account of the ill-fated Donner Party and the events and decisions that conspired against this early wagon train headed from Springfield, IL, to California. . . . Photos, reproductions, drawings, and primary-source documents as well as a detailed chronology make this an excellent resource." SLJ

   Includes bibliographical references

Olson, Tod

   ★ **How** to get rich in the California Gold Rush; an adventurer's guide to the fabulous riches discovered in 1848 . . . illustrations by Scott Allred; afterword by Marc Aronson. National Geographic 2008 47p il map (How to get rich) $16.95; lib bdg $25.90

Grades: 4 5 6 7   **979.4**

   1. Gold mines and mining 2. Prospecting 3. Frontier and pioneer life -- California

   ISBN 1-4263-0315-7; 1-4263-0316-5 lib bdg; 978-1-4263-0315-9; 978-1-4263-0316-6 lib bdg

                        LC 2008-19601

   This is a personal account of the California Gold Rush from the point-of-view of the fictitious character Thomas Hartley.

   This "deftly blends story with history to not only give readers an understanding of a gold rush but also to provide a lighthearted and engaging entry point into frontier life. . . . Period lithographs are reproduced alongside original illustrations. . . . A ledger on each page tracks the young men's finances in a genuinely exciting way, adding a sly element of math to this well-conceived and compulsively appealing book." Booklist

   Includes bibliographical references

Orr, Tamra

   California;   by Tamra B. Orr. Children's Press 2008 144p il map (America the beautiful, third series) lib bdg $38

Grades: 4 5 6 7   **979.4**

   ISBN 978-0-531-18557-5; 0-531-18557-5

                        LC 2006-36021

   Describes the history, geography, ecology, people, economy, cities, and sights of the state of California.

   Includes glossary and bibliographical references

Slavicek, Louise Chipley

The **San** Francisco earthquake and fire of 1906; [by] Louise Chipley Slavicek. Chelsea House 2008 128p il (Great historic disasters) lib bdg $35

Grades: 5 6 7 8   **979.4**

1. Fires 2. Earthquakes -- California

ISBN 978-0-7910-9650-5; 0-7910-9650-5

LC 2008-4896

This is a history of the 1906 earthquake and fire in San Francisco.

"Combining first-hand accounts, photographs, and other primary sources with a detailed and lively text, [this] fact-packed [resource offers] much to both report writers and history buffs." Horn Book Guide

Includes glossary and bibliographical references

Yep, Laurence, 1948-

★ The **lost** garden; by Laurence Yep. Messner 1991 xi, 117 p.p ill. (In my own words) (library) $14.98; (hardcover) $12.95

Grades: 6 7 8 9 10 11 12   **979.4**

1. Authors 2. Novelists 3. Chinese Americans 4. College teachers 5. Authors, American 6. Children's authors 7. Young adult authors 8. Chinese Americans -- Biography

ISBN 9780671741594; 9780671741600

LC 90040647

This is a volume in the In My Own Words series. The author of Dragonwings (BRD 1976), Child of The Owl (BRD 1977), The Rainbow People (BRD 1989), and The Star Fisher (BRD 1991) discusses his life and his writing.

"The writing is warm, wry, and humorous. . . . The Lost Garden will be welcomed as a literary autobiography for children and, more, a thoughtful probing into what it means to be an American." SLJ

979.5   Oregon

Kent, Deborah

Oregon. Children's Press 2008 144p il map (America the beautiful, third series) lib bdg $39

Grades: 4 5 6 7   **979.5**

ISBN 978-0-531-18587-2; 0-531-18587-7

LC 2007038691

Presents an introduction to the geography, natural resources, history, economy, important sites, daily life, and people of Oregon.

Includes glossary and bibliographical references

979.6   Idaho

Kent, Deborah

Idaho. Children's Press 2010 144p il map (America the beautiful, third series) lib bdg $39

Grades: 4 5 6 7   **979.6**

ISBN 978-0-531-18598-8; 0-531-18598-2

LC 2008005647

Takes readers on a tour of Idaho, describing the state's history, culture, land, economy, government, and sights,

and including unique facts, color maps and photos, the state song, suggested activities, lists of famous people, cultural institutions, and annual events, and other resources.

Includes glossary and bibliographical references

Stefoff, Rebecca

Idaho; by Rebecca Stefoff. 2nd ed.; Marshall Cavendish Benchmark 2008 144p il map (Celebrate the states) lib bdg $39.93

Grades: 4 5 6 7   **979.6**

ISBN 978-0-7614-3003-2; 0-7614-3003-2

LC 2007-29496

First published 2000

"Provides comprehensive information on the geography, history, wildlife, governmental structure, economy, cultural diversity, peoples, religion, and landmarks of Idaho." Publisher's note

Includes bibliographical references

979.7   Washington

Jankowski, Susan

Olympic National Park; adventure, explore, discover. [by] Susan Jankowski. MyReportLinks.com Books 2009 128p il map (America's national parks) lib bdg $33.27

Grades: 5 6 7 8   **979.7**

1. Olympic National Park (Wash.) 2. National parks and reserves -- United States

ISBN 978-1-59845-092-7 lib bdg; 1-59845-092-1 lib bdg

LC 2007-17341

This "informative, well-written book contains a physical description of the park; a summary of its history including the Native peoples of the area; activities such as hiking trails, campsites, and visitor centers; information about the park's plants, animals, and weather; full-color photographs; and numerous approved links available through the publisher's Web page. . . . Thorough, useful, and appealing, this . . . is a great update for collections." SLJ

Includes glossary and bibliographical references

Kirkpatrick, Katherine

★ **Mysterious** bones; the story of Kennewick Man. by Katherine Kirkpatrick; illustrated by Emma Stevenson. Holiday House 2011 60p il map $17.95

Grades: 6 7 8 9   **979.7**

1. Skeleton 2. Kennewick Man 3. Native Americans

ISBN 978-0-8234-2187-9; 0-8234-2187-2

LC 2009025575

Kennewick Man "was found in remarkable condition near the Columbia River in Washington . . . in 1996—one of the oldest and most complete skeletons found in America. Kirkpatrick addresses the controversy surrounding the treatment of his remains. . . . Excellent illustrations accompany the story, with crisp line-drawings of tools, skeletons, maps and possible facial reconstructions." Kirkus

Includes glossary and bibliographical references

Stefoff, Rebecca

Washington; [by] Rebecca Stefoff. 2nd ed.;
Marshall Cavendish Benchmark 2008 144p il map
(Celebrate the states) lib bdg $39.93
Grades: 4 5 6 7   **979.7**
ISBN 978-0-7614-2561-8; 0-7614-2561-6
LC 2006-32436
First published 1999
"Provides comprehensive information on the geography,
history, wildlife, governmental structure, economy, cultural
diversity, peoples, religion, and landmarks of Washington."
Publisher's note
Includes bibliographical references

979.8   Alaska

Orr, Tamra

Alaska; by Tamra B. Orr. Children's Press 2008
144p il map (America the beautiful, third series) lib
bdg $38
Grades: 4 5 6 7   **979.8**
ISBN 978-0-531-18569-8; 0-531-18569-9
LC 2007-22220
Describes the history, geography, ecology, people, econ-
omy, cities, and sights of the state of Alaska.
Includes glossary and bibliographical references

980   History of South America

Gorrell, Gena K.

★ **In** the land of the jaguar; South America and
its people. illustrated by Andrej Krystoforski. Tundra Books 2007 149p il $22.95
Grades: 5 6 7 8 9   **980**
1. South America
ISBN 978-0-88776-756-2
"This beautifully designed volume, with an engaging
narrative, combines a highly informative overview of the
continent with country-by-country detail. . . . The spacious
design includes big maps, clear type on thick paper, and
small, beautiful, fully captioned illustrations." Booklist

980.03   1830-1999

Kallen, Stuart A.

Che Guevara; by Stuart A. Kallen. Twenty-First
Century Books 2013 88 p. (lib. bdg.: alk. paper)
$33.27
Grades: 8 9 10 11 12   **980.03**
1. Cuba -- History -- 1958-1959, Revolution 2.
Revolutionaries -- Cuba -- Biography 3. Guerrillas --
Latin America -- Biography
ISBN 0822590352; 9780822590354
LC 2011045480
In author Stuart A. Kallen's book on Che Guevara, "the
charismatic Argentinian revolutionary had been leading gue-
rilla fighters in the jungles of Bolivia and was captured by

the Bolivian army. Mario Terán, a sergeant in the Bolivian
army, volunteered to execute the prisoner. He carried out the
bloody assignment with nine point-blank shots to Guevara's
body . . . In this chronicle of an assassination, find out what
inspired the myth of Che Guevara and what brought him to
this bloody crossroads of history." (Publisher's note)
Includes bibliographical references and index.

981   Brazil

Berkenkamp, Lauri

Discover the Amazon; the world's largest rainforest. illustrated by Blair Shedd. Nomad Press 2008
90p il map pa $16.95
Grades: 4 5 6 7   **981**
1. Rain forests 2. Rain forest ecology
ISBN 978-1-9346702-7-9 pa; 1-9346702-7-8 pa
"Berkenkamp's introduction to the [Amazon] river basin
incorporates maps, drawings, and photos in various shades
of green and brown on recycled paper. . . . The conversational style provides a 'you are there' feeling, conveying
information and anecdotes while stressing outdoor survival
skills. . . . Even readers who never travel to Amazonia will
appreciate the region's complexity and significance after perusing this book." SLJ

Deckker, Zilah

★ **Brazil**; [by] Zilah Deckker; David Robinson
and Joao Cezar de Castro Rocha, consultants. National Geographic 2008 64p il (Countries of the
world) lib bdg $27.90
Grades: 4 5 6 7   **981**
ISBN 978-1-4263-0298-5 lib bdg; 1-4263-0298-3
lib bdg
This describes the geography, nature, history, people and
culture, government, and economy of Brazil.
Includes glossary and bibliographical references

Heinrichs, Ann

The **Amazon** rain forest. Marshall Cavendish
Benchmark 2009 96p il (Nature's wonders) lib
bdg $35.64
Grades: 6 7 8 9   **981**
1. Rain forests
ISBN 978-0-7614-3932-5; 0-7614-3932-3
LC 2008017562
Provides information on the geography, history, wild-
life, peoples, and environmental issues of the Amazon
Rain Forest.
Includes glossary and bibliographical references

982   Argentina

Fearns, Les

Argentina; [by] Les and Daisy Fearns. Facts on
File 2005 61p il map (Countries of the world) $30
Grades: 7 8 9 10   **982**
ISBN 0-8160-6008-8
LC 2005040675

This is an introduction to Argentina's "culture, history, geography, government, and economy. [It is] competently written and [contains] current information. [The text is] clear but the level of vocabulary is quite high, which might prove challenging for less competent readers. Visually, the [book is] quite impressive, with full-color photographs, maps, tables, and graphs distributed throughout." SLJ

Includes bibliographical references

984 Bolivia

Pateman, Robert

Bolivia; [by] Robert Pateman & Marcus Cramer. 2nd ed.; Marshall Cavendish Benchmark 2006 144p il map (Cultures of the world) lib bdg $42.79

Grades: 5 6 7 8 **984**

ISBN 978-0-7614-2066-8 lib bdg; 0-7614-2066-5 lib bdg

LC 2006002425

First published 1995

This is "well organized, informative, and entertaining. . . . Excellent-quality full-color photographs and reproductions show the people, landforms, buildings, and everyday activities." SLJ

Includes bibliographical references

985 Peru

Bingham, Jane

The **Inca** empire; [by] Jane Bingham. Raintree 2007 64p il map (Time travel guide) lib bdg $34.29; pa $9.99

Grades: 6 7 8 9 **985**

1. Incas

ISBN 978-1-4109-2731-6 lib bdg; 1-4109-2731-8 lib bdg; 978-1-4109-2738-5 pa; 1-4109-2738-5 pa

LC 2006033877

This describes life in the ancient Inca empire in the form of a travel guide.

Includes glossary and bibliographical references

Calvert, Patricia

★ The **ancient** Inca; written by Patricia Calvert. Franklin Watts 2004 128p il (People of the ancient world) lib bdg $30.50; pa $9.95

Grades: 5 6 7 8 **985**

1. Incas

ISBN 0-531-12358-8 lib bdg; 0-531-16740-2 pa

LC 2004-1956

This "well-written, attractive [title has] extensive collections of quality color photographs of ruins and artifacts." SLJ

Includes bibliographical references

Donovan, Sandra, 1967-

Teens in Peru; by Sandy Donovan. Compass Point Books 2009 95p il (Global connections) lib bdg $33.26

Grades: 6 7 8 9 **985**

1. Teenagers 2. Peru

ISBN 978-0-7565-3852-1 lib bdg; 0-7565-3852-1 lib bdg

LC 2008-6503

Uncovers the challenges, pastimes, customs and culture of teens in Peru

This book is "concise and highly readable. . . . Clear, colorful photos and sidebars on a range of topics provide further context. . . . [This title] will enrich young adult collections." SLJ

Includes glossary and bibliographic references

Falconer, Kieran

★ **Peru**; [by] Kieran Falconer & Lynette Quek. 2nd ed.; Marshall Cavendish Benchmark 2006 144p il map (Cultures of the world) lib bdg $42.79

Grades: 5 6 7 8 **985**

ISBN 978-0-7614-2068-2 lib bdg; 0-7614-2068-1 lib bdg

First published 1995

This provides "information on the geography, history, governmental structure, economy, cultural diversity, peoples, religion, and culture of Peru." Publisher's note

Includes glossary and bibliographical references

Gruber, Beth

★ **Ancient** Inca; archaeology unlocks the secrets of the Inca's past. by Beth Gruber; Johan Reinhard, consultant. National Geographic 2007 64p il map (National Geographic investigates) $17.95; lib bdg $27.90

Grades: 5 6 7 8 **985**

1. Incas 2. Excavations (Archeology) -- Peru

ISBN 978-0-7922-7827-6; 978-0-7922-7873-3 lib bdg

LC 2006032104

This describes how archeologists have found out about ancient Incan civilization.

This offers "the beautiful photography and illustrations characteristic of the National Geographic Society, [a] well-written [text] and sidebars, and information on recent archaeological finds." SLJ

Includes bibliographical references

986.1 Colombia

Croy, Anita

★ **Colombia**; [by] Anita Croy; Ulrich Oslender and Mauricio Pardo, consultants. National Geographic 2008 64p il map (Countries of the world) lib bdg $27.90

Grades: 4 5 6 7 **986.1**

ISBN 978-1-4263-0257-2 lib bdg; 1-4263-0257-6 lib bdg

This describes the geography, nature, history, people and culture, government, and economy of Colombia

Includes glossary and bibliographical references

986.6   Ecuador

Foley, Erin

★ **Ecuador**; [by] Erin L. Foley & Leslie Jermyn. 2nd ed.; Marshall Cavendish Benchmark 2006 144p il map (Cultures of the world) lib bdg $42.79

Grades: 5 6 7 8   **986.6**
    ISBN 0-7614-2050-9
                                LC 2005022671
    First published 1995

This briefly describes Ecuador's "history, government, economy, and geography. . . . Particularly useful is the information on religion, the arts, food, leisure activities, and social roles. The [book has] great visual appeal with excellent full-color photographs on every page. [It] is especially successful in explaining social and economic hierarchies within the country." SLJ

Includes glossary and bibliographical references

Kras, Sara Louise

The **Galapagos** Islands; [by] Sara Louise Kras. Marshall Cavendish Benchmark 2008 96p il map (Nature's wonders) lib bdg $35.64

Grades: 5 6 7 8   **986.6**
    ISBN 978-0-7614-2856-5 lib bdg; 0-7614-2856-9 lib bdg
                                LC 2007020416

"Provides comprehensive information on the geography, history, wildlife, peoples, and environmental issues of the Galapagos Islands." Publisher's note

Includes glossary and bibliographical references

Lourie, Peter

★ **Lost** treasure of the Inca. Boyds Mills Press 1999 48p il map $18.95

Grades: 4 5 6 7   **986.6**
    1. Gold 2. Incas 3. Buried treasure 4. Incas -- Antiquities 5. Inca goldwork -- Ecuador 6. Treasure-trove -- Ecuador
    ISBN 1-56397-743-5

The author describes his search in the mountains of Ecuador for gold hidden by the Incas

Lourie "succumbed to altitude sickness and had to descend without discovering a glimmer of the gold. But he did return with a ripping good yarn to tell . . . and some breathtaking photographs of the mist-shrouded volcanic peaks. This should be a hot pick for armchair travelers." Bull Cent Child Books

    Includes glossary

988.1   Guyana

Jermyn, Leslie

Guyana; by Leslie Jermyn and Winnie Wong. Marshall Cavendish Benchmark 2010 144 p. col. ill., col. maps (library) $47.07

Grades: 5 6 7 8   **988.1**
    1. Guyana
    ISBN 1608700232; 9781608700233
                                LC 2010000724

This book by Leslie Jermyn is part of the Cultures of the World series and looks at the South American nation of Guyana. "Touching upon everything from its history to religion to architecture, this book . . . highlights the country's rich diversity and unique qualities. With a population that includes many different ethnic groups, the author . . . examines the contributions of each to Guyana's development and to its present culture." Children's Literature

Includes bibliographical references

Morrison, Marion

Guyana. Children's Press 2003 144p il map (Enchantment of the world, Second series) lib bdg $38

Grades: 5 6 7 8   **988.1**
    ISBN 978-0-516-22377-3 lib bdg; 0-516-22377-1 lib bdg
                                LC 2001-6915

Describes the geography, history, culture, religion, and people of Guyana

Includes bibliographical references

989.2   Paraguay

Jermyn, Leslie

Paraguay; [by] Leslie Jermyn and Yong Jui Lin. 2nd ed.; Marshall Cavendish Benchmark 2010 144p il map (Cultures of the world) lib bdg $42.79

Grades: 5 6 7 8   **989.2**
    ISBN 978-0-7614-4858-7 lib bdg; 0-7614-4858-6 lib bdg
                                LC 2009046495
    First published 2000

This offers information on the geography, history, wildlife, governmental structure, economy, cultural diversity, peoples, religion, and culture of Paraguay

Includes glossary and bibliographical references

989.5   Uruguay

Jermyn, Leslie

Uruguay; by Leslie Jermyn and Winnie Wong. 2nd ed.; Marshall Cavendish Benchmark 2009 144p il map (Cultures of the world) lib bdg $42.79

Grades: 5 6 7 8   **989.5**
    ISBN 978-0-7614-4482-4 lib bdg; 0-7614-4482-3 lib bdg
                                LC 2009007127
    First published 1999

Provides information on the geography, history, wildlife, governmental structure, economy, cultural diversity, peoples, religion, and culture of Uruguay

Includes glossary and bibliographical references

993 New Zealand

Gillespie, Carol Ann

New Zealand; [by] Carol Ann Gillespie. updated ed.; Chelsea House Publishers 2005 100p il map (Modern world nations) lib bdg $30

Grades: 7 8 9 10   **993**

     ISBN 0-7910-8708-5

                        LC 2005045445

First published 1992

This describes the natural landscapes, unique plant and animal life, history, culture, people, government and politics, and future outlook of New Zealand

Includes bibliographical references

Jackson, Barbara

★ New Zealand; [by] Barbara Jackson; Vaughan Wood and Simon Milne, consultants. National Geographic 2008 64p il map (Countries of the world) lib bdg $27.90

Grades: 4 5 6 7   **993**

     ISBN 978-1-4263-0301-2 lib bdg; 1-4263-0301-7 lib bdg

This describes the geography, nature, history, people and culture, government, and economy of New Zealand.

Smelt, Roselynn

New Zealand; by Roselynn Smelt. 2nd ed.; Marshall Cavendish Benchmark 2009 128p il map (Cultures of the world) lib bdg $42.79

Grades: 5 6 7 8   **993**

     ISBN 978-0-7614-3415-3 lib bdg; 0-7614-3415-1 lib bdg

                        LC 2008028792

First published 1998

"Provides comprehensive information on the geography, history, wildlife, governmental structure, economy, cultural diversity, peoples, religion, and culture of New Zealand." Publisher's note

Includes glossary and bibliographical references

994 Australia

Arnold, Caroline

★ Uluru, Australia's Aboriginal heart; photographs by Arthur Arnold. Clarion Books 2003 64p il $16

Grades: 5 6 7 8   **994**

     1. Aboriginal Australians 2. Australian aborigines -- Australia -- Uluru National Park

     ISBN 0-618-18181-4

                        LC 2002-15542

Describes Uluru, formerly known as Ayers Rock, in Australia's Uluru-Kata Tjuta National Park, its plant and animal life, and the country's Aboriginal people for whom the site is sacred

"The book's greatest accomplishment . . . is to give readers a sense of the ongoing spiritual importance of Uluru to the Anangu, who have lived around it for 10,000 years. Clear, colorful photos of Uluru and its surroundings appear on nearly every page, illustrating the text with beauty and finesse." Booklist

Einfeld, Jann

Life in the Australian Outback. Lucent Bks. 2003 112p il map (Way people live) lib bdg $21.96

Grades: 6 7 8 9   **994**

     1. Australian aborigines

     ISBN 1-59018-014-3

                        LC 2001-7504

"An in-depth look at a unique culture that exists in Australia's remote interior. Well detailed and meticulously documented, this book does an excellent job of illustrating the diversity of the outback population as well as the challenges faced by its inhabitants." SLJ

Includes glossary and bibliographical references

Leppman, Elizabeth J.

Australia and the Pacific; series consulting editor Charles F. Gritzner. Chelsea House Pubs. 2006 118p il map (Modern world cultures) lib bdg $30

Grades: 7 8 9 10   **994**

     1. Oceania 2. Australia

     ISBN 0-7910-8150-8

This describes the natural landscapes, history, people, culture, geopolitics, economy, regional contrasts, and future outlook of Australia and the Pacific.

Includes bibliographical references

Turner, Kate

★ Australia; [by] Kate Turner; Elaine Stratford and Joseph Powell, consultants. National Geographic 2007 64p il map (Countries of the world) lib bdg $27.90

Grades: 4 5 6 7   **994**

     ISBN 978-1-4263-0055-4

Describes the geography, nature, history, people and culture, government and economy of Australia

This "appealing [title has] wonderful photographs and maps. . . . [This book is a] reliable [source] for country research, and the interesting current material hold browsing potential as well." SLJ

Includes glossary and bibliographical references

995.3 Papua New Guinea

Gascoigne, Ingrid

Papua New Guinea; [by] Ingrid Gascoigne. 2nd ed.; Marshall Cavendish Benchmark 2009 144p il map (Cultures of the world) lib bdg $42.79

Grades: 5 6 7 8   **995.3**

     ISBN 978-0-7614-3416-0 lib bdg; 0-7614-3416-X lib bdg

                        LC 2008028794

First published 1998

"Provides comprehensive information on the geography, history, wildlife, governmental structure, economy, cultural diversity, peoples, religion, and culture of Papua New Guinea." Publisher's note

Includes glossary and bibliographical references

996   Polynesia and other Pacific Ocean islands

NgCheong-Lum, Roseline

Tahiti; [by] Roseline NgCheong-Lum. 2nd ed.; Marshall Cavendish Benchmark 2008 144p il map (Cultures of the world) lib bdg $42.79

Grades: 5 6 7 8   **996**

ISBN 978-0-7614-2089-7

LC 2007014901

"Provides comprehensive information on the geography, history, wildlife, governmental structure, economy, cultural diversity, peoples, religion, and culture of Tahiti." Publisher's note

Includes glossary and bibliographical references

Pelta, Kathy

Rediscovering Easter Island. Lerner Publs. 2000 112p il maps (How history is invented) lib bdg $23.93

Grades: 5 6 7 8   **996**

1. Easter Island
ISBN 0-8225-4890-9

LC 00-9163

Discusses the many visits made by explorers, missionaries, businessmen, scientists, and others to Easter Island since the late 1600s and what they revealed about life on this remote Pacific island

"Coverage is serious, generally evenhanded, and smoothly presented, making this a fine foundation for readers who enjoy digging up the past." Bull Cent Child Books

Includes bibliographical references

996.9   Hawaii and neighboring north central Pacific Ocean islands

Kent, Deborah

Hawaii; by Deborah Kent. Children's Press 2008 144p il map (America the beautiful, third series) lib bdg $38

Grades: 4 5 6 7   **996.9**

ISBN 978-0-531-18573-5; 0-531-18573-7

LC 2007-5705

Describes the history, geography, ecology, people, economy, cities, and sights of the state of Hawaii.

Includes glossary and bibliographical references

998   Arctic islands and Antarctica

Bledsoe, Lucy Jane

★ **How** to survive in Antarctica; written and photographed by Lucy Jane Bledsoe. Holiday House 2006 101p il map $16.95

Grades: 5 6 7 8   **998**

1. Authors 2. Novelists 3. Editors 4. Short story writers 5. Young adult authors
ISBN 0-8234-1890-1

LC 2004-60639

"Bledsoe, who made three trips to study Antarctica, bases her informal, chatty narrative on her thrilling adventure, bringing close the amazing science and geography as well as the gritty facts of human survival in the frigid environment. . . . Bledsoe's own black-and-white photos . . . will grab students across the curriculum." Booklist

Includes glossary

Johnson, Kristin

The **Endurance** expedition. ABDO Pub. Co. 2011 112p il map (Essential events) lib bdg $23.95

Grades: 7 8 9 10 11 12   **998**

1. Explorers 2. Antarctica -- Exploration
ISBN 978-1-61714-764-7; 1-61714-764-8

LC 2010043851

This book "about the race to be the first to reach the South Pole, focuses on the incredible rescue story—a grim survival adventure. The spacious . . . design is inviting, with many color illustrations and screens, and the extensive back matter includes a detailed time line, glossary, bibliography and source notes." Booklist

Includes glossary and bibliographical references

Latta, Sara L.

Ice scientist; careers in the frozen Antarctic. Enslow Publishers 2009 128p il (Wild science careers) lib bdg $31.93

Grades: 5 6 7 8   **998**

1. Scientists 2. Vocational guidance
ISBN 978-0-7660-3048-0 lib bdg; 0-7660-3048-2 lib bdg

LC 2008-4652

The book's "greatest strength is in the variety of first-hand accounts and the scientists' breadth of experience. [The book has] appealing color photographs and an attractive design." SLJ

Includes glossary and bibliographical references

Lourie, Peter

Arctic thaw; the people of the whale in a changing climate. Boyds Mills Press 2007 47p il map $17.95

Grades: 5 6 7 8   **998**

1. Inupiat 2. Whaling 3. Human ecology 4. Greenhouse effect 5. Human ecology -- Alaska
ISBN 978-1-59078-436-5; 1-59078-436-7

LC 2006-20045

"A somewhat sobering, yet upbeat examination of the probable effects of global warming on the culture of the Iñupiaq whale hunters of Alaska's North Slope. . . . [Lourie's] lively, straightforward text describes the mixture of traditional and modern ways of the present-day Iñupiaq, as well as the work of [Paul] Shepson and his team to record weather and climate changes and to predict what effect they will have locally and globally." SLJ

Includes bibliographical references

Lynch, Wayne

Arctic; text and photographs by Wayne Lynch; assisted by Aubrey Lang. NorthWord Books for

Young Readers 2007 64p il map (Our wild world: ecosystems) hardcover o.p. pa $8.95
Grades: 4 5 6 7   **998**
1. Animals -- Arctic regions
ISBN 978-1-55971-960-5; 978-1-55971-961-2 pa
LC 2006021920
"With accessible first-person writing, Lynch describes the Arctic ecosystem, discussing both the high and low Arctic. . . . Stunning photographs include close-ups and more expansive views." Horn Book Guide
Includes bibliographical references

Myers, Walter Dean, 1937-
★ **Antarctica**; journeys to the South Pole. Scholastic Press 2004 134p il maps $18.95
Grades: 6 7 8 9   **998**
1. Antarctica
ISBN 0-439-22001-7
LC 2004-2501
This book tracks "the explorers of the South Pole—including James Cook, Ernest Shackleton, and Richard Evelyn Byrd—and the dangers they encountered there, as well as their contributions to science." (Publisher's note)
This is "a lucid, well-written text." SLJ
Includes bibliographical references

Revkin, Andrew
★ The **North** Pole was here; puzzles and perils at the top of the world. [by] Andrew C. Revkin. 1st ed.; Kingfisher 2006 128p il map $15.95
Grades: 7 8 9 10   **998**
1. Greenhouse effect 2. North Pole
ISBN 0-7534-5993-0; 978-0-7534-5993-5
LC 2005-24307
The author "relates his journey to the top of the world in the company of scientists studying climate changes. The informative chapters weave together accounts of his experiences and observations with details about the environment, its exploration, and scientific concepts. . . . The illustrations include full-color photographs of the author's trek, archival reproductions and photos of previous excursions, original diagrams that clarify concepts, and maps. . . . The wonderfully written narrative will pull youngsters into the book and hold them there willingly until the last page." SLJ
Includes bibliographical references

Tulloch, Coral
Antarctica; the heart of the world. 1st American ed.; Enchanted Lion Books 2006 48p il map $17.95
Grades: 6 7 8 9   **998**
1. Antarctica
ISBN 1-59270-054-3
LC 2005-40162
"Tulloch writes out of her experiences as a voyager on an Antarctic resupply ship to illuminate the continent's geologic history, its flora and fauna, and its importance to the global ecosystem. She also addresses the early and continuing human explorations and their impact on the region as well as the area's rich potential and possible future problems. The writing is clear, and the science is comprehensible

without the slightest sense of talking down to youthful readers." Voice Youth Advocates
Includes bibliographical references

Wade, Rosalyn
Polar worlds. Simon & Schuster Books for Young Readers 2011 64p il (Insiders) $16.99
Grades: 4 5 6 7   **998**
1. Arctic regions 2. Antarctica
ISBN 978-1-4424-3275-8; 1-4424-3275-6
This "takes a look at the nether regions of the globe in this browser-friendly resource. . . . 'Introducing' opens with a geographic look at the Arctic and Antarctic regions, then moves on to the related topics of icebergs, plant and animal life, exploration, survival measures, and environmental threats. The 'In Focus' section zeroes in on 12 specific animals found in polar regions. . . . Each spread is dominated by a sharply rendered, often dramatic digital illustration. . . . A fine introduction to the world's deep freezers." Booklist

Walker, Sally M.
★ **Frozen** secrets; Antarctica revealed. Carolrhoda Books 2010 104p il map $20.95
Grades: 7 8 9 10   **998**
1. Antarctica
ISBN 978-1-58013-607-5; 1-58013-607-9
LC 2009-34282
This is an "account of the rich scientific findings coming out of the planet's southernmost continent. . . . It's an excellent overview that manages to pack a lot of technical and scientific information into a small space, but it's sufficiently well structured conceptually and well laid out visually . . . that it all goes down pretty easily. The photographic images reveal the stunning beauty of the continent in shot after shot, but there are also illuminating views of the scientists at work, and diagrams and maps round out the view." Bull Cent Child Books

Fic   FICTION

50 Cent (Musician), 1975-
Playground; with Aura Moser. Razorbill 2011 314p $17.99
Grades: 5 6 7 8   **Fic**
1. Bullies -- Fiction
ISBN 978-1-59514-434-8; 1-59514-434-X
Thirteen-year-old Butterball doesn't have much going for him. He's teased about his weight. He hates the Long Island suburb his mom moved them to so she could go to nursing school and start her life over. He wishes he still lived with his dad in New York City where there's always something happening, even if his dad doesn't have much time for him. Still, that's not why he beat up Maurice on the playground.
"Readers who were ever confused about having a gay parent, or being overweight, or going through a parental breakup, or just wanting to fit in and be accepted by their peers, will relate to Butterball. 50 Cents's debut young adult novel is a quick read that will be great for discussions on a variety of important and timely topics." Voice Youth Advocates

Abbott, Ellen Jensen

Watersmeet. Marshall Cavendish 2009 341p il $16.99

Grades: 6 7 8 9 10   **Fic**

1. Fantasy fiction
ISBN 978-0-7614-5536-3; 0-7614-5536-1

LC 2008-315

Fourteen-year-old Absina escapes the escalating violence, prejudice, and religious fervor of her home town, Vranille, and sets out with a dwarf, Haret, to seek the father she has never met in a place called Watersmeet.

"The relationship between Abisina and Haret is warm and engaging, and the dialogue between them cleverly captures the slow development of their camaraderie. . . . Fans of Ursula Le Guin's character-driven fantasies will enjoy this story of Abisina's quest to unify both her divided country and her divided self." Bull Cent Child Books

Abbott, Tony

Lunch-box dream. Farrar Straus Giroux 2011 178p $16.99

Grades: 6 7 8 9   **Fic**

1. Family life -- Fiction 2. Segregation -- Fiction 3. Race relations -- Fiction 4. Missing children -- Fiction 5. African Americans -- Fiction 6. Voyages and travels -- Fiction
ISBN 978-0-374-34673-7; 0-374-34673-9

LC 2010-33105

Told from multiple points of view, a white family on a 1959 road trip between Ohio and Florida, visiting Civil War battlefields along the way, crosses paths with a black family near Atlanta, where one of their children has gone missing.

"Throughout, Abbott . . . builds an increasingly disturbing undercurrent of racial conflict, sibling distrust, and marital discord. Although beautifully crafted and written, the book's emotional complexity and unsettling tone will likely prove challenging." Publ Wkly

★ The **postcard**. Little, Brown 2008 358p il $15.99; pa $5.99

Grades: 5 6 7 8   **Fic**

1. Mystery fiction 2. Grandmothers -- Fiction 3. Books and reading -- Fiction
ISBN 978-0-316-01172-3; 0-316-01172-X; 978-0-316-01173-0 pa; 0-316-01173-8 pa

LC 2007-31074

While in St. Petersburg, Florida, to help clean out his recently-deceased grandmother's house, thirteen-year-old Jason finds an old postcard which leads him on an adventure that blends figures from an old, unfinished detective story with his family's past.

"Mystery fans will appreciate the depth and intrigue of the dual level mysteries, and will also enjoy the wit and banter of the main characters." Libr Media Connect

Abdel-Fattah, Randa

★ **Does** my head look big in this? Orchard Books 2007 360p $16.99

Grades: 7 8 9 10 11 12   **Fic**

1. School stories 2. Muslims -- Fiction 3. Clothing and dress -- Fiction
ISBN 978-0-439-91947-0; 0-439-91947-9

LC 2006-29117

Year Eleven at an exclusive prep school in the suburbs of Melbourne, Australia, would be tough enough, but it is further complicated for Amal when she decides to wear the hijab, the Muslim head scarf, full-time as a badge of her faith—without losing her identity or sense of style.

"While the novel deals with a number of serious issues, it is extremely funny and entertaining." SLJ

Ten things I hate about me. Orchard Books 2009 297p $16.99

Grades: 7 8 9 10   **Fic**

1. School stories 2. Muslims -- Fiction 3. Lebanese -- Fiction 4. Prejudices -- Fiction
ISBN 978-0-5450-5055-5; 0-5450-5055-3

LC 2008-13667

This novel is set in Australia. Jamilia, known in school as Jamie, tries to hide her Muslim heritage from her classmates, until her conflicted feelings become too difficult for her to bear.

A "message of the importance of self-disclosure to maintain loving relationships of all kinds plays itself out as Jamie learns to negotiate her roles as daughter, sister, and friend. Readers will also get an enlightening look at post-9/11 racial tensions outside the U.S. and the problems they pose for Muslim teens." Bull Cent Child Books

★ **Where** the streets had a name; Randa Abdel-Fattah. Scholastic Press 2010 313p (reinforced binding) $17.99

Grades: 5 6 7 8   **Fic**

1. Jerusalem -- Fiction 2. Voyages and travels -- Fiction 3. Jewish-Arab relations -- Fiction 4. Muslims -- Fiction 5. Family life -- Fiction 6. Palestinian Arabs -- Fiction 7. Israel-Arab conflicts -- Fiction
ISBN 0545172926; 9780545172929; 978-0-545-17292-9; 0-545-17292-6

LC 2009043122

This book tells the story of 13-year-old Hayaat, who "lives behind the Israeli-built Separation Wall in the West Bank City of Bethlehem. When her beloved grandmother falls ill . . . [she] decides to make her way to Jerusalem to fill an empty hummus jar with soil from the land of her grandmother's ancestral home. She is certain that this will mend her heart. Unfortunately, although Jerusalem is merely minutes away, curfews, checkpoints, and an identity card that doesn't allow her to cross the border mean that Hayaat and her soccer-loving, troublemaker friend Samy face a perilous journey." (School Lib J)

"Hayaat chronicles this life-altering journey in the first-person, present tense, giving readers an intimate glimpse into the life of her warm, eccentric Muslim family, who survive despite the volatile political environment. A refreshing and hopeful teen perspective on the Israeli-Palestinian dilemma." Kirkus

Abela, Deborah

The **ghosts** of Gribblesea Pier. Farrar Straus Giroux 2011 232p $16.99

Grades: 4 5 6   **Fic**
1. Ghost stories 2. Circus -- Fiction 3. Family life -- Fiction 4. Swindlers and swindling -- Fiction 5. Eccentrics and eccentricities -- Fiction
ISBN 978-0-374-36239-3; 0-374-36239-4
LC 2010022517
Aurelie Bonhoffen, who has grown up in the circus, discovers a remarkable family secret on her twelfth birthday that may help in dealing with a sinister man who wants to take over her family's pier.

This is a "charmer of a ghostly adventure tale. . . . This fast-paced, engaging, and charming story has echoes of Jeanne Birdsall's 'Penderwicks' . . . and some Dickensian elements, but in the end this is just a finely executed story of family and friendship and the ties that bind a community." SLJ

Abrahams, Peter
Behind the curtain; an Echo Falls mystery. 1st ed.; Laura Geringer Books 2006 346p $15.99; lib bdg $16.89
Grades: 6 7 8   **Fic**
1. Mystery fiction
ISBN 9780060737047; 0-06-073704-2; 9780060737054 lib bdg; 0-06-073705-0 lib bdg
LC 2005-17774
An avid Sherlock Holmes fan, eighth grader Ingrid Levin-Hill is kidnapped while investigating mysterious happenings in her home town.

"This is a fast-paced mystery with well-defined characters and a plausible plotline and ending." SLJ

Down the rabbit hole; an Echo Falls mystery. Laura Geringer Books 2005 375p $15.99; lib bdg $16.89; pa $6.99
Grades: 6 7 8   **Fic**
1. Mystery fiction
ISBN 0-06-073701-8; 0-06-073702-6 lib bdg; 0-06-073703-4 pa
LC 2004-14778
"Ingrid Levin-Hill . . . has just been cast as the lead in Alice in Wonderland when she finds herself in a different role—murder detective. The corpse is that of 'Cracked-Up Katie,' whom Ingrid encountered when she attempted to get from her orthodontist to soccer practice." Publ Wkly

Into the dark; an Echo Falls mystery. Laura Geringer Books 2008 300p $15.99; lib bdg $16.89
Grades: 6 7 8   **Fic**
1. Mystery fiction
ISBN 978-0-06-073708-5; 0-06-073708-5; 978-0-06-073709-2 lib bdg; 0-06-073709-3 lib bdg
LC 2006-103018
Thirteen-year-old Sherlock Holmes aficionado Ingrid Levin-Hill tries to clear her grandfather's name when he is accused of murdering an environmental activist on his farm.

"This third installment of the enjoyable Echo Falls mysteries reaffirms the series' quality." Voice Youth Advocates

Reality check. HarperTeen 2009 330p $16.99; lib bdg $17.89; pa $8.99

Grades: 7 8 9 10   **Fic**
1. School stories 2. Gambling -- Fiction 3. Social classes -- Fiction 4. Missing persons -- Fiction
ISBN 978-0-06-122766-0; 0-06-122766-8; 978-0-06-122767-7 lib bdg; 0-06-122767-6 lib bdg; 978-0-06-122768-4 pa; 0-06-122768-4 pa
LC 2008-22593
After a knee injury destroys sixteen-year-old Cody's college hopes, he drops out of high school and gets a job in his small Montana town, but when his ex-girlfriend disappears from her Vermont boarding school, Cody travels cross-country to join the search.

"Abrahams writes a fine thriller that is pitched to attract everyone from reluctant readers to sports fans to romantic idealists." Voice Youth Advocates

Acampora, Paul
Rachel Spinelli punched me in the face. Roaring Brook Press 2011 168p $15.99
Grades: 5 6 7 8   **Fic**
1. Moving -- Fiction 2. Trumpet -- Fiction 3. Musicians -- Fiction 4. Friendship -- Fiction 5. Family life -- Fiction 6. Single parent family -- Fiction
ISBN 978-1-59643-548-3; 1-59643-548-8
LC 2010027436
When fourteen-year-old Zachary and his father move to Falls, Connecticut, he spends a summer falling in love, coming to terms with his mother's absence, and forming eclectic friendships.

"Realistic dialogue and poignantly amusing situations . . . all come together to gently flesh out a few months in the lives of people readers will savor getting to know. . . . An outstanding, humane coming-of-age tale of loss, yearning and forgiveness." Kirkus

Ackley, Amy
Sign language; a novel. Viking 2011 392p $16.99
Grades: 7 8 9 10   **Fic**
1. School stories 2. Death -- Fiction 3. Fathers -- Fiction 4. Bereavement -- Fiction 5. Family life -- Fiction
ISBN 978-0-670-01318-0; 0-670-01318-8
LC 2011003001
Teenaged Abby must deal with her feelings about her father's cancer and its aftermath while simultaneously navigating the difficult problems of growing up.

"This is an amazing debut novel for readers who appreciate contemporary teen fiction. It is both moving and realistic, a result of the well-crafted family relationships. The author succeeds in creating genuine connections that manage not to feel forced or rushed, despite the pace of the story, which spans three years." Voice Youth Advocates

Ada, Alma Flor, 1938-
Yes! we are Latinos; by Alma Flor Ada and F. Isabel Campoy; illustrated by David Diaz. Charlesbridge 2013 96 p. ill. (reinforced) $18.95
Grades: 7 8 9 10   **Fic**
1. Hispanic Americans -- Poetry 2. American poetry -- Latino authors 3. Short stories 4. Immigrants -- Fiction 5. Emigration and immigration -- Fiction 6. Latin

Americans -- United States -- Fiction 7. Immigrants -- United States -- fiction 8. Latin Americans -- United States -- fiction 9. Latin Americans -- Cultural assimilation -- fiction
ISBN 158089383X; 9781580893831

LC 2012027214

In this book, the authors "shape fictional portraits of 13 young people living in the U.S., who have diverse experiences and backgrounds but share a Latino heritage. The first-person narrative poems range from reflective to free-spirited, methodical to free-association. . . . Informative nonfictional interludes . . . address relevant subjects, including immigration, the challenges migrant workers face, and Cuba-U.S. history." (Publishers Weekly)

Includes bibliographical references and index

Adam, Paul

Max Cassidy: escape from Shadow Island. Walden Pond Press 2010 295p $16.99; pa $5.99
Grades: 6 7 8 9   **Fic**
1. Mystery fiction 2. Adventure fiction 3. Missing persons -- Fiction
ISBN 978-0-06-186323-3; 0-06-186323-8; 978-0-06-186325-7 pa; 0-06-186325-4 pa

LC 2009-12031

First published 2009 in the United Kingdom with title: Escape from Shadow Island

British fourteen-year-old Max Cassidy calls on his skills and training as a professional escape artist when he attempts to clear his mother of murdering his father, who disappeared two years earlier in the Central American country of Santo Domingo.

"With a cliffhanger ending, look for much more of this series and be sure to hand it to your reluctant readers." Voice Youth Advocates

Adams, Douglas

Life, the universe, and everything. Harmony Bks. 1982 227p hardcover o.p. pa $12.95
Grades: 11 12 Adult   **Fic**
1. Satire 2. Science fiction 3. Interplanetary voyages 4. Humor
ISBN 0-517-54874-7; 0-345-41890-6 pa

LC 82-15470

"Arthur Dent and his motley crew do tie up most of the loose ends and manage to prevent the destruction of the universe, but the first two novels . . . 'must' be read to understand the situation, and even then it's confusing." Libr J

Mostly harmless. Harmony Bks. 1992 277p hardcover o.p. pa $12.95
Grades: 11 12 Adult   **Fic**
1. Science fiction 2. Satirical fiction 3. Space flight -- Fiction
ISBN 0-517-57740-2; 0-345-37933-0 pa

LC 92-25457

"A Grebulon reconnaissance ship with faulty programming, a news reporter suffering from a bad case of missed opportunities, a fugitive from the new 'improved' offices of the Hitchhiker's Guide to the Galaxy, and a hitchhiker lost in a parallel universe come together in grand style in the fifth installment of Adams's best-selling 'trilogy.'" Libr J

So long, and thanks for all the fish. Harmony Bks. 1985 204p hardcover o.p. pa $7.99
Grades: 11 12 Adult   **Fic**
1. Satire 2. Wit and humor 3. Science fiction 4. Interplanetary voyages 5. Humor
ISBN 0-517-55439-9; 0-345-39183-4 pa

LC 84-19350

Arthur Dent "returns to a supposedly destroyed Earth to build a hyperspace bypass. The night of his return, Arthur falls in love with a sedated girl (her brother says she's 'barking mad'), only to lose her, then accidentally find her twice more. She is Fenchurch, the girl who in . . . 'Guide' . . . discovered the secret of Earth's potential happiness moments before it was demolished. Her 'madness' stems from the time when Earth should have been destroyed, and wasn't, but when all the dolphins disappeared. . . . The humor is still off-the-wall, but less forced and more gentle than the other books. . . . The series seems to be winding down, but it is still an addictive commodity to its fans." SLJ

★ The **hitchhiker's** guide to the galaxy; 25th anniversary illustrated collector's ed.; Harmony Books 2004 271p il $35
Grades: 7 8 9 10 11 12 Adult   **Fic**
1. Satire 2. Wit and humor 3. Science fiction 4. Interplanetary voyages 5. Humor
ISBN 1-4000-5293-9

LC 2004-558987

First published 1980

"Based on a BBC radio series, . . . this is the episodic story of Arthur Dent, a contemporary Englishman who discovers first that his unpretentious house is about to be demolished to make way for a bypass, and second that a good friend is actually an alien galactic hitchhiker who announces that Earth itself will soon be demolished to make way for an intergalactic speedway. A suitably bewildered Dent soon finds himself hitching . . . rides throughout space, aided by a . . . reference book, The Hitchhiker's Guide to the Galaxy, a compendium of 'facts,' philosophies, and wild advice." Libr J

The **restaurant** at the end of the universe. Harmony Bks. 1981 250p hardcover o.p. pa $12.95
Grades: 11 12 Adult   **Fic**
1. Satire 2. Wit and humor 3. Science fiction 4. Interplanetary voyages 5. Humor
ISBN 0-517-54535-7; 0-345-41892-1 pa

LC 81-6563

First published 1980 in the United Kingdom

"Poor uprooted Arthur Dent finds himself swept along in the wake of Zaphod Beeblebrox, former President of the Galaxy, as Zaphod searches for the man who rules the Universe. They and their companions tumble from one scrape into another, with the erratic aid of Zaphod's dead great-grandfather and Marvin, their perpetually depressed robot. Adams's lively sense of the ridiculous has concocted many hilarious episodes, though the inspired lunacy of the first book has become rather uneven here. Still, this is one of the best pieces of sf humor available." Libr J

Adams, Richard

Watership Down; Scribner classics ed.; Scribner 1996 429p $30; pa $15

Grades: 6 7 8 9 10   **Fic**

1. Allegories 2. Rabbits -- Fiction

ISBN 0-684-83605-X; 0-7432-7770-8 pa

First published 1972 in the United Kingdom; first United States edition 1974 by Macmillan

"Faced with the annihilation of its warren, a small group of male rabbits sets out across the English downs in search of a new home. Internal struggles for power surface in this intricately woven, realistically told adult adventure when the protagonists must coordinate tactics in order to defeat an enemy rabbit fortress. It is clear that the author has done research on rabbit behavior, for this tale is truly authentic." Shapiro Fic for Youth. 3d edition

Adams, S. J.

Sparks; the epic, completely true blue, (almost) holy quest of Debbie. 1; Flux 2011 256p pa $9.95

Grades: 8 9 10 11 12   **Fic**

1. Lesbians -- Fiction 2. Religion -- Fiction

ISBN 978-0-7387-2676-2; 0-7387-2676-1

LC 2011022913

Stonewall Honor Book (2013)

A sixteen-year-old lesbian tries to get over a crush on her religious best friend by embarking on a 'holy quest' with a couple of misfits who have invented a wacky, made-up faith called the Church of Blue.

"Adams has an easy sense of humor . . . and Debbie and her offbeat cohorts are nuanced and authentic as they follow a circuitous path to greater self-awareness and self-reliance." Publ Wkly

Adler, David A.

Don't talk to me about the war. Viking 2008 216p $15.99; pa $6.99

Grades: 4 5 6 7   **Fic**

1. Friendship -- Fiction 2. Family life -- Fiction 3. World War, 1939-1945 -- Fiction

ISBN 978-0-670-06307-9; 0-670-06307-X; 978-0-14-241372-2 pa; 0-14-241372-0 pa

LC 2007-17889

In 1940, thirteen-year-old Tommy's routine of school, playing stickball in his Bronx, New York, neighborhood, talking with his friend Beth, and listening to Dodgers games on the radio changes as his mother's illness and his increasing awareness of the war in Europe transform his world.

"An engaging and very accessible historical novel." Booklist

Adler, Emily

Sweet 15; by Emily Adler and Alex Echevarria. Marshall Cavendish 2009 240p $16.99

Grades: 7 8 9 10   **Fic**

1. School stories 2. Family life -- Fiction 3. Puerto Ricans -- Fiction 4. Quinceañera (Social custom) -- Fiction

ISBN 978-0-7614-5584-4; 0-7614-5584-1

LC 2008-21391

Shortly before her fifteenth birthday, Destiny Lozada's traditional Puerto Rican mother and feminist older sister hijack her quinceanera, each pushing her own agenda and ignoring the possibility that Destiny, a skateboarding tomboy, might have her own ideas about the coming-of-age ritual she is about to participate in.

"Destiny's resolution, the engaging dialogue, boys, gossip, best friends, fashion, texting, the first kiss and the city of New York all play a part in this charming, fresh and funny coming-of-age novel that will entertain teen readers, especially girls." Kirkus

Adlington, L. J.

Cherry Heaven. Greenwillow Books 2008 458p $16.99; lib bdg $17.89

Grades: 7 8 9 10   **Fic**

1. Science fiction 2. Orphans -- Fiction

ISBN 978-0-06-143180-7; 0-06-143180-X; 978-0-06-143181-4 lib bdg; 0-06-143181-8 lib bdg

LC 2007-24679

Kat and Tanka J leave the wartorn city, move with their adoptive parents to the New Frontier, and are soon settled into a home called Cherry Heaven, but Luka, an escaped factory worker, confirms their suspicion that New Frontier is not the utopia it seems to be.

"In this complex, absorbing, and sometimes disquieting novel, Adlington creates a world that is distinctly different from our own, yet chillingly familiar." Booklist

★ The **diary** of Pelly D. Greenwillow Books 2005 282p hardcover o.p. pa $8.99

Grades: 7 8 9 10   **Fic**

1. Science fiction

ISBN 0-06-076615-8; 0-06-076617-4 pa

LC 2004-52258

"On the planet Home From Home, Toni V is a brute laborer, a barely educated member of the Demolition Crew that is busy pulverizing the bombed-out remains of City Five's central plaza. Pelly D is a hip member of the swank elite who used to live in an exclusive apartment fronting the plaza. Their stories come together when Toni V uncovers Pelly D's diary in the debris. . . . Middle school, high school." Horn Book

"Adlington has crafted an original and disturbing dystopian fantasy told in a smart and sympathetic teen voice." Booklist

Agard, John

★ The **young** inferno; written by John Agard; illustrated by Satoshi Kitamura. Frances Lincoln Children's 2009 un il $19.95

Grades: 8 9 10 11 12   **Fic**

1. Novels in verse 2. Hell -- Fiction

ISBN 978-1-84507-769-3; 1-84507-769-5

"The narrative poems in this short book are accessible and have important things to say about the state of the human race. . . . The hoodie-wearing protagonist . . . awakens in a strange and frightening forest. A dark man appears and introduces himself as the tale-teller Aesop: he is to be the teen's escort through Hell. . . . As the pair travels through the Circles of Hell, they see the sins of mankind. . . . The scribbled, heavy-lined black ink and watercolor illustrations convey exactly the right mood for a book about a modern-day expedition into Hell. This will be a great book to pair with a discussion about Dante's Inferno and/or poetic structure." SLJ

Agell, Charlotte

Shift. Henry Holt and Co. 2008 230p $16.95

Grades: 7 8 9 10   Fic

1. Science fiction 2. Religion -- Fiction 3. Family life -- Fiction 4. Resistance to government -- Fiction 5. Environmental degradation -- Fiction

ISBN 978-0-8050-7810-7; 0-8050-7810-X

LC 2007-46942

In fifteen-year-old Adrian Havoc's world, HomeState rules every aspect of society and religious education is enforced but Adrian, refusing to believe that the Apocalypse is at hand, goes north through the Deadlands and joins a group of insurgents.

"The story is made particularly compelling by the economy and lyricism of the writing style. . . . Readers seeking contemplative and philosophical science fiction will find this a haunting exploration of government gone awry and one boy's steadfast pursuit of justice." Bull Cent Child Books

Aguiar, Nadia

Secrets of Tamarind. Feiwel and Friends 2011 373p map (The Book of Tamarind) $16.99

Grades: 5 6 7 8   Fic

1. Adventure fiction 2. Magic -- Fiction 3. Islands -- Fiction 4. Siblings -- Fiction 5. Environmental degradation -- Fiction

ISBN 978-0-312-38030-4; 0-312-38030-5

LC 2010050898

Four years after leaving the lost island of Tamarind, Maya, Simon, and Penny Nelson return to stop the Red Coral Project, a sinister group mining the magical mineral ophalla there and, in the process, ruining the magnificent island.

"Replete with ecological warnings applicable to real as well as fantasy worlds and glossed with lush descriptions of imaginary flora and fauna, the rapid-fire plot bristles with danger." Kirkus

The **lost** island of Tamarind; [by] Nadia Aguiar. Feiwel and Friends 2008 437p il map (The Book of Tamarind) $17.95

Grades: 5 6 7 8   Fic

1. War stories 2. Adventure fiction 3. Magic -- Fiction 4. Giants -- Fiction 5. Islands -- Fiction 6. Pirates -- Fiction 7. Siblings -- Fiction

ISBN 978-0-312-38029-8; 0-312-38029-1

LC 2008-5623

Thirteen-year-old Maya, who has spent her life at sea with her marine biologist parents, yearns for a normal life, but when a storm washes her parents overboard, life becomes anything but normal for Maya, her younger brother and baby sister, as they land at a mysterious, uncharted island filled with danger.

"Each detail of this fantasy is crafted with care; readers will be drawn into this dangerous, magical world where anything is possible and nothing can be fully explained." SLJ

Aguirre, Ann

Enclave. Feiwel & Friends 2011 262p $16.99

Grades: 8 9 10   Fic

1. Horror fiction 2. Fantasy fiction 3. Dystopian fiction 4. Apocalyptic fiction 5. Zombies -- Fiction

ISBN 978-0-312-65008-7; 0-312-65008-6

LC 2010031039

In a post-apocalyptic future, fifteen-year-old Deuce, a loyal Huntress, brings back meat while avoiding the Freaks outside her enclave, but when she is partnered with the mysterious outsider, Fade, she begins to see that the strict ways of the elders may be wrong—and dangerous. Bull Cent Child Books

"In this skilled though violent postapocalyptic thriller, Deuce has newly earned the rank of Huntress. . . . It's her duty to provide meat for her loveless, draconian enclave, deep beneath the streets of a ruined city, as well as to defend it against cannibalistic Freaks, who are gradually eliminating the scattered human survivors of a vaguely remembered plague. . . . Aguirre . . . has created a gritty and highly competent heroine, an equally deadly sidekick/love interest, and a fascinating if unpleasant civilization." Publ Wkly

Aiken, Joan

★ The **wolves** of Willoughby Chase; illustrated by Pat Marriott. Delacorte Press 2000 181p il hardcover o.p. pa $6.99

Grades: 5 6 7 8   Fic

1. Great Britain -- Fiction

ISBN 0-385-32790-0; 0-440-49603-9 pa

First published 1962 in the United Kingdom; first United States edition 1963 by Doubleday

"Plot, characterization, and background blend perfectly into an amazing whole. . . . Highly recommended." SLJ

Other titles in this series are:

Black hearts in Battersea (1964)
Cold Shoulder Road (1996)
The cuckoo tree (1971)
Dangerous games (1999)
Is underground (1993)
Midwinter nightingale (2003)
Nightbirds on Nantucket (1966)
The stolen lake (1981)
The witch of Clatteringshaws (2005)

Alban, Andrea

Anya's war. Feiwel and Friends 2011 188p $16.99

Grades: 7 8 9 10   Fic

1. Jews -- China -- Fiction 2. Jewish refugees -- Fiction 3. Abandoned children -- Fiction 4. Sino-Japanese Conflict, 1937-1945 -- Fiction

ISBN 978-0-312-37093-0; 0-312-37093-8

LC 2010-37089

In 1937, the privileged and relatively carefee life of a fourteen-year-old Jewish girl, whose family emigrated from Odessa, Ukraine, to Shanghai, China, comes to an end when she finds an abandoned baby, her hero, Amelia Earhart, goes missing, and war breaks out with Japan. Based on the author's family history.

"Most moving are the scenes with the full cast of family characters, who are irritating, irritable, funny, surprising, mean, and prejudiced. Alban also explores the complexities of Anya's Jewish community. . . . An important addition to literature about WWII refugees." Booklist

Albin, Gennifer

Crewel; Gennifer Albin. by Gennifer Albin. Farrar Straus Giroux 2012 368 p. (hardcover) $17.99

Grades: 8 9 10 11   **Fic**

1. Spiritual gifts 2. Secrecy -- Fiction 3. Psychics -- Fiction 4. Science fiction

ISBN 0374316414; 9780374316419; 9780374316440

LC 2011043930

In author Gennifer Albin's book, "sixteen year-old Adelice Lewys has a secret: she wants to fail. Gifted with the ability to weave time with matter, she's exactly what the Guild is looking for, and in the world of Arras, being chosen as a Spinster is everything a girl could want. . . . It also means the power to embroider the very fabric of life . . . [and] Adelice isn't interested. Not that her feelings matter, because she slipped and wove a moment at testing, and they're coming for her--tonight. Now she has one hour . . . to escape." (genniferalbin.com)

Alcott, Louisa May

Little women; illustrated by Scott McKowen. Sterling Pub. 2004 525p il $9.95

Grades: 5 6 7 8   **Fic**

1. Sisters -- Fiction 2. Family life -- Fiction

ISBN 978-1-4027-1458-0; 1-4027-1458-0

LC 2004-15669

First published 1868

Chronicles the joys and sorrows of the four March sisters as they grow into young women in mid-nineteenth-century New England.

Other titles about members of the March family are:

Eight cousins (1875)

Jo's boys (1886)

Little men (1871)

Rose in bloom (1876)

Alegria, Malin

Estrella's quinceanera. Simon & Schuster Books for Young Readers 2006 272p $14.95

Grades: 7 8 9 10   **Fic**

1. Mexican Americans -- Fiction 2. Quinceañera (Social custom) -- Fiction

ISBN 0-689-87809-5

Estrella's mother and aunt are planning a gaudy, traditional quinceañera for her, even though it is the last thing she wants.

"Alegria writes about Mexican American culture, first love, family, and of moving between worlds with poignant, sharp-sighted humor and authentic dialogue." Booklist

Alender, Katie

Bad girls don't die. Hyperion Books 2009 352p $15.99

Grades: 7 8 9 10   **Fic**

1. School stories 2. Sisters -- Fiction 3. Demoniac possession -- Fiction

ISBN 978-1-4231-0876-4; 1-4231-0876-0

LC 2008-46179

When fifteen-year-old Lexi's younger sister Kasey begins behaving strangely and their old Victorian house seems to take on a life of its own, Lexi investigates and discovers some frightening facts about previous occupants of the house, leading her to believe that many lives are in danger.

This "novel is both a mystery and a trip into the paranormal. . . . With just enough violence, suspense, and romance to keep readers turning pages, this . . . will be a popular addition to any YA collection." Booklist

Alexander, Jill S.

Paradise. Feiwel and Friends 2011 246p $16.99

Grades: 7 8 9 10   **Fic**

1. Love stories 2. Drums -- Fiction 3. Family life -- Fiction 4. Bands (Music) -- Fiction 5. Country music -- Fiction

ISBN 0312605412; 9780312605414

LC 2010050900

Teenaged Paisley Tillery dreams a career as a professional drummer will take her out of her small Texas town, but when her country rock band gets a handsome new lead singer from Paradise, Texas, those dreams may change.

"Strong, rural Southern storytelling and mother-daughter conflict are integral parts of the plot. . . . Alexander's simmering plot is . . . driven by a complex story and multiple, complex characters." SLJ

★ The sweetheart of Prosper County. Feiwel and Friends 2009 212p $16.99

Grades: 7 8 9 10   **Fic**

1. Bullies -- Fiction 2. Bereavement -- Fiction 3. Mother-daughter relationship -- Fiction

ISBN 978-0-312-54856-8; 0-312-54856-7

LC 2008-34757

In a small East Texas town largely ruled by prejudices and bullies, fourteen-year-old Austin sets out to win a ride in the next parade and, in the process, grows in her understanding of friendship and helps her widowed mother through her mourning.

"This is a warm, humorous story. . . . A refreshing picture of teen angst, with realistic dialogue and memorable characters." SLJ

Alexander, Lloyd

★ Westmark. Dutton 1981 184p hardcover o.p. pa $5.99

Grades: 5 6 7 8   **Fic**

1. Adventure fiction

ISBN 0-14-131068-5

A boy fleeing from criminal charges falls in with a charlatan, his dwarf attendant, and an urchin girl, travels with them about the kingdom of Westmark, and ultimately arrives at the palace where the king is grieving over the loss of his daughter

The author "peoples his tale with a marvelous cast of individuals, and weaves an intricate story of high adventure that climaxes in a superbly conceived conclusion, which, though predictable, is reached through carefully built tension and subtly added comic relief." Booklist

Other titles in this series are:

The Beggar Queen (1984)

The Kestrel (1982)

★ The **book** of three; rev ed.; Holt & Co. 1999
190p (Chronicles of Prydain) $19.95; pa $6.99
Grades: 5 6 7 8   **Fic**
    1. Fantasy fiction
    ISBN 978-0-8050-6132-1; 0-8050-6132-0; 978-0-
    8050-8048-3 pa; 0-8050-8048-1 pa
                     LC 98-40901

First published 1964
"Related in a simple, direct style, this fast-paced tale of
high adventure has a well-balanced blend of fantasy, realism, and humor." SLJ
    Other titles about the mythical land of Prydain are:
    The black cauldron (1965)
    The castle of Llyr (1966)
    The foundling and other tales of Prydain (1999)
    The high king (1968)
    Taran Wanderer (1967)

★ The **golden** dream of Carlo Chuchio. Henry
Holt & Co. 2007 306p il $16.95
Grades: 5 6 7 8 9   **Fic**
    1. Fantasy fiction 2. Buried treasure -- Fiction 3.
    Voyages and travels -- Fiction 4. Young adult literature
    -- Works
    ISBN 978-0-8050-8333-0; 0-8050-8333-2
                     LC 2006-49710
    Naive and bumbling Carlo, his shady camel-puller Bak-
sheesh, and Shira, a girl determined to return home, follow a
treasure map through the deserts and cities of the infamous
Golden Road, as mysterious strangers try in vain to point
them toward real treasures
    This "is an exuberant and compassionate tale of adven-
ture." Publ Wkly

★ The **iron** ring. Dutton Children's Bks. 1997
283p hardcover o.p. pa $5.99
Grades: 5 6 7 8   **Fic**
    1. Adventure fiction
    ISBN 0-14-130348-4 pa
                     LC 96-29730
    "Young Tamar, ruler of a small Indian kingdom, wagers
with a visiting king and loses his kingdom and his freedom.
Traveling to the king's land to make good on his debt, he
collects quite an entourage and eventually overcomes his
enemies with his friends' help. This tale offers delightful
characters, a philosophical interest in the meaning of life,
a thoughtful look at the caste system, and a clever use of
Indian animal folktales." Horn Book Guide

★ The **remarkable** journey of Prince Jen. Dutton Children's Bks. 1991 273p hardcover o.p. pa
$6.99
Grades: 5 6 7 8   **Fic**
    1. Adventure fiction
    ISBN 0-14-240225-7 pa
                     LC 91-13720
    Bearing six unusual gifts, young Prince Jen in Tang Dy-
nasty China embarks on a perilous quest and emerges trium-
phantly into manhood

"Alexander satisfies the taste for excitement, but his vivid characters and the food for thought he offers will nourish
long after the last page is turned." SLJ

Alexie, Sherman, 1966-
    ★ The **absolutely** true diary of a part-time In-
dian; art by Ellen Forney. Little, Brown 2007 229p
il $18.99
Grades: 8 9 10   **Fic**
    1. School stories 2. Friendship -- Fiction 3. Family life
    -- Fiction 4. Native Americans -- Fiction
    ISBN 0316013684; 9780316013680
                     LC 2007-22799
    National Book Award for Young People's Literature
(2007)
    Boston Globe-Horn Book Award: Fiction and Poetry
(2008)
    Budding cartoonist Junior leaves his troubled school on
the Spokane Indian Reservation to attend an all-white farm
town school where the only other Indian is the school mascot.
    "The many characters, on and off the rez, with whom he
has dealings are portrayed with compassion and verve. . . .
Forney's simple pencil cartoons fit perfectly within the story
and reflect the burgeoning artist within Junior." Booklist

Allison, Jennifer
    ★ **Gilda** Joyce, psychic investigator. Sleuth/
Dutton 2005 321p $13.99; pa $6.99
Grades: 5 6 7 8   **Fic**
    1. Mystery fiction 2. Cousins -- Fiction
    ISBN 978-0-525-47375-6; 0-525-47375-0; 978-0-14-
    240698-4 pa; 0-14-240698-8 pa
                     LC 2004-10834
    During the summer before ninth grade, intrepid Gilda
Joyce invites herself to the San Francisco mansion of distant
cousin Lester Splinter and his thirteen-year-old daughter,
where she uses her purported psychic abilities and detective skills to solve the mystery of the mansion's boarded-
up tower.
    "Allison pulls off something special here. She not only
offers a credible mystery . . . but also . . . provides particularly strong characterizations." Booklist
    Other titles about Gilda Joyce are:
    Gilda Joyce: the Ladies of the Lake (2006)
    Gilda Joyce: the ghost sonata (2007)
    Gilda Joyce: the dead drop (2009)
    Gilda Joyce: the bones of the holy (2011)

Almond, David, 1951-
    Clay. Delacorte Press 2006 247p hardcover o.p.
pa $8.99
Grades: 7 8 9 10   **Fic**
    1. Horror fiction 2. Supernatural -- Fiction
    ISBN 0-385-73171-X; 0-440-42013-X pa
                     LC 2005-22681
    The developing relationship between teenager Davie and
a mysterious new boy in town morphs into something darker
and more sinister when Davie learns firsthand of the boy's
supernatural powers.

"Rooted in the ordinariness of a community and in one boy's chance to play God, this story will grab readers with its gripping action and its important ideas." Booklist

★ **Kit's** wilderness; 10th-anniversary edition; Delacorte Press 2009 229p $16.99

Grades: 6 7 8 9 10   **Fic**

1. Ghost stories 2. Coal mines and mining -- Fiction
ISBN 978-0-385-32665-0; 0-385-32665-3
First published 1999
Michael L. Printz Award, 2001

Thirteen-year-old Kit goes to live with his grandfather in the decaying coal mining town of Stoneygate, England, and finds both the old man and the town haunted by ghosts of the past

The author "explores the power of friendship and family, the importance of memory, and the role of magic in our lives. This is a highly satisfying literary experience." SLJ

Mouse bird snake wolf; David Almond, illustrated by David McKean. Candlewick Press 2013 80 p. (reinforced) $17.99

Grades: 4 5 6 7   **Fic**

1. Animals 2. Fantasy fiction
ISBN 0763659126; 9780763659127
LC 2012950556

In this book, "Harry, Sue, and Little Ben live in a world whose lazy gods have made creatures like whales and camels but have given up their work, leaving blank spaces . . . . The children discover that they can create animals themselves, using sticks, leaves, and clay; Little Ben makes a mouse; Sue, a bird; and Harry, a snake. But Harry and Sue aren't satisfied. They create a terrifying wolf that turns on them and eats them, and Little Ben must summon the courage to save them." (Publishers Weekly)

★ **My** name is Mina. Delacorte Press 2011 300p $15.99; lib bdg $18.99

Grades: 5 6 7 8   **Fic**

1. Authorship -- Fiction
ISBN 978-0-385-74073-9; 0-385-74073-5; 978-0-375-98964-3 lib bdg; 0-375-98964-1 lib bdg; 978-0-375-98965-0 e-book
LC 2010040143

"This intimate prequel to Skellig is built around Mina McKee, the curious and brilliant home-schooled child who eventually befriends that book's protagonist, Michael. Mina, a budding writer, reveals her love of words in her journal; most of the book unfolds in a handwritten-looking font, with Mina's more emphatic entries exploding onto the pages in massive display type. Her lyrical, nonlinear prose records her reflections on her past, existential musings . . . and self-directed writing exercises. . . . Almond gives readers a vivid picture of the joyfully freeform workings of Mina's mind and her mixed emotions about being an isolated child. Her gradual emergence from the protective shell of home is beautifully portrayed. . . . This novel will inspire children to let their imaginations soar." Publ Wkly

★ **Raven** summer. Delacorte Press 2009 198p $19.99

Grades: 7 8 9 10 11 12   **Fic**

1. Orphans -- Fiction 2. Fate and fatalism -- Fiction
ISBN 978-0-385-73806-4; 0-385-73806-4
LC 2009-1661

Led to an abandoned baby by a raven, fourteen-year-old Liam seems fated to meet two foster children who have experienced the world's violence in very different ways as he struggles to understand war, family problems, and friends who grow apart.

"The tension builds to a shocking and totally believable ending. . . . A haunting story, perfect for group discussion." Booklist

★ **Skellig**; 10th anniversary ed.; Delacorte Press 2009 182p $16.99; pa $6.99

Grades: 5 6 7 8 9 10   **Fic**

1. Fantasy fiction
ISBN 978-0-385-32653-7; 0-385-32653-X; 978-0-440-41602-9 pa; 0-440-41602-7 pa
First published 1998 in the United Kingdom; first United States edition 1999
Michael L. Printz Award honor book

Unhappy about his baby sister's illness and the chaos of moving into a dilapidated old house, Michael retreats to the garage and finds a mysterious stranger who is something like a bird and something like an angel.

"The plot is beautifully paced and the characters are drawn with a graceful, careful hand. . . . A lovingly done, thought-provoking novel." SLJ

Slog's dad; illustrated by Dave McKean. Candlewick Press 2011 52p il $15.99

Grades: 5 6 7 8   **Fic**

1. Death -- Fiction 2. Future life -- Fiction 3. Father-son relationship -- Fiction
ISBN 978-0-7636-4940-1; 0-7636-4940-6
LC 2010-38700

When Slog's father died he promised to return for one last visit in the spring, but when Slog spots a scruffy man on a bench outside the butcher shop and identifies him as his father, his best friend Davie is skeptical.

"This grief-strafed wonder tale is brilliantly matched by some of McKean's most moving artwork yet. Text pages, featuring a voice steeped on Northern English flavor, are counterpoised against wordless illustration sequences that move readers from heaven to earth and back again, beginning with a celestial descent from the sky to a park bench by a man trailing clouds of watercolor glory." Bull Cent Child Books

★ The **fire**-eaters. Delacorte Press 2004 218p $15.95

Grades: 7 8 9 10   **Fic**

1. Great Britain -- Fiction
ISBN 0-385-73170-1
LC 2003-55709

First published 2003 in the United Kingdom

In 1962 England, despite observing his father's illness and the suffering of the fire-eating Mr. McNulty, as well as enduring abuse at school and the stress of the Cuban Missile Crisis, Bobby Burns and his family and friends still find reasons to rejoice in their lives and to have hope for the future.

"The author's trademark themes . . . are here in full, and resonate long after the last page is turned." SLJ

★ The **savage**; illustrated by Dave McKean. Candlewick Press 2008 79p il $17.99

Grades: 5 6 7 8   **Fic**

  1. Death -- Fiction 2. Fathers -- Fiction

  ISBN 978-0-7636-3932-7; 0-7636-3932-X

             LC 2008-928388

A boy tells about a story he wrote when dealing with his father's death about a savage kid living in a ruined chapel in the woods-and the tale about the savage kid coming to life in the real world.

"This illustrated novella, a graphic novel within a novel, will satisfy Almond's fans and newcomers alike. McKean's illustrations-ink and watercolor in black, blues, and greens-add an appropriately eerie touch." Horn Book Guide

Alonzo, Sandra

  ★ **Riding** invisible; written by Sandra Alonzo; illustrated by Nathan Huang. Hyperion 2010 234p il lib bdg $15.99

Grades: 7 8 9 10   **Fic**

  1. Horses -- Fiction 2. Brothers -- Fiction 3. Family life -- Fiction 4. Personality disorders -- Fiction

  ISBN 978-1-4231-1898-5; 1-4231-1898-7

             LC 2010-05041

After his older brother Will attacks his horse, Shy, Yancey runs away into the desert. Follow his adventures as he returns home to face life with a brother who has "conduct disorder."

"Written in a journal style and punctuated with sketches depicting Yancy's experiences, there's a lot here to engage readers." Horn Book Guide

Alter, Stephen

  Ghost letters. Bloomsbury 2008 227p $16.95

Grades: 5 6 7 8   **Fic**

  1. Ghost stories 2. Letters -- Fiction 3. Grandfathers -- Fiction 4. Space and time -- Fiction

  ISBN 1-58234-739-5; 978-1-58234-739-4

             LC 2007-30844

While exploring the area around his grandfather's home Gil discovers a bottle that carries messages into the past, finds a genie in a letter, and three letters that were never delivered but would have changed the course of history.

"Readers will find the book scary enough to thrill and clever enough to challenge their deductive reasoning." SLJ

Alvarez, Julia

  ★ **Before** we were free. Knopf 2002 167p $15.95; lib bdg $17.99; pa $5.99

Grades: 7 8 9 10   **Fic**

  1. Family life -- Fiction 2. Dominican Republic -- History -- 1930-1961

  ISBN 0-375-81544-9; 0-375-91544-3 lib bdg; 0-440-23784-X pa

             LC 2001-50520

In the early 1960s in the Dominican Republic, twelve-year-old Anita learns that her family is involved in the underground movement to end the bloody rule of the dictator, General Trujillo

This "is a realistic and compelling account of a girl growing up too quickly while coming to terms with the cost of freedom." Horn Book

  ★ **How** Tia Lola came to visit/stay. Knopf 2001 147p $15.95; pa $5.50

Grades: 4 5 6 7   **Fic**

  1. Aunts -- Fiction 2. Divorce -- Fiction 3. Dominican Americans -- Fiction

  ISBN 0-375-80215-0; 0-440-41870-4 pa

             LC 00-62932

Although ten-year-old Miguel is at first embarrassed by his colorful aunt, Tia Lola, when she comes to Vermont from the Dominican Republic to stay with his mother, his sister, and him after his parents' divorce, he learns to love her.

"Readers will enjoy the funny situations, identify with the developing relationships and conflicting feelings of the characters, and will get a spicy taste of Caribbean culture in the bargain." SLJ

Other titles about Tia Lola are:

How Tia Lola learned to teach (2010)

How Tia Lola saved the summer (2011)

How Tia Lola ended up starting over (2011)

  ★ **Return** to sender. Alfred A. Knopf 2009 325p $16.99; lib bdg $19.99

Grades: 4 5 6 7   **Fic**

  1. Farm life -- Fiction 2. Friendship -- Fiction 3. Migrant labor -- Fiction 4. Illegal aliens -- Fiction

  ISBN 978-0-375-85838-3; 0-375-85838-5; 978-0-375-95838-0 lib bdg; 0-375-95838-X lib bdg

             LC 2008-23520

Awarded the Belpre Author Medal (2010)

After his family hires migrant Mexican workers to help save their Vermont farm from foreclosure, eleven-year-old Tyler befriends the oldest daughter, but when he discovers they may not be in the country legally, he realizes that real friendship knows no borders.

"Readers will be moved by small moments. . . . A tender, well-constructed book." Publ Wkly

Amateau, Gigi

  A **certain** strain of peculiar. Candlewick Press 2009 261p $16.99

Grades: 6 7 8 9   **Fic**

  1. Ranch life -- Fiction 2. Grandmothers -- Fiction

  ISBN 978-0-7636-3009-6; 0-7636-3009-8

Tired of the miserable life she lives, Mary Harold leaves her mother behind and moves back to Alabama and her grandmother, where she receives support and love and starts to gain confidence in herself and her abilities.

"Mary Harold is a wonderfully complex and honest character. . . . [Her] narrative is heartfelt and poignant, and the message that being 'different' is nothing to be ashamed of will resonate with readers." Voice Youth Advocates

Amato, Mary

  Invisible lines; illustrations by Antonio Caparo. Egmont USA 2009 319p il $15.99; lib bdg $18.99

Grades: 6 7 8 9   **Fic**

  1. School stories 2. Moving -- Fiction 3. Social classes

-- Fiction 4. Single parent family -- Fiction
ISBN 978-1-60684-010-8; 1-60684-010-X; 978-1-60684-043-6 lib bdg; 1-60684-043-6 lib bdg

LC 2009-14639

Coming from a poor, single-parent family, seventh-grader Trevor must rely on his intelligence, artistic ability, quick wit, and soccer prowess to win friends at his new Washington, D.C. school, but popular and rich Xander seems determined to cause him trouble.

"The author's subtle sense of humor is at work here. . . . This fresh story is enhanced by notes and drawings from Trevor's fungi notebook. With its short chapters, snappy dialogue, and scientific extras, the novel should find a wide audience." SLJ

Anderson, Jodi Lynn

May Bird among the stars; book two. [by] Jodi Lynn Anderson. 1st ed.; Atheneum Books for Young Readers 2006 260p $16.95

Grades: 5 6 7 8   **Fic**
1. Fantasy fiction
ISBN 978-0-689-86924-2; 0-689-86924-X

LC 2005028832

Still trapped in The Ever After, ten-year-old May Bird struggles to decide whether to save the world of her ghostly friends from the evil Bo Cleevil or to return to her West Virginia home.

"Anderson has clearly had a great deal of fun creating a world not so different from our own where spirits go after death, and readers will love her humorous jabs at popular culture." SLJ

★ **Tiger** Lily; Jodi Lynn Anderson. HarperTeen 2012 304 p. (trade bdg.) $17.99

Grades: 8 9 10 11   **Fic**
1. Love stories 2. Jealousy -- Fiction 3. Fairy tales -- Fiction 4. Peter Pan (Fictional character) 5. Love -- Fiction 6. Magic -- Fiction 7. Fairies -- Fiction
ISBN 0062003259; 9780062003256

LC 2011032659

This is the story of Tiger Lily, the girl Peter Pan spurned for Wendy. "Told from the perspective of Tinker Bell, the novel explores how Tiger Lily meets and falls in love with Peter, despite being betrothed to another villager, a man Tiger Lily despises. Tiger Lily and Peter's complicated inner conflicts emerge as they sort out their feelings about freedom, power, loyalty, and responsibility. When a girl from England arrives, Tiger Lily" feels jealous for the first time. (Publishers Weekly)

Anderson, John David

★ **Standard** hero behavior; [by] John David Anderson. Clarion Books 2007 273p $16

Grades: 6 7 8   **Fic**
1. Fantasy fiction 2. Adventure fiction 3. Heroes and heroines -- Fiction
ISBN 0-618-75920-4; 978-0-618-75920-0

LC 2007013059

When fifteen-year-old Mason Quayle finds out that their town of Darlington is about to be attacked by orcs, goblins, ogres, and trolls, he goes in search of some heroes to save the day.

"Mason is thoroughly believable. . . . Using imaginative details, witty language with a scattering of modern idiom, and lots of allusions, Anderson manages the difficult task of constructing a satisfying story while poking large fun at all genre traditions. Fantasy fans are ensured a good laugh." Booklist

Anderson, Katie D.

Kiss & Make Up. Amazon Childrens Pub 2012 307 p. (hardcover) $16.99

Grades: 7 8 9 10   **Fic**
1. Occult fiction 2. School stories
ISBN 076146316X; 9780761463160

This book focuses on Emerson Taylor, who "has a gift—or a curse. She can read a person's mind with the lightest of kisses. When her financially strapped aunt announces that Emerson will not be attending private school the following year if her grades don't improve, Emerson initializes Operation Liplock. She will begin study sessions with the geeky Ivys—those destined to attend Ivy League colleges—where she will kiss them, allowing their knowledge to transfer to her mind." (School Library Journal)

Anderson, Laurie Halse, 1961-

★ **Chains**; seeds of America. Simon & Schuster Books for Young Readers 2008 316p $17.99

Grades: 6 7 8 9 10   **Fic**
1. Spies -- Fiction 2. Slavery -- Fiction 3. African Americans -- Fiction
ISBN 1-4169-0585-5; 1-4169-0586-3 pa; 978-1-4169-0585-1; 978-1-4169-0586-8 pa

LC 2007-52139

After being sold to a cruel couple in New York City, a slave named Isabel spies for the rebels during the Revolutionary War.

"This gripping novel offers readers a startlingly provocative view of the Revolutionary War. . . . [Anderson's] solidly researched exploration of British and Patriot treatment of slaves during a war for freedom is nuanced and evenhanded, presented in service of a fast-moving, emotionally involving plot." Publ Wkly

★ **Fever,** 1793. Simon & Schuster Bks. for Young Readers 2000 251p $17.99; pa $6.99

Grades: 5 6 7 8 9   **Fic**
1. Epidemics -- Fiction 2. Yellow fever -- Fiction 3. Yellow fever -- Pennsylvania -- Philadelphia
ISBN 978-0-689-83858-3; 0-689-83858-1; 978-0-689-84891-9 pa; 0-689-84891-9 pa

LC 00-32238

ALA YALSA Margaret A. Edwards Award (2009)

In 1793 Philadelphia, sixteen-year-old Matilda Cook, separated from her sick mother, learns about perseverance and self-reliance when she is forced to cope with the horrors of a yellow fever epidemic.

"A vivid work, rich with well-drawn and believable characters. Unexpected events pepper the top-flight novel that combines accurate historical detail with a spellbinding story line." Voice Youth Advocates

★ **Forge.** Atheneum Books for Young Readers 2010 297p (Seeds of America) $16.99

Grades: 6 7 8 9 10   **Fic**
1. Slavery -- Fiction 2. Soldiers -- Fiction 3. African Americans -- Fiction
ISBN 978-1-4169-6144-4; 1-4169-6144-5
LC 2010-15971

Separated from his friend Isabel after their daring escape from slavery, fifteen-year-old Curzon serves as a free man in the Continental Army at Valley Forge until he and Isabel are thrown together again, as slaves once more.

"Weaving a huge amount of historical detail seamlessly into the story, Anderson creates a vivid setting, believable characters both good and despicable and a clear portrayal of the moral ambiguity of the Revolutionary age. Not only can this sequel stand alone, for many readers it will be one of the best novels they have ever read." Kirkus

Speak; 10th anniversary ed.; Speak 2009 197p pa $11.99
Grades: 7 8 9 10   **Fic**
1. School stories 2. Rape -- Fiction
ISBN 978-0-14-241473-6
LC 2009-502164

First published 1999

A traumatic event near the end of the summer has a devastating effect on Melinda's freshman year in high school.

The novel is "keenly aware of the corrosive details of outsiderhood and the gap between home and daily life at high school; kids whose exclusion may have less concrete cause than Melinda's will nonetheless find the picture recognizable. This is a gripping account of personal wounding and recovery." Bull Cent Child Books

★ **Wintergirls**. Viking 2009 288p $17.99
Grades: 8 9 10 11 12   **Fic**
1. Death -- Fiction 2. Friendship -- Fiction 3. Self-mutilation -- Fiction 4. Anorexia nervosa -- Fiction
ISBN 978-0-670-01110-0; 0-670-01110-X
LC 2008-37452

Eighteen-year-old Lia comes to terms with her best friend's death from anorexia as she struggles with the same disorder.

"As events play out, Lia's guilt, her need to be thin, and her fight for acceptance unravel in an almost poetic stream of consciousness in this startlingly crisp and pitch-perfect first-person narrative." SLJ

Anderson, M. T., 1968-
Burger Wuss; M.T. Anderson. Candlewick Press 1999 192p (pbk.) $7.99
Grades: 7 8 9 10 11 12   **Fic**
1. Teenagers -- Fiction 2. Conformity -- Fiction 3. Fast food restaurants -- Fiction
ISBN 0763606804; 9780763631789; 9781439530726
LC 99014257

In this book that is set "[i]n a world where every teenager works at one fast food chain or another and likes it, Anthony just doesn't fit in. His first real girlfriend has dumped him for a meathead named Turner who works at O'Dermott's, so Anthony plots revenge. He gets a job at the restaurant and embarks on a complicated plot to pit the kids from Burger Queen against the kids from O'Dermott's--and thereby draw the BQ wrath down on company-man Turner's head. . . .

[T]his book is a burlesque of teenage angst and conformist culture. . . . Anarchist vagabond Shunt is Anthony's partner in his anti-conformity crimes." (Publishers Weekly)

The **chamber** in the sky. Scholastic Press 2012 282 p. (hardcover) $17.99
Grades: 5 6 7 8   **Fic**
1. American satire 2. Fantasy fiction 3. Human-alien encounters -- Fiction
ISBN 0545334934; 9780545334938

This novel, by National Book Award and Printz Honor winner M. T. Anderson, is book four of "The Norumbegan Quartet" series. "Brian and Gregory have . . . . gone to investigate intergalactic suburban sprawl that was infringing on the Vermont forests, and landed in the empire of New Norumbega inside the huge body of an alien. They've escaped certain death . . . and wreaked small amounts of havoc of their own. And finally, they're going to make sense of all their travels and adventures." (Publisher's note)

Feed. Candlewick Press 2002 237p hardcover o.p. pa $7.99
Grades: 8 9 10 11 12   **Fic**
1. Satire 2. Science fiction
ISBN 0-7636-1726-1; 0-7636-2259-1 pa
LC 2002-23738

In a future where most people have computer implants in their heads to control their environment, a boy meets an unusual girl who is in serious trouble

"An ingenious satire of corporate America and our present-day value system." Horn Book Guide

The **Game** of Sunken Places; [by] M. T. Anderson. Scholastic Press 2004 260p (The Norumbegan quartet) $16.95; pa $5.99
Grades: 5 6 7 8   **Fic**
1. Games -- Fiction
ISBN 0-439-41660-4; 0-439-41661-2 pa
LC 2003-20055

When two boys stay with an eccentric relative at his mansion in rural Vermont, they discover an old-fashioned board game that draws them into a mysterious adventure.

"Deliciously scary, often funny, and crowned by a pair of deeply satisfying surprises, this tour de force leaves one marveling at Anderson's ability to slip between genres as fluidly as his middle-grade heroes straddle worlds." Booklist

Other titles in this series are:
The suburb beyond the stars (2010)
The empire of gut and bone (2011)

★ **Whales** on stilts; illustrations by Kurt Cyrus. Harcourt 2005 188p il (Pals in peril) $15; pa $5.95
Grades: 4 5 6 7   **Fic**
1. Science fiction
ISBN 0-15-205340-9; 0-15-205394-8 pa
LC 2004-17754

Racing against the clock, shy middle-school student Lily and her best friends, Katie and Jasper, must foil the plot of her father's conniving boss to conquer the world using an army of whales.

"A story written with the author's tongue shoved firmly into his cheek. . . . It's full of witty pokes at other series novels and Jasper's nutty inventions." SLJ

Other titles in this series are:

The clue of the linoleum lederhosen (2006)

Jasper Dash and the Flame-pits of Delaware (2009)

Agent Q., or the smell of danger! (2010)

Zombie mommy (2011)

The **empire** of gut and bone. Scholastic 2011 324p (The Norumbegan quartet) $17.99

Grades: 5 6 7 8   **Fic**

1. Games -- Fiction 2. Supernatural -- Fiction

ISBN 978-0-545-13884-0; 0-545-13884-1

"Bent on tracking down the elven Norumbegans in order to save Vermont from an invasion of dream-sucking Thusser, Brian, Gregory and the mechanical troll Kalgrash pass through an interdimensional curtain—to find themselves inside an organic alien body. . . . Returning fans will find the unapologetically intellectual looniness uncannily, happily familiar." Kirkus

The **suburb** beyond the stars. Scholastic Press 2010 223p (The Norumbegan quartet) $17.99

Grades: 5 6 7 8   **Fic**

1. Games -- Fiction 2. Supernatural -- Fiction

ISBN 978-0-545-13882-6; 0-545-13882-5

LC 2009051836

Friends Brian and Gregory have survived the Game of Sunken Places, but are once again drawn back to cousin Prudence's house in Vermont, where they discover that something has gone very wrong with time, people have disappeared, and danger is lurking everywhere.

"This is a fun and gripping read, with action, suspense, and creepy monsters." SLJ

Anderson, R. J.

Spell Hunter. HarperCollinsPublishers 2009 329p (Faery rebels) $16.99

Grades: 7 8 9 10 11 12   **Fic**

1. Fantasy fiction 2. Magic -- Fiction 3. Fairies -- Fiction

ISBN 978-0-06-155474-2; 0-06-155474-X; 978-0-06-155475-9 lib bdg; 0-06-155475-8 lib bdg

LC 2008-27469

In a dying faery realm, only the brave and rebellious faery Knife persists in trying to discover how her people's magic was lost and what is needed to restore their powers and ensure their survival, but her quest is endangered by her secret friendship with a human named Paul.

"Filled with delicate, fantastical creatures; evil and dangerous crows; and a human who believes in love, this is a highly readable, sophisticated tale of romance and self-sacrifice." Booklist

Another title in this series is:

Wayfarer (2010)

Andrews, Jesse

Me & Earl & the dying girl; by Jesse Andrews. Amulet Books 2012 295 p. $16.95

Grades: 8 9 10   **Fic**

1. Leukemia -- Fiction 2. Friendship -- Fiction 3.

Family life -- Fiction 4. Pittsburgh (Pa.) -- Fiction 5. High school students -- Fiction 6. Humorous stories 7. Schools -- Fiction 8. High schools -- Fiction 9. Jews -- United States -- Fiction 10. Family life -- Pennsylvania -- Fiction

ISBN 9781419701764

LC 2011031796

This book is a "confessional from a teen narrator who won't be able to convince readers he's as unlikable as he wants them to believe." It covers "[h]is filmmaking ambitions . . . his unlikely friendship with the . . . Earl of the title. And his unlikelier friendship with Rachel, the titular 'dying girl'. . . . He chronicles his senior year, in which his mother guilt-trips him into hanging out with Rachel, who has acute myelogenous leukemia." (Kirkus Reviews)

Angleberger, Tom.

Darth Paper strikes back; an Origami Yoda book. Tom Angleberger. Amulet Books 2011 159p il $12.95

Grades: 4 5 6 7   **Fic**

1. School stories 2. Origami -- Fiction 3. Puppets and puppet plays -- Fiction 4. Eccentrics and eccentricities -- Fiction

ISBN 978-1-4197-0027-9; 1-4197-0027-8

LC 2011010388

Harvey, upset when his Darth Paper finger puppet brings humiliation, gets Dwight suspended, but Origami Yoda asks Tommy and Kellan, now in seventh grade, to make a new casefile to persuade the School Board to reinstate Dwight.

This is "a satisfying tale of friendship and just resistance to authority. Pitch-perfect middle-school milieu and enough Star Wars references (and laughs) to satisfy fans and win new ones." Kirkus

Horton Halfpott; or, The fiendish mystery of Smugwick Manor, or, The loosening of M'Lady Luggertuck's corset. Tom Angleberger with illustrations by the author. Amulet Books 2011 206p il $14.95

Grades: 4 5 6 7   **Fic**

1. Mystery fiction 2. Social classes -- Fiction 3. Household employees -- Fiction 4. Eccentrics and eccentricities -- Fiction

ISBN 978-0-8109-9715-8; 0-8109-9715-0

LC 2010-38096

Horton, an upstanding kitchen boy in a castle in nineteenth-century England, becomes embroiled in a mystery surrounding a series of thefts.

"Readers will enjoy Angleberger's . . . penchant for the absurd as well as his many droll asides. . . . The ending satisfies, and with Angleberger's many eclectic characters, his wild-and-witty storytelling, and a lighthearted but perplexing mystery . . . readers are in for a treat." Publ Wkly

Angus, Jennifer

In search of Goliathus hercules; by Jennifer Angus. Albert Whitman 2012 350 p. (hardcover) $17.99

Grades: 3 4 5 6 7   **Fic**

1. Fantasy fiction 2. Insects -- Fiction 3. Human-animal communication -- Fiction 4. Metamorphosis

-- Fiction
ISBN 0807529907; 9780807529904

LC 2011037135

In this novel, by Jennifer Angus, "Henri Bell, . . . in 1890 . . . strikes up a conversation with a friendly fly on the windowsill and discovers he possesses the astounding ability to speak with insects. Thus commences an epic journey for Henri as he manages a flea circus, commands an army of beetles, and ultimately sets out to British Malaya to find the mythical giant insect known as Goliathus Hercules." (Publisher's note)

Anthony, Joelle

Restoring harmony. G.P. Putnam's Sons 2010 307p $17.99

Grades: 6 7 8 9   **Fic**

1. Science fiction 2. Voyages and travels -- Fiction 3. Environmental degradation -- Fiction
ISBN 978-0-399-25281-5; 0-399-25281-9

LC 2009-29501

Ten years after the Great Collapse of 2031, sixteen-year-old Molly McClure, with only her fiddle for company, leaves the safety of her family's island home to travel through a dangerous and desolate wasteland on her way to Oregon to find her grandparents and persuade them to return with her to Canada.

"Adeptly combining adventure and romance, Anthony's debut is a tense and often charming tale that never lets its use of the oh-so-trendy dystopian future trope overwhelm some great characters." Publ Wkly

Antieau, Kim

Ruby's imagine; written by Kim Antieau. Houghton Mifflin Co. 2008 201p $16

Grades: 6 7 8 9   **Fic**

1. African Americans -- Fiction 2. Hurricane Katrina, 2005 -- Fiction
ISBN 978-0-618-99767-1; 0-618-99767-9

LC 2007047736

Tells the story of Hurricane Katrina from the point of view of Ruby, an unusually intuitive girl who lives with her grandmother in New Orleans but has powerful memories of an earlier life in the swamps.

"Antieau offers a complex, personal account of Katrina and its aftermath. . . . Ruby's atmospheric narrative is as dense and pungent as the bayou." Booklist

Appelbaum, Susannah

The **Hollow** Bettle; illustrated by Jennifer Taylor. Alfred A. Knopf 2009 399p il (The Poisons of Caux) $16.99; lib bdg $19.99

Grades: 4 5 6 7   **Fic**

1. Fantasy fiction 2. Uncles -- Fiction 3. Poisons and poisoning -- Fiction
ISBN 978-0-375-85173-5; 0-375-85173-9; 978-0-375-95173-2 lib bdg; 0-375-95173-3 lib bdg

LC 2008-22626

Eleven-year-old Ivy Manx sets out with her new friend, a young "taster," to find her missing uncle, an outlawed healer, in the dangerous kingdom of Caux where magic, herbs, and poisons rule.

This "is a deeply satisfying, humor-laced quest with elements of wizardry and herbology, deeds of a dastardly nature, and, ultimately, redemption." Booklist

Other titles in this series are:
The Taster's Guild (2010)
The Shepherd of Weeds (2011)

Appelt, Kathi

★ **Keeper**; illustrations by August Hall. Atheneum Books for Young Readers 2010 399p il $16.99

Grades: 5 6 7 8   **Fic**

1. Ocean -- Fiction 2. Sailing -- Fiction 3. Mermaids and mermen -- Fiction 4. Mother-daughter relationship -- Fiction
ISBN 978-1-4169-5060-8; 1-4169-5060-5

LC 2010000795

On the night of the blue moon when mermaids are said to gather on a sandbar in the Gulf of Mexico, ten-year-old Keeper sets out in a small boat, with her dog BD and a seagull named Captain, determined to find her mother, a mermaid, as Keeper has always believed, who left long ago to return to the sea.

"Deftly spinning together mermaid lore, local legend and natural history, this stunning tale proves 'every landscape has its magical beings,' and the most unlikely ones can form a perfect family. Hall's black-and-white illustrations lend perspective and immediacy. Beautiful and evocative—an absolute 'keeper.' " Kirkus

★ The **true** blue scouts of Sugarman Swamp; by Kathi Appelt. 1st ed. Atheneum Books for Young Readers 2013 336 p. (hardcover) $16.99

Grades: 5 6 7 8   **Fic**

1. Swamps -- Fiction 2. Raccoons -- Fiction 3. Humorous stories 4. Swamp animals -- Fiction 5. Land developers -- Fiction 6. Scouting (Youth activity) -- Fiction
ISBN 1442421053; 9781442421059; 9781442481213

LC 2012023723

This book is "told from the perspectives of animals and humans. . . .The main concern of Bingo and Jeremiah, two raccoon Swamp Scouts, is the approaching brood of feral hogs, which could destroy the precious canebrake sugar used to make fried pies at the local Paradise Pies cafe. Meanwhile, 12-year-old Chap Brayburn, the cafe proprietor's son, is worried about rich, horrible Sonny Boy Beaucoup, who wants to turn the swamp into the 'Gator World Wrestling Arena and Theme Park.'" (Publishers Weekly)

★ The **underneath**; illustrated by David Small. Atheneum Books for Young Readers 2008 313p il $16.99; pa $7.99

Grades: 3 4 5 6   **Fic**

1. Cats -- Fiction 2. Dogs -- Fiction
ISBN 978-1-4169-5058-5; 1-4169-5058-3; 978-1-4169-5059-2 pa; 1-4169-5059-1 pa

LC 2007031969

A Newbery Medal honor book, 2009

An abandoned "calico cat, about to have kittens, hears the lonely howl of [Ranger], a chained-up hound deep in the backwaters of the bayou. . . . Ranger urges the cat to hide underneath the porch, to raise her kittens there because Gar-

Face, the man living inside the house, will surely use them as alligator bait should he find them." (Publisher's note)

"Well realized in Small's excellent full-page drawings, this fine book is most of all distinguished by the originality of the story and the fresh beauty of its author's voice." Horn Book

Applegate, Katherine

Eve & Adam; by Michael Grant and Katherine Applegate. Feiwel and Friends 2012 291p. $17.99

Grades: 7 8 9 10 **Fic**

1. Mother-daughter relationship -- Fiction
ISBN 0312583516; 9780312583514

In this book by authors Michael Grant and Katherine Applegate, "a run-in with a streetcar left Evening Spiker's body seriously mangled . . . [H]er widowed mother, Terra, insists on moving her from the hospital to . . . [the] biotech company . . . Spiker Biopharmaceuticals. . . . Eve's healing is strangely swift [and] Terra drops a project . . . in her lap: Design a virtual human being from scratch. With help from her feisty, reckless friend Aislin, Eve takes up the challenge." (Kirkus Reviews)

★ **Home** of the brave. Feiwel & Friends 2007 249p $16.95

Grades: 5 6 7 8 **Fic**

1. Novels in verse 2. Cattle -- Fiction 3. Africans -- Fiction 4. Refugees -- Fiction 5. Immigrants -- Fiction
ISBN 0-312-36765-1; 978-0-312-36765-7
LC 2006-32053

Kek, an African refugee, is confronted by many strange things at the Minneapolis home of his aunt and cousin, as well as in his fifth grade classroom, and longs for his missing mother, but finds comfort in the company of a cow and her owner.

"This beautiful story of hope and resilience is written in free verse." Voice Youth Advocates

★ The **one** and only Ivan; illustrated by Patricia Castelao, Harper 2012 il $16.99

Grades: 3 4 5 6 **Fic**

1. Gorillas -- Fiction 2. Elephants -- Fiction 3. Animal welfare -- Fiction
ISBN 978-0-06-199225-4; 0-06-199225-9
LC 2011010034

John Newbery Medal (2013)

"Ivan narrates his tale in short, image-rich sentences and acute, sometimes humorous, observations that are all the more heartbreaking for their simple delivery. . . . Spot art captures poignant moments throughout. Utterly believable, this bittersweet story, complete with an author's note identifying the real Ivan, will inspire a new generation of advocates." Kirkus

Arbuthnott, Gill

The **Keepers'** tattoo. Chicken House 2010 425p $17.99

Grades: 6 7 8 9 **Fic**

1. Fantasy fiction 2. Dreams -- Fiction 3. Uncles -- Fiction 4. Tattooing -- Fiction
ISBN 978-0-545-17166-3; 0-545-17166-0
LC 2009-26327

Months before her fifteenth birthday, Nyssa learns that she is a special member of a legendary clan, the Keepers of Knowledge, as she and her uncle try to escape from Alaric, the White Wolf, who wants to use lines tattooed on her to destroy the rest of her people.

Arbuthnott "writes with restraint and thoughtfulness, never condescending to her readers. Nyssa is a convincing mixture of ignorance, courage, and resourcefulness." Publ Wkly

Archer, E.

Geek: fantasy novel. Scholastic Press 2011 310p $17.99

Grades: 7 8 9 10 **Fic**

1. Fantasy fiction 2. Aunts -- Fiction 3. Wishes -- Fiction 4. Cousins -- Fiction
ISBN 978-0-545-16040-7; 0-545-16040-5

This "is a stunning, often befuddling, and wildly amusing novel that will likely confound and enchant sci-fi and fantasy fans alike." Bull Cent Child Books

Archer, Jennifer

Through her eyes. HarperTeen 2011 377p $16.99

Grades: 7 8 9 10 **Fic**

1. School stories 2. Mystery fiction 3. Moving -- Fiction 4. Family life -- Fiction 5. Grandfathers -- Fiction 6. Supernatural -- Fiction
ISBN 978-0-06-183458-5; 0-06-183458-0
LC 2010-18440

Sixteen-year-old Tansy is used to moving every time her mother starts writing a new book, but in the small Texas town where her grandfather grew up, she is lured into the world of a troubled young man whose death sixty years earlier is shrouded in mystery.

"Archer's engrossing story gracefully weaves together the contemporary and historical into an eerie mystery, while examining relationships, reality, and the power of the mind." Publ Wkly

Armistead, Cal

Being Henry David; by Cal Armistead. Albert Whitman 2013 312 p. (hardcover) $16.99

Grades: 8 9 10 11 12 **Fic**

1. Mystery fiction 2. Amnesia -- Fiction 3. Guilt -- Fiction 4. Runaways -- Fiction 5. Family problems -- Fiction 6. Street children -- Fiction
ISBN 080750615X; 9780807506158
LC 2012017377

In this book, a "boy wakes up in Penn Station, remembering nothing. He guesses that he's about 17, he has a head injury, and he is carrying only 10 dollars. Near at hand is a copy of Walden, so for want of anything better he calls himself Henry David (Hank). He heads to Concord, Massachusetts, to find, he hopes, some clues at Walden Pond. As his memories slowly return, he remembers who he was; as he copes with the memories, he discovers who he is and can be." (School Library Journal)

Armstrong, Alan

Looking for Marco Polo; illustrated by Tim Jessell. Random House 2009 286p $16.99

Grades: 4 5 6 7   **Fic**
1. Travelers 2. Travel writers 3. Missing persons --
Fiction
ISBN 978-0-375-83321-2; 0-375-83321-8
When they lose touch with his father's Gobi Desert expedition, eleven-year-old Mark accompanies his mother to
Venice, Italy, and there, while waiting for news of his father,
learns about the legendary Marco Polo and his adventures
in the Far East.
"Armstrong ably conjures up the atmosphere of damp,
foggy Venice in late December while blowing some dust
off of the accounts of Marco Polo's travels with his lively
storytelling. . . . Whether or not readers know the specifics
of Marco Polo's voyages, they will enjoy this entertaining
blend of contemporary and historical adventure." Booklist

Racing the moon; by Alan Armstrong; illustrated
by Tim Jessell. Random House 2012 214 p. $16.99
Grades: 5 6 7 8   **Fic**
1. Adventure fiction 2. Historical fiction 3. Siblings
-- Fiction 4. Aeronautics -- Fiction 5. Space flight
-- Fiction 6. Brothers and sisters -- Fiction 7. Rockets
(Aeronautics) -- Fiction 8. Adventure and adventurers
-- Fiction
ISBN 037585889X; 9780375858895;
9780375858901; 9780375893094
LC 2012016261
In this children's book by Alan Armstrong "Twelve-
year-old Alex hangs out with her reckless 17-year-old brother Chuck, who's always getting them in trouble. . . . Alex
wants to be another Amelia Earhart [and][m]eeting her new
neighbor, Captain Ebbs, Alex finds a mentor. . . . She arranges for Alex to meet pioneer rocket scientist Wernher von
Braun, organizes a sailing trip to a Chesapeake Bay island
near a rocket launch and provides needed direction for the
risk-taking duo." Kirkus

Whittington; illustrated by S. D. Schindler. Random House 2005 191p il $14.95; lib bdg $16.99;
pa $6.50
Grades: 4 5 6   **Fic**
1. Cats -- Fiction 2. Domestic animals -- Fiction
ISBN 0-375-82864-8; 0-375-92864-2 lib bdg; 0-375-
82865-6 pa
LC 2004-05789
A Newbery Medal honor book, 2006
"A battered cat who calls himself Whittington takes up
residence in a shabby barn already inhabited by a variety of
scruffy livestock, owned by Bernie. . . . Bernie offers refuge
not only to his animals but also to his parentless grandchildren, Abby and Ben, who carry burdens of their own. The
children [can] communicate . . . with the animals, so Abby
and Ben join the audience when Whittington the cat retells
the story of Dick Whittington and his cat." (Bull Cent Child
Books)
"The story works beautifully, both as historical fiction
about medieval street life and commerce and as a witty, engaging tale of barnyard camaraderie and survival." Booklist

Armstrong, K. L.
Loki's wolves; by K.L. Armstrong and M.A.
Marr. 1st ed. Little, Brown and Co. 2013 368 p. ill.
(The Blackwell pages) (hardcover) $16.99
Grades: 4 5 6 7 8   **Fic**
1. Norse mythology -- Fiction 2. Adventure fiction 3.
Gods -- Fiction 4. Monsters -- Fiction 5. Supernatural
-- Fiction 6. Shapeshifting -- Fiction 7. Mythology,
Norse -- Fiction 8. Adventure and adventurers -- Fiction
ISBN 031620496X; 9780316204965
LC 2012029851
This juvenile fantasy novel, by K. L. Armstrong and
M. A. Marr, is the first book in the "Blackwell Pages" se-
ries. "Matt hears the words, but he can't believe them. He's
Thor's representative? Destined to fight trolls, monstrous
wolves and giant serpents . . . or the world ends? He's only
thirteen. . . . But now Ragnarok is coming, and it's up to
the champions to fight in the place of the long-dead gods."
(Publisher's note)
"It is so methodically constructed that readers will welcome the action Ragnarök will offer. . . . Norse mythology
brought to life with engaging contemporary characters and
future volumes that promise explosive action; ideal for Percy Jackson fans who want to branch out." Kirkus

The **summoning**. HarperCollinsPublishers 2008
390p (Darkest powers) $17.99; lib bdg $18.89
Grades: 7 8 9 10   **Fic**
1. Ghost stories 2. Supernatural -- Fiction
ISBN 978-0-06-166269-0; 0-06-166269-0; 978-0-06-
166272-0 lib bdg; 0-06-166272-0 lib bdg
LC 2008-14221
After fifteen-year-old Chloe starts seeing ghosts and is
sent to Lyle House, a mysterious group home for mentally
disturbed teenagers, she soon discovers that neither Lyle
House nor its inhabitants are exactly what they seem, and
that she and her new friends are in danger.
"Suspenseful, well-written, and engaging, this page-
turning . . . [novel] will be a hit." Voice Youth Advocates
Other titles in this series are:
The awakening (2009)
The reckoning (2010)
The gathering (2011)

Armstrong, William Howard
★ **Sounder**; [by] William H. Armstrong; illustrations by James Barkley. Harper & Row 1969 116p
il $15.99; pa $5.99
Grades: 5 6 7 8   **Fic**
1. Dogs -- Fiction 2. Family life -- Fiction 3. African
Americans -- Fiction
ISBN 0-06-020143-6; 0-06-440020-4 pa
Awarded the Newbery Medal, 1970
"Set in the South in the era of sharecropping and segregation, this succinctly told tale poignantly describes the
courage of a father who steals a ham in order to feed his
undernourished family; the determination of the eldest son,
who searches for his father despite the apathy of prison authorities; and the devotion of a coon dog named Sounder."
Shapiro. Fic for Youth. 3d edition

Arnston, Steven

★ The **Wikkeling**; illustrated by Daniela Jaglen-
ka Terrazzini. Running Press Kids 2011 256p il $18

Grades: 4 5 6   **Fic**

    1. Science fiction

    ISBN 978-0-7624-3903-4; 0-7624-3903-3

"In Henrietta's world, every part of life is monitored
and regulated by computers. House cats are considered wild
and dangerous animals. Old houses and old books can make
children sick. The girl's orderly and safe life is disrupted
the day she discovers a secret attic above her bedroom. . .
. Soon after this discovery, she starts seeing the Wikkeling,
a menacing yellow creature that gives children headaches
with the touch of a finger. . . . Arntson has created a detailed
and fascinating dystopian world that seems eerily similar to
our own, and Terrazzini's illustrations strike just the right
note." SLJ

Arntson, Steven

The **wrap**-up list; by Steven Arntson. Houghton
Mifflin Harcourt 2013 240 p. (hardcover) $15.99

Grades: 7 8 9 10   **Fic**

    1. Fantasy fiction 2. Death -- Fiction 3. Hispanic
Americans -- Fiction

    ISBN 0547824106; 9780547824109

                              LC 2012014035

This paranormal young adult novel, by Steven Arntson,
is set in a "modern-day suburban town, [where] one percent
of all fatalities come about in the most peculiar way. Deaths
. . . send a letter . . . to whomever is chosen . . . , telling them
to wrap up their lives and do the things they always wanted
to do before they have to 'depart.' When sixteen-year-old
Gabriela receives her notice, she is, of course devastated.
Will she kiss her crush Sylvester before it's too late?" (Publisher's note)

Aronson, Sarah

Beyond lucky. Dial Books for Young Readers
2011 250p $16.99

Grades: 4 5 6 7   **Fic**

    1. Mystery fiction 2. Chance -- Fiction 3. Soccer --
Fiction 4. Brothers -- Fiction 5. Jews -- United States
-- Fiction

    ISBN 978-0-8037-3520-0; 0-8037-3520-0

                              LC 2010-28800

Twelve-year-old Ari Fish is sure that the rare trading
card he found has changed his luck and that of his soccer
team, but after the card is stolen he comes to know that we
make our own luck, and that heroes can be fallible.

"Aronson skillfully dodges the predictability of sports-
themed books by creating multilayered characters and an
intriguing whodunit. . . . Aronson . . . includes a lot of fun
on-field action, but the off-field story is just as interesting. .
. . Aronson's graceful storytelling will keep even nonsoccer
buffs turning pages." Publ Wkly

Ashby, Amanda

Fairy bad day. Speak 2011 336p pa $7.99

Grades: 7 8 9 10 11 12   **Fic**

    1. School stories 2. Fantasy fiction 3. Ability -- Fiction

    4. Fairies -- Fiction 5. Supernatural -- Fiction

    ISBN 978-0-14-241259-6; 0-14-241259-7

                              LC 2010-046286

High schooler Emma is devastated to learn that she may
not follow in her mother's footsteps as a dragon slayer, but
with an unlikely band of allies she discovers that she may,
indeed, be more adept at slaying giant killer fairies.

"The characters are nicely developed, the dialogue is
fresh and engaging, the author's irreverent take on good versus evil will hook readers, and the satisfying plot twists will
keep them involved till the end." SLJ

Zombie queen of Newbury High. Speak 2009
199p pa $7.99

Grades: 7 8 9 10   **Fic**

    1. School stories 2. Zombies -- Fiction

    ISBN 978-0-14-241256-5; 0-14-241256-5

                              LC 2008-41035

While trying to cast a love spell on her date on the eve
of the senior prom, Mia inadvertently infects her entire high
school class with a virus that will turn them all into zombies.

"Zombie Queen is light, fast-paced, and . . . will quench
the thirst of the Christopher Pike and R. L. Stine set." SLJ

Asher, Jay

Thirteen reasons why; a novel. Razorbill 2007
288p $16.99

Grades: 8 9 10 11 12   **Fic**

    1. School stories 2. Suicide -- Fiction

    ISBN 9781595141712

                              LC 2007-03097

When high school student Clay Jenkins receives a box
in the mail containing thirteen cassette tapes recorded by his
classmate Hannah, who committed suicide, he spends a bewildering and heartbreaking night crisscrossing their town,
listening to Hannah's voice recounting the events leading up
to her death.

"Clay's pain is palpable and exquisitely drawn in gripping casually poetic prose. The complex and soulful characters expose astoundingly rich and singularly teenage inner
lives." SLJ

★ The **future** of us; [by] Jay Asher and Carolyn
Mackler. Razorbill 2011 356p $18.99

Grades: 8 9 10 11 12   **Fic**

    1. School stories 2. Computers -- Fiction 3.
Supernatural -- Fiction

    ISBN 978-1-59514-491-1; 1-59514-491-9

In this book by Jay Asher and Carolyn Mackler, "it's
1996, before Facebook's been invented. Yet Emma's first
computer leads her to her Facebook page from fifteen years
in the future. She tells only her friend and would-be boyfriend Josh, and they contemplate their futures with concern.
Can their current actions change who they become?" (Voice
of Youth Advocates)

"It's 1996, and Emma Nelson has just received her first
computer. . . . When Emma powers up the computer, she
discovers her own Facebook page (even though Facebook
doesn't exist yet) and herself in an unhappy marriage—15
years in the future. Alternating chapters from Josh and
Emma over the course of five days propel this riveting read,

as Emma discovers she can alter her future by adjusting her present actions and intentions." Booklist

Ashton, Brodi

Everbound; an Everneath novel. Brodi Ashton. Balzer + Bray 2013 368 p. (Everneath) (hardcover bdg: alk. paper) $17.99

Grades: 7 8 9 10   **Fic**

1. Love stories 2. Occult fiction 3. Future life -- Fiction 4. Hell -- Fiction 5. Love -- Fiction 6. Supernatural -- Fiction

ISBN 0062071165; 9780062071163

LC 2012028327

This young adult paranormal story, by Brodi Ashton, is the sequel to "Everneath." "Nikki Beckett could only watch as . . . Jack . . . sacrificed himself to save her, taking her place in the Tunnels of the Everneath for eternity. . . . Desperate for answers, Nikki turns to Cole, the immortal bad boy who wants to make her his queen. . . . But his heart has been touched by everything about Nikki, and he agrees to help in the only way he can: by taking her to the Everneath himself." (Publisher's note)

Everneath; Brodi Ashton. 1st ed; Balzer + Bray 2012 370p $17.99

Grades: 7 8 9 10   **Fic**

1. Love stories 2. Occult fiction 3. Fantasy fiction

ISBN 9780062071132 (trade bdg.)

LC 2011022892

This book tells the story of "Nikki Beckett [who] vanished, sucked into an underworld known as the Everneath. Now she's returned—to her old life, her family, her boyfriend—before she's banished back to the underworld . . . this time forever. She has six months before the Everneath comes to claim her, six months for good-byes she can't find the words for, six months to find redemption, if it exists. Nikki longs to spend these precious months forgetting the Everneath and trying to reconnect with her boyfriend, Jack, the person most devastated by her disappearance—and the one person she loves more than anything. But there's just one problem: Cole, the smoldering immortal who enticed her to the Everneath in the first place, has followed Nikki home. Cole wants to take over the throne in the underworld and is convinced Nikki is the key to making it happen." (Publisher's note)

Atkins, Catherine

Alt ed. Putnam 2003 198p $17.99; pa $6.99

Grades: 7 8 9 10   **Fic**

1. School stories

ISBN 0-399-23854-9; 0-14-240235-4 pa

LC 2002-16942

Participating in a special after-school counseling class with other troubled students, including a sensitive gay classmate, helps Susan, an overweight tenth grader, develop a better sense of herself

"Most of the characters . . . come to life in new and interesting ways, and Susan's story is strong, because she is reinventing family relationships as well as trying to communicate with her peers." Booklist

Atkinson, E. J.

★ **I,** Emma Freke; [by] Elizabeth Atkinson. Carolrhoda Books 2010 234p $16.95

Grades: 4 5 6 7   **Fic**

1. Family life -- Fiction 2. Family reunions -- Fiction 3. Single parent family -- Fiction 4. Eccentrics and eccentricities -- Fiction

ISBN 978-0-7613-5604-2; 0-7613-5604-5

LC 2009-38923

Growing up near Boston with her free-spirited mother and old-world grandfather, twelve-year-old Emma has always felt out of place but when she attends the family reunion her father's family holds annually in Wisconsin, she is in for some surprises.

"This rich story of self-acceptance offers readers much to think about. . . . The first-person narrative moves along briskly, with believable dialogue and plenty of humor." Booklist

Atkinson, Elizabeth

From Alice to Zen and everyone in between; a novel. Carolrhoda Books 2008 247p $16.95

Grades: 5 6 7   **Fic**

1. School stories 2. Moving -- Fiction 3. Popularity -- Fiction 4. Family life -- Fiction 5. Eccentrics and eccentricities -- Fiction

ISBN 978-0-8225-7271-8; 0-8225-7271-0

LC 2007-9659

Upon moving from Boston to the suburbs, eleven-year-old tomboy Alice meets Zen, a very strange neighbor who is determined to help her become popular when they both begin middle school, although he himself is a loner.

"Atkinson describes Alice's ethical development credibly and engagingly." Booklist

Atwater-Rhodes, Amelia

Persistence of memory. Delacorte Press 2008 212p $15.99; lib bdg $18.99; pa $8.99

Grades: 8 9 10 11 12   **Fic**

1. Witches -- Fiction 2. Vampires -- Fiction 3. Supernatural -- Fiction 4. Schizophrenia -- Fiction

ISBN 978-0-385-73437-0; 0-385-73437-9; 978-0-385-90443-8 lib bdg; 0-385-90443-6 lib bdg; 978-0-440-24004-4 pa; 0-440-24004-2 pa

LC 2008-16062

Diagnosed with schizophrenia as a child, sixteen-year-old Erin has spent half of her life in therapy and on drugs, but now must face the possibility of weird things in the real world, including shapeshifting friends and her "alter," a centuries-old vampire.

"What sets this novel apart . . . are the two narrators—Erin, grown used to, and even comfortable with, the idea that she is mentally ill; and Shevaun, willing to do anything to protect the family she's cobbled together. Secondary characters are equally compelling, and the world that Atwater-Rhodes has created is believable and intriguing." SLJ

Snakecharm; [by] Amelia Atwater-Rhodes. Delacorte Press 2004 167p (The Kiesha'ra) $14.95; pa $5.99

Grades: 7 8 9 10   Fic
1. Fantasy   2. Fantasy fiction
ISBN 0-385-73072-1; 0-385-90199-2 lib bdg; 978-0-385-73072-3; 978-0-440-23804-1 pa

LC 2003-20709

The peace forged by the love between Zane and Danica, leaders of the avian and serpiente realms that had been at war for generations, is threatened by the arrival of Syfka, an ancient falcon who claims one of her people is hidden in their midst.

"There is enough suspense to keep readers interested. This book is a must-have for libraries with fans of Hawksong." SLJ

Auch, Mary Jane

Ashes of roses. Holt & Co. 2002 250p $16.95; pa $6.50
Grades: 7 8 9 10 11 12 Adult   Fic
1. Immigrants -- Fiction   2. Irish Americans -- Fiction
ISBN 0-8050-6686-1; 0-440-23851-X pa

LC 2001-51896

Sixteen-year-old Margaret Rose Nolan, newly arrived from Ireland, finds work at New York City's Triangle Shirtwaist Factory shortly before the 1911 fire in which 146 employees died

"Fast-paced, populated by distinctive characters, and anchored in Auch's convincing sense of time and place, this title is a good choice for readers who like historical fiction." SLJ

Guitar boy. Henry Holt 2010 260p $16.99
Grades: 6 7 8 9   Fic
1. Guitars -- Fiction   2. Musicians -- Fiction   3. Family life -- Fiction
ISBN 978-0-8050-9112-0; 0-8050-9112-2

LC 2009-50782

After his mother is severely injured in an accident and his father kicks him out of the house, thirteen-year-old Travis attempts to survive on his own until he meets a guitar maker and some musicians who take him in and help him regain his confidence so that he can try to patch his family back together.

"Budding musicians will be fascinated by the details, but all readers will find their heartstrings plucked by this story." Booklist

Wing nut; [by] MJ Auch. Henry Holt & Co. 2005 231p $16.95
Grades: 4 5 6   Fic
1. Birds -- Fiction   2. Moving -- Fiction   3. Old age -- Fiction
ISBN 0-8050-7531-3

LC 2004-54046

When twelve-year-old Grady and his mother relocate yet again, they find work taking care of an elderly man, who teaches Grady about cars, birds, and what it means to have a home

"Auch's story . . . is engaging. . . . What will attract readers . . . is the author's careful integration of bird lore and the unusual challenges of creating and maintaining a purple martin colony." Booklist

Augarde, Steve

X-Isle. David Fickling Books 2010 476p $17.99
Grades: 7 8 9 10   Fic
1. Science fiction   2. Islands -- Fiction
ISBN 978-0-385-75193-3; 0-385-75193-1

LC 2010-281037

Baz and Ray, survivors of an apocalyptic flood, win places on X-Isle, an island where life is rumored to be better than on the devastated mainland, but they find the island to be a violent place ruled by religious fanatic Preacher John, and they decide they must come up with a weapon to protect themselves from impending danger.

"Augarde's near-future apocalyptic world is gruesomely hardscrabble without being overly graphic. . . . A gripping tale of fighting for the slenderest chance of hope." Publ Wkly

Austen, Catherine

All good children. Orca Book Publishers 2011 300p $19.95
Grades: 7 8 9 10 11 12   Fic
1. Siblings -- Fiction   2. Individualism -- Fiction   3. Totalitarianism -- Fiction
ISBN 978-1-55469-824-0; 1-55469-824-3

In the not-too-distant future, Max tries to maintain his identity in a world where the only way to survive is to conform and obey.

"Action packed, terrifying, and believable, this entertaining novel will provoke important discussions about subservience, resistance, and individual freedom." Booklist

Walking backward. Orca 2009 167p pa $9.95
Grades: 6 7 8 9   Fic
1. Bereavement -- Fiction
ISBN 978-1-55469-147-0 pa; 1-55469-147-8 pa

After his mother dies in a phobia-related car crash, twelve-year-old Josh tries to make sense of this grief while he looks after his little brother and watches his father retreat into a fantasy world

"In this impressive debut novel, Josh keeps a journal to chart his feelings and thoughts, allowing readers to follow his journey from sadness to acceptance and the eventual return of cohesion in his family. Given the subject matter, the story is never maudlin, and Josh's voice rings natural and true. An elegantly crafted volume of lasting power." Kirkus

Auxier, Jonathan

Peter Nimble and his fantastic eyes; a story. Amulet Books 2011 381p il $16.95
Grades: 4 5 6 7   Fic
1. Eye -- Fiction   2. Blind -- Fiction   3. Magic -- Fiction   4. Orphans -- Fiction   5. Thieves -- Fiction
ISBN 978-1-4197-0025-5; 1-4197-0025-1

LC 2010048692

Raised to be a thief, blind orphan Peter Nimble, age ten, steals from a mysterious stranger three pairs of magical eyes, that lead him to a hidden island where he must decide to become a hero or resume his life of crime.

"The fast-paced, episodic story, accompanied by Auxier's occasional pen-and-ink drawings, is inventive, unpredictable, and—like its hero—nimble." Publ Wkly

Avi, 1937-

The **Book** Without Words; a fable of medieval magic. Hyperion Books for Children 2005 203p hardcover o.p. pa $5.99

Grades: 5 6 7 8   **Fic**

1. Magic -- Fiction 2. Middle Ages -- Fiction 3. Supernatural -- Fiction

ISBN 0-7868-0829-2; 0-7868-1659-7 pa

"At the dawning of the Middle Ages, Thorston, an old al-chemist, works feverishly to create gold and to dose himself with a concoction that will enable him to live forever. The key to his success lies in a mysterious book with blank pages that can only be read by desperate, green-eyed people. . . . Avi's compelling language creates a dreary foreboding. . . . Clearly this is a story with a message, a true fable. Thoughtful readers will devour its absorbing plot and humorous elements, and learn a 'useful truth' along the way." SLJ

★ **City** of orphans; with illustrations by Greg Ruth. Atheneum Books for Young Readers 2011 350p il $16.99

Grades: 5 6 7 8   **Fic**

1. Mystery fiction 2. Gangs -- Fiction 3. Immigrants -- Fiction 4. Family life -- Fiction 5. Homeless persons -- Fiction

ISBN 978-1-4169-7102-3; 1-4169-7102-5

LC 2010049229

In 1893 New York, thirteen-year-old Maks, a newsboy, teams up with Willa, a homeless girl, to clear his older sister, Emma, from charges that she stole from the brand new Waldorf Hotel, where she works. Includes historical notes.

"Avi's vivid recreation of the sights and sounds of that time and place is spot on, masterfully weaving accurate historical details with Maks' experiences." Kirkus

Includes bibliographical references

★ **Crispin**: the cross of lead. Hyperion Bks. for Children 2002 $15.99; pa $6.99

Grades: 5 6 7 8   **Fic**

1. Orphans -- Fiction 2. Middle Ages -- Fiction

ISBN 0-7868-0828-4; 0-7868-1658-9 pa

LC 2001-51829

Awarded the Newbery Medal, 2001

Falsely accused of theft and murder, an orphaned peasant boy in fourteenth-century England flees his village and meets a larger-than-life juggler who holds a dangerous secret

This "book is a page-turner from beginning to end. . . . A meticulously crafted story, full of adventure, mystery, and action." SLJ

Other titles in this series are:

Crispin at the edge of the world (2006)

Crispin: the end of time (2010)

★ **Don't** you know there's a war on? HarperCollins Pubs. 2001 200p hardcover o.p. pa $5.99

Grades: 4 5 6 7   **Fic**

1. Teachers -- Fiction 2. World War, 1939-1945 -- Fiction 3. World War, 1939-1945 -- United States

ISBN 0-380-97863-6; 0-380-81544-3 pa

LC 00-46102

In wartime Brooklyn in 1943, eleven-year-old Howie Crispers mounts a campaign to save his favorite teacher from being fired

"The 1943 Brooklyn setting is well evoked in Howie's lively, slang-spangled narration. The novel's uncomplicated, compact structure invites reading aloud." Horn Book Guide

★ **Iron** thunder; the battle between the Monitor and the Merrimac, a civil war novel. Hyperion 2007 205p il $15.99; pa $5.99

Grades: 4 5 6   **Fic**

1. Ships -- Fiction

ISBN 978-1-4231-0446-9; 1-4231-0446-3; 978-1-4231-0518-3 pa; 1-4231-0518-4 pa

"This fascinating adventure taken from U.S. history begins in Brooklyn in 1862, when Tom Carroll, 13, is hired at the Iron Works in Greenpoint for a secret project, derisively known around the borough as Ericsson's Folly. John Ericsson, a Swedish inventor, is trying to build an ironclad ship that can battle the Merrimac, a Confederate ship being outfitted with metal plates in Virginia. . . . Illustrated with period engravings, this is gripping historical fiction from a keenly imagined perspective." Publ Wkly

The **man** who was Poe; a novel. Orchard Bks. 1989 208p hardcover o.p. pa $5.99

Grades: 4 5 6 7   **813**

1. Poets 2. Authors 3. Mystery fiction 4. Essayists 5. Short story writers

ISBN 0-531-08433-7; 0-380-73022-7 pa

LC 89-42537

In Providence, R.I., in 1848, Edgar Allan Poe reluctantly investigates the problems of eleven-year-old Edmund, whose family has mysteriously disappeared and whose story suggests a new Poe tale with a ghastly final twist

Avi blends "drama, history, and mystery without a hint of pastiche or calculation. And, as in the best mystery stories, readers will be left in the end with both the comfort of puzzles solved and the unease of mysteries remaining." Bull Cent Child Books

Midnight magic. Scholastic Press 1999 249p hardcover o.p. pa $5.99

Grades: 5 6 7 8   **Fic**

1. Magicians -- Fiction 2. Renaissance -- Fiction

ISBN 0-590-36035-3; 0-439-24219-3 pa

LC 98-50192

In Italy in 1491, Mangus the magician and his apprentice are summoned to the castle of Duke Claudio to determine if his daughter is indeed being haunted by a ghost.

An "entertaining tale of mystery and intrigue." SLJ

Another title about Mangus and Fabrizio is:

Murder at midnight (2009)

★ **Nothing** but the truth; a documentary novel. Scholastic Inc. 2010 177p pa $6.99

Grades: 6 7 8 9   **Fic**

1. School stories

ISBN 978-0-545-17415-2

First published 1991 by Orchard Bks.

A Newbery Medal honor book, 1992

A ninth-grader's suspension for singing "The Star-Spangled Banner" during homeroom becomes a national news story.

"The book is effectively set entirely in monologue or dialogue; conversations, memos, letters, diary entries, talk-radio transcripts, and newspaper articles are all interwoven to present an uninterrupted plot. The construction is nearly flawless; the characters seem painfully human and typically ordinary. . . . A powerful, explosive novel that involves the reader from start to finish." Horn Book

★ **Sophia's** war; a tale of the Revolution. Avi. Beach Lane Books 2012 302 p. (hardcover) $16.99
Grades: 5 6 7 8 **Fic**
1. Traitors -- Fiction 2. Women spies -- Fiction 3. United States -- History -- 1775-1783, Revolution -- Fiction 4. Spies -- Fiction
ISBN 1442414413; 9781442414419; 9781442414426; 9781442414433
LC 2012007962
In this novel by Avi "Sophia Calderwood witnesses the execution of Nathan Hale in New York City, which is newly occupied by the British army . . . in 1776. . . . Recruited as a spy, . . . she becomes aware that someone in the American army might be switching sides, and she uncovers a plot that will grievously damage the Americans if it succeeds. But the identity of the would-be traitor is so shocking that no one believes her, and so Sophia decides to stop the treacherous plot herself." (Publisher's note)
Includes bibliographical references

★ **Traitor's** gate. Atheneum Books for Young Readers 2007 351p $17.99
Grades: 5 6 7 8 **Fic**
1. Spies -- Fiction 2. Poverty -- Fiction 3. Family life -- Fiction
ISBN 0-689-85335-1
When his father is arrested as a debtor in 1849 London, fourteen-year-old John Huffman must take on unexpected responsibilities, from asking a distant relative for help to determining why people are spying on him and his family.
"With plenty of period detail, this action-packed narrative of twists, turns, and treachery is another winner from a master craftsman." SLJ

The **fighting** ground. Lippincott 1984 157p hardcover o.p. lib bdg $16.89; pa $5.99; rpt $5.99
Grades: 5 6 7 8 **Fic**
ISBN 0-397-32073-6; 0-397-32074-4 lib bdg; 0-06-440185-5 pa; 9780064401852 rpt
LC 82-47719
"It's April 1776, and the fighting ground is both the farm country of Pennsylvania and the heart of a boy which is 'wonderful ripe for war.' Twenty-four hours transform Jonathan from a cocky 13-year-old, eager to take on the British, into a young man who now knows the horror, the pathos, the ambiguities of war." Voice Youth Advocates

★ The **seer** of shadows. HarperCollinsPublishers 2008 202p $16.99; lib bdg $17.89; pa $6.99
Grades: 4 5 6 7 **Fic**
1. Ghost stories 2. Photography -- Fiction 3. Swindlers

and swindling -- Fiction
ISBN 978-0-06-000015-8; 0-06-000015-5; 978-0-06-000016-5 lib bdg; 0-06-000016-3 lib bdg; 978-0-06-000017-2 pa; 0-06-000017-1 pa
LC 2007-10891
In New York City in 1872, fourteen-year-old Horace, a photographer's apprentice, becomes entangled in a plot to create fraudulent spirit photographs, but when Horace accidentally frees the real ghost of a dead girl bent on revenge, his life takes a frightening turn.
"Fast-paced yet haunting. . . . This engaging novel has great immediacy and strong narrative drive." Booklist

★ The **true** confessions of Charlotte Doyle; decorations by Ruth E. Murray. Orchard Bks. 1990 215p $16.95; pa $5.99; rpt $16.99
Grades: 5 6 7 **Fic**
1. Sea stories
ISBN 0-531-05893-X; 0-380-72885-0 pa; 9780545477116 rpt
LC 90-30624
A Newbery Medal honor book, 1991
This is a "seafaring adventure, set in 1832. Charlotte Doyle, 13, returning from school in England to join her family in Rhode Island, is deposited on a seedy ship with a ruthless, mad captain and a mutinous crew. Refusing to heed warnings about Captain Jaggery's brutality, Charlotte seeks his guidance and approval only to become his victim, a pariah to the entire crew, and a convicted felon for the murder of the first mate." SLJ

Axelrod, Amy
Your friend in fashion, Abby Shapiro. Holiday House 2011 261p il $17.95
Grades: 4 5 6 **Fic**
1. Letters -- Fiction 2. Family life -- Fiction 3. Fashion designers -- Fiction 4. Jews -- United States -- Fiction
ISBN 978-0-8234-2340-8; 0-8234-2340-9
LC 2010-24185
Beginning in 1959, Abby, nearly eleven, writes a series of letters to Jackie Kennedy, each with sketches of outfits she has designed, as she faces family problems, concerns about neighbors, and her own desperate desire for both her first bra and a Barbie doll.
"Abby is an especially memorable protagonist, but all [Axelrod's] characters vibrate with life. . . . Funny, lively, sensitive—a real winner." Kirkus

Ayarbe, Heidi
★ **Compromised**. HarperTeen 2010 452p $16.99
Grades: 8 9 10 11 12 **Fic**
1. Foster home care -- Fiction 2. Runaway teenagers -- Fiction 3. Tourette syndrome -- Fiction 4. Voyages and travels -- Fiction
ISBN 978-0-06-172849-5; 0-06-172849-7
LC 2009-23545
With her con-man father in prison, fifteen-year-old Maya sets out from Reno, Nevada, for Boise, Idaho, hoping to stay out of foster care by finding an aunt she never knew existed, but a fellow runaway complicates all of her scientifically-devised plans.

"Ayarbe offers a gut-wrenching, terrifyingly authentic story and memorably etched, courageous characters whose influence on each other is palpable." Booklist

Ayres, Katherine

Macaroni boy. Delacorte Press 2003 182p hardcover o.p. pa $5.99

Grades: 5 6 7 8   **Fic**

1. School stories 2. Great Depression, 1929-1939 -- Fiction

ISBN 0-385-73016-0; 0-440-41884-4 pa

LC 2002-6768

In Pittsburgh in 1933, sixth-grader Mike Costa notices a connection between several strange occurrences, but the only way he can find out the truth about what's happening is to be nice to the class bully. Includes historical facts

"Actual places and events are interwoven with a heart-warming story of a close-knit family facing difficult times." Voice Youth Advocates

North by night; a story of the Underground Railroad. Delacorte Press 1998 176p hardcover o.p. pa $4.99

Grades: 6 7 8 9   **Fic**

1. Diaries -- Fiction 2. Slavery -- Fiction 3. Fugitive slaves -- Fiction 4. Underground railroad -- Fiction

ISBN 0-385-32564-9; 0-440-22747-x pa

LC 98-10039

Presents the journal of Lucinda, a sixteen-year-old girl whose family operates a stop on the Underground Railroad

This "is an absorbing tale. Ayres slips in a lot of evocative detail about the hard work of running a farm and a household before the Civil War, as well as some rather charming musing about kissing and its myriad effects on the psyche." Booklist

Babbitt, Natalie

The **moon** over High Street; Natalie Babbitt. Scholastic 2012 148 p $15.95

Grades: 3 4 5 6 7   **Fic**

1. Family -- fiction 2. Friendship -- fiction 3. Decision making -- fiction 4. Adopted children -- fiction

ISBN 054537636X; 9780545376365

LC 2011926886

This children's novel by Natalie Babbitt "presents 12-year-old Joe. . . . Orphaned shortly after his birth, Joe, who loves the moon, has been raised by his Gran, but after she breaks a hip, he's sent to spend some of the summer with his father's cousin. . . . In nearly idyllic Midville, . . . he inadvertently comes to the attention of the very wealthy factory owner Mr. Boulderwall . . . who decides that he will adopt Joe and raise him to take over his company." (Kirkus)

Baccalario, Pierdomenico

Ring of fire; translated by Leah D. Janeczko; illustrations by Iacopo Bruno. Random House 2009 293p il (Century quartet) $16.99; lib bdg $19.99

Grades: 5 6 7 8   **Fic**

1. Good and evil -- Fiction

ISBN 978-0-375-85895-6; 0-375-85895-4; 978-0-375-95895-3 lib bdg; 0-375-95895-9 lib bdg

LC 2009-08204

Original Italian edition, 2006

Four seemingly unrelated children are brought together in a Rome hotel where they discover that they are destined to become involved in a deep and ancient mystery involving a briefcase full of artifacts that expose them to great danger

"There are some genuinely exciting moments and the premise is intriguing." Publ Wkly

Other titles in this series are:
Star of Stone (2010)
City of Wind (2011)

Bacigalupi, Paolo

★ **Ship** Breaker; Bacigalupi, Paolo. Little, Brown and Co. 2010 326p $17.99

Grades: 8 9 10 11 12   **Fic**

1. Science fiction 2. Recycling -- Fiction

ISBN 0316056219; 9780316056212

LC 2009-34424

Michael L. Printz Award, 2011

In a futuristic world, teenaged Nailer scavenges copper wiring from grounded oil tankers for a living, but when he finds a beached clipper ship with a girl in the wreckage, he has to decide if he should strip the ship for its wealth or rescue the girl.

"Bacigalupi's cast is ethnically and morally diverse, and the book's message never overshadows the storytelling, action-packed pacing, or intricate world-building. At its core, the novel is an exploration of Nailer's discovery of the nature of the world around him and his ability to transcend that world's expectations." Publ Wkly

★ The **drowned** cities; by Paolo Bacigalupi. Little, Brown and Company 2012 448p. paperback $11.00

Grades: 9 10 11 12   **Fic**

1. Science fiction 2. Apocalyptic fiction 3. Refugees -- Fiction 4. War -- Fiction 5. Orphans -- Fiction 6. Soldiers -- Fiction 7. Survival -- Fiction 8. Genetic engineering -- Fiction

ISBN 9780316056243; 9780316056229 paperback

LC 2011031762

This book takes place "[i]n a dark future America where violence, terror, and grief touch everyone, young refugees Mahlia and Mouse have managed to leave behind the war-torn lands of the Drowned Cities by escaping into the jungle outskirts. But when they discover a wounded half-man--a bioengineered war beast named Tool--who is being hunted by a vengeful band of soldiers, their fragile existence quickly collapses." (Publisher's note)

Baggott, Julianna

The **Prince** of Fenway Park. HarperCollinsPublishers 2009 322p $16.99; lib bdg $17.89

Grades: 4 5 6 7   **Fic**

1. Orphans -- Fiction 2. Baseball -- Fiction 3. Supernatural -- Fiction 4. Father-son relationship -- Fiction

ISBN 978-0-06-087242-7; 0-06-087242-X; 978-0-06-087243-4 lib bdg; 0-06-087243-8 lib bdg

LC 2008-19666

In the fall of 2004, twelve-year-old Oscar Egg is sent to live with his father in a strange netherworld under Boston's

Fenway Park, where he joins the fairies, pooka, banshee, and other beings that are trapped there, waiting for someone to break the eighty-six-year-old curse that has prevented the Boston Red Sox from winning a World Series

"Both whimsical and provocative (the 'N' word crops up in some historical references), this story will engage readers who like clever tales, and also those who enjoy chewing over controversial themes." SLJ

Bailey, Em

Shift; Em Bailey. Random House Distribution Childrens 2012 304 p. (hardcover) $16.99

Grades: 7 8 9 10 11 12   **Fic**
1. Human behavior -- Fiction 2. Female friendship -- Fiction 3. High school students -- Fiction 4. Orphans -- Fiction 5. Schools -- Fiction 6. Popularity -- Fiction 7. High schools -- Fiction 8. Mental illness -- Fiction 9. Interpersonal relations -- Fiction
ISBN 1606843583; 9781606843581; 9781606843598
LC 2011034349

Author Em Bailey's character "Olive keeps it simple: take her meds, keep a low profile at school, stay away from the ocean (with its horrible memories), and try not to cause trouble since she's pretty sure her selfish, unruly behavior is what made her father take off six months ago. But then strange and mysterious Miranda Vaile shows up at her high school, and Olive's safeguards start to crumble. Miranda begins insinuating herself into the life of Olive's former best friend, Katie."

Baldwin, James

Go tell it on the mountain. Knopf 1953 303p $15.95; pa $6.99

Grades: 8 9 10 11 12 Adult   **Fic**
1. Family life -- Fiction 2. Autobiographical stories 3. African Americans -- Fiction 4. African Americans -- New York (N.Y.)
ISBN 0-679-60154-6; 0-440-33007-6 pa

This novel is an "autobiographical story of a Harlem child's relationship with his father against the background of his being saved in the pentecostal church." Benet's Reader's Ency of Am Lit

Balliett, Blue

The **Calder** game; illustrated by Brett Helquist. Scholastic Press 2008 379p il $17.99

Grades: 5 6 7 8   **Fic**
1. Mystery fiction 2. Sculpture -- Fiction 3. Missing persons -- Fiction
ISBN 978-0-439-85207-4; 0-439-85207-2
LC 2007031385

When seventh-grader Calder Pillay disappears from a remote English village—along with an Alexander Calder sculpture to which he has felt strangely drawn—his friends Petra and Tommy fly from Chicago to help his father find him.

Balliett "outdoes herself with this ambitious novel. . . . The mystery is crafted more solidly than in either of Balliett's previous titles, and the setting . . . proves completely enticing. And once again Helquist encodes his b&w illustrations with puzzle pieces." Publ Wkly

★ **Chasing** Vermeer; illustrated by Brett Helquist. Scholastic Press 2004 254p il $16.95

Grades: 5 6 7 8   **Fic**
1. Mystery fiction 2. Art -- Fiction
ISBN 0-439-37294-1
LC 2002-152106

When seemingly unrelated and strange events start to happen and a precious Vermeer painting disappears, eleven-year-olds Petra and Calder combine their talents to solve an international art scandal.

Balliett's purpose "seems to be to get children to think—about relationships, connections, coincidences, and the subtle language of artwork. . . . [This is] a book that offers children something new upon each reading. . . . Helquist . . . outdoes himself here, providing an interactive mystery in his pictures." Booklist

Other titles about Petra and Calder are:
The Wright 3 (2006)
The Calder game (2008)

★ The **Danger** Box. Scholastic Press 2010 306p $16.99

Grades: 5 6 7 8   **Fic**
1. Diaries -- Fiction 2. Antiques -- Fiction 3. Family life -- Fiction 4. Grandparents -- Fiction
ISBN 978-0-439-85209-8; 0-439-85209-9
LC 2010-16622

In small-town Michigan, twelve-year-old Zoomy and his new friend Lorrol investigate the journal found inside a mysterious box and find family secrets and a more valuable treasure, while a dangerous stranger watches and waits.

"This highly satisfying story will enlighten readers even as it inspires them to think about their own danger boxes." SLJ

★ **Hold** fast; by Blue Balliett. Scholastic Press 2013 288 p. (jacketed hardcover) $17.99

Grades: 3 4 5 6   **Fic**
1. Theft -- fiction 2. Mystery fiction -- fiction 3. Smuggling -- Fiction 4. Kidnapping -- Fiction 5. Missing persons -- Fiction 6. Homeless persons -- Fiction 7. Mystery and detective stories 8. Fathers and daughters -- Fiction 9. Homeless families -- fiction 10. Kidnapping victims -- fiction 11. Fathers and daughters -- fiction 12. Family life -- Illinois -- Chicago -- Fiction
ISBN 0545299888; 9780545299886
LC 2012041035

This book focuses on "the Pearl family: Dash, Summer, 11-year-old Early, and the little Jubie. Do they have a lot? Well, yes, they have Dash's love of words, their devotion to each other, and their dream: to have a home. Trying to help that dream along, Dash, a page at the Chicago Public Library, makes extra money inventorying a private collection of old books. One . . . day, Dash disappears, and the family must move to a shelter after an odd robbery sees their . . . apartment destroyed." Booklist

The **Wright** 3; illustrated by Brett Helquist. Scholastic Press 2006 318p il $16.99

Grades: 5 6 7 8   **Fic**
1. School stories 2. Mystery fiction
ISBN 0-439-69367-5

LC 2005-19608

In the midst of a series of unexplained accidents and mysterious coincidences, sixth-graders Calder, Petra, and Tommy lead their classmates in an attempt to keep Frank Lloyd Wright's famous Robie House from being demolished.

"The mystery itself and the perfectly realized setting make this an essential purchase." SLJ

Bancks, Tristan

Mac Slater hunts the cool. Simon & Schuster Books for Young Readers 2010 203p $15.99
Grades: 6 7 8 9   **Fic**
1. School stories 2. Beaches -- Fiction 3. Weblogs -- Fiction 4. Video recording -- Fiction
ISBN 978-1-4169-8574-7; 1-4169-8574-3

LC 2009-00152

Mac, an Australian youth, has one week to prove that he can be a "coolhunter," identifying emerging trends and posting images on a website, but he is competing against a classmate on whom he has a crush and dealing with resistance from his best friend and his own confusion over what "cool" means.

"Mac is a likable character who will appeal to a wide range of readers." Booklist

Mac Slater vs. the city. Simon & Schuster Books for Young Readers 2011 184p $15.99
Grades: 6 7 8 9   **Fic**
1. Inventors -- Fiction 2. Web sites -- Fiction 3. Inventions -- Fiction
ISBN 1-4169-8576-X; 978-1-4169-8576-1

LC 2010006858

Mac and his reluctant friend Paul head from Australia to Manhattan to continue their work for the Coolhunter website, and once there they discover a group of young inventors whose work is meant to be kept top-secret.

"The story takes twists and turns that are both surprising and rewarding. . . . An easy sell to many middle graders." SLJ

Banks, Kate

Walk softly, Rachel. Farrar, Straus & Giroux 2003 149p $16
Grades: 7 8 9 10   **Fic**
1. Death -- Fiction 2. Family life -- Fiction
ISBN 0-374-38230-1

LC 2002-26503

When fourteen-year-old Rachel reads the journal of her brother, who died when she was seven, she learns secrets that help her understand her parents and herself

"While Banks's poetic prose may consist of simple words, its effect on the ear and heart is remarkable." SLJ

Baratz-Logsted, Lauren

Crazy beautiful. Houghton Mifflin Harcourt 2009 191p $16
Grades: 7 8 9 10   **Fic**
1. School stories 2. Bullies -- Fiction 3. Amputees --

Fiction 4. Physically handicapped -- Fiction
ISBN 978-0-547-22307-0; 0-547-22307-2

LC 2008-40463

In this contemporary retelling of "Beauty and the Beast," a teenaged boy whose hands were amputated in an explosion and a gorgeous girl whose mother has recently died form an instant connection when they meet on their first day as new students.

"This romance transcends all of its potential pitfalls to create a powerful story about recovery and friendship." Kirkus

Twin's daughter. Bloomsbury 2010 390p $16.99
Grades: 7 8 9 10   **Fic**
1. Mystery fiction 2. Aunts -- Fiction 3. Twins -- Fiction 4. Homicide -- Fiction
ISBN 978-1-59990-513-6; 1-59990-513-2

LC 2010-08234

In Victorian London, thirteen-year-old Lucy's comfortable world with her loving parents begins slowly to unravel the day that a bedraggled woman who looks exactly like her mother appears at their door.

"Baratz-Logsted's gothic murder mystery is rife with twists and moves swiftly and elegantly. . . . The ending will intrigue and delight readers." Booklist

Bardugo, Leigh

Shadow and bone; Leigh Bardugo. Henry Holt 2012 358 p. (Grisha trilogy) (hc) $17.99
Grades: 8 9 10 11   **Fic**
1. Fantasy fiction 2. Magic -- Fiction 3. Monsters -- Fiction 4. Slavic mythology -- fiction 5. Ability -- Fiction 6. Orphans -- Fiction
ISBN 0805094598; 9780805094596

LC 2011034012

In this young adult novel, "[Leigh] Bardugo draws inspiration from Russian and Slavic myth and culture to kick off her 'Grisha' trilogy. In the nation of Ravka, Alina Starkov is a junior cartographer's assistant in the army, while her best friend Mai is an expert tracker. When a perilous mission into the magically created Shadow Fold goes wrong, Mai is gravely wounded and Alina manifests the rare ability to summon light. Immediately recruited into the order of the magic-using Grisha, Alina is taken under the wing of its intimidating and powerful leader, the Darkling, and heralded as the potential destroyer of the Shadow Fold. As she navigates Grisha politics and uncovers well-hidden secrets, she realizes that the fate of the nation rests on her shoulders and she may be in grave danger." (Publishers Weekly)

Siege and storm; Leigh Bardugo. 1st ed. Henry Holt and Co. 2013 448 p. (Grisha trilogy) (hardcover) $17.99
Grades: 8 9 10 11 12   **Fic**
1. Fantasy fiction 2. Russia -- Fiction 3. Monsters -- Fiction 4. Magic -- Fiction 5. Orphans -- Fiction
ISBN 0805094601; 9780805094602

LC 2012046361

This fantasy novel, by Leigh Bardugo, is book 2 of the "Grisha Trilogy." "Alina must try to make a life with Mal in an unfamiliar land, all while keeping her identity as the Sun Summoner a secret. But she can't outrun her past or her destiny for long. The Darkling has emerged from the

Shadow Fold with a terrifying new power and a dangerous plan that will test the very boundaries of the natural world." (Publisher's note)

Barker, M. P.

A **difficult** boy. Holiday House 2008 298p $16.95; pa $7.95

Grades: 5 6 7 8 **Fic**

1. Contract labor -- Fiction 2. Irish Americans -- Fiction 3. Swindlers and swindling -- Fiction

ISBN 978-0-8234-2086-5; 0-8234-2086-8; 978-0-8234-2244-9 pa; 0-8234-2244-5 pa

LC 2007-37059

In Farmington, Massachusetts, in 1839, nine-year-old Ethan experiences hardships as an indentured servant of the wealthy Lyman family alongside Daniel, a boy scorned simply for being Irish, and the boys bond as they try to right a terrible wrong.

"A memorable tale of friendship and a fascinating glimpse into mid-19th-century Massachusetts." SLJ

Barkley, Brad

Dream factory; [by] Brad Barkley + Heather Hepler. Dutton Books 2007 250p $16.99; pa $8.99

Grades: 8 9 10 11 12 **Fic**

1. Love stories 2. Summer employment -- Fiction

ISBN 978-0-525-47802-7; 0-525-47802-7; 978-0-14-241298-5 pa; 0-14-241298-8 pa

Alternating chapters present the view points of two teenagers who find summer employment as costumed cartoon characters at Disney World and try to resist falling in love.

"Able writing moves the story along while strong characterization makes even secondary players come alive." SLJ

Jars of glass; [by] Brad Barkley & Heather Hepler. Dutton Childrens Books 2008 246p $16.99

Grades: 7 8 9 10 11 12 **Fic**

1. Adoption -- Fiction 2. Siblings -- Fiction 3. Family life -- Fiction 4. Mental illness -- Fiction

ISBN 978-0-525-47911-6; 0-525-47911-2

LC 2007-52657

Two sisters, aged fourteen and fifteen, offer their views of events that occur during the year after their mother is diagnosed with schizophrenia and their family, including a recently adopted Russian orphan, begins to disintegrate.

"Barkley and Hepler are the masters of alternating narration, with Chloe's and Shana's voices both believable, clearly different, and usefully complementary. . . . This is an affecting story about families struggling to readjust in the face of one member's affliction." Bull Cent Child Books

Scrambled eggs at midnight; by Brad Barkley, Heather Hepler. Dutton Books 2006 262p $16.99

Grades: 7 8 9 10 **Fic**

1. Love stories 2. Fairs -- Fiction

ISBN 0-525-47760-8

LC 2005029187

Calliope and Eliot, two fifteen-year-olds in Asheville, North Carolina, begin to acknowledge some unpleasant truths about their parents and form their own ideas about love.

"This coauthored love story unfolds in alternating chapters narrated in Cal and Elliot's hilarious, heart-tugging voices. . . . The authors raise a potentially routine summer romance into a refreshing, poetic, memorable story." Booklist

Barnaby, Hannah

Wonder show; by Hannah Barnaby. Houghton Mifflin Books for Children 2012 viii, 274 p.p $16.99

Grades: 7 8 9 10 11 12 **Fic**

1. Fathers -- Fiction 2. Runaways -- Fiction 3. Sideshows -- Fiction 4. Orphanages -- Fiction 5. Depressions -- 1929 -- United States -- Fiction

ISBN 0547599803; 9780547599809

LC 2011052426

William C. Morris Award Finalist (2013)

In this book by Hannah Barnaby, "Portia Remini, 13 . . . escapes . . . from the McGreavey Home for Wayward Girls to search for her father. . . . She joins a carnival. . . . On the lam from sinister 'Mister,' who runs McGreavey's, Portia learns the stories of some of the carnival's strange troupe. . . . But . . . when Mister's dragnet closes in, Portia decides that to find the answers she seeks she must return to the horror of The Home."

Barnes, Jennifer Lynn

The **Squad**: perfect cover. Delacorte Press 2008 275p pa $6.99

Grades: 7 8 9 10 **Fic**

1. School stories 2. Spies -- Fiction 3. Computers -- Fiction 4. Cheerleading -- Fiction

ISBN 978-0-385-73454-7 pa; 0-385-73454-9 pa

LC 2007-09352

High school sophomore Toby Klein enjoys computer hacking and wearing combat boots, so she thinks it is a joke when she is invited to join the cheerleading squad but soon learns cheering is just a cover for an elite group of government operatives known as the Squad.

"In addition to offering crafty plotting and time-honored, typical teen conflicts and rivalries, Barnes maintains a sharp sense of humor in this action-adventure series." Bull Cent Child Books

Another title in this series is:

The Squad: killer spirit (2008)

Barnhill, Kelly Regan

★ The **mostly** true story of Jack; by Kelly Barnhill. Little, Brown 2011 323p il $16.99

Grades: 5 6 7 8 **Fic**

1. Magic -- Fiction 2. Friendship -- Fiction 3. Family life -- Fiction

ISBN 978-0-316-05670-0; 0-316-05670-7

LC 2010044934

Jack is practically invisible at home, but when his parents send him to Hazelwood, Iowa, to spend a summer with his odd aunt and uncle, he suddenly makes friends, is beaten up by the town bully, and is plotted against by the richest man in town.

"A truly splendid amalgamation of mystery, magic and creeping horror will spellbind the middle-grade set. . . . The mystery deepens with each chapter, revealing exactly the right amount with each step. Answers are doled out so meticulously that readers will be continually intrigued rather than frustrated. The result is the ultime page-turner." Kirkus

Barnholdt, Lauren

Girl meets ghost; by Lauren Barnholdt. Aladdin 2013 224 p. (alk. paper) $15.99

Grades: 4 5 6 7   **Fic**

1. Ghost stories 2. School stories 3. Mystery fiction 4. Dead -- Fiction 5. Ghosts -- Fiction 6. Schools -- Fiction 7. Middle schools -- Fiction 8. Psychic ability -- Fiction 9. Mystery and detective stories

ISBN 1442442468; 9781442442467

LC 2012032234

In this children's story, by Lauren Barnholt, "a tween girl becomes a reluctant medium. . . . There's an old saying that 'dead men tell no tales'--but that saying is definitely not true. Just ask twelve-year-old Kendall Williams, who can't get dead people to stop talking to her. . . . It's pretty frustrating being able to hear and see people that no one else can. . . . But Kendall is going to have to learn how to deal, because the only way to quiet the dead is to help them." (Publisher's note)

Sometimes it happens. Simon Pulse 2011 312p $16.99

Grades: 7 8 9 10   **Fic**

1. School stories 2. Dating (Social customs) -- Fiction

ISBN 978-1-4424-1314-6; 1-4424-1314-X

With help from her best friend Ava and Ava's boyfriend Noah, Hannah is recovering from being dumped by her boyfriend Sebastian, but on the first day of their senior year in high school, Ava learns that Hannah and Noah betrayed her while she was away.

"The writing style is smooth, featuring believable dialogue and first-person narration from Hannah's perspective. Hannah is a sympathetic character struggling with a relatable dilemma of liking your friend's significant other, yet wanting to be a faithful friend. The underlying message is captured by the title, Sometimes It Happens, as Hannah grows to understand that part of being human is hurting people without meaning to and then needing to ask for forgiveness." Voice Youth Advocates

Barnhouse, Rebecca

The book of the maidservant. Random House 2009 232p map $16.99; lib bdg $19.99

Grades: 7 8 9 10   **Fic**

1. Mystics 2. Memoirists 3. Writers on religion 4. Middle Ages -- Fiction 5. Religious life -- Fiction 6. Voyages and travels -- Fiction 7. Pilgrims and pilgrimages -- Fiction

ISBN 978-0-375-85856-7; 0-375-85856-3; 978-0-375-95856-4 lib bdg; 0-375-95856-8 lib bdg

LC 2008-28820

In 1413, a young maidservant accompanies her deeply religious mistress, Dame Margery Kempe, on a pilgrimage to Rome. Includes author's note on Kempe, writer of "The Book of Margery Kempe," considered by some to be the first autobiography in the English language

"Earthy, authentic, and engrossing, this fast-paced, easy read belongs on the shelf with Karen Cushman's The Midwife's Apprentice." Voice Youth Advocates

Includes bibliographical references

Barratt, Mark

Joe Rat. Eerdmans Books for Young Readers 2009 307p pa $9

Grades: 7 8 9 10   **Fic**

1. Crime -- Fiction 2. Orphans -- Fiction 3. Mental illness -- Fiction

ISBN 978-0-8028-5356-1; 0-8028-5356-0

LC 2008055972

First published 2008 in the United Kingdom

In the dark, dank sewers of Victorian London, a boy known as Joe Rat scrounges for valuables which he gives to "Mother," a criminal mastermind who considers him a favorite, but a chance meeting with a runaway girl and "the Madman" transforms all their lives.

"The unraveling of the Madman's identity is but one of the pleasures of Barratt's leisurely and convincing historical fiction." Booklist

The wild man. Eerdmans Books for Young Readers 2010 341p pa $9

Grades: 7 8 9 10   **Fic**

1. Crime -- Fiction 2. Fathers -- Fiction 3. Orphans -- Fiction 4. Social classes -- Fiction 5. Impostors and imposture -- Fiction

ISBN 978-0-8028-5377-6 pa; 0-8028-5377-3 pa

LC 2010010937

In Victorian England, Joe Rat has escaped the clutches of the criminal mastermind, Mother, and is trying to make an honest living in a better part of London, but when a rich philanthropist tracks down a man claiming to be Joe's missing father—a British army deserter—he must determine where his loyalties lie.

"Barratt writes as if he is keeping an adjacent berth to Dickens; here's hoping scrappy Joe has a few more tricks up his ratty sleeves." Booklist

Barrett, Tracy

The 100-year-old secret. Henry Holt and Co. 2008 157p (The Sherlock files) $15.95

Grades: 4 5 6 7   **Fic**

1. Mystery fiction 2. Siblings -- Fiction

ISBN 978-0-8050-8340-8; 0-8050-8340-5

LC 2007034004

Xena and Xander Holmes, an American brother and sister living in London for a year, discover that Sherlock Holmes was their great-great-great grandfather when they are inducted into the Society for the Preservation of Famous Detectives and given his unsolved casebook, from which they attempt to solve the case of a famous missing painting

"The main characters are observant, bright, and gifted with powers of deduction." SLJ

Other titles in this series are:
The beast of Blackslope (2009)
The case that time forgot (2010)
The missing heir (2011)

Dark of the moon. Harcourt 2011 310p $16.99

Grades: 7 8 9 10   **Fic**
  1. Classical mythology -- Fiction 2. Theseus (Greek Mythology) -- Fiction
  ISBN 978-0-547-58132-3; 0-547-58132-7
                LC 2011009597
Retells the story of the minotaur through the eyes of his fifteen-year-old sister, Ariadne, a lonely girl destined to become a goddess of the moon, and her new friend, Theseus, the son of Athens' king who was sent to Crete as a sacrifice to her misshapen brother.

"This retelling of the myth of the Minotaur is deft, dark, and enthralling. Barrett spares readers none of the gore and violence of the Kretan goddess-worship, which involves both human and animal sacrifice. Ariadne's beliefs, though alien to modern readers, are given sufficient context to make them comprehensible. . . . This thoughtful, well-written reimagining of a classic myth is a welcome addition to the genre." SLJ

  King of Ithaka. Henry Holt and Company 2010 261p map $16.99
Grades: 7 8 9 10   **Fic**
  1. Classical mythology -- Fiction 2. Odysseus (Greek mythology) -- Fiction
  ISBN 978-0-8050-8969-1; 0-8050-8969-1
                LC 2009-50770
Sixteen-year-old Telemachos and his two best friends leave their life of privilege to undertake a quest to find Telemachos's father Odysseus. "Grades six to ten." (Bull Cent Child Books)

"The exotic climes and vivid descriptions . . . give the story a sense of immediacy and color." Booklist

Barron, T. A.
  Merlin's dragon. Philomel Books 2008 305p (Merlin's dragon) $19.99
Grades: 6 7 8 9   **Fic**
  1. Fantasy fiction 2. Magic -- Fiction 3. Dragons -- Fiction
  ISBN 978-0-399-24750-7; 0-399-24750-5
                LC 2008-2469
Basil, a small, flying lizard who is searching for others like himself, discovers that there is more to him than he knows, as he becomes engaged in Avalon's great war between the evil Rhita Gawr and the forces of good.

"Basil is an appealing, complex character. . . . This first book in a new series will captivate readers already familiar with the fantasist's Merlin chronicles." Booklist

  Other titles in this series are:
  Doomraga's revenge (2009)
  Utlimate magic (2010)

  The **book** of magic; illustrated by August Hall. Philomel Books 2011 il (Merlin) $17.99 **Fic**
  1. Fantasy fiction 2. Magic -- Fiction 3. Merlin (Legendary character) -- Fiction
  ISBN 978-0-399-24741-5; 0-399-24741-6
                LC 2011013552
A compendium of maps, character descriptions, magical terms, timelines, and other tidbits from the author's Merlin saga.

"Guides to long-running series have two important jobs. They should remind fans of all the things they particularly love about the books, and they should whet the appetites of newcomers, thus creating more fans. Barron's guide to his 12-book saga about Merlin succeeds in both objectives." SLJ

  ★ The **lost** years of Merlin. Philomel Bks. 1996 326p $19.99; pa $7.99
Grades: 5 6 7 8   **Fic**
  1. Fantasy fiction 2. Merlin (Legendary character) -- Fiction
  ISBN 978-0-399-23018-1; 978-0-441-00668-7 pa
                LC 96-33920
"A boy, hurled on the rocks by the sea, regains consciousness unable to remember anything—not his parents, not his own name. He is sure that the secretive Branwen is not his mother, despite her claims, and that Emrys is not his real name. The two soon find themselves feared because of Branwen's healing abilities and Emrys' growing powers. . . . Barron has created not only a magical land populated by remarkable beings but also a completely magical tale, filled with ancient Celtic and Druidic lore, that will enchant readers." Booklist

  Other titles in this series are:
  The seven songs of Merlin (1997)
  The fires of Merlin (1998)
  The mirror of Merlin (1999)
  The wings of Merlin (2000)
  The book of magic (2011)

Barrow, Randi G.
  Saving Zasha; by Randi Barrow. Scholastic Press 2011 229p $16.99
Grades: 4 5 6 7   **Fic**
  1. Dogs -- Fiction 2. Journalists -- Fiction 3. Single parent family -- Fiction 4. World War, 1939-1945 -- Fiction
  ISBN 978-0-545-20632-7; 0-545-20632-4
                LC 2010-16899
In 1945 Russia, those who own German shepherds are considered traitors, but thirteen-year-old Mikhail and his family are determined to keep the dog a dying man brought them, while his classmate Katia strives to learn his secret.

"Mikhail's sense of humor, concern for his family, and love of Zasha are all readily apparent in his narration, which smoothly incorporates background information for readers unfamiliar with 20th-century Russian life and history. . . . Barrow's novel is quick reading yet weighty, and captures the prejudices and aftereffects of war." Publ Wkly

Barry, Dave
  Peter & the shadow thieves; by Dave Barry and Ridley Pearson; illustrations by Greg Call. Disney Editions/Hyperion Books for Children 2006 556p il $18.99
Grades: 5 6 7   **Fic**
  1. Fairy tales 2. Adventure fiction
  ISBN 0-7868-3787-X
                LC 2005-56033
Realizing that Molly and the other Starcatchers are in danger when the sinister being Lord Ombra visits the island

and seems to control people through their shadows, Peter and Tinker Bell travel to England to help save the stardust.

This "is filled with enough rollicking, death-defying adventure to satisfy anyone." SLJ

Peter and the Sword of Mercy; by Dave Barry and Ridley Pearson; illustrations by Greg Call. Disney/Hyperion Books 2009 515p il $18.99

Grades: 5 6 7   **Fic**

1. Fairy tales 2. Adventure fiction
ISBN 978-1-4231-2134-3; 1-4231-2134-1

James, one of Peter's original Lost Boys, is now working for Scotland Yard and suspects that the heir to England's throne, Prince Albert Edward, is under the influence of shadow creatures who are after starstuff hidden in an underground vault which has only one key: the Sword of Mercy.

"This adventure is fast and intense, and readers will feel compelled to find out what happens next."

Peter and the secret of Rundoon; by Dave Barry and Ridley Pearson; illustrations by Greg Call. Disney Editions/Hyperion Books for Children 2007 482p il $18.99

Grades: 5 6 7   **Fic**

1. Fairy tales 2. Adventure fiction
ISBN 0-7868-3788-8; 978-0-7868-3788-5
           LC 2007006306

Fearing that the sinister Lord Ombra was not destroyed, Peter and Molly travel to the land of Rundoon, which is ruled by the evil King Zarboff.

"This is a fun, intense, and totally worthwhile adventure." SLJ

Peter and the starcatchers; by Dave Barry and Ridley Pearson; illustrations by Greg Call. Hyperion 2004 451p il $17.99; pa $7.99

Grades: 5 6 7   **Fic**

1. Fairy tales 2. Adventure fiction 3. Pirates -- Fiction
ISBN 0-7868-5445-6; 0-7868-4907-X pa
           LC 2004-55275

Soon after Peter, an orphan, sets sail from England on the ship Never Land, he befriends Molly, a young Starcatcher, whose mission is to guard a trunk of magical stardust from a greedy pirate and the native inhabitants of a remote island. "Age ten and up." (N Y Times Book Rev)

"The authors plait multiple story lines together in short, fast-moving chapters. . . . Capitalizing on familiar material, this adventure is carefully crafted to set the stage for Peter's later exploits. This smoothly written page-turner just might send readers back to the original." SLJ

The **bridge** to Never Land; [by] Dave Barry and Ridley Pearson. Disney/Hyperion 2011 438p $18.99

Grades: 5 6 7   **Fic**

1. Fairy tales 2. Adventure fiction
ISBN 978-1-4231-3865-5; 1-4231-3865-1

"Bringing the Starcatchers series into the twenty-first century, this novel features Sarah and her brother, Aidan, who find a cryptic note in an antique desk and follow the clues to London, Princeton, and Orlando. Along the way,

they clash with evil Lord Ombra, find an ally in Molly Darling's great-great-great nephew, and discover Einstein's part in the plan. The plot is a thrill ride of action and adventure, with plenty of chase scenes and (no surprise here) a trip to Never Land." Booklist

Bartoletti, Susan Campbell

★ The **boy** who dared. Scholastic Press 2008 202p $16.99

Grades: 5 6 7 8   **Fic**

1. Courage -- Fiction 2. National socialism -- Fiction
ISBN 978-0-439-68013-4; 0-439-68013-1
           LC 2007014166

In October, 1942, seventeen-year-old Helmuth Hübener, imprisoned for distributing anti-Nazi leaflets, recalls his past life and how he came to dedicate himself to bringing the truth about Hitler and the war to the German people.

Bartoletti "does and excellent job of conveying the political climate surrounding Hitler's ascent to power, seamlessly integrating a complex range of socioeconomic conditions into her absorbing drama." Publ Wkly

Baskin, Nora Raleigh

All we know of love. Candlewick Press 2008 201p $16.99

Grades: 6 7 8 9 10   **Fic**

1. Mothers -- Fiction 2. Loss (Psychology) -- Fiction 3. Voyages and travels -- Fiction
ISBN 978-0-7636-3623-4; 0-7636-3623-1
           LC 2007-22396

Natalie, almost sixteen, sneaks away from her Connecticut home and takes the bus to Florida, looking for the mother who abandoned her father and her when she was ten years old.

"Baskin takes a familiar story line and examines it in a new and interesting way that will engage readers." Voice Youth Advocates

★ **Anything** but typical. Simon & Schuster Books for Young Readers 2009 195p il $15.99

Grades: 4 5 6 7   **Fic**

1. School stories 2. Autism -- Fiction 3. Authorship -- Fiction 4. Family life -- Fiction
ISBN 978-1-4169-6378-3; 1-4169-6378-2
           LC 2008-20994

ALA Schneider Family Book Award Honor Book (2010)

Jason, a twelve-year-old autistic boy who wants to become a writer, relates what his life is like as he tries to make sense of his world

"This is an enormously difficult subject, but Baskin, without dramatics or sentimentality, makes it universal." Booklist

★ The **summer** before boys. Simon & Schuster Books for Young Readers 2011 196p $15.99

Grades: 6 7 8   **Fic**

1. Girls -- Fiction 2. Friendship -- Fiction 3. Dating (Social customs) -- Fiction
ISBN 978-1-4169-8673-7; 1-4169-8673-1
           LC 2010045688

Twelve-year-old best friends and relatives, Julia and Eliza are happy to spend the summer together while Julia's mother is serving in the National Guard in Iraq but when they meet a neighborhood boy, their close relationship begins to change.

"A poignant story of children on the homefront and the ways that a first love can break up longtime friendships and change things forever." Booklist

The **truth** about my Bat Mitzvah. Simon & Schuster Books for Young Readers 2008 138p $15.99; pa $5.99

Grades: 5 6 7 8 **Fic**

1. Jews -- Fiction 2. Bat mitzvah -- Fiction 3. Grandmothers -- Fiction

ISBN 978-1-4169-3558-2; 1-4169-3558-4; 978-1-4169-7469-7 pa; 1-4169-7469-5 pa

LC 2007-01248

After her beloved grandmother, Nana, dies, non-religious twelve-year-old Caroline becomes curious about her mother's Jewish ancestry.

"Readers will identify with Caroline and her preoccupations. . . . This quick read will be a hit with preteens contemplating their own identities." Booklist

Bastedo, Jamie

On thin ice. Red Deer Press 2006 348p pa $10.95

Grades: 8 9 10 11 12 **Fic**

1. Inuit -- Fiction 2. Polar bear -- Fiction 3. Greenhouse effect -- Fiction

ISBN 978-0-88995-337-6; 0-88995-337-6

"Set in the remote Arctic village of Nanurtalik, this novel follows Ashley as she journeys on the shaman path chosen for her through the Inuit line of her father. Disturbed by haunting—sometimes frightening—dreams of a gigantic polar bear that seems bent on destroying her, Ashley furiously draws her dreams onto paper, capturing the very essence of the bear within. . . . This novel is told with richness of language, culture, and emotion, but its sense of place sparkles brightest." Voice Youth Advocates

Basye, Dale E.

Heck; where the bad kids go. by Dale E. Basye; illustrated by Bob Dob. Random House 2008 304p il $16.99; lib bdg $19.99

Grades: 5 6 7 8 **Fic**

1. School stories 2. Siblings -- Fiction 3. Future life -- Fiction

ISBN 978-0-375-84075-3; 0-375-84075-3; 978-0-375-94075-0 lib bdg; 0-375-94075-8 lib bdg

LC 2007-8379

When timid Milton and his older, scofflaw sister Marlo die in a marshmallow bear explosion at Grizzly Mall, they are sent to Heck, an otherworldly reform school from which they are determined to escape.

"The author's umpteen clever allusions—characters' eternal fates are decided by standardized 'Soul Aptitude Tests'; Mr. R. Nixon teaches ethics to evildoers in room 1972—make this book truly sparkle." Publ Wkly

Other titles in this series are:
Rapacia: the second circle of Heck (2009)
Blimpo: the third circle of Heck (2010)
Fibble: the fourth circle of Heck (2011)

Bates, Marni

Awkward. Kensington 2012 259p pa $9.95

Grades: 7 8 9 10 **Fic**

1. School stories 2. Fame -- Fiction 3. Popularity -- Fiction

ISBN 978-0-7582-6937-9; 0-7582-6937-4

"A brilliant but socially inept girl finds herself starring in a YouTube video gone viral when she knocks over a football player and tries to give him CPR. . . . Mackenzie tries to keep her head down as the entire nation laughs at her for her awkward video moves. . . . But her notoriety takes a positive turn when the hottest rock group around turns her film into a music video with a new hit song, boosting her fame even further. . . . Bates keeps her prose light, always focusing on the comedy as she lampoons high-school popularity, and gives narrator Mackenzie some good one-liners. . . . Very funny. Should please lots of readers, awkward or not." Kirkus

Bateson, Catherine

★ **Being** Bee. Holiday House 2007 126p il $16.95; pa $7.95

Grades: 4 5 6 **Fic**

1. Family life -- Fiction 2. Guinea pigs -- Fiction 3. Father-daughter relationship -- Fiction

ISBN 978-0-8234-2104-6; 0-8234-2104-X; 978-0-8234-2208-1 pa; 0-8234-2208-9 pa

LC 2006-101561

Bee faces friction at home and at school when her widowed father begins seriously dating Jazzi, who seems to take over the house and their lives, but as shared secrets and common interests finally begin to draw them together, Jazzi accidentally makes a terrible mistake.

"Bee's emotions are perspectives are honest and clearly presented. . . . She is a likable, believable character." SLJ

Magenta McPhee. Holiday House 2010 170p $16.95

Grades: 4 5 6 7 **Fic**

1. Authorship -- Fiction 2. Single parent family -- Fiction 3. Dating (Social customs) -- Fiction 4. Father-daughter relationship -- Fiction

ISBN 978-0-8234-2253-1; 0-8234-2253-4

LC 2009-10854

First published 2009 in Australia

Thinking her father needs a new interest in his life after he is laid-off of work, teenaged Magenta, who envisions herself as a future fantasy author, decides to dabble in matchmaking which brings unexpected results.

"With a personality as colorful as her name, Bateson's . . . eponymous heroine has a narrative voice that is smart, wry, and down-to-earth. . . . This [is a] real and ultimately reassuring story." Publ Wkly

Baucom, Ian

Through the skylight; a Venice tale. Ian Baucom. 1st ed. Atheneum Books for Young Readers 2013 400 p. ill. (hardcover) $17.99

Grades: 5 6 7 8 **Fic**

1. Fantasy fiction 2. Time travel -- Fiction 3. Venice (Italy) -- Fiction 4. Magic -- Fiction 5. Americans -- Italy -- Fiction 6. Mystery and detective stories 7.

Brothers and sisters -- Fiction
ISBN 1416917772; 9781416917779

LC 2012010642

In this juvenile novel, by Ian Baucom, illustrated by Justin Gerard, "when Jared, Shireen, and Miranda are each given one glittering gift from an old Venetian shopkeeper, they never fathom the powers they are now able to unleash. . . . For in another time, centuries earlier, another trio . . . have been kidnapped and, along with hundreds of other children, will be sold into child slavery. Unless, that is, they can find some way to save them all." (Publisher's note)

"Frequent black-and-white illustrations support the narrative. Baucom's familiarity with the setting and use of Italian words heighten the atmosphere. . . . The mix of protagonists' genders, historical details, and interesting magic creates a story with broad appeal and a message about the power of words. . ." SLJ

Bauer, A. C. E.

★ **Come** Fall. Random House 2010 231p $15.99; lib bdg $18.99

Grades: 4 5 6 7   **Fic**

1. School stories 2. Crows -- Fiction 3. Fairies -- Fiction 4. Friendship -- Fiction 5. Foster home care -- Fiction

ISBN 978-0-375-85825-3; 0-375-85825-3; 978-0-375-95855-7 lib bdg; 0-375-95855-X lib bdg

LC 2009-32419

Drawn together by a mentoring program and an unusual crow, middle school misfits Salman, Lu, and Blos form a strong friendship despite teasing by fellow students and the maneuverings of fairies Oberon, Titania, and Puck.

"Weaving in magic, dreams, doubles, contrasts, and other elements from the original play, Bauer spins an enticing variant." Booklist

No castles here. Random House 2007 270p $15.99; lib bdg $18.99

Grades: 4 5 6 7   **Fic**

1. Magic -- Fiction 2. Choirs (Music) -- Fiction 3. Books and reading -- Fiction 4. City and town life -- Fiction

ISBN 978-0-375-83921-4; 978-0-375-93921-1 lib bdg

LC 2006023601

Eleven-year-old Augie Boretski dreams of escaping his rundown Camden, New Jersey, neighborhood, but things start to turn around with help from a Big Brother, a music teacher, and a mysterious bookstore owner, so when his school is in trouble, he pulls the community together to save it

This is a "heartwarming novel." Booklist

Bauer, Joan

Almost home; by Joan Bauer. Viking 2012 264 p. (hardcover) $16.99

Grades: 5 6 7 8   **Fic**

1. Pets -- Fiction 2. Homeless persons -- Fiction 3. Mother-daughter relationship -- Fiction 4. Mothers and daughters -- Fiction

ISBN 0670012890; 9780670012893

LC 2011050483

In this book by Joan Bauer, "when twelve-year-old Sugar's grandfather dies and her gambling father takes off yet again, Sugar and her mother . . . head to Chicago for a fresh start, only to discover that fresh starts aren't so easy to come by for the homeless. . . .With the help of a rescue dog . . . a foster family . . . and her own grace and good humor, Sugar comes to understand that while she can't control the hand life deals her, she can control how she responds." (Publisher's note)

Close to famous. Viking 2011 250p $16.99

Grades: 5 6 7 8   **Fic**

1. Baking -- Fiction 2. Literacy -- Fiction 3. Country life -- Fiction 4. Single parent family -- Fiction

ISBN 0-670-01282-3; 978-0-670-01282-4

LC 2010030022

Twelve-year-old Foster McFee and her mother escape from her mother's abusive boyfriend and end up in the small town of Culpepper, West Virginia, where they use their strengths and challenge themselves to build a new life, with the help of the friends they make there.

"Bauer skillfully brings readers to the heart of Culpepper with rich depictions of contemporary small town and its residents and rhythms." Publ Wkly

★ **Peeled**. G.P. Putnam's Sons 2008 256p $16.99

Grades: 6 7 8 9 10   **Fic**

1. Ghost stories 2. School stories 3. Farm life -- Fiction 4. Journalism -- Fiction

ISBN 978-0-399-23475-0; 0-399-23475-6

LC 2007-42835

In an upstate New York farming community, high school reporter Hildy Biddle investigates a series of strange occurrences at a house rumored to be haunted.

This is "a warm and funny story full of likable, offbeat characters led by a strongly voiced, independently minded female protagonist on her way to genuine, well-earned maturity." SLJ

★ **Squashed**; [by] Joan Bauer. 1st G.P. Putnam's Sons ed; Puffin Books 2001 194p hardcover o.p. pa $7.99

Grades: 6 7 8 9   **Fic**

1. Country life -- Fiction

ISBN 0-399-23750-X; 0-14-240426-8 pa

LC 2001-18595

A reissue of the title first published 1992 by Delacorte Press

As sixteen-year-old Ellie pursues her two goals—growing the biggest pumpkin in Iowa and losing twenty pounds herself—she strengthens her relationship with her father and meets a young man with interests similar to her own.

"Skillful plot development and strong characterization are real stengths here. Ellie's perspetive, intelligent, and funny narrative keeps the story lively right up to its satisfying conclusion." SLJ

Stand tall. Putnam 2002 182p $16.99; pa $6.99

Grades: 5 6 7 8   **Fic**
  1. Divorce -- Fiction 2. Grandfathers -- Fiction
  ISBN 0-399-23473-X; 0-14-240148-X pa
                                          LC 2002-23876
Tree, a six-foot-three-inch twelve-year-old, copes with his parents' recent divorce and his failure as an athlete by helping his grandfather, a Vietnam vet and recent amputee, and Sophie, a new girl at school

The "swiftly paced story artfully blends poignant and outright funny moments, resulting in a triumphant tale that will resonate with many young readers." Publ Wkly

Bauer, Marion Dane
  ★ **On** my honor. Clarion Bks. 1986 90p $15
Grades: 4 5 6 7   **Fic**
  1. Accidents -- Fiction
  ISBN 0-89919-439-7
                                          LC 86-2679
A Newbery Medal honor book, 1987

When his best friend drowns while they are both swimming in a treacherous river that they had promised never to go near, Joel is devastated and terrified at having to tell both sets of parents the terrible consequences of their disobedience

"Bauer's association of Joel's guilt with the smell of the polluted river on his skin is particularly noteworthy. Its miasma almost rises off the pages. Descriptions are vivid, characterization and dialogue natural, and the style taut but unforced. A powerful, moving book." SLJ

Bauer, Marion Dane, 1938-
  Little dog, lost; Marion Dane Bauer; with illustrations by Jennifer Bell. Atheneum Books for Young Readers 2012 197 p. ill. (hardcover) $14.99
Grades: 4 5 6 7   **Fic**
  1. Dogs -- Fiction 2. Interpersonal relations -- Fiction
  3. Novels in verse 4. Parks -- Fiction 5. Loneliness
  -- Fiction 6. City and town life -- Fiction
  ISBN 1442434236; 9781442434233; 9781442434257
                                          LC 2011034024
This book tells the tale of "three needy creatures." Buddy the dog is "re-homed with a clueless though kind woman" after her family moves; Mark "feels his life is empty without the dog he desperately needs but his mother won't permit"; and "Charles Larue, the aging caretaker of a nearby mansion . . . spends his lonely days waiting for something—anything—to bring meaning to his life." The story is written in "[l]ong, thin lines of free-verse text." Additionally, "black-and-white illustrations" are included. (Kirkus)

Beaty, Andrea
  Cicada summer. Amulet Books 2008 167p $15.95
Grades: 4 5 6 7   **Fic**
  1. Siblings -- Fiction 2. Bereavement -- Fiction
  ISBN 978-0-8109-9472-0; 0-8109-9472-0
                                          LC 2007-22266
Twelve-year-old Lily mourns her brother, and has not spoken since the accident she feels she could of prevented but the summer Tinny comes to town she is the only one who realizes Lily's secret.

"This is compelling fiction that will be a hit with young readers. . . . Rich and thought-provoking and yet . . . accessible." Horn Book

  Dorko the magnificent; by Andrea Beaty. Amulet Books 2013 213 p $16.95
Grades: 3 4 5 6   **Fic**
  1. Magicians -- Fiction 2. Grandmothers -- Fiction 3. Humorous stories 4. Family life -- Fiction 5. Magic tricks -- Fiction
  ISBN 1419706381; 9781419706387
                                          LC 2012045674
In this book by Andrea Beaty "Robbie loves magic and he's good at it—sort of. When Grandma Melvyn moves in and takes over his room, Robbie discovers that she was once an internationally renowned magician and learns about the heartache that turned her into a bitter woman. Against all odds, Robbie and Grandma Melvyn form an uneasy alliance to show the world—or at least the kids of Hobson Elementary School—that he is a true magician." (Publisher's note)

Beaufrand, Mary Jane
  Primavera; by Mary Jane Beaufrand. 1st ed.; Little, Brown 2007 260p $16.99
Grades: 6 7 8 9   **Fic**
  1. Artists -- Fiction 2. Renaissance -- Fiction
  ISBN 978-0-316-01644-5; 0-316-01644-6
                                          LC 2006025288
Growing up in Renaissance Italy, Flora sees her family's fortunes ebb, but encounters with the artist Botticelli and the guidance of her nurse teach her to look past the material world to the beauty already in her life.

"Political, historical, and art historical details provide a canvas on which this tale of murder, intrigue, and young romance is played out, but are painted with a broad stroke." SLJ

  The **river**. Little, Brown 2010 215p il $16.99
Grades: 8 9 10 11 12   **Fic**
  1. Mystery fiction 2. Moving -- Fiction 3. Hotels and motels -- Fiction
  ISBN 978-0-316-04168-3; 0-316-04168-8
                                          LC 2008-50222
Teenager Ronnie's life is transformed by the murder of a ten-year-old neighbor for whom she babysat, and who had helped Ronnie adjust to living at a country inn on the banks of the Santiam River in Hoodoo, Oregon.

"With its blend of richly realistic character and slightly uncanny ambience, this will be a favorite with fans of mysteries that tug the heartstrings." Bull Cent Child Books

Beck, Ian
  Pastworld. Bloomsbury Children's Books 2009 355p $16.99
Grades: 7 8 9 10   **Fic**
  1. Science fiction 2. Homicide -- Fiction 3. Amusement parks -- Fiction 4. Genetic engineering -- Fiction
  ISBN 1-59990-040-8; 978-1-59990-040-7
                                          LC 2009-8706
In 2050, while visiting Pastworld, a Victorian London theme park, teenaged Caleb meets seventeen-year-old Eve, a Pastworld inhabitant who has no knowledge of the modern

world, and both become pawns in a murderer's diabolical plan that reveals disturbing truths about the teenagers' origins.

"Suspenseful and gripping. This spellbinding page-turner will keep readers on the edge of their seats." SLJ

The **secret** history of Tom Trueheart. Greenwillow Books 2007 341p il hardcover o.p. lib bdg $17.89; pa $6.99

Grades: 4 5 6 7   **Fic**

1. Fairy tales 2. Brothers -- Fiction 3. Storytelling -- Fiction

ISBN 978-0-06-115210-8; 0-06-115210-2; 978-0-06-115211-5 lib bdg; 0-06-115211-0 lib bdg; 978-0-06-115212-2 pa; 0-06-115212-9 pa

LC 2006043362

When young Tom Trueheart's seven older brothers all go missing during their adventures in the Land of Stories, he embarks on a perilous mission to save them and to capture the rogue story-writer who wants to do away with the heroes.

This "is a charming twist on fairy tales. . . . Silhouette drawings interspersed throughout add a wonderfully nostalgic touch." SLJ

Another title about Tom Trueheart is:
Tom Trueheart and the Land of Dark Stories (2008)

Becker, Tom

Darkside; [by] Tom Becker. Orchard Books 2008 294p (Darkside) $16.99

Grades: 7 8 9 10   **Fic**

1. Horror fiction 2. Supernatural -- Fiction
ISBN 978-0-545-03739-6; 0-545-03739-5

LC 2007-23634

Jonathan Starling's father is in an asylum and his home has been attacked when, while running away from kidnappers, he stumbles upon Darkside, a terrifying and hidden part of London ruled by the descendents of Jack the Ripper, where Jonathan is in mortal danger if he cannot find the way out.

"This fast-paced, unrelentingly entertaining story has plenty of suspense and lots of scares." Booklist

Lifeblood. Orchard Books 2008 279p (Darkside) $16.99

Grades: 7 8 9 10   **Fic**

1. Horror fiction 2. Supernatural -- Fiction
ISBN 978-0-545-03742-6; 0-545-03742-5

LC 2007051180

As Jonathan searches London's Darkside for the same murderer that his mother was seeking when she disappeared twelve years earlier, it becomes clear that it is Jonathan who is being hunted.

"Horror lovers will thrill to this gleeful gothic bloodbath." Horn Book Guide

Bedford, Martyn

★ **Flip**. Wendy Lamb Books 2011 261p $16.99; lib bdg $19.99; ebook $10.99

Grades: 8 9 10 11 12   **Fic**

1. Supernatural -- Fiction
ISBN 978-0-385-73990-0; 0-385-73990-7; 978-0-385-90808-5 lib bdg; 0-385-90808-3 lib bdg; 978-0-375-89855-6 ebook; 0-375-89855-7 ebook

LC 2010-13158

A teenager wakes up inside another boy's body and faces a life-or-death quest to return to his true self or be trapped forever in the wrong existence.

"Bedford packs so much exhilarating action and cleanly cut characterizations into his teen debut that readers will be catapulted head-first into Alex's strange new world." Kirkus

Beil, Michael

The **Red** Blazer Girls: the mistaken masterpiece. Alfred A. Knopf 2011 309p $16.99; lib bdg $19.99

Grades: 5 6 7 8   **Fic**

1. School stories 2. Mystery fiction 3. Puzzles -- Fiction 4. Art thefts -- Fiction

ISBN 978-0-375-86740-8; 0-375-86740-6; 978-0-375-96740-5 lib bdg; 0-375-96740-0 lib bdg

LC 2010030006

Sophie and her friends, who call themselves The Red Blazer Girls, embark on solving a case involving mistaken identities, switched paintings, and some priceless family heirlooms.

"Sophie narrates with humor and self-effacing aplomb. Visual evidence inserted in the text invites reader participation." Kirkus

Beil, Michael D.

★ The **Red** Blazer Girls: the ring of Rocamadour. Alfred A. Knopf 2009 299p $15.99; lib bdg $18.99

Grades: 5 6 7 8   **Fic**

1. School stories 2. Mystery fiction 3. Puzzles -- Fiction 4. Friendship -- Fiction

ISBN 978-0-375-84814-8; 0-375-84814-2; 978-0-375-94814-5 lib bdg; 0-375-94814-7 lib bdg

LC 2008-25254

Catholic-schooled seventh-graders Sophie, Margaret, Rebecca, and Leigh Ann help an elderly neighbor solve a puzzle her father left for her estranged daughter twenty years ago.

"The dialogue is fast and funny, the clues are often solvable." Booklist

Other titles about the Red Blazer Girls are:
The Red Blazer Girls: the vanishing violin (2010)
The Red Blazer Girls: the mistaken masterpiece (2011)

Bell, Braden

The **kindling**; Braden Bell. Sweetwater Books 2012 291 p. (alk. paper) $14.99

Grades: 5 6 7 8 9   **Fic**

1. Occult fiction 2. Puberty -- Fiction 3. Magic -- Fiction 4. Kidnapping -- Fiction 5. Middle schools -- Fiction

ISBN 1462110274; 9781462110278

LC 2012011285

In this book, the three pubescent main characters discover they have magic powers. "This trio, under the watchful eyes of their teachers, is 'kindling,' meaning special powers they did not know they had are igniting. They are slated to join their teachers as Magi, Warriors of the Light, and will need to learn the tricks of the trade from them to fight off the darkhands from the Otherwhere, who have been kidnapping random children." (Voice of Youth Advocates)

Bell, Cathleen Davitt

Little blog on the prairie. Bloomsbury 2010 276p $16.99

Grades: 6 7 8   **Fic**

1. Camps -- Fiction 2. Weblogs -- Fiction 3. Frontier and pioneer life -- Fiction

ISBN 978-1-59990-286-9; 1-59990-286-9

LC 2009-46897

Thirteen-year-old Genevieve's summer at a frontier family history camp in Laramie, Wyoming, with her parents and brother is filled with surprises, which she reports to friends back home on the cell phone she sneaked in, and which they turn into a blog.

This is a "a lively journey with empathetic characters." Publ Wkly

Slipping. Bloomsbury 2008 215p $16.95

Grades: 6 7 8 9   **Fic**

1. Ghost stories 2. Death -- Fiction 3. Grandfathers -- Fiction

ISBN 978-1-59990-258-6; 1-59990-258-3

LC 2008-04420

Thirteen-year-old Michael and an unlikely group of allies journey to the river of the dead to help Michael's grandfather release his hold on a ghostly life and, in the process, heal wounds that have kept Michael's father distant.

"The balance between the supernatural and genuine human feelings creates a compelling mix." Booklist

Bell, Hilari

Fall of a kingdom; by Hilari Bell. Simon Pulse 2005 422 p. map (Simon Pulse teen fantasy) (paperback) $6.99

Grades: 7 8 9 10   **Fic**

1. Fantasy fiction 2. Persian mythology -- Fiction

ISBN 0689854145; 9780689854149

LC 2005588003

This is the first book in Hilari Bell's Farsala trilogy. "Stories are told of a hero who will come to Farsala's aid when the need is greatest. But for thousands of years the prosperous land of Farsala has felt no such need. . . . Three young people are less sure of Farsala's invincibility. Jiaan, Soraya, and Kavi see Time's Wheel turning, with Farsala headed toward the Flames of Destruction. What they cannot see is how inextricably their lives are linked to Farsala's fate." (Publisher's note)

Forging the sword. Simon & Schuster Books for Young Readers 2006 494p (Farsala trilogy) $17.99

Grades: 7 8 9 10   **Fic**

1. Fantasy fiction

ISBN 978-0-689-85416-3; 0-689-85416-1

LC 2005017730

Farsalans, including Lady Soraya and her half-brother, Jiaan, Kavi, and others, work relentlessly and often secretly in their shared strategies regarding the ultimate defeat of the Hrum.

"Bell brings the Farsala Trilogy to a rousing conclusion. . . . The author maintains the complexity of her main characters and the intensity of the story line." Booklist

The **Goblin** Wood. Eos/HarperCollins Pubs. 2003 294p hardcover o.p. pa $7.99

Grades: 5 6 7 8   **Fic**

1. Fantasy fiction

ISBN 0-06-051371-3; 0-06-51373-3 pa

LC 2002-15281

A young Hedgewitch, an idealistic knight, and an army of clever goblins fight against the ruling hierarchy that is trying to rid the land of all magical creatures.

"Leavened by humor and a dollop of romance, this well-crafted fantasy adventure demonstrates Bell's talent for creating enduring characters and worlds." Booklist

Other titles in this trilogy are:

The Goblin Gate (2010)

The Goblin War (2011)

Rise of a hero. 2005 462p (Farsala trilogy) $16.95; pa $6.99

Grades: 7 8 9 10   **Fic**

1. Fantasy fiction

ISBN 0-689-85415-3; 0-689-85417-X pa

LC 2003-25164

Although the Hrum believe their war against Farsala is nearly over, Soraya has strategic information that will help if she can reach Jiaan and Kavi and their separate resistance movements, but discord and Time's Wheel seem destined to keep them apart.

"With a palpable sense of danger and an ending that promises much to be revealed, this is a sequel that will fly off the shelf." Booklist

Shield of stars. Simon & Schuster Books For Young Readers 2007 267p (The shield, the sword and the crown) $16.99

Grades: 6 7 8 9   **Fic**

1. Fantasy fiction

ISBN 978-1-4169-0594-3; 1-4169-0594-4

LC 2005-35571

When the Justice he works for is condemned for treason, fourteen-year-old and semi-reformed pickpocket Weasel sets out to find a notorious bandit who may be able to help save his master's life.

"Bell's trademark shades of gray help shift readers' perceptions of the characters and their motivations, adding an unusual layer of depth that moves this story beyond simple adventure. Weasel's choices are complex and believable." SLJ

Other titles in this series are:

Sword of waters (2008)

Crown of earth (2009)

Traitor's son; by Hilari Bell. Houghton 2012 250 p (The Raven duet) $16.99

Grades: 7 8 9 10 11 12   **Fic**

1. Science fiction 2. Magic -- Fiction 3. Bioterrorism -- Fiction 4. Environmental degradation -- Fiction 5.

Native Americans -- Alaska -- Fiction 6. Shapeshifting
-- Fiction 7. Indians of North America -- Alaska --
Fiction
ISBN 9780547196213

LC 2011012241

Terrorists "have released a bioplague that, unchecked,
will destroy the world's trees and humanity along with them.
. . . Raven, the shape-shifter . . . must persuade the reluctant
16-year-old Jason to accept Atalhanes' quest or doom will
follow." (Booklist) Author

"[Hilari] Bell blends an advanced technological society
with a traditional tribal one." (School Libr J)

Trickster's girl. Houghton Mifflin Harcourt
2011 281p (The Raven duet) $16
Grades: 7 8 9 10   Fic

1. Fantasy fiction 2. Magic -- Fiction 3. Bereavement
-- Fiction 4. Environmental degradation -- Fiction
ISBN 978-0-547-19620-6; 0-547-19620-2

LC 2010-06785

In the year 2098, grieving her father and angry with her
mother, fifteen-year-old Kelsa joins the magical Raven on an
epic journey from Utah to Alaska to heal the earth by restoring the flow of magic that humans have disrupted.

The "degree of nuance will sit especially well with
readers who prefer their speculative fiction to be character-
driven, and they'll appreciate the compelling exploration of
the ways the hopeful can cope with uncertainty." Bull Cent
Child Books

★ The **last** knight. Eos 2007 357p (Knight and
rogue) $16.99; lib bdg $17.89
Grades: 7 8 9 10   Fic

1. Fantasy fiction 2. Knights and knighthood -- Fiction
ISBN 978-0-06-082503-4; 0-06-082503-0; 978-0-06-
082504-1 lib bdg; 0-06-082504-9 lib bdg

LC 2006-36427

In alternate chapters, eighteen-year-old Sir Michael Sev-
enson, an anachronistic knight errant, and seventeen-year-
old Fisk, his streetwise squire, tell of their noble quest to
bring Lady Ceciel to justice while trying to solve her husband's murder.

"The novel is brimming with saved-by-a-hair escapades
and fast-paced realistic action. . . . This well-created fantasy
is a great read with worthwhile moral issues pertinent to its
intended audience." SLJ

Other titles in this series are:
Rogue's home (2008)
Player's ruse (2010)

Bell, Joanne
Juggling fire. Orca Book Publishers 2009 171p
pa $12.95
Grades: 7 8 9 10   Fic

1. Missing persons -- Fiction 2. Wilderness survival --
Fiction 3. Father-daughter relationship -- Fiction
ISBN 978-1-55469-094-7; 1-55469-094-3

"Sixteen-year-old Rachel's father disappeared years
earlier from her family's home in the Yukon wilderness. .
. . The teen sets off on a trek through the tundra and forest
with only her dog as a companion, hoping to find clues about
her father's disappearance. . . . Bell beautifully captures the

natural world through descriptions of the mountainous terrain as well as nail-biting encounters with bears and wolves.
Rachel is a smart, resourceful narrator." SLJ

Bell, Juliet
Kepler's dream; Juliet Bell. G. P. Putnam's Sons
2012 242 p. (hardcover) $16.99
Grades: 5 6 7 8   Fic

1. Mystery fiction 2. Leukemia -- Fiction 3.
Dysfunctional families -- Fiction 4. Cancer -- Fiction
5. Grandmothers -- Fiction 6. Books and reading --
Fiction 7. Mystery and detective stories 8. Swindlers
and swindling -- Fiction 9. Family life -- New Mexico
-- Fiction
ISBN 0399256458; 9780399256455

LC 2011024136

This book tells the story of "Ella Mackenzie, a . . . fifth-
going-on-sixth grader, [who] is sent to what she calls Broken
Family Camp. Ella's family is broken . . . . Her mother has
leukemia . . . and is about to have a stem cell transplant. Her
father, who works as a guide at an outdoor travel adventure
company, has literally gone fishing, as he has for most of
Ella's childhood. . . . Ella is forced to spend the summer
with the paternal grandmother she has never met." (New
York Times)

Bell, Ted
★ **Nick** of time. St. Martin's Griffin 2008 434p
il (Nick McIver time adventure) $17.95; pa $7.99
Grades: 6 7 8   Fic

1. Fantasy fiction 2. Adventure fiction 3. Pirates --
Fiction 4. World War, 1939-1945 -- Fiction
ISBN 978-0-312-38068-7; 0-312-38068-2; 978-0-312-
58143-5 pa; 0-312-58143-2 pa

LC 2008-13634

First published 2000 by Xlibris

This novel is set in "England, 1939, on the eve of war.
[12-year-old] Nick and his younger sister, Kate, live in a
lighthouse on the smallest of the Channel Islands. Nick and
Kate come to the aid of their father who is engaged in a . .
. war of espionage with German U-boat wolf packs." (Publisher's note)

"This is an immensely appealing book. . . . [The book is
filled] with great battle scenes; lots of nautical jargon; and
themes of courage, integrity, and honor." SLJ

Bellairs, John
★ The **curse** of the blue figurine. Dial Bks. for
Young Readers 1983 200p hardcover o.p. pa $5.99
Grades: 5 6 7 8   Fic

1. Mystery fiction
ISBN 0-8446-7138-4; 0-14-240258-3 pa

LC 82-73217

The author "intertwines real concerns with sorcery
in a seamless fashion, bringing dimension to his characters and events with expert timing and sharply honed
atmosphere." Booklist

Other titles about Johnny Dixon and Professor Childer-
mass are:
The chessmen of doom (1989)
The eyes of the killer robot (1986)
The mummy, the will and the crypt (1983)

The revenge of the wizard's ghost (1985)
The secret of the underground room (1990)
The spell of the sorcerer's skull (1984)
The trolley to yesterday (1989)

Bemis, John Claude

The **nine** pound hammer. Random House 2009
357p (The clockwork dark) $16.99; lib bdg $19.99
Grades: 6 7 8 9   **Fic**

1. Fantasy fiction 2. John Henry (Legendary character)
3. Orphans -- Fiction 4. Siblings -- Fiction
ISBN 978-0-375-85564-1; 0-375-85564-5; 978-0-375-
95564-8 lib bdg; 0-375-95564-X lib bdg; 978-0-375-
85565-8 pa; 0-375-85565-3 pa
                               LC 2008-22503
Drawn by the lodestone his father gave him years before,
twelve-year-old orphan Ray travels south, meeting along
the way various characters from folklore who are battling
against an evil industry baron known as the Gog.

"If readers still possess a twinkle of wonder for the step-
right-up days of side-show hucksterism, Bemis' debut will
shock and amaze them." Booklist

Other books in this series are:
The Wolf Tree (2010)
The White City (2011)

Bennett, Holly

Shapeshifter. Orca Book Publishers 2010 244p
il pa $9.95
Grades: 7 8 9 10   **Fic**

1. Fantasy fiction
ISBN 978-1-55469-158-6; 1-55469-158-3
In order to escape the sorceror who wants to control her
gift of song, Sive must transform herself into a deer, leave
the Otherworld and find refuge in Eire, the land of mortals.

This is a "rich, slightly revisionist retelling of an ancient
Irish legend. Basic human emotions—fear, love, greed—
move the tale along, and short first-person narratives that
personalize the action are interspersed throughout." Booklist

Bennett, Olivia

The **Allegra** Biscotti collection. Sourcebooks
2010 246p pa $8.99
Grades: 5 6 7 8   **Fic**

1. School stories 2. Fashion -- Fiction
ISBN 978-1-4022-4391-2; 1-4022-4391-X
By day, Emma Rose is a quiet, under-the-radar student
who doesn't mix with the popular set. But when school's
out, she becomes Queen of the Runway—whipping up cutting-edge designs.

"Credible characterizations and dialogue keep the novel
real. . . . Bennett slips in detailed descriptions of the teens'
outfits and Emma's designs, which appear in spot art."
Publ Wkly

Who what wear; illustrated by Georgia Rucker.
Sourcebooks Jabberwocky 2011 231p il (The Al-
legra Biscotti collection) pa $8.99
Grades: 5 6 7 8   **Fic**

1. Fashion designers -- Fiction
ISBN 978-1-4022-4392-9; 1-4022-4392-8

"Emma Rose, 14, is still trying to hide her identity as
New York City's up-and-coming fashion designer, Allegra
Biscotti, while juggling the pitfalls of friendship and middle
school. . . . The novel . . . comes to a satisfying, if predictable, conclusion. Interspersed throughout are illustrations of
Allegra's designs. . . . Who What Wear is a great recommendation for kids who dream of a career in fashion." SLJ

Benoit, Charles

★ **You**. HarperTeen 2010 223p $16.99
Grades: 8 9 10 11 12   **Fic**

1. School stories
ISBN 978-0-06-194704-9; 0-06-194704-0
                               LC 2009-43990
Fifteen-year-old Kyle discovers the shattering ramifications of the decisions he makes, and does not make, about
school, the girl he likes, and his future.

"The rapid pace is well suited to the narrative. . . . In
the end, Benoit creates a fully realized world where choices
have impact and the consequences of both action and inaction can be severe." SLJ

Benway, Robin

Also known as; by Robin Benway. Walker Books
For Young Readers 2013 320 p. (hardcover) $16.99
Grades: 7 8 9 10   **Fic**

1. School stories 2. Spies -- Fiction 3. Schools --
Fiction 4. High schools -- Fiction 5. Adventure and
adventurers -- Fiction
ISBN 0802733905; 9780802733900
                               LC 2012026254
In this book, "Maggie is a safecracking prodigy and the
only child of parents who work as spies for an organization
called the Collective. When the family relocates to New
York City, 16-year-old Maggie lands her first assignment:
befriending Jesse, a cute private school boy, to gain access
to the e-mail belonging to his magazine editor father, who is
suspected to be planning a revealing story about the Collective." (Publishers Weekly)

The **extraordinary** secrets of April, May and
June. Razorbill 2010 281p $16.99
Grades: 6 7 8 9 10   **Fic**

1. School stories 2. Sisters -- Fiction 3. Parapsychology
-- Fiction
ISBN 978-1-59514-286-3; 1-59514-286-X
                               LC 2010-22777
When they recover supernatural powers from their childhoods in the aftermath of their parents' divorce, three sisters
use their foretelling, invisibility, and mind-reading abilities
to tackle school and family challenges.

"The sisters take turns narrating, and their distinct personalities and extremely funny, often barbed dialogue will
keep readers laughing as each sibling learns to trust another
amazing power: the strength of sisterhood." Publ Wkly

Berk, Ari

Death watch. Simon & Schuster Books for
Young Readers 2011 527p (The Undertaken trilogy) $17.99

Grades: 7 8 9 10   **Fic**

1. Fantasy fiction 2. Father-son relationship -- Fiction
ISBN 978-1-4169-9115-1; 1-4169-9115-8

LC 2011006332

When seventeen-year-old Silas Umber's father disappears, Silas is sure it is connected to the powerful artifact he discovers, combined with his father's hidden hometown history, which compels Silas to pursue the path leading to his destiny and ultimately, to the discovery of his father, dead or alive.

"Berk's setting is atmospheric and creepy, fleshed out with a wealth of funereal traditions and folklore." Publ Wkly

Mistle child; Ari Berk. Simon & Schuster Books for Young Readers 2013 352 p. (The Undertaken trilogy) (hardcover) $17.99

Grades: 7 8 9 10   **Fic**

1. Fantasy 2. Ghosts -- Fiction 3. Families -- Fiction
ISBN 1416991174; 9781416991175; 9781442439160

LC 2012002977

This children's fantasy story, by Ari Berk, is book 2 of the "Understaken" series. "Silas Umber makes his way to the thoroughly haunted ancestral estate of Arvale to continue his training as a psychopomp. There he meets the specters of family going back thousands of years, becomes enmeshed in their subtle intrigues and undergoes a ritual that gives him the ability to banish the restless dead from this world forever. He also inadvertently frees a mad, ancient spirit." (Kirkus Reviews)

Berk, Josh

Guy Langman, crime scene procrastinator; Josh Berk. Alfred A. Knopf 2012 230 p. $19.99

Grades: 7 8 9 10 11 12   **Fic**

1. Clubs -- Fiction 2. Teenagers -- Fiction 3. Bereavement -- Fiction 4. Forensic sciences -- Fiction 5. Father-son relationship -- Fiction 6. Death -- Fiction 7. Grief -- Fiction 8. Humorous stories 9. Fathers and sons -- Fiction 10. Mystery and detective stories
ISBN 037585701X; 9780375857010; 9780375897757; 9780375957017

LC 2011023864

This young adult presents "wisecracking humor, teenage insecurity, and the occasional corpse. When underachieving class clown Guy Langman joins his school's forensics club, it's both to help deal him with the death of his father and to meet girls. Unfortunately, his plan to get closer to the lovely Raquel Flores fails when she falls for his best friend, Anoop. Guy throws himself into the lesson plan, mastering the art of fingerprinting and using his knowledge to pry into the mysteries of his father's checkered past. Then, during a forensics competition, he finds a real dead body. Convinced that recent events tie into one another, Guy tries to get to the heart of the matter, with help from the rest of the club." (Publishers Weekly)

★ The **dark** days of Hamburger Halpin. Alfred A. Knopf 2010 250p $16.99; lib bdg $19.99

Grades: 8 9 10 11 12   **Fic**

1. School stories 2. Deaf -- Fiction
ISBN 978-0-375-85699-0; 0-375-85699-4; 978-0-375-95699-7 lib bdg; 0-375-95699-9 lib bdg

LC 2009-3118

"A coming-of-age mash-up of satire, realistic fiction, mystery, and ill-fated teen romance, The Dark Days of Hamburger Halpin is a genre-bending breakthrough that teens are going to love." SLJ

Berkeley, Jon

The **lightning** key. HarperCollins Pub. 2009 399p (The Wednesday tales) $16.99

Grades: 4 5 6 7   **Fic**

1. Adventure fiction 2. Angels -- Fiction 3. Orphans -- Fiction
ISBN 978-0-06-075513-3; 0-06-075513-X

Now that Miles Wednesday has discovered his link to a magical Tiger's Egg, he's suddenly at the wheel of a great voyage. Determined to recover the stolen stone and free the trapped soul within, Miles sets off with Little, a Song Angel, and the wisecracking blind explorer Baltinglass of Araby.

"Middle and junior high students will delight in this story, the most lyrical and sharply written of the series." Voice Youth Advocates

The **tiger's** egg; [by] Jon Berkeley; illustrated by Brandon Dorman. HarperCollinsPublishers 2007 400p il (The Wednesday tales) $16.99; lib bdg $17.89

Grades: 4 5 6 7   **Fic**

1. Adventure fiction 2. Angels -- Fiction 3. Circus -- Fiction 4. Tigers -- Fiction 5. Orphans -- Fiction
ISBN 978-0-06-075510-2; 0-06-075510-5; 978-0-06-075511-9 lib bdg; 0-06-075511-3 lib bdg

LC 2006039842

While working for the newly revamped circus, orphaned eleven-year-old Miles gains information about his past and sets off with his angel companion, Little, on a quest to find a mystical tiger's egg before it falls into the hands of their nemesis, Cortado.

"This novel is engaging from beginning to end. Fantasy lovers will enjoy a variety of plot twists that will surprise even the most perceptive reader." Voice Youth Advocates

Berlin, Eric

The **potato** chip puzzles; Eric Berlin; [drawings by Katrina Damkoehler] G.P. Putnam's Sons 2009 244p il $16.99; pa $7.99

Grades: 4 5 6 7   **Fic**

1. Mystery fiction 2. Puzzles -- Fiction 3. Contests -- Fiction
ISBN 978-0-399-25198-6; 0-399-25198-7; 978-0-14-241637-2 pa; 0-14-241637-1 pa

LC 2008-33698

Winston and his friends enter an all-day puzzle contest to win fifty-thousand dollars for their school, but they must also figure out who is trying to keep them from winning. Puzzles for the reader to solve are included throughout the text.

"The pace is suspenseful but allows for pauses for problem-solving. The joy for both contestants and readers of this brain-teasing mystery will be in the process." Kirkus

★ The **puzzling** world of Winston Breen; the secret in the box. Putnam 2007 215p il $16.99; pa $7.99

Grades: 4 5 6 7   **Fic**
1. Mystery fiction 2. Puzzles -- Fiction 3. Siblings -- Fiction
ISBN 978-0-399-24693-7; 0-399-24693-2; 978-0-14-241388-3 pa; 0-14-241388-7 pa
LC 2006-20531

Puzzle-crazy, twelve-year-old Winston and his ten-year-old sister Katie find themselves involved in a dangerous mystery involving a hidden ring. Puzzles for the reader to solve are included throughout the text
"A delightfully clever mystery. . . . There is plenty of suspense to engage readers." SLJ

Bernobich, Beth
Fox & Phoenix. Viking 2011 360p $17.99
Grades: 7 8 9 10   **Fic**
1. Fantasy fiction 2. Magic -- Fiction 3. Princesses -- Fiction 4. Apprentices -- Fiction 5. Kings and rulers -- Fiction
ISBN 978-0-670-01278-7; 0-670-01278-5
LC 2011009388

Sixteen-year-old Kai, a magician's apprentice and former street tough, must travel to the Phoenix Empire, where his friend Princess Lian is studying statecraft, and help her escape so she can return home before her father, the king, dies.
"The characters and creatures in this book are interesting and believable; the plot is a compelling mixture of adventure, mystery, and fantasy. The most remarkable element, however, is the world Beth Bernobich has created." Voice Youth Advocates

Berry, Julie
The **Amaranth** enchantment. Bloomsbury U.S.A. Children's Books 2009 308p $16.99
Grades: 6 7 8 9   **Fic**
1. Fantasy fiction 2. Orphans -- Fiction 3. Extraterrestrial beings -- Fiction
ISBN 978-1-59990-334-7; 1-59990-334-2
LC 2008-22354

Orphaned at age five, Lucinda, now fifteen, stands with courage against the man who took everything from her, aided by a thief, a clever goat, and a mysterious woman called the Witch of Amaranth, while the prince she knew as a child prepares to marry, unaware that he, too, is in danger.
"A lively, quick, stylish, engaging first novel with some lovely, familiar fairy-tale elements." Publ Wkly

Bertagna, Julie
★ **Exodus**; [by] Julie Bertagna. Walker 2008 345p $16.95
Grades: 6 7 8 9 10   **Fic**
1. Science fiction 2. Floods -- Fiction 3. Greenhouse

effect -- Fiction 4. Voyages and travels -- Fiction
ISBN 978-0-8027-9745-2; 0-8027-9745-8
LC 2007-23116

In the year 2100, as the island of Wing is about to be covered by water, fifteen-year-old Mara discovers the existence of New World sky cities that are safe from the storms and rising waters, and convinces her people to travel to one of these cities in order to save themselves.
"Astonishing in its scope and exhilarating in both its action and its philosophical inquiry." Booklist

Zenith. Walker & Co. 2009 340p $16.99
Grades: 6 7 8 9 10   **Fic**
1. Science fiction 2. Floods -- Fiction 3. Greenhouse effect -- Fiction 4. Voyages and travels -- Fiction
ISBN 978-0-8027-9803-9; 0-8027-9803-9

After finding that New Mungo is not the refuge they sought, Mara, leaving Fox behind, again sets out to sea with a ship full of refugees and, with the help of the "Gipsea" boy Tuck, tries to find land at the top of the world that will be safe from storms and rising water.
"This is mostly Mara's story—a plucky, imperfect heroine leading the way to an uncertain future in a hostile world." Booklist

Beyer, Kat
The **demon** catchers of Milan; by Kat Beyer. Egmont, USA 2012 288 p. (Demon catchers of Milan trilogy) (hardcover) $16.99
Grades: 7 8 9 10 11   **Fic**
1. Occult fiction 2. Italy -- Fiction 3. Demoniac possession -- Fiction 4. Demonology -- Fiction 5. Americans -- Italy -- Fiction 6. Family life -- Italy -- Fiction
ISBN 1606843141; 9781606843147; 9781606843154
LC 2011034348

This book is "a tale of demonic possession and a centuries-old family trade in exorcism." Mia's life "is upended when a horrifying demon enters and nearly kills her. After Giuliano Della Torre and his grandson Emilio, long-estranged relatives from Milan, arrive and drive it out, they talk Mia's reluctant parents into letting her return to Italy with them." She shows a talent for the family business of exorcism. (Kirkus Reviews)

Bick, Ilsa J.
Ashes. Egmont USA 2011 465p $17.99; ebook $9.99
Grades: 8 9 10 11 12   **Fic**
1. Science fiction 2. Zombies -- Fiction 3. Wilderness survival -- Fiction
ISBN 978-1-60684-175-4; 978-1-60684-231-7 ebook
LC 2010-51825

Alex, a resourceful seventeen-year-old running from her incurable brain tumor, Tom, who has left the war in Afghanistan, and Ellie, an angry eight-year-old, join forces after an electromagnetic pulse sweeps through the sky and kills most of the world's population, turning some of those who remain into zombies and giving the others superhuman senses.
"Bick delivers an action-packed tale of an apocalypse unfolding. . . . [She] doesn't shy away from gore—one woman's guts 'boiled out in a dusky, desiccated tangle, like

limp spaghetti'—but it doesn't derail the story's progress." Publ Wkly

Bickle, Laura

The **hallowed** ones; Laura Bickle. Graphia 2012 311 p. (paperback) $8.99

Grades: 7 8 9 10 11 12   **Fic**

1. Horror stories 2. Amish -- Fiction 3. Terrorism -- Fiction 4. Family life -- Fiction 5. Bioterrorism -- Fiction 6. Coming of age -- Fiction 7. Christian life -- Fiction 8. Communicable diseases -- Fiction

ISBN 0547859260; 9780547859262

LC 2012014800

This book follows "Katie [who] is [about] to taste the freedom of rumspringa, [when] the elders close the gates of her small Amish community. . . . Katie daringly ventures Outside to find true horror: vampires have decimated a small nearby town and apparently much of the world's population. . . . Her situation is further complicated when she rescues Alex, a handsome Outsider who may or may not be a carrier of the contagion that seemingly caused the vampirism epidemic."

The **outside**; Laura Bickle. Houghton Mifflin Harcourt 2013 320 p. (hardcover) $16.99

Grades: 7 8 9 10 11 12   **Fic**

1. Horror fiction 2. Occult fiction 3. Vampires -- Fiction 4. Horror stories 5. Amish -- Fiction 6. Coming of age -- Fiction 7. Christian life -- Fiction

ISBN 0544000137; 9780544000131

LC 2012040065

This book is a sequel to Laura Bickle's "The Hallowed Ones." Katie, an exile from an Amish community, travels with "Alex and Ginger, the two outsiders she's befriended, seeking other survivors of the vampire plague that's unmade their world. . . . Discovering a group that's genetically engineered with immunity to vampires raises tension between them, pitting science against religion: Are these vampires aliens or mutants spawned in labs, rather than manifestations of demonic evil?" Kirkus

Bigelow, Lisa Jenn

Starting from here; by Lisa Jenn Bigelow. Marshall Cavendish Children 2012 282 p. (hardcover) $16.99

Grades: 8 9 10 11 12   **Fic**

1. School stories 2. Lesbians -- Fiction 3. Self-realization -- Fiction 4. Dogs -- Fiction 5. Schools -- Fiction 6. High schools -- Fiction 7. Fathers and daughters -- Fiction 8. Dating (Social customs) -- Fiction

ISBN 0761462333; 9780761462330; 9780761462347

LC 2011040129

In this book by Lisa Jenn Bigelow, "Colby is about ready to give up on people: her girlfriend Rachel dumps her and immediately moves onto Colby's opposite (a nice Jewish guy who does well in school), her mom is dead, and her dad is a frequently absent truck driver to whom she still hasn't come out. Only her best friend, Van, can bring her out of her shell. Then she adopts Mo, a friendly but wary stray dog, and life starts to move again." (Bulletin of the Center for Children's Books)

Billingsley, Franny

★ **Chime**. Dial Books for Young Readers 2011 361p $17.99

Grades: 7 8 9 10 11 12   **Fic**

1. Guilt -- Fiction 2. Twins -- Fiction 3. Sisters -- Fiction 4. Stepmothers -- Fiction 5. Supernatural -- Fiction

ISBN 0-8037-3552-9; 978-0-8037-3552-1

LC 2010-12140

"Filled with eccentric characters—self-hating Briony foremost—and oddly beautiful language, this is a darkly beguiling fantasy." Publ Wkly

The **Folk** Keeper. Atheneum Bks. for Young Readers 1999 162p hardcover o.p. pa $4.99; pa $5.99

Grades: 5 6 7 8   **Fic**

1. Fantasy fiction 2. Fairies -- Fiction 3. Orphans -- Fiction 4. Selkies -- Fiction

ISBN 0-689-82876-4; 0-689-84461-1 pa; 9780689844614 pa

LC 98-48778

Boston Globe Horn Book Winner (2000)

Orphaned Corinna disguises herself as a boy to pose as a Folk Keeper, one who keeps the supernatural Folk underground at bay. She discovers her heritage as a seal maiden when she is summoned to become the Folk Keeper for a wealthy family in their manor by the sea. "Ages ten to fourteen." (N Y Times Book Rev)

"The intricate plot, vibrant characters, dangerous intrigue, and fantastical elements combine into a truly remarkable novel steeped in atmosphere." Horn Book

Binding, Tim

★ **Sylvie** and the songman; with illustrations by Angela Barrett. Random House 2009 339p il $15.99; lib bdg $18.99

Grades: 5 6 7 8   **Fic**

1. Fantasy fiction

ISBN 978-0-385-75157-5; 0-385-75159-1; 978-0-385-75159-9 lib bdg; 0-385-75159-1 lib bdg

"Sylvie's composer father . . . goes missing and that's the first odd thing that interrupts her happy routine. Next, the animals seem to have lost their voices. The third is the arrival of the eerie, malevolent Woodpecker Man. . . . The dense narrative is packed with surreal imagery. . . . It's a testament to Binding's assured writing that the abstractions become visceral thrills, like a dream you just can't shake. . . . An unforgettable tale." Booklist

Bingham, Kelly

★ **Shark** girl. Candlewick Press 2007 276p $16.99; pa $8.99

Grades: 7 8 9 10   **Fic**

1. Novels in verse 2. Artists -- Fiction 3. Amputees -- Fiction

ISBN 978-0-7636-3207-6; 0-7636-3207-4; 978-0-7636-4627-1 pa; 0-7636-4627-X pa

LC 2006049120

After a shark attack causes the amputation of her right arm, fifteen-year-old Jane, an aspiring artist, struggles to come to terms with her loss and the changes it imposes on her day-to-day life and her plans for the future.

"In carefully constructed, sparsely crafted free verse, Bingham's debut novel offers a strong view of a teenager struggling to survive and learn to live again." Booklist

Birdsall, Jeanne

★ The **Penderwicks**; a summer tale of four sisters, two rabbits, and a very interesting boy. Knopf 2005 262p (The Penderwicks) $15.95; lib bdg $17.77; pa $6.99

Grades: 3 4 5 6   **Fic**
1. Sisters -- Fiction 2. Single parent family -- Fiction
ISBN 0-375-83143-6; 0-375-93143-0 lib bdg; 0-440-42047-4 pa

LC 2004-20364

"Four sisters—Rosalind, Skye, Jane, and Batty—spend a few weeks with their father and dog at a cottage on the grounds of a stately home in the Berkshires, where they complicate the lives of a handsome gardener, a lonely boy, and the boy's officious mother. . . . Grades four to seven." (Bull Cent Child Books)

"This comforting family story . . . [offers] . . . four marvelously appealing sisters, true childhood behavior . . . , and a writing style that will draw readers close." Booklist

The **Penderwicks** at Point Mouette. Alfred A. Knopf 2011 295p (The Penderwicks) $16.99

Grades: 4 5 6 7   **Fic**
1. Summer -- Fiction 2. Vacations -- Fiction 3. Family life -- Fiction
ISBN 978-0-375-85851-2; 0-375-85851-2

This is the third book about the Penderwick family, who appeared previously in The Penderwicks (2005) and The Penderwicks on Gardam Street (2008). "When summer comes around, it's off to the beach for Rosalind . . . and off to Maine with Aunt Claire for the rest of the Penderwick girls, as well as their old friend, Jeffrey. That leaves Skye as OAP (oldest available Penderwick). . . . Things look good as they settle into their cozy cottage. . . . But can Skye hold it together long enough to figure out Rosalind's directions about not letting Batty explode? Will Jane's Love Survey come to a tragic conclusion after she meets the alluring Dominic? . . . And will Jeffrey be able to keep peace between the girls?" (Publisher's note)

"Balancing the novel's comedy is an affecting, neatly crafted subplot that builds up to the emotionally charged revelation involving Jeffrey. From start to finish, this is a summer holiday to savor." Publ Wkly

The **Penderwicks** on Gardam Street; [illustrations by David Frankland] Alfred A. Knopf 2008 307p il $15.99; lib bdg $18.99

Grades: 3 4 5 6 7   **Fic**
1. Sisters -- Fiction 2. Family life -- Fiction 3. Dating (Social customs) -- Fiction
ISBN 978-0-3758-4090-6; 978-0-375-94090-3 lib bdg

LC 2007-49232

The four Penderwick sisters are faced with the unimaginable prospect of their widowed father dating, and they hatch a plot to stop him.

"Laugh-out-loud moments abound and the humor comes naturally from the characters and situations. . . . This is a book to cherish." SLJ

Birdseye, Tom

Storm Mountain. Holiday House 2010 135p $16.95

Grades: 4 5 6 7   **Fic**
1. Adventure fiction 2. Cousins -- Fiction 3. Blizzards -- Fiction 4. Mountaineering -- Fiction 5. Wilderness survival -- Fiction
ISBN 978-0-8234-2130-5; 0-8234-2130-9

LC 2010005768

Two thirteen-year-old cousins Cat and Ty are trapped in a blizzard on the same treacherous mountain in the Cascades that claimed the lives of their world-famous, mountain-climber, twin fathers exactly two years earlier.

"Birdseye's prose, full of careening action, melodrama and overwrought similes, reflects Ty's bulldozing personality. Add believable characters, the author's mountain-climbing expertise and a tear-jerking conclusion, and there's plenty here for young adventure enthusiasts." Kirkus

Black, Bekka

★ **IDrakula**. Sourcebooks/Fire 2010 150p pa $9.99

Grades: 7 8 9 10   **Fic**
1. Horror fiction 2. Vampires -- Fiction
ISBN 978-1-4022-4465-0 pa; 1-4022-4465-7 pa

This is a "take on Bram Stoker's Dracula—told exclusively through text messages, web browser screens, e-mails, and various photo and PDF attachments. . . . Black's storytelling instinct . . . consistently proves itself able to transcend gimmick. The format . . . actually lends the book a chilling sort of one-shock-per-page pulse. . . . Fast, inventive, creepy, and sure to be popular." Booklist

Black, Holly, 1971-

Black heart; Holly Black. Margaret K. McElderry Books 2012 296 p. (The curse workers) $17.99

Grades: 7 8 9 10   **Fic**
1. Love stories 2. Science fiction 3. Brothers -- Fiction 4. Organized crime -- Fiction 5. Love -- Fiction 6. Criminals -- Fiction
ISBN 9781442403468; 9781442403482

LC 2011028143

This book, the final volume of the Curse Workers trilogy, continues to follow "Cassel . . . [who has] figured out the truth about himself and signed on as a Fed-in-training, as has his charming and utterly unreliable older brother. But of course things don't go as planned; there are a lot of long cons Cassel has set in play or disrupted whose ripples are still being felt. And there's Lila, Cassel's best friend and the love of his life, who is also the rising head of a crime family and who hates Cassel's guts." (Kirkus)

★ **Doll** bones; Holly Black. 1st ed. Margaret K. McElderry Books 2013 256 p. (hardcover) $16.99

Grades: 5 6 7 8   **Fic**
1. Ghost stories 2. Dolls -- Fiction 3. Adventure fiction 4. Ghosts -- Fiction 5. Friendship -- Fiction 6. Family problems -- Fiction 7. Adventure and adventurers --

Fiction
ISBN 1416963987; 9781416963981; 9781442474871
LC 2012018299

In this book, by Holly Black, illustrated by Eliza Wheeler, "a doll that may be haunted leads three friends on a thrilling adventure. . . . Zach, Poppy, and Alice have been . . . playing one continuous, ever-changing game. . . . Ruling over all is the Great Queen, . . . cursing those who displease her. . . . Zach and Alice and Poppy set off on one last adventure to lay the Queen's ghost to rest. But nothing goes according to plan, and . . . creepy things begin to happen." (Publisher's note)

"Veteran Black packs both heft and depth into a deceptively simple (and convincingly uncanny) narrative. . . . A few rich metaphors . . . are woven throughout the story, as every encounter redraws the blurry lines between childishness and maturity, truth and lies, secrecy and honesty, magic and madness. Spooky, melancholy, elegiac and ultimately hopeful; a small gem." Kirkus

★ The **white** cat. Margaret K. McElderry Books 2010 310p (The curse workers) $17.99
Grades: 7 8 9 10　　　　　　　　　　　　　**Fic**
1. Science fiction 2. Memory -- Fiction 3. Brothers -- Fiction 4. Criminals -- Fiction
ISBN 978-1-416-96396-7; 1-416-96396-0
LC 2009-33979

When Cassel Sharpe discovers that his older brothers have used him to carry out their criminal schemes and then stolen his memories, he figures out a way to turn their evil machinations against them.

This "starts out with spine-tingling terror, and information is initially dispensed so sparingly, readers will be hooked." Booklist

Another title in this series is:
Red glove (2011)

Blacker, Terence
Boy2girl. Farrar, Straus and Giroux 2005 296p $16
Grades: 7 8 9 10　　　　　　　　　　　　　**Fic**
1. Cousins -- Fiction 2. Sex role -- Fiction
ISBN 0-374-30926-4
LC 2004-53268

After the death of his mother, thirteen-year-old Sam comes to live with his cousin and as a prank, he dresses up as a girl for school, but it soon gets out of hand.

"Sam's tale is told in very short chapters, each narrated by one of the many lively supporting characters who Sam meets. This unconventional technique works exceptionally well, telling the fast-paced story from different perspectives while delving into the ever-complicated world of sex roles." Booklist

Blackwood, Gary
Around the world in 100 days; [by] Gary Blackwood. Dutton Children's Books 2010 358p
Grades: 6 7 8 9　　　　　　　　　　　　　**Fic**
1. Adventure fiction 2. Automobiles -- Fiction 3. Journalists -- Fiction 4. Automobile travel -- Fiction 5. Young adult literature -- Works 6. Voyages around the

world -- Fiction
ISBN 0-525-42295-1; 978-0-525-42295-2
LC 2009-53236

When seventeen-year-old Harry Fogg undertakes a race against time to win a wager with a member of his famous father's club, he puts to good use the recklessness and fascination with all things mechanical that have caused him trouble in Victorian England.

"The journey is fun and suspenseful." Booklist

Blackwood, Gary L.
★ The **Shakespeare** stealer; [by] Gary Blackwood. Dutton Children's Bks. 1998 216p $15.99; pa $5.99
Grades: 5 6 7 8　　　　　　　　　　　　　**Fic**
1. Orphans -- Fiction 2. Theater -- Fiction 3. Actors and actresses -- Fiction 4. Great Britain -- History -- Elizabeth, 1558-1603 -- Fiction
ISBN 0-525-45863-8; 0-14-130595-9 pa
LC 97-42987

A young orphan boy is ordered by his master to infiltrate Shakespeare's acting troupe in order to steal the script of "Hamlet," but he discovers instead the meaning of friendship and loyalty

"Wry humor, cliffhanger chapter endings, and a plucky protagonist make this a fitting introduction to Shakespeare's world." Horn Book

Other titles in this series are:
Shakespeare's scribe (2000)
Shakespeare's spy (2003)

The **year** of the hangman; [by] Gary Blackwood. Dutton Children's Bks. 2002 261p $16.99; pa $5.99
Grades: 8 9 10 11 12　　　　　　　　　　　**Fic**
1. United States -- History -- Revolution, 1775-1783 -- fiction
ISBN 0-525-46921-4; 0-14-240078-5 pa
LC 2002-67498

In 1777, having been kidnapped and taken forcibly from England to the American colonies, fifteen-year-old Creighton becomes part of developments in the political unrest there that may spell defeat for the patriots and change the course of history

"Packed with action, convincing historical speculation, and compelling portrayals of real-life and fictional characters, this page-turner will appeal to fans of both history and fantasy." SLJ

Blackwood, Sage
Jinx; Sage Blackwood. Harper 2013 368 p. (Jinx) (trade bdg.) $16.99
Grades: 4 5 6　　　　　　　　　　　　　　**Fic**
1. Fantasy fiction 2. Magic -- Fiction 3. Voyages and travels -- Fiction
ISBN 0062129902; 9780062129901
LC 2012005249

This fantasy book is set "in the Urwald, an enormous, sentient forest where humans exist on sufferance . . . . After Jinx's brutal stepfather decides to abandon him in the forest, the boy is saved by a crusty, morally ambiguous wizard named Simon, who takes him in as a servant, eventually teaching him some magic. Years later, a 12-year-old Jinx and two new friends set off to find another wizard, the monstrous Bonemaster, in hopes he can help them overcome their respective magical troubles."

Blake, Kendare

★ **Anna** Dressed in Blood. Tor 2011 320p $17.99

Grades: 8 9 10 11 12   **Fic**
    1. Ghost stories 2. Horror fiction 3. Cats -- Fiction 4. Witches -- Fiction
    ISBN 978-0-7653-2865-6; 0-7653-2865-8
                 LC 2011018985

"Blake populates the story with a nice mixture of personalities, including Anna, and spices it with plenty of gallows humor, all the while keeping the suspense pounding. . . . Abundantly original, marvelously inventive and enormous fun, this can stand alongside the best horror fiction out there. We demand sequels." Kirkus

Blazanin, Jan

A **&** L do summer. Egmont USA 2011 273p pa $8.99

Grades: 7 8 9 10   **Fic**
    1. Summer -- Fiction 2. Bullies -- Fiction 3. Friendship -- Fiction 4. Family life -- Fiction 5. Domestic animals -- Fiction
    ISBN 978-1-60684-191-4 pa; 1-60684-191-2 pa; 978-1-60684-243-0 ebook
                 LC 2010-43616

In Iowa farm country, sixteen-year-old Aspen and her friend Laurel plan to get noticed the summer before their senior year and are unwittingly aided by pig triplets, a skunk, a chicken, bullies, a rookie policeman, and potential boyfriends.

"A series of mishaps add hilarity to the story. . . . All's well that ends well in this read perfectly suited for light refreshment on a hot summer day." Booklist

Block, Francesca Lia

The **waters** & the wild. HarperTeen 2009 113p $16.99; lib bdg $17.89

Grades: 7 8 9 10   **Fic**
    1. School stories 2. Fairies -- Fiction
    ISBN 978-0-06-145244-4; 0-06-145244-0; 978-0-06-145245-1 lib bdg; 0-06-145245-9 lib bdg
                 LC 2008031452

Thirteen-year-old Bee realizes that she is a fairy who has been switched at birth with another girl who now wants her life back.

"Fragments of poems by Yeats and Shelley are eerily apropos (and may provide an irresistible invitation for further reading). Haunting and thought provoking." Publ Wkly

Bloor, Edward

London calling; 1st ed.; Alfred A. Knopf 2006 289p $16.96; lib bdg $18.99

Grades: 6 7 8 9   **Fic**
    1. School stories 2. Science fiction 3. World War, 1939-1945 -- Fiction
    ISBN 0-375-83635-7; 0-375-93635-1 lib bdg
                 LC 2005-33330

Seventh-grader Martin Conway believes that his life is monotonous and dull until the night the antique radio he uses as a night-light transports him to the bombing of London in 1940.

"Evocative descriptions and elegant phrasings make the writing most enjoyable, and because the author uses a first-person voice, the story seems very personal." SLJ

★ **Taken**. Alfred A. Knopf 2007 247p $17; pa $8.99

Grades: 6 7 8 9 10   **Fic**
    1. Science fiction 2. Kidnapping -- Fiction 3. Social classes -- Fiction
    ISBN 978-0-375-83636-7; 0-375-83636-5; 978-0-440-42128-3 pa; 0-440-42128-4 pa
                 LC 2006-35561

In 2036 kidnapping rich children has become an industry, but when thirteen-year-old Charity Meyers is taken and held for ransom, she soon discovers that this particular kidnapping is not what it seems.

"Deftly constructed, this is as riveting as it is thought-provoking." Publ Wkly

★ **Tangerine**. Harcourt Brace & Co. 1997 294p $17

Grades: 7 8 9 10   **Fic**
    1. Soccer -- Fiction 2. Brothers -- Fiction
    ISBN 0-15-201246-X
                 LC 96-34182

Twelve-year-old Paul, who lives in the shadow of his football hero brother Erik, fights for the right to play soccer despite his near blindness and slowly begins to remember the incident that damaged his eyesight

"Readers will cheer for this bright, funny, decent kid." Horn Book Guide

A **plague** year. Alfred A. Knopf 2011 305p $15.99; lib bdg $10.99

Grades: 6 7 8 9 10   **Fic**
    1. School stories 2. Drug abuse -- Fiction 3. Supermarkets -- Fiction 4. Coal mines and mining -- Fiction
    ISBN 978-0-375-85681-5; 0-375-85681-1; 978-0-375-95681-2 lib bdg; 0-375-95681-6 lib bdg
                 LC 2010050651

A ninth-grader who works with his father in the local supermarket describes the plague of meth addiction that consumes many people in his Pennsylvania coal mining town from 9/11 and the nearby crash of United Flight 93 in Shanksville to the Quecreek Mine disaster in Somerset the following summer.

"The plot is message-heavy but goes down easily because Bloor excels at writing vivid scenes. Tom is a thoroughly sympathetic narrator as he grows to realize there is value in 'blooming where you are planted.'" Publ Wkly

Blos, Joan W.

★ **Letters** from the corrugated castle; a novel of gold rush California, 1850-1852. Atheneum Books for Young Readers 2007 310p $17.99; pa $5.99

Grades: 5 6 7 8   **Fic**
    1. Mexican Americans -- Fiction 2. Gold mines and

mining -- Fiction 3. Frontier and pioneer life -- Fiction
4. Mother-daughter relationship -- Fiction
ISBN 978-0-689-87077-4; 0-689-87077-9; 978-0-689-
87078-1 pa; 0-689-87078-7 pa

LC 2007-02673

A series of letters and newspaper articles reveals life in
California in the 1850s, especially for thirteen-year-old El-
dora, who was raised in Massachusetts as an orphan only to
meet her influential mother in San Francisco, and Luke, who
hopes to find a fortune in gold.

"It is Blos' sturdy characters, whose experiences reveal the complexity of human relationships and wisdom
about 'the salt and the sweet of life,' who will make this
last." Booklist

Blubaugh, Penny
  Serendipity Market. HarperTeen 2009 268p
$16.99; pa $8.99
Grades: 7 8 9 10   **Fic**
  1. Fairy tales 2. Magic -- Fiction 3. Storytelling --
Fiction
ISBN 978-0-06-146875-9; 0-06-146875-4; 978-0-06-
146877-3 pa; 0-06-146877-0 pa

LC 2008-10187

When the world begins to seem unbalanced, Mama Inez
calls ten storytellers to the Serendipity Market and, through
the power of their magical tales, the balance of the world is
corrected once again.

"In this debut storytelling tour de force, Blubaugh re-
packages familiar folk and fairy-tale themes with contemporary verve and wit." Kirkus

Blume, Judy, 1938-
  Are you there God?, it's me, Margaret; rev for-
mat ed.; Atheneum 2001 149p pbk. $8.99
Grades: 4 5 6 7   **Fic**
  1. Religion -- Fiction
ISBN 9780385739863; 0-689-84158-2
A reissue of the title first published 1970 by
Bradbury Press

A "story about the emotional, physical, and spiritual ups
and downs experienced by 12-year-old Margaret, child of
a Jewish-Protestant union." Natl Counc of Teach of Engl.
Adventuring with Books. 2d edition

  Here's to you, Rachel Robinson. Orchard Bks.
1993 196p hardcover o.p. pa $5.99
Grades: 5 6 7 8   **Fic**
  1. Siblings -- Fiction 2. Friendship -- Fiction 3. Gifted
children -- Fiction
ISBN 0-531-06801-3; 0-440-21974-4 pa

LC 93-9631

Expelled from boarding school, Charles' presence at
home proves disruptive, especially for sister Rachel, a gifted
seventh grader juggling friendships and school activities

"Blume once again demonstrates her ability to shape
multidimensional characters and to explore—often through
very convincing dialogue—the tangled interactions of believable, complex people." Publ Wkly

  Tiger eyes; a novel. Bradbury Press 1981 206p
$16.95; pa $6.99

Grades: 7 8 9 10   **Fic**
  1. Death -- Fiction
ISBN 0-689-85872-8; 0-440-98469-6 pa

LC 81-6152

Resettled in the "Bomb City" with her mother and brother, Davey Wexler recovers from the shock of her father's
death during a holdup of his 7-Eleven store in Atlantic City

"The plot is strong, interesting and believable. . . . The
story though intense and complicated flows smoothly and
easily." Voice Youth Advocates

Blume, Lesley M. M.
  Tennyson. Alfred A. Knopf 2008 288p $15.99;
lib bdg $18.99; pa $6.99
Grades: 6 7 8 9 10 11 12   **Fic**
  1. Family life -- Fiction
ISBN 978-0-375-84703-5; 978-0-375-94703-2 lib
bdg; 978-0-440-24061-7 pa

LC 2007-25983

After their mother abandons them during the Great Depression, eleven-year-old Tennyson Fontaine and her little
sister Hattie are sent to live with their eccentric Aunt Henrietta in a decaying plantation house

"Many readers will respond to this novel's Southern gothic sensibility, especially Blume's beautiful, poetic writing about how the past resonates through the
generations." Booklist

  ★ The **rising** star of Rusty Nail; [by] Lesley
M.M. Blume. Alfred A. Knopf 2007 270p $15.99;
lib bdg $18.99; pa $6.50
Grades: 4 5 6   **Fic**
  1. Pianists -- Fiction 2. Musicians -- Fiction 3. Russian
Americans -- Fiction
ISBN 978-0-375-83524-7; 978-0-375-93524-4 lib
bdg; 978-0-440-42111-5 pa

LC 2006024252

In the small town of Rusty Nail, Minnesota, in the early
1950s, musically talented ten-year-old Franny wants to take
advanced piano lessons from newcomer Olga Malenkov, a
famous Russian musician suspected of being a communist
spy by gossipy members of the community

"Blume has skillfully combined humor, history, and music to create an enjoyable novel that builds to a surprising
crescendo." SLJ

Blundell, Judy
  Strings attached. Scholastic Press 2011 310p
$17.99
Grades: 7 8 9 10   **Fic**
  1. Dance -- Fiction 2. Mafia -- Fiction 3. Homicide
-- Fiction 4. Italian Americans -- Fiction
ISBN 978-0-545-22126-9; 0-545-22126-9

LC 2010-41078

Blundell "successfully constructs a complex web of intrigue that connects characters in unexpected ways. History
and theater buffs will especially appreciate her attention to
detail—Blundell again demonstrates she can turn out first-
rate historical fiction." Publ Wkly

  ★ **What** I saw and how I lied. Scholastic Press
2008 284p $16.99

Grades: 8 9 10 11 12   **Fic**
  1. Mystery fiction
  ISBN 978-0-439-90346-2; 0-439-90346-7
                          LC 2008-08503

In 1947, with her jovial stepfather Joe back from the war and family life returning to normal, teenage Evie, smitten by the handsome young ex-GI who seems to have a secret hold on Joe, finds herself caught in a complicated web of lies whose devastating outcome change her life and that of her family forever.

"Using pitch-perfect dialogue and short sentences filled with meaning, Blundell has crafted a suspenseful, historical mystery." Booklist

A **city** tossed and broken; the diary of Minnie Bonner. Judy Blundell. Scholastic Inc. 2013 224 p. (paper over board) $12.99
Grades: 4 5 6 7   **Fic**
  1. San Francisco (Calif.) -- History -- Fiction 2. Diaries -- Fiction 3. Earthquakes -- Fiction 4. Household employees -- Fiction 5. Family life -- California -- Fiction 6. San Francisco Earthquake and Fire, Calif., 1906 -- Fiction
  ISBN 0545310229; 9780545310222
                          LC 2012014742

This novel, by Judy Blundell, presents the diary of the girl Minnie Bonner during the San Francisco, California earthquake of 1906 as part of the "Dear America" series. A "wealthy gentleman . . . offers Minnie a chance to work as a lady's maid. . . . But when a powerful earthquake strikes, Minnie finds herself the sole survivor among them. . . . Minnie has turned into an heiress overnight . . . and she is soon wrapped up in a deception that leads her down a dangerous path." (Publisher's note)

"The author deftly incorporates true events, circumstances and key historical figures into the rapidly unfolding fictional plot... Exciting, suspenseful, absorbing and informative." Kirkus

Bock, Caroline
  ★ **LIE**. St. Martin's Griffin 2011 211p pa $9.99
Grades: 8 9 10 11 12   **Fic**
  1. Homicide -- Fiction 2. Violence -- Fiction 3. Immigrants -- Fiction 4. Prejudices -- Fiction
  ISBN 978-0-312-66832-7; 0-312-66832-5
                          LC 2011019824

Seventeen-year-old Skylar Thompson is being questioned by the police. Her boyfriend, Jimmy, stands accused of brutally assaulting two young El Salvadoran immigrants from a neighboring town, and she's the prime witness.

"This effective, character-driven, episodic story examines the consequences of a hate crime on the teens involved in it. . . . Realistic and devastatingly insightful, this novel can serve as a springboard to classroom and family discussions. Unusual and important." Kirkus

Bodeen, S. A.
  The **Compound**. Feiwel and Friends 2008 248p $16.95; pa $8.99
Grades: 7 8 9 10   **Fic**
  1. Twins -- Fiction 2. Fathers -- Fiction 3. Survival

after airplane accidents, shipwrecks, etc. -- Fiction
  ISBN 0-312-37015-6; 0-312-57860-1 pa; 978-0-312-37015-2; 978-0-312-57860-2 pa
                          LC 2007-36148

After his parents, two sisters, and he have spent six years in a vast underground compound built by his wealthy father to protect them from a nuclear holocaust, fifteen-year-old Eli, whose twin brother and grandmother were left behind, discovers that his father has perpetrated a monstrous hoax on them all.

"The audience will feel the pressure closing in on them as they, like the characters, race through hairpin turns in the plot toward a breathless climax." Publ Wkly

The **gardener**. Feiwel and Friends 2010 233p $16.99
Grades: 7 8 9 10   **Fic**
  1. Science fiction 2. Fathers -- Fiction 3. Genetic engineering -- Fiction 4. Single parent family -- Fiction
  ISBN 978-0-312-37016-9; 0-312-37016-4
                          LC 2009-48802

When high school sophmore Mason finds a beautiful but catatonic girl in the nursing home where his mother works, the discovery leads him to revelations about a series of disturbing human experiments that have a connection to his own life.

"This is a fast-paced read that keeps readers guessing what the turn of a page will reveal." Voice Youth Advocates

The **raft**; S.A. Bodeen. Feiwel and Friends 2012 231 p. $16.99
Grades: 7 8 9 10   **Fic**
  1. Survival skills -- Fiction 2. Wilderness survival -- Fiction 3. Survival after airplane accidents, shipwrecks, etc. -- Fiction
  ISBN 0312650108; 9780312650100

This novel, by S. A. Bodeen, is a plane crash survival story. "All systems are go until a storm hits during the flight. The only passenger, Robie doesn't panic until the engine suddenly cuts out and Max shouts at her to put on a life jacket. . . . And then . . . she's in the water. Fighting for her life. Max pulls her onto the raft. . . . They have no water. Their only food is a bag of Skittles. There are sharks. There is an island. But there's no sign of help on the way." (Publisher's note)

Boie, Kirsten
  The **princess** plot; translated by David Henry Wilson. Scholastic 2009 378p $17.99
Grades: 5 6 7 8   **Fic**
  1. Princesses -- Fiction 2. Conspiracies -- Fiction
  ISBN 978-0-545-03220-9; 0-545-03220-2
                          LC 2008-24403

Original German edition, 2005

Believing that she is on a film set after auditioning and winning the role of a princess, fourteen-year-old Jenna becomes the unsuspecting pawn in a royal conspiracy

"This novel takes simple, straightforward writing and layers it with kidnappings, political intrigue, and an abundance of secret plots. Readers will enjoy leisurely uncovering the mystery of Jenna's heritage, right along with Jenna herself." Booklist

Another title about Jenna is:
The princess trap (2010)

Bolden, Tonya

★ **Finding** family. Bloomsbury 2010 181p il $15.99

Grades: 4 5 6 7   **Fic**

1. Aunts -- Fiction 2. Family life -- Fiction 3. Grandfathers -- Fiction 4. African Americans -- Fiction

ISBN 978-1-59990-318-7; 1-59990-318-0

LC 2010-00535

Raised in Charleston, West Virginia, at the turn of the twentieth century by her grandfather and aunt on off-putting tales of family members she has never met, twelve-year-old Delana is shocked when, after Aunt Tilley dies, she learns the truth about her parents and some of her other relatives.

"This richly lyrical and historically persuasive coming-of-age story explores the ties that bind, break and renew an affuent African-American family. . . . Period photographic portraits from Bolden's personal collection illustrate the book. Each carefully posed subject is a fascinating enigma." Kirkus

Boles, Philana Marie

Little divas. Amistad 2006 164p $15.99; lib bdg $16.89; pa $5.99

Grades: 5 6 7 8   **Fic**

1. Cousins -- Fiction 2. Divorce -- Fiction 3. African Americans -- Fiction 4. Father-daughter relationship -- Fiction

ISBN 0-06-073299-7; 0-06-073300-4 lib bdg; 0-06-073301-2 pa

The summer before seventh grade, Cassidy Carter must come to terms with living with her father, practically a stranger, as well as her relationships with her cousins, all amidst the overall confusion of adolescence.

"Boles portrays this variable age well, and readers will feel for Cassidy's trials." SLJ

Boll, Rosemarie

The **second** trial. Second Story Press 2010 319p pa $11.95

Grades: 6 7 8 9 10   **Fic**

1. Wife abuse -- Fiction 2. Family life -- Fiction 3. Domestic violence -- Fiction 4. Parent-child relationship -- Fiction

ISBN 978-1-897187-72-2 pa; 1-897187-72-6 pa

When his father's sentencing for domestic abuse isn't enough to protect them, Danny and his family are put into protective custody.

"This is a great story of upheaval and change, as well as the conflict a young person feels when his life is abruptly changed and he feels like he has lost control." Libr Media Connect

Bond, Victoria

Zora and me; the song of Ivory. [by] Victoria Bond and T. R. Simon. Candlewick Press 2010 170p $16.99; pa $6.99

Grades: 4 5 6 7   **Fic**

1. Race relations -- Fiction 2. African Americans --

Fiction

ISBN 978-0-7636-4300-3; 0-7636-4300-9; 978-0-7636-5814-4 pa; 0-7636-5814-6 pa

LC 2009-47410

Coretta Scott King/John Steptoe New Talent Award (Author), 2011

This is a fictionalized account of Zora Neale Hurston's childhood with her best friend Carrie, in Eatonville, Florida. Annotated bibliography.

"The brilliance of this novel is its rendering of African-American child life during the Jim Crow era as a time of wonder and imagination, while also attending to its harsh realities. Absolutely outstanding." Kirkus

Bondoux, Anne-Laure

★ **A time** of miracles. Delacorte Press 2010 180p map $17.99; lib bdg $20.99

Grades: 5 6 7 8   **Fic**

1. War stories 2. Refugees -- Fiction

ISBN 978-0-385-73922-1; 0-385-73922-2; 978-0-385-90777-4 lib bdg; 0-385-90777-X lib bdg

LC 2010008539

"Readers will find themselves mesmerized not only by the eloquent language but by a plot every bit as harrowing and surprising as Koumail's cherished bedtime story." Horn Book

Boniface, William

The **hero** revealed; [by] William Boniface; illustrations by Stephen Gilpin. HarperCollins Pub. 2006 294p il (The extraordinary adventures of Ordinary Boy) $15.99; lib bdg $16.89; pa $6.99

Grades: 4 5 6 7   **Fic**

1. Superheroes -- Fiction

ISBN 978-0-06-077464-6; 0-06-077464-9; 978-0-06-077465-3 lib bdg; 0-06-077465-7 lib bdg; 978-0-06-077466-0 pa; 0-06-077466-5 pa

LC 2005018676

Ordinary Boy, the only resident of Superopolis without a superpower, uncovers and foils a sinister plot to destroy the town

"This first book in a new series is great fun. . . . Boniface wields a cynical, but definitely kid-friendly, sense of humor, and Gilpin's illustrations are sharp and witty." SLJ

Other titles in this series are:
The return of Meteor Boy? (2007)
The great powers outage (2008)

Booraem, Ellen

★ **Small** persons with wings. Dial Books for Young Readers 2011 302p $16.99

Grades: 4 5 6 7   **Fic**

1. Fantasy fiction 2. Magic -- Fiction 3. Fairies -- Fiction 4. Grandfathers -- Fiction 5. Young adult literature -- Works 6. Lost and found possessions -- Fiction

ISBN 978-0-8037-3471-5; 0-8037-3471-9

LC 2010008400

When Mellie Turpin's grandfather dies and leaves her family his run-down inn and bar, she learns that for generations her family members have been fairy guardians. "Grades five to eight." (Bull Cent Child Books)

"In a fairy story that's wistful, humorous, and clever, Booraem . . . suggests that the real world—with its disappointments and failings—is still better than living with illusions. . . . The theme of making progress, rather than ignoring problems, is a strong one, gently presented." Publ Wkly

Texting the underworld; by Ellen Booraem. Dial Books for Young Readers 2013 319 p. (hardcover) $16.99

Grades: 5 6 7 8 **Fic**
1. Death -- Fiction 2. Humorous stories 3. Schools -- Fiction 4. Banshees -- Fiction 5. Future life -- Fiction 6. Supernatural -- Fiction 7. Middle schools -- Fiction
ISBN 0803737041; 9780803737044
LC 2012032488

In this book by Ellen Booraem, "Conor O'Neill is a smart but timid seventh-grader. . . . When a banshee straight out of his Irish-born grandfather's stories appears in Conor's room, he's terrified that someone he loves is going to die soon. The banshee, Ashling, is new at her job, and . . . she's curious about the present day, [so] she masquerades as a new student at Conor's school." (Publishers Weekly)

The **unnameables**. Harcourt 2008 317p $16
Grades: 6 7 8 9 **Fic**
1. Fantasy fiction 2. Utopias -- Fiction 3. Friendship -- Fiction
ISBN 978-0-1520-6368-9; 0-1520-6368-4
LC 2007-48844

On an island in whose strict society only useful objects are named and the unnamed are ignored or forbidden, thirteen-year-old Medford encounters an unusual and powerful creature, half-man, half-goat, and together they attempt to bring some changes to the community.

"Island, a creepy and restrictive world masquuerading as a utopia, is as memorable as the intricately developed inhabitants." Bull Cent Child Books

Boos, Ben
Fantasy: an artist's realm. Candlewick Press 2010 83p il $19.99
Grades: 6 7 8 9 **Fic**
1. Fantasy fiction
ISBN 978-0-7636-4056-9; 0-7636-4056-5
LC 2010007511

"This tour of New Perigord begins by presenting the fictional realm's geography, warriors, enemies, common weapons, and mages, including full details of their abilities and spells. . . . [Boos] reveals 'commonly encountered spirits,' such as elves, undines, and banshees. . . . The large spreads are filled with authentically ancient-looking, digitally produced pictures of the many imagined inhabitants and elements, all described in densely packed, short blocks of text. . . . This offers plenty of entertainment for even those with a more casual interest in the fantasy genre." Booklist

Bow, Erin
★ **Plain** Kate. Arthur A. Levine Books 2010 314p $17.99
Grades: 7 8 9 10 **Fic**
1. Fantasy fiction 2. Cats -- Fiction 3. Magic -- Fiction 4. Orphans -- Fiction 5. Witchcraft -- Fiction 6. Wood

carving -- Fiction
ISBN 978-0-545-16664-5; 0-545-16664-0
LC 2009-32652

Plain Kate's odd appearance and expertise as a woodcarver cause some to think her a witch, but friendship with a talking cat and, later, with humans help her to survive and even thrive in a world of magic, charms, and fear.

"Despite the talking animal . . . and graceful writing . . . this is a dark and complex tale, full of violence—knives cut a lot more than wood. . . . Kate is undeniably a sympathetic character deserving of happiness." Publ Wkly

Bowen, Fred
Quarterback season; written by Fred Bowen. Peachtree 2011 132p pa $5.95
Grades: 4 5 6 7 **Fic**
1. Diaries -- Fiction 2. Football -- Fiction
ISBN 978-1-56145-594-2; 1-56145-594-6
LC 2011002673

As a school assignment, eighth-grader Matt Monroe keeps a journal about his team's football season.

This is "another absorbing sports tale from the prolific and dependable Bowen. . . . The author expertly balances the subplots and football action." Booklist

Bowers, Laura
Beauty shop for rent; --fully equipped, inquire within. [by] Laura Bowers. 1st ed.; Harcourt 2007 328p $17; pa $6.95
Grades: 6 7 8 9 **Fic**
1. Beauty shops -- Fiction 2. Mother-daughter relationship -- Fiction
ISBN 0-15-205764-1; 978-0-15-205764-0; 978-0-15-206385-6 pa; 0-15-206385-4 pa
LC 2006016761

Raised by a great-grandmother and a bunch of beauty shop buddies, fourteen-year-old Abbey resolves to overcome her unhappy childhood and disillusionment with the mother who deserted her.

"This deceptively simple book reveals Abbey as a wonderful character who will appeal to a broad spectrum of readers." SLJ

Bowler, Tim
Blade: playing dead. Philomel Books 2009 231p $16.99; pa $7.99
Grades: 7 8 9 10 **Fic**
1. Gangs -- Fiction 2. Violence -- Fiction 3. Homeless persons -- Fiction
ISBN 978-0-399-25186-3; 0-399-25186-3; 978-0-14-241600-6 pa; 0-14-241600-2 pa
LC 2008-37813

First published 2008 in the United Kingdom

A fourteen-year-old British street person with extraordinary powers of observation and self-control must face murderous thugs connected with a past he has tried to forget, when his skills with a knife earned him the nickname, Blade.

"Bowler delivers an intense, gripping novel. . . . Readers who like their thrillers brutally realistic will find much to enjoy." Publ Wkly

Other books about Blade are:
Blade: fighting back (2011)

Blade: out of the shadows (2010)

Frozen fire; [by] Tim Bowler. Philomel Books 2008 328p $17.99

Grades: 7 8 9 10　　　　　　　　　　　　**Fic**

1. Brothers -- Fiction 2. Supernatural -- Fiction 3. Missing children -- Fiction

ISBN 978-0-399-25053-8; 0-399-25053-0

LC 2007-43880

First published 2006 in the United Kingdom

Fifteen-year-old Dusty gets a mysterious call from a boy who says he is going to kill himself, and while he claims to have called her randomly, he seems to know her intimately.

"Bowler plunges readers into a mystery of psychological, supernatural, and sociological dimensions. . . . The book's wintry setting is brittle and otherworldly, and the story never lacks for tension." Horn Book Guide

Boyd, Maria

★ **Will**. Alfred A. Knopf 2010 300p $16.99; lib bdg $19.99

Grades: 8 9 10 11 12　　　　　　　　　　**Fic**

1. School stories 2. Theater -- Fiction 3. Musicals -- Fiction 4. Homosexuality -- Fiction

ISBN 978-0-375-86209-0; 0-375-86209-9; 978-0-375-96209-7 lib bdg; 0-375-96209-3 lib bdg

LC 2009-39888

Seventeen-year-old Will's behavior has been getting him in trouble at his all-boys school in Sydney, Australia, but his latest punishment, playing in the band for a musical production, gives him new insights into his fellow students and helps him cope with an incident he has tried to forget.

"Readers should find it easy to sympathize with Will's vibrant, deadpan narration and his frequent use of slang, while recognizing that his jocular exterior hides a deeper vulnerability. . . . Boyd effectively handles Will's final outpouring of repressed emotions: the personal growth achieved by her realistic, likeable protagonist is abundantly clear." Publ Wkly

Bradbury, Jennifer

★ **Shift**. Atheneum Books for Young Readers 2008 245p $16.99

Grades: 7 8 9 10 11 12　　　　　　　　　**Fic**

1. Travel -- Fiction 2. Cycling -- Fiction 3. Friendship -- Fiction 4. Missing persons -- Fiction

ISBN 978-1-4169-4732-5; 1-4169-4732-9

LC 2007-23558

When best friends Chris and Win go on a cross country bicycle trek the summer after graduating and only one returns, the FBI wants to know what happened.

"Bradbury's keen details . . . add wonderful texture to this exciting [novel.] . . . Best of all is the friendship story." Booklist

Wrapped. Atheneum Books for Young Readers 2011 309p $16.99

Grades: 7 8 9 10　　　　　　　　　　　　**Fic**

1. Mystery fiction 2. Spies -- Fiction 3. Supernatural -- Fiction

ISBN 978-1-4169-9007-9; 1-4169-9007-0

"An 1815 parlor diversion leads to a fizzy, frothy caper. Agnes is a Regency debutante. . . . When she pockets the trinket she finds among the linens at her neighbor's mummy-wrapping party, she unwittingly sets off a series of catastrophes . . . that include burglaries, violent attacks and murder. . . . Bradbury weaves Egyptology, Napoleanic conquest and a flirtation with the supernatural into a spy thriller." Kirkus

Bradbury, Ray

The **Halloween** tree; [by] Ray Bradbury; illustrated by Joseph Mugnaini. Alfred A. Knopf 2007 145p il $15.99

Grades: 6 7 8 9　　　　　　　　　　　　**Fic**

1. Fantasy fiction 2. Halloween -- Fiction

ISBN 0-394-82409-1; 978-0-394-82409-3

A reissue of the title first published 1972

A group of boys meet a spirit-being and are carried back in time to the origins of Halloween celebrations.

This is "fast-moving, genuinely eerie." Booklist

Something wicked this way comes. Avon Bks. 1999 293p $15.95; pa $7.99

Grades: 7 8 9 10　　　　　　　　　　　　**Fic**

1. Horror fiction 2. Fantasy fiction 3. Horror stories 4. Boys -- Fiction 5. Carnival -- Fiction 6. Male friendship -- Fiction 7. Fathers and sons -- Fiction

ISBN 0-380-97727-3; 0-380-72940-7 pa

A reissue of the title first published 1962 by Simon and Schuster

"We read here of the loss of innocence, the recognition of evil, the bond between generations, and the purely fantastic. These forces enter Green Town, Illinois, on the wheels of Cooger and Dark's Pandemonium Shadow Show. Will Halloway and Jim Nightshade, two 13-year-olds, explore the sinister carnival for excitement, which becomes desperation as the forces of the dark threaten to engulf-them. Bradbury's gentle humanism and lyric style serve this fantasy well." Shapiro. Fic for Youth. 3d edition

Bradford, Chris

Young samurai: the way of the sword. Disney-Hyperion Books 2010 422p $16.99

Grades: 4 5 6 7　　　　　　　　　　　　**Fic**

1. Adventure fiction 2. Ninja -- Fiction 3. Orphans -- Fiction 4. Samurai -- Fiction 5. Martial arts -- Fiction

ISBN 978-1-4231-2025-4; 1-4231-2025-6

LC 2009008309

In 1611 Japan, English orphan Jack Fletcher continues his difficult training at Niten Ichi Ryu Samurai School, while also trying to get back the rutter, his father's navigational logbook, that an evil ninja wants to possess.

"With straightforward prose, [Bradford] has managed to pen lively and exciting fight sequences and is slowly beginning to develop a keen edge to his cast of characters, laying significant groundwork for future installments." Booklist

★ **Young** samurai: the way of the warrior. Hyperion Books for Children 2009 359p $16.99

Grades: 4 5 6 7　　　　　　　　　　　　**Fic**

1. Adventure fiction 2. Samurai -- Fiction 3. Martial

arts -- Fiction
ISBN 978-1-4231-1871-8; 1-4231-1871-5
LC 2008-46180
First published 2008 in the United Kingdom

Orphaned by a ninja pirate attack off the coast of Japan in 1611, twelve-year-old English lad Jack Fletcher is determined to prove himself, despite the bullying of fellow students, when the legendary sword master who rescued him begins training him as a samurai warrior.

"Jack's story alone makes for a page-turner, but coupling it with intriguing bits of Japanese history and culture, Bradford produces an adventure novel to rank among the genre's best." Publ Wkly

Includes bibliographical references

Bradley, Alex

24 girls in 7 days. Dutton 2005 265p $15.99
Grades: 7 8 9 10   **Fic**
1. Dating (Social customs) -- Fiction
ISBN 0-525-47369-6

"When the love of his life rejects his invitation to the senior prom, Jack Grammar's so-called best friends pose as Jack and run a personal ad in the online school newspaper soliciting a date. . . . The result is a hilarious adventure as Jack tries to speed-date 24 girls in 7 days. . . . This entertaining guy's eye view on dating, friendship, and understanding one's self is one that most libraries will want to own." SLJ

Bradley, Kimberly Brubaker

★ **Jefferson's** sons; a founding father's secret children. Dial Books for Young Readers 2011 368p $17.99
Grades: 5 6 7 8   **Fic**
1. Slavery -- Fiction 2. African Americans -- Fiction
ISBN 978-0-8037-3499-9; 0-8037-3499-9
LC 2010049650

"The characters spring to life. . . . [This is a] fascinating story of an American family that represents so many of the contradictions of our history. The afterword is as fascinating as the novel." Kirkus

The **lacemaker** and the princess. Margaret K. McElderry Books 2007 199p $16.99; pa $6.99
Grades: 4 5 6 7 8   **Fic**
1. Friendship -- Fiction 2. Lace and lace making -- Fiction
ISBN 978-1-4169-1920-9; 1-4169-1920-1; 978-1-4169-8583-9 pa; 1-4169-8583-2 pa

In 1788, eleven-year-old Isabelle, living with her lacemaker grandmother and mother near the palace of Versailles, becomes close friends with Marie Antoinette's daughter, Princess Therese, and finds their relationship complicated not only by their different social class but by the growing political unrest and resentment of the French people.

"Skillfully integrated historical facts frame this engrossing, believable story." Booklist

Brande, Robin

Evolution, me, & other freaks of nature. Alfred A. Knopf 2007 268p hardcover o.p. pa $7.99
Grades: 7 8 9 10   **Fic**
1. School stories 2. Evolution -- Fiction 3. Christian

life -- Fiction
ISBN 978-0-375-84349-5; 0-375-84349-3; 978-0-375-94349-2 lib bdg; 0-375-94349-8 lib bdg; 978-0-440-24030-3 pa; 0-440-24030-1 pa
LC 2006-34158

Following her conscience leads high school freshman Mena to clash with her parents and former friends from their conservative Christian church, but might result in better things when she stands up for a teacher who refuses to include "Intelligent Design" in lessons on evolution.

"Readers will appreciate this vulnerable but ultimately resilient protagonist who sees no conflict between science and her own deeply rooted faith." Booklist

★ **Fat** Cat. Alfred A. Knopf 2009 330p $16.99; lib bdg $19.99
Grades: 8 9 10 11 12   **Fic**
1. School stories 2. Obesity -- Fiction 3. Friendship -- Fiction 4. Science -- Experiments -- Fiction
ISBN 978-0-375-84449-2; 0-375-84449-X; 978-0-375-94449-9 lib bdg; 0-375-94449-4 lib bdg
LC 2008-50619

Overweight teenage Catherine embarks on a high school science project in which she must emulate the ways of hominins, the earliest ancestors of human beings, by eating an all-natural diet and foregoing technology.

The author "offers a fresh, funny portrait of a strong-minded young woman hurdling obstacles and fighting cravings to reach her goal." Publ Wkly

Brandeis, Gayle

My life with the Lincolns. Holt & Co. 2010 248p $16.99
Grades: 4 5 6 7   **Fic**
1. Family life -- Fiction 2. Race relations -- Fiction 3. African Americans -- Fiction
ISBN 978-0-8050-9013-0; 0-8050-9013-4
LC 2009-24151

"Twelve-year-old Mina Edelman is convinced that her family members are the Lincolns reincarnate, and she has many coincidences to back her up. . . . The strong theme of social justice creates a unifying thread in this informative, clear, personal, and passionate novel." Booklist

Brashares, Ann

3 willows; the sisterhood grows. Delacorte Press 2009 318p $18.99; lib bdg $21.99
Grades: 6 7 8 9 10   **Fic**
1. Friendship -- Fiction
ISBN 978-0-385-73676-3; 0-385-73676-2; 978-0-385-90628-9 lib bdg; 0-385-90628-5 lib bdg
LC 2008-34873

Ama, Jo, and Polly, three close friends from Bethesda, Maryland, spend the summer before ninth grade learning about themselves, their families, and the changing nature of their friendship.

"Brashares gets her characters' emotions and interactions just right." Publ Wkly

The **sisterhood** of the traveling pants. Delacorte Press 2001 294p $14.95; pa $8.95; pa $9.99

Grades: 8 9 10   **Fic**
1. Friendship 2. Jeans (Clothing) 3. Friendship -- Fiction
ISBN 0-385-72933-2; 0-385-73058-6 pa; 9780385730587 pa

LC 2002-282046

"Four teenagers—best friends since babyhood—have different destinations for the summer and are distressed about disbanding. When they find a pair of 'magic pants'—secondhand jeans that fit each girl perfectly, despite their different body types—they take a solemn vow that the Pants 'will travel to all the places we're going, and they will keep us together when we are apart.' . . . Middle school, high school." (Horn Book)

"Four lifelong high-school friends and a magical pair of jeans take summer journeys to discover love, disappointment, and self-realization." Booklist

Brauner, Barbara

The **glitter** trap; Barbara Brauner, James Iver Mattson. 1st ed. Disney-Hyperion Books 2013 240 p. (Oh my godmother) (reinforced) $16.99
Grades: 4 5 6 7   **Fic**
1. Fairies -- fiction 2. Middle schools -- fiction 3. Humorous fiction -- fiction
ISBN 1423163737; 9781423163732

LC 2013930976

In this children's novel, by Barbara Brauner, James Iver Mattson, and illustrated by Abigail Halpin, "middle school is far from a fairytale for adorkable misfit Lacey Unger-Ware. When Lacey ends up with popular girl Paige Harrington's smart-mouthed fairy godmother, Katarina, trapped in her hair, life gets more magical--just not in a 'prince charming' kind of way. Katarina's wings are too damaged to continue her fairy duties, and Lacey must take over as Paige's fairy godmother." (Publisher's note)

Bray, Libba

★ **Beauty** queens. Scholastic Press 2011 396p $44.99; $18.99
Grades: 8 9 10 11 12   **Fic**
1. Beauty contests -- Fiction 2. Survival after airplane accidents, shipwrecks, etc. -- Fiction
ISBN 978-0-545-31523-4; 978-0-439-89597-2; 0-439-89597-9

LC 2011-02321

In this book by Libba Bray, "on their way to the Miss Teen Dream competition, a planeload of beauty pageant contestants crashes on what appears to be a deserted island. While the surviving Teen Dreamers valiantly cope with the basics (finding food, water, and shelter; practicing their pageant skills), they become pawns in a massive global conspiracy involving a rogue former Miss Teen Dream winner; a megalomaniacal dictator; and a Big Brother-ish pageant sponsor, The Corporation." Horn Book Magazine

"A full-scale send-up of consumer culture, beauty pageants, and reality television: . . . it makes readers really examine their own values while they are laughing, and shaking their heads at the hyperbolic absurdity of those values gone seriously awry." Bull Cent Child Books

Breen, M. E.

★ **Darkwood**. Bloomsbury 2009 273p il $16.99
Grades: 5 6 7 8   **Fic**
1. Fantasy fiction 2. Adventure fiction 3. Wolves -- Fiction 4. Orphans -- Fiction 5. Sisters -- Fiction
ISBN 978-1-59990-259-3; 1-59990-259-1

LC 2008-44413

A clever and fearless orphan endures increasing danger while trying to escape from greedy, lawless men and elude the terrifying "kinderstalks"—animals who steal children—before discovering her true destiny.

"Breen's finely tuned storytelling—pithy description, quick and keen emotion, broad trust of readers' intelligence—offers equal gratification whether readers spot clues and connections early or late. Both grounded and wondrous." Kirkus

Brenna, Beverly

Waiting for no one. Red Deer 2011 187p pa $12.95
Grades: 7 8 9 10   **Fic**
1. Asperger's syndrome -- Fiction
ISBN 978-0-88995-437-3; 0-88995-437-2

Taylor Jane Smith is "taking a biology class at college and applying for a job at a local bookstore. Her Asperger's syndrome gives her an advantage in the class, but it's making the job-application process torture. . . . Taylor, with her flinty, exasperated approach to the world, remains a fascinating character and narrator." Bull Cent Child Books

Brennan, Caitlin

House of the star. Tor 2010 282p $17.99
Grades: 7 8 9 10   **Fic**
1. Fantasy fiction 2. Magic -- Fiction 3. Horses -- Fiction 4. Princesses -- Fiction 5. Ranch life -- Fiction
ISBN 978-0-7653-2037-7; 0-7653-2037-1

LC 2010-36678

"Princess Elen of Ymbria has always wanted to be a rider of a worldrunner—a magical horse that can travel safely on faerie roads between worlds. She is invited to Earth to stay at the House of Star, an Arizona ranch where these animals are bred. The only catch is that someone from the royal family of Caledon has been invited as well. . . . Brennan creates a magical world based around a realistic ranch setting. The two main characters are complex and avoid the common clichés about princesses. Fans of fantasy and horses will find an intriguing premise and a galloping plot." SLJ

Brennan, Herbie

The **Doomsday** Box; a Shadow Project adventure. Balzer & Bray 2011 328p $16.99
Grades: 6 7 8 9   **Fic**
1. Spies -- Fiction 2. Plague -- Fiction 3. Cold war -- Fiction 4. Time travel -- Fiction 5. Extrasensory perception -- Fiction
ISBN 978-0-06-175647-4; 0-06-175647-4

LC 2010-15947

Working on a highly-classified espionage project, four English teenagers go back in time to the Cold War in 1962 to prevent a global outbreak of the bubonic plague in the twenty-first century.

"Readers who enjoy their action/adventure laced with weird science and real politics will enjoy this fast-paced, exciting second in the series." Bull Cent Child Books

The **secret** prophecy; Herbie Brennan. Balzer + Bray 2012 322 p. (hardback) $27.95
Grades: 5 6 7 8   **Fic**
1. Murder -- Fiction 2. Conspiracies -- Fiction 3. Secret societies -- Fiction 4. Mystery and detective stories 5. Adventure and adventurers -- Fiction
ISBN 0691155895; 9780062071804
LC 2012024991

The **Shadow** Project. Balzer & Bray 2010 355p $16.99
Grades: 6 7 8 9   **Fic**
1. Spies -- Fiction 2. Supernatural -- Fiction
ISBN 978-0-06-175642-9; 0-06-175642-3
LC 2009-14276
A young English thief stumbles on, and subsequently is recruited for, a super-secret operation that trains teenagers in remote viewing and astral projection techniques in order to engage in spying.
"The action has a ready-for-its-close-up cinematic quality, and there's a manageable blend of stock and original, fully fleshed characters to guarantee investment and relatability. This is the kind of mind candy that action/adventure junkies will gobble right up." Bull Cent Child Books

Brennan, Sarah Rees
Team Human; Justine Larbalestier and Sarah Rees Brennan. HarperTeen 2012 344 p. (tr. bdg.) $17.99
Grades: 8 9 10 11 12   **Fic**
1. Love stories 2. School stories 3. Vampires -- Fiction 4. Female friendship -- Fiction 5. Schools -- Fiction 6. High schools -- Fiction
ISBN 0062089641; 9780062089649
LC 2011026149
In this book, "[h]igh school senior Mel Duan is not impressed when a 150-year old vampire (who looks like a teenager and talks like a 19th-century poet) enrolls in her school. Sure, New Whitby, Maine, is known for its large vampire population, but the vamps and humans keep to their own. Mel finds Francis merely annoying until her best friend Cathy falls for him and decides to become a vampire herself, at which point Mel shifts into full-blown protective mode." (Publishers Weekly)

Unspoken; by Sarah Rees Brennan. Random House Books for Young Readers 2012 p. cm. (The Lynburn legacy) (hardcover) $18.99
Grades: 7 8 9 10   **Fic**
1. Gothic novels -- fiction 2. Fantasy fiction 3. Mystery fiction 4. Horror stories 5. Magic -- Fiction 6. Magicians -- Fiction
ISBN 9780375870415; 9780375970412
LC 2012001954
This juvenile gothic mystery, by Sarah Rees Brennan, starts The Lynburn Legacy series. "Kami Glass knows that she could be a great reporter. . . . The aristocratic, secretive Lynburns are coming home, . . . and Kami is determined

. . . [to] get the scoop. Soon, two gorgeous, near-identical Lynburn cousins . . . join her journalistic team--not to mention Kami's imaginary best friend, . . . who turns out to be not quite so imaginary after all. And that's when the grisly murders start." Kirkus

Brewer, Heather
First kill. Dial Books for Young Readers 2011 309p il (The Slayer chronicles) $17.99
Grades: 6 7 8 9   **Fic**
1. Horror fiction 2. Vampires -- Fiction
ISBN 0-8037-3741-6; 978-0-8037-3741-9
LC 2011006061
The summer before ninth grade, when Joss sets off to meet his uncle and hunt down the beast that murdered his younger sister three years earlier, he learns he is destined to join the Slayer Society.
"This companion volume to Brewer's Vlad Tod series (Twelfth Grade Kills, 2010, etc.) provides a simple entry point into the opposite side of the vampire world—those tasked with killing the undead. . . . Action flows seamlessly into drama, and a betrayal comes after a series of clever misdirections." Kirkus

The **chronicles** of Vladimir Tod: eighth grade bites. Dutton Children's Books 2007 182p (The chronicles of Vladimir Tod) $16.99
Grades: 6 7 8 9   **Fic**
1. School stories 2. Orphans -- Fiction 3. Vampires -- Fiction
ISBN 978-0-525-47811-9; 0-525-47811-6
LC 2006030455
For thirteen years, Vlad, aided by his aunt and best friend, has kept secret that he is half-vampire, but when his missing teacher is replaced by a sinister substitute, he learns that there is more to being a vampire, and to his parents' deaths, than he could have guessed.
This "is an exceptional current-day vampire story. The mix of typical teen angst and dealing with growing vampiric urges make for a fast-moving, engaging story." Voice Youth Advocates
Other titles in this series are:
Ninth grade slays (2008)
Tenth grade bleeds (2009)
Eleventh grade burns (2010)

Brewster, Alicia Wright
Echo; Alicia Wright Brewster. Dragonfairy Press 2013 291 p. (paperback) $14.95
Grades: 7 8 9 10 11 12   **Fic**
1. Magic -- Fiction 2. End of the world -- Fiction
ISBN 0985023023; 9780985023027
LC 2012951596
In this book by Alicia Wright Brewster, "Earth-Two . . . will end in 10 days. Calling up all elemental practitioners to help, the Council elders have averted catastrophe only by repeatedly rewinding time back 10 days before the end. With each rewind, they become weakened echoes of their original selves. . . . Their efforts focus on eliminating the Mages--formerly human 'ether manipulators' whose elemental energies have consumed their humanity--causing the crisis." (Kirkus Reviews)

"Fully realized characters from Asha to the walk-ons lend their intense authenticity to the plot, which straddles the line between fantasy and science fiction, and deflect attention from the rubber science. This world has depth, mirroring the memorable characters who populate it." Kirkus

Brezenoff, Steve

Brooklyn, burning. Carolrhoda Lab 2011 202p $17.95

Grades: 8 9 10 11   **Fic**

1. Musicians -- Fiction 2. Runaway teenagers -- Fiction
ISBN 978-0-7613-7526-5

LC 2010051447

"Homelessness, queerness and the rougher sides of living on the street are handled without a whiff of sensationalism, and the moments between Kid, the first-person narrator, and Scout, addressed as 'you,' are described in language so natural and vibrant that readers may not even notice that neither character's gender is ever specified. . . . Overall, the tone is as raw, down-to-earth and transcendent as the music Scout and Kid ultimately make together." Kirkus

Brian, Kate, 1974-

Geek magnet; a novel in five acts. G.P. Putnam's Sons 2008 308p $16.99

Grades: 7 8 9 10   **Fic**

1. School stories 2. Theater -- Fiction 3. Dating (Social customs) -- Fiction
ISBN 978-0-399-24760-6; 0-399-24760-2

LC 2007-28707

Seventeen-year-old KJ Miller is determined to lose the label of "geek magnet" and get the guy of her dreams, all while stage managing the high school musical, with the help of the most popular girl in school.

"An enjoyable, touching read about self-discovery with a hopeful ending that avoids too-neat resolutions." Booklist

The **princess** & the pauper; [by] Kate Brian. Simon & Schuster Bks. for Young Readers 2003 266p hardcover o.p. pa $8.99

Grades: 7 8 9 10   **Fic**

1. Princesses -- Fiction
ISBN 0-689-86173-7; 1-4169-5369-8 pa

LC 2003-7380

When sixteen-year-old Julia, of Los Angeles, and sixteen-year-old Princess Carina, of Vineland, switch places, Julia dances at the ball with the incredible Markus and Carina escapes rigid protocol to spend time with a rock star

"Although the plot is pure fairy tale, the humor is incisive, the characters of the two girls are well drawn, and the touch of sweet, G-rated romance will thrill the intended audience." Booklist

Briant, Ed

Choppy socky blues. Flux 2010 259p pa $9.95

Grades: 7 8 9 10   **Fic**

1. Karate -- Fiction 2. Dating (Social customs) -- Fiction 3. Father-son relationship -- Fiction
ISBN 978-0-7387-1897-2; 0-7387-1897-1

LC 2009-30491

In the South of England, fourteen-year-old Jay resumes contact with his father, a movie stuntman and karate instruc-

tor, after two years of estrangement to impress a girl who turns out to be the girlfriend of Jay's former best friend.

"Jason's insecurities, resentment toward (and gradual peacemaking with) his father, and obsession with girls are believably rendered—he's the kind of awkward hero readers will be glad to see come into his own." Publ Wkly

I am (not) the walrus; Ed Briant. 1st ed. Flux 2012 280 p. (pbk.) $9.95

Grades: 8 9 10 11   **Fic**

1. Love stories 2. Rock music -- Fiction 3. Bands (Music) -- Fiction
ISBN 073873246X; 9780738732466

LC 2012004314

This novel, by Ed Briant, describes how "Toby and Zack's first gig could make or break their Beatles cover band, the Nowhere Men. But ever since getting dumped by his girlfriend, lead singer Toby can't quite pull off the Beatles' feel-good vibe. When Toby finds a note hidden inside his brother's bass claiming the instrument was stolen, he embarks on a quest to find the true owner--and hopes a girl named Michelle will help him recover his lost mojo along the way." (Publisher's note)

Bridges, Robin

The **gathering** storm. Delacorte Press 2012 387p (The Katerina trilogy) $17.99; lib bdg $20.99; ebook $10.99

Grades: 7 8 9 10   **Fic**

1. Vampires -- Fiction 2. Supernatural -- Fiction 3. Good and evil -- Fiction 4. Courts and courtiers -- Fiction
ISBN 978-0-385-74022-7; 0-385-74022-0; 978-0-385-90829-0 lib bdg; 0-385-90829-6 lib bdg; 978-0-375-89901-0 ebook

LC 2011026175

In St. Petersburg, Russia, in 1888, royal debutante Katerina Alexandrovna, Duchess of Oldenburg, tries to hide a dark secret—that she has the ability to raise the dead—but when she uses her special skill to protect a member of the Imperial Family, she finds herself caught in a web of intrigue.

"The fully realized setting, a fantastical version of pre-revolutionary Russia, adds a level of believability to this [book]. . . . An atmospheric and complicated vampire tale." Kirkus

Brittain, Bill

The **wish** giver; three tales of Coven Tree. drawings by Andrew Glass. Harper & Row 1983 181p il $16.89; pa $5.99

Grades: 5 6 7 8   **Fic**

1. Magic -- Fiction 2. Wishes -- Fiction
ISBN 0-06-020687-X; 0-06-440168-5 pa

LC 82-48264

A Newbery Medal honor book, 1984

"Captivating, fresh, and infused with homespun humor." Horn Book

"Witchy and devilish things happen in Coven Tree, New England, and their chronicler is Stew Meat, proprietor of the Coven Tree store. . . . Stew relates the King Midas luck that came to three young people, each of whom had a wish fulfilled, and each of whom rued that fulfillment." SLJ

Other titles about Coven Tree are:
Dr. Dredd's wagon of wonders (1987)
Professor Popkin's prodigious polish (1990)

Broach, Elise
★ **Masterpiece**; illustrated by Kelly Murphy. Henry Holt & Co. 2008 292p il $16.95
Grades: 4 5 6 7   **Fic**
1. Mystery fiction 2. Artists -- Fiction 3. Beetles -- Fiction
ISBN 978-0-8050-8270-8; 0-8050-8270-0

After Marvin, a beetle, makes a miniature drawing as an eleventh birthday gift for James, a human with whom he shares a house, the two new friends work together to help recover a Durer drawing stolen from the Metropolitan Museum of Art.

Broach "packs this fast-moving story with perennially seductive themes: hidden lives and secret friendships, miniature worlds lost to disbelievers. . . . Loosely implying rather than imitating the Old Masters they reference, the finely hatched drawings depict the settings realistically and the characters, especially the beetles, with joyful comic license." Publ Wkly

★ **Shakespeare's** secret; [by] Elise Broach. Henry Holt 2005 250p il $16.95; pa $5.99
Grades: 5 6 7 8   **Fic**
1. Mystery fiction
ISBN 0-8050-7387-6; 0-312-37132-2 pa
LC 2004-54020

Named after a character in a Shakespeare play, misfit sixth-grader Hero becomes interested in exploring this unusual connection because of a valuable diamond supposedly hidden in her new house, an intriguing neighbor, and the unexpected attention of the most popular boy in school.

"The mystery alone will engage readers. . . . The main characters are all well developed, and the dialogue is both realistic and well planned." SLJ

Brody, Jessica
My life undecided. Farrar, Straus and Giroux 2011 299p $16.99
Grades: 6 7 8 9   **Fic**
1. School stories 2. Weblogs -- Fiction 3. Decision making -- Fiction 4. Books and reading -- Fiction
ISBN 978-0-374-39905-4; 0-374-39905-0
LC 2009051277

Fifteen-year-old Brooklyn has been making bad decisions since, at age two, she became famous for falling down a mine shaft, and so she starts a blog to let others make every decision for her, while her community-service hours are devoted to a woman who insists Brooklyn read her 'Choose the Story' books.

"Brooklyn is a sympathetic protagonist with whom teens will identify. Her journey is fun to read, and decision-challenged readers will learn an important lesson about self-acceptance along the way." SLJ

Brooks, Bruce
All that remains. Atheneum Bks. for Young Readers 2001 168p $16; pa $6.99

Grades: 7 8 9 10   **Fic**
1. Short stories 2. Death -- Fiction
ISBN 0-689-83351-2; 0-689-83442-X pa
LC 00-56912

"All three offerings feature believable dialogue and attitudes true to the emotions of their young characters as well as intriguingly offbeat events." Horn Book Guide

What hearts. HarperCollins Pubs. 1992 194p $14/Can$18.75; lib bdg $13.89; rpt $6.99 **Fic**
1. Remarriage -- Fiction
ISBN 0-06-021131-8; 0-06-021132-6 lib bdg; 9780064471275 rpt
LC 92-5305

Newbery Honor Book (1993)

"This novel is composed of four short stories that begin when the main character, Asa, is just graduating from the first grade and ends when Asa is an adolescent. The stories are about love—within a family, among friends, between boy and girl, husband and wife. . . . Age twelve and up." (Horn Book)

"This present-day saga traces the formative years of Asa, who has spent most of his life moving from one town to another with his emotionally fragile mother and bullying stepfather. . . . Asa takes on the role of protector as he chooses to make sacrifices in order to save his mother's marriage or prevent her from falling into a depressive state." Publ Wkly

The **moves** make the man; a novel. HarperCollins Pubs. 1984 280p hardcover o.p. pa $6.99
Grades: 7 8 9 10 11 12   **Fic**
1. Friendship -- Fiction 2. African Americans -- Fiction
ISBN 0-06-020679-9; 0-06-440564-8 pa
A Newbery Medal honor book, 1985

This is an "excellent novel about values and the way people relate to one another." N Y Times Book Rev

Brooks, Laurie
Selkie girl; a novel. Alfred A. Knopf 2008 262p $15.99; lib bdg $18.99
Grades: 7 8 9 10   **Fic**
1. Fantasy fiction 2. Seals (Animals) -- Fiction
ISBN 978-0-375-85170-4; 0-375-85170-4; 978-0-375-95170-1 lib bdg; 0-375-95170-9 lib bdg
LC 2008-03547

When sixteen-year-old Elin Jean finds a seal pelt hidden at home and realizes that her mother is actually a selkie, she returns the pelt to her mother, only to find her life taking many unexpected turns.

"An extraordinary, beautifully written tale about belonging, love, and the laws of nature. . . . Brooks's rich prose reverberates with vivid, cinematic images." SLJ

Brooks, Martha
★ **Mistik** Lake. Farrar, Straus and Giroux 2007 207p $16
Grades: 8 9 10   **Fic**
1. Mothers -- Fiction 2. Family life -- Fiction
ISBN 978-0-374-34985-1; 0-374-34985-1
LC 2006-37391

After Odella's mother leaves her, her sisters, and their father in Manitoba and moves to Iceland with another man, she then dies there, and the family finally learns some of the secrets that have haunted them for two generations. "Grades seven to ten." (Bull Cent Child Books)

"All of the characters seem distinct and real, thanks to the author's exceptional skill with details." Publ Wkly

★ **Queen** of hearts. Farrar Straus Giroux 2011 224p $16.99

Grades: 7 8 9 10   Fic
1. Sick -- Fiction 2. Hospitals -- Fiction 3. Family life -- Fiction 4. Tuberculosis -- Fiction
ISBN 978-0-374-34229-6; 0-374-34229-6
LC 2010-52661

Shortly after her first kiss but before her sixteenth birthday in December, 1941, Marie Claire and her younger brother and sister are sent to a tuberculosis sanatorium near their Manitoba farm.

"Readers will be held by the story's heartbreaking truths, right to the end." Booklist

Brothers, Meagan
★ **Debbie** Harry sings in French. Henry Holt 2008 232p $16.95

Grades: 8 9 10 11 12   Fic
1. Sex role -- Fiction 2. Rock music -- Fiction 3. Transvestites -- Fiction
ISBN 978-0-8050-8080-3; 0-8050-8080-5
LC 2007-27322

When Johnny completes an alcohol rehabilitation program and his mother sends him to live with his uncle in North Carolina, he meets Maria, who seems to understand his fascination with the new wave band Blondie, and he learns about his deceased father's youthful forays into "glam rock," which gives him perspective on himself, his past, and his current life.

"The brisk pace and the strong-willed, empathetic narrator will keep readers fully engaged." Publ Wkly

Brouwer, Sigmund
Devil's pass; Sigmund Brouwer. Orca Book Publishers 2012 237 p. (pbk) $9.95

Grades: 6 7 8 9 10   Fic
1. Grandfathers -- Fiction 2. Voyages and travels -- Fiction 3. Grandparent-grandchild relationship -- Fiction 4. Street musicians -- Fiction
ISBN 155469938X; 9781554699384
LC 2012938220

In author Sigmund Brouwer's book, "seventeen-year-old Webb's abusive stepfather has made it impossible for him to live at home, so Webb survives on the streets of Toronto. . . . When Webb's grandfather dies, his will stipulates that his grandsons fulfill specific requests. Webb's task takes him to the Canol Trail in Canada's Far North. . . . With a Native guide, two German tourists and his guitar for company, Webb is forced to confront terrible events in his grandfather's past and somehow deal with the pain and confusion of his own life." (Publisher's note)

Brown, Don
The **train** jumper. Roaring Brook Press 2007 122p $16.95

Grades: 6 7 8 9   Fic
1. Tramps -- Fiction 2. Poverty -- Fiction 3. Great Depression, 1929-1939 -- Fiction
ISBN 978-1-59643-218-5; 1-59643-218-7
LC 2007-03440

Jumping freight trains during the Great Depression leads fourteen-year-old Collie to a friendship with men and boys on their way to "somewhere else."

"The matter-of-fact dialogue is easy to follow and draws readers into an accurate picture of life on the rails during the Depression." SLJ

Bruchac, Joseph, 1942-
Bearwalker; [by] Joseph Bruchac; illustrations by Sally Wern Comport. HarperCollinsPublishers 2007 208p il $15.99; lib bdg $16.89; pa $5.99

Grades: 5 6 7 8   Fic
1. Bears -- Fiction 2. Camping -- Fiction 3. Mohawk Indians -- Fiction
ISBN 978-0-06-112309-2; 0-06-112309-9; 978-0-06-112311-5 lib bdg; 0-06-112311-0 lib bdg; 978-0-06-112315-3 pa; 0-06-112315-3 pa
LC 2006-30420

Although the littlest student in his class, thirteen-year-old Baron Braun calls upon the strength and wisdom of his Mohawk ancestors to face both man and beast when he tries to get help for his classmates, who are being terrorized during a school field trip in the Adirondacks.

"This exciting horror story, illustrated with b/w drawings, is based on Native American folklore." Kliatt

★ **Code** talker; a novel about the Navajo Marines of World War Two. Dial 2005 240p $16.99

Grades: 6 7 8 9 10   Fic
1. Navajo Indians -- Fiction 2. World War, 1939-1945 -- Fiction
ISBN 0-8037-2921-9

After being taught in a boarding school run by whites that Navajo is a useless language, Ned Begay and other Navajo men are recruited by the Marines to become Code Talkers, sending messages during World War II in their native tongue.

"Bruchac's gentle prose presents a clear historical picture of young men in wartime. . . . Nonsensational and accurate, Bruchac's tale is quietly inspiring." SLJ

Includes bibliographical references

Dragon castle. Dial Books for Young Readers 2011 346p $16.99

Grades: 4 5 6 7   Fic
1. Fairy tales 2. Dragons -- Fiction 3. Princes -- Fiction 4. Kings and rulers -- Fiction
ISBN 978-0-8037-3376-3; 0-8037-3376-3
LC 2010028798

Young prince Rashko, aided by wise old Georgi, must channel the power of his ancestor, Pavol the great, and harness a magical dragon to face the evil Baron Temny after the foolish King and Queen go missing.

Bruchac "spins a good-natured and humorous fairy tale. . . . With its subtle focus on peaceful resistance and use of classic folk-tale elements, this story exudes a gentle sense of fun." Publ Wkly

Night wings; illustrations by Sally Wern Comport. HarperCollins 2009 194p $15.99; lib bdg $16.89

Grades: 5 6 7 8   Fic
1. Monsters -- Fiction 2. Abnaki Indians -- Fiction
ISBN 978-0-06-112318-4; 0-06-112318-8; 978-0-06-112319-1 lib bdg; 0-06-112319-6 lib bdg
LC 2008032096

After being taken captive by a band of treasure seekers, thirteen-year-old Paul and his Abenaki grandfather must face a legendary Native American monster at the top of Mount Washington.

"The intriguing Native lore, the realistic teen narrative, and cliffhanger sentences that build suspense at the end of each chapter are signature Bruchac and will captivate readers." SLJ

★ The **winter** people. Dial Bks. 2002 168p $16.99; pa $5.99

Grades: 5 6 7 8   Fic
1. Abnaki Indians -- Fiction
ISBN 0-8037-2694-5; 0-14-240229-X pa
LC 2002-338

As the French and Indian War rages in October of 1759, Saxso, a fourteen-year-old Abenaki boy, pursues the English rangers who have attacked his village and taken his mother and sisters hostage

"The narrative itself is thrilling, its spiritual aspects enlightening." Booklist

Wolf mark. Lee & Low/Tu Books 2011 377p $17.95

Grades: 6 7 8 9   Fic
1. Spies -- Fiction 2. Supernatural -- Fiction 3. Native Americans -- Fiction 4. Father-son relationship -- Fiction
ISBN 1-60060-661-X; 978-1-60060-661-8; 978-1-60060-878-0 e-book
LC 2011014252

When Lucas King's covert-ops father is kidnapped and his best friend Meena is put in danger, Luke's only chance to save them—a skin that will let him walk as a wolf—is hidden away in an abandoned mansion guarded by monsters.

"Bruchac has created a tense, readable novel. He combines Native American lore, supernatural elements, genetic engineering, romance, geopolitics, and adventure in one story. . . . The mystery and edge-of-your-seat action are enough to keep readers hooked." SLJ

Bryant, Jennifer
Kaleidoscope eyes; [by] Jen Bryant. Alfred A. Knopf 2009 264p $15.99; lib bdg $18.99

Grades: 5 6 7 8   Fic
1. Mystery fiction 2. Novels in verse 3. Buried treasure -- Fiction 4. Vietnam War, 1961-1975 -- Fiction
ISBN 978-0-375-84048-7; 0-375-84048-6; 978-0-375-94048-4 lib bdg; 0-375-94048-0 lib bdg
LC 2008027345

In 1968, with the Vietnam War raging, thirteen-year-old Lyza inherits a project from her deceased grandfather, who had been using his knowledge of maps and the geography of Lyza's New Jersey hometown to locate the lost treasure of Captain Kidd.

"Bryant weaves an emotional novel in poems based on a true story of buried treasure. Tensions among families are drawn with heart-wrenching prose, and her depiction of segregation is flawless. . . . The characters are witty and well developed." Voice Youth Advocates

Pieces of Georgia; a novel. [by] Jen Bryant. Knopf 2006 166p $15.95; lib bdg $17.99

Grades: 6 7 8 9   Fic
1. Artists -- Fiction 2. Bereavement -- Fiction
ISBN 0-375-83259-9; 0-375-93259-3 lib bdg
LC 2005-43593

In journal entries to her mother, a gifted artist who died suddenly, thirteen-year-old Georgia McCoy reveals how her life changes after she receives an anonymous gift membership to a nearby art museum.

"This is a remarkable book. . . . [The] story is a universal one of love, friendship, and loss and will be appreciated by a wide audience." SLJ

★ **Ringside,** 1925; views from the Scopes trial, a novel. [by] Jen Bryant. Alfred A. Knopf 2008 228p $15.99; lib bdg $18.99

Grades: 8 9 10 11 12   Fic
1. Geologists 2. Novels in verse 3. Science teachers 4. Evolution -- Study and teaching -- Fiction
ISBN 978-0-375-84047-0; 0-375-84047-8; 978-0-375-94047-7 lib bdg; 0-375-94047-2 lib bdg
LC 2007-7177

Visitors, spectators, and residents of Dayton, Tennessee, in 1925 describe, in a series of free-verse poems, the Scopes 'monkey trial' and its effects on that small town and its citizens.

"Bryant offers readers a ringside seat in this compelling and well-researched novel. It is fast-paced, interesting, and relevant to many current first-amendment challenges." SLJ

Bryce, Celia
Anthem for Jackson Dawes; by Celia Bryce. Bloomsbury USA Childrens 2013 240 p. (hardback) $16.99

Grades: 7 8 9 10   Fic
1. Hospitals -- Fiction 2. Cancer -- Patients -- Fiction 3. Cancer -- Fiction 4. Friendship -- Fiction 5. Family life -- Fiction 6. Medical care -- Fiction
ISBN 1599909758; 9781599909752
LC 2012024989

In this book, "after 13-year-old Megan Bright is diagnosed with a cancerous brain tumor, she's . . . determined to have everything remain as normal as possible during her time in the hospital. . . . Megan gets closer to the only other teenager there . . . and begins to acknowledge the emotions she's been keeping buried. Initially, Jackson rubs her the wrong way, but his positivity and determined interest in Megan teach her about optimism and taking control of what she can." (Publishers Weekly)

"Sensitive and honest, this novel addresses meaningful questions concerning mortality and soul searching, and its content is appropriate for younger teens." SLJ

Buckingham, Royce

Demonkeeper. G. P. Putnam's Sons 2007 216p hardcover o.p. pa $7.99

Grades: 4 5 6 7   Fic

1. Horror fiction 2. Supernatural -- Fiction

ISBN 978-0-399-24649-4; 0-399-24649-5; 978-0-14-241166-7 pa; 0-14-241166-3 pa

LC 2006-26541

When Nat, the weirdest boy in Seattle, leaves for a date with the plainest girl in town, chaos breaks out in the houseful of demons of which he is the sole guardian.

"This is horror on the mild side. . . . The easygoing, breezy humor adds appeal to an already engaging premise." Bull Cent Child Books

Budhos, Marina

Ask me no questions; [by] Marina Budhos. Atheneum Books for Young Readers 2006 162p $16.95; pa $8.99

Grades: 7 8 9 10   Fic

1. School stories 2. Family life -- Fiction 3. Asian Americans -- Fiction

ISBN 1-4169-0351-8; 1-4169-4920-8 pa

LC 2005-1831

Fourteen-year-old Nadira, her sister, and their parents leave Bangladesh for New York City, but the expiration of their visas and the events of September 11, 2001, bring frustration, sorrow, and terror for the whole family.

"Nadira and Aisha's strategies for surviving and succeeding in high school offer sharp insight into the narrow margins between belonging and not belonging." Horn Book Guide

Budhos, Marina Tamar

Tell us we're home; [by] Marina Budhos. Atheneum 2010 297p $16.95

Grades: 6 7 8 9 10   Fic

1. Immigrants -- Fiction 2. Social classes -- Fiction 3. Household employees -- Fiction 4. Mother-daughter relationship -- Fiction

ISBN 978-1-4169-0352-9; 1-4169-0352-6

LC 2009-27386

Three immigrant girls from different parts of the world meet and become close friends in a small New Jersey town where their mothers have found domestic work, but their relationships are tested when one girl's mother is accused of stealing a precious heirloom.

"These fully realized heroines are full of heart, and their passionate struggles against systemic injustice only make them more inspiring. Keenly necessary." Kirkus

Buffie, Margaret

Winter shadows; a novel. Tundra Books 2010 327p $19.95

Grades: 7 8 9 10   Fic

1. Prejudices -- Fiction 2. Family life -- Fiction 3. Stepmothers -- Fiction 4. Racially mixed people --

Fiction

ISBN 978-0-88776-968-9; 0-88776-968-3

"Hatred for their wicked stepmothers bonds two girls living in a stone house in Manitoba, Canada, more than 150 years apart. Grieving for her dead mother, high-school senior Cass is furious that she has to share a room with the daughter of her dad's new, harsh-tempered wife. Then she finds the 1836 diary of Beatrice, who is part Cree and faces vicious racism as a 'half-breed' in her mostly white community. . . . The alternating narratives are gripping, and the characters are drawn with rich complexity." Booklist

Bukiet, Melvin Jules

Undertown; Melvin Jules Bukiet. Amulet Books 2013 304 p. (hardcover) $16.95

Grades: 6 7 8   Fic

1. Sewerage -- Fiction 2. Sailing -- Fiction 3. Homeless persons -- Fiction 4. Adventure and adventurers -- Fiction

ISBN 141970589X; 9781419705892

LC 2012039246

In this adventure novel, by Melvin Jules Bukiet, "Timothy and Jessamyn are towed through the streets of Manhattan riding in Timothy's family's sailboat, . . . The teens . . . then fall down a huge construction site hole and into the vast sewer system below. . . . The kids navigate waterfalls and rapids as they travel through the rain sewers. They meet a graffiti artist their own age, a homeless person named You, and rats the size of large dogs." (Publisher's note)

"Bukiet's first children's outing veers between language carefully designed to appeal to its intended audience and occasionally sophisticated sentence structure and subjects that should instead engage far older readers. Dramatic and imaginative, this will probably most appeal to readers with a taste for the esoteric." BookList

Bullen, Alexandra

Wish; a novel. Point 2010 323p $17.99

Grades: 8 9 10 11 12   Fic

1. Fantasy fiction 2. Magic -- Fiction 3. Twins -- Fiction 4. Wishes -- Fiction 5. Sisters -- Fiction 6. Bereavement -- Fiction

ISBN 978-0-545-13905-2; 0-545-13905-8

LC 2009-22730

After her vivacious twin sister dies, a shy teenaged girl moves with her parents to San Francisco, where she meets a magical seamstress who grants her one wish.

"The detailed descriptions of San Francisco and above all the sisters' relationship provide solid grounding for a touching, enjoyable read." Kirkus

Bunce, Elizabeth C.

Liar's moon. Arthur A. Levine Books 2011 356p $17.99

Grades: 8 9 10 11 12   Fic

1. Fantasy fiction 2. Mystery fiction 3. Magic -- Fiction 4. Thieves -- Fiction 5. Homicide -- Fiction 6. Social classes -- Fiction

ISBN 978-0-545-13608-2; 0-545-13608-3

LC 2011005071

"A solid fantasy sequel embroils its irresistible heroine in mystery, intrigue and romance. . . . A darn good read." Kirkus

★ **Star** crossed. Arthur A. Levine Books 2010 359p $17.99

Grades: 8 9 10 11 12   **Fic**
1. Fantasy fiction 2. Magic -- Fiction 3. Thieves -- Fiction 4. Religion -- Fiction 5. Social classes -- Fiction 6. Kings and rulers -- Fiction
ISBN 978-0-545-13605-1; 0-545-13605-9
                                                    LC 2010-730
In a kingdom dominated by religious intolerance, sixteen-year-old Digger, a street thief, has always avoided attention, but when she learns that her friends are plotting against the throne she must decide whether to join them or turn them in.

"Couching her characters and setting in top-notch writing, Bunce . . . hooks readers into an intelligent page-turner with strong themes of growth, determination, and friendship." Publ Wkly

★ A **curse** dark as gold; [by] Elizabeth C. Bunce. Arthur A. Levine Books 2008 395p $17.99

Grades: 7 8 9 10   **Fic**
1. Magic -- Fiction 2. Uncles -- Fiction 3. Orphans -- Fiction 4. Sisters -- Fiction 5. Factories -- Fiction
ISBN 978-0-439-89576-7; 0-439-89576-6
                                                    LC 2007019759
ALA YALSA Morris Award, 2009
Upon the death of her father, seventeen-year-old Charlotte struggles to keep the family's woolen mill running in the face of an overwhelming mortgage and what the local villagers believe is a curse, but when a man capable of spinning straw into gold appears on the scene she must decide if his help is worth the price.

"This is a rich, compelling story that fleshes out the fairy tale, setting it in the nonspecific past of the Industrial Revolution. Readers unfamiliar with 'Rumplestilskin' will not be at a disadvantage here." KLIATT

Bunting, Eve
Blackwater. HarperCollins Pubs. 1999 146p hardcover o.p. pa $5.99

Grades: 5 6 7 8   **Fic**
1. Death -- Fiction 2. Guilt -- Fiction
ISBN 0-06-027843-9 lib bdg; 0-06-440890-6 pa
                                                    LC 99-24895
When a boy and girl are drowned in the Blackwater River, thirteen-year-old Brodie must decide whether to confess that he may have caused the accident

"Bunting's thought-provoking theme, solid characterization and skillful juggling of suspense and pathos make this a top-notch choice." Publ Wkly

The **pirate** captain's daughter; written by Eve Bunting. Sleeping Bear Press 2011 208p $15.95; pa $8.95

Grades: 7 8 9 10   **Fic**
1. Pirates -- Fiction 2. Sex role -- Fiction 3. Seafaring

life -- Fiction 4. Father-daughter relationship -- Fiction
ISBN 978-1-58536-526-5; 1-58536-526-2; 978-1-58536-525-8 pa; 1-58536-525-4 pa
                                                    LC 2010032409
Upon her mother's death, fifteen-year-old Catherine puts her courage and strength to the test by disguising herself as a boy to join her father, a pirate captain, on a ship whose crew includes men who are trying to steal a treasure from him.

"This is a gripping and entertaining novel that will have readers sucked in until the last page. Even teens who are not fond of historical fiction will enjoy." Voice Youth Advocates

The **summer** of Riley. HarperCollins Pubs. 2001 170p $15.95; lib bdg $16.89; pa $5.99

Grades: 4 5 6   **Fic**
1. Dogs -- Fiction 4. Divorce -- Fiction
ISBN 0-06-029141-9; 0-06-029142-7 lib bdg; 0-06-440927-9 pa
                                                    LC 00-63203
"William is still adjusting to his parents' separation and his father's engagement when his beloved grandfather dies. He knows his mother is letting him adopt a dog so he'll start feeling better, and Riley appears to be a perfect pet. . . . But when Riley violates a state law by chasing a neighbor's horse, William has to convince the county commissioners not to destroy his friend. . . . Bunting's story will have strong appeal for middle-graders who will relish the bittersweet but satisfying resolution." Booklist

Burg, Ann E.
★ **All** the broken pieces; a novel in verse. Scholastic Press 2009 218p $16.99

Grades: 7 8 9 10   **Fic**
1. Novels in verse 2. Adoption -- Fiction 3. Vietnamese Americans -- Fiction 4. Vietnam War, 1961-1975 -- Fiction
ISBN 978-0-545-08092-7; 0-545-08092-4
                                                    LC 2008-12381
Two years after being airlifted out of Vietnam in 1975, Matt Pin is haunted by the terrible secret he left behind and, now, in a loving adoptive home in the United States, a series of profound events forces him to confront his past.

This is written "in rapid, simple free verse. . . . The intensity of the simple words . . . will make readers want to rush to the end and then return to the beginning again to make connections between past and present, friends and enemies." Booklist

Burg, Shana
A **thousand** never evers. Delacorte Press 2008 301p $15.99; lib bdg $18.99

Grades: 6 7 8 9   **Fic**
1. Race relations -- Fiction 2. African Americans -- Fiction
ISBN 978-0-385-73470-7; 978-0-385-90468-1 lib bdg
As the civil rights movement in the South gains momentum in 1963—and violence against African Americans intensifies—the black residents, including seventh-grader Addie Ann Pickett, in the small town of Kuckachoo, Mississippi, begin their own courageous struggle for racial justice.

This is "gripping. . . . References to significant historical events . . . add authenticity and depth, while Addie's frank, expertly modulated voice delivers an emotional wallop." Publ Wkly

Burgis, Stephanie

Kat, incorrigible. Atheneum Books for Young Readers 2011 298p (The unladylike adventures of Kat Stephenson) $16.99
Grades: 6 7 8 9 10   Fic
   1. Magic -- Fiction 2. Sisters -- Fiction
ISBN 1416994475; 9781416994473
                                      LC 2009032543

In Regency England, when twelve-year-old Kat discovers she has magical powers, she tries to use them to rescue her sister from marrying a man she does not love.

"Regency romance and fantasy adventure all in one, this is a satisfying read and a promising beginning to a trilogy that is sure to be popular with middle school girls." SLJ

Renegade Magic. Atheneum 2012 304p (The unladylike adventures of Kat Stephenson) $16.99
Grades: 6 7 8 9 10   Fic
   1. Magic -- Fiction 2. Sisters -- Fiction
ISBN 9781416994497

Twelve-year-old Kat tries to use her untrained magical powers to prevent use of the wild magic of Sulis Minerva found in Bath, England, where Stepmama has brought the family in hopes of finding Kat's sister a proper match.

"This combination of history and fantasy is sure to please." SLJ

Stolen magic; Stephanie Burgis. 1st ed. Atheneum Books for Young Readers 2013 400 p. (hardcover) $17.99
Grades: 6 7 8 9 10   Fic
   1. Magic -- Fiction 2. Nobility -- Fiction 3. Marriage -- Fiction 4. Witchcraft -- Fiction 5. Family problems -- Fiction 6. Brothers and sisters -- Fiction
ISBN 1416994513; 9781416994510; 9781416994527; 9781442433823
                                      LC 2011042347

In this book by Stephanie Burgis, "[w]ith just days to go before her sister Angeline's long-delayed wedding to Frederick Carlyle, the impetuous Kat Stephenson has resigned herself to good behavior. But Kat's initiation into the magical Order of the Guardians is fast approaching, and trouble seems to follow her everywhere," including "the arrival of the mysterious Marquise de Valmont, who bears suspicious resemblance to Kat's late mother." (Publisher's note)

"Though Kat's longing for the mother she never knew sounds a note of gravitas, the now-too-familiar characters and predictable plotting call for freshening. A final plot twist that moves the series action beyond lives of the rich and titled could do the trick next time around. Kat's fans will want to hang on for Book 4." Kirkus

Burnett, Frances Hodgson

The **secret** garden; illustrated by Inga Moore. Candlewick Press 2008 278p il $21.99
Grades: 3 4 5 6   Fic
   1. Gardens -- Fiction 2. Orphans -- Fiction
ISBN 0-7636-3161-2; 978-0-7636-3161-1
                                      LC 2006051838

First published 1911

A ten-year-old orphan comes to live in a lonely house on the Yorkshire moors where she discovers an invalid cousin and the mysteries of a locked garden.

"Burnett's tale . . . is presented in an elegant, oversize volume and handsomely illustrated with Moore's detailed ink and watercolor paintings. Cleanly laid-out text pages are balanced by artwork ranging from delicate spot images to full-page renderings." SLJ

Burtenshaw, Jenna

Shadowcry. Greenwillow Books 2011 311p (The secrets of Wintercraft) $16.99
Grades: 8 9 10 11 12   Fic
   1. Fantasy fiction 2. Dead -- Fiction
ISBN 978-0-06-202642-2; 0-06-202642-9
                                      LC 2010025823

Pursued by two ruthless men of the High Council of Albiom, fifteen-year-old Kate Winters discovers that she is one of the Skilled, a rare person who can see through the veil between the living and the dead.

"Elegant, complex prose sweeps readers along." Horn Book

Burton, Rebecca

Leaving Jetty Road; [by] Rebecca Burton. 1st ed.; Knopf 2006 248p $15.95; lib bdg $17.99
Grades: 8 9 10 11 12   Fic
   1. School stories 2. Friendship -- Fiction 3. Anorexia nervosa -- Fiction
ISBN 0-375-83488-5; 0-375-93488-X lib bdg
                                      LC 2005018140

"In their final year of high school, best friends Lise, Nat, and Sofia make a New Year's resolution to become vegetarians. . . . As they prepare for the next steps in their lives, the girls become so wrapped up in themselves that they fail to see how their friends are growing, changing, and . . . hurting. Burton does an effective job of weaving the symptoms and personality characteristics of anorexia into an absorbing story about the tug and pull of old friendships as a teen's world expands." Booklist

Butcher, Kristin

Cheat; written by Kristin Butcher. Orca Book Publishers 2010 107p (Orca currents) pa $9.95
Grades: 7 8 9 10   Fic
   1. School stories 2. Cheating (Education) -- Fiction
ISBN 978-1-55469-274-3; 1-55469-274-1

Laurel investigates a cheating scam at her high school.

"This novel is a realistic portrayal of high school students' attitudes towards cheating. . . . This is a well-written narrative that will challenge readers to make a decision about what's right and what's wrong." Libr Media Connect

Butler, Dori Hillestad

The **truth** about Truman School; by Dori Hillestad Butler. Albert Whitman 2008 170p $15.95; pa $7.99
Grades: 5 6 7 8   Fic
   1. School stories 2. Bullies -- Fiction 3. Journalism

-- Fiction 4. Newspapers -- Fiction
ISBN 978-0-8075-8095-0; 0-8075-8095-3; 978-0-8075-8096-7 pa; 0-8075-8096-1 pa

LC 2007-29977

Tired of being told what to write by the school newspaper's advisor, Zibby and her friend Amr start an underground newspaper online where everyone is free to post anything, but things spiral out of control when a cyberbully starts using the site to harrass one popular girl.

"The story moves at a good pace and the timely subject of cyberbullying will be relevant to readers. The language is accessible and the students' voices ring true." SLJ

Buyea, Rob

★ **Because** of Mr. Terupt. Delacorte Press 2010 269p $16.99; lib bdg $19.99

Grades: 4 5 6   Fic

1. School stories 2. Teachers -- Fiction 3. Family life -- Fiction
ISBN 0-385-73882-X; 0-385-90749-4 lib bdg; 978-0-385-73882-8; 978-0-385-90749-1 lib bdg

LC 2010-03414

Seven fifth-graders at Snow Hill School in Connecticut relate how their lives are changed for the better by "rookie teacher" Mr. Terupt.

"Introducing characters and conflicts that will be familiar to any middle-school student, this powerful and emotional story is likely to spur discussion." Publ Wkly

Mr. Terupt falls again; Rob Buyea. Delacorte Press 2012 356 p. (hc) $16.99

Grades: 4 5 6   Fic

1. Love stories 2. School stories 3. Teacher-student relationship -- Fiction 4. Summer -- Fiction 5. Classrooms -- Fiction 6. Moving, Household -- Fiction 7. Teacher-student relationships -- Fiction
ISBN 0385742053; 9780375989100; 9780375990380; 9780385742054

LC 2012010897

This book is a follow-up to Rob Buyea's "Because of Mr. Terupt." Here, "looping with his students into sixth grade, Mr. Terupt continues to surprise them with challenging projects and perfect reading suggestions." For the seven students who narrate the story, "family worries go along with lingering questions about the health of their teacher. Sixth-grade relationships and a grown-up romance" are also explored. (Kirkus)

Buzbee, Lewis

The **haunting** of Charles Dickens; [illustrated by] Greg Ruth. Feiwel and Friends 2009 357p il $17.99

Grades: 5 6 7 8   Fic

1. Authors 2. Novelists 3. Mystery fiction 4. Authors -- Fiction 5. Kidnapping -- Fiction 6. Family life -- Fiction 7. Missing persons -- Fiction
ISBN 978-0-312-38256-8; 0-312-38256-1

LC 2008028553

Twelve-year-old Meg travels the rooftops and streets of 1862 London, England, in search of her missing brother, Orion, accompanied by a family friend, the famed author Charles Dickens, whose quest is to find his next novel.

"Buzbee creates solid characters . . . and an authentic flavor of Dickensian London, enhanced by Ruth's striking and evocative b&w drawings . . . , while addressing issues of feminism, the search for identity, and child abuse." Publ Wkly

Byars, Betsy Cromer

Cracker Jackson; [by] Betsy Byars. Viking Kestrel 1985 147p hardcover o.p. pa $5.99

Grades: 5 6 7 8   Fic

1. Wife abuse -- Fiction 2. Child abuse -- Fiction
ISBN 0-670-80546-7; 0-14-031881-X pa

LC 84-24684

"Suspense, danger, near-tragedy, heartbreak and tension-relieving, unwittingly comic efforts at seriously heroic action mark this as the best of middle-grade fiction to highlight the problems of wife-battering and child abuse." SLJ

★ The **dark** stairs; a Herculeah Jones mystery. by Betsy Byars. Viking 1994 130p hardcover o.p. pa $5.99

Grades: 4 5 6   Fic

1. Mystery fiction
ISBN 0-670-85487-5; 0-14-240592-2 pa

LC 94-14012

The intrepid Herculeah Jones helps her mother, a private investigator, solve a puzzling and frightening case

"There is plenty to laugh at in this book, including classic chapter headings guaranteed to cause shivers for the uninitiated; practiced mystery readers may feel that they are in on a bit of a joke and appreciate the hint of parody. This is a page-turner that is sure to entice the most reluctant readers." SLJ

Other titles about Herculeah Jones are:
Tarot says beware (1995)
Dead letter (1996)
Death's door (1997)
Disappearing acts (1998)
The black tower (2006)
King of murder (2006)

The **keeper** of the doves; by Betsy Byars. Viking 2002 121p $14.99; pa $5.99

Grades: 4 5 6 7   Fic

1. Sisters -- Fiction 2. Family life -- Fiction
ISBN 0-670-03576-9; 0-14-240063-7 pa

LC 2002-9283

In the late 1800s in Kentucky, Amie McBee and her four sisters both fear and torment the reclusive and seemingly sinister Mr. Tominski, but their father continues to provide for his needs

"This is Byars at her best—witty, appealing, thought-provoking." Horn Book

Cabot, Meg

★ **Airhead**. Scholastic/Point 2008 340p $16.99

Grades: 7 8 9 10   Fic

1. Fashion models -- Fiction 2. Transplantation of organs, tissues, etc. -- Fiction
ISBN 978-0-545-04052-5; 0-545-04052-3

LC 2007-38269

Sixteen-year-old Emerson Watts, an advanced placement student with a disdain for fashion, is the recipient of a "whole body transplant"; and finds herself transformed into one of the world's most famous teen supermodels.

"Cabot's portrayal of Emerson is brilliant. . . . Pure fun, this first series installment will leave readers clamoring for the next." Publ Wkly

Other titles in this series are:
Being Nikki (2009)
Runaway (2010)

★ **All**-American girl. HarperCollins Pubs. 2002 247p hardcover o.p. pa $7.99
Grades: 7 8 9 10   Fic
1. Presidents -- Fiction
ISBN 0-06-029469-8; 0-06-029470-1 lib bdg; 0-06-147989-6 pa
LC 2002-19049

A sophomore girl stops a presidential assassination attempt, is appointed Teen Ambassador to the United Nations, and catches the eye of the very cute First Son. "Grades six to ten." (Bull Cent Child Books)

There's "surprising depth in the characters and plenty of authenticity in the cultural details and the teenage voices—particularly in Sam's poignant, laugh-out-loud narration." Booklist

★ The **princess** diaries. Avon Bks. 2000 238p $15.95; lib bdg $15.89; pa $6.99
Grades: 6 7 8 9   Fic
1. Fathers and daughters 5. Princesses -- Fiction
ISBN 0-380-97848-2; 0-06-029210-5 lib bdg; 0-380-81402-1 pa
LC 99-46479

Fourteen-year-old Mia, who is trying to lead a normal life as a teenage girl in New York City, is shocked to learn that her father is the Prince of Genovia, a small European principality, and that she is a princess and the heir to the throne

"Readers will relate to Mia's bubbly, chatty voice and enjoy the humor of this unlikely fairy tale." SLJ

Other titles about Princess Mia are:
Forever princess (2008)
Party princess (2006)
Princess in pink (2004)
Princess in the spotlight (2001)
Princess in training (2005)
Princess in waiting (2003)
The princess present (2004)
Sweet sixteen princess (2006)
Valentine princess (2006)

Cadnum, Michael
Peril on the sea. Farrar, Straus and Giroux 2009 245p $16.95
Grades: 7 8 9 10   Fic
1. Adventure fiction 2. Pirates -- Fiction
ISBN 978-0-374-35823-5; 0-374-35823-0
LC 2008-5421

In the tense summer of 1588, eighteen-year-old Sherwin Morris, after nearly perishing in a shipwreck, finds himself aboard the privateer Vixen, captained by the notorious and

enigmatic Brandon Fletcher who offers him adventure and riches if Sherwin would write and disseminate a flattering account of the captain's exploits.

"Cadnum's prose is vivid and evocative, brilliantly recreating life at sea in the Elizabethan era. . . . The tale is expertly paced, the varied threads of the tale elegantly woven. There's plenty here to appeal to a wide audience." Kirkus

The **book** of the Lion. Viking 2000 204p hardcover o.p. pa $5.99
Grades: 7 8 9 10   Fic
1. Crusades -- Fiction 2. Middle Ages -- Fiction 3. Knights and knighthood -- Fiction
ISBN 0-670-88386-7; 0-14-230034-9 pa
LC 99-39370

In twelfth-century England, after his master, a maker of coins for the king, is brutally punished for alleged cheating, seventeen-year-old Edmund finds himself traveling to the Holy Land as squire to a knight crusader on his way to join the forces of Richard Lionheart

"Cadnum brilliantly captures both the grisly horror and the taut, sinewy excitement of hard travel and battle readiness. . . . There's bawdy and violent talk, but religion as part of the heart and bone of life is present, too." Booklist

Calkhoven, Laurie
Michael at the invasion of France, 1943; by Laurie Calkhoven. Dial Books for Young Readers 2012 231 p $16.99
Grades: 4 5 6 7   Fic
1. Children and war -- Fiction 2. Nazi persecution -- Fiction 3. France -- History -- 1940-1945, German occupation -- Fiction 4. World War, 1939-1945 -- Underground movements -- France -- Fiction
ISBN 0803737246; 9780803737242
LC 2011021634

In this young adult novel, a "young Parisian joins the French Resistance in this Boys of Wartime series entry. . . . Michael joins a friend in distributing taunting leaflets. His involvement in Resistance activities soon escalates into helping captured British and American airmen make their way to Spain. At first he acts only as a courier of forged identity documents, but later he helps first to slip a Jewish neighbor's child out of the city, then hides an ailing American. . . . Meanwhile, he serves as a witness to . . . wartime life under the Nazis, while seeing friends, neighbors and his own older brother taken away and ultimately earning sufficient self-esteem to lose his dependence on his father's regard." (Kirkus

Includes bibliographical references

Will at the Battle of Gettysburg, 1863. Dutton Children's Books 2011 230p (Boys of wartime) $16.99
Grades: 4 5 6 7   Fic
1. Gettysburg (Pa.), Battle of, 1863 -- Fiction
ISBN 978-0-525-42145-0; 0-525-42145-9
LC 2010013307

In 1863, twelve-year-old Will, who longs to be a drummer in the Union army, is stuck in his sleepy hometown of Gettysburg, Pennsylvania, but when the Union and Confederate armies meet right there in his town, he and his family are caught up in the fight. Includes historical notes, glossary, and a timeline of events.

"This solid piece of fiction will appeal to history buffs and reluctant readers alike." SLJ

Includes glossary and bibliographical references

Calloway, Cassidy

Confessions of a First Daughter. HarperTeen 2009 214p pa $8.99

Grades: 6 7 8 9 10   **Fic**
  1. School stories 2. Dating (Social customs) -- Fiction
  3. Presidents -- United States -- Fiction
  ISBN 978-0-06-172439-8; 0-06-172439-4
                                         LC 2009-1402

High school senior Morgan Abbott pretends to be her mother, the President of the United States, as a decoy, while she also tries to lead the life of a normal teenager.

"This is a light and entertaining read for teens who like some politics with their romance." SLJ

Calvert, Patricia

★ **Bigger**. Scribner 1994 137p hardcover o.p. pa $4.99

Grades: 5 6 7 8   **Fic**
  1. Dogs -- Fiction 2. Father-son relationship -- Fiction
  3. Frontier and pioneer life -- Fiction
  ISBN 0-684-19685-9; 0-689-86003-X pa
                                         LC 93-14415

When his father disappears near the Mexican border at the end of the Civil War, twelve-year-old Tyler decides to go after him and bring him home, acquiring on the journey a strange dog which he names Bigger

"Calvert's story has many tantalizing elements: Tyler is likable and realistically portrayed, the book raises some provocative issues, and the ending is sad but satisfying. . . . This is an entertaining story even reluctant readers will relish." Booklist

Other titles in this series are:
Betrayed! (2002)
Sooner (1998)

Cameron, Sharon

The **dark** unwinding; by Sharon Cameron. Scholastic Press 2012 318 p. (jacketed hardcover) $17.99

Grades: 6 7 8 9   **Fic**
  1. Fantasy fiction 2. Eccentrics and eccentricities -- Fiction 3. Toys -- Fiction 4. Uncles -- Fiction 5. Inventions -- Fiction 6. Inheritance and succession -- Fiction
  ISBN 0545327865; 9780545327862
                                         LC 2011044431

This steampunk novel, by Sharon Cameron, begins "when Katharine Tulman's inheritance is called into question by the rumor that her eccentric uncle is squandering away the family fortune. . . . But . . . Katharine discovers . . . [he is a] genius inventor with his own set of rules, who employs a village of . . . people rescued from the workhouses of London. Katharine is now torn between protecting her own inheritance and preserving the . . . community she grows to care for deeply." (Publisher's note)

Canales, Viola

★ The **tequila** worm. Wendy Lamb Books 2005 199p hardcover o.p. pa $7.99

Grades: 6 7 8 9 10   **Fic**
  1. Mexican Americans -- Fiction
  ISBN 0-385-74674-1; 0-375-84089-3 pa
                                         LC 2004-24533

Sofia grows up in the close-knit community of the barrio in McAllen, Texas, then finds that her experiences as a scholarship student at an Episcopal boarding school in Austin only strengthen her ties to family and her "comadres."

"The explanations of cultural traditions . . . are always rooted in immediate, authentic family emotions, and in Canales' exuberant storytelling, which . . . finds both humor and absurdity in sharply observed, painful situations." Booklist

Cantor, Jillian

The **September** sisters. HarperTeen 2009 361p $16.99

Grades: 7 8 9 10 11 12   **Fic**
  1. Sisters -- Fiction 2. Family life -- Fiction 3. Missing persons -- Fiction
  ISBN 978-0-06-168648-1; 0-06-168648-4
                                         LC 2008-7120

A teenaged girl tries to keep her family and herself together after the disappearance of her younger sister.

"Cantor treats the shape of Abby's agony with poignant credibility. . . . This is a sensitive and perceptive account of the way tragedy unfolds both quickly and slowly and life reassembles itself around it." Bull Cent Child Books

The **life** of glass. HarperTeen 2010 340p $16.99

Grades: 7 8 9 10 11 12   **Fic**
  1. Fathers -- Fiction 2. Bereavement -- Fiction 3. Family life -- Fiction
  ISBN 978-0-06-168651-1; 0-06-168651-4
                                         LC 2009-1758

Throughout her freshman year of high school, fourteen-year-old Melissa struggles to hold onto memories of her deceased father, cope with her mother's return to dating, get along with her sister, and sort out her feelings about her best friend, Ryan.

"Themes of memory, beauty, and secrets come together in this thoughtful, uplifting book that skillfully avoids Cinderella-tale predictability. . . . A gentle portrait of a girl growing through her grief." Booklist

Carbone, Elisa

★ **Jump**; [by] Elisa Carbone. Viking 2010 258p $16.99

Grades: 7 8 9 10 11 12   **Fic**
  1. Mountaineering -- Fiction 2. Runaway teenagers -- Fiction
  ISBN 0-670-01185-1; 978-0-670-01185-8
                                         LC 2009-30175

In this book by Elisa Carbone, "P.K. rebels against her parents and runs away from home with Critter, a boy she's just met. Their shared love of climbing takes them to Nevada and California, pursued by police. As they get acquainted in exciting circumstances, . . . romantic tension builds." (Voice Youth Advocates)

"Chapters range from a few sentences to a few pages, and the descriptions of the pair's climbs are riveting . . . The narrators' psychological explorations are as exhilarating as their physical exploits. . . . An incisive reflection on endurance, independence, belonging, self-knowledge, and love, this story should find a wide audience." Publ Wkly

Stealing freedom; [by] Elisa Carbone. Knopf 1998 258p hardcover o.p.

Grades: 6 7 8 9   **Fic**

1. Slavery -- Fiction 2. African Americans -- Fiction 3. Underground railroad -- Fiction

ISBN 0440417074; 0679893075

LC 98-36929

This historical novel is "based on the life of Ann Maria Weems, who was born into slavery in Maryland in the 1840s. . . . Her master's debts are many and so her beloved brothers are sold without warning. Abolitionists are able to buy the freedom of the rest of her family, but the master refuses to part with Ann Maria. . . . She surreptitiously teaches herself to read and falls in love with a neighbor's slave, Alfred. She promises never to leave without him, but there is nothing she can do when she is 'kidnapped' by abolitionists and has no way to contact him." (SLJ) "Grades seven to ten." (Booklist)

"This is a fine piece of historical fiction with a strong, appealing heroine." SLJ

Carbone, Elisa Lynn

Blood on the river; James Town 1607. [by] Elisa Carbone. Viking 2006 237p $16.99; pa $6.99

Grades: 5 6 7 8   **Fic**

1. Powhatan Indians -- Fiction

ISBN 0-670-06060-7; 0-14-240932-4 pa

LC 2005023646

Traveling to the New World in 1606 as the page to Captain John Smith, twelve-year-old orphan Samuel Collier settles in the new colony of James Town, where he must quickly learn to distinguish between friend and foe.

"A strong, visceral story of the hardship and peril settlers faced, as well as the brutal realities of colonial conquest." Booklist

Card, Orson Scott, 1951-

★ **Ender's** game. TOR Bks. 1991 xxi, 226p $24.95; pa $6.99

Grades: 7 8 9 10 11 12 Adult   **Fic**

1. Science fiction 2. Interplanetary wars 3. Interplanetary voyages -- Fiction

ISBN 0-312-93208-1; 0-8125-5070-6 pa

A reissue of the title first published 1985

ALA YALSA Margaret A. Edwards Award (2008)

"The key, of course, is Ender Wiggin himself. Mr. Card never makes the mistake of patronizing or sentimentalizing his hero. Alternately likable and insufferable, he is a convincing little Napoleon in short pants." N Y Times Book Rev

Other titles in the author's distant future series about Ender Wiggin include:

Children of the mind (1996)

Ender in exile (2008)

Ender's shadow (1999)

Shadow of the giant (2005)

Shadow of the Hegemon (2001)

Shadow of the giant (2005)

Shadow puppets (2002)

Speaker for the dead (1986)

A war of gifts (2007)

Xenocide (1991)

★ **Pathfinder**. Simon Pulse 2010 662p $18.99

Grades: 6 7 8 9 10   **Fic**

1. Science fiction 2. Time travel -- Fiction 3. Parapsychology -- Fiction 4. Young adult literature -- Works 5. Interplanetary voyages -- Fiction

ISBN 978-1-4169-9176-2; 1-4169-9176-X

LC 2010-23243

Thirteen-year-old Rigg has a secret ability to see the paths of others' pasts, but revelations after his father's death set him on a dangerous quest that brings new threats from those who would either control his destiny or kill him.

"While Card delves deeply into his story's knotted twists and turns, readers should have no trouble following the philosophical and scientific mysteries, which the characters are parsing right along with them. An epic in the best sense, and not simply because the twin stories stretch across centuries." Publ Wkly

Ruins; by Orson Scott Card. Simon Pulse 2012 544 p. (hardback) $18.99

Grades: 7 8 9 10 11 12   **Fic**

1. Evolution -- Fiction 2. Time travel -- Fiction 3. Space colonies -- Fiction 4. Science fiction

ISBN 1416991778; 9781416991779

LC 2011052745

In this book by Orson Scott Card, part of the Pathfinders series, "three time-shifters discover that the secrets of the past threaten their world with imminent obliteration. Rigg, his sister, Param, and best friend, Umbo, have joined their abilities to slip through time . . . circumventing the invisible Wall that divides their planet into 19 independent evolutionary experiments." Kirkus

Cardenas, Teresa

Letters to my mother; translated by David Unger. Groundwood Books/House of Anansi Press 2006 103p $15.95; pa $7.95

Grades: 7 8 9 10   **Fic**

1. Blacks -- Fiction 2. Race relations -- Fiction

ISBN 0-88899-720-5; 0-88899-721-3 pa

A young African-Cuban girl is sent to live with her aunt and cousins after the death of her mother and begins to write letters to her deceased mother telling of the misery, racial prejudice, and mistreatment at the hands of those around her.

"The main character's voice is authentic, and the other characters, sketched with spare lines, are believable and sympathetic. . . . Short chapters and lucid writing will appeal to reluctant readers." SLJ

Old dog; translated by David Unger. Groundwood Books/House of Anansi Press 2007 144p $16.95

Grades: 7 8 9 10 11 12   **Fic**

1. Slavery -- Fiction

ISBN 978-0-88899-757-9; 0-88899-757-4

Perro Viejo, an elderly slave on a Cuban sugar plantation, "recalls his life and the endless acts of atrocity and inhumanity he has witnessed. . . . [This is a] slender but powerful story that will invite classroom discussion." Booklist

Carey, Benedict

Poison most vial; a mystery. by Benedict Carey.
Amulet Books 2012 215 p. $16.95

Grades: 5 6 7 8   **Fic**

1. Mystery fiction 2. Forensic sciences -- Fiction 3.
Murder -- Fiction 4. Neighbors -- Fiction 5. Mystery
and detective stories 6. Fathers and daughters -- Fiction
ISBN 1419700316; 9781419700316

LC 2011038222

In this novel by Benedict Carey "Ruby's janitor father
becomes the prime suspect in a murder . . . [of] [f]orensics
expert Dr. Ramachandran . . . [and] the eighth grader decides it's up to her to clear his name. . . . [She] enlists the
aid of her large, Jamaican buddy, Rex, and reclusive, retired
toxicologist Clara Whitmore, who lives in Ruby's building.
What with hacking into computers, evading gangs and like
spy-jinx, the mystery demands a lot of brain work." (Kirkus)

★ The **unknowns**. Amulet Books 2009 259p
il map $16.95

Grades: 6 7 8 9   **Fic**

1. Mystery fiction 2. Mathematics -- Fiction 3.
Conspiracies -- Fiction 4. Missing persons -- Fiction
ISBN 978-0-8109-7991-8; 0-8109-7991-8

LC 2008-33914

When people start vanishing from a godforsaken trailer
park next to the Folsom Energy Plant, two eleven-year-olds
investigate using mathematical clues that were hastily planted by their friend Mrs. Clarke before she disappeared.

"Successfully working in the concepts of pi and the Pythagorean theorem into an adventure story is no easy task,
but . . . Carey succeeds because of his lively and unique writing." Voice Youth Advocates

Carey, Janet Lee

★ **Dragon's** Keep. Harcourt 2007 302p $17

Grades: 7 8 9 10   **Fic**

1. Fantasy fiction 2. Dragons -- Fiction 3. Princesses
-- Fiction 4. Mother-daughter relationship -- Fiction
ISBN 978-0-15-205926-2; 0-15-205926-1

LC 2006-24669

In 1145 A.D., as foretold by Merlin, fourteen-year-old
Rosalind, who will be the twenty-first Pendragon Queen of
Wilde Island, has much to accomplish to fulfill her destiny,
while hiding from her people the dragon's claw she was born
with that reflects only one of her mother's dark secrets.

This is told "in stunning, lyrical prose. . . . Carey smoothly blends many traditional fantasy tropes here, but her telling
is fresh as well as thoroughly compelling." Booklist

Dragons of Noor. Egmont USA 2010 421p
$17.99

Grades: 6 7 8 9   **Fic**

1. Fantasy fiction 2. Dragons -- Fiction
ISBN 978-1-60684-035-1; 1-60684-035-5

LC 2010011311

Seven hundred years after the days of the dragon wars,
magic again is stirring and three teenagers join forces to help
bind the broken kingdoms of Noor and Otherworld.

"The world building and tone are just right, and the
themes of friendship, loyalty, responsibility, and protection
of the planet are never intrusive. Hanna and Miles are realistic teens. . . . Most of the secondary characters are equally
compelling." SLJ

Dragonswood; by Janet Lee Carey. Dial Books
2012 403p.

Grades: 7 8 9   **Fic**

1. Love stories 2. Occult fiction 3. Fantasy fiction 4.
Fantasy 5. Dragons -- Fiction 6. Fairies -- Fiction
ISBN 9780803735040

LC 2011021638

This juvenile fantasy novel tells the story of "Wilde Island [which] is not at peace. The kingdom mourns the dead
Pendragon king and awaits the return of his heir; the uneasy
pact between dragons, fairies, and humans is strained; and
the regent is funding a bloodthirsty witch hunt, hoping to
rid the island of half-fey maidens. Tess, daughter of a blacksmith, has visions of the future, but she still doesn't expect
to be accused of witchcraft, forced to flee with her two best
friends, or offered shelter by the handsome and enigmatic
Garth Huntsman, a warden for Dragonswood. But Garth is
the younger prince in disguise and Tess soon learns that her
true father was fey." (Publisher's note)

★ **Stealing** death. Egmont USA 2009 354p
map $16.99; lib bdg $19.99

Grades: 7 8 9 10   **Fic**

1. Fantasy fiction 2. Death -- Fiction 3. Siblings --
Fiction
ISBN 978-1-60684-009-2; 1-60684-009-6; 978-1-
60684-045-0 lib bdg; 1-60684-045-2 lib bdg

LC 2009-16240

After losing his family, except for his younger sister
Jilly, and their home in a tragic fire, seventeen-year-old Kipp
Corwin, a poor farmer, must wrestle with death itself in or-
der to save Jilly and the woman he loves.

"Carey's wonderful language weaves family, love, wise
teachers, and petty villains together in a vast landscape. . . .
This is quite simply fantasy at its best—original, beautiful,
amazing, and deeply moving." SLJ

The **beast** of Noor. Atheneum Books for Young
Readers 2006 497p $16.95

Grades: 6 7 8 9   **Fic**

1. Fantasy fiction
ISBN 978-0-689-87644-8; 0-689-87644-0

LC 2005-17731

Fifteen-year-old Miles Ferrell uses the rare and special
gift he is given to break the curse of the Shriker, a murderous
creature reportedly brought to Shalem Wood by his family's
clan centuries

"Carey delivers an eerie, atmospheric tale, full of terror and courage, set in a convincingly realized magical
realm." Booklist

Carman, Patrick

The **Dark** Hills divide; [by] Patrick Carman. Orchard Books 2005 253p (The land of Elyon) $11.95
Grades: 4 5 6 7   **Fic**
1. Fantasy fiction
ISBN 0-439-70093-0

LC 2004-16312
When she finds the key to a secret passageway leading out of the walled city of Bridewell, twelve-year-old Alexa realizes her lifelong wish to explore the mysterious forests and mountains that lie beyond the wall

"Narrator Aasne Vigesaa clearly portrays Alexa's thoughtful, inquisitive nature and unsettled feelings. . . . Vigesaa's excellent use of pace, pitch, and tone help differentiate each character." SLJ

Other titles in this series are:
Beyond the Valley of Thorns (2005)
The tenth city (2006)
Into the mist (2007)
Stargazer (2008)

Rivers of fire; [by] Patrick Carman. 1st ed.; Little, Brown & Co. 2008 303p il (Atherton) $16.99
Grades: 5 6 7 8   **Fic**
1. Science fiction 2. Monsters -- Fiction 3. Friendship -- Fiction 4. Social classes -- Fiction
ISBN 978-0-316-16672-0; 0-316-16672-3

LC 2007048366
After Atherton's three-tiered world collapses, ending the geographical division of the social classes, Edgar, Samuel, and Isabel try to restore the flow of water and uncover the world's mysterious origins in the process.

"There's plenty of surface excitement in the book's giant, electric eels; carniverous centipedes; and biblically rising floodwaters." Booklist

The **dark** planet. Little, Brown 2009 350p il (Atherton) $16.99
Grades: 5 6 7 8   **Fic**
1. Science fiction
ISBN 978-0-316-16674-4; 0-316-16674-X

LC 2008-45348
After the destruction of the planet Atherton, Edgar must journey to a dark and damaged world named Earth in order to find the secrets of his civilization's past.

"This is primarily action-driven sci-fi with unique settings populated by creative creatures. Familiar and new characters (including one very cool dragon) maintain readers' interest. . . . Once again, Carman's introduction provides background information and character biographies for readers unfamiliar with the series. . . . Pencil illustrations, many appearing like full-page notes, better explain Atherton and Dark Planet phenomena." SLJ

The **house** of power. Little, Brown & Co. 2007 330p il (Atherton) $16.99; pa $5.99
Grades: 5 6 7 8   **Fic**
1. Science fiction 2. Orphans -- Fiction 3. Friendship -- Fiction 4. Earthquakes -- Fiction 5. Social classes

-- Fiction
ISBN 978-0-316-16670-6; 0-316-16670-7; 978-0-316-16671-3 pa; 0-316-16671-5 pa

LC 2006025976
Edgar, an eleven-year-old orphan, finds a book that reveals significant secrets about Atherton, the strictly divided world on which he lives, even as geological changes threaten to shift the power structure that allows a select few to live off the labor of others.

This "is a fast-paced novel with a unique setting, fascinating plot, and cliffhanger ending. It shines because of the author's imagination and skill." SLJ

Carmichael, Clay

★ **Wild** things; [written and illustrated by Clay Carmichael] Front Street 2009 248p il $18.95
Grades: 5 6 7 8   **Fic**
1. Cats -- Fiction 2. Uncles -- Fiction 3. Artists -- Fiction 4. Orphans -- Fiction 5. Family life -- Fiction
ISBN 978-1-59078-627-7; 1-59078-627-0

LC 2007-49911
Stubborn, self-reliant, eleven-year-old Zoe, recently orphaned, moves to the country to live with her prickly half-uncle, a famous doctor and sculptor, and together they learn about trust and the strength of family

"Carmichael gives a familiar plot a fresh new life in this touching story with a finely crafted sense of place." Booklist

Carriger, Gail

★ **Etiquette** & espionage; by Gail Carriger. Little, Brown 2013 320 p. (alk. paper) $17.99
Grades: 7 8 9 10 11 12   **Fic**
1. Spy stories 2. School stories 3. Assassins -- Fiction 4. Science fiction 5. Robots -- Fiction 6. Schools -- Fiction 7. Espionage -- Fiction 8. Etiquette -- Fiction 9. Boarding schools -- Fiction
ISBN 031619008X; 9780316190084

LC 2012005498
In this book, Sophronia's mother is "desperate for her daughter to become a proper lady. So she enrolls Sophronia in Mademoiselle Geraldine's Finishing Academy for Young Ladies of Quality. But Sophronia soon realizes the school is not quite what her mother might have hoped. At Mademoiselle Geraldine's, young ladies learn to finish . . . everything. Certainly, they learn the fine arts of dance, dress, and etiquette, but they also learn to deal out death, diversion, and espionage." (Publisher's note)

Carroll, Michael Owen, 1966-

Super human; Michael Carroll. Philomel Books 2010 325 p. ill. (hardcover) $16.99; (paperback) $8.99
Grades: 5 6 7 8 9   **Fic**
1. Superheroes -- Fiction 2. Good and evil -- Fiction
ISBN 9780399252976; 9780142419052; 0142419052; 0399252975

LC 2009-29965
A group of teenage superheroes tackle a powerful warrior who has been brought back from 4,000 years in the past to enslave the modern world.

The "exuberant prose is just right for setting, story, and characters alike-this is basically a novel-length superhero comic, sans illustrations, and should easily appeal to fans of the X-Men, Justice League, etc." Publ Wkly

"There is enough fighting in this book to appeal to middle school boys, and the telekinetic Roz, with a controlling superhero big brother, will appeal to girls. This title is a fast read with tension, suspense, and likeable characters." Libr Media Connect

The **ascension**; a Super human clash. Philomel Books 2011 378p (Super human) $16.99
Grades: 6 7 8 9   Fic
    1. Superheroes -- Fiction
    ISBN 978-0-399-25624-0; 0-399-25624-5
                  LC 2010029600
Teenagers with super powers must try to stop a villain who has travelled from the past in order to irreversibly alter reality.

"The characters are much less absolute in their morality than in their first outing, making the narrative even more engaging. . . . One of those rare sequels that exceed the first." Kirkus

Carson, Rae
   ★ The **bitter** kingdom; by Rae Carson. Greenwillow Books 2013 448 p. (hardcover) $17.99
Grades: 8 9 10 11 12   Fic
    1. Fantasy fiction 2. Magic -- Fiction 3. Queens -- Fiction 4. Love -- Fiction 5. Prophecies -- Fiction 6. Kings, queens, rulers, etc. -- Fiction
    ISBN 0062026542; 9780062026545
                  LC 2013011912
This is the final book in Rae Carson's Girl of Fire and Thorns trilogy. Here, "young Queen Elisa and her companions trek into enemy territory to rescue the man she loves, while a traitor back home attempts to overthrow her. Elisa's journeys take her to . . . Invierne, where she hopes to destroy the source of the Inviernos' magic and bargain for peace; to the Basajuan desert, where only her most audacious plans have any chance to stop the war; and home to try to regain her throne." (Publishers Weekly)

   ★ The **crown** of embers; by Rae Carson. Greenwillow Books 2012 410 p. (hardcover) $17.99
Grades: 8 9 10 11 12   Fic
    1. Love -- Fiction 2. Magic -- Fiction 3. Prophecies -- Fiction 4. Kings, queens, rulers, etc. -- Fiction
    ISBN 0062026518; 9780062026514
                  LC 2012014125
This young adult fantasy novel, by Rae Carson, is the sequel to the Morris, Cybils, and Andre Norton Award finalist book "The Girl of Fire and Thorns." "Elisa is a hero. . . . [But] to conquer the power she bears once and for all, Elisa must follow the trail of long-forgotten--and forbidden--clues from the deep, undiscovered catacombs of her own city to the treacherous seas. With her goes a one-eyed spy, a traitor, and the man who--despite everything--she is falling in love with." (Publisher's note)

   ★ The **girl** of fire and thorns. Greenwillow Books 2011 423p $17.99

Grades: 8 9 10 11 12   Fic
    1. Fantasy fiction 2. Magic -- Fiction 3. Prophecies -- Fiction 4. Kings and rulers -- Fiction
    ISBN 978-0-06-202648-4; 0-06-202648-8
                  LC 2010042021
"This fast-moving and exciting novel is rife with political conspiracies and machinations." SLJ

Carter, Ally
   Heist Society. Hyperion 2010 287p il map
Grades: 7 8 9 10   Fic
    1. Thieves -- Fiction
    ISBN 1-4231-1639-9; 978-1-4231-1639-4
                  LC 2009-40377
A group of teenagers conspire to re-steal several priceless paintings and save Kat Bishop's father from a vengeful collector who is accusing him of art theft. "Grades six to ten." (Bull Cent Child Books)

Carter "skillfully maintains suspense. . . . This is a thoroughly enjoyable, cinema-ready adventure." Booklist
   Another title about Kat is:
   Uncommon criminals (2011)

   Perfect scoundrels; a Heist society novel. by Ally Carter. 1st ed. Disney/Hyperion Books 2013 328 p. (hardcover) $17.99
Grades: 7 8 9 10   Fic
    1. Crime -- Fiction 2. Theft -- Fiction 3. Wealth -- Fiction 4. Detective and mystery stories 5. Dating (Social customs) -- Fiction 6. Swindlers and swindling -- Fiction 7. Inheritance and succession -- Fiction
    ISBN 1423166000; 9781423166009
                  LC 2012032405
This book is an installment of Ally Carter's Heist Society series. "When Hale suddenly inherits his grandmother's billion-dollar company, it's pretty obvious that he and Kat can't be up to their old tricks anymore. But can Hale trust Kat not to dip her hand in the cookie jar and steal the company's fortune—even though he knows she's prepared to do the impossible?" (Dolly Magazine)

Carter, Anne
   The **shepherd's** granddaughter; [by] Anne Laurel Carter. Groundwood Books 2008 224p $17.95; pa $12.95
Grades: 5 6 7 8   Fic
    1. Shepherds -- Fiction
    ISBN 978-0-88899-902-3; 0-88899-902-X; 978-0-88899-903-0 pa; 0-88899-903-8 pa
Amani longs to be a shepherd like her grandfather, Seedo. Like many Palestinians, her family has grazed sheep above the olive groves of the family homestead for generations, and she has been steeped in Seedo's stories, especially one about a secret meadow called the Firdoos-and the wolf that once showed him the path there.

"Carter strikes a splendid balance in character development, portraying both parties' flaws while demonstrating Palestinian sympathies. Background and cultural information are seamlessly woven into the narrative, which is written simply and clearly in a skillful depiction of sensitive situation." SLJ

Carvell, Marlene

Sweetgrass basket. Dutton Childrens Books 2005 243p $16.99

Grades: 7 8 9 10   **Fic**

  1. School stories 2. Sisters -- Fiction 3. Mohawk Indians -- Fiction

ISBN 0-525-47547-8

LC 2004-24374

In alternating passages, two Mohawk sisters describe their lives at the Carlisle Indian Industrial School, established in 1879 to educate Native Americans, as they try to assimilate into white culture and one of them is falsely accused of stealing.

"Carvell has put together a compelling, authentic, and sensitive portrayal of a part of our history that is still not made accurately available to young readers." SLJ

Who will tell my brother? Hyperion Bks. for Children 2002 150p hardcover o.p. pa $5.99

Grades: 7 8 9 10   **Fic**

  1. School stories 2. Mohawk Indians -- Fiction

ISBN 0-7868-0827-6; 0-7868-1657-0 pa

LC 2001-51759

During his lonely crusade to remove offensive mascots from his high school, Evan, part-Mohawk Indian, learns more about his heritage, his ancestors, and his place in the world

"The blank verse format will be appealing, especially to reluctant readers. . . . [A] lovely, heart-wrenching and profound little book." Voice Youth Advocates

Cary, Kate

Bloodline; a novel. Razor Bill 2005 324p hardcover o.p. pa $9.99

Grades: 7 8 9 10   **Fic**

  1. Horror fiction 2. Vampires -- Fiction 3. World War, 1914-1918 -- Fiction

ISBN 1-59514-012-3; 1-59514-078-6 pa

In this story told primarily through journal entries, a British soldier in World War I makes the horrifying discovery that his regiment commander is descended from Count Dracula.

"This story is an interesting blend of mystery, horror, and romance, and readers who love vampire novels will find it a refreshing twist to the classic story." SLJ

Bloodline: reckoning. Razorbill 2007 311p (Bloodline) hardcover o.p. pa $9.99

Grades: 7 8 9 10   **Fic**

  1. Horror fiction 2. Vampires -- Fiction 3. World War, 1914-1918 -- Fiction

ISBN 978-1-59514-013-5; 1-59514-013-1; 978-1-59514-179-8 pa; 1-59514-179-0 pa

LC 2006-101841

In this story told primarily through journal entries, Quincey Harker, the heir to Dracula's bloodline, returns to England in 1918 to pursue Nurse Mary Seward, whose fiance has been transformed into a monstrous vampire.

"This novel about good, evil, and the gray areas in between will be a favorite with fans of the vampire genre." SLJ

Casanova, Mary

Frozen; Mary Casanova. University of Minnesota Press 2012 264 p. (hc/j: alk. paper) $16.95

Grades: 7 8 9 10   **Fic**

  1. Voice -- Fiction 2. Mother-daughter relationship -- Fiction 3. Memory -- Fiction 4. Families -- Fiction 5. Identity -- Fiction 6. Selective mutism -- Fiction

ISBN 0816680566; 9780816680566; 9780816680573

LC 2012019376

Author Mary Casanova tells the story of a young girl's life after her mother dies. "Sixteen-year-old Sadie Rose hasn't spoken in eleven years—ever since she was found in a snowbank the night her mother died under strange circumstances . . . Like her voice, her memories of her mother and what happened that night were frozen . . . [The book] is a suspenseful, moving testimonial to the power of family and memory and the extraordinary strength of a young woman who has lost her voice in nearly every way, but is determined to find it again." (Publisher's note)

Includes bibliographical references

The **klipfish** code; by Mary Casanova. Houghton Mifflin Company 2007 227p map $16

Grades: 4 5 6 7   **Fic**

  1. Family life -- Fiction 2. World War, 1939-1945 -- Norway -- Fiction 3. World War, 1939-1945 -- Underground movements -- Fiction

ISBN 978-0-618-88393-6; 0-618-88393-2

LC 2007012752

Sent with her younger brother to Godøy Island to live with her aunt and grandfather after Germans bomb Norway in 1940, ten-year-old Merit longs to join her parents in the Resistance and when her aunt, a teacher, is taken away two years later, she resents even more the Nazis' presence and her grandfather's refusal to oppose them.

"Casanova spins an adventure-filled and harrowing story." SLJ

Includes glossary and bibliographical references

Cashore, Kristin

★ **Fire**; a novel. Dial Books 2009 461p map $17.99

Grades: 9 10 11 12   **Fic**

  1. Fantasy fiction

ISBN 978-0-8037-3461-6; 0-8037-3461-1

LC 2009-5187

In a kingdom called the Dells, Fire is the last human-shaped monster, with unimaginable beauty and the ability to control the minds of those around her, but even with these gifts she cannot escape the strife that overcomes her world.

"Many twists propel the action . . . [and] Cashore's conclusion satisfies, but readers will clamor for a sequel to the prequel—a book bridging the gap between this one and Graceling." Publ Wkly

★ **Graceling**. Harcourt 2008 471p map $17; pa $9.99

Grades: 8 9 10 11 12   **Fic**

  1. Fantasy fiction

ISBN 978-0-15-206396-2; 0-15-206396-X; 978-0-547-25830-0 pa; 0-547-25830-5 pa

LC 2007045436

ALA YALSA Morris Award Finalist, 2009

In a world where some people are born with extreme skills called Graces, Katsa struggles for redemption from her own horrifying Grace, the Grace of killing. She teams up with another young fighter to save their land from a corrupt king.

"This is gorgeous storytelling: exciting, stirring, and accessible. Fantasy and romance readers will be thrilled." SLJ

Castan, Mike

Fighting for Dontae; Mike Castan. Holiday House 2012 150 p. (hardcover) $16.95

Grades: 6 7 8 9 10 11 12 **Fic**
1. Gangs -- Fiction 2. Reading -- Fiction 3. Children with disabilities -- Fiction 4. Schools -- Fiction 5. Middle schools -- Fiction 6. Family problems -- Fiction 7. Mexican Americans -- Fiction 8. People with disabilities -- Fiction 9. People with mental disabilities -- Fiction
ISBN 0823423484; 9780823423484
LC 2011042115

This book is the story of seventh-grader Javier, who "does not really want to be in a gang," but thinks he must join the Playaz gang to be cool, which he desperately wants to be. "When he is assigned to work with the special-ed class at school, Javier knows that his days as a cool kid are officially over. He does not expect to enjoy it, but reading to Dontae, a severely disabled boy, becomes the one thing Javier looks forward to." (Children's Literature)

The **price** of loyalty. Holiday House 2011 150p $17.95

Grades: 7 8 9 10 **Fic**
1. School stories 2. Gangs -- Fiction 3. Mexican Americans -- Fiction
ISBN 978-0-8234-2268-5; 0-8234-2268-2
LC 2010024065

Mexican American middle-schooler Manny finds himself caught between going along with his friends who are set on forming a gang and cutting his ties to them and following his own inclination to stay out of trouble.

"Kids will recognize the peer pressure and how authorities contribute to it. . . . But the drama is never simplistic. . . . Readers will want to discuss it all." Booklist

Castellucci, Cecil

Boy proof. Candlewick Press 2005 203p $15.99; pa $7.99

Grades: 7 8 9 10 **Fic**
1. Motion pictures -- Fiction
ISBN 0-7636-2333-4; 0-7636-2796-6 pa
LC 2004-50256

Feeling alienated from everyone around her, Los Angeles high school senior and cinephile Victoria Denton hides behind the identity of a favorite movie character until an interesting new boy arrives at school and helps her realize that there is more to life than just the movies.

This "novel's clipped, funny, first-person, present-tense narrative will grab teens . . . with its romance and the screwball special effects, and with the story of an outsider's struggle both to belong and to be true to herself." Booklist

First day on Earth. Scholastic Press 2011 150p $17.99

Grades: 7 8 9 10 **Fic**
1. Children of alcoholics -- Fiction 2. Extraterrestrial beings -- Fiction
ISBN 978-0-545-06082-0; 0-545-06082-6

"Mal's spare first-person narration is wistful and raw, reflecting the feelings of anyone who's ever felt misunderstood or abandoned. . . . Castellucci also creates vibrant secondary characters. . . . A simple, tender work that speaks to the alien in all of us." Kirkus

Rose sees red. Scholastic Press 2010 197p $17.99

Grades: 7 8 9 10 **Fic**
1. School stories 2. Ballet -- Fiction 3. Russians -- Fiction 4. Friendship -- Fiction
ISBN 978-0-545-06079-0; 0-545-06079-6
LC 2009-36850

In the 1980s, two teenaged ballet dancers—one American, one Russian—spend an unforgettable night in New York City, forming a lasting friendship despite their cultural and political differences.

"The protagonist is a complexly layered character who suffers from crippling sensitivity, and her difficulty feeling at home in her body will resonate with teens. She is honest, funny, and completely authentic. . . . The prose is poetic and rich." SLJ

Castle, Jennifer

The **beginning** of after. HarperTeen 2011 425p $17.99

Grades: 8 9 10 **Fic**
1. School stories 2. Bereavement -- Fiction
ISBN 978-0-06-198579-9; 0-06-198579-1
LC 2011016614

"The friends' relationship rings true. . . . The journey offers a complex look at the aftermath of a tragedy." Voice Youth Advocates

Catanese, P. W.

Dragon games. Aladdin 2010 373p il (The books of Umber) $16.99

Grades: 5 6 7 8 **Fic**
1. Fantasy fiction 2. Adventure fiction
ISBN 1-4169-7521-7; 978-1-4169-7521-2
LC 2009018743

This is a sequel to Happenstance Found (2009). Having learned more about his mysterious past, Happenstance accompanies Lord Umber on a journey that could affect the future of Kuraharen.

"The fast-paced and high-energy action of this video-game-like quest will please fantasy adventure fans." Kirkus

Happenstance found. Aladdin 2009 342p il (The books of Umber) $16.99

Grades: 5 6 7 8 **Fic**
1. Fantasy fiction 2. Adventure fiction 3. Magic -- Fiction
ISBN 978-1-4169-7519-9; 1-4169-7519-5
LC 2008-45966

A boy awakens, blindfolded, with no memory of even his name, but soon meets Lord Umber, an adventurer and inventor, who calls him Happenstance and tells him that he has a very important destiny—and a powerful enemy.

"Catanese packs a lot into the book: rich characterizations, . . . well-choreographed action sequences and genuinely surprising twists at the end." Publ Wkly

Catmull, Katherine

Summer and Bird; by Katherine Catmull. Dutton Children's Books 2012 344 p. (hardback) $16.99

Grades: 5 6 7 8   **Fic**

1. Fairy tales 2. Birds -- Fiction 3. Sisters -- Fiction 4. Puppeteers -- Fiction 5. Adventure and adventurers -- Fiction

ISBN 0525953469; 9780525953463

LC 2012015587

This children's book, by Katherine Catmull, is "an enchanting--and twisted--tale of two sisters' quest to find their parents. When their parents disappear in the middle of the night, young sisters Summer and Bird set off on a quest to find them. A cryptic picture message from their mother leads them to a familiar gate in the woods, but comfortable sights quickly give way to a new world entirely--Down--one inhabited by talking birds and the evil Puppeteer queen." (Publisher's note)

Cavanaugh, Nancy J.

★ **This** journal belongs to Ratchet; by Nancy J. Cavanaugh. Sourcebooks Jabberwocky 2013 320 p. (hardcover) $12.99

Grades: 4 5 6 7   **Fic**

1. Diaries -- Fiction 2. Home schooling -- Fiction 3. Father-daughter relationship -- Fiction 4. Self-acceptance -- Fiction 5. Fathers and daughters -- Fiction 6. Environmental protection -- Fiction

ISBN 1402281064; 9781402281068

LC 2012041339

This juvenile novel, by Nancy Cavanaugh, begins on "the first day of school for all the kids in the neighborhood. But not for me. I'm homeschooled. . . . The best I've got is this notebook. I'm supposed to use it for my writing assignments, but my dad never checks. Here's what I'm really going to use it for: Ratchet's Top Secret Plan . . . turn my old, recycled, freakish, friendless, motherless life into something shiny and new." (Publisher's note)

"At first it seems artificial, with observations that are too on-the-nose. But as the novel's unexpectedly multifaceted plot comes together, it becomes increasingly compelling, suspenseful and moving. Triumphant enough to make readers cheer; touching enough to make them cry." Kirkus

Caveney, Philip

Sebastian Darke: Prince of Fools. Delacorte Press 2008 338p $15.99; lib bdg $18.99

Grades: 7 8 9 10   **Fic**

1. Fantasy fiction 2. Princesses -- Fiction 3. Fools and jesters -- Fiction

ISBN 978-0-385-73467-7; 978-0-385-90465-0 lib bdg

LC 2006-25262

First published 2007 in the United Kingdom

Accompanied by his sardonic buffalope Max, seventeen-year-old Sebastian Darke meets a spoiled princess and a diminutive soldier who aid in his quest to become court jester to the evil King Septimus.

"In a very plot-driven book, the central characters are nonetheless well developed. Max is a particularly creative invention. . . . There are enough sword fights, treachery, and wicked creatures for any adventure reader. The sense of humor . . . makes it a fun read." Voice Youth Advocates

Other titles about Sebastian Darke are:

Sebastian Darke: Prince of Pirates (2009)

Sebastian Darke: Prince of Explorers (2010)

Ceccarelli, David

The **Yawning** Rabbit River Chronicle; by Janine Layton Kimmel, David Ceccarelli. Spring Tree Press 2012 296 p. (hardcover) $17.99

Grades: 5 6 7   **Fic**

1. Fantasy fiction 2. Rivers -- Fiction 3. Forest animals -- Fiction

ISBN 0978500717; 9780978500719

In this novel, by Janine Layton Kimmel and David Ceccarelli, "the Yawning Rabbit River was returned to the forest by an act of love and sacrifice. . . . But now old enemies and old ghosts rise again to threaten its existence. . . . When young Nub meets Nil he doesn't realize the dangers that they are about to face. . . . When the truth of who they are is revealed the powers of good and evil that are swirling around Briarwood moves them towards an ultimate confrontation." (Publisher's note)

Cerrito, Angela

The **end** of the line. Holiday House 2011 213p $17.95

Grades: 6 7 8 9   **Fic**

1. Guilt -- Fiction 2. Uncles -- Fiction 3. Reformatories -- Fiction 4. Iraq War, 2003- -- Fiction

ISBN 978-0-8234-2287-6; 0-8234-2287-9

LC 2010-23475

"In the prison-like school that is his last chance, thirteen-year-old Robbie tries to recover from events that brought him there, including his uncle's war injuries and the death of [Ryan], a classmate." (Publisher's note)

"The author does an outstanding job of revealing compelling and complex characters through Robbie's narrative. . . . This book would work well as a class read-aloud or a literature circle title." Voice Youth Advocates

Cervantes, Jennifer

Tortilla sun. Chronicle Books 2010 224p $16.99

Grades: 5 6 7 8   **Fic**

1. Grandmothers -- Fiction 2. Father-daughter relationship -- Fiction

ISBN 978-0-8118-7015-3; 0-8118-7015-4

While spending a summer in New Mexico with her grandmother, twelve-year-old Izzy makes new friends, learns to cook, and for the first time hears stories about her father, who died before she was born.

"Cervantes evokes the beauty of the setting and develops a memorable cast of characters, brought to life through

Izzy's heartfelt narration. A beautiful and engaging debut novel." Kirkus

Chabon, Michael

Summerland. Hyperion Bks. for Children 2002 500p hardcover o.p. pa $8.95

Grades: 5 6 7 8   **Fic**

1. Fantasy fiction 2. Magic -- Fiction 3. Baseball -- Fiction

ISBN 0-7868-0877-2; 0-7868-1615-5 pa

LC 2002-27497

Ethan Feld, the worst baseball player in the history of the game, finds himself recruited by a 100-year-old scout to help a band of fairies triumph over an ancient enemy

"Much of the prose is beautifully descriptive as Chabon navigates vividly imagined other worlds and offers up some timeless themes." Horn Book

Chadda, Sarwat

The **devil's** kiss. Disney/Hyperion Books 2009 327p $17.99

Grades: 8 9 10   **Fic**

1. Supernatural -- Fiction 2. Good and evil -- Fiction

ISBN 978-1-4231-1999-9; 1-4231-1999-1

LC 2009-8313

Fifteen-year-old Billi SanGreal has grown up knowing that being a member of the Knights Templar puts her in danger, but if she is to save London from catastrophe she must make sacrifices greater than she imagined.

"Scenes of spiritual warfare are gripping (and often gruesome), as is the undercurrent of supernatural romance. Chadda offers an original take on familiar creatures like vampires, the undead and fallen angels, but it's Billi's personality and tumult of emotions that will keep readers hooked." Publ Wkly

Chaltas, Thalia

Because I am furniture. Viking Children's Books 2009 352p $16.99

Grades: 8 9 10 11   **Fic**

1. School stories 2. Novels in verse 3. Guilt -- Fiction 4. Child abuse -- Fiction 5. Child sexual abuse -- Fiction

ISBN 978-0-670-06298-0; 0-670-06298-7

LC 2008-23235

The youngest of three siblings, fourteen-year-old Anke feels both relieved and neglected that her father abuses her brother and sister but ignores her, but when she catches him with one of her friends, she finally becomes angry enough to take action.

"Incendiary, devastating, yet—in total—offering empowerment and hope, Chaltas's poems leave an indelible mark." Publ Wkly

Chambers, Veronica

Fifteen candles. Hyperion 2010 187p (Amigas) pa $7.99

Grades: 6 7 8 9 10   **Fic**

1. Friendship -- Fiction 2. Cuban Americans -- Fiction 3. Business enterprises -- Fiction 4. Quinceañera (Social custom) -- Fiction

ISBN 978-1-4231-2362-0; 1-4231-2362-X

"It's Alicia's quince años, and even though her thoroughly modern parents took her to Spain for her quinceañera, most of her friends are having elaborate parties to celebrate their entry into womanhood. When she realizes that a fellow intern in the mayor's office needs help in planning her quince, Alicia envisions a new business venture for her and her three best friends, Amigas Inc. . . . A warm celebration of Latin culture, especially the traditional quinceañera, this is the first in a series that is sure to draw a large audience." Booklist

Chan, Gillian

A **foreign** field. Kids Can Press 2002 184p $16.95; pa $5.95

Grades: 7 8 9 10   **Fic**

1. Love stories 2. World War, 1939-1945 -- Fiction

ISBN 1-55337-349-9; 1-55337-350-2 pa

"Fourteen-year-old Ellen, who lives near a Canadian air base that the Royal Air Force is using for training during WWII, has what she considers a tedious job as her war work: looking after her disobedient, airplane-mad younger brother, Colin. Colin introduces her to Stephen, a very young RAF trainee. . . . They find common ground and their friendship grows and deepens into love. . . . Chan beautifully captures the particular tensions and intensity of wartime relationships in this quiet, absorbing novel." Booklist

Chandler, Kristen

Girls don't fly. Viking 2011 300p $16.99

Grades: 7 8 9 10   **Fic**

1. Contests -- Fiction 2. Pregnancy -- Fiction 3. Family life -- Fiction 4. Dating (Social customs) -- Fiction

ISBN 978-0-670-01331-9; 0-670-01331-5

LC 2011010563

Myra, a high school senior, will do almost anything to win a contest and earn money for a study trip to the Galapagos Islands, which would mean getting away from her demanding family life in Utah and ex-boyfriend Erik, but Erik is set on winning the same contest.

"As Myra navigates from one trauma to the next, we know she is a princess in a scullery maid's disguise. Her cast of supporting characters is equally entertaining: sniveling Erik, sarcastic Melyssa, rough and tumble siblings, and, of course, Prince Charming, incognito as a graduate student. Funny, sensitive, loyal and endearing, Myra is a heroine to remember." Voice Youth Advocates

Wolves, boys, & other things that might kill me. Viking 2010 371p $17.99; pa $8.99

Grades: 7 8 9 10 11 12   **Fic**

1. Wolves -- Fiction

ISBN 978-0-670-01142-1; 0-670-01142-8; 978-0-14-241883-3 pa; 0-14-241883-8 pa

LC 2009-30179

Two teenagers become close as the citizens of their town fight over the packs of wolves that have been reintroduced into the nearby Yellowstone National Park.

This "is a lively drama, saturated with multifaceted characters and an environmental undercurrent. She writes persuasively about the great outdoors, smalltown dynamics and politics, and young love." Publ Wkly

Chapman, Fern Schumer

★ **Is** it night or day? Farrar, Straus, Giroux 2010 205p $17.99

Grades: 6 7 8 9 10   **Fic**

1. Jewish refugees -- Fiction 2. Jews -- Germany -- Fiction 3. Holocaust, 1933-1945 -- Fiction 4. World War, 1939-1945 -- Fiction 5. Jews -- United States -- Fiction

ISBN 0-374-17744-9; 978-0-374-17744-7

LC 2008055602

In 1938, Edith Westerfeld, a young German Jew, is sent by her parents to Chicago, Illinois, where she lives with an aunt and uncle and tries to assimilate into American culture, while worrying about her parents and mourning the loss of everything she has ever known. Based on the author's mother's experience, includes an afterword about a little-known program that brought twelve hundred Jewish children to safety during World War II.

"In Edith's bewildered, sad, angry voice, the words are eloquent and powerful." Booklist

Chapman, Lara

Flawless. Bloomsbury 2011 258 p. $16.99; pa $9.99

Grades: 7 8 9 10   **Fic**

1. Love stories 2. School stories 3. Friendship -- Fiction 4. Personal appearance -- Fiction

ISBN 1599906317; 1599905965; 9781599906317; 9781599905969

LC 2010049102

In this modern take on the Cyrano story, brilliant and witty high school student Sarah Burke, who is cursed with an enormous nose, helps her beautiful best friend try to win the heart of a handsome and smart new student, even though Sarah wants him for herself.

"This retelling of Cyrano de Bergerac is great fun. . . . The ending is predictable but satisfying. Each chapter begins with thoughtful quotes about love. This novel will attract both reluctant readers and literature lovers." SLJ

Charbonneau, Joelle

★ The **Testing**; by Joelle Charbonneau. Houghton Mifflin Harcourt 2013 344 p. (hardcover) $17.99

Grades: 7 8 9 10 11 12   **Fic**

1. Examinations -- Fiction 2. Survival skills -- Fiction 3. Schools -- Fiction 4. Missing persons -- Fiction 5. Graduation (School) -- Fiction 6. Universities and colleges -- Fiction

ISBN 0547959109; 9780547959108

LC 2012018090

In this book by Joelle Charbonneau, "Cia Vale is one of four teens chosen to represent her small colony at the annual Testing, an intensive mental and physical examination aimed at identifying the best and brightest, who will go on to the University and help rebuild their shattered world. Forewarned not to trust anyone, Cia nonetheless forms a tentative partnership with resourceful Tomas, with whom she shares an unexpected emotional connection." (Publishers Weekly)

Chari, Sheela

Vanished. Disney/Hyperion Books 2011 240p $16.99

Grades: 5 6 7 8   **Fic**

1. Mystery fiction 2. East Indian Americans -- Fiction 3. Lost and found possessions -- Fiction

ISBN 978-1-4231-3163-2; 1-4231-3163-0

LC 2010019660

Eleven-year-old Neela must solve the mystery when her beautiful, but cursed, veena, a classical Indian musical instrument, goes missing.

"Well-paced and with moments of family humor . . . the novel offers a strong cast of characters and richly-described settings; both the legend and the contemporary come alive for readers. . . . Chari . . . strikes the right note with this engaging, intricate story that spans generations and two countries." Kirkus

Includes bibliographical references

Chatterton, Martin

The **Brain** finds a leg. Peachtree Publishers 2009 212p $16.95

Grades: 4 5 6   **Fic**

1. School stories 2. Mystery fiction 3. Animals -- Fiction 4. Intellect -- Fiction 5. Inventions -- Fiction

ISBN 978-1-56145-503-4; 1-56145-503-2

LC 2009-00304

First published 2007 in Australia

In Farrago Bay, Australia, thirteen-year-old Sheldon is recruited by a new student, Theo Brain, to help investigate a murder, which is tied not only to bizzare animal behavior but also to a diabolical plot to alter human intelligence.

"Several deaths in the story war against the comedy but the laughs win. Readers shouldn't expect anything remotely realistic and instead surrender themselves to the industrial-strength zaniness." Kirkus

Another title about The Brain is:
The Brain full of holes (2010)

Cheaney, J. B.

The **middle** of somewhere. Alfred A. Knopf 2007 218p $15.99; lib bdg $18.99; pa $6.50

Grades: 5 6 7 8   **Fic**

1. Siblings -- Fiction 2. Grandfathers -- Fiction 3. Automobile travel -- Fiction 4. Attention deficit disorder -- Fiction

ISBN 978-0-375-83790-6; 978-0-375-93790-3 lib bdg; 978-0-440-42165-8 pa

LC 2006-29202

Twelve-year-old Ronnie loves organization, especially because her brother has attention-deficit hyperactivity disorder, but traveling with their grandfather who is investigating wind power in Kansas brings some pleasant, if chaotic, surprises.

"The main characters are particularly well drawn and believable, and readers will root for both children as they attempt to overcome the obstacles placed in front of them." Booklist

Chen, Justina

Return to me; by Justina Chen. Little, Brown and Co. 2013 352 p. (hardcover) $17.99

Grades: 7 8 9 10   **Fic**

1. Moving -- Fiction 2. Family life -- Fiction 3. Clairvoyance -- Fiction 4. Love -- Fiction 5.

Architecture -- Fiction 6. Family problems -- Fiction 7. Moving, Household -- Fiction 8. Self-actualization (Psychology) -- Fiction
ISBN 0316102555; 9780316102551

LC 2012001549

In this book, "moving away from her Washington home seems to be a logical part of Reb's life plan; after the summer, she'll start at Columbia University, studying to be a corporate architect in the family firm, while her family moves to New Jersey for her father's new job. All that unravels upon their arrival on the East Coast, when her father announces that he's leaving the family to be with another woman, forcing Reb to question everything." (Bulletin of the Center for Children's Books)

Cheng, Andrea

Brushing Mom's hair; illustrations by Nicole Wong. Wordsong 2009 59p il $17.95
Grades: 4 5 6 7 8   **Fic**
1. Novels in verse 2. Sick -- Fiction 3. Cancer -- Fiction 4. Mother-daughter relationship -- Fiction
ISBN 978-1-59078-599-7; 1-59078-599-1

LC 2009021965

A fourteen-year-old girl, whose mother's breast cancer diagnosis and treatment have affected every aspect of their lives, finds release in ballet and art classes.

"With one or two words on each line, the poems are a fast read, but the chatty voice packs in emotion. . . . Wong's small black-and-white pencil drawings on every page extend the poetry through the characters' body language." Booklist

Where do you stay? Boyds Mills Press 2011 134p $17.95
Grades: 4 5 6 7   **Fic**
1. Aunts -- Fiction 2. Cousins -- Fiction 3. Pianists -- Fiction 4. Bereavement -- Fiction 5. Homeless persons -- Fiction
ISBN 1-59078-707-2; 978-1-59078-707-6

Jerome is staying with his Aunt Geneva and her family, now that his mother has passed away. Aunt Geneva tries to make Jerome feel welcome, but his cousins are not happy about the new "member" of their family. Though Jerome has a place to stay, he doesn't feel he has a home, until he meets Mr. Willie, who lives in a ramshackle carriage house.

"In short chapters of lyrical prose, Cheng . . . provides a moving tribute to a multigenerational community's ability to sustain and recreate itself in times of change through resilience, hard work, and a commitment to beauty and kindness." Publ Wkly

Cheva, Cherry

DupliKate; a novel. HarperTeen 2009 242p $16.99
Grades: 7 8 9 10   **Fic**
1. School stories 2. Computer games -- Fiction 3. Virtual reality -- Fiction
ISBN 978-0-06-128854-8; 0-06-128854-3

LC 2009-18292

When she wakes up one morning to find her double in her room, seventeen-year-old Kate, already at wit's end with college applications, finals, and extracurricular activities, decides to put her to work.

This is a "light and funny novel. . . . Though this is lightweight territory, there is a strong message here about being true to yourself and balancing fun and work in your life. . . . This is sure to fly off the shelves." SLJ

Chibbaro, Julie

Deadly. Atheneum Books for Young Readers 2011 293 p. $16.99
Grades: 6 7 8 9 10   **Fic**
1. Diaries -- Fiction 2. Diaries -- Fiction 3. Sex role -- Fiction 4. Epidemiology -- Fiction 5. Typhoid fever -- Fiction 6. Interpersonal relations -- Fiction
ISBN 978-0-689-85738-6; 0-689-85738-1

LC 2010002291

"A deeply personal coming-of-age story set in an era of tumultuous social change, this is topnotch historical fiction that highlights the struggle between rational science and popular opinion as shaped by a sensational, reactionary press." SLJ

Childs, Tera Lynn

Oh. My. Gods. Dutton Books 2008 224p $16.99
Grades: 7 8 9 10   **Fic**
1. School stories 2. Running -- Fiction 3. Stepfamilies -- Fiction 4. Classical mythology -- Fiction
ISBN 978-0-525-47942-0; 0-525-47942-2

LC 2007-28294

When her mother suddenly decides to marry a near-stranger, Phoebe, whose passion is running, soon finds herself living on a remote Greek island, completing her senior year at an ancient high school where the students and teachers are all descended from gods or goddesses.

"Childs does a great job of character development and creating a fast-paced plot to keep readers engaged." Voice Youth Advocates

Sweet venom. Katherine Tegen Books 2011 345p $17.99
Grades: 7 8 9 10   **Fic**
1. Sisters -- Fiction 2. Monsters -- Fiction 3. Fate and fatalism -- Fiction 4. Classical mythology -- Fiction 5. Medusa (Greek mythology) -- Fiction
ISBN 978-0-06-200181-8; 0-06-200181-7

LC 2010050525

As monsters walk the streets of San Francisco, unseen by humans, three teenaged descendants of Medusa, the once-beautiful gorgon maligned in Greek mythology, must reunite and embrace their fates.

"Childs clearly has a sequel (or more) in mind and uses this book to ably set up an appealing conflict, introduce quite likable characters, and get readers ready for intrigue in the romance and fate-of-the-world departments." Booklist

Chima, Cinda Williams

The **Crimson** Crown; a Seven Realms novel. Cinda Williams Chima. Hyperion 2012 598 p. (hardback) $18.99
Grades: 7 8 9 10 11 12   **Fic**
1. Fantasy fiction 2. Queens -- Fiction 3. Magicians -- Fiction 4. Wizards -- Fiction 5. Kings, queens, rulers,

etc. -- Fiction
ISBN 1423144333; 9781423144335

LC 2011053079

In this fantasy novel by Cinda Williams Chima, book 4 of the Seven Realms series, "the Queendom of the Fells seems likely to shatter apart. For young queen Raisa . . . , maintaining peace even within her own castle walls is nearly impossible; tension between wizards and Clan has reached a fevered pitch. . . . Raisa's best hope is to unite her people against a common enemy. But that enemy might be the person with whom she's falling in love." (Publisher's note)

★ The **Demon** King; a Seven Realms novel. Disney Hyperion 2009 506p map (Seven Realms) $17.99

Grades: 7 8 9 10 11 12   **Fic**
1. Fantasy fiction 2. Princesses -- Fiction 3. Witchcraft -- Fiction
ISBN 978-1-4231-1823-7; 1-4231-1823-5

LC 2008-46178

Relates the intertwining fates of former street gang leader Han Alister and headstrong Princess Raisa, as Han takes possession of an amulet that once belonged to an evil wizard and Raisa uncovers a conspiracy in the Grey Wolf Court.

"With full-blooded, endearing heroes, a well-developed supporting cast and a detail-rich setting, Chima explores the lives of two young adults, one at the top of the world and the other at the bottom, struggling to find their place and protect those they love." Publ Wkly

Other titles in this series are:
The exiled queen (2010)
The Gray Wolf Throne (2011)

★ The **warrior** heir. Hyperion Books for Children 2006 426p hardcover o.p.

Grades: 7 8 9 10 11 12   **Fic**
1. Fantasy fiction 2. Magic -- Fiction
ISBN 0-7868-3916-3; 0-7868-3917-1 pa; 978-0-7868-3916-2; 978-0-7868-3917-9 pa

LC 2005-52720

After learning about his magical ancestry and his own warrior powers, sixteen-year-old Jack embarks on a training program to fight enemy wizards. "Grades seven to ten." (Bull Cent Child Books)

"Twists and turns abound in this remarkable, nearly flawless debut novel that mixes a young man's coming-of-age with fantasy and adventure. Fast paced and brilliantly plotted." Voice Youth Advocates

Other titles in this series are:
The dragon heir (2008)
The wizard heir (2007)

Choat, Beth

Soccerland. Marshall Cavendish 2010 231p (The International Sports Academy) $16.99

Grades: 7 8 9 10   **Fic**
1. Soccer -- Fiction
ISBN 978-0-7614-5724-4; 0-7614-5724-0

"Flora Dupre loves soccer, and before her mom died of cancer, she made a promise that one day she was going to play for the U.S. Women's National Team. . . . Choat's background in sports journalism is obvious. While soccer action takes precedence over any deep character development, readers will enjoy following Flora's new friendships, budding romance, and changing relationship with her father." SLJ

Choi, Sook Nyul

★ **Year** of impossible goodbyes. Houghton Mifflin 1991 171p hardcover o.p. pa $5.99

Grades: 5 6 7 8   **Fic**
1. Korea -- Fiction
ISBN 0-395-57419-6; 978-0-440-40759-1 pa

LC 91-10502

Sookan, a young Korean girl survives the oppressive Japanese and Russian occupation of North Korea during the 1940s, to later escape to freedom in South Korea

"Tragedies are not masked here, but neither are they overdramatized. . . . The observations are honest, the details authentic, the characterizations vividly developed." Bull Cent Child Books

Other titles about Sookan are:
Echoes of the white giraffe (1993)
Gathering of pearls (1994)

Choldenko, Gennifer

Al Capone does my homework; by Gennifer Choldenko. Dial Books for Young Readers 2013 224 p. (Al Capone Trilogy) (hardcover) $17.99

Grades: 5 6 7 8   **Fic**
1. Fires -- Fiction 2. Autism -- Fiction 3. Brothers and sisters -- Fiction 4. Swindlers and swindling -- Fiction
ISBN 0803734727; 9780803734722

LC 2012039138

This book, set on Alcatraz Island in the 1930s, is the third in Gennifer Choldenko's Al Capone trilogy. Moose lives with his parents and autistic sister on the island. "When Moose's dad gets promoted to Associate Warden, . . . it's a big deal. But the cons have a point system for targeting prison employees, and his dad is now in serious danger. After a fire starts in the Flanagan's apartment. Natalie is blamed, and Moose bands with the other kids to track down the possible arsonist." (Publisher's note)

Includes bibliographical references

★ **Al** Capone does my shirts. G.P. Putnam's Sons 2004 225p il $15.99; pa $6.99

Grades: 5 6 7 8   **Fic**
1. Autism -- Fiction 2. Siblings -- Fiction 3. Alcatraz Island (Calif.) -- Fiction
ISBN 0-399-23861-1; 0-14-240370-9 pa

LC 2002-31766

A Newbery Medal honor book, 2005

A twelve-year-old boy named Moose moves to Alcatraz Island in 1935 when guards' families were housed there, and has to contend with his extraordinary new environment in addition to life with his autistic sister.

"With its unique setting and well-developed characters, this warm, engaging coming-of-age story has plenty of appeal, and Choldenko offers some fascinating historical background on Alcatraz Island in an afterword." Booklist

Al Capone shines my shoes. Dial Books for Young Readers 2009 274p $16.99

Grades: 5 6 7 8 **Fic**
1. Autism -- Fiction 2. Siblings -- Fiction
ISBN 978-0-8037-3460-9; 0-8037-3460-3
LC 2009-04157
Moose Flanagan, who lives on Alcatraz along with his
family and the families of the other prison guards, is frightened when he discovers that noted gangster Al Capone, a
prisoner there, wants a favor in return for the help that he
secretly gave Moose.
"Effortless period dialogue, fully developed secondary
characters and a perfectly paced plot combine to create a
solid-gold sequel that will not disappoint." Kirkus
Includes bibliographical references

No passengers beyond this point. Dial Books for
Young Readers 2011 244p $16.99
Grades: 5 6 7 8 **Fic**
1. Fantasy fiction 2. Siblings -- Fiction 3. Space and
time -- Fiction
ISBN 978-0-8037-3534-7; 0-8037-3534-0
LC 2009-51661
With their house in foreclosure, sisters India and Mouse
and brother Finn are sent to stay with an uncle in Colorado
until their mother can join them, but when the plane lands,
the children are welcomed by cheering crowds to a strange
place where each of them has a perfect house and a clock
that is ticking down the time.
"Choldenko keeps the plot moving rapidly and constantly shifts the point of view, with each chapter narrated by one
of the three siblings, so that both readers and characters feel
discombobulated—everything is both concrete yet dreamlike. . . . No one can write a hormonal teenage girl at war
with her family like Choldenko, but in the end the family relationships and the determination each sibling has to protect
the others is what saves them all." Horn Book

Notes from a liar and her dog. Putnam 2001
216p hardcover o.p. pa $5.99
Grades: 5 6 7 8 **Fic**
1. Family life -- Fiction 2. Truthfulness and falsehood
-- Fiction
ISBN 0-399-23591-4; 0-14-250068-2 pa
LC 00-55354
Eleven-year-old Ant, stuck in a family that she does not
like, copes by pretending that her "real" parents are coming
to rescue her, by loving her dog Pistachio, by volunteering at
the zoo, and by bending the truth and telling lies
"Choldenko's writing is snappy and tender, depicting
both Ant's bravado and her isolation with sympathy." Bull
Cent Child Books

Chotjewitz, David
Daniel half human; and the good Nazi. trans-
lated by Doris Orgel. Atheneum Books for Young
Readers 2004 298p hardcover o.p. pa $6.99
Grades: 7 8 9 10 **Fic**
1. Jews -- Fiction 2. National socialism -- Fiction
ISBN 0-689-85747-0; 0-689-85748-9 pa
LC 2003-25554
In 1933, best friends Daniel and Armin admire Hitler,
but as anti-Semitism buoys Hitler to power, Daniel learns
he is half Jewish, threatening the friendship even as life in

their beloved Hamburg, Germany, is becoming nightmarish. Also details Daniel and Armin's reunion in 1945 in
interspersed chapters.
"Orgel's translation reads smoothly and movingly. An
outstanding addition to the large body of World War II/Ho-
locaust fiction." SLJ

Choyce, Lesley
Deconstructing Dylan. Boardwalk Books/Dun-
durn Press 2006 174p pa $12.99
Grades: 7 8 9 10 11 12 **Fic**
1. Science fiction 2. Cloning -- Fiction
ISBN 1-55002-603-8
"The year is 2014. . . . The only child of well-known
genetics researchers, Dylan has always felt that he is different from his peers in some fundamental way that he cannot
define. . . . [His parents] confess that Dylan is a clone of
his dead brother. . . . Choyce uses a tantalizing story line to
ask some difficult questions about the consequences of scientific progress. Dylan is an unforgettable character." Voice
Youth Advocates

Christopher, John
★ The **White** Mountains; 35th anniversary
ed; Simon & Schuster Bks. for Young Readers 2003
164p hardcover o.p. pa $5.99
Grades: 5 6 7 8 **Fic**
1. Science fiction
ISBN 0-689-85504-4; 0-689-85672-5 pa
LC 2002-70808
A reissue of the title first published 1967 by Macmillan
Young Will Parker and his companions make a perilous
journey toward an outpost of freedom where they hope to
escape from the ruling Tripods, who capture mature human
beings and make them docile, obedient servants
This "remarkable story . . . belongs to the school of sci-
ence-fiction which puts philosophy before technology and
is not afraid of telling an exciting story." Times Lit Suppl
Other titles about the Tripods are:
The city of gold and lead (2003 c1967)
The pool of fire (2003 c1968)
When the Tripods came (2003 c1988)

Christopher, Lucy
★ **Flyaway**; Lucy Christopher. Chicken House
2011 314p $16.99
Grades: 5 6 7 8 **Fic**
1. Sick -- Fiction 2. Swans -- Fiction 3. Hospitals
-- Fiction 4. Wildlife conservation -- Fiction 5. Family
life -- Fiction 6. Father-daughter relationship -- Fiction
ISBN 0545317711; 9780545317719
LC 2010051425
In this young adult novel, "when newly constructed
power lines ruin the annual return of the whooping swans
Isla and her father rise early to witness, the death of several
of the wild creatures and her father's sudden and severe illness both confound Isla and emphasize her loneliness. At
the hospital where her father awaits a heart operation, Harry,
waiting there for a bone-marrow transplant, befriends Isla
and points out the young swan he can see from his bed. .
. . News broadcasts . . . about deadly outbreaks of bird flu
contrast with the small unfolding of Isla's widowed grand-

father's stiff grief as he helps her construct an art project--a harness and wings from an ancient stuffed swan--and innocent romance flutters between Isla and Harry even as the young swan regains flight and her father begins to recover." Kirkus

Christopher offers "readers a quiet but compelling story with several well-realized, idiosyncratic characters. She skillfully develops the novel's varied elements and weaves them into a unified narrative. . . . This sensitive novel will resonate with many readers." Booklist

Churchyard, Kathleen

Bye for now; a Wishers story. Egmont USA 2011 264p $15.99

Grades: 4 5 6   **Fic**

1. Wishes -- Fiction

ISBN 978-1-60684-190-7; 1-60684-190-4; 978-1-60684-278-2 e-book

LC 2011005895

While blowing out the candles on her birthday cake, eleven-year-old Robin wishes she were someone else, and wakes up to find herself in the body of an eleven-year-old British actress.

"Robin's an engaging character whose lively narrative incorporates issues such as self-esteem and self-discovery." Booklist

Cisneros, Sandra

★ The **house** on Mango Street. Knopf 1994 134p $24

Grades: 7 8 9 10   **Fic**

1. Mexican Americans -- Fiction

ISBN 0-679-43335-X

LC 93-43564

Originally published by Arte Público Press in 1984. This is "a composite of evocative snapshots that manages to passionately recreate the milieu of the poor quarters of Chicago." Commonweal

Clare, Cassandra

Clockwork prince; Cassandra Clare. 1st ed. Margaret K. McElderry Books 2011 528 p. (The infernal devices) $19.99

Grades: 6 7 8 9 10 11 12   **Fic**

1. Orphans -- Fiction 2. Demonology -- Fiction 3. Supernatural -- Fiction 4. London (England) -- Fiction 5. Secret societies -- Fiction 6. Identity -- Fiction 7. London (England) -- History -- 19th century -- Fiction

ISBN 9781416975885; 9781442431348

LC 2011017869

In this book, a #1 New York Times Bestseller, set "[i]n the magical underworld of Victorian London, Tessa Gray has at last found safety with the Shadowhunters. But that safety proves fleeting when rogue forces in the Clave plot to see her protector, Charlotte, replaced as head of the Institute. If Charlotte loses her position, Tessa will be out on the street and easy prey for the mysterious Magister, who wants to use Tessa's powers for his own dark ends. With the help of the handsome, self-destructive Will and the fiercely devoted Jem, Tessa discovers that the Magister's war on the Shadowhunters is deeply personal. . . . To unravel the secrets of the past, the trio journeys from mist-shrouded Yorkshire

to a manor house that holds untold horrors, from the slums of London to an enchanted ballroom where Tessa discovers that the truth of her parentage is more sinister than she had imagined." (Publisher's note)

Clockwork princess; Cassandra Clare. 1st ed. Margaret K. McElderry Books 2013 592 p (The infernal devices) (hardcover) $19.99

Grades: 6 7 8 9 10 11 12   **Fic**

1. Love stories 2. Fantasy fiction 3. Orphans -- Fiction 4. Demonology -- Fiction 5. Supernatural -- Fiction 6. Secret societies -- Fiction 7. London (England) -- History -- 19th century -- Fiction

ISBN 141697590X; 9781416975908

LC 2012048910

This is the third installment of Cassandra Clare's The Infernal Devices trilogy. Here, "Tessa leads the fight against Mortmain (a.k.a. the Magister) and his army of clockwork automatons that threaten to wipe out the Shadowhunter race," automatons that are "reanimated with demon souls." Also of note are "Tessa's tangled relationships with her fiancé, Jem Carstairs, who has a terminal demon-related illness, and Jem's blood brother, Will Herondale, who's also in love with her." (Entertainment Weekly)

Clark, Clara Gillow

Secrets of Greymoor. Candlewick Press 2009 166p $15.99

Grades: 4 5 6 7   **Fic**

1. School stories 2. Wealth -- Fiction 3. Grandmothers -- Fiction

ISBN 978-0-7636-3249-6; 0-7636-3249-X

LC 2008019063

As her grandmother's financial situation worsens, Hattie is forced to attend a "common school," in late nineteenth-century Kingston, New York, where she stands up to a show-off, shares embellished stories about life as a rich girl, and tries to recover her family's wealth.

"Even readers new to Hattie's story will cheer. . . . [This is an] accessible first-person narrative." Booklist

Clark, Kathy

★ **Guardian** angel house. Second Story Press 2009 225p il map (Holocaust remembrance book for young readers) pa $14.95

Grades: 6 7 8 9 10   **Fic**

1. Nuns -- Fiction 2. Jews -- Hungary -- Fiction 3. Holocaust, 1933-1945 -- Fiction

ISBN 978-1-89718-758-6; 1-89718-758-0

When Mama decides to send Susan and Vera to a Catholic convent to hide from the Nazi soldiers, Susan is shocked. Will the two Jewish girls be safe in a building full of strangers?

"Based on the experiences of her mother and aunt, Clark provides a compelling, fictionalized account documenting the courage and compassion of these nuns. . . . Black-and-white photographs and an afterword help to bring the story and history to life." SLJ

Clarke, Arthur C.

2001: a space odyssey. New Am. Lib. 1968 221p hardcover o.p. pa $7.99

Grades: 7 8 9 10 11 12 Adult   **Fic**
1. Science fiction
ISBN 0-451-45799-4 pa

Astronauts of the spaceship Discovery, aided by their computer, HAL, blast off in search of proof that extraterrestrial beings had a part in the development of intelligent life forms on Earth millions of years ago.

"By standing the universe on its head, the author makes us see the ordinary universe in a different light. . . . [This novel becomes] a complex allegory about the history of the world." New Yorker

Clarke, Judith

One whole and perfect day. Front Street 2007 250p $16.95

Grades: 7 8 9 10   **Fic**
1. Family life -- Fiction 2. Grandfathers -- Fiction
ISBN 978-1-932425-95-6; 1-932425-95-0

LC 2006-20126

Michael L. Printz Award honor book, 2008

As her irritating family prepares to celebrate her grandfather's eightieth birthday, sixteen-year-old Lily yearns for just one whole perfect day together.

The author's "sharp, poetic prose evokes each character's inner life with rich and often amusing vibrancy." Horn Book

Starry nights. Front St. 2003 148p $15.95
Grades: 6 7 8 9   **Fic**
1. Ghost stories 2. Death -- Fiction
ISBN 1-88691-082-0

LC 2002-192884

Guilty over their older brother's drowning and their mother's subsequent breakdown, fourteen-year-old Vida ventures into the occult but it is ten-year-old Jess who meets the ghost who is trying to help them

"This tantalizing ghost story . . . will keep readers on the edge of their seats. . . . A spine-tingler with staying power." Publ Wkly

Clayton, Emma

The **Whisper**; Clayton, Emma. Chicken House/ Scholastic 2012 309 p $17.99

Grades: 5 6 7 8   **Fic**
1. Science fiction 2. Twins -- Fiction 3. Youth -- Fiction 4. Telepathy -- Fiction 5. Revolutions -- Fiction
ISBN 9780545433655; 0545433657; 054531772X; 9780545317726

LC 2011278492

In this book, "the story opens with the mutant Chosen Ones (Mika; his twin sister, Ellie; Audrey; and four other kids who remain entirely interchangeable) making their plans to stop Gorman (who has overdosed on Everlife-9 and is now a 13-year-old himself) and his equally scary counterpart, Raphael Mose, by taking control of . . . pretty much everything. Meanwhile Kobi (maybe the last free 13-year-old in London) and his father fall in with terrorists who will stop at nothing to blow up the towers where the rich people live. . . . Mika and company, with the help of Kobi, Grace (Raphael's mutant daughter), and a few functional adults actually do exactly what they set out to do—save the world." (School Libr J)

"Clayton writes for young people, and you can tell. The dialogue is authentic, and there is not a labored sentence or abrupt transition in sight." VOYA

The **roar**. Chicken House/Scholastic Inc. 2009 481p $17.99

Grades: 5 6 7 8   **Fic**
1. Science fiction 2. Twins -- Fiction
ISBN 978-0-439-92593-8; 0-439-92593-2

LC 2008-8311

"Mika and Ellie live in a future behind a wall: Solid concrete topped with high-voltage razor wire and guarded by a battalion of Ghengis Borgs, it was built to keep out the animals, because animals carry the plague. At least that's what Ellie, who was kidnapped as a child, has always been taught. But when she comes to suspect the truth behind her captivity, she's ready to risk exposure to the elements and answer the call of the wild." (Publisher's note)

"This is an unusually gripping adventure that targets a younger audience than most young adult sci-fi." Bull Cent Child Books

Cleary, Beverly

Dear Mr. Henshaw; illustrated by Paul O. Zelinsky. Morrow 1983 133p il $15.99; lib bdg $16.89; pa $5.99

Grades: 4 5 6 7   **Fic**
1. School stories 2. Divorce -- Fiction 3. Parent-child relationship -- Fiction
ISBN 0-688-02405-X; 0-688-02406-8 lib bdg; 0-380-70958-9 pa

LC 83-5372

Awarded the Newbery Medal, 1984

"Leigh Botts lives with his recently divorced mother and writes to his favorite author, Boyd Henshaw. When Henshaw answers his letters and encourages him to keep a journal, he does so, and in the process solves the mystery of who is stealing food from his lunchbox, tries to write a novel, and in the end, writes a prize-winning short story about an experience with his father. . . . Grades four to seven." (SLJ)

"Leigh Botts started writing letters to his favorite author, Boyd Henshaw, in the second grade. Now, Leigh is in the sixth grade, in a new school, and his parents are recently divorced. This year he writes many letters to Mr. Henshaw, and also keeps a journal. Through these the reader learns how Leigh adjusts to new situations, and of his triumphs." Child Book Rev Serv

Strider; illustrated by Paul O. Zelinsky. Morrow Junior Bks. 1991 179p il hardcover o.p. lib bdg $16.89; pa $5.99

Grades: 4 5 6 7   **Fic**
1. Dogs -- Fiction 2. Divorce -- Fiction
ISBN 0-688-09900-9; 0-688-09901-7 lib bdg; 0-380-71236-9 pa

LC 90-6608

In a series of diary entries, Leigh tells how he comes to terms with his parents' divorce, acquires joint custody of an abandoned dog, and joins the track team at school

"The development of the narrative is vintage Beverly Cleary, an inimitable blend of comic and poignant moments." Horn Book

Cleaver, Vera

★ **Where** the lillies bloom; [by] Vera & Bill Cleaver; illustrated by Jim Spanfeller. Lippincott 1969 174p il hardcover o.p. pa $5.99

Grades: 5 6 7 8   **Fic**

1. Orphans -- Fiction 2. Siblings -- Fiction

ISBN 0-397-31111-7; 0-06-447005-9 pa

"The setting is fascinating, the characterization good, and the style of the first-person story distinctive." Bull Cent Child Books

Clement-Moore, Rosemary

★ **Texas** gothic. Delacorte Press 2011 406p $17.99; lib bdg $20.99

Grades: 6 7 8 9 10   **Fic**

1. Ghost stories 2. Sisters -- Fiction 3. Farm life -- Fiction 4. Witchcraft -- Fiction

ISBN 978-0-385-73693-0; 0-385-73693-2; 978-0-385-90636-4 lib bdg; 0-385-90636-6 lib bdg

LC 2010-47923

"This engaging mystery has plenty of both paranormal and romance, spiced with loving families and satisfyingly packed with self-sufficient, competent girls." Kirkus

Clements, Andrew, 1949-

Extra credit; illustrations by Mark Elliott. Atheneum Books for Young Readers 2009 183p il $16.99

Grades: 4 5 6   **Fic**

1. Letters -- Fiction 2. Family life -- Fiction

ISBN 978-1-4169-4929-9; 1-4169-4929-1

LC 2008-42877

"Unless [Abby] wants to repeat the sixth grade, she'll have to meet some specific conditions, including taking on an extra-credit project: find a pen pal in a foreign country. Simple enough (even for a girl who hates homework). Abby's first letter arrives at a small school in Afghanistan, and Sadeed Bayat is chosen to be her pen pal.... Well, kind of. He is the best writer, but he is also a boy, and in his village it is not appropriate for a boy to correspond with a girl. So his younger sister dictates and signs the letter. Until Sadeed decides what his sister is telling Abby isn't what he'd like Abby to know." (Publisher's note)

Clements "successfully bridges two cultures in this timely and insightful dual-perspective story." Publ Wkly

The **school** story; illustrated by Brian Selznick. Simon & Schuster Bks. for Young Readers 2001 196p il $16; pa $5.99

Grades: 4 5 6 7   **Fic**

1. Authorship -- Fiction 2. Publishers and publishing -- Fiction

ISBN 0-689-82594-3; 0-689-85186-3 pa

LC 00-49683

After twelve-year-old Natalie writes a wonderful novel, her friend Zoe helps her devise a scheme to get it accepted at the publishing house where Natalie's mother works as an editor

"The girls are believable characters. . . . Selznick's black-and-white illustrations add humorous details. A comic novel that's a sure winner." SLJ

Things not seen. Philomel Bks. 2002 251p $15.99; pa $5.99

Grades: 7 8 9 10   **Fic**

1. Science fiction 2. Blind -- Fiction 3. People with disabilities

ISBN 0-399-23626-0; 0-14-240076-9 pa

LC 00-69900

When fifteen-year-old Bobby wakes up and finds himself invisible, he and his parents and his new blind friend Alicia try to find out what caused his condition and how to reverse it.

"The author spins a convincing and affecting story." Publ Wkly

Other titles in this series are:

Things hoped for (2006)

Things that are (2008)

Things that are; [by] Andrew Clements. Philomel Books 2008 224p $16.99

Grades: 7 8 9 10   **Fic**

1. Science fiction 2. Blind -- Fiction

ISBN 978-0-399-24691-3; 0-399-24691-6

Still adjusting to being blind, Alicia must outwit an invisible man who is putting her family and her boyfriend, who was once invisible himself, in danger.

"Clements tells a riveting tale, made all the more intriguing by the choice of narrator, who experiences and describes the world differently because she cannot see."

Troublemaker; Andrew Clements; illustrated by Mark Elliott. Atheneum Books for Young Readers 2011 p. cm. $16.99

Grades: 4 5 6 7   **Fic**

1. Schools -- Fiction 2. Behavior -- Fiction 3. Brothers -- Fiction

ISBN 978-1-4169-4930-5; 1-4169-4930-5

LC 2010045018

When his older brother gets in serious trouble, sixth-grader Clay decides to change his own mischief-making ways, but he cannot seem to shake his reputation as a troublemaker.

"Clements here enters into provocative territory and pulls it off like the pro he is. Kids will easily relate to Clay, and the secondary characters come alive as well." Kirkus

Clifton, Lutricia

Freaky Fast Frankie Joe; Lutricia Clifton. Holiday House 2012 248 p. (hardcover) $16.95

Grades: 4 5 6   **Fic**

1. Boys -- Fiction 2. Family -- Fiction 3. Brothers -- Fiction 4. Stepfamilies -- Fiction 5. Mothers and sons -- Fiction 6. Delivery of goods -- Fiction 7. Family life -- Illinois -- Fiction 8. Community life -- Illinois -- Fiction

ISBN 0823423670; 9780823423675

LC 2011019976

This is the story of Frankie Joe. While "his mom is in jail, Frankie Joe tries to adjust to living with his newly surfaced father, FJ, his stepmother and 'the four legitimate Huckaby sons.' The brothers tease Frankie Joe because, academically, he is 'freaky slow,' which is at odds with how fast he is when he runs or bikes. . . . Frankie Joe . . . launches Frankie Joe's Freaky Fast Delivery Service. With his income, he plans his escape back home from Illinois to Texas. But with each day Frankie Joe becomes more integrated into—and essential to—the town and the family, starting with his friendship with another town oddball, elderly Miss Peachcott. She tells Frankie Joe his family history." (Kirkus)

Clinton, Cathryn

A **stone** in my hand. Candlewick Press 2002 191p hardcover o.p. pa $6.99

Grades: 8 9 10 11   **Fic**
1. Family life -- Fiction 2. Palestinian Arabs -- Fiction
ISBN 0-7636-1388-6; 0-7636-4772-1 pa
LC 2001-58423

Eleven-year-old Malaak and her family are touched by the violence in Gaza between Jews and Palestinians when first her father disappears and then her older brother is drawn to the Islamic Jihad

"With a sharp eye for nuances of culture and the political situation in the Middle East, Clinton has created a rich, colorful cast of characters and created an emotionally charged novel." SLJ

Coakley, Lena

★ **Witchlanders**. Atheneum Books for Young Readers 2011 400p $16.99

Grades: 7 8 9 10 11 12   **Fic**
1. War stories 2. Fantasy fiction 3. Witches -- Fiction
ISBN 978-1-4424-2004-5; 1-4424-2004-9
LC 2010051922

After the prediction of Ryder's mother, once a great prophet and powerful witch, comes true and their village is destroyed by a deadly assassin, Ryder embarks on a quest that takes him into the mountains in search of the destroyer.

"Plot twists unfold at a riveting pace, the boys' characters are compellingly sketched, and Coakley explores her subject matter masterfully without falling prey to safe plot choices." Publ Wkly

Coats, J. Anderson

The **wicked** and the just; by Jillian Anderson Coats. Harcourt 2012 344 p. $16.99

Grades: 7 8 9 10 11 12   **Fic**
1. Daughters -- Fiction 2. Prejudices -- Fiction 3. Middle Ages -- Fiction 4. Wales -- History -- Fiction 5. Household employees -- Fiction
ISBN 0547688377; 9780547688374
LC 2011027315

In this young adult historical novel, "two girls of very different degree are brought together unwillingly by the English conquest of Wales. Cecily is in a pet at having to leave the home of her youth . . . and relocate to the Welsh frontier. . . . Cecily hates Caernarvon. She hates its weather, its primitive appointments and its natives, especially Gwinny, the servant girl who doesn't obey, and the young man who stares at her." (Kirkus Review)

Coben, Harlan, 1962-

★ **Seconds** away; a Mickey Bolitar novel. Harlan Coben. G. P. Putnam's Sons 2012 352 p. (hardback) $18.99

Grades: 8 9 10 11 12   **Fic**
1. Murder -- Fiction 2. Uncles -- Fiction 3. Schools -- Fiction 4. High schools -- Fiction 5. Mystery and detective stories 6. Adventure and adventurers -- Fiction
ISBN 9780399256516; 0399256512
LC 2012026728

This young adult adventure novel, by Harlan Coben, is the second book in his Mickey Bolitar series. "Mickey . . . continues to hunt for clues about the Abeona Shelter and the mysterious death of his father--all while trying to navigate the challenges of a new high school. . . . Now, not only does Mickey need to keep himself and his friends safe from the Butcher of Lodz, but he needs to figure out who shot [his classmate] Rachel." (Publisher's note)

Shelter; a Mickey Bolitar novel. G. P. Putnam's Sons 2011 304p $18.99

Grades: 8 9 10 11 12   **Fic**
1. School stories 2. Mystery fiction 3. Moving -- Fiction 4. Uncles -- Fiction 5. Missing persons -- Fiction
ISBN 9780399256509
LC 2011009004

After tragic events tear Mickey Bolitar away from his parents, he is forced to live with his estranged Uncle Myron and switch high schools, where he finds both friends and enemies, but when his new girlfriend, Ashley, vanishes, he follows her trail into a seedy underworld that reveals she is not what she seems to be.

This is a "suspenseful, well-executed spin-off of [the author's] bestselling Myron Bolitar mystery series for adults. . . . Coben's semi-noir style translates well to YA, and the supporting cast is thoroughly entertaining." Publ Wkly

Cochrane, Mick

The **girl** who threw butterflies. Alfred A. Knopf 2009 177p $15.99; $18.99

Grades: 6 7 8 9   **Fic**
1. Baseball -- Fiction 2. Sex role -- Fiction 3. Bereavement -- Fiction 4. Mother-daughter relationship -- Fiction
ISBN 978-0-375-85682-2; 0-375-85682-X; 978-0-375-95682-9 lib bdg; 0-375-95682-4 lib bdg
LC 2008-15986

Eighth-grader Molly's ability to throw a knuckleball earns her a spot on the baseball team, which not only helps her feel connected to her recently deceased father, who loved baseball, it helps in other aspects of her life, as well.

"Cochrane crafts an awkward yet engaging heroine whose perceptions and interactions with family, friends, and supporting characters ring true. Crisply written sports action balances the internal drama." SLJ

Cody, Matthew

Powerless. Alfred A. Knopf 2009 279p $15.99; lib bdg $18.99

Grades: 5 6 7 8   **Fic**
1. School stories 2. Moving -- Fiction 3. Bullies

-- Fiction 4. Family life -- Fiction 5. Superheroes -- Fiction 6. Supernatural -- Fiction
ISBN 978-0-375-85595-5; 0-375-85595-5; 978-0-375-95595-2 lib bdg; 0-375-95595-X lib bdg

LC 2008-40885

Soon after moving to Noble's Green, Pennsylvania, twelve-year-old Daniel learns that his new friends have super powers that they will lose when they turn thirteen, unless he can use his brain power to protect them.

"This first novel has an intriguing premise, appealing characters, and a straightforward narrative arc with plenty of action as well as some serious moments." Booklist

Super; Matthew Cody. Alfred A. Knopf 2012 298 p. (Sequel to Powerless) (trade) $16.99; (lib. bdg.) $19.99

Grades: 5 6 7 8   **Fic**

1. Superheroes -- Fiction 2. Supernatural -- Fiction 3. Supervillains -- Fiction
ISBN 0375968946; 9780375868948; 9780375899799; 9780375968945

LC 2012008220

In this children's novel, by Matthew Cody, "Daniel Corrigan is as regular as can be, especially when compared to the Supers: kids in his new hometown with actual powers like flight and super strength. But . . . only he was able to stop the Shroud, a supervillian bent on stealing his newfound friends' powers. . . . Now Daniel himself is starting to display powers, while . . . his friends are losing theirs. . . . Daniel worries there may be something . . . sinister at work." (Publisher's note)

Cohn, Rachel

The **Steps**. Simon & Schuster Bks. for Young Readers 2003 137p hardcover o.p. pa $4.99

Grades: 5 6 7 8   **Fic**

1. Family life -- Fiction 2. Stepfamilies -- Fiction
ISBN 978-0-689-84549-9; 0-689-84549-9; 978-0-689-87414-7 pa; 0-689-87414-6 pa

LC 2001-57566

Over Christmas vacation, Annabel goes from her home in Manhattan to visit her father, his new wife, and her half- and step-siblings in Sydney, Australia

"Packed with humorous incident, life lessons learned, Australian travel tidbits, and a litany of preteen-girl touchstones." Horn Book

Another title about this family is:
Two steps forward (2006)

★ **You** know where to find me. Simon & Schuster Books for Young Readers 2008 208p $15.99; pa $8.99

Grades: 8 9 10 11 12   **Fic**

1. Cousins -- Fiction 2. Obesity -- Fiction 3. Suicide -- Fiction 4. Drug abuse -- Fiction
ISBN 978-0-689-87859-6; 0-689-87859-1; 978-0-689-87860-2 pa; 0-689-87860-5 pa

LC 20070-0851

In the wake of her cousin's suicide, overweight and introverted seventeen-year-old Miles experiences significant changes in her relationships with her mother and father, her best friend Jamal and his family, and her cousin's

father, while gaining insights about herself, both positive and negative.

"Cohn once again excels at crafting a multidimensional, in-the-moment teenage world. . . . Her work is heartbreaking . . . but it rings with authenticity." Publ Wkly

Colasanti, Susane

So much closer. Viking 2011 241p $17.99

Grades: 7 8 9 10   **Fic**

1. School stories 2. Moving -- Fiction 3. Divorce -- Fiction
ISBN 978-0-670-01224-4; 0-670-01224-6

LC 2010-31962

Seventeen-year-old Brooke has a crush on Scott so big that when he heads for New York City, she moves into her estranged father's Greenwich Village apartment, but soon she begins to focus on knowing herself and finding her future path.

"Colasanti has once again formulated a teen romance that feels realistic, which will make this novel a hit with readers." SLJ

Something like fate. Viking 2010 268p il $17.99

Grades: 7 8 9 10   **Fic**

1. Love stories 2. School stories 3. Guilt -- Fiction 4. Friendship -- Fiction
ISBN 978-0-670-01146-9; 0-670-01146-0

Lani and Jason, who is her best friend's boyfriend, fall in love, causing Lani tremendous anguish and guilt.

"Colasanti provides credible and engaging character development for each cast member and interactions that spark just the right amount of tension to make this a romantic page-turner." Booklist

Cole, Brock

The **goats**; written and illustrated by Brock Cole. Farrar, Straus & Giroux 1987 184p il hardcover o.p. pa $5.99

Grades: 7 8 9 10   **Fic**

1. Camps -- Fiction 2. Friendship -- Fiction
ISBN 0-374-32678-9; 0-374-42575-2 pa

LC 87-45362

"This is an unflinching book, and there is a quality of raw emotion that may score some discomfort among adults. Such a first novel restores faith in the cultivation of children's literature." Bull Cent Child Books

Cole, Stephen

Thieves like us. Bloomsbury 2006 349p $16.95

Grades: 8 9 10 11 12   **Fic**

1. Adventure fiction
ISBN 978-1-58234-653-3; 1-58234-653-4

LC 2005030616

A mysterious benefactor hand-picks a group of teen geniuses to follow a set of clues leading to the secrets of everlasting life, secrets which they must steal and for which they risk being killed.

"This novel relies on fast action, cool gadgets, and clever problem solving." Booklist

Thieves till we die. Bloomsbury 2007 311p $16.95

Grades: 8 9 10 11 12   **Fic**
    1. Adventure fiction
    ISBN 978-1-59990-082-7; 1-59990-082-3
                      LC 2006-28419

Teen geniuses Jonah, Motti, Con, Tye, and Patch, working for their mysterious benefactor, Coldhardt, are out to recover more stolen artifacts when one of their members is kidnapped, and they must add a rescue operation to the mission.

"The page-turning mystery's fun comes from the terrifying escapes, clever gadgetry and detailed Aztec lore, and, of course, the central cast of death-defying teen savants who discover that home is wherever they are, together." Booklist

Z. Raptor; [by] Steve Cole. Philomel Books 2011 265p (The hunting) $16.99

Grades: 5 6 7 8   **Fic**
    1. Science fiction 2. Islands -- Fiction 3. Dinosaurs -- Fiction 4. Virtual reality -- Fiction 5. Father-son relationship -- Fiction
    ISBN 978-0-399-25254-9; 0-399-25254-1
                      LC 2010041650

In New York City to spend Christmas with his father, thirteen-year-old Adam Adlar discovers that he and his father are still targets of sinister forces and, despite his father's objections, Adam finds himself drawn back into the struggle against hyper-evolved, deadly velociraptors determined to wreak havoc and spread terror.

"A non-stop ride from beginning to end, this installment is well constructed, larded with frequent and often violent action and reads even better than the first." Kirkus

Z. Rex; [by] Steve Cole. Philomel Books 2009 245p (The hunting) $16.99; pa $7.99

Grades: 5 6 7 8   **Fic**
    1. Science fiction 2. Dinosaurs -- Fiction 3. Virtual reality -- Fiction 4. Father-son relationship -- Fiction
    ISBN 978-0-399-25253-2; 0-399-25253-3; 978-0-14-241712-6 pa; 0-14-241712-2 pa
                      LC 2009-6637

From Santa Fe, New Mexico, to Edinburgh, Scotland, thirteen-year-old Adam Adlar must elude police while being hunted by a dinosaur come-to-life from a virtual reality game invented by his father, who has gone missing.

"Cole has created a likable character who manages to come out on top in an extraordinary situation. The science aspects offer an interesting perspective and dilemma for a discussion on genetic engineering. In addition, the adventure, video gaming, and the perilous, sometimes bloody scenes will capture reluctant readers who may not normally devour their reading materials." SLJ

Colfer, Eoin, 1965-
  ★ **Airman**; [by] Eoin Colfer. Hyperion Books for Children 2008 412p $17.99; pa $7.99

Grades: 5 6 7 8 9   **Fic**
    1. Adventure fiction 2. Airplanes -- Fiction 3. Inventors -- Fiction 4. Prisoners -- Fiction
    ISBN 978-1-4231-0750-7; 1-4231-0750-0; 978-1-4231-0751-4 pa; 1-4231-0751-9 pa
                      LC 2007-38415

In the late nineteenth century, when Conor Broekhart discovers a conspiracy to overthrow the king, he is branded a traitor, imprisoned, and forced to mine for diamonds under brutal conditions while he plans a daring escape from Little Saltee prison by way of a flying machine that he must design, build, and, hardest of all, trust to carry him to safety.

This is "polished, sophisticated storytelling. . . . A tour de force." Publ Wkly

Half-Moon investigations. Miramax Books/Hyperion Books for Children 2006 290p $16.95; pa $7.99

Grades: 4 5 6 7   **Fic**
    1. Mystery fiction 2. Young adult literature -- Works
    ISBN 0-7868-4957-6; 0-7868-4960-6 pa

"The private-eye lingo has a great, comical grade-school snap, and . . . the kid's goofy charm and stubborn dedication to crime solving will win him a hefty, enthusiastic following." Booklist

The **reluctant** assassin; Eoin Colfer. Hyperion Book CH 2013 352 p. (W.A.R.P.) (hardcover) $17.99

Grades: 5 6 7 8   **Fic**
    1. Science fiction 2. Assassins -- Fiction 3. Time travel -- Fiction
    ISBN 1423161629; 9781423161622
                      LC 2012048160

This is the first book in the time-travel W.A.R.R. series from Eoin Colfer. "After a bungled mission, [FBI agent] Chevie has been sent to London where she is 'babysitting a metal capsule,' which she learns is one end of a wormhole to the year 1898, when [young assassin] Riley (and a corpse) materialize, direct from the Victorian era." (Publishers Weekly)

Collard, Sneed B.
  Double eagle. Peachtree 2009 245p $15.95

Grades: 4 5 6 7   **Fic**
    1. Coins -- Fiction 2. Hurricanes -- Fiction 3. Buried treasure -- Fiction
    ISBN 978-1-56145-480-8; 1-56145-480-X
                      LC 2008036746

In 1973, Michael and Kyle's discovery of a rare Confederate coin near an old Civil War fort turns into a race against time as the boys try to find more coins before a hurricane hits Alabama's Gulf coast.

"Mike's narrative moves quickly with likable and believable characters. The story will have particular appeal to readers with an interest in historical places and artifacts." SLJ

Includes bibliographical references

Collier, James Lincoln
  ★ **Jump** ship to freedom; [by] James Lincoln Collier, Christopher Collier. Delacorte Press 1981 198p hardcover o.p. pa $5.99

Grades: 6 7 8 9 **Fic**
1. Slavery -- Fiction 2. African Americans -- Fiction
ISBN 0-440-44323-7 pa
LC 81-65492

In 1787 Dan Arabus, a fourteen-year-old slave, anxious to buy freedom for himself and his mother, escapes from his dishonest master and tries to find help in cashing the soldier's notes received by his father, Jack Arabus, for fighting in the Revolution

"The period seems well researched, and the speech has an authentic ring without trying to imitate a dialect." SLJ

★ **My** brother Sam is dead; by James Lincoln Collier and Christopher Collier. Four Winds Press 1985 216p $17.95
Grades: 6 7 8 9 **Fic**
1. United States -- History -- 1775-1783, Revolution -- Fiction
ISBN 0-02-722980-7
LC 84-28787

A reissue of the title first published 1974
A Newbery Medal honor book, 1975

"In 1775 the Meeker family lived in Redding, Connecticut, a Tory community. Sam, the eldest son, allied himself with the Patriots. The youngest son, Tim, watched a rift in the family grow because of his brother's decision. Before the war was over the Meeker family had suffered at the hands of both the British and the Patriots." Shapiro. Fic for Youth. 3d edition

★ **War** comes to Willy Freeman; [by] James Lincoln Collier, Christopher Collier. Delacorte Press 1983 178p hardcover o.p. pa $5.99
Grades: 6 7 8 9 **Fic**
1. Slavery -- Fiction 2. African Americans -- Fiction
ISBN 0-440-49504-0 pa
LC 82-70317

This deals with events prior to those in Jump ship to freedom, and involves members of the same family. "Willy is thirteen when she begins her story, which takes place during the last two years of the Revolutionary War; her father, a free man, has been killed fighting against the British, her mother has disappeared. Willy makes her danger-fraught way to Fraunces Tavern in New York, her uncle, Jack Arabus, having told her that Mr. Fraunces may be able to help her. She works at the tavern until the war is over, goes to the Arabus home to find her mother dying, and participates in the trial (historically accurate save for the fictional addition of Willy) in which her uncle sues for his freedom and wins." Bull Cent Child Books

With every drop of blood; [by] James Lincoln Collier, Christopher Collier. Delacorte Press 1994 235p maps hardcover o.p. pa $6.99
Grades: 5 6 7 8 **Fic**
1. Race relations -- Fiction 2. African Americans -- Fiction
ISBN 0-385-32028-0; 0-440-21983-3 pa
LC 93-37655

"The relationship of Cush and Johnny and the convincingly conversational tone of Johnny's voice make this book an effectively immediate evocation of a distant and sometimes difficult-to-understand time." Horn Book

Collins, P. J. Sarah
What happened to Serenity? Red Deer Press 2011 222p pa $12.95
Grades: 7 8 9 10 **Fic**
1. Science fiction 2. Missing persons -- Fiction
ISBN 978-0-88995-453-3; 0-88995-453-4

Katherine lives in a post-apocalyptic community completely cut off from the rest of the world and when her best friend's sister Serenity suddenly disappears, Katherine must break out of town to find her.

"The story is set in 2021 and paints a unique picture of what lack of freedom and free speech could look like if this reality existed. Collins moves beyond the basic mystery and explores the intricate workings of the mind, the body, and the power of basic knowledge. Her story will keep readers engaged from beginning to end." SLJ

Collins, Pat Lowery
Daughter of winter. Candlewick Press 2010 272p $16.99
Grades: 4 5 6 7 **Fic**
1. Winter -- Fiction 2. Wampanoag Indians -- Fiction 3. Wilderness survival -- Fiction
ISBN 978-0-7636-4500-7; 0-7636-4500-1
LC 2009049099

In the mid-nineteenth-century shipbuilding town of Essex, Massachusetts, twelve-year-old Addie learns a startling secret about her past when she escapes servitude by running away to live in the snowy woods and meets an elderly Wampanoag woman.

"Collins' sense of place, incorporation of cultural and historical details, and the richly evoked winter setting make for a vividly imagined novel. An engaging survival story intertwined with a search for identity." Booklist

Hidden voices; the orphan musicians of Venice. Candlewick Press 2009 345p $17.99
Grades: 8 9 10 11 12 **Fic**
1. Orphans -- Fiction 2. Musicians -- Fiction
ISBN 978-0-7636-3917-4; 0-7636-3917-6
LC 2008-18762

Anetta, Rosalba, and Luisa, find their lives taking unexpected paths while growing up in eighteenth century Venice at the orphanage Ospedale della Pieta, where concerts are given to support the orphanage as well as expose the girls to potential suitors.

"Collins's descriptive prose makes Venice and a unique slice of history come alive as the three connecting narrative strains create a rich story of friendship and self-realization." SLJ

Collins, Suzanne, 1962-
★ **Catching** fire. Scholastic Press 2009 391p $17.99
Grades: 7 8 9 10 **Fic**
1. Science fiction
ISBN 978-0-439-02349-8; 0-439-02349-1
LC 2008-50493

This dystopian young adult novel, volume 2 of the Hunger Games trilogy, takes place after a televised, state-sponsored duel known as the Hunger Games. "Katniss Everdeen has won . . . with fellow district tribute Peeta Mellark. But it was a victory won by defiance of the Capitol and their harsh rules. Katniss and Peeta should be happy. After all, they have just won for themselves and their families a life of safety and plenty. But there are rumors of rebellion among the subjects, and Katniss and Peeta, to their horror, are the faces of that rebellion." (Publisher's note)

"Beyond the expert world building, the acute social commentary and the large cast of fully realized characters, there's action, intrigue, romance and some amount of hope in a story readers will find completely engrossing." Kirkus

Gregor the Overlander. Scholastic Press 2003 311p (Underland chronicles) $16.95; pa $5.99
Grades: 4 5 6 7   **Fic**
   1. Fantasy fiction 2. Children's literature -- Works -- Grades two through six
   ISBN 0-439-43536-6; 0-439-67813-7 pa
                                LC 2002-155865
When eleven-year-old Gregor and his two-year-old sister are pulled into a strange underground world, they trigger an epic battle involving men, bats, rats, cockroaches, and spiders while on a quest foretold by ancient prophecy

"Collins creates a fascinating, vivid, highly original world and a superb story to go along with it." Booklist

Other titles in this series are:
Gregor and the prophecy of Bane (2004)
Gregor and the curse of the warmbloods (2005)
Gregor and the marks of secret (2006)
Gregor and the code of claw (2007)

★ The **Hunger** Games. Scholastic Press 2008 374p $17.99; pa $8.99
Grades: 7 8 9 10   **Fic**
   1. Science fiction
   ISBN 978-0-439-02348-1; 0-439-02348-3; 978-0-439-02352-8 pa; 0-439-02352-1 pa
                                LC 2007-39987
In this dystopian young adult novel, "in the ruins of a place once known as North America lies the nation of Panem, a shining Capitol surrounded by twelve outlaying districts. The Capitol . . . keeps the districts in line by forcing them all to send one girl and one boy between the ages of twelve and eighteen to participate in the annual Hunger Games, a fight to the death on live TV. Sixteen-year-old Katniss Everdeen . . . regards it as a death sentence when she is forced to represent her district in the Games." (Publisher's note)

"Collins's characters are completely realistic and sympathetic. . . . The plot is tense, dramatic, and engrossing." SLJ

Mockingjay. Scholastic Press 2010 390p (Hunger Games) $17.99
Grades: 7 8 9 10   **Fic**
   1. Science fiction
   ISBN 978-0-439-02351-1; 0-439-02351-3
                                LC 2008-50493
This dystopian novel, volume 3 of the Hunger Games trilogy, takes place after heroine Katniss Everdeen has "survived the Hunger Games twice. But now that she's made it

out of the bloody arena alive, she's still not safe. . . . The Capitol wants revenge. Who do they think should pay for the unrest? Katniss. And what's worse, President Snow has made it clear that no one else is safe either. Not Katniss's family, not her friends, not the people of District 12." (Publisher's note)

"This concluding volume in Collins's Hunger Games trilogy accomplishes a rare feat, the last installment being the best yet, a beautifully orchestrated and intelligent novel that succeeds on every level." Publ Wkly

Collins, Tim
  Notes from a totally lame vampire; because the undead have feelings too. written by Tim Collins; illustrated by Andrew Pinder. Aladdin 2010 328p il $12.99
Grades: 6 7 8 9   **Fic**
   1. School stories 2. Love -- Fiction 3. Diaries -- Fiction 4. Vampires -- Fiction
   ISBN 978-1-4424-1183-8; 1-4424-1183-X
                                LC 2010-10634
Published in the United Kingdom with title: Diary of a wimpy vampire

Nigel Mullet, a 100-year-old vampire doomed to spend eternity in the body of a socially awkward fifteen-year-old boy, records his attempts to impress the love of his life, Chloe, while battling an embarrassingly overwhelming desire to sink his fangs into her.

"This book has a witty, laugh-out-loud story line and cartoon illustrations that are liberally sprinkled throughout. Readers will sympathize with Nigel and his teen angst, and the great ending makes this a satisfying and entertaining read." SLJ

Collins, Yvonne
  Now starring Vivien Leigh Reid: Diva in training; by Yvonne Collins and Sandy Rideout. Griffin 2006 242p pa $9.95
Grades: 7 8 9 10   **Fic**
   1. Actors -- Fiction 2. Mother-daughter relationship -- Fiction
   ISBN 0-312-33839-2
"Leigh Reid, who first appeared in Introducing Vivien Leigh Reid, . . . spent the summer she was 15 with Annika Anderson, her estranged, actress mother who left the family when Leigh was just a toddler. . . . In this book, Leigh . . . is recommended for a soap-opera audition that she nails due to her varied accents and versatility. . . . This volume is pop-culture fun with a moral." SLJ

  The **new** and improved Vivien Leigh Reid; diva in control. [by] Yvonne Collins and Sandy Rideout. 1st ed.; St. Martin's Griffin 2007 231p pa $9.95
Grades: 7 8 9 10   **Fic**
   1. Actors -- Fiction 2. Remarriage -- Fiction 3. Mother-daughter relationship -- Fiction
   ISBN 978-0-312-35828-0 pa; 0-312-35828-8 pa
                                LC 2006050570
When she arrives to spend Thanksgiving with her actress mother, sixteen-year-old Leigh is horrified to discover that her mother is planning to marry the producer who had fired Leigh the summer before and whose daughters are deter-

mined to sabotage their father's relationship as well as any hopes of reviving Leigh's budding acting career.

"Leigh is a likeable, funny, and realistic heroine" Kliatt

Collomore, Anna

The **ruining**; Anna Collomore. Razorbill 2013 272 p. $17.99

Grades: 7 8 9 10 11 12   **Fic**

1. Nannies -- Fiction 2. Mental illness -- Fiction 3. Psychopaths -- Fiction 4. Emotional problems -- Fiction
ISBN 1595144706; 9781595144706

                LC 2012032007

In this novel, by Anna Collomore, "Annie Phillips is thrilled to . . . begin . . . as a nanny for the picture-perfect Cohen family. In no time at all, she falls in love with the Cohens. . . . All too soon cracks appear in Annie's . . . perfect world. She's blamed for mistakes she doesn't remember making . . . and she feels like she's always being watched. . . . Annie's fear gives way to . . . hallucinations. Is she tumbling into madness, or is something sinister at play?" (Publisher's note)

Columbus, Chris

House of secrets; Chris Columbus; Ned Vizzini. 1st ed. Balzer + Bray 2013 496 p. (hardcover) $17.99

Grades: 5 6 7 8   **Fic**

1. Dwellings -- Fiction 2. Supernatural -- Fiction 3. Books and reading -- Fiction 4. Brothers and sisters -- Fiction 5. Adventure and adventurers -- Fiction
ISBN 0062192469; 9780062192462

                LC 2012051815

In this juvenile fantasy story, by Chris Columbus and Ned Vizzini, three siblings "relocate to an old Victorian house that used to be the home of occult novelist Denver Kristoff. . . . By the time the Walkers realize that one of their neighbors has sinister plans for them, they're banished to a primeval forest way off the grid. . . . Bloodthirsty medieval warriors patrol the woods around them, supernatural pirates roam the neighboring seas, and a power-hungry queen rules the land." (Publisher's note)

Combres, Elisabeth

Broken memory; a novel of Rwanda. translated by Shelley Tanaka. Groundwood Books/House of Anansi Press 2009 139p $17.95

Grades: 6 7 8 9 10   **Fic**

1. Orphans -- Fiction 2. Genocide -- Fiction 3. Hutu (African people) -- Fiction 4. Tutsi (African people) -- Fiction
ISBN 978-0-88899-892-7; 0-88899-892-9
Original French edition, 2007

"This is a quiet, reflective story; neither laden with detail nor full of historical descriptions, it is simply one girl's horrific tale of personal tragedy. . . . Combres' story offers readers intimate access to this chapter of history as well as considerable potential for discussion." Bull Cent Child Books

Comerford, Lynda B.

Rissa Bartholomew's declaration of independence. Scholastic Press 2009 250p $16.99

Grades: 4 5 6 7   **Fic**

1. School stories 2. Friendship -- Fiction
ISBN 978-0-545-05058-6; 0-545-05058-8

                LC 2008-26618

Having told off all of her old friends at her eleventh birthday party, Rissa starts middle school determined to make new friends while being herself, not simply being part of a herd.

"Rissa's troubles are ones that many middle-schoolers will identify with: new schools, shifting allegiances, new feelings, and changing bodies. First-time novelist Comerford gives her readers an appealing heroine who, despite her flaws and quirks, finds herself along the way." Booklist

Compestine, Ying Chang

Revolution is not a dinner party; a novel. Henry Holt and Company 2007 256p map $16.95; pa $7.99

Grades: 5 6 7 8   **Fic**

1. Communism -- Fiction 2. Persecution -- Fiction
ISBN 978-0-8050-8207-4; 0-8050-8207-7; 978-0-312-58149-7 pa; 0-312-58149-1 pa

                LC 2006035465

Starting in 1972 when she is nine years old, Ling, the daughter of two doctors, struggles to make sense of the communists' Cultural Revolution, which empties stores of food, homes of appliances deemed "bourgeois," and people of laughter.

"Readers should remain rapt by Compestine's storytelling throughout this gripping account of life during China's Cultural Revolution." Publ Wkly

Condie, Allyson Braithwaite.

Crossed; Ally Condie. Dutton Books 2011 367p map $17.99

Grades: 7 8 9 10   **Fic**

1. Fantasy fiction 2. Resistance to government -- Fiction
ISBN 978-0-525-42365-2; 0-525-42365-6

                LC 2011016442

Seventeen-year-old Cassia sacrifices everything and heads to the Outer Provinces in search of Ky, where she is confronted with shocking revelations about Society and the promise of rebellion.

"Newcomers will need to read the first book for background, but vivid, poetic writing will pull fans through as Condie immerses readers in her characters' yearnings and hopes." Publ Wkly

★ **Matched**; Ally Condie. Dutton Books 2010 369p $17.99

Grades: 7 8 9 10   **Fic**

1. Fantasy fiction
ISBN 978-0-525-42364-5; 0-525-42364-8

All her life, Cassia has never had a choice. The Society dictates everything: when and how to play, where to work, where to live, what to eat and wear, when to die, and most importantly to Cassia as she turns 17, who to marry. When she is Matched with her best friend Xander, things couldn't be more perfect. But why did her neighbor Ky's face show up on her match disk as well?

"Condie's enthralling and twisty dystopian plot is well served by her intriguing characters and fine writing. While the ending is unresolved . . . , Cassia's metamorphosis is gripping and satisfying." Publ Wkly

Reached; Ally Condie. Dutton 2012 512 p. (Matched trilogy) (hardcover) $17.99
Grades: 7 8 9 10   **Fic**
1. Science fiction 2. Epidemics -- Fiction 3. Resistance to government -- Fiction 4. Government, Resistance to -- Fiction
ISBN 9780525423669; 0525423664
LC 2012031916
"This final story in the 'Matched' trilogy finds Cassia, Ky, and Xander all working for the Rising, but in different locations and for different reasons. The Rising has introduced a plague into the cities for which they have the cure. They are easily able to take control as they cure people. An unexpected mutation of the illness catches the Rising off guard, and the Pilot (the Rising's leader) realizes he could quickly lose all that has been gained." (Voice of Youth Advocates)

Conly, Jane Leslie
★ **Murder** afloat. Hyperion Books for Children 2010 164p $17.99
Grades: 5 6 7 8   **Fic**
1. Adventure fiction 2. Kidnapping -- Fiction 3. Seafaring life -- Fiction
ISBN 978-1-4231-0416-2; 1-4231-0416-1
Benjamin Franklin Orville is caught up in a scuffle, kidnapped with a group of immigrants and forced to work aboard the Ella Dawn—one of the most ill-reputed oystering vessels in Baltimore.
"With compelling characters and details of the little-known process of oystering woven throughout, Conly's tale touches on the hardships of many German immigrants to the U.S., whose desperate plights offer parallels to contemporary immigration issues. Short chapters and suspenseful plot twists will keep readers turning the pages in this engaging historical adventure." Booklist

Connelly, Neil O.
★ The **miracle** stealer; [by] Neil Connelly. Arthur A. Levine Books 2010 230p $17.99
Grades: 8 9 10 11 12   **Fic**
1. Camps -- Fiction 2. Faith -- Fiction 3. Miracles -- Fiction 4. Siblings -- Fiction 5. Family life -- Fiction
ISBN 978-0-545-13195-7; 0-545-13195-2
LC 2010-727
In small-town Pennsylvania, nineteen-year-old Andi Grant will do anything to protect her six-year-old brother Daniel from those who believe he has a God-given gift as a healer—including their own mother.
"Neil Connelly has written a deeply thought provoking novel. . . . Throughout this gripping novel the climax builds from a slow burn to a tension packed conclusion." Libr Media Connect

Connor, Leslie
★ **Crunch**. Katherine Tegen Books 2010 330p $16.99; lib bdg $17.89

Grades: 5 6 7 8   **Fic**
1. Bicycles -- Fiction 2. Siblings -- Fiction 3. Family life -- Fiction 4. Energy conservation -- Fiction 5. Business enterprises -- Fiction
ISBN 978-0-06-169229-1; 0-06-169229-8; 978-0-06-169233-8 lib bdg; 0-06-169233-6 lib bdg
LC 2009-24339
This novel concerns "the trials and tribulations of 14-year-old Dewey Mariss and his family. His parents are away from home, unable to return because of a gasoline shortage. Running their small family business, the Bike Barn, with his younger brother and helping older sister Lil look after the five-year-old twins keeps Dewey plenty busy. . . . Characters are colorful but believable, dialogue crisp and amusing. The New England setting is attractively realized, and the underlying energy crisis treated seriously but not sensationally." Kirkus

Dead on town line; illustrations by Gina Triplett. Dial Books 2005 131p il $15.99
Grades: 7 8 9 10   **Fic**
1. Ghost stories 2. Homicide -- Fiction
ISBN 0-8037-3021-7
LC 2004-15312
"Cassie's body lies hidden in a crevice, where she tries to figure out what happens next. She meets the ghost of Birdie, another murdered girl who was hidden in the same crevice years earlier. . . . Each verse/chapter adds a piece to the puzzle of Cassie's death until her body is found and the crime is solved. . . . This is an absorbing and moving story." SLJ

★ **Waiting** for normal. Katherine Tegen Books 2008 290p $16.99; lib bdg $17.89
Grades: 5 6 7 8   **Fic**
1. Mothers -- Fiction 2. Family life -- Fiction
ISBN 978-0-06-089088-9; 0-06-089088-6; 978-0-06-089089-6 lib bdg; 0-06-089089-4 lib bdg
LC 2007-06881
Twelve-year-old Addie tries to cope with her mother's erratic behavior and being separated from her beloved stepfather and half-sisters when she and her mother go to live in a small trailer by the railroad tracks on the outskirts of Schenectady, New York.
"Connor . . . treats the subject of child neglect with honesty and grace in this poignant story. . . . Characters as persuasively optimistic as Addie are rare, and readers will gravitate to her." Publ Wkly

Conrad, Pam
★ **My** Daniel. Harper & Row 1989 137p pa $5.99
Grades: 5 6 7 8   **Fic**
1. Nebraska -- Fiction
ISBN 0-06-440309-2 pa
LC 88-19850
"Rendering scenes from both the past and the present with equal skill, Conrad is at the peak of her storytelling powers." Publ Wkly

Constable, Kate
The **singer** of all songs. Arthur A. Levine Books 2004 297p hardcover o.p. pa $6.99

Grades: 7 8 9 10   **Fic**
1. Fantasy fiction 2. Magic -- Fiction
ISBN 0-439-55478-0; 0-439-55479-9 pa
                                        LC 2003-9034
First published 2002 in Australia

Calwyn, a young priestess of ice magic, or chantment, joins with other chanters who have different magical skills to fight a sorcerer who wants to claim all powers for his own

"An impressive debut by an author who clearly has much to contribute to the fantasy genre." Booklist

Other available titles in this series are:
The waterless sea (2005)
The tenth power (2006)

Coombs, Kate

★ The **runaway** princess. Farrar, Straus and Giroux 2006 279p $17
Grades: 5 6 7 8   **Fic**
1. Fairy tales 2. Dragons -- Fiction 3. Princesses -- Fiction
ISBN 0-374-35546-0
                                        LC 2005-51225
Fifteen-year-old Princess Meg uses magic and her wits to rescue a baby dragon and escape the unwanted attentions of princes hoping to gain her hand in marriage through a contest arranged by her father, the king.

"This witty, humorous tale will be popular with fantasy buffs who enjoy takeoffs on fairy tales." Booklist

Another title about Princess Meg is:
The runaway dragon (2009)

Cooney, Caroline B., 1947-

Code orange. Delacorte 2005 200p hardcover o.p. pa $6.99
Grades: 7 8 9 10   **Fic**
1. School stories 2. Smallpox -- Fiction
ISBN 0-385-90277-8; 0-385-73260-0 pa
                                        LC 2004-26422
While conducting research for a school paper on smallpox, Mitty finds an envelope containing 100-year-old smallpox scabs and fears that he has infected himself and all of New York City.

"Readers won't soon forget either the profoundly disturbing premise of this page-turner or its likable, ultimately heroic slacker protagonist." Booklist

Diamonds in the shadow. Delacorte Press 2007 228p $15.99; pa $8.99
Grades: 7 8 9 10 11 12   **Fic**
1. Refugees -- Fiction 2. Family life -- Fiction 3. Africans -- United States -- Fiction
ISBN 978-0-385-73261-1; 978-0-385-73262-8 pa
                                        LC 2006-27811
The Finches, a Connecticut family, sponsor an African refugee family of four, all of whom have been scarred by the horrors of civil war, and who inadvertently put their benefactors in harm's way.

"Tension mounts in a novel that combines thrilling suspense and a story about innocence lost." Booklist

The **face** on the milk carton. Delacorte Press 2006 184p $15.95; pa $6.99

Grades: 7 8 9 10   **Fic**
1. Kidnapping -- Fiction
ISBN 978-0-385-32328-4; 0-385-32328-X; 978-0-440-22065-7 pa; 0-440-22065-3 pa
A reissue of the title first published 1990 by Bantam Books

A photograph of a missing girl on a milk carton leads Janie on a search for her real identity.

Cooney "demonstrates an excellent ear for dialogue and a gift for portraying responsible middle-class teenagers trying to come to terms with very real concerns." SLJ

Hit the road. Delacorte Press 2006 183p $15.95; lib bdg $17.99
Grades: 6 7 8 9   **Fic**
1. Old age -- Fiction 2. Kidnapping -- Fiction 3. Grandmothers -- Fiction 4. Automobile travel -- Fiction
ISBN 0-385-72944-8; 0-385-90174-7 lib bdg
                                        LC 2004-10106
Sixteen-year-old Brittany acts as chauffeur for her grandmother and three other eighty-plus-year-old women going to what is supposedly their college reunion, on a long drive that involves lies, theft, and kidnappings.

"Cooney masterfully combines nonstop, cleverly plotted action with heartfelt emotion." Booklist

If the witness lied. Delacorte Press 2009 213p $16.99; lib bdg $19.99
Grades: 6 7 8 9 10   **Fic**
1. Orphans -- Fiction 2. Siblings -- Fiction 3. Bereavement -- Fiction
ISBN 978-0-385-73448-6; 0-385-73448-4; 978-0-385-90451-3 lib bdg; 0-385-90451-7 lib bdg
                                        LC 2008-23959
Torn apart by tragedies and the publicity they brought, siblings Smithy, Jack, and Madison, aged fourteen to sixteen, tap into their parent's courage to pull together and protect their brother Tris, nearly three, from further media exploitation and a much more sinister threat.

"The pacing here is pure gold. Rotating through various perspectives to follow several plot strands . . . Cooney draws out the action, investing it with the slow-motion feel of an impending collision. . . . This family-drama-turned-thriller will have readers racing, heart in throat, to reach the conclusion." Horn Book

Janie face to face; Caroline B. Cooney. Delacorte Press 2013 352 p. (Janie Johnson) (ebk) $20.99; (trade hardcover) $17.99
Grades: 7 8 9 10   **Fic**
1. Love stories 2. Kidnapping -- Fiction 3. Family life -- Fiction 4. Love -- Fiction 5. Identity -- Fiction 6. Authorship -- Fiction 7. Universities and colleges -- Fiction
ISBN 0385742061; 9780375979972; 9780375990397; 9780385742061
                                        LC 2012006145
This book, by Caroline B. Cooney, is the conclusion to the "Janie Johnson" series which begun in 1990. "All will be revealed as readers find out if Janie and Reeve's love has endured, and whether or not the person who brought Janie and

her family so much emotional pain and suffering is brought to justice." (Publisher's note)

Three black swans. Delacorte Press 2010 276p $17.99; lib bdg $20.99

Grades: 7 8 9 10   **Fic**

1. Cousins -- Fiction 2. Sisters -- Fiction 3. Adoption -- Fiction 4. Triplets -- Fiction 5. Impostors and imposture -- Fiction

ISBN 978-0-385-73867-5; 0-385-73867-6; 978-0-385-90741-5 lib bdg; 0-385-90741-9 lib bdg

LC 2009-41990

When sixteen-year-old Missy Vianello decides to try to convince her classmates that her cousin Claire is really her long-lost identical twin, she has no idea that the results of her prank will be so life-changing.

"Cooney's psychologically probing story darts among multiple characters, forming a complex web of mistrust, economic stress, and parental sins that will keep readers guessing." Booklist

The **voice** on the radio. Delacorte Press 1996 183p hardcover o.p. pa $6.99

Grades: 7 8 9 10   **Fic**

1. Radio programs -- Fiction

ISBN 0-385-32213-5; 0-440-21977-9 pa

LC 96-3688

"Janie is a high-school junior and in love with Reeve. She finally feels that her life is somewhat normal and begins to reconcile with her biological family, but the voice on the radio destroys her trust. Cooney plots an engaging and realistic picture of betrayal, commitment, unconditional love, and forgiveness." ALAN

What Janie found. Delacorte Press 2000 181p pa $6.99

Grades: 7 8 9 10   **Fic**

1. Kidnapping -- Fiction 2. Parent-child relationship -- Fiction

ISBN 0-385-32611-4; 0-440-22772-0 pa

LC 99-37409

While still adjusting to the reality of having two families, her birth family and the family into which she was kidnapped as a small child, seventeen-year-old Janie makes a shocking discovery about her long-gone kidnapper

"Readers of the previous books will find this a satisfying closure to the unsettling circumstances of Janie's life." Booklist

Whatever happened to Janie? Delacorte Press 1993 199p hardcover o.p. pa $6.99

Grades: 7 8 9 10   **Fic**

1. Kidnapping -- Fiction

ISBN 0-385-31035-8; 0-440-21924-8 pa

LC 92-32334

The members of two families have their lives disrupted when Jane who had been kidnapped twelve years earlier discovers that the people who raised her are not her biological parents

"However strange the events of this book, the emotions of its characters remain excruciatingly real." Publ Wkly

Cooper, Ilene

Angel in my pocket. Feiwel and Friends 2011 278p $16.99

Grades: 4 5 6 7   **Fic**

1. School stories 2. Charms -- Fiction 3. Loss (Psychology) -- Fiction

ISBN 978-0-312-37014-5; 0-312-37014-8

LC 2010-34756

When seventh-grader Bette finds an angel coin she puts it in her pocket and forgets it but soon the mysterious and kind Gabby moves into her building and helps her face her major losses, and then the coin connects her with three classmates who all find new ways to believe in themselves.

"The characters and setting are lovingly crafted, and readers will be left contemplating the roles of luck, magic, and inner strength in the kids' transformed lives." Publ Wkly

Cooper, Michelle

The **FitzOsbornes** at war; Michelle Cooper. Alfred A. Knopf 2012 560 p. (hardcover) $17.99

Grades: 7 8 9 10   **Fic**

1. Exiles -- Fiction 2. Diaries -- Fiction 3. Historical fiction 4. World War, 1939-1945 -- Fiction 5. War -- Fiction 6. Family life -- England -- Fiction 7. World War, 1939-1945 -- England -- Fiction

ISBN 0375870504; 9780307974044; 9780375870507; 9780375970504

LC 2012009094

In this historical novel, by Michelle Cooper, "Sophie FitzOsborne and the royal family of Montmaray escaped their remote island home when the Nazis attacked. But as war breaks out in England and around the world, nowhere is safe. Sophie fills her journal with tales of a life during wartime. . . . But even as bombs rain down on London, hope springs up, and love blooms for this most endearing princess." (Publisher's note)

The **FitzOsbornes** in exile. Alfred A. Knopf 2011 457p $17.99; lib bdg $20.99

Grades: 7 8 9 10   **Fic**

1. Diaries -- Fiction 2. Princesses -- Fiction 3. Family life -- Fiction

ISBN 0-375-85865-2; 0-375-95865-7 lib bdg; 978-0-375-85865-9; 978-0-375-89802-0 e-book; 978-0-375-95865-6 lib bdg

LC 2010-34706

In this second volume of the Montmaray Journals series, "forced to leave their island kingdom, Sophie FitzOsborne and her eccentric family take shelter in England. . . . Aunt Charlotte is ruthless in her quest to see Sophie and Veronica married off by the end of the Season, Toby is as charming and lazy as ever, Henry is driving her governess to the brink of madness, and the battle of wills between Simon and Veronica continues." (Publisher's note)

"Readers who enjoy their history enriched by immersion into the social milieu of the time period will find this a fascinating, utterly absorbing venture into English society of the late '30s." Bull Cent Child Books

★ A **brief** history of Montmaray. Alfred A. Knopf 2009 296p $16.99; lib bdg $19.99

Grades: 7 8 9 10   **Fic**

1. Diaries -- Fiction 2. Islands -- Fiction 3. Princesses -- Fiction 4. Family life -- Fiction
ISBN 0-375-85864-4; 0-375-95864-9 lib bdg; 978-0-375-85864-2; 978-0-375-95864-9 lib bdg
LC 2008-49800

This book features "Sophie FitzOsborne [who] lives in a crumbling castle in the tiny island kingdom of Montmaray, along with her tomboy younger sister Henry, her beautiful, intellectual cousin Veronica, and Veronica's father, the completely mad King John. When Sophie receives a leather journal for her sixteenth birthday, she decides to write about her life on the island. But it is 1936 and bigger events are on the horizon." (Publisher's note)

"Cooper has crafted a sort of updated Gothic romance where sweeping adventure play equal with fluttering hearts." Booklist

Cooper, Susan

The **Boggart**. Margaret K. McElderry Bks. 1993 196p hardcover o.p. pa $5.99

Grades: 4 5 6 7   **Fic**

1. Supernatural -- Fiction
ISBN 0-689-50576-0; 0-689-86930-4 pa
LC 92-15527

After visiting the castle in Scotland which her family has inherited and returning home to Canada, twelve-year-old Emily finds that she has accidentally brought back with her a boggart, an invisible and mischievous spirit with a fondness for practical jokes

"Using both electronics and theater as metaphors for magic, Cooper has extended the world of high fantasy into contemporary children's lives through scenes superimposing the ordinary and the extraordinary." Bull Cent Child Books

Another title about the Boggart is:
The Boggart and the monster (1997)

★ **Ghost** Hawk; by Susan Cooper. 1st ed. Margaret K. McElderry Books 2013 328 p. map (hardcover) $16.99

Grades: 5 6 7 8   **Fic**

1. Ghosts -- Fiction 2. Survival -- Fiction 3. Coming of age -- Fiction 4. Wampanoag Indians -- Fiction 5. Indians of North America -- Massachusetts -- Fiction
ISBN 1442481412; 9781442481411; 9781442481435
LC 2012039892

This novel by Susan Cooper is "a story of adventure and friendship between a young Native American and a colonial New England settler. Little Hawk is sent into the woods alone [and] if [he] survives three moons by himself, he will be a man. John Wakely is only ten when his father dies, but he has already experienced . . . friendship of the nearby tribes. John sees how quickly the relationships between settlers and natives are deteriorating. His friendship with Little Hawk will put both boys in grave danger." (Publisher's note)

★ **King** of shadows. Margaret K. McElderry Bks. 1999 186p $16; pa $4.99; pa $6.99

Grades: 5 6 7 8   **Fic**

1. Actors -- Fiction 2. Time travel -- Fiction 3. Actors and actresses -- Fiction
ISBN 0-689-82817-9; 0-689-84445-X pa; 9780689844454 pa
LC 98-51127

Boston Globe Horn Book Honor Book (2000)

"Nat Field is thrilled when theater director Richard Babbage chooses him to become a player in the Company of Boys, an American summer drama troupe that will appear in Shakespeare's A Midsummer Night's Dream at the new replica of the Globe Theater in London. Shortly after his arrival in England, though, Nat feels ill and falls into a troubled sleep. To the doctor's astonishment, he seems to be suffering from the effects of the bubonic plague. He awakens in 1599 as another Nat Field, a child actor from St. Paul's School who is about to go to the Globe to rehearse A Midsummer Night's Dream in the role of Puck." (Booklist)

"Cleverly explicating old and new acting and performance techniques, Susan Cooper entertains her contemporary readers while giving them a first-rate theatrical education." N Y Times Book Rev

★ **Over** sea, under stone; illustrated by Margery Gill. Harcourt Brace Jovanovich 1966 252p il $19; pa $5.99

Grades: 5 6 7 8   **Fic**

1. Fantasy fiction 2. Good and evil -- Fiction
ISBN 0-15-259034-X; 0-689-84035-7 pa
First published 1965 in the United Kingdom

Three children on a holiday in Cornwall find an ancient manuscript which sends them on a dangerous quest for a grail that would reveal the true story of King Arthur and that entraps them in the eternal battle between the forces of the Light and the forces of the Dark.

"The air of mysticism and the allegorical quality of the continual contest between good and evil add much value to a fine plot, setting, and characterization." Horn Book

Other titles in this series are:
The dark is rising (1973)
Greenwitch (1974)
The grey king (1975)
Silver on the tree (1977)

Corbett, Sue

Free baseball; [by] Sue Corbett. Dutton Children's Books 2006 152p $15.99; pa $5.99

Grades: 5 6 7 8   **Fic**

1. Baseball -- Fiction 2. Cuban Americans -- Fiction
ISBN 0-525-47120-0; 0-14-241080-2 pa
LC 2005004792

Angry with his mother for having too little time for him, eleven-year-old Felix takes advantage of an opportunity to become bat boy for a minor league baseball team, hoping to someday be like his father, a famous Cuban outfielder. Includes glossaries of baseball terms and Spanish words and phrases

"An engaging, well-written story with a satisfying ending." SLJ

The **last** newspaper boy in America. Dutton Childrens Books 2009 199p $16.99

Grades: 4 5 6 7   **Fic**

1. Mystery fiction 2. Newspaper carriers -- Fiction
ISBN 978-0-525-42205-1; 0-525-42205-6

When the newspaper company cancels his route, Wil David is prepared to fight to get his job back, but his focus changes when he stumbles upon a carnival mystery and a plot by a con man that could destroy the town.

"Corbett's graceful dialogue, lovingly drawn characters and clever plot form a timely and refreshing tale." Publ Wkly

Cormier, Robert

★ **After** the first death. Dell Publishing 1991 233p pa $6.50

Grades: 7 8 9 10   **Fic**

1. Terrorism -- Fiction

ISBN 0-440-20835-1

First published 1979 by Pantheon Bks.

ALA YALSA Margaret A. Edwards Award (1991)

"A busload of children is hijacked by a band of terrorists whose demands include the exposure of a military brainwashing project. The narrative line moves from the teenage terrorist Milo to Kate the bus driver and the involvement of Ben, whose father is the head of the military operation, in this confrontation. The conclusion has a shocking twist." Shapiro. Fic for Youth. 2d edition

Beyond the chocolate war; a novel. Dell 1986 278p pa $6.99

Grades: 9 10 11 12   **Fic**

1. School stories

ISBN 0-440-90580-X

First published 1985

Dark deeds continue at Trinity High School, climaxing in a public demonstration of one student's homemade guillotine. Sequel to "The Chocolate War."

★ **I** am the cheese; a novel. Pantheon Bks. 1977 233p hardcover o.p. pa $6.50

Grades: 7 8 9 10 11 12 Adult   **Fic**

1. Intelligence service -- Fiction

ISBN 0-394-83462-3; 0-440-94060-5 pa

LC 76-55948

ALA YALSA Margaret A. Edwards Award (1991)

"The suspense builds relentlessly to an ending that, although shocking, is entirely plausible." Booklist

"Adam Farmer's mind has blanked out; his past is revealed in bits and pieces—partly by Adam himself, partly through a transcription of Adam's interviews with a government psychiatrist. Adam's father, a newspaper reporter, gave evidence at the trial of a criminal organization which had infiltrated the government itself. He and his family, marked for death, came under the protection of the super-secret Department of Re-Identification, which changed the family's name and kept them under constant surveillance. Now an adolescent, Adam is finally let in on his parents' terrible secret." SLJ

★ The **chocolate** war; a novel. Pantheon Bks. 1974 253p rpt $8.99; $19.95

Grades: 7 8 9 10   **Fic**

1. School stories

ISBN 9780375829871 rpt; 0-394-82805-4

ALA YALSA Margaret A. Edwards Award (1991)

"In the Trinity School for Boys the environment is completely dominated by an underground gang, the Vigils. During a chocolate candy sale Brother Leon, the acting headmaster of the school, defers to the Vigils, who reign with terror in the school. Jerry Renault is first a pawn for the Vigils' evil deeds and finally their victim." Shapiro. Fic for Youth. 3d edition

Cornish, D. M.

Factotum. Putnam Pub. 2010 684p (Monster blood tattoo) $19.99

Grades: 8 9 10 11 12   **Fic**

1. Fantasy fiction 2. Orphans -- Fiction 3. Monsters -- Fiction 4. Tattooing -- Fiction

ISBN 978-0-399-24640-1; 0-399-24640-1

Accused of being a monster instead of human, Rossamünd Bookchild looks to monster-hunter Branden Rose for help, but powerful forces are after them both, believing that Rossamünd holds the secret to perpetual youth.

"Along with many splendid names . . . and linguistic fancies . . . the author laces his rococo but fluent narrative with moral and ethical conundrums, twists both terrible and tongue in cheek, startling revelations about humans and 'monsters' alike and sturdy themes of loyalty, courage and self-realization. Readers new to the series should start with the first volume; fans will be more than satisfied." Kirkus

Cornwell, Autumn

★ **Carpe** diem. Feiwel & Friends 2007 360p $16.95; pa $8.99

Grades: 7 8 9 10   **Fic**

1. Artists -- Fiction 2. Authorship -- Fiction 3. Grandmothers -- Fiction

ISBN 0-312-36792-9; 978-0-312-36792-3; 978-0-312-56129-1 pa; 0-312-56129-6 pa

LC 2006-32054

Sixteen-year-old Vassar Spore's detailed plans for the next twenty years of her life are derailed when her bohemian grandmother insists that she join her in Southeast Asia for the summer, but as she writes a novel about her experiences, Vassar discovers new possibilities.

"Suspenseful and wonderfully detailed, the well-crafted story maintains its page-turning pace while adding small doses of insight and humor." SLJ

Correa, Shan

Gaff; written by Shan Correa. Peachtree 2010 212p $15.95

Grades: 4 5 6 7   **Fic**

1. Roosters -- Fiction 2. Animal welfare -- Fiction

ISBN 978-1-56145-526-3; 1-56145-526-1

In Hawaii, thirteen-year-old Paul Silva is determined to find a way to get his family out of the illegal cockfighting business.

"Correa's debut evokes the lush melange of sights, sounds and smells in 13-year-old Paulie's multicultural neighborhood in Hawaii. . . . Also woven into this ethical debate, rooted in economics and traditions, is Hawaiian pidgin English, which may challenge even experienced readers. . . . A fascinating look at the United States most mainlanders have never seen." Kirkus

Corrigan, Eireann

★ **Accomplice**. Scholastic Press 2010 296p $17.99

Grades: 7 8 9 10   **Fic**
1. School stories 2. Fraud -- Fiction 3. Friendship
-- Fiction
ISBN 978-0-545-05236-8; 0-545-05236-X
LC 2009-53869

High school juniors and best friends Finn and Chloe
hatch a daring plot to fake Chloe's disappearance from their
rural New Jersey town in order to have something compelling to put on their college applications, but unforeseen
events complicate matters.

"Corrigan has crafted a complex, heart-wrenchingly
plausible YA thriller. . . . A fascinating character study of
individuals and an entire town, this tension-filled story will
entice readers with a single booktalk." Booklist

Cotler, Steve

Cheesie Mack is cool in a duel; Steve Cotler ; illustrated by Adam McCauley. Random House 2012
229 p. (hardcover library binding) $18.99
Grades: 4 5 6   **Fic**
1. Camps -- Fiction 2. Siblings -- Fiction 3.
Interpersonal relations -- Fiction 4. Contests -- Fiction
ISBN 9780375864384; 9780375895715;
9780375964381
LC 2011016921

This book is the second in the Cheesie Mack series.
"Ronald 'Cheesie' Mack and his best friend Georgie secured the funds to go to summer camp on Bufflehead Lake
in Maine. Days later, the duo climbs aboard a bus and head
off to Camp Windward. Unfortunately Cheesie's older sister,
June . . . will be none too far away at Camp Leeward. . . . T late
registration results in both boys being stuck in a cabin with
the older guys... including Kevin, [June"]s boyfriend. When
Kevin gives Cheesie a hard time once too often, Cheesie suggests a Cool Duel. Each night the boys in the cabin will vote
on who did the coolest thing; in a week, the loser will have to
embarrass himself in front of the whole camp by bowing to
the winner. Can Cheesie prevail and still have fun at the camp
he worked so hard to attend?" (Kirkus Reviews)

Cheesie Mack is not a genius or anything; illustrated by Adam McCauley. Random House 2011
229p il $15.99; lib bdg $18.99
Grades: 4 5 6   **Fic**
1. Mystery fiction 2. Summer -- Fiction 3. Friendship
-- Fiction
ISBN 978-0-375-86437-7; 0-375-86437-7; 978-0-375-
96437-4 lib bdg; 0-375-96437-1 lib bdg; 978-0-375-
89570-8 e-book
LC 2009-33329

Ronald, aka Cheesie, Mack and his best friend Georgie
find opportunies for summertime mischief "when Georgie
finds a nearly century-old letter containing a worn penny
and a locket, a mystery that eventually leads the pals to the
Haunted Toad, a local rundown mansion. . . . Cheesie's . . .
easygoing, accessible voice will certainly appeal to middle-
grade readers. . . . The action . . . is all fun and games. . . .
A light-hearted and fast-moving read for kids looking for
middle-school shenanigans." Bull Cent Child Books

Cheesie Mack is running like crazy! by Steve
Cotler ; illustrated by Douglas Holgate. 1st ed.
Random House Inc. 2013 256 p. ill. (hardcover)

$15.99; (library) $18.99; (ebook) $47.97; (paper-
back) $6.99
Grades: 4 5 6   **Fic**
1. Schools -- Fiction 2. Elections -- Fiction 3.
Friendship -- Fiction 4. Best friends -- Fiction 5.
Middle schools -- Fiction 6. Track and field -- Fiction
7. Brothers and sisters -- Fiction
ISBN 0307977145; 9780307977137; 9780307977144;
9780307977151; 9780307977168
LC 2012017978

In this book by Steve Colter, "Cheesie and his best
friend, Georgie, are off to the middle school, where there
will be lots of new kids and new teachers. Cheesie has a
terrific idea--what better way to meet all the new kids than
to run for class president? Plus, if he wins, it'll drive his evil
older sister nuts! Then Cheesie gets bad news. One of his
friends from his old school is also running for president."
(Publisher's note

Cottrell Boyce, Frank

★ **Cosmic**. Walden Pond Press 2010 311p
$16.99; lib bdg $17.89
Grades: 4 5 6 7   **Fic**
1. Size -- Fiction 2. Outer space -- Exploration --
Fiction
ISBN 978-0-06-183683-1; 0-06-183683-4; 978-0-06-
183686-2 lib bdg; 0-06-183686-9 lib bdg
LC 2008277816

Boyce "knows how to tell a compellingly good story.
But in his latest extravagantly imaginative and marvelously
good-natured novel he has also written one that is bound to
win readers' hearts." Booklist

Framed. HarperCollins 2006 306p $16.99; lib
bdg $17.89; pa $6.99
Grades: 5 6 7 8   **Fic**
1. Art -- Fiction 2. Automobiles -- Fiction 3. Family
life -- Fiction 4. Business enterprises -- Fiction
ISBN 0-06-073402-7; 0-06-073403-5 lib bdg; 0-06-
073404-3 pa
LC 2006-00557

Dylan and his sisters have some ideas about how to
make Snowdonia Oasis Auto Marvel into a more profitable
business, but it is not until some strange men arrive in their
small town of Manod, Wales with valuable paintings, and
their father disappears, that they consider turning to crime.

"The colorful characters steal the show—even the secondary players are cleverly drawn. But it is Dylan's narrative
voice . . . that is truly a masterpiece." SLJ

★ The **un** -forgotten coat. Candlewick Press
2011 92p il $15.99
Grades: 5 6 7 8 9   **Fic**
1. Refugees -- Fiction 2. Immigrants -- Fiction
ISBN 978-0-7636-5729-1; 0-7636-5729-8
LC 2010048224

"Funny, sad, haunting and original, Cottrell Boyce's story leaves important elements unexpressed. . . . To complete
the narrative, readers must actively participate. They'll find
myriad paths to follow—immigration, demons, social networking, the mystery of cultural difference and the nature of
enchantment. A tricky, magical delight." Kirkus

Couloumbis, Audrey

★ **Love** me tender. Random House 2008 209p $16.99; lib bdg $19.99; pa $6.50

Grades: 5 6 7 8 **Fic**
1. Pregnancy -- Fiction 2. Family life -- Fiction 3. Grandmothers -- Fiction
ISBN 978-0-375-83839-2; 0-375-83839-2; 978-0-375-93839-9 lib bdg; 0-375-93839-7 lib bdg; 978-0-375-83840-8 pa; 0-375-83840-6 pa

LC 2006033162

Thirteen-year-old Elvira worries about her future when, after a fight, her father heads to Las Vegas for an Elvis impersonator competition and her pregnant mother takes her and her younger sister to Memphis to visit a grandmother the girls have never met.

"Tart characterizations, lively dialogue and Elvira's frank narration keep this perceptive novel both credible and buoyant." Publ Wkly

Maude March on the run! or, Trouble is her middle name. Random House 2007 309p $15.99; lib bdg $17.99

Grades: 4 5 6 7 **Fic**
1. Adventure fiction 2. Orphans -- Fiction 3. Frontier and pioneer life -- Fiction
ISBN 978-0-375-83246-8; 978-0-375-93246-5 lib bdg; 978-0-375-83248-2 pa

LC 2005036133

Due to a misunderstanding over her involvement in a botched robbery, Maude, with younger sister Sallie, hides out at the home of an uncle, but when she is discovered and arrested, the orphaned sisters flee, trying to clear Maude's name.

"The excitement of the Wild West comes to life in this action-packed sequel to The Misadventures of Maude March." SLJ

★ **War** games; a novel based on a true story. [by] Audrey Couloumbis & Akila Couloumbis. Random House Children's Books 2009 232p $16.99; lib bdg $19.99

Grades: 5 6 7 8 **Fic**
1. Cousins -- Fiction 2. Brothers -- Fiction 3. World War, 1939-1945 -- Underground movements -- Fiction
ISBN 978-0-375-85628-0; 0-375-85628-5; 978-0-375-95628-7 lib bdg; 0-375-95628-X lib bdg

LC 2008-46784

"For 12-year-old Petros, World War II feels unreal and far away. . . . But when the Germans invade Greece, the war suddenly comes impossibly close. Overnight, neighbors become enemies. People begin to keep secrets (Petros's family most of all). And for the first time, Petros has the chance to show Zola that he"s not just a little brother but that he can truly be counted on." (Publisher's note)

"The climactic violence is believable, and the resolution—though it takes place offstage—is deeply satisfying. Memorable." SLJ

★ The **misadventures** of Maude March; or, Trouble rides a fast horse. [by] Audrey Couloumbis.

Random House 2005 295p hardcover o.p. lib bdg $17.99; pa $7.50

Grades: 4 5 6 7 **Fic**
1. Adventure fiction 2. Orphans -- Fiction 3. Frontier and pioneer life -- Fiction
ISBN 0-375-83245-9; 0-375-93245-3 lib bdg; 0-375-83247-5 pa

LC 2004-16464

After the death of the stern aunt who raised them since they were orphaned, eleven-year-old Sallie and her fifteen-year-old sister escape their self-serving guardians and begin an adventure resembling those in the dime novels Sallie loves to read.

"Sallie's narration is delightful, with understatements that are laugh-out-loud hilarious. . . . Hard to put down, and a fun read-aloud." SLJ

Couvillon, Jacques

The **chicken** dance; [by] Jacques Couvillon. 1st U.S. ed.; Bloomsbury Children's Books 2007 326p $16.95

Grades: 6 7 8 9 **Fic**
1. Chickens -- Fiction 2. Family life -- Fiction 3. Country life -- Fiction
ISBN 978-1-59990-043-8; 1-59990-043-2

LC 2006102093

When eleven-year-old Don Schmidt wins a chicken-judging contest in his small town of Horse Island, Louisiana and goes from outcast to instant celebrity, even his neglectful mother occasionally takes notice of him and eventually he discovers some shocking family secrets.

"A funny, sometimes poignant novel. . . . [This offers] strong characters, interesting concepts, and a deft comedic touch." SLJ

Coventry, Susan

The **queen's** daughter. Henry Holt and Company 2010 373p map $16.99

Grades: 8 9 10 11 12 **Fic**
1. Queens 2. Princesses -- Fiction 3. Middle Ages -- Fiction
ISBN 978-0-8050-8992-9; 0-8050-8992-6

LC 2009-24154

A fictionalized biography of Joan of England, the youngest child of King Henry II of England and his queen consort, Eleanor of Aquitaine, chronicling her complicated relationships with her warring parents and many siblings, particularly with her favorite brother Richard the Lionheart, her years as Queen consort of Sicily, and her second marriage to Raymond VI, Count of Toulouse.

"Fans of historical fiction, and especially historical romance, will devour this volume." SLJ

Coville, Bruce

★ **Aliens** ate my homework; illustrated by Katherine Coville. Pocket Bks. 1993 179p il hardcover o.p. pa $5.99

Grades: 4 5 6 **Fic**
1. Science fiction 2. Extraterrestrial beings -- Fiction
ISBN 1-4169-3883-4 pa

LC 93-3945

Rod is surprised when a miniature spaceship lands in his school science project and reveals five tiny aliens, who ask his help in apprehending an interstellar criminal

"A funny and suspenseful romp, with appealing illustrations throughout." Horn Book Guide

Other titles in this series are:

Aliens stole my body (1998)

I left my sneakers in dimension X (1994)

The search for Snout (1995)

★ **Juliet** Dove, Queen of Love; a magic shop book. Harcourt 2003 190p $17; pa $5.95

Grades: 4 5 6   **Fic**

1. Magic -- Fiction 2. Classical mythology -- Fiction

ISBN 0-15-204561-9; 0-15-205217-8 pa

LC 2003-11846

A shy twelve-year-old girl must solve a puzzle involving characters from Greek mythology to free herself from a spell which makes her irresistible to boys

"Although humorous, the story has surprising depth. . . . Coville capably interweaves mythological characters with realistic modern ones, keeping readers truly absorbed." SLJ

The **monster's** ring; by Bruce Coville ; illustrated by Katherine Coville. Harcourt Brace & Co. 2002 105 p. ill. (reinforced) $16

Grades: 4 5 6   **Fic**

1. Magic -- Fiction 2. Bullies -- Fiction 3. Schools -- Fiction 4. Monsters -- Fiction 5. Halloween -- Fiction

ISBN 0152046186; 9780152046187

LC 2002003537

In this book by Bruce Coville, "Russell, the main character, has problems with the class bully. But then Russell gets a magic ring from a mysterious magic shop. He isn't careful with the ring's directions, and this leads to big problems." Namely, Russell begins turning into a monster. (Scholastic News)

The **monsters** of Morley Manor. Harcourt 2001 224p $16; pa $5.95

Grades: 4 5 6   **Fic**

1. Science fiction 2. Monsters -- Fiction 3. Extraterrestrial beings -- Fiction

ISBN 0-15-216382-4; 0-15-204705-0 pa

LC 00-12912

Anthony and his younger sister discover that the monster figures he got in an unusual box at an estate sale are alive, but they have no way of knowing that the "monsters" will lead them on fantastical adventures to other worlds in an effort to try to save Earth

"Coville's rollicking tale has an unbelievable plot and exaggerated characters, but this is exactly what makes it so entertaining." Horn Book Guide

★ The **skull** of truth; a magic shop book. illustrated by Gary A. Lippincott. Harcourt Brace & Co. 1997 195p il $17

Grades: 4 5 6 7   **Fic**

1. Fantasy fiction 2. Truthfulness and falsehood -- Fiction

ISBN 0-15-275457-1

LC 97-9264

Charlie, a sixth-grader with a compulsion to tell lies, acquires a mysterious skull that forces its owner to tell only the truth, causing some awkward moments before he understands its power

"Coville has structured the story very carefully, with a great deal of sensitivity to children's thought processes and emotions. The mood shifts from scary to funny to serious are fused with understandable language and sentence structures." SLJ

Cowing, Sue

You will call me Drog. Carolrhoda Books 2011 281p $16.95

Grades: 4 5 6 7   **Fic**

1. Aikido -- Fiction 2. Divorce -- Fiction 3. Supernatural -- Fiction 4. Puppets and puppet plays -- Fiction

ISBN 978-0-7613-6076-6; 0-7613-6076-X

LC 2010050891

Unless eleven-year-old Parker can find a way to remove the sinister puppet that refuses to leave his hand, he will wind up in military school or worse but first he must stand up for himself to his best friend Wren, his mother, and his nearly-absent father.

"There is nothing else out there quite like this, and Cowing shifts fluidly from sensitive drama to startling violence to high comedy. . . . A unique look at speaking your mind." Booklist

Cox, Suzy

The **Dead** Girls Detective Agency; Suzy Cox. Harper 2012 355 p. (trade bdg.) $9.99

Grades: 7 8 9 10   **Fic**

1. Dead -- Fiction 2. Murder -- Fiction 3. Mystery and detective stories

ISBN 0-06-202064-1; 9780062020642

LC 2012006567

This novel, by Suzy Cox, follows the ghost of a teenager seeking to solve her own murder. "Meet the Dead Girls Detective Agency: Nancy, Lorna, and Tess--not to mention Edison, the really cute if slightly hostile dead boy. Apparently, the only way out of this limbo is to figure out who killed me, or I'll have to spend eternity playing Nancy Drew. Considering I was fairly invisible in life, who could hate me enough to want me dead? And what if my murderer is someone I never would have suspected?" (Publisher's note)

Coy, John

★ **Box** out. Scholastic Press 2008 276p $16.99

Grades: 6 7 8 9 10   **Fic**

1. School stories 2. Prayer -- Fiction 3. Basketball -- Fiction

ISBN 978-0-439-87032-0; 0-439-87032-1

LC 2007-45354

High school sophomore Liam jeopardizes his new position on the varsity basketball team when he decides to take a stand against his coach who is leading prayers before games and enforcing teamwide participation.

"Plainly acquainted with teenagers and well as b-ball play and lingo, Coy adds subplots and supporting characters to give Liam's life dimension, but he weaves plenty of breathlessly compelling game action too." Booklist

★ **Crackback**. Scholastic 2005 201p $16.99

Grades: 7 8 9 10 **Fic**

1. School stories 2. Football -- Fiction 3. Drug abuse
-- Fiction 4. Father-son relationship -- Fiction
ISBN 0-439-69733-6

LC 2004-30972

Miles barely recalls when football was fun after being
sidelined by a new coach, constantly criticized by his father, and pressured by his best friend to take performance-
enhancing drugs.

The author "writes a moving, nuanced portrait of a teen
struggling with adults who demand, but don't always deserve, respect." Booklist

Love of the game. Feiwel and Friends 2011
182p $16.99

Grades: 4 5 6 7 **Fic**

1. School stories 2. Football -- Fiction 3. Family life
-- Fiction
ISBN 978-0-312-37331-3; 0-312-37331-7

LC 2010050897

Sixth-grader Jackson has a rough start in middle school,
with bullies on the bus, few classes with his friends, and
changes at home but some good teachers, meeting a girl,
joining a club, and playing football soon turn things around.

"Realistic characters, believable dialogue and a genuine
feel for the rhythms and issues of middle-schoolers make
this a satisfying addition to a solid middle-grade set." Kirkus

Craig, Colleen

★ **Afrika**. Tundra Books 2008 233p pa $9.95

Grades: 7 8 9 10 **Fic**

1. Fathers -- Fiction 2. Mothers -- Fiction
ISBN 978-0-88776-807-1; 0-88776-807-5

"Growing up in Canada with her white South African
mother, Kim van der Merwe does not know who her father
is. Now, at 13, she goes to Cape Town for the first time,
shortly after independence in the mid-1990s, because her
mother, a journalist, is going to report on the Truth and Reconciliation Commission. . . . Visiting and meeting her family for the first time, she decides that her mission will be to
discover her father's identity. . . . . The realities of the society
are carefully and skillfully portrayed, so that Kim's story is
truly the emotional heart of the book, and not a vehicle for
ideas." SLJ

Crane, Dede

Poster boy. Groundwood Books 2009 214p
$18.95

Grades: 8 9 10 11 **Fic**

1. Cancer -- Fiction 2. Siblings -- Fiction 3. Family
life -- Fiction
ISBN 978-0-88899-855-2; 0-88899-855-4

"Cruising along on the fringes of stoner life is cool with
16-year-old Gray Fallon. . . . Life's all good until Gray's
younger sister, 12-year-old Maggie, begins to complain
about aches in her legs and arms. It's a rare form of terminal cancer. . . . Crane effectively shows a family unraveling, and Gray's authentic teen narration springs from the
pages." Kirkus

Crane, E. M.

Skin deep; [by] E. M. Crane. Delacorte Press
2008 273p $16.99; lib bdg $19.99

Grades: 7 8 9 10 11 12 **Fic**

1. Dogs -- Fiction 2. Death -- Fiction 3. Friendship
-- Fiction
ISBN 978-0-385-73479-0; 0-385-73479-4; 978-0-385-
90477-3 lib bdg; 0-385-90477-0 lib bdg

When sixteen-year-old Andrea Anderson begins caring
for a sick neighbor's dog, she learns a lot about life, death,
pottery, friendship, hope, and love.

"Teenage girls who can empathize with Andrea's journey of self-discovery and its triumphs and losses will find
a well-written story, with lyrical explorations of nature, and
memorable characters." Voice Youth Advocates

Crawford, Brent

★ **Carter** finally gets it. Disney Hyperion Books
2009 300p $15.99; pa $8.99

Grades: 7 8 9 10 **Fic**

1. School stories
ISBN 978-1-4231-1246-4; 1-4231-1246-6; 978-1-
4231-1247-1 pa; 1-4231-1247-4 pa

LC 2008-46541

Awkward freshman Will Carter endures many painful
moments during his first year of high school before realizing
that nothing good comes easily, focus is everything, and the
payoff is usually incredible.

"Crawford expertly channels his inner 14-year-old for
this pitch-perfect comedy. . . . His stream-consciousness,
first-person narrative flails around in an excellent imitation
of a freshman." Booklist

Carter's big break. Hyperion 2010 231p
$15.99; pa $8.99

Grades: 8 9 10 11 12 **Fic**

1. Actors -- Fiction 2. Drug abuse -- Fiction 3. Self-
perception -- Fiction 4. Motion pictures -- Production
and direction -- Fiction
ISBN 978-1-4231-1243-3; 1-4231-1243-3; 978-1-
4231-1244-0 pa; 1-4231-1244-X pa

LC 2010-5040

Fourteen-year-old Will Carter's summer gets off to a bad
start when his girlfriend leaves him, but then he is cast opposite a major star, Hilary Idaho, in a small movie being filmed
in his town and things start looking up.

"This fast and fun read will definitely appeal to reluctant readers who want to see the underdog succeed in life
and love. A must-have, especially where the first book is
popular." SLJ

Carter's unfocused, one-track mind; a novel. by
Brent Crawford. Hyperion 2012 296 p. (Carter)
(hardback) $16.99

Grades: 7 8 9 10 **Fic**

1. High school students -- Fiction 2. Schools -- Fiction
3. High schools -- Fiction 4. Self-perception -- Fiction
5. Dating (Social customs) -- Fiction 6. Interpersonal
relations -- Fiction
ISBN 1423144457; 9781423144458

LC 2012001231

This young adult novel, by Brent Crawford, is the third book in the author's "Carter" series. "After an eventful freshman year and disastrous summer, fifteen-year-old Will Carter returns to Merrian High none the wiser. His sophomore year will present a host of new problems. . . . When Abby announces that she might be transferring to a New York arts school, Carter's world is turned upside down and he'll be forced to make the biggest decision of his life." (Publisher's note)

Creech, Sharon

Absolutely normal chaos. HarperCollins Pubs. 1995 230p $16.99; pa $5.99

Grades: 5 6 7 8   Fic

1. Family life -- Fiction

ISBN 0-06-026989-8; 0-06-440632-6 pa

LC 95-22448

First published 1990 in the United Kingdom

"Those in search of a light, humorous read will find it; those in search of something a little deeper will also be rewarded." SLJ

Bloomability. HarperCollins Pubs. 1998 273p hardcover o.p. pa $5.99

Grades: 5 6 7 8   Fic

1. School stories

ISBN 0-06-026993-6; 0-06-440823-X pa

LC 98-14601

When her aunt and uncle take her from New Mexico to Lugano, Switzerland, to attend an international school, thirteen-year-old Dinnie discovers her world expanding

"As if fresh, smart characters in a picturesque setting weren't engaging enough, Creech also poses an array of knotty questions, both personal and philosophical. . . . A story to stimulate both head and heart." Booklist

The **Castle** Corona; illuminated by David Diaz. Joanna Cotler Books 2007 320p il $18.99; lib bdg $19.89; pa $7.99

Grades: 4 5 6 7   Fic

1. Orphans -- Fiction 2. Siblings -- Fiction 3. Kings and rulers -- Fiction

ISBN 978-0-06-084621-3; 0-06-084621-6; 978-0-06-084622-0 lib bdg; 0-06-084622-4 lib bdg; 978-0-06-084623-7 pa; 0-06-084623-2 pa

LC 2006-32004

Two orphaned peasant children discover a mysterious pouch, the contents of which lead them to the majestic Castle Corona, where their lives may be transformed forever.

"The engaging, puzzle-like plot will attract readers, as the novel's heady themes, from wisdom to empathy to the fate-changing power of story, prompt them to deeper thought. Diaz's full-color chapter-heading artwork and ornamental flourishes lend the novel substantial aesthetic appeal." Booklist

Love that dog. HarperCollins Pubs. 2001 86p $15.99; lib bdg $14.89; pa $5.99

Grades: 4 5 6 7   Fic

1. Poetry 2. School stories 3. Poetry -- Fiction

ISBN 0-06-029287-3; 0-06-029289-X lib bdg; 0-06-440959-7 pa

LC 00-54233

"Creech has created a poignant, funny picture of a child's encounter with the power of poetry. . . . This book is a tiny treasure." SLJ

Another title about Jack is:

Hate that cat (2008)

Replay; a new book. Joanna Cotler Books 2005 $15.99; pa $5.99

Grades: 5 6 7 8   Fic

1. Theater -- Fiction 2. Family life -- Fiction 3. Italian Americans -- Fiction

ISBN 0-06-054019-2; 0-06-054021-4 pa

While preparing for a role in the school play, twelve-year-old Leo finds an autobiography that his father wrote as a teenager and ponders the ways people change as they grow up. Includes the text for the play, "Rumpopo's Porch."

"Both uproarious and tender, this story . . . captures [Leo's] big, noisy, extended Italian family with pitch-perfect dialogue that will sweep readers right to the end of the story." Booklist

★ **Walk** two moons. HarperCollins Pubs. 1994 280p $16.99; lib bdg $17.89; pa $6.99

Grades: 6 7 8 9   Fic

1. Death -- Fiction 2. Friendship -- Fiction 3. Family life -- Fiction 4. Grandparents -- Fiction

ISBN 0-06-023334-6; 0-06-023337-0 lib bdg; 0-06-440517-6 pa

LC 93-31277

Awarded the Newbery Medal, 1995

After her mother leaves home suddenly, thirteen-year-old Sal and her grandparents take a car trip retracing her mother's route. Along the way, Sal recounts the story of her friend Phoebe, whose mother also left

"An engaging story of love and loss, told with humor and suspense. . . . A richly layered novel about real and metaphorical journeys." SLJ

The **great** unexpected; Sharon Creech ; edited by Alyson Day. HarperCollins 2012 240 p. (lib. bdg.) $17.89

Grades: 4 5 6 7   Fic

1. Ireland -- Fiction 2. Orphans -- Fiction 3. Friendship -- Fiction

ISBN 0061892335; 9780061892325; 9780061892332

LC 2012942431

In this book by Sharon Creech, "best friends and orphans Naomi Deane and Lizzie Scatterding are surprised when a strange boy falls out of a tree in their little town of Blackbird Tree, USA. His name is Finn, and Naomi falls immediately under his spell. . . . Meanwhile, in Ireland, an old woman and her companion talk of murder and revenge." (Horn Book Magazine)

★ The **unfinished** angel. Joanna Cotler Books 2009 164p

Grades: 4 5 6   **Fic**
1. Angels -- Fiction 2. Orphans -- Fiction 3. Villages -- Fiction 4. Young adult literature -- Works 5. Children's literature -- Works -- Grades two through six
ISBN 0-06-143095-1; 0-06-143096-X lib bdg; 0-06-143097-8 pa; 978-0-06-143095-4; 978-0-06-143096-1 lib bdg; 978-0-06-143097-8 pa
                                        LC 2009-02796
In a tiny village in the Swiss Alps, an angel meets an American girl named Zola who has come with her father to open a school, and together Zola and the angel rescue a group of homeless orphans. "Ages eight to twelve." (Publisher's note)

"Some books are absolute magic, and this is one of them. . . . Creech's protagonist is hugely likable. . . . Creech's offering deserves to be read out loud and more than once to truly enjoy the angel's hilarious malapropisms and outright invented words, and to appreciate the book's tender, comical celebration of the human spirit." SLJ

Cremer, Andrea
Invisibility; Andrea Cremer and David Levithan. Philomel Books 2013 320 p. (hardcover) $18.99
Grades: 7 8 9 10 11 12   **Fic**
1. Love -- Fiction 2. Invisibility -- Fiction 3. Magic -- Fiction 4. Charms -- Fiction 5. Friendship -- Fiction 6. Family problems -- Fiction
ISBN 0399257608; 9780399257605
                                        LC 2012024514
This book by Andrea Cremer and David Levithan chronicles the "romance between a boy cursed with invisibility and the one girl who can see him. . . . Stephen is used to invisibility. He was born that way. . . . Elizabeth sometimes wishes for invisibility. . . . To Stephen"s amazement, she can see him. And to Elizabeth"s amazement, she wants him to be able to see her--all of her. But as the two become closer, an invisible world gets in their way." (Publisher's note)

"hough it begins as a stumbling, near–coming-out story (for Stephen), the novel deftly switches gears to a fast-paced supernatural thriller that will surely leave readers wanting more." Kirkus

Crewe, Megan
Give up the ghost. Henry Holt and Co. 2009 244p $17.99
Grades: 7 8 9 10   **Fic**
1. Ghost stories 2. School stories 3. Sisters -- Fiction 4. Bereavement -- Fiction
ISBN 978-0-8050-8930-1; 0-8050-8930-6
                                        LC 2008-50274
Sixteen-year-old Cass's only friends are her dead sister and the school ghosts who feed her gossip that she uses to make students face up to their bad behavior, but when a popular boy asks for her help, she begins to reach out to the living again.

The story "provides page-turning action. . . . Mysterious plot elements and the budding relationship between Cass and the VP will quickly engage reluctant readers." Publ Wkly

The **lives** we lost; a Way we fall novel. Megan Crewe. Hyperion 2013 288 p. (The fallen world) (alk. paper) $16.99

Grades: 7 8 9 10 11 12   **Fic**
1. Science fiction 2. Epidemics -- Fiction 3. Survival skills -- Fiction 4. Survival -- Fiction 5. Virus diseases -- Fiction
ISBN 1423146174; 9781423146179
                                        LC 2012032510
This novel, by Megan Crewe, is book two of "The Fallen World Trilogy." "A deadly virus has destroyed Kaelyn's small island community and spread beyond the quarantine. No one is safe. But when Kaelyn finds samples of a vaccine in her father's abandoned lab, she knows there must be someone, somewhere, who can replicate it. . . . How much will Kaelyn risk for an unproven cure, when the search could either destroy those she loves or save the human race?" (Publisher's note)

Crichton, Michael
Jurassic Park; a novel. Knopf 1990 399p $28.95; pa $7.99
Grades: 7 8 9 10 11 12 Adult   **Fic**
1. Science fiction 2. Dinosaurs -- Fiction 3. Scientists -- Fiction 4. Genetic engineering -- Fiction
ISBN 0-394-58816-9; 0-345-37077-5 pa
                                        LC 90-52960
"Crichton is a master at blending technology with fiction. . . . Suspense, excitement, and good adventure pervade this book." SLJ

Crocker, Nancy
★ **Billie** Standish was here. Simon & Schuster Books for Young Readers 2007 281p $16.99
Grades: 6 7 8 9   **Fic**
1. Rape -- Fiction 2. Friendship -- Fiction 3. Child abuse -- Fiction
ISBN 978-1-4169-2423-4; 1-4169-2423-X
                                        LC 2006-32688
When the river jeopardizes the levee and most of the town leaves, Miss Lydia, an elderly neighbor, and Billie form a friendship that withstands tragedy and time.

"This story is beautiful, painful, and complex, and the descriptions of people, events, and emotions are graphic and tangible. The rape scene is described but not sensationalized." SLJ

Crockett, S. D.
After the snow; S. D. Crockett. Feiwel & Friends 2012 304 p. $22.55
Grades: 6 7 8 9 10 11 12   **Fic**
1. Science fiction 2. Adventure fiction 3. Winter -- Fiction 4. Missing persons -- Fiction 5. Children and war -- Fiction 6. Survival -- Fiction 7. Voyages and travels -- Fiction 8. Adventure and adventurers -- Fiction
ISBN 9780312641696
                                        LC 2011036122
William C. Morris Award Finalist (2013)
In this book, "Willo"s father can still remember what life was like in Great Britain before the country entered a new ice age. . . . When his father and the rest of his family mysteriously disappear, Willo leaves the scant safety of home to search for them. . . . [He] saves a . . . girl he encounters along the way, and together they find their way into the city, in

which a long-dormant resistance movement is preparing for a final desperate exodus." (Bulletin of the Center for Children's Books)

Cross, Gillian, 1945-
   Where I belong. Holiday House 2011 245p $17.95

Grades: 7 8 9 10   **Fic**
   1. Refugees -- Fiction 2. Kidnapping -- Fiction 3. Fashion designers -- Fiction
   ISBN 978-0-8234-2332-3; 0-8234-2332-8
                       LC 2010-23671

This is a "fast-paced adventure. . . . The fashion element will engage readers who would otherwise not read this genre. . . . This broadly appealing title has an engaging cover and is a worthy addition to any collection." SLJ

Cross, Julie
   Tempest; Julie Cross. St. Martin's Griffin 2012 339p. $17.99

Grades: 8 9 10 11 12   **Fic**
   1. Love stories 2. Science fiction 3. Suspense fiction 4. Young men -- Fiction 5. Time travel -- Fiction 6. Spies -- Fiction
   ISBN 9780312568894
                       LC 2011032799

This novel follows "[n]ineteen-year-old Jackson Meyer . . . [who is] able to jump a couple of hours back in time . . . [and decides to] keep his . . . skill set a secret from his overprotective father and his beloved girlfriend Holly. When two armed men attempt to kidnap Jackson, shooting and most likely killing Holly in the process, Jackson time-jumps in a panic and inexplicably finds himself in 2007, where he is stuck until he can figure out how to get back to the future and save Holly. In the meantime, Jackson discovers that the man he has called Dad all these years is not in fact his father but rather a CIA agent and part of a shadowy government experiment called Tempest—an experiment that includes Jackson as one of its results." (Bulletin of the Center for Children's Books)

Cross, Sarah
   Dull boy. Dutton Childrens Books 2009 308p $17.99

Grades: 7 8 9 10   **Fic**
   1. Science fiction 2. Superheroes -- Fiction 3. Supernatural -- Fiction
   ISBN 978-0-525-42133-7; 0-525-42133-5
                       LC 2008-34208

Avery, a teenaged boy with frightening super powers that he is trying to hide, discovers other teenagers who also have strange powers and who are being sought by the icy and seductive Cherchette, but they do not know what she wants with them.

"Avery's narration, generously peppered with swear words, is hip, witty, funny, and sarcastic." SLJ

Crossan, Sarah
   Breathe; Sarah Crossan. Greenwillow Books 2012 373 p. (hardback) $17.99

Grades: 7 8 9 10 11 12   **Fic**
   1. Friendship -- Fiction 2. Science fiction 3. Survival

-- Fiction 4. Insurgency -- Fiction 5. Adventure and adventurers -- Fiction 6. Environmental degradation -- Fiction
   ISBN 0062118692; 9780062118691
                       LC 2012017496

In author Sarah Crossan's book, "Alina has been stealing for a long time . . . Quinn should be worried about Alina and a bit afraid for himself, too, but . . . it isn't every day that the girl of your dreams asks you to rescue her. Bea wants to tell him that none of this is fair; they'd planned a trip together, the two of them, and she'd hoped he'd discover her out here, not another girl. And as they walk into the Outlands with two days' worth of oxygen in their tanks, everything they believe will be shattered. Will they be able to make it back? Will they want to?" (Publisher's note)

   ★ The **Weight** of Water; by Sarah Crossan. Bloomsbury USA 2013 224 p. $16.99

Grades: 5 6 7 8   **Fic**
   1. Novels in verse 2. Swimming -- Fiction 3. Race relations -- Fiction 4. Immigrants -- England -- Fiction 5. Mothers and daughters -- Fiction
   ISBN 1599909677; 9781599909677
                       LC 2012038645

In this book, "12-year-old Kasienka moves with Mama from Gdansk, Poland, to Coventry, England, to find Tata, her father. The adjustment is difficult. At school, Kasienka is ostracized. At home, she questions why they are searching for a man who ran from them. When Kasienka complains, Mama questions her love. Kasienka feels powerful only when she swims at the pool—something Tata taught her to do. That is also where William, a schoolmate, first notices her." (Kirkus Reviews)

Crossley-Holland, Kevin
   ★ **Crossing** to Paradise. Arthur A. Levine Books 2008 339p $17.99

Grades: 7 8 9 10   **Fic**
   1. Singing -- Fiction 2. Literacy -- Fiction 3. Middle Ages -- Fiction 4. Christian life -- Fiction 5. Pilgrims and pilgrimages -- Fiction
   ISBN 978-0-545-05866-7; 0-545-05866-X; 978-0-545-05868-1 pa; 0-545-05868-6 pa
                       LC 2007-51853

First published 2006 in the United Kingdom with title: Gatty's tale

Gatty, the field-girl who appeared in the author's trilogy about King Arthur, is now an orphan. When she is selected for a pilgrimage, she travels from her home on an English estate to London, Venice, and eventually Jerusalem.

"Gatty, the irrepressible peasant girl first introduced in Crossley-Holland's 'Arthur' trilogy . . . comes into her own in this sweeping, vibrant story." SLJ

Crowe, Chris
   Mississippi trial, 1955. Penguin Putnam 2002 231p pa $5.99; $17.99

Grades: 7 8 9 10   **Fic**
   1. Racism -- Fiction 2. Grandfathers -- Fiction
   ISBN 0-14-250192-1 pa; 0-8037-2745-3
                       LC 2001-40221

In Mississippi in 1955, a sixteen-year-old finds himself at odds with his grandfather over issues surrounding the kidnapping and murder of a fourteen-year-old African American from Chicago.

"By combining real events with their impact upon a single fictional character, Crowe makes the issues in this novel hard-hitting and personal. The characters are complex." Voice Youth Advocates

Crowley, Cath

A **little** wanting song. Knopf 2010 265p $16.99; lib bdg $19.99

Grades: 8 9 10 11 12   **Fic**
1. Shyness -- Fiction 2. Musicians -- Fiction 3. Friendship -- Fiction 4. Loneliness -- Fiction
ISBN 978-0-375-86096-6; 0-375-86096-7; 978-0-375-96096-3 lib bdg; 0-375-96096-1 lib bdg
LC 2009-20305

First published 2005 in Australia with title: Chasing Charlie Duskin

One Australian summer, two very different sixteen-year-old girls—Charlie, a talented but shy musician, and Rose, a confident student longing to escape her tiny town—are drawn into an unexpected friendship, as told in their alternating voices

"Crowley's prose is lyrical and lovely, her characters are beautifully crafted, and her portrayal of teen life in Australia is a delight. . . . Female readers especially will enjoy this upbeat tale." Voice Youth Advocates

Crowley, James

Starfish; illustrations by Jim Madsen. Disney/Hyperion Books 2010 310p il $16.99

Grades: 4 5 6 7   **Fic**
1. Adventure fiction 2. Siblings -- Fiction 3. Siksika Indians -- Fiction 4. Runaway children -- Fiction
ISBN 978-1-4231-2588-4; 1-4231-2588-6

In the early part of the 1900s, Beatrice and Lionel, two Blackfeet Indian children, escape from the Chalk Bluff Indian Boarding School in Montana to find their grandfather, and must elude their pursuers and make a life for themselves in the wilderness.

"This is a fast-paced and interesting novel that will maintain reader interest. Readers will be drawn into the plight of Native Americans trying to survive brutal conditions." Libr Media Connect

Crowley, Suzanne

The **stolen** one. Greenwillow Books 2009 406p $17.99; lib bdg $18.89

Grades: 8 9 10 11 12   **Fic**
1. Orphans -- Fiction
ISBN 978-0-06-123200-8; 0-06-123200-9; 978-0-06-123201-5 lib bdg; 0-06-123201-7 lib bdg
LC 2008-15039

After the death of her foster mother, sixteen-year-old Kat goes to London to seek the answers to her parentage, and surprisingly finds herself invited into Queen Elizabeth's court.

"Intrigue, romance, and period details abound in this riveting story of Tudor England. . . . The sophisticated writing flows well, and the author does a terrific job of integrating historical details." SLJ

Crutcher, Chris

★ **Deadline**. Greenwillow Books 2007 316p $16.99; lib bdg $17.89; pa $8.99

Grades: 8 9 10 11 12   **Fic**
1. School stories 2. Death -- Fiction 3. Terminally ill -- Fiction
ISBN 978-0-06-085089-0; 0-06-085089-2; 978-0-06-085090-6 lib bdg; 0-06-085090-6 lib bdg; 978-0-06-085091-3 pa; 0-06-085091-4 pa
LC 2006-31526

Given the medical diagnosis of one year to live, high school senior Ben Wolf decides to fulfill his greatest fantasies, ponders his life's purpose and legacy, and converses through dreams with a spiritual guide known as "Hey-Soos."

"Ben's sensitive voice uses self-deprecating humor, philosophical pondering, and effective dramatic irony." Voice Youth Advocates

Ironman; a novel. Greenwillow Bks. 1995 181p $16.99; pa $6.99

Grades: 8 9 10 11 12   **Fic**
1. School stories 2. Triathlon -- Fiction 3. Father-son relationship -- Fiction
ISBN 0-688-13503-X; 0-06-059840-9 pa
LC 94-1657

While training for a triathlon, seventeen-year-old Bo attends Mr. Nak's anger management group at school which leads him to examine his relationship with his father.

"Through Crutcher's masterful character development, readers will believe in Bo, empathize with the other members of the anger-management group, absorb the wisdom of Mr. Nak and despise, yet at times pity, the boy's father. This is not a light read, as many serious issues surface, though the author's trademark dark humor (and colorful use of street language) is abundant." SLJ

Running loose. Greenwillow Bks. 1983 190p hardcover o.p. pa $8.99; pa $6.99

Grades: 7 8 9 10   **Fic**
1. School stories
ISBN 9780060094911 pa; 0-688-02002-X; 0-06-009491-5 pa
LC 82-20935

ALA YALSA Margaret A. Edwards Award (2000)

"Louie Banks tells what happened to him in his senior year in a small town Idaho high school. Besides falling in love with Becky and losing her in a senseless accident, Louie takes a stand against the coach when he sets the team up to injure a black player on an opposing team, and learns that you can't be honorable with dishonorable men. . . . Grade seven and up." (Voice Youth Advocates)

"Louie Banks tells what happened to him in his senior year in a small town Idaho high school. Besides falling in love with Becky and losing her in a senseless accident, Louie takes a stand against the coach when he sets the team up to injure a black player on an opposing team, and learns that you can't be honorable with dishonorable men." Voice Youth Advocates

Staying fat for Sarah Byrnes. Greenwillow Bks. 1993 216p hardcover o.p. pa $6.99

Grades: 7 8 9 10   **Fic**
1. Obesity -- Fiction 2. Swimming -- Fiction 3. Friendship -- Fiction 4. Child abuse -- Fiction
ISBN 0-688-11552-7; 0-06-009489-3 pa
LC 91-40097
ALA YALSA Margaret A. Edwards Award (2000)
"An obese boy and a disfigured girl suffer the emotional scars of years of mockery at the hands of their peers. They share a hard-boiled view of the world until events in their senior year hurl them in very different directions. A story about a friendship with staying power, written with pathos and pointed humor." SLJ

Stotan! HarperTempest 2003 261p pa $6.99
Grades: 7 8 9 10   **Fic**
1. Swimming -- Fiction
ISBN 0-06-009492-3
LC 85-12712
First published 1986
ALA YALSA Margaret A. Edwards Award (2000)
A high school coach invites members of his swimming team to a memorable week of rigorous training that tests their moral fiber as well as their physical stamina.
"A subplot involving the boys' fight against local Neo-Nazi activists provides some immediate action, while the various characters' conflicts tighten the middle and ending. The pace lags through the story's introduction; nevertheless, this is a searching sports novel, with a tone varying from macho-tough to sensitive." Bull Cent Child Books

Whale talk. Greenwillow Bks. 2001 220p $15.99; pa $8.99
Grades: 7 8 9 10   **Fic**
1. School stories 2. Swimming -- Fiction 3. Racially mixed people -- Fiction
ISBN 0-688-18019-1; 0-06-177131-7 pa
LC 00-59292
Intellectually and athletically gifted, TJ, a multiracial, adopted teenager, shuns organized sports and the gung-ho athletes at his high school until he agrees to form a swimming team and recruits some of the school's less popular students
"This remarkable novel is vintage Crutcher: heart-pounding athletic competitions, raw emotion, an insufferable high school atmosphere that allows bullying and reveres athletes, and a larger-than-life teen hero who champions the underdog while skewering both racists and abusers with his rapier-sharp wit." Book Rep

Cullen, Lynn
★ **I** am Rembrandt's daughter. Bloomsbury Children's Books 2007 307p $16.95
Grades: 7 8 9 10   **Fic**
1. Plague -- Fiction 2. Artists -- Fiction 3. Poverty -- Fiction 4. Father-daughter relationship -- Fiction
ISBN 978-1-59990-046-9; 1-59990-046-7
LC 2006-28197
In Amsterdam in the mid-1600s, Cornelia's life as the illegitimate child of renowned painter Rembrandt is marked by plague, poverty, and despair at ever earning her father's love, until she sees hope for a better future in the eyes of a weathy suitor.

"Historical fiction, mystery, and romance are masterfully woven. . . . Cullen's novel is a reader's delight." Voice Youth Advocates

Cummings, Priscilla
★ **Blindsided**. Dutton Children's Books 2010 226p $16.99
Grades: 7 8 9 10   **Fic**
1. School stories 2. Blind -- Fiction
ISBN 978-0-525-42161-0; 0-525-42161-0
LC 2009-25092
"Natalie, 14, knows that her future is becoming dimmer as the loss of her eyesight is a nightmare she can't avoid. . . . Part of going from denial to acceptance is attending a boarding school for the blind. . . . Natalie is a credible character and her fear is palpable and painful. . . . Readers will enjoy the high drama and heroics." SLJ

Red kayak; Priscilla Cummings. 1st ed; Dutton Children's Books 2004 209p $15.99; pa $6.99
Grades: 7 8 9 10   **Fic**
1. Death -- Fiction 2. Friendship -- Fiction
ISBN 0-525-47317-3; 0-14-240573-4 pa
LC 2003-63532
Living near the water on Maryland's Eastern Shore, thirteen-year-old Brady and his best friends J.T. and Digger become entangled in a tragedy which tests their friendship and their ideas about right and wrong.
"This well-crafted story will have broad appeal." SLJ

The **journey** back; Priscilla Cummings. Dutton Children's Books 2012 243 p. (hardcover) $16.99
Grades: 7 8 9 10   **Fic**
1. Camping -- Fiction 2. Coming of age -- Fiction 3. Voyages and travels -- Fiction 4. Fugitives from justice -- Fiction 5. Juvenile detention homes -- Fiction
ISBN 0525423621; 9780525423621
LC 2012003818
In this novel by Priscilla Cummings Digger is "escaped and on the run. . . His bold escape from a juvenile detention facility nearly kills him, but soon an angry fourteen-year-old Digger is . . . hijacking a tractor trailer, 'borrowing' a bicycle, and stealing a canoe. When injuries stop him, Digger hides at a riverside campground . . . New friends, a job caring for rescued horses, and risking his life to save another make Digger realize that the journey back is not just about getting home." (Publisher's note)

Currier, Katrina Saltonstall
Kai's journey to Gold Mountain; an Angel Island story. illustrated by Gabhor Utomo. Angel Island Association 2005 39p il $16.95
Grades: 4 5 6 7   **Fic**
1. Immigrants -- Fiction 2. Chinese Americans -- Fiction
ISBN 0-9667352-4-2
LC 2004-14821
In 1934, twelve-year-old Kai leaves China to join his father in America, but first he must take a long sea voyage, then endure weeks of crowded conditions and harsh examinations on Angel Island, fearing that he or his new friend will be sent home.

"The character Kai is based on a real person, whose photos, then and now, are part of the historical notes at the back of the book. Opposite each page of the intensely moving, detailed text are beautiful full-page watercolor-and-pencil illustrations that capture the crowded holding place, and, in unforgettable closeups, the characters' heartbreak and strength." Booklist

Curry, Jane Louise

The **Black** Canary. Margaret K. McElderry Books 2005 279p $16.95

Grades: 5 6 7 8   **Fic**

1. Singers -- Fiction 2. Racially mixed people -- Fiction

ISBN 0-689-86478-7

LC 2003-26150

As the child of two musicians, twelve-year-old James has no interest in music until he discovers a portal to seventeenth-century London in his uncle's basement, and finds himself in a situation where his beautiful voice and the fact that he is biracial might serve him well.

"A genuinely good story that conveys a sense of darkness and mystery in the textured backdrop of a storied time and place." Booklist

Curtis, Christopher Paul

★ **Bud,** not Buddy. Delacorte Press 1999 245p $16.95; pa $6.50

Grades: 4 5 6 7   **Fic**

1. Orphans -- Fiction 2. African Americans -- Fiction 3. Great Depression, 1929-1939 -- Fiction

ISBN 0-385-32306-9; 0-440-41328-1 pa

LC 99-10614

Awarded the Newbery Medal, 2000

Coretta Scott King Award for text

Ten-year-old Bud, a motherless boy living in Flint, Michigan, during the Great Depression, escapes a bad foster home and sets out in search of the man he believes to be his father—the renowned bandleader, H. E. Calloway of Grand Rapids

"Curtis says in a afterword that some of the characters are based on real people, including his own grandfathers, so it's not surprising that the rich blend of tall tale, slapstick, sorrow, and sweetness has the wry, teasing warmth of family folklore." Booklist

★ **Elijah** of Buxton. Scholastic 2007 341p $16.99; pa $7.99

Grades: 5 6 7 8   **Fic**

1. Slavery -- Fiction

ISBN 0-439-02344-0; 978-0-439-02344-3; 0-439-02345-9 pa; 978-0-439-02345-0 pa

LC 2007-05181

A Newbery Medal honor book, 2008

In 1859, eleven-year-old Elijah Freeman, the first free-born child in Buxton, Canada, which is a haven for slaves fleeing the American south, uses his wits and skills to try to bring to justice the lying preacher who has stolen money that was to be used to buy a family's freedom.

"Many readers drawn to the book by humor will find themselves at times on the edges of their seats in suspense and, at other moments, moved to tears." Booklist

★ The **Watsons** go to Birmingham--1963; a novel. Delacorte Press 1995 210p $16.95; pa $6.50

Grades: 4 5 6 7   **Fic**

1. Prejudices -- Fiction 2. Family life -- Fiction 3. African Americans -- Fiction

ISBN 0-385-32175-9; 0-440-41412-1 pa

LC 95-7091

A Newbery Medal honor book, 1996

The ordinary interactions and everyday routines of the Watsons, an African American family living in Flint, Michigan, are drastically changed after they go to visit Grandma in Alabama in the summer of 1963

"Curtis's ability to switch from fun and funky to pinpoint-accurate psychological imagery works unusually well. . . . Ribald humor, sly sibling digs, and a totally believable child's view of the world will make this book an instant hit." SLJ

Cushman, Karen

★ **Alchemy** and Meggy Swann. Clarion Books 2010 167p $16

Grades: 5 6 7 8   **Fic**

1. Alchemy -- Fiction 2. Poverty -- Fiction 3. Handicapped -- Fiction 4. Father-daughter relationship -- Fiction

ISBN 978-0-547-23184-6; 0-547-23184-9

LC 2009-16387

In 1573, the crippled, scorned, and destitute Meggy Swann goes to London, where she meets her father, an impoverished alchemist, and eventually discovers that although her legs are bent and weak, she has many other strengths.

"Writing with admirable economy and a lively ability to recreate the past believably, Cushman creates a memorable portrayal of a troubled, rather mulish girl who begins to use her strong will in positive ways." Booklist

★ **Catherine,** called Birdy. Clarion Bks. 1994 169p $16

Grades: 6 7 8 9   **Fic**

1. Middle Ages -- Fiction

ISBN 0-395-68186-3

LC 93-23333

A Newbery Medal honor book, 1995

The fourteen-year-old daughter of an English country knight keeps a journal in which she records the events of her life, particularly her longing for adventures beyond the usual role of women and her efforts to avoid being married off

"In the process of telling the routines of her young life, Birdy lays before readers a feast of details about medieval England. . . . Superb historical fiction." SLJ

★ **Rodzina**. Clarion Bks. 2003 215p $16; pa $6.50

Grades: 5 6 7 8   **Fic**

1. Orphans -- Fiction 2. Polish Americans -- Fiction

ISBN 0-618-13351-8; 0-440-41993-X pa

LC 2002-15976

A twelve-year-old Polish American girl is boarded onto an orphan train in Chicago with fears about traveling to the West and a life of unpaid slavery

"The story features engaging characters, a vivid setting, and a prickly but endearing heroine. . . . Rodzina's musings and observations provide poignancy, humor, and a keen sense of the human and topographical landscape." SLJ

Includes bibliographical references

★ **Will** Sparrow's road; Karen Cushman. Clarion Books 2012 216 p. (hardback) $16.99

Grades: 5 6 7 8   **Fic**

1. Historical fiction 2. Runaway children -- Fiction 3. Swindlers and swindling -- Fiction 4. Runaways -- Fiction 5. Freak shows -- Fiction

ISBN 0547739621; 9780547739625

LC 2011045898

In this book by Karen Cushman, set in Elizabethan England, "Will Sparrow, liar and thief, becomes a runaway. On the road, he encounters a series of con artists . . . and learns that others are more adept than he at lying and thieving. Then he reluctantly joins a traveling troupe of 'oddities,' including a dwarf and a cat-faced girl. . . . At last Will is forced to understand that appearances are misleading and that he has been his own worst deceiver." (Publisher's note)

Includes bibliographical references

The **ballad** of Lucy Whipple. Clarion Bks. 1996 195p $15; $16.00

Grades: 5 6 7 8   **Fic**

1. Family life -- Fiction 2. Frontier and pioneer life -- Fiction

ISBN 0-395-72806-1; 9780395728062

LC 95-45257

"Twelve-year-old Lucy is taken by her mother from their comfortable 19th-century home in Massachusetts to the rough-and-tumble California goldfields. Lucy's younger siblings don't object to this new life, but Lucy dislikes the dirt, hard work, and lack of civilization—especially reading material. When not helping Mama run Mr. Scatter's boarding house for miners, Lucy spends her time complaining or scheming a return to her beloved Massachusetts. Despite the losses she suffers in the makeshift town of Lucky Diggins, Lucy makes some surprising discoveries about herself and what she's gained in the West." (Christ Sci Monit)

"Cushman's heroine is a delightful character, and the historical setting is authentically portrayed." SLJ

The **loud** silence of Francine Green. Clarion Books 2006 225p $16

Grades: 6 7 8 9   **Fic**

1. School stories 2. Family life -- Fiction

ISBN 978-0-618-50455-8; 0-618-50455-9

LC 2005-29774

In 1949, thirteen-year-old Francine goes to Catholic school in Los Angeles where she becomes best friends with a girl who questions authority and is frequently punished by the nuns, causing Francine to question her own values.

Readers will "savor the story of friends and family tensions, the sly humor, and the questions about patriotism, activism, and freedom." Booklist

★ The **midwife's** apprentice. Clarion Bks. 1995 122p $12; pa $5.99

Grades: 6 7 8 9   **Fic**

1. Midwives -- Fiction 2. Middle Ages -- Fiction

ISBN 0-395-69229-6; 0-06-440630-X pa

LC 94-13792

Awarded the Newbery Medal, 1996

In medieval England, a nameless, homeless girl is taken in by a sharp-tempered midwife, and in spite of obstacles and hardship, eventually gains the three things she most wants: a full belly, a contented heart, and a place in this world

"Earthy humor, the foibles of humans both high and low, and a fascinating mix of superstition and genuinely helpful herbal remedies attached to childbirth make this a truly delightful introduction to a world seldom seen in children's literature." SLJ

Cypess, Leah

Mistwood. Greenwillow Books 2010 304p $16.99

Grades: 7 8 9 10   **Fic**

1. Fantasy fiction 2. Magic -- Fiction 3. Kings and rulers -- Fiction

ISBN 978-0-06-195699-7; 0-06-195699-6

LC 2009-23051

Brought back from the Mistwood to protect the royal family, a girl who has no memory of being a shape-shifter encounters political and magical intrigue as she struggles with her growing feelings for the prince.

"A traditional premise is transformed into a graceful meditation on the ramifications of loyalty, duty and purpose. . . . Astonishing and inspiring." Kirkus

Nightspell. Greenwillow Books 2011 326p $16.99

Grades: 7 8 9 10   **Fic**

1. Ghost stories 2. Dead -- Fiction 3. Sisters -- Fiction 4. Kings and rulers -- Fiction

ISBN 978-0-06-195702-4; 0-06-195702-X

LC 2010012637

Sent by her father, the king of Raellia, who is trying to forge an empire out of warring tribes, Darri arrives in Ghostland and discovers that her sister, whom she planned to rescue, may not want to leave this land where the dead mingle freely with the living.

"Swordfights, blood, and double-dealing pack the pages as this action-filled story races to a surprising conclusion." Booklist

D'Adamo, Francesco

Iqbal; a novel. written by Francesco D'Adamo; translated by Ann Leonori. Atheneum Bks. for Young Readers 2003 120p $15.95; pa $4.99

Grades: 5 6 7 8   **Fic**

1. Child labor -- Fiction

ISBN 0-689-85445-5; 1-4169-0329-1 pa

LC 2002-153498

Original Italian edition, 2001

A fictionalized account of the Pakistani child who escaped from bondage in a carpet factory and went on to help liberate other children like him before being gunned down at the age of thirteen

"The situation and setting are made clear in this novel. Readers cannot help but be moved by the plight of these youngsters. . . . This readable book will certainly add breadth to most collections." SLJ

D'Lacey, Chris

The **fire** within. Orchard Books 2005 340p $15.99

Grades: 6 7 8 9   **Fic**
     1. Dragons -- Fiction 2. Authorship -- Fiction 3. Supernatural -- Fiction
     ISBN 0-439-67244-9
                   LC 2004-58327

When college student David Rain rents a room in an unusual boardinghouse full of clay dragons, he has no idea that they, along with some lively squirrels, will help jumpstart his writing career.

This "has a satisfying domestic reality, spiced with some very unusual dragons." SLJ

     Other titles in this series are:
     Icefire (2006)
     Fire star (2007)
     The fire eternal (2008)
     Dark fire (2010)
     Fire world (2011)
     The Fire ascending (2012)

Dagg, Carole Estby

   ★ The **year** we were famous. Clarion Books 2011 250p $16.99

Grades: 6 7 8 9 10   **Fic**
     1. Adventure fiction 2. Voyages and travels -- Fiction 3. Mother-daughter relationship -- Fiction
     ISBN 978-0-618-99983-5; 0-618-99983-3

"Dagg writes a captivating story about the determination of a mother and daughter, who in 1896 walked from Washington State to New York City. . . . Clara's free-spirited but unreliable mother suggests that they walk nearly 4,000 miles to save their farm from foreclosure (a publisher offers them a 10,000 advance if they make it in seven months) and bring attention to the suffragist movement. . . . The pages go by quickly. . . . The journey in itself is amazing, but Dagg's tender portrayal of a mother and daughter who learn to appreciate and forgive each other makes it unforgettable." Publ Wkly

Dakin, Glenn

The **Society** of Dread. Egmont USA 2010 318p (Candle Man) $15.99

Grades: 5 6 7 8   **Fic**
     1. Adventure fiction 2. Superheroes -- Fiction
     ISBN 978-1-60684-019-1; 1-60684-019-3
                   LC 2010023104

Now head of the Society of Good Works, teenaged Theo must reluctantly use his mysterious ability to melt evil when he ventures underground to face villains of old.

"This appealing contemporary fantasy has a fast-paced plot and enough inventive monsters and villains to captivate even the most reluctant readers." SLJ

The **Society** of Unrelenting Vigilance; [illustrations by Greg Swearingen] Egmont 2009 300p il (Candle Man) $15.99; lib bdg $18.99

Grades: 4 5 6 7   **Fic**
     1. Adventure fiction 2. Superheroes -- Fiction
     ISBN 978-1-60684-015-3; 1-60684-015-0; 978-1-60684-047-4 lib bdg; 1-60684-047-9 lib bdg
                   LC 2009-14035

Thirteen-year-old Theo, who has lived in seclusion his entire life, discovers he is the descendant of the Candle Man, a Victorian vigilante with the ability to melt criminals with a single touch.

This is a "lighthearted, action-driven adventure. . . . With the help of a cast of appealing characters, the nonstop action rolls to a satisfying conclusion." SLJ

Dallas, Sandra

The **quilt** walk; by Sandra Dallas. Sleeping Bear Press 2012 213 p. (hardcover) $15.95

Grades: 3 4 5 6 7   **Fic**
     1. Quilts -- Fiction 3. Quilting -- Fiction 4. Friendship -- Fiction 5. Wagon trains -- Fiction 6. Frontier and pioneer life -- Fiction
     ISBN 1585368008; 9781585367993; 9781585368006
                   LC 2012005863

This children's historical story, by Sandra Dallas, begins in "1863 and Emily Blue Hatchett has been told by her father that, come spring, their family will leave their farm . . . in Quincy, Illinois and travel the Overland Trail to a new home in Golden, Colorado. . . . When Emmy s grandmother comes to say goodbye, she gives Emmy a special gift, something to occupy her time along the trail. The journey by wagon train is long and full of hardships." (Publisher's note)

Daly, Cathleen

   ★ **Flirt** Club. Roaring Brook Press 2011 281p $15.99

Grades: 5 6 7 8   **Fic**
     1. School stories 2. Clubs -- Fiction 3. Friendship -- Fiction
     ISBN 978-1-59643-572-8; 1-59643-572-0
                   LC 2010-27473

Through notes and journal entries, best friends and self-proclaimed "drama geeks" Cisco (Izzy) and the Bean (Annie) write of the trials of middle school, as well as their efforts to attract boys by forming a Flirt Club.

"Told through very funny notes to each other, journal entries, and minutes from Flirt Club meetings, Daly's debut sparkles with wit, and her protagonists brim with enthusiasm and heart. . . . It's refreshing to see these girls counter middle-school drama with silliness rather than angst and hand-wringing." Publ Wkly

Damico, Gina

Croak; by Gina Damico. Houghton Mifflin Harcourt 2012 311 p. $8.99

Grades: 7 8 9 10   **Fic**
     1. Mystery fiction 2. Soul -- Fiction 3. Death -- Fiction 4. Justice -- Fiction 5. Future life -- Fiction
     ISBN 9780547608327
                   LC 2011017125

This book tells the story of "sixteen-year-old bad girl Lex Bartleby [who] is shipped off to her uncle Mort's farm, supposedly to figure out her anger issues with the help of manual labor. Instead, she learns that "farmer" Mort is a reaper of another kind entirely and that, as mayor of Croak, a small collection of Grim Reapers, he will be teaching Lex the family business. Although she initially takes to ferrying souls into the Afterlife with aplomb, Lex begins to question the roles of Reapers as silent witnesses to the world's injustices, especially when their knowledge of people's deaths would allow them to wreak karmic justice upon the murderers and rapists that otherwise get away with their crimes." (Bulletin of the Center for Children's Books)

Rogue; by Gina Damico. Graphia 2013 336 p. (paperback) $8.99

Grades: 8 9 10   **Fic**

    1. Future life -- Fiction 2. Grim Reaper (Symbolic character) -- Fiction 3. Death -- Fiction 4. Humorous stories 5. Ghosts -- Fiction
    ISBN 0544108841; 9780544108844

                   LC 2013004154

This book by Gina Damico follows a "band of surly teenage grim reapers risking everything on their mission to save the Afterlife. Uncle Mort's plan to save the Afterlife by enlisting Junior Grims to help destroy the portals that access it is full of risks, loopholes and secrets—and fiery-tempered, impulsive Lex is the plan's unstable lynchpin." (Kirkus Reviews)

Scorch; Gina Damico. Houghton Mifflin Harcourt 2012 332 p. $8.99

Grades: 7 8 9 10   **Fic**

    1. Fantasy fiction 2. Death -- Fiction 3. Humorous stories 4. Future life -- Fiction
    ISBN 0547624573; 9780547624570

                   LC 2012014799

In this novel by Gina Damico "Lex is a full-time teenage grim reaper -- but now has the bizarre ability to Damn souls.... [S]he and her friends embark on a wild road trip to DeMyse. Though this sparkling desert oasis is full of luxuries and amusements, it feels like a prison to Lex. Her best chance at escape would be to stop all the senseless violence that she caused—but how can she do that from DeMyse, where the Grims seem mysteriously oblivious to the bloodshed?" (Publisher's note)

Daneshvari, Gitty

    Class is not dismissed! [illustrations by Carrie Gifford] Little, Brown and Company 2010 307p il $16.99

Grades: 4 5 6   **Fic**

    1. School stories 2. Phobias -- Fiction
    ISBN 978-0-316-03328-2; 0-316-03328-6

                   LC 2010006889

Thirteen-year-olds Madeleine, Theo, and Lulu, fourteen-year-old Garrison, and ten-year-old new "contestant" Hyacinth, must face their phobias and join forces to learn who is stealing wigs and pageant trophies from the School of Fear.

    "Filled with an eclectic, and often eccentric, cast of characters, this sequel uses the wry humor and outrageous situations that characterized the first book and makes for an entertaining read." SLJ

School of Fear; illustrated by Carrie Gifford. Little, Brown Books for Young Readers 2009 339p il $15.99

Grades: 4 5 6   **Fic**

    1. School stories 2. Phobias -- Fiction
    ISBN 978-0-316-03326-8; 0-316-03326-X

                   LC 2008051309

Twelve-year-olds Madeleine, Theo, and Lulu, and thirteen-year-old Garrison, are sent to a remote Massachusetts school to overcome their phobias, but tragedy strikes and the quartet must work together—with no adult assistance—to face their fears.

    This is "tautly paced, spine-tingling and quite funny." Publ Wkly

Danziger, Paula

    The **Divorce** Express. Delacorte Press 1982 148p il hardcover o.p. pa $5.99

Grades: 6 7 8 9   **Fic**

    1. Divorce -- Fiction 2. Parent-child relationship -- Fiction
    ISBN 0-14-240712-7 pa

                   LC 82-70318

This is "a warm, tender book for adolescents who must deal with the complexities of growing up." Child Book Rev Serv

    The **cat** ate my gymsuit; [by] Paula Danziger. 30th anniversary edition; G.P. Putnam's Sons 2004 151p $15.99; pa $5.99

Grades: 4 5 6 7   **Fic**

    1. School stories 2. Teachers -- Fiction
    ISBN 0-399-24307-0; 0-14-240654-6 pa

                   LC 2004001892

A reissue of the title first published 1974 by Delacorte Press

When the unconventional English teacher who helped her conquer many of her feelings of insecurity is fired, thirteen-year-old Marcy Lewis uses her new found courage to campaign for the teacher's reinstatement.

    "Paula Danziger's compassionate and accurate portrayal of a young girl struggling to find her own voice rings as true today as it did 30 years ago. A full cast brings this modern American classic of teenage angst to life with humor and pathos." SLJ

Dashner, James

    The **kill** order; James Dashner. Delacorte Press 2012 329 p. $17.99

Grades: 7 8 9 10 11 12   **Fic**

    1. Viruses -- Fiction 2. Survival skills -- Fiction 3. Natural disasters -- Fiction 4. Science fiction 5. Survival -- Fiction 6. Virus diseases -- Fiction
    ISBN 9780307979117; 9780375990823; 9780385742887; 0385742886

                   LC 2012016790

In this book by James Dashner "sun flares hit the earth and mankind fell to disease. Mark and Trina were there when it happened, and they survived. But surviving the sun flares was easy compared to what came next. Now a disease of rage and lunacy races across the eastern United States, and there's something suspicious about its origin. Worse yet, it's mutating, and all evidence suggests that it will bring humanity to its knees." (Publisher's note)

★ The **maze** runner. Delacorte Press 2009 375p $16.99; lib bdg $19.99

Grades: 7 8 9 10 11 12   **Fic**

1. Science fiction 2. Amnesia -- Fiction

ISBN 0-385-73794-7; 0-385-90702-8 lib bdg; 978-0-385-73794-4; 978-0-385-90702-6 lib bdg

LC 2009-1345

Sixteen-year-old Thomas wakes up with no memory in the middle of a maze and realizes he must work with the community in which he finds himself if he is to escape.

"With a fast-paced narrative steadily answering the myriad questions that arise and an ever-increasing air of tension, Dashner's suspenseful adventure will keep readers guessing until the very end." Publ Wkly

Other titles in this series are:

The scorch trials (2010)

The death cure (2011)

Daswani, Kavita

Indie girl. Simon Pulse 2007 232p pa $8.99

Grades: 7 8 9 10   **Fic**

1. Fashion -- Fiction 2. Journalists -- Fiction 3. East Indian Americans -- Fiction

ISBN 1-4169-4892-9

"What sets this novel apart is Daswani's nuanced take on her character's Indian-American subculture, the pressure she feels to be like her more conventional cousins, her desire for independence, American-style, and her pride in her heritage. Indie is a heroine worth meeting." Publ Wkly

David, Keren

★ **When** I was Joe. Frances Lincoln 2010 364p $16.95; pa $8.95

Grades: 7 8 9 10   **Fic**

1. Crime -- Fiction 2. Witnesses -- Fiction

ISBN 978-1-84780-131-9; 1-84780-131-5; 978-1-84780-100-5 pa; 1-84780-100-5 pa

After he witnesses a murder by some ruthless gangsters, Ty and his mother go into hiding under police protection. Even with a new identity, the killers will stop at nothing to silence him.

"This book has an intriguing premise and a cast of likable and realistic characters." SLJ

Davies, Jacqueline

Lost. Marshall Cavendish 2009 242p $16.99

Grades: 7 8 9 10   **Fic**

1. Sisters -- Fiction 2. Factories -- Fiction 3. Bereavement -- Fiction

ISBN 978-0-7614-5535-6; 0-7614-5535-3

LC 2008-40560

In 1911 New York, sixteen-year-old Essie Rosenfeld must stop taking care of her irrepressible six-year-old sister when she goes to work at the Triangle Waist Company, where she befriends a missing heiress who is in hiding from her family and who seems to understand the feelings of heartache and grief that Essie is trying desperately to escape.

The "unusual pacing adds depth and intrigue as the plot unfolds. There are many layers to this story, which will appeal to a variety of interests and age levels." SLJ

Where the ground meets the sky. Marshall Cavendish 2002 224p hardcover o.p. pa $5.95

Grades: 5 6 7 8   **Fic**

1. Interpersonal relations 2. World War, 1939-1945 -- Fiction

ISBN 0-7614-5105-6; 0-7614-5187-0 pa

LC 2001-32519

During World War II, a twelve-year-old girl is uprooted from her quiet, East coast life and moved to a secluded army post in the New Mexico desert where her father and other scientists are working on a top secret project

"The story is told in Hazel's lively, if self-conscious voice. . . . Davies skillfully describes the secrecy and intensity of the work and how it affected every aspect of the researchers' and their families' lives." Booklist

Davies, Stephen

Hacking Timbuktu. Clarion Books 2010 264p map $16.00

Grades: 7 8 9 10   **Fic**

1. Adventure fiction 2. Computers -- Fiction 3. Buried treasure -- Fiction

ISBN 0-547-39016-5; 978-0-547-39016-1

LC 2009-45352

London sixteen-year-old Danny Temple and friend Omar use their computer and parkour skills to elude pursuers as they follow clues in an Arabic manuscript to the mysterious cliffs of Bandiagara in sub-Saharan Africa seeking an ancient treasure.

"Davies delivers a satisfying mix of history, exotic locales, computer hacking, and parkour in this well-constructed adventure story." Booklist

★ **Outlaw.** Clarion Books 2011 192p $16.99

Grades: 7 8 9 10   **Fic**

1. Siblings -- Fiction 2. Terrorism -- Fiction 3. Kidnapping -- Fiction 4. Social problems -- Fiction

ISBN 978-0-547-39017-8; 0-547-39017-3

LC 2011009643

The children of Britain's ambassador to Burkina Faso, fifteen-year-old Jake, who loves technology and adventure, and thirteen-year-old Kas, a budding social activist, are abducted and spend time in the Sahara desert with Yakuuba Sor, who some call a terrorist but others consider a modern-day Robin Hood.

"Stephen Davies has crafted a novel full of intrigue, fast-paced action, and sly humor. The fast moving story will draw in many readers, including those who usually shy away from books." Voice Youth Advocates

Davis, Heather

Never cry werewolf. HarperTeen 2009 216p $16.99

Grades: 7 8 9 10   **Fic**

1. Camps -- Fiction 2. Werewolves -- Fiction

ISBN 978-0-06-134923-2; 0-06-134923-2

LC 2008-51967

Forced to attend a camp for teens with behavior problems, sixteen-year-old Shelby Locke's attempts to follow the rules go astray when she meets a handsome British werewolf.

"Davis weaves together a fast-paced action adventure story with issues of peer pressure, divorce, betrayal, friendship, acceptance, and, of course, romance." SLJ

Davis, Katie

The **curse** of Addy McMahon. Greenwillow Books 2008 271p $16.99; lib bdg $17.89

Grades: 4 5 6 **Fic**

1. Authorship -- Fiction 2. Friendship -- Fiction 3. Bereavement -- Fiction 4. Family life -- Fiction 5. Cartoons and caricatures -- Fiction

ISBN 978-0-06-128711-4; 0-06-128711-3; 978-0-06-128712-1 lib bdg; 0-06-128712-1 lib bdg

LC 2007041154

After her father's death, aspiring sixth-grade writer Addy McMahon feels like she is cursed with bad luck, and when she temporarily loses her best friend, and is forced to admit that her mother is dating again, she vows she will never write another word

"Peppered with authentic preteen conversations, the novel combines traditional narrative with graphic-novel stories, emails, and IMs. . . . The book is a fast-paced and interesting read." SLJ

Davis, Rebecca Fjelland

Chasing AllieCat. Flux 2011 277p pa $9.95

Grades: 7 8 9 10 **Fic**

1. Violence -- Fiction 2. Bereavement -- Fiction 3. Mountain biking -- Fiction

ISBN 978-0-7387-2130-9; 0-7387-2130-1

LC 2010038217

When she is left with relatives in rural Minnesota for the summer, Sadie meets Allie, a spiky-haired off-road biker, and Joe, who team up to train for a race, but when they find a priest badly beaten and near death in the woods, Allie mysteriously disappears leaving Sadie and Joe to discover the dangerous secrets she is hiding.

Davis "constructs a succinct, compelling story that combines romance, suspense, and the theme of overcoming challenges. The strong sense of place, character development, and love triangle dynamics should engage cycling enthusiasts as well as a broader audience." Publ Wkly

Davis, Tanita S.

Mare's war. Alfred A. Knopf 2009 341p $16.99; lib bdg $19.99

Grades: 7 8 9 10 **Fic**

1. Sisters -- Fiction 2. Grandmothers -- Fiction 3. African Americans -- Fiction 4. Automobile travel -- Fiction 5. World War, 1939-1945 -- Fiction

ISBN 978-0-375-85714-0; 0-375-85714-1; 978-0-375-95714-7 lib bdg; 0-375-95714-6 lib bdg

LC 2008-33744

ALA EMIERT Coretta Scott King Author Award Honor Book (2010)

Teens Octavia and Tali learn about strength, independence, and courage when they are forced to take a car trip with their grandmother, who tells about growing up Black in

1940s Alabama and serving in Europe during World War II as a member of the Women's Army Corps.

"The parallel travel narratives are masterfully managed, with postcards from Octavia and Tali to the folks back home in San Francisco signaling the shift between 'then' and 'now.' Absolutely essential reading." Kirkus

A **la** carte. Alfred A. Knopf Books for Young Readers 2008 288p $15.99; lib bdg $18.99

Grades: 7 8 9 10 **Fic**

1. Cooking -- Fiction 2. African Americans -- Fiction

ISBN 978-0-375-84815-5; 0-375-84815-0; 978-0-375-94815-2 lib bdg; 0-375-94815-5 lib bdg

LC 2007-49656

Lainey, a high school senior and aspiring celebrity chef, is forced to question her priorities after her best friend (and secret crush) runs away from home.

"The relationships and characters in this book are authentic. The actions and dialogue seem true to those represented. Even though it is a quick read, the story is a meaningful one." Voice Youth Advocate

Day, Karen

No cream puffs; 1st ed.; Wendy Lamb Books 2008 209p $15.99; lib bdg $18.99

Grades: 6 7 8 9 **Fic**

1. Baseball -- Fiction 2. Sex role -- Fiction 3. Friendship -- Fiction

ISBN 978-0-375-83775-3; 0-375-83775-2; 978-0-375-93775-0 lib bdg; 0-375-93775-7 lib bdg

LC 2007030018

In 1980, when twelve-year-old Madison, who loves to play baseball, decides to play in her town's baseball league, she never envisions the uproar it causes when she becomes the first girl to join.

This is a "perceptive, enjoyable title, packed with exciting baseball." Booklist

A **million** miles from Boston. Wendy Lamb Books 2011 215p $15.99; lib bdg $18.99

Grades: 4 5 6 7 **Fic**

1. Dogs -- Fiction 2. Summer -- Fiction 3. Vacations -- Fiction 4. Friendship -- Fiction 5. Family life -- Fiction 6. Single parent family -- Fiction

ISBN 978-0-385-73899-6; 0-385-73899-4; 978-0-385-90763-7 lib bdg; 0-385-90763-X lib bdg

LC 2010-16475

Rising seventh-grader Lucy plans on a perfect summer at the Maine lake where her family has owned a cottage for decades, but family of a classmate she dislikes has bought a home there and her widowed father is bringing a girlfriend to visit.

"Day delivers a well-paced, realistic 'summer of change' story. . . . Day persuasively renders Lucy's uneasiness with her complex shifting emotions and memories." Publ Wkly

De Goldi, Kate

★ The **10** p.m. question. Candlewick Press 2010 245p $15.99

Grades: 7 8 9 10 11 12 **Fic**

1. School stories 2. Worry -- Fiction 3. Agoraphobia -- Fiction 4. Family life -- Fiction 5. Eccentrics and

eccentricities -- Fiction
ISBN 978-0-7636-4939-5; 0-7636-4939-2

LC 2009-49726

First published 2008 in New Zealand

Twelve-year-old Frankie Parsons has a quirky family, a wonderful best friend, and a head full of worrying questions that he shares with his mother each night, but when free-spirited Sydney arrives at school with questions of her own, Frankie is forced to face the ultimate ten p.m. question.

"De Goldi's novel is an achingly poignant, wryly comic story of early adolescence. . . . Nearly every character . . . is a loving, talented, unforgettable eccentric whose dialogue, much like De Goldi's richly phrased narration, combines heart-stopping tenderness with perfectly timed, deliciously zany humor." Booklist

De Lint, Charles

The **blue** girl; Charles de Lint. Viking 2004 368p hardcover o.p. pa $7.99

Grades: 7 8 9 10   **Fic**

1. Ghost stories 2. School stories 3. Fairies -- Fiction
ISBN 0-670-05924-2; 0-14-240545-0 pa

LC 2004-19051

New at her high school, Imogene enlists the help of her introverted friend Maxine and the ghost of a boy who haunts the school after receiving warnings through her dreams that soul-eaters are threatening her life

"The book combines the turmoil of high school inter-twined with rich, detailed imagery drawn from traditional folklore and complex characters with realistic relation-ships. . . . This book is not just another ghost story, but a novel infused with the true sense of wonder and magic that is De Lint at his best. It is strongly recommended." Voice Youth Advocates

De Quidt, Jeremy

★ The **toymaker**; with illustrations by Gary Blythe. David Fickling Books 2010 356p il $16.99; lib bdg $19.99

Grades: 5 6 7 8   **Fic**

1. Adventure fiction 2. Toys -- Fiction
ISBN 978-0-385-75180-3; 0-385-75180-X; 978-0-385-75181-0 lib bdg; 0-385-75181-8 lib bdg

"Mathias . . . upon the death of his conjurer grandfa-ther, is spirited away from the decrepit carnival they called home. His unknown new guardian appears to be after the secret contained on an inherited piece of paper, which is now in Mathias' possession. . . . Moving briskly across an atmospheric Germanic setting, the characters are chased by howling wolves, a dangerous dwarf, and unforgiving cold in a bloody, mysterious, and darkly thrilling quest." Booklist

De la Pena, Matt

We were here. Delacorte Press 2009 357p $17.99; lib bdg $20.99

Grades: 7 8 9 10 11 12   **Fic**

1. Brothers -- Fiction 2. Friendship -- Fiction 3. Runaway teenagers -- Fiction 4. Juvenile delinquency -- Fiction
ISBN 978-0-385-73667-1; 0-385-73667-3; 978-0-385-90622-7 lib bdg; 0-385-90622-6 lib bdg

LC 2008-44568

Haunted by the event that sentences him to time in a group home, Miguel breaks out with two unlikely compan-ions and together they begin their journey down the Califor-nia coast hoping to get to Mexico and a new life.

"The contemporary survival adventure will keep read-ers hooked, as will the tension that builds from the story's secrets." Booklist

DeFelice, Cynthia C.

★ **Signal**. Farrar, Straus and Giroux 2009 151p $16.99

Grades: 5 6 7 8   **Fic**

1. Moving -- Fiction 2. Friendship -- Fiction 3. Loneliness -- Fiction 4. Child abuse -- Fiction 5. Country life -- Fiction
ISBN 978-0-374-39915-3; 0-374-39915-8

LC 2008-09278

After moving with his emotionally distant father to the Finger Lakes region of upstate New York, twelve-year-old Owen faces a lonely summer until he meets an abused girl who may be a space alien.

"Well-drawn secondary characters create a threatening backdrop to the developing mystery, while Owen's poignant relationship with his work-driven father elicits sympathy. The tension builds on several fronts to a gripping climax and satisfying conclusion. Owen's likable voice, the plot's quick pace and the science fiction overtones make this a winner." Publ Wkly

The **ghost** and Mrs. Hobbs; [by] Cynthia DeFe-lice. Farrar, Straus & Giroux 2001 180p $16; pa $5.99

Grades: 4 5 6   **Fic**

1. Ghost stories 2. Mystery and detective stories
ISBN 0-374-38046-5; 0-06-001172-6 pa

LC 00-52827

Hindered by a fight with her friend Dub and a series of mysterious fires, eleven-year-old Allie investigates the fire seventeen years earlier which claimed the lives of the hus-band and infant son of a school cafeteria worker, as well as the handsome young man whose ghost asks Allie for help

"This is a diverting and suspenseful ghost story offer-ing a likable protagonist and a thrilling romantic spark." Horn Book

The **ghost** of Cutler Creek; [by] Cynthia DeFe-lice. 1st ed; Farrar, Straus and Giroux 2004 181p $16; pa $5.95

Grades: 4 5 6   **Fic**

1. Ghost stories 2. Mystery fiction 3. Dogs -- Fiction 4. Mystery and detective stories
ISBN 0-374-38058-9; 0-374-40004-0 pa

LC 2003-49051

When Allie is contacted by the ghost of a dog, she and Dub investigate the surly new boy at school and his father, who may be running a puppy mill, to see if they are involved.

"DeFelice has created a suspenseful tale that will leave readers rapidly turning pages." SLJ

★ The **ghost** of Fossil Glen; by Cynthia De-Felice. Farrar, Straus & Giroux 1998 167p (Ghost Mysteries) $16; pa $7.99

Grades: 4 5 6   **Fic**

1. Ghost stories 2. Ghosts -- Fiction 3. Diaries -- Fiction 4. Imagination -- Fiction

ISBN 0-374-31787-9; 9780312602130 pa

LC 97-33230

"Strange events begin when a calm, unknown voice prevents Allie from panicking and falling from a dangerous cliff while fossil hunting. Then, an old journal mysteriously appears in her mailbox. Allie often feels a presence nearby and dreams of a girl falling from the cliff. She then discovers the grave marker of an 11-year-old girl who was missing and presumed dead in 1994. Because of her reputation for telling stories, Allie cannot convince anyone to believe her except her longtime friend and fellow fossil hunter, Dub. Driven to pursue the mystery, Allie finds an old diary that provides her with facts about the girl's death. Foolishly, she reveals what she knows and endangers her own life. . . . Grades four to six." (SLJ)

"Sixth-grader Allie Nichols encounters the ghost of Lucy Stiles and becomes involved with Lucy's unsolved death, eventually finding proof that Lucy was murdered." Horn Book Guide

The **ghost** of Poplar Point; [by] Cynthia DeFelice. 1st ed.; Farrar, Straus and Giroux 2007 183p $16

Grades: 4 5 6 7   **Fic**

1. Ghost stories 2. Seneca Indians -- Fiction

ISBN 0-374-32540-5; 978-0-374-32540-4

LC 2006047329

Prompted by the ghost of a young Seneca Indian girl, twelve-year-old Allie and her friend Dub are determined, despite the opposition of an unscrupulous property developer, that the historical pageant celebrating the founding of their town tells the truth about the fate of the Seneca people who lived there during the Revolutionary War.

"This engaging book moves along quickly to a satisfying conclusion." Booklist

DeKeyser, Stacy

The **Brixen** Witch; Stacy DeKeyser. Margaret K. McElderry Books 2012 208 p. (hardcover) $15.99

Grades: 4 5 6 7 8   **Fic**

1. Horror fiction 2. Occult fiction 3. Witches -- Fiction 4. Rats -- Fiction 5. Magic -- Fiction 6. Witchcraft -- Fiction 7. Community life -- Fiction

ISBN 9781442433281; 9781442433304

LC 2011033680

In this book, "12-year-old Rudi Bauer thinks he's found a treasure, [but] no good can come from taking something that belongs to the Brixen Witch. His sleep is plagued by nightmares, but when they stop there's no relief--the village is infested with rats. . . . As his Oma points out, young Rudi, the one child left behind after the children disappear and the one who precipitated the crisis, is the one to make things right." (Kirkus Reviews)

DeMatteis, J. M.

Imaginalis. Katherine Tegen Books 2010 248p $16.99

Grades: 5 6 7 8   **Fic**

1. Fantasy fiction 2. Magic -- Fiction 3. Imagination -- Fiction 4. Books and reading -- Fiction

ISBN 978-0-06-173286-7; 0-06-173286-9

Devastated that her favorite fantasy book series will not be completed, twelve-year-old Mehera discovers that only her belief, imagination, and courage will save the land of Imaginalis and its inhabitants from being lost forever.

This is "a sure-footed fantasy. . . . The well-drawn characters, abundant action and humor, and hopeful message about the power of reading and belief keep it afloat." Publ Wkly

DeVillers, Julia

Lynn Visible. Dutton Children's Books 2010 278p il $16.99

Grades: 6 7 8 9   **Fic**

1. School stories 2. Fashion -- Fiction

ISBN 978-0-525-47691-7; 0-525-47691-1

LC 2009-23058

"Lynn Vincent knows all the latest trends and isn't afraid to flaunt her funky style. The problem is, in small-town Pennsylvania, being fashion forward makes Lynn socially backward. . . . But when one of Lynn's unique creations makes it into the hands of a famous designer and onto the runway, it seems that Lynn might finally get her moment in the spotlight." Publisher's note

Dee, Barbara

Just another day in my insanely real life; a novel. Margaret K. McElderry Books 2006 252p $15.95; pa $5.99

Grades: 5 6 7 8   **Fic**

1. Authorship -- Fiction 2. Single parent family -- Fiction

ISBN 978-1-4169-0861-6; 1-4169-0861-7; 978-1-4169-4739-4 pa; 1-4169-4739-6 pa

With her father "out of the picture" and her mother working long hours, twelve-year-old Cassie unconsciously describes her anger and confusion in a fantasy novel she is writing for school.

"It's the drama and seething anger in Cassie's first-person narrative that's so compelling." Booklist

Deebs, Tracy

Tempest rising. Walker & Co. 2011 344p $16.99

Grades: 8 9 10 11 12   **Fic**

1. War stories 2. Mermaids and mermen -- Fiction

ISBN 978-0-8027-2231-7; 0-8027-2231-8

LC 2010-34339

On her seventeenth birthday, Tempest must decide whether to remain a human and live on land or submit to her mermaid half, like her mother before her, and enter into a long-running war under the sea.

"Tempest is a gutsy, independent heroine with more than enough agency to save herself from danger. . . . For readers wanting a solid, familiar, but slightly different paranormal romance." Booklist

Deedy, Carmen Agra

★ The **Cheshire** Cheese cat; a Dickens of a tale. Peachtree Publishers 2011 228p il $16.95

Grades: 5 6 7 8 **Fic**

1. Cats -- Fiction 2. Mice -- Fiction
ISBN 978-1-56145-595-9; 1-56145-595-4

LC 2010052275

"The vagaries of tavern life in 19th-century London come alive in this delightful tale. . . . The fast-moving plot is a masterwork of intricate detail that will keep readers enthralled, and the characters are well-rounded and believable. Language is a highlight of the novel; words both elegant and colorful fill the pages. . . . Combined with Moser's precise pencil sketches of personality-filled characters, the book is a success in every way." SLJ

Defoe, Daniel

Robinson Crusoe; edited with an introduction by Thomas Keymer and notes by Thomas Keymer and James Kelly. New ed.; Oxford University Press 2009 lii, 321p il (Oxford world's classics) pa $7.95

Grades: 8 9 10 11 12 Adult **Fic**

1. Adventure fiction 2. Islands -- Fiction 3. Survival after airplane accidents, shipwrecks, etc. -- Fiction
ISBN 978-0-19-955397-6

LC 2006-26022

First published 1719

"A minutely circumstantial account of the hero's shipwreck and escape to an uninhabited island, and the methodical industry whereby he makes himself a comfortable home. The story is founded on the actual experiences of Alexander Selkirk, who spent four years on the island of Juan Fernandez in the early 18th century." Lenrow. Reader's Guide to Prose Fic

Delaney, Joseph

★ **Revenge** of the witch; illustrations by Patrick Arrasmith. Greenwillow Bks. 2005 344p il (The last apprentice) $14.99; lib bdg $15.89; pa $7.99

Grades: 5 6 7 8 **Fic**

1. Witches -- Fiction 2. Supernatural -- Fiction
ISBN 0-06-076618-2; 0-06-076619-0 lib bdg; 0-06-076620-4 pa

LC 2004-54003

Young Tom, the seventh son of a seventh son, starts work as an apprentice for the village spook, whose job is to protect ordinary folk from "ghouls, boggarts, and all manner of wicked beasties"

"Delaney grabs readers by the throat and gives them a good shake in a smartly crafted story. . . . This is a gristly thriller. . . . Yet the twisted horror is amply buffered by an exquisitely normal young hero, matter-of-fact prose, and a workaday normalcy." Booklist

Other titles in this series are:
Curse of the bane (2006)
Night of the soul-stealer (2007)
Attack of the fiend (2008)
Wrath of the Bloodeye (2008)
Clash of the demons (2009)
Rise of the huntress (2010)
Rage of the fallen (2011)
The Spook's Bestiary (2011)

de la Peña, Matt

Mexican whiteboy. Delacorte Press 2008 249p $15.99; lib bdg $18.99

Grades: 8 9 10 11 12 **Fic**

1. Cousins -- Fiction 2. Mexican Americans -- Fiction 3. Racially mixed people -- Fiction
ISBN 978-0-385-73310-6; 0-385-73310-0; 978-0-385-90329-5 lib bdg; 0-385-90329-4 lib bdg

LC 2007-32302

Sixteen-year-old Danny searches for his identity amidst the confusion of being half-Mexican and half-white while spending a summer with his cousin and new friends on the baseball fields and back alleys of San Diego County, California.

"The author juggles his many plotlines well, and the portrayal of Danny's friends and neighborhood is rich and lively." Booklist

Delsol, Wendy

Flock; Wendy Delsol. Candlewick Press 2012 384 p. (hardback) $16.99

Grades: 7 8 9 10 **Fic**

1. Occult fiction 2. Infants -- Fiction 3. Sisters -- Fiction 4. Schools -- Fiction 5. High schools -- Fiction 6. Supernatural -- Fiction 7. Students, Foreign -- Fiction 8. Interpersonal relations -- Fiction
ISBN 0763660108; 9780763660109

LC 2011048371

This book is the final in the "Stork" trilogy. Protagonist Katla has returned to her high school life after saving her boyfriend Jack in Iceland. But "her hopes of dodging unfinished business are dashed by the arrival of two Icelandic exchange students: Marik . . . and Jinky . . . . It seems Katla not only enraged the Snow Queen by rescuing . . . Jack, she also was tricked into promising her frail baby sister to the water queen — and Marik has come to collect. What"s worse, Katla doesn"t dare confide in anyone lest she endanger them, so even her soul mate, Jack, is growing suspicious, And now Katla"s stork dreams, her guide for matching babies with mothers, have become strange and menacing as well. (Amazon.com)

Frost. Candlewick Press 2011 376p $15.99

Grades: 7 8 9 10 **Fic**

1. School stories 2. Snow -- Fiction 3. Supernatural -- Fiction
ISBN 978-0-7636-5386-6; 0-7636-5386-1

LC 2010047656

After her boyfriend Jack conjures up a record-breaking snow storm, sixteen-year-old Kat LeBlanc finds herself facing an unusual rival in the form of an environmental researcher from Greenland who is drawn to their small town of Norse Falls, Minnesota, by the storm.

"Well-paced narration will keep readers interested—a superior paranormal adventure." Kirkus

Stork. Candlewick Press 2010 357p $15.99; pa $8.99

Grades: 7 8 9 10   **Fic**
1. School stories 2. Supernatural -- Fiction
ISBN 978-0-7636-4844-2; 0-7636-4844-2; 978-0-
7636-5687-4 pa; 0-7636-5687-9 pa
                                        LC 2009-51357
After her parents' divorce, Katla and her mother move
from Los Angeles to Norse Falls, Minnesota, where Kat immediately alienates two boys at her high school and, improbably, discovers a kinship with a mysterious group of elderly
women—the Icelandic Stork Society—who "deliver souls."
"This snappy, lighthearted supernatural romance blends
Norse mythology and contemporary issues with an easy
touch." Booklist

Dennard, Susan
    Something strange and deadly; Susan Dennard.
1st ed. Harpercollins Childrens Books 2012 388 p.
(hardback) $17.99; (paperback) $9.99
Grades: 7 8 9 10 11 12   **Fic**
1. Ghost stories 2. Zombies -- Fiction 3. Horror stories
4. Dead -- Fiction 5. Magic -- fiction 6. Brothers and
sisters -- Fiction
ISBN 0062083260; 9780062083265; 9780062083272
                                        LC 2011042114
Author Susan Dennard's protagonist Eleanor Fitt "and
her dear Mama have just about run out of funds, and she
misses [her brother] Elijah terribly [while he is on a] . . .
three-year odyssey abroad. So when . . . he's been detained,
she is mightily distressed. The next day, the determined teen
is off for some help from the Spirit-Hunters. . . . Her can-
do attitude finds her at one point systematically disabling
a throng of zombies by smashing their kneecaps with her
parasol." (Kirkus Reviews)

Derby, Sally
    Kyle's island. Charlesbridge 2010 191p $16.95
Grades: 5 6 7 8   **Fic**
1. Lakes -- Fiction 2. Islands -- Fiction 3. Siblings
-- Fiction 4. Family life -- Fiction 5. Young adult
literature -- Works 6. Children's literature -- Works --
Grades two through six
ISBN 978-1-58089-316-9; 1-58089-316-3
                                        LC 2009-17581
Kile, almost thirteen, spends much of the summer yearning to explore a nearby island, striving to be a good brother,
fishing with an elderly neighbor, and fuming at his parents
over their separation that is forcing his mother to sell the
family's cabin on a Michigan lake.
"Derby writes a subtle coming-of-age novel that is
engaging from start to finish. Kyle's character is so well
developed that many readers will be able to understand
the realistic emotions and situations taking place." Libr
Media Connect

Deriso, Christine Hurley
    Then I met my sister. Flux 2011 269p pa $9.95
Grades: 8 9 10 11 12   **Fic**
1. Death -- Fiction 2. Diaries -- Fiction 3. Sisters
-- Fiction
ISBN 978-0-7387-2581-9; 0-7387-2581-1
                                        LC 2010-45239

Summer Stetson has always lived in the shadow of her
dead sister, knowing she can never measure up in any way,
but on her seventeenth birthday her aunt gives her Shannon's
diary, which reveals painful but liberating truths about Summer's family and herself.
"The journey Summer goes on to 'meet' her sister is
compelling, but equally interesting are her discoveries about
herself and her relationships. . . . This is a book intriguing
enough to read in one sitting." SLJ

Derting, Kimberly
    Desires of the dead. HarperCollins 2011 358p
$16.99
Grades: 7 8 9 10   **Fic**
1. School stories 2. Homicide -- Fiction 3. Friendship
-- Fiction 4. Supernatural -- Fiction 5. Extrasensory
perception -- Fiction
ISBN 978-0-06-177984-8; 0-06-177984-9
                                        LC 2010017838
Sixteen-year-old Violet Ambrose's ability to find murder
victims and their killers draws the attention of the FBI just as
her relationship with Jay, her best-friend-turned-boyfriend,
heats up.
"The author paces the story beautifully, weaving together several story lines as she inches up to the final, desperate scene. . . . Imaginative, convincing and successful
suspense." Kirkus

★ The **body** finder. Harper 2009 329p $16.99
Grades: 7 8 9 10 11 12   **Fic**
1. Mystery fiction 2. Dead -- Fiction 3. Supernatural
-- Fiction 4. Extrasensory perception -- Fiction
ISBN 978-0-06-177981-7; 0-06-177981-4
                                        LC 2009-39675
"Violet Ambrose can find dead bodies. Their aura of
sound, color, or even taste imprints itself on their murderers, and Violet's extrasensory perception picks up on those
elements. . . . Derting has written a suspenseful mystery
and sensual love story that will captivate readers who enjoy
authentic high-school settings, snappy dialogue, sweet romance, and heart-stopping drama." Booklist

The **last** echo; Kimberly Derting. Harper 2012
360 p. (hbk.) $17.99
Grades: 7 8 9 10 11 12   **Fic**
1. Love stories 2. Parapsychology -- Fiction 3. Serial
killers -- Fiction 4. Dead -- Fiction 5. Schools -- Fiction
6. Friendship -- Fiction 7. Best friends -- Fiction 8.
High schools -- Fiction 9. Serial murders -- Fiction 10.
Psychic ability -- Fiction
ISBN 0062082191; 9780062082190
                                        LC 2011044633
This book, "the third installment of the Body Finder series," begins with protagonist Violet "working for a secret
agency that specializes in using paranormal powers to fight
crime. . . . She still loves her normal boyfriend Jay, so she
worries about the strong physical response she feels whenever she touches Rafe, a member of the team. Meanwhile,
Violet doesn"t know she"s become the target of a terrifying
serial killer." (Kirkus Reviews)

"As always, this author writes a gripping tale... Personalities come across quite strongly, as several of the characters tend toward the eccentric." Kirkus

The pledge. Margaret K. McElderry Books 2011
323p $16.99

Grades: 7 8 9 10 **Fic**
1. Fantasy fiction 2. Ability -- Fiction 3. Social classes -- Fiction 4. Language and languages -- Fiction
ISBN 978-1-4424-2201-8; 1-4424-2201-7; 978-1-4424-2202-5 e-book
LC 2010053773

In a dystopian kingdom where the classes are separated by the languages they speak, Charlaina 'Charlie' Hart has a secret gift that is revealed when she meets a mysterious young man named Max.

Derting "keeps her story consistently engaging through vivid description and brisk pacing.... Great suspense from a prolific new writer with a vibrant imagination." Kirkus

Despain, Bree

The **dark** Divine. Egmont USA 2010 372p
$17.99; lib bdg $20.99

Grades: 7 8 9 10 11 **Fic**
1. School stories 2. Family life -- Fiction 3. Supernatural -- Fiction 4. Christian life -- Fiction
ISBN 978-1-60684-057-3; 1-60684-057-6; 978-1-60684-065-8 lib bdg; 1-60684-065-7 lib bdg
LC 2009-18680

Grace Divine, almost seventeen, learns a dark secret when her childhood friend—practically a brother—returns, upsetting her pastor-father and the rest of her family, around the time strange things are happening in and near their small Minnesota town.

"Despain raises complex issues of responsibility and forgiveness and offers no easy answers. Atmospheric and compelling." Booklist

Despeyroux, Denise

The **big** book of vampires; by Denise Despeyroux. Tundra Books of Northern New York 2013
108 p. (hardcover) $17.95

Grades: 5 6 7 **Fic**
1. Vampires -- Fiction
ISBN 1770493719; 9781770493711
LC 2011932738

"The most noted and significant terror/vampire stories and legends are adapted and included in this large and elaborately illustrated book. There are nine adaptations of this literary genre of the nineteenth century and four legends in the folk tradition. The legends, all about the adventures of vampires, originated in China, Spain, Poland, and Denmark.... Each of the two sections has a page listing the books along with several sentences of information." (Children's Literature)

Dessen, Sarah, 1970

★ **Along** for the ride; a novel. Viking 2009
383p $19.99

Grades: 7 8 9 10 **Fic**
1. Divorce -- Fiction 2. Infants -- Fiction 3. Stepfamilies -- Fiction 4. Dating (Social customs) -- Fiction
ISBN 978-0-670-01194-0; 0-670-01194-0
LC 2009-5661

When Auden impulsively goes to stay with her father, stepmother, and new baby sister the summer before she starts college, all the trauma of her parents' divorce is revived, even as she is making new friends and having new experiences such as learning to ride a bike and dating.

"Dessen explores the dynamics of an extended family headed by two opposing, flawed personalities, revealing their parental failures with wicked precision yet still managing to create real, even sympathetic characters. . . . [This book] provides the interpersonal intricacies fans expect from a Dessen plot." Horn Book

Lock and key; a novel. Viking Children's Books
2008 422p $18.99

Grades: 7 8 9 10 **Fic**
1. Child abuse -- Fiction 2. Family life -- Fiction 3. Abandoned children -- Fiction
ISBN 978-0-670-01088-2; 0-670-01088-X
LC 2007-25370

When she is abandoned by her alcoholic mother, high school senior Ruby winds up living with Cora, the sister she has not seen for ten years, and learns about Cora's new life, what makes a family, how to allow people to help her when she needs it, and that she too has something to offer others.

"The dialogue, especially between Ruby and Cora, is crisp, layered, and natural. The slow unfolding adds to an anticipatory mood. . . . Recommend this one to patient, sophisticated readers." SLJ

That summer. Orchard Books 1996 198p hardcover o.p. pa $8.99

Grades: 7 8 9 10 **Fic**
1. Sisters -- Fiction 2. Weddings -- Fiction
ISBN 0-531-09538-X; 0-531-08888-X lib bdg; 978-0-14-240172-9 pa; 0-14-240172-2 pa
LC 96-7643

During the summer of her divorced father's remarriage and her sister's wedding, fifteen-year-old Haven comes into her own by letting go of the myths of the past

"Dessen adds a fresh twist to a traditional sister-of-the-bride story with her keenly observant narrative full of witty ironies. Her combination of unforgettable characters and unexpected events generates hilarity as well as warmth." Publ Wkly

The **moon** and more; by Sarah Dessen. Viking
2013 384 p. (hardcover) $19.99

Grades: 7 8 9 10 **Fic**
1. Bildungsromans 2. Dating (Social customs) -- Fiction 3. Father-daughter relationship -- Fiction 4. Beaches -- Fiction 5. Resorts -- Fiction 6. Coming of age -- Fiction 7. Fathers and daughters -- Fiction 8. Family-owned business enterprises -- Fiction 9. Documentary films -- Production and direction -- Fiction
ISBN 0670785601; 9780670785605
LC 2012035720

In this novel, by Sarah Dessen, "Luke is the perfect boyfriend. . . . But now, in the summer before college, Emaline wonders if perfect is good enough. Enter Theo, a super-ambitious outsider.... Emaline's ... father, too, thinks Emaline should have a bigger life. . . . Emaline is attracted to the bright future that Theo and her father promise. But she also clings to the deep roots of her loving mother, stepfather, and sisters." (Publisher's note)

"Dessen's characters behave as deliciously unpredictably as people do in real life, and just as in real life, they sometimes have to make difficult choices with not-so-predictable outcomes... Completely engaging." Kirkus

The **truth** about forever. Viking 2004 382p $16.99; pa $6.50
Grades: 7 8 9 10   **Fic**
1. Death -- Fiction 2. Catering -- Fiction
ISBN 0-670-03639-0; 0-440-21928-0 pa
LC 2003-28298
The summer following her father's death, Macy plans to work at the library and wait for her brainy boyfriend to return from camp, but instead she goes to work at a catering business where she makes new friends and finally faces her grief.

"All of Dessen's characters . . . are fully and beautifully drawn. Their dialogue is natural and believable, and their care for one another is palpable. . . . Dessen charts Macy's navigation of grief in such an honest way it will touch every reader who meets her. " SLJ

What **happened** to goodbye. Viking 2011 402p $19.99
Grades: 8 9 10 11 12   **Fic**
1. School stories 2. Divorce -- Fiction
ISBN 978-0-670-01294-7; 0-670-01294-7
LC 2010-41041
"The novel nimbly weaves together familiar story lines of divorce, high-school happiness and angst, and teen-identity struggles with likable, authentic adult and teen characters and intriguing yet credible situations." Booklist

Detorie, Rick
★ The **accidental** genius of Weasel High. Egmont USA 2011 197p il pa $9.99
Grades: 5 6 7 8   **Fic**
1. Motion pictures -- Fiction
ISBN 1-60684-149-1 pa; 978-1-60684-149-5 pa
LC 2011-02776
Larkin Pace, a film-obsessed high school freshman, chronicles his experiences as he tries to raise money for a new camcorder and get a date with the girl who has been his best friend since third grade.

"Larkin serves as a relatable 'everykid,' and many readers will enjoy spending some time with him." SLJ

Deuker, Carl
★ **Gym** candy. Houghton Mifflin Company 2007 313p $16
Grades: 7 8 9 10 11 12   **Fic**
1. School stories 2. Football -- Fiction 3. Steroids -- Fiction 4. Father-son relationship -- Fiction
ISBN 978-0-618-77713-6; 0-618-77713-X
LC 2007-12749
Groomed by his father to be a star player, football is the only thing that has ever really mattered to Mick Johnson,

who works hard for a spot on the varsity team his freshman year, then tries to hold onto his edge by using steroids, despite the consequences to his health and social life.

"Deuker skillfully complements a sobering message with plenty of exciting on-field action and locker-room drama, while depicting Mick's emotional struggles with loneliness and insecurity as sensitively and realistically as his physical ones." Booklist

High heat. Houghton Mifflin 2003 277p $16; pa $6.99
Grades: 7 8 9 10   **Fic**
1. School stories 2. Fathers -- Fiction
ISBN 0-618-31117-3; 0-06-057248-5 pa
LC 2002-15324
When high school sophomore Shane Hunter's father is arrested for money laundering at his Lexus dealership, the star pitcher's life of affluence and private school begins to fall apart

This is "a story that delivers baseball action along with a rich psychological portrait, told through a compelling first-person narration." SLJ

Night hoops. Houghton Mifflin 2000 212p $15; pa $8.99
Grades: 7 8 9 10   **Fic**
1. Basketball -- Fiction 2. Friendship -- Fiction
ISBN 0-395-97936-6; 0-547-24891-1 pa
LC 99-47882
While trying to prove that he is good enough to be on his high school's varsity basketball team, Nick must also deal with his parents' divorce and erratic behavior of a troubled classmate who lives across the street

"The descriptions of the games are well written and accurate. Best of all, the complexities of basketball are contrasted with the complexities of life." SLJ

Painting the black. Avon Books 1999 248p pa $5.99
Grades: 8 9 10 11 12   **Fic**
1. School stories 2. Baseball -- Fiction
ISBN 0-380-73104-5
First published 1997 by Houghton Mifflin
"After a disastrous fall from a tree, senior Ryan Ward wrote off baseball. But he is swept back into the game when cocky, charismatic Josh Daniels—a star quarterback with the perfect spiral pass as well as a pitcher with a mean slider—moves into the neighborhood. . . . The well-written sports scenes—baseball and football—will draw reluctant readers, but it is Ryan's moral courage that will linger when the reading is done." Booklist

★ **Payback** time. Houghton Mifflin Harcourt 2010 298p $16
Grades: 7 8 9 10   **Fic**
1. School stories 2. Courage -- Fiction 3. Obesity -- Fiction 4. Football -- Fiction 5. Journalists -- Fiction
ISBN 978-0-547-27981-7; 0-547-27981-7
LC 2010-6779
Deuker "really cranks up the suspense in his newest page-turner. . . . The game action alone is riveting . . . but

Deuker enriches the tale with several well-tuned subplots and memorable narrator/protagonist." Booklist

Devlin, Ivy

Low red moon. Bloomsbury Children's Books 2010 244p $16.99

Grades: 7 8 9 10   **Fic**

1. Wolves -- Fiction 2. Homicide -- Fiction 3. Grandmothers -- Fiction 4. Supernatural -- Fiction 5. Forests and forestry -- Fiction

ISBN 978-1-59990-510-5; 1-59990-510-8

LC 2010-03480

Seventeen-year-old Avery can remember nothing to explain her parents' violent death in the woods where they live, but after meeting Ben, a mysterious new neighbor, she begins to believe some of the stories she has heard about creatures of the forest.

This is "an eerie and engrossing paranormal murder mystery. . . . The emotion pouring off the pages should sweep readers into this haunting story." Publ Wkly

DiCamillo, Kate, 1964-

★ **Because** of Winn-Dixie. Candlewick Press 2000 182p $15.99; pa $6.99

Grades: 4 5 6 7   **Fic**

1. Dogs -- Fiction

ISBN 978-0-7636-0776-0; 0-7636-0776-2; 978-0-7636-4432-1 pa; 0-7636-4432-3 pa

LC 99-34260

A Newbery honor book, 2001

Ten-year-old India Opal Buloni describes her first summer in the town of Naomi, Florida, and all the good things that happen to her because of her big ugly dog Winn-Dixie

"This well-crafted, realistic, and heartwarming story will be read and reread as a new favorite deserving a long-term place on library shelves." SLJ

★ **Flora** and Ulysses; The Illuminated Adventures. by Kate DiCamillo ; illustrated by K. G. Campbell. Candlewick Press 2013 240 p. ill. (reinforced) $17.99

Grades: 5 6 7 8   **Fic**

1. Occult fiction -- fiction 2. Children of divorced parents -- fiction

ISBN 076366040X; 9780763660406

LC 2012947748

In this book by Newbury Medalist Kate DiCamillo, "bitter about her parents' divorce. Flora Buckman has withdrawn into her favorite comic book The Amazing Incandesto! and memorized the advisories in its ongoing bonus feature, Terrible Things Can Happen to You! She puts those life-saving tips into action when a squirrel is swallowed whole by a neighbor's new vacuum cleaner. . . . Flora resuscitates the squirrel," who now has superpowers. (Publishers Weekly)

★ The **magician's** elephant; illustrated by Yoko Tanaka. Candlewick Press 2009 201p il $16.99

Grades: 4 5 6 7   **Fic**

1. Adventure fiction 2. Orphans -- Fiction 3. Siblings -- Fiction 4. Elephants -- Fiction 5. Missing children

-- Fiction

ISBN 978-0-7636-4410-9; 0-7636-4410-2

LC 2009-07359

When ten-year-old orphan Peter Augustus Duchene encounters a fortune teller in the marketplace one day and she tells him that his sister, who is presumed dead, is in fact alive, he embarks on a remarkable series of adventures as he desperately tries to find her.

"The profound and deeply affecting emotions at work in the story are bouyed up by the tale's succinct, lyrical text; gentle touches of humor; and uplifting message." Booklist

DiTerlizzi, Tony

A **hero** for WondLa; by Tony DiTerlizzi ; with illustrations by the author. Simon & Schuster Books for Young Readers 2012 445 p. (hardcover) $17.99

Grades: 5 6 7 8   **Fic**

1. Science fiction 2. Rescue work -- Fiction 3. Life on other planets -- Fiction 4. Identity -- Fiction 5. Human-alien encounters -- Fiction

ISBN 1416983120; 9781416983125; 9781442450844

LC 2011037031

Author Tony DiTerlizzi tells a science fiction story. "Eva Nine had never seen another human, but after a human boy named Hailey rescues her along with her companions, she couldn't be happier. Eva thinks she has everything she's ever dreamed of, especially when Hailey brings her and her friends to the colony of New Attica, where humans of all shapes and sizes live in apparent peace and harmony. But all is not idyllic in New Attica, and Eva Nine soon realizes that something sinister is going on . . . [that] could mean the end of everything and everyone on planet Orbona." (Publisher's note)

★ The **search** for WondLa; with illustrations by the author. Simon & Schuster Books for Young Readers 2010 477p il $17.99

Grades: 5 6 7 8   **Fic**

1. Science fiction 2. Extraterrestrial beings -- Fiction

ISBN 978-1-4169-8310-1; 1-4169-8310-4

LC 2010-01326

Living in isolation with a robot on what appears to be an alien world populated with bizarre life forms, a twelve-year-old human girl called Eva Nine sets out on a journey to find others like her.

"The abundant illustrations, drawn in a flat, two-tone style, are lush and enhance readers' understanding of this unique universe. . . . DiTerlizzi is pushing the envelope in his latest work, nearly creating a new format that combines a traditional novel with a graphic novel and with the interactivity of the computer. Yet, beneath this impressive package lies a theme readers will easily relate to: the need to belong, to connect, to figure out one's place in the world. The novel's ending is a stunning shocker that will leave kids frantically awaiting the next installment." SLJ

Dial, Connie

★ **Fallen** angels; Connie Dial. The Permanent Press 2012 296 p. hardcover o.p. $29

Grades: 8 9 10 11 12 Adult   **Fic**

1. Mystery fiction 2. Policewomen -- Fiction 3. Police corruption -- Fiction 4. Police -- California -- Los

Angeles -- Fiction
ISBN 1579622747; 9781579622749

LC 2011051392

ALA YALSA Margaret A. Edwards Award (1994)

This crime novel features Capt. Josie Corsino, who is investigating the death of starlet Hillary Dennis. Since the main suspect "Cory is L.A. city councilman Eli Goldman's son, Deputy Chief Eric Bright tells Corsino to go easy on Cory. Other pressures arise: Corsino's son, David, is tied to Cory; Corsino's husband, Jake, is unhappy; and too many incompetent or corrupt cops hamper her investigation." (Publishers Weekly)

"Black, seventeen, perceptive and sensitive, Richie (the narrator) has enlisted and been sent to Vietnam; in telling the story of his year of active service, Richie is candid about the horror of killing and the fear of being killed, the fear and bravery and confusion and tragedy of the war." Bull Cent Child Books

Diamand, Emily

Flood and fire. Chicken House/Scholastic 2011 351p il (Raiders' ransom) $17.99

Grades: 4 5 6 7   **Fic**

1. Science fiction 2. Adventure fiction 3. Cats -- Fiction 4. Robots -- Fiction 5. Computers -- Fiction 6. Terrorism -- Fiction

ISBN 978-0-545-24268-4; 0-545-24268-1

LC 2010023544

In 22nd-century Cambridge, England, thirteen-year-old Lilly Melkun must try to stop the strange, uncontrollable robots that were activated when a sinister-looking chip in her hand-held computer triggered a false anti-terrorist alert.

"The rare combination of action at breakneck speed and significant, believable character development makes this just about impossible to put down." Kirkus

★ **Raiders'** ransom. Chicken House/Scholastic 2009 334p map $17.99

Grades: 4 5 6 7   **Fic**

1. Science fiction 2. Adventure fiction 3. Pirates -- Fiction 4. Kidnapping -- Fiction 5. Environmental degradation -- Fiction

ISBN 978-0-545-14297-7; 0-545-14297-0

LC 2008-43692

It's the 22nd century and, because of climate change, much of England is underwater. Poor Lilly is out fishing with her trusty sea-cat when greedy raiders pillage the town—and kidnap the prime minister's daughter. Her village blamed, Lilly decides to find the girl.

This is a "captivating story. . . . A well-drawn world, plot twists galore and spunky characters make this one a true page-turner." Kirkus

Dickens, Charles

A **Christmas** carol; [by] Charles Dickens; illustrated by P.J. Lynch. Candlewick Press 2006 156p il $19.99

Grades: 5 6 7 8   **Fic**

1. Ghost stories 2. Christmas -- Fiction

ISBN 978-0-7636-3120-8; 0-7636-3120-5

LC 2005058122

A miser learns the true meaning of Christmas when three ghostly visitors review his past and foretell his future

Lynch's "watercolor-and-gouache illustrations lavishly enhance this handsome edition." SLJ

Dickerson, Melanie

The **merchant's** daughter. Zondervan 2011 284p pa $9.99

Grades: 7 8 9 10 11 12   **Fic**

1. Love -- Fiction 2. Middle Ages -- Fiction 3. Christian life -- Fiction 4. Contract labor -- Fiction

ISBN 978-0-31072761-3

LC 2011034338

In 1352 England, seventeen-year-old Annabel, granddaughter of a knight and a would-be nun, eludes a lecherous bailiff but falls in love with Lord Le Wyse, the ferocious and disfigured man to whom her family owes three years of indentured servitude, in this tale loosely based on Beauty and the Beast.

Dickerson "manages a heartfelt romance that will stick with readers, not only for its morality but also for the exploration of a woman's place within fourteenth-century English Christianity." Booklist

Dickinson, Peter

★ **Angel** Isle; illustrations by Ian Andrew. Wendy Lamb Books 2007 500p il $17.99; lib bdg $20.99

Grades: 7 8 9 10   **Fic**

1. Fantasy fiction 2. Magic -- Fiction

ISBN 978-0-385-74690-8; 978-0-385-90928-0 lib bdg

LC 2007-7053

While seeking the Ropemaker to restore the ancient magic that will protect their valley, Saranja, Maja, and Ribek must outwit twenty-four of the empire's most powerful and evil magicians.

"The characters are as well developed as those in the first book, and the complex, multilayered story includes more heady explorations of time and magic, joined here by thoughts on the meaning of true love." Booklist

★ **Eva**. Delacorte Press 1989 219p hardcover o.p. pa $6.50; pa $7.99

Grades: 7 8 9 10   **Fic**

1. Science fiction 2. Chimpanzees -- Fiction

ISBN 0-385-29702-5; 0-440-20766-5 pa; 9780440207665 pa

LC 88-29435

"Eva wakes up from a deep coma that was the result of a terrible car accident and finds herself drastically altered. The accident leaves her so badly injured that her parents consent to a radical experiment to transplant her brain and memory into the body of a research chimpanzee. With the aid of a computer for communication, Eva slowly adjusts to her new existence while scientists monitor her progress, feelings, and insight into the animal world." Voice Youth Advocates

★ The **ropemaker**. Delacorte Press 2001 375p $15.95; pa $7.95

Grades: 7 8 9 10   **Fic**
1. Fantasy fiction 2. Magic -- Fiction
ISBN 0-385-72921-9; 0-385-73063-2 pa
LC 2001-17422
Michael L. Printz Award honor book, 2002
When the magic that protects their Valley starts to fail, Tilja and her companions journey into the evil Empire to find the ancient magician Faheel, who originally cast those spells

"The suspense does not let up until the very last pages. While on one level this tale is a fantasy, it is also a wonderful coming-of-age story." SLJ

Dionne, Erin
Models don't eat chocolate cookies. Dial Books for Young Readers 2009 243p pa $7.99
Grades: 6 7 8 9   **Fic**
1. Obesity -- Fiction 2. Fashion models -- Fiction
ISBN 978-0-8037-3296-4; 0-8037-3296-1
LC 2008-20612
Overweight thirteen-year-old Celeste begins a campaign to lose weight in order to make sure she does not win the Miss HuskeyPeach modeling challenge, in which her mother and aunt have entered her--against her wishes.

"Wry first-person narrative also provides convincing views of middle-school friendships, family dynamics, and incremental personal growth. . . . A light, well-paced first novel." Booklist

The **total** tragedy of a girl named Hamlet. Dial Books for Young Readers 2010 290p $16.99
Grades: 6 7 8 9   **Fic**
1. School stories 2. Sisters -- Fiction 3. Theater -- Fiction
ISBN 978-0-8037-3298-8; 0-8037-3298-8
"Some sisterly bonding, the sweet flutterings of a first romance, and a creatively contrived comeuppance for the mean girls make this a cheerful read for younger middle-schoolers." Booklist

Divakaruni, Chitra Banerjee
The **conch** bearer. Roaring Brook Press 2003 265p (Brotherhood of the conch) $16.95; lib bdg $23.90
Grades: 5 6 7 8   **Fic**
1. Magic -- Fiction
ISBN 978-0-7613-1935-1; 0-7613-1935-2; 978-0-7613-2793-6 lib bdg; 0-7613-2793-2 lib bdg
LC 2003-8578
In India, a healer invites twelve-year-old Anand to join him on a quest to return a magical conch to its safe and rightful home, high in the Himalayan mountains

"Divakaruni keeps her tale fresh and riveting." Publ Wkly
Other titles in this series are:
The mirror of fire and dreaming (2005)
Shadowland (2009)

Dixon, Heather
★ **Entwined**. Greenwillow Books 2011 472p
Grades: 7 8 9 10   **Fic**
1. Fantasy fiction 2. Dance -- Fiction 3. Death -- Fiction 4. Magic -- Fiction 5. Princesses -- Fiction

6. Kings and rulers -- Fiction 7. Father-daughter relationship -- Fiction
ISBN 0-06-200103-5; 978-0-06-200103-0
LC 2010-11686
Confined to their dreary castle while mourning their mother's death, Princess Azalea and her eleven sisters join The Keeper, who is trapped in a magic passageway, in a nightly dance that soon becomes nightmarish.

"The story gracefully explores significant themes of grief and loss, mercy and love. Full of mystery, lush settings, and fully orbed characters, Dixon's debut is both suspenseful and rewarding." Booklist

Dobkin, Bonnie
Neptune's children; [by] Bonnie Dobkin. Walker & Co. 2008 262p map $16.99
Grades: 7 8 9 10   **Fic**
1. Terrorism -- Fiction 2. Amusement parks -- Fiction 3. Resistance to government -- Fiction
ISBN 978-0-8027-9734-6; 0-8027-9734-2
LC 2008-2680
When a biological terrorist attack kills all adults on Earth, children stranded at an amusement park work together to survive, led by Milo whose father was an engineer there, but when new threats arise and suspicions grow, rebellion erupts.

"This thriller has gripping writing that makes it hard to put down. The characterizations of the older children are well done. . . . Even with the large number of survival stories on the market, this is one worth adding to your collection." SLJ

Docherty, James
The **ice** cream con; [by] Jimmy Docherty. Scholastic 2008 250p $16.99
Grades: 5 6 7 8 9   **Fic**
1. Bullies -- Fiction 2. Thieves -- Fiction
ISBN 978-0-545-02885-1; 0-545-02885-X
LC 2007-35321
In Glasgow, Scotland, after getting mugged twice in ten minutes, thirteen-year-old Jake comes up with a plan to con the criminals on his estate with the help of his closest friends, until events start to snowball out of control.

"Docherty keeps the action coming fast and furious from beginning to end. . . . It is bound to be a huge hit with tween boys and especially reluctant readers." Voice Youth Advocates

Doctorow, Cory
★ **Little** brother. Tor Teen 2008 380p
Grades: 8 9 10 11 12   **Fic**
1. Computers -- Fiction 2. Terrorism -- Fiction 3. Civil rights -- Fiction
ISBN 0765319853; 9780765319852
LC 2008-1827
After being interrogated for days by the Department of Homeland Security in the aftermath of a terrorist attack on San Francisco, California, 17-year-old Marcus, released into what is now a police state, decides to use his expertise in computer hacking to set things right. "High school." (Horn Book)

"The author manages to explain naturally the necessary technical tools and scientific concepts in this fast-paced and well-written story. . . . The reader is privy to Marcus's gut-wrenching angst, frustration, and terror, thankfully offset by his self-awareness and humorous observations." Voice Youth Advocates

Pirate cinema; Cory Doctorow. 1st ed. Tor Teen 2012 384 p. (hardback) $19.99; (paperback) $9.99; (audiobook) $24.00

Grades: 7 8 9 10   **Fic**
   1. Copyright   2. Runaway teenagers -- Fiction 3. Science fiction 4. Internet -- Fiction 5. Protest movements -- Fiction 6. Motion pictures -- Production and direction -- Fiction
   ISBN 0765329085; 9780765329080; 9781429943185; 9780765329097; 9780307879585
                LC 2012019871

In this book, author Cory Doctorow tells the story of Trent McCauley, a boy who "has an irrepressible drive to create . . . [films] through illegal downloading, and when he's caught, . . . [he] runs away to London, where he's taken under the wing of streetwise Jem Dodger. . . . He meets 26 and creates the persona Cecil B. DeVil. Pulled by 26 into the politics of copyright and the lobbyist money that purchases laws, Cecil becomes a creative figurehead for reform against escalating laws that aggressively jail kids." (Kirkus Reviews)

Dogar, Sharon

   ★ **Annexed**. Houghton Mifflin Harcourt 2010 333p $17

Grades: 8 9 10 11 12   **Fic**
   1. Holocaust, 1933-1945 -- Fiction
   ISBN 978-0-547-50195-6; 0-547-50195-1
                LC 2010-282410

"On July 13, 1942, 15-year-old Peter van Pels and his parents entered the attic that became their home for two years. Peter is angry that he is hiding and not fighting Nazis. He is also not happy to be sharing cramped living quarters with the Franks, especially know-it-all Anne. In this novel, Dogar 'reimagines' what happened between the families who lived in the secret annex immortalized in Anne Frank's diary. In doing so, she creates a captivating historical novel and fully fleshes out the character of Peter, a boy whom teens will easily relate to." SLJ

Doherty, Berlie

The **girl** who saw lions. Roaring Brook Press 2008 249p $16.95

Grades: 6 7 8 9   **Fic**
   1. Adoption -- Fiction 2. AIDS (Disease) -- Fiction
   ISBN 978-1-59643-377-9; 1-59643-377-9
                LC 2007-44054

In alternating voices, thirteen-year-old Rosa and her mother are trying to adopt a Tanzanian child in England, while in Tanzania, nine-year-old Abela watches her family die and her uncle illegally sends her to England, in the hopes of selling her.

"Packs in a great deal of information about the AIDS crisis in Africa, female genital mutilation, international adoptions, the foster care system, and the many challenges facing parentless children and the social workers who try to

place them. Girls will love this emotionally powerful novel." Voice Youth Advocates

Doktorski, Jennifer Salvato

   Famous last words; Jennifer Salvato Doktorski. Henry Holt and Company 2013 288 p. (hardcover) $17.99

Grades: 7 8 9 10   **Fic**
   1. Women journalists -- Fiction 2. Internship programs -- Fiction 3. Journalism -- Fiction 4. Newspapers -- Fiction 5. Self-perception -- Fiction 6. Dating (Social customs) -- Fiction
   ISBN 0805093672; 9780805093674
                LC 2012046312

In this book, "aspiring reporter Sam D'Angelo, 16, is interning at her local New Jersey paper for the summer, stuck writing obituaries with her occasionally annoying, college-age fellow intern AJ. When she's not taking phone calls about dead people, Sam writes humorous imaginary obits (including one for herself); spends time with her grandmother; lusts after the 'incredibly hot' features intern, Tony Roma; and covertly investigates the shady mayor with AJ." (Publishers Weekly)

"Something of a love note to print journalism, the story is nevertheless snappy and contemporary, furthered by Sam's wry, self-deprecating narration and convincingly colloquial dialogue. Cleverly titled, realistically written, and on the whole engaging and sympathetic, this story rings true." Kirkus

Dolamore, Jaclyn

   ★ **Magic** under glass. Bloomsbury Children's Books 2010 225p $16.99

Grades: 7 8 9 10 11 12   **Fic**
   1. Fantasy fiction 2. Magic -- Fiction 3. Robots -- Fiction 4. Fairies -- Fiction 5. Singers -- Fiction
   ISBN 978-1-59990-430-6; 1-59990-430-6
                LC 2009-20944

A wealthy sorcerer's invitation to sing with his automaton leads seventeen-year-old Nimira, whose family's disgrace brought her from a palace to poverty, into political intrigue, enchantments, and a friendship with a fairy prince who needs her help.

"Delamore successfully juggles several elements that might have stymied even a more experienced writer: intriguing plot elements, sophisticated characterizations, and a subtle boost of girl power." Booklist

Dominy, Amy Fellner

   OyMG. Walker & Co. 2011 247p $16.99

Grades: 6 7 8 9   **Fic**
   1. Camps -- Fiction 2. Prejudices -- Fiction 3. Jews -- United States -- Fiction
   ISBN 978-0-8027-2177-8; 0-8027-2177-X
                LC 2010-34581

Fourteen-year-old Ellie will do almost anything to win a scholarship to the best speech school in the country, but must decide if she is willing to hide her Jewish heritage while at a Phoenix, Arizona, summer camp that could help her reach her goal.

"Readers will be pulled into the thoughtful exploration of one girl's emotional connection to her religion and family heritage, her struggle to balance ambition with honesty and self respect, and her delicate negotiation of being different when that difference isn't outwardly apparent." Bull Cent Child Books

Donaldson, Joan

On Viney's mountain. Holiday House 2009 231p $16.95

Grades: 6 7 8 9   **Fic**
1. Weaving -- Fiction 2. Family life -- Fiction 3. Mountain life -- Fiction
ISBN 978-0-8234-2129-9; 0-8234-2129-5
LC 2009-01062

In the Cumberland Mountains during the fall of 1879, sixteen-year-old Viney is shocked to hear that English-men will arrive on her mountain and build a new com-munity, demolishing the beautiful area that inspires her weaving designs.

"Based on actual events, this is historical romance with strong characters and plot development that illuminates without romanticizing the past." Booklist

Donaldson, Julia

Running on the cracks. Henry Holt 2009 218p $16.99

Grades: 6 7 8 9   **Fic**
1. Orphans -- Fiction 2. Runaway teenagers -- Fiction 3. Child sexual abuse -- Fiction 4. Racially mixed people -- Fiction
ISBN 978-0-8050-9054-3; 0-8050-9054-1
LC 2008-50278

After her parents are killed in an accident, English teen-ager Leonora Watts-Chan runs away to Glasgow, Scotland, to find her Chinese grandparents

"The characters in Donaldson's . . . YA debut are well drawn and their imperfections are authentic, particularly Mary's battle with mental illness. Despite heavy themes, the story is neither bleak nor gritty. The fast pace and short chap-ters should appeal to readers, who will celebrate the hopeful ending." Publ Wkly

Donovan, John

I'll get there, it better be worth the trip; 40th an-niversary edition; Flux 2010 228p pa $9.95

Grades: 7 8 9 10 11   **Fic**
1. Alcoholism -- Fiction 2. Friendship -- Fiction 3. Homosexuality -- Fiction
ISBN 978-0-7387-2134-7 pa; 0-7387-2134-4 pa
LC 2010014266

First published 1969 by Harper & Row

While trying to cope with his alcoholic mother and ab-sent father, a lonely New York City teenager develops a con-fusing crush on another boy.

"Donovan's novel is startlingly outspoken and honest in its presentation of a young teen questioning his sexuality. . . . Such is the author's skill that the reader knows this young man's journey of self-discovery will get him to his 'there,' wherever it may be. This welcome fortieth-anniversary edi-tion of a YA classic is an essential purchase for all libraries." Voice Youth Advocates

Dooley, Sarah

Body of water. Feiwel and Friends 2011 324p $16.99

Grades: 7 8 9   **Fic**
1. Arson -- Fiction 2. Camping -- Fiction 3. Family life -- Fiction 4. Homeless persons -- Fiction
ISBN 978-0-312-61254-2; 0-312-61254-0
LC 2011023523

After their trailer home and all their belongings are burned, twelve-year-old Ember and her Wiccan family move to a lakeside campground where Ember's anguish over losing her dog, as well as her friendship with the boy she fears started the fire, stops her from making new friends and moving on.

"Dooley puts readers directly into the center of Ember's plight with a heartfelt first-person narration. An enthralling tale that demystifies Wicca, humanizes homeless families and inspires reflection on friendship, forgiveness and mov-ing forward." Kirkus

Dorris, Michael

Morning Girl. Hyperion Bks. for Children 1992 74p hardcover o.p. pa $4.99

Grades: 4 5 6 7   **Fic**
1. Taino Indians -- Fiction
ISBN 0-7868-1358-X pa
LC 92-52989

Twelve year old Morning Girl, a Taino Indian who loves the day, and her younger brother Star Boy, who loves the night, take turns describing their life on a Bahamian island in 1492; in Morning Girl's last narrative, she witnesses the arrival of the first Europeans to her world

"The author uses a lyrical, yet easy-to-follow, style to place these compelling characters in historical context. . . . Dorris does a superb job of showing that family dynamics are complicated, regardless of time and place. . . . A touching glimpse into the humanity that connects us all." Horn Book

Sees Behind Trees. Hyperion Bks. for Children 1996 104p hardcover o.p. pa $4.99

Grades: 4 5 6 7   **Fic**
1. Native Americans -- Fiction 2. Vision disorders -- Fiction
ISBN 0-7868-1357-1 pa
LC 96-15859

"For the partially sighted Walnut, it is impossible to prove his right to a grown-up name by hitting a target with his bow and arrow. With his highly developed senses, how-ever, he demonstrates that he can do something even better: he can see 'what cannot be seen' which earns him the name Sees Behind Trees. . . . Set in sixteenth-century America, this richly imagined and gorgeously written rite-of-passage story has the gravity of legend. Moreover, it has buoyant humor and the immediacy of a compelling story that is peopled with multidimensional characters." Booklist

Dowd, Siobhan

★ **Bog** child. David Fickling Books 2008 321p

Grades: 8 9 10 11 12   **Fic**
1. Mummies -- Fiction 2. Prisoners -- Fiction 3.

Terrorism -- Fiction 4. Family life -- Fiction
ISBN 0-385-75170-2 lib bdg; 978-0-385-75169-8;
0-385-75169-9; 978-0-385-75170-4 lib bdg

LC 2008-2998

This novel is set in Northern Ireland in 1981. 18-year-old
Fergus is distracted from his upcoming A-level exams by
the discovery of a girl's body in a peat bog, his imprisoned
brother's hunger strike, and the stress of being a courier for
Sinn Fein.

"Dowd raises questions about moral choices within a
compelling plot that is full of surprises, powerfully bringing
home the impact of political conflict on innocent bystanders." Publ Wkly

★ The **London** Eye mystery. David Fickling
Books 2008 322p $15.99; lib bdg $18.99; pa $7.50
Grades: 5 6 7 8   **Fic**
1. Mystery fiction 2. Cousins -- Fiction 3. Siblings
-- Fiction 4. Missing children -- Fiction 5. Asperger's
syndrome -- Fiction
ISBN 978-0-375-84976-3; 0-375-84976-9; 978-0-375-
94976-0 lib bdg; 0-375-84976-3 lib bdg; 978-0-385-
75184-1 pa; 0-385-75184-2 pa

LC 2007-15119

First published 2007 in the United Kingdom

When Ted and Kat's cousin Salim disappears from the
London Eye ferris wheel, the two siblings must work together—Ted with his brain that is "wired differently" and
impatient Kat—to try to solve the mystery of what happened
to Salim.

"Everything rings true here, the family relationships, the
quirky connections of Ted's mental circuitry, and . . . the
mystery. . . . A page turner with heft." Booklist

Dowell, Frances O' Roark

Ten miles past normal. Atheneum Books for
Young Readers 2011 211p $16.99
Grades: 6 7 8 9 10   **Fic**
1. School stories 2. Farm life -- Fiction 3. Bands
(Music) -- Fiction
ISBN 1-4169-9585-4; 978-1-4169-9585-2

LC 2010-22041

Because living with "modern-hippy" parents on a goat
farm means fourteen-year-old Janie Gorman cannot have a
normal high school life, she tries joining Jam Band, making
friends with Monster, and spending time with elderly former
civil rights workers.

"Janie narrates her first year in high school with her sure,
smart, sarcastic voice. . . . Dowell gets all the details of ninth
grade right." Horn Book

Dowell, Frances O'Roark

Chicken boy. Atheneum Books for Young Read-
ers 2005 201p $15.95; pa $5.99
Grades: 4 5 6 7   **Fic**
1. Chickens -- Fiction 2. Friendship -- Fiction 3.
Family life -- Fiction
ISBN 0-689-85816-7; 1-4169-3482-0 pa

LC 2004-10928

Since the death of his mother, Tobin's family life and
school life have been in disarray, but after he starts raising

chickens with his seventh-grade classmate, Henry, everything starts to fall into place.

"There is no glib resolution, here. But the strong narration and the child's struggle with forgiveness make for poignant, aching drama." Booklist

★ **Dovey** Coe. Atheneum Bks. for Young Read-
ers 2000 181p $16; pa $5.99
Grades: 5 6 7 8   **Fic**
1. Brothers and sisters 2. Mountain life -- Fiction 3.
Mountain life -- North Carolina
ISBN 0-689-83174-9; 0-689-84667-3 pa

LC 99-46870

When accused of murder in her North Carolina mountain
town in 1928, Dovey Coe, a stronged-willed twelve-year-old
girl, comes to a new understanding of others, including her
deaf brother

"Dowell has created a memorable character in Dovey,
quick-witted and honest to a fault. . . . This is a delightful
book, thoughtful and full of substance." Booklist

★ **Falling** in. Atheneum Books for Young Readers 2010 245p il $16.99
Grades: 4 5 6 7   **Fic**
1. Fantasy fiction
ISBN 978-1-4169-5032-5; 1-4169-5032-X

LC 2009-10412

Middle-schooler Isabelle Bean follows a mouse's squeak
into a closet and falls into a parallel universe where the children believe she is the witch they have feared for years, finally come to devour them.

"This perfectly paced story has enough realistic elements to appeal even to nonfantasy readers." Booklist

★ **Shooting** the moon. Atheneum Books for
Young Readers 2008 163p $16.99; pa $5.99
Grades: 4 5 6 7   **Fic**
1. Soldiers -- Fiction 2. Family life -- Fiction 3.
Vietnam War, 1961-1975 -- Fiction
ISBN 978-1-4169-2690-0; 1-4169-2690-9; 978-1-
4169-7986-9 pa; 1-4169-7986-7 pa

LC 2006-100347

Boston Globe-Horn Book Award honor book: Fiction
and Poetry (2008)

When her brother is sent to fight in Vietnam, twelve-
year-old Jamie begins to reconsider the army world that she
has grown up in.

"The clear, well-paced first-person prose is perfectly
matched to this novel's spare setting and restrained plot. .
. . This [is a] thoughtful and satisfying story. . . . Readers
will find beauty in its resolution, and will leave this eloquent
heroine reluctantly." SLJ

The **kind** of friends we used to be. Atheneum
Books for Young Readers 2009 234p $16.99
Grades: 5 6 7 8   **Fic**
1. School stories 2. Friendship -- Fiction
ISBN 978-1-4169-5031-8; 1-4169-5031-1

LC 2008-22245

Twelve-year-olds Kate and Marylin, friends since preschool, draw further apart as Marylin becomes involved in
student government and cheerleading, while Kate wants

to play guitar and write songs, and both develop unlikely friendships with other girls and boys.

"Dowell gets middle-school dynamics exactly right, and while her empathetic portraits of Kate and Marylin are genuine and heartfelt, even secondary characters are memorable. A realistic and humorous look at the trials and tribulations of growing up and growing independent." SLJ

★ The **second** life of Abigail Walker; Frances O'Roark Dowell. Atheneum Books for Young Readers 2012 228 p. (hardcover) $16.99

Grades: 4 5 6 7   **Fic**

   1. Self-confidence -- Fiction 2. Friendship -- Fiction 3. Overweight persons -- Fiction 4. Human-animal relationships -- Fiction

   ISBN 1442405937; 9781442405936

LC 2012010646

This novel, by Frances O'Roark Dowell, follows a youth struggling with popularity. "Seventeen pounds. That's the difference between . . . chubby and slim, between teased and taunting. Abby is fine with her body, . . . so she speaks out against Kristen and her groupies--and becomes officially unpopular. Embracing her new status, Abby heads to an abandoned lot across the street and crosses an unfamiliar stream that leads her to a boy who's as different as they come." (Publisher's note)

Downer, Ann

  ★ **Hatching** magic. Atheneum Bks. for Young Readers 2003 242p $16.95; pa $5.99

Grades: 4 5 6 7   **Fic**

   1. Magic -- Fiction 2. Dragons -- Fiction

   ISBN 0-689-83400-4; 0-689-87057-4 pa

LC 00-56570

When a thirteenth-century wizard confronts twenty-first century Boston while seeking his pet dragon, he is followed by a rival wizard and a very unhappy demon, but eleven-year-old Theodora Oglethorpe may hold the secret to setting everything right

"With likable characters, and laced with plenty of humor and adventure, Downer's fantasy will have solid appeal for young genre fans." Booklist

Another title about Theodora is:

The dragon of never-was (2006)

Downham, Jenny

  ★ **Before** I die. David Fickling Books 2007 326p hardcover o.p. pa $9.99

Grades: 8 9 10 11 12   **Fic**

   1. Death -- Fiction 2. Terminally ill -- Fiction

   ISBN 978-0-385-75155-1; 978-0-385-75183-4 pa

LC 2007-20284

A terminally ill teenaged girl makes and carries out a list of things to do before she dies.

"Downham holds nothing back in her wrenchingly and exceptionally vibrant story." Publ Wkly

Dowswell, Paul

  The **Auslander**. Bloomsbury Children's Books 2011 295p $16.99

Grades: 7 8 9 10   **Fic**

   1. Orphans -- Fiction 2. Adoption -- Fiction 3.

Insurgency -- Fiction 4. National socialism -- Fiction 5. World War, 1939-1945 -- Fiction

   ISBN 1599906333; 9781599906331

LC 2010035626

First published 2009 in the United Kingdom

German soldiers take Peter from a Warsaw orphanage, and soon he is adopted by Professor Kaltenbach, a prominent Nazi, but Peter forms his own ideas about what he sees and hears and decides to take a risk that is most dangerous in 1942 Berlin.

"The characters are rich and nuanced; . . . the action is swift and suspenseful; and the juxtaposition of wartime nobility and wartime cruelty is timeless." Horn Book

Powder monkey; adventures of Sam Witchall. [by] Paul Dowswell. 1st U.S. ed.; Bloomsbury Pub. 2005 275p $16.95

Grades: 6 7 8 9   **Fic**

   1. Sea stories 2. Adventure fiction

   ISBN 978-1-58234-675-5; 1-58234-675-5

LC 2005013049

Thirteen-year-old Sam endures harsh conditions, battles, and a shipwreck after being pressed into service aboard the HMS Miranda during the Napoleonic Wars.

"Readers will be absorbed in the day-to-day life of young Sam, and his vivid tale will keep them on edge." SLJ

Other titles in this series are:

Prison ship (2006)

Battle fleet (2008)

Doyle, Arthur Conan, Sir, 1859-1930

The **adventures** and the memoirs of Sherlock Holmes; by Arthur Conan Doyle ; illustrated by Scott McKowen. Sterling Pub. Co. 2004 vi, 569 p.p ill. (hardcover) $9.95

Grades: 7 8 9 10 11 12 Adult   **Fic**

   1. Mystery fiction 2. Holmes, Sherlock (Fictional character) 3. Detective and mystery stories, English 4. Private investigators -- England -- Fiction 5. Holmes, Sherlock (Fictitious character) -- Fiction

   ISBN 140271453X; 9781402714535

LC 2004016067

This book is a collection of Sir Arthur Conan Doyle's mystery stories featuring detective "Sherlock Holmes, with his unequalled powers of deduction." This edition has illustrations created by Scott McKowen "in scratchboard, an engraving medium which evokes the look of popular art from the period of these stories." (Publisher's note)

Doyle, Brian

Boy O'Boy. Douglas & McIntyre 2003 161p hardcover o.p. pa $12.95

Grades: 6 7 8 9   **Fic**

   1. Child sexual abuse -- Fiction

   ISBN 0-88899-588-1; 0-88899-590-3 pa

Living in Ottawa in 1945, Martin O'Boy must deal with a drunken father, an overburdened mother, a disabled twin brother, and a sexual predator at his church.

"Martin O'Boy is an expert observer and narrator. . . . Martin's world is believably real. Even the description of the sexual encounter seems like what a confused 11 or 12-year-old might say. " SLJ

Pure Spring. Groundwood Books 2007 158p $16.95; pa $8.95

Grades: 6 7 8 9   **Fic**

1. Canada -- Fiction
ISBN 978-0-88899-774-6; 978-0-88899-775-3 pa

It's spring in post-World War II Ottawa and Martin has found a true home. He's also working even though he had to lie about his age to get the job. Martin is also in love, but his boss is robbing the family of the one he loves.

"Doyle lovingly shapes his characters. . . . Doyle rounds out the grimness with comedic scenes." Horn Book

Doyle, Eugenie F.

According to Kit; [by] Eugenie Doyle. Front Street 2009 215p $17.95

Grades: 7 8 9 10   **Fic**

1. Ballet -- Fiction 2. Farm life -- Fiction 3. Family life -- Fiction 4. Home schooling -- Fiction 5. Mother-daughter relationship -- Fiction
ISBN 978-1-59078-474-7; 1-59078-474-X

LC 2009-7032

As fifteen-year-old Kit does chores on her family's Vermont farm, she puzzles over her mother's apparent unhappiness, complains about being homeschooled after a minor incident at school, and strives to communicate just how important dance is to her.

Doyle's "characters are complicated and authentic. . . . Kit's obsession with ballet . . . will ring true for all teens equally focused on their own talents." Booklist

Doyle, Marissa

Betraying season. Henry Holt and Co. 2009 330p $16.99

Grades: 7 8 9 10   **Fic**

1. Magic -- Fiction 2. Witches -- Fiction
ISBN 978-0-8050-8252-4; 0-8050-8252-2

LC 2008-40593

In 1838, Penelope Leland goes to Ireland to study magic and prove to herself that she is as good a witch as her twin sister Persy, but when Niall Keating begins to pay her court, she cannot help being distracted.

"This is a full-bodied story that wonderfully combines elements of romance, fantasy, and history. . . . Whether Doyle is describing the Irish countryside, a magical incantation, or a lover's kiss, her writing is compelling, and it will be hard for readers not to be swept away by this invigorating story." Booklist

★ **Bewitching** season. Henry Holt 2008 346p $16.95; pa $8.99

Grades: 7 8 9 10   **Fic**

1. Magic -- Fiction 2. Twins -- Fiction 3. Sisters -- Fiction 4. Missing persons -- Fiction
ISBN 978-0-8050-8251-7; 0-8050-8251-4; 978-0-312-59695-8 pa; 0-312-59695-2 pa

In 1837, as seventeen-year-old twins, Persephone and Penelope, are starting their first London Season they find that their beloved governess, who has taught them everything they know about magic, has disappeared.

"Doyle takes as much care with characters . . . as with story details. This [is a] delightful mélange of genres." Booklist

Courtship and curses; Marissa Doyle. Henry Holt 2012 343 p. (hc) $17.99

Grades: 7 8 9 10   **Fic**

1. Regency novels 2. Mystery fiction 3. Magic -- Fiction 4. Witches -- Fiction 5. Self-acceptance -- Fiction 6. People with disabilities -- Fiction 7. Aristocracy (Social class) -- Fiction
ISBN 0805091874; 9780805091878

LC 2011031999

This book tells the story of "Lady Sophronia Rosier (Sophie)," who is preparing "for her entrance into London society," despite a disability incurred from illness. She has help from "her new best friend, Parthenope" and "begins her procession into society." It soon becomes clear that someone is using magic to target her and her father. "Sophie and Parthenope begin to investigate while playing their roles in society, dreadfully aware that lives are at stake." (Voice of Youth Advocates)

Doyle, Roddy

Wilderness. Arthur A. Levine Books 2007 211p $16.99

Grades: 6 7 8 9   **Fic**

1. Mothers -- Fiction 2. Sledding -- Fiction 3. Wilderness survival -- Fiction
ISBN 978-0-439-02356-6; 0-439-02356-4

LC 2007-11688

As Irish teenager Gráinne anxiously prepares for a reunion with her mother, who abandoned the family years before, Gráinne's half-brothers and their mother take a dog-sledding vacation in Finland.

"The drama and adventure are leavened by generous helpings of Doyle's characteristic charm, laugh-out-loud humor, and wonderful way with words." SLJ

★ **A greyhound** of a girl; Roddy Doyle. Amulet Books 2012 208 p. $16.95

Grades: 7 8 9 10 11 12   **Fic**

1. Dog racing -- Fiction 2. Family life -- Fiction 3. Dublin (Ireland) -- Fiction 4. Women -- Ireland -- Fiction 5. Death -- Fiction 6. Ghosts -- Fiction 7. Grandmothers -- Fiction 8. Voyages and travels -- Fiction 9. Mothers and daughters -- Fiction
ISBN 9781407129334 Marion Lloyd; 1407129333 Marion Lloyd; 9781419701689 Amulet; 1419701681 Amulet

LC 2011042200

This book tells the story of "Twelve-year-old Mary O'Hara," an Irish girl who "is surrounded by good-humored women . . . her mum at home, her mum's mum, who is dying in Dublin's Sacred Heart Hospital, and her mum's mum's mum, who has just materialized as a ghost on her street. . . . [Roddy] Doyle divides up the novel by character, giving readers first-hand glimpses into the nature of each woman through time." (Kirkus)

Draanen, Wendelin van

Runaway. Knopf 2006 250p $15.95; lib bdg $17.99

Grades: 6 7 8 9   **Fic**
  1. Orphans -- Fiction 2. Homeless persons -- Fiction 3. Runaway children -- Fiction
  ISBN 0-375-83522-9; 0-375-93522-3 lib bdg
                 LC 2005-33276

After running away from her fifth foster home, Holly, a twelve-year-old orphan, travels across the country, keeping a journal of her experiences and struggle to survive.

"The ending of this taut, powerful story seems possible and deeply hopeful." Booklist

★ **Sammy** Keyes and the hotel thief. Knopf 1998 163p il hardcover o.p. pa $6.50
Grades: 4 5 6 7   **Fic**
  1. Mystery fiction 2. Grandmothers -- Fiction 3. Mystery and detective stories 4. Robbers and outlaws -- Fiction
  ISBN 978-0-679-88839-0; 0-679-89264-8 pa
                 LC 97-40776

Thirteen-year-old Sammy's penchant for speaking her mind gets her in trouble when she involves herself in the investigation of a robbery at the "seedy" hotel across the street from the seniors' building where she is living with her grandmother

"This is a breezy novel with vivid characters." Bull Cent Child Books

  Other titles about Sammy Keyes are:
  Sammy Keyes and the art of deception (2003)
  Sammy Keyes and the cold hard cash (2008)
  Sammy Keyes and the curse of Moustache Mary (2000)
  Sammy Keyes and the dead giveaway (2005)
  Sammy Keyes and the Hollywood mummy (2001)
  Sammy Keyes and the night of skulls (2011)
  Sammy Keyes and the psycho Kitty Queen (2004)
  Sammy Keyes and the runaway elf (1999)
  Sammy Keyes and the search for snake eyes (2002)
  Sammy Keyes and the Sisters of Mercy (1999)
  Sammy Keyes and the skeleton man (1998)
  Sammy Keyes and the wedding crasher (2010)
  Sammy Keyes and the wild things (2007)

Drago, Ty
The **Undertakers** : rise of the Corpses. Sourcebooks Jabberwocky 2011 465p pa $10.99
Grades: 4 5 6 7   **Fic**
  1. Horror fiction 2. Zombies -- Fiction
  ISBN 978-1-4022-4785-9; 1-4022-4785-0

"Whatever you do, do not call them zombies! These are Corpses 'reanimated bodies that have been possessed,' and they are everywhere, although they are only visible to a select few, including 12-year-old Will Ritter. After realizing suddenly that he is able to see, Will is taken in by the Undertakers, a rogue group that rescues other, similarly targeted teens and fights to defeat the Corpses' evil plans to conquer Phildelphia and, ultimately, the world. . . . Calling into action a cast of distinctive characters with authentic voices and behaviors, . . . Will's breathless adventures . . . are thoughtful and exciting, and the descriptions of decaying flesh will likely both disgust and delight readers." Booklist

The **dragon's** lair; the lost journals of Van Polypheme. text compiled by Elizabeth Haydon ; il-

lustrations restored by Jason Chan. 1st ed. Tom Doherty Associates 2008 349 p. ill. (paperback) $7.99; (hardcover) $17.95
Grades: 5 6 7 8   **Fic**
  1. Fantasy 2. Dragons -- Fiction 3. Adventure and adventurers -- Fiction
  ISBN 9780765347749; 076530869X; 9780765308696
                 LC 2008003001

In this book, the third in Elizabeth Haydon's Lost Journals of Ven Polypheme series, it is only days "after Ven Polypheme and his friends escape from the Thieves Quarter, [and] the Thief Queen is sending her raven minions after them. The companions travel by cart to seek shelter with Saeli's family. Meanwhile on assignment from the king, Ven is secretly trying to discover why a dragon is attacking Nain villages and sowing discord between the Nain and the Lirin." (Publisher's note)

Draper, Sharon M. (Sharon Mills), 1948-
The **Battle** of Jericho. Atheneum Books for Young Readers 2003 297p $16.95; pa $6.99
Grades: 7 8 9 10   **Fic**
  1. School stories 2. Clubs -- Fiction 3. Death -- Fiction 4. Cousins -- Fiction
  ISBN 0-689-84232-5; 0-689-84233-3 pa
                 LC 2002-8612

"This title is a compelling read that drives home important lessons about making choices." SLJ

  Other titles in this series are:
  Just another hero (2009)
  November blues (2007)

Double Dutch. Atheneum Bks. for Young Readers 2002 183p $16; pa $4.99
Grades: 6 7 8 9   **Fic**
  1. Friendship -- Fiction 2. Rope skipping -- Fiction 3. African Americans -- Fiction
  ISBN 0-689-84230-9; 0-689-84231-7 pa
                 LC 00-50247

Three eighth-grade friends, preparing for the International Double Dutch Championship jump rope competition in their home town of Cincinnati, Ohio, cope with Randy's missing father, Delia's inability to read, and Yo Yo's encounter with the class bullies

"Teens will like the high-spirited, authentic dialogue . . . the honest look at tough issues, and the team workout scenes that show how sports can transform young lives." Booklist

★ **Fire** from the rock. Dutton Children's Books 2007 229p $16.99
Grades: 6 7 8 9   **Fic**
  1. School stories 2. Race relations -- Fiction 3. African Americans -- Fiction
  ISBN 978-0-525-47720-4; 0-525-47720-9
                 LC 2006-102952

In 1957, Sylvia Patterson's life is disrupted by the impending integration of Little Rock's Central High when she is selected to be one of the first black students to attend the previously all white school.

"This historical fiction novel is a must have. It keeps the reader engaged with vivid depictions of a time that most young people can only imagine." Voice Youth Advocates

★ **Out** of my mind. Atheneum 2010 295p $16.99

Grades: 5 6 7 8   **Fic**
1. Cerebral palsy -- Fiction
ISBN 978-1-4169-7170-2; 1-4169-7170-X
LC 2009-18404

Josette Frank Award for Fiction, 2011

"Fifth-grader Melody has cerebral palsy, a condition that affects her body but not her mind. Although she is unable to walk, talk, or feed or care for herself, she can read, think, and feel. A brilliant person is trapped inside her body, determined to make her mark in the world despite her physical limitations. . . . Told in Melody's voice, this highly readable, compelling novel quickly establishes her determination and intelligence and the almost insurmountable challenges she faces. . . . Uplifting and upsetting." Booklist

DuPrau, Jeanne
★ The **city** of Ember. Random House 2003 270p (Books of Ember) $15.95; lib bdg $17.99; pa $6.99

Grades: 5 6 7 8   **Fic**
1. Science fiction
ISBN 0-375-82273-9; 0-375-92274-1 lib bdg; 0-385-73628-2 pa
LC 2002-10239

"More than 200 years after an unspecified holocaust, the residents of Ember have lost all knowledge of anything beyond the area illuminated by the floodlamps on their buildings. . . . Food and other supplies are running low, and the power failures that plunge the town into impenetrable darkness are becoming longer and more frequent. Then Lina, a young foot messenger, discovers a damaged document from the mysterious Builders that hints at a way out." SLJ

Other titles in this series are:
The people of Sparks (2004)
The prophet of Yonwood (2006)
The diamond of Darkhold (2008)

Duble, Kathleen Benner
Hearts of iron. Margaret K. McElderry Books 2006 248p $15.95

Grades: 6 7 8 9   **Fic**
1. Iron industry -- Fiction
ISBN 1-4169-0850-1
LC 2005-29258

In early 1800s Connecticut, fifteen-year-old Lucy tries to decide whether to marry her childhood friend who unhappily toils at the Mt. Riga iron furnace or the young man from Boston who has come to work in her father's store.

"Well-written historical fiction with a unique setting and a touch of mystery, Lucy's story will both inform and entertain readers." SLJ

Phantoms in the snow. Scholastic Press 2011 226p $17.99

Grades: 6 7 8 9   **Fic**
1. Uncles -- Fiction 2. Orphans -- Fiction 3. Pacifism -- Fiction 4. Soldiers -- Fiction 5. Military bases -- Fiction 6. World War, 1939-1945 -- Italy -- Fiction
ISBN 978-0-545-19770-0; 0-545-19770-8
LC 2010016898

In 1944, fifteen-year-old Noah Garrett, recently orphaned, is sent to live at Camp Hale, Colorado, with an uncle he has never met, and there he finds his pacifist views put to the test.

"Duble has created a likable character in Noah, whose struggles to find out who he is and where he belongs in a world at war are convincingly portrayed and realistically resolved." Kirkus

Quest; 1st ed.; Margaret K. McElderry Books 2008 240p $16.99

Grades: 7 8 9 10   **Fic**
1. Spies -- Fiction 2. Explorers -- Fiction 3. Seafaring life -- Fiction
ISBN 978-1-4169-3386-1; 1-4169-3386-7
LC 2006102712

Relates events of explorer Henry Hudson's final voyage in 1602 from four points of view, those of his seventeen-year-old son aboard ship, a younger son left in London, a crewmember, and a young English woman acting as a spy in Holland in hopes of restoring honor to her family's name.

"The author's skillful juxtaposition of these four narratives creates an absorbing work of historical fiction that manages to incorporate the viewpoints of explorers, investors, sailors, governments, family members, and neighbors of those who played a part in this fascinating era." SLJ

The **sacrifice**. Margaret K. McElderry Books 2005 211p $15.95

Grades: 6 7 8 9   **Fic**
1. Puritans -- Fiction 2. Witchcraft -- Fiction
ISBN 0-689-87650-5
LC 2004-18355

Two sisters, aged ten and twelve, are accused of witchcraft in Andover, Massachusetts, in 1692 and await trial in a miserable prison while their mother desperately searches for some way to obtain their freedom.

"Well written with accessible language, this book will appeal to a wide range of readers." SLJ

Includes bibliographical references

Dudley, David L.
Caleb's wars. Clarion Books 2011 263p $16.99
Grades: 7 8 9 10   **Fic**
1. Germans -- Fiction 2. Family life -- Fiction 3. Segregation -- Fiction 4. Race relations -- Fiction 5. Prisoners of war -- Fiction 6. African Americans -- Fiction 7. World War, 1939-1945 -- Fiction
ISBN 978-0-547-23997-2; 0-547-23997-1
LC 2011009644

Fifteen-year-old Caleb's courageous commitment to justice grows as he faces a power struggle with his father, fights to keep both his temper and self-respect in dealing with whites, and puzzles over the German prisoners of war brought to his rural Georgia community during World War II.

"Caleb is compelling and believable, and Dudley's rich writing is impressive, clearly showing the various wars black Americans were fighting in the 1940s, both abroad and closer to home." SLJ

Duey, Kathleen

Sacred scars. Atheneum Books for Young Readers 2009 554p il (A resurrection of magic) $17.99

Grades: 7 8 9 10   Fic

1. School stories 2. Fantasy fiction 3. Magic -- Fiction
ISBN 978-0-689-84095-1; 0-689-84095-0

LC 2008-56044

In alternate chapters, Sadima works to free captive boys forced to copy documents in the caverns of Limori, and Hahp makes a pact with the remaining students of a wizards' academy in hopes that all will survive their training, as both learn valuable lessons about loyalty.

"The text so successfully portrays Hahp's experience in this grueling, cold-blooded wizard 'academy'—isolation, starvation, abuse and constant, unsolvable puzzles—that readers may absorb his strain, confusion and desolation themselves. . . . Absorbing and unwaveringly suspenseful." Kirkus

Skin hunger. Atheneum Books for Young Readers 2007 357p (Resurrection of magic) hardcover o.p. pa $9.99

Grades: 7 8 9 10   Fic

1. Fantasy fiction 2. Magic -- Fiction
ISBN 978-0-689-84093-7; 0-689-84093-4; 978-0-689-84094-4 pa; 0-689-84094-2 pa

LC 2006-34819

In alternate chapters, Sadima travels from her farm home to the city and becomes assistant to a heartless man who is trying to restore knowledge of magic to the world, and a group of boys fights to survive in the academy that has resulted from his efforts.

This is a "compelling new fantasy. . . . Duey sweeps readers up in the page-turning excitement." Horn Book

Dumas, Alexandre

The **three** musketeers; translated by Jacques Le Clercq. Modern Library 1999 xxi, 598 p.p (hardcover) $26.00

Grades: 7 8 9 10 11 12 Adult   Fic

1. Adventure 2. France -- Gascony 3. France -- 17th century 4. Courts and courtiers -- France
ISBN 0679603328; 9780679603320
Original French edition, 1844

"D'Artagnan arrives in Paris one day in 1625 and manages to be involved in three duels with three musketeers . . . Athos, Porthos and Aramis. They become d'Artagnan's best friends. The account of their adventures from 1625 on develops against the rich historical background of the reign of Louis XIII and the early part of that of Louis XIV, the main plot being furnished by the antagonism between Cardinal de Richelieu and Queen Anne d'Autriche." Haydn. Thesaurus of Book Dig

Duncan, Lois

I know what you did last summer. Little, Brown 1973 199p hardcover o.p. pa $6.50

Grades: 7 8 9 10 11 12   Fic

1. Mystery fiction
ISBN 0-440-22844-1 pa
ALA YALSA Margaret A. Edwards Award (1992)

This book "has vivid characterization, good balance, and the boding sense of impending danger that adds excitement to the best mystery stories." Bull Cent Child Books

★ **Killing** Mr. Griffin. Dell 1990 223p hardcover o.p. pa $6.50

Grades: 7 8 9 10   Fic

1. School stories 2. Kidnapping -- Fiction
ISBN 0-440-94515-1 pa
First published 1978 by Little, Brown
ALA YALSA Margaret A. Edwards Award (1992)

The author's "skillful plotting builds layers of tension that draws readers into the eye of the conflict. The ending is nicely handled in a manner which provides relief without removing any of the chilling implications." SLJ

Locked in time. Little, Brown 1985 210p hardcover o.p. pa $6.50

Grades: 7 8 9 10   Fic

1. Mystery fiction
ISBN 0-316-19555-3; 0-440-94942-4 pa

LC 85-23

This "is the story of a domineering mother, Lisette, and her two teenage children, Gabe and Josie, who have all drunk from the cup of eternal youth. Seventeen-year-old Nore Robbins goes to visit her father, Charles, and her new stepfamily, Lisette, Gabe and Josie, at Lisette's beautiful old estate deep in the Louisiana bayou country. Nore discovers her stepfamily's secret and, in an attempt to expose this knowledge, becomes Lisette's target for death. . . . Grades seven to ten." (SLJ)

"The writing style is smooth, the characters strongly developed, and the plot, which has excellent pace and momentum, is an adroit blending of fantasy and realism." Bull Cent Child Books

Stranger with my face. Little, Brown 1981 250p hardcover o.p. pa $8.95

Grades: 7 8 9 10   Fic

1. Twins -- Fiction 2. Supernatural -- Fiction
ISBN 0-440-98356-8

LC 81-8299

"The ghostly Lia is deliciously evil; the idea of astral projection—Lia's method of travel—is novel; the island setting is vivid; and the relationships among the young people are realistic in the smoothly written supernatural tale." Horn Book

Dunkle, Clare B.

The **house** of dead maids; illustrations by Patrick Arrasmith. Henry Holt and Co. 2010 146p il $15.99

Grades: 8 9 10 11 12   Fic

1. Ghost stories 2. Orphans -- Fiction 3. Household employees -- Fiction
ISBN 978-0-8050-9116-8; 0-8050-9116-5

LC 2009-50769

Eleven-year-old Tabby Aykroyd, who would later serve as housekeeper for thirty years to the Brontë sisters, is taken from an orphanage to a ghost-filled house, where she and a wild young boy are needed for a pagan ritual.

"The author manages to stay true to the essence of Wuthering Heights while creating a deliciously chilling ghost story that stands on its own. Readers do not have to be at all familiar with Brontë's gothic story of destructive love to be scared out of their wits by this one: cognoscenti, though, will recognize a few sly nods to the original." Bull Cent Child Books

★ The **sky** inside. Atheneum Books for Young Readers 2008 229p $16.99
Grades: 6 7 8 9   **Fic**
1. Science fiction
ISBN 978-1-41692-422-7; 1-41692-422-1
After the disappearance of his sister, Cassie, and other children who ask questions about their carefully choreographed life in a domed suburb cut off from the outside world, Martin and his intelligent dog investigate.

"Dunkle surrounds her protagonists with an enthralling range of settings, a memorable cast of characters. . . . Fans of the author will . . . recognize her evocative storytelling and intricate plotting." Bull Cent Child Books

The **walls** have eyes. Atheneum Books for Young Readers 2009 225p $16.99
Grades: 6 7 8 9   **Fic**
1. Science fiction 2. Dogs -- Fiction 3. Robots -- Fiction 4. Family life -- Fiction 5. Genetic engineering -- Fiction
ISBN 978-1-41695-379-1; 1-41695-379-5
                 LC 2008038298
Having spirited his parents out of their domed suburb, Martin goes to the school for help and finds that his sister, Cassie, and the other Wonder Babies are gone again, but his AllDog, Chip, may hold the means to save them all.

"Throughout, Dunkle creates a vivid sense of imminent danger. . . . The book is recommended for readers who enjoyed the first volume." Booklist

Dunlap, Susanne
In the shadow of the lamp; [by] Susanne Dunlap. Bloomsbury Children's Books 2011 293p $16.99
Grades: 7 8 9 10   **Fic**
1. Nurses -- Fiction 2. Crimean War, 1853-1856 -- Fiction
ISBN 978-1-59990-565-5; 1-59990-565-5
                 LC 2010-21158
Sixteen-year-old Molly Fraser works as a nurse with Florence Nightingale during the Crimean War to earn a salary to help her family survive in nineteenth-century England.

"Dunlap has written a story with roots deep in research about Florence Nightingale and the women who served as nurses during the Crimean War. . . . [She] . . . delivers another extraordinary novel that feels relevant even today." Libr Media Connect

Dunlap, Susanne Emily
The **musician's** daughter; [by] Susanne Dunlap. Bloomsbury 2009 322p $16.99

Grades: 8 9 10 11 12   **Fic**
1. Mystery fiction 2. Gypsies -- Fiction 3. Homicide -- Fiction 4. Musicians -- Fiction
ISBN 978-1-59990-332-3; 1-59990-332-6
                 LC 2008-30307
In eighteenth-century Vienna, Austria, fifteen-year-old Theresa seeks a way to help her mother and brother financially while investigating the murder of her father, a renowned violinist in Haydn's orchestra at the court of Prince Esterhazy, after his body is found near a gypsy camp.

"Dunlap skillfully builds suspense until the final page. . . . Readers will root for courageous Theresa through the exciting intrigue even as they absorb deeper messages about music and art's power to lift souls and inspire change." Booklist

Dunmore, Helen
Ingo. HarperCollins Pubs. 2005 328p $16.99; lib bdg $17.89
Grades: 6 7 8 9   **Fic**
1. Mermaids and mermen -- Fiction
ISBN 978-0-06-081852-4; 0-06-081852-2; 978-0-06-081853-1 lib bdg; 0-06-081853-0 lib bdg
                 LC 2005-19079
As they search for their missing father near their Cornwall home, Sapphy and her brother Conor learn about their family's connection to the domains of air and of water.

"Strong character development combines with an engaging plot and magical elements to make this a fine choice for fantasy readers, who will look forward to the next installments in this planned trilogy." SLJ
Other titles about Sapphire are:
The tide knot (2008)
The deep (2009)

Durango, Julia
The **walls** of Cartagena; by Julia Durango; illustrated by Tom Pohrt. Simon & Schuster Books for Young Readers 2008 152p il $15.99
Grades: 5 6 7 8   **Fic**
1. Leprosy -- Fiction 2. Slavery -- Fiction 3. Catholic Church -- Fiction
ISBN 978-1-4169-4102-6; 1-4169-4102-9
                 LC 2007041861
Thirteen-year-old Calepino, an African slave in the seventeenth-century Caribbean city of Cartagena, works as a translator for a Jesuit priest who tends to newly-arrived slaves and, after working for a Jewish doctor in a leper colony and helping an Angolan boy and his mother escape, he realizes his true calling

"Illustrated with occasional small ink sketches, the ultimate rescue adventure is gripping, but more compelling is the authentic history of people desperate and brave." Booklist

Durbin, William
The **Winter** War; [by] William Durbin. 1st ed.; Wendy Lamb Books 2008 231p $15.99; lib bdg $18.99
Grades: 6 7 8 9   **Fic**
1. Soldiers -- Fiction 2. Poliomyelitis -- Fiction 3.

Russo-Finnish War, 1939-1940 -- Fiction
ISBN 978-0-385-74652-6; 0-385-74652-0; 978-0-385-90889-4 lib bdg; 0-385-90889-X lib bdg
LC 2007007048

When Russian troops invade Finland during the winter of 1939–40, Marko, a young polio victim determined to keep his homeland free, joins the Finnish Army as a messenger boy.

"Durbin's graphic depictions of the realities of war are not for the faint of heart. . . . More than a war story, though, this is a tale of resilience and self-discovery. . . . An engaging novel for adventure lovers and fans of historical fiction alike." SLJ

Includes bibliographical references

The **broken** blade. Delacorte Press 1997 163p hardcover o.p. pa $5.50
Grades: 5 6 7 8   Fic
1. Fur trade -- Fiction
ISBN 0-385-32224-0; 0-440-41184-X
LC 96-22114

When an injury prevents his father from going into northern Canada with fur traders, thirteen-year-old Pierre decides to take his father's place as a voyageur

"This look at the early nineteenth-century Canadian fur trade should appeal to reluctant readers as well as adventure buffs, and it may be a welcome suggestion for middle-school historical fiction reports." Bull Cent Child Books

The **darkest** evening. Orchard Books 2004 232p $15.95
Grades: 6 7 8 9   Fic
1. Communism -- Fiction 2. Finnish Americans -- Fiction
ISBN 0-439-37307-7
LC 2003-20255

In the 1930s, a young Finnish-American boy reluctantly moves with his family to Karelia, a communist-Finnish state founded in Russia, where his idealistic father soon realizes that his conception of a communist utopia is flawed.

"Many readers who enjoy tales of courage under fire . . . will find this exciting stuff." Booklist

Durrant, Lynda
Imperfections. Clarion Books 2008 172p $16
Grades: 6 7 8 9   Fic
1. Shakers -- Fiction 2. Siblings -- Fiction 3. Abandoned children -- Fiction
ISBN 978-0-5470-0357-3; 0-5470-0357-9
LC 2008-23533

In 1862 Pleasant Hill, Kentucky, fourteen-year-old Rosemary Elizabeth strives to fit in with the Shaker sisters of this "Heaven on Earth," but yearns to be reunited with her mother and siblings from whom she was separated when they sought refuge from her abusive father. Includes facts about Shakers and Morgan's Raiders.

"This fine coming-of-age novel rewards readers with an unusual glimpse into a rarely portrayed religion as well as a different perspective on the Civil War." Booklist

Includes bibliographical references

My last skirt; the story of Jennie Hodgers, Union soldier. by Lynda Durrant. Clarion Books 2006 199p $16
Grades: 6 7 8 9   Fic
1. Sex role -- Fiction 2. Irish Americans -- Fiction
ISBN 978-0-618-57490-2; 0-618-57490-5
LC 2005027746

Enjoying the freedom afforded her while dressing as a boy in order to earn higher pay after emigrating from Ireland, Jennie Hodgers serves in the 95th Illinois Infantry as Private Albert Cashier, a Union soldier in the American Civil War.

"Based on a true story, Jennie's tale is gripping. . . . Her loneliness, longing, and missed opportunities will resonate deeply with readers." SLJ

Includes bibliographical references

Durst, Sarah Beth
Ice. Margaret K. McElderry Books 2009 308p $16.99
Grades: 7 8 9 10   Fic
1. Fairy tales 2. Polar bear -- Fiction 3. Scientists -- Fiction 4. Supernatural -- Fiction
ISBN 978-1-4169-8643-0; 1-4169-8643-X
LC 2009-8618

A modern-day retelling of "East o' the Sun, West o' the Moon" in which eighteen-year-old Cassie learns that her grandmother's fairy tale is true when a Polar Bear King comes to claim her for his bride and she must decide whether to go with him and save her long-lost mother, or continue helping her father with his research

"Told in a descriptive style that perfectly captures the changing settings, Durst's novel is a page-turner that readers who enjoy adventure mixed with fairy-tale romance will find hard to put down." Booklist

Into the Wild. Razorbill 2007 260p $15.99
Grades: 6 7 8 9   Fic
1. Fairy tales 2. Magic -- Fiction
ISBN 978-1-59514-156-9; 1-59514-156-1
LC 2007-01942

Having escaped from the Wild and the preordained fairy tale plots it imposes, Rapunzel, along with her daughter Julie Marchen, tries to live a fairly normal life, but when the Wild breaks free and takes over their town, it is Julie who has to prevent everyone from being trapped in the events of a story.

"The novel is a creative romp through the fairy tale genre, highlighting the strength of the female characters whose stories we all know so well." Kliatt

Another title about Julie is:
Out of the wild (2008)

Vessel; Sarah Beth Durst. Margaret K. McElderry Books 2012 424 p. $16.99
Grades: 7 8 9 10   Fic
1. Deserts -- Fiction 2. Survival -- Fiction 3. Goddesses -- Fiction 4. Fate and fatalism -- Fiction
ISBN 1442423765; 9781442423763; 9781442423787
LC 2011044691

In this book by Sarah Beth Durst, "Liyana has trained all her life to be the vessel for her desert tribe's goddess Bayla. . . . "Bayla never shows up, but the trickster god Korbyn appears in human form and gives Liyana some startling news: the gods have all been imprisoned in false vessels, and he and Liyana must retrieve the various tribes' unsuccessful vessels, figure out where the deities are being held, and rescue them." (Bulletin of the Center for Children's Books)

Eames, Brian

The **dagger** Quick. Simon & Schuster Books for Young Readers 2011 320p $15.99

Grades: 4 5 6 7 **Fic**
1. Sea stories 2. Adventure fiction 3. Pirates -- Fiction 4. Handicapped -- Fiction
ISBN 978-1-4424-2311-4; 1-4424-2311-0
LC 2011-04405

Twelve-year-old Christopher "Kitto" Wheale, a club-footed boy seemingly doomed to follow in the boring footsteps of his father as a cooper in seventeenth-century England, finds himself on a dangerous seafaring adventure with his newly discovered uncle, the infamous pirate William Quick.

"Thoroughly researched, fast-paced, and tense, this coming-of-age adventure doesn't sugarcoat the dangers of the era, even as it embraces the mythical glamour of a pirate's life." Publ Wkly

Edgar, Elsbeth

The **Visconti** house. Candlewick Press 2011 287p $16.99

Grades: 4 5 6 7 **Fic**
1. Houses -- Fiction 2. Family life -- Fiction
ISBN 0-7636-5019-6; 978-0-7636-5019-3
LC 2010-39172

Laura Horton has always been an outsider, more interested in writing, drawing, or spending time with her free-spirited family than in her fellow teens, but she is drawn to Leon, a new student, as together they explore the mysteries of her eccentric old house.

"Convincing dialogue and well-drawn characters, both major and minor, bring energy to the story. . . . A fine, sensitive first novel." Booklist

Edwardson, Debby Dahl

★ **Blessing's** bead. Farrar, Straus & Giroux 2009 178p $16.99

Grades: 6 7 8 9 10 **Fic**
1. Inupiat -- Fiction 2. Villages -- Fiction 3. Influenza -- Fiction 4. Alcoholism -- Fiction
ISBN 978-0-374-30805-6; 0-374-30805-5
LC 2008-26726

In 1917, Aaluk leaves for Siberia while her sister Nutaaq remains in their Alaskan village and becomes one of the few survivors of an influenza epidemic, then in 1986, Nunaaq's great-granddaughter leaves her mother due to a different kind of sickness and returns to the village where they were born

"It's the Nutaag's rhythmic, indelible voices—both as steady and elemental as the beat of a drum or a heart—that will move readers most. A unique, powerful debut." Booklist

★ **My** name is not easy. Marshall Cavendish 2011 248p $17.99; e-book $17.99

Grades: 7 8 9 10 **Fic**
1. School stories 2. Native Americans -- Fiction
ISBN 978-0-7614-5980-4; 0-7614-5980-4; 978-0-7614-6091-6 e-book
LC 2011002108

"Edwardson's skillful use of dialogue and her descriptions of rural Alaska as well as boarding-school life invoke a strong sense of empathy and compassion in readers. . . Edwardson is to be applauded for her depth of research and her ability to portray all sides of the equation in a fair and balanced manner while still creating a very enjoyable read." SLJ

Efaw, Amy

Battle dress. HarperCollins Pubs. 2000 291p hardcover o.p. lib bdg $16.89

Grades: 7 8 9 10 **Fic**
1. Military education -- Fiction 2. Women in the armed forces -- Fiction 3. Military education -- New York (State) -- West Point
ISBN 0-06-028411-0 lib bdg; 0-06-053520-2
LC 99-34516

As a newly arrived freshman at West Point, seventeen-year-old Andi finds herself gaining both confidence and self esteem as she struggles to get through the grueling six weeks of new cadet training known as the Beast

"This book by a West Point graduate is a gripping, hard-to-put-down look at a young woman's struggle to succeed in a traditionally all-male environment." Voice Youth Advocates

Ehrenberg, Pamela

★ **Ethan,** suspended; written by Pamela Ehrenberg. Eerdmans Books for Young Readers 2007 266p $16

Grades: 7 8 9 10 **Fic**
1. Jews -- Fiction 2. Grandparents -- Fiction 3. Race relations -- Fiction
ISBN 978-0-8028-5324-0
LC 2006032697

After a school suspension and his parents' separation, Ethan is sent to live with his grandparents in Washington, D.C., which is worlds apart from his home in a Philadelphia suburb.

"Ehrenberg focuses on themes of race and class without sounding preachy. . . . Best of all are the portraits of [Ethan's] scrappy Jewish grandparents." Booklist

Ehrenhaft, Daniel

Friend is not a verb; a novel. HarperTeen 2010 241p $16.99

Grades: 7 8 9 10 **Fic**
1. Siblings -- Fiction 2. Rock music -- Fiction 3. Family life -- Fiction 4. Bands (Music) -- Fiction
ISBN 978-0-06-113106-6; 0-06-113106-7
LC 2009-44006

While sixteen-year-old Hen's family and friends try to make his supposed dreams of becoming a rock star come true, he deals with the reality of being in a band with an ex-girlfriend, a friendship that may become love, and his older sister's mysterious disappearance and reappearance.

"Offbeat characters, an intriguing mystery, and a sweet romance make Ehrenhaft's . . . coming-of-age story stand out. . . . The mystery—and romance—wrap up rather neatly, but readers should be impressed by the clever surprise ending." Publ Wkly

Elkeles, Simone

How to ruin my teenage life. Flux 2007 281p pa $8.95

Grades: 7 8 9 10 11 12   **Fic**

1. Jews -- Fiction 2. Israelis -- Fiction 3. Father-daughter relationship -- Fiction

ISBN 978-0-7387-0961-1; 0-7387-1019-9

LC 2007005535

Living with her Israeli father in Chicago, seventeen-year-old Amy Nelson-Barak feels like a walking disaster, worried about her "non-boyfriend" in the Israeli army, her mother, new stepfather, and the baby they are expecting, a new boy named Nathan who has moved into her apartment building and goes to her school, and whether or not she really is the selfish snob that Nathan says she is.

"This book has laugh-out-loud moments. . . . Amy's thoughtfulness and depth raise this book above most of the chick-lit genre." Voice Youth Advocates

Other titles in this series are:

How to ruin a summer vacation (2006)

How to ruin your boyfriend's reputation (2009)

Elliott, Laura

Give me liberty; [by] L. M. Elliott. Katherine Tegen Books 2006 376p $16.99; lib bdg $17.89; pa $7.99

Grades: 5 6 7 8   **Fic**

ISBN 0-06-074421-9; 0-06-074422-7 lib bdg; 0-06-074423-5 pa

Follows the life of thirteen-year-old Nathaniel Dunn, from May 1774 to December 1775, as he serves his indentureship with a music teacher in Williamsburg, Virginia, and witnesses the growing rift between patriots and loyalists, culminating in the American Revolution.

"Elliott packs a great deal of historical detail into a novel already filled with action, well-drawn characters, and a sympathetic understanding of many points of view." Booklist

Under a war-torn sky; [by] L.M. Elliott. Hyperion Bks. for Children 2001 284p hardcover o.p. pa $5.99

Grades: 7 8 9 10   **Fic**

1. World War, 1939-1945 -- Fiction

ISBN 0-7868-0755-5; 0-7868-1753-4 pa

LC 2001-16633

After his plane is shot down by Hitler's Luftwaffe, nineteen-year-old Henry Forester of Richmond, Virginia, strives to walk across occupied France, with the help of the French Resistance, in hopes of rejoining his unit

"It's packed with action, intrigue, and suspense, but this novel celebrates acts of kindness and heroism without glorifying war." Booklist

A **troubled** peace; by L. M. Elliott. Katherine Tegen Books 2009 289p $16.99; lib bdg $17.89

Grades: 7 8 9 10   **Fic**

1. Veterans -- Fiction 2. World War, 1939-1945 -- Fiction

ISBN 978-0-06-074427-4; 0-06-074427-8; 978-0-06-074428-1 lib bdg; 0-06-074428-6 lib bdg

"It's near the end of World War II. Nineteen-year-old bomber pilot hero Henry Forester is back home in Virginia, suffering from nightmares and starting at every loud noise. . . . [He needs] to go back to France and search for the young boy who jeopardized his own life helping Henry escape. Returning and new readers alike will find action, well-developed characters, and deep details about the privations war brings." Booklist

Elliott, Patricia

★ The **Pale** Assassin. Holiday House 2009 336p $17.95

Grades: 7 8 9 10   **Fic**

1. Adventure fiction 2. Siblings -- Fiction

ISBN 978-0-8234-2250-0; 0-8234-2250-X

LC 2009-7554

In early 1790s Paris, as the Revolution gains momentum, young and sheltered Eugenie de Boncoeur finds it difficult to tell friend from foe as she and the royalist brother she relies on become the focus of "le Fantome," the sinister spymaster with a long-held grudge against their family.

"The best aspect of this excellent work of historical fiction is Eugenie herself. Her gradual coming of age and growing political awareness provides resonant depth to what becomes a highly suspenseful survival tale." Booklist

The **traitor's** smile. Holiday House 2011 304p $17.95

Grades: 7 8 9 10   **Fic**

1. Adventure fiction 2. Cousins -- Fiction

ISBN 978-0-8234-2361-3; 0-8234-2361-1

First published 2010 in the United Kingdom

As the French Revolutin rages around her, wealthy and beautiful Eugenie de Boncoeur is no longer safe in her own country. She flees the bloody streeets of Paris for her cousin Hetta's house in England, narrowly excaping the clutches of the evil Pale Assassin, who is determined to force her to marry him.

Ellis, Ann Dee

Everything is fine. Little, Brown and Co. Books for Young Readers 2009 154p il $16.99

Grades: 6 7 8 9 10   **Fic**

1. Mothers -- Fiction 2. Bereavement -- Fiction 3. Family life -- Fiction 4. Depression (Psychology) -- Fiction

ISBN 978-0-316-01364-2; 0-316-01364-1

LC 2008-5847

When her father leaves for a job out of town, Mazzy is left at home to try to cope with her mother, who has been severely depressed since the death of Mazzy's baby sister.

"What makes [this book] so extraordinary is the narrative device that Ellis employs to searing effect. . . . [This] is a story so painful you want to read it with your eyes closed. It is a stunning novel." Voice Youth Advocates

★ **This** is what I did. Little, Brown 2007 157p
$16.99

Grades: 6 7 8 9   **Fic**
    1. School stories 2. Bullies -- Fiction
    ISBN 978-0-316-01363-5; 0-316-01363-3

LC 2006-01388

Bullied because of an incident in his past, eighth-grader
Logan is unhappy at his new school and has difficulty relating to others until he meets a quirky girl and a counselor who
believe in him.

"Part staccato prose, part transcript, this haunting first
novel will grip readers right from the start. . . . A particularly
attractive book design incorporates small drawings between
each segment of text." Publ Wkly

Ellis, Deborah

Bifocal; [by] Deborah Ellis and Eric Walters.
Fitzhenry & Whiteside 2007 280p $18.95; pa
$12.95

Grades: 7 8 9 10   **Fic**
    1. School stories 2. Muslims -- Fiction 3. Prejudices
    -- Fiction
    ISBN 978-1-55455-036-4; 1-55455-036-X; 978-1-
    55455-062-3 pa; 1-55455-062-9 pa

When a Muslim boy is arrested at a high school on suspicion of terrorist affiliations, growing racial tensions divide
the student population.

"The story is told in the alternating voices of two students. . . . Their individual struggles to understand the flaring
prejudice and their journeys toward self-discovery are subtle
and authentic. . . . This is a story that will leave readers looking at their schools and themselves with new eyes." Booklist

My name is Parvana. Groundwood Books/House
of Anansi Press 2012 201 p. $16.95

Grades: 5 6 7 8   **Fic**
    1. Afghanistan -- Fiction 2. Interrogation -- Fiction 3.
    Women -- Afghanistan -- Fiction
    ISBN 1554982979; 9781554982974

In this novel by Deborah Ellis "15-year-old Parvana is
imprisoned and interrogated as a suspected terrorist in Afghanistan. . . . Parvana's captors" read "aloud the words in
her notebook to decide if the angry written sentiments of a
teenage girl can be evidence of guilt. . . . The interrogation,
the words of the notebook and the effective third-person narration combine for a . . . portrait of a girl and her country."
(Kirkus Reviews)

★ **No** ordinary day. Groundwood Books 2011
160p $16.95

Grades: 5 6 7   **Fic**
    1. Leprosy -- Fiction 2. Orphans -- Fiction 3. Poverty
    -- Fiction 4. Homeless persons -- Fiction
    ISBN 978-1-55498-134-2; 1-55498-134-4

"Valli, about 10, lives in the poverty-stricken town of
Jharia, India, where she is a coal picker. When she makes
a shocking discovery about her family, she runs away and,
after a series of harrowing events, reaches the bustling city
of Kolkata. . . . While begging for change one day, she is befriended by a kind doctor who recognizes Valli's symptoms
of leprosy. . . . With the help of the doctor and other leprosy
patients, Valli gets treatment and education, learns tolerance

for people different from herself, and simultaneously realizes her own self-worth. Although many important lessons are
presented in this even-paced, clearly written story, it is never
heavyhanded or didactic. Valli is a well-developed, realistic,
and engaging narrator. . . . An important, inspiring tale." SLJ

Ellis, Sarah

Odd man out. Groundwood Books/House of Anansi Press 2006 162p $18.95; pa $9.95

Grades: 5 6 7 8   **Fic**
    1. Cousins -- Fiction 2. Fathers -- Fiction 3.
    Grandmothers -- Fiction
    ISBN 0-88899-702-7; 978-0-88899-703-6 pa;
    0-88899-703-5 pa

"This is a thoughtful and often funny book of a boy on
the verge of adolescence challenged to think—of his father,
mother, cousins, life—in a different way." SLJ

Ellsworth, Loretta

★ **Unforgettable**. Walker Books for Young
Readers 2011 256p $16.99

Grades: 6 7 8 9   **Fic**
    1. School stories 2. Memory -- Fiction 3. Synesthesia
    -- Fiction 4. Dating (Social customs) -- Fiction
    ISBN 978-0-8027-2305-5; 0-8027-2305-5

LC 2010049590

When Baxter Green was three years old he developed
a condition that causes him to remember absolutely everything, and now that he is fifteen, he and his mother have
moved to Minnesota to escape her criminal boyfriend and,
Baxter hopes, to reconnect with a girl he has been thinking
about since kindergarten.

"A lot is going here—an exploration of of synesthesia
and memory, a crime story, an environmental drama, family
relationships and a sweet, earnest love story. . . . But everything works." Kirkus

Elston, Ashley

The **rules** for disappearing; Ashley Elston. 1st
ed. Hyperion 2013 320 p. (reinforced) $16.99

Grades: 7 8 9 10 11 12   **Fic**
    1. Witnesses -- Fiction 2. Friendship -- Fiction 3.
    Dysfunctional families -- Fiction 4. Schools -- Fiction
    5. High schools -- Fiction 6. Moving, Household --
    Fiction 7. Family life -- Louisiana -- Fiction 8. Witness
    protection programs -- Fiction
    ISBN 1423168976; 9781423168973

LC 2012035122

In this book by Ashley Elston, "seventeen-year-old
Meg Jones . . . and her family are in the witness protection
program, and they've changed towns six times in less than
a year. . . . Meg's mother is an alcoholic, her father is depressed and secretive, and her 11-year-old sister is having
trouble coping with all of the change. Fed up, Meg wants
out of the program and will do anything to save her family,
including digging up what her father did to get them into this
mess." (Publishers Weekly)

"The fresh first-person narration serves the story well,
providing grounding in reality as events spin out of control.
Though the plot may seem a bit far-fetched at times, the realistic setting, believable romance and spunky protagonist

will make this one worth the trip for mystery and romance fans." Kirkus

Emond, Stephen
★ **Happyface**. Little, Brown and Co. 2010 307p il $16.99

Grades: 7 8 9 10   Fic
1. School stories 2. Diaries -- Fiction 3. Divorce -- Fiction 4. Dating (Social customs) -- Fiction
ISBN 978-0-316-04100-3; 0-316-04100-9
LC 2008-47386

After going through traumatic times, a troubled, socially awkward teenager moves to a new school where he tries to reinvent himself.

"The illustrations range from comics to more fleshed-out drawings. Just like Happyface's writing, they can be whimsical, thoughtful, boyishly sarcastic, off-the-cuff, or achingly beautiful." Publ Wkly

★ **Winter** town; Story and art by Stephen Emond. Little, Brown 2011 336p il $17.99

Grades: 7 8 9   Fic
1. Love stories 2. Teenagers -- Fiction 3. High school students -- Fiction 4. Cartoons and caricatures -- Fiction
ISBN 9780316133326; 978-0-316-13332-6
LC 2011012966

Evan and Lucy, childhood best friends who grew apart after years of seeing one another only during Christmas break, begin a romance at age seventeen but his choice to mindlessly follow his father's plans for an Ivy League education rather than becoming the cartoonist he longs to be, and her more destructive choices in the wake of family problems, pull them apart.

This is a "remarkable illustrated work of contemporary fiction. . . . Interspersed throughout are both realistic illustrations and drawings of a comic strip being created by Evan and Lucy; these black-and-white, almost chibi-style panels form an effective parallel with the plot and appeal mightily on their own. Compelling, honest and true—this musing about art and self-discovery, replete with pitch-perfect dialogue, will have wide appeal." Kirkus

Enderle, Dotti
Crosswire. Calkins Creek 2010 143p $17.95

Grades: 5 6 7 8   Fic
1. Brothers -- Fiction 2. Droughts -- Fiction 3. Ranch life -- Fiction 4. Father-son relationship -- Fiction
ISBN 978-1-59078-751-9; 1-59078-751-X
LC 2010-07522

When an 1883 drought drives free-range cattlemen to shred Texas ranchers' barbed wire fences and steal water, thirteen-year-old Jesse works hard to help while dealing with his father and brother's falling-out and his own fear of guns.

"Enderle writes with restraint, her research neatly woven into the story, her characters carefully drawn. A small gem of a story." Kirkus
Includes bibliographical references

Engdahl, Sylvia Louise
★ **Enchantress** from the stars; foreword by Lois Lowry. Firebird 2003 288p pa $6.99

Grades: 7 8 9 10 11 12   Fic
1. Science fiction
ISBN 0-14-250037-2

A reissue of the title first published 1970 by Atheneum Pubs.

A Newbery Medal honor book, 1971

When young Elana unexpectedly joins the team leaving the spaceship to study the planet Andrecia, she becomes an integral part of an adventure involving three very different civilizations, each one centered on the third planet from the star in its own solar system

"Emphasis is on the intricate pattern of events rather than on characterization, and readers will find fascinating symbolism—and philosophical parallels to what they may have observed or thought. The book is completely absorbing and should have a wider appeal than much science fiction." Horn Book

Engle, Margarita
★ **Firefly** letters; a suffragette's journey to Cuba. Henry Holt & Co. 2010 151p $16.99

Grades: 7 8 9 10 11 12   Fic
1. Novels in verse 2. Slavery -- Fiction 3. Sex role -- Fiction
ISBN 978-0-8050-9082-6; 0-8050-9082-7
LC 2009-23445

"This engaging title documents 50-year-old Swedish suffragette and novelist Fredrika Bremer's three-month travels around Cuba in 1851. Based in the home of a wealthy sugar planter, Bremer journeys around the country with her host's teenaged slave Cecilia, who longs for her mother and home in the Congo. Elena, the planter's privileged 12-year-old daughter, begins to accompany them on their trips into the countryside. . . . Using elegant free verse and alternating among each character's point of view, Engle offers powerful glimpses into Cuban life at that time. Along the way, she comments on slavery, the rights of women, and the stark contrast between Cuba's rich and poor." SLJ

Hurricane dancers; the first Caribbean pirate shipwreck. Henry Holt and Co. 2011 145p $16.99

Grades: 6 7 8 9 10   Fic
1. Novels in verse 2. Children's poetry 3. Pirates -- Fiction 4. Shipwrecks -- Fiction 5. Native Americans -- West Indies -- Fiction
ISBN 978-0-8050-9240-0; 0-8050-9240-4
LC 2010-11690

This is an "accomplished historical novel in verse set in the Caribbean. . . . The son of a Taíno Indian mother and a Spanish father, [Quebrado] is taken in 1510 from his village on the island that is present-day Cuba and enslaved on a pirate's ship, where a brutal conquistador . . . is held captive for ransom. When a hurricane destroys the boat, Quebrado is pulled from the water by a fisherman, Naridó, whose village welcomes him, but escape from the past proves nearly impossible. . . . Engle fictionalizes historical fact in a powerful, original story. . . . Engle distills the emotion in each episode with potent rhythms, sounds, and original, unforgettable imagery." Booklist

★ The **Lightning** Dreamer; Cuba's Greatest Abolitionist. Margarita Engle. Houghton Mifflin Harcourt 2013 192 p. $16.99

Grades: 6 7 8 9 10   **Fic**

1. Historical fiction 2. Novels in verse 3. Authors -- Fiction 4. Feminists -- Fiction 5. Abolitionists -- Fiction

ISBN 0547807430; 9780547807430

LC 2013003913

This book is a "work of historical fiction about Cuban poet, author, antislavery activist and feminist Gertrudis Gómez de Avellaneda. Written in free verse, the story tells of how Tula, which was her childhood nickname, grows up in libraries, which she calls 'a safe place to heal/ and dream . . .,' influenced by the poetry of Jose Maria Heredia." (School Library Journal)

Includes bibliographical references.

★ **Tropical** secrets; Holocaust refugees in Cuba. Henry Holt 2009 199p $16.95

Grades: 7 8 9 10 11   **Fic**

1. Novels in verse 2. Jews -- Fiction 3. Refugees -- Fiction 4. Holocaust, 1933-1945 -- Fiction

ISBN 978-0-8050-8936-3; 0-8050-8936-5

LC 2008-36782

Escaping from Nazi Germany to Cuba in 1939, a young Jewish refugee dreams of finding his parents again, befriends a local girl with painful secrets of her own, and discovers that the Nazi darkness is never far away.

"Readers who think they might not like a novel in verse will be pleasantly surprised at how quickly and smoothly the story flows. . . . The book will provide great fodder for discussion of the Holocaust, self-reliance, ethnic and religious bias, and more." Voice Youth Advocates

The **wild** book; Margarita Engle. Harcourt Children's Books 2012 133p $16.99

Grades: 5 6 7 8   **Fic**

1. Novels in verse 2. Children's stories 3. Dyslexia -- Fiction

ISBN 9780547581316

LC 2011027320

This book tells the story of "Josefa 'Fefa' de la Caridad Uría Peña. . . . Diagnosed with 'word blindness' (a misnomer for dyslexia), Fefa struggles at school. . . . Discounting a doctor''s opinion . . . her mother gives her a blank diary: 'Let the words sprout / like seedlings, / then relax and watch / as your wild diary / grows.' . . . Her reading difficulties are heightened when bandits begin roving the countryside, kidnapping local children for ransom." (Kirkus Reviews)

English, Karen

★ **Francie**. Farrar, Straus & Giroux 1999 199p hardcover o.p. $17

Grades: 5 6 7 8   **Fic**

1. Race relations -- Fiction 2. African Americans -- Fiction

ISBN 0-374-32456-5; 0-374-42459-4 pa

LC 98-53047

Coretta Scott King honor book for text, 2000

"The best student in her small, all-black school in pre-integration Alabama, 12-year-old Francie hopes for a better

life. . . . When Jessie, an older school friend who is without family, is forced on the run by a racist employer, Francie leaves her mother's labeled canned food for him in the woods. Only when the sheriff begins searching their woods . . . does she realize the depth of the danger she may have brought to her family. Francie's smooth-flowing, well-paced narration is gently assisted by just the right touch of the vernacular. Characterization is evenhanded and believable, while place and time envelop readers." SLJ

Ephron, Delia

Frannie in pieces; drawings by Chad W. Beckerman. HarperTeen 2007 374p il $16.99; pa $8.99

Grades: 7 8 9 10   **Fic**

1. Puzzles -- Fiction 2. Bereavement -- Fiction 3. Father-daughter relationship -- Fiction

ISBN 978-0-06-074716-9; 0-06-074716-1; 978-0-06-074718-3 pa; 0-06-074718-8 pa

LC 2007-10909

When fifteen-year-old Frannie's father dies, only a mysterious jigsaw puzzle that he leaves behind can help her come to terms with his death.

"This is a tender, moving story dealing with grief and growing up and the power of art to heal." SLJ

The **girl** with the mermaid hair. HarperTeen 2010 312p $16.99

Grades: 7 8 9 10   **Fic**

1. Family life -- Fiction 2. Personal appearance -- Fiction 3. Perfectionism (Personality trait) -- Fiction

ISBN 978-0-06-154260-2; 0-06-154260-1

LC 2009-03061

A vain teenaged girl is obsessed with beauty and perfection until she uncovers a devastating family secret.

"A solid and perceptive realistic drama, this will particularly satisfy readers beginning to reconsider their own familial assumptions." Bull Cent Child Books

Epstein, Robin

God is in the pancakes. Dial Books 2010 265p $16.99

Grades: 7 8 9 10   **Fic**

1. Old age -- Fiction 2. Sisters -- Fiction 3. Religion -- Fiction 4. Euthanasia -- Fiction 5. Dating (Social customs) -- Fiction

ISBN 978-0-8037-3382-4; 0-8037-3382-8

Fifteen-year-old Grace, having turned her back on religion when her father left, now finds herself praying for help with her home and love life, and especially with whether she should help a beloved elderly friend die with dignity.

"Everything comes together in an authentic, breezy read that asks difficult questions and doesn't shy away from direct answers, or the reality that answers may not exist. With well-developed adults and a teen seeking help from God and anyone she perceives as wise, this memorable novel offers food for thought and sustenance for the soul." Booklist

Erdrich, Louise, 1954-

★ The **birchbark** house. Hyperion Bks. for Children 1999 244p il hardcover o.p. pa $6.99

Grades: 5 6 7 8   **Fic**
  1. Ojibwa Indians -- Fiction
  ISBN 0-7868-0300-2; 0-7868-1454-3 pa
                                        LC 98-46366
Omakayas, a seven-year-old Native American girl of the
Ojibwa tribe, lives through the joys of summer and the perils
of winter on an island in Lake Superior in 1847.
  "Erdrich crafts images of tender beauty while weaving
Ojibwa words seamlessly into the text. Her gentle spot art
throughout complements this first of several projected sto-
ries that will 'attempt to retrace [her] own family's history.'"
Horn Book Guide

  ★ **Chickadee**; Louise Erdrich. Harper 2012
256p. (trade bdg.) $16.99
Grades: 5 6 7 8   **Fic**
  1. Brothers -- Fiction 2. Ojibwe Indians -- Fiction
  3. Voyages and travels -- Fiction 4. Kidnapping --
  Fiction 5. Family life -- Fiction 6. Métis -- Fiction 7.
  Ojibwa Indians -- Fiction 8. Indians of North America
  -- Great Plains -- Fiction 9. Indians of North America
  -- Superior, Lake, Region -- Fiction
  ISBN 9780060577902; 9780060577919
                                     LC 2012006565
Scott O'Dell Award for Historical Fiction (2013)
This book is the "fourth book of The Birchbark House
Series. Omakayas is now a young mother with lively 8-year-
old twins named Chickadee and Makoons." Makoons plays
a trick on the tribe"s bully, resulting in the bully"s sons kid-
napping Chickadee. He escapes, then "runs into his Uncle
Quill driving an ox cart of furs to sell in St. Paul. Quill and
Chickadee travel with fellow traders on the Red River ox
cart trail, arriving in Pembina to find Makoons seriously ill."
(Kirkus)

  ★ The **game** of silence; [by] Louise Erdrich.
HarperCollins 2004 256p $15.99; lib bdg $16.89;
pa $5.99
Grades: 5 6 7 8   **Fic**
  1. Ojibwa Indians -- Fiction
  ISBN 0-06-029789-1; 0-06-029790-5 lib bdg; 0-06-
  441029-3 pa
                                      LC 2004-6018
Nine-year-old Omakayas, of the Ojibwa tribe, moves
west with her family in 1849
  "Erdrich's captivating tale of four seasons portrays a
deep appreciation of our environment, our history, and our
Native American sisters and brothers." SLJ

  ★ The **porcupine** year. HarperCollinsPublishers 2008 193p $15.99; lib bdg $16.89
Grades: 5 6 7 8   **Fic**
  1. Family life -- Fiction 2. Ojibwa Indians -- Fiction 3.
  Voyages and travels -- Fiction
  ISBN 978-0-06-029787-9; 0-06-029787-5; 978-0-06-
  029788-6 lib bdg; 0-06-029788-3 lib bdg
                                     LC 2008000757
In 1852, forced by the United States government to leave
their beloved Island of the Golden Breasted Woodpecker,
fourteen-year-old Omokayas and her Ojibwe family travel
in search of a new home.

"Based on Erdrich's own family history, this celebration
of life will move readers with its mischief, its anger, and its
sadness. What is left unspoken is as powerful as the story
told." Booklist

Ernst, Kathleen
  Hearts of stone; [by] Kathleen Ernst. 1st ed.;
Dutton Children's Books 2006 248p $16.99
Grades: 6 7 8 9   **Fic**
  1. Orphans -- Fiction
  ISBN 0-525-47686-5
                                    LC 2005032756
Orphaned when her father dies fighting for the Union
and her mother expires from exhaustion, and also estranged
from their Confederate neighbors, fifteen-year-old Hannah
struggles to find a way for her family to survive during the
Civil War in Tennessee.
  "Ernst movingly shows that the calamity and upheaval
of war extends far beyond the battlefields." Booklist

Erskine, Kathryn
  Quaking. Philomel Books 2007 236p $16.99
Grades: 7 8 9 10   **Fic**
  1. School stories 2. Patriotism -- Fiction 3. Toleration
  -- Fiction 4. Family life -- Fiction 5. Society of Friends
  -- Fiction
  ISBN 978-0-399-24774-3; 0-399-24774-2
                                     LC 2006-34563
In a Pennsylvania town where antiwar sentiments are
treated with contempt and violence, Matt, a fourteen-year-
old girl living with a Quaker family, deals with the demons
of her past as she battles bullies of the present, eventually
learning to trust in others as well as herself.
  "This is a compelling story, which enfolds the political issues into a deeper focus on the characters' personal
stories." Booklist

  The **absolute** value of Mike. Philomel Books
2011 247p $16.99
Grades: 5 6 7 8   **Fic**
  1. Business enterprises -- Fiction 2. Father-son
  relationship -- Fiction 3. Eccentrics and eccentricities
  -- Fiction
  ISBN 978-0-399-25505-2; 0-399-25505-2
                                     LC 2010-13333
Fourteen-year-old Mike, whose father is a brilliant mathematician but who has no math aptitude himself, spends the
summer in rural Pennsylvania with his elderly and eccentric relatives Moo and Poppy, helping the townspeople raise
money to adopt a Romanian orphan.
  "Erskine weaves together a large but entertaining cast of
characters. . . . Despite many laugh-out-loud moments, the
heart of the book is essentially serious." Horn Book

Eskilsen, Erik E.
  The **last** mall rat. Houghton Mifflin 2003 182p
$15; pa $5.95
Grades: 7 8 9 10   **Fic**
  1. Shopping centers and malls -- Fiction
  ISBN 0-618-23417-9; 0-618-60896-6 pa
                                     LC 2002-14436

Too young to get a job at the Onion River Mall, fifteen-year-old Mitch earns money from salesclerks to harrass rude shoppers

"Realistic dialogue and a keen sense of what matters to teens will draw them to this quick read." Booklist

Eulberg, Elizabeth

Revenge of the Girl With the Great Personality; Elizabeth Eulberg. Scholastic 2013 272 p. (hardcover) $17.99

Grades: 7 8 9 10   **Fic**

1. Sisters -- Fiction 2. Beauty contests -- Fiction
ISBN 9780545476997; 0545476992

In this novel, by Elizabeth Eulberg, "Everybody loves Lexi. She's popular, smart, funny . . . but she's never been one of . . . the pretty ones who get all the attention from guys. And on top of that, her seven-year-old sister, Mackenzie, is a terror in a tiara. . . . Lexi's sick of it. . . . The time has come for Lexi to step out from the sidelines. Girls without great personalities aren't going to know what hit them. Because Lexi's going to play the beauty game." (Publisher's note)

Evangelista, Beth

Gifted. Walker & Co. 2005 180p $16.95; pa $6.95

Grades: 5 6 7 8   **Fic**

1. Bullies -- Fiction 2. Camping -- Fiction 3. Gifted children -- Fiction
ISBN 0-8027-8994-3; 0-8027-9644-3 pa

Arrogant, mentally gifted George Clark has dreaded the eighth-grade class camping trip and its inevitable bullying, but a hurricane and a friend's loyalty make him realize what is important in life.

"It's hard to write a successful book with an unlikable protagonist . . . but that's what first-time author Evangelista has done. . . . Fresh and funny." Booklist

Evans, Lissa

Horten's miraculous mechanisms; magic, mystery & a very strange adventure. by Lissa Evans. Sterling 2012 270 p. $14.95

Grades: 3 4 5 6 7   **Fic**

1. Mystery fiction 2. Adventure fiction 3. Children's stories 4. Inventors -- Fiction 5. Magicians -- Fiction
ISBN 9781402798061

In this book, author Lissa Evans borrows several classic tropes and themes: magic, riddles, a quest, and even a night at a museum "for the . . . story of 10-year-old Stuart Horten . . . who stumbles into a family mystery when he and his parents move to the small British town of Beeton. There, Stuart discovers that his Great-Uncle Tony Horten, who disappeared years ago without a trace, was both an inventor of mechanical devices and a magician. A chance phone call in a broken phone booth is the first step in a journey that leads Stuart around town, as he unearths his great-uncle's legacy and secrets. Stuart also draws the attention of April, May, and June (the journalistically inclined triplets next door), as well as Beeton residents with more sinister intentions." (Publishers Weekly)

Evans, Richard Paul

Michael Vey; the prisoner of Cell-25. Mercury Ink/Simon Pulse 2011 326p $17.99

Grades: 6 7 8 9   **Fic**

1. Friendship -- Fiction 2. Electricity -- Fiction 3. Superheroes -- Fiction 4. Tourette syndrome -- Fiction
ISBN 978-1-4516-5650-3; 1-4516-5650-5

To everyone at Meridian High School, fourteen-year-old Michael Vey is nothing special, just the kid who has Tourette's syndrome. But in truth, Michael is extremely special-he has electric powers.

"Short chapters with intriguing titles, excellent writing, and engaging characters make this action-packed story a compulsively entertaining read. The tale progresses with altering points of view. Michael tells his story in first-person and Taylor's tale is narrated in third-person. . . . Though contemporary and edgy, this book contains no bad language, sex, or gratuitous violence. This is a book Rick Riordan's fans will want to read." Voice Youth Advocates

Explorer; the mystery boxes. edited by Kazu Kibuishi. Amulet Books 2012 126 p.

Grades: 4 5 6 7 8   **Fic**

1. Short stories 2. Graphic novels 3. Boxes -- Fiction 4. Mystery graphic novels 6. Children's stories, American
ISBN 9781419700095; 9781419700101

LC 2011025343

This collection of short stories offers "[s]even . . . stories [which] answer one simple question: what's in the box? . . . [E]ach of these . . . illustrated short graphic works revolves around a central theme: a mysterious box and the marvels--or mayhem--inside. Artists include . . . Kazu Kibuishi, Raina Telgemeier ('Smile'), and Dave Roman ('Astronaut Academy'), as well as Jason Caffoe, Stuart Livingston, Johane Matte, Rad Sechrist (all contributors to the . . . comics anthology series 'Flight'), and . . . artist Emily Carroll." (Publisher's note)

Fagan, Deva

Circus Galacticus. Harcourt 2011 291p $16.99

Grades: 6 7 8 9   **Fic**

1. Science fiction 2. Circus -- Fiction 3. Orphans -- Fiction
ISBN 978-0-547-58136-1; 0-547-58136-X

LC 2011009594

Trix's life in boarding school as an orphan charity case has been hard but when an alluring young Ringmaster invites her, a gymnast, to join Circus Galacticus she gains an entire universe of deadly enemies and potential friends, along with a chance to unravel secrets of her own past.

"Fagan's story makes SF fun. It's loaded with wild coincidences and easily spotted inspirations (X-Men, Doctor Who), yet the underlying idea of valuing diversity, friendship, and self-esteem shines, carried by Fagan's solid writing, appealing characters, and sprinkles of whimsy." Publ Wkly

Fortune's folly. Henry Holt 2009 260p $17.95

Grades: 5 6 7 8   **Fic**

1. Fairy tales 2. Adventure fiction 3. Prophecies --

Fiction
ISBN 978-0-8050-8742-0; 0-8050-8742-7

LC 2008-36780

Ever since her mother died and her father lost his shoe-making skills, Fortunata has survived by pretending to tell fortunes, but when she is tricked into telling the fortune of a prince, she is faced with the impossible task of fulfilling her wild prophecy to save her father's life.

"Fagan's language evokes images of fairy tales and legends, and the protagonist's first-person narrative sparkles with humor. In this book, words are powerful, impressive, mystical, and, sometimes, downright silly." SLJ

Fahy, Thomas Richard

The **unspoken**; [by] Tom Fahy. Simon & Schuster Books for Young Readers 2008 166p $15.99
Grades: 8 9 10 11 12   **Fic**
1. Horror fiction 2. Cults -- Fiction
ISBN 978-1-4169-4007-4; 1-4169-4007-3

LC 2007-00850

Six teens are drawn back to the small, North Carolina town where they once lived and, one by one, begin to die of their worst fears, as prophesied by the cult leader they killed five years earlier, and who they believe poisoned their parents.

"Teeth-clenching suspenseful at times and deliciously creepy at others, Fahy . . . delivers a classic horror story." Publ Wkly

Fairlie, Emily

The **lost** treasure of Tuckernuck; Emily Fairlie. Katherine Tegen Books 2012 283 p. (hardback) $16.99
Grades: 4 5 6 7 8   **Fic**
1. Mystery fiction 2. Buried treasure -- Fiction 3. Historic buildings -- Fiction 4. Schools -- Fiction 5. Mystery and detective stories 6. Treasure hunt (Game) -- Fiction
ISBN 0062118900; 9780062118905

LC 2012025279

This book by Emily Fairlie "tells the story of Bud and Laurie's quest to find the infamous Tutweiler Treasure. They're hot (or at least lukewarm) on the trail of clues, but time is running out -- the school board wants to tear down Tuckernuck Hall. Can Bud and Laurie find the treasure before it's lost forever?" (Publisher's note)

Falkner, Brian

The **project**. Random House 2011 275p $17.99
Grades: 6 7 8 9 10   **Fic**
1. Adventure fiction 2. Time travel -- Fiction 3. National socialism -- Fiction 4. World War, 1939-1945 -- Fiction
ISBN 978-0-375-96945-4; 0-375-96945-4

LC 2010033449

After discovering a terrible secret hidden in the most boring book in the world, Iowa fifteen-year-olds Luke and Tommy find out that members of a secret Nazi organization intend to use this information to rewrite history.

"The wacky unbelievability of this story in no way detracts from its enjoyment. It reads like an action movie, with plenty of chases, explosions, and by-a-hair escapes." SLJ

Falls, Kat

Dark life. Scholastic Press 2010 297p $16.99; pa $6.99
Grades: 4 5 6 7   **Fic**
1. Science fiction 2. Ocean -- Fiction
ISBN 978-0-545-17814-3; 0-545-17814-2; 978-0-545-17815-0 pa; 0-545-17815-0 pa

LC 2009-24907

"Ty has lived subsea his entire life. His family members moved below the water to make a better life for themselves. In this future, the climate changes on Earth have been so drastic that hardly any solid ground exits anymore. . . . This book will appeal to middle grade readers, who will enjoy the novel's mystery and suspense. It is a definite must-read for SF fans." Voice Youth Advocates

Rip tide. Scholastic Press 2011 320p $16.99
Grades: 4 5 6 7   **Fic**
1. Science fiction 2. Ocean -- Fiction
ISBN 0-545-17843-6; 978-0-545-17843-3

"While preparing to sell the season's seaweed crop, Ty stumbles across an abandoned township, its doors chained shut and its residents murdered. Soon after, the colonists' deal with another township goes bad, and Ty's parents are kidnapped. As Ty and Gemma try to track down those responsible and save their loved ones, they're forced to join up with the notorious Seablite Gang, infiltrate the rough-and-tumble town of Rip Tide, fight for their lives against sea monsters and human predators, and discover who's killing entire townships—and why. . . . There's no shortage of action, intrigue, or daring exploits in this aquatic thriller. Atmospheric and tense, built around an expertly used postapocalyptic meets Wild West setting, this story's a whole lot of fun." Publ Wkly

Fama, Elizabeth

Overboard; Elizabeth Fama. Cricket Books 2002 158p. maps (Cloth : alk. paper) $15.95
Grades: 7 8 9 10   **Fic**
1. Muslims -- Fiction 2. Indonesia -- Fiction 3. Shipwrecks -- Fiction 4. Survival after airplane accidents, shipwrecks, etc. -- Fiction 5. Survival -- Fiction
ISBN 0812626524; 9780553494365

LC 20020592

In this "novel based on a 1996 ferry accident off the coast of Sumatra, Emily, a 14-year-old American living in Indonesia with her doctor parents, boards an overcrowded, tilting ferry (without her parents' knowledge) after her uncle invites her to visit him on a nearby island. As the ship lists to 'an unnatural angle,' the captain distributes life vests. Emily hands hers to a younger boy who is trying to hang on to the railing. . . . The girl then becomes trapped in the life-vest locker, which immediately fills with water. . . . [The plot continues with a] chronicle of Emily's nightlong struggle to survive. . . . During the course of the evening, she [encounters] . . . a Muslim child who explains some of the tenets of his faith as they bob along in the water." (Publishers Weekly)

Fantaskey, Beth

Jessica's guide to dating on the dark side. Harcourt 2009 354p $17

Grades: 8 9 10 11 12   **Fic**
1. Vampires -- Fiction
ISBN 978-0-15-206384-9; 0-15-206384-6
LC 2007-49002
Seventeen-year-old Jessica, adopted and raised in Pennsylvania, learns that she is descended from a royal line of Romanian vampires and that she is betrothed to a vampire prince, who poses as a foreign exchange student while courting her.

"Fantaskey makes this premise work by playing up its absurdities without laughing at them. . . . The romance sizzles, the plot develops ingeniously and suspensefully, and the satire sings." Publ Wkly

Fardell, John
The **7** professors of the Far North. G. P. Putnam's Sons 2005 217p il hardcover o.p. pa $6.99
Grades: 4 5 6 7   **Fic**
1. Science fiction 2. Adventure fiction
ISBN 0-399-24381-X; 0-14-240735-6 pa
Eleven-year-old Sam finds himself involved in a dangerous adventure when he and his new friends, brother and sister Ben and Zara, set off for the Arctic to try and rescue the siblings' great-uncle and five other professors from the mad scientist holding them prisoner.

"Action is nonstop and very exciting. This inventive, funny, suspenseful, and exciting book will appeal to most readers." SLJ

Farinango, Maria Virginia
★ The **Queen** of Water. Delacorte Press 2011 352p $16.99; lib bdg $19.99
Grades: 8 9 10 11 12   **Fic**
1. Social classes -- Fiction
ISBN 978-0-385-73897-2; 0-385-73897-8; 978-0-385-90761-3 lib bdg; 0-385-90761-3 lib bdg
LC 2010-10512
"The complexities of class and ethnicity within Ecuadorian society are explained seamlessly within the context of the first-person narrative, and a glossary and pronunciation guide further help to plunge readers into the novel's world. By turns heartbreaking, infuriating and ultimately inspiring." Kirkus

Farizan, Sara
★ **If** you could be mine; a novel. Sara Farizan. Algonquin 2013 256 p. (hardcover) $16.95
Grades: 8 9 10 11 12   **Fic**
1. Sex reassignment surgery -- Fiction 2. Iran -- Social conditions -- Fiction 3. Love -- Fiction 4. Lesbians -- Fiction 5. Friendship -- Fiction 6. Best friends -- Fiction
ISBN 1616202513; 9781616202514
LC 2013008931
This novel, set in Iran, 17-year-old Sahar, who has wanted to marry her best friend Nasrin since they were six years old, dreams of living openly with her lover. Nasrin prefers to accept an arranged marriage, while intending to continue their illicit affair. Exposed to a world of sexual diversity by her gay cousin and made desperate by Nasrin's impending marriage, Sahar explores the one legal option for the two

of them to be together: her own sex reassignment surgery." (Publishers Weekly)

"Rich with details of life in contemporary Iran, this is a GLBTQ story that we haven't seen before in YA fiction." SLJ

Farmer, Nancy
★ The **Ear,** the Eye, and the Arm; a novel. Puffin Books 1995 311p pa $6.99
Grades: 6 7 8 9 10   **Fic**
1. Science fiction
ISBN 978-0-14-131109-8; 0-14-131109-6
LC 95019982
First published 1994 by Orchard Books
A Newbery Medal honor book, 1995
In 2194 in Zimbabwe, General Matsika's three children are kidnapped and put to work in a plastic mine while three mutant detectives use their special powers to search for them

"Throughout the story, it's the thrilling adventure that will grab readers, who will also like the comic, tender characterizations." Booklist

★ The **Sea** of Trolls. Atheneum Books for Young Readers 2004 459p $17.95; pa $9.99
Grades: 5 6 7 8 9   **Fic**
1. Fantasy fiction 2. Vikings -- Fiction 3. Norse mythology -- Fiction 4. Druids and Druidism -- Fiction
ISBN 0-689-86744-1; 0-689-86746-8 pa
LC 2003-19091
After Jack becomes apprenticed to a Druid bard, he and his little sister Lucy are captured by Viking Berserkers and taken to the home of King Ivar the Boneless and his half-troll queen, leading Jack to undertake a vital quest to Jotunheim, home of the trolls.

"This exciting and original fantasy will capture the hearts and imaginations of readers." SLJ
Includes bibliographical references
Other titles in this series are:
The Land of the Silver Apples (2007)
The Islands of the Blessed (2009)

A **girl** named Disaster. Orchard Bks. 1996 309p $19.95; pa $7.99
Grades: 6 7 8 9   **Fic**
1. Adventure fiction 2. Supernatural -- Fiction
ISBN 0-531-09539-8; 0-14-038635-1 pa
LC 96-15141
A Newbery Medal honor book, 1997
While journeying from Mozambique to Zimbabwe to escape an arranged marriage, eleven-year-old Nhamo struggles to escape drowning and starvation and in so doing comes close to the luminous world of the African spirits

"This story is humorous and heartwrenching, complex and multilayered." SLJ

★ The **house** of the scorpion. Atheneum Bks. for Young Readers 2002 380p $17.95; pa $7.99
Grades: 7 8 9 10   **Fic**
1. Science fiction 2. Cloning -- Fiction
ISBN 0-689-85222-3; 0-689-85223-1 pa
LC 2001-56594
A Newbery Medal honor book, 2003

In a future where humans despise clones, Matt enjoys special status as the young clone of El Patrón, the 140-year-old leader of a corrupt drug empire nestled between Mexico and the United States.

"This is a powerful, ultimately hopeful, story that builds on today's sociopolitical, ethical, and scientific issues and prognosticates a compelling picture of what the future could bring." Booklist

★ The **lord** of Opium; Nancy Farmer. Atheneum Books for Young Readers 2013 432 p. (hardcover) $17.99

Grades: 7 8 9 10   **Fic**
  1. Fantasy fiction 2. Drug traffic -- Fiction 3. Science fiction 4. Cloning -- Fiction 5. Environmental degradation -- Fiction
  ISBN 1442482540; 9781442482548
                                                        LC 2012030418

This book is the sequel to Nancy Farmer's "The House of the Scorpion." Here, "Matt was a clone of El Patrón, drug lord of Opium, but with El Patrón dead, Matt is now considered by international law to be fully human and El Patrón's rightful heir. But it's a corrupt land, now part of a larger Dope Confederacy carved out of the southeastern United States and northern Mexico, ruled over by drug lords and worked by armies of Illegals turned into 'eejits,' or zombies. Matt wants to bring reform." (Kirkus Reviews)

Farr, Richard
  Emperors of the ice; a true story of disaster and survival in the Antarctic, 1910-13. Farrar, Straus & Giroux 2008 215p il map $19.95

Grades: 6 7 8 9   **Fic**
  1. Penguins -- Fiction 2. Explorers -- Fiction
  ISBN 978-0-374-31975-5; 0-374-31975-8
                                                        LC 2007-52347

Apsley 'Cherry' Cherry-Garrard shares his adventures as the youngest member of Robert Scott's expedition to Antarctica in the early twentieth century, during which he and Edward Wilson try to learn the evolutionary history of emperor penguins. Includes historical notes.

"Heavily illustrated with paintings, photos, and documents from the actual expedition, the book brings vividly to life the explorers and scientists of nearly a century ago." Voice Youth Advocates

Includes bibliographical references

Farrant, Natasha
  After Iris; by Natasha Farrant. Dial Books for Young Readers 2013 272 p. (hardcover) $16.99

Grades: 5 6 7 8   **Fic**
  1. Grief -- Fiction 2. Babysitters -- Fiction 3. Twins -- Fiction 4. Diaries -- Fiction 5. Au pairs -- Fiction 6. Brothers and sisters -- Fiction 7. Family life -- England -- London -- Fiction 8. Video recordings -- Production and direction -- Fiction
  ISBN 0803739826; 9780803739826
                                                        LC 2012039136

In this book, 12-year-old "Bluebell Gadsby's family has been collapsing ever since Blue's twin sister. Iris, died three years ago. Blue's father is working on the other side of the country, and their mother is traveling overseas, which leaves

new au pair Zoran in charge. Between Blue's older sister Flora's rebelliousness, her two younger siblings' antics, and the family's pet rats, which live in the garden of their London home, Zoran has his hands full." (Publishers Weekly)

Farrar, Josh
  Rules to rock by. Walker Books for Young Readers 2010 244p $16.99

Grades: 4 5 6 7   **Fic**
  1. Moving -- Fiction 2. Bullies -- Fiction 3. Rock music -- Fiction 4. Rock musicians -- Fiction
  ISBN 978-0-8027-2079-5; 0-8027-2079-X

Annabella Cabrera tries to start a rock band at her new middle school in Providence, Rhode Island, but has trouble when the members of a rival band bully her and she develops a case of writer's block.

"Rock prevails in this spirited, never-say-die story about a girl and her dream. Farrar's first novel hits home about tween life, especially among the creative set, and for anyone who has ever been bullied." SLJ

Farrey, Brian
  The **Vengekeep** prophecies; Brian Farrey ; illustrated by Brett Helquist. Harper 2012 390 p. (hardback) $16.99

Grades: 4 5 6 7   **Fic**
  1. Magic -- Fiction 2. Prophecies -- Fiction 3. Swindlers and swindling -- Fiction 4. Monsters -- Fiction
  ISBN 0062049283; 9780062049285
                                                        LC 2012025282

In this book by Brian Farrey, "12-year-old Jaxter Grimjinx is anxious to prove himself at the family business: thievery. Jaxter's first attempt at burglary ends with . . . his family being jailed, but his parents have . . . replaced the prophetic tapestry that predicts the year ahead . . . with one that shows the Grimjinx family as heroes. The family quickly discovers, however, that the fake tapestry is actually enchanted, and every disaster it depicts is coming true." (Publishers Weekly)

Fawcett, Katie Pickard
  To come and go like magic. Alfred A. Knopf 2010 263p $16.99; lib bdg $19.99

Grades: 5 6 7 8   **Fic**
  1. Family life -- Fiction 2. Country life -- Fiction
  ISBN 978-0-375-85846-8; 0-375-85846-6; 978-0-375-95846-5 lib bdg; 0-375-95846-0 lib bdg
                                                        LC 2008-52188

In the 1970s, twelve-year-old Chili Sue Mahoney longs to escape her tiny Kentucky home town and see the world, but she also learns to recognize beauty in the people and places around her.

"Chili's first-person narrative stretches from poetic thoughts . . . to more down-to-earth observations. Her insights are absorbing and her setbacks heartbreaking, as she weighs the only home she's ever known against the possibilities that loom farther afield." Publ Wkly

Federle, Tim
  Better Nate than ever; Tim Federle. Simon & Schuster Books for Young Readers 2013 288 p. (hardcover) $16.99

Grades: 5 6 7 8   **Fic**
1. Theater -- Fiction 2. Musicals -- Fiction 3. Auditions
-- Fiction
ISBN 1442446897; 9781442446892; 9781442446908
LC 2011050388

In author Tim Federle's book, "Nate Foster has big dreams. His whole life, he's wanted to star in a Broadway show. (Heck, he'd settle for seeing a Broadway show.) But how is Nate supposed to make his dreams come true when he's stuck in Jankburg, Pennsylvania . . . ? With Libby's help, Nate plans a daring overnight escape to New York. There's an open casting call for 'E.T.: The Musical,' and Nate knows this could be the difference between small-town blues and big-time stardom." (Publisher's note)

Fehler, Gene
Beanball; by Gene Fehler. Clarion Books 2008 119p $16
Grades: 7 8 9 10   **Fic**
1. School stories 2. Novels in verse 3. Baseball -- Fiction
ISBN 0-618-84348-5; 978-0-618-84348-0
LC 2007013058

Relates, from diverse points of view, events surrounding the critical injury of popular and talented high school athlete, Luke "Wizard" Wallace, when he is hit in the face by a fastball.

This is a "moving baseball novel in free verse. . . . This swift read will appeal to both reluctant readers and baseball players." KLIATT

Feinstein, John
Last shot; a Final Four mystery. Knopf 2005 251p $16.95; lib bdg $18.99
Grades: 6 7 8 9   **Fic**
1. Mystery fiction 2. Basketball -- Fiction 3. Journalists -- Fiction
ISBN 0-375-83168-1; 0-375-93168-6 lib bdg
LC 2004-26535

After winning a basketball reporting contest, eighth graders Stevie and Susan Carol are sent to cover the Final Four tournament, where they discover that a talented player is being blackmailed into throwing the final game.

"The action on the court is vividly described. . . . Mystery fans will find enough suspense in this fast-paced narrative to keep them hooked." SLJ

Other titles in this series are:
Vanishing act (2006)
Cover-up (2007)
Change-up (2009)
Rivalry (2010)

Feldman, Ruth Tenzer
Blue thread; Ruth Tenzer Feldman. Ooligan Press 2012 302 p. $12.95
Grades: 7 8 9 10   **Fic**
1. Historical fiction 2. Jewish women -- Fiction 3. Women's rights -- Fiction
ISBN 1932010416; 9781932010411
LC 2011024382

This young adult novel focuses on Miriam, a young Jewish girl in 1912 Portland, Oregon. "While her mother plans

their trip to New York City to find her a husband, Miriam gets caught up in the fight for women's suffrage. At first she's nervous about going against her parents' wishes, but curiosity gets the better of her . . . . However, after a mysterious girl named Serakh whisks Miriam back to biblical times, her desire to be a larger part of the movement becomes stronger." (School Library Journal)

Fergus, Maureen
Ortega. Kids Can Press 2010 224p $16.95
Grades: 5 6 7 8   **Fic**
1. Science fiction 2. Gorillas -- Fiction
ISBN 978-1-55453-474-6; 1-55453-474-7

Eleven years ago, an infant lowland gorilla was acquired by a privately funded laboratory. An elite surgical team undertook a series of radical procedures designed to make it physically possible for the infant gorilla to acquire speech.

"The story's excitement and suspense as well as the emotional drama will ensnare readers. This interesting, affecting novel will definitely find an audience." SLJ

Recipe for disaster. Kids Can Press 2009 252p $18.95; pa $8.95
Grades: 7 8 9   **Fic**
1. Baking -- Fiction 2. Friendship -- Fiction
ISBN 978-1-55453-319-0; 1-55453-319-8; 978-1-55453-320-6 pa; 1-55453-320-1 pa

Francie was born to bake and dreams of one day starring in her own baking show. Her life is almost perfect until the new girl at school shows up.

"Francie is a delight. Her own special brand of humor touches every aspect of the tale. . . . This breezy, appealing read covers personal growth, the sacrifices of friendship, and the mistakes made along the way." SLJ

Ferraiolo, Jack D.
★ **Sidekicks**. Amulet 2011 309p $16.95
Grades: 6 7 8 9   **Fic**
1. Superheroes -- Fiction
ISBN 978-0-8109-9803-2; 0-8109-9803-3

"By all outward appearances, Bright Boy is an average middle-school student, but at night, he becomes the sidekick to superhero Rogue Warrior. . . . Ferraiolo is delightfully unafraid to inject irreverence into the superhero formula, adding plenty of humor to the high-adventure high jinks." Booklist

The **big** splash; by Jack D. Ferraiolo. Amulet Books 2008 277p $15.95
Grades: 4 5 6 7   **Fic**
1. School stories 2. Mystery fiction
ISBN 978-0-8109-7067-0; 0-8109-7067-8
LC 2007-49978

Matt Stevens, an average middle schooler with a glib tongue and a knack for solving crimes, uncovers a mystery while working with "the organization," a mafia-like syndicate run by seventh-grader Vincent "Mr. Biggs" Biggio, specializing in forged hall passes, test-copying rings, black market candy selling, and taking out hits with water guns.

This "novel delivers plenty of laughs, especially in the opening chapters, and fans of private-eye spoofs will enjoy this entertaining read." Booklist

Ferris, Jean

Much ado about Grubstake. Harcourt 2006 265p $17

Grades: 5 6 7 8   **Fic**
1. Orphans -- Fiction 2. City and town life -- Fiction 3. Gold mines and mining -- Fiction
ISBN 0-15-205706-4

When two city folks arrive in the depressed mining town of Grubstake, Colorado in 1888, sixteen-year-old orphaned Arley tries to discover why they want to buy the supposedly worthless mines in the area

"Ferris combines adventure, love, and off-the-wall characters in a page-turning story full of good laughs and common sense messages." Voice Youth Advocates

Twice upon a Marigold. Harcourt 2008 297p $17

Grades: 5 6 7 8   **Fic**
1. Fairy tales 2. Princesses -- Fiction 3. Kings and rulers -- Fiction
ISBN 978-0-15-206382-5; 0-15-206382-X
           LC 200735761

After a quiet, happy year in a small town, Queen Olympia regains her memory and initiates new plots and manipulations, as the residents of Zandelphia and Beaurivage, now ruled by Christian, Marigold, and Swithbert, feel the effects of her bad energy.

"Appealing new characters and fresh plot twists give this sequel a life of its own, though fans of the earlier book will enjoy the continuation of its story line, wry humor, and offbeat sense of fun." Booklist

Fforde, Jasper

★ The **last** Dragonslayer; Jasper Fforde. Hodder & Stoughton 2010 281 p. (The Chronicles of Kazam) $16.99; (hbk.) $16.99

Grades: 7 8 9 10   **Fic**
1. Magic -- Fiction 2. Dragons -- Fiction 3. Employment agencies -- Fiction
ISBN 978-0547738475; 1444707175; 1444707191; 9781444707175; 9781444707199
           LC 2010551874

In this book by Jasper Fforde, part of the Chronicles of Kazam series, "magic is fading. . . . Fifteen-year-old foundling Jennifer Strange runs Kazam, an employment agency for magicians -- but it's hard to stay in business when magic is drying up. And then the visions start, predicting the death of the world"s last dragon at the hands of an unnamed Dragonslayer. If the visions are true, everything will change for Kazam -- and for Jennifer." (Publisher's note)

Fienberg, Anna

Number 8. Walker 2007 288p $16.95

Grades: 7 8 9 10   **Fic**
1. Singers -- Fiction 2. Family life -- Fiction 3. Mathematics -- Fiction 4. Organized crime -- Fiction
ISBN 978-0-8027-9660-8; 0-8027-9660-5
           LC 2007-14706

While hiding out from the mob in the suburbs with his mother, a singer, Jackson uses his fascination with math and numbers to make friends, but strange phone calls and even greater threats endanger not only Jackson and his mother, but his new girlfriend, as well.

"The fact that each character has an idiosyncratic passion that somehow helps them understand the others adds dimension to an already effective suspense plot." Bull Cent Child Books

Fink, Mark

The **summer** I got a life. WestSide 2009 196p $15.95

Grades: 7 8 9   **Fic**
1. Love stories 2. Handicapped -- Fiction
ISBN 978-1-934813-12-6; 1-934813-12-5

"Andy is pumped that his freshman year is over and his vacation is about to begin. Then his dad's promotion changes everything. Instead of Hawaii, Andy is spending two weeks on a farm in Wisconsin with his somewhat odd, but well-meaning, aunt and uncle. Once there, though, he finds that things aren't so bad particularly when he spots 'the most incredible-looking girl he has ever seen.' . . . Andy discovers that an accident at age four has left Laura confined to a wheelchair. . . . This is an engaging novel filled with life lessons, a little romance, humor, sports, and fraternal love." SLJ

Finn, Mary

★ **Belladonna**. Candlewick Press 2011 371p $16.99

Grades: 7 8 9 10   **Fic**
1. Artists 2. Painters 3. Horses -- Fiction
ISBN 978-0-7636-5106-0; 0-7636-5106-0
           LC 2010038707

The audiobook is set "[i]n rural England in 1757, [where] Thomas Rose is on the verge-of becoming a man. Clever, but unable to learn reading and writing . . . Tom meets the enigmatic Hélène, a circus performer who goes by the name of Ling . . .Enchanted with Ling's stories of her life in the circus as much as with the girl herself, Tom commits to helping her find her beloved horse, Belladonna . . . Their search leads them to George Stubbs, known in the village as a horse butcher . . . the teens discover that Stubbs is a painter who is completing an anatomical study of horses that involves dissection of the animals. Stubbs takes Tom on as an apprentice and secures Ling a position in the household of the wealthy family that purchased Belladonna, not knowing that the girl's ultimate goal is to escape with her horse." (School Libr J)

"A touch of intrigue and interesting details about horses, early necropsy, and everyday life add a rich frame to this historical coming-of-age story, unique in both its setting and subject." Booklist

Finneyfrock, Karen

The **sweet** revenge of Celia Door; by Karen Finneyfrock. Viking 2013 272 p. (hardcover) $16.99

Grades: 7 8 9 10   **Fic**
1. School stories 2. Revenge -- Fiction 3. Teenagers -- Fiction 4. Gays -- Fiction 5. Poetry -- Fiction 6. Schools -- Fiction 7. High schools -- Fiction 8. Family

life -- Pennsylvania -- Hershey -- Fiction
ISBN 0670012750; 9780670012756

LC 2011047221

In this teen novel, by Karen Finneyfrock, "Celia Door enters her freshman year . . . with giant boots, dark eyeliner, and a thirst for revenge against Sandy Firestone. . . . But then Celia meets Drake, the cool new kid from New York City who entrusts her with his deepest, darkest secret. When Celia's quest for justice threatens her relationship with Drake, she's forced to decide which is sweeter: revenge or friendship." (Publisher's note)

Fisher, Catherine

Darkwater; by Catherine Fisher. Penguin Group USA 2012 229p $16.99

Grades: 6 7 8 9 10 11 12   **Fic**

1. Sin 2. Teenagers -- Fiction 3. Private schools -- Fiction 4. Soul -- Fiction 5. Twins -- Fiction 6. Schools -- Fiction 7. Brothers -- Fiction 8. Supernatural -- Fiction
ISBN 9780803738188

LC 2011048063

In author Catherine Fisher's book, "Sarah Trevelyan would give anything to regain the power and wealth her family has lost, so she makes a bargain with Azrael, Lord of Darkwater Hall. He gives her one hundred years and the means to accomplish her objective--in exchange for her soul. Fast-forward a hundred years to Tom, a fifteen-year-old boy who dreams of attending Darkwater Hall School but doesn't believe he has the talent. Until he meets a professor named Azrael, who offers him a bargain. Will Sarah be able to stop Tom from making the same mistake she did a century ago?" (Publisher's note)

★ **Incarceron**. Dial Books 2010 442p $17.99

Grades: 7 8 9 10   **Fic**

1. Fantasy fiction 2. Prisoners -- Fiction
ISBN 978-0-8037-3396-1; 0-8037-3396-8

LC 2008-46254

First published 2007 in the United Kingdom

To free herself from an upcoming arranged marriage, Claudia, the daughter of the Warden of Incarceron, a futuristic prison with a mind of its own, decides to help a young prisoner escape.

"Complex and inventive, with numerous and rewarding mysteries, this tale is certain to please." Publ Wkly

The **Margrave**. Dial Books for Young Readers 2011 464p (Relic master) $16.99

Grades: 6 7 8 9   **Fic**

1. Fantasy fiction 2. Apprentices -- Fiction
ISBN 978-0-8037-3676-4; 0-8037-3676-2

LC 2010043237

Their quest to find a secret relic with great power leads Master Galen and his sixteen-year-old apprentice Raffi into the Pit of Maar and the deep evil world at the heart of the Watch.

"The conclusion to Fisher's science-fantasy quartet satisfies." Kirkus

Sapphique. Dial Books 2011 460p $17.99

Grades: 7 8 9 10   **Fic**

1. Fantasy fiction 2. Computers -- Fiction 3. Prisoners -- Fiction 4. Identity (Psychology) -- Fiction
ISBN 978-0-8037-3397-8; 0-8037-3397-6

LC 2009-31479

After his escape from the sentient prison, Incarceron, Finn finds that the Realm is not at all what he expected, and he does not know whether he is to be its king, how to free his imprisoned friends, or how to stop Incarceron's quest to be free of its own nature.

"Fisher's superb world-building marks this title, effectively drawing the reader in to a place so rife with secrets even its inhabitants don't entirely understand the depth of its illusions." Bull Cent Child Books

The **dark** city. Dial Books for Young Readers 2011 376p (Relic master) $16.99

Grades: 6 7 8 9   **Fic**

1. Fantasy fiction 2. Apprentices -- Fiction
ISBN 978-0-8037-3673-3; 0-8037-3673-8

LC 2010028801

"Relic Master Galen injured both his body and his mind when he dismantled an ancient technological artifact. While his physical injuries have healed, the loss of his psychic gifts has left him reluctantly dependent on his talented young apprentice, Raffi. Together they travel the dangerous road to the ruined Antaran city of Tasceron, where Galen hopes to reclaim his abilities from a shadowy figure known only as the Crow." Booklist

The **hidden** Coronet. Dial Books for Young Readers 2011 421p (Relic master) $16.99

Grades: 6 7 8 9   **Fic**

1. Fantasy fiction 2. Apprentices -- Fiction
ISBN 978-0-8037-3675-7; 0-8037-3675-4

LC 2010039315

Sixteen-year-old Raffi and Master Galen continue to evade the Watch as they seek the Coronet, a potent ancient relic that could be their only hope for defeating the power that is destroying Anara.

"The climactic integration of visionary mysticism and gee-whiz gadgetry, rendered bittersweet by all-too human failures, leads directly to a cliffhanger ending." Kirkus

The **lost** heiress. Dial Books for Young Readers 2011 375p (Relic master) $16.99

Grades: 6 7 8 9   **Fic**

1. Fantasy fiction 2. Apprentices -- Fiction
ISBN 978-0-8037-3674-0; 0-8037-3674-6

LC 2010038156

Even though the city of Tasceron and its emperor have fallen, when Master Galen and his sixteen-year-old apprentice Raffi hear a rumor that the heiress to the throne still lives, they must try to find her and keep her safe.

"Separate plot threads intertwine in a satisfying climax, posing puzzles to keep readers ensnared while providing pleasing narrative momentum to the overall series." Kirkus

The **obsidian** mirror; by Catherine Fisher. Dial Books 2013 384 p. (hardcover) $17.99

Grades: 7 8 9 10 11 12   **Fic**
1. Fantasy fiction 2. Science fiction 3. Fathers -- Fiction 4. Time travel -- Fiction 5. Missing persons -- Fiction
ISBN 0803739699; 9780803739697

LC 2012019459

This book is the first in a trilogy from Catherine Fisher. The "mirror of the title, a dangerous gateway to other time periods, is being pursued by not one but three equally unpleasant and obsessive mad scientists. One of them, Oberon Venn, is the master of spooky Wintercombe Abbey. . . . Jake Wilde, Venn's teenage godson and his equal in arrogance, has been expelled from boarding school and shipped off to Wintercombe, where the boy plans to accuse Venn of having murdered Jake's father." (Publishers Weekly)

The **oracle** betrayed; book one of The Oracle Prophecies. by Catherine Fisher. 1st American ed; Greenwillow Books 2004 341p (Oracle prophecies) $16.99; lib bdg $17.89; pa $6.99
Grades: 7 8 9 10   **Fic**
1. Fantasy fiction
ISBN 0-06-057157-8; 0-06-057158-6 lib bdg; 0-06-057159-4 pa

LC 2003-48498

After she is chosen to be "Bearer-of-the-god," Mirany questions the established order and sets out, along with a musician and a scribe, to find the legitimate heir of the religious leader known as the Archon.
"This [is] a well-developed world with its own culture, some sharply realized settings, and several strong, distinctive characters." Booklist
Other titles in this series :
Day of the scarab: book three of The Oracle Prophecies (2006)
The Sphere of Secrets: book two of The Oracle Prophecies (2005)

Fitzgerald, Dawn
Soccer chick rules. Roaring Brook Press 2006 150p $16.95
Grades: 5 6 7 8   **Fic**
1. School stories 2. Soccer -- Fiction 3. Politics -- Fiction
ISBN 1-59643-137-7

While trying to focus on a winning soccer season, thirteen-year-old Tess becomes involved in local politics when she learns that all sports programs at her school will be stopped unless a tax levy is passed. "Grades five to eight." (Bull Cent Child Books)
This is "a fast-moving, true-to-life, amusing take on school life. The dialogue is especially spot-on." Booklist

Fitzmaurice, Kathryn
Destiny, rewritten; Kathryn Fitzmaurice ; [edited by] Molly O'Neill. Katherine Tegen Books 2013 352 p. (hardcover) $16.99
Grades: 4 5 6 7   **Fic**
1. Father-daughter relationship -- fiction
ISBN 0061625019; 9780061625015

LC 2012945971

In this novel, sixth-grader Emily, named for the poet Emily Dickinson, is pushed to become a poet by her mother "(she even commemorates the important moments of Emily's life in a first edition of Dickinson's poetry). Emily, however, thrives on predictability and order, and has no feel for poetry." She wants to find "her unknown father. . . . Just as Emily learns his name is hidden in the Dickinson book, it is accidentally taken and Emily sets out to find it." (Publishers Weekly)

A **diamond** in the desert; Kathryn Fitzmaurice. Viking 2012 258 p. (hardcover) $16.99
Grades: 5 6 7 8   **Fic**
1. Baseball -- Fiction 2. Father-son relationship -- Fiction 3. World War, 1939-1945 -- United States -- Fiction 4. Japanese Americans -- Evacuation and relocation, 1942-1945 -- Fiction 5. Guilt -- Fiction
ISBN 0670012920; 9780670012923

LC 2011012041

In this book, "Tetsu is twelve when he and his mother and sister are relocated by World War II's infamous Executive Order 9066, which justified the internment of Japanese-Americans, to the camp at Gila River. His father, a leader in the Japanese-American community, is detained separately in another location, and Tetsu generally takes his responsibility as the oldest male in the immediate family very seriously. He's particularly solicitous of his younger sister, Kimi, who is . . . traumatized by the lack of privacy in the camp. . . . Kimi . . . wanders out into the desert, where she nearly dies. Guilt-stricken, Tetsu withdraws from baseball and from his friends, until his father arrives at Gila River and rekindles his sonss interest in life." (Bulletin of the Center for Children's Books)
Includes bibliographical references (p. 255)

Fixmer, Elizabeth
★ **Saint** training. Zonderkidz 2010 239p $14.99
Grades: 5 6 7 8   **Fic**
1. School stories 2. Catholics -- Fiction 3. Family life -- Fiction 4. Christian life -- Fiction
ISBN 978-0-310-72018-8; 0-310-72018-4

LC 2010010831

During the turbulent 1960s, sixth-grader Mary Clare makes a deal with God: she will try to become a saint if He provides for her large, cash-strapped family.
"The politically fervent period of the late 1960s, with its dramatic upheavals in family, gender, social, and religious conventions, comes to life with pathos and humor in this powerful debut." Publ Wkly

Flack, Sophie
★ **Bunheads**. Poppy 2011 294p $17.99
Grades: 8 9 10 11 12   **Fic**
1. Ballet -- Fiction 2. Dating (Social customs) -- Fiction
ISBN 978-0-316-12653-3; 0-316-12653-5

LC 2011009715

Hannah Ward, nineteen, revels in the competition, intense rehearsals, and dazzling performances that come with being a member of Manhattan Ballet Company's corps de ballet, but after meeting handsome musician Jacob she begins to realize there could be more to her life.

"Readers, both dancers and 'pedestrians' (the corps' term for nondancers), will find Hannah's struggle a gripping read." Publ Wkly

Flake, Sharon G.

Bang! Jump at the Sun/Hyperion Books for Children 2005 298p hardcover o.p. pa $7.99

Grades: 8 9 10 11 12　　　　　　　　　　　　　**Fic**

1. Violence -- Fiction　2. Family life -- Fiction　3. African Americans -- Fiction

ISBN 0-7868-1844-1; 0-7868-4955-X pa

LC 2005-47434

A teenage boy must face the harsh realities of inner city life, a disintegrating family, and destructive temptations as he struggles to find his identity as a young man.

"This disturbing, thought-provoking novel will leave readers with plenty of food for thought and should fuel lively discussions." SLJ

★ The **broken** bike boy and the Queen of 33rd Street. Jump at the Sun/Hyperion Books for Children 2007 132p il $15.99; pa $5.99

Grades: 4 5 6 7　　　　　　　　　　　　　　**Fic**

1. School stories　2. Friendship -- Fiction　3. African Americans -- Fiction

ISBN 978-1-4231-0032-4; 1-4231-0032-8; 978-1-4231-0035-5 pa; 1-4231-0035-2 pa

LC 2006-35590

Ten-year-old Queen, a spoiled and conceited African American girl who is disliked by most of her classmates, learns a lesson about friendship from an unlikely "knight in shining armor."

"Complex intergenerational characters and a rich urban setting defy stereotyping. . . . Infrequent detailed pencil illustrations . . . add a welcome dimension." Horn Book

The **skin** I'm in. Jump at the Sun 1998 171p $14.95; pa $5.99

Grades: 6 7 8 9　　　　　　　　　　　　　　**Fic**

1. School stories　2. Teachers -- Fiction　3. African Americans -- Fiction

ISBN 0-7868-0444-0; 0-7868-1307-5 pa

LC 98-19615

Thirteen-year-old Maleeka, uncomfortable because her skin is extremely dark, meets a new teacher with a birthmark on her face and makes some discoveries about how to love who she is and what she looks like

This "novel is fast-paced and realistic." Horn Book Guide

Flanagan, John

The **hunters**; John Flanagan. Philomel 2012 403 p. (hardback) $18.99

Grades: 5 6 7 8　　　　　　　　　　　　　　**Fic**

1. Courage -- Fiction　2. Pirates -- Fiction　3. Friendship -- Fiction　4. Seafaring life -- Fiction　5. Adventure and adventurers -- Fiction

ISBN 0399256210; 9780399256219

LC 2012020986

This book by John Flanagan is part of the Brotherband Chronicles series. "Hal and his brotherband crew are hot on the trail of the pirate Zavac and they have one thing only on their minds: Stopping the bloodthirsty thief before he can do

more damage. Of course, they also know Zavac has the Andomal, the priceless Skandian artifact stolen when the brotherband let down their guard. The chase leads down mighty rivers, terrifying rapids, to the lawless fortress of Ragusa." (Publisher's note)

The **invaders**; John Flanagan. Philomel Books 2012 429 p. (The Brotherband chronicles) (hardback) $18.99

Grades: 5 6 7 8　　　　　　　　　　　　　　**Fic**

1. Courage -- Fiction　2. Pirates -- Fiction　3. Friendship -- Fiction　4. Seafaring life -- Fiction　5. Adventure and adventurers -- Fiction

ISBN 0399256202; 9780399256202

LC 2012000424

This book by John Flanagan is part of the Brotherband Chronicles series. "Hal and the Herons have done the impossible. This group of outsiders has beaten out the strongest, most skilled young warriors in all of Skandia to win the Brotherband competition. But their celebration comes to an abrupt end when the Skandians' most sacred artifact, the Andomal, is stolen--and the Herons are to blame." (Publisher's note)

★ The **outcasts**. Philomel Books 2011 434p (Brotherband chronicles) $18.99

Grades: 5 6 7 8　　　　　　　　　　　　　　**Fic**

1. Fantasy fiction　2. Adventure fiction　3. Friendship -- Fiction

ISBN 978-0-399-25619-6; 0-399-25619-9

Hal, who does not fit into Skandian society, ends up in a brotherband, a group of boys learning the skills that they need to become warriors, with other outcasts, and they compete with other brotherbands in a series of challenges.

"This enjoyable, old-fashioned tale should have easy appeal for Flanagan's many fans, who are already invested in the world he's created." Publ Wkly

★ The **ruins** of Gorlan. Philomel Books 2005 249p (Ranger's apprentice) $15.99; pa $7.99

Grades: 5 6 7 8　　　　　　　　　　　　　　**Fic**

1. Fantasy fiction

ISBN 0-399-24454-9; 0-14-240663-5 pa

When fifteen-year-old Will is rejected by battleschool, he becomes the reluctant apprentice to the mysterious Ranger Halt, and winds up protecting the kingdom from danger.

"Flanagan concentrates on character, offering readers a young protagonist they will care about and relationships that develop believably over time." Booklist

Other titles in this series are:

The burning bridge (2006)

The icebound land (2007)

The battle for Skandia (2008)

The socerer of the north (2008)

The siege of Macindaw (2009)

Erak's ransom (2010)

The kings of Clonmel (2010)

Halt's peril (2010)

The Emperor of Nihon-Ja (2011)

Flavin, Teresa

The **Blackhope** enigma. Candlewick Press 2011
280p $15.99

Grades: 5 6 7 8   **Fic**

1. Adventure fiction 2. Magic -- Fiction 3. Painting
-- Fiction 4. Space and time -- Fiction

ISBN 978-0-7636-5694-2; 0-7636-5694-1

LC 2010047654

Fourteen-year-old Sunni, her stepbrother Dean, and an
art-student friend trace the footsteps of a labyrinth built in
Blackhope Tower by a mysterious and brilliant sixteenth-
century artist, and suddenly find themselves trapped inside
his enchanted painting, trying desperately to get out.

"The settings are described in detail, and interesting
facts about painting techniques are cleverly interwoven. . .
. Readers . . . will be delighted with Flavin's fully-realized,
action-packed debut." Kirkus

Fleischman, Paul

★ **Bull** Run; woodcuts by David Frampton.
HarperCollins Pubs. 1993 104p il pa $4.99

Grades: 6 7 8 9   **Fic**

1. Bull Run, 1st Battle of, 1861 -- Fiction

ISBN 0-06-440588-5 pa

LC 92-14745

"Abandoning the conventions of narrative fiction, Fleischman tells a vivid, many-sided story in this original and
moving book. An excellent choice for readers' theater in the
classroom or on stage." Booklist

Seek. Simon Pulse 2003 167p pa $7.99

Grades: 7 8 9 10   **Fic**

1. Radio -- Fiction 2. Fathers -- Fiction

ISBN 0-689-85402-1

First published 2001 by Front St./Cricket Bks.

"Fleischman has orchestrated a symphony that is both
joyful and poignant with this book designed for reader's theatre." Voice Youth Advocates

Fleischman, Sid

The **entertainer** and the dybbuk. Greenwillow
Books 2007 180p lib bdg $17.89; pa $6.99; $16.99

Grades: 6 7 8 9   **Fic**

1. Ghost stories 2. Jews -- Fiction 3. Supernatural
-- Fiction 4. Ventriloquism -- Fiction 5. Holocaust,
1933-1945 -- Fiction

ISBN 0-06-13444-1; 978-0-06-134446-6 lib bdg;
0-06-134446-X lib bdg; 978-0-06-177140-8 pa;
0-06-177140-6 pa; 978-0-06-134445-9

LC 2007-17267

A struggling American ventriloquist in post-World War
II Europe is possessed by the mischievous spirit of a young
Jewish boy killed in the Holocaust.

"This exciting and thought-provoking book belongs in
every collection." SLJ

The **whipping** boy; illustrations by Peter Sis.
Greenwillow Bks. 1986 90p il $16.99; pa $5.99

Grades: 5 6 7 8   **Fic**

1. Adventure fiction 2. Thieves -- Fiction

ISBN 0-688-06216-4; 0-06-052122-8 pa

LC 85-17555

Awarded the Newbery Medal, 1987

"A round tale of adventure and humor, this follows the
fortunes of Prince Roland (better known as Prince Brat) and
his whipping boy, Jemmy, who has received all the hard
knocks for the prince's mischief. . . . There's not a moment's
lag in pace, and the stock characters, from Hold-Your-Nose
Billy to Betsy's dancing bear Petunia, have enough inventive
twists to project a lively air to it all." Bull Cent Child Books

Fletcher, Charlie

Stoneheart. Hyperion Books for Children 2007
450p (Stoneheart trilogy) $16.99; pa $7.99

Grades: 5 6 7 8   **Fic**

1. Fantasy fiction

ISBN 978-1-4231-0175-8; 1-4231-0175-8; 978-1-
4231-0176-5 pa; 1-4231-0176-6 pa

LC 2007-01138

When twelve-year-old George accidentally decapitates
a stone statue in London, England, he falls into a parallel
dimension where he must battle ancient "live" statues and
solve a dangerous riddle.

This "is an action-packed fantasy filled with battles,
chases, and an intriguing variety of characters." SLJ

Other titles in this series are:

Ironhand (2008)
Silvertongue (2009)

Fletcher, Ralph

The **one** o'clock chop; [by] Ralph Fletcher. 1st
ed.; Henry Holt 2007 183p $16.95

Grades: 7 8 9 10   **Fic**

1. Cousins -- Fiction 2. Boats and boating -- Fiction

ISBN 978-0-8050-8143-5; 0-8050-8143-7

LC 2006035470

In New York, fourteen-year-old Matt spends the summer
of 1973 digging clams to earn money for his own boat and
falling for Jazzy, a beautiful and talented girl from Hawaii
who happens to be his first cousin.

"Plenty of universal teen fascinations and concerns exist for those readers willing to enter Matt's world and give
themselves over to this smoothly paced and competently
written novel." SLJ

Fletcher, Susan

Alphabet of dreams. Atheneum Books for Young
Readers 2006 294p map $16.95

Grades: 6 7 8 9 10   **Fic**

1. Dreams -- Fiction 2. Zoroastrianism -- Fiction

ISBN 0-689-85042-5

Fourteen-year-old Mitra, of royal Persian lineage, and
her five-year-old brother Babak, whose dreams foretell
the future, flee for their lives in the company of the ma-
gus Melchoir and two other Zoroastrian priests, traveling
through Persia as they follow star signs leading to a newly-
born king in Bethlehem. Includes historical notes

"The characters are vivid and whole, the plot compelling, and the setting vast." Voice Youth Advocates

Ancient, strange, and lovely. Atheneum Books for Young Readers 2010 315p il (The dragon chronicles) $16.99

Grades: 6 7 8 9   **Fic**

1. Fantasy fiction 2. Dragons -- Fiction 3. Poaching -- Fiction

ISBN 978-1-4169-5786-7; 1-4169-5786-3

LC 2009053797

Fourteen-year-old Bryn must try to find a way to save a baby dragon from a dangerous modern world that seems to have no place for something so ancient.

"This book offers a wondrous mix of dystopic science fiction and magical fantasy. . . . Fletcher has done an outstanding job of creating a believable place and space for this story to unfold. The plot flows smoothly and quickly with a lot of action." SLJ

Dragon's milk. Atheneum Pubs. 1989 242p hardcover o.p. pa $5.99

Grades: 7 8 9 10   **Fic**

1. Fantasy fiction 2. Dragons -- Fiction

ISBN 0-689-31579-1; 0-689-71623-0 pa

LC 88-35059

Kaeldra, an outsider adopted by an Elythian family as a baby, possesses the power to understand dragons and uses this power to try to save her younger sister who needs dragon's milk to recover from an illness

"High-fantasy fans will delight in the clash of swords, the flash of magic, the many escape-and-rescue scenes." Booklist

Other titles in this series are:

Flight of the Dragon Kyn (1993)

Sign of the dove (1996)

Walk across the sea. Atheneum Bks. for Young Readers 2001 214p hardcover o.p. pa $4.99

Grades: 5 6 7 8   **Fic**

1. Prejudices -- Fiction 2. Chinese Americans -- Fiction

ISBN 0-689-84133-7; 0-689-85707-1 pa

LC 00-50246

In late nineteenth-century California, when Chinese immigrants are being driven out or even killed for fear they will take jobs from whites, fifteen-year-old Eliza Jane McCully defies the townspeople and her lighthouse-keeper father to help a Chinese boy who has been kind to her

"This is a gripping and complex story, and Fletcher's lyrical depiction of 19th-century life, her exceptionally well-drawn protagonist, and her deft analysis of racial discrimination make the book even more powerful." SLJ

Flinn, Alex

Beastly. HarperTeen 2007 304p $16.99; lib bdg $17.89; pa $8.99

Grades: 6 7 8 9 10   **Fic**

1. Fantasy fiction

ISBN 978-0-06-087416-2; 0-06-087416-3; 978-0-06-087417-9 lib bdg; 0-06-087417-1 lib bdg; 978-0-06-196328-5 pa; 0-06-196328-3 pa

LC 2006-36241

A modern retelling of "Beauty and the Beast" from the point of view of the Beast, a vain Manhattan private school student who is turned into a monster and must find true love before he can return to his human form.

This "is creative enough to make it an engaging read. . . . [This is an] engrossing tale that will have appeal for fans of fantasy and realistic fiction." Voice Youth Advocates

Cloaked. HarperTeen 2011 341p $16.99

Grades: 6 7 8 9   **Fic**

1. Fairy tales 2. Magic -- Fiction 3. Shoes -- Fiction 4. Animals -- Fiction 5. Princesses -- Fiction 6. Missing persons -- Fiction

ISBN 978-0-06-087422-3; 0-06-087422-8

LC 2009-53387

Seventeen-year-old Johnny is approached at his family's struggling shoe repair shop in a Miami, Florida, hotel by Alorian Princess Victoriana, who asks him to find her brother who was turned into a frog.

"A diverting, whimsical romp through fairy-tale tropes." Bull Cent Child Books

A kiss in time. HarperTeen 2009 384p $16.99; pa $8.99

Grades: 7 8 9 10 11 12   **Fic**

1. Witches -- Fiction 2. Princesses -- Fiction

ISBN 978-0-06-087419-3; 0-06-087419-8; 978-0-06-087421-6 pa; 0-06-087421-X pa

LC 2008-22582

Sixteen-year-old Princess Talia persuades seventeen-year-old Jack, the modern-day American who kissed her awake after a 300-year sleep, to take her to his Miami home, where she hopes to win his love before the witch who cursed her can spirit her away.

This is a "clever and humorous retelling of 'Sleeping Beauty.' . . . Alternating between the teenagers' distinctive points of view, Flinn skillfully delineates how their upbringings set them apart while drawing parallels between their family conflicts. Fans of happily-ever-after endings will delight in the upbeat resolution." Publ Wkly

Flood, Nancy Bo

★ **Warriors** in the crossfire. Front Street 2010 142p $17.95

Grades: 6 7 8 9   **Fic**

1. World War, 1939-1945 -- Fiction

ISBN 978-1-59078-661-1; 1-59078-661-0

Twelve-year-old Joseph helps his family to survive when the natives of Saipan are caught in the crossfire between Japanese and American soldiers towards the end of World War II.

"Intense and powerful reading that avoids bleakness by celebrating family, culture, and a longing for peace." Booklist

Flores-Gabis, Enrique

★ **90** miles to Havana. Roaring Brook Press 2010 292p $17.99

Grades: 5 6 7 8   **Fic**

1. Cuban refugees -- Fiction

ISBN 978-1-59643-168-3; 1-59643-168-7

"Drawing on his own experience as a child refugee from Cuba, Flores-Galbis offers a gripping historical novel about children who were evacuated from Cuba to the U.S. during Operation Pedro Pan in 1961. Julian, a young Cuban boy, experiences the violent revolution and watches mobs throw out his family's furniture and move into their home. For his safety, his parents send him to a refugee camp in Miami. . . . This is a seldom-told refugee story that will move readers with the first-person, present-tense rescue narrative, filled with betrayal, kindness, and waiting for what may never come." Booklist

Fogelin, Adrian

The **big** nothing; 1st ed; Peachtree 2004 235p $14.95

Grades: 7 8 9 10   **Fic**

1. Pianists -- Fiction 2. Family life -- Fiction
ISBN 1-56145-326-9

LC 2004-6327

Thirteen-year-old Justin Riggs struggles to cope with major family problems, including a brother who might be heading for the Persian Gulf, but finds an escape in piano lessons and the dream of a romance with a popular girl.

"Serious and humorous by turns, this seemingly simple story is actually quite complex but not weighty and will be enthusiastically embraced." SLJ

The **real** question. Peachtree 2006 234p $15.95

Grades: 7 8 9 10   **Fic**

1. Father-son relationship -- Fiction
ISBN 1-56145-383-8

LC 2006013996

Fisher Brown, a sixteen-year-old over-achiever, is on the verge of academic burnout when he impulsively decides to stop cramming for the SATs for one weekend and accompany his ne'erdowell neighbor to an out-of-town job repairing a roof.

"Fisher's first-person narration is dead-on. . . . This amazing title . . . should be required reading for every teen . . . who feels the weight of a parent's expectations but cannot quite figure out what to do about it." Voice Youth Advocates

Foley, Lizzie K.

Remarkable; a novel. by Lizzie K. Foley. Dial Books for Young Readers 2012 325 p. $16.99

Grades: 3 4 5 6 7   **Fic**

1. Fantasy fiction 2. Humorous fiction 3. Ability -- Fiction 4. Community life -- Fiction 5. Humorous stories 6. Pirates -- Fiction 7. Secrets -- Fiction 8. Eccentrics and eccentricities -- Fiction
ISBN 9780803737068

LC 2011021641

This book presents the story of an average girl named Jane Doe who lives in "the town of Remarkable, so named for its abundance of talented citizens, everyone lives up to its reputation. . . . Jane should be just as remarkable. Instead, this average 10-year-old girl is usually overlooked. . . . Mix in a rival town's dispute over jelly, hints of a Loch Ness Monster-like creature and a psychic pizzeria owner who sees the future in her reflective pizza pans. . . . With the help of her quiet Grandpa John, who's also forgotten most of the time, Jane learns to be true to herself and celebrate the ordinary in life." (Kirkus)

Fombelle, Timothee de

Toby alone; translated by Sarah Ardizzone; illustrated by Francois Place. Candlewick Press 2009 384p il $17.99; pa $8.99

Grades: 5 6 7 8   **Fic**

1. Fantasy fiction 2. Trees -- Fiction
ISBN 978-0-7636-4181-8; 0-7636-4181-2; 978-0-7636-4815-2 pa; 0-7636-4815-9 pa
Original French edition 2006

Toby is just one and a half millimeters tall, and he's the most wanted person in his world of the great oak Tree. When Toby's father discovers that the Tree is alive, he realizes that exploiting it could do damage to their world. Refusing to reveal the secret to an enraged community, Toby's parents have been imprisoned. Only Toby has managed to escape, but for how long?

"The impressive debut novel from French playwright de Fombelle deftly weaves mature political commentary, broad humor and some subtle satire into a thoroughly enjoyable adventure." Publ Wkly

Toby and the secrets of the tree; illustrated by Francois Place; translated by Sarah Ardizzone. Candlewick Press 2010 414p il $16.99

Grades: 5 6 7 8   **Fic**

1. Fantasy fiction 2. Trees -- Fiction
ISBN 978-0-7636-4655-4; 0-7636-4655-5

LC 2009014833

Thirteen-year-old Toby's tiny world is under greater threat than ever as Leo Blue holds Elisha prisoner while hunting the Grass People and anyone who stands in the way of his devastating plans for the oak Tree in which they all live, but this time Toby is not alone.

"Place's pen-and-ink illustrations are scattered generously throughout and enhance the overall quirkiness. . . . This interesting piece of eco-fantasy provides a satisfying conclusion for those who enjoyed the first book." SLJ

Fontes, Justine

Benito runs. Darby Creek 2011 104p (Surviving Southside) lib bdg $27.93; pa $7.99

Grades: 7 8 9 10   **Fic**

1. Fathers -- Fiction 2. Hispanic Americans -- Fiction 3. Post-traumatic stress disorder -- Fiction
ISBN 978-0-7613-6151-0 lib bdg; 0-7613-6151-0; 978-0-7613-6165-7 pa; 0-7613-6165-0 pa

LC 2010023820

This "well-written [story reinforces] the importance of family, friends, values, and thoughtful decision-making. . . . [An] excellent [purchase, this book] will attract and engage reluctant readers." SLJ

Forbes, Esther

Johnny Tremain; a novel for old & young. with illustrations by Lynd Ward. Houghton Mifflin Books for Children 1943 256p il $17; pa $6.99

Grades: 5 6 7 8   **Fic**

ISBN 978-0-395-06766-6; 0-395-06766-9; 978-0-440-44250-9 pa; 0-440-44250-8 pa
Awarded the Newbery Medal, 1944

"Johnny, an orphan, works as a favored apprentice to an aging silversmith until he burns his hand severely while working on an important project. During the Revolutionary War he serves as a dispatch rider for the Committee on Public Safety, meeting such men as Paul Revere and John Hancock. An outcast for a time, he finally learns on the battlefield of Lexington that his crippled hand can be put to use." Shapiro. Fic for Youth. 3d edition

Ford, John C.

The **morgue** and me. Viking 2009 313p $17.99

Grades: 8 9 10 11 12   Fic

1. Mystery fiction 2. Homicide -- Fiction 3. Journalists -- Fiction 4. Criminal investigation -- Fiction

ISBN 978-0-670-01096-7; 0-670-01096-0

LC 2009-1956

Eighteen-year-old Christopher, who plans to be a spy, learns of a murder cover-up through his summer job as a morgue assistant and teams up with Tina, a gorgeous newspaper reporter, to investigate, despite great danger.

"Ford spins a tale that's complex but not confusing, never whitewashing some of the harsher crimes people commit. The result is a story that holds its own as a mainstream mystery as well as a teen novel." Publ Wkly

Ford, Michael

The **Fire** of Ares. Walker & Co. 2008 244p (Spartan quest) $16.95; pa $7.99

Grades: 6 7 8 9   Fic

1. Slavery -- Fiction 2. Social classes -- Fiction 3. Sparta (Extinct city) -- Fiction

ISBN 978-0-8027-9744-5; 0-8027-9744-X; 978-0-8027-9827-5 pa; 0-8027-9827-6 pa

LC 2007024237

When slaves rebel in ancient Sparta, twelve-year-old Lysander, guarded by an heirloom amulet, the Fire of Ares, is caught between the Spartan ruling class, with whom he has been training as a warrior since his noble heritage was revealed, and those among whom he was recently laboring as a slave.

"Middle-grade boys who love action and vividly depicted battles will seize upon Ford's children's book debut . . . and they'll encounter a large number of interesting facts about ancient Greece along the way." Booklist

Other titles in this series are:

Birth of a warrior (2008)

Legacy of blood (2009)

★ The **poisoned** house. Albert Whitman 2011 319p $16.99

Grades: 6 7 8 9 10   Fic

1. Ghost stories 2. Supernatural -- Fiction 3. Household employees -- Fiction

ISBN 978-0-8075-6589-6; 0-8075-6589-X

LC 2010048250

As the widowed master of an elegant house in Victorian-era London slips slowly into madness and his tyrannical housekeeper takes on more power, a ghostly presence distracts a teenaged maidservant with clues to a deadly secret.

"This ghost story is light fare, chilling, and suspenseful." SLJ

Ford, Michael Thomas

Z. HarperTeen 2010 276p $16.99; lib bdg $17.89

Grades: 7 8 9 10   Fic

1. Science fiction 2. Games -- Fiction 3. Zombies -- Fiction

ISBN 978-0-06-073758-0; 0-06-073758-1; 978-0-06-073759-7 lib bdg; 0-06-073759-X lib bdg

LC 2009-44005

In the year 2032, after a virus that turned people into zombies has been eradicated, Josh is invited to join an underground gaming society, where the gamers hunt zombies and the action is more dangerous than it seems.

"This book is a thriller, and the clever plot and characters will have readers hoping for more." SLJ

Forester, Victoria

★ The **girl** who could fly. Feiwel and Friends 2008 329p $16.95

Grades: 4 5 6 7   Fic

1. School stories 2. Science fiction 3. Flight -- Fiction

ISBN 978-0-312-37462-4; 0-312-37462-3

LC 2008-06882

When homeschooled farm girl Piper McCloud reveals her ability to fly, she is quickly taken to a secret government facility to be trained with other exceptional children, but she soon realizes that something is very wrong and begins working with brilliant and wealthy Conrad to escape.

"The story soars, just like Piper, with enough loop-de-loops to keep kids uncertain about what will come next. . . . Best of all are the book's strong, lightly wrapped messages about friendship and authenticity and the difference between doing well and doing good." Booklist

Forman, Gayle

★ **If** I stay; a novel. Dutton Children's Books 2009 201p $16.99

Grades: 7 8 9 10   Fic

1. Coma -- Fiction 2. Death -- Fiction 3. Medical care -- Fiction

ISBN 978-0-525-42103-0; 0-525-42103-3

LC 2008-23938

While in a coma following an automobile accident that killed her parents and younger brother, seventeen-year-old Mia, a gifted cellist, weights whether to live with her grief or join her family in death.

"Intensely moving, the novel will force readers to take stock of their lives and the people and things that make them worth living." Publ Wkly

Where she went. Dutton Books 2011 264p $16.99

Grades: 7 8 9 10   Fic

1. Musicians -- Fiction 2. Rock music -- Fiction 3. Violoncellos -- Fiction

ISBN 978-0-525-42294-5; 0-525-42294-3

LC 2010-13474

"Both characters spring to life, and their pain-filled back story and current realities provide depth and will hold readers fast." Kirkus

Foxlee, Karen

★ The **anatomy** of wings. Alfred A. Knopf 2009 361p $16.99; lib bdg $19.99

Grades: 8 9 10 11 12   **Fic**
1. Sisters -- Fiction 2. Suicide -- Fiction 3. Bereavement -- Fiction 4. Family life -- Fiction

ISBN 978-0-375-85643-3; 0-375-85643-9; 978-0-375-95643-0 lib bdg; 0-375-95643-3 lib bdg

            LC 2008-19373

First published 2007 in Australia

After the suicide of her troubled teenage sister, eleven-year-old Jenny struggles to understand what actually happened.

Jenny's "observations are . . . poetic and washed with magic realism. . . . With heart-stopping accuracy and sly symbolism, Foxlee captures the small ways that humans reveal themselves, the mysterious intensity of female adolescence, and the surreal quiet of a grieving house, which slowly and with astonishing resilience fills again with sound and music." Booklist

Frank, E. R.

Life is funny; a novel. Puffin Books 2002 263p pa $7.99

Grades: 7 8 9 10   **Fic**
1. Family life -- Fiction

ISBN 0-14-230083-7

            LC 2001-48436

First published 2000 by DK Ink

The lives of a number of young people of different races, economic backgrounds, and family situations living in Brooklyn, New York, become intertwined over a seven year period.

"The voices ring true, and the talk is painful, vulgar, rough, sexy, funny, fearful, furious, gentle." Booklist

Wrecked. Atheneum Books for Young Readers 2005 247p $15.95

Grades: 8 9 10 11 12   **Fic**
1. Bereavement -- Fiction 2. Traffic accidents -- Fiction

ISBN 0-689-87383-2

            LC 2004-18448

After a car accident seriously injures her best friend and kills her brother's girlfriend, sixteen-year-old Anna tries to cope with her guilt and grief, while learning some truths about her family and herself.

"This story is compulsively readable both because Anna is likable and imperfect and because Frank's writing is so fluid." SLJ

Franklin, Emily

The **other** half of me. Delacorte Press 2007 247p $15.99; pa $6.50

Grades: 8 9 10 11 12   **Fic**
1. Artists -- Fiction 2. Sisters -- Fiction 3. Identity (Psychology) -- Fiction

ISBN 978-0-385-73445-5; 0-385-73445-X; 978-0-385-73446-2 pa; 0385-73446-8 pa

            LC 2006-36825

Feeling out of place in her athletic family, artistic sixteen-year-old Jenny Fitzgerald, whose biological father was a sperm donor, finds her half sister through the Sibling Do-

nor Registry and contacts her, hoping that this will finally make her feel complete.

"Franklin offers readers an engaging protagonist whose humor and unusual situation highlight the lonely and displaced feelings common to many teens." SLJ

Frazier, Angie

The **Eternal** Sea. Scholastic Press 2011 362p $17.99

Grades: 8 9 10 11 12   **Fic**
1. Adventure fiction 2. Supernatural -- Fiction

ISBN 978-0-545-11475-2; 0-545-11475-6

Realizing that the magic of Umandu, the stone that grants immortality, is not done, seventeen-year-old Camille accompanies Oscar, Ira, and Randall to Egypt, where all their lives are in grave danger.

"Readers who enjoy sea romances won't go wrong." SLJ

Everlasting. Scholastic Press 2010 329p $17.99

Grades: 8 9 10 11 12   **Fic**
1. Adventure fiction 2. Shipwrecks -- Fiction 3. Supernatural -- Fiction 4. Seafaring life -- Fiction 5. Father-daughter relationship -- Fiction

ISBN 978-0-545-11473-8; 0-545-11473-X

            LC 2009-20519

In 1855, seventeen-year-old Camille sets out from San Francisco, California, on her last sea voyage before entering a loveless marriage, but when her father's ship is destroyed, she and a friend embark on a cross-Australian quest to find her long-lost mother who holds a map to a magical stone.

"Although this novel takes place in the nineteenth century, many of the themes are relevant for today's teens. The author does a nice job of developing strong and funny characters while keeping the plot moving at a readable pace." Voice Youth Advocates

The **mastermind** plot; by Angie Frazier. Scholastic Press 2012 231 p. $16.99 (Suzanna Snow mysteries)

Grades: 4 5 6 7   **Fic**
1. Mystery fiction 2. Adventure fiction 3. Children's stories 4. Arson -- Fiction 5. Uncles -- Fiction 6. Schools -- Fiction 7. Grandmothers -- Fiction 8. Mystery and detective stories 9. Family life -- Massachusetts -- Boston -- Fiction

ISBN 0545208645; 9780545208642

            LC 2011003770

This children's mystery by Angie Frazier continues the adventures of Suzanna Snow. "She's just arrived in Boston, the city she's wanted to visit for as long as she can remember. . . . Her grandmother and cousin, Will, welcome her warmly, but her famous detective uncle, Bruce Snow, seems anything but pleased. He doesn't want [her] meddling in his current case involving a string of mysterious warehouse fires along the harbor front. But Zanna can't help herself. Is someone setting the fires? Just when she thinks she's on to something, a strange man starts following her. Is he a threat? Zanna needs to solve the case before she has the chance to find out." (Publisher's note)

The **midnight** tunnel; a Suzanna Snow mystery. Scholastic Press 2011 283p $16.99

Grades: 4 5 6 7　　　　　　　　　　　　Fic
1. Mystery fiction 2. Uncles -- Fiction 3. Missing children -- Fiction 4. Hotels and motels -- Fiction
ISBN 978-0-545-20862-8; 0-545-20862-9
LC 2010-26770

In 1905, Suzanna is in training to be a well-mannered hostess at a Loch Harbor, New Brunswick, hotel, but her dream of being a detective gets a boost when a seven-year-old guest goes missing and Suzanna's uncle, a famous detective, comes to solve the case.

"What Zanna lacks in grace and composure, she makes up for in pluck, persistence and cleverness, emerging a likely and likable Edwardian Nancy Drew." Kirkus

Frazier, Sundee Tucker
★ The **other** half of my heart; [by] Sundee T. Frazier. Delacorte Press 2010 296p $16.99
Grades: 5 6 7 8　　　　　　　　　　　　Fic
1. Twins -- Fiction 2. Sisters -- Fiction 3. Prejudices -- Fiction 4. Grandmothers -- Fiction 5. Beauty contests -- Fiction 6. African Americans -- Fiction 7. Racially mixed people -- Fiction
ISBN 978-0-385-73440-0; 0-385-73440-9
LC 2009013209

Twin daughters of interracial parents, eleven-year-olds Keira and Minna have very different skin tones and personalities, but it is not until their African American grandmother enters them in the Miss Black Pearl Pre-Teen competition in North Carolina that red-haired and pale-skinned Minna realizes what life in their small town in the Pacific Northwest has been like for her more outgoing, darker-skinned sister.

"Frazier addresses issues faced by mixed-race children with a grace and humor that keep her from being pedantic. The story is enjoyable in its own right, and will also encourage readers to rethink racial boundries and what it means to be black or white in America." SLJ

Frederick, Heather Vogel
The **voyage** of Patience Goodspeed. Simon & Schuster Bks. for Young Readers 2002 219p hardcover o.p. pa $4.99
Grades: 5 6 7 8　　　　　　　　　　　　Fic
1. Whaling -- Fiction 2. Navigation -- Fiction 3. Seafaring life -- Fiction
ISBN 0-689-84851-X; 0-689-84869-2 pa
LC 2001-49039

Following their mother's death in Nantucket, Captain Goodspeed brings twelve-year-old Patience and six-year-old Tad aboard his whaling ship, where a new crew member incites a mutiny and Patience puts her mathematical ability to good use

"This is an exciting voyage of peril and self-discovery." N Y Times Book Rev

Another title about Patience is:
The education of Patience Goodspeed (2004)

Fredericks, Mariah
Head games. Atheneum Books for Young Readers 2004 260p $15.95

Grades: 7 8 9 10　　　　　　　　　　　　Fic
1. School stories 2. Dating (Social customs) -- Fiction
ISBN 0-689-85532-X
LC 2003-17012

Two teenagers connect online in a roleplaying game which leads them into their own face-to-face, half-acknowledged courtship.

"This novel realistically portrays young adults trying to find themselves, fit in, and resist the labels put on them." SLJ

Love; illustrated by Liselotte Watkins. Atheneum Books for Young Readers 2007 270p il (In the cards) $15.99
Grades: 5 6 7 8　　　　　　　　　　　　Fic
1. School stories 2. Tarot -- Fiction 3. Friendship -- Fiction 4. Fortune telling -- Fiction
ISBN 978-0-689-87654-7; 0-689-87654-8
LC 2005-31956

Thirteen-year-old Anna hopes that her newly inherited tarot cards will predict an exciting future, including becoming the girlfriend of eighth-grade hottie, Declan Kelso.

"Fredericks displays a keen ear for dialogue and a knack for expressing some complex, real middle school emotions." SLJ

Other titles in this series are:
Fame (2008)
Life (2008)

Freitas, Donna
The **Survival** Kit. Farrar Straus Giroux 2011 351p $16.99
Grades: 7 8 9 10　　　　　　　　　　　　Fic
1. Death -- Fiction 2. Bereavement -- Fiction
ISBN 978-0-374-39917-7; 0-374-39917-4
LC 2010041294

"The premise of the survival kit, a real-life tradition from Freitas's own mother, begs to be discussed and glued-and-scissored with friends, students, teachers, and librarians. A copy of The Survival Kit would be a worthy addition for a teen coping with her own loss or struggling to help friends or family cope with theirs." Voice Youth Advocates

★ The **possibilities** of sainthood. Farrar, Straus & Giroux 2008 272p $16.95
Grades: 7 8 9 10 11 12　　　　　　　　　Fic
1. School stories 2. Saints -- Fiction 3. Catholics -- Fiction 4. Family life -- Fiction 5. Italian Americans -- Fiction
ISBN 978-0-374-36087-0; 0-374-36087-1
LC 2007-33298

While regularly petitioning the Vatican to make her the first living saint, fifteen-year-old Antonia Labella prays to assorted patron saints for everything from help with preparing the family's fig trees for a Rhode Island winter to getting her first kiss from the right boy.

"With a satisfying ending, this novel about the realistic struggles of a chaste teen is a great addition to all collections." SLJ

French, Vivian

The **robe** of skulls; [illustrated by] Ross Collins. Candlewick Press 2008 208p il $14.99 (Tales from the five kingdoms)

Grades: 4 5 6   **Fic**
1. Fairy tales 2. Bats -- Fiction 3. Magic -- Fiction 4. Trolls -- Fiction
ISBN 0-7636-3531-6; 0-7636-4364-5 pa; 978-0-7636-3531-2; 978-0-7636-4364-5 pa
LC 2007-38290

The sorceress Lady Lamorna has her heart set on a very expensive new robe, and she will stop at nothing—including kidnapping and black magic—to get the money to pay for it.

"Collins' black-and-white line drawings, dropped haphazardly into the text, perfectly complement the story, offering visual metaphors for the heady narrative mix of melodrama and humor." Bull Cent Child Books

Other titles in this series are:
The bag of bones (2009)
The heart of glass (2010)
The flight of dragons (2011)

Freymann-Weyr, Garret

My heartbeat. Houghton Mifflin 2002 154p $15

Grades: 7 8 9 10   **Fic**
1. Siblings -- Fiction 2. Homosexuality -- Fiction
ISBN 0-618-14181-2
LC 2001-47059

Michael L. Printz Award honor book, 2003

As she tries to understand the closeness between her older brother and his best friend, fourteen-year-old Ellen finds her relationship with each of them changing

"This beautiful novel tells a frank, upbeat story of teen bisexual love in all its uncertainty, pain, and joy. . . . The fast, clipped dialogue will sweep teens into the story, as will Ellen's immediate first-person, present-tense narrative." Booklist

Fridrik Erlingsson

Benjamin Dove. North-South 2007 206p $15.95; pa $7.95

Grades: 6 7 8 9   **Fic**
1. Friendship -- Fiction
ISBN 978-0-7358-2150-7; 0-7358-2150-X; 978-0-7358-2149-1 pa; 0-7358-2149-6 pa

"Benjamin tells the story of the summer her was 12, when free-spirited Roland moved into the neighborhood and changed the lives of Benjamin and his friends Jeff and Manny forever. . . . This is a well-written, attention-grabbing tale of desire for acceptance, conflict between good and evil, and coming-of-age." SLJ

Friedman, Aimee

The **year** my sister got lucky. Scholastic 2008 370p $16.99

Grades: 7 8 9 10   **Fic**
1. Moving -- Fiction 2. Sisters -- Fiction 3. Country life -- Fiction 4. City and town life -- Fiction
ISBN 978-0-439-92227-2; 0-439-92227-5
LC 2007-16416

When fourteen-year-old Katie and her older sister, Michaela, move from New York City to upstate New York,

Katie is horrified by the country lifestyle but is even more shocked when her sister adapts effortlessly, enjoying their new life, unlike Katie.

"Friedman gets the push and pull of the sister bond just right in this delightful, funny, insightful journey." Booklist

Friedman, D. Dina

Escaping into the night. Simon & Schuster for Young Readers 2006 199p $17.99; pa $7.99

Grades: 6 7 8 9   **Fic**
1. Jewish refugees -- Fiction 2. Holocaust, 1933-1945 -- Fiction 3. World War, 1939-1945 -- Fiction
ISBN 978-1-4169-0258-4; 1-4169-0258-9; 978-1-4169-8648-5 pa; 1-4169-86480 pa

"Halina, a Jewish teen, is expelled from her Polish ghetto just before residents are being exterminated or sent to concentration camps. She joins a group of refugees who have banded together in an underground encampment in the Belorussian forests during World War II. . . . This compelling story offers an unusual insight into a different war experience." Voice Youth Advocates

Friend, Catherine

Barn boot blues. Marshall Cavendish 2011 142p $16.99

Grades: 5 6 7 8   **Fic**
1. Moving -- Fiction 2. Farm life -- Fiction
ISBN 978-0-7614-5827-2; 0-7614-5827-1
LC 2011001909

When her parents swap urban life in Minneapolis for rural life on a farm 100 miles away, twelve-year-old Taylor feels as if she is living on another planet.

"In this refreshingly compact novel, readers learn interesting, authentic details about everything from spinning wool to collecting eggs to in a kind-of-gross, kind-of-wonderful climax birthing lambs. In Taylor, Friend has created a plucky, lightly sarcastic protagonist whose frustration at her situation is palpable but who never comes off as unlikable or bratty." Horn Book

Friend, Natasha

★ **Bounce**; [by] Natasha Friend. Scholastic Press 2007 188p $16.99

Grades: 6 7 8 9   **Fic**
1. Moving -- Fiction 2. Remarriage -- Fiction 3. Stepfamilies -- Fiction
ISBN 978-0-439-85350-7; 0-439-85350-8
LC 2006038126

Thirteen-year-old Evyn's world is turned upside-down when her father, widowed since she was a toddler, suddenly decides to remarry a woman with six children, move with Ev and her brother from Maine to Boston, and enroll her in private school.

The author "presents, through hip conversations and humor, believable characters and a feel-good story with a satisfying amount of pathos." SLJ

Lush. Scholastic Press 2006 178p $16.99

Grades: 7 8 9 10   **Fic**
1. Fathers -- Fiction 2. Alcoholism -- Fiction
ISBN 0-439-85346-X
LC 2005-031333

Unable to cope with her father's alcoholism, thirteen-year-old Sam corresponds with an older student, sharing her family problems and asking for advice.

"Friend adeptly takes a teen problem and turns it into a believable, sensitive, character-driven story, with realistic dialogue." Booklist

My life in black and white; by Natasha Friend. Penguin Group USA 2012 294 p. (hardcover) $17.99; (paperback) $8.99

Grades: 8 9 10 11   **Fic**

1. Boxing -- Fiction 2. Friendship -- Fiction 3. Peer pressure -- Fiction 4. Self-acceptance -- Fiction 5. Beauty, Personal -- Fiction 6. Dating (Social customs) -- Fiction

ISBN 067001303X; 9780670013036; 9780670784943

LC 2011021436

Author Natasha Friend tells the story of Lexi and her best friend Taylor. "After finding her boyfriend . . . and Taylor making out at a party, . . . an argument quickly escalates, leading to an accident that changes Lexi's life forever. . . . It isn't until her sister, Ruthie, and [friend] Theo . . . are honest with her that Lexi starts peeling away the plastic life she once had and discovers the real one underneath." (Kirkus Reviews)

Perfect. Milkweed Editions 2004 172p $16.95; pa $6.95

Grades: 6 7 8 9   **Fic**

1. Bulimia -- Fiction 2. Bereavement -- Fiction

ISBN 1-57131-652-3; 1-57131-651-5 pa

LC 2004-6371

Following the death of her father, thirteen-year-old Isabelle uses bulimia as a way to avoid her mother's and ten-year-old sister's grief, as well as her own.

"Isabelle's grief and anger are movingly and honestly portrayed, and her eventual empathy for her mother is believable and touching." Booklist

Friesen, Gayle

The **Isabel** factor. KCP Fiction 2005 252p $16.95; pa $6.95

Grades: 7 8 9 10   **Fic**

1. Camps -- Fiction 2. Friendship -- Fiction

ISBN 1-55337-737-0; 1-55337-738-9 pa

"Anna and Zoe are inseparable—at least until Zoe breaks her arm and Anna finds herself on her way to summer camp without her best friend. . . . By the time Zoe arrives at camp (with her arm still in a sling), Anna is already embroiled in keeping peace between the individualistic Isabel and everyone else in Cabin 7. . . . Girls addicted to friendship stories will welcome this particularly well-crafted novel." Booklist

Friesen, Jonathan

★ The **last** Martin. Zonderkidz 2011 266p $14.99

Grades: 4 5 6 7   **Fic**

1. Family life -- Fiction

ISBN 978-0-310-72080-5; 0-310-72080-X

LC 2010-48275

Thirteen-year-old Martin Boyle struggles to break a family curse after discovering that he has twelve weeks to live.

"Spiced with plenty of slapstick, the yarn speeds its protagonist through a succession of highs, lows and improbable triumphs on the way to a hilariously melodramatic finish." Kirkus

Friesner, Esther M.

Nobody's princess; [by] Esther Friesner. Random House 2007 305p hardcover o.p. pa $7.99

Grades: 6 7 8 9 10   **Fic**

1. Adventure fiction 2. Sex role -- Fiction 3. Classical mythology -- Fiction 4. Helen of Troy (Legendary character) -- Fiction

ISBN 978-0-375-87528-1; 0-375-87528-X; 978-0-375-87529-8 pa; 0-375-87529-8 pa

LC 2006-06515

Determined to fend for herself in a world where only men have real freedom, headstrong Helen, who will be called queen of Sparta and Helen of Troy one day, learns to fight, hunt, and ride horses while disguised as a boy, and goes on an adventure throughout the Mediterranean world.

This "is a fascinating portrait. . . . Along the way, Friesner skillfully exposes larger issues of women's rights, human bondage, and individual destiny. It's a rollicking good story." Booklist

Nobody's prize. Random House 2008 320p $16.99; lib bdg $19.99

Grades: 6 7 8 9   **Fic**

1. Adventure fiction 2. Sex role -- Fiction 3. Jason (Greek mythology) -- Fiction 4. Helen of Troy (Legendary character) -- Fiction

ISBN 978-0-375-87531-1; 0-375-87531-X; 978-0-375-97531-8 lib bdg; 0-375-97531-4 lib bdg

LC 2007-08395

Still longing for adventure, Princess Helen of Sparta maintains her disguise as a boy to join her unsuspecting brothers as part of the crew of the Argo, the ship commanded by Prince Jason in his quest for the Golden Fleece.

"Friesner is an accomplished writer who is able to interweave a contemporary feel for these ancient characters with pieces of history and mythology. She can also be funny. . . . It is possible for readers to begin with this book. . . . But it is surely best enjoyed as part of a series, and libraries with the first book will want to make sure fans get their second helping." Voice Youth Advocates

Sphinx's princess. Random House 2009 370p il map $17.99; lib bdg $20.99

Grades: 8 9 10 11 12   **Fic**

1. Queens -- Fiction

ISBN 978-0-375-85654-9; 0-375-85654-4; 978-0-375-95654-6 lib bdg; 0-375-95654-9 lib bdg

LC 2009-13719

Although she is a dutiful daughter, Nefertiti's dancing abilities, remarkable beauty, and intelligence garner attention near and far, so much so that her family is summoned to the Egyptian royal court, where Nefertiti becomes a pawn in the power play of her scheming aunt, Queen Tiye.

"Dramatic plot twists, a powerful female subject, and engrossing details of life in ancient Egypt make for lively historical fiction." Booklist

Sphinx's queen. Random House 2010 352p
$17.99; lib bdg $29.99
Grades: 8 9 10 11 12   **Fic**
   1. Queens -- Fiction
   ISBN 978-0-375-85657-0; 0-375-85657-9; 978-0-375-
   95657-7 lib bdg; 0-375-95657-3 lib bdg
                      LC 2010-13769
Chased after by the prince and his soldiers for a crime
she did not commit, Nefertiti finds temporary refuge in the
wild hills along the Nile's west bank before returning to the
royal court to plead her case to the Pharaoh.

This is written "in fine prose that expresses the questioning of religion that most young people experience as
they approach maturity. . . . This deeply moral book tells a
good story; or, rather, this good story reveals deeply moral
truths." SLJ

Spirit's princess; Esther Friesner. 1st ed. Random House Childrens Books 2012 449 p. (trade)
$17.99; (paperback) $10.99; (ebook) $53.97; (lib
bdg.) $20.99
Grades: 7 8 9 10   **Fic**
   1. Family -- Fiction 2. Father-daughter relationship
   -- Fiction 3. Physically handicapped children -- Fiction
   4. Magic -- Fiction 5. Shamans -- Fiction 6. Spirits
   -- Fiction 7. Sex role -- Fiction
   ISBN 0375869077; 9780375869075; 9780375873140;
   9780375873157; 9780375899904; 9780375969072
                      LC 2011010468
In the book by Esther Friesner, "Himiko's chieftain
father adores her, as do her older brother and her father's
wives. Despite their love and affection, none of them takes
Himiko seriously when she insists she is a shaman. Himiko
herself isn't sure she can achieve her goal; with one leg
lame since she was a child, she can't do a shaman's dances.
Though the current shaman insists Himiko will be her heir, it
can't happen until Himiko is ready to stand up to her father."
(Kirkus Reviews)

Threads and flames. Viking 2010 390p $17.99
Grades: 6 7 8 9 10   **Fic**
   1. Jews -- Fiction 2. Fires -- Fiction 3. Immigrants
   -- Fiction 4. Polish Americans -- Fiction
   ISBN 978-0-670-01245-9; 0-670-01245-9
"Friesner's sparkling prose makes the immigrant ex-
perience in New York's Lower East Side come alive. . . .
Readers will turn the pages with rapt attention to follow
the characters' intrepid, risk-all adventures in building new
lives." Booklist

Frost, Helen
  ★ **Crossing** stones. Farrar, Straus and Giroux
2009 184p $16.99
Grades: 6 7 8 9 10   **Fic**
   1. War stories 2. Novels in verse 3. Soldiers -- Fiction
   4. Family life -- Fiction 5. Women -- Suffrage -- Fiction
   6. World War, 1914-1918 -- Fiction
   ISBN 978-0-374-31653-2; 0-374-31653-8
                      LC 2008-20755
In their own voices, four young people, Muriel, Frank,
Emma, and Ollie, tell of their experiences during the first
World War, as the boys enlist and are sent overseas, Emma

finishes school, and Muriel fights for peace and wom-
en's suffrage.

"Beautifully written in formally structured verse. . .
. This [is a] beautifully written, gently told story." Voice
Youth Advocates

Diamond Willow. Farrar, Straus and Giroux
2008 111p $16
Grades: 5 6 7 8   **Fic**
   1. Novels in verse 2. Dogs -- Fiction 3. Athapascan
   Indians -- Fiction
   ISBN 978-0-374-31776-8; 0-374-31776-3
                      LC 2006-37438
In a remote area of Alaska, twelve-year-old Willow helps
her father with their sleigh dogs when she is not at school,
all the while unaware that the animals surrounding her carry
the spirits of dead ancestors and friends who care for her.

"Willow relates her story in one-page poems, each of
which contains a hidden message printed in darker type. .
. . Her poems offer pensive imagery and glimpses of character, and strong emotion. This complex and elegant novel
will resonate with readers who savor powerful drama and
multifaceted characters." SLJ

  ★ **Hidden**. Farrar Straus Giroux 2011 147p
$16.99
Grades: 6 7 8 9 10   **Fic**
   1. Novels in verse 2. Camps -- Fiction 3. Friendship
   -- Fiction
   ISBN 0-374-38221-2; 978-0-374-38221-6
                      LC 2010-24854
When Wren Abbott and Darra Monson are eight years
old, Darra's father steals a minivan. He doesn't know that
Wren is hiding in the back. Years later, in a chance encounter
at camp, the girls face each other for the first time.

"This novel in verse stands out through its deliberate use
of form to illuminate emotions and cleverly hide secrets in
the text." Booklist

Keesha's house. Frances Foster Bks./Farrar,
Straus & Giroux 2003 116p hardcover o.p. pa $8
Grades: 7 8 9 10   **Fic**
   1. Home -- Fiction
   ISBN 0-374-34064-1; 0-374-40012-1 pa
                      LC 2002-22698
Michael L. Printz Award honor book, 2004
Seven teens facing such problems as pregnancy, clos-
eted homosexuality, and abuse each describe in poetic forms
what caused them to leave home and where they found
home again

"Spare, eloquent, and elegantly concise. . . . Public, private, or correctional educators and librarians should put this
must-read on their shelves." Voice Youth Advocates

The braid. Farrar, Straus and Giroux 2006 95p
$16
Grades: 7 8 9 10   **Fic**
   1. Novels in verse 2. Sisters -- Fiction 3. Immigrants
   -- Fiction
   ISBN 0-374-30962-0
                      LC 2005-40148

Two Scottish sisters, living on the western island of Barra in the 1850s, relate, in alternate voices and linked narrative poems, their experiences after their family is forcible evicted and separated with one sister accompanying their parents and younger siblings to Cape Breton, Canada, and the other staying behind with other family on the small island of Mingulay.

"The book will inspire both students and teachers to go back and study how the taut poetic lines manage to contain the powerful feelings." Booklist

Fry, Michael

The **Odd** Squad; Bully Bait. by Michael Fry. Disney Hyperion 2013 224 p. (hardcover) $12.99
Grades: 4 5 6 7   **Fic**
    1. Bullies -- Fiction 2. Schools -- Fiction 3. Middle schools -- Fiction 4. Interpersonal relations -- Fiction
    ISBN 1423169247; 9781423169246
                      LC 2012014286

This children's story, by Michael Fry, is part of the "Odd Squad" series. "Nick is the shortest seventh-grader in the history of the world . . . , doesn't fit in . . . , and spends more time inside than outside his locker. . . . When a well-intentioned guidance counselor forces Nick to join the school's lamest club . . . , what starts off as a reluctant band of hopeless oddballs morphs into an effective and empowered team ready to face whatever middle school throws at them." (Publisher's note)

"Cartoonist Fry humorously mines the world of middle school as seen through the eyes of bullied Nick to answer the question: Can three oddballs team together to take down the school bully? ...Abundant cartoon-style illustrations enhance the book's silly yet sensitive portrayal of bullying and unlikely friendships." Kirkus

Fukuda, Andrew

The **Prey**; Andrew Fukuda. St Martins Press 2013 336 p. $18.99
Grades: 7 8 9 10 11 12   **Fic**
    1. Horror fiction 2. Occult fiction 3. Survival skills -- Fiction
    ISBN 1250005116; 9781250005113
                      LC 2013002667

This teen horror thriller, by Andrew Fukuda, is book 2 of the "Hunt" series. "With death only a heartbeat away, Gene and the remaining humans must find a way . . . to escape the hungry predators chasing them through the night. . . . Their escape takes them to a refuge of humans living high in the mountains. Gene and his friends think they're finally safe, but not everything here is as it seems." (Publisher's note)

Funke, Cornelia, 1958-

  ★ **Inkheart**; [by] Cornelia Funke; translated from the German by Anthea Bell. Scholastic 2003 534p $19.95; pa $9.99
Grades: 5 6 7 8   **Fic**
    1. Fantasy fiction 2. Books and reading -- Fiction
    ISBN 0-439-53164-0; 0-439-70910-5 pa
                      LC 2003-45844

Twelve-year-old Meggie learns that her father, who repairs and binds books for a living, can "read" fictional char-

acters to life when one of those characters abducts them and tries to force him into service.

The author "proves the power of her imagination; readers will be captivated by the chilling and thrilling world she has created here." Publ Wkly
    Other titles in this series are:
    Inkspell (2005)
    Inkdeath (2008)

  Fearless; Cornelia Funke. Little, Brown Books for Young Readers 2013 432 p. (hardcover) $19.99
Grades: 6 7 8 9   **Fic**
    1. Fantasy fiction 2. Brothers -- Fiction 3. Blessing and cursing -- Fiction 4. Magic -- Fiction 5. Adventure and adventurers -- Fiction
    ISBN 0316056103; 9780316056106
                      LC 2012028742

This fantasy novel, by Cornelia Funke, translated by Oliver Latsch, is part of the "Mirrorworld" series. "Jacob Reckless has . . . tried everything to shake the Fairy curse that traded his life for his brother's. . . . But . . . they hear of one last possibility . . . : a crossbow that can kill thousands, or heal one, when shot through the heart. But a Goyl treasure hunter is also searching for the prized crossbow." (Publisher's note)

"Adroitly building on layers of European fairy tale, Funke's original, rapid-fire narrative fearlessly transports Jacob and a bevy of ominous, multifaceted fantastical characters through a dark, decaying landscape in which death waits and honor is rare. Provocative, harrowing, engrossing." Kirkus

  ★ **Reckless**; written and illustrated by Cornelia Funke; translated by Oliver Latsch. Little, Brown 2010 394p il $19.99
Grades: 6 7 8 9   **Fic**
    1. Fantasy fiction 2. Adventure fiction 3. Magic -- Fiction 4. Brothers -- Fiction
    ISBN 978-0-316-05609-0; 0-316-05609-X; 031605609X; 9780316056090
                      LC 2010006877

Jacob and Will Reckless have looked out for each other ever since their father disappeared, but when Jacob discovers a magical mirror that transports him to a warring world populated by witches, giants, and ogres, he keeps it to himself until Will follows him one day, with dire consequences.

"The fluid, fast-paced narrative exposes Jacob's complex character, his complicated sibling relationship and a densely textured world brimming with vile villains and fairy-tale detritus." Kirkus

Fuqua, Jonathon Scott

The **Willoughby** Spit wonder. Candlewick 2004 145p $15.99
Grades: 5 6 7 8   **Fic**
    1. Sick -- Fiction 2. Father-son relationship -- Fiction
    ISBN 0-7636-1776-8
                      LC 2002-41141

In 1950s Norfolk, Virginia, as Carter and his sister watch their dying father struggle to remain cheerful, Carter decides to emulate Prince Namor, comic superhero, in order to inspire his father to stay alive.

"Carter . . . is a compelling character, and his growing understanding and acceptance of the world is shown quietly through an array of accurately observed details. A subtle, engaging novel." Booklist

Fusco, Kimberly Newton

★ The **wonder** of Charlie Anne. Alfred A. Knopf 2010 272p $16.99; lib bdg $19.99

Grades: 5 6 7 8   **Fic**

1. Farm life -- Fiction 2. Friendship -- Fiction 3. Race relations -- Fiction 4. African Americans -- Fiction 5. Great Depression, 1929-1939 -- Fiction

ISBN 978-0-375-86104-8; 0-375-86104-1; 978-0-375-96104-5 lib bdg; 0-375-96104-6 lib bdg

LC 2009-38831

In a 1930s Massachusetts farm town torn by the Depression, racial tension, and other hardships, Charlie Anne and her black next-door neighbor Phoebe form a friendship that begins to transform their community.

"Good humor, kindness and courage triumph in this warm, richly nuanced novel that cheers the heart like a song sweetly sung." Kirkus

Fusilli, Jim

Marley Z and the bloodstained violin. Dutton Children's Books 2008 164p $16.99

Grades: 5 6 7 8   **Fic**

1. School stories 2. Mystery fiction 3. Theft -- Fiction 4. Violins -- Fiction

ISBN 978-0-525-47907-9; 0-525-47907-4

Fourteen-year-old Marley Zimmerman is convinced that her friend did not steal a valuable violin from the Julliard School, despite surveillance video evidence, and enlists the other members of her would-be band, the Kingston Cowboys, to help her find the truth.

"Marley is a fully drawn character, and the supporting cast members are developed well enough to make them compelling and interesting. This mystery keeps pages turning to its surprise ending." SLJ

Gagnon, Michelle

Don't turn around; by Michelle Gagnon. Harper 2012 320 p. (trade bdg.) $17.99

Grades: 7 8 9 10 11 12   **Fic**

1. Dystopian fiction 2. Teenagers -- Fiction 3. Conspiracies -- Fiction 4. Computer hackers -- Fiction 5. Experiments -- Fiction 6. Foster home care -- Fiction 7. Abandoned children -- Fiction

ISBN 0062102907; 9780062102904

LC 2012009691

This book tells the story of "[t]eenage hackers Noa and Peter." Orphan Noa escapes a hospital after waking up from an operation she has no memory of. After having his computer seized when he investigated his father's files, "Peter enlists his hacktivist group /ALLIANCE/ (of which Noa is a member) to" investigate and counterattack. "The attack only serves to dig the teens in deeper when they uncover a frightening conspiracy of human experimentation and corporate malfeasance." (Kirkus Reviews)

Gaiman, Neil, 1960-

★ **Coraline**; [by] Neil Gaiman; with illustrations by Dave McKean. HarperCollins Pubs. 2002 162p il $16.99 pa $6.99

Grades: 5 6 7 8   **Fic**

1. Horror fiction 2. Supernatural -- Fiction

ISBN 0-380-80734-3 pa; 0-380-97778-8

LC 2002-18937

Looking for excitement, Coraline ventures through a mysterious door into a world that is similar, yet disturbingly different from her own, where she must challenge a gruesome entity in order to save herself, her parents, and the souls of three others

"Gaiman twines his taut tale with a menacing tone and crisp prose fraught with memorable imagery . . . yet keeps the narrative just this side of terrifying." Publ Wkly

★ The **graveyard** book; with illustrations by Dave McKean. HarperCollins 2008 312p il $17.99; lib bdg $18.89

Grades: 5 6 7 8 9 10   **Fic**

1. Death -- Fiction 2. Cemeteries -- Fiction 3. Supernatural -- Fiction

ISBN 0-06-053092-8; 0-06-053093-6 lib bdg; 978-0-06-053092-1; 978-0-06-053093-8 lib bdg

LC 2008-13860

Awarded the Newbery Medal (2009)

Nobody Owens, nicknamed Bod, is a normal boy, except that he has been raised by in a graveyard by ghosts.

"Gaiman writes with charm and humor, and again he has a real winner." Voice Youth Advocates

Interworld; [by] Neil Gaiman [and] Michael Reaves. Eos 2007 239p $16.99; lib bdg $17.89

Grades: 6 7 8 9 10   **Fic**

1. Science fiction 2. Space and time -- Fiction

ISBN 978-0-06-123896-3; 978-0-06-123897-0 lib bdg

LC 2007-08617

At nearly fifteen years of age, Joey Harker learns that he is able to travel between dimensions. Soon, he joins a team of different versions of himself, each from another dimension, to fight the evil forces striving to conquer all the worlds.

This offers "vivid, well-imagined settings and characters. . . . [A] rousing sf/fantasy hybrid." Booklist

Stardust. Avon Bks. 1999 238p hardcover o.p. pa $13.95; $30.00

Grades: 8 9 10 11 12 Adult   **Fic**

1. Fantasy fiction

ISBN 0-380-97728-1; 0-06-114202-6 pa; 9780062200396

LC 98-8773

"Young Tristran Thorn has grown up in the isolated village of Wall, on the edge of the realm of Faerie. When Tristran and the lovely Victoria see a falling star during the special market fair, Victoria impulsively offers him his heart's desire if he will retrieve the star for her. Tristran crosses the border into Faerie and encounters witches, unicorns, and other strange creatures." Libr J

Galante, Cecilia

Willowood. Simon & Schuster 2010 265p $16.99

Grades: 4 5 6 7   **Fic**

1. Geckos -- Fiction 2. Moving -- Fiction 3. Friendship -- Fiction 4. Single parent family -- Fiction

ISBN 978-1-4169-8022-3; 1-4169-8022-9

Eleven-year-old Lily has trouble leaving her best friend behind and moving to the city when her mother changes jobs, but she makes some very unlikely friends that soon become like family members.

"The characters . . . are fully realized individuals. . . . [This book has a] finely tuned plot and poetic language. . . . Children will enjoy the story of Lily's first few months in the big city." SLJ

The **patron** saint of butterflies. Bloomsbury 2008 292p $16.95

Grades: 6 7 8 9 10   **Fic**

1. Cults -- Fiction 2. Christian life -- Fiction

ISBN 978-1-59990-249-4; 1-59990-249-4

LC 2007-51368

When her grandmother takes fourteen-year-old Agnes, her younger brother, and best friend Honey and escapes Mount Blessing, a Connecticut religious commune, Agnes clings to the faith she loves while Honey looks toward a future free of control, cruelty, and preferential treatment.

"If both girls occasionally seem wise beyond their years, readers will nevertheless cheer them on as they ponder the limits of faith and duty." SLJ

The **summer** of May. Aladdin 2011 252p $16.99

Grades: 5 6 7 8   **Fic**

1. Anger -- Fiction 2. Summer -- Fiction 3. Teachers -- Fiction 4. Loss (Psychology) -- Fiction 5. Mother-daughter relationship -- Fiction

ISBN 1-4169-8023-7; 978-1-4169-8023-0

LC 2010-15879

An angry thirteen-year-old girl and her hated English teacher spend a summer school class together, learning surprising things about each other.

"May's voice is sometimes humorous, at times heartbreaking, and always authentic. . . . A taut and believable novel." SLJ

Gale, Eric Kahn

The **Bully** Book; Eric Kahn Gale. Harpercollins Childrens Books 2012 240 p. $16.99

Grades: 4 5 6 7 8   **Fic**

1. School stories 2. Bullies

ISBN 0062125117; 9780062125118

This juvenile novel, by Eric Kahn Gale, is about school bullying. "When the author was eleven, he was bullied. This book is loosely based on incidents that happened to him in sixth grade. Eric Haskins, the new sixth-grade bully target, is searching for answers. And unlike many of us who experienced something awful growing up, he finds them. Though they may not be what he expected." (Publisher's note)

Gantos, Jack

★ **Dead** end in Norvelt; Jack Gantos. Farrar Straus Giroux 2011 341p. $15.99

Grades: 4 5 6 7   **Fic**

1. Old age -- Fiction

ISBN 978-0-374-37993-3; 0-374-37993-9

LC 2010054009

Newbery Medal (2012)

Scott O'Dell Historical Fiction Award (2012)

In the historic town of Norvelt, Pennsylvania, twelve-year-old Jack Gantos spends the summer of 1962 grounded for various offenses until he is assigned to help an elderly neighbor with a most unusual chore involving the newly dead, molten wax, twisted promises, Girl Scout cookies, underage driving, lessons from history, typewriting, and countless bloody noses.

This is a "wildly entertaining meld of truth and fiction. . . . Memorable in every way." Publ Wkly

★ **Jack** on the tracks; four seasons of fifth grade. Farrar, Straus & Giroux 1999 182p il $16; pa $5.95

Grades: 5 6 7 8   **Fic**

1. School stories 2. Self-perception 3. Moving, Household 4. Brothers and sisters 5. Family life -- Fiction

ISBN 0-374-33665-2; 0-374-43717-3 pa

LC 99-27897

Moving with his unbearable sister to Miami, Florida, Jack tries to break some of his bad habits but finds himself irresistibly drawn to things disgusting, gross, and weird

"Jack is a likable and appealing fifth grader. His first-person preadolescent musings and worries are poignant, funny, and real." SLJ

Other titles in this series are:

Jack adrift (2003)

Jack on the tracks (1999)

Jack's black book (1997)

Jack's new power (1995)

Heads or tails (1994)

★ **Joey** Pigza swallowed the key. Farrar, Straus & Giroux 1998 153p $16.99

Grades: 5 6 7 8   **Fic**

1. School stories 2. Schools -- Fiction 3. Single-parent families -- Fiction 4. Attention deficit disorder -- Fiction 5. Attention-deficit hyperactivity disorder -- Fiction

ISBN 0-374-33664-4

LC 98-24264

To the constant disappointment of his mother and his teachers, Joey has trouble paying attention or controlling his mood swings when his prescription meds wear off and he starts getting worked up and acting wired

This "frenetic narrative pulls at heartstrings and tickles funny bones." SLJ

Other titles about Joey Pigza are:

Joey Pigza loses control (2000)

What would Joey do? (2002)

I am not Joey Pigza (2007)

Garcia, Cristina

★ **I** wanna be your shoebox. Simon & Schuster Books for Children 2008 198p $16.99; pa $6.99

Grades: 4 5 6 7   **Fic**
1. Jews -- Fiction 2. Family life -- Fiction 3. Grandfathers -- Fiction 4. Cuban Americans -- Fiction 5. Racially mixed people -- Fiction
ISBN 978-1-4169-3928-3; 1-4169-3928-8; 978-1-4169-7904-3 pa; 1-4169-7904-2 pa

Thirteen-year-old, clarinet-playing, Southern California surfer, Yumi Ruiz-Hirsch, comes from a complex family—her father is Jewish-Japanese, her mother is Cuban, and her parents are divorced—and when her grandfather Saul is diagnosed with terminal cancer, Yumi asks him to tell her his life story, which helps her to understand her own history and identity.

"García's . . . exceptional ability to channel a range of voices lights up her first children's novel. . . . The large personalities propel the story and bring tenderness and credibility to a classic message about change." Publ Wkly

Garcia, Kami

Beautiful creatures; by Kami Garcia & Margie Stohl. Little, Brown and Co. 2010 563p $17.99
Grades: 7 8 9 10   **Fic**
1. Love stories 2. School stories 3. Supernatural -- Fiction 4. Extrasensory perception -- Fiction
ISBN 0-316-04267-6; 978-0-316-04267-3
LC 2008-51306

ALA YALSA Morris Award Finalist, 2010

This novel is set in a small South Carolina town. Ethan is powerfully drawn to Lena, a new classmate with whom he shares a psychic connection and whose family hides a secret that my be revealed on her sixteenth birthday.

"The intensity of Ethan and Lena's need to be together is palpable, the detailed descriptions create a vivid, authentic world, and the allure of this story is the power of love. The satisfying conclusion is sure to lead directly into a sequel." SLJ

Beautiful darkness; by Kami Garcia & Margaret Stohl. Little, Brown 2010 503p $17.99; pa $9.99
Grades: 8 9 10 11 12   **Fic**
1. Love stories 2. Supernatural -- Fiction 3. Extrasensory perception -- Fiction
ISBN 978-0-316-07705-7; 0-316-07705-7; 978-0-316-07704-0 pa; 0-316-07704-6 pa
LC 2010-7015

In a small southern town with a secret world hidden in plain sight, sixteen-year-old Lena, who possesses supernatural powers and faces a life-altering decision, draws away from her true love, Ethan, a mortal with frightening visions.

"The southern gothic atmosphere, several new characters, and the surprising fate of one old favorite will keep readers going until the next book, which promises new surprises as '18 moons' approaches." Booklist

Garden, Nancy

Endgame. Harcourt 2006 287p $17
Grades: 8 9 10 11 12   **Fic**
1. School stories 2. Bullies -- Fiction 3. Violence -- Fiction 4. Family life -- Fiction
ISBN 0-15-205416-2; 978-0-15-205416-8
LC 2005-19486

Fifteen-year-old Gray Wilton, bullied at school and ridiculed by an unfeeling father for preferring drums to hunting, goes on a shooting rampage at his high school.

"This is a hard-hitting and eloquent look at the impact of bullying, and the resulting destruction of lives touched by the violence." SLJ

Gardner, Lyn

★ **Into** the woods; pictures by Mini Grey. David Fickling Books 2007 427p il $16.99; lib bdg $19.99; pa $7.50
Grades: 4 5 6 7 8   **Fic**
1. Fantasy fiction 2. Sisters -- Fiction
ISBN 978-0-385-75115-5; 0-385-75115-X; 978-0-385-75116-2 lib bdg; 0-385-75116-8 lib bdg; 978-0-440-42223-5 pa; 0-440-42223-X pa
LC 2006-24350

Pursued by the sinister Dr. DeWilde and his ravenous wolves, three sisters—Storm, the inheritor of a special musical pipe, the elder Aurora, and the baby Any—flee into the woods and begin a journey filled with danger as they try to find a way to defeat their pursuer and keep him from taking the pipe and control of the entire land.

"Gardner's fast-paced fantasy-adventure cleverly borrows from well-known fairy tales, and astute readers will enjoy identifying the many folkloric references. . . . Grey's appealing black-and-white illustrations add humor and detail to the story." Booklist

Out of the woods; pictures by Mini Grey. David Fickling Books 2010 348p il $17.99; lib bdg $20.99
Grades: 4 5 6 7 8   **Fic**
1. Fantasy fiction 2. Sisters -- Fiction
ISBN 978-0-385-75154-4; 0-385-75154-0; 978-0-385-75156-8 lib bdg; 0-385-75156-7 lib bdg

This is a sequel to Into the Woods (2007). The Eden sisters "are being lured into a wicked witch's lair. . . . Belladonna wants Aurora's heart and Storm's all-powerful musical pipe, and she will stop at nothing to get them." (Publisher's note)

"Aurora, Storm, and Any Eden thought their troubles were over when Storm tossed the Pied Piper's powerful, seductive pipe . . . into the sea and defeated the pipe's erstwhile owner, the villainous Dr. DeWilde. . . . But it seems their troubles have only begun. . . . A missing prince, a cowardly lion, a marauding dragon, seven dwarfs, and even the Grimm brothers all make appearances, and while the fractured fairy-tale stew is considerably more haphazard than that of the sisters' first outing, it's a well-conceived and entertaining mash-up nonetheless." Horn Book

Gardner, Sally

I, Coriander; [illustrations by Lydia Corry] Dial Bks. 2005 280p il $16.99
Grades: 6 7 8 9   **Fic**
1. Magic -- Fiction 2. Fairies -- Fiction
ISBN 0-8037-3099-3
LC 2005--06050

In 17th century London, Coriander, a girl who has inherited magic from her mother, must find a way to use this magic in order to save both herself and an inhabitant of the fairy world where her mother was born

"Seamlessly meshing fact and fantasy, the author composes a suspenseful masterpiece that will have audience members gladly suspending their disbelief." Publ Wkly

★ **Maggot** moon; Sally Gardner. Candlewick Press 2013 288 p. (reinforced) $16.99

Grades: 7 8 9 10 11 12   **Fic**

1. Dystopian fiction 2. Alternative histories -- fiction
ISBN 0763665533; 9780763665531

LC 2012947247

Costa Children's Book Award Winner 2012

In this dystopian novel, "Standish Treadwell, 15, has lost parents, neighbors, best friend: All disappeared from Zone Seven, a post-war occupied territory, into the hellish clutches of the Motherland. Now a new horror approaches. . . . Standish and [his friend] Hector spin fantasies about the far-off tantalizing consumer culture they glimpsed on television (now banned), but they lack a vision of the future beyond vague dreams of rescue." (Kirkus Reviews)

The **Silver** Blade. Dial Books 2009 362p $16.99

Grades: 8 9 10 11 12   **Fic**

1. Adventure fiction 2. Magic -- Fiction
ISBN 978-0-8037-3377-0; 0-8037-3377-1

LC 2009-9282

As the Revolution descends into the ferocious Reign of Terror, Yann, now an extraordinary practioner of magic, uses his skills to confound his enemies and help spirit refugees out of France, but the question of his true identity and the kidnapping of his true love, Sido, expose him to dangers that threaten to destroy him.

"A luscious melodrama, rich in sensuous detail from horrific to sublime, with an iridescent overlay of magic." Kirkus

★ The **red** necklace; a story of the French Revolution. Dial Books 2008 378p $16.99

Grades: 8 9 10 11 12   **Fic**

1. Adventure fiction 2. Gypsies -- Fiction 3. Orphans -- Fiction 4. Social classes -- Fiction
ISBN 978-0-8037-3100-4; 0-8037-3100-0

LC 2007-39813

In the late eighteenth-century, Sido, the twelve-year-old daughter of a self-indulgent marquis, and Yann, a fourteen-year-old Gypsy orphan raised to perform in a magic show, face a common enemy at the start of the French Revolution.

"Scores are waiting to be settled on every page; this is a heart-stopper." Booklist

Garner, Em

Contaminated; by Em Garner. Egmont USA 2013 336 p. (hardcover) $17.99; (ebook) $17.99

Grades: 7 8 9 10   **Fic**

1. Horror fiction 2. Dystopian fiction 3. Horror stories 4. Science fiction 5. Mothers -- Fiction
ISBN 1606843540; 9781606843543; 9781606843550

LC 2012024472

This book is set two years after "a diet drink with genetically modified ingredients transformed countless Americans into mindlessly violent animals" Now, "the Contaminated

are controlled by electronic collars, and the unclaimed are housed in kennels like that in which Velvet Ellis, 17, finds her mother." Velvet and her sister's "shaky hold on normal life is finally upended when Velvet brings their mother home, facing anger and fear from neighbors and eviction from their landlord." (Kirkus Reviews)

Garretson, Dee

Wildfire run. Harper 2010 261p $16.99; pa $6.99

Grades: 5 6 7 8   **Fic**

1. Adventure fiction 2. Fires -- Fiction 3. Presidents -- Fiction 4. Earthquakes -- Fiction 5. Wilderness survival -- Fiction
ISBN 978-0-06-195347-7; 0-06-195347-4; 978-0-06-195350-7 pa; 0-06-195350-4 pa

LC 2009049482

A relaxing retreat to Camp David turns deadly after a faraway earthquake sets off a chain of disastrous events that traps the president's twelve-year-old son, Luke, and his two friends within the compound.

"Along with a breathlessly paced plot, Garretson crafts a preteen protagonist who grows out of being a whiny, moody sort and, with his companions, displays generous measures of courage and ingenuity in rising to the occasion." Booklist

Gavin, Jamila

See no evil. Farrar, Straus and Giroux 2009 198p $16.95

Grades: 5 6 7 8 9   **Fic**

1. Spies -- Fiction 2. Wealth -- Fiction 3. Illegal aliens -- Fiction 4. Organized crime -- Fiction 5. Household employees -- Fiction
ISBN 978-0-374-36333-8; 0-374-36333-1

LC 2008-5123

First published 2008 in the United Kingdom with title: Robber baron's daughter

Twelve-year-old Nettie's sheltered and privileged life changes after her beloved tutor mysteriously disappears and Nettie, aided by the son of a household employee, begins to learn the truth about her father, whose wealth began with trafficking in illegal aliens.

"This well-written novel has descriptive language, atmosphere, and lots of intrigue as it moves to a stunning conclusion." SLJ

Gear, Kathleen O'Neal

Children of the Dawnland; [by] Kathleen O'Neal Gear and W. Michael Gear. Starscape 2009 336p $17.95

Grades: 6 7 8 9   **Fic**

1. Prehistoric peoples -- Fiction
ISBN 978-0-7653-2019-3; 0-7653-2019-3

LC 2008035761

13,000 years ago in the Great Lakes Region, twelve-year-old Twig, a Spirit Dreamer who can see into the future, teams up with best friend Greyhawk and the unpopular shaman Screech Owl to warn villagers of an impending natural disaster that could have devastating environmental effects.

"Those looking for an exciting fantasy novel will be pleased by the unusual setting, the well-paced action and the individual lens on culture change at a massive scale." Kirkus

Gee, Maurice

★ **Salt**. Orca Book Publishers 2009 252p map (The Salt trilogy) $18; pa $12.95

Grades: 6 7 8 9 10   **Fic**

1. Fantasy fiction 2. Extrasensory perception -- Fiction

ISBN 978-1-55469-209-5; 1-55469-209-1; 978-1-55469-369-6 pa; 1-55469-369-1 pa

"Hari lives in Blood Burrow, a hellacious, rat-infested slum. . . . Pearl is a pampered daughter of Company, her only purpose in life to be married off to cement one of her father's political alliances. When both young people, who share rare psychic gifts, revolt against their fates, they find themselves on a desperate journey across a hostile landscape, with the forces of Company at their heels. . . . A compelling tale of anger and moral development that also powerfully explores the evils of colonialism and racism." Publ Wkly

Other titles in this series are:
Gool (2010)
The Limping Man (2011)

Gensler, Sonia

The **revenant**. Alfred A. Knopf 2011 336p $16.99; lib bdg $19.99

Grades: 7 8 9 10   **Fic**

1. Ghost stories 2. School stories 3. Teachers -- Fiction 4. Cherokee Indians -- Fiction

ISBN 978-0-375-86701-9; 0-375-86701-5; 978-0-375-96701-6 lib bdg; 0-375-96701-X lib bdg

LC 2010-28701

When seventeen-year-old Willemina Hammond fakes credentials to get a teaching position at a school for Cherokee girls in nineteenth-century Oklahoma, she is haunted by the ghost of a drowned student.

"Gensler makes a solid debut with an eerie and suspenseful work of historical fiction in which everyone is a murder suspect. . . . The layers of detail address the complex social structure of the period, and Gensler's characters and dialogue are believably crafted." Publ Wkly

George, Jean Craighead

Charlie's raven; written and illustrated by Jean Craighead George. Dutton Children's Books 2004 190p il hardcover o.p. pa $6.99

Grades: 5 6 7 8   **Fic**

1. Ravens -- Fiction 2. Naturalists -- Fiction 3. Grandfathers -- Fiction

ISBN 0-525-47219-3; 0-14-240547-7 pa

Charlie's friend, Singing Bird, a Teton Sioux, tells him that ravens have curing powers, so Charlie steals a baby bird from its nest, hoping to heal his ailing Granddad, a retired naturalist.

"The story is technically accurate and offers a vivid sense of place and a window into Native American beliefs through storytelling." SLJ

George, Jessica Day

Dragon flight; [by] Jessica Day George. 1st U.S. ed.; Bloomsbury Children's Books 2008 262p $16.95

Grades: 5 6 7 8   **Fic**

1. Fantasy fiction 2. Dragons -- Fiction

ISBN 978-1-59990-110-7; 1-59990-110-2

LC 2007050762

Young seamstress Creel finds herself strategizing with the dragon king Shardas once again when a renegade dragon in a distant country launches a war against their country, bringing an entire army of dragons into the mix.

"Fans of the first book will find the same strengths here: the imaginatively detailed scenes; the thrilling, spell-fueled action; the possibility of romance with a prince; and the appealing, brave heroine." Booklist

Dragon slippers. Bloomsbury Children's Books 2007 324p $16.95; pa $7.99

Grades: 5 6 7 8   **Fic**

1. Fantasy fiction 2. Dragons -- Fiction 3. Orphans -- Fiction

ISBN 978-1-59990-057-5; 1-59990-057-2; 978-1-59990-275-3 pa; 1-59990-275-3 pa

LC 2006-21142

Orphaned after a fever epidemic, Creel befriends a dragon and unknowingly inherits an object that can either save or destroy her kingdom.

"The plot is fast paced with all the right touches of romance and adventure. . . . The characters are wonderfully drawn." Voice Youth Advocates

★ **Princess** of glass. Bloomsbury Children's Books 2010 266p $16.99

Grades: 6 7 8 9 10   **Fic**

1. Fairy tales 2. Princesses -- Fiction

ISBN 978-1-59990-478-8; 1-59990-478-0

In the midst of maneuverings to create political alliances through marriage, sixteen-year-old Poppy, one of the infamous twelve dancing princesses, becomes the target of a vengeful witch while Prince Christian tries to save her.

"In a clever reworking of the Cinderella story, George once again proves adept at spinning her own magical tale." Booklist

★ **Princess** of the midnight ball. Bloomsbury Children's Books 2009 280p $16.99

Grades: 6 7 8 9 10   **Fic**

1. Fairy tales

ISBN 978-1-59990-322-4; 1-59990-322-9

LC 2008-30310

A retelling of the tale of twelve princesses who wear out their shoes dancing every night, and of Galen, a former soldier now working in the king's gardens, who follows them in hopes of breaking the curse.

"Fans of fairy-tale retellings . . . will enjoy this story for its magic, humor, and touch of romance." SLJ

Sun and moon, ice and snow. Bloomsbury 2008 336p $16.95

Grades: 7 8 9 10 11 12   **Fic**

1. Fairy tales 2. Fantasy fiction

ISBN 1-59990-109-9; 978-1-59990-109-1

LC 2007030848

A girl travels east of the sun and west of the moon to free her beloved prince from a magic spell.

"George has adapted Norse myths and fairy tales to create this eerily beautiful, often terrifying world. . . . Mystery, adventure, and the supernatural, and a touch of love are woven together to create a vivid, well-crafted, poetic fantasy." Booklist

George, Madeleine

★ **Looks**. Viking 2008 240p $16.99; pa $7.99

Grades: 8 9 10 11 12   **Fic**

1. School stories 2. Obesity -- Fiction 3. Friendship -- Fiction 4. Anorexia nervosa -- Fiction

ISBN 978-0-670-06167-9; 0-670-06167-0; 978-0-14-241419-4 pa; 0-14-241419-0 pa

LC 2007-38218

"Meghan and Aimee are on opposite ends of the outcast spectrum. Meghan is extremely overweight. . . . Aimee, on the other hand, is classic anorexic. Both girls have been hurt by one of the popular girls at school. They join forces to bring Cara down in a stunning bit of public humiliation. . . . The story will make readers think about the various issues touched upon, and it is difficult to put down." SLJ

The **difference** between you and me; by Madeleine George. Viking 2012 256 p. (hardcover) $16.99

Grades: 7 8 9 10 11 12   **Fic**

1. Secrecy -- Fiction 2. Lesbians -- Fiction 3. High school students -- Fiction 4. Schools -- Fiction 5. High schools -- Fiction 6. Protest movements -- Fiction

ISBN 0446573450; 9780670011285

LC 2011012192

This young adult novel uses a trio of alternating narrators to tell the story of "self-proclaimed misfit and outspoken manifesto-author Jesse [who] deals daily with the hazards of being out and proud in high school. She's also carrying on a secret affair with image-conscious Emily, the girlfriend of a popular boy at school. Meeting weekly in the bathroom of the local public library, the two experience an inexplicable chemistry, even though Emily will barely acknowledge Jesse at any other time. Switching perspective among Emily, Jesse and a third girl, Esther, this . . . tale . . . explor[es] . . . attraction and shame. Jesse hides her relationship from her warmly quirky and accepting parents not because it is with a girl, but because she knows they will disapprove of its secrecy." (Kirkus)

Gephart, Donna

★ **How** to survive middle school. Delacorte Press 2010 247p $15.99; lib bdg $18.99

Grades: 5 6 7 8   **Fic**

1. School stories 2. Family life -- Fiction

ISBN 978-0-385-73793-7; 0-385-73793-9; 978-0-385-90701-9 lib bdg; 0-385-90701-X lib bdg

LC 2009-21809

When thirteen-year-old David Greenberg's best friend makes the start of middle school even worse than he feared it could be, David becomes friends with Penny, who shares his love of television shows and posts one of their skits on YouTube, making them wildly popular—online, at least.

"Gephart crafts for her likable protagonist an engaging, feel-good transition into adolescence that's well stocked with tears and laughter." Booklist

Olivia Bean, trivia queen; Donna Gephart. Delacorte Press 2012 278 p. $16.99

Grades: 3 4 5 6 7   **Fic**

1. Game shows -- Fiction 2. Children of divorced parents -- Fiction 3. Father-daughter relationship -- Fiction 4. Divorce -- Fiction 5. Fathers -- Fiction 6. Curiosities and wonders -- Fiction

ISBN 0385740522; 9780385740524

LC 2011006023

In this book, "Olivia Bean has watched 'Jeopardy!' every evening since she was a little girl, but the nightly tradition just hasn"t been the same since her father . . . took off for California two years ago. When the show announces auditions for Kids Week, Olivia is intent on making the cut, not only to compete but, more importantly, to get a plane ticket out to the show's taping in L.A. with the hopes of meeting up with her estranged dad." (Bulletin of the Center for Children's Books).

Geras, Adele

★ **Ithaka**. Harcourt 2006 360p $17; pa $6.95

Grades: 7 8 9 10   **Fic**

1. Trojan War -- Fiction 2. Classical mythology -- Fiction 3. Odysseus (Greek mythology) -- Fiction

ISBN 0-15-205603-3; 0-15-206104-5 pa

LC 2005-7569

The island of Ithaka is overrun with uncouth suitors demanding that Penelope choose a new husband, as she patiently awaits the return of Odysseus from the Trojan War.

This book "can introduce young people to the power of story in Homer's epics as well as being a beautifully written story in its own right." Voice Youth Advocates

★ **Troy**. Harcourt 2001 340p hardcover o.p. pa $6.95

Grades: 7 8 9 10   **Fic**

1. Trojan War -- Fiction

ISBN 0-15-216492-8; 0-15-204570-8 pa

LC 00-57262

"Mythology buffs will savor the author's ability to embellish stories of old without diminishing their original flavor, while the uninitiated will find this a captivating introduction to a pivotal event in classic Greek literature." Publ Wkly

Geus, Mireille

Piggy; translated by Nancy Forest-Flier. Front Street 2008 110p $14.95

Grades: 6 7 8 9 10   **Fic**

1. Autism -- Fiction 2. Bullies -- Fiction 3. Friendship -- Fiction 4. Criminal investigation -- Fiction

ISBN 978-1-59078-636-9; 1-59078-636-X

LC 2007-48847

Original Dutch edition 2005

Lizzie struggles to overcome the closed, internal world of autism when a new girl moves into her neighborhood, befriends her, then insists that Lizzie join her in seeking revenge on the boys who tease them.

"The title's compactness adds accessibility for readers who prefer sprint reads to distance, and this would be a natural discussion-starter for readers ranging from reluctant to adventurous." Bull Cent Child Books

Gewirtz, Adina Rishe

Zebra forest; Adina Rishe Gewirtz. Candlewick Press 2013 208 p. (reinforced) $15.99

Grades: 5 6 7 8   **Fic**

1. Hostages -- Fiction 2. Siblings -- Fiction
ISBN 0763660418; 9780763660413

LC 2012947251

In this novel, by Adina Rishe Gewirtz, "an escaped fugitive upends everything two siblings think they know about their family, their past, and themselves. . . . A rattling at the back door, an escapee from the prison holding them hostage in their own home, four lives that will never be the same. . . . [The book] portrays an unfolding standoff of truth against family secrets." (Publisher's note)

"Debut author Gewirtz successfully conveys the terror and tedium of being trapped. . . While the situation may frighten some readers, the matter-of-fact way [the protagonists] make the best of difficult circumstances . . . may be comforting to those whose families don"t match the ideal. An emotionally honest family story with an ending that"s hopeful without being implausibly upbeat." Pub Wkly

Gibbs, Stuart

Belly up. Simon & Schuster Books for Young Readers 2010 294p $15.99; pa $6.99

Grades: 4 5 6 7   **Fic**

1. Mystery fiction 2. Zoos -- Fiction 3. Hippopotamus -- Fiction
ISBN 978-1-4169-8731-4; 1-4169-8731-2; 978-1-4169-8732-1 pa; 1-4169-8732-0 pa

LC 2009-34860

Twelve-year-old Teddy investigates when a popular Texas zoo's star attraction, Henry the hippopotamus, is murdered.

"The characters are well-developed and believable, making this book appealing to reluctant readers and those who enjoy animal stories and mysteries." Libr Media Connect

The **last** musketeer. Harper 2011 244p $16.99

Grades: 5 6 7 8   **Fic**

1. Adventure fiction 2. Time travel -- Fiction
ISBN 978-0-06-204838-7; 0-06-204838-4

LC 2011019376

In Paris with his parents to sell family heirlooms, fourteen-year-old Greg Rich suddenly finds himself four hundred years in the past, and is aided by boys who will one day be known as 'The Three Musketeers.'

"From the gripping first sentence . . . the excitement never flags in this newly imagined Musketeer adventure. . . . Using Alexandre Dumas' stories as a jumping-off point, Gibbs mixes fact, fantasy and thrills to create a galloping swashbuckler." Kirkus

Gidwitz, Adam

★ A **tale** dark & Grimm. Dutton 2010 256p il $16.99

Grades: 5 6 7 8   **Fic**

1. Fairy tales 2. Siblings -- Fiction
ISBN 978-0-525-42334-8; 0-525-42334-6; 9780525425816

LC 2009-53289

This book follows Hansel and Gretel as they walk out of their own story and into eight more tales. "Age ten and up." (N Y Times Book Rev)

"An audacious debut that's wicked smart and wicked funny." Publ Wkly

Gier, Kerstin

★ **Ruby** red. Henry Holt 2011 330p $16.99

Grades: 7 8 9 10   **Fic**

1. Family life -- Fiction 2. Time travel -- Fiction 3. Secret societies -- Fiction
ISBN 978-0-8050-9252-3; 0-8050-9252-8

LC 2010-49223

Original German edition, 2009

"Adventure, humor, and mystery all have satisfying roles here." Booklist

Sapphire blue; Kerstin Gier ; translated from the German by Anthea Bell. Henry Holt 2012 362 p. (hc) $16.99

Grades: 7 8 9 10   **Fic**

1. Fantasy fiction 2. Time travel -- Fiction 3. Secret societies -- Fiction 4. Family life -- England -- London -- Fiction
ISBN 0805092668; 9780805092660

LC 2011034011

In this young adult fantasy novel, by Kerstin Gier, "16-year-old Gwen continues her time-traveling adventures as the newest member of the Circle of Twelve. . . . Her life's now controlled by . . . a secret society monitoring time travel. . . . All 12 time travelers must be introduced into the chronograph so the Circle can be closed, and the Guardians have assigned Gwen and irresistible Gideon de Villiers the task of locating four missing time travelers." (Kirkus Reviews)

Giff, Patricia Reilly

Eleven. Wendy Lamb Books 2008 164p $15.99; lib bdg $18.99; pa $6.50

Grades: 4 5 6 7   **Fic**

1. Woodwork -- Fiction 2. Friendship -- Fiction 3. Kidnapping -- Fiction 4. Learning disabilities -- Fiction
ISBN 978-0-385-73069-3; 978-0-385-90098-0 lib bdg; 978-0-440-23802-7 pa

LC 2007-12638

When Sam, who can barely read, discovers an old newspaper clipping just before his eleventh birthday, it brings forth memories from his past, and, with the help of a new friend at school and the castle they are building for a school project, his questions are eventually answered.

This is an "exquisitely rendered story of self-discovery." Publ Wkly

Lily's crossing. Delacorte Press 1997 180p $15.95; pa $6.50; $15.95

Grades: 4 5 6 7   **Fic**

1. Friendship -- Fiction 2. World War, 1939-1945 --

Fiction
ISBN 0-385-32142-2; 0-440-41453-9 pa;
9780385321426

LC 96-23021

A Newbery Medal honor book, 1998

"Set during World War II, this . . . story tells of the war's impact on two children, one an American and one a Hungarian refugee. Lily Mollahan, a spirited, sensitive youngster being raised by her grandmother and Poppy, her widower father, has a comfortable routine that includes the family's annual summer migration to Gram's beach house in Rockaway, NY. Lily looks forward to summer's freedom and fishing outings with Poppy. She meets Albert, a Hungarian boy who is staying at a neighbor's house. . . . Eventually the two become good friends. The war interferes directly with Lily's life when Poppy, an engineer, is sent to Europe to help with clean-up operations." (SLJ)

"Gentle elements of danger and suspense . . . keep the plot moving forward, while the delicate balance of characters and setting gently coalesces into an emotional whole that is fully satisfying." Bull Cent Child Books

★ **Nory** Ryan's song. Delacorte Press 2000 148p hardcover o.p. pa $5.99
Grades: 5 6 7 8   **Fic**
1. Famines -- Fiction 2. Ireland -- History -- Famine, 1845-1852
ISBN 0-385-32141-4; 0-440-41829-1 pa

LC 00-27690

When a terrible blight attacks Ireland's potato crop in 1845, twelve-year-old Nory Ryan's courage and ingenuity help her family and neighbors survive

"Giff brings the landscape and the cultural particulars of the era vividly to life and creates in Nory a heroine to cheer for. A beautiful, heart-wrenching novel that makes a devastating event understandable." Booklist

Another title about Nory is:
Maggie's door (2003)

Pictures of Hollis Woods. Wendy Lamb Bks. 2002 166p $15.95; pa $6.50
Grades: 5 6 7 8   **Fic**
1. Artists -- Fiction 2. Old age -- Fiction 3. Foster home care -- Fiction
ISBN 0-385-32655-6; 0-440-41578-0 pa

LC 2002-426

A Newbery Medal honor book, 2003

"She was named for the place where she was found as an abandoned baby. Twelve-year-old Hollis Woods has been through many foster homes—and she runs away, every time. In her latest placement, with an artist named Josie, the tightly wound Hollis begins to relax ever so slightly. . . . But Josie is slowly slipping into dementia, and Hollis knows that she'll be taken away from her if Josie is found out. . . . Giff has a sure hand with language, and the narrative is taut and absorbing." Booklist

Storyteller. Wendy Lamb Books 2010 166p $15.99; lib bdg $18.99
Grades: 5 6 7 8   **Fic**
1. Aunts -- Fiction 2. Family life -- Fiction 3. Father-

daughter relationship -- Fiction
ISBN 978-0-375-83888-0; 0-375-83888-0; 978-0-375-93888-7 lib bdg; 0-375-93888-5 lib bdg

LC 2009-48130

Forced to spend months at an aunt's house, Elizabeth feel a connection to her ancestor Zee, whose picture hangs on the wall, and who reveals her story of hardships during the Revolutionary War as Elizabeth comes to terms with her own troubles

"As she brings these characters and history alive, Giff again demostrates her own gift for storytelling." Publ Wkly

Water Street. Wendy Lamb Books 2006 164p $15.95; lib bdg $17.99; pa $6.50
Grades: 5 6 7 8   **Fic**
1. Family life -- Fiction 2. Irish Americans -- Fiction
ISBN 978-0-385-90097-3; 0-385-73068-3; 978-0-385-90097-3 lib bdg; 0-385-90097-X lib bdg; 978-0-440-41921-1 pa; 0-440-41921-2 pa

LC 2006-02024

In the shadow of the construction of the Brooklyn Bridge, eighth-graders and new neighbors Bird Mallon and Thomas Neary make some decisions about what they want to do with their lives.

"Continuing the Irish American immigration story begun in Nory Ryan's Song (2000) and Maggie's Door (2003), [this] novel, set in 1875, is about the next generation. . . . A poignant immigration story of friendship, work, and the meaning of home." Booklist

Giff, Patricia Reilly, 1935-
R my name is Rachel. Wendy Lamb Books 2011 166p $15.99; lib bdg $18.99; e-book $10.99
Grades: 4 5 6 7   **Fic**
1. Moving -- Fiction 2. Siblings -- Fiction 3. Farm life -- Fiction 4. Great Depression, 1929-1939 -- Fiction
ISBN 978-0-375-83889-7; 0-375-83889-9; 978-0-375-93889-4 lib bdg; 0-375-93889-3; 978-0-375-98389-4 e-book

LC 2011004303

Three city siblings, now living on a farm during the Great Depression, must survive on their own when their father takes a construction job miles away.

"Rachel's searing, present-tense narrative exposes her fears, determination, and hopefulness in the face of wrenching challenges. Recurring motifs—color, flowers, and drawings by a neighbor that Rachel discovers in unlikely places—add lyricism to this story of family solidarity." Publ Wkly

Giles, Gail
Right behind you. Little, Brown 2007 292p hardcover o.p. pa $7.99
Grades: 8 9 10 11 12   **Fic**
1. Homicide -- Fiction 2. Family life -- Fiction 3. Psychotherapy -- Fiction
ISBN 978-0-316-16636-2; 0-316-16636-7; 978-0-316-16637-9 pa; 0-316-16637-5 pa

LC 2007-12336

After spending over four years in a mental institution for murdering a friend in Alaska, fourteen-year-old Kip begins a completely new life in Indiana with his father and stepmother under a different name, but not only has trouble fitting in, he finds there are still problems to deal with from his childhood.

"The story-behind-the-headlines flavor gives this a voyeuristic appeal, while the capable writing and sympathetic yet troubled protagonist will suck readers right into the action." Bull Cent Child Books

Gill, David Macinnis

★ **Black** hole sun. Greenwillow Books 2010 340p $16.99

Grades: 8 9 10 11 12   **Fic**

1. Science fiction 2. Miners -- Fiction

ISBN 978-0-06-167304-7; 0-06-167304-8

LC 2009-23050

"Durango is the 16-year-old chief of a team of mercenaries who eke out a living on Mars by earning meager commissions for their dangerous work. Their current job, and the main thrust of this high-energy, action-filled, science-fiction romp, is to protect South Pole miners from the Dræu, a cannibalistic group who are after the miners' treasure. . . . Throughout the novel, the dialogue crackles with expertly delivered sarcastic wit and venom. . . . Readers will have a hard time turning the pages fast enough as the body count rises to the climactic, satisfying ending." Booklist

Invisible sun; by David Macinnis Gill. 1st ed. Greenwillow Books 2012 370 p. (Black Hole Sun Trilogy) (paperback) $9.99; (trade bdg.) $16.99

Grades: 8 9 10 11   **Fic**

1. Science fiction 2. Mars (Planet) -- Fiction 3. Adventure and adventurers -- Fiction

ISBN 9780062073334; 006207332X; 9780062073327

LC 2011002841

This science fiction adventure story, by David Macinnis Gill, is the sequel to "Black Hole Sun," continuing to describe how "Martian freedom fighters Durango and Vienne infiltrate an evil government compound in search of missing data they hope will render the planet safe from future harm. This . . . novel is packed with . . . death-defying escapes, ambushes and . . . shootouts." (Kirkus)

Shadow on the sun; David Macinnis Gill. 1st ed. Greenwillow Books, an imprint of HarperCollins Publishers 2013 432 p. (Black Hole Sun Trilogy) (hardcover) $17.99

Grades: 8 9 10 11   **Fic**

1. Science fiction 2. Mars (Planet) -- Fiction

ISBN 0062073354; 9780062073358

LC 2013008361

This young adult science fiction novel, by David Macinnis Gill, is the sequel to "Invisible Sun." "Ex-Regulators Durango and Vienne are at it again in a race against time on a dangerous Martian landscape. Shocked to have learned that his father heads up the enemy forces who captured him at the end of the previous book, wisecracking teen soldier Durango fights to escape the clutches of his evil dad and to reunite with his ex-assassin sidekick and love interest, Vienne." (Kirkus Reviews)

"This sequel doesn't stand alone, and Gill inserts just enough left turns and red herrings to keep seasoned series readers guessing. . . . A refreshingly nondystopic sci-fi adventure." Kirkus

Gilman, Charles

Professor Gargoyle; Charlie Ward. Quirk Books 2012 175 p. $13.99

Grades: 7 8 9 10   **Fic**

1. Horror fiction 2. School stories 3. Monsters -- fiction 4. Teachers -- fiction 5. Middle schools -- fiction

ISBN 1594745919; 9781594745911

LC 2011946052

In this novel by Charles Gilman "Strange things are happening at Lovecraft Middle School. Rats are leaping from lockers. Students are disappearing. The school library is a labyrinth of secret corridors. And the science teacher is acting very peculiar -- in fact, he just might be a monster-in-disguise. Twelve-year-old Robert Arthur knew that seventh grade was going to be weird, but this is ridiculous!"(Publisher's note)

Gilman, David

The **devil's** breath. Delacorte Press 2008 391p (Danger zone) $15.99; lib bdg $18.99

Grades: 7 8 9 10 11 12   **Fic**

1. Adventure fiction 2. Environmental protection -- Fiction

ISBN 978-0-385-73560-5; 978-0-385-90546-6 lib bdg

LC 2007-46744

When fifteen-year-old Max Gordon's environmentalist-adventurer father goes missing while working in Namibia and Max becomes the target of a would-be assassin at his school in England, he decides he must follow his father to Africa and find him before they both are killed.

"The action is relentless. . . . Gilman has a flair for making the preposterous seem possible." Booklist

Other titles in this series are:

Ice claw (2010)

Blood sun (2011)

Gilman, Laura Anne

Grail quest: the Camelot spell; book one. HarperCollins 2006 291p $10.99; lib bdg $14.89

Grades: 5 6 7 8   **Fic**

1. Kings 2. Magic -- Fiction 3. Middle Ages -- Fiction 4. Knights and knighthood -- Fiction

ISBN 0-06-077279-4; 0-06-077280-8 lib bdg

Three teenagers living in Camelot are forced to undertake a dangerous mission when King Arthur's court falls under a mysterious enchantment on the eve of the quest for the Holy Grail.

"The believable dialogue, succint plot, and uncomplicated references to court life will appeal to middle graders who are beginning to explore Aurthurian legend." Voice Youth Advocates

Other titles in this series are:

Grail quest: Morgain's revenge (2006)

Grail quest: The shadow companion (2006)

Gilmore, Kate

The **exchange** student. Houghton Mifflin 1999 216p $15; pa $6.95

Grades: 7 8 9 10   **Fic**

1. Science fiction 2. Endangered species -- Fiction 3. Wildlife conservation -- Fiction 4. Extraterrestrial

beings -- Fiction
ISBN 0-395-57511-7; 0-618-68948-6 pa
                                         LC 97-47162

When her mother arranges to host one of the young people coming to Earth from Chela, Daria is both pleased and
intrigued by the keen interest shown by the Chelan in her
work breeding endangered species

"Gilmore makes a farfetched premise seem more reasonable with everyday details of life in the twenty-first century,
sympathetic characters, and logical consequences. . . . A
story that will appeal to readers on many levels." Booklist

Gipson, Frederick Benjamin

Old Yeller; [by] Fred Gipson; drawings by Carl
Burger. Harper & Row 1956 158p il $23; pa $5.99
Grades: 6 7 8 9   **Fic**
    1. Dogs -- Fiction 2. Frontier and pioneer life -- Fiction
ISBN 0-06-011545-9; 0-06-440382-3 pa
                                         LC 56-8780

A Newbery Medal honor book, 1957

"Travis at fourteen was the man of the family during the
hard summer of 1860 when his father drove his herd of cattle
from Texas to the Kansas market. It was the summer when
an old yellow dog attached himself to the family and won
Travis' reluctant friendship. Before the summer was over,
Old Yeller proved more than a match for thieving raccoons,
fighting bulls, grizzly bears, and mad wolves. This is a skillful tale of a boy's love for a dog as well as a description of
a pioneer boyhood and it can't miss with any dog lover."
Horn Book

Glatstein, Jacob

Emil and Karl; by Yankev Glatshteyn; translated by Jeffrey Shandler. Roaring Brook Press 2006
194p $17.95; pa $6.99
Grades: 5 6 7 8   **Fic**
    1. Jews -- Fiction 2. Friendship -- Fiction 3. Holocaust,
1933-1945 -- Fiction
ISBN 1-59643-119-9; 0-312-37387-2 pa
                                         LC 2005-26800

Original Yiddish edition 1940

A story about the dilemma faced by two young boys—
one Jewish, the other not—when they suddenly find themselves without homes or families in Vienna on the eve of
World War II.

"The fast-moving prose is stark and immediate.
Glatshteyn was, of course, writing about what was happening to children in his time. . . . The translation, 65 years
after the novel's original publication, is nothing short of
haunting." Booklist

Gleitzman, Morris

Now; Morris Gleitzman. Henry Holt 2012 184
p. $16.99
Grades: 7 8 9 10   **Fic**
    1. Psychological fiction 2. Family life -- Fiction 3.
Grandfathers -- Fiction 4. Holocaust survivors -- Fiction
5. Wildfires -- Fiction 6. Jews -- Australia -- Fiction 7.
Separation (Psychology) -- Fiction
ISBN 0805093788; 9780805093780
                                         LC 2011033496

This novel by Morris Gleitzman is "[s]et in the current
day, this is the final book in the series that began with Once,
continued with Then and is . . . Now. . . . While her phy-
sician-parents are working in Africa, eleven-year-old Zelda
is living with her grandfather, eighty-year-old Holocaust-
survivor Felix Salinger, in Australia . . . He has achieved
much in his life and is widely admired in the community.
He has mostly buried the painful memories of his childhood
. . . when a disaster leads them both to deal with unresolved
feelings about the first Zelda, Felix's childhood friend."
(Publisher's note)

★ **Once**. Henry Holt and Company 2010 163p
$16.99
Grades: 7 8 9 10   **Fic**
    1. Jews -- Poland -- Fiction 2. Holocaust, 1933-1945
-- Fiction
ISBN 978-0-8050-9026-0; 0-8050-9026-6
                                         LC 2009-24153

"The horror of the Holocaust is told here through the
eyes of a Polish Jewish child, Felix, who loses his innocence
as he witnesses Nazi-led roundups, shootings, and deportations. . . . Most moving is the lack of any idealization. . . .
Felix escapes, but one and a half million Jewish children did
not, and this gripping novel will make readers want to find
out more about them." Booklist

Then. Henry Holt 2010 198p $16.99
Grades: 7 8 9 10   **Fic**
    1. Orphans -- Fiction 2. Jews -- Poland -- Fiction 3.
Holocaust, 1933-1945 -- Fiction 4. World War, 1939-
1945 -- Fiction
ISBN 978-0-8050-9027-7; 0-8050-9027-4
                                         LC 2009050774

In early 1940s Poland, ten-year-old Felix and his friend
Zelda escape from a cattle car headed to the Nazi death camps
and struggle to survive, first on their own and then with Ge-
nia, a farmer with her own reasons for hating Germans.

"There is no triumphant climax, and right up until
the shocking end, the story of hidden children will grab
readers with its details of the daily tension of rescue and
betrayal." Booklist

Godbersen, Anna

Envy; a Luxe novel. Harpercollins 2009 405p
$17.99; pa $9.99
Grades: 8 9 10 11 12   **Fic**
    1. Love -- Fiction 2. Wealth -- Fiction 3. Sisters --
Fiction 4. Social classes -- Fiction
ISBN 978-0-06-134572-2; 0-06-134572-5; 978-0-06-
134574-6 pa; 0-06-134574-1 pa
                                         LC 2009-275632

"Possibly the best book of Godbersen's three, this
lengthy tome will still leave readers wanting more." Voice
Youth Advocates

Goeglein, T. M.

Cold fury; T.M. Goeglein. G.P. Putnam's Sons
2012 312 p. (hardcover) $17.99
Grades: 8 9 10 11 12   **Fic**
    1. Mafia -- Fiction 2. Chicago (Ill.) -- Fiction 3.
Missing persons -- Fiction 4. Violence -- Fiction 5.

Secret societies -- Fiction 6. Mystery and detective stories
ISBN 0399257209; 9780399257209

LC 2011025824

This book by T. M. Goeglein follows "Sara Jane Rispoli . . . a normal sixteen-year-old coping with school and a budding romance--until her parents and brother are kidnapped and she discovers her family is deeply embedded in the Chicago Outfit (aka the mob). Now on the run from a masked assassin, rogue cops and her turncoat uncle, Sara Jane is chased and attacked at every turn, fighting back with cold fury as she searches for her family." (Publisher's note)

Going, K. L.

★ **Fat** kid rules the world. Putnam 2003 187p $17.99; pa $6.99

Grades: 7 8 9 10　　　　　　　　　Fic

1. Obesity -- Fiction 2. Musicians -- Fiction 3. Friendship -- Fiction
ISBN 0-399-23990-1; 0-14-240208-7 pa

LC 2002-67956

Michael L. Printz Award honor book, 2004

Seventeen-year-old Troy, depressed, suicidal, and weighing nearly 300 pounds, gets a new perspective on life when a homeless teenager who is a genius on guitar wants Troy to be the drummer in his rock band

"Going has put together an amazing assortment of characters. . . . This is an impressive debut that offers hope for all kids." Booklist

The **garden** of Eve. Harcourt 2007 234p $17; pa $6.99

Grades: 4 5 6 7　　　　　　　　　Fic

1. Death -- Fiction 2. Magic -- Fiction 3. Bereavement -- Fiction
ISBN 978-0-15-205986-6; 0-15-205986-5; 978-0-15-206614-7 pa; 0-15-206614-4 pa

LC 2007-05074

Eve gave up her belief in stories and magic after her mother's death, but a mysterious seed given to her as an eleventh-birthday gift by someone she has never met takes her and a boy who claims to be a ghost on a strange journey, to where their supposedly cursed town of Beaumont, New York, flourishes.

"Believably and with delicacy, Going paints a suspenseful story suffused with the poignant questions of what it means to be alive, and what might await on the other side." Horn Book

Goldblatt, Stacey

Stray; a novel. Delacorte Press 2007 276p $15.99; lib bdg $18.99

Grades: 7 8 9 10 11 12　　　　　　　　　Fic

1. Dogs -- Fiction 2. Dating (Social customs) -- Fiction 3. Mother-daughter relationship -- Fiction
ISBN 978-0-385-73443-1; 0-385-73443-3; 978-0-385-90448-3 lib bdg; 0-385-90448-7 lib bdg

LC 2006-31828

Natalie's mother, a veterinarian with a dogs-only practice, has the sixteen-year-old on such a short leash that, when the teenaged son of her old school friend comes to stay with

them for the summer, Natalie is tempted to break her mother's rules and follow her own instincts for a change.

"This fresh treatment of a familiar teen feeling will attract readers who love dogs as well as a good first-love story." Booklist

Golden, Christopher

The **sea** wolves; by Christopher Golden & Tim Lebbon ; with illustrations by Greg Ruth. Harper 2012 384 p. $16.99

Grades: 7 8 9 10　　　　　　　　　Fic

1. Sea stories 2. Adventure fiction 3. Pirates -- Fiction 4. Supernatural -- Fiction 5. Adventure and adventurers -- Fiction
ISBN 0061863203; 9780061863202; 9780061863219

LC 2011010031

This young adult fantasy adventure novel by Christopher Golden and Tim Lebbon follows "Jack London . . . a writer who lived his own real-life adventures. But . . . even he couldn't set down [all his adventures] in writing. Terrifying, mysterious, bizarre, and magical. . . . Clinging to life after he is captured in an attack by savage pirates, Jack is unprepared for what he faces at the hands of the crew and their charismatic, murderous captain, Ghost. For these mariners are not mortal men but hungry beasts chasing gold and death across the North Pacific. Jack's only hope lies with Sabine—a sad, sultry captive of Ghost's insatiable hunger. But on these waters, nothing is as it seems, and Sabine may be hiding dangerous secrets of her own." (Publisher's note)

The **wild**; by Christopher Golden & Tim Lebbon; with illustrations by Greg Ruth. Harper 2011 348p il (The secret journeys of Jack London) $15.99; lib bdg $16.89

Grades: 7 8 9 10　　　　　　　　　Fic

1. Adventure fiction 2. Wolves -- Fiction 3. Supernatural -- Fiction 4. Wilderness survival -- Fiction 5. Gold mines and mining -- Fiction
ISBN 978-0-06-186317-2; 0-06-186317-3; 978-0-06-186318-9 lib bdg; 0-06-186318-1 lib bdg

LC 2010-07475

Seventeen-year-old Jack London makes the arduous journey to the Yukon's gold fields in 1893, becoming increasingly uneasy about supernatural forces in the wilderness that seem to have taken a special interest in him.

"Golden and Lebbon write with a gritty assurance that brings the fantasy elements . . . down to earth. . . . Occasional sketches add a bit of cinematic drama." Booklist

Golden, Laura

Every day after; Laura Golden. 1st ed. Delacorte Press 2013 216 p. (ebook) $47.97; (library) $18.99; (hardcover) $15.99

Grades: 5 6 7　　　　　　　　　Fic

1. Self-reliance -- Fiction 2. Family problems -- Fiction 3. Abandoned children -- Fiction 4. Depressions -- 1929 -- Fiction
ISBN 0385743262; 9780307983121; 9780375991035; 9780385743266

LC 2012015770

This book, set in 1932 in small-town Alabama, "details the struggles and injustices facing 11-year-old Lizzie

Hawkins after her father loses his job and leaves town. Stuck with an overdue mortgage and a mother paralyzed by depression, Lizzie believes she just has to hold it together until her father returns, as she is sure he will." (Publishers Weekly)

Golding, Julia

Secret of the sirens; [by] Julia Golding. 1st Marshall Cavendish ed.; Marshall Cavendish 2007 357p (The companions quartet) $16.99

Grades: 7 8 9 10   **Fic**

1. Supernatural -- Fiction 2. Mythical animals -- Fiction 3. Environmental protection -- Fiction

ISBN 978-0-7614-5371-0; 0-7614-5371-7

LC 2006052799

First published 2006 in the United Kingdom

Upon moving to her aunt's seaside home in the British Isles, Connie becomes part of a secret society that shelters mythical creatures, and must use her ability to communicate with these beings to protect them from evil and the incursions of humans.

This "packs a serious environmental message, yet never feels heavyhanded. . . . The contemporary setting and its modern villains . . . make for an entertaining read." Publ Wkly

Other titles in this series are:
The gorgon's gaze (2007)
Mines of the minotaur (2008)
The chimera's curse (2008)

★ The **diamond** of Drury Lane. Roaring Brook Press 2008 424p (Cat Royal Quartet) $16.99; pa $7.99

Grades: 6 7 8 9   **Fic**

1. Orphans -- Fiction 2. Theater -- Fiction

ISBN 978-1-59643-351-9; 1-59643-351-5; 978-0-312-56123-9 pa; 0-312-56123-7 pa

LC 2007-23604

Orphan Catherine "Cat" Royal, living at the Drury Lane Theater in 1790s London, tries to find the "diamond" supposedly hidden in the theater, which unmasks a treasonous political cartoonist, and involves her in the street gangs of Covent Garden and the world of nobility.

This is "a story with as many cliff-hangers as there are chapters. But the real thrills also come from the varied, sharply drawn cast. . . . [Golding] offers a view of London readers can grasp with all their senses." Booklist

Other titles in this series are:
Cat among the pigeons (2008)
Den of thieves (2009)
Cat o' nine tails (2009)

The **silver** sea. Marshall Cavendish 2010 334p $17.99

Grades: 6 7 8 9   **Fic**

1. Pirates -- Fiction 2. Slavery -- Fiction 3. Vikings -- Fiction 4. Middle Ages -- Fiction 5. Father-daughter relationship -- Fiction

ISBN 978-0-7614-5725-1; 0-7614-5725-9

LC 2009-51263

When pirates raid a village in ninth-century Norway, eighteen-year-old Toki is captured as a prize, while Freydis, his younger sister, is taken to a friendly village where she

and her African slave, Enno, learn that their fates are linked by prophecy.

"The straightforward emotions and lack of complicated politics enable younger readers to traverse the landscapes of the Dark Ages with ease, . . . while following a well-wrought story of romance, revenge, and familial loyalty." Bull Cent Child Books

Golding, William

Lord of the flies; introduction by E. M. Forster; with a biographical and critical note by E. L. Epstein; illustrated by Ben Gibson. 50th anniversary ed; Berkley 2003 315p $23.95; pa $13

Grades: 8 9 10 11 12   **Fic**

1. Boys -- Fiction 2. Survival after airplane accidents, shipwrecks, etc. -- Fiction

ISBN 0-399-52920-9; 0-399-50148-7 pa

LC 2003-54825

First published 1954 in the United Kingdom; first United States edition, 1955, by Coward-McCann

"Stranded on an island, a group of English schoolboys leave innocence behind in a struggle for survival. A political structure modeled after English government is set up and a hierarchy develops, but forces of anarchy and aggression surface. The boys' existence begins to degenerate into a savage one. They are rescued from their microcosmic society to return to an adult, stylized milieu filled with the same psychological tensions and moral voids. Adventure and allegory are brilliantly combined in this novel." Shapiro. Fic for Youth. 3d edition

Golds, Cassandra

The **museum** of Mary Child. Kane Miller 2009 329p $16.99

Grades: 6 7 8 9 10   **Fic**

1. Dolls -- Fiction 2. Museums -- Fiction

ISBN 978-1-935279-13-6; 1-935279-13-0

LC 2009-922719

"Lonely Heloise wants only to be loved, but lives as if jailed in the house of her stern and sometimes cruel godmother. One day Heloise uncovers a beautiful doll, Maria, hidden under the floorboards of her room, and it is love at first sight. Heloise hides Maria from her godmother, whose personal Ten Commandments include forbidding play, 'pretty clothes' and the possession of a doll. . . . Once Maria is discovered, Heloise finds out the horrible truth about the museum that adjoins her godmother's cottage and is thrust down a strange and magical path that reveals how sheltered she has been. . . . Golds's novel is pure fun, filled with mystery and nearly impossible to put down." Publ Wkly

Gonzalez, Christina Diaz

★ The **red** umbrella. Alfred A. Knopf 2010 284p $19.99

Grades: 6 7 8 9   **Fic**

1. Family life -- Fiction

ISBN 0375861904; 0375961909 lib bdg; 9780375861901; 9780375961908 lib bdg

LC 2009022309

In 1961 after Fidel Castro comes to power in Cuba, fourteen-year-old Lucia and her seven-year-old brother are sent to the United States because her parents fear that the children will be taken away from them as others have been.

"The pain of the revolution for those who disagreed is made clear and pressing, and the text manages to balance between being informative and entertaining. This could prove a helpful tie-in for classroom history lessons or a solid recommendation for fans of quietly engaging historical fiction." Bull Cent Child Books

Gonzalez, Julie

Imaginary enemy. Delacorte Press 2008 241p $15.99; lib bdg $18.99

Grades: 6 7 8 9 10   **Fic**

1. Imaginary playmates -- Fiction

ISBN 978-0-385-73552-0; 0-385-73552-9; 978-0-385-90530-5 lib bdg; 0-385-90530-0 lib bdg

LC 2007-45752

Although her impetuous behavior, smart-mouthed comments, and slacker ways have landed her in trouble over the years, sixteen-year-old Jane has always put the blame on her "imaginary enemy," until a new development forces her to decide whether or not to assume responsibility for her actions.

"Gonzalez has written a witty, realistic novel . . . peppered with funny, authentic dialogue." Booklist

Goobie, Beth

Before wings; a novel. Orca Bk. Pubs. 2001 203p hardcover o.p. pa $8.95

Grades: 7 8 9 10   **Fic**

1. Camps -- Fiction 2. Death -- Fiction

ISBN 1-55143-161-0; 1-55143-163-7 pa

LC 00-105582

"Full of magic realism and beautifully written, this is a story of good triumphing over evil, life triumphing over death, the power of love, friendship, and the hope for an afterlife." Booklist

Goodman, Alison

★ **Eon** : Dragoneye reborn. Viking 2009 531p $19.99

Grades: 7 8 9 10   **Fic**

1. Fantasy fiction 2. Magic -- Fiction 3. Dragons -- Fiction 4. Sex role -- Fiction 5. Apprentices -- Fiction

ISBN 978-0-670-06227-0; 0-670-06227-8

LC 2008-33223

Sixteen-year-old Eon hopes to become an apprentice to one of the twelve energy dragons of good fortune and learn to be its main interpreter, but to do so will require much, including keeping secret that she is a girl.

"Entangled politics and fierce battle scenes provide a pulse-quickening pace, while the intriguing characters add interest and depth." Booklist

Eona : the last Dragoneye. Viking 2011 637p il $19.99

Grades: 7 8 9 10   **Fic**

1. Fantasy fiction 2. Magic -- Fiction 3. Dragons -- Fiction 4. Apprentices -- Fiction

ISBN 978-0-670-06311-6; 0-670-06311-8

LC 2011-02997

Eon has been revealed as Eona, the first female Dragoneye in hundreds of years. Along with fellow rebels Ryko and Lady Dela, she is on the run from High Lord Sethon's army. The renegades are on a quest for the black folio, stolen by the drug-riddled Dillon; they must also find Kygo, the young Pearl Emperor, who needs Eona's power and the black folio if he is to wrest back his throne from the self-styled "Emperor" Sethon.

"One of those rare and welcome fantasies that complicate black-and-white morality." Kirkus

Singing the Dogstar blues. Viking 2003 261p $16.99

Grades: 7 8 9 10   **Fic**

1. Time travel 2. Science fiction

ISBN 0-670-03610-2

LC 2002-12161

First published 1998 in Australia

In a future Australia, the saucy eighteen-year-old daughter of a famous newscaster and a sperm donor teams up with a hermaphrodite from the planet Choria in a time travel adventure that may significantly change both of their lives

"This wildly entertaining novel successfully mixes adventure, humor, mystery, and sf into a fast-paced, thrilling story that will appeal to a wide audience." Booklist

Goodman, Allegra

The **other** side of the island. Razorbill 2008 280p $16.99

Grades: 6 7 8 9   **Fic**

1. Science fiction

ISBN 978-1-59514-195-8; 1-59514-195-2

LC 2007-50915

Born in the eighth year of Enclosure, ten-year-old Honor lives in a highly regulated colony with her defiant parents, but when they have an illegal second child and are taken away, it is up to Honor and her friend Helix, another 'Unpredictable,' to uncover a terrible secret about their Island and the Corporation that runs everything.

"A satisfying and compelling read." Bull Cent Child Books

Gordon, Roderick

Tunnels; [by] Roderick Gordon, Brian Williams. Chicken House/Scholastic 2008 480p il $17.99

Grades: 6 7 8 9   **Fic**

1. Adventure fiction

ISBN 978-0-439-87177-8; 0-439-87177-8

LC 2007-09169

When Will Burrows and his friend Chester embark on a quest to find Will's archaeologist father, who has inexplicably disappeared, they are led to a labyrinthine world underneath London, full of sinister inhabitants with evil intentions toward "Topsoilers" like Will and his father.

This is "compelling. . . . The authors add distinctive, vivid touches to the . . . premise . . . and the murderous, refreshingly competant Styx makes an uncommonly challenging adversary." Booklist

Other titles in this series are:

Deeper (2009)

Freefall (2010)

Closer (2011)

Gorman, Carol

Games. HarperCollinsPublishers 2007 279p
$16.99; lib bdg $17.89

Grades: 6 7 8 9   **Fic**

1. School stories 2. Games -- Fiction

ISBN 978-0-06-057027-9; 0-06-057027-X; 978-0-06-
057028-6 lib bdg; 0-06-057028-8 lib bdg

LC 2006-31759

When fourteen-year-old rivals Boot Quinn and Mick
Sullivan fight once too often, the new principal devises the
punishment of having to play games together at his office,
where they learn which battles are worth fighting.

"This novel is a great book for middle school students,
well scripted, realistic, and entertaining. The characters are
true and understandable." Voice Youth Advocates

Gosselink, John

The **defense** of Thaddeus A. Ledbetter; a novel.
drawings by Jason Rosenstock. Amulet Books 2010
231p il $14.95

Grades: 4 5 6 7   **Fic**

1. School stories

ISBN 978-0-8109-8977-1; 0-8109-8977-8

LC 2009052209

Twelve-year-old Thaddeus A. Ledbetter, who considers
it a duty to share his knowledge and talent with others, re-
futes each of the charges which have sent him to "In-School
Suspension" for the remainder of seventh grade.

"This original and entertaining book, with its smarty-
pants narrator and case-file format, will draw comparisons
to the Wimpy Kid series." Booklist

Goto, Hiromi

★ **Half** World; illustrations by Jillian Tamaki.
Viking 2010 221p il $16.99

Grades: 7 8 9 10   **Fic**

1. Fantasy fiction 2. Mother-daughter relationship --
Fiction

ISBN 978-0-670-01220-6; 0-670-01220-3

"Raised in impoverished circumstances by her single
mother, overweight 14-year-old Melanie is the target of
ridicule at school and leads a lonely, introverted life. Then
an evil being named Mr. Glueskin kidnaps her mother, forcing Melanie to travel to Half World, a colorless land that
has been sundered from the realms of flesh and spirit, its
deceased inhabitants cursed to relive the most traumatic moments of their lives. . . . Goto writes the hellish Half World
as miserably surreal yet horrifyingly believable. . . . It's a
fast-moving and provocative journey with cosmically high
stakes, and one that should readily appeal to fans of dark,
nightmarish fantasy." Publ Wkly

Gourlay, Candy

★ **Tall** story. David Fickling Books 2011 295p
lib bdg $19.99

Grades: 6 7 8 9   **Fic**

1. Size -- Fiction 2. Giants -- Fiction 3. Siblings --
Fiction 4. Basketball -- Fiction 5. Culture conflict --
Fiction

ISBN 0385752172; 0385752180 lib bdg; 978-0-385-
75217-6; 9780385752183 lib bdg

LC 2010011891

In this book, "Bernardo, who suffers from gigantism,
lives in a world where real life and magic collide. . . . To his
younger sister, Andi, born and raised in London, Bernardo
is both the brother she has always loved and the freakishly
tall boy who is going to draw way too much attention at
school. . . . When an earthquake devastates San Andres just
after Bernardo leaves, he's sure it's his fault. He believes
that he brings destruction and danger wherever he goes, but
everyone else thinks that Bernardo brings miracles." (School
Library Journal)

"This will capture the hearts and minds of sports lovers—and just about everyone else as well." Booklist

Grabenstein, Chris

Escape from Mr. Lemoncello's library; Chris
Grabenstein. 1st ed. Random House Inc. 2013 304
p. (hardcover) $16.99; (library) $19.99

Grades: 5 6 7   **Fic**

1. Games -- Fiction 2. Libraries -- Fiction 3. Books
and reading -- Fiction

ISBN 037587089X; 9780375870897; 9780375970894

LC 2012048122

In this book, twelve "seventh-graders win a chance to
spend an overnight lock-in previewing their town's new
public library," which was "conceived by Luigi Lemoncello,
the . . . founder of Mr. Lemoncello's Imagination Factory,
which is a source for every kind of game imaginable. During the lock-in the winners . . . are offered a further challenge: 'Find your way out of the library using only what's
in the library.' The winner will become spokesperson for the
Imagination Factory." (Publishers Weekly)

The **crossroads**. Random House 2008 325p
(Haunted places mystery) $16.99; lib bdg $19.99;
pa $6.99

Grades: 5 6 7 8   **Fic**

1. Ghost stories 2. Stepmothers -- Fiction

ISBN 978-0-375-84697-7; 0-375-84697-2; 978-0-375-
94697-4 lib bdg; 0-375-94697-7 lib bdg; 978-0-375-
84698-4 pa; 0-375-84698-0 pa

LC 2007024803

When eleven-year-old Zack Jennings moves to Connecticut with his father and new stepmother, they must deal
with the ghosts left behind by a terrible accident, as well as
another kind of ghost from Zack's past

"An absorbing psychological thriller . . . as well as a
rip-roaring ghost story, this switches points of view among
humans, trees, and ghosts with astonishing élan." Booklist

Other titles in this series are:

The Hanging Hill (2009)

The smoky corridor (2010)

The Black Heart Crypt (2011)

Grace, Amanda

In too deep; Amanda Grace. Flux 2012 228
p. $9.95

Grades: 7 8 9 10 11 12   **Fic**

1. Rape -- Fiction 2. Honesty -- Fiction 3. False
accusation -- Fiction 4. High school students -- Fiction
5. Teenagers -- Conduct of life -- Fiction 6. Rumor --

Fiction 7. Schools -- Fiction 8. High schools -- Fiction
ISBN 0738726001; 9780738726007

LC 2011028806

In this young adult novel, a "girl gets caught in a lie she didn't tell but doesn't have the courage to correct. . . . Samantha wants to spark some romantic interest from her best friend and secret heartthrob Nick, so she makes a play for popularity-magnet Carter. He rebuffs her, but someone sees her leaving his bedroom in tears and jumps to the false conclusion that Carter assaulted her. Sam doesn't hear about the resulting rumors until she returns to school. Soon she feels too overwhelmed by social pressure to deny them. Sam finds many opportunities to confess the truth, but she can't bring herself to exonerate Carter. . . . Complicating matters, Sam knows that because of the deception, she's likely to lose Nick, who finally has declared his love for her." (Kirkus)

Graff, Lisa

A **tangle** of knots; Lisa Graff. Philomel Books 2013 240 p. $16.99

Grades: 3 4 5 6 **Fic**
1. Baking -- Fiction 2. Ability -- Fiction 3. Orphans -- Fiction 4. Identity -- Fiction 5. Family life -- New York -- Fiction
ISBN 0399255176; 9780399255175

LC 2012009573

This juvenile novel, by Lisa Graff, is set "in a slightly magical world where everyone has a Talent. . . . Eleven-year-old Cady is an orphan with a phenomenal Talent for cake baking. . . . And her destiny leads her to a mysterious address that houses a lost luggage emporium, an old recipe, a family of children searching for their own Talents, and a Talent Thief who will alter her life forever. However, these encounters hold the key to Cady's past and how she became an orphan." (Publisher's note)

Grant, K. M.

Blood red horse. Walker & Co. 2005 277p $16.95; pa $8.99

Grades: 6 7 8 9 **Fic**
1. Horses -- Fiction 2. Crusades -- Fiction 3. Middle Ages -- Fiction
ISBN 0-8027-8960-9; 0-8027-7734-8 pa

LC 2005-42280

First published 2004 in the United Kingdom

A special horse named Hosanna changes the lives of two English brothers and those around them as they fight with King Richard I against Saladin's armies during the Third Crusades.

This "story . . . transcends boundaries of gender and genre, with something to offer fans of equestrian fare, historical fiction, and battlefield drama alike." Booklist

Other titles in this series are:
Green jasper (2006)
Blaze of silver (2007)

★ **Blue** flame; book one of the Perfect Fire trilogy. Walker & Co. 2008 246p (Perfect fire trilogy) $16.99

Grades: 7 8 9 10 **Fic**
1. Middle Ages -- Fiction 2. Knights and knighthood

-- Fiction
ISBN 978-0-8027-9694-3; 0-8027-9694-X

LC 2007-51384

In 1242 in the restive Languedoc region of France, Parsifal, having been charged as a child to guard an important religious relic, has lived in hiding for much of his life until he befriends a young couple on opposite sides of the escalating conflict between the Catholics and the Cathars.

"Characters are as complex as the moral issues they face, and Grant's nuanced, thought-provoking look at the religious conflicts they face will resonate today." Booklist

Other books in this series are:
Paradise red (2010)
White heat (2009)

★ **How** the hangman lost his heart. Walker & Co. 2007 244p $16.95

Grades: 7 8 9 10 **Fic**
1. Adventure fiction
ISBN 978-0-8027-9672-1; 0-8027-9672-9

LC 2006-53182

When her Uncle Frank is executed for treason against England's King George in 1746, and his severed head is mounted on a pike for public viewing, daring Alice tries to reclaim the head for a proper burial, finding an unlikely ally in the softhearted executioner, while incurring the wrath of the royal guard.

"The story is filled with action and interesting characters. . . . This is a rousing read." SLJ

Grant, Katy

Hide and seek. Peachtree 2010 230p $15.95

Grades: 5 6 7 8 **Fic**
1. Divorce -- Fiction 2. Kidnapping -- Fiction 3. Family life -- Fiction 4. Wilderness survival -- Fiction
ISBN 978-1-56145-542-3; 1-56145-542-3

LC 2009040519

In the remote mountains of Arizona where he lives with his mother, stepfather, and two sisters, fourteen-year-old Chase discovers two kidnapped boys and gets caught up in a dangerous adventure when he comes up with a plan to get them to safety.

"Mystery and adventure propel this readable survival story that will hit the spot with Gary Paulsen's fans and may also entice reluctant readers." SLJ

Grant, Michael, 1954-

★ **Gone**. HarperTeen 2008 576p $17.99; lib bdg $18.89; pa $9.99

Grades: 7 8 9 10 **Fic**
1. Supernatural -- Fiction 2. Good and evil -- Fiction
ISBN 978-0-06-144876-8; 978-0-06-144877-5 lib bdg; 978-0-06-144878-2 pa

LC 2007-36734

In a small town on the coast of California, everyone over the age of fourteen suddenly disappears, setting up a battle between the remaining town residents and the students from a local private school, as well as those who have "The Power" and are able to perform supernatural feats and those who do not.

"A tour de force that will leave readers dazed, disturbed, and utterly breathless." Booklist

Other titles in this series are:
Hunger (2009)
Lies (2010)
Plague (2011)
Fear (2012)

★ The **call**; Michael Grant. 1st ed. Katherine Tegen Books 2010 243 p. ill. (The Magnificent 12) (hardcover) $16.99

Grades: 4 5 6   **Fic**
1. Fantasy fiction 2. Adventure fiction 3. Humorous stories 4. Good and evil -- Fiction 5. Adventure and adventurers -- Fiction
ISBN 0061833665; 9780061833663
LC 2009044815
A seemingly average twelve-year-old learns that he is destined to gather a team of similarly gifted children to try to save the world from a nameless evil, which is threatening to reappear after an absence of three thousand years. "Age ten and up." (Publisher's note)
"The author keeps the story moving at a brisk pace with suspenseful action and laugh-out-loud humor." Kirkus

The **trap**. Katherine Tegen Books 2011 294p $16.99 (The Magnificent 12)

Grades: 4 5 6   **Fic**
1. Fantasy fiction 2. Adventure fiction 3. Good and evil -- Fiction
ISBN 0-06-183368-1; 978-0-06-183368-7
LC 2010040580
Mack MacAvoy, an average-seeming twelve-year-old boy who happens to have special powers, travels to China in an effort to assemble an elite team of his peers to help him thwart the evil Pale Queen.

Grant, Vicki

Quid pro quo. Orca 2005 160p $16.95; pa $7.95

Grades: 7 8 9 10   **Fic**
1. Mystery fiction 2. Lawyers -- Fiction 3. Missing persons -- Fiction 4. Mother-son relationship -- Fiction
ISBN 1-55143-394-X; 1-55143-370-2 pa
"Cyril Floyd MacIntyre, 13, is perplexed over the disappearance of his mother, a 28-year-old law-school graduate. . . . Cyril becomes involved in a web of intrigue and deceit searching for her. His discovery of resurfacing shady characters who played a role in Andy's disappearance makes for a suspense-filled, well-plotted legal thriller." SLJ

Res judicata. Orca Book Publishers 2008 172p pa $9.95

Grades: 7 8 9 10   **Fic**
1. Mystery fiction 2. Lawyers -- Fiction 3. Criminals -- Fiction 4. Mother-son relationship -- Fiction
ISBN 978-1-55143940-2; 1-55143940-9
Cyril MacIntyre is on the case again, working for his eccentric mother and giving new meaning to the term "legal aid" in this sequel to Quid Pro Quo.
"The novel features laugh-out-loud bits between mother and son and plenty of hilarious insights from Cyril about life and the law. Students who enjoy quick-witted writing and good mysteries will enjoy how well Vicki Grant cracks the case." Libr Media Connect

Gratz, Alan

★ The **Brooklyn** nine; a novel in nine innings. Dial Books 2009 299p $16.99

Grades: 5 6 7 8 9   **Fic**
1. Baseball -- Fiction 2. Family life -- Fiction 3. German Americans -- Fiction
ISBN 978-0-8037-3224-7; 0-8037-3224-4
LC 2008-21263
This novel follows the fortunes of a German immigrant family through nine generations, beginning in 1845, as they experience American life and play baseball.
Gratz "builds this novel upon a clever . . . conceit . . . and executes it with polish and precision." Booklist

Samurai shortstop. Dial Books 2006 280p hardcover o.p. pa $7.99

Grades: 7 8 9 10   **Fic**
1. School stories 2. Baseball -- Fiction 3. Father-son relationship -- Fiction
ISBN 0-8037-3075-6; 978-0-8037-3075-5; 0-14-241099-3 pa; 978-0-14-24099-8 pa
LC 2005-22081
While obtaining a Western education at a prestigious Japanese boarding school in 1890, sixteen-year-old Toyo also receives traditional samurai training which has profound effects on both his baseball game and his relationship with his father. This book features some scenes of graphic violence.
"This is an intense read about a fascinating time and place in world history." Publ Wkly

Graves, Keith

The **orphan** of Awkward Falls. Chronicle Books 2011 337p $16.99

Grades: 4 5 6 7   **Fic**
1. Mystery fiction 2. Orphans -- Fiction 3. Homicide -- Fiction 4. Inventors -- Fiction 5. Mentally ill -- Fiction 6. Science -- Experiments -- Fiction
ISBN 978-0-8118-7814-2; 0-8118-7814-7
LC 2011008008
Josephine Cravitz, the new girl in Awkward Falls, and her neighbor Thaddeus Hibble, a reclusive and orphaned boy inventor, become the targets of a mad cannibal from the local asylum for the criminally insane.
"Graves crafts a quick-moving plot composed of macabre twists. . . . Wordless opening and closing sequences, plus a handful of interior illustrations, both fill in background detail and intensify the overall macabre atmosphere." Kirkus

Gray, Claudia

Spellcaster; Claudia Gray. HarperTeen 2013 400 p. (hardback) $17.99

Grades: 8 9 10 11 12   **Fic**
1. Occult fiction 2. Witches -- Fiction 3. Horror stories 4. Magic -- Fiction 5. Schools -- Fiction 6. High schools -- Fiction 7. Blessing and cursing -- Fiction 8. Family life -- Rhode Island -- Fiction
ISBN 0061961205; 9780061961205
LC 2012025331

This young adult paranormal romance story, by Claudia Gray, follows a teenage girl with magical powers. "Descended from witches, Nadia can sense that a spell has been cast over the tiny Rhode Island town--a sickness infecting everyone and everything in it. The magic at work is darker and more powerful than anything she's come across and has sunk its claws most deeply into Mateo . . . her rescuer, her friend, and the guy she yearns to get closer to even as he pushes her away." (Publisher's note)

Gray, Dianne E.

Tomorrow, the river; [illustrations by Stephanie Cooper] Houghton Mifflin Company 2006 233p il $16

Grades: 6 7 8 9   **Fic**
  1. Sisters -- Fiction 2. Steamboats -- Fiction 3. Photography -- Fiction
  ISBN 978-0-618-56329-6; 0-618-56329-6
                LC 2005038068
In 1896, fourteen-year-old Megan joins her sister and family on their steamboat for the summer riding up the Mississippi River towards St. Paul, Minnesota, and through all of their adventures, Megan realizes what is her "true calling."

"History and river life are skillfully woven into the fast-moving plot, and the characters are fully realized." SLJ

Gray, Keith

★ **Ostrich** boys. Random House 2010 297p $17.99; lib bdg $20.99

Grades: 8 9 10 11 12   **Fic**
  1. Death -- Fiction 2. Friendship -- Fiction
  ISBN 978-0-375-85843-7; 0-375-85843-1; 978-0-375-95843-4 lib bdg; 0-375-95843-6 lib bdg
                LC 2008-21729
After their best friend Ross dies, English teenagers Blake, Kenny, and Sim plan a proper memorial by taking his ashes to Ross, Scotland, an adventure-filled journey that tests their loyalty to each other and forces them to question what friendship means.

"Gray's writing is cheeky, crisp, and realistic. He has created funny, bright characters whom readers cannot help but root for." SLJ

Green, Tim, 1963-

Baseball great. HarperCollinsPublishers 2009 250p $16.99; lib bdg $17.89

Grades: 5 6 7 8   **Fic**
  1. School stories 2. Baseball -- Fiction 3. Father-son relationship -- Fiction
  ISBN 978-0-06-162686-9; 0-06-162686-4; 978-0-06-162687-6 lib bdg; 0-06-162687-2 lib bdg
                LC 2008051778
All twelve-year-old Josh wants to do is play baseball but when his father, a minor league pitcher, signs him up for a youth championship team, Josh finds himself embroiled in a situation with potentially illegal consequences.

"Issues of peer and family pressure are well handled, and the short, punchy chapters and crisp dialogue are likely to hold the attention of young baseball fans." SLJ

Other titles in this series are:
Rivals (2010)

Best of the best (2011)

Football genius. HarperCollinsPublishers 2007 244p $16.99; lib bdg $17.89; pa $6.99

Grades: 5 6 7 8   **Fic**
  1. Football -- Fiction
  ISBN 978-0-06-112270-5; 0-06-112270-X; 978-0-06-112272-9 lib bdg; 0-06-112272-6 lib bdg; 978-0-06-112273-6 pa; 0-06-112273-4 pa
                LC 2006-29470
Troy, a sixth-grader with an unusual gift for predicting football plays before they occur, attempts to use his ability to help his favorite team, the Atlanta Falcons, but he must first prove himself to the coach and players.

The author "imparts many insider details that football fans will love. Green makes Troy a winning hero, and he ties everything together with a fast-moving plot." Booklist

Other titles in this series are:
Football champ (2009)
The big time (2010)
Deep zone (2011)

Football hero. HarperCollinsPublishers 2008 297p $16.99; lib bdg $17.89; pa $6.99

Grades: 5 6 7 8   **Fic**
  1. Mafia -- Fiction 2. Football -- Fiction
  ISBN 978-0-06-112274-3; 0-06-112274-2; 978-0-06-112275-0 lib bdg; 0-06-112275-0 lib bdg; 978-0-06-112276-7 pa; 0-06-112276-9 pa
                LC 2007-24184
When twelve-year-old Ty's brother Thane is recruited out of college to play for the New York Jets, their Uncle Gus uses Ty to get insider information for his gambling ring, landing Ty and Thane in trouble with the Mafia.

"The novel is briskly paced and undemanding, and might be a good bet for sports-minded reluctant readers." SLJ

Force out; Tim Green. 1st ed. Harper 2013 288 p. (hardcover) $16.99

Grades: 4 5 6   **Fic**
  1. Baseball -- Fiction 2. Friendship -- Fiction 3. Best friends -- Fiction 4. Competition (Psychology) -- Fiction
  ISBN 0062089595; 9780062089595
                LC 2012026752
In this juvenile novel, by Tim Green, "Joey and Zach have always been best friends. They're also two of the best baseball players in their league, and shoo-ins for the all-star team at the end of the season. Their dream is to play together on the Center State select team, and they will do anything to help each other get there. . . . Then the unthinkable happens: The boys learn there's only one open spot on the select team." (Publisher's note)

"Though Green is no stylist, he does a better job of avoiding the sports fantasy and sticking to real life than usual. There's plenty of play-by-play for those who want the sports to be the focus, but the interactions off the field are never shortchanged. . . . A slice of life for middle school readers who know that their sport is a microcosm of the larger world." Kirkus

Greenwald, Lisa

★ **My** life in pink and green. Amulet Books 2010 288 p. $16.95

Grades: 4 5 6 7 **Fic**

1. Cosmetics -- Fiction 2. Environmental protection -- Fiction 3. Mother-daughter relationship -- Fiction
ISBN 0810983524; 0810989840 pa; 9780810983526; 9780810989849

LC 2008025577

When the family's drugstore is failing, seventh-grader Lucy uses her problem solving talents to come up with solution that might resuscitate the business, along with helping the environment.

"Greenwald deftly blends eco-facts and makeup tips, friendship dynamics, and spot-on middle-school politics into a warm, uplifting story." Booklist

Sweet treats, secret crushes. Amulet Books 2010 291p $16.95

Grades: 5 6 7 8 **Fic**

1. Friendship -- Fiction 2. Valentine's Day -- Fiction 3. Apartment houses -- Fiction
ISBN 978-0-8109-8990-0; 0-8109-8990-5

LC 2009052208

When a snowstorm keeps thirteen-year-old best friends Olivia, Kate, and Georgia inside their Brooklyn, New York, apartment building on Valentine's Day, they connect with their neighbors by distributing homemade fortune cookies and uncover one another's secrets along the way.

"An affectionate, insightful ode to friendship. An enjoyable, sure-to-be popular read." Booklist

Greenwald, Tommy

★ **Charlie** Joe Jackson's guide to not reading. Roaring Brook Press 2011 220p il $14.99

Grades: 4 5 6 7 **Fic**

1. School stories 2. Books and reading -- Fiction
ISBN 978-1-59643-691-6; 1-59643-691-3

LC 2010-24079

Middle schooler Charlie Joe is proud of his success at avoiding reading, but eventually his schemes go too far.

"With its subversive humor and contemporary details drawn straight from kids' worlds, this clever title should attract a wide following." Booklist

Charlie Joe Jackson's guide to summer vacation; by Tommy Greenwald ; illustrated by J. P. Coovert. 1st ed. Roaring Brook Press 2013 231 p. ill. (hardcover) $14.99

Grades: 4 5 6 7 **Fic**

1. Camps -- Fiction 2. Humorous stories 3. Interpersonal relations -- Fiction
ISBN 159643757X; 9781596437579; 9781596438804

LC 2012034249

In this graphic novel by Tommy Greenwald "Charlie Joe Jackson finds himself in a terrible dream he can't wake up from: Camp Rituhbukkee . . . a place filled with grammar workshops, Read-a-Ramas, and kids who actually like reading. But Charlie Joe is determined to convince the entire camp to hate reading and writing—one genius at a time. Tommy Greenwald's 'Charlie Joe Jackson's Guide to Sum-

mer Vacation' is another . . . installment in the life of a reluctant reader." (Publisher's note)

Griffin, Adele

The **Julian** game. G.P. Putnam's Sons 2010 200p $16.99

Grades: 8 9 10 11 12 **Fic**

1. School stories 2. Bullies -- Fiction
ISBN 978-0-399-25460-4; 0-399-25460-9

LC 2010-2281

In an effort to improve her social status, a new scholarship student at an exclusive girls' school uses a fake online profile to help a popular girl get back at her ex-boyfriend, but the consequences are difficult to handle.

This is a "perceptive novel. . . . Canny use of details makes Griffin's characters fully realized and believable. . . . Strong pacing and a sympathetic protagonist ought to keep readers hooked." Publ Wkly

Where I want to be. G.P. Putnam's Sons 2005 150p pa $6.99

Grades: 7 8 9 10 **Fic**

1. Death -- Fiction 2. Sisters -- Fiction 3. Mental illness -- Fiction
ISBN 0-399-23783-6; 0-14-240948-0 pa

LC 2004-1887

Two teenaged sisters, separated by death but still connected, work through their feelings of loss over the closeness they shared as children that was later destroyed by one's mental illness, and finally make peace with each other

"Thoughtful, unique, and ultimately life-affirming, this is a fascinating take on the literary device of a main character speaking after death." SLJ

Griffin, Claire J.

Nowhere to run; Claire J. Griffin. 1st ed. Namelos llc 2013 118 p. (hardcover) $18.95

Grades: 7 8 9 10 **Fic**

1. School stories 2. Juvenile delinquency -- Fiction
ISBN 1608981444; 9781608981441; 9781608981458

LC 2012951212

In this novel, by Claire J. Griffin, "Calvin has Deej--and a coach who thinks Calvin can win the championship in the 100-meter dash, a little brother who looks up to him, a boss who trusts him with the keys to the car shop, and Momma, who made him promise to stay in school. And then there's Junior, the girlfriend of Calvin's dreams. . . . But when Calvin and Deej get suspended from school on a trumped-up charge, things start to fall apart." (Publisher's note)

Griffin, Paul

Ten Mile River. Dial Books 2008 188p $16.99

Grades: 8 9 10 11 12 **Fic**

1. Homeless persons -- Fiction 2. Runaway teenagers -- Fiction 3. Juvenile delinquency -- Fiction
ISBN 978-0-8037-3284-1; 0-8037-3284-8

LC 2007-047870

Having escaped from juvenile detention centers and foster care, two teenaged boys live on their own in an abandoned shack in a New York City park, making their way by stealing, occasionally working, and trying to keep from being arrested.

"The language is tough but convincing, the setting authentic, the characters memorable and their struggles played out with a complexity that respects the audience's intelligence." Publ Wkly

Griffin, Peni R.

The **ghost** sitter. Dutton Children's Bks. 2001 131p $14.99; pa $5.99

Grades: 4 5 6 7   **Fic**

1. Ghost stories

ISBN 0-525-46676-2; 0-14-230216-3 pa

LC 00-65859

When she realizes that her new house is haunted by the ghost of a ten-year-old girl who used to live there, Charlotte tries to help her find peace

"Griffin's book has several strong appeals: new best friends solving a mystery together, a just-scary-enough ghost girl, and a deathless bond between sisters that provides the book with its resoundingly satisfying conclusion and bang-up last sentence." Horn Book

Grimes, Nikki

★ **Bronx** masquerade. Dial Bks. 2002 167p $16.99; pa $5.99

Grades: 7 8 9 10   **Fic**

1. School stories 2. African Americans -- Fiction

ISBN 0-8037-2569-8; 0-14-250189-1 pa

LC 00-31701

While studying the Harlem Renaissance, students at a Bronx high school read aloud poems they've written, revealing their innermost thoughts and fears to their formerly clueless classmates

"Funny and painful, awkward and abstract, the poems talk about race, abuse, parental love, neglect, death, and body image. . . . Readers will enjoy the lively, smart voices that talk bravely about real issues and secret fears. A fantastic choice for readers' theater." Booklist

Dark sons. Jump at the Sun 2005 216p $15.99

Grades: 6 7 8 9 10   **Fic**

1. Novels in verse 2. Stepfamilies -- Fiction 3. Father-son relationship -- Fiction

ISBN 0-7868-1888-3

LC 2004-54208

Alternating poems compare and contrast the conflicted feelings of Ishmael, son of the Biblical patriarch Abraham, and Sam, a teenager in New York City, as they try to come to terms with being abandoned by their fathers and with the love they feel for their younger stepbrothers.

"The simple words eloquently reveal what it's like to miss someone. . . . but even more moving is the struggle to forgive and the affection each boy feels for the baby that displaces him. The elemental connections and the hope . . . will speak to a wide audience." Booklist

★ **Jazmin's** notebook. Dial Bks. 1998 102p $15.99

Grades: 6 7 8 9   **Fic**

1. Authorship -- Fiction 2. African Americans -- Fiction

ISBN 0-8037-2224-9

LC 97-5850

A Coretta Scott King honor book for text, 1999

Jazmin, an Afro-American fourteen-year-old who lives with her older sister in a small Harlem apartment in the 1960s, finds strength in writing poetry and keeping a record of the events in her sometimes difficult life

"An articulate, admirable heroine, Jazmin leaps over life's hurdles with agility and integrity." Publ Wkly

★ **Planet** Middle School. Bloomsbury Childrens 2011 154p $15.99

Grades: 4 5 6 7   **Fic**

1. School stories 2. Novels in verse 3. Basketball -- Fiction 4. Friendship -- Fiction 5. Family life -- Fiction

ISBN 978-1-59990-284-5; 1-59990-284-2

LC 2010050744

A series of poems describes all the baffling changes at home and at school in twelve-year-old Joylin's transition from tomboy basketball player to not-quite-girly girl.

"In freeflowing free-verse poems, multi–awardwinning author and poet Grimes . . . explores the riot of hormones and expected gender roles that can make negotiating the preteen years such a challenge. . . . A work that should help adolescent readers find the courage and humor to grow into the individuals they already are." Kirkus

A **girl** named Mister. Zondervan 2010 223p $15.99

Grades: 8 9 10 11   **Fic**

1. Novels in verse 2. Pregnancy -- Fiction 3. Christian life -- Fiction 4. African Americans -- Fiction

ISBN 978-0-310-72078-2; 0-310-72078-8

LC 2010-10830

A pregnant teenager finds support and forgiveness from God through a book of poetry presented from the Virgin Mary's perspective.

"Writing in lovely prose with lyrical, forthright language that avoids over-moralizing while driving home the big issues of teen pregnancy, award-winning Nikki Grimes just may help a few young women make different choices. At the same time, she effectively makes the case for parents and schools to continue to educate, educate, educate." Voice Youth Advocates

The **road** to Paris. G. P. Putnam's Sons 2006 153p $15.99; pa $6.99

Grades: 4 5 6 7   **Fic**

1. Siblings -- Fiction 2. Foster home care -- Fiction 3. Racially mixed people -- Fiction

ISBN 0-399-24537-5; 978-0-399-24537-4; 978-0-14-241082-0 pa; 0-14-241082-9 pa

LC 2005-28920

Inconsolable at being separated from her older brother, eight-year-old Paris is apprehensive about her new foster family but just as she learns to trust them, she faces a life-changing decision.

"In clear, short chapters, Grimes tells a beautiful story of family, friendship, and faith from the viewpoint of a child in search of home in a harsh world." Booklist

Grisham, John, 1955-

Theodore Boone: kid lawyer. Dutton Children's Books 2010 263p $16.99

Grades: 4 5 6 7   **Fic**
1. Mystery fiction 2. Lawyers -- Fiction 3. Young adult
literature -- Works 4. Children's literature -- Works --
Grades two through six
ISBN 0-525-42384-2; 978-0-525-42384-3

With two attorneys for parents, thirteen-year-old Theodore Boone knows more about the law than most lawyers do.
But when a high profile murder trial comes to his small town
and Theo gets pulled into it, it's up to this amateur attorney
to save the day.

"Grisham serves up a dandy legal adventure that moves
along quickly. Without intruding on the story's trajectory, he
gives plenty of background about the legal process and explores various ethical questions." Horn Book Guide

Another title about Theodore Boone is:
Theodore Boone: the abduction (2011)
Theodore Boone: The accused (2012)

Grossman, Nancy

A **world** away; Nancy Grossman. Hyperion
2012 394 p. $16.99
Grades: 7 8 9 10   **Fic**
1. Bildungsromans 2. Amish -- Fiction 3. Adolescence
-- Fiction 4. Aunts -- Fiction 5. Self-realization --
Fiction
ISBN 1423151534; 9781423151531
                                    LC 2011032890

This book is the story of 16-year-old Eliza, who "feels
trapped by the conservative traditions of her Amish community. During her 'rumspringa,' a time when Amish teenagers
are allowed to 'step out of the plain world,' she" works as
"a nanny . . . . Eliza is thrilled with her new contemporary
wardrobe and the modern conveniences available to her, but
she didn't anticipate falling in love with a neighbor . . . or
discovering secrets that will significantly change her view of
her family." (Publishers Weekly)

Guibord, Maurissa

★ **Warped**. Delacorte Press 2011 339p $16.99;
lib bdg $19.99
Grades: 7 8 9 10   **Fic**
1. Magic -- Fiction 2. Tapestry -- Fiction 3. Time
travel -- Fiction
ISBN 0-385-73891-9; 0-385-90758-3 lib bdg; 978-0-
385-73891-0; 978-0-385-90758-3 lib bdg
                                    LC 2009-53654

When seventeen-year-old Tessa Brody comes into possession of an ancient unicorn tapestry, she is thrust into sixteenth-century England, where her life is intertwined with
that of a handsome nobleman.

"This has it all—fantasy, romance, witchcraft, life-
threatening situations, detective work, chase scenes, and a
smattering of violence. Imaginative and compelling, it's impossible to put down." SLJ

Gulledge, Laura Lee

Will & whit; Laura Lee Gulledge. Abrams Book
2013 192 p. ill. (paperback) $12.95
Grades: 7 8 9 10   **Fic**
1. Grief -- Graphic novels 2. Fear of the dark -- Graphic
novels
ISBN 1419705466; 9781419705465
                                    LC 2012955192

In this graphic novel, by Laura Lee Gulledge, "Wilhelmina 'Will' Huxstep is a creative soul struggling to come
to terms with a family tragedy. She crafts whimsical lamps,
in part to deal with her fear of the dark. . . . She longs for
unplugged adventures with her fellow creative friends, Autumn, Noel, and Reese. Little does she know that she will
get her wish in the form of an arts carnival and a blackout
. . . which forces Will to face her fear of darkness." (Publisher's note)

Gurtler, Janet

I'm not her. Sourcebooks Fire 2011 288p pa
$9.99
Grades: 7 8 9 10   **Fic**
1. Cancer -- Fiction 2. Sisters -- Fiction 3. Identity
(Psychology) -- Fiction
ISBN 978-1-4022-5636-3; 1-4022-5636-1

Brainy Tess Smith is the younger sibling of the beautiful,
popular, volleyball-scholarship-bound Kristina. When Kristina is diagnosed with bone cancer, it drastically changes
both sisters' lives.

"This quick and heartbreaking read realistically shows
how one person's illness affects an entire community." SLJ

Gutman, Dan

Mission unstoppable. Harper 2011 293p (The
genius files) $16.99; lib bdg $17.89
Grades: 5 6 7 8   **Fic**
1. Adventure fiction 2. Twins -- Fiction 3. Genius --
Fiction 4. Siblings -- Fiction 5. Family life -- Fiction
ISBN 0-06-182764-9; 0-06-182765-7 lib bdg; 978-0-
06-182764-8; 978-0-06-182765-5 lib bdg
                                    LC 2010-09390

On a cross-country vacation with their parents, twins
Coke and Pepsi, soon to be thirteen, fend off strange assassins as they try to come to terms with their being part
of a top-secret government organization known as The
Genius Files.

"Gutman's novel offers a quirky look at Americana that
will engage curious minds. . . . Those looking for a fun and
suspenseful read . . . will not be disappointed." Booklist

Another title in this series is:
Never say genius (2012)

Shoeless Joe & me; a baseball card adventure.
HarperCollins Pubs. 2002 163p (Baseball card adventures) hardcover o.p. lib bdg $17.89; pa $5.99
Grades: 4 5 6 7   **Fic**
1. Baseball players 2. Baseball -- Fiction
ISBN 0-06-029253-9; 0-06-029254-7 lib bdg; 0-06-
447259-0 pa
                                    LC 2001-24638

Joe Stoshack travels back to 1919, where he meets Shoeless Joe Jackson and tries to prevent the fixing of the World
Series in which Jackson was wrongly implicated

"Shoeless Joe is compelling, and Joe's adventures are
exciting." Voice Youth Advocates

Other titles in the Baseball card adventures series are:
Abner & me (2005)

Babe & me (2000)
Honus & me (1997)
Jackie & me (1999)
Jim & me (2008)
Mickey & me (2003)
Ray & me (2009)
Roberto & me (2010)
Satch & me (2006)

The **million** dollar shot. Hyperion Bks. for Children 1997 114p hardcover o.p. pa $5.99
Grades: 4 5 6 7   **Fic**
   1. Contests -- Fiction 2. Basketball -- Fiction
   ISBN 0-7868-2275-9; 1-4231-0084-0 pa
                               LC 97-6461
Eleven-year-old Eddie gets a chance to win a million dollars by sinking a foul shot at the National Basketball Association finals
This "will appeal to both sports readers and general audiences. Gutman's subtle humor, exciting sports action, and excruciating suspense make this title an outstanding choice for reluctant readers." SLJ

Gwaltney, Doris
  Homefront. Simon & Schuster Books for Young Readers 2006 310p $16.99; pa $6.99
Grades: 5 6 7 8   **Fic**
   1. Family life -- Fiction 2. World War, 1939-1945 -- Fiction
   ISBN 0-689-86842-1; 1-4169-9572-2 pa
                            LC 2006-283492
"As Margaret Ann Motley looks forward to seventh grade, the only changes she sees on the horizon are her sister's leaving for college and, immediately afterwards, moving . . . into her sister's old room. With the U.S. on the brink of World War II, though, greater changes are in store. . . . Gwaltney provides vivid character portrayals. . . . Well grounded in the Tidewater area of Virginia, the novel's social context is made real." Booklist

Haber, Melissa Glenn
  Dear Anjali. Aladdin 2010 282p $16.99
Grades: 5 6 7 8   **Fic**
   1. Letters -- Fiction 2. Friendship -- Fiction 3. Bereavement -- Fiction
   ISBN 978-1-4169-9599-9; 1-4169-9599-4
When her best friend dies at the age of thirteen, Meredith writes letters to her as she tries to endure her grief and other confusing emotions.
"Haber skillfully handles the child's heartache, her loneliness, and the conflicting desires. . . . By placing the story between the keys of Meredith's dad's old typewriter, the author gives the narrative a believable realism. . . . The realistic, not-too-tidy ending brings truth to this novel, underscoring that life is complicated." SLJ

Haddix, Margaret Peterson
  ★ **Among** the hidden. Simon & Schuster Bks. for Young Readers 1998 153p $16.95; pa $5.99

Grades: 5 6 7 8   **Fic**
   1. Science fiction
   ISBN 0-689-81700-2; 0-689-82475-0 pa
                            LC 97-33052
In a future where the Population Police enforce the law limiting a family to only two children, Luke has lived all his twelve years in isolation and fear on his family's farm, until another 'third' convinces him that the government is wrong
"The fully realized setting, honest characters, and fast paced plot combine for a suspenseful tale." ALAN
Other titles in this series are:
Among the Barons (2003)
Among the betrayed (2002)
Among the brave (2004)
Among the enemy (2005)
Among the free (2006)
Among the impostors (2001)

  ★ **Double** identity. Simon & Schuster Books for Young Readers 2005 218p $15.95
Grades: 5 6 7 8   **Fic**
   1. Science fiction 2. Cloning -- Fiction
   ISBN 0-689-87374-3
                           LC 2004-13448
Thirteen-year-old Bethany's parents have always been overprotective, but when they suddenly drop out of sight with no explanation, leaving her with an aunt she never knew existed, Bethany uncovers shocking secrets that make her question everything she thought she knew about herself and her family.
This is a "suspenseful sf novel guaranteed to keep readers riveted." Booklist

  ★ **Found**. Simon & Schuster Books for Young Readers 2008 314p (The missing) $15.99; pa $6.99
Grades: 5 6 7 8 9   **Fic**
   1. Science fiction 2. Adoption -- Fiction
   ISBN 978-1-4169-5417-0; 1-4169-5417-1; 978-1-4169-5421-7 pa; 1-4169-5421-X pa
                           LC 2007-23614
When thirteen-year-olds Jonah and Chip, who are both adopted, learn they were discovered on a plane that appeared out of nowhere, full of babies with no adults on board, they realize that they have uncovered a mystery involving time travel and two opposing forces, each trying to repair the fabric of time.
This is "a tantalizing opener to a new series. . . . Readers will be hard-pressed to wait for the next installment." Publ Wkly
Other titles in this series are:
Sent (2009)
Sabotaged (2010)
Torn (2011)
Caught (2012)

  Just Ella. Simon & Schuster Bks. for Young Readers 1999 185p hardcover o.p. pa $5.99
Grades: 7 8 9 10   **Fic**
   1. Sex role -- Fiction 2. Princesses -- Fiction
   ISBN 0-689-82186-7; 0-689-83128-5 pa
                            LC 98-8384

In this continuation of the Cinderella story, fifteen-year-old Ella finds that accepting Prince Charming's proposal ensnares her in a suffocating tangle of palace rules and royal etiquette, so she plots to escape

"In lively prose, with well-developed characters, creative plot twists, wit, and drama, Haddix transforms the Cinderella tale into an insightful coming-of-age story." Booklist

Leaving Fishers. Simon & Schuster Bks. for Young Readers 1997 211p hardcover o.p. pa $5.99
Grades: 7 8 9 10 **Fic**
  1. Cults -- Fiction
  ISBN 0-689-81125-X; 0-689-86793-X pa
                 LC 96-47857
After joining her new friends in the religious group called Fishers of Men, Dorry finds herself immersed in a cult from which she must struggle to extricate herself

"The novel does a credible job of showing the effect of a cult on a vulnerable person, without disavowing strong religious beliefs." Child Book Rev Serv

★ **Uprising**. Simon & Schuster Books for Young Readers 2007 346p $16.99; pa $7.99
Grades: 6 7 8 9 10 **Fic**
  1. Fires -- Fiction 2. Strikes -- Fiction
  ISBN 978-1-4169-1171-5; 1-4169-1171-5; 978-1-4169-1172-2 pa; 1-4169-1172-3 pa
                 LC 2006-34870
In 1927, at the urging of twenty-one-year-old Harriet, Mrs. Livingston reluctantly recalls her experiences at the Triangle Shirtwaist factory, including miserable working conditions that led to a strike, then the fire that took the lives of her two best friends, when Harriet, the boss's daughter, was only five years old. Includes historical notes.

"This deftly crafted historical novel unfolds dramatically with an absorbing story and well-drawn characters who readily evoke empathy and compassion." SLJ

The **always** war. Simon & Schuster Books for Young Readers 2011 197p $16.99
Grades: 7 8 9 10 **Fic**
  1. War stories 2. Science fiction 3. Computers -- Fiction 4. Heroes and heroines -- Fiction 5. Post-traumatic stress disorder -- Fiction
  ISBN 978-1-4169-9526-5; 1-4169-9526-9
                 LC 2010033344
In a war-torn future United States, fifteen-year-old Tessa, her childhood friend Gideon, now a traumatized military hero, and Dek, a streetwise orphan, enter enemy territory and discover the shocking truth about a war that began more than seventy-five years earlier.

"The short chapters with cliff-hanger endings and the action-packed plot make this book and excellent choice for reluctant readers." SLJ

Hagerup, Klaus
  Markus and the girls; translated by Tara Chace. Front Street 2009 208p $17.95
Grades: 6 7 8 9 **Fic**
  1. School stories 2. Love -- Fiction
  ISBN 978-1-59078-520-1; 1-59078-520-7
                 LC 2007048850

Only two months into his first year of junior high school, Markus has already fallen in love with all of the girls in his class.

"Hagerup's romp of Shakespearean comedic complexity is balanced by a healthy dose of slapstick." Horn Book Guide

Hahn, Mary Downing, 1937-
  ★ **Hear** the wind blow. Clarion Bks. 2003 212p $15
Grades: 5 6 7 8 **Fic**
  1. Siblings -- Fiction
  ISBN 0-618-18190-3
                 LC 2002-15977
With their mother dead and their home burned, a thirteen-year-old boy and his little sister set out across Virginia in search of relatives during the final days of the Civil War

The author "gives readers an entertaining and thought-provoking combination: a strong adventure inextricably bound to a specific time and place, but one that resonates with universal themes." Horn Book

Promises to the dead. Clarion Bks. 2000 202p hardcover o.p. pa $5.99
Grades: 5 6 7 8 **Fic**
  1. Slavery -- Fiction
  ISBN 0-395-96394-X; 0-547-25838-0 pa
                 LC 99-48525
Twelve-year-old Jesse leaves his home on Maryland's Eastern Shore to help a young runaway slave find a safe haven in the early days of the Civil War

"Hahn skillfully blends the language and customs of the Civil War era with an exciting plot." Voice Youth Advocates

★ **Stepping** on the cracks. Clarion Bks. 1991 216p $16; pa $6.99
Grades: 5 6 7 8 **Fic**
  1. World War, 1939-1945 -- Fiction
  ISBN 0-395-58507-4; 0-547-07660-6 pa
                 LC 91-7706
In 1944, while her brother is overseas fighting in World War II, eleven-year-old Margaret gets a new view of the school bully Gordy when she finds him hiding his own brother, an army deserter, and decides to help him

"Well-drawn characters and a satisfying plot. . . . There is plenty of action and page-turning suspense to please those who want a quick read, but there is much to ponder and reflect on as well." SLJ

★ **Wait** till Helen comes; a ghost story. Clarion Bks. 1986 184p $15; pa $5.95; pa $6.99
Grades: 4 5 6 **Fic**
  1. Ghost stories 2. Stepchildren -- Fiction
  ISBN 0-89919-453-2; 0-547-02864-4 pa; 9780380704422 pa
                 LC 86-2648
"Molly, the 12-year-old narrator, and her brother Michael dislike their bratty 5-year-old stepsister Heather and resent the family move to an isolated converted church in the country. The adjourning graveyard frightens Molly, but Heather seems drawn to it. Molly discovers that the ghost of a child (Helen) who died in a fire a century ago wants to lure Heather to her doom. Molly determines to save her

stepsister. In so doing, she learns that Heather's strange behavior stems from her feelings of guilt at having accidentally caused her mother's death by playing near a stove and starting a fire. Eventually, Molly wrests Heather from Helen's arms as the ghost attempts to drown them. The girls discover the skeletons of Helen's parents, and their burial finally puts to rest Helen's spirit. . . . Grades four to seven." (SLJ)

"Intertwined with the ghost story is the question of Molly's moral imperative to save a child she truly dislikes. Though the emotional turnaround may be a bit quick for some, this still scores as a first-rate thriller." Booklist

★ The **ghost** of Crutchfield Hall. Clarion Books 2010 153p $17

Grades: 5 6 7 8   **Fic**
1. Ghost stories 2. Cousins -- Fiction 3. Orphans -- Fiction
ISBN 978-0-547-38560-0; 0-547-38560-9

In the nineteenth century, ten-year-old Florence Crutchfield leaves a London orphanage to live with her great-uncle, great-aunt, and sickly cousin James, but she soon realizes the home has another resident, who means to do her and James harm.

"A deliciously spine-tingling tale that even the most reluctant readers will enjoy." SLJ

Mister Death's blue-eyed girls; Mary Downing Hahn. Clarion Books 2012 330 p. $16.99

Grades: 8 9 10 11 12   **Fic**
1. Mystery fiction 2. Historical fiction 3. Homicide -- Fiction 4. Grief -- Fiction 5. Murder -- Fiction 6. Coming of age -- Fiction
ISBN 0547760620; 9780547760629
        LC 2011025950

In this work of historical fiction, "[t]he high-school year is almost over, there's a party in the park and Mister Death will soon be there, rifle in hand. . . . Two girls, Cheryl and Bobbi Jo, never make it to school the next day, their bloody bodies found in the park where they were shot. [Mary Downing] Hahn's . . . story traces the effects of a crime on everyone involved, including Buddy Novak, accused of a crime he didn't commit." (Kirkus Reviews)

Haines, Kathryn Miller
★ The **girl** is murder. Roaring Brook Press 2011 352p $16.99

Grades: 7 8 9 10   **Fic**
1. Mystery fiction 2. Social classes -- Fiction 3. Missing persons -- Fiction 4. Father-daughter relationship -- Fiction
ISBN 978-1-59643-609-1; 1-59643-609-3
        LC 2010-32935

In 1942 New York City, fifteen-year-old Iris grieves for her mother who committed suicide, and secretly helps her father with his detective business since he, having lost a leg at Pearl Harbor, struggles to make ends meet.

This is "a smart offering that gives both mysteries and historical fiction a good name. . . . The mystery is solid, but what makes this such a standout is the cast. . . . The characters, young and old, leap off the pages." Booklist

The **girl** is trouble; Kathryn Miller Haines. Roaring Brook Press 2012 336p. $17.99

Grades: 6 7 8   **Fic**
1. Mystery fiction 2. Historical fiction 3. Women detectives -- Fiction
ISBN 9781596436107
        LC 2011031806

This book is set in "the Fall of 1942 and Iris's world is rapidly changing. Her Pop is back from the war with a missing leg, limiting his ability to do the physically grueling part of his detective work. Iris is dying to help, especially when she discovers that one of Pop's cases involves a boy at her school. Now, instead of sitting at home watching Deanna Durbin movies, Iris is sneaking out of the house, double crossing her friends, and dancing at the Savoy till all hours of the night. There's certainly never a dull moment in the private eye business." (Publisher's note)

Halam, Ann
Snakehead. Wendy Lamb Books 2008 289p il map $16.99; lib bdg $19.99

Grades: 6 7 8 9 10   **Fic**
1. Gods and goddesses -- Fiction 2. Classical mythology -- Fiction 3. Medusa (Greek mythology) -- Fiction 4. Perseus (Greek mythology) -- Fiction
ISBN 978-0-375-84108-8; 978-0-375-94108-5 lib bdg
        LC 2007-28318

Compelled by his father Zeus to accept the evil king Polydectes's challenge to bring the head of the monstrous Medusa to the Aegean island of Serifos, Perseus, although questioning the gods' interference in human lives, sets out, accompanied by his beloved Andromeda, a princess with her own harsh destiny to fulfill.

"Mythology buffs will appreciate the plethora of classical figures, while periodic references to contemporary culture (e.g., a band of rich, rowdy teens are dubbed the Yacht Club kids) and occasional slang drive the story home for the target audience without sacrificing its heroic dimensions." Publ Wkly

Hale, Marian
The **goodbye** season. Henry Holt and Co. 2009 271p $16.99

Grades: 7 8 9 10   **Fic**
1. Bereavement -- Fiction 2. Family life -- Fiction 3. Household employees -- Fiction 4. Mother-daughter relationship -- Fiction
ISBN 978-0-8050-8855-7; 0-8050-8855-5
        LC 2008-50275

In Canton, Texas, seventeen-year-old Mercy's dreams of a different life than her mother's are postponed by harsh circumstances, including the influenza epidemic of 1918-19, which forces her into doing domestic work for a loving, if troubled, family.

This is a "compelling, tautly written novel." SLJ

The **truth** about sparrows. Henry Holt & Co. 2004 260p $16.95; pa $6.99

Grades: 5 6 7 8   **Fic**
1. Moving -- Fiction 2. Friendship -- Fiction 3. Great

Depression, 1929-1939 -- Fiction
ISBN 0-8050-7584-4; 0-312-37133-0 pa
LC 2003-56981

Twelve-year-old Sadie promises that she will always be Wilma's best friend when their families leave drought-stricken Missouri in 1933, but once in Texas, Sadie learns that she must try to make a new home—and new friends, too

"Rich with social history, this first novel is informative, enjoyable, and evocative." SLJ

Hale, Shannon

★ **Book** of a thousand days; illustrations by James Noel Smith. Bloomsbury Children's Books 2007 305p il $17.95

Grades: 7 8 9 10   Fic

1. Love stories 2. Fantasy fiction
ISBN 978-1-59990-051-3; 1-59990-051-3
LC 2006-36999

Fifteen-year-old Dashti, sworn to obey her sixteen-year-old mistress, the Lady Saren, shares Saren's years of punishment locked in a tower, then brings her safely to the lands of her true love, where both must hide who they are as they work as kitchen maids.

This is a "captivating fantasy filled with romance, magic, and strong female characters." Booklist

The **Goose** girl. Bloomsbury Children's Books 2003 383p $17.95; pa $8.99

Grades: 6 7 8 9   Fic

1. Fairy tales 2. Princesses -- Fiction
ISBN 1-58234-843-X; 1-58234-990-8 pa
LC 2002-28336

On her way to marry a prince she's never met, Princess Anidori is betrayed by her guards and her lady-in-waiting and must become a goose girl to survive until she can reveal her true identity and reclaim the crown that is rightfully hers

"A fine adventure tale full of danger, suspense, surprising twists, and a satisfying conclusion." Booklist

Other titles in this series are:
Enna burning (2004)
River secrets (2006)
Forest born (2009)

Princess Academy; palace of stone. Shannon Hale. Bloomsbury 2012 321 p. (hardcover) $16.99

Grades: 6 7 8 9   Fic

1. Schools -- Fiction 2. Sex role -- Fiction 3. Mountains -- Fiction 4. Telepathy -- Fiction 5. Self-confidence -- Fiction 6. Kings, queens, rulers, etc. -- Fiction
ISBN 1599908735; 9781599908731
LC 2012003875

A Newbery Medal honor book, 2006

While attending a strict academy for potential princesses with the other girls from her mountain village, fourteen-year-old Miri discovers unexpected talents and connections to her homeland.

"Hale weaves an intricate, multilayered story about families, relationships, education, and the place we call home." SLJ

Other titles in this series are:
Palace of Stone

Hall, C. Aubrey

Crystal bones. Marshall Cavendish Children's Books 2011 313p (The Faelin chronicles) $17.99

Grades: 7 8 9 10   Fic

1. Fantasy fiction 2. Fairies -- Fiction 3. Orphans -- Fiction
ISBN 0-7614-5828-X; 978-0-7614-5828-9
LC 2010015435

Suddenly and violently orphaned, Diello and his sister Cynthe learn secrets about their heritage when their parents' goblin enemies come searching for a powerful sword that has been kept hidden for many years.

"Though these are somewhat serious, heavy issues, the book has an underlying innocence that makes it amenable for a wide range of readers." Booklist

Hall, Teri

Away. Dial Books 2011 234 p. $16.99

Grades: 5 6 7 8   Fic

1. Science fiction 2. Resistance to government -- Fiction
ISBN 9780803735026; 0803735022
LC 2011001163

After helping heal Malgam, Rachel learns that her father is still living in the devastated territory of Away, captured by members of another clan who are planning to use him to make a deal with the government on the other side of the Line, and she joins the rescue party that must risk much to save him.

"This worthy sequel . . . continues to build a dystopian world rich with suspense and moral choices." Kirkus

The **Line.** Dial Books 2010 219p $16.99

Grades: 5 6 7 8   Fic

1. Science fiction
ISBN 978-0-8037-3466-1; 0-8037-3466-2
LC 2009-12301

Rachel thinks that she and her mother are safe working for Ms. Moore at her estate close to The Line, an invisible border of the Unified States, but when Rachel has an opportunity to Cross into the forbidden zone, she is both frightened and intrigued

This "sets readers up for a series about another world that might have come from situations too close to our own." Libr Media Connect

Halpern, Julie

Get well soon. Feiwel & Friends 2007 193p $16.95; pa $8.99

Grades: 7 8 9 10   Fic

1. Mental illness -- Fiction 2. Psychiatric hospitals -- Fiction
ISBN 0-312-36795-3; 978-0-312-36795-4; 0-312-58148-3 pa; 978-0-312-58148-0 pa
LC 2006-32358

When her parents confine her to a mental hospital, Anna, an overweight teenage girl who suffers from panic attacks, describes her experiences in a series of letters to a friend.

"Halpern creates a narrative that reflects the changes in Anna with each passing day that includes self-reflection and a good dose of humor." Voice Youth Advocates

Have a nice day; Julie Halpern. Feiwel and Friends 2012 325 p. $16.99

Grades: 7 8 9 10 11 12   **Fic**

1. Mental illness -- Fiction

ISBN 0312606605; 9780312606602

In author Julie Halpern's book, "Anna Bloom has just come home from a three-week stay in a mental hospital. She feels...okay. It's time to get back to some sort of normal life, whatever that means. She has to go back to school, where teachers and friends are dying to know what happened to her, but are too afraid to ask. And Anna is dying to know what's going on back at the hospital with her crush, Justin, but is too afraid to ask. Meanwhile, Anna's parents aren't getting along, and she wonders if she's the cause of her family's troubles." (Publisher's note)

Halpin, Brendan

★ **Shutout**. Farrar, Straus and Giroux 2010 183p $16.99

Grades: 6 7 8 9   **Fic**

1. Soccer -- Fiction 2. Friendship -- Fiction

ISBN 978-0-374-36899-9; 0-374-36899-6

                      LC 2009-32972

Fourteen-year-old Amanda and her best friend Lena start high school looking forward to playing on the varsity soccer team, but when Lena makes varsity and Amanda only makes junior varsity, their long friendship rapidly changes.

"The dialogue is spot-on, and the characters are fully fleshed out. . . . While there is plenty of soccer action for fans of the sport, the book will also appeal to teens looking for a solid friendship story." SLJ

Hamilton, K. R.

In the forests of the night; by Kersten Hamilton. Clarion Books 2011 295p (Goblin wars) $16.99

Grades: 7 8 9 10   **Fic**

1. Zoos -- Fiction 2. Magic -- Fiction 3. Goblins -- Fiction 4. Irish Americans -- Fiction 5. Mythical animals -- Fiction 6. Mentally handicapped children -- Fiction

ISBN 978-0-547-43560-2; 0-547-43560-6

                      LC 2011009846

Teagan, Finn, and Aiden have made it out of Mag Mell alive, but the Dark Man's forces follow them to Chicago, where Tea's goblin cousins cause all sorts of trouble while she is torn between the life she wants and the future she is drawn to as a wild Stormrider, born to reign.

"The straightforwardness of the story and spurts of humor arising from situations and characters will sustain readers' interest and keep them involved. Teagan has a plan for what comes next; fans will have a hard time waiting for her to bring it on." Kirkus

★ **Tyger** tyger; by Kersten Hamilton. Clarion Books 2010 308p (Goblin wars) $17

Grades: 7 8 9 10   **Fic**

1. Fantasy fiction 2. Magic -- Fiction 3. Goblins -- Fiction 4. Irish Americans -- Fiction 5. Mentally handicapped children -- Fiction

ISBN 978-0-547-33008-2; 0-547-33008-1

                      LC 2010-01337

Soon after the mysterious and alluring Finn arrives at her family's home, sixteen-year-old Teagan Wylltson and her disabled brother are drawn into the battle Finn's family has fought since the thirteenth century, when Finn MacCumhaill angered the goblin king.

"Laced with humor, packed with surprises and driven by suspense, the plot grabs readers from the start using the stylistic tactics of the best fantasy writing. Major characters are beautifully drawn, and many of the secondary characters are equally distinct." Kirkus

Hamilton, Kiki

The **faerie** ring. Tor Teen 2011 343p $17.99

Grades: 7 8 9 10   **Fic**

1. Fantasy fiction 2. Fairies -- Fiction 3. Orphans -- Fiction 4. Thieves -- Fiction

ISBN 978-0-7653-2722-2; 0-7653-2722-8

                      LC 2011021577

"In 1871 London, a ragged girl pickpocket steals a ring that enforces a truce between the British Crown and the Faery world, setting off a struggle between the realms. . . . The story keeps suspense high with one crisis after another, until it escalates into a final exciting showdown." Kirkus

Hamilton, Virginia

★ The **house** of Dies Drear; illustrated by Eros Keith. Macmillan 1968 246p il hardcover o.p. pa $5.99

Grades: 5 6 7 8   **Fic**

1. Mystery fiction 2. African Americans -- Fiction

ISBN 0-02-742500-2; 1-4169-1405-6 pa

"The answer to the mystery comes in a startling dramatic dénouement that is pure theater. This is gifted writing; the characterization is unforgettable, the plot imbued with mounting tension." Saturday Rev

★ The **planet** of Junior Brown. Macmillan 1971 210p hardcover o.p. pa $5.99

Grades: 6 7 8 9   **Fic**

1. Friendship -- Fiction 2. African Americans -- Fiction

ISBN 0-689-71721-0; 1-4169-1410-2 pa

A Newbery Medal honor book, 1972

"This is the story of a crucial week in the lives of two black, eighth-grade dropouts who have been spending their time with the school janitor. Each boy is presented as a distinct individual. Jr. is a three-hundred pound musical prodigy as neurotic as his overprotective mother. Buddy has learned to live by his wits in a world of homeless children. Buddy becomes Jr. Brown's protector and says to the other boys, 'We are together because we have to learn to live for each other.'" Read Ladders for Hum Relat. 6th edition

Hamley, Dennis

Without warning; Ellen's story 1914-1918. [by] Dennis Hamley. 1st U.S. ed.; Candlewick Press 2007 326p $17.99

Grades: 6 7 8 9   **Fic**

1. World War, 1914-1918 -- Fiction

ISBN 978-0-7636-3338-7; 0-7636-3338-0

                      LC 2007025248

First published 2006 in the United Kingdom with title: Ellen's people

During World War I, an English teenager leaves the safety of home and begins a journey of self-discovery that takes her close to the front lines to pursue her calling as a nurse.

"This intense narrative dramatically offers insight into the effects of World War I on the English home front. . . . This is a highly readable selection with many well-drawn characters." SLJ

Han, Jenny

Shug; [by] Jenny Han. 1st ed.; Simon & Schuster Books for Young Readers 2006 248p $14.95

Grades: 5 6 7 8   **Fic**

1. School stories 2. Family life -- Fiction
ISBN 978-1-4169-0942-2; 1-4169-0942-7

LC 2005009367

"Tall, freckled, gawky seventh-grader Annemarie Wilcox (whose family calls her Shug) has a beautiful, popular older sister; a gorgeous, alcoholic mother who doesn't fit in their small Georgia town; and a father who's always away on business. She also has a huge crush on Mark, the neighborhood boy who has always been her best friend. . . . Shug's direct, honest narration reveals a wholly believable, endearing, hot-tempered young woman who faces painful truths and survives." Booklist

★ The **summer** I turned pretty. Simon & Schuster Books for Young Readers 2009 276p $16.99

Grades: 7 8 9 10   **Fic**

1. Summer -- Fiction 2. Beaches -- Fiction 3. Vacations -- Fiction 4. Friendship -- Fiction
ISBN 978-1-4169-6823-8; 1-4169-6823-7

LC 2008-27070

Belly spends the summer she turns sixteen at the beach just like every other summer of her life, but this time things are very different.

"Romantic and heartbreakingly real. . . . The novel perfectly blends romance, family drama, and a coming-of-age tale, one that is substantially deeper than most." SLJ

Other titles in this series are:

It's not summer without you (2010)
We'll always have summer (2011)

Handler, Daniel, 1970-

★ **Why** we broke up; art by Maira Kalman. Little, Brown 2012 354p il $19.99

Grades: 8 9 10 11 12   **Fic**

1. Man-woman relationship -- Fiction 2. Letters -- Fiction 3. Dating (Social customs) -- Fiction
ISBN 978-0-316-12725-7

LC 2011009714

Printz Honor Book (2012)

Sixteen-year-old Min Green writes a letter to Ed Slaterton in which she breaks up with him, documenting their relationship and how items in the accompanying box, from bottle caps to a cookbook, foretell the end.

Hannan, Peter

My big mouth; 10 songs I wrote that almost got me killed. Scholastic Press 2011 235p il $16.99

Grades: 6 7 8 9   **Fic**

1. School stories 2. Bullies -- Fiction 3. Rock music

-- Fiction 4. Bands (Music) -- Fiction
ISBN 978-0-545-16210-4; 0-545-16210-6

LC 2010034426

"Hannan's abundant cartoons set the tone for the misadventures of Davis Delaware, the new kid in ninth grade. Davis's attempts to blend in quickly land him on the wrong side of school bully Gerald 'the Butcher' when he forms a band with Gerald's cute girlfriend, Molly, and her dweeby friend, Edwin. . . . Hannan's edgy, exaggerated style suits the humor-driven narrative well. Give this to readers who enjoy light, entertaining realistic fiction." SLJ

Hannigan, Katherine

True (. . . sort of) Greenwillow Books 2011 360p $16.99; lib bdg $17.89

Grades: 4 5 6   **Fic**

1. School stories 2. Siblings -- Fiction 3. Friendship -- Fiction 4. Family life -- Fiction
ISBN 978-0-06-196873-0; 0-06-196873-0; 978-0-06-196874-7 lib bdg; 0-06-196874-9 lib bdg

For most of her eleven years, Delly has been in trouble without knowing why, until her little brother, R. B., and a strange, silent new friend, Ferris, help her find a way to be good—and happy—again.

"Told in carefully crafted language that begs to be read aloud, the story runs the gamut from laugh-out-loud funny to emotionally wrenching." SLJ

Hansen, Joyce

Home is with our family; [illustrated by] E. B. Lewis. Hyperion 2010 272p il (Black pioneers) $16.99

Grades: 4 5 6 7   **Fic**

1. Abolitionists -- Fiction 2. African Americans -- Fiction
ISBN 978-0-7868-5217-8; 0-7868-5217-8

Maria Peterson is looking forward to turning 13. She envisions new adult prestige and responsibility, like attending abolitionist meetings and listening to inspiring speakers like Sojourner Truth. However, she doesn't bank on all the unexpected changes that her 13th year brings.

"The plot flows quickly and has enough action to hold a reader's attention. Teachers can use this book to provide their students with a deeper understanding of the Fugitive Slave Act." Libr Media Connect

One true friend. Clarion Bks. 2001 154p hardcover o.p. pa $6.95

Grades: 4 5 6 7   **Fic**

1. Friendship -- Fiction 2. Foster home care -- Fiction 3. African Americans -- Fiction
ISBN 0-395-84983-7; 0-618-60991-1 pa

LC 2001-28483

Fourteen-year-old orphan Amir, living in Syracuse, exchanges letters with his friend Doris, still living in their old Bronx neighborhood, in which they share their lives and give each other advice on friendship, family, foster care, and making decisions

"Both sad and hopeful, this story dramatizes the struggle for survival, the primal pull of family, and the gift of 'one true friend.'" Booklist

Other titles about Amir and Doris are:

The gift-giver (1980)
Yellow Bird and me (1985)

Hardinge, Frances

★ **Fly** by night. HarperCollinsPublishers 2006
487p hardcover o.p. lib bdg $17.89; pa $7.99
Grades: 5 6 7 8   **Fic**
1. Fantasy fiction
ISBN 978-0-06-087627-2; 0-06-087627-1; 978-0-06-
087629-6 lib bdg; 0-06-087629-8 lib bdg; 978-0-06-
087630-2 pa; 0-06-087630-1 pa
LC 2005-20598
Mosca Mye and her homicidal goose, Saracen, travel to
the city of Mandelion on the heels of smooth-talking con-
man, Eponymous Clent.
"Through rich, colorful language and a sure sense of plot
and pacing, Hardinge has created a distinctly imaginative
world full of engaging characters, robust humor, and true
suspense." SLJ

Fly trap. Harper 2011 584p $16.99
Grades: 5 6 7 8   **Fic**
1. Fantasy fiction
ISBN 978-0-06-088044-6; 0-06-088044-9
LC 2010027755
Adventurous orphan Mosca Mye, her savage goose,
Saracen, and their sometimes-loyal companion, Eponymous
Clent, become embroiled in the intrigues of Toll, a town that
changes entirely as day turns to night.
Crammed with eccentric, Dickensian characters, unex-
pected plot turns, and numerous very niche gods and god-
desses . . . , Hardinge's world is rich enough to fuel two or
three fantasy novels. It's a beautifully written tale, by turns
humorous and heartbreaking and a sheer pleasure to read.
Publ Wkly

★ The **lost** conspiracy. Harper 2009 568p
$16.99; lib bdg $17.89
Grades: 6 7 8 9 10   **Fic**
1. Fantasy fiction 2. Sisters -- Fiction
ISBN 978-0-06-088041-5; 0-06-088041-4; 978-0-06-
088042-2 lib bdg; 0-06-088042-2 lib bdg
LC 2008-45380
Published in the United Kingdom with title:
Gullstruck Island
When a lie is exposed and their tribe turns against them,
Hathin must find a way to save her sister Arilou—once con-
sidered the tribe's oracle—and herself.
"A deeply imaginative story, with nuanced characters,
intricate plotting, and an amazingly original setting. . . .
A perfectly pitched, hopeful ending caps off this standout
adventure." Booklist

Hardy, Janice

The **shifter**. Balzer + Bray 2009 370p (The
Healing Wars) $16.99; pa $7.99
Grades: 5 6 7 8   **Fic**
1. War stories 2. Fantasy fiction 3. Orphans -- Fiction
4. Sisters -- Fiction
ISBN 978-0-06-174704-5; 0-06-174704-1; 978-0-06-
174708-3 pa; 0-06-174708-4 pa
LC 2008-47673

Nya is an orphan struggling for survival in a city crippled
by war. She is also a Taker—with her touch, she can heal
injuries, pulling pain from another person into her own body.
But unlike her sister, Tali, and the other Takers who become
Healers' League apprentices, Nya's skill is flawed: She can't
push that pain into pynvium, the enchanted metal used to
store it. All she can do is shift it into another person
"The ethical dilemmas raised . . . provide thoughtful discussion material and also make the story accessible to more
than just fantasy readers." Booklist
Other titles in this series are:
Blue fire (2010)
Darkfall (2011)

Harland, Richard

Liberator; Richard Harland. 1st ed. Simon &
Schuster Book for Young Readers 2012 487 p. maps
(paperback) $9.99; (hardcover) $17.99
Grades: 6 7 8 9 10   **Fic**
1. Steampunk fiction 2. Revolutions -- Fiction 3.
Social conflict -- Fiction 4. Social classes -- Fiction
ISBN 9781442423343; 1442423331; 9781442423336;
9781442423350
LC 2010050911
This is the "second of [Richard] Harland's steampunk
series." Here, "[a]fter the Filthies revolted, Col Porpentine
and his family were among the few swanks to stay aboard
the juggernaut now called the 'Liberator.' But the new regime has troubles galore: A saboteur stalks the halls, an anti-
Swank zealot joins the Revolutionary Council and people
are disappearing. It's hard for Col to maintain a blossoming
romance with revolutionary Filthy Riff in this atmosphere."
(Kirkus Reviews)

Worldshaker. Simon & Schuster Books for
Young Readers 2010 388p $16.99
Grades: 6 7 8 9 10   **Fic**
1. Fantasy fiction 2. Social classes -- Fiction
ISBN 978-1-4169-9552-4; 1-4169-9552-8
LC 2009-16924
Sixteen-year-old Col Porpentine is being groomed as the
next Commander of Worldshaker, a juggernaut where elite
families live on the upper decks while the Filthies toil below,
but when he meets Riff, a Filthy girl on the run, he discovers
how ignorant he is of his home and its residents.
"Harland's steampunk alternate history is filled with oppression, class struggle, and war, showing their devastation
on a personal level through Col's privileged eyes. . . . The
writing is sharp and the story fast-paced, demonstrating that,
despite his elite status, Col may be just as trapped as any
Filthy." Publ Wkly

Harmel, Kristin

When you wish; [by] Kristin Harmel. 1st ed.;
Delacorte Press 2008 273p $15.99; lib bdg $18.99
Grades: 7 8 9 10   **Fic**
1. Fame -- Fiction 2. Singers -- Fiction 3. Father-
daughter relationship -- Fiction 4. Mother-daughter
relationship -- Fiction
ISBN 978-0-385-73475-2; 0-385-73475-1; 978-0-385-
90474-2 lib bdg; 0-385-90474-6 lib bdg
LC 2007020472

When sixteen-year-old pop singing sensation Star Beck learns that her father, who left when she was three, has been writing to her for six years, she disguises herself, leaves her controlling mother and adoring fans behind, and goes to find him—and, perhaps, a normal life—in St. Petersburg, Florida.

"Harmel has created a character and a story that will have wide appeal. There is enough complexity to hold the interest of a more demanding reader, even while remaining basically an entertaining reading experience." KLIATT

Harness, Cheryl

Just for you to know. HarperCollins 2006 308p $16.99; lib bdg $17.89

Grades: 5 6 7 8 **Fic**

1. Death -- Fiction 2. Family life -- Fiction
ISBN 0-06-078313-3; 0-06-078314-1 lib bdg
LC 2006-281855

In Independence, Missouri, in 1963, twelve-year-old Carmen already has her hands full dealing with a dreamy mother, a sometimes reckless father, and five noisy little brothers, but must find a way to hold onto her own dreams when tragedy strikes.

"Carmen's pain and loneliness are brought to life through her narrative. The writing flows nicely." SLJ

Harper, Suzanne

The **Juliet** club. Greenwillow Books 2008 402p $17.99; lib bdg $18.89

Grades: 8 9 10 11 12 **Fic**

1. Letters -- Fiction
ISBN 978-0-06-136691-8; 0-06-136691-9; 978-0-06-136692-5 lib bdg; 0-06-136692-7 lib bdg
LC 2007-41315

When high school junior Kate wins an essay contest that sends her to Verona, Italy, to study Shakespeare's 'Romeo and Juliet' over the summer, she meets both American and Italian students and learns not just about Shakespeare, but also about star-crossed lovers—and herself.

"An amalgam of familiar Shakespearean plot elements, character names, and devices make up this delightful, light, and romantic read. . . . The chapter titles are each given act and scene designations to keep the structure of a play. Following the formula of a Shakespearean comedy, the novel ends with a grand ball where misunderstandings are resolved and couples are revealed in a magical evening." Voice Youth Advocates

The **secret** life of Sparrow Delaney. Greenwillow Books 2007 364p $16.99; lib bdg $17.89

Grades: 7 8 9 10 **Fic**

1. Family life -- Fiction 2. Spiritualism -- Fiction
ISBN 978-0-06-113158-5; 0-06-113158-X; 978-0-06-113159-2 lib bdg; 0-06-113159-8 lib bdg
LC 2006-41339

In Lily Dale, New York, a community dedicated to the religion of Spiritualism, tenth-grader Sparrow Delaney, the youngest daughter in an eccentric family of psychics, agonizes over whether or not to reveal her special abilities in order to help a friend.

"For all of the imagination the author displays in inventing a spirit world, she shows equal skill in probing the nuances of tender emotions, too." Publ Wkly

Harrington, Karen

Sure signs of crazy; by Karen Harrington. 1st ed. Little Brown & Co 2013 288 p. (hardcover) $17

Grades: 4 5 6 7 8 **Fic**

1. Coming of age -- Fiction 2. Mental illness -- Fiction
3. Family problems -- Fiction
ISBN 0316210587; 9780316210584
LC 2012030683

In this book, "worried that she will grow up to be crazy like her mother or alcoholic like her father, rising seventh-grader Sarah Nelson takes courage from Harper Lee's 'To Kill a Mockingbird,' writing letters to Atticus Finch and discovering her own strengths. . . . She describes the events of the summer she turns 12, gets her period, develops a crush on a neighbor and fellow word lover, and comes to terms with her parents' failings." (Kirkus Reviews)

Harris, Joanne

Runemarks. Alfred A. Knopf 2008 526p map $18.99; lib bdg $21.99

Grades: 7 8 9 10 11 12 **Fic**

1. Fantasy fiction 2. Magic -- Fiction 3. Norse mythology -- Fiction
ISBN 978-0-375-84444-7; 978-0-375-94444-4 lib bdg; 0-375-84444-9; 0-375-94444-3 lib bdg
LC 2007-28928

Maddy Smith, who bears the mysterious mark of a rune on her hand, learns that she is destined to join the gods of Norse mythology and play a role in the fate of the world.

"Harris demonstrates a knack for moving seamlessly between the serious and comic. . . . She creates a glorious and complex world replete with rune-based magic spells, bickering gods, exciting adventures, and difficult moral issues." Publ Wkly

Harris, Lewis

A **taste** for red. Clarion Books 2009 169p $16

Grades: 4 5 6 **Fic**

1. Vampires -- Fiction 2. Friendship -- Fiction 3. Missing children -- Fiction
ISBN 978-0-547-14462-7; 0-547-14462-8
LC 2008-25318

When some of her classmates disappear, sixth-grader Svetlana, along with her new friends go in search of the missing students using her newfound ability as an Olfactive, one who has heightened smell, hearing, and the ability to detect vampires.

"Svetlana comes across as a strong character. . . . Her first-person narrative is fast-paced and witty, and her mild scorn for everything she encounters at school will appeal to angst-ridden tweens. Sure to be a crowd-pleaser." SLJ

Harrison, Cora

I was Jane Austen's best friend; illustrated by Susan Hellard. Delacorte Press 2010 342p il $17.99; lib bdg $20.99

Grades: 7 8 9 10 **Fic**

1. Cousins -- Fiction 2. Diaries -- Fiction 3. Friendship

-- Fiction

ISBN 978-0-385-73940-5; 0-385-73940-0; 978-0-385-90787-3 lib bdg; 0-385-90787-7 lib bdg

LC 2010-15309

In a series of journal entries, Jenny Cooper describes her stay with cousin Jane Austen in the 1790s, and her entrance into Jane's world of beautiful dresses, dances, secrets, gossip, and romance.

"This is a lovely, simple coming-of-age story with a strong historical setting. . . . The situations and locations are unmistakable and will be pleasingly familiar to readers of Austen's works." Voice of Youth Advocates

Harrison, Michelle

13 curses. Little, Brown 2011 486p (13 Treasures Trilogy) $15.99; pa $6.99

Grades: 5 6 7 8   **Fic**

1. Magic -- Fiction 2. Fairies -- Fiction 3. Orphans -- Fiction 4. Kidnapping -- Fiction

ISBN 978-0-316-04150-8; 0-316-04150-5; 978-0316041492 pa

When fairies steal her brother, thirteen-year-old Rowan Fox promises that in exchange for his return she will find the thirteen charms that the fairies have enchanted and hidden in the human world.

"The sure-handed storytelling creates a completely credible setting—by turns violent and tender, sinister and poignant. . . . Contrasts between human emotion and commitment and the cold, often cruel magic and mischief of the fairy realm create terrific tension and afford opportunities for heroism for the young protagonists." Kirkus

★ **13** treasures. Little, Brown Books for Young Readers 2010 355p il $15.99

Grades: 5 6 7 8   **Fic**

1. Mystery fiction 2. Fairies -- Fiction 3. Grandmothers -- Fiction

ISBN 978-0-316-04148-5; 0-316-04148-3

LC 2008-45511

Bedeviled by evil fairies that only she can see, thirteen-year-old Tanya is sent to stay with her cold and distant grandmother at Elvesden Manor, where she and the caretaker's son solve a disturbing mystery that leads them to the discovery that Tanya's life is in danger.

"Harrison writes with great assuredness, creating a seductive setting and memorable, fully developed characters. . . . It's an excellent choice for fans of the Spiderwick Chronicles and other modern-day fairy tales." Publ Wkly

Harrison, Troon

The **horse** road; by Troon Harrison. Bloomsbury 2012 320 p. (alk. paper) $16.99

Grades: 4 5 6 7   **Fic**

1. Horses -- Fiction 2. Historical fiction 3. Horsemanship -- Fiction

ISBN 1599908468; 9781599908465

LC 2012014010

This book is "the first of a projected trio of horse-centered historical novels. . . . Kalli, shy and stammering everywhere but on a horse, begins to prove herself when she and her friend Batu catch a glimpse over a mountainside of thousands of Middle Kingdom warriors preparing to attack

their town. . . . When her own mare, Swan, is stolen, she dons armor and weapons and rides to the rescue. In the end, she wins Swan not in battle, but through shrewd bargaining." (Kirkus Reviews)

"Densely descriptive prose, rife with historical and equine detail for horse-fiction fans, vividly portrays aspects of daily life and culture." Booklist

Hart, Alison

Gabriel's horses; by Alison Hart. 1st ed.; Peachtree 2007 161p (Racing to freedom) $14.95

Grades: 6 7 8 9   **Fic**

1. Slavery -- Fiction 2. Horse racing -- Fiction 3. African Americans -- Fiction

ISBN 978-1-56145-398-6; 1-56145-398-6

LC 2006027697

In Kentucky, during the Civil War, the twelve-year-old slave Gabriel, contends with a cruel new horse trainer and skirmishes with Confederate soldiers as he pursues his dream of becoming a jockey.

"The author grounds this fast-paced tale in historical fact by providing a nonfiction epilogue. Readers will find this wonderful blend of history and horses appealing." SLJ

Another title in this series is:

Gabriel's triumph (2007)

Hartinger, Brent

Project Sweet Life. HarperTeen 2009 282p $16.99

Grades: 6 7 8 9   **Fic**

1. Friendship -- Fiction 2. Summer employment -- Fiction

ISBN 978-0-06-082411-2; 0-06-082411-5

LC 2008-19644

When their fathers insist that they get summer jobs, three fifteen-year-old friends in Tacoma, Washington, dedicate their summer vacation to fooling their parents into thinking that they are working, which proves to be even harder than having real jobs would have been.

This "will keep readers laughing and engaged." SLJ

Hartman, Rachel

★ **Seraphina**; a novel. by Rachel Hartman. Random House 2012 465 p. (hardcover) $17.99

Grades: 7 8 9 10 11 12   **Fic**

1. Fantasy fiction 2. Dragons -- Fiction 3. Kings and rulers -- Fiction 4. Fantasy 5. Music -- Fiction 6. Secrets -- Fiction 7. Identity -- Fiction 8. Courts and courtiers -- Fiction 9. Self-actualization (Psychology) -- Fiction

ISBN 9780375866562; 9780375896583; 9780375966569; 0375866566

LC 2011003015

William C. Morris Award (2013)

Boston Globe-Horn Book Honor: Fiction (2013).

In this book, "[a]fter 40 years of peace between human and dragon kingdoms, their much-maligned treaty is on the verge of collapse. Tensions are already high with an influx of dragons, reluctantly shifted to human forms, arriving for their ruler Ardmagar Comonot's anniversary. But when Prince Rufus is found murdered in the fashion of dragons-

-that is, his head has been bitten off--things reach a fever pitch." (Booklist)

Hartnett, Sonya, 1968-
★ **Butterfly**. Candlewick Press 2010 232p $16.99

Grades: 7 8 9 10 11 12   Fic
1. Family life -- Fiction
ISBN 0-7636-4760-8; 978-0-7636-4760-5
LC 2009046549

In 1980s Australia, nearly fourteen-year-old Ariella "Plum" Coyle fears the disapproval of her friends, feels inferior to her older brothers, and hates her awkward, adolescent body but when her glamorous neighbor befriends her, Plum starts to become what she wants to be—until she discovers her neighbor's ulterior motive.

"The deliberate pacing, insight into teen angst, and masterful word choice make this a captivating read to savor." SLJ

What the birds see. Candlewick Press 2003 196p $15.99

Grades: 7 8 9 10   Fic
1. Missing children -- Fiction
ISBN 0-7636-2092-0
LC 2002-73717

While the residents of his town concern themselves with the disappearance of three children, a lonely, rejected nine-year-old boy worries that he may inherit his mother's insanity

"Tightly composed and ripe with symbolism, this complex book will offer opportunities for rich discussion." SLJ

Hartry, Nancy
Watching Jimmy. Tundra Books 2009 152p $16.95

Grades: 5 6 7 8   Fic
1. Child abuse -- Fiction 2. Brain -- Wounds and injuries -- Fiction
ISBN 0-88776-871-7; 978-0-88776-871-2

This story takes place in Canadia in 1958. Eleven-year-old Carolyn walks an emotional tightrope knowing what really happened to her best friend, Jimmy, the day his Uncle Ted chose to teach him a lesson that left Jimmy brain-damaged. But when Uncle Ted threatens his beleaguered family with even more abuse and the loss of their home, Carolyn must find the courage to match wits with him and to speak out, using the truth as her only weapon.

"Like a steady beat that pulses louder and louder, the story unfolds against a backdrop of postwar social and political concerns and Remembrance Day. Carolyn is a passionate and feisty character, delineated with love and precision, and readers will be drawn to her. A compelling and satisfying novel." SLJ

Harvey, Alyxandra
Haunting Violet. Walker Books for Young Readers 2011 352p $17.99

Grades: 6 7 8 9   Fic
1. Ghost stories 2. Mystery fiction 3. Spiritualism -- Fiction 4. Social classes -- Fiction
ISBN 978-0-8027-9839-8; 0-8027-9839-X
LC 2010-31077

Sixteen-year-old Violet Willoughby has been part of her mother's Spiritualist scam since she was nine, but during an 1872 house party in Hampshire, England, she is horrified to learn that she can actually see ghosts, one of whom wants Violet to solve her murder.

"A well-paced, clever and scary supernatural-suspense story." Kirkus

Hearts at stake. Walker & Co. 2010 248p (The Drake chronicles) $16.99; pa $9.99

Grades: 8 9 10 11 12   Fic
1. Siblings -- Fiction 2. Vampires -- Fiction 3. Friendship -- Fiction
ISBN 978-0-8027-9840-4; 0-8027-9840-3; 978-0-8027-2074-0 pa; 0-8027-2074-9 pa
LC 2009-23156

As her momentous sixteenth birthday approaches, Solange Drake, the only born female vampire in 900 years, is protected by her large family of brothers and her human best friend Lucy from increasingly persistent attempts on her life by the powerful vampire queen and her followers.

"Witty, sly, and never disappointing." Booklist
Other titles in this series are:
Blood feud (2010)
Out for blood (2011)

Harvey, Sarah N.
Death benefits. Orca Book Publishers 2010 212p pa $12.95

Grades: 6 7 8 9   Fic
1. Old age -- Fiction 2. Grandfathers -- Fiction
ISBN 978-1-55469-226-2 pa; 1-55469-226-1 pa

Royce is pressed into service as a caregiver for his ninety-five-year-old grandfather and gradually comes to appreciate the cantankerous old man.

"Harvey's writing is energetic, and Royce's snarky narration is sure to keep readers' attention." Publ Wkly

Haskell, Merrie
The **princess** curse. Harper 2011 325p $16.99

Grades: 4 5 6 7   Fic
1. Fairy tales 2. Magic -- Fiction 3. Princesses -- Fiction
ISBN 978-0-06-200813-8; 0-06-200813-7
LC 2010040424

"Author Haskell has her way with the story of 'The Twelve Dancing Princesses,' incorporating references to other myths and legends and adding many twists of her own, not least of which is making the royals' attempted rescuer a strong-willed, 13-year-old apprentice herbalist, Reveka. . . . When Vasile offers the hand of any of his daughters in marriage to anyone who banishes the curse (or a 'fabulous dowry' if the curse-breaker is female), Reveka is determined to win the reward. . . . With a good sense of humor, an able and empowered protagonist, and a highly original take on this tale, Haskell's story gives readers much to enjoy." Publ Wkly

Hathaway, Barbara
Letters to Missy Violet. Houghton Mifflin 2012 157p $15.99

Grades: 4 5 6 **Fic**
1. Letters -- Fiction 2. African Americans -- Fiction
ISBN 9780547363004

LC 2011012162

While her friend Missy Violet, the town midwife, is away in Florida, eleven-year-old Viney concerns herself with ailing neighbors, schoolmates, and her irrepressible cousin Charles, who feels superior because he has been to Harlem in New York City.

"This Depression-era gem . . . offers a child's-eye view on America's racial inequities. . . . Like a warm cup of alphabet soup, this offering packs several essential ingredients-hope, love, despair, courage, family, honor-into a hearty, child-size blend." Kirkus

Missy Violet & me. Houghton 2004 100p $15
Grades: 4 5 6 **Fic**
1. Midwives -- Fiction 2. Childbirth -- Fiction 3. African Americans -- Fiction
ISBN 978-0-618-37163-1; 0-618-37163-X
Coretta Scott King/John Steptoe New Talent Award, 2005

During the early 1900s, eleven-year-old Viney spends her summer working for the local midwife and learns first-hand about birth, death, and "catchin' babies."

"Unspooled as leisurely as a summer afternoon spent on the front porch, this appealingly nostalgic tale conveys the tenor of the time as well as the affable narrator's growth during one momentous summer." Publ Wkly

Hausman, Gerald
A **mind** with wings; the story of Henry David Thoreau. [by] Gerald & Loretta Hausman. 1st ed; Trumpeter Books for Young Readers 2006 148p $15.95
Grades: 6 7 8 9 **Fic**
1. Naturalists -- Fiction
ISBN 1-59030-228-1

LC 2005018094

"This well-researched novel expertly captures Thoreau's character and life in mid-19th-century Massachusetts. . . . Careful readers will have much to mull over, and they will savor the adventures of this great American thinker." SLJ
Includes bibliographical references

Hautman, Pete, 1952-
★ **All** -in. Simon & Schuster Books for Young Readers 2007 181p hardcover o.p. pa $5.99
Grades: 7 8 9 10 **Fic**
1. Poker -- Fiction 2. Gambling -- Fiction 3. Young adult literature -- Works
ISBN 978-1-4169-1325-2; 1-4169-1325-4; 978-1-4169-1326-9 pa; 1-4169-1326-9 pa

LC 2006-23871

Having won thousands of dollars playing high-stakes poker in Las Vegas, seventeen-year-old Denn Doyle hits a losing streak after falling in love with a young casino card dealer named Cattie Hart.

"Skillfully using the multiple-voice approach, Hautman brings to life the intricacies of poker, crafting a thrill-ing story of loss, good versus evil, and redemption." Voice Youth Advocates

Blank confession. Simon & Schuster Books for Young Readers 2010 170p $16.99
Grades: 7 8 9 10 **Fic**
1. School stories 2. Bullies -- Fiction 3. Drug traffic -- Fiction
ISBN 978-1-4169-1327-6; 1-4169-1327-0

LC 2009-50169

A new and enigmatic student named Shayne appears at high school one day, befriends the smallest boy in the school, and takes on a notorious drug dealer before turning himself in to the police for killing someone.

"Masterfully written with simple prose, solid dialogue and memorable characters, the tale will grip readers from the start and keep the reading in one big gulp, in the hope of seeing behind Shayne's mask. A sure hit with teen readers." Kirkus

★ The **Cydonian** pyramid; Pete Hautman. Candlewick Press 2013 368 p. (The Klaatu Diskos) (reinforced) $16.99
Grades: 7 8 9 10 11 12 **Fic**
1. Science fiction 2. Time travel -- Fiction
ISBN 0763654043; 9780763654047

LC 2012942673

This novel, by Pete Hautman, is part of the "Klaatu Diskos" series. "More than half a millennium in the future, in the shadow of the looming Cydonian Pyramid, a pampered girl named Lah Lia has been raised for one purpose: to be sacrificed. . . . But just as she is about to be killed, a strange boy appears from the diskos, providing a cover of chaos that allows her to escape and launching her on a time-spinning journey in which her fate is irreversibly linked to his." (Publisher's note)

★ **Godless**. Simon & Schuster Books for Young Readers 2004 208p $15.95; pa $8.99
Grades: 7 8 9 10 **Fic**
1. Religion -- Fiction
ISBN 0-689-86278-4; 1-4169-0816-1 pa

LC 2003-10468

When sixteen-year-old Jason Bock and his friends create their own religion to worship the town's water tower, what started out as a joke begins to take on a power of its own

"The witty text and provocative subject will make this a supremely enjoyable discussion-starter as well as pleasurable read." Bull Cent Child Books

Hole in the sky. Simon & Schuster Bks. for Young Readers 2001 179p $16; pa $11.95
Grades: 7 8 9 10 **Fic**
1. Science fiction
ISBN 0-689-83118-8; 1-4169-6822-9 pa

LC 00-58324

In a future world ravaged by a mutant virus, sixteen-year-old Ceej and three other teenagers seek to save the Grand Canyon from being flooded, while trying to avoid capture by a band of renegade Survivors

"Readers will appreciate the novel's intense action and fascinating premise." Horn Book Guide

How to steal a car. Scholastic Press 2009 170p $16.99

Grades: 7 8 9 10   **Fic**

1. Theft -- Fiction 2. Family life -- Fiction
ISBN 978-0-545-11318-2; 0-545-11318-0

LC 2008-54146

Fifteen-year-old, suburban high school student Kelleigh, who has her learner's permit, recounts how she began stealing cars one summer, for reasons that seem unclear even to her.

"A sharply observed, subversive coming-of-age tale." Kirkus

Snatched; [by] Pete Hautman and Mary Logue. Putnam 2006 200p (Bloodwater mysteries) $15.99

Grades: 7 8 9 10   **Fic**

1. Mystery fiction 2. Kidnapping -- Fiction
ISBN 0-399-24377-1

LC 2005-28558

Too curious for her own good, Roni, crime reporter for her high school newspaper, teams up with Brian, freshman science geek, to investigate the beating and kidnapping of a classmate.

"Give this solid marks for plotting and characterization, as well as for suspense." Booklist

Other titles in this series are:
Skullduggery (2007)
Doppelganger (2008)

★ **Sweetblood**. Simon & Schuster Bks. for Young Readers 2003 180p $16.95; pa $6.99

Grades: 7 8 9 10   **Fic**

1. Diabetes -- Fiction
ISBN 0-689-85048-4; 0-689-87324-7 pa

LC 2002-11179

"Hautman does an outstanding job of making Lucy's theory and her struggle to accept herself credible. . . . Lucy's clever, self-deprecating voice is endlessly original." Booklist

★ The **big** crunch. Scholastic Press 2011 280p $17.99

Grades: 8 9 10 11 12   **Fic**

1. School stories 2. Dating (Social customs) -- Fiction
ISBN 978-0-545-24075-8; 0-545-24075-1

LC 2010-40011

"Wes Andrews has just ended a suffocating relationship with Izzy. June is new to the school—her sixth in the last four years. Like Wes, she's not looking to get entangled. . . . But in the high-school world of 'users, posers, geeks, skanks, preps, gangstas, macho-morons, punks, burnouts, and so forth,' the two relatively normal, nice kids do find each other . . . eventually. Hautman uses a third-person point of view to weave a humorous and bittersweet tale of romance and the convoluted, uncertain paths that bring two people together. A poignant and quiet tale in which the only special effect is love—refreshing." Kirkus

The **obsidian** blade. Candlewick Press 2012 308p $16.99

Grades: 7 8 9 10   **Fic**

1. Uncles -- Fiction 2. Religion -- Fiction 3. Supernatural -- Fiction 4. Space and time -- Fiction 5. Missing persons -- Fiction
ISBN 978-0-7636-5403-0

LC 2011018617

After thirteen-year-old Tucker Feye's parents disappear, he suspects that the strange disks of shimmering air that he keeps seeing are somehow involved, and when he steps inside of one he is whisked on a time-twisting journey trailed by a shadowy sect of priests and haunted by ghostlike figures.

Hawkins, Aaron R.

The **year** money grew on trees; written and illustrated by Aaron R. Hawkins. Houghton Mifflin 2010 293p il $16

Grades: 5 6 7 8   **Fic**

1. Apples -- Fiction 2. Cousins -- Fiction 3. Siblings -- Fiction 4. Farm life -- Fiction 5. Money-making projects for children -- Fiction
ISBN 978-0-547-27977-0; 0-547-27977-9

In early 1980s New Mexico, thirteen-year-old Jackson Jones recruits his cousins and sisters to help tend an elderly neighbor's neglected apple orchard for the chance to make big money and, perhaps, to own the orchard.

"Hawkins's children's book debut is rich with details that feel drawn from memory, . . . and Jackson's narration sparkles. His hard work, setbacks, and motivations make this a highly relatable adventure in entrepreneurship." Publ Wkly

Hawkins, Rachel

Demonglass; a Hex Hall novel. Hyperion 2011 359p $16.99

Grades: 7 8 9 10   **Fic**

1. Ghost stories 2. Magic -- Fiction 3. Witches -- Fiction 4. Supernatural -- Fiction 5. Father-daughter relationship -- Fiction
ISBN 978-1-4231-2131-2; 1-4231-2131-7

LC 2010-10511

After learning that she is capable of dangerous magic, Sophie Mercer goes to England with her father, friend Jenna, and Cal hoping to have her powers removed, but soon she learns that she is being hunted by the Eye—and haunted by Elodie.

"Narrator Sophie's delivery is . . . delightfully bold, and the many action scenes lend a cinematic feel." Booklist

Hex Hall. Disney/Hyperion Books 2010 323p $16.99

Grades: 7 8 9 10   **Fic**

1. School stories 2. Witches -- Fiction 3. Supernatural -- Fiction
ISBN 1423121309; 9781423121305

When Sophie attracts too much human attention for a prom-night spell gone horribly wrong, she is exiled to Hex Hall, an isolated reform school for witches, faeries, and shapeshifters.

"Sixteen-year-old Sophie Mercer, whose absentee father is a warlock, discovered both her heritage and her powers at age 13. While at her school prom, Sophie happens upon a miserable girl sobbing in the bathroom and tries to perform a love spell to help her out. It misfires, and Sophie finds herself at Hecate (aka Hex) Hall, a boarding school for delinquent Prodigium (witches, warlocks, faeries, shape-shifters, and the occasional vampire). What makes this fast-paced romp work is Hawkins' wry humor and sharp eye for teen dynamics." Booklist

Haydon, Elizabeth

The **Floating** Island; the lost journals of Ven Polypheme. illustrated by Brett Helquist. Starscape 2006 368p il $17.95; pa $5.99

Grades: 5 6 7 8   **Fic**
   1. Fantasy fiction
   ISBN 0-7653-0867-3; 0-7653-4772-5 pa
                   LC 2006005768

Ven, the youngest son of a long line of famous shipwrights, dreams of sailing to far-off lands where magic thrives. He gets his chance when he is chosen to direct the Inspection of his family's latest ship and sets sail on the journey of a lifetime

The author's "world building is as successful as her characters, with Helquist's occasional loose sketches providing some visual distraction and additional atmosphere. A delightful epic fantasy." Booklist

The **Thief** Queen's daughter; 1st hardcover ed.; Tom Doherty Associates 2007 319p (Lost journals of Ven Polypheme) $17.95; pa $6.99

Grades: 5 6 7 8   **Fic**
   1. Fantasy fiction
   ISBN 978-0-7653-0868-9; 0-7653-0868-1; 978-0-7653-4773-2 pa; 0-7653-4773-3 pa
                   LC 2007007933

Young Ven Polypheme is sent on a secret mission within the walls of the Gated City, a former penal colony in the land of Serendair, where he and his friends face kidnapping and even worse dangers from the ruthless Thief Queen, who is trying to reclaim her runaway daughter.

"Haydon uses snippets of Ven's diary entries, fast-paced action, and plenty of humorous touches to keep readers engaged." SLJ

Hayes, Rosemary

Payback. Frances Lincoln 2009 207p pa $8.95

Grades: 7 8 9 10   **Fic**
   1. Muslims -- Fiction
   ISBN 978-1-84507-935-2 pa; 1-84507-935-3 pa

Halima, a teenaged Muslim girl living in London, discovers her father owes a favor to a distant relative in Pakistan and must repay the debt by forcing Halima into marriage

"In this tale of clashing cultures set against a backdrop of strong family ties and traditional Muslim faith, Hayes writes clearly and concisely, switching the narrative voice among the characters and letting the dynamics of the story simmer and build realistically." SLJ

Hayles, Marsha

Breathing room; Marsha Hayles. Henry Holt and Co. 2012 244 p. (hc) $17.99

Grades: 5 6 7 8   **Fic**
   1. Bildungsromans 2. Historical fiction 3. Teenagers -- Fiction 4. Tuberculosis -- Fiction 5. Sick -- Fiction

6. Hospitals -- Fiction 7. Coming of age -- Fiction
   ISBN 0805089616; 9780805089615
                   LC 2011034055

Author Marsha Hayles" book is "set in 1940 at a sanitarium in Loon Lake, Minn. . . . Thirteen-year-old Evvy Hoffmeister has tuberculosis and feels abandoned by her family when she"s sent to the sanitarium to be cured. The cold nurses, strict rules, mind-numbing routines, and endless bed rest are dispiriting for Evvy and her roommates: kind Beverly, glamorous Pearl, and defensive Dena. . . . Nonetheless, the girls find strength in each other and discover creative ways to bring cheer." (Publishers Weekly)

Headley, Justina Chen

★ **North** of beautiful. Little, Brown 2009 373p $16.99

Grades: 7 8 9 10 11 12   **Fic**
   1. Aesthetics -- Fiction
   ISBN 978-0-316-02505-8; 0-316-02505-4
                   LC 2008-09260

Headley's "finely crafted novel traces a teen's uncharted quest to find beauty. Two things block Terra's happiness: a port-wine stain on her face and her verbally abusive father. . . . A car accident brings her together with Jacob, an Asian-born adoptee with unconventional ideas. . . . The author confidently addresses very large, slippery questions about the meaning of art, travel, love and of course, beauty." Publ Wkly

Healey, Karen

When we wake; Karen Healey. Little, Brown Books for Young Readers 2013 304 p. (hardcover) $17.99

Grades: 7 8 9 10 11 12   **Fic**
   1. Science fiction 2. Dystopian fiction
   ISBN 031620076X; 9780316200769
                   LC 2012028739

In this science fiction novel, by Karen Healy, "Sixteen-year-old Tegan is just like every other girl living in 2027-- But on what should have been the best day of Tegan's life, she dies--and wakes up a hundred years in the future, locked in a government facility with no idea what happened. . . . But the future isn't all she hoped it would be, and when . . . secrets come to light, Tegan must make a choice: Does she keep her head down and survive, or fight for a better future?" (Publisher's note)

The **shattering**. Little, Brown 2011 311p $17.99

Grades: 7 8 9 10   **Fic**
   1. Mystery fiction 2. Suicide -- Fiction 3. Homicide -- Fiction 4. Supernatural -- Fiction
   ISBN 978-0-316-12572-7; 0-316-12572-5
                   LC 2010047996

When a rash of suicides disturbs Summerton, an oddly perfect tourist town on the west coast of New Zealand, the younger siblings of the dead boys become suspicious and begin an investigation that reveals dark secrets and puts them in grave danger.

"Juggling multiple viewpoints, Healey skillfully keeps her characters on an emotional roller-coaster even as they deal with physical threats. The climax delivers a gut punch that only underscores the sensitivity of the subject matter (without lessening the thrill at all)." Publ Wkly

Healy, Christopher

The **hero's** guide to saving your kingdom; written by Christopher Healy ; with drawings by Todd Harris. Walden Pond Press 2012 438 p. ill., map $16.99

Grades: 4 5 6 7   **Fic**
    1. Princes -- Fiction 2. Fairy tales -- Fiction 3. Heroes and heroines -- Fiction 4. Fairy tales 5. Humorous stories 6. Witches -- Fiction
    ISBN 0062117432; 9780062117434
                                        LC 2011053347

In this book, "four Princes . . . must team up on a . . . quest to save their kingdoms. . . . Cinderella wants adventure more than sheltered Prince Frederic does. Prince Gustav's pride is still badly damaged from having needed Rapunzel's teary-eyed rescue. Through Sleeping Beauty, Prince Liam learns kissing someone out of enchanted sleep doesn't guarantee compatibility. . . . Although she loves wacky Prince Duncan, Snow White needs some solitude." (Kirkus Reviews)

The **hero's** guide to storming the castle; by Christopher Healy ; with drawings by Todd Harris. Walden Pond Press, an imprint of HarperCollinsPublishers 2013 496 p. (Hero's Guide) (hardcover) $16.99

Grades: 4 5 6 7   **Fic**
    1. Fractured fairy tales 2. Fairy tales 3. Humorous stories 4. Heroes -- Fiction 5. Princes -- Fiction 6. Characters in literature -- Fiction
    ISBN 0062118455; 9780062118455
                                        LC 2012050668

In this humorous, middle-grade fantasy story, by Christopher Healy, illustrated by Todd Harris, "the charming princes from the fairy tales of Cinderella, Rapunzel, Snow White, and Briar Rose, saved the countryside from an evil witch in 'The Hero's Guide to Saving Your Kingdom.' And now, they have to save the day again, by keeping a magical object from falling into the hands of power-mad warlords who would use it for evil." (Publisher's note)

Hearn, Julie

Hazel; a novel. Atheneum Books for Young Readers 2009 389p $17.99

Grades: 8 9 10 11   **Fic**
    1. Slavery -- Fiction 2. Social classes -- Fiction 3. Racially mixed people -- Fiction
    ISBN 978-1-4169-2504-0; 1-4169-2504-X
                                        LC 2008-53961

Thirteen-year-old Hazel leaves her comfortable, if somewhat unconventional, London home in 1913 after her father has a breakdown, and goes to live in the Caribbean on her grandparents' sugar plantation where she discovers some shocking family secrets.

"Hearn's characters vividly reveal class distinctions and racial prejudices prevalent in 1913." Voice Youth Advocates

★ **Ivy**; a novel. Atheneum Books for Young Readers 2008 355p $17.99; pa $9.99

Grades: 8 9 10 11 12   **Fic**
    1. Artists -- Fiction 2. Criminals -- Fiction 3. Drug abuse -- Fiction
    ISBN 978-1-4169-2506-4; 1-4169-2506-6; 978-1-4169-2507-1 pa; 1-4169-2507-4 pa
                                        LC 2007-045463

In mid-nineteenth-century London, young, mistreated, and destitute Ivy, whose main asset is her beautiful red hair, comes to the attention of an aspiring painter of the pre-Raphaelite school of artists who, with the connivance of Ivy's unsavory family, is determined to make her his model and muse.

"Quirky characters, darkly humorous situations, and quick action make this enjoyable historical fiction." SLJ

The **minister's** daughter. Atheneum Books for Young Readers 2005 263p hardcover o.p. pa $7.99

Grades: 7 8 9 10   **Fic**
    1. Witchcraft -- Fiction 2. Supernatural -- Fiction
    ISBN 0-689-87690-4; 0-689-87691-2 pa
                                        LC 2004-18324

In 1645 in England, the daughters of the town minister successfully accuse a local healer and her granddaughter of witchcraft to conceal an out-of-wedlock pregnancy, but years later during the 1692 Salem trials their lie has unexpected repercussions.

"With its thought-provoking perceptions about human nature, magic and persecution, this tale will surely cast a spell over readers." Publ Wkly

Heath, Jack

The **Lab**. Scholastic Press 2008 311p $17.99

Grades: 7 8 9 10   **Fic**
    1. Science fiction 2. Adventure fiction 3. Spies -- Fiction 4. Genetic engineering -- Fiction
    ISBN 978-0-545-06860-4; 0-545-06860-6

"A gritty dystopic world exists under the iron rule of the mega-corporation Chao-Sonic, with only a few vigilante groups around to act as resistance. Six of Hearts is easily the best agent on one such group, the Deck, and he is fiercely dedicated to justice, using his extensive genetic modifications to his advantage. . . . The compelling and memorable protagonist stands out even against the intricately described and disturbing city whose vividness makes the place's questionable fate a suspenseful issue in its own right." Bull Cent Child Books

Money run; by Jack Heath. 1st American ed. Scholastic Press 2013 245 p. (hardcover) $17.99

Grades: 8 9 10   **Fic**
    1. Crime -- Fiction 2. Adventure fiction 3. Stealing -- Fiction 4. Assassins -- Fiction 5. Robbers and outlaws -- Fiction
    ISBN 0545512662; 9780545512664
                                        LC 2013004005

In this book, "Ashley and Benjamin are two teen partners in crime--real crime, as in major heists--who rely on their youth to avoid suspicion. . . . Their prey today happens to be a billionaire businessman who has sponsored an essay contest with a prize of $10,000 (Ash has won with an essay ghostwritten by Benjamin), but that's peanuts compared to the $2 million they hope to loot." (Kirkus Reviews)

Remote control. Scholastic Press 2010 326p $17.99

Grades: 7 8 9 10   **Fic**
1. Science fiction 2. Adventure fiction 3. Spies -- Fiction 4. Genetic engineering -- Fiction
ISBN 978-0-545-07591-6; 0-545-07591-2
First published 2007 in Australia

Agent Six of Hearts, 16-year-old superhuman, is on a mission. His brother Kyntak has been kidnapped. A strange and sinister new figure is rising in power. Six is suspected of being a double agent. The Deck has been put into lockdown by the Queen of Spades. A mysterious girl has appeared who acts as Six's guardian angel. Who can he trust?

"The technothriller begun in The Lab (2008) takes several intriguing twists . . . on its way to a satisfying, if temporary, resolution." Booklist

Hegamin, Tonya
M +O 4evr; [by] Tonya Cherie Hegamin. Houghton Mifflin Co. 2008 165p $16

Grades: 8 9 10 11   **Fic**
1. Death -- Fiction 2. Slavery -- Fiction 3. Lesbians -- Fiction 4. Friendship -- Fiction 5. Family life -- Fiction
ISBN 978-0-618-49570-2; 0-618-49570-3
                                                         LC 2007-34293

In parallel stories, Hannah, a slave, finds love while fleeing a Maryland plantation in 1842, and in the present, Opal watches her life-long best friend, Marianne, pull away and eventually lose her life in the same Pennsylvania ravine where Hannah died.

"Hegamin's first novel is richly imaginative as it deals with difficult subjects. . . . [The] parallel stories of love and loss blend seamlessly in this small book that packs a big wallop." SLJ

Pemba's song; a ghost story. [by] Tonya Hegamin & Marilyn Nelson. Scholastic Press 2008 109p $16.99

Grades: 7 8 9 10   **Fic**
1. Moving -- Fiction 2. Slavery -- Fiction 3. Parapsychology -- Fiction 4. African Americans -- Fiction
ISBN 978-0-545-02076-3; 0-545-02076-X
                                                        LC 2007051044

As fifteen-year-old Pemba adjusts to leaving her Brooklyn, New York, home for small-town Connecticut, a Black history researcher helps her understand the paranormal experiences drawing her into the life of a mulatto girl who was once a slave in her house.

"Written in shifting voices and styles, this vivid, collaborative novella tells a supernatural story of a young girl's connection with history." Booklist

Hegedus, Bethany
Between us Baxters. WestSide Books 2009 306p $17.95

Grades: 7 8 9 10   **Fic**
1. Friendship -- Fiction 2. Race relations -- Fiction
ISBN 978-1-934813-02-7; 1-934813-02-8

"In 1959, in Holcolm County, GA, there is a palpable tension. Times are slowly changing, causing resentment among some folks and optimism among others. The volatile mix sets the tone for this story of family, friendship, and racial discrimination. . . .When suspicious fires, vandalism, and threats to successful black business owners cause fear and distrust among the townspeople, the strength of Polly and Timbre Ann's bond is tested. . . . The connection between the two girls and their families is beautifully described and believable, and the richness of the characters is apparent. The pacing of the story is deliberate and suspenseful with twists and turns that add to the bittersweet conclusion." SLJ

Heldring, Thatcher
Roy Morelli steps up to the plate. Delacorte Press 2010 229p $15.99; lib bdg $18.99

Grades: 5 6 7 8   **Fic**
1. School stories 2. Divorce -- Fiction 3. Baseball -- Fiction
ISBN 978-0-385-73391-5; 0-385-73391-7; 978-0-385-90406-3 lib bdg; 0-385-90406-1 lib bdg
                                                        LC 2009033845

When eighth-grader Roy Morelli's divorced parents find out he is failing history, they ban him from playing on his beloved all-star baseball team, and, even worse, he winds up being tutored by his father's new girlfriend.

"The novel features good characterization and some sizzling dialogue. . . . The game action is fast paced and exciting, the depiction of middle school dynamics rings true, and the main character shows genuine emotional growth over the course of the novel." SLJ

Helgerson, Joseph
Crows & cards; a novel. written with diligence by Mr. Joseph Helgerson; to which are added fine illustrations by Mr. Peter Desève; also included is Dictionarium Americannicum; being the words herein most arcane and alien and their definitions. Houghton Mifflin Harcourt 2009 344p il $16; pa $5.99

Grades: 4 5 6 7   **Fic**
1. Slavery -- Fiction 2. Gambling -- Fiction 3. Apprentices -- Fiction 4. Native Americans -- Fiction
ISBN 978-0-618-88395-0; 0-618-88395-9; 978-0-547-33909-2 pa; 0-547-33909-7 pa
                                                        LC 2008013308

In 1849, Zeb's parents ship him off to St. Louis to become an apprentice tanner, but the naive twelve-year-old rebels, casting his lot with a cheating riverboat gambler, while a slave and an Indian medicine man try to get Zeb back on the right path. Includes historical notes, glossary, and bibliographical references

"Helgerson surrounds Zeb with a lively cast. . . . A solid choice for fans of high-spun yarns and not-too-tall tales." Booklist

★ **Horns** & wrinkles. Houghton Mifflin 2006 357p il $16; pa $4.95

Grades: 4 5 6 7   **Fic**
1. Magic -- Fiction 2. Trolls -- Fiction 3. Bullies -- Fiction
ISBN 0-618-61679-9; 0-618-98178-0 pa
                                                        LC 2005025448

Along a magic-saturated stretch of the Mississippi River near Blue Wing, Minnesota, twelve-year-old Claire and her bullying cousin Duke are drawn into an adventure involving Bodacious Deepthink the Great Rock Troll, a helpful fairy, and a group of trolls searching for their fathers.

"Tongue-in-cheek humor brings a delightful zing to the playfully inventive storytelling and fast-paced plot. Enchanting sketches foreshadow each chapter, adding to the wonder." SLJ

Hemingway, Edith Morris

Road to Tater Hill; [by] Edith M. Hemingway. Delacorte Press 2009 213p map $16.99; lib bdg $19.99

Grades: 5 6 7 8   Fic

1. Friendship -- Fiction 2. Bereavement -- Fiction 3. Grandparents -- Fiction 4. Mountain life -- Fiction 5. Depression (Psychology) -- Fiction

ISBN 978-0-385-73677-0; 0-385-73677-0; 978-0-385-90627-2 lib bdg; 0-385-90627-7 lib bdg

LC 2008-24906

At her grandparents' North Carolina mountain home during the summer of 1963, eleven-year-old Annie Winters, grief-stricken by the death of her newborn sister and isolated by her mother's deepening depression, finds comfort in holding an oblong stone 'rock baby' and in the friendship of a neighbor boy and a reclusive mountain woman with a devastating secret

"Drawing on the author's childhood roots, the heart of this first novel is the sense of place, described in simple lyrical words. . . . True to Annie's viewpoint, the particulars tell a universal drama of childhood grief, complete in all its sadness, anger, loneliness, and healing." Booklist

Hemphill, Helen

Long gone daddy. Front Street 2006 176p $16.95

Grades: 8 9 10 11 12   Fic

1. Grandfathers -- Fiction 2. Christian life -- Fiction 3. Father-son relationship -- Fiction

ISBN 1-932425-38-1

LC 2005-25105

Young Harlan Q. Stank gets a taste of life in the fast lane when he accompanies his preacher father on a road trip to Las Vegas to bury his grandfather and to fulfill the terms of the old man's will.

"Many teens will see their own questions about faith, worship, and independence in Harlan's heart-twisting feelings." Booklist

★ The **adventurous** deeds of Deadwood Jones. Front Street 2008 228p $16.95

Grades: 5 6 7 8   Fic

1. Cousins -- Fiction 2. Cowhands -- Fiction 3. Race relations -- Fiction 4. African Americans -- Fiction

ISBN 978-1-59078-637-6; 1-59078-637-8

LC 2008005422

Thirteen-year-old Prometheus Jones and his eleven-year-old cousin Omer flee Tennessee and join a cattle drive that will eventually take them to Texas, where Prometheus hopes his father lives, and they find adventure and face challenges as African Americans in a land still recovering from the Civil War.

"Prometheus is an always sympathetic and engaging character, and the dangers and misadventures he encounters . . . make for compelling reading." Booklist

Hemphill, Michael

Stonewall Hinkleman and the Battle of Bull Run; [by] Michael Hemphill and Sam Riddleburger. Dial Books for Young Readers 2009 168p $16.99

Grades: 4 5 6   Fic

1. Time travel -- Fiction 2. Bull Run, 1st Battle of, 1861 -- Fiction

ISBN 978-0-8037-3179-0; 0-8037-3179-5

LC 2008-15795

While participating in a reenactment of the Battle of Bull Run, twelve-year-old Stonewall Hinkleman is transported back to the actual Civil War battle by means of a magic bugle.

This is a "well-paced time-travel novel. . . . Stonewall is a likable character whose attitude changes for the better in the story. . . . A good choice for historical fiction fans." SLJ

Hemphill, Stephanie

Sisters of glass; Stephanie Hemphill. Alfred A. Knopf 2012 150 p. $16.99

Grades: 7 8 9 10   Fic

1. Love stories 2. Novels in verse 3. Historical fiction 4. Families -- Fiction 5. Family life -- Fiction 6. Glass blowing and working -- Fiction

ISBN 0375861092; 0375961097; 9780375861093; 9780375961090

LC 2011277551

This book presents "[a] . . . tale of destiny, fidelity, and true love" set in "fourteenth-century Murano, Italy (of glass-making renown) and . . . told through verse. . . . Maria is disdainful of her training to be a society woman and yearns instead to spend her time with her art or in the family"s furnaces with Luca, an employee whose skill with glass is the marvel that leads Maria, who once aspired to be a glassblower, to fall in love with him." (Booklist)

★ **Wicked** girls; a novel of the Salem witch trials. Balzer + Bray 2010 408p il $17.99

Grades: 7 8 9 10 11 12   Fic

1. Novels in verse 2. Trials -- Fiction 3. Witchcraft -- Fiction

ISBN 0-06-185328-3; 0-06-185329-1 lib bdg; 978-0-06-185328-9; 978-0-06-185329-6 lib bdg

LC 2010-9593

This is "a fictionalized account of the Salem witch trials told from the perspectives of three of the real young women living in Salem in 1692. Ann Putnam Jr. plays the queen bee. When her father suggests that a spate of illnesses within the village is the result of witchcraft, Ann . . . puts in motion a chain of events that will change the lives of the people around her forever. Mercy Lewis, the beautiful servant in Ann's house, inspires adulation in some and envy in others. With a troubled past, she seizes her only chance at safety. Margaret Walcott, Ann's cousin, is desperately in love and consumed with fiery jealousy. She is torn between staying loyal to her friends and pursuing the life she dreams of with her betrothed." (Publisher's note)

"Hemphill's raw, intimate poetry probes behind the abstract facts and creates characters that pulse with complex emotion." Booklist

Includes bibliographical references

Henderson, Jan-Andrew

Bunker 10. Harcourt 2007 253p $17

Grades: 7 8 9 10   **Fic**

1. Virtual reality -- Fiction 2. Genetic engineering -- Fiction

ISBN 978-0-15-206240-8; 0-15-206240-8

LC 2006-38694

Something is going terribly wrong at the top secret Pinewood Military Installation as the teenage geniuses who study and work there are about to discover a horrible truth.

"Henderson ably balances intriguing plot twists and hauntingly well-developed characters with gripping pace and dramatic showdowns." Bull Cent Child Books

Henderson, Jason

★ **Vampire** rising. HarperTeen 2010 249p (Alex Van Helsing) $16.99

Grades: 6 7 8 9 10   **Fic**

1. Horror fiction 2. School stories 3. Vampires -- Fiction 4. Supernatural -- Fiction

ISBN 978-0-06-195099-5; 0-06-195099-8

LC 2009-39663

At a boarding school in Switzerland, fourteen-year-old Alex Van Helsing learns that vampires are real, that he has a natural ability to sense them, and that an agency called the Polidorium has been helping his family fight them since 1821.

"Henderson references Mary Shelley's Frankenstein to weave a great story line full of action, suspense, and adventure. The satisfying story captivates readers with a modern-day spin of James Bond meets Dracula." SLJ

Another title about Alex Van Helsing is:

Voice of the undead (2011)

The Triumph of Death (2012)

Heneghan, James

Payback. Groundwood/House of Anansi Press 2007 184p $16.95; pa $8.95

Grades: 6 7 8 9   **Fic**

1. Guilt -- Fiction 2. Bullies -- Fiction 3. Suicide -- Fiction 4. Immigrants -- Fiction 5. Irish -- Canada -- Fiction

ISBN 0-88899-701-9; 978-0-88899-701-2; 978-0-88899-704-3 pa; 0-88899-704-3 pa

"After his eighth-grade classmate Benny commits suicide, Charley blames himself. . . . Why did he do nothing when he saw the bullies torment Benny and call him 'fag'? Was it because, as a new Irish immigrant in Vancouver, Charley himself was threatened and bullied? . . . The drama of guilt, sorrow, and redemption is honest and heartfelt, told in Charley's spare, fast, first-person narrative." Booklist

Safe house. Orca Book Publishers 2006 151p pa $7.95

Grades: 6 7 8 9   **Fic**

1. Belfast (Northern Ireland) -- Fiction

ISBN 1-55143-640-X pa; 978-1-55143-640-1 pa

"Readers will be drawn by the fast action and the breathless escape adventure, but they'll also respond to the politics of war in Belfast." Booklist

Henkes, Kevin

★ **Bird** Lake moon. Greenwillow Books 2008 179p $15.99; lib bdg $16.89; pa $5.99

Grades: 4 5 6 7   **Fic**

1. Lakes -- Fiction 2. Divorce -- Fiction 3. Friendship -- Fiction 4. Bereavement -- Fiction 5. Family life -- Fiction

ISBN 978-0-06-147076-9; 0-06-147076-7; 978-0-06-147078-3 lib bdg; 0-06-147078-3 lib bdg; 978-0-06-147079-0 pa; 0-06-147079-1 pa

LC 2007-36564

Twelve-year-old Mitch and his mother are spending the summer with his grandparents at Bird Lake after his parents separate, and ten-year-old Spencer and his family have returned to the lake where Spencer's little brother drowned long ago, and as the boys become friends and spend time together, each of them begins to heal

"Characters are gently and believably developed as the story weaves in and around the beautiful Wisconsin setting. The superbly crafted plot moves smoothly and unhurriedly, mirroring a slow summer pace." SLJ

★ **Olive's** ocean. Greenwillow Bks. 2003 217p $15.99; pa $6.99

Grades: 5 6 7 8   **Fic**

1. Family life -- Fiction 2. Grandmothers -- Fiction

ISBN 0-06-053543-1; 0-06-053545-8 pa

LC 2002-29782

A Newbery Medal honor book, 2004

On a summer visit to her grandmother's cottage by the ocean, twelve-year-old Martha gains perspective on the death of a classmate, on her relationship with her grandmother, on her feelings for an older boy, and on her plans to be a writer.

"Rich characterizations move this compelling novel to its satisfying and emotionally authentic conclusion." SLJ

Protecting Marie. Greenwillow Bks. 1995 195p $18.99; pa $5.99

Grades: 5 6 7 8   **Fic**

1. Dogs -- Fiction 2. Father-daughter relationship -- Fiction

ISBN 0-688-13958-2; 0-06-053545-8 pa

LC 94-16387

Relates twelve-year-old Fanny's love-hate relationship with her father, a temperamental artist, who has given Fanny a new dog

"The characters ring heartbreakingly true in this quiet, wise story; they are complex and difficult—like all of us—and worthy of our attention." Horn Book

Henry, April

Torched. G.P. Putnam's Sons 2009 224p $16.99

Grades: 8 9 10 11   **Fic**

1. Terrorism -- Fiction 2. Environmental movement

-- Fiction

ISBN 978-0-399-24645-6; 0-399-24645-2

LC 2008-01145

In order to save her parents from going to jail for possession of marijuana, sixteen-year-old Ellie must help the FBI uncover the intentions of a radical environmental group by going undercover.

"The mix of politics and thrilling action will grab teens. . . . This suspenseful story will spark discussion about what it means to fight for right 'by any means necessary.'" Booklist

Henry, O.

The **gift** of the Magi; illustrations by P.J. Lynch. Candlewick Press 2008 un il $15.99

Grades: 5 6 7 8   Fic

1. Gifts -- Fiction 2. Christmas -- Fiction

ISBN 978-0-7636-3530-5; 0-7636-3530-8

LC 2007052028

A husband and wife sacrifice treasured possessions in order to buy each other Christmas presents.

The story "enjoys a gentle new interpretation through watercolor illustrations in worn grays and warm brown tones. . . . Lynch's illustrations of wintry landscapes and the protagonists' animated faces add an accessible level of storytelling to the sophisticated prose." Horn Book Guide

Henson, Heather

Dream of Night. Atheneum 2010 218p $15.99

Grades: 6 7 8 9   Fic

1. Horses -- Fiction 2. Child abuse -- Fiction 3. Foster home care -- Fiction

ISBN 978-1-4169-4899-5; 1-4169-4899-6

"Once Dream of Night was a champion racehorse, but by the time Jess DiLima gets him he's nearly dead from starvation and pneumonia, and his thin hide is covered in scars. Twelve-year-old Shiloh is scarred, too, both from physical abuse and from the emotional withering of years in foster care. . . . [Henson's] novel, like her characters, shimmers with anger and hope. She doesn't pull her punches—the scenes and flashbacks of abuse are realistically graphic—but she also never lets the details overwhelm the narrative, always offering the possibility of redemption." Kirkus

Hepler, Heather

The **cupcake** queen. Dutton 2009 242p $16.99; pa $7.99

Grades: 6 7 8 9   Fic

1. Baking -- Fiction 2. Moving -- Fiction 3. Family life -- Fiction

ISBN 978-0-525-42157-3; 0-525-42157-2; 978-0-14-241668-6 pa; 0-14-241668-1 pa

LC 2008-48971

While longing to return to life in New York City, thirteen-year-old Penny helps her mother and grandmother run a cupcake bakery in Hog's Hollow, tries to avoid the beastly popular girls, to be a good friend to quirky Tally, and to catch the eye of enigmatic Marcus.

"An endearing and poignant story about standing up to adversity and finding peace in what it is, rather than holding out for what it could be." Publ Wkly

Herbach, Geoff

Nothing special; Geoff Herbach. Sourcebooks Inc. 2012 290 p. (paperback) $9.99; (ebook) $9.99

Grades: 6 7 8 9 10   Fic

1. Friendship -- Fiction 2. Dysfunctional families -- Fiction 3. Teenagers -- Conduct of life -- Fiction

ISBN 1402265077; 9781402265075; 9781402265099

In this book, author Geoff Herbach tells the story of Felton, a football and track star who deals with his girlfriend Aleah abroad in Germany and "the possibility that his younger brother Andrew could be falling apart. Andrew has convinced their mother to let him go to band camp, but Felton discovers that Andrew, usually the sane member of the family, has in fact run away to Florida. An impromptu road trip with erstwhile best friend Gus turns up surprising reasons for Andrew's escape." (Kirkus Reviews)

Stupid fast. Sourcebooks 2011 311p pa $9.99

Grades: 6 7 8 9 10   Fic

1. Boys -- Fiction 2. Football -- Fiction

ISBN 978-1-4022-5630-1; 1-4022-5630-2

"Herbach is at his peak limning the confusion and frustration of a young man who no longer recognizes his own body, and Felton's self-deprecating take on his newly awarded A-list status is funny and compelling." Bull Cent Child Books

Herlong, Madaline

The **great** wide sea; [by] M. H. Herlong. Viking Children's Books 2008 283p $16.99; pa $6.99

Grades: 7 8 9 10   Fic

1. Sailing -- Fiction 2. Brothers -- Fiction 3. Bereavement -- Fiction 4. Father-son relationship -- Fiction 5. Survival after airplane accidents, shipwrecks, etc. -- Fiction

ISBN 978-0-670-06330-7; 0-670-06330-4; 978-0-14-241670-9 pa; 0-14-241670-3 pa

LC 2008-08384

Still mourning the death of their mother, three brothers go with their father on an extended sailing trip off the Florida Keys and have an adventure at sea

"Herlong makes the most of the three boys' characters, each exceptionally well developed here, to make this as much a novel of brotherhood as a sea story." Bull Cent Child Books

Herrick, Steven

By the river. Front Street 2006 238p $16.95

Grades: 8 9 10 11 12   Fic

1. Death -- Fiction 2. Brothers -- Fiction 3. Single parent family -- Fiction

ISBN 1-932425-72-1

LC 2005-23967

First published 2004 in the United Kingdom

A fourteen-year-old describes, through prose poems, his life in a small Australian town in 1962, where, since their mother's death, he and his brother have been mainly on their own to learn about life, death, and love.

"The poems are simple but potent in their simplicity, blending together in a compelling, evocative story of a gentle, intelligent boy growing up and learning to deal with a sometimes-ugly little world that he . . . will eventually escape." Voice Youth Advocates

Hesse, Karen

★ **Brooklyn** Bridge; a novel. Feiwel and Friends 2008 229p il map $17.95

Grades: 5 6 7 8 9 10   **Fic**

1. Immigrants -- Fiction 2. Family life -- Fiction 3. Social classes -- Fiction 4. Homeless persons -- Fiction 5. Russian Americans -- Fiction

ISBN 978-0-312-37886-8; 0-312-37886-6

LC 2008-05624

In 1903 Brooklyn, fourteen-year-old Joseph Michtom's life changes for the worse when his parents, Russian immigrants, invent the teddy bear and turn their apartment into a factory, while nearby the glitter of Coney Island contrasts with the dismal lives of children dwelling under the Brooklyn Bridge.

Hesse "applies her gift for narrative voice to this memorable story. . . . The novel explodes with dark drama before its eerie but moving resolution." Publ Wkly

★ **Letters** from Rifka. Holt & Co. 1992 148p $16.95; pa $6.99

Grades: 5 6 7 8   **Fic**

1. Jews -- Fiction 2. Letters -- Fiction 3. Immigrants -- Fiction 4. Young adult literature -- Works 5. Children's literature -- Works -- Grades two through six

ISBN 0-8050-1964-2; 0-312-53561-9 pa

LC 91-48007

In letters to her cousin, Rifka, a young Jewish girl, chronicles her family's flight from Russia in 1919 and her own experiences when she must be left in Belgium for a while when the others emigrate to America

"Based on the true story of the author's great-aunt, the moving account of a brave young girl's story brings to life the day-to-day trials and horrors experienced by many immigrants as well as the resourcefulness and strength they found within themselves." Horn Book

★ **Out** of the dust. Scholastic 1997 227p $16.95; pa $6.99

Grades: 5 6 7 8   **Fic**

1. Novels in verse 2. Farm life -- Fiction 3. Dust storms -- Fiction

ISBN 0-590-36080-9; 0-590-37125-8 pa

LC 96-40344

Awarded the Newbery Medal, 1998

"Hesse's writing transcends the gloom and transforms it into a powerfully compelling tale of a girl with enormous strength, courage, and love. The entire novel is written in very readable blank verse." Booklist

Safekeeping; Karen Hesse. Feiwel and Friends 2012 294 p. ill., map $17.99

Grades: 7 8 9 10 11 12   **Fic**

1. Revolutions -- Fiction 2. Voyages and travels -- Fiction

ISBN 1250011345; 9781250011343

LC 2012288414

In this book, a "group of rebels called the American People's Party has taken control" in the U.S. "Radley, an American teenager returning home from doing volunteer work in Haiti, finds her parents gone and her Vermont home abandoned. Not knowing whom to trust or where she"ll be safe, she sets out on foot to Canada, befriending a reticent girl along the way. The two form a tentative friendship and manage to cross into Canada." (Publishers Weekly)

Witness. Scholastic Press 2001 161p $16.95; pa $5.99

Grades: 6 7 8 9   **Fic**

1. Novels in verse 2. Ku Klux Klan 3. Prejudices -- Fiction

ISBN 0-439-27199-1; 0-439-27200-9 pa

LC 00-54139

A series of poems express the views of eleven people in a small Vermont town, including a young black girl and a young Jewish girl, during the early 1920s when the Ku Klux Klan is trying to infiltrate the town

"The story is divided into five acts, and would lend itself beautifully to performance. The plot unfolds smoothly, and the author creates multidimensional characters." SLJ

Hesser, Terry Spencer

Kissing doorknobs. Delacorte Press 1998 149p hardcover o.p. pa $6.50

Grades: 7 8 9 10   **Fic**

1. Friendship -- Fiction 2. Family life -- Fiction 3. Mental illness -- Fiction 4. Obsessive-compulsive disorder -- Fiction

ISBN 0-385-32329-8; 0-440-41314-1 pa

LC 97-26937

Fourteen-year-old Tara describes how her increasingly strange compulsions begin to take over her life and affect her relationships with her family and friends

"An honest, fresh, and multilayered story to which readers will instantly relate. . . . The prose is forthright, economical, and peppered with wry humor." SLJ

Hiaasen, Carl

★ **Flush**. Knopf 2005 263p $16.95; lib bdg $18.99; pa $8.99

Grades: 5 6 7 8   **Fic**

1. Boats and boating -- Fiction 2. Environmental protection -- Fiction

ISBN 0-375-82182-1; 0-375-92182-6 lib bdg; 0-375-84185-7 pa

LC 2005-05259

With their father jailed for sinking a river boat, Noah Underwood and his younger sister, Abbey, must gather evidence that the owner of this floating casino is emptying his bilge tanks into the protected waters around their Florida Keys home

"This quick-reading, fun, family adventure harkens back to the Hardy Boys in its simplicity and quirky characters." SLJ

★ **Hoot**. Knopf 2002 292p $15.95; pa $8.95

Grades: 5 6 7 8   **Fic**

1. Owls -- Fiction 2. Environmental protection -- Fiction

ISBN 0-375-82181-3; 0-375-82916-4 pa

LC 2002-25478

A Newbery Medal honor book, 2003

Roy, who is new to his small Florida community, becomes involved in another boy's attempt to save a colony of burrowing owls from a proposed construction site

"The story is full of offbeat humor, buffoonish yet charming supporting characters, and genuinely touching scenes of children enjoying the wildness of nature." Booklist

★ **Scat**. Knopf 2009 371p $16.99; lib bdg $19.99; pa $8.99

Grades: 5 6 7 8   **Fic**

1. Teachers -- Fiction 2. Missing persons -- Fiction 3. Wildlife conservation -- Fiction

ISBN 978-0-375-83486-8; 0-375-83486-9; 978-0-375-93486-5 lib bdg; 0-375-93486-3 lib bdg; 978-0-375-83487-5 pa; 0-375-83487-7 pa

LC 2008-28266

Nick and his friend Marta decide to investigate when a mysterious fire starts near a Florida wildlife preserve and an unpopular teacher goes missing.

"Once again, Hiaasen has written an edge-of-the-seat eco-thriller. . . . From the first sentence, readers will be hooked. . . . This well-written and smoothly plotted story, with fully realized characters, will certainly appeal to mystery lovers." SLJ

Hickam, Homer H., 1943-

Crater; a Helium-3 novel. Homer Hickam. Thomas Nelson 2012 311 p.

Grades: 6 7 8   **Fic**

1. Moon -- Fiction 2. Science fiction 3. Orphans -- Fiction 4. Trucking -- Fiction 5. Space flight -- Fiction

ISBN 1595546642; 9781595546647

LC 2011051931

This young adult science fiction novel tells the story of "[l]ong-haul trucking on the Moon with raiders, romance and a secret mission. Teenage orphan Crater Trueblood was plucked from the Helium-3 mines by lunar kingpin Colonel Medaris. . . . Trueblood suddenly finds himself scouting for a convoy headed for Armstrong City and charged with picking up a mysterious package. In the course of an eventful trip, Crater survives numerous natural hazards out in the 'big suck,' learns how to deal with rambunctious truckers (much like herding cats) and plays various high-speed low-gravity sports. He also hooks up with the Colonel's mercurial granddaughter Maria and battles genetically altered superwarriors with help from a vacuum-suited horse and a Tribble-like supercomputer." (Kirkus)

Crescent; second in the Helium-3 series. by Homer Hickam. Thomas Nelson 2013 336 p. (A Helium-3 novel) (pbk.) $9.99

Grades: 7 8 9 10 11 12   **Fic**

1. Moon -- Fiction 2. Fugitives from justice -- Fiction 3. War -- Fiction 4. Science fiction 5. Prejudices -- Fiction 6. Prisoners of war -- Fiction

ISBN 1595546634; 9781595546630

LC 2012051410

This book is the sequel to author Homer Hickam's "Crater". "Weary of the war with the Unified Countries of the World . . . Crater Trueblood captures Crescent--a short, mouthy and thoroughly deadly genetically altered superwar-

rior from Earth. He is then faced with the tall task of keeping her from killing, or being killed by, the vengeful citizens of Moontown. Meanwhile, his estranged sweetheart, Maria, . . . barely blasts her way out of a UCW kidnap attempt." (Kirkus Reviews)

"Expertly blending space opera and hard sci-fi, romance, and even mystery (there's a detour for a nifty whodunit), this is fast paced, packed with intriguing ideas." Booklist

Hicks, Deron R.

The **secrets** of Shakespeare's grave; by Deron R. Hicks ; [illustrated by Mark Edward Geyer] Houghton Mifflin Harcourt 2012 273 p. (hardcover) $16.99

Grades: 4 5 6   **Fic**

1. Mystery fiction 2. Shakespeare, William, 1564-1616 -- Fiction 3. Cousins -- Fiction 4. Mystery and detective stories 5. Brothers and sisters -- Fiction 6. Adventure and adventurers -- Fiction 7. Family-owned business enterprises -- Fiction

ISBN 0547840349; 9780547840345

LC 2012014801

In this book by Deron R. Hicks "Twelve-year-old Colophon Letterford has a serious mystery on her hands. Will she discover the link between her family's literary legacy and Shakespeare's tomb before it's too late? Antique paintings, secret passages, locked mausoleums, a four-hundred-year-old treasure, and a cast of quirky (and some ignoble) characters all add up to a . . . journey through literary time and space in real-world locales from Mont St. Michel to Stratford-Upon-Avon to Central Park!" (Publisher's note)

Higgins, F. E.

★ The **Black** Book of Secrets. Feiwel and Friends 2007 273p $14.95

Grades: 4 5 6 7   **Fic**

1. Apprentices -- Fiction 2. Pawnbrokers -- Fiction

ISBN 978-0-312-36844-9; 0-312-36844-5

LC 2007-32559

When Ludlow Fitch runs away from his thieving parents in the City, he meets up with the mysterious Joe Zabbidou, who calls himself a secret pawnbroker, and who takes Ludlow as an apprentice to record the confessions of the townspeople of Pagus Parvus, where resentments are many and trust is scarce.

This is "an intriguing blend of adventure and historical fiction spiced with a light touch of the fantastic." Voice Youth Advocates

The **Eyeball** Collector. Feiwel & Friends 2009 251p $14.99

Grades: 7 8 9 10   **Fic**

1. Horror fiction 2. Mystery fiction

ISBN 978-0-312-56681-4; 0-312-56681-6

"In what the author dubs a 'polyquel' that partially bridges her Black Book of Secrets (2007) and its prequel Bone Magician (2008), Higgins sends a suddenly penniless young orphan from the filthy streets of Urbs Umida's South Side to an extravagantly rococo estate house in search of vengeance for his family's ruin. . . . Readers with a taste for lurid prose, macabre twists, riddles, exotic poisons, high-society caricatures, murderous schemes and scenes of stomach-churning degeneracy will find some or all of these in every chapter, and though the author trots in multiple characters and references from previous episodes, this one stands sturdily on its own." Kirkus

The **lunatic's** curse. Feiwel and Friends 2011 336p $15.99

Grades: 6 7 8 9 **Fic**

1. Horror fiction

ISBN 978-0-312-56682-1; 0-312-56682-4

"The prosperous town of Oppum Oppidulum, the deep and cold adjacent Lake Beluarum and the Asylum for the Peculiar and Bizarre that sits on an island in said lake all hold horrifying secrets. Young Rex discovers this when his father is confined to the Asylum after suddenly going mad and eating his own hand—to the open glee of Rex's sinister new stepmother Acantha Grammaticus. . . . Strewing her narrative with dark hints, obscure clues, assorted lunatics and, in particular, both macabre cuisine and a panoply of noxious or tantalizingly evocative odors, the author contrives a highly atmospheric experience. Readers with strong stomachs and a taste for melodramatic narratives . . . will devour this yarn with relish." Kirkus

Higgins, Jack

★ **Sure** fire; [by] Jack Higgins with Justin Richards. G.P. Putnam's Sons 2007 237p $16.99

Grades: 6 7 8 9 **Fic**

1. Adventure fiction 2. Spies -- Fiction 3. Twins -- Fiction 4. Fathers -- Fiction

ISBN 978-0-399-24784-2; 0-399-24784-X

LC 2007008144

First published 2006 in the United Kingdom

Resentful of having to go and live with their estranged father after the death of their mother, fifteen-year-old twins, Rich and Jade, soon find they have more complicated problems when their father is kidnapped and their attempts to rescue him involve them in a dangerous international plot to control the world's oil.

This is a "standout YA spy novel. . . . Each chapter ends with a cliff-hanger, maintaining the high level of suspense." Publ Wkly

Other titles in this series are:
Death run (2008)
Sharp shot (2009)
First strike (2010)

Higgins, M. G.

Bi -Normal; M. G. Higgins. Saddleback Pub 2013 191 p. (paperback) $9.95

Grades: 7 8 9 10 11 12 **Fic**

1. School stories 2. Gay teenagers -- Fiction

ISBN 1622500040; 9781622500048

In this book, "a teen football player with a girlfriend discovers he has feelings for another boy. When Brett first notices his attraction to Zach, a boy who sits next to him in art class, he wants to push it away Brett and his friends are the kind of guys who ogle girls' bodies and pick on boys they perceive as gay. As his feelings intensify, however, Brett is torn between acting on his attraction and acting out of his denial." (Kirkus Reviews)

Higgins, Simon

Moonshadow; rise of the ninja. Little Brown & Co. 2010 325p il $15.99

Grades: 4 5 6 7 **Fic**

1. Ninja -- Fiction 2. Spies -- Fiction 3. Secret societies -- Fiction

ISBN 978-0-316-05531-4; 0-316-05531-X

First published 2008 in Australia with title: Moonshadow: eye of the beast

It's the dawn of an age of peace in medieval Japan. But a power-hungry warlord is plotting to plunge the national into a deadly civil war. Enter Moonshadow, the newest agent for the Grey Light Order, a secret brotherhood of ninja spy warriors. Can Moonshadow defeat the evil warlord or will his first mission be his last?

"The swordplay is fast and furious, and Japanese terms and places are integrated in a manner that reluctant readers will find accessible. This adventure is part spy novel, part magic, and all fun." SLJ

The **nightmare** ninja. Little, Brown 2011 368p (Moonshadow) $15.99

Grades: 4 5 6 7 **Fic**

1. Ninja -- Fiction 2. Orphans -- Fiction 3. Supernatural -- Fiction

ISBN 978-0-316-05533-8; 0-316-05533-6

LC 2010043177

Battling a power-hungry warlord in medieval Japan, teenaged Moonshadow, an orphaned ninja in the shogun's secret service with the ability to see through the eyes of animals, encounters a weaponless assassin who enters the mind of his victims during their sleep.

"Higgins effectively uses this work to set the stage for a compelling third installment." Kirkus

Hill, C. J.

Erasing time; C. J. Hill. Katherine Tegen Books 2012 361 p. $17.99

Grades: 8 9 10 11 **Fic**

1. Secrecy -- Fiction 2. Resistance to government 3. Future life -- Fiction 4. Science fiction 5. Twins -- Fiction 6. Sisters -- Fiction 7. Time travel -- Fiction

ISBN 0062123920; 9780062123923

LC 2011044624

Slayers. Feiwel and Friends 2011 373p $16.99

Grades: 7 8 9 10 11 12 **Fic**

1. Fantasy fiction 2. Camps -- Fiction 3. Ability -- Fiction 4. Dragons -- Fiction 5. Supernatural -- Fiction

ISBN 978-0-312-61414-0; 0-312-61414-4

LC 2011023559

At a rustic summer camp, sixteen-year-old Tori, a senator's daughter, learns that she is descended from medieval dragon slayers, that dragons still exist, and that she is expected to hone her special abilities to join her fellow campers in battling the beasts and the man who controls them.

"The dragon mythos has a good dollop of modern science, and Hill offers cunning peeks into the minds of characters on all sides of the power struggle. . . . The character development, plotting, and ethical quandries make this more than a worthy equal to the works of Rick Riordan or Christopher Paolini." Booklist

Hill, Kirkpatrick

Do not pass go. Margaret K. McElderry Books
2007 229p $15.99

Grades: 6 7 8 9   **Fic**

1. Fathers -- Fiction 2. Prisoners -- Fiction
ISBN 978-1-4169-1400-6; 1-4169-1400-5

LC 2006-03254

When Deet's father is jailed for using drugs, Deet learns
that prison is not what he expected, nor are other people necessarily the way he thought they were.

"Hill does not sugar-coat the hardships that plague
Deet's family. . . . Deet emerges as a sensitive, courageous
protagonist who is smart enough and open-minded enough
to look past people's mistakes." Publ Wkly

Hilmo, Tess

★ **With** a name like Love. Margaret Ferguson
Books/Farrar Straus Giroux 2011 249p $16.99

Grades: 5 6 7 8   **Fic**

1. Mystery fiction 2. Country life -- Fiction 3. Christian
life -- Fiction 4. Conduct of life -- Fiction
ISBN 978-0-374-38465-4; 0-374-38465-7

LC 2010036314

Thirteen-year-old Olivene Love gets tangled up in a
murder mystery when her itinerant preaching family arrives
in the small town of Binder, Arkansas in 1957.

"Hilmo creates a family, town and a mystery that readers
won't soon forget." Kirkus

Hinton, S. E.

★ The **outsiders**. Viking 1967 188p $17.99;
pa $9.99

Grades: 7 8 9 10   **Fic**

1. Social classes -- Fiction 2. Juvenile delinquency --
Fiction
ISBN 0-670-53257-6; 0-14-038572-X pa
ALA YALSA Margaret A. Edwards Award (1988)

"This remarkable novel by a seventeen-year-old girl
gives a moving, credible view of the outsiders from the
inside—their loyalty to each other, their sensitivity under tough crusts, their understanding of self and society."
Horn Book

Hinwood, Christine

The **returning**. Dial Books 2011 302p map
$17.99

Grades: 6 7 8 9 10   **Fic**

1. War stories 2. Villages -- Fiction
ISBN 978-0-8037-3528-6; 0-8037-3528-6

LC 2010-08398

First published 2009 in Australia with title: Bloodflower

When the twelve-year war between the Uplanders and
Downlanders is over and Cam returns home to his village,
questions dog him, from how he lost an arm to why he was
the only one of his fellow soldiers to survive, such that he
must leave until his own suspicions are resolved.

"Themes of rebuilding and redemption are powerful, but
it is in the small, acutely observed details of debut author
Hinwood's world that her story truly shines." Publ Wkly

Hirahara, Naomi

1001 cranes. Delacorte Press 2008 230p $15.99;
lib bdg $18.99; pa $6.50

Grades: 5 6 7 8   **Fic**

1. Family life -- Fiction 2. Grandparents -- Fiction 3.
Japanese Americans -- Fiction
ISBN 978-0-385-73556-8; 0-385-73556-1; 978-0-385-
90541-1 lib bdg; 0-385-90541-6 lib bdg; 978-0-440-
42234-1 pa; 0-440-42234-5 pa

LC 2007-27655

With her parents on the verge of separating, Angela, a
twelve-year-old Japanese American girl, spends the summer in Los Angeles with her grandparents, where she folds
paper cranes into wedding displays, becomes involved with
a young skateboarder, and learns how complicated relationships can be.

Angela's "colorful, bold voice captures the excitement
of her first love as well as the anxiety of not understanding
the many secrets of the adults around her. By experiencing
her family's support, by learning about her Japanese heritage, and by acknowledging the various ways that love is expressed, Angela emerges into a strong, caring person." SLJ

Hiranandani, Veera

★ The **whole** story of half a girl. Delacorte Press
2012 $16.99; lib bdg $19.99

Grades: 4 5 6 7   **Fic**

1. School stories 2. East Indian Americans -- Fiction
3. Racially mixed people -- Fiction 4. Depression
(Psychology) -- Fiction
ISBN 978-0-385-74128-6; 0-385-74128-6; 978-0-375-
98995-7 lib bdg; 0-375-98995-1 lib bdg; 978-0-375-
98441-9 ebook

LC 2011026178

In this book, "[w]hen Sonia"s father loses his job at the
end of her fifth-grade year, it means she can't return to her
beloved private school and instead must navigate the rocky
waters of public school for the first time. Up until this point,
eleven-year-old Sonia has never thought that much about her
identity as the daughter of an Indian father and a Jewish-
American mother, but she is suddenly faced with questions
that she can"t always answer about her race, her ethnicity,
and her core values. She . . . begins two friendships: with
Kate, a very perky, popular girl who encourages Sonia to
try out for cheerleading but seems very keen on transforming her into something she isn't, and with Alisha, who, like
Sonia, aspires to be a writer." (Bulletin of the Center for
Children"s Books).

"Sonia's struggles are painfully realistic. . . True to life,
her problems do not wrap up neatly, but Sonia's growth is
deeply rewarding in this thoughtful and beautifully wrought
novel." Publ Wkly

Hirsch, Jeff

The **eleventh** plague. Scholastic Press 2011
278p $17.99

Grades: 7 8 9 10   **Fic**

1. Science fiction
ISBN 978-0-545-29014-2; 0-545-29014-7

LC 2010048966

Twenty years after the start of the war that caused the
Collapse, fifteen-year-old Stephen, his father, and grandfa-

ther travel post-Collapse America scavenging, but when his grandfather dies and his father decides to risk everything to save the lives of two strangers, Stephen's life is turned upside down.

This "novel is an impressive story with strong characters. . . . Hirsch delivers a tight, well-crafted story." Publ Wkly

Hirsch, Odo

Darius Bell and the glitter pool. Kane/Miller 2010 214p $15.99

Grades: 4 5 6 7   **Fic**

    1. Gifts -- Fiction 2. Poverty -- Fiction
    ISBN 978-1-935279-65-5; 1-935279-65-3
    First published 2009 in Australia

The Bell family's ancestors were showered with honours, gifts and grants of land. In exchange, they have bestowed a Gift, once every 25 years, on the town. Now it's Darius's father's turn and there is no money for an impressive gift. When an earthquake reveals a glorious cave, with the most beautiful minerals lining the walls, he thinks he's found the answer.

"With an inventive cast of characters and a surprise twist at the end, this gentle, appealing story would make a terrific read-aloud for a young audience." Booklist

Hitchcock, Shannon

The **ballad** of Jessie Pearl; Shannon Hitchcock. 1st ed. Namelos llc 2012 131 p. ill. (hardcover) $18.95

Grades: 5 6 7 8   **Fic**

    1. Love stories 2. Historical fiction 3. Tuberculosis -- Fiction
    ISBN 160898141X; 9781608981410; 9781608981427
    LC 2012936706

In this novel, by Shannon Hitchcock, "it's 1922, and Jessie has big plans for her future, but that's before tuberculosis strikes. Though she has no talent for cooking, cleaning, or nursing, Jessie puts her dreams on hold to help her family. She falls in love for the first time ever, and suddenly what she wants is not so simple anymore." (Publisher's note)

Hobbs, Valerie

★ The **last** best days of summer. Frances Foster Books 2010 197p $16.99

Grades: 5 6 7 8   **Fic**

    1. Artists -- Fiction 2. Old age -- Fiction 3. Popularity -- Fiction 4. Grandmothers -- Fiction 5. Down syndrome -- Fiction
    ISBN 978-0-374-34670-6; 0-374-34670-4
    LC 2008-47145

During a summer visit, twelve-year-old Lucy must come to terms with both her grandmother's failing memory and how her mentally-challenged neighbor will impact her popularity when both enter the same middle school in the fall.

"The story's finely tuned realism is refreshing, particularly in Lucy's yearning for social acceptance and in the fully drawn and wholly memorable characters." Booklist

Hobbs, Will

Beardance. Atheneum Pubs. 1993 197p il pa $5.99

Grades: 7 8 9 10   **Fic**

    1. Bears -- Fiction 2. Ute Indians -- Fiction
    ISBN 0-689-31867-7; 0-689-87072-8 pa
    LC 92-44874

While accompanying an elderly rancher on a trip into the San Juan Mountains, Cloyd, a Ute Indian boy, tries to help two orphaned grizzly cubs survive the winter and, at the same time, completes his spirit mission.

"The story offers plenty of action and memorable characters, and the descriptions of Ute rituals and legends, the setting, and Cloyd's first experiences with spirit dreams are particularly well done." Horn Book Guide

★ **Bearstone**. Atheneum Pubs. 1989 154p hardcover o.p. pa $4.99

Grades: 7 8 9 10   **Fic**

    1. Ute Indians -- Fiction
    ISBN 0-689-87071-X pa
    LC 89-6641

"The growth and maturity that Cloyd acquires as the summer progresses is juxtaposed poetically against the majestic Colorado landscape. Hobbs has creatively blended myth and reality as Cloyd forges a new identity for himself." Voice Youth Advocates

Crossing the wire. HarperCollins 2006 216p $15.99; lib bdg $16.89; pa $5.99

Grades: 5 6 7 8   **Fic**

    1. Mexicans -- Fiction 2. Illegal aliens -- Fiction
    ISBN 978-0-06-074138-9; 0-06-074138-4; 978-0-06-074139-6 lib bdg; 0-06-074139-2 lib bdg; 978-0-06-074140-2 pa; 0-06-074140-6 pa
    LC 2005-19697

Fifteen-year-old Victor Flores journeys north in a desperate attempt to cross the Arizona border and find work in the United States to support his family in central Mexico.

This is "an exciting story in a vital contemporary setting." Voice Youth Advocates

Downriver. Atheneum Pubs. 1991 204p hardcover o.p. pa $6.99

Grades: 7 8 9 10   **Fic**

    1. White-water canoeing -- Fiction
    ISBN 0-689-31690-9; 0-440-22673-2 pa
    LC 90-1044

Fifteen-year-old Jessie and the other rebellious teenage members of a wilderness survival school team abandon their adult leader, hijack his boats, and try to run the dangerous white water at the bottom of the Grand Canyon

"The book is exquisitely plotted, with nail-biting suspense and excitement." SLJ

Ghost canoe. Morrow Junior Bks. 1997 195p $16.99

Grades: 5 6 7 8   **Fic**

    1. Adventure fiction 2. Buried treasure -- Fiction
    ISBN 0-688-14193-5
    LC 96-34417

Fourteen-year-old Nathan, fishing with the Makah in the Pacific Northwest, finds himself holding a vital clue when a mysterious stranger comes to town looking for Spanish treasure

"Hobbs blends together a number of elements to create an exciting adventure set in 1874. . . . A winning tale that artfully combines history, nature, and suspense." SLJ

★ **Go** big or go home. HarperCollinsPublishers 2008 185p $15.99; lib bdg $16.89; pa $5.99

Grades: 6 7 8 9   **Fic**

1. Science fiction 2. Cousins -- Fiction 3. Meteorites -- Fiction

ISBN 0-06-074141-4; 0-06-074142-2 lib bdg; 0-06-074143-0 pa; 978-0-06-074141-9; 978-0-06-074142-6 lib bdg; 978-0-06-074143-3 pa

LC 2006100440

Fourteen-year-old Brady and his cousin Quinn love extreme sports, but nothing could prepare them for the aftermath of Brady's close encounter with a meteorite after it crashes into his Black Hills, South Dakota, bedroom.

"The sense of place is powerful, with bits of lore about the region making the reader feel immersed in the story and its setting, and the characterizations are especially strong." Voice Youth Advocates

★ **Jason's** gold. Morrow Junior Bks. 1999 221p $16.99; pa $5.99

Grades: 5 6 7 8   **Fic**

1. Orphans -- Fiction 2. Voyages and travels -- Fiction 3. Klondike River Valley (Yukon) -- Gold discoveries -- Fiction

ISBN 0-688-15093-4; 0-380-72914-8 pa

LC 99-17973

When news of the discovery of gold in Canada's Yukon Territory in 1897 reaches fifteen-year-old Jason, he embarks on a 10,000-mile journey to strike it rich

"The successful presentation of a fascinating era, coupled with plenty of action, makes this a good historical fiction choice." SLJ

Leaving Protection. HarperCollins 2004 178p il map $15.99; pa $5.99

Grades: 7 8 9 10   **Fic**

1. Fishing -- Fiction 2. Buried treasure -- Fiction

ISBN 0-688-17475-2; 0-380-73312-9 pa

LC 2003-15545

Sixteen-year-old Robbie Daniels, happy to get a job aboard a troller fishing for king salmon off southeastern Alaska, finds himself in danger when he discovers that his mysterious captain is searching for long-buried Russian plaques that lay claim to Alaska and the Northwest

This "nautical thriller brims with detail about the fishing life and weaves in historical facts as well. . . . Robbie's doubts build to a climactic finale involving a dramatic and fateful storm at sea, grippingly rendered. Fans of maritime tales will relish the atmosphere and the bursts of action." Publ Wkly

Never say die; by Will Hobbs. HarperCollins Children's Books 2012 224 p. (trade bdg.) $16.99

Grades: 4 5 6 7   **Fic**

1. Canada -- Fiction 2. Wilderness survival -- Fiction 3. Adventure fiction 4. Bears -- Fiction 5. Caribou -- Fiction 6. Eskimos -- Fiction 7. Brothers -- Fiction 8. Inuit -- Canada -- Fiction 9. Photojournalism -- Fiction

10. Climatic changes -- Fiction

ISBN 006170878X; 9780061708787; 9780061708794

LC 2011053289

This juvenile adventure novel, by Will Hobbs, is set "in Canada's Arctic, [where] Nick Thrasher is an accomplished Inuit hunter at fifteen. . . . Ryan Powers . . . invites Nick to come along and help him find the caribou. Barely down the river, disaster strikes. . . . With nothing but the clothes on his back and the knife on his hip, Nick is up against it in a world of wolves, caribou, and grizzlies. All the while, the monstrous grolar bear stalks the land." (Publisher's note)

Take me to the river. HarperCollins 2011 184p $15.99; lib bdg $16.89

Grades: 5 6 7 8   **Fic**

1. Cousins -- Fiction 2. Canoes and canoeing -- Fiction

ISBN 978-0-06-074144-0; 0-06-074144-9; 978-0-06-074145-7 lib bdg; 0-06-074145-7 lib bdg

LC 2010003147

When North Carolina fourteen-year-old Dylan Sands joins his fifteen-year-old cousin Rio in running the Rio Grande River, they face a tropical storm and a fugitive kidnapper.

"The story unfolds in a disarming manner. The pace is quick, and the challenges are relentless, but the writing is so grounded in physical details and emotional realism that every turn of events seems convincing within the context of the story." Booklist

Wild Man Island. HarperCollins Pubs. 2002 184p $15.99; lib bdg $16.89; pa $5.99

Grades: 6 7 8 9   **Fic**

1. Wilderness survival -- Fiction

ISBN 0-688-17473-6; 0-06-029810-3 lib bdg; 0-380-73310-2 pa

LC 2001-39818

After fourteen-year-old Andy slips away from his kayaking group to visit the wilderness site of his archaeologist father's death, a storm strands him on Admiralty Island, Alaska, where he manages to survive, encounters unexpected animal and human inhabitants, and looks for traces of the earliest prehistoric immigrants to America

"A well-paced adventure, this novel combines survival saga, mystery, and archaeological expedition." Voice Youth Advocates

Hocking, Amanda

Wake; Amanda Hocking. St. Martin's Griffin 2012 309 p. (hardback) $17.99

Grades: 7 8 9 10   **Fic**

1. Occult fiction 2. Fantasy fiction 3. Sirens (Mythology) -- Fiction 4. Love -- Fiction 5. Sisters -- Fiction 6. Supernatural -- Fiction 7. Seaside resorts -- Fiction

ISBN 1250008123; 9781250008121; 9781429956581

LC 2012014630

This is the first in Amanda Hocking's Watersong series. Here, "Gemma Fisher is happy—she's a star on the swim team, her family is loving and supportive, and the crushworthy boy next door returns her interest. The only downside: three gorgeous but creepy new girls who have her in their sights." These girls ultimately turn out to be Sirens who trick Gemma into drinking potion that turns her into a Siren as well. (Publishers Weekly)

Hodkin, Michelle

The **evolution** of Mara Dyer; Michelle Hodkin. Simon & Schuster Books for Young Readers 2012 527 p. (hardcover) $17.99

Grades: 7 8 9 10 11 12   **Fic**

  1. Stalkers -- Fiction 2. Supernatural -- Fiction 3. Post-traumatic stress disorder -- Fiction 4. Love -- Fiction

  ISBN 1442421797; 9781442421790; 9781442421813

                          LC 2012019195

In this novel by Michelle Hodkin, part of the Mara Dyer Trilogy, "Mara continues her relationship with wealthy Noah. . . . Meanwhile, Mara insists that her supposedly dead former boyfriend, Jude, continues to stalk her. She is being treated as an outpatient for PTSD after causing (as she originally believed) the deaths of Jude and her friends. . . . Noah uses his wits and wealth to try to protect her and to investigate the possibility that Jude indeed survived." (Kirkus)

The **unbecoming** of Mara Dyer. Simon & Schuster 2011 456p $16.99

Grades: 7 8 9 10 11 12   **Fic**

  1. School stories 2. Family life -- Fiction 3. Supernatural -- Fiction 4. Post-traumatic stress disorder -- Fiction

  ISBN 978-1-4424-2176-9; 1-4424-2176-2

                          LC 2010050862

Seventeen-year-old Mara cannot remember the accident that took the lives of three of her friends but, after moving from Rhode Island to Florida, finding love with Noah, and more deaths, she realizes uncovering something buried in her memory might save her family and her future.

"The characters are real and wonderful, and the supernatural story is riveting." SLJ

Hof, Marjolijn

Mother number zero. Groundwood Books 2011 179p $16.95

Grades: 4 5 6 7   **Fic**

  1. Adoption -- Fiction 2. Siblings -- Fiction 3. Family life -- Fiction

  ISBN 978-1-55498-078-9; 1-55498-078-X

Fay "and his older sister An Bing Wa were both adopted; she was an abandoned baby in China, and he was born to a mother traumatized in the Bosnian conflict. A new girl in the neighborhood, Maud, takes a keen interest in Fay's story and urges him to find his birth mother. . . . Hof . . . writes Fay's narration with a calm, matter-of-fact voice that possesses a literalness and simplicity in keeping with his youth. . . . The story nonetheless treats the characters with quiet percipience. . . . Younger fans of domestic novels who like a tale with more gravitas if not reading difficulty will appreciate this thoughtful family story." Bull Cent Child Books

Hoffman, Alice

Green angel. Scholastic Press 2003 116p pa $5.99

Grades: 7 8 9 10   **Fic**

  1. Gardening -- Fiction

  ISBN 0-439-44384-9; 0-545-20411-9 pa

                          LC 2002-6980

Haunted by grief and by her past after losing her family in a fire, fifteen-year-old Green retreats into her ruined garden as she struggles to survive emotionally and physically on her own

"A powerfully written and thought-provoking selection." SLJ

★ **Green** witch. Scholastic Press 2010 135p $17.99

Grades: 7 8 9 10 11 12   **Fic**

  1. Orphans -- Fiction 2. Gardening -- Fiction 3. Bereavement -- Fiction 4. Storytelling -- Fiction 5. Supernatural -- Fiction 6. Missing persons -- Fiction

  ISBN 978-0-545-14195-6; 0-545-14195-8

                          LC 2009-17606

A year after her world was nearly destroyed, sixteen-year-old Green has become the one villagers turn to for aid, especially to record their stories, but Green will need the help of other women who, like herself, are believed to be witches if she is to find her best friend and her one true love.

"Haunting, philosophical, and filled with poetic imagery . . . this book will leave an indelible mark." Publ Wkly

Hoffman, Mary

★ The **falconer's** knot; a story of friars, flirtation and foul play. Bloomsbury Children's Books 2007 297p $16.95

Grades: 7 8 9 10   **Fic**

  1. Love stories 2. Renaissance -- Fiction 3. Religious life -- Fiction

  ISBN 978-1-59990-056-8; 1-59990-056-4

                          LC 2006-16365

Silvano and Chiara, teens sent to live in a friary and a nunnery in Renaissance Italy, are drawn to one another and dream of a future together, but when murders are committed in the friary, they must discover who is behind the crimes before they can realize their love.

"Hoffman creates utterly engaging characters and vivid settings, and she skillfully turns up the suspense, wrapping her varied plot threads into a satisfying whole." Booklist

Hoffman, Nina Kiriki

A **stir** of bones. Viking 2003 211p $15.99

Grades: 7 8 9 10   **Fic**

  1. Ghost stories 2. Wife abuse -- Fiction

  ISBN 0-670-03551-3

                          LC 2003-5029

Fourteen-year-old Susan Blackstrom "begins the painful process of breaking away from her abusive father, with help from allies both human and supernatural. A chance encounter with three classmates leads Susan to an abandoned house that . . . harbors an uncommonly substantial ghost named Nathan. . . . Richly endowed with complex relationships, a strange and subtle brand of magic, evocative language, and suspenseful storytelling, this will draw readers into a world less safe and simple than it seems at first glance." Booklist

Hokenson, Terry

The **winter** road; 1st ed.; Front Street 2006
175p $16.95

Grades: 7 8 9 10   **Fic**
1. Survival after airplane accidents, shipwrecks, etc. --
Fiction
ISBN 1-932425-45-4
LC 2005027030

Seventeen-year-old Willa, still grieving over the death
of her older brother and the neglect of her father, decides
to fly a small plane to fetch her mother from Northern
Ontario, but when the plane crashes she is all alone in the
snowy wilderness.

"The mortal challenges Willa faces make for a gripping
narrative, one sharpened by visceral details." Booklist

Holder, Nancy

Crusade; by Nancy Holder and Debbie Viguie.
Simon Pulse 2010 470p $16.99

Grades: 7 8 9 10 11   **Fic**
1. Horror fiction 2. Sisters -- Fiction 3. Vampires --
Fiction 4. Supernatural -- Fiction
ISBN 978-1-4169-9802-0; 1-4169-9802-0
LC 2010-9094

An international team of six teenaged vampire hunters,
trained in Salamanca, Spain, goes to New Orleans seeking to
rescue team-member Jenn's younger sister as the vampires
escalate their efforts to take over the Earth.

"The cinematic writing and apocalyptic scenario should
find a ready audience." Publ Wkly

Damned; by Nancy Holder and Debbie Viguie.
Simon Pulse 2011 $16.99; pa $9.99

Grades: 7 8 9 10   **Fic**
1. Horror fiction 2. Vampires -- Fiction 3. Supernatural
-- Fiction
ISBN 978-1-4169-9804-4; 1-4169-9804-7; 978-1-
4169-9805-1 pa; 1-4169-9805-5 pa
LC 2011005474

As the newly appointed Hunter, teenager Jenn leads the
fighting teams who defend against the Cursed Ones--the
vampires who are taking over Earth--but an even more sinister force now threatens the teams of hunters, with the fate
of humanity at stake.

Holm, Jennifer L.

★ **Boston** Jane: an adventure. HarperCollins
Pubs. 2001 273p hardcover o.p. pa $6.99

Grades: 6 7 8 9   **Fic**
1. Chinook Indians -- Fiction 2. Frontier and pioneer
life -- Fiction
ISBN 0-06-028738-1; 0-06-028739-X; 0-06-440849-
3 pa
LC 2001-16753

Schooled in the lessons of etiquette for young ladies
of 1854, Miss Jane Peck of Philadelphia finds little use for
manners during her long sea voyage to the Pacific Northwest
and while living among the American traders and Chinook
Indians of Washington Territory

"Strong characterizations, meticulous attention to historical details . . . and a perceptive understanding of human
nature make this a first-rate story not to be missed." Booklist

Other titles about Boston Jane are:
Boston Jane: the claim (2004)
Boston Jane: wilderness days (2002)

★ **Middle** school is worse than meatloaf; a year
told through stuff. by Jennifer L. Holm; pictures by
Elicia Castaldi. Atheneum Books for Young Readers
2007 un il $12.99

Grades: 5 6 7 8   **Fic**
1. School stories 2. Family life -- Fiction
ISBN 0-689-85281-9

"Ginny Davis begins seventh grade with a list of items
to accomplish. This list, along with lots of other 'stuff'—including diary entries, refrigerator notes, cards from Grandpa, and IM screen messages—convey a year full of ups and
downs. Digitally rendered collage illustrations realistically
depict the various means of communication, and the story
flows easily from one colorful page to the next. . . . The story
combines honesty and humor to create a believable and appealing voice." SLJ

★ **Our** only May Amelia. HarperCollins Pubs.
1999 253p il hardcover o.p. pa $5.99

Grades: 5 6 7 8   **Fic**
1. Sex role -- Fiction 2. Family life -- Fiction 3. Finnish
Americans -- Fiction 4. Brothers and sisters -- Fiction
5. Frontier and pioneer life -- Fiction 6. Frontier and
pioneer life -- Washington (State) -- Fiction
ISBN 0-06-027822-6; 0-06-440856-6 pa
LC 98-47504

A Newbery Medal honor book, 2000

As the only girl in a Finnish American family of seven
brothers, May Amelia Jackson resents being expected to act
like a lady while growing up in Washington State in 1899

"The voice of the colloquial first-person narrative rings
true and provides a vivid picture of frontier and pioneer life.
. . . An afterword discusses Holm's research into her own
family's history and that of other Finnish immigrants." Horn
Book Guide

★ **Penny** from heaven. Random House 2006
274p il $15.95; lib bdg $17.99; pa $6.99

Grades: 5 6 7 8   **Fic**
1. Family life -- Fiction 2. Italian Americans -- Fiction
ISBN 0-375-83687-X; 0-375-93687-4 lib bdg; 0-375-
83689-6 pa
LC 2005-13896

A Newbery Medal honor book, 2007

As she turns twelve during the summer of 1953, Penny
gains new insights into herself and her family while also
learning a secret about her father's death.

"Holm impressively wraps pathos with comedy in
this coming-of-age story, populated by a cast of vivid
characters." Booklist

The **trouble** with May Amelia; illustrated by
Adam Gustavson. Atheneum Books for Young Readers 2011 204p il $15.99

Grades: 5 6 7 8   **Fic**
1. Sex role -- Fiction 2. Siblings -- Fiction 3. Finnish
Americans -- Fiction 4. Frontier and pioneer life --

Fiction
ISBN 1-4169-1373-4; 978-1-4169-1373-3

LC 2010042092

Living with seven brothers and her father, who thinks girls are useless, a thirteen-year-old Finnish American farm girl is determined to prove her worth when a enterprising gentleman tries to purchase their cash-strapped family settlement in Washington State in 1900.

"Holm gets her heroine just right. Narrating events in dryly witty, plainspoken first-person, this indomitable teen draws readers in with her account, through which her world comes alive." Kirkus

Holmes, Sara Lewis

★ **Operation** Yes. Arthur A. Levine Books 2009 234p $16.99

Grades: 5 6 7 8   **Fic**

1. School stories 2. Acting -- Fiction 3. Cousins -- Fiction 4. Teachers -- Fiction 5. Military bases -- Fiction
ISBN 978-0-545-10795-2; 0-545-10795-4; 978-0-545-10796-9 pa; 0-545-10796-2 pa

LC 2008053732

In her first ever teaching job, Miss Loupe uses improvisational acting exercises with her sixth-grade students at an Air Force base school, and when she experiences a family tragedy, her previously skeptical class members use what they have learned to help her, her brother, and other wounded soldiers

"Quick, funny, sad, full of heart, and irresistibly absorbing." Booklist

Holt, Kimberly Willis

★ **When** Zachary Beaver came to town. Holt & Co. 1999 227p $17.99

Grades: 5 6 7 8   **Fic**

1. Obesity -- Fiction 2. Friendship -- Fiction
ISBN 0-8050-6116-9

LC 99-27998

During the summer of 1971 in a small Texas town, thirteen-year-old Toby and his best friend Cal meet the star of a sideshow act, 600-pound Zachary, the fattest boy in the world

"Holt writes with a subtle sense of humor and sensitivity, and reading her work is a delightful experience." Voice Youth Advocates

★ The **water** seeker. Henry Holt 2010 309p $16.99

Grades: 4 5 6 7   **Fic**

1. Father-son relationship -- Fiction 2. Frontier and pioneer life -- Fiction 3. Overland journeys to the Pacific -- Fiction
ISBN 978-0-8050-8020-9; 0-8050-8020-1

LC 2009-24149

Traces the hard life, filled with losses, adversity, and adventure, of Amos, son of a trapper and dowser, from 1833 when his mother dies giving birth to him until 1859, when he himself has grown up and has a son of his own.

"Drawing on such diverse themes as Manifest Destiny, personal identity and cross-cultural relationships, the author has crafted a satisfying all-ages story that hosts a dazzling

array of richly realized secondary characters . . . and flows as effortlessly as the Platte River." Kirkus

Holub, Josef

An **innocent** soldier; translated by Michael Hofmann. Arthur A. Levine Books 2005 231p $16.99

Grades: 8 9 10 11 12   **Fic**

1. War stories
ISBN 0-439-62771-0

A sixteen-year-old farmhand is tricked into fighting in the Napoleonic Wars by the farmer for whom he works, who secretly substitutes him for the farmer's own son.

"This is a well-wrought psychological tale. . . . [It] has a lot to offer to those seeking to build a deep historical fiction collection." SLJ

Holyoke, Polly

The **Neptune** Project; Polly Holyoke. 1st ed. Disney-Hyperion Books 2013 352 p. (reinforced) $16.99

Grades: 4 5 6 7   **Fic**

1. Science fiction 2. Ocean -- Fiction 3. Genetic engineering -- Fiction 4. Survival -- Fiction 5. Undersea colonies -- Fiction 6. Environmental degradation -- Fiction
ISBN 1423157567; 9781423157564

LC 2013000353

In this novel, by Polly Holyoke, "Nere . . . is one of a group of kids who . . . have been genetically altered to survive in the ocean. . . . In order to reach the safe haven of the Neptune colony, Nere and her fellow mutates must swim through hundreds of miles of dangerous waters, relying only on their wits, dolphins, and each other to evade terrifying undersea creatures and a government that will stop at nothing to capture the Neptune kids." (Publisher's note)

Hoobler, Dorothy

★ The **ghost** in the Tokaido Inn; [by] Dorothy and Thomas Hoobler. Philomel Bks. 1999 214p $17.99; pa $6.99

Grades: 6 7 8 9   **Fic**

1. Mystery fiction 2. Mystery and detective stories 3. Japan -- History -- Tokugawa period, 1600-1868
ISBN 0-399-23330-X; 0-698-11879-0 pa

LC 98-14089

While attempting to solve the mystery of a stolen jewel, Seikei, a merchant's son who longs to be a samurai, joins a group of kabuki actors in eighteenth-century Japan

"Precise characterization, suspenseful plot twists, and a pace defined by swift and sometimes violent action make this a lively period thriller." Bull Cent Child Books

Other titles about Seikei are:
The demon in the teahouse (2001)
In darkess, death (2004)
The sword that cut the burning grass (2005)
A samurai never fears death (2007)
Seven paths to death (2008)

Hooper, Mary

Fallen Grace. Bloomsbury 2011 309p $16.99

Grades: 7 8 9 10   **Fic**

1. Orphans -- Fiction 2. Poverty -- Fiction 3. Sisters

-- Fiction 4. Mentally handicapped -- Fiction 5. Swindlers and swindling -- Fiction 6. Funeral rites and ceremonies -- Fiction
ISBN 978-1-59990-564-8; 1-59990-564-7

LC 2010-25498

In Victorian London, impoverished fifteen-year-old orphan Grace takes care of her older but mentally unfit sister Lily, and after enduring many harsh and painful experiences, the two become the victims of a fraud perpetrated by the wealthy owners of several funeral businesses.

Hooper "packs her brisk Dickensian fable with colorful characters and suspenseful, satisfying plot twists. The sobering realities of child poverty and exploitation are vividly conveyed, along with fascinating details of the Victorian funeral trade." Kirkus

Includes bibliographical references

Hopkinson, Deborah

Into the firestorm; a novel of San Francisco, 1906. Alfred A. Knopf 2006 200p hardcover o.p. pa $5.99

Grades: 5 6 7 8 **Fic**

1. Orphans -- Fiction 2. Earthquakes -- Fiction
ISBN 0-375-83652-7; 0-440-42129-2 pa

LC 2005-37189

Days after arriving in San Francisco from Texas, eleven-year-old orphan Nicholas Dray tries to help his new neighbors survive the 1906 San Francisco earthquake and the subsequent fires.

"The terror of the 1906 disaster is brought powerfully alive in this fast-paced tale. . . . Nick is a thoroughly developed protagonist, as are the supporting characters." SLJ

Includes bibliographical references

Hopkinson, Nalo

The **Chaos**; Nalo Hopkinson. Margaret K. McElderry Books 2012 241p. $16.99

Grades: 7 8 9 10 11 12 **Fic**

1. Science fiction 2. Toronto (Ont.) -- Fiction 3. Racially mixed people -- Fiction 4. Identity -- Fiction 5. Supernatural -- Fiction 6. Brothers and sisters -- Fiction 7. Family life -- Canada -- Fiction 8. Interpersonal relations -- Fiction
ISBN 1416954880; 9781416954880; 9781442409552

LC 2011018154

In this young adult science fiction novel, "Scotch"s womanly build and mixed heritage (white Jamaican dad, black American mom) made her the target of small-town school bullies. Since moving to Toronto, she"s found friends and status. . . . When a giant bubble appears at an open-mic event, Scotch dares her brother, Rich, to touch it. He disappears, a volcano rises from Lake Ontario and chaos ripples across city and world, transforming reality in ways bizarre." (Kirkus Reviews)

Horowitz, Anthony

★ **Public** enemy number two; a Diamond brothers mystery. Philomel Books 2004 190p $16.99; pa $5.99

Grades: 5 6 7 8 **Fic**

1. Mystery fiction
ISBN 0-399-24154-X; 0-14-240218-4 pa

LC 2004-10418

When thirteen-year-old Nick is framed for a jewel robbery, he and his brother, the bumbling detective Tim Diamond, attempt to clear his name by capturing the master criminal known as the Fence.

"Horowitz has a knack for puns and humor, and he successfully combines it with a nonstop action mystery that has everything from hydraulically controlled buses to secret caverns. A readable and exciting adventure." SLJ

Other titles in the Diamond Brothers Mystery series are:
The falcon's Maltester (2004)
South by southeast (2005)
Three of Diamonds (2005)
The Greek who stole Christmas (2008)

Raven's gate; book one of the Gatekeepers. [by] Anthony Horowitz. 1st ed; Scholastic Press 2005 254p (Gatekeepers) $17.95; pa $7.99

Grades: 6 7 8 9 **Fic**

1. Witchcraft -- Fiction 2. Supernatural -- Fiction
ISBN 0-439-67995-8; 0-439-68009-7 pa

LC 2004-21512

Sent to live in a foster home in a remote Yorkshire village, Matt, a troubled fourteen-year-old English boy, uncovers an evil plot involving witchcraft and the site of an ancient stone circle.

"The creepy activities and the overall atmosphere of fear are well defined, and once the action starts, it doesn't let up. . . . This powerful struggle between good and evil is a real page-turner." SLJ

Other titles in the Gatekeepers series are:
Evil star (2006)
Nightrise (2007)
Necropolis (2009)

★ **Stormbreaker**. Philomel Books 2001 192p (An Alex Rider adventure) $17.99; pa $7.99

Grades: 5 6 7 8 **Fic**

1. Adventure fiction 2. Spies -- Fiction 3. Orphans -- Fiction 4. Terrorism -- Fiction
ISBN 0-399-23620-1; 0-14-240611-2 pa

LC 00-63683

First published 2000 in the United Kingdom

After the death of the uncle who had been his guardian, fourteen-year-old Alex Rider is coerced to continue his uncle's dangerous work for Britain's intelligence agency, MI6

"Horowitz thoughtfully balances Alex's super-spy finesse with typical teen insecurities to create a likable hero living a fantasy come true. An entertaining, nicely layered novel." Booklist

Other titles about Alex Rider are:
Point blank (2002)
Skeleton key (2003)
Eagle strike (2004)
Scorpia (2005)
Alex Rider, the gadgets (2006)
Ark angel (2006)
Snakehead (2007)
Crocodile tears (2009)

Scorpia rising (2011)

Horvath, Polly

The **Corps** of the Bare-Boned Plane. Farrar, Straus and Giroux 2007 261p $17

Grades: 7 8 9 10 11 12 **Fic**

1. Death -- Fiction 2. Uncles -- Fiction 3. Cousins -- Fiction 4. Islands -- Fiction 5. Airplanes -- Fiction 6. Bereavement -- Fiction

ISBN 978-0-374-31553-5; 0-374-31553-1

LC 2006-41281

When their parents are killed in a train accident, cousins Meline and Jocelyn, who have little in common, are sent to live with their wealthy, eccentric, and isolated Uncle Marten on his island off the coast of British Columbia, where they are soon joined by other oddly disconnected and troubled people.

"The savagely dark humor allows Horvath to place her characters in increasingly bizarre psychic positions, building to an almost painful crescendo in a remarkable examination of the extremes of emotional distress." Horn Book

Everything on a waffle. Farrar, Straus & Giroux 2001 149p hardcover o.p. $16

Grades: 4 5 6 7 **Fic**

1. Uncles -- Fiction

ISBN 0-374-32236-8; 0-374-42208-7 pa

LC 00-35399

A Newbery Medal honor book, 2002

Eleven-year-old Primrose living in a small fishing village in British Columbia recounts her experiences and all that she learns about human nature and the unpredictability of life in the months after her parents are lost at sea

"The story is full of subtle humor and wisdom, presented through the eyes of a uniquely appealing young protagonist." SLJ

★ **My** one hundred adventures. Schwartz & Wade Books 2008 260p $16.99; lib bdg $19.99; pa $7.99

Grades: 4 5 6 7 **Fic**

1. Summer -- Fiction 2. Beaches -- Fiction 3. Siblings -- Fiction 4. Babysitters -- Fiction 5. Single parent family -- Fiction

ISBN 978-0-375-84582-6; 0-375-84582-8; 978-0-375-95582-2 lib bdg; 0-375-95582-8 lib bdg; 978-0-375-85526-9 pa; 0-375-85526-2 pa

LC 2008-02243

Twelve-year-old Jane, who lives at the beach in a run-down old house with her mother, two brothers, and sister, has an eventful summer accompanying her pastor on bible deliveries, meeting former boyfriends of her mother's, and being coerced into babysitting for a family of ill-mannered children.

With writing as foamy as waves, as gritty as sand, or as deep as the sea, this book may startle readers with the freedom given the heroine. . . . Unconventionality is Horvath's stock and trade, but here the high quirkiness quotient rests easily against Jane's inner story with its honest, childlike core. Booklist

Northward to the moon. Schwartz & Wade Books 2010 244p $17.99; lib bdg $20.99

Grades: 4 5 6 7 **Fic**

1. Ranch life -- Fiction 2. Family life -- Fiction 3. Grandmothers -- Fiction 4. Automobile travel -- Fiction

ISBN 978-0-375-86110-9; 0-375-86110-6; 978-0-375-96110-6 lib bdg; 0-375-96110-0 lib bdg

LC 2009-10133

When her stepfather loses his job in Saskatchewan, Jane and the rest of the family set off on a car trip, ending up in Nevada after improbably being given a bag full of possibly stolen money.

"Many characters here are distinct, wonderfully idiosyncratic individuals, and Horvath's fine-tuned observations are conveyed with subtlety and precision." Booklist

★ **One** year in Coal Harbor; Polly Horvath. Schwartz & Wade Books 2012 216 p. (hardcover) $16.99

Grades: 5 6 7 **Fic**

1. Cookbooks -- Fiction 2. Friendship -- Fiction 3. British Columbia -- Fiction 4. Self-reliance -- Fiction 5. Family problems -- Fiction 6. Foster home care -- Fiction 7. Interpersonal relations -- Fiction 8. Eccentrics and eccentricities -- Fiction

ISBN 0375869700; 9780375869709; 9780375969706

LC 2011023591

In this book by Polly Horvath, "Primrose Squab . . . chronicl[es] the latest goings-on in her British Columbian fishing village. Now 12 and happily reunited with her parents, Primrose has set her sights on compiling a cookbook. . . . When Ked, a foster child, arrives in town, Primrose gains an accomplice in her culinary efforts and an ally in opposing a local logging operation. More importantly, she hopes she has found a true best friend." (Publishers Weekly)

The **canning** season. Farrar, Straus & Giroux 2003 195p $16; pa $6.95

Grades: 6 7 8 9 **Fic**

1. Aunts -- Fiction

ISBN 0-374-39956-5; 0-374-41042-9 pa

LC 2002-66296

Thirteen-year-old Ratchet spends a summer in Maine with her eccentric great-aunts Tilly and Penpen, hearing strange stories from the past and encountering a variety of unusual and colorful characters

"Offbeat, slapstick humor is mitigated by poignancy in Horvath's distinctive rollicking style. There is occasional use of strong language, and the family stories are woven with death, often gruesomely described. . . . Readers are in for a wise and wacky ride when they open this novel." SLJ

The **vacation**; [by] Polly Horvath. 1st ed; Farrar, Straus & Giroux 2005 197p $16

Grades: 6 7 8 9 **Fic**

1. Aunts -- Fiction 2. Vacations -- Fiction 3. Family life -- Fiction 4. Automobile travel -- Fiction

ISBN 0-374-38070-8

LC 2004-57667

When his parents go to Africa to work as missionaries, twelve-year-old Henry's eccentric aunts, Pigg and Mag, take him on a cross-country car trip, allowing him to gain insight into his family and himself.

"Horvath spins another delightfully offbeat yarn, complete with her signature cast of eccentric characters, wacky situations, poignant moments, and snappy dialogue." SLJ

House, Silas

★ **Eli** the Good. Candlewick Press 2009 295p $16.99

Grades: 5 6 7 8   **Fic**

1. Aunts -- Fiction 2. Veterans -- Fiction 3. Friendship -- Fiction 4. Family life -- Fiction 5. Post-traumatic stress disorder -- Fiction

ISBN 978-0-7636-4341-6; 0-7636-4341-6

LC 2009004589

In the summer of 1976, ten-year-old Eli Book's excitement over Bicentennial celebrations is tempered by his father's flashbacks to the Vietnam War and other family problems, as well as concern about his tough but troubled best friend, Edie.

"House writes beautifully, with a gentle tone. He lays out Eli's world in exquisite detail. . . . The story flows along as steadily as a stream. . . . Eli is good company and children will enjoy accompanying him on his journey." SLJ

Houston, Julian

New boy. Houghton Mifflin Co. 2005 282p $16

Grades: 8 9 10 11 12   **Fic**

1. School stories 2. Prejudices -- Fiction 3. African Americans -- Fiction

ISBN 0-618-43253-1

LC 2004-27207

"As the first black student in an elite Connecticut boarding school in the late 1950s, Rob Garrett, 16, knows he is making history. . . . When his friends in the South plan a sit-in against segregation, he knows he must be part of it. . . . The honest first-person narrative makes stirring drama. . . . This brings up much for discussion about then and now." Booklist

Houtman, Jacqueline

The **reinvention** of Edison Thomas. Front Street 2010 189p $17.95

Grades: 6 7 8 9   **Fic**

1. School stories 2. Friendship -- Fiction 3. Inventions -- Fiction

ISBN 978-1-59078-708-3; 1-59078-708-0

Middle school student Eddy Thomas loves science and inventing, but has trouble with people. Finally he meets some friends who appreciate his abilities and respect his unique view of the world.

"A perceptive look at a complicated mind, the novel is steeped in the world of science (binomial nomenclature appears throughout), and the quirky humor and authentic characters should have wide appeal." Publ Wkly

Houts, Michelle

The **Beef** Princess of Practical County. Delacorte Press 2009 226p $16.99; lib bdg $19.99

Grades: 6 7 8 9   **Fic**

1. Cattle -- Fiction 2. Farm life -- Fiction

ISBN 978-0-385-73584-1; 978-0-385-90568-8 lib bdg

LC 2008-34712

Twelve-year-old Libby, the daughter of an Indiana cattle farmer, raises two calves in hopes of winning the annual steer competition at the county fair, but fails to follow her father's warning about developing a bond with animals that are destined to be sold at auction.

"Houts paints an idyllic yet authentic picture of farm life as she takes Libby and her family through the ups and downs of cattle raising and fair showing with sly humor and a flair for description and characterization." Booklist

Howard, Ellen

The **crimson** cap. Holiday House 2009 177p $16.95

Grades: 5 6 7 8   **Fic**

1. Explorers -- Fiction 2. Native Americans -- Fiction

ISBN 978-0-8234-2152-7; 0-8234-2152-X

LC 2009-25551

In 1684, wearing his father's faded cap, eleven-year-old Pierre Talon joins explorer Rene-Robert Cavelier on an ill-fated expedition to seek the Mississippi River, but after the expedition falls apart Pierre, deathly ill, is taken in by Hasinai Indians. Includes historical facts.

"A riveting adventure that will prove to be hard to put down. Howard's fast-paced writing brings the story to life. This solid coming-of-age story is based on real events and historical figures." SLJ

Howe, James, 1946-

★ **Addie** on the inside. Atheneum Books for Young Readers 2011 206p $16.99

Grades: 5 6 7 8   **Fic**

1. School stories 2. Novels in verse 3. Grandmothers -- Fiction 4. Self-acceptance -- Fiction

ISBN 141691384X; 9781416913849

LC 2010024497

Outspoken thirteen-year-old Addie Carle learns about love, loss, and staying true to herself as she navigates seventh grade, enjoys a visit from her grandmother, fights with her boyfriend, and endures gossip and meanness from her former best friend.

"Howe's artfully crafted lines show Addie's intelligence and wit, and his imagery evokes the aura of sadness surrounding 'this purgatory of/ the middle school years/ when so many things/ that never mattered before/ and will never matter again/ matter.' Readers will empathize with Addie's anguish and admire her courage to keep fighting." Publ Wkly

Totally Joe. Atheneum Books for Young Readers 2005 189p $15.95

Grades: 6 7 8 9   **Fic**

1. Homosexuality -- Fiction

ISBN 0-689-83957-X

LC 2004-22242

As a school assignment, a thirteen-year-old boy writes an alphabiography—life from A to Z—and explores issues of friendship, family, school, and the challenges of being a gay teenager.

"Howe deals with weighty issues, but uses Joe's affable personality to interject ample humor." Publ Wkly

The **misfits**. Atheneum Bks. for Young Readers 2001 274p $16; pa $5.99

Grades: 5 6 7 8 **Fic**

1. School stories 2. Elections -- Fiction 3. Friendship -- Fiction

ISBN 0-689-83955-3; 0-689-83956-1 pa

LC 00-66390

Four students who do not fit in at their small-town middle school decide to create a third party for the student council elections to represent all students who have ever been called names

This is a "timely, sensitive, laugh-out-loud must-read for all middle school students and teachers." Voice Youth Advocates

Howe, Peter

Waggit again; drawings by Omar Rayyan. HarperCollinsPublishers 2009 292p il $16.99; lib bdg $17.89

Grades: 5 6 7 **Fic**

1. Dogs -- Fiction

ISBN 978-0-06-124264-9; 0-06-124264-0; 978-0-06-124265-6 lib bdg; 0-06-124265-9 lib bdg

LC 2008020213

After being left in the country by his owner, Waggit sets out on the long journey to New York City and meets some unexpected friends along the way.

Felicia's "relationship with the dogs is made wonderfully plausible. Waggit's growth in self-understanding is also fully developed and well handled, and the ending will satisfy readers deeply." Kirkus

Waggit's tale; drawings by Omar Rayyan. HarperCollinsPublishers 2008 288p il $16.99; lib bdg $17.89; pa $6.99

Grades: 5 6 7 **Fic**

1. Dogs -- Fiction

ISBN 978-0-06-124261-8; 0-06-124261-6; 978-0-06-124262-5 lib bdg; 0-06-124262-4 lib bdg; 978-0-06-124263-2 pa; 0-06-124263-2 pa

LC 2007020878

When Waggit is abandoned by his owner as a puppy, he meets a pack of wild dogs who become his friends and teach him to survive in the city park, but when he has a chance to go home with a kind woman who wants to adopt him, he takes it

"The novel celebrates the wild freedom of the feral dog pack, while also emphasizing the many hazards of urban life for homeless companion animals." Voice Youth Advocates

Howell, Troy

The **dragon** of Cripple Creek; a novel. Amulet Books 2011 385p $19.95

Grades: 5 6 7 8 **Fic**

1. Fantasy fiction 2. Adventure fiction 3. Gold -- Fiction 4. Dragons -- Fiction

ISBN 978-0-8109-9713-4; 0-8109-9713-4

LC 2010-34362

When Kat, her father, and brother visit an old gold mine that has been turned into an amusement park, she falls down a shaft and meets an ancient dragon, the last of his kind, and inadvertently triggers a twenty-first century gold rush.

"Writing in Kat's first person narrative, which is wry and funny, clipped and eloquent, Howell, best known as an illustrator, mixes fantasy adventure with a moving conservation story in a debut that blends sadness, secrecy, and pure fantasy." Booklist

Howland, Leila

Nantucket blue; Leila Howland. 1st ed. Hyperion 2013 304 p. (reinforced) $16.99

Grades: 8 9 10 11 12 **Fic**

1. Summer -- Fiction 2. Female friendship -- Fiction 3. Interpersonal relations -- Fiction 4. Grief -- Fiction 5. Divorce -- Fiction 6. Friendship -- Fiction 7. Best friends -- Fiction

ISBN 1423160517; 9781423160519

LC 2012035121

This novel, by Leila Howland, follows a girl named "Cricket Thompson. . . . When Jules and her family suffer a devastating tragedy that forces the girls apart, Jules becomes a stranger whom Cricket wonders whether she ever really knew. . . . But it's the things Cricket hadn't counted on—most of all, falling hard for someone who should be completely off-limits—that turn her dreams into an exhilarating, bittersweet reality." (Publisher's note)

Hrdlitschka, Shelley

Allegra; by Shelley Hrdlitschka. Orca Book Publishers 2013 280 p. (paperback) $12.95; (ebook) $12.99

Grades: 7 8 9 10 **Fic**

1. School stories 2. Teacher-student relationship -- Fiction

ISBN 1459801970; 9781459801974; 9781459801981 pdf; 9781459801998

LC 2012952952

In this book, Allegra, daughter of two musicians, is thrilled to be at Deer Lake School for the Fine and Performing Arts. She "has her sights set on becoming a professional dancer. However, her excitement is dimmed by the school's requirement that she take a music-theory class. Despite her initial reluctance, Allegra soon begins to enjoy the class due to the charisma of its young and attractive teacher," Mr. Rocchelli. Is their relationship too close? (School Library Journal)

★ **Sister** wife. Orca 2008 269p pa $12.95

Grades: 8 9 10 11 12 **Fic**

1. Polygamy -- Fiction

ISBN 978-1-55143-927-3; 1-55143-927-1

In a remote polygamist community, Celeste struggles to accept her destiny while longing to be free to live her life her way.

"This compelling story combines with authentic characters to pique the interest of a wide array of teens and get them talking about faith and free will." Voice Youth Advocates

Hubbard, Amanda

Ripple; [by] Mandy Hubbard. Razorbill 2011
260p $16.99

Grades: 8 9 10 11 12   **Fic**

1. Love stories 2. Fantasy fiction 3. Sirens (Mythology)
ISBN 978-1-59514-423-2; 1-59514-423-4

"Lexi, 18, is responsible for the death of Steven, her
friend Siena's brother and the only boy she ever loved.
That was two years ago, right before discovering that she
is a siren, cursed to swim each night and sing out haunting
melodies that will lure men to their deaths in the water. She
has been protecting herself and those around her by keeping everyone at a distance and swimming in an isolated lake
where no one will hear her song. But as the new school year
begins, Lexi finds herself pursued by two boys whom she
can't ignore. . . . In this new twist on a supernatural romance,
Hubbard expands the genre by including both a siren and a
nix in among the high school drama. . . . Fans of girl dramas,
mysteries, and fantasy romance will devour the story." SLJ

Hudson, Tara

Hereafter. HarperTeen 2011 407p $17.99

Grades: 8 9 10 11 12   **Fic**

1. Ghost stories 2. Family life -- Fiction 3. Future life
-- Fiction 4. Good and evil -- Fiction 5. Near-death
experiences -- Fiction
ISBN 978-0-06-202677-4; 0-06-202677-1

LC 2010045622

Amelia, long a ghost, forms a strong bond with eighteen-
year-old Joshua, who nearly drowned where she did and
who awakens in her long-forgotten senses and memories
even as Eli, a spirit, tries to draw her away.

"A must for collections given the genre's
popularity." Booklist

Hughes, Dean

Missing in action. Atheneum Books for Young
Readers 2010 228p $16.99; pa $6.99

Grades: 6 7 8 9   **Fic**

1. Baseball -- Fiction 2. Prejudices -- Fiction 3. Family
life -- Fiction 4. Grandparents -- Fiction 5. World
War, 1939-1945 -- Fiction 6. Racially mixed people
-- Fiction 7. Japanese Americans -- Evacuation and
relocation, 1942-1945 -- Fiction
ISBN 978-1-4169-1502-7; 1-4169-1502-8; 978-1-
4424-1248-4 pa; 1-4424-1248-8 pa

LC 2009-11276

While his father is missing in action in the Pacific during World War II, twelve-year-old Jay moves with his
mother to small-town Utah, where he sees prejudice from
both sides, as a part-Navajo himself and through an unlikely
friendship with Japanese American Ken from the nearby
internment camp.

"Jay's pain and eventual resolution will touch readers in
this sure-to-be-popular work of historical fiction." Booklist

Search and destroy. Atheneum Books for Young
Readers 2006 216p $16.95

Grades: 7 8 9 10   **Fic**

1. Vietnam War, 1961-1975 -- Fiction
ISBN 0-689-87023-X

LC 2005-11255

Recent high school graduate Rick Ward, undecided about
his future and eager to escape his unhappy home life, joins
the army and experiences the horrors of the war in Vietnam.

"This is a compelling, insightful story about the emotional, physical, and psychological scars that wars leave
upon soldiers." Booklist

Soldier boys. Atheneum Bks. for Young Readers
2001 162p $16.95; pa $5.99

Grades: 7 8 9 10   **Fic**

1. Soldiers -- Fiction 2. World War, 1939-1945 --
Fiction 3. Ardennes, Battle of the, 1944-1945 -- Fiction
ISBN 0-689-81748-7; 0-689-86021-8 pa

LC 00-46920

"This World War II novel tells the parallel stories of two
young soldiers fighting on opposite sides of the conflict—
a paratrooper from Utah and a Hitler Youth who joins the
German army. Spence and Dieter's paths cross briefly on a
snow-covered Belgian hill in a scene both compassionate
and tragic. Hughes tells their tales in assured prose that's
harrowing without being exploitive." Horn Book Guide

Hughes, Gregory

Unhooking the moon; by Gregory Hughes.
Quercus 2010 374 p. (hardcover) $16.95

Grades: 6 7 8   **Fic**

1. Orphans -- fiction 2. Voyages and travels -- fiction
ISBN 1623650208; 9781623650209

LC 2010478376

In this book, orphans Bob and Marie Claire (aka Rat)
travel from Winnipeg to New York City in search of their
drug dealer uncle. "For lack of a better plan, they wander
Manhattan and the Bronx asking passersby if they know
him. This strategy leads to encounters with a host of colorful
city types, notably a pair of softhearted con men and a lonely
rising rap star." (Kirkus Reviews)

Hughes, Mark Peter

A crack in the sky. Delacorte Press 2010 405p
il $16.99; lib bdg $19.99

Grades: 5 6 7 8   **Fic**

1. Science fiction
ISBN 978-0-385-73708-1; 0-385-73708-4; 978-0-385-
90645-6 lib bdg; 0-385-90645-5 lib bdg

LC 2009-43532

In a post-apocalyptic world, thirteen-year-old Eli, part of
the most powerful family in the world, keeps noticing problems with the operations of his domed city but his family
denies them, while in the surrounding desert, the Outsiders
struggle to survive while awaiting a prophesied savior.

"Hughes keeps his protagonist an individual, and in fact
an amiable, scrappy one with whom readers will identify."
Bull Cent Child Books

Hughes, Pat Raccio

★ Five 4ths of July; by Pat Raccio Hughes. Viking 2011 278p $16.99

Grades: 7 8 9 10   **Fic**

1. Adventure fiction
ISBN 978-0-670-01207-7; 0-670-01207-6

LC 2010-49521

On July 4th, 1777, fourteen-year-old Jake Mallory and his friends are celebrating their new nation's independence, but over the next four years Jake finds himself in increasingly adventurous circumstances as he battles British forces, barely survives captivity on a prison ship, and finally returns home to Connecticut, war-torn and weary, but hopeful for America's future.

This is a "straightforward and well-conceived novel. . . . A fine addition to collections on the war and an eye-opening look at the horrors of British prison ships." Kirkus

Hughes, Shirley, 1927-

★ **Hero** on a bicycle; Shirley Hughes. Candlewick Press 2013 224 p. $15.99

Grades: 5 6 7   **Fic**

1. Historical fiction 2. World War, 1939-1945 -- Fiction
ISBN 076366037X; 9780763660376

         LC 2012943650

This book is set in Italy during World War II. "The narrative focuses on a city under German occupation, events being perceived principally through the eyes of three members of the Crivelli family: teenager Paolo, his older sister Constanza and Rosemary, their English-born mother. . . . When an opportunity arises for Paolo, Constanza and Rosemary to lend their practical support to the Partisan cause Paolo, in particular, seizes it enthusiastically." (School Librarian)

Hull, Nancy L.

On rough seas; [by] Nancy L. Hull. Clarion Books 2008 261p $16

Grades: 6 7 8 9   **Fic**

1. World War, 1939-1945 -- Fiction 2. Dunkerque (France), Battle of, 1940 -- Fiction
ISBN 978-0-618-89743-8; 0-618-89743-8

         LC 2007-37933

In Dover, England in 1940, fourteen-year-old Alec Curtis wants nothing more than to go to sea, to absolve himself of the guilt he feels over the earlier drowning of his cousin and to help the war effort, but when he sneaks aboard a small boat going across the English Channel to Dunkirk, his experience changes him forever.

"Hull offers a sensitive portrayal of Alec's seesawing emotions and gradual recognition of what matters to him, culminating in subtle changes that show his newfound maturity in sometimes unexpected yet wholly convincing ways. A well-researched historical novel." Booklist

Hulme, John

★ The **glitch** in sleep; [by] John Hulme and Michael Wexler; illustrations by Gideon Kendall. Bloomsbury Children's Books 2007 277p il (The Seems) $16.95; pa $7.99

Grades: 4 5 6 7   **Fic**

1. Science fiction 2. Sleep -- Fiction
ISBN 978-1-59990-129-9; 1-59990-129-3; 978-1-59990-298-2 pa; 1-59990-298-2 pa

         LC 2007-2598

When twelve-year-old Becker Drane is recruited by The Seems, a parallel universe that runs everything in The World, he must fix a disastrous glitch in the Department of Sleep that threatens everyone's ability to ever fall asleep again

"The story is upbeat and full of humor. . . . Dynamic full-page illustrations appear throughout." SLJ
Another title in this series is:
The split second (2008)
The lost train of thought (2009)

Humphreys, Chris

The **hunt** of the unicorn. Alfred A. Knopf 2011 345p $16.99; lib bdg $19.99; e-book $16.99

Grades: 6 7 8 9   **Fic**

1. Fantasy fiction 2. Unicorns -- Fiction
ISBN 978-0-375-85872-7; 0-375-85872-7; 978-0-375-95872-4 lib bdg; 0-375-95872-4; 978-0-375-89624-8 e-book

         LC 2010-30852

Despite strange dreams and her ailing father's firm belief in the family lore of a long-ago ancestor's connection to the mythical unicorn, fifteen-year-old New Yorker Elayne remains skeptical until, during a school visit to the unicorn tapestries in the Cloisters, she finds herself entering a tumultuous world where she must fulfill the legacy of her ancestors by taming the unicorn and bringing a tyrant to justice.

"This is wish fulfillment at its finest, with Elayne playing the everyday gal turned spunky heroine. . . . With references to our world's overpopulation and pollution, there is a heady dose of environmentalism here, but it is nicely tempered with a fair amount of humor and adventure." Bull Cent Child Books

Hunt, Lynda Mullaly

One for the Murphys; Lynda Mullaly Hunt. Nancy Paulsen Books 2012 224 p. $16.99

Grades: 5 6 7 8   **Fic**

1. Stepfathers -- Fiction 2. Family problems -- Fiction 3. Foster home care -- Fiction 4. Mothers and daughters -- Fiction 5. Family life -- Connecticut -- Fiction
ISBN 0399256156; 9780399256158

         LC 2011046708

This book by Lynda Mullaly Hunt follows "eighth-grader Carley Connors [as she] learns about a different kind of family life, first resisting and then resisting having to leave the loving, loyal Murphys. . . . She's torn between her love for her mother and her memory of the fight that sent her to the hospital, when her mother caught and held her for her stepfather. Slowly won over at home . . . Carley also finds a friend at school in the prickly, Wicked-obsessed Toni." (Kirkus Reviews)

Hunter, Erin

Dawn; [by] Erin Hunter. 1st ed.; HarperCollins 2005 335p (Warriors: the new prophecy) $15.99; lib bdg $17.89; pa $6.99

Grades: 6 7 8 9   **Fic**

1. Fantasy fiction 2. Cats -- Fiction
ISBN 978-0-06-074455-7; 0-06-074455-3; 978-0-06-074456-4 lib bdg; 0-06-074456-1 lib bdg; 978-0-06-074457-1 pa; 0-06-074457-X pa

         LC 2005009175

The questing cats return to a forest devastated by the Twolegs, where they must find a way to convince their Clans to leave in search of a new home, even though they have no idea where they are going.

"Fans will relish this eminently satisfying episode." Booklist

★ **Into** the wild. HarperCollins Pubs. 2003 272p il map (Warriors) $15.99; lib bdg $16.89; pa $5.99

Grades: 6 7 8 9   **Fic**

1. Fantasy fiction 2. Cats -- Fiction

ISBN 0-06-000002-3; 0-06-052548-7 lib bdg; 0-06-052550-9 pa

For generations, four clans of wild cats have shared the forest. When their warrior code is threatened by mysterious deaths, a house cat named Rusty may turn out to be the bravest warrior of all.

"The author has created an intriguing world with an intricate structure and mythology, and an engaging young hero." SLJ

Other titles in the Warriors series are:
Code of the clans (2009)
A dangerous path (2004)
The darkest hour (2004)
Fire and ice (2003)
Forest of secrets (2003)
Rising storm (2004)

The **sight**; [by] Erin Hunter. HarperCollins Pub. 2007 363p (Warriors: power of three) $16.99; lib bdg $17.89

Grades: 6 7 8 9   **Fic**

1. Fantasy fiction 2. Cats -- Fiction

ISBN 978-0-06-089201-2; 0-06-089201-3; 978-0-06-089203-6 lib bdg; 0-06-089203-X lib bdg

LC 2007-11860

In a troubled time for the Clans, three young cats, grandchildren of the legendary Firestar, begin their training as warriors and, in the course of many adventures, discover their true destiny.

"Plenty of action and solid characterizations make this an enticing choice for fans of the long-running enterprise." Booklist

Other titles in this series are:
Dark river (2008)
Outcast (2008)
Eclipse (2008)
Long shadows (2009)
Sunrise (2009)

Huntley, Amy

The **everafter**. Balzer + Bray 2009 144p $16.99; lib bdg $17.89; pa $8.99

Grades: 7 8 9 10   **Fic**

1. Dead -- Fiction 2. Death -- Fiction 3. Friendship -- Fiction 4. Lost and found possessions -- Fiction

ISBN 978-0-06-177679-3; 0-06-177679-3; 978-0-06-177680-9 lib bdg; 0-06-177680-7 lib bdg; 978-0-06-177681-6 pa; 0-06-177681-5 pa

LC 2008-46149

ALA YALSA Morris Award Finalist, 2010

Madison Stanton doesn't know where she is or how she got there. But she does know this—she is dead. And alone in a vast, dark space. The only company Maddy has in this place are luminescent objects that turn out to be all the things

she lost while she was alive. And soon she discovers that, with these artifacts, she can re-experience—and even—change moments from her life.

"This fresh take on a teen's journey of self-exploration is a compelling and highly enjoyable tale. Huntley expertly combines a coming-of-age story with a supernatural mystery that keeps readers engrossed until the climactic ending. This touching story will appeal to those looking for a ghost story, romance, or family drama." SLJ

Hurley, Tonya

★ **Ghostgirl**. Little, Brown 2008 328p $17.99

Grades: 7 8 9 10   **Fic**

1. Ghost stories 2. School stories 3. Death -- Fiction 4. Popularity -- Fiction

ISBN 978-0-316-11357-1; 0-316-11357-3

LC 2007-31541

After dying, high school senior Charlotte Usher is as invisible to nearly everyone as she always felt, but despite what she learns in a sort of alternative high school for dead teens, she clings to life while seeking a way to go to the Fall Ball with the boy of her dreams.

"Hurley combines afterlife antics, gothic gore, and high school hell to produce an original, hilarious satire. . . . Tim Burton and Edgar Allan Poe devotees will die for this fantastic, phantasmal read." SLJ

Other titles in this series are:
Ghostgirl: Homecoming (2009)
Ghostgirl: Lovesick (2010)

Hurst, Carol Otis

Through the lock. Houghton Mifflin 2001 160p $15

Grades: 5 6 7 8   **Fic**

1. Canals -- Fiction 2. Orphans -- Fiction

ISBN 0-618-03036-0

LC 99-28510

Etta, a twelve-year-old orphan in nineteenth-century Connecticut, meets Walter, a boy living in an abandoned cabin on the New Haven and Northampton Canal and has adventures with him while trying to be reunited with her siblings

"Etta and Walter's terse conversations, anguished and funny, are the best part of the book, and the history is fascinating." Booklist

Huxley, Aldous

Brave new world. Harper & Row 1946 xx, 311p hardcover o.p. pa $13.95

Grades: 7 8 9 10   **Fic**

1. Satire 2. Utopias -- Fiction 3. Technology and civilization -- Fiction

ISBN 0-06-085052-3 pa

First published 1932 by Doubleday, Doran & Company

"The ironic title, which Huxley has taken from Shakespeare's 'The Tempest,' describes a world in which science has taken control over morality and humaneness. In this utopia humans emerge from test tubes, families are obsolete, and even pleasure is regulated. When a so-called savage who believes in spirituality is found and is imported to the community, he cannot accomodate himself to this world and ends his life." Shapiro. Fic for Youth. 3d edition

Hyde, Catherine Ryan

The **year** of my miraculous reappearance. Alfred A. Knopf 2007 228p $15.99; lib bdg $18.99

Grades: 7 8 9 10 **Fic**

1. Siblings -- Fiction 2. Alcoholism -- Fiction 3. Down syndrome -- Fiction

ISBN 978-0-375-83257-4; 978-0-375-93257-1 lib bdg; 0-375-83257-2; 0-375-93257-7 lib bdg

LC 2006-29194

Thirteen-year-old Cynnie has had to deal with her mother's alcoholism and stream of boyfriends all her life, but when her grandparents take custody of her brother, Bill, who has Down Syndrome, Cynnie becomes self-destructive and winds up in court-mandated Alcoholics Anonymous meetings.

"Cynnie's love for and devotion to Bill are wholly believable, as are her attempts to snare a stable adult presence in her life. Secondary characters are multidimensional and well drawn." Booklist

Ibbitson, John

★ The **Landing**; a novel. KCP Fiction 2008 160p $17.95; pa $7.95

Grades: 7 8 9 10 **Fic**

1. Uncles -- Fiction 2. Violinists -- Fiction

ISBN 978-1-55453-234-6; 1-55453-234-5; 978-1-55453-238-4 pa; 1-55453-238-8 pa

Ben thinks he will always be stuck at Cook's Landing, barely making ends meet like his uncle. But when he meets a wealthy widow from New York City, he sees himself there too. When she hires him to play his violin, he realizes his gift could unlock the possibilities of the world. Then, during a stormy night on Lake Muskoka, everything changes.

"With lovely prose, Ibbitson brings to life the rugged beauty and the devastating poverty of the Lake Muskoka region. His characters are as strong and remote as their surroundings." Voice Youth Advocates

Ibbotson, Eva

★ The **Ogre** of Oglefort; [illustrations by Lisa K. Weber] Dutton Children's Books 2011 246p il $16.99

Grades: 4 5 6 **Fic**

1. Fairy tales 2. Magic -- Fiction 3. Orphans -- Fiction 4. Princesses -- Fiction

ISBN 978-0-525-42382-9; 0-525-42382-6

LC 2010038137

When the Hag of Dribble, an orphan boy, and a troll called Ulf are sent to rescue a princess from an ogre, it turns out to be far from the routine magical mission they expect.

"Magical creatures abound in this effervescent fairy tale that effectively merges classic tropes with modern sensibilities." Bull Cent Child Books

One dog and his boy; by Eva Ibbotson. Scholastic Press 2012 271 p. $16.99

Grades: 3 4 5 6 **Fic**

1. Children's stories 2. Dogs -- Fiction 3. Wealth -- Fiction 4. Voyages and travels -- Fiction 5. Human-animal relationships -- Fiction 6. Family life -- England

-- London -- Fiction

ISBN 0545351960; 9780545351966

LC 2011003773

In this book, by Eva Ibbotson, "[all] Hal has ever wanted is a dog. His busy parents, hoping that he'll tire of the idea, rent a dog from Easy Pets, run by the heartless Mr. and Mrs. Carker. Hal and Fleck, the dog he chooses, bond immediately, and they are both heartbroken when Hal's mother, realizing that Hal's interest isn't waning, sneaks the dog back to Easy Pets. Hal decides to get Fleck back and run away to his grandparents." (Bulletin of the Center for Children's Books)

The **beasts** of Clawstone Castle; illustrated by Kevin Hawkes. Dutton Children's Books 2006 243p il hardcover o.p. $16.99

Grades: 4 5 6 **Fic**

1. Ghost stories 2. Cattle -- Fiction 3. Castles -- Fiction

ISBN 0-14-240931-6 pa; 0-525-47719-5

LC 2005-29188

While spending the summer with elderly relatives at Clawstone Castle in northern England, Madlyn and her brother Rollo, with the help of several ghosts, attempt to save the rare cattle that live on the castle grounds.

"Ibbotson's charismatic ghosts are great. . .—as human as they are horrific—and there's plenty of quirky humor in this energetic, diverting read, loaded with charm." Booklist

★ The **dragonfly** pool; illustrated by Kevin Hawkes. Dutton Children's Books 2008 377p il $17.99; pa $7.99

Grades: 5 6 7 8 **Fic**

1. School stories 2. World War, 1939-1945 -- Fiction

ISBN 978-0-525-42064-4; 0-525-42064-9; 978-0-14-241486-6 pa; 0-14-241486-7 pa

"Ibbotson's trademark eccentric characters and strongly contrasted principles of right and wrong brighten and broaden this uplifting tale." Booklist

★ The **star** of Kazan; illustrated by Kevin Hawkes. Dutton 2004 405p il $16.99; pa $7.99

Grades: 5 6 7 8 **Fic**

1. Mystery fiction

ISBN 0-525-47347-5; 0-14-240582-5 pa

LC 2004-45455

After twelve-year-old Annika, a foundling living in late nineteenth-century Vienna, inherits a trunk of costume jewelry, a woman claiming to be her aristocratic mother arrives and takes her to live in a strangely decrepit mansion in Germany

"This is a rich saga . . . full of stalwart friends, sly villains, a brave heroine, and good triumphing over evil. . . . An intensely satisfying read." SLJ

Ingold, Jeanette

The **Big** Burn. Harcourt 2002 295p $17; pa $6.95

Grades: 7 8 9 10 **Fic**

1. Forest fires -- Fiction

ISBN 0-15-216470-7; 0-15-204924-X pa

LC 2001-5667

Three teenagers battle the flames of the Big Burn of 1910, one of the century's biggest wildfires

"A solid adventure story with a well-realized setting." Booklist

Includes bibliographical references (p. {293}-295)

Hitch. Harcourt, Inc 2005 272p $17; pa $6.95

Grades: 7 8 9 10   **Fic**

1. Montana -- Fiction 2. Great Depression, 1929-1939 -- Fiction

ISBN 0-15-204747-6; 0-15-20561-9 pa

LC 2004-19447

To help his family during the Depression and avoid becoming a drunk like his father, Moss Trawnley joins the Civilian Conservation Corps, helps build a new camp near Monroe, Montana, and leads the other men in making the camp a success.

This is "a credible, involving story. . . . Both [the author's] writing style and her 1930s setting feels totally true to the time." Booklist

Mountain solo. Harcourt 2003 309p $17; pa $6.95

Grades: 7 8 9 10   **Fic**

1. Violinists -- Fiction 2. Family life -- Fiction

ISBN 0-15-202670-3; 0-15-205358-1 pa

LC 2003-42326

Back at her childhood home in Missoula, Montana, after a disastrous concert in Germany, a teenage violin prodigy contemplates giving up life with her mother in New York City and her music as she, her father, stepmother, and step-sister hike to a pioneer homesite where another violinist once faced difficult decisions of his own

"Mountain Solo is a good read for anyone fascinated by the power of music and its effects on individuals' lives." SLJ

Includes bibliographical references (p. {307}-309)

Irving, Washington

The **Legend** of Sleepy Hollow; illustrated by Gris Grimly. Atheneum Books for Young Readers 2007 un il $16.99

Grades: 4 5 6   **Fic**

1. Ghost stories

ISBN 1-4169-0625-8; 978-1-4169-0625-4

LC 2005-27502

A superstitious schoolmaster, in love with a wealthy farmer's daughter, has a terrifying encounter with a headless horseman.

"The tale, . . . slightly condensed but with language and ambiguities intact, is reimagined here with humor, vigor, [and] clarity. . . . Irving's language is challenging . . . but Grimly's numerous Halloween-hued panel and spot illustrations . . . parse it into comprehensible tidbits. The comically amplified emotions and warm yellow and orange tones balance the horror aspects of the text." Horn Book

Jackson, Alison

Rainmaker. Boyds Mills Press 2005 192p $16.95

Grades: 5 6 7 8   **Fic**

1. Droughts -- Fiction 2. Great Depression, 1929-1939 -- Fiction

ISBN 1-59078-309-3

"For 13-year-old Pidge Martin, the summer of 1939 brings changes and challenges. Her town, Frostfree, Florida, faces its longest drought in 40 years, and if it doesn't rain soon, area families . . . may lose their farms. A miracle is in order, and Pidge's father hopes a rainmaker can provide one. . . . Pidge is a well-characterized, sympathetic protagonist that readers will connect with." Booklist

Jacobson, Jennifer

The **complete** history of why I hate her; [by] Jennifer Richard Jacobson. Atheneum Books for Young Readers 2010 181p $16.99

Grades: 7 8 9 10   **Fic**

1. Cancer -- Fiction 2. Resorts -- Fiction 3. Sisters -- Fiction 4. Personality disorders -- Fiction

ISBN 978-0-689-87800-8; 0-689-87800-1

LC 2008-42959

Wanting a break from being known only for her sister's cancer, seventeen-year-old Nola leaves Boston for a waitressing job at a summer resort in Maine, but soon feels as if her new best friend is taking over her life.

"A compelling story of self-discovery with plenty of insights into the motivations that drive relationships." Booklist

Jacobson, Jennifer Richard, 1958-

★ **Small** as an elephant; [by] Jennifer Richard Jacobson. Candlewick Press 2011 275p $15.99

Grades: 5 6 7 8   **Fic**

1. Adventure fiction 2. Abandoned children -- Fiction 3. Mother-son relationship -- Fiction

ISBN 0-7636-4155-3; 978-0-7636-4155-9

LC 2010039175

When his mother disappears from an Acadia National Park campground, Jack tries to make his way back home to Boston, with only a small toy elephant for company.

"Jacobson masterfully puts readers into Jack's mind—he loves and understands his mother, but sometimes his judgments are not always good, and readers understand. . . . Jack's journey to a new kind of family is inspiring and never sappy." Kirkus

Jacques, Brian

The **Bellmaker**; illustrated by Allan Curless. Philomel Bks. 1994 336p il pa $7.99

Grades: 5 6 7 8 9   **Fic**

1. Fantasy fiction 2. Animals -- Fiction

ISBN 0-399-22805-5; 978-0-441-00315-0 pa; 0-441-00315-X pa

LC 94-9730

Worried about his daughter Mariel, Joseph the Bellmaker is led by a dream from Redwall Abbey to Southsward, where he is caught up in the battle between Squirrelking Gael and the vicious Foxwolf Nagru

Castaways of the Flying Dutchman; illustrated by Ian Schoenherr. Philomel Bks. 2001 327p il $22.95; pa $7.99

Grades: 6 7 8 9   **Fic**

1. Adventure fiction 2. Dogs -- Fiction 3. Angels -- Fiction 4. Orphans -- Fiction

ISBN 0-399-23601-5; 0-14-250118-2 pa

LC 00-59822

In 1620, a boy and his dog are rescued from the doomed ship, Flying Dutchman, by an angel who guides them in travelling the world, eternally helping those in great need

"The swashbuckling language brims with color and melodrama; the villains are dastardly and stupid; and buried treasure, mysterious clues, and luscious culinary descriptions . . . keep the pages turning." Booklist

Other titles in this series are:

The angel's command (2003)

Voyage of slaves (2006)

★ **Redwall**; illustrated by Gary Chalk. 20th anniversary ed.; Philomel 2007 351p il $23.99; pa $7.99

Grades: 5 6 7 8 9   **Fic**

1. Fantasy fiction 2. Mice -- Fiction 3. Animals -- Fiction

ISBN 978-0-399-24794-1; 0-399-24794-7; 978-0-441-00548-2 pa; 0-441-00548-9 pa

First published 1986

"Thoroughly engrossing, this novel captivates despite its length. . . . The theme will linger long after the story is finished." Booklist

Other titles in this series are:

The Bellmaker (1995)

Doomwyte (2008)

Eulalia! (2007)

High Rhulain (2005)

The legend of Luke (2000)

Loamhedge (2003)

The long patrol (1998)

Lord Brocktree (2000)

Mariel of Redwall (1992)

Marlfox (1998)

Martin the Warrior (1994)

Mattimeo (1990)

Mossflower (1998)

The outcast of Redwall (1996)

Pearls of Lutra (1997)

Rakkety Tam (2004)

The Rogue Crew (2011)

Sable Quean (2009)

Salamandastron (1993)

Taggerung (2001)

Triss (2002)

Jaden, Denise

Losing Faith. Simon Pulse 2010 381p pa $9.99

Grades: 7 8 9 10 11 12   **Fic**

1. School stories 2. Cults -- Fiction 3. Death -- Fiction 4. Sisters -- Fiction 5. Bereavement -- Fiction 6. Christian life -- Fiction

ISBN 978-1-4169-9609-5; 1-4169-9609-5

LC 2010-7296

Brie tries to cope with her grief over her older sister Faith's sudden death by trying to learn more about the religious "home group" Faith secretly joined and never talked about with Brie or her parents.

"With pitch-perfect portrayals of high school social life and a nuanced view into a variety of Christian experiences of faith, this first novel gives readers much to think about." SLJ

James, Helen Foster

Paper son; Lee's journey to America. written by Helen Foster James and Virginia Shin-Mui Loh ; illustrated by Wilson Ong. Sleeping Bear Press 2013 32 p. ill. (reinforced) $16.99

Grades: 5 6 7 8   **Fic**

1. Orphans -- Fiction 2. Immigrants -- Fiction 3. Chinese Americans -- Fiction 4. Emigration and immigration -- Fiction

ISBN 1585368334; 9781585368334

LC 2012033691

This historical novel, by Helen Foster James, Virginia Shin-Mui Loh, and illustrated by Wilson Ong, is part of the "Tales of Young Americans" series. "In 1926, 12-year-old Fu Lee['s] . . . parents . . . spent all of their money buying a 'paper son slot' for Lee to go to America. Being a 'paper son' means pretending to be the son of a family already in America. . . . But first he must pass the test at Angel Island Immigration Station in San Francisco." (Publisher's note)

Jansen, Hanna

Over a thousand hills I walk with you; translated from the German by Elizabeth D. Crawford. Carolrhoda Books 2006 342p $16.95

Grades: 7 8 9 10   **Fic**

1. Adopted children 2. Genocide -- Rwanda

ISBN 1-57505-927-4; 978-1-57505-927-3

LC 2005-21123

Original German edition, 2002

"Eight-year-old Jeanne was the only one of her family to survive the 1994 Rwanda genocide. Then a German family adopted her, and her adoptive mother now tells Jeanne's story in a compelling fictionalized biography that stays true to the traumatized child's bewildered viewpoint." Booklist

Jaramillo, Ann

La linea. Roaring Brook Press 2006 131p $16.95; pa $7.99

Grades: 5 6 7 8   **Fic**

1. Mexicans -- Fiction 2. Siblings -- Fiction 3. Immigrants -- Fiction

ISBN 1-59643-154-7; 0-312-37354-6 pa

LC 2005-20133

When fifteen-year-old Miguel's time finally comes to leave his poor Mexican village, cross the border illegally, and join his parents in California, his younger sister's determination to join him soon imperils them both.

"A gripping contemporary survival adventure, this spare first novel is also a heart-wrenching family story of courage, betrayal, and love." Booklist

Jarzab, Anna

All unquiet things. Delacorte Press 2010 339p $17.99

Grades: 8 9 10 11 12   **Fic**

1. School stories 2. Mystery fiction 3. Homicide -- Fiction 4. Social classes -- Fiction

ISBN 978-0-385-73835-4; 0-385-73835-8; 978-0-385-90723-1 lib bdg; 0-385-90723-0 lib bdg

LC 2009-11557

After the death of his ex-girlfriend Carly, northern California high school student Neily joins forces with Carly's cousin Audrey to try to solve her murder.

The **opposite** of hallelujah; Anna Jarzab. Delacorte Press 2012 452 p. (hc) $16.99

Grades: 7 8 9 10   **Fic**

1. Ex-nuns -- Fiction 2. Secrets -- Fiction 3. Sisters -- Fiction 4. Nuns -- Fiction 5. Guilt -- Fiction

ISBN 0385738366; 9780375894084; 9780385738361; 9780385907248

LC 2012010882

In this book by Anna Jarzab "Caro's parents drop the bombshell news that [her sister] Hannah is returning to live with them. . . . Unable to understand Hannah, Caro resorts to telling lies about her mysterious reappearance. . . . And as she unearths a clue from Hannah's past--one that could save Hannah from the dark secret that possesses her--Caro begins to see her sister in a whole new light." (Publisher's note)

Jeffrey, Mark

Max Quick: the pocket and the pendant. Harper 2011 294p $15.99

Grades: 4 5 6 7   **Fic**

1. Science fiction 2. Time -- Fiction 3. Voyages and travels -- Fiction 4. Identity (Psychology) -- Fiction

ISBN 978-0-06-198892-9; 0-06-198892-8

LC 2010-42663

First released 2005 as a podcast audiobook

Young Max, a troubled boy with a mysterious past, joins two other youths unaffected when the rest of the world was frozen in time on a journey across America—and time itself—seeking the source of the "Time-stop."

"This fast-paced adventure . . . will keep readers turning pages." SLJ

Jenkins, A. M.

Night road. HarperTeen 2008 362p $16.99; lib bdg $17.89; pa $8.99

Grades: 8 9 10 11 12   **Fic**

1. Horror fiction 2. Vampires -- Fiction 3. Automobile travel -- Fiction

ISBN 978-0-06-054604-5; 0-06-054604-2; 978-0-06-054605-2 lib bdg; 0-06-054605-0 lib bdg; 978-0-06-054606-9 pa; 0-06-054606-9 pa

LC 2007-31703

Battling his own memories and fears, Cole, an extraordinarily conscientious vampire, and Sandor, a more impulsive acquaintance, spend a few months on the road, trying to train a young man who recently joined their ranks.

"The real strength of the novel lies in the noirish atmosphere, accessible prose, and crisp, sharp dialogue." Horn Book

Repossessed. HarperTeen 2007 218p $15.99

Grades: 7 8 9 10   **Fic**

1. School stories 2. Devil -- Fiction 3. Demoniac possession -- Fiction

ISBN 978-0-06-083568-2; 0-06-083568-0

LC 2007-09142

Michael L. Printz Award honor book, 2008

A fallen angel, tired of being unappreciated while doing his pointless, demeaning job, leaves Hell, enters the body of a seventeen-year-old boy, and tries to experience the full range of human feelings before being caught and punished, while the boy's family and friends puzzle over his changed behavior.

"Funny and clever. . . . It's a quick, quirky and entertaining read, with some meaty ideas in it, too." Kliatt

Jennings, Richard W.

Ghost town. Houghton Mifflin 2009 167p $16

Grades: 7 8 9 10   **Fic**

1. Ghost towns -- Fiction 2. Imaginary playmates -- Fiction 3. Business enterprises -- Fiction

ISBN 978-0-547-19471-4; 0-547-19471-4

LC 2008036781

Thirteen-year-old Spencer Honesty and his imaginary friend, an Indian called Chief Leopard Frog, improbably achieve fame and riches in the abandoned town of Paisley, Kansas, when Spencer begins taking photographs with his deceased father's ancient camera and Chief Leopard Frog has his poems published by a shady businessman in the Cayman Islands.

"Jennings has a dry wit, and the protagonist's matter-of-fact observations make the most outlandish scenes seem possible. This is a coming-of-age story/tall tale that's full of charm." SLJ

★ **Orwell's** luck; [by] Richard Jennings. Houghton Mifflin 2000 146p $15; pa $6.95

Grades: 5 6 7 8   **Fic**

1. Magic -- Fiction 2. Rabbits -- Fiction

ISBN 0-618-03628-8; 0-618-69335-1 pa

LC 99-33501

While caring for an injured rabbit which becomes her confidant, horoscope writer, and source of good luck, a thoughtful seventh grade girl learns to see things in more than one way

"This absolutely captivating tale is about everyday magic . . . filled with quiet humor and seamless invention. The characters . . . are the sort that readers fall in love with." Booklist

Stink City. Houghton Mifflin Company 2006 186p $16

Grades: 5 6 7 8   **Fic**

1. Fishing -- Fiction 2. Animal rights movement -- Fiction

ISBN 978-0-618-55248-1; 0-618-55248-0

LC 2006-05863

As fifteen-year-old Cade gets involved in animal rights activism in his struggle to atone for the suffering of fish used in his family's smelly catfish bait business, his neighbor Leigh Ann tries to keep him out of trouble

"Many kids will enjoy the fishing lore, eccentric diversions, and exaggerated humor in this whopper of a yarn." Booklist

Jeschonek, Robert T.

My favorite band does not exist. Clarion Books 2011 327p $16.99

Grades: 8 9 10 11 12   **Fic**
  1. Fantasy fiction
  ISBN 978-0-547-37027-9; 0-547-37027-X
  Sixteen-year-old Idea Deity, who believes that he is a character in a novel who will die in the sixty-fourth chapter, has created a fictional underground rock band on the internet which, it turns out, may actually exist, and whose members are wondering who is broadcasting all their personal information.
  "Jeschonek has created a quirky, time and space-bending adventure that might just gather a cult following of its own. . . . Libraries looking for a strong addition to their science-fiction collections will want to invest in this sophisticated novel." SLJ

Jimenez, Francisco
  ★ **Breaking** through. Houghton Mifflin 2001 195p il $15; pa $6.95
Grades: 7 8 9 10 11 12   **Fic**
  1. Migrant labor -- Fiction 2. Mexican Americans -- Fiction
  ISBN 0-618-01173-0; 0-618-34248-6 pa
                       LC 2001-16941
  Having come from Mexico to California ten years ago, fourteen-year-old Francisco is still working in the fields but fighting to improve his life and complete his education
  "For all its recounting of deprivation, this is a hopeful book, told with rectitude and dignity." Horn Book

  ★ **Reaching** out. Houghton Mifflin 2008 196p $16; pa $6.99
Grades: 7 8 9 10 11 12   **Fic**
  1. Mexican Americans -- Fiction 2. Father-son relationship -- Fiction
  ISBN 978-0-618-03851-0; 0-618-03851-5; 978-0-547-25030-4 pa; 0-547-25030-4 pa
  A Pura Belpre Author Award honor book, 2009
  "Papa's raging depression intensifies young Jiménez's personal guilt and conflict in the 1960s. . . . He is the first in his Mexican American migrant family to attend college in California. . . . Like his other fictionalized autobiographies, The Circuit (1997) and Breaking Through (2001), this sequel tells Jiménez's personal story in self-contained chapters that join together in a stirring narrative. . . . The spare episodes will draw readers with the quiet daily detail of work, anger, sorrow, and hope." Booklist

  ★ The **circuit** : stories from the life of a migrant child. Houghton Mifflin 1999 $16
Grades: 7 8 9 10 11 12   **Fic**
  1. Family life -- Fiction 2. Migrant labor -- Fiction 3. Mexican Americans -- Fiction
  ISBN 0-395-7902-1; 978-0-395-97902-0
  First published 1997 by University of New Mexico Press
  The story "begins in Mexico when the author is very young and his parents inform him that they are going on a very long trip to 'El Norte.' What follows is a series of stories of the family's unending migration from one farm to another as they search for the next harvesting job. Each story is told from the point of view of the author as a young child. The simple and direct narrative stays true to this perspective. . . . Lifting the story up from the mundane, Jiménez

deftly portrays the strong bonds of love that hold this family together." Publ Wkly

Jinks, Catherine
  Babylonne; [by] Catherine Jinks. Candlewick Press 2008 384p map $18.99
Grades: 7 8 9 10 11 12   **Fic**
  1. War stories 2. Orphans -- Fiction 3. Middle Ages -- Fiction
  ISBN 978-0-7636-3650-0; 0-7636-3650-9
                       LC 2007-21958
  In the violent and predatory world of thirteenth-century Languedoc, Pagan's sixteen-year-old daughter disguises herself as a boy and runs away with a priest who claims to be a friend of her dead father and mother, not knowing whether or not she can trust him, or anyone.
  "Complete with snappy dialogue, humorous asides, and colorful descriptions . . . this novel stands on its own as a very fine historical fiction book about a period in history that is not commonly written about for teens." Voice Youth Advocates

  ★ **Evil** genius. Harcourt 2007 486p $17
Grades: 7 8 9 10   **Fic**
  1. School stories 2. Crime -- Fiction 3. Genius -- Fiction 4. Good and evil -- Fiction
  ISBN 978-0-15-205988-0; 0-15-205988-1
                       LC 2006-14476
  First published 2005 in Australia
  Child prodigy Cadel Piggot, an antisocial computer hacker, discovers his true identity when he enrolls as a first-year student at an advanced crime academy.
  "Cadel's turnabout is convincingly hampered by his difficulty recognizing appropriate outlets for rage, and Jinks' whiplash-inducing suspense writing will gratify fans of Anthony Horowitz's high-tech spy scenarios." Booklist
  Other titles about Cadel Piggot are:
  Genius squad (2008)
  Genius wars (2010)

  Living hell. Harcourt 2010 256p $17
Grades: 7 8 9 10   **Fic**
  1. Science fiction
  ISBN 978-0-15-206193-7; 0-15-206193-2
                       LC 2009-18938
  Chronicles the transformation of a spaceship into a living organism, as seventeen-year-old Cheney leads the hundreds of inhabitants in a fight for survival while machines turn on them, treating all humans as parasites.
  "Jinks' well-thought-out environs and rational characters help ground this otherwise out-of-control interstellar thriller." Booklist

  The **abused** werewolf rescue group. Harcourt 2011 409p $16.99
Grades: 8 9 10 11 12   **Fic**
  1. Mystery fiction 2. Werewolves -- Fiction
  ISBN 978-0-15-206615-4; 0-15-206615-2
  When Tobias wakes up in a hospital with no memory of the night before, a mysterious man tells him he has a dangerous condition, and he finds himself involved with a group of werewolves convinced he needs their help.

Jinks "weaves an action-packed story that has a tempo all its own. The constant plot twists and turns thrust the characters into bizarre situations that are at times as humorous as they are scary." SLJ

The **reformed** vampire support group. Houghton Mifflin Harcourt 2009 362p $17; pa $8.99

Grades: 8 9 10 11 12   **Fic**

1. Mystery fiction 2. Vampires -- Fiction

ISBN 978-0-15-206609-3; 0-15-206609-8; 978-0-547-41166-8 pa; 0-547-41166-9 pa

LC 2008-25115

Fifteen-year-old vampire Nina has been stuck for fifty-one years in a boring support group for vampires, and nothing exciting has ever happened to them—until one of them is murdered and the others must try to solve the crime.

"Those tired of torrid bloodsucker stories or looking for a comic riff on the trend will feel refreshed by the vomitous, guinea-pig-drinking accidental heroics of Nina and her pals." Kirkus

Jobling, Curtis

The **rise** of the wolf. Viking Childrens Books 2011 (Wereworld) 421p $16.99

Grades: 4 5 6 7   **Fic**

1. Fantasy fiction 2. Adventure fiction 3. Werewolves -- Fiction

ISBN 978-0-670-01330-2; 0-670-01330-7

LC 2010049517

When a vicious beast invades his father's farm and sixteen-year-old Drew suddenly transforms into a werewolf, he runs away from his family, seeking refuge in the most out of the way parts of Lyssia, only to be captured by Lord Bergan's men and forced to battle numerous werecreatures while trying to prove that he is not the enemy.

"Jobling's characterizations are solid, his world-building is complex and fascinating, and the combat scenes are suitably exciting. The book's themes are familiar—lost prince in exile, voyage of self-discovery, young heroes rebelling against injustice and evil—but Jobling uses them to tell a thoroughly enjoyable adventure that makes particularly inventive use of its shapeshifter elements and mythology." Publ Wkly

Jocelyn, Marthe

Folly. Wendy Lamb Books 2010 249p $15.99; lib bdg $18.99

Grades: 8 9 10 11 12   **Fic**

1. Abandoned children -- Fiction 2. Household employees -- Fiction

ISBN 978-0-385-73846-0; 0-385-73846-3; 978-0-385-90731-6 lib bdg; 0-385-90731-1 lib bdg

LC 2009-23116

In a parallel narrative set in late nineteenth-century England, teenaged country girl Mary Finn relates the unhappy conclusion to her experiences as a young servant in an aristocratic London household while, years later, young James Nelligan describes how he comes to leave his beloved foster family to live and be educated at London's famous Foundling Hospital.

"Mary's spry narration (James's chapters unfold in third-person) combined with the tale's texture and fervent emotion will seduce readers." Horn Book Guide

★ **How** it happened in Peach Hill. Wendy Lamb Books 2007 232p $15.99; lib bdg $18.99

Grades: 6 7 8 9   **Fic**

1. Clairvoyance -- Fiction 2. Swindlers and swindling -- Fiction 3. Mother-daughter relationship -- Fiction

ISBN 978-0-375-83701-2; 0-375-93701-9; 978-0-375-93701-9 lib bdg; 0-375-93701-3 lib bdg

LC 2006-26688

When fifteen-year-old Annie Grey and her "clairvoyant" mother arrive in Peach Hill, New York, in 1924, each finds a reason for wanting to finally settle down, but to reach their goals they will have to do some serious lying and Annie will have to stand up for herself.

"The blend of coming-of-age, adventure, and intrigue, framed by details of small-town life and a classic con, will appeal to fans of spunky female characters and readers of historical fiction alike." Booklist

Mable Riley; a reliable record of humdrum, peril, and romance. Candlewick Press 2004 279p $15.99; pa $6.99

Grades: 5 6 7 8   **Fic**

1. Teachers -- Fiction 2. Women's rights -- Fiction

ISBN 0-7636-2120-X; 0-7636-3287-2 pa

LC 2003-55322

In 1901, fourteen-year-old Mable Riley dreams of being a writer and having adventures while stuck in Perth County, Ontario, assisting her sister in teaching school and secretly becoming friends with a neighbor who holds scandalous opinions on women's rights.

"This book is a funny and inspiring tale of a young girl finding her voice and the courage to make it heard." Voice Youth Advocates

★ **Would** you. Wendy Lamb Books 2008 165p $15.99; lib bdg $18.99; pa $6.50

Grades: 8 9 10 11 12   **Fic**

1. Coma -- Fiction 2. Sisters -- Fiction 3. Family life -- Fiction 4. Medical care -- Fiction 5. Traffic accidents -- Fiction

ISBN 978-0-375-83703-6; 0-375-83703-5; 978-0-375-93703-3 lib bdg; 0-375-93703-X lib bdg; 978-0-375-83704-3 pa; 0-375-83704-3 pa

LC 2007-18913

When her beloved sister, Claire, steps in front of a car and winds up in a coma, Nat's anticipated summer of working, hanging around with friends, and seeing Claire off to college is transformed into a nightmare of doctors, hospitals, and well-meaning neighbors.

"Jocelyn captures a teen's thoughts and reactions in a time of incredible anguish without making her overly dramatic. Readers will fly through the pages of this book, crying, laughing, and crying some more." SLJ

John, Antony

Five flavors of dumb. Dial Books 2010 337p $16.99

Grades: 7 8 9 10   **Fic**
1. Deaf -- Fiction 2. Rock musicians -- Fiction 3. Seattle (Wash.) -- Fiction
ISBN 978-0-8037-3433-3; 0-8037-3433-6
         LC 2009-44449
Eighteen-year-old Piper is profoundly hearing impaired and resents her parent's decision raid her college fund to get cochlear implants for her baby sister. She becomes the manager for her classmates' popular rock band, called Dumb, giving her the chance to prove her capabilities to her parents and others, if only she can get the band members to get along.
"Readers interested in any of the narrative strands . . . will find a solid, satisfyingly complex story here." Bull Cent Child Books

Johnson, Angela, 1961-
★ A **certain** October; Angela Johnson. Simon & Schuster Books For Young Readers 2012 176 p. (hardback) $16.99
Grades: 7 8 9 10 11 12   **Fic**
1. Bildungsromans 2. Death -- Fiction 3. Guilt -- Fiction 4. Teenagers -- Fiction 5. Autism -- Fiction 6. Friendship -- Fiction 7. High schools -- Fiction
ISBN 9781442417267; 9780689865053; 9780689870651
         LC 2012001595
In this book, "when a terrible accident occurs, Scotty feels responsible for the loss of someone she hardly knew, and the world goes wrong. She cannot tell what is a dream and what is real. Her friends are having a hard time getting through to her and her family is preoccupied with their own trauma. But the prospect of a boy, a dance, and the possibility that everything can fall back into place soon help Scotty realize that she is capable of adding her own flavor to life." (Publisher's note)

★ **Heaven**. Simon & Schuster Bks. for Young Readers 1998 138p $16.95; pa $7.99
Grades: 6 7 8 9   **Fic**
1. Parent and child 2. Adoption -- Fiction 3. African Americans -- Fiction
ISBN 0-689-82229-4; 1-4424-0342-X pa
         LC 98-3291
Coretta Scott King Award for text, 1999
Fourteen-year-old Marley's seemingly perfect life in the small town of Heaven is disrupted when she discovers that her father and mother are not her real parents
"In spare, often poetic prose . . . Johnson relates Marley's insightful quest into what makes a family." SLJ

★ **Sweet,** hereafter; Angela Johnson. 1st ed. Simon and Schuster Books for Young Readers 2010 118 p. (paperback) $7.99; (hardcover) $16.99
Grades: 7 8 9 10   **Fic**
1. Iraq War, 2003- -- Fiction 2. African Americans -- Fiction
ISBN 0689873859; 9780689873867; 9780689873850; 0689873867
         LC 2009027618
"Johnson concludes the trilogy that began with Heaven (1998) and The First Part Last (2003). . . . Johnson's stripped-

down, poetic prose is filled with shattering emotional truths about war's incalculable devastation, love's mysteries, and the bewildering, necessary search for happiness." Booklist

"With heartfelt empathy, we share in Shoogy's personal loss and her need for a new direction. Characters from the two other titles reappear, and we get a glimpse of how their lives are moving forward. This book belongs in all junior and senior high school collections, especially those who already own the first two titles. . . . Johnson now has one more well-woven character development novel to her name." Libr Media Connect

★ **Toning** the sweep. Orchard Bks. 1993 103p hardcover o.p. pa $5.99
Grades: 6 7 8 9   **Fic**
1. Death -- Fiction 2. Family life -- Fiction 3. Grandmothers -- Fiction 4. African Americans -- Fiction
ISBN 0-531-05476-4; 0-531-08626-7 lib bdg; 978-0-590-48142-7 pa; 0-590-48142-8 pa
         LC 92-34062
Coretta Scott King Award for text
On a visit to her grandmother Ola, who is dying of cancer in her house in the desert, fourteen-year-old Emmie hears many stories about the past and her family history and comes to a better understanding of relatives both dead and living
"Full of subtle nuance, the novel is overlaid with meaning about the connections of family and the power of friendship." SLJ

★ A **cool** moonlight. Dial Bks. 2003 133p hardcover o.p. pa $6.99
Grades: 4 5 6   **Fic**
1. Skin -- Diseases -- Fiction
ISBN 0-8037-2846-8; 0-14-240284-2 pa
         LC 2002-31521
Nine-year-old Lila, born with xeroderma pigmentosum, a skin disease that make her sensitive to sunlight, makes secret plans to feel the sun's rays on her tenth birthday
"The book's real magic resides in the spell cast by Johnson's spare, lucid, lyrical prose. Using simple words and vivid sensory images, she creates Lila's inner world as a place of quiet intensity." Booklist

★ The **first** part last. Simon & Schuster Bks. for Young Readers 2003 131p $15.95
Grades: 7 8 9 10   **Fic**
1. Infants -- Fiction 2. Teenage fathers -- Fiction 3. African Americans -- Fiction
ISBN 0-689-84922-2
         LC 2002-36512
Michael L. Printz Award, 2004
Bobby's carefree teenage life changes forever when he becomes a father and must care for his adored baby daughter.
"Brief, poetic, and absolutely riveting." SLJ

Johnson, J. J.
★ The **theory** of everything; by Jen Wichman. Peachtree Publishers 2012 334 p. ill. (hardcover) $16.95
Grades: 7 8 9 10   **Fic**
1. Bereavement -- Fiction 2. Interpersonal relations

-- Fiction 3. Grief -- Fiction 4. Friendship -- Fiction 5. Best friends -- Fiction 6. Loss (Psychology) -- Fiction 7. Family life -- New York (State) -- Fiction
ISBN 1561456233; 9781561456239

LC 2011020973

In this novel, by J. J. Johnson, "ever since Sarah Jones's best friend Jamie died in a freak accident, life has felt sort of . . . random. Sarah has always followed the rules. . . . Now what? . . . In a last ditch effort to pull it together, Sarah ends up working for Roy, a local eccentric who owns a Christmas tree farm, and who might also be trying to understand the rules, patterns, and connections in life." (Publisher's note)

Johnson, Lindsay Lee

Worlds apart. Front Street 2005 166p il $16.95
Grades: 7 8 9 10   **Fic**
1. Moving -- Fiction 2. Psychiatric hospitals -- Fiction
ISBN 1-932425-28-4

LC 2005-12052

A thirteen-year-old daughter of a surgeon finds herself wrenched away from a comfortable lifestyle to a home on the grounds of a mental hospital, where her father has accepted a five year contract.

"This story brings bias and prejudice to the forefront in a discussable and readable narrative." SLJ

Johnson, Maureen

13 little blue envelopes. HarperCollins Publishers 2005 317p $15.99; pa $8.99
Grades: 8 9 10 11 12   **Fic**
1. Aunts -- Fiction 2. Voyages and travels -- Fiction 3. Young adult literature -- Works
ISBN 0-06-054141-5; 0-06-054143-1 pa

LC 2005-02658

When seventeen-year-old Ginny receives a packet of mysterious envelopes from her favorite aunt, she leaves New Jersey to criss-cross Europe on a sort of scavenger hunt that transforms her life.

"Equal parts poignant, funny and inspiring, this tale is sure to spark wanderlust." Publ Wkly

★ **Suite** Scarlett. Scholastic Point 2008 353p $16.99
Grades: 6 7 8 9 10   **Fic**
1. Authorship -- Fiction 2. Family life -- Fiction 3. Hotels and motels -- Fiction
ISBN 978-0-439-89927-7; 0-439-89927-3

LC 2007-041903

Fifteen-year-old Scarlett Marvin is stuck in New York City for the summer working at her quirky family's historic hotel, but her brother's attractive new friend and a seasonal guest who offers her an intriguing and challenging writing project improve her outlook.

"Utterly winning, madcap Manhattan farce, crafted with a winking, urbane narrative and tight, wry dialogue." Booklist
Another title about Scarlett is:
Scarlett fever (2010)

The **last** little blue envelope. HarperTeen 2011 282p $16.99
Grades: 8 9 10 11 12   **Fic**
1. Aunts -- Fiction 2. Artists -- Fiction 3. Letters --

Fiction 4. Voyages and travels -- Fiction 5. Young adult literature -- Works 6. Swindlers and swindling -- Fiction
ISBN 978-0-06-197679-7; 0-06-197679-2

LC 2010033580

"Ginny's narrative, told in an intelligent, third-person voice, establishes her firmly as a sympathetic, often hilarious everygirl, whose efforts to understand herself and who she'd like to be are fraught with moments both romantic and heartbreaking. Johnson's skill in creating secondary characters that are unusual, realistically flawed and utterly believable is again on display here. . . . This is an appealingly smart and honest read that fans of the first will find deeply satisfying." Kirkus

★ The **madness** underneath; Maureen Johnson. G. P. Putnam's Sons 2013 304 p. (Shades of London) (hardback) $17.99
Grades: 6 7 8 9 10   **Fic**
1. Ghost stories 2. Occult fiction 3. Mystery fiction 4. Ghosts -- Fiction 5. Murder -- Fiction 6. Schools -- Fiction 7. Boarding schools -- Fiction
ISBN 039925661X; 9780399256615

LC 2012026755

This paranormal mystery novel, by Maureen Johnson, is book two of "The Shades of London Trilogy." "After her near-fatal run-in with the Jack the Ripper copycat, Rory Devereaux . . . [has] become a human terminus, with the power to eliminate ghosts on contact. . . . The Ripper may be gone, but now there is a string of new inexplicable deaths threatening London. Rory has evidence that the deaths are no coincidence. Something much more sinister is going on." (Publisher's note)

The **name** of the star. G. P. Putnam's Sons 2011 384p $16.99
Grades: 6 7 8 9 10   **Fic**
1. Ghost stories 2. School stories 3. Homicide -- Fiction 4. Witnesses -- Fiction
ISBN 978-0-399-25660-8; 0-399-25660-1; 9780399256608; 0399256601

LC 2011009003

"Johnson's trademark sense of humor serves to counterbalance some grisly murders in this page-turner, which opens her Shades of London series. . . . As one mutilated body after another turns up, Johnson . . . amplifies the story's mysteries with smart use of and subtle commentary on modern media shenanigans and London's infamously extensive surveillance network. . . . Readers looking for nonstop fun, action, and a little gore have come to the right place." Publ Wkly

Johnson, Peter

★ **What** happened. Front Street 2007 133p $16.95
Grades: 8 9 10 11 12   **Fic**
1. Traffic accidents -- Fiction 2. Father-son relationship -- Fiction
ISBN 978-1-932425-67-3; 1-932425-67-5

LC 2006-12028

When Duane is involved in a hit-and-run accident during a snowstorm, passengers Kyle and his younger brother must face Duane's powerful father, a man whose hatred of their own absent father may lead him to harm the boys.

"The voice that Johnson has given this boy . . . is breathtakingly good, each word conspiring with every other word to create an irresistibly seductive tone that is a haunting combination of sadness and fragile hope." Booklist

Johnson-Shelton, Nils

The **Invisible** Tower. HarperCollins 2011 (Otherworld chronicles) 335p $16.99

Grades: 4 5 6 7   **Fic**
1. Adventure fiction 2. Kings
ISBN 978-0-06-207086-9; 0-06-207086-X
LC 2011022928

A twelve-year-old boy learns that he is actually King Arthur brought back to life in the twenty-first century—and that the fate of the universe rests in his hands.

"This new take on the Arthurian legends, told in third-person, pits wisecracking contemporary teens with their contemporary banter. . . . against all manner of obstacles. . . . It's always high-spirited and fun. Gives new life to Arthurian legends and may just send readers back to more traditional tellings." Kirkus

The **seven** swords; Nils Johnson-Shelton. HarperCollins 2013 368 p. (Otherworld chronicles) (hardback) $16.99

Grades: 4 5 6 7   **Fic**
1. Arthurian romances -- Adaptations 2. Adventure and adventurers -- Fiction
ISBN 0062070940; 9780062070944
LC 2012019088

This juvenile adventure fantasy, by Nils Johnson-Shelton, second in the "Otherworld Chronicles," follows "Artie Kingfisher, the new King Arthur. On a quest to recover seven magical swords of the Dark Ages, Artie and Kay gather 'New Knights of the Round Table' and try to unite two worlds. Standing in their way is Lordess Morgaine. . . . Artie and his band travel from Ohio via crossover points between worlds in search of swords in Sweden, France and Japan." (Kirkus Reviews)

Johnston, Julie

A **very** fine line. Tundra Books 2006 198p $18.95; pa $10.95

Grades: 5 6 7 8   **Fic**
1. Clairvoyance -- Fiction
ISBN 978-0-88776-746-3; 0-88776-746-X; 978-0-88776-829-3 pa; 0-88776-829-6 pa

Then thirteen-year-old Rosalind's "aunt informs her that as the seventh daughter of a seventh daughter, she can . . . see glimpses of the future, she balks. . . . The story begins in Kepston, Ontario, in 1941. . . . Readers who come to the book intrigued by the idea of clairvoyance will fine much more: several vivid characters, a well-realized setting, and a sensitively nuanced resolution." Booklist

Johnston, Tony

Any small goodness; a novel of the barrio. illustrations by Raúl Colón. Blue Sky Press (NY) 2001 128p il $16.95; pa $4.99

Grades: 4 5 6 7   **Fic**
1. Mexican Americans -- Fiction
ISBN 0-439-18936-5; 0-439-23384-4 pa
LC 99-59877

Arturo and his family and friends share all kinds of experiences living in the barrio of East Los Angeles—reclaiming their names, playing basketball, championing the school librarian, and even starting their own gang

"The characters are likable and warm. . . . The message is positive and the episodes, while occasionally serious, are more often humorous and gratifying." SLJ

Jolin, Paula

In the name of God. Roaring Brook Press 2007 208p $16.95

Grades: 8 9 10 11 12   **Fic**
1. Muslims -- Fiction 2. Family life -- Fiction 3. Islamic fundamentalism -- Fiction
ISBN 978-1-59643-211-6; 1-59643-211-X
LC 2006-23834

Determined to follow the laws set down in the Qur'an, seventeen-year-old Nadia becomes involved in a violent revolutionary movement aimed at supporting Muslim rule in Syria and opposing the Western politics and materialism that increasingly affect her family.

"The well-written prose and short chapters give stories in the news a face and a character. Readers of this book will not be able to read or watch the news in the same way." Voice Youth Advocates

Jones, Allan Frewin

Destiny's path; [by] Frewin Jones. HarperTeen 2009 329p $16.99

Grades: 8 9 10 11 12   **Fic**
1. War stories 2. Magic -- Fiction 3. Princesses -- Fiction 4. Fate and fatalism -- Fiction
ISBN 978-0-06-087146-8; 0-06-087146-6
LC 2009-14587

When fifteen-year-old Princess Branwen tries to turn away from her destiny as the one who will save Wales from the Saxons, the Shining Ones send an owl in the form of a young girl called Blodwedd to guide her and Rhodri on the right path.

"Branwen's compelling story leaves readers waiting for the sequel." Booklist

Jones, Diana Wynne, 1934-2011

★ **Enchanted** glass. Greenwillow Books 2010 292p $16.99

Grades: 6 7 8 9   **Fic**
1. Magic -- Fiction 2. Orphans -- Fiction 3. Villages -- Fiction
ISBN 978-0-06-186684-5; 0-06-186684-9
LC 2009006195

After his grandfather dies, Andrew Hope inherits a house and surrounding land in an English village, but things become very complicated when young orphan Aidan shows up and suddenly a host of variously magical townsfolk and interlopers start intruding on their lives.

"Jones hits all the bases, combining fluid storytelling, sly humor, and exquisitely drawn characters." Booklist

House of many ways. Greenwillow Books 2008 404p $17.99; lib bdg $18.89; pa $8.99

Grades: 5 6 7 8   **Fic**

1. Fantasy fiction 2. Magic -- Fiction 3. Houses -- Fiction 4. Uncles -- Fiction

ISBN 978-0-06-147795-9; 0-06-147795-8; 978-0-06-147796-6 lib bdg; 0-06-147796-6 lib bdg; 978-0-06-147797-3 pa; 0-06-147797-4 pa

LC 2007036147

When Charmain is asked to housesit for Great Uncle William, the Royal Wizard of Norland, she is ecstatic to get away from her parents, but finds that his house is much more than it seems.

This is "a buoyantly entertaining read. . . . [Jones'] comic pacing and wit are amply evident." Horn Book

★ **Howl's** moving castle. Greenwillow Books 1986 212p hardcover o.p. pa $6.99

Grades: 5 6 7 8   **Fic**

1. Fantasy fiction

ISBN 0-06-147878-4 pa; 0-688-06233-4; 978-0-06-147878-9 pa

LC 85-21981

Sophie "resigns herself to making a living as a hatter and helping her younger sisters prepare to make their fortunes. But adventure seeks her out in the shop where she sits alone dreaming over her hats. The wicked Witch of the Waste, angered by 'competition' in the area, turns her into an old woman, so she seeks refuge inside the strange moving castle of the wizard Howl. Howl, advertised by his apprentice as an eater of souls, lives a mad, frantic life trying to escape the curse the witch has placed on him, find the perfect girl of his dreams and end the contract he and his fire demon have entered. Sophie, against her best instincts and at first unaware of her own powers, falls in love. . . . Grade six and up." (SLJ)

"Satisfyingly, Sophie meets a fate far exceeding her dreary expectations. This novel is an exciting, multi-faceted puzzle, peopled with vibrant, captivating characters. A generous sprinkling of humor adds potency to this skillful author's spell." Voice Youth Advocates

Jones, Kimberly K.

Sand dollar summer. Margaret K. McElderry Books 2006 206p $15.95; pa $5.99

Grades: 5 6 7 8   **Fic**

1. Islands -- Fiction 2. Family life -- Fiction

ISBN 978-1-4169-0362-8; 1-4169-0362-3; 978-1-4169-5834-5 pa; 1-4169-5834-7 pa

LC 2005012740

When twelve-year-old Lise spends the summer on an island in Maine with her self-reliant mother and bright—but oddly mute—younger brother, her formerly safe world is complicated by an aged Indian neighbor, her mother's childhood friend, and a hurricane.

"The drama in [the] smart, tough, first-person narrative is understated; the spaces between the words are as eloquent as what is said. . . . The family story . . . is exquisitely told." Booklist

Jones, Traci L.

Finding my place. Farrar Straus Giroux 2010 181p $16.99

Grades: 6 7 8 9   **Fic**

1. School stories 2. Moving -- Fiction 3. Friendship -- Fiction 4. Prejudices -- Fiction 5. Race relations -- Fiction 6. African Americans -- Fiction

ISBN 978-0-374-33573-1; 0-374-33573-7

LC 2008-54433

After moving to an affluent suburb of Denver in 1975, ninth-grader Tiphanie feels lonely at her nearly all-white high school until she befriends another "outsider" and discovers that prejudice exists in many forms.

"Tiphanie is refreshingly witty and open-minded. . . . Jones handles the intricacies of race relations splendidly and excels in the frankness of her prose. . . . This immediate, engaging novel will appeal to readers of all backgrounds." Booklist

★ **Silhouetted** by the blue. Farrar, Straus & Giroux 2011 200p $16.99

Grades: 5 6 7 8   **Fic**

1. School stories 2. Theater -- Fiction 3. Bereavement -- Fiction 4. African Americans -- Fiction 5. Depression (Psychology) -- Fiction

ISBN 978-0-374-36914-9; 0-374-36914-3

LC 2010008419

After the death of her mother in an automobile accident, seventh-grader Serena, who has gotten the lead in her middle school play, is left to handle the day-to-day challenges of caring for herself and her younger brother when their father cannot pull himself out of his depression.

"Jones has written another winner with this beautiful, haunting tale rich in story and characterization." Booklist

Standing against the wind; 1st ed.; Farrar, Straus and Giroux 2006 184p $16

Grades: 6 7 8 9   **Fic**

1. School stories 2. African Americans -- Fiction 3. City and town life -- Fiction

ISBN 978-0-374-37174-6; 0-374-37174-1

LC 2005-51226

As she tries to escape her poor Chicago neighborhood by winning a scholarship to a prestigious boarding school, shy and studious eighth-grader Patrice discovers that she has more options in life than she previously realized.

"Handled without obscenity, the lively street talk will draw readers to the gripping story of a contemporary kid who works to make her dreams come true." Booklist

Jordan, Rosa

Lost Goat Lane. Peachtree Publisher 2004 197p $14.95

Grades: 5 6 7 8   **Fic**

1. Goats -- Fiction 2. Race relations -- Fiction 3. African Americans -- Fiction

ISBN 1-56145-325-0

LC 2004-5343

Two families—one white, one black—living near one another in rural Florida overcome their suspicions of each other and find ways to work together, with the help of their children and a few goats

"The fully realized characters and the warmth of the story make up for the small sermons. A tender, satisfying offering." SLJ

Other titles in this series are:
The goatnappers (2007)
The last wild place (2008)

Joseph, Lynn

Flowers in the sky; by Lynn Joseph. HarperTeen 2013 240 p. (hardcover) $17.99

Grades: 8 9 10 11 12   **Fic**

1. Bildungsromans 2. New York (N.Y.) -- Fiction 3. Brothers and sisters -- Fiction 4. Love -- Fiction 5. Immigrants -- Fiction 6. Coming of age -- Fiction 7. Dominican Americans -- Fiction

ISBN 0060297948; 9780060297947

LC 2012038122

In this novel, by Lynn Joseph, "fifteen-year-old Nina Perez . . . must leave her . . . lush island home in Samana, Dominican Republic, when she's sent . . . to live with her brother, Darrio, in New York, to seek out a better life. . . . But then she meets . . . [a] tall, green-eyed boy . . . , who just might help her learn to see beauty in spite of tragedy." (Publisher's note)

The **color** of my words. HarperCollins Pubs. 2000 138p hardcover o.p. pa $5.99

Grades: 5 6 7 8   **Fic**

1. Siblings -- Fiction 2. Family life -- Fiction

ISBN 0-06-028232-0; 0-06-447204-3 pa

LC 00-22440

When life gets difficult for Ana Rosa, a twelve-year-old would-be writer living in a small village in the Dominican Republic, she can depend on her older brother to make her feel better—until the life-changing events on her thirteenth birthday

"A finely crafted novel, lovely and lyrical." SLJ

Joyce, Graham, 1954-

The **exchange**. Viking 2008 241p $16.99

Grades: 7 8 9 10   **Fic**

1. Tattooing -- Fiction 2. Supernatural -- Fiction 3. Single parent family -- Fiction 4. Dating (Social customs) -- Fiction

ISBN 978-0-670-06207-2; 0-670-06207-3

LC 2007-32160

Cursed by the elderly recluse whose home she and a friend were creeping through late one night, fourteen-year-old Caz soon finds her life disintegrating and realizes she must find a way of lifting the curse—or at least understanding its power.

"Joyce has crafted a bizarre, magically realistic tale. . . . It's a wild ride with subtly moralistic undertones and a surprisingly happy ending that will stay with readers." Booklist

Juby, Susan

Another kind of cowboy. HarperTeen 2007 344p $16.99

Grades: 8 9 10 11 12   **Fic**

1. Horses -- Fiction 2. Friendship -- Fiction 3.

Horsemanship -- Fiction 4. Homosexuality -- Fiction

ISBN 0-06-076517-8; 978-0-06-076517-0

LC 2006-36336

In Vancouver, British Columbia, two teenage dressage riders, one a spoiled rich girl and the other a closeted gay sixteen-year-old boy, come to terms with their identities and learn to accept themselves.

"Wry humor infuses this quiet story with a gentle warmth, and the secondary characters are well developed." Booklist

Getting the girl; a guide to private investigation, surveillance, and cookery. [by] S. Juby. HarperTeen 2008 341p $16.99; lib bdg $17.89; pa $8.99

Grades: 6 7 8 9 10   **Fic**

1. School stories 2. Mystery fiction 3. Popularity -- Fiction

ISBN 978-0-06-076525-5; 0-06-076525-9; 978-0-06-076527-9 lib bdg; 0-06-076527-5 lib bdg; 978-0-06-076528-6 pa; 0-06-076528-3 pa

LC 2008-00788

Ninth-grader Sherman Mack investigates the "Defilers," a secret group at his British Columbia high school that marks certain female students as pariahs, at first because he is trying to protect the girl he has a crush on, but later as a matter of principle.

Juby "applies her signature brand of humor to a detective novel. . . . [This offers a] strong and memorable female cast. . . . Here's hoping that Juby delivers on the promise of sequels." Horn Book

Jung, Mike

Geeks, girls, and secret identities; by Mike Jung ; with illustrations by Mike Maihack. Arthur A. Levine Books 2012 307 p. (hardcover : alk. paper) $16.99

Grades: 3 4 5 6 7   **Fic**

1. Secrecy -- Fiction 2. Science fiction 3. Clubs -- Fiction 4. Humorous stories 5. Robots -- Fiction 6. Schools -- Fiction 7. Superheroes -- Fiction 8. Middle schools -- Fiction

ISBN 0545335485; 9780545335485; 9780545335492; 9780545392518

LC 2011042548

In author Mike Jung's book, "Vincent Wu is Captain Stupendous's No. 1 Fan, but even he has to admit that Captain Stupendous has been a little off lately. During Professor Mayhem's latest attack, Captain Stupendous barely made it out alive, although he did manage to save Vincent from a giant monster robot. It's Vincent's dream come true . . . until he finds out Captain Stupendous's secret identity: It's Polly Winnicott-Lee, the girl Vincent happens to have a crush on." (Publisher's note)

Kade, Stacey

Queen of the dead. Hyperion 2011 266p $16.99

Grades: 8 9 10 11 12   **Fic**

1. Ghost stories 2. Family life -- Fiction 3. Secret societies -- Fiction

ISBN 978-1-4231-3467-1; 1-4231-3467-2

LC 2010029226

Will gets involved with The Order, a group consisting of ghost-talkers like himself, as he continues to help spirits into the light, while Alona, his vain, self-centered, and cranky spirit guide begins to learn the value of helping others.

"This sequel to The Ghost and the Goth (2010) has exchanged some of the lighter humor for a more complex story line. Characters are more fully developed, and the momentum is stronger." Booklist

The **ghost** and the goth. Hyperion 2010 281p $16.99

Grades: 8 9 10 11 12   **Fic**
1. Ghost stories 2. School stories
ISBN 1-4231-2197-X; 978-1-4231-2197-8
LC 2010-8135

After being hit by a bus and killed, a high school homecoming queen gets stuck in the land of the living, with only a loser classmate—who happens to be able to see and hear ghosts—to help her.

"The tale is absorbing, and Kade successfully portrays a typical present-day high school. This novel will appeal to fans of romances and ghost stories alike." SLJ

Kadohata, Cynthia

Cracker! the best dog in Vietnam. Atheneum Books for Young Readers 2007 312p $16.99; pa $7.99

Grades: 5 6 7 8   **Fic**
1. Dogs -- Fiction 2. Vietnam War, 1961-1975 -- Fiction
ISBN 978-1-4169-0637-7; 1-4169-0637-1; 978-1-4169-0638-4 pa; 1-4169-0638-X pa
LC 2006-22022

The author "tells a stirring, realistic story of America's war in Vietnam, using the alternating viewpoints of an army dog named Cracker and her 17-year-old handler, Rick Hanski. . . . The heartfelt tale explores the close bond of the scout-dog team." Booklist

★ **Kira** -Kira. Atheneum Bks. for Young Readers 2004 244p $15.95; pa $6.99

Grades: 5 6 7 8   **Fic**
1. Death -- Fiction 2. Sisters -- Fiction 3. Japanese Americans -- Fiction
ISBN 0-689-85639-3; 0-689-85640-7 pa
Awarded the Newbery Medal, 2005

Chronicles the close friendship between two Japanese-American sisters growing up in rural Georgia during the late 1950s and early 1960s, and the despair when one sister becomes terminally ill.

"This beautifully written story tells of a girl struggling to find her own way in a family torn by illness and horrendous work conditions. . . . All of the characters are believable and well developed." SLJ

★ **Outside** beauty. Atheneum Books for Young Readers 2008 265p $16.99; pa $8.99

Grades: 5 6 7 8   **Fic**
1. Sisters -- Fiction 2. Japanese Americans -- Fiction 3. Father-daughter relationship -- Fiction 4. Mother-daughter relationship -- Fiction
ISBN 978-0-689-86575-6; 0-689-86575-9; 978-1-4169-9818-1 pa; 1-4169-9818-7 pa
LC 2007-39711

Thirteen-year-old Shelby and her three sisters must go to live with their respective fathers while their mother, who has trained them to rely on their looks, recovers from a car accident that scarred her face

Kadohata's "gifts for creating and containing drama and for careful definition of character prove as powerful as ever in this wise, tender and compelling novel." Publ Wkly

Weedflower. Atheneum Books for Young Readers 2006 260p $16.95; pa $5.99

Grades: 5 6 7 8   **Fic**
1. World War, 1939-1945 -- Fiction 2. Japanese Americans -- Evacuation and relocation, 1942-1945 -- Fiction
ISBN 0-689-86574-0; 1-4169-7566-7 pa
LC 2004-24912

After twelve-year-old Sumiko and her Japanese-American family are relocated from their flower farm in southern California to an internment camp on a Mojave Indian reservation in Arizona, she helps her family and neighbors, becomes friends with a local Indian boy, and tries to hold on to her dream of owning a flower shop.

Sumiko "is a sympathetic heroine, surrounded by well-crafted, fascinating people. The concise yet lyrical prose conveys her story in a compelling narrative." SLJ

★ A **million** shades of gray. Atheneum Books for Young Readers 2010 216p $16.99

Grades: 5 6 7 8   **Fic**
1. Elephants -- Fiction 2. Wilderness survival -- Fiction
ISBN 978-1-4169-1883-7; 1-4169-1883-3
LC 2009-33307

In 1975 after American troops pull out of Vietnam, a thirteen-year-old boy and his beloved elephant escape into the jungle when the Viet Cong attack his village.

"Kadohata delves deep into the soul of her protagonist while making a faraway place and stark consequences of war seem very near." Publ Wkly

★ The **thing** about luck; Cynthia Kadohata ; illustrated by Julia Kuo. 1st ed. Atheneum Books for Young Readers 2013 288 p. (hardcover) $16.99

Grades: 5 6 7 8   **Fic**
1. Luck -- Fiction 2. Japanese Americans -- Fiction 3. Brothers and sisters -- Fiction 4. Grandparents -- Fiction 5. Farm life -- Kansas -- Fiction
ISBN 1416918825; 9781416918820; 9781442474673
LC 2012021287

National Book Award Finalist (2013)

In this novel, by Newbery Medalist Cynthia Kadohata, "Summer knows that kouun means 'good luck' in Japanese, and this year her family has none of it. Just when she thinks nothing else can possibly go wrong, an emergency whisks her parents away to Japan--right before harvest season. Summer and her little brother, Jaz, are left in the care of their grandparents, who come out of retirement in order to harvest wheat and help pay the bills." (Publisher's note)

"Kadohata expertly captures the uncertainties of the tween years as Summer navigates the balance of childlike concerns with the onset of increasingly grown-up responsibilities." (SLJ)

Kagawa, Julie

The **Eternity** Cure; Julie Kagawa. Harlequin Books 2013 448 p. (hardcover) $16.99

Grades: 7 8 9 10 11 12   **Fic**

  1. Science fiction 2. Vampires -- Fiction 3. Epidemics -- Fiction

  ISBN 0373210698; 9780373210695

This vampire novel, by Julie Kagawa, is part of the "Blood of Eden" series. "Allie will follow the call of blood to save her creator, Kanin, from the psychotic vampire Sarren. But when the trail leads to Allie's birthplace in New Covington, what Allie finds there will change the world forever. . . . There's a new plague on the rise, a strain of the Red Lung virus that wiped out most of humanity generations ago--and this strain is deadly to humans and vampires alike." (Publisher's note)

★ The **immortal** rules; a legend begins. Julie Kagawa. Harlequin Teen 2012 504 p. (Blood of Eden) (hardcover) $18.99

Grades: 7 8 9 10 11 12   **Fic**

  1. Love stories 2. Diseases -- Fiction 3. Vampires -- Fiction

  ISBN 0373210515; 9780373210510

          LC 2011279454

In this book, "[r]abids, vicious hybrid creatures born of the plague, prowl the land beyond the walled vampire cities. . . . When Allie is savagely attacked by a rabid, . . . a mysterious vampire offers her the choice of a human death or 'life' as a vampire. . . . Allie's determination to remain more human than monster is put to the test, particularly when she joins a band of humans on a desperate journey to safety on the island of Eden. Particularly when she falls in love." (Kirkus)

"Kagawa wraps excellent writing and skillful plotting around a well-developed concept and engaging characters, resulting in a fresh and imaginative thrill-ride that deserves a wide audience." Pub Wkly

Kang, Hildi

Chengli and the Silk Road caravan. Tanglewood 2011 178p $14.95

Grades: 5 6 7 8   **Fic**

  1. Fathers -- Fiction 2. Princesses -- Fiction 3. Trade routes -- Fiction

  ISBN 978-1-933718-54-5; 1-933718-54-4

          LC 2010047359

Called to follow the wind and search for information about his father who disappeared many years ago, thirteen-year-old Chengli, carrying a piece of jade with strange writing that had belonged to his father, joins a caravan charged with giving safe passage to the Emperor's daughter as it navigates the constant dangers of the Silk Road in 630 A.D.

"This fast-paced adventure is filled with friendship, historical detail, changing scenery, and action. It will appeal to a wide range of readers." SLJ

Kantor, Melissa

Girlfriend material. Disney/Hyperion Books 2009 251p $15.99

Grades: 7 8 9 10   **Fic**

  1. Summer -- Fiction

  ISBN 978-1-4231-0849-8; 1-4231-0849-3

Kate has never had a boyfriend. But while crashing at her mother's wealthy friends' home at Cape Cod for the summer, Kate meets Adam. But when her breezy summer romance with Adam becomes more complicated, Kate asks herself if she is girlfriend material.

"The changes in Kate are both gradual and realistic. . . . Her emotional journey and acute self-consciousness are likely to strike a chord." Publ Wkly

The **breakup** bible; a novel. Hyperion Books for Children 2007 272p $15.99

Grades: 8 9 10 11 12   **Fic**

  1. Dating (Social customs) -- Fiction

  ISBN 978-0-7868-0962-2

Jennifer thinks she and Max are the perfect couple, until he decides he just wants to be friends.

"Written with wit and featuring a few fine plot twists, this will have teen girls nodding sympathetically." Booklist

Karim, Sheba

Skunk girl. Farrar, Straus & Giroux 2009 231p $16.95

Grades: 8 9 10 11 12   **Fic**

  1. School stories 2. Muslims -- Fiction 3. Family life -- Fiction 4. Pakistani Americans -- Fiction 5. Dating (Social customs) -- Fiction

  ISBN 978-0-374-37011-4; 0-374-37011-7

          LC 2008-7482

Nina Khan is not just the only Asian or Muslim student in her small-town high school in upstate New York, she is also faces the legacy of her "Supernerd" older sister, body hair, and the pain of having a crush when her parents forbid her to date.

This novel is "rife with smart, self-deprecating humor." Kirkus

Karr, Kathleen

Fortune's fool. Alfred A. Knopf 2008 201p $15.99; lib bdg $18.99; pa $6.50

Grades: 5 6 7 8   **Fic**

  1. Middle Ages -- Fiction 2. Fools and jesters -- Fiction

  ISBN 978-0-375-84816-2; 0-375-84816-9; 978-0-375-94816-9 lib bdg; 0-375-84816-3 lib bdg; 978-0-375-84307-5 pa; 0-375-84307-8 pa

          LC 2007-49034

In medieval Germany, fifteen-year-old Conrad, a court jester, and his beloved Christa, a servant girl, escape from a cruel master and journey through the countryside on a quest to find a kind lord who will give them sanctuary.

"Karr does an splendid job of recreating the medieval milieu, especially the life of a professional entertainer with all of its challenges and hardships." Booklist

Katcher, Brian

Playing with matches. Delacorte Press 2008 294p $15.99; lib bdg $18.99

Grades: 8 9 10 11 12   **Fic**

  1. School stories 2. Burns and scalds -- Fiction 3.

Dating (Social customs) -- Fiction
ISBN 978-0-385-73544-5; 0-385-73544-8; 978-0-385-90525-1 lib bdg; 0-385-90525-4 lib bdg

LC 2007-27654

While trying to find a girl who will date him, Missouri high school junior Leon Sanders befriends a lonely, disfigured female classmate.

"This is a strong debut novel with a cast of quirky, multidimensional characters struggling with issues of acceptance, sexuality, identity, and self-worth." SLJ

Kehret, Peg

Abduction! Dutton Children's Books 2004 215p $16.99; pa $6.99

Grades: 5 6 7 8   Fic
1. Kidnapping -- Fiction
ISBN 0-525-47294-0; 0-14-240617-1 pa

LC 2003-63531

Thirteen-year-old Bonnie has a feeling of foreboding on the very day that her six-year-old brother Matt and their dog Pookie are abducted, and she becomes involved in a major search effort as well as a frightening adventure

"This novel has enough suspense to keep children interested, and it will also appeal to reluctant readers." SLJ

The **ghost's** grave. Dutton Children's Books 2005 210p $16.99; pa $5.99

Grades: 5 6 7 8   Fic
1. Ghost stories 2. Coal miners -- Fiction
ISBN 0-525-46162-0; 0-14-240819-0 pa

LC 2004022064

Apprehensive about spending the summer in Washington State with his Aunt Ethel when his parents get an overseas job, twelve-year-old Josh soon finds adventure when he meets the ghost of a coal miner.

"This fast-paced and engaging book should be a hit with fans of ghost stories. Josh is a rich character to whom readers can relate." SLJ

Keith, Harold

★ **Rifles** for Watie. Crowell 1957 332p $16.89; pa $5.99

Grades: 6 7 8 9   Fic
1. Generals 2. Indian leaders 3. United States -- History -- 1861-1865
ISBN 0-690-04907-2; 0-06-447030-X pa
Awarded the Newbery Medal, 1958

"An exceptionally well-written story of the Civil War as it was fought in the western states." Bull Cent Child Books

Keller, Julia

★ **Back** home. Egmont USA 2009 194p $15.99; lib bdg $18.99

Grades: 6 7 8 9   Fic
1. Fathers -- Fiction 2. Soldiers -- Fiction 3. Family life -- Fiction 4. Iraq War, 2003- -- Fiction 5. Brain -- Wounds and injuries -- Fiction
ISBN 978-1-60684-005-4; 1-60684-005-3; 978-1-60684-048-1 lib bdg; 1-60684-048-7 lib bdg

LC 2009-15877

Thirteen-year-old Rachel Browning understands that her father will be different after being injured in the Iraq War,

but no one is prepared for the impact that his traumatic brain injury and other wounds have on the entire family

"No one who reads this heartbreaking book will ever forget it. With integrity, authenticity, and immediacy, Keller has captured the extraordinary complexity and challenge of unexpected change and, to her everlasting credit, unsparingly shares the whole truth of it with her readers." Booklist

Kelley, Jane

The **girl** behind the glass; [by] Jane Kelley. Random House 2011 183p $16.99; lib bdg $19.99; e-book $16.99

Grades: 4 5 6 7   Fic
1. Ghost stories 2. Twins -- Fiction 3. Moving -- Fiction 4. Sisters -- Fiction 5. Family life -- Fiction
ISBN 978-0-375-86220-5; 0-375-86220-X; 978-0-375-96220-2 lib bdg; 0-375-96220-4 lib bdg; 978-0-375-88996-7 e-book

LC 2010-43568

Moving from Brooklyn to a rental house in the country strains the relationship between eleven-year-old identical twins Hannah and Anna Zimmer, a situation made worse by the ghost of a girl who is trapped in the house because of problems with her own sister eighty years before.

"Both chilling and lyrical. . . . The tensions within the Zimmer family are especially well-observed, and Kelley . . . conveys an impressive amount of emotion with few words. The ethereal tone and steady parceling out of warning, clues, and bits of information . . . maintain the novel's intrigue and will keep readers invested in the unfolding mystery." Publ Wkly

Kelly, Jacqueline

★ The **evolution** of Calpurnia Tate. Henry Holt and Co. 2009 340p $16.99

Grades: 4 5 6 7   Fic
1. Nature -- Fiction 2. Family life -- Fiction 3. Naturalists -- Fiction 4. Grandfathers -- Fiction
ISBN 978-0-8050-8841-0; 0-8050-8841-5

LC 2008-40595

A Newbery Medal honor book (2010)

In central Texas in 1899, eleven-year-old Callie Vee Tate is instructed to be a lady by her mother, learns about love from the older three of her six brothers, and studies the natural world with her grandfather, the latter of which leads to an important discovery.

"Callie is a charming, inquisitive protagonist; a joyous, bright, and thoughtful creation. . . . Several scenes . . . mix gentle humor and pathos to great effect." SLJ

Kelly, Lynne

Chained; Lynne Kelly. Farrar Straus Giroux 2012 248 p. (hardcover) $16.99

Grades: 4 5 6   Fic
1. Debt 2. Circus performers -- Fiction 3. Human-animal relationship -- Fiction 4. Circus -- Fiction 5. Elephants -- Fiction 6. Child labor -- Fiction 7. Animals -- Treatment -- Fiction
ISBN 0374312370; 9780374312374; 9780374312503

LC 2011031767

In author Lynne Kelly's book, "after ten-year-old Hastin's family borrows money to pay for his sister's hospital bill, he leaves his village in northern India to take a job as an elephant keeper and work off the debt. . . . The crowds that come to the circus see a lively animal . . . but Hastin sees Nandita, a sweet elephant and his best friend, who is chained when she's not performing and hurt with a hook until she learns tricks perfectly. Hastin protects Nandita as best as he can, knowing that the only way they will both survive is if he can find a way for them to escape." (Publisher's note)

Kelsey, Marybeth

A **recipe** 4 robbery. Greenwillow Books 2009 282p $16.99; lib bdg $17.89

Grades: 4 5 6   **Fic**
1. Mystery fiction
ISBN 978-0-06-128843-2; 0-06-128843-8; 978-0-06-128845-6 lib bdg; 0-06-128845-4 lib bdg
LC 2008-29145

An unsupervised goose, missing family heirlooms, and some suspicious characters turn the annual cucumber festival into a robbery investigation for three sixth-grade friends.

"The novel is full of likable characters and fun twists and turns. The plot moves quickly, and Kelsey writes with wit and verve." SLJ

Kennedy, James

The **Order** of Odd-Fish; [by] James Kennedy. Delacorte Press 2008 403p $15.99; lib bdg $18.99

Grades: 6 7 8 9   **Fic**
1. Adventure fiction 2. Aunts -- Fiction
ISBN 978-0-385-73543-8; 0-385-73543-X; 978-0-385-90524-4 lib bdg; 0-385-90524-6 lib bdg
LC 2008-00711

Thirteen-year-old Jo suddenly finds her humdrum life turned upside down when Colonel Anatoly Kordakov shows up at her aunt's party and announces he has come to protect her.

"This clever, creative story will keep readers engaged and laughing." Libr Media Connect

Kent, Rose

Kimchi & calamari. HarperCollinsPublishers 2007 220p $15.99; lib bdg $16.89

Grades: 4 5 6 7   **Fic**
1. Adoption -- Fiction 2. Korean Americans -- Fiction 3. Italian Americans -- Fiction
ISBN 978-0-06-083769-3; 0-06-083769-1; 978-0-06-083770-9 lib bdg; 0-06-083770-5 lib bdg
LC 2006-20041

"Fourteen-year-old Korean adoptee Joseph Calderaro is stumped when his social studies teacher assigns an ancestry essay. . . . Kent's debut novel humorously captures the feelings of a young teen who thoroughly enjoys his Italian-American family but still wonders about his birth parents." Booklist

Kent, Trilby

★ **Medina** Hill. Tundra Books 2009 172p $19.95

Grades: 6 7 8 9   **Fic**
1. Great Britain -- Fiction
ISBN 978-0-88776-888-0; 0-88776-888-1
"In the grimy London of 1935, eleven-year-old Dominic

Walker has lost his voice. His mother is sick and his father's unemployed. Rescue comes in the form of his Uncle Roo, who arrives to take him and his young sister, Marlo, to Cornwall." Publisher's note
This is a "highly original debut." Booklist

Stones for my father. Tundra Books 2011 170p $19.95

Grades: 6 7 8 9   **Fic**
1. Afrikaners -- Fiction 2. South African War, 1899-1902 -- Fiction
ISBN 978-1-77049-252-3; 1-77049-252-6

"This meticulously researched novel about a white Afrikaner girl caught up in the Boer War at the turn of the 19th century brings to light a hitherto overlooked aspect of South African history. Corlie Roux is living with her harsh mother and younger brothers on an isolated farm in what was the South African Republic (now Mpumalanga). As the war reaches their farm, they flee, but are captured and interned in a concentration camp. . . . Kent tackles the challenge of depicting the complex relationships between Afrikaner colonists and English imperialists, and also the relationships of both these groups to the indigenous Africans." SLJ

Kephart, Beth

Dangerous neighbors; a novel. Egmont USA 2010 176p $16.99; lib bdg $19.99

Grades: 7 8 9 10   **Fic**
1. Death -- Fiction 2. Guilt -- Fiction 3. Twins -- Fiction 4. Sisters -- Fiction 5. Bereavement -- Fiction
ISBN 978-1-60684-080-1; 1-60684-080-0; 978-1-60684-106-8 lib bdg; 1-60684-106-8 lib bdg
LC 2010-11249

Set against the backdrop of the 1876 Centennial Exhibition in Philadelphia, Katherine cannot forgive herself when her beloved twin sister dies, and she feels that her only course of action is to follow suit.

"Exceptionally graceful prose . . . and flashbacks are so realistically drawn and deftly integrated that readers will be as startled as Katherine to find themselves yanked out of morose memories and surrounded by noisy fairgoers." Bull Cent Child Books

Dr. Radway's Sarsaparilla Resolvent; by Beth Kephart ; illustrated by William Sulit. Temple Univ Pr 2013 198 p. ill. (paperback) $15.95

Grades: 6 7 8 9   **Fic**
1. Grief -- Fiction 2. Police brutality -- Fiction
ISBN 0984042962; 9780984042968

This book by Beth Kephart follows 14-year-old protagonist William Quinn. "With his father in the Cherry Hill prison and his genially wayward older brother, Francis, recently beaten to death by a brutal policeman, his mother has ground herself into unbearable, paralyzing grief, and the boy has to find a way to save them both. . . . Gradually, William finds a way to make right some terrible wrongs." (Kirkus Reviews)

★ **House** of Dance. HarperTeen 2008 263p $16.99; lib bdg $17.89; pa $10.99

Grades: 7 8 9 10   **Fic**
1. Death -- Fiction 2. Cancer -- Fiction 3. Dancers -- Fiction 4. Grandfathers -- Fiction 5. Mother-daughter

relationship -- Fiction
ISBN 978-0-06-142928-6; 0-06-142928-7; 978-0-06-142929-3 lib bdg; 0-06-142929-5 lib bdg; 978-0-06-142930-9 pa; 0-06-142930-9 pa

LC 2007-26011

During one of her daily visits across town to visit her dying grandfather, fifteen-year-old Rosie discovers a dance studio that helps her find a way to bring her family members together.

This is "distinguished more by its sharp, eloquent prose than by its plot. . . . Poetically expressed memories and moving dialogue both anchor and amplify the characters' emotions." Publ Wkly

Nothing but ghosts. HarperTeen 2009 278p $17.95

Grades: 8 9 10 11 12   **Fic**

1. Art -- Fiction 2. Mothers -- Fiction 3. Gardening -- Fiction 4. Bereavement -- Fiction 5. Loss (Psychology) -- Fiction
ISBN 978-0-06-166796-1; 0-06-166796-X

LC 2008-26024

After her mother's death, sixteen-year-old Katie copes with her grief by working in the garden of an old estate, where she becomes intrigued by the story of a reclusive millionaire, while her father, an art restorer, manages in his own way to come to terms with the death of his wife.

"Kephart's evocative writing and gentle resolution offer healing and hope as her characters come to terms with their losses." Publ Wkly

★ **Undercover**. HarperTeen 2007 278p $16.99; lib bdg $17.89; pa $8.99

Grades: 8 9 10 11 12   **Fic**

1. School stories 2. Poetry -- Fiction 3. Family life -- Fiction
ISBN 978-0-06-123893-2; 0-06-123893-7; 978-0-06-123894-9 lib bdg; 0-06-123894-5 lib bdg; 978-0-06-123895-6 pa; 0-06-123895-3 pa

LC 2007-2981

High school sophomore Elisa is used to observing while going unnoticed except when classmates ask her to write love notes for them, but a teacher's recognition of her talent, a "client's" desire for her friendship, a love of ice skating, and her parent's marital problems draw her out of herself.

"Kephart tells a moving story. . . . Readers will fall easily into the compelling premise and Elisa's memorable, graceful voice." Booklist

You are my only; a novel. Egmont USA 2011 240p $16.99

Grades: 7 8 9 10   **Fic**

1. Kidnapping -- Fiction 2. Home schooling -- Fiction 3. Mother-daughter relationship -- Fiction
ISBN 978-1-60684-272-0; 1-60684-272-2

LC 2010052662

Tells, in their separate voices and at a space of fourteen years, of Emmy, whose baby has been stolen, and Sophie, a teenager who defies her nomadic, controlling mother by making friends with a neighbor boy and his elderly aunts.

This is a "a psychologically taut novel. . . . Succinct, emotionally packed chapters capture similarities between mother and daughter, the depth of their despair, their common desire to be free, and their poetic vision of the world." Publ Wkly

★ The **heart** is not a size. HarperTeen 2010 244p $16.99

Grades: 7 8 9 10   **Fic**

1. Poverty -- Fiction 2. Friendship -- Fiction 3. Volunteer work -- Fiction
ISBN 978-0-06-147048-6; 0-06-147048-1

LC 2008-55721

Fifteen-year-old Georgia learns a great deal about herself and her troubled best friend Riley when they become part of a group of suburban Pennsylvania teenagers that go to Anapra, a squatters village in the border town of Juarez, Mexico, to undertake a community construction project.

"Kephart's prose is typically poetic. She pens a faster-paced novel that explores teens' inner selves. . . . The writing is vivid, enabling readers to visualize Anapra's desolation and hope." Voice Youth Advocates

Kerley, Barbara

Greetings from planet Earth. Scholastic Press 2007 246p $16.99

Grades: 5 6 7 8   **Fic**

1. Family life -- Fiction 2. Vietnam War, 1961-1975 -- Fiction 3. Father-son relationship -- Fiction 4. Children's literature -- Works -- Grades two through six
ISBN 0-439-80203-2; 978-0-439-80203-1

LC 2006-11300

In 1977, as twelve-year-old Theo struggles with a science class project on space exploration, questions emerge about why his father never returned from Vietnam and why Theo's mother has been keeping secrets for many years.

"The novel convincingly portrays a family overshadowed by secrets." Booklist

Kerr, M. E.

Gentlehands. Harper & Row 1978 183p hardcover o.p. pa $5.99

Grades: 7 8 9 10   **Fic**

1. Criminals -- Fiction 2. Grandfathers -- Fiction 3. Social classes -- Fiction
ISBN 978-0-06-447067-4 pa; 0-06-447067-9 pa

LC 77-11860

ALA YALSA Margaret A. Edwards Award (1993)

"Buddy Boyle falls for Skye and her affluent, breezy way of life. Finding his own parents not 'cultured' enough for this new relationship, Buddy turns to his grandfather, whose love of opera and other refinements make him more suitable to make Skye's acquaintance. A shocking surprise awaits Buddy when Mr. DeLucca, pursuer of an infamous Nazi, finally identifies his quarry." Shapiro. Fic for youth. 3rd edition

If I love you, am I trapped forever? Marshall Cavendish 2008 178p $16.99

Grades: 8 9 10 11 12   **Fic**

1. School stories 2. Newspapers -- Fiction 3. Dating (Social customs) -- Fiction 4. Father-son relationship

-- Fiction
ISBN 978-0-7614-5545-5

LC 2007051768

A reissue of the title first published 1973 by Harper & Row

Alan, a popular senior high school student, faces painful changes after a new student, Duncan "Doomed" Stein, comes to town and starts an influential underground newspaper.

"Extremely humorous at times, the story is also occasionally touched with sadness and poignancy." Horn Book Guide

Kerz, Anna

Better than weird. Orca Book Publishers 2011 218p pa $9.95

Grades: 4 5 6 7 **Fic**

1. School stories 2. Autism -- Fiction 3. Bullies -- Fiction 4. Father-son relationship -- Fiction
ISBN 978-1-55469-362-7 pa; 1-55469-362-4 pa

When Aaron's long-absent father returns, Aaron must cope with bullying at school, his grandmother's illness and his father's pregnant new wife.

"Yet another in a long line of recent books about kids with autism, Kerz's effort nevertheless shines. . . . A heartwarming read for fans of realistic fiction." Booklist

The **gnome's** eye. Orca Book Publishers 2010 210p pa $12.95

Grades: 4 5 6 7 **Fic**

1. Fear -- Fiction 2. Immigrants -- Fiction
ISBN 978-1-55469-195-1 pa; 1-55469-195-8 pa

When Theresa and her family immigrate to Canada after World War II, she confronts her many fears with the help of a talisman given to her by a friend in Austria.

"Both laughter and genuine concern will be evident through Theresa's imaginative storytelling and descriptive narrative." SLJ

Kessler, Jackie Morse

Breath; Jackie Morse Kessler. Graphia 2013 336 p. (paperback) $8.99

Grades: 8 9 10 11 12 **Fic**

1. Death -- Fiction 2. Depression (Psychology) -- Fiction 3. Four Horsemen of the Apocalypse -- Fiction
ISBN 0547970439; 9780547970431

LC 2012023509

In this book by Jackie Morse Kessler, "the fourth and final title in the 'Riders of the Apocalypse' series, Death is suicidal. Because his soul mate did not follow him into the world of sadness and dying, the Grim Reaper has decided to end it all, a decision that will mean the end of humanity. Fortunately, he doesn't consider the fact that high-school senior Xander Atwood, although similarly depressed, might worm his way into Death's heart and provide insight that could change his mind." (Booklist)

"Kessler once again highlights a common teen affliction, this time depression, in her allegory of hopelessness turned to hope. . . . The series is a strong and unique attempt to encourage troubled teens to consider their options and accept the help they need, while exposing all readers to the pain their friends may be experiencing." Booklist

Loss; Jackie Morse Kessler. Graphia 2012 258 p. $8.99

Grades: 8 9 10 11 12 **Fic**

1. Fantasy fiction 2. Plague -- Fiction 3. Bullies -- Fiction 4. Apocalyptic fiction 5. Schools -- Fiction 6. Diseases -- Fiction 7. Self-esteem -- Fiction 8. Time travel -- Fiction 9. High schools -- Fiction 10. Four Horsemen of the Apocalypse -- Fiction
ISBN 0547712154; 9780547712154

LC 2011031490

This young adult novel is part of Jackie Morse Kessler's Riders of the Apocalypse series in which "[f]ifteen-year-old Billy Ballard is the kid that everyone picks on. But things change drastically when Death tells Billy he must stand in as Pestilence, the White Rider of the Apocalypse. Now armed with a Bow that allows him to strike with disease from a distance, Billy lashes out at his tormentors . . . and accidentally causes an outbreak of meningitis. Horrified by his actions, Billy begs Death to take back the Bow. For that to happen, says Death, Billy must track down the real White Rider, and stop him from unleashing something awful on humanity . . . that could make the Black Plague look like a summer cold. Does one bullied teenager have the strength to stand his ground—and the courage to save the world?" (Publisher's note)

Key, Watt

Alabama moon. Farrar, Straus & Giroux 2006 294p $16; pa $6.99

Grades: 5 6 7 8 **Fic**

1. Orphans -- Fiction 2. Wilderness survival -- Fiction
ISBN 0-374-30184-0; 0-312-38428-9 pa

LC 2005-40165

After the death of his father, ten-year-old Moon leaves their forest shelter home and is sent to an Alabama institution, becoming entangled in the outside world he has never known and making good friends, a relentless enemy, and finally a new life

"The book is well written with a flowing style, plenty of dialogue, and lots of action. The characters are well drawn and three-dimensional." SLJ

Dirt road home. Farrar Straus Giroux 2010 211p $16.99

Grades: 5 6 7 8 **Fic**

1. Gangs -- Fiction 2. Violence -- Fiction 3. Reformatories -- Fiction 4. Father-son relationship -- Fiction
ISBN 978-0-374-30863-6; 0-374-30863-2

LC 2010-11319

At Hellenweiler, a reformatory for second-offenders, fourteen-year-old Hal Mitchell will soon be free if he can avoid the gang violence of his fellow inmates, but the real enemy may lie elsewhere.

"With authentic characters and a candid first-person narrative, Key's story offers a disturbing appraisal of life in a juvenile facility, and a riveting battle for justice." Publ Wkly

★ **Fourmile**; Watt Key. Farrar Straus Giroux 2012 227 p, $16.99

Grades: 5 6 **Fic**

1. Child abuse -- Fiction 2. Father-son relationship

-- Fiction 3. Mother-son relationship -- Fiction 4.
Violence -- Fiction 5. Loss (Psychology) -- Fiction 6.
Farm life -- Alabama -- Fiction
ISBN 0374350957; 9780374324414; 9780374350956
          LC 2012003220

In the book by Watt Key, "[m]iddle schooler Foster and
his mother have been barely getting by since his father's
death a year ago. . . . Mother has begun a relationship with
dangerous, unpleasant Dax, a man she seems powerless to
keep from abusing both Foster and his dog, Joe. Then Gary
shows up, hiking along the rural road. . . . Foster, desperate
to find some steady ground in his life, connects to Gary immediately." (Kirkus Reviews)

Khan, Rukhsana
 Wanting Mor. Groundwood/House of Anansi
Books 2009 190p $17.95
Grades: 6 7 8 9   **Fic**
 1. Sex role -- Fiction 2. Bereavement -- Fiction 3.
Birth defects -- Fiction
ISBN 0-88899-858-9; 978-0-88899-858-3; 978-0-
88899-862-0 pa

Jameela and her family live in a poor, war-torn village in
Afghanistan. Even with her cleft lip and lack of educational
opportunities, Jameela feels relatively secure, sustained by
her Muslim faith and the love of her mother, Mor. But when
Mor dies, Jameela's father impulsively decides to start a new
life in Kabul.

"This compelling story is based on real incidents. Jameela's matter-of-fact, first person narrative will awaken young
readers to life and conditions in Afghanistan." Booklist

Khoury, Jessica
 Origin; Jessica Khoury. Razorbill 2012 393 p.
$17.99
Grades: 6 7 8   **Fic**
 1. Science fiction 2. Immortality -- Fiction 3. Science
-- Experiments -- Fiction 4. Rain forests -- Fiction 5.
Indigenous peoples -- Fiction
ISBN 1595145958; 9781595145956
          LC 2012014447

In this young adult novel by Jessica Khoury "Pia has
grown up in a secret laboratory hidden deep in the Amazon
rainforest. She was raised by a team of scientists who have
created her to be the start of a new immortal race. But on
the night of her seventeenth birthday . . . and sneaks outside
the compound for the first time in her life . . . Pia meets
Eio, a boy from a nearby village. Together, they embark on
a race against time to discover the truth about Pia's origin."
(Publisher's note)

Kidd, Ronald
 The **year** of the bomb. Simon & Schuster Books
for Young Readers 2009 202p $15.99
Grades: 6 7 8 9   **Fic**
 1. Fear -- Fiction 2. Cold war -- Fiction 3. Blacklisting
of entertainers -- Fiction 4. Motion pictures --
Production and direction -- Fiction
ISBN 978-1-4169-5892-5; 1-4169-5892-4
          LC 2008023646

In 1955 California, as "Invasion of the Body Snatchers"
is filmed in their hometown, thirteen-year-old Arnie dis-

covers a real enemy when he and three friends go against a
young government agent determined to find communists at a
neaby university or on the movie set.

"The book is vividly imbued with historical detail; parallels between the Red Scare witch hunters and the movie's body-invading aliens are particularly effective." Horn
Book Guide

Kilworth, Garry
 Attica. Little, Brown 2009 334p pa $11.95
Grades: 5 6 7 8   **Fic**
 1. Fantasy fiction 2. Stepfamilies -- Fiction
ISBN 978-1-904233-56-5 pa; 1-904233-56-2 pa

"The children have distinct personalities and react to
Attica in realistic ways, finding their own strengths in this
exhilarating, unpredictable environment. This book is a rare
find." Booklist

Kimmel, Elizabeth Cody
 ★ The **reinvention** of Moxie Roosevelt. Dial
Books for Young Readers 2010 256p $16.99
Grades: 4 5 6 7   **Fic**
 1. School stories
ISBN 978-0-8037-3303-9; 0-8037-3303-8
          LC 2009-37939

On her first day of boarding school, a thirteen-year-old
girl who feels boring and invisible decides to change her personality to match her unusual name.

"Kimmel's sharply observed novel reflects a keen understanding of the agony of self-definition that is adolescence.
Readers will cheer for Moxie as she charts her path toward
self-acceptance." Kirkus

Kinard, Kami
 The **Boy** Project; notes and observations of Kara
McAllister. Scholastic Press 2012 $12.99
Grades: 6 7 8 9   **Fic**
 1. School stories 2. Science projects -- Fiction 3.
Dating (Social customs) -- Fiction
ISBN 978-0-545-34515-6; 0-545-34515-4
          LC 2011008332

Eighth-grader Kara McAllister chronicles her efforts
when she tries to use the scientific method to transform her
social blunders into romantic victories.

"This middle-school drama is hip to the moment, with
breakup texting, kissing and popularity tug of wars. . . . Kara's irrepressible spirit, clever wit and introspection save this
story from vapidity." Kirkus

Kindl, Patrice
 Keeping the castle; a tale of romance, riches, and
real estate. by Patrice Kindl. Viking Childrens Books
2012 261 p. $16.99; (hardcover)
Grades: 7 8 9 10 11   **Fic**
 1. Love stories 2. Regency novels 3. Marriage --
Fiction 4. Castles -- Fiction 5. Courtship -- Fiction 6.
Social classes -- Fiction
ISBN 0670014389; 9780670014385
          LC 2011033185

In this book, "[s]eventeen-year-old Althea Crawley is . .
. on a quest to marry rich so that she may secure the family"s
only inheritance, a dilapidated castle on the edge of the

North Sea. . . . Marriage prospects in tiny Lesser Hoo are slim, to say the least, until dashing and wealthy Lord Boring arrives on the scene. Matters are further complicated by a revolving cast of potential suitors, including Lord Boring"s cousin, Mr. Fredericks." (Booklist)

King, Caro

Seven sorcerers. Aladdin 2011 324p $15.99

Grades: 5 6 7 8   **Fic**

1. Fantasy fiction 2. Adventure fiction 3. Siblings -- Fiction 4. Missing children -- Fiction

ISBN 978-1-4424-2042-7; 1-4424-2042-1

LC 2011001432

First published 2009 in the United Kingdom

When eleven-year-old Nin Redfern wakes up one rainy Wednesday morning to discover that her younger brother has ceased to exist, she must venture into a magical land called the Drift where she grapples with bogeymen, tombfolk, mudmen, and the spirits of sorcerers to try and rescue him.

"King has written a complex, intelligent fantasy that is at turns funny and terrifying." Booklist

Kinney, Jeff

★ **Diary** of a wimpy kid: Greg Heffley's journal. Amulet Books 2007 217p pa $14.95

Grades: 5 6 7 8   **Fic**

1. School stories 2. Friendship -- Fiction

ISBN 978-0-8109-9313-6 pa; 0-8109-9313-9 pa

LC 2006-31847

Greg records his sixth grade experiences in a middle school where he and his best friend, Rowley, undersized weaklings amid boys who need to shave twice daily, hope just to survive, but when Rowley grows more popular, Greg must take drastic measures to save their friendship

"Kinney's background as a cartoonist is apparent in this hybrid book that falls somewhere between traditional prose and graphic novel. . . . The pace moves quickly. The first of three installments, it is an excellent choice for reluctant readers, but more experienced readers will also find much to enjoy and relate to." SLJ

Other titles about Greg are:

Diary of a wimpy kid: Rodrick rules (2008)

Diary of a wimpy kid: the last straw (2009)

Diary of a wimpy kid: dog days (2009)

Diary of a wimpy kid; the ugly truth (2010)

Diary of a wimmpy kid:The third wheel (2012)

Kinsey-Warnock, Natalie

True colors; by Natalie Kinsey-Warnock. Alfred A. Knopf Books for Young Readers 2012 242 p. (hard cover) $15.99

Grades: 4 5 6 7   **Fic**

1. Absent mothers -- Fiction 2. Abandoned children -- Fiction 3. Identity -- Fiction 4. Foundlings -- Fiction 5. Farm life -- Vermont -- Fiction 6. People with mental disabilities -- Fiction

ISBN 0375860991; 9780375854538; 9780375860997; 9780375897061; 9780375960994

LC 2011037863

This book by Natalie Kinsey-Warnock "tells the story of one girl's journey to find the mother she never had, set against the period backdrop of a small farming town in 1950s Vermont. For her entire life, 10-year-old Blue has never known her mother. . . . Over the course of one summer, she resolves to finally find out who she is. . . . Her search leads her down a road of self-discovery that will change her life forever." (Publisher's note)

Kipling, Rudyard, 1865-1936

★ The **jungle** book; by Rudyard Kipling; illustrated by Robert R. Ingpen. Sterling Children's Books 2012 192 p. ill. (hardcover) $19.95

Grades: 4 5 6 7   **Fic**

1. Fantasy fiction

ISBN 1402782845; 9781402782848

This book is an illustrated version of Rudyard Kipling's 1894 children's story collection "The Jungle Book." Illustrations by Robert Ingpen accompany the stories "of the boy Mowgli, rescued and raised by tigers in the heart of the jungle. The tales feature such . . . creatures such as Bagheera, the graceful black panther; Baloo, the kindly brown bear; and Kaa, the snake with the hypnotic stare." The stories 'Rikki-Tikki-Tavi,' 'The White Seal,' and 'Toomai of the Elephants'" are included, too. (Publisher's note)

Kirby, Jessi

Golden; Jessi Kirby. 1st ed. Simon & Schuster Books for Young Readers 2013 288 p. (hardcover) $16.99

Grades: 7 8 9 10 11 12   **Fic**

1. Love stories 2. Mystery fiction 3. Diaries -- Fiction 4. Love -- Fiction 5. Choice -- Fiction 6. Family problems -- Fiction 7. Mothers and daughters -- Fiction

ISBN 1442452161; 9781442452169; 9781442452183; 9781442452251

LC 2012042216

In this novel, by Jessi Kirby, "seventeen-year-old Parker Frost has never taken the road less traveled. . . . Julianna Farnetti and Shane Cruz are remembered as the golden couple of Summit Lakes High . . . but Julianna's journal tells . . . . the secrets that were swept away with her the night that Shane's jeep plunged into an icy river. . . . Reading Julianna's journal gives Parker . . . reasons to question what really happened the night of the accident." (Publisher's note)

"Kirby"s . . . third novel is inspirational and contemplative in its mood and tone. Multifaceted characters and dashes of mystery and romance come together in a successful mediation on the value of taking an active role in one"s life." Pub Wkly

Moonglass. Simon & Schuster Books for Young Readers 2011 232p $16.99; ebook $9.99

Grades: 8 9 10 11 12   **Fic**

1. Guilt -- Fiction 2. Moving -- Fiction 3. Beaches -- Fiction 4. Suicide -- Fiction 5. Father-daughter relationship -- Fiction

ISBN 978-1-4424-1694-9; 1-4424-1694-7; 978-1-4424-1696-3 ebook; 1-4424-1696-3 ebook

LC 2010-37389

At age seven, Anna watched her mother walk into the surf and drown, but nine years later, when she moves with her father to the beach where her parents fell in love, she joins the cross-country team, makes new friends, and faces her guilt.

"Kirby creates a cast of sympathetic and credible characters, each imperfect but well intentioned. There's action as well as introspection here." Booklist

Kirby, Matthew J.

Icefall. Scholastic Press 2011 325p $17.99

Grades: 5 6 7 8   **Fic**

1. Fantasy fiction 2. Ice -- Fiction 3. Winter -- Fiction 4. Storytelling -- Fiction

ISBN 978-0-545-27424-1; 0-545-27424-9

LC 2011000890

"Kirby turns in a claustrophobic, thought-provoking coming-of-age adventure that shows a young woman growing into her own, while demonstrating the power of myth and legend. Kirby's attention to detail and stark descriptions make this an effective mood piece." Publ Wkly

★ The **clockwork** three. Scholastic Press 2010 391p $17.99

Grades: 5 6 7 8   **Fic**

1. Fantasy fiction 2. Friendship -- Fiction 3. Clocks and watches -- Fiction

ISBN 978-0-545-20337-1; 0-545-20337-6

LC 2009-37879

As mysterious circumstances bring Giuseppe, Frederick, and Hannah together, their lives soon interlock like the turning gears in a clock and they realize that each one holds a key to solving the others' mysteries

This is a "riveting historical fantasy. . . . Kirby has assembled all the ingredients for a rousing adventure, which he delivers with rich, transporting prose." Publ Wkly

Kittle, Katrina

Reasons to be happy. Sourcebooks Jabberwocky 2011 281p pa $7.99

Grades: 7 8 9 10   **Fic**

1. School stories 2. Bulimia -- Fiction 3. Popularity -- Fiction 4. Bereavement -- Fiction 5. Personal appearance -- Fiction

ISBN 978-1-4022-6020-9; 1-4022-6020-2

LC 2011020276

Eighth-grader Hannah Carlisle feels unattractive compared to her movie star parents and cliquish Beverly Hills classmates, and when her mother's cancer worsens and her father starts drinking heavily, Hannah's grief and anger turn into bulimia, which only her aunt, a documentary filmmaker, understands.

"Hannah's believability as a character as well as the realistic, painful depiction of bulimia make this a standout." Booklist

Kittredge, Caitlin

The **Iron** Thorn. Delacorte Press 2011 493p (Iron Codex) $17.99; lib bdg $20.99

Grades: 7 8 9 10   **Fic**

1. Fantasy fiction

ISBN 0-385-73829-3; 0-385-90720-6 lib bdg; 978-0-385-73829-3; 978-0-385-90720-0 lib bdg

LC 2010-00972

In an alternate 1950s, mechanically gifted fifteen-year-old Aoife Grayson, whose family has a history of going mad at sixteen, must leave the totalitarian city of Lovecraft and

venture into the world of magic to solve the mystery of her brother's disappearance and the mysteries surrounding her father and the Land of Thorn.

"Steampunk fans will delight in this first title in the sure-to-be-popular Iron Codex series. . . . There's plenty of tame but satisfying romance, too, and plot twists galore. Aoife is a caustic-tongued, feisty, and independent young woman, with plenty of nerve and courage." Booklist

The **nightmare** garden; Caitlin Kittredge. Delacorte Press 2012 417 p. (The iron codex) (hardback) $17.99

Grades: 7 8 9 10   **Fic**

1. Fantasy fiction 2. Adventure fiction 3. Steampunk fiction 4. Metaphysics -- Fiction 5. Voyages and travels -- Fiction 6. Magic -- Fiction

ISBN 9780375985690; 9780385738316; 9780385907217

LC 2011038306

This book is the second novel in Caitlin Kittredge's "Iron Codex" series. "Spoiled, inconsistent, often-thoughtless heroine Aoife Grayson nearly destroyed the world when she broke the Lovecraft Engine and sundered the gates between the worlds of human and Fae. But she's not going to let a little thing like that stop her, so she sets off on an exhausting, somewhat episodic adventure through the steampunk-horror '50s nightmare that is her world . . . . The ending promises even bigger adventures to come." (Kirkus)

Kizer, Amber

Meridian. Delacorte Press 2009 305p $16.99; lib bdg $19.99

Grades: 7 8 9 10   **Fic**

1. Death -- Fiction 2. Angels -- Fiction 3. Supernatural -- Fiction 4. Good and evil -- Fiction

ISBN 978-0-385-73668-8; 0-385-73668-1; 978-0-385-90621-0 lib bdg; 0-385-90621-8 lib bdg

LC 2008-35666

On her sixteenth birthday, Meridian is whisked off to her great-aunt's home in Revelation, Colorado, where she learns that she is a Fenestra, the half-human, half-angel link between the living and the dead, and must learn to help human souls to the afterlife before the dark forces reach them.

"The author brings a fresh voice to the realm of teen paranormal romantic fiction. . . . The characters are compelling and the themes of good and evil, life and death will keep readers engaged." SLJ

Wildcat fireflies. Delacorte Press 2011 508p $16.99

Grades: 7 8 9 10   **Fic**

1. Death -- Fiction 2. Angels -- Fiction 3. Supernatural -- Fiction 4. Good and evil -- Fiction

ISBN 978-0-385-73971-9; 0-385-73971-0

LC 2010-30405

Teenaged Meridian Sozu, a half-human, half-angel link between the living and the dead known as a Fenestra, hits the road with Tens, her love and sworn protector, in hopes of finding another person with Meridian's ability to help souls transition safely into the afterlife.

"Some of the day-to-day events may be hard to believe, but this is a book about angels and demons after all; fans will forgive." Kirkus

A **matter** of days; Amber Kizer. 1st ed. Delacorte Press 2013 288 p. (ebook) $50.97; (hardcover) $16.99; (library) $19.99

Grades: 7 8 9 10   **Fic**

1. Science fiction 2. Survival -- Fiction 5. Epidemics -- Fiction 3. Virus diseases -- Fiction 4. Brothers and sisters -- Fiction

ISBN 0385908040; 9780375898259; 9780385739733; 9780385908047

LC 2012012200

In this book, "Nadia and Rabbit's military doctor uncle, Bean, visited them and insisted on injecting them with a vaccine for a 'new bug.' Not long afterward, the disease XRD TB . . . starts ravaging the world, and 16-year-old Nadia and 11-year-old Rabbit are the only survivors in their entire town. With the assorted survival gear their uncle ordered for them, they attempt to make their way from their Seattle suburb to their grandfather in West Virginia." (Publishers Weekly)

Klages, Ellen

White sands, red menace. Viking 2008 337p $16.99

Grades: 5 6 7 8   **Fic**

1. Cold war -- Fiction 2. Scientists -- Fiction 3. Atomic bomb -- Fiction

ISBN 978-0-670-06235-5; 0-670-06235-9

"The groundbreaking science is part of daily life for the smart techno-teens, and the adult characters are as compelling as the kids. . . . Along with . . . global issues, Klages' compelling story explores personal relationships and what it means to be a family." Booklist

★ The **green** glass sea. Viking 2006 321p $16.99; pa $7.99

Grades: 5 6 7 8   **Fic**

1. Scientists -- Fiction 2. Atomic bomb -- Fiction 3. World War, 1939-1945 -- Fiction

ISBN 0-670-06134-4; 0-14-241149-3 pa

It is 1943, and 11-year-old Dewey Kerrigan is traveling west on a train to live with her scientist father—but no one will tell her exactly where he is. When she reaches Los Alamos, New Mexico, she learns why: he's working on a top secret government program.

"Many readers will know as little about the true nature of the project as the girls do, so the gradual revelation of facts is especially effective, while those who already know about Los Alamos's historical significance will experience the story in a different, but equally powerful, way." SLJ

Klass, David

Firestorm. Frances Foster Books 2006 289p (The Caretaker trilogy) $17

Grades: 8 9 10 11 12   **Fic**

1. Science fiction

ISBN 0-374-32307-0

LC 2005-52112

After learning that he has been sent from the future for a special purpose, eighteen-year-old Jack receives help from an unusual dog and a shape-shifting female fighter.

"The sobering events and tone are leavened with engaging humor, and the characters are multidimensional. The relentless pace, coupled with issues of ecology, time travel, self-identity, and sexual awakening, makes for a thrilling and memorable read." SLJ

Other books in the Caretaker Trilogy are:
Whirlwind (2008)
Timelock (2009)

★ **Stuck** on Earth. Farrar Straus & Giroux 2010 227p $16.99

Grades: 4 5 6 7   **Fic**

1. Science fiction 2. Bullies -- Fiction 3. Extraterrestrial beings -- Fiction

ISBN 978-0-374-39951-1; 0-374-39951-4

LC 2008--48133

On a secret mission to evaluate whether the human race should be annihilated, a space alien inhabits the body of a bullied fourteen-year-old boy.

"Klass's . . . thoughtful, often wrenching book offers plenty to think about, from what's really going on in Tom's head to questions about human responsibility to the planet and each other. It takes 'alienation' to a whole new level." Publ Wkly

Klass, Sheila Solomon

★ **Soldier's** secret; the story of Deborah Sampson. Henry Holt 2009 215p $17.95

Grades: 6 7 8 9 10   **Fic**

1. Soldiers 2. Memoirists 3. Soldiers -- Fiction

ISBN 978-0-8050-8200-5; 0-8050-8200-X

LC 2008-36783

During the Revolutionary War, a young woman named Deborah Sampson disguises herself as a man in order to serve in the Continental Army.

In this novel, Sampson "is strong, brave, and witty. . . . Klass doesn't shy away from the horrors of battle; she also is blunt regarding details young readers will wonder about, like how Sampson dealt with bathing, urination, and menstruation. . . . Sampson's romantic yearnings for a fellow soldier . . . is given just the right notes or restraint and realism." Booklist

Klause, Annette Curtis

The **silver** kiss. Delacorte Press 1990 198p hardcover o.p. pa $5.99

Grades: 8 9 10 11 12   **Fic**

1. Death -- Fiction 2. Vampires -- Fiction

ISBN 0-385-30160-X; 0-440-21346-0 pa

LC 89-48880

"There's inherent romantic appeal in the vampire legend, and Klause weaves all the gory details into a poignant love story that becomes both sensuous and suspenseful." Booklist

Klein, Lisa M.

Cate of the Lost Colony; by Lisa Klein. Bloomsbury 2010 329p $16.99

Grades: 8 9 10 11 12　　　　　　　　　**Fic**
　1. Orphans -- Fiction 9. Lumbee Indians -- Fiction
ISBN 978-1-59990-507-5; 1-59990-507-8
　　　　　　　　　　　　　　　LC 2010-8299
　When her dalliance with Sir Walter Ralegh is discovered by Queen Elizabeth in 1587, lady-in-waiting Catherine Archer is banished to the struggling colony of Roanoke, where she and the other English settlers must rely on a Croatoan Indian for their survival. Includes author's note on the mystery surrounding the Lost Colony.
　"This robust, convincing portrait of the Elizabethan world with complex, rounded characters wraps an intriguingly plausible solution to the 'lost colony' mystery inside a compelling love story of subtle thematic depth." Kirkus
　Includes bibliographical references

Lady Macbeth's daughter. Bloomsbury 2009
291p $16.99
Grades: 7 8 9 10　　　　　　　　　　　**Fic**
　1. Homicide -- Fiction 2. Witchcraft -- Fiction 3. Kings and rulers -- Fiction 4. Physically handicapped -- Fiction
ISBN 978-1-59990-347-7; 1-59990-347-4
　　　　　　　　　　　　　　　LC 2009-6717
　In alternating chapters, ambitious Lady Macbeth tries to bear a son and win the throne of Scotland for her husband, and Albia, their daughter who was banished at birth and raised by three weird sisters, falls in love, learns of her parentage, and seeks to free Scotland from tyranny in this tale based on Shakespeare's Macbeth.
　"The writing is crisp and clear and makes good use of Shakespeare's language and its times. The characters are well-developed and the story being told from the perspective of the mother and daughter makes for age-old conflict. This tale will keep readers asking the ultimate question of whether or not power is ultimately worth the price." Libr Media Connect

Klise, Kate
　★ **Grounded**. Feiwel and Friends 2010 196p
$16.99
Grades: 4 5 6 7　　　　　　　　　　　**Fic**
　1. Death -- Fiction 2. Bereavement -- Fiction 3. Swindlers and swindling -- Fiction
ISBN 978-0-312-57039-2; 0-312-57039-2
　　　　　　　　　　　　　　　LC 2010013008
　After her father, brother, and sister are killed in a plane crash, twelve-year-old Daralynn's life in tiny Digginsville, Missouri, proceeds as her mother turns angry and embittered, her grandmother becomes senile, and her flamboyant aunt continues to run the Summer Sunset Retirement Home for Distinguished Gentlemen, while being courted by the owner of the town's new crematorium.
　"Dark humor melds with genuine pathos in Klise's moving novel. . . . This quiet story illuminates and celebrates the human need for connection beyond the grave." Booklist

Homesick; Kate Klise. 1st ed. Feiwel and Friends 2012 192 p. (hardcover) $16.99
Grades: 4 5 6 7 8　　　　　　　　　　**Fic**
　1. Divorce -- Fiction 2. Family life -- Fiction
ISBN 1250008425; 9781250008428

In this book by Kate Klise, "Benny's parents are splitting up. . . . Benny's dad has always liked clutter, but now, he begins hoarding everything. . . . As his house grows more cluttered and his father grows more distant, Benny tries to sort out whether he can change anything at all. Meanwhile, a local teacher enters their quiet Missouri town in America's Most Charming Small Town contest, and the pressure is on to clean up the area, especially Benny's ramshackle of a house." (Publisher's note)

Letters from camp; illustrated by M. Sarah Klise. Avon Bks. 1999 178p il hardcover o.p. pa $5.99
Grades: 4 5 6 7　　　　　　　　　　　**Fic**
　1. Camps -- Fiction 2. Letters -- Fiction 3. Siblings -- Fiction 4. Mystery and detective stories 5. Brothers and sisters -- Fiction
ISBN 0-380-97539-4; 0-380-79348-2 pa
　　　　　　　　　　　　　　　LC 98-52315
　Sent to Camp Happy Harmony to learn how to get along with each other, pairs of brothers and sisters chronicle in letters home how they come to suspect the intentions of the singing family running the camp
　This is a "delightfully wacky story. . . . The humor is very gentle and tongue-in-cheek. . . . An entirely satisfying camp adventure." Booklist

Regarding the sink; where, oh where, did Waters go? illustrated by M. Sarah Klise. Harcourt 2004
127p il $15
Grades: 4 5 6 7　　　　　　　　　　　**Fic**
　1. School stories
ISBN 0-15-205019-1
　　　　　　　　　　　　　　　LC 2003-26560
　A series of letters reveals the selection of the famous fountain designer, Florence Waters, to design a new sink for the Geyser Creek Middle School cafeteria, her subsequent disappearance, and the efforts of a class of sixth-graders to find her
　"Piecing the story and clues together is satisfying. Introduce this book to savvy readers who are ready for the jump to a clever, unconventional reading experience." SLJ
　Other titles in this series are:
　Regarding the bathrooms (2006)
　Regarding the bees (2007)
　Regarding the fountain (1998)
　Regarding the trees (2005)

Kluger, Jeffrey
　★ **Freedom** stone. Philomel Books 2011 316p
$16.99
Grades: 4 5 6　　　　　　　　　　　　**Fic**
　1. Magic -- Fiction 2. Slavery -- Fiction 3. African Americans -- Fiction
ISBN 978-0-399-25214-3; 0-399-25214-2
　　　　　　　　　　　　　　　LC 2010-06028
　With the help of a magical stone from Africa, a thirteen-year-old slave travels to the battle of Vicksburg to clear her father's name and free her family from bondage.
　Kluger "adeptly mixes drama, fantasy, romance, and history, while creating characters so determined to survive that readers can't help being drawn into their plights. In a climax that breaks with reality but that will keep readers hungry to

learn the outcome, Kluger proves his storytelling prowess." Publ Wkly

Kluger, Steve

★ **My** most excellent year; a novel of love, Mary Poppins, & Fenway Park. Dial Books 2008 403p $16.99; pa $8.99

Grades: 8 9 10 11 12   **Fic**
   1. Friendship -- Fiction
   ISBN 978-0-8037-3227-8; 0-8037-3227-9; 978-0-14-241343-2 pa; 0-14-2413437 pa
                LC 2007-26651

"Three bright and funny Brookline, MA, eleventh graders look back on their most excellent year—ninth grade—for a school report. Told in alternating chapters by each of them, this enchanting, life-affirming coming-of-age story unfolds through instant messages, emails, memos, diary entries, and letters. . . . This is a rich and humorous novel for older readers." SLJ

Knowles, Jo

See you at Harry's; Jo Knowles. 1st ed. Candlewick Press 2012 310 p. $16.99

Grades: 6 7 8 9 10 11   **Fic**
   1. Siblings -- Fiction 2. Bereavement -- Fiction 3. Restaurants -- Fiction 4. Gay teenagers -- Fiction 5. Family -- Fiction 6. Grief -- Fiction 7. Family life -- Fiction 8. Homosexuality -- Fiction 9. Family problems -- Fiction 10. Brothers and sisters -- Fiction
   ISBN 9780763654078
                LC 2011018619

In this children's novel, "seventh grader Fern . . . relates the . . . tragedies of her family. Her high-school-freshman older brother Holden has come to the place in his life where he's acknowledged that he's gay. . . . Fern offers him support and love. . . . And then there's 3-year-old Charlie, always messy, often annoying, but deeply loved. Fern's busy, distracted parents leave all of the kids wanting for more attention--until a tragic accident tears the family apart." (Kirkus Reviews)

Knox, Elizabeth

Dreamhunter; book one of the Dreamhunter duet. Farrar, Straus & Giroux 2006 365p (Dreamhunter duet) $19; pa $8.99

Grades: 7 8 9 10   **Fic**
   1. Fantasy fiction 2. Dreams -- Fiction
   ISBN 0-374-31853-0; 0-312-53571-6 pa
                LC 2005-46366

First published 2005 in the United Kingdom

In a world where select people can enter "The Place" and find dreams of every kind to share with others for a fee, a fifteen-year-old girl is training to be a dreamhunter when her father disappears, leaving her to carry on his mysterious mission. "Grades nine to twelve." (Bull Cent Child Books)

This first of a two-book series is "a highly original exploration of the idea of a collective unconscious, mixed with imagery from the raising of Lazarus and with the brave, dark qualities of the psyche of an adolescent female." Horn Book Guide

Dreamquake; book two of the Dreamhunter duet. Farrar, Straus & Giroux 2007 449p map (Dreamhunter duet) $19

Grades: 7 8 9 10   **Fic**
   1. Fantasy fiction 2. Dreams -- Fiction
   ISBN 978-0-374-31854-3; 0-374-31854-9
                LC 2006-48109

Michael L. Printz Award honor book, 2008

Aided by her family and her creation, Nown, Laura investigates the powerful Regulatory Body's involvement in mysterious disappearances and activities and learns, in the process, the true nature of the Place in which dreams are found.

The author's "haunting, invigorating storytelling will leave readers eager to return to its puzzles—and to reap its rewards." Booklist

Mortal fire; by Elizabeth Knox. 1st ed. Frances Foster Books 2013 448 p. (hardcover) $17.99

Grades: 7 8 9 10 11   **Fic**
   1. Occult fiction 2. Fantasy fiction 3. Magic -- Fiction 4. Identity -- Fiction 5. Stepbrothers -- Fiction
   ISBN 0374388296; 9780374388294
                LC 2012040872

This novel, set in a fictional area of New Zealand, stars Canny, a "16-year-old Ma'eu, taciturn, antisocial, and exceptionally gifted in math." She has what she calls "Extra," an "ethereal script that Canny alone can see, attached to plants, buildings, or nothing at all." When she and friends "come upon a valley dense with the Extra, Canny realizes that there is more to her visions than her own oddness— there are people, the Zarenes, whose existence is interwoven with this magical language." (Publishers Weekly)

Knudsen, Michelle

★ The **dragon** of Trelian. Candlewick Press 2009 407p $16.99

Grades: 4 5 6 7   **Fic**
   1. Fantasy fiction 2. Magic -- Fiction 3. Dragons -- Fiction 4. Princesses -- Fiction
   ISBN 978-0-7636-3455-1; 0-7636-3455-7
                LC 2008025378

A mage's apprentice, a princess, and a dragon combine their strength and magic to bring down a traitor and restore peace to the kingdom of Trelian.

"Knudsen does a fantastic job of creating sympathetic and realistic characters that really drive the story. The tale is adventurous and exciting with many twists and turns along the way." SLJ

The **princess** of Trelian; Michelle Knudsen. Candlewick Press 2012 437 p. $16.99

Grades: 4 5 6 7   **Fic**
   1. Magic -- Fiction 2. Dragons -- Fiction 3. Princesses -- Fiction
   ISBN 0763650625; 9780763650629
                LC 2011047174

In this juvenile fantasy novel, by Michelle Knudsen, a "sequel to 'The Dragon of Trelian,' . . . Princess Meg is now heir to the throne, but her subjects are uneasy about her . . . dragon, and it only becomes worse when a neighboring king accuses the dragon of ravaging the countryside. . . . Meanwhile, Meg's best friend Calen has earned his mage's mark, but a mysterious, magical attack occurs. . . . [T]he deposed villain from the previous book is behind all the mischief." (Horn Book Magazine)

Knutsson, Catherine

Shadows cast by stars; Catherine Knutsson. 1st ed. Atheneum Books for Young Readers 2012 456 p. (hardcover) $17.99; (paperback) $9.99

Grades: 7 8 9 10   **Fic**
1. Blood 2. Science fiction 3. Plague -- Fiction 4. Twins -- Fiction 5. Spirits -- Fiction 6. Family life -- Fiction 7. Brothers and sisters -- Fiction 8. Indians of North America -- Fiction
ISBN 1442401915; 9781442401914; 9781442401938; 9781442401921
      LC 2011038419

Author Catherine Knutsson tells the story of Native American Cassandra Mercredi. The "sixteen-year-old . . . [may] be immune to Plague, but that doesn't mean she's safe--government forces are searching for those of aboriginal heritage to harvest their blood. When a search threatens Cassandra and her family, they flee to the Island: a mysterious and idyllic territory protected by the Band, a group of guerilla warriors--and by an enigmatic energy barrier that keeps outsiders out and the spirit world in." (Publisher's note)

Koertge, Ronald

Now playing; Stoner & Spaz II. [by] Ron Koertge. Candlewick Press 2011 208p $16.99

Grades: 8 9 10 11 12   **Fic**
1. School stories 2. Drug abuse -- Fiction 3. Cerebral palsy -- Fiction 4. Self-acceptance -- Fiction 5. Dating (Social customs) -- Fiction
ISBN 978-0-7636-5081-0; 0-7636-5081-1
      LC 2010040151

High schooler Ben Bancroft, a budding filmmaker with cerebral palsy, struggles to understand his relationship with drug-addict Colleen while he explores a new friendship with A.J., who shares his obsession with movies and makes a good impression on Ben's grandmother.

"Koertge writes sharp dialogue and vivid scenes." Publ Wkly

★ **Shakespeare** makes the playoffs; [by] Ron Koertge. Candlewick Press 2010 170p lib bdg $15.99; pa $5.99

Grades: 6 7 8 9   **Fic**
1. Novels in verse 2. Poetry -- Fiction 3. Baseball -- Fiction
ISBN 978-0-7636-4435-2 lib bdg; 0-7636-4435-8 lib bdg; 978-0-7636-5852-6 pa
      LC 2009-14519

Fourteen-year-old Kevin Boland, poet and first baseman, is torn between his cute girlfriend Mira and Amy, who is funny, plays Chopin on the piano, and is also a poet.

"The well-crafted poetry is firmly rooted in the experiences of regular teens and addresses subjects that range from breakups to baseball. . . . Appealing and accessible." Booklist

★ **Stoner** & Spaz; [by] Ron Koertge. Candlewick Press 2002 169p hardcover o.p. pa $6.99

Grades: 8 9 10 11 12   **Fic**
1. School stories 2. Cerebral palsy -- Fiction
ISBN 0-7636-1608-7; 0-7636-2150-1 pa
      LC 2001-43050

A troubled youth with cerebral palsy struggles toward self-acceptance with the help of a drug-addicted young woman

"Funny, touching, and surprising, it is a hopeful yet realistic view of things as they are and as they could be." Booklist

★ **Strays**; [by] Ron Koertge. Candlewick Press 2007 167p $16.99

Grades: 7 8 9 10 11 12   **Fic**
1. Orphans -- Fiction 2. Foster home care -- Fiction
ISBN 978-0-7636-2705-8; 0-7636-2705-4
      LC 2007-24096

After his parents are killed in a car accident, high school senior Sam wonders whether he will ever feel again or if he will remain numbed by grief.

"Though Koertge never soft pedals the horrors faced by some foster children, this thoughtful novel about the lost and abandoned is a hopeful one." Booklist

Koja, Kathe

★ **Buddha** boy. Speak 2004 117p pa $5.99

Grades: 7 8 9 10   **Fic**
1. School stories 2. Artists -- Fiction 3. Buddhism -- Fiction 4. Conduct of life -- Fiction
ISBN 0-14-240209-5
      LC 2004041669

First published 2003 by Farrar, Straus & Giroux

Justin spends time with Jinsen, the unusual and artistic new student whom the school bullies torment and call Buddha Boy, and ends up making choices that impact Jinsen, himself, and the entire school.

"A compelling introduction to Buddhism and a credible portrait of how true friendship brings out the best in people." Publ Wkly

★ **Headlong**. Farrar, Straus and Giroux 2008 195p $16.95

Grades: 8 9 10 11 12   **Fic**
1. School stories 2. Orphans -- Fiction 3. Social classes -- Fiction
ISBN 978-0-374-32912-9; 0-374-32912-5
      LC 2007-23612

High school sophomore Lily opens herself to new possibilities when, despite warnings, she becomes friends with 'ghetto girl' Hazel, a new student at the private Vaughn School which Lily, following in her elitist mother's footsteps, has attended since preschool.

"Class, identity and friendship are the intersecting subjects of this intelligent novel. . . . [The author] relays this story with her usual insight and, through her lightning-fast characterizations, an ability to project multiple perspectives simultaneously." Publ Wkly

★ **Kissing** the bee. Farrar, Straus and Giroux 2007 121p $16

Grades: 8 9 10 11 12   **Fic**
1. Love stories 2. School stories 3. Bees -- Fiction 4.

Friendship -- Fiction
ISBN 978-0-374-39938-2; 0-374-39938-7

LC 2006-37378

While working on a bee project for her advanced biology class, quiet high school senior Dana reflects on her relationship with gorgeous best friend Avra and Avra's boyfriend Emil, whom Dana secretly loves.

The "understated, tightly focused language evokes vivid scenes and heady emotions." Publ Wkly

Konigsberg, Bill

★ **Openly** straight; Bill Konigsberg. Arthur A. Levine Books 2013 336 p. (hard cover : alk. paper) $17.99

Grades: 8 9 10 11   **Fic**
1. School stories 2. Gay teenagers -- Fiction 3. Schools -- Fiction 4. Identity -- Fiction 5. Homosexuality -- Fiction 6. Preparatory schools -- Fiction
ISBN 0545509890; 9780545509893; 9780545509909

LC 2012030552

In this book, "Coloradan Rafe Goldberg has always been the token gay kid. He's been out since eighth grade. His parents and community are totally supportive. . . . On the outside, Rafe seems fine, but on the inside, he's looking for change, which comes with the opportunity to reinvent himself at the prestigious Natick Academy in Massachusetts. There for his junior year, Rafe cloaks his gayness in order to be just like one of the other guys." All is well until he falls for a straight friend. (Kirkus Reviews)

Konigsburg, E. L.

Silent to the bone. Atheneum Bks. for Young Readers 2000 261p hardcover o.p. pa $5.99
Grades: 7 8 9 10   **Fic**
1. Mystery fiction 2. Siblings -- Fiction
ISBN 0-689-83601-5; 0-689-83602-3 pa

LC 00-20043

When he is wrongly accused of gravely injuring his baby half-sister, thirteen-year-old Branwell loses his power of speech and only his friend Connor is able to reach him and uncover the truth about what really happened

"A compelling mystery that is also a moving story of family, friendship, and seduction." Booklist

The **mysterious** edge of the heroic world. Atheneum Books for Young Readers 2007 244p $16.99; pa $5.99
Grades: 5 6 7 8   **Fic**
1. Friendship -- Fiction 2. Art museums -- Fiction
ISBN 978-1-4169-4972-5; 1-4169-4972-0; 978-1-4169-5353-1 pa; 1-4169-5353-1 pa
"This humorous, poignant, tragic, and mysterious story has intertwining plots that peel away like the layers of an onion." SLJ

The **outcasts** of 19 Schuyler Place. Atheneum Bks. for Young Readers 2004 296p $16.95
Grades: 5 6 7 8   **Fic**
1. Social action -- Fiction
ISBN 0-689-86636-4

LC 2003-8067

Upon leaving an oppressive summer camp, twelve-year-old Margaret Rose Kane spearheads a campaign to preserve three unique towers her grand uncles have been building in their back yard for over forty years

"The plot is well paced and has excellent foreshadowing. Konigsburg's characters are particularly well motivated. . . . Funny and thought-provoking by turns, this is Konigsburg at her masterful best." SLJ

★ The **view** from Saturday. Atheneum Bks. for Young Readers 1996 163p $16.95; pa $5.99
Grades: 4 5 6 7   **Fic**
1. School stories 2. Friendship -- Fiction 3. Physically handicapped -- Fiction
ISBN 0-689-80993-X; 0-689-81721-5 pa

LC 95-52624

Awarded the Newbery Medal, 1997

Four students, with their own individual stories, develop a special bond and attract the attention of their teacher, a paraplegic, who choses them to represent their sixth-grade class in the Academic Bowl competition

"Glowing with humor and dusted with magic. . . . Wrought with deep compassion and a keen sense of balance." Publ Wkly

Korman, Gordon

★ The **Juvie** three. Hyperion 2008 249p lib bdg $15.99
Grades: 7 8 9 10   **Fic**
1. Friendship -- Fiction 2. Juvenile delinquency -- Fiction
ISBN 978-1-4231-0158-1; 1-4231-0158-8

LC 2008-19087

Gecko, Arjay, and Terence, all in trouble with the law, must find a way to keep their halfway house open in order to stay out of juvenile detention.

"Korman keeps lots of balls in the air as he handles each boy's distinct voice and character—as well as the increasingly absurd situation—with humor and flashes of sadness." Booklist

No more dead dogs. Hyperion Bks. for Children 2000 180p $15.99; pa $5.99
Grades: 5 6 7 8   **Fic**
1. Schools 2. Theater 3. Football 4. School stories 5. Humorous stories 6. Theater -- Fiction
ISBN 0-7868-0531-5; 0-7868-1601-5 pa

LC 00-24313

Eighth-grade football hero Wallace Wallace is sentenced to detention attending rehearsals of the school play where, in spite of himself, he becomes wrapped up in the production and begins to suggest changes that improve not only the play but his life as well

"Humor abounds here, but underlying is the true angst of the middle school student." Voice Youth Advocates

★ **Schooled**. Hyperion Books for Children 2007 208p $15.99
Grades: 6 7 8 9   **Fic**
1. School stories 2. Hippies -- Fiction
ISBN 0-7868-5692-0

Homeschooled by his hippie grandmother, Capricorn (Cap) Anderson has never watched television, tasted a pizza, or even heard of a wedgie. But when his grandmother lands in the hospital, Cap is forced to move in with a guidance counselor and attend the local middle school.

"This rewarding novel features an engaging main character and some memorable moments of comedy, tenderness, and reflection." Booklist

★ **Son** of the mob. Hyperion Bks. for Children 2002 262p hardcover o.p. pa $7.99

Grades: 7 8 9 10   **Fic**

1. Organized crime 2. Mafia -- Fiction
ISBN 0-7868-0769-5; 0-7868-1593-0 pa

LC 2002-68672

Seventeen-year-old Vince's life is constantly complicated by the fact that he is the son of a powerful Mafia boss, a relationship that threatens to destroy his romance with the daughter of an FBI agent

"The fast-paced, tightly focused story addresses the problems of being an honest kid in a family of outlaws—and loving them anyway. Korman doesn't ignore the seamier side of mob life, but even when the subject matter gets violent . . . he keeps things light by relating his tale in the first-person voice of a humorously sarcastic yet law-abiding wise guy." Horn Book

Another title about Vince is:
Son of the mob: Hollywood hustle (2004)

Swindle. Scholastic Press 2008 252p (Swindle)

Grades: 4 5 6   **Fic**

1. Baseball cards -- Fiction 2. Swindlers and swindling -- Fiction
ISBN 0-439-90344-0; 0-439-90345-9 pa; 978-0-439-90344-8; 978-0-439-90345-5 pa

LC 2007-17225

After unscrupulous collector S. Wendell Palomino cons him out of a valuable baseball card, sixth-grader Griffin Bing puts together a band of misfits to break into Palomino's store and steal the card back, planning to use the money to finance his father's failing invention, the SmartPick fruit picker. "Grades four to six." (Bull Cent Child Books)

"The plot is the main attraction, and its clever intricacies—silly, deceptively predictable, and seasoned with the occasional unexpected twist—do not disappoint." Booklist

Ungifted; Gordon Korman. Balzer + Bray 2012 280 p. $16.99

Grades: 4 5 6   **Fic**

1. School stories 2. Humorous stories 3. Robots -- Fiction 4. Schools -- Fiction 5. Behavior -- Fiction 6. Robotics -- Fiction 7. Middle schools -- Fiction 8. Gifted children -- Fiction
ISBN 006174266X; 9780061742668

LC 2012008408

In this children's book, "hyperactive, heedless Donovan Curtis whacks a school statue of Atlas with a stick, which sends the huge metal globe on Atlas's shoulders rolling into the gym during a basketball game, which lands Donovan in the superintendent's office, where his name is mistakenly entered by the irate administrator onto a list of candidates for the district's middle-school gifted program." The plot

includes "Donovan's shallow yet indispensable contribution to his team's robotics competition." (Bulletin of the Center for Children's Books)

Zoobreak. Scholastic Press 2009 230p $16.99; pa $6.99

Grades: 3 4 5 6   **Fic**

1. Adventure fiction 2. Zoos -- Fiction 3. Theft -- Fiction 4. Lost and found possessions -- Fiction
ISBN 978-0-545-12499-7; 0-545-12499-9; 978-0-545-12500-0 pa; 0-545-12500-6 pa

LC 2009015456

After a class trip to a floating zoo where animals are mistreated and Savannah's missing pet monkey is found in a cage, Long Island sixth-grader Griffin Bing and his band of misfits plan a rescue.

"Both children and adults will find the story fast moving and enjoyable. The often-unpredictable plot is interesting, full of humor, and good fun." Voice Youth Advocates

Kositsky, Lynne

The **thought** of high windows. Kids Can Press 2004 175p hardcover o.p. pa $6.95

Grades: 7 8 9 10   **Fic**

1. Jews -- Fiction 2. Holocaust, 1933-1945 -- Fiction
ISBN 1-55337-621-8; 1-55337-622-6 pa

"Esther describes her life as one of a group of Jewish children taken from Germany to France by the Red Cross during World War II. The novel begins when she is 15 and living in a French castle; her childhood in Berlin is described through flashbacks. . . . Based on true events, this is an immediate, painfully honest story." SLJ

Koss, Amy Goldman

Poison Ivy. Roaring Brook Press 2006 166p $16.96

Grades: 7 8 9 10   **Fic**

1. School stories 2. Bullies -- Fiction
ISBN 1-59643-118-0

LC 2005-17256

In a government class three popular girls undergo a mock trial for their ruthless bullying of a classmate.

"Realistic dialogue and fast-paced action will hold interest, and the final verdict is unsettling, but not unexpected." SLJ

Side effects; 1st ed.; Roaring Brook Press 2006 143p $16.95

Grades: 6 7 8 9   **Fic**

1. Cancer -- Fiction
ISBN 978-1-59643-167-6; 1-59643-167-9

LC 2005-31473

Everything changes for Isabelle, not quite fifteen, when she is diagnosed with lymphoma—but eventually she survives and even thrives.

"Koss refuses to glamorize Issy's illness or treatment. Instead, she settles for an honesty and frankness that will both challenge and enlighten readers." Booklist

The **girls**. Dial Bks. for Young Readers 2000 121p $16.99; pa $5.99

Grades: 5 6 7 8   **Fic**
   1. Friendship -- Fiction
   ISBN 0-8037-2494-2; 0-14-230033-0 pa
                     LC 99-19318
"This provocative page-turner will be passed from one girl to the next." SLJ

Kostick, Conor
   ★ **Epic**. Viking 2007 364p $17.99
Grades: 7 8 9 10   **Fic**
   1. Fantasy fiction 2. Video games -- Fiction
   ISBN 0-670-06179-4; 978-0-670-06179-2
                   LC 2006-19958
On New Earth, a world based on a video role-playing game, fourteen-year-old Erik pursuades his friends to aid him in some unusual gambits in order to save his father from exile and safeguard the futures of each of their families.
   "There is intrigue and mystery throughout this captivating page-turner. Veins of moral and ethical social situations and decisions provide some great opportunities for discussion. Well written and engaging." SLJ
   Other titles in this series are:
   Edda (2011)
   Saga (2008)

Krieg, Jim
   ★ **Griff** Carver, hallway patrol. Razorbill 2010 224p $15.99
Grades: 4 5 6 7   **Fic**
   1. School stories 2. Counterfeits and counterfeiting -- Fiction
   ISBN 978-1-59514-276-4; 1-59514-276-2
                   LC 2009-32553
Legendary Griff Carver joins the Rampart Middle School Hallway Patrol and, with the help of his friend Tommy, Griff solves the case of counterfeit hall passes.
   "With comically over-the-top cop lingo . . . Griff and Tommy tell their stories through incident reports and interviews, adding drama and humor to the most mundane aspects of school. . . . Krieg will keep readers chuckling through the hilarious but action-packed showdown." Publ Wkly

Krisher, Trudy
   Fallout. Holiday House 2006 315p $17.95
Grades: 7 8 9 10   **Fic**
   1. Friendship -- Fiction 2. Prejudices -- Fiction
   ISBN 978-0-8234-2035-3; 0-8234-2035-3
                   LC 2006-41193
The move of an unconventional Hollywood family to a coastal North Carolina town in the early 1950s results not only in an unlikely friendship between high school age Genevieve and newcomer Brenda but also in a challenge to traditional ways of thinking.
   "This is an excellent novel for teens searching for a good story with a well-paced and action-filled plot that challenges them to think about the importance of voicing their opinions." SLJ

Krishnaswami, Uma
   ★ The **grand** plan to fix everything; [illustrations by Abigail Halpin] Atheneum Books for Young Readers 2011 224p il $16.99

Grades: 4 5 6 7   **Fic**
   1. Actors -- Fiction 2. Moving -- Fiction 3. Friendship -- Fiction 4. East Indian Americans -- Fiction
   ISBN 978-1-4169-9589-0; 1-4169-9589-7
                   LC 2010035145
Eleven-year-old Dini loves movies, and so when she learns that her family is moving to India for two years, her devastation over leaving her best friend in Maryland is tempered by the possibility of meeting her favorite actress, Dolly Singh.
   "An out-of-the-ordinary setting, a distinctive middle-grade character with an unusual passion, and the pace of a lively Bollywood 'fillum' make this novel a delight." Publ Wkly

Krokos, Dan
   False memory; Dan Krokos. Disney Press 2012 327 p. $17.99
Grades: 6 7 8 9   **Fic**
   1. Secrecy -- Fiction 2. Teenagers -- Fiction 3. Science fiction 4. Memory -- Fiction 5. Genetic engineering -- Fiction
   ISBN 1423149769; 9781423149767
                   LC 2011053532
In author Dan Krokos" book, "Miranda North wakes up alone on a park bench with no memory. In her panic, she releases a mysterious energy that incites pure terror in everyone around her . . . Miranda discovers she was trained to be a weapon and is part of an elite force of genetically-altered teens who possess flawless combat skills and powers strong enough to destroy a city . . . Then Miranda uncovers a dark truth that sets her team on the run. Suddenly her past doesn"t seem to matter…when there may not be a future." Publisher's Note

Kuhlman, Evan
   ★ The **last** invisible boy; written by Evan Kuhlman; illustrated by J. P. Coovert. Atheneum Books for Young Readers 2008 233p il $16.99; pa $5.99
Grades: 4 5 6 7   **Fic**
   1. School stories 2. Bereavement -- Fiction 3. Family life -- Fiction 4. Father-son relationship -- Fiction
   ISBN 978-1-4169-5797-3; 1-4169-5797-9; 978-1-4169-6089-8 pa; 1-4169-6089-9 pa
                   LC 2007-40258
In the wake of his father's sudden death, twelve-year-old Finn feels he is becoming invisible as his hair and skin become whiter by the day, and so he writes and illustrates a book to try to understand what is happening and to hold on to himself and his father
   "Vivid details . . . add depth to the characterizations and grow in meaning as the story progresses. . . . Finn's distinct narrative voice, and the sweet precision with which the story unfolds, give this title a touching resonance." Booklist

Kurtz, Chris
   The **adventures** of a South Pole pig; a novel of snow and courage. Chris Kurtz ; illustrations by Jennifer Black Reinhardt. Harcourt Children's Books, Houghton Mifflin Harcourt 2013 288 p. $16.99
Grades: 4 5 6 7   **Fic**
   1. Dogs -- Fiction 2. Pigs -- Fiction 3. Sled dogs

-- Fiction 4. Dogsledding -- Fiction 5. Adventure and adventurers -- Fiction
ISBN 0547634552; 9780547634555

LC 2012027226

In this children's story, by Chris Kurtz, illustrated by Jennifer Black Reinhardt, "the day Flora spots a team of sled dogs is the day she sets her heart on becoming a sled pig. Before she knows it, she's on board a ship to Antarctica for the most exhilarating--and dangerous--adventure of her life." (Publisher's note)

Kwasney, Michelle D.

Itch; [by] Michelle D. Kwasney. Henry Holt 2008 240p $16.95

Grades: 5 6 7 8   **Fic**

1. School stories 2. Mothers -- Fiction 3. Friendship -- Fiction 4. Child abuse -- Fiction 5. Grandparents -- Fiction
ISBN 978-0-8050-8083-4; 0-8050-8083-X

LC 2007027573

In 1968, after the death of her beloved Gramps, Delores "Itch" Colchester and her grandmother move from Florida to an Ohio trailer park, where she meets new people and, when she learns that a friend is being abused by her mother, tries her best to emulate her plain-spoken grandfather

"The 1960s references provide the realistic backdrop for this moving, believable story. Sympathetic well-drawn characters draw the reader into Delores' personal struggles." Booklist

L'Engle, Madeleine

★ A **wrinkle** in time. Farrar, Straus & Giroux 1962 211p $17; pa $7.99

Grades: 5 6 7 8 9 10   **Fic**

1. Fantasy fiction
ISBN 0-374-38613-7; 0-312-36754-6 pa
ALA YALSA Margaret A. Edwards Award (1998)
Awarded The Newbery Medal, 1963
This book "makes unusual demands on the imagination and consequently gives great rewards." Horn Book
Other titles in this series are:
A swiftly tilting planet (1978)
A wind in the door (1973)

La Fevers, R. L.

Theodosia and the Serpents of Chaos; illustrated by Yoko Tanaka. Houghton Mifflin 2007 343p il $16; pa $6.99

Grades: 4 5 6 7   **Fic**

1. Adventure fiction 2. Magic -- Fiction 3. Museums -- Fiction
ISBN 978-0-618-75638-4; 0-618-75638-8; 978-0-618-99976-7 pa; 0-618-99976-0 pa

LC 2006-34284

Set in 1906 London and Cairo, this mystery adventure introduces an intrepid heroine—Theodosia Throckmorton, who is thrust into the heart of a mystery when she learns an ancient Egyptian amulet carries a curse that threatens to crumble the British Empire

"It's the delicious, precise, and atmospheric details (nicely extended in Tanaka's few, stylized illustrations) that will capture and hold readers." Booklist

Other titles about Theodosia are:
Theodosia and the Staff of Osiris (2008)
Theodosia and the Eyes of Horus (2010)
Theodosia and the last Pharoah (2011)

La Valley, Josanne

The **Vine** basket; by Josanne La Valley. Clarion Books 2013 252 p. (hardcover) $16.99

Grades: 4 5 6 7 8   **Fic**

1. China -- Fiction 2. Farm life -- Fiction 3. Basket making -- Fiction 4. Ethnic relations -- Fiction 5. Farm life -- China -- Fiction 6. Fathers and daughters -- Fiction 7. Uighur (Turkic people) -- Fiction
ISBN 0547848013; 9780547848013

LC 2012021007

In this novel, by Josanne La Valley, "things aren't looking good for fourteen-year-old Mehrigul. She yearns to be in school, but she"s needed on the family farm. . . . Her only hope is an American woman who buys one of her decorative vine baskets for a staggering sum and says she will return in three weeks for more. Mehrigul must brave terrible storms, torn-up hands from working the fields, and her father's scorn to get the baskets done." (Publisher's note)

"The vivid and authentic sense of place, custom, and politics serves as an effective vehicle for the skillfully characterized, emotionally charged story. . . . The realistic and satisfying resolution will resonate with readers . . . An absorbing read and an excellent choice for expanding global understanding." SLJ

LaFaye, A.

Stella stands alone; [by] A. LaFaye. Simon & Schuster Books for Young Readers 2008 245p map $16.99

Grades: 7 8 10   **Fic**

1. Orphans -- Fiction 2. African Americans -- Fiction 3. Swindlers and swindling -- Fiction 4. Reconstruction (1865-1876) -- Fiction
ISBN 978-1-4169-1164-7; 1-4169-1164-2

LC 2007-38725

Fourteen-year-old Stella, orphaned just after the Civil War, fights to keep her family's plantation and fulfill her father's desire to turn land over to the people who have worked on it for generations, but first she must find her father's hidden deed and will.

"Readers will be drawn along by Stella's refusal to act helpless and sweet and her discovery of strength and kindness in unexpected places. The sadness and anger, and the wrenching legacy of slavery are present throughout." Booklist

Water steps. Milkweed Editions 2009 175p $16.95; pa $6.95

Grades: 4 5 6 7   **Fic**

1. Water -- Fiction 2. Phobias -- Fiction 3. Irish Americans -- Fiction
ISBN 978-1-57131-687-5; 1-57131-687-6; 978-1-57131-686-8 pa; 1-57131-686-8 pa

LC 2008011684

Eleven-year-old Kyna, terrified of water since her family drowned in a storm that nearly took her life as well, works to overcome her phobia when her adoptive parents, Irish immigrants with a mysterious past, rent a cabin on Lake Champlain for the summer.

"The language is almost poetic with its use of sensory detail, alliteration, and precise word choices. A satisfying story of overcoming one's fears and discovering secrets." SLJ

LaFleur, Suzanne M.

★ **Love,** Aubrey. Wendy Lamb Books 2009 262p $15.99; lib bdg $18.99

Grades: 5 6 7 8   **Fic**
1. School stories 2. Letters -- Fiction 3. Friendship -- Fiction 4. Bereavement -- Fiction 5. Grandmothers -- Fiction 6. Abandoned children -- Fiction 7. Depression (Psychology) -- Fiction
ISBN 978-0-385-73774-6; 0-385-73774-2; 978-0-385-90686-9 lib bdg; 0-385-90686-2 lib bdg
           LC 2008-31742

While living with her Gram in Vermont, eleven-year-old Aubrey writes letters as a way of dealing with losing her father and sister in a car accident, and then being abandoned by her grief-stricken mother.

Aubrey's "detailed progression from denial to acceptance makes her both brave and credible in this honest and realistic portrayal of grief." Kirkus

Laban, Elizabeth

The **Tragedy** Paper; Elizabeth LaBan. Alfred A. Knopf 2013 320 p. $17.99

Grades: 7 8 9 10 11 12   **Fic**
1. Love stories 2. School stories 3. Albinos and albinism -- Fiction 4. Schools -- Fiction 5. High schools -- Fiction 6. Boarding schools -- Fiction 7. Dating (Social customs) -- Fiction 8. Interpersonal relations -- Fiction
ISBN 0375870407; 9780375870408; 9780375970405; 9780375989124
           LC 2012011294

This novel by Elizabeth Laban "follows the story of Tim Macbeth, a seventeen-year-old albino and a recent transfer to the prestigious Irving School. . . . He finds himself falling for the quintessential 'It' girl, Vanessa Sheller. . . . Vanessa is into him, too, but she can kiss her social status goodbye if anyone ever finds out. Tim and Vanessa begin a clandestine romance, but looming over them is the Tragedy Paper, Irving's version of a senior year thesis." (Publisher's note)

Lacey, Josh

Island of Thieves; Josh Lacey. Houghton Mifflin 2012 228 p.

Grades: 4 5 6 7 8   **Fic**
1. Peru -- Fiction 2. Adventure fiction 3. Uncles -- Fiction 4. Pirates -- Fiction 5. Buried treasure -- Fiction 6. Islands -- Fiction 7. Mystery and detective stories 8. Adventure and adventurers -- Fiction
ISBN 0547763271; 9780547763279
           LC 2011033893

In this children's novel, a boy takes part in "swashbuckling adventures in faraway places, freed from the strictures of parents, school, siblings and caregivers. . . . Tom nearly ruins his parents' vacation by accidentally burning down the shed in his backyard. . . . Harvey welcomes Tom . . . but as soon as Tom's parents leave, he starts packing for Peru. . . .

When he tells Tom it's because he has an opportunity to hunt for pirate treasure, Tom blackmails his uncle into taking him along." (Kirkus)

Lai, Thanhha

★ **Inside** out and back again. Harper 2011 262p $15.99

Grades: 4 5 6 7   **Fic**
1. Novels in verse 2. Immigrants -- Fiction 3. Vietnamese Americans -- Fiction
ISBN 978-0-06-196278-3; 0-06-196278-3
           LC 2010007855

"Based on Lai's personal experience, this first novel captures a child-refugee's struggle with rare honesty. Written in accessible, short free-verse poems." Booklist

Lairamore, Dawn

Ivy and the meanstalk. Holiday House 2011 227p $16.95

Grades: 4 5 6 7   **Fic**
1. Fairy tales 2. Giants -- Fiction 3. Dragons -- Fiction 4. Princesses -- Fiction
ISBN 978-0-8234-2392-7; 0-8234-2392-1
           LC 2010048627

Fourteen-year-old Princess Ivy wants nothing more than to have a little fun in the company of her dragon friend, Elridge, but unless she can recover the magical harp snatched by a thieving youth named Jack long ago, her entire kingdom will suffer an unspeakable fate.

This is "delightful and humorous. . . . Lairamore's well-developed characters are excellent riffs on fairy-tale traditions. . . . Various settings are depicted in rich detail while never detracting from the narrative. The plot is filled with action-packed scenes." SLJ

★ **Ivy's** ever after. Holiday House 2010 311p $16.95

Grades: 4 5 6 7   **Fic**
1. Fairy tales 2. Dragons -- Fiction 3. Princesses -- Fiction
ISBN 978-0-8234-2261-6; 0-8234-2261-5
           LC 2009-43288

Fourteen-year-old Ivy, a most unroyal princess, befriends Elridge, the dragon sent to keep her in a tower, and together they set out on a perilous quest to find Ivy's fairy godmother, who may be able to save both from their dire fates.

"Ivy is an engaging alternative to the standard damsel-in-distress figure, and with a lushly vivid setting, witty dialogue, and lots of adventure, this well-plotted first novel will appeal to fans of Vivian Vande Velde's A Hidden Magic (1985) and A Well-Timed Enchantment (1990)." Booklist

Laird, Elizabeth

The **betrayal** of Maggie Blair. Houghton Mifflin 2011 423p il $16.99

Grades: 7 8 9 10   **Fic**
1. Uncles -- Fiction 2. Witchcraft -- Fiction
ISBN 978-0-547-34126-2; 0-547-34126-1
           LC 2010-25120

In seventeenth-century Scotland, sixteen-year-old Maggie Blair is sentenced to be hanged as a witch but escapes to the home of her uncle, placing him and his family in great danger as she risks her life to save them all from the King's men.

"Laird seamlessly weaves a fairly comprehensive history lesson into an engaging, lively story." Bull Cent Child Books

A **little** piece of ground; [by] Elizabeth Laird; with Sonia Nimr. Haymarket Books 2006 216p pa $9.95

Grades: 6 7 8 9 10   **Fic**

1. Israel-Arab conflicts -- Fiction
ISBN 978-1-931859-38-7; 1-931859-38-8
LC 2006008707

During the Israeli occupation of Ramallah in the West Bank of Palestine, twelve-year-old Karim and his friends create a secret place for themselves where they can momentarily forget the horrors of war.

"Throughout this powerful narrative, the authors remain true to Karim's character and reactions. He is a typical self-centered adolescent. . . . [This book] deserves serious attention and discussion." SLJ

Lake, Nick

Blood ninja II: the revenge of Lord Oda. Simon and Schuster Books for Young Readers 2010 377p $16.99

Grades: 7 8 9 10 11   **Fic**

1. Ninja -- Fiction 2. Vampires -- Fiction
ISBN 978-1-4169-8629-4; 1-4169-8629-4
LC 2010-10110

In sixteenth-century Japan, Taro, a vampire like all ninja warriors, tries to protect his mother and defeat the power-hungry Lord Oda, who he believed was dead.

"Ghosts and Zen Buddhist philosophy add a surprising and sometimes effective depth to the story." Booklist

Lancaster, Mike A.

★ **Human.4**. Egmont USA 2011 231p $16.99

Grades: 7 8 9 10   **Fic**

1. Science fiction 2. Computers -- Fiction 3. Family life -- Fiction
ISBN 978-1-6068-4099-3; 1-6068-4099-1
LC 2010030313

Twenty-first century fourteen-year-old Kyle was hypnotized when humanity was upgraded to 1.0 and he, incompatible with the new technology, exposes its terrifying impact in a tape-recording found by the superhumans of the future.

"Lancaster fashions a fast-paced, upsetting little thriller punctuated by ominous editorial notes that translate Kyle's details for the futuristic audience." Booklist

The **future** we left behind; Mike A. Lancaster. Egmont USA 2012 367 p. (hardback) $16.99

Grades: 7 8 9 10   **Fic**

1. Science fiction 2. Cults -- Fiction 3. Computer programs -- Fiction 4. Family life -- England -- Fiction 5. Technological innovations -- Fiction
ISBN 1606844105; 9781606844106; 9781606844113
LC 2012003794

This sequel to "Human.4" is set in the future. Here, "Peter is the son of the man who saved the world by inventing robot bees. Destined by his wealthy genius father for a future in science, Peter rebels against both by enrolling in

a literature class and befriending Alpha, a girl in a wacky religious cult. Alpha is a Strakerite, following the ancient tapes of Kyle Straker. Kyle and his girlfriend Lilly believed humans are regularly upgraded by aliens. Skeptical at first, Peter is soon convinced." (Kirkus)

Landon, Kristen

The **limit**. Aladdin 2010 291p $15.99

Grades: 6 7 8 9   **Fic**

1. Science fiction
ISBN 978-1-4424-0271-3; 1-4424-0271-7
LC 2010-12707

When his family exceeds its legal debt limit, thirteen-year-old Matt is sent to the Federal Debt Rehabilitation Agency workhouse, where he discovers illicit activities are being carried out using the children who have been placed there.

"From the first sentence . . . Landon captures readers' attention and keeps it. This first-person, part realistic fiction, part fantasy should appeal to readers looking for high-action adventure." Booklist

Landy, Derek

★ **Skulduggery** Pleasant. HarperCollinsPublishers 2007 392p $17.99; lib bdg $18.89; pa $7.99

Grades: 4 5 6 7   **Fic**

1. Fantasy fiction 2. Magic -- Fiction 3. Young adult literature -- Works
ISBN 978-0-06-123115-5; 0-06-123115-0; 978-0-06-123116-2 lib bdg; 0-06-123116-9 lib bdg; 978-0-06-123117-9 pa; 0-06-123117-7 pa
LC 2006-29403

When twelve-year-old Stephanie inherits her weird uncle's estate, she must join forces with Skulduggery Pleasant, a skeleton mage, to save the world from the Faceless Ones

This "is a rich fantasy that is as engaging in its creative protagonists and villains as it is in the lightning-paced plot and sharp humor." Bulletin Cent Child Books

Other titles in this series are:
Playing with fire (2008)
The faceless ones (2009)

Lane, Andrew

Black ice; Andrew Lane. Farrar Straus Giroux 2013 288 p. (Sherlock Holmes. The legend begins) (hardcover) $17.99

Grades: 5 6 7 8   **Fic**

1. Mystery fiction 2. Holmes, Sherlock (Fictional character) -- Fiction 3. Murder -- Fiction 4. Mystery and detective stories
ISBN 0374387699; 9780374387693
LC 2012004996

This novel, by Andrew Lane, is the third book of the "Sherlock Holmes: The Legend Begins" series. "When Sherlock and Amyus Crowe, his American tutor, visit Sherlock's brother, Mycroft, in London, all they are expecting is lunch and some polite conversation. What they find shocks both of them to the core: a locked room, a dead body, and Mycroft holding a knife. . . . Threatened with the gallows, Mycroft needs Sherlock to save him." (Publisher's note)

Rebel fire; Andrew Lane. Farrar Straus Giroux 2012 343 p. (Sherlock Holmes. The legend begins) $16.99

Grades: 5 6 7 8   **Fic**

1. Mystery fiction 2. Holmes, Sherlock (Fictional character) -- Fiction 3. Mystery and detective stories
ISBN 0374387680; 9780374387686

LC 2011000124

This novel, by Andrew Lane, is part of the "Sherlock Holmes: The Legend Begins" series. "Fourteen-year-old Sherlock Holmes knows that Amyus Crowe, his mysterious American tutor, has some dark secrets. But he didn't expect to find John Wilkes Booth, the notorious assassin, apparently alive and well in England--and Crowe somehow mixed up in it. . . . And so begins an adventure that will take Sherlock across the Atlantic, to the center of a deadly web." (Publisher's note)

Includes bibliographical references

Lane, Dakota

Gothic Lolita; a mystical thriller. words and photographs by Dakota Lane. Atheneum Books for Young Readers 2008 194p il $17.99

Grades: 8 9 10 11 12   **Fic**

1. Weblogs -- Fiction 2. Bereavement -- Fiction 3. Racially mixed people -- Fiction
ISBN 978-1-4169-1396-2; 1-4169-1396-3

LC 2008-15390

Lane "focuses on two half-Japanese, half-American girls who forge an unusual bond over their blogs, loneliness and fascination with the gothic Lolita subculture. Chelsea is in L.A. and Miya is in Japan. . . . Readers will find themselves quickly engrossed." Publ Wkly

Langrish, Katherine

★ The **shadow** hunt. Harper 2010 322p $16.99

Grades: 6 7 8 9   **Fic**

1. Fantasy fiction
ISBN 978-0-06-111676-6; 0-06-111676-9

LC 2009-930446

First published 2009 in the United Kingdom

"Thirteen-year-old Wolf is running away from the abbey where he was raised when he unexpectedly meets renowned knight Sir Hugo. Together, they capture a mysterious elf-child and return to Hugo's castle, where Wolf will be allowed to stay—if he gets the elf-child to speak. . . . In this medieval fantasy, Langrish . . . provides a vividly rendered, engrossing tale. Epic themes—good and evil, faith and doubt, sin and redemption—are made personal and poignant through the losses and longings of the notably well-drawn, dimensional main characters." Booklist

Larbalestier, Justine

How to ditch your fairy. Bloomsbury 2008 307p $16.99

Grades: 6 7 8 9 10   **Fic**

1. Magic -- Fiction 2. Fairies -- Fiction
ISBN 978-1-59990-301-9; 1-59990-301-6

LC 2008-02408

In a world in which everyone has a personal fairy who tends to one aspect of daily life, fourteen-year-old Charlie decides she does not want hers—a parking fairy—and embarks on a series of misadventures designed to rid herself of the invisible sprite and replace it with a better one, like her friend Rochelle's shopping fairy.

"Charlie is totally likable, smart, and sarcastic, a perfectly self-involved, insecure teen. At its core, this is a typical coming-of-age story, but the addition of the fairies, the slightly alternative setting, and the made-up slang make it much more." SLJ

Magic or madness. Razorbill 2005 288p $16.99; pa $7.99

Grades: 8 9 10 11 12   **Fic**

1. Magic -- Fiction 2. Grandmothers -- Fiction 3. Space and time -- Fiction
ISBN 1-59514-022-0; 1-59514-124-3 pa

LC 2004-18263

From the Sydney, Australia home of a grandmother she believes is a witch, fifteen-year-old Reason Cansino is magically transported to New York City, where she discovers that friends and foes can be hard to distinguish

"Readers looking for layered, understated fantasy will follow the looping paths of Larbalestier's fine writing . . . with gratitude and awe." Booklist

Other titles about Reason Cansino are:
Magic lessons (2006)
Magic's child (2007)

Larson, Kirby

Hattie Big Sky. Delacorte Press 2006 289p hardcover o.p. pa $6.99

Grades: 6 7 8 9 10   **Fic**

1. Montana -- Fiction 2. Orphans -- Fiction 3. World War, 1914-1918 -- Fiction 4. Frontier and pioneer life -- Fiction
ISBN 0-385-73313-5; 0-385-73595-2 pa

LC 2005-35039

A Newbery Medal honor book, 2007

After inheriting her uncle's homesteading claim in Montana, sixteen-year-old orphan Hattie Brooks travels from Iowa in 1917 to make a home for herself and encounters some unexpected problems related to the war being fought in Europe.

This is "a richly textured novel full of memorable characters." Booklist

Hattie ever after; Kirby Larson. Delacorte Press 2013 240 p. (hc) $16.99

Grades: 6 7 8 9 10   **Fic**

1. Historical fiction 2. Orphans -- Fiction 3. Reporters and reporting -- Fiction 4. Self-reliance -- Fiction
ISBN 0385737467; 9780307979681; 9780385737463; 9780385906685

LC 2012007068

In this novel, by Newbury Honor award-winning author Kirby Larson, "after leaving Uncle Chester's homestead claim, orphan Hattie Brooks throws a lasso around a new dream, even bigger than the Montana sky. She wants to be a reporter . . . , go to Grand Places, and do Grand Things, like Hattie's hero Nellie Bly. Another girl might be stymied by this, but . . . nothing can squash her desire to write for a big city newspaper." (Publisher's note)

Includes bibliographical references

Laskas, Gretchen Moran

The **miner's** daughter. Simon & Schuster Books for Young Readers 2007 250p $15.99

Grades: 8 9 10 11 12   Fic

1. Family life -- Fiction 2. Coal mines and mining -- Fiction 3. Great Depression, 1929-1939 -- Fiction

ISBN 978-1-4169-1262-0; 1-4169-1262-2

LC 2006-00684

Sixteen-year-old Willa, living in a Depression-era West Virginia mining town, works hard to help her family, experiences love and friendship, and finds an outlet for her writing when her family becomes part of the Arthurdale, West Virginia, community supported by Eleanor Roosevelt.

"Richly drawn characters and plot make this an excellent novel that explores the struggles endured by many in America in the 1930s." SLJ

Lasky, Kathryn

★ **Ashes**. Viking 2010 318p $16.99

Grades: 6 7 8 9 10 11 12   Fic

1. National socialism -- Fiction

ISBN 978-0-670-01157-5; 0-670-01157-6

LC 2009-33127

In 1932 Berlin, thirteen-year-old Gaby Schramm witnesses the beginning of Hitler's rise to power, as soldiers become ubiquitous, her beloved literature teacher starts wearing a jewelled swastika pin, and the family's dear friend, Albert Einstein, leaves the country while Gaby's parents secretly bury his books and papers in their small yard.

"Gaby's questioning but assertive nature helps form a compelling, readable portrait of pre-WWII Germany." Publ Wkly

Chasing Orion. Candlewick Press 2010 362p $17.99

Grades: 6 7 8 9   Fic

1. Friendship -- Fiction 2. Poliomyelitis -- Fiction

ISBN 978-0-7636-3982-2; 0-7636-3982-6

LC 2009007327

In 1952, when Georgie is eleven years old, her family moves to a new Indiana neighborhood where her teenaged neighbor has polio and is in an iron lung.

"A truly extraordinary page-turner that embraces life's big and small aspects with humor and a healthy respect for its profound contradictions." Kirkus

Hawksmaid; the untold story of Robin Hood and Maid Marian. Harper 2010 292p $16.99

Grades: 5 6 7 8   Fic

1. Falconry -- Fiction 2. Robin Hood (Legendary character) -- Fiction 3. Maid Marian (Legendary character) -- Fiction

ISBN 978-0-06-000071-4; 0-06-000071-6

In twelfth-century England, Matty grows up to be a master falconer, able to communicate with the devoted birds who later help her and Fynn, also known as Robin Hood, to foil Prince John's plot to steal the crown.

"Lasky nicely weaves details of 12th-century life into this suspenseful adventure whose fantasy ending may surprise but will certainly please readers." SLJ

Lone wolf. Scholastic Press 2010 219p il map (Wolves of the Beyond) $16.99

Grades: 5 6 7 8   Fic

1. Fantasy fiction 2. Wolves -- Fiction

ISBN 978-0-545-09310-1; 0-545-09310-4

LC 2009-17007

Abandoned by his pack, a baby wolf with a mysterious mark on his deformed paw survives and embarks on a journey that will change the world of the wolves of the Beyond.

"Lasky merges anthropomorphic fantasy with realistic details about wolves and bears to produce an almost plausible emotional narrative, complete with dialogue and personalities. . . . The author builds a captivating world of forest, snow and volcanoes populated by intelligent animals and weaves a compelling story sure to bring readers back for the second installment." Kirkus

Other titles in this series are:

Shadow wolf (2010)

Watch wolf (2011)

Frost worlf (2011)

Latham, Irene

Leaving Gee's Bend. G.P. Putnam's Sons 2010 230p $16.99

Grades: 5 6 7 8   Fic

1. Quilts -- Fiction 2. African Americans -- Fiction

ISBN 978-0-399-25179-5; 0-399-25179-0

LC 2009-08732

Ludelphia Bennett, a determined, ten-year-old African American girl in 1932 Gee's Bend, Alabama, leaves home in an effort to find medical help for her sick mother, and she recounts her ensuing adventures in a quilt she is making.

"Ludelphia's voice is authentic and memorable, and Latham captures the tension of her dangerous journey and the racism she encounters." Booklist

Lavender, William

Aftershocks. Harcourt 2006 344p $17

Grades: 8 9 10 11 12   Fic

1. Sex role -- Fiction 2. Earthquakes -- Fiction 3. Chinese Americans -- Fiction 4. Father-daughter relationship -- Fiction

ISBN 0-15-205882-6

LC 2005-19695

In San Francisco from 1903 to 1908, teenager Jessie Wainwright determines to reach her goal of becoming a doctor while also trying to care for the illegitimate child of a liaison between her father and their Chinese maid.

This "is readable historical fiction about an engrossing event in U.S. history." Voice Youth Advocates

Law, Ingrid

★ **Savvy**. Dial Books for Young Readers 2008 342p $16.99

Grades: 4 5 6 7   Fic

1. Magic -- Fiction 2. Family life -- Fiction 3. Voyages and travels -- Fiction

ISBN 978-0-8037-3306-0; 0-8037-3306-2

LC 2007-39814

A Newbery Medal honor book, 2009

Boston Globe-Horn Book Award honor book: Fiction and Poetry (2008)

Recounts the adventures of Mississippi (Mibs) Beaumont, whose thirteenth birthday has revealed her "savvy"—a magical power unique to each member of her family—just as her father is injured in a terrible accident.

"Short chapters and cliffhangers keep the pace quick, while the mix of traditional language and vernacular helps the story feel both fresh and timeless. . . . [This is] a vibrant and cinematic novel that readers are going to love." Publ Wkly

★ **Scumble**. Dial Books for Young Readers 2010 400p il $16.99

Grades: 4 5 6 7   **Fic**
1. Magic -- Fiction 2. Ranch life -- Fiction
ISBN 978-0-8037-3307-7; 0-8037-3307-0
            LC 2010-02444

Mibs's cousin Ledge is disappointed to discover that his "savvy" —the magical power unique to each member of their family—is to make things fall apart, which endangers his uncle Autry's ranch and reveals the family secret to future reporter Sarah.

This provides a "satisfying plot, delightful characters, alliterative language, and rich imagery." Booklist

Lawlor, Laurie

Dead reckoning; a pirate voyage with Captain Drake. Simon & Schuster Books for Young Readers 2005 254p $15.95

Grades: 7 8 9 10   **Fic**
1. Orphans -- Fiction 2. Pirates -- Fiction 3. Seafaring life -- Fiction
ISBN 0-689-86577-5
            LC 2004-21682

Emmet, a fifteen-year-old orphan, learns hard lessons about survival when he sails from England in 1577 as a servant aboard the Golden Hind—the ship of his cousin, the explorer and pirate Francis Drake—on its three-year circumnavigation of the world.

"The tone is dark and grim, and there are scenes that might horrify younger readers. . . . But the story is authentic and harrowing, and the historical details are well done. This book would be perfect for older teens who love historical fiction, or want more on pirates." SLJ

He will go fearless; [by] Laurie Lawlor. Simon & Schuster Books for Young Readers 2006 210p $15.95

Grades: 5 6 7 8   **Fic**
1. Father-son relationship -- Fiction 2. Overland journeys to the Pacific -- Fiction
ISBN 0-689-86579-1
            LC 2005-06129

With the Civil War ended and Reconstruction begun, fifteen-year-old Billy resolves to make the dangerous and challenging journey West in search of real fortune – his true father.

"Danger, adventure, and survival combine to make this a richly detailed story." SLJ

Lawrence, Caroline

★ **P.K.** Pinkerton and the petrified man; Caroline Lawrence. G.P. Putnam's Sons 2013 320 p. (hardcover) $16.99

Grades: 4 5 6   **Fic**
1. Mystery fiction 2. Western stories 3. Orphans -- Fiction 4. Disguise -- Fiction 5. Mystery and detective stories 6. Racially mixed people -- Fiction
ISBN 0399256342; 9780399256349
            LC 2012026737

This western mystery adventure novel, by Caroline Lawrence, is "starring Master-of-Disguise, P.K. Pinkerton. After vanquishing three notorious Desperados, twelve-year-old P.K. Pinkerton opens a private-eye business in Virginia City. P.K.'s skills are quickly put to the test: When a maid named Martha witnesses a murder, she hires the young detective to track the killer before he finds her too." (Publisher's note)

The **case** of the deadly desperados; Caroline Lawrence. G.P. Putnam's Sons 2011 279 p. (Western mysteries) $16.99

Grades: 5 6 7 8   **Fic**
1. Mystery fiction 2. Western stories 3. Orphans -- Fiction 4. Racially mixed people -- Fiction 5. Disguise -- Fiction
ISBN 9780399256332
            LC 2011013305

In this book, Caroline "Lawrence shifts her sleuthing . . . [to] Virginia City, Montana in the 1860s. . . . Whittlin' Walt . . . has just scalped and slain the foster parents of twelve-year-old P. K. (Pinky) Pinkerton, . . . who holds a coveted deed to an entire region of silver mines. Pinky hightails it to Virginia City . . . to register his claim, . . . [then] to Chicago, where he wants to join the detective whom he believes to be his father." (Bulletin of the Center for Children's Books)

Lawrence, Iain

★ The **giant** -slayer. Delacorte Press 2009 292p $16.99

Grades: 5 6 7 8   **Fic**
1. Imagination -- Fiction 2. Medical care -- Fiction 3. Storytelling -- Fiction 4. Poliomyelitis -- Fiction 5. Father-daughter relationship -- Fiction
ISBN 978-0-385-73376-2; 0-385-73376-3
            LC 2008-35409

When her eight-year-old neighbor is stricken with polio in 1955, eleven-year-old Laurie discovers that there is power in her imagination as she weaves a story during her visits with him and other patients confined to iron lung machines.

This is "compelling. . . . This effectively shows how children face life-changing challenges with incredible determination." Booklist

The **seance**. Delacorte Press 2008 262p il $15.99; lib bdg $18.99; pa $6.99

Grades: 4 5 6 7   **Fic**
1. Mystery fiction 2. Magicians -- Fiction 3. Spiritualism -- Fiction
ISBN 978-0-385-73375-5; 0-385-73375-5; 978-0-385-90392-9 lib bdg; 0-385-90392-8 lib bdg; 978-0-440-23970-3 pa; 0-440-23970-2 pa
            LC 2007-27994

In 1926, magician Harry Houdini arrives in the city to perform magic and to expose fradulent mediums but thirteen-year-old Scooter King, who works for his mother making her seances seem real, needs Houdini's help to solve a murder.

"Mystery lovers will get a kick out of this rollicking whodunit featuring swashbuckling soothsayers, outlandish séances, magic tricks and more." Publ Wkly

★ The **wreckers**. Delacorte Press 1998 196p hardcover o.p. pa $5.99

Grades: 5 6 7 8   **Fic**
    1. Adventure fiction   2. Survival -- Fiction   3. Shipwrecks -- Fiction
    ISBN 0-385-32535-5; 0-440-41545-4 pa

                                                LC 97-31625
"In 1799 fourteen-year-old John Spencer survives a shipwreck on the coast of Cornwall. To his horror, he soon learns that the villagers are not rescuers, but pirates who lure ships ashore in order to plunder their cargoes. . . . Lawrence creates an edge-of-the-chair survival/mystery story. Fast-moving, mesmerizing." Horn Book Guide

    Other titles in this series are:
    The smugglers (1999)
    The buccaneers (2001)

Le Guin, Ursula K.

Gifts. Harcourt 2004 274p $17; pa $7.95

Grades: 7 8 9 10   **Fic**
    1. Fantasy fiction
    ISBN 9780152051235; 0-15-205123-6; 0-15-205124-4 pa

                                                LC 2003-21449
"Brantors, or chiefs, of the various clans of the Uplands have powers passed down through generations, powers to call animals to the hunt, start fires, cast a wasting disease, or undo the very essence of a life or thing. The clans live isolated from the inhabitants of the Lowland cities in an uneasy truce, where each people's ambitions are kept at bay by fear of the other's vengeance. Two Upland teenagers, Gry and Orrec, have grown from childhood friendship into romance and also into a repudiation of their hereditary powers. . . . Rejecting traditions that bind them to roles unwanted and undesired, Gry and Orrec decide to leave their homes and seek a freer if less privileged life in the Lowlands." (Bull Cent Child Books)

"Although intriguing as a coming-of-age allegory, Orrec's story is also rich in . . . earthy magic and intelligent plot twists." Booklist

Powers. Harcourt 2007 502p map $17; pa $7.99

Grades: 7 8 9 10   **Fic**
    1. Fantasy fiction
    ISBN 978-0-15-205770-1; 0-15-205770-6; 978-0-15-206674-1 pa; 0-15-206674-8 pa

                                                LC 2006-13549
When young Gavir's sister is brutally killed, he escapes from slavery and sets out to explore the world and his own psychic abilities.

"Le Guin uses her own prodigious power as a writer to craft lyrical, precise sentences, evoking a palpable sense of place and believable characters." SLJ

Voices. Harcourt 2006 341p $17

Grades: 7 8 9 10   **Fic**
    1. Fantasy fiction
    ISBN 978-015-205678-0; 0-15-205678-5

                                                LC 2005020753
Young Memer takes on a pivotal role in freeing her war-torn homeland from its oppressive captors.

"While her prose is simple and unadorned, Le Guin's superior narrative voice and storytelling power make even small moments ring with truth, and often with beauty." SLJ

The **farthest** shore. Pocket Books 2004 259p $15

Grades: 6 7 8 9   **Fic**
    1. Fantasy fiction
    ISBN 978-1-416-50964-6; 1-416-50964-X
    First published 1972 by Atheneum Pubs.

This book continues "the story of Ged and introduces a new hero, Arren, the young prince who travels with the Archmage Ged on his last perilous mission. The writing has, as the concept has, a majestic intricacy; to appreciate it the reader must enjoy ornate language, the grave discussion of life and death and love, and courage, and the tongue-rolling exotic names of a legendary land." Bull Cent Child Books

★ A **wizard** of Earthsea; [by] Ursula K. Le Guin; illustrated by Ruth Robbins. Bantam trade pbk. ed.; Bantam Books 2004 182p il pa $15

Grades: 6 7 8 9   **Fic**
    1. Fantasy fiction 2. Science fiction 3. Magic -- Fiction
    ISBN 0-553-38304-3; 978-0-553-38304-1

                                                LC 2004558962
A reissue of the title first published 1968 by Parnassus Press

    ALA YALSA Margaret A. Edwards Award (2004)
A "powerful fantasy-allegory. Though set as prose, the rhythms of the langauge are truly and consistently poetical." Read Ladders for Hum Relat. 5th edition

    Other titles in this series are:
    The Tombs of Atuan (1971)
    The farthest shore (1972)
    Tehanu (1990)

LeZotte, Ann Clare

T4; a novel in verse. written by Ann Clare LeZotte. Houghton Mifflin Co. 2008 108p $14

Grades: 6 7 8 9 10   **Fic**
    1. Novels in verse 2. Deaf -- Fiction 3. Euthanasia -- Fiction
    ISBN 978-0-547-04684-6; 0-547-04684-7

                                                LC 2007-47737
When the Nazi party takes control of Germany, thirteen-year-old Paula, who is deaf, finds her world-as-she-knows-it turned upside down, as she is taken into hiding to protect her from the new law nicknamed T4.

"This novel will have a lasting effect on readers, giving insight into an often-forgotten aspect of the horrors of the Third Reich." SLJ

Leal, Ann Haywood

Also known as Harper. Henry Holt 2009 246p $16.95

Grades: 4 5 6 7 **Fic**

1. Poets -- Fiction 2. Siblings -- Fiction 3. Handicapped -- Fiction 4. Single parent family -- Fiction

ISBN 978-0-8050-8881-6; 0-8050-8881-4

LC 2008-36940

Writing poetry helps fifth-grader Harper Lee Morgan cope with her father's absence, being evicted, and having to skip school to care for her brother while their mother works, and things look even brighter after she befriends a mute girl and a kindly disabled woman.

"The characters are memorable as are the descriptive passages. . . . Most touching are Harper's pithy poems that expose the raw emotions of a bright but disadvantaged girl. This book is rich with discussion opportunity for middle school students." Voice Youth Advocates

A **finders**-keepers place. Henry Holt 2010 259p $16.99

Grades: 5 6 7 **Fic**

1. School stories 2. Sisters -- Fiction 3. Mental illness -- Fiction 4. Missing persons -- Fiction 5. Single parent family -- Fiction 6. Manic-depressive illness -- Fiction

ISBN 978-0-8050-8882-3; 0-8050-8882-2

LC 2009-50771

As their mother's manic-depression grows worse, eleven-year-old Esther and her sister Ruth visit various churches hoping to find their father, a preacher named Ezekiel who left them seven years before in 1966.

"Leal excels in pithy characterization, mainly through spot-on dialogue, yielding sympathetic characters, a gripping plot, and no shortage of heartbreaking moments." Publ Wkly

Lean, Sarah

★ A **dog** called Homeless; Sarah Lean. Katherine Tegen Books 2012 202 p. (trade bdg) $16.99

Grades: 3 4 5 6 7 **Fic**

1. Dogs -- Fiction 2. Blind -- Fiction 3. Grief -- Fiction 4. Hearing impaired -- Fiction 5. Selective mutism -- Fiction 6. Single-parent families -- Fiction 7. People with disabilities -- Fiction

ISBN 0062122207; 9780062122209

LC 2011044628

Schneider Family Book Award (2013)

In this book by Sarah Lean, "a girl grieving for her dead mother gives up talking when she becomes convinced that what she says doesn't matter. . . . Cally begins to see her mother . . . dressed in a red raincoat and sometimes accompanied by a very large dog. . . . Cally also meets Mrs. Cooper, a neighbor in their new apartment building who lovingly cares for her blind, nearly deaf 11-year-old son, Sam." (Kirkus Reviews)

Leavitt, Lindsey

Going vintage; by Lindsey Leavitt. 1st U.S. ed. Bloomsbury 2013 320 p. (hardcover) $16.99

Grades: 7 8 9 10 **Fic**

1. School stories 2. Sisters -- Fiction 3. Dating (Social customs) -- Fiction 4. Lists -- Fiction 5. Schools --

Fiction 6. High schools -- Fiction 7. Family life -- California -- Fiction

ISBN 1599907879; 9781599907871

LC 2012023269

In this book, "after discovering her boyfriend has a serious online relationship with another girl, Mallory very publicly dumps him on his social media site. She complicates the situation by deciding to try to fulfill a to-do list her grandmother crafted at the beginning of her junior year of high school in 1962, a time Mallory thinks must have been much simpler than today. . . . She's aided by her loyal younger sister, Ginnie, and the growing affection of her ex's cousin, charming Oliver." (Kirkus)

Sean Griswold's head. Bloomsbury 2011 276p $16.99

Grades: 7 8 9 10 **Fic**

1. School stories 2. Family life -- Fiction 3. Multiple sclerosis -- Fiction

ISBN 978-1-59990-498-6; 1-59990-498-5

LC 2010-06949

"Leavitt capably handles the issues of chronic illness with sensitivity, making this an insightful, humorous, and ultimately uplifting family drama." Bull Cent Child Books

Leavitt, Martine

My book of life by Angel; Martine Leavitt. Farrar, Straus and Giroux Books for Young Readers 2012 252 p. $17.99; (hardback) $17.99; (ebook) $12.95

Grades: 8 9 10 11 **Fic**

1. Novels in verse 2. Runaway teenagers -- Fiction 3. Juvenile prostitution -- Fiction 4. Runaways -- Fiction 5. Drug abuse -- Fiction 6. Prostitution -- Fiction

ISBN 0374351236; 9780374351236; 9781554983179

LC 2011044563

This "novel in verse tells the story of 16-year-old Angel, who has been working as a prostitute in Vancouver. . . . After Angel's friend Serena disappears, Angel decides to give up" the drugs her pimp Call feeds her "and try to return home. Angel's withdrawal is severe . . . but it's nothing compared to the pain she feels when Call brings home an 11-year-old girl, Melli, to follow in Angel's footsteps. Angel is determined to keep Melli safe, even while other women continue to disappear." (Publishers Weekly)

Lecesne, James

★ **Absolute** brightness. HarperTeen 2008 472p $17.99; lib bdg $18.89

Grades: 7 8 9 10 **Fic**

1. Cousins -- Fiction 2. Good and evil -- Fiction 3. Homosexuality -- Fiction

ISBN 978-0-06-125627-1; 0-06-125627-7; 978-0-06-125628-8 lib bdg; 0-06-125628-5 lib bdg

LC 2007-02988

ALA YALSA Morris Award Finalist, 2009

In the beach town of Neptune, New Jersey, Phoebe's life is changed irrevocably when her gay cousin moves into her house and soon goes missing.

"This thoughtful novel is beautifully written; its themes are haunting, and in spite of the central tragedy, it's often laugh-out-loud funny." Kliatt

Leck, James

★ The **adventures** of Jack Lime; written by James Leck. Kids Can Press 2010 126p $16.95; pa $8.95

Grades: 5 6 7 8   **Fic**

1. Mystery fiction 2. Narcolepsy -- Fiction
ISBN 978-1-55453-364-0; 1-55453-364-3; 978-1-55453-365-7 pa; 1-55453-365-1 pa

"Jack Lime is the guy you come to if you've got a problem. . . . He'll find out what needs finding out. . . . This slim volume contains three cases. In the first, Jack susses out the whereabouts of a missing bike. In the second, he shakes down a hamster-napping and blackmail scheme. And in the final, he recounts his first case on the job. . . . All the touchstones that make for great noir are translated for kids. . . . The lingo that makes hard-boiled reading so much fun is here, but never schticky, and Leck knows that a great hero needs a debilitating flaw: for Jack, it's his narcolepsy." Booklist

Lee, Harper

★ To kill a **mockingbird**; Harper Lee. 50th anniversary ed; Harper 2010 323p $25.00

Grades: 8 9 10 11 12 Adult   **Fic**

1. Race relations -- Fiction
ISBN 9780061743528

"Scout, as Jean Louise is called, is a precocious child. She relates her impressions of the time when her lawyer father, Atticus Finch, is defending a black man accused of raping a white woman in a small Alabama town during the 1930's. Atticus's courageous act brings the violence and injustice that exists in their world sharply into focus as it intrudes into the lighthearted life that Scout and her brother Jem have enjoyed until that time." Shapiro. Fic for Youth. 3d edition

Lee, Tanith

Piratica; being a daring tale of a singular girl's adventure upon the high seas. Presented most handsomely by the notorious Tanith Lee. Dutton Children's Books 2004 288p $17.99

Grades: 6 7 8 9   **Fic**

1. Adventure fiction 2. Pirates -- Fiction 3. Sex role -- Fiction
ISBN 0-525-47324-6

First published 2003 in the United Kingdom

A bump on the head restores Art's memories of her mother and the exciting life they led, so the sixteen-year-old leaves Angels Academy for Young Maidens, seeks out the pirates who were her family before her mother's death, and leads them back to adventure on the high seas.

"Piratica is a refreshing, tongue-in-cheek, tangled tale that will entice readers who crave adventure and fantasy." SLJ

Piratica II: return to Parrot Island; being the return of a most intrepid heroine to sea and secrets. Dutton Children's Books 2006 320p $17.99

Grades: 6 7 8 9   **Fic**

1. Adventure fiction 2. Pirates -- Fiction 3. Sex role -- Fiction
ISBN 0-525-47769-1

Art Blastside is bored with life ashore, so she jumps at the chance to return to sea.

"Lee's writing is complex, and she uses her skill to craft subtle pundit humor and lush description." Voice Youth Advocates

Lee, Ying S.

A **spy** in the house. Candlewick Press 2010 335p (The Agency) $16.99

Grades: 8 9 10 11 12   **Fic**

1. Mystery fiction 2. Orphans -- Fiction 3. Household employees -- Fiction 4. Swindlers and swindling -- Fiction
ISBN 978-0-7636-4067-5; 0-7636-4067-0

LC 2009-32736

Rescued from the gallows in 1850s London, young orphan and thief Mary Quinn is offered a place at Miss Scrimshaw's Academy for Girls where she is trained to be part of an all-female investigative unit called The Agency and, at age seventeen, she infiltrates a rich merchant's home in hopes of tracing his missing cargo ships.

"Lee fills the story with classic elements of Victorian mystery and melodrama. Class differences, love gone awry, racial discrimination, London's growing pains in the 1850s, and the status of women in society are all addressed. Historical details are woven seamlessly into the plot, and descriptive writing allows readers to be part of each scene." SLJ

Other titles in this series are:
The body at the tower (2010)
The traitor in the tunnel (2012)

Leeds, Constance

The **unfortunate** son; by Constance Leeds. Viking Childrens Books 2012 302 p. (hardcover) $16.99

Grades: 4 5 6 7   **Fic**

1. Bildungsromans 2. Historical fiction 3. Pirates -- Fiction 4. Kidnapping -- Fiction 5. Luck -- Fiction 6. Fishing -- Fiction 7. Slavery -- Fiction 8. Identity -- Fiction 9. Abnormalities, Human -- Fiction
ISBN 0670013986; 9780670013982

LC 2011027530

This book is the story of Luc, whose "father hates him, seemingly without reason, so" the boy runs away "to apprentice with a local fisherman. . . . Living with the fisherman's family he grows close to their ward, the beautiful Beatrice, and things seem to be looking up . . . until he's kidnapped by pirates and sold to a Tunisian in North Africa. While Luc receives an education from his learned master, Beatrice" attempts to unravel Luc's past. (Kirkus Reviews)

Lennon, Tom

When love comes to town; Tom Lennon. Albert Whitman 2013 304 p. (reinforced) $15.99

Grades: 8 9 10 11 12   **Fic**

1. Historical fiction 2. Gay teenagers -- Fiction 3. Gays -- Fiction 4. Coming out (Sexual orientation) -- Fiction
ISBN 0807589160; 9780807589168

LC 2012020160

In this novel, by Tom Lennon, "the year is 1990, and in his hometown of Dublin, Ireland, Neil Byrne plays rugby, keeps up with the in-crowd at his school, and is just a regular guy. A guy who's gay. It's a secret he keeps from the wider world as he explores the city at night and struggles to figure out how to reveal his real self--and to whom." (Publisher's note)

Leonard, Julia Platt

Cold case. Aladdin 2011 281p $15.99

Grades: 6 7 8 9   **Fic**

1. Mystery fiction 2. Spies -- Fiction 3. Brothers -- Fiction 4. Homicide -- Fiction 5. Family life -- Fiction 6. Restaurants -- Fiction

ISBN 978-1-4424-2009-0; 1-4424-2009-X

LC 2010041854

When thirteen-year-old Oz Keillor finds a dead body in his family's Santa Fe, New Mexico, restaurant, he is determined to solve the mystery in which his older brother is implicated, but which also involves their long-dead father, who was accused of being a spy.

"The well-plotted double mystery is propped up by a few choice details about restaurant life, some sly red herrings, and a cast of nicely rounded characters." Booklist

Les Becquets, Diane

Season of ice. Bloomsbury U.S.A. Children's Books 2008 281p $16.95

Grades: 8 9 10 11 12   **Fic**

1. Lakes -- Fiction 2. Stepfamilies -- Fiction 3. Missing persons -- Fiction 4. Father-daughter relationship -- Fiction

ISBN 978-1-59990-063-6; 1-59990-063-7

LC 2007-30845

When seventeen-year-old Genesis Sommer's father disappears on Moosehead Lake near their small-town Maine home in mid-November, she must cope with the pressure of keeping her family together, even while rumors about the event plague her.

This is "a heartbreaking story from the very beginning, but Les Becquets turns it into something well beyond a mere tearjerker. . . . It's a tender story of a tough, smart, loving girl who finds that she can rise to the challenge of what she's lost because of what she's gained. Readers will understand her and admire her, and find her difficult indeed to forget." Bull Cent Child Books

Lester, Alison

Quicksand pony. Houghton Mifflin 1998 136p $15

Grades: 5 6 7 8   **Fic**

1. Horses -- Fiction 2. Ponies -- Fiction

ISBN 0-395-93749-3

LC 98-6930

First published 1997 in Australia

After her pony Bella, trapped in quicksand, is rescued by a mysterious unseen person, ten-year-old Biddy follows the trail into the Australian bush and discovers the solution to a disappearance that happened years ago

"A multilayered story of survival, love, mystery, and family relationships." SLJ

Lester, Joan Steinau

★ **Black,** white, other. Zondervan 2011 222p $15.99

Grades: 7 8 9 10   **Fic**

1. Divorce -- Fiction 2. Slavery -- Fiction 3. Family life -- Fiction 4. Grandmothers -- Fiction 5. Race relations -- Fiction 6. Racially mixed people -- Fiction

ISBN 978-0-310-72763-7; 0-310-72763-4

LC 2011015208

Twenty miles from Oakland, California, where fires have led to racial tension, multi-racial fifteen-year-old Nina faces the bigotry of long-time friends, her parents' divorce, and her brother's misbehavior, while learning of her great-great grandmother Sarah's escape from slavery.

"Lester . . . conjures a credible plot and complications; divorce is a fact of life and racially mixed heritage is conspicuously becoming one. The simple contrapuntal narrative of Sarah Armstrong's escaping slavery distinguishes the book emotionally and psychologically, raising it above other issue-oriented YA novels. Lester writes with social sensitivity and an ear for teen language and concerns. This is engaging treatment of a challenging subject that comes with little precedent." Publ Wkly

Includes bibliographical references

Lester, Julius

Day of tears; a novel in dialogue. Hyperion 2005 177p hardcover o.p. pa $7.99

Grades: 7 8 9 10   **Fic**

1. Slavery -- Fiction 2. African Americans -- Fiction

ISBN 0-7868-0490-4; 1-42310-409-9 pa

Coretta Scott King Award for text

Emma has taken care of the Butler children since Sarah and Frances's mother, Fanny, left. Emma wants to raise the girls to have good hearts, as a rift over slavery has ripped the Butler household apart. Now, to pay off debts, Pierce Butler wants to cash in his slave "assets", possibly including Emma.

"The horror of the auction and its aftermath is unforgettable. . . . The racism is virulent (there's widespread use of the n-word). The personal voices make this a stirring text for group discussion." Booklist

★ **Guardian.** Amistad/HarperTeen 2008 129p $16.99; lib bdg $17.89

Grades: 7 8 9 10   **Fic**

1. Lynching -- Fiction 2. Race relations -- Fiction 3. African Americans -- Fiction

ISBN 978-0-06-155890-0; 0-06-155890-7; 978-0-06-155891-7 lib bdg; 0-06-155891-5 lib bdg

LC 2008-14251

In a rural southern town in 1946, a white man and his son witness the lynching of an innocent black man. Includes historical note on lynching.

"The author's understated, haunting prose is as compelling as it is dark; . . . [the story] leaves a deep impression." Publ Wkly

Includes bibliographical references

Time's memory. Farrar, Straus & Giroux 2006 230p $17

Grades: 8 9 10 11 12   **Fic**

1. Slavery -- Fiction 2. African Americans -- Fiction

ISBN 0-374-37178-4; 978-0-374-37178-4

LC 2005-47716

Ekundayo, a Dogon spirit brought to America from Africa, inhabits the body of a young African American slave on a Virginia plantation, where he experiences loss, sorrow, and reconciliation in the months preceding the Civil War.

"More than a picture of slavery through the eyes of those enslaved or their captors, Lester's narrative evokes spiritual images of Mali's Dogon people." SLJ

Levine, Gail Carson, 1947-

Ella enchanted. HarperCollins Pubs. 1997 232p $16.99; lib bdg $17.89; pa $6.50

Grades: 5 6 7 8   **Fic**

1. Fairy tales 2. Fantasy fiction
ISBN 0-06-027510-3; 0-06-027511-1 lib bdg; 0-06-440705-5 pa

LC 96-30734

A Newbery Medal honor book, 1998

"Ella is blessed by a fairy at birth with the gift of obedience. But the blessing is a horror for Ella, who must literally do what everyone tells her, from sweeping the floor to giving up a beloved heirloom necklace. After her mother dies, and her covetous, caustic father leaves on a trading trip, Ella's world is turned upside down. She battles both ogres and wicked stepsisters, makes friends and loses them, and must deny her love for her prince, Charmont, to save his life and his realm. In making this ultimate sacrifice, she breaks the curse." (Booklist)

"As finely designed as a tapestry, Ella's story both neatly incorporates elements of the original tale and mightily expands them." Booklist

Ever. HarperCollinsPublishers 2008 256p $16.99; lib bdg $17.89; pa $6.99

Grades: 5 6 7 8   **Fic**

1. Winds -- Fiction 2. Immortality -- Fiction 3. Fate and fatalism -- Fiction 4. Gods and goddesses -- Fiction
ISBN 978-0-06-122962-6; 0-06-122962-8; 978-0-06-122963-3 lib bdg; 0-06-122963-6 lib bdg; 978-0-06-122964-0 pa; 0-06-122964-4 pa

LC 2007-32289

Fourteen-year-old Kezi and Olus, Akkan god of the winds, fall in love and together try to change her fate—to be sacrificed to a Hyte god because of a rash promise her father made—through a series of quests that might make her immortal.

"Levine conducts a riveting journey, offering passion and profound pondering along the way." Publ Wkly

Fairest. HarperCollins 2006 326p $16.99

Grades: 6 7 8 9   **Fic**

1. Fairy tales 2. Singing -- Fiction
ISBN 978-0-06-073408-4; 0-06-073408-6

LC 2006-00337

In a land where beauty and singing are valued above all else, Aza eventually comes to reconcile her unconventional appearance and her magical voice, and learns to accept herself for who she truly is.

"The plot is fast-paced, and Aza's growth and maturity are well crafted and believable." SLJ

★ A **tale** of Two Castles. Harper 2011 328p $16.99; lib bdg $17.89

Grades: 4 5 6   **Fic**

1. Fantasy fiction 2. Mystery fiction 3. Dragons -- Fiction 4. Apprentices -- Fiction 5. Kings and rulers -- Fiction
ISBN 978-0-06-122965-7; 0-06-122965-2; 978-0-06-122966-4 lib bdg; 0-06-122966-0 lib bdg

LC 2010027756

"Hoping to apprentice as an actor, Elodie travels from her rural home to the city of Two Castles. . . . When she's robbed and then rejected as an actor, she apprentices herself to crafty dragon Meenore as a detective. Shape-shifting Count Jonty Um, a kindly ogre, is their first client. . . . But who is to be trusted and who isn't? . . . Intermediate, middle school." (Horn Book)

"Readers are certain to be pulled, like Elodie herself, right into the midst of the rich and swirling life of Two Castles." SLJ

Levine, Kristin

★ The **best** bad luck I ever had. Putnam 2009 266p $16.99

Grades: 5 6 7 8   **Fic**

1. Friendship -- Fiction 2. Prejudices -- Fiction 3. Family life -- Fiction 4. Country life -- Fiction 5. Race relations -- Fiction
ISBN 978-0-399-25090-3; 0-399-25090-5

LC 2008-11570

In Moundville, Alabama, in 1917, twelve-year-old Dit hopes the new postmaster will have a son his age, but instead he meets Emma, who is black, and their friendship challenges accepted ways of thinking and leads them to save the life of a condemned man.

"Tension builds just below the surface of this energetic, seamlessly narrated . . . novel. . . . Levine handles the setting with grace and nuance." Publ Wkly

★ The **lions** of Little Rock; Kristin Levine. G. P. Putnam's Sons 2012 298p.

Grades: 5 6 7 8   **Fic**

1. School stories 2. African Americans -- Fiction 3. School integration -- Fiction 4. Schools -- Fiction 5. Friendship -- Fiction 6. Bashfulness -- Fiction 7. Middle schools -- Fiction 8. Race relations -- Fiction 9. Family life -- Arkansas -- Fiction
ISBN 9780399256448

LC 2011031835

This book presents a "portrait of 1958 Little Rock, Ark., the tumultuous year when the governor refused integration by closing local high schools. The story is told through the . . . voice of painfully quiet 12-year-old Marlee Nisbett, who makes a rare friend in Liz, a new student at her middle school. Liz instills some much-needed confidence in Marlee, but when it's revealed that Liz is 'passing' as a white student, Liz must leave school abruptly, putting their friendship to the test. The girls meet in secret, and Marlee joins an antisegregationist organization, both actions inviting serious risk amid escalating racist threats." (Publishers Weekly)

Levitin, Sonia

★ **Strange** relations. Alfred A. Knopf 2007 298p hardcover o.p. pa $6.50

Grades: 7 8 9 10 **Fic**

1. Jews -- Fiction 2. Cousins -- Fiction 3. Religion -- Fiction

ISBN 978-0-375-83751-7; 0-375-83751-5; 978-0-440-23963-5 pa; 0-440-23963-X pa

LC 2006-33275

Fifteen-year-old Marne is excited to be able to spend her summer vacation in Hawaii, not realizing the change in her lifestyle it would bring staying with her aunt, seven cousins, and uncle who is a Chasidic rabbi.

"It's rare to find such well-developed characters, empathetic and sensitive religious treatment, and carefully crafted plotlines in one novel." SLJ

Lewis, C. S.

★ The **lion,** the witch, and the wardrobe; illustrated by Pauline Baynes. HarperCollins Pubs. 1994 189p il (The chronicles of Narnia) $17.99; lib bdg $18.89; pa $7.99

Grades: 4 5 6 7 **Fic**

1. Fantasy fiction

ISBN 0-06-023481-4; 0-06-023482-2 lib bdg; 0-06-440499-4 pa

LC 93-8889

A reissue of the title first published 1950 by Macmillan

Four English schoolchildren find their way through the back of a wardrobe into the magic land of Narnia and assist Aslan, the golden lion, to triumph over the White Witch, who has cursed the land with eternal winter

This begins "the 'Narnia' stories, outstanding modern fairy tales with an underlying theme of good overcoming evil." Child Books Too Good to Miss

Other titles in this series are:

Prince Caspian (1951)

The voyage of the Dawn Treader (1952)

The silver chair (1953)

The horse and his boy (1954)

The magician's nephew (1956)

The last battle (1956)

Lewis, Gill

One white dolphin; Gill Lewis ; illustrated by Raquel Aparicio. Atheneum Books for Young Readers 2012 p. cm. (hardback) $15.99

Grades: 5 6 7 **Fic**

1. Ecology -- Fiction 2. Dolphins -- Fiction 3. Seashore -- Fiction 4. Marine ecology -- Fiction 5. Wildlife rescue -- Fiction 6. Environmental protection -- Fiction

ISBN 9781442414471; 9781442414501

LC 2012009182

In this book, "a boy with cerebral palsy and an injured albino dolphin calf help Kara Wood come to terms with her mother's death and the sale of the family's boat, Moana. Kara's mother vanished a year ago on a dolphin-saving trip to the South Pacific. With debts mounting, her father plans to sell the sailboat they built. . . . The temporary protection of the reef near their British coastal home is about to expire." (Kirkus Reviews)

★ **Wild** wings; illustrated by Yuta Onoda. Atheneum Books for Young Readers 2011 287p il $15.99

Grades: 4 5 6 7 **Fic**

1. Ospreys -- Fiction 2. Farm life -- Fiction 3. Friendship -- Fiction

ISBN 1-4424-1445-6; 978-1-4424-1445-7

LC 2010-49228

Callum becomes friends with Iona, a practically feral classmate who has discovered an osprey, thought to be gone from Scotland, on Callum's family farm, and they eventually share the secret with others, including Jeneba who encounters the same bird at her home in Gambia.

This is a "rich, moving tale. . . . The suspenseful story line is surrounded with precise details. . . . Short chapters, some with cliffhanging endings, will read-aloud well. . . . A powerfully memorable story." Kirkus

Lieberman, Leanne

Lauren Yanofsky hates the holocaust; Leanne Lieberman. Orca Book Publishers 2013 240 p. (paperback) $12.95; (ebook) $12.99

Grades: 7 8 9 10 **Fic**

1. Jews -- Fiction 2. Holocaust, 1933-1945 -- Fiction

ISBN 1459801091; 9781459801097; 9781459801103 pdf; 9781459801110

LC 2012952950

In this novel, by Leanne Lieberman, "Lauren Yanofsky doesn't want to be Jewish anymore. Her father, a noted Holocaust historian, keeps giving her Holocaust memoirs to read, and her mother doesn't understand why Lauren hates the idea of Jewish youth camps and family vacations to Holocaust memorials. But when Lauren sees some of her friends . . . playing Nazi war games, she is faced with a terrible choice: betray her friends or betray her heritage." (Publisher's note)

"Lieberman . . . smoothly weaves humor and knowledge about Judaism through Lauren"s story. Lauren"s narration is contemplative and from the heart, and readers should relate to her attempts to identify her beliefs and tackle life"s big questions." Pub Wkly

Lieurance, Suzanne

The **locket**; surviving the Triangle Shirtwaist fire. [by] Suzanne Lieurance. Enslow Publishers 2008 160p il (Historical fiction adventures) lib bdg $27.93

Grades: 4 5 6 7 **Fic**

1. Sisters -- Fiction 2. Factories -- Fiction 3. Immigrants -- Fiction 4. Jews -- United States -- Fiction

ISBN 978-0-7660-2928-6 lib bdg; 0-7660-2928-X lib bdg

LC 2007-5281

After Galena, an eleven-year-old Russian immigrant, survives a terrible fire at the non-unionized Triangle Shirtwaist factory while her older sister and many others do not, she begins fighting for improved working conditions in New York City factories.

"Woven together in perfect compatibility, the historical background and fictional plot give readers a clear insight into Jewish immigrants and . . . unfair labor practices, and there is excellent foreshadowing of the fire." SLJ

Includes bibliographical references

Lin, Grace

★ **Starry** River of the Sky; by Grace Lin. Little, Brown 2012 288 p. col. ill. $17.99

Grades: 3 4 5 6   **Fic**

1. Fairy tales 2. Moon -- Fiction 3. Villages -- Fiction 4. Storytelling -- Fiction

ISBN 0316125954; 9780316125956

LC 2012012651

In this novel by Grace Lin, "the moon is missing from the remote Village of Clear Sky, but only a young boy named Rendi seems to notice! Rendi has run away from home and is now working as a chore boy at the village inn. He can't help but notice the village's peculiar inhabitants and their problems . . . but one day, a mysterious lady arrives at the Inn with the gift of storytelling, and slowly transforms the villagers and Rendi himself." (Publisher's note)

Includes bibliographical references.

★ **Where** the mountain meets the moon. Little, Brown and Co. 2009 278p il $16.99

Grades: 4 5 6 7   **Fic**

1. Fairy tales 2. Dragons -- Fiction

ISBN 978-0-316-11427-1; 0-316-11427-8

LC 2008-32818

A Newbery Medal honor book, 2010

Minli, an adventurous girl from a poor village, buys a magical goldfish, and then joins a dragon who cannot fly on a quest to find the Old Man of the Moon in hopes of bringing life to Fruitless Mountain and freshness to Jade River

"With beautiful language, Lin creates a strong, memorable heroine and a mystical land. . . . Children will embrace this accessible, timeless story about the evil of greed and the joy of gratitude." Booklist

Lipsyte, Robert

★ **One** fat summer. Harper & Row 1977 152p hardcover o.p. pa $5.99

Grades: 7 8 9 10   **Fic**

1. Obesity -- Fiction 2. Weight loss -- Fiction

ISBN 0-06-023895-X; 0-06-447073-3 pa

LC 76-49746

ALA YALSA Margaret A. Edwards Award (2001)

"This is far superior to most of the summer-of-change stories; any change that takes place is logical and the protagonist learns by action and reaction to be both self-reliant and compassionate." Bull Cent Child Books

★ The **contender**. Harper & Row 1967 182p hardcover o.p. pa $5.99

Grades: 7 8 9 10   **Fic**

1. Boxing -- Fiction 2. African Americans -- Fiction

ISBN 0-06-447039-3

ALA YALSA Margaret A. Edwards Award (2001)

"After a street fight in which he is the chief target, Alfred wanders into a gym in his neighborhood. He decides not only to improve his physical condition but also to become a boxer. Because of this interest Alfred's life is completely changed. He assumes a more positive outlook on his im-

mediate future, even within the confines of a black ghetto." Shapiro. Fic for Youth. 3d edition

The **twinning** project; by Robert Lipsyte. Clarion Books 2012 269 p. (hardback) $16.99

Grades: 4 5 6 7   **Fic**

1. Science fiction 2. Twins -- Fiction 3. Parallel universes -- Fiction 4. Schools -- Fiction 5. Middle schools -- Fiction 6. Space and time -- Fiction

ISBN 0547645716; 9780547645711

LC 2011050252

This book by Robert Lipsyte follows protagonist Tom, who has been "expelled from school after school for fighting bullies. . . . The boy's only comfort comes from talking through his problems with his imaginary twin, Eddie, a jock who lives on a version of Earth 50 years behind Tom's. . . . When the boys' 'grandfather' on both Earths reveals that the twin planets were created by alien scientists, the boys switch places to fight for the survival of both Earths." (Publishers Weekly)

Lisle, Holly

★ The **Ruby** Key. Orchard Books 2008 361p (Moon & sun) $16.99; pa $7.99

Grades: 5 6 7 8   **Fic**

1. Fantasy fiction 2. Siblings -- Fiction

ISBN 978-0-545-00012-3; 0-545-00012-2; 978-0-545-00013-0 pa; 0-545-00013-0 pa

LC 2007-30217

In a world where an uneasy peace binds Humans and Nightlings, fourteen-year-old Genna and her twelve-year-old brother Dan learn of their uncle's plot to gain immortality in exchange for human lives, and the two strike their own bargain with the Nightling lord, which sets them on a dangerous journey along the Moonroads in search of a key.

"Lisle's fertile imagination provides the nightworlds with monsters . . . but it is her clever plotting in this . . . fantasy, leading up to a thrilling finish . . . That will bewitch her audience." Horn Book

The **silver** door. Orchard Books 2009 366p (Moon & sun) $17.99

Grades: 5 6 7 8   **Fic**

1. War stories 2. Fantasy fiction

ISBN 978-0-545-00014-7; 0-545-00014-9

LC 2008-40153

When Genna is chosen as the Sunrider of prophecy, her destiny is to unite the magic of the sun and the moon for the good of both Nightlings and humans.

"This second book of the Moon & Sun series has jarring stop-start feel, but the complexities of the interlaced human and nightling societies continue to unfold in fascinating way, creating a multi-hued, fully realized world for readers to explore." Horn Book

Littke, Lael

Lake of secrets. Holt & Co. 2002 202p $16.95

Grades: 7 8 9 10   **Fic**

1. Mystery fiction 2. Reincarnation -- Fiction 3. Mystery and detective stories

ISBN 0-8050-6730-2

LC 2001-39933

Having arrived in her mother's home town to try to find her long-missing brother, who disappeared three years before she was born, fifteen-year-old Carlene finds herself haunted by memories from a past life

"The realistic characters and plot make the idea compelling, and the story will intrigue teens." Booklist

Little, Kimberley Griffiths

★ **Circle** of secrets. Scholastic Press 2011 326p $17.99

Grades: 5 6 7 8 **Fic**

1. Ghost stories 2. Guilt -- Fiction 3. Mother-daughter relationship -- Fiction

ISBN 978-0-545-16561-7; 0-545-16561-X

LC 2011000889

A year after her mother has deserted the family, eleven-year-old Shelby goes to stay with her, deep in the Louisiana bayou, where they both confront old hurts and regrets.

"The gently spooky ghost angle is handled nicely with some religious overtones. A very dramatic climax leads to a sweet, satisfying ending with some surprising twists and with reconciliation occurring for several characters." Kirkus

The **healing** spell. Scholastic Press 2010 354p $17.99

Grades: 5 6 7 8 **Fic**

1. Coma -- Fiction 2. Guilt -- Fiction

ISBN 978-0-545-16559-4; 0-545-16559-8

LC 2009-28016

Twelve-year-old Livie is living with a secret and it's crushing her. She knows she is responsible for her mother's coma, but she can't tell anyone. It's up to her to find a way to wake her momma up.

"Little explores the extremes of childhood guilt and its consequences in this harsh yet well-crafted story about fully drawn people. The bayou, with its rich culture, is an atmospheric character that overlays the story with mystery and dread." Booklist

Littman, Sarah

Life, after; [by] Sarah Darer Littman. Scholastic Press 2010 281p $17.99

Grades: 7 8 9 10 11 12 **Fic**

1. Terrorism -- Fiction 2. Immigrants -- Fiction

ISBN 978-0-545-15144-3; 0-545-15144-9

After a terrorist attack kills Dani's aunt and unborn cousin, life in Argentina—private school, a boyfriend, a loving family—crumbles quickly. In order to escape a country that is sinking under their feet, Dani and her family move to the United States.

The author "weaves sensitively articulated themes . . . and credible teen banter into an emotionally complex tale." Booklist

Llewellyn, Sam

Darksolstice. Orchard Books 2010 365p map (Lyonesse) $17.99

Grades: 5 6 7 8 **Fic**

1. Fantasy fiction 2. Kings

ISBN 978-0-439-93471-8; 0-439-93471-0

LC 2009006283

While Idris Limpet, Rightful King of the Land of Lyonesse, is making the treacherous journey to the distant land of Aegypt to rescue his dear friend and sister, Morgan, he meets a company of friends who shall become his Knights of the Round Table and lead armies to battle the evil regent, Fisheagle.

The **well** between the worlds. Orchard Books 2009 339p (Lyonesse) $17.99

Grades: 5 6 7 8 **Fic**

1. Fantasy fiction 2. Kings

ISBN 978-0-439-93469-5; 0-439-93469-9

LC 2008-20075

Eleven-year-old Idris Limpet, living with his family in the once noble but now evil and corrupt island country of Lyonesse, finds his life taking a dramatic turn when, after a near-drowning incident, he is accused of being allied to the feared sea monsters and is rescued from a death sentence by a mysterious and fearsome stranger.

"Seldom does one find a new fantasy that is so richly textured, so original in concept, and with such a wonderfully interesting story. . . . Fantasy lovers will be impatient to find out where their paths take them." Voice Youth Advocates

Lloyd, Alison

Year of the tiger. Holiday House 2010 194p $16.95

Grades: 5 6 7 8 **Fic**

1. Adventure fiction 2. Archery -- Fiction 3. Social classes -- Fiction

ISBN 978-0-8234-2277-7; 0-8234-2277-1

LC 2009033651

First published 2008 in Australia

In ancient China, Hu and Ren forge an unlikely alliance in an effort to become expert archers and, ultimately, to save their city from invading barbarians.

"Brimming with details of daily life in the Han Dynasty, this fast-paced story alternates in the third person between Hu and Ren." Kirkus

Lloyd, Saci

★ The **carbon** diaries 2015. Holiday House 2009 330p il map $17.95

Grades: 8 9 10 11 12 **Fic**

1. Science fiction 2. Family life -- Fiction 3. Conservation of natural resources -- Fiction

ISBN 978-0-8234-2190-9; 0-8234-2190-2

LC 2008-19712

First published 2008 in the United Kingdom

In 2015, when England becomes the first nation to introduce carbon dioxide rationing in a drastic bid to combat climate change, sixteen-year-old Laura documents the first year of rationing as her family spirals out of control.

"Deeply compulsive and urgently compulsory reading." Booklist

Includes bibliographical references

The **carbon** diaries 2017. Holiday House 2010 326p il map $17.95

Grades: 8 9 10 11 12 **Fic**

1. Science fiction 2. College students -- Fiction 3.

Conservation of natural resources -- Fiction
ISBN 978-0-8234-2260-9; 0-8234-2260-7
First published 2009 in the United Kingdom
Two years after England introduces carbon dioxide rationing to combat climatic change, eighteen-year-old Laura chronicles her first year at a London university as natural disasters and political upheaval disrupt her studies.
"The friction of living life in times of radical upheaval remains potent, sobering, and awfully exciting." Booklist

Lockhart, E.
★ **Dramarama**. Hyperion 2007 311p $15.99
Grades: 7 8 9 10 11 12   **Fic**
1. School stories 2. Actors -- Fiction 3. Friendship -- Fiction
ISBN 0-7868-3815-9; 978-0-7868-3815-8
LC 2006-49599
Spending their summer at Wildewood Academy, an elite boarding school for the performing arts, tests the bond between best friends Sadye and Demi.
"Teens will identify strongly with both the heartbreak and the humor in this authentic portrayal of friendships maturing and decaying." SLJ

★ The **disreputable** history of Frankie Landau-Banks. Hyperion 2008 352p $16.99; pa $8.99
Grades: 7 8 9 10 11 12   **Fic**
1. School stories
ISBN 0-7868-3818-3; 0-7868-3819-1 pa; 978-0-7868-3818-9; 978-0-7868-3819-6 pa
Michael L. Printz Award honor book, 2009
"Frankie Landau-Banks at age 14: Debate Club. Her father's 'bunny rabbit.' A mildly geeky girl attending a highly competitive boarding school. Frankie Landau-Banks at age 15: A knockout figure. A sharp tongue. A chip on her shoulder. And a gorgeous new senior boyfriend: . . . Matthew Livingston. Frankie Landau-Banks. No longer the kind of girl to take 'no' for an answer. Especially when 'no' means she's excluded from her boyfriend's all-male secret society. . . . Not when she knows she's smarter than any of them. When she knows Matthew's lying to her. . . . Frankie Banks at age 16: Possibly a criminal mastermind. This is the story of how she got that way." (Publisher's note)
"On her return to Alabaster Prep . . . [Frankie] attracts the attention of gorgeous Matthew . . . [who] is a member of the Loyal Order of the Basset Hounds, an all-male Alabaster secret society. . . . Frankie engineers her own guerilla membership by assuming a false online identity. . . . Lockhart creates a unique, indelible character. . . . Teens will be galvanized." Booklist

Loizeaux, William
★ **Clarence** Cochran, a human boy; pictures by Anne Wilsdorf. Farrar, Straus and Giroux 2009 152p il $16
Grades: 4 5 6   **Fic**
1. Toleration -- Fiction 2. Cockroaches -- Fiction 3. Environmental protection -- Fiction
ISBN 978-0-374-31323-4; 0-374-31323-7
LC 2007-35358
With the threat of extermination looming, a cockroach who has been transformed into a tiny human learns to communicate with his human hosts, leading to an agreement both sides can live with, and a friendship between Clarence and ten-year-old Mimi, a human environmentalist.
"There's a serious message here about environmentalism and the power of words, and the action and suspense make this a good read-aloud or classroom-discussion choice." SLJ

London, Jack
White Fang; Jack London. Scholastic 2001 252p. hardcover o.p. rpt $5.99
Grades: 7 8 9 10 11 12 Adult   **Fic**
1. Dogs -- Fiction
ISBN 9780439236195 rpt
LC 98-19241
First published 1906
White Fang "is about a dog, a cross-breed, sold to Beauty Smith. This owner tortures the dog to increase his ferocity and value as a fighter. A new owner Weedom Scott, brings the dog to California, and, by kind treatment, domesticates him. White Fang later sacrifices his life to save Scott." Haydn. Thesaurus of Book Dig

★ The **call** of the wild; pictures by Wendell Minor. Atheneum Books for Young Readers 1999 112p il $24; pa $4.95
Grades: 5 6 7 8 9 10 11 12 Adult   **Fic**
1. Dogs -- Fiction
ISBN 0-689-81836-X; 1-4165-0019-7 pa
LC 97-45019
First published 1903 by Macmillan
"Buck, half-St. Bernard, half-Scottish sheepdog, is stolen from his comfortable home in California and pressed into service as a sledge dog in the Klondike. At first he is abused by both man and dog, but he learns to fight ruthlessly. He becomes lead dog on a sledge team, after bettering Spitz, the vicious old leader, in a brutal fight to the death. In John Thornton, he finally finds a master whom he can respect and love. When Thornton is killed by Indians, Buck breaks away to the wilds and becomes the leader of a wolf pack, returning each year to the site of Thornton's death." Reader's Ency. 4th edition

Long, Ruth Frances
The **treachery** of beautiful things; by Ruth Frances Long. Dial Books 2012 363 p. (hardcover) $17.99
Grades: 7 8 9 10 11 12   **Fic**
1. Fantasy fiction 2. Fairies -- Fiction 3. Forests and forestry -- Fiction 4. Love -- Fiction 5. Kings, queens, rulers, etc. -- Fiction
ISBN 0803735804; 9780803735804
LC 2011027165
In this book by Ruth Long, "the trees swallowed her brother whole, and Jenny was there to see it. Now seventeen, she revisits the woods where Tom was taken. . . . She's lured into the trees, where she finds strange and dangerous creatures. . . . Among them is Jack, mercurial and magnetic, with secrets of his own. Determined to find her brother, with or without Jack's help, Jenny struggles to navigate a faerie world where stunning beauty masks some of the most treacherous evils." (Publisher's note)

Lopez, Diana

Ask my mood ring how I feel; by Diana Lopez. 1st ed. Little, Brown and Co. 2013 324 p. (hardcover) $17

Grades: 4 5 6 7   **Fic**
   1. Cancer -- Fiction 2. Promises -- Fiction 3. Friendship -- Fiction 4. Fund-raising -- Fiction 5. Christian life -- Fiction 6. Hispanic Americans -- Fiction 7. Family life -- Texas -- Fiction
   ISBN 0316209961; 9780316209960
                                                        LC 2012029856
In this book, Chia's "mother is diagnosed with breast cancer, which spurs . . . changes throughout their family. . . . After visiting the Basilica of Our Lady of San Juan del Valle in southern Texas, Chia dedicates herself to a promesa, vowing to secure 500 sponsors for a Walk for the Cure in exchange (she hopes) for her mother's recovery." (Publishers Weekly)

Confetti girl. Little, Brown and Company 2009 198p $15.99

Grades: 4 5 6 7   **Fic**
   1. School stories 2. Friendship -- Fiction 3. Bereavement -- Fiction 4. Mexican Americans -- Fiction 5. Father-daughter relationship -- Fiction
   ISBN 978-0-316-02955-1; 0-316-02955-6
                                                        LC 2008032819
After the death of her mother, Texas sixth-grader Lina's grades and mood drop as she watches her father lose himself more and more in books, while her best friend uses Lina as an excuse to secretly meet her boyfriend.
"Lopez effectively portrays the Texas setting and the characters' Latino heritage. . . . This . . . novel puts at its center a likable girl facing realistic problems on her own terms." Booklist

Lord, Cynthia

★ **Rules**; [by] Cynthia Lord. Scholastic Press 2006 200p $15.99; pa $6.99

Grades: 4 5 6 7   **Fic**
   1. Autism -- Fiction 2. Siblings -- Fiction 3. Handicapped -- Fiction
   ISBN 0-439-44382-2; 0-439-44383-0 pa
                                                        LC 2005017519
A Newbery Medal honor book, 2007
Frustrated at life with an autistic brother, twelve-year-old Catherine longs for a normal existence but her world is further complicated by a friendship with an young paraplegic
"The details of autistic behavior are handled well, as are depictions of relationships. . . . A heartwarming first novel." Booklist

★ **Touch** blue. Scholastic Press 2010 186p $16.99

Grades: 4 5 6 7   **Fic**
   1. Islands -- Fiction 2. Foster home care -- Fiction
   ISBN 978-0-545-03531-6; 0-545-03531-7
                                                        LC 2009042306
When the state of Maine threatens to shut down their island's one-room schoolhouse because of dwindling enrollment, eleven-year-old Tess, a strong believer in luck, and her

family take in a trumpet-playing foster child named Aaron to increase the school's population.
"Aaron's relationship with his foster family . . . develops believably. The tight-knit community and lobster-catching details make for a warm, colorful environment. This is a feel-good story." Booklist

Lottridge, Celia Barker

The **listening** tree. Fitzhenry & Whiteside 2011 172p $11.95

Grades: 4 5 6 7   **Fic**
   1. Courage -- Fiction 2. Great Depression, 1929-1939 -- Fiction
   ISBN 978-1-55455-052-4; 1-55455-052-1
It's 1935, and Ellen and her mother must leave their dried-up Saskatchewan farm to board with Aunt Gladys in Toronto. Intimidated by her new surroundings, Ellen chooses to hide in the branches of the large leafy tree outside her window and watch the neighbourhood children playing, rather than joining in their games. But when Ellen overhears a plan to evict the family-next-door from their home, she must overcome her fears and help her neighbours.
"Lottridge provides a wealth of well-developed, believable characters, especially Ellen. The story is a deftly-written, heartbreaking, and heartwarming tale of friendship and the perseverance to withstand hardships. This is a great book to introduce young readers to the impact of the Great Depression." Voice Youth Advocates

Love, D. Anne

Defying the diva; [by] D. Anne Love. Margaret K. McElderry Books 2008 257p $16.99

Grades: 7 8 9 10   **Fic**
   1. School stories 2. Bullies -- Fiction
   ISBN 978-1-4169-3481-3; 1-4169-3481-2
                                                        LC 2007-10945
During Haley's freshman year of high school, a campaign of gossip and bullying causes her to be socially ostracized, but after spending the summer living with her aunt, working at a resort, making new friends, and dating a hunky lifeguard, she learns how to stand up for herself and begins to trust again.
"Concluding with a serious author's note on harassment, which includes information on getting help, this text skillfully captures the painful reality of teen bullying while also telling Haley's humorous and sincere story of growing up." Kirkus

Semiprecious. Margaret K. McElderry Books 2006 293p $16.95; pa $6.99

Grades: 5 6 7 8   **Fic**
   1. Family life -- Fiction
   ISBN 978-0-689-85638-9; 0-689-85638-5; 978-0-689-87389-8 pa; 0-689-87389-1 pa
                                                        LC 2005-14906
Uprooted and living with an aunt in 1960s Oklahoma, thirteen-year-old Garnet and her older sister Opal brave their mother's desertion and their father's recovery from an accident, learning that "the best home of all is the one you make inside yourself"
"An involving novel of hurt, healing, and adjustment." Booklist

Low, Dene

The **entomological** tales of Augustus T. Percival; Petronella saves nearly everyone. Houghton Mifflin 2009 196p $16.00

Grades: 7 8 9 10   **Fic**

1. Uncles -- Fiction 2. Insects -- Fiction 3. Missing persons -- Fiction

ISBN 0-547-15250-7; 978-0-547-15250-9

Petronella's fashionable friends are arriving at her country estate near London to celebrate her sixteenth birthday and her coming out party. During the festivities, important guests are disappearing, kidnapping notes are appearing, many of the clues are insects, and Uncle Augustus (who has developed a bug eating compulsion) is surreptitiously devouring evidence.

"Archetypical characters are skillfully drawn, time and place are clearly evoked, and excitement and intrigue abound amid the hilarity." SLJ

Lowry, Lois, 1937-

★ **Anastasia** Krupnik. Houghton Mifflin 1979 113p $17; pa $5.99

Grades: 4 5 6   **Fic**

1. Family life -- Fiction

ISBN 0-395-28629-8; 0-440-40852-0 pa

Anastasia's 10th year has some good things like falling in love and really getting to know her grandmother and some bad things like finding out about an impending baby brother

"Anastasia's father and mother—an English professor and an artist—are among the most humorous, sensible, and understanding parents to be found in . . . children's fiction, and Anastasia herself is an amusing and engaging heroine." Horn Book

Other titles about Anastasia Krupnik are:
Anastasia again! (1981)
Anastasia at your service (1982)
Anastasia, ask your analyst (1984)
Anastasia on her own (1985)
Anastasia has the answers (1986)
Anastasia's chosen career (1987)
Anastasia at this address (1991)
Anastasia, absolutely (1995)

Gathering blue. Houghton Mifflin 2000 215p $16; pa $8.95

Grades: 5 6 7 8   **Fic**

1. Artists 2. Orphans 3. Science fiction 4. Physically handicapped

ISBN 0-618-05581-9; 0-385-73256-2 pa

LC 00-24359

Lame and suddenly orphaned, Kira is mysteriously removed from her squalid village to live in the palatial Council Edifice, where she is expected to use her gifts as a weaver to do the bidding of the all-powerful Guardians

"Lowry has once again created a fully realized world full of drama, suspense, and even humor." SLJ

★ **Number** the stars. Houghton Mifflin 1989 137p $16

Grades: 4 5 6 7   **Fic**

1. Jews -- Fiction 2. Friendship -- Fiction 3. World

War, 1939-1945 -- Fiction

ISBN 0-395-51060-0

LC 88-37134

Awarded the Newbery Medal, 1990

In 1943, during the German occupation of Denmark, ten-year-old Annemarie learns how to be brave and courageous when she helps shelter her Jewish friend from the Nazis

"The appended details the historical incidents upon which Lowry bases her plot. . . . The whole work is seamless, compelling, and memorable." Horn Book

★ The **giver**. Houghton Mifflin 1993 180p $17; pa $8.95

Grades: 6 7 8 9 10   **Fic**

1. Science fiction

ISBN 0-395-64566-2; 0-385-73255-4 pa

LC 92-15034

Awarded the Newbery Medal, 1994

Given his lifetime assignment at the Ceremony of Twelve, Jonas becomes the receiver of memories shared by only one other in his community and discovers the terrible truth about the society in which he lives.

"A riveting, chilling story that inspires a new appreciation for diversity, love, and even pain. Truly memorable." SLJ

The **silent** boy. Houghton Mifflin 2003 178p $15

Grades: 4 5 6 7   **Fic**

1. Unmarried mothers 2. Mentally handicapped -- Fiction

ISBN 0-618-28231-9

LC 2002-9072

Katy, the precocious eight-year-old daughter of the town doctor, befriends a retarded boy

"The author balances humor and generosity with the obstacles and injustice of Katy's world to depict a complete picture of the turn of the 20th century." Publ Wkly

★ **Son**; by Lois Lowry. Houghton Mifflin 2012 393 p. $17.99

Grades: 6 7 8 9 10 11 12   **Fic**

1. Science fiction 2. Dystopian fiction 3. Amnesia -- Fiction 4. Mothers -- Fiction 5. Secrecy -- Fiction 6. Identity -- Fiction 7. Mother-child relationship -- Fiction 8. Mother and child -- Fiction 9. Separation (Psychology) -- Fiction

ISBN 0547887205; 9780547887203

LC 2012014034

Author Lois Lowry tells the story of "14-year-old Claire, [who] has no contact with her baby Gabe until she surreptitiously bonds with him in the community Nurturing Center. . . . After living for years with Alys, a childless healer, Claire's memory returns. Intent on finding Gabe, she . . . encounters the sinister Trademaster and exchanges her youth for his help in finding her child, now living in the same village as middle-aged Jonas and his wife Kira. Elderly and failing, Claire reveals her identity to Gabe, who must use his unique talent to save the village." (Kirkus Reviews)

Lu, Marie

★ **Legend**. G. P. Putnam's Sons 2011 305p $17.99

Grades: 8 9 10 11 12 **Fic**
1. War stories 2. Science fiction 3. Plague -- Fiction 4. Siblings -- Fiction 5. Soldiers -- Fiction 6. Criminals -- Fiction 7. Resistance to government -- Fiction
ISBN 978-0-399-25675-2; 0-399-25675-X
LC 2011002003
"The characters are likable, the plot moves at a good pace, and the adventure is solid." SLJ

Lubar, David
Hidden talents. TOR Bks. 1999 213p il hardcover o.p. pa $5.99
Grades: 6 7 8 9 **Fic**
1. School stories 2. Extrasensory perception -- Fiction
ISBN 0-312-86646-1; 0-7653-4265-0 pa
LC 99-24560
When thirteen-year-old Martin arrives at an alternative school for misfits and problem students, he falls in with a group of boys with psychic powers and discovers something surprising about himself
The author "serves up great fun, along with an insight or two for those whose powers are only too human." Publ Wkly

★ **Sleeping** freshmen never lie. Dutton Books 2005 279p $16.99; pa $6.99
Grades: 7 8 9 10 **Fic**
1. School stories 2. Authorship -- Fiction
ISBN 0-525-47311-4; 0-14-240780-1 pa
LC 2004-23067
While navigating his first year of high school and awaiting the birth of his new baby brother, Scott loses old friends and gains some unlikely new ones as he hones his skills as a writer
"The plot is framed by Scott's journal of advice for the unborn baby. The novel's absurd, comical mood is evident in its entries. . . . The author brings the protagonist to three-dimensional life by combining these introspective musings with active, hilarious narration." SLJ

True talents. Tom Doherty Associates 2007 315p $17.95; pa $5.99
Grades: 6 7 8 9 **Fic**
1. Friendship -- Fiction 2. Kidnapping -- Fiction 3. Extrasensory perception -- Fiction
ISBN 978-0-7653-0977-8; 0-7653-0977-7; 978-0-7653-4856-2 pa; 0-7653-4856-X pa
LC 2006-39763
Over a year after fourteen-year-old Eddie "Trash" Thalmeyer and his friends from Edgeview Alternative School find out about their psychic abilities, Trash is kidnapped and Torchie, Cheater, Lucky, Flinch, and Martin must join forces to rescue their friend, discovering their true talents in the process.
This is "a gripping page-turner, with a flawlessly structured plot and compelling, struggling characters who never let each other down." Voice Youth Advocates

Luddy, Karon
★ **Spelldown**. Simon & Schuster Books for Young Readers 2007 211p $15.99; pa $5.99

Grades: 5 6 7 8 **Fic**
1. School stories 2. Spelling bees -- Fiction
ISBN 1-4169-1610-5; 978-1-4169-1610-9; 1-4169-5452-X pa; 978-1-4169-5452-1 pa
LC 2006-21956
In 1969, the town of Red Clover, South Carolina, led by an enthusiastic new Latin teacher, supports thirteen-year-old Karlene as she wins her school spelling bee and strives to qualify for the National Bee, despite family problems and a growing desire for romance.
"This heartrending and funny debut novel deftly evokes place, time and character." Publ Wkly

Luper, Eric
Bug boy. Farrar, Straus and Giroux 2009 248p $16.99
Grades: 7 8 9 10 **Fic**
1. Gambling -- Fiction 2. Horse racing -- Fiction 3. Father-son relationship -- Fiction 4. Swindlers and swindling -- Fiction
ISBN 978-0-374-31000-4; 0-374-31000-9
LC 2008-26730
In 1934 Saratoga, New York, just as fifteen-year-old Jack Walsh finally realizes his dream of becoming a jockey, complications arise in the form of a female bookie, an unexpected visit from his father, and a man who wants him to "fix" a race.
"This well-written, engaging story effectively captures the desperate times of the Depression and the hard-edged world of horse racing." SLJ

Lupica, Mike
Heat. Philomel Books 2006 220p $16.99
Grades: 5 6 7 8 **Fic**
1. Cubans -- Fiction 2. Orphans -- Fiction 3. Baseball -- Fiction 4. Illegal aliens -- Fiction
ISBN 0-14-240757-7 pa; 0-399-24301-1
LC 2005013521
Pitching prodigy Michael Arroyo is on the run from social services after being banned from playing Little League baseball because rival coaches doubt he is only twelve years old and he has no parents to offer them proof.
"The dialogue crackles, and the rich cast of supporting characters' . . . nearly steals the show. Topnotch entertainment." Booklist

Hero. Philomel Books 2010 289p $17.99
Grades: 6 7 8 9 **Fic**
1. Adventure fiction 2. Death -- Fiction 3. Politics -- Fiction 4. Family life -- Fiction 5. Superheroes -- Fiction 6. Father-son relationship -- Fiction
ISBN 978-0-399-25283-9; 0-399-25283-5
LC 2010-01772
Fourteen-year-old Zach learns he has the same special abilities as his father, who was the President's globe-trotting troubleshooter until "the Bads" killed him, and now Zach must decide whether to use his powers in the same way at the risk of his own life.
"Lupica effectively unfolds this high-adventure story." Booklist

Miracle on 49th Street. Philomel Books 2006 246p $17.99; pa $7.99

Grades: 5 6 7 8   **Fic**

1. Basketball -- Fiction 2. Father-daughter relationship -- Fiction

ISBN 0-399-24488-3; 0-14-240942-1 pa

LC 2005-32648

After her mother's death, twelve-year-old Molly learns that her father is a basketball star for the Boston Celtics.

"Lupica creates intriguing, complex characters . . . and he paces his story well, with enough twists and cliff-hangers to keep the pages turning." SLJ

Play Makers; Mike Lupica. Scholastic 2013 224 p. (hardcover) $16.99

Grades: 3 4 5 6 7   **Fic**

1. School stories 2. Basketball -- Fiction 3. Competition (Psychology) -- Fiction

ISBN 0545381835; 9780545381833

This novel, by Mike Lupica, is the book 2 of the "Game Changers" series. "Ben McBain and his crew must now prepare for basketball season. . . . But there is a new kid in town, Chase Braggs, a point guard like Ben who seems to be better, stronger, and faster. . . . Ben's rivalry with Chase seems to take the fun out of playing ball with his best friends. Will Ben be able to pull it together for his team and for himself?" (Publisher's note)

Summer ball; [by] Mike Lupica. Philomel Books 2007 244p $17.99

Grades: 6 7 8 9   **Fic**

1. Camps -- Fiction 2. Basketball -- Fiction

ISBN 978-0-399-24487-2

LC 2006021781

Thirteen-year-old Danny must prove himself all over again for a disapproving coach and against new rivals at a summer basketball camp.

"Lupica breathes life into both characters and story. Danny is . . . sympathetic and engaging. He is surrounded by a cast of supporting characters who add humor and whose interactions ring true." SLJ

The **batboy**. Philomel Books 2010 247p $17.99

Grades: 5 6 7 8   **Fic**

1. Baseball -- Fiction 2. Mother-son relationship -- Fiction

ISBN 978-0-399-25000-2; 0-399-25000-X

LC 2009015067

Even though his mother feels baseball ruined her marriage to his father, she allows fourteen-year-old Brian to become a bat boy for the Detroit Tigers, who have just drafted his favorite player back onto the team.

Lupica gives "his readers a behind-the-scenes look at major league sports. In this novel, he adds genuine insights into family dynamics and the emotional state of his hero." Booklist

The **big** field. Philomel Books 2008 243p $17.99

Grades: 5 6 7 8   **Fic**

1. Baseball -- Fiction 2. Father-son relationship --

Fiction

ISBN 978-0-399-24625-8; 0-399-24625-8

LC 2007-23647

When fourteen-year-old baseball player Hutch feels threatened by the arrival of a new teammate named Darryl, he tries to work through his insecurities about both Darryl and his remote and silent father, who was once a great ballplayer too.

"Writing in typically fluid prose and laying in a strong supporting lineup, Lupica strikes the right balance between personal issues and game action." Booklist

Lurie, April

The **latent** powers of Dylan Fontaine. Delacorte Press 2008 208p $15.99; lib bdg $18.99

Grades: 8 9 10 11 12   **Fic**

1. Family life -- Fiction

ISBN 978-0-385-73125-6; 978-0-385-90153-6 lib bdg

LC 2007-32313

Fifteen-year-old Dylan's friend Angie is making a film about him while he is busy trying to keep his older brother from getting caught with drugs, to deal with his mother having left the family, and to figure out how to get Angie to think of him as more than just a friend.

"This is a story about guys, primarily . . . brothers; fathers and sons; lonely young men who are feeling somewhat lost. Any reader will care for each one of them. Lurie does a wonderful job of making them real." KLIATT

Ly, Many

Roots and wings; [by] Many Ly. Delacorte Press 2008 262p $15.99; lib bdg $18.99

Grades: 6 7 8 9 10   **Fic**

1. Buddhism -- Fiction 2. Cambodian Americans -- Fiction

ISBN 978-0-385-73500-1; 978-0-385-90494-0 lib bdg; 0-385-73500-6; 0-385-90494-0 lib bdg

LC 2008-00474

While in St. Petersburg, Florida, to give her grandmother a Cambodian funeral, fourteen-year-old Grace, who was raised in Pennsylvania, finally gets some answers about the father she never met, her mother's and grandmother's youth, and her Asian-American heritage.

"The book is beautifully written . . . [and] the author allows family secrets to unfold carefully and explores them with sincerity." SLJ

Lyga, Barry

Archvillain. Scholastic Press 2010 180p $16.99

Grades: 4 5 6 7   **Fic**

1. Science fiction 2. Superheroes -- Fiction 3. Good and evil -- Fiction 4. Extraterrestrial beings -- Fiction

ISBN 978-0-545-19649-9; 0-545-19649-3

LC 2010-05291

Twelve-year-old Kyle Camden develops greater mental agility and superpowers during a plasma storm that also brings Mighty Mike, an alien, to the town of Bouring, but while each does what he thinks is best, Kyle is labeled a villain and Mike a hero.

"Comic book fans in particular will appreciate this clever origin story, first in a new series. . . . Lyga . . . laces his story with ample humor. . . . Readers will find plenty to ponder." Publ Wkly

Goth girl rising. Houghton Mifflin Harcourt 2009 390p $17

Grades: 8 9 10 11 12   Fic
1. School stories 2. Psychotherapy -- Fiction
ISBN 978-0-547-07664-5; 0-547-07664-9

"After six months in a mental hospital, Kyra, the newly shaven-headed heroine of The Astonishing Adventures of Fan Boy and Goth Girl (2006), has only one plan: to exact embarrassing revenge on sweet, loyal Fan Boy for not contacting her while she was away. . . . Goth teens and fans of the first novel will be drawn into the darkness that is her life." Kirkus

Hero -type. Houghton Mifflin Co. 2008 295p $16

Grades: 7 8 9 10   Fic
1. School stories 2. Patriotism -- Fiction 3. Heroes and heroines -- Fiction
ISBN 978-0-547-07663-8; 0-547-07663-0
LC 2008-7276

Feeling awkward and ugly is only one reason sixteen-year-old Kevin is uncomfortable with the publicity surrounding his act of accidental heroism, but when a reporter photographs him apparently being unpatriotic, he steps into the limelight to encourage people to think about what the symbols of freedom really mean.

"Leavened by much humor . . . this neatly plotted look at what real patriotism and heroism mean will get readers thinking." KLIATT

★ The **astonishing** adventures of Fanboy & Goth Girl. Houghton Mifflin 2006 311p $16.95

Grades: 8 9 10 11 12   Fic
1. School stories 2. Friendship -- Fiction 3. Cartoons and caricatures -- Fiction
ISBN 0-618-72392-7
LC 2005-33259

A fifteen-year-old "geek" who keeps a list of the high school jocks and others who torment him, and pours his energy into creating a great graphic novel, encounters Kyra, Goth Girl, who helps change his outlook on almost everything, including himself.

"This engaging first novel has good characterization with genuine voices. . . . The book is compulsively readable." Voice Youth Advocates

Lynch, Chris

Angry young man. Simon & Schuster BFYR 2011 167p $16.99

Grades: 7 8 9 10   Fic
1. Brothers -- Fiction 2. Single parent family -- Fiction 3. Mother-son relationship -- Fiction
ISBN 0-689-84790-4; 978-0-689-84790-5
LC 2009-52832

Eighteen-year-old Robert tries to help his half-brother Xan, a seventeen-year-old misfit, to make better choices as he becomes increasingly attracted to a variety of protesters, anarchists, and the like.

"For those who wonder about the roots of homegrown terror and extremism, . . . Lynch pushes the spotlight from the individual to society in a story that can be brutal and ugly, yet isn't devoid of hope." Publ Wkly

The **Big** Game of Everything. HarperTeen 2008 275p $16.99; lib bdg $17.89

Grades: 7 8 9 10   Fic
1. Golf -- Fiction 2. Family life -- Fiction 3. Grandfathers -- Fiction 4. Summer employment -- Fiction
ISBN 978-0-06-074034-4; 0-06-074034-5; 978-0-06-074035-1 lib bdg; 0-06-074035-3 lib bdg
LC 2007-49578

Jock and his eccentric family spend the summer working at Grampus's golf complex, where they end up learning the rules of "The Big Game of Everything."

"This Printz Honor-winning author offers up another touching and offbeat novel full of delightfully skewed humor." Voice Youth Advocates

Casualties of war; Chris Lynch. Scholastic Press 2013 192 p. (hc) $16.99

Grades: 8 9 10 11 12   Fic
1. War stories 2. Soldiers -- Fiction 3. Vietnam War, 1961-1975 -- Fiction 4. Airmen -- Fiction 5. Agent Orange -- Fiction
ISBN 0545270235; 9780545270236; 9780545270243
LC 2012014434

This book concludes "[Chris] Lynch's Vietnam War series . . . with the final narrative of four friends caught in the chaos of war. Morris, Ivan and Rudi have told their stories; it's Beck's turn. Beck, now in the Air Force, was always the smart one, the one bound for college. . . . And in Vietnam, Beck does feel as if he has 'just been handed the keys to the universe itself.' He is, literally, above it all, as he watches the war from on high in his C-123 aircraft." (Kirkus)

★ **Hothouse**. HarperTeen 2010 198p $16.99

Grades: 8 9 10 11 12   Fic
1. Death -- Fiction 2. Friendship -- Fiction 3. Bereavement -- Fiction 4. Fire fighters -- Fiction 5. Father-son relationship -- Fiction
ISBN 978-0-06-167379-5; 0-06-167379-X
LC 2010-3145

Teens D.J. and Russell, life-long friends and neighbors, had drifted apart but when their firefighter fathers are both killed, they try to help one another come to terms with the tragedy and its aftermath.

"Lynch fully commits to the first-person voice, giving into Russ' second-by-second conflicts and contradictions. The author also has a strong grasp of the garrulous slaps and punches that make up many male relationships. Russ' friendships are so real they hurt. The story hurts, too, but that's how it should be." Booklist

★ **Inexcusable**. Atheneum Books for Young Readers 2005 165p $16.95; pa $6.99

Grades: 8 9 10 11 12   Fic
1. School stories 2. Rape -- Fiction 3. Football --

Fiction

ISBN 0-689-84789-0; 1-416-93972-5 pa

LC 2004-30874

High school senior and football player Keir sets out to enjoy himself on graduation night, but when he attempts to comfort a friend whose date has left her stranded, things go terribly wrong

"This finely crafted and thought-provoking page-turner carefully conveys that it is simply inexcusable to whitewash wrongs, and that those responsible should (and hopefully will) pay the price." SLJ

Lynch, Chris, 1962-

Pieces; Chris Lynch. Simon & Schuster Books for Young Readers 2013 176 p. (hardcover) $16.99

Grades: 7 8 9 10 11 12   **Fic**

1. Death -- Fiction 2. Grief -- Fiction 3. Brothers -- Fiction 4. Interpersonal relations -- Fiction 5. Donation of organs, tissues, etc. -- Fiction

ISBN 1416927034; 9781416927037; 9781442453111

LC 2011042049

In this book, "a year after his 20-year-old brother Duane died in a diving accident, 18-year-old Eric still can't seem to move forward. In an attempt to keep the 'nothingness that is filling the Duane space' from taking hold, he reaches out to three of the donors who received his brother's 'pieces.' After meeting shy, redheaded Phil, brassy Barry and sweet single mom Melinda, Eric finds himself constantly asking the questions, 'Who are these people? Who are they, to me? Who am I, to them?'" (Kirkus Reviews)

Lyon, Annabel

All -season Edie. Orca Book Publishers 2008 179p pa $8.95

Grades: 5 6 7 8   **Fic**

1. Family life -- Fiction 2. Grandfathers -- Fiction

ISBN 978-1-55143-713-2 pa; 1-55143-713-9 pa

"Wry, fast, and funny. . . . Set in a Vancouver suburb . . . [this book] gets the preteen voice perfectly." Booklist

Lyon, Steve

The **gift** moves. Houghton Mifflin 2004 230p $15

Grades: 5 6 7 8   **Fic**

1. Science fiction

ISBN 0-618-39128-2

LC 2003-12293

In a futuristic United States devoid of wealth and material things, a teenage baker befriends a talented weaver's apprentice who holds a dark secret.

"Lyon mixes elements of magical realism with a coming-of-age story, incorporating issues that teens will relate to. . . . This is an unusual story that is sure to inspire much thought and contemplation." SLJ

Lyons, Mary E.

Letters from a slave boy; the story of Joseph Jacobs. Atheneum Books for Young Readers 2007 197p il map $15.99; pa $5.99

Grades: 6 7 8 9   **Fic**

1. Letters -- Fiction 2. Slavery -- Fiction 3. African

Americans -- Fiction

ISBN 978-0-689-87867-1; 0-689-87867-2; 978-0-689-87868-8 pa; 0-689-87868-0 pa

LC 2006-01277

A fictionalized look at the life of Joseph Jacobs, son of a slave, told in the form of letters that he might have written during his life in pre-Civil War North Carolina, on a whaling expedition, in New York, New England, and finally in California during the Gold Rush.

"The 'letters' are short and the pace is quick. The dialect and spelling give authenticity without making the text difficult to read and understand. . . . This title stands on its own, but children who appreciated the forthright perspective of the first book will want to read this one as well." SLJ

★ **Letters** from a slave girl; the story of Harriet Jacobs. Scribner 1992 146p il hardcover o.p. pa $5.99; pa $5.99

Grades: 6 7 8 9   **Fic**

1. Slaves 2. Letters -- Fiction 3. African Americans -- Fiction

ISBN 0-684-19446-5; 1-4169-3637-8 pa; 9781416936374 pa

LC 91-45778

This is a fictionalized version of the life of Harriet Jacobs, told in the form of letters that she might have written during her slavery in North Carolina and as she prepared for escape to the North in 1842. Glossary. Bibliography.

This "is historical fiction at its best. . . . Mary Lyons has remained faithful to Jacobs's actual autobiography throughout her readable, compelling novel. . . . Her observations of the horrors of slavery are concise and lucid. The letters are written in dialect, based on Jacobs's own writing and on other slave narrations of the period." Horn Book

MacColl, Michaela

Nobody's secret; by Michaela MacColl. Chronicle Books 2013 288 p. (reinforced) $16.99

Grades: 7 8 9 10   **Fic**

1. Mystery fiction 2. Historical fiction 3. Poets -- Fiction 4. Mystery and detective stories

ISBN 1452108609; 9781452108605

LC 2012030364

In this book, when "15-year-old Emily Dickinson meets and flirts with a handsome stranger, she feels the first flicker of romance. Then the young man is found dead in her family's pond, and the budding poet is sure that he was a victim of foul play. Determined to see that justice is done, she and her younger sister, Vinnie, investigate and discover that he is James Wentworth, heir to a fortune from which his aunt and uncle have defrauded him. Suspecting murder, Emily sets out to solve the case." (School Library Journal)

★ **Prisoners** in the palace; how Victoria became queen with the help of her maid, a reporter, and a scoundrel; a novel of intrigue and romance. Chronicle Books 2010 367p $16.99

Grades: 7 8 9 10   **Fic**

1. Queens 2. Orphans -- Fiction 3. Household employees -- Fiction

ISBN 978-0-8118-7300-0; 0-8118-7300-5

LC 2010-8257

Recently orphaned and destitute, seventeen-year-old Liza Hastings earns a position as a lady's maid to sixteen-year-old Princess Victoria at Kensington Palace in 1836, the year before Victoria becomes Queen of England.

"This novel is full of historical detail, vivid settings, and richly drawn characters, and themes of friendship and romance give the story teen appeal." Booklist

Promise the night. Chronicle Books 2011 $16.99
Grades: 6 7 8 9 **Fic**
1. Women air pilots -- Fiction
ISBN 978-0-8118-7625-4; 0-8118-7625-X
LC 2011010938
This novel explores the early life of Beryl Markham, who grew up on a farm in Kenya, and became the first person to fly solo across the Atlantic from east to west.

"MacColl vividly portrays her headstrong protagonist . . . with fierce, exuberant spirit." Booklist

MacCullough, Carolyn
Always a witch. Clarion Books 2011 276p $16.99
Grades: 8 9 10 11 12 **Fic**
1. Witches -- Fiction 2. Time travel -- Fiction 3. Good and evil -- Fiction
ISBN 978-0-547-22485-5; 0-547-22485-0
LC 2011008148
Haunted by her grandmother's prophecy that she will soon be forced to make a terrible decision, witch Tamsin Greene risks everything to travel back in time to 1887 New York to confront the enemy that wants to destroy her family.

This is "an enjoyable magical adventure." Kirkus

Drawing the ocean. Roaring Brook Press 2006 170p $16.95
Grades: 7 8 9 10 **Fic**
1. Ghost stories 2. Death -- Fiction 3. Twins -- Fiction 4. Siblings -- Fiction
ISBN 978-1-59643-092-1; 1-59643-092-3
LC 2005-31471
A gifted artist, Sadie is determined to fit in at her new school, but her deceased twin brother Ollie keeps appearing to her.

"Characters of every age come to life with vivid descriptions and dialogue that make this spare mood piece work." SLJ

★ **Once** a witch. Clarion Books 2009 292p $16
Grades: 8 9 10 11 12 **Fic**
1. Sisters -- Fiction 2. Witches -- Fiction 3. Time travel -- Fiction 4. Good and evil -- Fiction
ISBN 978-0-547-22399-5; 0-547-22399-4
LC 2008-49234
Born into a family of witches, seventeen-year-old Tamsin is raised believing that she alone lacks a magical "Talent," but when her beautiful and powerful sister is taken by an age-old rival of the family in an attempt to change the balance of power, Tamsin discovers her true destiny.

"The book will appeal to teen readers who enjoy stories with romance, magic, or time travel, along with hardcore fantasy aficionados, and it is appropriate for all young adult collections." Voice Youth Advocates

MacDonald, Anne Louise
Seeing red. KCP Fiction 2009 220p $17.95; pa $8.95
Grades: 6 7 8 9 **Fic**
1. Dreams -- Fiction 2. Extrasensory perception -- Fiction
ISBN 978-1-55453-291-9; 1-55453-291-4; 978-1-55453-292-6 pa; 1-55453-292-2 pa
"From the time he was a young child, Frankie's dreams invoked meaningful colors and seemed like premonitions that he was powerless to change. . . . He develops an unexpected friendship with an unpopular classmate whom he is convinced is a mind reader and who also sees colors. The dilemmas faced by Frankie and some of the other characters are intriguing as they struggle with their fears, disappointments, and aspirations. The story has several touching moments and unexpected turns in a plot." SLJ

MacDonald, Bailey
Wicked Will. Aladdin 2009 201p $16.99
Grades: 5 6 7 **Fic**
1. Mystery fiction 2. Orphans -- Fiction 3. Theater -- Fiction
ISBN 1-4169-8660-X; 978-1-4169-8660-7
LC 2008-50818
Performing in the English town of Stratford-on-Avon in 1576, Viola, a young actress (disguised as a boy) and a local lad named Will Shakespeare uncover a murder mystery.

"The chapters themselves logically reveal the twists and turns of the plot in concise, readable prose. The realistic details put flesh on the bones of not only the primary characters, but also of the secondary personages as well." SLJ

The **secret** of the sealed room; a mystery of young Benjamin Franklin. Aladdin 2010 208p $16.99
Grades: 4 5 6 7 **Fic**
1. Mystery fiction
ISBN 978-1-4169-9760-3; 1-4169-9760-1
When she runs away after her master dies, indentured servant Patience Martin is accused of stealing and needs the help of a young Benjamin Franklin to prove her innocence.

"MacDonald creates a series of events that could very well be factual and leaves the reader curious to know more. Replete with historical facts without being blatant, the well-developed plot will keep mystery lovers guessing until the very last chapter." Booklist

MacHale, D. J.
Raven rise; [by] D.J. MacHale. 1st ed.; Simon & Schuster Books for Young Readers 2008 544p (Pendragon) $17.99
Grades: 7 8 9 10 **Fic**
1. Fantasy fiction 2. Adventure fiction
ISBN 978-1-4169-1418-1; 1-4169-1418-8
LC 2007046886
While Pendragon is trapped on Ibara, Alder returns to Denduron and reluctantly goes into battle again, and other Travelers face obstacles of various sorts, Saint Dane gains the power he seeks on Second Earth and makes his push to destroy and rebuild Halla.

SYLO; by D.J. MacHale. Penguin Group USA 2013 416 p. (hardcover) $17.99

Grades: 5 6 7 8 9　　　　　　　　　　　　　**Fic**

1. Dystopian fiction 2. Adventure fiction
ISBN 1595146652; 9781595146656

This is the first book in a proposed trilogy from D.J. MacHale. Here, Tucker Pierce has a small but satisfying life on a small island. But when the island is quarantined by the U.S. Navy, things start to fall apart. . . . People start dying. The girl he wants to get to know a whole lot better, Tori, is captured along with Tucker and imprisoned behind barbed wire." They must escape to the mainland and try to figure out what this SYLO organization that is imprisoning them is. (Kirkus Reviews)

★ The **pilgrims** of Rayne. Simon & Schuster Books for Young Readers 2007 547p (Pendragon) $16.99; pa $8.99

Grades: 7 8 9 10　　　　　　　　　　　　　**Fic**

1. Fantasy fiction 2. Adventure fiction
ISBN 978-1-4169-1416-7; 1-4169-1416-1; 978-1-4169-1417-4 pa; 1-4169-1417-X pa

　　　　　　　　　　　　　　　LC 2006038131

With Saint Dane seemingly on the verge of toppling all of the territories, Pendragon and Courtney set out to rescue Mark and find themselves traveling—and battling—their way through different worlds as they try to save all of Halla.

This is "packed . . . with nonstop action, mind-boggling plot twists, and well-imagined locales." Voice Youth Advocates

Other titles in this series are:
The merchant of death (2002)
The lost city of Faar (2003)
The never war (2003)
The reality bug (2003)
Black water (2004)
The rivers of Zadaa (2005)
Quillan games (2006)
Raven rise (2008)
The soldiers of Halla (2009)

MacLachlan, Patricia, 1938-

Kindred souls; Patricia MacLachlan. Harper-Collins 2012 119 p. $16.99

Grades: 4 5 6　　　　　　　　　　　　　　**Fic**

1. Bereavement -- Fiction 2. Family life -- Fiction 3. Family farms -- Fiction 4. Grandfathers -- Fiction 5. Houses -- Remodeling -- Fiction 6. Dogs -- Fiction 7. Old age -- Fiction 8. Prairies -- Fiction 9. Farm life -- Fiction 10. Sod houses -- Fiction
ISBN 9780060522971; 9780060522988

　　　　　　　　　　　　　　　LC 2011016617

This book follows narrator Jake and his 88-year-old grandfather Billy, the eponymous kindred souls of the story's title. The pair "live on a farm that their family has owned for generations; in fact, Billy was born in a sod house he remembers fondly, the ruins of which still exist on the property." To comfort their dying grandfather, "Jake and his siblings undertake a remarkably ambitious project: They rebuild the sod house; Billy moves into it, and he eventually passes away there." The "first-person account of a boy coping with

his grandfather's death . . . portrays . . . the opportunity to grieve for a loved one even while he is still alive." (Kirkus)

MacLean, Jill

Nix Minus One; by Jill Maclean. Pajama Press 2013 296 p. (hardcover) $21.95

Grades: 7 8 9 10　　　　　　　　　　　　　**Fic**

1. School stories 2. Novels in verse
ISBN 192748524X; 9781927485248

This novel in verse focuses on 15-year-old Nix. "Formerly known as 'Fatty Humbolt,' he is struggling with his crush on Loren Cody, the girlfriend of the best player on the hockey team, and his love-hate relationship with his older sister, Roxy." Nix is shy while Roxy is the opposite. "Then Roxy falls for Bryan Sykes, a popular but notorious cad and politician's son, and Nix is forced to come out of his shell and find his voice." (School Library Journal)

★ The **nine** lives of Travis Keating. Fitzhenry & Whiteside 2008 217p pa $11.95

Grades: 5 6 7 8　　　　　　　　　　　　　**Fic**

1. Cats -- Fiction 2. Bullies -- Fiction
ISBN 978-1-55455-104-0; 1-55455-104-8

After his mother's death, Travis Keating and his father move to Ratchet, Newfoundland, to start a new life. Things are tough for Travis (Hud, the school bully, being the toughest) until, putting aside his own problems, he starts to care for a colony of feral cats.

"This is a solid piece of contemporary fiction with an interesting story. It should have broad appeal." SLJ

Macdonald, Maryann

Odette's secrets; by Maryann Macdonald. Bloomsbury 2013 240 p. (hardback) $16.99

Grades: 6 7 8 9　　　　　　　　　　　　　**Fic**

1. Novels in verse 2. Hidden children (Holocaust) -- Fiction 3. France -- History -- 1940-1945, German occupation -- Fiction 4. Identity -- Fiction 5. Jews -- France -- Fiction 6. Holocaust, Jewish (1939-1945) -- Fiction 7. World War, 1939-1945 -- France -- Fiction
ISBN 159990750X; 9781599907505

　　　　　　　　　　　　　　　LC 2012015549

This biographical story-in-verse, by Maryann Macdonald, takes place in Nazi-occupied France. "Odette is a young Jewish girl living in Paris during a dangerous time. . . . After Odette's father enlists in the French army and her mother joins the Resistance, Odette is sent to the countryside until it is safe to return. On the surface, she leads the life of a regular girl . . . but inside, she is burning with secrets about the life she left behind and her true identity." (Publisher's note)

Mack, Tracy

The **fall** of the Amazing Zalindas; casebook no. 1. by Tracy Mack and Michael Citrin; illustrations by Greg Ruth. Orchard Books 2006 259p il (Sherlock Holmes and the Baker Street irregulars) $16.99; pa $6.99

Grades: 4 5 6 7　　　　　　　　　　　　　**Fic**

1. Mystery fiction 2. Circus -- Fiction
ISBN 0-439-82836-8; 0-545-06939-4 pa

　　　　　　　　　　　　　　　LC 2005-34000

The ragamuffin boys known as the Baker Street Irregulars help Sherlock Holmes solve the mysterious deaths of a family of circus tightrope walkers.

"Colorful, well-defined characters . . . and plenty of historical detail, Cockney slang . . . and Sherlockian references bring Victorian England to life. Vintage-style design elements and evocative black-and-white illustrations further the effect." Booklist

The **mystery** of the conjured man; [by] Tracy Mack & Michael Citrin; [illustrations by Greg Ruth] Orchard Books 2009 il (Sherlock Holmes and the Baker Street Irregulars) hardcover o.p.

Grades: 4 5 6   Fic
   1. Mystery fiction 2. Spiritualism -- Fiction 3. Swindlers and swindling -- Fiction
   ISBN 978-0-439-83667-8 pa
                       LC 2006035701

The ragtag group of orphan boys known as the Baker Street Irregulars faces shady characters and seemingly real ghosts when they assist the famous detective, Sherlock Holmes, in investigating the mysterious death of Greta Berlinger during a seance.

"A great addition to an entertaining series." SLJ

Mackall, Dandi Daley
   The **silence** of murder. Alfred A. Knopf 2011 327p $16.99; lib bdg $19.99

Grades: 7 8 9 10   Fic
   1. Mystery fiction 2. Homicide -- Fiction 3. Siblings -- Fiction 4. Mentally handicapped -- Fiction
   ISBN 978-0-375-86896-2; 978-0-375-96896-9 lib bdg
                       LC 2010035991

Sixteen-year-old Hope must defend her developmentally disabled brother (who has not spoken a word since he was seven) when he is accused of murdering a beloved high school baseball coach.

"The well-plotted mystery is intriguing, and Hope's determined efforts to solve it have an authentic feel." Booklist

Mackel, Kathy
   ★ **Boost**. Dial Books 2008 248p $16.99; pa $7.99

Grades: 6 7 8 9   Fic
   1. Steroids -- Fiction 2. Basketball -- Fiction
   ISBN 978-0-8037-3240-7; 0-8037-3240-6; 978-0-14-241539-9 pa; 0-14-241539-1 pa
                       LC 2007-49441

Thirteen-year-old Savvy's dreams of starting for her elite basketball team are in danger when she is accused of taking steroids

"Mackel has turned a tough subject in the world of teen competitive sports into a highly readable blend of intense action, interfamily relationships, and intrigue." SLJ

Mackey, Weezie Kerr
   Throwing like a girl; [by] Weezie Kerr Mackey. Marshall Cavendish 2007 271p $16.99

Grades: 6 7 8 9   Fic
   1. School stories 2. Softball -- Fiction 3. Family life

-- Fiction
   ISBN 978-0-7614-5342-0
                       LC 2006030233

After moving from Chicago to Dallas in the spring of her sophomore year, fifteen-year-old Ella finds that joining the softball team at her private school not only helps her make friends, it also provides unexpected opportunities to learn and grow.

"Readers will be delighted with how well the athletics and the girly stuff work in tandem." Booklist

Mackler, Carolyn
   Tangled. HarperTeen 2010 308p $16.99

Grades: 8 9 10 11 12   Fic
   1. Vacations -- Fiction 2. Friendship -- Fiction
   ISBN 978-0-06-173104-4; 0-06-173104-8
                       LC 2009-7286

The lives of four very different teenagers become entangled in ways that none of them could have imagined after a short stay at a Caribbean resort

"The various viewpoints weave together to create a compelling and cohesive whole. Themes of understanding, respecting others, and the power of good communication are carefully and effectively woven throughout a story that begs for discussion." SLJ

The **earth,** my butt, and other big, round things. Candlewick Press 2003 246p $15.99; pa $8.99

Grades: 7 8 9 10   Fic
   1. School stories 2. Obesity -- Fiction 3. Family life -- Fiction
   ISBN 0-7636-1958-2; 0-7636-2091-2 pa
                       LC 2002-73921

Michael L. Printz Award honor book, 2004

Feeling like she does not fit in with the other members of her family, who are all thin, brilliant, and good-looking, fifteen-year-old Virginia tries to deal with her self-image, her first physical relationship, and her disillusionment with some of the people closest to her

"The e-mails [Virginia] exchanges . . . and the lists she makes (e.g., 'The Fat Girl Code of Conduct') add both realism and insight to her character. The heroine's transformation into someone who finds her own style and speaks her own mind is believable—and worthy of applause." Publ Wkly

Madden, Kerry
   Gentle's Holler. Viking 2005 237p $16.99; pa $6.99

Grades: 5 6 7 8   Fic
   1. Poverty -- Fiction 2. Family life -- Fiction
   ISBN 0-670-05998-6; 0-14-240751-8 pa
                       LC 2004-18424

In the early 1960s, twelve-year-old songwriter Livy Two Weems dreams of seeing the world beyond the Maggie Valley, North Carolina, holler where she lives in poverty with her parents and eight brothers and sisters, but understands that she must put family first.

"Livy's narration rings true and is wonderfully voiced, and Madden's message about the importance of forgiveness will be well received." SLJ

Other titles in this series are:

Louisiana's song (2007)
Jessie's mountain (2008)

Maddox, Jake

Free throw; by Jake Maddox; illustrated by Sean Tiffany; text by Anastasia Suen. Stone Arch Books 2007 65p il lib bdg $22.60; pa $5.95

Grades: 4 5 6 7   **Fic**
  1. Basketball -- Fiction
ISBN 978-1-59889-060-0 lib bdg; 1-59889-060-3 lib bdg; 978-1-59889-238-3 pa; 1-59889-238-X pa
                          LC 2006006076

Since Derek is now the tallest player on his basketball team, the coach decides to have him play center but Jason, the former center, has little confidence in Derek and will not pass him the ball.

"The clear descriptions, realistic dialogue, abundant action, and touches of humor will appeal to younger children, as well as to middle school or older readers who are working to bolster their skills. They will appreciate the large font and the comic-book-style drawings that illuminate the [text]." SLJ

Madigan, L. K.

★ The **mermaid's** mirror. Houghton Mifflin Harcourt 2010 316p $16

Grades: 8 9 10 11 12   **Fic**
  1. Magic -- Fiction 2. Surfing -- Fiction 3. Family life -- Fiction 4. Mermaids and mermen -- Fiction 5. Father-daughter relationship -- Fiction
ISBN 978-0-547-19491-2; 0-547-19491-9
                          LC 2010-6771

Lena, almost sixteen, has always felt drawn to the waters of San Francisco Bay despite the fears of her father, a former surfer, but after she glimpses a beautiful woman with a tail, nothing can keep Lena from seeking the mermaid in the dangerous waves at Magic Crescent Cove.

"The characters . . . are well rounded and integrated into the plot. . . . With highly imagistic descriptions and savvy dialogue, Madigan offers a rewarding and credible story that uses fantasy elements to bare truths about family ties." Booklist

Madison, Bennett

Lulu Dark and the summer of the Fox; a mystery. by Bennett Madison. Razorbill 2006 $10.99

Grades: 7 8 9 10   **Fic**
  1. Mystery fiction
ISBN 1-59514-086-7
                          LC 2006004960

When a mysterious person called the Fox begins to threaten young starlets, Lulu Dark investigates, even though she suspects that her own mother—an aging actress—might be behind it all.

"Teens will enjoy this smart, funny chick-lit heroine who has real problems and a satirical outlook." SLJ

Magnin, Joyce

Carrying Mason; [by] Joyce Magnin. Zonderkidz 2011 153p $14.99

Grades: 5 6 7 8   **Fic**
  1. Family life -- Fiction 2. Country life -- Fiction 3.

Mentally handicapped -- Fiction
ISBN 978-0-310-72681-4; 0-310-72681-6
                          LC 2011014462

In rural Pennsylvania in 1958, when thirteen-year-old Luna's best friend Mason dies, she decides to move in with his mentally disabled mother and care for her as Mason did.

"Gently, deliberately paced, Luna's first-person tale provides a fresh look at mental disabilities and the additional burden of negative attitudes. While Ruby's disability is apparent, this effort also celebrates her capabilities. Although the primary focus is Luna, her quirky father, supportive mother and boy-crazy older sister are also sufficiently developed to provide additional depth. A quiet coming-of-age tale with heart offers a fresh look at mentally disabled adults." Kirkus

Magoon, Kekla

Camo girl. Aladdin 2010 218p $16.99

Grades: 5 6 7 8   **Fic**
  1. Friendship -- Fiction 2. Prejudices -- Fiction 3. Racially mixed people -- Fiction
ISBN 978-1-4169-7804-6; 1-4169-7804-6

A novel about a biracial girl living in the suburbs of Las Vegas examines the friendships that grow out of, and despite, her race.

"Magoon . . . offers a sensitive and articulate portrayal of a pair of middle-school outsiders. . . . This poetic and nuanced story addresses the courage it takes to truly know and support someone, as well as the difficult choices that come with growing up." Publ Wkly

Fire in the streets; by Kekla Magoon. 1st Aladdin hardcover ed. Aladdin 2012 336 p. $15.99

Grades: 7 8 9 10   **Fic**
  1. Historical fiction 2. Black nationalism -- Fiction 3. African Americans -- Civil rights -- Fiction 4. Racism -- Fiction 5. African Americans -- Fiction 6. Brothers and sisters -- Fiction 7. Civil rights movements -- Fiction 8. United States -- History -- 20th century -- Fiction
ISBN 9781416990734; 9781442422308
                          LC 2011039129

This historical novel by Kekla Magoon, is set "in the sweltering Chicago summer of 1968. [Maxie] is a Black Panther--or at least she wants to be one. . . . At fourteen, she"s allowed to help out in the office, but she certainly can"t help patrol the streets. Then Maxie realizes that there is a traitor in their midst, and if she can figure out who it is, it may be her ticket to becoming a real Panther. But when she learns the truth, the knowledge threatens to destroy her world." (Publisher"s note)

★ The **rock** and the river. Aladdin 2009 290p $15.99

Grades: 7 8 9 10   **Fic**
  1. Brothers -- Fiction 2. African Americans -- Fiction
ISBN 978-1-4169-7582-3; 1-4169-7582-9
                          LC 2008-29170

ALA EMIERT Coretta Scott King John Steptoe New Talent Award (2010)

In 1968 Chicago, fourteen-year-old Sam Childs is caught in a conflict between his father's nonviolent approach to seeking civil rights for African Americans and his older brother, who has joined the Black Panther Party.

This "novel will make readers feel what it was like to be young, black, and militant 40 years ago, including the seething fury and desperation over the daily discrimination that drove the oppressed to fight back." Booklist

Maguire, Gregory
What -the-Dickens; the story of a rogue tooth fairy. Candlewick Press 2007 295p $15.99; pa $6.99

Grades: 4 5 6 7   **Fic**
1. Storms -- Fiction 2. Cousins -- Fiction 3. Fairies -- Fiction 4. Orphans -- Fiction 5. Storytelling -- Fiction
ISBN 978-0-7636-2961-8; 0-7636-2961-8; 978-0-7636-4307-2 pa; 0-7636-4307-6 pa
LC 2007-24186
As a terrible storm rages, ten-year-old Dinah and her brother and sister listen to their cousin Gage's tale of a newly-hatched, orphaned, skibberee, or tooth fairy, called What-the-Dickens, who hopes to find a home among the skibbereen tribe, if only he can stay out of trouble.

"The immediacy of the story and combination of fantasy and reality will grip even reluctant readers." SLJ

Mah, Adeline Yen
Chinese Cinderella and the Secret Dragon Society; [by] Adeline Yen Mah. 1st ed; HarperCollins 2005 242p $15.99; lib bdg $16.89

Grades: 5 6 7 8   **Fic**
1. Martial arts -- Fiction 2. World War, 1939-1945 -- Fiction
ISBN 0-06-056734-1; 0-06-056735-X lib bdg
LC 2004-8852
During the Japanese occupation of parts of China, twelve-year-old Ye Xian is thrown out of her father's and stepmother's home, joins a martial arts group, and tries to help her aunt and the Americans in their struggle against the Japanese invaders.

"Full of adventure and contrivance, this somewhat old-fashioned, plot-driven novel is clear about the values that are important to the author. . . . These young people are courageous, creative, and open-minded." SLJ

Mahoney, Karen
The **iron** witch. Flux 2011 299p $9.95

Grades: 6 7 8 9 10   **Fic**
1. Magic -- Fiction 2. Alchemy -- Fiction 3. Orphans -- Fiction 4. Kidnapping -- Fiction
ISBN 0-7387-2582-X; 978-0-7387-2582-6
LC 2010037692
Seventeen-year-old Donna Underwood is considered a freak, cursed by the magical heritage that destroyed her alchemist parents, but when vicious wood elves abduct her best friend Navin, Donna must betray all her parents fought for and join the battle between the humans and the fey.

"Adventurous, dark and dangerous. The Iron Witch will have teen readers clamoring for more." Libr Media Connect

Mahy, Margaret
Maddigan's Fantasia. Margaret K. McElderry Books 2007 499p $15.99

Grades: 4 5 6 7   **Fic**
1. Fantasy fiction 2. Magic -- Fiction 3. Circus -- Fiction
ISBN 1-4169-1812-4; 978-1-4169-1817-7
LC 2006-15512
In a world made uncertain by "the Chaos," two time-traveling boys, fifteen-year-old Timon and eleven-year-old Eden, seek to protect a magic talisman, aided by twelve-year-old Garland, a member of a traveling circus known as Maddigan's Fantasia.

"A well-drawn character, Garland resembles other Mahy protagonists—cranky, assertive and filled with self-doubt—and her adventures are invariably exciting." Publ Wkly

The **Magician** of Hoad. Margaret K. McElderry Books 2009 411p $18.99

Grades: 7 8 9 10   **Fic**
1. Fantasy fiction 2. Magicians -- Fiction
ISBN 978-1-4169-7807-7; 1-4169-7807-0
LC 2008-23000
A young farm boy who possesses mysterious powers is chosen by the king to be the court's royal magician.

"Mahy majestically deploys the poetic language of fantasy to portray the changes and challenges of adolescence; here, and epic quest for identity is wrapped up in terror, romance, surprise, and suspense—always sustained by luminous imagery and intelligent, musical prose." Horn Book

Maizel, Rebecca
Infinite days; a vampire queen novel. St. Martin's Griffin 2010 325p (Vampire queen) pa $9.99

Grades: 7 8 9 10   **Fic**
1. School stories 2. Vampires -- Fiction 3. Supernatural -- Fiction
ISBN 978-0-312-64991-3; 0-312-64991-6
At a New England boarding school, Lenah Beaudonte tries to act like a normal sixteen-year-old although she was, before a hundred-year hibernation, a centuries-old vampire queen whose bloodthirsty, abandoned coven is seeking her.

"The story is filled with action, romance, longing, deception, and sacrifice. It will leave vampire fans thirsting for more." SLJ

Stolen nights; a Vampire queen novel. Rebecca Maizel. St. Martin's Griffin 2013 303 p. (paperback) $9.99

Grades: 7 8 9 10   **Fic**
1. Love -- Fiction 2. Vampires -- Fiction 3. Supernatural -- Fiction 4. Schools -- Fiction 5. Boarding schools -- Fiction
ISBN 0312649924; 9780312649920
LC 2012038339
This book, the second in author Rebecca Maizel's Vampire Queen series, follows Lenah Beaudonte . . . a vampire who has just become human again. . . . Lenah and her lover, Rhode, are now both human teens. . . . [T]hey are confronted . . . by the Aeris, a sort of supernatural communion of the elements, who . . .give them a choice: they can either go back to their original times . . . or stay in the present day with the caveat of not being able to be romantically linked to each other." (VOYA)

"At first, this novel seems to lack luster in its genre, but timeless themes of love and the search for identity, in addition to the cliff-hanger ending, leave readers pondering Lenah's choices and keenly anticipating the next installment." SLJ

Malaghan, Michael

Greek ransom. Andersen Press 2010 264p pa $9.99

Grades: 5 6 7 8   **Fic**

1. Adventure fiction 2. Siblings -- Fiction 3. Kidnapping -- Fiction

ISBN 978-184270-786-9; 1-84270-786-8

"Nick and Callie Latham are on the Greek island of Theta with their archaeologist parents for a working vacation. Then the children discover that Mum and Dad have lost the family's money in a reckless bid to locate the lost treasure of King Akanon. A shifty businessman kidnaps the couple in order to acquire it for himself. After Nick and Callie barely escape capture themselves, it's up to them to find a way to free their parents. . . . Readers will be on the edge of their seats throughout to see what happens next. . . . The relationship between Nick and Callie is spot-on, and kids will enjoy this high-spirited tale." SLJ

Malchow, Alex

The **Sword** of Darrow; [by] Alex and Hal Malchow. BenBella 2011 531p map $17.99

Grades: 5 6 7 8   **Fic**

1. Fantasy fiction 2. Magic -- Fiction 3. Fairies -- Fiction 4. Princesses -- Fiction

ISBN 978-1-9356-1846-1; 1-9356-1846-6

LC 2011012233

"For 10 years the people of Sonnencrest endured the cruel and tyrannical rule of the Goblins. Then Princess Babette, the only surviving member of the royal family, and Darrow, a crippled boy, become the unlikely forces in the fight against the oppressors. The authors paint convincing portraits of the characters. . . . Readers will be drawn to this fledgling rebellion and follow it to its spectacular success. Magic, monsters, and wizards add to the excitement." SLJ

Maldonado, Torrey

Secret Saturdays. G.P. Putnam's Sons 2010 195p $16.99

Grades: 6 7 8 9   **Fic**

1. School stories 2. African Americans -- Fiction 3. Single parent family -- Fiction 4. Racially mixed people -- Fiction

ISBN 978-0-399-25158-0; 0-399-25158-8

LC 2009-10361

Twelve-year-old boys living in a rough part of New York confront questions about what it means to be a friend, a father, and a man.

"Maldonado convincingly portrays roughneck playgrounds where boys are expected to be 'hard' and . . . Justin's narration resonates with the authenticity of a preteen doing his best in an urban landscape that has taught him all he knows. . . . The book remains a moving portrayal of the hope to be found through honest relationships." Publ Wkly

Malley, Gemma

The **Declaration**. Bloomsbury 2007 300p $16.95

Grades: 7 8 9 10   **Fic**

1. Science fiction 2. Immortality -- Fiction

ISBN 978-1-59990-119-0; 1-59990-119-6

LC 2006-102138

In 2140 England, where drugs enable people to live forever and children are illegal, teenaged Anna, an obedient "Surplus" training to become a house servant, discovers that her birth parents are trying to find her.

This is "gripping. . . . The indoctrinated teen's awakening to massive injustice makes compulsive reading." Booklist

Other titles in this series are:

The legacy (2011)

The resistance (2008)

Mangum, Lisa

After hello; Lisa Mangum. Shadow Mountain 2012 272 p. (hardbound : alk. paper) $17.99

Grades: 7 8 9 10   **Fic**

1. Friendship -- Fiction 2. Photographers -- Fiction 3. Man-woman relationship -- Fiction 4. Trust -- Fiction 5. Dating (Social customs) -- Fiction 6. Interpersonal relations -- Fiction

ISBN 1609070100; 9781609070106

LC 2012017735

Author Lisa Mangum focuses on Sara, a girl whose "first trip to New York City . . . turns into 24 hours she will never forget. An amateur photographer, Sara walks around the city taking pictures; when a boy named Sam wanders into her lens, she is intrigued by him and follows him on his missions to find and trade things for people . . . As Sam and Sara travel from St. John the Divine Cathedral to Central Park and Times Square, they meet a string of artists and musicians and reluctantly discuss their turbulent pasts." (Barnes & Noble)

Manivong, Laura

Escaping the tiger. Harper 2010 216p il $15.99

Grades: 6 7 8 9   **Fic**

1. Refugees -- Fiction 2. Family life -- Fiction

ISBN 978-0-06-166177-8; 0-06-166177-5

LC 2009-24095

In 1982, twelve-year-old Vonlai, his parents, and sister, Dalah, escape from Laos to a Thai refugee camp, where they spend four long years struggling to survive in hopes on one day reaching America.

"This compelling novel offers significant historical background. This is certainly a book to prompt purposeful discussion to increase historical and multicultural awareness." SLJ

Mankell, Henning

★ A **bridge** to the stars. Delacorte Press 2007 164p $15.99; lib bdg $18.99; pa $8.99

Grades: 6 7 8 9   **Fic**

1. Father-son relationship -- Fiction

ISBN 978-0-385-73495-0; 0-385-73495-6; 978-0-385-90489-6 lib bdg; 0-385-90489-4 lib bdg; 978-0-440-24042-6 pa; 0-440-24042-5 pa

LC 2006-26901

In Sweden in 1956, eleven-year-old Joel and his father, a logger who was once a sailor, live alone with their secrets, including Joel's secret society that meets at night and his father's new romantic interest.

This is a "quiet but deeply satisfying coming-of-age story. . . . Those who welcome character-driven fiction will treasure this beautifully realized novel." Booklist

Other titles in this series are:
Shadows in the twilight (2008)
When the snow fell (2009)

Mantchev, Lisa

Eyes like stars. Feiwel and Friends 2009 356p $16.99

Grades: 8 9 10 11 12   **Fic**

1. Magic -- Fiction 2. Actors -- Fiction 3. Orphans -- Fiction 4. Theater -- Fiction 5. Books and reading -- Fiction

ISBN 978-0-312-38096-0; 0-312-38096-8

LC 2008-15317

Thirteen-year-old Bertie strives to save Theater Illuminata, the only home she has ever known, but is hindered by the Players who magically live on there, especially Ariel, who is willing to destroy the Book at the center of the magic in order to escape into the outside world.

"The story contains enough mystery and mayhem to keep readers engaged, even as they analyze." Voice Youth Advocates

Other titles in this series include:
Perchance to dream (2010)
So silver bright (2011)

Manzano, Sonia

★ The **revolution** of Evelyn Serrano; Sonia Manzano. Scholastic 2012 205 p. $17.99

Grades: 6 7 8 9 10   **Fic**

1. Historical fiction 2. Puerto Ricans -- Fiction 3. Identity -- Fiction 4. Grandmothers -- Fiction 5. Protest movements -- Fiction 6. Family life -- New York (State) -- Harlem -- Fiction 7. Puerto Ricans -- New York (State) -- New York -- Fiction

ISBN 0545325056; 9780545325059; 9780545325066

LC 2012009240

Pura Belpré Author Honor Book (2013)

This novel, by Sonia Manzano, is set "in New York's El Barrio in 1969. . . . The Young Lords, a Puerto Rican activist group, dump garbage in the street and set it on fire, igniting a powerful protest. When Abuela steps in to take charge, Evelyn is thrust into the action. . . . Evelyn learns important truths about her Latino heritage and the history makers who shaped a nation." (Publisher's note)

Includes bibliographical references

Marchetta, Melina

★ **Finnikin** of the rock. Candlewick Press 2010 399p map $18.99

Grades: 8 9 10 11 12   **Fic**

1. Fantasy fiction

ISBN 0-7636-4361-0; 978-0-7636-4361-4

LC 2009-28046

In this fantasy novel, "Finnikin was only a child during the five days of the unspeakable, when the royal family of Lumatere were brutally murdered, and an imposter seized the throne. . . . Finnikin, now on the cusp of manhood, is

compelled to join forces with an arrogant and enigmatic young novice named Evanjalin, who claims that her dark dreams will lead the exiles to a surviving royal child and a way to pierce the cursed barrier and regain the land of Lumatere." (Publisher's note)

"The skillful world building includes just enough detail to create a vivid sense of place, and Marchetta maintains suspense with unexpected story arcs. It is the achingly real characters, though, and the relationships that emerge through the captivating dialogue that drive the story. Filled with questions about the impact of exile and the human need to belong, this standout fantasy quickly reveals that its real magic lies in its accomplished writing." Booklist

★ **Froi** of the exiles. Candlewick 2012 608 p.

Grades: 8 9 10 11 12   **Fic**

1. Exiles 2. War stories 3. Fantasy fiction

ISBN 9780763647599

In this fantasy book, "Froi, a former street thief who has started a new life in Lumatere, is sent to Charyn in disguise to assassinate its king, but his worldview is shaken by revelations about his own unknown past. Tensions between the two kingdoms ratchet up, and Froi"s loyalties are tested as he becomes entrenched in the chaotic political situation in Charyn and is drawn to its unpredictable princess, Quintana, who has been horribly abused in an attempt to break Charyn"s curse." (Publishers Weekly)

★ **Quintana** of Charyn; Melina Marchetta. Candlewick Press 2013 528 p. (Lumatere chronicles) $18.99

Grades: 8 9 10 11 12   **Fic**

1. War stories 2. Fantasy fiction

ISBN 0763658359; 9780763658359

LC 2012955120

This is the conclusion of Melina Marchetta's trilogy which began with "Finnikin of the Rock." Here, "the kingdoms of Lumatere and Charyn attempt to bridge past atrocities through a new generation of leaders. Although tragedies arise, unity and healing are core themes, compared to the horrors of the previous books. As the title suggests, Quintana--the rightful ruler of Charyn, hidden following the uprising in the kingdom in Froi of the Exiles--is at the center of this final book." (Publishers Weekly)

Marcus, Kimberly

Exposed. Random House 2011 260p $16.99; lib bdg $19.99

Grades: 8 9 10   **Fic**

1. School stories 2. Novels in verse 3. Rape -- Fiction 4. Guilt -- Fiction 5. Friendship -- Fiction 6. Photography -- Fiction

ISBN 0-375-86693-0; 0-375-96693-5 lib bdg; 978-0-375-86693-7; 978-0-375-89724-5 e-book; 978-0-375-96693-4 lib bdg

LC 2009-51545

High school senior Liz, a gifted photographer, can no longer see things clearly after her best friend accuses Liz's older brother of a terrible crime.

"The narrative largely zooms in on Liz's pain and her struggle to ground herself in her photography and gain admission to art school as events swirl around her. As a result of tethering the narrative to Liz's perspective, the ongoing discussion of Kate's rape and ensuing trial are not heavy-handed or gratuitous. In Liz, Marcus has created a sympathetic lead. A worthy addition to any collection." SLJ

Margolis, Leslie

Everybody bugs out. Bloomsbury Children's Books 2011 195p $15.99

Grades: 4 5 6   **Fic**

    1. School stories 2. Friendship -- Fiction 3. Family life -- Fiction

    ISBN 1-59990-526-4; 978-1-59990-526-6

                           LC 2010035628

Sixth-grader Annabelle realizes that she has a crush on Oliver, with whom she is doing a science fair project, just before the Valentine's Day dance—and just before her friend Claire announces her crush on him.

"Margolis' breezy tone nicely conveys the peaks and valleys of middle-school life." Kirkus

Girl's best friend. Bloomsbury USA Childrens Books 2010 261p $14.99

Grades: 4 5 6 7   **Fic**

    1. School stories 2. Mystery fiction 3. Dogs -- Fiction 4. Twins -- Fiction 5. Siblings -- Fiction 6. Family life -- Fiction

    ISBN 978-1-59990-525-9; 1-59990-525-6

                           LC 2010000562

In Brooklyn, New York, twelve-year-old dog-walker Maggie, aided by her twin brother Finn and best friend Lucy, investigates someone she believes is stealing pets.

"Characters are well-developed, typical preteens. Readers will easily identify with these seventh graders, and they will love the eccentric landlady who adds a bit of humor. Mystery fans will enjoy this lighthearted whodunit." SLJ

Girls acting catty. Bloomsbury 2009 179p $15.99

Grades: 4 5 6   **Fic**

    1. School stories 2. Remarriage -- Fiction 3. Family life -- Fiction

    ISBN 978-1-59990-237-1; 1-59990-237-0

                           LC 2009002144

Sixth-grader Annabelle spends autumn coping with competing groups of friends at school, her mother's pre-wedding stress, learning to get along with a cute stepbrother-to-be, and such momentous events as wearing her first bra and learning to shave her legs.

"Margolis handles Annabelle's minor crises with sensitivity and humor." SLJ

Marillier, Juliet

★ **Cybele's** secret. Alfred A. Knopf 2008 432p $17.99; lib bdg $20.99

Grades: 7 8 9 10   **Fic**

    1. Magic -- Fiction 2. Sisters -- Fiction 3. Supernatural -- Fiction

    ISBN 978-0-375-83365-6; 0-375-83365-X; 978-0-375-93365-3 lib bdg; 0-375-93365-4 lib bdg

                           LC 2008-4758

Scholarly eighteen-year-old Paula and her merchant father journey from Transylvania to Istanbul to buy an ancient

pagan artifact rumored to be charmed, but others, including a handsome Portuguese pirate and an envoy from the magical Wildwood, want to acquire the item, as well.

This is a "honeyed draught of a [novel]. . . . Marillier embroiders Ottoman Empire cultural details into every fold and drape of her story." Booklist

Shadowfell; Juliet Marillier. Alfred A. Knopf 2012 410 p. map (trade) $16.99

Grades: 7 8 9 10 11 12   **Fic**

    1. Fantasy fiction 2. Magic -- Fiction 3. Adventure fiction 4. Fantasy 5. Orphans -- Fiction 6. Insurgency -- Fiction 7. Voyages and travels -- Fiction

    ISBN 0375869549; 9780375869549; 9780375969546; 9780375983665

                           LC 2011041050

Originally published: Sydney, N.S.W. : Pan Macmillan, 2012.

In this novel by Juliet Marillier "Fifteen-year-old Neryn is alone in the land of Alban, where the oppressive king has ordered anyone with magical strengths captured and brought before him. Eager to hide her own canny skill--a uniquely powerful ability to communicate with the fairy-like Good Folk--Neryn sets out for the legendary Shadowfell, a home and training ground for a secret rebel group determined to overthrow the evil King Keldec." (Publisher's note)

Wildwood dancing. Knopf 2007 416p $16.99; lib bdg $18.99

Grades: 7 8 9 10   **Fic**

    1. Magic -- Fiction 2. Sisters -- Fiction 3. Supernatural -- Fiction

    ISBN 0-375-83364-1; 0-375-93364-6 lib bdg

                           LC 2006-16075

Five sisters who live with their merchant father in Transylvania use a hidden portal in their home to cross over into a magical world, the Wildwood.

This is told "with a striking sense of place, magical elements, beautifully portrayed characters, strong heroines, and an emotional core that touches the heart." Voice Youth Advocates

Mariz, Rae

The **Unidentified**. Balzer + Bray 2010 296p $16.99

Grades: 7 8 9 10   **Fic**

    1. School stories 2. Science fiction

    ISBN 978-0-06-180208-9; 0-06-180208-5

                           LC 2009-54254

In a futuristic alternative school set in a shopping mall where video game-playing students are observed and used by corporate sponsors for market research, Katey "Kid" Dade struggles to figure out where she fits in and whether she even wants to.

"An all-too-logical extrapolation of today's trends, this story of conformity, rebellion, and seeking one's identity is evocative of Scott Westerfeld and Cory Doctorow, injecting a dystopian setting with an optimistic, antiestablishment undercurrent." Publ Wkly

Marr, Melissa

Wicked lovely. HarperTeen 2007 328p il $16.99; lib bdg $17.89

Grades: 8 9 10 11 12   Fic

1. Fantasy fiction 2. Fairies -- Fiction 3. Kings and rulers -- Fiction

ISBN 978-0-06-121465-3; 0-06-121465-5; 978-0-06-121466-0 lib bdg; 0-06-121466-3 lib bdg

LC 2007-09143

Seventeen-year-old Aislinn, who has the rare ability to see faeries, is drawn against her will into a centuries-old battle between the Summer King and the Winter Queen, and the survival of her life, her love, and summer all hang in the balance.

"This story explores the themes of love, commitment, and what it really means to give of oneself for the greater good to save everyone else. It is the unusual combination of past legends and modern-day life that gives a unique twist to this 'fairy' tale." SLJ

Other titles in this series are:

Darkest mercy (2011)
Fragile eternity (2009)
Ink exchange (2008)
Radiant shadows (2010)

Marriott, Zoe

The **swan** kingdom. Candlewick Press 2008 272p $16.99; pa $8.99

Grades: 6 7 8 9 10 11 12   Fic

1. Fantasy fiction 2. Magic -- Fiction

ISBN 978-0-7636-3481-0; 0-7636-3481-6; 978-0-7636-4293-8 pa; 0-7636-4293-2 pa

LC 2007-38291

When Alexa's mother is killed, her father marries a cunning and powerful woman and her brothers disappear, sending Alexa on a long, dangerous journey as she attempts to harness the mystical power she inherited from her mother and restore the kingdom to its proper balance.

"The mix of magic, royalty and romance will compel many teens." Publ Wkly

Marsden, Carolyn, 1950-

My Own Revolution; Carolyn Marsden. Candlewick Press 2012 174 p. $16.99

Grades: 7 8 9 10 11 12   Fic

1. Czechoslovakia -- Fiction 2. Communist countries -- Fiction 3. Resistance to government -- Fiction

ISBN 0763653950; 9780763653958

LC 2012942296

This young adult novel, by Carolyn Marsden, takes place "in 1960s Czechoslovakia, [where] . . . fourteen-year-old Patrik rebels against the communist regime in small ways whenever he gets the chance. . . . But anti-Party sentiment is risky, and when party interference cuts a little too close to home, Patrik and his family find themselves faced with a decision . . . that will change everything." (Publisher's note)

Sahwira; an African friendship. [by] Carolyn Marsden and Philip Matzigkeit. Candlewick Press 2009 189p $15.99

Grades: 5 6 7 8   Fic

1. Clergy -- Fiction 2. Friendship -- Fiction 3. Race relations -- Fiction

ISBN 978-0-7636-3575-6; 0-7636-3575-8

The strong friendship between two boys, one black and one white, who live on a mission in Rhodesia, begins to unravel as protests against white colonial rule intensify in 1964.

"The book looks beyond race to examine questions about the meaning of being Christian, fear of Communism, family loyalty, and ethical choices. Marsden and Matzigkeit . . . deftly navigate the dynamic forces at play in the two boys' lives. . . . The story crosses genres to bring in elements of historical fiction, intrigue, and mystery." Bull Cent Child Books

★ **Take** me with you. Candlewick Press 2010 160p $14.99

Grades: 4 5 6 7   Fic

1. Orphans -- Fiction 2. Friendship -- Fiction 3. Racially mixed people -- Fiction

ISBN 978-0-7636-3739-2; 0-7636-3739-4

LC 2009-38053

This story is set in "Italy after World War II. Pina and Susanna have lived at their Naples orphanage since they were babies. . . . Pina, pretty and blonde, . . . is sure the nuns tell prospective parents she is bad. Susanna is the daughter of an Italian woman and a black American solider. . . ; no one looks like her. Then two very different parents come into the girls' lives. . . . Both satisfy the girls' dreams in unexpected ways. Marsden often puts crafts like sewing or crocheting into her stories, and in many ways she is like a master craftsman, using words instead of stitches for her deceptively simple design." Booklist

Marsden, John, 1950-

★ **Tomorrow,** when the war began. Houghton Mifflin 1995 286p $9.99

Grades: 7 8 9 10   Fic

1. War stories

ISBN 0395706734

LC 94-29299

First published 1993 in Australia

"Australian teenager Ellie and six of her friends return from a winter break camping trip to find their homes burned or deserted, their families imprisoned, and their country occupied by a foreign military force in league with a band of disaffected Australians. As their shock wears off, the seven decide they must stick together if they are to survive. After a life-threatening skirmish with the occupiers, the teens retreat to their isolated campsite in the bush country and make plans to fight a guerilla war against the invaders. . . . Grade eight and up." (SLJ)

"The novel is a riveting adventure through which Marsden explores the capacity for evil and the necessity of working together to oppose it." Horn Book

Other available titles in this series are:

Burning for revenge (2000)
Darkness, be my friend (1999)
The dead of night (1997)
A killing frost (1998)
The night is for hunting (2001)
The other side of dawn (2002)

While I live. Scholastic 2007 299p (The Ellie chronicles) $16.99

Grades: 7 8 9 10   **Fic**
1. War stories 2. Young adult literature -- Works
ISBN 978-0-439-78318-7; 0-439-78318-6

Officially the war is over, but Ellie can not seem to escape it and resume a normal life especially after her parents are murdered and she becomes the ward of an unscrupulous lawyer who wants to acquire her family's property.

"Fans of 16-year-old Ellie Linton . . . will be overjoyed that she's back in an exciting series of her own. The realistic and shocking war-related violence that characterized the earlier titles is just as prevalent here." SLJ

Other titles about Ellie Linton are:
Circle of flight (2009)
Incurable (2008)

Marsh, Katherine

★ **Jepp,** who defied the stars; Katherine Marsh. Hyperion 2012 385 p. (hardback) $16.99

Grades: 6 7 8 9 10   **Fic**
1. Bildungsromans 2. Dwarfs -- Fiction 3. Historical fiction 4. Renaissance -- Fiction 5. Voyages and travels -- Fiction 6. Courts and courtiers -- Fiction
ISBN 1423135008; 9781423135005

LC 2011053065

This book tells the story of "a 15-year-old dwarf named Jepp. . . . The first of the book's three sections finds a battered and beaten Jepp being transported ignobly in a cage to an unknown destination; along the way, he recalls the events that led him there, from his humble upbringing in an inn to becoming a court dwarf in Brussels. . . . Jepp's fortunes continue to wax and wane in the later sections, as he arrives at the island castle of astronomer Tycho Brahe." (Publishers Weekly)

★ The **night** tourist; [by] Katherine Marsh. 1st ed.; Hyperion Books for Children 2007 232p $17.99

Grades: 6 7 8 9   **Fic**
1. Death -- Fiction 2. Classical mythology -- Fiction
ISBN 978-1-4231-0689-0; 1-4231-0689-X

LC 2007013311

After fourteen-year-old classics prodigy Jack Perdu has a near fatal accident he meets Euri, a young ghost who introduces him to New York's Underworld, where those who died in New York reside until they are ready to move on, and Jack vows to find his dead mother there.

"Mixing numerous references to mythology and classical literature with deft touches of humor and extensive historical details . . . this intelligent and self-assured debut will compel readers from its outset and leave them satisfied." Publ Wkly

The **twilight** prisoner; [by] Katherine Marsh. 1st ed.; Hyperion Books for Children 2009 246p $17.99

Grades: 6 7 8 9   **Fic**
1. Death -- Fiction 2. Classical mythology -- Fiction
ISBN 978-1-4231-0693-7; 1-4231-0693-8

LC 2008013938

In an effort to impress a female classmate, high school sophomore Jack Perdu endangers both of their lives by taking her to New York City's Underworld, where those who died in New York reside until they are ready to move on.

"Readers should be drawn in by the complex relationships between Marsh's protagonists and Jack's continuing existential struggles, caught between the worlds of the living and the dead." Publ Wkly

Martin, Ann M., 1955-

Better to wish; Ann M. Martin. 1st ed. Scholastic 2013 240 p. (Family tree) (hardcover) $16.99

Grades: 3 4 5 6 7   **Fic**
1. Depressions -- 1929 -- Fiction 2. Family life -- Maine -- Fiction
ISBN 0545359422; 9780545359429

LC 2012047940

This is the first book in Ann M. Martin's Family Tree series. "Growing up in Maine, eight-year-old Abby Nichols is the oldest daughter of an ambitious carpenter eager to realize the American Dream. But his prejudices are strong, too: he won't let Abby associate with her Irish Catholic neighbor, Orrin. . . . As Abby's father gains success, she enjoys more privileges, . . . but the family's newfound prosperity doesn't ease her outrage over her father's mistreatment of the less fortunate." (Publishers Weekly)

Everything for a dog. Feiwel and Friends 2009 211p $16.99

Grades: 5 6 7 8   **Fic**
1. Dogs -- Fiction 2. Loneliness -- Fiction 3. Bereavement -- Fiction
ISBN 978-0-312-38651-1; 0-312-38651-6

LC 2008-34747

In parallel stories, Bone, an orphaned dog, finds and loses a series of homes, Molly, a family pet, helps Charlie through the grief and other after-effects of his brother's death, and lonely Henry pleads for a dog of his own

"This is a sensitive, gentle read that surrounds its occasional heartbreak with plenty of hope and warm feelings." Booklist

Here today. Scholastic 2004 308p $16.95; pa $5.99

Grades: 5 6 7 8   **Fic**
1. Mothers -- Fiction 2. Family life -- Fiction
ISBN 0-439-57944-9; 0-439-57945-7 pa

LC 2004-41620

In 1963, Ellie's mother was crowned a grocery store beauty queen, her classmates treated her cruelly, and President Kennedy was killed. It was also when Ellie realized that in trying to keep her life together she had to let pieces of it go

"Martin paints a well-articulated picture of the times, but it is her memorable child and adult characters that shine here." SLJ

A **corner** of the universe. Scholastic Press 2002 189p $15.95; pa $5.99

Grades: 5 6 7 8   **Fic**
1. Uncles -- Fiction 2. Friendship -- Fiction 3. Mentally

handicapped -- Fiction
ISBN 0-439-38880-5; 0-439-38881-3 pa

LC 2001-57611

A Newbery Medal honor book, 2003

The summer that Hattie turns twelve, she meets the childlike uncle she never knew and becomes friends with a girl who works at the carnival that comes to Hattie's small town

"Martin delivers wonderfully real characters and an engrossing plot through the viewpoint of a girl who tries so earnestly to connect with those around her." SLJ

Martin, Rafe

Birdwing; [by] Rafe Martin. 1st ed; Arthur A. Levine Books 2005 359p $16.99

Grades: 6 7 8 9   Fic

1. Fairy tales 2. Young adult literature -- Works
ISBN 0-439-21167-0

LC 2004-11695

Prince Ardwin, known as Birdwing, the youngest of six brothers turned into swans by their stepmother, is unable to complete the transformation back into human form, so he undertakes a journey to discover whether his feathered arm will be a curse or a blessing to him.

"The many original characters and unusual adventure scenes ensure that readers will remember this well-paced fantasy." Booklist

Martinez, Claudia Guadalupe

The **smell** of old lady perfume. Cinco Puntos Press 2008 249p il $15.95

Grades: 5 6 7 8   Fic

1. School stories 2. Death -- Fiction 3. Grandmothers -- Fiction 4. Hispanic Americans -- Fiction 5. Young adult literature -- Works 6. Children's literature -- Works -- Grades two through six
ISBN 978-1-9336-9318-7; 1-9336-9318-5

LC 2007-38296

When sixth-grader Chela Gonzalez's father has a stroke and her grandmother moves in to help take care of the family, her world is turned upside down.

"Short, well-crafted chapters offer perceptive glimpses into life on the border, the dynamics of middle-grade girls, and a family in turmoil." Horn Book Guide

Martinez, Jessica

★ **Virtuosity**. Simon Pulse 2011 294p $16.99

Grades: 8 9 10 11 12   Fic

1. Musicians -- Fiction 2. Drug abuse -- Fiction 3. Violinists -- Fiction 4. Mother-daughter relationship -- Fiction
ISBN 978-1-4424-2052-6; 1-4424-2052-9

LC 2010042513

This is a "riveting novel. . . . The portrayal of Carmen's world . . . is unique and convincing. . . . Even readers without much interest in music will enjoy this exceptional novel." SLJ

Mary-Todd, Jonathan

Shot down; Jonathan Mary-Todd. Darby Creek 2012 92 p. (lib. bdg. : alk. paper) $27.93

Grades: 7 8 9 10 11 12   Fic

1. Adventure fiction 2. Apocalyptic fiction 3. Survival skills -- Fiction 4. Survival after airplane accidents, shipwrecks, etc. -- Fiction 5. Science fiction 6. Hunting -- Fiction 7. Survival -- Fiction
ISBN 0761383298; 9780761383291

LC 2012006864

This young adult novel, by Jonathan Mary-Todd, is a post-apocalyptic adventure story. "When a bullet knocks Malik and the Captain's hot-air balloon out of the sky, Malik goes into wilderness survival mode. . . . Whatever the crisis, he's always counted on the Gene Matterhorn Wilderness Survival Guidebook when things got crazy. Now he and the Captain are in the middle of miles of Kentucky wilderness, being chased by manhunters." (Publisher's note)

Mason, Prue

Camel rider; [by] Prue Mason. 1st U.S. ed.; Charlesbridge 2007 204p $15.95

Grades: 6 7 8 9   Fic

1. War stories 2. Deserts -- Fiction 3. Wilderness survival -- Fiction
ISBN 978-1-58089-314-5; 1-58089-314-7

LC 2006034125

Two expatriates living in a Middle Eastern country, twelve-year-old Adam from Australia and Walid from Bangladesh, must rely on one another when war breaks out and they find themselves in the desert, both trying to reach the same city with no water, little food, and no common language.

"The suspense is sustained and the wildly improbable happy ending is very satisfying." SLJ

Mason, Timothy

The **last** synapsid. Delacorte Press 2009 311p il $16.99; lib bdg $19.99

Grades: 5 6 7 8   Fic

1. Time travel -- Fiction 2. Space and time -- Fiction 3. Prehistoric animals -- Fiction
ISBN 978-0-385-73581-0; 0-385-73581-2; 978-0-385-90567-1 lib bdg; 0-385-90567-X lib bdg

LC 2008-35678

On a mountain near their tiny town of Faith, Colorado, best friends Rob and Phoebe discover a squat, drooly creature from thirty million years before the dinosaurs, that needs their help in tracking down a violent carnivore that must be returned to its proper place in time, or humans will never evolve.

"Mason has written a highly engaging fantasy that includes something for all readers. . . . Readers will find it difficult to put this book down until they have reached the last page." Libr Media Connect

Mass, Wendy

★ **Every** soul a star; a novel. Little, Brown and Co. 2008 322p $15.99; pa $6.99

Grades: 5 6 7 8   Fic

1. Friendship -- Fiction 2. Solar eclipses -- Fiction
ISBN 978-0-316-00256-1; 0-316-00256-9; 978-0-316-00257-8 pa; 0-316-00257-7 pa

LC 2008009259

Ally, Bree, and Jack meet at the one place the Great Eclipse can be seen in totality, each carrying the burden of different personal problems, which become dim when compared to the task they embark upon and the friendship they find.

Mass "combines astronomy and storytelling for a well-balanced look at friendships and the role they play in shaping identity. . . . Information about solar eclipses and astronomy is carefully woven into the plot to build drama and will almost certainly intrigue readers." Publ Wkly

Includes bibliographical references

Heaven looks a lot like the mall; a novel. Little, Brown 2007 251p $16.99

Grades: 8 9 10 11 12   **Fic**
1. School stories 2. Coma -- Fiction 3. Shopping centers and malls -- Fiction
ISBN 978-0-316-05851-3; 0-316-05851-3
LC 2007-12333

When high school junior Tessa Reynolds falls into a coma after getting hit in the head during gym class, she experiences heaven as the mall where her parents work, and she revisits key events from her life, causing her to reevaluate herself and how she wants to live.

"Tessa's journey and authentic voice is one that readers will appreciate. . . . Funny, thought-provoking, and at times heartbreaking, this story will entertain and inspire readers." SLJ

Jeremy Fink and the meaning of life. Little, Brown 2006 289p $15.99; pa $6.99

Grades: 5 6 7 8   **Fic**
1. Conduct of life -- Fiction 2. Father-son relationship -- Fiction
ISBN 978-0-316-05829-2; 0-316-05829-7; 978-0-316-05849-0 pa; 0-316-05849-1 pa
LC 2005037291

Just before his thirteenth birthday, Jeremy Fink receives a keyless locked box—set aside by his father before his death five years earlier—that purportedly contains the meaning of life.

"Mass fashions an adventure in which both journey and destination are worth the trip." Horn Book

Pi in the sky; Wendy Mass. 1st ed. Little, Brown and Co. 2013 256 p. (hardcover) $17

Grades: 3 4 5 6 7   **Fic**
1. Creation -- Fiction 2. Science fiction
ISBN 0316089168; 9780316089166
LC 2012030638

In this humorous children's novel, by Wendy Mass, "Joss is the seventh son of the Supreme Overlord of the Universe, and all he gets to do is deliver pies. . . . But when Earth suddenly disappears, Joss is tasked with the not-so-simple job of bringing it back. With the help of an outspoken girl from Earth named Annika, Joss embarks on the adventure of a lifetime and learns that the universe is an even stranger place than he'd imagined." (Publisher's note)

A **mango** -shaped space; a novel. Little, Brown 2003 220p $16.95

Grades: 5 6 7 8   **Fic**
1. School stories 2. Synesthesia -- Fiction
ISBN 0-316-52388-7
LC 2002-72989

Afraid that she is crazy, thirteen-year-old Mia, who sees a special color with every letter, number, and sound, keeps this a secret until she becomes overwhelmed by school, changing relationships, and the loss of something important to her

"Mass skillfully conveys Mia's emotions, and readers will be intrigued with this fictional depiction of an actual, and fascinating, condition." Horn Book Guide

Masson, Sophie
Snow, fire, sword; 1st American ed.; Eos 2006 359p $15.99; lib bdg $16.89

Grades: 6 7 8 9   **Fic**
1. Fantasy fiction 2. Magic -- Fiction
ISBN 978-0-06-079091-2; 0-06-079091-1; 978-0-06-079092-9 lib bdg; 0-06-079092-X lib bdg
LC 2005-18149

In the mythical, Indonesia-like country of Jayangan, a village girl and an apprentice swordmaker embark on a magical journey to defeat a hidden evil that threatens their land.

"The sense of a permeable membrane between spirit worlds and contemporary reality will fascinate many readers, as will the shifting images of water buffaloes and motorbikes, villages and cities, and sacred and secular ways." Booklist

The **madman** of Venice. Delacorte Press 2010 276p $17.99; lib bdg $20.99

Grades: 6 7 8 9   **Fic**
1. Missing persons -- Fiction
ISBN 978-0-385-73843-9; 0-385-73843-9; 978-0-385-90729-3 lib bdg; 0-385-90729-X lib bdg
LC 2009022369

First published 2009 in the United Kingdom

"An exotic setting and delicious intrigue combine to make intense historical fiction in this tale of missing persons, murder, and, of course, romance. English merchant Master Ashby heads to Venice in 1602 to investigate the murder of his agent Salerio and the strange disappearance of a young Jewish girl accused of witchcraft by the cruel, conniving wife of the Count of Montemaro. . . . Ashby and his alchemist friend Dr. Leone soon find themselves entangled in a morass that involves Venetian pirates, mistaken identities, and the poisoning of the Count." SLJ

Master, Irfan
★ A **beautiful** lie; by Irfan Master. Albert Whitman 2012 301 p. (hardcover) $16.99

Grades: 7 8 9 10   **Fic**
1. Deception -- Fiction 2. India -- History -- Fiction 3. Father-son relationship -- Fiction 4. Honesty -- Fiction 5. Terminally ill -- Fiction
ISBN 0807505978; 9780807505977
LC 2011051132

In this book by Irfan Master, set "in India in 1947, the country is coming apart -- and so is thirteen-year-old Bilal's life. He is determined to protect his dying father from the news of Partition, news that he knows will break his father's heart. With spirit and determination, and with the help of his good friends, Bilal builds an elaborate deception, even printing false pages of the local newspaper to hide the signs of national unrest." (Publisher's note)

Matas, Carol

After the war. Simon & Schuster Bks. for Young Readers 1996 116p map hardcover o.p. pa $4.99

Grades: 7 8 9 10   **Fic**

1. Jews -- Fiction 2. Holocaust, 1933-1945 -- Fiction
ISBN 0-689-80350-8; 0-689-80722-8

LC 95-43613

After being released from Buchenwald at the end of World War II, fifteen-year-old Ruth risks her life to lead a group of children across Europe to Palestine

"Rich in texture and simple in its honesty, this story resonates with feeling." Voice Youth Advocates

Sparks fly upward. Clarion Bks. 2002 180p $15

Grades: 4 5 6 7   **Fic**

1. Jews -- Fiction 2. Moving, Household 3. Family life -- Canada 4. Prejudices -- Fiction
ISBN 0-618-15964-9

LC 2001-47188

In 1910, when a family of Russian Jews moves from Saskatchewan to Winnipeg, Canada, twelve-year-old Rebecca must live with Christians temporarily and struggles with anti-Semitism, confusion about God, and changing relationships with family and friends

"There's no sentimentality in the characterization . . . and the history is well researched. Most compelling, though, is Rebecca's personal struggle with faith, friendship, and loyalty." Booklist

The whirlwind. Orca 2007 128p pa $8.95

Grades: 6 7 8 9   **Fic**

1. Jews -- Fiction 2. Immigrants -- Fiction 3. World War, 1939-1945 -- Fiction
ISBN 978-1-55143-703-3 pa; 1-55143-703-1 pa

"Benjamin Friedman, a 15-year-old Jewish boy, fears for his life in Nazi Germany. Fortunately, his family is able to escape Hitler, arriving in Seattle in the summer of 1941. Ben is relieved to be there but is upset and confused by his experiences. . . . This unique and thought-provoking story shows what prejudice and indifference to suffering and wrongdoing can lead to. It imparts an understanding of the Holocaust and World War II." SLJ

Matthews, Andrew

The **way** of the warrior. Dutton Children's Books 2008 152p $15.99

Grades: 7 8 9 10   **Fic**

1. Samurai -- Fiction
ISBN 978-0-525-42063-7; 0-525-42063-0

"In 1565, when Jimmu is 10 years old, he witnesses his father commit seppuku, a ritual suicide, to avoid bringing dishonor to his family. . . . Jimmu spends the next seven years learning the art of the samurai . . . with the sole intention of avenging his father . . . . The . . . story is an honest and engaging portrayal of a young man's struggle to do the right thing. . . . The vivid depictions of a soldier's life in 16th-century Japan will captivate samurai enthusiasts, and the amount of action that Matthews packs into this relatively short novel will appeal to reluctant readers." SLJ

Matthews, L. S.

Lexi. Delacorte Press 2008 200p $14.99; lib bdg $17.99

Grades: 4 5 6 7   **Fic**

1. Twins -- Fiction 2. Amnesia -- Fiction 3. Orphans -- Fiction 4. Sisters -- Fiction 5. Homeless persons -- Fiction
ISBN 978-0-385-73574-2; 0-385-73574-X; 978-0-385-90563-3 lib bdg; 0-385-90563-7 lib bdg

LC 2007-46745

When twelve-year-old Lexi wakes up in the middle of a forest with no memory of her name or anything else, she slowly reconstructs her forgotten life with the help of some shelter workers, an ex-boxer, and her long-lost grandmother.

"This is a story of improbable, sometimes frightening events told by a child narrator, in which extraordinary things seem perfectly plausible. . . . Fans of Matthews's previous work will appreciate its sense of childlike wonder and fantasy." SLJ

The outcasts. Delacorte Press 2007 259p $15.99; lib bdg $18.99

Grades: 7 8 9 10   **Fic**

1. School stories 2. Supernatural -- Fiction
ISBN 978-0-385-73367-0; 978-0-385-90382-0 lib bdg

LC 2006-50872

First published 2005 in the United Kingdom

A much-anticipated school trip to England's West Country turns into a life-changing adventure for five high school misfits when they fall into another dimension while exploring the house in which they are staying.

"A fun, wild, and thoughtfully layered adventure." Booklist

Matthews, Tom L.

Danger in the dark; a Houdini & Nate mystery. [by] Tom Lalicki; pictures by Carlyn Cerniglia. Farrar, Straus and Giroux 2006 186p il $14.95

Grades: 4 5 6 7   **Fic**

1. Magicians 2. Mystery fiction 3. Nonfiction writers 4. Magicians -- Fiction 5. Spiritualism -- Fiction
ISBN 0-374-31680-5

LC 2005052111

Thirteen-year-old Nathaniel, aided by the famous magician Harry Houdini, plots to unmask a phony spirit advisor attempting to relieve the boy's great-aunt of her fortune.

"The action is nonstop, and even a flurry of enormous coincidences won't spoil enthusiasm for this entertaining story." Booklist

Other titles in this series are:
Shots at sea (2007)
Frame-up on the Bowery (2009)

Matti, Truus

★ **Departure** time; translated from the Dutch by Nancy Forest-Flier. Namelos 2010 214p $18.95; pa $9.95

Grades: 5 6 7 8   **Fic**
1. Memory -- Fiction 2. Father-daughter relationship
-- Fiction
ISBN 978-1-60898-087-1; 1-60898-087-1; 978-1-
60898-009-3 pa; 1-60898-009-X pa
Original Dutch edition 2009
"A 10-year-old girl is lost in a surrealistic landscape—a
red-earth desert threatened by an approaching storm. Nothing looks familiar. She can't remember how she got to this
place. Alternating with this classic bad-dream setting, which
is narrated in the third person, is a first-person, furious tirade
by a girl who feels abandoned by her father and neglected
by her mother. Readers will be intrigued by the way Matti
interweaves these stories and tantalizes with the possible
connections between them. . . . Remarkable and arresting
and wholly original, this novel lingers in the mind long after
the last page has been read." SLJ

Mister Orange; Truus Matti ; translated from the
Dutch by Laura Watkinson. Enchanged Lion Books
2013 156 p. (hardcover) $16.95
Grades: 5 6 7 8   **Fic**
1. Artists -- Fiction 5. Friendship -- Fiction 2. World
War, 1939-1945 -- Fiction
ISBN 159270123X; 9781592701230
                                          LC 2012051313
This children's story, by Truus Matti, translated by Laura
Watkinson, is set in Manhattan in "1943. . . . Linus Muller
works at the family grocery store in the east 70s. . . . One of
his customers . . . arranges to have a crate of oranges delivered every other week. Over the course of these deliveries,
an intimacy develops between Linus and . . . Mister Orange.
In the peacefulness of Mister Orange's spare kitchen, they
discuss the war, the future, freedom and imagination." (Publisher's note)

Mayall, Beth
Mermaid Park. Razorbill 2005 248p $16.99
Grades: 7 8 9 10   **Fic**
1. Swimming -- Fiction 2. Family life -- Fiction 3.
Summer employment -- Fiction
ISBN 1-59514-029-8
Sixteen-year-old Amy escapes family difficulties by im-
mersing herself in her job at a mermaid-themed water show.
"This is a good read that deals with real growing-up
issues." SLJ

Mazer, Harry
My brother Abe; Sally Lincoln's story. Simon
& Schuster Books for Young Readers 2009 202p
$15.99
Grades: 4 5 6 7   **Fic**
1. Frontier and pioneer life -- Fiction
ISBN 978-1-4169-3884-2; 1-4169-3884-2
                                          LC 2008-01106
Forced off their land in Kentucky in 1816, nine-year-old
Sarah Lincoln, known as Sally, and her family, including
younger brother Abe, move to the Indiana frontier.
"Drawing on a limber imagination and knack for story-
telling, Mazer . . . turns a few facts from Abraham Lincoln's
childhood into a vivid historical novel. . . . Abe's older sister,

Sally, about whom little is known, serves as the personable
narrator and protagonist." Publ Wkly

★ **Snow** bound. Delacorte Press 1973 146p
hardcover o.p. pa $5.99
Grades: 7 8 9 10   **Fic**
1. Runaway children -- Fiction 2. Wilderness survival
-- Fiction
ISBN 0-440-96134-3
                                          LC 72-7958
"Tony Laporte is angry when his parents will not allow
him to keep a stray dog, so he takes off in his mother's old
car. Driving without a license in the middle of a snowstorm
that soon becomes a blizzard, Tony picks up a hitchhiker,
Cindy Reichert. Trying to impress the slightly older girl
with his driving skill, Tony wrecks the car, leaving the two
stranded in a desolate area far from a main highway, with
little likelihood of rescue for days." Shapiro. Fic for Youth.
3d edition

A **boy** at war; a novel of Pearl Harbor. Simon
& Schuster Bks. for Young Readers 2001 104p il
hardcover o.p. pa $4.99
Grades: 7 8 9 10   **Fic**
1. Pearl Harbor (Oahu, Hawaii), Attack on, 1941 --
Fiction
ISBN 0-689-84161-2; 0-689-84160-4 pa
                                          LC 00-49687
While fishing with his friends off Honolulu on December 7, 1941, teenaged Adam is caught in the midst of the
Japanese attack and through the chaos of the subsequent
days tries to find his father, a naval officer who was serving
on the U.S.S. Arizona when the bombs fell
"Mazer's graphic, sensory descriptions give the narrative immediacy, putting readers alongside Adam, watching
with him as 'pieces of the ship and pieces of men rained
down around him.' . . . This is a thought-provoking, sobering
account of the human costs of war." Horn Book Guide
Other titles in this series are:
A boy no more (2004)
Heroes don't run (2005)

★ **The** last mission. Dell 1981 188p pa $5.99
Grades: 7 8 9 10   **Fic**
1. Jews -- Fiction 2. Prisoners of war -- Fiction 3.
World War, 1939-1945 -- Fiction
ISBN 0-440-94797-9
First published 1979 by Delacorte Press
In 1944 a 15-year-old Jewish boy tells his family he will
travel in the West but instead, enlists in the United States Air
Corps and is subsequently taken prisoner by the Germans.
"Told in a rapid journalistic style, occasionally peppered
with barrack-room vulgarities, the story is a vivid and moving account of a boy's experience during World War II as
well as a skillful, convincing portrayal of his misgivings as
a Jew on enemy soil and of his ability to size up—in mature
human fashion—the misery around him." Horn Book

Mazer, Norma Fox
After the rain. Morrow 1987 291p hardcover
o.p. pa $5.99

Grades: 6 7 8 9   **Fic**
1. Death -- Fiction 2. Grandfathers -- Fiction
ISBN 0-688-06867-7; 0-380-75025-2 pa

LC 86-33270

A Newbery Medal honor book, 1988
"A powerful book, dealing with death and dying and the strength of family affection." Horn Book

Girlhearts. HarperCollins Pubs. 2001 210p hardcover o.p. lib bdg $16.89; pa $6.99
Grades: 6 7 8 9   **Fic**
1. Death -- Fiction 2. Orphans -- Fiction 3. Mothers and daughters
ISBN 0-688-13350-9; 0-688-06866-9 lib bdg; 0-380-72290-9 pa

LC 00-63202

Thirteen-year-old Sarabeth Silver's life is turned upside-down when her mother dies suddenly, leaving her orphaned, confused, and at the mercy of everyone who seems to know what is best for her
"Mazer's intimate portrait of grief is convincing and well drawn." Horn Book Guide

The **missing** girl. HarperTeen 2008 288p $16.99; lib bdg $17.89
Grades: 7 8 9 10   **Fic**
1. Sisters -- Fiction 2. Kidnapping -- Fiction 3. Child sexual abuse -- Fiction
ISBN 978-0-06-623776-3; 978-0-06-623777-0 lib bdg

LC 2007-09136

In Mallory, New York, as five sisters, aged eleven to seventeen, deal with assorted problems, conflicts, fears, and yearnings, a mysterious middle-aged man watches them, fascinated, deciding which one he likes the best.
"Fans of . . . classic tales of high-tension peril will appreciate the way this successfully plays on their deepest fears." Bull Cent Child Books

McBride, Regina
The **fire** opal. Delacorte Press 2010 293p $16.99; lib bdg $19.99
Grades: 7 8 9 10   **Fic**
1. Family life -- Fiction 2. Supernatural -- Fiction 3. Celtic mythology -- Fiction 4. Young adult literature -- Works
ISBN 978-0-385-73781-4; 0-385-73781-5; 978-0-385-90692-0 lib bdg; 0-385-90692-7 lib bdg

LC 2009-07573

While invading English soldiers do battle in sixteenth-century Ireland, Maeve grows up with a mystical connection to a queen who, centuries before, faced enemies of her own.
"Filled with fantastic creatures and hair-raising adventure, this mystical, imaginative tale should appeal to fantasy fans of all ages. A compelling, addictive read." Voice Youth Advocates

McCaffrey, Anne
Dragonflight; volume 1 of The Dragonriders of Pern. Ballantine Bks. 1978 337p il (Dragonriders of Pern) hardcover o.p. pa $12.95
Grades: 8 9 10 11 12 Adult   **Fic**
1. Dragons 2. Fantasy fiction 3. Science fiction 4.

Life on other planets 5. Fantasies 6. Dragons -- Fiction
ISBN 0-345-27749-X; 0-345-48426-6 pa

LC 78-16707

First published 1968 in paperback. Based on two award winning stories entitled: Weyr search and Dragonrider. Many titles co-written by Todd McCaffrey
ALA YALSA Margaret A. Edwards Award (1999)
The planet Pern, originally colonized from Earth but long out of contact with it, has been periodically threatened by the deadly silver Threads which fall from the wandering Red Star. To combat them a life form on the planet was developed into winged, fire-breathing dragons. Humans with a high degree of empathy and telepathic power are needed to train and preserve these creatures. As the story begins, Pern has fallen into decay, the threat of the Red Star has been forgotten, the Dragonriders and dragons are reduced in number and in disrepute, and the evil Lord Fax has begun conquering neighboring holds.
Fantasy titles set on Pern include:
All the Weyrs of Pern (1991)
The chronicles of Pern: first fall (1993)
Dragon Harper (2007)
Dragon's fire (2006)
Dragon's kin (2003)
Dragon's time (2011)
Dragondrums (1979)
Dragonquest (1971)
Dragonsdawn (1988)
Dragonseye (1997)
Dragonsinger (1977)
Dragonsong (1976)
The masterharper of Pern (1998)
Morets: Dragonlady of Pern (1983)
Nerilka's story (1986)
The Renegades of Pern (1989)
The skies of Pern (2001)
White dragon (1978)

McCarthy, Maureen
When you wish upon a rat; by Maureen McCarthy. Amulet Books 2012 281 p. $16.95
Grades: 4 5 6   **Fic**
1. Wishes -- Fiction 5. Family life -- Fiction
ISBN 1419701614; 9781419701610

LC 2012015626

In this Middle school novel, by Maureen McCarthy, "With an absentminded inventor for a father and a flighty artist for a mother, it's always reliable Ruth [Craze] who ends up doing the dishes, paying the bills, and finding lost socks. . . . So when Rodney the Rat--a slightly sinister stuffed animal that was a gift from her favorite aunt--suggests a way out, Ruth is ready to risk everything. Three wishes. Three chances to create her perfect life. A million ways to get it wrong." (Publisher's note)

McCaughrean, Geraldine
Not the end of the world; a novel. HarperTempest 2005 244p $16.99; lib bdg $17.89
Grades: 7 8 9 10   **Fic**
1. Noah's ark -- Fiction
ISBN 0-06-076030-3; 0-06-076031-1 lib bdg

LC 2004-14786

Noah's daughter, daughters-in-law, sons, wife, and the animals describe what it was like to be aboard the ark while they watched everyone around them drown.

"This frightening retelling of the biblical Noah's Ark story is written beautifully and with brutal clarity." Voice Youth Advocates

★ The **death** -defying Pepper Roux. Harper 2010 328p $16.99; lib bdg $17.89

Grades: 5 6 7 8   **Fic**
  1. Adventure fiction 2. Fate and fatalism -- Fiction
  ISBN 978-0-06-183665-7; 0-06-183665-6; 978-0-06-183666-4 lib bdg; 0-06-183666-4 lib bdg
                     LC 2009-39665

Having been raised believing he will die before he reaches the age of fourteen, Pepper Roux runs away on his fourteenth birthday in an attempt to elude his fate, assumes another identity, and continues to try to outrun death, no matter the consequences.

"McCaughrean's exuberant prose and whirling humor animate an unforgettable cast of characters." Booklist

★ The **glorious** adventures of the Sunshine Queen. Harper 2011 325p $16.99

Grades: 5 6 7 8   **Fic**
  1. Adventure fiction 2. Theater -- Fiction
  ISBN 978-0-06-200806-0; 0-06-200806-4
                     LC 2010021958

When a diphtheria outbreak forces twelve-year-old Cissy to leave her Oklahoma hometown in the 1890s, she and her two classmates embark on a wild adventure down the Missouri River with a team of traveling actors who are living on a dilapidated paddle steamer.

"McCaughrean invests her characters with humanity and shows a farcical sense for dialogue, while her arch narrative voice, includes the theatrical and clever turns of phrase." Booklist

★ The **kite** rider; a novel. HarperCollins Pubs. 2002 272p maps hardcover o.p. pa $6.99

Grades: 5 6 7 8   **Fic**
  1. Kites -- Fiction 2. China -- History -- Yüan dynasty, 1260-1368
  ISBN 0-06-623874-9; 0-06-441091-9 pa
                     LC 2001-39522

In thirteenth-century China, after trying to save his widowed mother from a horrendous second marriage, twelve-year-old Haoyou has life-changing adventures when he takes to the sky as a circus kite rider and ends up meeting the great Mongol ruler Kublai Khan

"The story is a genuine page-turner. . . . McCaughrean fully immerses her memorable characters in the culture and lore of the ancient Chinese and Mongols, which make this not only a solid adventure story but also a window to a fascinating time and place." Booklist

McClain, Lee

Sizzle. Marshall Cavendish 2011 190p $17.99

Grades: 6 7 8 9   **Fic**
  1. Moving -- Fiction 2. Cooking -- Fiction 3. Orphans -- Fiction 4. Foster home care -- Fiction 5. Mexican

Americans -- Fiction
  ISBN 978-0-7614-5981-1; 0-7614-5981-2
                     LC 2011001234

When the aunt she lives with becomes ill, orphaned Linda Delgado must leave Arizona for Philadelphia, where she struggles to adapt to a huge foster family, eating canned food, and finding an outlet for her love of cooking.

"Linda's friendly narration is compelling and easy to read. Chapters are broken up with screen shots of her food blog. With a light but honest touch, this book addresses many serious matters." SLJ

McClintock, Norah

Masked; written by Norah McClintock. Orca Book Publishers 2010 108p (Orca soundings) pa $9.95

Grades: 7 8 9 10   **Fic**
  1. Mystery fiction
  ISBN 978-1-55469-364-1; 1-55469-364-0

Rosie walks in on an armed robbery in her father's convenience store. Who is that masked man? And why is the loser from school there?

"Tight plotting, swift pacing, and tension that intensifies with each page mark this entry in the always-reliable Orca Soundings series for reluctant readers." Booklist

She said/she saw. Orca Book Publishers 2011 211p pa $12.95

Grades: 7 8 9 10   **Fic**
  1. Homicide -- Fiction 2. Witnesses -- Fiction 3. Criminal investigation -- Fiction
  ISBN 1-55469-335-7 pa; 978-1-55469-335-1 pa

When Tegan's two best friends are gunned down in front of her, nobody believes her that she didn't see who did it and doesn't know why.

"The brisk pace, solid character development and inventive structuring make for fast, page-turning reading, and at all wraps up with an unpredictable plot twist and ending. Mysterious and haunting, packed with hard truths about adolescence." Kirkus

Taken. Orca Book Publishers 2009 166p pa $12.95

Grades: 7 8 9 10   **Fic**
  1. Kidnapping -- Fiction 2. Wilderness survival -- Fiction
  ISBN 978-1-55469-152-4; 1-55469-152-4

"After two girls from a nearby town go missing everyone goes on high alert, suspecting a serial killer, and while walking home, Stephanie is grabbed from behind and injected with a drug that knocks her out. She awakens hours later to find herself tied up in an abandoned cabin deep in a densely wooded area. . . . Her harrowing journey back to safety propels this plot-driven, fast-paced tale forward. . . . Told in the first person, this suspenseful survival story is sure to have strong appeal." Kirkus

McClymer, Kelly

Must love black. Simon Pulse 2008 167p pa $8.99

Grades: 6 7 8 9   **Fic**
  1. Twins -- Fiction 2. Sisters -- Fiction 3. Babysitters

-- Fiction
ISBN 978-1-4169-6994-5; 1-4169-4903-8

"Philippa does not consider herself a Goth but she loves the color black. When she answers a classified ad for a summer nanny position, it is the advertisement's one specification 'must love black' that attracts her to the job. . . . McClymer's novel combines understated gothic elements with traditional teen romance tropes and succeeds as a light and funny read." SLJ

McCormick, Patricia

Cut. Front St. 2000 168p $16.95
Grades: 7 8 9 10   Fic
1. Self-mutilation -- Fiction 2. Psychiatric hospitals -- Fiction
ISBN 1-88691-061-8

LC 00-34840

While confined to a mental hospital, thirteen-year-old Callie slowly comes to understand some of the reasons behind her self-mutilation, and gradually starts to get better

"Realistic, sensitive, and heartfelt." Voice Youth Advocates

My brother's keeper. Hyperion Books for Children 2004 187p $15.99
Grades: 7 8 9 10   Fic
1. Baseball -- Fiction 2. Brothers -- Fiction 3. Drug abuse -- Fiction
ISBN 0-7868-5173-2

LC 2004-55233

Thirteen-year-old Toby, a prematurely gray-haired Pittsburgh Pirates fan and baseball card collector, tries to cope with his brother's drug use, his father's absence, and his mother dating Stanley the Food King.

"This is a clever and believable first-person narrative by a responsible, caring, and appealing kid who is doing his utmost to hold together people he loves." Booklist

Purple Heart. Balzer + Bray 2009 198p $16.99; lib bdg $17.89; pa $8.99
Grades: 7 8 9 10   Fic
1. Memory -- Fiction 2. Soldiers -- Fiction 3. Hospitals -- Fiction 4. Iraq War, 2003- -- Fiction 5. Brain -- Wounds and injuries -- Fiction
ISBN 978-0-06-173090-0; 0-06-173090-4; 978-0-06-173091-7 lib bdg; 0-06-173091-2 lib bdg; 978-0-06-173092-4 pa; 0-06-173092-0 pa

LC 2009-1757

While recuperating in a Baghdad hospital from a traumatic brain injury sustained during the Iraq War, eighteen-year-old soldier Matt Duffy struggles to recall what happened to him and how it relates to his ten-year-old friend, Ali.

"Strong characters heighten the drama. . . . McCormick raises moral questions without judgment and will have readers examining not only this conflict but the nature of heroism and war." Publ Wkly

McCoy, Chris

Scurvy Goonda. Alfred A. Knopf 2009 324p $16.99; lib bdg $19.99

Grades: 4 5 6 7 8   Fic
1. Adventure fiction 2. Pirates -- Fiction 3. Family life -- Fiction 4. Imaginary playmates -- Fiction
ISBN 978-0-375-85598-6; 0-375-85598-X; 978-0-375-95598-3 lib bdg; 0-375-95598-4 lib bdg

LC 2008-39290

At age fourteen, Ted Merritt is eager to replace his imaginary friend, a bacon-loving pirate, with real friends but soon he is led from Cape Cod, Massachusetts, into a world of discarded 'abstract companions' who are intent on wreaking vengeance on the human race.

"Refreshingly hilarious, slighty disgusting, and utterly original, this nutty underdog caper finishes with a rousing climax and a satisfying resolution." Bull Cent Child Books

McCrite, K. D.

In front of God and everybody. Thomas Nelson 2011 298p (Confessions of April Grace) pa $9.99
Grades: 4 5 6 7   Fic
1. Farm life -- Fiction 2. Christian life -- Fiction 3. Swindlers and swindling -- Fiction
ISBN 978-1-4003-1722-6; 1-4003-1722-3

LC 2011005583

In the summer of 1986, eleven-year-old April Grace, who lives on a rural Arkansas farm with her family, across a field from her grandmother, has her sense of Christian charity tested when a snooty couple from San Francisco moves into a dilapidated house down the road and her grandmother takes up with a loud, obnoxious, and suspicious-acting Texan.

"With keen eyes and good humor, April Grace notes the quirks, presumptions, and motivations of family and neighbors; she has plenty of fodder—the characters' personalities are dialed up to 11." Publ Wkly

McDaniel, Lurlene

Breathless. Delacorte Press 2009 165p $13.99
Grades: 8 9 10 11 12   Fic
1. Cancer -- Fiction 2. Suicide -- Fiction 3. Siblings -- Fiction 4. Friendship -- Fiction
ISBN 978-0-385-90458-2; 0-385-90458-4

LC 2008-18427

A high school diving champion develops bone cancer in this story told from the points of view of the diver, his best friend, his sister, and his girlfriend.

"This is a heartstrings-tugging read that retains the central character's dignity and peace in the face of insurmountable odds. A sensitive book on a delicate topic." SLJ

Hit and run; [by] Lurlene McDaniel. 1st ed.; Delacorte Press 2007 180p $10.99
Grades: 8 9 10 11 12   Fic
1. School stories 2. Traffic accidents -- Fiction
ISBN 978-0-385-73161-4

LC 2006012738

Events surrounding the hit and run accident of a popular high school student are told from the viewpoints of those involved, including the victim.

This "demonstrates the power of love and making choices. McDaniel, known for her inspiring novels, has a simplistic style, but a weighty message—it's the way you respond to a given situation that defines who you are and who you will be." SLJ

McDonald, Abby

The **anti** -prom. Candlewick Press 2011 280p $16.99

Grades: 8 9 10 11   **Fic**
1. School stories
ISBN 978-0-7636-4956-2; 0-7636-4956-2
        LC 2010-39170

On prom night, Bliss, Jolene, and Meg, students from the same high school who barely know one another, band together to get revenge against Bliss's boyfriend and her best friend, whom she caught together in the limousine they rented.

"McDonald instills more intelligence than you'd expect from such a plot while not skimping on the simple pleasures, either." Booklist

McDonald, Ian

Be my enemy; by Ian McDonald. Pyr 2012 280 p. (hardcover) $16.95

Grades: 7 8 9 10   **Fic**
1. Science fiction 2. Kidnapping -- Fiction 3. Technology -- Fiction 4. Father-son relationship -- Fiction
ISBN 1616146788; 9781616146788
        LC 2012018572

This book by Ian McDonald is the second in the Everness Series. "Everett Singh has escaped with the Infundibulum from the clutches of Charlotte Villiers and the Order, but at a terrible price. His father is missing, banished to one of the billions of parallel universes of the Panoply of All Worlds, and Everett and the crew of the airship Everness have taken a wild Heisenberg jump to a random parallel plane." (Publisher's note)

★ **Planesrunner**. Pyr 2011 (Everness) 269p $16.95

Grades: 6 7 8 9   **Fic**
1. Science fiction
ISBN 978-1-61614-541-5; 1-61614-541-2
        LC 2011032751

When fourteen-year-old Everett Singh's scientist father is kidnapped from the streets of London, he leaves a mysterious app on Everett's computer giving him access to the Infundibulum—a map of parallel earths—which is being sought by technologically advanced dark powers that Everett must somehow elude while he tries to rescue his father.

"McDonald writes with scientific and literary sophistication, as well as a wicked sense of humor. Add nonstop action, eccentric characters, and expert universe building, and this first volume of the Everness series is a winner." Publ Wkly

McDonald, Janet

Harlem Hustle. Frances Foster Books 2006 182p $16

Grades: 8 9 10 11   **Fic**
1. Rap music -- Fiction 2. African Americans -- Fiction
ISBN 978-0-374-37184-5; 0-374-37184-9
        LC 2005-52108

Eric "Hustle" Samson, a smart and streetwise seventeen-year-old dropout from Harlem, aspires to rap stardom, a dream he naively believes is about to come true.

"The author nails the hip-hop lingo and the street slang, and her characters strike just the right attitude. . . . Young adults will love this book." SLJ

★ **Off** -color. Farrar, Straus and Giroux 2007 163p $16

Grades: 7 8 9 10 11 12   **Fic**
1. Single parent family -- Fiction 2. Racially mixed people -- Fiction 3. Mother-daughter relationship -- Fiction
ISBN 0-374-37196-2
        LC 2006-47334

Fifteen-year-old Cameron living with her single mother in Brooklyn finds her search for identity further challenged when she discovers that she is the product of a biracial relationship.

"McDonald dramatizes the big issues from the inside, showing the hard times and the joy in fast-talking dialogue that is honest, insulting, angry, tender, and very funny." Booklist

McDonnell, Margot

Torn to pieces. Delacorte Press 2008 258p $15.99; lib bdg $18.99

Grades: 8 9 10 11 12   **Fic**
1. Friendship -- Fiction 2. Grandparents -- Fiction 3. Missing persons -- Fiction 4. Mother-daughter relationship -- Fiction
ISBN 978-0-385-73559-9; 0-385-73559-6; 978-0-385-90542-8 lib bdg; 0-385-90542-4 lib bdg
        LC 2007-41536

When her mother disappears during a business trip, seventeen-year-old Anne discovers that her family harbors many dark secrets.

"This teen thriller . . . builds to a gripping conclusion with a final twist that will shock and satisfy teen readers." Booklist

McDowell, Marilyn Taylor

★ **Carolina** Harmony. Delacorte 2009 288p $16.99; lib bdg $19.99

Grades: 4 5 6 7   **Fic**
1. Orphans -- Fiction 2. Farm life -- Fiction
ISBN 978-0-385-73590-2; 0-385-73590-1; 978-0-385-90575-6 lib bdg; 0-385-90575-0 lib bdg

"After Carolina's beloved Auntie Shen suffers a stroke, Carolina escapes from an unpleasant foster placement. The orphaned 10-year-old finds love at Harmony Farm, but the web of lies she spins almost leads to losing that home too. . . . This third-person narrative unwinds leisurely, with plenty of backtracking to fill in details of Carolina's life and the glories of her world in the Blue Ridge Mountains. . . . McDowell reveals her love for this part of the world, savoring the language, the environment, and the traditions of mountain culture." Booklist

McElligott, Matthew

Benjamin Franklinstein lives! [by] Matthew McElligott & Larry Tuxbury; illustrated by Mat-

thew McElligott. G. P. Putnam's Sons 2010 121p
il $12.99

Grades: 4 5 6 7   **Fic**
    1. Science fiction 2. Zombies -- Fiction 3. Members
of Congress
    ISBN 978-0-399-25229-7; 0-399-25229-0
    While working on a science fair project, a Philadelphia
school boy discovers both a secret laboratory in his basement and Benjamin Franklin, who comes to life after receiving a jolt of electricity.
    "It's a light fun read, and McElligott's many diagrams,
graphs, and drawings are a nice addition." Booklist

    Benjamin Franklinstein meets the Fright broth-
ers; by Matthew McElligott and Larry Tuxbury;
[illustrated by Matthew McElligott] G. P. Putnam's
Sons 2011 147p il $16.99

Grades: 4 5 6 7   **Fic**
    1. Scientists -- Fiction 2. Secret societies -- Fiction
    ISBN 978-0-399-25480-2; 0-399-25480-3
                    LC 2010040431
    Victor and his friends, aided by Benjamin Franklin, un-
cover an evil scheme involving giant bats and two mysterious brothers, and learn more about the secretive Modern
Order of Prometheus.
    "Enhanced by frequent charts, diagrams, lists and other
visual aids, a spirit of rational (if often reckless) scientific
inquiry pervades the tale, as Ben and his allies translate
coded messages, analyze evidence, get a lesson in meteorology and conduct experiments using both real and science-
fictional gear on the way to a literally electrifying climax. .
. . The authors have way too much fun taking the opener's
premise and evil conspiracy to the next level. Readers will
too." Kirkus

McEntire, Myra
    Hourglass. Egmont USA 2011 390p $17.99

Grades: 7 8 9 10   **Fic**
    1. Science fiction 2. Orphans -- Fiction 3. Homicide
-- Fiction 4. Siblings -- Fiction 5. Parapsychology --
Fiction 6. Space and time -- Fiction
    ISBN 1-60684-144-0; 978-1-60684-144-0
                    LC 2010-43618
    Seventeen-year-old Emerson uses her power to manipu-
late time to help Michael, a consultant hired by her brother,
to prevent a murder that happened six months ago.
    "Em is an entertainingly cheeky narrator and appeal-
ingly resilient heroine. . . . McEntire deftly juggles plot,
characters and dialogue; her portrait of grief is particularly
poignant." Kirkus

McGhee, Alison
    All rivers flow to the sea. Candlewick Press 2005
168p $15.99

Grades: 8 9 10 11 12   **Fic**
    1. Sisters -- Fiction 2. Bereavement -- Fiction 3.
Traffic accidents -- Fiction
    ISBN 0-7636-2591-4
                    LC 2004-54609
    After a car accident in the Adirondacks leaves her older
sister Ivy brain-dead, seventeen-year-old Rose struggles with
her grief and guilt as she slowly learns to let her sister go.

    "This somber, philosophical look at loss and the rees-
tablishment of identity is sensitive and perceptive, and includes passages of beautiful writing. Supporting characters
are complex and lovingly rendered." Booklist

McGowan, Keith
    The **witch's** guide to cooking with children; il-
lustrated by Yoko Tanaka. Henry Holt and Co. 2009
180p il $15.99

Grades: 5 6 7 8   **Fic**
    1. Witches -- Fiction 2. Siblings -- Fiction
    ISBN 978-0-8050-8668-3; 0-8050-8668-4
                    LC 2008-50269
    Eleven-year-old inventor Sol must recover his self-
confidence if he and his eight-year-old sister, Connie, are to
escape the clutches of Hansel and Gretel's witch, to whom
they have been led by their new stepmother and the man they
believe to be their father.
    "McGowan's modern retelling of the Hansel and Gretel
plot is nuanced, fascinating, and gratifyingly dark without
being graphic or horrific. . . . Tanaka's frequent softly shaded
monochromatic illustrations are atmospheric and haunting,
and the human figures' oversized eyes and exaggerated noses echo the disturbing strangeness of the story. Hand this to
kids who like their folktales on the scary side." Bull Cent
Child Books

McGraw, Eloise Jarvis
    The **moorchild**; [by] Eloise McGraw. Margaret
K. McElderry Bks. 1996 241p $17; pa $5.99

Grades: 4 5 6 7   **Fic**
    1. Fantasy fiction 2. Fairies -- Fiction
    ISBN 0-689-80654-X; 1-4169-2768-9 pa
                    LC 95-34107
    A Newbery Medal honor book, 1997
    "Incorporating some classic fantasy motifs and icons,
McGraw . . . conjures up an appreciably familiar world that,
as evidence of her storytelling power, still strikes an original
chord." Publ Wkly

McGuigan, Mary Ann
    Morning in a different place. Front Street 2009
195p $17.95

Grades: 7 8 9 10   **Fic**
    1. Friendship -- Fiction 2. Race relations -- Fiction 3.
African Americans -- Fiction
    ISBN 978-1-59078-551-5; 1-59078-551-7
                    LC 2007-17547
    In 1963 in the Bronx, New York, eighth-graders Fiona
and Yolanda help one another face hard decisions at home
despite family and social opposition to their interracial
friendship, but Fiona is on her own when popular classmates
start paying attention to her and give her a glimpse of both a
different way of life and a new kind of hatefulness.
    This book is "never didactic. McGuigan's writing is
spare and low-key, and her metaphors are acute." Booklist

McKay, Hilary
    ★ **Saffy's** angel. Margaret K. McElderry Bks.
2002 152p $16; pa $4.99

Grades: 5 6 7 8   **Fic**
1. Adoption -- Fiction 5. Family life -- Fiction
ISBN 0-689-84933-8; 0-689-84934-6 pa
                                    LC 2001-44110
First published 2001 in the United Kingdom

After learning that she was adopted, thirteen-year-old
Saffron's relationship with her eccentric, artistic family
changes, until they help her go back to Italy where she was
born to find a special momento of her past

"Like the Casson household itself, the plot is a chaotic
whirl that careens off in several directions simultaneously.
But McKay always skillfully draws each clearly defined
character back into the story with witty, well-edited details;
rapid dialogue; and fine pacing." Booklist

Other titles in this series are:
Indigo's star (2004)
Permanent Rose (2005)
Caddy ever after (2006)
Forever Rose (2008)

McKay, Sharon E.
Enemy territory; Sharon McKay. Annick Press
2012 184 p. $21.95
Grades: 6 7 8 9 10 11 12   **Fic**
1. Toleration -- Fiction 2. Israel-Arab conflicts --
Fiction
ISBN 1554514312; 9781554514311

In author Sharon E. McKay's book, "Sam, an Israeli teen
whose leg may have to be amputated, and Yusuf, a Palestinian teen who has lost his left eye, find themselves uneasy
roommates in a Jerusalem hospital. One night, the boys decide to slip away while the nurses aren't looking and go on
an adventure to the Old City. . . . They band together to find
their way home and to defend themselves against unfriendly
locals, arrest by the military police, and an encounter with a
deadly desert snake." (Publisher's note)

Thunder over Kandahar; photographs by Rafal
Gerszak. Annick Press 2010 260p il $21.95; pa
$12.95
Grades: 7 8 9 10 11 12   **Fic**
1. Afghan War, 2001- -- Fiction
ISBN 978-1-55451-267-6; 1-55451-267-0; 978-1-
55451-266-9 pa; 1-55451-266-2 pa

"When her British and American-educated parents' return to Afghanistan is cut short by a terrible attack, 14-year-
old Yasmine is sent to Kandahar for safety. Instead, the driver abandons her and her friend Tamanna along the way, and
they must travel on their own through Taliban-controlled
mountains. . . . In spite of unrelenting violence, along with
grinding poverty, restrictive customs, and the horrors of
war, what shines through this sad narrative is the love Af-
ghans have for their country. . . . [The author] traveled to
Afghanistan and provides numerous credits for this gripping
tale." SLJ

McKenzie, Nancy
Guinevere's gift. Alfred A. Knopf 2008 327p
(The Chrysalis Queen quartet) $15.99; lib bdg
$18.99
Grades: 7 8 9 10   **Fic**
1. Cousins -- Fiction 2. Guinevere (Legendary

character) -- Fiction
ISBN 978-0-375-84345-7; 0-375-84345-0; 978-0-375-
94345-4 lib bdg; 0-375-94345-5 lib bdg
                                    LC 2007-28782

When the orphaned Guinevere is twelve years old, living with Queen Alyse and King Pellinore of Gwynedd, she
fearlessly helps rescue her cousin from kidnappers who are
plotting to seize the palace and overthrow the king, even as
the queen despairs of Guinevere's rebellious nature.

"Adventure seekers can be content with this tale of a
heroine and her castle while dedicated legend fans will
appreciate where it fits in the overall tapestry." Bull Cent
Child Books

Another title in this series is:
Guinevere's gamble (2009)

McKernan, Victoria
Shackleton's stowaway. Knopf 2005 336p
$15.95; lib bdg $17.99
Grades: 7 8 9 10   **Fic**
1. Explorers 2. Adventure fiction 3. Survival after
airplane accidents, shipwrecks, etc. -- Fiction
ISBN 0-375-82691-2; 0-375-92691-7 lib bdg
                                    LC 2004-10313

A fictionalized account of the adventures of eighteen-
year-old Perce Blackborow, who stowed away for the 1914
Shackleton Antarctic expedition and, after their ship Endurance was crushed by ice, endured many hardships, including
the loss of the toes of his left foot to frostbite, during the
nearly two-year return journey across sea and ice

"This book provides historical information for history
and geography classes who are interested in exploration,
the Antarctic, and early history of great sea voyages." Libr
Media Connect

★ The **devil's** paintbox. Alfred A. Knopf 2009
359p $16.99; lib bdg $19.99
Grades: 6 7 8 9 10   **Fic**
1. Orphans -- Fiction 2. Siblings -- Fiction 3. Frontier
and pioneer life -- Fiction 4. Overland journeys to the
Pacific -- Fiction
ISBN 978-0-375-83750-0; 0-375-83750-7; 978-0-375-
93750-7 lib bdg; 0-375-93750-1 lib bdg
                                    LC 2008-4749

In 1866, fifteen-year-old Aidan and his thirteen-year-
old sister Maddy, penniless orphans, leave drought-stricken
Kansas on a wagon train hoping for a better life in Seattle,
but find there are still many hardships to be faced.

This is a "gripping novel. . . . Attention to detail and
steady pacing keep readers fully engaged." Publ Wkly

McKinlay, Meg
Below; Meg McKinlay. Candlewick Press 2013
224 p. (reinforced) $15.99
Grades: 4 5 6 7   **Fic**
1. Reservoirs -- Fiction 2. Extinct cities -- Fiction
ISBN 0763661260; 9780763661267
                                    LC 2012943652

In this book by Meg McKinlay, "Cassie was . . . the first
baby born in the Australian town of New Lower Grange,
which was established after the intentional flooding of the
previous town to accommodate a dam. . . . [S]he feels the

pull of the forbidden lake above Old Lower Grange. There, she is joined by Liam, a classmate whose life was altered in a tragic accident, and together they search for the truth about the town"s past as its centenary celebration approaches." (Publishers Weekly)

"Although the author does a masterful job of making sure all the pieces fit at the end, the central mystery is hard to buy. This is mitigated by a reasonably suspenseful climax, an earned family solidarity message and the lesson: that to find the truth, one must delve below the surface. A quietly intriguing meditation on history and truth." Kirkus

McKinley, Robin

★ **Beauty**; a retelling of the story of Beauty & the beast. Harper & Row 1978 247p $15.99; pa $5.99

Grades: 7 8 9 10   Fic
    1. Fairy tales
    ISBN 0-06-024149-7; 0-06-440477-3 pa
                                    LC 77-25636

"McKinley's version of this folktale is embellished with rich descriptions and settings and detailed characterizations. The author has not modernized the story but varied the traditional version to attract modern readers. The values of love, honor, and beauty are placed in a magical setting that will please the reader of fantasy." Shapiro. Fic for Youth. 3d edition

Chalice. G.P. Putnam's Sons 2008 263p $18.99
Grades: 7 8 9 10 11 12   Fic
    1. Fantasy fiction 2. Bees -- Fiction
    ISBN 978-0-399-24676-0; 0-399-24676-2
                                    LC 2008-704

A beekeeper by trade, Mirasol's life changes completely when she is named the new Chalice, the most important advisor to the new Master, a former priest of fire.

"The fantasy realm is evoked in thorough and telling detail. . . . A lavish and lasting treat." Publ Wkly

Dragonhaven. G.P. Putnam's Sons 2007 342p $17.99
Grades: 7 8 9 10 11 12   Fic
    1. Fantasy fiction 2. Dragons -- Fiction
    ISBN 978-0-399-24675-3; 0-399-24675-4
                                    LC 2007-8197

When Jake Mendoza, who lives in the Smokehill National Park where his father runs the Makepeace Institute of Integrated Dragon Studies, goes on his first solo overnight in the park, he finds an infant dragon whose mother has been killed by a poacher.

Readers "will be engaged by McKinley's well-drawn characters and want to root for the Smokehill community's fight to save the ultimate endangered species." SLJ

Pegasus. G.P. Putnam's Sons 2010 404p $18.99
Grades: 8 9 10 11 12   Fic
    1. Fantasy fiction 2. Magic -- Fiction 3. Princesses -- Fiction 4. Pegasus (Greek mythology) -- Fiction
    ISBN 0-399-24677-0; 978-0-399-24677-7
                                    LC 2010-2279

Because of a thousand-year-old alliance between humans and pegasi, Princess Sylvi is ceremonially bound to Ebon, her own pegasus, on her twelfth birthday, but the closeness of their bond becomes a threat to the status quo and possibly to the safety of their two nations.

"McKinley's storytelling is to be savored. She lavishes page after page upon rituals and ceremonies, basks in the awe of her intricately constructed world, and displays a masterful sense of pegasi physicality and mannerisms." Booklist

Rose daughter. Greenwillow Bks. 1997 306p pa $7.99
Grades: 7 8 9 10   Fic
    1. Fairy tales
    ISBN 0-688-15439-5; 0-441-00583-7 pa
                                    LC 96-48783

Compared to Beauty, this "is fuller bodied, with richer characterizations and a more mystical, darker edge. . . . There is more background on the Beast in this version . . . and Beauty's choice at the end, a departure from that in Beauty, is just so right. Readers will be enchanted, in the best sense of the word." Booklist

★ The **blue** sword. Greenwillow Bks. 1982 272p $17.99; pa $6.99
Grades: 7 8 9 10   Fic
    1. Fantasy fiction
    ISBN 0-688-00938-7; 0-441-06880-4 pa
                                    LC 82-2895

A Newbery Medal honor book, 1983

Harry, bored with her sheltered life in the remote orange-growing colony of Daria, discovers magic in herself when she is kidnapped by a native king with mysterious powers.

"This is a zesty, romantic, heroic fantasy with an appealing stalwart heroine, a finely realixed mythical kingdom, and a grounding in reality." Booklist

★ The **hero** and the crown. Greenwillow Bks. 1985 246p lib bdg $16.99
Grades: 6 7 8 9   Fic
    1. Fantasy fiction
    ISBN 0-688-02593-5
                                    LC 84-4074

Awarded the Newbery Medal, 1985

The author "has in this suspenseful prequel . . . created an utterly engrossing fantasy, replete with a fairly mature romantic subplot as well as adventure." N Y Times Book Rev

McKinnon, Hannah Roberts

★ **Franny** Parker. Farrar Straus Giroux 2009 149p $16
Grades: 5 6 7 8   Fic
    1. Droughts -- Fiction 2. Violence -- Fiction 3. Family life -- Fiction
    ISBN 978-0-374-32469-8; 0-374-32469-7
                                    LC 2008-01702

Through a hot, dry Oklahoma summer, twelve-year-old Franny tends wild animals brought by her neighbors, hears gossip during a weekly quilting bee, befriends a new neighbor who has some big secrets, and learns to hope.

"Franny is a relatable and consistent narrator, the homey rural setting is throughtfully rendered and the easy prose should appeal to reluctant readers." Publ Wkly

The **properties** of water. Farrar, Straus, and Giroux 2010 166p $16.99

Grades: 5 6 7 8   **Fic**

1. Sisters -- Fiction 2. Accidents -- Fiction

ISBN 978-0-374-36145-7; 0-374-36145-2

When her older sister, Marni, is paralyzed jumping off the cliffs into the lake near their house, twelve-year-old Lace feels responsible for the accident and struggles to find a way to help heal her family.

McKinnon "has created a cast of believably imperfect characters, and Lace's emotions ring true." Publ Wkly

McKissack, Fredrick

★ **Shooting** star. Atheneum Books for Young Readers 2009 273p $16.99

Grades: 8 9 10 11 12   **Fic**

1. School stories 2. Football -- Fiction 3. Steroids -- Fiction 4. African Americans -- Fiction

ISBN 978-1-4169-4745-5; 1-4169-4745-0

LC 2008-55525

Jomo Rogers, a naturally talented athlete, starts taking performance enhancing drugs in order to be an even better high school football player, but finds his life spinning out of control as his game improves.

"Profane and scatological language abounds, but it is not outside the realm of what one could hear any day in a school locker room. Top-notch sports fiction." SLJ

McKissack, Patricia C.

Cyborg; a Clone codes novel. [by] Patricia C. McKissack, Fredrick L. McKissack, John P. McKissack. Scholastic Press 2011 107p $16.99

Grades: 4 5 6 7   **Fic**

1. Science fiction 2. Civil rights -- Fiction 3. Artificial intelligence -- Fiction

ISBN 978-0-439-92985-1; 0-439-92985-7

LC 2010016075

Seventeen-year-old Houston, a cyborg since the age of seven, and a fugitive living on the Moon, joins with other cyborgs all over the world in non-violent protest marches to challenge the Cyborg Act 2130 and hopefully secure increased civil liberties.

"The McKissacks continue to successfully draw parallels between a futuristic world that tries to control those considered different and historic racial struggles. . . . The worldbuilding is intriguing, there is plenty of action and ethnic diversity in a science-fiction tale is welcome." Kirkus

★ **Let** my people go; Bible stories told by a freeman of color to his daughter, Charlotte, in Charleston, South Carolina, 1806-16. by Patricia and Fredrick McKissack; illustrated by James Ransome. Atheneum Bks. for Young Readers 1998 134p il $20

Grades: 4 5 6 7   **Fic**

1. Bible stories 2. Slavery -- Fiction 3. African Americans -- Fiction

ISBN 0-689-80856-9

LC 97-19983

Charlotte, the daughter of a free black man who worked as a blacksmith in Charleston, South Carolina, in the early 1800s recalls the stories from the Bible that her father shared with her, relating them to the experiences of African Americans

"The poignant juxtaposition of the Biblical characters and Charlotte's personal narrative is authentic and moving. . . . The occasional illustrations are powerful oil paintings in rich colors, emotional and evocative." SLJ

Includes bibliographical references

★ **Nzingha,** warrior queen of Matamba; by Patricia McKissack. Scholastic 2000 136p (Royal diaries) $10.95

Grades: 5 6 7 8   **Fic**

1. Princesses -- Fiction 2. Slave trade -- Fiction 3. Mbundu (African people)

ISBN 0-439-11210-9

LC 00-24216

Presents the diary of thirteen-year-old Nzingha, a sixteenth-century West African princess who loves to hunt and hopes to lead her kingdom one day against the invasion of the Portuguese slave traders

"The diary format will appeal to readers and the author's use of time lines, seasons, and actual place names makes the story believable and interesting." SLJ

The **clone** codes; [by] Patricia C. McKissack, Fredrick L. McKissack [and] John McKissack. Scholastic 2010 173p $16.99

Grades: 4 5 6 7   **Fic**

1. Science fiction 2. Cloning -- Fiction 3. Segregation -- Fiction 4. Identity (Psychology) -- Fiction

ISBN 978-0-439-92983-7; 0-439-92983-0

LC 2009-24076

On the run from a bounty hunter who arrested her mother for being part of a secret society devoted to freeing clones, thirteen-year-old Leanna learns amazing truths about herself and her family as she is forced to consider the value of freedom and what it really means to be human in 2170 America.

"The story is tight and fast-paced, yet makes room for historical parallels that are vivid without being preachy. An intriguing start to a planned trilogy." Publ Wkly

A **friendship** for today. Scholastic Press 2007 172p $16.99

Grades: 4 5 6 7   **Fic**

1. Divorce -- Fiction 2. Friendship -- Fiction 3. Race relations -- Fiction 4. African Americans -- Fiction 5. School integration -- Fiction

ISBN 978-0-439-66098-3

LC 2006-29293

In 1954, when desegregation comes to Kirkland, Missouri, ten-year-old Rosemary faces many changes and challenges at school and at home as her parents separate.

"A real, at times raw tale about a winning and insightful young heroine during a bittersweet era." Publ Wkly

McLaren, Clemence

Inside the walls of Troy; a novel of the women who lived the Trojan War. Atheneum Bks. for Young Readers 1996 199p hardcover o.p. pa $5.99

Grades: 7 8 9 10   **Fic**

1. Helen of Troy (Legendary character) -- Fiction
ISBN 0-689-31820-0; 0-689-87397-2 pa

LC 93-8127

The events surrounding the famous battle between the Greeks and the Trojans are told from the points of view of two women, the beautiful Helen and the prophetic Cassandra

"These ancient stories are made as fresh and vivid as any modern tale by the electrifying characters and sensual details." Booklist

McLoughlin, Jane

At Yellow Lake. Frances Lincoln Children's Books 2012 358 p. (paperback) $8.99

Grades: 7 8 9 10   **Fic**

1. Mystery fiction 2. Teenagers -- Fiction 3. Native Americans -- Fiction
ISBN 1847802877; 9781847802873

In this book by Jane McLoughlin, "Etta, Peter and Jonah all find themselves at a cabin by the shore of Yellow Lake. . . . Jonah has come to Yellow Lake to try to get in touch with his Ojibwe roots. Peter is there to bury a lock of his mother's hair -- her final request. Etta is on the run from her mother's creepy boyfriend. . . . But as the three take shelter in the cabin . . . they soon realise that they have inadvertently stumbled onto the scene of a horrifying crime." (Publisher's note)

McMann, Lisa

Cryer's Cross. Simon Pulse 2011 232p $16.99

Grades: 7 8 9 10   **Fic**

1. Mystery fiction 2. Supernatural -- Fiction 3. Missing persons -- Fiction 4. Obsessive-compulsive disorder -- Fiction
ISBN 978-1-4169-9481-7; 1-4169-9481-5; 978-1-4169-9483-1 ebook

LC 2010-15410

"Kendall is a unique character, and the details of her OCD compulsions are well drawn. Haunting passages from another world, which provide just enough detail to intrigue and disturb readers, are intertwined with Kendall's story. Part mystery, part ghost story, and part romance, this book has enough to satisfy a variety of readers." Booklist

Wake. Simon Pulse 2008 210p $15.99; pa $8.99

Grades: 7 8 9 10   **Fic**

1. School stories 2. Dreams -- Fiction
ISBN 978-1-4169-5357-9; 1-4169-5357-4; 978-1-4169-7447-5 pa; 1-4169-7447-4 pa

LC 2007036267

Ever since she was eight years old, high school student Janie Hannagan has been uncontrollably drawn into other people's dreams, but it is not until she befriends an elderly nursing home patient and becomes involved with an enigmatic fellow-student that she discovers her true power.

"A fast pace, a great mix of teen angst and supernatural experiences, and an eerie, attention-grabbing cover will make this a hit." Booklist

Other titles in this series are:
Fade (2009)
Gone (2010)

McMullan, Margaret

Cashay. Houghton Mifflin Harcourt 2009 166p $15

Grades: 7 8 9 10   **Fic**

1. Anger -- Fiction 2. Mentoring -- Fiction 3. Bereavement -- Fiction 4. Racially mixed people -- Fiction
ISBN 978-0-547-07656-0; 0-547-07656-8

LC 2008-36111

When her world is turned upside down by her sister's death, a mentor is assigned to fourteen-year-old Cashay to help her through her anger and grief.

"Cashay's spirited voice and non-frothy prose will draw both confirmed and newer fans of inner-city drama." Kirkus

★ How I found the Strong; a Civil War story. Houghton Mifflin 2004 136p $15

Grades: 5 6 7 8   **Fic**

1. Slavery -- Fiction
ISBN 0-618-35008-X

LC 2003-12294

Frank Russell, known as Shanks, wishes he could have gone with his father and brother to fight for Mississippi and the Confederacy, but his experiences with the war and his changing relationship with the family slave, Buck, change his thinking.

"The crisply written narrative is full of regional speech and detail, creating a vivid portrait." Voice Youth Advocates

★ Sources of light. Houghton Mifflin 2010 233p $15

Grades: 6 7 8 9   **Fic**

1. Photography -- Fiction 2. Race relations -- Fiction 3. African Americans -- Civil rights -- Fiction
ISBN 978-0-547-07659-1; 0-547-07659-2

LC 2009-49708

"When 14-year-old Samantha Thomas moves to Jackson, Miss., in 1962, following her father's death in Vietnam, she learns about love and hate all in the same year. Her mother meets Perry Walker, a photographer who teaches Sam about taking photographs and seeing the world in new ways, but what she begins seeing and pondering is the racial situation in Jackson—lunch-counter sit-ins, voter-registration protests and the violent reprisals of many in the white community, including the father of the boy she begins to like. . . . This offers a superb portrait of a place and time and a memorable character trying to make sense of a world both ugly and beautiful." Kirkus

★ When I crossed No-Bob. Houghton Mifflin Company 2007 209p $16

Grades: 5 6 7 8   **Fic**

1. Farm life -- Fiction 2. Race relations -- Fiction 3. Abandoned children -- Fiction 4. Reconstruction (1865-1876) -- Fiction
ISBN 978-0-618-71715-6; 0-618-71715-3

LC 2007-12753

Ten years after the Civil War's end, twelve-year-old Addy, abandoned by her parents, is taken from the horrid town of No-Bob by schoolteacher Frank Russell and his bride, but when her father returns to claim her she must find another way to leave her O'Donnell past behind.

"The simple prose can be pure poetry. . . . Readers will be drawn by the history close-up and by the elemental moral choice." Booklist

McNab, Andy

Traitor; [by] Andy McNab and Robert Rigby. G.P. Putnam's Sons 2005 265p $15.99

Grades: 7 8 9 10   **Fic**
  1. Spies -- Fiction 2. Orphans -- Fiction 3. Grandfathers -- Fiction
  ISBN 0-399-24464-6

                                        LC 2005-6701

"Orphaned Londoner Danny Watts wants nothing to do with his estranged grandfather, a traitor who went MIA years ago, until the British military offers Danny a proposition: find his grandfather and he'll receive a scholarship. . . . With help from his best friend, Elena, he sets off to find his relative and the truth. . . . The well-crafted language includes a few coarse phrases. . . . With its brisk plot and unpredictable characters, this story of intrigue rises above many standard adventure stories." Booklist

  Other titles in this series are:
  Payback (2006)
  Avenger (2007)
  Meltdown (2008)

McNamee, Eoin

The Navigator. Wendy Lamb Books 2007 342p il (Navigator trilogy) $15.99; pa $6.99

Grades: 6 7 8 9   **Fic**
  1. Fantasy fiction 2. Time -- Fiction
  ISBN 978-0-375-83910-8; 0-375-83910-0; 978-0-385-73554-4 pa; 0-385-73554-5 pa

                                        LC 2006-26691

Owen has always been different, and not only because his father committed suicide, but he is not prepared for the knowledge that he has a mission to help the Wakeful—the custodians of time—to stop the Harsh from reversing the flow of time.

McNamee "shows a deft hand in writing for children. Excellent world-building, a thrilling and propulsive plot, internal consistency and a multitude of child heroes guarantee a following for this exciting fantasy." Kirkus

  Other titles in this series are:
  City of Time (2008)
  The Frost Child (2009)

McNamee, Graham

Acceleration. Wendy Lamb Bks. 2003 210p hardcover o.p. pa $6.99

Grades: 8 9 10 11 12   **Fic**
  1. Mystery fiction 2. Homicide -- Fiction
  ISBN 0-385-73119-1; 0-440-23836-6 pa

                                        LC 2003-3708

Stuck working in the Lost and Found of the Toronto Transit Authority for the summer, seventeen-year-old Duncan finds the diary of a serial killer and sets out to stop him

"Never overexploits the sensational potential of the subject and builds suspense layer upon layer, while injecting some surprising comedy relief." Booklist

Bonechiller; [by] Graham McNamee. 1st ed.; Wendy Lamb Books 2008 294p $15.99; lib bdg $18.99

Grades: 7 8 9 10 11 12   **Fic**
  1. Monsters -- Fiction 2. Bereavement -- Fiction 3. Supernatural -- Fiction
  ISBN 978-0-385-74658-8; 0-385-74658-X; 978-0-385-90895-5 lib bdg; 0-385-90895-4 lib bdg

                                        LC 2007039383

Four high school students face off against a soul-stealing beast that has been making young people disappear their small Ontario, Canada, town for centuries.

"This will be an easy booktalk and a spendidly enjoyable read sure to please those who respond with both hope and dread when things go bump in the night." Bull Cent Child Books

McNaughton, Janet

An earthly knight. HarperCollins Publishers 2004 261p $15.99; lib bdg $16.89

Grades: 7 8 9 10   **Fic**
  1. Fantasy fiction
  ISBN 0-06-008992-X; 0-06-008993-8 lib bdg

                                        LC 2003-9561

First published 2003 in Canada

In 1162 in Scotland, sixteen-year-old Jenny Avenel falls in love with the mysterious Tam Lin while being courted by the king's brother and must navigate the tides of tradition and the power of ancient magic to define her own destiny.

"The author does an excellent job of interweaving legend and history to create an exciting and engaging tale." SLJ

McNeal, Laura

★ Dark water. Alfred A. Knopf 2010 287p $16.99; lib bdg $19.99

Grades: 7 8 9 10   **Fic**
  1. Fires -- Fiction 2. Divorce -- Fiction 3. Family life -- Fiction 4. Illegal aliens -- Fiction 5. Homeless persons -- Fiction
  ISBN 978-0-375-84973-2; 0-375-84973-4; 978-0-375-94973-9 lib bdg; 0-375-94973-9 lib bdg

                                        LC 2009-43249

Living in a cottage on her uncle's southern California avocado ranch since her parent's messy divorce, fifteen-year-old Pearl Dewitt meets and falls in love with an illegal migrant worker, and is trapped with him when wildfires approach his makeshift forest home.

"Notable for well-drawn characters, an engaging plot and, especially, hauntingly beautiful language, this is an outstanding book." Kirkus

The decoding of Lana Morris; [by] Laura & Tom McNeal. Alfred A. Knopf 2007 289p $15.99

Grades: 7 8 9 10 11 12   **Fic**
  1. Drawing -- Fiction 2. Handicapped -- Fiction 3. Supernatural -- Fiction 4. Foster home care -- Fiction
  ISBN 0-375-83106-1; 978-0-375-83106-5

                                        LC 2006-23950

For sixteen-year-old Lana life is often difficult, with a flirtatious foster father, an ice queen foster mother, a houseful of special needs children to care for, and bullies harrass-ing her, until the day she ventures into an antique shop and buys a drawing set that may change her life.

This is "a colorful character drama with genuine spice and impact." Bull Cent Child Books

McNeal, Tom

★ **Far** far away; by Tom McNeal. 1st ed. Alfred A. Knopf Books for Young Readers 2013 371 p. (hardcover) $17.99; (ebook) $53.97; (library) $20.99

Grades: 7 8 9 10   **Fic**
1. Occult fiction 2. Fantasy fiction 3. Ghosts -- Fiction 4. Friendship -- Fiction 5. Supernatural -- Fiction 6. Missing persons -- Fiction
ISBN 0375849726; 9780375849725; 9780375896989; 9780375949722

LC 2012020603

This book "is narrated by the ghost of Jacob Grimm . . . , unhappily caught in the Zwischenraum (a plane of existence between life and death). For now, he is the nearly constant companion of Jeremy Johnson," who hears voices. This ability "has made him an object of derision for many in his little town, though—thrillingly—not to the electrifyingly vibrant Ginger Boultinghouse, who is more than happy to lure Jeremy into more trouble than he's ever encountered." (School Library Journal)

McNicoll, Sylvia

Last chance for Paris. Fitzhenry & Whiteside 2008 204p pa $11.95

Grades: 6 7 8 9   **Fic**
1. Twins -- Fiction 2. Wolves -- Fiction 3. Siblings -- Fiction
ISBN 978-1-5545-5061-6 pa; 1-5545-5061-0 pa

Fourteen-year-old Zanna goes to the Alberta ice fields with her father and twin brother, Martin, where they find a wolf pup which they name Paris. When Martin is lost, Paris helps find him.

"Written with elements of wry humor and romance, this Canadian novel features a narrator whose disarmingly candid opinions make her an appealing guide for readers who usually veer away from backwoods or survival stories." Booklist

McNish, Cliff

★ **Angel**. Carolrhoda Books 2008 312p $16.95

Grades: 7 8 9 10   **Fic**
1. School stories 2. Angels -- Fiction 3. Bullies -- Fiction 4. Popularity -- Fiction 5. Mental illness -- Fiction
ISBN 978-0-8225-8900-6; 0-8225-8900-1

LC 2007-9664

An unlikely friendship develops between fourteen-year-olds Stephanie, an angel-obsessed social outcast, and Freya, a popular student whose visions of angels sent her to a mental institution and who is now seeing a dark angel at every turn.

"The author beautifuly melds a tale of the fantastic and the mundane." Voice Youth Advocates

The **silver** child; by Cliff McNish. 1st American ed; Carolrhoda Books 2005 192p lib bdg $15.95

Grades: 6 7 8 9   **Fic**
1. Fantasy fiction
ISBN 1-57505-825-1

LC 2004-12407

Drawn to a wasteland of garbage dumps called Coldharbour, six children undergo mysterious transformations and band together to face an unknown enemy.

The author "writes a darkly compelling fantasy, using alternating narratives to add to the suspense. His vivid, often lyrical prose will engage readers." Booklist
Other titles in this series are:
Silver City (2006)
Silver world (2007)

McPhee, Peter

New blood. James Lorimer 2008 167p pa $8.95

Grades: 6 7 8 9 10   **Fic**
1. School stories 2. Bullies -- Fiction
ISBN 978-1-55028-996-1; 1-55028-996-9

When his family moves from the tough streets of Glasgow to Winnipeg, Canada, Callum finds that his high school days of dealing with bullies are far from over.

"The Scottish culture, which becomes a colorful character, adds to the fullness of the story. The writing, rich in dialogue, does not waste words and keeps the reader involved and cheering for this gutsy hero who fights his fear to stand against abuse aimed at himself and others." Voice Youth Advocates

McQuein, Josin L.

Arclight; Josin L. McQuein. 1st ed. Greenwillow Books, an imprint of HarperCollins Publishers 2013 416 p. (hardcover) $17.99

Grades: 8 9 10 11 12   **Fic**
1. Science fiction 2. Amnesia -- Fiction 3. Identity -- Fiction
ISBN 0062130145; 9780062130143

LC 2013002929

In this book, "Marina was pulled from the Dark at the cost of nine lives, and she is paying the price. Ostracized and abused by those whose parents died for her sake, Marina is all but alone in the Arclight, a safe zone where it is never dark. The Fade live in the Dark—chameleons, they steal humans from the light to an unknown fate. Marina dreams of their voices and frets that she has no memory of her life before her rescue." She seeks answers about her past. (Publishers Weekly)

McQuerry, Maureen Doyle

The **Peculiars**; a novel. Maureen Doyle McQuerry. Amulet Books 2012 359 p. (hardback) $16.95

Grades: 7 8 9 10 11 12   **Fic**
1. Fantasy fiction 2. Voyages and travels -- Fiction 3. Father-daughter relationship -- Fiction 4. Goblins -- Fiction 5. Identity -- Fiction 6. Abnormalities, Human -- Fiction 7. Adventure and adventurers -- Fiction
ISBN 1419701789; 9781419701788

LC 2012000844

This is the story of Lena Mattacascar, who at age 18 "travel[s] to Scree, an uncharted wilderness of 'indigenous folks' and deported convicts," sitting on the train with young librarian "Jimson Quiggley," with "marshal Thomas Sal-tre" watching them. "Lena cannot stop thinking about her mysterious father" or the possibility that she's part Peculiar (goblin). "Scree is the place where Lena's questions might be answered, but arriving there just multiplies them." (Publishers Weekly)

McWilliams, Kelly

Doormat; a novel. Delacorte Press 2004 131p $15.95; lib bdg $17.99

Grades: 6 7 8 9   **Fic**

1. Theater -- Fiction 2. Pregnancy -- Fiction 3. Friendship -- Fiction

ISBN 0-385-73168-X; 0-385-90204-2 lib bdg

LC 2003-19675

Fourteen-year-old Jaime has always been a doormat, but her diary reveals how getting the lead in a school play, finding her first boyfriend, discovering her dream, and helping her best friend cope with being pregnant transform her life.

"McWilliams' first-person, present-tense vignettes are taut, funny, and touching, the dialogue is authentic, and both the teen and adult characters ring true." Booklist

Mccall, Guadalupe Garcia

★ **Under** the mesquite. Lee & Low Books 2011 224p $17.95

Grades: 7 8 9 10 11 12   **Fic**

1. Cancer -- Fiction 2. Family life -- Fiction 3. Mexican Americans -- Fiction

ISBN 978-1-60060-429-4; 1-60060-429-3; 978-1-60060-875-9 ebook

LC 2010052567

"With poignant imagery and well-placed Spanish, the author effectively captures the complex lives of teenagers in many Latino and/or immigrant families." Kirkus

Mead, Alice

Dawn and dusk. Farrar, Straus and Giroux 2007 151p $16

Grades: 6 7 8 9   **Fic**

1. Refugees -- Fiction 2. Iran-Iraq War, 1980-1988 -- Fiction

ISBN 0-374-31708-9; 978-0-374-31708-9

LC 2006-40850

As thirteen-year-old Azad tries desperately to cling to the life he has known, the political situation in Iran during the war with Iraq finally forces his family to flee their home and seek safety elsewhere.

"Azad is an appealing protagonist, and it is his simple and direct story that will draw readers through the complexities of a multinational ethnic longing for self-determination that remains at the heart of an international tinderbox." SLJ

★ **Swimming** to America; Alice Mead. 1st ed; Farrar, Straus and Giroux 2005 153p $16

Grades: 6 7 8 9   **Fic**

1. Immigrants -- Fiction

ISBN 0-374-38047-3

LC 2004-53249

Eighth grader Linda Berati struggles to understand who she is within the context of her mother's secrecy about the family background, her discomfort with her old girlfriends,

her involvement with the family problems of her Cuban-American friend Ramon, and an opportunity to attend a school for "free spirits" like herself.

Written with "sensitivity and optimism. . . . [This is] an informative, empathetic, contemporary portrait of the immigrant experience." SLJ

Mebus, Scott

Gods of Manhattan. Dutton Children's Books 2008 372p (Gods of Manhattan) $17.99

Grades: 6 7 8 9   **Fic**

1. Fantasy fiction 2. Adventure fiction 3. Space and time -- Fiction 4. Gods and goddesses -- Fiction

ISBN 978-0-525-47955-0; 0-525-47955-4

LC 2007-18113

"Rory, 13, and his sister Bridget, 9, live in present-day New York City unaware of the spirits from Manhattan's or 'Mannahatta's' past that coexist alongside them. Rory has a gift for seeing this other world but has repressed this ability until the day he notices a cockroach riding a rat, an ancient Indian warrior, a papier-mâché boy, and other oddities. . . . The use of real historical figures and events lends authenticity to this compulsively readable and fast-paced fantasy." SLJ

Other titles in this series are:

Spirits in the park (2009)

The sorcerer's secret (2010)

Medina, Meg

★ **Milagros**; girl from Away. Henry Holt and Co. 2008 279p $17.89

Grades: 6 7 8 9   **Fic**

1. Magic -- Fiction 2. Islands -- Fiction 3. Rays (Fishes) -- Fiction 4. Mother-daughter relationship -- Fiction

ISBN 978-0-8050-8230-2; 0-8050-8230-1

LC 2007-46939

Twelve-year-old Milagros barely survives an invasion of her tiny, Caribbean island home, escapes with the help of mysterious sea creatures, reunites briefly with her pirate-father, and learns about a mother's love when cast ashore on another island.

"Medina's use of magical realism keeps readers tantalizingly off-balance as she navigates among settings. . . . [This] haunting tale . . . will remain with readers." Horn Book

Meehan, Kierin

★ **Hannah's** winter. Kane/Miller Book Publishers 2009 212p $15.95

Grades: 5 6 7 8   **Fic**

1. Adventure fiction

ISBN 978-1-933605-98-2; 1-933605-98-7

First published 2001 in Australia

Hannah would much rather be back in Australia, starting high school with her friends. But Japan turns out to be nothing like she'd imagined. When Hannah and her new friend Miki find an ancient message in the stationery shop, they are drawn into involving a mysterious riddle.

"Meehan utilizes beautifully crafted similes and metaphors as she creates a loving and detailed portrayal of Japan and its people. . . . The tale remains so grounded in reality that it never defies belief. A fine fantasy." Kirkus

Meehl, Brian

★ **Suck** it up. Delacorte Press 2008 323p $15.99; pa $8.99

Grades: 8 9 10 11   **Fic**

1. Vampires -- Fiction

ISBN 978-0-385-73300-7; 0-385-73300-3; 978-0-440-42091-0 pa; 0-440-42091-1 pa

LC 2007-27995

After graduating from the International Vampire League, a scrawny, teenaged vampire named Morning is given the chance to fulfill his childhood dream of becoming a superhero when he embarks on a League mission to become the first vampire to reveal his identity to humans and to demonstrate how peacefully-evolved, blood-substitute-drinking vampires can use their powers to help humanity.

This "an original and light variation on the current trend in brooding teen vampire protagonists. . . . Puns abound in this lengthy, complicated romp. . . . Teens will find it delightful." Booklist

Melling, O. R.

The **Hunter's** Moon. Amulet Books 2005 284p (Chronicles of Faerie) $16.95; pa $7.95

Grades: 7 8 9 10   **Fic**

1. Magic -- Fiction

ISBN 0-8109-5857-0; 0-8109-9214-0 pa

LC 2004-22216

First published 1992 in Ireland

Two teenage cousins, one Irish, the other from the United States, set out to find a magic doorway to the Faraway Country, where humans must bow to the little people.

"This novel is a compelling blend of Irish mythology and geography. Characters that breathe and connect with readers, and a picturesque landscape that shifts between the present and the past, bring readers into the experience." SLJ

Other available titles in this series are:

The book of dreams (2009)

The Light-Bearer's daughter (2007)

The Summer King (2006)

Meloy, Colin

Under Wildwood; Colin Meloy ; illustrated by Carson Ellis. Balzer + Bray 2012 559 p. (hardback) $17.99

Grades: 5 6 7 8   **Fic**

1. Fantasy fiction 2. Adventure fiction 3. Fantasy 4. Animals -- Fiction

ISBN 006202471X; 9780062024718

LC 2012019040

This children's picture book is a sequel to "Wildwood." Here, bookish "Prue and bandit-in-training Curtis team up once again to fight a nefarious governess and evil science teacher in this fast-paced fantasy set in Oregon. . . . In this strange land, it can be difficult to tell friend from foe, making for deliciously suspenseful adventures with a rat named Septimus and a circus bear with hooks instead of paws." (Children's Literature)

★ **Wildwood**; illustrations by Carson Ellis. Balzer + Bray 2011 541p il $16.99

Grades: 5 6 7 8   **Fic**

1. Fantasy fiction 2. Animals -- Fiction 3. Siblings

-- Fiction 4. Missing persons -- Fiction

ISBN 978-0-06-202468-8; 0-06-202468-X

LC 2011010072

When her baby brother is kidnapped by crows, seventh-grader Prue McKeel ventures into the forbidden Impassable Wilderness—a dangerous and magical forest in the middle of Portland, Oregon—and soon finds herself involved in a war among the various inhabitants.

"Illustrations by Ellis . . . bring forest and inhabitants to gently whimsical life. A satisfying blend of fantasy, adventure story, eco-fable and political satire with broad appeal." Kirkus

Meloy, Maile

★ The **apothecary**. G. P. Putnam's Sons 2011 353p $16.99

Grades: 6 7 8 9   **Fic**

1. Adventure fiction 2. Alchemy -- Fiction 3. Cold war -- Fiction

ISBN 978-0-399-25627-1; 0-399-25627-X

LC 2010045003

"With evocative, confident prose and equally atmospheric spot art from Schoenherr, adult author Meloy's first book for young readers is an auspicious one." Publ Wkly

The **apprentices**; by Maile Meloy ; illustrated by Ian Schoenherr. G.P. Putnam's Sons, an imprint of Penguin Group (USA) Inc. 2013 432 p. (hardcover) $16.99

Grades: 6 7 8 9   **Fic**

1. Magic -- Fiction 2. Alchemy -- Fiction 3. Voyages and travels -- Fiction

ISBN 9780399162459

LC 2012048715

In this book by Maile Meloy is the sequel to "The Apothecary". "Janie, now 16, is alone at an elite American boarding school, unaware of the whereabouts of her first boyfriend, Benjamin, and his apothecary father. After she is wrongly expelled, she realizes she is the victim of a nefarious scheme, which again poses a threat to world peace. The . . . plot spans the globe as the heroes find their way back to each other." (Publishers Weekly)

Meltzer, Milton

Tough times; by Milton Meltzer. Clarion Books 2007 168p $16

Grades: 5 6 7 8   **Fic**

1. Jews -- Fiction 2. Family life -- Fiction 3. Great Depression, 1929-1939 -- Fiction

ISBN 978-0-618-87445-3; 0-618-87445-3

LC 2006102765

In 1931 Worcester, Massachusetts, Joey Singer, the teenaged son of Jewish immigrants, suffers with his family through the early part of the Great Depression, trying to finish high school, working a milk delivery route, marching on Washington, and eventually even becoming a hobo, all the while trying to figure out how to go to college and realize his dream of becoming a writer.

"Joey's strong voice makes this a valuable addition to the historical-fiction shelves." Booklist

Meminger, Neesha

Shine, coconut moon. Margaret K. McElderry Books 2009 256p $16.99; pa $8.99

Grades: 7 8 9 10 **Fic**

1. School stories 2. Prejudices -- Fiction 3. East Indian Americans -- Fiction 4. September 11 terrorist attacks, 2001 -- Fiction

ISBN 978-1-4169-5495-8; 1-4169-5495-3; 978-1-4424-0305-5 pa; 1-4424-0305-5 pa

LC 2008-9836

In the days and weeks following the terrorist attacks on September 11, 2001, Samar, who is of Punjabi heritage but has been raised with no knowledge of her past by her single mother, wants to learn about her family's history and to get in touch with the grandparents her mother shuns.

"Meminger's debut book is a beautiful and sensitive portrait of a young woman's journey from self-absorbed navet to selfless, unified awareness." SLJ

Merrill, Jean

★ The **pushcart** war; by Jean Merrill; with illustrations by Ronni Solbert. Bantam Doubleday Dell Books for Young Readers 1987 222p il pa $6.50

Grades: 5 6 7 8 **Fic**

1. Trucks -- Fiction

ISBN 0-440-47147-8

A reissue of the title first published 1964 by W. R. Scott

The outbreak of a war between truck drivers and pushcart peddlers brings the mounting problems of traffic to the attention of both the city of New York and the world.

"A book that is both humorous and downright funny. . . . Such a lively book will need little introducing." Horn Book

Messer, Stephen

★ **Windblowne**. Random House 2010 304p $16.99

Grades: 4 5 6 7 **Fic**

1. Fantasy fiction 2. Kites -- Fiction 3. Uncles -- Fiction 4. Space and time -- Fiction

ISBN 978-0-375-86195-6; 0-375-86195-5

LC 2008-43777

Hapless Oliver, who lives in the trees in the town of Windblowne, seeks his eccentric great-uncle Gilbert's help in creating a kite for the all-important kite festival, but when Gilbert suddenly disappears, Oliver is guided by one of Gilbert's kites in a quest through different worlds to find him.

"Messer constructs a tale that moves along at a powerful, steady pace to a climactic faceoff, and Oliver's realization that the gateway to worlds is open for those who can truly listen to the wind's voices sparks a memorable sea change in his self-image." Kirkus

The **death** of Yorik Mortwell; illustrated by Gris Grimly. Random House Children's Books 2011 173p il $15.99; lib bdg $18.99; e-book $15.95

Grades: 5 6 7 8 **Fic**

1. Ghost stories 2. Fantasy fiction 3. Magic -- Fiction 4. Siblings -- Fiction 5. Demonology -- Fiction 6.

Good and evil -- Fiction 7. Social classes -- Fiction

ISBN 978-0-375-86858-0; 978-0-375-96858-7 lib bdg; 978-0-375-89928-7 e-book

LC 2010014255

Following his death at the hands of fellow twelve-year-old, Lord Thomas, Yorik returns as a ghost to protect his sister from a similar fate but soon learns of ancient magical beings, both good and evil, who are vying for power at the Estate.

"Full-page, macabre illustrations appear throughout. Lemony Snicket, Harry Potter, and Neil Gaiman enthusiasts will appreciate this engaging, eccentric adventure." SLJ

Messner, Kate

Sugar and ice. Walker & Co. 2010 275p $16.99

Grades: 4 5 6 7 **Fic**

1. Ice skating -- Fiction

ISBN 978-0-8027-2081-8; 0-8027-2081-1

LC 2009-54217

When Russian skating coach Andrei Grosheva offers farm girl Claire a scholarship to train with the elite in Lake Placid, she encounters a world of mean girls on ice, where competition is everything

"The dialogue between classmates and siblings is realistic, and the intergenerational or extended family relationships are interesting. The author shows the intensity of the world of competitive skating without dwelling on its rough edges, making it accessible not only to tween readers, but also to those who might have Olympic aspirations." SLJ

The **brilliant** fall of Gianna Z. Walker 2009 198p $16.99

Grades: 5 6 7 8 **Fic**

1. Trees -- Fiction 2. Old age -- Fiction 3. Running -- Fiction 4. Grandmothers -- Fiction

ISBN 978-0-8027-9842-8; 0-8027-9842-X

Gianna has less than one week to complete her leaf project if she wants to compete in the upcoming cross-country sectionals, but issues like procrastination, disorganization—and her grandmother's declining health—seem destined to keep her from finishing.

"Youngsters will find much to relate to in this likable protagonist's struggle to balance family and academic commitments. . . . Plot twists keep readers engaged, and Messner's warm and humorous tone will capture even reluctant readers." SLJ

Meyer, Carolyn

Beware, Princess Elizabeth. Harcourt 2001 214p (Young royals) hardcover o.p. pa $5.95

Grades: 7 8 9 10 **Fic**

1. Queens 2. Sisters 3. Princesses

ISBN 0-15-202659-2; 0-15-204556-2 pa

LC 00-11700

After the death of her father, King Henry VIII, in 1547, thirteen-year-old Elizabeth must endure the political intrigues and dangers of the reigns of her half-brother Edward and her half-sister Mary before finally becoming Queen of England eleven years later

"The story moves along swiftly with hints of romance, life-and-death plots, and snippets of everyday life." Book Rep

Cleopatra confesses. Simon & Schuster Books for Young Readers 2011 289p $16.99

Grades: 6 7 8 9   **Fic**
    1. Queens -- Fiction 2. Princesses -- Fiction
ISBN 978-1-4169-8727-7; 1-4169-8727-4
                 LC 2010025989

Princess Cleopatra, the third (and favorite) daughter of King Ptolemy XII, comes of age in ancient Egypt, accumulating power and discovering love.

Meyer's "lush, detail-rich prose ably evokes Cleopatra's life as a young princess, beginning at age 10 and continuing on until she turns 22. . . . Narrating with the poise and confidence of a born leader, this Cleopatra should win readers over." Publ Wkly

Includes bibliographical references

Duchessina; a novel of Catherine de' Medici. Harcourt 2007 261p (Young royals) $17

Grades: 7 8 9 10   **Fic**
    1. Queens -- Fiction 2. Orphans -- Fiction
ISBN 978-0-15-205588-2; 0-15-205588-6
                 LC 2006028876

While her tyrannical family is out of favor in Italy, young Catherine de Medici is raised in convents, then in 1533, when she is fourteen, her uncle, Pope Clement VII, arranges for her marriage to prince Henri of France, who is destined to become king.

"With meticulous historical detail, sensitive characterizations, and Catherine's strong narration, Meyer's memorable story of a fascinating young woman who relies on her intelligence, rather than her beauty, will hit home with many teens." Booklist

The **true** adventures of Charley Darwin. Harcourt 2009 321p il $17

Grades: 7 8 9 10   **Fic**
    1. Naturalists 2. Travel writers 3. Writers on science 4. Natural history -- Fiction 5. Voyages around the world -- Fiction
ISBN 978-0-15-206194-4; 0-15-206194-0
                 LC 2008-17451

In nineteenth-century England, young Charles Darwin rejects the more traditional careers of physician and clergyman, choosing instead to embark on a dangerous five-year journey by ship to explore the natural world.

"Meyer's writing has a light touch that capitalizes on the humorous, romantic, and exciting events in the man's life while introducing his scientific pursuits and the beliefs of his time. . . . This novel paints a readable and detailed portrait of the young Charles Darwin." SLJ

Includes bibliographical references

Meyer, Kai

The **water** mirror; translated by Elizabeth D. Crawford. Margaret K. McElderry Books 2005 250p (Dark reflections) $15.95

Grades: 5 6 7 8   **Fic**
    1. Fantasy fiction 2. Orphans -- Fiction 3. Mermaids

and mermen -- Fiction
ISBN 0-689-87787-0
                 LC 2005-11943

Original German edition 2001

In Venice two teenaged orphans, apprenticed to a maker of magic mirrors, begin to realize that their fates are tied to the magical protector of the city known as the Flowing Queen and to the ruler of Hell, respectively.

An "inventive and original fantasy . . . A powerful mix of political intrigue, adventure, and magic." SLJ
    Other titles in this series are:
    The stone light (2007)
    The glass word (2008)

Meyer, L. A.

★ **Bloody** Jack; being an account of the curious adventures of Mary Jacky Faber, ship's boy. Harcourt 2002 278p hardcover o.p. pa $6.95

Grades: 7 8 9 10   **Fic**
    1. Adventure fiction 2. Orphans -- Fiction 3. Pirates -- Fiction 4. Sex role -- Fiction 5. Seafaring life -- Fiction
ISBN 0-15-216731-5; 0-15-205085-X pa
                 LC 2002-759

Reduced to begging and thievery in the streets of 18th-century London, a thirteen-year-old orphan disguises herself as a boy and connives her way onto a British warship set for high sea adventure in search of pirates

"From shooting a pirate in battle to foiling a shipmate's sexual attack to surviving when stranded alone on a Caribbean island, the action in Jacky's tale will entertain readers with a taste for adventure." Booklist
    Other titles in this series are:
    Curse of the blue tattoo (2004)
    In the belly of The Bloodhound (2006)
    The mark of the golden dragon (2011)
    Mississippi Jack (2007)
    My bonny light horseman (2008)
    Rapture of the deep (2009)
    Under the Jolly Roger (2005)
    The wake of the Lorelei Lee (2010)

Viva Jacquelina! being an account of the further adventures of Jacky Faber, over the hills and far away. written by L.A. Meyer. Harcourt 2012 p. cm. $16.99

Grades: 7 8 9 10   **Fic**
    1. Spain -- History -- Fiction 2. Sex role -- Fiction 3. Seafaring life -- Fiction 4. Adventure and adventurers -- Fiction
ISBN 9780547763507
                 LC 2011041931

This young adult adventure novel, by L. A. Meyer, continues the "Bloody Jack Adventures" series. "Once again under the thumb of British Intelligence, Jacky is sent to Spain to spy for the Crown during the early days of the nineteenth-century Peninsular War. She finds herself in the company of guerilla freedom fighters, poses for the famous artist Goya, runs with the bulls, is kidnapped by the Spanish Inquisition, and travels with a caravan of gypsies." (Publisher's note)

Meyer, Marissa, 1984-

★ **Cinder**; Marissa Meyer. Feiwel & Friends 2012 320 p. $17.99

Grades: 7 8 9 10 11 12   **Fic**
1. Fairy tales 2. Science fiction 3. Robots -- Fiction
ISBN 9780312641894

LC 2011036123

In this book, "as plague ravages the overcrowded Earth, observed by a ruthless lunar people, Cinder, a gifted mechanic and cyborg, becomes involved with handsome Prince Kai and must uncover secrets about her past in order to protect the world in this futuristic take on the Cinderella story." (Publisher's note)

★ **Scarlet**; Marissa Meyer. Feiwel and Friends 2013 464 p. $17.99
Grades: 7 8 9 10 11 12   **Fic**
1. Science fiction 2. Cyborgs -- Fiction 3. Missing persons -- Fiction 4. Extraterrestrial beings -- Fiction
ISBN 0312642962; 9780312642969

LC 2012034060

This novel, by Marissa Meyer, is the second book of the "Lunar Chronicles" series. "Cinder, the cyborg mechanic, . . . [is] trying to break out of prison. . . . [Meanwhile,] Scarlet Benoit's grandmother is missing. . . . When Scarlet encounters Wolf, a street fighter who may have information . . . , she is loath to trust this stranger. . . . As Scarlet and Wolf unravel one mystery, they encounter another when they meet Cinder." (Publisher's note)

Meyer, Stephenie
★ **Twilight**. Little, Brown and Co. 2005 498p $17.99; pa $8.99
Grades: 8 9 10 11 12   **Fic**
1. School stories 2. Vampires -- Fiction
ISBN 0-316-16017-2; 0-316-01584-9 pa

LC 2004-24730

When seventeen-year-old Bella leaves Phoenix to live with her father in Forks, Washington, she meets an exquisitely handsome boy at school for whom she feels an overwhelming attraction and who she comes to realize is not wholly human.
"Realistic, subtle, succinct, and easy to follow, . . . [this book] will have readers dying to sink their teeth into it." SLJ
Other titles in this series are:
Breaking dawn (2008)
Eclipse (2007)
New moon (2006)

Meyer, Susan
Black radishes; [by] Susan Lynn Meyer. Delacorte Press 2010 228p map $16.99; lib bdg $19.99
Grades: 5 6 7 8   **Fic**
1. Jews -- France -- Fiction 2. Holocaust, 1933-1945 -- Fiction
ISBN 978-0-385-73881-1; 0-385-73881-1; 978-0-385-90748-4 lib bdg; 0-385-90748-6 lib bdg

LC 2009-47613

"Set in France during World War II, this historical novel follows eleven-year-old Gustave as his family escapes Paris for safer quarters in the small, provincial town of Saint-Georges. . . . Not long after Gustave's family arrives in Saint-Georges, the Nazis invade and occupy Paris and establish a demarcation line between occupied northern France and unoccupied Vichy France in the south. . . . The episodic

narrative offers abundant detail, and the wartime dangers, especially Gustave's father's illicit travel between occupied and unoccupied zones, adds considerable suspense. Gustave's growth over the course of the novel is both realistic and relatable, making this an appealing topical entry for the upper elementary/middle school set." Bull Cent Child Books

Meyerhoff, Jenny
Queen of secrets. Farrar, Straus and Giroux 2010 230p $16.99
Grades: 8 9 10 11 12   **Fic**
1. School stories 2. Cousins -- Fiction 3. Orphans -- Fiction 4. Grandparents -- Fiction 5. Jews -- United States -- Fiction
ISBN 978-0-374-32628-9; 0-374-32628-2

LC 2008-55561

Fifteen-year-old Essie Green, an orphan who has been raised by her secular Jewish grandparents in Michigan, experiences conflicting loyalties and confusing emotions when her aunt, uncle, and cousin move back from New York, and her very religious cousin tries to fit in with the other football players at Essie's high school, one of whom is Essie's popular new boyfriend.
"Compelling characters, dramatic tension, and thoughtful exploration of how teenagers create their own identity amid familial and cultural influences should give this story wide appeal." Publ Wkly

Michael, Jan
★ **City** boy. Clarion Books 2009 186p $16
Grades: 5 6 7 8   **Fic**
1. Orphans -- Fiction 2. Country life -- Fiction
ISBN 978-0-547-22310-0; 0-547-22310-2

LC 2008-37418

First published in the United Kingdom with title: Leaving home
In the southern African country of Malawi, after the AIDS-related deaths of both of his parents, a boy leaves his affluent life in the city to live in a rural village, sharing a one-roomed hut with his aunt, his cousins, and other orphans.
"This is a powerful portrait of poverty and hardship, evenly balanced with shades of hope. Michael's simple prose subtly layers detail, building full-bodied descriptions of landscapes and characters, leaving no room for shortcuts. . . . A stoic tale of surviving life's uncertainties." Kirkus

Michael, Livi
City of dogs. G. P. Putnam's Sons 2007 250p $16.99
Grades: 5 6 7 8   **Fic**
1. Fantasy fiction 2. Dogs -- Fiction 3. Norse mythology -- Fiction
ISBN 978-0-399-24356-1; 0-399-24356-9

LC 2006-26539

Jenny, a mysterious dog, shows up on Sam's birthday and pulls many of the other dogs in the neighborhood into her quest to prevent the destruction of the world.
"Fantasy readers seeking a thoughtful novel into which to sink their teeth will especially appreciate the unhurried pace, the frequently shifting perspectives . . . and the offbeat but quite effective dogcentric narration." Bull Cent Child Books

Michaelis, Antonia

★ **Tiger** moon; translated from the German by Anthea Bell. Amulet Books 2008 453p $19.95 pa$9.95

Grades: 8 9 10 11 12   **Fic**

1. Tigers -- Fiction 2. Thieves -- Fiction 3. Princesses -- Fiction 4. Storytelling -- Fiction
ISBN 0-8109-4499-5 pa; 0-8109-9481-X; 978-0-8109-4499-2 pa; 978-0-8109-9481-2

LC 2007-22823

Sold to be the eighth wife of a rich and cruel merchant, Safia, also called Raka, tries to escape her fate by telling stories of Farhad the thief, his companion Nitish the white tiger, and their travels across India to retrieve a famous jewel that will save a kidnapped princess from becoming the bride of a demon king.

"The plot is fast paced and exciting, and the story gives an excellent overview of the conflicts of India at the time of British occupation, and of Hindu religious beliefs." SLJ

Michaels, Rune

★ **Genesis** Alpha; [by] Rune Michaels. 1st ed.; Atheneum Books for Young Readers 2007 193p $15.99

Grades: 7 8 9 10   **Fic**

1. Brothers -- Fiction 2. Homicide -- Fiction 3. Video games -- Fiction 4. Genetic engineering -- Fiction
ISBN 978-1-4169-1886-8; 1-4169-1886-8

LC 2007001446

When thirteen-year-old Josh's beloved older brother, Max, is arrested for murder, the victim's sister leads Josh to evidence of Max's guilt—and her own—hidden in their favorite online role-playing game. Josh, who was conceived to save Max's life years earlier, must consider whether he shares that guilt.

"Skillfully interweaving science fiction and cyberspace into a murder mystery, Michaels gives readers a story that is not only difficult to put down but also poses questions that will linger long after the last page is turned." Voice Youth Advocates

Nobel genes. Simon & Schuster 2010 181p $16.99

Grades: 6 7 8 9 10   **Fic**

1. Mentally ill -- Fiction 2. Mother-son relationship -- Fiction 3. Manic-depressive illness -- Fiction
ISBN 978-1-4169-1259-0; 1-4169-1259-2

LC 2009-36665

A boy whose manic-depressive mother has always told him that his father won a Nobel Prize, spends his time taking care of her and searching for clues to the identity of the Nobel Prizewinning sperm donor, eventually finding a truth he must learn to accept.

This is a "skillful, deeply disconcerting tale. . . . Michaels . . . makes effective use of first-person narration to give readers a highly believable protagonist and a riveting, from-the-trenches look at what it is like to live with a parent who suffers from a serious mental illness." Publ Wkly

The **reminder**. Atheneum Books for Young Readers 2008 182p $16.99; pa $8.99

Grades: 6 7 8 9 10   **Fic**

1. Robots -- Fiction 2. Mothers -- Fiction 3. Bereavement -- Fiction
ISBN 978-1-4169-4131-6; 1-4169-4131-2; 978-1-4424-0253-9 pa; 1-4424-0253-9 pa

LC 2008-15391

A teenaged girl who hears her dead mother's voice makes a startling discovery after breaking into her father's industrial robotics lab and finding his latest secret project: a lifelike replica of her mother's head that looks, talks, moves, and even smiles just like her mother.

"An intriguing story about loss and survival, with elements of science fiction." Booklist

Mieville, China

★ **Un** Lun Dun. Ballantine Books 2007 432p il hardcover o.p. pa $9

Grades: 5 6 7 8 9   **Fic**

1. Fantasy fiction 2. Young adult literature -- Works
ISBN 978-0-345-49516-7; 0-345-49516-0; 978-0-345-45844-5 pa; 0-345-45844-3 pa

LC 2007-296921

When 12-year-old Zanna and her friend Deeba find a secret entrance leading out of London and into the strange city of Un Lun Dun, it appears that an ancient prophesy is coming true at last

"Miéville's fantastical city is vivid and splendidly crafted. . . . The story is exceptional and the action moves along at a quick pace." SLJ

Mikaelsen, Ben

Ghost of Spirit Bear; [by] Ben Mikaelsen. 1st ed.; HarperCollins Publishers 2008 154p $16.99; lib bdg $17.89

Grades: 6 7 8 9   **Fic**

1. School stories 2. Bullies -- Fiction
ISBN 978-0-06-009007-4; 0-06-009007-3; 978-0-06-009008-1 lib bdg; 0-06-009008-1 lib bdg

LC 2007036732

After a year in exile on an Alaskan island as punishment for severely beating a fellow student, Cole Matthews returns to school in Minneapolis having made peace with himself and his victim--but he finds that surviving the violence and hatred of high school is even harder than surviving in the wilderness.

This is "gripping and fast moving. . . [this novel] will appeal to boys especially and to reluctant readers." KLIATT

Touching Spirit Bear. HarperCollins Pubs. 2001 241p $15.99; lib bdg $16.89; pa $5.99

Grades: 6 7 8 9   **Fic**

1. Bears -- Fiction 2. Wilderness survival -- Fiction 3. Indians of North America -- Alaska 4. Juvenile delinquents -- Rehabilitation
ISBN 0-380-97744-3; 0-06-029149-4 lib bdg; 0-380-80560-X pa

LC 00-40702

After his anger erupts into violence, Cole, in order to avoid going to prison, agrees to participate in a sentencing alternative based on the native American Circle Justice, and he is sent to a remote Alaskan Island where an encounter with a huge Spirit Bear changes his life

"Mikaelsen's portrayal of this angry, manipulative, damaged teen is dead on. . . . Gross details about Cole eating raw worms, a mouse, and worse will appeal to fans of the outdoor adventure/survival genre." SLJ

Miklowitz, Gloria D.

The **enemy** has a face. Eerdmans Bks. for Young Readers 2003 139p $16; pa $8

Grades: 7 8 9 10   Fic

1. Missing persons 2. Palestinian Arabs 3. Arab-Israeli conflict 4. Jews -- United States 5. Missing persons -- Fiction

ISBN 0-8028-5243-2; 0-8028-5261-0 pa

LC 2002-9233

Netta and her family have relocated temporarily from Israel to Los Angeles, and when her seventeen-year-old brother mysteriously disappears, she becomes convinced that he has been abducted by Palestinian terrorists

"Almost unbearably suspenseful, the plot will keep readers turning pages as fast as they can. Nicely interspersed with the events is a thoughtful examination of some of the reasons behind the age-old strife between Palestinians and Israelis. Readers come away with a greater understanding of the conflict, and Netta is given the opportunity to modify her attitude about her former enemies." SLJ

Milford, Kate

★ The **Boneshaker**; [illustrations by Andrea Offermann] Clarion Books 2010 372p il $17

Grades: 5 6 7 8 9   Fic

1. Bicycles -- Fiction 2. Demonology -- Fiction 3. Supernatural -- Fiction

ISBN 978-0-547-24187-6; 0-547-24187-9

LC 2009-45350

When Jake Limberleg brings his traveling medicine show to a small Missouri town in 1913, thirteen-year-old Natalie senses that something is wrong and, after investigating, learns that her love of automata and other machines make her the only one who can set things right.

"Natalie is a well-drawn protagonist with sturdy supporting characters around her. The tension built into the solidly constructed plot is complemented by themes that explore the literal and metaphorical role of crossroads and that thin line between good and evil." Kirkus

The **Broken** Lands; by Kate Milford ; with illustrations by Andrea Offermann. Clarion Books 2012 455 p. ill. (hardback) $16.99

Grades: 5 6 7 8 9 10   Fic

1. Bridges -- Fiction 2. Supernatural -- Fiction 3. New York (N.Y.) -- Fiction 4. Orphans -- Fiction 5. Demonology -- Fiction 6. Good and evil -- Fiction

ISBN 0547739664; 9780547739663

LC 2011049466

This book, a prequel to "Kate Milford's 'The Boneshaker,' [is] set in . . . nineteenth-century Coney Island and New York City. Few crossroads compare to the one being formed by the Brooklyn Bridge and the East River, and as the bridge's construction progresses, forces of unimaginable evil seek to bend that power to their advantage. . . . Can the teenagers Sam, a card sharp, and Jin, a fireworks expert, stop them before it's too late?" (Publisher's note)

Millard, Glenda

★ A **small** free kiss in the dark. Holiday House 2010 180p $16.95

Grades: 6 7 8 9   Fic

1. War stories 2. Infants -- Fiction 3. Refugees -- Fiction 4. Homeless persons -- Fiction

ISBN 978-0-8234-2264-7; 0-8234-2264-X

LC 2009-27212

First published 2009 in Australia

Skip "narrates with an artist's attention to detail and rich use of visual metaphor. . . . Skip's optimism against the apocalyptic background lends the story a haunting quality that is not to be easily forgotten." SLJ

Miller, Kirsten

All you desire; can you trust your heart? Razorbill 2011 423p $17.99

Grades: 6 7 8 9 10   Fic

1. Love stories 2. Reincarnation -- Fiction 3. Fate and fatalism -- Fiction

ISBN 978-1-59514-323-5; 1-59514-323-8

Haven Moore and Iain Morrow have been living a blissful life in Rome, an ocean way from the Ouroboros Society and its diabolical leader. But paradise is not to last. The mysterious disappearance of Haven's best friend, Beau, sends the pair running back to New York, where they encounter the Horae, an underground group of women who have spent centuries scheming to destroy Adam Rosier.

"A multi-layered mystery with (mostly) rounded characters." Kirkus

★ **Kiki** Strike: inside the shadow city; [by] Kirsten Miller. Bloomsbury Children's Books 2006 387p $16.95

Grades: 5 6 7 8   Fic

1. Mystery fiction

ISBN 978-1-58234-960-2; 1-58234-960-6

LC 2005030945

Life becomes more interesting for Ananka Fishbein when, at the age of twelve, she discovers an underground room in the park across from her New York City apartment and meets a mysterious girl called Kiki Strike who claims that she, too, wants to explore the subterranean world

"If a 12-year-old can be a hardboiled detective, Ananka Fishbein is one. Her narration is fresh and funny, and the author's unadorned, economical, yet descriptive style carries her character through with verve." SLJ

Another title about Kiki Strike is:

Kiki Strike: The empress's tomb (2007)

Kiki Strike; the darkness dwellers (2013)

★ The **eternal** ones. Razorbill 2010 411p $17.99

Grades: 6 7 8 9 10   Fic

1. Love stories 2. Faith -- Fiction 3. Reincarnation -- Fiction 4. Fate and fatalism -- Fiction

ISBN 978-1-59514-308-2; 1-59514-308-4

LC 2010-22775

Seventeen-year-old Haven Moore leaves East Tennessee to attend the Fashion Institute of Technology in New York City, where she meets playboy Iain Morrow, whose fate may be tied to hers through a series of past lives.

"Miller's writing elevates the supernatural romance well beyond typical fare, and Haven's mix of naïveté and determination makes her a solid, credible heroine." Publ Wkly

Miller, Sarah

★ **Miss** Spitfire; reaching Helen Keller. Atheneum Books for Young Readers 2007 208p $16.99
Grades: 7 8 9 10 11 **Fic**
1. Deaf -- Fiction 2. Blind -- Fiction 3. Teachers -- Fiction
ISBN 978-1-4169-2542-2; 1-4169-2542-2
LC 2006014738
At age twenty-one, partially-blind, lonely but spirited Annie Sullivan travels from Massachusetts to Alabama to try and teach six-year-old Helen Keller, deaf and blind since age two, self-discipline and communication skills. Includes historical notes and timeline.
"This excellent novel is compelling reading even for those familiar with the Keller/Sullivan experience." SLJ
Includes bibliographical references

The **lost** crown. Atheneum Books for Young Readers 2011 412p $17.99
Grades: 8 9 10 11 12 **Fic**
1. Sisters -- Fiction 2. Kings and rulers -- Fiction 3. World War, 1914-1918 -- Fiction
ISBN 978-1-4169-8340-8; 1-4169-8340-6
LC 2010037001
In alternating chapters, Grand Duchesses Olga, Tatiana, Maria, and Anastasia tell how their privileged lives as the daughters of the tsar in early twentieth-century Russia are transformed by world war and revolution.
"Each Grand Duchess comes across as a unique personality. . . . Like the best historical novels, this allows modern-day teens to see themselves in very different people." Booklist

Millet, Lydia

The **fires** beneath the sea. Big Mouth House 2011 256p (The dissenters) $16.95
Grades: 4 5 6 7 **Fic**
1. Otters -- Fiction 2. Mothers -- Fiction 3. Supernatural -- Fiction
ISBN 978-1-931520-71-3; 1-931520-71-2
"Mom vanished two months ago, and summer's ending. While swimming in the ocean, Cara spots a sea otter—but sea otters don't belong on Atlantic beaches. Cara reaches out her fingertips, and the otter streams words into Cara's mind. . . . Millet's prose is lyrically evocative. . . . A lush and intelligent opener for a topical eco-fantasy series." Kirkus

Mills, Claudia

One square inch. Farrar, Straus and Giroux 2010 168p $16.99
Grades: 4 5 6 7 **Fic**
1. Mothers -- Fiction 2. Siblings -- Fiction 3. Imagination -- Fiction 4. Manic-depressive illness -- Fiction
ISBN 978-0-374-35652-1; 0-374-35652-1
When their mother's behavior changes and she starts to neglect her children, seventh-grader Cooper and his little sister take refuge in Inchland, an imaginary country inspired by deeds to one square inch of land that their grandfather gave them.
Mills "delivers a compassionate story about life with a bipolar parent. . . . The twist of [Cooper's] emotions and depth of his concern for his mother and sister are believable and deeply moving." Publ Wkly

Mills, Rob

Charlie's key. Orca Book Publishers 2011 254p pa $9.99
Grades: 5 6 7 8 9 **Fic**
1. Mystery fiction 2. Orphans -- Fiction
ISBN 978-1-55469-872-1; 1-55469-872-3
A young orphan struggles to unlock the significance of an old key left by his dying father.
"A fast-paced, often riveting mystery with a plausible, thrilling climax." Kirkus

Mills, Sam

The **viper** within; [by] Sam Mills. 1st American ed.; Alfred A. Knopf 2008 296p $16.99; lib bdg $19.99
Grades: 7 8 9 10 **Fic**
1. Cults -- Fiction 2. Divorce -- Fiction 3. Religion -- Fiction 4. Kidnapping -- Fiction
ISBN 978-0-375-84465-2; 0-375-84465-1; 978-0-375-94465-9 lib bdg; 0-375-94465-6 lib bdg
LC 2007031952
Bitter and angry after his parents' divorce, Jon joins a cult, The Religion of Hebetheus, at his high school and soon becomes embroiled in a plot to kidnap a fellow student and suspected terrorist, but their plans go terribly wrong.
"Thought provoking, tension packed, and suspenseful, Mill's novel forces readers to grapple with multiple perspectives on terrorism, cults, religion, victimization, fidelity, embedded misogyny and conscience." Voice Youth Advocates

Milway, Alex

The **mousehunter**; written and illustrated by Alex Milway. Little, Brown 2009 422p il map $15.99
Grades: 4 5 6 7 **Fic**
1. Adventure fiction 2. Mice -- Fiction 3. Pirates -- Fiction
ISBN 978-0-316-02454-9; 0-316-02454-6
Captain Mousebeard is a feared mousehunting pirate. He seeks out the rarest and most precious breeds of mice to collect and trade. Emeline, a mousekeeper, wants the bounty her master puts on Mousebeard's head. So she heads off to adventure to capture the pirate.
"Milway has created an atmospheric and engaging world filled with hundreds of varieties of mice with different coloring, temperaments, and abilities. New creatures are introduced both within the text and in pages with information and illustrations from The Mousehunter's Almanac interspersed between chapters. Readers will enjoy the action, chases, and plot twists." SLJ

Mitchard, Jacquelyn

★ **All** we know of heaven; a novel. HarperTeen 2008 312p $16.99; lib bdg $17.89

Grades: 7 8 9 10 11 12   **Fic**
1. Death -- Fiction 2. Bereavement -- Fiction 3. Traffic accidents -- Fiction
ISBN 978-0-06-134578-4; 0-06-134578-4; 978-0-06-134579-1 lib bdg; 0-06-134579-2 lib bdg

When Maureen and Bridget, two sixteen-year-old best friends who look like sisters, are in a terrible car accident and one of them dies, they are at first incorrectly identified at the hospital, and then, as Maureen achieves a remarkable recovery, she must deal with the repercussions of the accident, the mixup, and some choices she made while she was getting better.

"Riveting, compassionate and psychologically nuanced. . . . Utterly gripping." Publ Wkly

The **midnight** twins. Razorbill 2008 235p $16.99; pa $8.99
Grades: 6 7 8 9   **Fic**
1. Twins -- Fiction 2. Telepathy -- Fiction 3. Clairvoyance -- Fiction
ISBN 978-1-59514-160-6; 1-59514-160-X; 978-1-59514-226-9 pa; 1-59514-226-6 pa
LC 2007-31139

Identical twins Meredith and Mallory Brynn have always shared one another's thoughts, even as they dream, but their connection diminishes as they approach their thirteenth birthday, and one begins to see the future, the other the past, leading them to discover that a high school student they know is doing horrible things that place the twins, and others, in grave danger.

"The plot moves quickly, propelled by the mysteries of the sisters' relationship. . . . The girls' supernatural knowledge is a delicious bonus." Publ Wkly

Other titles about Meredith and Mallory are:
Look both ways (2009)
Watch for me by moonlight (2010)

Mitchell, Saundra
The **vespertine**. Harcourt 2011 296p $16.99
Grades: 8 9 10 11 12   **Fic**
1. Clairvoyance -- Fiction
ISBN 978-0-547-48247-7; 0-547-48247-7

It's the summer of 1889, and Amelia van den Broek is new to Baltimore and eager to take in all the pleasures the city has to offer. But her gaiety is interrupted by disturbing, dreamlike visions she has only at sunset—visions that offer glimpses of the future. Soon, friends and strangers alike call on Amelia to hear her prophecies. However, a forbidden romance with Nathaniel, an artist, threatens the new life Amelia is building in Baltimore.

"Nathaniel's forbidden charms will most certainly have readers swooning. . . . There's . . . considerable fun to be had here, and Amelia's supernatural power is believably portrayed." Bull Cent Child Books

Miéville, China, 1972-
★ **Railsea**; China Mieville. Del Rey/Ballantine Books 2012 424 p. ill. (hbk. : alk. paper) $18.00
Grades: 7 8 9 10   **Fic**
1. Adventure fiction 2. Steampunk fiction 3. Railroads

-- Fiction 4. Imaginary places -- Fiction
ISBN 0345524527; 9780345524522; 9780345524546
LC 2012009516

This book presents "a steampunk spin on 'Moby-Dick' . . . . Instead of chasing whales on the sea, the crew of the diesel train Medes hunt moldywarpes—enormous, man-eating, molelike creatures who are only one of the countless menacing species who burrow in the perilous earth beneath a tangled ocean of train tracks. And it is one moldywarpe in particular, the great Mocker-Jack, that Captain Naphi is after—it"s trendy for any captain worth her iron to have such a defining obsession, and she is fully aware that they hunt metaphor in beast form. Aboard for the grand adventure is your hero, young Sham (don"t call him Ishmael)." (Booklist)

Mlawski, Shana
Hammer of witches; by Shana Mlawski. Tu Books 2013 400 p. (reinforced) $18.95
Grades: 6 7 8 9   **Fic**
1. Fantasy fiction 2. Storytelling -- Fiction 3. America -- Exploration -- Fiction 4. Magic -- Fiction 5. Wizards -- Fiction 6. Explorers -- Fiction
ISBN 1600609872; 9781600609879
LC 2012048627

In this novel, by Shana Mlawski, "Baltasar Infante . . . encounters a monster straight out of stories one night . . . . Captured by . . . a mysterious witch-hunting arm of the Spanish Inquisition, . . . the Inquisitor demands he reveal the whereabouts of Amir al-Katib, a legendary Moorish sorcerer who can bring myths and the creatures within them to life. Now Baltasar must escape, find al-Katib, and defeat a dreadful power that may destroy the world." (Publisher's note)

"Newcomer Mlawski delivers a fast-paced coming-of-age adventure, respectfully evoking the complexities and cultural landscape of the period. She draws from a variety of sources, including Jewish and Biblical myth, offering an accessible, attention-grabbing story that seamlessly inserts its magical elements into historical fact." Pub Wkly

Mlynowski, Sarah
Gimme a call. Delacorte Press 2010 301p $17.99; lib bdg $20.99
Grades: 7 8 9 10   **Fic**
1. School stories 2. Time travel -- Fiction
ISBN 978-0-385-73588-9; 0-385-73588-X; 978-0-385-90574-9 lib bdg; 0-385-90574-2 lib bdg
LC 2009-20020

"When Devi's high-school sweetheart breaks up with her right before their senior prom, she is devastated. Not only is she dateless but she is also friendless and relegated to a mediocre college because she has concentrated on her boyfriend instead of academics. . . . In a fresh twist on time travel, she contacts her freshman self via cell phone and proceeds to change their future. Of course, one small change leads to others, and both girls begin to wonder about the wisdom of this collaboration. Mlynowski has given herself a complicated, challenging story, and she is particularly effective in conveying the differences in maturity and perspective between a freshman and a senior." Booklist

Ten things we did (and probably shouldn't have) HarperTeen 2011 357p $16.99; ebook $9.99

Grades: 7 8 9 10   Fic
1. Friendship -- Fiction
ISBN 978-0-06-170124-5; 0-06-170124-6; 978-0-06-
208461-3 ebook; 0-06-208461-5 ebook
                                        LC 2010-45556
Sixteen-year-old April, a high school junior, and her
friend Vi, a senior, get a crash course in reality as the list
of things they should not do becomes a list of things they
did while living parent-free in Westport, Connecticut, for
the semester.

"With wit, energy, and an uncanny understanding of
teenage logic, Mlynowski . . . weighs the pros and cons of
independence in this modern cautionary tale. . . . Mlynowski
avoids sermonizing, offering 10 madcap and remarkably
tense escapades that will have readers laughing, cringing,
and guessing how April will get out of the next pickle."
Publ Wkly

Mobley, Jeannie
★ **Katerina's** wish; Jeannie Mobley. Marga-
ret K. McElderry Books 2012 256 p. (hardcover)
$15.99
Grades: 4 5 6 7   Fic
1. Wishes -- Fiction 2. Historical fiction 3. Immigrants
-- Fiction 4. Czech Americans -- Fiction 5. Coal mines
and mining -- Fiction 6. Family life -- Colorado --
Fiction
ISBN 1442433434; 9781442433434; 9781442433458
                                        LC 2011044392
In this young adult novel, Katerina and her family have
immigrated from Bohemia and "settled in a coal mining
camp, [where] they are still buried in work and trapped
by debt. Then Trina sees a fish that reminds her of a fairy
tale about a magic carp; soon after, her two younger sisters'
frivolous wishes are granted. Initially skeptical, Trina eventually makes her wish: for a farm that will make her family
happy." (Publishers Weekly)

Mochizuki, Ken
Beacon Hill boys. Scholastic Press 2002 201p
$16.95; pa $5.99
Grades: 7 8 9 10   Fic
1. Japanese Americans -- Fiction
ISBN 0-439-26749-8; 0-439-24906-6 pa
                                        LC 2002-2343
In 1972 in Seattle, a teenager in a Japanese American
family struggles for his own identity, along with a group of
three friends who share his anger and confusion
"The author nicely balances universal experiences of
male adolescence . . . with scenes that bring readers right
into the complicated era, and his important, thought-provoking story asks tough questions about racial and cultural
identity, prejudice, and family." Booklist

Molloy, Michael
Peter Raven under fire. Scholastic 2005 502p
il maps $17.95
Grades: 6 7 8 9   Fic
1. Sea stories 2. Adventure fiction
ISBN 0-439-72454-6
"In 1800, continuous war has depleted France's trea-
sury, but Napoleon still wants to expand his empire. To this

end, he needs money to defeat the superior British Navy
and to exploit Louisiana for the greatest gain. In England,
midshipman Peter Raven, 13, is assigned to HMS Torren.
When powerful, sadistic pirates murder everyone on the ship
except Peter and jack-of-all-trades Matthew Book, the protagonist finds himself apprenticed to a British spy. . . . Fast
paced with multiple plot twists. . . . Molloy's writing is intelligent and engaging." SLJ

Moloney, James
The **Book** of Lies. HarperCollinsPublishers
2007 360p $16.99; lib bdg $17.89
Grades: 5 6 7 8   Fic
1. Fantasy fiction 2. Magic -- Fiction 3. Orphans
-- Fiction
ISBN 978-0-06-057842-8; 0-06-057842-4; 978-0-06-
057843-5 lib bdg; 0-06-057843-2 lib bdg
                                        LC 2006-29874
On the night he was brought to an orphanage, Marcel's
memories were taken by a sorceror and replaced with new
ones by his Book of Lies, but Bea, a girl with the ability to
make herself invisible, was watching and is determined to
help him discover his true identity.
"Readers who enjoy the mixture of mystery, riddles, action, and camaraderie will be pleased that the open-ended
conclusion leads to a planned sequel." Booklist

Monaghan, Annabel
A **girl** named Digit; by Annabel Monaghan.
Houghton Mifflin Harcourt 2012 187 p. $16.99
Grades: 7 8 9   Fic
1. School stories 2. Terrorism -- Fiction 3.
Cryptography -- Fiction 4. Kidnapping -- Fiction 5.
Interpersonal relations -- Fiction 6. Adventure and
adventurers -- Fiction
ISBN 054766852X; 9780547668529; 9780544022485
                                        LC 2011012239
In this book, "saddled with the nickname Digit, Farrah
resolved to fit in once she reached high school by hiding
her math skills. Then Farrah stumbles upon an eco-terrorist
organization after their suicide bomb attack on JFK Airport,
and the terrorists want her dead. . . . Farrah's FBI protector,
the cute, young rookie agent John Bennett, . . . works with
Farrah to uncover a blackmail scheme involving the attack's
bomber." (Kirkus Reviews)

Mone, Gregory
Fish. Scholastic Press 2010 241p $16.99
Grades: 4 5 6 7   Fic
1. Adventure fiction 2. Ciphers -- Fiction 3. Pirates
-- Fiction 4. Buried treasure -- Fiction
ISBN 978-0-545-11632-9; 0-545-11632-5
Eleven-year-old Fish, seeking a way to help his family
financially, becomes a reluctant cabin boy on a pirate ship,
where he soon makes friends—and enemies—and is asked
to help decipher clues that might lead to a legendary treasure.
"Mone seamlessly integrates factual information into his
tale of friendship, loyalty, and exploration. . . . Fish makes a
splashing good addition to adventure fiction." SLJ

Monninger, Joseph

★ **Finding** somewhere. Delacorte Press 2011
$17.99; lib bdg $20.99; e-book $17.99

Grades: 7 8 9 10   **Fic**

1. Horses -- Fiction 2. Friendship -- Fiction 3.
Automobile travel -- Fiction
ISBN 978-0-385-73942-9; 978-0-385-90789-7 lib
bdg; 978-0-375-86214-4 e-book

            LC 2010053551

Sixteen-year-old Hattie and eighteen-year-old Delores
set off on a road trip that takes unexpected turns as they
discover the healing power of friendship and confront what
each of them is fleeing from.

"Monninger's writing is delicious, evocative and, especially during horse-focused scenes, moving. Horse story,
road trip, coming-of-age tale: It's any and all of these, but
mostly a tender and authentic voyage into the mind of a
wise, funny and wholly likable protagonist." Kirkus

★ **Hippie** chick. Front Street 2008 156p $16.95

Grades: 8 9 10 11 12   **Fic**

1. Manatees -- Fiction 2. Shipwrecks -- Fiction 3.
Survival after airplane accidents, shipwrecks, etc. --
Fiction
ISBN 978-1-59078-598-0; 1-59078-598-3

            LC 2007-51976

After her sailboat capsizes, fifteen-year-old Lolly Em-
merson is rescued by manatees and taken to a mangrove key
in the Everglades, where she forms a bond with her aquatic
companions while struggling to survive.

"It's an affecting account, beautifully told." SLJ

Wish. Delacorte Press 2010 193p $17.99; lib
bdg $20.99

Grades: 6 7 8 9 10   **Fic**

1. Sharks -- Fiction 2. Wishes -- Fiction 3. Siblings
-- Fiction 4. Cystic fibrosis -- Fiction
ISBN 978-0-385-73941-2; 0-385-73941-9; 978-0-385-
90788-0 lib bdg; 0-385-90788-5 lib bdg

            LC 2010-09958

Bee's brother, Tommy, knows everything there is to
know about sharks. He also knows that his life will be cut
short by cystic fibrosis. And so does Bee. That's why she
wants to make his wish-foundation-sponsored trip to swim
with a great white shark an unforgettable memory. Only
when Bee takes Tommy to meet a famous shark attack survivor and hard-core surfer does Tommy have the chance to
live one day to the fullest.

"Fans of Monninger's other works will recognize the
fluid, thoughtful writing and vivid characters, and this could
be an eye-opener for shark aficionados looking to take
their interest beyond the glitz of shark week." Bull Cent
Child Books

Moodie, Craig

Into the trap. Roaring Brook Press 2011 199p
$15.99

Grades: 5 6 7 8   **Fic**

1. Adventure fiction 2. Islands -- Fiction 3. Thieves
-- Fiction 4. Lobsters -- Fiction
ISBN 978-1-59643-585-8; 1-59643-585-2

            LC 2010029238

Twelve-year-old Eddie Atwell accidentally learns who
has been stealing lobsters from Fog Island lobstermen and
enlists thirteen-year-old Briggs Fairfield, a summer visitor,
to help foil their plans.

"Set over a single, tense day, the novel's chapter titles
track the hours and give the book an immediate, real-time
pace. An exciting drama." Booklist

Moore, Carley

The **stalker** chronicles; Carley Moore. Farrar
Straus Giroux 2012 230 p. (hardcover) $16.99

Grades: 8 9 10 11 12   **Fic**

1. School stories 2. Divorce -- Fiction 3. Interpersonal
relations -- Fiction 4. Schools -- Fiction 5. Friendship
-- Fiction 6. Best friends -- Fiction 7. High schools
-- Fiction 8. Family life -- New York (State) -- Fiction
ISBN 9780374371807; 9781429961752

            LC 2011013093

This book features "Cammie, a high-school sophomore,
whose history has involved such intense interest in guys . .
. that she"s now known around school as a stalker. When
cute new guy Toby turns up in her small town, Cammie"s
determined that she"ll change her ways, . . . and finally get
the relationship she"s been longing for. . . . The dissolution
of Cammie"s parents" marriage . . . brings her dysfunctional patterns into sharp relief." (Bulletin of the Center for
Children"s Books)

Moore, Derrick

Always upbeat / All that; Stephanie Perry Moore
; All that / Stephanie Perry Moore & Derrick Moore.
Saddleback 2012 314 p. $14.95

Grades: 7 8 9 10 11 12   **Fic**

1. Football players 2. Cheerleading -- Fiction 3. High
school students -- Fiction
ISBN 1616518847; 9781616518844

This book by Stephanie Perry Moore and Derrick Moore
"deliver[s] a pair of intersecting but distinct stories from the
points of view of a cheerleader and a quarterback at a predominantly African-American Atlanta high school. Spoiled,
confident Charli Black and driven athlete Blake Strong have
been together for two years. Now, at the start of their junior
year, they are growing apart. Blake wants to 'take [their]
relationship to the next level,' but Charli wants to wait."
(Kirkus Reviews)

Moore, Perry

Hero. Hyperion 2007 428p $16.99

Grades: 7 8 9 10 11 12   **Fic**

1. Science fiction 2. Superheroes -- Fiction 3.
Homosexuality -- Fiction 5. Father-son relationship --
Fiction
ISBN 978-1-4231-0195-6; 1-4231-0195-2

Thom Creed, the gay son of a disowned superhero, finds
that he, too, has special powers and is asked to join the very
League that rejected his father, and it is there that Thom finds
other misfits whom he can finally trust.

"The combination of mystery, fantasy, thriller, and romance create a delightful and compelling read." Voice
Youth Advocates

Moore, Peter

Red moon rising. Hyperion 2011 328p $16.99

Grades: 7 8 9 10   **Fic**

1. Vampires -- Fiction 2. Werewolves -- Fiction
ISBN 978-1-4231-1665-3; 1-4231-1665-8

LC 2009-40375

In a world where vampires dominate and werewolves are despised, a teenaged half-vampire discovers his recessive werewolf genes are developing with the approaching full moon.

"The details are imaginative and believable, as are the social interactions at school and in Danny's home." Booklist

Moran, Katy

Bloodline. Candlewick Press 2009 297p il map $16.99

Grades: 7 8 9 10   **Fic**

1. War stories 2. Adventure fiction 3. Middle Ages -- Fiction
ISBN 978-07636-4083-5; 0-7636-4083-2

LC 2008-21413

While traveling through early seventh-century Britain trying to stop an impending war, Essa, who bears the blood of native British tribes and of the invading Anglish, makes discoveries that divide his loyalties.

"Essa is a complex, sympathetic protagonist: prickly and quick of temper, but also clever, determined and of unflinching integrity. If his struggle is authentically gory and ultimately tragic, it is not without glimpses of love and hope." Kirkus

Bloodline rising. Candlewick Press 2011 328p map $16.99

Grades: 7 8 9 10   **Fic**

1. Slaves -- Fiction 2. Criminals -- Fiction 3. Middle Ages -- Fiction
ISBN 978-0-7636-4508-3; 0-7636-4508-7

LC 2010-46692

Cai, a thief in seventh-century Constantinople, finds himself held captive on a trading ship bound for Britain—the home his father, a ruthless barbarian assassin, fled long ago—where he discovers that his Anglish captors know more about the secrets of his family than he does.

"At its heart, this is the story of a boy's turbulent relationship with his father, torn between resentment and admiration, rivalry and respect, which renders the tale both as intimate as heartbreak and universal as hope. Grim, lyrical and unforgettable." Kirkus

Mordecai, Martin

Blue Mountain trouble. Arthur A. Levine Books 2009 341p $16.99

Grades: 5 6 7 8   **Fic**

1. Twins -- Fiction 2. Siblings -- Fiction 3. Family life -- Fiction 4. Mountain life -- Fiction
ISBN 978-0-545-04156-0; 0-545-04156-2

LC 2008042648

After being saved from a disastrous landslide by an extraordinary goat that blocks their usual way to school, twins Pollyread and Jackson, living with their parents high in the mountains of Jamaica, find the strange goat reappearing at crucial intervals as their day-to-day life is changed by series of mysterious events involving the return of a local troublemaker and secrets from their family's past.

"Mordecai has written a nostalgic valentine to his native island that is . . . always rich in characterization with a beautifully realized setting. The elements of magic and mystery intriguing, too." Booklist

Morden, Simon

The **lost** art. David Fickling Books 2008 521p $16.99; lib bdg $19.99

Grades: 8 9 10 11 12   **Fic**

1. Science fiction 2. Religion and science -- Fiction
ISBN 978-0-385-75147-6; 0-385-75147-8; 978-0-385-75148-3 lib bdg; 0-385-75148-6 lib bdg

LC 2007-35591

A millennium after a devastating war changed the direction of Earth's rotation, when the Church keeps science and technology suppressed, magician-like Benzamir and Va, a killer-for-hire turned monk, seek Solomon, who is surreptitiously spreading technology for nefarious purposes.

"This original and engaging science fiction adventure features adult protagonists, though they deal with classic coming-of-age questions about their place in the world." Horn Book Guide

Morgan, Nicola

The **highwayman's** footsteps. Candlewick Press 2007 354p $16.99

Grades: 6 7 8 9   **Fic**

1. Adventure fiction
ISBN 978-0-7636-3472-8; 0-7636-3472-7

LC 2007-25997

In eighteenth-century England, William runs away from his father, only to be captured by an armed highwayman who turns out to be a girl. Together, they seek vengeance against William's cruel father and the soldiers who killed the girl's parents.

"Alfred Noyes' romantic epic . . . provides the jumping off point for this beautifully written historical novel. . . . Excellent for both recreational reading and curriculum support in the humanities." Booklist

Morgan, Page

The **beautiful** and the cursed; by Page Morgan. 1st ed. Delacorte Press 2013 352 p. (library) $21.99; (hardcover) $18.99

Grades: 7 8 9 10 11 12   **Fic**

1. Love stories 2. Gargoyles -- Fiction 3. Brothers and sisters -- Fiction 4. Sisters -- Fiction 5. Supernatural -- Fiction
ISBN 0385743114; 9780375990953; 9780385743112

LC 2012022378

In this book by Page Morgan, "Ingrid, her sister Gabby, and their mom arrive at the abandoned abbey that they plan to turn into an art gallery. Grayson, Ingrid's twin brother, had procured the place and was supposed to meet them there. Grayson, however, does not show up and the girls are surprised to learn that he has actually been missing for several days. . . . [Ingrid] and Gabby . . .discover a world of living gargoyles that can transform into humans." (Children's Literature)

Morgenstern, Susie Hoch

Secret letters from 0 to 10; translated by Gill Rosner. Viking 1998 137p $16.99; pa $4.99

Grades: 4 5 6   **Fic**

1. School stories 2. Schools -- Fiction 3. Friendship -- Fiction

ISBN 0-670-88007-8; 0-14-130819-2 pa

LC 98-5559

Ten-year-old Ernest lives a boring existence in Paris with his grandmother until a lively girl named Victory enters his class at school

"Morgenstern has created extremely well-drawn, distinct, and sometimes quirky characters with eloquent dialogue." SLJ

Moriarty, Chris

The **inquisitor's** apprentice; illustrations by Mark Edward Geyer. Harcourt Children's Books 2011 345p il $16.99

Grades: 4 5 6 7   **Fic**

1. Inventors 2. Gangs -- Fiction 3. Magic -- Fiction 4. Witches -- Fiction 5. Apprentices -- Fiction 6. Jews -- United States -- Fiction

ISBN 978-0-547-58135-4; 0-547-58135-1

In early twentieth-century New York, Sacha Kessler's ability to see witches earns him an apprenticeship to the police department's star Inquisitor, Maximillian Wolf, to help stop magical crime and, with fellow apprentice Lily Astral, Sacha investigates who is trying to kill Thomas Edison, whose mechanical witch detector that could unleash the worst witch-hunt in American history.

"Sacha, Lily and Inspector Wolf are all fully developed and multilayered characters, as are the many other distinctive personalities that appear in the tale. The author employs rich language and syntax that please the ear and touch the senses, making it all come alive." Kirkus

The **watcher** in the shadows; Chris Moriarty ; [illustrated by] Mark Edward Geyer. Harcourt Children's Books 2013 336 p. (hardcover) $16.99

Grades: 4 5 6 7   **Fic**

1. Fantasy fiction 2. Jews -- Fiction 3. Mystery fiction

ISBN 0547466323; 9780547466323

LC 2013003919

This juvenile novel, by Chris Moriarty, is part of the "Inquisitor's Apprentice" series. "New York's Bowery District becomes the scene of a terrible murder when the Klezmer King gets fried to a crisp by his Electric Tuxedo--on stage! The Inquisitor's apprentice, thirteen-year-old Sacha Kessler, tries to help find the killer, but the closer he gets to solving the crime, the more it sounds as if the creature that haunted him in his first adventure is back." (Publisher's note)

"Rich language, colorful syntax, vivid description and a brilliant cast of characters beckon readers right into both the adventure and the heartfelt emotional landscape. Exciting, action-packed and absolutely marvelous." Kirkus

Moriarty, Jaclyn

★ A **corner** of white; Jaclyn Moriarty. Arthur A. Levine Books 2013 384 p. (Colors of Madeleine trilogy) (hardcover) $17.99

Grades: 7 8 9 10 11 12   **Fic**

1. Fantasy fiction 2. Epistolary fiction 3. Color -- Fiction 4. Magic -- Fiction 5. Princesses -- Fiction 6. Missing persons -- Fiction 7. Interpersonal relations -- Fiction

ISBN 0545397367; 9780545397360

LC 2012016582

Boston Globe-Horn Book Honor: Fiction (2013).

This opening volume of a fantasy series from Jaclyn Moriarty focuses on 14-year-old Madeleine, who "lives in Cambridge, England, with her zany mother in uncertain circumstances, having run away from their fabulously privileged international existence. Meanwhile, Elliot lives in Bonfire, The Farms, Cello, a parallel reality. . . . Through a crack between their worlds, they begin exchanging letters." (Kirkus Reviews)

"Australian writer Moriarty"s marvelously original fantasy is quirky and clever... [she] captures the proud iconoclasm of many homeschoolers and does not shy away from tenderness and poignancy." BookList

The **year** of secret assignments. Arthur A. Levine Books 2004 340p $16.95; pa $7.99

Grades: 8 9 10 11 12   **Fic**

1. School stories 2. Friendship -- Fiction

ISBN 0-439-49881-3; 0-439-49882-1 pa

LC 2003-14278

Three female students from Ashbury High write to three male students from rival Brookfield High as part of a pen pal program, leading to romance, humiliation, revenge plots, and war between the schools

"There are a few coarse moments—a reference to a blow job and some caustic outbursts. . . . This is an unusual novel with an exhilarating pace, irrepressible characters, and a screwball humor that will easily attract teens." Booklist

Other titles set at Ashbury High are:

The ghosts of Ashbury High (2010)

The murder of Bindy Mackenzie (2006)

Morpurgo, Michael

★ **Kensuke's** kingdom. Scholastic Press 2003 164p hardcover o.p. pa $5.99

Grades: 4 5 6 7   **Fic**

1. Islands 2. Japanese 3. Survival 4. Castaways 5. Survival after airplane accidents, shipwrecks, etc. -- Fiction

ISBN 0-439-38202-5; 0-439-59181-3 pa

LC 2002-9078

First published 1999 in the United Kingdom

When Michael is swept off his family's yacht, he washes up on a desert island, where he struggles to survive—until he finds he is not alone

This is "highly readable. . . . The end is bittersweet but believable, and the epilogue is a sad commentary on the long-lasting effects of war." Booklist

The **Mozart** question; [by] Michael Morpurgo; illustrated by Michael Foreman. Candlewick Press 2008 66p il $15.99

Grades: 4 5 6 7   **Fic**

1. Violinists -- Fiction 2. Holocaust, 1933-1945 --

Fiction
ISBN 978-0-7636-3552-7; 0-7636-3552-9

A young journalist goes to Venice, Italy, to interview a famous violinist, who tells the story of his parents' incarceration by the Nazis, and explains why they can no longer listen to the music of Mozart.

"Morpurgo breathes life into this touching tale, which is conveyed with compassion and honesty. Foreman's watercolors enrich the narrative." SLJ

Private Peaceful. Scholastic Press 2004 202p $16.95; pa $5.99

Grades: 7 8 9 10   Fic

1. World War, 1914-1918 -- Fiction
ISBN 0-439-63648-5; 0-439-63653-1 pa

LC 2003-65347

First published 2003 in the United Kingdom

When Thomas Peaceful's older brother is forced to join the British Army, Thomas decides to sign up as well, although he is only fourteen years old, to prove himself to his country, his family, his childhood love, Molly, and himself

"In this World War I story, the terse and beautiful narrative of a young English soldier is as compelling about the world left behind as about the horrific daily details of trench warfare. . . . Suspense builds right to the end, which is shocking, honest, and unforgettable." Booklist

War horse; by Michael Morpurgo. Scholastic 2007 165p $16.99

Grades: 5 6 7 8   Fic

1. Horses -- Fiction 2. World War, 1914-1918 -- Fiction
ISBN 978-0-439-79663-7; 0-439-79663-6

LC 2006044368

First published 1982 in the United Kingdom

Joey the horse recalls his experiences growing up on an English farm, his struggle for survival as a cavalry horse during World War I, and his reunion with his beloved master

"At times deeply affecting, the story balances the horror with moments of respite and care." Horn Book Guide

The **amazing** story of Adolphus Tips; [by] Michael Morpurgo. Scholastic Press 2006 140p $15.99

Grades: 4 5 6 7   Fic

1. Cats -- Fiction 2. Grandmothers -- Fiction 3. World War, 1939-1945 -- Fiction
ISBN 0-439-79661-X

LC 2005049038

When Boowie reads the diary that his grandmother sends him, he learns of her childhood in World War II England when American and British soldiers practiced for D-Day's invasion in the area of her home, and about her beloved cat, Adolphus Tips, and the cat's namesake

"The personal story of anger and love is as gripping as the war drama, and Morpurgo includes a fascinating note about the invasion rehearsal and why its history is seldom told." Booklist

An **elephant** in the garden. Feiwel and Friends 2011 199p $16.99

Grades: 6 7 8 9   Fic

1. Zoos -- Fiction 2. Elephants -- Fiction 3. World War,

1939-1945 -- Fiction
ISBN 978-0-312-59369-8; 0-312-59369-4

Lizzie and Karl's mother is a zoo keeper; the family has become attached to an orphaned elephant named Marlene, who will be destroyed as a precautionary measure so she and the other animals don't run wild should the zoo be hit by bombs. The family persuades the zoo director to let Marlene stay in their garden instead. When the city is bombed, the family flees with thousands of others, but how can they walk the same route when they have an elephant in tow, and keep themselves safe?

"This well-paced, heartwarming narrative by a master storyteller will appeal to readers on several levels—as a tale of adventure and suspense, as a commentary on human trauma and animal welfare during war, as a perspective on the hardships facing the German people in the final months of World War II, and as a tribute to the rich memories and experiences of an older generation." SLJ

Morris, Gerald

★ The **squire's** tale. Houghton Mifflin 1998 212p (The squire's tales) $15; pa $5.50

Grades: 6 7 8 9   Fic

1. Magic -- Fiction 2. Knights and knighthood -- Fiction 3. Gawain (Legendary character) -- Fiction 4. Gawain (Legendary character) -- Fiction
ISBN 0-395-86959-5; 0-440-22823-9 pa

LC 97-12447

In medieval England, fourteen-year-old Terence finds his tranquil existence suddenly changed when he becomes the squire of the young Gawain of Orkney and accompanies him on a long quest, proving Gawain's worth as a knight and revealing an important secret about his own true identity

"Well-drawn characters, excellent, snappy dialogue, detailed descriptions of medieval life, and a dry wit put a new spin on this engaging tale of the characters and events of King Arthur's time." Booklist

Other titles in this series are:
The squire, his knight, & his lady (1999)
The savage damsel and the dwarf (2000)
Parsifal's page (2001)
The ballad of Sir Dinadan (2003)
The princess, the crone, and the dung-cart knight (2004)
The lionness & her knight (2005)
The quest of the Fair Unknown (2006)
The squire's quest (2009)
The legend of the king (2010)

Morris, Paula

Ruined; a novel. Point 2009 309p $16.99

Grades: 6 7 8 9 10   Fic

1. Ghost stories
ISBN 978-0-545-04215-4; 0-545-04215-1

Set in New Orleans, this is "the story of 15-year-old Rebecca Brown, a proud New Yorker sent to live with a family friend while her father travels overseas. Ostracized as an outsider, Rebecca struggles to fit in and cope with her new surroundings. When she befriends Lisette, a ghost who has haunted the cemetery ever since her mysterious death 155 years earlier, Rebecca is drawn into an eerie story of betrayal, loss, old curses and family secrets. . . . This moody tale thoroughly embraces the rich history, occult lore and complex issues of race, ethnicity, class and culture that have defined New Orleans for centuries." Publ Wkly

Morton-Shaw, Christine

The **hunt** for the seventh. HarperCollins 2008 273p il map $16.99; lib bdg $17.89; pa $6.99
Grades: 6 7 8 9   **Fic**
1. Ghost stories 2. Mystery fiction 3. Father-son relationship -- Fiction
ISBN 978-0-06-072822-9; 0-06-072822-1; 978-0-06-072823-6 lib bdg; 0-06-072823-X lib bdg; 978-0-06-072824-3 pa; 0-06-072824-8 pa
     LC 2007-38885
When his father starts a new job at Minerva Hall as gardener, twelve-year-old Jim discovers an ancient curse that needs to be unraveled before disaster happens.

"Morton-Shaw skillfully weaves ancient lore into a gripping mystery. The fine plotting keeps readers turning the pages as suspense builds to the surprising end." SLJ

The **riddles** of Epsilon. Katherine Tegen Books 2005 375p $16.99; lib bdg $17.89
Grades: 7 8 9 10   **Fic**
1. Supernatural -- Fiction
ISBN 0-06-072819-1; 0-06-072820-5 lib bdg
     LC 2004-14641
After moving with her parents to a remote English island, fourteen-year-old Jess attempts to dispel an ancient curse by solving a series of riddles, aided by Epsilon, a supernatural being.

Moses, Shelia P.

Joseph. Margaret K. McElderry Books 2008 174p $16.99; pa $8.99
Grades: 7 8 9 10   **Fic**
1. Drug abuse -- Fiction 2. African Americans -- Fiction 3. Mother-son relationship -- Fiction
ISBN 978-1-4169-1752-6; 1-4169-1752-7; 978-4169-9442-8 pa; 1-4169-9442-4 pa
Fourteen-year-old Joseph tries to avoid trouble and keep in touch with his father, who is serving in Iraq, as he and his alcoholic, drug-addicted mother move from one homeless shelter to another.

"Moses creates a compelling character in Joseph. His struggle to survive his current situation intact is fascinating to read. . . . Negative influences such as drug dealers and users are described in a clear, cold light. Education and hard work are praised for their positive influences. Middle school and junior high teens will enjoy this story." Voice Youth Advocates

The **legend** of Buddy Bush. Margaret K. McElderry Books 2004 216p $15.95
Grades: 6 7 8 9   **Fic**
1. Race relations 2. African Americans -- Fiction 3. Family life -- North Carolina
ISBN 0-689-85839-6
     LC 2003-8024
In 1947, twelve-year-old Pattie Mae is sustained by her dreams of escaping Rich Square, North Carolina, and moving to Harlem when her Uncle Buddy is arrested for attempt-

ed rape of a white woman and her grandfather is diagnosed with a terminal brain tumor.

"Patti Mae's first-person voice, steeped in the inflections of the South, rings true, and her observations richly evoke a time, place, and a resilient African American community." Booklist
Another title about Buddy Bush is:
The return of Buddy Bush (2005)

Mosley, Walter

47. Little, Brown 2005 232p $16.99
Grades: 7 8 9 10   **Fic**
1. Magic -- Fiction 2. Slavery -- Fiction 3. African Americans -- Fiction
ISBN 0-316-11035-3
     LC 2004-12500
Number 47, a fourteen-year-old slave boy growing up under the watchful eye of a brutal master in 1832, meets the mysterious Tall John, who introduces him to a magical science and also teaches him the meaning of freedom.

"Time travel, shape-shifting, and intergalactic conflict add unusual, provocative elements to this story. And yet, well-drawn characters; lively dialogue filled with gritty, regional dialect; vivid descriptions; and poignant reflections ground it in harsh reality." SLJ

Moss, Jenny

Shadow. Scholastic Press 2010 377p $17.99
Grades: 7 8 9 10   **Fic**
1. Fairy tales 2. Kings and rulers -- Fiction
ISBN 978-0-545-03641-2; 0-545-03641-0
     LC 2009-14209
When Shadow, whose job all her life has been to stay close to the young queen and prevent her prophecied death at the age of sixteen, fails in her task and the castle is thrown into chaos, she escapes along with a young knight, embarking upon a journey that eventually reveals her true identity.

"With its dashing knights, pretentious queen, and put-upon protagonist, the story starts out like any other garden-variety fairytale, but it soon takes a turn for the darkly subversive world of pagan religions and political scheming. . . . A nuanced coming of age story with a fairy-tale setting, this is sure to please." Bull Cent Child Books

Winnie's war. Walker & Co. 2009 178p $16.99
Grades: 5 6 7 8   **Fic**
1. Epidemics -- Fiction 2. Influenza -- Fiction 3. Family life -- Fiction
ISBN 978-0-8027-9819-0; 0-8027-9819-5
     LC 2008-23233
Living in the shadow of a Texas cemetery, twelve-year-old Winnie Grace struggles to keep the Spanish influenza of 1918 from touching her family—her coffin-building father, her troubled mother, and her two baby sisters.

"The small town of Coward Creek comes to life in Moss's writing. . . . Winnie and the others populate a solid plot, but it is the setting and the characters that will make this book last as a popular favorite with a space on shelves well into the future." Voice Youth Advocates

Moulton, Courtney Allison

Angelfire; 1st ed. Katherine Tegen Books 2011 453 p. $17.99

Grades: 7 8 9 10   **Fic**

1. Horror fiction 2. Horror stories 3. Souls -- Fiction 4. Angels -- Fiction 5. Monsters -- Fiction 6. Reincarnation -- Fiction

ISBN 9780062002327; 9780062002341

LC 2010012821

A seventeen-year-old girl discovers that she has the reincarnated soul of an ancient warrior destined to battle the reapers --creatures who devour humans and send their souls to Hell.

"The author has introduced a dark and compelling world of action and intrigue, albeit with enough 'normal' drama and humor sprinkled throughout to lighten it. . . . Older junior and senior high school readers will find themselves engrossed in the story until its powerful conclusion— then anxiously awaiting the second installment." Voice Youth Advocates

Mourlevat, Jean-Claude

★ Winter's end; translated by Anthea Bell. Candlewick Press 2009 415p lib bdg $21.99

Grades: 8 9 10 11 12   **Fic**

1. Fantasy fiction 2. Adventure fiction 3. Orphans -- Fiction 4. Despotism -- Fiction 5. Resistance to government -- Fiction

ISBN 978-0-7636-4450-5; 0-7636-4450-1

LC 2009-8456

Fleeing across icy mountains from a pack of terrifying dog-men sent to hunt them down, four teenagers escape from their prison-like boarding schools to take up the fight against the tyrannical government that murdered their parents fifteen years earlier.

"Teeming with heroic acts, heartbreaking instances of sacrifice and intriguing characters . . . the book will keep readers absorbed and set imaginations spinning." Publ Wkly

★ The pull of the ocean; [by] Jean-Claude Mourlevat; translated from the French by Y. Maudet. Delacorte Press 2006 190p hardcover o.p. lib bdg $17.99; pa $6.50

Grades: 5 6 7   **Fic**

1. Size -- Fiction 2. Twins -- Fiction 3. Brothers -- Fiction

ISBN 978-0-385-73348-9; 0-385-73348-8; 978-0-385-90364-6 lib bdg; 0-385-90364-2 lib bdg; 978-0-385-73666-4 pa; 0-385-73666-5 pa

LC 2006001802

Loosely based on Charles Perrault's "Tom Thumb," seven brothers in modern-day France flee their poor parents' farm, led by the youngest who, although mute and unusually small, is exceptionally wise.

This "is a memorable novel that readers will find engaging and intellectually satisfying." SLJ

Mulder, Michelle

Out of the box. Orca Book Publishers 2011 150p pa $9.95

Grades: 6 7 8 9   **Fic**

1. Aunts -- Fiction 2. Family life -- Fiction 3. Mother-daughter relationship -- Fiction

ISBN 978-1-55469-328-3 pa; 1-55469-328-4 pa

Ellie's passion for tango music leads to an interest in Argentine history and a desire to separate herself from her parents' problems.

"Ellie's narration authentically conveys her gradual growth, the insecurities that surround her developing friendships, her role in a dysfunctional family, and the pleasure she takes in music. Adults and their relationships are portrayed credibly. . . . A bit of Argentine history rounds out the believable plot." SLJ

Mull, Brandon

★ A world without heroes. Aladdin 2011 454p (Beyonders) $19.99

Grades: 4 5 6 7   **Fic**

1. Fantasy fiction 2. Magic -- Fiction 3. Space and time -- Fiction 4. Heroes and heroines -- Fiction

ISBN 978-1-4169-9792-4; 1-4169-9792-X

LC 2010-23437

Fourteen-year-old Jason Walker is transported to a strange world called Lyrian, where he joins Rachel, who was also drawn there from our world, and a few rebels, to piece together the Word that can destroy the malicious wizard emperor, Surroth.

"Mull moves his story at a brisk pace, preventing the tragedies from overwhelming the adventure, while offering ample action and feisty dialogue to keep fantasy lovers entertained." Publ Wkly

Muller, Rachel Dunstan

Squeeze; written by Rachel Dunstan Muller. Orca Book Publishers 2010 166p (Orca sports) pa $9.95

Grades: 6 7 8 9   **Fic**

1. Caves -- Fiction 2. Brothers -- Fiction 3. Accidents -- Fiction

ISBN 978-1-55469-324-5; 1-55469-324-1

On a caving trip with his older brother, Byron discovers a new cave but has to make some life-or-death decisions when his brother is seriously injured.

"A fast-paced, compulsively readable book. . . . Information about caving is woven seamlessly into the narrative, and descriptions of the beauty of underground rock formations are often quite lyrical." SLJ

Mulligan, Andy

★ Trash. David Fickling Books 2010 232p $16.99; lib bdg $19.99

Grades: 6 7 8 9   **Fic**

1. Mystery fiction 2. Poverty -- Fiction 3. Political corruption -- Fiction 4. Refuse and refuse disposal -- Fiction

ISBN 978-0-385-75214-5; 0-385-75214-8; 978-0-385-75215-2 lib bdg; 0-385-75215-6 lib bdg

LC 2010-15940

Fourteen-year-olds Raphael and Gardo team up with a younger boy, Rat, to figure out the mysteries surrounding a bag Raphael finds during their daily life of sorting through trash in a third-world country's dump.

"While on the surface the book reads like a fast-paced adventure title, it also makes a larger statement about the horrors of poverty and injustice in the world. . . . Trash is a compelling read." SLJ

Murdock, Catherine Gilbert
★ **Dairy** Queen; a novel. Houghton Mifflin 2006 275p $16
Grades: 7 8 9 10   Fic
1. Football -- Fiction 2. Farm life -- Fiction
ISBN 0-618-68307-0
                                    LC 2005-19077
After spending her summer running the family farm and training the quarterback for her school's rival football team, sixteen-year-old D.J. decides to go out for the sport herself, not anticipating the reactions of those around her.
"D. J.'s voice is funny, frank, and intelligent, and her story is not easily pigeonholed." Voice Youth Advocates
Other titles about D.J. Schwenk are:
Front and center (2009)
The off season (2007)

★ **Princess** Ben; being a wholly truthful account of her various discoveries and misadventures, recounted to the best of her recollection, in four parts. written by Catherine Gilbert Murdock. Houghton Mifflin 2008 344p $16; pa $8.99
Grades: 7 8 9 10   Fic
1. Fairy tales 2. Magic -- Fiction 3. Princesses -- Fiction 4. Courts and courtiers -- Fiction 5. Young adult literature -- Works
ISBN 978-0-618-95971-6; 0-618-95971-8; 978-0-547-22325-4 pa; 0-547-22325-0 pa
                                    LC 2007-34300
A girl is transformed, through instruction in life at court, determination, and magic, from sullen, pudgy, graceless Ben into Crown Princess Benevolence, a fit ruler of the kindgom of Montagne as it faces war with neighboring Drachensbett.
"Murdock's prose sweeps the reader up and never falters, blending a formal syntax and vocabulary with an intimate tone that bonds the reader with Ben." Horn Book

★ **Wisdom's** kiss; a thrilling and romantic adventure, incorporating magic, villany and a cat. written by Catherine Gilbert Murdock. Houghton Mifflin 2011 284p $16.99
Grades: 7 8 9 10   Fic
1. Fairy tales 2. Cats -- Fiction 3. Orphans -- Fiction 4. Soldiers -- Fiction 5. Princesses -- Fiction 6. Supernatural -- Fiction 7. Household employees -- Fiction
ISBN 978-0-547-56687-0; 0-547-56687-5
                                    LC 2011003708
Princess Wisdom, who yearns for a life of adventure beyond the kingdom of Montagne, Tips, a soldier keeping his true life secret from his family, Fortitude, an orphaned maid who longs for Tips, and Magic the cat form an uneasy alliance as they try to save the kingdom from certain destruction. Told through diaries, memoirs, encyclopedia entries, letters, biographies, and a stage play.
"Packed with double entendres, humorous dialogue and situations, and a black cat that will capture the reader's

imagination, this is a joyful, timeless fantasy that teens will savor." Booklist

Murphy, Claire Rudolf
Free radical. Clarion Bks. 2002 198p $15
Grades: 7 8 9 10   Fic
1. Baseball -- Fiction 2. Fugitives from justice
ISBN 0-618-11134-4
                                    LC 2001-42268
In Fairbanks, Alaska, in the middle of the summer Little League baseball season, fifteen-year-old Luke is stunned when his mother confesses that she is wanted by the FBI for her role in the death of a student during an anti-Vietnam War protest thirty years ago
"The fast action of the baseball scenes will lure teens to the sports story, and the thought-provoking issues of guilt and responsibility will hold their interest." Booklist

Murphy, Jim
Desperate journey. Scholastic Press 2006 278p il map $16.99
Grades: 5 6 7 8   Fic
1. Family life -- Fiction
ISBN 0-439-07806-7
                                    LC 2006-02526
In the mid-1800s, with both her father and her uncle in jail on an assault charge, Maggie, her brother, and her ailing mother rush their barge along the Erie Canal to deliver their heavy cargo or lose everything.
This is a "gripping novel." Booklist

Murphy, Rita
Bird. Delacorte Press 2008 151p $15.99; lib bdg $18.99
Grades: 5 6 7 8   Fic
1. Kites -- Fiction 2. Flight -- Fiction 3. Houses -- Fiction 4. Supernatural -- Fiction
ISBN 978-0-385-73018-1; 0-385-73018-7; 978-0-385-90557-2 lib bdg; 0-385-90557-2 lib bdg
                                    LC 2008-04690
Miranda, a small, delicate girl easily carried off by the wind, lands at Bourne Manor on the coast of Lake Champlain and is raised by the dour Wysteria Barrows, but she begins to believe rumors that the Manor is cursed and, aided by a new friend and kites secreted in an attic, seeks to escape.
"This enchanting novel is well written with lyrical text and beautiful descriptions. . . . Good for middle school students, this book will make a nice addition to school and public libraries alike." Libr Media Connect

Looking for Lucy Buick. Delacorte Press 2005 165p $15.95; lib bdg $17.99
Grades: 7 8 9 10   Fic
1. Family life -- Fiction 2. Abandoned children -- Fiction
ISBN 0-385-72939-1; 0-385-90176-3 lib bdg
                                    LC 2004-20128
Following the death of her favorite adoptive aunt, Lucy goes searching for her biological family who abandoned her in an old Buick eighteen years before.
"What wins the day are the people in Lucy's life, living and dead . . . who pop off the pages, and Murphy's

voice . . . which tells the story with a steadfastness and sweetness." Booklist

Murray, Kirsty

The **secret** life of Maeve Lee Kwong; by Kirsty Murray. Allen & Unwin 2008 252p (Children of the wind) pa $8.95

Grades: 5 6 7 8 **Fic**

1. Chinese -- Fiction 2. Racially mixed people -- Fiction
ISBN 978-1-86508-737-5 pa; 1-86508-737-8 pa

"Being half-Chinese and half-Irish never bothered Maeve Lee Kwong much. A lot of Australians have mixed heritages, and she considers herself fully Aussie. Then her mother dies in a car accident, and Maeve no longer knows who she is, or where she belongs. . . . This book has a lot going for it, including short and highly varied scenes that propel the story forward at a brisk pace. With settings in Australia, Hong Kong, and Ireland, the descriptions are lush and appealing." SLJ

Murray, Martine

How to make a bird. Arthur A. Levine Books 2010 233p $17.99

Grades: 7 8 9 10 **Fic**

1. Bereavement -- Fiction 2. Family life -- Fiction 3. Runaway teenagers -- Fiction
ISBN 978-0-439-66951-1; 0-439-66951-0

LC 2009-27453

When seventeen-year-old, small-town Australian girl Manon Clarkeson leaves home in the middle of the night, wearing her mother's long, inappropriate red silk dress and riding her bike, she is heading for Melbourne, not exactly sure what she is looking for but not wanting to stay at home alone with her father anymore.

"Although Mannie's defining attributes—acute self-consciousness and claustrophobic intensity—are hallmarks of many YA heroines, Murray's powerful lyrical voice and close observation breathe new life into them. . . . The novel offers an especially vivid sense of place—the harsh but open rural landscape and densely populated yet lonely, urban Melbourne." Kirkus

Mussi, Sarah

★ The **door** of no return. Margaret K. McElderry Books 2008 394p $17.99; pa $8.99

Grades: 8 9 10 11 12 **Fic**

1. Adventure fiction 2. Blacks -- Fiction 3. Homicide -- Fiction 4. Buried treasure -- Fiction
ISBN 978-1-4169-1550-8; 1-4169-1550-8; 978-1-4169-6825-2 pa; 1-4169-6825-3 pa

LC 2007-18670

Sixteen-year-old Zac never believed his grandfather's tales about their enslaved ancestors being descended from an African king, but when his grandfather is murdered and the villains come after Zac, he sets out for Ghana to find King Baktu's long-lost treasure before the murderers do.

"This exciting narrative takes place in England and Africa; in jungles, dark caves, and on the sea. . . . Overall, this is a complex, masterful story for confident readers." SLJ

Myers, Anna

Assassin; [by] Anna Myers. Walker & Company 2005 212p $16.95

Grades: 7 8 9 10 **Fic**

1. Actors 2. Lawyers 3. Presidents 4. Murderers 5. State legislators 6. Members of Congress
ISBN 0-8027-8989-7

LC 2005042275

In alternating passages, a young White House seamstress named Bella and the actor John Wilkes Booth describe the events that lead to the latter's assassination of Abraham Lincoln.

"The novel offers a good opportunity for discussion about the assassin, his motivations, and, in this case, how he drew an unsuspecting girl into his scheme." SLJ

Spy! [by] Anna Myers. Walker & Co. 2008 211p $16.99

Grades: 5 6 7 8 9 **Fic**

1. Revolutionaries 2. Spies -- Fiction 3. Orphans -- Fiction 4. Teachers -- Fiction
ISBN 978-0-8027-9742-1; 0-8027-9742-3

LC 2008-254

In 1774, twelve-year-old Jonah becomes a pupil of Nathan Hale, who inspires him to question his beliefs about the impending revolution, and two years later, Jonah makes a decision that leads to Nathan's execution.

"Set against clearly delineated historical events, the story employs personal thoughts and feelings to show the conflicts facing the colonists. This well-written novel is a good supplement to American history studies." SLJ

Time of the witches. Walker & Co. 2009 197p $16.99

Grades: 6 7 8 9 **Fic**

1. Trials -- Fiction 2. Orphans -- Fiction 3. Witchcraft -- Fiction
ISBN 978-0-8027-9820-6; 0-8027-9820-9

LC 2008-54278

Orphaned Drucilla finds a home with the beautiful but troubled Mistress Putnam as accusations of witchcraft start to swirl in Salem Village.

"Myers brings a time of mass hysteria to life. . . . Myers draws heavily from the actual participants in the events. . . . A solid piece of historical fiction." SLJ

Tulsa burning. Walker & Co. 2002 152p $16.95; pa $6.95

Grades: 7 8 9 10 **Fic**

1. Riots -- Fiction 2. Race relations -- Fiction
ISBN 0-8027-8829-7; 0-8027-7696-5 pa

LC 2002-23457

In 1921, fifteen-year-old Noble Chase hates the sheriff of Wekiwa, Oklahoma, and is more than willing to cross him to help his best friend, a black man, who is injured during race riots in nearby Tulsa

"In this emotional page-turner, Myers expertly captures an era of poisonous racism while conveying the strong, true voice of a courageous young man." Booklist

Wart; [by] Anna Myers. Walker & Co. 2007 215p $16.95

Grades: 5 6 7 8   **Fic**

1. Remarriage -- Fiction 2. Witchcraft -- Fiction
ISBN 978-0-8027-8977-8; 0-8027-8977-3

LC 2007006218

Regretting his part in his father's decision not to marry the town librarian, Stewart has many misgivings about the latest woman in their lives, although her spells and charms might make Stewart popular and improve his basketball game.

"The plot moves quickly and the characters are appealing and unique." SLJ

The **grave** robber's secret. Walker & Co. 2011 196p $16.99

Grades: 7 8 9 10   **Fic**

1. Homicide -- Fiction 2. Grave robbing -- Fiction
ISBN 978-0-8027-2183-9; 0-8027-2183-4

LC 2010018097

In Philadelphia in the 1800s, twelve-year-old Robbie is forced to help his father rob graves, then when he suspects his dad of murder, Robbie makes a life-changing decision.

"The story is well written and the characterization is excellent. Readers will connect to Robby on several levels and will feel for Martha Burke." Libr Media Connect

Myers, Edward

★ **Storyteller**; by Edward Myers. Clarion Books 2008 283p $16

Grades: 6 7 8 9   **Fic**

1. Fairy tales 2. Storytelling -- Fiction 3. Kings and rulers -- Fiction
ISBN 978-0-618-69541-6; 0-618-69541-9

LC 2007031031

Jack, a seventeen-year-old storyteller, goes to the royal city seeking his fortune and soon attracts the attention of the grief-stricken king, his beautiful eldest daughter, and his cruel young son, and he attempts to help them—and the entire kingdom—through his stories.

"This old-fashioned story has the timeless appeal of adventure, humor, and light romance, all woven together by an able teller of tales." Booklist

Myers, Walter Dean

A **star** is born; Walter Dean Myers. Scholastic 2012 176 p. (Cruisers) (ebook) $17.99; (hardcover) $17.99

Grades: 6 7 8 9   **Fic**

1. School stories 2. Autism -- Fiction 3. Siblings -- Fiction 4. Gifted children -- Fiction 5. Schools -- Fiction 6. Theater -- Fiction 7. Middle schools -- Fiction 8. African Americans -- Fiction 9. Brothers and sisters -- Fiction
ISBN 9780545512688; 9780439916288

LC 2011030333

This book is the third in the Cruisers series. "For 14-year-old LaShonda Powell, real life is a lot tougher than solving for x and y in algebra class. She's been offered a full scholarship to the Virginia Woolf Society Program for Young Ladies, thanks to her costume designs for the recent class play, and if she completes the program, she'll qualify for future college scholarships. The problem is that LaShonda lives in a group home with her autistic brother, Chris, and the two are inseparable." (Kirkus)

Myers, Walter Dean, 1937-

Amiri & Odette; a love story. a poem by Walter Dean Myers; paintings by Javaka Steptoe. Scholastic Press 2009 un il $17.99

Grades: 7 8 9 10   **Fic**

1. Fairy tales 2. Love stories 3. Novels in verse 4. African Americans -- Fiction 5. Young adult literature -- Works
ISBN 978-0-590-68041-7; 0-590-68041-2

LC 2008-11563

Presents a modern, urban retelling in verse of the ballet in which brave Amiri falls in love with beautiful Odette and fights evil Big Red for her on the streets of the Swan Lake Projects.

"Myers's verse is almost overwrought—as it should be to suit the story, and the intensity of teenage love. The melodrama combines with an energy and beat that—heightened by dynamic text design—makes this ideal for performance. Steptoe's collage-on-cinderblock illustrations have a roughness, darkness, and density that suit the tone." SLJ

Carmen; an urban adaptation of the opera. Egmont USA 2011 various pagings $16.99

Grades: 8 9 10 11 12   **Fic**

1. Love -- Fiction 2. Hispanic Americans -- Fiction 3. Young adult literature -- Works
ISBN 978-1-60684-115-0; 1-60684-115-7; 978-1-60684-199-0 e-book

LC 2011002491

A policeman's obsessive love for a tempestuous wig factory worker ends in tragedy in this updated version of Bizet's Carmen, set in Spanish Harlem, and told in screenplay format.

"Myers seamlessly pulls off the drama's transportation to a contemporary urban setting and, true to form, renders it accessible to today's teens. . . . An excellent choice for reluctant readers, urban or otherwise." SLJ

★ The **Cruisers**; Walter Dean Myers. Scholastic Press 2010 126 p. $15.99

Grades: 6 7 8 9   **Fic**

1. Schools -- Fiction 2. Newspapers -- Fiction 3. Middle schools -- Fiction 4. Race relations -- Fiction 5. African Americans -- Fiction 6. Freedom of speech -- Fiction
ISBN 978-0-439-91626-4; 0-439-91626-7; 9780439916264

LC 2009052426

Friends Zander, Kambui, LaShonda, and Bobbi, caught in the middle of a mock Civil War at DaVinci Academy, learn the true cost of freedom of speech when they use their alternative newspaper, The Cruiser, to try to make peace.

"A finely crafted look at smart, urban underachievers. . . . [The book offers] fleet pacing, a spot-on voice, good characters, great dialogue, smart ideas, and an unusual story that can maneuver whip-quick from light to heavy and right back again." Booklist

Another title in this series is:

The Cruisers: checkmate (2011)

★ **Darius** & Twig; Walter Dean Myers. 1st ed. Harper, an imprint of HarperCollinsPublishers 2013 208 p. (hardcover) $17.99
Grades: 8 9 10 11 12   **Fic**
1. Friendship -- Fiction 2. Harlem (New York, N.Y.) -- Fiction 3. Running -- Fiction 4. Authorship -- Fiction 5. Best friends -- Fiction 6. African Americans -- Fiction 7. Dominican Americans -- Fiction
ISBN 0061728233; 9780061728235; 9780061728242
                                         LC 2012050678
In this book by Walter Dean Myers, "Harlem teenager Darius, a writer, wants to get out of his neighborhood and make it to college, but his grades aren't good enough. He's hoping that if he can get a story published, he might nab a college scholarship. His best friend Twig is a track star, and sees athletics as his escape. Both are skeptical of the hype they are fed about how hard work pays off, and they face obstacles ranging from school bullies . . . to indifferent educators." (Publishers Weekly)
"This encouraging text may inspire teens who feel trapped by their surroundings...Told in Darius's voice, the prose is poetic but concise. This would be a worthwhile addition to any middle or high school media center or public library shelf and would make a valuable book for discussion in a middle school classroom.—" VOYA

Dope sick. HarperTeen/Amistad 2009 186p $16.99; lib bdg $17.89
Grades: 8 9 10 11 12   **Fic**
1. Drug abuse -- Fiction 2. Supernatural -- Fiction 3. African Americans -- Fiction
ISBN 978-0-06-121477-6; 0-06-121477-9; 978-0-06-121478-3 lib bdg; 0-06-121478-7 lib bdg
                                         LC 2008-10568
Seeing no way out of his difficult life in Harlem, seventeen-year-old Jeremy "Lil J" Dance flees into a house after a drug deal goes awry and meets a weird man who shows different turning points in Lil J's life when he could have made better choices.
"Myers uses street-style lingo to cover Lil J's sorry history of drug use, jail time, irresponsible fatherhood and his own childhood grief. A didn't-see-that-coming ending wraps up the story on a note of well-earned hope and will leave readers with plenty to think about." Publ Wkly

Game. HarperTeen 2008 218p $16.99; lib bdg $17.89
Grades: 8 9 10 11 12   **Fic**
1. School stories 2. Basketball -- Fiction 3. Czech Americans -- Fiction 4. African Americans -- Fiction
ISBN 978-0-06-058294-4; 978-0-06-058295-1 lib bdg
                                         LC 2007-18370
If Harlem high school senior Drew Lawson is going to realize his dream of playing college, then professional, basketball, he will have to improve at being coached and being a team player, especially after a new—white—student threatens to take the scouts' attention away from him.
"Basketball fans will love the long passages of detailed court action. . . . The authentic thoughts of a strong, likable, African American teen whose anxieties, sharp insights,

and belief in his own abilities will captivate readers of all backgrounds." Booklist

Harlem summer. Scholastic Press 2007 176p il $16.99
Grades: 6 7 8 9   **Fic**
1. African Americans -- Fiction 2. Harlem Renaissance -- Fiction
ISBN 978-0-439-36843-8; 0-439-36843-X
                                         LC 2006-46812
In 1920s Harlem, sixteen-year-old Mark Purvis, an aspiring jazz saxophonist, gets a summer job as an errand boy for the publishers of the groundbreaking African American magazine, "The Crisis," but soon finds himself on the enemy list of mobster Dutch Shultz.
"Readers will be delighted to accompany the teen on his action-packed adventures." Booklist

★ **Hoops**; a novel. Delacorte Press 1981 183p hardcover o.p. pa $5.99
Grades: 7 8 9 10   **Fic**
1. Basketball -- Fiction 2. African Americans -- Fiction
ISBN 0-440-93884-8 pa
                                         LC 81-65497
ALA YALSA Margaret A. Edwards Award (1994)
"This story offers the reader some fast, descriptive basketball action, a love story between Lonnie and girlfriend Mary-Ann, peer friendship problems, and gangster intrigues. Most importantly, however, it portrays the growth of a trusting and deeply caring father-son relationship between [the coach] Cal and [fatherless] Lonnie." Voice Youth Advocates

Kick; [by] Walter Dean Myers and Ross Workman. HarperTeen 2011 197p $16.99; lib bdg $17.89
Grades: 7 8 9 10   **Fic**
1. Police -- Fiction 2. Soccer -- Fiction 3. Mentoring -- Fiction 4. Family life -- Fiction 5. Criminal investigation -- Fiction
ISBN 978-0-06-200489-5; 0-06-200489-1; 978-0-06-200490-1 lib bdg; 0-06-200490-5 lib bdg
                                         LC 2010-18441
Told in their separate voices, thirteen-year-old soccer star Kevin and police sergeant Brown, who knew his father, try to keep Kevin out of juvenile hall after he is arrested on very serious charges.
"Workman is a genuine talent, writing short, declarative sentences that move that narrative forward with assurance and a page-turning tempo. Myers, of course, is a master. . . . The respective voices and characters play off each other as successfully as a high-stakes soccer match." Booklist

Lockdown. Amistad 2010 247p $16.99; lib bdg $17.89
Grades: 8 9 10 11 12   **Fic**
1. Old age -- Fiction 2. Friendship -- Fiction 3. African Americans -- Fiction 4. Juvenile delinquency -- Fiction
ISBN 978-0-06-121480-6; 0-06-121480-9; 978-0-06-121481-3 lib bdg; 0-06-121481-7 lib bdg
                                         LC 2009-7287
Coretta Scott King Author Award honor book, 2011

Teenage Reese, serving time at a juvenile detention facility, gets a lesson in making it through hard times from an unlikely friend with a harrowing past.

"Reese's first-person narration rings with authenticity. . . . Myers' storytelling skills ensure that the messages he offers are never heavy-handed." Booklist

★ **Monster**; illustrations by Christopher Myers. HarperCollins Pubs. 1999 281p il $14.95; lib bdg $14.89; pa $8.99

Grades: 7 8 9 10   **Fic**

1. Trials -- Fiction 2. African Americans -- Fiction
ISBN 0-06-028077-8; 0-06-028078-6 lib bdg; 0-06-440731-4 pa

LC 98-40958

Michael L. Printz Award honor book

While on trial as an accomplice to a murder, sixteen-year-old Steve Harmon records his experiences in prison and in the courtroom in the form of a film script as he tries to come to terms with the course his life has taken.

"Balancing courtroom drama and a sordid jailhouse setting with flashbacks to the crime, Myers adeptly allows each character to speak for him or herself, leaving readers to judge for themselves the truthfulness of the defendants, witnesses, lawyers, and, most compellingly, Steve himself." Horn Book Guide

Oh, Snap! by Walter Dean Myers. Scholastic 2013 128 p. (hardcover) $17.99

Grades: 6 7 8 9   **Fic**

1. Theft -- Fiction 2. Journalists -- Fiction
ISBN 0439916291; 9780439916295

This is the fourth book in Walter Dean Myers's Cruisers series. Here, the "four budding urban journalists are psyched that their underground publication, 'The Cruiser,' was named the third-best school newspaper in the city, an honor that doesn't sit well with the official school newspaper, which ups its game. This pushes narrator Zander to hastily get involved with the case of Phat Tony, a wannabe rapper classmate who may be involved in a robbery." (Booklist)

★ **Riot**. Egmont 2009 164p $16.99; lib bdg $19.99; pa $8.99

Grades: 7 8 9 10 11 12   **Fic**

1. Riots -- Fiction 2. Race relations -- Fiction 3. Irish Americans -- Fiction 4. African Americans -- Fiction 5. Racially mixed people -- Fiction
ISBN 978-1-60684-000-9; 1-60684-000-2; 978-1-60684-042-9 lib bdg; 1-60684-042-8 lib bdg; 978-1-60684-209-6 pa; 1-60684-209-9 pa

LC 2009-14638

In 1863, fifteen-year-old Claire, the daughter of an Irish mother and a black father, faces ugly truths and great danger when Irish immigrants, enraged by the Civil War and a federal draft, lash out against blacks and wealthy "swells" of New York City.

"In this fast, dramatic novel told in screenplay format, Myers takes on a controversial historical conflict that is seldom written about. . . . There are no easy resolutions, idealized characters, or stereotypes, and the conflicts are unforgettable." Booklist

Scorpions. Harper & Row 1988 216p $16.99; lib bdg $16.89; pa $5.99

Grades: 6 7 8 9   **Fic**

1. African Americans -- Fiction 2. Juvenile delinquency -- Fiction
ISBN 0-06-024364-3; 0-06-024365-1 lib bdg; 0-06-447066-0 pa

LC 85-45815

A Newbery Medal honor book, 1989

Set in Harlem, this "story presents a brutally honest picture of the tragic influence of gang membership and pressures on a young black adolescent. Jamal Hicks, age twelve, reluctantly follows the orders of his older brother, now serving time in prison for robbery, and takes his place as leader of the Scorpions. When Jamal's leadership is challenged, disaster follows and Jamal learns some tragic lessons about friendship and owning a gun." Child Book Rev Serv

★ **Slam!** Scholastic Press 1996 266p hardcover o.p. pa $5.99

Grades: 7 8 9 10   **Fic**

1. School stories 2. Basketball -- Fiction 3. African Americans -- Fiction
ISBN 0-590-48667-5; 0-590-48668-3 pa

LC 95-46647

Coretta Scott King Award for text

Seventeen-year-old "Slam" Harris is counting on his noteworthy basketball talents to get him out of the inner city and give him a chance to succeed in life, but his coach sees things differently

Myers "descriptions of Slam on the court . . . use crisp details, not flowery language, to achieve their muscular poetry, and Myers is equally vivid in relating the torment Slam feels as he stares at a page of indecipherable algebra formulas. . . . [This is an] admirably realistic coming-of-age novel." Booklist

Street love. Amistad/Harper Tempest 2006 134p $15.99; lib bdg $16.89

Grades: 8 9 10 11 12   **Fic**

1. Novels in verse 2. Love -- Fiction 3. African Americans -- Fiction
ISBN 978-0-06-028079-6; 0-06-028079-4; 978-0-06-028080-2 lib bdg; 0-06-028080-8 lib bdg

LC 2006-02457

This story told in free verse is set against a background of street gangs and poverty in Harlem in which seventeen-year-old African American Damien takes a bold step to ensure that he and his new love will not be separated.

"The realistic drama on the street and at home tells a gripping story." Booklist

★ **Sunrise** over Fallujah. Scholastic Press 2008 290p $17.99

Grades: 8 9 10 11 12   **Fic**

1. Iraq War, 2003- -- Fiction 2. African Americans -- Fiction
ISBN 978-0-439-91624-0; 0-439-91624-0

LC 2007-25444

"Instead of heading to college as his father wishes, Robin leaves Harlem and joins the army to stand up for his country after 9/11. While stationed in Iraq with a war looming that he hopes will be averted, he begins writing letters home to his parents and to his Uncle Richie. . . . Myers brilliantly freeze-frames the opening months of the current Iraq War by realistically capturing its pivotal moments in 2003 and creating a vivid setting. Memorable characters share instances of wry levity that balance the story without deflecting its serious tone." SLJ

Myklusch, Matt

Jack Blank and the Imagine Nation. Aladdin 2010 480p $16.99

Grades: 4 5 6 7   **Fic**

1. Fantasy fiction 2. Science fiction 3. Orphans -- Fiction 4. Superheroes -- Fiction

ISBN 978-1-4169-9561-6; 1-4169-9561-7

Twelve-year-old Jack, freed from a dismal orphanage, makes his way to the elusive and impossible Imagine Nation, where a mentor saves him from dissection and trains him to use his superpower, despite the virus he carries that makes him a threat.

This creates "a richly imagined world with strong appeal to fans of comics. The island is populated by a fun cast of heroes and villains. . . . Brisk narration captures the superhero world with a mixture of fast-paced action, wry humor, and occasional heartfelt speeches about courage and friendship." SLJ

The **secret** war. Aladdin 2011 529p $16.99

Grades: 4 5 6 7   **Fic**

1. Fantasy fiction 2. Orphans -- Fiction 3. Viruses -- Fiction 4. Superheroes -- Fiction

ISBN 978-1-4169-9564-7; 1-4169-9564-1

LC 2010041779

Twelve-year-old Jack may be the Imagine Nation's only hope of fending off a new Rustov attack, with the help of his fellow superheroes-in-training, but the virus he carries, and Jonas's suspicions, provide new complications.

Myracle, Lauren

Eleven. Dutton Children's Books 2004 201p (The Winnie years) $16.99; pa $6.99

Grades: 4 5 6 7   **Fic**

1. Schools 2. Friendship 3. Family life 4. Best friends 5. Friendship -- Fiction 6. Family life -- Fiction

ISBN 0-525-47165-0; 0-14-240346-6 pa

LC 2003-49076

The year between turning eleven and turning twelve bring many changes for Winnie and her friends

"The inclusion of details about the everyday lives of these girls . . . will make this novel enjoyable, even for reluctant readers. However, it's the book's occasional revelation of harder truths that lifts it out of the ordinary." SLJ

Other titles in this series are:
Twelve (2007)
Thirteen (2008)
Thirteen plus one (2010)
Ten (2011)

★ **Luv** ya bunches. Amulet Books 2009 335p $15.95

Grades: 4 5 6   **Fic**

1. School stories 2. Friendship -- Fiction

ISBN 978-0-8109-4211-0; 0-8109-4211-9

LC 2009012585

Four friends—each named after a flower—navigate the ups and downs of fifth grade. Told through text messages, blog posts, screenplay, and straight narrative

Myracle "displays a shining awareness of and sensitivity to the highly textured society of tween girls. . . . This is a fun, challenging, and gently edifying story." Booklist

Another title about these characters is:
Violet in bloom (2010)

Peace, love, and baby ducks. Dutton Children's Books 2009 292p $16.99; pa $8.99

Grades: 8 9 10 11 12   **Fic**

1. Sisters -- Fiction

ISBN 978-0-525-47743-3; 0-525-47743-8; 978-0-14-241527-6 pa; 0-14-241527-8 pa

LC 2008-34221

Fifteen-year-old Carly's summer volunteer experience makes her feel more real than her life of privilege in Atlanta ever did, but her younger sister starts high school pretending to be what she is not, and both find their relationships suffering.

"Myracle empathetically explores issues of socioeconomic class, sibling rivalry, and parental influence in a story that is deeper and more nuanced than the title and cutesy cover." Booklist

Na, An

Wait for me. Putnam 2006 169p hardcover o.p. pa $7.99

Grades: 8 9 10 11 12   **Fic**

1. Deaf -- Fiction 2. Sisters -- Fiction 3. Korean Americans -- Fiction 4. Mother-daughter relationship -- Fiction

ISBN 0-399-24275-9; 0-14-240918-9 pa

LC 2005-30931

As her senior year in high school approaches, Mina yearns to find her own path in life but working at the family business, taking care of her little sister, and dealing with her mother's impossible expectations are as stifling as the southern California heat, until she falls in love with a man who offers a way out.

"This is a well-crafted tale, sensitively told. . . . The mother-daughter conflict will resonate with teens of any culture who have wrestled parents for the right to choose their own paths." Bull Cent Child Books

★ **A** step from heaven. Front St. 2000 156p $15.95

Grades: 7 8 9 10   **Fic**

1. Family life -- Fiction 2. Emigration and immigration 3. Korean Americans -- Fiction

ISBN 1-88691-058-8

LC 00-41083

Michael L. Printz Award, 2002

A young Korean girl and her family find it difficult to learn English and adjust to life in America

"This isn't a quick read, especially at the beginning when the child is trying to decipher American words and customs, but the coming-of-age drama will grab teens and make them think of their own conflicts between home and outside. As in the best writing, the particulars make the story universal." Booklist

Naftali, Joel

The **rendering**; [by] Joel Naftali. Egmont USA 2011 275p $15.99

Grades: 5 6 7 8   **Fic**

1. Science fiction 2. Adventure fiction 3. Weblogs -- Fiction

ISBN 978-1-60684-118-1; 1-60684-118-1

LC 2010-36640

Thirteen-year-old Doug relates in a series of blog posts the story of how he saved the world but was falsely branded a terrorist and murderer, forced to fight the evil Dr. Roach and his armored biodroid army with an electronics-destroying superpower of his own.

"Naftali balances tragedy and absurd humor with aplomb, not an easy task when dealing with horrific explosions and giant wisecracking skunks. Readers seeking a fast-paced, action-packed adventure will find this eminently suitable." Bull Cent Child Books

Naidoo, Beverley

★ **Burn** my heart. HarperCollins 2009 209p $15.99; lib bdg $16.89

Grades: 7 8 9 10 11 12   **Fic**

1. Friendship -- Fiction 2. Race relations -- Fiction

ISBN 978-0-06-143297-2; 0-06-143297-0; 978-0-06-143298-9 lib bdg; 0-06-143298-9 lib bdg

LC 2008-928322

First published 2007 in the United Kingdom

This "is an interesting story of which few people will be aware but might wish to know more. This solid novel would be a good multicultural addition to a teen collection." Voice Youth Advocates

★ **Journey** to Jo'burg; a South African story. illustrations by Eric Velasquez. Lippincott 1986 80p il hardcover o.p. pa $4.99

Grades: 5 6 7 8   **Fic**

ISBN 0-06-440237-1 pa

LC 85-45508

"This touching novel graphically depicts the plight of Africans living in the horror of South Africa. Thirteen-year-old Maledi and her 9-year-old brother leave their small village, take the perilous journey to the city, and encounter, firsthand, the painful struggle for justice, freedom, and dignity in the 'City of Gold.' A provocative story with a message readers will long remember." Soc Educ

Web of lies. HarperCollins Pub. 2006 256p lib bdg $16.89; $15.99

Grades: 6 7 8 9   **Fic**

1. Gangs -- Fiction 2. Africans -- Fiction 3. Refugees -- Fiction

ISBN 0-06-076077-X lib bdg; 0-06-076075-3

"In The Other Side of Truth (2001), Naidoo brings politics close through the eyes of Sade, who, following the assassination of her mother in Nigeria, flees to London with her brother, Femi. Now, two years later, the children have

been reunited with their father, as the refugee family waits for asylum. The focus this time is on Femi, 12, who succumbs to pressure to join a violent gang. . . . Readers will want to talk about the issues Naidoo raises here." Booklist

★ The **other** side of truth. HarperCollins Pubs. 2001 252p hardcover o.p. pa $5.99

Grades: 5 6 7 8   **Fic**

1. Africans -- Fiction 2. Refugees -- Fiction 4. Brothers and sisters

ISBN 0-06-029628-3; 0-06-441002-1 pa

LC 00-54112

First published 2000 in the United Kingdom

Smuggled out of Nigeria after their mother's murder, Sade and her younger brother are abandoned in London when their uncle fails to meet them at the airport and they are fearful of their new surroundings and of what may have happened to their journalist father back in Nigeria

"Part survival adventure, part docudrama, the narrative stays true to Sade's viewpoint. . . . This powerful novel brings the news images very close." Booklist

Nails, Jennifer

Next to Mexico; by Jennifer Nails. Houghton Mifflin Harcourt 2008 235p $16

Grades: 4 5 6   **Fic**

1. School stories 2. Friendship -- Fiction 3. Mexican Americans -- Fiction

ISBN 978-0-618-96635-6; 0-618-96635-8

LC 2008007268

Outspoken, impulsive Lylice has skipped fifth grade, but she finds that getting along at Susan B. Anthony Middle School is more difficult than she expected, until she is assigned to be the English Buddy to Mexico Mendoza, a recent immigrant.

"Lylice humorously narrates this lively, thought-provoking story, becoming increasingly likeable and endearing." Voice Youth Advocates

Namioka, Lensey

Mismatch; a novel. Delacorte Press 2006 217p $15.95; lib bdg $17.99

Grades: 7 8 9 10   **Fic**

1. Prejudices -- Fiction 2. Chinese Americans -- Fiction 3. Japanese Americans -- Fiction 4. Dating (Social customs) -- Fiction

ISBN 0-385-73183-3; 0-385-90220-4 lib bdg

Their families clash when Andy, a Japanese-American teenaged boy, starts dating Sue, a Chinese-American teenaged girl.

"A story that is current, relevant, and upbeat." SLJ

Ties that bind, ties that break; a novel. Delacorte Press 1999 154p hardcover o.p. pa $5.50

Grades: 5 6 7 8   **Fic**

1. Sex role -- Fiction 2. Footbinding -- Fiction 3. Individuality -- Fiction

ISBN 0-385-32666-1; 0-440-41599-3 pa

LC 98-27877

"In lyrical, descriptive prose, Namioka compassionately portrays a young girl's coming-of-age in a repressive, challenging time." Booklist

★ An **ocean** apart, a world away. Delacorte Press 2002 197p hardcover o.p. pa $5.50
Grades: 5 6 7 8 **Fic**
1. Chinese -- United States -- Fiction
ISBN 0-385-73002-0; 0-440-22973-1 pa
LC 2002-73550
Despite the odds facing her decision to become a doctor in 1920's Nanking, China, teenaged Yanyan leaves her family to study at Cornell University where, along with hard work, she finds prejudice and loneliness as well as friendship and a new sense of accomplishment
"Without heavy messages, Namioka explores what it means to be independent." Booklist

Nance, Andrew
Daemon Hall; [by] Andrew Nance; with illustrations by Coleman Polhemus. Henry Holt 2007 259p $16.95
Grades: 7 8 9 10 **Fic**
1. Horror fiction 2. Authorship -- Fiction
ISBN 978-0-8050-8171-8; 0-8050-8171-2
LC 2006-31044
Famous horror story writer R. U. Tremblin comes to the town of Maplewood to hold a short story writing contest, offering the five finalists the chance to spend what turns out to be a terrifying—and deadly—night with him in a haunted house.
"Readers looking for creepy chills and thrills will find plenty of satisfaction in this fast-paced book." Booklist

Return to Daemon Hall: evil roots; with illustrations by Coleman Polhemus. Henry Holt 2011 240p il $16.99
Grades: 7 8 9 10 **Fic**
1. Horror fiction 2. Authors -- Fiction 3. Contests -- Fiction 4. Authorship -- Fiction 5. Storytelling -- Fiction
ISBN 978-0-8050-8748-2; 0-8050-8748-6
LC 2010048609
Wade and Demarius go to author Ian Tremblin's home as judges of the second writing contest but soon are mysteriously transported to Daemon Hall, where they and the three finalists must tell—and act out—the stories each has written.
"Polhemus' stark artwork builds the mood, with heavy lines and crosshatching complementing the campfire nature of the tales." Kirkus

Nanji, Shenaaz
Child of dandelions. Front Street 2008 214p $17.95
Grades: 7 8 9 10 11 12 **Fic**
1. Generals 2. Presidents 3. Family life -- Fiction 4. East Indians -- Fiction
ISBN 978-1-93242-593-2; 1-93242-593-4
LC 2007-31576
In Uganda in 1972, fifteen-year-old Sabine and her family, wealthy citizens of Indian descent, try to preserve their normal life during the ninety days allowed by President Idi Amin for all foreign Indians to leave the country, while soldiers and others terrorize them and people disappear.
"This is an absorbing story rich with historical detail and human dynamics." Bull Cent Child Books

Napoli, Donna Jo
Alligator bayou. Wendy Lamb Books 2009 280p $16.99; lib bdg $19.99
Grades: 6 7 8 9 10 **Fic**
1. Uncles -- Fiction 2. Prejudices -- Fiction 3. Country life -- Fiction 4. Italian Americans -- Fiction
ISBN 978-0-385-74654-0; 0-385-74654-7; 978-0-385-90891-7 lib bdg; 0-385-90891-1 lib bdg
LC 2008-14504
Fourteen-year-old Calogero Scalise and his Sicilian uncles and cousin live in small-town Louisiana in 1898, when Jim Crow laws rule and anti-immigration sentiment is strong, so despite his attempts to be polite and to follow American customs, disaster dogs his family at every turn.
"Napoli's skillful pacing and fascinating detail combine in a gripping story that sheds cold, new light on Southern history and on the nature of racial prejudice." Booklist

★ **Beast**. Atheneum Bks. for Young Readers 2000 260p hardcover o.p. pa $8
Grades: 7 8 9 10 **Fic**
1. Fairy tales
ISBN 0-689-83589-2; 0-689-87005-1 pa
LC 99-89923
"The reader is immersed in the imagery and spirituality of ancient Persia. . . . Although Napoli uses Farsi (Persian) and Arabic words in the text (there is a glossary), this only adds to the texture and richness of her remarkable piece of writing." Book Rep

Bound. Atheneum Books for Young Readers 2004 186p hardcover o.p. pa $5.99
Grades: 8 9 10 11 12 **Fic**
1. Sex role -- Fiction
ISBN 0-689-86175-3; 0-689-86178-8 pa
LC 2004-365
In a novel based on Chinese Cinderella tales, fourteen-year-old stepchild Xing-Xing endures a life of neglect and servitude, as her stepmother cruelly mutilates her own child's feet so that she alone might marry well
The author "fleshes out and enriches the story with well-rounded characters and with accurate information about a specific time and place in Chinese history; the result is a dramatic and masterful retelling." SLJ

Fire in the hills. Dutton Children's Books 2006 215p hardcover o.p. pa $7.99
Grades: 5 6 7 8 **Fic**
1. World War, 1939-1945 -- Fiction
ISBN 0-525-47751-9; 0-14-241200-7 pa
Upon returning to Italy, fourteen-year-old Roberto struggles to survive, first on his own, then as a member of the resistance, fighting against the Nazi occupiers while yearning to reach home safely and for an end to the war.

"This well-written book grips the reader from the beginning and on through Roberto's adventures." Voice Youth Advocates

★ **Hush**; an Irish princess' tale. Atheneum Books for Young Readers 2007 308p $16.99

Grades: 8 9 10 11 12   **Fic**

1. Slavery -- Fiction 2. Princesses -- Fiction 3. Middle Ages -- Fiction

ISBN 978-0-689-86176-5; 0-689-86176-1

LC 2007-2676

Fifteen-year-old Melkorka, an Irish princess, is kidnapped by Russian slave traders and not only learns how to survive but to challenge some of the brutality of her captors, who are fascinated by her apparent muteness and the possibility that she is enchanted.

This is a "powerful survival story. . . . Napoli does not shy from detailing practices that will make readers wince . . . and the Russian crew repeatedly gang-rapes an older captive. . . . The tension over Mel's hopes for escape paces this story like a thriller." Publ Wkly

Lights on the Nile. HarperCollins 2011 278p $16.99; lib bdg $17.89

Grades: 4 5 6 7   **Fic**

1. Baboons -- Fiction 2. Fairies -- Fiction 3. Kidnapping -- Fiction

ISBN 978-0-06-166793-0; 0-06-166793-5; 978-0-06-166794-7 lib bdg; 0-06-166794-3 lib bdg

LC 2011010179

Ten-year-old Kepi, a young girl in ancient Egypt, embarks on a journey to save her family when she is unexpectedly taken captive, along with the baby baboon she has rescued from a crocodile.

Napoli "crafts a mystical coming-of-age tale and a love letter of sorts to Egypt, saturated with proverbs, intriguing details of everyday life at the time, and rich descriptions of the places Kepi visits. . . . Kepi's survival skills and perspective are challenged in this absorbing adventure." Publ Wkly

★ **Stones** in water. Dutton Children's Bks. 1997 209p hardcover o.p. pa $5.99

Grades: 5 6 7 8   **Fic**

1. World War, 1939-1945 -- Fiction

ISBN 0-525-45842-5; 0-14-130600-9 pa

LC 97-14253

After being taken by German soldiers from a local movie theater along with other Italian boys including his Jewish friend, Roberto is forced to work in Germany, escapes into the Ukrainian winter, before desperately trying to make his way back home to Venice

This is a "gripping, meticulously researched story (loosely based on the life of an actual survivor)." Publ Wkly

The **great** god Pan. Wendy Lamb Bks. 2003 149p $15.95; lib bdg $17.99

Grades: 7 8 9 10   **Fic**

1. Pan (Greek deity) -- Fiction 2. Classical mythology -- Fiction

ISBN 0-385-32777-3; 0-385-90120-8 lib bdg

LC 2002-13139

A retelling of the Greek myths about Pan, both goat and god, whose reed flute frolicking leads him to a meeting with Iphigenia, a human raised as the daughter of King Agamemnon and Queen Clytemnestra

"Filling in gaps that appear in other myths about Pan and Iphigenia, Napoli creates a novel filled with breathtaking language about nature, music, and desire. Teen readers will swoon." Booklist

The **smile**. Dutton Children's Books 2008 260p $17.99

Grades: 7 8 9 10   **Fic**

1. Artists -- Fiction 2. Renaissance -- Fiction

ISBN 978-0-525-47999-4; 0-525-47999-6

LC 2007-48522

In Renaissance Italy, Elisabetta longs for romance, and when Leonardo da Vinci introduces her to Guiliano de Medici, whose family rules Florence but is about to be deposed, she has no inkling of the romance—and sorrow—that will ensue.

"Napoli skillfully draws readers into the vibrant settings . . . with tangible, sensory details that enliven the novel's intriguing references to history and art. Elisabetta's strength and individuality . . . will captivate readers." Booklist

The **wager**. Henry Holt 2010 262p il $16.99

Grades: 8 9 10 11 12   **Fic**

1. Fairy tales 2. Devil -- Fiction

ISBN 978-0-8050-8781-9; 0-8050-8781-8

LC 2009-23436

Having lost everything in a tidal wave in 1169 Sicily, nineteen-year-old Don Giovanni makes a simple-sounding wager with a stranger he recognizes as the devil but, while desperate enough to surrender his pride and good looks for three years, he is not willing to give up his soul.

"Evocative of Hermann Hesse's Siddhartha, this marvelous story is well told, and the rich, sophisticated language will grip skilled readers." SLJ

Naylor, Phyllis Reynolds

Alice in April. Atheneum Pubs. 1993 164p hardcover o.p. pa $5.99

Grades: 5 6 7 8   **Fic**

1. School stories 2. Family life -- Fiction

ISBN 0-689-31805-7; 978-1-442-42757-0 pa; 1-442-42757-4 pa

LC 92-17016

While trying to survive seventh grade, Alice discovers that turning thirteen will make her the Woman of the House at home, so she starts a campaign to get more appreciated for taking care of her father and older brother

"Deftly written dialogue and an empathetic tone neatly balance substantial themes with plain good fun." Publ Wkly

Alice in rapture, sort of. Atheneum Pubs. 1989 166p hardcover o.p. pa $5.99

Grades: 5 6 7 8   **Fic**

1. Family life -- Fiction

ISBN 0-689-31466-3; 1-442-42362-5 pa

LC 88-8174

The summer before she enters the seventh grade becomes the summer of Alice's first boyfriend, and she discovers that love is about the most mixed-up thing that can possibly happen to you, especially since she has no mother to go to for advice

"A book that is wise, perceptive, and hilarious." SLJ

Cricket man. Atheneum Books for Young Readers 2008 208p $16.99

Grades: 6 7 8 9   **Fic**

1. School stories 2. Pregnancy -- Fiction 3. Family life -- Fiction 4. Skateboarding -- Fiction 5. Heroes and heroines -- Fiction

ISBN 978-1-416-94981-7; 1-416-94981-X

                                LC 2008-05889

Thirteen-year-old Kenny secretly calls himself "Cricket Man" after a summer of rescuing creatures from his family's Bethesda, Maryland, pool, which gives him more self-confidence and an urge to be a hero, especially for his depressed sixteen-year-old neighbor, Jodie.

"Naylor sketches a sensitive portrayal of life in middle school. . . . An involving novel by a fine storyteller." Booklist

Faith, hope, and Ivy June. Delacorte Press 2009 280p $16.99; lib bdg $19.99

Grades: 5 6 7 8   **Fic**

1. School stories 2. Young adult literature -- Works

ISBN 978-0-385-73615-2; 0-385-73615-0; 978-0-385-90588-6 lib bdg; 0-385-90588-2 lib bdg

                                LC 2008-19625

During a student exchange program, seventh-graders Ivy June and Catherine share their lives, homes, and communities, and find that although their lifestyles are total opposites they have a lot in common.

"This finely crafted novel . . . depicts a deep friendship growing slowly through understanding. As both girls wait out tragedies at the book's end, they cling to hope—and each other—in a thoroughly real and unaffected way. Naylor depicts Appalachia with sympathetic realism." Kirkus

Incredibly Alice. Atheneum Books for Young Readers 2011 278p $16.99

Grades: 7 8 9 10   **Fic**

1. School stories 2. Theater -- Fiction 3. Family life -- Fiction 4. Young adult literature -- Works 5. Dating (Social customs) -- Fiction

ISBN 978-1-4169-7553-3; 1-4169-7553-5

                                LC 2010036982

Maryland teenager Alice McKinley spends her last semester of high school performing in the school play, working on the student paper, worrying about being away from her boyfriend, who will be studying in Spain, and anticipating her future in college.

"Realistic and satisfying, Alice and friends' bittersweet senior year's ending and their preparations for adulthood's exciting and uncertain world will resonate with any high school female." Voice Youth Advocates

★ **Reluctantly** Alice. Atheneum Pubs. 1991 182p $16; pa $4.99

Grades: 7 8 9 10   **Fic**

1. School stories 2. Family life -- Fiction 3. Young adult literature -- Works 4. Children's literature --

Works -- Grades two through six

ISBN 0-689-31681-X; 0-689-81688-X pa

                                LC 90-37956

Alice experiences the joys and embarrassments of seventh grade while advising her father and older brother on their love lives

"Naylor combines laugh-out-loud scenes with moments of sudden gentleness. . . . The characters are complex, the dialogue is droll, the junior high world authentic." Booklist

Other titles about Alice are:
Achingly Alice (1998)
Alice alone (2001)
Alice in-between (1994)
Alice in lace (1996)
Alice in the know (2006)
Alice on her way (2005)
Alice on the outside (1999)
Alice the brave (1995)
All but Alice (1992)
Almost Alice (2008)
Intensely Alice (2009)
Dangerously Alice (2007)
The grooming of Alice (2000)
Including Alice (2004)
Outrageously Alice (1997)
Patiently Alice (2003)
Simply Alice (2002)

★ **Shiloh**. Atheneum Pubs. 1991 144p $16.95; pa $6.99

Grades: 4 5 6   **Fic**

1. Dogs -- Fiction 2. Children's literature -- Works -- Grades two through six

ISBN 0-689-31614-3; 0-689-83582-5 pa

                                LC 90-603

Awarded the Newbery Medal, 1992

When he finds a lost beagle in the hills behind his West Virginia home, Marty tries to hide it from his family and the dog's real owner, a mean-spirited man known to shoot deer out of season and to mistreat his dogs

"A credible plot and characters, a well-drawn setting, and nicely paced narration combine in a story that leaves the reader feeling good." Horn Book

Other titles about Shiloh are:
Shiloh season (1996)
Saving Shiloh (1997)

Neely, Cynthia

Unearthly; [by] Cynthia Hand. HarperTeen 2011 435p $17.99

Grades: 7 8 9 10   **Fic**

1. School stories 2. Angels -- Fiction 3. Moving -- Fiction 4. Supernatural -- Fiction

ISBN 978-0-06-199616-0; 0-06-199616-5

                                LC 2010-17849

Sixteen-year-old Clara Gardner's purpose as an angel-blood begins to manifest itself, forcing her family to pull up stakes and move to Jackson, Wyoming, where she learns that danger and heartbreak come with her powers.

"Hand avoids overt discussion of religion while telling an engaging and romantic tale with a solid backstory. Her characters deal realistically with the uncertainty of being on

the cusp of maturity without wrapping themselves in angst."
Publ Wkly

Neff, Henry H.
  The **hound** of Rowan. Random House 2007
414p il (The tapestry) $17.99; lib bdg $20.99; pa
$6.99
  Grades: 6 7 8 9   **Fic**
    1. School stories 2. Magic -- Fiction
    ISBN 978-0-375-83894-1; 0-375-83894-5; 978-0-375-
93894-8 lib bdg; 0-375-93894-4 lib bdg; 978-0-375-
83895-8 pa; 0-375-83895-3 pa
                                       LC 2006-20970
  After glimpsing a hint of his destiny in a mysterious tapestry, twelve-year-old Max McDaniels becomes a student at
Rowan Academy, where he trains in "mystics and combat"
in preparation for war with an ancient enemy that has been
kidnapping children like him.
  "Max's intelligence and goodhearted nature give the
story a solid emotional core even as the surprising twists and
turns keep the pages turning." Voice Youth Advocates
    Other titles in this series are:
    The second siege (2008)
    The fiend and the forge (2011)

Nelson, Blake
  Destroy all cars. Scholastic Press 2009 218p
$17.99
  Grades: 7 8 9 10   **Fic**
    1. School stories 2. Ecology -- Fiction 3. Social action
-- Fiction
    ISBN 978-0-545-10474-6; 0-545-10474-2
                                       LC 2008-34850
  Through assignments for English class, seventeen-year-
old James Hoff rants against consumerism and his classmates' apathy, puzzles over his feelings for his ex-girlfriend,
and expresses disdain for his emotionally-distant parents.
  Nelson "offers an elegant and bittersweet story of a teenager who is finding his voice and trying to make meaning in
a world he often finds hopeless." Publ Wkly

  They came from below. Tor 2007 299p $17.95
  Grades: 7 8 9 10   **Fic**
    1. Beaches -- Fiction 2. Supernatural -- Fiction 3.
Marine pollution -- Fiction
    ISBN 978-0-7653-1423-9; 0-7653-1423-1
                                       LC 2007-09542
  While vacationing on Cape Cod, best friends Emily, age
sixteen, and Reese, seventeen, meet Steve and Dave, who
seem too good to be true, and whose presence turns out to be
related to a dire threat of global pollution.
  "Offering wittiness, suspense and ideologies borrowed
from Eastern religions, Nelson reaches a new level of depth
and creativity with this intriguing depiction of one very
weird summer." Publ Wkly

Nelson, James
  On the volcano. G.P. Putnam's Sons 2011 275p
$16.99
  Grades: 7 8 9 10   **Fic**
    1. Violence -- Fiction 2. Volcanoes -- Fiction 3.
Wilderness areas -- Fiction 4. Frontier and pioneer life

-- Fiction
    ISBN 978-0-399-25282-2; 0-399-25282-7
                                       LC 2008-53557
  In the 1870s, sixteen-year-old Katie has grown up in a
remote cabin on the edge of a volcano with her father and
their friend Lorraine, the only people she has ever seen, but,
after eagerly anticipating it for so long, her first trip into a
town ultimately brings tragedy into their lives.
  "Nelson has created a moving tale of frontier life. Katie
shows tremendous fighting spirit as she deal with the trials
in her life. . . . [This] is perfect for historical fiction fans."
Voice Youth Advocates

Nelson, Nina
  Bringing the boy home; by N.A. Nelson. HarperCollinsPublishers 2008 211p $15.99; lib bdg
$16.89
  Grades: 5 6 7 8   **Fic**
    1. Rain forests -- Fiction 2. Senses and sensation --
Fiction 3. Extrasensory perception -- Fiction
    ISBN 978-0-06-088698-1; 0-06-088698-6; 978-0-06-
088699-8 lib bdg; 0-06-088699-4 lib bdg
                                       LC 2007-31702
  As two Takunami youths approach their thirteenth birth-
days, Luka reaches the culmination of his mother's training
for the tribe's manhood test while Tirio, raised in Miami,
Florida, by his adoptive mother, feels called to begin preparations to prove himself during his upcoming visit to the
Amazon rain forest where he was born.
  "The vivid setting, imagined cultural particulars . . . and
magical realism will captivate readers." Booklist

Nelson, R. A.
  Days of Little Texas. Alfred A. Knopf 2009
388p $16.99; lib bdg $19.99
  Grades: 8 9 10 11 12   **Fic**
    1. Ghost stories 2. Slavery -- Fiction 3. Supernatural
-- Fiction 4. Good and evil -- Fiction 5. Christian life
-- Fiction 6. Evangelistic work -- Fiction
    ISBN 978-0-375-85593-1; 0-375-85593-9; 978-0-375-
95593-8 lib bdg; 0-375-95593-3 lib bdg
                                       LC 2008-33855
  Sixteen-year-old Ronald Earl King, who has been a charismatic evangelist since he was ten years old, is about to
preach at a huge revival meeting on the grounds of an old
plantation, where, with confusing help from the ghost of a
girl he could not heal, he becomes engaged in an epic battle
between good and evil.
  "Chapters are brief, the pace is rapid, and the tension
is high as Ronald wrestles with demons both temporal and
spiritual to find his place in the world. An affecting and
sharply written story." SLJ

Nelson, Theresa
  Ruby electric; a novel. Atheneum Bks. for
Young Readers 2003 264p hardcover o.p. pa $5.99
  Grades: 5 6 7 8   **Fic**
    1. Fathers -- Fiction 2. Siblings -- Fiction 3. Authorship
-- Fiction
    ISBN 0-689-83852-2; 0-689-87146-5 pa
                                       LC 2002-8034

Twelve-year-old Ruby Miller, movie buff and aspiring screen writer, tries to resolve the mysteries surrounding her little brother's stuffed woolly mammoth and their father's five year absence

"Ruby's voice is electric, and she is an unforgettable character with courage, a cause, and imagination." Booklist

Nemeth, Sally

The **heights,** the depths, and everything in between. Alfred A. Knopf 2006 263p hardcover o.p. lib bdg $17.99; pa $6.99

Grades: 5 6 7 8   **Fic**
1. Size -- Fiction 2. Dwarfism -- Fiction 3. Friendship -- Fiction
ISBN 0-375-83458-3; 0-375-93458-8 lib bdg; 0-553-49499-6 pa

LC 2005-33273

In 1977, best friends Lucy Small, a seventh grader from Wilmington, Delaware, who is five feet ten inches tall, and Jake Little, a dwarf, try unsuccessfully to go unnoticed during their first year of junior high school

"Playwright Nemeth has a real gift for capturing teen dialogue and emotions. . . . Readers will relate to this satisfying tale." Booklist

Neri, G.

Ghetto cowboy; [by] G. Neri; illustrated by Jesse Joshua Watson. Candlewick Press 2011 218p il $15.99

Grades: 4 5 6 7   **Fic**
1. Horses -- Fiction 2. Moving -- Fiction 3. African Americans -- Fiction 4. City and town life -- Fiction 5. Father-son relationship -- Fiction
ISBN 978-0-7636-4922-7; 0-7636-4922-8

LC 2010007565

Twelve-year-old Cole's behavior causes his mother to drive him from Detroit to Philadelphia to live with a father he has never known, but who soon has Cole involved with a group of African-American "cowboys" who rescue horses and use them to steer youths away from drugs and gangs.

"This well-written book is based on a true story of urban cowboys in Philadelphia and New York. Cole's spot-on emotional insight is conveyed through believable dialogue. . . . Watson's illustrations punctuate the intriguing aspects of the story and make the novel more appealing." SLJ

Neri, Greg

Chess rumble; by G. Neri; art by Jesse Joshua Watson. Lee & Low Books 2007 64p il $18.95

Grades: 5 6 7 8   **Fic**
1. Chess -- Fiction 2. African Americans -- Fiction
ISBN 978-1-58430-279-7

LC 2007010772

Branded a troublemaker due to his anger over everything from being bullied to his sister's death a year before, Marcus begins to control himself and cope with his problems at home and at his inner-city school when an unlikely mentor teaches him to play chess

"Neri expertly captures Marcus's voice and delicately teases out his alternating vulnerability and rage. The cadence and emotion of the verse are masterfully echoed through Watson's expressive acrylic illustrations." SLJ

Ness, Patrick, 1971-

The **Ask** and the Answer; a novel. Candlewick Press 2009 519p (Chaos walking) $18.99

Grades: 8 9 10 11 12   **Fic**
1. Science fiction 2. Telepathy -- Fiction 3. Space colonies -- Fiction 4. Social problems -- Fiction
ISBN 978-0-7636-4490-1; 0-7636-4490-0

LC 2009-7329

Alternate chapters follow teenagers Todd and Viola, who become separated as the Mayor's oppressive new regime takes power in New Prentisstown, a space colony where residents can hear each other's thoughts.

"Provocative questions about gender bias, racism, the meaning of war and the price of peace are thoughtfully threaded throughout a breathless, often violent plot peopled with heartbreakingly real characters." Kirkus

★ A **monster** calls; a novel. Candlewick Press 2011 204p il $15.99

Grades: 6 7 8 9 10   **Fic**
1. School stories 2. Cancer -- Fiction 3. Monsters -- Fiction 4. Loss (Psychology) -- Fiction 5. Mother-son relationship -- Fiction
ISBN 978-0-7636-5559-4; 0-7636-5559-7

LC 2010040741

This is a "profoundly moving, expertly crafted tale of unaccountable loss. . . . A singular masterpiece, exceptionally well-served by Kay's atmospheric and ominous illustrations." Publ Wkly

Monsters of men. Candlewick Press 2010 603p (Chaos walking) $18.99; pa $9.99

Grades: 8 9 10 11 12   **Fic**
1. War stories 2. Science fiction 3. Telepathy -- Fiction 4. Space colonies -- Fiction 5. Social problems -- Fiction
ISBN 978-0-7636-4751-3; 0-7636-4751-9; 978-0-7636-5665-2 pa; 0-7636-5665-8 pa

As a world-ending war surges to life around them, Todd and Viola face monstrous decisions, questioning all they have ever known as they try to step back from the darkness and find the best way to achieve peace.

"The Chaos Walking trilogy comes to a powerful conclusion in this grueling but triumphant tale." Publ Wkly

★ The **knife** of never letting go. Candlewick Press 2008 479p (Chaos walking) $18.99

Grades: 8 9 10 11 12   **Fic**
1. Boys -- Fiction 2. Science fiction 3. Dystopian fiction 4. Psychics -- Fiction 5. Telepathy -- Fiction 6. Space colonies -- Fiction
ISBN 978-0-7636-3931-0; 0-7636-3931-1

LC 2007-52334

Pursued by power-hungry Prentiss and mad minister Aaron, young Todd and Viola set out across New World searching for answers about his colony's true past and seeking a way to warn the ship bringing hopeful settlers from Old World.

"This troubling, unforgettable opener to the Chaos Walking trilogy is a penetrating look at the ways in which we reveal ourselves to one another, and what it takes to be a man in a society gone horribly wrong." Booklist

Neumeier, Rachel

★ The **City** in the Lake. Alfred A. Knopf 2008 304p $15.99; lib bdg $18.99

Grades: 8 9 10 11 12   **Fic**
1. Fantasy fiction 2. Magic -- Fiction
ISBN 978-0-375-84704-2; 0-375-84704-9; 978-0-375-94704-9 lib bdg; 0-375-94704-3 lib bdg
LC 2008-08941

Seventeen-year-old Timou, who is learning to be a mage, must save her mysterious, magical homeland, The Kingdom, from a powerful force that is trying to control it.

"Neumeier structures her story around archetypal fantasy elements. . . . It's the poetic, shimmering language and fascinating unfolding of worlds that elevates this engrossing story beyond its formula." Booklist

The **Floating** Islands. Alfred A. Knopf 2011 388p map $16.99; lib bdg $19.99

Grades: 5 6 7   **Fic**
1. Fantasy fiction 2. Magic -- Fiction 3. Flight -- Fiction 4. Cousins -- Fiction
ISBN 0-375-84705-7; 0-375-94705-1 lib bdg; 978-0-375-84705-9; 978-0-375-94705-6 lib bdg
LC 2010-12772

The adventures of two teenaged cousins who live in a place called The Floating Islands, one of whom is studying to become a mage and the other one of the legendary island flyers.

"The author delineates complex characters, geographies and societies alike with a dab hand, deftly weaves them all—along with dragons of several sorts, mouthwatering kitchen talk, flashes of humor and a late-blooming romance—into a suspenseful plot and delivers and outstanding tale that is self-contained but full of promise for sequels." Kirkus

Newbery, Linda

At the firefly gate. David Fickling Books 2007 152p hardcover o.p. pa $6.50

Grades: 5 6 7 8   **Fic**
1. Supernatural -- Fiction 2. World War, 1939-1945 -- Fiction
ISBN 978-0-385-75113-1; 978-0-440-42188-7 pa
LC 2006-01796

After moving with his parents from London to Suffolk near a former World War II airfield , Henry sees the shadowy image of a man by the orchard gate and feels an unusual affinity with an eldery woman who lives next door

"This is a well-written book, with an old-fashioned tone, that emphasizes character and feelings over plot. It's for thoughtful readers who appreciate a book that lingers in their minds." SLJ

Catcall; illustrated by Ian P. Benfold Haywood. David Fickling Books 2008 179p il $15.99; lib bdg $18.99

Grades: 5 6 7 8   **Fic**
1. Cats -- Fiction 2. Family life -- Fiction 3.

Stepfamilies -- Fiction
ISBN 978-0-385-75164-3; 0-385-75164-8; 978-0-385-75165-0 lib bdg; 0-385-75165-6 lib bdg
LC 2008-1910

When eight-year-old Jamie becomes almost possessed by a lion he encountered in a wild animal park, his blended family, especially his cat-loving older brother Josh, struggles to connect with the boy they love

"In addition to the likable characters, the story provides an example of people working through problems without yelling or abuse. It is refreshing to read about this loving family, reminiscent of those created by Madeleine L'Engle." SLJ

Flightsend. David Fickling Books 2010 241p $15.99; lib bdg $18.99

Grades: 7 8 9 10   **Fic**
1. Moving -- Fiction 2. Bereavement -- Fiction
ISBN 978-0-385-75203-9; 0-385-75203-2; 978-0-385-75205-3 lib bdg; 0-385-75205-9 lib bdg
First published 1999 in the United Kingdom

Just when her life seems to be falling apart, an English teen named Charlie gains a fresh perspective when she and her mother relocate to a rural village.

"The characters are wonderfully developed. The leisurely plot unfolds quietly, meandering through Charlie's life and endearing her to readers." SLJ

Lost boy. David Fickling Books 2008 194p $15.99; lib bdg $18.99

Grades: 4 5 6 7   **Fic**
1. Ghost stories 2. Mystery fiction 3. Traffic accidents -- Fiction
ISBN 978-0-375-84574-1; 978-0-375-93617-3 lib bdg
LC 2007-15041
First published 2005 in the United Kingdom

After Matt moves to Hay-on-Wye in Wales, a boy his age who bears the same initials and was killed in a car accident many years earlier, appears to Matt.

"With its imaginative melding of present-day concerns, good storytelling, lush descriptions of the landscape and even a faithful dog, this novel will ensnare readers." Publ Wkly

Newbound, Andrew

Ghoul strike! Chicken House 2010 309p $16.99

Grades: 4 5 6 7   **Fic**
1. Angels -- Fiction 2. Monsters -- Fiction 3. Supernatural -- Fiction
ISBN 978-0-545-22938-8; 0-545-22938-3
LC 2010013580

When twelve-year-old, psychic ghost hunter Alannah Malarra faces demons from another dimension, rather than the treasure-hoarding ghosts she is used to, she needs the help of protectors from the Attack-ready Network of Global Evanescent Law-enforcers (A.N.G.E.L.) police force to help her quell the dangerous uprising

"Alannah is a great female hero. . . . The other main characters are also multidimensional, and descriptions of the various creatures are detailed and entertaining. Readers will enjoy the fast-paced plot and the friendship between Alannah and Wortley." SLJ

Newton, Robert

Runner. Alfred A. Knopf 2007 209p $15.99; lib bdg $18.99

Grades: 6 7 8 9   **Fic**

1. Poverty -- Fiction 2. Running -- Fiction 3. Criminals -- Fiction

ISBN 978-0-375-83744-9; 978-0-375-93744-6 lib bdg; 0-375-83744-2; 0-375-93744-7 lib bdg

LC 2006-29275

In Richmond, Australia, in 1919, fifteen-year-old Charlie Feehan becomes an errand boy for a notorious mobster, hoping that his ability to run will help him, his widowed mother, and his baby brother to escape poverty.

"Rich dialogue in Australian dialect creates a colorful picture of the historical urban setting, suspenseful plot, and warm characterizations." SLJ

Nicholls, Sally

★ **Season** of secrets. Arthur A. Levine Books 2011 225p $16.99

Grades: 4 5 6   **Fic**

1. Sisters -- Fiction 2. Bereavement -- Fiction 3. Family life -- Fiction

ISBN 978-0-545-21825-2; 0-545-21825-X

LC 2010017070

Sent by their father to live in the country with their grandparents after the sudden death of their mother, Molly's older sister Hannah expresses her grief in a raging rebellion while imaginative Molly finds herself increasingly distracted by visions, that seemingly only she can see, of a strange hunt in the nearby forest.

"Written in gently flowing prose, the plot appropriately transitions from autumn into summer as Molly emerges from grief to acceptance and hope. A poignant story of healing tinged with mystery." Kirkus

★ **Ways** to live forever; [by] Sally Nicholls. Arthur A. Levine Books 2008 212p il $16.99

Grades: 4 5 6 7   **Fic**

1. Death -- Fiction 2. Leukemia -- Fiction 3. Authorship -- Fiction 4. Family life -- Fiction

ISBN 978-0-545-06948-9; 0-545-06948-3

LC 2007047341

Eleven-year-old Sam McQueen, who has leukemia, writes a book during the last three months of his life, in which he tells about what he would like to accomplish, how he feels, and things that have happened to him.

This "skirts easy sentiment to confront the hard questions head-on, intelligently and realistically and with an enormous range of feeling." Publ Wkly

Nichols, Janet

★ **Messed** up; [by] Janet Nichols Lynch. Holiday House 2009 250p $17.95

Grades: 7 8 9 10   **Fic**

1. School stories 2. Family life -- Fiction 3. Abandoned children -- Fiction 4. Hispanic Americans -- Fiction

ISBN 978-0-8234-2185-5; 0-8234-2185-6

LC 2008-22577

Fifteen-year-old RD is repeating the eighth grade, planning to have an easy year, but after his grandmother walks out her boyfriend is no longer able to care for him, which leaves RD to fend for himself while avoiding being caught.

"A memorable story of grit and survival, and helping hands along the way." Kirkus

Nicholson, William

Seeker. Harcourt 2006 413p (Noble warriors) $17; pa $7.95

Grades: 7 8 9 10   **Fic**

1. Fantasy fiction

ISBN 978-0-15-205768-8; 0-15-205768-4; 978-0-15-205866-1 pa; 0-15-205866-4 pa

LC 2005-17171

"The classic coming-of-age tale is combined with a rich setting of cold villains, strange powers, and disturbing warriors." Voice Youth Advocates

Other titles in this series are:

Jango (2007)

Noman (2008)

Nielsen, Jennifer A.

Elliot and the Yeti threat; illustrated by Gideon Kendall. Sourcebooks Jabberwocky 2012 il $12.99

Grades: 4 5 6 7   **Fic**

1. Fantasy fiction 2. Yeti -- Fiction

ISBN 978-1-4022-4021-8; 1-4022-4021-X

Being King of the Brownies is no easy job! Elliot outsmarted the Goblins and foiled the Pixie Plot, but now he's being threatened by a giant Yeti. Oh, and there's a mermaid hiding in his bathtub. Elliot might be able to survive some unusual self-defense lessons and a kingnapping plot, but can he withstand the friendship of the neighbor girl—his arch—nemesis–Cami Wortson?

Nielsen, Susin

Dear George Clooney; please marry my mom. Tundra Books 2010 229p $15.95

Grades: 5 6 7 8   **Fic**

1. Divorce -- Fiction 2. Letters -- Fiction

ISBN 978-0-88776-977-1; 0-88776-977-2

"Smarting from her parent's divorce—her director father left her mother to marry an actress—Violet is fed up with all the 'losers' her mother has since dated. . . . She pens a letter to George Clooney . . . explaining that she's trying to find a suitable suitor for her parent. . . . Nielsen skillfully balances her story's keen humor . . . with poignancy." Publ Wkly

★ **Word** nerd. Tundra Books 2008 248p $18.95; pa $12.95

Grades: 5 6 7 8   **Fic**

1. Friendship -- Fiction 2. Scrabble (Game) -- Fiction 3. Mother-son relationship -- Fiction

ISBN 978-0-88776-875-0; 0-88776-875-X; 978-0-88776-990-0 pa; 0-88776-990-X pa

"Twelve-year-old Ambrose Bukowski and his widowed, overprotective mother . . . move frequently. When he almost dies after he bites into a peanut that bullies put in his sandwich, just to see if he is really allergic, Irene . . . decides to homeschool him. . . . Ambrose gets to know 25-year-old Cosmo, recently released from jail and the son of the Bukowskis' . . . landlords. . . . Ambrose . . . talks Cosmo into taking him to a Scrabble Club. . . . This is a tender, often funny story with some really interesting characters. It will appeal to word nerds, but even more to anyone who has ever longed for acceptance or had to fight unreasonable parental restrictions." SLJ

The **reluctant** journal of Henry K. Larsen; Susin Nielsen. Tundra Books of Northern New York 2012 243 p. $17.95

Grades: 7 8 9 10 11 12   **Fic**
   1. Bullies -- Fiction 2. Grief -- Fiction
   ISBN 1770493727; 9781770493728
                        LC 2011938782

In this novel, by Susin Nielsen, "thirteen-year-old Henry's happy life abruptly ends when his older brother kills the boy who bullied him in school and then takes his own life. Henry refers to this tragedy as 'IT.' He moves to a new city . . . for a fresh start. To help him cope with IT, Henry's therapist recommends he keep a journal. Henry hates the suggestion but soon finds himself recording his thoughts and feelings constantly, even updating it multiple times per day." (Kirkus Reviews)

Nielson, Sheila A.

Forbidden sea. Scholastic 2010 296p $17.99

Grades: 5 6 7 8   **Fic**
   1. Fantasy fiction 2. Islands -- Fiction 3. Superstition -- Fiction 4. Mermaids and mermen -- Fiction
   ISBN 978-0-545-09734-5; 0-545-09734-7
                        LC 2009-22993

When a mermaid attempts to lure her into the sea, fourteen-year-old Adrianne, who lives in a superstitious island community, must choose between the promise of an underwater paradise and those she loves.

"The plot pacing is steady and suspenseful as more details about the protagonist's current life and past are revealed through her absorbing first-person narration. Nielsen's new spin on a traditional fantasy setup is sure to appeal." SLJ

Nigg, Joe

How to raise and keep a dragon; by John Topsell; executive editor, Joseph Nigg; illustrations, Dan Malone. Barron's 2006 128p il $18.99

Grades: 5 6 7 8   **Fic**
   1. Dragons -- Fiction
   ISBN 0-7641-5920-8

"Posing as dragon-breeder John Topsell . . . Nigg instructs readers in selecting and caring for a breed of dragon suited for them. . . . While not intended as a serious book on mythology, Nigg does share many bits of real dragon lore while spinning out details of what it might be like to live in a world where people breed, register, and show these creatures. Malone's full-color illustrations on every page offer fans many cool pictures to copy or sketch. With its tongue firmly in cheek, this book is a lot of lighthearted fun." SLJ

Nimmo, Jenny

Emlyn's moon. Orchard Books 2007 152p (Magician trilogy) $9.99

Grades: 4 5 6 7   **Fic**
   1. Magic -- Fiction
   ISBN 978-0-439-84676-9; 0-439-84676-5
                        LC 2006-09855

First published 1986 in the United Kingdom; first U.S. edition 1989 by Dutton with title: Orchard of the crescent moon

Nia, the middle girl in a large Welsh family, discovers her own special artistic talent as she uncovers the dark secret shared by the Llewelyn and Griffiths families.

"The book's manageable length, sympathetic characters, and appealing jacket art will lure readers." Booklist

Midnight for Charlie Bone. Orchard Bks. 2003 401p (Children of the Red King) $12.99

Grades: 5 6 7 8   **Fic**
   1. School stories 2. Magic -- Fiction
   ISBN 978-0-439-47429-0; 0-439-47429-9
                        LC 2002-30738

First published 2002 in the United Kingdom

Charlie Bone's life with his widowed mother and two grandmothers undergoes a dramatic change when he discovers that he can hear people in photographs talking.

"This marvelous fantasy is able to stand on its own despite inevitable comparisons to the students of Hogwarts." Voice Youth Advocates

Other titles in this series are:
Charlie Bone and the time twister (2003)
Charlie Bone and the invisible boy (2004)
Charlie Bone and the castle of mirrors (2005)
Charlie Bone and the hidden king (2006)
Charlie Bone and the beast (2007)
Charlie Bone and the shadow (2008)
Charlie Bone and the Red Knight (2010)

★ The **snow** spider; [by] Jenny Nimmo. Orchard Books 2006 146p (Magician trilogy) $9.99

Grades: 4 5 6 7   **Fic**
   1. Magic -- Fiction 2. Father-son relationship -- Fiction
   ISBN 978-0-439-84675-2; 0-439-84675-7
                        LC 2006009445

A reissue of the title first published 1987 by Dutton

Gifts from Gwyn's grandmother on his ninth birthday open up a whole new world to him, as he discovers he has magical powers that help him heal the breach with his father that has existed ever since his sister's mysterious disappearance four years before

"The narration is paced well and builds in excitement along with the tale." SLJ

Other titles in this series are:
Emlyn's moon (2007)
Chestnut solider (2007)

Nix, Garth, 1963-

Mister Monday; Keys to the kingdom, book one. Scholastic 2003 361p (Keys to the kingdom) $15.99; pa $5.99

Grades: 6 7 8 9   **Fic**
   1. Fantasy fiction 2. Young adult literature -- Works
   ISBN 0-439-70370-0; 0-439-55123-4 pa
                        LC 2004-540574

Arthur Penhaligon is supposed to die at a young age, but is saved by a key that is shaped like the minute hand of a clock. The key causes bizarre creatures to come from another realm, bringing with them a plague. A man named Mister Monday will stop at nothing to get the key back. Arthur goes to a mysterious house that only he can see, so that he can learn the truth about himself and the key

"The first in a seven part series for middle graders is every bit as exciting and suspenseful as the author's previous young adult novels." SLJ

Other titles in the Keys to the Kingdom series are:

Grim Tuesday (2004)

Drowned Wednesday (2005)

Sir Thursday (2006)

Lady Friday (2007)

Superior Saturday (2008)

Lord Sunday (2010)

★ **Sabriel**. HarperCollins Pubs. 1996 292p hardcover o.p. pa $7.99

Grades: 7 8 9 10   **Fic**

1. Fantasy fiction 2. Young adult literature -- Works
ISBN 0-06-027322-4; 0-06-447183-7 pa

LC 96-1295

First published 1995 in Australia

Sabriel, daughter of the necromancer Abhorsen, must journey into the mysterious and magical Old Kingdom to rescue her father from the Land of the Dead.

"The final battle is gripping, and the bloody cost of combat is forcefully presented. The story is remarkable for the level of originality of the fantastic elements . . . and for the subtle presentation, which leaves readers to explore for themselves the complex structure and significance of the magic elements." Horn Book

Other titles in this series are:

Abhorsen (2003)

Across the wall (2005)

Lirael, daughter of the Clayr (2001)

Shade's children. HarperCollins Pubs. 1997 310p $18.99; pa $6.99

Grades: 7 8 9 10   **Fic**

1. Science fiction
ISBN 0-06-027324-0; 0-06-447196-9 pa

LC 97-3841

In a savage postnuclear world, four young fugitives attempt to overthrow the bloodthirsty rule of the Overlords with the help of Shade, their mysterious mentor

"Grim, unusual, and fascinating." Horn Book

Troubletwisters; [by] Garth Nix and Sean Williams. Scholastic Press 2011 293p $16.99

Grades: 5 6 7 8   **Fic**

1. Fantasy fiction 2. Magic -- Fiction 3. Twins -- Fiction 4. Siblings -- Fiction 5. Grandmothers -- Fiction
ISBN 978-0-545-25897-5; 0-545-25897-9

LC 2011015765

When their house mysteriously explodes and they are sent to live with an unknown relative named Grandma X, twelve-year-old twins Jaide and Jack Shield learn that they are troubletwisters, young Wardens just coming into their powers, who must protect humanity from The Evil trying to break into Earth's dimension.

"Full of adventure and the unexpected, . . . [this] is delightfully twisted. The pacing is perfect, the setting is ee-

rily dark, the faceless Evil rings true, and the resolution is satisfying." Booklist

Nixon, Joan Lowery

Laugh till you cry. Delacorte Press 2004 99p hardcover o.p. lib bdg $17.99

Grades: 5 6 7 8   **Fic**

1. School stories 2. Moving -- Fiction 3. Family life -- Fiction
ISBN 0-385-73027-6; 0-385-90186-0 lib bdg

LC 2004-9557

Thirteen years old and a budding comedian, Cody has little to laugh about after he and his mother move from California to Texas to help his sick grandmother and he finds himself framed by his jealous cousin for calling in bomb threats to their school.

"The pacing of the story, Cody's humorous side, and the book's length make this mystery ideal for reluctant readers." SLJ

Nightmare. Delacorte Press 2003 166p hardcover o.p. lib bdg $17.99; pa $5.99

Grades: 6 7 8 9   **Fic**

1. Mystery fiction 2. Camps -- Fiction 3. Homicide -- Fiction
ISBN 0-385-73026-8; 0-385-90151-8 lib bdg; 0-4402-3773-4 pa

LC 2003-43434

Emily is sent to a camp for underachievers where she discovers a murderer on the staff who might provide an explanation for her recurring nightmares

"Elements of suspense and mystery are cleverly integrated with the teen's problems resulting from what she witnessed as a child. Readers will once again fall under Nixon's spell as they enjoy this page-turner." SLJ

The **haunting**. Delacorte Press 1998 184p hardcover o.p. pa $5.50

Grades: 7 8 9 10   **Fic**

1. Ghost stories 2. Ghosts -- Fiction 3. Haunted houses -- Fiction
ISBN 0-385-32247-X; 0-440-22008-4 pa

LC 97-32658

When her mother inherits an old plantation house in the Louisiana countryside, fifteen-year-old Lia seeks to rid it of the evil spirit that haunts it

"This title has it all - a hint of romance, some really scary scenes, and a plucky heroine who successfully routs both outer and inner demons." Horn Book Guide

No crystal stair; a documentary novel of the life and work of Lewis Michaux, Harlem bookseller. by Vaunda Micheaux Nelson ; art work by R. Gregory Christie. Carolrhoda Lab 2012 188p. ill.

Grades: 6 7 8 9 10 11 12   **Fic**

1. African American authors 2. New York (N.Y.) -- Harlem 3. Booksellers and bookselling
ISBN 9780761361695

LC 2011021251

Coretta Scott King Author Honor Book (2013)

This "biographical novel presents the life and work of a man whose Harlem bookstore became an intellectual, literary haven for African Americans from 1939 until 1975. [The book proceeds t]hrough alternating voices of actual family members, acquaintances, journalists, and the subject himself, [Lewis] Michaux. . . . Influenced by the nationalism of Marcus Garvey and the intellect of Frederick Douglass, he believed that black people needed to educate themselves . . . [and h]e opened the National Memorial African Bookstore. . . . He accumulated works by black writers and talked to customers and passersby about cultural awareness and self-improvement. His bookstore attracted Harlem residents; civil-rights activists, including Malcolm X and Muhammad Ali; and political attention." (School Libr J)

Noel, Alyson

Radiance. Square Fish 2010 183p pa $7.99

Grades: 5 6 7 8   **Fic**

1. Ghost stories 2. Dead -- Fiction 3. Future life -- Fiction

ISBN 978-0-312-62917-5; 0-312-62917-6

LC 2010015840

After crossing the bridge into the afterlife, a place called Here where the time is always Now, Riley's existence continues in much the same way as when she was alive until she is given the job of Soul Catcher and, together with her teacher Bodhi, returns to earth for her first assignment, a ghost called the Radiant Boy who has been haunting an English castle for centuries and resisted all previous attempts to get him across the bridge.

"Narrating in a contemporary voice with an honest and comfortable cadence, Riley is imperfect, but always likable. . . . In the midst of this wildly fanciful setting, Noël is able to capture with nail-on-the-head accuracy common worries and concerns of today's tweens." SLJ

Other titles in this series are:
Dreamland (2011)
Shimmer (2011)

Nolan, Han

★ **Crazy**. Harcourt 2010 348p $17

Grades: 7 8 9 10   **Fic**

1. School stories 2. Friendship -- Fiction 3. Bereavement -- Fiction 4. Mental illness -- Fiction 5. Father-son relationship -- Fiction

ISBN 978-0-15-205109-9; 0-15-205109-0

LC 2009-49969

Fifteen-year-old loner Jason struggles to hide father's declining mental condition after his mother's death, but when his father disappears he must confide in the other members of a therapy group he has been forced to join at school.

"Nolan leavens this haunting but hopeful story with spot-on humor and a well-developed cast of characters." Booklist

A **face** in every window. Harcourt Brace & Co. 1999 264p hardcover o.p. pa $6.95

Grades: 7 8 9 10   **Fic**

1. Family problems 2. Mentally handicapped -- Fiction 3. People with mental disabilities

ISBN 0-15-201915-4; 0-15-206418-4 pa

LC 99-14230

After the death of his grandmother, who held the family together, teenage JP is left with a mentally challenged father

and a mother who seems ineffectual and constantly sick, and he feels everything sliding out of control

"Only a writer as talented as Nolan could make this improbable story line and bizarre cast of characters not only believable but also ultimately uplifting, intriguing, and memorable." Booklist

A **summer** of Kings. Harcourt 2006 334p $17

Grades: 6 7 8 9   **Fic**

1. Black Muslims -- Fiction 2. Race relations -- Fiction 3. African Americans -- Fiction

ISBN 0-15-205108-2

LC 2005-19487

Over the course of the summer of 1963, fourteen-year-old Esther Young discovers the passion within her when eighteen-year-old King-Roy Johnson, accused of murdering a white man in Alabama, comes to live with her family.

"Infused with rhetoric that is as meaningful today as it was two generations ago, this young teen's account of a life-changing summer not only opens a window to history, but also displays Nolan's brilliant gift for crafting profoundly appealing protagonists." SLJ

Nolen, Jerdine

Eliza's freedom road; an Underground Railroad diary. Simon & Schuster Books for Young Readers 2011 139p il map $14.99

Grades: 4 5 6 7   **Fic**

1. Diaries -- Fiction 2. Slavery -- Fiction 3. African Americans -- Fiction 4. Underground railroad -- Fiction

ISBN 1-4169-5814-2; 978-1-4169-5814-7

LC 2010-20931

A twelve-year-old slave girl begins writing in a journal where she documents her journey via the Underground Railroad from Alexandria, Virginia, to freedom in St. Catharines, Canada.

"Nolen reveals some of the traumas and tragedies of slavery but keeps her focus on those things that allow Eliza the power to escape: literacy, her mother's legacy, a bit of luck and a great deal of courage." Kirkus

Includes bibliographical references

Norcliffe, James

The **boy** who could fly. Egmont USA 2010 312p $15.99

Grades: 5 6 7 8   **Fic**

1. Fantasy fiction 2. Flight -- Fiction 3. Siblings -- Fiction 4. Abandoned children -- Fiction

ISBN 978-1-60684-084-9; 1-60684-084-3

LC 2009-41167

First published 2009 in New Zealand with title: The loblolly boy

Having grown up in a miserable home for abandoned children, a young boy jumps at the chance to exchange places with the mysterious, flying "loblolly boy," but once he takes on this new identity, he discovers what a harsh price he must pay.

"Norcliffe has written an imaginative and richly atmospheric fantasy with sympathetic characters. . . . This is . . . a haunting tale that will capture most readers' imaginations." Booklist

Nordin, Sofia

In the wild; translated by Maria Lundin. House of Anansi Press 2005 115p hardcover o.p. pa $6.95
Grades: 4 5 6 7   **Fic**
   1. Bullies -- Fiction 2. Wilderness survival -- Fiction
   ISBN 0-88899-648-9; 0-88899-663-2 pa
   Originally published in Swedish
   "Amanda, the target of harassment by her classmates, is on an adventure trip with her sixth-grade class. When she and one of the bullies, Philip, are separated from the group and become lost in the wilderness, they are forced to work together to survive. . . . Nordin realistically depicts the psychological effects of relentless hounding. . . . The translation is smooth and the text flows naturally. . . . Well written, and a lightning-fast read." SLJ

North, Pearl

Libyrinth. Tor Teen 2009 332p $17.95
Grades: 7 8 9 10   **Fic**
   1. Fantasy fiction 2. Books and reading -- Fiction
   ISBN 978-0-7653-2096-4; 0-7653-2096-7
                                              LC 2009-1514
   In a distant future where Libyrarians preserve and protect the ancient books that are housed in the fortress-like Libyrinth, Haly is imprisoned by Eradicants, who believe that the written word is evil, and she must try to mend the rift between the two groups before their war for knowledge destroys them all.
   "Among this novel's pleasures are the many anonymous quotations scattered throughout, snatches of prose that Haly hears as she goes about her chores . . . all of which are carefully identified at the end. The complex moral issues posed by this thoughtful and exciting tale are just as fascinating." Publ Wkly

The **boy** from Ilysies. Tor 2010 316p $17.99
Grades: 7 8 9 10   **Fic**
   1. Fantasy fiction 2. Books and reading -- Fiction
   ISBN 978-0-7653-2097-1; 0-7653-2097-5
                                              LC 2010-36676
   Cast out of the Libyrinth after being tricked into committing a crime, young Po may return only if he completes a dangerous mission to retrieve a legendary artifact that could either be the answer to all of the Libyrinth's problems, or could destroy the world.
   "North has created that rare thing: a second book in a series that is stronger than the first." SLJ

North, Phoebe

Starglass; by Phoebe North. 1st ed. Simon & Schuster Books for Young Readers 2013 448 p. (hardcover) $17.99
Grades: 7 8 9 10   **Fic**
   1. Jews -- Fiction 2. Underground movements -- Fiction 3. Interplanetary voyages -- Fiction 4. Science fiction 5. Insurgency -- Fiction 6. Fathers and daughters -- Fiction
   ISBN 1442459530; 9781442459533; 9781442459557
                                              LC 2012021171
   In this book by Phoebe North, "[o]n a generation ship that left Earth 500 years ago, a teenager grapples with disillusionment and emotional isolation as her society nears the planet it intends to land on. Terra lives with her harsh, alcoholic father and awaits her adult job assignment . . . from the strict ruling Council." She "discovers a secret rebellion aboard the Asherah." (Kirkus Reviews)

Northrop, Michael

Plunked; Michael Northrop. Scholastic Press 2012 247 p. $16.99
Grades: 4 5 6 7 8   **Fic**
   1. Fear -- Fiction 2. Schools -- Fiction 3. Baseball -- Fiction 4. Perseverance (Ethics) -- Fiction
   ISBN 0545297141; 9780545297141
                                              LC 2011032737
   This children's story by Michael Northrop centers on the "Sixth grader Jack Mogens [who] has it all figured out: He's got his batting routine down, and his outfielding earns him a starting spot alongside his best friend Andy on their Little League team, the Tall Pines Braves. He even manages to have a not-totally-embarrassing conversation with Katie, the team's killer shortstop. But in the first game of the season, a powerful stray pitch brings everything Jack's worked so hard for crashing down around his ears. . . ." Jack then has to face his fears and anxieties and return to the game. (Publisher's note)

Trapped. Scholastic Press 2011 225p $17.99
Grades: 7 8 9 10   **Fic**
   1. School stories 2. Blizzards -- Fiction
   ISBN 978-0-545-21012-6; 0-545-21012-7
                                              LC 2010-36595
   Seven high school students are stranded at their New England high school during a week-long blizzard that shuts down the power and heat, freezes the pipes, and leaves them wondering if they will survive.
   "Northrop is cooly brilliant in his setup, amassing the tension along with the snow, shrewdly observing the shifting social dynamics within the group." Bull Cent Child Books

Norville, Rod

Moonshine express; with a history of moonshine today and yesterday. Four Seasons Pub. 2003 xxix, 195p pa $13.95
Grades: 6 7 8 9   **Fic**
   1. Moonshining -- Fiction
   ISBN 1-89129-99-2
   "This is an edge-of-the-seat thriller." SLJ

Nuzum, K. A.

A **small** white scar; [by] K.A. Nuzum. 1st ed.; Joanna Cotler Books 2006 180p $15.99; lib bdg $16.89
Grades: 6 7 8 9   **Fic**
   1. Twins -- Fiction 2. Brothers -- Fiction 3. Cowhands -- Fiction 4. Mentally handicapped -- Fiction
   ISBN 978-0-06-075639-0; 0-06-075639-X; 978-0-06-075640-6 lib bdg; 0-06-075640-3 lib bdg
                                              LC 2005017721
   Fifteen-year-old Will Bennon leaves his family and begins life as a cowboy, but his mentally retarded twin brother follows him and joins the journey.
   "The images of the stark 1940s Colorado countryside suffering from drought, and the wild animals that popu-

late it, are clearly drawn with poetic turns of phrase. Characters, plot, and theme all combine to make a compelling story." SLJ

Nye, Naomi Shihab

Going going. Greenwillow Books 2005 232p il $15.99; lib bdg $16.89

Grades: 7 8 9 10   **Fic**

1. Small business -- Fiction 2. Political activists -- Fiction

ISBN 0-688-16185-5; 0-06-029366-7 lib bdg

LC 2004-10146

In San Antonio, Texas, sixteen-year-old Florrie leads her friends and a new boyfriend in a campaign which supports small businesses and protests the effects of chain stores.

The "novel's strong message belongs honestly to Florrie, whose vivid individualism will engage readers. Nye evokes history through small details, inviting readers to view their own cities and towns with a new perspective." Horn Book Guide

★ **Habibi**. Simon & Schuster Bks. for Young Readers 1997 259p $16; pa $5.99

Grades: 7 8 9 10   **Fic**

1. Jewish-Arab relations -- Fiction

ISBN 0-689-80149-1; 0-689-82523-4 pa

LC 97-10943

When fourteen-year-old Liyanne Abboud, her younger brother, and her parents move from St. Louis to a new home between Jerusalem and the Palestinian village where her father was born, they face many changes and must deal with the tensions between Jews and Palestinians

"Poetically imaged and leavened with humor, the story renders layered and complex history understandable through character and incident." SLJ

Nylund, Eric S.

The **Resisters**; [by] Eric Nylund. Random House 2011 210p $16.99; lib bdg $19.99

Grades: 5 6 7 8   **Fic**

1. Science fiction 2. Brainwashing -- Fiction 3. Extraterrestrial beings -- Fiction

ISBN 978-0-375-86856-6; 0-375-86856-9; 978-0-375-96856-3 lib bdg; 0-375-96856-3 lib bdg

LC 2010-19230

When twelve-year-olds Madison and Felix kidnap him, Ethan learns that the Earth has been taken over by aliens and that all the adults in the world are under mind control.

"Ethan, Felix, and Madison are multidimensional characters with authentic emotions and realistic attitudes and motives. This book mixes considerable background exposition with fast-moving action. While the immediate plot issues are resolved, there are plenty of threads left dangling. Middle school boys will enjoy the high-tech battle action and will look forward to the next installment." SLJ

Nyoka, Gail

Mella and the N'anga; an African tale. Sumach Press 2006 158p pa $9.95

Grades: 5 6 7 8   **Fic**

1. Fantasy fiction

ISBN 1-894549-49-X

In ancient mythical Zimbabwe, Mella and two other girls train with the N'anga, a mysterious, spiritual advisor, to become Daughters of the Hunt and rescue their people.

"The language reinforces the sense of the ancient court setting, and many passages glimmer with mysticism linked to the beauty of the natural world. Mella's thrilling, magical, girl-powered quest will attract many readers." Booklist

O Guilin, Peadar

The **inferior**. David Fickling Books 2008 439p $16.99

Grades: 8 9 10 11 12   **Fic**

1. Science fiction 2. Hunting -- Fiction 3. Cannibalism -- Fiction

ISBN 978-0-385-75145-2; 0-385-75145-1

LC 2007-34496

In a brutal world where hunting and cannibalism are necessary for survival, something is going terribly wrong as even the globes on the roof of the world are fighting, but one young man, influenced by a beautiful and mysterious stranger, begins to envision new possibilities.

This is an "epic story of survival, betrayal, and community. . . . This well-paced fantasy/science fiction blend perfectly introduces community conflict at a base level. . . . Easy to follow and intriguing at every turn, TheInferior will hold readers from page to page, chapter to chapter, to the very end." SLJ

O'Brien, Annemarie

Lara's gift; by Annemarie O'Brien. Alfred A. Knopf 2013 176 p. (hardcover) $16.99; (ebook) $50.97; (library binding) 19.99

Grades: 5 6 7 8 9   **Fic**

1. Dogs -- Fiction 2. Borzoi -- Fiction 3. Visions -- Fiction 4. Sex role -- Fiction 5. Family life -- Russia -- Fiction 6. Fathers and daughters -- Fiction

ISBN 0307931749; 9780307931740; 9780307975485; 9780375971051

LC 2012034070

In this book, on "a remote estate in 1910s Russia, Lara must prove herself capable of following in her father's footsteps as the head of a prestigious borzoi breeding kennel. There are so many things between her and the realization of her dream. That she is female is the biggest obstacle, but she must also hide the fact that she has visions of future occurrences that involve the dogs and the dangerous wolves that populate the estate." (Kirkus Reviews)

O'Brien, Caragh M.

★ **Birthmarked**. Roaring Brook Press 2010 362p map $16.99

Grades: 6 7 8 9 10   **Fic**

1. Science fiction 2. Midwives -- Fiction 3. Genetic engineering -- Fiction

ISBN 978-1-59643-569-8; 1-59643-569-0

LC 2010-281716

In a future world baked dry by the sun and divided into those who live inside the wall and those who live outside it, sixteen-year-old midwife Gaia Stone is forced into a difficult choice when her parents are arrested and taken into the city.

"Readers who enjoy adventures with a strong heroine standing up to authority against the odds will enjoy this compelling tale." SLJ

O'Brien, Johnny

Day of the assassins; a Jack Christie novel. [illustrated by Nick Hardcastle] Templar Books 2009 211p il $15.99

Grades: 5 6 7 8   **Fic**

1. Princes 2. Science fiction 3. Adventure fiction 4. Time travel -- Fiction 5. World War, 1914-1918 -- Fiction

ISBN 978-0-7636-4595-3; 0-7636-4595-8

LC 2009023630

Fifteen-year-old Jack is sent to 1914 Europe as a pawn in the battle between his long-lost father, who has built a time machine, and a secret network of scientists who want to prevent him from trying to use it to change history for the better.

"From an explosive escape out of captivity to a much-anticipated scene that decides the fate of World War I, the end of the book has plenty of action. Historical information and photographs about the events and people central to the period enhance this title even more." SLJ

Another title about Jack is:
Day of deliverance (2010)

O'Brien, Robert C.

★ **Mrs.** Frisby and the rats of NIMH; [by] Robert C. O'Brien; illustrated by Zena Bernstein. Atheneum Books for Young Readers 2006 233p il $18; pa $6.99

Grades: 4 5 6 7   **Fic**

1. Mice -- Fiction 2. Rats -- Fiction

ISBN 978-0-689-20651-1; 0-689-20651-8; 978-0-689-71068-1 pa; 0-689-71068-2 pa

A reissue of the title first published 1971

Awarded the Newbery Medal, 1972

Having no one to help her with her problems, a widowed mouse visits the rats whose former imprisonment in a laboratory made them wise and long lived.

"The story is fresh and ingenious, the style witty, and the plot both hilarious and convincing." Saturday Rev

★ **Z** for Zachariah. Atheneum Pubs. 1975 246p hardcover o.p. pa $7.99

Grades: 7 8 9 10   **Fic**

1. Science fiction

ISBN 0-689-30442-0; 1-416-93921-0 pa

Seemingly the only person left alive after a nuclear war, a sixteen-year-old girl is relieved to see a man arrive into her valley until she realizes that he is a tyrant and she must somehow escape.

"The journal form is used by O'Brien very effectively, with no lack of drama and contrast, and the pace and suspense of the story are adroitly maintained until the dramatic and surprising ending." Bull Cent Child Books

O'Connell, Tyne

True love, the sphinx, and other unsolvable riddles; a comedy in four voices. [by] Tyne O'Connell. 1st U.S. ed.; Bloomsbury 2007 225p $16.95

Grades: 7 8 9 10   **Fic**

1. Love stories 2. School stories 3. Friendship -- Fiction

ISBN 978-1-59990-050-6; 1-59990-050-5

LC 2007002596

While on a class trip in Egypt, two teenaged best friends from an American private boys' school and two teenaged best friends from a British private girls' school meet each other, and must endure many misunderstandings on their path to true love.

"This flirty, fun romcom, told from four distinctive points of view, reads like an old-time comedy of errors. O'Connell describes Egypt with such vitality and richness that it shines as a separate character." SLJ

O'Connor, Barbara

Fame and glory in Freedom, Georgia. Farrar, Straus & Giroux 2003 104p $16; pa $6.95

Grades: 4 5 6 7   **Fic**

1. School stories 2. Contests -- Fiction

ISBN 0-374-32258-9; 0-374-40018-0 pa

LC 2002-190212

Unpopular sixth-grader Burdette Bird Weaver persuades the new boy at school, whom everyone thinks is mean and dumb, to be her partner for a spelling bee that might win her everything she's ever wanted

"An idiosyncratic group of characters play out this touching and well-paced story about friendship, family, and connection." Horn Books

Greetings from nowhere. Farrar, Straus and Giroux 2008 198p $16

Grades: 4 5 6 7   **Fic**

1. Hotels and motels -- Fiction

ISBN 978-0-374-39937-5; 0-374-39937-9

LC 2006-37439

In North Carolina's Great Smoky Mountains, a troubled boy and his mother, a happy family seeking adventure, a man and his lonely daughter, and the widow who must sell the rundown motel that has been her home for decades, meet and are transformed by their shared experiences.

"The plainspoken text is clean, direct, and honest in its portrayal of pain and hope." Booklist

★ **How** to steal a dog; a novel. Farrar, Straus & Giroux 2007 170p pa $6.99; $16

Grades: 4 5 6   **Fic**

1. Dogs -- Fiction 2. Siblings -- Fiction 3. Homeless persons -- Fiction

ISBN 0-312-56112-1 pa; 0-374-33497-8; 978-0-312-56112-3 pa; 978-0-374-33497-0

LC 2005-40166

Living in the family car in their small North Carolina town, Georgina persuades her younger brother to help her in an elaborate scheme to get money by stealing a dog and then claiming the reward that the owners are bound to offer

This is told "in stripped-down, unsentimental prose. . . . The myriad effects of homelessness and the realistic picture of a moral quandary will surely generate discussion." Booklist

O'Connor, Sheila

★ **Sparrow** Road. G. P. Putnam's Sons 2011 247p $16.99

Grades: 5 6 7 8   Fic

1. Artists -- Fiction
ISBN 978-0-399-25458-1; 0-399-25458-7
LC 2010-28290

Twelve-year-old Raine spends the summer at a mysterious artists colony and discovers a secret about her past.

This is a "beautifully written novel. . . . Readers finding themselves in this quiet world will find plenty of space to imagine and dream for themselves." Kirkus

O'Dell, Kathleen

Agnes Parker . . . girl in progress. Dial Bks. 2003 156p hardcover o.p. pa $6.99

Grades: 4 5 6 7   Fic

1. Bullies 2. Friendship -- Fiction
ISBN 0-8037-2648-1; 0-14-240228-1 pa
LC 2001-58256

As she starts in the sixth grade, Agnes faces challenges with her old best friend, a longtime bully, a wonderful new classmate and neighbor, and herself

"This is a thoughtful, gently humorous, and resonant cusp-of-coming-of-age novel." Horn Book Guide

Other titles about Agnes Parker are:

Agnes Parker . . . Happy camper? (2005)

Agnes Parker . . . Keeping cool in middle school (2007)

O'Dell, Scott

★ **Island** of the Blue Dolphins; illustrated by Ted Lewin. 50th anniversary ed.; Houghton Mifflin Books for Children 2010 177p il $22

Grades: 5 6 7 8   Fic

1. Native Americans -- Fiction 2. Wilderness survival -- Fiction
ISBN 978-0-547-42483-5; 0-547-42483-3

A reissue of the newly illustrated edition published 1990; first published 1960

Awarded the Newbery Medal, 1961

Left alone on a beautiful but isolated island off the coast of California, a young Indian girl spends eighteen years, not only merely surviving through her enormous courage and self-reliance, but also finding a measure of happiness in her solitary life.

The edition illustrated by Ted Lewin "features twelve full-page, full-color watercolors in purple and blue hues that are appropriate to the island setting. This handsome gift-edition version includes a new introduction by Lois Lowry to commemorate the book's fiftieth anniversary." Horn Book Guide

Sing down the moon. Houghton Mifflin 1970 137p hardcover o.p. pa $6.99

Grades: 5 6 7 8   Fic

1. Navajo Indians -- Fiction
ISBN 0-395-10919-1; 978-0-547-40632-9 pa; 0-547-40632-0 pa

A Newbery Medal honor book, 1971

"There is a poetic sonority of style, a sense of identification, and a note of indomitable courage and stoicism that is touching and impressive." Saturday Rev

Streams to the river, river to the sea; a novel of Sacagawea. Houghton Mifflin 1986 191p hardcover o.p. pa $6.99

Grades: 5 6 7 8   Fic

1. Interpreters 2. Guides (Persons) 3. Native Americans -- Fiction
ISBN 0-395-40430-4; 0-618-96642-0 pa
LC 86-936

"An informative and involving choice for American history students and pioneer-adventure readers." Bull Cent Child Books

Thunder rolling in the mountains; [by] Scott O'Dell and Elizabeth Hall. Houghton Mifflin 1992 128p map $17

Grades: 5 6 7 8   Fic

1. Nez Perce Indians -- Fiction
ISBN 0-395-59966-0
LC 91-15961

"This is a sad, dark-hued story told in Mr. O'Dell's lean, affecting prose." Child Book Rev Serv

★ **Zia.** Houghton Mifflin 1976 179p hardcover o.p. pa $6.95

Grades: 5 6 7 8   Fic

1. Native Americans -- Fiction 2. Christian missions -- Fiction
ISBN 0-395-24393-9; 978-0-547-40633-6 pa; 0-547-40633-9 pa
LC 75-44156

"Zia is an excellent story in its own right, written in a clear, quiet, and reflective style which is in harmony with the plot and characterization." SLJ

O'Hearn, Kate

Kira. Kane Miller 2009 309p (Shadow of the dragon) $16.99

Grades: 6 7 8 9   Fic

1. Fantasy fiction 2. Dragons -- Fiction 3. Prisoners -- Fiction
ISBN 978-1-935279-05-1; 1-935279-05-X

"With plenty of exciting action sequences, this debut fantasy will appeal to girls clamoring for a hearty heroine, and the cliff-hanger ending will have readers checking the release date for the next book." Booklist

Another title in this series is:

Elspeth (2010)

O'Neal, Eilis

★ The **false** princess. Egmont USA 2010 319p $16.99

Grades: 6 7 8 9   Fic

1. Magic -- Fiction 2. Princesses -- Fiction 3. Witchcraft -- Fiction 4. Conspiracies -- Fiction
ISBN 978-1-60684-079-5; 1-60684-079-7
LC 2009040903

This is a "compelling fantasy, which is filled with magic, political drama, and romance." Publ Wkly

O'Rourke, Erica

Tangled; Erica O'Rourke. KTeen/Kensington 2012 ix, 326 p.p (trade pbk.) $9.95

Grades: 7 8 9 10   Fic
    1. Occult fiction 2. Magic -- Fiction 3. Interpersonal relations -- Fiction 4. Secrets -- Fiction 5. Friendship -- Fiction
ISBN 0758267053; 9780758267054
       LC 2011277358
This is the second in the "Torn" trilogy. To help her dead friend"s sister, Mo must "summon Luc for help. But help for Constance comes with a price—the Quartoren, leaders of the Arcs, want Mo to repair the ley lines from which they draw their power." Several others require her attention as well, pulling Mo in several directions and exacerbating her struggle of living in both the human and magical worlds. (Kirkus)

Torn. Kensington 2011 310p pa $9.95

Grades: 7 8 9 10   Fic
    1. Magic -- Fiction 2. Homicide -- Fiction 3. Friendship -- Fiction
ISBN 978-0-7582-6703-0; 0-7582-6703-7
Mo Fitzgerald knows about secrets. But when she witnesses her best friend's murder, she discovers Verity was hiding things she never could have guessed. To find the answers she needs and the vengeance she craves, Mo will have to enter a world of raw magic and shifting alliances. And she'll have to choose between two very different, equally dangerous guys.
    "O'Rourke's heroine is refreshing: determined, spunky, and unpredictable. . . . Torn should . . . satisfy readers with an insatiable thirst for well-written, fast-paced fantasy and leave them eager for the next installment in the series." SLJ

Oaks, J. Adams

    ★ **Why** I fight; a novel. Atheneum Books for Young Readers 2009 228p $16.99; pa $8.99

Grades: 8 9 10 11 12   Fic
    1. Uncles -- Fiction 2. Violence -- Fiction 3. Criminals -- Fiction
ISBN 978-1-4169-1177-7; 1-4169-1177-4; 978-1-4424-0254-6 pa; 1-4424-0254-7 pa
       LC 2007-46433
After his house burns down, twelve-year-old Wyatt Reaves takes off with his uncle, and the two of them drive from town to town for six years, earning money mostly by fighting, until Wyatt finally confronts his parents one last time.
    "Oaks' first novel is a breathtaking debut with an unforgettable protagonist. . . . The voice Oaks has created for Wyatt to tell his painful and poignant story is a wonderful combination of the unlettered and the eloquent." Booklist

Oates, Joyce Carol

    ★ **Big** Mouth & Ugly Girl. HarperCollins Pubs. 2002 265p hardcover o.p. pa $7.99

Grades: 7 8 9 10   Fic
    1. School stories 2. Friendship -- Fiction
ISBN 0-06-623756-4; 0-06-447347-3 pa
       LC 2001-24601
When sixteen-year-old Matt is falsely accused of threatening to blow up his high school and his friends turn against him, an unlikely classmate comes to his aid.
    "Readers will be propelled through these pages by an intense curiosity to learn how events will play out. Oates has written a fast-moving, timely, compelling story." SLJ

Freaky green eyes. Harper Tempest 2003 341p hardcover o.p. pa $6.99

Grades: 7 8 9 10   Fic
    1. Domestic violence -- Fiction
ISBN 0-06-623757-2 lib bdg; 0-06-447348-1 pa
       LC 2002-32868
Fifteen-year-old Frankie relates the events of the year leading up to her mother's mysterious disappearance and her own struggle to discover and accept the truth about her parents' relationship.
    "Oates pulls readers into a fast-paced, first-person thriller. . . . An absorbing page-turner." Booklist

Okimoto, Jean Davies

    Maya and the cotton candy boy. Endicott and Hugh 2011 $16.99; pa $9.99

Grades: 4 5 6 7   Fic
    1. School stories 2. Siblings -- Fiction 3. Immigrants -- Fiction
ISBN 978-0-9823167-4-0; 0-9823167-4-7; 978-0-9823167-5-7 pa; 0-9823167-5-5 pa
Newly arrived from Kazakhstan, twelve-year-old Maya Alazova resents the way her mother babies her brother, but when she leaves her English Language Learner program for mainstream classes and has to deal with a boy, a bully, and conflict at home, she finds her brother can help with their new culture in ways their parents can't.
    "Maya tells her story well, and observant readers will come away with a better understanding of the sacrifices made by similar families." SLJ

Okorafor, Nnedi

    Akata witch. Viking 2011 349p $16.99

Grades: 6 7 8 9   Fic
    1. Fantasy fiction 2. Witchcraft -- Fiction 3. Albinos and albinism -- Fiction
ISBN 978-0-670-01196-4; 0-670-01196-7
"Although 12-year-old Sunny is Nigerian, she was born in America, and her Nigerian classmates see her as an outsider. Worse, she's an albino, an obvious target for bullies and suspected of being a ghost or a witch. Things change, however, when she has a vision of impending nuclear war. Then her classmate Orlu and his friend Chichi turn out to be Leopard People—witches—and insist that she is, too. . . . This tale is filled with marvels and is sure to appeal to teens whose interest in fantasy goes beyond dwarves and fairies." Publ Wkly

Okorafor, Nnedimma

    Zahrah the Windseeker; by Nnedi Okorafor-Mbachu. Houghton Mifflin 2005 308p il $16

Grades: 5 6 7 8   **Fic**
   1. Fantasy fiction
   ISBN 0-618-34090-4
                                      LC 2004-15783
   Zahrah, a timid thirteen-year-old girl, undertakes a dangerous quest into the Forbidden Greeny Jungle to seek the
antidote for her best friend after he is bitten by a snake, and
finds knowledge, courage, and hidden powers along the way.
   "Okorafor-Mbachu's evocative setting will draw experienced fantasy readers with its heady mix of the familiar and
the strange." Booklist

The **shadow** speaker; [by] Nnedi Okorafor-Mbachu. Jump at the Sun/Hyperion Books for Children
2007 336p hardcover o.p. pa $8.99
Grades: 7 8 9 10   **Fic**
   1. Fantasy fiction 2. Science fiction
   ISBN 978-1-4231-0033-1; 1-4231-0033-6; 978-1-
   4231-0036-2 pa; 1-4231-0036-0 pa
                                      LC 2007-13313
   In West Africa in 2070, after fifteen-year-old "shadow
speaker" Ejii witnesses her father's beheading, she embarks
on a dangerous journey across the Sahara to find Jaa, her
father's killer, and upon finding her, she also discovers
a greater purpose to her life and to the mystical powers
she possesses.
   "Okorafor-Mbachu does an excellent job of combining
both science fiction and fantasy elements into this novel. .
. . The action moves along at a quick pace and will keep
most readers on their toes and wanting more at the end of the
novel." Voice Youth Advocates

Oliver, Jana G.
   The **demon** trapper's daughter; a demon trapper
novel. [by] Jana Oliver. St. Martin's Griffin 2011
355p pa $9.99
Grades: 7 8 9 10   **Fic**
   1. Demonology -- Fiction 2. Apprentices -- Fiction 3.
   Supernatural -- Fiction 4. Father-daughter relationship
   -- Fiction
   ISBN 978-0-312-61478-2; 0-312-61478-0
                                      LC 2010-38860
   In 2018 Atlanta, Georgia, after a demon threatens seventeen-year-old Riley Blackthorne's life and murders her
father, a legendary demon trapper to whom she was apprenticed, her father's partner, Beck, steps in to care for her,
knowing she hates him.
   "With a strong female heroine, a fascinating setting, and
a complex, thrill-soaked story, this series is off to a strong
start." Publ Wkly

Soul thief; [by] Jana Oliver. St. Martin's Griffin
2011 339p (A demon trappers novel) pa $9.99
Grades: 7 8 9 10   **Fic**
   1. Orphans -- Fiction 2. Demonology -- Fiction 3.
   Apprentices -- Fiction 4. Supernatural -- Fiction
   ISBN 978-0-312-61479-9
                                      LC 2011019930
   In 2018 Atlanta, Georgia, seventeen-year-old apprentice
Demon Trapper Riley Blackthorne must deal with unwanted
fame, an unofficial bodyguard, an overprotective friend, the

Vatican's own Demon Trappers, and an extremely powerful
Grade Five demon who is stalking her.

Oliver, Lauren
   ★ **Liesl** & Po; illustrated by Kei Acedera. Harper 2011 307p il $16.99
Grades: 4 5 6 7   **Fic**
   1. Ghost stories 2. Fantasy fiction 3. Magic -- Fiction
   4. Bereavement -- Fiction
   ISBN 978-0-06-201451-1; 0-06-201451-X
   Liesl lives in a tiny attic bedroom, locked away by her
cruel stepmother. Her only friends are the shadows and the
mice—until one night a ghost appears from the darkness.
It is Po, who comes from the Other Side. That same night,
an alchemist's apprentice, Will, accidentally bungles an
important delivery. He switches a box containing the most
powerful magic in the world with one containing something
decidedly less remarkable.
   This is a "charming, insightful fantasy. . . . This original
fairy tale, told by a wise and humorous omniscient narrator
and peopled with broadly drawn but instantly recognizable
characters, avoids sentimentality to show the magic of accepting loss without letting go and finding joy in the lives
left behind." Booklist

Pandemonium; Lauren Oliver. 1st ed.; Harper-
CollinsPublishers 2012 375p $17.99
Grades: 8 9 10 11   **Fic**
   1. Science fiction 2. Love -- Fiction 3. Resistance to
   government -- Fiction
   ISBN 978-0-06-197806-7
                                      LC 2011024241
   After falling in love, Lena and Alex flee their oppressive
society where love is outlawed and everyone must receive
"the cure"—an operation that makes them immune to the
delirium of love—but Lena alone manages to find her way
to a community of resistance fighters, and although she is
bereft without the boy she loves, her struggles seem to be
leading her toward a new love.

Requiem; Lauren Oliver. Harper 2013 432 p.
(hardcover) $18.99
Grades: 8 9 10 11 12   **Fic**
   1. Science fiction 2. Resistance to government -- Fiction
   3. Love -- Fiction 4. Marriage -- Fiction 5. Friendship
   -- Fiction 6. Best friends -- Fiction 7. Government,
   Resistance to -- Fiction
   ISBN 0062014536; 9780062014535
                                      LC 2012030236
   This young adult novel, by Lauren Oliver, is the conclusion to the "Delirium" trilogy. "The nascent rebellion . . . has
ignited into an all-out revolution . . . , and Lena is at the center of the fight. After rescuing Julian from a death sentence,
Lena and her friends fled to the Wilds. But the Wilds are no
longer a safe haven. . . . As Lena navigates the increasingly
dangerous terrain of the Wilds, her best friend, Hana, lives a
safe, loveless life in Portland." (Publisher's note)

   ★ The **spindlers**; Lauren Oliver ; illustrated
by Iacopo Bruno. 1st ed. Harper 2012 246 p. ill.
(hardcover) $16.99

Grades: 4 5 6   **Fic**

1. Soul -- Fiction 2. Brothers and sisters -- Fiction
ISBN 0061978086; 9780061978081

LC 2012009698

This children's fantasy novel, by Lauren Oliver, is about a young girl who travels to a fantasy realm to rescue her younger brother from monsters. "When Liza's brother, Patrick, changes overnight, Liza knows exactly what has happened: The spindlers have gotten to him and stolen his soul. . . . To rescue Patrick, Liza must go Below, armed with little more than her wits and a broom. There, she uncovers a vast world populated with . . . terrible dangers." (Publisher's note)

Olsen, Sylvia

White girl. Sono Nis Press 2004 235p pa $8.95
Grades: 7 8 9 10   **Fic**

1. Prejudices -- Fiction 2. Native Americans -- Fiction
ISBN 1-5503-9147-X

"The talk is contemporary and relaxed, and the characters will hold readers as much as the novel's extraordinary sense of place." Booklist

The **girl** with a baby. Sono Nis Press 2004 203p pa $8.95

Grades: 7 8 9 10   **Fic**

1. Teenage mothers -- Fiction 2. Native Americans -- Fiction
ISBN 1-55039-142-9

This "novel tells of teenage mother Jane, 14, who wants to stay in school and raise her baby, Destiny, to be respectful of tradition and smart in the new ways. Jane's family left the reservation because of resentment against Dad, who is white; now in a white area, they face prejudice for being Indian. . . . Jane's home . . . is drawn without romanticism, and . . . Jane's first-person narrative never denies how hard life is, and how thrilling." Booklist

Olson, Gretchen

Call me Hope; a novel. by Gretchen Olson. Little, Brown & Company 2007 272p hardcover o.p. pa $5.99

Grades: 4 5 6   **Fic**

1. Child abuse -- Fiction 2. Mother-daughter relationship -- Fiction
ISBN 978-0-316-01236-2; 0-316-01236-X; 978-0-316-01239-3 pa; 0-316-01239-4 pa

LC 2006027896

In Oregon, eleven-year-old Hope begins coping with her mother's verbal abuse by devising survival strategies for herself based on a history unit about the Holocaust, and meanwhile she works toward buying a pair of purple hiking boots by helping at a second-hand shop

"Hope is a winsome character whose bravery and determination will resonate with middle-grade readers." Booklist

Omololu, Cynthia Jaynes

Dirty little secrets; [by] C.J. Omololu. Walker & Co. 2010 212p $16.99

Grades: 8 9 10 11 12   **Fic**

1. School stories 2. Death -- Fiction 3. Compulsive behavior -- Fiction 4. Mother-daughter relationship -- Fiction
ISBN 978-0-8027-8660-9; 0-8027-8660-X

LC 2009-22461

When her unstable mother dies unexpectedly, sixteen-year-old Lucy must take control and find a way to keep the long-held secret of her mother's compulsive hoarding from being revealed to friends, neighbors, and especially the media.

"As a valuable new addition to heartbreaking but honest books about teens immersed in emotionally distressed families, . . . this potent and creatively woven page-turner brings a traumatic situation front and center." SLJ

Oppel, Kenneth

Airborn. Eos 2004 355p $16.99; lib bdg $17.89
Grades: 7 8 9 10   **Fic**

1. Fantasy fiction 2. Airships -- Fiction 3. Imaginary creatures
ISBN 0-06-053180-0; 0-06-053181-9 lib bdg

LC 2003-15642

Michael L. Printz Award honor book, 2005

Matt, a young cabin boy aboard an airship, and Kate, a wealthy young girl traveling with her chaperone, team up to search for the existence of mysterious winged creatures reportedly living hundreds of feet above the Earth's surface.

"This rousing adventure has something for everyone: appealing and enterprising characters, nasty villains, and a little romance." SLJ

Other titles in this series are:
Skybreaker (2005)
Starclimber (2009)

★ **Half** brother. Scholastic Press 2010 375p $17.99

Grades: 7 8 9 10   **Fic**

1. Research -- Fiction 2. Chimpanzees -- Fiction 3. Family life -- Fiction
ISBN 978-0-545-22925-8; 0-545-22925-1

LC 2010-2696

In 1973, when a renowned Canadian behavioral psychologist pursues his latest research project—an experiment to determine whether chimpanzees can acquire advanced language skills—he brings home a baby chimp named Zan and asks his thirteen-year-old son to treat Zan like a little brother.

"Oppel has taken a fascinating subject and molded it into a topnotch read. Deftly integrating family dynamics, animal-rights issues, and the painful lessons of growing up, Half Brother draws readers in from the beginning and doesn't let go." SLJ

Silverwing. Simon & Schuster Bks. for Young Readers 1997 217p hardcover o.p. pa $6.99
Grades: 5 6 7 8   **Fic**

1. Bats -- Fiction
ISBN 0-689-81529-8; 1-4169-4998-4 pa

LC 97-10977

When a newborn bat named Shade but sometimes called "Runt" becomes separated from his colony during migration, he grows in ways that prepare him for even greater journeys

"Oppel's bats are fully developed characters who, if not quite cuddly, will certainly earn readers' sympathy and re-

spect. In Silverwing the author has created an intriguing microcosm of rival species, factions, and religions." Horn Book
Other titles in this series are:
Sunwing (2000)
Firewing (2003)
Darkwing (2007)

Skybreaker. Eos 2005 369p il hardcover o.p. lib bdg $17.89; pa $6.99
Grades: 7 8 9 10   **Fic**
1. Fantasy fiction 2. Airships -- Fiction
ISBN 0-06-053227-0; 0-06-053228-9 lib bdg; 0-06-053229-7 pa
LC 2005-08386
Matt Cruse, a student at the Airship Academy, and Kate de Vries, a young heiress, team up with a gypsy and a daring captain, to find a long-lost airship, rumored to carry a treasure beyond imagination.
This "starts with a bang and doesn't let up until the satisfying ending. . . . This worthy companion to Airborn maintains its roller-coaster thrills in true swashbuckling style." SLJ

Starclimber. Eos 2009 390p $17.99; lib bdg $18.89
Grades: 7 8 9 10   **Fic**
1. Fantasy fiction 2. Airships -- Fiction 3. Outer space -- Exploration -- Fiction
ISBN 978-0-06-085057-9; 0-06-085057-4; 978-0-06-085058-6 lib bdg; 0-06-085058-2 lib bdg
LC 2008019747
As members of the first crew of astralnauts, Matt Cruse and Kate De Vries journey into outer space on the Starclimber and face a series of catastrophes that threaten the survival of all on board.
This "is a thrilling roller-coaster ride of a book, full of humor and derring-do and guaranteed to keep readers up long past midnight." SLJ

Such wicked intent; Kenneth Oppel. Simon & Schuster Books For Young Readers 2012 320 p. (hardback) $16.99; (paperback) $9.99
Grades: 7 8 9 10   **Fic**
1. Love stories 2. Death -- Fiction 3. Friendship -- Fiction 4. Horror stories 5. Dead -- Fiction 6. Twins -- Fiction 7. Alchemy -- Fiction 8. Brothers -- Fiction 9. Supernatural -- Fiction
ISBN 1442403187; 9781442403185; 9781442403208; 9781442403192
LC 2011042843
This book by Kenneth Oppel is part of the "Apprenticeship of Victor Frankenstein" series. "[T]hree weeks after [his twin] Konrad's death, Victor plucks a mysterious box from the still-warm ashes of the books of the Dark Library. Demonstrating tremendous hubris, Victor aims to return Konrad to the living world and still win Elizabeth, Konrad"s grief-stricken love and the boys" childhood friend." (Kirkus Reviews)

★ **This** dark endeavor; the apprenticeship of Victor Frankenstein. Simon & Schuster Books for Young Readers 2011 298p $17.99

Grades: 7 8 9 10   **Fic**
1. Horror fiction 2. Twins -- Fiction 3. Alchemy -- Fiction 4. Brothers -- Fiction
ISBN 1-4424-0315-2; 1-4424-0317-9 ebook; 978-1-4424-0315-4; 978-1-4424-0317-8 ebook
LC 2011016974
When his twin brother falls ill in the family's chateau in the independent republic of Geneva in the eighteenth century, sixteen-year-old Victor Frankenstein embarks on a dangerous and uncertain quest to create the forbidden Elixir of Life described in an ancient text in the family's secret Biblioteka Obscura.
"Written in a readable approximation of early 19th-century style, Oppel's . . . tale is melodramatic, exciting, disquieting, and intentionally over the top." Publ Wkly

Orenstein, Denise Gosliner
Unseen companion. Katherine Tegen Bks. 2003 357p lib bdg $16.89; pa $7.99
Grades: 7 8 9 10   **Fic**
1. Inuit -- Fiction
ISBN 0-06-052057-4 lib bdg; 0-06-052058-2 pa
LC 2002-152944
"In distinctive voices, the four narrators tell their own involving stories. . . . A sensitive observer and a compelling storyteller, Orenstein offers a novel that is both touching and harsh." Booklist

★ The **secret** twin. Katherine Tegen Books 2007 385p $16.99; lib bdg $17.89
Grades: 7 8 9 10   **Fic**
1. Twins -- Fiction 2. Orphans -- Fiction 3. Siamese twins -- Fiction
ISBN 978-0-06-078564-2; 0-06-078564-0; 978-0-06-078565-9 lib bdg; 0-06-078565-9 lib bdg
LC 2006-03876
Born a conjoined twin, thirteen-year-old Noah bears the secret guilt of being the only survivor, and now finds himself in the care of a stranger with a secret of her own.
"This spellbinding story will entangle readers at the first sentence. . . . Orenstein's writing is magic—every word and phrase precisely chosen." Booklist

Orlev, Uri
Run, boy, run; a novel. translated from the Hebrew by Hillel Halkin. Houghton Mifflin 2003 186p $15
Grades: 7 8 9 10   **Fic**
1. Holocaust survivors 2. Jews -- Poland -- Fiction 3. Holocaust, 1933-1945 -- Fiction
ISBN 0-618-16465-0
LC 2003-1550
Original Hebrew edition, 2001
Based on the true story of a nine-year-old boy who escapes the Warsaw Ghetto and must survive throughout the war in the Nazi-occupied Polish countryside
"The story is totally engrossing as it vividly describes the hardships faced by so many youngsters during the war. Orlev has . . . successfully used historical fiction to illustrate the Holocaust experience." SLJ

★ The **song** of the whales; translated by Hillel Halkin. Houghton Mifflin Books for Children 2010 108p $16

Grades: 5 6 7 8   **Fic**
1. Jews -- Fiction 2. Dreams -- Fiction 3. Old age -- Fiction 4. Family life -- Fiction 5. Grandfathers -- Fiction
ISBN 978-0-547-25752-5; 0-547-25752-X
LC 2009-49720

At age eight, Mikha'el knows he is different from other boys, but over the course of three years as he helps his parents care for his elderly grandfather in Jerusalem, Grandpa teaches Mikha'el to use the gift they share of making other people's dreams sweeter.

This is "the sort of story that operates on many different levels. . . . With a clean sense that less is more, Orlev has crafted a sweetly mysterious and quietly moving read." Booklist

Ortiz Cofer, Judith
Call me Maria; a novel. Orchard Books 2004 127p $16.95

Grades: 7 8 9 10   **Fic**
1. Identity 2. Puerto Ricans -- Fiction
ISBN 0-439-38577-6
LC 2004-2674

Fifteen-year-old Maria leaves her mother and their Puerto Rican home to live in the barrio of New York with her father, feeling torn between the two cultures in which she has been raised.

"Through a mixture of poems, letters, and prose, María gradually reveals herself as a true student of language and life. . . . Understated but with a brilliant combination of all the right words to convey events, Cofer aptly relates the complexities of María's two homes, her parents' lives, and the difficulty of her choice between them." SLJ

If I could fly. Farrar Straus & Giroux 2011 195p $16.99

Grades: 8 9 10 11 12   **Fic**
1. Pigeons -- Fiction 2. Singers -- Fiction 3. Family life -- Fiction 4. Puerto Ricans -- Fiction
ISBN 978-0-374-33517-5; 0-374-33517-6
LC 2010022309

When fifteen-year-old Doris's mother, a professional singer, returns to Puerto Rico and her father finds a girlfriend, Doris cares for a neighbor's pigeons and relies on friends as she begins to find her own voice and wings.

"A familiar story of mother/daughter relationships delivered lyrically, simply and inspirationally." Kirkus

Orwell, George, 1903-1950
Animal farm; a fairy story. with a foreword to the Centennial edition by Ann Patchett; with a preface by Russell Baker; introduction by C.M. Woodhouse. Centennial ed.; Harcourt Brace 2003 xxix, 97p $14
Grades: 7 8 9 10 11 12 Adult   **Fic**
1. Animals -- Fiction 2. Totalitarianism -- Fiction
ISBN 978-0-45228-424-1; 0-45228-424-4
First published 1945 in the United Kingdom; first United States edition 1946

Orwell's 1945 fable about the power struggles among animals on a farm parallels the situation in Russia at the time as Orwell saw it; the characters include the ruthless pig Stalin, his idealistic Trotsky-like adversary, and the simple, kindly horse who represents the common man.

Nineteen eighty-four; with an introduction by Julian Symonds. Knopf 1992 xlii, 325p $19
Grades: 8 9 10 11 12 Adult   **Fic**
1. Satire 2. Individualism 3. Totalitarianism -- Fiction
ISBN 0-679-41739-7
LC 92-52906

First published 1949 by Harcourt, Brace
"A dictatorship called Big Brother rules the people in a collectivist society where Winston Smith works in the Ministry of Truth. The Thought Police persuade the people that ignorance is strength and war is peace. Winston becomes involved in a forbidden love affair and joins the underground to resist this mind control." Shapiro. Fic for Youth. 3d edition

Osa, Nancy
Cuba 15. Delacorte Press 2003 277p hardcover o.p. pa $7.95
Grades: 7 8 9 10   **Fic**
1. Cuban Americans -- Fiction
ISBN 0-385-73021-7; 0-385-73233-3 pa
LC 2002-13389

Violet Paz, who is half Cuban American, half Polish American, reluctantly prepares for her upcoming "quince," a Spanish nickname for the celebration of an Hispanic girl's fifteenth birthday

"Violet's hilarious, cool first-person narrative veers between slapstick and tenderness, denial and truth." Booklist

Osterlund, Anne
Aurelia. Speak 2008 246p pa $8.99
Grades: 8 9 10 11   **Fic**
1. Mystery fiction 2. Princesses -- Fiction
ISBN 978-0-14-240579-6; 0-14-240579-5
LC 2007-36074

The king sends for Robert, whose father was a trusted spy, when someone tries to assassinate Aurelia, the stubborn and feisty crown princess of Tyralt.

"Osterlund's characters are both believable, relatable, and enviable, which makes this book enjoyable to read. Even though the book might seem to fit the mold of a quintessential princess fairy tale, Aurelia's spitfire attitude and her resulting actions lend the story a unique twist." Voice Youth Advocates

Exile. Speak 2011 295p pa $8.99
Grades: 8 9 10 11   **Fic**
1. Princesses -- Fiction 2. Voyages and travels -- Fiction
ISBN 978-0-14-241739-3; 0-14-241739-4
LC 2010009645

In exile, Princess Aurelia is free of responsibilities, able to travel the country and meet the people of Tyralt, but when her journey erupts in a fiery conflagration that puts the fate of the kingdom in peril, she and her companion Robert must determine whether they have the strength and the will to complete their mission.

Ostlere, Cathy

★ **Karma**; a novel in verse. Razorbill 2011
517p map $18.99

Grades: 7 8 9 10 11 12   **Fic**

1. Novels in verse 2. Violence -- Fiction 3. Culture
conflict -- Fiction

ISBN 978-1-59514-338-9; 1-59514-338-6

"The novel's pace and tension will compel readers to
read at a gallop, but then stop again and again to turn a finely
crafted phrase, whether to appreciate the richness of the
language and imagery or to reconsider the layers beneath
a thought. This is a book in which readers will consider the
roots and realities of destiny and chance. Karma is a spectacular, sophisticated tale that will stick with readers long
after they're done considering its last lines." SLJ

Ostow, Micol

Emily Goldberg learns to salsa. Razorbill 2006
200p $16.99

Grades: 7 8 9 10   **Fic**

1. Jews -- Fiction 2. Family life -- Fiction 3. Puerto
Ricans -- Fiction 4. Racially mixed people -- Fiction

ISBN 1-59514-081-6

LC 2006-14651

Forced to stay with her mother in Puerto Rico for weeks
after her grandmother's funeral, half-Jewish Emily, who has
just graduated from a Westchester, New York high school,
does not find it easy to connect with her Puerto Rican heritage and relatives she had never met.

This is "a moving story that has a solid plotline and plenty of family secrets." Booklist

★ **So** punk rock (and other ways to disappoint
your mother) a novel. with art by David Ostow. Flux
2009 246p il pa $9.95

Grades: 8 9 10 11 12   **Fic**

1. School stories 2. Rock music -- Fiction 3. Bands
(Music) -- Fiction 4. Jews -- United States -- Fiction

ISBN 978-0-7387-1471-4; 0-7387-1471-2

LC 2009-8216

Four suburban New Jersey students from the Leo R. Git-
tleman Jewish Day School form a rock band that becomes
inexplicably popular, creating exhiliration, friction, confrontation, and soul-searching among its members.

The "comic-strip-style illustrations are true show-stoppers. . . . A rollicking, witty, and ultra-contemporary book
that drums on the funny bone and reverberates through the
heart." Booklist

Oswald, Nancy

Nothing here but stones; a Jewish pioneer story.
[by] Nancy Oswald. Henry Holt 2004 215p $16.95

Grades: 5 6 7 8   **Fic**

1. Jews -- Fiction 2. Immigrants -- Fiction 3. Frontier
and pioneer life -- Fiction

ISBN 0-8050-7465-1

LC 2003-56969

In 1882, ten-year-old Emma and her family, along with
other Russian Jewish immigrants, arrive in Cotopaxi, Colorado, where they face inhospitable conditions as they attempt to start an agricultural colony, and lonely Emma is
comforted by the horse whose life she saved

"This well-paced, vivid account should capture readers'
attention." SLJ

Owen, James A.

Here, there be dragons; written and illustrated by
James A. Owen. Simon & Schuster Books for Young
Readers 2006 326p il (The Chronicles of the Imagi-
narium Geographica) $17.95

Grades: 8 9 10 11 12   **Fic**

1. Poets 2. Fantasy fiction

ISBN 978-1-4169-1227-9; 1-4169-1227-4

LC 2005-30486

Three young men are entrusted with the Imaginarium
Geographica, an atlas of fantastical places to which they
travel in hopes of defeating the Winter King whose bid
for power is related to the First World War raging in the
Real World.

"From the arresting prologue, the reader is gripped by
a finely crafted fantasy tale and compelled to continue. . .
. This superb saga has interesting characters and plenty of
action." Voice Youth Advocates

Other titles in this series are:

The search for the Red Dragon (2007)
The indigo king (2008)
The shadow dragons (2009)
The dragon's apprentice (2010)

Oz, Amos

★ **Suddenly** in the depths of the forest; translated from the Hebrew by Sondra Silverston. Harcourt
2011 134p $15.99

Grades: 4 5 6 7   **Fic**

1. Fables 2. Animals -- Fiction

ISBN 978-0-547-55153-1; 0-547-55153-3

LC 2011-08664

In a gray and gloomy village, all of the animals—from
dogs and cats to fish and snails—disappeared years before.
No one talks about it and no one knows why, though everyone agrees that the village has been cursed. But when two
children see a fish—a tiny one and just for a second—they
become determined to unravel the mystery of where the animals have gone.

"In this swiftly moving fable . . . Oz creates palpable
tension with a repetitive, almost hypnotic rhythm and lyrical language that twists a discussion-provoking morality tale
into something much more enchanting." Booklist

Padian, Maria

Brett McCarthy: work in progress. Knopf 2008
276p $15.99; lib bdg $18.99

Grades: 5 6 7 8   **Fic**

1. School stories 2. Cancer -- Fiction 3. Friendship
-- Fiction 4. Family life -- Fiction 5. Grandmothers
-- Fiction

ISBN 978-0-375-84675-5; 0-375-84675-1; 978-0-375-
94675-2 lib bdg; 0-375-94675-6 lib bdg

LC 2007-04415

Eighth-grader Brett McCarthy—once good student
and best-friend-to-Diane, now suspended and friendless—
faces school and family troubles as she grapples with her
redefined life.

"It is Padian's fully developed characters and ear for teenage voices that make this a story that will resonate with anyone who has ever felt isolated in the middle of a crowd." SLJ

Jersey tomatoes are the best. Alfred A. Knopf 2011 344p $16.99; lib bdg $19.99

Grades: 7 8 9 10   **Fic**
1. Camps -- Fiction 2. Ballet -- Fiction 3. Tennis -- Fiction 4. Friendship -- Fiction 5. Anorexia nervosa -- Fiction
ISBN 978-0-375-86579-4; 0-375-86579-9; 978-0-375-96579-1 lib bdg; 0-375-96579-3 lib bdg
LC 2010-11827
When fifteen-year-old best friends Henry and Eve leave New Jersey, one for tennis camp in Florida and one for ballet camp in New York, each faces challenges that put her long-cherished dreams of the future to the test.

"Padian's writing and plotting are clean and clear, and her handling of the duo's dilemmas never stoops to melodrama. An excellent read for sports lovers who desire some meaty beefsteak in their stories." Booklist

Palacio, R. J.
★ **Wonder**; by R.J. Palacio. Alfred A. Knopf 2012 315 p. $15.99

Grades: 3 4 5 6   **Fic**
1. Birth defects -- Fiction 2. Schools -- Fiction 3. Middle schools -- Fiction 4. Self-acceptance -- Fiction 5. Abnormalities, Human -- Fiction
ISBN 9780375869020; 9780375899881; 9780375969027
LC 2011027133
In this book, "[a]fter being homeschooled for years, Auggie Pullman is about to start fifth grade, but he's worried: How will he fit into middle-school life when he looks so different from everyone else? Auggie has had 27 surgeries to correct facial anomalies he was born with, but he still has a face that has earned him such cruel nicknames as Freak, Freddy Krueger, Gross-out and Lizard face. . . . Palacio divides the novel into eight parts, interspersing Auggie's first-person narrative with the voices of family members and classmates, . . . expanding the story beyond Auggie's viewpoint and demonstrating that Auggie's arrival at school doesn't test only him, it affects everyone in the community." (Kirkus)

Paley, Sasha
Huge. Simon & Schuster Books for Young Readers 2007 259p $15.99

Grades: 7 8 9   **Fic**
1. Camps -- Fiction 2. Obesity -- Fiction 3. Friendship -- Fiction
ISBN 978-1-4169-3517-9; 1-4169-3517-7
LC 2007-03510
When Wilhelmina and April find themselves roommates at a fat camp, both with very different goals, they find they have very little in common until they are both humiliated by the same person.

"The characters are sharply drawn, and the often-amusing story does a good job of showing how everyday concerns are often overshadowed by the issue of weight." Booklist

Palma, Felix J.
The **map** of the sky; a novel. by Felix J. Palma. 1st Atria Books hardcover ed. Atria Books 2012 594 p. (hardcover : alk. paper) $26.00; (paperback) $16.00; (ebook) $24.99

Grades: 6 7 8 9 10 11 12 Adult   **Fic**
1. Time travel -- Fiction 2. Extraterrestrial beings -- Fiction 3. Wells, H. G. (Herbert George), 1866-1946/ Fiction 4. Fiances -- Fiction 5. Writers -- Fiction
ISBN 1451660316; 9781451660319; 9781451660326; 9781921942907
LC 2012028794
In this book by Felix J. Palma, "H. G. Wells . . . meet[s] . . . Garrett Serviss, the man who dared write a sequel to his 'War of the Worlds.'. . . An alcohol-infused sense of camaraderie and adventure inspire the two men to set off to view a hidden secret -- a Martian kept in a locked room in the Natural History Museum. As alien forces converge on London, a group of citizens struggle to preserve the once-proud city against destruction." (Library Journal)

The **map** of time; Félix J. Palma ; translated by Nick Caistor. Atria Books 2011 611p. $26.00

Grades: 6 7 8 9 10 11 12 Adult   **Fic**
1. Science fiction 2. Historical fiction 3. Time travel -- Fiction
ISBN 9781439167397; 1439167397; 143916746X; 9781439167465
LC 2010047304
Originally published in Spain in 2008.
Col. ill. on lining papers.
This book, the first in a trilogy is a "thriller that explores the ramifications of time travel in three intersecting narratives. In the opening chapter, set in 1896 England, aristocratic Andrew Harrington plans to take his own life, despondent over the death years earlier of his lover, the last victim of Jack the Ripper. Meanwhile, 21-year-old Claire Haggerty plots to escape her restrictive role as a woman in Victorian society by journeying to the year 2000. A new commercial concern, Murray's Time Travel, offers such a trip for a hefty fee. Finally, Scotland Yarder Colin Garrett believes that the fatal wound on a murder victim could only have been caused by a weapon from the future. Linking all three stories is H.G. Wells, the author of The Time Machine." (Publisher"s Wkly)

Palmer, Robin
The **Corner** of Bitter and Sweet; by Robin Palmer. Penguin Group USA 2013 400 p. $9.99

Grades: 7 8 9 10 11 12   **Fic**
1. Children of alcoholics -- Fiction 2. Television personalities -- Fiction 3. Mother-daughter relationship -- Fiction
ISBN 0142412503; 9780142412503
In this book by Robin Palmer, "a teenage girl and her showbiz mom are forced to re-evaluate their relationship after rehab. . . . To learn how to cope, Annabelle joins Alateen. But when Janie scores a role in a new movie with hot young superstar Billy Barrett, Annabelle frets that if anything goes wrong, it could put her mom right back on the bottle. Fortunately she's distracted by her own crush on small-town

boy Matt and the lure of a college photography fellowship."
(Kirkus Reviews)

Yours truly, Lucy B. Parker: girl vs. superstar. G.
P. Putnam's Sons 2010 215p $15.99; pa $6.99
Grades: 5 6 7 8   **Fic**
1. Celebrities -- Fiction 2. Stepfamilies -- Fiction
ISBN 978-0-399-25489-5; 0-399-25489-7; 978-0-14-
241500-9 pa; 0-14-241500-6 pa
"Lucy B. Parker, 12, is having a difficult time. Her best
friend dumps her, she still hasn't gotten her period, and her
mom insists that she wear a bra. Just when things can't get
any worse, her mom announces that she's going to marry
the father of Laurel Moses, a TV-music-movie star . . . who
happens to hate Lucy's guts. . . . Readers will relate to the
lessons learned, but they aren't preachy or in-your-face. The
writing is easy to follow, and this book will definitely be
enjoyed by preteens who long for Laurel's glamorous life,
while also appreciating with Lucy's stable home." SLJ
Another title about Lucy is:
Sealed with a kiss (2010)

Paolini, Christopher
★ **Eragon**. Knopf 2003 509p (Inheritance)
$18.95; lib bdg $20.99; pa $6.99
Grades: 7 8 9 10   **Fic**
1. Fantasy fiction 2. Dragons -- Fiction
ISBN 0-375-82668-8; 0-375-92668-2 lib bdg; 0-440-
23848-X pa
LC 2003-47481
First published 2002 in different form by
Paolini International
In Aagaesia, a fifteen-year-old boy of unknown lineage
called Eragon finds a mysterious stone that weaves his life
into an intricate tapestry of destiny, magic, and power, peo-
pled with dragons, elves, and monsters
"This unusual, powerful tale . . . is the first book in the
planned Inheritance trilogy. . . . The telling remains con-
stantly fresh and fluid, and [the author] has done a fine job of
creating an appealing and convincing relationship between
the youth and the dragon." Booklist
Other titles in this series are:
Brisningr (2008)
Eldest (2005)

Papademetriou, Lisa
Drop. Alfred A. Knopf 2008 169p $15.99; lib
bdg $18.99
Grades: 8 9 10 11 12   **Fic**
1. Gambling -- Fiction
ISBN 978-0-375-84244-3; 0-375-84244-6; 978-0-375-
94244-0 lib bdg; 0-375-94244-0 lib bdg
LC 2008-02568
Sixteen-year-old math prodigy Jerrica discovers she has
the ability to predict outcomes in blackjack and roulette,
and joins forces with Sanjay and Kat to develop her theories
while helping them get the money they desperately need.
"The characters are well drawn and the excitement of
the gambling scenes is well executed. Additionally, some
surprising details about the teens turn the story upside down,

unraveling everything that readers thought they knew about
them. A page-turner." SLJ

M or F? a novel. [by] Lisa Papademetriou and
Chris Tebbetts. Razorbill 2005 296p $16.99
Grades: 8 9 10 11 12   **Fic**
1. Friendship -- Fiction 2. Homosexuality -- Fiction
ISBN 1-59514-034-4
LC 2005008149
Gay teen Marcus helps his friend Frannie chat up her
crush online, but then becomes convinced that the crush is
falling for him instead.
"This is a creative, funny romance, written with style
and sophistication." Booklist

Paquette, Ammi-Joan
Nowhere girl. Walker & Co. 2011 246p $16.99
Grades: 6 7 8 9   **Fic**
1. Fathers -- Fiction 2. Voyages and travels -- Fiction
ISBN 978-0-8027-2297-3; 0-8027-2297-0
LC 2010049591
Fair-skinned and blond-haired, thirteen-year-old Luchi
was born in a Thai prison where her American mother was
being held and she has never had any other home, but when
her mother dies Luchi sets out into the world to search for
the family and home she has always dreamed of.
"The classic quest story gets expanded here with contemporary details in spare lyrical prose that intensify the
perilous, archetypal journey. . . . The realistic specifics . .
. make the story of betrayal and kindness immediate and
universal." Booklist

Paratore, Coleen
The **wedding** planner's daughter; [by] Coleen
Murtagh Paratore. Simon & Schuster Books for
Young Readers 2005 200p $15.95; pa $5.99
Grades: 5 6 7 8   **Fic**
1. Weddings -- Fiction 2. Mother-daughter relationship
-- Fiction
ISBN 0-689-87340-9; 1-4169-1854-X pa
LC 2004-14502
Willa, a romantic girl who wants a father, tries to
find a husband for her mother, Cape Cod's most popular
wedding planner.
"This book is as sweet a confection as the cherry cordials
its 12-year-old protagonist is so fond of eating. . . . The girl's
letter to her mother . . . provides emotional heft to what has
up to that point been just a pleasant story." SLJ
Other titles about Willa are:
The cupid chronicles (2007)
Willa by heart (2008)
Forget me not (2009)

Park, Barbara
The **graduation** of Jake Moon. Atheneum Bks.
for Young Readers 2000 115p $15; pa $4.99
Grades: 4 5 6 7   **Fic**
1. Grandfathers -- Fiction 2. Alzheimer's disease --
Fiction
ISBN 0-689-83912-X; 0-689-83985-5 pa
LC 99-87475

Fourteen-year-old Jake recalls how he has spent the last four years of his life watching his grandfather descend slowly but surely into the horrors of Alzheimer's disease

"Jake is a well-rounded and believable character surrounded by colorful and equally realistic supporting characters. . . . This novel . . . is written in an accessible style that will appeal to a wide audience." SLJ

Park, Linda Sue

Archer's quest. Clarion Books 2006 167p $16; pa $6.50

Grades: 4 5 6 7   **Fic**

1. Science fiction 2. Korean Americans -- Fiction
ISBN 978-0-618-59631-7; 0-618-59631-3; 978-0-440-42204-4 pa; 0-440-42204-3 pa

LC 2005-29789

Twelve-year-old Kevin Kim helps Chu-mong, a legendary king of ancient Korea, return to his own time

This "is a breezy, fun read." Voice Youth Advocates

Click; [by] Linda Sue Park [et al.] Arthur A. Levine Books 2007 217p $16.99

Grades: 7 8 9 10   **Fic**

1. Adventure fiction 2. Photojournalism -- Fiction
ISBN 0-439-41138-6; 978-0-439-41138-7

LC 2006-100069

"Ten distinguished authors each write a chapter of this intriguing novel of mystery and family, which examines the lives touched by a photojournalist George Keane, aka Gee. . . . The authors' distinctive styles remain evident; although readers expecting a more straightforward or linear story may find the leaps through time and place challenging, the thematic currents help the chapters gel into a cohesive whole." Publ Wkly

Project Mulberry; a novel. Clarion 2005 225p $16; pa $6.99

Grades: 5 6 7 8   **Fic**

1. Korean Americans -- Fiction
ISBN 0-618-47786-1; 0-440-42163-2 pa

LC 2004-18159

While working on a project for an afterschool club, Julia, a Korean American girl, and her friend Patrick learn not just about silkworms, but also about tolerance, prejudice, friendship, patience, and more. Between the chapters are short dialogues between the author and main character about the writing of the book

"The unforgettable family and friendship story, the quiet, almost unspoken racism, and the excitement of the science make this a great cross-curriculum title." Booklist

Storm warning. Scholastic 2010 190p (The 39 clues) $12.99

Grades: 4 5 6 7   **Fic**

1. Ciphers -- Fiction
ISBN 978-0-545-06049-3; 0-545-06049-4

Amy and Dan hit the high seas as they follow the trail of some infamous ancestors to track down a long lost treasure. However, the real prize isn't hidden in a chest. It's the discovery of the Madrigals' most dangerous secret and, even

more shockingly, the true identity of the mysterious man in black.

When my name was Keoko. Clarion Bks. 2002 199p $16; pa $6.99

Grades: 5 6 7 8   **Fic**

1. Courage 2. Patriotism 3. Military occupation 4. Family life -- Korea 5. World War, 1939-1945 -- Fiction
ISBN 0-618-13335-6; 0-440-41944-1 pa

LC 2001-32487

With national pride and occasional fear, a brother and sister face the increasingly oppressive occupation of Korea by Japan during World War II, which threatens to suppress Korean culture entirely

"Park is a masterful prose stylist, and her characters are developed beautifully. She excels at making traditional Korean culture accessible to Western readers." Voice Youth Advocates

Includes bibliographical references

★ A **long** walk to water; based on a true story. Clarion Books 2010 121p map $16

Grades: 6 7 8 9 10   **Fic**

1. Refugees 2. Relief workers 3. Water -- Fiction 4. Africans -- Fiction
ISBN 978-0-547-25127-1; 0-547-25127-0

LC 2009-48857

When the Sudanese civil war reaches his village in 1985, eleven-year-old Salva becomes separated from his family and must walk with other Dinka tribe members through southern Sudan, Ethiopia, and Kenya in search of safe haven. Based on the life of Salva Dut, who, after emigrating to America in 1996, began a project to dig water wells in Sudan.

This is a "spare, immediate account. . . . Young readers will be stunned by the triumphant climax of the former refugee who makes a difference." Booklist

★ A **single** shard. Clarion Bks. 2001 152p $15; pa $6.99

Grades: 5 6 7 8   **Fic**

1. Pottery -- Fiction
ISBN 0-395-97827-0; 0-440-41851-8 pa

LC 00-43102

Awarded the Newbery Medal, 2002

Tree-ear, a thirteen-year-old orphan in medieval Korea, lives under a bridge in a potters' village, and longs to learn how to throw the delicate celadon ceramics himself

"This quiet, but involving, story draws readers into a very different time and place. . . . A well-crafted novel with an unusual setting." Booklist

Park, Linda Sue, 1960-

Keeping score. Clarion Books 2008 202p map $16; pa $6.99

Grades: 4 5 6 7   **Fic**

1. Baseball -- Fiction 2. Family life -- Fiction
ISBN 978-0-618-92799-9; 0-618-92799-9; 978-0-547-24897-4 pa; 0-547-24897-0 pa

LC 2007-46522

"Maggie's perspective is authentically childlike and engaging, and her relations with her family and friends ring true. . . . This finely crafted novel should resonate with a wide audience of readers." SLJ

Trust no one; Linda Sue Park. 1st ed. Scholastic Press 2013 190 p. (reinforced) $12.99
Grades: 4 5 6 7   Fic
   1. Spy stories 2. Mystery fiction
   ISBN 0545298431; 9780545298438
                       LC 2012939109
   This is the fifth installment of Linda Sue Park's Cahills vs. Vespers series. Here, "Amy and Dan discover that one of their friends is a spy for the Vespers, a group of evil agents who kidnapped seven of their family members. But which friend is it? The shocking secrets continue when the Cahill siblings finally figure out the Vespers' real plan, and it's much worse than they originally thought." (Owl Magazine)

Parker, Marjorie Hodgson
   David and the Mighty Eighth; a British boy and a Texas airman in World War II. by Marjorie Hodgson Parker; illustrated by Mark Postlethwaite. Bright Sky Press 2007 176p il $17.95
Grades: 4 5 6 7   Fic
   1. World War, 1939-1945 -- Fiction
   ISBN 978-1-931721-93-6; 1-931721-93-9
                       LC 2007025999
   When, during the London Blitz, he and his older sister are evacuated to go live on their grandparents' East Anglia farm, a young English boy finds it difficult to adjust to his new life until the arrival of the pilots and crews of the U.S. Eight Air Force at nearby airfields brings excitement, friendship, and hope for the future.
   This is an "exciting novel, based on a true story. . . . The story is framed by extensive historical notes. . . . Spacious type, thick paper, and an occasional black-and-white drawings make this an appealing package all around." Booklist

Parker, Robert B.
   Chasing the bear; a young Spenser novel. Philomel Books 2009 169p $14.99
Grades: 7 8 9 10   Fic
   1. Bullies -- Fiction 2. Friendship -- Fiction 3. Kidnapping -- Fiction 4. Child abuse -- Fiction
   ISBN 978-0-399-24776-7; 0-399-24776-9
                       LC 2008-52725
   Spenser reflects back to when he was fourteen-years-old and how he helped his best friend Jeannie when she was abducted by her abusive father.
   "A clean, sharp jab of a read." Booklist

   The **Edenville** Owls. Philomel Books 2007 194p $17.99
Grades: 6 7 8 9   Fic
   1. Mystery fiction 2. Teachers -- Fiction 3. Basketball -- Fiction 4. Friendship -- Fiction
   ISBN 978-0-399-24656-2; 0-399-24656-8
                       LC 2006-34533
   Fourteen-year-old Bobby, living in a small Massachusetts town just after World War II, finds himself facing many new challenges as he tries to pull together his coachless basketball team, cope with new feelings for his old friend

Joanie, and discover the identity of the mysterious stranger who seems to be threatening his teacher.
   "The poignant, well-articulated coming-of-age moments deepen the heart-pounding suspense." Booklist

Parkinson, Curtis
   Domenic's war; a story of the Battle of Monte Cassino. Tundra Books 2006 191p pa $9.95
Grades: 6 7 8 9   Fic
   1. World War, 1939-1945 -- Fiction
   ISBN 0-88776-751-6
   "Based on actual experiences, this World War II novel tells the stories of Italians living near Monte Cassino, caught between the German army and the Allied forces. Young Domenic Luppino and his family live north of the fighting, but fear the advancing troops. Fifteen-year-old Antonio lost his entire family when fighting moved into the town, and now he's on his own. Both boys face hardships and risk their lives for friends and family. Their stories of strength, resourcefulness, and survival are deftly placed within the context of the Monte Cassino campaign and will give readers a poignant look at the ways in which the war affected average citizens." SLJ

Parkinson, Siobhán
   Blue like Friday. Roaring Brook Press 2008 160p $16.95
Grades: 4 5 6 7   Fic
   1. Family life -- Fiction 2. Synesthesia -- Fiction 3. Missing persons -- Fiction
   ISBN 978-1-59643-340-3; 1-59643-340-X
   When Olivia helps her quirky friend Hal, whose synesthesia causes him to experience everything in colors, with a prank intended to get rid of Hal's potential stepfather, there are unexpected consequences, including the disappearance of Hal's mother.
   "Parkinson creates a warm, moving story of real families facing real problems. . . . The economy of her prose is admirable; all the characters are well drawn." Booklist

   Long story short. Roaring Brook Press 2011 160p $16.99
Grades: 6 7 8 9 10   Fic
   1. Siblings -- Fiction 2. Runaway children -- Fiction
   ISBN 978-1-59643-647-3; 1-59643-647-6
                       LC 2010-29023
   Fourteen-year-old Jono and his eight-year-old sister Julie run away when, soon after their grandmother's death, their alcoholic mother hits Julie, but when the police find them in Galway, Jono learns he is in big trouble.
   "A deeply affecting story about what can go wrong when adults fail children and the choices available to go them are all bad." Publ Wkly

Parnell, Robyn
   The **mighty** Quinn; by Robyn Parnell ; illustrated by Aaron and Katie DeYoe. 1st ed. Scarletta Press 2013 263 p. ill. (paperback) $10.95
Grades: 4 5 6 7   Fic
   1. Bullies -- Fiction 2. Schools -- Fiction 3. Friendship

-- Fiction
ISBN 1938063104; 9781938063107

LC 2012031518

In this story, by Robyn Parnell, "Quinn Andrews-Lee . . . faces a dismal school year. His little sister outshines him . . . , he yearns for a service award his peers disdain, and charismatic bigot Matt Barker's goal in life is to torment Quinn. . . . When Quinn reports an act of vandalism, he is accused of injuring Matt. . . . A free-spirited new kid in Quinn's class, helps Quinn deduce who hurt Matt, but Matt would probably die . . . before admitting the truth." (Publisher's note)

Parry, Rosanne

Heart of a shepherd; [by] Rosanne Parry. Random House Children's Books 2009 161p lib bdg $18.99; $15.99

Grades: 4 5 6 7   **Fic**
   1. Ranch life -- Fiction 2. Family life -- Fiction 3. Christian life -- Fiction 4. Iraq War, 2003- -- Fiction
ISBN 0-375-84802-9; 978-0-375-94802-2 lib bdg; 0-375-94802-3 lib bdg; 978-0-375-84802-5

LC 2007-48094

Ignatius 'Brother' Alderman, nearly twelve, promises to help his grandparents keep the family's Oregon ranch the same while his brothers are away and his father is deployed to Iraq, but as he comes to accept the inevitability of change, he also sees the man he is meant to be

There is "more action than introspection afoot, with sibling tensions, a wildfire, and the grandfather's death along the journey. It's refreshing . . . to find a protagonist with his eyes and heart open to positive adult examples . . . and who matches his mettle to theirs." Bull Cent Child Books

Second fiddle. Random House 2011 233p map $16.99; lib bdg $19.99

Grades: 5 6 7 8   **Fic**
   1. Music -- Fiction 2. Soldiers -- Fiction
ISBN 978-0-375-86196-3; 0-375-86196-3; 978-0-375-96196-0 lib bdg; 0-375-96196-8 lib bdg; 978-0-375-89350-6 e-book

LC 2009-33324

Six months after the fall of the Berlin Wall, three eighth-grade girls living on an American military base with their families in Berlin try to save a Russian soldier, who has been beaten and left for dead, by smuggling him to Paris, where they are going to perform in a music competition.

"This reads like first-class historical fiction; Parry . . . vividly conjures the political tensions of the period, the challenges of life as an army brat, and the redemptive power of music." Publ Wkly

Partridge, Elizabeth

★ **Dogtag** summer. Bloomsbury Books for Young Readers 2011 226p $16.99

Grades: 4 5 6 7   **Fic**
   1. Hippies -- Fiction 2. Adoption -- Fiction 3. Family life -- Fiction 4. Vietnamese Americans -- Fiction 5. Racially mixed people -- Fiction 6. Vietnam War, 1961-1975 -- Fiction
ISBN 978-1-59990-183-1; 1-59990-183-8

LC 2010-25515

In the summer of 1980 before she starts junior high school in Santa Rosa, California, Tracy, who was adopted from Vietnam when she was six years old, finds an old ammo box with a dog tag and picture that bring up painful memories for both her Vietnam-veteran father and her.

"This gripping yet tender coming-of-age story reveals multiple nuanced perspectives of the Vietnam War and its aftermath. . . . Powerful historical fiction." Publ Wkly

Paterson, Katherine

Bread and roses, too. Clarion Books 2006 275p $16; pa $6.99

Grades: 5 6 7 8   **Fic**
   1. Strikes -- Fiction 2. Immigrants -- Fiction
ISBN 978-0-618-65479-6; 0-618-65479-8; 978-0-547-07651-5 pa; 0-547-07651-7 pa

LC 2005-31702

Jake and Rosa, two children, form an unlikely friendship as they try to survive and understand the 1912 Bread and Roses strike of mill workers in Lawrence, Massachusetts.

"Paterson has skillfully woven true events and real historical figures into the fictional story and created vivid settings, clearly drawn characters, and a strong sense of the hardship and injustice faced by the mostly immigrant mill workers." SLJ

★ **Bridge** to Terabithia; illustrated by Donna Diamond. Crowell 1977 128p il $15.99; lib bdg $16.89; pa $5.99

Grades: 4 5 6 7   **Fic**
   1. Death -- Fiction 2. Friendship -- Fiction
ISBN 0-690-01359-0; 0-690-04635-9 lib bdg; 0-06-440184-7 pa

LC 77-2221

Awarded the Newbery Medal, 1978

The life of Jess, a ten-year-old boy in rural Virginia expands when he becomes friends with a newcomer who subsequently meets an untimely death trying to reach their hideaway, Terabithia, during a storm

"Jess and his family are magnificently characterized; the book abounds in descriptive vignettes, humorous sidelights on the clash of cultures, and realistic depictions of rural school life." Horn Book

★ **Jacob** have I loved. Crowell 1980 216p $15.99; lib bdg $17.89; pa $6.99

Grades: 5 6 7 8   **Fic**
   1. Twins -- Fiction 2. Sisters -- Fiction
ISBN 0-690-04078-4; 0-690-04079-2 lib bdg; 0-06-440368-8 pa

LC 80-668

Awarded the Newbery Medal, 1981

Filled with resentment over the attention showered upon her twin sister, and awaiting the day she can leave her town behind, young Louise meets a wise old sea captain and begins learning how to let go of her anger.

"Each incident and feeling in the life of her young protagonist rings true because the younger voice is so alive and direct. This is a book full of humor and compassion and sharpness." Bull Cent Child Books

Jip; his story. Lodestar Bks. 1996 181p hardcover o.p. pa $6.99

Grades: 5 6 7 8   **Fic**

1. Slavery -- Fiction 2. African Americans -- Fiction 3. Racially mixed people -- Fiction

ISBN 0-525-67543-4; 0-14-240411-X pa

LC 96-2680

While living on a Vermont poor farm during 1855 and 1856, Jip learns that his mother was a runaway slave, and that his father, the plantation owner, plans to reclaim him as property

"This historically accurate story is full of revelations and surprises, one of which is the return appearance of the heroine of Lyddie.... The taut, extremely readable narrative and its tender depictions of friendship and loyalty provide first-rate entertainment." Publ Wkly

★ **Lyddie**. Lodestar Bks. 1991 182p $17.99; pa $6.99

Grades: 5 6 7 8 9   **Fic**

1. Factories -- Fiction

ISBN 0-525-67338-5; 0-14-240254-0 pa

LC 90-42944

Impoverished Vermont farm girl Lyddie Worthen is determined to gain her independence by becoming a factory worker in Lowell, Massachusetts, in the 1840s

"Not only does the book contain a riveting plot, engaging characters, and a splendid setting, but the language—graceful, evocative, and rhythmic—incorporates the rural speech patterns of Lyddie's folk, the simple Quaker expressions of the farm neighbors, and the lilt of fellow mill girl Bridget's Irish brogue.... A superb story of grit, determination, and personal growth." Horn Book

Park's quest. Lodestar Bks. 1988 148p hardcover o.p. pa $5.99

Grades: 5 6 7 8   **Fic**

1. Farm life -- Fiction 2. Vietnamese Americans -- Fiction

ISBN 0-14-034262-1 pa

LC 87-32422

Eleven-year-old Park makes some startling discoveries when he travels to his grandfather's farm in Virginia to learn about his father who died in the Vietnam War and meets a Vietnamese-American girl named Thanh

The author "confronts the complexity, the ambiguity, of the war and the emotions of those it involved with an honesty that young readers are sure to recognize and appreciate." N Y Times Book Rev

Preacher's boy. Clarion Bks. 1999 168p $15; pa $4.95

Grades: 5 6 7 8   **Fic**

1. Family life -- Fiction 2. Christian life -- Fiction 3. Fathers and sons -- Fiction 4. Family life -- Vermont -- Fiction

ISBN 0-395-83897-5; 0-06-447233-7 pa

LC 98-50083

In 1899, ten-year-old Robbie, son of a preacher in a small Vermont town, gets himself into all kinds of trouble when he decides to give up being Christian in order to make the most of his life before the end of the world

"With warmth, humor, and her powerful yet plain style, Paterson draws empathetic and memorable characters." SLJ

The **day** of the pelican. Clarion Books 2009 145p $16

Grades: 6 7 8 9   **Fic**

1. Muslims -- Fiction 2. Refugees -- Fiction 3. Albanians -- Fiction

ISBN 978-0-547-18188-2; 0-547-18188-4

LC 2009-14998

In 1998 when the Kosovo hostilities escalate, thirteen-year-old Meli's life as an ethnic Albanian, changes forever after her brother escapes his Serbian captors and the entire family flees from one refugee camp to another until they are able to immigrate to America.

"Paterson offers a realistic and provocative account of these refugees' plight, balanced by the hope of new beginnings and the resilience of the human spirit." Publ Wkly

★ The **great** Gilly Hopkins. Crowell 1978 148p $15.99; lib bdg $16.89; pa $5.99

Grades: 5 6 7 8   **Fic**

1. Foster home care -- Fiction

ISBN 0-690-03837-2; 0-690-03838-0 lib bdg; 0-06-440201-0 pa

LC 77-27075

A Newbery Medal honor book, 1979

"A well-structured story, [this] has vitality of writing style, natural dialogue, deep insight in characterization, and a keen sense of the fluid dynamics in human relationships." Bull Cent Child Books

The **same** stuff as stars. Clarion Bks. 2002 242p $15

Grades: 5 6 7 8   **Fic**

1. Brothers and Sisters -- Fiction

ISBN 0-618-24744-0

LC 2002-3967

When Angel's self-absorbed mother leaves her and her younger brother with their poor great-grandmother, the eleven-year-old girl worries not only about her mother and brother, her imprisoned father, the frail old woman, but also about a mysterious man who begins sharing with her the wonder of the stars

"Paterson's deft hand at characterization, her insight into the human soul, and her glorious prose make this book one to rejoice over." Voice Youth Advocates

Patneaude, David

Thin wood walls. Houghton Mifflin 2004 231p $16

Grades: 7 8 9 10   **Fic**

1. World War, 1939-1945 -- Fiction 2. Japanese Americans -- Evacuation and relocation, 1942-1945 -- Fiction

ISBN 0-618-34290-7

LC 2004-1014

When the Japanese bomb Pearl Harbor, Joe Hamada and his family face growing prejudice, eventually being torn away from their home and sent to a relocation camp in California, even as his older brother joins the United States Army to fight in the war.

"Basing his story on extensive research and interviews, the author does a fine job of bringing the daily experience up close through the story of an American kid torn from home." Booklist

A **piece** of the sky; [by] David Patneaude; [cover illustration by Layne Johnson] Albert Whitman 2007 178p il $15.95

Grades: 5 6 7 8   **Fic**
  1. Meteorites -- Fiction 2. Mountaineering -- Fiction
  ISBN 978-0-8075-6536-0
  LC 2006023529
Fourteen-year-old Russell, his friend Phoebe, and her brother Isaac must find a legendary meteor in the Oregon mountains before it is exploited
  "This old-fashioned adventure story has contemporary appeal." Booklist

Paton Walsh, Jill
  A **parcel** of patterns. Farrar, Straus & Giroux 1983 136p hardcover o.p. pa $5.95

Grades: 7 8 9 10   **Fic**
  1. Plague -- Fiction
  ISBN 0-374-35750-1; 0-374-45743-3 pa
  LC 83-48143
Mall Percival tells how the plague came to her Derbyshire village of Eyam in the year 1665, how the villagers determined to isolate themselves to prevent further spread of the disease, and how three-fourths of them died before the end of the following year.
  "Historical in broad outline, the narrative blends superb characterizations, skillful plotting, and convincing speech for a hauntingly memorable story that offers a richly textured picture of the period." Child Book Rev Serv

Paton, Alan
  Cry, the beloved country. Scribner Classics 2003 316p $28; pa $15

Grades: 7 8 9 10 11 12 Adult   **Fic**
  1. Zulus (African people) 2. Race relations -- Fiction 3. Anglican and Episcopal clergy
  ISBN 0-7432-6195-X; 0-7432-6217-4 pa
  First published 1948
  "Reverend Kumalo, a black South African preacher, is called to Johannesburg to rescue his sister. There he learns that his son Absalom has been accused of murdering a young white attorney whose interests and sympathies had been with the natives. Despite this, the attorney's father comes to the aid of the minister to help the natives in their struggle to survive a drought." Shapiro. Fic for Youth. 3d edition

Patrick, Cat
  Forgotten; a novel. Little, Brown 2011 288p $17.99

Grades: 7 8 9 10 11   **Fic**
  1. School stories 2. Memory -- Fiction 3. Family life -- Fiction 4. Dating (Social customs) -- Fiction
  ISBN 978-0-316-09461-0; 0-316-09461-7
  LC 2010-43032
Sixteen-year-old London Lane forgets everything each night and must use notes to struggle through the day, even to recall her wonderful boyfriend, but she "remembers" future

events and as her "flashforwards" become more disturbing she realizes she must learn more about the past lest it destroy her future.
  "Patrick raises philosophical issues of real interest. . . . Thoughtful readers will enjoy the mind games, romance readers will enjoy the relationship dynamics, and all readers will find themselves inexorably pulled into a logical yet surprising and compelling finish." Booklist

The **Originals**; Cat Patrick. 1st ed. Little, Brown and Co. 2013 304 p. (hardcover) $18

Grades: 8 9 10 11 12   **Fic**
  1. Sisters -- Fiction 2. Human cloning -- Fiction 3. Dating (Social customs) -- Fiction 4. Cloning -- Fiction 5. Individuality -- Fiction 6. Single-parent families -- Fiction
  ISBN 0316219436; 9780316219433
  LC 2012029853
In this novel, by Cat Patrick, "17-year-olds Lizzie, Ella, and Betsey Best grew up as identical triplets . . . until they discovered a shocking family secret. They're actually closer than sisters, they're clones . . . , hiding from a government agency that would expose them. . . . Then Lizzie meets Sean Kelly. . . . As their relationship develops, Lizzie realizes that she's not a carbon copy of her sisters; she's an individual with unique dreams and desires." (Publisher's note)

Revived; by Cat Patrick. 1st ed. Little, Brown & Co. 2012 336 p. (hardcover) $17.99; (paperback) $8.99

Grades: 7 8 9 10 11 12   **Fic**
  1. Drugs -- Testing 2. Secrecy -- Fiction 3. Science -- Experiments -- Fiction 4. Death -- Fiction 5. Drugs -- Fiction 6. Schools -- Fiction 7. High schools -- Fiction 8. Moving, Household -- Fiction
  ISBN 0316094625; 9780316094627; 9780316094634
  LC 2011026950
This book, by Cat Patrick, follows Daisy, who since the age of five has been "part of a top-secret clinical trial for a drug called Revive that can bring the deceased back to life. . . . Daisy uncovers some secrets within the program: a mysterious extra case file, a new test batch of Revive, some unexplained car crashes, and the erratic behavior of the mysterious man at the top, nicknamed God." (Bulletin of the Center for Children"s Books)

Patron, Susan
  Behind the masks; the diary of Angeline Reddy. Susan Patron. Scholastic 2012 293 p. ill., map $12.99

Grades: 5 6 7 8 9   **Fic**
  1. Mystery fiction 2. Diaries -- Fiction 3. Thieves -- Fiction 4. Gold mines and mining -- Fiction 5. Frontier and pioneer life -- California -- Fiction 6. Lawyers -- Fiction 7. Mystery and detective stories 8. Robbers and outlaws -- Fiction
  ISBN 9780545304375
  LC 2011023826
"[T]his Dear America series title [is] set in Bodie, California, in 1880. Fourteen-year-old diarist and would-be dramatist Angeline Reddy does not believe her father, criminal lawyer Patrick Reddy, has been murdered. Convinced his

disappearance is purposeful, Angie investigates his 'demise' and tries to bring him back to their rough-and-tumble mining community. Assisted by friends, a dashing young Wells Fargo clerk, and the members of a local theater troupe, . . . Angie offers a revealing look at frontier life "especially pre-occupations with thespian entertainments, racial and social prejudices, and vigilante justice."(Booklist)

Patt, Beverly

★ **Best** friends forever; a World War II scrap-book. with illustrations by Shula Klinger. Marshall Cavendish 2010 92p il $17.99

Grades: 5 6 7 8   **Fic**
  1. Friendship -- Fiction 2. World War, 1939-1945 -- Fiction 3. Japanese Americans -- Evacuation and relocation, 1942-1945 -- Fiction
  ISBN 978-0-7614-5577-6; 0-7614-5577-9
                                    LC 2008-20875
Fourteen-year-old Louise keeps a scrapbook detailing the events in her life after her best friend, Dottie, a Japanese-American girl, and her family are sent to a relocation camp during World War II.

"If the drama of the girls separation isn't enough, a romantic subplot and the antics of Dottie's goofy dog (living with Louise in her absence) will surely keep young readers interested. This heartwarming tale of steadfast friendship makes a wonderful access point for learning more about World War II and Japanese internment." SLJ

Includes bibliographical references

Patten, E. J.

Return to Exile; illustrated by John Rocco. Simon & Schuster 2011 512p (The Hunter chronicles) $16.99

Grades: 5 6 7 8   **Fic**
  1. Fantasy fiction 2. Uncles -- Fiction 3. Monsters -- Fiction
  ISBN 978-1-4424-2032-8; 1-4424-2032-4; 978-1-4169-8259-3 e-book
                                    LC 2010053480
"Sky's twelfth birthday is a mix. His mother's delicious homemade goulash cannot overshadow the disappearance of his beloved uncle, Phineas, or the family's return to the small town of Exile. Sky has grown up reading about the Hunters of Legend, but he never dreamed that they were real until monsters appear in Exile and make Sky their target. . . . Patten's first novel excels at world building and pacing; the monsters . . . are fully formed and vividly drawn. . . . Interspersed with humor to keep an otherwise dark story from becoming overbearing, the balance is just right." Booklist

Patterson, James

Maximum Ride: the angel experiment. Little, Brown 2005 422p (Maximum Ride) $16.99

Grades: 7 8 9 10   **Fic**
  1. Science fiction 2. Genetic engineering -- Fiction
  ISBN 0-316-15556-X
                                    LC 2004-18623
After the mutant Erasers abduct the youngest member of their group, the "bird kids," who are the result of genetic experimentation, take off in pursuit and find themselves struggling to understand their own origins and purpose.

"Smart-mouthed sympathetic characters and copious butt-kicking make this fast read pure escapist pleasure." Horn Book Guide
  Other titles in this series are:
  School's out - forever (2006)
  Saving the world and other extreme sports (2007)
  Final warning (2008)
  Max (2009)
  Fang (2010)
  Angel (2011)

★ **Middle** school, the worst years of my life. Little, Brown 2011 281p il $15.99

Grades: 4 5 6 7   **Fic**
  1. School stories 2. Bereavement -- Fiction 3. Family life -- Fiction
  ISBN 978-0-316-10187-5; 0-316-10187-7
                                    LC 2010022852
"The book's ultrashort chapters, dynamic artwork, and message that 'normal is boring' should go a long way toward assuring kids who don't fit the mold that there's a place for them, too." Publ Wkly

Patterson, Valerie O.

The **other** side of blue. Clarion Books 2009 223p $16

Grades: 7 8 9 10   **Fic**
  1. Artists -- Fiction 2. Bereavement -- Fiction 3. Mother-daughter relationship -- Fiction
  ISBN 978-0-547-24436-5; 0-547-24436-3
                                    LC 2008-49233
The summer after her father drowned off the island of Curacao, Cyan and her mother, a painter, return to the house they stay at every summer, along with the daughter of her mother's fiance, but Cyan blames her mother and spends her time trying to find out what really happened to her father

"In her memorable first-person voice, filled with the minute observations of a young artist, Cyan sketches out with believable detail the beautiful setting, the unspoken family tension, and her fragile recovery of hope after loss." Booklist

Pattou, Edith

East. Harcourt 2003 498p hardcover o.p. pa $8.95

Grades: 7 8 9 10   **Fic**
  1. Fairy tales 2. Bears -- Fiction
  ISBN 0-15-204563-5; 0-15-205221-6 pa
                                    LC 2003-2338
A young woman journeys to a distant castle on the back of a great white bear who is the victim of a cruel enchantment

"Readers with a taste for fantasy and folklore will embrace Pattou's . . . lushly rendered retelling of 'East of the Sun and West of the Moon'." Publ Wkly

Pauley, Kimberly

Cat Girl's day off; Kimberly Pauley. Tu Books 2012 334 p. $17.95

Grades: 6 7 8 9 10   **Fic**
  1. Cats -- Fiction 2. Mystery fiction 3. Adventure fiction 4. High school students -- Fiction 5. Family life -- Illinois -- Chicago -- Fiction 6. Motion pictures

-- Production and direction -- Fiction
ISBN 1600608833; 9781600608834; 9781600608841

LC 2011042997

In this young adult novel, "High school sophomore Natalie 'Nat' Ng has a 'Talent she's not proud of: the ability to talk to cats. Her younger sister is a "supergenius" with chameleonlike abilities; her older sister is proficient in truth divination and levitation, and has X-ray vision; and her parents work for the Bureau of Extrasensory Regulation and Management. When a film crew comes to Nat's Chicago high school to shoot a takeoff of "Ferris Bueller's Day Off" things get fishy: the female star isn't acting like herself, and Nat learns from a cat that celebrity blogger Easton West may not be who she claims to be. Along with her friends Oscar and Melly, Nat gets dragged into a whirlwind adventure to find out what happened to the real Easton." (Publishers Weekly)

Paulsen, Gary

Crush; the theory, practice, and destructive properties of love. Gary Paulsen. Wendy Lamb Books 2012 136 p.

Grades: 5 6 7 8   **Fic**
1. Love -- Fiction 2. Humorous fiction 3. Crushes -- Fiction 4. High school students -- Fiction 5. Dating (Social customs) -- Fiction 6. Humorous stories 7. Interpersonal relations -- Fiction
ISBN 0385742304; 9780307974532; 9780375990540; 9780385742306; 9780385742313

LC 2011028915

In this book, "Tina, aka the most beautiful girl he's ever seen, has stolen Kevin's heart, although she's blissfully oblivious to the effect she has on him. . . . Rather than reveal his ardor outright, Kevin decides it's safer to first make a scientific study of just how love works by setting up romantic opportunities for his victims (otherwise known as study subjects). He starts by trying to create a candlelit dinner for his parents, although he accidentally causes a fire." (Kirkus Reviews)

★ **Dogsong**. Atheneum Books for Young Readers 2000 177p $17.99; pa $6.99

Grades: 6 7 8 9   **Fic**
1. Inuit -- Fiction 2. Sled dog racing -- Fiction
ISBN 0-689-83960-X; 1-416-93962-8 pa

A reissue of the title first published 1985 by Bradbury Press

A Newbery Medal honor book, 1986

A fourteen-year-old Eskimo boy who feels assailed by the modernity of his life takes a 1400-mile journey by dog sled across ice, tunda, and mountains seeking his own "song" of himself

The author's "mystical tone and blunt prose style are well suited to the spare landscape of his story, and his depictions of Russell's icebound existence add both authenticity and color to a slick rendition of the vision-quest plot, which incorporates human tragedy as well as promise." Booklist

Flat broke. Wendy Lamb Books 2011 118p $12.99; lib bdg $15.99

Grades: 4 5 6   **Fic**
1. Friendship -- Fiction 2. Family life -- Fiction 3. Business enterprises -- Fiction 4. Money-making

projects for children -- Fiction
ISBN 978-0-385-74002-9; 0-385-74002-6; 978-0-385-90818-4 lib bdg; 0-385-90818-0 lib bdg

LC 2010049415

Fourteen-year-old Kevin is a hard worker, so when his income is cut off he begins a series of businesses, from poker games to selling snacks, earning money to take a girl to a dance, but his partners soon tire of his methods.

"A jocular, fast-paced voyage into the sometimes simple but never quiet mind of an ambitious eighth grader." Kirkus

★ **Harris** and me; a summer remembered. Harcourt Brace & Co. 1993 157p $16

Grades: 5 6 7 8   **Fic**
1. Cousins -- Fiction 2. Farm life -- Fiction
ISBN 0-15-292877-4

LC 93-19788

Sent to live with relatives on their farm because of his unhappy home life, an eleven-year-old city boy meets his distant cousin Harris and is given an introduction to a whole new world

"Readers will experience hearts as large as farmers' appetites, humor as broad as the country landscape and adventures as wild as boyhood imaginations. All this adds up to a hearty helping of old-fashioned, rip-roaring entertainment." Publ Wkly

★ **Hatchet**; [by] Gary Paulsen; illustrated by Drew Willis. 20th anniversary ed.; Simon & Schuster Books for Young Readers 2007 188p il $19.99; pa $6.99

Grades: 6 7 8 9   **Fic**
1. Divorce -- Fiction 2. Survival after airplane accidents, shipwrecks, etc. -- Fiction
ISBN 978-1-416-92508-8; 1-416-92508-2; 978-1-416-93647-3 pa; 1-416-93647-5 pa

A reissue of the title first published 1987 by Bradbury Press

A Newbery Medal honor book, 1988

After a plane crash, thirteen-year-old Brian spends fifty-four days in the wilderness, learning to survive initially with only the aid of a hatchet given him by his mother, and learning also to survive his parents' divorce

"Paulsen's knowledge of our national wilderness is obvious and beautifully shared." Voice Youth Advocates

Other titles in this series are:
The river (1991)
Brian's winter (1996)
Brian's return (1999)
Brian's hunt (2003)

Liar, liar; the theory, practice, and destructive properties of deception. Wendy Lamb Books 2011 120p $12.99; lib bdg $15.99

Grades: 4 5 6   **Fic**
1. School stories 2. Family life -- Fiction 3. Truthfulness and falsehood -- Fiction
ISBN 0-385-74001-8; 0-385-90817-2 lib bdg; 978-0-385-74001-2; 978-0-385-90817-7 lib bdg

LC 2010-28356

Fourteen-year-old Kevin is very good at lying and doing so makes life easier, until he finds himself in big trouble with his friends, family, and teachers. "Ages eight to twelve." (Publisher's note)

"Kevin's grappling with family troubles adds . . . emotional dimension to Paulsen's novel." Publ Wkly

Nightjohn. Delacorte Press 1993 92p $15.95; pa $5.99

Grades: 7 8 9 10   **Fic**
  1. Reading -- Fiction 2. Slavery -- Fiction 3. African Americans -- Fiction
  ISBN 0-385-30838-8; 0-440-21936-1 pa
                                              LC 92-1222

Twelve-year-old Sarny's brutal life as a slave becomes even more dangerous when a newly arrived slave offers to teach her how to read

"Paulsen is at his best here: the writing is stark and bare-boned, without stylistic pretensions of any kind. The narrator's voice is strong and true, the violence real but stylized with an almost mythic tone. . . . The simplicity of the text will make the book ideal for older reluctant readers who can handle violence but can't or won't handle fancy writing in long books. Best of all, the metaphor of reading as an act of freedom speaks for itself through striking action unembroidered by didactic messages." Bull Cent Child Books

Notes from the dog. Wendy Lamb Books 2009 133p $15.99; lib bdg $18.99

Grades: 5 6 7 8   **Fic**
  1. Cancer -- Fiction 2. Gardening -- Fiction
  ISBN 0-385-73845-5; 0-385-90730-3 lib bdg; 978-0-385-73845-3; 978-0-385-90730-9 lib bdg
                                              LC 2009-13300

When Johanna shows up at the beginning of summer to house-sit next door to Finn, he has no idea of the profound effect she will have on his life by the time summer vacation is over.

"The plot is straightforward, but Paulsen's thoughtful characters are compelling and their interactions realistic. This emotional, coming-of-age journey about taking responsibilty for one's own happiness and making personal connections will not disappoint." Publ Wkly

The **Schernoff** discoveries. Delacorte Press 1997 103p pa $4.99

Grades: 5 6 7 8   **Fic**
  1. School stories 2. Friendship -- Fiction
  ISBN 0440414636
                                              LC 96045390

This "novel, narrated by a 14-year-old, self-confessed geek, focuses on the narrator's friend, Harold. Equally geeky and brainy as well, Harold takes the lead in {a} . . . series of adventures ranging from the unusual but pragmatic (enrolling in home economics to meet girls) to the sneaky and possibly suicidal (taking revenge on the football players who broke his slide rule by giving them a cake flavored with 43 boxes of chocolate laxatives)." (Booklist)

"The tone is breezy, funny, and sometimes touching (but not too mushy) and bound to keep the most reluctant reader chuckling." Bull Cent Child Books

Soldier's heart; a novel of the Civil War. Delacorte Press 1998 106p $15.95; pa $5.99

Grades: 7 8 9 10   **Fic**
  1. Post-traumatic stress disorder -- Fiction 2. United States -- History -- Civil War, 1861-1865
  ISBN 0-385-32498-7; 0-440-22838-7 pa
                                              LC 98-10038

"This compelling and realistic depiction of war is based on a true story. . . . Paulsen's writing is crisp and fast-paced, and this soldier's story will haunt readers long after they finish reading the novel." Book Rep

The **Transall** saga. Delacorte Press 1998 248p pa $6.50

Grades: 5 6 7 8   **Fic**
  1. Science fiction 2. Survival -- Fiction 3. Time travel -- Fiction
  ISBN 0-440-21976-0 pa
                                              LC 97-40773

While backpacking in the desert, thirteen-year-old Mark falls into a tube of blue light and is transported into a more primitive world, where he must use his knowledge and skills to survive

"A riveting tale of adventure and action." Voice Youth Advocates

Vote; the theory, practice, and destructive properties of politics. Gary Paulsen. 1st ed. Wendy Lamb Books 2013 144 p. (hardcover) $12.99; (ebook) $38.97

Grades: 5 6 7 8   **Fic**
  1. School stories 2. Humorous fiction 3. Elections -- Fiction 4. Humorous stories 5. Schools -- Fiction 6. Middle schools -- Fiction 7. Politics, Practical -- Fiction 8. Interpersonal relations -- Fiction
  ISBN 0385742282; 9780307974525; 9780375990533; 9780385742283 trade; 9780385742290
                                              LC 2012023059

In this humorous children's novel, by Gary Paulsen, the author's lead character from previous stories is reprised when he runs for school office. "Kevin Spencer . . . has a knack for tackling big ideas and goofing up, so what's next? Politics, of course! He's running for office, and his campaign is truly unique." (Publisher's note)

"Those who started this four-book series at the beginning may sense that our protagonist is maturing a wee bit, but not so much as to dampen the humor for fans or newcomers. . . . Fast-paced action and Kevin"s penchant for getting into ridiculous situations make this the perfect book bait for not-so-eager readers." BookList

★ **Woods** runner. Wendy Lamb Books 2010 164p $15.99; lib bdg $18.99

Grades: 6 7 8 9   **Fic**
  1. Spies -- Fiction 2. Soldiers -- Fiction 3. Kidnapping -- Fiction 4. Native Americans -- Fiction 5. Frontier and pioneer life -- Fiction
  ISBN 978-0-385-73884-2; 0-385-73884-6; 978-0-385-90751-4 lib bdg; 0-385-90751-6 lib bdg
                                              LC 2009-27397

From his 1776 Pennsylvania homestead, thirteen-year-old Samuel, who is a highly-skilled woodsman, sets out toward New York City to rescue his parents from the band of British soldiers and Indians who kidnapped them after slaughtering most of their community. Includes historical notes.

"Paulsen fortifies this illuminating and gripping story with interspersed historical sections that offer details about frontier life and the war (such as technology, alliances, and other period information), helping place Sam's struggles in context." Publ Wkly

The **island**. Orchard Bks. 1988 202p hardcover o.p. pa $5.99

Grades: 8 9 10 11 12   **Fic**
  1. Islands -- Fiction
  ISBN 0-531-05749-6; 0-439-78662-2 pa
                                            LC 87-24761
"With humor and psychological genius, Paulsen develops strong adolescent characters who lend new power to youth's plea to be allowed to apply individual skills in their risk-taking." Voice Youth Advocates

The **winter** room. Orchard Bks. 1989 103p $16.95; pa $5.99

Grades: 5 6 7 8   **Fic**
  1. Farm life -- Fiction
  ISBN 0-531-05839-5; 0-545-08534-9 pa
                                            LC 89-42541
A Newbery Medal honor book, 1990

A young boy growing up on a northern Minnesota farm describes the scenes around him and recounts his old Norwegian uncle's tales of an almost mythological logging past

"While this seems at first to be a collection of anecdotes organized around the progression of the farm calendar, Paulsen subtly builds a conflict that becomes apparent in the last brief chapters, forceful and well-prepared. . . . Lyrical and only occasionally sentimental, the prose is clean, clear, and deceptively simple." Bull Cent Child Books

Pausewang, Gudrun
  Dark hours; translated by John Brownjohn. Annick Press 2006 208p $21.95

Grades: 6 7 8 9   **Fic**
  1. Refugees -- Fiction 2. World War, 1939-1945 -- Fiction
  ISBN 1-55451-042-2
"Well written with suspense and powerful sentiments, this story will spark discussion." SLJ

Traitor; translated from the German by Rachel Ward. Carolrhoda Books 2006 220p hardcover o.p. pa $9.95

Grades: 7 8 9 10   **Fic**
  1. Prisoners of war -- Fiction 2. World War, 1939-1945 -- Fiction
  ISBN 0-8225-6195-6; 0-7613-6571-0 pa
                                            LC 2005-33379
During the closing months of World War II, a fifteen-year-old German girl must decide whether or not to help an escaped Russian prisoner of war, despite the serious consequences if she does so.

"Pausewang presents an exciting and thought-provoking novel." SLJ

Paver, Michelle
  Wolf brother. HarperCollins 2005 295p (Chronicles of ancient darkness) $16.99; lib bdg $17.89; pa $6.99

Grades: 5 6 7 8   **Fic**
  1. Bears -- Fiction 2. Wolves -- Fiction 3. Demoniac possession -- Fiction 4. Prehistoric peoples -- Fiction
  ISBN 0-06-072825-6; 0-06-072826-4 lib bdg; 0-06-072827-2 pa
                                            LC 2004-8857
First published 2004 in the United Kingdom

6,000 years in the past, twelve-year-old Tarak and his guide, a wolf cub, set out on a dangerous journey to fulfill an oath the boy made to his dying father—to travel to the Mountain of the World Spirit seeking a way to destroy a demon-possessed bear that threatens all the clans

"Paver's depth of research into the spiritual world of primitive peoples makes this impressive British import, slated to be the first in a six-book series, intriguing and believable." SLJ

Other titles in this series are:
Spirit walker (2006)
Soul eater (2007)
Outcast (2008)
Oath breaker (2009)
Ghost hunter (2010)

Peacock, Carol Antoinette
  Red thread sisters; by Carol Antoinette Peacock. Viking 2012 236 p. (hardcover) $15.99

Grades: 4 5 6 7 8   **Fic**
  1. Adoptees -- Fiction 2. Friendship -- Fiction 3. Chinese Americans -- Fiction 4. Adoption -- Fiction 5. Family life -- Fiction 6. Interracial adoption -- Fiction 7. Intercountry adoption -- Fiction
  ISBN 0670013862; 9780670013869
                                            LC 2012019511
This novel, by Carol Antoinette Peacock, offers a "story of friendship, family, and love. Wen has spent the first eleven years of her life at an orphanage in rural China . . . [with] her best friend, Shu Ling. When Wen is adopted by an American couple, she struggles . . . knowing that Shu Ling remains back at the orphanage, alone. Wen knows that her best friend deserves a family and a future, too. But finding a home for Shu Ling isn't easy, and time is running out." (Publisher's note)

Peacock, Shane
  ★ **Eye** of the crow. Tundra Books 2007 264p (The boy Sherlock Holmes) $24.99; pa $9.95

Grades: 6 7 8 9 10   **Fic**
  1. Mystery fiction
  ISBN 978-0-88776-850-7; 0-88776-850-4; 978-0-88776-919-1 pa; 0-88776-919-5 pa
"A young woman is brutally murdered in a dark back street of Whitechapel; a young Arab is discovered with the bloody murder weapon; and a thirteen-year-old Sherlock Holmes, who was seen speaking with the alleged killer as he was hauled into jail, is suspected to be his accomplice. . . . Although imaginative reconstruction of Holmes childhood has been the subject of literary and cinematic endeavors,

Peacock's take ranks among the most successful." Bull Cent Child Books

Other titles in this series are:

Death in the air (2008)
The dragon turn (2011)
The secret fiend (2010)
Vanishing girl (2009)

Pearce, Jackson

As you wish. HarperTeen 2009 298p $16.99
Grades: 6 7 8 9   **Fic**
1. School stories 2. Wishes -- Fiction 3. Artists -- Fiction 4. Popularity -- Fiction 5. Homosexuality -- Fiction
ISBN 006166152X; 0061661538; 0061661546; 9780061661525; 9780061661532; 9780061661549
LC 2008-44033

When a genie arrives to grant sixteen-year-old Viola's wish to feel she belongs, as she did before her best friend/boyfriend announced that he is gay, her delay in making wishes gives her and the mysterious Jinn time to fall in love.

"Written in alternating chapters between Jinn and Viola, the story unfolds to rapidly change from the regular 'genie in the bottle' saga to a poignant tale of love and sacrifices made in the name of love. . . . The result is a fabulous fantasy from a first time author." Voice Youth Advocates

Pearce, Jacqueline

Manga touch; [by] Jacqueline Pearce. Orca Books 2007 105p pa $8.95
Grades: 6 7 8   **Fic**
1. Travel -- Fiction
ISBN 978-1-55143-746-0 pa; 1-55143-746-5 pa

Dana takes a school trip to Japan to learn about Japanese culture and artwork. She surprisingly discovers she has a lot to learn about people as well as manga art.

"Readers will enjoy the skillful way Pearce weaves in facts regarding Japanese culture while still keeping things interesting." Voice Youth Advocates

Pearsall, Shelley

All of the above; a novel. illustrations by Javaka Steptoe. Little, Brown 2006 234p il hardcover o.p. pa $5.99
Grades: 5 6 7 8   **Fic**
1. School stories 2. City and town life -- Fiction
ISBN 0-316-11524-X; 978-0-316-11524-7; 978-0-316-11526-1 pa; 0-316-11526-6 pa
LC 2005-33109

Five urban middle school students, their teacher, and other community members relate how a school project to build the world's largest tetrahedron affects the lives of everyone involved.

"Pearsall's novel, based on a real event in 2002—is a delightful story about the power of a vision and the importance of a goal. The authentic voices of the students and the well-intentioned, supportive adults surrounding them illustrate all that is good about schools, family, friendship, and community." Booklist

All shook up; [by] Shelley Pearsall. Alfred A. Knopf 2008 261p il $15.99; lib bdg $18.99
Grades: 6 7 8 9   **Fic**
1. Father-son relationship -- Fiction
ISBN 978-0-375-83698-5; 0-375-83698-5; 978-0-375-93698-2 lib bdg; 0-375-93698-X lib bdg
LC 2007-22931

When thirteen-year-old Josh goes to stay with his father in Chicago for a few months, he discovers—to his horror—that his dad has become an Elvis impersonator.

"This affecting story of a typical, clever middle-school boy dealing with divorce and the new families that sometimes replace the old is also a very funny tale told by a terrifically engaging young narrator." Voice Youth Advocates

Jump into the sky; Shelley Pearsall. Alfred A. Knopf 2012 344 p. $16.99
Grades: 4 5 6 7   **Fic**
1. Historical fiction 2. Father-son relationship -- Fiction 3. World War, 1939-1945 -- Children -- Fiction 4. World War, 1939-1945 -- African Americans -- Fiction 5. Prejudices -- Fiction 6. Segregation -- Fiction 7. Fathers and sons -- Fiction 8. African Americans -- Fiction
ISBN 0375836993; 0375895485; 0375936998; 0440421403; 9780375836992; 9780375895487; 9780375936999; 9780440421405
LC 2011024935

This novel by Shelley Pearsall presents a "tale of the 555th Parachute Infantry Battalion, little known all-black paratroopers serving during WWII. . . . Her tale of 13-year-old Levi Battle's struggle to find his place in the world during World War II . . . [is the] story of a displaced boy hungry to connect with the war-hero father who is more legend than parent. . . . Levi is [sent to] his father at a base in North Carolina. . . . [and] is plunged into the racist South." (Kirkus Reviews)

Pearson, Joanna

The **rites** & wrongs of Janice Wills. Arthur A. Levine Books 2011 218p $16.99
Grades: 8 9 10 11 12   **Fic**
1. School stories 2. Anthropology -- Fiction
ISBN 978-0-545-19773-1; 0-545-19773-2
LC 2010029348

Aspiring anthropologist Janice Wills reports on the sociocultural ordeals of being an almost-seventeen-year-old in Melva, North Carolina, including "Beautiful Rich Girls," parties, and the Miss Livermush pageant.

"This anthropological observation-style novel is unique and provides a great social commentary on the life of teenagers. It is a cute story that includes mentions of bisexuality, some strong language, and the hint that the Hot Theater Guy might push Janice too far, but it remains a fun look at life in small town Southern society." Voice Youth Advocates

Pearson, Mary E.

Fox forever; Mary E. Pearson. Henry Holt and Company 2013 304 p. (hardcover) $17.99
Grades: 7 8 9 10 11 12   **Fic**
1. Science fiction 2. Dystopian fiction 3. Bioethics -- Fiction 4. Biotechnology -- Fiction 5. Medical ethics

-- Fiction 6. Government, resistance to -- Fiction
ISBN 0805094342; 9780805094343

LC 2012027677

This young adult novel, by Mary E. Pearson, is the conclusion to the "Jenna Fox Chronicles." "After . . . 260 years as a disembodied mind in a little black box, [Lock Jenkins] has a . . . body. But . . . he'll have to return the Favor he accepted from the . . . Network. Locke must infiltrate the home of a government official by gaining the trust of his daughter, seventeen-year-old Raine, and he soon finds himself pulled deep into the world of the resistance--and into Raine's life." (Publisher's note)

The **Fox** Inheritance; [by] Mary E. Pearson. Henry Holt 2011 384p $16.99

Grades: 7 8 9 10 11 12   **Fic**
1. Science fiction 2. Bioethics -- Fiction
ISBN 0805088296; 9780805088298

LC 2011004800

Two-hundred-sixty years after a terrible accident destroyed their bodies, sixteen-year-old Locke and seventeen-year-old Kara have been brought back to life in newly bioengineered bodies, with many questions about the world they find themselves in and more than two centuries of horrible memories of being trapped in a digital netherworld wondering what would become of them.

"Pearson delivers another spellbinding thriller. . . . A dazzling blend of science fiction, mystery, and teen friendship drama." Publ Wkly

★ The **adoration** of Jenna Fox; [by] Mary E. Pearson. Henry Holt and Co. 2008 272p $16.95; pa $8.99

Grades: 7 8 9 10 11 12   **Fic**
1. Science fiction 2. Bioethics -- Fiction
ISBN 978-0-8050-7668-4; 0-8050-7668-9; 978-0-312-59441-1 pa; 0-312-59441-0 pa

LC 2007-27314

In the not-too-distant future, when biotechnological advances have made synthetic bodies and brains possible but illegal, a seventeen-year-old girl, recovering from a serious accident and suffering from memory lapses, learns a startling secret about her existence.

"The science . . . and the science fiction are fascinating, but what will hold readers most are the moral issues of betrayal, loyalty, sacrifice, and survival." Booklist

Peck, Richard, 1934-
Are you in the house alone? Viking 1976 156p pa $5.99

Grades: 8 9 10 11 12   **Fic**
1. Rape -- Fiction
ISBN 0-14-130693-9 pa

LC 76-28810

ALA YALSA Margaret A. Edwards Award (1990)

"Gail is frightened by the obscene telephone calls she receives and the notes that are left on her school locker. It is after she has been raped by a classmate while she is babysitting that she begins to understand the real meaning of fear. Although she is a victim, she is doubted by her family, friends, and the police. Most unendurable is the fact that she is forced frequently to cross the path of her attacker, the son

of a prominent member of the community." Shapiro. Fic for Youth. 2d edition

Fair weather; a novel. Dial Bks. 2001 130p il $16.99; pa $5.99

Grades: 5 6 7 8   **Fic**
1. Actors 2. Singers 3. Family life 4. Scouts 5. Hunters 6. Circus executives 7. Circus performers -- Fiction
ISBN 0-8037-2516-7; 0-14-250034-8 pa

LC 00-55561

In 1893, thirteen-year-old Rosie and members of her family travel from their Illinois farm to Chicago to visit Aunt Euterpe and attend the World's Columbian Exposition which, along with an encounter with Buffalo Bill and Lillian Russell, turns out to be a life-changing experience for everyone

"Peck's unforgettable characters, cunning dialogue and fast-paced action will keep readers in stitches." Publ Wkly

Here lies the librarian. Dial Books 2006 145p $16.99; pa $6.99

Grades: 4 5 6   **Fic**
1. Librarians -- Fiction 2. Automobiles -- Fiction 3. Country life -- Fiction
ISBN 0-8037-3080-2; 0-14-240908-1 pa

LC 2005-20279

Fourteen-year-old Eleanor "Peewee" McGrath, a tomboy and automobile enthusiast, discovers new possibilities for her future after the 1914 arrival in her small Indiana town of four young librarians.

"Another gem from Peck, with his signature combination of quirky characters, poignancy, and outrageous farce." SLJ

★ A **long** way from Chicago; a novel in stories. Dial Bks. for Young Readers 1998 148p pa $5.99; $15.99

Grades: 5 6 7 8   **Fic**
1. Grandmothers -- Fiction 2. Depressions -- 1929 -- Fiction 3. Country life -- Illinois -- Fiction 4. Great Depression, 1929-1939 -- Fiction
ISBN 0-14-240110-2 pa; 0-8037-2290-7

LC 98-10953

A Newbery Medal honor book, 1999

Joe recounts his annual summer trips to rural Illinois with his sister during the Great Depression to visit their larger-than-life grandmother

"The novel reveals a strong sense of place, a depth of characterization, and a rich sense of humor." Horn Book

★ **On** the wings of heroes. Dial Books 2007 148p $16.99; pa $6.99

Grades: 4 5 6 7   **Fic**
1. World War, 1939-1945 -- Fiction
ISBN 0-8037-3081-0; 0-14-241204-X pa

LC 2006011906

A boy in Illinois remembers the homefront years of World War II, especially his two heroes, his brother in the Air Force and his father, who fought in the previous war.

"Peck's masterful, detail-rich prose describes wartime in the United States. . . . Peck's characters are memorable. . . . This book is an absolute delight." SLJ

Three -quarters dead. Dial Books 2010 193p $16.99

Grades: 7 8 9 10 11 12   **Fic**
1. Ghost stories 2. Horror fiction 3. Dead -- Fiction 4. Friendship -- Fiction

ISBN 978-0-8037-3454-8; 0-8037-3454-9
LC 2009-49362

Sophomore loner Kerry is overjoyed when three popular senior girls pick her to be in their clique, until a shocking accident sets off a string of supernatural occurrences that become more and more threatening.

"This staccato-sentenced chiller is not so much a ghost story as it is a smart, sly treatise on friendship, bullying and the timeless power of high-school hierarchies. . . . [The author's] real-life depictions of adolescent egotism and backstabbing cruelty are spot-on." Kirkus

The **river** between us. Dial Bks. 2003 164p $16.99; pa $6.99

Grades: 7 8 9 10   **Fic**
1. Race relations -- Fiction 2. Racially mixed people -- Fiction

ISBN 0-8037-2735-6; 0-14-240310-5 pa
LC 2002-34815

During the early days of the Civil War, the Pruitt family takes in two mysterious young ladies who have fled New Orleans to come north to Illinois

"The harsh realities of war are brutally related in a complex, always surprising plot that resonates on mutiple levels." Horn Book Guide

★ A **season** of gifts. Dial Books for Young Readers 2009 156p $16.99

Grades: 5 6 7 8   **Fic**
1. Moving -- Fiction

ISBN 978-0-8037-3082-3; 0-8037-3082-9
LC 2008-48050

Relates the surprising gifts bestowed on twelve-year-old Bob Barnhart and his family, who have recently moved to a small Illinois town in 1958, by their larger-than-life neighbor, Mrs. Dowdel.

"The type of down-home humor and vibrant characterizations Peck fans have come to adore re-emerge in full as Peck resurrects Mrs. Dowdel, the irrepressible, self-sufficient grandmother featured in A Year Down Yonder and A Long Way from Chicago." Publ Wkly

★ The **teacher's** funeral; a comedy in three parts. Dial Books 2004 190p $16.99; pa $6.99

Grades: 5 6 7 8   **Fic**
1. Teachers -- Fiction 2. Country life -- Fiction

ISBN 0-8037-2736-4; 0-14-240507-8 pa
LC 2004-4361

In rural Indiana in 1904, fifteen-year-old Russell's dream of quitting school and joining a wheat threshing crew is disrupted when his older sister takes over the teaching at his one-room schoolhouse after mean, old Myrt Arbuckle "hauls off and dies."

"The dry wit and unpretentious tone make the story's events comical, its characters memorable, and its conclusion unexpectedly moving." Booklist

★ A **year** down yonder. Dial Bks. for Young Readers 2000 130p $16.99; pa $5.99

Grades: 5 6 7 8   **Fic**
1. Grandmothers 2. Depressions -- 1929 3. Grandmothers -- Fiction 4. Country life -- Illinois 5. Great Depression, 1929-1939 -- Fiction

ISBN 0-8037-2518-3; 0-14-230070-5 pa
LC 99-43159

Awarded the Newbery Medal, 2001

"Peck has created a delightful, insightful tale that resounds with a storyteller's wit, humor, and vivid description." SLJ

Peck, Robert Newton

★ A **day** no pigs would die. Knopf 1973 150p $25; pa $5.50

Grades: 6 7 8 9   **Fic**
1. Pigs -- Fiction 2. Shakers -- Fiction 3. Family life -- Fiction 4. Autobiographical stories 5. Father-son relationship -- Fiction

ISBN 0-394-48235-2; 0-679-85306-5 pa

"Rob lives a rigorous life on a Shaker farm in Vermont in the 1920s. Since farm life is earthy, this book is filled with Yankee humor and explicit descriptions of animals mating. A painful incident that involves the slaughter of Rob's beloved pet pig is instrumental in urging him toward adulthood. The death of his father completes the process of his accepting responsibility." Shapiro. Fic for Youth. 3d edition

Peet, Mal

★ **Tamar**. Candlewick Press 2007 424p $17.99

Grades: 8 9 10 11 12   **Fic**
1. Grandfathers -- Fiction 2. World War, 1939-1945 -- Fiction

ISBN 978-0-7636-3488-9; 0-7636-3488-3
LC 2006-51837

In 1995, 15-year-old Tamar inherits a box containing a series of coded messages from his late grandfather. The messages show Tamar the life that his grandfather lived during World War II the life of an Allied undercover operative in Nazi-occupied Holland.

"Peet's plot is tightly constructed, and striking, descriptive language, full of metaphor, grounds the story." Booklist

Pellegrino, Marge

Journey of dreams. Frances Lincoln Children's Books 2009 250p map $15.95

Grades: 6 7 8 9   **Fic**
1. Refugees -- Fiction

ISBN 978-1-84780-061-9; 1-84780-061-0

"This novel will captivate both Latin American survivors of civil war and their peers. Outstanding." Kirkus

Includes glossary

Pennington, Kate

Brief candle; [by] Kate Pennington. Hodder Children's 2004 262p pa $12.95

Grades: 6 7 8 9   **Fic**
1. Poets 2. Authors 3. Novelists
ISBN 0-12-92965-2

"Along with losing herself in romantic poetry, 14-year-old Emily Bronte loves to wander the wild landscape around her father's parsonage. . . . Her two passions thrillingly collide when she encounters a distraught young man, whose courtship of a girl outside his station has left him jobless and desperate. . . . Pennington's homage offers the most to teens familiar with Bronte's Wuthering Heights. . . . But even readers without much previous knowledge about the book's underpinnings . . . will enjoy the universally accessible view of an ill-fated love and the dreamy restless teen who acts on its behalf." SLJ

Pennypacker, Sara, 1951-
★ The **summer** of the gypsy moths; Sara Pennypacker. Balzer + Bray 2012 275 p. $15.99
Grades: 4 5 6   **Fic**
1. Death -- Fiction 2. Secrets -- Fiction 3. Great aunts -- Fiction 4. Loss (Psychology) -- Fiction
ISBN 0061964204; 9780061964206
LC 2011026095

This middle reader story by Sara Pennypacker follows "Stella[, who] loves living with Great-aunt Louise in her big old house near the water on Cape Cod . . . since her mom is . . . unreliable. So while Mom 'finds herself,' Stella fantasizes that someday she'll come back to the Cape and settle down. The only obstacle to her plan? Angel, the foster kid Louise has taken in. . . . [T]he girls hardly speak to each other. But when tragedy unexpectedly strikes, Stella and Angel are forced to rely on each other to survive." (Publisher's note)

Perera, Anna
★ **Guantanamo** boy. Albert Whitman 2011 339p $17.99
Grades: 7 8 9 10 11 12   **Fic**
1. Cousins -- Fiction 2. Muslims -- Fiction 3. Torture -- Fiction 4. Prisoners -- Fiction 5. Prejudices -- Fiction
ISBN 978-0-8075-3077-1; 0-8075-3077-8
LC 2010048016

"Readers will feel every ounce of Khalid's terror, frustration, and helplessness in this disturbing look at a sad, ongoing chapter in contemporary history." Publ Wkly

Perez, Ashley Hope
What can(t) wait. Carolrhoda 2011 234p $17.95
Grades: 7 8 9 10   **Fic**
1. Family life -- Fiction 2. Mexican Americans -- Fiction 3. Young adult literature -- Works
ISBN 978-0-7613-6155-8; 0-7613-6155-3
LC 2010-28175

"Pérez fills a hole in YA lit by giving Marisa an authentic voice that smoothly blends Spanish phrases into dialogue and captures the pressures of both Latina life and being caught between two cultures." Kirkus

Perez, L. King
Remember as you pass me by. Milkweed 2007 184p $16.95; pa $6.95
Grades: 5 6 7 8   **Fic**
1. Friendship -- Fiction 2. Race relations -- Fiction 3.

African Americans -- Fiction
ISBN 978-1-57131-677-6; 978-1-57131-678-3 pa

In small-town Texas in the mid-1950s, twelve-year-old Silvy tries to make sense of her parent's financial problems, a Supreme Court ruling that will integrate her school, the prejudice of her family and friends, and her own behavior, which always seems to be wrong

"The story flows chronologically with enough drama to keep readers turning the pages." SLJ

Perez, Marlene
Dead is the new black. Harcourt 2008 190p pa $7.95
Grades: 7 8 9 10   **Fic**
1. School stories 2. Cheerleading -- Fiction 3. Supernatural -- Fiction 4. Extrasensory perception -- Fiction
ISBN 978-0-15-206408-2; 0-15-206408-7
LC 2007027677

While dealing with her first boyfriend and suddenly being pressed into service as a substitute cheerleader, seventeen-year-old Daisy Giordano, daughter and sister of psychics but herself a 'normal', attempts to help her mother discover who is behind a series of bizarre attacks on teenage girls in their little town of Nightshade, California.

"This is the witty and humorous first installment in a series; it provides romance, mystery, friendship, adventure, and the supernatural all rolled up in a fast-paced, plot-twisting story." SLJ

Other titles in this series are:
Dead is a state of mind (2009)
Dead is so last year (2009)
Dead is just a rumor (2010)
Dead is not an option (2011)

Perkins, Lynne Rae
All alone in the universe. Greenwillow Bks. 1999 140p il hardcover o.p. pa $5.99
Grades: 5 6 7 8   **Fic**
1. Friendship -- Fiction 2. Best friends -- Fiction
ISBN 0-688-16881-7; 0-380-73302-1 pa
LC 98-50093

Debbie is dismayed when her best friend Maureen starts spending time with ordinary, boring Glenna

"A poignant story written with sensitivity and tenderness." SLJ

★ **As** easy as falling off the face of the earth. Greenwillow Books 2010 352p il $16.99
Grades: 8 9 10 11 12   **Fic**
1. Adventure fiction 2. Chance -- Fiction 3. Accidents -- Fiction
ISBN 978-0-06-187090-3; 0-06-187090-0
LC 2009-42524

A teenaged boy encounters one comedic calamity after another when his train strands him in the middle of nowhere, and everything comes down to luck.

"The real pleasure is Perkins' relentlessly entertaining writing. . . . Wallowing in the wry humor, small but potent truths, and cheerful implausibility is an absolute delight." Booklist

★ **Criss** cross. Greenwillow Books 2005 337p
$16.99; lib bdg $17.89; pa $6.99

Grades: 6 7 8 9   **Fic**

1. Nineteen sixties -- Fiction
ISBN 0-06-009272-6; 0-06-009273-4 lib bdg; 0-06-
009274-2 pa

LC 2004-54023

Awarded the Newbery Medal, 2006

Teenagers in a small town in the 1960s experience new
thoughts and feelings, question their identities, connect, and
disconnect as they search for the meaning of life and love.

"Debbie . . . and Hector . . . narrate most of the novel.
Both are 14 years old. Hector is a fabulous character with
a wry humor and an appealing sense of self-awareness. . .
. The descriptive, measured writing includes poems, prose,
haiku, and question-and-answer formats. There is a great
deal of humor in this gentle story." SLJ

Perkins, Mitali

★ **Bamboo** people. Charlesbridge 2010 272p
$16.95

Grades: 5 6 7 8   **Fic**

1. Wilderness survival -- Fiction
ISBN 978-1-58089-328-2; 1-58089-328-7

LC 2009005495

Two Burmese boys, one a Karenni refugee and the other
the son of an imprisoned Burmese doctor, meet in the jungle
and in order to survive they must learn to trust each other.

"Perkins seamlessly blends cultural, political, religious,
and philosophical context into her story, which is distinguished by humor, astute insights into human nature, and
memorable characters." Publ Wkly

Secret keeper. Delacorte Press 2009 225p
$16.99; lib bdg $19.99

Grades: 7 8 9 10   **Fic**

1. Sisters -- Fiction 2. Family life -- Fiction
ISBN 978-0-385-73340-3; 0-385-73340-2; 978-0-385-
90356-1 lib bdg; 0-385-90356-1 lib bdg

LC 2008-21475

In 1974 when her father leaves New Delhi, India, to seek
a job in New York, Ashi, a tomboy at the advanced age of
sixteen, feels thwarted in the home of her extended family
in Calcutta where she, her mother, and sister must stay, and
when her father dies before he can send for them, they must
remain with their relatives and observe the old-fashioned
traditions that Ashi hates.

"The plot is full of surprising secrets rooted in the characters' conflicts and deep connections with each other. The
two sisters and their mutual sacrifices are both heartbreaking
and hopeful." Booklist

Perkins, Stephanie

Anna and the French kiss. Dutton 2010 372p
$16.99

Grades: 7 8 9 10   **Fic**

1. School stories
ISBN 978-0-525-42327-0; 0-525-42327-3

LC 2009-53290

"Perkin's debut surpasses the usual chick-lit fare with
smart dialogue, fresh characters and plenty of tingly interac-

tions, all set amid pastries, parks and walks along the Seine
in arguably the most romantic city in the world." Kirkus

Perro, Bryan

The **key** of Braha; Bryan Perro ; translated from
the French by Y. Maudet. Delacorte Press 2012 184
p. $16.99

Grades: 4 5 6 7   **Fic**

1. Fantasy fiction 2. Adventure fiction 3. Dead --
Fiction 4. Good and evil -- Fiction
ISBN 0385907672; 9780375896941; 9780385739047;
9780385907675

LC 2011026173

This book is the second in Bryan Perro's 'Amos Daragon' young adult fantasy series, translated from French, in
which a 12-year-old sorcerer named Amos, "unwittingly
takes on a hazardous mission: He's killed so he can pass into
and fix a netherworld crowded with dead souls who aren't
being permitted to pass on to their appointed fates. . . . Once
there Amos receives aid against numerous enemies from a
varied cast of . . . characters, many of whom are figures from
mythology (explained in a lexicon)." (Kirkus)

The **mask** wearer; translated from the French
by Y. Maudet. Delacorte Press 2011 167p (Amos
Paragon) $16.99; lib bdg $19.99

Grades: 4 5 6 7   **Fic**

1. Fantasy fiction 2. Adventure fiction 3. Good and
evil -- Fiction
ISBN 0-385-73903-6; 0-385-90766-4 lib bdg; 978-0-
385-73903-0; 978-0-385-90766-8 lib bdg

LC 2010023725

To defeat the forces of evil which threaten his world,
young Amos Daragon, aided by mythical animal friends,
sets out on a journey to find four masks that harness the
forces of nature and sixteen powerful stones that give the
masks their magic.

"Amos's journey of self-discovery and his quick thinking are sure to keep readers turning the pages to discover the
truth behind the never-ending chaos." SLJ

Peters, Julie Anne, 1952-

★ **By** the time you read this, I'll be dead. Disney/
Hyperion Books 2010 200p $16.99

Grades: 8 9 10 11 12   **Fic**

1. Bullies -- Fiction 2. Obesity -- Fiction 3. Suicide
-- Fiction 4. Depression (Psychology) -- Fiction
ISBN 1-4231-1618-6; 978-1-4231-1618-9

LC 2009-8315

High school student Daelyn Rice, who has been bullied throughout her school career and has more than once
attempted suicide, again makes plans to kill herself, in spite
of the persistent attempts of an unusual boy to draw her out.

"Powerfully portrayed in the first person, the protagonist's account offers compelling insight into just how spiri-
tually and emotionally devastating bullying can be." Voice
Youth Advocates

Between Mom and Jo. Little, Brown 2006 232p
$16.99

Grades: 7 8 9 10 **Fic**
1. Lesbians -- Fiction 2. Prejudices -- Fiction 3. Family life -- Fiction 4. Mother-son relationship -- Fiction
ISBN 0-316-73906-5

LC 2005-22012

Fourteen-year-old Nick has a three-legged dog named Lucky 2, some pet fish, and two mothers, whose relationship complicates his entire life as they face prejudice, work problems, alcoholism, cancer, and finally separation.

"A powerful, moving examination of the relationships we forge within the family we are given." Horn Book Guide

Define normal; a novel. Little, Brown 2000 196p $14.95; pa $5.95
Grades: 7 8 9 10 **Fic**
1. Friendship 2. School stories 3. Peer counseling 4. Family problems 5. Parent and child
ISBN 0-316-70631-0; 0-316-73489-6 pa

LC 99-42774

When she agrees to meet with Jasmine as a peer counselor at their middle school, Antonia never dreams that this girl with the black lipstick and pierced eyebrow will end up helping her deal with the serious problems she faces at home and become a good friend

"Readers who are looking for believable characters and a good story about friendship, being different, and growing wiser will appreciate Define 'Normal'" Voice Youth Advocates

Petersen, P. J.
Wild river. Delacorte Press 2009 120p $14.99; lib bdg $17.99
Grades: 4 5 6 7 **Fic**
1. Brothers -- Fiction 2. Kayaks and kayaking -- Fiction 3. Wilderness survival -- Fiction
ISBN 978-0-385-73724-1; 0-385-73724-6; 978-0-385-90656-2 lib bdg; 0-385-90656-0 lib bdg

LC 2008-24921

Considered lazy and unathletic, twelve-year-old Ryan discovers a heroic side of himself when a kayak trip with his older brother goes horribly awry.

"The compelling first-person narration sets this apart from other adventure stories. . . . With sharp pacing, short sentences, and an unintimidating length, this is a strong, accessible choice for younger readers." Booklist

Peterson, Lois J.
Beyond repair; [by] Lois Peterson. Orca Book Publishers 2011 121p (Orca currents) pa $9.95
Grades: 6 7 8 9 **Fic**
1. Bereavement -- Fiction
ISBN 978-1-55469-816-5; 1-55469-816-2

Cam, still grieving over the death of his father, is worried that he is being stalked.

"Compact, dialogue driven writing keeps the atmosphere tense as Cam races toward a confrontation with his father's killer. . . . A resonant, quick read from a reliable reluctant reader series." Booklist

Silver rain; [by] Lois Peterson. Orca Book Publishers 2010 181p pa $9.95

Grades: 6 7 8 9 **Fic**
1. Missing persons -- Fiction 2. Great Depression, 1929-1939 -- Fiction
ISBN 978-1-55469-280-4; 1-55469-280-6

Elsie's father has disappeared and, as the Depression wears on, the family becomes desperate for money.

"Terse, grim, and funny, the plainspoken narrative from Elsie's viewpoint beautifully conveys a child's sense of the times." Booklist

Peterson, Will
Triskellion; [by] Will Peterson. Candlewick Press 2008 365p $16.99
Grades: 6 7 8 9 **Fic**
1. Twins -- Fiction 2. Siblings -- Fiction 3. Supernatural -- Fiction
ISBN 978-0-7636-3971-6; 0-7636-3971-0

After their parents' divorce, Rachel and Adam are sent to live with their grandmother in the English village of Triskellion, where they find danger and paranormal activity as they discover hidden secrets that some will kill to keep buried.

"The plot moves along at a brisk pace, and there's plenty of adventure, dark and creepy atmosphere, and a touch of the paranormal." SLJ

Triskellion 2: The burning. Candlewick Press 2009 461p $16.99
Grades: 6 7 8 9 **Fic**
1. Twins -- Fiction 2. Siblings -- Fiction 3. Archeology -- Fiction 4. Supernatural -- Fiction
ISBN 978-0-7636-4223-5; 0-7636-4223-1

LC 2009006657

Fourteen-year-old twins Adam and Rachel, pursued by both their former 'Hope Project' benefactors and followers of a zombie-like figure, flee London for Paris, Seville, and finally Morocco, where they unearth an ancient secret more startling than the first.

This is an "action-packed sequel. . . . [It is] imaginative and centered on two likable teens." SLJ

Petrucha, Stefan
The **Rule** of Won. Walker & Co. 2008 227p $16.99
Grades: 8 9 10 11 12 **Fic**
1. School stories 2. Clubs -- Fiction 3. Supernatural -- Fiction 4. Books and reading -- Fiction
ISBN 978-0-8027-9651-6; 0-8027-9651-6

LC 2008-00255

Caleb Dunne, the quintessential slacker, is pressured by his girlfriend to join a high school club based on The Rule of Won, which promises to fulfill members' every "crave," but when nonbelievers start being ostracized and even hurt, Caleb must act.

"The book is fast paced and gripping enough to draw in reluctant readers. . . . Raising questions about issues such as personal responsibility, freedom of speech and the press, and standing up for unpopular beliefs, this novel would be a terrific choice for book-group and class discussions." SLJ

Split. Walker Books for Young Readers 2010 257p $16.99

Grades: 7 8 9 10   **Fic**
  1. Computers -- Fiction 2. Space and time -- Fiction
  ISBN 978-0-8027-9372-0; 0-8027-9372-X
                                              LC 2009-8889

After his mother dies, Wade Jackson cannot decide whether to become a musician or a scholar, so he does both—splitting his consciousness into two distinct worlds.

"The shifting action keeps the fast-paced dual plots moving, and teens will be entertained by the two Wades' embodiment of the tension between being success oriented and following your whims." Booklist

★ **Teen,** Inc. [by] Stefan Petrucha. Walker 2007 244p $16.95

Grades: 8 9 10 11 12   **Fic**
  1. Orphans -- Fiction 2. Pollution -- Fiction 3. Business ethics -- Fiction
  ISBN 978-0-8027-9650-9; 0-8027-9650-8
                                              LC 2007-2368

Fourteen-year-old Jaiden has been raised by NECorp. since his parents were killed when he was a baby, so when he discovers that the corporation has been lying about producing illegal levels of mercury emissions, he and his two friends decide to try to do something about it.

"Witty and provocative without being preachy, this novel has both daring characters and a heady plot." Booklist

Pfeffer, Susan Beth
  Life as we knew it. Harcourt 2006 337p $17

Grades: 7 8 9 10   **Fic**
  1. Science fiction 2. Family life -- Fiction 3. Natural disasters -- Fiction
  ISBN 0-15-205826-5; 978-0-15-205826-5
                                              LC 2005-36321

Through journal entries sixteen-year-old Miranda describes her family's struggle to survive after a meteor hits the moon, causing worldwide tsunamis, earthquakes, and volcanic eruptions.

"Each page is filled with events both wearying and terrifying and infused with honest emotions. Pfeffer brings cataclysmic tragedy very close." Booklist

  Other titles in this series are:
  The dead & gone (2008)
  This world we live in (2010)

Philbin, Joanna
  The **daughters**. Little, Brown 2010 275p il $16.99

Grades: 6 7 8 9   **Fic**
  1. School stories 2. Fame -- Fiction 3. Wealth -- Fiction 4. Friendship -- Fiction
  ISBN 978-0-316-04900-9; 0-316-04900-X

In New York City, three fourteen-year-old best friends who are all daughters of celebrities watch out for each other as they try to strike a balance between ordinary high school events, such as finding a date for the homecoming dance, and family functions like walking the red carpet with their famous parents.

This is a "fun, quick read. . . . Readers will be intrigued by the well-drawn characters and their growth over the course of several months." SLJ

  Other titles in this series are:

The daughters break the rules (2010)
The daughters take the stage (2011)

Philbrick, W. R.
  ★ The **mostly** true adventures of Homer P. Figg; [by] Rodman Philbrick. Blue Sky Press 2009 224p $16.99

Grades: 5 6 7 8   **Fic**
  1. Adventure fiction 2. Orphans -- Fiction 3. Brothers -- Fiction
  ISBN 978-0-439-66818-7; 0-439-66818-2
                                              LC 2008-16925

A Newbery Medal honor book, 2010

Twelve-year-old Homer, a poor but clever orphan, has extraordinary adventures after running away from his evil uncle to rescue his brother, who has been sold into service in the Civil War

"The book wouldn't be nearly as much fun without Homer's tall tales, but there are serious moments, too, and the horror of war and injustice of slavery ring clearly above the din of playful exaggerations." Publ Wkly

Pierce, Tamora
  ★ **First** test. Random House 1999 216p (Protector of the small) hardcover o.p. pa $5.99

Grades: 6 7 8 9   **Fic**
  1. Fantasy fiction 2. Sex role -- Fiction 3. Knights and knighthood -- Fiction
  ISBN 0-679-88914-0; 0-679-98914-5 lib bdg; 0-679-88917-5 pa
                                              LC 98-30903

First title in the Protector of the small series. Ten-year-old Keladry of Mindalen, daughter of nobles, serves as a page but must prove herself to the males around her if she is ever to fulfill her dream of becoming a knight

"Pierce spins a whopping good yarn, her plot balanced on a solid base of action and characterization." Bull Cent Child Books

  Other titles in this series are:
  Page (2001)
  Squire (2002)
  Lady knight (2002)

  Mastiff. Random House 2011 593p (Beka Cooper) $18.99; lib bdg $21.99; e-book $10.99

Grades: 7 8 9 10   **Fic**
  1. Fantasy fiction 2. Police -- Fiction 3. Kidnapping -- Fiction 4. Kings and rulers -- Fiction
  ISBN 978-0-375-81470-9; 978-0-375-91470-6 lib bdg; 978-0-375-89328-5 e-book
                                              LC 2011024152

Beka, having just lost her fiance in a slaver's raid, is able to distract herself by going with her team on an important hunt at the queen's request, unaware that the throne of Tortall depends on their success.

"This novel provides both crackerjack storytelling and an endearingly complex protagonist." Kirkus

  ★ **Melting** stones. Scholastic Press 2008 312p $17.99

Grades: 8 9 10 11 12 **Fic**
1. Fantasy fiction 2. Magic -- Fiction
ISBN 978-0-545-05264-1; 0-545-05264-5
LC 2007045036
Residents of the island of Starns send for help from Winding Circle temple, and when prickly green mage Rosethorn and young stone mage trainee Evvy respond, Evvy finds that the problem is with a long-dormant volcano and tries to use her talents to avert the looming destruction.

This "is a riveting story that has many inventive and exciting plot twists and turns. . . . The story features excellent character development." SLJ

★ **Sandry's** book. Scholastic Press 1997 252p (Circle of magic) hardcover o.p. pa $6.99
Grades: 6 7 8 9 **Fic**
1. Fantasy fiction 2. Magic -- Fiction
ISBN 0-590-55356-9; 0-590-55408-5 pa
LC 95-39540
Four young misfits find themselves living in a strictly disciplined temple community where they become friends while also learning to do crafts and to use their powers, especially magic

"Pierce has created an excellent new world where magic is a science and utterly believable and populated it with a cast of well-developed characters." Booklist

Other available titles in this series are:
Tris's book (1998)
Daja's book (1998)
Briar's book (1999)

★ **Terrier**. Random House 2006 581p il map (Beka Cooper) hardcover o.p. pa $9.99
Grades: 7 8 9 10 **Fic**
1. Fantasy fiction 2. Magic -- Fiction 3. Police -- Fiction
ISBN 978-0-375-81468-6; 0-375-81468-X; 978-0-375-83816-3 pa; 0-375-83816-3 pa
LC 2006-14834
When sixteen-year-old Beka becomes "Puppy" to a pair of "Dogs," as the Provost's Guards are called, she uses her police training, natural abilities and a touch of magic to help them solve the case of a murdered baby in Tortall's Lower City.

"Pierce deftly handles the novel's journal structure, and her clear homage to the police-procedural genre applies a welcome twist to the girl-legend-in-the-making story line." Booklist

Other titles featuring Beka Cooper are:
Bloodhound (2009)
Mastiff (2011)

★ **Trickster's** choice. Random House 2003 422p $17.95; pa $8.95
Grades: 7 8 9 10 **Fic**
1. Fantasy fiction
ISBN 0-375-81466-3; 0-375-82879-6 pa
LC 2003-5202
Alianne must call forth her mother Alanna's courage and her father's wit in order to survive on the Copper Isles in a royal court rife with political intrigue and murderous conspiracy

"This series opener is packed with Pierce's alluring mix of fantasy, adventure, romance, and humor, making the book an essential purchase for school and public libraries." Voice Youth Advocates

Another title in this series is:
Trickster's queen (2004)

★ The **will** of the empress. Scholastic Press 2005 550p $17.99; pa $8.99
Grades: 8 9 10 11 12 **Fic**
1. Fantasy fiction
ISBN 0-439-44171-4; 0-439-44172-2 pa
LC 2005-02874
On visit to Namorn to visit her vast landholdings and her devious cousin, Empress Berenene, eighteen-year-old Sandry must rely on her childhood friends and fellow mages, Daja, Tris, and Briar, despite the distance that has grown between them

"This novel begins two years after the Circle of Magic and The Circle Opens series. . . . Readers will enjoy being reacquainted with these older but still very well-developed characters." SLJ

Pierson, D. C.
Crap kingdom; by DC Pierson. Viking 2013 368 p. (hardcover) $17.99
Grades: 7 8 9 10 11 12 **Fic**
1. Fantasy fiction 2. Humorous fiction 3. Heroes -- Fiction
ISBN 067001432X; 9780670014323
LC 2012015578
In this comic novel, by D. C. Pierson, "with [a] . . . mysterious yet oddly ordinary-looking prophecy, Tom's fate is sealed: he's . . . whisked away to a magical kingdom to be its Chosen One. There's just one problem: The kingdom is mostly made of garbage from Earth. . . . When Tom turns down the job of Chosen One, he thinks he's making a smart decision. But when Tom discovers he's been replaced by his best friend Kyle, . . . Tom wants Crap Kingdom back--at any cost." (Publisher's note)

The **boy** who couldn't sleep and never had to; a novel. DC Pierson. Vintage Books 2010 226 p. ill. $14.95
Grades: 11 12 Adult **Fic**
1. Science fiction 2. Teenagers -- Fiction 3. Friendship -- Fiction 4. Sleep disorders -- Fiction
ISBN 9780307474612
LC 2009021984
Alex Award (2011)
In this book, the recipient of a 2010 ALA Alex Award, "[w]hen [high-school student] Darren Bennett meets [classmate] Eric Lederer, there's an instant connection. They share a love of drawing, the bottom rung on the cruel high school social ladder and a pathological fear of girls. Then Eric reveals a secret: He doesn"t sleep. Ever. When word leaks out about Eric's condition, he and Darren find themselves on the run. Is it the government trying to tap into Eric"s mind, or something far darker? It could be that not sleeping is only part of what Eric's capable of, and the truth is both better and worse than they could ever imagine." (Publisher's note)

Pignat, Caroline

★ **Greener** grass; the famine years. Red Deer Press 2009 276p pa $12.95

Grades: 7 8 9 10   **Fic**

1. Famines -- Fiction

ISBN 978-0-88995-402-1; 0-88995-402-X

"In 1847, 15-year-old Kit is jailed for digging up potatoes on confiscated land to feed her starving family, and during the three weeks that she is incarcerated, she reflects on the past year in Ireland: the blight, the famine, evictions, and deaths. . . . True to Kat's voice, the plain, rhythmic language . . . is lyrical but never ornate. The tension in the story and in the well-developed characters is always rooted in daily detail." Booklist

Wild geese. Red Deer Press 2010 335p pa $12.95

Grades: 7 8 9 10   **Fic**

1. Irish -- Fiction 2. Immigrants -- Fiction 3. Seafaring life -- Fiction

ISBN 978-0-88995-432-8 pa; 0-88995-432-1 pa

"Kit, pursued as a criminal, has safely made it on board an immigrant 'coffin' ship bound for Canada, disguised as a boy and accompanied by Mick, her best friend. Along the way, with historically gritty authenticity, she encounters a lethal fever, near-starvation conditions and terrifying storms. . . . When she finally reaches Canada, there is more disease and separation." Kirkus

Pike, Aprilynne

Earthbound. Penguin Group USA 2013 352 p. $17.99

Grades: 7 8 9 10   **Fic**

1. Occult fiction 2. Science fiction

ISBN 1595146504; 9781595146502

This is the first book in a series from Aprilynne Pike. Here, plane crash survivor Tavia "is in rehab and finishing her senior year online. She has time to look at the world with attentive eyes, and what she sees is often unnerving: glowing triangles on the historic houses of Portsmouth, N.H., or pedestrians who flicker. She tries to attribute these visions to the brain injury she sustained in the crash, but she can't dismiss the stalker with a blond ponytail so easily." (Publishers Weekly)

"The characters are well developed and the narrative is easy to follow... Pike does take a while to get to the heart of the matter, but overall the story is compelling. Readers of supernatural romances will be clamoring." SLJ

Wings. HarperTeen 2009 294p $16.99; lib bdg $17.89; pa $8.99

Grades: 7 8 9 10   **Fic**

1. Fantasy fiction 2. Plants -- Fiction 3. Trolls -- Fiction 4. Fairies -- Fiction

ISBN 978-0-06-166803-6; 0-06-166803-6; 978-0-06-166804-3 lib bdg; 0-06-166804-4 lib bdg; 978-0-06-166805-0 pa; 0-06-166805-2 pa

LC 2008-24653

When a plant blooms out of fifteen-year-old Laurel's back, it leads her to discover the fact that she is a faerie and that she has a crucial role to play in keeping the world safe from the encroaching enemy trolls.

"Replete with budding romance, teen heroics, a good smattering of evil individuals, and an ending that serves up a ready sequel, this novel nonetheless provides an unusual approach to middle level fantasy through its startlingly creative premise that faeries are of the plant world and not the animal world. . . . Both male and female fantasy readers will enjoy this fast-paced action fantasy." Voice Youth Advocates

Other titles in this series are:

Illusions (2011)

Spells (2010)

Pinkney, Andrea Davis

★ **Bird** in a box; illustrations by Sean Qualls. Little, Brown Books for Young Readers 2011 278p il $16.99

Grades: 4 5 6 7   **Fic**

1. Boxing -- Fiction 2. African Americans -- Fiction 3. Radio broadcasting -- Fiction 4. Great Depression, 1929-1939 -- Fiction

ISBN 978-0-316-07403-2; 0-316-07403-9

LC 2010-22851

In 1936, three children meet at the Mercy Home for Negro Orphans in New York State, and while not all three are orphans, they are all dealing with grief and loss which together, along with the help of a sympathetic staff member and the boxing matches of Joe Louis, they manage to overcome.

"Pinkney weaves quite a bit of 1930s history into her story and succeeds admirably in showing how Louis came to represent so much more than his sport. Her detailed notes make this an accessible and inspiring piece of historical fiction that belongs in most collections." SLJ

With the might of angels; the diary of Dawnie Rae Johnson. Scholastic 2011 324p il map (Dear America) $12.99

Grades: 5 6 7 8   **Fic**

1. School stories 2. Diaries -- Fiction 3. Family life -- Fiction 4. Race relations -- Fiction 5. African Americans -- Fiction 6. School integration -- Fiction

ISBN 0-545-29705-2; 978-0-545-29705-9

LC 2011001363

In 1955 Hadley, Virginia, twelve-year-old Dawnie Rae Johnson, a tomboy who excels at baseball and at her studies, becomes the first African American student to attend the all-white Prettyman Coburn school, turning her world upside down. Includes historical notes about the period.

"Dawnie's journal is realistic, encompassing thoughts and emotions one would expect of someone so stressed. . . . The author seamlessly incorporates historical events into the child's journal. The end matter contains age-appropriate photographs, a time line, and brief biographical sketches of the people mentioned. A first purchase." SLJ

Pinkwater, Daniel Manus, 1941-

Adventures of a cat-whiskered girl; illustrations by Calef Brown. Houghton Mifflin Books for Children 2010 268p il $16

Grades: 4 5 6   **Fic**

1. Science fiction 2. Cats -- Fiction 3. Extraterrestrial beings -- Fiction

ISBN 978-0-547-22324-7; 0-547-22324-2

Big Audrey, who has catlike whiskers, and her telepathic friend Molly set out on a journey to find out why flying saucers are landing behind the old stone barn in Poughkeepsie, New York, and, more importantly, to determine whether another cat-whiskered girl really exists.

"Mixing the absurd with the profound, Pinkwater's odd narration will have even the most serious readers laughing at the chaos." Booklist

Bushman lives! written by Daniel Pinkwater ; illustrated by Calef Brown. Houghton Mifflin Harcourt 2012 247 p. $16.99

Grades: 5 6 7 8   **Fic**
   1. Gorillas -- Fiction 2. Teenagers -- Fiction 3. Friendship -- Fiction 4. Humorous stories 5. Artists -- Fiction 6. Coming of age -- Fiction 7. Adventure and adventurers -- Fiction
   ISBN 0547385390; 9780547385396
                      LC 2011048211
In author Daniel Pinkwater's book, "Harold Knishke has no idea he wants to be an artist until the guy in the army cap in Bughouse Square just asks him. Almost immediately Harold is taking drawing classes from a taxidermist and acquires a studio of his own in a building so mysterious he can't tell a soul about it . . . He also has a best friend who is convinced that Bushman, the 427-pound gorilla who once lived in the Lincoln Park Zoo and is now stuffed and on display in the Field Museum of Natural History, is still alive." (Kirkus)

The **Neddiad**; how Neddie took the train, went to Hollywood, and saved civilization. by Daniel Pinkwater; illustrations by Calef Brown. Houghton Mifflin 2007 307p il $16

Grades: 5 6 7 8   **Fic**
   1. Turtles -- Fiction
   ISBN 978-0-618-59444-3; 0-618-59444-2
                      LC 2006033944
When shoelace heir Neddie Wentworthstein and his family take the train from Chicago to Los Angeles in the 1940s, he winds up in possession of a valuable Indian turtle artifact whose owner is supposed to be able to prevent the impending destruction of the world, but he is not sure exactly how.

"A bright and breezy adventure with a smart and funny narrator. . . . [This is a] goofy and lovingly nostalgic historical fantasy." SLJ

The **Yggyssey**; how Iggy wondered what happened to all the ghosts, found out where they went, and went there. illustrations by Calef Brown. Houghton Mifflin Co. 2009 245p il $16

Grades: 4 5 6   **Fic**
   1. Ghost stories 2. Hotels and motels -- Fiction
   ISBN 978-0-618-59445-0; 0-618-59445-0
                      LC 2008-01874
In the mid-1950s, Yggdrasil Birnbaum and her friends, Seamus and Neddie, journey to Old New Hackensack, which is on another plane, to try to learn why ghosts are disappearing from the Birnbaum's hotel and other Hollywood, California, locations.

"Once again, Pinkwater combines a goofy plot, myth and fairy tale references, and an obvious affection for yesteryear Los Angeles in a supernaturally funny read." Booklist

Pinter, Jason
  Zeke Bartholomew, superspy. Sourcebooks Jabberwocky 2011 256p pa $7.99

Grades: 4 5 6 7   **Fic**
   1. Adventure fiction 2. Spies -- Fiction
   ISBN 978-1-4022-5755-1; 1-4022-5755-4
Zeke Bartholomew has always dreamed of being a spy. But when a case of mistaken identity goes horribly wrong, he's thrust into a world of real-life espionage beyond his wildest dreams. Soon this 7th grade nobody finds himself hunted by the lava-powered behemoth Ragnarok, aided by a mysterious butt-kicking girl who goes only by the codename 'Sparrow.'

"Zeke's first-person narration and ample one-liners provide plenty of laughs in a novel that combines espionage, wild sci-fi, and a satiric take on the ever-growing kids-save-the-world subgenre." Booklist

Pitcher, Annabel
  My sister lives on the mantelpiece; a novel. Annabel Pitcher. 1st US ed. Little, Brown & Co. 2012 214 p. (hardcover) $17.99

Grades: 6 7 8 9 10   **Fic**
   1. Bullies 2. Religions 3. Prejudices 4. Grief -- Fiction 5. Family problems -- Fiction
   ISBN 0316176907; 9780316176903
                      LC 2011027350
In this book, Annabel Pitcher tells a story about "grief, prejudice, religion, bullying, and familial instability. . . . Jamie and his family are still dealing with his sister Rose's death in a terrorist bombing five years earlier. . . . The family falls apart--their mother runs off with another man, and their alcoholic father moves from London to the Lake District with the children, where he lavishes attention on Rose's urn. . . . Jamie's pivotal friendship with a Muslim girl, Sunya, is a standout." (Publishers Weekly)

Pixley, Marcella
  ★ **Freak**. Farrar, Straus and Giroux 2007 131p $16

Grades: 6 7 8 9 10   **Fic**
   1. School stories 2. Bullies -- Fiction
   ISBN 0-374-32453-0; 978-0-374-32453-7
                      LC 2006-50683
Twelve-year-old Miriam, poetic, smart, and quirky, is considered a freak by the popular girls at her middle school, and she eventually explodes in response to their bullying, revealing an inner strength she did not know she had.

"The story's conflicts are exceptionally riveting and believable." Booklist

  ★ **Without** Tess. Farrar Straus Giroux 2011 280p $16.99

Grades: 7 8 9 10   **Fic**
   1. Death -- Fiction 2. Guilt -- Fiction 3. Sisters -- Fiction 4. Mental illness -- Fiction 5. Jews -- United States -- Fiction
   ISBN 978-0-374-36174-7; 0-374-36174-6
                      LC 2011001469
Fifteen-year-old Lizzie Cohen recalls what it was like growing up with her imaginative but disturbed older sister

Tess, and how she is striving to reclaim her own life since Tess died.

The author "plumbs the emotional depths of a tough subject with sensitivity and insight into the complexities of human nature and sibling bonds." Kirkus

Platt, Chris

Astra. Peachtree 2010 144p $15.95

Grades: 5 6 7 8   Fic

1. Horses -- Fiction 2. Father-daughter relationship -- Fiction

ISBN 978-1-56145-541-6; 1-56145-541-5
LC 2010001654

Forbidden to ride after her mother's death in a riding accident, thirteen-year-old Lily nurses her mother's beloved horse, Astra, back to health, hoping that someday Astra will win the Tevis Cup endurance race

"Filled with information about endurance racing as well as a cast of interesting supporting characters, including the dishy new boy in town, this novel is a quick and enjoyable read." SLJ

Platt, Randall Beth

Hellie Jondoe; [by] Randall Platt. Texas Tech University Press 2009 216p pa $16.95

Grades: 5 6 7 8   Fic

1. Orphans -- Fiction

ISBN 978-0-89672-663-5 pa; 0-89672-663-0 pa
LC 2009-21514

In 1918, as the Great War ends and the Spanish influenza pandemic begins, thirteen-year-old Hellie Jondoe survives on the streets of New York as a beggar and pickpocket until she boards the orphan train to Oregon, where she learns about loyalty, honesty, and the meaning of family

"This is solid historical fiction with a scrappy heroine who is genuinely tough and a true survivor. Irrepressible and irreverent." Kirkus

Plum, Amy

Die for me. HarperTeen 2011 344p $17.99

Grades: 8 9 10 11   Fic

1. Love stories 2. Dead -- Fiction 3. Sisters -- Fiction 4. Bereavement -- Fiction 5. Supernatural -- Fiction

ISBN 978-0-06-200401-7; 0-06-200401-8
LC 2010-30785

After their parents are killed in a car accident, sixteen-year-old Kate Mercier and her older sister Georgia, each grieving in her own way, move to Paris to live with their grandparents and Kate finds herself powerfully drawn to the handsome but elusive Vincent who seems to harbor a mysterious and dangerous secret.

"Plum deftly navigates the real world and the fantastical. Her characters are authentic, and their romances are believable. Plum introduces a world and a story that are sure to intrigue teen readers and will easily attract fans of the Twilight series." Booklist

Poblocki, Dan

The **nightmarys**. Random House 2010 325p $16.99; lib bdg $19.99

Grades: 6 7 8 9   Fic

1. Mystery fiction 2. Supernatural -- Fiction

ISBN 978-0-375-84256-6; 0-375-84256-X; 978-0-375-94256-3 lib bdg; 0-375-94256-4 lib bdg
LC 2009-50690

Seventh-grader Timothy July and his new friend Abigail try to break a curse that is causing them and others to be tormented by their greatest fears brought to life.

Poblocki "offers plenty of grisly, cinematically creepy imagery for readers who like a good scare, and the tightly wound narrative and ongoing tension between Timothy and Abigail will keep readers holding their breath until even after what they think is the climax." Publ Wkly

The **stone** child. Random House 2009 274p $15.99; lib bdg $18.99

Grades: 5 6 7 8   Fic

1. Authors -- Fiction 2. Monsters -- Fiction 3. Supernatural -- Fiction 4. Books and reading -- Fiction

ISBN 978-0-375-84254-2; 0-375-84254-3; 978-0-375-94254-9 lib bdg; 0-375-94254-8 lib bdg
LC 2008-21722

When friends Eddie, Harris, and Maggie discover that the scary adventures in their favorite author's fictional books come true, they must find a way to close the portal that allows evil creatures and witches to enter their hometown of Gatesweed.

"The creep factor is high but not graphic, and the kids act and react like real kids. . . . This briskly paced novel is sure to be popular with fans of scary stuff." SLJ

Polak, Monique

★ **What** world is left. Orca Book Pub. 2008 215p pa $12.95

Grades: 7 8 9 10 11 12   Fic

1. Jews -- Netherlands -- Fiction 2. Holocaust, 1933-1945 -- Fiction 3. World War, 1939-1945 -- Netherlands -- Fiction

ISBN 978-1-5514-3847-4; 1-5514-3847-X

"Growing up in a secular Jewish home in Holland, Anneke cares little about Judaism, so she has no faith to lose when, in 1943, her family is deported to Theresienstadt, the Nazi concentration camp. . . . Based on the experiences of the author's mother . . . this novel is narrated in Anneke's first-person, present-tense voice. The details are unforgettable. . . . An important addition to the Holocaust curriculum." Booklist

The **middle** of everywhere. Orca Book Publishers 2009 200p pa $12.95

Grades: 7 8 9 10   Fic

1. Inuit -- Fiction 2. Wilderness survival -- Fiction

ISBN 978-1-55469-090-9; 1-55469-090-0

Noah spends a school term in George River, in Quebec's Far North, trying to understand the Inuit culture, which he finds both threatening and puzzling.

"Although the survival-adventure details will engage reluctant readers, the story has elements of romance when Noah strives to impress an Inuit classmate." SLJ

Polisner, Gae

The **pull** of gravity. Frances Foster Books 2011
202p $16.99

Grades: 6 7 8 9   **Fic**
1. Death -- Fiction 2. Bereavement -- Fiction 3. Family
life -- Fiction 4. Father-son relationship -- Fiction
ISBN 978-0-374-37193-7; 0-374-37193-8

LC 2010-21749

When their friend Scooter dies of a rare disease, teenagers Nick Gardner and Jaycee Amato set out on a secret
journey to find the father who abandoned "The Scoot" when
he was an infant, and give him a signed first edition of "Of
Mice and Men."

"Polisner's first novel begins with a bang and ends with
another . . . . There is a great deal to enjoy throughout, and
literary kids will surely enjoy a subplot involving John
Steinbeck." Booklist

Pollock, Tom

★ The **city's** son; Tom Pollock. Flux 2012
460p $16.99

Grades: 6 7 8   **Fic**
1. London (England) -- Fiction 2. Magic -- Fiction 3.
Supernatural -- Fiction 4. Family problems -- Fiction
ISBN 9780738734309

LC 2012010589

This novel, by Tom Pollock, follows "teenage graffiti
artist Beth Bradley . . . [and] Filius, the ragged crown prince
of London's underworld. . . . Reach, the malign god of demolition, is on a rampage . . . to lay claim to the skyscraper
throne. Caught up in helping Filius raise an alleyway army
to battle Reach, Beth soon forgets her old life. But when
the enemy claims her best friend, Beth must choose between
the acceptance she finds in the streets and the life she left
behind." (Publisher's note)

Porter, Sarah

Lost voices. Houghton Mifflin Harcourt 2011
291p $16.99

Grades: 7 8 9 10   **Fic**
1. Singing -- Fiction 2. Supernatural -- Fiction 3.
Mermaids and mermen -- Fiction
ISBN 978-0-547-48250-7; 0-547-48250-7

LC 2011008438

Assaulted and left on the cliffs outside of her grim Alaskan fishing village by her abusive, alcoholic uncle, fourteen-
year-old Luce expects to die when she tumbles into the icy
waters below, but when she instead transforms into a mermaid she is faced with struggles and choices she could never
have imagined.

"Porter's writing is expressive and graceful. . . . A captivatingly different story." Booklist

Porter, Tracey

★ **Billy** Creekmore. Joanna Cotler Books 2007
305p $16.99; lib bdg $17.89; pa $6.99

Grades: 5 6 7 8   **Fic**
1. Circus -- Fiction 2. Orphanages -- Fiction 3. Coal

mines and mining -- Fiction
ISBN 978-0-06-077570-4; 0-06-0-77570-X; 978-0-06-
077571-1 lib bdg; 0-06-077571-8 lib bdg; 978-0-06-
077572-8 pa; 0-06-077572-6 pa

LC 2007-00001

In 1905, ten-year-old Billy is taken from an orphanage
to live with an aunt and uncle he never knew he had, and he
enjoys his first taste of family life until his work in a coal
mine and involvement with a union brings trouble, then he
joins a circus in hopes of finding his father.

"Porter's writing is strong, and the story, told in Billy's
steadfast yet child-true voice, makes the shocking history
about the lives of children at the turn of the last century
come alive for today's readers." Booklist

Potter, Ellen

★ **Slob.** Philomel Books 2009 199p $16.99

Grades: 5 6 7 8   **Fic**
1. Obesity -- Fiction 2. Orphans -- Fiction 3. Siblings
-- Fiction 4. Inventions -- Fiction 5. Bereavement --
Fiction
ISBN 978-0-399-24705-7; 0-399-24705-X

LC 2008-40476

Picked on, overweight genius Owen tries to invent a television that can see the past to find out what happened the day
his parents were killed.

"An intriguingly offbeat mystery, . . . at turns humorous,
suspenseful and poignant." Kirkus

The **humming** room; Ellen Potter. 1st ed. Feiwel & Friends 2012 184 p. $16.99

Grades: 4 5 6 7   **Fic**
1. Gardens -- Fiction 2. Islands -- Fiction 3. Orphans
-- Fiction
ISBN 0312644388; 9780312644383

LC 2011033583

In this book by Ellen Potter, "[h]idden under the family
trailer, Roo hears . . . the murder of her drug-dealing father. .
. . [S]he is sent to live with her . . . reclusive uncle on Cough
Rock, a spooky old house named for its former use as a sanitarium. . . . [The cast of characters includes a] personal assistant, a cheerful local servant, a mysterious wild boy, and a
secluded boy cousin with a fearful temper who is not expected to live." (Bulletin of the Center for Children''s Books)

Powell, Laura

Burn mark; by Laura Powell. Bloomsbury Children's Books 2012 403p. (hardback) $17.99

Grades: 7 8 9 10 11 12   **Fic**
1. Occult fiction 2. Witches -- Fiction 3. Supernatural
-- Fiction
ISBN 1599908433; 9781599908434

LC 2011034464

This young adult fantasy, by Laura Powell, is set "in a
modern world where witches are hunted down and burned
at the stake. . . . Glory is from a family of witches, and is
desperate to develop her 'Fae' powers. . . . Lucas is the son
of the Chief Prosecutor for the Inquisition with a privileged
life very different from the witches he is being trained to
prosecute. And then one day, both Glory and Lucas develop

the Fae . . . [and] their lives are inextricably bound together."
(Publisher's note)

The **Master** of Misrule; Laura Powell. Alfred A.
Knopf 2012 363 p. (trade hardcover) $16.99
Grades: 7 8 9 10 11 12   Fic
1. Games -- Fiction 2. Tarot -- Fiction 3. Supernatural
-- Fiction 4. Role playing -- Fiction 5. Space and time
-- Fiction
ISBN 0375865888; 9780375865664; 9780375865886;
9780375897849; 9780375965883
LC 2011021135
In this book, "despite holding the Triumphs that promise
answers to their various back stories (including the murder
of Cat's parents, Blaine's abusive stepfather and Flora's co-
matose sister, all related to the Game of Triumphs), resolution eludes Cat and her friends. They must fight the Fool,
now the Master of Misrule, whom they released in the first
volume, not only for their own success, but to save the
world." (Kirkus Reviews)
"This fast-paced novel mixes fantasy and reality in an
intricately described setting... Packed with mystery, action,
and even a hint of romance, The Master of Misrule will appeal to fans of role-playing games or anyone seeking an adventurous read.—" VOYA

The **game** of triumphs. Alfred A. Knopf 2011
269p $16.99; lib bdg $19.99; ebook $10.99
Grades: 7 8 9 10   Fic
1. Games -- Fiction 2. Tarot -- Fiction 3. Supernatural
-- Fiction 4. Space and time -- Fiction
ISBN 978-0-375-86587-9; 0-375-86587-X; 978-0-
375-96587-6 lib bdg; 0-375-96587-4 lib bdg; 978-0-
375-89774-0 ebook
LC 2010021813
Fifteen-year-old Cat and three other London teens are
drawn into a dangerous game in which Tarot cards open
doorways into a different dimension and while there is everything to win, losing can be fatal.
"Original and engrossing." Kirkus

Powell, Randy
Swiss mist. Farrar, Straus & Giroux 2008 210p
$16.95
Grades: 6 7 8 9 10   Fic
1. Divorce -- Fiction
ISBN 978-0-374-37356-6; 0-374-37356-6
LC 2007-27680
Follows Milo from fifth grade, when his mother and philosopher father get divorced, through tenth grade, when his
mother has married a wealthy businessman and Milo is still
a bit of a loner, looking for the meaning of life.
"This book is rewardingly remarkable for the characters
and bits of truth that Milo never stops pursuing, even as he
learns that truth is not what matters most." SLJ

Three clams and an oyster. Farrar, Straus & Giroux 2002 216p hardcover o.p. pa $6.95
Grades: 7 8 9 10   Fic
1. Humorous stories 2. Football -- Fiction 3. Friendship

-- Fiction
ISBN 0-374-37526-7; 0-374-40007-5 pa
LC 2001-54833
During their humorous search to find a fourth player for
their flag football team, three high school juniors are forced
to examine their long friendship, their individual flaws, and
their inability to try new experiences
"Sometimes philosophical, sometimes comical, but always touching, Randy Powell writes an unusually moving
story of adolescent male friends." Book Rep

Powers, J. L.
This thing called the future; a novel. Cinco Pun-
tos 2011 213p $15.95
Grades: 8 9 10 11 12   Fic
1. Sick -- Fiction 2. Mother-daughter relationship --
Fiction
ISBN 978-1-933693-95-8; 1-933693-95-9
Powers "composes a compelling, often harrowing por-
trait of a struggling country, where old beliefs and rituals
still have power, but can't erase the problems of the present.
Readers will be fully invested in Khosi's efforts to secure a
better future." Publ Wkly

Pratchett, Terry
★ **Dodger**; by Terry Pratchett. HarperCollins
2012 360 p. (hardback) $17.99
Grades: 7 8 9 10   Fic
1. Love -- Fiction 2. Humorous stories 3. Adventure
and adventurers -- Fiction
ISBN 0062009494; 9780062009494; 9780062009500
LC 2012022155
Michael L. Printz Honor Book (2013)
Author Terry Pratchett presents a story of historical fiction. "Dodger is a guttersnipe and a tosher . . . [and] a petty
criminal but also (generally) one of the good guys. One night
he rescues a beautiful young woman and finds himself hob-
nobbing quite literally with the likes of Charlie Dickens .
. . and Ben Disraeli . . . And when he attempts to smarten
himself up to impress the damsel in distress, he unexpectedly comes face to face with . . . Sweeney Todd." (Kirkus)

★ **I** shall wear midnight. Harper 2010 355p
$16.99
Grades: 7 8 9 10   Fic
1. Ghost stories 2. Fantasy fiction 3. Fairies -- Fiction
4. Witches -- Fiction
ISBN 978-0-06-143304-7; 0-06-143304-7
LC 2010-24442
Fifteen-year-old Tiffany Aching, the witch of the Chalk,
seeks her place amid a troublesome populace and tries
to control the ill-behaved, six-inch-high Wee Free Men
who follow her as she faces an ancient evil that agitates
against witches.
"The final adventure in Pratchett's Tiffany Aching series brings this subset of Discworld novels to a moving and
highly satisfactory conclusion." Publ Wkly

★ **Nation**. HarperCollins 2008 367p $16.99;
lib bdg $17.89; pa $8.99
Grades: 7 8 9 10 11 12   Fic
1. Islands -- Fiction 2. Tsunamis -- Fiction 3. Young

adult literature -- Works 4. Survival after airplane accidents, shipwrecks, etc. -- Fiction
ISBN 978-0-06-143301-6; 0-06-143301-2; 978-0-06-143302-3 lib bdg; 0-06-143302-0 lib bdg; 978-0-06-143303-0 pa; 0-06-143303-9 pa

LC 2008-20211

Boston Globe-Horn Book Award: Fiction (2009)

After a devastating tsunami destroys all that they have ever known, Mau, an island boy, and Daphne, an aristocratic English girl, together with a small band of refugees, set about rebuilding their community and all the things that are important in their lives.

"Quirky wit and broad vision make this a fascinating survival story on many levels." Booklist

★ **Only** you can save mankind. HarperCollins 2005 207p hardcover o.p. lib bdg $16.89; pa $6.99
Grades: 5 6 7 8   **Fic**
1. War stories 2. Computer games -- Fiction
ISBN 0-06-054185-7; 0-06-054186-5 lib bdg; 0-06-054187-3 pa

First published 1992 in the United Kingdom

Twelve-year-old Johnny endures tensions between his parents, watches television coverage of the Gulf War, and plays a computer game called Only You Can Save Mankind, in which he is increasingly drawn into the reality of the alien ScreeWee

This is "a wild ride, full of Pratchett's trademark humor; digs at primitive, low-resolution games . . . ; and some not-so-subtle philosophy about war and peace." Booklist

Other titles in this trilogy are:
Johnny and the dead (2006)
Johnny and the bomb (2006)

The **Wee** Free Men. HarperCollins Pubs. 2003 263p hardcover o.p. pa $9.99
Grades: 7 8 9 10   **Fic**
1. Fantasy fiction 2. Witches -- Fiction
ISBN 0-06-001236-6; 0-06-201217-7 pa

LC 2002-15396

A young witch-to-be named Tiffany teams up with the Wee Free Men, a clan of six-inch-high blue men, to rescue her baby brother and ward off a sinister invasion from Fairyland

"Pratchett invites readers into his well-established realm of Discworld where action, magic, and characters are firmly rooted in literary reality. Humor ripples throughout, making tense, dangerous moments stand out in stark contrast." Bull Cent Child Books

Other titles about Tiffany are:
A hat full of sky (2004)
I shall wear midnight (2010)
Wintersmith (2006)

★ The **amazing** Maurice and his educated rodents. HarperCollins Pubs. 2001 241p hardcover o.p. pa $6.99
Grades: 7 8 9 10   **Fic**
1. Fantasy fiction 2. Cats -- Fiction 3. Rats -- Fiction
ISBN 0-06-001233-1; 0-06-001235-8 pa

LC 2001-42411

A talking cat, intelligent rats, and a strange boy cooperate in a Pied Piper scam until they try to con the wrong town and are confronted by a deadly evil rat king

"In this laugh-out-loud fantasy, his first 'Discworld' novel for younger readers, Pratchett rethinks a classic story and comes up with a winner." SLJ

Preller, James
★ **Bystander**. Feiwel and Friends 2009 226p $16.99
Grades: 5 6 7 8   **Fic**
1. School stories 2. Moving -- Fiction 3. Bullies -- Fiction 4. Divorce -- Fiction 5. Family life -- Fiction
ISBN 0312379064; 9780312379063

LC 2008-28554

Thirteen-year-old Eric discovers there are consequences to not standing by and watching as the bully at his new school hurts people, but although school officials are aware of the problem, Eric may be the one with a solution.

"Although there are no pat answers, the message (that a bystander is hardly better than an instigator) is clear, and Preller's well-shaped characters, strong writing, and realistic treatment of middle-school life deliver it cleanly." Booklist

★ **Six** innings; a game in the life. Feiwel and Friends 2008 147p $16.95
Grades: 4 5 6 7   **Fic**
1. Cancer -- Fiction 2. Baseball -- Fiction
ISBN 978-0-312-36763-3; 0-312-36763-5

LC 2007-32846

Earl Grubb's Pool Supplies plays Northeast Gas & Electric in the Little League championship game, while Sam, who has cancer and is in a wheelchair, has to call the play-by-play instead of participating in the game.

"The outcome is predictable but the journey is nailbitingly tense. Kids will be nodding in agreement at the truths laid bare." Publ Wkly

Preus, Margi
★ **Heart** of a samurai; based on the true story of Nakahama Manjiro. Abrams/Amulet 2010 301p il $15.95
Grades: 7 8 9 10 11 12   **Fic**
1. Japanese -- United States -- Fiction 2. Survival after airplane accidents, shipwrecks, etc. -- Fiction
ISBN 978-0-8109-8981-8; 0-8109-8981-6

LC 2009-51634

A Newbery Medal honor book, 2011

In 1841, rescued by an American whaler after a terrible shipwreck leaves him and his four companions castaways on a remote island, fourteen-year-old Manjiro, who dreams of becoming a samurai, learns new laws and customs as he becomes the first Japanese person to set foot in the United States.

The author "mixes fact with fiction in a tale that is at once adventurous, heartwarming, sprawling, and nerve-racking in its depictions of early anti-Asian sentiment. She succeeds in making readers feel every bit as 'other' as Manjiro, while showing America at its best and worst through his eyes." Publ Wkly

Includes bibliographical references

Shadow on the mountain; a novel inspired by the true adventures of a wartime spy. by Margi Preus. Amulet Books 2012 286 p. (alk. paper) $16.95

Grades: 6 7 8 9   Fic

1. Spies -- Fiction 2. World War, 1939-1945 -- Underground movements -- Norway -- Fiction
ISBN 1419704249; 9781419704246

LC 2012015623

This juvenile historical fiction novel, by Margi Preus, "recounts the adventures of a 14-year-old Norwegian boy named Espen during World War II. After Nazi Germany invades and occupies Norway, Espen and his friends are swept up in the Norwegian resistance movement. Espen gets his start by delivering illegal newspapers, then graduates to the role of courier and finally becomes a spy, dodging the Gestapo along the way." (Publisher's note)

Includes bibliographical references.

Prevost, Guillaume

The **book** of time; [by] Guillaume Prévost; translated by William Rodarmor. Arthur A. Levine Books 2007 213p $16.99; pa $6.99

Grades: 5 6 7 8   Fic

1. Science fiction 2. Missing persons -- Fiction
ISBN 978-0-439-88375-7; 0-439-88375-X; 978-0-439-88379-5 pa; 0-439-88379-2 pa

LC 2006-38446

Original French edition 2006

Sam Faulkner travels back in time to medieval Ireland, ancient Egypt and Renaissance Bruges in search of his missing father

"The appeal of the novel . . . comes from both well-drawn characters and a swiftly moving story." Booklist

Other titles in this series are:
The gate of days (2008)
The circle of gold (2009)

Price, Charlie

★ **Desert** Angel. Farrar Straus Giroux 2011 176p $15.99

Grades: 8 9 10 11 12   Fic

1. Violence -- Fiction 2. Illegal aliens -- Fiction 3. Mexican Americans -- Fiction
ISBN 978-0-374-31775-1; 0-374-31775-5

LC 2010044122

"Price's pacing is tight, aided by direct, clipped prose that underscores Scotty's brutality and Angel's fragile emotional state. Both the best and worst of humanity shine through in this gripping novel." Publ Wkly

Price, Lissa

Starters; Lissa Price. Delacorte Press 2012 336 p. (paperback) $9.99; (ebook) $53.97; (glb) $20.99; (hardcover) $17.99

Grades: 7 8 9 10   Fic

1. Science fiction 2. Orphans -- Fiction 3. Intergenerational relations -- Fiction 4. Brothers and sisters -- Fiction
ISBN 9780385742481; 0385742371; 9780307975232; 9780375990601; 9780385742375

LC 2011040820

In this book, "[w]hen a deadly virus wipes out the entire population of the U.S. save the elderly and the young, . . . the result is a dysfunctional society polarized between young 'Starters' and the increasingly long-lived 'Enders.' Children who are unclaimed by surviving relatives are institutionalized, and many -- like Callie and her little brother, Tyler -- learn to fend for themselves in virtual hiding from the law to escape that fate." (Bulletin of the Center for Children's Books)

Price, Nora

Zoe letting go; Nora Price. Razorbill 2012 279 p. $17.99

Grades: 8 9 10 11 12   Fic

1. Rehabilitation -- Fiction 2. Eating disorders -- Fiction 3. Diaries -- Fiction 4. Letters -- Fiction 5. Friendship -- Fiction 6. Anorexia nervosa -- Fiction 7. Emotional problems -- Fiction
ISBN 1595144668; 9781595144669

LC 2012012257

This book tells the story of 16-year-old Zoe, who "finds herself in a small rehabilitation center for girls with eating disorders," which she feels "must be some kind of mistake" because "she feels in control of her cautious dietary habits. Through letters to her mysteriously silent best friend, Elise, as well as a personal journal," it becomes clear that Zoe is in denial and "that she is, in fact, a girl with a disorder that is spiraling out of control." (School Library Journal)

Priestly, Chris

Mister Creecher. Bloomsbury 2011 390p $16.99

Grades: 6 7 8 9   Fic

1. Horror fiction 2. Frankenstein's monster (Fictional character)
ISBN 978-1-59990-703-1; 1-59990-703-8

Billy is a street urchin, a pickpocket, and a petty thief. Mister Creecher is a giant of a man whose appearance terrifies everyone he meets. A bond develops between these two misfits as they embark on a bloody journey that will take them from London northward on the trail of their target . . . Doctor Victor Frankenstein.

"Priestly's love of Shelley is evident. Here, he restores Shelley's original creature—not a lurching, moaning monster but an eloquent, profoundly flawed being—imbuing him with the deep desire to be loved and accepted." Booklist

Prineas, Sarah

★ The **magic** thief; illustrations by Antonio Javier Caparo. HarperCollins Pubs. 2008 419p il map

Grades: 4 5 6 7   Fic

1. Fantasy fiction 2. Magic -- Fiction 3. Thieves -- Fiction 4. Apprentices -- Fiction
ISBN 0-06-137587-X; 0-06-137588-8 lib bdg; 0-06-137590-X pa; 978-0-06-137587-3; 978-0-06-137588-0 lib bdg; 978-0-06-137590-3 pa

LC 2007031704

Conn is a young thief who is drawn into a life of adventure after picking the pocket of the wizard Nevery Flinglas. Finglas has returned from exile to try to reverse the decline of magic in Wellmet City. "Grades five to nine." (Bull Cent Child Books)

"Conn is a thief but, through desire and inevitability, becomes a wizard . . . This evolution begins when Conn picks the pocket of the wizard Nevery. . . . What works wonderfully well here is the boy's irresistable voice." Booklist

Other titles in this series are:

Lost (2009)

Found (2010)

Prinz, Yvonne

The **Vinyl** Princess. HarperTeen 2010 313p $16.99

Grades: 8 9 10 11 12 **Fic**

1. Music -- Fiction 2. Zines -- Fiction 3. Weblogs -- Fiction 4. Sound recordings -- Fiction

ISBN 978-0-06-171583-9; 0-06-171583-2

LC 2009-14270

Allie, a sixteen-year-old who is obsessed with LPs, works at the used record store on Telegraph Ave. and deals with crushes—her own and her mother's—her increasingly popular blog and zine, and generally grows up over the course of one summer in her hometown of Berkeley, California.

Prinz "writes with a genuine passion for music that readers who live to listen will recognize, and in this heartfelt, often-hilarious story, she shows the profound ways that music can shape lives." Booklist

Proimos, James

12 things to do before you crash and burn. Roaring Brook Press 2011 121p $14.99

Grades: 7 8 9 10 **Fic**

1. Uncles -- Fiction 2. Bereavement -- Fiction 3. Father-son relationship -- Fiction

ISBN 978-1-59643-595-7; 1-59643-595-X

LC 2010043935

Sixteen-year-old James 'Hercules' Martino completes twelve tasks while spending two weeks in Baltimore with his Uncle Anthony, and gains insights into himself, his uncle, and his recently deceased father, a self-help author and daytime talk show host who was beloved by the public but a terrible father.

"Proimos fully inhabits the mind and voice of his hero, whose almost mythic journey offers moments hilarious, heartbreaking, and triumphant." Publ Wkly

Prose, Francine

After. HarperCollins Pubs. 2003 330p $15.99; lib bdg $16.89

Grades: 7 8 9 10 **Fic**

1. School stories 2. Conspiracies -- Fiction 3. School violence -- Fiction

ISBN 0-06-008081-7; 0-06-008082-5 lib bdg

LC 2002-14386

In the aftermath of a nearby school shooting, a grief and crisis counselor takes over Central High School and enacts increasingly harsh measures to control students, while those who do not comply disappear

"This drama raises all-too-relevant questions about the fine line between safety as a means of protection versus encroachment on individual rights and free will. Sure to spur heated discussions." Publ Wkly

Touch. HarperTeen 2009 262p $16.99; lib bdg $17.89

Grades: 7 8 9 10 **Fic**

1. School stories 2. Friendship -- Fiction 3. Family life -- Fiction 4. Stepmothers -- Fiction

ISBN 978-0-06-137517-0; 0-06-137517-9; 978-0-06-137518-7 lib bdg; 0-06-137518-7 lib bdg

LC 2008-20208

Ninth-grader Maisie's concepts of friendship, loyalty, self-acceptance, and truth are tested to their limit after a schoolbus incident with the three boys who have been her best friends since early childhood.

"Readers will be fascinated by this convincing tale and the questions that it raises, from its gripping first chapter to its poignant and surprising conclusion." Voice Youth Advocates

The **turning**; by Francine Prose. HarperTeen 2012 256 p. (hardcover) $17.99

Grades: 7 8 9 10 **Fic**

1. Ghost stories 2. Horror fiction 3. Babysitters -- Fiction 4. Ghosts -- Fiction

ISBN 0061999660; 9780061999666

LC 2012019090

This book by Francine Prose is an "epistolary retelling of Henry James's 'The Turn of the Screw' [which] traces a contemporary babysitter's supernatural encounters. The protagonist, Jack, is hoping to earn some money for college when he agrees to care for orphan siblings on Crackstone's Landing, a remote island without phones, Internet, or TV. . . . Jack is spooked by two ethereal figures, perhaps the ghosts of the children's former governess and her beau." (Publishers Weekly)

Pryor, Bonnie

Simon's escape; a story of the Holocaust. Enslow Publishers 2010 160p (Historical fiction adventures) lib bdg $27.93; pa $14.95

Grades: 4 5 6 **Fic**

1. Jews -- Poland -- Fiction 2. Holocaust, 1933-1945 -- Fiction 3. World War, 1939-1945 -- Fiction

ISBN 978-0-7660-3388-7 lib bdg; 0-7660-3388-0 lib bdg; 978-1-59845-216-7 pa; 1-59845-216-9 pa

LC 2009029322

Simon, a young Polish Jew, and his family are forced by Nazis to leave their home for the filth and hunger of the Warsaw ghetto then, when his family is all taken away, he escapes to fight for survival in the countryside. Includes facts about the Holocaust

This "is a compelling, informative introduction to Holocaust history." Booklist

The **iron** dragon; the courageous story of Lee Chin. Enslow Publishers 2010 160p (Historical fiction adventures) lib bdg $27.93; pa $14.95

Grades: 4 5 6 **Fic**

1. Railroads -- Fiction 2. Immigrants -- Fiction 3. Chinese Americans -- Fiction

ISBN 978-0-7660-3389-4 lib bdg; 0-7660-3389-9 lib bdg; 978-1-59845-215-0 pa; 1-59845-215-0 pa

LC 2009017930

In the mid-nineteenth century, teenager Lee Chin and his father leave China for California to work on the transcontinental railroad, where Lee defies his father's wishes and saves money to free his younger sister from slavery in China, then brings her to join him in beginning a new life in America. Includes historical note about the Chinese who helped build the transcontinental railroad

"Lee Chin's tale is compellingly told. . . . Historical information is accurate and honest about the period depicted." SLJ

Pullman, Philip, 1946-

★ **Once** upon a time in the North; illustrated by John Lawrence. Knopf 2008 95p il $12.99

Grades: 7 8 9 10 11 12   **Fic**
   1. Fantasy fiction
   ISBN 978-0-375-84510-9; 0-375-84510-0
                    LC 2007-43993

In a time before Lyra Silvertongue was born, the tough American balloonist Lee Scoresby and the great armoured bear Iorek Byrnison meet when Lee and his hare daemon Hester crash-land their trading balloon onto a port in the far Arctic North and find themselves right in the middle of a political powder keg.

"The precise narrative prose is spiced up with Lee's flights of 'oratorical flamboyancy,' and the sardonic banter between Lee and his daemon Hester is as amusing as ever. [Illustrated with] engraved spot illustrations and 'reproduced' documents." Horn Book

Two crafty criminals! and how they were captured by the daring detectives of the New Cut Gang ; including Thunderbolt's Waxwork & the gas-fitters' ball. Philip Pullman. Alfred A. Knopf 2012 281 p. $16.99

Grades: 5 6 7 8   **Fic**
   1. Mystery fiction 2. Crime -- Fiction 3. Gangs -- Fiction 4. Humorous stories 5. Adventure and adventurers -- Fiction
   ISBN 9780375870293; 9780375970290; 9780375988684
                    LC 2011042391

This children's book by Philip Pullman was published in 1994 as two novellas: "Thunderbolt's Waxwork" and "The Gas-Fitters' Ball," which are set in "1894 London . . . [and] star . . . the intrepid boy and girl detectives of the New Cut Gang. . . . Thunderbolt Dobney sees his own father hauled off to jail for what he thinks must be 'coining.' . . . [H]e and the New Cut Gang expose the real criminal. . . . In 'The Gas-Fitters' Ball,' . . . the Gas-Fitters' Hall is burgled." (Kirkus Reviews)

★ The **golden** compass; his dark materials book I. [appendix illustrations by Ian Beck] Deluxe 10th anniversary ed.; Alfred A. Knopf 2006 399p il $22.95

Grades: 7 8 9 10 11 12   **Fic**
   1. Fantasy fiction
   ISBN 978-0-375-83830-9; 0-375-83830-9
                    LC 2005-32556

First published 1995 in the United Kingdom with title: Northern lights

This first title in a fantasy trilogy "introduces the characters and sets up the basic conflict, namely, a race to unlock the mystery of a newly discovered type of charged particles simply called 'dust' that may be a bridge to an alternate universe. The action follows 11-year-old protagonist Lyra Belacqua from her home at Oxford University to the frozen wastes of the North on a quest to save dozens of kidnapped children from the evil 'Gobblers,' who are using them as part of a sinister experiment involving dust." Libr J [review of 1996 edition]

Other titles in the His dark materials series are:
The amber spyglass (2000)
The subtle knife (1997)

Pyron, Bobbie

★ A **dog's** way home. Katherine Tegen Books 2011 321p lib bdg $17.89; $16.99

Grades: 4 5 6 7   **Fic**
   1. Dogs -- Fiction 2. Traffic accidents -- Fiction
   ISBN 0-06-198673-9 lib bdg; 0-06-198674-7; 978-0-06-198673-4 lib bdg; 978-0-06-198674-1
                    LC 2010006960

After a car accident strands them at opposite ends of the Blue Ridge Parkway, eleven-year-old Abby and her beloved sheltie Tam overcome months filled with physical and emotional challenges to find their way back to each other.

"A heartwarming, suspenseful tale. . . . With vibrant, sympathetic characterizations, Pyron creates an inspiring portrayal of devotion and survival against all odds." Publ Wkly

The **dogs** of winter; by Bobbie Pyron. Arthur A. Levine Books 2012 312 p. (hardcover : alk. paper) $16.99

Grades: 5 6 7 8   **Fic**
   1. Wild dogs -- Fiction 2. Abandoned children -- Fiction 3. Wilderness survival -- Fiction 4. Gangs -- Fiction 5. Street children -- Fiction 6. Homeless persons -- Fiction 7. Human-animal relationships -- Fiction
   ISBN 0545399300; 9780545399302; 9780545399319; 9780545469852
                    LC 2011051519

In this book by Bobbie Pyron "Ivan's mother disappears, [and] he's abandoned on the streets of Moscow, with little chance to make it through the harsh winter. But help comes in an unexpected form: Ivan is adopted by a pack of dogs, and the dogs quickly become more than just his street companions: They become his family. Soon Ivan, who used to love reading fairytales, is practically living in one." But "when help is finally offered to him, will he be able to accept it?" (Publisher's note)

Qamar, Amjed

Beneath my mother's feet. Atheneum Books for Young Readers 2008 198p $16.99

Grades: 7 8 9 10   **Fic**
   1. Poverty -- Fiction 2. Sex role -- Fiction 3. Household employees -- Fiction
   ISBN 978-1-4169-4728-8; 1-4169-4728-0
                    LC 2007-19001

When her father is injured, fourteen-year-old Nazia is pulled away from school, her friends, and her preparations for an arranged marriage, to help her mother clean houses in a wealthy part of Karachi, Pakistan, where she finally rebels against the destiny that is planned for her.

This novel "provides a fascinating glimpse into a world remarkably distant from that of most American teens, and would be an excellent suggestion for readers who want to know about how other young people live." SLJ

Quick, Barbara

A **golden** web. HarperTeen 2010 266p $16.99

Grades: 7 8 9 10   **Fic**

1. Anatomy -- Fiction 2. Sex role -- Fiction 3. Middle Ages -- Fiction
ISBN 978-0-06-144887-4; 0-06-144887-7

            LC 2009-14265

In fourteenth-century Bologna, Alessandra Giliani, a brilliant young girl, defies convention and risks death in order to attend medical school at the university so that she can study anatomy.

"Alessandra's intellectual curiosity is wonderfully depicted, her philosophical musings are entertaining, and her commitment to the pursuit of biological knowledge enlivens the plot. Quick's prose is fluid and authentic, bright and engaging." Publ Wkly

Quick, Matthew

★ **Sorta** like a rockstar; a novel. Little, Brown 2010 355p $16.99; pa $8.99

Grades: 7 8 9 10 11   **Fic**

1. School stories 2. Homeless persons -- Fiction 3. Depression (Psychology) -- Fiction
ISBN 978-0-316-04352-6; 0-316-04352-4; 978-0-316-04353-3 pa; 0-316-04353-2 pa

            LC 2008-46746

Although seventeen-year-old Amber Appleton is homeless, living in a school bus with her unfit mother, she is a relentless optimist who visits the elderly at a nursing home, teaches English to Korean Catholic women with the use of rhythm and blues music, and befriends a solitary Vietnam veteran and his dog, but eventually she experiences one burden more than she can bear and slips into a deep depression.

"This book is the answer to all those angst-ridden and painfully grim novels in the shortcut lingo of short attention-span theater. Hugely enjoyable." SLJ

Quintero, Sofia

★ **Efrain's** secret. Alfred A. Knopf 2010 265p $16.99; lib bdg $19.99

Grades: 8 9 10 11 12   **Fic**

1. School stories 2. Violence -- Fiction 3. Drug traffic -- Fiction 4. Hispanic Americans -- Fiction
ISBN 978-0-375-84706-6; 0-375-84706-5; 978-0-375-94706-3 lib bdg; 0-375-94706-X lib bdg

            LC 2009-8493

Ambitious high school senior and honor student Efrain Rodriguez makes some questionable choices in pursuit of his dream to escape the South Bronx and attend an Ivy League college.

"Quintero imbues her characters with unexpected grace and charm. . . . Mostly, though, it is Quintero's effortless grasp of teen slang that gives her first-person story its heart." Booklist

Rabin, Staton

Black powder. Margaret K. McElderry Books 2005 245p $16.95

Grades: 6 7 8 9   **Fic**

1. Science fiction 2. African Americans -- Fiction
ISBN 0-689-86876-4

This is "a touching story of two great scientific minds discovering the humanity behind the ideas. Langston is particularly well-developed as an intelligent, mostly responsible African-American finding his way." SLJ

Raedeke, Christy

The **daykeeper's** grimoire. Flux 2010 352p (Prophecy of days) pa $9.95

Grades: 7 8 9 10   **Fic**

1. Mayas -- Fiction 2. Prophecies -- Fiction 3. Conspiracies -- Fiction 4. Secret societies -- Fiction
ISBN 978-0-7387-1576-6; 0-7387-1576-X

            LC 2009-30668

Caity Mac Fireland of San Francisco accompanies her parents to an isle off the coast of Scotland where she finds a Mayan relic and, guided by a motley crew of advisors, uncovers an incredible secret that an elite group of power-brokers will stop at nothing to control.

"A delightful heroine, she's funny, frank, and mostly true to the way a real teen would act if she found herself in such an odd circumstance. Readers will want to follow Caity's adventure." Booklist

The **serpent's** coil. Flux 2011 298p (Prophecy of days) $9.95

Grades: 7 8 9 10   **Fic**

1. Travel -- Fiction 2. Prophecies -- Fiction 3. Conspiracies -- Fiction 4. Native Americans -- Fiction
ISBN 978-0-7387-1577-3; 0-7387-1577-8

            LC 2011004573

While attending a boarding school that allows her to travel around the globe, Caity continues her mission to fulfill a Mayan prophecy and mobilize the world's young people to stop the devastating global reign of the Fraternitas.

"Conspiracies abound in the second book of the Prophecy of Days series, which, if possible, moves at an even greater pace than the first. Raedeke weaves together an impressive array of mysticism, ancient knowledge, and conspiracy theories while keeping the main plot, if not all the details, easy to follow." Voice Youth Advocates

Raf, Mindy

The **symptoms** of my insanity; Mindy Raf. Dial 2013 384 p. (hardcover) $17.99

Grades: 8 9 10 11 12   **Fic**

1. School stories 2. Puberty -- Fiction 3. Teenage girls -- Fiction 4. Mothers -- Fiction 5. Schools -- Fiction 6. High schools -- Fiction 7. Hypochondria -- Fiction
ISBN 0803732414; 9780803732414

            LC 2012024708

In this novel, by Mindy Raf, "a teenage hypochondriac with large breasts learns to deal with life's pressure and find self-acceptance." Izzy's "ever-expanding chest is the brunt of ogling and inappropriate jokes." She is then pranked by a basketball player, exposing a picture of her on the Internet. "Her internal questioning of the incident exemplifies what many teenage girls feel about sexual expectations and misguided culpability in sexual assaults." (Kirkus Reviews)

"While the plot is predictable . . . Izzy's self-deprecating humor and wry observations bring fresh air to tired tropes. Raf's background in comedy serves her well and gives her protagonist an authenticity that will make readers feel invested in her story. A fairly standard contribution to the genre, but a solid one." SLJ

Railsback, Lisa

Noonie's masterpiece; art by Sarajo Frieden. Chronicle Books 2010 208p il $18.99

Grades: 4 5 6 7   **Fic**

1. School stories 2. Artists -- Fiction 3. Family life -- Fiction 4. Father-daughter relationship -- Fiction 5. Eccentrics and eccentricities -- Fiction

ISBN 978-0-8118-6654-5; 0-8118-6654-8

LC 2008-26831

Upon learning that her deceased mother, an artist, went through a "Purple Period," ten-year-old Noonie decides to do the same, hoping that this will bring her archaeologist father home to see her win a school art contest and that the aunt, uncle, and cousin she lives with will come to understand her just a little.

"Noonie may be an unreliable and even unlikable narrator at times, but her pain and vulnerability are as evident as her belief in herself as an artist, and by the end of the story, she'll have readers in her corner. The ink-and-watercolor illustrations, appearing throughout the book, have a 1960s-retro look." Booklist

Rallison, Janette

Just one wish. G. P. Putnam's Sons 2009 264p $16.99; pa $7.99

Grades: 7 8 9 10   **Fic**

1. Actors -- Fiction 2. Cancer -- Fiction 3. Siblings -- Fiction

ISBN 978-0-399-24618-0; 0-399-24618-5; 978-0-14-241599-3 pa; 0-14-241599-5 pa

LC 2008-9297

Seventeen-year-old Annika tries to cheer up her little brother Jeremy before his surgery to remove a cancerous tumor by bringing home his favorite television actor, Steve Raleigh, the star of "Teen Robin Hood"

"Annika's wacky encounters . . . and anxiety for her brother make the story both comical and poignant." Horn Book Guide

Randall, Thomas

Dreams of the dead. Bloomsbury Children's Books 2009 276p (The waking) pa $8.99

Grades: 8 9 10 11 12   **Fic**

1. School stories 2. Death -- Fiction 3. Supernatural -- Fiction

ISBN 978-1-59990-250-0; 1-59990-250-8

LC 2008-30844

After her mother dies, sixteen-year-old Kara and her father move to Japan, where he teaches and she attends school, but she is haunted by a series of frightening nightmares and deaths that might be revenge—or something worse

"The story has suspense, mystery, and horror. It will be a great hit with fans of manga, anime, or Japanese culture." SLJ

Spirits of the Noh. Bloomsbury U.S.A. Children's Books 2010 264p (The waking) $8.99

Grades: 8 9 10 11 12   **Fic**

1. Horror fiction 2. School stories 3. Monsters -- Fiction 4. Supernatural -- Fiction

ISBN 978-1-59990-251-7; 1-59990-251-6

LC 2009018251

Just as Kara and her friends at the Monju-no-Chie school in Japan are beginning to get over the horrifying deaths of two students, another monster emerges to terrorize the school.

"Using all the usual horror elements, Randall constructs a fine teen chiller complete with mean-girl drama, a dash of romance and the angst of teens who believe that adults do not understand them." Kirkus

Ransom, Candice

Rebel McKenzie; Candice Ransom. Disney Hyperion 2012 270 p. $16.99

Grades: 4 5 6 7   **Fic**

1. Country life -- Fiction 2. Beauty contests -- Fiction 3. Money-making projects for children -- Fiction 4. Nephews -- Fiction 5. Trailer camps -- Fiction 6. Loss (Psychology) -- Fiction 7. Country life -- Virginia -- Fiction

ISBN 1423145399; 9781423145394

LC 2011032729

In this novel by Candice Ransom "Rebel McKenzie wants to spend her summer attending . . . a camp where kids discover prehistoric bones, right alongside real paleontologists. But digs cost money, and Rebel is broker than four o'clock. When she finds out her annoying neighbor Bambi Lovering won five hundred dollars by playing a ukulele behind her head in a beauty contest, Rebel decides to win the Frog Level Volunteer Fire Department's beauty pageant." (Publisher's note)

Rapp, Adam

The **children** and the wolves; Adam Rapp. Candlewick Press 2011 152 p. $16.99

Grades: 8 9 10   **Fic**

1. Kidnapping -- Fiction 2. Psychological fiction 3. Juvenile delinquency -- Fiction 4. Drug abuse -- Fiction 5. Single parent family -- Fiction

ISBN 0763653373; 9780763653378

LC 2011013676

This book by Printz Honor-winning author Adam Rapp presents a story "about three disaffected teens and a kidnapped child. Three teenagers—a sharp, well-to-do girl named Bounce and two struggling boys named Wiggins and Orange—are holding a four-year old girl hostage in Orange's basement. The little girl answers to 'the Frog'and seems content to play a video game about wolves all day long, a game that parallels the reality around her. As the stakes grow higher and the guilt and tension mount, Wiggins cracks and finally brings Frog to a trusted adult." (Publisher's note)

Raskin, Joyce

My misadventures as a teenage rock star; written by Joyce Raskin; illustrations by Carol Chu. Graphia 2011 107p il pa $8.99

Grades: 7 8 9 10   **Fic**

1. Popularity -- Fiction 2. Rock music -- Fiction 3. Family life -- Fiction 4. Bands (Music) -- Fiction
ISBN 978-0-547-39311-7 pa; 0-547-39311-3 pa
LC 2010-27456

Fourteen-year-old Alex, a short, pasty, shy, greasy-haired girl with acne, gains self-confidence when her brother convinces her to play bass in a rock band, but she finds that being 'cool' has its drawbacks.

"The unintimidating length and layout, direct prose, and swift-moving plot make thsi a particularly fine choice for reluctant readers." Bull Cent Child Books

Ravel, Edeet

The **saver**. Groundwood Books/House of Anansi Press 2008 214p $17.95; pa $8.95

Grades: 7 8 9 10 11   **Fic**

1. Death -- Fiction 2. Uncles -- Fiction 3. Orphans -- Fiction
ISBN 978-0-88899-882-8; 0-88899-882-1; 978-0-88899-883-5 pa; 0-88899-883-X pa

When 17-year-old Fern's mother dies of a heart attack, she has to make her own way in the world. She takes over her mother's housecleaning jobs, takes a job as a janitor, and adds two other part-time jobs. Then her Uncle Jack, whom she's never met, shows up to help her.

"Written as a series of letters to an imaginary friend on another planet, this is a compelling story of determination and the will to survive." SLJ

Rawlings, Marjorie Kinnan

The **yearling**; with pictures by N. C. Wyeth. Scribner 1985 400p il hardcover o.p. pa $5.95

Grades: 5 6 7 8   **Fic**

1. Deer -- Fiction
ISBN 0-684-18461-3; 0-02-044931-3 pa
LC 85-40301

Reissue of the title first published 1938; awarded Pulitzer Prize, 1939

"With its excellent descriptions of Florida scrub landscapes, its skillful use of native vernacular, its tender relation between Jody and his pet fawn, The Yearling is a simply written, picturesque story of boyhood." Time

Rawls, Wilson

Where the red fern grows; the story of two dogs and a boy. Bantam Bks. 1996 212p $16.95; pa $5.99

Grades: 4 5 6 7   **Fic**

1. Dogs -- Fiction
ISBN 0-385-32330-1; 0-440-41267-6 pa
First published 1961 by Doubleday

"Looking back more than 50 years to his boyhood in the Ozarks, the narrator, recalls how he achieved his heart's desire in the ownership of two redbone hounds, how he taught them all the tricks of hunting, and how they won the championship coon hunt before Old Dan was killed by a mountain lion and Little Ann died of grief. Although some readers may find this novel hackneyed and entirely too sentimental, others will enjoy the fine coonhunting episodes and appreciate the author's feelings for nature." Booklist

Ray, Delia

Ghost girl; a Blue Ridge Mountain story. Clarion Bks. 2003 216p il $15

Grades: 5 6 7 8   **Fic**

1. Presidents 2. School stories 3. Philanthropists 4. Teachers -- Fiction 5. Spouses of presidents 6. Secretaries of commerce
ISBN 0-618-33377-0
LC 2003-4115

Eleven-year-old April is delighted when President and Mrs. Hoover build a school near her Madison County, Virginia, home but her family's poverty, grief over the accidental death of her brother, and other problems may mean that April can never learn to read from the wonderful teacher, Miss Vest

"This excellent portrayal of four important years in a girl's life rises to the top. Based on a real school and teacher, this novel seamlessly incorporates historical facts into the narrative." SLJ

Here lies Linc. Alfred A. Knopf 2011 308p $16.99; lib bdg $19.99

Grades: 5 6 7 8   **Fic**

1. School stories 2. Death -- Fiction 3. Cemeteries -- Fiction 4. Family life -- Fiction
ISBN 978-0-375-86757-6; 0-375-86757-0; 978-0-375-96756-6 lib bdg; 0-375-96756-7 lib bdg
LC 2010030004

While researching a rumored-to-be-haunted grave for a local history project, twelve-year-old Lincoln Crenshaw unearths some startling truths about his own family.

"Ray's tale, which centers around a real legend, strikes the perfect balance of humor, realistic chills and near-teen angst." Kirkus

Singing hands. Clarion Books 2006 248p il $16

Grades: 4 5 6 7   **Fic**

1. Deaf -- Fiction 2. Clergy -- Fiction 3. Family life -- Fiction
ISBN 0-618-65762-2
LC 2005-22972

In the late 1940s, twelve-year-old Gussie, a minister's daughter, learns the definition of integrity while helping with a celebration at the Alabama School for the Deaf—her punishment for misdeeds against her deaf parents and their boarders.

"While the portrayal of a signing household is natural and convincing, the focus is on Gussie's rebellion and growth, the real heart of the story." Horn Book Guide

Reedy, Trent

Words in the dust. Arthur A. Levine Books 2011 266p $17.99

Grades: 5 6 7 8   **Fic**

1. Literacy -- Fiction 2. Sex role -- Fiction 3. Birth

defects -- Fiction
ISBN 0-545-26125-2; 978-0-545-26125-8

LC 2010-26160

Zulaikha, a thirteen-year-old girl in Afghanistan, faces a series of frightening but exhilarating changes in her life as she defies her father and secretly meets with an old woman who teaches her to read, her older sister gets married, and American troops offer her surgery to fix her disfiguring cleft lip.

"The evolution of key relationships presents a nuanced look at family dynamics and Afghan culture. Though unsentimental and fraught with tragedy, Reedy's narrative offers hope and will go a long way toward helping readers understand the people behind the headlines." Publ Wkly

Rees, Celia

The **fool's** girl. Bloomsbury 2010 297p $16.99
Grades: 8 9 10 11 12   **Fic**
1. Poets 2. Authors 3. Dramatists 4. Adventure fiction
ISBN 978-1-59990-486-3; 1-59990-486-1

LC 2009-51894

Violetta and Feste have come to London to rescue a holy relic taken from a church in Illyria by the evil Malvolio, and once there, they tell the story of their adventures to playwright William Shakespeare, who turns it into a play.

"Expertly livening the proceedings with intrigues, japes, kisses, mildly bawdy comments, . . . colorful characters, plot twists, quick violence, and an occasional breath of the supernatural, Rees dishes up a quick-paced tale that builds to a suspenseful climax." Booklist

Rees, Douglas

Vampire High: sophomore year. Delacorte 2010 247p $16.99; lib bdg $17.89
Grades: 7 8 9 10   **Fic**
1. School stories 2. Vampires -- Fiction
ISBN 978-0-385-73725-8; 0-385-73725-4; 978-0-385-90657-9 lib bdg; 0-385-90657-9 lib bdg

When Cody's Goth cousin Turk moves into his house, enrolls at Vlad Dracul, and decides to turn an abandoned nineteenth-century mill into an art center, the vampire (Jenti) students are not pleased, and Cody's hopes for a great sophomore year are blighted.

"Rees's fast-paced and action-packed story line tackles important teen issues like identity, belonging, friendship, and acceptance in a way that is not overbearing or preachy. With lots of humor and strong, engaging characters, this novel has an appeal factor that is sure to make its mark (or bite) on readers of this genre." SLJ

Rees, Douglas C.

Vampire High. Delacorte Press 2003 226p $15.95; lib bdg $17.99
Grades: 7 8 9 10   **Fic**
1. School stories 2. Vampires -- Fiction
ISBN 0-385-73117-5; 0-385-90143-7 lib bdg

LC 2003-41992

When his family moves from California to New Sodom, Massachusetts and Cody enters Vlad Dracul Magnet School, many things seem strange, from the dark-haired, pale-skinned, supernaturally strong students to Charon, the wolf who guides him around campus on the first day

"There's barely a false note in this rollicking tale of horror, humor, and light romance that will appeal to both girls and boys." Booklist

Another title in this series is:
Vampire High: sophomore year (2010)

Reeve, Philip, 1966-

★ **Fever** Crumb. Scholastic Press 2010 325p $17.99
Grades: 6 7 8 9 10   **Fic**
1. Science fiction 2. Orphans -- Fiction 3. Sex role -- Fiction
ISBN 978-0-545-20719-5; 0-545-20719-3

LC 2009-15457

Foundling Fever Crumb has been raised as an engineer although females in the future London, England, are not believed capable of rational thought, but at age fourteen she leaves her sheltered world and begins to learn startling truths about her past while facing danger in the present.

"Reeve's captivating flights of imagination play as vital a role in the story as his endearing heroine, hiss-worthy villains, and nifty array of supporting characters." Booklist

★ **Here** lies Arthur. Scholastic Press 2008 339p $16.99
Grades: 7 8 9 10   **Fic**
1. Kings 2. Magic -- Fiction
ISBN 978-0-545-09334-7; 0-545-09334-1

LC 2008-05787

When her village is attacked and burned, Gwyna seeks protection from the bard Myrddin, who uses Gwyna in his plan to transform young Arthur into the heroic King Arthur.

"Powerfully inventive. . . . Events rush headlong toward the inevitable ending, but Gwyna's observations illuminate them in a new way." Booklist

Mothstorm; or the horror from beyond Georgium Sidus!; or a tale of two shapers. as told by Art Mumby to Philip Reeve; decorated throughout by David Wyatt. Bloomsbury U.S.A. Children's Books 2008 390p il $16.99; pa $7.99
Grades: 5 6 7 8   **Fic**
1. Science fiction 2. Adventure fiction 3. Siblings -- Fiction
ISBN 978-1-59990-303-3; 1-59990-303-2; 978-1-59990-382-8 pa; 1-59990-382-2 pa

LC 2008008192

Reports of a strange phenomenon at the fringe of the galaxy and its connection to one of Father's old friends send the entire Mumby family, accompanied by Jack and other friends, to a far-off planet where they must find a way to prevent a new invasion of the solar system by giant moths.

This "is a clever blending of genres including science fiction, historical fiction, fantasy, and adventure with a liberal dash of British humor and style." SLJ

No such thing as dragons. Scholastic Press 2010 186p $16.99
Grades: 4 5 6 7   **Fic**
1. Fantasy fiction 2. Dragons -- Fiction
ISBN 978-0-545-22224-2; 0-545-22224-9

A young, mute boy who is apprenticed to a dragon-slayer suspects that the winged beasts do not exist, until he—and his master—learn the truth.

"This is certainly different from anything that Reeve has done previously, but is still shot through with his trademark imagination and feel for action. It will be eagerly devoured by young readers." SLJ

Scrivener's moon; the third book in the Fever Crumb series. Philip Reeve. Scholastic Press 2012 341 p. (Fever Crumb series) (hardcover) $17.99
Grades: 6 7 8 9 10   **Fic**
1. Steampunk fiction 2. Technology -- Fiction 3. Science fiction 4. Identity -- Fiction
ISBN 0545222184; 9780545222181
LC 2012008124
This young adult steampunk adventure novel, by Philip Reeve, is the conclusion to the "Fever Crumb" trilogy. "The Scriven people are brilliant, mad--and dead. All except one, whose monstrous creation is nearly complete--a giant city on wheels. New London terrifies the rest of the world, and an army of mammoth-riders gathers to fight it. Meanwhile, young Fever Crumb begins a hunt for Ancient technology in the icy strongholds of the north." (Publisher's note)

Starcross; or The coming of the moobs!, or, Our adventures in the fourth dimension: a stirring adventure of spies, time travel and curious hats. as narrated by Art Mumby, (& Miss Myrtle Mumby) to their amanuensis, Philip Reeve & illustrated throughout by David Wyatt. Bloomsbury U.S.A. Children's Books 2007 368p il $16.95; pa $7.99
Grades: 5 6 7 8   **Fic**
1. Science fiction
ISBN 978-1-59990-121-3; 1-59990-121-8; 978-1-59990-296-8 pa; 1-59990-296-6 pa
LC 2007-12002
Young Arthur Mumby, his sister Myrtle, and their mother accept an invitation to take a holiday at an up-and-coming resort in the asteroid belt, where they become involved in a dastardly plot involving spies, time travel, and mind-altering clothing

"It's all very tongue-in-cheek with plenty of jokes and puns in the best traditions of British humor." Booklist

A **Web** of Air. Scholastic Press 2011 293p $17.99
Grades: 6 7 8 9 10   **Fic**
1. Science fiction 2. Flight -- Fiction 3. Orphans -- Fiction
ISBN 0-545-22216-8; 978-0-545-22216-7
LC 2010043341
Two years ago, Fever Crumb escaped the wartorn city of London in a traveling theater. Now, she arrives in the extraordinary city of Mayda, where buildings ascend the cliffs on funicular rails, and a mysterious recluse is building a machine that can fly.

"It's clear that Reeve . . . is building toward an epic, and his remarkable storytelling gifts, coupled with a trenchant understanding of human nature, make these projected volumes worth the wait." Horn Book

Reger, Rob
Emily the Strange: the lost days; [by] Rob Reger and Jessica Gruner; illustrated by Rob Reger and Buzz Parker. Harper 2009 266p il $16.99; lib bdg $17.89
Grades: 7 8 9 10   **Fic**
1. Adventure fiction 2. Amnesia -- Fiction 3. Runaway teenagers -- Fiction
ISBN 978-0-06-145229-1; 0-06-145229-7; 978-0-06-145230-7 lib bdg; 0-06-145230-0 lib bdg
LC 2008027225
Emily the Strange has lost her memory and finds herself in the town of Blackrock with nothing more than her diary, her slingshot, and the clothes on her back

"The action moves along with no lulls, and none of the entries or illustrations are superfluous. This is a highly enjoyable read." SLJ

Other titles about Emily the Strange are:
Emily the Strange: stranger and stranger (2010)
Emily the Strange: dark times (2010)

Reh, Rusalka
Pizzicato; the abduction of the magic violin. translated by David Henry Wilson. AmazonCrossing 2011 124p pa $9.95
Grades: 4 5 6 7   **Fic**
1. Magic -- Fiction 2. Orphans -- Fiction 3. Violins -- Fiction
ISBN 978-1-6110-9004-8; 1-6110-9004-0
Darius is none too pleased to be paired with Archibald Archinola, a master violinmaker, for a school project, especially when he thinks about his rival—fellow orphan and constant nemesis Max—being surrounded by Porsches at Auto Frederick for the same assignment. But when Darius discovers an old violin in a glass case and strikes the chords, a cut on his hand magically disappears, and suddenly studying with the violinmaker proves to be anything but dull.

This story "has an Old World European charm, from the cast of eccentric, lovable characters to the scenes of café life. Readers will delight in watching the buffoonish villains get their comeuppance, but it's Darius' wish-fulfillment . . . that will satisfy readers most." Booklist

Reichs, Kathleen J.
Seizure; [by] Kathy Reichs. 2011 491p $17.99
Grades: 6 7 8 9 10   **Fic**
1. Adventure fiction 2. Supernatural -- Fiction
ISBN 9781595143945; 1595143947
"Tory Brennan, 14, and her friends are still trying to determine exactly what happened to them following the events of the series opener (Virals, 2010). The teens have been exposed to an experimental virus that altered their DNA, giving them characteristics comparable to wolves, enhancing their natural senses and creating a human pack. . . . Due to the economy, funding has been pulled on [Kit's father's] research project, necessitating a change of job and a move away from South Carolina and her pack mates. . . . Dodging bullets, slipping out after curfew, following obscure clues into underground tunnels, not to mention Cotillion duties and snarky classmates, are just part of the adventure. . . . Reichs taps into the angst of teens, fear of separation and the uncer-

tainty of today's economy and wraps it all in an entertaining yarn of history, pirates and modern technology." Kirkus

★ **Virals**; [by] Kathy Reichs. Penguin/Razorbill 2010 454p map $17.99

Grades: 6 7 8 9 10   **Fic**
1. Mystery fiction 2. Viruses -- Fiction 3. Missing persons -- Fiction
ISBN 978-1-59514-342-6; 1-59514-342-4
           LC 2010-42384

Tory Brennan is the leader of a band of teenage "sci-philes" who live on an island off the coast of South Carolina and when the group rescues a dog caged for medical testing, they are exposed to an experimental strain of canine parvovirus that changes their lives forever.

"From the opening sentence to the last word, readers will be absorbed in Tory Brennan's world. . . . Reichs has found a pitch-perfect voice for Tory that will ring true with today's teens, capturing and entirely new audience." Kirkus

Reinhardt, Dana
★ **How** to build a house; a novel. Wendy Lamb Books 2008 227p $15.99; lib bdg $18.99

Grades: 8 9 10 11 12   **Fic**
1. Divorce -- Fiction 2. Building -- Fiction 3. Stepfamilies -- Fiction 4. Volunteer work -- Fiction
ISBN 978-0-375-84453-9; 0-375-84453-8; 978-0-375-94454-3 lib bdg; 0-375-94454-0 lib bdg
           LC 2007-33403

Seventeen-year-old Harper Evans hopes to escape the effects of her father's divorce on her family and friendships by volunteering her summer to build a house in a small Tennessee town devastated by a tornado.

"This meticulously crafted book illustrates how both homes and relationships can be resurrected through hard work, hope and teamwork." Publ Wkly

Odessa again; Dana Reinhardt. 1st ed. Wendy Lamb Books 2013 208 p. (ebook) $47.97; (hardcover) $15.99; (library) $18.99

Grades: 4 5 6 7   **Fic**
1. Remarriage -- Fiction 2. Time travel -- Fiction
ISBN 0385739567; 9780375897887; 9780385739566; 9780385907934
           LC 2012008231

In this children's novel, by Dana Reinhardt, "fourth grader Odessa Green-Light lives with her mom and her toad of a little brother, Oliver. Her dad is getting remarried. . . . Meanwhile, Odessa moves into the attic room of their new house. One day [it] . . . turns out that Odessa has gone back in time a whole day! With this new power she can fix all sorts of things--embarrassing moments, big mistakes, and even help Oliver be less of a toad. Her biggest goal: reunite Mom and Dad." (Publisher's note)

"Realistically drawn, Odessa is a believable, likable kid on the brink of growing up, struggling with family changes. . . . With humor as well as depth, this is an endearing story of a spunky girl who realizes that life gets more, not less, confusing as she grows up." Kirkus

The **summer** I learned to fly. Wendy Lamb Books 2011 216p $15.99; lib bdg $18.99; e-book $15.99

Grades: 5 6 7 8   **Fic**
1. Rats -- Fiction 2. Family life -- Fiction 3. Retail trade -- Fiction 4. Single parent family -- Fiction
ISBN 978-0-385-73954-2; 0-385-73954-0; 978-0-385-90792-7 lib bdg; 0-385-90792-3 lib bdg; 978-0-375-89787-0 e-book; 0-375-89787-9 e-book
           LC 2010029412

Thirteen-year-old Drew starts the summer of 1986 helping in her mother's cheese shop and dreaming about co-worker Nick, but when her widowed mother begins dating, Drew's father's book of lists, her pet rat, and Emmett, a boy on a quest, help her cope.

"This quiet novel invites readers to share in its heroine's deepest yearnings, changing moods, and difficult realizations." Publ Wkly

★ The **things** a brother knows. Wendy Lamb Books 2010 245p $16.99; lib bdg $19.99

Grades: 7 8 9 10 11 12   **Fic**
1. Brothers -- Fiction 2. Soldiers -- Fiction 3. Family life -- Fiction 4. Jews -- United States -- Fiction
ISBN 978-0-375-84455-3; 0-375-84455-4; 978-0-375-94455-9 lib bdg; 0-375-94455-9 lib bdg

Although they have never gotten along well, seventeen-year-old Levi follows his older brother Boaz, an ex-Marine, on a walking trip from Boston to Washington, D.C. in hopes of learning why Boaz is completely withdrawn.

"Reinhardt's poignant story of a soldier coping with survivor's guilt and trauma, and his Israeli American family's struggle to understand and help, is timely and honest." Booklist

Reisman, Michael
★ **Simon** Bloom, the gravity keeper. Dutton Children's Books 2007 298p $15.99; pa $8.99

Grades: 5 6 7 8   **Fic**
1. Science fiction 2. Physics -- Fiction 3. Extraterrestrial beings -- Fiction
ISBN 978-0-525-47922-2; 978-0-14-241368-5 pa
           LC 2006039046

Nerdy sixth-grader Simon Bloom finds a book that enables him to control the laws of physics, but when two thugs come after him, he needs the formulas in the book to save himself

This is a "fast-paced, cinematic . . . novel. . . . It makes scientific concepts interesting and accessible." Publ Wkly

Another title about Simon Bloom is:
Simon Bloom, the octopus effect (2009)

Renn, Diana
Tokyo heist; by Diana Renn. Viking 2012 373 p. (hardcover) $17.99

Grades: 7 8 9 10 11 12   **Fic**
1. Mystery fiction 2. Art thefts -- Fiction 3. Tokyo (Japan) -- Fiction 4. Mystery and detective stories 5. Fathers and daughters -- Fiction
ISBN 0670013323; 9780670013326
           LC 2011043364

In this book "when sixteen-year-old Violet agrees to spend the summer with her father, an up-and-coming artist in Seattle, she has no idea what she's walking into. Her father's newest clients, the Yamada family, are the victims of a high-profile art robbery: van Gogh sketches have been stolen from their home, and, until they can produce the corresponding painting, everyone's lives are in danger." (Publisher's note)

"The plot has lots of twists and turns, leaving readers on edge, and a hint of romance... Teens will learn about Japanese culture, and fans of manga and art students will rejoice that they can relate to the protagonist and story." LJ

Rennison, Louise

Withering tights. HarperTeen 2011 274p (Misadventures of Tallulah Casey) $16.99

Grades: 7 8 9 10 **Fic**
1. Camps -- Fiction 2. Acting -- Fiction
ISBN 0-06-179931-9; 978-0-06-179931-0
LC 2010045552

Self-conscious about her knobby knees but confident in her acting ability, fourteen-year-old Tallulah spends the summer at a Yorkshire performing arts camp that, she is surprised to learn, is for girls only.

"Tallulah is a vivacious and hilarious character who will speak to every girl." SLJ

Repka, Janice

The **clueless** girl's guide to being a genius. Dutton Children's Books 2011 218p $16.99

Grades: 4 5 6 **Fic**
1. School stories 2. Genius -- Fiction 3. Teachers -- Fiction 4. Friendship -- Fiction 5. Mathematics -- Fiction 6. Baton twirling -- Fiction
ISBN 978-0-525-42333-1; 0-525-42333-8
LC 2010038139

When Aphrodite Wigglesmith, a thirteen-year-old, Harvard-educated mathematics genius, returns home to teach remedial math to middle school students, both she and her students end up getting unexpected lessons.

"A lighthearted, funny and often bizarre saga of middle-school mayhem.... Equal parts silly and endearing." Kirkus

Resau, Laura

★ **Red** glass. Delacorte Press 2007 275p $15.99; lib bdg $18.99

Grades: 7 8 9 10 **Fic**
1. Orphans -- Fiction 2. Family life -- Fiction 3. Automobile travel -- Fiction
ISBN 978-0-385-73466-0; 0-385-73466-2; 978-0-385-90464-3 lib bdg; 0-385-90464-9 lib bdg
LC 2007-02408

Sixteen-year-old Sophie has been frail and delicate since her premature birth, but discovers her true strength during a journey through Mexico, where the six-year-old orphan her family hopes to adopt was born, and to Guatemala, where her would-be boyfriend hopes to find his mother and plans to remain.

"The vivid characters, the fine imagery, and the satisfying story arc make this a rewarding novel." Booklist

★ **What** the moon saw; a novel. Delacorte Press 2006 258p $15.95; pa $5.99

Grades: 5 6 7 8 **Fic**
1. Country life -- Fiction 2. Grandparents -- Fiction
ISBN 0-385-73343-7; 0-440-23957-5 pa
LC 2006-04571

Fourteen-year-old Clara Luna spends the summer with her grandparents in the tiny, remote village of Yucuyoo, Mexico, learning about her grandmother's life as a healer, her father's decision to leave home for the United States, and her own place in the world.

This is an "exquisitely crafted narrative.... The characters are well developed.... Resau does an exceptional job of portraying the agricultural society sympathetically and realistically." SLJ

The **indigo** notebook. Delacorte Press 2009 324p $16.99; lib bdg $19.99; pa $9.99

Grades: 7 8 9 10 11 12 **Fic**
1. Fathers -- Fiction 2. Single parent family -- Fiction 3. Mother-daughter relationship -- Fiction
ISBN 978-0-385-73652-7; 0-385-73652-5; 978-0-385-90614-2 lib bdg; 0-385-90614-5 lib bdg; 978-0-375-84524-6 pa; 0-375-84524-0 pa
LC 2008-40519

Fifteen-year-old Zeeta comes to terms with her flighty mother and their itinerant life when, soon after moving to Ecuador, she helps an American teenager find his birth father in a nearby village

"Observant, aware, and occasionally wry, Zeeta's first-person narration will attract readers and hold them." Booklist

The **ruby** notebook. Delacorte Press 2010 373p $16.99; lib bdg $19.99

Grades: 7 8 9 10 **Fic**
1. Single parent family -- Fiction 2. Mother-daughter relationship -- Fiction
ISBN 978-0-385-73653-4; 0-385-73653-3; 978-0-385-90615-9 lib bdg; 0-385-90615-3 lib bdg
LC 2009-51965

When sixteen-year-old Zeeta and her itinerant mother move to Aix-en-Provence, France, Zeeta is haunted by a mysterious admirer who keeps leaving mementoes for her, and when her Ecuadorian boyfriend comes to visit, their relationship seems to have changed.

"Weaving bits of magic, city lore and bittersweet romance into each of the many plot lines, Resau has again crafted a complex and satisfying novel.... Characters are rich and vibrant." Kirkus

Restrepo, Bettina

★ **Illegal**. Katherine Tegen Books 2011 251p $16.99

Grades: 7 8 9 10 **Fic**
1. Mexicans -- Fiction 2. Illegal aliens -- Fiction 3. Young adult literature -- Works
ISBN 978-0-06-195342-2; 0-06-195342-3
LC 2010-19451

Nora, a fifteen-year-old Mexican girl, faces the challenges of being an illegal immigrant in Texas when she and her mother cross the border in search of Nora's father.

"Restrepo's novel offers an unsparing immigrant story that is both gritty and redemptive. . . . This is urban realism meets quest tale, told with great emotional immediacy, and it will appeal to many teen readers." Bull Cent Child Books

Revis, Beth

Across the universe. Razorbill 2011 398p $17.99

Grades: 7 8 9 10   **Fic**

1. Science fiction 2. Dictators -- Fiction 3. Space vehicles -- Fiction 4. Young adult literature -- Works
ISBN 978-1-59514-397-6; 1-59514-397-1
LC 2010-51834

Amy, a cryogenically frozen passenger aboard the vast spaceship Godspeed, is nearly killed when her cyro chamber is unplugged fifty years before Godspeed's scheduled landing. All she knows is that she must race to unlock Godspeed's hidden secrets before whoever woke her tries to kill again—and she doesn't know who she can trust on a ship ruled by a tyrant.

"Revis's tale hits all of the standard dystopian notes, while presenting a believable romance and a series of tantalizing mysteries that will hold readers' attention." Publ Wkly

Rex, Adam

★ **Cold** cereal. Balzer + Bray 2012 421 p il $16.99

Grades: 4 5 6 7   **Fic**

1. Adventure fiction 2. Food -- Fiction 3. Magic -- Fiction 4. Twins -- Fiction 5. Siblings -- Fiction
ISBN 978-0-06-206002-0; 0-06-206002-3
LC 2011019538

A boy who may be part changeling, twins involved in a bizarre secret experiment, and a clurichaun in a red tracksuit try to save the world from an evil cereal company whose ultimate goal is world domination.

"The author tucks in portrait illustrations and hilariously odd TV-commercial storyboards, along with a hooded Secret Society, figures from Arthurian legend, magical spells and potions, a certain amount of violence, many wonderful throwaway lines. . . . All in all, it's a mad scramble that culminates in the revelation of a dastardly plot that will require sequels to foil." Kirkus

Unlucky charms; Adam Rex. Balzer + Bray 2013 400 p. (The cold cereal saga) (hardback) $16.99

Grades: 4 5 6 7   **Fic**

1. Magic -- Fiction 2. Twins -- Fiction
ISBN 0062060058; 9780062060051
LC 2012026714

This humorous juvenile fantasy book, by Adam Rex, is part of the "Cold Cereal Saga." "In this hectic middle volume, [Adam] Rex's notably diverse crew of human, part-human and nonhuman allies splits up in hopes of scotching the schemes of the sorceress Nimue, who is out to create a worldwide army of mind-controlled 'sugar zombies' through magically enhanced breakfast cereal." (Kirkus Reviews)

★ **The true** meaning of Smekday. Hyperion Books for Children 2007 423p il $16.99; pa $6.99

Grades: 5 6 7 8   **Fic**

1. Science fiction 2. End of the world -- Fiction 3. Extraterrestrial beings -- Fiction
ISBN 0-7868-4900-2; 978-0-7868-4900-0; 0-7868-4901-0 pa; 978-0-7868-4901-7 pa

When her mother is abducted by aliens on Christmas Eve (or "Smekday" Eve since the Boov invasion), 11 year-old Tip hops in the family car and heads south to find her and meets an alien Boov mechanic who agrees to help her and save the planet from disaster.

"Incorporating dozens of his weird and wonderful illustrations and fruitfully manipulating the narrative structure, Rex skewers any number of subjects." Publ Wkly

Reynolds, Marilyn

Shut up! Morning Glory Press 2009 245p $15.95; pa $9.95

Grades: 8 9 10 11 12   **Fic**

1. Brothers -- Fiction 2. Child sexual abuse -- Fiction
ISBN 978-1-932538-93-9; 1-932538-93-3; 978-1-932538-88-5 pa; 1-932538-88-7 pa
LC 2008-933535

This book "presents a marginalized issue—sexual abuse of boys—in a frank, thoughtful, and sensitive manner." Voice Youth Advocates

Rhodes, Jewell Parker

★ **Ninth** Ward. Little, Brown 2010 217p $15.99

Grades: 5 6 7 8   **Fic**

1. Extrasensory perception -- Fiction 2. Hurricane Katrina, 2005 -- Fiction
ISBN 978-0-316-04307-6; 0-316-04307-9
LC 2009-34423

Coretta Scott King Author Award honor book, 2011

In New Orleans' Ninth Ward, twelve-year-old Lanesha, who can see spirits, and her adopted grandmother have no choice but to stay and weather the storm as Hurricane Katrina bears down upon them.

"The dynamics of the diverse community enrich the survival story, and the contemporary struggle of one brave child humanizes the historic tragedy." Booklist

Sugar; Jewell Parker Rhodes. 1st ed. Little, Brown and Co. 2013 288 p. (hardcover) $16.99

Grades: 3 4 5 6 7 8   **Fic**

1. Race relations -- Fiction 2. African Americans -- Fiction 3. Chinese Americans -- Fiction 4. Plantation life -- Louisiana -- Fiction 5. Reconstruction (U.S. history, 1865-1877) -- Fiction
ISBN 0316043052; 9780316043052
LC 2012026218

In this historical novel, by Jewell Parker Rhodes, "ten-year-old Sugar lives on the River Road sugar plantation along the banks of the Mississippi. Slavery is over, but laboring in the fields all day doesn't make her feel very free. . . . Here's another tale of a strong, spirited young girl who rises beyond her circumstances and inspires others to work toward a brighter future." (Publisher's note)

"Sugar's clipped narration is personable and engaging, strongly evoking the novel's historical setting and myriad racial tensions, making them accessible and meaningful to beginning readers." Pub Wkly

Rhuday-Perkovich, Olugbemisola

8th grade superzero. Arthur A. Levine Books 2010 324p $16.99

Grades: 6 7 8 9   **Fic**
1. School stories 2. Politics -- Fiction 3. Volunteer work -- Fiction 4. Homeless persons -- Fiction 5. African Americans -- Fiction
ISBN 978-0-545-09676-8; 0-545-09676-6
          LC 2009-19850

After halfheartedly joining his church youth group's project at a homeless shelter near his Brooklyn middle school, eighth-grade "loser" Reggie McKnight is inspired to run for school office on a platform of making a real difference in the community.

The author "manages to bring both passion and compassion to a story that has its moments of humor and genuine emotion, and will be highly useful for classroom discussion." Booklist

Rich, Naomi

★ **Alis**. Viking Children's Books 2009 274p $17.99

Grades: 7 8 9 10   **Fic**
1. Marriage -- Fiction 2. Religion -- Fiction 3. Runaway teenagers -- Fiction
ISBN 978-0-670-01125-4; 0-670-01125-8
          LC 2008-23234

Raised within the strict religious confines of the Community of the Book, Alis flees from an arranged marriage to the much older Minister of her town and her life takes a series of unexpected twists before she returns to accept her fate.

"Rich's sympathetic portrayal of Alis and her desperate struggle to exercise free will in a theocracy will have audiences firmly gripped." Publ Wkly

Richards, Jame

★ **Three** rivers rising; a novel of the Johnstown flood. Alfred A. Knopf 2010 293p $16.99; lib bdg $19.99

Grades: 6 7 8 9 10   **Fic**
1. Novels in verse 2. Floods -- Fiction 3. Social classes -- Fiction
ISBN 978-0-375-85885-7; 0-375-85885-7; 978-0-375-95885-4 lib bdg; 0-375-95885-1 lib bdg
          LC 2009-4251

Sixteen-year-old Celestia is a wealthy member of the South Fork Fishing and Hunting Club, where she meets and falls in love with Peter, a hired hand who lives in the valley below, and by the time of the torrential rains that lead to the disastrous Johnstown flood of 1889, she has been disowned by her family and is staying with him in Johnstown. Includes an author's note and historical timeline.

This is a "striking novel in verse. . . . Richards builds strong characters with few words and artfully interweaves the lives of these independent thinkers." Publ Wkly

Includes bibliographical references

Richards, Jasmine

The **book** of wonders. HarperCollins 2012 400p $14.99

Grades: 4 5 6 7   **Fic**
1. Fantasy fiction 2. Adventure fiction 3. Friendship -- Fiction
ISBN 978-0-06-201007-0; 0-06-201007-7
          LC 2011009153

In a tale loosely based on the Arabian nights, thirteen-year-old Zardi and her best friend, Ridhan, join forces with Captain Sinbad to defeat an evil sultan and restore magic to the world of Arribitha.

"This buoyant debut offers a fresh plot, brisk pacing and engaging characters. . . . Richards deftly borrows from lesser-known tales of the 1001 Arabian Nights to enrich her complex storyline while keeping style and syntax simple and direct." Kirkus

Richter, Conrad

The **light** in the forest. Everyman's Library 2005 176p $14.95; pa $6.50

Grades: 7 8 9 10   **Fic**
1. Delaware Indians -- Fiction 2. Frontier and pioneer life -- Fiction
ISBN 1-4000-4426-X; 1-4000-7788-5 pa
First published 1953 by Knopf

"A boy stolen in early childhood and brought up by the Delawares is at fifteen suddenly returned to the family he has forgotten. He resents his loss of independence, hates the brutality of the white man's civilization, and longs only for a return to the Indians whom he remembers as peace-loving and kind. His return to the Delawares does not, however, bring him peace; rather, he must make a bitter choice between helping his indian brothers kill agroup of unsuspecting white men or helping the white men escape. This is both vivid re-creation of outdoor life and a provocative study in conflicting loyalties." Horn Book

Richter, Jutta

Beyond the station lies the sea; translated from the German by Anna Brailovsky. Milkweed Editions 2009 81p $14

Grades: 4 5 6 7   **Fic**
1. Angels -- Fiction 2. Homeless persons -- Fiction
ISBN 978-1-57131-690-5; 1-57131-690-6
          LC 2009018135

Trying to get to the beach where it is warm, two homeless boys enlist the aid of a rich woman who gives them money in exchange for a guardian angel.

"Richter presents a darkly poetic, masterfully crafted view of life on the streets." Publ Wkly

Riel, Jorn

The **shipwreck**; translated from Danish by John Mason; illustrated by Helen Cann. Barefoot Books 2011 il (The Inuk quartet) pa $12.99

Grades: 4 5 6   **Fic**
1. Adventure fiction 2. Inuit -- Fiction 3. Vikings -- Fiction
ISBN 978-1-84686-335-6; 1-84686-335-X

"This beautifully illustrated epic adventure, set circa 1000 CE, begins with the shocking, retaliatory beheading of young Viking Leiv's father by Thorstein Gunnarsson. The playful boy becomes withdrawn and vows to take revenge. When Thorstein casts off from Iceland for Greenland to serve out his sentence of exile, Leiv stows away onboard but is swept into the sea during a storm. An Inuit brother and sister, Apuluk, 12, and Narua, 11, find him and care for him in secret. . . . The narrative is straightforward and well paced, with several engaging dramatic episodes. Riel skillfully interweaves information about the Inuit culture, language, and environment without being didactic. . . . Vocabulary may pose a challenge for less-advanced readers, and mention of beheadings and amputations may be unsuitable for others. But Cann's ethereal watercolor, graphite, and collage illustrations in cool blue tones and browns have a calmer mood that will enchant readers with the beauty of the Arctic landscape." SLJ

Riggs, Ransom

Miss Peregrine's home for peculiar children. Quirk Books 2011 352p il $17.99

Grades: 6 7 8 9   **Fic**

1. Ghost stories

ISBN 978-1-59474-476-1; 1-59474-476-9

"When Jacob's grandfather, Abe, a WWII veteran, is savagely murdered, Jacob has a nervous breakdown, in part because he believes that his grandfather was killed by a monster that only they could see. On his psychiatrist's advice, Jacob and his father travel from their home in Florida to Cairnholm Island off the coast of Wales, which, during the war, housed Miss Peregrine's Home for Peculiar Children. . . . Nearly 50 unsettling vintage photographs appear throughout, forming the framework of this dark but empowering tale, as Riggs creates supernatural backstories and identities for those pictured in them. . . . It's an enjoyable, eccentric read, distinguished by well-developed characters, a believable Welsh setting, and some very creepy monsters." Publ Wkly

Riley, James

Half upon a time. Aladdin 2010 385p $15.99

Grades: 5 6 7 8   **Fic**

1. Fairy tales 2. Adventure fiction

ISBN 978-1-4169-9593-7; 1-4169-9593-5

LC 2010012714

In the village of Giant's Hand Jack's grandfather has been pushing him to find a princess and get married, so when a young lady falls out of the sky wearing a shirt that says "Punk Princess," and she tells Jack that her grandmother, who looks suspiciously like the long-missing Snow White, has been kidnapped, Jack decides to help her.

"Riley does a wonderful job of combining the 21st century with the world in which fairies are alive, as well as creating characters that middle school students will relate to." Libr Media Connect

Rinaldi, Ann

Come Juneteenth. Harcourt 2007 246p (Great episodes) $17; pa $6.99

Grades: 6 7 8 9   **Fic**

1. Slavery -- Fiction 2. Juneteenth -- Fiction 3. Family life -- Fiction 4. African Americans -- Fiction

ISBN 978-0-15-05947-7; 0-15-205947-4; 978-0-15-206392-4 pa; 0-15-206392-7 pa

LC 2006-21458

Fourteen-year-old Luli and her family face tragedy after failing to tell their slaves that President Lincoln's Emancipation Proclamation made them free.

"Luli's authentic voice demonstrates Rinaldi's ability to evoke the human side of history." SLJ

Girl in blue. Scholastic Press 2001 310p hardcover o.p. pa $5.99

Grades: 6 7 8 9   **Fic**

1. Spies 2. Gender role 3. Sex role 4. Spies -- Fiction 5. Sex role -- Fiction 6. United States -- History -- Civil War, 1861-1865

ISBN 0-439-07336-7; 0-439-67646-0 pa

LC 00-41945

To escape an abusive father and an arranged marriage, fourteen-year-old Sarah, dressed as a boy, leaves her Michigan home to enlist in the Union Army, and becomes a soldier on the battlefields of Virginia as well as a Union spy working in the house of Confederate sympathizer Rose O'Neal Greenhow in Washington, D.C.

"This first-person novel will engage readers through its sympathetic main character and exciting action." Booklist

★ The **fifth** of March; a story of the Boston Massacre. Harcourt Brace & Co. 1993 335p (Great episodes) pa $6.95

Grades: 7 8 9 10   **Fic**

1. Political leaders 2. Boston Massacre, 1770 -- Fiction

ISBN 0-15-205078-7 pa

LC 93-17821

Fourteen-year-old Rachel Marsh, an indentured servant in the Boston household of John and Abigail Adams, is caught up in the colonists' unrest that eventually escalates into the massacre of March 5, 1770.

"The story moves along briskly, and details of life in 18th-century Boston are woven into the narrative." SLJ

The **redheaded** princess. HarperCollinsPublishers 2008 214p $15.99; lib bdg $16.89

Grades: 6 7 8 9   **Fic**

1. Queens

ISBN 978-0-06-073374-2; 0-06-073374-8; 978-0-06-073375-9 lib bdg; 0-06-073375-6 lib bdg

LC 2007-18577

In 1542, nine-year-old Lady Elizabeth lives on an estate near London, striving to get back into the good graces of her father, King Henry VIII, and as the years pass she faces his death and those of other close relatives until she finds herself next in line to ascend the throne of England in 1558.

"The rich scene-setting and believable, appealing heroine will satisfy Rinaldi's many fans." Booklist

An **unlikely** friendship; a novel of Mary Todd Lincoln and Elizabeth Keckley. Harcourt 2007 241p $17

Grades: 6 7 8 9   **Fic**

1. Memoirists 2. Dressmakers 3. Slavery -- Fiction 4. Friendship -- Fiction 5. Spouses of presidents

ISBN 0-15-205597-5

LC 2005-30210

Relates the lives of Mary Todd Lincoln, raised in a wealthy Virginia family, and Lizzy Keckley, a dressmaker born a slave, as they grow up separately then become best friends when Mary's childhood dream of living in the White House comes true.

This "story is fascinating and filled with remarkable gems of historical memorabilia to create a very satisfying read." Voice Youth Advocates

Riordan, Rick

The **Serpent's** Shadow; Rick Riordan. Disney/ Hyperion Books 2012 viii, 406 p.p (hardcover) $19.99

Grades: 4 5 6 7   **Fic**
   1. Adventure fiction 2. Supernatural -- Fiction 3. Mythology 4. Magic -- Fiction 5. Mythology, Egyptian -- Fiction 6. Voyages and travels -- Fiction 7. Brothers and sisters -- Fiction
   ISBN 1423140575; 9781423140573
                           LC 2012454979

This book by Rick Riordan is the third installment of the Kane Chronicles series. "Despite their best efforts, Carter and Sadie Kane can't seem to keep Apophis, the chaos snake, down. Now Apophis is threatening to plunge the world into eternal darkness, and the Kanes are faced with the impossible task of having to destroy him once and for all." (Publisher's note)

Vespers rising; [by] Rick Riordan, Peter Lerangis, Gordon Korman, Jude Watson. Scholastic 2011 238p (The 39 clues) $12.99

Grades: 4 5 6 7   **Fic**
   1. Ciphers -- Fiction
   ISBN 978-0-545-29059-3; 0-545-32606-0

Fourteen-year-old Amy Cahill and her younger brother Dan thought they could return to their regular lives when they found the 39 clues. But the Vespers, powerful enemies, will stop at nothing to get the clues. And with the Vespers rising, the world is in jeopardy.

★ The **lightning** thief. Miramax Books/Hyperion Books for Children 2005 377p (Percy Jackson & the Olympians) $19.99 pa$7.99

Grades: 5 6 7 8 9   **Fic**
   1. Classical mythology -- Fiction
   ISBN 0-7868-5629-7; 1-4231-3494-X pa; 978-0-6417-2344-5; 978-1-4231-3494-7 pa
                           LC 2005-299400

Twelve-year-old Percy Jackson learns he is a demigod, the son of a mortal woman and Poseidon, god of the sea. His mother sends him to a summer camp for demigods where he and his new friends set out on a quest to prevent a war between the gods.

"Riordan's fast-paced adventure is fresh, dangerous, and funny." Booklist

Other titles in this series are:
The Sea of Monsters (2006)
The Titan's curse (2007)
The battle of the Labyrinth (2008)
The last Olympian (2009)

The **lost** hero. Disney/Hyperion Books 2010 553p $18.99

Grades: 5 6 7 8   **Fic**
   1. Camps -- Fiction 2. Monsters -- Fiction 3. Classical mythology -- Fiction
   ISBN 978-1-4231-1339-3; 1-4231-1339-X
                           LC 2010015469

"Completely in control of pacing and tone, . . . [Riordan] . . . balances a faultless comic banter against deeper notes that reveal the characters' vulnerabilities." Horn Book

★ The **maze** of bones. Scholastic 2008 220p il (The 39 clues) $12.99

Grades: 4 5 6 7   **Fic**
   1. Family -- Fiction 2. Ciphers -- Fiction
   ISBN 978-0-545-06039-4; 0-545-06039-7

At the reading of their grandmother's will, Dan and Amy Cahill are given the choice of receiving a million dollars or uncovering the 39 clues hidden around the world that will lead to the source of the family's power, but by taking on the clues, they end up in a dangerous race against their own family members.

"Adeptly incorporating a genuine kids' perspective, the narrative unfolds like a boulder rolling downhill and keeps readers glued to the pages. . . . The book dazzles with suspense, plot twists, and snappy humor." SLJ

Other titles in this series are:
One false note by Gordon Korman (2008)
The sword thief by Peter Lerangis (2009)
The black circle by Patrick Carman (2009)
Beyond the grave by Jude Watson (2009)
In too deep by Jude Watson (2010)
The viper's nest by Peter Lerangis (2010)
The emperor's code by Gordon Korman (2010)
Storm warning by Linda Sue Park (2010)
Into the gauntlet by Margaret Peterson Haddix (2010)

The **son** of Neptune. Disney/Hyperion Books 2011 521p (The heroes of Olympus) $19.99

Grades: 5 6 7 8   **Fic**
   1. Camps -- Fiction 2. Monsters -- Fiction 3. Prophecies -- Fiction 4. Classical mythology -- Fiction
   ISBN 978-1-4231-4059-7; 1-4231-4059-1
                           LC 2011017658

Demigod Percy Jackson, still with no memory, and his new friends from Camp Jupiter, Hazel and Frank, go on a quest to free Death, but their bigger task is to unite the Greek and Roman camps so that the Prophecy of Seven can be fulfilled.

The **throne** of fire; Rick Riordan. Disney/Hyperion Books 2011 (Kane chronicles) $18.99

Grades: 4 5 6 7   **Fic**
   ISBN 978-1-4231-4056-6; 1-4231-4056-7; 1423140567; 9781423140566

Carter and Sadie, offspring of the brilliant Egyptologist Dr. Julius Kane, embark on a worldwide search for the Book of Ra, but the House of Life and the gods of chaos are determined to stop them.

"Lit by flashes of humor, this fantasy adventure is an engaging addition to the Kane Chronicles series." Booklist

Ritter, John H.

Choosing up sides. Philomel Bks. 1998 166p
$17.99; pa $5.99

Grades: 6 7 8 9   **Fic**
1. Baseball -- Fiction 2. Self-acceptance -- Fiction 3.
Fathers and sons -- Fiction 4. Father-son relationship
-- Fiction 5. Left- and right-handedness -- Fiction
ISBN 0-399-23185-4; 0-689-11840-5 pa
LC 97-39779

"This is an entertaining and thought-provoking coming-
of-age story." Book Rep

The **boy** who saved baseball. Philomel Books
2003 216p $17.99; pa $6.99

Grades: 5 6 7 8   **Fic**
1. Baseball -- Fiction
ISBN 0-399-23622-8; 0-14-240286-9 pa
LC 2002-15792

The fate of a small California town rests on the outcome
of one baseball game, and Tom Gallagher hopes to lead his
team to victory with the secrets of the now disgraced player,
Dante Del Gato

"This tale is peppered with both optimism and dilemmas; it has plenty of play-by-play action, lots of humor, and
a triumphant ending." SLJ

The **desperado** who stole baseball. Philomel
Books 2009 260p il $17.99

Grades: 5 6 7 8   **Fic**
1. Outlaws 2. Orphans -- Fiction 3. Baseball -- Fiction
4. Frontier and pioneer life -- Fiction
ISBN 978-0-399-24664-7; 0-399-24664-9
LC 2008-16901

In 1881, the scrappy, rough-and-tumble baseball team in
a California mining town enlists the help of a quick-witted
twelve-year-old orphan and the notorious outlaw Billy the
Kid to win a big game against the National League Champion Chicago White Stockings

"This tall-tale page-turner stands alone though it will be
most appreciated by fans of Ritter's earlier works." SLJ

Robert, Na'ima bint

Boy vs. girl. Frances Lincoln Children's 2011
260p $15.95

Grades: 6 7 8 9 10   **Fic**
1. Twins -- Fiction 2. Muslims -- Fiction 3. Ramadan
-- Fiction 4. Siblings -- Fiction 5. Pakistanis -- Great
Britain -- Fiction
ISBN 978-1-84780-150-0; 1-84780-150-1

"Twins Farhana and Faraz determine to fast during Ramadan now that they are 16. . . . As first-generation Brits,
they must respond to the demands of their Pakistani family, their secular schools, and their friends. . . . The characters are realistic. . . . A well-balanced chord is struck
here between storytelling and exploring the complex and
sometimes conflicting pulls of tradition, family, friends, and
lifestyle." Booklist

From Somalia with love; [by] Na'ima B. Robert. Frances Lincoln Children's Books 2008 159p
$15.95; pa $7.95

Grades: 7 8 9 10   **Fic**
1. Muslims -- Fiction 2. Father-daughter relationship
-- Fiction
ISBN 978-1-84507-831-7; 1-84507-831-4; 978-1-
84507-832-4 pa; 1-84507-832-2 pa

"Safia has grown up believing her father died in the
fighting in Somalia. When she finds out that he is alive and
on his way to London to join the family, she is apprehensive
about the difference his presence will make in her life. . . .
This is a unique title that will be popular in regions that have
large Somali populations or where Randa Abdel-Fattah's
books are popular." SLJ

Includes glossary

Roberts, Jeyn

Dark inside. Simon & Schuster Books for Young
Readers 2011 327p $17.99

Grades: 7 8 9 10   **Fic**
1. Science fiction 2. Monsters -- Fiction 3. Good and
evil -- Fiction
ISBN 978-1-4424-2351-0; 1-4424-2351-X
LC 2011008642

After tremendous earthquakes destroy the Earth's major
cities, an ancient evil emerges, turning ordinary people into
hunters, killers, and insane monsters but a small group of
teens comes together in a fight for survival and safety.

"Well-balanced, realistic suspense." Kirkus

Rage within; Jeyn Roberts. Simon & Schuster
Books for Young Readers 2012 357 p. $17.99

Grades: 7 8 9 10   **Fic**
1. Science fiction 2. Apocalyptic fiction 3. Monsters
-- Fiction 4. Survival -- Fiction 5. Good and evil --
Fiction
ISBN 1442423544; 9781442423541; 9781442423565
LC 2011047396

In author Jeyn Roberts' "apocalyptic sequel to 'Dark Inside'. . . Aries, Clementine, Michael, and Mason have survived the first wave of the apocalypse that wiped out most
of the world's population and turned many of the rest into
murderous Baggers. Now they're hiding out in an abandoned house . . . trying to figure out their next move. As the
Baggers begin to create a new world order, these four teens
will have to trust and rely on each other in order to survive."
(Publisher's note)

Roberts, Laura Peyton

Green. Delacorte Press 2010 261p $16.99; lib
bdg $19.99

Grades: 5 6 7 8   **Fic**
1. Fantasy fiction 2. Leprechauns -- Fiction 3.
Grandmothers -- Fiction
ISBN 978-0-385-73558-2; 0-385-73558-8; 978-0-385-
90543-5 lib bdg; 0-385-90543-2 lib bdg
LC 2008-54241

Abducted by leprechauns on her thirteenth birthday, Lilybet Green learns that there is more to her family
tree—and to her bond with her late grandmother—than she
ever imagined.

"A fun, fresh take on leprechaun lore that pushes well
past typical depictions to embrace banking transactions,
lepro-human relations, and some creative problem-solving.

Lily is a credible hero, by turns scared and confident, and definitely one young readers will enjoy following." Booklist

Roberts, Marion

Sunny side up. Wendy Lamb Books 2009 244p il $15.99; lib bdg $18.99

Grades: 4 5 6 7   **Fic**

    1. Friendship -- Fiction 2. Family life -- Fiction

    ISBN 978-0-385-73672-5; 0-385-73672-X; 978-0-385-90624-1 lib bdg; 0-385-90624-2 lib bdg

LC 2008-08633

First published 2008 in Australia

As the hot Australian summer draws to an end, eleven-year-old Sunny, content to be an only child with amicably divorced parents, finds her life getting much too complicated when her mother's boyfriend moves in with his two children, her best friend begins to develop an interest in boys, and she is contacted by her long-estranged grandmother.

"Character development is strong, as the girl is quick to observe and comment on the people in her life, and the setting forms an interesting backdrop. Small black-and-white photos are liberally scattered throughout." SLJ

Roberts, Willo Davis

The **kidnappers**. Atheneum Bks. for Young Readers 1998 137p hardcover o.p. pa $4.99

Grades: 4 5 6 7   **Fic**

    1. Wealth -- Fiction 2. Bullies -- Fiction 3. Kidnapping -- Fiction

    ISBN 0-689-81394-5; 0-689-81393-7 pa

LC 96-53677

No one believes eleven-year-old Joey, who has a reputation for telling tall tales, when he claims to have witnessed the kidnapping of the class bully outside their expensive New York City private school

"The combination of a witty narrative and a suspenseful plot makes this a good page-turner that will leave even the most reluctant readers glued to their seats." Booklist

Robinet, Harriette Gillem

Walking to the bus-rider blues. Atheneum Bks. for Young Readers 2000 146p hardcover o.p. pa $4.99

Grades: 5 6 7 8   **Fic**

    1. Race relations -- Fiction 2. African Americans -- Fiction

    ISBN 0-689-83191-9; 0-689-83886-7 pa

LC 99-29054

Twelve-year-old Alfa Merryfield, his older sister, and their grandmother struggle for rent money, food, and their dignity as they participate in the Montgomery, Alabama bus boycott in the summer of 1956

"Ingredients of mystery, suspense, and humor enhance and personalize this well-constructed story that offers insight into a troubled era." SLJ

Robinson, A. M.

Vampire crush. HarperTeen 2011 404p pa $8.99

Grades: 7 8 9 10   **Fic**

    1. Vampires -- Fiction

    ISBN 978-0-06-198971-1 pa; 0-06-198971-1 pa

LC 2010-09397

Sixteen-year-old journalist Sophie McGee's junior year is filled with unexpected drama—and romance—when she discovers that her new classmates are hiding a dark secret, while the "boy next door" from her childhood re-enters her life.

"Sophie is smart, funny, and determined, and her narration adds humor and wit to the story. The quirky supporting cast is pretty much what you'd expect in a teen vampire tale. An original and entertaining entry to the genre that won't disappoint." Booklist

Robinson, Barbara

★ The **best** Christmas pageant ever; pictures by Judith Gwyn Brown. Harper & Row 1972 80p il $15.99; lib bdg $16.89; pa $5.99

Grades: 4 5 6   **Fic**

    1. Pageants -- Fiction 2. Christmas -- Fiction

    ISBN 0-06-025043-7; 0-06-025044-5 lib bdg; 0-06-440275-4 pa

In this story the six Herdmans, "absolutely the worst kids in the history of the world," discover the meaning of Christmas when they bully their way into the leading roles of the local church nativity play

The story "romps through the festive preparations with comic relish, and if the Herdmans are so gauche as to seem exaggerated, they are still enjoyable, as are the not-so-subtle pokes at pageant-planning in general." Bull Cent Child Books

Other titles about the Herdmans are:

The best Halloween ever (2004)

The best school year ever (1994)

Rodda, Emily

★ The **key** to Rondo. Scholastic Press 2008 342p $16.99; pa $6.99

Grades: 5 6 7 8   **Fic**

    1. Fantasy fiction 2. Magic -- Fiction 3. Cousins -- Fiction 4. Young adult literature -- Works

    ISBN 0-545-03535-X; 978-0-545-03535-4; 0-545-03536-8 pa; 978-0-545-03536-1 pa

LC 2007-16873

Through an heirloom music box, Leo, a serious, responsible boy, and his badly-behaved cousin Mimi enter the magical world of Rondo to rescue Mimi's dog from a sorceress, who wishes to exchange him for the key that allows free travel between worlds.

"Rodda fills the cousins' quest with image-rich prose and compelling action." Bull Cent Child Books

Another title about Rondo is:

The Wizard of Rondo (2009)

Rodgers, Mary

Freaky Friday. Harper & Row 1972 145p hardcover o.p. pa $5.99

Grades: 4 5 6 7   **Fic**

    1. Mother-daughter relationship -- Fiction

    ISBN 0-06-025048-8; 0-06-025049-6 lib bdg; 0-06-057010-5 pa

"A fresh, imaginative, and entertaining story." Bull Cent Child Books

Rodman, Mary Ann

★ **Jimmy's** stars. Farrar, Straus & Giroux 2008 257p $16.95

Grades: 5 6 7 8   **Fic**

1. Siblings -- Fiction 2. Soldiers -- Fiction 3. Family life -- Fiction 4. World War, 1939-1945 -- Fiction
ISBN 978-0-374-33703-2; 0-374-33703-9

LC 2007-05091

In 1943, eleven-year-old Ellie is her brother Jimmy's "best girl," and when he leaves Pittsburgh just before Thanksgiving to fight in World War II, he promises he will return, asks her to leave the Christmas tree up until he does, and reminds her to "let the joy out."

Rodman "finds beauty in every emotional nuance. . . . The lively spirit of working-class Pittsburgh . . . extends Ellie's person story with a broader sense of home-front life." Booklist

Rodman, Sean

Infiltration. Orca Book Publishers 2011 130p (Orca soundings) lib bdg $16.95; pa $9.95

Grades: 7 8 9 10   **Fic**

1. City and town life -- Fiction
ISBN 978-1-55469-986-5 lib bdg; 1-55469-986-X lib bdg; 978-1-55469-985-8 pa; 1-55469-985-1 pa

Bex breaks into locked and abandoned buildings just because he can, but when a new friend's behavior becomes more and more risky, he has to do the right thing.

This "is a fast-paced action-adventure story. . . . The page-turning suspense it generates and the fascinating hook of urban-exploration should grab any reader." Booklist

Roecker, Laura

★ The **Liar** Society; by Lisa and Laura Roecker. Sourcebooks Fire 2011 361p pa $9.99

Grades: 7 8 9 10   **Fic**

1. School stories 2. Mystery fiction 3. Secret societies -- Fiction
ISBN 978-1-4022-5633-2; 1-4022-5633-7

When Kate receives a mysterious e-mail from her dead friend Grace, she must prove that Grace's death was not an accident, but finds that her elite private school holds secrets so big people are willing to kill to protect them.

This is a "smartly paced and plotted first novel, full of twists, clues, and sleuthing. Add this to your go-to list of mysteries." Booklist

The **lies** that bind; Lisa and Laura Roecker. Sourcebooks Fire 2012 314 p. (The Liar Society) (tp : alk. paper) $9.99

Grades: 7 8 9 10   **Fic**

1. School stories 2. Missing persons -- Fiction 3. Secret societies -- Fiction 4. Schools -- Fiction 5. High schools -- Fiction
ISBN 1402270240; 9781402270246

LC 2012035855

This young adult school mystery, by Lisa and Laura Roecker, is part of "The Liar Society" series. "Kate has heard of messages from beyond the grave, but she never ex-

pected to find one in a fortune cookie. Especially from her best friend, Grace--who's supposed to be dead. At the elite Pemberly Brown Academy, . . . a popular girl has gone missing, and Kate owes it to Grace's memory to find out what happened. But in a school ruled by secret societies, who can she trust?" (Publisher's note)

Rollins, James

Jake Ransom and the Skull King's shadow. HarperCollins 2009 399p il map $16.99; lib bdg $17.89; pa $7.99

Grades: 5 6 7 8   **Fic**

1. Adventure fiction 2. Mayas -- Fiction 3. Siblings -- Fiction 4. Archeology -- Fiction
ISBN 978-0-06-147379-1; 0-06-147379-0; 978-0-06-147380-7 lib bdg; 0-06-147380-4 lib bdg; 978-0-06-147381-4 pa; 0-06-147381-2 pa

LC 2009-14570

Connecticut middle-schooler Jake and his older sister Kady are transported by a Mayan artifact to a strange world inhabited by a mix of people from long-lost civilizations who are threatened by prehistoric creatures and an evil alchemist, the Skull King.

This is an "exciting time-travel adventure. . . . Rollins . . . presents a wide range of interesting historical information while telling a rollicking good story that should please a wide range of readers." Publ Wkly

Another title about Jake Ransom is:
Jake Ransom and the howling sphinx (2011)

Rorby, Ginny

Lost in the river of grass. Carolrhoda Lab 2011 255p $17.95

Grades: 7 8 9 10   **Fic**

1. Wilderness survival -- Fiction
ISBN 978-0-7613-5685-1; 0-7613-5685-1

LC 2009-53999

"In this authentic survival adventure, Sarah, a 13-year-old scholarship student, leaves her preppy classmates on a weekend trip to the Everglades and takes off with Andy, 15 . . . who offers her a brief guided tour in his airboat. After the boat sinks, they walk for three days through the swamp . . . until, finally, helicopters rescue them. What comes through best here is not only the teens' courage and mutual support but also the realism of their fights and weaknesses." Booklist

The **outside** of a horse; a novel. Dial Books for Young Readers 2010 343p $16.99

Grades: 7 8 9 10   **Fic**

1. Horses -- Fiction 2. Amputees -- Fiction 3. Veterans -- Fiction 4. Father-daughter relationship -- Fiction
ISBN 978-0-8037-3478-4; 0-8037-3478-6

LC 2009-25101

When her father returns from the Iraq War as an amputee with post-traumatic stress disorder, Hannah escapes by volunteering to work with rescued horses, never thinking that the abused horses could also help her father recover.

Hannah "comes across as a believable teen. As a backdrop to the story, Rorby has interwoven a good deal of disturbing information about animal cruelty. Horse lovers and most others will saddle up right away with this poignant tale." Booklist

Rose, Caroline Starr

★ **May** B. a novel-in-verse. Schwartz & Wade Books 2012 $15.99; lib bdg $18.99

Grades: 4 5 6 7 **Fic**
1. Novels in verse 2. Frontier and pioneer life -- Fiction
ISBN 978-1-58246-393-3; 1-58246-393-X; 978-1-58246-412-1 lib bdg; 1-58246-412-X lib bdg
LC 2010033222

When a failed wheat crop nearly bankrupts the Betterly family, Pa pulls twelve-year-old May from school and hires her out to a couple new to the Kansas frontier.

"If May is a brave, stubborn fighter, the short, free-verse lines are one-two punches in this Laura Ingalls Wilder-inspired ode to the human spirit." Kirkus

Rosen, Michael J.

Sailing the unknown; around the world with Captain Cook. written by Michael J. Rosen ; illustrated by Maria Cristina Pritelli. Creative Editions 2012 37 p. $17.99

Grades: 3 4 5 6 7 **Fic**
1. Sea stories 2. Explorers -- Fiction 3. Voyages around the world -- Fiction 4. Diaries -- Fiction
ISBN 1568462166; 9781568462165
LC 2011040840

This children's book, by Michael J. Rosen, illustrated by Maria Cristina Pritelli, tells the story of "an 11-year-old sailor named Nicholas, . . . [who in 1768] took to the seas with British explorer James Cook on a 3-year expedition of discovery, venturing into an uncharted world filled with strange lands, mysterious peoples, and peculiar creatures." (Publisher's note)

Rosen, Renee

★ **Every** crooked pot. St. Martin's Griffin 2007 227p pa $8.95

Grades: 7 8 9 10 **Fic**
1. Birth defects -- Fiction 2. Father-daughter relationship -- Fiction
ISBN 978-0-312-36543-1; 0-312-36543-8
LC 2007-10457

"Rosen looks back at the life of Nina Goldman, whose growing up is tied to two pillars: a port-wine stain around her eye and her inimitable father, Artie. The birthmark, she hates; her father, she loves. Both shape her in ways that merit Rosen's minute investigation. . . . There's real power in the writing." Booklist

Rosoff, Meg

★ **There** is no dog; Meg Rosoff. G. P. Putnam's Sons 2011 243p. $17.99

Grades: 7 8 9 **Fic**
1. Love stories 2. God -- Fiction 3. Man-woman relationship -- Fiction
ISBN 9780399257643
LC 2011020651

This book "looks at the world's natural disasters, injustices, and chaos and presents a[n] . . . explanation: God is a horny teenage boy. According to this . . . account, God, aka 'Bob,' was given Earth by his mother, who won the planet in a poker game. Bob showed flashes of brilliance during Cre-

ation, but he feels little responsibility for the planet. When he falls head-over-heels in lust with a beautiful zoo employee, Lucy, Bob's passion and growing anger toward those who would keep them apart is manifested through wildly fluctuating weather and rampant flooding." (Publishers Weekly)

Ross, Elizabeth

Belle epoque; Elizabeth Ross. Delacorte Press 2013 336 p. (ebook) $53.97; (library) $20.99; (hardcover) $17.99

Grades: 7 8 9 10 11 12 **Fic**
1. Love stories 2. Historical fiction 3. Female friendship -- Fiction 4. Runaways -- Fiction 5. Social classes -- Fiction 6. Conduct of life -- Fiction 7. Beauty, Personal -- Fiction 8. Interpersonal relations -- Fiction
ISBN 0375990054; 9780375985270; 9780375990052; 9780385741460
LC 2012034694

In this book, "sixteen-year-old runaway Maude Pichon is ugly—so much so that she lands a job as a 'repoussoir,' an unattractive girl paid to be seen with a lovelier girl to make her appear even more beautiful by comparison . . . . Maude is humiliated by the idea, but her poverty leaves her few options." Then "chance sends a dashing composer Maude's way, and a countess hires her to befriend her independent-minded daughter, Isabelle." (Publishers Weekly)

"Ross models her plot on an 1866 story by Zola, "Les Repoussoirs," expanding its focus to highlight Maude's plight and using that to illuminate the chasm that existed between the wealthy and the poor... A refreshingly relevant and inspiring historical venture." Kirkus

Ross, Jeff

The **drop**. Orca Book Publishers 2011 157p (Orca sports) pa $9.95

Grades: 6 7 8 9 **Fic**
1. Snowboarding -- Fiction
ISBN 978-1-55469-392-4; 1-55469-392-6

When Alex and three other snowboarders find themselves in trouble in the remote mountains of British Columbia, Alex must confront his fears and lead them to safety.

"Readers need not be regular snowboarders to appreciate the extended descriptions of the sport: they will feel the exhilaration of every turn and jump. The writing is crisp, and the plot moves along quickly." SLJ

Rossetti, Rinsai

The **girl** with borrowed wings; by Rinsai Rossetti. Dial Books 2012 300 p. (hardcover) $17.99

Grades: 7 8 9 10 11 12 **Fic**
1. Cats -- Fiction 2. Voyages and travels -- Fiction 3. Father-daughter relationship -- Fiction 4. Love -- Fiction 5. Flying -- Fiction 6. Deserts -- Fiction 7. Shapeshifting -- Fiction
ISBN 0803735669; 9780803735668
LC 2011027164

This is Rinsai Rossetti's debut, a coming-of-age novel. Of "Thai descent, 17-year-old Frenenqer Paje has grown up" with "her coldly overbearing father . . . . [S]he disobeys her father by rescuing a mistreated cat" who "is actually a shapeshifting 'Free person' named Sangris . . . . By night, he flies Frenenqer around the world to places both real and magical, slowly chipping away at the defenses she has built up to withstand her father's callous cruelty." (Publishers Weekly)

Rossi, Veronica

Under the never sky; Veronica Rossi. Harper-Collins 2012 376 p. $17.99

Grades: 6 7 8 9 10 11 12   **Fic**

1. Science fiction 2. Apocalyptic fiction 3. Cannibalism -- Fiction 4. Man-woman relationship -- Fiction

ISBN 9780062072030

LC 2011044631

This book tells the story of "Aria [who] knows her chances of surviving in the outer wasteland--known as The Death Shop--are slim. . . . Then Aria meets an Outsider named Perry. He's wild--a savage--and her only hope of staying alive. A hunter for his tribe in a merciless landscape, Perry views Aria as sheltered and fragile--everything he would expect from a Dweller. . . . Opposites in nearly every way, Aria and Perry must accept each other to survive." (Publisher's note)

Rottman, S. L.

Out of the blue; written by S.L. Rottman. Peachtree Publishers 2009 297p $16.95

Grades: 6 7 8 9   **Fic**

1. Moving -- Fiction 2. Child abuse -- Fiction 3. Military bases -- Fiction

ISBN 978-1-56145-499-0; 1-56145-499-0

LC 2008052839

After moving to Minot, North Dakota, with his mother, the new female base commander, Air Force dependent Stu Ballentyne gradually becomes aware that something terrible is going on in his neighbor's house.

"The story offers both a realistic interpretation of teenage life on an Air Force base and the teen's feeling of powerlessness upon witnessing child abuse—both physical and verbal—in action." SLJ

Rowen, Michelle

Reign check. Walker 2010 292p (Demon princess) $16.99; pa $9.99

Grades: 7 8 9 10   **Fic**

1. School stories 2. Fairies -- Fiction 3. Demonology -- Fiction 4. Friendship -- Fiction

ISBN 978-0-8027-2093-1; 0-8027-2093-5; 978-0-8027-9549-6 pa; 0-8027-9549-8 pa

LC 2009028796

Sixteen-year-old Nikki is again summoned to the Underworld to appear before the Demon Council, the king of the faerie realm enrolls at her small-town Canada high school to experience human life, and her mother begins dating one of her teachers.

"Another chilling, sometimes violent, romantic fantasy that moves from the mundane world to the Shadowlands to the dungeons of the Underground before Nikki can finish her Christmas shopping." Booklist

Reign or shine. Walker & Co. 2009 284p (Demon princess) $16.99; pa $9.99

Grades: 7 8 9 10   **Fic**

1. School stories 2. Moving -- Fiction 3. Demonology

-- Fiction 4. Remarriage -- Fiction

ISBN 978-0-8027-8492-6; 0-8027-8492-5; 978-0-8027-9534-2 pa; 0-8027-9534-X pa

LC 2009000205

In small-town Canada after her mother's fourth marriage, sixteen-year-old Nikki learns that her long-lost father is king of the demons, a fact that threatens to destroy her newfound popularity and sense of belonging.

Rowen "skillfully balances a lighthearted teen voice with emotional maturity. . . . Nikki's engaging voice and several intriguing secondary characters make this a winner." Publ Wkly

Rowling, J. K., 1965-

★ **Harry** Potter and the Sorcerer's Stone; illustrations by Mary Grandpré. Arthur A. Levine Bks. 1998 309p il $22.99; pa $8.99

Grades: 4 5 6 7 8 9 10   **Fic**

1. Fantasy fiction 2. Witches -- Fiction

ISBN 0-590-35340-3; 0-590-35342-X pa

LC 97-39059

First published 1997 in the United Kingdom with title: Harry Potter and the Philosopher's Stone

Rescued from the outrageous neglect of his aunt and uncle, a young boy with a great destiny proves his worth while attending Hogwarts School for Witchcraft and Wizardry.

This "is a brilliantly imagined and beautifully written fantasy." Booklist

Other titles in this series are:

Harry Potter and the Chamber of Secrets (1999)

Harry Potter and the Deathly Hallows (2007)

Harry Potter and Goblet of Fire (2000)

Harry Potter and the Half-Blood Prince (2005)

Harry Potter and the Order of the Phoenix (2003)

Harry Potter and the prisoner of Azkaban (1999)

Roy, James

Max Quigley; technically not a bully. written and illustrated by James Roy. Houghton Mifflin Harcourt 2009 202p il $12.95

Grades: 4 5 6   **Fic**

1. Bullies -- Fiction 2. Friendship -- Fiction

ISBN 978-0-547-15263-9; 0-547-15263-9

LC 2008-36110

First published 2007 in Australia

After playing a prank on one of his "geeky" classmates, sixth-grader Max Quigley's punishment is to be tutored by him.

"Straightforward chronology, believable dialogue, self-contained chapters, and plenty of humor make this accessible to reluctant readers and particularly appealing to boys who may see a bit of themselves in this realistic school story." Booklist

Roy, Jennifer

★ **Yellow** star; by Jennifer Roy. Marshall Cavendish 2006 227p $16.95

Grades: 5 6 7 8   **Fic**

1. Jews -- Fiction 2. Holocaust, 1933-1945 -- Fiction

ISBN 0-7614-5277-X; 978-0-7614-5277-5

LC 2005-50788

From 1939, when Syvia is four and a half years old, to 1945 when she has just turned ten, a Jewish girl and her family struggle to survive in Poland's Lodz ghetto during the Nazi occupation.

"In a thoughtful, vividly descriptive, almost poetic prose, Roy retells the true story of her Aunt Syvia's experiences. . . . This book is a standout in the genre of Holocaust literature." SLJ

Roy, Jennifer Rozines

★ **Mindblind**; [by] Jennifer Roy. Marshall Cavendish 2010 248p il $15.99

Grades: 7 8 9 10 11   **Fic**

1. Genius -- Fiction 2. Bands (Music) -- Fiction 3. Asperger's syndrome -- Fiction

ISBN 978-0-7614-5716-9; 0-7614-5716-X

LC 2010-6966

Fourteen-year-old Nathaniel Clark, who has Asperger's Syndrome, tries to prove that he is a genius by writing songs for his rock band, so that he can become a member of the prestigious Aldus Institute, the premier organization for the profoundly gifted.

"Mature readers will empathize with Nathaniel as his friends, Jessa and Cooper, do. This book is for teens who appreciate a story about self-discovery, dreams, and friendship." Voice Youth Advocates

Rubens, Michael

Sons of the 613; Mike Rubens. Clarion Books 2012 305 p. (hardcover) $16.99

Grades: 7 8 9 10   **Fic**

1. Brothers -- Fiction 2. Bar mitzvah -- Fiction 3. Masculinity -- Fiction 4. Schools -- Fiction 5. Coming of age -- Fiction 6. Junior high schools -- Fiction 7. Jews -- United States -- Fiction 8. Family life -- Minnesota -- Fiction

ISBN 0547612168; 9780547612164

LC 2011044352

In this book by Michael Rubens, "Isaac's parents have abandoned him for a trip to Italy in the final days before his bar mitzvah. And even worse, his hotheaded older brother, Josh, has been left in charge. . . . When Josh declares that there is more to becoming a man than memorization, the mad 'quest' begins for Isaac. . . . But when Isaac begins to fall for Josh's girlfriend, Leslie, the challenges escalate from bad to worse." (Publisher's note)

Ruby, Laura

Bad apple. HarperTeen 2009 247p $16.99; pa $8.99

Grades: 8 9 10 11 12   **Fic**

1. School stories 2. Bullies -- Fiction 3. Divorce -- Fiction 4. Teacher-student relationship -- Fiction

ISBN 978-0-06-124330-1; 0-06-124330-2; 978-0-06-124333-2 pa; 0-06-124333-7 pa

LC 2009-1409

Tola Riley, a high school junior, struggles to tell the truth when she and her art teacher are accused of having an affair.

"Tola and her family are fascinating, quirky-yet-believable, and wholly likable. Ruby works in traditional fairy-tale elements . . . with wry humor." Booklist

Ruby, Lois

Shanghai shadows. Holiday House 2006 284p $16.95

Grades: 7 8 9 10   **Fic**

1. Jews -- Fiction 2. World War, 1939-1945 -- Fiction 3. Young adult literature -- Works

ISBN 0-8234-1960-6; 978-0-8234-1960-9

LC 2005-50342

From 1939 to 1945, a Jewish family struggles to survive in occupied China; young Ilse by remaining optimistic, her older brother by joining a resistance movement, her mother by maintaining connections to the past, and her father by playing the violin that had been his livelihood.

The author's "careful research, courageous characters, low-key descriptions of fear and misery, and understated examples of love, friendship, and courage will further readers' understanding and personalize the often-horrifying epoch." Booklist

Includes bibliographical references

The **secret** of Laurel Oaks. Tom Doherty Associates 2008 282p $16.95

Grades: 6 7 8 9   **Fic**

1. Ghost stories 2. Slavery -- Fiction

ISBN 978-0-7653-1366-9; 0-7653-1366-9

LC 2008-28395

While staying with her family in Louisiana's Laurel Oaks Plantation, purported to be one of the most haunted places in America, thirteen-year-old Lila is contacted by the ghost of a slave girl unjustly convicted of murder. Story inspired by the author's visit to the Myrtles Plantation in Louisiana.

"Ruby succeeds in writing a captivating story about a time long gone, portraying the horror of slavery effectively." Libr Media Connect

Rue, Ginger

Brand new Emily; a novel. Tricycle Press 2009 240p $14.99

Grades: 7 8 9 10   **Fic**

1. School stories 2. Poets -- Fiction 3. Publicity -- Fiction 4. Popularity -- Fiction

ISBN 978-1-58246-269-1; 1-58246-269-0

LC 2008011357

Tired of being picked on by a trio of popular girls, fourteen-year-old poet Emily hires a major public relations firm to change her image and soon finds herself "re-branded" as Em, one of the most important teens not only in her middle school, but in celebrity magazines, as well.

"It's a smart premise, and besides having something pertinent to say about kindness, hubris and the perils of popularity, Rue also imparts insight into how celebrities are designed and marketed. . . . The material is so enjoyable that readers might not even notice that they've learned something." Kirkus

Ruiz Zafon, Carlos, 1964-

The **Midnight** Palace; translated by Lucia Graves. Little, Brown 2011 298p $17.99

Grades: 7 8 9 10   **Fic**

1. Twins -- Fiction 2. Orphans -- Fiction 3. Siblings -- Fiction 4. Demonology -- Fiction 5. Secret societies

-- Fiction
ISBN 978-0-316-04473-8; 0-316-04473-3

LC 2010-43131

Original Spanish edition 1994

When a mysterious threat reenters the lives of twins Ben and Sheere, separated as babies and reunited as teenagers in 1930s Calcutta, the siblings must confront an unspeakable terror, with the help of their secret society of fellow orphans.

"The sense of dread and mystery that pervades the story, and the themes of lost innocence and sacrifice keep readers turning the pages." SLJ

★ The **Prince** of Mist; translated by Lucia Graves. Little, Brown 2010 320p $17.99

Grades: 6 7 8 9 10   **Fic**

1. Dead -- Fiction 2. Magic -- Fiction 3. Siblings -- Fiction 4. Shipwrecks -- Fiction 5. Supernatural -- Fiction

ISBN 978-0-316-04477-6; 0-316-04477-6

LC 2009-51256

In 1943, in a seaside town where their family has gone to be safe from war, thirteen-year-old Max Carver and sister, fifteen-year-old Alicia, with new friend Roland, face off against an evil magician who is striving to complete a bargain made before he died.

"Zafon is a master storyteller. From the first page, the reader is drawn into the mystery and suspense that the young people encounter when they move into the Fleischmann house. . . . This book can be read and enjoyed by every level of reader." Voice Youth Advocates

Rumley, Crickett

Never sit down in a hoopskirt and other things I learned in Southern belle hell. Egmont USA 2011 296p pa $8.99

Grades: 8 9 10 11 12   **Fic**

1. Etiquette -- Fiction 2. Grandmothers -- Fiction 3. Beauty contests -- Fiction 4. Father-daughter relationship -- Fiction

ISBN 978-1-60684-131-0; 1-60684-131-9

LC 2010043617

After being ousted from yet another elite boarding school, seventeen-year-old Jane returns to her Alabama hometown, where her grandmother persuades her to enter the Magnolia Maid pageant.

"Rumley works in nice points about shaking up the status quo while still keeping things light and bright." Booklist

Runholt, Susan

The **mystery** of the third Lucretia. Viking Childrens Books 2008 288p $16.99; pa $6.99

Grades: 5 6 7 8   **Fic**

1. Mystery fiction 2. Art -- Fiction 3. Friendship -- Fiction

ISBN 978-0-670-06252-2; 0-670-06252-9; 978-0-14-241338-8 pa; 0-14-241338-0 pa

LC 2007-24009

While traveling in London, Paris, and Amsterdam, fourteen-year-old best friends Kari and Lucas solve an international art forgery mystery.

"There are enough artistic details for fans of art mysteries and enough spying and fleeing for fans of detective adventure." Bull Cent Child Books

Other titles about Kari and Lucas are:
Rescuing Seneca Crane (2009)
The adventure at Simba Hill (2011)

Runyon, Brent

Surface tension; a novel in four summers. Alfred A. Knopf 2009 197p $16.99; lib bdg $19.99

Grades: 8 9 10 11   **Fic**

1. Vacations -- Fiction 2. Family life -- Fiction

ISBN 978-0-375-84446-1; 0-375-84446-5; 978-0-375-94446-8 lib bdg; 0-375-94446-X lib bdg

LC 2008-9193

During the summer vacations of his thirteenth through his sixteenth year at the family's lake cottage, Luke realizes that although some things stay the same over the years that many more change.

"With sensitivity and candor, Runyon reveals how life changes us all and how these unavoidable changes can be full of both turmoil and wonder." Kirkus

Rupp, Rebecca

After Eli; Rebecca Rupp. 1st ed. Candlewick 2012 245 p. (hardcover) $15.99; (ebook) $15.99

Grades: 4 5 6 7 8   **Fic**

1. Bildungsromans 2. Family -- Fiction 3. Brothers -- Fiction 4. Bereavement -- Fiction 5. Death -- Fiction 6. Books and reading -- Fiction 7. Interpersonal relations -- Fiction

ISBN 0763658103; 9780763658106; 9780763661946

LC 2011048344

In this book, "Daniel, a wry and thoughtful narrator, looks back on the summer when he was 14, three years after his older brother, Eli, died in Iraq at age 22." Daniel's "memories of larger-than-life Eli and his lingering anger about his death" are interwoven with "Daniel's day-to-day challenges, including his dysfunctional family . . . ; his frustrations with his . . . friends; his attraction to Isabelle, a . . . newcomer to town; and his nascent friendship with school outcast Walter." (Publishers Weekly)

★ **Octavia** Boone's big questions about life, the universe, and everything. Candlewick Press 2010 185p $15.99

Grades: 5 6 7 8   **Fic**

1. School stories 2. Religion -- Fiction 3. Family life -- Fiction 4. Christian life -- Fiction

ISBN 978-0-7636-4491-8; 0-7636-4491-9

LC 2009-47408

Seventh-grader Octavia puzzles over life's biggest questions when her mother seems to find the answers in a conservative Christian church, while her artist father believes the writings of Henry David Thoreau hold the key.

"This hopeful novel highlights the resilience of children and the courage of those who seek truth in a complicated world." Publ Wkly

Rush, Jennifer

Altered; by Jennifer Rush. 1st ed. Little, Brown and Co. 2013 336 p. (hardcover) $17.99

Grades: 7 8 9 10 11 12   **Fic**
1. Science fiction 2. Runaway teenagers -- Fiction 3. Memory -- Fiction 4. Identity -- Fiction 5. Runaways -- Fiction 6. Genetic engineering -- Fiction 7. Fathers and daughters -- Fiction
ISBN 0316197084; 9780316197083

LC 2012007545

This is the debut novel in a series from Jennifer Rush. Here, "homeschooled 18-year-old Anna Mason has a life ruled by secrecy. Her widower father works for a clandestine organization called the Branch, and four gorgeous genetically altered teenage boys live in the basement laboratory of their New York State farmhouse. . . . When the Branch tries to collect 'the units,' chaos erupts, and Sam, Anna, and the others take off on the run." (Publishers Weekly)

Russell, Christopher
Dogboy. Greenwillow Books 2006 259p $15.99; $15.99; lib bdg $16.89
Grades: 5 6 7 8   **Fic**
1. Dogs -- Fiction 2. Orphans -- Fiction 3. Middle Ages -- Fiction 4. Knights and knighthood -- Fiction 5. Hundred Years' War, 1339-1453 -- Fiction
ISBN 978-0-06-084116-4; 0-06-084116-8; 978-0-06-084117-1 lib bdg; 0-06-084117-6 lib bdg

LC 2005-08525

First published 2005 in the United Kingdom
In 1346, twelve-year-old Brind, an orphaned kennel boy raised with hunting dogs at an English manor, accompanies his master, along with half of the manor's prized mastiffs, to France, where he must fend for himself when both his master and the dogs are lost at the decisive battle of Crécy
"The action is fast-paced with narrow escapes at every turn and elements of dry humor at the most unlikely times." SLJ

Russell, Krista
Chasing the Nightbird. Peachtree 2011 200p $15.95
Grades: 5 6 7 8   **Fic**
1. Sailors -- Fiction 2. Slavery -- Fiction 3. Abolitionists -- Fiction
ISBN 1561455970; 9781561455973

LC 2011002665

In 1851 New Bedford, Massachusetts, fourteen-year-old Cape Verdean sailor Lucky Valera is kidnapped by his estranged half-brother and forced to work in a mill, but while Lucky is plotting his escape he meets a former slave and a young Quaker girl who influence his plans.
"Without slowing the story's pace, Russell gives readers plenty to think about regarding the turbulent racial dynamics of the period—Lucky, who is dark-skinned yet free, initially sees little connection between his life and the plight of slaves. Strong-willed and goodhearted, Lucky is an especially vibrant hero in this multifaceted and suspenseful historical adventure." Publ Wkly

Russell, Randy
Dead rules. HarperTeen 2011 376p $16.99
Grades: 7 8 9 10   **Fic**
1. School stories 2. Dead -- Fiction 3. Future life --

Fiction 4. Supernatural -- Fiction
ISBN 978-0-06-19867-03; 0-06-19867-04

LC 2010032452

When high school junior Jana Webster dies suddenly, she finds herself in Dead School, where she faces choices that will determine when she, a Riser, will move on, but she strives to become a Slider instead, for the chance to be with the love of her life—even if it means killing him.
"Sarcastic quips and double entendres drive the story's humor, but it's the sensitivity of the supporting characters . . . that allows Jana (and readers) to see laughter within tragedy." Kirkus

Rutkoski, Marie
★ The **Cabinet** of Wonders; [by] Marie Rutkoski. Farrar Straus Giroux 2008 258p (The Kronos Chronicles) $16.95; pa $6.99
Grades: 5 6 7 8   **Fic**
1. Fantasy fiction 2. Magic -- Fiction 3. Gypsies -- Fiction 4. Princes -- Fiction
ISBN 978-0-374-31026-4; 0-374-31026-2; 978-0-312-60239-0 pa; 0-312-60239-1 pa

LC 2007037702

Twelve-year-old Petra, accompanied by her magical tin spider, goes to Prague hoping to retrieve the enchanted eyes the Prince of Bohemia took from her father, and is aided in her quest by a Roma boy and his sister.
"Add this heady mix of history and enchantment to the season's list of astonishingly accomplished first novels. . . . Infusions of folklore (and Rutkowski's embellishments of them) don't slow the fast plot but more deeply entrance readers." Publ Wkly
Other titles in this series are:
The Celestial Globe (2009)
The Jewel of the Kalderash (2011)

★ The **shadow** society; Marie Rutkoski. Farrar, Straus and Giroux 2012 408 p. $17.99
Grades: 7 8 9 10 11 12   **Fic**
1. Science fiction 2. Alternative histories 3. Supernatural -- Fiction 4. Schools -- Fiction 5. Identity -- Fiction 6. High schools -- Fiction 7. Foster home care -- Fiction
ISBN 0374349053; 9780374349059

LC 2011033158

In this novel by Marie Rutkoski "Darcy Jones doesn't remember anything before the day she was abandoned as a child outside a Chicago firehouse. . . . But she couldn't have guessed that she comes from an alternate world where the Great Chicago Fire didn't happen and deadly creatures called Shades terrorize the human population. Memories begin to haunt Darcy when a new boy arrives at her high school, and he makes her feel both desire and desired in a way she hadn't thought possible." (Publisher's note)

Ryan, Amy Kathleen
★ **Glow**. St. Martin's Griffin 2011 307p (Sky chasers) $17.99
Grades: 8 9 10 11 12   **Fic**
1. Science fiction
ISBN 978-0-312-59056-7; 0-312-59056-3

LC 2011020385

Part of the first generation to be conceived in deep space, fifteen-year-old Waverly is expected to marry young and have children to populate a new planet, but a violent betrayal by the dogmatic leader of their sister ship could have devastating consequences.

"The themes of survival, morality, religion, and power are well developed, and the characters are equally complex. The author has also created a unique and vivid outer-space setting that is exciting and easy to imagine." SLJ

Spark; a Sky chasers novel. Amy Kathleen Ryan. 1st ed. St. Martin's Press 2012 309 p. (hardcover) $17.99; (paperback) $9.99

Grades: 8 9 10 11 12   **Fic**
1. Mystery fiction 2. Friendship -- Fiction 3. Parent-child relationship -- Fiction 4. Science fiction
ISBN 0312621353; 9780312621353; 9781250014160; 9781250031952

LC 2012004631

Author Amy Kathleen Ryan's character "Waverly Marshall has endured and committed terrible acts aboard the 'New Horizon.' . . . [Kieran] delivers sermons designed to promote both unity and loyalty. . . . Meanwhile, Seth . . . escapes the brig under mysterious circumstances and discovers a major threat to the ship. As Waverly, Kieran, [and] Seth . . . work . . . to keep the peace, secure the ship and rescue their parents from the 'New Horizon,' . . . political and moral questions arise." (Kirkus Reviews)

Ryan, Pam Muñoz
★ The **dreamer**; drawings by Peter Sís. Scholastic Press 2010 372p il $17.99

Grades: 4 5 6 7   **Fic**
1. Father-son relationship -- Fiction
ISBN 978-0-439-26970-4; 0-439-26970-9
Boston Globe-Horn Book Award honor book: Fiction (2010)

Neftali finds beauty and wonder everywhere. He loves to collect treasures, daydream, and write—pastimes his authoritarian father thinks are for fools. Against all odds, Neftali prevails against his father's cruelty and his own crippling shyness to become one of the most widely read poets in the world, Pablo Neruda.

"Ryan loads the narrative with vivid sensory details. And although it isn't poetry, it eloquently evokes the sensation of experiencing the world as someone who savors the rhythms of words and gets lost in the intricate surprises of nature. The neat squares of Sis' meticulously stippled illustrations, richly symbolic in their own right, complement and deepen the lyrical quality of the book." Booklist

Esperanza rising. Scholastic Press 2000 262p $15.95; pa $4.99

Grades: 5 6 7 8   **Fic**
1. Mexican Americans -- Fiction 2. Agricultural laborers -- Fiction
ISBN 0-439-12041-1; 0-439-12042-X pa

LC 00-24186

Esperanza and her mother are forced to leave their life of wealth and privilege in Mexico to go work in the labor camps of Southern California, where they must adapt to the harsh circumstances facing Mexican farm workers on the eve of the Great Depression

"Ryan writes movingly in clear, poetic language that children will sink into, and the [book] offers excellent opportunities for discussion and curriculum support." Booklist

Rylander, Chris
The **fourth** stall. Walden Pond Press 2011 314p $15.99

Grades: 4 5 6 7   **Fic**
1. School stories 2. Bullies -- Fiction 3. Friendship -- Fiction 4. Business enterprises -- Fiction
ISBN 978-0-06-199496-8; 0-06-199496-0

LC 2010016280

Sixth-graders Mac and Vince operate a business charging schoolmates for protection from bullies and for help to negotiate conflicts peacefully, with amazing challenges and results.

"Rylander mines a substantial amount of humor and heart from this combination hardboiled crime novel and middle-grade character piece. . . . A light and enjoyable caper." Publ Wkly

Rylant, Cynthia
★ **Missing** May. Orchard Bks. 1992 89p hardcover o.p. pa $5.99

Grades: 5 6 7 8   **Fic**
1. Death -- Fiction
ISBN 0-531-05996-0; 0-439-61383-3 pa

LC 91-23303

Awarded the Newbery Medal, 1993

After the death of the beloved aunt who has raised her, twelve-year-old Summer and her uncle Ob leave their West Virginia trailer in search of the strength to go on living

"There is much to ponder here, from the meaning of life and death to the power of love. That it all succeeds is a tribute to a fine writer who brings to the task a natural grace of language, an earthly sense of humor, and a well-grounded sense of the spiritual." SLJ

★ A **fine** white dust. Simon & Schuster 2000 106p $25; pa $4.99

Grades: 5 6 7 8   **Fic**
1. Religion -- Fiction 2. Friendship -- Fiction 3. Family life -- Fiction
ISBN 978-0-689-84087-6; 0-689-84087-X; 978-1-4169-2769-3 pa; 1-4169-2769-7 pa
A reissue of the title first published 1986 by Bradbury Press
A Newbery Medal honor book, 1987

The visit of the traveling Preacher Man to his small North Carolina town gives new impetus to thirteen-year-old Peter's struggle to reconcile his own deeply felt religious belief with the beliefs and non-beliefs of his family and friends

"Blending humor and intense emotion with a poetic use of language, Cynthia Rylant has created a taut, finely drawn portrait of a boy's growth from seeking for belief, through seduction and betrayal, to a spiritual acceptance and a readiness 'for something whole.'" Horn Book

Sachar, Louis

★ **Holes**; [by] Louis Sachar. 10th anniversary ed.; Farrar, Straus and Giroux 2008 265p $18

Grades: 5 6 7 8 **Fic**

1. Friendship -- Fiction 2. Buried treasure -- Fiction 3. Homeless persons -- Fiction 4. Juvenile delinquency -- Fiction

ISBN 978-0-374-33266-2; 0-374-33266-5

LC 2007045430

A reissue of the title first published 1998. Includes additional information about the author and his Newbery acceptance speech

Awarded the Newbery Medal, 1999

As further evidence of his family's bad fortune which they attribute to a curse on a distant relative, Stanley Yelnats is sent to a hellish correctional camp in the Texas desert where he finds his first real friend, a treasure, and a new sense of himself

"This delightfully clever story is well-crafted and thought-provoking, with a bit of a folklore thrown in for good measure." Voice Youth Advocates

Small steps; [by] Louis Sachar. Delacorte Press 2006 257p $16.95; lib bdg $19.99

Grades: 5 6 7 8 **Fic**

1. Cerebral palsy -- Fiction 2. African Americans -- Fiction 3. Juvenile delinquency -- Fiction

ISBN 0-385-73314-3; 0-385-90333-2 lib bdg

LC 2005-09102

Three years after being released from Camp Green Lake, Armpit is trying hard to keep his life on track, but when his old pal X-Ray shows up with a tempting plan to make some easy money scalping concert tickets, Armpit reluctantly goes along.

This "is a story of redemption, of the triumph of the human spirit, of self-sacrifice, and of doing the right thing. Sachar is a master storyteller who creates memorable characters." SLJ

★ The **cardturner**; a novel about a king, a queen, and a joker. Delacorte Press 2010 336p $17.99; lib bdg $20.99

Grades: 8 9 10 11 12 **Fic**

1. Uncles -- Fiction 2. Family life -- Fiction 3. Bridge (Game) -- Fiction

ISBN 978-0-385-73662-6; 0-385-73662-2; 978-0-385-90619-7 lib bdg; 0-385-90619-6 lib bdg

LC 2009-27585

"Alton gets roped into serving as a card turner for his great-uncle, Lester Trapp, a bridge whizz who recently lost his eyesight. . . . To Alton's surprise, he becomes enamored of the game and begins to bond with his crusty uncle. . . . With dry, understated humor, Alton makes the intricacies of bridge accessible, while his relationships with and observations about family members and friends . . . form a portrait of a reflective teenager whose life is infinitely enriched by connections he never expected to make." Publ Wkly

Saenz, Benjamin Alire

★ **He** forgot to say good-bye. Simon & Schuster 2008 321p $16.99

Grades: 8 9 10 11 **Fic**

1. Drug abuse -- Fiction 2. Mexican Americans -- Fiction

ISBN 978-1-4169-4963-3; 1-4169-4963-1

LC 2007-21959

Two teenaged boys with very different lives find that they share a common bond—fathers they have never met who left when they were small boys—and in spite of their differences, they become close when they each need someone who understands.

"The affirming and hopeful ending is well-earned for the characters and a great payoff for the reader. . . . Characters are well-developed and complex. . . . Overall it is a strong novel with broad teenage appeal." Voice Youth Advocates

Sage, Angie

★ **Magyk**; Septimus Heap, book one. illustrations by Mark Zug. Katherine Tegen Books 2005 576p il $16.99; lib bdg $17.89; pa $7.99

Grades: 5 6 7 8 **Fic**

1. Fantasy fiction 2. Magic -- Fiction 3. Children's literature -- Works -- Grades two through six

ISBN 0-06-057731-2; 0-06-057732-0 lib bdg; 0-06-057733-9 pa

LC 2003-28185

After learning that she is the Princess, Jenna is whisked from her home and carried toward safety by the Extraordinary Wizard, those she always believed were her father and brother, and a young guard known only as Boy 412, pursued by agents of those who killed her mother ten years earlier.

"Youngsters will lose themselves happily in Sage's fluent, charismatic storytelling, which enfolds supportive allies and horrific enemies, abundant quirky details, and poignant moments of self-discovery." Booklist

Other titles in this series are:
Flyte (2006)
Physik (2007)
Queste (2008)
Syren (2009)
Darke (2011)

The **Magykal** papers; illustrations by Mark Zug. Katherine Tegen Books 2009 167p il (Septimus Heap)

Grades: 5 6 7 8 **Fic**

1. Fantasy fiction 2. Magic -- Fiction 3. Princesses -- Fiction

ISBN 0-06-170416-4; 978-0-06-170416-1

LC 2008027110

Purports to be a compilation of pamphlets, journals, restaurant reviews, maps, historical information, and other never-before-published papers from the world of the apprentice alchemist, Septimus Heap.

"Fans of Sage's saga will rejoice in the little pieces if 'magyk' collected here. Beautifully rendered in full color." SLJ

Saint-Exupery, Antoine de

The **little** prince; written and illustrated by Antoine de Saint-Exupery; translated from the French by Richard Howard. Harcourt 2000 83p il $18; pa $12

Grades: 4 5 6 7 8 9 10 11 12 Adult   **Fic**
1. Fairy tales 2. Fantasy fiction 3. Princes -- Fiction 4. Philosophical novels 5. Air pilots -- Fiction
ISBN 0-15-202398-4; 0-15-601219-7 pa
LC 99-50439

A new translation of the title first published 1943 by Reynal & Hitchcock

"This many-dimensional fable of an airplane pilot who has crashed in the desert is for readers of all ages. The pilot comes upon the little prince soon after the crash. The prince tells of his adventures on different planets and on Earth as he attempts to learn about the universe in order to live peacefully on his own small planet. A spiritual quality enhances the seemingly simple observations of the little prince." Shapiro. Fic for Youth. 3d edition

Saldana, Rene

Dancing with the devil and other tales from beyond; = Bailando con el diablo y otros cuentos del más allá. by René Saldaña, Jr. ; Spanish translation by Gabriela Baeza Ventura. Piñata Books 2012 81 p. (alk. paper) $9.95
Grades: 5 6 7 8 9   **Fic**
1. Short stories 2. Mexican Americans -- Fiction
ISBN 1558857443; 9781558857445
LC 2012008729

Author Rene Saldaña Jr. presents a book of short stories. "Lauro and Miguel run for their lives--with La Llorona's cold breath on their necks-- after being caught smoking cigarettes down by the river. There's Felipe, who's so determined to win back the Peñitas Grand Master Marble Champion title that he's willing to make a deal for a shooter with a supernatural edge. And when Louie's leg swells up after he cuts his toe playing with a knife, he can't help but wonder if his mom's warning could be true." (Publisher's note)

Saldin, Erin

★ The **girls** of No Return. Arthur A. Levine Books 2012 345 p $17.99
Grades: 7 8 9 10   **Fic**
1. School stories 2. Wilderness areas -- Fiction
ISBN 978-0-545-31026-0; 0-545-31026-1; 978-0-545-39253-2 e-book
LC 2011024214

A troubled sixteen-year-old girl attending a wilderness school in the Idaho mountains must finally face the consequences of her complicated friendships with two of the other girls at the school.

"Teen and adult characters that matter are complex and intriguing. Saldin keeps readers intrigued by both withholding information and sharing Lida's retrospective thoughts without ever seeming manipulative. This debut is richly rewarding and will linger for its subtle examination of human behavior and emotions-love, trust, guilt and forgiveness." Kirkus

Salerni, Dianne K.

We hear the dead. Sourcebooks Fire 2010 422p pa $9.99
Grades: 7 8 9 10   **Fic**
1. Mediums 2. Sisters -- Fiction 3. Spiritualism --

Fiction
ISBN 978-1-4022-3092-9; 1-4022-3092-3

The author "paints vivid scenes of life in upstate New York during a time when exposed ankles were shocking and the Underground Railroad offered a dangerous route to freedom for both conductors and slaves. Historical fiction at its best." SLJ

Sales, Leila

Past perfect. Simon Pulse 2011 306p $16.99
Grades: 7 8 9 10   **Fic**
1. Summer employment -- Fiction 2. Dating (Social customs) -- Fiction
ISBN 978-1-4424-0682-7; 1-4424-0682-8
LC 2011025811

"Chelsea is an appealing narrator with a sharp sense of humor, and readers will tear through this novel to find out whether she reunites with Ezra or gets together with Dan from the rival museum. . . . This is a satisfying and fun read." SLJ

Salisbury, Graham

★ **Eyes** of the emperor. Wendy Lamb Books 2005 228p hardcover o.p. pa $6.99
Grades: 7 8 9 10   **Fic**
1. Japanese Americans -- Fiction 2. World War, 1939-1945 -- Fiction
ISBN 0-385-72971-5; 0-440-22956-1 pa
LC 2004-15142

Following orders from the United States Army, several young Japanese American men train K-9 units to hunt Asians during World War II.

"Based on the experiences of 26 Hawaiian-Americans of Japanese ancestry, this novel tells an uncomfortable story. Yet it tells of belief in honor, respect, and love of country." Libr Media Connect

★ **House** of the red fish. Wendy Lamb Books 2006 291p $16.95; lib bdg $17.99
Grades: 6 7 8 9   **Fic**
1. Japanese Americans -- Fiction 2. World War, 1939-1945 -- Fiction
ISBN 0-385-73121-3; 0-385-90145-3 lib bdg
LC 2006-07544

Over a year after Japan's attack on Pearl Harbor and the arrest of Tomi's father and grandfather, Tomi and his friends, battling anti-Japanese-American sentiment in Hawaii, try to find a way to salvage his father's sunken fishing boat.

"Many readers, even those who don't enjoy historical fiction, will like the portrayal of the work and the male camaraderie." Booklist

Lord of the deep. Delacorte Press 2001 182p hardcover o.p. pa $7.99
Grades: 5 6 7 8   **Fic**
1. Fishing 2. Stepfathers 3. Fishing -- Fiction 4. Stepfathers -- Fiction
ISBN 0-385-72918-9; 0-440-22911-1 pa
LC 00-60280

Working for Bill, his stepfather, on a charter fishing boat in Hawaii teaches thirteen-year-old Mikey about fishing, and about taking risks, making sacrifices, and facing some of life's difficult choices

"With its vivid Hawaiian setting, this fine novel is a natural for book-discussion groups that enjoy pondering moral ambiguity. Its action-packed scenes will also lure in reluctant readers." SLJ

★ **Night** of the howling dogs; a novel. Wendy Lamb Books 2007 191p $16.99; lib bdg $19.99; pa $6.50

Grades: 5 6 7 8   **Fic**
   1. Camping -- Fiction 2. Tsunamis -- Fiction 3. Earthquakes -- Fiction 4. Survival after airplane accidents, shipwrecks, etc. -- Fiction
   ISBN 978-0-385-73122-5; 978-0-385-90146-8 lib bdg; 978-0-440-23839-3 pa
                         LC 2007-07054

In 1975, eleven Boy Scouts, their leaders, and some new friends camping at Halape, Hawaii, find their survival skills put to the test when a massive earthquake strikes, followed by a tsunami.

This is a "vivid adventure. . . . Salisbury weaves Hawaiian legend into the modern-day narrative to create a haunting, unusual novel." Booklist

Under the blood-red sun. Delacorte Press 1994 246p hardcover o.p. pa $5.99

Grades: 5 6 7 8 9 10   **Fic**
   1. Japanese Americans -- Fiction 2. World War, 1939-1945 -- Fiction 3. Pearl Harbor (Oahu, Hawaii), Attack on, 1941 -- Fiction
   ISBN 0-385-32099-X; 0-440-41139-4 pa
                         LC 94-444

Tomikazu Nakaji's biggest concerns are baseball, homework, and a local bully, until life with his Japanese family in Hawaii changes drastically after the bombing of Pearl Harbor in December 1941

"Character development of major figures is good, the setting is warmly realized, and the pace of the story moves gently though inexorably forward." SLJ

Saller, Carol Fisher

Eddie's war; [by] Carol Fisher Saller. Namelos 2011 ix, 194p $18.95

Grades: 5 6 7 8   **Fic**
   1. Novels in verse 2. Brothers -- Fiction 3. Farm life -- Fiction 4. World War, 1939-1945 -- Fiction
   ISBN 1-60898-108-8; 1-60898-109-6 pa; 978-1-60898-108-3; 978-1-60898-109-0 pa

"When we meet him in 1934, Eddie is five, Tom ten. In the next ten years the brothers develop friendships, discover family secrets, . . . and ponder the causes of European conflict . . . as well as the virulent prejudice rife in their own farming community. Tom's enlisting in 1943 unveils the real nature of war that has inspired the boys' games. Narrated by Eddie, these seventy-six vignettes are beautifully phrased and vividly revealing of character." Horn Book

Sanchez, Alex

★ **Bait**. Simon & Schuster Books for Young Readers 2009 239p $16.99

Grades: 7 8 9 10   **Fic**
   1. Stepfathers -- Fiction 2. Mexican Americans -- Fiction 3. Child sexual abuse -- Fiction
   ISBN 978-1-4169-3772-2; 1-4169-3772-2
                         LC 2008-38815

Diego keeps getting into trouble because of his explosive temper until he finally finds a probation officer who helps him get to the root of his anger so that he can stop running from his past.

"This groundbreaking novel brings to life an appealing young man who is neither totally a victim nor a victimizer, one who struggles to handle conflicts that derail many young lives. . . . High interest and accessible, this coming-of-age story belongs in every collection." SLJ

So hard to say; Alex Sanchez. 1st ed; Simon & Schuster Books for Young Readers 2004 230p $14.95

Grades: 6 7 8 9   **Fic**
   1. Homosexuality -- Fiction 2. Mexican Americans -- Fiction
   ISBN 0-689-86564-3
                         LC 2003-21128

Thirteen-year-old Xio, a Mexican American girl, and Frederick, who has just moved to California from Wisconsin, quickly become close friends, but when Xio starts thinking of Frederick as her boyfriend, he must confront his feelings of confusion and face the fear that he might be gay.

"Adventurous, multifaceted, funny, and unpredictably insightful, Sanchez's novel . . . gels well-rounded characterizations with the universal excitement of first love." SLJ

Sandell, Lisa Ann

A **map** of the known world. Scholastic Press 2009 273p $16.99

Grades: 7 8 9 10   **Fic**
   1. School stories 2. Art -- Fiction 3. Bereavement -- Fiction 4. Family life -- Fiction
   ISBN 978-0-545-06970-0; 0-545-06970-X
                         LC 2008-50745

Devastated, along with her parents, by the death of her older brother and apprehensive about being a freshman in the same high school he attended, fourteen-year-old Cora finds unexpected solace in art.

Sandell's "fluid phrasing and choice of metaphors give her prose a quiet poetic ambience." Publ Wkly

Sanders, Scott Loring

Gray baby; a novel. Houghton Mifflin Harcourt 2009 321p $17

Grades: 7 8 9 10   **Fic**
   1. Homicide -- Fiction 2. Alcoholism -- Fiction 3. Country life -- Fiction 4. Single parent family -- Fiction 5. Racially mixed people -- Fiction
   ISBN 978-0-547-07661-4; 0-547-07661-4
                         LC 2008-36810

Clifton has grown up in rural Virginia with the memory of his African American father being beaten to death by policemen, causing his white mother to slip into alcoholism and depression, but after befriending an old man who listens to his problems, Clifton finally feels less alone in the world.

"Unflinching and raw, the story, set in the late 1980s, explores the destructiveness of racism." Horn Book Guide

Sanders, Shelly

Rachel's secret. Second Story Press 2012 248 p. $12.95

Grades: 6 7 8 9 10   Fic

1. Historical fiction 2. Antisemitism -- Fiction 3. Judaism -- Relations -- Christianity -- Fiction

ISBN 1926920376; 9781926920375

This book follows "14-year-old Rachel . . . living under Russian rule in Kishinev in 1903, [she] was one of the last people to see her Christian friend Mikhail alive when she witnessed his murder at the hands of disgruntled relatives who stood to lose out on an inheritance. His death is blamed on Jews, however, and a vicious pogrom is unleashed on the city. Rachel"s anguish about knowing what happened stems from a justified fear of not being believed if she comes forward, thus evoking more turmoil. She also harbors guilt that her somewhat risky friendship with a non-Jewish boy somehow triggered the calamity. . . . [W]hile Rachel does act courageously and courtroom justice is meted out, virulent anti-Semitism still rules the day." (Booklist)

Sanderson, Brandon

★ Alcatraz versus the evil Librarians. Scholastic Press 2007 308p $16.99; pa $6.99

Grades: 4 5 6 7   Fic

1. Fantasy fiction 2. Librarians -- Fiction 3. Grandfathers -- Fiction

ISBN 0-439-92550-9; 978-0-439-92550-1; 0-439-92552-5 pa; 978-0-439-92552-5 pa

LC 2006-38378

On his thirteenth birthday, foster child Alcatraz Smedry receives a bag of sand which is immediately stolen by the evil Librarians who are trying to take over the world. Soon, Alcatraz is introduced to his grandfather and his own special talent, and told that he must use it to save civilization.

"Readers whose sense of humor runs toward the subversive will be instantly captivated. . . . This nutty novel isn't for everyone, but it's also sure to win passionate fans." Publ Wkly

Other titles about Alcatraz are:

Alcatraz versus the scrivener's bones (2008)

Alcatraz versus the Knights of Crystallia (2009)

Alcatraz versus the shattered lens (2010)

Sandler, Karen

Tankborn. Tu Books 2011 373p map $17.95

Grades: 7 8 9 10   Fic

1. Science fiction 2. Genetic engineering -- Fiction

ISBN 978-1-60060-662-5; 1-60060-662-8

LC 2011014589

Kayla and Mishalla, two genetically engineered non-human slaves (GENs), fall in love with higher-status boys, discover deep secrets about the creation of GENs, and in the process find out what it means to be human.

"Sandler has created a fascinating dystopian world. . . . The author's speculative vision of the darker side of future possibilities in genetic engineering and mind control is both chilling and thought-provoking." SLJ

Saunders, Kate

★ Beswitched. Delacorte Press 2011 244p $16.99

Grades: 4 5 6 7   Fic

1. School stories 2. Magic -- Fiction 3. Time travel -- Fiction

ISBN 978-0-385-74075-3

LC 2011000747

First published 2010 in the United Kingdom

On her way, reluctantly, to a boarding school in present-day England, Flora suddenly finds herself in 1935, the new girl at St. Winifred's, having been summoned via a magic spell by her new dormitory mates.

"This absorbing novel . . . features a dimensional, delightful protagonist, whose personality and growth ring true. . . . Along with the entertaining magical elements, the universal themes of self-discovery and looking beyond appearances combine into a wholly engaging and enjoyable read." Booklist

The **Whizz** Pop Chocolate Shop; Kate Saunders. 1st ed. Delacorte Press 2013 293 p. (hardcover) $16.99

Grades: 5 6 7 8   Fic

1. Chocolate -- Fiction 2. Cats -- Fiction 3. Magic -- Fiction 4. Twins -- Fiction 5. Immortality -- Fiction 6. Brothers and sisters -- Fiction 7. Adventure and adventurers -- Fiction

ISBN 0385743017; 9780385743013

LC 2011053081

In this children's story, by Kate Saunders, "the family of eleven-year-old twins Oz and Lily have inherited [a house], together with the mysterious shop downstairs. Long ago, the shop's famous chocolate-makers . . . were clever sorcerers. Now evil villains are hunting for the secret of their greatest recipe. . . . This magic chocolate [has] the ability to destroy the world. . . . It's up to them to stop the villains and keep the magical chocolate recipe out of harm's way." (Publisher's note)

Scaletta, Kurtis

Mamba Point. Alfred A. Knopf 2010 268p il $16.99; lib bdg $19.99

Grades: 5 6 7 8   Fic

1. Fear -- Fiction 2. Snakes -- Fiction

ISBN 978-0-375-86180-2; 0-375-86180-7; 978-0-375-96180-9 lib bdg; 0-375-96180-1 lib bdg

LC 2009-22084

After moving with his family to Liberia, twelve-year-old Linus discovers that he has a mystical connection with the black mamba, one of the deadliest snakes in Africa, which he is told will give him some of the snake's characteristics. Includes facts about the author's experiences as a thirteen-year-old American living in Liberia in 1982

Scaletta "has created an appealing, well-written protagonist whose everyday and extraordinary experiences . . . change his life in unexpected, positive ways. . . . The engaging first-person narrative and array of diversely drawn characters further enliven the novel." Booklist

Mudville. Alfred A. Knopf 2009 265p $16.99; lib bdg $19.99; pa $7.99

Grades: 5 6 7 8   **Fic**
   1. Rain -- Fiction 2. Baseball -- Fiction 3. Family life
-- Fiction 4. Dakota Indians -- Fiction 5. Foster home
care -- Fiction
   ISBN 978-0-375-85579-5; 0-375-85579-3; 978-0-375-
95579-2 lib bdg; 0-375-95579-8 lib bdg; 978-0-375-
84472-0 pa; 0-375-84472-4 pa
                   LC 2008000166
   For twenty-two years, since a fateful baseball game
against their rival town, it has rained in Moundville, so when
the rain finally stops, twelve-year-old Roy, his friends, and
foster brother Sturgis dare to face the curse and form a team
   The author "balances perceptive explorations of personal and domestic issues perfectly with fine baseball talk and .
. . absorbing play-by-play." SLJ

Scalzi, John
   Fuzzy nation. Tor 2011 301p $24.99
Grades: 8 9 10   **Fic**
   1. Science fiction 2. Space colonies -- Fiction 3. Life
on other planets -- Fiction
   ISBN 978-0-7653-2854-0; 0-7653-2854-2
                   LC 2010038178
   Jack Holloway, prospecting on Zara XXIII for ZaraCorp,
finds an immensely valuable stream of sunstone. But when
he forwards footage of the planet's catlike, native "fuzzies"
to a biologist friend who believes the "fuzzies" are sentient-
hired company thugs, murder, and arson soon follow to protect ZaraCorp's mining interests
   "Readers drawn to books with themes related to ethics,
ecology, and science will appreciate this smart novel." Voice
Youth Advocates

Scarrow, Alex
   TimeRiders. Walker & Co. 2010 405p $16.99
Grades: 7 8 9 10   **Fic**
   1. Science fiction 2. Time travel -- Fiction 3.
Environmental protection -- Fiction 4. September 11
terrorist attacks, 2001 -- Fiction
   ISBN 978-0-8027-2172-3; 0-8027-2172-9
                   LC 2009-53166
   Rescued from imminent death, teens Maddy, Liam,
and Sal join forces in 2001 Manhattan to correct changes
in history made by other time travelers, using a "time
bubble" surrounding the attack on the Twin Towers to hide
their journeys.
   "The characters are expertly developed, each displaying vulnerabilities and quirks that make them memorable
as individuals. . . . This is a brilliantly paced, fascinating
look at the ways in which one seemingly small change can
ripple out to—literally—the end of the world." Bull Cent
Child Books
   Another title in this series is:
   Day of the predator (2011)

Scheibe, Lindsey
   Riptide; one summer, endless possibilities. Lind-
sey Scheibe. 1st ed. Flux 2013 277 p. (paperback)
$9.99
Grades: 7 8 9 10 11 12   **Fic**
   1. Surfing -- Fiction 2. Teenage girls -- Fiction 3.
Friendship -- Fiction 4. Child abuse -- Fiction 5. Best

friends -- Fiction 6. Dating (Social customs) -- Fiction
   ISBN 0738735949; 9780738735948
                   LC 2012048951
   In this novel, by Lindsey Scheibe, "signing up for her
first surf competition, Grace has just one summer to train
and impress the university scouts who will be judging the
comp. But summer is about more than just big waves. As romances ignite and her feelings for Ford threaten to reach the
point of no return, Grace must face the biggest challenges of
her life." (Publisher's note)

Schindler, Holly
   Playing hurt. Flux 2011 303p pa $9.95
Grades: 7 8 9 10   **Fic**
   1. Love stories 2. Resorts -- Fiction 3. Loss
(Psychology) -- Fiction
   ISBN 978-0-7387-2287-0; 0-7387-2287-1
                   LC 2010-44173
   Chelsea Keyes, a high school basketball star whose
promising career has been cut short by a terrible accident on
the court, and Clint Morgan, a nineteen-year-old ex-hockey
player who gave up his sport following a game-related tragedy, meet at a Minnesota lake resort and find themselves
drawn together by the losses they have suffered.
   "Both heartbreaking and thrilling, the emotional journey
that Clint and Chelsea embark on together is more than a
heady romance; the characters are realistically drawn, and
the book does not shy away from the reality of the characters' experiences: anger and grief mixed with desire and
yearning. The book speaks to personal struggles and triumphs and the ability of the human spirit to heal." Voice
Youth Advocates

Schlitz, Laura Amy
   ★ **Splendors** and glooms; Laura Amy Schlitz.
Candlewick 2012 384 p. $17.99
Grades: 4 5 6 7   **Fic**
   1. Mystery fiction 2. Orphans -- Fiction 3. Kidnapping
-- Fiction 4. Puppets and puppet plays -- Fiction 5.
Puppets -- Fiction 6. Witches -- Fiction 7. Blessing
and cursing -- Fiction
   ISBN 0763653802; 9780763653804
                   LC 2011048366
   John Newbery Honor Book (2013)
   In this book by Laura Amy Schlitz "Clara Wintermute .
. . invites . . . the master puppeteer, Gaspare Grisini, . . . to
entertain at her birthday party. . . . When Clara vanishes that
night, suspicion of kidnapping falls upon the puppeteer and,
by association, Lizzie Rose and Parsefall. As they seek to
puzzle out Clara's whereabouts, Lizzie and Parse uncover
Grisini's criminal past." (Publisher's note)

   ★ A **drowned** maiden's hair; a melodrama.
Candlewick Press 2006 389p $15.99
Grades: 5 6 7 8   **Fic**
   1. Orphans -- Fiction 2. Spiritualism -- Fiction
   ISBN 978-0-7636-2930-4; 0-7636-2930-8
                   LC 2006-49056
   At the Barbary Asylum for Female Orphans, eleven-
year-old Maud is adopted by three spinster sisters moon-
lighting as mediums who take her home and reveal to her the
role she will play in their seances.

"Filled with heavy atmosphere and suspense, this story recreates life in early-20th-century New England. . . . Maud is a charismatic, three-dimensional character." SLJ

Schmatz, Pat
★ **Bluefish**. Candlewick Press 2011 226p $15.99
Grades: 5 6 7 8   Fic
1. School stories 2. Literacy -- Fiction 3. Teachers -- Fiction
ISBN 978-0-7636-5334-7; 0-7636-5334-9
LC 2010044815
"A cast of richly developed characters peoples this work of contemporary fiction, told in the third person from Travis' point of view, with first-person vignettes from Velveeta's perspective peppered throughout. . . . A story rife with unusual honesty and hope." Kirkus

Schmid, Susan Maupin
Lost time. Philomel Books 2008 169p $16.99
Grades: 6 7 8 9   Fic
1. Science fiction 2. Missing persons -- Fiction
ISBN 978-0-399-24460-5; 0-399-24460-3
LC 2007-42095
Violynne, the twelve-year-old daughter of missing archaeologists on the planet Lindos, must solve the puzzle of her parents' disappearance before the dictatorial Arbiter captures her and forces her to do his bidding.
"Lively, descriptive prose incorporates mystery, action-adventure, and sci-fi elements, including exotic beings, landscapes, and devices. . . . [An] enjoyable, suspenseful read." Booklist

Schmidt, Gary D.
★ **Lizzie** Bright and the Buckminster boy. Clarion Books 2004 219p $15; pa $6.99
Grades: 7 8 9 10   Fic
1. Race relations -- Fiction
ISBN 0-618-43929-3; 0-553-49495-3 pa
LC 2003-20967
A Newbery Medal honor book, 2005
In 1911, Turner Buckminster hates his new home of Phippsburg, Maine, but things improve when he meets Lizzie Bright Griffin, a girl from a poor, nearby island community founded by former slaves that the town fathers—and Turner's—want to change into a tourist spot
"Although the story is hauntingly sad, there is much humor, too. Schmidt's writing is infused with feeling and rich in imagery. With fully developed, memorable characters and a fascinating, little-known piece of history, this novel will leave a powerful impression on readers." SLJ

★ **Okay** for now. Clarion Books 2011 360p il $16.99
Grades: 4 5 6 7   Fic
1. Moving -- Fiction 2. City and town life -- Fiction
ISBN 978-0-547-15260-8; 0-547-15260-4
LC 2010942981
"It's 1968. The Vietnam War and Apollo 11 are in the background, and . . . Doug Swieteck starts a new life in tiny Marysville, N.Y. . . . He may have moved away, but his cruel father and abusive brothers are still with him. . . . This is

Schmidt's best novel yet—darker than The Wednesday Wars and written with more restraint, but with the same expert attention to voice, character and big ideas." Kirkus

★ **Trouble**. Clarion Books 2008 297p $16
Grades: 6 7 8 9 10   Fic
1. Death -- Fiction 2. Prejudices -- Fiction 3. Family life -- Fiction 4. Traffic accidents -- Fiction 5. Cambodian Americans -- Fiction
ISBN 978-0-618-92766-1; 0-618-92766-2
LC 2007-40104
Fourteen-year-old Henry, wishing to honor his brother Franklin's dying wish, sets out to hike Maine's Mount Katahdin with his best friend and dog, but fate adds another companion—the Cambodian refugee accused of fatally injuring Franklin—and reveals troubles that predate the accident.
"Schmidt creates a rich and credible world peopled with fully developed characters who have a lot of complex reckoning to do. . . . [The author's prose] is flawless, and Henry's odyssey of growth and understanding is pitch-perfect and deeply satisfying." Bull Cent Child Books

★ The **Wednesday** wars. Clarion Books 2007 264p pa $6.99; $16
Grades: 5 6 7 8   Fic
1. Poets 2. School stories
ISBN 054723760X; 0618724834; 9780547237602; 9780618724833
LC 2006-23660
A Newbery Medal honor book, 2008
During the 1967 school year, on Wednesday afternoons when all his classmates go to either Catechism or Hebrew school, seventh-grader Holling Hoodhound stays in Mrs. Baker's classroom where they read the plays of William Shakespeare and Holling learns something of value about the world he lives in.
"The serious issues are leavened with ample humor, and the supporting cast . . . is fully dimensional. Best of all is the hero." Publ Wkly

Schneider, Robyn
Knightley Academy; by Violet Haberdasher. Aladdin 2010 469p $15.99
Grades: 5 6 7 8   Fic
1. School stories 2. Orphans -- Fiction 3. Knights and knighthood -- Fiction
ISBN 978-1-4169-9143-4; 1-4169-9143-3
LC 2009-23443
In an alternate Victorian England, fourteen-year-old orphan Henry Grim, a maltreated servant at an exclusive school for the "sons of Gentry and Quality," begins a new life when he unexpectedly becomes the first commoner to be accepted at Knightley Academy, a prestigious boarding school for knights.
"Robyn Schneider . . . writing as the pseudonymous Haberdasher, delivers a cute novel that balances its simple plot with a solid lead character, witty dialogue, and a jaunty narrative voice. . . . The nebulous historical setting and focus on military training and chivalry are a welcome change of pace from fictional academies that revolve around magic." Publ Wkly

The **secret** prince; [by] Violet Haberdasher. Aladdin 2011 503p $16.99

Grades: 5 6 7 8   **Fic**
1. School stories 2. Orphans -- Fiction 3. Secret societies -- Fiction 4. Knights and knighthood -- Fiction
ISBN 978-1-4169-9145-8; 1-4169-9145-X
LC 2010038855

Fourteen-year-old orphan Henry Grim's schooling at the prestigious Knightley Academy continues, as he and some friends discover an old classroom filled with forgotten weapons which lead them into a dangerous adventure.

"Though some of the past events can be gleaned from this book, it's more enjoyable for those who have read Knightley Academy. . . . The fast-moving plotline in this installment is wrapped up nicely, but enough is left hanging and the characters are interesting enough to make readers eagerly anticipate the next in the series." SLJ

Schraff, Anne E.

A **boy** called Twister; [by] Anne Schraff. Saddleback Educational 2010 180p (Urban underground) pa $8.95

Grades: 6 7 8 9 10   **Fic**
1. Moving -- Fiction 2. Fathers -- Fiction 3. Prisoners -- Fiction 4. Track athletics -- Fiction
ISBN 978-1-61651-002-2 pa; 1-61651-002-1 pa

"After his beloved mother dies, Kevin, 16, moves from Texas to his grandparents' home in California. He quickly settles in and makes new friends, begins a romance, stars on the track team, and confronts the school bully, Marco. Throughout it all, though, he keeps the secret that his dad was sent to prison for second-degree murder and died in a prison riot when Kevin was 6. . . . This small, fast-paced paperback will grab even reluctant readers with the suspenseful story, cool dialogue, and sports action, which never distracts from Kevin's personal struggle." Booklist

Schreck, Karen

While he was away; Karen Schreck. Sourcebooks Fire 2012 249 p. $8.99

Grades: 7 8 9 10   **Fic**
1. Love stories 2. Loneliness -- Fiction 3. Iraq War, 2003-2011 -- Fiction
ISBN 140226402X; 9781402264023

This book follows a couple, Penna and David, as David "leaves for a stint in Iraq. . . . Penna is anxious and devastated, but eventually she finds ways to cope. . . . In Iraq, David struggles with the mind-numbing work of patrols and the terror that interrupts it, and he focuses on an orphanage for Iraqi refugee children as a way to be useful. . . . Paralleling Penna's story is her discovery of a grandmother who lost her first husband in World War II." (Kirkus Reviews)

"With realistic characters and interesting dialogue, While He Was Away is both insightful and tragic." VOYA

Schrefer, Eliot

★ **Endangered**; Eliot Schrefer. Scholastic Press 2012 264 p. (reinforced) $17.99

Grades: 7 8 9 10 11 12   **Fic**
1. Animal sanctuaries -- Fiction 2. Wildlife conservation -- Fiction 3. Congo (Democratic Republic) -- Fiction 4. Apes -- Fiction 5. Bonobo -- Fiction 6. Divorce --

Fiction 7. Wildlife rescue -- Fiction 8. Racially mixed people -- Fiction
ISBN 0545165768; 9780545165761
LC 2012030877

This book by Eliot Schrefer was a 2012 National Book Award Finalist for Young People's Literature. "When one girl has to follow her mother to her sanctuary for bonobos, she's not thrilled to be there. It's her mother's passion, and she'd rather have nothing to do with it. But when revolution breaks out and their sanctuary is attacked, she must rescue the bonobos and hide in the jungle. Together, they will fight to keep safe, to eat, and to survive." (Publisher's note)

The **deadly** sister. Scholastic Press 2010 310p $17.99

Grades: 8 9 10 11 12   **Fic**
1. Mystery fiction 2. Sisters -- Fiction 3. Homicide -- Fiction
ISBN 978-0-545-16574-7; 0-545-16574-1
LC 2010-281733

Abby Goodwin has always covered for her sister, Maya, but now Maya has been accused of murder, and Abby's not sure she'll be able to cover for her sister anymore. Abby helps Maya escape. But when Abby begins investigating the death, she find that you can't trust anyone, not even the people you think you know.

"Well-drawn characters, realistic dialogue, and suspenseful twists and turns add to the appeal. Teens crave mystery, and this book will suit them just fine." SLJ

Schreiber, Ellen

Vampire kisses. Katherine Tegen Books 2003 197p $15.99; lib bdg $16.89

Grades: 7 8 9 10   **Fic**
1. Vampires -- Fiction
ISBN 0-06-009334-X; 0-06-009335-8 lib bdg
LC 2002-155506

Sixteen-year-old Raven, an outcast who always wears black and hopes to become a vampire some day, falls in love with the mysterious new boy in town, eager to find out if he can make her dreams come true

"Schreiber uses a careful balance of humor, irony, pathos, and romance." Booklist
Other titles in this series are:
Vampire kisses 2: Kissing coffins (2005)
Vampire kisses 3: Vampireville (2006)
Vampire kisses 4: Dance with a vampire (2007)
Vampire kisses 5: The Coffin Club (2008)
Vampire kisses 6: Royal Blood (2009)
Vampire kisses 7: Love bites (2010)
Vampire kisses 8: Cryptic cravings (2011)

Schroder, Monika

Saraswati's way. Farrar Straus Giroux 2010 233p $15.99

Grades: 5 6 7 8   **Fic**
1. Education -- Fiction 2. Mathematics -- Fiction
ISBN 978-0-374-36411-3; 0-374-36411-7
LC 2009-37286

Leaving his village in rural India to find a better education, mathematically gifted, twelve-year-old Akash ends up at the New Delhi train station, where he relies on Saraswati, the Hindu goddess of knowledge, to guide him as he negotiates life on the street, resists the temptations of easy money, and learns whom he can trust.

"With skillfully integrated cultural details . . . and a fully realized child's story, Schröder presents a view, sobering and inspiring, of remarkably resilient young people surviving poverty without losing themselves." Booklist

The **dog** in the wood. Front Street 2009 163p $17.95

Grades: 6 7 8 9   **Fic**
1. Russians -- Fiction 2. Family life -- Fiction 3. Political prisoners -- Fiction 4. World War, 1939-1945 -- Fiction
ISBN 978-1-59078-701-4; 1-59078-701-3
LC 2009-04970

As World War II draws to an end, Russian soldiers occupy Schwartz, Germany, bringing both friendship and hardship to the family of ten-year-old Fritz, whose grandfather was a Nazi sympathizer, eventually forcing them to leave their farm, then arresting Fritz's mother and her hired hand.

"The action in this important addition of WWII literature will grab readers, and Schröder's story is an excellent, authentic portrait of children in war." Booklist

Schroeder, Lisa
Chasing Brooklyn. Simon Pulse 2010 412p $15.99

Grades: 7 8 9 10   **Fic**
1. Novels in verse 2. Dreams -- Fiction 3. Bereavement -- Fiction
ISBN 978-1-4169-9168-7; 1-4169-9168-9
LC 2009-19442

As teenagers Brooklyn and Nico work to help each other recover from the deaths of Brooklyn's boyfriend—Nico's brother Lucca—and their friend Gabe, the two begin to rediscover their passion for life, and a newly blossoming passion for one another.

"Chasing Brooklyn is told in a verse format that enables the author to cut right to the emotional quick. The short sentences and minimal dialogue keep the focus on the pain and fear of the two main characters. . . . While the wrenching impact will leave readers raw, the ultimately hopeful ending is comforting. A quick read, but one with substance." SLJ

Schröder, Monika
My brother's shadow. Farrar Straus Giroux 2011 217p $16.99

Grades: 6 7 8 9 10   **Fic**
1. Journalism -- Fiction 2. Family life -- Fiction 3. Political activists -- Fiction 4. World War, 1914-1918 -- Fiction
ISBN 978-0-374-35122-9; 0-374-35122-8
LC 2010033107

In 1918 Berlin, Germany, sixteen-year-old Moritz struggles to do what is right on his newspaper job, in his relationship with his mother and sister who are outspoken socialists, and with his brother, who returns from the war physically and emotionally scarred.

"In this nuanced and realistic work of historical fiction, Schröder . . . immerses readers in her setting with meticulous

details and dynamic characters that contribute to a palpable sense of tension." Publ Wkly

Schumacher, Julie
★ **Black** box; a novel. Delacorte Press 2008 168p $15.99; lib bdg $18.99

Grades: 8 9 10 11 12   **Fic**
1. School stories 2. Sisters -- Fiction 3. Family life -- Fiction 4. Depression (Psychology) -- Fiction
ISBN 978-0-385-73542-1; 0-385-73542-1; 978-0-385-90523-7 lib bdg; 0-385-90523-8 lib bdg
LC 2007-45774

When her sixteen-year-old sister is hospitalized for depression and her parents want to keep it a secret, fourteen-year-old Elena tries to cope with her own anxiety and feelings of guilt that she is determined to conceal from outsiders.

"The writing is spare, direct, and honest. Written in the first person, this is a readable, ultimately uplifting book about a difficult subject." SLJ

Schwab, Victoria
The **Near** Witch. Hyperion Books 2011 282p $16.99

Grades: 7 8 9 10   **Fic**
1. Witches -- Fiction 2. Villages -- Fiction 3. Supernatural -- Fiction
ISBN 978-1-4231-3787-0; 1-4231-3787-6
LC 2010036289

Sixteen-year-old Lexi, who lives on an enchanted moor at the edge of the village of Near, must solve the mystery when, the day after a mysterious boy appears in town, children start disappearing.

"Part fairy tale, part legend with a little romance, this well-written mystery will capture the attention of teens." SLJ

Schwabach, Karen
The **storm** before Atlanta. Random House 2010 307p $16.99; lib bdg $19.99

Grades: 5 6 7 8   **Fic**
1. Freedom -- Fiction 2. Slavery -- Fiction 3. Soldiers -- Fiction 4. Runaway children -- Fiction
ISBN 978-0-375-85866-6; 0-375-85866-0; 978-0-375-95866-3 lib bdg; 0-375-95866-5 lib bdg
LC 2010014514

In 1863 northwestern Georgia, an unlikely alliance forms between ten-year-old New York drummer boy Jeremy, fourteen-year-old Confederate Charlie, and runaway slave Dulcie as they learn truths about the Civil War, slavery, and freedom.

"Richly detailed and well paced, the story provides both well-developed characters and plenty of suspense and gore. For those who like to know the facts behind historical fiction, the author provides historical notes and selected sources. An appealing Civil War title for readers with strong stomachs." Kirkus

Schwartz, Ellen
Cellular; written by Ellen Schwartz. Orca Book Publishers 2010 115p (Orca soundings) pa $9.95

Grades: 7 8 9 10   **Fic**
1. Leukemia -- Fiction 2. Friendship -- Fiction
ISBN 978-1-55469-296-5; 1-55469-296-2

When Brendan is diagnosed with leukemia, his life is turned upside down. With smothering family, and distant friends, all seems hopeless until he meets Lark, terminally ill, and yet full of life.

"In this emotional entry in the Orca Soundings series, Lark's sweetness and wisdom spin out on a trajectory that readers just know will not end happily for her, even though Brendan realizes she has touched his life mightily." Booklist

Stealing home. Tundra Books 2006 217p pa $8.95

Grades: 5 6 7 8   **Fic**
  1. Jews -- Fiction 2. Orphans -- Fiction 3. Family life -- Fiction 4. Racially mixed people -- Fiction
  ISBN 978-0-88776-765-4 pa; 0-88776-765-6 pa

"Joey, an orphaned, mixed-race 10-year-old isn't the only one who has to make adjustments after he's taken in by Jewish relatives he never knew he had. Wondering why his mother never told him about her side of the family, Joey moves to Brooklyn—to find a warm welcome from Aunt Frieda, an instant ally in baseball-loving cousin Bobbie, and a decidedly cold shoulder from his grandfather. . . . Keenly felt internal conflicts, lightened by some sparky banter, put this more than a cut above the average." Booklist

Schwartz, Virginia Frances
  Send one angel down. Holiday House 2000 163p $15.95 **Fic**
  1. Cousins -- Fiction 2. Slavery -- Fiction 3. Racially-mixed people 4. African Americans -- Fiction 5. Racially mixed people -- Fiction
  ISBN 0-8234-1484-1

                        LC 99-52818

Abram, a young slave tries to hide the horrors of slavery from his younger cousin Eliza, a light-skinned slave who is the daughter of the plantation owner

"Schwartz's well-developed characters are full of humanity and personality, and the story vividly acknowledges the sustaining power of music . . . in the lives of the slaves. This is a profoundly moving tale that is ultimately hopeful but never glosses over the horrific treatment of slaves." Booklist

Scott, Elaine
  Secrets of the Cirque Medrano. Charlesbridge 2008 216p lib bdg $15.95

Grades: 4 5 6 7   **Fic**
  1. Artists 2. Painters 3. Circus -- Fiction 4. Orphans -- Fiction 5. Restaurants -- Fiction
  ISBN 978-1-57091-712-7 lib bdg; 1-57091-712-4 lib bdg

                        LC 2007-2329

In the Paris village of Montmartre in 1904, fourteen-year-old Brigitte works long hours in her aunt's cafe, where she serves such regular customers as the young artist Pablo Picasso, encounters Russian revolutionaries, and longs to attend the exciting circus nearby. Includes author's note on the Picasso painting "Family of Saltimbanques"

This "places an interesting historical moment within the grasp of middle-schoolers." Kirkus

Scott, Elizabeth
  Perfect you. Simon Pulse 2008 304p pa $9.99

Grades: 7 8 9 10   **Fic**
  1. School stories 2. Friendship -- Fiction 3. Family life -- Fiction
  ISBN 978-1-4169-5355-5 pa; 1-4169-5355-8 pa

                        LC 2007-929324

"Kate's father quit his job and is now living his dream by selling infomercial vitamins at a mall kiosk. The teen's college-graduate brother is living on the couch, her mother is working two jobs, and her friend Anna isn't talking to her now that Anna has lost weight and become popular. Making Kate's life completely miserable, her overbearing grandmother has moved in, and Will, the boy Kate tries to pretend she doesn't like because of their contentious history, is constantly making approaches. . . . Scott does a good job portraying a teen who is simultaneously self-centered and sympathetic. . . . Supporting characters are well fleshed out, and the ending, while encouraging, isn't all sunshine and roses, making it believable as well as hopeful." SLJ

Stealing Heaven. HarperTeen 2008 307p $16.99; lib bdg $17.89; pa $8.99

Grades: 7 8 9 10   **Fic**
  1. Thieves -- Fiction 2. Mother-daughter relationship -- Fiction
  ISBN 978-0-06-112280-4; 0-06-112280-7; 978-0-06-112281-1 lib bdg; 0-06-112281-5 lib bdg; 978-0-06-112282-8 pa; 0-06-112282-3 pa

Eighteen-year-old Dani grows weary of her life as a thief when she and her mother move to a town where Dani feels like she can put down roots.

"Witty dialogue gives a new perspective full of hope to YAs who feel trapped between family and friends." KLIATT

Scott, Kieran
  This is so not happening; Kieran Scott. Simon & Schuster BFYR. 2012 315 p. (hardcover) $16.99

Grades: 7 8 9 10   **Fic**
  1. Love stories 2. Teenage parents -- Fiction 3. Dating (Social customs) -- Fiction 4. Babies -- Fiction 5. Schools -- Fiction 6. High schools -- Fiction 7. Social classes -- Fiction 8. Teenage fathers -- Fiction 9. Teenage mothers -- Fiction 10. Family life -- New Jersey -- Fiction
  ISBN 1416999558; 9781416999553

                        LC 2011041612

In this book, the third in a series, "constantly thwarted lovers Ally and Jake finally establish a firm boyfriend-girlfriend relationship during their senior year in high school. . . . Ally learns that her former best friend Chloe is pregnant and saying that Jake is the father. Because the brief encounter between the two occurred outside of their formal relationship, Ally decides to forgive Jake and stick with him, even as he becomes ever more obsessed with the baby." (Kirkus Reviews)

Scott, Michael
  ★ The **alchemyst**. Delacorte Press 2007 375p (The secrets of the immortal Nicholas Flammel) $16.99; lib bdg $19.99

Grades: 7 8 9 10　　　　　　　　　　**Fic**

1. Magic -- Fiction 2. Twins -- Fiction 3. Alchemy -- Fiction 4. Writers on science 5. Siblings -- Fiction
ISBN 978-0-385-73357-1; 0-385-73357-7; 978-0-385-90372-1 lib bdg; 0-385-90372-3 lib bdg

LC 2006-24417

While working at pleasant but mundane summer jobs in San Francisco, fifteen-year-old twins, Sophie and Josh, suddenly find themselves caught up in the deadly, centuries-old struggle between rival alchemists, Nicholas Flamel and John Dee, over the possession of an ancient and powerful book holding the secret formulas for alchemy and everlasting life.

"Scott uses a gigantic canvas for this riveting fantasy. . . . A fabulous read." SLJ

Other titles in this series are:

The magician (2008)

The sorceress (2009)

The necromancer (2010)

The warlock (2011)

The **enchantress**; Michael Scott. Delacorte Press 2012 517 p. $18.99

Grades: 7 8 9 10　　　　　　　　　　**Fic**

1. Atlantis -- Fiction 2. Monsters -- Fiction 3. Time travel -- Fiction 4. Flamel, Nicolas, d. 1418 -- Fiction 5. Magic -- Fiction 6. Twins -- Fiction 7. Alchemists -- Fiction 8. Supernatural -- Fiction 9. Brothers and sisters -- Fiction
ISBN 0385735359; 9780385735353

LC 2012006497

In this book, the final installment of the "Secrets of the Immortal Nicholas Flamel" series, "Nicholas Flamel and his beloved wife, Perenelle, are making a final stand to save San Francisco from an attack of monsters large and small, launched from Alcatraz Island by Quetzalcoatl. Twins Josh (Gold) and Sophie (Silver) are being staged to take power from Aten and become rulers of an overthrown Danu Talis 10,000 years earlier." (Booklist)

"[Scott] fully fleshes out his main characters in their final roles, realistically and sometimes surprisingly melding their lives, their deaths, and their futures. This is a powerful and tidy conclusion to [the] series." Booklist

Scott, Mindi

Freefall. Simon Pulse 2010 315p pa $7.99

Grades: 8 9 10 11 12　　　　　　　　　**Fic**

1. Alcoholism -- Fiction 2. Bereavement -- Fiction 3. Rock musicians -- Fiction
ISBN 978-1-4424-0278-2; 1-4424-0278-4

LC 2010-12663

Seth, a bass guitar player in a teen rock band, deals with alcoholism, his best friend's death, and first love.

"Seth's character arc is fully realized, without the burden of too much introspection or weighty insight to bog down the pace of the narrative. . . . This is a solid exploration of what you can and can't do to help your friends, built on top of an engaging story of boy meets girl." Bull Cent Child Books

Scotto, Michael

Postcards from Pismo; Michael Scotto ; [edited by] Ashley Mortimer. Midlandia Press 2012 180 p. pa$10.99

Grades: 4 5 6　　　　　　　　　　　**Fic**

1. Afghan War, 2001- -- Fiction 2. Filipino Americans -- Fiction 3. Military personnel -- United States -- Correspondence -- Fiction
ISBN 0983724369; 9780983724360

LC 2011943050

In this book, a "class assignment blossoms into friendship as a fourth-grade (later fifth-) Californian showers a young soldier stationed in Afghanistan with letters, e-mail messages and postcards. [Michael] Scotto supplies only chatty Felix's side of the continuing correspondence. . . . Felix queries his pen pal about what soldiers do while detailing his own interests, teachers, town, hard-working Filipino American parents (and their reactions when his restless big brother enlists)." (Kirkus)

Scrimger, Richard

Me & death; an afterlife adventure. Tundra Books 2010 187p pa $12.95

Grades: 7 8 9 10　　　　　　　　　　**Fic**

1. Death -- Fiction 2. Future life -- Fiction
ISBN 978-0-88776-796-8 pa; 0-88776-796-6 pa

"Jim isn't an easy guy to like. . . . While he is chasing another kid, he falls in front of an oncoming car. So begins his epic journey into the afterlife, in which he is shown scenes from his past by three different ghosts, all of whom have a key to his future in the real world. . . . Scrimger creates unpredictable, sad, and authentic scenes that enliven the story. . . . Scrimger's novel is a difficult, compelling read that taps into teens' fascination with death, as well as the line between good and bad behavior." Booklist

Sedgwick, Marcus

★ **My** swordhand is singing. Wendy Lamb Books 2007 205p hardcover o.p. pa $6.99

Grades: 7 8 9 10　　　　　　　　　　**Fic**

1. Horror fiction 2. Gypsies -- Fiction 3. Vampires -- Fiction 4. Supernatural -- Fiction
ISBN 978-0-375-84689-2; 978-0-375-84690-8 pa

LC 2007-07051

In the dangerous dark of winter in an Eastern European village during the early seventeenth century, Peter learns from a gypsy girl that the Shadow Queen is behind the recent murders and reanimations, and his father's secret past may hold the key to stopping her.

"Sedgwick writes a compellingly fresh vampire story, combining elements from ancient myths and legends to create a believable and frightening tale." Voice Youth Advocates

★ **Revolver**. Roaring Brook Press 2010 204p $16.99

Grades: 7 8 9 10　　　　　　　　　　**Fic**

1. Death -- Fiction 2. Siblings -- Fiction
ISBN 978-1-59643-592-6; 1-59643-592-5
First published 2009 in the United Kingdom
A Michael L. Printz honor book, 2011

In an isolated cabin, fourteen-year-old Sig is alone with a corpse: his father, who has fallen through the ice and frozen to death only hours earlier. Then comes a stranger claiming that Sig's father owes him a share of a horde of stolen gold. Sig's only protection is a loaded Colt revolver hidden in the cabin's storeroom.

"Tight plotting and a wealth of moral concerns—good versus evil; faith, love, and hope; the presence of God; survival in a bleak landscape; trusting the lessons parents teach—make this a memorable tale." Horn Book

★ **White** crow. Roaring Brook Press 2011 234p $15.99

Grades: 8 9 10 11 12 **Fic**

1. Horror fiction 2. Villages -- Fiction 3. Friendship -- Fiction 4. Good and evil -- Fiction

ISBN 978-1-59643-594-0; 1-59643-594-1

LC 2010034053

"Showing his customary skill with a gothic setting and morally troubled characters, Sedgwick keeps readers guessing to the very end." Publ Wkly

Selfors, Suzanne

Coffeehouse angel. Walker & Co. 2009 276p $16.99

Grades: 7 8 9 10 **Fic**

1. School stories 2. Angels -- Fiction 3. Wishes -- Fiction 4. Grandmothers -- Fiction

ISBN 978-0-8027-9812-1; 0-8027-9812-8

LC 2008-33333

Sixteen-year-old Katrina's kindness to a man she finds sleeping behind her grandmother's coffeehouse leads to a strange reward as Malcolm, who is actually a teenage guardian angel, insists on rewarding her by granting her deepest wish.

"This light read is right for teens struggling with self-confidence issues. . . . Although the protagonist deals with loneliness, illness, aging, and competition in this coming-of-age novel, it is a humorous read." Voice Youth Advocates

Fortune's magic farm; illustrated by Catia Chien. Little, Brown 2009 264p il $14.99; pa $5.99

Grades: 4 5 6 **Fic**

1. Farms -- Fiction 2. Magic -- Fiction 3. Orphans -- Fiction

ISBN 978-0-316-01818-0; 0-316-01818-X; 978-0-316-01819-7 pa; 0-316-01819-8 pa

LC 2008-12493

Rescued from a rainy, boggy town where she works in a dismal factory, ten-year-old orphan Isabelle learns that she is the last surviving member of a family that tends the world's only remaining magic-producing farm.

"Readers will cozy up to the tale's quirky characters and enjoy the many twists and turns of this magical adventure." Kirkus

★ **Saving** Juliet. Walker & Co. 2008 242p $16.95

Grades: 7 8 9 10 11 12 **Fic**

1. Actors -- Fiction 2. Theater -- Fiction 3. Space and time -- Fiction

ISBN 978-0-8027-9740-7; 0-8027-9740-7

LC 2007-18528

Seventeen-year-old Mimi Wallingford's stage fright and fight with her mother on the closing night of Romeo and Juliet are nothing compared to the troubles she faces when she and her leading man are transported to Shakespeare's Verona, where she decides to give the real Juliet a happy ending.

This is "hilarious and often very clever. . . . Readers will have fun with the characters. . . . Mimi . . . is an honest savvy narrator." Publ Wkly

Smells like dog. Little, Brown 2010 360p $15.99

Grades: 4 5 6 7 **Fic**

1. Dogs -- Fiction 2. Uncles -- Fiction 3. Buried treasure -- Fiction

ISBN 978-0-316-04398-4; 0-316-04398-2

When farm boy Homer Pudding's explorer-uncle dies and leaves him a droopy dog with a mysterious coin hidden on its collar, it leads him to The City, where they meet Madame La Directeur, the conniving head of the Natural History Museum, who is trying to steal the coin and take Homer's place in a secret society of adventurers.

"Full of fantasy, fun, and humorous dialogue, this will attract dog lovers, mystery enthusiasts, adventure addicts, and reluctant readers. A thoroughly enjoyable read." Voice Youth Advocates

Another title about Homer Pudding is:
Smells like treasure (2011)

The **sweetest** spell; Suzanne Selfors. Walker & Co. 2012 404 p. (hardback) $16.99

Grades: 7 8 9 10 11 12 **Fic**

1. Love stories 2. Fantasy fiction 3. Physically handicapped -- Fiction 4. Fantasy 5. Magic -- Fiction 6. Chocolate -- Fiction 7. Prejudices -- Fiction 8. People with disabilities -- Fiction

ISBN 0802723764; 9780802723765

LC 2011034591

This book follows "Emmeline . . . an outcast among her people, the Kell. When the king enslaves the men and her village is destroyed in a flood, Emmeline is taken in by Owen Oak and his family. She discovers that she can churn butter into chocolate -- a food that's been lost for years in the land of Anglund. Romance blossoms, but the two are separated when the girl is kidnapped for her magical abilities." (School Library Journal)

"Selfors"s story line initially comes across as chaotic, but the pacing is strong, and the elements of her tale fall into place in a logical and entirely satisfying manner. An exhilarating, romantic, and frequently funny story of self-discovery." Pub Wkly

Selzer, Adam

How to get suspended and influence people; a novel. Delacorte Press 2007 183p $15.99; lib bdg $18.99

Grades: 6 7 8 9 **Fic**

1. School stories 2. Censorship -- Fiction 3. Motion pictures -- Fiction

ISBN 978-0-385-73369-4; 978-0-385-90384-4 lib bdg

LC 2006-20438

Gifted eighth-grader Leon Harris becomes an instant celebrity when the film he makes for a class project sends him to in-school suspension.

"This funny, fast-paced novel is filled with characters who epitomize the middle school experience, and it presents a lesson or two about free speech as well." SLJ

Another title about Leon is:

Pirates of the retail wasteland (2008)

I kissed a zombie, and I liked it. Delacorte Press 2010 177p lib bdg $12.99; pa $7.99

Grades: 7 8 9 10   **Fic**

1. Zombies -- Fiction 2. Vampires -- Fiction 3. Dating (Social customs) -- Fiction

ISBN 978-0-385-90497-1 lib bdg; 0-385-90497-5 lib bdg; 978-0-385-73503-2 pa; 0-385-73503-0 pa

LC 2009-24052

Living in the post-human era when the undead are part of everyday life, high schooler Alley breaks her no-dating rule when Doug catches her eye, but classmate Will demands to turn her into a vampire and her zombie boyfriend may be unable to stop him.

"With snappy dialogue and a light, funny touch, Selzer creates a readable examination of love, self-sacrifice, and where to draw the line before you lose yourself." Publ Wkly

I put a spell on you; from the files of Chrissie Woodward, spelling bee detective. Delacorte Press 2008 247p $15.99; lib bdg $18.99

Grades: 4 5 6 7   **Fic**

1. School stories 2. Mystery fiction 3. Spelling bees -- Fiction

ISBN 978-0-385-73504-9; 0-385-73504-9; 978-0-385-90498-8 lib bdg; 0-385-90498-3 lib bdg

LC 2008035673

When Gordon Liddy Community School's resident tattletale-detective, Chrissie Woodward, realizes that the adults are out to fix the big spelling bee, she transfers her loyalty to her fellow students and starts collecting evidence. Told through in-class letters, administrative memos, file notes from Chrissie's investigation, and testimony from spelling bee contestants

"The wit in this school story is directed almost entirely against the grownups in a scathingly funny indictment of a shady principal and insanely competitive parents." Horn Book

Selznick, Brian

★ **Wonderstruck**; a novel in words and pictures. Scholastic Press 2011 637p il $29.99

Grades: 4 5 6 7   **Fic**

1. Deaf -- Fiction 2. Museums -- Fiction 3. Runaway children -- Fiction

ISBN 978-0-545-02789-2; 0-545-02789-6

LC 2011009113

"Readers know that the two stories will converge, but Selznick keeps them guessing, cutting back and forth with expert precision. . . . Both stories are equally immersive and impeccably paced. . . . Visually stunning, completely compelling." Kirkus

★ The **invention** of Hugo Cabret; a novel in words and pictures. Scholastic Press 2007 533p il $22.95

Grades: 4 5 6 7   **Fic**

1. Robots -- Fiction 2. Orphans -- Fiction 3. Motion picture directors 4. Motion pictures -- Fiction

ISBN 0-439-81378-6

LC 2006-07119

Awarded the Caldecott Medal, 2008

When twelve-year-old Hugo, an orphan living and repairing clocks within the walls of a Paris train station in 1931, meets a mysterious toyseller and his goddaughter, his undercover life and his biggest secret are jeopardized.

"With characteristic intelligence, exquisite images, and a breathtaking design, Selznick shatters conventions related to the art of bookmaking." SLJ

Sensel, Joni

The **Farwalker's** quest. Bloomsbury U.S.A Children's Books 2009 372p $16.99

Grades: 5 6 7 8   **Fic**

1. Fantasy fiction

ISBN 978-1-59990-272-2; 1-59990-272-9

LC 2008-30523

When twelve-year-old Ariel and her friend Zeke find a mysterious artifact the like of which has not been seen in a long time, it proves to be the beginning of a long and arduous journey that will untimately reveal to them their true identities.

"This is a solid and well-paced fantasy in which the journey is more important than the conclusion." SLJ

The **timekeeper's** moon; [drawings by Yelena Safronova] Bloomsbury 2010 339p il $16.99

Grades: 5 6 7 8   **Fic**

1. Fantasy fiction

ISBN 978-1-59990-457-3; 1-59990-457-8

LC 2009-16690

Summoned by the moon to embark on a dangerous journey, thirteen-year-old Ariel Farwalker, knowing she must obey or risk destruction, sets out with her guardian, Scarl, to follow a mysterious map to an unknown entity called "Timekeeper"

"Vivid world building and tight pacing mark this sequel . . . further distinguished by rich characters with believable relationships." Booklist

Sepetys, Ruta

★ **Between** shades of gray. Philomel Books 2011 344p map $17.99

Grades: 8 9 10 11 12   **Fic**

1. Lithuania – Fiction 2. Soviet Union -- Fiction

ISBN 978-0-399-25412-3; 0-399-25412-9

LC 2009-50092

"A harrowing page-turner, made all the more so for its basis in historical fact, the novel illuminates the persecution suffered by Stalin's victims (20 million were killed), while presenting memorable characters who retain their will to survive even after more than a decade in exile." Publ Wkly

Service, Pamela F.

Tomorrow's magic; [by] Pamela F. Service. 1st ed.; Random House 2007 437p $15.99; lib bdg $18.99; pa $7.99

Grades: 7 8 9 10   **Fic**

1. Fantasy fiction 2. Science fiction 3. Kings 4. Magic -- Fiction 5. Merlin (Legendary character) -- Fiction 6.

Morgan le Fay (Legendary character) -- Fiction
ISBN 978-0-375-84087-6; 0-375-84087-7; 978-0-375-94087-3 lib bdg; 0-375-94087-1 lib bdg; 978-0-375-84087-6 pa; 0-375-84088-5 pa

LC 2006016131

First published in two volumes by Atheneum: Winter of magic's return (1985), Tomorrow's magic (1987)

Two novels in which a young, resurrected Merlin and two friends attempt to bring King Arthur back to Britain, then struggle against the evil plots of Morgan Le Fey to build a new and better civilization in the wake of a nuclear holocaust.

"Service has done a terrific job melding futuristic science fiction with ancient Arthurian legend." Horn Book Guide

Yesterday's magic; [by] Pamela F. Service. Random House 2008 216p $16.99

Grades: 7 8 9 10 **Fic**
1. Fantasy fiction 2. Science fiction 3. Kings 4. Magic -- Fiction 5. Merlin (Legendary character) -- Fiction 6. Morgan le Fay (Legendary character) -- Fiction
ISBN 978-0-375-85577-1; 0-375-85577-7

"When Heather McKenna is kidnapped by the sorceress Morgan LeFay, it is up to Heather's friend Welly and the wizard Merlin . . . to rescue her. Set 500 years in the future, following a nuclear devastation, the technological world has ground to a halt, but magic is beginning to take hold again." Publisher's note

Shahan, Sherry

Death mountain; [by] Sherry Shahan. 1st ed.; Peachtree 2005 202p $15.95

Grades: 5 6 7 8 **Fic**
1. Wilderness survival -- Fiction
ISBN 1-56145-353-6

LC 2005010820

"A day trip to a mountain lake turns to disaster when lightning strikes a pack mule, a mud slide kills a horse, and hikers scatter, seeking shelter. Erin, 14, leaves her new friend Levi with the injured hikers to search for his sister, Mae, who has run off-trail in the confusion. . . . A great addition to the adventure-survival genre." SLJ

Ice island. Delacorte Press 2012 $10.99; lib bdg $18.99; ebook $10.99

Grades: 4 5 6 7 **Fic**
1. Dogs -- Fiction 2. Sled dog racing -- Fiction 3. Wilderness survival -- Fiction 4. Iditarod Trail Sled Dog Race, Alaska -- Fiction
ISBN 978-0-385-74154-5; 0-385-74154-5; 978-0-375-99009-0 lib bdg; 0-375-99009-7 lib bdg; 978-0-375-98575-1 ebook

LC 2011003838

Thirteen-year-old Tatum's dream of competing in the grueling 1,049-mile Iditerod Trail Sled Dog Race may be at an end when she becomes lost in a freak snowstorm during a training run on Alaska's remote Santa Ysabel Island.

"Riveting and atmospheric. . . . This survival adventure creates an almost otherworldly experience within a treacherous and bracingly beautiful landscape." Kirkus

Shan, Darren

Lord Loss; [by] Darren Shan. 1st U.S. ed.; Little, Brown 2005 233p (Demonata) hardcover o.p. pa $8.99

Grades: 7 8 9 10 **Fic**
1. Horror fiction 2. Young adult literature -- Works
ISBN 0-316-11499-5; 0-316-01233-5 pa

LC 2005-0145

Presumably the only witness to the horrific and bloody murder of his entire family, a teenage boy must outwit not only the mental health professionals determined to cure his delusion, but also the demonic forces only he can see.

"The plot rolls along at high speed, but Shan is still quite adept when it comes to capturing Grubbs' roller-coaster emotions." Booklist

Other titles in this series are:
Demon thief (2006)
Slawter (2006)
Bec (2007)
Blood beast (2007)
Demon apocalypse (2008)
Death's shadow (2008)
Wolf island (2009)
Dark calling (2009)

Shanahan, Lisa

★ The **sweet,** terrible, glorious year I truly, completely lost it. Delacorte Press 2007 297p $15.99; lib bdg $18.99

Grades: 7 8 9 10 **Fic**
1. School stories 2. Theater -- Fiction 3. Family life -- Fiction
ISBN 978-0-385-73516-2; 0-385-73516-2; 978-0-385-90505-3 lib bdg; 0-385-90505-X lib bdg

LC 2006-101158

Fourteen-year-old Gemma Stone struggles to understand her shifting emotions as her older sister plans her wedding, she overcomes her nerves and tries out for the school play, and she gets to know one of the most notorious boys in her class.

"Shanahan's quirky characters are a riot, but the depth of Gemma's growth and heartbreak is profound." SLJ

Sharenow, Rob

My mother the cheerleader; a novel. Laura Geringer Books 2007 288p hardcover o.p. pa $8.99

Grades: 7 8 9 10 **Fic**
1. Race relations -- Fiction 2. School integration -- Fiction 3. Mother-daughter relationship -- Fiction
ISBN 978-0-06-114896-5; 0-06-114896-2; 978-0-06-114898-9 pa; 0-06-114898-9 pa

LC 2006-21716

Thirteen-year-old Louise uncovers secrets about her family and her neighborhood during the violent protests over school desegregation in 1960 New Orleans.

"Through inquisitive Louise's perspective, readers get a wrenching look at the era's turmoil and pervasive racism." Publ Wkly

Sharenow, Robert

★ The **Berlin** Boxing Club. HarperTeen 2011 404p il $17.99

Grades: 7 8 9 10   **Fic**

1. Boxers (Persons) 2. Boxing -- Fiction 3. Family life -- Fiction 4. Jews -- Germany -- Fiction 5. National socialism -- Fiction 6. Holocaust, 1933-1945 -- Fiction

ISBN 978-0-06-157968-4; 0-06-157968-8

LC 2010024446

"Readers will be drawn by the sports detail and by the close-up narrative of the daily oppression." Booklist

Shaw, Liane

Fostergirls. Second Story Press 2011 256p pa $11.95

Grades: 6 7 8 9   **Fic**

1. Foster home care -- Fiction

ISBN 978-1-897187-90-6; 1-897187-90-4

"Her name is Sadie, but she might as well be called Fostergirl. Grouphomegirl. That's how everyone thinks of her. Sadie doesn't care. . . . Her goal is to go unnoticed, to disappear. Nothing good comes from being noticed, especially if you're a fostergirl. Another new high school, another new group home. This one is lucky number 13, but who's counting? Except, this time there's a girl at her school named Rhiannon who won't let Sadie be invisible. In fact, she insists on being her friend. This friendship, and the dawning feeling that she finally belongs, might be able to restore Sadie's belief in others, and—ultimately—herself." (Publisher's note)

"Shaw's biggest challenge is making caustic, self-deprecating, and distrustful Sadie likable. Fortunately, she succeeds. Sadie, though tough as nails, narrates her story with an amusing edginess that works. Shaw keeps things PG-rated . . . while highlighting the reality of life as a foster child. . . . Readers seeking an honest account of how a girl without parents survives, this story delivers." Publ Wkly

Shaw, Susan

One of the survivors. Margaret K. McElderry Books 2009 199p $15.99

Grades: 6 7 8 9   **Fic**

1. School stories 2. Anger -- Fiction 3. Death -- Fiction 4. Fires -- Fiction 5. Guilt -- Fiction 6. Bereavement -- Fiction

ISBN 978-1-4169-6129-1; 1-4169-6129-1

LC 2008035965

When his classmates die in a school fire, fourteen-year-old Joey is haunted by their deaths and struggles to survive amidst suspicion and anger from the town.

"Shaw tackles a gut-wrenching situation in honest, solution-oriented terms that should appeal to reluctant readers. The novel is short, the plot and suspense build slowly, and the decisions required by the teens make for thought-provoking discussions." SLJ

★ **Safe**. Dutton Books 2007 168p $16.99

Grades: 7 8 9 10   **Fic**

1. Rape -- Fiction 2. Mothers -- Fiction

ISBN 978-0-525-47829-4; 0-525-47829-9

LC 2006-36428

When thirteen-year-old Tracy, whose mother died when she was three years old, is raped and beaten on the last day of school, all her feelings of security disappear and she does not know how to cope with the fear and dread that engulf her.

This is an "extraordinarily tender novel. . . . Intimate, first-person narrative honestly expresses Tracy's full range of emotions." Publ Wkly

Tunnel vision. Margaret K. McElderry Books 2011 272p $16.99

Grades: 5 6 7 8   **Fic**

1. Crime -- Fiction 2. Homicide -- Fiction 3. Witnesses -- Fiction 4. Organized crime -- Fiction

ISBN 978-1-4424-0839-5; 1-4424-0839-1

LC 2010036306

After witnessing her mother's murder, sixteen-year-old high school student Liza Wellington and her father go into the witness protection program.

"The author creates a completely believable character in Liza, who often reverts to childlike emotions only to learn the hard way that cold reality takes precedence over even dearly held wishes. Kudos for the unexpected double ending, both illusory and realistic, giving readers a choice." Kirkus

Shecter, Vicky Alvear

Cleopatra's moon. Arthur A. Levine Books 2011 353p $18.99

Grades: 8 9 10 11 12   **Fic**

1. Queens 2. Generals 3. Statesmen 4. Orators 5. Princesses -- Fiction

ISBN 978-0-545-22130-6; 0-545-22130-7

LC 2010028818

Cleopatra Selene, the only surviving daughter of Cleopatra and Marc Antony, recalls her life of pomp and splendor in Egypt and, after her parents' deaths, capitivity and treachery in Rome.

"This novel has romance, drama, heartbreak, and adventure, all rooted in an accurate and descriptive historical setting. Shecter writes about the world of ancient Egypt and Rome with wonderful detail. . . . Her characters are skillfully fictionalized." SLJ

Sheinmel, Alyssa B.

The **lucky** kind. Alfred A. Knopf 2011 201p $16.99; lib bdg $19.99

Grades: 8 9 10 11 12   **Fic**

1. Adoption -- Fiction 2. Friendship -- Fiction 3. Family life -- Fiction

ISBN 978-0-375-86785-9; 0-375-86785-6; 978-0-375-96785-6 lib bdg; 0-375-96785-0 lib bdg; 978-0-375-89866-2 e-book

LC 2010-27967

Having always felt secure within his small family, Manhattan high school junior Nick is unsettled to discover the existence of an older brother that his father put up for adoption many years ago.

"Nick's narration, ruminative yet straightforward, gives him a credible voice as he lurches unwillingly toward adulthood, and the book deftly conveys that he's really a good guy even if the situation is causing him to sink below his usual standards. The well-crafted family story offers an excellent stage for depicting the challenge facing every young adult—how to accept human responsibilty and fraility as we go through life." Bull Cent Child Books

Sheinmel, Courtney

All the things you are. Simon & Schuster Books for Young Readers 2011 244p $15.99

Grades: 5 6 7 8   **Fic**

1. Theft -- Fiction 2. Friendship -- Fiction 3. Family life -- Fiction 4. Stepfamilies -- Fiction
ISBN 978-1-4169-9717-7; 1-4169-9717-2

LC 2010010090

When Carly Wheeler's mother is arrested for embezzling, Carly's perfect life begins to fall apart as friends at her prestigious private school stop talking to her, her beloved stepfather starts worrying about finances, and her image of herself and her family changes.

"Sheinmel persuasively and sensitively conveys Carly's conflicting emotions and her attempts to make sense of what's been thrust upon her." Publ Wkly

Positively. Simon & Schuster Books for Young Readers 2009 216p $15.99

Grades: 6 7 8 9 10   **Fic**

1. Camps -- Fiction 2. Death -- Fiction 3. Friendship -- Fiction 4. Bereavement -- Fiction 5. Stepfamilies -- Fiction 6. AIDS (Disease) -- Fiction
ISBN 978-1-4169-7169-6; 1-4169-7169-6

LC 2008-35447

Thirteen-year-old Emmy, grieving over her mother who died of AIDS, resentful of having to live with her father and pregnant stepmother, and despairing about her future, finds hope at a summer camp for HIV-positive girls like herself. Includes facts about Elizabeth Glaser, one of the founders of the Pediatric AIDS Foundation.

"This valuable story discusses uncertainty, very human fears, and most important, hope. . . . It is a terrific introduction to a complex and important topic." Voice Youth Advocates

Sheldon, Dyan

Confessions of a Hollywood star. Candlewick Press 2006 202p $15.99

Grades: 7 8 9 10   **Fic**

1. Actors -- Fiction 2. Motion pictures -- Fiction
ISBN 0-7636-3075-6

Upon learning at the end of her senior year of high school that a Hollywood film is being made in her hometown, Lola stops at nothing to get a part and upstage her nemesis, Carla Santini.

"Lola's voice is once again an uproariously funny delight." Booklist

My perfect life. Candlewick Press 2002 201p $16.99; pa $5.99

Grades: 7 8 9 10   **Fic**

1. School stories 2. Interpersonal relations 3. Elections -- Fiction
ISBN 0-7636-1839-X; 0-7636-2436-5 pa

LC 2001-58118

Ella has no interest in running for class president at her suburban high school, but her off-beat friend Lola tricks her into challenging the rich and overbearing Carla Santini in a less-than-friendly race

"The story is entertaining and well written. The characters reflect the personalities and cliques of kids in any high school." SLJ

The **crazy** things girls do for love. Candlewick Press 2011 $15.99

Grades: 7 8 9 10   **Fic**

1. School stories 2. Environmental protection -- Fiction
ISBN 978-0-7636-5018-6; 0-7636-5018-8

LC 2010048434

When fashionista Sicilee, arty Maya, and antisocial Waneeda risk their reputations by joining Clifton Springs High School's Environmental Club to be near gorgeous new student Cody Lightfoot, each finds a new way of looking at the world.

"The details are laugh-out-loud funny. . . . With plenty of wry romance, the story builds to a save-the-trees climax that also brings a change in Cody." Booklist

Sherlock, Patti

Letters from Wolfie. Viking 2004 232p $16.99; pa $6.99

Grades: 5 6 7 8   **Fic**

1. Dogs -- Fiction 2. Vietnam War, 1961-1975 -- Fiction
ISBN 0-670-03694-3; 0-14-240358-X pa

LC 2003-24316

Certain that he is doing the right thing by donating his dog, Wolfie, to the Army's scout program in Vietnam, thirteen-year-old Mark begins to have second thoughts when the Army refuses to say when and if Wolfie will ever return.

"In this topnotch novel, Sherlock weaves together numerous threads of emotion, information, and plot so seamlessly that readers will be surprised by how much they've learned by the time they finish this deceptively simple story." SLJ

Sherman, Deborah

The **BEDMAS** conspiracy. Fitzhenry & Whiteside 2011 170p pa $9.95

Grades: 4 5 6 7   **Fic**

1. School stories 2. Bands (Music) -- Fiction
ISBN 978-1-55455-181-1; 1-55455-181-1

Adam's band, Sick on a Snow Day, is challenged by more than just an unusual name: Adam is mistakenly accused of cheating on a test and must maintain a clean record and B-average if he wants to stay in the band. Then his lead singer, Daniela, gets stage fright.

"Adam's academic difficulties and Daniela's stage fright are only two of the challenges thrown their way, but both are handled imaginatively and with humor. . . . A genial read." SLJ

Sherman, Delia

Changeling. Viking 2006 292p $16.99; pa $8.99

Grades: 5 6 7 8   **Fic**

1. Fantasy fiction
ISBN 0-670-05967-6; 0-14-241188-4 pa

"Neef is a changeling, a human baby stolen by fairies. She lives in 'New York Between,' an invisible parallel city, and she was raised under the protection of her godmother (a white rat) and the Green Lady of Central Park. . . . After breaking Fairy Law, Neef is expelled, and she must complete a heroic quest . . . in order to regain entry to her community. . . . Silly, profound, and lightning paced all at once, this novel will please adventure fans and fantasy readers alike." Bull Cent Child Books

Another title about Neef is:

The Magic Mirror of the Mermaid Queen (2009)

★ The **freedom** maze. Big Mouth House 2011 267p $16.95

Grades: 7 8 9 10   **Fic**

1. Slavery -- Fiction 2. Time travel -- Fiction 3. Race relations -- Fiction 4. Plantation life -- Fiction

ISBN 978-1-931520-30-0; 1-931520-30-5

"It's 1960, but on the decayed Fairchild sugar plantation in rural Louisiana, vestiges of a grimmer past remain-the old cottage, overgrown garden maze, relations between white and black races. Stuck for the summer in the family ancestral home under the thumb of her cranky, imperious grandmother, Sophie, 13, makes a reckless wish that lands her in 1860, enslaved-by her own ancestors. . . . Plantation life for whites and blacks unfolds in compelling, often excruciating detail. . . . Multilayered, compassionate and thought-provoking." Kirkus

Sherrard, Valerie

The **glory** wind. Fitzhenry & Whiteside 2011 222p pa $12.95

Grades: 5 6 7 8   **Fic**

1. Prejudices -- Fiction 2. Country life -- Fiction

ISBN 978-1-55455-170-5; 1-55455-170-6

Eleven-year-old Luke must come to terms with the moral prejudices of his small town in rural 1950s Ontario when he befriends Gracie, the daughter of a young widow who moves in next door.

"Luke's first person narration is fresh and emotionally true. . . . The haunting depiction of small-mindedness will leave readers wondering, as Luke comes to, about Gracie's true nature: heavenly child—or angel?" Kirkus

Sherry, Maureen

Walls within walls; illustrated by Adam Stower. Katherine Tegen Books 2010 349p il $16.99

Grades: 4 5 6 7   **Fic**

1. Mystery fiction 2. Siblings -- Fiction

ISBN 978-0-06-176700-5; 0-06-176700-X

LC 2010-09494

When the Smithfork family moves into a lavish Manhattan apartment building, they discover clues to a decades-old mystery hidden behind the walls of their new home.

This "packs all sorts of interesting information about topics like history and architecture into a mystery that kids can (almost) solve. . . . Readers will get a real feel for the uniqueness that is New York City." Booklist

Sheth, Kashmira

Blue jasmine; [by] Kashmira Sheth. Hyperion Books for Children 2004 186p $15.99; pa $5.99

Grades: 5 6 7 8   **Fic**

1. Immigrants -- Fiction 2. East Indians -- Fiction

ISBN 0-7868-1855-7; 0-7868-5565-7 pa

LC 2003-50818

When twelve-year-old Seema moves to Iowa City with her parents and younger sister, she leaves friends and family behind in her native India but gradually begins to feel at home in her new country

"Seema's story, which articulates the ache for distant home and family, will resonate with fellow immigrants and enlighten their classmates." Booklist

Boys without names. Balzer & Bray 2010 316p $15.99

Grades: 4 5 6 7   **Fic**

1. Slavery -- Fiction 2. Child labor -- Fiction 3. Missing persons -- Fiction

ISBN 978-0-06-185760-7; 0-06-185760-2

LC 2009-11747

Eleven-year-old Gopal and his family leave their rural Indian village for life with his uncle in Mumbai, but when they arrive his father goes missing and Gopal ends up locked in a sweatshop from which there is no escape.

"Readers quickly come to care for this clever, perceptive boy who tries hard to do the right thing. . . . The author includes more about child labor at the end of this well-told survival story with a social conscience." SLJ

★ **Keeping** corner. Hyperion 2007 281p hardcover o.p. pa $5.99

Grades: 7 8 9 10 11 12   **Fic**

1. Widows -- Fiction 2. Writers on politics 3. Women's rights -- Fiction

ISBN 978-0-7868-3859-2; 0-7868-3859-0; 978-0-7868-3860-8 pa; 0-7868-3860-4 pa

LC 2007-15314

In India in the 1940s, twelve-year-old Leela's happy, spoiled childhood ends when her husband since age nine, whom she barely knows, dies, leaving her a widow whose only hope of happiness could come from Mahatma Ghandi's social and political reforms.

Sheth "sets up a thrilling premise in which politics become achingly personal." Booklist

Shimko, Bonnie

★ The **private** thoughts of Amelia E. Rye. Farrar, Straus Giroux 2010 234p $16.99

Grades: 5 6 7 8   **Fic**

1. Friendship -- Fiction 2. Mother-daughter relationship -- Fiction

ISBN 978-0-374-36131-0; 0-374-36131-2

LC 2008048092

Growing up in a small town in upstate New York during the 1960s, 13-year-old Amelia E. Ryel, unwanted by her mother, searches for love and acceptance.

"The book is peopled with believable, multilayered characters. . . . Shimko's . . . story is original, and Amelia's distinctive voice and likable nature will have readers rooting for her in times of trouble and cheering her ultimate good fortune." Publ Wkly

Shimura Takako

Wandering son; Shimura Takako ; translated by Matt Thorn. Fantagraphics Books 2012 200 p. ill. (hardcover) $19.99

Grades: 7 8 9 10 **Fic**
1. Manga 2. Puberty -- Graphic novels 3. Bildungsromans -- Graphic novels 4. Transgendered people -- Graphic novels 5. Graphic novels 6. Sex role -- Graphic novels
ISBN 1606995332; 9781606995334
This manga "tells the story of a friendship between Shuichi, a young boy who wishes he were a girl, and Yoshino, a young girl who wishes she were a boy. . . . Shuichi's impulses toward a female identity feel confusing and shameful to him, and it's the girls in his life—first Yoshino, and then Saori—who point out his difference and encourage it. . . . Both children are teased mercilessly by their classmates, whose sexual development, while perhaps more socially normative, is just as confusing to them." (Publishers Weekly)

This graphic novel "tells the story of a friendship between Shuichi, a young boy who wishes he were a girl, and Yoshino, a young girl who wishes she were a boy." Publ Wkly

Shinn, Sharon
★ **Gateway**. Viking 2009 280p $17.99
Grades: 6 7 8 9 10 **Fic**
1. Space and time -- Fiction 2. Chinese Americans -- Fiction
ISBN 978-0-670-01178-0; 0-670-01178-9
LC 2009-14002
While passing through the Arch in St. Louis, Missouri, a Chinese American teenager is transported to a parallel world where she is given a dangerous assignment.

The author's "fantasy finds the right balance between adventure and romance, while illuminating how seductive evil can be and that sometimes the best weapon one can possess is a skeptical mind." Publ Wkly

Shoemaker, Tim
Back before dark; Timothy Shoemaker. Zondervan 2013 384 p. (hardcover) $14.99
Grades: 7 8 9 10 **Fic**
1. Friendship -- Fiction 2. Kidnapping -- Fiction 3. Best friends -- Fiction 4. Christian life -- Fiction 5. Conduct of life -- Fiction 6. Mystery and detective stories
ISBN 0310734991; 9780310734994
LC 2012049855

Code of silence; Tim Shoemaker. Zondervan 2012 331 p. $14.99
Grades: 7 8 9 10 **Fic**
1. Youth -- Fiction 2. Secrecy -- Fiction 3. Deception -- Fiction 4. Witnesses -- Fiction 5. Christian life -- Fiction 6. Conduct of life -- Fiction 7. Robbers and outlaws -- Fiction
ISBN 9780310726531
LC 2011048880
In this crime novel for young adults by Tim Shoemaker, "thirteen-year-olds Cooper, Gordy, and Hiro are snacking at their favorite burger joint, Frank 'n Stein's, when they witness a brutal robbery. Two men, masked as a clown and Elvis, savagely beat the owner and steal his considerable stash of cash. The kids manage to escape, and with the security camera hard drive to boot, but Clown gets a good look at

Cooper and swears he'll find him. Afraid to go to the police (the robbers were wearing cop pants), Cooper convinces his friends to enact a code of silence. As the maybe-crooked police and other possible suspects get closer to identifying the witnesses, the kids" lies to their parents, their teachers, and one another set off increasingly desperate maneuvers and dangerous infighting" (Booklist)

Showalter, Gena
Intertwined. Harlequin Teen 2009 440p $15.99
Grades: 7 8 9 10 **Fic**
1. Vampires -- Fiction 2. Werewolves -- Fiction 3. Supernatural -- Fiction
ISBN 978-0-373-21002-2; 0-373-21002-7
"This fast-paced, action-driven plot has many unexpected twists and turns. Well written, with a unique story line and strong characters." SLJ
Other titles in this series are:
Unraveled (2010)
Twisted (2011)

Shreve, Susan
The **lovely** shoes; [by] Susan Shreve. Arthur A. Levine Books 2011 252p $16.99
Grades: 6 7 8 9 **Fic**
1. Shoemakers 2. School stories 3. Birth defects -- Fiction 4. Mother-daughter relationship -- Fiction
ISBN 978-0-439-68049-3; 0-439-68049-2
LC 2010027937
In 1950s Ohio, ninth-grader Franny feels isolated and self-conscious at high school because of her deformed leg and feet, but her irrepressibly high-spirited mother is determined to find shoes for Franny to wear at the school dances.

"Celebrating the rewards of determination and a positive attitude, this atmospheric novel credibly depicts Franny's internal growth and changing attitude. The contrast between smalltown Ohio and splendorous Florence provides an intriguing framework for the book's classic themes." Publ Wkly

Shulman, Mark
★ **Scrawl**. Roaring Brook Press 2010 234p $16.99
Grades: 6 7 8 9 10 **Fic**
1. School stories 2. Bullies -- Fiction 3. Diaries -- Fiction 4. Poverty -- Fiction 5. Self-perception -- Fiction
ISBN 978-1-59643-417-2; 1-59643-417-1
LC 2010-10521
When eighth-grade school bully Tod and his friends get caught committing a crime on school property, his penalty— staying after school and writing in a journal under the eye of the school guidance counsellor—reveals aspects of himself that he prefers to keep hidden.

"Blackmail, cliques, and a sense of hopelessness from both students and teachers sets up an unexpected ending that will leave readers with a new appreciation for how difficult high school can be. With the potential to occupy the rarified air of titles like S.E. Hinton's The Outsiders and Chris Crutcher's Staying Fat for Sarah Byrnes . . ., Scrawl paints the stereotypical school bully in a different, poignant light." Voice Youth Advocates

Shulman, Polly

Enthusiasm. G. P. Putnam's Sons 2006 198p
hardcover o.p. pa $7.99

Grades: 7 8 9 10   **Fic**
  1. School stories
  ISBN 0-399-24389-5; 0-14-240935-9 pa
                            LC 2005-13490

Julie and Ashleigh, high school sophomores and Jane
Austen fans, seem to fall for the same Mr. Darcy-like boy
and struggle to hide their true feelings from one another
while rehearsing for a school musical.

"While familiarity with Austen's world through her
books or, more likely, the movie renditions will deepen readers' appreciation for Shulman's impressive . . . novel, it is by
no means a prerequisite to enjoying this involving and often
amusing narrative of friendship, courtship, and (of course)
true love." Booklist

★ The **Grimm** Legacy. G. P. Putnam's Sons
2010 325p $16.99

Grades: 5 6 7 8   **Fic**
  1. Fantasy fiction 2. Magic -- Fiction 3. Libraries
-- Fiction
  ISBN 0-399-25096-4; 978-0-399-25096-5
                            LC 2009028919

New York high school student Elizabeth gets an after-
school job as a page at the "New-York Circulating Material Repository," and when she gains coveted access to its
Grimm Collection of magical objects, she and the other
pages are drawn into a series of frightening adventures involving mythical creatures and stolen goods.

"This modern fantasy has intrigue, adventure, and romance, and the magical aspects of the tale are both clever
and intricately woven. . . . Shulman's prose is fast paced,
filled with humor, and peopled with characters who are either true to life or delightfully bizarre." SLJ

The **Wells** Bequest; by Polly Shulman. Nancy
Paulsen Books, an imprint of Penguin Group (USA)
Inc. 2013 272 p. (hardcover) $16.99

Grades: 5 6 7 8   **Fic**
  1. Science fiction 2. Time travel -- Fiction
  ISBN 0399256466; 9780399256462
                            LC 2012036571

This book is a companion to Polly Shulman's "The
Grimm Legacy." Here, New York Circulating Material Repository page "Leo notices an object materializing on the
floor. The glittering, football-sized machine has 'gears and
rods and knobs and a little saddle' —and two miniscule humans, one of whom is himself." He discovers that he and his
fellow page Jaya must travel in time to prevent another page
from misusing Nikola Tesla's death ray. (Kirkus Reviews)

Shurtliff, Liesl

Rump; the true story of Rumpelstiltskin. Liesl
Shurtliff. 1st ed. Alfred A. Knopf 2013 272 p.
(hardcover) $16.99

Grades: 3 4 5 6 7   **Fic**
  1. Fractured fairy tales 2. Gold -- Fiction 3. Humorous

stories 4. Magic -- Fiction
  ISBN 0307977935; 9780307977939 trade;
9780307977946; 9780307977953; 9780307977960
                            LC 2012005093

In this fractured fairy tale, by Liesl Shurtliff, "12-year-
old [Rumpelstiltskin] . . . finds an old spinning wheel, . . .
[and] discovers he has a gift for spinning straw into gold. His
best friend, Red Riding Hood, warns him that magic is dangerous, and she's right. With each thread he spins, he weaves
himself deeper into a curse. To break the spell, Rump must
go on a perilous quest, fighting off pixies, trolls, poison apples, and a wickedly foolish queen." (Publisher's note)

"Debut author Shurtliff upends the traditional characterization of this fairy tale's antihero, recasting Rumpelstiltskin
as a sympathetic and tragically doomed protagonist. . . . [T]
he picaresque-style narrative gives the maligned character a
refreshingly plainspoken voice, while honoring the original
story's hauntingly strange events." Pub Wkly

Shusterman, Neal

★ **Antsy** does time. Dutton Children's Books
2008 247p $16.99

Grades: 5 6 7 8   **Fic**
  1. School stories 2. Death -- Fiction
  ISBN 978-0-525-47825-6; 0-525-47825-6
                            LC 2008-00459

Fourteen-year-old Anthony "Antsy" Bonano learns
about life, death, and a lot more when he tries to help a friend
with a terminal illness feel hopeful about the future.

"Featuring a terrific supporting cast led by Antsy's wise,
acerbic mother, an expert blend of comedy and near tragedy,
and the wry observations of a narrator . . . this will keep
tween readers hooked from start to finish." Booklist

Bruiser. HarperTeen 2010 328p $16.99; lib
bdg $17.89

Grades: 8 9 10 11 12   **Fic**
  1. Twins -- Fiction 2. Siblings -- Fiction 3. Child abuse
-- Fiction 4. Supernatural -- Fiction
  ISBN 978-0-06-113408-1; 0-06-113408-2; 978-0-06-
113409-8 lib bdg; 0-06-113409-0 lib bdg
                            LC 2009-30930

Inexplicable events start to occur when sixteen-year-old
twins Tennyson and Bronte befriend a troubled and misunderstood outcast, aptly nicknamed Bruiser, and his little
brother, Cody.

"Narrated in turns by Tennyson, Bronte, Bruiser, and
Bruiser's little brother, Cody, the story is a fascinating study
in the art of self-deception and the way our best intentions
for others are often based in the selfish desires of our deepest selves. . . . This eloquent and thoughtful story will most
certainly leave its mark." Bull Cent Child Books

★ **Downsiders**. Simon & Schuster Bks. for
Young Readers 1999 246p hardcover o.p. pa $8.99

Grades: 9 10 11 12   **Fic**
  1. Subways -- Fiction 2. Subways -- New York (State)
-- New York
  ISBN 0-689-80375-3; 1-4169-9747-4 pa
                            LC 98-38555

When fourteen-year-old Lindsay meets Talon and discovers the Downsiders world which had evolved from the

subway built in New York in 1867 by Alfred Ely Beach, she and her new friend experience the clash of their two cultures.

"Shusterman has invented an alternate world in the Downside that is both original and humorous." Voice Youth Advocates

★ **Everlost**. Simon & Schuster Books for Young Readers 2006 313p (The Skinjacker trilogy) $16.95; pa $8.99

Grades: 8 9 10 11 12   **Fic**
    1. Death -- Fiction 2. Future life -- Fiction 3. Traffic accidents -- Fiction 4. Young adult literature -- Works
    ISBN 978-0-689-87237-2; 0-689-87237-2; 978-1-4169-9749-8 pa; 1-4169-9749-0 pa
                            LC 2005-32244

When Nick and Allie are killed in a car crash, they end up in Everlost, or limbo for lost souls, where although Nick is satisfied, Allie will stop at nothing—even skinjacking—to break free.

"Shusterman has reimagined what happens after death and questions power and the meaning of charity. While all this is going on, he has also managed to write a rip-roaring adventure complete with monsters, blimps, and high-diving horses." SLJ

    Other titles in this series are:
    Everfound (2011)
    Everwild (2009)

Full tilt; a novel. Simon & Schuster Bks. for Young Readers 2003 201p $16.95; pa $8.99

Grades: 7 8 9 10   **Fic**
    1. Horror fiction 2. Brothers -- Fiction 3. Amusement parks -- Fiction
    ISBN 0-689-80374-5; 1-4169-9748-2 pa
                            LC 2002-13867

"Shusterman has created a surreal, scary fantasy, packed with suspenseful psychological drama." Booklist

The **Schwa** was here; [by] Neal Shusterman. 1st ed; Dutton Children's Books 2004 228p $15.99

Grades: 5 6 7 8   **Fic**
    1. Friendship -- Fiction
    ISBN 0-525-47182-0
                            LC 2004-45072

A Brooklyn eighth-grader nicknamed Antsy befriends the Schwa, an "invisible-ish" boy who is tired of blending into his surroundings and going unnoticed by nearly everyone.

"Antsy is one funny narrator. . . . Shusterman has created yet another very readable and refreshingly different story." Voice Youth Advocates

Shusterman, Neal, 1962-

UnWholly; Neal Shusterman. Simon & Schuster Books For Young Readers 2012 402 p. (hardback) $17.99

Grades: 6 7 8 9 10 11 12   **Fic**
    1. Science fiction 2. Identity -- Fiction 3. Survival skills -- Fiction 4. Survival -- Fiction 5. Revolutionaries -- Fiction 6. Fugitives from justice -- Fiction
    ISBN 1442423668; 9781442423664; 9781442423688
                          LC 2012002729

This sequel to Neal Shusterman"s book "Unwind" follows "Cam . . . a product of unwinding; made entirely out of the parts of other unwinds, he is a teen who does not technically exist. A futuristic Frankenstein, Cam struggles with a search for identity and meaning. . . . And when the actions of a sadistic bounty hunter cause Cam's fate to become inextricably bound with the fates of Connor, Risa, and Lev, he"ll have to question humanity itself." (Publisher's note)

★ **Unwind**. Simon & Schuster Books for Young Readers 2007 335p $17.99

Grades: 6 7 8 9 10 11 12   **Fic**
    1. Science fiction
    ISBN 1-4169-1204-5; 1-4169-1205-3 pa; 978-1-4169-1204-0; 978-1-4169-1205-7 pa
                          LC 2006032689

In a future world where those between the ages of thirteen and eighteen can have their lives "unwound" and their body parts harvested for use by others, three teens go to extreme lengths to uphold their beliefs—and, perhaps, save their own lives.

"Poignant, compelling, and ultimately terrifying." Voice Youth Advocates

Siegelson, Kim L.

Honey Bea; [by] Kim L. Siegelson. 1st ed; Jump at the Sun/Hyperion Books for Children 2006 276p $15.99

Grades: 7 8 9 10   **Fic**
    1. Magic -- Fiction 2. Slavery -- Fiction 3. Plantation life -- Fiction
    ISBN 0-7868-0853-5
                          LC 2003-61888

On a Louisiana sugar plantation, a young slave girl struggles with the magical powers that have been passed down from her grandmother and mother to her, unsure of the responsibilities and consequences that accompany this power.

"Siegelson crafts a mesmerizing tale heavy with the scent of honey and flowers and rooted in Louisiana soil." Booklist

Silberberg, Alan

★ **Milo**; sticky notes and brain freeze. written and illustrated by Alan Silberberg. Aladdin 2010 275p il $15.99

Grades: 5 6 7 8   **Fic**
    1. Death -- Fiction 2. Mothers -- Fiction 3. Friendship -- Fiction 4. Bereavement -- Fiction
    ISBN 978-1-4169-9430-5; 1-4169-9430-0
                          LC 2010012708

"This is more than just another funny story about a middle school misfit who is the new kid in the neighborhood. While Milo does struggle with all the normal tween anxieties and self-consciousness about his family, there is more. Silberberg details the daily events with Wimpy Kid-like drawings and quick-witted humor that will keep the pages turning. Milo's new friendships with classmates Marshall and Hillary and elderly neighbor Sylvia Poole allow readers to glimpse at the deeper truth–Milo's mother's death–as it emerges between laugh lines. Silberberg takes on a tough topic and always stays true to the age of the character through dialogue and artwork while maintaining that wisecracking, 12-year-old humor." SLJ

Silvey, Craig

★ **Jasper** Jones; a novel. Alfred A. Knopf 2011
312p $16.99

Grades: 6 7 8 9 10   **Fic**

1. Mystery fiction 2. Homicide -- Fiction 3. Family
life -- Fiction 4. Young adult literature -- Works

ISBN 0-375-86666-3; 0-375-96666-8 lib bdg; 978-0-
375-86666-1; 978-0-375-96666-8 lib bdg

LC 2010-9364

In small-town Australia, teens Jasper and Charlie form
an unlikely friendship when one asks the other to help him
cover up a murder until they can prove who is responsible.

"Silvey infuses his prose with a musician's sensibility—Charlie's pounding heart is echoed in the terse staccato sentences of the opening scenes, alternating with legato
phrases laden with meaning. The author's keen ear for dialogue is evident in the humorous verbal sparring between
Charlie and Jeffrey, typical of smart 13-year-old boys. . . . A
richly rewarding exploration of truth and lies by a masterful
storyteller." Kirkus

Simmons, Michael

Alien feast; [by] Michael Simmons; illustrated
by George O'Connor. Roaring Brook Press 2008
240p il (Chronicles of the first invasion) $9.95

Grades: 5 6 7 8   **Fic**

1. Science fiction 2. Orphans -- Fiction 3. Kidnapping
-- Fiction 4. Extraterrestrial beings -- Fiction

ISBN 978-1-59643-281-9; 1-59643-281-0

LC 2007-44050

In 2017, human-eating aliens have kidnapped two scientists who might cure the disease that is destroying them,
and twelve-year-old William Aitkin, his elderly, ailing Uncle Maynard, and the scientists' daughter, Sophie, set out to
rescue them.

"The youngsters are nicely developed, and, refreshingly,
they act as you'd expect kids to behave in such a stressful
situation, not like miniature adults. O'Connor's artwork
adds to the humor." SLJ

Simner, Janni Lee

Bones of Faerie. Random House 2009 247p
$16.99; lib bdg $19.99

Grades: 7 8 9 10   **Fic**

1. Fantasy fiction 2. Magic -- Fiction 3. Fairies --
Fiction

ISBN 978-0-375-84563-5; 978-0-375-94563-2 lib bdg

LC 2008-2022

Fifteen-year-old Liza travels through war-ravaged territory, accompanied by two companions, in a struggle to
bridge the faerie and human worlds and to bring back her
mother while learning of her own powers and that magic
can be controlled.

This is a "compelling developed, highly vulnerable trio
whose resolute defiance against the status quo will resonate
with readers long after specific details of the story may be
forgotten." Bull Cent Child Books

Faerie after; Janni Lee Simner. Random House
Inc. 2013 272 p. (ebook) $50.97; (hardcover)
$16.99; (library) $19.99

Grades: 7 8 9 10   **Fic**

1. Occult fiction 2. Fantasy fiction 3. Fairies -- Fiction
4. Magic -- Fiction 5. Coming of age -- Fiction

ISBN 0375870695; 9780307974556; 9780375870699;
9780375970696

LC 2012006430

This is the third book in Janni Lee's Bones of Faerie
trilogy. "Relative peace has descended upon Liza's town,
where she practices her summoner magic and waits for her
half-faerie baby sister to be born. But the forest is showing new dangers, though subtle ones," particularly a strange
dust. "Liza's quest to find out what's wrong reveals fresh
disasters." (Kirkus)

Faerie winter. Random House Children's Books
2011 270p $16.99; lib bdg $19.99

Grades: 7 8 9 10   **Fic**

1. Magic -- Fiction 2. Fairies -- Fiction 3. Mother-
daughter relationship -- Fiction

ISBN 978-0-375-86671-5; 0-375-86671-X; 978-0-
375-96671-2 lib bdg; 0-375-96671-4 lib bdg

LC 2010014250

Unable to get answers from her mother, sixteen-year-
old Liza learns from Karin that while her own actions may
have doomed the fairy and human worlds, she may be able
to save them with more training, if the Faerie Queen can first
be stopped.

"Simner tells a more streamlined story this time around
and keeps up the dark atmospherics of her high-appeal blend
of unsettling speculative-fiction scenarios." Booklist

Thief eyes. Random House 2010 272p $16.99

Grades: 7 8 9 10   **Fic**

1. Fantasy fiction 2. Magic -- Fiction 3. Missing
persons -- Fiction

ISBN 978-0-375-86670-8; 0-375-86670-1

LC 2009-18166

Haley's mother disappeared while on a trip to Iceland,
and a year later, when her father takes her there to find out
what happened, Haley finds herself deeply involved in an
ancient saga that began with her Nordic ancestors.

"Simner skillfully weaves Haley and Ari's modern
emotional struggles into the ancient saga and enlivens the
story with an intriguing cast of characters from the original
tale." Booklist

Simon, Charnan

Plan B. Darby Creek 2011 104p (Surviving
Southside) lib bdg $27.93; pa $7.95

Grades: 7 8 9 10   **Fic**

1. School stories 2. Pregnancy -- Fiction

ISBN 978-0-7613-6149-7 lib bdg; 0-7613-6149-9 lib
bdg; 978-0-7613-6163-3 pa; 0-7613-6163-4 pa

LC 2010023819

Lucy has her life planned out: she'll graduate and then
join her boyfriend, Luke, at college in Austin. She'll become
a Spanish teacher and of course they'll get married. But then
Lucy gets pregnant. Together, she and Luke will have to
make the most difficult decision of their lives.

This "well-written [story reinforces] the importance of
family, friends, values, and thoughtful decision-making. . . .

[An] excellent [purchase, this book] will attract and engage reluctant readers." SLJ

Singer, Nicky

Gem X. Holiday House 2008 311p $16.95

Grades: 7 8 9 10   **Fic**

1. Science fiction 2. Cloning -- Fiction 3. Genetic engineering -- Fiction 4. Political corruption -- Fiction

ISBN 978-0-8234-2108-4; 0-8234-2108-2

LC 2007-14975

Sixteen-year-old Maxo Strang, the most perfect human ever made, suddenly discovers a 'crack' in his face, which leads him to expose his community's dark underworld of secret scientific research and the city's corrupt supreme leader.

"This intelligent, fast-paced novel will appeal to those teens who . . . want speculative fiction with bite and satire." SLJ

Singleton, Linda Joy

Dead girl dancing; Linda Joy Singleton. Flux 2009 259 p. $9.95

Grades: 8 9 10 11 12   **Fic**

1. Fantasy fiction 2. Stalkers -- Fiction 3. Supernatural -- Fiction 4. Identity -- Fiction 5. Friendship -- Fiction 6. Future life -- Fiction 7. Self-esteem -- Fiction 8. Best friends -- Fiction 9. Emotional problems -- Fiction

ISBN 9780738714066

LC 2008044037

This paranormal young adult book, the second book in Linda Joy Singleton's "Dead Girl" series after "Dead Girl Watching," continues the story of Amber, who is a "Temp Lifer," or someone who has the ability to "step[. . .] into someone's life--and their body." In this installment, Amber is stuck in the body of "[her] boyfriend's older sister, who is getting ready to go wild on spring break--while being pursued by a psycho stalker and a Dark Lifer." (Publisher's note)

Dead girl in love; Linda Joy Singleton. Flux 2009 283 p. $9.95

Grades: 8 9 10 11 12   **Fic**

1. Fantasy fiction 2. Supernatural -- Fiction 3. Female friendship -- Fiction 4. Identity -- Fiction 5. Friendship -- Fiction 6. Future life -- Fiction 7. Best friends -- Fiction 8. Grandmothers -- Fiction 9. Mothers and daughters -- Fiction

ISBN 0738714070; 9780738714073

LC 2009009049

This paranormal young adult book, the third book in Linda Joy Singleton's "Dead Girl" series after "Dead Girl Dancing," continues the story of Amber, whose "dead grandmother keeps finding people who have big problems and then [Amber has] the freaky experience of stepping into their life—and their body!—to provide help. This time, [she's] in the body of [her] BFF, Alyce. Since Alyce and [Amber] know everything about each other," Amber thinks she "won't have to do a lot of detective work" with this case. However, she's alarmed to discover that a question she does have to answer is why Alyce's body is in a coffin. (Publisher's note)

Dead girl walking; [by] Linda Joy Singleton. Flux 2008 308p (Dead girl) $9.95

Grades: 8 9 10 11 12   **Fic**

1. School stories 2. Death -- Fiction 3. Future life -- Fiction

ISBN 978-0-7387-1405-9; 0-7387-1405-4

LC 2008012991

When Amber, a smart, middle-class, high school student, is hit by a truck, she meets her deceased grandmother in a dreamlike place, then takes a wrong turn and awakens in the body of a wealthy, beautiful, popular classmate with serious problems.

"This page-turner has wit, love, courage, adventure, and remarkable insight." SLJ

Sitomer, Alan Lawrence

★ The **downside** of being up. G.P. Putnam's Sons 2011 215p $16.99

Grades: 6 7 8 9   **Fic**

1. School stories 2. Puberty -- Fiction 3. Family life -- Fiction

ISBN 978-0-399-25498-7; 0-399-25498-6

LC 2010044203

All Bobby Connor wants is to survive middle school, but puberty is making that difficult for him as his body conspires against him.

"It is impossible to dislike this pun-filled tale. . . . This fiction provides some long-needed realism, served up by a narrator who knows what he is talking about." Booklist

The **secret** story of Sonia Rodriguez. Jump at the Sun/Hyperion Books For Children 2008 312p lib bdg $17.99

Grades: 7 8 9 10   **Fic**

1. Family life -- Fiction 2. Mexican Americans -- Fiction

ISBN 978-1-4231-1072-9; 1-4231-1072-2

LC 2007-45265

Tenth-grader Sonia reveals secrets about her life and her Hispanic family as she studies hard to become the first Rodriguez to finish high school.

"Sonia's immediate voice will hold teens with its mix of anger, sorrow, tenderness, and humor." Booklist

Skelton, Matthew

★ **Endymion** Spring. Delacorte Press 2006 392p il $17.95; lib bdg $19.99; pa $9.99

Grades: 5 6 7 8   **Fic**

1. Inventors 2. Printers 3. Magic -- Fiction 4. Books and reading -- Fiction

ISBN 0-385-73380-1; 0-385-90397-9 lib bdg; 0-385-73456-5 pa

LC 2006-46259

Having reluctantly accompanied his academic mother and pesky younger sister to Oxford, twelve-year-old Blake Winters is at loose ends until he stumbles across an ancient and magical book, secretly brought to England in 1453 by Gutenberg's mute apprentice to save it from evil forces, and which now draws Blake into a dangerous and life-threatening quest

"This book is certain to reach an audience looking for a page-turner, and it just might motivate readers to explore the . . . facts behind the fiction." SLJ

★ The **story** of Cirrus Flux. Delacorte Press 2010 288p il $17.99; lib bdg $20.99

Grades: 4 5 6 7   Fic
1. Adventure fiction 2. Orphans -- Fiction 3. Supernatural -- Fiction
ISBN 978-0-385-73381-6; 0-385-73381-X; 978-0-385-90398-1 lib bdg; 0-385-90398-7 lib bdg
LC 2009-18987

In 1783 London, the destiny of an orphaned boy and girl becomes intertwined as the boy, Cirrus Flux, is pursued by a sinister woman mesmerist, a tiny man with an all-seeing eye, and a skull-collecting scoundrel, all of whom believe that he possesses an orb containing a divine power.

Skelton "neatly weaves touches of fantasy into a late-eighteenth century London setting. . . . His literary sensibility and grubby atmospherics are strong enough to carry the tale." Booklist

Skurzynski, Gloria

The **Virtual** War. Simon & Schuster Bks. for Young Readers 1997 152p hardcover o.p. pa $10.95

Grades: 6 7 8 9   Fic
1. Science fiction 2. Virtual reality -- Fiction
ISBN 0-689-81374-0; 1-4169-7577-2 pa
LC 96-35346

In a future world where global contamination has necessitated limited human contact, three young people with unique genetically engineered abilities are teamed up to wage a war in virtual reality

"Skurzynski's anti-war message is clear yet never didactic; her characters are complex and fully realized, the pacing brisk, and the story compelling." Bull Cent Child Books

Other titles in this series are:
The choice (2006)
The clones (2002)
The revolt (2005)

Slade, Arthur G,

★ The **hunchback** assignments; [by] Arthur Slade. Wendy Lamb Books 2009 278p $15.99; lib bdg $18.99

Grades: 7 8 9 10   Fic
1. Science fiction 2. Spies -- Fiction 3. Supernatural -- Fiction 4. Physically handicapped -- Fiction
ISBN 978-0-385-73784-5; 0-385-73784-X; 978-0-385-90694-4 lib bdg; 0-385-90694-3 lib bdg
LC 2008-54378

In Victorian London, fourteen-year-old Modo, a shape-changing hunchback, becomes a secret agent for the Permanent Association, which strives to protect the world from the evil machinations of the Clockwork Guild.

"A solid story line and well-crafted writing make for a pleasing and evocative adventure." Booklist

Other titles in the series are:
The dark deeps (2010)
Empire of ruins (2011)

Jolted; Newton Starker's rules for survival. [by] Arthur Slade. Wendy Lamb Books 2009 227p $15.99; lib bdg $18.99

Grades: 5 6 7 8   Fic
1. School stories 2. Lightning -- Fiction
ISBN 978-0-385-74700-4; 0-385-74700-4; 978-0-385-90944-0 lib bdg; 0-385-90944-6 lib bdg
LC 2008-8632

First published 2008 in Canada

Many of Newton Starker's ancestors, including his mother, have been killed by lightning strikes, so when he enrolls at the eccentric Jerry Potts Academy of Higher Learning and Survival in Moose Jaw, Saskatchewan, he tries to be a model student so that he can avoid the same fate.

"The premise will snag readers immediately [and] . . . Slade's portrayal of Newton's sweep of emotions as he deals with his perceived fate–fear, fury, dogged determination–is especially convincing." Publ Wkly

Slater, Adam

The **Shadowing** : Hunted. Egmont 2011 208p $16.99

Grades: 7 8 9 10   Fic
1. Ghost stories 2. Horror fiction 3. Supernatural -- Fiction
ISBN 978-1-6068-426-1; 1-60684-261-7

"Callum Scott sees ghosts. . . . It's because he is a 'chime child,' born on a full moon between midnight Friday and dawn Saturday. . . . When a huge, particularly evil-looking black dog and a pale boy dripping blood start following him, he is unnerved. . . . The barrier between the human world and the demon realm is disintegrating like it does every hundred years, and only the chime children can keep humanity safe. Slater shows a knack for building tension and terror and readers . . . will gulp this series opener and ask for more." Booklist

Slayton, Fran Cannon

★ **When** the whistle blows. Philomel Books 2009 162p $16.99

Grades: 7 8 9 10   Fic
1. Railroads -- Fiction 2. Family life -- Fiction 3. Country life -- Fiction
ISBN 978-0-399-25189-4; 0-399-25189-8
LC 2008-38435

Jimmy Cannon tells about his life in the 1940s as the son of a West Virginia railroad man, loving the trains and expecting one day to work on the railroad like his father and brothers.

"Telling details and gentle humor help set the scene and reveal a great deal about these characters and their lives. . . . A polished paean to a bygone time and place." SLJ

Sleator, William

★ **Interstellar** pig. Dutton 1984 197p hardcover o.p. pa $6.99

Grades: 5 6 7 8   Fic
1. Science fiction
ISBN 0-14-037595-3 pa
LC 84-4132

Barney's boring seaside vacation suddenly becomes more interesting when the cottage next door is occupied by three exotic neighbors who are addicted to a game they call "Interstellar Pig."

The author "draws the reader in with intimations of danger and horror, but the climactic battle is more slapstick than horrific, and the victor's prize could scarcely be more ironic. Problematic as straight science fiction but great fun as a spoof on human-alien contact." Booklist

Another title about Barney is:

Parasite Pig (2002)

Singularity. Dutton 1985 170p hardcover o.p. pa $5.99

Grades: 7 8 9 10   **Fic**

1. Science fiction 2. Twins -- Fiction

ISBN 0-525-44161-1; 0-14-037598-8 pa

LC 84-26075

Sixteen-year-old twins Harry and Barry stumble across a gateway to another universe, where a distortion in time and space causes a dramatic change in their competitive relationship

"The book has a title with a fine double entendre and is an unusual, suspenseful yarn told by a master storyteller." Horn Book

★ The **duplicate**. Dutton 1988 154p hardcover o.p. pa $5.99

Grades: 7 8 9 10   **Fic**

1. Science fiction

ISBN 0-14-130431-6

LC 87-30562

Sixteen-year-old David, finding a strange machine that creates replicas of living organisms, duplicates himself and suffers the horrible consequences when the duplicate turns against him

"There are some points in the story when the roles of the clones (referred to as Duplicates A and B) become congested to the detriment of the book's pace, but fantasy fans will doubtless find the concept fresh enough and eerie enough to compensate for this, and Sleator is, as always, economical in casting and structuring his story." Bull Cent Child Books

Sloan, Holly Goldberg

★ **I'll** be there. Little, Brown 2011 392p $17.99

Grades: 7 8 9 10   **Fic**

1. Brothers -- Fiction 2. Family life -- Fiction 3. Mental illness -- Fiction 4. Young adult literature -- Works 5. Father-son relationship -- Fiction

ISBN 978-0-316-12279-5; 0-316-12279-3

LC 2010-42994

"This riveting story will keep readers interested and guessing until the end." SLJ

Smelcer, John E.

The **Great** Death; [by] John Smelcer. Henry Holt and Co. 2009 166p $15.99

Grades: 6 7 8 9   **Fic**

1. Death -- Fiction 2. Orphans -- Fiction 3. Sisters -- Fiction 4. Epidemics -- Fiction 5. Native Americans -- Fiction 6. Voyages and travels -- Fiction

ISBN 978-0-8050-8100-8; 0-8050-8100-3

LC 2008-51113

As their Alaskan village's only survivors of sickness brought by white men one winter early in the twentieth century, sisters Millie, aged thirteen, and Maura, ten, make their way south in hopes of finding someone alive.

"An engaging tale of survival." Kirkus

The **trap**; [by] John Smelcer. Henry Holt and Co. 2006 170p $15.95

Grades: 6 7 8 9   **Fic**

1. Grandfathers -- Fiction 2. Native Americans -- Fiction 3. Survival after airplane accidents, shipwrecks, etc. -- Fiction

ISBN 978-0-8050-7939-5; 0-8050-7939-4

LC 2005035740

In alternating chapters, seventeen-year-old Johnny Least-Weasel worries about his missing grandfather, and the grandfather, Albert Least-Weasel, struggles to survive, caught in his own steel trap in the Alaskan winter.

"In this story, Smelcer . . . seems to straddle the line flawlessly between an ancient legend and contemporary fiction. . . . His characters act with quiet dignity. . . . The suspense is played on an everyday level, which is why it works." Voice Youth Advocates

Smibert, Angie

Memento Nora. Marshall Cavendish 2011 184p $16.99

Grades: 8 9 10 11 12   **Fic**

1. Science fiction 2. Memory -- Fiction 3. Terrorism -- Fiction 4. Cartoons and caricatures -- Fiction 5. Resistance to government -- Fiction

ISBN 0-7614-5829-8; 978-0-7614-5829-6

LC 2010011816

In a near future in which terrorism is commonplace but memories of horrors witnessed can be obliterated by a pill, teens Nora, Winter, and Micah, create an underground comic to share with their classmates the experiences they want to remember.

This offers "a multi-threaded plot that manages to be both complex and comfortably easy to follow. . . . The fast pace encourages readers to fall headfirst into a gripping suspense-adventure ride." Bull Cent Child Books

Smiley, Jane

★ The **Georges** and the Jewels; with illustrations by Elaine Clayton. Alfred A. Knopf 2009 232p il $16.99; lib bdg $19.99

Grades: 4 5 6 7   **Fic**

1. Horses -- Fiction 2. Ranch life -- Fiction 3. Christian life -- Fiction

ISBN 978-0-375-86227-4; 0-375-86227-7; 978-0-375-96227-1 lib bdg; 0-375-96227-1 lib bdg

LC 2009-06241

Seventh-grader Abby Lovitt grows up on her family's California horse ranch in the 1960s, learning to train the horses her father sells and trying to reconcile her strict religious upbringing with her own ideas about life.

"As might be expected from the skilled hands of Smiley . . . there are synchronous storylines . . . [and] many will find it difficult to say goodbye to Abby, Jack and especially to Ornery George." Publ Wkly

Other titles in this series are:

A good horse (2010)
True blue (2011)

Smith, Alexander Gordon

Lockdown. Farrar, Straus and Giroux 2009 273p
(Escape from Furnace) $14.99

Grades: 7 8 9 10   **Fic**
1. Science fiction 2. Escapes -- Fiction 3. Prisoners
-- Fiction
ISBN 978-0-374-32491-9; 0-374-32491-3
LC 2008-43439

When fourteen-year-old Alex is framed for murder, he
becomes an inmate in the Furnace Penitentiary, where brutal
inmates and sadistic guards reign, boys who disappear in the
middle of the night sometimes return weirdly altered, and
escape might just be possible.

"Once a plot is hatched, readers will be turning pages
without pause, and the cliffhanger ending will have them
anticipating the next installment. Most appealing is Smith's
flowing writing style, filled with kid-speak, colorful adjectives, and amusing analogies." SLJ

Other titles in this series are:
Death sentence (2011)
Solitary (2010)

Smith, Cynthia Leitich

Feral nights; Cynthia Leitich Smith. Candlewick Press 2013 304 p. $17.99

Grades: 9 10 11 12   **Fic**
1. Occult fiction 2. Monsters -- Fiction
ISBN 0763659096; 9780763659097
LC 2012942377

This young adult paranormal fantasy story, by Cynthia
Leitich Smith, is the first entry in the series "Feral." "When
sexy, free-spirited werecat Yoshi tracks his sister, Ruby, to
Austin, he discovers that she is not only MIA, but also the
key suspect in a murder investigation. Meanwhile, werepos-
sum Clyde and human Aimee have set out to do a little detective work of their own, sworn to avenge the brutal killing
of werearmadillo pal Travis." (Publisher's note)

Rain is not my Indian name. HarperCollins Pubs.
2001 135p $15.99; lib bdg $16.89

Grades: 6 7 8 9   **Fic**
1. Death -- Fiction 2. Photography -- Fiction 3. Native
Americans -- Fiction
ISBN 0-688-17397-7; 0-06-029504-X lib bdg
LC 00-59705

Tired of staying in seclusion since the death of her best
friend, a fourteen-year-old Native American girl takes on a
photographic assignment with her local newspaper to cover
events at the Native American summer youth camp

"The engaging first-person narrative convincingly portrays Rain's grieving process and addresses the varying degrees of prejudice she encounters." Horn Book Guide

Smith, D. James

The **boys** of San Joaquin; a novel. Atheneum
Books for Young Readers 2005 231p $15.95; pa
$5.99

Grades: 5 6 7 8   **Fic**
1. Deaf -- Fiction 2. Family life -- Fiction 3. Italian

Americans -- Fiction
ISBN 0-689-87606-8; 1-4169-1619-9 pa
LC 2004-3075

In a small California town in 1951, twelve-year-old
Paolo and his deaf cousin Billy get caught up in a search
for money missing from the church collection, leading them
to complicated discoveries about themselves, other family
members, and townspeople they thought they knew

"Narrator Paolo has an appealingly distinctive voice and
a keen eye for observing people, and the supporting characters are equally memorable." Booklist

Other titles about Paolo and Billy are:
Probably the world's best story about a dog and the girl
who loved me (2006)
It was September when we ran away the first time (2008)

Smith, Emily Wing

Back when you were easier to love. Dutton
Books 2011 296p $16.99

Grades: 8 9 10 11 12   **Fic**
1. Love stories 2. Mormons -- Fiction 3. Automobile
travel -- Fiction
ISBN 978-0-525-42199-3; 0-525-42199-8
LC 2010-13469

When her boyfriend Zan leaves high school in Utah a
year early to attend Pitzer College, a broken-hearted Joy and
Zan's best friend Noah take off on a road trip to California
seeking "closure."

Smith "effectively reconstructs Zan and Joy's relationship. . . . Joy's voice is sturdy, and her articulations about
loss and belief are thoughtful and often moving. Self-acceptance and both the comforts and restrictions of the Mormon
religion and identity are central themes in this sweet story."
Publ Wkly

★ The **way** he lived; [by] Emily Wing Smith.
1st ed.; Flux 2008 232p pa $9.95

Grades: 8 9 10 11 12   **Fic**
1. Death -- Fiction 2. Mormons -- Fiction
ISBN 978-0-7387-1404-2 pa
LC 2008024416

"The author preserves each narrator's complexity. . .
It's a testament to Smith's skills that although her central
character speaks only through other people's recollections,
his identity emerges distinctly by the end of the novel."
Publ Wkly

Smith, Hope Anita

★ **Keeping** the night watch; with illustrations by
E.B. Lewis. Henry Holt 2008 73p il $18.95

Grades: 4 5 6 7   **Fic**
1. Novels in verse 2. Fathers -- Fiction 3. Family life
-- Fiction 4. African Americans -- Fiction
ISBN 978-0-8050-7202-0; 0-8050-7202-0
LC 2007-12372

Coretta Scott King honor book for text, 2009

A thirteen-year-old African American boy chronicles
what happens to his family when his father, who temporarily
left, returns home and they all must deal with their feelings
of anger, hope, abandonment, and fear.

"The words are simple . . . and the beautiful watercolor
pictures of the African American family have the same quiet

intensity as pictures in the first book. . . . Although mainly in free verse, there's also a sonnet." Booklist

The **way** a door closes; [by] Hope Anita Smith; with illustrations by Shane W. Evans. Holt & Co. 2003 52p il $18.95

Grades: 4 5 6 7   **Fic**
  1. Novels in verse 2. Fathers -- Fiction 3. Family life -- Fiction 4. African Americans -- Fiction
  ISBN 0-8050-6477-X
                         LC 2002-67884
In this novel in verse "readers are drawn into the thoughts and feelings of a 13-year-old African American as he tries to understand and cope with a parent's departure from the family. . . . In carefully chosen, straightforward language, Smith conveys the boy's roller-coaster emotions with pinpoint accuracy. The results are poems that are heartbreaking, angry, and tender. Done in warm shades of mostly brown, blue, and gold, Evans's color spot and full-page paintings have a realistic, slightly sculptural appearance and are a perfect complement to the poems." SLJ

Smith, Icy
  Half spoon of rice; a survival story of the Cambodian genocide. written by Icy Smith; illustrated by Sopaul Nhem. East West Discovery Press 2010 42p il $19.95

Grades: 5 6 7 8   **Fic**
  1. Genocide -- Fiction
  ISBN 0-9821675-8-X; 978-0-9821675-8-8
                         LC 2009002973
Nine-year-old Nat and his family are forced from their home on April 17, 1975, marched for many days, separated from each other, and forced to work in the rice fields, where Nat concentrates on survival. Includes historical notes and photographs documenting the Cambodian genocide
  "Bold, impressionistic oil paintings, mainly full page but some full spreads, speak volumes, and archival photographs are appended. This powerful child's eye view of war is harsh and realistic—like its subject—though accessible and thought-provoking." SLJ

Smith, Jennifer E.
  The **comeback** season. Simon & Schuster Books for Young Readers 2008 246p $15.99

Grades: 6 7 8 9 10   **Fic**
  1. Baseball -- Fiction 2. Bereavement -- Fiction 3. Family life -- Fiction 4. Father-daughter relationship -- Fiction
  ISBN 978-1-4169-3847-7; 1-4169-3847-8
                         LC 2007-17067
High school freshman Ryan Walsh, a Chicago Cubs fan, meets Nick when they both skip school on opening day, and their blossoming relationship becomes difficult for Ryan when she discovers that Nick is seriously ill and she again feels the pain of losing her father five years earlier.
  "Smith deftly twines strands of grief, romance, baseball, family, and friendships lost and regained into this tale. . . . The present-tense narrative has an immediacy that will engage readers and the supporting cast is unusually vivid." Booklist

Smith, Patricia Clark
  Weetamoo, heart of the Pocassets. Scholastic 2003 203p il (Royal diaries) $10.95

Grades: 6 7 8 9   **Fic**
  1. Pocasset Indians 2. Native Americans -- Fiction
  ISBN 0-439-12910-9
                         LC 00-49243
The 1653-1654 diary of a fourteen-year-old Pocasset Indian girl, destined to become a leader of her tribe, describes how her life changes with the seasons, after a ritual fast she undertakes, and with her tribe's interaction with the English "Coat-men" of the nearby Plymouth Colony
  This is "a lively yet ultimately tragic tale that vividly evokes the time period." Booklist

Smith, Roland
  Cryptid hunters. Hyperion Books for Children 2005 348p $15.99; pa $5.99

Grades: 5 6 7 8   **Fic**
  1. Adventure fiction 2. Twins -- Fiction
  ISBN 0-7868-5161-9; 0-7868-5162-7 pa
Twins, Grace and Marty, along with a mysterious uncle, are dropped into the middle of the Congolese jungle in search of their missing photojournalist parents.
  "The action is nonstop in this well-paced jungle adventure, and Smith adds a deeper layer in scenes of Marty and Grace discovering truths about their complicated family relationships." Booklist

  Elephant run. Hyperion Books for Children 2007 318p $15.99

Grades: 6 7 8 9 10 11 12   **Fic**
  1. Elephants -- Fiction 2. Prisoners of war -- Fiction 3. World War, 1939-1945 -- Fiction
  ISBN 978-1-4231-0402-5; 1-4231-0402-1
                         LC 2007-13310
Nick endures servitude, beatings, and more after his British father's plantation in Burma is invaded by the Japanese in 1941.
  "The Burmese setting and the role of elephants in the lumbering industry are exceptionally well integrated into this wartime adventure tale." Bull Cent Child Books

  Eruption; Roland Smith. Scholastic Press 2012 156 p. (Storm runners.)

Grades: 5 6 7 8   **Fic**
  1. Circus -- Fiction 2. Rescue work -- Fiction 3. Volcanoes -- Mexico -- Fiction 4. Earthquakes -- Mexico -- Fiction 5. Father-son relationship -- Fiction 6. Survival -- Fiction 7. Volcanoes -- Fiction 8. Earthquakes -- Fiction 9. Storm chasers -- Fiction 10. Circus animals -- Fiction 11. Fathers and sons -- Fiction
  ISBN 0545081742; 9780545081740
                         LC 2011042743
In the third "installment in the 'Storm Runners' series, Chase and his father are off to Mexico to find the missing Rossi Family Circus. . . . [T]hey end up near a rumbling volcano. [Roland] Smith . . . gives the survival story an extra dose of octane with some escaped wild animals—in this case, a tiger that nearly devours Chase." (Booklist) ". . . [A]ll contact has been lost with the Rossi Brothers' Circus, on tour near Mexico City, in the wake of a major earthquake.

This sends a crew headed by catastrophe experts Chase and his father John to the rescue. . . . [They find themselves on] Popocatepetl's shaking, landslide ridden slopes amid clouds of ash to discover human corpses, dead elephants and big cats, desperados, trapped refugees, dozens of badly injured villagers and . . . an escaped tiger." (Kirkus)

I, Q.: book one, Independence Hall. Sleeping Bear Press 2008 302p pa $8.95

Grades: 5 6 7 8   **Fic**
    1. Adventure fiction 2. Spies -- Fiction 3. Terrorism -- Fiction
    ISBN 978-1-58536-325-4 pa; 1-58536-325-1 pa
In Philadelphia, Angela realizes she's being followed, and Q soon learns the secret about Angela's real mother, a former Secret Service agent
    "Adventure, suspense, humor, fascinating characters, and plot twists galore will draw middle-graders to this series starter." Booklist

I. Q.: book two, The White House. Sleeping Bear Press 2010 pa $8.95

Grades: 5 6 7 8   **Fic**
    1. Spies -- Fiction 2. Siblings -- Fiction 3. Terrorism -- Fiction 4. Remarriage -- Fiction
    ISBN 978-1-58536-456-5; 1-58536-456-8
                                                  LC 2011378292
Q (Quest) and Angela make it to the White House in Washington, D.C. to find that it is even harder to determine who are the 'good' and 'bad' guys than ever before.
    "This spellbinding James Bond genre espionage novel for the middle school set will leave readers breathlessly waiting for the next installment." Voice Youth Advocates

★ **Peak.** Harcourt 2007 246p $17

Grades: 7 8 9 10   **Fic**
    1. Mountaineering -- Fiction 2. Fathers and sons -- Fiction 3. Father-son relationship -- Fiction
    ISBN 978-0-15-202417-8
                                                  LC 2006024325
After fourteen-year-old Peak Marcello is arrested for scaling a New York City skyscraper, he is sent to live with his long-lost father, who wants him to be the youngest person to reach the Everest summit.
    "This is a thrilling, multifaceted adventure story. Smith includes plenty of mountaineering facts told in vivid detail. . . . But he also explores other issues, such as the selfishness that nearly always accompanies the intensely single-minded." Booklist

Storm runners. Scholastic Press 2011 143p $16.99

Grades: 5 6 7 8   **Fic**
    1. Hurricanes -- Fiction 2. Father-son relationship -- Fiction
    ISBN 978-0-545-08175-7; 0-545-08175-0
                                                  LC 2010-32720
Twelve-year-old Chase Masters travels the country with his father, a "storm runner," but he is tested in ways he never could have imagined when he and a new friend are caught in a hurricane near St. Petersburg, Florida.

"This is an exciting, quick read. . . . Readers will feel engaged with Chase and his friends in their struggles to survive." SLJ

Tentacles. Scholastic Press 2009 318p $16.99

Grades: 5 6 7 8   **Fic**
    1. Mystery fiction 2. Adventure fiction 3. Squids -- Fiction
    ISBN 978-0-545-16688-1; 0-545-16688-8
                                                  LC 2009011125
After the mysterious disappearance of their parents, Marty and Grace go to live with their scientist uncle and accompany him on, what soon becomes, an increasingly dangerous expedition to New Zealand to track a giant squid.

The **surge.** Scholastic Press 2011 133p il (Storm runners) $16.99

Grades: 5 6 7 8   **Fic**
    1. Circus -- Fiction 2. Storms -- Fiction 3. Hurricanes -- Fiction
    ISBN 978-0-545-08179-5; 0-545-08179-3
                                                  LC 2011017358
After barely surviving a terrifying hurricane, Chase and his friends Nicole and Rashawn have made it to the safety of Nicole's family farm, which is also the winter home of the Rossi Brothers Circus, where flood waters are rising and dangerous circus animals are on the loose.
    "A high-velocity page-turner." Kirkus

Smith, Sarah
The **other** side of dark. Atheneum Books for Young Readers 2010 312p $16.99

Grades: 6 7 8 9 10   **Fic**
    1. Ghost stories 2. Orphans -- Fiction 3. Supernatural -- Fiction 4. Race relations -- Fiction 5. African Americans -- Fiction
    ISBN 978-1-4424-0280-5; 1-4424-0280-6
                                                  LC 2010-14690
Since losing both of her parents, fifteen-year-old Katie can see and talk to ghosts, which makes her a loner until fellow student Law sees her drawing of a historic house and together they seek a treasure rumored to be hidden there by illegal slave-traders.
    The author "weaves complicated racial issues into a romantic, mysterious novel." Booklist

Smith, Sherri L.
★ **Flygirl.** G.P. Putnam's Sons 2009 275p $16.99

Grades: 7 8 9 10   **Fic**
    1. Air pilots -- Fiction 2. Women air pilots -- Fiction 3. African Americans -- Fiction 4. World War, 1939-1945 -- Fiction
    ISBN 978-0-399-24709-5; 0-399-24709-2
                                                  LC 2008-25407
During World War II, a light-skinned African American girl "passes" for white in order to join the Women Airforce Service Pilots.
    "The details about navigation are exciting, but tougher than any flight maneuver are Ida Mae's loneliness, shame, and fear that she will be thrown out of the the military, feelings that culminate in an unforgettable climax." Booklist

Snicket, Lemony, 1970-

★ **Who** could that be at this hour? by Lemony Snicket ; art by Seth. Little, Brown 2012 272 p. $15.99

Grades: 3 4 5 6 7   **Fic**
1. Bildungsromans 2. Humorous stories 3. Statues -- Fiction 4. Stealing -- Fiction 5. Apprentices -- Fiction 6. Mystery and detective stories
ISBN 0316123080; 9780316123082

LC 2012012657

This children's adventure mystery, by Lemony Snicket, begins in "Stain'd-by-the-Sea, the mostly deserted town where 12-year-old Lemony Snicket takes his first case as apprentice to chaperone S. Theodora Markson. They have been hired by Mrs. Murphy Sallis to retrieve a vastly valuable statue of the local legend, the Bombinating Beast. . . . With the help and/or hindrance of girls Moxie and Ellington, can Snicket keep his promises and come close to solving a mystery?" (Kirkus Reviews)

Sniegoski, Tom

Quest for the Spark; Book 2 written by Tom Sniegoski ; illustrated by Jeff Smith ; color by Steve Hamaker. Graphix 2012 234 p. $22.99

Grades: 4 5 6 7   **Fic**
1. Fantasy fiction 2. Magic -- Fiction 3. Adventure fiction 4. Dreams -- Fiction 5. Dragons -- Fiction 6. Fantasy 7. Humorous stories 8. Heroes -- Fiction 9. Adventure and adventurers -- Fiction
ISBN 9780545141031; 9780545141048

LC 2011020281

This book is set in the world of illustrator Jeff Smith's "Bone" graphic novels. Here, author Tom Sniegoski tells the story of "Tom, a Valley turnip farmer" who "receives a vision that the peaceful otherworld of the Dreaming is under attack. The evil Nacht, a renegade Dragon, seeks to control the dreamland, and through it, the Waking World as well. A mysterious forest woman tells Tom that he has been chosen to lead a quest to find the scattered pieces of the Spark--the light of creation that can drive back the dark power. When his family falls under the Nacht's corrupted sleep spell, Tom realizes that he has no choice and sets out with his best friend, a talking raccoon." (School Libr J)

Quest for the spark; book one. written by Tom Sniegoski; illustrated by Jeff Smith; color by Steve Hamaker. Graphix 2011 218p il (Bone) $22.99; pa $10.99

Grades: 4 5 6 7   **Fic**
1. Fantasy fiction 2. Adventure fiction 3. Magic -- Fiction 4. Dreams -- Fiction 5. Heroes and heroines -- Fiction
ISBN 978-0-545-14101-7; 0-545-14101-X; 978-0-545-14102-4 pa; 0-545-14102-8 pa

LC 2010017002

Twelve-year-old Tom Elm, his raccoon friend Roderick, Percival, Abbey, and Barclay Bone, warrior-priest Randolf, and forest-woman Lorimar join in a quest to find the pieces of the Spark that can save Dreaming—and the Waking World—from a Darkness created by the Nacht.

"At long last . . . we return to the Valley that was the setting for Smith's comics-landscape-changing Bone, though this adventure takes place in prose rather than panels. . . . As long as fans are not expecting a repeat of the old magic and not too disappointed that there isn't nearly enough of Smith's always excellent full-color, full-page artwork helping out, it looks as if they're in for a cheery jaunt back through a beloved world." Booklist

Sleeper code; by Tom Sniegoski. Razorbill 2006 278p (Sleeper conspiracy) pa $6.99

Grades: 8 9 10 11 12   **Fic**
1. Conspiracies -- Fiction 2. Sleep disorders -- Fiction 3. Multiple personality -- Fiction
ISBN 1-59514-052-2

LC 2006009102

Just when he has met a beautiful girl and his outlook is improving, sixteen-year-old narcoleptic Tom Lovett begins to suspect that his dreams and hallucinations of killing people may be something more real and terrifying.

"Readers looking for fast-paced action and espionage will enjoy this first book in the two-part Sleeper Conspiracy." SLJ

Snow, Alan

Here be monsters! an adventure involving magic, trolls, and other creatures. written and illustrated by Alan Snow. Atheneum Books for Young Readers 2006 529p il (The Ratbridge chronicles) $17.95; pa $8.99

Grades: 4 5 6 7   **Fic**
1. Fantasy fiction 2. Monsters -- Fiction
ISBN 978-0-689-87047-7; 0-689-87047-7; 978-0-689-87048-4 pa; 0-689-87048-5 pa

LC 2005-24438

While gathering food to bring to his grandfather, young Arthur becomes trapped in the city of Ratbridge, where he and some new friends try to stop a plot to shrink the monsters of Arthur's home, the Underworld, for a nefarious purpose

"Helpful in creating the settings and bringing the more fantastic characters to life, the illustrations, which are often amusing, also make the book accessible to younger children who like lengthy books. Snow's inventive fantasy . . . combines stout hearts, terrible troubles, and inspired lunacy." Booklist

Snow, Carol

Snap. HarperTeen 2009 221p $16.99

Grades: 7 8 9 10   **Fic**
1. Beaches -- Fiction 2. Cameras -- Fiction 3. Friendship -- Fiction 4. Family life -- Fiction 5. Photography -- Fiction 6. Supernatural -- Fiction
ISBN 978-0-06-145211-6; 0-06-145211-4

LC 2009-14581

When fifteen-year-old Madison's parents, who are having problems, bring her to a seedy beachside town, she relies on some quirky new friends for help figuring out how her camera is taking pictures of people who are not there, and who later suffer tragedies.

"Snow's novel is a page-turning blend of romance, mystery, and the supernatural. . . . Characters are well developed." SLJ

Switch. HarperTeen 2008 215p $16.99; pa $8.99

Grades: 8 9 10 11 12   **Fic**

1. Supernatural -- Fiction
ISBN 978-0-06-145208-6; 0-06-145208-4; 978-0-06-145210-9 pa; 0-06-145210-6 pa

LC 2008020220

Living in a small beach community with her mother, fifteen-year-old Claire, an accomplished swimmer, discovers that, like her long-dead but, still very much present, grandmother, she has the ability to inhabit other people's bodies while asleep.

"Claire's quick-paced narration comes laced with bolts of sarcasm; the realistic problems blend successfully into a suspenseful, mystical story." Kirkus

Snow, Maya

Sisters of the sword. HarperCollins 2008 275p (Sisters of the sword) $16.99; lib bdg $17.89; pa $6.99

Grades: 5 6 7 8   **Fic**

1. Samurai -- Fiction 2. Sisters -- Fiction 3. Sex role -- Fiction 4. Young adult literature -- Works
ISBN 978-0-06-124387-5; 0-06-124387-6; 978-0-06-124388-2 lib bdg; 0-06-124388-4 lib bdg; 978-0-06-124389-9 pa; 0-06-124389-2 pa

LC 2007-029610

Two aristocratic sisters in ancient Japan disguise themselves as samurai warriors to take revenge on the uncle who betrayed their family.

"This rousing new series . . . starts off with a bang, or more accurately, the silent thrust of a sword." Booklist

Other titles in this series are:
Chasing the secret (2009)
Journey through fire (2009)

Snyder, Laurel

Any which wall; drawings by LeUyen Pham. Random House 2009 242p il $16.99; lib bdg $19.99

Grades: 4 5 6 7   **Fic**

1. Magic -- Fiction 2. Wishes -- Fiction 3. Siblings -- Fiction 4. Space and time -- Fiction
ISBN 978-0-375-85560-3; 0-375-85560-2; 978-0-375-95560-0 lib bdg; 0-375-95560-7 lib bdg

LC 2008-22605

In the middle of an Iowa cornfield, four children find a magic wall that enables them to travel through time and space.

"Snyder's fresh, down-to-earth voice is complemented by Pham's energetic illustrations, which seem at once retro and modern. Fantasy fans will enjoy this novel, but so will readers who like stories about ordinary kids." SLJ

Snyder, Zilpha Keatley

William S. and the great escape. Atheneum Books for Young Readers 2009 214p $16.99

Grades: 5 6 7 8   **Fic**

1. Acting -- Fiction 2. Siblings -- Fiction
ISBN 978-1-4169-6763-7; 1-4169-6763-X

LC 2008-10377

In 1938, twelve-year-old William has already decided to leave home when his younger sister informs him that she and their brother and sister are going too, and right away, but complications arise when an acquaintance decides to "help" them.

"Wit and pluck are rewarded in this quick-paced, high-drama adventure, which may also whet young appetites for Shakespeare." Publ Wkly

William's midsummer dreams. Atheneum Books for Young Readers 2011 209p $17.99

Grades: 5 6 7 8   **Fic**

1. Aunts -- Fiction 2. Acting -- Fiction 3. Theater -- Fiction 4. Adoption -- Fiction 5. Siblings -- Fiction
ISBN 978-1-4424-1997-1; 9781442419995 e-book

LC 2010036958

Now permanently settled with Aunt Fiona, who has adopted him and his siblings, thirteen-year-old William gets the chance to play Puck in a professional production of A Midsummer Night's Dream.

"An adventure story with a lot to say about identity, ambition and character." Kirkus

The **magic** nation thing; [by] Zilpha Keatley Snyder. Delacorte Press 2005 164p hardcover o.p. pa $6.50

Grades: 4 5 6 7   **Fic**

1. Extrasensory perception -- Fiction
ISBN 0-385-73085-3; 0-440-41931-X pa

LC 2004-10105

Although twelve-year-old Abby has always tried to deny that she has some kind of weird psychic power, she takes advantage of it to help her mother, a struggling private investigator, and, more importantly, to find her best friend's little brother when he goes missing at a ski resort

"Readers will delight in Snyder's vivid descriptions of Abby's special powers, but what will draw them most is the warm, believable story." Booklist

Somper, Justin

Demons of the ocean. Little, Brown 2006 330p (Vampirates) $15.99

Grades: 6 7 8 9   **Fic**

1. Adventure fiction 2. Twins -- Fiction 3. Pirates -- Fiction 4. Vampires -- Fiction
ISBN 0-316-01373-0

When twins Connor and Grace's ship is wrecked in a storm and Connor is rescued by pirates, he believes that Grace has been taken aboard the mythical Vampirate's ship, and he is determined to find her.

"This winning fantasy features both pirates and vampires with adventure, bloodcurling action, and sinister characters." Voice Youth Advocates

Other titles in this series are:
Tide of terror (2007)
Blood Captain (2008)
Black heart (2009)
Empire of night (2010)

Son, John

Finding my hat. Orchard Bks. 2003 185p (First person fiction) $16.95; pa $6.99

Grades: 5 6 7 8   **Fic**
1. Family life -- Fiction 2. Korean Americans -- Fiction
ISBN 0-439-43538-2; 0-439-43539-0 pa
LC 2002-44998
Jin-Han describes his life growing up with his mother and father, immigrants from Korea, and his little sister as they move to different cities with his parents' business
This is "a beautifully written and deeply personal account of growing up." SLJ

Sones, Sonya
Stop pretending; what happened when my big sister went crazy. HarperCollins Pubs. 1999 149p lib bdg $14.89; pa $6.99
Grades: 6 7 8 9   **Fic**
1. Sisters -- Fiction 2. Mental illness -- Fiction
ISBN 0-06-028386-6 lib bdg; 0-06-446218-8 pa
LC 99-11473
"Based on the journals Sones wrote at the age of 13 when her 19-year-old sister was hospitalized due to manic depression, the simply crafted but deeply felt poems reflect her thoughts, fears, hopes, and dreams during that troubling time." SLJ

★ **What** my girlfriend doesn't know. Simon & Schuster Books for Young Readers 2007 291p $16.99
Grades: 7 8 9 10   **Fic**
1. School stories 2. Artists -- Fiction 3. Dating (Social customs) -- Fiction
ISBN 978-0-689-87602-8; 0-689-87602-5
LC 2006-14682
Fourteen-year-old Robin Murphy is so unpopular at high school that his name is slang for "loser," and so when he begins dating the beautiful and popular Sophie her reputation plummets, but he finds acceptance as a student in a drawing class at Harvard.
"Robin's believable voice is distinctive, and Sones uses her spare words (and a few drawings) to expert effect." Booklist

What my mother doesn't know. Simon & Schuster Bks. for Young Readers 2001 259p hardcover o.p. pa $7.99
Grades: 7 8 9 10   **Fic**
1. Love 2. Novels in verse 3. Dating (Social customs) -- Fiction
ISBN 0-689-84114-0; 0-689-85553-2 pa
LC 00-52634
This is "a fast, funny, touching book. . . . The very short, sometimes rhythmic lines make each page fly. Sophie's voice is colloquial and intimate." Booklist

Sonnenblick, Jordan
★ **After** ever after. Scholastic Press 2010 260p $16.99
Grades: 5 6 7 8   **Fic**
1. School stories 2. Cancer -- Fiction 3. Friendship -- Fiction 4. Family life -- Fiction
ISBN 978-0-439-83706-4; 0-439-83706-5

Jeffery's cancer is in remission but the chemotherapy and radiation treatments have left him with concentration problems, and he worries about school work, his friends, his family, and a girl who likes him
"Sonnenblick imbues Jeffrey with a smooth, likable, and unaffected voice. . . . As hilarious as it is tragic, and as honest as it is hopeful . . . [this book is] irresistable reading." Booklist

Drums, girls, & dangerous pie. Scholastic Press 2005 273p $16.99
Grades: 5 6 7 8   **Fic**
1. Brothers -- Fiction 2. Leukemia -- Fiction
ISBN 0-439-75519-0
LC 2004-62563
First published 2004 by Turning Tide Press
When his younger brother is diagnosed with leukemia, thirteen-year-old Steven tries to deal with his complicated emotions, his school life, and his desire to support his family.
"A story that could have morphed into melodrama is saved by reality, rawness, and the wit Sonnenblick infuses into Steven's first-person voice." Booklist

★ **Notes** from the midnight driver. Scholastic Press 2006 265p $16.99
Grades: 8 9 10 11 12   **Fic**
1. Old age -- Fiction 2. Musicians -- Fiction 3. Friendship -- Fiction
ISBN 0-439-75779-7
LC 2005-27972
After being assigned to perform community service at a nursing home, sixteen-year-old Alex befriends a cantankerous old man who has some lessons to impart about jazz guitar playing, love, and forgiveness.
The author "deftly infiltrates the teenage mind to produce a first-person narrative riddled with enough hapless confusion, mulish equivocation, and beleaguered deadpan humor to have readers nodding with recognition, sighing with sympathy, and gasping with laughter—often on the same page." Horn Book

★ **Zen** and the art of faking it. Scholastic Press 2007 264p $16.99; pa $7.99
Grades: 5 6 7 8   **Fic**
1. School stories 2. Zen Buddhism -- Fiction 3. Asian Americans -- Fiction
ISBN 978-0-439-83707-1; 0-439-83707-3; 978-0-439-83709-5 pa; 0-439-83709-X pa
LC 2006-28841
When thirteen-year-old San Lee moves to a new town and school for the umpteenth time, he is looking for a way to stand out when his knowledge of Zen Buddhism, gained in his previous school, provides the answer—and the need to quickly become a convincing Zen master.
The author gives readers "plenty to laugh at. . . . Mixed with more serious scenes, . . . lighter moments take a basic message about the importance of honesty and forgiveness and treat it with panache." Publ Wkly

Sorrells, Walter
Erratum; 1st ed.; Dutton 2008 298p $17.99

Grades: 4 5 6 7 **Fic**
1. Science fiction 2. Space and time -- Fiction 3. Books and reading -- Fiction
ISBN 978-0-525-47832-4; 0-525-47832-9
LC 2007052647

When Jessica finds--and then loses--an unfinished book about her life, she learns that if she cannot keep it from falling into the wrong hands, the balance of the universe is in peril.

"Highly imaginative, fast-paced and a bit disorienting. . . . Sorrell presents a stew of hearty concepts, including string theory, alternate dimensions and mind control. Readers with a taste for science or science fiction will be especially intrigued." Publ Wkly

★ **First** shot. Dutton Children's Books 2007 279p hardcover o.p. pa $7.99
Grades: 7 8 9 10 11 12 **Fic**
1. Mystery fiction 2. Homicide -- Fiction 3. Father-son relationship -- Fiction
ISBN 978-0-525-47801-0; 0-525-47801-9; 978-0-14-241421-7 pa; 0-14-241421-2 pa

As David enters his senior year of high school, a family secret emerges that could solve the mystery of why his mother was murdered two years ago.

"David's first person narration pulls readers into the young man's torment. . . . This is a fast-paced, intriguing read." Booklist

Whiteout. Dutton Children's Books 2009 312p (Hunted) $15.99
Grades: 7 8 9 10 **Fic**
1. Mystery fiction 2. Homicide -- Fiction 3. Blizzards -- Fiction 4. Mother-daughter relationship -- Fiction
ISBN 978-0-525-42141-2; 0-525-42141-6

Sixteen-year-old Chass makes her way through a Minnesota blizzard, seeking not only the murderer of a beloved music teacher, but also something belonging to the killer who has been chasing her mother and herself around the country.

"There is . . . plenty of suspense to propel even a reluctant reader, and a number of false turns to keep the reader guessing." Voice Youth Advocates

Soto, Gary, 1952-
Accidental love; [by] Gary Soto. Harcourt 2006 179p $16
Grades: 6 7 8 9 **Fic**
1. Love stories 2. School stories 3. Hispanic Americans -- Fiction
ISBN 0-15-205497-9
LC 2004-29900

After unexpectedly falling in love with a "nerdy" boy, fourteen-year-old Marisa works to change her life by transferring to another school, altering some of her behavior, and losing weight.

This is a "warmhearted, humorous novel." SLJ

★ **Buried** onions. Harcourt Brace & Co. 1997 149p hardcover o.p. pa $6.95

Grades: 8 9 10 11 12 **Fic**
1. Violence -- Fiction 2. Mexican Americans -- Fiction
ISBN 0-15-201333-4; 0-15-206265-3 pa
LC 96-53112

When nineteen-year-old Eddie drops out of college, he struggles to find a place for himself as a Mexican American living in a violence-infested neighborhood of Fresno, California.

"Soto has created a beautiful, touching, and truthful story. . . . The lyrical language and Spanish phrases add to the immediacy of setting and to the sensitivity the author brings to his character's life." Voice Youth Advocates

★ **Taking** sides. Harcourt Brace Jovanovich 1991 138p hardcover o.p. pa $5.95
Grades: 5 6 7 8 **Fic**
1. Basketball -- Fiction 2. Hispanic Americans -- Fiction
ISBN 0-15-284076-1; 0-15-204694-1 pa
LC 91-11082

Fourteen-year-old Lincoln Mendoza, an aspiring basketball player, must come to terms with his divided loyalties when he moves from the Hispanic inner city to a white suburban neighborhood

This is a "light but appealing story. . . . Because of its subject matter and its clear, straightforward prose, it will be especially good for reluctant readers." SLJ

Includes glossary

Sparrow, Rebecca
The **year** Nick McGowan came to stay; [by] Rebecca Sparrow. 1st American ed.; Alfred A. Knopf 2008 198p $15.99; lib bdg $18.99
Grades: 8 9 10 11 **Fic**
1. School stories
ISBN 978-0-375-84570-3; 0-375-84570-4; 978-0-375-94570-0 lib bdg; 0-375-84570-9 lib bdg
LC 2007020758

First published 2006 in Australia

In her final year of high school in 1989, Australian teenager Rachel has her world turned upside down when the most popular (and disturbed) boy in school comes to live with her family for a semester.

"This book is full of laugh-out-loud moments. . . . Sparrow is adept at accurately portraying her teenage characters and placing them in realistic scenarios that most readers will find pertinent." SLJ

Speare, Elizabeth George
★ The **sign** of the beaver. Houghton Mifflin 1983 135p $16
Grades: 5 6 7 8 **Fic**
1. Friendship -- Fiction 2. Native Americans -- Fiction 3. Frontier and pioneer life -- Fiction
ISBN 0-395-33890-5
LC 83-118

A Newbery Medal honor book, 1984

Left alone to guard the family's wilderness home in eighteenth-century Maine, Matt is hard-pressed to survive until local Indians teach him their skills

Matt "begins to understand the Indians' ingenuity and respect for nature and the devastating impact of the encroachment of the white man. In a quiet but not unsuspenseful story . . . the author articulates historical facts along with the adventures and the thoughts, emotions, and developing insights of a young adolescent." Horn Book

★ The **witch** of Blackbird Pond. Houghton Mifflin 1958 249p $17

Grades: 6 7 8 9   **Fic**

1. Puritans -- Fiction 2. Witchcraft -- Fiction
ISBN 0-395-07114-3

LC 58-11063

Awarded the Newbery Medal, 1959

"Headstrong and undisciplined, Barbados-bred Kit Tyler is an embarrassment to her Puritan relatives, and her sincere attempts to aid a reputed witch soon bring her to trial as a suspect." Child Books Too Good to Miss

Speare, Elizabeth George, 1908-1994

Calico Captive; illustrated by W. T. Mars. Sandpiper 2001 274p ill. (pbk.) $6.95

Grades: 6 7 8   **Fic**

1. Historical fiction 2. Prisoners -- Fiction 3. Native Americans -- Fiction 4. United States -- History -- 1755-1763, French and Indian War -- Fiction
ISBN 9780618150762

LC 57009017

In this book, set "[i]n the year 1754, the stillness of Charlestown, New Hampshire, is shattered by the terrifying cries of an Indian raid. Young Miriam Willard . . . finds herself . . . a captive on a forest trail, caught up in the ebb and flow of the French and Indian War. It is a harrowing march north. . . . At the end of the trail waits a life of hard work and, perhaps, even a life of slavery. . . . Miriam and her companions finally reach Montreal, a city of shifting loyalties filled with the intrigue of war, and here, by a sudden twist of fortune, Miriam meets the prominent Du Quesne family, who introduce her to a life she has never imagined. Based on an actual narrative diary published in 1807, . . . [the book] reenacts a . . . facet of history." (Publisher's note)

Spillebeen, Geert

Age 14; translated by Terese Edelstein. Houghton Mifflin 2009 216p $16

Grades: 8 9 10 11 12   **Fic**

1. Soldiers -- Fiction 2. World War, 1914-1918 -- Fiction
ISBN 978-0-547-05342-4; 0-547-05342-8

LC 2010-277732

"Based on a true story, this spare, powerful novel . . . focuses on Patrick, a poor Irish kid who is just 13 when war breaks out. He dreams of escaping his dreary future and abusive dad and finding adventure and glory in the army. . . . The recruiters knowingly accept him into the service when he claims that he is a 17-year-old named John. . . . Spillebeen brings to the story to a realistic, grim conclusion." Booklist

Kipling's choice; written by Geert Spillebeen; translated by Terese Edelstein. Houghton Mifflin Co 2005 147p $16; pa $7.99

Grades: 7 8 9 10   **Fic**

1. Army officers 2. Children of prominent persons 3.

World War, 1914-1918 -- Fiction
ISBN 0-618-43124-1; 0-618-80035-2 pa

LC 2004-20856

In 1915, mortally wounded in Loos, France, eighteen-year-old John Kipling, son of writer Rudyard Kipling, remembers his boyhood and the events leading to what is to be his first and last World War I battle.

"This well-written novel combines facts with speculation about John Kipling's short life and gruesome death. A riveting account of World War I." SLJ

Spinelli, Jerry

★ **Crash**. Knopf 1996 162p hardcover o.p. pa $6.99; lib bdg $17.99

Grades: 5 6 7 8   **Fic**

1. Football -- Fiction 2. Friendship -- Fiction 3. Grandfathers -- Fiction
ISBN 0440238579; 0679879579; 0679979573

LC 95030942

"Crash is a star football player. He torments Penn, a classmate who is everything Crash is not—friendly, small, and a pacifist. When his beloved grandfather comes to live with his family and suffers a debilitating stroke, Crash begins to see value in many of the things he has scorned." Horn Book Guide

Hokey Pokey; by Jerry Spinelli. Alfred A. Knopf Books for Young Readers 2013 304 p. (hard cover) $15.99

Grades: 5 6 7 8   **Fic**

1. Bildungsromans 2. Fantasy fiction 3. Imaginary places 4. Play -- Fiction 5. Growth -- Fiction
ISBN 0375831983; 9780307975706; 9780375831980; 9780375832017; 9780375931987

LC 2012004177

In this book, Jerry Spinelli "creates a surreal landscape." There are no adults in "Hokey Pokey, where boys and girls dine on flavored ice and spend their days watching cartoons, playing cowboy games, and using their bicycles as trusty steeds. Jack's bike, Scramjet, is . . . stolen by his archenemy, Jubilee. This marks the first of a series of unsettling events that give Jack, a boy on the brink of adolescence, the eerie impression that 'things have shifted.'" (Publishers Weekly)

Jake and Lily; Jerry Spinelli. 1st ed. Balzer + Bray 2012 335 p. (hardback) $15.99

Grades: 3 4 5 6 7   **Fic**

1. Twins -- Fiction 2. Bullies -- Fiction 3. Children's stories 4. Friendship -- Fiction 5. Individuality -- Fiction 6. Brothers and sisters -- Fiction
ISBN 9780060281359; 9780060281366

LC 2011053362

This book offers a "story about a pair of twins growing apart. For almost as long as they can remember, Jake and Lily have shared a 'special sense,' which they call 'goombla.' . . . Lily tries to find out who she is without her brother, but it's hard work, and most of her attempts are unsuccessful. . . . Though the twins eventually rediscover their 'goombla,' . . . [author Jerry] Spinelli doesn't suggest that the two will go back to being the people they once were." (Publishers Weekly)

★ **Maniac** Magee; a novel. Little, Brown 1990
184p $16.99; pa $6.99

Grades: 5 6 7 8 **Fic**

1. Orphans -- Fiction 2. Race relations -- Fiction 3.
Homeless persons -- Fiction

ISBN 0-316-80722-2; 0-316-80906-3 pa

LC 89-27144

Awarded the Newbery Medal, 1991

"Orphaned at three, Jeffery Lionel Magee, after eight
unhappy years with relatives, one day takes off running. A
year later, he ends up 200 miles away in Two Mills, a highly
segregated community. Part tall tale and part contemporary
realistic fiction, this unusual novel magically weaves timely issues of homelessness, racial prejudice, and illiteracy
into an energetic story that bursts with creativity, enthusiasm, and hope for the future. In short, it's a celebration of
life." Booklist

Smiles to go. Joanna Cotler Books 2008 248p
$16.99; lib bdg $17.89; pa $6.99

Grades: 6 7 8 9 10 **Fic**

1. School stories 2. Siblings -- Fiction 3. Friendship
-- Fiction 4. Family life -- Fiction

ISBN 978-0-06-028133-5; 0-06-028133-2; 978-0-06-
028134-2 lib bdg; 0-06-028134-0 lib bdg; 978-0-06-
447197-8 pa; 0-06-447197-7 pa

LC 2007-29563

Will Tuppence's life has always been ruled by science
and common sense but in ninth grade, shaken up by the discovery that protons decay, he begins to see the entire world
differently and gains new perspective on his relationships
with his little sister and two closest friends.

"What makes a Spinelli novel isn't plotting so much as
character, dialogue, voice and humor. The Spinelli touch
remains true in this funny and thoroughly enjoyable read."
Publ Wkly

★ **Stargirl**. Knopf 2000 186p $15.95; lib bdg
$17.99; pa $8.95

Grades: 7 8 9 10 **Fic**

1. School stories

ISBN 0-679-88637-0; 0-679-98637-5 lib bdg; 0-375-
82233-X pa

LC 99-87944

In this story about the perils of popularity, the courage
of nonconformity, and the thrill of first love, an eccentric
student named Stargirl changes Mica High School forever

"As always respectful of his audience, Spinelli poses
searching questions about loyalty to one's friends and
oneself and leaves readers to form their own answers."
Publ Wkly

Another title about Stargirl is:
Love, Stargirl (2007)

There's a girl in my hammerlock. Simon &
Schuster Bks. for Young Readers 1991 199p hardcover o.p. pa $5.99

Grades: 5 6 7 8 **Fic**

1. School stories 2. Sex role -- Fiction 3. Wrestling
-- Fiction

ISBN 1-4169-3937-7 pa

LC 91-8765

Thirteen-year-old Maisie joins her school's formerly
all-male wrestling team and tries to last through the season,
despite opposition from other students, her best friend, and
her own teammates

The author "tackles a meaty subject—traditional gender
roles—with his usual humor and finesse. The result, written
in a breezy, first-person style, is a rattling good sports story
that is clever, witty and tightly written." Publ Wkly

★ **Wringer**. HarperCollins Pubs. 1997 228p
$16.99; lib bdg $16.89; pa $6.50

Grades: 4 5 6 7 **Fic**

1. Courage -- Fiction 2. Pigeons -- Fiction 3. Violence
-- Fiction

ISBN 0-06-024913-7; 0-06-024914-5 lib bdg; 0-06-
440578-8 pa

LC 96-37897

A Newbery Medal honor book, 1998

"During the annual pigeon shoot, it is a town tradition
for 10-year-old boys to break the necks of wounded birds.
In this riveting story told with verve and suspense, Palmer
rebels." SLJ

Spinner, Stephanie

Damosel; in which the Lady of the Lake renders
a frank and often startling account of her wondrous
life and times. Alfred A. Knopf 2008 198p $16.99;
lib bdg $19.99

Grades: 7 8 9 10 **Fic**

1. Kings 2. Magic -- Fiction 3. Dwarfs -- Fiction 4.
Fools and jesters -- Fiction

ISBN 978-0-375-83634-3; 0-375-83634-9; 978-0-375-
93634-0 lib bdg; 0-375-93634-3 lib bdg

LC 2007-43519

Damosel, a rule-bound Lady of the Lake, and Twixt, a
seventeen-year-old dwarf, relate their experiences as they
strive to help King Arthur face Morgause, Morgan, and
Mordred, one through her magic and the other through his
humble loyalty.

"The magic is exciting and palpable. . . . Spinner's elegant language, strong characterizations, energetic dialogue, and lively plot combine in a memorable, accessible
novel." Booklist

Quicksilver. Knopf 2005 229p hardcover o.p.
pa $5.99

Grades: 7 8 9 10 **Fic**

1. Classical mythology -- Fiction

ISBN 0-375-82638-6; 0-440-23845-5 pa

LC 2004-10311

Hermes, Prince of Thieves and son of Zeus, relates why
the seasons change, the history of the Trojan War, his friendship with Pegasus, and many more adventures.

"Spinner seamlessly weaves necessary background information about the cast of celestial characters into a narrative filled with thrilling action and violence that is drawn
straight from the original stories. Teens will connect with
Hermes' immediate, often very funny voice." Booklist

Quiver. Knopf 2002 177p $15.95; lib bdg
$17.99; pa $5.99

Grades: 7 8 9 10 **Fic**

1. Atalanta (Greek mythology) -- Fiction
ISBN 0-375-81489-2; 0-375-91489-7 lib bdg; 0-440-23819-6 pa

LC 2002-5451

When her father commands that she produce an heir, the huntress Atalanta gives her suitors a seemingly impossible task in order to uphold her pledge of chastity, as the gods of ancient Greece look on

"Spinner gives this Greek myth a fresh face and makes Atalanta a strong heroine." SLJ

Spooner, Michael

Last Child. Henry Holt 2005 230p $16.95

Grades: 7 8 9 10 **Fic**

1. Smallpox -- Fiction 2. Mandan Indians -- Fiction
ISBN 0-8050-7739-1

LC 2005-9957

"Action-packed prose; sharp, witty dialogue; and strong characterization make this novel an entertaining read." Voice Youth Advocates

Spradlin, Michael P.

Keeper of the Grail. G.P. Putnam's Sons 2008 248p (The youngest Templar) $17.99

Grades: 6 7 8 9 **Fic**

1. Grail -- Fiction 2. Crusades -- Fiction 3. Middle Ages -- Fiction
ISBN 978-0-399-24763-7; 0-399-24763-7

LC 2007-36143

In 1191, fifteen-year-old Tristan, a youth of unknown origin raised in an English abbey, becomes a Templar Knight's squire during the Third Crusade and soon finds himself on a mission to bring the Holy Grail to safety.

"The deadly action, uncompromising in many of its descriptions, may take center stage, but Spradlin smartly doesn't neglect story. . . . The stirring story ends with a true cliff-hanger, priming fans for the next installment." Booklist

Other titles in this series are:

Trail of fate (2009)

Orphan of destiny (2010)

Springer, Kristina

My fake boyfriend is better than yours. Farrar, Straus and Giroux 2010 180p $15.99

Grades: 5 6 7 **Fic**

1. Honesty -- Fiction 2. Friendship -- Fiction 3. Imagination -- Fiction
ISBN 978-0-374-39910-8; 0-374-39910-7

LC 2009-32981

When her best friend Sea returns from her summer vacation claiming to have a boyfriend, twelve-year-old Tori is sure she is lying and makes up her own boyfriend, who just so happens to do everything better than Sea's boyfriend.

"Springer writes in authentic tween language. . . . Tori is a well-rounded character, both likable and relatable. The themes will resonate with any girl who's ever gone through the hardships of middle school. . . . A fun read." SLJ

Springer, Nancy

I am Mordred; a tale from Camelot. Philomel Bks. 1998 184p hardcover o.p. pa $6.99

Grades: 7 8 9 10 **Fic**

1. Mordred (Legendary character) -- Fiction
ISBN 0-399-23143-9; 0-698-11841-3 pa

LC 97-39740

"Springer humanizes Arthurian archvillain Mordred in a thoroughly captivating and poignant tale." Booklist

I am Morgan le Fay; a tale from Camelot. Philomel Bks. 2001 227p hardcover o.p. pa $5.99

Grades: 7 8 9 10 **Fic**

1. Morgan le Fay (Legendary character)
ISBN 0-399-23451-9; 0-698-11974-6 pa

LC 99-52847

In a war-torn England where her half-brother Arthur will eventually become king, the young Morgan le Fay comes to realize that she has magic powers and links to the faerie world

"Introspective, yet threaded with intrigue and adventure, this compelling study of the legendary villainess explores the ways that love, hate, jealousy, and the desire for power shape one young woman's fate and affect the destiny of others." Horn Book

★ **Rowan** Hood, outlaw girl of Sherwood Forest. Philomel Bks. 2001 170p hardcover o.p. pa $5.99

Grades: 4 5 6 7 **Fic**

1. Adventure fiction 2. Middle Ages -- Fiction 3. Robin Hood (Legendary character) -- Fiction
ISBN 0-399-23368-7; 0-698-11972-X pa

LC 00-63694

In her quest to connect with Robin Hood, the father she has never met, thirteen-year-old Rosemary disguises herself as a boy, befriends a half-wolf, half-dog, a runaway princess, and an overgrown boy whose singing is hypnotic, and makes peace with her elfin heritage

"This tale is a charmer, filled with exciting action, plenty of humor, engaging characters, and a nice fantasy twist." Booklist

Other titles about Rowan Hood are:

Lionclaw (2002)

Outlaw princess of Sherwood (2003)

Wild boy (2004)

Rowan Hood returns (2005)

★ The **case** of the missing marquess; an Enola Holmes mystery. Philomel Books 2006 216p pa $6.99; $10.99

Grades: 5 6 7 8 **Fic**

1. Mystery fiction 2. Missing persons -- Fiction
ISBN 0-14-240933-2 pa; 0-399-24304-6

Enola Holmes, much younger sister of detective Sherlock Holmes, must travel to London in disguise to unravel the disappearance of her missing mother. "Grades four to eight." (Bull Cent Child Books)

"Enola's loneliness, intelligence, sense of humor, and sheer pluck make her an extremely appealing heroine." SLJ

Other titles about Enola Holmes are:

The case of the left-handed lady (2007)

The case of the bizarre bouquets (2008)

The case of the peculiar pink fan (2008)

The case of the cryptic crinoline (2009)

The case of the gypsy good-bye (2010)

St. Crow, Lili

Strange angels. Razorbill 2009 293p pa $9.99
Grades: 8 9 10 11 12   **Fic**
  1. Orphans -- Fiction 2. Vampires -- Fiction 3.
Werewolves -- Fiction 4. Supernatural -- Fiction 5.
Extrasensory perception -- Fiction
ISBN 978-1-59514-251-1; 1-59514-251-7
                                      LC 2008-39720
Sixteen-year-old Dru's psychic abilities helped her fa-
ther battle zombies and other creatures of the "Real World,"
but now she must rely on herself, a "werwulf"-bitten friend,
and a half-human vampire hunter to learn who murdered her
parents, and why.
  "The book grabs readers by the throat, sets hearts beating
loudly and never lets go." Kirkus
  Other titles in this series are:
  Betrayals (2009)
  Defiance (2011)
  Jealousy (2010)

St. John, Lauren

The **white** giraffe; illustrated by David Dean.
Dial Books for Young Readers 2007 180p il $16.99;
pa $6.99
Grades: 4 5 6 7   **Fic**
  1. Orphans -- Fiction 2. Giraffes -- Fiction 3. Mythical
animals -- Fiction
ISBN 978-0-8037-3211-7; 0-8037-3211-2; 978-0-14-
241152-0 pa; 0-14-241152-3 pa
                                      LC 2006-21323
After a fire kills her parents, eleven-year-old Martine
must leave England to live with her grandmother on a wild-
life game reserve in South Africa, where she befriends a
mythical white giraffe
  "The story is captivating and well spun." SLJ
  Other titles in this series are:
  Dolphin song (2008)
  Last leopard (2009)
  The elephant's tale (2010)

Stahler, David

Doppelganger; [by] David Stahler, Jr. Harper-
Collins Publishers 2006 258p hardcover o.p. pa
$8.99
Grades: 8 9 10 11 12   **Fic**
  1. Horror fiction 2. Child abuse -- Fiction 3. Family
life -- Fiction 4. Supernatural -- Fiction
ISBN 978-0-06-087232-8; 0-06-087232-2; 978-0-06-
087234-2 pa; 0-06-087234-9 pa
                                      LC 2005-28484
When a sixteen-year-old member of a race of shape-
shifting killers called doppelgangers assumes the life of a
troubled teen, he becomes unexpectedly embroiled in human
life—and it is nothing like what he has seen on television.
  "This brooding story of literally stepping into someone
else's shoes combines romance, horror, and angst to create
a distinctive story of redemption. The abusive relationships
in Chris's family are portrayed with realism and sensitivity."
Voice Youth Advocates

Spinning out; by David Stahler Jr. Chronicle
Books 2012 285p $16.99

Grades: 7 8 9 10   **Fic**
  1. School stories 2. Theater -- Fiction 3. Friendship
-- Fiction 4. Schizophrenia -- Fiction 5. Television
scriptwriters 6. Mental illness -- Fiction
ISBN 978-0-8118-7780-0; 0-8118-7780-9
                                      LC 2010039392
Frenchy and Stewart, two Northern Vermont high school
seniors, try out for the school musical, 'Man of La Mancha,'
but when Stewart is cast as Don Quixote he soon becomes
obsessed with his role and Frenchy must try to overcome
his own demons to help his friend stay grounded in reality.
  "Stahler creates a solid narrator in Frenchy, ably balancing his grief, confusion over Stewart's deteriorating mental
state, and elation at his dawning relationship with stage manager Kaela. The resulting denouement is chaotic and heart-
wrenching." Publ Wkly

Standiford, Natalie

The **secret** tree; Natalie Standiford. Scholastic
Press 2012 245 p. $16.99
Grades: 4 5 6 7   **Fic**
  1. Bildungsromans 2. Mystery fiction
ISBN 0545334799; 9780545334792
  This coming of age story combines "[m]iddle-school dynamics, pesky sibling relations, a rumored haunted house, .
. . and a mystery. . . . When 10-year-old Minty discovers a
hollow tree in the woods . . . [and] find[s] a secret written on
a scrap of paper stashed inside, it sets the stage for a . . . mystery. . . . [W]hile Minty tries to figure out what's going on,
she . . . befriend[s] an apparently parentless kid, Raymond,
who seems to live in an abandoned spec house." (Kirkus)

Staniszewski, Anna

My very unfairy tale life. Sourcebooks Jabberwocky 2011 198p pa $6.99
Grades: 4 5 6 7   **Fic**
  1. Fairy tales 2. Magic -- Fiction
ISBN 978-1-4022-5946-3; 1-4022-5946-8
Jenny, a professional adventurer, would prefer spending
time with her friends over helping magical kingdoms around
the universe, but soon she is given the choice to return to her
normal life or go into a battle she doesn't think she can win.
  "An eye for imaginative detail mixes with these likable
characters and a theme of empathy for others to keep the
story appropriate to a younger audience, who easily will
identify with Jenny. Charming." Kirkus

Stanley, Diane

★ **Bella** at midnight; illustrated by Bagram Ibatoulline. HarperCollins Pubs. 2006 278p il $15.99;
lib bdg $16.89; pa $6.99
Grades: 5 6 7 8   **Fic**
  1. Fairy tales 2. Knights and knighthood -- Fiction
ISBN 978-0-06-077573-5; 0-06-077573-4; 978-0-06-
077574-2 lib bdg; 0-06-077574-2 lib bdg; 978-0-06-
077575-9 pa; 0-06-077575-0 pa
                                      LC 2005-05906
Raised by peasants, Bella discovers that she is actually
the daughter of a knight and finds herself caught up in a terrible plot that will change her life and the kingdom forever
  "What raises this above other recreated fairy tales
is the quality of the writing, dotted with jeweled descrip-

tion and anchored by the strong values—loyalty, truth, honor." Booklist

★ **Saving** Sky. Harper 2010 199p $15.99

Grades: 5 6 7 8   **Fic**

1. Terrorism -- Fiction 2. Immigrants -- Fiction 3. Prejudices -- Fiction 4. Ranch life -- Fiction 5. Family life -- Fiction
ISBN 978-0-06-123905-2; 0-06-123905-4

LC 2010-09393

In an America that has suffered continual terrorist attacks since 9/11, seventh-grader Sky stands up for what is right and helps a classmate of Middle Eastern descent, although doing so places her and her family at great risk.

"Readers will have much to discuss after finishing this beautifully written, disturbing book." Booklist

The **cup** and the crown; Diane Stanley. Harper 2012 344 p. (hardback) $16.99

Grades: 5 6 7 8   **Fic**

1. Fantasy fiction 2. Magic -- Fiction 3. Identity -- Fiction 4. Clairvoyance -- Fiction
ISBN 0061963216; 9780061963216

LC 2012025280

In this fantasy novel by Diane Stanley "Molly has visions of a beautiful goblet: one of her grandfather's loving cups, which he filled with magic that bound people together. So it hardly surprises Molly when handsome King Alaric asks her to find a loving cup to help him win the heart of the beautiful Princess of Cortova. As Molly and her friends Winifred and Tobias journey far beyond the safe borders of Westria, a mysterious raven appears to guide their quest." (Publisher's note)

The **mysterious** matter of I.M. Fine. HarperCollins Pubs. 2001 201p hardcover o.p. pa $5.99

Grades: 4 5 6 7   **Fic**

1. Magic 2. Mystery fiction 3. Books and reading 4. Magic -- Fiction 5. Books and reading -- Fiction 6. Mystery and detective stories
ISBN 0-688-17546-5; 0-380-73327-7 pa

LC 00-54040

Noticing that a popular series of horror novels is having a bizarre effect on the behavior of its readers, Franny and Beamer set out to find the mysterious author

"The solidly constructed mystery, well-rounded characters, and playful jab at wildly successful horror writers go down a treat." Horn Book Guide

Another title about Franny and her friends is:
The mysterious case of the Allbright Academy (2008)

★ The **silver** bowl. Harper 2011 307p $16.99

Grades: 5 6 7 8   **Fic**

1. Fantasy fiction 2. Clairvoyance -- Fiction
ISBN 978-0-06-157543-3; 0-06-157543-7

"Molly is a young scullery maid in the castle of King Edmund, and like her mother before her, she sees visions and hears voices that offer glimpses of the future. But is this a blessing or a curse?. . . . The girl's choice of silence . . . is challenged when she learns that a rumored curse on the royal family is true and only by sharing her visions might they be saved. Combining carefully chosen details of setting with a richly realized fantasy premise, Stanley succeeds in creating a believable world large enough to accommodate not only menace and evil but also loyalty, enduring friendship, and love." Booklist

Stanley, George Edward

Night fires; a novel. Aladdin 2009 183p $15.99

Grades: 7 8 9 10   **Fic**

1. Moving -- Fiction 2. Bereavement -- Fiction 3. Race relations -- Fiction
ISBN 978-1-4169-7559-5; 1-4169-7559-4

LC 2008051607

In 1922, thirteen-year-old Woodrow Harper and his recently-widowed mother move to his father's childhood home in Lawton, Oklahoma, where he is torn between the "right people" of the Ku Klux Klan and those who encourage him to follow the path of his "nigra-loving" father.

"A thought-provoking novel. . . . Stanley's highly charged, emotional story tells of a very dark period in this country's history." SLJ

Staples, Suzanne Fisher

Dangerous skies. Farrar, Straus & Giroux 1996 231p hardcover o.p. pa $7.95

Grades: 7 8 9 10   **Fic**

1. Friendship -- Fiction 2. Prejudices -- Fiction 3. African Americans -- Fiction
ISBN 0-374-31694-5; 0-374-41670-2 pa

LC 95-45529

"At twelve, white boy Buck and black girl Tunes Smith are best friends. . . . The adolescents' idyllic world of fishing and observing nature is shattered when their much older friend Jorge Rodrigues is murdered, and Tunes is accused of the crime. . . . Staples's beautifully written and chilling tale of contemporary racism should keep young adult readers turning pages until they reach the heart-breaking end." Voice Youth Advocates

Shabanu; daughter of the wind. Knopf 1989 240p hardcover o.p. pa $6.50

Grades: 8 9 10 11 12   **Fic**

1. Sex role -- Fiction
ISBN 0-394-84815-2; 0-440-23856-0 pa

LC 89-2714

A Newbery Medal honor book, 1990

When eleven-year-old Shabanu, the daughter of a nomad in the Cholistan Desert of present-day Pakistan, is pledged in marriage to an older man whose money will bring prestige to the family, she must either accept the decision, as is the custom, or risk the consequences of defying her father's wishes

"Interspersing native words throughout adds realism, but may trip up readers, who must be patient enough to find meaning through context. This use of language is, however, an important element in helping Staples paint an evocative picture of life in the desert that includes references to the hard facts of reality." Booklist

Other titles in this series are:
Haveli (1993)
The house of djinn (2008)

★ **Under** the Persimmon tree. Farrar, Straus & Giroux 2005 275p $17

Grades: 78 9 10   **Fic**

1. Afghanistan – Fiction

2. Pakistan -- Fiction
ISBN 0-374-38025-2

During the 2001 Afghan War, the lives of Najmal, a young refugee from Kunduz, Afghanistan, and Nusrat, an American-Muslim teacher who is awaiting her huband's return from Mazar-i-Sharif, intersect at a school in Peshawar, Pakistan.

"Staples weaves a lot of history and politics into her story. . . . But . . . it's the personal story . . . that compels as it takes readers beyond the modern stereotypes of Muslims as fundamentalist fanatics. There are no sweet reunions, but there's hope in heartbreaking scenes of kindness and courage." Booklist

Starke, Ruth

Noodle pie. Kane Miller 2010 il 187p $15.99

Grades: 4 5 6 7   **Fic**

1. Vietnamese -- Fiction
ISBN 978-1-935279-25-9; 1-935279-25-4

"Eleven-year-old Andy's first trip to Vietnam with his father, a 'Viet Kieu' (someone born in Vietnam who now lives overseas), exposes him to internalized prejudices about his heritage. . . . Andy distinguishes himself from his pushy relatives by emphasizing his Australian citizenship and criticizing customs that seem unfair. . . . This humorous, touching novel is a delicious cross-cultural treat, and includes an appendix of Vietnamese recipes." Publ Wkly

Starmer, Aaron

The **only** ones. Delacorte Press 2011 321p $17.99; lib bdg $20.99; e-book $17.99

Grades: 4 5 6 7   **Fic**

1. Supernatural -- Fiction
ISBN 978-0-385-74043-2; 0-385-74043-3; 978-0-385-90839-9 lib bdg; 0-385-90839-3 lib bdg; 978-0-375-89919-5 e-book

LC 2010040383

After setting off from the island where he has been leading a solitary existence, thirteen-year-old Martin discovers a village with other children who have been living similarly without any adults, since the grown-ups have all been spirited away.

"Both literary and engaging, this is the kind of book readers will want to return to for new discoveries." Kirkus

Stauffacher, Sue

Harry Sue. Knopf 2005 288p hardcover o.p. lib bdg $17.99; pa $6.50

Grades: 5 6 7 8   **Fic**

1. Prisoners -- Fiction 2. Handicapped -- Fiction 3. Mother-daughter relationship -- Fiction
ISBN 0-375-83274-2; 0-375-93274-7 lib bdg; 0-440-42064-4 pa

LC 2004-16945

Although tough-talking Harry Sue would like to start a life of crime in order to be "sent up" and find her incarcerated mother, she must first protect the children at her ne-

glectful grandmother's home day care center and befriend a paralyzed boy.

"This is a riveting story, dramatically and well told, with characters whom readers won't soon forget." SLJ

Stead, Rebecca

First light. Wendy Lamb Books 2007 328p $15.99; lib bdg $18.99; pa $6.99

Grades: 5 6 7 8   **Fic**

1. Supernatural -- Fiction 2. Greenhouse effect -- Fiction 3. Young adult literature -- Works
ISBN 978-0-375-84017-3; 0-375-84017-6; 987-0-375-094017-0 lib bdg; 0-375-94017-0 lib bdg; 978-0-440-42222-8 pa; 0-440-42222-1 pa

LC 2006-39733

This "novel is an exciting, engaging mix of science fiction, mystery, and adventure. . . . Peter and Thea are fully developed main characters." SLJ

Liar & spy; by Rebecca Stead. Wendy Lamb Books 2012 180 p. (hardback) $15.99

Grades: 4 5 6 7 8   **Fic**

1. Spy stories 2. Boys -- Fiction 3. Neighbors -- Fiction 4. Friendship -- Fiction 5. Spies -- Fiction 6. Schools -- Fiction 7. Middle schools -- Fiction 8. Apartment houses -- Fiction 9. Family life -- New York (State) -- New York -- Fiction
ISBN 0385737432; 9780375899539; 9780385737432; 9780385906654

LC 2011042674

In this book, protagonist "Georges has a lot going on. Dad was laid off so Mom has started working extra shifts at the hospital, and they had to sell their house in Brooklyn and move into an apartment. One good thing about the new building is Safer, an unusual boy who lives on the top floor. He's determined to teach Georges how to be a spy. Their main case: spy on the mysterious Mr. X in the apartment above Georges. As Georges and Safer go deeper into their Mr. X plan, the line between games, lies, and reality begin to blur." (Barnes and Noble)

★ **When** you reach me. Wendy Lamb Books 2009 199p $15.99; lib bdg $18.99

Grades: 5 6 7 8   **Fic**

1. Space and time -- Fiction
ISBN 978-0-385-73742-5; 0-385-73742-4; 978-0-385-90664-7 lib bdg; 0-385-90664-1 lib bdg

LC 2008-24998

Boston Globe-Horn Book Award: Fiction (2010)

Awarded the Newbery Medal, 2010

As her mother prepares to be a contestant on the 1980s television game show, "The $20,000 Pyramid," a twelve-year-old New York City girl tries to make sense of a series of mysterious notes received from an anonymous source that seems to defy the laws of time and space

"The '70s New York setting is an honest reverberation of the era; the mental gymnastics required of readers are invigorating; and the characters . . . are honest bits of humanity." Booklist

Steele, Allen

Apollo's outcasts; by Allen Steele. Pyr 2012 311 p. (hardcover) $16.99

Grades: 7 8 9 10 **Fic**

1. Space colonies -- Fiction 2. Coups d'état -- Fiction 3. Regression (Civilization) -- Fiction 4. Children with disabilities -- Fiction

ISBN 1616146869; 9781616146863

LC 2012023582

This book from Hugo Award-winning author Allen Steele sends "a handful of kids to the Moon in the wake of a political coup in America. Jamey Barlowe, 16, was born on the Moon but raised on Earth; as a result of a low-gravity infancy, Jamey uses a multifunctional 'mobil' chair to get around. . . . Anxious to do something productive upon arriving in Apollo (and able to walk for the first time), Jamey joins the elite Lunar Search and Rescue, just in time to end up on the front lines." (Publishers Weekly)

Steer, Dugald

The dragon diary; [by] Dugald A. Steer; illustrated by Douglas Carrel. Candlewick Press 2009 248p il (Dragonology chronicles) $16.99

Grades: 5 6 7 8 **Fic**

1. Fantasy fiction 2. Dragons -- Fiction 3. Siblings -- Fiction

ISBN 978-0-7636-3425-4; 0-7636-3425-5

LC 2009005795

Apprentice dragonologists Daniel and Beatrice Cook's mentor is called away at a crucial time, leaving the brother and sister alone to search for an ancient diary that could cure some gravely ill dragons

"This fast-paced fantasy features sibling rivalry, multitudes of dragons, and mid-air heroics." Horn Book Guide

Stein, Tammar

High dive. Alfred A. Knopf 2008 201p $15.99; lib bdg $18.99

Grades: 7 8 9 10 **Fic**

1. Vacations -- Fiction 2. Friendship -- Fiction 3. Loss (Psychology) -- Fiction 4. Single parent family -- Fiction

ISBN 978-0-375-83024-2; 0-375-83024-3; 978-0-375-93024-9 lib bdg; 0-375-93024-8 lib bdg

LC 2007049657

With her mother stationed in Iraq as an Army nurse, Vanderbilt University student Arden Vogel, whose father was killed in a traffic accident a few years earlier, impulsively ends up on a tour of Europe with a group of college girls she meets on her way to attend to some family business in Sardinia.

"Ideal for the thoughtful armchair traveler, this story is engaging enough for readers on the long flight to the enduring wonders of Europe and emerging adulthood." SLJ

Kindred. Alfred A. Knopf 2011 266p $16.99; lib bdg $19.99

Grades: 7 8 9 10 **Fic**

1. Twins -- Fiction 2. Angels -- Fiction 3. Siblings -- Fiction 4. Supernatural -- Fiction 5. Good and evil

-- Fiction

ISBN 978-0-375-85871-0; 0-375-85871-7; 978-0-375-95871-7 lib bdg; 0-375-95871-1 lib bdg

LC 2010-07071

Spiritual warfare breaks out when the Archangel Raphael and the Devil deliver assignments to eighteen-year-old fraternal twins Miriam and Moses.

"Skillfully intertwining family, medical, and supernatural dramas with a sweet romantic subplot, Stein . . . unleashes cosmic battles to play out among the inhabitants of smalltown Hamilton, Tenn., a setting replete with Civil War history. . . . Miriam's initial interpretation of her illness as divine punishment gives way to more complex theological reflections in this riveting tale, an angel book that stands out from the chorus." Publ Wkly

Light years; a novel. Knopf 2005 263p hardcover o.p. pa $6.99

Grades: 7 8 9 10 **Fic**

1. Bereavement -- Fiction 2. Israel-Arab conflicts -- Fiction

ISBN 0-375-83023-5; 0-440-23902-8 pa

LC 2004-7776

Maya Laor leaves her home in Israel to study astronomy at the University of Virginia after the tragic death of her boyfriend in a suicide bombing.

"This well-paced first novel, a moving study of grief and recovery, is also a love story that should appeal particularly to students interested in other ways of seeing the world." SLJ

Includes bibliographical references

Steinbeck, John

The pearl; John Steinbeck centennial ed; Penguin Books 2002 87p pa $11

Grades: 7 8 9 10 **Fic**

1. Poverty -- Fiction

ISBN 0-14-200069-8

LC 2001-56113

First published 1947

"Kino, a poor pearl-fisher, lives a happy albeit spartan life with his wife and their child. When he finds a magnificent pearl, the Pearl of the World, he is besieged by dishonest pearl merchants and envious neighbors. Even a greedy doctor ties his professional treatment of their baby when it is bitten by a scorpion to the possible acquisition of the pearl. After a series of disasters, Kino throws the pearl away since it has brought him only unhappiness." Shapiro. Fic for Youth. 3d edition

The red pony. Viking 1993 100p pa $9

Grades: 4 5 6 7 **Fic**

1. Horses -- Fiction 2. Ranch life -- Fiction

ISBN 0-670-59184-X; 0-14-017736-1 pa

LC 86-1610

First published 1937

"Jody Tiflin, ten years old, begins to grow up in these four vignettes describing his life on a farm in California. He takes responsibility for his red pony and suffers when it dies. An old man arouses Jody's curiosity about what is beyond the mountains, and he anxiously awaits the birth of a colt.

His grandfather's tales are a source of interest and wonder for Jody." Shapiro. Fic for Youth. 3d edition

Steinmetz, Karen

The **mourning** wars. Roaring Brook Press 2010 232p $17.99

Grades: 7 8 9 10   **Fic**
1. Mohawk Indians -- Fiction
ISBN 978-1-59643-290-1; 1-59643-290-X
LC 2010-11735

In 1704, Mohawk Indians attack the frontier village of Deerfield, Massachusetts, kidnapping over 100 residents, including seven-year-old Eunice Williams. Based on a true story.

"Eunice's largely imagined life makes a fascinating story with a setting that is vividly and dramatically evoked. The book will be especially useful in the classroom." Booklist

Includes bibliographical references

Stellings, Caroline

The **contest**. Seventh Generation 2009 123p pa $9.95

Grades: 4 5 6 7   **Fic**
1. Poverty -- Fiction 2. Contests -- Fiction 3. Friendship -- Fiction 4. Books and reading -- Fiction 5. Racially mixed people -- Fiction
ISBN 978-0-9779183-5-5 pa; 0-9779183-5-1 pa
LC 2009-20294

Rosy, a poor, eleven-year-old, half-Mohawk girl from Hamilton, Ontario, Canada enters an Anne of Green Gables look-alike contest in hopes of winning a set of Anne books, and gains a new friend and deeper understanding of Anne's character

"Readers will enjoy Rosy and her spunky attitude. . . . Some readers will finish this book and go seeking the Anne series to read, and those already familiar with the Anne books will enjoy the connection." Libr Media Connect

Stemple, Adam

B.U.G. (Big Ugly Guy) by Jane Yolen and Adam Stemple. Dutton Children's Books 2013 344 p. $16.99

Grades: 4 5 6 7 8   **Fic**
1. Golem -- Fiction 2. Magic -- Fiction 3. Bullies -- Fiction 4. Friendship -- Fiction 5. Bands (Music) -- Fiction 6. Klezmer music -- Fiction 7. Jews -- United States -- Fiction
ISBN 9780525422389
LC 2012018217

A constant target for bullies, Sammy Greenburg is glad to make friends with a boy named Skink, who even agrees to "start up a Klezmer fusion garage band after Sammy introduces Skink to the unique combination of jazz and Jewish folk music. When the bullies beat up Skink, however, Sammy decides enough is enough, and, using a formula he finds in his rabbi's study, he creates a golem to take vengeance on his enemies—and fill the missing drummer spot in his new band." (Bulletin of the Center for Children's Books)

Stephens, John

★ The **emerald** atlas. Alfred A. Knopf 2011 417p (The books of beginning) $17.99; lib bdg $20.99

Grades: 4 5 6   **Fic**
1. Magic -- Fiction 2. Monsters -- Fiction 3. Siblings -- Fiction 4. Prophecies -- Fiction 5. Space and time -- Fiction 6. Books and reading -- Fiction
ISBN 978-0-375-86870-2; 0-375-86870-4; 978-0-375-96870-9 lib bdg; 0-375-96870-9 lib bdg
LC 2010029100

Kate, Michael, and Emma have passed from one orphanage to another in the ten years since their parents disappeared to protect them, but now they learn that they have special powers, a prophesied quest to find a magical book, and a fearsome enemy.

"This fast-paced, fully imagined fantasy is by turns frightening and funny, and the siblings are well-crafted and empathetic heroes. Highly enjoyable, it should find many readers." Publ Wkly

★ The **fire** chronicle; John Stephens. Alfred A. Knopf 2012 437 p. (hardback) $17.99

Grades: 4 5 6   **Fic**
1. Fantasy fiction 2. Adventure fiction 3. Time travel 4. Magic -- Fiction 5. Identity -- Fiction 6. Monsters -- Fiction 7. Prophecies -- Fiction 8. Space and time -- Fiction 9. Books and reading -- Fiction 10. Brothers and sisters -- Fiction
ISBN 0375868712; 9780375868719; 9780375899560; 9780375968716
LC 2012016139

In this novel by John Stephens, part of the Books of Beginning series, "Kate, Michael, and Emma long to continue the hunt for their missing parents. . . . A frantic chase sends Kate a hundred years into the past, to a perilous, enchanted New York City. . . . Meanwhile, Michael and Emma have set off to find the second of the Books of Beginning. A series of clues leads them into a hidden world where they must brave harsh polar storms, track down an ancient order of warriors, and confront terrible monsters." (Publisher's note)

Sternberg, Libby

The **case** against my brother. Bancroft Press 2007 201p $19.95

Grades: 6 7 8 9   **Fic**
1. Brothers -- Fiction 2. Prejudices -- Fiction 3. Polish Americans -- Fiction
ISBN 978-1-890862-51-0; 1-890862-51-7

"In 1922, when their widowed mother dies, Carl Matiuski and his older brother, Adam, move to Portland, OR, to live with an uncle. . . . When [Adam] is accused of a crime he didn't commit, Carl steps in . . . to try to clear his brother's name. . . . Readers are easily swept up in the adventure as the eye-opening mystery unfolds." SLJ

Stevenson, Robert Louis

Kidnapped; [by] Robert Louis Stevenson; with an introduction by Sid Hite. F. Watts 2007 213p (Scholastic classics) $25.50

Grades: 7 8 9 10 11 12 Adult   **Fic**
1. Adventure fiction 2. Kidnapping -- Fiction
ISBN 978-0-531-16990-2; 0-531-16990-1
LC 2006006816
First published 1886
A sixteen-year-old orphan is kidnapped by his villainous uncle, but later escapes and becomes involved in the struggle of the Scottish highlanders against English rule.

Treasure Island; by Robert Louis Stevenson ; illustrated by N.C. Wyeth. Scribner 1981 xvi, 273 p., [13] leaves of platesp col. ill. (paperback) $6.99; (reinforced) $29.99
Grades: 5 6 7 8 9 10 11 12 Adult   **Fic**
1. Adventure fiction 2. Pirates -- Fiction 3. Buried treasure -- Fiction
ISBN 0689832125; 9780689832123; 9780684171609; 0684171600
LC 81008788
Originally published: 1911.
Young Jim Hawkins discovers a treasure map in the chest of an old sailor who dies under mysterious circumstances at his mother's inn. He shows it to Dr. Livesey and Squire Trelawney who agree to outfit a ship and sail to Treasure Island. Among the crew is the pirate Long John Silver and his followers who are in pursuit of the treasure

The **strange** case of Dr. Jekyll and Mr. Hyde; with an introduction by Joyce Carol Oates. Vintage Books 1991 97p pa $8.95
Grades: 7 8 9 10 11 12 Adult   **Fic**
1. Allegories 2. Physicians 3. Horror fiction 4. Novelettes 5. Horror stories 6. Dual personality 7. Good and evil -- Fiction
ISBN 0-679-73476-7
LC 90-50600
First published 1886. Variant title: Dr. Jekyll and Mr. Hyde
"The disturbing tale of the dual personality of Dr. Jekyll, a physician. A generous and philanthropic man, he is preoccupied with the problems of good and evil and with the possibility of separating them into two distinct personalities. He develops a drug that transforms him into the demonic Mr. Hyde, in whose person he exhausts all the latent evil in his nature. He also creates an antidote that will restore him to his respectable existence as Dr. Jekyll. Gradually, however, the unmitigated evil of his darker self predominates, until finally he performs an atrocious murder. . . . The novel is of great psychological perception and strongly concerned with ethical problems." Reader's Ency. 4th edition

Stevenson, Robin H.
Dead in the water; [by] Robin Stevenson. Orca Book Publishers 2008 169p (Orca sports) pa $9.95
Grades: 6 7 8 9   **Fic**
1. Adventure fiction 2. Sailing -- Fiction 3. Endangered species -- Fiction
ISBN 978-1-5514-3962-4 pa; 1-5514-3962-X pa
"Simon ('Spacey') joins three other teenagers for a weeklong sailing course in British Columbia, Canada. . . . His weird shipmate, Olivia, insists that the men on a nearby cabin cruiser are smuggling abalone, a threatened shellfish

species, and she persuades Simon to help her investigate. . . . Stevenson . . . delivers plenty of realistic, gripping detail about handling a boat in screaming winds and crashing waves, as well as a solid story about a crucial environmental issue." Booklist

Escape velocity. Orca Book Publishers 2011 232p pa $12.95
Grades: 6 7 8 9   **Fic**
1. Mother-daughter relationship -- Fiction
ISBN 978-1-55469-866-0; 1-55469-866-9
Forced to live with the mother who abandoned her at birth, Lou goes looking for truth in her mother's fiction.
"Lou is a fully rounded, attractive character. Zoe's emotional insensitivity toward her, while painful, becomes understandable as her believable back story emerges. Other characters are also nicely, authentically fleshed out, adding depth and a strong sense of reality. A quiet, moving exploration of what it means to be a mother—or a daughter—even when the relationship is unconventional." Kirkus

Liars and fools; written by Robin Stevenson. Orca Book Publishers 2010 246p pa $9.95
Grades: 5 6 7 8   **Fic**
1. Bereavement -- Fiction
ISBN 978-1-55469-248-4 pa; 1-55469-248-2 pa
Still grieving the loss of her mother, Fiona resists the idea of moving on with her life, especially when her father starts dating a psychic.
"Fiona is a believable character trying to deal with her grief. . . . Her relationship with her best (and only) friend, Abby, is realistic, and the banter between the two girls adds humor." Booklist

Out of order; written by Robin Stevenson. Orca Book Publishers 2007 221p pa $8.95
Grades: 8 9 10 11 12   **Fic**
1. School stories 2. Friendship -- Fiction
ISBN 978-1-55143-693-7; 1-55143-693-0
When Sophie moves to Victoria, she hopes to leave the bullying she experienced in Ontario behind, but when she makes two new friends who are polar opposites, she finds that friendships can both help and harm her sense of self.
"The visceral, emotional reactions of the characters ring true. . . . Despite weighty themes, this story is about friendship and self-worth." Voice Youth Advocates

Stevermer, Caroline
Magic below stairs. Dial Books for Young Readers 2010 199p $16.99
Grades: 4 5 6 7   **Fic**
1. Magic -- Fiction 2. Orphans -- Fiction 3. Household employees -- Fiction
ISBN 978-0-8037-3467-8; 0-8037-3467-0
LC 2009-25100
Ten-year-old Frederick, who is surreptitiously watched over by a household elf, is plucked from a London orphanage to be a servant to a wealthy wizard, and eventually his uncanny abilities lead him to become the wizard's apprentice.
"A well-developed fictional world and the many concrete details of belowstairs life make the magical events in this engaging chapter book more believable." Booklist

Stewart, Alex

Dragonwood; Alex Stewart. Evans 2010 56 p. $7.99

Grades: 7 8 9 10   **Fic**

1. Fantasy fiction 2. Mystery fiction 3. Elves -- Fiction 4. Criminals -- Fiction

ISBN 0237541351; 145174465X; 9780237541354; 9781451744651

LC 2011287528

This book is part of "the Shades series . . . from Britain" and "presents a fantasy story that dispenses with the massive casting and large chunks of world building" found in other fantasy stories. The story "follows a Halfling bounty hunter, Pip, who has been paid by an elven prince to track down and return the head of an orcish outlaw, who is rumored to have slain the prince's sister. He soon enough finds reason to doubt his employer's word, but Pip is sworn to carry out his mission one way or another." Author Alex Stewart offers "a conflicted-private-eye story in a fantasy setting." (Booklist)

Stewart, Paul

Phantom of Blood Alley; [by] Paul Stewart & Chris Riddell; illustrated by Chris Riddell. David Fickling Books 2010 201p il (Barnaby Grimes) $16.99

Grades: 4 5 6 7   **Fic**

1. Mystery fiction 2. Photography -- Fiction 3. Supernatural -- Fiction

ISBN 978-0-385-75134-6; 0-385-75134-6

First published 2009 in the United Kingdom

Barnaby finds himself in the fiercely competitive world of early photography, where the rewards are immense but so are the risks. After an experiment goes disastrously wrong, Barnaby is on the trail of a mad chemist with a talent for disappearing into thin air.

The **curse** of the night wolf; [by] Paul Stewart and Chris Riddell; illustrated by Chris Riddell. David Fickling Books 2008 204p il (Barnaby Grimes) $15.99; lib bdg $18.99

Grades: 4 5 6 7   **Fic**

1. Mystery fiction 2. Physicians -- Fiction 3. Werewolves -- Fiction

ISBN 978-0-385-75125-4; 0-385-75125-7; 978-0-385-75126-1 lib bdg; 0-385-75126-5 lib bdg

LC 2008-01697

Soon after Victorian messenger Barnaby Grimes is attacked by a huge beast while crossing London's rooftops, he becomes entangled in a mystery involving patent medicine, impoverished patients, and very expensive furs.

"Moody, highly detailed pen-and-ink drawings provide ornamentation throughout, lending a classic Victorian feel to help punctuate the drama. . . . Possessing an easy confidence and quick wit . . . Barnaby is an appealing character." Booklist

Other titles in this series are:

Return of the emerald skull (2009)

Legion of the Dead (2010)

Phantom of the Blood Alley (2010)

Stewart, Trenton Lee

The **extraordinary** education of Nicholas Benedict; by Trenton Lee Stewart ; illustrated by Diana Sudyka. Little, Brown 2012 470 p. $17.99

Grades: 4 5 6 7 8   **Fic**

1. Bullies -- Fiction 2. Orphans -- Fiction 3. Friendship -- Fiction 4. Narcolepsy -- Fiction 5. Orphanages -- Fiction 6. Genius -- Fiction 7. Mystery and detective stories 8. Adventure and adventurers -- Fiction

ISBN 9780316176194

LC 2011031690

This book tells the story of Nicholas Benedict who "is just 9 years. . . . Small in physical stature but intellectually gifted, he has an 'unfortunate' nose . . . and a medical condition that prompts 'unpredictable sleeping episodes' that drop him from consciousness like a trapdoor into a black dungeon at the least opportune of times. . . . What has long made him a nuisance to less intelligent adults and target practice for bullies also makes him a curiosity for a slightly older boy who befriends him at his new home—the ominously named Rothschild's End. The orphanage is housed in a two-story mansion. . . . [The book] revolves around . . . the . . . themes . . . [of] orphans, friendship and the sorts of surrogate families that form as a result." (LA Times)

★ The **mysterious** Benedict Society; illustrated by Carson Ellis. Little, Brown 2007 485p il $16.99; pa $6.99

Grades: 5 6 7 8   **Fic**

1. Science fiction 2. Adventure fiction

ISBN 978-0-316-05777-6; 0-316-05777-0; 978-0-316-00395-7 pa; 0-316-00395-6 pa

LC 2006-09925

After passing a series of mind-bending tests, four children are selected for a secret mission that requires them to go undercover at the Learning Institute for the Very Enlightened, where the only rule is that there are no rules

"Stewart's unusual characters, threatening villains, and dramatic plot twists will grab and hold readers' attention." SLJ

Other titles about the Benedict Society are:

The mysterious Benedict Society and the perilous journey (2008)

The mysterious Benedict Society and the prisoner's dilemma (2009)

Stiefvater, Maggie

★ The **Scorpio** Races. Scholastic Press 2011 409p $17.99

Grades: 8 9 10 11 12   **Fic**

1. Love stories 2. Fantasy fiction 3. Horses -- Fiction 4. Racing -- Fiction 5. Orphans -- Fiction

ISBN 978-0-545-22490-1; 0-545-22490-X

LC 2011015775

"Stiefvater's narration is as much about atmospherics as it is about event, and the water horses are the environment in which Sean and Puck move, allies and rivals to the end. It's not a feel-good story—dread, loss, and hard choices are the islanders' lot. As a study of courage and loyalty tested, however, it is an utterly compelling read." Publ Wkly

★ The **raven** boys; Maggie Stiefvater. Scholastic Press 2012 409 p. $18.99

Grades: 8 9 10 11 12 **Fic**

1. Magic -- Fiction 2. Supernatural -- Fiction 3. Private schools -- Fiction 4. Paranormal fiction 5. Occultism -- Fiction 6. Clairvoyance -- Fiction

ISBN 0545424925; 9780545424929

LC 2012030880

This book is the first in Maggie Stiefvater's series the "Raven Cycle". It follows "16-year-old Blue Sargent, daughter of a small-town psychic, [who] has lived her whole life under a prophecy: If she kisses her true love, he will die. . . . She sees a vision of a dying Raven boy named Gansey. The Raven Boys--students at Aglionby, a nearby prep school, so-called because of the ravens on their school crest--soon encounter Blue in person." (Kirkus Reviews)

Stier, Catherine

The **terrible** secrets of the Tell-All Club. Albert Whitman & Co. 2009 125p $14.99

Grades: 4 5 6 **Fic**

1. School stories 2. Clubs -- Fiction 3. Friendship -- Fiction

ISBN 978-0-8075-7798-1; 0-8075-7798-7

LC 2008055704

When four fifth-grade friends complete a "tell-all" survey, tensions arise and come to a head during an overnight class trip

"Told in the four voices of the club members, the story shows the characters' insecurities and the family issues they face. Reluctant readers will find it fast paced, easy to follow, and populated with likable personalities." SLJ

Stoffels, Karlijn

★ **Heartsinger**; translated by Laura Watkinson. Arthur A. Levine Books 2009 134p $16.99

Grades: 8 9 10 11 **Fic**

1. Fantasy fiction 2. Love -- Fiction 3. Voyages and travels -- Fiction

ISBN 978-0-545-06929-8; 0-545-06929-7; 978-0-545-06968-7 pa; 0-545-06968-8 pa

LC 2008-17785

In this meditation on various kinds of love, Mee travels across the country to the court of the Princess Esperanza, singing the life stories of some of the people he meets.

"Written with clarity and grace. . . . This unusual novel offers readers limpid writing, strong storytelling, and the unblinking recognition of love in many forms." Booklist

Stolz, Joelle

The **shadows** of Ghadames; translated from the French by Catherine Temerson. Delacorte Press 2004 119p $15.95; lib bdg $17.99

Grades: 5 6 7 8 **Fic**

1. Muslims -- Fiction 2. Sex role -- Fiction

ISBN 0-385-73104-3; 0-385-90131-3 lib bdg

LC 2003-21656

At the end of the nineteenth century in Libya, eleven-year-old Malika simultaneously enjoys and feels constricted by the narrow world of women, but an injured stranger enters her home and disrupts the traditional order of things.

"Stolz invigorates her tale with elegant prose and a deft portrayal of a girl verging on adolescence. The vivid backdrop is intoxicating." Booklist

Stone, Phoebe

Deep down popular; a novel. by Phoebe Stone. Arthur A. Levine Books 2008 280p $16.99; pa $4.99

Grades: 4 5 6 7 **Fic**

1. School stories 2. Friendship -- Fiction 3. Family life -- Fiction 4. Country life -- Fiction

ISBN 978-0-439-80245-1; 0-439-80245-8; 978-0-439-80244-4 pa; 0-439-80244-X pa

LC 2007017198

In a small Virginia town, sixth-grader Jessie Lou Ferguson has a crush on the hugely popular Conrad Parker Smith, and when he suddenly develops a medical problem and the teacher asks Jessie Lou to help him, they become friends, to her surprise

"Jessie Lou tells her tale with the strong, rough-edged purity of a young poet, which she is; equally strong are the story's underpinnings, longing and laughter, and a willingness to believe in something despite the facts." Booklist

★ The **Romeo** and Juliet code. Arthur A. Levine Books 2011 300p $16.99

Grades: 4 5 6 7 **Fic**

1. Ciphers -- Fiction 2. Family life -- Fiction 3. World War, 1939-1945 -- United States -- Fiction 4. World War, 1939-1945 -- Evacuation of civilians -- Fiction

ISBN 978-0-545-21511-4; 0-545-21511-0

LC 2010-30005

During World War II, eleven-year-old Felicity is sent from London to Bottlebay, Maine, to live with her grandmother, aunt, uncle, and a reclusive boy who helps her decode mysterious letters that contain the truth about her missing parents.

Felicity "is endearingly portrayed, and the back story, so gradually revealed, provides a peek into the depths of the souls of some of the adults. The pacing is deliberately slow, yet Felicity's growing awareness of how she can help heal the troubled adults makes this an eminently satisfying read." Kirkus

Romeo blue; by Phoebe Stone. 1st ed. Arthur A. Levine Books 2013 352 p. (hardcover) $16.99

Grades: 4 5 6 7 **Fic**

1. Espionage -- Fiction 2. World War, 1939-1945 -- Evacuation of civilians -- Fiction 3. Identity -- Fiction 4. Foster children -- Fiction

ISBN 0545443601; 9780545443609

LC 2012038060

"In this sequel to the WWII historical mystery 'The Romeo and Juliet Code,' . . . twelve-year old . . . Flissy now knows her Uncle Gideon is actually her biological father. . . . And she knows her whole family are some kind of spies, but she does not know . . . if they are still alive. And she has no idea why the creepy neighbor, Mr. Fitzwilliam, has invited her and adopted cousin Derek for tea, how he seems to know about her parents' secret activities." (Children's Literature)

The **boy** on Cinnamon Street; by Phoebe Stone. Arthur A. Levine Books 2012 234 p. $16.99

Grades: 3 4 5 6 7 8 **Fic**

1. Friendship -- Fiction 2. Memory -- Fiction 3. Schools -- Fiction 4. Grandparents -- Fiction
ISBN 0545215129; 9780545215121

LC 2011017862

This book tells the story of "seventh-grader [Louise who] lives with her grandparents in their condo and she"s quit [gymnastics], . . . instead spending her time with friends Reni and her brother Henderson Elliot, whose warm and embracing family she adores. When a cute ninth-grader turns up on her doorstep delivering pizza, and she then finds a note under the mat confessing interest in Louise, she"s transported into her first serious crush." (Bulletin of the Center for Children"s Books)

Stone, Tamara Ireland

Time between us; Tamara Ireland Stone. Hyperion 2012 384 p. (hardcover) $17.99

Grades: 7 8 9 10 **Fic**

1. Love stories 2. Time travel -- Fiction 3. High schools -- Fiction 4. Space and time -- Fiction
ISBN 142315956X; 9781423159568

LC 2011053368

This book by Tamara Ireland Stone follows "Anna and Bennett," a couple who "were never supposed to meet: she lives in 1995 Chicago and he lives in 2012 San Francisco. But Bennett's unique ability to travel through time and space brings him into Anna's life, and with him, a new world of adventure and possibility. As their relationship deepens, they face the reality that time might knock Bennett back where he belongs." (Publisher's note)

Stork, Francisco X.

★ **Marcelo** in the real world. Arthur A. Levine Books 2009 312p $17.99

Grades: 8 9 10 11 12 **Fic**

1. Autism -- Fiction 2. Asperger's syndrome -- Fiction
ISBN 0-545-05474-5; 978-0-545-05474-4

LC 2008-14729

ALA Schneider Family Book Award Honor Book (2010)

This book features "Marcelo Sandoval [who] is a 17-year-old looking forward to his senior year in high school. Living with something akin to Asperger's syndrome, Marcelo has spent his life learning step by step how to do things that many people learn intuitively. . . . Marcelo's father makes a deal with him: if he will spend the summer working at his father's law firm and successfully follow the rules of the real world, he can choose where he will spend his senior year." (Christian Century)

"Stork introduces ethical dilemmas, the possibility of love, and other 'real world" conflicts, all the while preserving the integrity of his characterizations and intensifying the novel's psychological and emotional stakes." Publ Wkly

★ The **last** summer of the death warriors. Arthur A. Levine Books 2010 344p $17.99

Grades: 8 9 10 11 12 **Fic**

1. Death -- Fiction 2. Orphans -- Fiction 3. Mexican

Americans -- Fiction
ISBN 978-0-545-15133-7; 0-545-15133-3

LC 2009-19853

"This novel, in the way of the best literary fiction, is an invitation to careful reading that rewards serious analysis and discussion. Thoughtful readers will be delighted by both the challenge and Stork's respect for their abilities." Booklist

Strasser, Todd

Boot camp. Simon & Schuster Books for Young Readers 2007 238p hardcover o.p. pa $6.99

Grades: 8 9 10 11 12 **Fic**

1. Torture -- Fiction 2. Juvenile delinquency -- Fiction
ISBN 978-1-4169-0848-7; 1-4169-0848-X; 978-1-4169-5942-7 pa; 1-4169-5942-4 pa

LC 2006-13634

After ignoring several warnings to stop dating his former teacher, Garrett is sent to Lake Harmony, a boot camp that uses brutal methods to train students to obey their parents.

"The ending is both realistic and disturbing. . . . Writing in the teen's mature and perceptive voice, Strasser creates characters who will provoke strong reactions from readers. . . . [This is a] fast-paced and revealing story." SLJ

Can't get there from here. Simon & Schuster Books for Young Readers 2004 198p $15.95

Grades: 7 8 9 10 **Fic**

1. Homeless persons -- Fiction 2. Runaway teenagers -- Fiction
ISBN 0-689-84169-8

LC 2003-170

Tired of being hungry, cold, and dirty from living on the streets of New York City with a tribe of other homeless teenagers who are dying, one by one, a girl named Maybe ponders her future and longs for someone to care about her

"While the events described in this cautionary tale are shocking, the language is not, making these all-too-real problems accessible to a wide readership." SLJ

Famous. Simon & Schuster Books for Young Readers 2011 257p $15.99

Grades: 7 8 9 10 **Fic**

1. Fame -- Fiction 2. Actors -- Fiction 3. Celebrities -- Fiction
ISBN 978-1-4169-7511-3; 1-4169-7511-X

LC 2009-48163

Sixteen-year-old Jamie Gordon had a taste of praise and recognition at age fourteen when her unflattering photograph of an actress was published, but as she pursues her dream of being a celebrity photographer, she becomes immersed in the dark side of fame.

"The book makes some astute observations about America's reality-television culture and its obsession with fame. . . . This well-crafted novel clearly belongs in all public, junior high, and high school libraries." Voice Youth Advocates

If I grow up. Simon & Schuster Books for Young Readers 2009 222p $16.99

Grades: 7 8 9 10 **Fic**

1. Gangs -- Fiction 2. Poverty -- Fiction 3. Violence

-- Fiction 4. African Americans -- Fiction
ISBN 978-1-4169-2523-1; 1-4169-2523-6

LC 2008-00655

Growing up in the inner-city projects, DeShawn is reluctantly forced into the gang world by circumstances beyond his control.

"Strasser's writing puts the reader in the midst of the projects and offers totally real characters." Voice Youth Advocates

Includes bibliographical references

Stratton, Allan

★ **Borderline**. HarperTeen 2010 298p $16.99; lib bdg $17.89

Grades: 6 7 8 9 10   **Fic**
1. Muslims -- Fiction 2. Terrorism -- Fiction 3. Friendship -- Fiction 4. Prejudices -- Fiction
ISBN 978-0-06-145111-9; 0-06-145111-8; 978-0-06-145112-6 lib bdg; 0-06-145112-6 lib bdg

LC 2009-5241

Despite the strained relationship between them, teenaged Sami Sabiri risks his life to uncover the truth when his father is implicated in a terrorist plot.

This is "a powerful story and excellent resource for teaching tolerance, with a message that extends well beyond the timely subject matter." Publ Wkly

Chanda's secrets. Annick Press 2004 193p $19.95; pa $8.95

Grades: 7 8 9 10   **Fic**
1. AIDS (Disease) -- Fiction
ISBN 1-55037-835-X; 1-55037-834-1 pa

Michael L. Printz Award honor book, 2005

"The details of sub-Saharan African life are convincing and smoothly woven into this moving story of poverty and courage, but the real insight for readers will be the appalling treatment of the AIDS victims. Strong language and frank description are appropriate to the subject matter." SLJ

Another title about Chanda is:
Chanda's war (2007)

Strauss, Victoria

Passion blue; by Victoria Strauss. Marshall Cavendish Children 2012 346 p. (hardcover) $17.99

Grades: 7 8 9 10 11 12   **Fic**
1. Historical fiction 2. Convents -- Fiction 3. Women artists -- Fiction 4. Self-realization -- Fiction 5. Nuns -- Fiction 6. Magic -- Fiction 7. Artists -- Fiction 8. Talismans -- Fiction
ISBN 0761462309; 9780761462309; 9780761462316

LC 2011040133

In this book by Victoria Strauss, when "Giulia is forced into a convent . . . she is surprised to learn of the beauty within, and that nuns and novices have vocations. . . . Her world expands as she learns the tools, materials, and techniques of great Renaissance painters. By chance, she meets a young male artisan repairing a convent masterpiece. They begin a clandestine romance. Her two desires -- painting and a husband -- war within as she contemplates her future." (School Library Journal)

Strickland, Brad

The **sign** of the sinister sorcerer; [by] Brad Strickland. Dial Books for Young Readers 2008 168p $16.99

Grades: 4 5 6 7   **Fic**
1. Mystery fiction 2. Magic -- Fiction 3. Uncles -- Fiction 4. Orphans -- Fiction 5. Witches -- Fiction 6. Supernatural -- Fiction
ISBN 978-0-8037-3151-6; 0-8037-3151-5

LC 2008007698

In Michigan in the mid-1950s, Lewis Barnavelt is convinced that the series of accidents he and his uncle are experiencing are the result of a curse by a mysterious, hooded figure that may be part of his uncle's past.

"For readers who enjoy trying to solve the mystery as they read, there are abundant clues including an anagram. A quick, exciting read." SLJ

Other titles about Lewis Barnavelt by Brad Strickland are:
The beast under the wizard's bridge (2000)
The house where nobody lived (2006)
The spector from the magician's museum (1998)
The tower at the end of the world (2001)
The whistle, the grave, and the ghost (2003)

Stringer, Helen

★ **Spellbinder**. Feiwel and Friends 2009 372p $17.99

Grades: 5 6 7 8   **Fic**
1. Ghost stories 2. Dead -- Fiction
ISBN 978-0-312-38763-1; 0-312-38763-6

LC 2008-28552

Twelve-year-old Belladonna Johnson, who lives with the ghosts of her parents in the north of England, teams up with an always-in-trouble classmate to investigate why all of the ghosts in the world have suddenly disappeared.

"Magical creatures, amulets, and verses are all a part of this delightful tale. . . . Stringer maintains the humor and logic of preteens who are awkwardly coming into their magical destinies." SLJ

The **midnight** gate. Feiwel and Friends 2011 376p $17.99

Grades: 5 6 7 8   **Fic**
1. Ghost stories 2. School stories 3. Orphans -- Fiction 4. Supernatural -- Fiction
ISBN 0-312-38764-4; 978-0-312-38764-8

LC 2010036476

Twelve-year-old Belladonna Johnson, who lives with the ghosts of her parents, once again teams up with her classmate Steve, whose mother has suddenly disappeared, when they are given a dangerous assignment by a ghostly monk involving a return to the Dark Times.

"Stringer's vivid descriptions and irreverent nods to all sorts of mythology, along with well-paced cliff-hangers throughout, are just right for fantasy and adventure buffs." Booklist

Strohmeyer, Sarah

Smart girls get what they want; by Sarah Strohmeyer. 1st ed. Harpercollins Childrens Books 2012 348 p. (tr. bdg.) $17.99; (paperback) $9.99

Grades: 7 8 9 10 11 12   **Fic**
1. Female friendship -- Fiction 2. High school students
-- Fiction 3. Interpersonal relations -- Fiction
ISBN 0061953407; 9780061953408; 9780061953415
LC 2011026094

Author Sarah Strohmeyer tells the story of Gigi, Neerja,
and Bea, three friends who "stumble upon . . . [Neerja's sis-
ter] Parad's signature-less yearbook, making them think that
maybe studying isn't everything. . . . When Gigi is accused
of cheating on the AP Chemistry midterm along with Mike, a
Man Clan wannabe who calls her 'Einstein,' the girls launch
into action. Gigi finds herself running for student rep against
Will, the new guy from California. . . . Neerja tries out for
the lead in Romeo and Juliet and Bea convinces Gigi to join
the ski team with her." (Kirkus Reviews)

Stroud, Jonathan
★ The **Amulet** of Samarkand. Hyperion Bks. for
Children 2003 462p (Bartimaeus trilogy) $17.95;
pa $7.99
Grades: 7 8 9 10   **Fic**
1. Fantasy fiction
ISBN 0-7868-1859-X; 0-7868-5255-0 pa
LC 2003-49904

Nathaniel, a magician's apprentice, summons up the
djinni Bartimaeus and instructs him to steal the Amulet of
Samarkand from the powerful magician Simon Lovelace.

"There is plenty of action, mystery, and humor to keep
readers turning the pages. This title, the first in a trilogy, is a
must for fantasy fans." SLJ

Other titles in this series are:
The golem's eye (2004)
Ptolemy's gate (2006)

★ **Heroes** of the valley. Hyperion Books for
Children 2009 483p $17.99
Grades: 7 8 9 10   **Fic**
1. Adventure fiction 2. Middle Ages -- Fiction
ISBN 978-1-4231-0966-2; 1-4231-0966-X

"Twelve Houses control sections of a valley. Halli
Sveinsson—at 15, the youngest child of the rulers of the
House of Svein—goes against tradition when he sets out
to avenge the death of his murdered uncle, and his actions
result in warfare among Houses for the first time in generations. . . . Smart, funny dialogue and prose, revealing passages about the exploits of the hero Svein, bouts of action and a
touch of romance briskly move the story along." Publ Wkly

★ The **ring** of Solomon; a Bartimaeus novel.
Disney/Hyperion Books 2010 398p $17.99
Grades: 7 8 9 10   **Fic**
1. Fantasy fiction 2. Kings 3. Magic -- Fiction 4.
Witchcraft -- Fiction
ISBN 978-1-4231-2372-9; 1-4231-2372-7
LC 2010015468

Wise-cracking djinni Bartimaeus finds himself at the
court of King Solomon with an unpleasant master, a sinister
servant, and King Solomon's magic ring.

"In this exciting prequel set in ancient Israel, Stroud
presents an early adventure of his sharp-tongued djinn, Bartimaeus. . . . This is a superior fantasy that should have fans
racing back to those books." Publ Wkly

Strykowski, Marcia
Call Me Amy; Marcia Strykowski. Midpoint
Trade Books Inc 2013 180 p. (hardcover) $24.95
Grades: 6 7 8   **Fic**
1. Adolescence 2. Animal rescue
ISBN 1935462768; 9781935462767

In this novel, set in Maine in 1973, eighth-grader Amy
Henderson is dealing with acne, her faraway best friend, and
overall nervousness. "But the sudden appearance of an injured harbor seal brings her closer to two unlikely allies as
they care for the seal, dubbed 'Pup,' in secret: loudmouthed
Craig, whose carefree personality is a cover for underlying
insecurities and family problems, and elderly Miss Cogshell,
who proves to be worldly and kind." (Publishers Weekly)

"Well-drawn, sympathetic characters and the developing
spark between Amy and Craig combine to create a pleasant,
satisfying read." Kirkus

Stuber, Barbara
★ **Crossing** the tracks. Margarert K. McElderry
Books 2010 258p $16.99
Grades: 6 7 8 9   **Fic**
1. Household employees -- Fiction 2. Father-daughter
relationship -- Fiction
ISBN 978-1-4169-9703-0; 1-4169-9703-2
LC 2009-42672

In Missouri in 1926, fifteen-year-old Iris Baldwin discovers what family truly means when her father hires her
out for the summer as a companion to a country doctor's
invalid mother.

"Thought-provoking and tenderhearted, Iris's story is
one of a mature young woman who faces life with courage
and common sense. . . . This thoughtful novel offers strong
character development and an engaging protagonist." SLJ

Sturtevant, Katherine
The **brothers** story; Katherine Sturtevant. 1st
ed. Farrar, Straus & Giroux 2009 271 p. (rein-
forced) $16.99
Grades: 6 7 8   **Fic**
1. Twins -- Fiction 2. Brothers -- Fiction 3. Apprentices
-- Fiction 4. Mentally handicapped -- Fiction
ISBN 0374309922; 9780374309923
LC 2008035513

"Kit's wrestling with situations of moral complexity
leads him to question some of the era's culturally accepted
religious mores, providing a subtle but enlightening exploration of class and gender roles. . . . An era comes alive
in this tale of a young man's awakening to his life's call."
Publ Wkly

"Readers will quickly empathize with Kit; his conflicted
feelings toward his brother, a mixture of great tenderness
and shame, are sensitively drawn. He experiences the beginnings of his sexual awakening in scenes that are occasionally
ribald but never gratuitous. Sturtevant invokes the cacoph-
ony of noises, smells, and sights of London, along with the
sorrows and kindnesses found in daily life." SLJ

A **true** and faithful narrative. Farrar, Straus &
Giroux 2006 247p $17

Grades: 6 7 8 9   Fic

1. London (England)--Fiction

ISBN 0-374-37809-6

LC 2005046922

In London in the 1680s, Meg—now sixteen years old—tries to decide whether to marry either of the two men who court her, taking into account both love and her writing ambitions.

The author "offers readers a story depicted with great clarity and many vivid details of everyday life. Written in the first-person, the narrative reveals Meg as a strong-willed yet vulnerable young woman who emerges as a well-rounded, convincing individual." Booklist

Sullivan, Laura L.

Guardian of the Green Hill; [illustrations by David Wyatt] Henry Holt and Company 2011 293p il $16.99

Grades: 5 6 7 8   Fic

1. Fantasy fiction 2. Fairies -- Fiction 3. Siblings -- Fiction 4. Supernatural -- Fiction

ISBN 978-0-8050-8985-1; 0-8050-8985-3

LC 2010029231

After the Midsummer War ends, Meg Morgan faces a madman in the battle for control of the last bastion of fairies in England, aided by her siblings Rowan, Silly, and James, and American neighbors Dickie Rhys, and Finn Fachan.

"Sullivan's writing has a timelessness that contrasts nicely with Meg's distinctly modern ideas and weaves a compelling story that will pull readers along." SLJ

Under the green hill. Henry Holt and Company 2010 308p $16.99

Grades: 5 6 7 8   Fic

1. Fantasy fiction 2. Fairies -- Fiction 3. Siblings -- Fiction 4. Supernatural -- Fiction

ISBN 978-0-8050-8984-4; 0-8050-8984-5

LC 2009-50772

While staying with distant relatives in England, Americans Rowan, Meg, Silly, and James Morgan, with their neighbors Dickie Rhys and Finn Fachan, learn that one of them must fight to the death in the Midsummer War required by the local fairies

"Sullivan draws heavily on her knowledge of Middle English folklore and creates a story rich with memorable characters and evocative language." SLJ

Sullivan, Mary

Dear Blue Sky; Mary Sullivan. Nancy Paulsen Books 2012 248 $16.99

Grades: 4 5 6 7   Fic

1. Siblings -- Fiction 2. War -- Fiction 3. Pen pals -- Fiction 4. Family life -- Fiction 5. Down syndrome -- Fiction 6. Iraq War, 2003-2011 -- Fiction 7. Brothers and sisters -- Fiction

ISBN 0399256849; 9780399256844

LC 2011046952

In the book by Mary Sullivan, "Cassie's whole world changes when her beloved older brother, Sef, goes to war in Iraq . . . While her parents are preoccupied, her best friend, Sonia, inexplicably stops talking to her; her older sister, Van, tests out risky behaviors; and her developmentally delayed younger brother, Jack, becomes altogether silent. When a seventh-grade social-studies project leads her to a blog called Blue Sky, written by an Iraqi girl of similar age, Cassie starts to see the war from a different perspective." (Kirkus)

Sullivan, Tara

Golden boy; Tara Sullivan. G.P. Putnam's Sons, an imprint of Penguin Group (USA) Inc. 2013 368 p. (hardcover) $16.99

Grades: 7 8 9 10 11 12   Fic

1. Voyages and travels -- Fiction 2. Albinos and albinism -- Fiction 3. Survival -- Fiction 4. Human rights -- Fiction 5. Human skin color -- Fiction

ISBN 0399161120; 9780399161124

LC 2012043310

In this book, an albino boy named Habo does not fit in with his Tanzanian family, who shun him. "Only Habo's sister, Asu, protects and nurtures him. Poverty forces the family from their rural home near Arusha to Mwanza, hundreds of miles away, to stay with relatives. After their bus fare runs out, they hitch a ride across the Serengeti with an ivory poacher who sees opportunity in Habo. Forced to flee for his life, the boy eventually becomes an apprentice to Kweli, a wise, blind carver." (Kirkus)

Suma, Nova Ren

Dani noir. Aladdin 2009 266p $15.99

Grades: 6 7 8 9   Fic

1. Mystery fiction 2. Divorce -- Fiction 3. Remarriage -- Fiction 4. Motion pictures -- Fiction 5. Mother-daughter relationship -- Fiction

ISBN 978-1-4169-7564-9; 1-4169-7564-0

LC 2009-22270

Imaginative thirteen-year-old Dani feels trapped in her small mountain town with only film noir at the local art theater and her depressed mother for company, but while trying to solve a real mystery she learns much about herself and life.

"Suma's watertight debut displays an expert balance of the realities of teenage life, humor and intrigue." Publ Wkly

Summers, Courtney

This is not a test; Courtney Summers. St. Martin's Griffin 2012 336 p. $9.99; (pbk.) $9.99

Grades: 7 8 9 10 11 12   Fic

1. Adventure fiction 2. Zombies -- Fiction 3. Child abuse -- Fiction 4. Horror stories 5. Schools -- Fiction 6. Survival -- Fiction

ISBN 0312656742; 9780312656744; 9781250011817

LC 2012004633

In this book, "six teens who barely know or like each other seek refuge in their high school while the undead hordes lurk outside. . . . The end of the world unfolds through the eyes of high school junior Sloane Price, who has been contemplating suicide since her older sister ran away six months earlier, leaving Sloane with their physically abusive father. But these worries are pushed aside as Sloane tries to keep her fellow students alive." (Publishers Weekly)

Sun, Amanda

Ink; Amanda Sun. Harlequin Books 2013 304 p. (paperback) $9.99

Grades: 7 8 9 10 11 12   **Fic**

1. Love stories 2. Fantasy fiction 3. Japan -- Fiction
ISBN 037321071X; 9780373210718

In this teen romance novel, by Amanda Sun, part of "The Paper Gods" series, "Katie Greene must move halfway across the world. Stuck with her aunt in Shizuoka, Japan, Katie feels lost. Alone. . . . When Katie meets aloof but gorgeous Tomohiro, the star of the school's kendo team, she is intrigued by him. . . . Somehow Tomo is connected to the kami, powerful ancient beings who once ruled Japan--and as feelings develop between Katie and Tomo, things begin to spiral out of control." (Publisher's note)

"Katie's tendency to jump to conclusions, cry, and act before she thinks is frustrating, but it leaves plenty of room for growth. The descriptions of life in Japan—particularly teen life— create a strong sense of place, and set a vivid backdrop for this intriguing series opener by a debut author." BookList

Supplee, Suzanne

Somebody everybody listens to. Dutton 2010 245p $16.99

Grades: 7 8 9 10 11 12   **Fic**

1. Singers -- Fiction 2. Country music -- Fiction
ISBN 978-0-525-42242-6; 0-525-42242-0
LC 2009-25089

Retta Lee Jones is blessed with a beautiful voice and has big dreams of leaving her tiny Tennessee hometown. With a beaten down car, a pocketful of hard-earned waitressing money, and stars in her eyes, Retta sets out to make it big in Nashville.

"While a must read for country music lovers, . . . [this book] will appeal to a wide audience, especially those who long to pursue a dream against the odds." Publ Wkly

Sutcliff, Rosemary

Sword song. Farrar, Straus & Giroux 1998 271p hardcover o.p. pa $6.95

Grades: 7 8 9 10   **Fic**

1. Vikings -- Fiction
ISBN 0-374-37363-9; 0-374-46984-9 pa
LC 98-16827

At sixteen, Bjarni is cast out of the Norse settlement in the Angles' Land for an act of oath-breaking and spends five years sailing the west coast of Scotland and witnessing the feuds of the clan chiefs living there

"This is a well-crafted story that will appeal to sophisticated readers." SLJ

Sweeney, Joyce

The **guardian**. Henry Holt and Co. 2009 177p $16.95

Grades: 7 8 9 10   **Fic**

1. School stories 2. Bullies -- Fiction 3. Siblings -- Fiction 4. Foster home care -- Fiction 5. Father-son relationship -- Fiction
ISBN 978-0-8050-8019-3; 0-8050-8019-8
LC 2008-40602

When thirteen-year-old Hunter, struggling to deal with a harsh, money-grubbing foster mother, three challenging foster sisters, and a school bully, returns to his childhood faith and prays to St. Gabriel, he instantly becomes aware that he does, indeed, have a guardian.

"Sweeney's prose is insightful and realistic, with cleverly delivered descriptions. The peripheral characters are believable, and the religious undercurrent supports the plot. Well-paced, and with a satisfying conclusion." SLJ

Swift, Jonathan

Gulliver's travels; illustrated by Scott McKowen. Sterling Pub. Co. 2007 293p il (Sterling unabridged classics) $9.95

Grades: 7 8 9 10 11 12 Adult   **Fic**

1. Fantasy fiction 2. Voyages and travels -- Fiction
ISBN 978-1-4027-4339-9; 1-4027-4339-4
LC 2007003974

First published 1726

"In the account of his four wonder-countries Swift satirizes contemporary manners and morals, art and politics-in fact the whole social scheme-from four different points of view. The huge Brobdingnagians reduce man to his natural insignificance, the little people of Lilliput parody Europe and its petty broils, in Laputa philosophers are ridiculed, and finally all Swift's hatred and contempt find their satisfaction in degrading humanity to a bestial condition." Baker. Guide to the Best Fic

Swinburne, Stephen R.

Wiff and Dirty George: the Z.E.B.R.A. Incident. Boyds Mills Press 2010 167p il $17.95

Grades: 4 5 6 7   **Fic**

1. Great Britain -- Fiction
ISBN 978-1-59078-755-7; 1-59078-755-2

"London in 1969 was a trippy place, no doubt, but it's made even more psychodelic with the adventures of Wiff and Dirty George, two twelve-year-olds who follow their noses into a world of trouble. While on a morning train, the boys are slightly horrified when everyone's pants fall down, but instead of worrying overmuch about their own embarrassment, they take off after the large white rabbit who seems to be the instigator of the mass humiliation. . . . The humor is more situational than verbal; the characters are all comedic straight men in a twisted, absurd world. . . . Delightfully daft 'clues' precede each chapter, and a glossary of Britishisms will help young Yanks navigate the dialect." Bull Cent Child Books

Tak, Bibi Dumon

Soldier bear; written by Bibi Dumon Tak; illustrated by Philip Hopman; translated by Laura Watkinson. Eerdmans Books for Young Readers 2011 145p il $13

Grades: 4 5 6 7   **Fic**

1. Bears -- Fiction 2. Soldiers -- Fiction 3. World War, 1939-1945 -- Fiction
ISBN 978-0-8028-5375-2; 0-8028-5375-7
LC 2011013963

Original Dutch edition 2008

An orphaned Syrian brown bear cub is adopted by Polish soldiers during World War II and serves for five years as their mischievous mascot in Iran and Italy. Based on a true story.

"This is smoothly translated and engagingly illustrated with sketches and helpful maps. Funny, fresh and heartwarming." Kirkus

Tal, Eve

Cursing Columbus. Cinco Puntos Press 2009 248p $17.95

Grades: 7 8 9 10   **Fic**
   1. Jews -- Fiction 2. Immigrants -- Fiction 3. Family life -- Fiction 4. Russian Americans -- Fiction
   ISBN 978-1-933693-59-0; 1-933693-59-2
                         LC 2009-15834
In 1907, fourteen-year-old Raizel, who has lived in New York City for three years, and her brother Lemmel, newly-arrived, respond very differently to the challenges of living as Ukrainian Jews in the Lower East Side as Raizel works toward fitting in and getting ahead, while Lemmel joins a gang and lives on the streets
  "The story offers a realistic and poignant picture of a bygone time." SLJ

Double crossing. Cinco Puntos Press 2005 261p $16.95

Grades: 7 8 9 10   **Fic**
   1. Jews -- Fiction 2. Immigrants -- Fiction
   ISBN 0-938317-94-6
                         LC 2005-8188
In 1905, as life becomes increasingly difficult for Jews in Ukraine, eleven-year-old Raizel and her father flee to America in hopes of earning money to bring the rest of the family there, but her father's health and Orthodox faith become barriers.
  "Tal's fictionalized account of her grandfather's journey to America is fast paced, full of suspense, and highly readable." SLJ

Tanner, Lian

City of lies. Delacorte Press 2011 278 p. (The Keeper's trilogy) lib bdg $20.99; $17.99

Grades: 5 6 7 8   **Fic**
   1. Fantasy fiction 2. Adventure fiction 3. Thieves -- Fiction 4. Kidnapping -- Fiction
   ISBN 0385739060; 0385907699 lib bdg; 9780385907699 lib bdg; 9780385739061
                         LC 2010048579
Twelve-year-old Goldie, impulsive and bold, relies on her skills as a liar and a thief to try to rescue her captured friends from the child-stealers running rampant in the City of Spoke.

Museum of thieves. Delacorte Press 2010 312p (The Keepers Trilogy) $16.99; lib bdg $19.99

Grades: 5 6 7 8   **Fic**
   1. Fantasy fiction 2. Adventure fiction 3. Museums -- Fiction 4. Thieves -- Fiction
   ISBN 978-0-385-73905-4; 0-385-73905-2; 978-0-385-90768-2 lib bdg; 0-385-90768-0 lib bdg
                         LC 2009053655
Goldie, an impulsive and bold twelve-year-old, escapes the oppressive city of Jewel, where children are required to wear guardchains for their protection, and finds refuge in the extraordinary Museum of Dunt, an ever-shifting world where she discovers a useful talent for thievery and mysterious secrets that threaten her city and everyone she loves.
  "Readers will be quickly caught up in the highly dramatic chases, the intriguing museum that shifts layout at will, and the nifty otherworld elements. There's depth beneath that, though. . . . [The book] may set young readers thinking about their own world's choices." Bull Cent Child Books

Tarshis, Lauren

Emma -Jean Lazarus fell in love. Dial Books for Young Readers 2009 169p $16.99; pa $6.99

Grades: 5 6 7   **Fic**
   1. School stories 2. Friendship -- Fiction
   ISBN 978-0-8037-3321-3; 0-8037-3321-6; 978-0-14-241568-9 pa; 0-14-241568-5 pa
Seventh-grader Emma-Jean Lazarus uses her logical, scientific mind to navigate the mysteries of the upcoming Spring Fling, her friend Colleen's secret admirer, and other love-related dilemmas
  "Tarshis deftly weaves in important details from the previous book . . . providing those new to Emma-Jean some necessary back story. . . . Fans will appreciate the continuity and relish the reappearance of familiar characters, especially Ms Wright, the lovable school janitor, and the rest of Emma Jean's true blue friends. The story ends on a happy note with the possibility of more adventures to come." Kirkus

★ **Emma** -Jean Lazarus fell out of a tree. Dial Books for Young Readers 2007 199p $16.99

Grades: 5 6 7   **Fic**
   1. School stories 2. Friendship -- Fiction
   ISBN 978-0-8037-3164-6; 0-8037-3164-7
                         LC 2006-18428
A quirky and utterly logical seventh-grade girl named Emma-Jean Lazarus discovers some interesting results when she gets involved in the messy everyday problems of her peers.
  "Readers will be fascinated by Emma-Jean's emotionless observations and her adult-level vocabulary. Tarshis pulls off a balancing act, showing the child's detachment yet making her a sympathetic character. Exceptionally fleshed-out secondary characters add warmth to the story." SLJ

Tashjian, Janet

★ **My** life as a book; with cartoons by Jake Tashjian. Henry Holt 2010 211p il $16.99; pa $6.99

Grades: 4 5 6 7   **Fic**
   1. Summer -- Fiction 2. Animals -- Fiction 3. Family life -- Fiction 4. Books and reading -- Fiction
   ISBN 978-0-8050-8903-5; 0-8050-8903-9; 978-0-312-67289-8 pa; 0-312-67289-6 pa
                         LC 2009-18909
Dubbed a "reluctant reader" by his teacher, twelve-year-old Derek spends summer vacation learning important lessons even though he does not complete his summer reading list.
  "The protagonist is by turns likable and irritating, but always interesting. He is sure to engage fans of Jeff Kinney's 'Diary of a Wimpy Kid' books . . . as well as those looking for a spunky, contemporary boy with a mystery to solve.

Reluctant readers will appreciate the book's large print and quick-paced story." SLJ

"Another title about Derek is:
My life as a stuntboy (2011)

The **gospel** according to Larry. Holt & Co. 2001 227p il $16.95; pa $5.99

Grades: 7 8 9 10　　　　　　　　　　　　　　Fic
1. Fame 2. Web sites 3. Identity 4. Coming of age 5. Web sites -- Fiction
ISBN 0-8050-6378-1; 0-440-23792-0 pa
LC 2001-24568

Seventeen-year-old Josh, a loner-philosopher who wants to make a difference in the world, tries to maintain his secret identity as the author of a web site that is receiving national attention

"Tashjian fabricates a cleverly constructed scenario and expertly carries it out to the bittersweet end." Horn Book Guide

Other titles about Larry are:
Vote for Larry (2004)
Larry and the meaning of life (2008)

Tate, Eleanora E.

Celeste's Harlem Renaissance. Little, Brown 2007 279p $15.99; pa $5.99

Grades: 4 5 6 7　　　　　　　　　　　　　　Fic
1. Aunts -- Fiction 2. African Americans -- Fiction 3. Harlem Renaissance -- Fiction
ISBN 978-0-316-52394-3; 978-0-316-11362-5 pa

In 1921, thirteen-year-old Celeste leaves North Carolina to stay with her glamorous Aunt Valentina in Harlem, New York, where she discovers the vibrant Harlem Renaissance in full swing, even though her aunt's life is not exactly what she was led to believe.

"Both sobering and inspiring, Tate's novel is a moving portrait of growing up black and female in 1920s America." Booklist

Taub, Melinda

Still star-crossed; by Melinda Taub. 1st ed. Random House Childrens Books 2013 352 p. (library) $19.99; (hardcover) $16.99

Grades: 7 8 9 10 11 12　　　　　　　　　　Fic
1. Love stories 2. Historical fiction 3. Love -- Fiction 4. Families -- Fiction 5. Vendetta -- Fiction 6. Characters in literature -- Fiction
ISBN 0385743505; 9780375991189; 9780385743501
LC 2012032626

This young adult novel is a sequel to the events of the play "Romeo and Juliet." The "peace purchased with Romeo's and Juliet's deaths lasts two weeks before the Capulets and Montagues renew their fight in the streets of Verona. . . . Prince Escalus attempts to force the feuding families into concord by arranging a marriage between Rosaline and Benvolio." (Kirkus Reviews)

Tayleur, Karen

Chasing boys. Walker & Co. 2009 244p $16.99

Grades: 7 8 9 10 11　　　　　　　　　　　　Fic
1. School stories 2. Fathers -- Fiction
ISBN 978-0-8027-9830-5; 0-8027-9830-6
LC 2008-23241

First published 2007 by Black Dog Books

With her father gone and her family dealing with financial problems, El transfers to a new school, where she falls for one of the popular boys and then must decide whether to remain true to herself or become like the girls she scorns.

"All the ingredients of El's life are blended seamlessly, never downplaying the audience's intelligence, as Tayleur captures the all-consuming nature of a teenage crush without making El ridiculous. Moody, poetic, and intimate, this book is billed as the 'romance for girls who don't like pink,' but is much more than that." Booklist

Taylor, Greg

Killer Pizza. Feiwel and Friends 2009 346p $16.99

Grades: 6 7 8 9　　　　　　　　　　　　　　Fic
1. Horror fiction 2. Monsters -- Fiction
ISBN 978-0-312-37379-5; 0-312-37379-1
LC 2008028543

While working as summer employees in a local pizza parlor, three teenagers are recruited by an underground organization of monster hunters.

"Toby is an easygoing and relatable young adult, and young teens will enjoy the fun, slightly scary read." Voice Youth Advocates

Killer Pizza: the slice. Feiwel and Friends 2011 341p $16.99

Grades: 6 7 8 9　　　　　　　　　　　　　　Fic
1. Horror fiction 2. Adventure fiction 3. Monsters -- Fiction
ISBN 978-0-312-58088-9; 0-312-58088-6
LC 2010048928

Having passed the tests to become Monster Combat Officers, teens Toby, Annabel, and Strobe are sent on a secret mission to deliver to the Monster Protection Program a beautiful fourteen-year-old monster who wants to defect, regardless of the considerable dangers this poses.

The **girl** who became a Beatle. Feiwel and Friends 2011 281p $16.99; pa $9.99

Grades: 6 7 8 9　　　　　　　　　　　　　　Fic
1. Fame -- Fiction 2. Rock music -- Fiction 3. Space and time -- Fiction 4. Conduct of life -- Fiction
ISBN 978-0-312-65259-3; 0-312-65259-3; 978-0-312-60683-1 pa; 0-312-60683-4 pa
LC 2010-41450

Regina Bloomsbury, a sixteen-year-old, Beatles-obsessed rocker, takes a trip to an alternate reality where the Beatles never existed and her band, the Caverns, are the rock-and-roll superstars.

"Teens will likely skim over the fantasy's shaky logistical questions and enjoy the vicarious view of stardom's perks and pitfalls, which Taylor deepens with Regina's lingering, real-world sorrow over her parents' divorce." Booklist

Taylor, Laini

Blackbringer. G. P. Putnam's Sons 2007 437p (Faeries of Dreamdark) $17.99

Grades: 6 7 8 9   **Fic**

1. Fantasy fiction 2. Magic -- Fiction 3. Fairies -- Fiction

ISBN 978-0-399-24630-2; 0-399-24630-4

LC 2006026540

Magpie Windwitch, faerie, devil hunter, and granddaughter of the West Wind, must defeat an ancient evil creature, the Blackbringer, who has escaped from his bottle and threatens to unmake all of creation.

"Taylor drives the story forward by slowly teasing the reader with twists and turns in the plot. . . . Teen readers will identify with this faerie's humanness." Voice Youth Advocates

★ **Daughter** of smoke and bone. Little, Brown 2011 418p $18.99

Grades: 8 9 10 11 12   **Fic**

1. Love stories 2. Occult fiction 3. Fantasy fiction 4. School stories 5. Angels -- Fiction 6. Artists -- Fiction 7. Supernatural -- Fiction 8. Classical mythology -- Fiction

ISBN 978-0-316-13402-6; 0-316-13402-3; 9780316196192

LC 2010045802

Seventeen-year-old Karou, a lovely, enigmatic art student in a Prague boarding school, carries a sketchbook of hideous, frightening monsters—the chimaerae who form the only family she has ever known.

Taylor "again weaves a masterful mix of reality and fantasy with cross-genre appeal. Exquisitely written and beautifully paced." Publ Wkly

★ **Days** of blood & starlight; Laini Taylor. 1st ed. Little, Brown Books for Young Readers 2012 528 p. maps (Daughter of smoke and bone trilogy) (hardcover) $18.99

Grades: 9 10 11 12   **Fic**

1. Angels -- Fiction 2. Demonology -- Fiction 3. Supernatural -- Fiction 4. Mythology, Greek -- Fiction

ISBN 0316133973; 9780316133975

LC 2012028752

In this fantasy sequel to "Daughter of Smoke and Bone," "Karou . . . has taken up the resurrection work . . . under the direction of the dangerous chimaera leader, Thiago. . . . The angel army is menacing the countryside in an attempt to kill the remaining chimaera, so she is designing and resurrecting stronger, more effective winged warriors to protect her people." (Bulletin of the Center for Children's Books)

Silksinger; illustrations by Jim Di Bartolo. G.P. Putnam's Sons 2009 449p il (Dreamdark) $18.99

Grades: 6 7 8 9   **Fic**

1. Fantasy fiction 2. Fairies -- Fiction 3. Mercenary soldiers -- Fiction 4. Good and evil -- Fiction

ISBN 978-0-399-24631-9; 0-399-24631-2

LC 2008047981

While journeying by dragonfly caravan over the Sayash Mountains, warrior-faerie Whisper Silksinger, hunted by devils, meets a young mercenary with an ancient scimitar and secrets of his own.

"With excellent world-building and deft pacing, this story is difficult to put down. The characters are well developed, and their close relationships and rapid-fire dialogue enhance the story." SLJ

Taylor, Mildred D.

★ **Let** the circle be unbroken. Dial Bks. for Young Readers 1981 394p $17.99; pa $7.99

Grades: 4 5 6 7   **Fic**

1. African Americans -- Fiction 2. Great Depression, 1929-1939 -- Fiction

ISBN 0-8037-4748-9; 0-14-034892-1 pa

LC 81-65854

The author "provides her readers with a literal sense of witnessing important American history. . . . Moreover, [she] never neglects the details of her volatile 9-year-old heroine's interior life. The daydreams, the jealousy, the incredible ardor of that age come alive." N Y Times Book Rev

★ **Roll** of thunder, hear my cry; 25th anniversary ed; Phyllis Fogelman Books 2001 276p $17.99; pa $7.99

Grades: 4 5 6 7 8 9   **Fic**

1. African Americans -- Fiction

ISBN 0-8037-2647-3; 0-14-240112-9 pa

LC 00-39378

First published 1976 by Dial Press

Awarded the Newbery Medal, 1977

"The time is 1933. The place is Spokane, Mississippi where the Logans, the only black family who own their own land, wage a courageous struggle to remain independent, displeasing a white plantation owner bent on taking their land. But this suspenseful tale is also about the story's young narrator, Cassie, and her three brothers who decide to wage their own personal battles to maintain the self-dignity and pride with which they were raised. . . . Ms. Taylor's richly textured novel shows a strong, proud black family . . . resisting rather than succumbing to oppression." Child Book Rev Serv

The **friendship**; pictures by Max Ginsburg. Dial Bks. for Young Readers 1987 53p il $15.99; pa $4.99

Grades: 4 5 6 7   **Fic**

1. Race relations -- Fiction 2. African Americans -- Fiction

ISBN 0-8037-0417-8; 0-14-038964-4 pa

LC 86-29309

Coretta Scott King Award for text

This "story about race relations in rural Mississippi during the Depression focuses on an incident between an old Black man, Mr. Tom Bee, and a white storekeeper, Mr. John Wallace. Indebted to Tom for saving his life as a young man, John had promised they would always be friends. But now, years later, John insists that Tom call him 'Mister' and shoots the old man for defiantly—and publicly—calling him by his first name. Narrator Cassie Logan and her brothers . . . are verbally abused by Wallace's villainous sons before witnessing the encounter." Bull Cent Child Books

★ The **gold** Cadillac; pictures by Michael Hays. Dial Bks. for Young Readers 1987 43p il $16.99; pa $4.99

Grades: 4 5 6 7   **Fic**

1. Prejudices -- Fiction 2. Race relations -- Fiction 3. African Americans -- Fiction

ISBN 0-8037-0342-2; 0-14-038963-6 pa

LC 86-11526

"Full-page sepia paintings effectively portray the characters, setting, and mood of the story events as Hays ably demonstrates his understanding of the social and emotional environments which existed for blacks during this period." SLJ

★ The **land**. Phyllis Fogelman Bks. 2001 375p $17.99; pa $6.99

Grades: 7 8 9 10   **Fic**

1. Race relations -- Fiction 2. African Americans -- Fiction 3. Racially mixed people -- Fiction

ISBN 0-8037-1950-7; 0-14-250146-8 pa

LC 00-39329

Coretta Scott King Award for text

After the Civil War Paul-Edward Logan, the son of a white father and a black mother, finds himself caught between the two worlds of colored folks and white folks as he pursues his dream of owning land of his own.

"Taylor masterfully uses harsh historical realities to frame a powerful coming-of-age story that stands on its own merits." Horn Book Guide

★ The **road** to Memphis; by Mildred Taylor. Dial Bks. 1989 290p $18.99; pa $6.99

Grades: 4 5 6 7   **Fic**

1. Race relations -- Fiction 2. African Americans -- Fiction

ISBN 0-8037-0340-6; 0-14-036077-8 pa

LC 88-33654

Coretta Scott King Award for text

Sadistically teased by two white boys in 1940's rural Mississippi, Cassie Logan's friend, Moe, severely injures one of the boys with a tire iron and enlists Cassie's help in trying to flee the state

"Taylor's continued smooth, easy language provides readability for all ages, with a focus on universal human pride, worthy values, and individual responsibility. This action-packed drama is highly recommended." Voice Youth Advocates

The **well**; David's story. Dial Bks. for Young Readers 1995 92p hardcover o.p. pa $5.99

Grades: 4 5 6 7   **Fic**

1. Race relations -- Fiction 2. African Americans -- Fiction

ISBN 0-8037-1802-0; 0-14-038642-4 pa

LC 94-25360

This story "delivers an emotional wallop in a concentrated span of time and action. . . . This story reverberates in the heart long after the final paragraph is read." Horn Book

Taylor, S. S.

The **Expeditioners** and the Treasure of Drowned Man's Canyon; and the Treasure of Drowned Man's Canyon. by S. S. Taylor; illustrated by Katherine Roy. Pgw 2012 320 p. $22

Grades: 5 6 7 8   **Fic**

1. Adventure fiction

ISBN 1938073061; 9781938073069

In this book by S. S. Taylor, illustrated by Katherine Roy, "computers have failed, electricity is extinct, and the race to discover new lands is underway! Brilliant explorer Alexander West has just died under mysterious circumstances, but not before smuggling half of a strange map to his intrepid children--Kit the brain, M.K. the tinkerer, and Zander the brave. Why are so many government agents trying to steal the half-map? (And where is the other half?)" (Publisher's note)

Taylor, Theodore

★ **Timothy** of the cay. Harcourt Brace & Co. 1993 161p hardcover o.p. pa $5.95

Grades: 5 6 7 8   **Fic**

1. Blind -- Fiction 2. Race relations -- Fiction 3. Survival after airplane accidents, shipwrecks, etc. -- Fiction

ISBN 0-15-288358-4; 0-15-206320-X pa

LC 93-7898

Having survived being blinded and shipwrecked on a tiny Caribbean island with the old black man Timothy, twelve-year-old white Phillip is rescued and hopes to regain his sight with an operation. Alternate chapters follow the life of Timothy from his days as a young cabin boy

"Somewhat more thoughtful than its well-loved antecedent, this boldly drawn novel is no less commanding." Publ Wkly

★ The **cay**. Delacorte Press 1987 137p $16.95; pa $5.50

Grades: 5 6 7 8   **Fic**

1. Blind -- Fiction 2. Race relations -- Fiction 3. Survival after airplane accidents, shipwrecks, etc. -- Fiction

ISBN 0-385-07906-0; 0-440-22912-X pa

A reissue of the title first published 1969

When the freighter on which they are traveling is torpedoed by a German submarine during World War II, Phillip, an adolescent white boy blinded by a blow on the head, and Timothy, an old black man, are stranded on a tiny Caribbean island where the boy acquires a new kind of vision, courage, and love from his old companion

"Starkly dramatic, believable and compelling." Saturday Rev

Teague, Mark

★ The **doom** machine; a novel. Blue Sky Press 2009 376p $17.99

Grades: 4 5 6 7   **Fic**

1. Science fiction 2. Space and time -- Fiction 3. Extraterrestrial beings -- Fiction

ISBN 978-0-545-15142-9; 0-545-15142-2

LC 2009-14262

When a spaceship lands in the small town of Vern Hollow in 1956, juvenile delinquent Jack Creedle and prim, studious Isadora Shumway form an unexpected alliance as they try to keep a group of extraterrestrials from stealing eccentric Uncle Bud's space travel machine.

"This book is filled with humor and dramatic figurative language that makes the setting completely approachable. It is a great fit for science fiction, humor, and adventure genre fans." Voice Youth Advocates

Teller, Janne

★ **Nothing**; translated from the Danish by Martin Aitken. Atheneum Books for Young Readers 2010 227p $16.99

Grades: 7 8 9 10 11 12   **Fic**
1. School stories 2. Meaning (Philosophy) -- Fiction
ISBN 978-1-4169-8579-2; 1-4169-8579-4

LC 2009-19784

Michael J. Printz honor book, 2011

When thirteen-year-old Pierre Anthon leaves school to sit in a plum tree and train for becoming part of nothing, his seventh grade classmates set out on a desperate quest for the meaning of life.

"Indelible, elusive, and timeless, this uncompromising novel has all the marks of a classic." Booklist

TenNapel, Doug

Cardboard; Doug TenNapel. Graphix / Scholastic 2012 288 p. $24.99

Grades: 5 6 7 8   **Fic**
1. Boxes -- Fiction 2. Gifts -- Graphic novels 3. Magic -- Graphic novels 4. Bullies -- Graphic novels 5. Father-son relationship -- Graphic novels
ISBN 0545418720; 9780545418720; 9780545418737

LC 2011934533

In this graphic novel, "Cam Howerton's out-of-work father is so broke, the best he can do for Cam's birthday is an empty cardboard box purchased from a toy seller with two mysterious rules: return every unused scrap of cardboard and don't ask for any more. . . . [T]he box becomes a project. What should father and son make out of the box? 'A boxer,' Cam suggests. . . . 'Boxer Bill,' created from inanimate material, comes alive. Unfortunately, Marcus, the neighborhood bully . . . steals the scrap materials, and begins turning out a whole evil empire of cardboard monsters. . . . [A]fter losing control of them he must unite with Cam and his father to defeat the massive cardboard army. . . . [Q]uestions are raised about what it means to be a man, what makes a good man, and what forms people's character." (Horn Book)

Terry, Chris L.

Zero fade; Chris L Terry. Curbside Splendor Publishing 2013 294 p. $12

Grades: 7 8 9 10   **Fic**
1. School stories 2. Bullies -- Fiction 3. Historical fiction
ISBN 0988480433; 9780988480438

LC 2013944486

This book focuses on Kevin Phifer, "a black seventh-grader in 1990s Richmond, Va." He "wants a fade, thinking the stylish haircut will bolster his shaky standing in the cut-throat world of middle school, where he's just one friend away from eating lunch alone. But his mother, a church secretary and solo parent studying for a nursing degree at night, won't even try. Expressing his frustration leads to a week's grounding. Tyrell and his entourage of bullies make Kevin's life miserable at school." (Kirkus Reviews)

"Original, hilarious, thought-provoking and wicked smart: not to be missed." (Kirkus)

Terry, Teri

Slated; Teri Terry. Nancy Paulsen Books 2013 346 p. (hardcover) $17.99

Grades: 7 8 9 10   **Fic**
1. Science fiction 2. Memory -- Fiction 3. Identity -- Fiction 4. Schools -- Fiction 5. High schools -- Fiction 6. Family life -- England -- Fiction
ISBN 0399161724; 9780399161728

LC 2012020873

In this novel, by Teri Terry, "Kyla has been Slated--her memory and personality erased as punishment for committing a crime she can't remember. The government has taught her how to walk and talk again, given her a new identity and a new family, and told her to be grateful for this second chance that she doesn't deserve. It's also her last chance--because they'll be watching to make sure she plays by their rules." (Publisher's note)

Testa, Dom

★ The **comet's** curse. Tor Teen 2009 236p (Galahad) $16.95

Grades: 7 8 9 10 11 12   **Fic**
1. Science fiction 2. Interplanetary voyages -- Fiction
ISBN 978-0-7653-2107-7; 0-7653-2107-6

LC 2008-35620

First published 2005 by Profound Impact Group

Desperate to save the human race after a comet's deadly particles devastate the adult population, scientists create a ship that will carry a crew of 251 teenagers to a home in a distant solar system.

This book is "both a mystery and an adventure, combining a solid cast of characters with humor, pathos, growing pains and just a hint of romance." Kirkus

Other titles in this series are:
The Cassini code (2010)
Cosmic storm (2011)
The dark zone (2011)
The web of Titan (2009)

Tharp, Tim

Knights of the hill country. Alfred A. Knopf 2006 233p hardcover o.p. pa $6.99

Grades: 8 9 10 11 12   **Fic**
1. School stories 2. Football -- Fiction
ISBN 978-0-375-83653-4; 0-375-83653-5; 978-0-553-49513-3 pa; 0-553-49513-5 pa

LC 2005-33279

In his senior year, high school star linebacker Hampton Greene finally begins to think for himself and discovers that he might be interested in more than just football.

"Taut scenes on the football field and the dilemmas about choosing what feels right over what's expected are all made memorable by Hamp's unforgettable, colloquial voice." Booklist

Thomas, Erin

Boarder patrol; written by Erin Thomas. Orca Book Publishers 2010 170p (Orca sports) pa $9.95

Grades: 6 7 8 9   **Fic**

1. Mystery fiction 2. Skiing -- Fiction 3. Cousins -- Fiction 4. Snowboarding -- Fiction

ISBN 978-1-55469-294-1 pa; 1-55469-294-6 pa

"Ryan, 16, works as a Junior Ski Patrol volunteer in order to earn a free lift pass. His dream is to pursue snowboarding professionally. His cousin, Kevin, who works at the lifts, starts acting strangely, especially when Ryan begins investigating the disappearance of some ski equipment, including his own, on the mountain. . . . The story includes vivid descriptions of snowboarding and mountain rescue, and the mystery is involving." SLJ

Thomason, Mark

Moonrunner. Kane/Miller 2009 217p $15.95

Grades: 4 5 6 7   **Fic**

1. Horses -- Fiction

ISBN 978-1-935279-03-7; 1-935279-03-3

First published 2008 in Australia

"In the 1890s, Casey and his parents immigrate to Australia, to a homestead that they inherited from his grandfather. The 12-year-old finds the change difficult. He is bullied at school, and he misses his baseball team in Montana and his horse. Then he happens upon a magnificent wild stallion, and he is determined to befriend the brumby, whom he names Moonrunner. . . . This well-paced story effectively portrays the family's struggles. Casey is a strong, engaging protagonist whose interactions with the other characters are believable and interesting." SLJ

Thompson, Holly

★ **Orchards**. Delacorte Press 2011 327p il $17.99; lib bdg $20.99

Grades: 7 8 9 10   **Fic**

1. Novels in verse 2. Suicide -- Fiction 3. Bereavement -- Fiction 4. Family life -- Fiction 5. Racially mixed people -- Fiction

ISBN 978-0-385-73977-1; 0-385-73977-X; 978-0-385-90806-1 lib bdg; 0-385-90806-7 lib bdg

LC 2010-23724

"Kanako's urgent teen voice, written in rapid free verse and illustrated with occasional black-and-white sketches, will hold readers with its nonreverential family story." Booklist

The **language** inside; Holly Thompson. 1st ed. Delacorte Press 2013 528 p. (hardcover) $17.99

Grades: 7 8 9 10 11 12   **Fic**

1. Novels in verse 2. Moving -- Fiction 3. Interpersonal relations -- Fiction 4. Cancer -- Fiction 5. Tsunamis -- Fiction 6. Moving, Household -- Fiction 7. Family life -- Massachusetts -- Fiction

ISBN 0385739796; 9780375898358; 9780385739795; 9780385908078

LC 2012030596

Includes bibliographical references (p. 520).

In this novel in verse, by Holly Thompson, "Emma's family moves to a town outside Lowell, Massachusetts, to stay with Emma's grandmother while her mom undergoes treatment. Emma feels out of place in the United States. She begins to have migraines, and longs to be back in Japan. At her grandmother's urging, she volunteers in a long-term care center to help Zena, a patient with locked-in syndrome, write down her poems." (Publisher's note)

Thompson, Kate

Origins. Bloomsbury 2007 313p (Missing link trilogy) $17.95

Grades: 6 7 8 9   **Fic**

1. Science fiction 2. Animals -- Fiction 3. Future life -- Fiction 4. Genetic engineering -- Fiction 5. Young adult literature -- Works

ISBN 978-1-58234-652-6; 1-58234-652-6

LC 2007-06924

Christy 's souvenir stone from the yeti's cave proves to be fatal for many of the inhabitants of Fourth World leaving among the survivors a pair of genetically-altered twins whose eventual descendants face an uncertain future in a stone age world of nuclear devastation and disease.

This is "a post-apolcalyptic stunner. [It blends] weighty science fiction themes like genetic engineering and the future of human evolution with equally thought-provoking allegorical fable." Publ Wkly

★ The **new** policeman. Greenwillow Books 2007 442p hardcover o.p. pa $8.99

Grades: 7 8 9 10   **Fic**

1. Fantasy fiction 2. Music -- Fiction 3. Fairies -- Fiction 4. Space and time -- Fiction

ISBN 978-0-06-117427-8; 0-06-117427-0; 978-0-06-117429-2 pa; 0-06-117429-7 pa

LC 2006-8246

First published 2005 in the United Kingdom

Irish teenager JJ Liddy discovers that time is leaking from his world into Tir na nOg, the land of the fairies, and when he attempts to stop the leak he finds out a lot about his family history, the music that he loves, and a crime his great-grandfather may or may not have committed.

"Mesmerizing and captivating, this book is guaranteed to charm fantasy fans." Voice Youth Advocates

Other titles in this series are:

The last of the High Kings (2008)

The white horse trick (2010)

Thompson, Paul B.

The **devil's** door; a Salem witchcraft story. Enslow Publishers 2010 160p (Historical fiction adventures) lib bdg $27.93; pa $14.95

Grades: 4 5 6   **Fic**

1. Trials -- Fiction 2. Witchcraft -- Fiction

ISBN 978-0-7660-3387-0 lib bdg; 0-7660-3387-2 lib bdg; 978-1-59845-214-3 pa; 1-59845-214-2 pa

Sarah Wright and her father Ephraim move to Salem Village, Massachusetts, in 1692, where they witness the Salem witchcraft hysteria, during which Ephraim is arrested and Sarah must try to help him escape from jail.

"Factual material is incorporated into the narrative, creating a fast-paced, fascinating read." SLJ

Thompson, Ricki

City of cannibals. Front Street 2010 269p
$18.95

Grades: 8 9 10 11 12   **Fic**
   1. Monks -- Fiction 2. Persecution -- Fiction 3.
Runaway teenagers -- Fiction
ISBN 978-1-59078-623-9; 1-59078-623-8
                    LC 2010-2105
   In 1536 England, sixteen-year-old Dell runs away from
her brutal father and life in a cave carrying only a handmade
puppet to travel to London, where she learns truths about her
mother's death and the conflict between King Henry VIII
and the Catholic Church.
   "Thompson's England is authentically vulgar, and her
grasp of period slang—as well as Dell's burgeoning sexual
desires—is expert. Packed with rich metaphor, this is a challenging but rewarding read." Booklist

Thomson, Jamie

Dark Lord, the early years; by Jamie Thomson.
Walker & Co. 2012 290 p. (hardcover) $16.99

Grades: 6 7 8 9   **Fic**
   1. School stories 2. Fantasy fiction 3. Fantasy 4.
Humorous stories 5. Magic -- Fiction 6. Identity --
Fiction
ISBN 0802728499; 9780802728494
             LC 2012007152
   In this book by Jamie Thomson, "the Dark Lord" renamed Dirk Lloyd by confused, puny Earthlings is taken to
the Hospital Lockup and then to a House of Detention" after
waking up in a parking lot "trapped in the body of a 12-year-
old human." People think he's crazy, "but thankfully, Christopher, the child of his captors, agrees to be a minion, as does
goth girl Sooz. Dirk must find a way back to his Darklands"
before he loses his evil abilities. (Kirkus)

Thomson, Sarah L.

The **secret** of the Rose; 1st ed.; Greenwillow
Books 2006 296p $16.99; lib bdg $17.89

Grades: 6 7 8 9   **Fic**
   1. Authors 2. Dramatists 3. Theater -- Fiction 4. Sex
role -- Fiction 5. Catholics -- Fiction
ISBN 978-0-06-087250-2; 0-06-087250-0; 978-0-06-
087251-9 lib bdg; 0-06-087251-9 lib bdg
            LC 2005-22177
   When her father is imprisoned in 1592 England for being Catholic, fourteen-year-old Rosalind disguises herself as
a boy and finds an ultimately dangerous job as servant to
playwright Christopher Marlowe.
   "Part historical mystery, part suspense, this fast-paced
story is propelled by Rosalind's desire not just to survive but
also to learn who she is." Voice Youth Advocates

Thor, Annika

   ★ A **faraway** island; translated from the Swedish by Linda Schenck. Delacorte Press 2009 247p
map $16.99; lib bdg $19.99

Grades: 4 5 6 7   **Fic**
   1. Jews -- Fiction 2. Islands -- Fiction 3. Sisters --
Fiction 4. Refugees -- Fiction 5. World War, 1939-

1945 -- Fiction
ISBN 978-0-385-73617-6; 0-385-73617-7; 978-0-385-
90590-9 lib bdg; 0-385-90590-4 lib bdg
           LC 2009-15420
ALA ALSC Batchelder Award (2010)
   In 1939 Sweden, two Jewish sisters wait for their parents
to flee the Nazis in Austria, but while eight-year-old Nellie
settles in quickly, twelve-year-old Stephie feels stranded at
the end of the world, with a foster mother who is as cold and
unforgiving as the island on which they live.
   "Children will readily empathize with Stephie's courage.
Both sisters are well-drawn, likable characters. This is the
first of four books Thor has written about the two girls." SLJ

The **lily** pond. Delacorte Press 2011 217p
$16.99; lib bdg $19.99

Grades: 4 5 6 7   **Fic**
   1. School stories 2. Refugees -- Fiction 3. Friendship
-- Fiction 4. Jews -- Sweden -- Fiction 5. World War,
1939-1945 -- Fiction
ISBN 978-0-385-74039-5; 978-0-385-90838-2 lib
bdg; 978-0-375-89914-0 e-book
           LC 2010053548

Thurlo, Aimee

The **spirit** line; [by] Aimeé & David Thurlo.
Viking 2004 216p $15.99

Grades: 6 7 8 9   **Fic**
   1. Navajo Indians -- Fiction
ISBN 0-670-03645-5
   When the special rug Crystal Manyfeathers is weaving for her kinaaldá, the traditional Navajo womanhood
ceremony, is stolen from her loom, there are any number
of suspects.
   "Carefully combining humor and seriousness, this well-
paced story contains accurate portrayals of Navajo customs,
mostly believable teen dialogue, and a realistic depiction of
the conflicts modern Native young people face." SLJ

Tiernan, Cate

Balefire. Razorbill 2011 974p pa $8.99

Grades: 8 9 10 11 12   **Fic**
   1. Twins -- Fiction 2. Sisters -- Fiction 3. Witchcraft
-- Fiction
ISBN 978-1-59514-411-9
   An omnibus edition of four titles previously published
separately, the first three of which were first published 2005.
The last, A necklace of water, was first published 2006
   Separated since birth, seventeen-year-old twins Thais
and Clio unexpectedly meet in New Orleans where they
seem to be pursued by a coven of witches who want to harness the twins' magical powers for its own ends.

Tocher, Timothy

Bill Pennant, Babe Ruth, and me. Cricket Books
2009 178p $16.95

Grades: 5 6 7 8   **Fic**
   1. Baseball -- Fiction
ISBN 978-0-8126-2755-8; 0-8126-2755-5
           LC 2008026829
   In 1920, sixteen-year-old Hank finds his loyalties divided when he is assigned to care for the Giants' mascot, a

wildcat named Bill Pennant, as well as keep an eye on Babe Ruth in Ruth's first season with the New York Yankees.

The author "seamlessly blends fact and fiction. He recreates the era with scrupulous attention to its syntax and slang, as well as details of daily life. Ruth, McGraw and the other historical figures come alive for readers, and the fictional Hank is a sympathetic, fully developed character." Kirkus

Chief Sunrise, John McGraw, and me; Timothy Tocher. 1st ed; Cricket Books 2004 154p $15.95

Grades: 5 6 7 8   **Fic**
1. Baseball -- Fiction 2. Race relations -- Fiction 3. Runaway teenagers -- Fiction
ISBN 0-8126-2711-3

LC 2003-23407

In 1919, fifteen-year-old Hank escapes an abusive father and goes looking for a chance to become a baseball player, accompanied by a man who calls himself Chief Sunrise and claims to be a full-blooded Seminole.

"The story is both entertaining and thought-provoking." Booklist

Todd, Pamela

The **blind** faith hotel; [by] Pamela Todd. Margaret K. McElderry Books 2008 312p $16.99; pa $8.99

Grades: 8 9 10   **Fic**
1. Nature -- Fiction 2. Prairies -- Fiction 3. Family life -- Fiction
ISBN 978-1-4169-5494-1; 1-4169-5494-5; 978-1-4169-9509-8 pa; 1-4169-9509-9 pa

LC 2007-43912

When her parents separate and she and her siblings move with their mother from the northwest coast to a midwest prairie farmhouse, fourteen-year-old Zoe, miserably unhappy to be away from the ocean and her father, begins to develop a deep attachment to her new surroundings, when, after a shoplifting episode, she is assigned to work at a nature preserve.

"This touching novel tackles many difficult issues; beautiful imagery and language keep the story vibrant." Horn Book Guide

Toft, Di

Wolven. Scholastic 2010 322p $16.99; pa $7.99

Grades: 5 6 7 8   **Fic**
1. Werewolves -- Fiction 2. Supernatural -- Fiction
ISBN 978-0-545-17109-0; 0-545-17109-1; 978-0-545-17110-6 pa; 0-545-17110-5 pa

Twelve-year-old Nat, with help from his friends, and his "pet" Woody, a wolf that turns into a boy, must face werewolves that have been altered as part of a dastardly plan.

"Toft spins an incredible tale full of action, mystery, and suspense. This hair-raising adventure with its fresh perspective on werewolf lore is perfect for audiences not ready for some of the edgier material out there. A satisfying read with a fly-off-the-shelves cover." SLJ

Another title in this series is:
The twilight circus (2011)

Toksvig, Sandi

★ **Hitler's** canary. Roaring Brook Press 2007 191p $16.95

Grades: 5 6 7 8   **Fic**
1. Jews -- Fiction 2. World War, 1939-1945 -- Fiction
ISBN 978-1-59643-247-5; 1-59643-247-0

LC 2006-16607

Ten-year-old Bamse and his Jewish friend Anton participate in the Danish Resistance during World War II.

"Though . . . suspenseful episodes will thrill readers, it is Bamse's growing courage and deepening understanding that drive the story." Booklist

Tolan, Stephanie S.

★ **Surviving** the Applewhites. HarperCollins Pubs. 2002 216p $15.99; lib bdg $17.89; pa $5.99

Grades: 5 6 7 8   **Fic**
1. Theater -- Fiction 2. Family life -- Fiction 3. Eccentrics and eccentricities -- Fiction
ISBN 0-06-623602-9; 0-06-623603-7 lib bdg; 0-06-441044-7 pa

LC 2002-1474

A Newbery Medal honor book, 2003

Jake, a budding juvenile delinquent, is sent for home schooling to the arty and eccentric Applewhite family's Creative Academy, where he discovers talents and interests he never knew he had

This is a "thoroughly enjoyable book with humor, well-drawn characters, and a super cover." Voice Youth Advocates

Toliver, Wendy

Lifted. Simon Pulse 2010 309p pa $9.99

Grades: 7 8 9 10   **Fic**
1. School stories 2. Theft -- Fiction 3. Moving -- Fiction
ISBN 978-1-4169-9048-2; 1-4169-9048-8

"Poppy isn't happy with her single mother for moving her to Texas and enrolling the decidedly secular 16-year-old in a private Baptist high school. Soon, however, she becomes fascinated with the two most elite girls in class. . . . Her new friends, despite their pious attitudes, are shoplifters. Toliver does a good job of making clear the thefts are less about the desire for things like designer jeans than about the adrenaline rush of getting away with something. . . . Will appeal to all teens interested in wayward behavior." Booklist

Tolkien, J. R. R. (John Ronald Reuel), 1892-1973

★ The **hobbit**; or, There and back again. illustrated by Michael Hague. Houghton Mifflin 1984 290p il $29.95

Grades: 5 6 7 8 9 10 11 12 Adult   **Fic**
1. Magic 2. Satire 3. Allegories 4. Fantasy fiction 5. Fantasies 6. Imaginary kingdoms
ISBN 0-395-36290-3

LC 84-9023

First published 1937 in the United Kingdom; first United States edition 1938

Bilbo Baggins, a respectable, well-to-do hobbit, lives comfortably in his hobbit-hole until the day the wandering wizard Gandalf chooses him to share in an adventure from which he may never return. "Grades four to eight." (Bull Cent Child Books)

"It must be understood that this is a children's book only in the sense that the first of many readings can be undertaken in the nursery. . . . [The hobbit] will be funniest to its youngest readers, and only years later, at a tenth or twentieth reading, will they begin to realize what deft scholarship and profound reflection have gone to make everything in it so ripe, so friendly, and in its own way so true." Times Lit Suppl

★ The **lord** of the rings; 50th Anniversary ed; Houghton Mifflin 2004 xxv, 1157p il map slip case $100

Grades: 7 8 9 10 11 12 Adult   **Fic**
1. Fantasy fiction
ISBN 0-618-51765-0
                                        LC 2004-275215
First published 1954 in the United Kingdom
"This is a tale of imaginary gnomelike creatures who battle against evil. Led by Frodo, the hobbits embark on a journey to prevent a magic ring from falling into the grasp of the powers of darkness. The forces of good succeed in their fight against the Dark Lord of evil, and Frodo and Sam bring the Ring to Mount Doom, where it is destroyed." Shapiro. Fic for Youth. 3d edition

Tomlinson, Heather
★ **Aurelie**; a faerie tale. Henry Holt 2008 184p $16.95

Grades: 7 8 9 10   **Fic**
1. Fantasy fiction 2. Music -- Fiction 3. Fairies -- Fiction 4. Princesses -- Fiction
ISBN 978-0-8050-8276-0; 0-8050-8276-X
                                        LC 2007-41958
Heartsick at losing her two dearest companions, Princess Aurelie finds comfort in the glorious music of the faeries, but the duties of the court call her, as do the needs of her friends.
"Graceful prose leads the reader through a complex chronological narrative and a Shakespearean tangle of love stories." Booklist

★ **Toads** and diamonds. Henry Holt 2010 278p $16.99

Grades: 8 9 10 11 12   **Fic**
1. Fairy tales
ISBN 978-0-8050-8968-4; 0-8050-8968-3
                                        LC 2009-23448
A retelling of the Perrault fairy tale set in pre-colonial India, in which two stepsisters receive gifts from a goddess and each walks her own path to find her gift's purpose, discovering romance along the way.
The author "creates a vivid setting. Lavish details starkly contrast the two girls' lives and personalities. . . . The complexities of the cultural backstory pose a challenge to readers, but this beautifully embroidered adventure is well worth the effort." Booklist

★ The **swan** maiden. Henry Holt 2007 292p $16.95

Grades: 6 7 8 9   **Fic**
1. Fairy tales 2. Magic -- Fiction
ISBN 978-0-8050-8275-3; 0-8050-8275-1
                                        LC 2006-33774

Raised as a chastelaine-in-training unlike her sisters who are learning the arts of sorcery, Doucette discovers when she is sixteen years old that she too has magic in her blood, and she must brave her mother's wrath-and the loss of the man she loves-in order to follow her birthright.
"Layered, elegantly written, and filled with unexpected twists and turns, The Swan Maiden soars with grace and power." Booklist

Tooke, Wes
King of the mound; my summer with Satchel Paige. Simon & Schuster Books for Young Readers 2012 155p $15.99

Grades: 4 5 6   **Fic**
1. Baseball players 2. Baseball -- Fiction 3. Handicapped -- Fiction 4. Poliomyelitis -- Fiction 5. African Americans -- Fiction 6. Father-son relationship -- Fiction
ISBN 978-1-4424-3346-5; 1-4424-3346-9
                                        LC 2011012740
Twelve-year-old Nick loves baseball so after a year in the hospital fighting polio and with a brace on one leg, Nick takes a job with the minor league team for which his father is catcher and gets to see the great pitcher, Satchel Paige, play during the 1935 season. Includes historical notes.
"Tooke sticks closely to historical records, with the addition of a few extra Paige exploits and aphorisms, and . . . the fictional overlay offers a comfortably predictable 'hard work brings just rewards' arc. Nourishing fare for Matt Christopher graduates." Kirkus

Towell, Ann
Grease town. Tundra Books 2010 232p $19.99
Grades: 5 6 7 8   **Fic**
1. Race relations -- Fiction
ISBN 0-88776-983-7; 978-0-88776-983-2
"When twelve-year-old Titus Sullivan decides to run away to join his Uncle Amos and older brother, Lem, he finds an alien and exciting world in Oil Springs, the first Canadian oil boomtown of the 19th century. The Enniskillen swamp is slick with oil, and it takes enterprising folk to plumb its depths. The adventurers who work there are a tough lot of individuals. In this hard world, Titus becomes friends with a young black boy, the child of slaves who came to Canada on the Underground Railroad. When tragedy strikes in the form of a race riot, Titus's loyalties are tested." (Publisher's note)
"In 1863, oil has recently been discovered in Oil Springs, Ontario, and a variety of people, black and white, and from many different walks of life, are settling there. Orphans Lem and Titus Sullivan live in their aunt's stuffy and regimented house. When 19-year-old Lem sets out for Oil Springs, 13-year-old Titus stows away in his brother's wagon. . . . Towell skillfully creates the setting of this mucky little town and its colorful inhabitants. Titus, who narrates, has a voice that is believable and uncontrived. . . . Supporting characters are equally strong and well developed. . . . Towell has created a strong narrator and a compelling plot." SLJ

Towell, Katy
Skary childrin and the carousel of sorrow. Alfred A. Knopf 2011 265p $16.99; lib bdg $19.99; ebook $16.99

Grades: 4 5 6 7   **Fic**
1. Ghost stories 2. School stories 3. Supernatural
-- Fiction
ISBN 978-0-375-86859-7; 0-375-86859-3; 978-0-375-
96860-0 lib bdg; 0-375-96860-1 lib bdg; 978-0-375-
89931-7 e-book; 0-375-89931-6 e-book
                                    LC 2010-38830
In Widowsbury, an isolated village where people believe
"known is good, new is bad," three outcasts from the girls'
school join forces with a home-schooled boy to uncover and
combat the evil that is making people disappear.
"Towell tucks violent tempests, maggoty slime, hideous
transformations, nightmares, sudden terrors and like atmo-
sphere-building elements into a rousingly melodramatic literary debut." Kirkus

Townley, Roderick
Sky; a novel in three sets and an encore. by Rod-
erick Townley. 1st ed; Atheneum Books for Young
Readers 2004 265p $16.95
Grades: 7 8 9 10   **Fic**
1.. Jazz musicians -- Fiction 2. New York (N.Y.) --
History -- 20th century
ISBN 0-689-85712-8
                                    LC 2003-11354
In New York City in 1959, fifteen-year-old Alec Schuyler, at odds with his widowed father over his love of music,
finds a mentor and friend in a blind, black jazz musician.
"Townley presents a compassionate portrait of a young
man who is battling for his own place in life and sets the
story in the exciting time of the beat poets and the explosive
development of jazz music." SLJ

The **blue** shoe; a tale of thievery, villainy, sorcery, and shoes. by Roderick Townley; illustrated
by Mary GrandPré. Alfred A. Knopf 2009 254p il
$16.99; lib bdg $19.99
Grades: 4 5 6 7   **Fic**
1. Fables 2. Fairy tales
ISBN 978-0-375-85600-6; 0-375-85600-5; 978-0-375-
95600-3 lib bdg; 0-375-95600-X lib bdg
                                    LC 2008-43851
A mysterious stranger commissions a single, valuable
shoe from a humble cobbler, changing the cobbler's life and
the life of his young apprentice forever.
This is a "fun, whimsical fairy tale. . . . The good-versus-
evil plotline, dynamic cast of characters, . . . light romance
between Hap and Sophia, and copious amounts of magic and
intrigue will be a hit with a wide range of readers." Booklist

The **door** in the forest; [by] Roderick Townley.
Alfred A. Knopf 2011 245p $16.99; lib bdg $19.99
Grades: 4 5 6   **Fic**
1. Magic -- Fiction 2. Honesty -- Fiction 3. Soldiers
-- Fiction 4. Space and time -- Fiction
ISBN 0-375-85601-3; 0-375-95601-8 lib bdg; 978-0-
375-85601-3; 978-0-375-95601-0 lib bdg
                                    LC 2010034710
While trying to outwit the soldiers who are occupying
their small town, fourteen-year-old Daniel, who cannot lie,
and Emily, who discovers she has magical powers, are in-

explicably drawn to a mysterious island in the heart of the
forest where townsfolk have been warned never to go.
"Townley's fanciful story swings like a pendulum from
Wild West tall tale to a vague mysticism that is enlivened
by colorful imagery. . . . At its considerable best, it is quirky
and engaging; sentences hurry purposefully along, deepening atmosphere, theme, and plot." Horn Book

Townsend, Wendy
★ **Lizard** love; [by] Wendy Townsend. Front
Street 2008 196p $17.95
Grades: 6 7 8 9   **Fic**
1. Reptiles -- Fiction 2. Country life -- Fiction 3. City
and town life -- Fiction
ISBN 978-1-932425-34-5; 1-932425-34-9
                                    LC 2007017975
Grace, a teenager, and her mother have moved to Manhattan where she feels alienated and out of place, far from
the ponds and farm where she grew up playing with bull-
frogs and lizards, until she finds Fang & Claw, a reptile store,
and meets the owner's son, Walter.
"Townsend displays a remarkable narrative gift. . . . Her
sensitive herpetological descriptions are unflinching, evocative, and positively elegant. Even minor characterizations
are full and complex." Booklist

★ The **sundown** rule. Namelos 2011 128p
$18.95
Grades: 5 6 7 8   **Fic**
1. Aunts -- Fiction 2. Uncles -- Fiction 3. Wildlife
conservation -- Fiction 4. Father-daughter relationship
-- Fiction
ISBN 1-60898-099-5; 978-1-60898-099-4
Louise and her dad live an idyllic life surrounded by nature. When he gets an assignment to go to Brazil to write
an article for a magazine, Louise has to go live in a suburb
with her aunt and uncle, leaving her cat, Cash, behind, since
Aunt Kay is allergic to animals. Her dad says that it will be
for only six weeks, and that everything will be okay. But it
isn't, especially when Cash gets hit by a car and dies. And
when a new friend's dad shoots a crow for no reason. And
when her own dad gets sick, really sick, and might not be
coming home.
"Townsend builds a rich, moving story that is refreshing
for its subject matter and lyrical realism." Publ Wkly

Tracy, Kristen
Bessica Lefter bites back; by Kristen Tracy.
Delacorte Press 2012 263 p. $16.99
Grades: 4 5 6 7   **Fic**
1. Gifts -- Fiction 2. Mascots -- Fiction 3. Middle
schools -- Fiction 4. School children -- Fiction 5.
Friendship 6. Schools -- Fiction
ISBN 9780385740692; 0385740697
                                    LC 2011045677
In this children's book, "[s]ixth-grader Bessica's new
middle-school persona meets a host of problems, including mending a friendship damaged by mean text messages,
facing a bully in her first outing as team mascot and coming to terms with her grandmother's boyfriend. . . . Rumor
has it the opposing mascot in the first game will facebomb
her. Neither Bessica nor readers learn what facebombing

actually is in this context until after the disastrous event." (Kirkus Reviews)

Sharks & boys. Hyperion 2011 272p $16.99

Grades: 6 7 8 9   **Fic**

1. Ships -- Fiction 2. Twins -- Fiction 3. Siblings -- Fiction 4. Survival after airplane accidents, shipwrecks, etc. -- Fiction

ISBN 978-1-4231-4354-3; 1-4231-4354-X

LC 2011-04803

Feeling betrayed, fifteen-year-old Enid follows her boyfriend, Wick, from Vermont to Maryland where he and six others they know from twin studies rent a yacht, but after she sneaks aboard a storm sets them adrift without food or water, fighting for survival.

"A page-turning thriller, . . . this emotionally complex novel makes everyone's worst beach nightmare palpable and provides a fascinating character study that explores what happens when instincts are pitted against relationships." Booklist

The **reinvention** of Bessica Lefter. Delacorte Press 2011 305p $15.99

Grades: 4 5 6 7   **Fic**

1. School stories 2. Friendship -- Fiction

ISBN 978-0-385-90634-0; 0-385-90634-X

LC 2010-04844

Eleven-year-old Bessica's plans to begin North Teton Middle School as a new person begin to fall apart even before school begins.

Tracy "offers a positive and comforting message about learning to make adjustments, ending the book on a happy note, with Bessica finding her niche as school mascot." Publ Wkly

Trafton, Jennifer

★ The **rise** and fall of Mount Majestic; illustrations by Brett Helquist. Dial Books for Young Readers 2010 338p il $16.99

Grades: 4 5 6 7   **Fic**

1. Fairy tales 2. Adventure fiction 3. Giants -- Fiction

ISBN 978-0-8037-3375-6; 0-8037-3375-5

LC 2009-51659

Ten-year-old Persimmony Smudge, who longs for heroic adventures, overhears a secret that thrusts her into the middle of a dangerous mission that could destroy the island on which she lives.

"Trafton imbues her tale with a delightful sense of fun and fascinating, well-rounded characters-playful wordsmithing and flowing dialogue make this an excellent choice for bedtime read-aloud." Publ Wkly

Tregay, Sarah

Love and leftovers; a novel in verse. Katherine Tegen Books 2011 432p $17.99

Grades: 7 8 9 10   **Fic**

1. Novels in verse 2. Moving -- Fiction 3. Bisexuality -- Fiction 4. Family life -- Fiction

ISBN 978-0-06-202358-2; 0-06-202358-6

LC 2011019367

When her father starts dating a man, fifteen-year-old Marcie's depressed mother takes her to New Hampshire but just as Marcie starts falling for a great guy her father brings her back to Iowa, where all of her relationships have become strained.

"Tregay's choice to write in verse works well, her spare but effective language artfully evoking what otherwise might be a conventional highschool romance. . . . The father's completely accepted gay relationship, although mostly in the background, adds an element of interest. It all feels realistic and makes for an interesting, attractive novel. A verse novel with real depth." Kirkus

Treggiari, Jo

Ashes, ashes. Scholastic Press 2011 360p $17.99

Grades: 7 8 9 10   **Fic**

1. Science fiction 2. Dogs -- Fiction 3. Epidemics -- Fiction

ISBN 978-0-545-25563-9; 0-545-25563-5

LC 2010032398

In a future Manhattan devastated by environmental catastrophes and epidemics, sixteen-year-old Lucy survives alone until vicious hounds target her and force her to join Aidan and his band, but soon they learn that she is the target of Sweepers, who kidnap and infect people with plague.

"The tense plot, cinematic moments, and highly capable protagonists make this a fast, gripping read." Publ Wkly

Trigiani, Adriana

Viola in reel life. HarperTeen 2009 282p $16.99

Grades: 7 8 9 10   **Fic**

1. Ghost stories 2. School stories 3. Video recording -- Fiction 4. Dating (Social customs) -- Fiction

ISBN 978-0-06-145102-7; 0-06-145102-9

LC 2009-14269

When fourteen-year-old Viola is sent from her beloved Brooklyn to boarding school in Indiana for ninth grade, she overcomes her initial reservations as she makes friends with her roommates, goes on a real date, and uses the unsettling ghost she keeps seeing as the subject of a short film—her first.

This "is a sweet, character-driven story. Viola is very real, as are her feelings, hopes, desires, and dreams." SLJ

Viola in the spotlight. HarperTeen 2011 283p $16.99

Grades: 7 8 9 10   **Fic**

1. Theater -- Fiction 2. Family life -- Fiction 3. Dating (Social customs) -- Fiction

ISBN 978-0-06-145105-8; 0-06-145105-3

LC 2010045553

Back home in Brooklyn, fifteen-year-old Viola has big summer plans but with one best friend going to camp and the other not only working but experiencing her first crush, Viola is glad to be overworked as an unpaid lighting intern when her grandmother's play goes to Broadway.

"An equally enjoyable follow-up to Viola in Reel Life." Booklist

Trueman, Terry

★ **7** days at the hot corner. HarperTempest 2007 160p $15.99

Grades: 7 8 9 10 **Fic**
1. Baseball -- Fiction 2. Friendship -- Fiction 3. Homosexuality -- Fiction
ISBN 978-0-06-057494-9; 0-06-057494-1
LC 2006-03706

Varsity baseball player Scott Latimer struggles with his own prejudices and those of others when his best friend reveals that he is gay.

This "suspenseful story is enhanced by some late-inning surprises, the gay subplot is treated with honesty and integrity, and Scott and Travis are believable, sympathetic characters." Booklist

★ **Cruise** control; 1st ed; HarperTempest 2004 149p $15.99; lib bdg $16.89; pa $8.99
Grades: 7 8 9 10 **Fic**
1. Brothers -- Fiction 2. Basketball -- Fiction 3. People with disabilities 4. Cerebral palsy -- Fiction 5. Father-son relationship -- Fiction
ISBN 0-06-623960-5; 0-06-623961-3 lib bdg; 0-06-447377-5 pa
LC 2003-19822

A talented basketball player struggles to deal with the helplessness and anger that come with having a brother rendered completely dysfunctional by severe cerebral palsy and a father who deserted the family.

"This powerful tale is extremely well written and will give readers an understanding of what it's like to have a challenged sibling." SLJ

Hurricane; a novel. HarperCollins 2008 137p $15.99; lib bdg $16.89
Grades: 5 6 7 **Fic**
1. Hurricanes -- Fiction 2. Survival after airplane accidents, shipwrecks, etc. -- Fiction
ISBN 978-0-06-000018-9; 0-06-000018-X; 978-0-06-000019-6 lib bdg; 0-06-000019-8 lib bdg
LC 2007-02990

A revised edition of Swallowing the sun, published 2004 in the United Kingdom

"Thirteen-year-old Jose lives with his family in Honduras. A hurricane hits, causing the recently clear-cut hillside adjacent to his village to become a mudslide that smothers and kills most of its fifty inhabitants. . . . Jose quickly takes charge and becomes a resourceful member of his ailing community. This survival tale is concise but engaging. Trueman's descriptions of the village buried in mud and of the difficulties it creates for the survivors are vivid." Voice Youth Advocates

★ **Inside** out. HarperTempest 2003 117p hardcover o.p. pa $8.99
Grades: 7 8 9 10 **Fic**
1. Suicide -- Fiction 2. Hostages -- Fiction 3. Mentally ill -- Fiction 4. Schizophrenia -- Fiction 5. Juvenile delinquency -- Fiction
ISBN 0-06-623962-1; 0-06-447376-7 pa
LC 2002-151604

A sixteen-year-old with schizophrenia is caught up in the events surrounding an attempted robbery by two other teens who eventually hold him hostage.

"Trueman sometimes captures moments of heartbreaking truth, and his swift, suspenseful plot will have particular appeal to reluctant readers." Booklist

Life happens next; a novel. Terry Trueman. HarperTeen 2012 132 p. (trade bdg.) $17.99
Grades: 7 8 9 10 **Fic**
1. Love stories 2. Down syndrome -- Fiction 3. Cerebral palsy -- Fiction 4. Dogs -- Fiction 5. Communication -- Fiction 6. Special education -- Fiction 7. People with disabilities -- Fiction 8. Family life -- Washington (State) -- Seattle -- Fiction
ISBN 0062028030; 9780062028037; 9780062028051
LC 2011044627

This book is the sequel to author Terry Trueman's "Stuck in Neutral." Here, Shawn McDaniel, who has cerebral palsy, "fantasizes about his sister's best friend, Ally, and what it would be like if he ever got up the courage to tell her how he felt about her." He is also dealing with "Debi, [who] moves in with them. . . . Debi has Down's syndrome and is often disruptive, but . . . she becomes the first person to connect with Shawn on more than a surface level." (Voice of Youth Advocates)

★ **Stuck** in neutral. HarperCollins Pubs. 2000 114p $14.95; lib bdg $16.89; pa $6.99
Grades: 7 8 9 10 **Fic**
1. Euthanasia -- Fiction 2. People with disabilities 3. Cerebral palsy -- Fiction 4. Father-son relationship -- Fiction
ISBN 0-06-028519-2; 0-06-028518-4 lib bdg; 0-06-447213-2 pa
LC 99-37098

Michael L. Printz Award honor book, 2001

Fourteen-year-old Shawn McDaniel, who suffers from severe cerebral palsy and cannot function, relates his perceptions of his life, his family, and his condition, especially as he believes his father is planning to kill him.

"Trueman has created a compelling novel that poses questions about ability and existence while fostering sympathy for people with severe physical limitations." Bull Cent Child Books

Tubb, Kristin O'Donnell

The **13th** sign; Kristin O'Donnell Tubb. Feiwel and Friends 2013 272 p. $16.99
Grades: 6 7 8 9 **Fic**
1. Astrology -- Fiction 2. Zodiac -- Fiction 3. Occult fiction -- Fiction 4. Zodiac -- Fiction 5. Supernatural -- Fiction 6. Books and reading -- Fiction 7. Adventure and adventurers -- Fiction
ISBN 0312583524; 9780312583521
LC 2012034058

In this juvenile astrology-themed fantasy novel, by Kristin O'Donnell Tubb, "when a teen accidentally unlocks the lost 13th zodiac sign, everyone's personality shifts, and she must confront 12 Keepers of the zodiac to restore global order. . . . Unless she can find and restore Ophiuchus to the heavens within 23 hours, all personality changes will be permanent. To do this, Jalen must destroy 12 Keepers who protect Ophiuchus." (Kirkus Reviews)

★ **Selling** hope. Feiwel and Friends 2010 215p $16.99

Grades: 6 7 8 **Fic**
1. Comets -- Fiction 2. Mothers -- Fiction 3. Magic tricks -- Fiction 4. Single parent family -- Fiction
ISBN 978-0-312-61122-4; 0-312-61122-6
LC 2010-12571
In 1910, just before the earth passes through the tail of Halley's Comet, thirteen-year-old Hope McDaniels, whose father is a magician in a traveling vaudeville show, tries to earn enough money to quit the circuit by selling "anti-comet pills," with the help of fellow-performer Buster Keaton.

"Tubb deftly ingrains a thoughtful ethical question into the story . . . but never overdoes it in this bouncy tale populated by a terrific cast of characters." Booklist

Tullson, Diane
Riley Park. Orca Book Publishers 2009 102p (Orca soundings) $16.95; pa $9.95

Grades: 7 8 9 10 **Fic**
1. Homicide -- Fiction 2. Friendship -- Fiction 3. Bereavement -- Fiction 4. Brain -- Wounds and injuries -- Fiction
ISBN 978-1-55469-124-1; 1-55469-124-9; 978-1-55469-123-4 pa; 1-55469-123-0 pa
After Corbin and his best friend Darius are attacked in Riley Park, Corbin must cope with the loss of his friend, his physical impairments, and finding the culprit.

This is "a suspenseful, tightly plotted story that manages . . . to create both a memorable protagonist and a thought-provoking, emotionally involving story." Booklist

Tunnell, Michael O.
Wishing moon. Dutton Children's Books 2004 272p hardcover o.p. pa $9.99

Grades: 6 7 8 9 **Fic**
1. Magic -- Fiction 2. Orphans -- Fiction
ISBN 0-525-47193-6; 978-1-460-93919-2 pa; 1-460-93919-0 pa
LC 2003-62486
After a fourteen-year-old orphan named Aminah comes to possess a magic lamp, the wishes granted her by the genie inside it allow her to alter her life by choosing prosperity, purpose, and romance.

"Aminah strives to do good with her magic, and yet the tale skips preachiness and goes for rich characterizations and a strong, suspenseful plot worthy of the Arabian Nights." Booklist

Another title about Aminah is:
Moon without magic (2007)

Turnage, Sheila
★ **Three** times lucky; by Sheila Turnage. Dial Books for Young Readers 2012 256 p. (hardcover) $16.99

Grades: 5 6 7 8 **Fic**
1. Absent mothers -- Fiction 2. Adopted children -- Fiction 3. Abandoned children -- Fiction 4. Murder -- Fiction 5. Identity -- Fiction 6. Foundlings -- Fiction 7. Mystery and detective stories
ISBN 0803736703; 9780803736702
LC 2011035027

John Newbery Honor Book (2013)
This is the story of Mo LoBeau, who washed downstream as an infant 11 years ago and who has since been in the care of the Colonel, "a stranger who can"t remember anything about his own past," and "Miss Lana, owner of the Tupelo Cafe. Mo . . . loves the Colonel and Lana, but" wonders about her origins. She "send[s] messages in bottles to her 'Upstream Mother.'" Also featured are "an out-of-town detective, a dead body . . . , a long-forgotten bank robbery, and a kidnapping." (Publishers Weekly)

Turner, Ann Warren
Father of lies; [by] Ann Turner. HarperTeen 2011 247p $16.99

Grades: 7 8 9 10 **Fic**
1. Witchcraft -- Fiction 2. Manic-depressive illness -- Fiction
ISBN 978-0-06-137085-4; 0-06-137085-1
LC 2010-15224
In 1692 when a plague of accusations descends on Salem Village in Massachusetts and "witch fever" erupts, fourteen-year-old Lidda, who has begun to experience visions and hear voices, tries to expose the lies of the witch trials without being hanged as a witch herself. Includes author's notes about the Salem Witch Trials and bipolar disease.

"Turner perfectly captures the nightmare nature of Salem's witchcraft period and of some of the outside forces that may have fueled it. . . . Yet the town's issues play a secondary role in Lidda's own believable struggles with encrouching insanity—or an otherworldly paranormal force: an appraisal left for engaged readers to make." Kirkus

Includes bibliographical references

Hard hit; [by] Ann Turner. Scholastic Press 2006 167p $16.99

Grades: 7 8 9 10 **Fic**
1. Novels in verse 2. Death -- Fiction 3. Cancer -- Fiction 4. Baseball -- Fiction 5. Father-son relationship -- Fiction
ISBN 0-439-29680-3
LC 2005-49906
A rising high school baseball star faces his most difficult challenge when his father is diagnosed with pancreatic cancer.

This is a "novel in verse that speaks volumes long after the book is closed." Voice Youth Advocates

Turner, Max
End of days. St. Martin's Griffin 2010 296p (Night runner) pa $9.99

Grades: 7 8 9 10 **Fic**
1. Vampires -- Fiction 2. Supernatural -- Fiction
ISBN 978-0-312-59252-3; 0-312-59252-3
LC 2010-30191
While Charlie struggles with his vampirism, he, Zack, and their friends are pulled into a conflict with the mysterious Mr. Hyde, a creature who hunts vampires.

"The well-developed characters add dimension to the story line, and Zack's witty and sarcastic humor makes this a truly enjoyable read." SLJ

Night runner. St. Martin's Griffin 2009 261p pa $9.99

Grades: 7 8 9 10   **Fic**

   1. Vampires -- Fiction

   ISBN 978-0-312-59228-8; 0-312-59228-0

                LC 2009-16672

Fifteen-year-old Zach is quite content living in a mental ward because of his unusual allergies until dark secrets about his past, his parents, and his strange sickness slowly surface, placing him in great danger

"This fast-paced vampire story featuring a likable character with a strong voice will appeal to a broad teen audience." Booklist

Turner, Megan Whalen

  ★ The **thief**. Greenwillow Bks. 1996 219p $17.99; pa $6.99

Grades: 7 8 9 10   **Fic**

   1. Adventure fiction 2. Thieves -- Fiction

   ISBN 0-688-14627-9; 0-06-082497-2 pa

                LC 95-41040

A Newbery Medal honor book, 1997

"A tantalizing, suspenseful, exceptionally clever novel. . . . The author's characterization of Gen is simply superb." Horn Book

   Other titles in this series are:

   A conspiracy of kings (2010)

   The King of Attolia (2006)

   The Queen of Attolia (2000)

Twain, Mark

  ★ The **adventures** of Tom Sawyer; illustrated by Barry Moser; afterword by Peter Glassman. Books of Wonder 1989 261p il $24.99

Grades: 5 6 7 8   **Fic**

   1. Missouri – Fiction 2. Mississippi River -- Fiction

   ISBN 0-688-07510-X

   First published 1876

The adventures and pranks of a mischievous boy growing up in a Mississippi River town on the early nineteenth century.

The **prince** and the pauper; introduction by Christopher Paul Curtis. Modern Library 2003 211p (The Modern Library classics) pa $8.95

Grades: 5 6 7 8 9 10 11 12 Adult   **Fic**

   1. Edward VI, King of England, 1537-1553 – Fiction 2. Great Britain -- History -- 1485-1603, Tudors -- Fiction

   ISBN 0-375-76112-8

                LC 2002-26302

   First published 1881

"Edward VI of England and a little pauper change places a few days before Henry VIII's death. The prince wanders in rags, while Tom Canty suffers the horrors of princedom. At the last moment, the mistake is rectified." Reader's Ency. 4th edition

Twomey, Cathleen

  Beachmont letters. Boyds Mills Press 2003 223p $16.95

Grades: 7 8 9 10   **Fic**

   1. Fires -- Fiction 2. Burns and scalds -- Fiction

   ISBN 1-59078-050-7

                LC 2002-111301

Scarred by a fire that killed her father, a seventeen-year-old girl begins a correspondence with a young soldier in 1944

This "has plenty of atmosphere and an appealing, courageous heroine who gradually realizes her own strength. This unusual survivor/love story is certain to be a three-hanky read." Booklist

Uchida, Yoshiko

  ★ **Journey** to Topaz; a story of the Japanese-American evacuation. illustrated by Donald Carrick. Heyday Books 2005 149p il pa $9.95

Grades: 5 6 7 8   **Fic**

   1. World War, 1939-1945 -- Fiction 2. Japanese Americans -- Evacuation and relocation, 1942-1945 -- Fiction

   ISBN 978-1-890771-91-1 pa; 1-890771-91-0 pa

                LC 2004-16537

   First published 1971 by Scribner

After the Pearl Harbor attack an eleven-year-old Japanese-American girl and her family are forced to go to an aliens camp in Utah

  ★ A **jar** of dreams. Atheneum Pubs. 1981 131p hardcover o.p. pa $4.99

Grades: 5 6 7 8   **Fic**

   1. Prejudices -- Fiction 2. Family life -- Fiction 3. Japanese Americans -- Fiction

   ISBN 0-689-50210-9; 0-689-71672-9 pa

                LC 81-3480

"Rinko in her guilelessness is genuine and refreshing, and her worries and concerns seem wholly natural, honest, and convincing." Horn Book

   Other titles about Rinko Tsujimura and her family are:

   The best bad thing (1983)

   The happiest ending (1985)

Uehashi, Nahoko

  ★ **Moribito**; Guardian of the Spirit. [by] Nahoko Uehashi; translated by Cathy Hirano; illustrated by Yuko Shimizu. Arthur A. Levine Books 2008 248p il $17.99

Grades: 6 7 8 9   **Fic**

   1. Fantasy fiction 2. Martial arts -- Fiction

   ISBN 978-0-5450-0542-5; 0-5450-0542-6

The wandering warrior Balsa is hired to protect Prince Chagum from both a mysterious monster and the prince's father, the Mikado.

"This book is first in a series of ten that have garnered literary and popular success in Japan. . . . Balsa and Chagum's story is brought to America with a strong translation. . . . Readers who are fans of action manga, especially with strong female characters, will enjoy the ninja-like fighting scenes. . . . The exciting premise, combined with an attractive cover, should insure that this title will circulate well." Voice Youth Advocates

Moribito II; Guardian of the Darkness. by Na-hoko Uehashi; translated by Cathy Hirano; illustrated by Yuko Shimizu. Arthur A. Levine Books 2009 245p il $17.99

Grades: 6 7 8 9   Fic

1. Fantasy fiction

ISBN 978-0-545-10295-7; 0-545-10295-2

LC 2008-37444

ALA ALSC Batchelder Award Honor Book (2010)

The wandering female bodyguard Balsa returns to her native country of Kanbal, where she uncovers a conspiracy to frame her mentor and herself.

"Once again, Uehashi immerses readers in the culture, traditions, mythology–even diet–of the populace, creating a full, captivating world. . . . This growing series has something for everyone." Publ Wkly

Umansky, Kaye

Solomon Snow and the stolen jewel. Candlewick Press 2007 245p $12.99

Grades: 5 6 7 8   Fic

1. Orphans -- Fiction

ISBN 978-0-7636-2793-5; 0-7636-2793-3

LC 2006-47331

While trying to rescue Prudence's father from prison, Solomon, Prudence, the Infant Prodigy, and Mr. Skippy the rabbit find themselves caught up in the mad plans of the villainous Dr. Calimari to steal a fabulous and cursed ruby.

"Fans of Lemony Snicket will enjoy this fast-paced read. . . . Reluctant readers might find the short chapters, silly comedy, and simple characters attractive." SLJ

Under the moons of Mars; new adventures on Barsoom. edited by John Joseph Adams. Simon & Schuster Books for Young Readers 2012 xv, 352 p.p $16.99

Grades: 6 7 8 9 10 11 12   Fic

1. Science fiction 2. Adventure fiction 3. Short stories -- Collections 4. Short stories, American 5. Science fiction, American

ISBN 9781442420304; 1442420294; 9781442420298; 9781442420311

LC 2011034391

This anthology, edited by John Joseph Adams, features several science fiction stories set in Edgar Rice Burroughs' Barsoom series. "Fans of all ages have marveled at the adventures of John Carter, an Earthman who suddenly finds himself in a strange new world. A century later, readers can enjoy this compilation of brand-new stories starring John Carter of Mars." (Publisher's note)

Updale, Eleanor

★ **Montmorency**; thief, liar, gentleman? Orchard Books 2004 232p $16.95

Grades: 6 7 8 9 10   Fic

1. Thieves -- Fiction

ISBN 0-439-58035-8

LC 2003-56345

First published 2003 in the United Kingdom

In Victorian London, after his life is saved by a young physician, a thief utilizes the knowledge he gains in prison and from the scientific lectures he attends as the physician's case study exhibit to create a new, highly successful, double life for himself.

"Updale adroitly works the tradition of devilish schemes and narrow escapes, and the plot moves as nimbly as the master thief himself." Bull Cent Child Books

Other titles about Montmorency are:

Montmorency and the assassins (2006)

Montmorency on the rocks: doctor, aristocrat, murderer? (2005)

Montmorency's revenge (2007)

Upjohn, Rebecca

The **secret** of the village fool; by Rebecca Upjohn ; illustrated by Renne Benoit. Second Story Press 2012 32 p. $18.95

Grades: 5 6 7 8   Fic

1. World War, 1939-1945 -- Jews -- fiction 2. World War, 1939-1945 -- Poland -- fiction

ISBN 1926920759; 9781926920757

In this children's book by Rebecca Upjohn, illustrated by Renne Benoit, "Milek and his brother Munio live in a sleepy village in Poland. . . . They reluctantly do as their mother asks when she asks them to visit their neighbor Anton, knowing that the rest of the village laughs at him because of his strange habits of speaking to animals and only eating vegetables. Things change quickly when war comes to their town in the form of Nazi soldiers searching for Jewish families like that of Milek and Munio." (Publisher's note)

Urban, Linda

★ The **center** of everything; by Linda Urban. Houghton Mifflin Harcourt 2013 208 p. $15.99

Grades: 4 5 6 7   Fic

1. Wishes -- fiction 2. Bereavement -- fiction

ISBN 0547763484; 9780547763484

LC 2012954515

In this book, "months after her grandmother's death, 12-year-old Ruby Pepperdine composes a winning essay honoring her New Hampshire town's namesake" and will get to read it to the community. But she's more concerned that "she didn't listen to her grandmother's final words before she died. Ruby thinks that maybe if she wishes hard enough, 'everything will be back to how it is supposed to be,' but making a wish the right way is a tricky business." (Publishers Weekly)

Ursu, Anne

★ **Breadcrumbs**; drawings by Erin McGuire. Walden Pond Press 2011 313p il $16.99

Grades: 4 5 6 7   Fic

1. Fairy tales 2. Magic -- Fiction 3. Friendship -- Fiction

ISBN 978-0-06-201505-1; 0-06-201505-2

LC 2010045666

"Fifth-grader Hazel embarks on a memorable journey into the Minnesota woods to find her best friend Jack, who vanishes after a shard of glass pierces his eye. . . . Hazel enters the woods to find 'an entirely different place,' populated by creatures from the pages of Hans Christian Andersen. . . . [This is a] multi-layered, artfully crafted, transforming testament to the power of friendship." Kirkus

Usher, Mark David

The **golden** ass of Lucius Apuleius; adapted from the Latin original by M.D. Usher; illustrations by T. Motley. David R. Godine 2011 il $17.95

Grades: 4 5 6 7   **Fic**

1. Magic -- Fiction 2. Social classes -- Fiction 3. Classical mythology -- Fiction

ISBN 978-1-56792-418-3; 1-56792-418-2

LC 2010032978

Lucius Apuleius, a young nobleman fascinated by magic, accidentally turns himself into an ass and then sets out on a journey that reveals to him the conditions of peasants and slaves in and around Thessaly and leads him to find redemption as a follower of Isis and Osiris.

"A faithful (if relatively clean) version of the world's oldest surviving complete novel. . . . Though all of the sex and most of the dissolute behavior has been excised, the lad's first transformation is milked throughout for double entendres . . . and there are plenty of silly incidents and names . . . to lighten the overall tone. Motley's elaborate illustrated initials and pen-and-ink drawings add satiric bite. . . . An entertaining romp." Kirkus

Vail, Rachel

Kiss me again; Rachel Vail. HarperTeen 2013 256 p. (hardcover) $17.99

Grades: 7 8 9 10   **Fic**

1. Love stories 2. Kissing -- Fiction 3. Teenagers -- Sexual behavior -- Fiction 4. Schools -- Fiction 5. Remarriage -- Fiction

ISBN 0061947172; 9780061947179

LC 2012011521

In this book, "ninth-grader Charlie Collins has lived with her mother, a divorced Harvard professor, for many years. Now Mom's new husband, Joe, has moved into the spacious house, along with his sweet 9-year-old daughter, Samantha, and his notoriously flirtatious ninth-grade son, Kevin. . . . Charlie copes with a mutual crush on Kevin; an increasingly tenuous relationship with her best friend, Tess; her first paying job; and other trials and triumphs of growing up." (Kirkus)

Lucky. HarperTeen 2008 233p $16.99; lib bdg $17.89

Grades: 7 8 9 10   **Fic**

1. School stories 2. Wealth -- Fiction 3. Friendship -- Fiction

ISBN 978-0-06-089043-8; 978-0-06-089044-5 lib bdg

As Phoebe and her clique of privileged girlfriends get ready to graduate from eighth grade, a financial scandal threatens her family's security—as well as Phoebe's social status—but ultimately it teaches her the real meaning of friendship.

"Vail's insightful characterizations of teen girls and their shifting loyalties is right on target." Booklist

Other titles in this series are:

Gorgeous (2009)

Brilliant (2010)

Valente, Catherynne M.

★ The **girl** who circumnavigated Fairyland in a ship of her own making. Feiwel and Friends 2011 247p il $16.99

Grades: 4 5 6 7   **Fic**

1. Fantasy fiction

ISBN 978-0-312-64961-6; 0-312-64961-4

LC 2010050895

"The book's appeal is crystal clear from the outset: this is a kind of The Wonderful Wizard of Oz by way of Alice's Adventures in Wonderland, made vivid by Juan's Tenniel-inflected illustrations. . . . Those who thrill to lovingly wrought tales of fantasy and adventure . . . will be enchanted." Publ Wkly

The **girl** who fell beneath Fairyland and led the revels there; by Catherynne M. Valente ; with illustrations by Ana Juan. Feiwel and Friends 2012 258 p. $16.99

Grades: 4 5 6 7   **Fic**

1. Fantasy fiction

ISBN 0312649622; 9780312649623

In this book by Catherynne M. Valente, illustrated by Ana Juan, "September has longed to return to Fairyland after her first adventure there. And when she finally does, she learns that its inhabitants have been losing their shadows--and their magic--to the world of Fairyland Below. This underworld has a new ruler: Halloween, the Hollow Queen, who is September's shadow. And Halloween does not want to give Fairyland's shadows back." (Publisher's note)

Valentine, Allyson

How (not) to find a boyfriend; by Allyson Valentine. Philomel Books 2013 304 p. (hardcover) $16.99

Grades: 7 8 9 10   **Fic**

1. School stories 2. Popularity -- Fiction 3. Genius -- Fiction 4. Schools -- Fiction 5. Cheerleading -- Fiction 6. High schools -- Fiction 7. Dating (Social customs) -- Fiction

ISBN 0399257713; 9780399257711

LC 2012019316

In this book, former nerd Nora Fulbright has worked hard to shed her geeky image since starting high school. "As sophomore year begins, she's made the cheerleading squad, and it looks like the handsome fullback is taking notice of her. . . . Worried that the cheer captain will mock her for taking AP classes, she switches her schedule, then has to switch it back so she'll have classes with Adam, the brainy and adorable new boy in school." (Publishers Weekly)

Valentine, Jenny

Broken soup. HarperTeen 2009 216p $16.99

Grades: 7 8 9 10   **Fic**

1. Bereavement -- Fiction 2. Family life -- Fiction

ISBN 978-0-06-085071-5; 0-06-085071-X

LC 2008-11719

A photographic negative and two surprising new friends become the catalyst for healing as fifteen-year-old Rowan struggles to keep her family and her life together after her brother's death.

"The mystery Valentine sets in motion is quickly paced and packed with revelations. . . . The main appeal of the book, however, is her beautifully modulated tone. . . . Insightful details abound." Booklist

Double; Jenny Valentine. Disney-Hyperion 2012 246 p. (alk. paper) $16.99
Grades: 7 8 9 10 11 12   **Fic**
1. Mystery fiction 2. Identity -- Fiction 3. Homeless persons -- Fiction 4. London (England) -- Fiction 5. Missing children -- Fiction 6. Impersonation -- Fiction
ISBN 1423147146; 9781423147145
LC 2011010027
In this book, "[w]hat starts as a case of mistaken identity turns into a . . . mystery. . . . Homeless, 16-year-old Chap is . . . presented with . . . [the]opportunity of a lifetime: if he pretends to be Cassiel Roadnight, a teen who has been missing for two years and who looks just like Chap, Chap can have the life and family he's always dreamed of. As he tries to pass in his new identity . . . Chap begins to suspect that there"s more to Cassiel's disappearance than meets the eye." (Publishers Weekly)

★ **Me,** the missing, and the dead. HarperTeen 2008 201p $16.99; lib bdg $17.89
Grades: 8 9 10 11   **Fic**
1. Death -- Fiction 2. Fathers -- Fiction 3. Missing persons -- Fiction 4. Single parent family -- Fiction
ISBN 978-0-06-085068-5; 0-06-085068-X; 978-0-06-085069-2 lib bdg; 0-06-085069-8 lib bdg
LC 2007-14476
First published 2007 in the United Kingdom with title: Finding Violet Park
ALA YALSA Morris Award finalist, 2009
When a series of chance events leaves him in possession of an urn with ashes, sixteen-year-old Londoner Lucas Swain becomes convinced that its occupant, Violet Park, is communicating with him, initiating a voyage of self-discovery that forces him to finally confront the events surrounding his father's sudden disappearance.
"Part mystery, part magical realism, part story of personal growth, and in large part simply about a funny teenager making light of his and his family's pain, this short novel is engaging from start to finish." SLJ

Van Beirs, Pat

A **sword** in her hand; by Jean-Claude Van Rijckeghem and Pat Van Beirs; translated by John Nieuwenhuizen. Annick 2011 276p $21.95
Grades: 5 6 7 8   **Fic**
1. Plague -- Fiction 2. Princesses -- Fiction 3. Middle Ages -- Fiction 4. Father-daughter relationship -- Fiction
ISBN 978-1-55451-291-1; 1-55451-291-3
The Count of Flanders flies in a rage when his newborn child is not the expected male heir but a girl. Marguerite growing up under the disapproving eye of her heartless father learns to survive in the violent male world of the Middle Ages. Will she be able to resist the combined presure of politics, power and a foreign prince?

"The deft characterization of Marguerite and the sumptuous details woven throughout this captivating novel will engage readers." SLJ

Van Draanen, Wendelin, 1965-
Flipped. Knopf 2001 212p $14.95
Grades: 6 7 8 9   **Fic**
1. Family life 2. Conduct of life 3. Self-perception 4. Interpersonal relations
ISBN 9780375811746; 0-375-81174-5; 0-375-82544-4 pa
LC 2001-29238
In alternating chapters, two teenagers describe how their feelings about themselves, each other, and their families have changed over the years.
"There"s lots of laugh-out-loud egg puns and humor in this novel. There"s also, however, a substantial amount of serious social commentary woven in, as well as an exploration of the importance of perspective in relationships." SLJ

The **running** dream. Alfred A. Knopf 2011 336p $16.99; lib bdg $19.99
Grades: 7 8 9 10 11 12   **Fic**
1. School stories 2. Running -- Fiction 3. Amputees -- Fiction 4. Handicapped -- Fiction
ISBN 978-0-375-86667-8; 0-375-86667-1; 978-0-375-96667-5 lib bdg; 0-375-96667-6 lib bdg
LC 2010-07072
"It's a classic problem novel in a lot of ways. . . . Overall, though, this is a tremendously upbeat book. . . . Van Draanen's extensive research into both running and amputees pays dividends." Booklist

Sammy Keyes and the night of skulls. Alfred A. Knopf 2011 304p $15.99; lib bdg $18.99
Grades: 4 5 6 7   **Fic**
1. School stories 2. Mystery fiction 3. Skeleton -- Fiction 4. Halloween -- Fiction 5. Missing persons -- Fiction
ISBN 978-0-375-86108-6; 0-375-86108-4; 978-0-375-96108-3 lib bdg; 0-375-96108-9 lib bdg
LC 2011027485
Junior high detective Sammy Keyes and her friends take a detour through a graveyard on Halloween night and find themselves in the middle of a mystery involving missing people, human skulls, and a ghoulish embalmer, while school presents its own set of tricks and treats.
"Van Draanen has created a sometimes scary and sometimes funny story that realistically depicts young teen personalities, peer pressure, crushes, and some serious concepts." Voice Youth Advocates

Sammy Keyes and the showdown in Sin City; Wendelin Van Draanen. Alfred A. Knopf 2013 288 p. (trade) $16.99
Grades: 4 5 6 7   **Fic**
1. Las Vegas (Nev.) -- Fiction 2. Mystery fiction -- Fiction 3. Mother-daughter relationship -- Fiction 4. Fathers -- Fiction 5. Identity -- Fiction 6. Mystery and

detective stories
ISBN 0375870539; 9780307930613; 9780307974082; 9780375870538; 9780375970535

LC 2012013474

This book, by Wendelin Van Draanen, is part of the "Sammy Keyes" series. In it "Sammy tackles the persistent mysteries of her own life. Mysteries like: Who is her father? . . . How long can she manage to hide out in Grams' seniors-only building before someone catches on? Is her mother really planning to marry her boyfriend's father? . . . During one crazy weekend in Las Vegas, with the help of an entire army of Elvis impersonators, Sammy finally gets some answers." (Publisher's note)

Van Eekhout, Greg

The **boy** at the end of the world. Bloomsbury Children's Books 2011 212p $16.99

Grades: 4 5 6 7   **Fic**

1. Science fiction 2. Robots -- Fiction
ISBN 978-1-59990-524-2; 1-59990-524-8

LC 2010035741

Born half-grown in a world that is being destroyed, Fisher has instinctive knowledge of many things, including that he must avoid the robot that knows his name.

"A pleaser for readers who prefer their sf livened up with unpredictable elements and emotional complexity." Booklist

Van Etten, David

Likely story. Alfred A. Knopf 2008 230p il $15.99; lib bdg $18.99

Grades: 7 8 9 10   **Fic**

1. Television -- Fiction 2. Mother-daughter relationship -- Fiction
ISBN 978-0-375-84676-2; 0-375-84676-X; 978-0-375-94676-9 lib bdg; 0-375-94676-4 lib bdg

LC 2007-22724

Sixteen-year-old Mallory, daughter of the star of a long-running but faltering soap opera, writes her own soap opera script and becomes deeply involved in the day-to-day life of a Hollywood player, while trying to hold on to some shaky personal relationships.

"Strong-willed, quick-witted Mallory is a sympathetic heroine, and Van Etten engagingly weds melodrama to the more mundane, universal dramas of teenage life." Horn Book Guide

Other titles in this series are:
All that glitters (2008)
Red carpet riot (2009)

Van Leeuwen, Jean

★ **Cabin** on Trouble Creek. Dial Books for Young Readers 2004 119p $16.99; pa $6.99

Grades: 4 5 6 7   **Fic**

1. Brothers 2. Self-reliance 3. Brothers -- Fiction 4. Frontier and pioneer life -- Fiction
ISBN 0-8037-2548-5; 0-14-241164-7 pa

LC 2003-14151

In 1803 in Ohio, two young brothers are left to finish the log cabin and guard the land while their father goes back to Pennsylvania to fetch their mother and younger siblings.

"Excellent pacing is what makes this novel work so well. . . . The suspense builds consistently. The boys' strug-

gle is portrayed realistically, without sugarcoating nature's harshness." SLJ

Lucy was there-- Phyllis Fogelman Bks. 2002 165p $16.99

Grades: 4 5 6 7   **Fic**

1. Dogs 2. Grief 3. Friendship 4. Loss (Psychology) 5. Dogs -- Fiction 6. Family problems 7. Death -- Fiction 8. Friendship -- Fiction
ISBN 0-8037-2738-0

LC 2001-33974

With the help of new friends and a very special dog, Morgan begins to come to terms with the loss of her mother and five-year-old brother, who boarded a plane and never came back

"Morgan's anguish is palpable but never overwrought, and the short chapters, appealing heroine, and well-told story leavened with humor give this solid . . . appeal." Booklist

Van Tol, Alex

Knifepoint; written by Alex Van Tol. Orca Book Publishers 2010 113p (Orca soundings) $16.95; pa $9.95

Grades: 7 8 9 10   **Fic**

1. Kidnapping -- Fiction
ISBN 978-1-55469-306-1; 1-55469-06-3; 978-1-55469-305-4 pa; 1-55469-305-5 pa

Jill is enduring a brutal job on a mountain ranch, guiding wannabe-cowboys on trail rides. On a solo ride with a handsome stranger she ends up in a fight for her life with no one to help her.

"The suspense is palpable. Both reluctant and avid readers who enjoy nail-biting tension will race through." Booklist

Van de Ruit, John

Spud. Razorbill 2007 331p hardcover o.p. pa $9.99

Grades: 6 7 8 9 10   **Fic**

1. School stories
ISBN 978-1-59514-170-5; 0-14-302484-1; 978-1-59514-187-3 pa; 1-59514-187-1 pa

LC 2007-6065

In 1990, thirteen-year-old John "Spud" Milton, a prepubescent choirboy, keeps a diary of his first year at an elite, boys-only boarding school in South Africa.

"This raucous autobiographical novel about a scholarship boy in an elite boys' boarding school in 1990 is mainly farce but also part coming-of-age tale." Booklist

Vande Velde, Vivian

Heir apparent. Harcourt 2002 315p $17; pa $6.95

Grades: 6 7 8 9   **Fic**

1. Science fiction 2. Virtual reality -- Fiction
ISBN 0-15-204560-0; 0-15-205125-2 pa

LC 2002-2441

While playing a total immersion virtual reality game of kings and intrigue, fourteen-year-old Giannine learns that demonstrators have damaged the equipment to which she is connected, and she must win the game quickly or be damaged herself

"This adventure includes a cast of intriguing characters and personalities. The feisty heroine has a funny, sarcastic sense of humor and succeeds because of her ingenuity and determination." SLJ

Magic can be murder. Harcourt 2000 197p hardcover o.p. pa $6.99

Grades: 6 7 8 9   **Fic**

1. Witchcraft 2. Mystery fiction 3. Murder
ISBN 0-15-202665-7; 0-547-25872-0 pa

LC 00-8595

Nola and her mother have unusual abilities that have always set them apart from others, but when Nola sees a murder using her power to call up images using water and a person's hair, she finds herself in the worst danger ever

"The well-developed characters provide entertaining reading." SLJ

Remembering Raquel. Harcourt 2007 160p $16

Grades: 8 9 10 11   **Fic**

1. School stories 2. Death -- Fiction 3. Obesity -- Fiction
ISBN 978-0-15-205976-7

LC 2006-35769

Various people recall aspects of the life of Raquel Falcone, an unpopular, overweight freshman at Quail Run High School, including classmates, her parents, and the driver who struck and killed her as she was walking home from an animated film festival.

"Easily booktalked and deeper than it initially seems, this will be popular with reluctant readers." Booklist

★ **Stolen**. Marshall Cavendish 2008 158p $16.99

Grades: 6 7 8 9 10   **Fic**

1. Magic -- Fiction 2. Amnesia -- Fiction 3. Witches -- Fiction 4. Missing children -- Fiction
ISBN 978-0-7614-5515-8; 0-7614-5515-9

LC 2008-03184

A girl finds herself running through the forest at the edge of a village with no memory of anything, even her own name, and later learns that she might be twelve-year-old Isabelle, believed to be stolen by a witch six years before.

"Vande Velde, noted for her well-crafted riffs on fairy tales, has written her darkest yet, a story of greed, jealousy, and insidious evil that will haunt the reader for some time to come." Booklist

The **book** of Mordred; [illustrations by Justin Gerard] Houghton Mifflin 2005 342p hardcover o.p. pa $8.99

Grades: 8 9 10 11 12   **Fic**

1. Kings 2. Knights and knighthood -- Fiction 3. Mordred (Legendary character) -- Fiction
ISBN 0-618-50754-X; 0-618-80916-3 pa

LC 2004-28223

As the peaceful King Arthur reigns, the five-year-old daughter of Lady Alayna, newly widowed of the village-wizard Toland, is abducted by knights who leave their barn burning and their only servant dead.

"All of the characters are well developed and have a strong presence throughout. . . . [This] provides an intriguing counterpoint to anyone who is interested in Arthurian legend." SLJ

Vanderpool, Clare

★ **Moon** over Manifest. Delacorte Press 2010 351p $16.99; lib bdg $19.99

Grades: 5 6 7 8   **Fic**

1. Fathers -- Fiction 2. Great Depression, 1929-1939 -- Fiction
ISBN 978-0-385-73883-5; 0-385-73883-8; 978-0-385-90750-7 lib bdg; 0-385-90750-8 lib bdg

LC 2009-40042

Awarded the Newbery Medal, 2011

Twelve-year-old Abilene Tucker is the daughter of a drifter who, in the summer of 1936, sends her to stay with an old friend in Manifest, Kansas, where he grew up, and where she hopes to find out some things about his past.

"The absolute necessity of story as a way to redemption and healing past wounds is at the heart of this beautiful debut, and readers will cherish every word up to the heartbreaking yet hopeful and deeply gratifying ending." Kirkus

Vaughn, Carrie

Steel. HarperTeen 2011 294p $16.99; lib bdg $17.89

Grades: 7 8 9 10   **Fic**

1. Fencing -- Fiction 2. Pirates -- Fiction 3. Time travel -- Fiction
ISBN 978-0-06-154791-1; 0-06-154791-3; 978-0-06-195648-5 lib bdg; 0-06-195648-1 lib bdg

LC 2010012631

When Jill, a competitive high school fencer, goes with her family on vacation to the Bahamas, she is magically transported to an early-eighteenth-century pirate ship in the middle of the ocean.

This is "thoroughly enjoyable. . . . Through her assertive, appealing protagonist and a satisfying plot that sheds light on lesser-known aspects of pirate life, Vaughn introduces readers to an intriguing sport with an ancient pedigree." Kirkus

Voices of dragons. HarperTeen 2010 309p $16.99

Grades: 7 8 9 10   **Fic**

1. Fantasy fiction 2. Dragons -- Fiction
ISBN 978-0-06-179894-8; 0-06-179894-0

LC 2009-11604

In a parallel world where humans and dragons live in a state of cold war, seventeen-year-old Kay and her dragon friend, Artegal, struggle to find a way to show that dragons and humans can coexist.

"Vaughn's story is charming and fast paced with a strong, likable heroine." Publ Wkly

Vaught, Susan

Freaks like us; by Susan Vaught. Bloomsbury 2012 240 p. (hardcover) $16.99

Grades: 7 8 9 10 11 12   **Fic**

1. Friendship -- Fiction 2. Schizophrenia -- Fiction 3. Mental illness -- Fiction 4. Missing persons -- Fiction 5. Love -- Fiction 6. Missing children -- Fiction 7.

Mystery and detective stories
ISBN 1599908727; 9781599908724

LC 2012004227

This is the story of Jason, whose selectively mute friend Sunshine has "vanished, and Jason, whose schizophrenia has shaped his life, is a suspect in her disappearance. Seniors Jason, Drip and Sunshine have ridden the short bus and gone through school labeled SED--that's 'Severely Emotionally Disturbed.' Bullying at the hands of kids with behavioral disabilities goes unreported and unpunished, but the trio's alliance made life bearable in their catchall special ed program . . . . As the FBI investigates, Jason's always-shaky world threatens to come apart. Not taking "fuzzy pills" keeps his brain sharp, but the voices plaguing him grow louder. Jason carries Sunshine's secrets--should he break his promise not to tell?" (Kirkus)

Vaupel, Robin

My contract with Henry. Holiday House 2003 244p $16.95

Grades: 6 7 8 9   **Fic**
1. Friendship -- Fiction
ISBN 0-8234-1701-8

LC 2002-27471

A mission that begins as an eighth-grade project on Henry David Thoreau's experimental living at Walden Pond becomes a life-changing experience for a group of outsider students who become budding philosophers, environmental activists, and loyal friends
"Vaupel creates a painfully accurate portrayal of middle-school social dynamics." Booklist

The **rules** of the universe by Austin W. Hale. Holiday House 2007 265p $16.95

Grades: 4 5 6 7   **Fic**
1. Science fiction 2. Death -- Fiction 3. Grandfathers -- Fiction
ISBN 978-0-8234-1811-4; 0-8234-1811-1

LC 2003-56751

Thirteen-year-old Austin Hale, an aspiring scientist and disciple of his grandfather, a Nobel Prize-winning molecular physicist, finds himself in control of a powerful energy force that can turn back time and turn his orbit upside down
"The captivating blend of scientific research and magic is effectively balanced against the stark realism of a boy facing his first significant losses; the overall tone is one of cautious optimism." Bull Cent Child Books

Vawter, Vince

Paperboy; Vince Vawter. 1st ed. Delacorte Press 2013 240 p. (library) $19.99; (hardcover) $16.99

Grades: 5 6 7 8   **Fic**
1. Stuttering -- Fiction 2. Race relations -- Fiction 3. Newspaper carriers -- Fiction 4. Self-esteem -- Fiction 5. Interpersonal relations -- Fiction 6. Family life -- Tennessee -- Fiction
ISBN 0385742444; 9780307975058; 9780375990588; 9780385742443

LC 2012030546

In this book by Vince Vawter, "[a]fter an overthrown baseball busts his best friend's lip, 11-year-old Victor Vollmer takes over the boy's paper route. This is a particu-

larly daunting task for the able-armed Victor, as he has a prominent stutter that embarrasses him. . . .Through the paper route he meets a number of people, gains a much-needed sense of self and community, and has a life-threatening showdown with a local cart man." (School Library Journal)
"Carefully crafted language, authenticity of setting and quirky characters that ring fully true all combine to make this a worthwhile read. Although Little Man's stutter holds up dialogue, that annoyance also powerfully reflects its stultifying impact on his life. An engaging and heartfelt presentation that never whitewashes the difficult time and situation as Little Man comes of age." Kirkus

Veciana-Suarez, Ana

The **flight** to freedom. Orchard Bks. 2002 215p (First person fiction) $16.95; pa $6.99

Grades: 6 7 8 9   **Fic**
1. Immigrants -- Fiction 2. Cuban Americans -- Fiction
ISBN 0-439-38199-1; 0-439-38200-9 pa

LC 2001-58783

Writing in the diary which her father gave her, thirteen-year-old Yara describes life with her family in Havana, Cuba, in 1967 as well as her experiences in Miami, Florida, after immigrating there to be reunited with some relatives while leaving others behind
"The story and characters ring true in their portrayal of loss, longing, and the hope of starting a new life." SLJ

Venkatraman, Padma

★ **Climbing** the stairs. G.P. Putnam's Sons 2008 247p $16.99

Grades: 6 7 8 9 10   **Fic**
1. Prejudices -- Fiction 2. Family life -- Fiction 3. Brain -- Wounds and injuries -- Fiction
ISBN 978-0-399-24746-0; 0-399-24746-7

LC 2007-21757

In India, in 1941, when her father becomes brain-damaged in a non-violent protest march, fifteen-year-old Vidya and her family are forced to move in with her father's extended family and become accustomed to a totally different way of life.
"Venkatraman paints an intricate and convincing backdrop of a conservative Brahmin home in a time of change. . . . The striking cover art . . . will draw readers to this vividly told story." Booklist

★ **Island's** end. G.P. Putnam's Sons 2011 240p $16.99

Grades: 5 6 7 8 9   **Fic**
1. Islands -- Fiction 2. Apprentices -- Fiction
ISBN 978-0-399-25099-6; 0-399-25099-9

LC 2010036298

"Uido's clear, intelligent, present-tense voice consistently engrosses as she pushes through doubt and loss to find the right path. The beach, jungle and cliff settings are palpable. . . . There is very little information known about Andaman Islanders, making it hard to gauge the authenticity of this portrayal; the author's note indicates a respectful and diligent approach to her subject. . . . Refreshingly hopeful and beautifully written." Kirkus

Verday, Jessica

The **Hollow**. Simon Pulse 2009 515p $17.99

Grades: 7 8 9 10 11 12 **Fic**

1. Ghost stories 2. School stories 3. Bereavement -- Fiction 4. Supernatural -- Fiction

ISBN 1-4169-7893-3; 978-1-4169-7893-0

LC 2008042817

High-school junior Abbey struggles with the loss of her best friend Kristen, who vanished on a legendary bridge, but her grief is eased by Caspian, an attractive and mysterious stranger she meets in the Sleepy Hollow cemetery.

"Abbey's narration is heartfelt and authentically written." SLJ

Verne, Jules

★ **20,000** leagues under the sea; illustrated by the Dillons; translated by Anthony Bonner. Books of Wonder 2000 394p il $21.95

Grades: 5 6 7 8 9 10 11 12 Adult **Fic**

1. Sea stories 2. Science fiction 3. Submarines -- Fiction

ISBN 0-688-10535-1

LC 00-24336

Original French edition, 1870

Retells the adventures of a French professor and his two companions as they sail above and below the world's oceans as prisoners on the fabulous electric submarine of the deranged Captain Nemo

Vernick, Audrey

★ **Water** balloon. Clarion Books 2011 312p $16.99

Grades: 4 5 6 7 **Fic**

1. Dogs -- Fiction 2. Divorce -- Fiction 3. Friendship -- Fiction 4. Babysitters -- Fiction 5. Father-daughter relationship -- Fiction

ISBN 978-0-547-59554-2; 0-547-59554-9

LC 2011009847

With her best friends pulling away from her, her newly-separated parents deciding she should spend the summer at her father's new home, and a babysitting job she does not want, Marley's life is already as precarious as an overfull water balloon when a cute boy enters the picture.

"The book moves along at a pace that will keep tweens interested, and the dialogue among the characters feels real. Marley's relationships with her friends and family are complex, and even the most reluctant readers will relate to her and the choices that she makes." SLJ

Vernick, Shirley Reva

The **blood** lie; a novel. Cinco Puntos Press 2011 141p $15.95

Grades: 5 6 7 8 **Fic**

1. Love -- Fiction 2. Prejudices -- Fiction 3. Antisemitism -- Fiction 4. Jews -- United States -- Fiction

ISBN 978-1-933693-84-2; 1-933693-84-3

LC 2011011429

"Based on an actual incident in Massena in 1928, the slim novel effectively mines layers of ignorance, fear, intolerance and manipulation, and it connects the incident to Henry Ford's anti-Semitic writing and to the lynching of Jewish businessman Leo Frank in 1915." Kirkus

Vigilante, Danette

Trouble with half a moon. G. P. Putnam's Sons 2011 181p $16.99

Grades: 5 6 7 8 **Fic**

1. Faith -- Fiction 2. Friendship -- Fiction 3. Bereavement -- Fiction 4. Child abuse -- Fiction 5. Puerto Ricans -- Fiction 6. City and town life -- Fiction 7. Jamaican Americans -- Fiction

ISBN 978-0-399-25159-7; 0-399-25159-6

LC 2010-07377

Overwhelmed by grief and guilt over her brother's death and its impact on her mother, and at odds with her best friend, thirteen-year-old Dellie reaches out to a neglected boy in her building in the projects and learns from a new neighbor to have faith in herself and others.

"The story is told with considerable appeal and accessibility, and kids won't have to lead the same life as Dellie to recognize their travails." Bull Cent Child Books

Villareal, Ray

Body slammed! by Ray Villareal. Piñata Books 2012 194 p. (alk. paper) $11.95

Grades: 7 8 9 10 **Fic**

1. Wrestling -- Fiction 2. Schools -- Fiction 3. Fathers and sons -- Fiction 4. Mexican Americans -- Fiction

ISBN 1558857494; 9781558857490

LC 2012003181

This novel, by Ray Villareal, follows "[s]ixteen-year-old Jesse Baron . . . [who] is fed up with being cut down and dismissed, whether by the coach or his friends. . . . But it's through his dad that Jesse meets TJ Masters, a brash, new wrestling talent who's over 21, . . . TJ makes Jesse feel tough and confident. . . . But will Jesse listen to his family and friends when they warn him about hanging out with someone who's often reckless and irresponsible?" (Publisher's note)

Vincent, Zu

The **lucky** place. Front Street 2008 230p $17.95

Grades: 7 8 9 10 **Fic**

1. Death -- Fiction 2. Cancer -- Fiction 3. Alcoholism -- Fiction 4. Stepfathers -- Fiction 5. Father-daughter relationship -- Fiction

ISBN 978-1-932425-70-3; 1-932425-70-5

LC 2007-18357

"Readers meet Cassie when she is three years old and her inebriated father leaves her behind at the racetrack. . . . She is returned home by the police and their mother eventually realizes that this man is not a competent father. . . . Mom brings home Ellis, New Daddy, and Cassie can't help but feel his strength. . . . Cassie's voice changes as she grows into a 12-year-old who comes to know that inside herself is the real lucky place that she can truly count on. . . . Taking place in California in the late 1950s and early '60s . . . Vincent's novel ably creates a world that makes promises it can't keep. . . . A stunning fiction debut." SLJ

Vivian, Siobhan

The **list**; Siobhan Vivian. Scholastic 2012 333 p. $17.99

Grades: 7 8 9 10 11 12   **Fic**
1. Female friendship 2. Self-perception -- Fiction 3. Personal appearance -- Fiction 4. High school students -- Fiction 5. Identity (Psychology) -- Fiction 6. Schools -- Fiction 7. Identity -- Fiction 8. Friendship -- Fiction 9. Self-esteem -- Fiction 10. High schools -- Fiction 11. Beauty, Personal -- Fiction
ISBN 0545169178; 9780545169172
LC 2012004248

This young adult novel presents an "exploration of physical appearance and the status it confers. . . . Every year during homecoming week, a list is posted anonymously at Mount Washington High naming the prettiest and ugliest girls in each class. . . . The list confers instant status, transforming formerly homeschooled sophomore Lauren from geeky to hot while consigning her counterpart . . . Candace, to pariah. But what the label mainly confers is anxiety. Prettiest junior Bridget despairs that she"ll ever be thin enough to merit her title. . . . Jennifer, four-time 'ugliest' winner, tries to relish the notoriety. . . . Whether clued in or clueless to the intricate social complexities, boyfriends reinforce the status quo, while moms carry scars of their own past physical insecurities." (Kirkus)

A **little** friendly advice. Scholastic/Push 2008 248p $16.99
Grades: 7 8 9 10 11 12   **Fic**
1. Divorce -- Fiction 2. Friendship -- Fiction 3. Father-daughter relationship -- Fiction
ISBN 978-0-545-00404-6; 0-545-00404-7
LC 2007-9905

When Ruby's divorced father shows up unexpectedly on her sixteenth birthday, the week that follows is full of confusing surprises, including discovering that her best friend has been keeping secrets from her, her mother has not been truthful about the past, and life is often complicated.

"Readers will find themselves and their relationships reflected in Ruby's story—for better and worse." Publ Wkly

Voelkel, J.

Middleworld; [by] J & P Voelkel [i.e., Jon Voelkel, Pamela Craik Voelkel] Smith and Kraus Publishers 2007 397p il (The Jaguar stones) $17.95; pa $8.99
Grades: 4 5 6 7   **Fic**
1. Adventure fiction 2. Mayas -- Fiction
ISBN 978-1-57525-561-3; 1-57525-561-8; 978-1-60684-071-9 pa; 1-60684-071-1 pa

"Suspense and intrigue, human sacrifice, smuggling, and secret doors and escape routes through pyramids ensure that the novel, the first in a projected trilogy, is likely to win legions of fans." SLJ

The **end** of the world club; [by] J&P Voelkel. Egmont USA 2011 384p (The Jaguar stones) $16.99
Grades: 4 5 6 7   **Fic**
1. Adventure fiction 2. Mayas -- Fiction 3. Supernatural -- Fiction
ISBN 978-1-60684-072-6; 1-60684-072-X
LC 2010036641

With the end of the Mayan calendar fast approaching, fourteen-year-old Max Murphy and his friend Lola, the Maya girl who saved his life in the perilous jungle, race against time to outwit the twelve villainous Lords of Death, following the trail of the conquistadors into a forgotten land steeped in legend and superstition.

"The authors use Maya mythology and terms and add interesting facts about Spain and Spanish culture. This is a fast-paced book, and the action starts right away." SLJ

Voigt, Cynthia

Bad girls in love. Atheneum Bks. for Young Readers 2002 233p hardcover o.p. pa $11.99
Grades: 6 7 8 9   **Fic**
1. School stories 2. Friendship -- Fiction
ISBN 0-689-82471-8; 0-689-86620-8 pa
LC 2001-45898

Now in the eighth grade, best friends Mikey and Margalo try to figure out boys, crushes, and falling in love

It's the girls' "talk—insulting, furious, funny, needy, and smart—on the telephone, and in the school's cafeteria, bathrooms, and hallways that gets the junior-high jungle exactly right." Booklist
Other titles in this series are:
Bad, badder, baddest (1997)
Bad girls (1996)
Bad girls, bad girls, whatcha gonna do? (2006)
It's not easy being bad (2000)

★ **Dicey's** song. Atheneum Pubs. 1982 196p $17.95; pa $6.99
Grades: 5 6 7 8   **Fic**
1. Siblings -- Fiction 2. Grandmothers -- Fiction
ISBN 0-689-30944-9; 0-689-86362-4 pa
LC 82-3882

Awarded the Newbery Medal, 1983
"The vividness of Dicey is striking; Voigt has plumbed and probed her character inside out to fashion a memorable protagonist." Booklist

★ **Homecoming**. Atheneum Pubs. 1981 312p $18.95; pa $6.99
Grades: 6 7 8 9   **Fic**
1. Siblings -- Fiction 2. Abandoned children -- Fiction
ISBN 0-689-30833-7; 0-689-86361-6 pa
LC 80-36723

ALA YALSA Margaret A. Edwards Award (1995)
"The characterizations of the children are original and intriguing, and there are a number of interesting minor characters encountered in their travels." SLJ

★ **Izzy**, willy-nilly; Rev. format ed.; Atheneum Books for Young Readers 2005 327p $17.95; pa $6.99
Grades: 7 8 9 10   **Fic**
1. Amputees -- Fiction 2. Friendship -- Fiction 3. Drunk driving -- Fiction
ISBN 978-1-4169-0340-6; 1-4169-0340-2; 978-1-4169-0339-0 pa; 1-4169-0339-9 pa
LC 2005299062

A reissue of the title first published 1986
ALA YALSA Margaret A. Edwards Award (1995)
A car accident causes fifteen-year-old Izzy to lose one leg and face the need to start building a new life as an amputee.

"Voigt shows unusual insight into the workings of a 15-year-old girl's mind. . . . Just as Voigt's perceptive empathy brings Izzy to life, other characterizations are memorable, whether of Izzy's shallow former friends or of her egocentric 10-year-old sister." Pub Wkly [review of 1986 edition]

Mister Max; the book of lost things. by Cynthia Voigt ; illustrated by Iacopo Bruno. Alfred A. Knopf 2013 384 p. (hardcover) $16.99; (library) $19.99
Grades: 5 6 7 8   Fic
1. Abandoned children 2. Self-reliance -- Fiction 3. Problem solving -- Fiction
ISBN 0307976815; 9780307976819; 9780307976826; 9780375971235
LC 2012033823
In this book, Max "is left at the dock when he misses a boat to India, where his [actor] parents supposedly have been invited by a maharajah to start a theater. . . . Although his wise yet bossy librarian grandmother lives next door, 12-year-old Max wants to earn his keep and be independent. Cleverly donning the costumes and different roles performed by his missing parents, Max discovers an aptitude for finding lost things. . . . He is a 'solutioneer,' solving people's problems." (Kirkus Reviews)

★ A **solitary** blue. Atheneum Pubs. 1983 189p hardcover o.p. pa $6.99
Grades: 7 8 9 10   Fic
1. Divorce -- Fiction 2. Parent-child relationship -- Fiction
ISBN 0689310080; 0689863608
LC 83-6007
A Newbery honor book, 1984
"Jefferson Greene, a minor character from Dicey's Song {BRD 1983}, is the subject of the new novel. Beginning when Jeff was seven years old and ending when he was in high school, the book overlaps and goes beyond the earlier one. . . . {This novel} explores the relationships among Jeff, his mother Melody, and his father 'the Professor.' After Melody walked out on the family to pursue a long line of unrealistic causes, the Professor and his young son went on as if nothing had changed. Their . . . coexistence continued until Jeff at the age of eleven received an unexpected invitation to spend the summer with his mother and her family in South Carolina. . . . Age twelve and up." (Horn Book)
"This is the most mature and sophisticated of Voigt's novels. . . . Beautifully knit . . . compelling and intelligent." Bull Cent Child Books

Volponi, Paul
Black and white. Viking 2005 185p $15.99; pa $6.99
Grades: 7 8 9 10   Fic
1. Basketball -- Fiction 2. Race relations -- Fiction 3. African Americans -- Fiction
ISBN 0-670-06006-2; 0-14-240692-9 pa
LC 2004-24543
Two star high school basketball players, one black and one white, experience the justice system differently after committing a crime together and getting caught.

"These complex characters share a mutual respect and struggle with issues of loyalty, honesty, and courage. Social conflicts, basketball fervor, and tough personal choices make this title a gripping story." SLJ

★ **Homestretch**. Atheneum Books for Young Readers 2009 151p $16.99
Grades: 6 7 8 9 10   Fic
1. Death -- Fiction 2. Prejudices -- Fiction 3. Horse racing -- Fiction 4. Mexican Americans -- Fiction 5. Father-son relationship -- Fiction
ISBN 978-1-4169-3987-0; 1-4169-3987-3
LC 2008-30024
Five months after losing his mother, seventeen-year-old Gas runs away from an abusive father and gets a job working at an Arkansas race track, surrounded by the illegal Mexican immigrants that he and his father blame for her death.
"Volponi continues his streak of well-written novels in this simply written, coming-of-age story." Voice Youth Advocates

★ **Hurricane** song; a novel of New Orleans. Viking Childrens Books 2008 144p $15.99
Grades: 7 8 9 10 11 12   Fic
1. Jazz music -- Fiction 2. Father-son relationship -- Fiction 3. Hurricane Katrina, 2005 -- Fiction
ISBN 978-0-670-06160-0; 0-670-06160-3
LC 2007-38215
Twelve-year-old Miles Shaw goes to live with his father, a jazz musician, in New Orleans, and together they survive the horrors of Hurricane Katrina in the Superdome, learning about each other and growing closer through their painful experiences.
"A brilliant blend of reality and fiction, this novel hits every chord just right." Voice Youth Advocates

Rikers High. Viking 2010 216p $16.99
Grades: 8 9 10 11 12   Fic
1. Prisoners -- Fiction 2. African Americans -- Fiction 3. Juvenile delinquency -- Fiction
ISBN 978-0-670-01107-0; 0-670-01107-X
LC 2009-22471
Based on the adult novel, Rikers, published in 2002 by Black Heron Press
Arrested on a minor offense, a New York City teenager attends high school in the jail facility on Rikers Island, as he waits for his case to go to court.
"The author draws authentic situations and characters from his six years of teaching at Rikers. . . . An absorbing portrait of life in the stir. . . . Rare is the reader who won't find his narrative sobering." Booklist

★ **Rucker** Park setup. Viking 2007 149p $15.99
Grades: 7 8 9 10 11 12   Fic
1. Mystery fiction 2. Homicide -- Fiction 3. Basketball -- Fiction 4. African Americans -- Fiction
ISBN 978-0-670-06130-3; 0-670-06130-1
LC 2006-28463
While playing in a crucial basketball game on the very court where his best friend was murdered, Mackey tries to come to terms with his own part in that murder and decide

whether to maintain his silence or tell J.R.'s father and the police what really happened.

The author's "description of playing pickup ball on one of the toughest courts in the world feels wholly authentic. The characters also feel real." Voice Youth Advocates

The **hand** you're dealt. Atheneum Books for Young Readers 2008 176p $16.99

Grades: 8 9 10 11   **Fic**
1. School stories 2. Poker -- Fiction 3. Teachers -- Fiction
ISBN 978-1-4169-3989-4; 1-4169-3989-X
                          LC 2007-22988

When seventeen-year-old Huck's vindictive math teacher wins the town poker tournament and takes the winner's watch away from Huck's father while he is in a coma, Huck vows to get even with him no matter what it takes.

"The varied characters are unique and add to the book's interest quotient." Voice Youth Advocates

Voorhees, Coert
Lucky fools; Coert Voorhees. Hyperion Books 2012 293 p. $16.99

Grades: 8 9 10 11 12   **Fic**
1. College choice 2. Theater -- Fiction 3. Dating (Social customs) -- Fiction 4. Schools -- Fiction 5. College choice -- Fiction 6. Preparatory schools -- Fiction
ISBN 1423123980; 9781423123989
                          LC 2011026252

Author Coert Voorhees presents a story about an aspiring high school actor. "For the seniors at prestigious Oak Fields Prep, the pressure is on to get into an Ivy League school. . . . But David Ellison, star of the school play . . . wants to go to Juilliard instead. As David's Juilliard audition and the play's opening night approach, he is plagued with doubts about his acting ability and his relationships with two girls." (Publishers Weekly)

Vrettos, Adrienne Maria
★ **Sight**; [by] Adrienne Maria Vrettos. Margaret K. McElderry Books 2007 254p $16.99

Grades: 7 8 9 10   **Fic**
1. School stories 2. Parapsychology -- Fiction 3. Missing persons -- Fiction 4. Criminal investigation -- Fiction
ISBN 978-1-4169-0657-5; 1-4169-0657-6
                          LC 2006-35999

Sixteen-year-old Dylan uses her psychic abilities to help police solve crimes against children, but keeps her extracurricular activities secret from her friends at school.

"Vrettos has created a creepy scenario with a taut plot and a gripping climax. . . . She has crafted a believable setting and characters." Bull Cent Books

Skin. Margaret K. McElderry Books 2006 227p $16.95

Grades: 7 8 9 10   **Fic**
1. Siblings -- Fiction 2. Anorexia nervosa -- Fiction
ISBN 1-4169-0655-X
                          LC 2005001119

When his parents decide to separate, eighth-grader Donnie watches with horror as the physical condition of his sixteen-year old sister, Karen, deteriorates due to an eating disorder.

"The overwhelming alienation Donnie endures will speak to many teens, while his honest perspective will be welcomed by boys." Booklist

Wagner, Hilary
Nightshade City; [illustrations by Omar Rayyan] Holiday House 2010 262p il $17.95

Grades: 5 6 7 8   **Fic**
1. Fantasy fiction 2. Rats -- Fiction
ISBN 978-0-8234-2285-2; 0-8234-2285-2
                          LC 2010-02474

Eleven years after the cruel Killdeer took over the Catacombs far beneath the human's Trillium City, Juniper Belancourt, assisted by Vincent and Victor Nightshade, leads a maverick band of rats to escape and establish their own city.

"The themes of love, loss and loyalty resonate through the novel, and the moments of darkness and violence are ultimately overpowered by hope and redemption. A good story well-told." Kirkus

The **white** assassin. Holiday House 2011 il (The Nightshade chronicles) 242p $17.95

Grades: 5 6 7 8   **Fic**
1. Fantasy fiction 2. Rats -- Fiction
ISBN 978-0-8234-2333-0
                          LC 2011009579

Snakes, bats, and rats join forces to save Nightshade from Billycan and his horde of brutal swamp rats, aided by an antidote to the drug that made Billycan the way he is, but the revelation of secrets proves an even more powerful weapon in the fight for peace.

Waite, Michael P.
The **witches** of Dredmoore Hollow; by Riford McKenzie; with illustrations by Peter Ferguson. Marshall Cavendish Children 2008 264p il $16.99

Grades: 4 5 6 7   **Fic**
1. Aunts -- Fiction 2. Witches -- Fiction
ISBN 978-0-7614-5458-8; 0-7614-5458-6
                          LC 2007-29781

Strange things begin happening at Elijah's New England home just before his twelfth birthday in 1927, especially after two aunts he had never met whisk him away to Moaning Marsh, where he realizes that they are witches who need something from him in order to remove a curse.

"The book has continuous action and piles of demonic atmosphere." SLJ

Walden, Mark
H.I.V.E; The Higher Institute of Villainous Education. Simon & Schuster Books for Young Readers 2007 309p $15.99; pa $6.99

Grades: 5 6 7 8   **Fic**
1. Criminals -- Fiction
ISBN 1-4169-3571-1; 978-1-4169-3571-1; 978-1-4169-3572-8 pa; 1-4169-3572-X pa
                          LC 2007-16205

"H.I.V.E. is operated on a volcanic island in a distant ocean by G.L.O.V.E., a shadowy organization of worldwide wickedness. And, as 13-year-old master of mischief Otto Malpense soon discovers, here the slickest of young tricksters, thieves, and hackers have been brought against their will to be trained as the next generation of supervillains. . . . [This] novel is a real page-turner; those who love superhero stories will eat it up." SLJ

Another title about H.I.V.E. is:

H.I.V.E.: The Overlord protocol (2008)
H.I.V.E.: Escape velocity (2011)
H.I.V.E.: Dreadnought (2011)

Waldorf, Heather

Tripping. Red Deer Press 2008 342p pa $12.95

Grades: 8 9 10 11 12   **Fic**

1. Amputees -- Fiction 2. Voyages and travels -- Fiction 3. Wilderness survival -- Fiction

ISBN 978-0-88995-426-7; 0-88995-426-7

"Rainey and five other teens begin an eight-week school-sponsored educational/survival trek across Canada. . . . Rainey's challenge is heightened because she has an artificial leg and she learns that her mother, who abandoned her as a baby, lives near one of their stops and wants to meet her. As the trip progresses, the individuals bond and become part of a team. . . . Waldorf has written a unique story in which six very different young people are united in a common cause. Told with wit and humor, this fast-paced novel has character development that is extraordinary." SLJ

Wallace, Bill

Skinny -dipping at Monster Lake. Simon & Schuster Bks. for Young Readers 2003 212p hardcover o.p. pa $5.99

Grades: 4 5 6 7   **Fic**

ISBN 0-689-85150-2; 0-689-85151-0 pa

LC 2002-152820

When twelve-year-old Kent helps his father in a daring underwater rescue, he wins the respect he has always craved.

"This old-fashioned adventure has wide appeal, and the youngsters' games and camaraderie will hook even reluctant readers." SLJ

Wallace, Jason

Out of shadows. Holiday House 2011 282p $17.95

Grades: 7 8 9 10 11 12   **Fic**

1. School stories 2. Bullies -- Fiction 3. Race relations -- Fiction

ISBN 978-0-8234-2342-2; 0-8234-2342-5

LC 2010-24372

In 1983, at an elite boys' boarding school in Zimbabwe, thirteen-year-old English lad Robert Jacklin finds himself torn between his black roommate and the white bullies still bitter over losing power through the recent civil war.

"This thought-provoking narrative offers teens a window into a distinctive time and place in history that is likely to be unfamiliar to most of them. A first purchase for high schools, especially those with a strong world cultures curriculum." SLJ

Wallace, Rich

One good punch. Alfred A. Knopf 2007 114p $15.99

Grades: 7 8 9 10 11 12   **Fic**

1. School stories 2. Journalism -- Fiction 3. Track athletics -- Fiction

ISBN 978-0-375-81352-8; 0-375-81352-7

LC 2006-33270

Eighteen-year-old Michael Kerrigan, writer of obituaries for the Scranton Observer and captain of the track team, is ready for the most important season of his life—until the police find four joints in his school locker, and he is faced with a choice that could change everything.

"This novel's success is in creating a multidimensional male character in a format that will appeal to all readers. The moral dilemma . . . makes this novel ripe for ethical discussions." Voice Youth Advocates

Perpetual check. Alfred A. Knopf 2009 112p $15.99; lib bdg $18.99

Grades: 8 9 10 11   **Fic**

1. Chess -- Fiction 2. Brothers -- Fiction 3. Father-son relationship -- Fiction

ISBN 978-0-375-84058-6; 0-375-84058-3; 978-0-375-94058-3 lib bdg; 0-375-94058-8 lib bdg

LC 2008-04159

Brothers Zeke and Randy participate in an important chess tournament, playing against each other while also trying to deal with their father's intensely competitive tendencies.

"Wallace cleverly positions Randy and Zeke for a win-win conclusion in this satisfying, engaging, and deceptively simple story." SLJ

War and watermelon. Viking 2011 184p $15.99

Grades: 6 7 8 9   **Fic**

1. School stories 2. Brothers -- Fiction 3. Football -- Fiction 4. Family life -- Fiction

ISBN 978-0-670-01152-0; 0-670-01152-5

LC 2010-41043

As the summer of 1969 turns to fall in their New Jersey town, twelve-year-old Brody plays football in his first year at junior high while his older brother's protest of the war in Vietnam causes tension with their father.

"Sixties culture and events . . . are well integrated into the story, and humorous vignettes . . . help lighten the mood." Booklist

★ **Wrestling** Sturbridge. Knopf 1996 135p hardcover o.p. pa $4.99

Grades: 7 8 9 10   **Fic**

1. Wrestling -- Fiction 2. Friendship -- Fiction

ISBN 0-679-87803-3; 0-679-88555-2 pa

LC 95-20468

"The wresting scenes are thrilling. . . . Like Ben, whose voice is so strong and clear here, Wallace weighs his words carefully, making every one count in this excellent, under-stated first novel." Booklist

Wallenfels, Stephen

POD. Namelos 2009 212p $18.95; pa $9.95

Grades: 7 8 9 10   **Fic**
1. Science fiction 2. Extraterrestrial beings -- Fiction
ISBN 978-1-60898-011-6; 1-60898-011-1; 978-1-60898-010-9 pa; 1-60898-010-3 pa

LC 2008-29721

As alien spacecrafts fill the sky and zap up any human being who dares to go outside, fifteen-year-old Josh and twelve-year-old Megs, living in different cities, describe what could be their last days on Earth.

"The dire circumstances don't negate the humor, the hormones, or the humanity found in the young narrators. This is solid, straightforward sci-fi." Booklist

Walliams, David

★ The **boy** in the dress; illustrated by Quentin Blake. Razorbill 2009 231p il $15.99

Grades: 4 5 6 7   **Fic**
1. School stories 2. Soccer -- Fiction 3. Transvestites -- Fiction
ISBN 978-1-59514-299-3; 1-59514-299-1

"Dennis is a bit surprised—but not terribly nonplussed—to discover that he enjoys wearing dresses. The 12-year-old does, however, realize this is not the kind of revelation he wants to share with his truck-driving dad, his older brother, or his mates on the school football team, where he is the star player. . . . Walliams . . . has written a witty, high-spirited, and, well, sensible story about cross-dressing and other real-life issues." Booklist

Walsh, Alice

A **Long** Way from Home. Orca Book Pub 2012 232 p. (paperback) $11.95

Grades: 7 8 9 10   **Fic**
1. Immigrants -- Fiction 2. Prejudices -- Fiction 3. September 11 terrorist attacks, 2001 -- Fiction
ISBN 1926920791; 9781926920795

In this book by Alice Walsh, "thirteen-year-old Rabia, along with her mother and younger brother, flees Afghanistan. . . . They take part in a program that is relocating refugee widows and orphans to America. . . . After the terrorist attack on the World Trade Center in New York City, their plane is diverted to Gander, Newfoundland. Also on the plane is a boy named Colin, who struggles with his prejudices against Rabia and her family." (Publisher's note)

Walsh, Pat

★ The **Crowfield** curse. Chicken House 2010 326p il $16.99

Grades: 5 6 7 8   **Fic**
1. Magic -- Fiction 2. Orphans -- Fiction 3. Monasteries -- Fiction
ISBN 0-545-22922-7; 978-0-545-22922-7

LC 2009-51483

In 1347, when fourteen-year-old orphan William Paynel, an impoverished servant at Crowfield Abbey, goes into the forest to gather wood and finds a magical creature caught in a trap, he discovers he has the ability to see fays and becomes embroiled in a strange mystery involving Old Magic, a bitter feud, and ancient secrets.

"This suspenseful and spooky story will thrill readers. . . . With fascinating attention to detail and an edgy battle

between evil and good, Walsh sweeps readers almost effortlessly into another time and place." SLJ

The **Crowfield** demon; Pat Walsh. Scholastic 2012 360 p. $16.99

Grades: 5 6 7 8   **Fic**
1. Fantasy fiction 2. Adventure fiction 3. Children's stories 4. Demonology -- Fiction 5. Magic -- Fiction 6. Orphans -- Fiction 7. Identity -- Fiction 8. Monasteries -- Fiction 9. Blessing and cursing -- Fiction
ISBN 054531769X; 9780545317696; 9780545373500

LC 2011029246

This juvenile historical fantasy novel by Pat Walsh is the sequel to his earlier story "The Crowfield Curse." "In "The Crowfield Curse," young monks' apprentice Will learned he was gifted with the Sight: able to see beyond this mortal coil into the spirit realms of Old Magic. Protected by the warrior fay Shadlok -- and befriended by the wry, wary hobgoblin called Brother Walter -- the boy is just coming into his strange powers. But now, from its very foundations, Crowfield Abbey has begun to crumble. As Will slaves to salvage the chapel, he discovers something truly terrifying. A heathen creature from a pagan past is creeping up through the rubble -- avowed to unleash havoc on holy ground!" (Publisher's note)

Walters, Eric

Catboy. Orca Book Publishers 2011 229p pa $9.95

Grades: 4 5 6 7   **Fic**
1. Boys -- Fiction 2. Cats -- Fiction
ISBN 978-1-55469-953-7 pa; 1-55469-953-3 pa

The wild cat colony Taylor has been caring for is at risk of being destroyed, and in order to save it, Taylor will need the help of all his friends.

"Walters' story . . . moves fast and is plenty appealing. . . . Solid writing, strong kid characters, caring adults, and cute animals could make this a popular choice." Booklist

Sketches; by Eric Walters. Viking 2008 232p $15.99

Grades: 7 8 9 10   **Fic**
1. Artists -- Fiction 2. Homeless persons -- Fiction 3. Runaway teenagers -- Fiction
ISBN 978-0-670-06294-2; 0-670-06294-4

LC 2007-23123

After running away from home, fifteen-year-old Dana finds friends on the Toronto streets, and, eventually, a way to come to terms with what has happened to her.

"The characters' well-portrayed camaraderie, resourcefulness, and resiliency carry the tale, which ends on a note of promise." SLJ

Special Edward. Orca Book Publishers 2009 108p (Orca currents) $16.95; pa $9.95

Grades: 7 8 9 10   **Fic**
1. School stories 2. Learning disabilities -- Fiction
ISBN 978-1-55469-096-1; 1-55469-096-X; 978-1-55469-092-3 pa; 1-55469-092-7 pa

In an attempt to gain lower expectations and extra time for tests, Edward tries to fake a special education designation.

"Walters has a good ear for teen talk, and Edward is as charming to read about as he is in the classroom. The author deftly weaves subtle clues into Edward's character that will leave readers nodding in agreement with his true condition. . . . A refreshing read." SLJ

Splat! written by Eric Walters. Orca Book Publishers 2008 112p $16.95; pa $9.95
Grades: 7 8 9 10   **Fic**
    1. Tomatoes -- Fiction 2. Friendship -- Fiction
    ISBN 978-1-55143-988-4; 1-55143-988-3; 978-1-55143-986-0 pa; 1-55143-986-7 pa
"The relationship between Keegan and narrator Alex, with their relentless and often quite funny smartassed exhanges, is the core of this speedy and readable novel." Bull Cent Child Books

The **money** pit mystery. Fitzhenry & Whiteside 2011 289p pa $9.95
Grades: 4 5 6 7   **Fic**
    1. Mystery fiction 2. Islands -- Fiction 3. Family life -- Fiction 4. Buried treasure -- Fiction
    ISBN 978-1-55455-123-1; 1-55455-123-4
"Sam's grandfather and mother had a fight years ago, and now Sam, his sister, and their mother are visiting him for the first time in years. When they arrive on tiny Oak Island, they are shocked to discover how rundown the man's once-immaculate house has become. To make matters worse, he isn't even there. When Sam, Beth, and their friend, Buzz, do some exploring, they are surprised by some security guards at the town's 'money pit.' Some folks believe that Captain Kidd buried treasure here. . . . This is a well-thought-out mystery with lots of suspense and a fully realized picture of a struggling family." SLJ

Ward, David
  ★ **Escape** the mask. Amulet Books 2008 195p (The grassland trilogy) $15.95
Grades: 7 8 9 10   **Fic**
    1. Science fiction 2. Slavery -- Fiction
    ISBN 978-0-8109-9477-5; 0-8109-9477-1
                                   LC 2007028212
Six young friends, tortured by the Spears and forced to work as slaves in the harsh fields of Grassland, vow to escape to find the freedom that was stolen from them long ago, and their opportunity arises when Outsiders come and wage war against the Spears.
"Ward's novel bursts with action and is laden with tense scenes. His excellent descriptive writing allows the reader to visualize the action. In addition, Ward's fantasy world is so believable that the text almost reads as historical fiction." Voice Youth Advocates
    Other titles in this series are:
    Beneath the mask (2008)
    Beyond the mask (2010)

Ward, Rachel
The **Chaos**. Chicken House 2011 339p $17.99
Grades: 8 9 10 11 12   **Fic**
    1. Science fiction 2. Death -- Fiction 3. Orphans -- Fiction 4. Blacks -- Great Britain -- Fiction
    ISBN 978-0-545-24269-1; 0-545-24269-X

When rising flood waters force him and his grandmother to evacuate their coastal home and return to London, sixteen-year-old Adam, who has inherited his mother's curse of being able to see the day that someone will die when he looks into their eyes, becomes disturbed when he begins to see January 1, 2027, a date six months into the future, in nearly everyone around him.
"In this sequel to Numbers a fascinating premise is again worked out through gripping episodes and a lightly handled metaphysical dilemma." Horn Book

Infinity; Rachel Ward. Chicken House/Scholastic 2012 249 p. (Numbers) $17.99
Grades: 8 9 10 11 12   **Fic**
    1. Death -- Fiction 2. Psychic ability -- Fiction 3. Interpersonal relations -- Fiction 4. Blacks -- England -- London -- Fiction
    ISBN 0545350921; 9780545350921; 9780545381918
                                 LC 2011032709
This novel, by Rachel Ward, is the conclusion to the "Numbers" trilogy. "Sarah loves Adam, but can't bear the thought that every time he looks in her eyes, he can see her dying; can see her last day. It's 2029. Two years since the Chaos. . . . Little Mia was supposed to die that New Year's Day. The numbers don't lie. But somehow she changed her date. Mia's just a baby, oblivious to her special power. But ruthless people are hunting her down, determined to steal her secret." (Publisher's note)

★ **Numbers**. Chicken House/Scholastic 2010 325p $17.99
Grades: 8 9 10 11 12   **Fic**
    1. Science fiction 2. Death -- Fiction 3. Runaway teenagers -- Fiction 4. Blacks -- Great Britain -- Fiction
    ISBN 978-0-545-14299-1; 0-545-14299-7
                                 LC 2008-55440
"Ward's debut novel is gritty, bold, and utterly unique. Jem's isolation and pain, hidden beneath a veneer of toughness, are palpable, and the ending is a real shocker." SLJ

Wardlaw, Lee
101 ways to bug your friends and enemies. Dial Books for Young Readers 2011 $16.99; pa $6.99
Grades: 4 5 6 7   **Fic**
    1. School stories 2. Bullies -- Fiction
    ISBN 978-0-8037-3262-9; 978-0-14-241949-6 pa
                                 LC 2011001161
Steve "Sneeze" Wyatt takes half of his classes at the high school, where he attracts the attention of a bully on the varsity golf team, while at middle school all of his friends seem to be falling in love—including Sneeze, himself.
"With a unique cast of characters (including supportive parents) and plenty of conflict and humor, this is a good choice for reluctant readers." SLJ

101 ways to bug your teacher; Lee Wardlaw. Dial Books 2004 246p hardcover o.p. pa $6.99
Grades: 4 5 6 7   **Fic**
    1. Schools 2. Teachers
    ISBN 0-8037-2658-9; 0-14-240331-1 pa
                                 LC 2003-20068

Steve "Sneeze" Wyatt attempts to thwart his parents' plan to have him skip eighth grade, but he has bigger problems when his friends disapprove of his new list and Mrs. "Fierce" Pierce threatens to keep him from the Invention Convention.

"In spite of the title, the characters show respect for their teachers and parents, and for one another. A delightful read." SLJ

Warner, Sally

It's only temporary; written and illustrated by Sally Warner. Viking Childrens Books 2008 182p il $15.99

Grades: 4 5 6 7   Fic

1. Bullies -- Fiction 2. Siblings -- Fiction 3. Grandmothers -- Fiction 4. Brain -- Wounds and injuries -- Fiction

ISBN 978-0-670-06111-2; 0-670-06111-5

LC 2007-038220

When Skye's older brother comes home after a devastating accident, she moves from Albuquerque, New Mexico, to California to live with her grandmother and attend middle school, where she somewhat reluctantly makes new friends, learns to stand up for herself and those she cares about, and begins to craft a new relationship with her changed brother.

"Warner deftly handles Skye's anger toward her brain-injured brother, also infusing her with a convincingly developed sense of compassion. Witty line art decorates some pages." Horn Book Guide

Wasserman, Robin

★ **Awakening**. Scholastic 2007 207p (Chasing yesterday) pa $5.99

Grades: 6 7 8 9   Fic

1. Amnesia -- Fiction

ISBN 978-0-439-93338-4

"A teenager wakes up just yards away from a mysterious industrial accident. . . . Although she is seriously injured and has amnesia, she should be dead. . . . As Jane Doe, or J.D., she receives national news attention. Then a woman shows up, claiming to be her mother, and J.D. goes 'home' to a house she cannot remember and begins psychiatric treatment with an old family friend, who unnervingly looks exactly like the monstrous doctor of her nightmares. . . . [Wasserman's] characters are well developed and believable, her plot is suspenseful, and her backgrounds . . . are nicely detailed." Voice Youth Advocates

Another title in this series is:

Betrayal (2007)

The **book** of blood and shadow; by Robin Wasserman. Alfred A. Knopf 2012 352p. $17.99

Grades: 7 8 9   Fic

1. Mystery fiction 2. Suspense fiction 3. Homicide -- Fiction 4. Prague (Czech Republic) -- Fiction

ISBN 9780375868764; 9780375872778; 9780375899614; 9780375968761

LC 2011003920

In this book, "Nora . . . help[s] an eccentric professor translate a sixteenth-century book by a notable alchemist (and the letters left by his daughter, Elizabeth), . . . spending more time with her best friend, Chris, and his roommate, Max, who are also working on the project. Just as quickly as

Nora becomes invested in Elizabeth"s life, Max transforms from a slightly creepy tagalong to a sweet, solicitous boyfriend. Then Chris is brutally murdered, his girlfriend Adriane is left without memory of the night, and Max (the main suspect in the crime) disappears. . . . Nora . . . continu[es] her translation of the secrets encrypted in Elizabeth"s . . . communications and uncovering conspiracies . . . in which she herself is . . . a key figure." (Bulletin of the Center for Children"s Books)

Waters, Dan

★ **Generation** dead. Hyperion 2008 382p $16.99

Grades: 7 8 9 10   Fic

1. School stories 2. Death -- Fiction 3. Zombies -- Fiction 4. Prejudices -- Fiction

ISBN 978-1-4231-0921-1; 1-4231-0921-X

LC 2007-36361

When dead teenagers who have come back to life start showing up at her high school, Phoebe, a goth girl, becomes interested in the phenomenon, and when she starts dating a "living impaired" boy, they encounter prejudice, fear, and hatred.

This "is a classic desegregation story that also skewers adult attempts to make teenagers play nice. . . . Motivational speakers, politically correct speech and encounter groups come in for special ridicule." N Y Times Book Rev

Waters, Zack C.

Blood moon rider; [by] Zack C. Waters. Pineapple Press 2006 126p $13.95

Grades: 5 6 7 8   Fic

1. Ranch life -- Fiction 2. Grandfathers -- Fiction 3. World War, 1939-1945 -- Fiction

ISBN 978-1-56164-350-9; 1-56164-350-5

LC 2005030749

After his father's death in World War II, fourteen-year-old Harley Wallace tries to join the Marines but is, instead, sent to live with his grandfather in Peru Landing, Florida, where he soon joins a covert effort to stop Nazis from destroying a secret airbase on Tampa Bay

This is "an adventure filled with unexpected kindnesses and the irrepressibility of family ties, as well as a brush with espionage and a couple of suspenseful shoot'em-up scenes. A colorful cast of characters and a nod to teenage romance help make this a good choice for middle school boys." SLJ

Watkins, Steve

★ **Down** Sand Mountain. Candlewick Press 2008 327p $16.99

Grades: 7 8 9 10   Fic

1. School stories 2. Bullies -- Fiction 3. Family life -- Fiction 4. Race relations -- Fiction

ISBN 978-0-7636-3839-9; 0-7636-3839-0

LC 2007-52159

In a small Florida mining town in 1966, twelve-year-old Dewey faces one worst-day-ever after another, but comes to know that the issues he faces about bullies, girls, race, and identity are part of the adult world, as well.

"The simple, beautiful prose remains totally true to the child's bewildered viewpoint. . . . Readers will be haunted by the disturbing drama of harsh secrets close to home." Booklist

Watkins, Yoko Kawashima
★ **My** brother, my sister, and I. Bradbury Press 1994 275p hardcover o.p. pa $5.99
Grades: 6 7 8 9   **Fic**
1. World War, 1939-1945 -- Fiction
ISBN 0-02-792526-9; 0-689-80656-6 pa
LC 93-23535
"Watkins's first-person narrative is beautifully direct and emotionally honest." Publ Wkly

★ **So** far from the bamboo grove. Lothrop, Lee & Shepard Bks. 1986 183p map hardcover o.p. pa $5.99
Grades: 6 7 8 9   **Fic**
1. World War, 1939-1945 -- Fiction
ISBN 0-688-13115-8 pa
LC 85-15939
A fictionalized autobiography in which eight-year-old Yoko escapes from Korea to Japan with her mother and sister at the end of World War II
"An admirably told and absorbing novel." Horn Book

Watson, Cristy
Benched. Orca Book Publishers 2011 123p (Orca currents) pa $9.95
Grades: 6 7 8 9   **Fic**
1. Gangs -- Fiction 2. Brothers -- Fiction
ISBN 1-55469-408-6; 978-1-55469-408-2
Cody and his friends get caught up in gang activity when they steal a park bench.
"Reluctant readers, especially, will be hooked as the tension builds, and the realistic story, which avoids a slick resolution, will spark discussion." Booklist

Watson, Geoff
Edison's gold. Egmont USA 2010 312p $15.99; lib bdg $18.99
Grades: 4 5 6 7   **Fic**
1. Inventors 2. Mystery fiction 3. Adventure fiction 4. Electrical engineers 5. Inventors -- Fiction 6. Secret societies -- Fiction
ISBN 978-1-60684-094-8; 1-60684-094-0; 978-1-60684-095-5 lib bdg; 1-60684-095-9 lib bdg
LC 2010-11312
Tom Edison and his friends become embroiled in a mystery involving his 'double-great' grandfather's inventions, a secret society, and a vendetta being carried out by a descendant of inventor Nikola Tesla.
This "is a fast-paced adventure filled mystery that middle schoolers will like." SLJ

Watson, Jude
Beyond the grave. Scholastic 2009 190p (The 39 clues) $12.99
Grades: 4 5 6 7   **Fic**
1. Ciphers -- Fiction 2. Orphans -- Fiction 3. Siblings -- Fiction
ISBN 978-0-545-06044-8; 0-545-06044-3

A clue sends Amy and Dan jetting off to find out just what's behind the fierce rivalry between the Tomas and Ekaterina branches of the Cahill family. Was a Clue stolen from the Tomas branch? Where is it now? And most important, can Amy and Dan get their hands on it before their rivals do?
"Like the previous books, historical information is woven into the fast-paced adventure." SLJ

In too deep. Scholastic 2009 206p (The 39 clues) $12.99
Grades: 4 5 6 7   **Fic**
1. Adventure fiction 2. Ciphers -- Fiction 3. Orphans -- Fiction 4. Siblings -- Fiction
ISBN 978-0-545-09064-3; 0-545-09064-4
"Amy and Dan fly to Australia. Attemping to trace their late parents' journey eight years earlier, they link Amelia Earhart's last flight to their own family quest. . . . The spy-versus-spy mentality will keep readers guessing. . . . The series' fans will devour the breathless action scenes in this fast-paced adventure." Booklist

Watson, Renee
What Momma left me. Bloomsbury 2010 224p $15.99
Grades: 5 6 7 8   **Fic**
1. Orphans -- Fiction 2. Bereavement -- Fiction 3. Family life -- Fiction 4. Grandparents -- Fiction 5. Christian life -- Fiction 6. African Americans -- Fiction
ISBN 978-1-59990-446-7; 1-59990-446-2
LC 2009-18263
After the death of their mother, thirteen-year-old Serenity Evans and her younger brother go to live with their grandparents, who try to keep them safe from bad influences and help them come to terms with what has happened to their family.
"Serenity's struggles and insights, as she wrestles with her parents' legacy and an uncertain future, are inspiring, authentic, and told in a straighforward yet poetic style. The first-person narration is consistent, and the mystery of the painful circumstances of her mother's death—as well as additional tragedies—propels the story." Publ Wkly

Watts, Irene N.
★ **No** moon. Tundra Books 2010 234p pa $12.95
Grades: 6 7 8 9   **Fic**
1. Shipwrecks -- Fiction 2. Household employees -- Fiction
ISBN 978-0-88776-971-9; 0-88776-971-3
Louisa Gardener is the fourteen-year-old nursemaid to the young daughters of a wealthy, titled family living in London, England, in 1912. The family decides to sail to New York aboard the Titanic. An accident to the children's nanny, only days prior to the sailing, means that Louisa must go in her stead.
"Watts provides a fascinating account of what the great unsinkable ship was like. The catastrophe is rendered in a heartbreakingly graceful style. . . . [This is a] uniquely engaging and satisfying coming-of-age historical adventure." Booklist

Weatherford, Carole Boston

★ **Becoming** Billie Holiday; art by Floyd Cooper. Wordsong 2008 116p il $19.95

Grades: 7 8 9 10 Fic

1. Singers 2. Blues musicians 3. Novels in verse 4. Singers -- Fiction 5. Jazz music -- Fiction 6. African Americans -- Fiction

ISBN 978-1-59078-507-2; 1-59078-507-X

LC 2007-51214

Coretta Scott King honor book for text, 2009

Jazz vocalist Billie Holiday looks back on her early years in this fictional memoir written in verse.

"This captivating title places readers solidly into Holiday's world, and is suitable for independent reading as well as a variety of classroom uses." SLJ

Includes bibliographical references

Weatherly, Lee

Angel burn; [by] L.A. Weatherly. Candlewick Press 2011 449p $17.99

Grades: 8 9 10 11 12 Fic

1. Love -- Fiction 2. Angels -- Fiction 3. Supernatural -- Fiction

ISBN 978-0-7636-5652-2; 0-7636-5652-6

LC 2010-44819

In a world where angels are fierce stalkers whose irresistible force allows them to feed off humans and drain them of their vitality, a ruthless teenaged assassin of angels falls in love with a half-angel half-human girl, with devastating consequences.

"Weatherly's plot and writing are first-rate, adrenaline-fueled while still taking the time to thoughtfully develop the characters and build the romance. This elevated twist on the angel genre deserves to be spread far and wide." Publ Wkly

Kat got your tongue. David Fickling Books 2007 195p $15.99; lib bdg $18.99

Grades: 7 8 9 10 Fic

1. Amnesia -- Fiction

ISBN 978-0-385-75117-9; 0-385-75117-6; 978-0-385-75122-3 lib bdg; 0-385-75122-2 lib bdg

LC 2006-24408

After being hit by a car, thirteen-year-old Kat wakes up in the hospital with no memory of her previous life.

"Weatherby writes with fluid grace and makes this story line compelling, sprinkling bits of humor into Kat's journey toward recovery." Booklist

Weaver, Will

Defect. Farrar, Straus and Giroux 2007 199p $16

Grades: 7 8 9 10 11 12 Fic

1. School stories 2. Birth defects -- Fiction 3. Foster home care -- Fiction

ISBN 0-374-31725-9; 978-0-374-31725-6

LC 2006-49152

After spending most of his life in Minnesota foster homes hiding a bizarre physical abnormality, fifteen-year-old David is offered a chance at normalcy, but must decide if giving up what makes him special is the right thing to do.

The author "skillfully interweaves the improbable with twenty-first-century realities in this provocative novel of the ultimate cost of being so, so different." Voice of Youth Advocates

Full service. Farrar, Straus & Giroux 2005 231p hardcover o.p. pa $8.99

Grades: 7 8 9 10 Fic

1. Farm life -- Fiction 2. Service stations -- Fiction

ISBN 0-374-32485-9; 0-374-40022-9 pa

LC 2004-57671

In the summer of 1965, teenager Paul Sutton, a northern Minnesota farm boy, takes a job at a gas station in town, where his strict religious upbringing is challenged by new people and experiences.

"Weaver is a wonderful stylist and his beautifully chosen words put such a shine on his deeply felt story that most teens will be able to find their own faces reflected in its pages." Booklist

Saturday night dirt. Farrar, Straus and Giroux 2008 163p $14.95; pa $7.99

Grades: 8 9 10 11 Fic

1. Automobile racing -- Fiction

ISBN 978-0-374-35060-4; 0-374-35060-4; 978-0-312-56131-4 pa; 0-312-56131-8 pa

LC 2007-6988

In a small town in northern Minnesota, the much-anticipated Saturday night dirt-track race at the old-fashioned, barely viable, Headwaters Speedway becomes, in many ways, an important life-changing event for all the participants on and off the track.

"Weaver presents compelling character studies. . . . Young racing fans . . . will find much that rings true here." Booklist

Other titles in this series are Checkered flag cheater (2010)

Super stock rookie (2009)

Webb, Philip

Six days. Chicken House 2011 336p $17.99

Grades: 5 6 7 8 Fic

1. Science fiction 2. Siblings -- Fiction 3. Space and time -- Fiction

ISBN 978-0-545-31767-2; 0-545-31767-3

LC 2010054233

Cass and her brother Wilbur scavenge in the ruins of a future London seeking an artifact for their Russian masters, but the search takes on a new urgency after the arrival of Erin and Peyto, strangers from afar who claim to hold the key to locating the mysterious object.

Webb "has created a complex and intriguing dystopia filled with devastation, clever devices . . . and lots of local color. . . . The novel's rapid pacing will hook readers and keep them turning pages." Booklist

Weber, David

★ A **beautiful** friendship. Baen Books 2011 361p $18.99

Grades: 6 7 8 9 Fic

1. Science fiction 2. Animals -- Fiction 3. Space colonies -- Fiction

ISBN 978-1-4516-3747-2; 1-4516-3747-0

LC 2011015815

Twelve-year-old Stephanie Harrington, a genetically-enhanced girl on the pioneer planet of Sphinx, bonds with a treecat, a telepathic and fully sentient animal, putting her in danger from highly placed enemies who want to ensure that the planet remains entirely in human hands.

"The environmenatal messages, human-animal friendship, humor, action, and inventive techology will make this series starter an easy hit with teen sf readers." Booklist

Weber, Lori

If you live like me. Lobster Press 2009 331p pa $14.95

Grades: 7 8 9 10   **Fic**

1. Family life -- Fiction

ISBN 978-1-897550-12-0; 1-897550-12-X

Cheryl's unhappiness builds with each move as her family travels across Canada while her father does research for a book, and by the time they reach Newfoundland, she is planning her escape, but events cause her to re-examine her feelings

"Weber's depiction of Cheryl is true to life, an accurate account of an independent and intelligent teenager struggling with loneliness, acceptance of change, and her own approaching adulthood." SLJ

Wedekind, Annie

A **horse** of her own; by Annie Wedekind. Feiwel and Friends 2008 275p $16.95; pa $7.99

Grades: 5 6 7 8   **Fic**

1. Camps -- Fiction 2. Horses -- Fiction 3. Horsemanship -- Fiction

ISBN 978-0-312-36927-9; 0-312-36927-1; 978-0-312-58146-6 pa; 0-312-58146-7 pa

LC 2007032769

At summer camp Jane feels like an outsider among the cliquish rich girls who board their horses at Sunny Acres farm, and when the horse she has been riding is sold to another camper, she feels even worse until her teacher asks her to help train a beautiful but skittish new horse, and the experience brings out the best in her.

"Tenacious and thoughtful, Jane is an appealing protagonist who gradually recognizes that being accepted no longer matters to her. The plot . . . has enough twists, including a hint of romance, to sustain readers' interest." SLJ

Weeks, Sarah

As simple as it seems. Laura Geringer Books 2010 181p $15.99; lib bdg $16.89

Grades: 4 5 6   **Fic**

1. Ghost stories 2. Adoption -- Fiction 3. Friendship -- Fiction

ISBN 978-0-06-084663-3; 0-06-084663-1; 978-0-06-084664-0 lib bdg; 0-06-084664-X lib bdg

Eleven-year-old Verbena Polter gets through a difficult summer of turbulent emotions and the revelation of a disturbing family secret with an odd new friend who believes she is the ghost of a girl who drowned many years before.

"Weeks's characters are well rounded and her story line is engaging." Horn Book Guide

★ **Jumping** the scratch; a novel. Laura Geringer Books 2006 167p il $15.99; pa $5.99

Grades: 5 6 7 8   **Fic**

1. Aunts -- Fiction 2. Memory -- Fiction 3. Child sexual abuse -- Fiction

ISBN 978-0-06-054109-5; 0-06-054109-1; 978-0-06-054110-1 pa; 0-06-054111-3 pa

LC 2005-17776

After moving with his mother to a trailer park to care for an injured aunt, eleven-year-old Jamie Reardon struggles to cope with a deeply buried secret

"Weeks alludes to sexual abuse, but with a broad brush and no graphic details. . . . Weeks perfectly captures not only the guilt, shame, and pain of the abused boy but also the tenor of a fifth-grade classroom from the point of view of a new student who is friendless, targeted, and belittled by an insensitive teacher. Touches of humor ameliorate the pain and poignancy." SLJ

Pie. Scholastic Press 2011 183p $16.99

Grades: 4 5 6 7   **Fic**

1. Cats -- Fiction 2. Pies -- Fiction 3. Aunts -- Fiction

ISBN 978-0-545-27011-3; 0-545-27011-1

In the 1950s in the small town of Ipswitch, PA, Polly Portman dies and leaves the recipe for her prize-winning piecrust to her cat Lardo, in the care of her niece Alice, but then the cat is kidnapped and the bakery is trashed.

"Weeks deftly leavens moments of hilarity with the process of grieving in this sweet coming-of-age story in which Alice learns from Aunt Polly to follow her heart and to open it as well. Readers will close the book with a satisfied sigh and may seek out an adult to help them bake a pie. Recipes included." SLJ

Wein, Elizabeth E.

The **empty** kingdom. Viking 2008 217p (Mark of Solomon) $16.99

Grades: 7 8 9 10   **Fic**

1. Princes -- Fiction

ISBN 978-0-670-06273-7; 0-670-06273-1

LC 2007-29082

Telemakos, imprisoned on the upper levels of Abreha's, ruler of Himyar, twelve-story palace and lacking any way to communicate his predicament to his family in faraway Aksum, tries to find a subtle and effective way to regain his freedom.

"Wein deftly balances the political with the personal. . . . A unique, epic journey into adulthood." Horn Book

★ The **lion** hunter. Viking 2007 223p (Mark of Solomon) $16.99

Grades: 7 8 9 10   **Fic**

1. Kings 2. Princes -- Fiction

ISBN 978-0-670-06163-1; 0-670-03638-2

Still recovering from his ordeal as a government spy, twelve-year-old Telemakos, the half-Ethiopian grandson of King Artos of Britain, is sent with his sister to live with Abreha, the ruler of Himyar. His Aunt Goewin warns him that Abreha is a dangerous man, but just how dangerous remains to be seen.

"The vividly evoked setting provides a lush backdrop for the story's seemingly casual permutations, and readers' sympathies toward the embattled, wounded hero will draw them on willingly while Wein weaves her web of loyalty and intrigue." Horn Book

Weingarten, Lynn

Wherever Nina lies. Point 2009 316p $16.99
Grades: 8 9 10 11 12   Fic
1. Sisters -- Fiction 2. Missing persons -- Fiction
ISBN 978-0-545-06631-0; 0-545-06631-X
LC 2008-21527
"Sixteen-year-old Ellie Wrigley is desperate to find her unconventional, beloved older sister, Nina, who disappeared two years ago, seemingly without a trace. When Ellie uncovers a clue in a local secondhand shop . . . she is determined to investigate. . . . Ellie sets off on a cross-country chase with her new crush, Sean, who has also lost a sibling. . . . Weingarten's fast-paced, chatty style will keep readers tuned in." Publ Wkly

Weissman, Elissa Brent

The **short** seller; Elissa Brent Weissman. 1st ed. Atheneum Books for Young Readers 2013 256 p. (hardcover) $15.99
Grades: 3 4 5 6   Fic
1. Girls -- Fiction 2. Stocks -- Fiction 3. Friendship -- Fiction 4. Best friends -- Fiction 5. Mononucleosis -- Fiction 6. Electronic trading of securities -- Fiction
ISBN 1442452552; 9781442452558
LC 2012018632
In this middle-grade novel, by Elissa Brent Weissman, "a twelve-year-old takes on the stock market. . . . It all starts when seventh grader Lindy Sachs is granted $100 and access to her father's online trading account. . . . With trading talent and access to her parents' savings, the opportunity to make some real dough is too tempting to pass up. In fact, given how well Lindy's stocks are doing, it would be a disservice to not invest it all. . . . Right?" (Publisher's note)

The **trouble** with Mark Hopper. Dutton Children's Books 2009 227p $16.99
Grades: 5 6 7 8   Fic
1. School stories 2. Contests -- Fiction 3. Identity (Psychology) -- Fiction
ISBN 978-0-525-42067-5; 0-525-42067-3
LC 2008-34211
When two eleven-year-olds with the same name, similar looks, and very different personalities go to the same Maryland middle school, confusion and bad feelings ensue, but things improve after a teacher insists that they become study partners.
"Realistic school interactions give Weissman's novel a lot of kid appeal with substance." Horn Book Guide

Welch, Sheila Kelly

Waiting to forget. Namelos 2011 170p $18.95
Grades: 5 6 7 8   Fic
1. Siblings -- Fiction 2. Foster home care -- Fiction
ISBN 978-1-60898-114-4; 1-60898-114-2
T.J. and his sister, Angela, learn how to move forward and be happy while in foster care.
"T.J.'s authentic voice and the multilayered presentation of his memories, shifting between the waiting room

and his past, make for a poignant, realistic tale of child-survivors." Kirkus

Wells, H. G.

The **war** of the worlds; illustrated by Edward Gorey. New York Review Books 2005 251p il $16.95
Grades: 7 8 9 10 11 12 Adult   Fic
1. Science fiction 2. Interplanetary wars 3. Interplanetary visitors 4. Extraterrestrial beings -- Fiction
ISBN 1-59017-158-6
LC 2005-3693
First published 1898
In this novel the author "introduced the 'Alien' being into the role which became a cliché—a monstrous invader of Earth, a competitor in a cosmic struggle for existence. Though the Martians were a ruthless and terrible enemy, HGW was careful to point out that Man had driven many animal species to extinction, and that human invaders of Tasmania had behaved no less callously in exterminating their cousins." Sci Fic Ency

Wells, Ken

Rascal; a dog and his boy. illustrations by Christian Slade. Alfred A. Knopf 2010 201p il $16.99; lib bdg $19.99
Grades: 4 5 6 7   Fic
1. Dogs -- Fiction
ISBN 978-0-375-86652-4; 0-375-86652-3; 978-0-375-96652-1 lib bdg; 0-375-96652-8 lib bdg
LC 2009-37606
Rascal may be the happiest beagle ever to live. He used to live on Voclain's Farm, but now he lives with his very own boy, Meely. Together they explore the Louisiana bayou. But when Meely gets stuck on a rotting bridge deep in the bayou, it's up to Rascal to save his boy from danger.
"This is a cracking good animal story of classic pedigree. . . . Characterizations of both humans and animals are sharp and distinct. . . . [The] narration sings with the same lively Cajun-flavored spice as the dialogue, and it's an easy dialect to get the hang of." Bull Cent Child Books

Wells, Robison

Feedback; Robison Wells. HarperTeen 2012 312 p. (hardback) $17.99
Grades: 7 8 9 10   Fic
1. Private schools -- Fiction 2. School stories 3. Mystery fiction 4. Science fiction 5. Robots -- Fiction 6. Survival -- Fiction
ISBN 0062026100; 9780062026101; 9780062228307
LC 2012004296
In author Robison Wells" story, "Benson Fisher escaped from Maxfield Academy's deadly rules and brutal gangs. The worst was over. Or so he thought. But now he's trapped on the other side of the wall, in a different kind of prison. . . . [His friends] are all pawns in the school's twisted experiment, held captive and controlled by an unseen force. And while Benson struggles to figure out who, if anyone, can be trusted, he discovers that Maxfield Academy's plans are darker than anything he imagined--and they may be impossible to stop." (Publisher"s note)

Wells, Robison E.

Variant. HarperTeen 2011 376p $17.99

Grades: 7 8 9 10   **Fic**

1. School stories 2. Science fiction

ISBN 978-0-06-202608-8; 0-06-202608-9

LC 2010042661

After years in foster homes, seventeen-year-old Benson Fisher applies to New Mexico's Maxfield Academy in hopes of securing a brighter future, but instead he finds that the school is a prison and no one is what he or she seems.

"Hard to put down from the very first page, this fast-paced novel with Stepford overtones answers only some of the questions it poses, holding some of the most tantalizing open for the next installment in a series that is anything but ordinary." Kirkus

Wells, Rosemary

My Havana; [by] Rosemary Wells with Secundino Fernandez; illustrated by Peter Ferguson. Candlewick Press 2010 65p il $17.99

Grades: 4 5 6 7   **Fic**

1. Architects 2. Dictators -- Fiction 3. Family life -- Fiction

ISBN 978-0-7636-4305-8; 0-7636-4305-X

LC 2009-12053

Relates events in the childhood of architect Secundino Fernandez, who left his beloved Havana, Cuba, with his parents, first to spend a year in Spain, and later to move to New York City.

"Wells has chosen anecdotes wisely, and Ferguson's illustrations are atmospheric, capturing Dino's childlike enthusiasm and longing." Kirkus

★ **On** the Blue Comet; illustrated by Bagram Ibatoulline. Candlewick Press 2010 329p il $16.99

Grades: 5 6 7 8   **Fic**

1. Adventure fiction 2. Railroads -- Fiction 3. Space and time -- Fiction

ISBN 978-0-7636-3722-4; 0-7636-3722-X

LC 2009051358

During the Great Depression, Oscar's dad must sell their home and head west in search of work. Oscar meets a mysterious drifter and witnesses a crime so stunning it catapults Oscar on a train journey from coast to coast, from one decade to another.

"Ibatoulline's full-color, atmospheric Norman Rockwell-like vignettes enhance the nostalgic feel of this warm, cleverly crafted adventure." Kirkus

★ **Red** moon at Sharpsburg. Viking 2007 236p $16.99; pa $7.99

Grades: 6 7 8 9 10   **Fic**

1. United States -- History -- 1861-1865 2. Civil War -- Fiction

ISBN 0-670-03638-2; 978-0-670-03638-7; 0-14-241205-8 pa; 978-0-14-241205-3 pa

As the Civil War breaks out, India, a young Southern girl, summons her sharp intelligence and the courage she didn't know she had to survive the war that threatens to destroy her family, her Virginia home and the only life she has ever known.

"This powerful novel is unflinching in its depiction of war and the devastation it causes, yet shows the resilience and hope that can follow such a tragedy. India is a memorable, thoroughly believable character." SLJ

Welsh, M. L.

Heart of stone; a Verity Gallant tale. M.L. Welsh. David Fickling Books 2012 409 p. (hard cover) $16.99

Grades: 5 6 7 8   **Fic**

1. Love stories 2. Occult fiction 3. Witches -- Fiction 4. Fantasy 5. Sailing -- Fiction 6. Betrayal -- Fiction 7. Friendship -- Fiction 8. Family life -- Fiction 9. Books and reading -- Fiction

ISBN 0385752431; 9780375899164; 9780385752428; 9780385752435

LC 2011023878

This book is a "companion novel to 'Mistress Of The Storm' . . . tell[ing] the story of heroine Verity Gallant's fight against an evil force determined to put an end to all happily-ever-after stories. . . . The evil force appears to be trying to destroy Verity's cliffside hometown of Wellow, which is rapidly being eroded by white sand gathering as if it had a single motive—to erase all the 'Original Stories' with happy endings." (Voice of Youth Advocates)

★ **Mistress** of the Storm; a Verity Gallant tale. David Fickling Books 2011 318p $16.99; lib bdg $19.99

Grades: 5 6 7 8   **Fic**

1. Fantasy fiction 2. Sailing -- Fiction 3. Witches -- Fiction 4. Friendship -- Fiction 5. Family life -- Fiction 6. Books and reading -- Fiction

ISBN 978-0-385-75244-2; 0-385-75244-X; 978-0-385-75245-9 lib bdg; 0-385-75245-8 lib bdg

LC 2010018721

First published in the United Kingdom

After a stranger gives an ancient book to unpopular, twelve-year-old Verity Gallant, she and her new-found friends, Henry and Martha, uncover secrets stirring in the harbor town of Wellow and use them to face a powerful, vengeful witch.

"Welsh's prose is lovely, her characters are well-drawn, and the atmosphere of the town is palpable. In creating a place in the world where a story read aloud can become true, Welsh offers a benediction of sorts to readers, that 'every child who is alone or out of place will find the friends they need, and the love they deserve.'" Publ Wkly

Werlin, Nancy

Double helix. Dial Books 2004 252p hardcover o.p. pa $6.99

Grades: 7 8 9 10   **Fic**

1. Science fiction 2. Bioethics -- Fiction 3. Genetic engineering -- Fiction

ISBN 0-8037-2606-6; 0-14-240327-X pa

LC 2003-12269

Eighteen-year-old Eli discovers a shocking secret about his life and his family while working for a Nobel Prizewinning scientist whose specialty is genetic engineering.

"Werlin clearly and dramatically raises fundamental bioethical issues for teens to ponder. She also creates a riveting story with sharply etched characters and complex relationships that will stick with readers long after the book is closed." SLJ

★ **Extraordinary**. Dial Books for Young Readers 2010 393p il $17.99

Grades: 8 9 10 11 12 **Fic**

1. Fantasy fiction 2. Jews -- Fiction 3. Fairies -- Fiction 4. Friendship -- Fiction

ISBN 978-0-8037-3372-5; 0-8037-3372-0

LC 2010-2086

Phoebe, a member of the wealthy Rothschilds family, befriends Mallory, an awkward new girl in school, and the two become as close as sisters, but Phoebe does not know that Mallory is a faerie, sent to the human world to trap the ordinary human girl into fulfilling a promise made by her ancestor Mayer to the queen of the faeries.

"The carefully nuanced, often sensual prose delivers a highly effective narrative. Characterizations are arresting and complex." SLJ

★ **Impossible**; a novel. Dial Books 2008 376p $17.99

Grades: 7 8 9 10 **Fic**

1. Magic -- Fiction 2. Pregnancy -- Fiction 3. Teenage mothers -- Fiction

ISBN 978-0-8037-3002-1; 0-8037-3002-0

LC 2008-06633

When seventeen-year-old Lucy discovers her family is under an ancient curse by an evil Elfin Knight, she realizes to break the curse she must perform three impossible tasks before her daughter is born in order to save them both.

"Werlin earns high marks for the tale's graceful interplay between wild magic and contemporary reality." Booklist

★ The **killer's** cousin; [by] Nancy Werlin. Dial Books 2009 227p $16.99; pa $7.99

Grades: 7 8 9 10 **Fic**

1. Cousins -- Fiction 2. Homicide -- Fiction

ISBN 978-0-8037-3370-1; 0-8037-3370-4; 978-0-14-241373-9 pa; 0-14-241373-9 pa

LC 2008-24294

A reissue of the title first published 1998 by Delacorte

After being acquitted of murder, seventeen-year-old David goes to stay with relatives in Cambridge, Massachusetts, where he finds himself forced to face his past as he learns more about his strange young cousin Lily.

"Teens will find this tautly plotted thriller, rich in complex, finely drawn characters, an absolute page-turner." Booklist

The **rules** of survival. Dial Books 2006 259p $16.99

Grades: 8 9 10 11 12 **Fic**

1. Siblings -- Fiction 2. Child abuse -- Fiction

ISBN 0-8037-3001-2

LC 2006-1675

Seventeen-year-old Matthew recounts his attempts, starting at a young age, to free himself and his sisters from the grip of their emotionally and physically abusive mother.

The author "tackles the topic of child abuse with grace and insight. . . . Teens will empathize with these siblings and the secrets they keep in this psychological horror story." SLJ

West, Kasie

Pivot point; Kasie West. HarperTeen 2013 352 p. (hardback) $17.99

Grades: 7 8 9 10 **Fic**

1. Love stories 2. Occult fiction 3. Divorce -- Fiction 4. Love -- Fiction 5. Schools -- Fiction 6. High schools -- Fiction 7. Choice (Psychology) -- Fiction

ISBN 0062117378; 9780062117373

LC 2012019089

This book tells the story of Addie Coleman, who has the ability to see into the future and choose between the better of two options. "She is a Searcher living in the Compound, the southern Texas home of the most gifted individuals in the county. When her parents decide to divorce, with her mother staying in the Compound, and her father opting to live in the normal world, she decides to use her ability to help her chose with whom to live." (Booklist)

Westerfeld, Scott

Blue noon; [by] Scott Westerfeld. 1st ed.; Eos 2006 378p (Midnighters) $15.99; lib bdg $16.89

Grades: 7 8 9 10 **Fic**

1. Science fiction

ISBN 0-06-051957-6; 0-06-051958-4 lib bdg

LC 2005017597

The five midnighters from Bixby discover that the secret hour is starting to invade the daylight world, and if they cannot stop it, the darklings will soon be free to hunt again.

"The plot maintains an exciting pace. . . . This is fun recreational reading." SLJ

Extras. Simon Pulse 2011 399p $17.99; pa $9.99

Grades: 7 8 9 10 **Fic**

1. Science fiction

ISBN 978-1-4424-3007-5; 978-1-4424-1978-0 pa

First published 2007

Aya is "an 'extra' (face rank stuck in the mid-400,000s) in a city run on a 'reputation economy.' If Aya can win fame as a 'kicker,' reporting with her trusty hovercam on a story that captures the city's imagination, her face rank will soar. . . . Westerfeld shows he has a finger on the pulse of our reputation economy, alchemizing the cult of celebrity, advertising's constant competition for consumer attention." Horn Book

★ **Leviathan**; written by Scott Westerfeld; illustrated by Keith Thompson. Simon Pulse 2009 440p il map $19.99; pa $9.99

Grades: 7 8 9 10 **Fic**

1. War stories 2. Science fiction 3. Princes -- Fiction 4. Mythical animals -- Fiction 5. Genetic engineering -- Fiction

ISBN 978-1-4169-7173-3; 1-4169-7173-4; 978-1-4169-7174-0 pa; 1-4169-7174-2 pa

LC 2009-881

In an alternate 1914 Europe, fifteen-year-old Austrian Prince Alek, on the run from the Clanker Powers who are attempting to take over the globe using mechanical machinery, forms an uneasy alliance with Deryn who, disguised as a boy to join the British Air Service, is learning to fly genetically-engineered beasts.

"The protagonists' stories are equally gripping and keep the story moving, and Thompson's detail-rich panels bring Westerfeld's unusual creations to life." Publ Wkly

Other titles in this series are:
Behemoth (2010)
Goliath (2011)

Pretties. Simon Pulse 2011 348p $17.99; pa $9.99

Grades: 7 8 9 10   Fic
1. Science fiction
ISBN 978-1-4169-3639-8; 978-1-4424-1980-3 pa
First published 2005

Tally's transformation to perfect and popular including her totally hot boyfriend is everything she always wanted. But beneath the fun and freedom something is wrong and now Tally has to fight for her life because what she knows has put her in danger with the authorities.

"Riveting and compulsively readable, this action-packed sequel does not disappoint." Booklist

★ **So** yesterday; a novel. Razorbill 2004 225p $16.99; pa $7.99

Grades: 7 8 9 10   Fic
1. Mystery fiction 2. Missing persons -- Fiction
ISBN 1-59514-000-X; 1-59514-032-8 pa
LC 2004-2302

Hunter Braque, a New York City teenager who is paid by corporations to spot what is "cool," combines his analytical skills with girlfriend Jen's creative talents to find a missing person and thwart a conspiracy directed at the heart of consumer culture

"This hip, fascinating thriller aggressively questions consumer culture. . . . Teens will inhale this wholly entertaining, thought-provoking look at a system fueled by their purchasing power." Booklist

Specials. Simon Pulse 2011 350p $17.99; pa $9.99

Grades: 7 8 9 10   Fic
1. Science fiction
ISBN 978-1-4424-3008-2; 978-1-4424-1979-7 pa
First published 2006

Tally has been transformed from a repellent ugly to supermodel pretty. Now she's a super-amped fighting machine. Her mission is to keep the uglies down and the pretties stupid. But Tally's never been good at playing by the rules.

"Readers who enjoyed Uglies and Pretties . . . will not want to miss Specials. . . . Westerfeld's themes include vanity, environmental conservation, Utopian idealism, fascism, violence, and love." SLJ

Uglies. Simon Pulse 2005 425p rpt $17.99

Grades: 7 8 9 10   Fic
1. Science fiction
ISBN 9781416936381

"Tally is an ugly, waiting eagerly for her sixteenth birthday, when surgery will make her into a Pretty and she can

join her old friend Peris in the life of the beautiful in New Pretty Town. In the meantime, she revels in hoverboarding and pulling tricks with her rebellious friend, Shay, who doesn't share Tally's anticipation for joining the Pretty world. When Shay runs away to join dissidents outside the city, Tally is blackmailed by the city's Special Circumstances unit into following Shay and uncovering the location of the anti-establishment rebels, a task that becomes more difficult when Tally's sympathies begin to skew toward the rebels, especially their charismatic leader, David. . . . Grades six to ten." (Bull Cent Child Books)

"Fifteen-year-old Tally's eerily harmonious, postapocalyptic society gives extreme makeovers to teens on their sixteenth birthdays. . . . When a top-secret agency threatens to leave Tally ugly forever unless she spies on runaway teens, she agrees to infiltrate the Smoke, a shadowy colony of refugees from the 'tyranny of physical perfection.'" Booklist

Weston, Robert Paul

Dust city; a novel. by Robert Weston. Razorbill 2010 299p $16.99

Grades: 7 8 9 10   Fic
1. Magic -- Fiction 2. Wolves -- Fiction 3. Fairies -- Fiction 4. Father-son relationship -- Fiction
ISBN 978-1-59514-296-2; 1-59514-296-7
LC 2010-36067

Henry Whelp, son of the Big Bad Wolf, investigates what happened to the fairies that used to protect humans and animalia, and what role the corporation that manufactures synthetic fairy dust played in his father's crime.

"The premise is fractured fairy tale, but the play is pure noir. . . . The clever setup and gutting of fairy-tale tropes will garner plenty of enthusiasm." Booklist

★ **Zorgamazoo**. Razorbill 2008 281p il $15.99

Grades: 4 5 6 7   Fic
1. Novels in verse 2. Adventure fiction 3. Imagination -- Fiction
ISBN 978-1-59514-199-6; 1-59514-199-5
LC 2007-51682

Imaginative and adventurous Katrina eludes her maniacal guardian to help Morty, a member of a vanishing breed of zorgles, with his quest to uncover the fate of the fabled zorgles of Zorgmazoo as well as of other creatures that seem to have disappeared from the earth.

"This book is a natural descendant to the works of Dr. Seuss and Roald Dahl." Booklist

Weyn, Suzanne

Distant waves; a novel of the Titanic. Scholastic Press 2009 330p $17.99

Grades: 8 9 10 11   Fic
1. Sisters -- Fiction 2. Electrical engineers 3. Inventors -- Fiction 4. Spiritualism -- Fiction 5. Mother-daughter relationship -- Fiction
ISBN 978-0-545-08572-4; 0-545-08572-1
LC 2008-40708

In the early twentieth century, four sisters and their widowed mother, a famed spiritualist, travel from New York to London, and as the Titanic conveys them and their acquaintances, journalist W.T. Stead, scientist Nikola Tesla, and industrialist John Jacob Astor, home, Tesla's inventions will either doom or save them all.

"The interplay of science, spirituality, history and romance will satisfy." Publ Wkly

Empty. Scholastic Press 2010 183p $17.99

Grades: 7 8 9 10   **Fic**
    1. Science fiction 2. Ecology -- Fiction 3. Hurricanes -- Fiction 4. Energy resources -- Fiction 5. Environmental degradation -- Fiction
    ISBN 978-0-545-17278-3; 0-545-17278-0
                                        LC 2010-16743
When, just ten years in the future, oil supplies run out and global warming leads to devastating storms, senior high school classmates Tom, Niki, Gwen, Hector, and Brock realize that the world as they know it is ending and lead the way to a more environmentally-friendly society.

"The realistic and thought-provoking scenario is packaged into a speedy read, and given the popularity of dystopian fiction, it should find an audience." Booklist

Recruited. Darby Creek 2011 104p (Surviving Southside) lib bdg $27.93

Grades: 7 8 9 10   **Fic**
    1. School stories 2. Football -- Fiction 3. African Americans -- Fiction
    ISBN 978-0-7613-6153-4; 0-7613-6153-7
                                        LC 2010023662
"Kadeem is ecstatic when scouts shower him with gifts, dinners, and parties and he realizes that his dream of playing college football may be coming true. His happiness quickly turns to dread, though, as he learns that the incentives offered to him are violations of recruitment policy. . . . [This] well-written [story reinforces] the importance of family, friends, values, and thoughtful decision-making. . . . [An] excellent [purchase, this book] will attract and engage reluctant readers." SLJ

Reincarnation; [by] Suzanne Weyn. Scholastic Press 2008 293p $17.99

Grades: 7 8 9 10   **Fic**
    1. Love stories 2. Reincarnation -- Fiction 3. Space and time -- Fiction
    ISBN 978-0-545-01323-9; 0-545-01323-2
                                        LC 2007-08743
When a young couple dies in prehistoric times, their love—and link to various green stones—endures through the ages as they are reborn into new bodies and somehow find a way to connect.

"Readers with a romantic bent will be drawn to this story, which pushes the notion of eternal love to its limits: two spirits find each other again and again, at different moments in history." Publ Wkly

Wharton, Thomas

The **shadow** of Malabron. Candlewick Press 2009 382p (The perilous realm) $16.99

Grades: 5 6 7 8   **Fic**
    1. Fantasy fiction
    ISBN 978-0-7636-3911-2; 0-7636-3911-7
                                        LC 2009-7768

When Will, a rebellious teen, stumbles from the present into the realm where stories come from, he learns he has a mission concerning the evil Malabron and, aided by some of the story folk, he faces a host of perils while seeking the gateless gate that will take him home.

"Lush descriptive prose, cleverly sustained suspense, a sprinkling of humor and an exciting climax will keep readers riveted to the story, while those who know their folklore will be delighted by Wharton's twisting of the tropes and tales of myth and legend." Kirkus

Whelan, Gloria

After the train. HarperCollins 2009 152p $15.99; lib bdg $16.89

Grades: 6 7 8 9   **Fic**
    1. Antisemitism -- Fiction 2. Jews -- Germany -- Fiction
    ISBN 978-0-06-029596-7; 0-06-029596-1; 978-0-06-029597-4 lib bdg; 0-06-029597-X lib bdg
                                        LC 2008-10185
Ten years after the end of the Second World War, the town of Rolfen, West Germany, looks just as peaceful and beautiful as ever, until young Peter Liebig discovers a secret about his past that leads him to question everything, including the town's calm facade and his own sense of comfort and belonging.

"The story offers effective suspense in the mystery of Peter's situation and a dramatic climax. . . . Fans of Whelan's middle-school-aimed historical fiction . . . will definitely want to get their hands on this title." Bull Cent Child Books

All my noble dreams and then what happens; Gloria Whelan. 1st ed. Simon & Schuster Books for Young Readers 2013 272 p. (hardcover) $15.99

Grades: 6 7 8 9 10   **Fic**
    1. Aunts -- Fiction 2. Insurgency -- Fiction 3. Family life -- India -- Fiction
    ISBN 1442449764; 9781442449763; 9781442449770
                                        LC 2012018599
This novel is a sequel to Gloria Whelan's "Small Acts of Amazing Courage." Set "in India in the year 1921," here British-born protagonist Rosy has returned to "India, the land she considers home, after an extended stay in England. The household . . . is bustling with preparations for a visit by the Prince of Wales. Rosy has promised to deliver a letter written by Mahatma Gandhi, an appeal to Great Britain to give India its freedom." (Publishers Weekly)

Burying the sun. HarperCollins Publishers 2004 205p $15.99; lib bdg $16.89 **Fic**

Grades: 5 6 7 8   **Fic**
    1. Famines 2. Survival 3. World War, 1939-1945 -- Fiction 4. Saint Petersburg (Russia) -- Siege, 1941-1944 -- Fiction
    ISBN 0-06-054112-1; 0-06-054113-X lib bdg
                                        LC 2003-12487
In Leningrad in 1941, when Russia and Germany are at war, fourteen-year-old Georgi vows to help his family and his city during the terrible siege.

"Haunting images and elegant prose make this companion to The Impossible Journey . . . and Angel on the Square . . . memorable. . . . The lilting writing style and simple dignity of the characters help construct an honest portrait of everyday life in extraordinary circumstances." SLJ

Includes bibliographical references

Chu Ju's house. HarperCollins 2004 227p $15.99; lib bdg $16.89

Grades: 5 6 7 8   **Fic**

1. Gender role 2. Runaways 3. Sex role 4. Sex role -- Fiction 5. Runaway teenagers -- Fiction 6. China -- History -- 1976- -- Fiction

ISBN 0-06-050724-1; 0-06-050725-X lib bdg

LC 2003-6979

In order to save her baby sister, fourteen-year-old Chu Ju leaves her rural home in modern China and earns food and shelter by working on a sampan, tending silk worms, and planting rice seedlings, while wondering if she will ever see her family again.

"Whelan tells a compelling adventure story, filled with rich cultural detail, about a smart, likable teenage girl who overcomes society's gender restrictions." Booklist

★ The **Disappeared**. Dial Books 2008 136p $16.99; pa $6.99

Grades: 8 9 10 11 12   **Fic**

1. Siblings -- Fiction

ISBN 978-0-8037-3275-9; 0-8037-3275-9; 978-0-14-241540-5 pa; 0-14-241540-5 pa

LC 2007-43750

Teenaged Silvia tries to save her brother, Eduardo, after he is captured by the military government in 1970s Argentina

"The deftly handled voices of Silvia and Eduardo follow the well-intentioned, but often grievous, mistakes of youth. Their compelling tale is a chilling account of the manipulative power of corruption." SLJ

Includes bibliographical references

Goodbye, Vietnam. Knopf 1992 135p hardcover o.p. pa $5.50

Grades: 4 5 6 7   **Fic**

1. Refugees -- Fiction 2. Vietnamese -- Fiction

ISBN 0-679-82376-X; 0-679-92263-6 pa

LC 91-3660

Thirteen-year-old Mai and her family embark on a dangerous sea voyage from Vietnam to Hong Kong to escape the unpredictable and often brutal Vietnamese government

"While the book has the suspense and appeal of any good escape story, Whelan is neither melodramatic nor sentimental, and the sometimes horrific details of the scary voyage are plain but understated." Bull Cent Child Books

★ **Homeless** bird. HarperCollins Pubs. 2000 216p hardcover o.p. pa $5.99

Grades: 6 7 8 9 10   **Fic**

1. Courage 2. Women -- India -- Fiction

ISBN 0-06-028454-4; 0-06-440819-1 pa

LC 99-33241

When thirteen-year-old Koly enters into an ill-fated arranged marriage, she must either suffer a destiny dictated by India's tradition or find the courage to oppose it.

"This beautifully told, inspiring story takes readers on a fascinating journey through modern India and the universal intricacies of a young woman's heart." Booklist

★ **Listening** for lions. HarperCollins 2005 194p $15.99; lib bdg $16.89; pa $5.99

Grades: 5 6 7 8   **Fic**

1. Orphans -- Fiction 2. Physicians -- Fiction

ISBN 0-06-058174-3; 0-06-058175-1 lib bdg; 0-06-058176-X pa

Left an orphan after the influenza epidemic in British East Africa in 1918, thirteen-year-old Rachel is tricked into assuming a deceased neighbor's identity to travel to England, where her only dream is to return to Africa and rebuild her parents' mission hospital.

"In a straightforward, sympathetic voice, Rachel tells an involving, episodic story." Booklist

See what I see. HarperTeen 2011 199p $16.99

Grades: 7 8 9 10 11 12   **Fic**

1. Sick -- Fiction 2. Artists -- Fiction 3. Father-daughter relationship -- Fiction

ISBN 978-0-06-125545-8; 0-06-125545-9

LC 2010-03094

When eighteen-year-old Kate arrives on the Detroit doorstep of her long-estranged father, a famous painter, she is shocked to learn that he is dying and does not want to support her efforts to attend the local art school.

"With elegant prose, Whelan portrays a gradually developing and complex relationship built on guilt, curiosity, love, and a passion for art." Booklist

Small acts of amazing courage. Simon & Schuster Books for Young Readers 2011 217p $15.99

Grades: 6 7 8 9 10   **Fic**

1. Aunts -- Fiction 2. Bereavement -- Fiction

ISBN 978-1-4424-0931-6; 1-4424-0931-2

LC 2010-13164

In 1919, independent-minded fifteen-year-old Rosalind lives in India with her English parents, and when they fear she has fallen in with some rebellious types who believe in Indian self-government, she is sent "home" to London, where she has never been before and where her older brother died, to stay with her two aunts.

"Whelan balances the facts with distinctive, sometimes comical characterizations and vibrant, original sensory descriptions. . . . Whelan's vibrant, episodic story explores the tension between doing what's right, rather than what's expected, and the infinite complexities of colonialism." Booklist

★ The **locked** garden. HarperCollins Children's Books 2009 168p $15.99

Grades: 4 5 6 7   **Fic**

1. Family life -- Fiction 2. Mental illness -- Fiction 3. Psychiatric hospitals -- Fiction 5.

ISBN 978-0-06-079094-3; 0-06-079094-6

LC 2008-24637

After their mother dies of typhoid, Verna and her younger sister Carlie move with their father, a psychiatrist, and stern Aunt Maude to an asylum for the mentally ill in early-twentieth-century Michigan, where new ideas in the treatment of mental illness are being proposed, but old prejudices still hold sway.

"Whelan establishes a strong sense of time, unusual setting and characters. . . . This convincing melodrama portrays an atypical attitude toward treating mental illness." Kirkus

Whitaker, Alecia

The **queen** of Kentucky. Little, Brown 2011 375p $17.99

Grades: 7 8 9 10   **Fic**
1. School stories 2. Farm life -- Fiction 3. Friendship -- Fiction 4. Popularity -- Fiction 5. Dating (Social customs) -- Fiction
ISBN 978-0-316-12506-2; 0-316-12506-7
       LC 2010045840

In this book, "Ricki Jo is determined to give herself an extreme makeover as she enters high school, . . . expanding her horizons beyond her life as a hard-working farm girl. Another new girl, Mackenzie, becomes her ally, and . . . they join up with an established group of friends who are . . . in the cool crowd. Ricki Jo, now Ericka, becomes a cheerleader, develops a crush on a much sought after boy who teases her mercilessly, experiments with alcohol, and reinvents her sense of style through magazines. Her transformation doesn"t always go smoothly, and her best friend, Luke, tries his best to keep her grounded, but Ericka is determined to transform from her old self to what she considers her new and improved self." (Bulletin of the Center for Children"s Books)

"This is familiar territory, but Whitaker's setting is fresh, and readers from rural areas will recognize the class differences. . . . Ericka's first-person voice is sassy and quite believable as she tries to figure out who she is—and who everybody else is, too." Booklist

White, Amy Brecount

Forget -her-nots. Greenwillow Books 2010 374p $16.99; lib bdg $17.89

Grades: 7 8 9 10   **Fic**
1. School stories 2. Magic -- Fiction 3. Flowers -- Fiction 4. Mother-daughter relationship -- Fiction
ISBN 978-0-06-167298-9; 0-06-167298-X; 978-0-06-167299-6 lib bdg; 0-06-167299-8 lib bdg
       LC 2009-7105

At a Charlottesville, Virginia, boarding school, fourteen-year-old Laurel realizes that she shares her deceased mother's connection with flowers, but as she begins to learn their ancient language and share it with other students, she discovers powers that are beyond her control.

"A delicate sense of magical possibility and reverence for the natural world help elevate White's story from a typical prep-school drama into something more memorable." Publ Wkly

White, Andrea

Surviving Antarctica; reality TV 2083. HarperCollins Publishers 2005 327p hardcover o.p. pa $6.99

Grades: 7 8 9 10   **Fic**
1. Science fiction
ISBN 0-06-055454-1; 0-06-055456-8 pa
       LC 2004-6249

In the year 2083, five fourteen-year-olds who were deprived by chance of the opportunity to continue their educations reenact Scott's 1910-1913 expedition to the South Pole as contestants on a reality television show, secretly aided by a Department of Entertainment employee

"A real page-turner, this novel will give readers pause as they ponder the ethics of teens risking their lives in adult-contrived situations for the entertainment of the masses." Booklist

Window boy. Bright Sky Press 2008 255p $17.95

Grades: 6 7 8 9   **Fic**
1. School stories 2. Cerebral palsy -- Fiction 3. Imaginary playmates -- Fiction
ISBN 978-1-933979-14-4; 1-933979-14-3
       LC 2008-492

After his mother finally convinces the principal of Greenfield Junior High to admit him, twelve-year-old Sam arrives for his first day of school, along with his imaginary friend Winston Churchill, who encourages him to persevere with his cerebral palsy.

"Strong character development is combined with an accurate representation of the lack of educational opportunities for those who were physically and mentally disabled pre-IDEA." SLJ

Windows on the world. Namelos 2011 $18.95; pa $9.95

Grades: 6 7 8 9   **Fic**
1. School stories 2. Science fiction 3. Birds -- Fiction 4. Orphans -- Fiction 5. Time travel -- Fiction
ISBN 978-1-60898-105-2; 1-60898-105-3; 978-1-60898-106-9 pa; 1-60898-106-1 pa
       LC 2011003678

In 2083, orphan Shama Katooee, who has just stolen an expensive pet bird, is mysteriously selected to attend the elite Chronos Academy to be trained in the practice of Time-Watch, although she has no idea how or why she has been given this honor.

"The third-person narrative focuses mainly on Shama, with intermittent chapters on Maye Jones in NYC in 2001 and Lt. Bazel. White . . . subtly poses other questions surrounding advancements in technology and capitalism in this well-imagined and disturbing future." Kirkus

White, Ellen Emerson

The **President's** daughter. Feiwel and Friends 2008 304p pa $9.99

Grades: 7 8 9 10   **Fic**
1. Moving -- Fiction 2. Politics -- Fiction 3. Mother-daughter relationship -- Fiction
ISBN 0-312-37488-7; 978-0-312-37488-4
       LC 2008-6888

First published 1984

Sixteen-year-old Meghan Powers' happy life in Massachusetts changes drastically when her mother, one of the most prestigious senators in the country, becomes the front-runner in the race for United States President.

"Besides offering a solid look at the political system, this [book] has very strong characterizations." Booklist

Other titles about Meg are:

White House autumn (2008)
Long live the queen (2008)
Long may she reign (2007)

White, Kiersten
  Paranormalcy. HarperTeen 2010 335p $16.99
Grades: 7 8 9 10 11 12   **Fic**
  1. Police -- Fiction 2. Fairies -- Fiction 3. Prophecies
-- Fiction 4. Supernatural -- Fiction
  ISBN 978-0-06-198584-3; 0-06-198584-3
                                    LC 2010-07027
When a dark prophecy begins to come true, sixteen-
year-old Evie of the International Paranormal Containment
Agency must not only try to stop it, she must also uncover
its connection to herself and the alluring shapeshifter, Lend.
  "White shows the technique and polish of a pro in this
absorbing romance, which comes closer than most to hitting
the Buffy mark. . . . The action is fast; fun and fear are in
abundance; and Lend's father is actually a cool grownup."
Publ Wkly

  Supernaturally. HarperTeen 2011 342p $17.99
Grades: 7 8 9 10   **Fic**
  1. Fairies -- Fiction 2. Prophecies -- Fiction 3.
Supernatural -- Fiction
  ISBN 978-0-06-198586-7; 0-06-198586-4
                                    LC 2010040426
Sixteen-year-old Evie thinks she has left the International Paranormal Containment Agency, and her own paranormal activities, behind her when she is recruited to help at
the Agency, where she discovers more about the dark faerie
prophecy that threatens her future.
  "Evie's voice is the best part of the story, as she balances
her supernatural abilities against typical teen concerns and
obsessions." Kirkus

White, Ruth
  ★ **Belle** Prater's boy. Farrar, Straus & Giroux
1996 196p $17
Grades: 5 6 7 8   **Fic**
  1. Cousins -- Fiction
  ISBN 0-374-30668-0
                                    LC 94-43625
A Newbery Medal honor book, 1997
  "Gypsy and her cousin Woodrow become close friends
after Woodrow's mother disappears. Both sixth-graders feel
deserted by their parents—Gypsy discovers that her father
committed suicide—and need to define themselves apart
from these tragedies. White's prose evokes the coal mining
region of Virginia and the emotional quality of her characters' transformations." Horn Book Guide
  Another title about Belle Prater is:
  The search for Belle Prater (2005)

  ★ **Little** Audrey. Farrar, Straus & Giroux 2008
145p $16
Grades: 5 6 7 8   **Fic**
  1. Death -- Fiction 2. Coal miners -- Fiction 3. Country
life -- Fiction
  ISBN 978-0-374-34580-8; 0-374-34580-5
                                    LC 2007-29310

In 1948, eleven-year-old Audrey lives with her father,
mother, and three younger sisters in Jewell Valley, a coal
mining camp in Southwest Virginia, where her mother still
mourns the death of a baby, her father goes on drinking bing-
es on paydays, and Audrey tries to recover from the scarlet
fever that has left her skinny and needing to wear glasses.
  "The setting is perfectly portrayed and the characterizations ring true." Voice Youth Advocates

  Memories of Summer. Farrar, Straus & Giroux
2000 135p $16
Grades: 7 8 9 10   **Fic**
  1. Sisters 2. Mental illness 3. Sisters -- Fiction 4.
Mentally ill -- Fiction
  ISBN 0-374-34945-2
                                    LC 99-54793
In 1955, thirteen-year-old Lyric finds her whole life
changing when her family moves from the hills of Virginia
to a town in Michigan and her older sister Summer begins
descending into mental illness
  "A marvelous recreation of time and place and a poignant story that has much to say about compassion." SLJ

  ★ **Way** Down Deep. Farrar, Straus and Giroux
2007 197p $16
Grades: 5 6 7 8   **Fic**
  1. Orphans -- Fiction
  ISBN 0-374-38251-4; 978-0-374-38251-3
                                    LC 2006-46324
In the West Virginia town of Way Down Deep in the
1950s, a foundling called Ruby June is happily living with
Miss Arbutus at the local boarding house when suddenly, after the arrival of a family of outsiders, the mystery of Ruby's
past begins to unravel.
  This is "a story as tender as a breeze and as sharp as a
tack. . . . At the heart of the story are profound questions that
readers will enjoy puzzling out." Booklist

  You'll like it here (everybody does) Delacorte
Press 2011 272p $16.99; lib bdg $19.99
Grades: 4 5 6 7   **Fic**
  1. Science fiction 2. Family life -- Fiction 3.
Interplanetary voyages -- Fiction 4. Extraterrestrial
beings -- Fiction
  ISBN 978-0-385-73998-6; 0-385-73998-2; 978-0-385-
90813-9 lib bdg; 0-385-90813-X lib bdg
                                    LC 2010-32153
Although Meggie Blue seems to be an average sixth-
grader she is abnormally frightened when residents of her
small, North Carolina town become fixated on aliens, and
soon she and her family are forced to flee, making it clear
that all is not as it seems.
  White's "considerable writing skills elevate a story with
many familiar elements, including the importance of individuality, the pitfalls of conformity, and the tyranny of a dictatorship. Kids will like this, but it's also a fun jumping off
point for serious discussion." Booklist

  ★ A **month** of Sundays. Margaret Ferguson
Books/Farrar Straus Giroux 2011 168p $16.99
Grades: 6 7 8 9   **Fic**
  1. Sick -- Fiction 2. Family life -- Fiction 3. Country

life -- Fiction 4. Christian life -- Fiction
ISBN 978-0-374-39912-2; 0-374-39912-3
LC 2010036311

In the summer of 1956 while her mother is in Florida searching for a job, fourteen-year-old April Garnet Rose, who has never met her father, stays with her terminally ill aunt in Virginia and accompanies her as she visits different churches, looking for God.

"White captures life in small-town America. . . . This heartwarming story has more than a touch of wonder. Expanding one's emotional life . . . is beautifully captured here." Booklist

White, T. H.

★ The **once** and future king. Putnam 1958 677p $25.95

Grades: 8 9 10 11 12 Adult   **Fic**
1. Chivalry 2. Middle Ages 3. Fantasy fiction 4. Knights and knighthood 5. Kings 6. Fantasies 7. Legends and folk tales 8. Knights and knighthood -- Fiction
ISBN 0-399-10597-2
LC 58-10760

"White's contemporary retelling of Malory's Le Morte d'Arthur is both romantic and exciting." Shapiro. Fic for Youth. 3d edition

Whitley, David

Midnight charter. Roaring Brook Press 2009 319p $17.99

Grades: 7 8 9 10   **Fic**
1. Science fiction
ISBN 978-1-59643-381-6; 1-59643-381-7

"Deft world-building and crafty plotting combine for a zinger of an ending that will leave readers poised for book two. Surprisingly sophisticated upper-middle-grade fare, with enough meat to satisfy older readers as well." Kirkus

The **children** of the lost. Roaring Brook Press 2011 357p $16.99

Grades: 7 8 9 10   **Fic**
1. Fantasy fiction
ISBN 978-1-59643-614-5; 1-59643-614-X
LC 2010-28112

Banished from Agora, the ancient city-state where absolutely everything must be bartered, Mark and Lily are happy to find the apparently perfect land of Giseth except that the inhabitants seem fearful, something strange lurks in the surrounding forest, and a mysterious woman keeps appearing in their dreams urging them to find the children of the lost.

This "explores tantalizing new territory and solidifies the Agora Trilogy as one of the more literary ambitious and complex fantasies going." Booklist

Whitman, Emily

Wildwing. Greenwillow Books 2010 359p $16.99

Grades: 7 8 9 10   **Fic**
1. Falcons -- Fiction 2. Time travel -- Fiction 3. Social classes -- Fiction
ISBN 978-0-06-172452-7; 0-06-172452-1
LC 2009-44189

In 1913 London, fifteen-year-old Addy is a lowly servant, but when she gets inside an elevator car in her employer's study, she is suddenly transported to a castle in 1240 and discovers that she is mistaken for the lord's intended bride.

"Whitman populates both of her worlds with vivid, believable characters. . . . This historical novel with a time-travel twist of sci-fi will find an avid readership." SLJ

Whitney, Kim Ablon

The **other** half of life; a novel based on the true story of the MS St. Louis. Alfred A. Knopf 2009 237p $16.99; lib bdg $19.99

Grades: 6 7 8 9 10   **Fic**
1. Jews -- Germany -- Fiction 2. Holocaust, 1933-1945 -- Fiction
ISBN 978-0-375-85219-0; 0-375-85219-0; 978-0-375-95219-7 lib bdg; 0-375-95219-5 lib bdg
LC 2008-38949

In 1939, fifteen-year-old Thomas sails on a German ship bound for Cuba with more than nine hundred German Jews expecting to be granted safe haven in Cuba.

"The characters are intriguing enough, but it's the real-life history that provides the novel's energy." Horn Book Guide

Includes bibliographical references

Whittemore, Jo

Odd girl in. Simon & Schuster 2011 234p pa $6.99

Grades: 4 5 6   **Fic**
1. School stories 2. Siblings -- Fiction
ISBN 978-1-4424-1284-2; 1-4424-1284-4

"Spunky 12-year-old Alex doesn't really want friends or a social life. . . . She hates girly giggling parties and doesn't see any other girls in her middle school that she'd want to have as a friend, so she just concentrates on following in the footsteps of her prankster older twin brothers. . . . Alex's absent mother provides an element of drama in this otherwise witty, laugh-out-loud romp. Whittemore handles not only the comedy but deftly portrays Alex's and her brothers' advancement into a more mature state of mind. It should keep middle-schoolers laughing from start to finish." Kirkus

Whittenberg, Allison

Life is fine. Delacorte Press 2008 181p $15.99; lib bdg $18.99

Grades: 8 9 10 11 12   **Fic**
1. Child abuse -- Fiction 2. African Americans -- Fiction 3. Mother-daughter relationship -- Fiction
ISBN 978-0-385-73480-6; 978-0-385-90478-0 lib bdg
LC 2007-27604

With a neglectful mother who has an abusive, live-in boyfriend, life for fifteen-year-old Samara is not fine, but when a substitute teacher walks into class one day and introduces her to poetry, she starts to view life from a different perspective.

"Samara's voice is sharp and convincing." Publ Wkly

Sweet Thang. Delacorte Press 2006 149p $15.95

Grades: 5 6 7 8   **Fic**
1. School stories 2. Family life -- Fiction 3. African

Americans -- Fiction
ISBN 0-385-73292-9

LC 2005-03809

In 1975, life is not fair for fourteen-year-old Charmaine Upshaw, who shares a room with her brother, tries to impress a handsome classmate, and acts as caretaker for a rambunctious six-year-old cousin who has taken over the family.

"Whittenberg has created a refreshing cast and a good read." SLJ

Another title about the Upshaw family is:
Hollywood & Maine (2009)

Whyman, Matt

Goldstrike; a thriller. Atheneum Books for Young Readers 2010 262p $16.99

Grades: 7 8 9 10   **Fic**

1. Computer crimes -- Fiction
ISBN 978-1-4169-9510-4; 1-4169-9510-2

LC 2009-17830

After escaping Camp Twilight, eighteen-year-old Carl Hobbes and Beth, his girlfriend, begin a new life in London, England, where he attempts to program Sphynx Cargo's highly intelligent supercomputer to help protect them from the CIA and assassins.

"The action sequences are believable and often realistically brutal, and the climactic battle is intense and entertaining." Publ Wkly

Icecore; a Carl Hobbes thriller. Atheneum Books for Young Readers 2007 307p $16.99; pa $8.99

Grades: 7 8 9 10   **Fic**

1. Torture -- Fiction 2. Prisoners -- Fiction 3. Military bases -- Fiction 4. Computer crimes -- Fiction
ISBN 978-1-4169-4907-7; 1-4169-4907-0; 978-1-4169-8960-8 pa; 1-4169-8960-9 pa

LC 2007-02674

Seventeen-year-old Englishman Carl Hobbes meant no harm when he hacked into Fort Knox's security system, but at Camp Twilight in the Arctic Circle, known as the Guantanamo Bay of the north, he is tortured to reveal information about a conspiracy of which he was never a part.

"Powered by a fast-paced narrative, this exploration of numerous timely themes . . . gives the eminently readable adventure a degree of depth." Publ Wkly

Wiggins, Bethany

Stung; Bethany Wiggins. Walker & Company 2013 304 p. (hardcover) $17.99

Grades: 7 8 9 10 11 12   **Fic**

1. Science fiction 2. Epidemics -- Fiction 3. Survival -- Fiction
ISBN 0802734189; 9780802734181

LC 2012027183

In this novel, by Bethany Wiggins, "a worldwide pandemic occurred and the government tried to bio-engineer a cure. Only the solution was deadlier than the original problem-the vaccination turned people into ferocious, deadly beasts who were branded as a warning to un-vaccinated survivors. Key people needed to rebuild society are protected from disease and beasts inside a fortress-like wall. But Fiona has awakened branded, alone-and on the wrong side of the wall." (Publisher's note)

"Wiggins. . . muses on the dangers of science and medicine and deftly maps out the chain of events that has led to catastrophe, creating a violent world vastly different from ours but still recognizable. With a stirring conclusion and space for a sequel, it's an altogether captivating story." Kirkus

Wignall, K. J.

Blood; [by] K. J. Wignall. Egmont USA 2011 264p (Mercian triology) $16.99; ebook $16.99

Grades: 7 8 9 10 11 12   **Fic**

1. Vampires -- Fiction 2. Good and evil -- Fiction
ISBN 978-1-60684-220-1; 1-60684-220-X; 978-1-60684-258-4 ebook; 1-60684-258-7 ebook

LC 2011005899

A centuries-old vampire wakes up in the modern day to find he is being hunted by an unknown enemy, and begins to uncover the secrets of his origin and the path of his destiny.

Wignall "develops what could have been yet another vampire story into a promising series opener with a sophisticated plot and elegant prose." Booklist

Wild, K.

Fight game; [by] Kate Wild. Chicken House/Scholastic 2007 279p $16.99

Grades: 7 8 9 10   **Fic**

1. Science fiction 2. Spies -- Fiction 3. Martial arts -- Fiction 4. Genetic engineering -- Fiction
ISBN 978-0-439-87175-4; 0-439-87175-1

LC 2006-32889

Fifteen-year-old Freedom Smith is a fighter, just like all of his relatives who have the "Hercules gene," which leads him to a choice between being jailed for attempted murder or working with a covert law enforcement agency to break up a mysterious, illegal fight ring.

"Intriguing supporting characters pepper Wild's debut novel and bolster an already strong portagonist. . . . Wild's story pulsates with raw energy." Voice Youth Advocates

Wildavsky, Rachel

The **secret** of Rover. Amulet Books 2011 351p $16.95

Grades: 5 6 7 8   **Fic**

1. Twins -- Fiction 2. Uncles -- Fiction 3. Siblings -- Fiction 4. Inventions -- Fiction 5. Kidnapping -- Fiction 6. Voyages and travels -- Fiction
ISBN 0-8109-9710-X; 978-0-8109-9710-3

LC 2010-23450

Twelve-year-old twins Katie and David Bowen evade foreign militants and make their way from Washington, D.C. to their uncle's Vermont home, hoping he can help rescue their parents, who were kidnapped because of their secret invention, Rover.

"Kids making the transition from series mysteries to more sophisticated thrillers will do well by this suspenseful and age-appropriate drama." Bull Cent Child Books

Wiles, Deborah

★ The **Aurora** County All-Stars. Harcourt 2007 242p il $16; pa $5.99

Grades: 4 5 6   **Fic**

1. Death -- Fiction 2. Baseball -- Fiction 3. Race

relations -- Fiction
ISBN 978-0-15-206068-8; 0-15-206068-5; 978-0-15-206626-0 pa; 0-15-206626-8 pa

LC 2006-102551

In a small Mississippi town, after the death of the old man to whom twelve-year-old star pitcher House Jackson has been secretly reading for a year, House uncovers secrets about the man and the history of baseball in Aurora County.

"Quotations from Walt Whitman's poetry, baseball players and Aurora County news dispatches pepper the story and add color. . . . A home run for Wiles." Publ Wkly

★ **Countdown**. Scholastic 2010 377p il (The sixties trilogy) $17.99
Grades: 4 5 6 7   **Fic**
1. Cold war -- Fiction 2. Family life -- Fiction 3. Cuban Missile Crisis, 1962 -- Fiction
ISBN 978-0-545-10605-4; 0-545-10605-2

It's 1962, and it seems everyone is living in fear. Twelve-year-old Franny Chapman lives with her family in Washington, DC, during the days surrounding the Cuban Missile Crisis. Amidst the pervasive threat of nuclear war, Franny must face the tension between herself and her younger brother, figure out where she fits in with her family, and look beyond outward appearances.

"Wiles skillfully keeps many balls in the air, giving readers a story that appeals across the decades as well as offering enticing paths into the history." Booklist

Wilhelm, Doug
The **revealers**. Farrar, Straus & Giroux 2003 207p $16 **Fic**
Grades: 4 5 6 7   **Fic**
1. School stories 2. Internet -- Fiction 3. Friendship -- Fiction
ISBN 0-374-36255-6

LC 2002-35321

Tired of being bullied and picked on, three seventh-grade outcasts join forces and, using scientific methods and the power of the Internet, begin to create a new atmosphere at Parkland Middle School. "Grades five to nine." (Bull Cent Child Books)

"Briskly plotted, the novel shows how bringing the stories to light transforms stereotypes into real people and provides a vehicle for others to become involved. . . . The novel is effective and will fascinate even reluctant readers." SLJ

Wilkins, Ebony Joy
Sellout. Scholastic Press 2010 267p $17.99
Grades: 7 8 9 10   **Fic**
1. Social classes -- Fiction 2. African Americans -- Fiction
ISBN 978-0-545-10928-4; 0-545-10928-0

NaTasha loves her life of affluence in Park Adams, but her grandmother fears she has lost touch with her roots and whisks her off to Harlem, where NaTasha meets rough, streetwise girls at a crisis center and finds the courage to hold her own against them.

"Some elements of the story tie up too easily—NaTasha's greatest tormentors warm up to her a bit too quickly to be believed—but the message of staying true to oneself shines through." SLJ

Wilkinson, Lili
Pink. HarperTeen 2011 310p $16.99
Grades: 7 8 9 10 11 12   **Fic**
1. School stories 2. Theater -- Fiction 3. Homosexuality -- Fiction 4. Identity (Psychology) -- Fiction
ISBN 978-0-06-192653-2; 0-06-192653-1

LC 2010-9389

Sixteen-year-old Ava does not know who she is or where she belongs, but when she tries out a new personality—and sexual orientation—at a different school, her edgy girlfriend, potential boyfriend, and others are hurt by her lack of honesty.

"The novel is in turn laugh-out-loud funny, endearing, and heartbreaking as Ava repeatedly steps into teenage social land mines—with unexpected results. Because Wilkinson doesn't rely on stereotypes, the characters are well-developed, and interactions between them feel genuine." Voice Youth Advocates

Wilks, Mike
Mirrorscape. Egmont USA 2009 340p $16.99; lib bdg $19.99
Grades: 6 7 8 9   **Fic**
1. Fantasy fiction 2. Adventure fiction 3. Art -- Fiction 4. Artists -- Fiction 5. Apprentices -- Fiction
ISBN 978-1-60684-008-5; 1-60684-008-8; 978-1-60684-040-5 lib bdg; 1-60684-040-1 lib bdg

LC 2009-16245

In a world where all pleasures are severely restricted, Melkin Womper is apprenticed to a master painter where he discovers the Mirrorscape, a world inside paintings, and becomes entangled in a war between the restrictive Fifth Mystery and the rebels fighting to stop them

"In this innovative debut, readers will find an imaginative fantasy devoid of typical wizardry." Booklist

Williams, Alex
The **deep** freeze of Bartholomew Tullock. Philomel Books 2008 298p $16.99
Grades: 6 7 8 9   **Fic**
1. Adventure fiction 2. Dogs -- Fiction 3. Weather -- Fiction 4. Inventions -- Fiction
ISBN 978-0-399-25185-6; 0-399-25185-5

LC 2008-02663

Published in the United Kingdom with title: The storm maker

In a land of never-ending snow, Rufus Breeze and his mother must protect the family home from being seized by tyrant Bartholomew Tullock, while sister Madeline and her father, an inventor of fans that are now useless, join forces with a ne'er-do-well adventurer and his blue-haired terrier, hoping to make some money.

This offers "originality of setting, a full complement of truly heinous villains, insurmountable dangers cleverly surmounted, ingenious contraptions, and plucky, appealing underdogs. . . . William handles his material with fizz and verve." Bull Cent Child Books

The **talent** thief; an extraordinary tale of an ordinary boy. Philomel Books 2010 300p $16.99

Grades: 5 6 7 8   **Fic**

1. Adventure fiction 2. Orphans -- Fiction
ISBN 978-0-399-25278-5; 0-399-25278-9

Orphaned Cressida, a magnificent singer, and her twelve-year-old brother Adam attend the by-invitation-only Festival of Youthful Genius, where they join forces with a former race car driver to try to stop a bizarre creature from stealing the talents of the young prodigies.

"This is a story that fantasy and adventure fans will enjoy, and the well-paced action will propel them to the end." SLJ

Williams, Carol Lynch

Glimpse. Simon & Schuster Books for Young Readers 2010 484p $16.99

Grades: 7 8 9 10   **Fic**

1. Novels in verse 2. Sisters -- Fiction 3. Suicide -- Fiction 4. Child sexual abuse -- Fiction
ISBN 978-1-4169-9730-6; 1-4169-9730-X

LC 2009-41147

Living with their mother who earns money as a prostitute, two sisters take care of each other and when the older one attempts suicide, the younger one tries to uncover the reason.

"Williams leans hard on her free-verse line breaks for drama . . . and it works. A page-turner for Ellen Hopkins fans." Kirkus

Miles from ordinary; a novel. St. Martin's Press 2011 197p $16.99

Grades: 7 8 9 10   **Fic**

1. Family life -- Fiction 2. Mental illness -- Fiction 3. Mother-daughter relationship -- Fiction
ISBN 978-0-312-55512-2; 0-312-55512-1

LC 2010-40324

"The author has crafted both a riveting, unusual suspense tale and an absolutely convincing character in Lacey. The book truly is miles from ordinary, in the very best way. Outstanding." Kirkus

The **chosen** one. St. Martin's Griffin 2009 213p $16.95

Grades: 7 8 9 10   **Fic**

1. Cults -- Fiction 2. Polygamy -- Fiction 3. Family life -- Fiction
ISBN 978-0-312-55511-5; 0-312-55511-3

LC 2009-4800

In a polygamous cult in the desert, Kyra, not yet fourteen, sees being chosen to be the seventh wife of her uncle as just punishment for having read books and kissed a boy, in violation of Prophet Childs' teachings, and is torn between facing her fate and running away from all that she knows and loves.

"This book is a highly emotional, terrifying read. It is not measured or objective. Physical abuse, fear, and even murder are constants. It is a girl-in-peril story, and as such, it is impossible to put down and holds tremendous teen appeal." Voice Youth Advocates

Williams, Kathryn

Pizza, love, and other stuff that made me famous; Kathryn Williams. Henry Holt 2012 231 p. $16.99

Grades: 7 8 9 10   **Fic**

1. Cooking -- Fiction 2. Reality television programs -- Fiction 3. Restaurants -- Fiction 4. Interpersonal relations -- Fiction 5. Competition (Psychology) -- Fiction 6. Television -- Production and direction -- Fiction
ISBN 0805092854; 9780805092851

LC 2011034053

In this young adult novel by Kathryn Williams "Sixteen-year-old Sophie Nicolaides . . . audition[s] for a new reality show, 'Teen Test Kitchen.'. . . [T]he prize includes a full scholarship to one of America's finest culinary schools and a summer in Napa, California, not to mention fame. Once on set, Sophie immediately finds herself in the thick of the drama -- including a secret burn book, cutthroat celebrity judges, and a very cute French chef." (Publisher's note)

Williams, Katie

The **space** between trees. Chronicle Books 2010 274p $17.99

Grades: 8 9 10 11 12   **Fic**

1. School stories 2. Homicide -- Fiction
ISBN 978-0-8118-7175-4; 0-8118-7175-4

LC 2009-48561

When the body of a classmate is discovered in the woods, sixteen-year-old Evie's lies wind up involving her with the girl's best friend, trying to track down the killer.

"Evie's raw honesty and the choices she makes make for difficult reading, but also a darkly beautiful, emotionally honest story of personal growth." Publ Wkly

Williams, L. A.

The **witches'** kitchen; [by] Allen Williams. Little Brown 2010 276p il $16.99

Grades: 5 6 7 8   **Fic**

1. Magic -- Fiction 2. Toads -- Fiction 3. Witchcraft -- Fiction
ISBN 978-0-7595-2912-0; 0-7595-2912-4

LC 2009-45625

When Toad wakes up dangling over a bubbling witches' cauldron with no memory of her former life, she just manages to escape and, with the help of an imp, a fairy, and some other friends, she sets out to discover her identity.

Toad is "an engaging protagonist. . . . Her ragtag pals are elegantly described. . . . Intricate pencil drawings . . . pepper the text, adding details that elaborate on the spare descriptions." Bull Cent Child Books

Williams, Laura E.

Slant; [by] Laura E. Williams. Milkweed Editions 2008 149p $16.95; pa $6.95

Grades: 5 6 7 8 9   **Fic**

1. Mothers -- Fiction 2. Adoption -- Fiction 3. Friendship -- Fiction 4. Prejudices -- Fiction 5. Plastic surgery -- Fiction 6. Korean Americans -- Fiction
ISBN 978-1-57131-681-3; 1-57131-681-7; 978-1-57131-682-0 pa; 1-57131-682-5 pa

LC 2008007093

Thirteen-year-old Lauren, a Korean-American adoptee, is tired of being called "slant" and "gook," and longs to have plastic surgery on her eyes, but when her father finds out about her wish—and a long-kept secret about her mother's death is revealed—Lauren starts to question some of her own assumptions

"The characters are exceptionally well drawn, and the friendship between Julie and Lauren is not only believable, featuring humor, conflict, and true wit, but also captures both girls' gains in maturity." SLJ

Williams, Maiya

The **Fizzy** Whiz kid. Amulet Books 2010 273p $16.95

Grades: 5 6 7 8   **Fic**

1. Moving -- Fiction 2. Advertising -- Fiction
ISBN 978-0-8109-8347-2; 0-8109-8347-8

Moving to Hollywood with his academic parents, eleven-year-old Mitch feels like an outsider in his school where everyone has connections to the powerful and famous in the entertainment industry, until he is cast in a soda commercial that launches a popular catchphrase.

"Williams' breezy tale is as addictive and bubbly as a Fizzy Whiz itself, and her experience in the entertainment industry packs real value into her descriptions of auditions, movie sets, and agent negotiations. . . . Mitchell's realization that he is a product being assembled is both goofy and poignant." Booklist

Williams, Michael

★ **Now** is the time for running. Little, Brown 2011 233p $17.99

Grades: 6 7 8 9 10   **Fic**

1. Soccer -- Fiction 2. Brothers -- Fiction 3. Refugees -- Fiction 4. Homeless persons -- Fiction 5. Mentally handicapped -- Fiction
ISBN 978-0-316-07790-3; 0-316-07790-9

LC 2010043460

"There is plenty of material to captivate readers: fast-paced soccer matches every bit as tough as the players; the determination of Deo and his fellow refugees to survive unthinkably harsh conditions; and raw depictions of violence. . . . But it's the tender relationship between Deo and Innocent, along with some heartbreaking twists of fate, that will endure in readers' minds." Publ Wkly

Williams, Sarah DeFord

★ **Palace** beautiful. G.P. Putnam's Sons 2010 232p $16.99

Grades: 6 7 8 9   **Fic**

1. Moving -- Fiction 2. Diaries -- Fiction 3. Influenza -- Fiction 4. Family life -- Fiction
ISBN 978-0-399-25298-3; 0-399-25298-3

LC 2009-03213

After her move in 1985 to Salt Lake City, thirteen-year-old Sadie finds a journal in a hidey-hole in the attic, and along with her sister and new friend she reads about the influenza epidemic of 1918.

"Williams does a super job with the characters in this beautifully written book, and it is satisfying to see how they develop." SLJ

Williams, Susan

Wind rider. HarperCollins 2006 309p $16.99

Grades: 7 8 9 10   **Fic**

1. Horses -- Fiction 2. Sex role -- Fiction 3. Prehistoric peoples -- Fiction
ISBN 978-0-06-087236-6; 0-06-087236-5; 978-0-06-087237-3 lib bdg; 0-06-087237-3 lib bdg

LC 2005028595

Fern, a teenager living in 4000 B.C., defies the expectations of her people by displaying a unique and new ability to tame horses and by also questioning many of the traditional activities of women.

"Fern aggressively strains against her mother's expectations and her society's traditional gender roles, and it is these timeless struggles, narrated in Fern's poetic voice, that transform Williams' impressively researched details into a vividly imagined, wholly captivating world." Booklist

Williams, Suzanne

Bull rider; [by] Suzanne Morgan Williams. Margaret K. McElderry Books 2009 241p $16.99

Grades: 7 8 9 10   **Fic**

1. Brothers -- Fiction 2. Veterans -- Fiction 3. Bull riding -- Fiction 4. Wounds and injuries -- Fiction
ISBN 978-1-4169-6130-7; 1-4169-6130-5

LC 2007-52518

When his older brother, a bull-riding champion, returns from the Iraq War partially paralyzed, fourteen-year-old Cam takes a break from skateboarding to enter a bull-riding contest, in hopes of winning the $15,000 prize and motivating his depressed brother to continue with his rehabilitation.

"The mix of wild macho action with family anguish and tenderness will grab teens. . . . , [This is a] powerful contemporary story of family, community, and work." Booklist

Williams, Tad

The **dragons** of Ordinary Farm; by Tad Williams and Deborah Beale; pictures by Greg Swearingen. Harper 2009 412p il $16.99

Grades: 4 5 6 7   **Fic**

1. Farms -- Fiction 2. Uncles -- Fiction 3. Siblings -- Fiction 4. Supernatural -- Fiction 5. Mythical animals -- Fiction
ISBN 978-0-06-154345-6; 0-06-154345-4

LC 2008035298

When their great-uncle Gideon invites Tyler and Lucinda to his farm for the summer, they discover his animals are extremely unusual.

"Williams and Beale have created a gripping fantasy with realistic but appealing characters as well as scientific magic that explains the appearance of legendary creatures." SLJ

Williams-Garcia, Rita

★ **Jumped**. HarperTeen 2009 169p $16.99; lib bdg $17.89

Grades: 8 9 10 11 12   **Fic**

1. School stories 2. Bullies -- Fiction
ISBN 978-0-06-076091-5; 0-06-076091-5; 978-0-06-076092-2 lib bdg; 0-06-076092-3 lib bdg

LC 2008-22381

The lives of Leticia, Dominique, and Trina are irrevocably intertwined through the course of one day in an urban high school after Leticia overhears Dominique's plans to beat up Trina and must decide whether or not to get involved.

"In alternating chapters narrated by Leticia, Trina, and Dominique, Williams-Garcia has given her characters strong, individual voices that ring true to teenage speech, and she lets them make their choices without judgment or moralizing." SLJ

★ **Like** sisters on the homefront. Lodestar Bks. 1995 165p hardcover o.p. pa $5.99

Grades: 7 8 9 10 **Fic**

1. Family life -- Fiction 2. Teenage mothers -- Fiction 3. African Americans -- Fiction

ISBN 0-525-67465-9; 0-14-038561-4 pa

LC 95-3690

"Beautifully written, the text captures the cadence and rhythm of New York street talk and the dilemma of being poor, black, and uneducated. This is a gritty, realistic, well-told story." SLJ

No laughter here. HarperCollins 2004 133p $15.99; lib bdg $16.89

Grades: 7 8 9 10 **Fic**

1. Friendship -- Fiction 2. African Americans -- Fiction 3. Female circumcision -- Fiction

ISBN 0-688-16247-9; 0-688-16248-7 lib bdg

LC 2003-9331

In Queens, New York, ten-year-old Akilah is determined to find out why her closest friend, Victoria, is silent and withdrawn after returning from a trip to her homeland, Nigeria.

This is a "disturbing and poignant coming-of-age novel. . . . This contemporary tale about the ancient rite of female circumcision will no doubt leave an indelible mark on pre-teens." Publ Wkly

★ **One** crazy summer. Amistad 2010 218p $15.99; lib bdg $16.89

Grades: 4 5 6 7 **Fic**

1. Poets -- Fiction 2. Mothers -- Fiction 3. Sisters -- Fiction

ISBN 978-0-06-076088-5; 0-06-076088-5; 978-0-06-076089-2 lib bdg; 0-06-076089-3 lib bdg

LC 2009-09293

A Newbery Medal honor book, 2011

In the summer of 1968, after travelling from Brooklyn to Oakland, California, to spend a month with the mother they barely know, eleven-year-old Delphine and her two younger sisters arrive to a cold welcome as they discover that their mother, a dedicated poet and printer, is resentful of the intrusion of their visit and wants them to attend a nearby Black Panther summer camp.

"Delphine's growing awareness of injustice on a personal and universal level is smoothly woven into the story in poetic language that will stimulate and move readers." Publ Wkly

★ **P.S.** Be Eleven; Rita Williams-Garcia. Harpercollins Childrens Books 2013 288 p. $16.99

Grades: 4 5 6 7 8 **Fic**

1. Historical fiction 2. African American children -- fiction

ISBN 0061938629; 9780061938627

This book is a follow-up to Rita Williams-Garcia's Newbery Honor-winning "One Crazy Summer." Here, "Delphine and her sisters return to Brooklyn from visiting their estranged mother, Cecile, a poet . . . . Change and conflict have

the Gaither household in upheaval: Pa has a new girlfriend, Uncle Darnell returns from Vietnam a damaged young man, and the sixth-grade teacher Delphine hoped to get has been replaced by a man from Zambia." (Publishers Weekly)

"...Soars as a finely drawn portrait of a family in flux and as a memorable slice of a specific time in our nation''s history." Booklist

Williamson, Jill

By darkness hid. Marcher Lord Press 2009 490p map (Blood of kings) $14.99

Grades: 7 8 9 10 **Fic**

1. Fantasy fiction 2. Gifted children -- Fiction 3. Knights and knighthood -- Fiction

ISBN 978-0-9821049-5-8; 0-9821049-5-2

"With no family, Achan Cham is marked as a stray and lives the brutal life of a slave. When he is lucky enough to be chosen to begin training as a Kingsguard Knight, his life changes completely, but he is left to wonder if it is for the better. . . . Wonderfully written with a superb plot, this book is a sure-fire hit with almost any reader. . . . The novel is a solid choice for any collection." Voice Youth Advocates

To darkness fled. Marcher Lord Press 2010 680p map (Blood of kings) pa $17.99

Grades: 7 8 9 10 **Fic**

1. Fantasy fiction 2. Knights and knighthood -- Fiction

ISBN 978-0-9825987-0-2; 0-9825987-0-X

"Once again the superb writing enhances the thought-provoking story, making this package too good to miss. . . . Reading this will certainly leave the reader anxiously awaiting the next installment." Voice Youth Advocates

Willingham, Bill

Down the Mysterly River; illustrations by Mark Buckingham. Tor/Starscape 2011 333p il $15.99

Grades: 4 5 6 7 **Fic**

1. Fantasy fiction 2. Memory -- Fiction 3. Animals -- Fiction 4. Forests and forestry -- Fiction

ISBN 978-0-7653-2792-5; 0-7653-2792-9

LC 2011018958

Top notch Boy Scout Max "the Wolf" cannot remember how he came to be in a strange forest, but soon he and three talking animals are on the run from the Blue Cutters, hunters who will alter the foursome's very essence if they can catch them.

"Willingham roles out his themes slowly, only fully spelling them out in the final scene, but they don't interfere with the rollicking story, nasty (but fully realized) villains, and heroic camaraderie. . . . [This] is a stellar example of a novel working both as an adventure tale and as metafiction." Publ Wkly

Willis, Cynthia Chapman

Buck fever. Feiwel and Friends 2009 228p $16.99

Grades: 7 8 9 10 **Fic**

1. Artists -- Fiction 2. Hunting -- Fiction 3. Siblings -- Fiction 4. Family life -- Fiction 5. Father-son relationship -- Fiction

ISBN 978-0-312-38297-1; 0-312-38297-9

LC 2008034748

Twelve-year-old Joey and his fifteen-year-old sister Philly relate their experiences trying to cope in a family already strained by the mother's extended travel, and pushed further apart by the father's disappointment that Joey is more interested in drawing deer than hunting them.

"The quietness of nature and small-town life is wonderfully reflected in Willis' patient and artful prose, and every hunting detail feels authentic.... An unusually sensitive and reflective boy-centric book." Booklist

Willner-Pardo, Gina

The **hard** kind of promise. Clarion Books/Houghton Mifflin Harcourt 2010 200p $16

Grades: 4 5 6 7 Fic

1. School stories 2. Friendship -- Fiction 3. Popularity -- Fiction

ISBN 978-0-547-24395-5; 0-547-24395-2

California seventh-graders Sarah and Marjorie made a promise in kindergarten to always be friends, but Marjorie is weird and Sarah, wanting to be at least somewhat popular, makes friends with a fellow choir member.

"Willner-Pardo's avoidance of overblown crises and dramatic climaxes creates a steadily paced, authentic story" Publ Wkly

Willocks, Tim

Doglands. Random House 2011 308p $16.99; lib bdg $19.99; ebook $16.99

Grades: 5 6 7 8 Fic

1. Adventure fiction 2. Dogs -- Fiction 3. Supernatural -- Fiction 4. Animal welfare -- Fiction

ISBN 978-0-375-86571-8; 0-375-86571-3; 978-0-375-96571-5 lib bdg; 0-375-96571-8 lib bdg; 978-0-375-89604-0 ebook; 0-375-89604-X ebook

LC 2009033328

Furgal, a half-greyhound puppy, escapes a cruel dog-track owner and sets out in the hope of finding his father and the fabled Doglands, later returning to try to free his mother, sisters, and the other abused dogs.

"The dogs each have distinct personalities, and the mystic lore of the Doglands adds a secondary fantasy layer to the narrative. Humans are only sketched in, which is fitting, since the tale is told from the dog point of view. A riveting dog tale with a healthy serving of savagery, not all on the part of the four-legged characters." Kirkus

Wilson, Diane L.

Black storm comin' Margaret K. McElderry Books 2005 295p $17.99

Grades: 7 8 9 10 Fic

1. Pony express -- Fiction 2. Racially mixed people -- Fiction 3. Frontier and pioneer life -- Fiction

ISBN 0-689-87137-6; 0-689-87138-2

LC 2004-9438

Twelve-year-old Colton, son of a black mother and a white father, takes a job with the Pony Express in 1860 after his father abandons the family on their California-bound wagon train, and risks his life to deliver an important letter that may affect the growing conflict between the North and South.

"Wilson masterfully creates a multidimensional character in Colton.... Readers will absorb greater lessons as they become engrossed in the excitement, beauty, and terror of Colton's journey to California and manhood." Booklist

★ **Firehorse**. Margaret K. McElderry Books 2006 325p $16.95

Grades: 7 8 9 10 Fic

1. Arson -- Fiction 2. Horses -- Fiction 3. Sex role -- Fiction 4. Family life -- Fiction 5. Veterinary medicine -- Fiction

ISBN 1-4169-1551-6; 978-1-4169-1551-5

LC 2005-30785

Spirited fifteen-year-old horse lover Rachel Selby determines to become a veterinarian, despite the opposition of her rigid father, her proper mother, and the norms of Boston in 1872, while that city faces a serial arsonist and an epidemic spreading through its firehorse population.

"Wilson paces the story well, with tension building. . . . The novel's finest achievement, though, is the convincing depiction of family dynamics in an era when men ruled the household and and women, who had few opportunities, folded their dreams and put them away with the linens they embroidered." Booklist

Wilson, Jacqueline

Best friends. Roaring Brook Press 2008 229p $15.95; pa $7.99

Grades: 4 5 6 7 Fic

1. School stories 2. Friendship -- Fiction

ISBN 978-1-59643-278-9; 1-59643-278-0; 978-0-312-58144-2 pa; 0-312-58144-0 pa

LC 2006-39716

Rambunctious and irrepressible Gemma has been best friends with Alice ever since they were born on the same day, so when Alice moves miles away to Scotland, Gemma is distraught over the idea that Alice might find a new best friend.

"Believable, sympathetic characters; recognizable home and school situations; and plenty of humor . . . will ensure that this becomes . . . a popular read for middle-grade girls." Booklist

Kiss. Roaring Brook Press 2010 248p $16.99

Grades: 7 8 9 10 Fic

1. Friendship -- Fiction

ISBN 978-1-59643-242-0; 1-59643-242-X

"Sylvie, 14, has always assumed she would marry her best friend, Carl, but lately he has been distant and doesn't even seem interested in their secret fantasy, Glassworld. When a game of spin the bottle results in Carl kissing Sylvie's new friend, Miranda, and refusing to kiss her, Sylvie begins to doubt her attractiveness. But when Carl suddenly insists on including his new friend, Paul, on all their outings, especially his birthday party, Sylvie is even more confused.... With sharply drawn characters, Wilson handles the confusion and angst of teen love and sexuality with careful sensitivity." SLJ

Wilson, John

And in the morning. Kids Can Press 2003 198p $16.95

Grades: 7 8 9 10   **Fic**
1. World War, 1914-1918 -- Fiction
ISBN 1-55337-400-2

"Jim Hay, 16, is caught up in the patriotic fervor sweeping across Scotland as the British troops prepare to enter World War I. . . . His father is killed in action and 10 days later his mother dies from shock and grief. Within weeks, Jim has signed up and is soon in the trenches. . . . A compelling, fascinating, and ultimately disturbing book that is not to be missed." SLJ

Ghost moon. Orca 2011 (Desert legends trilogy) 172p pa $12.95
Grades: 6 7 8 9   **Fic**
1. Outlaws 2. Frontier and pioneer life -- Fiction
ISBN 978-1-55469-879-0; 1-55469-879-0

"A young wanderer lands in the middle of New Mexico's Lincoln County War. . . . 16-year-old James Doolen falls in with Bill Bonney (not yet known as 'Billy the Kid') a charming but decidedly mercurial teenager who hares off on a vicious killing spree after their new boss, John Tunstall, is murdered by a rival merchant's gang of hired gunmen. . . . Action fans will thrill to the gunplay and other dangers. James' conflicting feelings about his archetypically dangerous friend . . . introduce thought provoking elements. A tale of the Old West with a sturdy historical base and nary a dull moment." Kirkus

Victorio's war; John Wilson. Orca Book Publishers 2012 157p. $12.95
Grades: 6 7 8 9   **Fic**
1. Western stories 2. Historical fiction 3. Biographical fiction
ISBN 9781554698820; 9781554698837 (pdf); 9781554698844 (epub)
LC 2011942580

In this historical novel, by John Wilson, after "taking up a new job scouting for a troop of Buffalo Soldiers, Jim Doolen finds himself caught between friends in the military and friends riding with the Apaches they are chasing. . . . He is saved by his mystic old mentor Too-ah-yay-say from being killed . . . and held captive until a final massacre by Mexican soldiers." (Kirkus)

Written in blood. Orca Book Publishers 2010 157p (Desert legends trilogy) pa $12.95
Grades: 6 7 8 9   **Fic**
1. Fathers -- Fiction 2. Voyages and travels -- Fiction 3. Frontier and pioneer life -- Fiction
ISBN 978-1-55469-270-5 pa; 1-55469-270-9 pa

A young man's search for the father who abandoned him takes him through the wilds of the Arizona territory and northern Mexico during the 1870's and brings him in contact with an assortment of intriguing characters.

"Told in a terse, present-tense narrative, James' adventures will thrill all fans of traditional pulp-style oaters." Booklist

The **alchemist's** dream; [by] John Wilson. Key Porter Books 2007 248p pa $12.95
Grades: 7 8 9 10   **Fic**
1. Explorers 2. Magicians 3. Mathematicians 4.

Astrologers 5. Biographers 6. Writers on science 7. Explorers -- Fiction 8. Navigation -- Fiction
ISBN 978-1-55263-934-4 pa; 1-55263-934-7 pa

"Middle grade readers and high school readers who like historical fiction and stories of adventure with some mystery thrown in will be drawn to this book." Voice Youth Advocates

Wilson, N. D.
★ The **dragon's** tooth; [by] N. D. Wilson. Random House 2011 485p (Ashtown burials) $16.99; lib bdg $19.99; e-book $16.99
Grades: 5 6 7 8   **Fic**
1. Fantasy fiction 2. Magic -- Fiction 3. Siblings -- Fiction 4. Secret societies -- Fiction
ISBN 978-0-375-86439-1; 0-375-86439-3; 978-0-375-96439-8 lib bdg; 0-375-96439-8 lib bdg; 978-0-375-89572-2 e-book
LC 2009038651

"This fast-paced fantasy quickly draws readers in to its alternate reality. . . . Allusions to mythology and complex character development . . . make Wilson's first in a proposed series a gem." Booklist

Wilson, Nancy Hope
Mountain pose. Farrar, Straus & Giroux 2001 233p $17
Grades: 5 6 7 8   **Fic**
1. Wills 2. Diaries -- Fiction 3. Grandmothers -- Fiction
ISBN 0-374-35078-7
LC 00-57269

When twelve-year-old Ellie inherits an old Vermont farm from her cruel and heartless grandmother Aurelia, she reads a set of diaries written by an ancestor and discovers secrets from the past

"Beautifully written and suspenseful, this novel explores the many emotions associated with the tragedy of spousal and child abuse." Voice Youth Advocates

Wilson, Nathan D.
★ **Leepike** Ridge; [by] N. D. Wilson. Random House 2007 224p $15.99; lib bdg $18.99; pa $6.99
Grades: 4 5 6 7   **Fic**
1. Adventure fiction 2. Caves -- Fiction 3. Missing persons -- Fiction 4. Mother-son relationship -- Fiction
ISBN 978-0-375-83873-6; 0-375-83873-2; 978-0-375-93873-3 lib bdg; 0-375-93873-7 lib bdg; 978-0-375-83874-3 pa; 0-375-83874-0 pa
LC 2006-13352

While his widowed mother continues to search for him, eleven-year-old Tom, presumed dead after drifting away down a river, finds himself trapped in a series of underground caves with another survivor and a dog, and pursued by murderous treasure-hunters

"While Leepike Ridge is primarily an adventure story involving murder, treachery, and betrayal, Wilson's rich imagination and his quirky characters are a true delight." SLJ

Winerip, Michael
Adam Canfield of the Slash. Candlewick Press 2005 326p $15.99; pa $6.99

Grades: 5 6 7 8   **Fic**
1. School stories 2. Journalism -- Fiction
ISBN 0-7636-2340-7; 0-7636-2794-1 pa

While serving as co-editors of their school newspaper, middle-schoolers Adam and Jennifer uncover fraud and corruption in their school and in the city's government.

"This is a deceptively fun read that somehow manages to present kids with some of the most subtle social and ethical questions currently shaping their futures." SLJ

Other titles about Adam Canfield are:
Adam Canfield, watch you back! (2007)
Adam Canfield, the last reporter (2009)

Winston, Sherri
★ The **Kayla** chronicles; a novel. Little, Brown 2007 188p hardcover o.p. pa $7.99
Grades: 6 7 8 9 10   **Fic**
1. School stories 2. Dancers -- Fiction 3. Journalism -- Fiction 4. African Americans -- Fiction
ISBN 978-0-316-11430-1; 0-316-11430-8; 978-0-316-11431-8 pa; 0-316-11431-6 pa
LC 2006-933219

Kayla transforms herself from mild-mannered journalist to hot-trotting dance diva in order to properly investigate her high school's dance team, and has a hard time remaining true to her real self while in the role.

"Few recent novels for younger YAs mesh levity and substance this successfully." Booklist

Winters, Ben H.
The **secret** life of Ms. Finkleman. Harper 2010 247p $16.99
Grades: 4 5 6 7   **Fic**
1. School stories 2. Teachers -- Fiction 3. Musicians -- Fiction 4. Rock music -- Fiction
ISBN 978-0-06-196541-8; 0-06-196541-3
LC 2010-04601

Spurred by a special project from her social studies teacher, seventh-grader Bethesda Fielding uncovers the secret identity of her music teacher, which leads to a most unusual concert performance and a tutoring assignment.

"Liberally laced with humor and featuring an upbeat heroine, unexpected friendship and rock-music trivia, this witty middle-school drama offers a lighthearted lesson in the importance of getting the facts straight." Kirkus

Another title about Bethesda Fielding is:
The mystery of missing everything (2011)

Winters, Cat
★ **In** the shadow of blackbirds; Cat Winters. Amulet Books 2013 400 p. $16.95
Grades: 8 9 10 11 12   **Fic**
1. Occult fiction 2. Historical fiction 3. Ghosts -- Fiction 4. Spiritualism -- Fiction 5. World War, 1914-1918 -- Fiction 6. Influenza Epidemic, 1918-1919 -- Fiction
ISBN 141970530X; 9781419705304
LC 2012039262

In this book, sixteen-year-old Mary Shelley Black lives in 1918. "With WWI raging on and Mary's father on trial for treason, she goes to live with her Aunt Eva in San Diego, Calif. . . . Grieving for her childhood beau Stephen,

who died while fighting overseas with the Army, Mary goes outside during a thunderstorm and is struck dead by lightning—for a few minutes. When Mary comes to, she discovers she can communicate with the dead, including Stephen." (Publishers Weekly)

Winterson, Jeanette
Tanglewreck. Bloomsbury Children's Books 2006 414p $16.95; pa $6.95
Grades: 5 6 7 8   **Fic**
1. Science fiction 2. Space and time -- Fiction 3. Clocks and watches -- Fiction
ISBN 978-1-58234-919-0; 1-58234-919-3; 978-1-59990-081-0 pa; 1-59990-081-5 pa
LC 2005-30630

Eleven-year-old Silver sets out to find the Timekeeper—a clock that controls time—and to protect it from falling into the hands of two people who want to use the device for their own nefarious ends

"Winterson seamlessly combines rousing adventure with time warps, quantum physics, and a few wonderfully hapless flunkies." Booklist

Winthrop, Elizabeth
Counting on Grace. Wendy Lamb Books 2006 232p $15.95; lib bdg $17.99; pa $6.99
Grades: 5 6 7 8   **Fic**
1. Photographers 2. Factories -- Fiction 3. Child labor -- Fiction 4. Photographers -- Fiction
ISBN 0-385-74644-X; 0-385-90878-4 lib bdg; 0-553-48783-3 pa

It's 1910 in Pownal, Vermont. At 12 Grace and her best friend Arthur must go to work in the mill, helping their mothers work the looms. Together Grace and Arthur write a secret letter to the Child Labor Board about underage children working in the mill. A few weeks later, Lewis Hine, a famous reformer, arrives undercover to gather evidence. Grace meets him and appears in some of his photographs, changing her life forever.

"Much information on early photography and the workings of the textile mills is conveyed, and history and fiction are woven seamlessly together in this beautifully written novel." SLJ

Wiseman, Eva
★ **Puppet**; a novel. Tundra Books 2009 243p $17.95
Grades: 7 8 9 10 11 12   **Fic**
1. Prejudices -- Fiction 2. Jews -- Hungary -- Fiction
ISBN 978-0-88776-828-6; 0-88776-828-8

"Times are hard in Julie Vamosi's Hungarian village in the late nineteenth-century, and the townspeople . . . blame the Jews. After Julie's best friend, Esther, . . . disappears, the rumor spreads that the Jews cut her throat and drained her blood to drink with their Passover matzos. . . . Based on the records of a trial in 1883, this searing novel dramatizes virulent anti-Semitism from the viewpoint of a Christian child. . . . The climax is electrifying." Booklist

Wiseman, Rosalind
Boys, girls, and other hazardous materials. Putnam 2010 282p $17.99

Grades: 8 9 10 11 12 **Fic**
1. School stories
ISBN 978-0-399-247965; 0-399-24796-3
LC 2009-18446

Transferring to a new high school, freshman Charlotte "Charlie" Healey faces tough choices as she tries to shed her "mean girl" image.

Wiseman "succeeds in delivering realistic, likable characters whose challenges and mistakes are all too relatable." Bull Cent Child Books

Wisler, G. Clifton
Caleb's choice. Lodestar Bks. 1996 154p hardcover o.p. pa $4.99 **Fic**
Grades: 5 6 7 8 **Fic**
1. Slavery -- Fiction 2. Underground railroad -- Fiction
ISBN 0-14-038256-9 pa
LC 96-2339

While living in Texas in 1858, fourteen-year-old Caleb faces a dilemma in deciding whether or not to assist fugitive slaves in their run for freedom

"This fast-paced, easy-to-read novel proves that history can be intriguing and exciting, Wisler draws readers into this masterful, and often humorous tale." ALAN

Red Cap. Lodestar Bks. 1991 160p hardcover o.p. pa $5.99
Grades: 4 5 6 7 **Fic**
1. Powell, Ransom J., 1849-1899 – Fiction 2. Andersonville Prison – Fiction 3. United States -- History -- 1861-1865, Civil War -- Fiction
ISBN 0-14-036936-8 pa
LC 90-21944

A young Yankee drummer boy displays great courage when he's captured and sent to Andersonville Prison

The author "presents a well-researched view of the war. He effectively interweaves the known facts of Powell's life with first-person accounts of other soldiers and prisoners to create an exciting story." SLJ

Withers, Pam
First descent. Tundra Books 2011 265p $17.95
Grades: 7 8 9 10 **Fic**
1. Kayaks and kayaking -- Fiction
ISBN 978-1-77049-257-8; 1-77049-257-7

"Seventeen-year-old champion slalom kayaker Rex Scruggs is determined to kayak Colombia's Furioso River, when he meets a young woman, an Andean indigena, who both aids Rex in his quest and puts him in the crosshairs of Colombia's battling guerrillas and paramilitaries. . . . Withers flings the reader from one perilous adventure to another." Booklist

Wittlinger, Ellen
Hard love. Simon & Schuster Bks. for Young Readers 1999 224p hardcover o.p. pa $8.99
Grades: 7 8 9 10 **Fic**
1. Divorce -- Fiction 2. Identity -- Fiction 3. Lesbians -- Fiction 4. Authorship -- Fiction 5. Underground press publications -- Fiction
ISBN 0-689-82134-4; 0-689-84154-X pa
LC 98-6668

Michael L. Printz Award honor book, 2000

"John, cynical yet vulnerable, thinks he's immune to emotion until he meets bright, brittle Marisol, the author of his favorite zine. He falls in love, but Marisol, a lesbian, just wants to be friends. A love story of a different sort—funny, poignant, and thoughtful." Booklist

Love & lies; Marisol's story. Simon & Schuster Books for Young Readers 2008 245p $16.99
Grades: 7 8 9 10 **Fic**
1. Lesbians -- Fiction 2. Authorship -- Fiction
ISBN 978-1-4169-1623-9; 1-4169-1623-7
LC 2007-18330

When Marisol, a self-confident eighteen-year-old lesbian, moves to Cambridge, Massachusetts to work and try to write a novel, she falls under the spell of her beautiful but deceitful writing teacher, while also befriending a shy, vulnerable girl from Indiana.

"The emotional morass of Marisol's life . . . is complex and realistic; it will draw in both fans of the earlier novel . . . and realistic-fiction readers seeking a love story with depth." Bull Cent Child Books

Parrotfish. Simon & Schuster Books for Young Readers 2007 294p $16.99
Grades: 7 8 9 10 **Fic**
1. School stories 2. Family life -- Fiction 3. Transsexualism -- Fiction
ISBN 978-1-4169-1622-2; 1-4169-1622-9
LC 2006-9689

Grady, a transgendered high school student, yearns for acceptance by his classmates and family as he struggles to adjust to his new identity as a male.

"The author demonstrates well the complexity faced by transgendered people and makes the teen's frustration with having to fit into a category fully apparent." Publ Wkly

This means war! Simon & Schuster Books for Young Readers 2010 224p $16.99
Grades: 5 6 7 8 **Fic**
1. Fear -- Fiction 2. Contests -- Fiction 3. Friendship -- Fiction
ISBN 978-1-4169-97101-6; 1-4169-7101-7
LC 2008-32586

In 1962, when her best friend Lowell begins to hang around new friends who think girls are losers, Juliet, a fearful fifth-grader, teams up with bold, brave Patsy who challenges the boys to a series of increasingly dangerous contests

"Wittlinger latches on to a poignant metaphor for war in the lively and readable tale set against the backdrop of the 1962 Cuban missile crisis." Booklist

Zigzag. Simon & Schuster Bks. for Young Readers 2003 267p $16.95
Grades: 7 8 9 10 **Fic**
1. Cousins -- Fiction 2. Automobile travel -- Fiction
ISBN 0-689-84996-6
LC 2002-2145

A high-school junior makes a trip with her aunt and two cousins, discovering places she did not know existed and strengths she did not know she had

"Teens will easily hear themselves in Robin's hilarious, sharp observations and feel her excitement as she travels through new country and discovers her own strength." Booklist

Woelfle, Gretchen

All the world's a stage; a novel in five acts. illustrated by Thomas Cox. Holiday House 2011 163p il $16.95

Grades: 4 5 6 7   **Fic**

1. Actors -- Fiction 2. Orphans -- Fiction 3. Theater -- Fiction 4. Apprentices -- Fiction
ISBN 978-0-8234-2281-4; 0-8234-2281-X

LC 2010023474

Twelve-year-old orphan Christopher "Kit" Buckles becomes a stage boy in a London theater in 1598, tries his hand at acting, and later helps build the Globe Theater for playwright William Shakespeare and the Chamberlain's Men acting troupe.

"The most compelling drama is Kit's universal search for his calling and his shifting friendships. . . . Frequent charming drawings enhance the sense of time and place." Booklist
Includes glossary and bibliographical references

Wolf, Allan

New found land; Lewis and Clark's voyage of discovery: a novel. Candlewick Press 2004 500p map $18.99

Grades: 7 8 9 10   **Fic**

1. Lewis and Clark Expedition (1804-1806) -- Fiction
ISBN 0-7636-2113-7

LC 2003-65254

The letters and thoughts of Thomas Jefferson, members of the Corps of Discovery, their guide Sacagawea, and Captain Lewis's Newfoundland dog, all tell of the historic exploratory expedition to seek a water route to the Pacific Ocean.

"This is an extraordinary, engrossing book that would appeal most to serious readers, but it should definitely be added to any collection." SLJ
Includes glossary and bibliographical references

★ The **watch** that ends the night; voices from the Titanic. Candlewick Press 2011 466p $21.99

Grades: 7 8 9 10   **Fic**

1. Novels in verse 2. Shipwrecks -- Fiction
ISBN 978-0-7636-3703-3

LC 2010040150

"A lyrical, monumental work of fact and imagination that reads like an oral history revved up by the drama of the event." Kirkus

Wolf, Joan M.

★ **Someone** named Eva. Clarion Books 2007 200p $16; pa $6.99

Grades: 5 6 7 8   **Fic**

1. School stories 2. National socialism -- Fiction 3. World War, 1939-1945 -- Fiction
ISBN 0-618-53579-9; 0-547-23766-9 pa

LC 2006-26070

From her home in Lidice, Czechoslovakia, in 1942, eleven-year-old Milada is taken with other blond, blue-eyed

children to a school in Poland to be trained as "proper Germans" for adoption by German families, but all the while she remembers her true name and history.

"This amazing, eye-opening story, masterfully written, is an essential part of World War II literature and belongs on the shelves of every library." SLJ

Wolff, Virginia Euwer

★ **Make** lemonade. Holt & Co. 1993 200p $17.95; pa $7.95

Grades: 8 9 10 11 12   **Fic**

1. Novels in verse 2. Poverty -- Fiction 3. Babysitters -- Fiction 4. Teenage mothers -- Fiction
ISBN 978-0-8050-2228-5; 0-8050-2228-7; 978-0-8050-8070-4 pa; 0-8050-8070-8 pa

LC 92-41182

"Fourteen-year-old LaVaughn accepts the job of babysitting Jolly's two small children but quickly realizes that the young woman, a seventeen-year-old single mother, needs as much help and nurturing as her two neglected children. The four become something akin to a temporary family, and through their relationship each makes progress toward a better life. Sixty-six brief chapters, with words arranged on the page like poetry, perfectly echo the patterns of teenage speech." Horn Book Guide

Other titles in this trilogy are:
This full house (2009)
True believer (2001)

The **Mozart** season. Holt & Co. 1991 249p hardcover o.p. pa $6.99

Grades: 6 7 8 9   **Fic**

1. Violinists -- Fiction
ISBN 0-8050-1571-X; 0-312-36745-7 pa

LC 90-23635

Allegra spends her twelfth summer practicing a Mozart concerto for a violin competition and finding many significant connections in her world

"With a clear, fresh voice that never falters, Wolff gives readers a delightful heroine, a fully realized setting, and a slowly building tension that reaches a stunning climax." SLJ

★ **Probably** still Nick Swansen. Holt & Co. 1988 144p hardcover o.p. pa $7.99

Grades: 7 8 9 10   **Fic**

1. Learning disabilities -- Fiction
ISBN 0-8050-0701-6; 0-689-85226-6 pa

LC 88-13175

Sixteen-year-old learning-disabled Nick struggles to endure a life in which the other kids make fun of him, he has to take special classes, his date for the prom makes an excuse not to go with him, and he is haunted by the memory of his older sister who drowned while he was watching

"It is a poignant, gentle, utterly believable narrative." Booklist

Wolfson, Jill

Home, and other big, fat lies. Henry Holt 2006 281p $16.95

Grades: 5 6 7 8   **Fic**

1. Nature -- Fiction 2. Foster home care -- Fiction 3.

Environmental protection -- Fiction
ISBN 978-0-8050-7670-7; 0-8050-7670-0

LC 200035843

Eleven-year-old Termite, a foster child with an eye for the beauty of nature and a talent for getting into trouble, takes on the loggers in her new home town when she tries to save the biggest tree in the forest.

"Written with humor and sensitivity." Voice Youth Advocates

What I call life. Holt & Co. 2005 270p $16.95; pa $6.99

Grades: 5 6 7 8   **Fic**

1. Foster home care -- Fiction
ISBN 0-8050-7669-7; 0-312-37752-5 pa

Placed in a group foster home, eleven-year-old Cal Lavender learns how to cope with life from the four other girls who live there and from their storytelling guardian, the Knitting Lady.

"Wolfson paints her characters with delightful authenticity. Her debut novel is a treasure of quiet good humor and skillful storytelling that conveys subtle messages about kindness, compassion, and the gift of family regardless of its configuration." Booklist

Wolitzer, Meg

The **fingertips** of Duncan Dorfman. Dutton Childrens Books 2011 294p $16.99

Grades: 4 5 6 7   **Fic**

1. Contests -- Fiction 2. Individualism -- Fiction 3. Scrabble (Game) -- Fiction
ISBN 978-0-525-42304-1; 0-525-42304-4

LC 2011005228

"The novel is shot through with Scrabble words and rules in a way that is reminiscent of Louis Sachar's The Cardturner (2010). Readers will identify with and root for the characters as their tales intertwine to a satisfying if slightly too cheery close. Word wizards aren't the only ones who will enjoy this readable rumination on ethics, competition and identity." Kirkus

Wollman, Jessica

Switched. Delacorte Press 2007 249p $15.99

Grades: 6 7 8 9   **Fic**

1. School stories 2. Social classes -- Fiction 3. Household employees -- Fiction 4. Mother-daughter relationship -- Fiction
ISBN 978-0-385-73396-0

Laura and Willa, born the same night seventeen years ago on opposite sides of Darien, Connecticut, are both unhappy with their lives and when they discover they look remarkably alike, they decide to try out one another's lives for four months.

"Wollman turns a potentially clichéd premise . . . into an entertaining and thoughtful novel. . . . Wollman creates credible characters who should endear themselves to readers." Publ Wkly

Wood, Frances

When Molly was a Harvey Girl; by Frances M. Wood. Kane/Miller 2010 226p $15.99

Grades: 6 7 8 9   **Fic**

1. Sisters -- Fiction 2. Restaurants -- Fiction 3. Frontier and pioneer life -- Fiction
ISBN 978-1-935279-51-8; 1-935279-51-3

"Thirteen-year-old Molly Gerry and her older sister Colleen's world is rocked when their father dies, leaving them penniless. Their best hope seems to be leaving their small Illinois town to work at the Harvey Eating House in Raton, New Mexico. . . . Inspired by the author's great-grandmother's experiences, this historical bildungsroman shows life out west in the 1800s in all its flash and grittiness. Molly is a strongly drawn character. . . . [This is a] delightful tale." Booklist

Wood, June Rae

The **man** who loved clowns. Putnam 1992 224p hardcover o.p. pa $5.99

Grades: 5 6 7 8   **Fic**

1. Uncles -- Fiction 2. Down syndrome -- Fiction 3. Mentally handicapped -- Fiction
ISBN 0-14-240422-5 pa

LC 91-33861

Thirteen-year-old Delrita, whose unhappy life has caused her to hide from the world, loves her uncle Punky but sometimes feels ashamed of his behavior because he has Down's syndrome

"Wood's prose is strong and flowing, with a good balance of dialogue and narrative, and with several well-developed and memorable characters." SLJ

Another title about Delrita is:
Turtle on a fence post (1997)

Wood, Maggie L.

Captured. Lobster Press 2011 284p (The Divided Realms) $12.95

Grades: 6 7 8 9   **Fic**

1. Fantasy fiction 2. Young adult literature -- Works
ISBN 978-1-77080-071-7 pa; 1-77080-071-9 pa

"Willow was brought up believing she was just a normal girl with a grandmother that had a penchant for telling fantastic stories about another realm where she was a princess and magic and fairies were everyday occurrences. . . . Or, at least that is what Willow thought until the day her Nana died and she was transported to the home she never knew to save a family she never knew she had. . . . Wood's characters must think outside the game to save their world. Sometimes it takes an outsider to see things that those on the inside cannot. This is a wonderful book—well written and likely to fly off the shelves while fantasy is still the hot genre." Voice Youth Advocates

The **darkening**. Lobster Press 2011 283p (The Divided Realms) pa $12.95

Grades: 6 7 8 9   **Fic**

1. Fantasy fiction 2. Fairies -- Fiction
ISBN 978-1-77080-072-4 pa; 1-77080-072-7 pa

"Willow travels to the faery realm, but when Brand breaks the all-important rules by stowing away in the magical transport spell, the faeries turn the pair over to the dark lord Jarlath Thornheart, who throws them into the terrifying goblin's gauntlet. . . . This story remains entertaining." Kirkus

Wood, Maryrose

My life the musical; by Maryrose Wood. 1st ed.; Delacorte Press 2008 228p $15.99; lib bdg $18.99

Grades: 7 8 9 10   **Fic**

1. School stories 2. Theater -- Fiction 3. Musicals -- Fiction

ISBN 978-0-385-73278-9; 0-385-73278-3; 978-0-385-90297-7 lib bdg; 0-385-90297-2 lib bdg

LC 2007015034

Sixteen-year-old Emily Pearl's obsession with Broadway shows, and one musical in particular, lands her in trouble in school and at home, but it might also allow her and her best friend, Phillip, to find a dramatic solution to the problems.

"Teens will enjoy the fast pace and humor in this uplifting novel." SLJ

The **poison** diaries; based on a concept by the Duchess of Northumberland. Balzer + Bray 2010 278p $16.99

Grades: 8 9 10 11   **Fic**

1. Plants -- Fiction 2. Supernatural -- Fiction 3. Poisons and poisoning -- Fiction 4. Father-daughter relationship -- Fiction

ISBN 978-0-06-180236-2; 0-06-180236-0

LC 2009-54427

In late eighteenth-century Northumberland, England, sixteen-year-old Jessamine Luxton and the mysterious Weed uncover the horrible secrets of poisons growing in Thomas Luxton's apothecary garden.

"This intriguing fantasy has many tendrils to wrap around teen hearts. . . . The haunting ending will leave readers wanting to talk about the themes of cruelty, honesty, and loyalty." Booklist

Another title in this series is:
Nightshade (2011)

The **unseen** guest; by Maryrose Wood ; illustrated by Jon Klassen. Balzer + Bray 2012 340 p. (hardback) $15.99

Grades: 4 5 6   **Fic**

1. Mystery fiction 2. Wolves -- Fiction 3. Nannies -- Fiction 4. Wild children -- Fiction 5. Great Britain -- History -- 19th century -- Fiction 6. Orphans -- Fiction 7. Secrets -- Fiction 8. Governesses -- Fiction

ISBN 9780061791185

LC 2011053315

This young adult novel offers a "Victorian mystery [story about] teenage governess Penelope Lumley [who] takes on threats to her wolfish young charges that include a hustler after the Ashton fortune. . . . Once he meets the three feral children Penelope is charged with training up to be human, Faucet's scheme to finance the introduction of ostrich racing to the British Isles by marrying the Dowager Lady Ashton is transformed to visions of wolf racing and sideshow exhibitions. . . . Along with . . . pitching her plucky protagonist into one crisis after another . . . the author slips in a few more seemingly significant Clues to the Ashtons' curious history and Penelope's apparent involvement in it." (Kirkus)

Wooding, Chris

Havoc; illustrated by Dan Chernett. Scholastic Press 2010 396p il $16.99

Grades: 6 7 8 9   **Fic**

1. Magic -- Fiction 2. Good and evil -- Fiction 3. Comic books, strips, etc. -- Fiction

ISBN 978-0-545-16045-2; 0-545-16045-6

"As Seth makes his way back into Malice with the talismanic Shard and joins the effort to mount an attack on the dread Deadhouse, a new ally, Alicia, nervously tracks the House's sinister master Tall Jake to the decrepit English psychiatric hospital where Grendel—the mad, disturbed, misshapen graphic artist (and maybe god?) who has created both the comic and the world it depicts—is imprisoned. . . . This features expertly meshed multiple plotlines, colorful supporting characters . . . frequent eerie skitterings and sudden feelings of dread plus nonstop action that breaks, occasionally, from prose into graphic-novel–style panels festooned with noisy sound effects." Kirkus

★ **Malice**; illustrated by Dan Chernett. Scholastic Press 2009 377p il $14.99; pa $8.99

Grades: 6 7 8 9 10   **Fic**

1. Horror fiction 2. Comic books, strips, etc. -- Fiction

ISBN 978-0-545-16043-8; 0-545-16043-X; 978-0-545-16044-5 pa; 0-545-16044-8 pa

Everyone's heard the rumors. Call on Tall Jake and he'll take you to Malice, a world that exists inside a horrifying comic book. A place most kids never leave. Seth and Kady think it's all a silly myth. But then their friend disappears.

"This nail-biter will keep readers glued to the story until the very last page is turned. . . . Seth and Kady are strong and exciting characters." SLJ

Poison. Orchard Bks. 2005 273p $16.99; pa $7.99

Grades: 7 8 9 10   **Fic**

1. Fantasy fiction 2. Fairies -- Fiction 3. Storytelling -- Fiction

ISBN 0-439-75570-0; 0-439-75571-9 pa

LC 2005-02174

First published 2003 in the United Kingdom

When Poison leaves her home in the marshes of Gull to retrieve the infant sister who was snatched by the fairies, she and a group of unusual friends survive encounters with the inhabitants of various Realms, and Poison herself confronts a surprising destiny.

"Poison's story should please crowds of horror fans who like their books fast-paced, darkly atmospheric, and melodramatic." SLJ

★ The **haunting** of Alaizabel Cray. Orchard Bks. 2004 292p $16.95; pa $7.99

Grades: 7 8 9 10   **Fic**

1. Horror fiction 2. Supernatural -- Fiction

ISBN 0-439-54656-7; 0-439-59851-6 pa

LC 2003-69108

First published 2001 in the United Kingdom

In a world similar to Victorian London, Thaniel, a seventeen-year-old hunter of deadly, demonic creatures called the wych-kin, takes in a lost, possessed girl, and becomes embroiled in a plot to unleash evil on the world

"Eerie and exhilarating. . . . [The author] fuses together his best storytelling skills . . . to create a fabulously horrific and ultimately timeless underworld." SLJ

The **storm** thief. Orchard Books 2006 310p $16.99

Grades: 6 7 8 9 10   **Fic**
1. Science fiction
ISBN 0-439-86513-1

LC 2005-35993

With the help of a golem, two teenaged thieves try to survive on the city island of Orokos, where unpredictable probability storms continually change both the landscape and the inhabitants.

The author "delivers memorable characters, such as Vago, whose plight—Who am I and where do I belong in the world?—will be understood by many teens. Wooding also creates a unique world for his characters to explore, and the setting serves as an excellent backdrop for the author to develop his theme of order versus chaos and the need for balance between the two." Voice Youth Advocates

Woodruff, Elvira

Dear Austin; letters from the Underground Railroad. illustrated by Nancy Carpenter. Knopf 1998 137p il $16; lib bdg $17.99; pa $5.50

Grades: 4 5 6   **Fic**
1. Slavery -- Fiction 2. African Americans -- Fiction 3. Underground railroad -- Fiction
ISBN 0-679-88594-3; 0-679-98594-8 lib bdg; 0-375-80356-4 pa

LC 98-5314

In 1853, in letters to his older brother, eleven-year-old Levi describes his adventures in the Pennsylvania countryside with his black friend Jupiter and his experiences with the Underground Railroad

"The smoothly written text is fast paced." Horn Book Guide

Fearless. Scholastic Press 2008 224p il $16.99; pa $6.99

Grades: 5 6 7 8   **Fic**
1. Artists 2. Engravers 3. Inventors 4. Architects 5. Adventure fiction 6. Orphans -- Fiction 7. Lighthouses -- Fiction
ISBN 978-0-439-67703-5; 0-439-67703-3; 978-0-439-67704-2 pa; 0-439-67704-1 pa

LC 2006-10137

In late seventeenth-century England, eleven-year-old Digory, forced to leave his hometown after his father is lost at sea, becomes an apprentice to the architect Henry Winstanley, who built a lighthouse on the treacherous Eddystone Reef—the very rocks that sank Digory's grandfather's ship years before.

"This fascinating, well-written story is closely based on the life of the real Henry Winstanley. . . . The characters are finely drawn and the action is nonstop." SLJ

George Washington's spy; a time travel adventure. Scholastic Press 2010 229p $16.99

Grades: 4 5 6   **Fic**
1. Authors 2. Diplomats 3. Inventors 4. Statesmen

5. Scientists 6. Writers on science 7. Members of Congress 8. Time travel -- Fiction
ISBN 978-0-545-10487-6; 0-545-10487-4

LC 2009032700

Ten-year-old Matt and six other children travel to 1776 Boston, living out American history as they meet Benjamin Franklin, learn about colonial medicine, and become part of a rebel spy ring

"Woodruff does an excellent job of conveying the complexities of war. . . . This is a great introduction to the Revolutionary period. . . . The story is fast paced, exciting, and informative." SLJ

Woods, Brenda

Emako Blue. G. P. Putnam's Sons 2004 124p $15.99

Grades: 7 8 9 10   **Fic**
1. African Americans -- Fiction
ISBN 0-399-24006-3

LC 2003-16647

Monterey, Savannah, Jamal, and Eddie have never had much to do with each other until Emako Blue shows up at chorus practice, but just as the lives of the five Los Angeles high school students become intertwined, tragedy tears them apart.

"This short, succinct, and poignant story of friendship, family, and overwhelming sadness will leave some readers in tears." SLJ

My name is Sally Little Song. G.P. Putnam's Sons 2006 182p $15.99; pa $5.99

Grades: 4 5 6 7   **Fic**
1. Slavery -- Fiction 2. Seminole Indians -- Fiction 3. African Americans -- Fiction
ISBN 0-399-24312-7; 0-14-240943-X pa

LC 2005-32651

When their owner plans to sell one of them in 1802, twelve-year-old Sally and her family run away from their Georgia plantation to look for both freedom from slavery and a home in Florida with the Seminole Indians.

"Based on historical accounts, this novel provides readers with an alternative view of the realities of slavery—an escape to the South rather than North. . . . This accessible tale will prove a rich resource for study and discussion." SLJ

A star on the Hollywood Walk of Fame. G. P. Putnam's Sons 2010 164p il $16.99

Grades: 6 7 8 9 10 11 12   **Fic**
1. School stories 2. Authorship -- Fiction
ISBN 978-0-399-24683-8; 0-399-24683-5

LC 2009-08750

Nine Los Angeles high school students use a creative writing class assignment to shed light on their own lives.

"Woods is such a master of pace and voice that her storytelling will rivet even reluctant readers to the page. Her use of dialect is flawless, and her quick transitions from one character's perspective to the next keep things lively." Bull Cent Child Books

Woods, Ron

The **hero**. Knopf 2002 215p hardcover o.p. pa $4.99

Grades: 5 6 7 8   **Fic**

1. Death -- Fiction 2. Rafting (Sports) -- Fiction

ISBN 0-375-80612-1; 0-440-22978-2 pa

           LC 00-54460

In the summer of 1957 in Idaho, when 14 year old Jamie and his older cousin Jerry reluctantly include outsider Dennis in their rafting adventure, Dennis drowns and Jamie lies that Dennis made a heroic sacrifice

"The author deftly handles a convincing adventure with emotional depth and tenderness toward his characters." SLJ

Woodson, Jacqueline

★ **After** Tupac and D Foster. G.P. Putnam's Sons 2008 153p $15.99

Grades: 7 8 9 10   **Fic**

1. Poets 2. Actors 3. Rap musicians 4. Friendship -- Fiction 5. African Americans -- Fiction

ISBN 978-0-399-24654-8

          LC 2007-23725

A Newbery honor book, 2009

In the New York City borough of Queens in 1996, three girls bond over their shared love of Tupac Shakur's music, as together they try to make sense of the unpredictable world in which they live.

"The subtlety and depth with which the author conveys the girls' relationships lend this novel exceptional vividness and staying power." Publ Wkly

★ **Feathers**. G.P. Putnam's Sons 2007 118p $15.99; pa $6.99

Grades: 4 5 6 7   **Fic**

1. Religion -- Fiction 2. Race relations -- Fiction 3. African Americans -- Fiction

ISBN 978-0-399-23989-2; 0-399-23989-8; 978-0-14-241198-8 pa; 0-14-241198-1 pa

          LC 2006-24713

A Newbery Medal honor book, 2008

When a new, white student nicknamed "The Jesus Boy" joins her sixth grade class in the winter of 1971, Frannie's growing friendship with him makes her start to see some things in a new light.

"Woodson creates in Frannie a strong protagonist who thinks for herself and recognizes the value and meaning of family. The story ends with hope and thoughtfulness while speaking to those adolescents who struggle with race, faith, and prejudice." SLJ

★ **From** the notebooks of Melanin Sun. G.P. Putnam's Sons 2010 126p $17.99; pa $7.99

Grades: 7 8 9 10   **Fic**

1. Lesbians -- Fiction 2. African Americans -- Fiction 3. Mother-son relationship -- Fiction

ISBN 978-0-399-25280-8; 0-399-25280-0; 978-0-14-241641-9 pa; 0-14-241641-X pa

          LC 2009011314

A reissue of the title first published 1995 by Blue Sky Press

A Coretta Scott King honor book, 1996

Almost-fourteen-year-old Melanin Sun's comfortable, quiet life is shattered when his mother reveals she has fallen in love with a woman

"Offering no easy answers, Woodson teaches the reader that love can lead to acceptance of all manner of differences." Publ Wkly

Hush. Putnam 2002 181p $15.99; pa $5.99

Grades: 6 7 8 9   **Fic**

1. African Americans 2. Jehovah's Witnesses 3. Witnesses -- Fiction 4. Witness protection programs 5. African Americans -- Fiction

ISBN 0-399-23114-5; 0-14-250049-6 pa

          LC 2001-19710

Thirteen-year-old Toswiah finds her life changed when her family enters the witness protection program

The author's "poetic, low-key, yet vivid writing style perfectly conveys the story's atmosphere of quiet intensity." Horn Book

★ **If** you come softly. Putnam 1998 181p $15.99; pa $5.99

Grades: 7 8 9 10   **Fic**

1. African Americans 2. Interracial dating 3. Race relations -- Fiction 4. African Americans -- Fiction 5. Family life -- New York (State) -- New York

ISBN 0-399-23112-9; 0-698-11862-6 pa

          LC 97-32212

ALA YALSA Margaret A. Edwards Award (2006)

After meeting at their private school in New York, fifteen-year-old Jeremiah, who is black and whose parents are separated, and Ellie, who is white and whose mother has twice abandoned her, fall in love and then try to cope with people's reactions

"The gentle and melancholy tone of this book makes it ideal for thoughtful readers and fans of romance." Voice Youth Advocates

Another title about Jeremiah is:

Behind you (2004)

Lena; by Jacqueline Woodson. 1st G.P. Putnam's Sons ed.; G. P. Putnam's Sons 2006 135p $17.99

Grades: 6 7 8 9   **Fic**

1. Sisters -- Fiction 2. Runaway teenagers -- Fiction

ISBN 0-399-24469-7

          LC 2005032666

A reissue of the title first published 1999 by Delacorte Press

ALA YALSA Margaret A. Edwards Award (2006)

Thirteen-year-old Lena and her younger sister Dion mourn the death of their mother as they hitchhike from Ohio to Kentucky while running away from their abusive father.

"Soulful, wise and sometimes wrenching, this taut story never loses its grip on the reader." Publ Wkly

★ **Locomotion**. Putnam 2003 100p $17.99; pa $5.99

Grades: 4 5 6 7   **Fic**

1. Orphans 2. Novels in verse 3. African Americans -- Poetry 4. Foster home care -- Fiction 5. African Americans -- Fiction

ISBN 978-0-399-23115-5; 0-399-23115-3; 978-0-14-241552-8 pa; 0-14-241552-9 pa

          LC 2002-69779

In a series of poems, eleven-year-old Lonnie writes about his life, after the death of his parents, separated from his younger sister, living in a foster home, and finding his poetic voice at school

"In a masterful use of voice, Woodson allows Lonnie's poems to tell a complex story of loss and grief and to create a gritty, urban environment. Despite the spare text, Lonnie's foster mother and the other minor characters are three-dimensional, making the boy's world a convincingly real one." SLJ

★ **Peace,** Locomotion. G.P. Putnam's Sons 2009 134p $15.99; pa $7.99

Grades: 4 5 6 7   **Fic**
1. Letters -- Fiction 2. Orphans -- Fiction 3. Siblings -- Fiction 4. Foster home care -- Fiction 5. African Americans -- Fiction
ISBN 978-0-399-24655-5; 0-399-24655-X; 978-0-14-241512-2 pa; 0-14-241512-X pa

LC 2008-18583

Through letters to his little sister, who is living in a different foster home, sixth-grader Lonnie, also known as "Locomotion," keeps a record of their lives while they are apart, describing his own foster family, including his foster brother who returns home after losing a leg in the Iraq War

"Woodson creates a full-bodied character in kind, sensitive Lonnie. Readers will understand his quest for peace, and appreciate the hard work he does to find it." Publ Wkly

Woodworth, Chris
Double -click for trouble. Farrar, Straus and Giroux 2008 162p $16

Grades: 6 7 8 9   **Fic**
1. Uncles -- Fiction 2. Country life -- Fiction
ISBN 978-0-374-30987-9; 0-374-30987-6

LC 2006-38351

After he is caught viewing inappropriate websites on the Internet, a fatherless, thirteen-year-old Chicago boy is sent to rural Indiana to spend school break with his eccentric great-uncle.

"Woodworth perfectly captures an eighth-grade boy on the cusp of adolescence, struggling with his identity as he learns about himself, his family, and what is really important in relationships." SLJ

When Ratboy lived next door. Farrar, Straus and Giroux 2005 181p $16

Grades: 6 7 8 9   **Fic**
1. Raccoons -- Fiction 2. Friendship -- Fiction
ISBN 0-374-34677-1

LC 2004-50634

When his strange family moves into her quiet southern Indiana town, sixth-grader Lydia Carson initially despises her new neighbor and classmate, who seems as wild as the raccoon that is his closest companion.

"There are serious issues present, including poverty, alcoholism, abuse, learning disabilities, and bullying. The conflicts of the plot are effectively tied up, though not too neatly to lose believability. . . . An outstanding offering." SLJ

Woon, Yvonne
Dead beautiful. Disney/Hyperion 2010 456p $16.99; pa $9.99

Grades: 7 8 9 10 11 12   **Fic**
1. School stories 2. Immortality -- Fiction 3. Supernatural -- Fiction
ISBN 978-1-4231-1956-2; 1-4231-1956-8; 978-1-4231-1961-6 pa; 1-4231-1961-4 pa

LC 2009-42850

After her parents die under mysterious circumstances, sixteen-year-old Renee Winters is sent from California to an old-fashioned boarding school in Maine, where she meets a fellow student to whom she seems strangely connected.

"This hefty novel takes a new and unconventional look at the undead, focusing on story and interesting characters and leaving gore and mayhem hidden in the background. . . . Well written, intriguing and, above all, different." Kirkus

Wrede, Patricia C., 1953-
Across the Great Barrier; Patricia C. Wrede. Scholastic Press 2011 339p (Frontier magic) $16.99

Grades: 7 8 9 10 11 12   **Fic**
1. Fantasy 2. Magic -- Fiction 3. Twins -- Fiction 4. Brothers and sisters -- Fiction 5. Frontier and pioneer life -- Fiction
ISBN 978-0-545-03343-5; 0-545-03343-8; 9780545033435

LC 2011032260

Eff is an unlucky thirteenth child. Her twin brother, Lan, is a powerful seventh son of a seventh son. And yet, Eff is the one who saved the day for the settlements west of the Great Barrier. Her unique ways of doing magic and seeing the world, and her fascination with the magical creatures and land in the Great Plains push Eff to work toward joining an expedition heading west. But things are changing on the frontier.

"Splendid worldbuilding and deliciously complex characterization continue to be the hallmarks of this standout fantasy." Kirkus

Dealing with dragons. Harcourt Brace Jovanovich 1990 212p (The Enchanted Forest Chronicles) hardcover o.p. pa $6.99

Grades: 5 6 7 8   **Fic**
1. Fairy tales 2. Magic -- Fiction 3. Dragons -- Fiction
ISBN 0-15-222900-0; 0-15-204566-X pa

LC 89-24599

Bored with traditional palace life, a princess goes off to live with a group of dragons and soon becomes involved with fighting against some disreputable wizards who want to steal away the dragons' kingdom

"A decidedly diverting novel with plenty of action and many slightly skewed fairy-tale conventions that add to the laugh-out-loud reading pleasure and give the story a wide appeal." Booklist

Other titles in this series are:
Searching for dragons (1991)
Calling on dragons (1993)
Talking to dragons (1993)

The **Far** West; Patricia C. Wrede. Scholastic Press 2012 378 p. $17.99

Grades: 7 8 9 10 11 12   **Fic**
1. Steampunk fiction 2. Magic -- Fiction 3. Twins --
Fiction 4. Friendship -- Fiction
ISBN 0545033446; 9780545033442

LC 2012288790

This young adult speampunk novel, by Patricia C.
Wrede, concludes the "Frontier Magic" trilogy. "Eff is an
unlucky thirteenth child . . . but also the seventh daughter
in her family. Her twin brother, Lan, is a powerful double
seventh son. Her life at the edge of the Great Barrier Spell is
different from anyone else's that she knows. . . . With Lan,
William, Professor Torgeson, Wash, and Professor Ochiba,
Eff finds that nothing on the wild frontier is as they expected." (Publisher's note)

Sorcery and Cecelia, or, The enchanted chocolate
pot; being the correspondence of two young ladies of
quality regarding various magical scandals in London
and the country. [by] Patricia C. Wrede and Caroline
Stevermer. Harcourt 2003 316p $17; pa $6.95
Grades: 7 8 9 10   **Fic**
1. Cousins -- Fiction 2. Supernatural -- Fiction
ISBN 0-15-204615-1; 0-15-205300-X pa

LC 2002-38706

In 1817 in England, two young cousins, Cecilia living in
the country and Kate in London, write letters to keep each
other informed of their exploits, which take a sinister turn
when they find themselves confronted by evil wizards

"This is a fun story that quickly draws in the reader."
Voice Youth Advocates

Other titles about Kate and Cecilia are:
The grand tour (2004)
The mislaid magician (2006)

The **thirteenth** child. Scholastic Press 2009
344p (Frontier magic) $16.99
Grades: 7 8 9 10 11 12   **Fic**
1. School stories 2. Fantasy fiction 3. Magic -- Fiction
4. Twins -- Fiction 5. Frontier and pioneer life -- Fiction
ISBN 978-0-545-03342-8; 0-545-03342-X

LC 2008-34048

Eighteen-year-old Eff must finally get over believing she
is bad luck and accept that her special training in Aphrikan
magic, and being the twin of the seventh son of a seventh
son, give her extraordinary power to combat magical creatures that threaten settlements on the western frontier.

Wrede "creates a rich world where steam dragons seem
as normal as bears, and a sympathetic character in Eff."
Publ Wkly

Wright, Bil
Putting makeup on the fat boy. Simon & Schus-
ter Books for Young Readers 2011 219p $16.99
Grades: 7 8 9 10 11 12   **Fic**
1. School stories 2. Cosmetics -- Fiction 3.
Homosexuality -- Fiction 4. Hispanic Americans --
Fiction 5. Single parent family -- Fiction
ISBN 978-1-4169-3996-2; 1-4169-3996-2

LC 2010032450

"Obviously, there's a whole lot going on in Wright's
novel, but it's handled deftly and, for the most part, believ-

ably. Best of all, Carlos is not completely defined by his
homosexuality." Booklist

When the black girl sings; [by] Bil Wright. Simon & Schuster Books for Young Readers 2007
266p $16.99; pa $5.99
Grades: 6 7 8 9 10   **Fic**
1. Divorce -- Fiction 2. Adoption -- Fiction 3. African
Americans -- Fiction
ISBN 978-1-4169-3995-5; 1-4169-3995-4; 978-1-
4169-4003-6 pa; 1-4169-4003-0 pa

LC 2006030837

Adopted by white parents and sent to an exclusive Connecticut girls' school where she is the only black student,
fourteen-year-old Lahni Schuler feels like an outcast, particularly when her parents separate, but after attending a local church where she hears gospel music for the first time,
she finds her voice.

"Readers will enjoy the distinctive characters, lively dialogue, and palette of adolescent and racial insecurities in this
contemporary, upbeat story." SLJ

Wright, Denis
Violence 101; a novel. G. P. Putnam's Sons
2010 213p $16.99
Grades: 8 9 10   **Fic**
1. Genius -- Fiction 2. Violence -- Fiction 3.
Reformatories -- Fiction 4. Race relations -- Fiction
ISBN 978-0-399-25493-2; 0-399-25493-5

LC 2010-02851

First published 2007 in New Zealand

In a New Zealand reformatory, Hamish Graham, an extremely intelligent fourteen-year-old who believes in the
compulsory study of violence, learns that it is not always
the answer.

"Wright's novel is clever and biting, a tragedy of society's failure to deal with kids like Hamish and a satire of
society's winking condemnations of violence. Hamish's actions can be revolting, despite his justifications, but he still
draws empathy as a product of the environment at large.
Hardly a comfortable book to read, but a gripping one."
Publ Wkly

Wulffson, Don L.
Soldier X. Viking 2001 226p $15.99; pa $6.99
Grades: 7 8 9 10   **Fic**
1. World War, 1939-1945 -- Fiction 2. World War,
1939-1945 -- Campaigns -- Soviet Union
ISBN 0-670-88863-X; 0-14-250073-9 pa

LC 99-49418

In 1943 sixteen-year-old Erik experiences the horrors of
war when he is drafted into the German army and sent to
fight on the Russian front

"Erik's first-person narrative records battlefield sequences with an unflinching—and occasionally numbing—brutality, in a story notable for its unusual perspective." Horn
Book Guide

Wunder, Wendy
★ The **probability** of miracles. Razorbill 2011
360p $17.99

Grades: 8 9 10 11 12   **Fic**
1. Death -- Fiction 2. Cancer -- Fiction 3. Miracles -- Fiction
ISBN 978-1-59514-368-6; 1-59514-368-8

"Faced with death, one teen discovers life in this bittersweet debut. . . . Cynical and loner Campbell Cooper (an Italian-Samoan-American) gave up on magic after her parents divorced, her father died and she developed neuroblastoma. . . . Having exhausted Western medicine, her single mother suggests spending the summer after Cam's graduation in Promise, Maine, a hidden town . . . known to have mysterious healing powers. . . . Exploring both sides of Cam's heritage, the story unfolds through narration as beautiful as the sun's daily 'everlasting gobstopper descent behind the lighthouse.' Irreverent humor, quirky small-town charm and surprises along the way help readers brace themselves for the tearjerker ending." Kirkus

Wynne-Jones, Tim
The **boy** in the burning house. Farrar, Straus & Giroux 2001 213p hardcover o.p. pa $5.95
Grades: 6 7 8 9   **Fic**
1. Mystery fiction
ISBN 0-374-30930-2; 0-374-40887-4 pa
LC 99-89534

First published 2000 in Canada
Trying to solve the mystery of his father's disappearance from their rural Canadian community, fourteen-year-old Jim gets help from the disturbed Ruth Rose, who suspects her stepfather, a local pastor
"A gripping, fast-moving plot offers the pure adrenaline rush of a thriller." Horn Book Guide

Wyss, Thelma Hatch
Bear dancer; the story of a Ute girl. Margaret K. McElderry Books 2005 181p il $15.95
Grades: 5 6 7 8   **Fic**
1. Ute Indians -- Fiction
ISBN 1-4169-0285-6
LC 2005-40620

In late nineteenth-century Colorado, Elk Girl, sister of Ute chief Ouray, is captured by Cheyenne and Arapaho warriors, rescued by the white "enemy," and finally returned to her home. Includes historical notes.
"This fascinating story is based on a real person. . . . An excellent addition to historical-fiction collections." SLJ

Yancey, Richard
The **extraordinary** adventures of Alfred Kropp; by Rick Yancey. Bloomsbury Pub. 2005 339p $16.95; pa $7.95
Grades: 7 8 9 10   **Fic**
1. Adventure fiction 2. Kings 3. Orphans -- Fiction
ISBN 1-58234-693-3; 1-59990-044-0 pa
LC 2005-13044

Through a series of dangerous and violent misadventures, teenage loser Alfred Kropp rescues King Arthur's legendary sword Excalibur from the forces of evil.
"True to its action-adventure genre, the story is light-hearted, entertaining, occasionally half-witted, but by and large fun." SLJ
Other titles about Alfred Kropp are:

Alfred Kropp: the seal of Solomon (2007)
Alfred Kropp: the thirteenth skull (2008)

Yang, Dori Jones
Daughter of Xanadu. Delacorte Press 2011 336p map $17.99
Grades: 7 8 9 10 11 12   **Fic**
1. Travelers 2. Love stories 3. Kings 4. Travel writers 5. Sex role -- Fiction 6. Soldiers -- Fiction
ISBN 0385739230; 0385907788; 9780385739238; 9780385907781
LC 2009-53652

Emmajin, the sixteen-year-old granddaughter of Khublai Khan, becomes a warrior and falls in love with explorer Marco Polo in thirteenth-century China.
"Daughter of Xanadu offers rich descriptions and vivid depictions of fictional characters and historical figures, making them charming and believable. A colorful and compelling read." SLJ

Yee, Lisa
Absolutely Maybe. Arthur A. Levine Books 2009 274p $16.99
Grades: 8 9 10 11 12   **Fic**
1. Fathers -- Fiction 2. Runaway teenagers -- Fiction 3. Mother-daughter relationship -- Fiction
ISBN 978-0-439-83844-3; 0-439-83844-4
LC 2008-17787

When living with her mother, an alcoholic ex-beauty queen, becomes unbearable, almost seventeen-year-old Maybelline "Maybe" Chestnut runs away to California, where she finds work on a taco truck and tries to track down her birth father.
"The characters are complex and their friendships layered—they sweep readers up in their path." Publ Wkly

Millicent Min, girl genius. Arthur A. Levine Books 2003 248p $16.95; pa $4.99
Grades: 5 6 7   **Fic**
1. School stories 2. Gifted children -- Fiction 3. Chinese Americans -- Fiction
ISBN 0-439-42519-0; 0-439-42520-4 pa
LC 2003-3747

"At the tender age of eleven, Millicent Min has completed her junior year of high school. Summer school is Millie's idea of fun, so she is excited that her parents are allowing her to take a college poetry course. . . . The tension between Millie's formal, overly intellectual way of expressing herself and her emotional immaturity makes her a very funny narrator. . . . Readers considerably older than Millicent's eleven years will enjoy this strong debut novel." Voice Youth Advocates
Other titles about Millicent Min and her friends are:
Stanford Wong flunks big-time (2005)
So totally Emily Ebers (2007)

Warp speed. Arthur A. Levine Books 2011 310p $16.99
Grades: 5 6 7 8   **Fic**
1. School stories 2. Bullies -- Fiction 3. Popularity

-- Fiction 4. Family life -- Fiction
ISBN 978-0-545-12276-4; 0-545-12276-7

LC 2010-24228

"Yee's combination of humor and sympathy works a charm here, giving Marley a life of his own and a chance at success in this solid addition to her prismatic look at middle school." Kirkus

Yee, Paul

Learning to fly; [by] Paul Yee. Orca Book Pub. 2008 108p (Orca soundings) $16.95

Grades: 7 8 9 10   Fic

1. Chinese -- Fiction 2. Drug abuse -- Fiction 3. Friendship -- Fiction 4. Immigrants -- Fiction 5. Prejudices -- Fiction 6. Native Americans -- Fiction
ISBN 978-1-55143-955-6; 1-55143-955-7

"Jason Chen, 17, wants to leave his small town in Canada and return to China. . . . His white high-school teachers do not know how smart he is, and his classmates jeer at him. Driven to join the crowd of potheads, he bonds especially with his Native American classmate, Charles ('Chief'). Narrated in Jason's wry, first-person, present-tense narrative, Yee's slim novel packs in a lot. . . . The clipped dialogue perfectly echoes the contemporary scene, the harsh prejudice felt by the new immigrant and the Native American, and their gripping friendship story." Booklist

Yelchin, Eugene

★ **Breaking** Stalin's nose; written and illustrated by Eugene Yelchin. Henry Holt and Company 2011 140p il $15.99

Grades: 4 5 6 7   Fic

1. Communism -- Fiction 2. Father-son relationship -- Fiction
ISBN 0-8050-9216-1; 978-0-8050-9216-5

LC 2011005792

In the Stalinist era of the Soviet Union, ten-year-old Sasha idolizes his father, a devoted Communist, but when police take his father away and leave Sasha homeless, he is forced to examine his own perceptions, values, and beliefs.

"Readers will quickly pick up on the dichotomy between Sasha's ardent beliefs and the reality of life under Stalinism, and be glad for his ultimate disillusion, even as they worry for his future. An author's note concisely presents the chilling historical background and personal connection that underlie the story." Publ Wkly

Yeomans, Ellen

Rubber houses; a novel. Little, Brown and Company 2007 152p $15.99

Grades: 7 8 9 10   Fic

1. Novels in verse 2. Death -- Fiction 3. Siblings -- Fiction 4. Bereavement -- Fiction
ISBN 978-0-316-10647-4; 0-316-10647-X

LC 2005-37297

A novel in verse that relates seventeen-year-old Kit's experiences as her younger brother is diagnosed with and dies of cancer and as she withdraws into and gradually emerges from her grief.

"This slim work speaks volumes about the grieving process. Yeomans has very precisely selected her words to convey the fear and the grief that Kit feels." SLJ

Yep, Laurence, 1948-

City of fire. Tom Doherty Associates 2009 320p $15.99

Grades: 5 6 7 8   Fic

1. Fantasy fiction 2. Magic -- Fiction 3. Dragons -- Fiction
ISBN 978-0-7653-1924-1; 0-7653-1924-1

LC 2009016737

Twelve-year-old Scirye and her companions travel to Houlani, a new Hawaiian island created by magic, where they enlist the help of volcano goddess Pele in an attempt to stop an evil dragon and a mysterious man from altering the universe.

"Readers will be on tenterhooks awaiting the next episode of this exhilarating chase." Booklist

City of ice. Tor 2011 383p $17.99

Grades: 5 6 7 8   Fic

1. Fantasy fiction 2. Magic -- Fiction 3. Dragons -- Fiction
ISBN 978-0-7653-1925-8; 0-7653-1925-X

LC 2011007411

From the islands of Hawaii, Scirye and her loyal companions pursue the villainous Mr. Roland and evil dragon Badik all the way to the city of Nova Hafnia in the icy Arctic Circle, to prevent Roland from obtaining the power to alter the universe.

"Readers who enjoy inner conflicts, barbed dialogue, casts replete with supernatural creatures and fantasy epics that don't take themselves too seriously will find it a treat." Kirkus

★ **Dragon** road; Golden Mountain chronicles: 1939. HarperCollins 2008 291p $16.99; lib bdg $17.89

Grades: 6 7 8 9   Fic

1. Basketball -- Fiction 2. Chinese Americans -- Fiction 3. Great Depression, 1929-1939 -- Fiction
ISBN 978-0-06-027520-4; 0-06-027520-0; 978-0-06-027521-1 lib bdg; 0-06-027521-9 lib bdg

LC 2008-00784

In 1939, unable to find regular jobs because of the Great Depression, long-time friends Cal Chin and Barney Young tour the country as members of a Chinese American basketball team.

"As always, Yep's history is impeccable; now he's written an episode with appeal to basketball fans as well." Booklist

Includes bibliographical references

★ **Dragon's** gate; Golden Mountain chronicles: 1867. HarperCollins Pubs. 1993 273p $16.99; pa $6.99

Grades: 6 7 8 9   Fic

1. Railroads -- Fiction 2. Young adult literature -- Works 3. Chinese -- United States -- Fiction
ISBN 0-06-022971-3; 0-06-440489-7 pa

LC 92-43649

A Newbery Medal honor book, 1994

When he accidentally kills a Manchu, a fifteen-year-old Chinese boy is sent to America to join his father, an uncle, and other Chinese working to build a tunnel for the transcontinental railroad through the Sierra Nevada mountains in 1867

"Yep has succeeded in realizing the primary characters and the irrepressibly dramatic story. . . . The carefully researched details will move students to thought and discussion." Bull Cent Child Books

Dragons of silk. Harper 2011 339p $15.99

Grades: 6 7 8 9   **Fic**

1. Silkworms -- Fiction 2. Chinese Americans -- Fiction
ISBN 978-0-06-027518-1; 0-06-027518-9
LC 2011016553

Four generations of Chinese and Chinese-American girls, beginning in 1835, are tied together by the tradition of raising silkworms and the legacy of the legendary Weaving Maid.

"Yep doesn't shy away from some harsh historical truths: the pervasiveness of opium addiction, bloody battles erupting between silk-factory owners and independent weavers and severe exclusion laws. The earlier chapters, while slowly paced, are more interesting, as Yep deftly conjures the culture and spirit of long-ago China. . . . Overall, however, the author captures the world of women well, and lush silk is a prominent backdrop." Kirkus

★ **Dragonwings**; Golden Mountain chronicles: 1903. Harper & Row 1975 248p lib bdg $16.89; pa $6.99

Grades: 6 7 8 9   **Fic**

1. Chinese Americans -- Fiction
ISBN 0-06-026738-0 lib bdg; 0-06-440085-9 pa
A Newbery Medal honor book, 1976

"In 1903 Moon Shadow, eight years old, leaves China for the 'Land of the Golden Mountains,' San Francisco, to be with his father, Windrider, a father he has never seen. There, beset by the trials experienced by most foreigners in America, Moonrider shares his father's dream—to fly. This dream enables Windrider to endure the mockery of the other Chinese, the poverty he suffers in this hostile place—the land of the white demons—and his loneliness for his wife and his own country." Shapiro. Fic for Youth. 3d edition

Hiroshima; a novella. Scholastic 1995 56p hardcover o.p. pa $4.99

Grades: 4 5 6 7   **Fic**

1. Hiroshima (Japan) -- Bombardment, 1945 -- Fiction
ISBN 0-590-20832-2; 0-590-20833-0 pa
LC 94-18195

"This moving and detailed narrative chronicles the dropping of the atomic bomb on Hiroshima and its effects on its citizens, especially on twelve-year-old Sachi. Based on true accounts, this book describes the horrors and sadness as well as the courage and hope that result from war." Soc Educ

★ The **star** maker. Harper 2010 100p $15.99; lib bdg $16.89

Grades: 5 6 7 8   **Fic**

1. Uncles -- Fiction 2. Family life -- Fiction 3. Chinese New Year -- Fiction 4. Chinese Americans -- Fiction
ISBN 978-0-06-025315-8; 0-06-025315-0; 978-0-06-025316-5 lib bdg; 0-06-025316-9 lib bdg
LC 2010-07856

With the help of his popular Uncle Chester, a young Chinese American boy tries hard to fulfill a promise to have firecrackers for everyone on the Chinese New Year in 1954. Includes an afterword with information about the Chinese customs portrayed in the story.

"Yep skillfully portrays the significance and emotional nature of common childhood dramas, from fears of going back on one's word to worries of losing a favorite uncle to a new girlfriend. . . . Yep has crafted other memorable characters, including Chinatown itself, which sparkle with energy and camaraderie." Publ Wkly

Includes bibliographical references

★ The **traitor**; Golden Mountain chronicles, 1885. HarperCollins Pubs. 2003 310p hardcover o.p. pa $6.99

Grades: 5 6 7 8   **Fic**

1. Friendship -- Fiction 2. Illegitimate children 3. Prejudices -- Fiction 4. Chinese Americans -- Fiction 5. Rock Springs Massacre, Rock Springs, Wyo., 1885
ISBN 0-06-027522-7; 0-06-000831-8 pa
LC 2002-22534

In 1885, a lonely illegitimate American boy and a lonely Chinese American boy develop an unlikely friendship in the midst of prejudices and racial tension in their coal mining town of Rock Springs, Wyoming

"The short chapters read quickly, and readers will become involved through the first-person voices that capture each boy's feelings of being an outsider and a traitor." Booklist

Yhard, Jo Ann

The **fossil** hunter of Sydney Mines. Nimbus Pub. 2010 169p il pa $10.95

Grades: 4 5 6 7   **Fic**

1. Mystery fiction 2. Fossils -- Fiction
ISBN 978-1-55109-760-2; 1-55109-760-5

"When a mining company wants to strip mine, Grace's father disagrees due to the damage it would do to the area's irreplaceable fossils. Grace and her father lead the protests, but the protests stop once her father disappears and is presumed dead in an accident. . . . Yhard excels at providing enough information to allow the reader to follow the clues and solve the crime. Nothing is too far-fetched nor too obvious as the suspense builds to a satisfying resolution." Libr Media Connect

Yohalem, Eve

★ **Escape** under the forever sky; a novel. Chronicle Books 2009 220p $16.99

Grades: 4 5 6 7   **Fic**

1. Kidnapping -- Fiction 2. Wilderness survival -- Fiction 3. Mother-daughter relationship -- Fiction
ISBN 978-0-8118-6653-8; 0-8118-6653-X
LC 2008-19565

As a future conservation zoologist whose mother is the United States Ambassador to Ethiopia, thirteen-year-old Lucy uses her knowledge for survival when she is kidnapped and subsequently escapes.

"Lucy's past and present are gracefully woven together, through well-integrated flashbacks, into a powerful picture of the life of a foreigner in Ethiopia. The story should appeal to all with a sense of adventure." Publ Wkly

Yolen, Jane

★ **Briar** Rose. Doherty Assocs. 1992 190p (Fairy tale series) hardcover o.p. pa $6.99

Grades: 8 9 10 11 12 Adult   **Fic**

1. Grandmothers 2. Fantasy fiction 3. Holocaust, Jewish (1933-1945) -- Fiction
ISBN 0-312-85135-9; 0-7653-4230-8 pa

LC 92-25456

"Yolen takes the story of Briar Rose (commonly known as Sleeping Beauty) and links it to the Holocaust. . . . Rebecca Berlin, a young woman who has grown up hearing her grandmother Gemma tell an unusual and frightening version of the Sleeping Beauty legend, realizes when Gemma dies that the fairy tale offers one of the very few clues she has to her grandmother's past. . . . By interpolating Gemma's vivid and imaginative story into the larger narrative, Yolen has created an engrossing novel." Publ Wkly

Curse of the Thirteenth Fey; the True Tale of Sleeping Beauty. Jane Yolen. Philomel Books 2012 290 p. $16.99

Grades: 6 7 8 9 10   **Fic**

1. Curses -- Fiction 2. Fairy tales 3. Elves -- Fiction 4. Magic -- Fiction 5. Family life -- Fiction
ISBN 0399256644; 9780399256646

LC 2011038847

In author Jane Yolen's book, "Gorse is the thirteenth . . . in a family of fairies tied to the evil king's land and made to do his bidding. . . . When accident-prone Gorse falls ill just as the family is bid to bless the new princess . . . [she] races to the castle with the last piece of magic the family has left. . . . But that is when accident, mayhem, and magic combine to drive Gorse's story into the unthinkable, threatening the baby, the kingdom, and all." (Publisher's note)

Dragon's blood. Harcourt 2004 303p (Pit dragon chronicles) pa $6.95

Grades: 6 7 8 9   **Fic**

1. Fantasy fiction 2. Dragons -- Fiction
ISBN 0-15-205126-0

LC 2003-56661

A reissue of the title first published 1982 by Delacorte Press

Jakkin, a bond boy who works as a Keeper in a dragon nursery on the planet Austar IV, secretly trains a fighting pit dragon of his own in hopes of winning his freedom

"An original and engrossing fantasy." Horn Book

Other titles in this series are:

Heart's blood (2004)
Sending of dragons (2004)
Dragon's heart (2009)

Girl in a cage; [by] Jane Yolen & Robert J. Harris. Philomel Bks. 2002 234p hardcover o.p. pa $6.99

Grades: 7 8 9 10   **Fic**

1. Kings 2. Scotland -- History -- Robert I, 1306-1329
ISBN 0-399-23627-9; 0-14-240132-3 pa

LC 2001-55978

As English armies invade Scotland in 1306, eleven-year-old Princess Marjorie, daughter of the newly crowned Scottish king, Robert the Bruce, is captured by England's King Edward Longshanks and held in a cage on public display

"Marjorie's first-person narration of her captivity and the events leading up to it is exciting and moving, and her strategies for coping with a hideous imprisonment are models of ingenuity and staying true to oneself." SLJ

Merlin; the young Merlin trilogy, book three. Harcourt Brace & Co. 1997 91p (Young Merlin trilogy) $15

Grades: 4 5 6 7   **Fic**

1. Fantasy fiction 2. Merlin (Legendary character) -- Fiction
ISBN 0-15-200814-4

LC 96-11683

Merlin, now twelve years old, begins to come into his magic while being held captive by a band of wild folk

This book is "written in stark but poetic language that will challenge some readers." SLJ

Pay the piper; [by] Jane Yolen and Adam Stemple. Tor/Starscape 2005 175p $16.95

Grades: 6 7 8 9   **Fic**

1. Fantasy fiction 2. Rock music -- Fiction
ISBN 0-7653-1158-5

When Callie interviews the band, Brass Rat, for her school newspaper, her feelings are ambivalent, but when all the children of Northampton begin to disappear on Halloween, she knows where the dangerous search must begin.

The authors "have produced a rollicking good riff on the Pied Piper. . . . The authors keep the action moving. . . . An entertaining as well as meaty read." Booklist

★ The **Rogues**; [by] Jane Yolen & Robert J. Harris. Philomel Books 2007 277p $18.99

Grades: 7 8 9 10   **Fic**

1. Adventure fiction
ISBN 978-0-399-23898-7

LC 2006-26434

After his family is evicted from their Scottish farm, fifteen-year-old Roddy forms an unlikely friendship with a notorious rogue who helps him outwit a tyrant landlord in order to find a family treasure and make his way to America.

"The suspense mounts and the plot races along flawlessly in this excellent historical adventure." Booklist

Snow in Summer. Philomel Books 2011 243p $16.99

Grades: 4 5 6 7   **Fic**

1. Fairy tales 2. Magic -- Fiction 3. Stepmothers -- Fiction
ISBN 0-399-25663-6; 978-0-399-25663-9

LC 2010044242

Recasts the tale of Snow White, setting it in West Virginia in the 1940s with a stepmother who is a snake-handler.

"This story is beautifully written and deliciously scary, with just enough differences from familiar versions to keep readers guessing." Publ Wkly

Troll Bridge; a rock 'n' roll fairy tale. [by] Jane Yolen and Adam Stemple. 1st ed.; Starscape 2006 240p $16.95; pa $5.99

Grades: 7 8 9 10   **Fic**
  1. Fairy tales 2. Musicians -- Fiction
  ISBN 0-7653-1426-6; 0-7653-5284-2 pa
                                      LC 2005034517

Sixteen-year-old harpist prodigy Moira is transported to a strange and mystical wilderness, where she finds herself in the middle of a deadly struggle between a magical fox and a monstrous troll.

"The story ends with a grand twist that is totally satisfying. The writing is filled with humor and straightforward prose, and the song lyrics are so well written that one can almost hear the music that accompanies them." SLJ

The **queen's** own fool; a novel of Mary Queen of Scots. [by] Jane Yolen and Robert J. Harris. Philomel Bks. 2000 390p pa $7.99

Grades: 7 8 9 10   **Fic**
  1. Queens
  ISBN 0-399-23380-6; 0-698-11918-5 pa
                                      LC 99-55070

When twelve-year-old Nicola leaves Troupe Brufort and serves as the fool for Mary, Queen of Scots, she experiences the political and religious upheavals in both France and Scotland

"The authors have woven fiction and historical fact into a seamless tapestry." Horn Book Guide

Yoo, David
The **detention** club. Balzer + Bray 2011 299p $16.99

Grades: 5 6 7 8   **Fic**
  1. School stories 2. Siblings -- Fiction 3. Popularity -- Fiction 4. Korean Americans -- Fiction
  ISBN 978-0-06-178378-4; 0-06-178378-1
                                      LC 2010-46211

Sixth-grader Peter Lee, in a desperate attempt to regain the popularity he had in elementary school, discovers that serving detention can win him important friends, much to the dismay of his over-achieving eighth-grade sister, Sunny.

"Even readers who guess the thief's identity early on will be entertained by the boys' hijinks and empathize with their desire to fit in." Publ Wkly

Yoo, Paula
Good enough. HarperTeen 2008 322p $16.99; lib bdg $17.89

Grades: 7 8 9 10   **Fic**
  1. Violinists -- Fiction 2. Korean Americans -- Fiction
  ISBN 978-0-06-079085-1; 978-0-06-079086-8 lib bdg
                                      LC 2007-02985

A Korean American teenager tries to please her parents by getting into an Ivy League college, but a new guy in school and her love of the violin tempt her in new directions.

"The frequent lists, . . . SAT questions, and even spam recipes are, like Patti's convincing narration, filled with laugh-out-loud lines, but it's the deeper questions about growing up with immigrant parents, confronting racism, and how best to find success and happiness that will stay with readers." Booklist

Young, E. L.
STORM : The Infinity Code. Dial 2008 311p il $16.99

Grades: 6 7 8 9   **Fic**
  1. Adventure fiction 2. Spies -- Fiction
  ISBN 978-0-8037-3265-0

In London, the teenaged geniuses of STORM, a secret organization dedicated to eliminating the world's misery through science and technology, uncover plans for a deadly weapon and race to find and dismantle it, then confront the corrupt scientist behind the scheme.

"Young's debut novel is full of unusual scientific creations—all based on real inventions. The novel is plot-driven and packed with unlikely escapes and improbable plot twists—exactly what many middle school and junior high readers crave." Voice Youth Advocates
  Other titles in this series are:
  STORM: The ghost machine (2008)
  STORM: The black sphere (2009)

Young, Karen Romano
Doodlebug; a novel in doodles. Feiwel and Friends 2010 un il $14.99

Grades: 4 5 6 7   **Fic**
  1. School stories 2. Moving -- Fiction 3. Family life -- Fiction 4. Racially mixed people -- Fiction
  ISBN 978-0-312-56156-7; 0-312-56156-3

Doreen Bussey, aka Dodo, takes the nickname Doodlebug when her family moves from Los Angeles to San Francisco and she records her experiences in a notebook with words, scribbles, and drawings.

This offers "an engaging, originial heroine, a satisfying story and lots of great pictures. . . . Some details, like the fact that the family is interracial, are shown but not stated, rewarding careful examination of the artwork. . . . Charming and thoughtful." Kirkus

Young, Moira
Blood red road. Margaret K. McElderry Books 2011 512p (Dustlands trilogy) $17.99

Grades: 6 7 8 9 10   **Fic**
  1. Science fiction 2. Twins -- Fiction 3. Orphans -- Fiction 4. Siblings -- Fiction 5. Kidnapping -- Fiction
  ISBN 978-1-4424-2998-7; 1-4424-2998-4
                                      LC 2011-03423

"Readers will . . . be riveted by the book's fast-paced mix of action and romance. It's a natural for Hunger Games fans." Publ Wkly

Young, Suzanne
A **need** so beautiful. Balzer + Bray 2011 267p $16.99; ebook $9.99

Grades: 8 9 10 11 12   **Fic**
  1. Supernatural -- Fiction 2. Good and evil -- Fiction
  ISBN 978-0-06-200824-4; 0-06-200824-2; 978-0-06-208454-5 ebook; 0-06-208454-2 ebook
                                      LC 2010040810

A compelling Need that Charlotte has felt all her life is growing stronger, forcing her to connect with people in crisis, but at the same time other changes are taking place and she is terrified by what Monroe, a doctor and family friend, says must happen next.

"Charlotte is an exceptionally likable character who demonstrates an extraordinary amount of personal growth as she learns to accept her fate. . . . A unique take on the age-old struggle of good vs. evil." SLJ

Zadoff, Allen

Food, girls, and other things I can't have. Egmont USA 2009 311p $16.99; lib bdg $19.99

Grades: 7 8 9 10   **Fic**

1. School stories 2. Obesity -- Fiction 3. Football -- Fiction 4. Popularity -- Fiction

ISBN 978-1-60684-004-7; 1-60684-004-5; 978-1-60684-051-1 lib bdg; 1-60684-051-7 lib bdg

LC 2009-16242

Fifteen-year-old Andrew Zansky, the second fattest student at his high school, joins the varsity football team to get the attention of a new girl on whom he has a crush.

"The author does not lead Andy down the expected path. When forced to make a decision, his choice is unique and the conclusion satisfying. . . . The possibly offensive locker room language is typical and lends credibility. More importantly, Andy's character is thoughtful and refreshing." SLJ

My life, the theater, and other tragedies; a novel. Egmont USA 2011 282p $16.99

Grades: 7 8 9 10   **Fic**

1. School stories 2. Theater -- Fiction 3. Bereavement -- Fiction

ISBN 978-1-60684-036-8; 1-60684-036-3

LC 2010043619

While working backstage on a high school production of 'A Midsummer Night's Dream,' sixteen-year-old Adam develops feelings for a beautiful actress—which violates an unwritten code—and begins to overcome the grief that has controlled him since his father's death nearly two years earlier.

"Zadoff captures the confusion, torn loyalties, and overwrought drama of teenage life—not to mention student theater." Publ Wkly

Zahler, Diane

The **thirteenth** princess. Harper 2009 243p

Grades: 4 5 6 7   **Fic**

1. Fairy tales 2. Magic -- Fiction 3. Sisters -- Fiction 4. Princesses -- Fiction 5. Household employees -- Fiction

ISBN 0-06-182498-4; 0-06-182499-2 lib bdg; 978-0-06-182498-2; 978-0-06-182499-9 lib bdg

LC 2009-14575

Zita, cast aside by her father and raised as a kitchen maid, learns when she is nearly twelve that she is a princess and that her twelve sisters love her, and so when she discovers they are victims of an evil enchantment, she desperately tries to save them. Inspired by the Grimm fairy tale, "The twelve dancing princesses."

Zahler "deftly and thoughtfully embellishes the tale's classic elements. . . . Zahler takes a light story and gives it gratifying depth, rounding out the characters and their motivations without betraying the source material and wrapping it all together in a graceful and cohesive romantic drama." Publ Wkly

A **true** princess. Harper 2011 182p $15.99

Grades: 4 5 6   **Fic**

1. Fairy tales 2. Friendship -- Fiction 3. Princesses -- Fiction 4. Voyages and travels -- Fiction

ISBN 978-0-06-182501-9; 0-06-182501-8

LC 2010017846

Twelve-year-old Lilia goes north to seek the family she has never known, accompanied by her friends Kai and Karina and their dog Ove, on an adventure fraught with peril, especially when they become lost in Bitra Forest, the Elf King's domain. Inspired by the Hans Christian Andersen tale, The princess and the pea.

"Readers who enjoyed . . . Zahler's The Thirteenth Princess . . . will also relish this tale." SLJ

Zalben, Jane Breskin

Four seasons. Alfred A. Knopf 2011 322p $15.99; lib bdg $18.99

Grades: 6 7 8 9   **Fic**

1. Music -- Fiction 2. Pianists -- Fiction

ISBN 978-0-375-86222-9; 0-375-86222-6; 978-0-375-96222-6 lib bdg; 0-375-96222-0 lib bdg

LC 2010-12731

Over the course of a year, thirteen-year-old Allegra Katz, a student at the demanding Julliard School and the daughter of two musicians, tries to decide whether she wants to continue to pursue a career as a concert pianist or to do something else with her life.

"The warm, complicated relationships and respectful treatment of Ally's depression animate an involving, perceptive, and reassuring novel that will hit readers where they live." Bull Cent Child Books

Zarr, Sara

★ **How** to save a life; Sara Zarr. Little, Brown 2011 341 p. $17.99

Grades: 6 7 8 9 10 11 12   **Fic**

1. Adoption -- Fiction 2. Bereavement -- Fiction 3. Mother-daughter relationship -- Fiction 4. Pregnancy -- Fiction 5. Family life -- Fiction

ISBN 9780316036061

LC 2010045832

Told from their own viewpoints, seventeen-year-old Jill, in grief over the loss of her father, and Mandy, nearly nineteen, are thrown together when Jill's mother agrees to adopt Mandy's unborn child but nothing turns out as they had anticipated.

★ The **Lucy** variations; by Sara Zarr. 1st ed. Little, Brown and Co. 2013 320 p. (hardcover) $17.99

Grades: 7 8 9 10 11 12   **Fic**

1. Pianists -- Fiction 2. Brothers and sisters -- Fiction 3. Ability -- Fiction 4. Family life -- California -- Fiction 5. Self-actualization (Psychology) -- Fiction

ISBN 031620501X; 9780316205016

LC 2012029852

In this novel, by Sara Zarr, "Lucy Beck-Moreau once had a promising future as a concert pianist. . . . Now, at sixteen, it's over. A death, and a betrayal, led her to walk away. That leaves her talented ten-year-old brother, Gus, to shoulder the full weight of the Beck-Moreau family expectations. Then Gus gets a new piano teacher who is young, kind, and interested in helping Lucy rekindle her love of piano--on her own terms." (Publisher's note)

"The third-person narration focuses entirely on Lucy but allows readers enough distance to help them understand her behavior in ways Lucy cannot. Occasional flashbacks fill out the back story. The combination of sympathetic main character and unusual social and cultural world makes this satisfying coming-of-age story stand out." Kirkus

★ **Once** was lost. Little, Brown 2009 217p $16.99
Grades: 7 8 9 10 **Fic**
1. Clergy -- Fiction 2. Alcoholism -- Fiction 3. Kidnapping -- Fiction 4. Christian life -- Fiction
ISBN 978-0-316-03604-7; 0-316-03604-8
LC 2009-25187

As the tragedy of a missing girl unfolds in her small town, fifteen-year-old Samara, who feels emotionally abandoned by her parents, begins to question her faith.

"This multilayered exploration of the intersection of the spiritual life and imperfect people features suspense and packs an emotional wallop." SLJ

★ **Sweethearts**. Little, Brown and Co. 2008 217p $16.99
Grades: 8 9 10 11 12 **Fic**
1. Love stories 2. School stories 3. Weight loss -- Fiction
ISBN 978-0-316-01455-7; 0-316-01455-9
LC 2007-41099

After losing her soul mate, Cameron, when they were nine, Jennifer, now seventeen, transformed herself from the unpopular fat girl into the beautiful and popular Jenna, but Cameron's unexpected return dredges up memories that cause both social and emotional turmoil.

"Zarr's writing is remarkable. . . . She conveys great delicacy of feeling and shades of meaning, and the realistic, moving ending will inspire excellent discussion." Booklist

Zemser, Amy Bronwen
★ **Dear** Julia. Greenwillow Books 2008 327p $16.99; lib bdg $17.89
Grades: 7 8 9 10 **Fic**
1. Cooking -- Fiction 2. Contests -- Fiction 3. Feminism -- Fiction 4. Mother-daughter relationship -- Fiction
ISBN 978-0-06-029458-8; 0-06-029458-2; 978-0-06-029459-5 lib bdg; 0-06-029459-0 lib bdg
LC 2008-3824

Shy sixteen-year-old Elaine has long dreamed of being the next Julia Child, to the dismay of her feminist mother, but when her first friend, the outrageous Lucida Sans, convinces Elaine to enter a cooking contest, anything could happen.

"Readers will laugh throughout, but Zemser never loses sight of Elaine's frailties and hopes." Publ Wkly

Zenatti, Valerie
A **bottle** in the Gaza Sea; translated by Adriana Hunter. Bloomsbury Children's Books 2008 149p il $16.95

Grades: 7 8 9 10 11 12 **Fic**
1. Letters -- Fiction 2. Israel-Arab conflicts -- Fiction
ISBN 978-1-59990-200-5; 1-59990-200-1
LC 2007-42361
Original French edition, 2005

Seventeen-year-old Tal Levine of Jerusalem, despondent over the ongoing Arab-Israeli conflict, puts her hopes for peace in a bottle and asks her brother, a military nurse in the Gaza Strip, to toss it into the sea, leading ultimately to friendship and understanding between her and an 'enemy.'

"Zenatti uses short, riveting chapters, . . . to pack a punch with readers reluctant to voracious. The overall effect is one of a haunting relationship that will help teens understand both sides of the Israeli-Palestinian conflict." Kirkus

Zephaniah, Benjamin
Face. Bloomsbury Pub. 2002 207p $15.95; pa $6.95
Grades: 7 8 9 10 **Fic**
1. Prejudices 2. Traffic accidents 3. Disfigured persons 4. Burns and scalds -- Fiction
ISBN 1-58234-774-3; 1-58234-921-5 pa
LC 2002-22758
First published 1999 in the United Kingdom

"This book will not only be enjoyed by teen readers for its entertaining story, but also for its statement about prejudice." Voice Youth Advocates

Zettel, Sarah
Dust girl; Sarah Zettel. Random House 2012 292 p. (trade : alk. paper) $17.99
Grades: 6 7 8 9 **Fic**
1. Fairies -- Fiction 2. Voyages and travels -- Fiction 3. Father-daughter relationship -- Fiction 4. Magic -- Fiction
ISBN 9780375869389; 9780375873812; 9780375969386; 9780375983184
LC 2011043310

In this book, "a mixed-race girl in Dust Bowl Kansas discovers her long-lost father isn't just a black man: He's a fairy. . . . [A] strange man . . . tells Callie secrets of her never-met father. Soon Callie's walking the dusty roads with Jack, a ragged white kid. . . . Callie and Jack dodge fairy politics and dangers, from grasshopper people to enchanted food to magic movie theaters--but the conventional dangers are no less threatening." (Kirkus Reviews)

Golden girl; by Sarah Zettel. 1st ed. Random House Inc. 2013 308 p. (The American fairy trilogy) (hardcover) $17.99; (library) $20.99
Grades: 7 8 9 10 **Fic**
1. Magic -- Fiction 2. Fairies -- Fiction 3. Racially mixed people -- Fiction
ISBN 0375869395; 9780375869396; 9780375969393
LC 2013006238

In this book, it's 1935, and Callie LeRoux has journeyed to Hollywood from Slow Run, Kan., in search of her white human mother and black fairy father. A fairy kidnap attempt is foiled by none other than the famous Renaissance man Paul Robeson, a human who seems impervious to fairy magic. . . . Callie just wants to find her parents and get the heck out of Dodge, but with a prophecy hanging over her head, it won't be easy." (Kirkus Reviews)

Zevin, Gabrielle

Because it is my blood; Gabrielle Zevin. Farrar Straus Giroux 2012 350 p. $17.99

Grades: 7 8 9 10   **Fic**
1. Crime -- Fiction 2. Criminals -- Fiction 3. High school students -- Fiction 4. Science fiction 5. Violence -- Fiction 6. Chocolate -- Fiction 7. Celebrities -- Fiction 8. Organized crime -- Fiction 9. Family life -- New York (State) -- New York -- Fiction
ISBN 0374380740; 9780374380748
                                             LC 2011036991
In Gabrielle Zeven's book, "Anya Balanchine is determined to follow the straight and narrow . . . since her release from Liberty Children's Facility . . . Unfortunately, her criminal record is making it hard for her to do that. No high school wants her with a gun possession charge . . . But when old friends return demanding that certain debts be paid, Anya is thrown right back into the criminal world that she had been determined to escape." (Macmillan)

Elsewhere. Farrar, Straus & Giroux 2005 275p $16; pa $6.95

Grades: 7 8 9 10   **Fic**
1. Death -- Fiction 2. Future life -- Fiction
ISBN 0-374-32091-8; 0-312-36746-5 pa
                                             LC 2004-56279
After fifteen-year-old Liz Hall is hit by a taxi and killed, she finds herself in a place that is both like and unlike Earth, where she must adjust to her new status and figure out how to "live."
"Zevin's third-person narrative calmly, but surely guides readers through the bumpy landscape of strongly delineated characters dealing with the most difficult issue that faces all of us. A quiet book that provides much to think about and discuss." SLJ

★ **Memoirs** of a teenage amnesiac. Farrar, Straus and Giroux 2007 271p $17; pa $8.99

Grades: 7 8 9 10   **Fic**
1. School stories 2. Amnesia -- Fiction 3. Friendship -- Fiction
ISBN 978-0-374-34946-2; 0-374-34946-0; 978-0-312-56128-4 pa; 0-312-56128-8 pa
                                             LC 2006-35287
After a nasty fall, Naomi realizes that she has no memory of the last four years and finds herself reassessing every aspect of her life.
This is a "sensitive, joyful novel. . . . Pulled by the the heart-bruising love story, readers will pause to contemplate irresistible questions." Booklist

Zhang, Kat

What's left of me. Harper 2012 343 p. $17.99

Grades: 8 9 10 11 12   **Fic**
1. Twins 2. Dystopian fiction 3. Science fiction
ISBN 0062114875; 9780062114877
                                             LC 2012289047
This novel, by Kat Zhang, is the first book of the young adult science fiction "Hybrid Chronicles." "Eva and Addie

started out the same way as everyone else--two souls woven together in one body, taking turns controlling their movements. . . . Finally Addie was pronounced healthy and Eva was declared gone. Except, she wasn't. . . . For the past three years, Eva has clung to the remnants of her life, . . . for a chance to smile, to twirl, to speak, Eva will do anything." (Publisher's note)

Ziegler, Jennifer

How not to be popular. Delacorte Press 2008 339p $15.99; lib bdg $18.99

Grades: 7 8 9 10 11 12   **Fic**
1. School stories 2. Hippies -- Fiction 3. Popularity -- Fiction
ISBN 978-0-385-73465-3; 0-385-73465-4; 978-0-385-90463-6 lib bdg; 0-385-90463-0 lib bdg
                                             LC 2007-27603
Seventeen-year-old Sugar Magnolia Dempsey is tired of leaving friends behind every time her hippie parents decide to move, but her plan to be unpopular at her new school backfires when other students join her on the path to "supreme dorkdom."
This "balances laugh-out-loud, sardonic commentary with earnest reflections that will directly connect with teens." Booklist

Zielin, Lara

Donut days. G.P. Putnam's Sons 2009 246p $16.99

Grades: 7 8 9 10   **Fic**
1. Clergy -- Fiction 2. Sex role -- Fiction 3. Journalism -- Fiction 4. Christian life -- Fiction
ISBN 978-0-399-25066-8; 0-399-25066-2
                                             LC 2008-26138
During a camp-out promoting the opening of a donut shop in a small Minnesota town, sixteen-year-old Emma, an aspiring journalist, begins to connect an ongoing pollution investigation with the turmoil in the evangelical Christian church where her parents are pastors.
This is a "sweet, satisfying treat. . . . Teens will enjoy this lighter look at some serious issues of faith and family." SLJ

Zimmer, Tracie Vaughn

42 miles; illustrated by Elaine Clayton. Clarion Books 2008 73p il $16

Grades: 4 5 6   **Fic**
1. Novels in verse 2. Divorce -- Fiction 3. Farm life -- Fiction 4. Family life -- Fiction 5. City and town life -- Fiction
ISBN 978-0-618-61867-5; 0-618-61867-8
                                             LC 2007-31032
As her thirteenth birthday approaches, JoEllen decides to bring together her two separate lives—one as Joey, who enjoys weekends with her father and other relatives on a farm, and another as Ellen, who lives with her mother in an apartment near her school and friends.
"Using free verse, Zimmer shows the richness in both places, while black-and-white composit illustrations bright the bits and pieces together." Booklist

Reaching for sun. Bloomsbury Children's Books 2007 192p $14.95

Grades: 7 8 9 10   **Fic**
1. Novels in verse 2. Friendship -- Fiction 3. Cerebral palsy -- Fiction
ISBN 1-59990-037-8

LC 2006-13197

Josie, who lives with her mother and grandmother and has cerebral palsy, befriends a boy who moves into one of the rich houses behind her old farmhouse.

"Written in verse, this quick-reading, appealing story will capture readers' hearts with its winsome heroine and affecting situations." Booklist

Zindel, Paul

★ The **Pigman**; a novel. Harper & Row 1968 182p hardcover o.p. pa $6.99

Grades: 7 8 9 10   **Fic**
ISBN 0-06-026828-X; 0-06-0757353-3 pa
ALA YALSA Margaret A. Edwards Award (2002)

"John Conlan and Lorraine Jensen, high school sophomores, are both troubled young people who have problems at home. They become friendly with an elderly widower, Mr. Pignati, who welcomes them into his home and shares with them his simple pleasures, including his collection of ceramic pigs, of which he is proud. When the Pigman, as the young people call him, goes to the hospital after a heart attack, they take advantage of his house for a party that becomes destructive. The consequences are tragic and propel the two young friends into more responsible behavior." Shapiro. Fic for Youth. 3d edition

Another title about the Pigman is:
The Pigman's legacy (1980)

Zink, Michelle

Guardian of the Gate. Little, Brown 2010 340p $17.99

Grades: 7 8 9 10   **Fic**
1. Magic -- Fiction 2. Twins -- Fiction 3. Sisters -- Fiction 4. Supernatural -- Fiction 5. Good and evil -- Fiction
ISBN 978-0-316-03447-0; 0-316-03447-9

In 1891 London, sixteen-year-old orphan Lia Milthorpe continues her quest to end an ancient prophecy requiring her to search for missing pages and human "keys" and develop her powers for an inevitable final confrontation with her twin sister Alice.

"An intense and captivating story that gives a whole new meaning to sibling rivalry." Voice Youth Advocates

★ **Prophecy** of the sisters. Little, Brown 2009 343p $17.99

Grades: 7 8 9 10   **Fic**
1. Twins -- Fiction 2. Sisters -- Fiction 3. Supernatural -- Fiction 4. Good and evil -- Fiction 5. Young adult literature -- Works
ISBN 978-0-316-02742-7; 0-316-02742-1

LC 2008-45290

In late nineteenth-century New York state, wealthy sixteen-year-old twin sisters Lia and Alice Milthorpe find that they are on opposite sides of an ancient prophecy that has destroyed their parents and seeks to do even more harm.

"This arresting story takes readers to other planes of existence." Booklist

Zinn, Bridget

Poison; by Bridget Zinn. 1st ed. Disney/Hyperion Books 2013 276 p. (hardcover) $16.99

Grades: 7 8 9 10 11 12   **Fic**
1. Magic -- Fiction 2. Heroes -- Fiction 3. Princesses -- Fiction 4. Impersonation -- Fiction 5. Fugitives from justice -- Fiction
ISBN 1423139933; 9781423139935

LC 2012008693

In this novel, sixteen-year-old "Kyra is on the run. She may be one of the Kingdom of Mohr's most highly skilled potions masters, but she has also just tried—and failed—to poison Princess Ariana. And Kyra is determined to finish her mission even if it means killing her best friend. . . . In order to save her kingdom from a nefarious plot, Kyra will have to come to terms with all the gifts she possesses." (School Library Journal)

Zombie mommy; illustrations by Kurt Cyrus. Beach Lane Books 2011 il (Pals in peril) $16.99

Grades: 4 5 6 7   **Fic**
1. Adventure fiction 2. Zombies -- Fiction
ISBN 978-1-4169-8641-6; 1-4169-8641-3

LC 2010047668

Home from their latest Delaware crime-stopping adventures, Lily Gefelty and her friends Katie, Jasper, and Drgnan Pghlik face killer tarantulas and teenaged vampires when they try to rescue Lily's mother, who has been possessed by a menacing zombie that wants to take over the world.

"Ridiculous in all the best ways." Kirkus

Zucker, Naomi Flink

★ **Callie's** rules; by Naomi Zucker. Egmont USA 2009 240p $15.99; lib bdg $18.99

Grades: 4 5 6 7   **Fic**
1. School stories 2. Halloween -- Fiction 3. Family life -- Fiction
ISBN 978-1-60684-027-6; 1-60684-027-4; 978-1-60684-052-8 lib bdg; 1-60684-052-5 lib bdg

LC 2009-15419

Eleven-year-old Callie Jones tries to keep track of all the rules for fitting in that other middle schoolers seem to know, but when the town decides to replace Halloween with an Autumn Festival, Callie leads her large family in an unusual protest.

"Callie herself is both funny and resourceful. Worthwhile and entertaining." Kirkus

Write on, Callie Jones; by Naomi Zucker. Egmont USA 2010 188p $15.99

Grades: 4 5 6 7   **Fic**
1. School stories 2. Authorship -- Fiction 3. Newspapers -- Fiction
ISBN 978-1-60684-028-3; 1-60684-028-2

LC 2010-23134

As she continues to establish rules for navigating middle school, aspiring author Callie writes for the school newspaper until the principal cancels her article and Callie's quest to have her voice heard leads to a series of unexpected consequences.

"Playful, entertaining writing peppers this novel. . . . A quick, easy read for fans of the first book." SLJ

Zuckerman, Linda

A **taste** for rabbit. Arthur A. Levine Books 2007
310p $16.99

Grades: 7 8 9 10   **Fic**

1. Foxes -- Fiction 2. Animals -- Fiction 3. Rabbits
-- Fiction 4. Resistance to government -- Fiction
ISBN 0-439-86977-3; 978-0-439-86977-5

LC 2007-7787

Quentin, a rabbit who lives in a walled compound run
by a militaristic government, must join forces with Harry,
a fox, to stop the sinister disappearances of outspoken and
rebellious rabbit citizens.

"The blend of adventure, mystery and morality in this
heroic tale of honor and friendship will appeal to middle-
school fantasy fans." Publ Wkly

Zusak, Markus

★ The **book** thief. Knopf 2006 552p il $16.95;
lib bdg $18.99

Grades: 8 9 10 11 12   **Fic**

1. Death -- Fiction 2. Jews -- Germany -- Fiction 3.
Books and reading -- Fiction 4. Holocaust, 1933-1945
-- Fiction 5. World War, 1939-1945 -- Fiction
ISBN 0-375-83100-2; 0-375-93100-7 lib bdg

LC 2005-08942

Michael L. Printz Award honor book, 2007

Trying to make sense of the horrors of World War II,
Death relates the story of Liesel—a young German girl
whose book-stealing and storytelling talents help sustain
her family and the Jewish man they are hiding, as well as
their neighbors.

"This hefty volume is an achievement—a challenging
book in both length and subject, and best suited to sophisticated older readers." Publ Wkly

Zweig, Eric

Fever season. Dundurn Press 2009 254p $10

Grades: 7 8 9 10   **Fic**

1. Hockey -- Fiction 2. Orphans -- Fiction 3. Influenza
-- Fiction
ISBN 978-1-55488-432-2; 1-55488-432-2

When David is orphaned by the Spanish influenza outbreak in 1919 Montreal, he needs to find his long-lost uncle
if he wants to avoid the orphanage, and he gets his chance
when he gets a job with the Montreal Canadiens.

"Zweig tells a good story while he weaves a vibrant tapestry of life in the early 1900's. . . . Dramatic descriptions of
war nightmares and flu sick-rooms hung with bleach-dipped
sheets make history come alive. Interesting tidbits about
hockey and its stars such as Bad Joe Hall, coupled with play-
by-play action and French Canadian expressions, give the
story true hockey flavor." Voice Youth Advocates

Bad Island; created, written, and drawn by Doug
TenNapel. Graphix 2011 218p il $24.99

Grades: 6 7 8 9 10   **Fic**

1. Adventure graphic novels 2. Family life -- Graphic
novels 3. Extraterrestrial beings -- Graphic novels 4.
Father-son relationship -- Graphic novels 5. Survival
after airplane accidents, shipwrecks, etc. -- Graphic

novels
ISBN 0545314798; 0545314801 pa; 9780545314794;
9780545314800 pa

LC 2011276008

"Dad has decided to take Reese . . . and his sister, Janine, on a fishing trip. The vacation takes an unexpected
turn when their boat capsizes during a storm and they find
themselves marooned on a strange island. To their horror,
the family slowly realizes that the island is the submerged
body of a giant creature, escaped from another world. The
story alternates between the shipwreck survivors and the faraway world that created this 'island.'. . . The vibrant color
palette used in the family's story contrasts with the grays
and browns of the monster world. . . . Expressive wide-eyed
faces perfectly capture emotions while the effective use of
humor . . . keeps the tension from becoming overwhelming. TenNapel has crafted another rip-roaring adventure with
wide audience appeal." SLJ

Cornered; 14 stories of bullying and defiance. [edit-
ed by] Rhoda Belleza. Running Press Teens 2012
383 p. $9.95

Grades: 7 8 9 10 11 12   **Fic**

1. Short stories 2. School stories 3. Bullies -- Fiction
ISBN 9780762444281

LC 2011943133

This book is a "bully-themed anthology" of stories that
focus "not only on teens who are targets of bullying, but also
those who perpetrate it—and many . . . do both. Bullying [in
the stories] takes many forms, including a teacher ridiculing
students, a viral racist email and hazing on a soccer team.
The contributors largely delve into bullies' behavior without
resting on cliché . . . Most contributors also . . . observe
that family dynamics can have as much impact as those at
school." (Kirkus)

S C   STORY COLLECTIONS

13; thirteen stories that capture the agony and ecstasy of being thirteen. edited by James Howe.
Atheneum Books for Young Readers 2003 278p
$16.95; pa $7.99

Grades: 4 5 6 7   **S C**

1. Short stories
ISBN 0-689-82863-2; 1-416-92684-4 pa

"The stories are a mixture of humor, pathos, and poignancy, and most are based on personal experiences. . . .
Howe has chosen excellent authors for this volume and they
have written oh-so-true stories about that wonderful, terrible
first year of being a teenager. " SLJ

666: the number of the beast. Point 2007 330p
$14.99

Grades: 7 8 9 10 11 12   **S C**

1. Short stories 2. Horror fiction
ISBN 978-0-545-02117-3; 0-545-02117-0

LC 2007-20058

Eighteen winners of the Bram Stoker award contribute
tales of evil, darkness, and beasts.

"Vampires, werewolves, evil fairies—all the usual suspects line up in this horror-star-studded collection of stories

created to creep readers out. . . . The cover alone, featuring a beast with blood-red fangs, will have this book flying off the shelves. . . . Horror-seekers . . . will find something here to keep them up nights." Voice Youth Advocates

Abrahams, Peter

Up all night; a short story collection. [by] Peter Abrahams [et al.]; with an introduction by Laura Geringer. Laura Geringer Books/HarperTeen 2008 227p il $16.99; lib bdg $17.89; pa $8.99

Grades: 8 9 10 11 12   S C

1. Short stories 2. Night -- Fiction
ISBN 978-0-06-137076-2; 0-06-137076-2; 978-0-06-137077-9 lib bdg; 0-06-137077-0 lib bdg; 978-0-06-137078-6 pa; 0-06-137078-9 pa

LC 2007-21355

"Six top teen authors have contributed stories to this winning collection. Abrahams has written a modern ghost story, Libba Bray tells of a wild night partying with friends that changes a girl's relationship with her estranged father, and David Levithan gives readers a magical take on life in the city. Patricia McCormick takes a hard look at freedom and power, Sarah Weeks writes of responsibility with humor, and Yang tops off the book in his own graphic-novel style. Each story shines in its own way." SLJ

Alexander, Lloyd

★ The **foundling** and other tales of Prydain; rev & expanded ed; Holt & Co. 1999 98p hardcover o.p. pa $5.99

Grades: 5 6 7 8   S C

1. Fantasy 2. Short stories
ISBN 0-8050-6130-4; 0-8050-8053-8 pa

LC 98-42807

First published 1973; this revised and expanded edition includes two additional stories Coll and his white pig and The truthful harp, first published separately 1965 and 1967 respectively

Eight short stories dealing with events that preceded the birth of Taran, the Assistant Pig-Keeper and key figure in the author's five works on the Kingdom of Prydain which began with The book of three

"The stories are written with vivid grace and humor." Chicago. Children's Book Center [review of 1973 edition]

★ **American** eyes; new Asian-American short stories for young adults. introduction by Cynthia Kadohata. Fawcett Juniper 1996 138p pa $6.99

Grades: 7 8 9 10   S C

1. Short stories 2. Asian Americans -- Fiction
ISBN 0-449-70448-3

First published 1994 by Holt & Co.

These ten stories reflect the conflict Asian Americans face in balancing an ancient heritage and an unknown future.

This collection is distinguished by the "excellent quality of its writing, the acuteness of characterization, and the sophistication of its themes." SLJ

Amnesty International

Free? : stories about human rights; [edited by] Amnesty International. Candlewick Press 2010 202p il $17.99; pa $8.99

Grades: 7 8 9 10   S C

1. Short stories 2. Freedom -- Fiction 3. Human rights -- Fiction
ISBN 978-0-7636-4703-2; 0-7636-4703-9; 978-0-7636-4926-5 pa; 0-7636-4926-0 pa

LC 2009-14720

An anthology of fourteen stories by young adult authors from around the world, on such themes as asylum, law, education, and faith, compiled in honor of the sixtieth anniversary of the Universal Declaration of Human Rights.

"Margaret Mahy writes about class with wit and intensity, as does Jamila Gavin, who sets the class war in India, where a young girl's family throws her out for resisting an arranged marriage. . . . David Almond explores school power plays in a story about a boy who says no to a popular bully. Hurricane Katrina is Rita Williams-Garcia's setting. Two contemporary Palestinian stories compare the current occupation with Native American experiences of oppression. . . . Sure to spark discussion and perhaps participation in Amnesty International." Booklist

Appelt, Kathi

Kissing Tennessee and other stories from the Stardust Dance. Harcourt 2000 118p hardcover o.p. pa $5.95

Grades: 6 7 8 9   S C

1. Dance 2. Schools 3. Short stories 4. School stories 5. Interpersonal relations
ISBN 0-15-202249-X; 0-15-205127-9 pa

LC 99-50505

Graduating eighth graders relate their stories of love and heartbreak that have brought them to Dogwood Junior High's magical Stardust Dance.

"This collection will spark conversation in contemporary literature discussions, will quietly unsettle readers, and will elevate the quality of short-story collections." SLJ

Asimov, Isaac

I, robot; Bantam hardcover ed.; Bantam Books 2004 224p (Robot series) $24; pa $7.99

Grades: 7 8 9 10 11 12 Adult   S C

1. Robots 2. Short stories 3. Science fiction
ISBN 0-553-80370-0; 0-553-29438-5 pa

LC 2003-69139

First published 1950 by Gnome Press

"These loosely connected stories cover the career of Dr. Susan Calvin and United States Robots, the industry that she heads, from the time of the public's early distrust of these robots to its later dependency on them. This collection is an important introduction to a theme often found in science fiction: the encroachment of technology on our lives." Shapiro. Fic for Youth. 3d edition

Aspin, Diana

Ordinary miracles. Red Deer Press 2003 168p (Northern Lights young novels) pa $7.95

Grades: 7 8 9 10   S C
   1. Short stories
   ISBN 0-88995-277-9

A collection of 13 short stories concerning life in a small Canadian community, covering such topics as an old man's memories of abandonment by his mother and his abusive life as an orphan, a teen's struggle with his sexuality, and issues such as alcoholism, death, adultery, and poverty.

This is "a riveting collection. . . . The author has created a work that leaves readers awash with feelings of empathy for each young protagonist." SLJ

Avi
  Strange happenings; five tales of transformation. Harcourt 2006 147p $15; pa $5.95
Grades: 5 6 7 8   S C
   1. Short stories 2. Supernatural -- Fiction 3. Children's literature -- Works -- Grades two through six
   ISBN 0-15-205790-0; 0-15-206461-3 pa
                      LC 2004-29579

"In this short story collection, Avi offers five fantastical tales, set in both contemporary and fairy-tale lands, that explore the notion of transformation.... The pieces are vividly imagined and shot through with a captivating, edgy spookiness, which, along with their brevity and some droll, crackling dialogue, makes them great choices for sharing aloud in class or as inspiration in creative-writing units." Booklist

  What do fish have to do with anything? and other stories; illustrated by Tracy Mitchell. Candlewick Press 1997 202p il hardcover o.p. pa $6.99
Grades: 4 5 6 7   S C
   1. Short stories
   ISBN 0-7636-0329-5; 0-7636-2319-9 pa
                       LC 97-1354

"While Avi's endings are not tidy, they are effective: each story brings its protagonist beyond childhood self-absorption to the realization that one is an integral part of a bigger picture." Horn Book

★ **Baseball** crazy: ten short stories that cover all the bases; edited by Nancy E. Mercado. Dial Books for Young Readers 2008 191p $16.99; pa $6.99
Grades: 4 5 6 7   S C
   1. Short stories 2. Baseball -- Fiction
   ISBN 978-0-8037-3162-2; 0-8037-3162-0; 978-0-14-241371-5 pa; 0-14-241371-2 pa
                     LC 2007-26649

"There's no shortage of great writing in this collection of 10 stories. Baseball unifies the entries, but there the similarities end. . . . Readers will be drawn in by the masterful storytelling." Publ Wkly

The **beastly** bride; tales of the animal people. edited by Ellen Datlow & Terri Windling; introduction by Terri Windling; selected decorations by Charles Vess. Viking 2010 500p $19.99
Grades: 8 9 10 11 12   S C
   1. Short stories 2. Children's poetry 3. Supernatural

   -- Fiction
   ISBN 978-0-670-01145-2; 0-670-01145-2
                     LC 2009-14317

A collection of stories and poems relating to animal transfiguration legends from around the world, retold and reimagined by various authors. Includes brief biographies, authors' notes, and suggestions for further reading

"The majority of these beastly tales make for fun, thoughtful, occasionally gripping, reading." Voice Youth Advocates

★ **Best** shorts; favorite short stories for sharing. selected by Avi; assisted by Carolyn Shute; afterword by Katherine Paterson; [illustrations by Chris Raschka] Houghton Mifflin 2006 342p $16.95
Grades: 5 6 7 8   S C
   1. Short stories
   ISBN 978-0-618-47603-9; 0-618-47603-2
                     LC 2006011535

"There is no integrating theme in the 24 short stories included here—just fine writing, cultural diversity, and timeless creativity. With such strong writers as Richard Peck, Natalie Babbitt, Lloyd Alexander, and Rafe Martin, one would expect nothing less." SLJ

Book Wish Foundation
  ★ **What** you wish for; foreword by Mia Farrow. G.P. Putnam's Sons 2011 252p $17.99
Grades: 6 7 8 9   S C
   ISBN 978-0-399-25454-3; 0-399-25454-4
                     LC 2011003215

A collection of stories and poems with the theme of wishes.

This is a "moving anthology. . . . There isn't a weak story in the book, but, of course, a few are standouts. . . . Here's a wish: that this collection might find the widest readership possible." Booklist

★ **Brave** new words; the Oxford dictionary of science fiction. edited by Jeffrey Prucher; introduction by Gene Wolfe. Oxford University Press 2007 xxxi, 342p $29.95
Grades: 7 8 9 10 11 12 Adult   S C
   1. Reference books 2. Science fiction -- Dictionaries
   ISBN 978-0-19-530567-8; 0-19-530567-1
                     LC 2006-37280

"This new science fiction lexicon . . . is an important and entertaining reference source for any science fiction writer, magazine editor, fan, neophyte reader, or librarian." Choice
  Includes bibliographical references

Carter, Alden R.
  ★ **Love,** football, and other contact sports. Holiday House 2006 261p $16.95
Grades: 8 9 10 11 12   S C
   1. Short stories 2. School stories 3. Football -- Fiction
   ISBN 978-0-8234-1975-3; 0-8234-1975-4
                     LC 2005-46094

This "collection of short stories, which revolves around Argyle West High School's football team, features an ensemble cast of students during their sophomore, junior, and senior years. . . . Written with sensitivity and conviction, the realistic stories are leavened with occasional, often ironic humor." Booklist

★ The **chronicles** of Harris Burdick; 14 amazing authors tell the tales. Houghton Mifflin Harcourt 2011 un il $24.99

Grades: 5 6 7 8 9   S C

1. Short stories

ISBN 978-0-547-54810-4; 0-547-54810-9; 0547548109; 9780547548104

LC 2011006564

"Van Allsburg's The Mysteries of Harris Burdick, published in 1984, paired foreboding sentences with cryptic, highly detailed charcoal-pencil illustrations. With mostly stimulating, sometimes conventional results, seasoned authors (and Van Allsburg himself) play the game children have for decades, incorporating the sentences and visual cues into new stories . . . that expand on the original's enigmas. The liveliest entries pick up on Van Allsburg's haunting ambiguity: Jon Scieszka ends with a cliffhanger, Gregory Maguire weaves a complex tale of magic, and M.T. Anderson concocts a chilling Halloween offering. For a lakeside picture of two children, Sherman Alexie writes a sinister narrative about exasperating twins who pretend to have a third sibling, until their creepy prank backfires. . . . This star-studded exercise in creative writing tests the wits of favorite authors and shows readers how even the big shots hone their craft." Publ Wkly

Cleavage; breakaway fiction for real girls. edited by Deb Loughead & Jocelyn Shipley. Sumach Press 2008 186p il pa $12.95

Grades: 8 9 10 11 12   S C

1. Short stories 2. Teenage girls -- Fiction 3. Young adult literature -- Works 4. Mother-daughter relationship -- Fiction 5. Short stories -- Collections

ISBN 978-1-894549-76-9; 1-894549-76-7

"Alternately edgy, charming, funny, and sweet, these 15 stories address issues confronting adolescents. Integral to each selection is the complicated relationship between the girls and their mothers. . . . The selections touch on the multiple meanings of the word 'cleavage,' and together form an aptly named collection of stories about body image and mothers and daughters coming together and growing apart. A fresh, honest, and entertaining anthology." SLJ

The **Color** of absence; 12 stories about loss and hope. edited by James Howe. Atheneum Bks. for Young Readers 2001 238p hardcover o.p. pa $6.99

Grades: 7 8 9 10   S C

1. Short stories 2. Loss (Psychology) 3. Short stories, American

ISBN 0-689-82862-4; 0-689-8567-9 pa

LC 00-44206

A collection of stories dealing with different kinds of loss experienced by young people.

"A solid choice for all collections." SLJ

Compestine, Ying Chang

★ A **banquet** for hungry ghosts; a collection of deliciously frightening tales. illustrated by Coleman Polhemus. Henry Holt and Co. 2009 180p il $16.99

Grades: 6 7 8 9 10   S C

1. Ghost stories 2. Short stories

ISBN 978-0-8050-8208-1; 0-8050-8208-5

LC 2008-50273

Presents and eight-course banquet of ghost stories centering around Chinese cooking and culture. Each story is followed by a recipe and historical notes

"The stories are laced with beautiful (as well as lurid) images and chilling illustrations of the ghosts and their victims. Like the ghosts themselves, Compestine's memorable stories should prove difficult to shake." Publ Wkly

Corsets & clockwork; 13 steampunk romances. edited by Trisha Telep. Running Press Teens 2011 437p pa $9.95

Grades: 7 8 9 10   S C

1. Love stories 2. Short stories

ISBN 978-0-7624-4092-4; 0-7624-4092-9

Collects thirteen original stories set during the Victorian era, including tales of steam-powered machines, family secrets, and love.

"While not every story is exceptional, all are engaging. Some of them contain challenging vocabulary and concepts; however, the action and romance in the other selections would make them good choices for reluctant readers. The common flaw is that the stories end too soon, just when readers have begun to fall in love with the steampunk worlds the writers have created." SLJ

Coville, Bruce

Oddest of all; stories by Bruce Coville. Harcourt 2008 235p $16

Grades: 6 7 8 9   S C

1. Short stories 2. Horror fiction

ISBN 978-0-15-205808-1; 0-15-205808-7

LC 2007-50298

A collection of nine short stories featuring ghosts, half-humans, unicorns, and other unusual creatures.

"The variety of fiction subgenres, brilliant use of themes, the stories' brief lengths, strong character viewpoints, and fast-paced action and resolution of story line make this collection a must-have." Voice Youth Advocates

Cowboy stories; illustrated by Barry Moser; introduction by Peter Glassman. Chronicle Books 2007 181p il $16.95

Grades: 7 8 9 10   S C

1. Short stories 2. Cowhands -- Fiction

ISBN 978-0-8118-5418-4; 0-8118-5418-3

LC 2006-31568

"This collection of 20 stories by well-known writers features the most American of icons, the cowboy. . . . Some of the selections are excerpts from well-known novels such as Shane and The Virginian. Others are short stories by Western authors including Annie Proulx and Louis L'Amour. Actual cowboys, Nat Love and 'Teddy Blue' Abbott, offer exciting accounts of their lives. A significant feature here is Moser's artwork. Twenty-two stunning black-and-white engravings offer up the true grit of their cowboy subjects and galvanize readers." SLJ

Crutcher, Chris

★ **Athletic** shorts; six short stories. Greenwillow Bks. 1991 154p $17.99; pa $6.99

Grades: 7 8 9 10   S C

1. Short stories 2. Sports -- Fiction

ISBN 0-688-10816-4; 0-06-050783-7 pa

LC 91-4418

ALA YALSA Margaret A. Edwards Award (2000)

A collection of short stories about high school sports

"The author seamlessly blends humor with more serious elements... These Athletic Shorts will speak to YAs, touch them deeply, and introduce them to characters they'll want to know better." SLJ

Dahl, Roald

Skin and other stories. Viking 2000 212p $15.99; pa $8.99

Grades: 7 8 9 10   S C

1. Short stories

ISBN 0-670-89184-3; 0-14-131034-0 pa

LC 99-58600

A collection of 13 of the author's short stories written for adults. "Full of irony and unexpected twists, they smack of the master's touch—every word carefully chosen, characters fully fleshed out in only a few pages, the sense of place immediate." Booklist

Del Negro, Janice

★ **Passion** and poison; tales of shape-shifters, ghosts, and spirited women. Marshall Cavendish 2007 64p il $16.99

Grades: 5 6 7 8   S C

1. Ghost stories 2. Short stories 3. Supernatural -- Fiction

ISBN 978-0-7614-5361-1; 0-7614-5361-X

LC 2007-07237

"Including both original tales and retellings, this collection of seven stories . . . features diverse female protagonists facing challenges and perils—from human bullies to ghosts. More eerie than scary, the tales of bravery, revenge, grief, and redemption share a gothic sensibility. . . . The black-and-white illustrations . . . evoke bygone times." Booklist

Delacre, Lulu

★ **Salsa** stories; stories and linocuts by Lulu Delacre. Scholastic Press 2000 105p il hardcover o.p. $16.99

Grades: 4 5 6   S C

1. Short stories 2. Family life -- Fiction

ISBN 0-590-63118-7; 0-590-63121-7 pa

LC 99-25534

A collection of stories within the story of a family celebration where the guests relate their memories of growing up in various Latin American countries. Also contains recipes

"Kids will respond to both the warmth and the anxiety of the family life described in the vivid writing, and in Delacre's nicely composed linocuts." Booklist

Delaney, Joseph

The **Spook's** tale and other horrors; illustrations by Patrick Arrasmith. Greenwillow Books 2009 166p il (The last apprentice) $10.95; lib bdg $14.89

Grades: 5 6 7 8   S C

1. Short stories 2. Witches -- Fiction 3. Supernatural -- Fiction

ISBN 978-0-06-173028-3; 0-06-173028-9; 978-0-06-173030-6 lib bdg; 0-06-173030-0 lib bdg

LC 2008042235

As sixty-year-old John Gregory reflects on the past, he reveals how the world of ghosts, ghasts, witches, and boggarts was exposed to him and he later became the Spook, even though his first intention had been to join the priesthood.

"These short stories are narrated by secondary characters from the popular series, giving insight into some of Tom Ward's well-known companions. A 'Gallery of Villains' section identifies additional characters and gives a citation to the novels. . . . This book would be perfect for pulling reluctant readers into the series. The occasional black-and-white illustrations add a creepy, atmospheric touch." SLJ

Destination unexpected: short stories; collected by Donald R. Gallo. Candlewick Press 2003 240p hardcover o.p. pa $8.99

Grades: 7 8 9 10   S C

1. Short stories

ISBN 0-7636-1764-4; 0-7636-3119-1 pa

LC 2002-71599

This collection "features teen protagonists experiencing a transforming experience while on some kind of journey. . . . . Whether humorous or serious, the stories are consistently well written and engaging." Booklist

Does this book make me look fat? edited by Marissa Walsh. Clarion Books 2008 215p $16

Grades: 7 8 9 10 11 12   S C

1. Short stories 2. Obesity -- Fiction 3. Eating disorders -- Fiction 4. Young adult literature -- Works 5. Body image 6. Short stories -- Collections

ISBN 978-0-547-01496-8; 0-547-01496-1

LC 2008-25070

"This star-studded collection tackles a popular topic—body image—with humor, sensitivity, and creativity. . . . [It includes] Megan McCafferty's story narrated by a pair of skinny jeans. Other highlights are Matt de la Peña's wrenching story of a young man coming to terms with his sister's devastating eating disorder, and Sarra Manning's feisty protagonist, who helps a co-worker find her own style and later faces her own body issues." Booklist

Don't cramp my style; stories about that time of the month. edited by Lisa Rowe Fraustino. Simon & Schuster for Young Readers 2004 295p $15.95

Grades: 7 8 9 10   S C

1. Short stories 2. Menstruation -- Fiction

ISBN 0-689-85882-5

A collection of eleven stories concerning menstruation.

"This highly recommended collection . . . encompasses an impressive variety of times, cultures, attitudes, and moods. . . . The writing . . . is consistently excellent." Voice Youth Advocates

Ellis, Deborah

Lunch with Lenin and other stories. Fitzhenry & Whiteside 2008 169p pa $14.95

Grades: 7 8 9 10 11 12   **S C**

1. Short stories 2. Drug abuse -- Fiction

ISBN 978-1-55455-105-7; 1-55455-105-6

A collection of short stories that explore the lives of teen-agers affected directly or indirectly by drugs.

"The relatively short stories read quickly, offering neither judgment nor solutions but rather the opportunity for compassion and understanding. . . . The collection's quality . . . is high enough to justify placing this book in every library." Voice Youth Advocates

Enthralled; paranormal diversions. edited by Melissa Marr and Kelley Armstrong. HarperCollins 2011 452p $17.99; pa $9.99

Grades: 7 8 9 10   **S C**

1. Short stories 2. Supernatural -- Fiction 3. Voyages and travels -- Fiction

ISBN 978-0-06-201579-2; 0-06-201579-6; 978-0-06-201578-5 pa; 0-06-201578-8 pa

LC 2011019393

A collection of sixteen original short stories by writers of paranormal tales, featuring journeys made by teens and magical beings.

"These short stories are loosely connected by a very openly interpreted journey motif. Psychics, genies, angels and gargoyles join fairies and vampires to terrorize and romance their fellow characters. The diversity in authors allows for the sometimes-neglected horror implied in paranormal stories to be spotlighted. . . . This collection is ideal as a sampler tray for paranormal readers looking to pick up new authors to follow or to further explore the fictional worlds they already know." Kirkus

Estevis, Anne

Down Garrapata road; by Anne Estevis. Arte Piñata Books 2003 119p pa $12.95

Grades: 7 8 9 10   **S C**

1. Short stories 2. Mexican Americans -- Fiction

ISBN 1-55885-397-9

LC 2003-49837

A collection of short stories set in a small Mexican-American community in southern Texas during the 1940s and 1950s, revealing the traditions, love, and social concerns of the families living there.

"Sly, gentle, and written in lively, simple language, these are stories that will draw readers into the particulars of a culture while capturing universal family dramas." Booklist

★ **Every** man for himself; ten short stories about being a guy. edited by Nancy E. Mercado. Dial Books 2005 154p il hardcover o.p. pa $6.99

Grades: 7 8 9 10   **S C**

1. Short stories 2. Boys -- Fiction

ISBN 0-8037-2896-4; 0-14-240813-1 pa

LC 2004-24069

"This collection provides a refreshing look at the values, decisions, and friendships that ultimately shape a boy into a man. The stories themselves are diverse, ranging from humorous to serious." SLJ

Face relations; 11 stories about seeing beyond color. Simon & Schuster Books for Young Readers 2004 224p $17.95

Grades: 7 8 9 10   **S C**

1. Short stories 2. Race relations -- Fiction

ISBN 0-689-85637-7

"Contributed by familiar writers for young people, including Ellen Wittlinger, M. E. Kerr, Rita Williams-Garcia, Naomi Shihab Nye, and Jess Mowry, the stories ask challenging questions about what role race plays in family life, at school, in friendships, and in love. . . . This is a provocative collection." Booklist

Fear: 13 stories of suspense and horror; [selected by and with an] introduction by R.L. Stine. Dutton 2010 306p $16.99; pa $7.99

Grades: 7 8 9 10   **S C**

1. Short stories 2. Horror fiction

ISBN 978-0-525-42168-9; 0-525-42168-8; 978-0-14-241774-4 pa; 0-14-241774-2 pa

LC 2009-53284

"Thirteen highly suspenseful short stories. . . . [Stine] enlists some of the best in the business, such as Meg Cabot and F. Paul Wilson, Walter Sorrells and James Rollins, who offer plenty of heart-throbbing supernatural horror, crime suspense, shockers and sometimes a mixture of all three. . . . Fast-paced, shuddery-scary fun." Kirkus

Firebirds; an anthology of original fantasy and science fiction. edited by Sharyn November. Firebird Press 2003 420p il $19.99

Grades: 7 8 9 10 11 12   **S C**

1. Short stories 2. Fantasy fiction 3. Science fiction

ISBN 0-14-250142-5

"Teens will find much to savor and celebrate in this dazzling collection of 16 short stories by some of the best fantasy writers around." SLJ

Firebirds rising; an anthology of original science fiction and fantasy. edited by Sharyn November. Firebird 2006 530p hardcover o.p. pa $9.99

Grades: 7 8 9 10 11 12   **S C**

1. Short stories 2. Fantasy fiction 3. Science fiction

ISBN 0-14-240549-3; 978-0-14-240549-9; 0-14-240936-7 pa; 978-0-14-240936-7 pa

This is a collection of sixteen science fiction and fantasy stories.

"This anthology is a wonderful choice for any young adult collection." Voice Youth Advocates

Firebirds soaring; an anthology of original speculative fiction. [edited by Sharyn November; illustrated by Mike Dringenberg] Firebird 2009 574p il $19.99

Grades: 7 8 9 10 11 12   **S C**

1. Short stories 2. Fantasy fiction 3. Science fiction

ISBN 978-0-14-240552-9; 0-14-240552-3

LC 2008-29516

This anthology "contains 19 short stories by some of the top writers in this genre. . . . The selections vary in length, with some short stories, some novellas. Each work is introduced by an evocative illustration that beautifully sets the scene for the written work. The variety of styles and themes and a gathering together of so many talented writers in one work offer readers a banquet for the imagination. For fans of the genre, this is a must read." SLJ

Flake, Sharon G.

★ **Who** am I without him? short stories about girls and the boys in their lives. Jump at the Sun/ Hyperion Books for Children 2004 168p $15.99; pa $7.99

Grades: 7 8 9 10   **S C**
1. Short stories 2. African Americans -- Fiction
ISBN 0-7868-0693-1; 1-4231-0383-1 pa

Ten short stories about African American teenage girls and their relationships with boys.

"Addressing issues and situations that many girls face in today's often complex society, this book is provocative and thought-provoking." SLJ

Flanagan, John

The **lost** stories. Philomel 2011 422p (Ranger's apprentice) $17.99

Grades: 5 6 7 8   **S C**
1. Short stories 2. Fantasy fiction
ISBN 978-0-399-25618-9; 0-399-25618-0

This is "a collection of nine stories showing events not recorded in the books [of the Ranger's Apprentice series] and following the familiar characters during certain unrecorded times. In the framework story, set in 1896, an archaeologist discovers the fabled lost stories of the medieval Kingdom of Araluen. . . . Inspired by questions from readers, these short stories retain the adventure and the camaraderis of the novels." Booklist

Fleischman, Paul

Graven images; three stories. by Paul Fleischman; illustrations by Bagram Ibatoulline. Candlewick Press 2006 116p il $16.99; pa $5.99

Grades: 5 6 7 8   **S C**
1. Short stories 2. Supernatural -- Fiction
ISBN 0-7636-2775-5; 0-7636-2984-7 pa

LC 2005054283

A newly illustrated edition with a new afterword of the title first published 1982 by Harper & Row

A Newbery Medal honor book, 1983

A collection of three stories about a child who reads the lips of those who whisper secrets into a statue's ear; a daydreaming shoemaker's apprentice who must find ways to make the girl he loves notice him; and a stone carver who creates a statue of a ghost.

"Readers will be delighted with the return to print of [this title] with haunting new acrylic gouache illustrations . . . evoking the spinetingling aspects of this trio of tales. . . . Via a new afterword, the author explains the stories' inspiration and describes this book's significance early in his career." Publ Wkly

Friends; stories about new friends, old friends, and unexpectedly true friends. edited by Ann M. Mar-

tin and David Levithan. Scholastic Press 2005 185p $16.95

Grades: 5 6 7 8   **S C**
1. Short stories 2. Friendship -- Fiction
ISBN 0-439-72991-2

LC 2004-27758

"This collection of stories by well-known authors spans a broad definition of the term 'friend,' and also approaches the topic from a wide variety of viewpoints. . . . The selections by Ann M. Martin, Pam Muñoz Ryan, Rachel Cohn, David Levithan, and Patricia McCormick are among the more outstanding entries. . . . It is also likely that every reader will find at least one that hits home." SLJ

Full house; 10 stories about poker. edited by Pete Hautman. G. P. Putnam's Sons 2007 161p $17.99

Grades: 7 8 9 10   **S C**
1. Short stories 2. Poker -- Fiction 3. Young adult literature -- Works 4. Short stories -- Collections
ISBN 978-0-399-24528-2

LC 2007-14116

This is a "compilation of stories about teenage encounters with poker. The characters find themselves in high-stakes situations: playing with the Devil, competing in a scholarship game, fighting to defeat a deadbeat stepdad, and staying one step ahead of an Internet poker company. . . . The stories vary from the eerily realistic to amusingly farfetched. In all cases, teen poker players will recognize themselves and their opponents in this diverse collection." SLJ

Gaiman, Neil

★ **M** is for magic; illustrations by Teddy Kristiansen. HarperCollins Pub. 2007 260p il $16.99; lib bdg $17.89; pa $6.99

Grades: 7 8 9 10   **S C**
1. Short stories 2. Magic -- Fiction
ISBN 978-0-06-118642-4; 0-06-118642-2; 978-0-06-118645-5 lib bdg; 0-06-118645-7 lib bdg; 978-0-06-118647-9 pa; 0-06-118647-3 pa

LC 2007-14472

Gaiman "has selected nine of his short stories and a poem and added a segment from an upcoming children's title for this volume. . . . This well-chosen collection is sure to create a new generation of Gaiman fans who will not need to understand all the allusions to enjoy the stories." Booklist

Gallo, Donald R.

★ **Owning** it; stories about teens with disabilities. edited by Donald R. Gallo. Candlewick Press 2008 215p pbk. $6.99

Grades: 7 8 9 10   **S C**
1. Short stories 2. Diseases -- Fiction 3. Handicapped -- Fiction
ISBN 9780763646615

LC 2007-24963

This anthology presents ten stories of teenagers facing the challenges of school, parents, boyfriends and girlfriends, in addition to the additional complications that come with having a physical or psychological disability.

"Each of the stories is strong and will resonate with teens dealing with everything from drinking problems, migraines, Tourette's Syndrome, and even cancer." Libr Media Connect

Geektastic; stories from the nerd herd. edited by Holly Black and Cecil Castellucci. Little Brown & Co. 2009 403p il $16.99

Grades: 7 8 9 10   **S C**

1. Short stories 2. Young adult literature -- Works 3. Short stories -- Collections
ISBN 978-0-316-00809-9; 0-316-00809-5

LC 2009-455709

A collection of twenty-nine short stories about geeks.

"Although not all geekdoms are covered, topics include cosplay (dressing as characters), cons (conventions), SF television and movies, RPGs (roleplaying games), fantasy books, baton-twirling, astronomy, Rocky Horror, quiz bowl, and dinosaurs. Geek-themed comics by Hope Larson and Bryan Lee O'Malley separate the stories. . . . Although readers need not necessarily be geeks to appreciate this well-written collection, it will help. Buy for all the geeks in your library—including the librarian." Voice Youth Advocates

Give me shelter; stories about children who seek asylum. edited by Tony Bradman. Frances Lincoln 2007 220p $16.95

Grades: 5 6 7 8   **S C**

1. Short stories 2. Refugees -- Fiction
ISBN 978-1-84507-522-4; 1-84507-522-6

This is a "moving collection of 11 powerful narratives, quite different in their particulars but astonishingly similar in their sense of loss and loneliness. . . . While most of the stories focus on current asylum-seekers in Britain, one looks back to a Vietnamese child's trip to Australia, and another is set in an unnamed Eastern European country." SLJ

Gothic! ten original dark tales. edited by Deborah Noyes. Candlewick Press 2004 241p hardcover o.p. pa $7.99

Grades: 7 8 9 10   **S C**

1. Short stories 2. Horror fiction
ISBN 0-7636-2243-5; 0-7636-2737-2 pa

LC 2004-45188

This "collection features short stories by noted young adult authors such as M. T. Anderson, Caitlín R. Kiernan, Garth Nix, Celia Rees, Janni Lee Simner, and Barry Yourgrau. . . . These varied tales take place in the distant past and in the high-tech present. Some are humorous while others have surprising twists or are reminiscent of classic fairy tales full of malevolent characters, but all share a love of the surreal or supernatural. . . . A sophisticated, thought-provoking, and gripping read." SLJ

★ **Guys** read: funny business; edited and with an introduction by Jon Scieszka; stories by Mac Barnett [et al.]; with illustrations by Adam Rex. Walden Pond Press 2010 268p il $16.99; pa $5.99

Grades: 4 5 6 7   **S C**

1. Short stories 2. Humorous fiction 3. Boys -- Fiction 4. Short stories -- Collections 5. Children's literature

-- Works -- Grades two through six
ISBN 978-0-06-196374-2; 0-06-196374-7; 978-0-06-196373-5 pa; 0-06-196373-9 pa

LC 2010-08122

A collection of humorous stories featuring a teenaged mummy, a homicidal turkey, and the world's largest pool of chocolate milk.

"A must-have collection for the boys in your library—and while you're at it, get a copy for the girls too!" Booklist

★ **Half-human**; compiled & edited by Bruce Coville; photo illustrations by Marc Tauss. Scholastic Press 2001 212p il $16.95; pa $5.99

Grades: 7 8 9 10   **S C**

1. Metamorphosis 2. Short stories 3. Fantasy fiction 4. Identity 5. Animals, Mythical 6. Children's stories, American
ISBN 0-590-95944-1; 0-590-95588-8 pa

LC 00-50524

A collection of 9 stories and one poem about such creatures as mermaids and centaurs, who are part-human and part-animal or part-plant.

Readers "will be intrigued with this unusual collection of well-written fantasies that illustrate the adolescent challenge of discovering both our animal and human natures." Booklist

★ **Half-minute horrors**; edited by Susan Rich. HarperCollinsPublishers 2009 141p il $12.99

Grades: 5 6 7 8   **S C**

1. Short stories 2. Horror fiction 3. Young adult literature -- Works 4. Short stories -- Collections 5. Children's literature -- Works -- Grades two through six
ISBN 978-0-06-183379-3; 0-06-183379-7

LC 2009-18293

An anthology of very short, scary stories by an assortment of authors and illustrators including Chris Raschka, Joyce Carol Oates, Neil Gaiman, Jack Gantos, and Lane Smith.

"This collection of more than 70 chilling snippets is ideal for campfires and car trips. The stories—some a couple sentences, some a few pages—range from darkly humorous . . . to outright creepy. . . . These are inherently quick reads, but with enough plot and detail to encourage further imagining." Publ Wkly

Hearne, Betsy Gould

The **canine** connection: stories about dogs and people; [by] Betsy Hearne. Margaret K. McElderry Bks. 2003 113p hardcover o.p. pa $8.95

Grades: 5 6 7 8   **S C**

1. Dogs 2. Short stories 3. Human-animal relationships
ISBN 0-689-85258-4; 1-4169-6817-2 pa

LC 2001-58991

Twelve short stories that reflect the varied ways that dogs and humans relate

"The emotions and dialogue are pitch perfect. . . . A rewarding collection that will stay with readers." Booklist

Holt, Kimberly Willis

Part of me; stories of a Louisiana family. 1st ed.; H. Holt 2006 208p $16.95

Grades: 7 8 9 10 **S C**
1. Short stories 2. Family life -- Fiction
ISBN 978-0-8050-6360-8; 0-8050-6360-9
LC 2005-29676

Ten stories trace the connections between four generations of one Louisiana family from 1939 when a young girl leaves school to help support her family to 2006 when an eighty-year-old woman embarks on a book tour.

"Holt once again excels at creating character and an evocative sense of place." SLJ

Horowitz, Anthony
★ **Horowitz** horror; [by] Anthony Horowitz. 1st American ed.; Philomel Books 2006 217p $10.99
Grades: 7 8 9 10 **S C**
1. Short stories 2. Horror fiction
ISBN 0-399-24489-1
LC 2005058609

First published 1999 in the United Kingdom
"In this collection of nine macabre tales, Horowitz proves himself as adept at spooky psychological horror as he is at creating breakneck adventure-suspense." Booklist

★ **More** Horowitz horror; stories you'll wish you'd never read. [by] Anthony Horowitz. 1st American ed.; Philomel Books 2006 210p $11.99
Grades: 7 8 9 10 **S C**
1. Short stories 2. Horror fiction
ISBN 978-0-399-24519-0
LC 2006045583

A collection of frightening tales.
This "cements [Horowitz's] reputation in the horror genre by once again yanking young readers out of their safe, familiar world." Booklist

Join in; multiethnic short stories by outstanding writers for young adults. edited by Donald R. Gallo. Delacorte Press 1993 256p hardcover o.p. pa $5.99
Grades: 7 8 9 10 **S C**
1. Short stories 2. Short stories -- Collections
ISBN 0-440-21957-4 pa
LC 92-43169

"Diverse, thought-provoking, and consistently well-written." Kirkus

Kiss me deadly; 13 tales of paranormal love. edited by Trisha Telep. RP Teens 2010 430p pa $9.95
Grades: 7 8 9 10 **S C**
1. Love stories 2. Short stories 3. Supernatural -- Fiction
ISBN 978-0-7624-3949-2; 0-7624-3949-1
LC 2010-926067

A collection of short stories combining dark seduction and modern romance presents a variety of tales featuring the romantic lives of humans and werewolves, ghosts, fallen angels, zombies, and shape-shifters.

The stories "have varying lengths and tones, representing an impressive range of writing styles; it is likely that any fantasy reader will find at least one memorable story that speaks directly to his or her preferences." Bull Cent Child Books

Lay-ups and long shots; an anthology of short stories. by Joseph Bruchac . . . [et al.] Darby Creek Pub. 2008 112p il $15.95
Grades: 4 5 6 **S C**
1. Short stories 2. Sports -- Fiction
ISBN 978-1-58196-078-5; 1-58196-078-6

"These nine new short stories feature tweens or teens who, despite lack of skill or other obstacles, engage in athletic pursuits. Some . . . have autobiographical elements. . . . Consistently readable and engaging, the collection should have as much appeal for geeks as it does for jocks." Booklist

Le Guin, Ursula K.
Tales from Earthsea. Ace Books 2002 314p (The Earthsea cycle) rpt $16.99; pa $13.95
Grades: 11 12 Adult **S C**
1. Short stories 2. Fantasy fiction
ISBN 9780547851402 rpt; 0-441-00932-8
LC 2001-56673

"Inhabited by people no better or worse than ourselves, Earthsea is dominated by the practice of magic as precise as any science and as unpredictable in its social consequences. Since it is based entirely on language, Earthsea's magic serves as a metaphor for the writer's own sorcery. Yet despite Le Guin's strong bias toward the didactic there is no hint of by-the-numbers allegory here." N Y Times Book Rev

Lester, Julius
Long journey home: stories from black history. Dial Press (NY) 1972 147p hardcover o.p. pa $5.99
Grades: 6 7 8 9 **S C**
1. Short stories 2. African Americans -- Fiction
ISBN 0-14-038981-4 pa

"In a foreword, Julius Lester explains that he has chosen minor figures because the mass of people were the 'movers of history' while the great figures are their symbols. . . . The selections are diversified in their settings and alike in their sharply-etched effectiveness." Bull Cent Child Books

★ **Life** on Mars: tales from the new frontier; an original science fiction anthology. edited by Jonathan Strahan. Viking 2011 333p $19.99
Grades: 7 8 9 10 **S C**
1. Short stories 2. Science fiction
ISBN 978-0-670-01216-9; 0-670-01216-5
LC 2011-02998

"In this strong anthology, Strahan . . . collects stories by some of the most talented writers in science fiction. Ranging from the first Mars landing to the far future, they often make use of the most recent scientific data about the Red Planet. . . . Invoking some of the great authors of Martian tales, from Burroughs and Bradbury to Heinlein and Kim Stanley Robinson . . . , this anthology is sure to appeal to any teens who yearn to explore Earth's nearest neighbor." Publ Wkly

Love is hell; [by] Melissa Marr . . . [et al.] HarperTeen 2008 263p $16.99; pa $9.99
Grades: 7 8 9 10 **S C**
1. Love stories 2. Short stories 3. Supernatural --

Fiction

ISBN 978-0-06-144305-3; 0-06-144305-0; 978-0-06-144304-6 pa; 0-06-144304-2 pa

LC 2007-49574

"Supernatural romance is the well-chosen theme of five original stories by as many authors. . . . There's enough variety to round out the central theme, and consistently supple storytelling will lure readers through all five entries." Publ Wkly

Magic in the mirrorstone; tales of fantasy. edited by Steve Berman. Wizards of the Coast 2008 295p $14.95

Grades: 8 9 10 11   S C

1. Short stories 2. Fantasy fiction

ISBN 978-0-7869-4732-4

LC 2007-31357

An anthology of fifteen stories featuring such themes as amphibians that speak and enchanted jewelry.

"Ranging from funny to disquieting to bittersweet, the stories in this solid collection will appeal to most genre fans, including many adults." Booklist

Marston, Elsa

Santa Claus in Baghdad and other stories about teens in the Arab world. Indiana University Press 2008 198p pa $15.95

Grades: 6 7 8 9 10   S C

1. Short stories

ISBN 978-0-253-22004-2; 0-253-22004-1

LC 2007-50768

A collection of eight stories, most previously published in other anthologies, about what it is like to grow up in the Middle East today.

"Marston, who has lived and visited the countries of which she writes, offers a realistic portrait of the Middle East that mixes possiblity and bleakness in equal measure." Voice Youth Advocates

McKinley, Robin

★ **Fire** : tales of elemental spirits; [by] Robin McKinley and Peter Dickinson. G. P. Putnam's Sons 2009 297p $19.99

Grades: 7 8 9 10   S C

1. Short stories 2. Fire -- Fiction 3. Mythical animals -- Fiction

ISBN 978-0-399-25289-1; 0-399-25289-4

LC 2009-4730

"The settings of these five tales range from ancient to modern, but they are all united by encounters with magical creatures with an affinity for fire. . . . This collection of beautifully crafted tales will find a warm welcome from fans of either author, as well as from fantasy readers in general." SLJ

Water : tales of elemental spirits; [by] Robin McKinley, Peter Dickinson. Putnam 2002 266p $18.99; pa $6.99

Grades: 7 8 9 10   S C

1. Ocean 2. Short stories 3. Fantasy fiction 4. Mermen

5. Mermaids

ISBN 0-399-23796-8; 0-14-240244-3 pa

LC 2001-41642

"The masterfully written stories all feature distinct, richly detailed casts and settings . . . and focus as strongly on action as on character. There's plenty here to excite, enthrall, and move even the pickiest readers." SLJ

The **door** in the hedge. Greenwillow Bks. 1981 216p hardcover o.p. pa $6.99

Grades: 7 8 9 10   S C

1. Fairy tales 2. Short stories

ISBN 0-688-00312-5; 0-698-11960-6 pa

LC 80-21903

"These tales are well-written and enjoyable to read. It is too bad they lack illustrations." Child Book Rev Serv

McKissack, Patricia C.

★ **Porch** lies; tales of slicksters, tricksters, and other wily characters. [by] Patricia C. McKissack; illustrated by André Carrilho. Schwartz & Wade Books 2006 146p il $18.95; lib bdg $22.99

Grades: 4 5 6 7   S C

1. Short stories 2. African Americans -- Fiction

ISBN 0-375-83619-5; 0-375-93619-X lib bdg

LC 2005-22048

The "original tales in this uproarious collection draw on African American oral tradition and blend history and legend with sly humor, creepy horror, villainous characters, and wild farce. McKissack based the stories on those she heard as a child while sitting on her grandparents' porch. . . . Carrilho's full-page illustrations—part cartoon, part portrait in silhouette—combine realistic characters with scary monsters." Booklist

★ The **dark**-thirty; Southern tales of the supernatural. illustrated by Brian Pinkney. Knopf 1992 122p il $18.95; lib bdg $20.99; pa $6.50

Grades: 4 5 6 7   S C

1. Ghost stories 2. Short stories 3. African Americans -- Fiction

ISBN 0-679-81863-4; 0-679-91853-9 lib bdg; 0-679-89006-8 pa

LC 92-3021

Coretta Scott King Award for text, 1993; A Newbery honor book, 1993

A collection of ghost stories with African American themes, designed to be told during the Dark Thirty—the half hour before sunset—when ghosts seem all too believable

"Strong characterizations are superbly drawn in a few words. The atmosphere of each selection is skillfully developed and sustained to the very end. Pinkney's stark scratchboard illustrations evoke an eerie mood, which heightens the suspense of each tale." SLJ

McRobbie, David

A **whole** lot of Wayne; [by] David McRobbie. Allen & Unwin 2007 396p pa $12.95

Grades: 7 8 9 10   S C

1. Short stories 2. Boys -- Fiction

ISBN 978-1-74175-244-1; 1-74175-244-2

"McRobbie thoroughly entertains readers with this charming and heartwarming collection of stories starring Wayne Wilson. Accompanied by his friend Squocka Berrington, the teen finds himself in a variety of hilarious and oftentimes precarious situations." SLJ

★ **Moccasin** thunder; American Indians stories for today. edited by Lori Marie Carlson. HarperCollins 2005 156p $15.99

Grades: 7 8 9 10   S C
1. Short stories 2. Native Americans -- Fiction
ISBN 0-06-623957-5

LC 2004-22186

Presents ten short stories about contemporary Native American teens by members of tribes of the United States and Canada, including Louise Erdrich and Joseph Bruchac.

"This distinguished anthology offers powerful, beautifully written stories that are thoughtful and important for teens to hear." SLJ

Morpurgo, Michael

Singing for Mrs. Pettigrew; stories and essays from a writing life. illustrated by Peter Bailey. Candlewick Press 2009 263p il $18.99

Grades: 6 7 8 9   S C
1. Essays 2. Short stories 3. Voyages and travels -- Fiction
ISBN 978-0-7636-3624-1; 0-7636-3624-X

"Morpurgo's writing is thoroughly enjoyable in this collection of previously published short stories and poems with accompanying essays. The pieces cover a wide range of emotions. . . . Evocative fine-lined black-and-white illustrations appear throughout." Horn Book Guide

My dad's a punk; 12 stories about boys and their fathers. edited by Tony Bradman. Kingfisher 2006 271p pa $7.95

Grades: 7 8 9 10   S C
1. Short stories 2. Father-son relationship -- Fiction
ISBN 0-7534-5870-5

"Authors such as Ron Koertge, Tim Wynne-Jones, and Francis McCrickard explore father-son relationships in moving stories set in the past, present, and future. From bird watching to bird slaughter, divorced dads to gay dads, and close conversations to clandestine meetings on street corners, the situations and characters in each of these stories convey the depth and breadth of what it means to be a male in a family. A strong collection." Booklist

Myers, Walter Dean, 1937-

145th Street; short stories. Delacorte Press 2000 151p hardcover o.p. pa $5.50

Grades: 7 8 9 10   S C
1. Short stories 2. African Americans -- Fiction 3. Children's stories, American
ISBN 0-385-32137-6; 0-440-22916-2 pa

LC 99-36097

"These ten powerful stories create a vivid mosaic of life in the Harlem neighborhood of 145th Street. Memorable characters range from outgoing Big Joe, who decides to stage his own funeral party in Big Joe's funeral, to book-loving Monkeyman, who outsmarts the Tigros gang. . . .

Beautifully told, Myers's stories offer an enticing collection for teens." Voice Youth Advocates

★ **What** they found; love on 145th street. Wendy Lamb Books 2007 243p $15.99; lib bdg $18.99

Grades: 8 9 10 11 12   S C
1. Short stories 2. Family life -- Fiction 3. African Americans -- Fiction
ISBN 978-0-385-32138-9; 0-385-32138-4; 978-0-375-93709-5 lib bdg; 0-375-93709-9 lib bdg

LC 2007-7057

Fifteen interrelated stories explore different aspects of love, such as a dying father's determination to help start a family business—a beauty salon—and the relationship of two teens who plan to remain celibate until they marry.

"Rich in both character and setting, these urban tales combine heartbreak and hope into a vivid tableau of a community. A priority purchase for all libraries, especially those in urban settings." SLJ

Na, An

No such thing as the real world; a short story collection. [by] An Na [et al.]; introduction by Jill Santopolo; [compiled by Laura Geringer and Jill Santopolo] HarperTeen 2009 246p $16.99

Grades: 8 9 10   S C
1. Short stories
ISBN 978-0-06-147058-5; 0-06-147058-9

LC 2008-22583

Six young adult authors present short stories featuring teens who have to face the "real world" for the first time.

"This unique collection will challenge students' intellect and have them questioning their own decision-making skills. A fine balance is straddled between sophisticated prose and authentic teen voices, uninhibited and peppered with profanity." SLJ

Naidoo, Beverley

Out of bounds: seven stories of conflict and hope. HarperCollins Pubs. 2003 175p $16.99; pa $5.99

Grades: 5 6 7 8   S C
1. Short stories 2. Apartheid 3. Children's stories, South African (English)
ISBN 0-06-050799-3; 0-06-050801-9 pa

LC 2002-68901

First published 2001 in the United Kingdom

Seven stories, spanning the time period from 1948 to 2000, chronicle the experiences of young people from different races and ethnic groups as they try to cope with the restrictions placed on their lives by South Africa's apartheid laws

"Naidoo's book reveals our humanity and inhumanity with starkness and precision. . . . She honors her country's past, present, and future with these brave tales." Horn Book

Nayeri, Daniel

★ **Straw** house, Wood house, Brick house, Blow. Candlewick Press 2011 404p $19.99

Grades: 8 9 10 11 12   S C
1. Love stories 2. Short stories 3. Mystery fiction 4.

Science fiction
ISBN 9780763655266; 0763655260

LC 2011013675

A collection of four novellas in different genres, including a western about a farmer who grows living toys and a rancher who grows half-living people; a science fiction story of the near-future in which the world is as easy to manipulate as the Internet; a crime story in which every wish comes true and only the Imaginary Crimes Unit can stop them; and a comedic love story in which Death describes himself as a charismatic hero.

"Four stylistically brilliant novellas offer readers a range of exquisite reading experiences in this collection." Bull Cent Child Books

Nix, Garth

★ **Across** the wall; a tale of the Abhorsen and other stories. Eos 2005 305p hardcover o.p. pa $7.99

Grades: 7 8 9 10   S C

1. Short stories 2. Fantasy fiction
ISBN 0-06-074713-7; 0-06-074715-3 pa

In Nicholas Sayre and the creature of case, the opening novella, "Nick encounters a bloodsucking Free Magic monster during a visit to Ancelstierre's top-secret intelligence agency. The story teasingly refers to British mysteries and spy fiction, parodic elements that will appeal most to Nix's adult fans. Even less-experienced readers, though, will enjoy getting to know Nick on his own terms. . . . The remaining 11 stories . . . include selections clearly intended for middle-graders as well as more sophisticated offerings containing frank references to sex and violence spattered with 'blood and brains and urine.' Buy this with the understanding that the packaging will attract the full spectrum of Nix's fans but that the younger ones may get more than they bargained for." Booklist

Noyes, Deborah

★ The **ghosts** of Kerfol. Candlewick Press 2008 163p $16.99

Grades: 8 9 10 11 12   S C

1. Ghost stories 2. Short stories 3. Supernatural -- Fiction
ISBN 978-0-7636-3000-3; 0-7636-3000-4

LC 2007-51884

Over the centuries, the inhabitants of author Edith Wharton's fictional mansion, Kerfol, are haunted by the ghosts of dead dogs, fractured relationships, and the taste of bitter revenge.

This collection includes "five wonderfully chilling short stories." Publ Wkly

The **restless** dead; ten original stories of the supernatural. edited by Deborah Noyes. Candlewick Press 2007 253p pbk. $7.99; $16.99

Grades: 8 9 10 11 12   S C

1. Short stories 2. Horror fiction 3. Supernatural -- Fiction
ISBN 9780763636715; 0-7636-2906-5; 978-0-7636-2906-9

LC 2007-22114

This is a companion volume to Gothic!: Ten Original Dark Tales. This is a collection of ten stories by Kelly Link, Chris Wooding, Annette Curtis Klause, Marcus Sedgwick, Herbie Brennan, Deobrah Noyes, Libba Bray, M.A. Anderson, Holly Black, and Nancy Etchemendy. "Grades seven to nine." (Bull Cent Child Books)

This is a "collection of terrifying stories from some of the most well-known authors writing for teens, including M. T. Anderson, Holly Black, Libby Bray, and Annette Curtis Klause. From vampires to vindictive ghosts, this diverse anthology has it all, and then some." Booklist

Nye, Naomi Shihab, 1952-

★ **There** is no long distance now; very short stories. Greenwillow Books 2011 201p $17.99

Grades: 7 8 9 10 11 12   S C

1. Short stories
ISBN 0-06-201965-1; 978-0-06-201965-3

LC 2010025559

"Very short stories offer glimpses into the everyday lives of young people. . . . As she does in her poetry, Nye achieves a perfect marriage of theme and structure in stories that reflect the moments, glimpses and epiphones of growing up." Kirkus

On the fringe; edited by Donald R. Gallo. Dial Bks. for Young Readers 2001 224p hardcover o.p. pa $6.99

Grades: 7 8 9 10   S C

1. Schools 2. High schools 3. Short stories 4. Children's stories, American
ISBN 0-8037-2656-2; 0-14-250026-7 pa

LC 00-40521

"Kids who are geeks, unathletic, poor, emotionally fragile, loners, or unattractive by current standards form the heart of this collection of exceptional stories by well-known YA authors such as Joan Bauer, Chris Crutcher, and M. E. Kerr." SLJ

Once upon a cuento; edited by Lyn Miller-Lachman. Curbstone Press 2003 243p pa $15.95

Grades: 9 10 11 12   S C

1. Short stories 2. Hispanic Americans -- Fiction
ISBN 1-88068-499-3

LC 2003-14667

"Writing quality is consisently high throughout. . . . This book . . . succeeds admirably in proving, through literature, that there is no single 'Latino experience.'" Voice Youth Advocates

Ortiz Cofer, Judith

An **island** like you; stories of the barrio. Puffin Books 1996 165p $6.99; pa $6.99

Grades: 7 8 9 10 11 12   S C

1. Short stories 2. Puerto Ricans -- Fiction
ISBN 9780545131339; 0-14-038068-X

LC 96-23203

A collection of twelve stories about young people in Paterson New Jersey caught between their Puerto Rican heritage and their American surroundings.

"The combination of interweaving of characters, intensity of emotion, and deft control of language make this a rewarding collection." Bull Cent Child Books

★ **Outside** rules; short stories about nonconformist youth. edited, with an introduction by Claire Robson. Persea Books 2007 178p pa $9.95
Grades: 7 8 9 10   S C
1. Short stories 2. Young adult literature -- Works 3. Short stories -- Collections
ISBN 0-89255-316-2; 978-0-89255-316-7
     LC 2006-22548
An anthology of fourteen short stories about youth who do not quite fit in because they are too brainy, unathletic, poor, the "wrong" religion, emotionally fragile, from non-traditional families, not model-thin, or simply bent on following a unique path.

"The collection is broadly multicultural, and the stories are consistently insightful, original, and discussion provoking in addition to being well written." Bull Cent Child Books

Paulsen, Gary
Paintings from the cave; three novellas. Wendy Lamb Books 2011 161p $15.99; lib bdg $18.99
Grades: 4 5 6 7   S C
1. Short stories 2. Art -- Fiction 3. Dogs -- Fiction 4. Violence -- Fiction 5. Homeless persons -- Fiction
ISBN 978-0-385-74684-7; 978-0-385-90921-1 lib bdg; 978-0-375-89743-6 e-book
     LC 2011016287
"These novellas portray an unflinching look at children who have endured neglectful and abusive homes and are surviving on their own. The atmospheric first tale, 'Man of the Iron Heads,' is narrated by Jake, a boy of about 11, who hides from the local gang until he finds the courage to outsmart its violent leader. 'Jo-Jo the Dog-Faced Girl' presents a lonely girl with three adopted dogs who finds acceptance in befriending a girl with leukemia. Finally, 'Erik's Rules' celebrates the power of art and is told by Jamie, the younger of two homeless brothers, whose unstable existence changes after a chance encounter with a friendly volunteer at the animal shelter. By incorporating the solace found in dogs, art, libraries, and new friends into these tales of heartache and redemption, Paulsen provides his readers with hope of a better life." SLJ

Peck, Richard
Past perfect, present tense: new and collected stories. Dial Bks. 2004 177p hardcover o.p. pa $6.99
Grades: 7 8 9 10 11 12   S C
1. Short stories
ISBN 0-8037-2998-7; 0-14-240537-X pa
     LC 2003-10904
A collection of short stories, including two previously unpublished ones, that deal with the way things could be.

"The stories perfectly highlight Peck's range and expertise at characterization. Almost every one is a superb read-aloud. . . . This superior collection is a must for every library." SLJ

★ **Pick**-up game; a full day of full court. edited by Marc Aronson & Charles R. Smith Jr. Candlewick Press 2011 170p il $15.99; pbk. $6.99
Grades: 7 8 9 10   S C
1. Short stories 2. Basketball -- Fiction
ISBN 0-7636-4562-1; 978-0-7636-4562-5; 9780763660680
A series of short stories by such authors as Walter Dean Myers, Rita Williams-Garcia, and Joseph Bruchac, interspersed with poems and photographs, provides different perspectives on a game of streetball played one steamy July day at the West 4th Street court in New York City known as The Cage.

"This anthology squeaks out a win. . . . Sharp-elbow action alternates with an almost spiritual grace." Booklist

Pierce, Tamora
★ **Young** warriors; stories of strength. edited by Tamora Pierce and Josepha Sherman. Random House 2005 312p hardcover o.p. pa $9.99
Grades: 7 8 9 10   S C
1. Short stories 2. Fantasy fiction
ISBN 0-375-82962-8; 978-0-375-82962-8; 0-375-82963-6 pa; 978-0-375-82963-5 pa
     LC 2004-16432
This is a "collection of fifteen fantasy and alternative history stories featuring war and warriors. . . . Grades seven to twelve." (Bull Cent Child Books)

"This timely and appealing anthology will surely help swell the ranks of teenage fantasy readers." SLJ

★ **Places** I never meant to be; original stories by censored writers. edited by Judy Blume. Atheneum Bks. for Young Readers 1999 198p hardcover o.p. pa $10
Grades: 7 8 9 10   S C
1. Censorship 2. Short stories 3. Short stories, American
ISBN 0-689-82034-8; 0-689-84258-9 pa
     LC 98-30343
"The contributors are a stellar list of well-known YA authors. . . . The authors' notes about censorship add a thought-provoking dimension to the collection, as does Blume's introduction, and the stories themselves are emotionally intense." Bull Cent Child Books

Poe, Edgar Allan
★ **Edgar** Allan Poe; edited by Andrew Delbanco; illustrated by Gerard DuBois. Sterling 2006 80p il (Stories for young people) $14.95
Grades: 6 7 8 9   S C
1. Short stories 2. Horror fiction
ISBN 1-4027-1515-3
"Introductory comments and appropriately atmospheric paintings enhance this handsomely packaged collection of five of Poe's unsettling short stories. . . . The editor . . . provides glosses for unusual words and literary references within the narratives." Booklist

Edgar Allan Poe's tales of death and dementia; illustrated by Gris Grimly. Atheneum Books for Young Readers 2009 136p il $18.99

Grades: 7 8 9 10   **S C**

1. Short stories 2. Horror fiction

ISBN 978-1-4169-5025-7; 1-4169-5025-7

LC 2009003056

"Four of Poe's morbid short stories are adapted for teens in this heavily illustrated presentation: 'The Tell-Tale Heart,' 'The System of Dr. Tarr and Professor Fether,' 'The Oblong Box,' and 'The Facts in the Case of M. Valdemar.' Grimly intersperses his horror-infused ink-and-watercolor cartoon art throughout Poe's putrid prose. The effect is an offering that bridges graphic and traditional print formats. Great for readers who adore the gothic and the gruesome." SLJ

Edgar Allan Poe's tales of mystery and madness; illustrated by Gris Grimley. Atheneum Books for Young Readers 2004 135p il $17.95

Grades: 8 9 10 11 12   **S C**

1. Short stories 2. Horror fiction

ISBN 0-689-84837-4

LC 2003-10565

"With high-production values and gothic sensibilities thoroughly reflected in both text and art, this is an essential purchase for libraries. Adults can use it to lead young people to some great literature; readers will pluck it off the shelves themselves for creepy, entertaining fun." Booklist

★ **Tales** of terror; illustrated with an introduction and notes by Michael McCurdy. Knopf 2005 89p il $15.95; lib bdg $17.99

Grades: 7 8 9 10   **S C**

1. Short stories 2. Horror fiction

ISBN 0-375-83305-6; 0-375-93305-0 lib bdg

LC 2004-23204

"This collection includes six of Poe's most famous tales. . . . In the introduction, McCurdy discusses of Poe's life and remarks on the darkness of Poe's nature, reflected in his work, and the physical darkness of his world after sundown, reflected in the illustrations. The 18 full-page, black-and-white scratchboard-style pictures are suitably dramatic and often macabre. This handsome volume, . . . accompanied by a CD that features readings of four of the tales, offers a good introduction to Poe's fiction." Booklist

Priestley, Chris

Uncle Montague's tales of terror; [by] Chris Priestley; illustrations by David Roberts. Bloomsbury Children's Books 2007 238p il $12.95

Grades: 5 6 7 8 9   **S C**

1. Short stories 2. Horror fiction 3. Uncles -- Fiction 4. Storytelling -- Fiction

ISBN 978-1-59990-118-3; 1-59990-118-8

"Ghosts, demons, jinns, and deadly trees populate these 10 chilly short stories set in the late 19th century, with the language and black-and-white illustrations capturing the feel of Victorian times. Young Edgar hears these tales while visiting his eccentric Uncle Montague, and each one is connected to a strange object in his uncle's study. . . . An enjoy-able collection with enough creepy atmosphere (and some gruesome action) to hold readers' attention." SLJ

Rice, David

Crazy loco; stories about growing up Chicano in southern Texas. Dial Books for Young Readers 2001 135p hardcover o.p. pa $6.99

Grades: 7 8 9 10 11 12   **S C**

1. Short stories 2. Mexican Americans -- Fiction

ISBN 0-8037-2598-1; 0-14-250056-9 pa

LC 00-59042

A collection of nine stories about Mexican American kids growing up in the Rio Grande Valley of southern Texas.

"Two great strengths of these stories are the pitch-perfect sense for the speech and thought patterns of teens and the vivid depiction of the daily lives of Mexican-Americans in Texas's Rio Grande Valley." SLJ

Rowling, J. K.

The **tales** of Beedle the Bard; translated from the ancient runes by Hermione Granger; commentary by Albus Dumbledore; introduction, notes, and illustrations by J.K. Rowling. Arthur A. Levine 2008 111p il $12.99

Grades: 5 6 7 8 9 10 11 12   **S C**

1. Fairy tales 2. Short stories 3. Magic -- Fiction

ISBN 978-0-545-12828-5; 0-545-12828-5

A collection of tales from the world of Harry Potter.

"The introduction is captivating . . . [and] the tales themselves are entertaining. . . . Rowling is at the top of her game as a superb storyteller, providing her legions of fans with an enchanting collection of wizard folklore." Voice Youth Advocates

San Souci, Robert

★ **Dare** to be scared; thirteen stories to chill and thrill. illustrations by David Ouimet. Cricket Bks. 2003 159p il $15.95

Grades: 4 5 6 7   **S C**

1. Short stories 2. Horror fiction

ISBN 0-8126-2688-5

LC 2002-152827

"With crisp, straightforward delivery and some intriguing endings, these 13 tales are great fun for young readers who like to be spooked." Booklist

Dare to be scared 4; thirteen more tales of terror. [by] Robert D. San Souci; illustrations by David Ouimet. Cricket Books 2009 275p il $17.95

Grades: 4 5 6 7   **S C**

1. Short stories 2. Horror fiction

ISBN 978-0-8126-2754-1; 0-8126-2754-7

LC 2009018490

"These deliciously shivery tales are perfect for campfire spookiness or as Halloween read-alouds. As in the previous books in the series, San Souci relies heavily on folklore and urban legends, giving the stories an even more chilling impact. . . . Strong themes such as death and murder are prevalent throughout. Ouimet's dark illustrations are paired perfectly with this creepy collection." SLJ

★ **Double**-dare to be scared: another thirteen chilling tales; [by] Robert D. San Souci; illustrated by David Ouimet. Cricket Books 2004 170p il $15.95

Grades: 4 5 6 7   S C

1. Short stories 2. Horror fiction 3. Horror stories 4. Horror tales, American 5. Children's stories, American
ISBN 0-8126-2716-4

LC 2003-26610

"San Souci uses elements of urban legend and folklore to weave powerful and suspenseful yet age-appropriate stories that youngsters will revisit, finding new meaning with each reading." SLJ

Haunted houses; [by] Robert D. San Souci; illustrated by Kelly Murphy and Antoine Revoy. Henry Holt 2010 276p il (Are you scared yet?) $16.99

Grades: 4 5 6 7   S C

1. Ghost stories 2. Short stories 3. Horror fiction
ISBN 978-0-8050-8750-5; 0-8050-8750-8

LC 2009-50763

"These 10 spooky stories include a classic Halloween scare: visitors get their admission fee of $25 back if they make it to the top floor of a haunted house—but can they? In another, the primary occupant of a dollhouse is a ghost of a child who needs help moving from one consciousness to another. . . . The stories are well paced and satisfyingly startling. . . . This book won't stay on the shelves for long. Murphy and Revoy's black-and-white illustrations heighten the fright factor, making San Souci's collection even more riveting." SLJ

Triple-dare to be scared; thirteen further freaky tales. [by] Robert D. San Souci; illustrations by David Ouimet. Cricket Books 2007 229p il $16.95

Grades: 4 5 6 7   S C

1. Short stories 2. Horror fiction
ISBN 978-0-8126-2749-7; 0-8126-2749-0

LC 2006025899

"San Souci serves up 13 more spooky tales, and Ouimet's macabre black-and-white illustrations are a perfect complement to each one. The selections are short enough for read-alouds or for independent readers to complete in one sitting." SLJ

Scary stories; illustrations by Barry Moser; introduction by Peter Glassman. Chronicle Books 2006 184p il $16.95

Grades: 6 7 8 9   S C

1. Short stories 2. Horror fiction
ISBN 978-0-8118-5414-6; 0-8118-5414-0

LC 2005025226

"A collection of 20 previously published stories, some by well-known writers of horror such as Stephen King and H. P. Lovecraft, others by authors not generally associated with the genre, like Winston Churchill. Each selection includes a chilling black-and-white engraving, often placed near the end of the story for maximum effect." SLJ

Scieszka Jon, Ed

★ **Guys** read: thriller. Walden Pond Press 2011 viii, 272p $16.99; pa $6.99

Grades: 5 6 7 8   S C

1. Short stories 2. Adventure fiction
ISBN 978-0-06-196376-6; 0-06-196376-3; 978-0-06-196375-9 pa; 0-06-196375-5 pa

"Scieszka has gathered 10 thrilling stories from stellar writers. There are ghost stories, a deeply touching tale of a wish-granting machine and one about monsters that live in storm drains. . . . This anthology is brimming with choice stuff for guys who appreciate the uncanny, the uncouth and the unput-down-able." Kirkus

Sedgwick, Marcus

★ **Midwinterblood**; Marcus Sedgwick. Roaring Brook Press 2013 272 p. (hardcover) $17.99

Grades: 7 8 9 10 11 12   S C

1. Reincarnation -- Fiction 2. Love -- Fiction 3. Islands -- Fiction
ISBN 1596438002; 9781596438002

LC 2012013302

Author Marcus Sedgwick presents seven stories about "an archaeologist who unearths a mysterious artifact, an airman who finds himself far from home, a painter, a ghost, a vampire, and a Viking." The stories "take place on the remote Scandinavian island of Blessed where a curiously powerful plant that resembles a dragon grows. . . . What secrets lurk beneath the surface of this idyllic countryside? And what might be powerful enough to break the cycle of midwinterblood?" (Publisher's note)

Shards and Ashes; edited by Melissa Marr and Kelley Armstrong ; with additional stories by Veronica Roth, Kami Garcia, Margaret Stohl and more. Harpercollins Childrens Books 2013 x, 369 p.p (ebook) $7.99; (hardcover) $17.99

Grades: 7 8 9 10   S C

1. Science fiction 2. Dystopian fiction 3. Apocalyptic fiction
ISBN 9780062098474; 0062098462; 9780062098467

This book, edited by Melissa Marr and Kelley Armstrong, offers nine science fiction short stories. "The world is gone, destroyed by human, ecological, or supernatural causes. Survivors dodge chemical warfare and cruel gods; they travel the reaches of space and inhabit underground caverns. Their enemies are disease, corrupt corporations, and one another; their resources are few and their courage is tested." (Publisher's note)

Shattered: stories of children and war; edited by Jennifer Armstrong. Knopf 2002 166p hardcover o.p. pa $6.50

Grades: 7 8 9 10   S C

1. War 2. War stories 3. Short stories
ISBN 0-375-81112-5; 0-440-23765-3 pa

LC 2001-18609

"These selections will make teens cry, will make them angry, but most of all they will make them think." SLJ

★ **Shelf** life: stories by the book; edited by Gary Paulsen. Simon & Schuster Bks. for Young Readers 2003 173p $16.95

Grades: 5 6 7 8 S C

1. Short stories 2. Books and reading 3. Books and reading -- Fiction 4. Children's stories, American

ISBN 0-689-84180-9

LC 2002-66901

Ten short stories in which the lives of young people in different circumstances are changed by their encounters with books

"Covering almost every genre of fiction, including mystery, SF, fantasy and realism, these well-crafted stories by familiar authors offer sharply drawn characterizations and intriguing premises." Publ Wkly

Shusterman, Neal

Darkness creeping; twenty twisted tales. Puffin Books 2007 291p pa $7.99

Grades: 5 6 7 8 S C

1. Short stories 2. Horror fiction

ISBN 0-14-240721-6

"The author takes a walk on the dark side in this collection of spooky stories, some old, some new, all delightfully creepy. He knows his audience, providing enough horrific touches to appeal to the most challenging readers—those hard-to-reach middle school boys. Each story is introduced with a brief statement describing where he got the idea." Voice Youth Advocates

★ **Sideshow**; ten original tales of freaks, illusionists, and other matters odd and magical. edited by Deborah Noyes. Candlewick Press 2009 199p il $16.99

Grades: 7 8 9 10 S C

1. Short stories 2. Young adult literature -- Works 3. Short stories -- Collections

ISBN 978-0-7636-3752-1; 0-7636-3752-1

LC 2008-37420

"This is a masterpiece of 10 short stories by world-class authors. Contributors include David Almond, Annette Curtis Klause, and Vivian Vande Velde. . . . Not all of the stories are traditional prose; several are graphic renditions, including Matt Phelan's masterfully drawn 'Jargo!' . . . Suspending disbelief, readers of this fantastic anthology may start investing in psychics and sleeping with the light on." SLJ

Sleator, William

★ **Oddballs**; stories. Dutton Children's Bks. 1993 134p hardcover o.p. pa $5.99

Grades: 6 7 8 9 10 S C

1. Short stories 2. Friendship -- Fiction 3. Family life -- Fiction

ISBN 0-525-45057-2; 0-14-037438-8 pa

LC 92-27666

A collection of stories based on experiences from the author's youth and peopled with an unusual assortment of family and friends.

"Fresh, funny, and slightly gross, the quasi-autobiographical glimpses will grab the reader's attention." Horn Book Guide

Smith, Charles R., 1969-

Winning words; sports stories and photographs. [by] Charles R. Smith. Candlewick Press 2008 70p il $17.99

Grades: 5 6 7 8 S C

1. Short stories 2. Sports -- Fiction

ISBN 978-0-7636-1445-4; 0-7636-1445-9

In this collection of short stories and photographs, Charles R. Smith Jr. shows young athletes overcoming their fears and challenging themselves to do their best.

"This outstanding collection consists of six readable and engaging stories. . . . Smith does a fine job of evoking the action and character of the games, in words and in close-up photos." SLJ

Soto, Gary

★ **Baseball** in April, and other stories; 10th anniversary ed; Harcourt Brace Jovanovich 2000 111p $16; pa $6

Grades: 5 6 7 8 S C

1. Short stories 2. Mexican Americans -- Fiction

ISBN 0-15-202573-1; 0-15-202567-7 pa

A reissue of the title first published 1990

A collection of eleven short stories focusing on the everyday adventures of Hispanic young people growing up in Fresno, California

Each story "gets at the heart of some aspect of growing up. The insecurities, the embarrassments, the triumphs, the inequities of it all are chronicled with wit and charm. Soto's characters ring true and his knowledge of, and affection for, their shared Mexican-American heritage is obvious and infectious." Voice Youth Advocates

★ **Help** wanted; stories. by Gary Soto. Harcourt 2005 216p $17; pa $6.95

Grades: 6 7 8 9 S C

1. Short stories 2. Mexican Americans -- Fiction

ISBN 0-15-205201-1; 978-0-15-205663-6 pa

LC 2004-7510

"The stories are sometimes funny, often poignant, and occasionally provocative." Booklist

Hey 13! Holiday House 2011 197p $16.95

Grades: 6 7 8 9 S C

1. Short stories

ISBN 978-0-8234-2395-8; 0-8234-2395-6

LC 2011007709

A collection of thirteen short stories about the ups and downs of being thirteen years old.

"The author's skill and the short story format are both well utilized. . . . This title offers both comfort and fun for tween readers." Booklist

★ **Local** news. Harcourt Brace Jovanovich 1993 148p hardcover o.p. pa $5.95

Grades: 5 6 7 8 S C

1. Short stories 2. Mexican Americans -- Fiction

ISBN 0-15-248117-6; 0-15-204695-X pa

LC 92-37905

A collection of thirteen short stories about the everyday lives of Mexican American young people in California's Central Valley

"These stories resonate with integrity, verve, and compassion." Horn Book

Spilsbury, Richard

Jay -Z; Richard Spilsbury. Heinemann Library 2013 48 p. (Titans of business) (pbk.) $8.99

Grades: 4   5   6   7
1. Businessmen 2. Rap musicians 3. Success in business
ISBN 1432964305; 1432964372; 9781432964306; 9781432964375

                     LC 2011050758

This book, part of the Titans of Business series, looks at rapper and entrepreneur Jay-Z. "Starting with Jay-Z's early life as Shawn Corey Carter in a poor Brooklyn neighborhood, the biography recounts how he overcame his difficult adolescence as a drug dealer with his desire to be a musician." (Booklist)

Includes bibliographical references and index

Spinelli, Jerry

The **library** card. Scholastic 1997 148p pa $4.99

Grades: 4 5 6 7   **S C**
1. Short stories 2. Books and reading -- Fiction
ISBN 0-590-38633-6

                     LC 96-18412

"A library card is the magical object common to each of these four stories in which a budding street thug, a television addict, a homeless orphan, and a lonely girl are all transformed by the power and the possibilities that await them within the walls of the public library. Spinelli's characters . . . are unusual and memorable; his writing both humorous and convincing." Horn Book Guide

Sports shorts. Darby Creek Pub. 2005 127p il $15.99; pa $4.99

Grades: 5 6 7 8   **S C**
1. Short stories 2. Sports -- Fiction
ISBN 9780761385363; 1-58196-040-9; 1-58196-058-1 pa

A collection of eight semi-autobiographical stories about the authors' experiences with sports while growing up.

"Some of the vignettes are laugh-out-loud funny. . . . The book's smaller-than-standard trim size and inviting page design will help attract readers to this rewarding collection." Booklist

★ **Steampunk!** an anthology of fantastically rich and strange stories. edited by Kelly Link and Gavin J. Grant. Candlewick Press 2011 432p pbk. $12.99

Grades: 8 9 10 11 12   **S C**
1. Short stories 2. Fantasy fiction
ISBN 0763657972; 9780763657970

                     LC 2010040742

In this collection of short stories edited by Kelly Link and Gavin J. Grant "fourteen [authors] of speculative fiction, including two graphic storytellers, embrace the [steampunk]

genre"s established themes and refashion them in surprising ways and settings as diverse as Appalachia, ancient Rome, future Australia, and alternate California." (Publisher's note)

"Veteran editors Link and Grant serve up a delicious mix of original stories from 14 skilled writers and artists. . . . Chockful of gear-driven automatons, looming dirigibles, and wildly implausible time machines, these often baroque, intensely anachronistic tales should please steampunks of all ages." Publ Wkly

Tan, Shaun

★ **Lost** & found; 3 by Shaun Tan. Arthur A. Levine Books 2011 un il $21.99

Grades: 5 6 7 8   **S C**
1. Short stories
ISBN 978-0-545-22924-1; 0-545-22924-3

                     LC 2010030936

This book comprises three previously published stories by the Australian author-illustrator "In 'The Red Tree,' a young girl moves listlessly through her day with a sense of dreadful ennui that escalates with each page turn . . . until finally finding some hope at the end. In 'The Lost Thing,' a young boy discovers a most peculiar object and dutifully tries to find a proper home for it. . . . Finally, 'The Rabbits' (with a text by John Marsden) is a colonization fable, as rabbits invade and populate a new land, overwhelming the native animal population and severely altering the landscape. . . . Intermediate, middle school." (Horn Book)

"'The Red Tree' follows a solitary girl through a single, not very good day, exploring her feelings as they shift from disappointment and confusion to alienation and despair. The spare, lyrical text provides an anchor for Tan's large, moody, beautiful paintings. 'The Lost Thing' is a more upbeat tale of a boy who discovers an unusual object and then must decide what to do with it. Freedom and imagination are the themes in this story, and here the art includes fascinating and sometimes humorous bits of technical drawings. The prose of John Marsden's 'The Rabbits,' an allegory about imperialism, is so simple and melodic that it verges on poetry. The artist emphasizes the invasive foreignness of the rabbits by dressing them in baroque uniforms, drawing mystifying, gigantic machines and buildings for them to build and deploy in their inexorable drive to dominate." SLJ

★ **Tales** from outer suburbia. Arthur A. Levine Books 2009 92p il $19.99

Grades: 7 8 9 10   **S C**
1. Short stories 2. Suburban life -- Fiction
ISBN 0-545-05587-3; 978-0-545-05587-1

                     LC 2008-13784

This is a collection of fifteen illustrated stories set in the Australian suburbs.

"The term 'suburbia' may conjure visions of vast and generic sameness, but in his hypnotic collection of 15 short stories and meditations, Tan does for the sprawling landscape what he did for the metropolis in The Arrival . . . . Ideas and imagery both beautiful and disturbing will linger." Publ Wkly

★ **Talking** leaves; contemporary native American short stories. introduced and edited by Craig Lesley; associate editor, Katheryn Stavrakis. Dell 1991 xxvi, 385p pa $16.95

Grades: 8 9 10 11 12 Adult   **S C**

1. Short stories 2. Native Americans -- Fiction
ISBN 0-385-31272-5

LC 92-139334

This anthology includes contributions by such authors as Louise Erdrich, Diane Glancy, Michael Dorris, N. Scott Momaday, Paula Gunn Allen, and Mary Tallmountain

"All these stories have a strong sense of person and place and engagingly inform of the Native American condition." Libr J

Taylor, Laini

★ **Lips** touch; three times. illustrations by Jim Di Bartolo. Arthur A. Levine Books 2009 265p il $17.99

Grades: 8 9 10 11 12   **S C**

1. Short stories 2. Kissing -- Fiction 3. Supernatural -- Fiction
ISBN 978-0-545-05585-7; 0-545-05585-7

LC 2009-5458

These three stories about kissing feature elements of the supernatural.

"Taylor offers a powerful trio of tales, each founded upon the consequences of a kiss. . . . Contemporary Kizzy, who so yearns to be a normal, popular teenager that she forgets the rules of her Old Country upbringing and is seduced by a goblin in disguise; Anamique, living in British colonial India, silenced forever due to a spell cast upon her at birth; and Esmé, who at 14 discovers she is host to another—non-human—being. . . . Each is, in vividly distinctive fashion, a mesmerizing love story that comes to a satisfying but never predictable conclusion. Di Bartolo's illustrations provide tantalizing visual preludes to each tale." Publ Wkly

This family is driving me crazy; ten stories about surviving your family. edited by M. Jerry Weiss and Helen S. Weiss. G. P. Putnam's Sons 2009 224p $17.99

Grades: 6 7 8 9 10   **S C**

1. Short stories 2. Family life -- Fiction 3. Young adult literature -- Works 4. Short stories -- Collections
ISBN 978-0-399-25040-8; 0-399-25040-9

LC 2009-06821

"Ten authors contribute short stories about family life. . . . The diversity of authors really provides something for everyone. . . . Enough gems are included here to make it a worthwhile purchase." Booklist

This is PUSH; an anthology of new writing. edited by David Levithan. Scholastic 2007 232p (Push anthology) pa $6.99

Grades: 6 7 8 9   **S C**

1. Short stories 2. Young adult literature -- Works
ISBN 978-0-439-89028-1; 0-439-89028-4

"Fifteen new stories make up this first-class anthology. . . . Readers will be left speechless by Chris Wooding's jarring, horrific tale of two godlike beings . . . and they will no doubt be haunted by Markus Zusak's captivatingly poetic story of a gravedigger and his crush. . . . As a whole, they run the literary gamut from realistic fiction to memoir to romance to

mystery to horror, and each one will no doubt be devoured by teens." SLJ

Tomo; friendship through fiction : an anthology of Japan teen stories. edited by Holly Thompson ; cover and part-title illustrations by John Shelley. Stone Bridge Press 2012 383 p. pa $14.95

Grades: 7 8 9 10   **S C**

1. Japan -- Fiction 2. Young adult literature 3. Short stories -- Collections 4. Children's stories, Japanese
ISBN 1611720060; 9781611720068

LC 2011051530

This book of short stories, edited by Holly Thompson, is an "anthology of authors with direct or indirect Japanese 'heritage or experience.' The 36 tales (all but six of which are new) were gathered as contributions to the relief effort for victims of the 2011 earthquake and tsunami." The various entries focus on stories about Japanese and half-Japanese teenagers in a variety of genres, including historical fiction, contemporary teenage drama, and fantasy. Stories are indexed by plot themes, including friendship, ghosts, super-powers, and family relationships. (Kirkus)

★ **Troll's** eye view; a book of villainous tales. Viking 2009 200p $16.99; pa $7.99

Grades: 5 6 7 8   **S C**

1. Fairy tales 2. Short stories
ISBN 978-0-670-06141-9; 0-670-06141-7; 978-0-14-241673-0 pa; 0-14-241673-8 pa

Everyone thinks they know the real story behind the villains in fairy tales—evil, no two ways about it. But the villains themselves beg to differ. In this anthology for younger readers, you'll hear from the Giant's wife (from Jack and the Beanstalk), Rumpelstiltskin, the oldest of the Twelve Dancing Princesses, and more.

"A mixed bag of funny, quirky, and downright creepy entries. . . . The collection is largely accessible and very enjoyable." Booklist

Twain, Mark

★ **Mark** Twain; edited by Gregg Camfield; illustrated by Sally Wern Comport. Sterling 2005 80p il (Stories for young people) $14.95

Grades: 6 7 8 9   **S C**

1. Short stories
ISBN 1-4027-1178-6

"This collection of five stories includes 'An Encounter with an Interviewer,' 'The Invalid's Story,' 'Advice to Youth,' 'The L1,000,000 Banknote,' and 'A Fable.'. . . . Handsome illustrations with detailed, revealing facial expressions and body language appear on almost every page. The book opens with a biography, explaining the meaning of mark twain," briefly outlining Clemens's life, and quickly discussing his influence on American literature." SLJ

Ultimate sports; short stories by outstanding writers for young adults. edited by Donald R. Gallo. Delacorte Press 1995 333p hardcover o.p. pa $6.99

Grades: 7 8 9 10   **S C**

1. Short stories 2. Sports -- Fiction 3. Short stories

-- Collections
ISBN 0-440-22707-0; 0-440-22707-0 pa
LC 94-49610

A collection of sixteen short stories about teenage athletes.

"There is a terrific mix of the serious and the lighthearted, female and male characters, and traditional and nontraditional games. A winning collection." SLJ

Under my hat; tales from the cauldron. edited by Jonathan Strahan. Random House 2012 415 p. (trade) $16.99

Grades: 5 6 7 8   S C

1. Short stories 2. Witches -- Fiction

ISBN 0375868305; 9780375868047; 9780375868306; 9780375898815; 9780375968303

LC 2011031253

This book presents "eighteen short tales about witches. . . . Garth Nix"s 'A Handful of Ashes' features a library and librarian. Delia Sherman"s 'The Witch in the Woods' . . . [features] deer and bear shape-shifters and no small darkness. . . . Jane Yolen makes Hans Christian Andersen's life a tale itself." (Kirkus Reviews)

Under the weather; stories about climate change. edited by Tony Bradman. Frances Lincoln Children's 2009 215p pbk. $8.99; $16.95

Grades: 5 6 7 8   S C

1. Short stories 2. Greenhouse effect -- Fiction

ISBN 9781845079444; 1-84507-930-2; 978-1-84507-930-7

"Eight stories by a variety of authors attempt to make the facts about climate change and its global ramifications relevant to today's children. The majority of the selections are about youngsters enacting change and working toward solutions in tangible ways. For example, 'How to Build the Perfect Sandcastle" is about a Philippino boy who works to rebuild the coral reefs, which are dying due to the rise in ocean temperature. . . . Overall . . . this is a worthwhile effort that will appeal to children wanting to make a difference in their world as well as to teachers trying to make the scientific reality of climate change real to their students." SLJ

Unnatural creatures; stories. Neil Gaiman ; [edited by] Rosemary Brosnan. 1st ed. HarperCollins 2013 480 p. ill. (hardcover) $17.99

Grades: 8 9 10 11 12   S C

1. Short stories 2. Fantasy fiction 3. Monsters -- Fiction

ISBN 0062236296; 9780062236296; 9780062236302

LC 2013933032

This fantasy-horror short story collection, compiled by Neil Gaiman and edited by Maria Dahvana Headley, "is a collection of short stories about the fantastical things that exist only in our minds. . . . The sixteen stories . . . range from the whimsical to the terrifying. The magical creatures range from werewolves to sunbirds to beings never before classified. E. Nesbit, Diana Wynne Jones, Gahan Wilson, and other literary luminaries contribute to the anthology." (Publisher's note)

Vande Velde, Vivian

All Hallows' Eve; 13 stories. Harcourt 2006 225p $17

Grades: 7 8 9 10   S C

1. Short stories 2. Halloween -- Fiction 3. Supernatural -- Fiction

ISBN 978-0-15-205576-9; 0-15-205576-2

LC 2006-05439

Presents thirteen tales of Halloween horrors, including ghosts, vampires, and pranks gone awry.

"This mistress of the macabre draws readers in with her familiar conversational tone and easily recognizable situations . . . before skillfully shifting the narratives in unsettling, sometimes terrifying, directions. . . . Vande Velde's narrative tricks are a treat." Horn Book

★ **Being** dead; stories. Harcourt 2001 203p hardcover o.p. pa $6.95

Grades: 7 8 9 10   S C

1. Supernatural 2. Short stories 3. Horror fiction 4. Horror stories 5. Supernatural -- Fiction

ISBN 0-15-216320-4; 0-15-204912-6 pa

LC 00-12996

"Often humorous and sometimes evoking sympathy, this anthology will be enjoyed by lovers of mild horror as well as by those who like clever short stories." Voice Youth Advocates

Cloaked in red. Marshall Cavendish Children 2010 127p $15.99

Grades: 7 8 9 10   S C

1. Fairy tales 2. Short stories

ISBN 0-7614-5793-3; 978-0-7614-5793-0

LC 2009-51753

This book presents eight variations on the traditional tale of Little Red Riding Hood. "Grades five to eight." (Bull Cent Child Books)

The stories "blend wry contemporary commentary with fractured-fairy-tale elements, horror, and a subtle bit of sensuality. . . . The wacky tales can easily be used to inspire teens to make up versions of their own." Booklist

Visions: nineteen short stories by outstanding writers for young adults; edited by Donald R. Gallo. Delacorte Press 1987 228p hardcover o.p. pa $6.99

Grades: 7 8 9 10   S C

1. Short stories

ISBN 0-440-20208-6

LC 87-6787

"Information about the authors follows each of nineteen original short stories, most of them impressive examples of the genre, all of them written by established men and women. Among the familiar names: Joan Aiken, M.E. Kerr, Walter Dean Myers, Richard Peck. The tales are grouped under such headings as 'Adjustments' or 'Kinships,' and include both realistic and fanciful writing, most of the work being of fine quality and the rest only slightly less so." Bull Cent Child Books

Voices in first person; reflections on Latino identity. [edited by Lori Marie Carlson] Atheneum Books for Young Readers 2008 96p il $16.99

Grades: 6 7 8 9 10 11 12   S C

1. Short stories 2. American literature -- Hispanic American authors -- Collections

ISBN 978-1-4169-0635-3; 1-4169-0635-5

LC 2006-34161

A collection of brief fictional pieces about the experiences of Latinos in the United States, by such writers as Sandra Cisneros, Gary Soto, Oscar Hijuelos, and others.

"Carlson has drawn from both established and new writers, focusing on finding Latino voices that speak to contemporary readers. . . . This collection sparkles more than its predecessors because of its dynamic design, featuring black-and-white photographs and line illustrations incorporated with the text in a collage-like magazine layout." SLJ

Wallace, Rich

Losing is not an option: stories. Knopf 2003 127p hardcover o.p. pa $5.99

Grades: 7 8 9 10   S C

1. Short stories

ISBN 0-375-81351-9; 0-440-23844-7 pa

LC 2002-34036

Nine episodes in the life of a young man, from sneaking into his tenth football game in a row with his best friend in sixth grade to running his last high school race, the Pennsylvania state championships.

"Readers will nod with recognition as they follow this jock/poet/regular guy from the cusp of adolescence to the edge of adulthood." Horn Book Guide

What are you afraid of? stories about phobias. edited by Donald R. Gallo. Candlewick Press 2006 189p $16.99

Grades: 6 7 8 9   S C

1. Short stories 2. Phobias -- Fiction 3. Young adult literature -- Works 4. Short stories -- Collections

ISBN 0-7636-2654-6

LC 2004-62874

Presents ten short stories by well-known authors featuring teenagers with phobias, inluding fear of gaining weight, fear of clowns, and fear of cats.

"This is an excellent collection on a topic that holds a strange and fascinating allure." SLJ

Who do you think you are? stories of friends and enemies. selected by Hazel Rochman and Darlene Z. McCampbell. Little, Brown 1993 170p hardcover o.p. pa $9.99

Grades: 7 8 9 10   S C

1. Short stories 2. Friendship -- Fiction

ISBN 0-316-75320-3

LC 93-314

"Meticulously chosen and arranged, these works crystalize moments of vulnerability, sorrow and understanding; together, they serve as an excellent introduction to modern American writing." Publ Wkly

You don't have a clue; Latino mystery stories for teens. [edited by Sarah Cortez] Pinata Books 2011 310p pa $16.95

Grades: 6 7 8 9 10   S C

1. Short stories 2. Hispanic Americans -- Fiction 3. Young adult literature -- Works 4. Short stories -- Collections -- Juvenile literature

ISBN 1-55885-692-7; 978-1-55885-692-9

LC 2011-00117

These short stories are "set in schools and communities from New York City to Venice Beach, California." (Publisher's note) "Grades seven to ten." (Bull Cent Child Books)

You never did learn to knock; 14 stories about girls and their mothers. selected by Bel Mooney. Kingfisher 2006 254p pa $7.95

Grades: 7 8 9 10   S C

1. Short stories 2. Mother-daughter relationship -- Fiction

ISBN 0-7534-5877-2

In this collection of short stories about mothers and daughters "situations include adoption, girls manipulating their mothers, divorce, and terminal illness. . . . A solid, enjoyable collection due to its breezy style and content." SLJ

AUTHOR, TITLE, AND SUBJECT INDEX

This index to the books in the Classified Collection includes author, title, and subject entries; added entries for publishers' series, illustrators, joint authors, and editors of works entered under title; and name and subject cross-references; all arranged in one alphabet.

The number or symbol in bold face type at the end of each entry refers to the Dewey Decimal Classification or to the Fiction (Fic) or Story Collection (S C), or Easy Books (E) section where the main entry for the book will be found. Works classed in 92 will be found under the headings for the biographies' subject.

A

Wurdinger, S. D. Rock climbing **796.52**

ADVENTURE STORIES *See* Adventure fiction

ADVENTURE TRAVEL

See also Travel; Voyages and travels

Adventurers. Branzei, S. **920.72**

The **adventures** and the memoirs of Sherlock Holmes. Doyle, A. C. S. **Fic**

Adventures of a cat-whiskered girl. Pinkwater, D. M. **Fic**

The **adventures** of a South Pole pig. Kurtz, C. **Fic**

The **adventures** of Jack Lime. Leck, J. **Fic**

The **adventures** of Medical Man. Evans, M. **616**

The **adventures** of Molly Whuppie and other Appalachian folktales. Shelby, A. **398.2**

The **adventures** of Tom Sawyer. Twain, M. **Fic**

Adventures on the ancient Silk Road. Galloway, P. **950**

Adventurous aquarist guide [series]

Wood, K. The 101 best tropical fishes **639.34**

The **adventurous** book of outdoor games. Strother, S. **796**

The **adventurous** deeds of Deadwood Jones. Hemphill, H. **Fic**

The **adventurous** life of Myles Standish. Harness, C. **92**

ADVERTISING

Freese, S. M. Craigslist **381**

Sobel, D. What's the catch? **153.8**

ADVERTISING

See also Business; Retail trade

ADVERTISING -- FICTION

Williams, M. The Fizzy Whiz kid **Fic**

ADVERTISING -- LIBRARIES

Imhoff, K. R. Library contests **021.7**

ADVERTISING AND CHILDREN

See also Advertising; Children

ADVERTISING COPY

See also Advertising; Authorship

ADVERTISING EXECUTIVES

Molnar, H. L. Under a red sky **92**

ADVERTISING LAYOUT AND TYPOGRAPHY

See also Advertising; Printing; Typography

ADVICE COLUMNS

See also Counseling; Newspapers -- Sections, columns, etc.

AENEAS (LEGENDARY CHARACTER)

Hamilton, E. Mythology **292**

AERIAL BOMBS *See* Bombs

AERIAL PHOTOGRAPHY

See also Photography

Belmont, H. Looking at aerial photographs **910**

Collier, M. Over the mountains **557**

Delannoy, I. Our living Earth **779**

AERIAL PHOTOGRAPHY IN GEOLOGY

Collier, M. Over the mountains **557**

AERIAL PROPELLERS

See also Airplanes

AERIAL RECONNAISSANCE

See also Military aeronautics; Remote sensing

AERIAL ROCKETS *See* Rockets (Aeronautics)

An aerial view of geology [series]

Collier, M. Over the mountains **557**

AEROBICS

See also Exercise

AERODYNAMICS

See also Air; Dynamics; Pneumatics

AERONAUTICAL ENGINEERS

Richie, J. Space flight **629**

AERONAUTICAL SPORTS

See also Aeronautics; Sports

AERONAUTICS

See also Engineering; Locomotion

Carson, M. K. The Wright Brothers for kids **629.13**

Hense, M. How fighter pilots use math **629.13**

Mercer, B. The flying machine book **745.592**

Parker, S. By air **387.7**

Skurzynski, G. This is rocket science **629.4**

AERONAUTICS -- ACCIDENTS *See* Aircraft accidents

AERONAUTICS -- ENCYCLOPEDIAS

Flight and motion **629.13**

AERONAUTICS -- FICTION

Armstrong, A. Racing the moon **Fic**

AERONAUTICS -- FLIGHTS

See also Voyages and travels

Skrypuch, M. F. Last airlift **959.704**

AERONAUTICS -- HISTORY

Carson, M. K. The Wright Brothers for kids **629.13**

Collins, M. Airborne: a photobiography of Wilbur and Orville Wright **92**

Crompton, S. The Wright brothers **92**

Faber, H. The airplane **629.133**

Finkelstein, N. H. Three across **629.13**

Freedman, R. The Wright brothers: how they invented the airplane **92**

Hardesty, V. Epic flights **629.13**

Nahum, A. Flying machine **629.133**

AERONAUTICS -- VOYAGES *See* Aeronautics -- Flights

AERONAUTICS AND CIVILIZATION

See also Aeronautics; Civilization

AERONAUTICS IN AGRICULTURE

See also Aeronautics; Agriculture; Spraying and dusting

AERONAUTICS, MILITARY *See* Military aeronautics

AEROPLANES *See* Airplanes

Aerosmith. Burlingame, J. **781.66**

AEROSOL SNIFFING *See* Solvent abuse

AEROSOLS

See also Air pollution

Grimes, N. Jazmin's notebook   **Fic**
Pearsall, S. Jump into the sky   **Fic**

AFRICAN AMERICANS -- POETRY
Grimes, N. A dime a dozen   **811**
Weatherford, C. B. Remember the bridge   **811**

AFRICAN AMERICANS -- MARYLAND -- BAL-TIMORE -- SOCIAL CONDITIONS -- 20TH CENTURY
Moore, W. Discovering Wes Moore   **975.2**

AFRICAN AMERICANS -- MIGRATIONS -- HISTORY -- 20TH CENTURY
Harris, L. L. The great migration north, 1910-1970 **307.2**

AFRICAN AMERICANS -- MISSISSIPPI
Robson, D. The murder of Emmett Till   **364.152**
Wright, S. Simeon's story   **305.8**

AFRICAN AMERICANS -- MONUMENTS
Horton, J. O. Landmarks of African American history **305.8**

AFRICAN AMERICANS -- MUSIC
Cooper, M. L. Slave spirituals and the Jubilee Singers **782.421**

AFRICAN AMERICANS -- NEW YORK (N.Y.)
Bolden, T. Maritcha   **92**

AFRICAN AMERICANS -- POETRY
Alexander, E. Miss Crandall's School for Young Ladies and Little Misses of Color **811**
Angelou, M. Maya Angelou   **811**
Crisler, C. L. Tough boy sonatas   **811**
Flake, S. G. You don't even know me   **808.8**
Giovanni, N. Ego-tripping and other poems for young people **811**
Grimes, N. A dime a dozen   **811**
Hughes, L. The dream keeper and other poems   **811**
Hughes, L. Langston Hughes   **811**
I, too, sing America   **811**
My black me   **811**
Myers, W. D. Harlem   **811**
Myers, W. D. Here in Harlem   **811**
Nelson, M. Fortune's bones   **811**
Nelson, M. The freedom business   **811**
Nelson, M. A wreath for Emmett Till   **811**
Shange, N. Freedom's a-callin' me   **811**
Smith, H. A. Mother poems   **811**
Soul looks back in wonder   **811**
Spires, E. I heard God talking to me   **811**
Weatherford, C. B. Remember the bridge   **811**
Woodson, J. Locomotion   **Fic**
Words with wings   **811**

AFRICAN AMERICANS -- QUOTATIONS
Hudson, W. Powerful words   **081**

AFRICAN AMERICANS -- RELIGION
See also Blacks -- Religion; Religion
Haskins, J. African American religious leaders   **920**
Murphy, L. African-American faith in America   **200**

AFRICAN AMERICANS -- SEGREGATION

See also Blacks -- Segregation; Segregation
Osborne, L. B. Miles to go for freedom   **305.896**

AFRICAN AMERICANS -- SEGREGATION -- HISTORY -- 20TH CENTURY
Osborne, L. B. Miles to go for freedom   **305.896**

AFRICAN AMERICANS -- SOCIAL CONDITIONS
Hinman, B. Eternal vigilance: the story of Ida B. Wells-Barnett **92**

AFRICAN AMERICANS -- SUFFRAGE
See also African Americans -- Civil rights; Blacks -- Suffrage; Suffrage
Aretha, D. Selma and the Voting Rights Act   **324.6**

AFRICAN AMERICANS -- TENNESSEE -- MEMPHIS -- SOCIAL CONDITIONS -- 20TH CENTURY
Bausum, A. Marching to the mountaintop   **323**

AFRICAN AMERICANS -- WEST (U.S.) -- BIOGRAPHY -- CARTOONS AND COMICS
Best shot in the West   **978**

AFRICAN AMERICANS -- WEST (U.S.)
Schlissel, L. Black frontiers   **978**
African Americans and the Civil War. Reis, R. A. **973.7**
African Americans during Reconstruction. Worth, R. **973.8**
African Americans during the Civil War. DeFord, D. H. **973.7**

AFRICAN AMERICANS IN ART
Lawrence, J. The great migration   **759.13**
Words with wings   **811**

AFRICAN AMERICANS IN ART
Duggleby, J. Story painter: the life of Jacob Lawrence **759.13**

AFRICAN AMERICANS IN LITERATURE
Bernadowski, C. Teaching literacy skills to adolescents using Coretta Scott King Award winners **372.4**
Brooks, W. M. Embracing, evaluating, and examining African American children's and young adult literature **028.5**
Embracing, evaluating, and examining African American children's and young adult literature **028.5**
Litwin, L. B. A reader's guide to Zora Neale Hurston's Their eyes were watching god **813**
Loos, P. A reader's guide to Lorraine Hansberry's A raisin in the sun **812**
Stover, L. T. Jacqueline Woodson   **813**
Wilkin, B. T. African and African American images in Newbery Award winning titles **810**

AFRICAN AMERICANS IN MOTION PICTURES
See also Blacks in motion pictures; Minorities in motion pictures; Motion pictures
Lace, W. W. Blacks in film   **791.43**

Alexander, Sally Hobart
 She touched the world: Laura Bridgman, deaf-blind pioneer **92**

Alexander, the Great, 356-323 B.C.
 About
 Behnke, A. The conquests of Alexander the Great **92**
 Adams, S. Alexander **92**
 Demi Alexander the Great **92**

Alexie, Sherman, 1966-
 The absolutely true diary of a part-time Indian **Fic**

Alfred Blalock, Helen Taussig, and Vivien Thomas. Yount, L. **617.4**

Alfred Kropp: the seal of Solomon. Yancey, R. **Fic**

Alfred Kropp: the thirteenth skull. Yancey, R. **Fic**

ALGAE
 See also Marine plants
 Arato, R. Protists **579**
 Parker, S. Protozoans, algae & other protists **579**

ALGEBRA
 See also Mathematical analysis; Mathematics
 Caron, L. Pre-algebra and algebra smarts! **512**
 Green, D. Algebra & geometry **516.2**

Algebra & geometry. Green, D. **516.2**

Algeria. Kagda, F. **965**

ALGERIA -- HISTORY -- 1954-1962, REVOLUTION
 Wagner, H. L. The Algerian war **965**

The **Algerian** war. Wagner, H. L. **965**

Alhazen, 965-1039
 About
 Steffens, B. Ibn al-Haytham **92**

Ali Baba and the forty thieves. Manning, M. K. **741.5**

Ali, Muhammad, 1942-
 About
 Micklos, J. Muhammad Ali **92**
 Myers, W. D. The greatest: Muhammad Ali **92**
 Owens, T. Muhammad Ali **92**
 Smith, C. R. Twelve rounds to glory: the story of Muhammad Ali **92**
 Streissguth, T. Clay v. United States and how Muhammad Ali fought the draft **343**

Ali, Rubina
 Slumgirl dreaming **92**

Ali, Rubina
 About
 Ali, R. Slumgirl dreaming **92**

Ali, Sharifah Enayat
 Afghanistan **958.1**

Alice in April. Naylor, P. R. **Fic**

Alice in lace. Naylor, P. R. **Fic**

Alice in rapture, sort of. Naylor, P. R. **Fic**

Alice in-between. Naylor, P. R. **Fic**

Alice on her way. Naylor, P. R. **Fic**

Alice the brave. Naylor, P. R. **Fic**

Alicia Alonso. Bernier-Grand, C. T. **92**

Alien deep. Hague, B. **551.2**

Alien feast. Simmons, M. **Fic**

Alien Hunter's Handbook. Brake, M. **576.8**

ALIEN LABOR, CHINESE -- UNITED STATES -- HISTORY -- 19TH CENTURY
 Perl, L. To the Golden Mountain **305.8**

Alien snow. Dahl, M. **741.5**

ALIENATION (SOCIAL PSYCHOLOGY)
 Crossan, S. The Weight of Water **Fic**

ALIENS
 See also Minorities

Aliens ate my homework. Coville, B. **Fic**

ALIENS FROM OUTER SPACE *See* Extraterrestrial beings

Aliki
 William Shakespeare & the Globe **792.09**

ALIMONY
 See also Divorce

Alire, Camila
 Serving Latino communities **027.6**

Alis. Rich, N. **Fic**

Alive in the killing fields. Keat, N. **92**

Alkouatli, Claire
 Islam **297**

All aboard! Zimmermann, K. R. **385**

All about adoption. Lanchon, A. **362.7**

All about electric and hybrid cars. Bearce, S. **629.222**

All about Japan. Moore, W. **952**

All about Korea. Bowler, A. M. **951.9**

All about money. Simons, R. **332.4**

All about sleep from A to ZZZZ. Scott, E. **612.8**

All alone in the universe. Perkins, L. R. **Fic**

All but Alice. Naylor, P. R. **Fic**

All good children. Austen, C. **Fic**

All Hallows' Eve. Vande Velde, V. **S C**

All in the family. Otfinoski, S. **292**

All my noble dreams and then what happens. Whelan, G. **Fic**

All of the above. Pearsall, S. **Fic**

All our relatives. Goble, P. **970.004**

All rivers flow to the sea. McGhee, A. **Fic**

All shook up. Pearsall, S. **Fic**

ALL TERRAIN VEHICLES
 See also Vehicles

All that glitters. Van Etten, D. **Fic**

All that remains. Brooks, B. **Fic**

All the birds of North America. Griggs, J. L. **598**

All the broken pieces. Burg, A. E. **Fic**

All the things you are. Sheinmel, C. **Fic**

All the world's a stage. **Fic**

All the wrong people have self esteem. Rosenwald, L. **646.7**

All unquiet things. Jarzab, A. **Fic**

All we know of heaven. Mitchard, J. **Fic**

All we know of love. Baskin, N. R. **Fic**

All you desire. Miller, K. **Fic**

giero, A.   **973.917**

American voices from the new republic, 1783-1830. Stefoff, R.   **973.4**

American voices from the opening of the West. Stefoff, R.   **978**

American voices from the time of slavery. Sirimarco, E.   **326**

American voices from the Wild West. Stefoff, R.   **978**

American voices from the women's movement. Schomp, V.   **305.4**

American voices from-- [series]

Ruggiero, A. American voices from Reconstruction   **973.8**

Ruggiero, A. American voices from The Great Depression   **973.917**

Schomp, V. American voices from the women's movement   **305.4**

Sirimarco, E. American voices from the civil rights movement   **323.1**

Sirimarco, E. American voices from the time of slavery   **326**

Stefoff, R. American voices from a century of immigration: 1820-1924   **325**

Stefoff, R. American voices from Colonial life   **973.2**

Stefoff, R. American voices from the new republic, 1783-1830   **973.4**

Stefoff, R. American voices from the opening of the West   **978**

Stefoff, R. American voices from the Wild West   **978**

American war library, American Revolution [series]

Stewart, G. Life of a soldier in Washington's army   **973.3**

American war library, Cold War [series]

Campbell, G. A. The home front   **973.92**

American war series

Carey, C. W. The Mexican War   **973.6**

Warrick, K. C. The War of 1812   **973.5**

The **American** West. McEvoy, A.   **391**

AMERICAN WIT AND HUMOR

See also American literature; Wit and humor

American women scientists. Reynolds, M. D.   **509**

American workers [series]

Baker, J. The Bread and Roses strike of 1912 **331.8**

Getzinger, D. The Triangle Shirtwaist Factory fire   **974.7**

Laughlin, R. The Ludlow massacre of 1913-14   **331.8**

Laughlin, R. The Pullman strike of 1894   **331.8**

Whitelaw, N. The Homestead Steel Strike of 1892   **331.8**

AMERICAN-SPANISH WAR, 1898 *See* Spanish-American War, 1898

AMERICANA

See also Collectors and collecting; Popular culture -- United States; United States -- Civilization; United States -- History

AMERICANISMS

Dictionary of American slang   **427**

Little, B. &. C. I. Bartlett's Roget's thesaurus **423**

Ostler, R. Dewdroppers, waldos, and slackers **428**

AMERICANIZATION

See also Socialization

AMERICANS -- ITALY -- FICTION

Baucom, I. Through the skylight   **Fic**

Beyer, K. The demon catchers of Milan   **Fic**

Americans from India and other South Asian countries. Park, K.   **305.8**

Americans from Russia and Eastern Europe. Weiss, G. G.   **305.8**

Americans from the Caribbean and Central America. Keedle, J.   **305.8**

Americans: the spirit of a nation [series]

Schuman, M. Frederick Douglass   **92**

Schuman, M. Jim Thorpe   **92**

Worth, R. Johnny Appleseed   **92**

Americapedia. Anderson, J. L.   **320**

The **Americas** and the Pacific. Connolly, S. **970.004**

Americus.   **741.5**

Ames, Lee J.

Draw 50 aliens, UFO's galaxy ghouls, milky way marauders, and other extra terrestrial creatures **743**

Draw 50 animal 'toons   **741.5**

Draw 50 animals   **743**

Draw 50 athletes   **743**

Draw 50 baby animals   **743**

Draw 50 beasties and yugglies and turnover uglies and things that go bump in the night   **743**

Draw 50 birds   **743**

Draw 50 boats, ships, trucks & trains   **743**

Draw 50 buildings and other structures   **743**

Draw 50 cats   **743**

Draw 50 dinosaurs and other prehistoric animals   **743**

Draw 50 dogs   **743**

Draw 50 endangered animals   **743**

Draw 50 famous faces   **743**

Draw 50 flowers, trees, and other plants   **743**

Draw 50 holiday decorations   **743**

Draw 50 horses   **743**

Draw 50 monsters, creeps, superheroes, demons, dragons, nerds, dirts, ghouls, giants, vampires, zombies, and other curiosa   **743**

Draw 50 people   **743**

[Draw 50 series]   **743**

Drawing with Lee Ames   **741.2**

Amigas [series]

Chambers, V. Fifteen candles   **Fic**

Amigurumi world. Rimoli, A. P.   **746.43**

Amin, Idi, 1925-2003

About

Nanji, S. Child of dandelions   **Fic**

Amiri & Odette. Myers, W. D.   **Fic**

AMISH -- FICTION

Bickle, L. The outside   **Fic**

Grossman, N. A world away   **Fic**

The **Amistad.** Grayson, R.   326

AMNESIA

     See also Memory

AMNESIA -- FICTION

Armistead, C. Being Henry David   **Fic**

Lerangis, P. Somebody, please tell me who I am

Lowry, L. Son   **Fic**

AMNESTY

     See also Administration of criminal justice; Executive power

Amnesty International

Free?: stories about human rights   **S C**

Among the Barons. Haddix, M. P.   **Fic**

Among the betrayed. Haddix, M. P.   **Fic**

Among the brave. Haddix, M. P.   **Fic**

Among the enemy. Haddix, M. P.   **Fic**

Among the free. Haddix, M. P.   **Fic**

Among the hidden. Haddix, M. P.   **Fic**

Among the impostors. Haddix, M. P.   **Fic**

Amos Paragon [series]

The mask wearer   **Fic**

AMPHETAMINES

Menhard, F. R. The facts about amphetamines   362.29

Warburton, L. Amphetamines and other stimulants   362.29

AMPHETAMINES

     See also Stimulants

Amphetamines and other stimulants. Warburton, L.   362.29

The **amphibian** class. Stefoff, R.   597.8

AMPHIBIANS

Conant, R. A field guide to reptiles & amphibians   597.9

Gilpin, D. Tree frogs, mud puppies, & other amphibians   597.8

Reptiles and amphibians   333.95

Stebbins, R. C. A field guide to Western reptiles and amphibians   597.9

Stefoff, R. The amphibian class   597.8

AMPHIBIANS

     See also Animals

AMPHIBIANS -- CANADA -- IDENTIFICATION

Conant, R. A field guide to reptiles & amphibians   597.9

AMPHIBIANS -- NORTH AMERICA -- IDENTIFICATION

Stebbins, R. C. A field guide to Western reptiles and amphibians   597.9

AMPHIBIANS -- UNITED STATES -- IDENTIFICATION

Conant, R. A field guide to reptiles & amphibians   597.9

AMPHITHEATERS -- ROME

Mann, E. The Roman Colosseum   937

AMPLIFIERS (ELECTRONICS)

     See also Electronics

AMPUTEES -- FICTION

Baratz-Logsted, L. Crazy beautiful   **Fic**

Bingham, K. Shark girl   **Fic**

Rorby, G. The outside of a horse   **Fic**

Van Draanen, W. The running dream   **Fic**

Voigt, C. Izzy, willy-nilly   **Fic**

Waldorf, H. Tripping   **Fic**

Amstutz, Lorraine Stutzman

Zehr, H. What will happen to me?   362.82

The **Amulet** of Samarkand. Stroud, J.   **Fic**

The **Amulet** of Samarkand. Stroud, J.   741.5

Amulet, book four: The Last Council. Kibuishi, K.   741.5

Amulet, book one: The Stonekeeper. Kibuishi, K.   741.5

Amulet, book three: The Cloud Searchers. Kibuishi, K.   741.5

Amulet, book two: The Stonekeeper's curse. Kibuishi, K.   741.5

AMUNDSEN, ROALD, 1872-1928

Bodden, V. To the South Pole   919.8

AMUSEMENT PARKS -- FICTION

Beck, I. Pastworld   **Fic**

Bradbury, R. Something wicked this way comes **Fic**

Dobkin, B. Neptune's children   **Fic**

Shusterman, N. Full tilt   **Fic**

AMUSEMENTS

Bell-Rehwoldt, S. The kids' guide to building cool stuff   745.5

Buchanan, A. J. The daring book for girls   646.700

Glenn, J. Unbored   790

Hines-Stephens, S. Show off   790.1

Iggulden, C. The dangerous book for boys   031.02

Amy Tan. Mussari, M.   92

ANABOLIC STEROIDS *See* Steroids

ANALGESICS

Bjornlund, L. Oxycodone   615

Breguet, A. Vicodin, OxyContin, and other pain relievers   362.29

ANALYTIC GEOMETRY

     See also Geometry

ANALYTICAL CHEMISTRY

     See also Chemistry

ANARCHISTS

Bausum, A. Denied, detained, deported   325

Anastasia at your service. Lowry, L.   **Fic**

Anastasia Krupnik. Lowry, L.   **Fic**

Anatolios, Khaled

Ruby's imagine   **Fic**

ANTIETAM (MD.), BATTLE OF, 1862

Hughes, C. The Battle of Antietam   **973.7**

Murphy, J. A savage thunder   **973.7**

ANTIETAM, BATTLE OF, MD., 1862

Hughes, C. The Battle of Antietam   **973.7**

Murphy, J. A savage thunder   **973.7**

Antigua and Barbuda. Kras, S. L.   **972.9**

ANTINUCLEAR MOVEMENT

    See also Arms control; Nuclear weapons; Social movements

ANTIQUE AND CLASSIC CARS

    See also Automobiles

ANTIQUE AND VINTAGE MOTORCYCLES

    See also Motorcycles

ANTIQUES

    See also Antiquities; Collectors and collecting; Decoration and ornament; Decorative arts

ANTIQUES -- FICTION

Balliett, B. The Danger Box   **Fic**

ANTIQUITIES

Compoint, S. Buried treasures   **930.1**

Dumont-Le Cornec, E. Wonders of the world   **910**

ANTIQUITIES -- COLLECTION AND PRESERVATION

    See also Collectors and collecting

ANTIQUITIES

Barber, N. Tomb explorers   **930.1**

ANTIQUITY OF MAN *See* Human origins

ANTISEMITISM

Downing, D. The origins of the Holocaust   **940.53**

ANTISEMITISM

    See also Prejudices

ANTISEMITISM -- FICTION

Sanders, S. Rachel's secret   **Fic**

ANTISLAVERY *See* Abolitionists; Slavery; Slaves -- Emancipation

ANTISLAVERY MOVEMENTS

Edwards, J. Abolitionists and slave resistance   **326**

McNeese, T. The rise and fall of American slavery   **326**

Tackach, J. The abolition of American slavery   **326**

ANTISLAVERY MOVEMENTS -- UNITED STATES

Fradin, D. B. Bound for the North Star   **326**

ANTISLAVERY MOVEMENTS -- UNITED STATES -- HISTORY -- 19TH CENTURY

Cline-Ransome, L. Words set me free   **973.8**

Raatma, L. The Underground Railroad   **973.7**

Sanders, N. I. Frederick Douglass for kids   **973.8**

ANTISLAVERY MOVEMENTS -- UNITED STATES -- HISTORY

Edwards, J. Abolitionists and slave resistance   **326**

McNeese, T. The rise and fall of American slavery   **326**

Tackach, J. The abolition of American slavery   **326**

ANTISLAVERY MOVEMENTS -- UNITED STATES -- STUDY AND TEACHING -- ACTIVITY PROGRAMS

Sanders, N. I. Frederick Douglass for kids   **973.8**

Antoine Lavoisier. Van Gorp, L.   **92**

Anton, Mauricio

Turner, A. National Geographic prehistoric mammals   **569**

Antoni van Leeuwenhoek. Yount, L.   **92**

Antonio Lopez de Santa Anna. Lange, B.   **92**

Antonius, Marcus, ca. 83-30 B.C. -- Fiction

About

Shecter, V. A. Cleopatra's moon   **Fic**

ANTS

    See also Insects

Rodriguez, A. M. Secret of the plant-killing ants . . . and more!   **595.7**

Antsy does time. Shusterman, N.   **Fic**

Anwar, Merry

Cornell, K. A. Cooking the Indonesian way   **641.5**

ANXIETY

Levin, J. Anxiety and panic attacks   **616.85**

Parks, P. J. Anxiety disorders   **616.85**

Schutz, S. I don't want to be crazy   **92**

Tompkins, M. A. My anxious mind   **616.85**

The truth about anxiety and depression   **616.85**

ANXIETY

    See also Emotions; Neuroses; Stress (Psychology)

Anxiety and panic attacks. Levin, J.   **616.85**

Anxiety disorders. Parks, P. J.   **616.85**

ANXIETY IN ADOLESCENCE

Chesner, J. ADHD in HD   **618.92**

ANXIOUSNESS *See* Anxiety

Any small goodness. Johnston, T.   **Fic**

Any which wall. Snyder, L.   **Fic**

Anya's ghost. Brosgol, V.   **741.5**

Anya's war. Alban, A.   **Fic**

Anything but typical. Baskin, N. R.   **Fic**

Anzovin, Steven

Kane, J. N. Famous first facts   **031.02**

The **Apache.** Bial, R.   **970.004**

APACHE INDIANS

Bial, R. The Apache   **970.004**

Ehrlich, A. Wounded Knee: an Indian history of the American West   **970.004**

Jastrzembski, J. C. The Apache wars   **970.004**

Sullivan, G. Geronimo   **92**

The **Apache** wars. Jastrzembski, J. C.   **970.004**

APARTHEID

    See also Segregation; South Africa -- Race relations

Beecroft, S. The release of Nelson Mandela   **968.06**

Coster, P. The struggle against apartheid   **968**

Downing, D. Apartheid in South Africa   **968**

Sonneborn, L. The end of apartheid in South Africa **968.06**

APARTHEID -- FICTION

Naidoo, B. Out of bounds: seven stories of conflict and hope **S C**

Apartheid in South Africa. Downing, D. **968**

APARTMENT HOUSES

    See also Buildings; Domestic architecture; Houses; Housing

APARTMENT HOUSES -- FICTION

Greenwald, L. Sweet treats, secret crushes **Fic**

Stead, R. Liar & spy **Fic**

Ape-men. **001.9**

APES

    See also Primates

Barker, D. Top 50 reasons to care about great apes **599.8**

APES -- FICTION

Schrefer, E. Endangered **Fic**

Apfelbaum, Nina

Rosen, P. Bearing witness **016**

APHRODITE (GREEK DEITY)

    See also Gods and goddesses

APICULTURE *See* Beekeeping

APOCALYPTIC FICTION

Aguirre, A. Enclave **Fic**

Bacigalupi, P. The drowned cities **Fic**

Kessler, J. Loss **Fic**

Kizer, A. A matter of days **Fic**

Mary-Todd, J. Shot down **Fic**

Roberts, J. Rage within **Fic**

Rossi, V. Under the never sky **Fic**

Shards and Ashes **S C**

APOCALYPTIC FILMS

    See also Motion pictures

APOLLO (GREEK DEITY)

    See also Gods and goddesses

APOLLO 13 (SPACECRAFT)

Holden, H. M. Danger in space **629.45**

APOLLO PROJECT

    See also Life support systems (Space environment); Orbital rendezvous (Space flight); Space flight to the moon

Bodden, V. To the moon **629.45**

Holden, H. M. Danger in space **629.45**

APOLLO PROJECT -- GRAPHIC NOVELS

Ottaviani, J. T-Minus: the race to the moon **629.45**

Apollo's outcasts. Steele, A. **Fic**

Apolo Anton Ohno. Aldridge, R. **92**

Apolo Anton Ohno. Uschan, M. V. **796.91**

The **apothecary.** Meloy, M. **Fic**

Appalachia. Rylant, C. **974**

APPARATUS, ELECTRONIC *See* Electronic apparatus and appliances

APPARITIONS

Matthews, R. Ghosts and spirits **133.1**

APPARITIONS

    See also Parapsychology; Spirits

APPEARANCE, PERSONAL *See* Personal appearance

Appelbaum, Susannah

The Hollow Bettle **Fic**

The Shepherd of Weeds **Fic**

The Tasters Guild **Fic**

Appelt, Kathi

Keeper **Fic**

Kissing Tennessee and other stories from the Stardust Dance **S C**

Poems from homeroom **811**

The true blue scouts of Sugarman Swamp **Fic**

The underneath **Fic**

APPERCEPTION

    See also Educational psychology; Psychology

APPETITE DEPRESSANTS

Breguet, A. Diet pills **615**

APPETIZERS

    See also Cooking

Appignanesi, Richard

As you like it **741.5**

Hamlet **741.5**

A midsummer night's dream **741.5**

Romeo and Juliet **741.5**

The tempest **741.5**

(adapter) The merchant of Venice **741.5**

(adapter) Twelfth night **741.5**

APPLE *See* Apples

Apple for the teacher. Yolen, J. **782.42**

Applegate, Katherine

Eve & Adam **Fic**

Home of the brave **Fic**

The one and only Ivan **Fic**

APPLES

    See also Fruit

Worth, R. Johnny Appleseed **92**

APPLES -- FICTION

Hawkins, A. R. The year money grew on trees **Fic**

Appleseed, Johnny, 1774-1845

About

Worth, R. Johnny Appleseed **92**

APPLIANCES, ELECTRONIC *See* Electronic apparatus and appliances

APPLICATIONS FOR POSITIONS

    See also Job hunting; Personnel management

APPLIED PSYCHOLOGY

    See also Psychology

APPLIED SCIENCE *See* Technology

APPOMATTOX CAMPAIGN, 1865

Benoit, P. The surrender at Appomattox **973.7**

APPRAISAL OF BOOKS *See* Book reviewing; Books and reading; Criticism; Literature -- History and criticism

APPRECIATION OF ART *See* Art appreciation

APPRECIATION OF MUSIC *See* Music appreciation

The **apprentices.** Meloy, M.   **Fic**

APPRENTICESHIP NOVELS *See* Bildungsromans

APRIL FOOLS' DAY
   See also Holidays

Apte, Sunita
   Eating green   **630**

Apuleius
   Usher, M. D. The golden ass of Lucius Apuleius   **Fic**

AQUACULTURE
   See also Agriculture; Marine resources

Aquarium fish. Mills, D.   **639.34**

AQUARIUMS
   See also Freshwater biology; Natural history
   Indiviglio, F. The everything aquarium book **639.34**
   Mills, D. Aquarium fish   **639.34**
   Wood, K. The 101 best tropical fishes   **639.34**

AQUATIC ANIMALS
   See also Animals
   Basher, S. Oceans   **551.46**
   Markle, S. Fishing spiders   **595.4**

AQUATIC BIOLOGY
   Dawes, J. Exploring the world of aquatic life **591.7**

AQUATIC BIRDS *See* Water birds

AQUATIC EXERCISES
   See also Exercise

AQUATIC FAUNA *See* Aquatic animals

AQUATIC PLANTS *See* Freshwater plants; Marine plants

Aquatic turtles. Bartlett, R. D.   **639.3**

AQUEDUCTS
   See also Civil engineering; Hydraulic structures; Water supply

ARAB AMERICANS -- HISTORY
   Addasi, M. A kid's guide to Arab American history   **973**

ARAB AMERICANS -- HISTORY -- STUDY AND TEACHING -- ACTIVITY PROGRAMS
   Addasi, M. A kid's guide to Arab American history   **973**

ARAB AMERICANS -- SOCIAL LIFE AND CUSTOMS
   Addasi, M. A kid's guide to Arab American history   **973**

ARAB CIVILIZATION
   Blanchard, A. Arab science and invention in the golden age   **509**

The **Arab** Conquests of the Middle East. January, B.   **956**

ARAB COUNTRIES
   See also Islamic countries; Middle East

ARAB COUNTRIES -- POLITICS AND GOVERNMENT

   See also Politics

ARAB REFUGEES
   See also Refugees

Arab science and invention in the golden age. Blanchard, A.   **509**

ARAB-ISRAEL WAR, 1973 *See* Israel-Arab War, 1973

The **Arab-Israeli** War since 1948. Woolf, A. **956.04**

The **Arab-Israeli** conflict. Senker, C.   **956.04**

ARAB-ISRAELI CONFLICT
   See also Israel-Arab conflicts
   Barakat, I. Tasting the sky   **92**
   Frank, M. Understanding the Holy Land   **956.94**
   Woolf, A. The Arab-Israeli War since 1948 **956.04**

ARAB-JEWISH RELATIONS *See* Jewish-Arab relations

Arabian nights. Tarnowska, W.   **398.2**

ARABIC CIVILIZATION
   See also Civilization

ARABIC LITERATURE
   See also Literature

ARABS
   Ramen, F. Albucasis (Abu al-Qasim al-Zahrawi) **92**

ARABS -- FOLKLORE
   Tarnowska, W. Arabian nights   **398.2**

ARABS -- PALESTINE *See* Palestinian Arabs

The **arachnid** class. Stefoff, R.   **595.4**

Arachnid world [series]
   Markle, S. Mites   **595.4**
   Markle, S. Tarantulas   **595.4**
   Markle, S. Wind scorpions   **595.4**
   Markle, S. Black widows   **595.4**
   Markle, S. Harvestmen   **595.4**
   Markle, S. Orb weavers   **595.4**
   Markle, S. Scorpions   **595.4**
   Markle, S. Ticks   **595.4**
   Markle, S. Wolf spiders   **595.4**

ARACHNIDS
   See also Animals
   Markle, S. Mites   **595.4**
   Markle, S. Tarantulas   **595.4**
   Markle, S. Wind scorpions   **595.4**
   Markle, S. Crab spiders   **595.4**
   Markle, S. Fishing spiders   **595.4**
   Markle, S. Jumping spiders   **595.4**

ARACHNOLOGISTS
   Silk & venom   **595.4**

Arai, Kiyoko
   Beauty Pop, Vol. 1   **741.5**

Aranzi Aronzo Inc.
   Cute dolls   **745.592**

ARAPAHO INDIANS
   Ehrlich, A. Wounded Knee: an Indian history of the American West   **970.004**

Arato, Rona
   Design it!   **745.2**

AT RISK STUDENTS
> *See also* Students

At the crime scene! Ballard, C.   363.2
At the firefly gate. Newbery, L.   **Fic**
At the sea floor cafe. Bulion, L.   811
At Yellow Lake. McLoughlin, J.   **Fic**
ATALANTA (GREEK MYTHOLOGY) -- FICTION
> Spinner, S. Quiver   **Fic**

Atangan, Patrick
> The yellow jar   741.5

Atha, Antony
> Fitness for young people   613.7

ATHAPASCAN INDIANS -- FICTION
> Frost, H. Diamond Willow   **Fic**

ATHEISM
> *See also* Religion; Secularism; Theology

Athena. O'Connor, G.   741.5
ATHENA (GREEK DEITY)
> O'Connor, G. Athena   741.5

ATHENA (GREEK DEITY)
> *See also* Gods and goddesses

Atherton [series]
> Carman, P. The dark planet   **Fic**
> Carman, P. The house of power   **Fic**
> Carman, P. Rivers of fire   **Fic**

ATHLETES
> Bruchac, J. Jim Thorpe   92
> Frederick, S. Strength training for teen athletes   613.7
> Kent, D. Athletes with disabilities   371.9
> Labrecque, E. Jim Thorpe   92
> Schuman, M. Jim Thorpe   92
> Whitfield, S. Simon says gold: Simon Whitfield's pursuit of athletic excellence   92

ATHLETES -- DICTIONARIES
> Great athletes   920.003

ATHLETES -- DRUG USE
> Egendorf, L. K. Performance-enhancing drugs   362.29
> Freedman, J. Professional wrestling   362.29
> LeVert, S. The facts about steroids   362.29
> Porterfield, J. Doping   362.29
> Porterfield, J. Major League Baseball   362.29
> Schaefer, A. Steroids   362.29
> Sommers, A. L. College athletics   362.29
> Sommers, M. A. The NFL   362.29

ATHLETES -- WOUNDS AND INJURIES
> Sports injuries information for teens   617.1

ATHLETES IN ART
> Ames, L. J. Draw 50 athletes   743

Athletes with disabilities. Kent, D.   371.9
ATHLETES WITH DISABILITIES -- BIOGRAPHY
> Kent, D. Athletes with disabilities   371.9

Athletic shorts. Crutcher, C.   **S C**

Atkin, S. Beth
> Gunstories   363.33

Atkins, Catherine
> Alt ed   **Fic**

Atkins, Jeannine
> Borrowed names   811

Atkinson, E. J.
> I, Emma Freke   **Fic**

Atkinson, Elizabeth
> From Alice to Zen and everyone in between   **Fic**

Atkinson, Peter
> The Lion encyclopedia of the Bible   220

ATLANTIC OCEAN
> *See also* Ocean

The **Atlantic** slave trade. Nardo, D.   326
ATLANTIS (LEGENDARY PLACE)
> Hawkins, J. Atlantis and other lost worlds   001.94

ATLANTIS -- FICTION
> Scott, M. The enchantress   **Fic**

Atlantis and other lost worlds. Hawkins, J.   001.94
Atlas. Rafter, D.   741.5
Atlas of ancient worlds. Chrisp, P.   911
Atlas of Asia. Campbell, R.   950
The **atlas** of endangered animals. Hammond, P.   591.68
The **atlas** of endangered species. Mackay, R.   333.95
Atlas of Hispanic-American history. Ochoa, G.   305.8
Atlas of the universe. Garlick, M. A.   520
The **atlas** of the world's most dangerous animals. Hammond, P.   591.6
ATLASES
> *See also* Geography; Maps

Facts on File, I. Maps on file   912
Hammond, P. The atlas of endangered animals   591.68
National Geographic atlas of the world   912
National Geographic student atlas of the world   912
National Geographic United States atlas for young explorers   912
The new cultural atlas of Egypt   932
The new cultural atlas of the Greek world   938
Oxford Atlas of the world   912
Student atlas   912
Wojtanik, A. The National Geographic Bee ultimate fact book   910
ATLASES, ASTRONOMICAL *See* Stars -- Atlases
Atmosphere. Gallant, R. A.   551.51
The **atmosphere.** Vogt, G.   551.5
ATMOSPHERE
> *See also* Air; Earth

Casper, J. K. Water and atmosphere   553.7
Cosgrove, B. Weather   551.5
Gallant, R. A. Atmosphere   551.51
Vogt, G. The atmosphere   551.5

The **Bambino:** the story of Babe Ruth's legendary 1927 season. Yomtov, N.   **92**

Bamboo people. Perkins, M.   **Fic**

Bancks, Tristan
Mac Slater hunts the cool   **Fic**
Mac Slater vs. the city   **Fic**

A **band** of bears. Hunt, J. P.   **599.78**

BANDITS *See* Thieves

BANDMASTERS *See* Conductors (Music)

BANDS (MUSIC)
Goodmark, R. Girls rock   **781.66**
Marx, T. Steel drumming at the Apollo   **785**

BANDS (MUSIC) -- FICTION
Perez, M. Dead is a killer tune   **Fic**

BANDS (MUSIC)
Briant, E. I am (not) the walrus   **Fic**

Bang! Flake, S. G.   **Fic**

Bangladesh. Phillips, D. A.   **954.92**

BANJO
Ellis, R. M. With a banjo on my knee   **787.8**

BANJOISTS
Ellis, R. M. With a banjo on my knee   **787.8**

BANJOISTS -- UNITED STATES -- BIOGRA-PHY
Ellis, R. M. With a banjo on my knee   **787.8**

BANJOS
Ellis, R. M. With a banjo on my knee   **787.8**

BANK CREDIT CARDS *See* Credit cards

BANK FAILURES
Casil, A. S. Why banks fail   **332.1**

BANK FAILURES
See also Bankruptcy; Banks and banking; Business failures

BANKERS
Ransom, C. F. Maggie L. Walker   **92**

BANKING *See* Banks and banking

Banking basics. Fischer, J.   **332.1**

BANKRUPTCY
Bezdecheck, B. Bailout!   **338.6**

Banks and banking. Connolly, S.   **332.1**

BANKS AND BANKING
Bostick, N. Managing Money   **332**
Casil, A. S. Why banks fail   **332.1**
Connolly, S. Banks and banking   **332.1**
Fischer, J. Banking basics   **332.1**

BANKS AND BANKING -- CREDIT CARDS *See* Credit cards

Banks, Kate
Walk softly, Rachel   **Fic**

Banks, Tyra
About
Todd, A. M. Tyra Banks   **92**

Bankston, John
Nellie Bly   **070.92**
Ray Bradbury   **92**

Bankston, John

Christopher Paolini   **92**
Jacqueline Wilson   **92**
Katherine Paterson   **92**
Lois Lowry   **92**
Ray Bradbury   **92**
Stephen Hawking   **92**

BANNERS *See* Flags

Bannister
The Master of Shadows   **741.5**

Bannister (Person)
The shadow door   **741.5**
The Shadow Spies   **741.5**

Banqueri, Eduardo
Weather   **551.5**

A **banquet** for hungry ghosts. Compestine, Y. C.   **S C**

BANQUETS *See* Dining; Dinners

Bansavage, Lisa
(ed) Shakespeare, W. One hundred and eleven Shakespeare monologues   **822.3**

BANSHEES -- FICTION
Booraem, E. Texting the underworld   **Fic**

Banting, Erinn
Caves   **577.5**
England   **942**

Baptiste, Tracey
Al Gore   **92**
Sharon Creech   **92**

BAR *See* Lawyers

BAR MITZVAH
Metter, B. Bar mitzvah, bat mitzvah   **296.4**

BAR MITZVAH -- FICTION
Rubens, M. Sons of the 613   **Fic**

Bar mitzvah, bat mitzvah. Metter, B.   **296.4**

Barack Obama. Burgan, M.   **92**

Barack Obama. Zeiger, J.   **973.932**

Barack Obama. Krensky, S.   **92**

Barakat, Ibtisam
Tasting the sky   **92**

Barakat, Ibtisam
About
Barakat, I. Tasting the sky   **92**

Baratz-Logsted, Lauren
Crazy beautiful   **Fic**
Twin's daughter   **Fic**

Barbados. Elias, M. L.   **972.98**

Barbara Guth worlds of wonder science series for young readers [series]
Sequeira, M. Cell phone science   **621.384**

Barbara McClintock. Spangenburg, R.   **92**

Barbara McClintock, geneticist. Cullen, J. H.   **92**

Barbarians. Helget, N.   **940.1**

Barbarians! [series]
Hinds, K. Ancient Celts   **936**
Hinds, K. Early Germans   **936**
Hinds, K. Goths   **936**

Extreme biology 570
Human body 612
Budzik, M. Punctuation: the write stuff! 428
Dingle, A. The periodic table 546
Gilpin, D. Planet Earth 550
Green, D. Algebra & geometry 516.2
Green, D. Astronomy 520
Green, D. Chemistry 540
Green, D. Physics 530
Green, D. Rocks and minerals 552
Oceans 551.46

BASHFULNESS
Coville, B. Juliet Dove, Queen of Love Fic

BASHFULNESS -- FICTION
Levine, K. The lions of Little Rock Fic

Basic biology [series]
Walker, D. Inheritance and evolution 576

BASIC LIFE SKILLS *See* Life skills

BASIC RIGHTS *See* Civil rights; Human rights

The **basics** of quantum physics. Willett, E. 539

BASKET MAKING
See also Weaving

BASKET MAKING -- FICTION
La Valley, J. The Vine basket Fic

Basketball. Labrecque, E. 796.323
Basketball. Gifford, C. 796.323
Basketball. Robinson, T. 796.323
Basketball. Yancey, D. 796.323
Basketball. Slade, S. 796.323

BASKETBALL
See also Ball games; Sports

BASKETBALL
Burns, B. Basketball step-by-step 796.323
Doeden, M. The greatest basketball records 796.323
Gardner, R. Slam dunk! science projects with basketball 530
Gifford, C. Basketball 796.323
Labrecque, E. Basketball 796.323
Robinson, T. Basketball 796.323
Slade, S. Basketball 796.323
Stewart, M. Swish 796.323
Thomas, K. How basketball works 796.323
Yancey, D. Basketball 796.323

BASKETBALL -- BIOGRAPHY
Roselius, J. C. Magic Johnson 92
Yasuda, A. Lebron James 92

BASKETBALL -- FICTION
Lupica, M. Play Makers Fic

BASKETBALL
Burleigh, R. Hoops 811

BASKETBALL -- POETRY
Burleigh, R. Hoops 811
Smith, C. R. Hoop queens 811

BASKETBALL -- UNITED STATES -- HISTORY
Coy, J. Hoop genius E

BASKETBALL COACHES

Roselius, J. C. Magic Johnson 92

BASKETBALL PLAYERS
Roselius, J. C. Magic Johnson 92
Yasuda, A. Lebron James 92

BASKETBALL PLAYERS -- UNITED STATES -- BIOGRAPHY
Thornley, S. Tim Duncan 796.323

BASKETBALL PLAYERS -- UNITED STATES -- BIOGRAPHY
Thornley, S. Kevin Garnett 796.323
Thornley, S. Kobe Bryant 796.323
Thornley, S. Tim Duncan 796.323
Basketball step-by-step. Burns, B. 796.323

BASKETBALL TEAMS
See also Basketball; Sports teams

Baskin, Nora Raleigh
All we know of love Fic
Anything but typical Fic
The summer before boys Fic
The truth about my Bat Mitzvah Fic

Basman, Michael
Chess for kids 794.1

Bass, L. G.
(comp) Na, A. No such thing as the real world S C

Bassil, Andrea
Vincent van Gogh 92

Bassis, Volodymyr
Ukraine 947.7

Bastedo, Jamie
On thin ice Fic

Basye, Dale E.
Heck Fic

BAT MITZVAH
Metter, B. Bar mitzvah, bat mitzvah 296.4

BAT MITZVAH -- FICTION
Baskin, N. R. The truth about my Bat Mitzvah Fic

The **bat** scientists. Carson, M. K. 599.4

The **batboy.** Lupica, M. Fic

Bateman, Teresa
Red, white, blue, and Uncle who? 929.9

Bates, Daisy

About
Fradin, J. B. The power of one 323

Bates, Marni
Awkward Fic

Bateson, Catherine
Being Bee Fic
Magenta McPhee Fic

BATHS
See also Cleanliness; Hygiene; Physical therapy

BATHYSCAPHE
See also Oceanography -- Research; Submersibles

BATHYSCAPHE -- HISTORY -- 20TH CENTURY

Bodden, V. To the ocean deep | 551.46

BATIK
    See also Dyes and dyeing
BATMAN (FICTIONAL CHARACTER)
    Fisch, S. Super friends: for justice! | 741.5
Batmanglij, Najmieh
    Happy Nowruz | 641.5
Batmanglij, Najmieh
    About
    Major, J. S. Caravan to America | 745
BATON TWIRLING -- FICTION
    Repka, J. The clueless girl's guide to being a genius | Fic
Bats. Gish, M. | 599.4
BATS
    Carson, M. K. The bat scientists | 599.4
    Gish, M. Bats | 599.4
    Taschek, K. Hanging with bats | 599.4
    Williams, K. Stokes beginner's guide to bats | 599.4
BATS
    See also Mammals
BATS -- FICTION
    The flight of dragons | Fic
    French, V. The bag of bones | Fic
    French, V. The heart of glass | Fic
    Oppel, K. Darkwing | Fic
    Oppel, K. Firewing | Fic
    Oppel, K. Silverwing | Fic
    Oppel, K. Sunwing | Fic
    The robe of skulls | Fic
BATS -- FICTION
    Oppel, K. Firewing | Fic
    Oppel, K. Sunwing | Fic
BATS
    Carson, M. K. The bat scientists | 599.4
Batten, Jack
    Oscar Peterson | 786.2
    Silent in an evil time: the brave war of Edith Cavell | 92
    The war to end all wars | 940.3
BATTERED WIVES *See* Abused women
BATTERED WOMEN *See* Abused women
Battle dress. Efaw, A. | Fic
Battle Fleet. Dowswell, P. | Fic
The **battle** for Skandia. Flanagan, J. | Fic
The **Battle** of Antietam. Hughes, C. | 973.7
The **Battle** of Britain. Allport, A. | 940.54
The **Battle** of Britain. Moore, K. | 940.54
The **battle** of Iwo Jima. Hama, L. | 940.54
The **Battle** of Jericho. Draper, S. M. | Fic
The **Battle** of Midway. Torres, J. A. | 940.54
The **Battle** of Nashville. Bobrick, B. | 973.7
Battle of the dinosaur bones. Johnson, R. L. | 560.973
The **battle** of the Labyrinth. Riordan, R. | Fic
BATTLE SHIPS *See* Warships
BATTLES

    See also Military art and science; Military history; War
Battles & weapons: exploring history through art. Chapman, C. | 355
BATTLESHIPS *See* Warships
Baucom, Ian
    Through the skylight | Fic
Bauer, A. C. E.
    Come Fall | Fic
    No castles here | Fic
Bauer, Helen
    Beethoven for kids | 92
Bauer, Joan
    Almost home | Fic
    Close to famous | Fic
    Peeled | Fic
    Squashed | Fic
    Stand tall | Fic
Bauer, Marion Dane, 1938-
    Little dog, lost | Fic
    On my honor | Fic
    A writer's story | 808
Bauer, Marion Dane, 1938-
    About
    Bauer, M. D. A writer's story | 808
Baughan, Brian
    Russell Simmons | 92
Baughan, Michael Gray
    Shel Silverstein | 92
Baule, Steven M.
    Facilities planning for school library and technology centers | 027.8
Baumbach, Donna
    Less is more | 025.2
Bausum, Ann
    Denied, detained, deported | 325
    Marching to the mountaintop | 323
    Our Country's Presidents | 973.09
Bausum, Ann
    Denied, detained, deported | 325
    Dragon bones and dinosaur eggs: a photobiography of Roy Chapman Andrews | 92
    Freedom Riders | 323.1
    Muckrakers | 070.4
    Our country's first ladies | 920
    Our Country's Presidents | 973.09
    Unraveling freedom | 940.3
    With courage and cloth | 305.4
Baxter, Kathleen A.
    From cover to cover | 028.1
    Gotcha again for guys! | 028.5
    Gotcha good! | 028.5
Baxter, Roberta
    Ernest Rutherford and the birth of the atomic age | 530.092
    Illuminated progress | 92

John Dalton and the development of atomic theory **509.2**

The particle model of matter **530**

Skeptical chemist **92**

Baynes, Pauline

Questionable creatures **398.2**

Lewis, C. S. The horse and his boy **Fic**

Lewis, C. S. The last battle **Fic**

Lewis, C. S. The lion, the witch, and the wardrobe **Fic**

Lewis, C. S. The magician's nephew **Fic**

Lewis, C. S. Prince Caspian **Fic**

Lewis, C. S. The silver chair **Fic**

Lewis, C. S. The voyage of the Dawn Treader **Fic**

BAZAARS *See* Fairs

Bazelon, Emily

Sticks and stones **302.34**

Bazemore, Suzanne

Soccer: how it works **796.334**

Bazin, Maurice

Math and science across cultures **510**

Be a better babysitter. Buckley, A. **649**

Be confident in who you are. Fox, A. **158**

Be my enemy. McDonald, I. **Fic**

Beach, Alfred E., 1826-1896

About

Sandler, M. W. Secret subway **388.4**

BEACHES

See also Seashore

BEACHES -- FICTION

Bancks, T. Mac Slater hunts the cool **Fic**

Dessen, S. The moon and more **Fic**

Han, J. It's not summer without you **Fic**

Han, J. The summer I turned pretty **Fic**

Han, J. We'll always have summer **Fic**

Horvath, P. My one hundred adventures **Fic**

Kirby, J. Moonglass **Fic**

Nelson, B. They came from below **Fic**

Snow, C. Snap **Fic**

Beachmont letters. Twomey, C. **Fic**

Beacon Hill boys. Mochizuki, K. **Fic**

Beading. Boonyadhistarn, T. **745.58**

BEADWORK

Boonyadhistarn, T. Beading **745.58**

BEADWORK

See also Handicraft

The **beagle.** Schweitzer, K. **636.7**

Beagle, Peter S.

The last unicorn **741.5**

Beahm, George W.

Discovering The golden compass **823**

Beale, Deborah

Williams, T. The dragons of Ordinary Farm **Fic**

Beanball. Fehler, G. **Fic**

Bear dancer. Wyss, T. H. **Fic**

Bear rescue. Thomas, K. **599.78**

Bearce, Stephanie

All about electric and hybrid cars **629.222**

How to harness solar power for your home **621.47**

Beard, Hilary

Williams, V. Venus & Serena **92**

Beardance. Hobbs, W. **Fic**

Bearing witness. Rosen, P. **016**

BEARINGS (MACHINERY)

See also Machinery

BEARS

Hamilton, S. L. Mauled by a bear **599.78**

Hunt, J. P. A band of bears **599.78**

McAllister, I. Salmon bears **599.78**

Montgomery, S. Search for the golden moon bear **599.78**

Thomas, K. Bear rescue **599.78**

Ward, P. Bears of the world **599.78**

BEARS

See also Mammals

BEARS -- FICTION

Bruchac, J. Bearwalker **Fic**

D'Lacey, C. Fire star **Fic**

D'Lacey, C. Icefire **Fic**

Hobbs, W. Beardance **Fic**

Hobbs, W. Never say die **Fic**

Mikaelsen, B. Touching Spirit Bear **Fic**

Pattou, E. East **Fic**

Paulsen, G. Brian's hunt **Fic**

Paver, M. Wolf brother **Fic**

Tak, B. D. Soldier bear **Fic**

BEARS

McAllister, I. Salmon bears **599.78**

Montgomery, S. Search for the golden moon bear **599.78**

Bears of the world. Ward, P. **599.78**

Bearstone. Hobbs, W. **Fic**

Bearwalker. Bruchac, J. **Fic**

Beast. Napoli, D. J. **Fic**

Beast Friends Forever. Forbes, R. L. **811**

The **Beast** of Blackslope. Barrett, T. **Fic**

The **beast** of Noor. Carey, J. L. **Fic**

Beastly. Flinn, A. **Fic**

The **beastly** bride. **S C**

BEASTS *See* Animals

The **beasts** of Clawstone Castle. **Fic**

Beating depression. Zucker, F. **616.85**

The **Beatles.** Roberts, J. **781.66**

Beatty, Richard

Boron **546**

Copper **546**

The lanthanides **546**

Manganese **546**

Phosphorus **546**

Sulfur **546**

(ed) Exploring the world of mammals **599**

Beatty, Scott

Superman 741.5

Beaty, Andrea
Cicada summer Fic
Dorko the magnificent Fic

Beaudoin, Marie-Nathalie
Responding to the culture of bullying and disrespect 371.5

Beaufrand, Mary Jane
Primavera Fic
The river Fic

Beauties and beasts. Beauty and the beast 398.21

The **beautiful** and the cursed. Morgan, P. Fic

Beautiful creatures. Garcia, K. Fic

Beautiful darkness. Garcia, K. Fic

A **beautiful** friendship. Weber, D. Fic

A **beautiful** lie. Master, I. Fic

Beautiful me. Orr, T. 158

The **beautiful** stories of life. Rylant, C. 292

Beauty. McKinley, R. Fic

BEAUTY *See* Aesthetics

Beauty and the beast
Beauties and beasts 398.21

BEAUTY CONTESTS
See also Contests

BEAUTY CONTESTS -- FICTION
Eulberg, E. Revenge of the Girl With the Great Personality Fic
Ransom, C. Rebel McKenzie Fic

Beauty Pop, Vol. 1. Arai, K. 741.5

Beauty queens. Bray, L. Fic

Beauty shop for rent. Bowers, L. Fic

BEAUTY SHOPS
See also Business enterprises

BEAUTY SHOPS -- FICTION
Bowers, L. Beauty shop for rent Fic

BEAUTY, PERSONAL
Skin health information for teens 616.5

BEAUTY, PERSONAL *See* Personal appearance; Personal grooming

BEAUTY, PERSONAL -- FICTION
Friend, N. My life in black and white Fic
Ross, E. Belle epoque Fic
Uglies 741.5
Vivian, S. The list Fic
Westerfeld, S. Uglies Fic

BEAVERS
See also Furbearing animals; Mammals

Bec. Shan, D. Fic

Because I am furniture. Chaltas, T. Fic

Because it is my blood. Zevin, G. Fic

Because of Mr. Terupt. Buyea, R. Fic

Because of Winn-Dixie. DiCamillo, K. Fic

Beccaloni, George
Biggest bugs life-size 595.7

Beccia, Carlyn
The raucous royals 920

Matthews, T. L. Frame-up on the Bowery Fic

Beck, Glenn
About
Novak, A. Glenn Beck 320.52

Beck, Ian
Pastworld Fic
The secret history of Tom Trueheart Fic
Tom Trueheart and the Land of Dark Stories Fic

Becker, Helaine
Funny business 792

Becker, John E.
Wild cats: past & present 599.75

Becker, Tom
Darkside Fic
Lifeblood Fic

Beckman, Wendy Hart
Robert Cormier 92

Becoming Ben Franklin. Freedman, R. 973.309

Becoming Billie Holiday. Weatherford, C. B. Fic

Becoming Joe DiMaggio. Testa, M. 811

Bedard, Michael
The painted wall and other strange tales 398.2
William Blake 92

BEDBUGS
Gleason, C. Feasting bedbugs, mites, and ticks 614.4

Bedell, J. M.
Combating terrorism 363.32
Teens in Pakistan 305.23

Bedford, Martyn
Flip Fic

The **BEDMAS** conspiracy. Sherman, D. Fic

Bednar, Sylvie
Flags of the world

BEDOUINS
See also Arabs

BEDSPREADS
See also Interior design

BEDTIME
See also Night; Sleep

BEE CULTURE *See* Beekeeping
Burns, L. G. The hive detectives 638

Beebe, William, 1877-1962
About
Matsen, B. The incredible record-setting deep-sea dive of the bathysphere 551.46

Beechen, Adam
Justice League Unlimited: the ties that bind 741.5

Beecher family
About
Fritz, J. Harriet Beecher Stowe and the Beecher preachers 813

Beecroft, Simon
The release of Nelson Mandela 968.06

BEEF
See also Meat

Thompson, B. The young birder's guide to birds of eastern North America   **598**

BIRDBANDING
    See also Wildlife conservation
BIRDING *See* Bird watching
BIRDS
    Abramson, A. S. Inside dinosaurs   **567.9**
    Burnie, D. Bird   **598**
    Chin, J. Island   **508.866**
    Chu, M. Birdscapes   **598**
    Latimer, J. P. Backyard birds   **598**
    Latimer, J. P. Songbirds   **598**
    Long, J. A. Feathered dinosaurs   **567.9**
    Rodriguez, A. M. Secret of the puking penguins . . . and more!   **591.4**
    Sloan, C. How dinosaurs took flight   **567.9**
    Stefoff, R. The bird class   **598**
    Thompson, B. The young birder's guide to birds of eastern North America   **598**
    Webb, S. Looking for seabirds   **598**
    Wolf, S. The robin makes a laughing sound   **598**
BIRDS
    See also Animals
BIRDS -- ALASKA
    Webb, S. Looking for seabirds   **598**
BIRDS -- ANATOMY
    See also Anatomy
BIRDS -- BEHAVIOR
    See also Animal behavior
BIRDS -- COLOR
    See also Color
BIRDS -- EGGS
    See also Eggs
BIRDS -- ENCYCLOPEDIAS
    Birds of the world   **598**
    International Masters Publishers (Firm) The encyclopedia of birds   **598**
BIRDS -- FICTION
    Auch, M. J. Wing nut   **Fic**
    Catmull, K. Summer and Bird   **Fic**
    White, A. Windows on the world   **Fic**
BIRDS -- FOLKLORE
    Larson, J. C. Hummingbirds   **598**
    Norman, H. Between heaven and earth   **398.2**
BIRDS -- IDENTIFICATION
    Alderfer, J. National Geographic kids bird guide of North America   **598.097**
BIRDS
    Read, N. City critters   **591.75**
BIRDS -- MIGRATION
    Vogel, C. G. The man who flies with birds   **598**
BIRDS -- MIGRATION
    Vogel, C. G. The man who flies with birds   **598**
BIRDS -- NORTH AMERICA
    Alderfer, J. National Geographic kids bird guide of North America   **598.097**

BIRDS -- NORTH AMERICA -- IDENTIFICATION
    Robbins, C. S. Birds of North America   **598**
BIRDS -- NORTH AMERICA -- IDENTIFICATION
    Alderfer, J. National Geographic kids bird guide of North America   **598.097**
BIRDS -- NORTH AMERICA
    Thompson, B. The young birder's guide to birds of eastern North America   **598**
BIRDS -- ORIGIN
    Sloan, C. How dinosaurs took flight   **567.9**
BIRDS -- POETRY
    Fleischman, P. I am phoenix: poems for two voices   **811**
BIRDS -- PROTECTION
    Hoose, P. Moonbird   **598.072**
BIRDS -- PROTECTION
    See also Wildlife conservation
BIRDS -- SONG *See* Birdsongs
BIRDS -- UNITED STATES
    Sherman, P. John James Audubon   **92**
BIRDS -- WESTERN CANADA
    Peterson, R. T. Peterson field guide to birds of Western North America   **598**
BIRDS -- WESTERN STATES
    Peterson, R. T. Peterson field guide to birds of Western North America   **598**
BIRDS IN ART
    Ames, L. J. Draw 50 birds   **743**
    Nguyen, D. Origami birds   **736**
Birds of North America. Robbins, C. S.   **598**
Birds of prey. Latimer, J. P.   **598.9**
BIRDS OF PREY
    See also Birds; Predatory animals
BIRDS OF PREY
    Hickman, P. M. Birds of prey rescue   **598**
    Latimer, J. P. Birds of prey   **598.9**
    Laubach, C. M. Raptor! a kid's guide to birds of prey   **598**
BIRDS OF PREY -- IDENTIFICATION
    Latimer, J. P. Birds of prey   **598.9**
BIRDS OF PREY
    Latimer, J. P. Birds of prey   **598.9**
Birds of prey rescue. Hickman, P. M.   **598**
Birds of the world.   **598**
BIRDS, FOSSIL
    Sloan, C. How dinosaurs took flight   **567.9**
Birdsall, Jeanne
    The Penderwicks   **Fic**
    The Penderwicks at Point Mouette   **Fic**
    The Penderwicks on Gardam Street   **Fic**
Birdscapes. Chu, M.   **598**
Birdseye, Tom
    Storm Mountain   **Fic**
BIRDSONGS

Paprocki, S. B. Bob Marley   92
Partridge, K. Louis Armstrong   92
Slavicek, L. C. Paul Robeson   92
Black and white. Volponi, P.   Fic
BLACK ART
   See also Art
BLACK ART (MAGIC) *See* Magic; Witchcraft
BLACK ARTISTS
   See also Artists
The **Black** arts movement. Robson, D.   700
BLACK ATHLETES
   See also Athletes
BLACK AUTHORS
   See also Authors
The **Black** Book of Secrets. Higgins, F. E.   Fic
Black box. Schumacher, J.   Fic
BLACK BUSINESSPEOPLE
   See also Businesspeople
The **Black** Canary. Curry, J. L.   Fic
BLACK CANARY (FICTIONAL CHARACTER)
  Kreisberg, A. Green Arrow and Black Canary: five
   stages   741.5
Black cat bone. Lewis, J. P.   811
The **Black** Cauldron. Alexander, L.   Fic
BLACK CHILDREN
   See also Children
The **Black** Dahlia. Haugen, B.   364.152
The **Black** Death. Slavicek, L. C.   614.5
BLACK DEATH *See* Plague
The **black** death. Currie, S.   614.5
The **Black** Death. Zahler, D.   614.5
The **Black** Death. Nardo, D.   614.5
BLACK DEATH -- HISTORY
  Currie, S. The black death   614.5
Black Elk's vision. Nelson, S. D.   92
Black Elk, 1863-1950
      About
  Nelson, S. D. Black Elk's vision   92
The **Black** experience in America.   305.8
Black frontiers. Schlissel, L.   978
Black hands, white sails. McKissack, P. C. 639.2
Black Hawk and the War of 1832. Bowes, J. P. 973.5
BLACK HAWK WAR, 1832
  Bowes, J. P. Black Hawk and the War of 1832 973.5
Black Hawk, Sauk chief, 1767-1838
      About
  Bowes, J. P. Black Hawk and the War of 1832 973.5
Black heart. Black, H.   FIC
Black heart. Somper, J.   Fic
The **black** heart crypt. Grabenstein, C.   Fic
Black hearts in Battersea. Aiken, J.   Fic
A **black** hole is not a hole.   523.8
Black hole sun. Gill, D. M.   Fic
Black Hole Sun Trilogy [series]
  Gill, D. M. Invisible sun   Fic
  Gill, D. M. Shadow on the sun   Fic

BLACK HOLES (ASTRONOMY)
  Jackson, E. B. The mysterious universe   523.8
BLACK HOLES (ASTRONOMY)
   See also Astronomy; Astrophysics; Stars
  A black hole is not a hole   523.8
BLACK HUMOR (LITERATURE)
   See also Fiction; Literature; Wit and humor
Black ice. Lane, A.   Fic
Black Indians. Katz, W. L.   305.8
Black is for beginnings. Stolarz, L. F.   741.5
BLACK LIBRARIANS
   See also Librarians
BLACK MAGIC (WITCHCRAFT) *See* Magic;
  Witchcraft
Black magic and witches.   133.4
BLACK MUSIC
   See also Music
BLACK MUSICIANS
   See also Musicians
BLACK MUSLIM LEADERS
  Archer, J. They had a dream   323.1
  Burlingame, J. Malcolm X   92
  Draper, A. S. The assassination of Malcolm
   X   364.15
  Gunderson, J. X: the biography of Malcolm X 92
  Sharp, A. W. Malcolm X and Black pride   92
BLACK MUSLIMS
  Burlingame, J. Malcolm X   92
  Draper, A. S. The assassination of Malcolm
   X   364.15
  Gunderson, J. X: the biography of Malcolm X 92
  Sharp, A. W. Malcolm X and Black pride   92
BLACK MUSLIMS -- FICTION
  Nolan, H. A summer of Kings   Fic
BLACK NATIONALISM -- FICTION
  Magoon, K. Fire in the streets   Fic
Black pioneers [series]
  Hansen, J. Home is with our family   Fic
Black potatoes. Bartoletti, S. C.   941.508
Black powder. Rabin, S.   Fic
Black radishes. Meyer, S.   Fic
Black Sabbath. Aberback, B.   781.66
Black stars [series]
  Haskins, J. African American religious leaders 920
  Sullivan, O. R. African American millionaires 920
  Tate, E. E. African American musicians   920
Black stars in a white night sky. Lawson, J. 811
Black storm comin'. Wilson, D. L.   Fic
Black Tuesday. Doak, R. S.   330.9
Black water. MacHale, D. J.   Fic
Black widows. Markle, S.   595.4
BLACK WOMEN
   See also Women
Black, Angela
  Sheehan, S. Jamaica   972.92
Black, Ann N.

BLOOD GROUPS

    See also Blood

The **blood** lie. Vernick, S. R.   Fic

Blood moon rider. Waters, Z. C.   Fic

Blood ninja II: the revenge of Lord Oda. Lake, N.   Fic

Blood of Eden [series]

    Kagawa, J. The immortal rules   Fic

Blood of kings [series]

    Williamson, J. By darkness hid   Fic

    Williamson, J. To darkness fled   Fic

Blood on the river. Carbone, E. L.   Fic

BLOOD PRESSURE

    See also Blood

Blood red horse. Grant, K. M.   Fic

Blood red road. Young, M.   Fic

Blood sun. Gilman, D.   Fic

Bloodhound. Pierce, T.   Fic

Bloodline. Moran, K.   Fic

Bloodline [series]

    Cary, K. Bloodline: reckoning   Fic

Bloodline. Cary, K.   Fic

Bloodline rising. Moran, K.   Fic

Bloodline: reckoning. Cary, K.   Fic

BLOODSTAINS

    Rainis, K. G. Blood & DNA evidence   363.2

BLOODSUCKING ANIMALS

    Knapp, R. Bloodsucking creatures   591.5

Bloodsucking creatures. Knapp, R.   591.5

Bloodwater mysteries [series]

    Hautman, P. Doppelganger   Fic

    Hautman, P. Skullduggery   Fic

    Hautman, P. Snatched   Fic

Bloody Jack. Meyer, L. A.   Fic

Bloody times. Swanson, J. L.   973.7

Bloom, Barbara Lee

    Nat Love   92

Bloom, Ona

    Morgan, J. Cells of the nervous system   611

Bloomability. Creech, S.   Fic

Bloomberg, Michael

           About

    Shichtman, S. H. Michael Bloomberg   92

Bloomfield, Alan

    Jennings, M. Baseball step-by-step   796.357

Bloomfield, Jill

    Jewish holidays cookbook   641.5

Bloor, Edward

    London calling   Fic

    A plague year   Fic

    Taken   Fic

    Tangerine   Fic

Blos, Joan W.

    Letters from the corrugated castle   Fic

Blount, Marcellus

    (ed) African American Poetry   811.008

Blubaugh, Penny

    Serendipity Market   Fic

The **blue** book on information age inquiry, instruction and literacy. Callison, D.   028.7

BLUE COLLAR WORKERS *See* Labor; Working class

Blue fire. Hardy, J.   Fic

Blue flame. Grant, K. M.   Fic

The **blue** girl. De Lint, C.   Fic

Blue jasmine. Sheth, K.   Fic

The **blue** jean book. Kyi, T. L.   391

Blue like Friday. Parkinson, S.   Fic

Blue lipstick. Grandits, J.   811

Blue Mountain trouble. Mordecai, M.   Fic

Blue noon. Westerfeld, S.   Fic

The **blue** shoe. Townley, R.   Fic

The **blue** sword. McKinley, R.   Fic

Blue thread. Feldman, R. T.   Fic

Blue, Rose

    Naden, C. J. Dred Scott   342

    Naden, C. J. James Monroe   92

    Naden, C. J. John Muir   92

Bluefish. Schmatz, P.   Fic

BLUEGRASS MUSIC

    See also Music

Blues. Handyside, C.   781.643

BLUES MUSIC

    Handyside, C. Blues   781.643

    Mendelson, A. A. American R & B   781.644

BLUES MUSIC

    See also African American music; Folk music -- United States; Popular music

BLUES MUSIC -- POETRY

    Lewis, J. P. Black cat bone   811

BLUES MUSICIANS

    Duggleby, J. Uh huh!: the story of Ray Charles   92

    Lewis, J. P. Black cat bone   811

    Orgill, R. Shout, sister, shout!   920

    Weatherford, C. B. Becoming Billie Holiday   Fic

    Woog, A. Ray Charles and the birth of soul   92

BLUES SONGS *See* Blues music

Bluestein, Jane

    Katz, E. D. High school's not forever   373.1

Blumberg, Rhoda

    Commodore Perry in the land of the Shogun   952

    Shipwrecked!: the true adventures of a Japanese boy   92

Blume, Judy, 1938-

    Blume, J. Here's to you, Rachel Robinson   Fic

    Are you there God?, it's me, Margaret   Fic

    Here's to you, Rachel Robinson   Fic

    Tiger eyes   Fic

    (ed) Places I never meant to be   813

Blume, Lesley M. M.

    The rising star of Rusty Nail   Fic

    Tennyson   Fic

Blumenthal, Karen

Bootleg   363.4

Let me play   796

Mr. Sam   92

Six days in October   332.64

Steve Jobs   621.39

Blundell, Judy

A city tossed and broken   Fic

Strings attached   Fic

What I saw and how I lied   Fic

Bly, Nellie, 1864-1922

About

Bankston, J. Nellie Bly   070.92

Macy, S. Bylines: a photobiography of Nellie Bly   92

BOARD BOOKS FOR CHILDREN

See also Picture books for children

BOARD GAMES

Mayer, B. Libraries got game   025.2

BOARD GAMES

See also Games

BOARD GAMES -- GRAPHIC NOVELS

Hotta, Y. Hikaru No Go, Volume 1   741.5

Boarder patrol. Thomas, E.   Fic

BOARDING SCHOOLS *See* Private schools

BOARDING SCHOOLS -- FICTION

Carriger, G. Etiquette & espionage   Fic

Johnson, M. The madness underneath   Fic

Laban, E. The Tragedy Paper   Fic

Maizel, R. Stolen nights   Fic

BOAT RACING

See also Boats and boating; Racing

BOATING *See* Boats and boating

BOATS AND BOATING

Cummings, P. Red kayak   Fic

Paulsen, G. Caught by the sea   818

BOATS AND BOATING -- FICTION

Fletcher, R. The one o'clock chop   Fic

Hiaasen, C. Flush   Fic

BOATS AND BOATING

Paulsen, G. Caught by the sea   818

Boaz, John

(ed) Free speech   342

Bob Marley. Paprocki, S. B.   92

Bober, Natalie

Abigail Adams   973.4

Bobrick, Benson

A passion for victory: the story of the Olympics in ancient and early modern times   796.4

The Battle of Nashville   973.7

Fight for freedom   973.3

Bochner, Arthur Berg

The new totally awesome business book for kids (and their parents)   658

Bochner, R. The new totally awesome money book for kids (and their parents)   332.024

Bochner, Rose

Bochner, A. B. The new totally awesome business book for kids (and their parents)   658

The new totally awesome money book for kids (and their parents)   332.024

Bock, Caroline

LIE   Fic

Bockenhauer, Mark H.

Our fifty states   973

Bodart, Joni Richards

Radical reads 2   028.5

They suck, they bite, they eat, they kill   813

Bodden, Valerie

The Cold War   909.82

Concrete poetry   809.1

Creating the character   808.3

Critical plant life   581.7

Environmental law   344

Frank Gehry   92

Haiku   809.1

Limericks   809.1

Man walks on the Moon   629.45

Nursery rhymes   398.8

Painting the picture   808.3

Samuel Houston   92

Setting the style   808.3

Telling the tale   808.3

Through the American West   917.804

To the heart of Africa   916.704

To the moon   629.45

To the ocean deep   551.46

To the South Pole   919.8

To the top of Mount Everest   796.522

Using the Internet   025.042

Vincent van Gogh   92

Bodeen, S. A.

The Compound   Fic

The gardener   Fic

The raft   Fic

Bodies from the ash. Deem, J. M.   937

Bodies from the bog. Deem, J. M.   573.3

Bodies from the ice. Deem, J. M.   393

BODY *See* Human body

BODY ART

Bliss, J. Preening, painting, and piercing   391

The **body** at the tower. Lee, Y. S.   Fic

The **body** book for boys. Mar, J.   612.6

Body by design. Nagel, R.   612

BODY CARE *See* Hygiene

Body drama. Redd, N. A.   612

The **Body** eclectic.   808.81

The **body** finder. Derting, K.   Fic

BODY IMAGE

Baish, V. Self-image and eating disorders   616.85

Graydon, S. In your face   391

Libal, A. Social discrimination and body size   362.1

BOMBINGS -- ALABAMA -- BIRMINGHAM
Brimner, L. D. Birmingham Sunday   **323.1**

BOMBS
Newton, M. Bomb squad   **363.2**

Bonar, Samantha
Small wildcats   **599.75**

Bond, Victoria
Zora and me   **Fic**

Bondoux, Anne-Laure
A time of miracles   **Fic**

BONDS
See also Finance; Investments; Negotiable instruments; Securities; Stock exchanges

Bondy, Halley
Don't sit on the baby   **649.1**

Bone [series]
Sniegoski, T. Quest for the spark   **Fic**

Bone detective. Hopping, L. J.   **92**

Bone: crown of horns. Smith, J.   **741.5**

Bone: crown of horns. Smith, J.   **741.5**

Bone: out from Boneville. Smith, J.   **741.5**

Bone: Rose. Smith, J.   **741.5**

Bone: tall tales. Smith, J.   **741.5**

Bone: treasure hunters. Smith, J.   **741.5**

Bonechiller. McNamee, G.   **Fic**

BONES
Markle, S. Shattered bones   **617.1**

BONES
See also Musculoskeletal system

BONES -- DISEASES
See also Diseases

Bones Never Lie. MacLeod, E.   **363.25**

Bones of Faerie. Simner, J. L.   **Fic**

Bones rock! Larson, P. L.   **560**

Bones speak! Spilsbury, R.   **614**

Bones, brains and DNA. Tattersall, I.   **599.93**

The **Boneshaker.** Milford, K.   **Fic**

Bonhoeffer, Dietrich, 1906-1945
About
Martin, M. J. Champion of freedom   **230**

Boniface, William
The great powers outage   **Fic**
The hero revealed   **Fic**
The return of Meteor Boy?   **Fic**

Bonner, Hannah
When dinos dawned, mammals got munched, and Pterosaurs took flight   **567.9**

Bonnet, Robert L.
46 science fair projects for the evil genius   **507.8**
Home run!   **530**

Bonnin, Jenny
McKay, K. True green kids   **333.72**

BONOBO -- FICTION
Schrefer, E. Endangered   **Fic**

Book by book. Spiegel, C.   **011.6**

BOOK CLUBS (DISCUSSION GROUPS)

Kunzel, B. L. The teen-centered book club   **027.62**

BOOK CLUBS (DISCUSSION GROUPS)
See also Clubs

BOOK COLLECTING
See also Book selection; Collectors and collecting

BOOK DISCUSSION GROUPS
Kunzel, B. L. The teen-centered book club   **027.62**

BOOK DISCUSSION GROUPS See Book clubs (Discussion groups)

BOOK ILLUSTRATION See Illustration of books

BOOK LISTS See Best books

Book of a thousand days. Hale, S.   **Fic**

The **book** of blood. Newquist, H.   **612.1**

The **book** of blood and shadow. Wasserman, R. **Fic**

The **Book** of dragons. Hague, M.   **808.83**

The **book** of dreams. Melling, O. R.   **Fic**

The **book** of gardening projects for kids. Cohen, W.   **635**

The **Book** of Lies. Moloney, J.   **Fic**

The **book** of magic. Barron, T. A.   **Fic**

The **Book** of monologues for aspiring actors. **808.82**

The **book** of Mordred. Vande Velde, V.   **Fic**

The **Book** of Mormon. Book of Mormon   **289.3**

Book of Mormon
The Book of Mormon   **289.3**

The **book** of North American owls. Sattler, H. R.   **598.9**

The **book** of pirates. Rose, J.   **910.4**

The **book** of potentially catastrophic science. Connolly, S.   **507.8**

The Book of Tamarind [series]
Aguiar, N. The lost island of Tamarind   **Fic**
Aguiar, N. Secrets of Tamarind   **Fic**

The **book** of the Lion. Cadnum, M.   **Fic**

The **book** of the maidservant. Barnhouse, R.   **Fic**

The **book** of three. Alexander, L.   **Fic**

The **book** of time. Prevost, G.   **Fic**

The **book** of wonders. Richards, J.   **Fic**

BOOK REVIEWING
See also Books and reading; Criticism

BOOK SELECTION
Keane, N. J. 101 great, ready-to-use book lists for teens   **028.5**

BOOK SELECTION
See also Libraries -- Acquisitions; Libraries -- Collection development

BOOK TALKS
Baxter, K. A. Gotcha again for guys!   **028.5**
Bromann, J. Booktalking that works   **028.5**
Bromann, J. More booktalking that works   **028.5**
Cannon, T. C. Cooler than fiction   **027.62**
Cole, S. Booktalking around the world   **021.7**
Cox Clark, R. E. Tantalizing tidbits for middle schoolers   **028.5**
Diamant-Cohen, B. Booktalking bonanza   **028.5**

See also Weapons

Bow, Erin

Plain Kate — Fic

Bow, James

Earth's secrets — 550

Bow, Patricia

Chimpanzee rescue — 599.8

Bowden, Rob, 1973-

African culture — 960

Ancient Africa — 960

Changing Africa — 960

Energy sources — 333.79

Kenya — 967.62

Modern Africa — 960

Water supply — 363.6

Bowe, Brian J.

The Ramones — 781.66

BOWED INSTRUMENTS *See* Stringed instruments

BOWED STRINGED INSTRUMENTS -- CONSTRUCTION

Pagliaro, M. The musical instrument desk reference — 784.192

Bowen, Fred

Quarterback season — Fic

Bowers, Elizabeth Shimer

Ehrlich, P. Living with allergies — 616.97

Bowers, Laura

Beauty shop for rent — Fic

Bowers, Nathan

4-H guide to training horses — 636.1

Bowers, Rick

The spies of Mississippi — 323.1

Superman versus the Ku Klux Klan — 741.5

Bowes, John P.

Black Hawk and the War of 1832 — 973.5

BOWHEAD WHALE

Lourie, P. Whaling season — 599.5

BOWHUNTING

See also Hunting

Bowler, Ann Martin

All about Korea — 951.9

Bowler, Gerald

The world encyclopedia of Christmas — 394.26

Bowler, Tim

Blade: out of the shadows — Fic

Blade: playing dead — Fic

Fighting back — Fic

Frozen fire — Fic

BOWLING

See also Ball games

Bowling, beatniks, and bell-bottoms. — 306

Bowman's store. Bruchac, J. — 92

Bowman, John Stewart

(ed) Isserman, M. World War II — 940.53

Bowman, Vibiana

(ed) Teaching Generation M — 027.62

Box out. Coy, J. — Fic

Box turtles. Stone, L. M. — 597.92

Box, Matthew J.

(ed) Adoption — 362.7

(ed) Poverty — 362.5

BOXERS (PERSONS)

Micklos, J. Muhammad Ali — 92

Myers, W. D. The greatest: Muhammad Ali — 92

Owens, T. Muhammad Ali — 92

Smith, C. R. Twelve rounds to glory: the story of Muhammad Ali — 92

Streissguth, T. Clay v. United States and how Muhammad Ali fought the draft — 343

Sullivan, G. Knockout!: a photobiography of boxer Joe Louis — 92

BOXES -- COLLECTORS AND COLLECTING

See also Collectors and collecting

BOXES -- FICTION

Explorer — Fic

TenNapel, D. Cardboard — Fic

Boxing. Mason, P. — 796.8

BOXING

Mason, P. Boxing — 796.8

BOXING -- BIOGRAPHY

Micklos, J. Muhammad Ali — 92

Myers, W. D. The greatest: Muhammad Ali — 92

Owens, T. Muhammad Ali — 92

Smith, C. R. Twelve rounds to glory: the story of Muhammad Ali — 92

Sullivan, G. Knockout!: a photobiography of boxer Joe Louis — 92

BOXING -- FICTION

Friend, N. My life in black and white — Fic

Lipsyte, R. The contender — Fic

Pinkney, A. D. Bird in a box — Fic

Sharenow, R. The Berlin Boxing Club — Fic

The **boy** at the end of the world. Van Eekhout, G. — Fic

A **boy** at war. Mazer, H. — Fic

A **boy** called Twister. Schraff, A. E. — Fic

The **boy** from Ilysies. North, P. — Fic

The **boy** in the burning house. Wynne-Jones, T. — Fic

The **boy** in the dress. Walliams, D. — Fic

A **boy** no more. Mazer, H. — Fic

Boy O'Boy. Doyle, B. — Fic

The **boy** on Cinnamon Street. Stone, P. — FIC

The **Boy** Project. Kinard, K. — Fic

Boy proof. Castellucci, C. — Fic

BOY SCOUTS

See also Boys' clubs; Scouts and scouting

The **boy** Sherlock Holmes [series]

Peacock, S. Death in the air — Fic

Peacock, S. The dragon turn — Fic

Peacock, S. Eye of the crow — Fic

Peacock, S. The secret fiend — Fic

Peacock, S. Vanishing girl   **Fic**
Boy talk.   **612.6**
Boy vs. girl. Robert, N. B.   **Fic**
BOY WHALERS -- HISTORY
Murphy, J. Gone a-whaling   **306.3**
The **boy** who could fly. Norcliffe, J.   **Fic**
The **boy** who couldn't sleep and never had to. Pierson, D. C.   **Fic**
The **boy** who dared. Bartoletti, S. C.   **Fic**
The **boy** who saved baseball. Ritter, J. H.   **Fic**
Boy2girl. Blacker, T.   **Fic**
Boy: tales of childhood. Dahl, R.   **92**
BOYCOTTS
> *See also* Commerce; Consumers; Passive resistance

BOYCOTTS
Freedman, R. Freedom walkers   **323.1**
Boyd, Herb
Wright, S. Simeon's story   **305.8**
Boyd, Maria
Will   **Fic**
Boyle, Robert, 1627-1691
About
Baxter, R. Skeptical chemist   **92**
Boyne, John
Noah   Barleywater   runs   away
Boyology. Burningham, S. O.   **306.7**
BOYS
Aronson, M. For boys only   **031.02**
Boy talk   **612.6**
Dude!   **810**
Iggulden, C. The dangerous book for boys   **031.02**
Jukes, M. The guy book   **305.235**
Mar, J. The body book for boys   **612.6**
You hear me?   **810**
BOYS
> *See also* Children

BOYS -- BOOKS AND READING
Baxter, K. A. Gotcha again for guys!   **028.5**
Bilz, R. L. Life is tough   **028.5**
Knowles, E. Boys and literacy   **028.5**
Sullivan, M. Connecting boys with books 2   **028.5**
Sullivan, M. Serving boys through readers' advisory   **028.5**
Welch, R. J. The guy-friendly YA library   **027.62**
Zbaracki, M. D. Best books for boys   **028.5**
BOYS -- FICTION
Clifton, L. Freaky Fast Frankie Joe   **Fic**
Ness, P. The knife of never letting go   **Fic**
Stead, R. Liar & spy   **Fic**
BOYS -- HEALTH AND HYGIENE
Will puberty last my whole life?   **613**
BOYS
Aronson, M. For boys only   **031.02**
Baxter, K. A. Gotcha again for guys!   **028.5**
Sullivan, M. Serving boys through readers' advisory   **028.5**
Zbaracki, M. D. Best books for boys   **028.5**
BOYS -- POETRY
Flake, S. G. You don't even know me   **808.8**
BOYS -- PSYCHOLOGY
Burningham, S. O. Boyology   **306.7**
Saval, M. The secret lives of boys   **155.5**
BOYS -- SOCIETIES *See* Boys' clubs
Boys and literacy. Knowles, E.   **028.5**
The **boys** of San Joaquin. Smith, D. J.   **Fic**
Boys of Steel.   **741.5**
Boys of wartime [series]
Calkhoven, L. Will at the Battle of Gettysburg, 1863   **Fic**
Boys without names. Sheth, K.   **Fic**
BOYS' CLUBS
> *See also* Clubs; Societies

The **boys'** guide to growing up. Couwenhoven, T.   **613**
The **boys'** war. Murphy, J.   **973.7**
Boys, girls, and other hazardous materials. Wiseman, R.   **Fic**
Braafladt, Keith
Technology and literacy   **027.62**
Braasch, Gary
Cherry, L. How we know what we know about our changing climate   **363.7**
BRACHIOSAURUS
> *See also* Dinosaurs

Bradberry, Sarah
Kids knit!   **746.43**
Bradbury, Adrian
Walters, E. When elephants fight   **920**
Bradbury, Jennifer
Shift   **Fic**
Wrapped   **Fic**
Bradbury, Ray
The Halloween tree   **Fic**
Something wicked this way comes   **Fic**
Bradbury, Ray, 1920-
About
Bankston, J. Ray Bradbury   **92**
Bradford, Chris
Young samurai: the way of the sword   **Fic**
Young samurai: the way of the warrior   **Fic**
Bradford, William, 1590-1657
About
Doherty, K. William Bradford   **974.4**
Philbrick, N. The Mayflower and the Pilgrims' New World   **973.2**
Bradley, Alex
24 girls in 7 days   **Fic**
Bradley, James
Flags of our fathers   **940.54**
Bradley, Kimberly Brubaker
Jefferson's sons   **Fic**

The lacemaker and the princess **Fic**

Bradley, Timothy J.
Paleo bugs **560**

Bradman, Tony
(ed) Give me shelter **S C**
(ed) My dad's a punk **S C**
(ed) Under the weather **S C**

Brady, Hana
About
Levine, K. Hana's suitcase **940.53**

Brady, Hana
About
Levine, K. Hana's suitcase on stage **812**

Brady, Mathew B., ca. 1823-1896
About
Armstrong, J. Photo by Brady **973.7**
Rosenberg, A. The Civil War **920**

Brager, Bruce L., 1949-
John Paul Jones **92**

Bragg, Georgia
How they croaked **920**

Brahe, Tycho, 1546-1601
About
Boerst, W. J. Tycho Brahe **92**
Nardo, D. Tycho Brahe **92**

BRAHMANISM
See also Religions

The **braid.** Frost, H. **Fic**

BRAILLE BOOKS
See also Books

Braille, Louis, 1809-1852
About
Freedman, R. Out of darkness: the story of Louis Braille **92**

The **brain.** Simon, S. **612.8**

BRAIN
Hudmon, A. Learning and memory **153.1**
Newquist, H. P. The great brain book **612.8**
Rau, D. M. Freaking out! **612.8**
Simon, S. The brain **612.8**
Simpson, K. The human brain **612.8**
Wilson, M. R. Frequently asked questions about how the teen brain works **612.8**
Winston, R. M. L. What goes on in my head? **612.8**

BRAIN
See also Head; Nervous system

BRAIN -- CANCER
Freedman, J. Brain cancer **616.99**

BRAIN -- DISEASES
See also Diseases

BRAIN -- TUMORS
Gunther, J. Death be not proud **92**
Parks, P. J. Brain tumors **616.99**

BRAIN -- WOUNDS AND INJURIES
Fleischman, J. Phineas Gage: a gruesome but true story about brain science **362.1**

Markle, S. Wounded brains **617**

BRAIN -- WOUNDS AND INJURIES -- FICTION
Hartry, N. Watching Jimmy **Fic**
Keller, J. Back home **Fic**
McCormick, P. Purple Heart **Fic**
Tullson, D. Riley Park **Fic**
Venkatraman, P. Climbing the stairs **Fic**
Warner, S. It's only temporary **Fic**

Brain cancer. Freedman, J. **616.99**

BRAIN DAMAGE -- COMPLICATIONS
Fleischman, J. Phineas Gage: a gruesome but true story about brain science **362.1**

BRAIN DAMAGE -- PATIENTS -- UNITED STATES -- BIOGRAPHY
Fleischman, J. Phineas Gage: a gruesome but true story about brain science **362.1**

BRAIN DAMAGED CHILDREN
Esherick, J. The journey toward recovery **616.8**

BRAIN DAMAGED CHILDREN
See also Exceptional children; Handicapped children

BRAIN DEATH
See also Death

The **Brain** finds a leg. Chatterton, M. **Fic**
The **Brain** full of holes. Chatterton, M. **Fic**
Brain tumors. Parks, P. J. **616.99**
Brainstorm! Tucker, T. **609.2**

BRAINWASHING
See also Behavior modification; Mental suggestion; Psychological warfare; Psychology of learning

BRAINWASHING -- FICTION
Nylund, E. S. The Resisters **Fic**
Robbins, T. The drained brains caper **741.5**

Brake, Mark
Alien Hunter's Handbook **576.8**

Bram Stoker's Dracula. Raven, N. **741.5**

BRAND NAME PRODUCTS
Muharrar, A. More than a label **305.23**

BRAND NAME PRODUCTS
See also Commercial products; Manufactures

Brand new Emily. Rue, G. **Fic**

Brande, Robin
Evolution, me, & other freaks of nature **Fic**
Fat Cat **Fic**

BRANDED MERCHANDISE *See* Brand name products

Brandeis, Gayle
My life with the Lincolns **Fic**

Brannen, Daniel E.
Benson, S. UXL encyclopedia of U.S. history **973**
Supreme Court drama **347**

Branscomb, Leslie Wolf
Earl Warren **92**
Marc Jacobs **92**

Branzei, Sylvia

Burwell, Letitia M.
About
Cloud Tapper, S. Voices from slavery's past **326**
Bury my heart at Wounded Knee. Brown, D. A. **970.004**
BURYING GROUNDS See Burial; Cemeteries
Burying the sun. Whelan, G. **Fic**
Busby, Cylin
The year we disappeared **92**
(ed) First kiss (then tell) **808.8**
Busby, Cylin, 1970-
About
Busby, C. The year we disappeared **92**
Busby, John
Busby, C. The year we disappeared **92**
Busby, John, 1942-
About
Busby, C. The year we disappeared **92**
Buscemi, Karen
Split in two **306.874**
BUSES
See also Automobiles; Highway transportation; Local transit; Motor vehicles
BUSH SURVIVAL See Wilderness survival
Bush v. Gore. Sergis, D. K. **342**
Bush, Gail
Tales out of the school library **027.8**
Bush, George W.
About
The Election of 2000 and the administration of George W. Bush **324**
Sergis, D. K. Bush v. Gore **342**
Bush, George W. (George Walker), 1946-
About
Burgan, M. George W. Bush **973.931**
Bushman lives! **Fic**
Bushman, Claudia L.
Mormons in America **289.3**
Bushman, Richard L.
Bushman, C. L. Mormons in America **289.3**
BUSINESS
See also Commerce; Economics
BUSINESS -- INFORMATION RESOURCES
See also Information resources
BUSINESS -- INTERNET RESOURCES
See also Internet resources
BUSINESS AND POLITICS
See also Politics
Business builders [series]
Aaseng, N. Business builders in sweets and treats **920**
Business builders in sweets and treats. Aaseng, N. **920**
BUSINESS CYCLES
Hollander, B. Booms, bubbles, and busts **338.5**
BUSINESS CYCLES

See also Cycles; Economic conditions
BUSINESS DEPRESSION, 1929-1939 See Great Depression, 1929-1939
BUSINESS ENTERPRISES
Rankin, K. Start it up **338**
BUSINESS ENTERPRISES -- FICTION
Chambers, V. Fifteen candles **Fic**
Connor, L. Crunch **Fic**
Cottrell Boyce, F. Framed **Fic**
Erskine, K. The absolute value of Mike **Fic**
Jennings, R. W. Ghost town **Fic**
Paulsen, G. Flat broke **Fic**
Rylander, C. The fourth stall **Fic**
BUSINESS ETHICS
See also Ethics; Professional ethics
BUSINESS ETHICS -- FICTION
Petrucha, S. Teen, Inc. **Fic**
BUSINESS ETIQUETTE
See also Etiquette
BUSINESS FORECASTING
See also Economic forecasting; Forecasting
Business leaders [series]
Baughan, B. Russell Simmons **92**
Hasday, J. L. Facebook and Mark Zuckerberg **92**
Johnson, A. J. Warren Buffett **92**
Sapet, K. Google founders: Larry Page and Sergey Brin **92**
Scally, R. Jeff Bezos **92**
Smith, C. Twitter **92**
BUSINESS LETTERS
See also Letter writing
BUSINESS MATHEMATICS
See also Mathematics
BUSINESS MORTALITY See Bankruptcy; Business failures
BUSINESS ORGANIZATIONS See Business enterprises
BUSINESS PEOPLE See Businesspeople
BUSINESS RECESSIONS See Recessions
BUSINESS SCHOOLS
See also Schools
Business without borders. Andrews, D. **658**
BUSINESSES See Business enterprises
BUSINESSMEN
Blumenthal, K. Mr. Sam **92**
Copley, B. The tall Mexican: the life of Hank Aguirre, all-star pitcher, businessman, humanitarian **92**
Edge, L. B. Andrew Carnegie **92**
Ehrenhaft, D. Larry Ellison **338.7**
Ehrenhaft, D. Marc Andreessen **338.7**
Freese, S. M. Craigslist **381**
Hasday, J. L. Facebook and Mark Zuckerberg **92**
Mitchell, D. Driven **92**
Robinson, T. Jeff Bezos **92**
Scally, R. Jeff Bezos **92**

CAMOUFLAGE (BIOLOGY)
Frogs!   **597.8**
CAMOUFLAGE (BIOLOGY)
    See also Animal defenses
CAMOUFLAGE (MILITARY SCIENCE)
    See also Military art and science; Naval art
and science
CAMPAIGN FUNDS
    See also Elections; Politics
CAMPAIGN FUNDS -- UNITED STATES
Marzilli, A. Election reform   **324.6**
CAMPAIGN LITERATURE
    See also Literature; Politics
CAMPAIGNS, POLITICAL *See* Politics
Campbell's scoop. Campbell, P. J.   **809**
Campbell, Andrew
Cosmetic surgery   **617.9**
Organ transplants   **617.9**
Campbell, Andrew C.
Dawes, J. Exploring the world of aquatic life **591.7**
Campbell, Geoffrey A.
The home front   **973.92**
Campbell, Kimberly Edwina
Less is more   **809**
Lois Duncan   **92**
Richard Peck   **92**
Campbell, Margaret Christine
Discovering atoms   **539.7**
Campbell, Patricia J.
Campbell's scoop   **809**
Campbell, Ross
Shadoweyes   **741.5**
Campbell, Rusty
Atlas of Asia   **950**
Campfire Graphic Novels Series
Helfand, L. Conquering Everest   **741.5**
Campfire mythology [series]
Foley, R. Stolen hearts   **741.5**
CAMPING
Champion, N. Fire and cooking   **796.54**
George, J. C. Pocket guide to the outdoors **796.5**
CAMPING
    See also Outdoor recreation
CAMPING -- FICTION
Bruchac, J. Bearwalker   **Fic**
Cummings, P. The journey back   **Fic**
Dooley, S. Body of water   **Fic**
Evangelista, B. Gifted   **Fic**
Salisbury, G. Night of the howling dogs   **Fic**
CAMPING
Cummings, P. The journey back   **Fic**
Campoy, F. Isabel
(jt. auth) Ada, A. F. Yes! we are Latinos   **Fic**
CAMPS
    See also Recreation
CAMPS -- FICTION

Cotler, S. Cheesie Mack is cool in a duel   **Fic**
CAMPS -- FICTION
Charlie Joe Jackson's guide to summer vacation **Fic**
Can diets be harmful?   **613.2**
Can I change the way I look? Libal, A.   **613**
Can I see your I.D.? Barton, C.   **001.9**
Can the War on Terrorism be won?   **363.32**
Can we travel to the stars? Solway, A.   **629.45**
Can't get there from here. Strasser, T.   **Fic**
Canada. Williams, B.   **971**
Canada. Sonneborn, L.   **971**
CANADA -- FICTION
Hobbs, W. Never say die   **Fic**
CANADA -- HISTORY
Cryptic Canada   **971.1**
**CANADA -- HISTORY -- TO 1763 (NEW
FRANCE)**
Goodman, J. E. Despite all obstacles: La Salle and
the conquest of the Mississippi   **92**
CANADA
Sonneborn, L. Canada   **971**
CANADA -- SOCIAL LIFE AND CUSTOMS
Sonneborn, L. Canada   **971**
Canadian dinosaurs. Kelsey, E.   **567.909**
CANADIAN LITERATURE
    See also Literature
CANADIANS
Dublin, A. June Callwood   **92**
Canales, Viola
The tequila worm   **Fic**
Canaletto. Rice, E.   **92**
Canaletto, 1697-1768
               About
Rice, E. Canaletto   **92**
The **canals.** Bial, R.   **386**
CANALS
Bial, R. The canals   **386**
Roop, P. River roads west   **386**
CANALS
    See also Civil engineering; Hydraulic struc-
tures; Transportation; Waterways
CANALS -- FICTION
Hurst, C. O. Through the lock   **Fic**
CANALS -- UNITED STATES
Bial, R. The canals   **386**
CANARIES
    See also Birds; Cage birds
CANCER
Cancer information for teens   **616.99**
Dreyer, Z. Living with cancer   **362.1**
Goldsmith, C. Skin cancer   **616.99**
Grover, L. A. Loose threads   **811**
Gunther, J. Death be not proud   **92**
Lew, K. The truth about cancer   **616.99**
Skloot, R. The immortal life of Henrietta Lacks **616**
Thornton, D. Living with cancer   **616.99**

CANCER
> *See also* Diseases; Tumors

CANCER -- ENVIRONMENTAL ASPECTS
> *See also* Environmentally induced diseases

CANCER -- FICTION
Bell, J. Kepler's dream	Fic
Bryce, C. Anthem for Jackson Dawes	Fic
Cheng, A. Brushing Mom's hair	Fic
Crane, D. Poster boy	Fic
Gurtler, J. I'm not her	Fic
Jacobson, J. The complete history of why I hate her	Fic
Kephart, B. House of Dance	Fic
Koss, A. G. Side effects	Fic
Lopez, D. Ask my mood ring how I feel	Fic
Mccall, G. G. Under the mesquite	Fic
McDaniel, L. Breathless	Fic
A monster calls	Fic
Padian, M. Brett McCarthy: work in progress	Fic
Paulsen, G. Notes from the dog	Fic
Preller, J. Six innings	Fic
Rallison, J. Just one wish	Fic
Sonnenblick, J. After ever after	Fic
Thompson, H. The language inside	Fic
Turner, A. W. Hard hit	Fic
Vincent, Z. The lucky place	Fic
Wunder, W. The probability of miracles	Fic

CANCER -- GENETIC ASPECTS
> *See also* Medical genetics

CANCER
Sheen, B. Prostate cancer	616.99

CANCER -- POETRY
Grover, L. A. Loose threads	811

CANCER -- PATIENTS
Therrien, P. An enemy within	362.196

CANCER -- PATIENTS -- FICTION
Bryce, C. Anthem for Jackson Dawes	Fic

CANCER -- PSYCHOLOGICAL ASPECTS
Silver, M. My parent has cancer and it really sucks	616.99

CANCER -- SURGERY
> *See also* Surgery

Cancer and modern science [series]
Casil, A. S. Pancreatic cancer	616.99
Freedman, J. Brain cancer	616.99
Stokes, M. Colon cancer	616.99
Stokes, M. Prostate cancer	616.99

CANCER IN CHILDREN -- PATIENTS -- BIOGRAPHY
Therrien, P. An enemy within	362.196
Cancer information for teens.	616.99

CANCER PATIENTS *See* Cancer -- Patients

CANDIES *See* Candy

Candle Man [series]
Dakin, G. The Society of Dread	Fic
Dakin, G. The Society of Unrelenting Vigilance	Fic

CANDLEMAKING
Check, L. Create your own candles	745.5

CANDLES
Check, L. Create your own candles	745.5

CANDY
Love, A. Sweet!	641.8
Candy bomber. Tunnell, M.	92
Cane toad. Somervill, B. A.	597.8

Caney, Steven
Steven Caney's ultimate building book	624

Canfield, Jack
Chicken soup for the teenage soul [I-IV]	158
(comp) Chicken soup for the teenage soul's the real deal	158

The **canine** connection: stories about dogs and people. Hearne, B. G.   S C

CANNABIS *See* Marijuana

Cannarella, Deborah
Kansas	978.1

Cannavale, Matthew C.
Florida, 1513-1821	975.9
North Carolina, 1524-1776	975.6

CANNIBALISM
> *See also* Ethnology; Human behavior

CANNIBALISM -- FICTION
Rossi, V. Under the never sky	Fic

CANNING AND PRESERVING
> *See also* Cooking; Food -- Preservation; Industrial chemistry

The **canning** season. Horvath, P.   Fic

Cannon, Tara C.
Cooler than fiction	027.62

Cano-Murillo, Kathy
The crafty diva's lifestyle makeover	745.5
Canoeing and kayaking. Thorpe, Y.	797.1

CANOES AND CANOEING
Thorpe, Y. Canoeing and kayaking	797.1

CANOES AND CANOEING
> *See also* Boats and boating; Water sports

CANOES AND CANOEING -- FICTION
Hobbs, W. Take me to the river	Fic
Canterbury tales. Cohen, B.	821
Canto familiar. Soto, G.	811

Cantor, George
Usain Bolt	796.42

Cantor, Jillian
The life of glass	Fic
The September sisters	Fic
Canyons. Hanson, E. A.	551.4

CANYONS
Hanson, E. A. Canyons	551.4

Capaccio, George
ADD and ADHD	616.85
Jupiter	523.4
Mars	523.4
The sun	523.7

Cardboard. TenNapel, D.   **Fic**

Cardenas, Teresa
Letters to my mother   **Fic**
Old dog   **Fic**

CARDIAC DISEASES *See* Heart diseases

CARDIFF GIANT
Murphy, J. The giant and how he humbugged America   **974.7**

CARDINALS
Gibbs, S. The last musketeer   **Fic**

CARDIOVASCULAR SYSTEM
Bjorklund, R. Circulatory system   **612.1**
Markle, S. Faulty hearts   **612.1**
Simon, S. The heart   **612.1**

CARDIOVASCULAR SYSTEM
See also Anatomy; Physiology
Gold, J. C. Learning about the circulatory and lymphatic systems   **612.1**
Markle, S. Faulty hearts   **612.1**

The **cardturner.** Sachar, L.   **Fic**

The **care** & keeping of you 2.   **613**

CARE OF CHILDREN *See* Child care

CARE OF THE DYING *See* Terminal care

A **career** as a hairstylist. Heos, B.   **646.7**

CAREER CHANGES
See also Age and employment; Vocational guidance

CAREER COUNSELING *See* Vocational guidance

CAREER DEVELOPMENT *See* Personnel management; Vocational guidance

CAREER GUIDANCE *See* Vocational guidance

Career ideas for teens [series]
Reeves, D. L. Career ideas for teens in architecture and construction   **624**

Career ideas for teens in architecture and construction. Reeves, D. L.   **624**

CAREERS *See* Occupations; Professions; Vocational guidance

Careers in green energy. Flath, C.   **333.79**

Careers in the computer game industry. Gerardi, D.   **794.8**

Careers in the new economy [series]
Gerardi, D. Careers in the computer game industry   **794.8**

Careers in the U.S. Air Force. Dolan, E. F.   **358.4**
Careers in the U.S. Army. Dolan, E. F.   **355**
Careers in the U.S. Coast Guard. Dolan, E. F. **363.2**
Careers in the U.S. Marine Corps. Dolan, E. F. **359.9**
Careers in the U.S. Navy. Dolan, E. F.   **359**

CAREGIVERS
See also Volunteer work

The Caretaker trilogy [series]
Klass, D. Firestorm   **Fic**
Klass, D. Timelock   **Fic**
Klass, D. Whirlwind   **Fic**

Carey, Benedict
Poison most vial   **Fic**
The unknowns   **Fic**

Carey, Charles W.
The Mexican War   **973.6**
(ed) Castro's Cuba   **972.91**

Carey, Janet Lee
Dragonswood   **Fic**

Carey, Janet Lee
The beast of Noor   **Fic**
Dragon's Keep   **Fic**
Dragons of Noor   **Fic**
Stealing death   **Fic**

Carey, Mike
Re-Gifters   **741.5**

CARIBBEAN AMERICANS
Keedle, J. Americans from the Caribbean and Central America   **305.8**

CARIBBEAN COOKING
Mofford, J. H. Recipe and craft guide to the Caribbean   **641.5**

CARIBOU
Heuer, K. Being caribou   **599.65**

CARIBOU -- FICTION
Hobbs, W. Never say die   **Fic**

CARIBOU
Heuer, K. Being caribou   **599.65**

CARICATURES AND CARTOONS *See* Cartoons and caricatures

Caring for your mutt. Bolan, S.   **636.7**

Carl Linnaeus. Anderson, M. J.   **92**

Carle, Jill
Carle, M. Teens cook   **641.5**
Carle, M. Teens cook dessert   **641.8**

Carle, Judi
Carle, M. Teens cook   **641.5**
Carle, M. Teens cook dessert   **641.8**

Carle, Megan
Teens cook   **641.5**
Teens cook dessert   **641.8**

Carlisle, Rodney P.
Civil War and Reconstruction   **973.7**
Exploring space   **629.4**
World War I   **940.3**

Carlos Santana. Slavicek, L. C.   **92**

Carlowicz, Michael J.
The moon   **523.3**

Carlson, Laurie M.
Harry Houdini for kids   **92**
Thomas Edison for kids   **92**

Carlson, Lori M.
(ed) American eyes   **S C**
(ed) Cool salsa   **811**
(ed) Moccasin thunder   **S C**
(ed) Voices in first person   **S C**

Carlson, W. Bernard

CARTOONS AND COMICS

Becker, H. Funny business · 792

Caldwell, B. Fantasy! cartooning · 741.5

Giarrano, V. Comics crash course · 741.5

Greenberger, R. Will Eisner · 92

Hart, C. Mecha mania · 741.5

The Superhero book · 741.5

CARTOONS AND COMICS -- FICTION

Pierson, D. C. The boy who couldn't sleep and never had to · Fic

CARTOONS AND COMICS

Krensky, S. Comic book century · 741.5

CARTOONS, ANIMATED *See* Animated films

Carus, Marianne

(ed) 911: the book of help · 810

Carvalho, Solomon Nunes, 1815-1897

About

Hirschfelder, A. B. Photo odyssey: Solomon Carvalho's remarkable Western adventure, 1853-54 · 917

Carvell, Marlene

Sweetgrass basket · Fic

Who will tell my brother? · Fic

Carver, a life in poems. Nelson, M. · 811

Carver, George Washington, 1864?-1943

About

Abrams, D. George Washington Carver · 92

Harness, C. The groundbreaking, chance-taking life of George Washington Carver and science & invention in America · 92

MacLeod, E. George Washington Carver · 92

Nelson, M. Carver, a life in poems · 811

CARVING (MEAT, ETC.)

See also Dining; Entertaining; Meat

Cary, Kate

Bloodline · Fic

Bloodline: reckoning · Fic

Casanova, Mary

Frozen · Fic

The klipfish code · Fic

The **case** against my brother. Sternberg, L. · Fic

Case closed? Hughes, S. · 902

The **case** of the bizarre bouquets. Springer, N. · Fic

The **case** of the cryptic crinoline. Springer, N. · Fic

The **case** of the deadly desperados. Lawrence, C. · Fic

The **case** of the flesh-eating bacteria. Faulk, M. · 616.5

The **case** of the gypsy good-bye. Springer, N. · Fic

The **case** of the left-handed lady. Springer, N. · Fic

The **case** of the missing marquess. Springer, N. · Fic

The **case** of the monkeys that fell from the trees. Quinlan, S. E. · 577.3

The **case** of the peculiar pink fan. Springer, N. · Fic

The **case** of the vanishing golden frogs. Markle, S. · 597.8

The **case** that time forgot. Barrett, T. · Fic

Casey at the bat. Thayer, E. L. · 811

Cash, Johnny

About

Willett, E. Johnny Cash · 92

Cashay. McMullan, M. · Fic

Cashore, Kristin

Fire · Fic

Graceling · Fic

Casil, Amy Sterling

Pancreatic cancer · 616.99

Why banks fail · 332.1

Casper, Julie Kerr

Agriculture · 630

Animals · 590

Forests · 333.75

Lands · 333.73

Minerals · 549

Plants · 580

Water and atmosphere · 553.7

Cassady, Marsh

(ed) The Book of monologues for aspiring actors · 808.82

Cassell's French dictionary. Girard, D. · 443

Cassell's German-English, English-German dictionary. Betteridge, H. T. · 433

Cassell's Italian dictionary. · 453

Cassell's Latin dictionary. Simpson, D. P. · 473

Cassell's Spanish-English, English-Spanish dictionary. Gooch, A. · 463

CASSETTE BOOKS *See* Audiobooks

CASSETTE TAPES, AUDIO *See* Sound recordings

The **Cassini** code. Testa, D. · Fic

Castan, Mike

Fighting for Dontae · Fic

The price of loyalty · Fic

The **castaways.** Vollmar, R. · 741.5

CASTAWAYS *See* Survival after airplane accidents, shipwrecks, etc.

CASTAWAYS

Morpurgo, M. Kensuke's kingdom · Fic

Castaways of the Flying Dutchman. Jacques, B. · Fic

Castelao, Patricia

Applegate, K. The one and only Ivan · Fic

Castellucci, Cecil

Boy proof · Fic

First day on Earth · Fic

Janes in love · 741.5

The Plain Janes · 741.5

Rose sees red · Fic

(ed) Geektastic · S C

The **Castle** Corona. Creech, S. · Fic

Castle life. Durman, L. · 940.1

The **castle** of Llyr. Alexander, L. · Fic

Castle waiting. Medley, L. · 741.5

See also Christian sects; Christianity

CATHOLIC CHURCH -- CHARITIES

See also Charities

CATHOLIC CHURCH -- CLERGY

See also Clergy; Priests

CATHOLIC CHURCH -- FICTION

Durango, J. The walls of Cartagena   Fic

CATHOLIC COLLEGES AND UNIVERSITIES

See also Colleges and universities

CATHOLIC FAITH *See* Catholic Church

CATHOLIC LITERATURE

See also Christian literature; Literature

CATHOLIC SCHOOLS

Ayres, K. Macaroni boy   Fic

CATHOLICISM *See* Catholic Church

Catholicism & Orthodox Christianity. Brown, S. F.   **280**

CATHOLICS

Cooper, I. Jack   **973**

CATHOLICS -- FICTION

Fixmer, E. Saint training   Fic

Freitas, D. The possibilities of sainthood   Fic

Thomson, S. L. The secret of the Rose   Fic

Catlin, George, 1796-1872

About

Reich, S. Painting the wild frontier: the art and adventures of George Catlin   **92**

Worth, R. George Catlin   **92**

Catmull, Katherine

Summer and Bird   Fic

Cats. Stefoff, R.   **636.8**

CATS

See also Domestic animals; Mammals

CATS

Bidner, J. Is my cat a tiger?   **636.8**

Biniok, J. Mixed breed cats   **636.8**

Bonar, S. Small wildcats   **599.75**

Edney, A. T. B. ASPCA complete cat care manual   **636.8**

Myron, V. Dewey the library cat   **636.8**

Stefoff, R. Cats   **636.8**

Whitehead, S. How to speak cat   **636.8**

CATS -- FICTION

Pauley, K. Cat Girl's day off   Fic

Rossetti, R. The girl with borrowed wings   Fic

CATS -- GRAPHIC NOVELS

Brubaker, J. reMIND   **741.5**

Hunter, E. The lost warrior   **741.5**

Hunter, E. Warriors: Tiger & Sasha #1: into the woods   **741.5**

Pyle, K. C. Katman   **741.5**

CATS

Stefoff, R. Cats   **636.8**

CATS -- POETRY

Lear, E. The owl and the pussycat   **821**

CATS IN ART

Ames, L. J. Draw 50 cats   **743**

CATTLE

Montgomery, S. Temple Grandin   **636**

Steele, C. Cattle ranching in the American West   **636**

CATTLE

See also Domestic animals; Mammals

CATTLE -- FICTION

Applegate, K. Home of the brave   Fic

The beasts of Clawstone Castle   Fic

Houts, M. The Beef Princess of Practical County   Fic

CATTLE -- VACCINATION

See also Vaccination

Cattle ranching in the American West. Steele, C. **636**

Caught. Haddix, M. P.   Fic

Caught by the sea. Paulsen, G.   **818**

CAUSATION

See also Metaphysics; Philosophy

Cause: Reconstruction America, 1863-1877. Bolden, T.   **973.7**

The **causes** of school violence. Schier, H.   **371.7**

Causes of the Civil War. Mountjoy, S.   **973.7**

CAUTIONARY TALES AND VERSES *See* Didactic fiction; Didactic poetry; Fables; Parables

The **cavalry** during the Civil War. Uschan, M. V.   **973.7**

Cavanaugh, Nancy J.

This journal belongs to Ratchet   Fic

Cavanaugh, Terence W.

Bookmapping   **372.6**

Keane, N. J. The tech-savvy booktalker   **021.7**

CAVE DWELLERS

Miller, S. S. Secret lives of cave creatures   **591.7**

CAVE DWELLERS

See also Prehistoric peoples

CAVE ECOLOGY

Banting, E. Caves   **577.5**

CAVE ECOLOGY

See also Ecology

CAVE ECOLOGY

Banting, E. Caves   **577.5**

Cave paintings to Picasso. Sayre, H. M.   **709**

Cavell, Edith, 1865-1915

About

Batten, J. Silent in an evil time: the brave war of Edith Cavell   **92**

Caveney, Philip

Sebastian Darke: Prince of Fools   Fic

Caves. Banting, E.   **577.5**

CAVES

Banting, E. Caves   **577.5**

Hanson, J. K. Caves   **551.4**

Taylor, P. L. The secret of Priest's Grotto   **940.53**

Caves. Hanson, J. K.   **551.4**

CAVES -- FICTION

Muller, R. D. Squeeze   Fic

Cherry, Lynne

How we know what we know about our changing
climate **363.7**

Cherry-Garrard, Apsley, 1886-1959 -- Fiction

About

Farr, R. Emperors of the ice **Fic**

Cheryl Harness history [series]

Harness, C. The adventurous life of Myles
Standish **92**

Harness, C. The tragic tale of Narcissa Whitman
and a faithful history of the Oregon Trail **92**

The **Cheshire** Cheese cat. Deedy, C. A. **Fic**

Chesner, Jonathan

ADHD in HD **618.92**

Chess. King, D. **794.1**

CHESS

See also Board games

CHESS

Basman, M. Chess for kids **794.1**

King, D. Chess **794.1**

CHESS -- FICTION

Myers, W. D. The Cruisers: checkmate **Fic**

Neri, G. Chess rumble **Fic**

Wallace, R. Perpetual check **Fic**

CHESS FOR CHILDREN

Basman, M. Chess for kids **794.1**

Chess for kids. Basman, M. **794.1**

Chess rumble. Neri, G. **Fic**

Chesterman, Charles W.

The Audubon Society field guide to North American rocks and minerals **549**

Chetwynd, Josh

The secret history of balls **796.3**

Cheva, Cherry

DupliKate **Fic**

Chevat, Richard

Pollan, M. The omnivore's dilemma **338.1**

Chevat, Richie

Gore, A. Our choice **363.7**

Chew on this. Schlosser, E. **394.1**

CHEYENNE INDIANS

Ehrlich, A. Wounded Knee: an Indian history of the
American West **970.004**

Chiang, Yeng-Fong

Krasno, R. Cloud weavers **398.2**

Chiappe, Luis M.

Dingus, L. Dinosaur eggs discovered! **567.9**

Chibbaro, Julie

Deadly **Fic**

CHICAGO (ILL.) -- ANTIQUITIES

See also Antiquities

CHICAGO (ILL.) -- BIOGRAPHY

See also Biography

CHICAGO (ILL.) -- CLIMATE

See also Climate

CHICAGO (ILL.) -- ECONOMIC CONDITIONS

See also Economic conditions

CHICAGO (ILL.) -- FICTION

Goeglein, T. M. Cold fury **Fic**

CHICAGO (ILL.) -- MAPS

See also Maps

**CHICAGO (ILL.) -- POLITICS AND GOVERN-
MENT**

See also Municipal government; Politics

CHICAGO (ILL.) -- POPULATION

See also Population

CHICAGO (ILL.) -- RACE RELATIONS

See also Race relations

CHICAGO (ILL.) -- STATISTICS

See also Statistics

Chicago history for kids. Hurd, O. **977.3**

Chicagoland Detective Agency [series]

Robbins, T. The drained brains caper **741.5**

CHICANERY *See* Deception

CHICANOS *See* Mexican Americans

Chickadee. Erdrich, L. **Fic**

Chicken boy. Dowell, F. O. **Fic**

The **chicken** dance. Couvillon, J. **Fic**

Chicken pox. Hoffmann, G. **616.9**

CHICKEN POX *See* Chickenpox

Chicken soup for the teenage soul [I-IV] Canfield,
J. **158**

Chicken soup for the teenage soul's the real deal. **158**

CHICKENPOX

Hoffmann, G. Chicken pox **616.9**

CHICKENPOX

See also Diseases; Viruses

CHICKENS

Kindschi, T. 4-H guide to raising chickens **636.5**

CHICKENS -- FICTION

Couvillon, J. The chicken dance **Fic**

Dowell, F. O. Chicken boy **Fic**

Chico Mendes. Murphy, A. G. **92**

Chief Joseph. Hopping, L. J. **92**

CHIEF JUSTICES *See* Judges

Chief Sunrise, John McGraw, and me. Tocher, T. **Fic**

Chiggers. Larson, H. **741.5**

CHILD ABUSE

Gordon, S. M. Beyond bruises **362.7**

Medina, S. Abuse and neglect **362.7**

Stewart, S. When Daddy hit Mommy **362.82**

See also Child welfare; Domestic violence;
Parent-child relationship

CHILD ABUSE -- FICTION

Key, W. Fourmile **Fic**

Summers, C. This is not a test **Fic**

CHILD ACTORS

See also Actors

CHILD AND PARENT *See* Parent-child relationship

Child and youth security sourcebook. **362.7**

CHILD ARTISTS

Volavkova, H. --I never saw another butter-fly-- **741.9**

CHILD ARTISTS
   See also Artists; Gifted children
CHILD AUTHORS
   See also Authors; Gifted children
CHILD BEHAVIOR *See* Child psychology; Children -- Conduct of life; Etiquette for children and teenagers
CHILD BENEFACTORS
   Rhodes-Courter, A. M. Three little words **92**
CHILD BIRTH *See* Childbirth
CHILD CARE
   Bondy, H. Don't sit on the baby **649.1**
   McAlpine, M. Working with children **362.7**
CHILD CARE SERVICES
   See also Public welfare; Social work
CHILD CUSTODY
   See also Divorce mediation; Parent-child relationship
CHILD DEVELOPMENT
   McAlpine, M. Working with children **362.7**
CHILD DEVELOPMENT
   See also Children
Child labor. Gifford, C. **331.3**
CHILD LABOR
   See also Age and employment; Child welfare; Labor; Social problems
   Bartoletti, S. C. Growing up in coal country **331.3**
   Bartoletti, S. C. Kids on strike! **331.892**
   Chambers, C. Living as a child laborer **331.3**
   Farrell, C. Children's rights **305.23**
   Freedman, R. Kids at work **331.3**
   Gifford, C. Child labor **331.3**
CHILD LABOR -- FICTION
   D'Adamo, F. Iqbal **Fic**
   Kelly, L. Chained **Fic**
   Sheth, K. Boys without names **Fic**
   Winthrop, E. Counting on Grace **Fic**
CHILD LABOR -- HISTORY
   Bartoletti, S. C. Kids on strike! **331.892**
CHILD LABOR -- UNITED STATES
   Burgan, M. Breaker boys **331.3**
CHILD LABOR -- UNITED STATES -- HISTORY
   Bartoletti, S. C. Kids on strike! **331.892**
CHILD MOLESTING *See* Child sexual abuse
CHILD NEGLECT *See* Child abuse
Child of dandelions. Nanji, S. **Fic**
CHILD PLACING *See* Adoption; Foster home care
CHILD PORNOGRAPHY
   See also Pornography
CHILD PSYCHOLOGY
   See also Psychology
CHILD RAISING *See* Child rearing

CHILD REARING
   Simons, R. Grandparents raising kids **306.8**
CHILD REARING
   See also Child care; Child-adult relationship; Parent-child relationship
CHILD REFUGEES -- GREAT BRITAIN -- HISTORY
   Hodge, D. Rescuing the children **940.53**
CHILD SEX ABUSE *See* Child sexual abuse
CHILD SEXUAL ABUSE
   Farrell, C. Children's rights **305.23**
   Medina, S. Abuse and neglect **362.7**
   Mooney, C. Online predators **004.6**
   Strong at the heart **362.7**
CHILD SEXUAL ABUSE
   See also Child abuse; Incest; Sex crimes
CHILD SEXUAL ABUSE -- FICTION
   Chaltas, T. Because I am furniture **Fic**
   Donaldson, J. Running on the cracks **Fic**
   Doyle, B. Boy O'Boy **Fic**
   Mazer, N. F. The missing girl **Fic**
   Reynolds, M. Shut up! **Fic**
   Sanchez, A. Bait **Fic**
   Weeks, S. Jumping the scratch **Fic**
   Williams, C. L. Glimpse **Fic**
CHILD SEXUAL ABUSE
   Strong at the heart **362.7**
CHILD SEXUAL ABUSE -- PREVENTION
   Nelson, S. K. Stay safe! **613.6**
CHILD STUDY *See* Child development; Child psychology
CHILD SUPPORT
   See also Child welfare; Desertion and nonsupport; Divorce mediation
CHILD WELFARE
   Marsico, K. The Texas polygamist raid **364.1**
CHILD WELFARE
   See also Charities; Public welfare; Social work
A **child's** introduction to ballet. Lee, L. **792.8**
Child's World (Firm)
   Buckley, J. The Child's World encyclopedia of the NFL **796.332**
   The Child's World encyclopedia of baseball **796.357**
The **Child's** World encyclopedia of baseball. **796.357**
The **Child's** World encyclopedia of the NFL. Buckley, J. **796.332**
Child, Lydia Maria Francis, 1802-1880
About
   Abrams, D. Julia Child **92**
   Abrams, D. Julia Child, chef **641.509**
   Kenschaft, L. Lydia Maria Child **303.48**
CHILD-ADULT RELATIONSHIP
   See also Children
CHILD-ADULT RELATIONSHIP -- FICTION
   Matti, T. Mister Orange **Fic**

grade bites **Fic**

Brewer, H. The chronicles of Vladimir Tod: ninth grade slays **Fic**

Brewer, H. Eleventh grade burns **Fic**

Brewer, H. Tenth grade bleeds **Fic**

The **chronicles** of Vladimir Tod: eighth grade bites. Brewer, H. **Fic**

The **chronicles** of Vladimir Tod: ninth grade slays. Brewer, H. **Fic**

CHRONOLOGY
>*See also* Astronomy; History; Time

The Chrysalis Queen quartet [series]
McKenzie, N. Guinevere's gamble **Fic**
McKenzie, N. Guinevere's gift **Fic**

Chu Ju's house. Whelan, G. **Fic**

Chu, Miyoko
Birdscapes **598**

The **church.** Schomp, V. **274**

The **church.** Hinds, K. **274.2**

CHURCH -- GOVERNMENT POLICY *See* Church and state

CHURCH AND STATE
Mountjoy, S. Engel v. Vitale **344**

CHURCH AND STATE -- UNITED STATES
McIntosh, K. When religion & politics mix **201**

CHURCH ARCHITECTURE
>*See also* Architecture

CHURCH BUILDINGS
>*See also* Buildings

CHURCH DENOMINATIONS *See* Christian sects; Sects

CHURCH ENTERTAINMENTS
>*See also* Amusements; Church work

CHURCH FESTIVALS *See* Religious holidays

CHURCH HISTORY
Nardo, D. The birth of Christianity **270**

CHURCH HISTORY
>*See also* History

CHURCH HISTORY -- 600-1500, MIDDLE AGES
>*See also* Middle Ages

CHURCH LIBRARIES
>*See also* Libraries

CHURCH MUSIC
>*See also* Music

CHURCH OF ENGLAND
Hinds, K. The church **274.2**
Schomp, V. The church **274**

CHURCH OF JESUS CHRIST OF LATTER-DAY SAINTS
Bial, R. Nauvoo **289.3**
Book of Mormon The Book of Mormon **289.3**
Bushman, C. L. Mormons in America **289.3**

CHURCH SCHOOLS
>*See also* Private schools; Schools

CHURCH WORK WITH THE SICK

>*See also* Church work; Sick

CHURCH WORK WITH YOUTH
>*See also* Church work; Youth

CHURCH YEAR
>*See also* Calendars; Religious holidays; Worship

Church, Audrey P.
Leverage your library program to help raise test scores **027.8**

Church, Benjamin, 1639-1718
>About
Philbrick, N. The Mayflower and the Pilgrims' New World **973.2**

CHURCHES *See* Church buildings; Religious institutions

Churchill, Winston Sir, 1874-1965
>About
Bell, T. Nick of time **Fic**
Severance, J. B. Winston Churchill **941.084**
White, A. Window boy **Fic**

Churchill, Winston Sir, 1874-1965 -- Fiction
>About
White, A. Window boy **Fic**

Churchyard, Kathleen
Bye for now **Fic**

CHURCHYARDS *See* Cemeteries

Chwast, Seymour
The odyssey **741.5**

Chin Shih-huang, Emperor of China, 259-210 B.C.
>About
O'Connor, J. The emperor's silent army **931**

The **CIA** and other American spies. Goodman, M. E. **327.127**

Cianciotto, Jason
(jt. auth) Cahill, S. LGBT youth in America's schools **371.826**

Cibos, Lindsay
Hodges, J. Draw furries **743**

Cicada summer. Beaty, A. **Fic**

CIGARETTES
>*See also* Smoking; Tobacco

CIGARS
>*See also* Smoking; Tobacco

CINCO DE MAYO
Mattern, J. Celebrate Cinco de Mayo **394.26**

CINCO DE MAYO (HOLIDAY)
>*See also* Holidays

Cinder. Meyer, M. **Fic**

CINDERELLA (LEGENDARY CHARACTER)
Whipple, L. If the shoe fits **811**

CINEMA *See* Motion pictures

CINEMATOGRAPHY
Miller, R. Special effects **778.5**
>*See also* Photography

CIPHER AND TELEGRAPH CODES
>*See also* Ciphers; Telegraph

Smith, C. R.   The mighty 12 **398.209**
Steer, D.   The mythology handbook **292**
Tracy, K.   Cerberus **398.2**
Turnbull, A.   Greek myths **292**

CLASSICAL MYTHOLOGY
  See also Mythology

CLASSICAL MYTHOLOGY -- FICTION
Barrett, T.   Dark of the moon **Fic**
Barrett, T.   King of Ithaka **Fic**
Childs, T. L.   Oh. My. Gods. **Fic**
Childs, T. L.   Sweet venom **Fic**
Coville, B.   Juliet Dove, Queen of Love **Fic**
Friesner, E. M.   Nobody's princess **Fic**
Geras, A.   Ithaka **Fic**
Halam, A.   Snakehead **Fic**
Marsh, K.   The night tourist **Fic**
Marsh, K.   The twilight prisoner **Fic**
Napoli, D. J.   The great god Pan **Fic**
Riordan, R.   The battle of the Labyrinth **Fic**
Riordan, R.   The last Olympian **Fic**
Riordan, R.   The lightning thief **Fic**
Riordan, R.   The lost hero **Fic**
Riordan, R.   The Sea of Monsters **Fic**
Riordan, R.   The son of Neptune **Fic**
Riordan, R.   The Titan's curse **Fic**
Spinner, S.   Quicksilver **Fic**
Taylor, L.   Daughter of smoke and bone **Fic**
Usher, M. D.   The golden ass of Lucius Apuleius **Fic**

CLASSICAL MYTHOLOGY -- POETRY
Hovey, K.   Ancient voices **811**

CLASSICISM
  See also Aesthetics; Literature

CLASSICISM IN ARCHITECTURE
  See also Architecture; Classicism

CLASSICISTS
McClafferty, C. K.   In defiance of Hitler **92**

Classics illustrated [series]
Carroll, L.   Through the looking-glass **741.5**
Geary, R.   Great expectations **741.5**
Geary, R.   The invisible man **741.5**
Poe, E. A.   The raven and other poems **741.5**
Shelley, M. W.   Frankenstein **741.5**

CLASSIFICATION OF SCIENCES
Tyson, N. D. G.   The Pluto files **523.4**

CLASSROOM MANAGEMENT
  See also School discipline; Teaching

CLASSROOMS -- FICTION
Buyea, R.   Mr. Terupt falls again **Fic**

CLASSROOMS -- FICTION
Buyea, R.   Mr. Terupt falls again **Fic**
Claude Monet. Kallen, S. A. **92**
Claudette Colvin. Hoose, P. **92**
Clay. Almond, D. **Fic**

CLAY
  See also Ceramics; Soils

Clay v. United States and how Muhammad Ali fought the draft. Streissguth, T. **343**

Claybourne, Anna
Forms of energy **531**
Gut-wrenching gravity and other fatal forces **531**
The nature of matter **530.4**
The Renaissance **940.2**
Surrealism **709.04**
Who discovered natural selection? **576.8**
Who split the atom? **539**

Clayton, Elaine
Smiley, J.   The Georges and the Jewels **Fic**
Smiley, J.   A good horse **Fic**
Smiley, J.   True Blue **Fic**
Wayland, A. H.   Girl coming in for a landing **811**
Zimmer, T. V.   42 miles **Fic**

Clayton, Emma
The roar **Fic**
The Whisper **Fic**

Clean air. Bridges, A. **363.7**
Clean water. Geiger, B. **363.7**

CLEANING
  See also Sanitation

CLEANLINESS
  See also Hygiene; Sanitation

Cleare, John
Epic climbs **796.52**

Cleary, Beverly
Dear Mr. Henshaw **Fic**
A girl from Yamhill: a memoir **92**
Strider **Fic**

Cleary, Beverly
        About
Cleary, B.   A girl from Yamhill: a memoir **92**

Cleary, Brian P.
The laugh stand **817**

Cleavage. **S C**

Cleaver, Bill
Cleaver, V.   Where the lillies bloom **Fic**

Cleaver, Vera
Where the lillies bloom **Fic**

CLEMENCY
  See also Administration of criminal justice; Executive power

Clement-Moore, Rosemary
Texas gothic **Fic**

Clemente, Roberto, 1934-1972
        About
Freedman, L.   Roberto Clemente **92**
Gutman, D.   Roberto & me **Fic**
Marquez, H.   Roberto Clemente **92**

Clements, Andrew, 1949-
Clements, A.   Troublemaker **Fic**
Extra credit **Fic**
The school story **Fic**
Things hoped for **Fic**

Arnold, C. El Nino — **551.6**
Climate change. Oxlade, C. — **363.7**

CLIMATE CHANGE
Christie, P. 50 climate questions — **551.609**
Climate change. Hartman, E. — **551.6**
Climate change [series]
Baker, S. In temperate zones — **551.6**
Baker, S. In the Antarctic — **508**
Baker, S. In the Arctic — **971**
Baker, S. In the tropics — **508**

CLIMATE CHANGE
See also Climate
Climate change. Nardo, D. — **551.6**
Climate change research. George, C. — **551.6**
Climate crisis. Nardo, D. — **363.7**
Climate fever. Hanel, R. — **363.7**

CLIMATIC CHANGES -- FICTION
Hobbs, W. Never say die — Fic

CLIMATIC CHANGES -- HISTORY
Christie, P. The curse of Akkad — **551.6**

CLIMATIC CHANGES
Arnold, C. El Nino — **551.6**
Burgan, M. Not a drop to drink — **363.6**
Cherry, L. How we know what we know about our changing climate — **363.7**
Davies, N. Gaia warriors — **363.7**
Delano, M. F. Earth in the hot seat — **363.7**
Ride, S. K. Mission: planet Earth — **525**
Ride, S. K. Mission: save the planet — **333.72**
Townsend, J. Predicting the effects of climate change — **363.7**

CLIMATOLOGY *See* Climate
Cosgrove, B. Weather — **551.5**
Stille, D. R. The greenhouse effect — **363.7**

CLIMBING PLANTS
See also Gardening; Plants
Climbing the stairs. Venkatraman, P. — Fic
Cline, Eric H.
Digging for Troy — **939**
Cline-Ransome, Lesa
Words set me free — **973.8**
CLINICAL DRUG TRIALS *See* Drugs -- Testing
CLINICAL GENETICS *See* Medical genetics
CLINICAL IMAGING *See* Diagnostic imaging
CLINICAL TRIALS OF DRUGS *See* Drugs -- Testing
The **Clinton** view. Tracy, K. — **92**
Clinton, Catherine
(comp) I, too, sing America — **811**
(ed) A Poem of her own — **811**
Clinton, Cathryn
A stone in my hand — Fic
Clinton, Hillary Rodham, 1947-
About
Abrams, D. Hillary Rodham Clinton — **92**
Blashfield, J. F. Hillary Clinton — **92**

Tracy, K. The Clinton view — **92**
CLIPPER SHIPS
See also Ships
CLIQUES (SOCIOLOGY)
Romain, T. Cliques, phonies & other baloney — **158**
Cliques, crushes & true friends. Harris, A. R. — **158**
Cliques, phonies & other baloney. Romain, T. — **158**
Cloaked. Flinn, A. — Fic
Cloaked in red. Vande Velde, V. — S C
Clocks. Collier, J. L. — **681.1**
CLOCKS AND WATCHES
Collier, J. L. Clocks — **681.1**
Jenkins, M. The time book — **529**
Kagayame, J. Discovering the construct of time — **529**
Sullivan, N. Time — **529**
CLOCKS AND WATCHES
See also Time
CLOCKS AND WATCHES -- FICTION
Kirby, M. J. The clockwork three — Fic
Winterson, J. Tanglewreck — Fic
CLOCKS AND WATCHES -- HISTORY
Collier, J. L. Clocks — **681.1**
The clockwork dark [series]
Bemis, J. C. The nine pound hammer — Fic
Bemis, J. C. The White City — Fic
Bemis, J. C. The Wolf Tree — Fic
Clockwork prince. Clare, C. — Fic
Clockwork princess. Clare, C. — Fic
The **clockwork** three. Kirby, M. J. — Fic
CLOG DANCING
See also Dance
The **clone** codes. McKissack, P. C. — Fic
The **clones.** Skurzynski, G. — Fic
CLONES AND CLONING *See* Cloning
Cloning. — **176**
Cloning. — **176**
Cloning. Schafer, S. — **174.2**
Cloning. Aldridge, S. — **660.6**
CLONING
See also Genetic engineering
CLONING -- ETHICAL ASPECTS
See also Ethics
CLONING -- FICTION
Choyce, L. Deconstructing Dylan — Fic
Farmer, N. The house of the scorpion — Fic
Farmer, N. The lord of Opium — Fic
Haddix, M. P. Double identity — Fic
Horowitz, A. Point blank — Fic
McKissack, P. C. The clone codes — Fic
Patrick, C. The Originals — Fic
Singer, N. Gem X — Fic
Skurzynski, G. The clones — Fic
Close encounters of the wild kind [series]
Hamilton, S. L. Ambushed by a cougar — **599.75**
Hamilton, S. L. Attacked by a crocodile — **597.98**
Hamilton, S. L. Bitten by a rattlesnake — **597.96**

See also Aesthetics; Chemistry; Light; Optics; Painting; Photometry

COLOR -- FICTION

Moriarty, J. A corner of white   **Fic**

COLOR -- PSYCHOLOGICAL ASPECTS

See also Color sense; Psychology

The **Color** of absence.   **813**

The **color** of my words. Joseph, L.   **Fic**

COLOR PHOTOGRAPHY

See also Photography

COLOR SENSE

See also Psychophysiology; Senses and sensation; Vision

COLOR TELEVISION

See also Television

Colorado. Somervill, B. A.   **978.8**

COLORADO RIVER -- HOOVER DAM *See* Hoover Dam (Ariz. and Nev.)

COLORING BOOKS

See also Picture books for children

Colors of Madeleine trilogy [series]

Moriarty, J. A corner of white   **Fic**

COLOUR *See* Color

Colson, Mary

Forest furnace   **634.9**

Colston, Valerie

Teens go green!   **027.62**

Coltrane, John, 1926-1967

About

Golio, G. Spirit seeker   **788.7**

The **Columbia** space shuttle disaster. Cole, M. D.   **629.44**

The **Columbine** High School massacre. Marsico, K.   **364.152**

The **Columbine** School shooting. Mackay, J.   **364.152**

Columbus. Feinstein, S.   **92**

Columbus. Demi   **970.01**

COLUMBUS DAY

See also Holidays

Columbus, Chris

House of secrets   **Fic**

Columbus, Christopher

About

Berne, E. C. Christopher Columbus   **970.01**

Demi Columbus   **970.01**

Feinstein, S. Columbus   **92**

Fritz, J. Around the world in a hundred years   **910.92**

Mlawski, S. Hammer of witches   **Fic**

COLUMBUS, CHRISTOPHER, 1451-1506

Berne, E. C. Christopher Columbus   **970.01**

Demi Columbus   **970.01**

COLUMNISTS

Fleming, C. Our Eleanor   **92**

Freedman, R. Eleanor Roosevelt   **973.917**

Krull, K. Lives of extraordinary women   **920**

MacLeod, E. Eleanor Roosevelt   **92**

COLUMNISTS *See* Journalists

Colvin, Claudette

About

Freedman, R. Freedom walkers   **323.1**

Hoose, P. Claudette Colvin   **92**

COMA -- FICTION

Forman, G. If I stay   **Fic**

Jocelyn, M. Would you   **Fic**

Little, K. G. The healing spell   **Fic**

Mass, W. Heaven looks a lot like the mall   **Fic**

Comanche Chief Quanah Parker. Sanford, W. R.   **978.004**

COMANCHE INDIANS

Freedman, R. Indian chiefs   **970.004**

COMANCHE INDIANS -- HISTORY

Sanford, W. R. Comanche Chief Quanah Parker   **978.004**

COMANCHE INDIANS -- KINGS AND RULERS -- BIOGRAPHY

Sanford, W. R. Comanche Chief Quanah Parker   **978.004**

COMANCHE INDIANS -- WARS

Sanford, W. R. Comanche Chief Quanah Parker   **978.004**

Combat sports [series]

Mason, P. Boxing   **796.8**

Combating terrorism. Bedell, J. M.   **363.32**

Combres, Elisabeth

Broken memory   **Fic**

COMBUSTION

See also Chemistry

Come Fall. Bauer, A. C. E.   **Fic**

Come Juneteenth. Rinaldi, A.   **Fic**

The **comeback** season. Smith, J. E.   **Fic**

COMEDIANS

Fleischman, S. Sir Charlie   **92**

Friedman, L. S. Tina Fey   **92**

Paprocki, S. B. Ellen Degeneres   **92**

Tiger, C. Margaret Cho   **92**

COMEDIANS

See also Actors; Entertainers

COMEDIES

See also Drama; Wit and humor

COMEDY

See also Drama; Wit and humor

COMEDY FILMS

See also Comedies; Motion pictures

Comerford, Lynda B.

Rissa Bartholomew's declaration of independence   **Fic**

The **comet's** curse. Testa, D.   **Fic**

COMETS

Koppes, S. N. Killer rocks from outer space   **523.5**

Nardo, D. Asteroids and comets   **523.4**

Poynter, M. Doomsday rocks from space   **523.4**

COMMERCIAL GEOGRAPHY
> *See also* Commerce; Geography

COMMERCIAL PHOTOGRAPHY
> *See also* Photography

Commodore Perry in the land of the Shogun. Blumberg, R.   **952**

COMMONPLACES *See* Terms and phrases

COMMUNICABLE DISEASES
Ballard, C. AIDS and other epidemics   **614.5**
Brownlee, C. Cute, furry, and deadly   **614.4**
Duke, S. S. Infections, infestations, and disease   **616.9**
Epidemics: opposing viewpoints   **614.4**
Farrell, J. Invisible enemies   **614.4**
Goldsmith, C. Invisible invaders   **614.4**
Grady, D. Deadly invaders   **614.4**
Landau, E. Food poisoning and foodborne diseases   **615.9**
Miller, D. A. Pandemics   **614.4**
Tilden, T. E. L. Help! What's eating my flesh? **614.4**

COMMUNICABLE DISEASES
> *See also* Diseases; Public health

COMMUNICABLE DISEASES -- ENCYCLOPEDIAS
Allman, T. Infectious disease research   **616.9**

COMMUNICABLE DISEASES -- FICTION
Bickle, L. The hallowed ones   **Fic**

COMMUNICABLE DISEASES
Allman, T. Infectious disease research   **616.9**

COMMUNICABLE DISEASES -- PREVENTION
> *See also* Preventive medicine

COMMUNICABLE DISEASES -- TREATMENT
Blank, A. Invincible microbe   **616.9**

Communication. Solway, A.   **303.4**

COMMUNICATION
Marek, K. Organizational storytelling for librarians   **025.1**
Solway, A. Communication   **303.4**

COMMUNICATION -- FICTION
Trueman, T. Life happens next   **Fic**

COMMUNICATION AMONG ANIMALS *See* Animal communication

COMMUNICATION ARTS *See* Language arts

COMMUNICATION SATELLITES *See* Artificial satellites in telecommunication

COMMUNICATION SYSTEMS, WIRELESS
> *See* Wireless communication systems

Communications and broadcasting. Henderson, H.   **384**

COMMUNICATIONS RELAY SATELLITES
> *See* Artificial satellites in telecommunication

Communications satellites. Byers, A.   **384.5**

COMMUNISM
> *See also* Collectivism; Political science; Totalitarianism

COMMUNISM -- CHINA
Jiang Red scarf girl   **951.05**

COMMUNISM -- FICTION
Compestine, Y. C. Revolution is not a dinner party   **Fic**
Durbin, W. The darkest evening   **Fic**
Yelchin, E. Breaking Stalin's nose   **Fic**

COMMUNISM -- UNITED STATES
Fitzgerald, B. McCarthyism   **973.921**

COMMUNISM AND LITERATURE
> *See also* Communism; Literature

COMMUNISM AND RELIGION
> *See also* Communism; Religion

COMMUNIST COUNTRIES -- FICTION
Marsden, C. My Own Revolution   **Fic**

COMMUNIST LEADERS
Castro's Cuba   **972.91**
Heuston, K. B. Mao Zedong   **92**
Naden, C. J. Mao Zedong and the Chinese Revolution   **92**
Slavicek, L. C. Mao Zedong   **92**
Wyborny, S. Kim Jong Il   **921**

COMMUNITIES -- UNITED STATES -- HISTORY
DiPiazza, F. D. Friend me!   **302.3**

COMMUNITY AND LIBRARIES *See* Libraries and community

COMMUNITY AND SCHOOL
> *See also* Community life

COMMUNITY CENTERS
> *See also* Cities and towns -- Civic improvement; Community life; Community organization; Recreation; Social settlements

COMMUNITY DEVELOPMENT
> *See also* Domestic economic assistance; Social change; Urban renewal

COMMUNITY LIFE
O'Neal, C. Ways to help in your community **361.3**

COMMUNITY LIFE -- FICTION
Foley, L. K. Remarkable   **Fic**

COMMUNITY LIFE -- ILLINOIS -- FICTION
Clifton, L. Freaky Fast Frankie Joe   **Fic**

COMMUNITY LIFE -- NORTH CAROLINA -- FICTION
Turnage, S. Three times lucky   **Fic**

COMMUNITY LIFE -- UNITED STATES -- HISTORY
DiPiazza, F. D. Friend me!   **302.3**

COMMUNITY ORGANIZATION
> *See also* Community life; Social work

COMMUNITY RESOURCES -- INFORMATION SERVICES
Lukenbill, W. B. Community resources in the school library media center   **025.2**

Community resources in the school library media center. Lukenbill, W. B.   **025.2**

COMPOSERS -- UNITED STATES
Furstinger, N. Say it with music   92

COMPOSERS -- UNITED STATES -- BIOGRA-PHY
Roberts, R. Scott Joplin   780.92

COMPOSERS, AUSTRIAN
Bauer, H. Beethoven for kids   92

COMPOSITION (ART)
See also Art

COMPOSITION (MUSIC)
See also Music; Music -- Theory

COMPOSITION (RHETORIC) *See* Rhetoric

COMPOST
See also Fertilizers; Soils

The **Compound.** Bodeen, S. A.   Fic
Compromised. Ayarbe, H.   Fic

COMPULSIVE BEHAVIOR
See also Abnormal psychology; Human behavior

COMPULSIVE BEHAVIOR -- ENCYCLOPE-DIAS
Drugs, alcohol, and tobacco   362.29

COMPULSIVE BEHAVIOR -- FICTION
Omololu, C. J. Dirty little secrets   Fic

COMPULSIVE EXERCISING *See* Exercise addiction

COMPUTATION (MATHEMATICS) *See* Arithmetic

COMPUTER ANIMATION
Buckley, A. M. Pixar   338.7
Egan, J. How video game designers use math **794.8**

COMPUTER ANIMATION
See also Animation (Cinematography)

COMPUTER ART
See also Art; Computer graphics

COMPUTER ASSISTED INSTRUCTION *See* Computer-assisted instruction

COMPUTER BULLETIN BOARDS *See* Internet forums

COMPUTER CRIMES
Gray, L. Virtual crime!   363.2
Jacobs, T. A. Teen cyberbullying investigated **364.1**
Mooney, C. Online predators   004.6

COMPUTER CRIMES
See also Crime

COMPUTER CRIMES -- FICTION
Whyman, M. Goldstrike   Fic
Whyman, M. Icecore   Fic

COMPUTER CRIMES
Hynson, C. Cyber crime   364.16

COMPUTER CRIMES -- PREVENTION
Hunter, N. Internet safety   005.8
Hynson, C. Cyber crime   364.16

COMPUTER ENGINEERS -- UNITED STATES -- BIOGRAPHY
Blumenthal, K. Steve Jobs   621.39

COMPUTER FRAUD *See* Computer crimes
Computer game designer. Rauf, D.   **794.8**

COMPUTER GAMES
Egan, J. How video game designers use math **794.8**
Gerardi, D. Careers in the computer game industry   **794.8**
Jozefowicz, C. Video game developer   **794.8**
Oxlade, C. Gaming technology   **794.8**
Rauf, D. Computer game designer   **794.8**

COMPUTER GAMES
See also Computer software; Games

COMPUTER GAMES -- FICTION
Cheva, C. DupliKate   **Fic**
Pratchett, T. Only you can save mankind   **Fic**

COMPUTER HACKERS
See also Computer crimes; Criminals

COMPUTER HACKERS -- FICTION
Gagnon, M. Don't turn around   **Fic**

COMPUTER INDUSTRY
Goldsworthy, S. Steve Jobs   92
Hamen, S. E. Google   338.7
Isaacs, S. S. Bill and Melinda Gates   92
Lohr, S. Digital revolutionaries   004
Quinn, J. Steve Jobs   338.46

COMPUTER INDUSTRY -- UNITED STATES -- HISTORY
Blumenthal, K. Steve Jobs   621.39

COMPUTER INDUSTRY EXECUTIVES
Goldsworthy, S. Steve Jobs   92

COMPUTER KEYBOARDS *See* Keyboards (Electronics)

COMPUTER LITERACY
See also Computers and civilization; Literacy

COMPUTER LITERACY -- STUDY AND TEACHING
Braafladt, K. Technology and literacy   027.62

COMPUTER MUSIC
See also Music

COMPUTER NETWORK RESOURCES *See* Internet resources
Bodden, V. Using the Internet   025.042

COMPUTER NETWORKS
See also Data transmission systems; Telecommunication

COMPUTER PROGRAMMERS
Ehrenhaft, D. Marc Andreessen   338.7
Gold, S. D. Tinker v. Des Moines   342
Smith, C. Twitter   92

COMPUTER PROGRAMMERS -- UNITED STATES -- BIOGRAPHY
Henderson, H. Larry Page and Sergey Brin **005.109**

COMPUTER PROGRAMS -- FICTION
Lancaster, M. A. The future we left behind   Fic

COMPUTER SCIENCE
See also Science

COMPUTER SCIENCE -- DICTIONARIES

See also Encyclopedias and dictionaries

COMPUTER SCIENTISTS
Goldsworthy, S. Steve Jobs **92**
Hamen, S. E. Google **338.7**
Sapet, K. Google founders: Larry Page and Sergey Brin **92**
Thimmesh, C. Girls think of everything **920**

COMPUTER SECURITY
Sandler, C. Living with the Internet and online dangers **004.6**

COMPUTER SOFTWARE EXECUTIVES
Aronson, M. Bill Gates **92**
Ehrenhaft, D. Larry Ellison **338.7**
Ehrenhaft, D. Marc Andreessen **338.7**
Isaacs, S. S. Bill and Melinda Gates **92**
Lesinski, J. M. Bill Gates **92**
Smith, C. Twitter **92**

COMPUTER SOFTWARE INDUSTRY
Aronson, M. Bill Gates **92**
Ehrenhaft, D. Larry Ellison **338.7**
Flath, C. Tomorrow's enterprising scientists **004**
Lesinski, J. M. Bill Gates **92**

COMPUTER SOFTWARE INDUSTRY -- UNITED STATES
Ehrenhaft, D. Larry Ellison **338.7**

COMPUTER SOUND PROCESSING
See also Computers; Sound

COMPUTER VIRUSES
See also Computer crimes; Computer software

COMPUTER-ASSISTED INSTRUCTION
Braun, L. W. Teens, technology, and literacy; or, Why bad grammar isn't always bad **373.1**
Johnson, S. Digital tools for teaching **371.3**
November, A. C. Empowering students with technology **371.3**
Smith, S. S. Web-based instruction **025.5**
Teehan, K. Wikis **371.3**

COMPUTER-BASED MULTIMEDIA INFORMATION SYSTEMS *See* Multimedia

COMPUTER-GENERATED ANIMATION *See* Computer animation

COMPUTERS
Gifford, C. Cool tech **537.5**

COMPUTERS
See also Electronic apparatus and appliances

COMPUTERS -- ACCESS CONTROL *See* Computer security

COMPUTERS -- CARTOONS AND CARICATURES
See also Cartoons and caricatures

COMPUTERS -- EDUCATIONAL USE *See* Computer-assisted instruction

COMPUTERS -- FICTION
Asher, J. The future of us **Fic**
Barnes, J. L. The Squad: perfect cover **Fic**
Barnes, J. The Squad: killer spirit **Fic**
Davies, S. Hacking Timbuktu **Fic**
Diamand, E. Flood and fire **Fic**
Doctorow, C. Little brother **Fic**
Fisher, C. Sapphique **Fic**
Haddix, M. P. The always war **Fic**
Lancaster, M. A. Human.4 **Fic**
Petrucha, S. Split **Fic**

COMPUTERS -- HISTORY
Collier, B. Charles Babbage and the engines of perfection **510**
Henderson, H. Alan Turing **92**
Lohr, S. Digital revolutionaries **004**
Snedden, R. Who invented the computer? **004**

COMPUTERS
Gifford, C. Cool tech **537.5**

COMPUTERS -- SECURITY MEASURES *See* Computer security

COMPUTERS AND CHILDREN
See also Children; Computers

COMPUTERS AND CIVILIZATION
See also Civilization; Computers; Technology and civilization

COMPUTERS AND THE HANDICAPPED
See also Computers; Handicapped

CON ARTISTS *See* Swindlers and swindling

CON GAME *See* Swindlers and swindling

Conant, Roger
A field guide to reptiles & amphibians **597.9**

CONCEALMENT *See* Secrecy

CONCENTRATION CAMPS
Byers, A. Youth destroyed--the Nazi camps **940.53**

CONCEPT LEARNING
See also Concepts; Psychology of learning

CONCEPTION -- PREVENTION *See* Birth control

CONCERTS
See also Amusements; Music

The **conch** bearer. Divakaruni, C. B. **Fic**

CONCHOLOGY
Arthur, A. Shell **594**

The **concise** encyclopedia of World War II. Nolan, C. J. **940.53**

Concise guide to information literacy. Lanning, S. **020**

The **concise** Oxford dictionary of music. Bourne, J. **780**

CONCRETE CONSTRUCTION
See also Building

Concrete poetry. Bodden, V. **809.1**

CONCRETE POETRY, AMERICAN
A Poke in the I **811**

CONDENSERS (STEAM)
See also Steam engines

Condie, Allyson Braithwaite.
Crossed **Fic**

P.   028.5

Connecting young adults and libraries. Gorman,
M.   027.62

Connelly, Neil O.
The miracle stealer   Fic

Connikie, Yvonne
Fashions of a decade, The 1960s   391

Connolly, Sean
The Americas and the Pacific   970.004
Banks and banking   332.1
The book of potentially catastrophic science 507.8
New Testament miracles   226
The stock market   332.6

Connor, Leslie
Crunch   Fic
Dead on town line   Fic
Waiting for normal   Fic

Connor, Theophilus Eugene, 1897-1973
                        About
Brimner, L. D. Black & white   323.1

Conquering Everest. Helfand, L.   741.5

The **conquests** of Alexander the Great. Behnke,
A.   92

Conquistadors. Gunderson, J.   970.01

Conrad, Pam
My Daniel   Fic

CONSCIENCE
    See also Christian ethics; Duty; Ethics

CONSCIOUSNESS
    See also Apperception; Mind and body; Per-
    ception; Psychology

CONSCIOUSNESS EXPANDING DRUGS See
    Hallucinogens

Conservation. Green, J.   333.72

CONSERVATION BIOLOGY -- RESEARCH
Carson, M. K. The bat scientists   599.4

Conservation heroes [series]
Baptiste, T. Al Gore   92
Breguet, A. Steve and Bindi Irwin   92
Fitzpatrick, B. Theodore Roosevelt   92
Goldstein, N. John Muir   92
Knowles, J. Jacques Cousteau   92
Murphy, A. G. Chico Mendes   92
Sherman, P. John James Audubon   92
Welty, T. Jane Goodall   92
West, K. Ansel Adams   92

CONSERVATION MOVEMENT See Environ-
    mental movement

CONSERVATION OF ENERGY See Energy con-
    servation; Force and energy

CONSERVATION OF FORESTS See Forest con-
    servation

CONSERVATION OF NATURAL RESOURCES
Ravilious, K. Power   179

CONSERVATION OF NATURAL RESOURCES
    See also Environmental protection; Natural

resources

**CONSERVATION OF NATURAL RESOURCES
    -- BIBLIOGRAPHY**
Wesson, L. P. Green reads   016

**CONSERVATION OF NATURAL RESOURCES
    -- FICTION**
Lloyd, S. The carbon diaries 2015   Fic
Lloyd, S. The carbon diaries 2017   Fic

CONSERVATION OF NATURAL RESOURCES
Green, J. Conservation   333.72

CONSERVATION OF NATURE See Nature conservation

CONSERVATION OF POWER RESOURCES
See Energy conservation

CONSERVATION OF THE SOIL See Soil conservation

CONSERVATION OF WATER See Water conservation

CONSERVATION OF WILDLIFE See Wildlife
conservation

CONSERVATIONISTS
Baptiste, T. Al Gore   92
Breguet, A. Steve and Bindi Irwin   92
Byrnes, P. Environmental pioneers   363.7
Corwin, J. Jeff Corwin: a wild life   92
Ebersole, R. Gorilla mountain   92
Frydenborg, K. The wild horse scientists   599.66
Goldstein, N. John Muir   92
Heuer, K. Being caribou   599.65
Macgillivray, A. Understanding Rachel Carson's
    Silent Spring   363.7
Montgomery, S. Saving the ghost of the moun-
    tain   599.75
Murphy, A. G. Chico Mendes   92
Piddock, C. Rachel Carson   92
Scherer, G. Who on earth is Rachel Carson?   92
Sergis, D. K. Bush v. Gore   342
Vogel, C. G. The man who flies with birds   598

CONSERVATISM -- UNITED STATES
Novak, A. Glenn Beck   320.52

**CONSERVATIVES -- UNITED STATES -- BIOG-
    RAPHY**
Novak, A. Glenn Beck   320.52

**CONSERVATIVES -- UNITED STATES -- BIOG-
    RAPHY**
Novak, A. Glenn Beck   320.52

Conserving the environment.   333.7

CONSOLATION
    See also Emotions; Human behavior

CONSORTIA, LIBRARY See Library cooperation

CONSPIRACIES
    See also Crime; Political crimes and offenses

CONSPIRACIES -- FICTION
Gagnon, M. Don't turn around   Fic

A **conspiracy** of kings. Turner, M. W.   Fic

Constable, Kate

Crain, Cynthia D.
Adam Smith   92
John Maynard Keynes   92
Milton Friedman   92
Cramer, Marcus
Pateman, R. Bolivia   984
Crandall, Prudence, 1803-1890
About
Alexander, E. Miss Crandall's School for Young Ladies and Little Misses of Color   811
Jurmain, S. The forbidden schoolhouse   92
Crane, Beverley E.
Using WEB 2.0 tools in the K-12 classroom   371.3
Crane, Dede
Poster boy   Fic
Crane, E. M.
Skin deep   Fic
Crane, Stephen, 1871-1900
About
Lukes, B. L. Soldier's courage: the story of Stephen Crane   813
Vansant, W. The red badge of courage   741.5
CRANKS *See* Eccentrics and eccentricities
Crap kingdom. Pierson, D. C.   Fic
Crash. Spinelli, J.   Fic
Crash course [series]
Miller, D. P. Crash course in teen services   027.62
Crash course in teen services. Miller, D. P.   027.62
CRASHES (FINANCE) *See* Financial crises
Crater. Hickam, H. H.   Fic
Crawford, Andy
Adams, S. World War I   940.3
Adams, S. World War II   940.53
Hornby, H. Soccer   796.334
Crawford, Brent
Carter finally gets it   Fic
Carter's big break   Fic
Carter's unfocused, one-track mind   Fic
CRAYON DRAWING
See also Drawing
Crayton, Lisa A.
A student's guide to Toni Morrison   813
Crazy. Nolan, H.   Fic
Crazy beautiful. Baratz-Logsted, L.   Fic
Crazy Horse, ca. 1842-1877
About
Sanford, W. R. Oglala Sioux Chief Crazy Horse   978.004
Crazy Horse, Sioux Chief, ca. 1842-1877
About
Freedman, R. The life and death of Crazy Horse   978
Crazy loco. Rice, D.   S C
The **crazy** things girls do for love. Sheldon, D.   Fic
Create your own candles. Check, L.   745.5
Create, relate & pop @ the library. Helmrich, E.
Creating multimedia presentations. Orr, T.   005

Creating the character. Bodden, V.   808.3
CREATION
Hamilton, V. In the beginning; creation stories from around the world   201
CREATION (LITERARY, ARTISTIC, ETC.)
See also Genius; Imagination; Intellect; Inventions
Golio, G. Spirit seeker   788.7
CREATION -- FICTION
Mass, W. Pi in the sky   Fic
CREATIVE ABILITY
Raczka, B. Before they were famous   704
CREATIVE ACTIVITIES
Carson, M. K. Beyond the solar system   520.9
Kuskowski, A. Cool relaxing   613.7
See also Amusements; Elementary education; Kindergarten
Creative minds biography [series]
Cook, J. Natural writer: a story about Marjorie Kinnan Rawlings   813
CREATIVE THINKING
See also Creative ability
CREATIVE WRITING
Bodden, V. Creating the character   808.3
Bodden, V. Painting the picture   808.3
Bodden, V. Setting the style   808.3
Bodden, V. Telling the tale   808.3
Ellis, S. From reader to writer   028
Farrell, T. Write your own fantasy story   808.3
Farrell, T. Write your own mystery story   808.3
Farrell, T. Write your own science fiction story   808.3
Fletcher, R. How writers work   808
Fletcher, R. Poetry matters   808.1
Hanley, V. Seize the story   808.3
Hardesty, C. The teen-centered writing club   027.62
Levine, G. C. Writing magic   808.3
Mazer, A. Spilling ink   808.3
Mlynowski, S. See Jane write   808.3
Otfinoski, S. Extraordinary short story writing   808.3
Rosinsky, N. M. Write your own fairy tale   808.3
Rosinsky, N. M. Write your own myth   808.3
Rosinsky, N. M. Write your own tall tale   808.3
Saccardi, M. Books that teach kids to write   028.5
See also Authorship; Creation (Literary, artistic, etc.); Language arts
CREATIVITY *See* Creative ability
Creature scene investigation [series]
Emmer, R. Kraken   001.9
Creatures of the deep. Woodward, J.   591.7
CREDIT
Tomljanovic, T. Borrowing   332.7
CREDIT
See also Finance; Money
CREDIT CARD FRAUD

Crowley, Cath
A little wanting song — Fic
Crowley, James
Starfish — Fic
Crowley, Suzanne
The stolen one — Fic
Crown of earth. Bell, H. — Fic
The **crown** of embers. Carson, R. — Fic
Crows & cards. Helgerson, J. — Fic
CROWS -- FICTION
Bauer, A. C. E. Come Fall — Fic
CROWS -- GRAPHIC NOVELS
McAdoo, D. Red moon — 741.5
Crowther, Robert
Robert Crowther's pop-up house of inventions 609
Croy, Anita
(ed) Ancient Aztec and Maya — 972
(ed) Ancient Egypt — 932
(ed) Ancient Greece — 938
(ed) Ancient Rome — 937
Ancient Pueblo — 978
Colombia — 986.1
Exploring the past — 930.1
Guatemala — 972.81
Spain — 946
Croy, Elden
United States — 973
CRUDE OIL *See* Petroleum
CRUELTY
See also Ethics
CRUELTY TO ANIMALS *See* Animal welfare
CRUELTY TO CHILDREN *See* Child abuse
Cruise control. Trueman, T. — Fic
The **Cruisers.** Myers, W. D. — Fic
Cruisers [series]
Myers, W. D. A star is born — Fic
The **Cruisers:** checkmate. Myers, W. D. — Fic
CRUISES *See* Ocean travel
Crumbley, Paul
Student's Encyclopedia of Great American Writers — 810.9
Crump, Marty
The mystery of Darwin's frog — 597.8
Crunch. Connor, L. — Fic
Crusade. Holder, N. — Fic
CRUSADES
Crompton, S. The Third Crusade — 956
Lace, W. W. The unholy crusade — 956.1
CRUSADES -- FICTION
Cadnum, M. The book of the Lion — Fic
Grant, K. M. Blood red horse — Fic
Spradlin, M. P. Keeper of the Grail — Fic
CRUSADES
Currie, S. The Medieval crusades — 909.07
CRUSADES -- THIRD, 1189-1192
Cadnum, M. The book of the Lion — Fic

Crush. Paulsen, G. — Fic
Crush: love poems. — 808.81
CRUSHES
See also Friendship; Love
CRUSHES -- FICTION
Paulsen, G. Crush — Fic
Crust and spray. Larsen, C. S. — 612.8
CRUSTACEA
Gilpin, D. Lobsters, crabs & other crustaceans 595
Crutcher, Chris
Athletic shorts — S C
Deadline — Fic
Ironman — Fic
King of the mild frontier: an ill-advised autobiography — 92
Running loose — Fic
Staying fat for Sarah Byrnes — Fic
Stotan! — Fic
Whale talk — Fic
Crutcher, Chris, 1946-
About
Crutcher, C. King of the mild frontier: an ill-advised autobiography — 92
Sommers, M. A. Chris Crutcher — 92
Cruz, Barbara
Triumphs and struggles for Latino civil rights 323.1
Cruz, Celia, 1929-2003
About
Cartlidge, C. Celia Cruz — 92
Cruzan v. Missouri. Donnelly, K. J. — 344
Cruzan v. Missouri. Perl, L. — 344
Cruzan v. Missouri and the right to die debate.
Fridell, R. — 344
Cruzan, Joe, d. 1996
About
Donnelly, K. J. Cruzan v. Missouri — 344
Fridell, R. Cruzan v. Missouri and the right to die debate — 344
Perl, L. Cruzan v. Missouri — 344
Cruzan, Nancy
About
Donnelly, K. J. Cruzan v. Missouri — 344
Fridell, R. Cruzan v. Missouri and the right to die debate — 344
Perl, L. Cruzan v. Missouri — 344
Cry, the beloved country. Paton, A. — Fic
Cryer's Cross. McMann, L. — Fic
Cryobiology. Winner, C. — 571.4
CRYOBIOLOGY
Winner, C. Cryobiology — 571.4
See also Biology; Cold; Low temperatures
CRYONICS
See also Burial
CRYOSURGERY
See also Cold -- Therapeutic use; Surgery
Cryptic Canada. — 971.1

(ed) The Supreme Court justices   347.73

Cushman, Karen
- Alchemy and Meggy Swann   Fic
- The ballad of Lucy Whipple   Fic
- Catherine, called Birdy   Fic
- The loud silence of Francine Green   Fic
- The midwife's apprentice   Fic
- Rodzina   Fic
- Will Sparrow's road   Fic

Custer's last stand.   973.8

Custer, George Armstrong, 1839-1876
About
- Custer's last stand   973.8

Cut. McCormick, P.   Fic

Cut from the same cloth. San Souci, R.   398.2

Cute dolls. Aranzi Aronzo Inc.   745.592

Cute, furry, and deadly. Brownlee, C.   614.4

Cutting-edge medicine. Goldsmith, C.   610

Cutting-edge science [series]
- Aldridge, S. AIDS   616.97
- Aldridge, S. Cloning   660.6
- Green, C. Drug resistance   616.9
- Green, C. Stem cells   616.02
- Hodge, S. Global warming   363.7
- Mileham, R. Global pollution   363.7
- Rooney, A. Volcanoes   551.2

CYANIDES -- ENVIRONMENTAL ASPECTS -- DANUBE RIVER WATERSHED
- Bryan, N. Danube   363.7

Cybele's secret. Marillier, J.   Fic

Cyber crime. Hynson, C.   364.16

CYBERBULLYING
- Mooney, C. Online predators   004.6
- Myers, J. J. Responding to cyber bullying   371.5
  - *See also* Bullies; Computer crimes

CYBERBULLYING -- PREVENTION
- Bully   371.58

CYBERNETICS
- *See also* Communication; Electronics; System theory

Cybersafety [series]
- Gentry, S. E. Living with the Internet   303.48

CYBERSPACE
- *See also* Computer networks; Space and time

Cyborg. McKissack, P. C.   Fic

CYBORGS -- FICTION
- Meyer, M. Scarlet   Fic

CYCLING
- Cyclist bikelist   796.6
- Haduch, B. Go fly a bike!   629.227
- Macy, S. Wheels of change   796.6
- Mulder, M. Pedal it!   388

CYCLING
- *See also* Exercise; Outdoor recreation; Sports

CYCLING -- FICTION
- Bradbury, J. Shift   Fic

CYCLING FOR WOMEN
- Macy, S. Wheels of change   796.6

Cyclist bikelist.   796.6

CYCLISTS
- Brill, M. T. Marshall Major Taylor   92

CYCLONES
- Longshore, D. Encyclopedia of hurricanes, typhoons, and cyclones   551.55
  - *See also* Meteorology; Storms; Winds

CYCLONES -- ENCYCLOPEDIAS
- Longshore, D. Encyclopedia of hurricanes, typhoons, and cyclones   551.55

CYCLOPEDIAS *See* Encyclopedias and dictionaries

CYCLOTRONS
- *See also* Atoms; Nuclear physics; Transmutation (Chemistry)

The **Cydonian** pyramid. Hautman, P.   Fic

Cypess, Leah
- Mistwood   Fic
- Nightspell   Fic

Cyprus. Spilling, M.   956.93

Cystic fibrosis. Giddings, S.   616.2

CYSTIC FIBROSIS
- Bjorklund, R. Cystic fibrosis   616.3
- Giddings, S. Cystic fibrosis   616.2
- Powell, J. Explaining cystic fibrosis   616.3

Cystic fibrosis. Bjorklund, R.   616.3

CYSTIC FIBROSIS -- FICTION
- Monninger, J. Wish   Fic

CYTOLOGY *See* Cells
- Stewart, M. Cell biology   571.6

CZECH AMERICANS -- FICTION
- Mobley, J. Katerina's wish   Fic
- Myers, W. D. Game   Fic

Czech Republic. Sioras, E.   943.7

Czech Republic. Docalavich, H.   943.710

CZECH REPUBLIC
- Docalavich, H. Czech Republic   943.710

CZECHOSLOVAKIA -- FICTION
- Marsden, C. My Own Revolution   Fic

D

D DAY *See* Normandy (France), Attack on, 1944

D is for Dahl. Cooling, W.   823

D'Adamo, Anthony
- Ames, L. J. Draw 50 birds   743

D'Adamo, Francesco
- Iqbal   Fic

D'Agnese, Joseph
- Signing their rights away   920
- Kiernan, D. Signing our lives away   920

D'Aluisio, Faith
- Menzel, P. What the world eats   641.3

D'Amico, Joan
- The coming to America cookbook   641.5

Exploring the world of aquatic life   591.7

Dawn. Hunter, E.   Fic

Dawn and dusk. Mead, A.   Fic

Dawson, Ian
   Renaissance medicine   610

Dawson, Willow
   Lila & Ecco's do-it-yourself comics club   741.5

DAY
     See also Chronology; Time

A **day** at the New Amsterdam Theatre. Amendola, D.   792.6

DAY CARE CENTERS
     See also Child care; Child welfare; Children -- Institutional care

DAY DREAMS *See* Fantasy

A **day** no pigs would die. Peck, R. N.   Fic

DAY OF ATONEMENT *See* Yom Kippur

Day of deliverance. O'Brien, J.   Fic

Day of tears. Lester, J.   Fic

Day of the assassins. O'Brien, J.   Fic

DAY OF THE DEAD
     See also Holidays

The **day** of the pelican. Paterson, K.   Fic

Day of the predator. Scarrow, A.   Fic

Day of the scarab. Fisher, C.   Fic

The **day** the Rabbi disappeared: Jewish holiday tales of magic. Schwartz, H.   398.2

The **day** the world exploded. Winchester, S.   551.2

A **day** without immigrants. Ouellette, J.   331.6

Day, Alyson
   (ed) Creech, S. The great unexpected   Fic

Day, Karen
   A million miles from Boston   Fic
   No cream puffs   Fic

Day, Trevor
   DK guide to savage Earth   550
   Genetics   576.5
   Oceans   551.46

The **daykeeper's** grimoire. Raedeke, C.   Fic

DAYS
     See also Calendars

Days of blood & starlight. Taylor, L.   Fic

Days of change [series]
   Bodden, V. The Cold War   909.82
   Bodden, V. Man walks on the Moon   629.45
   Riggs, K. The French Revolution   944.04

Days of Little Texas. Nelson, R. A.   Fic

Days that changed the world [series]
   Beecroft, S. The release of Nelson Mandela   968.06

The **Daytona** 500. Pimm, N. R.   796.72

De Capua, Sarah
   The Tuskegee airmen   940.54

De Goldi, Kate
   The 10 p.m. question   Fic

De La Beckwith, Byron -- Trials, litigation, etc.
     About

Coleman, W. Racism on trial   345

De la Bedoyere, Camilla
   Balancing work and play   155.9
   The discovery of DNA   572.8
   Personal hygiene and sexual health   613

De la Pena, Matt
   de la Peña, M. Mexican whiteboy   Fic
   Mexican whiteboy   Fic
   We were here   Fic

De la Renta, Oscar
     About
   Darraj, S. M. Oscar de la Renta   92

De Lambilly, Elisabeth
   Gandhi   92

De Leal, Amy
   Howard, H. Living as a refugee in America 305.23

De Lint, Charles
   The blue girl   Fic

De Liz, Renae
   Beagle, P. S. The last unicorn   741.5

De Paola, Tomie
   Christmas remembered   92

De Paola, Tomie, 1934-
     About
   De Paola, T. Christmas remembered   92

De Quidt, Jeremy
   The toymaker   Fic

De Seve, Peter
   Helgerson, J. Crows & cards   Fic

DEAD
     See also Burial; Cremation; Death; Funeral rites and ceremonies; Obituaries

The **dead** & the gone. Pfeffer, S. B.   Fic

DEAD -- FICTION
   Barnholdt, L. Girl meets ghost   Fic
   Burtenshaw, J. Shadowcry   Fic
   Cox, S. The Dead Girls Detective Agency   Fic
   Cypess, L. Nightspell   Fic
   Dennard, S. Something strange and deadly   Fic
   Derting, K. The body finder   Fic
   Derting, K. The last echo   Fic
   Huntley, A. The everafter   Fic
   The key of Braha   Fic
   Noel, A. Radiance   Fic
   Noel, A. Shimmer   Fic
   Oppel, K. Such wicked intent   Fic
   Peck, R. Three-quarters dead   Fic
   Plum, A. Die for me   Fic
   Ruiz Zafon, C. The Prince of Mist   Fic
   Russell, R. Dead rules   Fic
   Shusterman, N. Everfound   Fic
   Shusterman, N. Everwild   Fic
   Stewart, P. Legion of the Dead   Fic
   Stringer, H. Spellbinder   Fic

DEAD -- FICTION
   The key of Braha   Fic

About

Paprocki, S. B. Ellen Degeneres   92

Deisler, Veronica

(jt. auth) Ambrose, M. Investigating eating disorders (anorexia, bulimia, and binge eating) **616.85**

DEISM

See also Religion; Theology

DEITIES *See* Gods and goddesses

DEJECTION *See* Depression (Psychology)

DeKeyser, Stacy

The Brixen Witch   Fic

Del Negro, Janice

Passion and poison   S C

Delacre, Lulu

Golden tales   398.209

Salsa stories   S C

DeLallo, Laura

Hammered by a heat wave!   551.5

Delaney, Joseph

Attack of the Fiend   Fic

Clash of the demons   Fic

Curse of the bane   Fic

Night of the soul-stealer   Fic

Rage of the fallen   Fic

Revenge of the witch   Fic

The Spook's Bestiary   Fic

The Spook's tale and other horrors   S C

Wrath of the Bloodeye   Fic

Rise of the huntress   Fic

Delannoy, Isabelle

Our living Earth   779

Delano, Marfe Ferguson

Earth in the hot seat   363.7

Genius   92

Helen's eyes   92

Delano, Poli

When I was a boy Neruda called me Policarpo   92

Délano, Poli, 1936-

About

Delano, P. When I was a boy Neruda called me Policarpo   92

Delaware. Schuman, M.   975.1

The **Delaware.** Bial, R.   974

DELAWARE INDIANS

Bial, R. The Delaware   974

DELAWARE INDIANS -- FICTION

Richter, C. The light in the forest   Fic

Delaware, 1638-1776. Price, K.   975.1

Delbanco, Andrew

(ed) Poe, E. A. Edgar Allan Poe   S C

DELINQUENCY, JUVENILE *See* Juvenile delinquency

DELINQUENTS *See* Criminals

DELIVERY OF GOODS -- FICTION

Clifton, L. Freaky Fast Frankie Joe   Fic

DELIVERY OF HEALTH CARE *See* Medical care

DELIVERY OF MEDICAL CARE *See* Medical care

Dell, Pamela

Hatshepsut   92

Man on the moon   629.45

Mississippi   976.2

Protecting the planet   333.72

Delsol, Wendy

Flock   Fic

Frost   Fic

Stork   Fic

DeMallie, H. R.

Behind enemy lines   940.54

DeMallie, H. R.

About

DeMallie, H. R. Behind enemy lines   940.54

DeMatteis, J. M.

Imaginalis   Fic

Dembicki, Matt

(ed) Trickster: Native American tales   398.2

Demi, 1942-

Alexander the Great   92

Buddha   294.3

Columbus   970.01

The Dalai Lama   294.3

Genghis Khan   92

The legend of Lao Tzu and the Tao te ching   299.5

Marco Polo   92

Muhammad   297

Rumi   92

Tutankhamun   92

Demilly, Christian

Pop art   709.04

Democracy. Lansford, T.   321.8

DEMOCRACY

See also Constitutional history; Constitutional law; Political science

Democracy. Laxer, J.   321.8

DEMOCRACY

Lansford, T. Democracy   321.8

Laxer, J. Democracy   321.8

DEMOCRACY -- BURMA

O'Keefe, S. Champion of freedom   959.105

DEMOCRACY -- UNITED STATES -- HISTORY

Han, L. C. Handbook to American democracy   320.4

Democratic Republic of the Congo. Heale, J. 967.51

Democritus

About

Macfarlane, K. The father of the atom   92

DEMOGRAPHY *See* Population

Demon apocalypse. Shan, D.   Fic

The **demon** catchers of Milan. Beyer, K.   Fic

Demon catchers of Milan trilogy [series]

Seba, J. A. Homosexuality around the world **306.76**

DEPRESSION, MENTAL *See* Depression (Psychology)

DEPRESSIONS

>*See also* Business cycles

DEPRESSIONS -- 1929

Burg, D. F. The Great Depression **973.91**

Collier, C. Progressivism, the Great Depression, and the New Deal, 1901 to 1941 **973.91**

Cooper, M. L. Dust to eat **973.917**

Freedman, R. Children of the Great Depression **305.23**

Marrin, A. Years of dust **978**

DEPRESSIONS -- 1929 -- FICTION

Golden, L. Every day after **Fic**

Martin, A. M. Better to wish **Fic**

Peck, R. A long way from Chicago **Fic**

DEPRESSIONS -- 1929 -- UNITED STATES -- FICTION

Barnaby, H. Wonder show **Fic**

DEPRESSIONS -- 1929 -- UNITED STATES

Collier, C. Progressivism, the Great Depression, and the New Deal, 1901 to 1941 **973.91**

DEPRESSIONS -- 1929 -- UNITED STATES -- SOURCES

McElvaine, R. S. The Depression and New Deal **973.91**

Ruggiero, A. American voices from The Great Depression **973.917**

DEPRESSIONS

Rylant, C. Something permanent **811**

DEPRESSIVE PSYCHOSES *See* Depression (Psychology)

Derby, Sally

Kyle's island **Fic**

Derek Jeter. Rappoport, K. **796.357**

Deriso, Christine Hurley

Then I met my sister **Fic**

DERMATITIS *See* Skin -- Diseases

Derting, Kimberly

The body finder **Fic**

Desires of the dead **Fic**

The last echo **Fic**

The pledge **Fic**

Des Chenes, Betz

American civil rights: primary sources **323.1**

(ed) Engelbert, P. American civil rights: biographies **305.8**

DeSaix, Debbi Durland

Hidden on the mountain **940.53**

DeSalle, Rob

Tattersall, I. Bones, brains and DNA **599.93**

Desaulniers, Kristi L.

Northern America **970**

DESCENT *See* Genealogy; Heredity

DESCRIPTIVE CATALOGING/STANDARDS

Oliver, C. Introducing RDA **025.3**

DESCRIPTIVE GEOMETRY

>*See also* Geometrical drawing; Geometry

DESEGREGATED SCHOOLS *See* School integration

DESEGREGATION *See* Segregation

DESEGREGATION IN EDUCATION *See* School integration

Desert. Warhol, T. **577.5**

Desert Angel. Price, C. **Fic**

DESERT ANIMALS

>*See also* Animals; Deserts

DESERT ECOLOGY

Allaby, M. Deserts **577.5**

Fridell, R. Life in the desert **577.5**

Lynch, W. Sonoran Desert **577.5**

Warhol, T. Desert **577.5**

DESERT ECOLOGY

>*See also* Ecology

Desert legends trilogy [series]

Wilson, J. Ghost moon **Fic**

Wilson, J. Written in blood **Fic**

DESERT PLANTS

>*See also* Deserts; Plant ecology; Plants

DESERTIFICATION

>*See also* Climate; Deserts

DESERTION AND NONSUPPORT

>*See also* Divorce; Domestic relations

Deserts. Aleshire, P. **551.4**

DESERTS

>*See also* Physical geography

DESERTS

Aleshire, P. Deserts **551.4**

Allaby, M. Deserts **577.5**

Fridell, R. Life in the desert **577.5**

Hinds, K. The countryside **909**

Warhol, T. Desert **577.5**

Deserts. Allaby, M. **577.5**

DESERTS -- FICTION

Durst, S. B. Vessel **Fic**

DESERTS

Allaby, M. Deserts **577.5**

Desetta, Al

(ed) The Courage to be yourself **305.23**

Design and engineering for STEM [series]

Oxlade, C. Gadgets and games **688.7**

Design it! Arato, R. **745.2**

Design your own butterfly garden. Harkins, S. S. **638**

DESIGN, INDUSTRIAL *See* Industrial design

Arato, R. Design it! **745.2**

DESIGNED GENETIC CHANGE *See* Genetic engineering

DESIGNER DRUGS

LeVert, S. Ecstasy **362.29**

>*See also* Drugs

DESIGNERS

Dinosaurs. Holtz, T. R.   567.9

DINOSAURS

  See also Fossil reptiles; Prehistoric animals

Abramson, A. S. Inside dinosaurs   **567.9**

Bacchin, M. Giant vs. giant   **567.9**

Bacchin, M. T. rex and the great extinction   **567.9**

Barrett, P. M. National Geographic dinosaurs **567.9**

Bausum, A. Dragon bones and dinosaur eggs: a photobiography of Roy Chapman Andrews   **92**

Berkowitz, J. Jurassic poop   **567.9**

Bonner, H. When dinos dawned, mammals got munched, and Pterosaurs took flight   **567.9**

Crichton, M. Jurassic Park   **Fic**

Dingus, L. Dinosaur eggs discovered!   **567.9**

Dixon, D. Meat-eating dinosaurs   **567.912**

Dixon, D. Plant-eating dinosaurs   **567.9**

Dixon, D. Prehistoric oceans   **567.9**

Dixon, D. Prehistoric skies   **567.9**

Funston, S. Dino-why?   **567.9**

Holtz, T. R. Dinosaurs   **567.9**

Lessem, D. The ultimate dinopedia   **567.9**

Long, J. A. Dinosaurs   **567.9**

Long, J. A. Feathered dinosaurs   **567.9**

Malam, J. Dinosaur atlas   **567.9**

Manning, P. L. Dinomummy   **567.9**

McGowan, C. Dinosaur discovery   **567.9**

Mehling, R. Great extinctions of the past   **576.8**

Peterson, S. Pterodactyl   **567.9**

Sloan, C. Bizarre dinosaurs   **567.9**

Sloan, C. How dinosaurs took flight   **567.9**

Woodward, J. 3-D dinosaur   **567.9**

Zoehfeld, K. W. Dinosaur parents, dinosaur young   **567.9**

DINOSAURS -- BEHAVIOR

Zoehfeld, K. W. Dinosaur parents, dinosaur young   **567.9**

DINOSAURS -- EGGS

  See also Eggs

Dingus, L. Dinosaur eggs discovered!   **567.9**

DINOSAURS -- FICTION

Cole, S. Z. Raptor   **Fic**

Cole, S. Z. Rex   **Fic**

Crichton, M. Jurassic Park   **Fic**

DINOSAURS -- GRAPHIC NOVELS

TenNapel, D. R. Tommysaurus Rex   **741.5**

DINOSAURS

Kelsey, E. Canadian dinosaurs   **567.909**

DINOSAURS IN ART

Ames, L. J. Draw 50 dinosaurs and other prehistoric animals   **743**

Miller, S. Dinosaurs: how to draw thunder lizards and other prehistoric beasts   **743**

Dinosaurs: how to draw thunder lizards and other prehistoric beasts. Miller, S.   **743**

Dionne, Erin

Models don't eat chocolate cookies   **Fic**

The total tragedy of a girl named Hamlet   **Fic**

DIONYSUS (GREEK DEITY)

  See also Gods and goddesses

Diorio, Mary Ann L.

A student's guide to Herman Melville   **813**

A student's guide to Mark Twain   **813**

DIPHTHERIA

  See also Diseases

DiPiazza, Francesca Davis

Friend me!   **302.3**

DIPLODOCUS

  See also Dinosaurs

DIPLOMATS

  See also Diplomacy; International relations; Statesmen

Adler, D. A. B. Franklin, printer   **973.3**

Blashfield, J. F. Golda Meir   **92**

Borden, L. His name was Raoul Wallenberg   **92**

Dash, J. A dangerous engine   **92**

Delano, P. When I was a boy Neruda called me Policarpo   **92**

Fleming, C. Ben Franklin's almanac   **92**

Fleming, C. Our Eleanor   **92**

Freedman, R. Eleanor Roosevelt   **973.917**

Krull, K. Lives of extraordinary women   **920**

Lagos, A. The sons of liberty 2   **741.5**

MacLeod, E. Eleanor Roosevelt   **92**

McElligott, M. Benjamin Franklinstein lives!   **Fic**

Miller, B. M. Benjamin Franklin, American genius   **92**

DiPrimio, Pete

The sphinx   **398.2**

We visit Iran   **955**

DIRECT MARKETING

  See also Mail-order business; Marketing

DIRECT SELLING

  See also Marketing; Retail trade; Selling

Directing. Bezdecheck, B.   **792.6**

DIRIGIBLE BALLOONS *See* Airships

Dirt road home. Key, W.   **Fic**

Dirty little secrets. Omololu, C. J.   **Fic**

DISABILITIES

  See also Diseases; Wounds and injuries

DISABLED *See* Handicapped

Disappearances. Matthews, R.   **001.9**

The **Disappeared.** Whelan, G.   **Fic**

DISAPPOINTMENT

  See also Emotions

Disaster in the Indian Ocean, Tsunami 2004. Torres, J. A.   **909.83**

Disaster planning. Halsted, D. D.   **025.8**

DISASTER PREPAREDNESS *See* Disaster relief

DISASTER RELIEF

Halsted, D. D. Disaster planning   **025.8**

Morley, D. Healing our world   **610**

Palser, B. Hurricane Katrina   **363.34**

Dizzy Gillespie. Boone, M.   **788.9**

Dizzy in your eyes. Mora, P.   **811**

DK biography [series]

  Buckley, J. Pele   **92**

  Burgan, M. Ronald Reagan   **92**

  Krensky, S. Barack Obama   **92**

  Krensky, S. Clara Barton   **92**

  Sawyer, K. K. Harriet Tubman   **92**

  Wills, C. A. Annie Oakley: a photographic story of a life   **92**

DK children's illustrated encyclopedia. DK Publishing, I.   **031**

DK eyewitness books [series]

  Adams, S. World War I   **940.3**

  Adams, S. World War II   **940.53**

  Bender, L. Invention   **609**

  Burnie, D. Bird   **598**

  Byam, M. Arms & armor   **355.8**

  Challoner, J. Hurricane & tornado   **551.55**

  Clutton-Brock, J. Horse   **636.1**

  Cosgrove, B. Weather   **551.5**

  Cribb, J. Money   **332.4**

  Fortey, J. Great scientists   **920**

  Gamlin, L. Evolution   **576.8**

  Greenaway, T. Jungle   **577.3**

  Hornby, H. Soccer   **796.334**

  James, S. Ancient Rome   **937**

  Lane, B. Crime and detection   **363.2**

  Langley, A. Medieval life   **940.1**

  Langley, M. Religion   **200**

  Lippincott, K. Astronomy   **520**

  McCarthy, C. Reptile   **597.9**

  Murdoch, D. H. North American Indian   **970.004**

  Nahum, A. Flying machine   **629.133**

  Newmark, A. Chemistry   **540**

  Parker, S. Seashore   **577.7**

  Redmond, I. Elephant   **599.67**

  Rowland-Warne, L. Costume   **391**

  Stott, C. Space exploration   **629.4**

  Taylor, P. D. Fossil   **560**

  Tubb, J. N. Bible lands   **220.9**

  Walker, R. Human body   **612**

  Woodward, J. Water   **553.7**

DK guide to savage Earth. Day, T.   **550**

DK Publishing (Company)

  (comp) Sharks   **597.3**

  (comp) Student atlas   **912**

DK Publishing, Inc.

  DK children's illustrated encyclopedia   **031**

DNA. Silverstein, A.   **572.8**

DNA

  See also Cells; Heredity; Nucleic acids

DNA. Ollhoff, J.   **929**

DNA

  Boon, K. A. The human genome project   **599.93**

  De la Bedoyere, C. The discovery of DNA   **572.8**

  Hall, L. E. DNA and RNA   **611**

  Johnson, R. L. Amazing DNA   **572.8**

  Polcovar, J. Rosalind Franklin and the structure of life   **92**

  Rand, C. DNA and heredity   **572.8**

  Silverstein, A. DNA   **572.8**

  Vaughan, J. Who discovered DNA?   **572.8**

DNA -- HISTORY

  Yount, L. Rosalind Franklin   **572.809**

DNA

  Johnson, R. L. Amazing DNA   **572.8**

DNA and body evidence. Innes, B.   **363.2**

DNA and heredity. Rand, C.   **572.8**

DNA and RNA. Hall, L. E.   **611**

DNA FINGERPRINTING

  See also Identification; Medical jurisprudence

  Innes, B. DNA and body evidence   **363.2**

  Rainis, K. G. Blood & DNA evidence   **363.2**

DNA FINGERPRINTS *See* DNA fingerprinting

DNA IDENTIFICATION *See* DNA fingerprinting

DNA PROFILING *See* DNA fingerprinting

Do all Indians live in tipis? National Museum of the American Indian (U.S.)   **970.004**

Do not open. Farndon, J.   **031.02**

Do not pass go. Hill, K.   **Fic**

Do you know where your food comes from? Morris, N.   **363.8**

Do you love me? Harris, A. R.   **613.9**

Do you read me? Webber, D.   **363.2**

DO-IT-YOURSELF WORK

  Backyard Biology   **570.78**

Doable renewables. Rigsby, M.   **333.79**

Doak, Robin S.

  Black Tuesday   **330.9**

  California, 1542-1850   **979.4**

  Georgia, 1521-1776   **975.8**

  Maryland, 1634-1776   **975.2**

  New Jersey 1609-1776   **974.9**

  South Carolina, 1540-1776   **975.7**

  Struggling to become American   **305.8**

Dobkin, Bonnie

  Neptune's children   **Fic**

Dobson, Clive

  Wind power   **333.9**

Dobson, Jolie

  The duct tape book   **745.5**

Doc Fizzix mousetrap racers. Balmer, A. J.   **629.22**

Docalavich, Heather

  Czech Republic   **943.710**

  Denmark   **948.9**

  The Netherlands   **949.2**

  Poland   **943.8**

  Sweden   **948.5**

Docherty, James

  The ice cream con   **Fic**

Doctorow, Cory

DRAWINGS *See* Drawing

Dreadnought. Walden, M.   **Fic**

A **dream** deferred. Sharp, A. W.   **323.1**

Dream factory. Barkley, B.   **Fic**

DREAM INTERPRETATION *See* Dreams

The **dream** keeper and other poems. Hughes, L. **811**

A **dream** of freedom. McWhorter, D.   **323.1**

Dream of Night. Henson, H.   **Fic**

Dreamdark [series]

  Taylor, L. Silksinger   **Fic**

The **dreamer.** Ryan, P. M.   **Fic**

Dreamhunter. Knox, E.   **Fic**

Dreamhunter duet [series]

  Knox, E. Dreamhunter   **Fic**

  Knox, E. Dreamquake   **Fic**

DREAMING *See* Dreams

Dreamland. Noel, A.   **Fic**

Dreamquake. Knox, E.   **Fic**

DREAMS

  Brynie, F. H. 101 questions about sleep and dreams that kept you awake nights . . . until now   **612.8**

DREAMS -- FICTION

  Quest for the Spark   **Fic**

DREAMS -- GRAPHIC NOVELS

  Stolarz, L. F. Black is for beginnings   **741.5**

DREAMS

  Brynie, F. H. 101 questions about sleep and dreams that kept you awake nights . . . until now   **612.8**

Dreams from my father. Obama, B.   **92**

Dreams of the dead. Randall, T.   **Fic**

Dred Scott. Naden, C. J.   **342**

Dred Scott v. Sandford. Van Zee, A.   **342.730**

DREDGING

  See also Civil engineering; Hydraulic engineering

Dreier, David Louis

  Baseball   **796.357**

  Electrical circuits   **537**

DRESS *See* Clothing and dress

DRESS ACCESSORIES

  Warwick, E. Everywear   **745.5**

DRESS ACCESSORIES

  See also Clothing and dress

  Warwick, E. Everywear   **745.5**

DRESSAGE *See* Horsemanship

Dressing a nation: the history of U.S. fashion [series]

  Behnke, A. The little black dress and zoot suits **391**

  Bix, C. O. Petticoats and frock coats   **391**

  Havelin, K. Buckskin dresses and pumpkin breeches   **391**

  Havelin, K. Hoopskirts, Union blues, and Confederate grays   **391**

  Krohn, K. E. Calico dresses and buffalo robes **391**

DRESSMAKERS

  Jones, L. Mrs. Lincoln's dressmaker: the unlikely friendship of Elizabeth Keckley and Mary Todd Lincoln   **92**

DRESSMAKING

  See also Clothing and dress; Clothing industry

Drew, Naomi

  The kids' guide to working out conflicts   **303.6**

Drewe, James

  Jennings, M. Tai chi step-by-step   **613.7**

Dreyer, ZoAnn

  Living with cancer   **362.1**

Drez, Ronald J.

  Remember D-day   **940.54**

DRIED FOODS

  See also Food

DRILLING PLATFORMS

  See also Ocean engineering; Offshore oil well drilling

DRILLING, OIL WELL *See* Oil well drilling

DRINKING AGE

  See also Age; Teenagers -- Alcohol use; Youth -- Alcohol use

DRINKING AND TEENAGERS *See* Teenagers -- Alcohol use

DRINKING CUPS -- FICTION

  Stanley, D. The cup and the crown   **Fic**

DRINKING OF ALCOHOLIC BEVERAGES

  Alcohol information for teens   **613.81**

  Gottfried, T. Alcohol   **362.292**

  Gottfried, T. The facts about alcohol   **362.292**

DRINKING OF ALCOHOLIC BEVERAGES -- UNITED STATES

  Gottfried, T. The facts about alcohol   **362.292**

DRINKING PROBLEM *See* Alcoholism; Drinking of alcoholic beverages

DRINKING WATER

  See also Water; Water supply

Driven. Mitchell, D.   **92**

Driver, Stephanie Schwartz

  Understanding the Declaration of Independence   **973.3**

DRIVING UNDER THE INFLUENCE OF ALCOHOL *See* Drunk driving

DRIVING WHILE INTOXICATED *See* Drunk driving

DRONE AIRCRAFT

  Mooney, C. Pilotless planes   **623.7**

The **drop.** Ross, J.   **Fic**

Drop. Papademetriou, L.   **Fic**

DROPOUTS

  See also Students; Youth

Droughts. Fradin, J. B.   **363.34**

DROUGHTS

  See also Meteorology

  Chin, J. Island   **508.866**

  Cooper, M. L. Dust to eat   **973.917**

(jt. auth) Broyles, J. Frequently asked questions about hate crimes **364.15**

DUNKERQUE (FRANCE), BATTLE OF, 1940 -- FICTION

Hull, N. L. On rough seas **Fic**

Dunkle, Clare B.

The sky inside **Fic**

The walls have eyes **Fic**

The house of dead maids **Fic**

Dunkleberger, Amy

A student's guide to Arthur Miller **812**

Dunlap, Susanne Emily

In the shadow of the lamp **Fic**

The musician's daughter **Fic**

Dunlap, S. In the shadow of the lamp **Fic**

Dunmore, Helen

The deep **Fic**

Ingo **Fic**

Tide knot **Fic**

Dunn, Danielle

Dunn, J. A teen's guide to getting published **808**

Dunn, Jessica

A teen's guide to getting published **808**

Dunn, Joeming W.

The phantom of the opera **741.5**

Dunning, Mark

Burns, B. Basketball step-by-step **796.323**

Dunning, Stephen

(comp) Reflections on a gift of watermelon pickle-
-and other modern verse **811**

Dunstan, Simon

Entebbe **967.61**

The **duplicate.** Sleator, W. **Fic**

DupliKate. Cheva, C. **Fic**

DuPrau, Jeanne

The city of Ember **Fic**

The diamond of Darkhold **Fic**

The people of Sparks **Fic**

The prophet of Yonwood **Fic**

Durango, Julia

The walls of Cartagena **Fic**

Durbin, William

The broken blade **Fic**

The darkest evening **Fic**

The Winter War **Fic**

Durman, Laura

Castle life **940.1**

Knights **940.1**

Siege **355.4**

Durrant, Lynda

Imperfections **Fic**

My last skirt **Fic**

Durst, Sarah Beth

Ice **Fic**

Into the Wild **Fic**

Vessel **Fic**

DUST

See also Air pollution

The **Dust** Bowl. Reis, R. A. **978**

DUST BOWL ERA, 1931-1939

Marrin, A. Years of dust **978**

Sandler, M. W. The Dust Bowl through the lens **973.9**

The **Dust** Bowl through the lens. Sandler, M. W. **973.9**

Dust city. Weston, R. P. **Fic**

Dust girl. Zettel, S. **Fic**

DUST STORMS

Marrin, A. Years of dust **978**

Reis, R. A. The Dust Bowl **978**

Sandler, M. W. The Dust Bowl through the lens **973.9**

DUST STORMS

See also Droughts; Erosion; Storms

DUST STORMS -- FICTION

Hesse, K. Out of the dust **Fic**

DUST STORMS -- GRAPHIC NOVELS

Phelan, M. The storm in the barn **741.5**

DUST STORMS -- GREAT PLAINS -- HISTORY -- 20TH CENTURY

Cooper, M. L. Dust to eat **973.917**

Marrin, A. Years of dust **978**

Dust to eat. Cooper, M. L. **973.917**

Dustlands trilogy [series]

Young, M. Blood red road **Fic**

Dut, Salva -- Fiction

About

Park, L. S. A long walk to water **Fic**

DUTCH AMERICANS

Huey, L. M. American archaeology uncovers the Dutch colonies **974.7**

DuTemple, Lesley A.

The Panama Canal **972.87**

The Pantheon **726**

The Taj Mahal **726**

DUTY

See also Ethics; Human behavior

Duwel, Lucretia I.

Simpson, M. S. Bringing classes into the public library **027.62**

Dvorak in America. Horowitz, J. **92**

Dvořák, Antonín, 1841-1904

About

Horowitz, J. Dvorak in America **92**

DWARF TREES

See also Trees

DWARFISM -- FICTION

Nemeth, S. The heights, the depths, and everything in between **Fic**

DWARFS

Sullivan, G. Tom Thumb **92**

DWARFS -- FICTION

dieval literature

Early civilizations. Kelly, K.   **610**

Early explorations: the 1500s. Hernandez, R. E.   **970.01**

Early Germans. Hinds, K.   **936**

The early human world. Robertshaw, P.   **599.93**

Early humans. Holmes, T.   **599.93**

Early medieval times. Malam, J.   **940.1**

Early national America, 1790-1850. McNeese, T.   **973.4**

EARLY PRINTED BOOKS
> *See also* Books

Earnest, Peter
> The real spy's guide to becoming a spy   **327.12**

Earning money. Fischer, J.   **650.1**

Earth.   **550**

Earth. Fuoco, G. D.   **333.72**

EARTH
> *See also* Planets; Solar system

EARTH -- GRAVITY *See* Gravity

EARTH -- MAPS
> Oxford Atlas of the world   **912**

Earth and the moon. Hicks, T. A.   **525**

Earth and the moon. Miller, R.   **525**

Earth chemistry. Cobb, A. B.   **551**

Earth heroes [series]
> Hodgkins, F. Champions of the ocean   **920**
> Malnor, B. Champions of the wilderness   **920**
> Malnor, C. Champions of wild animals   **920**

Earth in the hot seat. Delano, M. F.   **363.7**

Earth issues [series]
> Bodden, V. Critical plant life   **581.7**
> Bodden, V. Environmental law   **344**
> Gunderson, J. The energy dilemma   **333.79**
> Gunderson, J. Global warming   **363.7**

Earth science fair projects. Calhoun, Y.   **550**

Earth science projects using the scientific method [series]
> Calhoun, Y. Earth science fair projects   **550**
> Gardner, R. Planet Earth science fair projects **507.8**
> Gardner, R. Weather science fair projects   **551.6**
> Rybolt, T. R. Environmental science fair projects   **550**

EARTH SCIENCES
> Bow, J. Earth's secrets   **550**
> Calhoun, Y. Earth science fair projects   **550**
> Diagram Group The Facts on File Earth science handbook   **550**
> Gardner, R. Earth's cycles   **550**
> Gardner, R. Planet Earth science fair projects **507.8**
> Gilpin, D. Planet Earth   **550**
> Latham, D. Amazing biome projects you can build yourself   **577**
> Rybolt, T. R. Environmental science fair projects   **550**
> Solway, A. Understanding cycles and systems **550**

EARTH SCIENCES
> *See also* Physical sciences; Science
> VanCleave, J. P. Step-by-step science experiments in earth science   **550.78**

EARTH SCIENCES -- ENCYCLOPEDIAS
> Allaby, M. Visual encyclopedia of earth   **550**

EARTH SCIENCES -- EXPERIMENTS
> VanCleave, J. P. Step-by-step science experiments in earth science   **550.78**

Earth's biomes [series]
> Warhol, T. Chaparral and scrub   **577.3**
> Warhol, T. Desert   **577.5**
> Warhol, T. Tundra   **577.5**
> Warhol, T. Water   **577.6**

Earth's core and mantle. Vogt, G.   **551.1**

Earth's cycles. Gardner, R.   **550**

Earth's journey through space. Bell, T. E.   **525**

Earth's secrets. Bow, J.   **550**

Earth's shifting surface. Snedden, R.   **551.1**

Earth's spheres [series]
> Vogt, G. The atmosphere   **551.5**
> Vogt, G. Earth's core and mantle   **551.1**
> Vogt, G. The lithosphere   **551.1**

EARTH, EFFECT OF MAN ON *See* Human influence on nature

The **earth,** my butt, and other big, round things. Mackler, C.   **Fic**

Earth, sea, sun, and sky. Stieff, B.   **704.9**

Earth, space, and beyond [series]
> Solway, A. Why is there life on Earth?   **576.8**

Earth-friendly crafts. Ross, K.   **745.5**

Earth-friendly design. Welsbacher, A.   **745.2**

Earth-friendly energy. Fridell, R.   **333.79**

Earth-friendly waste management. Wilcox, C.   **363.7**

Earth: our planet in space. Simon, S.   **525**

Earthbound. Pike, A.   **Fic**

EarthEcho International
> (comp) Cousteau, P. Make a splash!   **577.7**

EARTHENWARE *See* Pottery

An **earthly** knight. McNaughton, J.   **Fic**

Earthquake in Haiti. Aronin, M.   **972.94**

EARTHQUAKE SEA WAVES *See* Tsunamis

Earthquakes. Fradin, J. B.   **551.2**

Earthquakes. Silverstein, A.   **551.2**

EARTHQUAKES
> *See also* Earth; Geology; Natural disasters; Physical geography
> Aronin, M. Earthquake in Haiti   **972.94**
> Day, T. DK guide to savage Earth   **550**
> Dwyer, H. Earthquakes!   **551.2**
> Fradin, J. B. Earthquakes   **551.2**
> Levy, M. Earthquakes, volcanoes, and tsunamis   **551.2**
> McCollum, S. Volcanic eruptions, earthquakes, and tsunamis   **551.2**

ECOLOGY -- FICTION
Klass, D. Timelock   **Fic**
Nelson, B. Destroy all cars   **Fic**
One white dolphin   **Fic**
Weyn, S. Empty   **Fic**
ECOLOGY
Ecology   **577**
VanCleave, J. P. Step-by-step science experiments
in ecology   **577.078**
ECOLOGY -- PHILIPPINES
Turner, P. S. Project Seahorse   **597**
ECOLOGY -- VOCATIONAL GUIDANCE
Power Scott, J. Green careers   **333.72**
ECOLOGY, HUMAN *See* Human ecology
ECOLOGY, SOCIAL *See* Human ecology
ECONOMIC BIOLOGY *See* Economic botany;
Economic zoology
ECONOMIC BOTANY
See also Agriculture; Botany
Young, K. J. Ethnobotany   **581.6**
ECONOMIC CONDITIONS
See also Business; Economics; Social condi-
tions; Wealth
McNeese, T. The Great Depression, 1929-
1940   **973.917**
ECONOMIC CYCLES *See* Business cycles
ECONOMIC DEVELOPMENT
See also Economic policy; Economics
ECONOMIC FORECASTING
See also Business cycles; Economics; Fore-
casting
ECONOMIC GEOLOGY
See also Geology
ECONOMIC HISTORY *See* Economic conditions
ECONOMIC INDICATORS
See also Economics
ECONOMIC POLICY
See also Economics; Planning
Laxer, J. Democracy   **321.8**
ECONOMIC POLICY -- UNITED STATES
Brezina, C. America's recession   **330.9**
Brezina, C. How stimulus plans work   **338.5**
Heinrichs, A. The great recession   **330.9**
ECONOMIC RECESSIONS *See* Recessions
ECONOMIC ZOOLOGY
See also Zoology
ECONOMICS
Hollander, B. Money matters   **330**
Simons, R. All about money   **332.4**
**ECONOMICS -- HANDBOOKS, MANUALS,
ETC.**
Bostick, N. Managing Money   **332**
ECONOMISTS
Crain, C. D. Adam Smith   **92**
Crain, C. D. John Maynard Keynes   **92**
Crain, C. D. Milton Friedman   **92**

ECONOMY *See* Saving and investment
Ecosystem [series]
Allaby, M. Deserts   **577.5**
Allaby, M. Temperate forests   **577.3**
Day, T. Oceans   **551.46**
Moore, P. D. Wetlands   **578.7**
Ecosystem science fair projects. Walker, P.   **577**
Ecosystems. Housel, D. J.   **577**
ECOSYSTEMS *See* Ecology
Ecosystems. Rompella, N.   **577**
ECOTERRORISM
See also Environmental movement; Terrorism
ECOTOURISM
See also Tourist trade
Ecstasy. LeVert, S.   **362.29**
ECSTASY (DRUG)
Koellhoffer, T. Ecstasy and other club drugs **362.29**
LeVert, S. Ecstasy   **362.29**
LeVert, S. The facts about ecstasy   **362.29**
Ecstasy and other club drugs. Koellhoffer, T. **362.29**
Ecuador. Foley, E.   **986.6**
EDAPHOLOGY *See* Soil ecology
Edda. Kostick, C.   **Fic**
EDDAS
See also Old Norse literature; Poetry; Scan-
dinavian literature
Eddie's war. Saller, C. F.   **Fic**
Edens, Cooper
(comp) Classic western stories   **808.8**
The **Edenville** Owls. Parker, R. B.   **Fic**
Edgar Allan Poe. Poe, E. A.   **S C**
Edgar Allan Poe. Meltzer, M.   **92**
EDGAR ALLAN POE AWARDS
See also Literary prizes; Mystery fiction
Edgar Allan Poe's tales of death and dementia. Poe,
E. A.   **S C**
Edgar Allan Poe's tales of mystery and madness.
Poe, E. A.   **S C**
Edgar, Elsbeth
The Visconti house   **Fic**
Edge books. Paper airplanes [series]
Harbo, C. L. Paper airplanes: Captain, level
4   **745.592**
Harbo, C. L. Paper airplanes: Copilot, level
2   **745.592**
Harbo, C. L. Paper airplanes: Flight school, level
1   **745.592**
Harbo, C. L. Paper airplanes: Pilot, level 3 **745.592**
Edge books: making and breaking codes [series]
Bell-Rehwoldt, S. Speaking secret codes   **652**
Gregory, J. Breaking secret codes   **652**
Gregory, J. Making secret codes   **652**
The **edge** of the sea. Carson, R.   **577.7**
Edge, Laura Bufano, 1953-
Edge, L. B. From jazz babies to generation
next   **305.23**

(ed) Is Islam a religion of war or peace? **297**

Einstein, Albert, 1879-1955
About
Delano, M. F. Genius **92**
Krull, K. Albert Einstein **92**
Haddix, M. P. Caught **Fic**
Pohlen, J. Albert Einstein and relativity for kids **530.092**

Einstein-Marić, Mileva, 1875-1948 -- Fiction
About
Haddix, M. P. Caught **Fic**

Eisenhower, Dwight D. (Dwight David), 1890-1969
About
Mara, W. Dwight Eisenhower **92**
Young, J. C. Dwight D. Eisenhower **973.921**

Eisner, Will, 1917-2005
About
Greenberger, R. Will Eisner **92**

Ejaz, Khadija
Recipe and craft guide to India **641.5**
We visit Oman **953.53**

EL NIÑO CURRENT
See also Ocean currents
El Nino. Arnold, C. **551.6**
EL NIÑO CURRENT
Arnold, C. El Nino **551.6**
El Salvador. Foley, E. **972.84**

ELDERLY -- COUNSELING OF
See also Counseling
ELDERLY -- DISEASES
See also Diseases
ELDERLY -- HEALTH AND HYGIENE
See also Health; Hygiene
ELDERLY -- HOUSING
See also Housing
ELDERLY -- LIBRARY SERVICES
See also Elderly; Library services
ELDERLY -- LIFE SKILLS GUIDES
See also Life skills
ELDERLY -- MEDICAL CARE
See also Elderly -- Care; Medical care
ELDERLY -- RECREATION
See also Recreation
ELDERLY ABUSE
See also Domestic violence
Eldest. Paolini, C. **Fic**
Eldredge, Niles
Charles Darwin and the mystery of mysteries **92**
Eleanor
About
Brooks, P. S. Queen Eleanor, Independent Spirit of the Medieval World **942.03**
Eleanor of Aquitaine. Kramer, A. **92**
Eleanor Roosevelt. Freedman, R. **973.917**
Eleanor Roosevelt. MacLeod, E. **92**

Eleanor, of Aquitaine, Queen, consort of Henry II, King of England, 1122?-1204
About
Krull, K. Lives of extraordinary women **920**
Eleanor, of Aquitaine, Queen, consort of Henry II, King of England, 1122?-1204
About
Kramer, A. Eleanor of Aquitaine **92**
ELECTION *See* Elections
ELECTION LAW
See also Constitutional law
ELECTION LAW -- UNITED STATES -- CRIMINAL PROVISIONS -- HISTORY -- 19TH CENTURY
Monroe, J. The Susan B. Anthony women's voting rights trial **324.6**
The **Election** of 2000 and the administration of George W. Bush. **324**
Election reform. Marzilli, A. **324.6**
ELECTIONEERING *See* Politics
ELECTIONS
See also Politics
Steele, P. Vote **324**
ELECTIONS -- FICTION
Cotler, S. Cheesie Mack is running like crazy! **Fic**
Paulsen, G. Vote **Fic**
ELECTIONS -- UNITED STATES
Marzilli, A. Election reform **324.6**
Electric and magnetic phenomena. Galiano, D. **537**
ELECTRIC AUTOMOBILES
See also Automobiles
Bearce, S. All about electric and hybrid cars **629.222**
Mackay, J. Electric cars **629.22**
Electric cars. Mackay, J. **629.22**
ELECTRIC CARS *See* Electric automobiles
ELECTRIC CIRCUITS
See also Electric lines; Electricity
Dreier, D. L. Electrical circuits **537**
ELECTRIC CONDUCTORS
See also Electronics
ELECTRIC CURRENTS
See also Electricity
ELECTRIC DISTRIBUTION *See* Electric lines; Electric power distribution
ELECTRIC GUITAR
See also Electronic musical instruments; Guitars
The **electric** light. Sonneborn, L. **621.32**
ELECTRIC LIGHT *See* Electric lighting; Photometry; Phototherapy
ELECTRIC LIGHTING
Collier, J. L. Electricity and the light bulb **621.32**
Sonneborn, L. The electric light **621.32**
ELECTRIC LINES
Macaulay, D. Underground **624**
ELECTRIC MACHINERY

Hirshfield, L. Girls gone green   **333.72**
Horn, G. Environmental engineer   **628**
Kaye, C. B. Going blue   **333.91**
Keithley, M. Eco-tracking   **577**
Kelsey, E. Not your typical book about the environment   **333.72**
Marcovitz, H. How serious a threat is climate change?   **363.7**
McKay, K. True green kids   **333.72**
Molland, J. Get out!   **333.72**
Nagle, J. Living green   **333.72**
Petronis, L. 47 things you can do for the environment   **333.72**
Power Scott, J. Green careers   **333.72**
Raatma, L. Green living   **333.72**
Rapp, V. Protecting Earth's land   **333.72**
Recycle this book   **333.72**
Ride, S. K. Mission: save the planet   **333.72**
Smalley, C. P. Green changes you can make around your home   **333.72**
Strange, C. Environmental science & protection   **333.72**
Try this at home   **333.72**
Welsbacher, A. Earth-friendly design   **745.2**
Welsbacher, A. Protecting Earth's rain forests **577.3**

ENVIRONMENTAL PROTECTION
See also Ecology; Environment

ENVIRONMENTAL PROTECTION -- BIBLIOGRAPHY
Wesson, L. P. Green reads   **016**

ENVIRONMENTAL PROTECTION -- FICTION
Cavanaugh, N. J. This journal belongs to Ratchet   **Fic**
Gilman, D. Blood sun   **Fic**
Gilman, D. The devil's breath   **Fic**
Golding, J. The gorgon's gaze   **Fic**
Golding, J. Mines of the minotaur   **Fic**
Golding, J. Secret of the sirens   **Fic**
Greenwald, L. My life in pink and green   **Fic**
Hiaasen, C. Flush   **Fic**
Hiaasen, C. Hoot   **Fic**
Loizeaux, W. Clarence Cochran, a human boy **Fic**
One white dolphin   **Fic**
Scarrow, A. TimeRiders   **Fic**
Sheldon, D. The crazy things girls do for love **Fic**
Wolfson, J. Home, and other big, fat lies   **Fic**

ENVIRONMENTAL PROTECTION
Spilsbury, R. Towns and cities   **307.76**

ENVIRONMENTAL PROTECTION -- LAW AND LEGISLATION *See* Environmental law

ENVIRONMENTAL PROTECTION -- VOCATIONAL GUIDANCE
Gazlay, S. Managing green spaces   **333.7**
Power Scott, J. Green careers   **333.72**

ENVIRONMENTAL QUALITY -- GOVERNMENT POLICY *See* Environmental policy

ENVIRONMENTAL RESPONSIBILITY
McKay, K. True green kids   **333.72**

ENVIRONMENTAL SCIENCE
Byers, A. Jobs as green builders and planners **690**
Walker, P. Environmental science experiments   **507.8**
Environmental science & protection. Strange, C.   **333.72**
Environmental science experiments. Walker, P.   **507.8**
Environmental science fair projects. Rybolt, T. R.   **550**

ENVIRONMENTAL SCIENCES
Cobb, A. B. Earth chemistry   **551**
The environment: opposing viewpoints   **363.7**
Gardner, R. Ace your ecology and environmental science project   **577**
Harmon, D. Jobs in environmental cleanup and emergency hazmat response   **628**
Reilly, K. M. Planet Earth   **333.72**
Rybolt, T. R. Environmental science fair projects   **550**
Strange, C. Environmental science & protection   **333.72**
Young, K. R. Junkyard science   **507.8**

ENVIRONMENTAL SCIENCES
See also Science
Kriesberg, D. A. Think green, take action **333.72**

ENVIRONMENTAL SCIENCES -- STUDY AND TEACHING
Kriesberg, D. A. Think green, take action **333.72**

ENVIRONMENTALISM
Green, J. Conservation   **333.72**

ENVIRONMENTALISM *See* Environmental movement; Environmental protection
Cousteau, P. Make a splash!   **577.7**
Ecology   **577**
Green, J. Food and farming   **338.1**
McKay, K. True green kids   **333.72**
Solway, A. Transportation   **363.73**

ENVIRONMENTALISTS
Baptiste, T. Al Gore   **92**
Byrnes, P. Environmental pioneers   **363.7**
Cousteau, P. Make a splash!   **577.7**
Hodgkins, F. Champions of the ocean   **920**
Housel, D. J. Ecologists   **920**
Malnor, B. Champions of the wilderness   **920**
Piddock, C. Rachel Carson   **92**
Rohmer, H. Heroes of the environment   **333.72**
Scherer, G. Who on earth is Rachel Carson?   **92**

ENVIRONMENTALISTS
Malnor, B. Champions of the wilderness   **920**

ENVIRONMENTALISTS -- UNITED STATES -- BIOGRAPHY
Byrnes, P. Environmental pioneers   **363.7**

Gow, M. Measuring the Earth 92

Erdoes, Richard
(ed) American Indian myths and legends 398.2
Brave Bird, M. Lakota woman 92

Erdrich, Louise, 1954-
The birchbark house Fic
Chickadee Fic
The game of silence Fic
The porcupine year Fic

ERGONOMICS *See* Human engineering

Erickson, Paul
Daily life in the Pilgrim colony, 1636 974.4

Erikson, Rolf
Designing a school library media center for the future 027.8

Eritrea. NgCheong-Lum, R. 963.5

Erlbach, Arlene
The middle school survival guide 373.1

Ernest Hemingway. Reef, C. 92
Ernest Hemingway. Whiting, J. 92
Ernest J. Gaines. Abrams, D. 92
Ernest Rutherford and the birth of the atomic age. Baxter, R. 530.092
Ernest Shackleton. Johnson, R. L. 92
Ernesto Che Guevara. Abrams, D. 92

Ernst, Kathleen
Hearts of stone Fic

Erosion. Stille, D. R. 551.3

EROSION
See also Geology
Stille, D. R. Erosion 551.3

EROTIC ART
See also Art; Erotica

EROTIC FILMS
See also Motion pictures

EROTIC LITERATURE
See also Erotica; Literature

EROTIC POETRY
See also Erotic literature; Poetry

Erratum. Sorrells, W. Fic

ERRORS, SCIENTIFIC
YES mag (Periodical) Hoaxed! 500

Erskine, Kathryn
The absolute value of Mike Fic
Quaking Fic

Eruption. Smith, R. Fic
Eruption! Rusch, E. 363.34
Escape and evasion. McIntosh, J. S. 335.4
Escape from Furnace [series]
Smith, A. G. Death sentence Fic
Smith, A. G. Lockdown Fic
Smith, A. G. Solitary Fic
Escape from Mr. Lemoncello's library. Grabenstein, C. Fic
Escape from Saigon. Warren, A. 92
Escape the mask. Ward, D. Fic

Escape under the forever sky. Yohalem, E. Fic
Escape velocity. Walden, M. Fic
Escape velocity. Stevenson, R. Fic
Escape! Fleischman, S. 92
Escape--teens on the run. Altman, L. J. 940.53

ESCAPES
See also Adventure and adventurers; Prisons

ESCAPES -- FICTION
Smith, A. G. Lockdown Fic

ESCAPES -- IRELAND -- HISTORY -- 19TH CENTURY
Fradin, D. B. The Irish potato famine 941.508

Escaping into the night. Friedman, D. D. Fic
Escaping slavery on the Underground Railroad. Stein, R. C. 973.7
Escaping the tiger. Manivong, L. Fic

Esckilsen, Erik E.
The last mall rat Fic

Esherick, Joan
Dying for acceptance 616.86
The FDA and psychiatric drugs 363
The journey toward recovery 616.8
No more butts 616.86

ESKIMOS *See* Inuit

ESKIMOS -- FICTION
Hobbs, W. Never say die Fic

Eskridge, Ann E.
Slave uprisings and runaways 326

ESP *See* Extrasensory perception

Espejo, Roman
(ed) Mass media: opposing viewpoints 302.23
(ed) What is a hate crime? 364.1

Espeland, Pamela
(ed) Fox, J. S. Get organized without losing it 371.3
(ed) Galas, J. C. The power to prevent suicide 362.28
Gootman, M. E. When a friend dies 155.9
Kincher, J. Psychology for kids vol. 1: 40 fun tests that help you learn about yourself 150
Kincher, J. Psychology for kids vol. 2: 40 fun experiments that help you learn about others 150

Esperanza rising. Ryan, P. M. Fic

ESPIONAGE
Abbott, D. Conflict in the Middle East 956
Earnest, P. The real spy's guide to becoming a spy 327.12
Janeczko, P. B. The dark game 327.12
Mitchell, S. K. Spies and lies 327.12
Mitchell, S. K. Spies, double agents, and traitors 327.12
Mitchell, S. K. Spy codes and ciphers 652
Mitchell, S. K. Spy gizmos and gadgets 327.12

ESPIONAGE
See also Intelligence service; Secret service; Subversive activities

Weinberg, L. What is terrorism? 303.6

Euclid

About

Hightower, P. The father of geometry: Euclid and his 3D world 92

EUGENICS

See also Genetics; Population

Eulberg, Elizabeth

Revenge of the Girl With the Great Personality **Fic**

EURO

See also Capital market; Money

Europe. Allen, P. 780.94

EUROPE -- ANTIQUITIES

Deem, J. M. Bodies from the bog 573.3

The **European** colonization of Africa. Nardo, D. 960

EUROPEAN FEDERATION

Ponsford, S. The European Union today 341.242

EUROPEAN FEDERATION

See also Europe -- Politics and government; Federal government; International organization

The **European** settlement of North America (1492-1763) Stanley, G. E. 973.2

EUROPEAN UNION

See also European federation

EUROPEAN UNION

Docalavich, H. Czech Republic 943.710

Docalavich, H. Denmark 948.9

Docalavich, H. Poland 943.8

Docalavich, H. Sweden 948.5

Etingoff, K. Greece 949.5

Etingoff, K. Portugal 946.9

Hanks, R. R. Spain 946

Indovino, S. C. Spain 946

The **European** Union today. Ponsford, S. 341.242

EUTHANASIA

Euthanasia: opposing viewpoints 179.7

Rebman, R. C. Euthanasia and the right to die **179.7**

Stefoff, R. The right to die 179.7

Suicide: opposing viewpoints 362.28

Terminal illness: opposing viewpoints 362.1

EUTHANASIA

See also Homicide; Medical ethics

EUTHANASIA -- FICTION

Epstein, R. God is in the pancakes **Fic**

LeZotte, A. C. T4 **Fic**

Trueman, T. Stuck in neutral **Fic**

Euthanasia and the right to die. Rebman, R. C. **179.7**

Euthanasia: opposing viewpoints. **179.7**

eV: vol. 1. Farr, J. 741.5

Eva. Dickinson, P. **Fic**

Eva Peron. Favor, L. J. 92

Eva's story. Schloss, E. 92

EVACUATION AND RELOCATION OF JAPA-NESE AMERICANS, 1942-1945 *See* Japanese Americans -- Evacuation and relocation, 1942-1945

EVACUATION OF CIVILIANS

See also Civil defense; Disaster relief

EVACUATION OF CIVILIANS -- VIETNAM

Skrypuch, M. F. Last airlift 959.704

Evaluating teen services and programs. Flowers, S. 027.62

EVALUATION

Nichols, B. Managing curriculum and assessment 375

Wilson, D. Strategies for evaluation 370.15

EVALUATION OF LITERATURE *See* Best books; Books and reading; Criticism; Literature -- History and criticism

EVANGELICALISM

See also Protestantism

Evangelista, Beth

Gifted **Fic**

EVANGELISTIC WORK -- FICTION

Nelson, R. A. Days of Little Texas **Fic**

Evans, Arthur V.

National Wildlife Federation field guide to insects and spiders & related species of North America 595.7

Evans, Bill

It's raining fish and spiders 551.6

Evans, Colin

Crime lab 363.2

Evidence 363.2

Interpol 363.2

New York Police Department 363.2

Evans, Kate

Weird weather 363.7

Evans, Lissa

Horten's miraculous mechanisms **Fic**

Evans, Michael

The adventures of Medical Man 616

Evans, Robert C.

(ed) Student's encyclopedia of great American writers 810.9

Evans-Martin, Fay

Down syndrome 616.85

Eve & Adam. Applegate, K. **Fic**

EVENING AND CONTINUATION SCHOOLS

See also Compulsory education; Continuing education; Education; Public schools; Schools; Secondary education; Technical education

Events. Butterfield, M. 796.48

Ever. Levine, G. C. **Fic**

The **everafter**. Huntley, A. **Fic**

Everbound. Ashton, B. **Fic**

Everfound. Shusterman, N. **Fic**

The **Everglades.** Lynch, W. 508

Everglades National Park. Jankowski, S. 975.9

EVERGLADES NATIONAL PARK (FLA.)
Jankowski, S. Everglades National Park 975.9

EVERGREENS
Stefoff, R. The conifer division 585

EVERGREENS
See also Landscape gardening; Shrubs; Trees

Everhart, Michael J.
Sea monsters 567.9

Everlasting. Frazier, A. Fic

Everlost. Shusterman, N. Fic

Everneath. Ashton, B. Fic

Everneath [series]
Ashton, B. Everbound Fic

Everness [series]
McDonald, I. Planesrunner Fic

Evers, Medgar Wiley, 1925-1963
About
Coleman, W. Racism on trial 345
Ribeiro, M. The assassination of Medgar Evers 976.2

Everwild. Shusterman, N. Fic

Every bone tells a story. Rubalcaba, J. 930.1

Every crooked pot. Rosen, R. Fic

Every day after. Golden, L. Fic

Every human has rights. National Geographic Society (U.S.) 323

Every man for himself. S C

Every soul a star. Mass, W. Fic

Every thing on it. Silverstein, S. 811

Everybody bugs out. Margolis, L. Fic

Everybody's revolution. Fleming, T. J. 973.3

Everyday economics [series]
Morrison, J. Investing 332.6
Morrison, J. Saving 332.024
Tomljanovic, T. Borrowing 332.7
Wiseman, B. Budgeting 332.024

Everyday life in medieval Europe. Hinds, K. 940.1

Everyday life in the Renaissance. Hinds, K. 940.2

Everyday life in the Roman Empire. Hinds, K. 937

Everyday science [series]
Rau, D. M. Freaking out! 612.8

The **everything** aquarium book. Indiviglio, F. 639.34

Everything for a dog. Martin, A. M. Fic

Everything is fine. Ellis, A. D. Fic

Everything on a waffle. Horvath, P. Fic

Everything series
Indiviglio, F. The everything aquarium book 639.34

Everything you need to know about creating your own support system. Kreiner, A. 158

Everything you need to know about dealing with sexual assault. Kaminker, L. 364.1

Everywear. Warwick, E. 745.5

Evidence. Evans, C. 363.2

Evil genius. Jinks, C. Fic

Evil genius series
Bonnet, R. L. 46 science fair projects for the evil genius 507.8

EVIL SPIRITS *See* Demonology

Evil star. Horowitz, A. Fic

Evolution. Holmes, T. 576.8

EVOLUTION
See also Philosophy
Anderson, D. How do we know the nature of human origins 599.93
Ashby, R. Young Charles Darwin and the voyage of the Beagle 92
Billions of years, amazing changes 576.8
Eamer, C. Spiked scorpions & walking whales 591.3
Eamer, C. Super crocs & monster wings 591.3
Evolution 576.8
Gallant, R. A. History 551.7
Gamlin, L. Evolution 576.8
Gardner, R. Genetics and evolution science fair projects 576
Gibbons, A. Charles Darwin 92
Gordon, S. M. The evolution debate 576.8
Hartman, E. Changing life on Earth 576.8
Holmes, T. Early humans 599.93
Holmes, T. Evolution 576.8
Johnson, S. A. Shaking the foundation 576.8
Kelly, E. Evolving planet 551
Krull, K. Charles Darwin 92
Leone, B. Origin 92
Schanzer, R. What Darwin saw 92
Sloan, C. The human story 599.93
Stefoff, R. Charles Darwin and the evolution revolution 575
Stefoff, R. Modern humans 599.93
Tattersall, I. Bones, brains and DNA 599.93
Walker, D. Inheritance and evolution 576
Walker, R. What is the theory of evolution? 576.8
Winston, R. M. L. Evolution revolution 576.8
Wood, A. J. Charles Darwin and the Beagle adventure 508

Evolution. Gamlin, L. 576.8

Evolution. 576.8

Evolution. Fleisher, P. 576.8

EVOLUTION (BIOLOGY)
Heiligman, D. Charles and Emma 92
Johnson, S. A. Shaking the foundation 576.8
Silverstein, A. Adaptation 578.4
Wood, A. J. Charles Darwin and the Beagle adventure 508

EVOLUTION -- FICTION
Card, O. S. Ruins Fic

EVOLUTION
Fleisher, P. Evolution 576.8

EVOLUTION -- STUDY AND TEACHING
Burgan, M. The Scopes trial 345

The **exchange** student. Gilmore, K.   **Fic**

EXCRETION
  Klosterman, L. Excretory system   **612.4**
Excretory system. Klosterman, L.   **612.4**
EXCUSES
  See also Etiquette; Manners and customs
EXECUTIONS AND EXECUTIONERS
  See also Criminal law; Criminal procedure
EXECUTIVE POWER
  See also Constitutional law; Political science
EXECUTIVES
  Gitlin, M. eBay   **338.7**
Exercise. Dicker, K.   **613.7**
EXERCISE
  Dicker, K. Exercise   **613.7**
  Frederick, S. Strength training for teen athletes   **613.7**
  Gardner, R. Ace your exercise and nutrition science project: great science fair ideas   **613**
  Gedatus, G. Exercise for weight management **613.7**
  Mason, P. Improving endurance   **613.7**
  Mason, P. Improving flexibility   **613.7**
  Mason, P. Improving speed   **613.7**
  Mason, P. Improving strength & power   **613.7**
  Nagle, J. Frequently asked questions about Wii and video game injuries and fitness   **617.1**
  Vedral, J. L. Toning for teens   **613.7**
EXERCISE
  See also Health; Hygiene
Exercise addiction. Currie-McGhee, L. K.   **616.85**
EXERCISE ADDICTION
  Currie-McGhee, L. K. Exercise addiction   **616.85**
Exercise for weight management. Gedatus, G. **613.7**
Exile. Osterlund, A.   **Fic**
The **exiled** queen. Chima, C. W.   **Fic**
EXILES
  Marchetta, M. Froi of the exiles   **Fic**
EXILES
  See also Persons; Political refugees
EXILES -- FICTION
  Cooper, M. The FitzOsbornes at war   **Fic**
EXOBIOLOGY
  Turner, P. S. Life on earth--and beyond   **576.8**
Exodus. Bertagna, J.   **Fic**
EXORCISM
  See also Supernatural
Expectations for women. Mills, J. E.   **305.4**
The **Expeditioners** and the Treasure of Drowned Man's Canyon. Taylor, S. S.   **Fic**
EXPEDITIONS, SCIENTIFIC *See* Scientific expeditions
Experiencing the American Civil War. Hillstrom, K.   **973.7**
Experiment with science [series]
  Just add water   **546**
EXPERIMENTAL FILMS

  See also Motion pictures
EXPERIMENTAL SCHOOLS
  See also Education -- Experimental methods; Schools
EXPERIMENTAL THEATER
  See also Theater
EXPERIMENTATION ON ANIMALS *See* Animal experimentation
EXPERIMENTATION ON HUMANS, MEDICAL *See* Human experimentation in medicine
Experimenting with chemistry. Farndon, J.   **540**
Experimenting with everyday science [series]
  Tomecek, S. Art & architecture   **701**
  Tomecek, S. Music   **781.2**
  Tomecek, S. Tools and machines   **621.9**
Experimenting with physics. Farndon, J.   **530**
Experimenting with science [series]
  Farndon, J. Experimenting with chemistry   **540**
  Farndon, J. Experimenting with physics   **530**
  Meiani, A. Air   **533**
  Meiani, A. Light   **535**
  Meiani, A. Magnetism   **538**
  Meiani, A. Water   **532**
EXPERIMENTS
  Farndon, J. Time   **529**
EXPERIMENTS -- FICTION
  Gagnon, M. Don't turn around   **Fic**
Experiments with electricity and magnetism. Woodford, C.   **537**
EXPERT SYSTEMS (COMPUTER SCIENCE)
  See also Artificial intelligence; Data processing; Information systems
Explaining [series]
  Ballard, C. Explaining food allergies   **616.97**
  Bender, L. Explaining blindness   **617.7**
  Bender, L. Explaining epilepsy   **616.8**
  Levete, S. Explaining cerebral palsy   **616.8**
  Levete, S. Explaining deafness   **617.8**
  Loughrey, A. Explaining diabetes   **616.4**
  Powell, J. Explaining cystic fibrosis   **616.3**
  Royston, A. Explaining asthma   **616.2**
  Royston, A. Explaining down syndrome   **616.85**
  Snedden, R. Explaining autism   **616.85**
Explaining asthma. Royston, A.   **616.2**
Explaining autism. Snedden, R.   **616.85**
Explaining blindness. Bender, L.   **617.7**
Explaining cerebral palsy. Levete, S.   **616.8**
Explaining cystic fibrosis. Powell, J.   **616.3**
Explaining deafness. Levete, S.   **617.8**
Explaining diabetes. Loughrey, A.   **616.4**
Explaining down syndrome. Royston, A.   **616.85**
Explaining epilepsy. Bender, L.   **616.8**
Explaining food allergies. Ballard, C.   **616.97**
Exploding ants. Settel, J.   **591.5**
EXPLORATION
  Aronson, M. The world made new   **910.4**

EXPLORERS

See also Adventure and adventurers; Heroes and heroines

EXPLORERS -- AFRICA, SOUTHERN -- BIOGRAPHY

Bodden, V. To the heart of Africa   **916.704**

EXPLORERS -- AMERICA -- BIOGRAPHY

Berne, E. C. Christopher Columbus   **970.01**

Demi Columbus   **970.01**

Edwards, J. Henry Hudson and his voyages of exploration in world history   **970.01**

Gaines, A. Hernando de Soto and the Spanish search for gold in world history   **970.01**

EXPLORERS -- BIOGRAPHY

Bodden, V. To the ocean deep   **551.46**

EXPLORERS -- FICTION

Sailing the unknown   **Fic**

EXPLORERS -- FRANCE -- BIOGRAPHY

Goodman, J. E. Despite all obstacles: La Salle and the conquest of the Mississippi   **92**

EXPLORERS -- GREAT BRITAIN -- BIOGRAPHY

Aronson, M. Sir Walter Ralegh and the quest for El Dorado   **942.05**

Edwards, J. Henry Hudson and his voyages of exploration in world history   **970.01**

Johnson, R. L. Ernest Shackleton   **92**

EXPLORERS

Fritz, J. Around the world in a hundred years **910.92**

Into the unknown   **910.4**

EXPLORERS -- MISSISSIPPI RIVER -- BIOGRAPHY

Goodman, J. E. Despite all obstacles: La Salle and the conquest of the Mississippi   **92**

EXPLORERS -- NORWAY -- BIOGRAPHY

Bodden, V. To the South Pole   **919.8**

EXPLORERS -- POETRY

Katz, B. Trailblazers   **811**

EXPLORERS -- POLAR REGIONS -- BIOGRAPHY

Nardo, D. Polar explorations   **910.911**

EXPLORERS -- PORTUGAL -- BIOGRAPHY

Calvert, P. Vasco da Gama   **92**

Goodman, J. E. A long and uncertain journey: the 27,000 mile voyage of Vasco da Gama   **910**

EXPLORERS -- SCOTLAND -- BIOGRAPHY

Bodden, V. To the heart of Africa   **916.704**

EXPLORERS -- SPAIN -- BIOGRAPHY

Berne, E. C. Christopher Columbus   **970.01**

Demi Columbus   **970.01**

Gaines, A. Hernando de Soto and the Spanish search for gold in world history   **970.01**

EXPLORERS -- WEST (U.S.) -- BIOGRAPHY

Green, C. R. Zebulon Pike   **978**

Hirschfelder, A. B. Photo odyssey: Solomon Carvalho's remarkable Western adventure, 1853-

54   **917**

EXPLORERS -- WEST (U.S.) -- DIARIES

Stille, D. R. The journals of Lewis and Clark   **917.804**

Explorers of new worlds [series]

Brennan, K. Sir Edmund Hillary, modern day explorer   **796.52**

Explorers of the New World. Mooney, C.   **970.01**

Explorers, trappers, and pioneers. Todras, E. H. **911**

Exploring American history: from colonial times to 1877.   **973**

Exploring Canada [series]

Ferry, S. Ontario   **971**

Ferry, S. Quebec   **971**

Ferry, S. Yukon Territory   **971**

Laws, G. D. Alberta   **971**

Laws, G. D. Manitoba   **971**

Laws, G. D. The Maritime Provinces   **971.5**

Laws, G. D. The Northwest Territories   **971**

Mayell, M. Newfoundland   **971**

Mayell, M. Saskatchewan   **971**

Palana, B. J. British Columbia   **971**

Exploring cultural history [series]

Living in Nazi Germany   **943.086**

Exploring ecosystems [series]

Martin, P. A. F. Prairies, fields, and meadows **577.4**

Exploring forces and motion. Solway, A.   **531**

Exploring immigration. Ollhoff, J.   **304.8**

Exploring mammals.   **599**

Exploring science [series]

Nardo, D. Force and motion   **531**

Stille, D. R. Erosion   **551.3**

Stille, D. R. The greenhouse effect   **363.7**

Stille, D. R. Manipulating light   **535**

Stille, D. R. Plate tectonics   **551.1**

Stille, D. R. Waves   **531**

Exploring science and medical discoveries [series]

Evolution   **576.8**

Exploring science: physical science [series]

Dreier, D. L. Electrical circuits   **537**

Solway, A. Exploring forces and motion   **531**

Exploring space. Carlisle, R. P.   **629.4**

Exploring the ancient world [series]

Rosinsky, N. M. Ancient China   **931**

Exploring the life, myth, and art of ancient Greece. Stafford, E. J.   **938**

Exploring the life, myth, and art of ancient China. Shaughnessy, E. L.   **931**

Exploring the life, myth, and art of ancient Egypt. Fletcher, J.   **932**

Exploring the life, myth, and art of ancient Rome. Allan, T.   **937**

Exploring the life, myth, and art of India. Ram-Prasad, C.   **954**

Exploring the life, myth, and art of Native Americans. Zimmerman, L. J.   **970.004**

EXTRATERRESTRIAL BEINGS
Allman, T. Are extraterrestrials a threat to mankind? **001.9**
Nardo, D. Martians **001.9**
EXTRATERRESTRIAL BEINGS
See also Life on other planets
EXTRATERRESTRIAL BEINGS -- FICTION
Palma, F. J. The map of the sky **Fic**
EXTRATERRESTRIAL BEINGS -- GRAPHIC NOVELS
Bad Island **Fic**
EXTRATERRESTRIAL BEINGS
Brake, M. Alien Hunter's Handbook **576.8**
EXTRATERRESTRIAL LIFE *See* Life on other planets
Extraterrestrial life [series]
Allman, T. Are extraterrestrials a threat to mankind? **001.9**
EXTRAVEHICULAR ACTIVITY (SPACE FLIGHT)
See also Space flight
Extreme animals. Davies, N. **590**
Extreme biology. **570**
The extreme Earth [series]
Aleshire, P. Deserts **551.4**
Aleshire, P. Mountains **551.4**
Aleshire, P. Ocean ridges and trenches **551.46**
Burnham, L. Rivers **551.48**
Carrigan, P. Waterfalls **551.48**
Hanson, E. A. Canyons **551.4**
Hanson, J. K. Caves **551.4**
Hanson, J. K. Lakes **551.48**
EXTREME ENVIRONMENTS
Davies, N. Extreme animals **590**
Extreme face painting. Wolfe, B. **745.5**
Extreme rocks & minerals! Smithsonian Institution **552**
Extreme scientists. Jackson, D. M. **509**
EXTREME SPORTS
Hile, L. Surviving extreme sports **796**
EXTREME SPORTS
See also Sports
Extreme survival [series]
Hile, L. Animal survival **591.5**
Hile, L. Surviving extreme sports **796**
Hurley, M. Surviving the wilderness **613.6**
Extreme teens. Anderson, S. B. **027.62**
Extreme threats [series]
Cunningham, K. Wildfires **363.3**
Nardo, D. Asteroids and comets **523.4**
Nardo, D. Climate change **551.6**
Nardo, D. Volcanoes **551.2**
Extreme weather. Streissguth, T. **551.5**
Extreme weather. Simpson, K. **551.6**
EXTREME WEATHER
Evans, B. It's raining fish and spiders **551.6**

EXTREMISM (POLITICAL SCIENCE) *See* Radicalism
EYE
Larsen, C. S. Crust and spray **612.8**
Markle, S. Lost sight **617.7**
Simon, S. Eyes and ears **612.8**
EYE -- FICTION
Auxier, J. Peter Nimble and his fantastic eyes **Fic**
EYE
Simon, S. Eyes and ears **612.8**
Eye of the crow. Peacock, S. **Fic**
The **eye** of the whale. O'Connell, J. **599.5**
Eye on art [series]
Emert, P. R. Art in glass **748.2**
Kallen, S. A. Claude Monet **92**
Kallen, S. A. Pablo Picasso **92**
Kallen, S. A. Photography **770**
Macfarlane, K. The jeweler's art **739.27**
Uschan, M. V. Graffiti **751.7**
Yancey, D. Art deco **709.04**
Eye on the universe. Cole, M. D. **522**
The **Eyeball** Collector. Higgins, F. E. **Fic**
Eyes and ears. Simon, S. **612.8**
Eyes like stars. Mantchev, L. **Fic**
Eyes of the emperor. Salisbury, G. **Fic**
Eyes on the prize: America's civil rights years, 1954-1965. Williams, J. **323.1**
Eyewitness books [series]
Steele, P. Vote **324**
Eyewitness companions [series]
Ridsdale, C. Trees **582.16**
Eyewitness disaster [series]
Dwyer, H. Earthquakes! **551.2**
Dwyer, H. Floods! **551.48**
Dwyer, H. Tsunamis! **551.46**
Royston, A. Hurricanes! **551.55**
Royston, A. Storms! **551.55**
Eyewitness history [series]
Burg, D. F. The Great Depression **973.91**
Carlisle, R. P. Civil War and Reconstruction **973.7**
Carlisle, R. P. World War I **940.3**
Wexler, S. The civil rights movement **323.1**

F

F. Scott Fitzgerald. Lazo, C. E. **813**
F. W. Prep [series]
Nobleman, M. T. Extraordinary e-mails, letters, and resumes **808**
Otfinoski, S. Extraordinary short story writing **808.3**
Orr, T. Extraordinary essays **808.4**
Ryan, M. Extraordinary oral presentations **808.5**
Faber, Harold
The airplane **629.133**
FABLES
Oz, A. Suddenly in the depths of the forest **Fic**

Levine, K. The lions of Little Rock   **Fic**

FAMILY LIFE -- CALIFORNIA -- FICTION

Blundell, J. A city tossed and broken   **Fic**

Leavitt, L. Going vintage   **Fic**

Zarr, S. The Lucy variations   **Fic**

FAMILY LIFE -- CANADA -- FICTION

Hopkinson, N. The Chaos   **Fic**

FAMILY LIFE -- COLORADO -- FICTION

Mobley, J. Katerina's wish   **Fic**

FAMILY LIFE -- CONNECTICUT -- FICTION

Hunt, L. M. One for the Murphys   **Fic**

FAMILY LIFE -- ENGLAND -- FICTION

Cooper, M. The FitzOsbornes at war   **Fic**

Lancaster, M. A. The future we left behind   **Fic**

Terry, T. Slated   **Fic**

FAMILY LIFE -- ENGLAND -- LONDON -- FICTION

Farrant, N. After Iris   **Fic**

Ibbotson, E. One dog and his boy   **Fic**

Sapphire blue   **Fic**

FAMILY LIFE -- FICTION

Andrews, J. Me & Earl & the dying girl   **Fic**

Chen, J. Return to me   **Fic**

Cooney, C. B. Janie face to face   **Fic**

Doyle, R. A greyhound of a girl   **Fic**

Gleitzman, M. Now   **Fic**

Klise, K. Homesick   **Fic**

MacLachlan, P. Kindred souls   **Fic**

FAMILY LIFE -- GRAPHIC NOVELS

Bad Island   **Fic**

FAMILY LIFE -- ILLINOIS -- CHICAGO -- FICTION

Balliett, B. Hold fast   **Fic**

Pauley, K. Cat Girl's day off   **Fic**

FAMILY LIFE -- ILLINOIS -- FICTION

Clifton, L. Freaky Fast Frankie Joe   **Fic**

Stone, T. I. Time between us   **Fic**

FAMILY LIFE -- INDIA -- FICTION

Whelan, G. All my noble dreams and then what happens   **Fic**

FAMILY LIFE -- ITALY -- FICTION

Beyer, K. The demon catchers of Milan   **Fic**

FAMILY LIFE -- FICTION

Pennypacker, S. The summer of the gypsy moths   **Fic**

Yolen, J. Curse of the Thirteenth Fey   **Fic**

FAMILY LIFE -- LOUISIANA -- FICTION

Elston, A. The rules for disappearing   **Fic**

FAMILY LIFE -- MAINE -- FICTION

Martin, A. M. Better to wish   **Fic**

Stone, P. Romeo blue   **Fic**

FAMILY LIFE -- MASSACHUSETTS -- BOSTON -- FICTION

Frazier, A. The mastermind plot   **Fic**

FAMILY LIFE -- MASSACHUSETTS -- FICTION

Thompson, H. The language inside   **Fic**

FAMILY LIFE -- MINNESOTA -- FICTION

Rubens, M. Sons of the 613   **Fic**

FAMILY LIFE -- NEW JERSEY -- FICTION

Scott, K. This is so not happening   **Fic**

FAMILY LIFE -- NEW MEXICO -- FICTION

Bell, J. Kepler's dream   **Fic**

FAMILY LIFE -- NEW YORK (STATE) -- FICTION

Johnson, J. J. The theory of everything   **Fic**

Moore, C. The stalker chronicles   **Fic**

FAMILY LIFE -- NEW YORK (STATE) -- HARLEM -- FICTION

Manzano, S. The revolution of Evelyn Serrano   **Fic**

FAMILY LIFE -- NEW YORK (STATE) -- NEW YORK -- FICTION

Matti, T. Mister Orange   **Fic**

Stead, R. Liar & spy   **Fic**

Zevin, G. Because it is my blood   **Fic**

FAMILY LIFE -- NEW YORK -- FICTION

Graff, L. A tangle of knots   **Fic**

FAMILY LIFE -- PENNSYLVANIA -- FICTION

Andrews, J. Me & Earl & the dying girl   **Fic**

FAMILY LIFE -- PENNSYLVANIA -- HERSHEY -- FICTION

Finneyfrock, K. The sweet revenge of Celia Door   **Fic**

FAMILY LIFE -- RHODE ISLAND -- FICTION

Gray, C. Spellcaster   **Fic**

FAMILY LIFE -- RUSSIA -- FICTION

O'Brien, A. Lara's gift   **Fic**

FAMILY LIFE -- TENNESSEE -- FICTION

Vawter, V. Paperboy   **Fic**

FAMILY LIFE -- TEXAS -- FICTION

Lopez, D. Ask my mood ring how I feel   **Fic**

FAMILY LIFE -- VERMONT -- FICTION

Paterson, K. Preacher's boy   **Fic**

FAMILY LIFE -- WASHINGTON (STATE) -- SEATTLE -- FICTION

Trueman, T. Life happens next   **Fic**

Family matters. Meese, R. L.   **011.6**

FAMILY MEDICINE

   See also Medicine

A **family** of readers. Sutton, R.   **809**

FAMILY PLANNING *See* Birth control

FAMILY PLANNING ADVOCATES

Bausum, A. Denied, detained, deported   **325**

FAMILY PROBLEMS -- FICTION

Armistead, C. Being Henry David   **Fic**

Black, H. Doll bones   **Fic**

Burgis, S. Stolen magic   **Fic**

Castan, M. Fighting for Dontae   **Fic**

Chen, J. Return to me   **Fic**

Cremer, A. Invisibility   **Fic**

Golden, L. Every day after   **Fic**

Harrington, K. Sure signs of crazy   **Fic**

Angus, J. In search of Goliathus hercules	**Fic**	Bunce, E. C. Liar's moon	**Fic**
Appelbaum, S. The Hollow Bettle	**Fic**	Bunce, E. C. Star crossed	**Fic**
Appelbaum, S. The Shepherd of Weeds	**Fic**	Burtenshaw, J. Shadowcry	**Fic**
Appelbaum, S. The Tasters Guild	**Fic**	Carey, J. L. The beast of Noor	**Fic**
Arbuthnott, G. The Keepers' tattoo	**Fic**	Carey, J. L. Dragon's Keep	**Fic**
Archer, E. Geek: fantasy novel	**Fic**	Carey, J. L. Dragons of Noor	**Fic**
Arntson, S. The wrap-up list	**Fic**	Carey, J. L. Dragonswood	**Fic**
Ashby, A. Fairy bad day	**Fic**	Carey, J. L. Stealing death	**Fic**
Ashton, B. Everneath	**Fic**	Carman, P. Beyond the Valley of Thorns	**Fic**
Atwater-Rhodes, A. Snakecharm	**Fic**	Carman, P. The Dark Hills divide	**Fic**
Bardugo, L. Shadow and bone	**Fic**	Carman, P. Into the mist	**Fic**
Bardugo, L. Siege and storm	**Fic**	Carman, P. Stargazer	**Fic**
Barron, T. A. The book of magic	**Fic**	Carman, P. The tenth city	**Fic**
Barron, T. A. Doomraga's revenge	**Fic**	Carson, R. The bitter kingdom	**Fic**
Barron, T. A. The fires of Merlin	**Fic**	Carson, R. The girl of fire and thorns	**Fic**
Barron, T. A. The lost years of Merlin	**Fic**	Cashore, K. Fire	**Fic**
Barron, T. A. Merlin's dragon	**Fic**	Cashore, K. Graceling	**Fic**
Barron, T. A. The mirror of Merlin	**Fic**	Catanese, P. W. Dragon games	**Fic**
Barron, T. A. The seven songs of Merlin	**Fic**	Catanese, P. W. Happenstance found	**Fic**
Barron, T. A. Ultimate magic	**Fic**	Caveney, P. Sebastian Darke: Prince of Fools	**Fic**
Barron, T. A. The wings of Merlin	**Fic**	Ceccarelli, D. The Yawning Rabbit River Chroni-	
Baucom, I. Through the skylight	**Fic**	cle	**Fic**
Bell, H. Crown of earth	**Fic**	Chabon, M. Summerland	**Fic**
Bell, H. Fall of a kingdom	**Fic**	Chima, C. W. The Crimson Crown	**Fic**
Bell, H. Forging the sword	**Fic**	Chima, C. W. The Demon King	**Fic**
Bell, H. The Goblin Gate	**Fic**	Chima, C. W. The dragon heir	**Fic**
Bell, H. The Goblin War	**Fic**	Chima, C. W. The exiled queen	**Fic**
Bell, H. The Goblin Wood	**Fic**	Chima, C. W. The Gray Wolf Throne	**Fic**
Bell, H. The last knight	**Fic**	Chima, C. W. The warrior heir	**Fic**
Bell, H. Player's ruse	**Fic**	Chima, C. W. The wizard heir	**Fic**
Bell, H. Rise of a hero	**Fic**	Choldenko, G. No passengers beyond this point	**Fic**
Bell, H. Rogue's home	**Fic**	Clare, C. Clockwork princess	**Fic**
Bell, H. Shield of stars	**Fic**	Coakley, L. Witchlanders	**Fic**
Bell, H. Sword of waters	**Fic**	Colfer, E. Artemis Fowl	**Fic**
Bell, H. Trickster's girl	**Fic**	Colfer, E. Artemis Fowl: the Arctic incident	**Fic**
Bell, T. Nick of time	**Fic**	Colfer, E. Artemis Fowl: The Atlantis complex	**Fic**
Bemis, J. C. The nine pound hammer	**Fic**	Colfer, E. Artemis Fowl: the Eternity code	**Fic**
Bemis, J. C. The White City	**Fic**	Colfer, E. Artemis Fowl: the lost colony	**Fic**
Bemis, J. C. The Wolf Tree	**Fic**	Colfer, E. Artemis Fowl: The opal deception	**Fic**
Bennett, H. Shapeshifter	**Fic**	Collins, S. Gregor and the Code of Claw	**Fic**
Berk, A. Death watch	**Fic**	Collins, S. Gregor and the curse of the warm-	
Bernobich, B. Fox & Phoenix	**Fic**	bloods	**Fic**
Berry, J. The Amaranth enchantment	**Fic**	Collins, S. Gregor and the marks of secret	**Fic**
Billingsley, F. The Folk Keeper	**Fic**	Collins, S. Gregor and the prophecy of Bane	**Fic**
Binding, T. Sylvie and the songman	**Fic**	Collins, S. Gregor the Overlander	**Fic**
Blackwood, S. Jinx	**Fic**	Condie, A. B. Crossed	**Fic**
Booraem, E. Small persons with wings	**Fic**	Condie, A. B. Matched	**Fic**
Booraem, E. The unnameables	**Fic**	Constable, K. The singer of all songs	**Fic**
Boos, B. Fantasy: an artist's realm	**Fic**	Constable, K. The tenth power	**Fic**
Bow, E. Plain Kate	**Fic**	Constable, K. The waterless sea	**Fic**
Bradbury, R. The Halloween tree	**Fic**	Cooper, S. The dark is rising	**Fic**
Bradbury, R. Something wicked this way comes	**Fic**	Cooper, S. Greenwitch	**Fic**
Breen, M. E. Darkwood	**Fic**	Cooper, S. The grey king	**Fic**
Brennan, C. House of the star	**Fic**	Cooper, S. Over sea, under stone	**Fic**
Brooks, L. Selkie girl	**Fic**	Cooper, S. Silver on the tree	**Fic**
Bullen, A. Wish	**Fic**	Cornish, D. M. Factotum	**Fic**

Hunter, E. Into the wild — Fic
Hunter, E. Rising storm — Fic
Hunter, E. The sight — Fic
Jacques, B. The Bellmaker — Fic
Jacques, B. Mariel of Redwall — Fic
Jacques, B. Martin the Warrior — Fic
Jacques, B. Mossflower — Fic
Jacques, B. Pearls of Lutra — Fic
Jacques, B. Redwall — Fic
Jacques, B. Salamandastron — Fic
Jeschonek, R. T. My favorite band does not exist — Fic
Jobling, C. The rise of the wolf — Fic
Jones, D. W. Howl's moving castle — Fic
Jones, D. W. House of many ways — Fic
Jones, D. W. The tough guide to Fantasyland — 828
Kessler, J. Loss — Fic
The key of Braha — Fic
Kilworth, G. Attica — Fic
King, C. Seven sorcerers — Fic
Kirby, M. J. The clockwork three — Fic
Kirby, M. J. Icefall — Fic
Kittredge, C. The Iron Thorn — Fic
Kittredge, C. The nightmare garden — Fic
Knox, E. Dreamhunter — Fic
Knox, E. Dreamquake — Fic
Knox, E. Mortal fire — Fic
Knudsen, M. The dragon of Trelian — Fic
Kostick, C. Epic — Fic
Kostick, C. Saga — Fic
Landy, D. The Faceless Ones — Fic
Landy, D. Playing with fire — Fic
Landy, D. Skulduggery Pleasant — Fic
Langrish, K. The shadow hunt — Fic
Lasky, K. Frost wolf — Fic
Lasky, K. Lone wolf — Fic
Lasky, K. Shadow wolf — Fic
Lasky, K. Watch wolf — Fic
Le Guin, U. K. The farthest shore — Fic
Le Guin, U. K. Gifts — Fic
Le Guin, U. K. Powers — Fic
Le Guin, U. K. Tales from Earthsea — S C
Le Guin, U. K. Tehanu — Fic
Le Guin, U. K. The Tombs of Atuan — Fic
Le Guin, U. K. Voices — Fic
Le Guin, U. K. A wizard of Earthsea — Fic
L'Engle, M. A swiftly tilting planet — Fic
L'Engle, M. A wind in the door — Fic
L'Engle, M. A wrinkle in time — Fic
Levine, G. C. A tale of Two Castles — Fic
Levine, G. C. Ella enchanted — Fic
Lewis, C. S. The horse and his boy — Fic
Lewis, C. S. The last battle — Fic
Lewis, C. S. The lion, the witch, and the wardrobe — Fic
Lewis, C. S. The magician's nephew — Fic

Lewis, C. S. Prince Caspian — Fic
Lewis, C. S. The silver chair — Fic
Lewis, C. S. The voyage of the Dawn Treader — Fic
Lisle, H. The Ruby Key — Fic
Lisle, H. The silver door — Fic
Llewellyn, S. Darksolstice — Fic
Llewellyn, S. The well between the worlds — Fic
Long, R. F. The treachery of beautiful things — Fic
MacHale, D. J. Black water — Fic
MacHale, D. J. The lost city of Faar — Fic
MacHale, D. J. The merchant of death — Fic
MacHale, D. J. The never war — Fic
MacHale, D. J. The pilgrims of Rayne — Fic
MacHale, D. J. The Quillan games — Fic
MacHale, D. J. Raven rise — Fic
MacHale, D. J. The reality bug — Fic
MacHale, D. J. The Rivers of Zadaa — Fic
MacHale, D. J. The soldiers of Halla — Fic
Magic in the mirrorstone — S C
The magic thief — Fic
Mahy, M. Maddigan's Fantasia — Fic
Mahy, M. The Magician of Hoad — Fic
Malchow, A. The Sword of Darrow — Fic
Marchetta, M. Finnikin of the rock — Fic
Marchetta, M. Froi of the exiles — Fic
Marchetta, M. Quintana of Charyn — Fic
Marillier, J. Shadowfell — Fic
Marr, M. Darkest mercy — Fic
Marr, M. Fragile eternity — Fic
Marr, M. Ink exchange — Fic
Marr, M. Radiant shadows — Fic
Marr, M. Wicked lovely — Fic
Marriott, Z. The swan kingdom — Fic
The mask wearer — Fic
Masson, S. Snow, fire, sword — Fic
McCaffrey, A. Dragonflight — Fic
McCaffrey, A. Dragon's fire — Fic
McGraw, E. J. The moorchild — Fic
McKinley, R. The blue sword — Fic
McKinley, R. Chalice — Fic
McKinley, R. Dragonhaven — Fic
McKinley, R. The hero and the crown — Fic
McKinley, R. Pegasus — Fic
McKinley, R. Water: tales of elemental spirits — S C
McNamee, E. City of Time — Fic
McNamee, E. The Frost Child — Fic
McNamee, E. The Navigator — Fic
McNaughton, J. An earthly knight — Fic
McNeal, T. Far far away — Fic
McNish, C. The silver child — Fic
McNish, C. Silver City — Fic
McNish, C. Silver world — Fic
McQuerry, M. D. The Peculiars — Fic
Mebus, S. Gods of Manhattan — Fic
Mebus, S. The sorcerer's secret — Fic
Mebus, S. Spirits in the park — Fic

Sage, A. Flyte	Fic
Sage, A. Magyk	Fic
Sage, A. The Magykal papers	Fic
Sage, A. Physik	Fic
Sage, A. Queste	Fic
Sage, A. Syren	Fic
Saint-Exupery, A. d. The little prince	Fic
Sanderson, B. Alcatraz versus the evil Librarians	Fic
Sanderson, B. Alcatraz versus the Knights of Crystallia	Fic
Sanderson, B. Alcatraz versus the Scrivener's Bones	Fic
Sanderson, B. Alcatraz versus the shattered lens	Fic
Sapphire blue	Fic
Selfors, S. The sweetest spell	Fic
Sensel, J. The Farwalker's quest	Fic
Sensel, J. The timekeeper's moon	Fic
Service, P. F. Tomorrow's magic	Fic
Service, P. F. Yesterday's magic	Fic
Sherman, D. Changeling	Fic
Sherman, D. The Magic Mirror of the Mermaid Queen	Fic
Shulman, P. The Grimm Legacy	Fic
Simner, J. L. Bones of Faerie	Fic
Simner, J. L. Faerie after	Fic
Simner, J. L. Thief eyes	Fic
Singleton, L. J. Dead girl dancing	Fic
Singleton, L. J. Dead girl in love	Fic
Sniegoski, T. Quest for the spark	Fic
Snow, A. Here be monsters!	Fic
Spinelli, J. Hokey Pokey	Fic
Stanley, D. The cup and the crown	Fic
Stanley, D. The silver bowl	Fic
Steampunk!	S C
Steer, D. The dragon diary	Fic
Stephens, J. The fire chronicle	Fic
Stewart, A. Dragonwood	Fic
Stiefvater, M. The Scorpio Races	Fic
Stoffels, K. Heartsinger	Fic
Stroud, J. The Amulet of Samarkand	Fic
Stroud, J. The golem's eye	Fic
Stroud, J. Ptolemy's gate	Fic
Stroud, J. The ring of Solomon	Fic
Sullivan, L. L. Guardian of the Green Hill	Fic
Sullivan, L. L. Under the green hill	Fic
Sun, A. Ink	Fic
Swift, J. Gulliver's travels	Fic
Tanner, L. City of lies	Fic
Tanner, L. Museum of thieves	Fic
Taylor, L. Blackbringer	Fic
Taylor, L. Daughter of smoke and bone	Fic
Taylor, L. Silksinger	Fic
Thompson, K. The last of the High Kings	Fic
Thompson, K. The new policeman	Fic
Thompson, K. The white horse trick	Fic

Thomson, J. Dark Lord, the early years	Fic
Tolkien, J. R. R. The hobbit, or, There and back again	Fic
Tolkien, J. R. R. The lord of the rings	Fic
Tomlinson, H. Aurelie	Fic
Uehashi, N. Moribito II	Fic
Under Wildwood	Fic
Unnatural creatures	S C
Vaughn, C. Voices of dragons	Fic
Wagner, H. Nightshade City	Fic
Wagner, H. The white assassin	Fic
Walsh, P. The Crowfield demon	Fic
The watcher in the shadows	Fic
Welcome to Bordertown	808
Welsh, M. L. Mistress of the Storm	Fic
Werlin, N. Extraordinary	Fic
Wharton, T. The shadow of Malabron	Fic
White, T. H. The once and future king	Fic
Whitley, D. The children of the lost	Fic
Wildwood	Fic
Wilks, M. Mirrorscape	Fic
Williamson, J. By darkness hid	Fic
Williamson, J. To darkness fled	Fic
Willingham, B. Down the Mysterly River	Fic
Wilson, N. D. The dragon's tooth	Fic
Wood, M. L. Captured	Fic
Wood, M. L. The darkening	Fic
Wooding, C. Poison	Fic
Wrede, P. C. The thirteenth child	Fic
Yep, L. City of fire	Fic
Yep, L. City of ice	Fic
Yolen, J. Briar Rose	Fic
Yolen, J. Dragon's blood	Fic
Yolen, J. Dragon's heart	Fic
Yolen, J. Heart's blood	Fic
Yolen, J. Hobby	813
Yolen, J. Merlin	Fic
Yolen, J. Passager	813
Yolen, J. Pay the piper	Fic
Yolen, J. A sending of dragons	Fic

FANTASY FICTION -- AUTHORSHIP

Jones, D. W. Reflections	823

FANTASY FICTION -- BIBLIOGRAPHY

Fichtelberg, S. Encountering enchantment	016

FANTASY FICTION -- HISTORY AND CRITICISM

Colbert, D. The magical worlds of Harry Potter	823
The wand in the word	813

FANTASY FICTION -- FICTION

Almond, D. Mouse bird snake wolf	Fic
Anderson, J. L. May Bird and The Ever After	
Booraem, E. Texting the underworld	Fic
Brennan, S. R. Unspoken	Fic
Bridges, R. The gathering storm	Fic
Cameron, S. The dark unwinding	Fic
Carroll, M. Quantum prophecy	

FARM LIFE
Rosen, M. J. Our farm   630
FARM LIFE -- KANSAS -- FICTION
Kadohata, C. The thing about luck   Fic
FARM LIFE -- MISCELLANEA
Rothman, J. Farm anatomy   630
FARM LIFE -- PICTORIAL WORKS
Rothman, J. Farm anatomy   630
FARM LIFE -- UNITED STATES
Rosen, M. J. Our farm   630
FARM LIFE -- VERMONT -- FICTION
Kinsey-Warnock, N. True colors   Fic
FARM MANAGEMENT
See also Farms; Management
FARM PRODUCE
Rothman, J. Farm anatomy   630
FARM PRODUCE
See also Food; Raw materials
FARM PRODUCE -- MARKETING
See also Marketing; Prices
FARM TENANCY
See also Farms; Land tenure
Farmer, Lesley S. Johnson
Collaborating with administrators and educational support staff   027.8
Neal-Schuman technology management handbook for school library media centers   025.1
Farmer, Nancy
The lord of Opium   Fic
Farmer, Nancy
The Ear, the Eye, and the Arm   Fic
A girl named Disaster   Fic
The house of the scorpion   Fic
The Islands of the Blessed   Fic
The Land of the Silver Apples   Fic
The Sea of Trolls   Fic
Farmer, Paul, 1959-
Kidder, T. Mountains beyond mountains   92
FARMERS
Collier, C. Indians, cowboys, and farmers and the battle for the Great Plains, 1865-1910   978
Nelson, M. The freedom business   811
Philbrick, N. The Mayflower and the Pilgrims' New World   973.2
FARMERS
See also Agriculture
Farming. Martin, C.   636
FARMING *See* Agriculture
Farming for the future. Bailey, G.   630
FARMING, ORGANIC *See* Organic farming
FARMS
Parker, S. Food and farming   630
Rothman, J. Farm anatomy   630
FARMS
See also Land use; Real estate
FARMS -- FICTION

Selfors, S. Fortune's magic farm   Fic
Williams, T. The dragons of Ordinary Farm   Fic
FARMS
Rosen, M. J. Our farm   630
Farndon, John
Aluminum   546
Do not open   031.02
Experimenting with chemistry   540
Experimenting with physics   530
Oxygen   546
Time   529
Farquhar, Jackie
(ed) Try this at home   333.72
Farr, James
eV: vol. 1   741.5
Farr, Richard
Emperors of the ice   Fic
Farrand, John
Bull, J. L. The National Audubon Society field guide to North American birds, Eastern region   598
Udvardy, M. D. F. National Audubon Society field guide to North American birds, Western region   598
Farrant, Natasha
After Iris   Fic
Farrar, Amy
ADHD   616.85
Farrar, Josh
Rules to rock by   Fic
Farrell, Courtney
Build it green   720
Children's rights   305.23
Green jobs   331.7
The Gulf of Mexico oil spill   363.7
Mental disorders   362.1
Plants out of place   581.6
Terror at the Munich Olympics   796.48
Farrell, Jeanette
Invisible enemies   614.4
Farrell, Tish
Write your own fantasy story   808.3
Write your own mystery story   808.3
Write your own science fiction story   808.3
Farrey, Brian
The Vengekeep prophecies   Fic
Farsala trilogy [series]
Bell, H. Forging the sword   Fic
Bell, H. Rise of a hero   Fic
The **farthest** shore. Le Guin, U. K.   Fic
The **Farwalker's** quest. Sensel, J.   Fic
Faryon, Cynthia J.
Guilty of being weird   364.152
The **fascinating** history of American Indians. McNeese, T.   970.004
FASCISM
See also Totalitarianism

MacHale, D. J. The soldiers of Halla   **Fic**

McCaughrean, G. The death-defying Pepper Roux   **Fic**

Miller, K. All you desire   **Fic**

Miller, K. The eternal ones   **Fic**

The **fate** of Achilles. Landmann, B.   **883**

Father Abraham. Holzer, H.   **92**

FATHER AND CHILD

Johnson, A. The first part last   **Fic**

The **father** of anatomy. Yount, L.   **92**

The **father** of geometry: Euclid and his 3D world. Hightower, P.   **92**

Father of lies. Turner, A. W.   **Fic**

The **father** of the atom. Macfarlane, K.   **92**

FATHER'S DAY

    See also Holidays

FATHER-CHILD RELATIONSHIP

    See also Children; Fathers; Parent-child relationship

FATHER-DAUGHTER RELATIONSHIP

Busby, C. The year we disappeared   **92**

FATHER-DAUGHTER RELATIONSHIP

    See also Daughters; Father-child relationship; Fathers

FATHER-DAUGHTER RELATIONSHIP -- FICTION

Cavanaugh, N. J. This journal belongs to Ratchet   **Fic**

Dessen, S. The moon and more   **Fic**

Friesner, E. Spirit's princess   **Fic**

Gephart, D. Olivia Bean, trivia queen   **Fic**

McQuerry, M. D. The Peculiars   **Fic**

Rossetti, R. The girl with borrowed wings   **Fic**

Zettel, S. Dust girl   **Fic**

FATHER-DAUGHTER RELATIONSHIP -- FICTION

Christopher, L. Flyaway   **Fic**

Fitzmaurice, K. Destiny, rewritten   **Fic**

FATHER-SON RELATIONSHIP

Peck, R. N. A day no pigs would die   **Fic**

    See also Father-child relationship; Fathers; Sons

FATHER-SON RELATIONSHIP -- FICTION

Berk, J. Guy Langman, crime scene procrastinator   **Fic**

Fitzmaurice, K. A diamond in the desert   **Fic**

Key, W. Fourmile   **Fic**

Master, I. A beautiful lie   **Fic**

McDonald, I. Be my enemy   **Fic**

Pearsall, S. Jump into the sky   **Fic**

Smith, R. Eruption   **Fic**

FATHER-SON RELATIONSHIP -- GRAPHIC NOVELS

Bad Island   **Fic**

TenNapel, D. Cardboard   **Fic**

FATHER-SON RELATIONSHIP -- FICTION

Villareal, R. Body slammed!   **Fic**

FATHERS

    See also Family; Men

FATHERS -- FICTION

Ackley, A. Sign language   **Fic**

Almond, D. The savage   **Fic**

Barnaby, H. Wonder show   **Fic**

Barratt, M. The wild man   **Fic**

Bodeen, S. A. The Compound   **Fic**

Bodeen, S. A. The gardener   **Fic**

Bouchard, H. Harvey   **741.5**

Cantor, J. The life of glass   **Fic**

Craig, C. Afrika   **Fic**

Deuker, C. High heat   **Fic**

Ellis, S. Odd man out   **Fic**

Fisher, C. The obsidian mirror   **Fic**

Fleischman, P. Seek   **Fic**

Fontes, J. Benito runs   **Fic**

Friend, N. Lush   **Fic**

Gantos, J. I am not Joey Pigza   **Fic**

Gephart, D. Olivia Bean, trivia queen   **Fic**

Higgins, J. Death run   **Fic**

Higgins, J. First strike   **Fic**

Higgins, J. Sharp shot   **Fic**

Higgins, J. Sure fire   **Fic**

Hill, K. Do not pass go   **Fic**

Kang, H. Chengli and the Silk Road caravan   **Fic**

Keller, J. Back home   **Fic**

Nelson, T. Ruby electric   **Fic**

Paquette Nowhere girl   **Fic**

Resau, L. The indigo notebook   **Fic**

Schraff, A. E. A boy called Twister   **Fic**

Smith, H. A. Keeping the night watch   **Fic**

Smith, H. A. The way a door closes   **Fic**

Tayleur, K. Chasing boys   **Fic**

Valentine, J. Me, the missing, and the dead   **Fic**

Van Draanen, W. Sammy Keyes and the showdown in Sin City   **Fic**

Vanderpool, C. Moon over Manifest   **Fic**

Wilson, J. Written in blood   **Fic**

Yee, L. Absolutely Maybe   **Fic**

FATHERS AND DAUGHTERS *See* Father-daughter relationship

FATHERS AND DAUGHTERS -- FICTION

Balliett, B. Hold fast   **Fic**

Bigelow, L. J. Starting from here   **Fic**

Carey, B. Poison most vial   **Fic**

Cavanaugh, N. J. This journal belongs to Ratchet   **Fic**

Dessen, S. The moon and more   **Fic**

La Valley, J. The Vine basket   **Fic**

North, P. Starglass   **Fic**

O'Brien, A. Lara's gift   **Fic**

Renn, D. Tokyo heist   **Fic**

Rush, J. Altered   **Fic**

FATHERS AND DAUGHTERS -- FICTION

Govenar, A. B. Extraordinary ordinary people **745**

FOLK BELIEFS *See* Folklore; Superstition

FOLK DANCING
> *See also* Dance

The **Folk** Keeper. Billingsley, F.   **Fic**

FOLK LITERATURE
Beauty and the beast Beauties and beasts **398.21**
> *See also* Folklore; Literature

FOLK LORE *See* Folklore

FOLK MUSIC
Handyside, C. Folk   **781.62**
> *See also* Music

FOLK MUSICIANS
Orgill, R. Shout, sister, shout!   **920**
Partridge, E. This land was made for you and me **92**

**FOLK SINGERS -- UNITED STATES -- BIOG-
RAPHY**
Partridge, E. This land was made for you and me **92**

FOLK SONGS
> *See also* Folklore; Songs; Vocal music

FOLK SONGS -- UNITED STATES
> *See also* American songs

Folk stories of the Hmong. Livo, N. J.   **398.2**

FOLK TALES *See* Folklore; Legends

FOLKLORE
The August House book of scary stories   **398.2**
Beauty and the beast Beauties and beasts **398.21**
Forest, H. Wisdom tales from around the world   **398.2**
Hausman, G. Horses of myth   **398.2**
Horowitz, A. Death and the underworld   **398.2**
Horowitz, A. Heroes and villains   **398.2**
Jaffe, N. The cow of no color: riddle stories and justice tales from around the world   **398.2**
Mitton, T. The storyteller's secrets   **398.2**
Norman, H. Between heaven and earth   **398.2**
Olson, A. N. Ask the bones: scary stories from around the world   **398.2**
Olson, A. N. More bones   **398.2**
Rapunzel and other magic fairy tales   **398.2**
San Souci, R. A terrifying taste of short & shivery   **398.2**
Schwartz, H. The day the Rabbi disappeared: Jewish holiday tales of magic   **398.2**
Tchana, K. H. Changing Woman and her sisters   **398.2**
Yolen, J. Mightier than the sword   **398.2**

FOLKLORE -- AFRICA
African folktales   **398.2**
African tales   **398.2**
Bryan, A. Ashley Bryan's African tales, uh-huh   **398.2**

FOLKLORE -- APPALACHIAN MOUNTAINS
Shelby, A. The adventures of Molly Whuppie and other Appalachian folktales   **398.2**

FOLKLORE -- CHINA

Bedard, M. The painted wall and other strange tales   **398.2**
Krasno, R. Cloud weavers   **398.2**
Yep, L. The rainbow people   **398.2**

FOLKLORE -- CHINA
Bedard, M. The painted wall and other strange tales   **398.2**
Yep, L. The rainbow people   **398.2**

FOLKLORE -- CUBA
Hayes, J. Dance, Nana, dance   **398.2**

FOLKLORE -- DICTIONARIES
Myths and legends   **398**

FOLKLORE -- ENGLAND
McKinley, R. The outlaws of Sherwood   **398.2**

FOLKLORE -- EUROPE
Morpurgo, M. Beowulf   **398.2**
Raven, N. Beowulf   **398.2**
Rumford, J. Beowulf   **398.2**

FOLKLORE -- GERMANY
Zahler, D. The thirteenth princess   **Fic**

FOLKLORE -- GRAPHIC NOVELS
Manning, M. K. Ali Baba and the forty thieves **741.5**
Powell, M. The seven voyages of Sinbad   **741.5**
Trickster: Native American tales   **398.2**

FOLKLORE -- GREAT BRITAIN
English folktales   **398.2**
Philip, N. Celtic fairy tales   **398.2**
Pyle, H. The merry adventures of Robin Hood **398.2**

FOLKLORE -- GUATEMALA
Menchu, R. The secret legacy   **398.2**

FOLKLORE -- INDEXES
Index to fairy tales   **398.2**

FOLKLORE -- INDIA
Gavin, J. Tales from India   **398.2**

FOLKLORE -- IRAQ
The epic of Gilgamesh   **398.2**

FOLKLORE -- IRELAND
Burns, B. The king with horse's ears and other Irish folktales   **398.2**

FOLKLORE -- JAPAN -- GRAPHIC NOVELS
Ichiro   **741.5**

FOLKLORE
Forest, H. Wisdom tales from around the world   **398.2**
Hague, M. The Book of dragons   **808.83**
Norman, H. Between heaven and earth   **398.2**
Schwartz, A. Scary stories 3   **398.2**

FOLKLORE -- LATIN AMERICA
Delacre, L. Golden tales   **398.209**
Sanna, E. Latino folklore and culture   **398.2**

FOLKLORE -- LATIN AMERICA
Delacre, L. Golden tales   **398.209**

FOLKLORE -- NORWAY
George, J. D. Sun and moon, ice and snow   **Fic**

FOLKLORE -- POLAND
Monte, R. The mermaid of Warsaw   **398.2**

FOOTBALL -- ENCYCLOPEDIAS
Buckley, J. The Child's World encyclopedia of the NFL **796.332**

FOOTBALL -- FICTION
Bowen, F. Quarterback season **Fic**
Carter, A. R. Love, football, and other contact sports **S C**
Coy, J. Crackback **Fic**
Coy, J. Love of the game **Fic**
Deuker, C. Gym candy **Fic**
Deuker, C. Payback time **Fic**
Feinstein, J. Cover-up **Fic**
Feinstein, J. The rivalry **Fic**
Green, T. The big time **Fic**
Green, T. Deep zone **Fic**
Green, T. Football champ **Fic**
Green, T. Football genius **Fic**
Green, T. Football hero **Fic**
Herbach, G. Stupid fast **Fic**
Lynch, C. Inexcusable **Fic**
McKissack, F. Shooting star **Fic**
Murdock, C. G. Dairy Queen **Fic**
Murdock, C. G. The off season **Fic**
Powell, R. Three clams and an oyster **Fic**
Spinelli, J. Crash **Fic**
Tharp, T. Knights of the hill country **Fic**
Wallace, R. War and watermelon **Fic**
Weyn, S. Recruited **Fic**
Zadoff, A. Food, girls, and other things I can't have **Fic**
Football champ. Green, T. **Fic**
Football genius. Green, T. **Fic**
Football genius [series]
Green, T. The big time **Fic**
Green, T. Deep zone **Fic**
Football hero. Green, T. **Fic**

FOOTBALL PLAYERS
Aaseng, N. You are the juror **345**
Pellowski, M. The O.J. Simpson murder trial **345**
Slavicek, L. C. Paul Robeson **92**

FOOTBALL PLAYERS -- UNITED STATES -- BIOGRAPHY
Rappoport, K. Peyton Manning **796.332**

FOOTBINDING -- FICTION
Namioka, L. Ties that bind, ties that break **Fic**
Footnotes. Augustyn, F. **792.8**
Footprints [series]
Mulder, M. Pedal it! **388**
For boys only. Aronson, M. **031.02**
For horse-crazy girls only. Wilsdon, C. **636.1**
For kids [series]
Stein, S. Duke Ellington **92**

FORAGE PLANTS
See also Economic botany; Feeds; Plants
Forbes, Esther
Johnny Tremain **Fic**

Forbes, Robert L.
Beast Friends Forever **811**
The **forbidden** schoolhouse. Jurmain, S. **92**
Forbidden sea. Nielson, S. A. **Fic**

FORCE AND ENERGY
Bonnet, R. L. Home run! **530**
Claybourne, A. Forms of energy **531**
Gardner, R. Ace your forces and motion science project **531**
Gardner, R. Forces and motion science fair projects **531**
Goodstein, M. Goal! science projects with soccer **507.8**
Nardo, D. Force and motion **531**
Orr, T. Motion and forces **531**
Pinna, S. d. Transfer of energy **531**
Silverstein, A. Forces and motion **531**
Solway, A. Exploring forces and motion **531**
Viegas, J. Kinetic and potential energy **531**

FORCE AND ENERGY -- EXPERIMENTS
VanCleave, J. P. Step-by-step science experiments in energy **531**

FORCE AND ENERGY
Claybourne, A. Gut-wrenching gravity and other fatal forces **531**
Silverstein, A. Forces and motion **531**

FORCE AND ENERGY -- STUDY AND TEACHING (MIDDLE SCHOOL)
Energy **531**

FORCE AND ENERGY.
Nardo, D. Force and motion **531**
Force and motion. Nardo, D. **531**
Force out. Green, T. **Fic**

FORCED MIGRATION
See also Internal migration
Forces and motion. Silverstein, A. **531**
Forces and motion science fair projects. Gardner, R. **531**

FORD AUTOMOBILE
See also Automobiles
Ford, Christopher
Stickman Odyssey **741.5**
Ford, Emily
What you must think of me **616.85**
Ford, Henry, 1863-1947
About
Mitchell, D. Driven **92**
Ford, John C.
The morgue and me **Fic**
Ford, Michael
Birth of a warrior **Fic**
The Fire of Ares **Fic**
Legacy of blood **Fic**
The poisoned house **Fic**
Ford, Michael Thomas
Z **Fic**

Wrecked	Fic	Reality rules!	028.5

Frank, Mitch
Understanding September 11th   973.931
Understanding the Holy Land   956.94

Frank, Otto
(ed) Frank, A. The diary of a young girl: the definitive edition   940.53

Frankenstein. Viney, B.   741.5
Frankenstein. Hirschmann, K.   813
Frankenstein. Shelley, M. W.   741.5

FRANKENSTEIN (FICTIONAL CHARACTER)
Priestly, C. Mister Creecher   Fic

FRANKENSTEIN (FICTITIOUS CHARACTER)
Nardo, D. Understanding Frankenstein   823

FRANKENSTEIN'S MONSTER (FICTIONAL CHARACTER)
Priestly, C. Mister Creecher   Fic

FRANKFURTERS
Watson, S. Mystery meat   613.2

Franklin Delano Roosevelt. Freedman, R.   973.917
Franklin Delano Roosevelt for kids. Panchyk, R.   92

Franklin, Benjamin, 1706-1790
About
Adler, D. A. B. Franklin, printer   973.3
Benjamin Franklinstein meets the Fright brothers   Fic
Dash, J. A dangerous engine   92
Fleming, C. Ben Franklin's almanac   92
Freedman, R. Becoming Ben Franklin   973.309
Lagos, A. The sons of liberty 2   741.5
MacDonald, B. The secret of the sealed room   Fic
McElligott, M. Benjamin Franklinstein lives!   Fic
Miller, B. M. Benjamin Franklin, American genius   92
Woodruff, E. George Washington's spy   Fic

Franklin, Emily
The other half of me   Fic

Franklin, Patricia
School library collection development   025.2

Franklin, Patricia
Stephens, C. G. Library 101   027.8

Franklin, Rosalind, 1920-1958
About
Polcovar, J. Rosalind Franklin and the structure of life   92
Yount, L. Rosalind Franklin   572.809

Frannie in pieces. Ephron, D.   Fic
Franny Parker. McKinnon, H. R.   Fic

Franz Ferdinand, Archduke of Austria, 1863-1914
About
O'Brien, J. Day of the assassins   Fic

Franz Ferdinand, Archduke of Austria, 1863-1914 -- Fiction
About
O'Brien, J. Day of the assassins   Fic

Fraser, Elizabeth

FRATERNITIES AND SORORITIES
See also Colleges and universities; Students -- Societies

FRAUD
Bell, S. Fakes and forgeries   363.2
Schroeder, A. Scams!   364.1
Spilsbury, R. Counterfeit!   363.2
YES mag (Periodical) Hoaxed!   500

FRAUD
See also Commercial law; Crime; Offenses against property; White collar crimes

FRAUD -- FICTION
Corrigan, E. Accomplice   Fic

FRAUD IN SCIENCE
See also Science
YES mag (Periodical) Hoaxed!   500

FRAUD, COMPUTER *See* Computer crimes

Fraustino, Lisa Rowe
(ed) Don't cramp my style   S C

Frazier, Angie
The Eternal Sea   Fic
Everlasting   Fic
The mastermind plot   Fic
The midnight tunnel   Fic

Frazier, Sundee Tucker
The other half of my heart   Fic

Freak. Pixley, M.   Fic

FREAK SHOWS -- FICTION
Cushman, K. Will Sparrow's road   Fic

Freaking out! Rau, D. M.   612.8
Freaks like us. Vaught, S.   Fic
Freaky Fast Frankie Joe. Clifton, L.   Fic
Freaky flowers. Souza, D. M.   582.13
Freaky Friday. Rodgers, M.   Fic
Freaky green eyes. Oates, J. C.   Fic
Frederick Douglass. Adler, D. A.   92
Frederick Douglass. Schuman, M.   92
Frederick Douglass for kids. Sanders, N. I.   973.8

Frederick, Heather Vogel
The voyage of Patience Goodspeed   Fic

Frederick, Shane
Football   796.332
Strength training for teen athletes   613.7

Fredericks, Carrie
Autism   616.85
Obesity   616.3

Fredericks, Mariah
Head games   Fic
Life   Fic
Love   Fic

Free at last. Bullard, S.   323.1
Free baseball. Corbett, S.   Fic

FREE DIVING *See* Scuba diving; Skin diving
FREE PRESS *See* Freedom of the press
Free radical. Murphy, C. R.   Fic

Free running. Eason, S.   613.7
Free speech.   342
FREE SPEECH *See* Freedom of speech
Free throw. Maddox, J.   Fic
FREE TRADE
     See also Commercial policy; International trade
FREE UNIVERSITIES
     See also Colleges and universities
FREE VERSE
     See also Poetry
FREE WILL AND DETERMINISM
     See also Philosophy
Free?: stories about human rights. Amnesty International   S C
Freedman, Jeri
     America debates stem cell research   174.2
     Brain cancer   616.99
     Professional wrestling   362.29
     Robots through history   629.8
     Sid Fleischman   92
     Tay-Sachs disease   616.8
Freedman, Lew
     Boston Red Sox   796.357
     Roberto Clemente   92
Freedman, Russell, 1929-
     Abraham Lincoln and Frederick Douglass   973.709
     Becoming Ben Franklin   973.309
     Freedman, R. Give me liberty!   973.3
     Children of the Great Depression   305.23
     Eleanor Roosevelt   973.917
     Franklin Delano Roosevelt   973.917
     Freedom walkers   323.1
     Give me liberty!   973.3
     In defense of liberty   342
     In the days of the vaqueros   636.2
     Indian chiefs   970.004
     Kids at work   331.3
     Lafayette and the American Revolution   92
     The life and death of Crazy Horse   978
     Lincoln: a photobiography   92
     Martha Graham, a dancer's life   792.8
     Out of darkness: the story of Louis Braille   92
     The voice that challenged a nation   92
     The war to end all wars   940.3
     Washington at Valley Forge   973.3
     Who was first?   970.01
     The Wright brothers: how they invented the airplane   92
FREEDMEN
     Blair, M. W. Liberty or death   973.3
FREEDOM
     See also Democracy; Political science
FREEDOM -- FICTION
     Amnesty International Free?: stories about human rights   S C

Schwabach, K. The storm before Atlanta   Fic
The freedom business. Nelson, M.   811
Freedom cannot rest. Bohannon, L. F.   92
The freedom maze. Sherman, D.   Fic
FREEDOM OF ASSEMBLY
     See also Civil rights; Freedom
FREEDOM OF ASSOCIATION
     See also Civil rights; Freedom
FREEDOM OF CONSCIENCE
     See also Conscience; Freedom; Toleration
Freedom of expression and the Internet. Dougherty, T.   323.44
Freedom of information. Stearman, K.   342
FREEDOM OF INFORMATION
     Adams, H. R. Ensuring intellectual freedom and access to information in the school library media program   027.8
     See also Civil rights; Intellectual freedom
FREEDOM OF INFORMATION -- UNITED STATES
     Stearman, K. Freedom of information   342
FREEDOM OF MOVEMENT
     See also Civil rights; Freedom
FREEDOM OF RELIGION
     Haynes, C. C. First freedoms   342
     Jones, M. The First Amendment   342
FREEDOM OF RELIGION
     See also Civil rights; Freedom; Toleration
FREEDOM OF SPEECH
     Axelrod-Contrada, J. Reno v. ACLU   344
     Dougherty, T. Freedom of expression and the Internet   323.44
     Free speech   342
     Fridell, R. U.S. v. Eichman   342
     Gold, S. D. Tinker v. Des Moines   342
     Haynes, C. C. First freedoms   342
     Icenoggle, J. Schenck v. United States and the freedom of speech debate   323
     Jones, M. The First Amendment   342
FREEDOM OF SPEECH
     See also Censorship; Civil rights; Freedom; Intellectual freedom
FREEDOM OF SPEECH -- FICTION
     Myers, W. D. The Cruisers   Fic
FREEDOM OF SPEECH -- UNITED STATES -- HISTORY -- SOURCES
     The Founding of America   973.3
FREEDOM OF TEACHING *See* Academic freedom
FREEDOM OF THE PRESS
     Gold, S. D. New York Times Co. v. Sullivan   342
     Gold, S. D. The Pentagon papers   342
     Haynes, C. C. First freedoms   342
     Jarrow, G. The printer's trial   345
     Jones, M. The First Amendment   342
     Phillips, T. A. Hazelwood v. Kuhlmeier and the

About

Whitelaw, N. The Homestead Steel Strike of 1892 — **331.8**

Frida. Bernier-Grand, C. — **811**

Frida Kahlo. Hillstrom, L. — **92**

Fridell, Ron

Cruzan v. Missouri and the right to die debate — **344**

Dictatorship — **321.9**

Earth-friendly energy — **333.79**

Gideon v. Wainwright — **345**

Life in the desert — **577.5**

Miranda law — **345**

Protecting Earth's water supply — **363.7**

Religious fundamentalism — **200.9**

Sports technology — **688.7**

U.S. v. Eichman — **342**

Fridrik Erlingsson

Benjamin Dove — **Fic**

Friedlander, Mark P.

Outbreak — **614.4**

Friedman, Aimee

The year my sister got lucky — **Fic**

Friedman, Cory

About

Patterson, J. Med head — **92**

Friedman, D. Dina

Escaping into the night — **Fic**

Friedman, Hal

Patterson, J. Med head — **92**

Friedman, Ian C.

Manny Ramirez — **92**

Friedman, Ina R.

The other victims — **940.53**

Friedman, Lauri S.

(ed) Civil liberties — **323**

(ed) Fast food — **362.1**

Energy alternatives — **333.79**

Terrorist attacks — **363.32**

Tina Fey — **92**

(ed) Oceans — **551.46**

(ed) Organic food and farming — **641.3**

(ed) Torture — **364.6**

Friedman, Milton, 1912-2006

About

Crain, C. D. Milton Friedman — **92**

Friend is not a verb. Ehrenhaft, D. — **Fic**

Friend me! DiPiazza, F. D. — **302.3**

Friend, Catherine

Barn boot blues — **Fic**

Friend, Natasha

My life in black and white — **Fic**

Friend, Natasha

Bounce — **Fic**

Lush — **Fic**

Perfect — **Fic**

FRIENDLY FIRE (MILITARY SCIENCE)

See also Military art and science

Friends. — **S C**

FRIENDS *See* Friendship

Friends forever? Amblard, O. — **158**

Friends with boys. Hicks, F. E. — **741.5**

FRIENDS, SOCIETY OF *See* Society of Friends

The **friendship.** Taylor, M. D. — **Fic**

FRIENDSHIP

See also Human behavior

Amblard, O. Friends forever? — **158**

Bezdecheck, B. Relationships — **158**

Fox, A. Real friends vs. the other kind — **158**

Freedman, R. Abraham Lincoln and Frederick Douglass — **973.709**

Hantman, C. 30 days to finding and keeping sassy sidekicks and BFFs — **158**

Harris, A. R. Cliques, crushes & true friends — **158**

Owens, L. L. Frenemies — **158**

Perrier, P. Flying solo — **158**

Romain, T. Cliques, phonies & other baloney — **158**

Taylor, J. The girls' guide to friends — **158**

Webber, D. Your space — **158**

FRIENDSHIP -- FICTION

Andrews, J. Me & Earl & the dying girl — **Fic**

Bushman lives! — **Fic**

Creech, S. The great unexpected — **Fic**

Crossan, S. Breathe — **Fic**

Elston, A. The rules for disappearing — **Fic**

Herbach, G. Nothing special — **Fic**

Horvath, P. One year in Coal Harbor — **Fic**

Mangum, L. After hello — **Fic**

Myers, W. D. Darius & Twig — **Fic**

Oppel, K. Such wicked intent — **Fic**

Peacock, C. A. Red thread sisters — **Fic**

Pierson, D. C. The boy who couldn't sleep and never had to — **Fic**

Ryan, A. K. Spark — **Fic**

Spinelli, J. Jake and Lily — **Fic**

Stead, R. Liar & spy — **Fic**

Stewart, T. L. The extraordinary education of Nicholas Benedict — **Fic**

Stone, P. The boy on Cinnamon Street — **Fic**

Vaught, S. Freaks like us — **Fic**

FRIENDSHIP -- GRAPHIC NOVELS

Castellucci, C. Janes in love — **741.5**

Castellucci, C. The Plain Janes — **741.5**

Crilley, M. Miki Falls, Book One: Spring — **741.5**

Gulledge, L. L. Page by Paige — **741.5**

Hicks, F. E. The war at Ellsmere — **741.5**

Larson, H. Chiggers — **741.5**

Pyle, K. C. Katman — **741.5**

Soo, K. Jellaby: monster in the city — **741.5**

Tamaki, M. Skim — **741.5**

Weinstein, L. Girl stories — **741.5**

Winick, J. Pedro & me — **362.1**

FRIENDSHIP -- FICTION

Babbitt, N. The moon over High Street **Fic**
Cooper, S. Ghost Hawk **Fic**
Cotler, S. Cheesie Mack is running like crazy! **Fic**
Dowell, F. O. The second life of Abigail Walker **Fic**
Flanagan, J. The hunters **Fic**
Flanagan, J. The invaders **Fic**
Fry, M. The Odd Squad **Fic**
Green, T. Force out **Fic**
Jung, M. Geeks, girls, and secret identities **Fic**
Matti, T. Mister Orange **Fic**
McKay, S. E. Enemy territory **Fic**
The mighty Quinn **Fic**
Standiford, N. The secret tree **Fic**
Tomo **S C**
Tracy, K. Bessica Lefter bites back **Fic**

FRIENDSHIP -- UNITED STATES
Freedman, R. Abraham Lincoln and Frederick Douglass **973.709**

FRIENDSHIP BETWEEN WOMEN *See* Female friendship
A **friendship** for today. McKissack, P. C. **Fic**

FRIENDSHIP IN WOMEN *See* Female friendship
FRIENDSHIP/FICTION
Markus and Diana
Friesen, Gayle
The Isabel factor **Fic**
Friesen, Jonathan
The last Martin **Fic**
Friesen, Ray
Cupcakes of doom! **741.5**
Friesner, Esther M.
Nobody's princess **Fic**
Nobody's prize **Fic**
Sphinx's princess **Fic**
Sphinx's queen **Fic**
Spirit's princess **Fic**
Threads and flames **Fic**

FRIIENDSHIP -- FICTION
Uglies **741.5**

Fritz, Jean
Alexander Hamilton **92**
Around the world in a hundred years **910.92**
Bully for you, Teddy Roosevelt! **92**
Fritz, J. Homesick: my own story **92**
Harriet Beecher Stowe and the Beecher preachers **813**
Homesick: my own story **92**
Traitor: the case of Benedict Arnold **92**
The **frog** scientist. Turner, P. S. **597.8**

FROGS
Beltz, E. Frogs: inside their remarkable world **597.8**
Frogs! **597.8**
Markle, S. The case of the vanishing golden frogs **597.8**
Turner, P. S. The frog scientist **597.8**

FROGS

See also Amphibians
Crump, M. The mystery of Darwin's frog **597.8**
Solway, A. Poison frogs and other amphibians **597.87**
Frogs! **597.8**
Frogs: inside their remarkable world. Beltz, E. **597.8**
Froi of the exiles. Marchetta, M. **FIC**
Frolund, Tina
(ed) The official YALSA awards guidebook **011.6**
From Alice to Zen and everyone in between. Atkinson, E. **Fic**
From boneshakers to choppers. Smedman, L. **629.227**
From China to America. O'Keefe, S. **92**
From cover to cover. Baxter, K. A. **028.1**
From Greek atoms to quarks. Morgan, S. **530**
From jazz babies to generation next. Edge, L. B. **305.23**
From locusts to...automobile anti-collision systems. Mara, W. **629.2**
From many cultures, one history [series]
Cruz, B. Triumphs and struggles for Latino civil rights **323.1**
Edwards, J. The history of the American Indians and the reservation **970.004**
Kent, D. The tragic history of the Japanese-American internment camps **940.53**
Miller, M. School desegregation and the story of the Little Rock Nine **379**
Stein, R. C. Escaping slavery on the Underground Railroad **973.7**
Worth, R. Puerto Rico in American history **972.95**
From Mendel's peas to genetic fingerprinting. Morgan, S. **576.5**
From mud huts to skyscrapers. **720**
From reader to writer. Ellis, S. **028**
From sea urchins to dolly the sheep. Morgan, S. **571.8**
From slave ship to freedom road. Lester, J. **306.3**
From Somalia with love. Robert, N. b. **Fic**
From steam engines to nuclear fusion. Ballard, C. **333.79**
From the notebooks of Melanin Sun. Woodson, J. **Fic**
From then to now. **909**
Front and center. Murdock, C. G. **Fic**
Front-page lives [series]
Burgan, M. Barack Obama **92**
Catel, P. Nelson Mandela **92**
Isaacs, S. S. Bill and Melinda Gates **92**
Price, S. Benazir Bhutto **92**

FRONTIER AND PIONEER LIFE
Anderson, W. T. Laura Ingalls Wilder **813**
Berne, E. C. Laura Ingalls Wilder **92**
Cook, J. Natural writer: a story about Marjorie Kinnan Rawlings **813**

(ed) Junior Worldmark encyclopedia of the Mexican states   **972**

(ed) Junior Worldmark encyclopedia of the states   **973**

(ed) Junior worldmark encyclopedia of the nations   **910.3**

Gall, Timothy L.

(ed) Junior worldmark encyclopedia of the nations   **910.3**

(ed) Junior Worldmark encyclopedia of the Canadian provinces   **971**

(ed) Junior Worldmark encyclopedia of the Mexican states   **972**

(ed) Junior Worldmark encyclopedia of the states   **973**

Gallant, Roy A.

Atmosphere   **551.51**

History   **551.7**

Water   **553.7**

The **Gallaudet** dictionary of American Sign Language.   **419**

Gallaudet University

The Gallaudet dictionary of American Sign Language   **419**

Gallaway, Beth

Game on!   **025.2**

Gallo, Donald R.

(ed) Destination unexpected: short stories   **S C**

Owning it   **S C**

Richard Peck   **813**

(ed) Join in   **813**

(ed) On the fringe   **S C**

(ed) Ultimate sports   **813**

(ed) Visions: nineteen short stories by outstanding writers for young adults   **S C**

(ed) What are you afraid of?   **S C**

Galloway, Priscilla

Adventures on the ancient Silk Road   **950**

Gallup guides for youth facing persistent prejudice. Seba, J.   **306.76**

Gallup Youth Survey [series]

Marcovitz, H. Teens & volunteerism   **361.3**

Gallup's guide to modern gay, lesbian, and transgender lifestyle [series]

Sanna, E. Gay believers   **306.76**

Seba, J. Coming out   **306.76**

Seba, J. Gay characters in theatre, movies, and television: new roles, new attitudes   **791.43**

Gama, Vasco da, 1469-1524

About

Calvert, P. Vasco da Gama   **92**

Fritz, J. Around the world in a hundred years **910.92**

Goodman, J. E. A long and uncertain journey: the 27,000 mile voyage of Vasco da Gama   **910**

Gamble, Cyndi

Leopards   **599.75**

GAMBLING

See also Games

GAMBLING -- FICTION

Abrahams, P. Reality check   **Fic**

Hautman, P. All-in   **Fic**

Helgerson, J. Crows & cards   **Fic**

Luper, E. Bug boy   **Fic**

Papademetriou, L. Drop   **Fic**

Game. Myers, W. D.   **Fic**

GAME AND GAME BIRDS

See also Animals; Birds; Wildlife

The **game** of silence. Erdrich, L.   **Fic**

The **Game** of Sunken Places. Anderson, M. T. **Fic**

The **game** of triumphs. Powell, L.   **Fic**

Game on! Gallaway, B.   **025.2**

GAME PROTECTION

See also Game and game birds; Hunting; Wildlife conservation

GAME RESERVES

See also Hunting; Wildlife conservation

GAME SHOWS -- FICTION

Gephart, D. Olivia Bean, trivia queen   **Fic**

GAME THEORY

See also Mathematical models; Mathematics; Probabilities

Games. Gorman, C.   **Fic**

GAMES

See also Entertaining; Physical education; Recreation

The art of stone skipping and other fun old-time games   **790.1**

Bell-Rehwoldt, S. The kids' guide to classic games   **790.1**

Danks, F. Run wild!   **790.1**

Rowell, V. Tag, toss & run   **790.1**

Strother, S. The adventurous book of outdoor games   **796**

GAMES -- FICTION

Powell, L. The Master of Misrule   **Fic**

GAMES -- GENERAL

Glenn, J. Unbored   **790**

GAMES

Gifford, C. Cool tech   **537.5**

Glenn, J. Unbored   **790**

Rowell, V. Tag, toss & run   **790.1**

GAMES IN MATHEMATICS EDUCATION

Salvadori, M. G. Math games for middle school **510**

Gaming technology. Oxlade, C.   **794.8**

Gamlin, Linda

Evolution   **576.8**

Gandhi. Wilkinson, P.   **92**

Gandhi.   **92**

Gandhi, Indira, 1917-1984

About

Ebine, K. Gandhi: a manga biography   **92**

Gandhi   **92**

The Full spectrum   **306.76**

Martin, H. J. Serving lesbian, gay, bisexual, transgender, and questioning teens   **027.62**

Seba, J. Gay characters in theatre, movies, and television: new roles, new attitudes   **791.43**

GAY MEN -- CIVIL RIGHTS

Aretha, D. No compromise: the story of Harvey Milk   **92**

GAY MEN -- CIVIL RIGHTS *See* Gay rights

GAY MEN'S WRITINGS

See also Literature

GAY PARENTS

Fields, J. Gay and lesbian parents   **306.8**

GAY PARENTS

See also Gay men; Lesbians; Parents

GAY RIGHTS

See also Civil rights

Seba, J. A. Homosexuality around the world **306.76**

GAY RIGHTS -- UNITED STATES

Littlefield, B. My two moms   **306.874**

GAY RIGHTS ACTIVISTS

Aretha, D. No compromise: the story of Harvey Milk   **92**

GAY STUDENTS -- UNITED STATES

Cahill, S. LGBT youth in America's schools **371.826**

GAY TEENAGERS

See also Gay youth; Teenagers

GAY TEENAGERS -- FICTION

Higgins, M. G. Bi-Normal   **Fic**

Knowles, J. See you at Harry's   **Fic**

Konigsberg, B. Openly straight   **Fic**

Lennon, T. When love comes to town   **Fic**

GAY WOMEN *See* Lesbians

GAY YOUTH

Cahill, S. LGBT youth in America's schools **371.826**

GAY YOUTH

See also Youth

GAY YOUTH

The Full spectrum   **306.76**

GAY YOUTH -- UNITED STATES

Seba, J. Gallup guides for youth facing persistent prejudice   **306.76**

Gay, Kathlyn

The aftermath of the Chinese nationalist revolution   **951.04**

The aftermath of the Russian Revolution   **947.084**

Epilepsy   **616.8**

The scoop on what to eat   **613.2**

Volunteering   **361.3**

GAYS -- FICTION

Finneyfrock, K. The sweet revenge of Celia Door   **Fic**

Lennon, T. When love comes to town   **Fic**

GAYS

Seba, J. A. Homosexuality around the world **306.76**

GAYS -- LEGAL STATUS, LAWS, ETC.

Seba, J. A. Homosexuality around the world **306.76**

GAYS AND LESBIANS IN THE MILITARY

See also Gay men; Lesbians; Military personnel

GAYS, FEMALE *See* Lesbians

GAYS, MALE *See* Gay men

GAZETTEERS

See also Geography

Gazlay, Suzy

Managing green spaces   **333.7**

GDYNIA (POLAND) -- BIOGRAPHY

Warren, A. Surviving Hitler   **940.53**

Gear, Kathleen O'Neal

Children of the Dawnland   **Fic**

Gear, W. Michael

Gear, K. O. Children of the Dawnland   **Fic**

GEARING

See also Machinery; Power transmission; Wheels

Geary, Rick

Great expectations   **741.5**

The invisible man   **741.5**

Geckos. Bartlett, R. D.   **639.3**

GECKOS

Bartlett, R. D. Geckos   **639.3**

GECKOS -- FICTION

Galante, C. Willowood   **Fic**

Gedatus, Gus

Exercise for weight management   **613.7**

Gedney, Mona

The life and times of Buddha   **294.3**

Gee, Joshua

Encyclopedia horrifica   **001.9**

Gee, Maurice

Gool   **Fic**

The Limping Man   **Fic**

Salt   **Fic**

Geek magnet. Brian, K.   **Fic**

Geek: fantasy novel. Archer, E.   **Fic**

Geeks, girls, and secret identities. Jung, M.   **Fic**

Geektastic.   **S C**

GEESE

See also Birds; Poultry

Gehrig, Lou, 1903-1941

About

Buckley, J. Lou Gehrig   **92**

Gehry, Frank

About

Bodden, V. Frank Gehry   **92**

Geiger, Beth

Clean water   **363.7**

GEISHAS

Hoobler, D. The demon in the teahouse   **Fic**

GEISHAS

See also Entertainers

Gelfand, Dale Evva

American West 970.004

Sullivan, G. Geronimo 92

Gerszak, Rafal, 1980-

About

Beyond bullets 958.1

GESTALT PSYCHOLOGY

See also Consciousness; Perception; Psychology; Senses and sensation; Theory of knowledge

Get hooked. Werker, K. P. 746.43

Get hooked again. Werker, K. P. 746.43

Get into Art! Brooks, S. E

Get organized without losing it. Fox, J. S. 371.3

Get out! Molland, J. 333.72

Get real. Rockliff, M. 333.7

Get real [series]

Tym, K. Coping with your emotions 152.4

Tym, K. School survival 371.8

Get smart with your money [series]

Byers, A. First credit cards and credit smarts 332.7

Harmon, D. First car smarts 629.222

Harmon, D. First job smarts 650.1

Peterson, J. M. First budget smarts 332.024

Get well soon. Halpern, J. Fic

Getting away with murder: the true story of the Emmett Till case. Crowe, C. 364.152

Getting graphic! Gorman, M. 741.5

Getting inked. Gerber, L. 391

Getting the girl. Juby, S. Fic

Gettysburg. Johnson, J. 973.7

Gettysburg. Gregory, J. 973.7

GETTYSBURG (PA.), BATTLE OF, 1863

Johnson, J. Gettysburg 973.7

Murphy, J. The long road to Gettysburg 973.7

Weber, J. L. Summer's bloodiest days 973.7

GETTYSBURG (PA.), BATTLE OF, 1863 -- FICTION

Calkhoven, L. Will at the Battle of Gettysburg, 1863 Fic

Gutman, D. Abner & me Fic

GETTYSBURG (PA.), BATTLE OF, 1863

Gregory, J. Gettysburg 973.7

Tarshis, L. I survived the Battle of Gettysburg, 1863 E

GETTYSBURG, BATTLE OF, GETTYSBURG, PA., 1863

Gregory, J. Gettysburg 973.7

Getz, David

Frozen man 930.1

Getzinger, Donna

George Frideric Handel and music for voices 92

The Triangle Shirtwaist Factory fire 974.7

Geus, Mireille

Piggy Fic

Gewirtz, Adina Rishe

Zebra forest Fic

Gewirtz, Elaine Waldorf

The bulldog 636.7

Fetch this book 636.7

Geyer, Mark

Moriarty, C. The inquisitor's apprentice Fic

GEYSERS

See also Geology; Geothermal resources; Physical geography; Water

Ghana. Levy, P. 966.7

Gherman, Beverly

Anne Morrow Lindbergh 92

Norman Rockwell 759.13

Sparky: the life and art of Charles Schulz 92

Ghetto cowboy. Neri, G. Fic

GHETTOS, INNER CITY *See* Inner cities

The **ghost** and Mrs. Hobbs. DeFelice, C. C. Fic

The **ghost** and the goth. Kade, S. Fic

Ghost canoe. Hobbs, W. Fic

GHOST DANCE

Ehrlich, A. Wounded Knee: an Indian history of the American West 970.004

Ghost girl. Ray, D. Fic

Ghost Hawk. Cooper, S. Fic

Ghost hunt. Hawes, J. 133.1

Ghost hunt 2. Hawes, J. 133.1

Ghost hunter. Paver, M. Fic

The **ghost** in the Tokaido Inn. Hoobler, D. Fic

Ghost letters. Alter, S. Fic

Ghost moon. Wilson, J. Fic

Ghost Mysteries [series]

DeFelice, C. C. The ghost of Fossil Glen Fic

The **ghost** of Crutchfield Hall. Hahn, M. D. Fic

The **ghost** of Cutler Creek. DeFelice, C. C. Fic

The **ghost** of Fossil Glen. DeFelice, C. C. Fic

The **ghost** of Poplar Point. DeFelice, C. C. Fic

Ghost of Spirit Bear. Mikaelsen, B. Fic

The **ghost** sitter. Griffin, P. R. Fic

GHOST STORIES

Abela, D. The ghosts of Gribblesea Pier Fic

Allison, J. Gilda Joyce, psychic investigator: the bones of the holy Fic

Almond, D. Kit's wilderness Fic

Alter, S. Ghost letters Fic

Armstrong, K. The awakening Fic

Armstrong, K. The reckoning Fic

Armstrong, K. The summoning Fic

Avi The seer of shadows Fic

Bauer, J. Peeled Fic

The beasts of Clawstone Castle Fic

Bell, C. D. Slipping Fic

Black, H. Doll bones Fic

Blake, K. Anna Dressed in Blood Fic

Clarke, J. Starry nights Fic

Clement-Moore, R. Texas gothic Fic

Compestine, Y. C. A banquet for hungry ghosts S C

Connor, L. Dead on town line Fic

Crewe, M. Give up the ghost   **Fic**
Cypess, L. Nightspell   **Fic**
De Lint, C. The blue girl   **Fic**
The death of Yorik Mortwell   **Fic**
DeFelice, C. C. The ghost and Mrs. Hobbs   **Fic**
DeFelice, C. C. The ghost of Cutler Creek   **Fic**
DeFelice, C. C. The ghost of Fossil Glen   **Fic**
DeFelice, C. C. The ghost of Poplar Point   **Fic**
Del Negro, J. Passion and poison   **S C**
Dennard, S. Something strange and deadly   **Fic**
Dickens, C. A Christmas carol   **Fic**
Fleischman, S. The entertainer and the dybbuk **Fic**
Ford, M. The poisoned house   **Fic**
Gensler, S. The revenant   **Fic**
Grabenstein, C. The black heart crypt   **Fic**
Grabenstein, C. The crossroads   **Fic**
Grabenstein, C. The Hanging Hill   **Fic**
Grabenstein, C. The smoky corridor   **Fic**
Griffin, P. R. The ghost sitter   **Fic**
Hahn, M. D. The ghost of Crutchfield Hall   **Fic**
Hahn, M. D. Wait till Helen comes   **Fic**
Harvey, A. Haunting Violet   **Fic**
Hawkins, R. Demonglass   **Fic**
Hicks, F. E. Friends with boys   **741.5**
Hoffman, N. K. A stir of bones   **Fic**
The house of dead maids   **Fic**
Hudson, T. Hereafter   **Fic**
Hurley, T. Ghostgirl   **Fic**
Irving, W. The Legend of Sleepy Hollow   **Fic**
Johnson, M. The madness underneath   **Fic**
Johnson, M. The name of the star   **Fic**
Kade, S. The ghost and the goth   **Fic**
Kade, S. Queen of the dead   **Fic**
Kehret, P. The ghost's grave   **Fic**
Kelley, J. The girl behind the glass   **Fic**
Little, K. G. Circle of secrets   **Fic**
MacCullough, C. Drawing the ocean   **Fic**
McKissack, P. C. The dark-thirty   **S C**
Morris, P. Ruined   **Fic**
Morton-Shaw, C. The hunt for the seventh   **Fic**
Nelson, R. A. Days of Little Texas   **Fic**
Newbery, L. Lost boy   **Fic**
Nixon, J. L. The haunting   **Fic**
Noel, A. Dreamland   **Fic**
Noel, A. Radiance   **Fic**
Noel, A. Shimmer   **Fic**
Noyes, D. The ghosts of Kerfol   **S C**
Oliver, L. Liesl & Po   **Fic**
Peck, R. Three-quarters dead   **Fic**
Pinkwater, D. M. The Yggyssey   **Fic**
Pratchett, T. I shall wear midnight   **Fic**
Pratchett, T. Johnny and the dead   **Fic**
Prose, F. The turning   **Fic**
Riggs, R. Miss Peregrine's home for peculiar children   **Fic**
Ruby, L. The secret of Laurel Oaks   **Fic**

San Souci, R. Haunted houses   **S C**
San Souci, R. A terrifying taste of short & shivery   **398.2**
Schwartz, A. More scary stories to tell in the dark   **398.2**
Schwartz, A. Scary stories 3   **398.2**
Schwartz, A. Scary stories to tell in the dark **398.25**
Slater, A. The Shadowing: Hunted   **Fic**
Smith, S. The other side of dark   **Fic**
Stringer, H. The midnight gate   **Fic**
Stringer, H. Spellbinder   **Fic**
Towell, K. Skary childrin and the carousel of sorrow   **Fic**
Trigiani, A. Viola in reel life   **Fic**
Verday, J. The Hollow   **Fic**
Weeks, S. As simple as it seems   **Fic**

GHOST STORIES
> *See also* Fantasy fiction; Horror fiction; Occult fiction

GHOST STORIES -- FICTION
Barnholdt, L. Girl meets ghost   **Fic**
Berk, A. Mistle child   **Fic**
Cox, S. The Dead Girls Detective Agency   **Fic**

GHOST STORIES
Compestine, Y. C. A banquet for hungry ghosts **S C**
Irving, W. The Legend of Sleepy Hollow   **Fic**
Ghost town. Jennings, R. W.   **Fic**

GHOST TOWNS
> *See also* Extinct cities

GHOST TOWNS -- FICTION
Jennings, R. W. Ghost town   **Fic**
Ghost trackers. Gudgeon, C.   **133.1**
The **ghost's** grave. Kehret, P.   **Fic**
Ghostgirl. Hurley, T.   **Fic**
Ghostopolis. TenNapel, D.   **741.5**

GHOSTS
Bardhan-Quallen, S. The real monsters   **001.9**
Gee, J. Encyclopedia horrifica   **001.9**
Gudgeon, C. Ghost trackers   **133.1**
Hawes, J. Ghost hunt   **133.1**
Hawes, J. Ghost hunt 2   **133.1**
Matthews, R. Ghosts and spirits   **133.1**
Paranormal phenomena: opposing viewpoints **133**
Stefoff, R. Ghosts and spirits   **133.1**
Wetzel, C. Haunted U.S.A.   **133.1**
> *See also* Apparitions; Folklore; Spirits

GHOSTS -- FICTION
Barnholdt, L. Girl meets ghost   **Fic**
Berk, A. Mistle child   **Fic**
Black, H. Doll bones   **Fic**
Cooper, S. Ghost Hawk   **Fic**
Damico, G. Rogue   **Fic**
DeFelice, C. C. The ghost of Fossil Glen   **Fic**
Doyle, R. A greyhound of a girl   **Fic**
Johnson, M. The madness underneath   **Fic**
McNeal, T. Far far away   **Fic**

Giovanni, Nikki

Ego-tripping and other poems for young people **811**

On my journey now   **782.25**

(ed) Shimmy shimmy shimmy like my sister Kate   **811**

Gipson, Frederick Benjamin

Old Yeller   **Fic**

Giraffes. Lockwood, S.   **599.63**

GIRAFFES

Lockwood, S. Giraffes   **599.63**

GIRAFFES -- FICTION

St. John, L. The white giraffe   **Fic**

Girard, Denis

Cassell's French dictionary   **443**

The **girl** behind the glass. Kelley, J.   **Fic**

Girl coming in for a landing. Wayland, A. H.   **811**

A **girl** from Yamhill: a memoir. Cleary, B.   **92**

Girl in a cage. Yolen, J.   **Fic**

Girl in blue. Rinaldi, A.   **Fic**

Girl in the know. Katz, A.   **612.6**

Girl in the mirror. Harris, A. R.   **158**

The **girl** is murder. Haines, K. M.   **Fic**

The **girl** is trouble. Haines, K. M.   **Fic**

Girl meets ghost. Barnholdt, L.   **Fic**

A **girl** named Digit. Monaghan, A.   **Fic**

A **girl** named Disaster. Farmer, N.   **Fic**

A **girl** named Faithful Plum. Bernstein, R. **792.802**

A **girl** named Mister. Grimes, N.   **Fic**

The **girl** of fire and thorns. Carson, R.   **Fic**

GIRL SCOUTS

Wadsworth, G. First Girl Scout   **369.463**

Girl stories. Weinstein, L.   **741.5**

The **girl** who became a Beatle. Taylor, G.   **Fic**

The **girl** who circumnavigated Fairyland in a ship of her own making.   **Fic**

The **girl** who could fly. Forester, V.   **Fic**

The **girl** who fell beneath Fairyland and led the revels there.   **Fic**

The **girl** who saw lions. Doherty, B.   **Fic**

The **girl** who threw butterflies. Cochrane, M.   **Fic**

The **girl** who was on fire.   **813**

The **girl** with a baby. Olsen, S.   **Fic**

The **girl** with borrowed wings. Rossetti, R.   **Fic**

The **girl** with the mermaid hair. Ephron, D.   **Fic**

Girl's best friend. Margolis, L.   **Fic**

The **girl's** body book. Dunham, K.   **613**

Girlfriend material. Kantor, M.   **Fic**

Girlhearts. Mazer, N. F.   **Fic**

Girlology's there's something new about you. Holmes, M.   **612.6**

Girlosophy: real girls eat. Paul, A.   **641.5**

The **girls.** Koss, A. G.   **Fic**

GIRLS

    See also Children

GIRLS

33 things every girl should know   **810**

Buchanan, A. J. The daring book for girls **646.700**

Cisneros, S. The house on Mango Street   **Fic**

Holmes, M. Girlology's there's something new about you   **612.6**

Jeffrie, S. The girls' book of glamour   **646.7**

Jukes, M. Growing up: it's a girl thing   **612.6**

Red   **814**

Shandler, S. Ophelia speaks   **305.235**

Things I have to tell you   **810**

GIRLS -- BIOGRAPHY

McCann, M. R. Girls who rocked the world **920.72**

GIRLS -- FICTION

Miller, K. Kiki Strike   **Fic**

Pearson, L. Hilda and the Midnight Giant   **741.5**

Weissman, E. B. The short seller   **Fic**

GIRLS -- GRAPHIC NOVELS

Weinstein, L. Girl stories   **741.5**

GIRLS -- HEALTH AND HYGIENE

Will puberty last my whole life?   **613**

GIRLS -- HEALTH AND HYGIENE

Katz, A. Girl in the know   **612.6**

GIRLS -- FICTION

Hunt, L. M. One for the Murphys   **Fic**

GIRLS -- POETRY

George, K. O. Swimming upstream   **811**

GIRLS -- LIFE SKILLS GUIDES

Buchanan, A. J. The daring book for girls **646.700**

The care & keeping of you 2   **613**

GIRLS -- PHYSIOLOGY

Jukes, M. Growing up: it's a girl thing   **612.6**

GIRLS -- POETRY

Nye, N. S. A maze me   **811**

GIRLS -- PSYCHOLOGY

Stone, P. The boy on Cinnamon Street   **Fic**

GIRLS -- PSYCHOLOGY

Katz, A. Girl in the know   **612.6**

Girls acting catty. Margolis, L.   **Fic**

Girls against girls. Burton, B.   **305.23**

Girls don't fly. Chandler, K.   **Fic**

Girls gone green. Hirshfield, L.   **333.72**

Girls got game.   **810**

GIRLS IN LITERATURE

Buchanan, A. J. The daring book for girls **646.700**

The **girls** of No Return. Saldin, E.   **Fic**

Girls play to win [series]

Gitlin, M. Softball   **796.357**

Hoblin, P. Swimming & diving   **797.2**

Kassouf, J. Soccer   **796.334**

Kenney, K. L. Skiing & snowboarding   **796.93**

McDougall, C. Figure skating   **796.91**

McDougall, C. Track & field   **796.42**

McDougall, C. Volleyball   **796.325**

McMahon, D. Hockey   **796.962**

Robinson, T. Basketball   **796.323**

Smolka, B. Lacrosse   **796.34**

Girls rock. Goodmark, R.   **781.66**

Invisible invaders 614.4
Skin cancer 616.99
Superbugs strike back 615
Goldsmith, Francisca
The readers' advisory guide to graphic novels 025.2
Goldsmith, Mike
Graham, I. Science rocks! 507.8
Universe 523.1
Goldstein, Margaret J.
Lindop, E. America in the 1920s 973.91
Lindop, E. America in the 1930s 973.917
Lindop, E. America in the 1940s 973.917
Lindop, E. America in the 1960s 973.923
Goldstein, Natalie
(jt. auth) Campbell, M. C. Discovering atoms 539.7
Animal hunting and feeding 591.5
John Muir 92
Parkinson's disease 616.8
Goldstrike. Whyman, M. Fic
Goldsworthy, Steve
Steve Jobs 92
Goldwasser, Amy
(ed) Red 814
GOLDWORK
See also Art metalwork; Gold; Metalwork
GOLEM
See also Jewish legends; Mysticism/Judaism
GOLEM -- FICTION
Stemple, A. B.U.G. Fic
The **golem's** eye. Stroud, J. Fic
Golf. Kelley, K. C. 796.352
GOLF
Gifford, C. Golf: from tee to green 796.352
Kelley, K. C. Golf 796.352
Roberts, J. Tiger Woods 92
GOLF
See also Sports
GOLF -- FICTION
Lynch, C. The Big Game of Everything Fic
Golf: from tee to green. Gifford, C. 796.352
GOLFERS
Lobby, M. Babe Didrikson Zaharias 92
Roberts, J. Tiger Woods 92
Van Natta, D. Wonder girl 92
Goliath. Westerfeld, S. Fic
Golio, Gary
Spirit seeker 788.7
Golio, Gary
Jimi: sounds like a rainbow: a story of young Jimi Hendrix
Gollon, Matilda
(ed) The big idea science book 500
Golus, Carrie
Take a stand! 302.3
Tupac Shakur 92
Gone. Grant, M. Fic

Gone. McMann, L. Fic
Gone [series]
Grant, M. Lies Fic
Grant, M. Plague Fic
Grant, M. Fear Fic
Gone a-whaling. Murphy, J. 306.3
Gonzalez, Christina Diaz
The red umbrella Fic
Gonzalez, Julie
Imaginary enemy Fic
Goobie, Beth
Before wings Fic
Gooch, Anthony
Cassell's Spanish-English, English-Spanish dictionary 463
GOOD AND EVIL
See also Ethics; Philosophy; Theology
GOOD AND EVIL -- POETRY
Wicked poems 811
Good as Lily. Kim, D. K. 741.5
Good brother, bad brother. Giblin, J. 92
Good enough. Yoo, P. Fic
The **good** fight. Ambrose, S. E. 940.53
GOOD FRIDAY
See also Christian holidays; Holy Week; Lent
GOOD GROOMING *See* Personal grooming
A **good** horse. Smiley, J. Fic
Good masters! Sweet ladies! Schlitz, L. A. 940.1
The Good Neighbors [series]
Black, H. The Good Neighbors, book two: Kith 741.5
Black, H. The Good Neighbors; book one: Kin 741.5
Black, H. Kind 741.5
The **Good** Neighbors, book two: Kith. Black, H. 741.5
The **Good** Neighbors; book one: Kin. Black, H. 741.5
Good news Bible. Bible 220.5
Good Queen Bess: the story of Elizabeth I of England. Stanley, D. 92
Good sports [series]
Stout, G. Yes she can! 920
Good vs evil [series]
Dahl, M. Alien snow 741.5
Good women of a well-blessed land. Miller, B. M. 305.4
The **good,** the bad, and the Barbie. Stone, T. L. 688.7
The **good,** the bad, the slimy. Latta, S. L. 579
Goodall, Jane
The chimpanzees I love 599.8
Goodall, Jane, 1934-
About
Bardhan-Quallen, S. Jane Goodall 92
Kozleski, L. Jane Goodall 590
Welty, T. Jane Goodall 92

The **goodbye** season. Hale, M.   Fic
Goodbye, gasoline. Lew, K.   621.31
Goodbye, Vietnam. Whelan, G.   Fic
Goodman, Alison
   Eon: Dragoneye reborn   Fic
   Eona: the last Dragoneye   Fic
   Singing the Dogstar blues   Fic
Goodman, Allegra
   The other side of the island   Fic
Goodman, Benny, 1909-1986
         About
   Mattern, J. Benny Goodman   781.650
Goodman, Joan E.
   Despite all obstacles: La Salle and the conquest of the Mississippi   92
   A long and uncertain journey: the 27,000 mile voyage of Vasco da Gama   910
Goodman, Michael E.
   The CIA and other American spies   327.127
   The KGB and other Russian spies   327.124
   The SIS and other British spies   327.124
Goodman, Susan
   Ultimate field trip 5   629.45
Goodmark, Robyn
   Girls rock   781.66
Goodstein, Madeline
   Gardner, R. Ace your forces and motion science project   531
   Gardner, R. Ace your physical science project   530
   Gardner, R. Ace your space science project   520
   Ace your sports science project   507.8
   Goal! science projects with soccer   507.8
   Plastics and polymers science fair projects   540.7
   Water science fair projects   546
   Wheels!   530
Google. Hamen, S. E.   338.7
GOOGLE
     See also Web search engines; Web sites
Google founders: Larry Page and Sergey Brin. Sapet, K.   92
Gool. Gee, M.   Fic
The **Goose** girl. Hale, S.   Fic
Gootman, Marilyn E.
   When a friend dies   155.9
Gordon, Cambria
   David, L. The down-to-earth guide to global warming   363.7
Gordon, Roderick
   Closer   Fic
   Deeper   Fic
   Freefall   Fic
   Tunnels   Fic
Gordon, Sherri Mabry
   Beyond bruises   362.7
   The evolution debate   576.8
   Peanut butter, milk, and other deadly threats   616.97

Gore, Al
   An inconvenient truth   363.7
   Our choice   363.7
Gore, Al, 1948-
         About
   Baptiste, T. Al Gore   92
   Sergis, D. K. Bush v. Gore   342
GORGE-PURGE SYNDROME See Bulimia
Gorgeous. Vail, R.   Fic
The **gorgon's** gaze. Golding, J.   Fic
GORILLA -- UGANDA
   Sobol, R. Breakfast in the rainforest   599.8
Gorilla mountain. Ebersole, R.   92
Gorillas. Gish, M.   599.8
GORILLAS
   Ebersole, R. Gorilla mountain   92
   Gish, M. Gorillas   599.8
   Kushner, J. M. Who on earth is Dian Fossey?   92
   Sobol, R. Breakfast in the rainforest   599.8
GORILLAS
     See also Apes
GORILLAS -- FICTION
   Bushman lives!   Fic
Gorman, Carol
   Games   Fic
Gorman, Jacqueline Laks
   Fossil fuels   333.8
   The modern feminist movement   305.4
Gorman, Michele
   Connecting young adults and libraries   027.62
   Getting graphic!   741.5
Gormley, Beatrice
   Maria Mitchell   92
Gorrell, Gena K.
   In the land of the jaguar   980
   Say what?   422
   Working like a dog   636.7
Gorrissen, Janina
   I love him to pieces   741.5
   Stolarz, L. F. Black is for beginnings   741.5
The **gospel** according to Larry. Tashjian, J.   Fic
GOSPEL MUSIC
     See also African American music; Church music; Popular music
Goss, Linda
   (ed) Talk that talk: an anthology of African-American storytelling   398.2
Gosselink, John
   The defense of Thaddeus A. Ledbetter   Fic
GOSSIP
     See also Journalism; Libel and slander
Gotcha again for guys! Baxter, K. A.   028.5
Gotcha good! Baxter, K. A.   028.5
Goth girl rising. Lyga, B.   Fic
GOTHIC ARCHITECTURE
   Macaulay, D. Building the book Cathedral   726.6

Gothic Lolita. Lane, D.   **Fic**

GOTHIC NOVELS

    See also Historical fiction; Horror fiction; Occult fiction

GOTHIC NOVELS -- FICTION

    Brennan, S. R. Unspoken   **Fic**

GOTHIC REVIVAL (ARCHITECTURE)

    See also Architecture

GOTHIC REVIVAL (ART)

    See also Art

GOTHIC REVIVAL (LITERATURE)

    See also Literature

Gothic!   **S C**

Goths. Hinds, K.   **936**

GOTHS

    Hinds, K. Goths   **936**

GOTHS

    See also Teutonic peoples

Goto, Hiromi

    Half World   **Fic**

Gottfried, Ted

    Alcohol   **362.292**

    Censorship   **363.31**

    The facts about alcohol   **362.292**

    The facts about marijuana   **362.29**

    The fight for peace   **303.6**

    Marijuana   **362.29**

    Millard Fillmore   **92**

    The road to Communism   **947**

Gould, William

    (ed) The Facts on File dictionary of astronomy **520**

Gourlay, Candy

    Tall story   **Fic**

Gourley, Catherine

    Flappers and the new American woman   **305.4**

    Gibson girls and suffragists   **305.4**

    Gidgets and women warriors   **305.4**

    The horrors of Andersonville   **973.7**

    Rosie and Mrs. America   **305.4**

Gourse, Leslie

    Sophisticated ladies   **920**

GOUT

    See also Arthritis; Rheumatism

Govenar, Alan B.

    Extraordinary ordinary people   **745**

GOVERNESSES -- FICTION

    The unseen guest   **Fic**

GOVERNMENT AID TO LIBRARIES

    See also Government aid; Libraries -- Government policy; Library finance

Government and social class in colonial America. Nardo, D.   **973.2**

GOVERNMENT BUDGETS *See* Budget

GOVERNMENT BUSINESS ENTERPRISES

    See also Business enterprises

GOVERNMENT OFFICIALS

Aronson, M. John Winthrop, Oliver Cromwell, and the Land of Promise   **92**

Brown, D. A. Bury my heart at Wounded Knee   **970.004**

Childress, D. Barefoot conquistador   **92**

Ehrlich, A. Wounded Knee: an Indian history of the American West   **970.004**

Hubbard-Brown, J. Condoleezza Rice   **92**

Jarrow, G. Robert H. Jackson   **92**

Lourie, P. On the Texas trail of Cabeza de Vaca   **92**

Rice, C. Condoleezza Rice   **92**

GOVERNMENT OWNERSHIP

    See also Economic policy; Industrial policy; Socialism

GOVERNMENT POLICY *See* Buy national policy; Commercial policy; Cultural policy; Economic policy; Energy policy; Environmental policy; Fiscal policy; Industrial policy; Labor policy; Medical policy; Military policy; Monetary policy; Social policy; Wage-price policy

GOVERNMENT PUBLICATIONS

    See also Library resources

GOVERNMENT, RESISTANCE TO *See* Resistance to government

GOVERNMENT, RESISTANCE TO -- FICTION

Condie, A. Reached   **Fic**

Hill, C. J. Erasing time   **Fic**

Oliver, L. Requiem   **Fic**

Pearson, M. E. Fox forever   **Fic**

GOVERNMENTAL INVESTIGATIONS

    See also Administration of justice

GOVERNORS

Allen, M. G. Calvin Coolidge   **973.91**

Bausum, A. Unraveling freedom   **940.3**

Bodden, V. Samuel Houston   **92**

Bolden, T. FDR's alphabet soup   **973.917**

Branscomb, L. W. Earl Warren   **92**

Brill, M. T. America in the 1980s   **973.927**

Burgan, M. Ronald Reagan   **92**

Byrnes, P. Environmental pioneers   **363.7**

Cooper, M. L. Theodore Roosevelt   **92**

The Election of 2000 and the administration of George W. Bush   **324**

Elish, D. Theodore Roosevelt   **92**

Fitzpatrick, B. Theodore Roosevelt   **92**

Freedman, R. Franklin Delano Roosevelt   **973.917**

Fritz, J. Bully for you, Teddy Roosevelt!   **92**

Harness, C. The remarkable, rough-riding life of Theodore Roosevelt and the rise of empire America   **92**

Hollihan, K. L. Theodore Roosevelt for kids   **92**

Kennedy, J. F. Profiles in courage   **920**

Kraft, B. H. Theodore Roosevelt   **973.91**

Lukes, B. L. Woodrow Wilson and the Progressive Era   **92**

Marsico, K. Ronald Reagan   **92**

Beaty, A. Dorko the magnificent **Fic**

GRANDMOTHERS -- GRAPHIC NOVELS

Heuvel, E. A family secret **741.5**

GRANDMOTHERS -- FICTION

Manzano, S. The revolution of Evelyn Serrano **Fic**

GRANDMOTHERS -- POETRY

Grover, L. A. Loose threads **811**

GRANDPARENT AND CHILD *See* Grandparent-grandchild relationship

GRANDPARENT AND CHILD -- FICTION

Manzano, S. The revolution of Evelyn Serrano **Fic**

GRANDPARENT-GRANDCHILD RELATION-SHIP

See also Family; Grandparents

GRANDPARENT-GRANDCHILD RELATION-SHIP -- FICTION

Brouwer, S. Devil's pass **Fic**

GRANDPARENTING

See also Grandparents; Parenting

GRANDPARENTS

Simons, R. Grandparents raising kids **306.8**

See also Family

GRANDPARENTS -- FICTION

Balliett, B. The Danger Box **Fic**
Creech, S. Walk two moons **Fic**
Ehrenberg, P. Ethan, suspended **Fic**
Hemingway, E. M. Road to Tater Hill **Fic**
Hirahara, N. 1001 cranes **Fic**
Hughes, D. Missing in action **Fic**
Kadohata, C. The thing about luck **Fic**
Kwasney, M. D. Itch **Fic**
McDonnell, M. Torn to pieces **Fic**
Meyerhoff, J. Queen of secrets **Fic**
Resau, L. What the moon saw **Fic**
Stone, P. The boy on Cinnamon Street **Fic**
Watson, R. What Momma left me **Fic**

GRANDPARENTS AS PARENTS

See also Grandparents; Parenting

Grandparents raising kids. Simons, R. **306.8**

Grandpre, Mary

Harry Potter and the deathly hallows **Fic**
Rowling, J. K. Harry Potter and the Chamber of Secrets **Fic**
Rowling, J. K. Harry Potter and the Goblet of Fire **Fic**
Rowling, J. K. Harry Potter and the Half-blood Prince **Fic**
Rowling, J. K. Harry Potter and the Order of the Phoenix **Fic**
Rowling, J. K. Harry Potter and the prisoner of Azkaban **Fic**
Rowling, J. K. Harry Potter and the Sorcerer's Stone **Fic**
Townley, R. The blue shoe **Fic**

GRANITE

See also Rocks; Stone

Grant, Alan

Robert Louis Stevenson's Kidnapped **741.5**
Robert Louis Stevenson's Strange case of Dr. Jekyll and Mr. Hyde **741.5**

Grant, Gavin J.

(ed) Steampunk! **S C**

Grant, K. M.

Paradise red **Fic**

Grant, K. M.

Blaze of silver **Fic**
Blood red horse **Fic**
Blue flame **Fic**
Green jasper **Fic**
How the hangman lost his heart **Fic**
White heat **Fic**

Grant, Katy

Hide and seek **Fic**

Grant, Michael, 1954-

(jt. auth) Applegate, K. Eve & Adam **Fic**
The call **Fic**
Fear **Fic**
Gone **Fic**
Hunger **Fic**
Lies **Fic**
Plague **Fic**
The trap **Fic**
Grant, M. Fear **Fic**
Grant, M. Hunger **Fic**

Grant, Neil

Ancient Egypt and Greece **932**
Renaissance Europe **940.2**

Grant, R. G.

The Cold War **909.82**
Why did Hiroshima happen? **940.54**
Why did the Great Depression happen? **330.9**
Why did World War I happen? **940.3**

Grant, Reg

Slavery **326**

Grant, Ulysses S. (Ulysses Simpson), 1822-1885

About

Benoit, P. The surrender at Appomattox **973.7**

Grant, Vicki

Quid pro quo **Fic**
Res judicata **Fic**

GRANTS *See* Grants-in-aid; Subsidies

GRANTS-IN-AID

Anderson, C. Write grants, get money **025.1**

GRAPES

See also Fruit

GRAPH THEORY

See also Algebra; Mathematical analysis; Topology

GRAPHIC ARTS

See also Art

Graphic battles of World War II [series]

Hama, L. The battle of Iwo Jima **940.54**

See also Ecology

The grassland trilogy [series]
Ward, D. Beneath the mask   Fic
Ward, D. Beyond the mask   Fic
Ward, D. Escape the mask   Fic
GRASSLANDS
Hoare, B. Temperate grasslands   577.4
GRASSLANDS
See also Land use
GRATITUDE
See also Emotions; Virtue
Gratz, Alan
The Brooklyn nine   Fic
Samurai shortstop   Fic
The **grave** robber's secret. Myers, A.   Fic
GRAVE ROBBING
Sheinkin, S. Lincoln's Grave Robbers   973.709
GRAVE ROBBING -- FICTION
Myers, A. The grave robber's secret   Fic
Gravelle, Jennifer
Gravelle, K. The period book   612.6
Gravelle, Karen
The period book   612.6
Graven images. Fleischman, P.   S C
GRAVES *See* Burial; Cemeteries; Epitaphs; Funeral rites and ceremonies; Mounds and mound builders; Tombs
Graves, Keith
The orphan of Awkward Falls   Fic
Gravett, Christopher
Going to war in Viking times   355
The **graveyard** book. Gaiman, N.   Fic
GRAVEYARDS *See* Cemeteries
GRAVITATION
See also Physics
GRAVITY
Phelan, G. Invisible force   531
Sullivan, N. Weight   530
GRAVITY
Claybourne, A. Gut-wrenching gravity and other fatal forces   531
Gray baby. Sanders, S. L.   Fic
Gray matter [series]
Hudmon, A. Learning and memory   153.1
Morgan, J. Cells of the nervous system   611
The **Gray** Wolf Throne. Chima, C. W.   Fic
Gray, Claudia
Spellcaster   Fic
Gray, Dianne E.
Tomorrow, the river   Fic
Gray, Edward G.
Colonial America   973.2
Gray, Judy Silverstein
The U.S. Coast Guard and military careers   359.9
Gray, Keith
Ostrich boys   Fic

Gray, Leon
Iodine   546
Tin   546
Virtual crime!   363.2
Zinc   546
(ed) The new cultural atlas of Egypt   932
Gray, Susan Heinrichs
Australian spotted jellyfish   593.5
Emerald ash borer   595.7
Living with juvenile rheumatoid arthritis   616.7
Gray, Virginia
Lee, C. The great number rumble   510
The **gray-eyed** goddess. Osborne, M. P.   883
Graydon, Shari
In your face   391
Grayson, Devin
Uglies   741.5
Grayson, Robert
The Amistad   326
Managing your digital footprint   004.6
Military   355.4
Performers   791.8
Transportation   636.088
GREASE *See* Lubrication and lubricants; Oils and fats
Grease town. Towell, A.   Fic
Great achievers [series]
Lyons, M. E. Sorrow's kitchen   92
The **great** and only Barnum. Fleming, C.   92
A **great** and sublime fool. Caravantes, P.   92
Great art thefts. Guillain, C.   364.16
Great artists and their world [series]
Spence, D. Cezanne   92
Spence, D. Degas   92
Spence, D. Gauguin   92
Spence, D. Manet   92
Spence, D. Michelangelo   709.2
Spence, D. Monet   92
Spence, D. Picasso   92
Spence, D. Renoir   92
Great athletes.   920.003
GREAT AUNTS -- FICTION
Pennypacker, S. The summer of the gypsy moths   Fic
The **Great** Barrier Reef. Kummer, P. K.   578.7
Great battles through the ages [series]
Crompton, S. The Third Crusade   956
The **great** brain book. Newquist, H. P.   612.8
GREAT BRITAIN -- COURT AND COURTIERS -- BIOGRAPHY
Aronson, M. Sir Walter Ralegh and the quest for El Dorado   942.05
GREAT BRITAIN -- HISTORY -- 1066-1485, MEDIEVAL PERIOD
Nardo, D. Medieval Europe   940.1

GREAT BRITAIN -- HISTORY -- 1558-1603, ELIZABETH

Kallen, S. A. Elizabethan England **942.05**

GREAT BRITAIN -- HISTORY -- 19TH CENTURY -- FICTION

The unseen guest **Fic**

GREAT BRITAIN -- HISTORY -- ELIZABETH, 1558-1603 -- FICTION

Blackwood, G. L. The Shakespeare stealer **Fic**

Cushman, K. Will Sparrow's road **Fic**

GREAT BRITAIN

Indovino, S. C. United Kingdom **941**

GREAT BRITAIN -- KINGS AND RULERS

See also Kings and rulers

Great building feats [series]

DuTemple, L. A. The Panama Canal **972.87**

DuTemple, L. A. The Pantheon **726**

DuTemple, L. A. The Taj Mahal **726**

The **great** Chicago fire of 1871. Bennie, P. **363.1**

The **great** circle. Philip, N. **970.004**

Great Civil War projects you can build yourself. Anderson, M. **973.7**

The **Great** Death. Smelcer, J. E. **Fic**

Great decisions [series]

Aaseng, N. You are the juror **345**

The **Great** Depression. Burg, D. F. **973.91**

The **Great** Depression. Bingham, J. **973.91**

GREAT DEPRESSION, 1929-1939

Bingham, J. The Great Depression **973.91**

Blumenthal, K. Six days in October **332.64**

Burg, D. F. The Great Depression **973.91**

Collier, C. Progressivism, the Great Depression, and the New Deal, 1901 to 1941 **973.91**

Cooper, M. L. Dust to eat **973.917**

Corrigan, J. The 1930s decade in photos **973.917**

Doak, R. S. Black Tuesday **330.9**

Freedman, R. Children of the Great Depression **305.23**

Grant, R. G. Why did the Great Depression happen? **330.9**

Lange, B. The Stock Market Crash of 1929 **330.9**

Marrin, A. Years of dust **978**

McElvaine, R. S. The Depression and New Deal **973.91**

McNeese, T. The Great Depression, 1929-1940 **973.917**

Nardo, D. Migrant mother **973.917**

Ruggiero, A. American voices from The Great Depression **973.917**

Stanley, J. Children of the Dust Bowl **371.9**

GREAT DEPRESSION, 1929-1939

See also Depressions; Economic conditions

GREAT DEPRESSION, 1929-1939 -- FICTION

Ayres, K. Macaroni boy **Fic**

Blume, L. M. M. Tennyson **Fic**

Brown, D. The train jumper **Fic**

Curtis, C. P. Bud, not Buddy **Fic**

Fusco, K. N. The wonder of Charlie Anne **Fic**

Giff, P. R. R my name is Rachel **Fic**

Hale, M. The truth about sparrows **Fic**

Hesse, K. Out of the dust **Fic**

Ingold, J. Hitch **Fic**

Jackson, A. Rainmaker **Fic**

Laskas, G. M. The miner's daughter **Fic**

Lottridge, C. B. The listening tree **Fic**

Meltzer, M. Tough times **Fic**

Peck, R. A long way from Chicago **Fic**

Peck, R. A year down yonder **Fic**

Peterson, L. J. Silver rain **Fic**

Pinkney, A. D. Bird in a box **Fic**

Taylor, M. D. Let the circle be unbroken **Fic**

Vanderpool, C. Moon over Manifest **Fic**

Vollmar, R. The castaways **741.5**

Yep, L. Dragon road **Fic**

GREAT DEPRESSION, 1929-1939

Golden, L. Every day after **Fic**

The **Great** Depression, 1929-1940. McNeese, T. **973.917**

Great displays for your library step by step. Phillips, S. P. **021.7**

Great episodes [series]

Rinaldi, A. Come Juneteenth **Fic**

Rinaldi, A. The fifth of March **Fic**

Great expectations. Geary, R. **741.5**

The **great** explainer. LeVine, H. **92**

Great explorations [series]

Calvert, P. Vasco da Gama **92**

Elish, D. Edmund Hillary **92**

Otfinoski, S. Henry Hudson **92**

Young, S. Richard Francis Burton **92**

Great explorers [series]

Crompton, S. Lewis and Clark **92**

Crompton, S. Robert de La Salle **92**

Crompton, S. Sir Edmund Hillary **92**

Koestler-Grack, R. A. Ferdinand Magellan **92**

Koestler-Grack, R. A. Sir Ernest Shackleton **92**

Lace, W. W. Captain James Cook **92**

Lace, W. W. Sir Francis Drake **92**

Wagner, H. L. Hernan Cortes **92**

Woog, A. Jacques Cartier **92**

Great explorers book [series]

Goodman, J. E. Despite all obstacles: La Salle and the conquest of the Mississippi **92**

Goodman, J. E. A long and uncertain journey: the 27,000 mile voyage of Vasco da Gama **910**

Great explorers of the world [series]

Aretha, D. La Salle **92**

Aretha, D. Magellan **92**

DeFries, C. L. Leif Eriksson **92**

Feinstein, S. Captain Cook **92**

Feinstein, S. Columbus **92**

Feinstein, S. Marco Polo **92**

man origins **599.93**

Great scientists. Fortey, J. **920**

Great scientists and famous inventors [series]

Graham, A. Astonishing ancient world scientists **920**

Young, J. C. Brilliant African-American scientists **920**

Young, J. C. Inspiring African-American inventors **920**

Great shakes. Stille, D. R. **551.2**

Great Smoky Mountains National Park. Graham, A. **976.8**

GREAT SMOKY MOUNTAINS NATIONAL PARK (N.C. AND TENN.)

Graham, A. Great Smoky Mountains National Park **976.8**

Great speeches in history series

Civil rights **323.1**

The Founding of America **973.3**

Great spiritual leaders of modern times [series]

Gandhi **92**

Great Supreme Court decisions [series]

Mountjoy, S. Engel v. Vitale **344**

VanMeter, L. A. Miranda v. Arizona **345**

The **great** thinker: Aristotle and the foundations of science. Gow, M. **92**

The **Great** Train Robbery. Haugen, B. **364.1**

Great trials of the 20th century [series]

Sorensen, L. The Scottsboro Boys Trial **345**

The **great** unexpected. Creech, S. **Fic**

The **great** whaleship disaster of 1871. Baker, J. **910.4**

The **great** wide sea. Herlong, M. **Fic**

Great Zimbabwe. Hall, M. **968.91**

The **greatest** basketball records. Doeden, M. **796.323**

The **greatest** doctor of ancient times: Hippocrates and his oath. Gow, M. **92**

The **greatest** football records. Dougherty, T. **796.332**

The **greatest** mathematician. Hightower, P. **92**

The **greatest** moments in sports. Berman, L. **796**

The **greatest** moments in sports. Berman, L. **796.097**

The **greatest** stories never told. Beyer, R. **904**

The **greatest**: Muhammad Ali. Myers, W. D. **92**

Greathouse, Lisa E.

Skygazers **920**

Solar system **523.2**

Greece. Etingoff, K. **949.5**

Greece. Heinrichs, A. **949.5**

Greece. Green, J. **949.5**

GREECE -- BIOGRAPHY

See also Biography

GREECE -- CIVILIZATION

Stafford, E. J. Exploring the life, myth, and art of ancient Greece **938**

GREECE -- CIVILIZATION

See also Classical civilization

Heinrichs, A. Greece **949.5**

Marcovitz, H. Ancient Greece **938**

Nardo, D. Classical civilization **938**

Steele, P. Ancient Greece **938**

GREECE -- GEOGRAPHY

See also Geography

GREECE -- HISTORICAL GEOGRAPHY

See also Ancient geography; Greece -- Geography; Historical geography

GREECE -- HISTORY -- 0-323

Stafford, E. J. Exploring the life, myth, and art of ancient Greece **938**

GREECE -- HISTORY -- GRAPHIC NOVELS

Marathon **741.5**

GREECE -- HISTORY

Heinrichs, A. Greece **949.5**

Marcovitz, H. Ancient Greece **938**

Nardo, D. Classical civilization **938**

Steele, P. Ancient Greece **938**

GREECE

Etingoff, K. Greece **949.5**

GREECE -- RELIGION

Stafford, E. J. Exploring the life, myth, and art of ancient Greece **938**

GREECE -- SOCIAL LIFE AND CUSTOMS

Orr, T. The food of Greece **394.1**

GREECE, ANCIENT See Greece -- History -- 0-323

GREED

See also Human behavior

Greek and Roman mythology, A to Z. Daly, K. N. **292**

GREEK ARCHITECTURE

See also Ancient architecture; Architecture

GREEK ART

Langley, A. Ancient Greece **709.3**

Stafford, E. J. Exploring the life, myth, and art of ancient Greece **938**

GREEK ART

See also Ancient art; Art; Classical antiquities

GREEK CIVILIZATION See Greece -- Civilization

GREEK COOKING

Orr, T. The food of Greece **394.1**

GREEK LITERATURE

See also Literature

GREEK MYTHOLOGY

Napoli, D. J. Treasury of Greek mythology **398.2**

O'Connor, G. Hades **398.209**

Stafford, E. J. Exploring the life, myth, and art of ancient Greece **938**

GREEK MYTHOLOGY

See also Classical mythology

GREEK MYTHOLOGY -- GRAPHIC NOVELS

Foley, R. Stolen hearts **741.5**

Ford, C. Stickman Odyssey 741.5
Hinds, G. The Odyssey 741.5
Hoena, B. A. Perseus and Medusa 741.5
Langridge, R. Thor, the mighty avenger, v.1. 741.5
Venditti, R. The lightning thief: the graphic novel 741.5
Greek myths. Turnbull, A. 292
GREEK ORTHODOX CHURCH
    See also Christian sects; Orthodox Eastern Church
Greek ransom. Malaghan, M. Fic
GREEK SCULPTURE
    See also Sculpture
The **Greek** who stole Christmas. Horowitz, A. Fic
Greeks. Kerrigan, M. 938
Green. Roberts, L. P. Fic
Green angel. Hoffman, A. Fic
GREEN ARROW (FICTIONAL CHARACTER)
    Kreisberg, A. Green Arrow and Black Canary: five stages 741.5
Green Arrow and Black Canary: five stages. Kreisberg, A. 741.5
Green Berets. Earl, C. F. 356
Green careers. Power Scott, J. 333.72
Green careers [series]
    Brezina, C. Jobs in sustainable energy 333.79
    Byers, A. Jobs as green builders and planners 690
    Ching, J. Jobs in green travel and tourism 910.2
    Harmon, D. Jobs in environmental cleanup and emergency hazmat response 628
    Hayhurst, C. Jobs in environmental law 344
    Johanson, P. Jobs in sustainable agriculture 630
Green changes you can make around your home. Smalley, C. P. 333.72
Green construction. Miller, M. 690
Green general contractor. Somervill, B. A. 690
Green generation [series]
    Dell, P. Protecting the planet 333.72
    Hanel, R. Climate fever 363.7
    Raatma, L. Green living 333.72
    Rau, D. M. Alternative energy beyond fossil fuels 333.79
The **green** glass sea. Klages, E. Fic
Green jasper. Grant, K. M. Fic
Green jobs. Farrell, C. 331.7
Green living. Raatma, L. 333.72
The **green** movement. 333.72
GREEN MOVEMENT *See* Environmental movement
Green reads. Wesson, L. P. 016
GREEN TECHNOLOGY
    See also Technology
Green witch. Hoffman, A. Fic
The **green world** [series]
    Gibson, J. P. Plant diversity 580
    Hopkins, W. G. Plant biotechnology 630

Young, K. J. Ethnobotany 581.6
Green, Carl R.
    Buffalo Bill Cody 978
    Calamity Jane 978
    Daniel Boone 976.9
    Davy Crockett 976.8
    Sacagawea 978.004
    Sam Houston 976.4
    Spacewalk 629.45
    Zebulon Pike 978
Green, Caroline
    Drug resistance 616.9
    Stem cells 616.02
Green, Dan
    (jt. auth) Basher, S. Oceans 551.46
    Basher, S. Human body 612
    Algebra & geometry 516.2
    Astronomy 520
    Chemistry 540
    The elements 546
    Extreme biology 570
    Physics 530
    Rocks and minerals 552
Green, Jen
    Ancient Celts 936
    Conservation 333.72
    Food and farming 338.1
    Greece 949.5
    Inside animals 571
    Jamaica 972.92
    Vietnam 959.7
Green, Julie
    Shooting video to make learning fun 778.5
    Write it down 371.3
Green, Michelle Y.
    A strong right arm: the story of Mamie Peanut Johnson 92
Green, Tim
    Baseball great Fic
    Best of the best Fic
    The big time Fic
    Deep zone Fic
    Football champ Fic
    Football genius Fic
    Football hero Fic
    Rivals Fic
Green, Tim, 1963-
    Force out Fic
Green-collar careers [series]
    Gazlay, S. Managing green spaces 333.7
Greenaway, Theresa
    Jungle 577.3
Greenberg, Dan
    Whales 599.5
Greenberg, Daniel A.
    Whales 599.5

Haiti. Yomtov, N.   **972.94**

HAITI

  Yomtov, N. Haiti   **972.94**

Hakim, Joy

  The story of science: Aristotle leads the way   **509**

  The story of science: Einstein adds a new dimension   **509**

  The story of science: Newton at the center   **509**

Halam, Ann

  Snakehead   **Fic**

Hale, Dean

  Rapunzel's revenge   **741.5**

  Hale, S. Calamity Jack   **741.5**

Hale, Marian

  The goodbye season   **Fic**

  The truth about sparrows   **Fic**

Hale, Nathan, 1755-1776 -- Fiction

About

  Myers, A. Spy!   **Fic**

Hale, Rosemary Drage

  Christianity   **230**

Hale, Shannon

  (jt. auth) Hale, D. Rapunzel's revenge   **741.5**

  Book of a thousand days   **Fic**

  Calamity Jack   **741.5**

  Enna burning   **Fic**

  Forest born   **Fic**

  The Goose girl   **Fic**

  Princess Academy   **Fic**

  River secrets   **Fic**

Haley, James L.

  Stephen F. Austin and the founding of Texas **976.4**

Half brother. Oppel, K.   **Fic**

Half spoon of rice.   **Fic**

Half upon a time. Riley, J.   **Fic**

Half World. Goto, H.   **Fic**

Half-human.   **S C**

Half-minute horrors.   **S C**

Half-Moon investigations. Colfer, E.   **Fic**

Halilbegovich, Nadja

  My childhood under fire   **949.7**

Halilbegovich, Nadja, 1979-

About

  Halilbegovich, N. My childhood under fire **949.7**

Hall, Alvin

  Show me the money   **332.024**

Hall, C. Aubrey

  Crystal bones   **Fic**

Hall, Derek

  (ed) Chemistry, Earth, and space sciences   **920**

  (ed) Life sciences   **920**

  (ed) Philosophy, invention, and engineering   **920**

  (ed) Physical sciences   **920**

Hall, Donald

  (ed) The Oxford book of children's verse in America   **811**

Hall, Elizabeth

  O'Dell, S. Thunder rolling in the mountains   **Fic**

Hall, Howard

  A charm of dolphins   **599.5**

Hall, Linley Erin

  DNA and RNA   **611**

  The transactinides   **546**

Hall, Margaret

  Skin deep   **612.7**

Hall, Martin

  Great Zimbabwe   **968.91**

Hall, Megan Kelley

  (ed) Dear bully   **302.3**

Hall, Susan

  Using picture storybooks to teach literary devices   **016**

Hall, Teri

  Away   **Fic**

  The Line   **Fic**

Halleck, Elaine

  (ed) Living in Nazi Germany   **943.086**

HALLEY'S COMET

    See also Comets

Halley, Edmond, 1656-1742

About

  Fox, M. V. Scheduling the heavens   **92**

The **hallowed** ones. Bickle, L.   **Fic**

HALLOWEEN

    See also Holidays

HALLOWEEN -- FICTION

  Bradbury, R. The Halloween tree   **Fic**

  Coville, B. The monster's ring   **Fic**

  Draanen, W. v. Sammy Keyes and the skeleton man   **Fic**

  Van Draanen, W. Sammy Keyes and the night of skulls   **Fic**

  Vande Velde, V. All Hallows' Eve   **S C**

  Zucker, N. F. Callie's rules   **Fic**

The **Halloween** tree. Bradbury, R.   **Fic**

Hallowell, Edward M.

  Positively ADD   **616.85**

Halls, Kelly Milner

  Mysteries of the mummy kids   **393**

  Saving the Baghdad Zoo   **636.088**

  Tales of the cryptids   **001.9**

  Wild dogs   **599.77**

  Wild horses   **599.66**

HALLUCINATIONS AND ILLUSIONS

    See also Abnormal psychology; Parapsychology; Subconsciousness; Visions

HALLUCINOGENIC DRUGS *See* Hallucinogens

  Barter, J. Hallucinogens   **362.29**

HALLUCINOGENIC PLANTS *See* Hallucinogens

  Barter, J. Hallucinogens   **362.29**

Hallucinogens. Barter, J.   **362.29**

Harper, Suzanne

Earnest, P. The real spy's guide to becoming a spy   327.12

The Juliet club   Fic

The secret life of Sparrow Delaney   Fic

Harper, Timothy

Harper, E. Your name in print   808

Harpur, James

Celtic myth   299

Harriet Beecher Stowe and the Beecher preachers. Fritz, J.   813

Harriet Tubman. Sawyer, K. K.   92

Harriet Tubman and the Underground Railroad. Adler, D. A.   973.7

Harriet Tubman, secret agent. Allen, T. B.   92

Harrington, Karen

Sure signs of crazy   Fic

Harris and me. Paulsen, G.   Fic

Harris, Ashley Rae

Cliques, crushes & true friends   158

Do you love me?   613.9

Girl in the mirror   158

Is this really my family?   646.7

Tupac Shakur   92

Txt me l8r   303.4

Harris, Blake

Ferry, S. Yukon Territory   971

Harris, Caroline

Wild weather   551.55

Harris, Christopher

Mayer, B. Libraries got game   025.2

Harris, Elizabeth Snoke

Crime scene science fair projects   363.2

Save the Earth science experiments   507.8

Harris, Frances Jacobson

I found it on the Internet   025.042

Harris, Joanne

Runemarks   Fic

Harris, John

Strong stuff   398.2

Harris, Joseph

Space exploration   629.4

Transportation   388

Harris, Laurie Lanzen

The great migration north, 1910-1970   307.2

Harris, Lewis

A taste for red   Fic

Harris, Nathaniel

Ancient Maya   972

Crime fighting   363.2

Drug trafficking   363.45

Mosaics   738.5

Wall paintings   751.7

Harris, Robert J.

Yolen, J. Girl in a cage   Fic

Yolen, J. The queen's own fool   Fic

Yolen, J. The Rogues   Fic

Harris, Robie H.

It's perfectly normal   613.9

Harris, Tim

(ed) Mammals of the Northern Hemisphere   599.168

(ed) Reptiles and amphibians   333.95

Harrison, Cora

I was Jane Austen's best friend   Fic

Harrison, David L.

(ed) Dude!   810

Mammoth bones and broken stones   970.01

Harrison, George

About

Spitz, B. Yeah! yeah! yeah!   920

Roberts, J. The Beatles   781.66

Harrison, Michael

(ed) The Oxford book of story poems   808.81

Harrison, Michelle

13 curses   Fic

13 treasures   Fic

Harrison, Paul

Why did the Cold War happen?   909.82

Harrison, Troon

The horse road   Fic

Harry Houdini for kids. Carlson, L. M.   92

Harry Potter and the Chamber of Secrets. Rowling, J. K.   Fic

Harry Potter and the deathly hallows.   Fic

Harry Potter and the Goblet of Fire. Rowling, J. K.   Fic

Harry Potter and the Half-blood Prince. Rowling, J. K.   Fic

Harry Potter and the Order of the Phoenix. Rowling, J. K.   Fic

Harry Potter and the prisoner of Azkaban. Rowling, J. K.   Fic

Harry Potter and the Sorcerer's Stone. Rowling, J. K.   Fic

HARRY POTTER BOOKS

Sickels, A. Mythmaker: the story of J.K. Rowling   92

Harry Sue. Stauffacher, S.   Fic

Hart, Alison

Gabriel's horses   Fic

Gabriel's triumph   Fic

Hart, Christopher

Drawing the new adventure cartoons   741.5

How to draw comic book bad guys and gals   741.5

Manga for the beginner   741.5

Manga mania romance   741.5

Mecha mania   741.5

Hart, John

Walking softly in the wilderness   796.51

Hart, Joyce

Baldwin, G. Oklahoma   976.6

Baldwin, G. Wyoming   978.7

Rooney, A. Health and medicine   **610**
Stoyles, P. The A-Z of health   **616**
HEALTH -- INFORMATION SERVICES
Lukenbill, W. B. Health information in a changing world   **372**
HEALTH
Rau, D. M. Going organic   **613.2**
HEALTH -- STUDY AND TEACHING See Health education
Health alert [series]
Bjorklund, R. Asthma   **616.2**
Bjorklund, R. Cerebral palsy   **616.8**
Bjorklund, R. Cystic fibrosis   **616.3**
Bjorklund, R. Epilepsy   **616.8**
Brill, M. T. Alzheimer's disease   **616.8**
Brill, M. T. Down syndrome   **616.85**
Calamandrei, C. Fever   **616**
Capaccio, G. ADD and ADHD   **616.85**
Colligan, L. H. Sleep disorders   **616.8**
Colligan, L. H. Tick-borne illnesses   **616.9**
Hicks, T. A. Obesity   **616.3**
Hoffmann, G. Chicken pox   **616.9**
Hoffmann, G. The flu   **616.2**
Hoffmann, G. Osteoporosis   **616.7**
Klosterman, L. Meningitis   **616.8**
Health and disease. Henningfeld, D. A.   **363.7**
Health and medicine. Rooney, A.   **610**
Health at risk [series]
Allman, T. Drugs   **616.86**
Allman, T. Obesity   **616.3**
Bjornlund, L. D. Alcohol   **362.292**
Currie, S. Junk food   **613.2**
Miller, H. Smoking   **616.86**
Schaefer, A. Steroids   **362.29**
Stewart, G. Anorexia   **616.85**
Stewart, G. Bulimia   **616.85**
HEALTH BEHAVIOR
Fullick, A. Understanding health and behavior **150**
HEALTH CARE See Medical care
HEALTH CARE DELIVERY See Medical care
Health care for everyone. Jones, M.   **362.1**
HEALTH CARE PERSONNEL See Medical personnel
HEALTH COUNSELING
See also Counseling; Health education
HEALTH EDUCATION
Lukenbill, W. B. Health information in a changing world   **372**
HEALTH EDUCATION
See also Education; Health
HEALTH FACILITIES
See also Medical care; Public health
HEALTH FOODS See Natural foods
Health information in a changing world. Lukenbill, W. B.   **372**
HEALTH INSURANCE

Jones, M. Health care for everyone   **362.1**
HEALTH MAINTENANCE ORGANIZATIONS
See also Health insurance; Medical practice
HEALTH PERSONNEL See Medical personnel
HEALTH PROFESSIONS See Medical personnel
Health science projects about psychology. Gardner, R.   **150**
HEALTH SCIENCES PERSONNEL See Medical personnel
HEALTH SELF-CARE
See also Alternative medicine; Health; Medical care
HEALTH SERVICES ACCESSIBILITY See Access to health care
HEALTH SERVICES PERSONNEL See Medical personnel
Health zone [series]
Doeden, M. Eat right!   **613.2**
Donovan, S. Keep your cool!   **616.85**
Golus, C. Take a stand!   **302.3**
Nelson, S. K. Stay safe!   **613.6**
Healthy eating: a guide to nutrition [series]
Allman, T. Nutrition and disease prevention **612.3**
Smolin, L. A. Nutrition and weight management   **613.2**
Healthy lifestyles [series]
De la Bedoyere, C. Balancing work and play **155.9**
De la Bedoyere, C. Personal hygiene and sexual health   **613**
Dicker, K. Diet and nutrition   **613**
Dicker, K. Exercise   **613.7**
Gifford, C. Sports   **796**
Rooney, A. Dealing with drugs   **615**
Healthy living [series]
Edwards, H. Talking about your weight   **613.2**
Healy, Christopher
The hero's guide to saving your kingdom   **Fic**
The hero's guide to storming the castle   **Fic**
Hear the wind blow. Hahn, M. D.   **Fic**
HEARING
Simon, S. Eyes and ears   **612.8**
HEARING
See also Senses and sensation; Sound
HEARING AIDS
See also Deafness
HEARING EAR DOGS
See also Animals and the handicapped; Deaf -- Means of communication; Working dogs
HEARING IMPAIRED
See also Physically handicapped
HEARING IMPAIRED -- FICTION
Lean, S. A dog called Homeless   **Fic**
HEARING IN ANIMALS
See also Hearing; Senses and sensation in animals
Hearn, Julie

Hazel **Fic**
Ivy **Fic**
The minister's daughter **Fic**
Hearne, Betsy Gould
Beauty and the beast Beauties and beasts **398.21**
The canine connection: stories about dogs and people **S C**
Hearst, Patricia Campbell
About
Aaseng, N. You are the juror **345**
The **heart.** Simon, S. **612.1**
HEART
Markle, S. Faulty hearts **612.1**
Simon, S. The heart **612.1**
HEART
See also Cardiovascular system
HEART -- ANATOMY
See also Anatomy
HEART -- DISEASES *See* Heart diseases
Markle, S. Faulty hearts **612.1**
Silverstein, A. Heart disease **616.1**
HEART
Markle, S. Faulty hearts **612.1**
HEART -- PHYSIOLOGY
See also Physiology
HEART -- SURGERY
Yount, L. Alfred Blalock, Helen Taussig, and Vivien Thomas **617.4**
HEART -- SURGERY
See also Surgery
HEART -- TRANSPLANTATION
See also Transplantation of organs, tissues, etc.
HEART ATTACK
See also Heart diseases
Heart disease. Silverstein, A. **616.1**
HEART DISEASE *See* Heart diseases
HEART DISEASES
Markle, S. Faulty hearts **612.1**
Silverstein, A. Heart disease **616.1**
HEART DISEASES
See also Diseases
HEART DISEASES -- PREVENTION
See also Preventive medicine
The **heart** has its reasons. Cart, M. **813**
The **heart** is not a size. Kephart, B. **Fic**
Heart of a samurai. Preus, M. **Fic**
Heart of a shepherd. Parry, R. **Fic**
The **heart** of glass. French, V. **Fic**
Heart of stone. Welsh, M. L. **Fic**
HEART SURGEONS -- UNITED STATES -- BIOGRAPHY
Yount, L. Alfred Blalock, Helen Taussig, and Vivien Thomas **617.4**
Heart to heart. **811**
Heart's blood. Yolen, J. **Fic**

Hearts at stake. Harvey, A. **Fic**
Hearts of iron. Duble, K. B. **Fic**
Hearts of stone. Ernst, K. **Fic**
Heartsinger. Stoffels, K. **Fic**
Heat. Lupica, M. **Fic**
HEAT
Gardner, R. Easy genius science projects with temperature and heat **536**
Heat **536**
Sullivan, N. Temperature **536**
Heat. **536**
HEAT
Heat **536**
HEAT -- POETRY
Singer, M. Central heating **811**
HEAT ENGINES
See also Engines; Thermodynamics
Heath Ledger. Watson, S. **92**
Heath, Alan
Windows on the world **394.2**
Heath, Jack
The Lab **Fic**
Money run **Fic**
Remote control **Fic**
Heaven. Johnson, A. **Fic**
HEAVEN
See also Eschatology; Future life
Heaven looks a lot like the mall. Mass, W. **Fic**
HEAVY METALS -- ENVIRONMENTAL ASPECTS -- DANUBE RIVER WATERSHED
Bryan, N. Danube **363.7**
HEBRAISTS
Bitton-Jackson, L. I have lived a thousand years **940.53**
Bitton-Jackson, L. My bridges of hope **940.53**
HEBREW LITERATURE
See also Literature
HEBREWS *See* Jews
Heck. Basye, D. E. **Fic**
The **hedge** knight. Avery, B. **741.5**
Hegamin, Tonya
M+O 4evr **Fic**
Pemba's song **Fic**
Hegedus, Bethany
Between us Baxters **Fic**
Height, Dorothy I., 1912-2010
About
Pinkney, A. D. Let it shine **920**
The **heights,** the depths, and everything in between.
Nemeth, S. **Fic**
Heiligman, Deborah
Charles and Emma **92**
High hopes **92**
Heinrichs, Ann
The Amazon rain forest **981**
Gerardus Mercator **92**

The great recession 330.9
Greece 949.5
The Japanese American internment 940.53
Maine 974.1
Nebraska 978.2
Nevada 979.3
The Nile 962
North Carolina 975.6
The Sahara 966
Vermont 974.3
Heir apparent. Vande Velde, V. Fic
Heist Society. Carter, A. Fic
Helbig, Alethea
Myths and hero tales 398.2
Heldring, Thatcher
Roy Morelli steps up to the plate Fic
Helen Keller. MacLeod, E. 92
Helen Keller. Sullivan, G. 92
Helen Keller: rebellious spirit. Lawlor, L. 92
HELEN OF TROY (LEGENDARY CHARAC-TER) -- FICTION
Friesner, E. M. Nobody's princess Fic
Friesner, E. M. Nobody's prize Fic
McLaren, C. Inside the walls of Troy Fic
Helen's eyes. Delano, M. F. 92
Helfand, Lewis
Conquering Everest 741.5
Kim 741.5
Helft, Claude
Chinese mythology 299.5
Helgerson, Joseph
Crows & cards Fic
Horns & wrinkles Fic
Helget, Nicole
Barbarians 940.1
Mongols 950
Helget, Nicole Lea
Swans 598
HELICOPTERS
See also Aeronautics; Airplanes
HELIUM
See also Chemical elements; Gases
A Helium-3 novel [series]
Hickam, H. Crescent Fic
HELL
See also Eschatology; Future life
HELL -- FICTION
Agard, J. The young inferno Fic
Ashton, B. Everbound Fic
HELLENISM
See also Greece -- Civilization
Heller, Tania
Overweight 613.2
Hellie Jondoe. Platt, R. B. Fic
Helmrich, Erin
Create, relate & pop @ the library

Help wanted. Soto, G. S C
Help! What's eating my flesh? Tilden, T. E. L. 614.4
Helpers. Martin, C. 362.4
HELPING BEHAVIOR
See also Human behavior; Interpersonal relations
HELPLESSNESS (PSYCHOLOGY)
See also Emotions
Helsby, Genevieve
Those amazing musical instruments 784.19
Hemings family
About
Lanier, S. Jefferson's children 973.4
Hemings, Sally, 1773-1835
About
Bradley, K. B. Jefferson's sons Fic
Lanier, S. Jefferson's children 973.4
Hemingway, Edith Morris
Road to Tater Hill Fic
Hemingway, Ernest, 1899-1961
About
Pingelton, T. J. A student's guide to Ernest Hemingway 813
Reef, C. Ernest Hemingway 92
Whiting, J. Ernest Hemingway 92
Hemophilia. Raabe, M. 616.1
HEMOPHILIA
Raabe, M. Hemophilia 616.1
HEMP
See also Fibers
Hemphill, Helen
The adventurous deeds of Deadwood Jones Fic
Long gone daddy Fic
Hemphill, Leaunda S.
Myers, J. J. Responding to cyber bullying 371.5
Hemphill, Michael
Stonewall Hinkleman and the Battle of Bull Run Fic
Hemphill, Stephanie
Sisters of glass Fic
Wicked girls Fic
Your own, Sylvia 811
Henaff, Carole
Tarnowska, W. Arabian nights 398.2
Henderson, Harry
Alan Turing 92
Artificial intelligence 006.3
Communications and broadcasting 384
The Curie family 539.7
Larry Page and Sergey Brin 005.109
Mathematics: powerful patterns in nature and society 510
Modern robotics 629.8
Richard Feynman 92
Henderson, Harry, 1951-
The Leakey family 599.909
Henderson, Helene

HIGH RISE BUILDINGS *See* Skyscrapers

HIGH SCHOOL LIBRARIES
> *See also* School libraries

HIGH SCHOOL LIBRARIES -- BOOK LISTS

Keane, N. J. 101 great, ready-to-use book lists for teens **028.5**

HIGH SCHOOL LIFE *See* High school students

High school musicals [series]

Bezdecheck, B. Directing **792.6**

HIGH SCHOOL STUDENTS

Katz, E. D. High school's not forever **373.1**

HIGH SCHOOL STUDENTS
> *See also* Students

HIGH SCHOOL STUDENTS -- BOOKS AND READING

Serritella, J. Look again! **373.1**

HIGH SCHOOL STUDENTS -- FICTION

Andrews, J. Me & Earl & the dying girl **Fic**
Bailey, E. Shift **Fic**
Crawford, B. Carter's unfocused, one-track mind **Fic**
Emond, S. Winter town **Fic**
George, M. The difference between you and me **Fic**
Grace, A. In too deep **Fic**
Moore, D. Always upbeat / All that **Fic**
Pauley, K. Cat Girl's day off **Fic**
Paulsen, G. Crush **Fic**
Perez, M. Dead is a battlefield **Fic**
Strohmeyer, S. Smart girls get what they want **Fic**
Vivian, S. The list **Fic**
Zevin, G. Because it is my blood **Fic**

HIGH SCHOOL STUDENTS -- GRAPHIC NOVELS

Akira, S. Monkey High!: vol. 1 **741.5**
Carey, M. Re-Gifters **741.5**
Castellucci, C. Janes in love **741.5**
Castellucci, C. The Plain Janes **741.5**
Crilley, M. Miki Falls, Book One: Spring **741.5**

HIGH SCHOOL STUDENTS -- POETRY

Appelt, K. Poems from homeroom **811**
Fields, T. After the death of Anna Gonzales **811**
Wayland, A. H. Girl coming in for a landing **811**

High school's not forever. Katz, E. D. **373.1**

HIGH SCHOOLS

Crutcher, C. Whale talk **Fic**
Deuker, C. High heat **Fic**
Fields, T. After the death of Anna Gonzales **811**
Koertge, R. Stoner & Spaz **Fic**
Naylor, P. R. Simply Alice **Fic**
Oates, J. C. Big Mouth & Ugly Girl **Fic**
On the fringe **S C**
Sheldon, D. My perfect life **Fic**
Spinelli, J. Stargirl **Fic**
Townley, R. Sky **Fic**
> *See also* Public schools; Schools

HIGH SCHOOLS -- ENTRANCE REQUIREMENTS

Elliott, K. How to prepare for the SSAT/ISEE, Secondary School Admissions Test/Independent School Entrance Exam **373.1**

HIGH SCHOOLS -- FICTION

Andrews, J. Me & Earl & the dying girl **Fic**
Bailey, E. Shift **Fic**
Benway, R. Also known as **Fic**
Bigelow, L. J. Starting from here **Fic**
Brennan, S. R. Team Human **Fic**
Coben, H. Seconds away **Fic**
Crawford, B. Carter's unfocused, one-track mind **Fic**
Delsol, W. Flock **Fic**
Derting, K. The last echo **Fic**
Elston, A. The rules for disappearing **Fic**
Finneyfrock, K. The sweet revenge of Celia Door **Fic**
George, M. The difference between you and me **Fic**
Grace, A. In too deep **Fic**
Gray, C. Spellcaster **Fic**
Johnson, A. A certain October **Fic**
Kessler, J. Loss **Fic**
Laban, E. The Tragedy Paper **Fic**
Leavitt, L. Going vintage **Fic**
Moore, C. The stalker chronicles **Fic**
Patrick, C. Revived **Fic**
Pauley, K. Cat Girl's day off **Fic**
Perez, M. Dead is a battlefield **Fic**
Perez, M. Dead is a killer tune **Fic**
Pierson, D. C. The boy who couldn't sleep and never had to **Fic**
Raf, M. The symptoms of my insanity **Fic**
Roecker, L. The lies that bind **Fic**
Rutkoski, M. The shadow society **Fic**
Scott, K. This is so not happening **Fic**
Stone, T. I. Time between us **Fic**
Strohmeyer, S. Smart girls get what they want **Fic**
Summers, C. This is not a test **Fic**
Terry, T. Slated **Fic**
Vail, R. Kiss me again **Fic**
Valentine, A. How (not) to find a boyfriend **Fic**
Villareal, R. Body slammed! **Fic**
Vivian, S. The list **Fic**
West, K. Pivot point **Fic**

HIGH SCHOOLS -- FICTION

Coben, H. Seconds away **Fic**

HIGH SCHOOLS -- STUDENTS *See* High school students

HIGH SPEED AERONAUTICS
> *See also* Aeronautics

HIGH TECH *See* Technology

HIGH TECHNOLOGY *See* Technology

HIGH-CARBOHYDRATE DIET
> *See also* Diet

HIGH-FIBER DIET
> *See also* Diet

High-tech babies. Winkler, K.   **618.1**

Hightower, Paul
> The father of geometry: Euclid and his 3D world **92**
> Galileo   **92**
> The greatest mathematician   **92**

HIGHWAY ACCIDENTS *See* Traffic accidents

HIGHWAY ENGINEERING
> *See also* Civil engineering; Engineering

HIGHWAY TRANSPORTATION
> *See also* Transportation

The **highwayman.** Noyes, A.   **821**
The **highwayman's** footsteps. Morgan, N.   **Fic**
Highwaymen. Blackwood, G. L.   **364.15**

HIGHWAYMEN *See* Thieves

HIJACKING OF AIRCRAFT *See* Hijacking of airplanes

HIJACKING OF AIRPLANES
> Olson, K. M. The D.B. Cooper hijacking   **364.1**

Hikaru No Go, Volume 1. Hotta, Y.   **741.5**

HIKERS
> Heuer, K. Being caribou   **599.65**

HIKING
> *See also* Outdoor life

Hilda and the Midnight Giant. Pearson, L.   **741.5**

Hile, Lori
> Animal survival   **591.5**
> Surviving extreme sports   **796**

Hill, C. J.
> Erasing time   **Fic**
> Slayers   **Fic**

Hill, Jeff
> Prohibition   **363.4**

Hill, Kirkpatrick
> Do not pass go   **Fic**

Hill, Laban Carrick
> America dreaming   **303.4**
> Harlem stomp!   **810**

Hillary Clinton. Blashfield, J. F.   **92**
Hillary Rodham Clinton. Abrams, D.   **92**

Hillary, Edmund Sir
About
> Bodden, V. To the top of Mount Everest   **796.522**
> Brennan, K. Sir Edmund Hillary, modern day explorer   **796.52**
> Crompton, S. Sir Edmund Hillary   **92**
> Elish, D. Edmund Hillary   **92**
> Helfand, L. Conquering Everest   **741.5**

HILLBILLY MUSIC *See* Country music

Hillman, Ben
> How weird is it   **500**

Hillman, Laura
> I will plant you a lilac tree   **940.53**

Hillstrom, Kevin
> American Civil War: almanac   **973.7**

American Civil War: biographies   **973.7**
American Civil War: primary sources   **973.7**
American Indian removal and the trail to Wounded Knee   **973.8**
Diego Rivera   **92**
Experiencing the American Civil War   **973.7**
Food allergies   **616.97**
The Harlem Renaissance   **810**
The September 11 terrorist attacks   **973.931**

Hillstrom, Laurie Collier
> Global positioning systems   **910.2**
> Hillstrom, K. American Civil War: almanac **973.7**
> Hillstrom, K. American Civil War: biographies   **973.7**
> Hillstrom, K. American Civil War: primary sources   **973.7**
> Hillstrom, K. American Indian removal and the trail to Wounded Knee   **973.8**
> Hillstrom, K. Experiencing the American Civil War   **973.7**
> The attack on Pearl Harbor   **940.54**
> Frida Kahlo   **92**
> Online social networks   **302.3**

Hilmo, Tess
> With a name like Love   **Fic**

The **Hindenburg** disaster. Sherman, J.   **363.1**
The **Hindenburg** disaster of 1937. Lace, W. W.   **363.1**

Hinds, Gareth
> Gifts from the gods   **401**
> Beowulf   **741.5**
> King Lear   **741.5**
> The merchant of Venice   **741.5**
> The Odyssey   **741.5**

Hinds, Maurene J.
> Furman v. Georgia and the death penalty debate **345**
> A reader's guide to Richard Wright's Black boy **813**

HINDU HOLIDAYS
> *See also* Religious holidays

HINDU MYTHOLOGY
> Gavin, J. Tales from India   **398.2**
> Schomp, V. Ancient India   **294.5**

HINDU MYTHOLOGY -- GRAPHIC NOVELS
> Arni, S. Sita's Ramayana   **741.5**

HINDU PHILOSOPHY
> *See also* Philosophy

Hinduism. Rosinsky, N. M.   **294.5**
Hinduism. Narayanan, V.   **294.5**
Hinduism. Wangu, M. B.   **294.5**

HINDUISM
> *See also* Religions
> Ganeri, A. The Ramayana and Hinduism   **294.5**
> Mann, G. S. Buddhists, Hindus, and Sikhs in America   **294**
> Narayanan, V. Hinduism   **294.5**
> Ollhoff, J. Indian mythology   **294**

trip **Fic**

Freymann-Weyr, G. My heartbeat **Fic**

Howe, J. Totally Joe **Fic**

Juby, S. Another kind of cowboy **Fic**

Knowles, J. See you at Harry's **Fic**

Konigsberg, B. Openly straight **Fic**

Lecesne, J. Absolute brightness **Fic**

Moore, P. Hero **Fic**

Papademetriou, L. M or F? **Fic**

Pearce, J. As you wish **Fic**

Sanchez, A. So hard to say **Fic**

Trueman, T. 7 days at the hot corner **Fic**

Wilkinson, L. Pink **Fic**

Wright, B. Putting makeup on the fat boy **Fic**

HOMOSEXUALITY -- FICTION
Konigsberg, B. Openly straight **Fic**

HOMOSEXUALITY AND EDUCATION -- UNITED STATES
Cahill, S. LGBT youth in America's schools **371.826**

Homosexuality around the world. Seba, J. A. **306.76**

HOMOSEXUALITY IN LITERATURE
Cart, M. The heart has its reasons **813**

Seba, J. Gay characters in theatre, movies, and television: new roles, new attitudes **791.43**

HOMOSEXUALITY IN MOTION PICTURES
Seba, J. Gay characters in theatre, movies, and television: new roles, new attitudes **791.43**

HOMOSEXUALITY ON TELEVISION
Seba, J. Gay characters in theatre, movies, and television: new roles, new attitudes **791.43**

HOMOSEXUALS, FEMALE *See* Lesbians

HOMOSEXUALS, MALE *See* Gay men

Honduras. Shields, C. J. **972.83**

Honduras. McGaffey, L. **972.83**

Honduras. Kras, S. L. **972.83**

HONESTY
Cheating **179**

Choldenko, G. Notes from a liar and her dog **Fic**

HONESTY
See also Ethics; Human behavior

HONESTY -- FICTION
Grace, A. In too deep **Fic**

HONEY
Buchmann, S. Honey bees **638**

HONEY
See also Food

Honey Bea. Siegelson, K. L. **Fic**

Honey bees. Buchmann, S. **638**

Honeybee. Nye, N. S. **811**

HONEYBEE
Burns, L. G. The hive detectives **638**

HONEYBEE CULTURE *See* Beekeeping

HONEYGUIDES
Miller, S. S. Woodpeckers, toucans, and their kin **598**

HONEYGUIDES (BIRDS)

Miller, S. S. Woodpeckers, toucans, and their kin **598**

Hong Kong. Kagda, F. **951.25**

Honnold, RoseMary
More teen programs that work **027.62**

The teen reader's advisor **028.5**

HONOR
See also Conduct of life

Honus & me. Gutman, D. **Fic**

Hoobler, Dorothy
The demon in the teahouse **Fic**

The ghost in the Tokaido Inn **Fic**

Seven paths to death **Fic**

The sword that cut the burning grass **Fic**

Hoobler, Thomas
Hoobler, D. The demon in the teahouse **Fic**

Hoobler, D. The ghost in the Tokaido Inn **Fic**

Hoobler, D. Seven paths to death **Fic**

Hoobler, D. The sword that cut the burning grass **Fic**

HOOKED RUGS
See also Handicraft; Rugs and carpets

Hoop genius. Coy, J. **E**

Hoop queens. Smith, C. R. **811**

Hooper, Mary
Fallen Grace **Fic**

Hoops. Myers, W. D. **Fic**

Hoops. Burleigh, R. **811**

Hoopskirts, Union blues, and Confederate grays. Havelin, K. **391**

Hoose, Phillip
Claudette Colvin **92**

Moonbird **598.072**

The race to save the Lord God Bird **598**

We were there, too! **973**

Hoose, P. Claudette Colvin **92**

Hoot. Hiaasen, C. **Fic**

The **Hoover** Dam. Aldridge, R. **627**

Hoover Dam. Mann, E. **627**

HOOVER DAM (ARIZ. AND NEV.)
Aaseng, N. Construction: building the impossible **624**

Aldridge, R. The Hoover Dam **627**

Mann, E. Hoover Dam **627**

See also Dams

HOOVER DAM (ARIZ. AND NEV.) -- HISTORY
Mann, E. Hoover Dam **627**

Hoover, Herbert, 1874-1964 -- Fiction
About
Ray, D. Ghost girl **Fic**

Hoover, Lou Henry, 1874-1944 -- Fiction
About
Ray, D. Ghost girl **Fic**

HOPE
See also Emotions; Spiritual life; Virtue

Hopeless Savages. Van Meter, J. **741.5**

Hopkins, Lee Bennett

(ed) America at war	811
Been to yesterdays: poems of a life	811
Pass the poetry, please!	372.6
(comp) Lives: poems about famous Americans	811
(comp) My America	811

Hopkins, William G.

Plant biotechnology	630

Hopkinson, Deborah

Into the firestorm	Fic
Titanic	910.916
Up before daybreak	331.7

Hopkinson, Nalo

The Chaos	Fic

Hoppa, Jocelyn

Isaac Asimov	92

Hoppe, Paul

Barton, C. Can I see your I.D.?	001.9

Hopper, Edward, 1882-1967
About

Rubin, S. G. Edward Hopper	92

Hopper, Grace, 1906-1992
About

Thimmesh, C. Girls think of everything	920

Hopping, Lorraine Jean

Bone detective	92
Chief Joseph	92
Space rocks	92

Horn, Geoffrey

Environmental engineer	628
Sojourner Truth	305.5

Hornby, Hugh

Soccer	796.334

Horne, Richard

101 things you wish you'd invented--and some you wish no one had	609

Horns & wrinkles. Helgerson, J.	Fic

HOROLOGY *See* Clocks and watches; Sundials; Time

HOROSCOPES

Jennings, R. W. Orwell's luck	Fic
Horowitz horror. Horowitz, A.	S C

Horowitz, Anthony

Ark angel	Fic
Crocodile tears	Fic
Death and the underworld	398.2
Eagle Strike	Fic
Evil star	Fic
The Falcon's Malteser	Fic
The Greek who stole Christmas	Fic
Heroes and villains	398.2
Horowitz horror	S C
More Horowitz horror	S C
Necropolis	Fic
Nightrise	Fic
Point blank	Fic

Point blank: the graphic novel	741.5
Public enemy number two	Fic
Raven's gate	Fic
Scorpia	Fic
Scorpia rising	Fic
Skeleton Key	Fic
Snakehead	Fic
South by southeast	Fic
Stormbreaker	Fic
Stormbreaker: the graphic novel	741.5
Three of diamonds	Fic

Horowitz, Anthony, 1955-
About

Abrams, D. Anthony Horowitz	92

Horowitz, Joseph

Dvorak in America	92

HORROR

See also Emotions; Fear

HORROR -- FICTION *See* Horror fiction

HORROR FICTION

666: the number of the beast	S C
Aguirre, A. Enclave	Fic
Almond, D. Clay	Fic
The August House book of scary stories	398.2
Becker, T. Darkside	Fic
Becker, T. Lifeblood	Fic
Beware!	808.8
Bickle, L. The outside	Fic
Black, B. iDrakula	Fic
Blake, K. Anna Dressed in Blood	Fic
Bradbury, R. Something wicked this way comes	Fic
Brewer, H. The chronicles of Vladimir Tod: ninth grade slays	Fic
Brewer, H. Eleventh grade burns	Fic
Brewer, H. First kill	Fic
Brewer, H. Tenth grade bleeds	Fic
Buckingham, R. Demonkeeper	Fic
Cary, K. Bloodline	Fic
Cary, K. Bloodline: reckoning	Fic
Coville, B. Oddest of all	S C
Dare to be scared	S C
DeKeyser, S. The Brixen Witch	Fic
Delaney, J. Rage of the fallen	Fic
Delaney, J. The Spook's Bestiary	Fic
Drago, T. The Undertakers: rise of the Corpses	Fic
Fahy, T. R. The unspoken	Fic
Fear: 13 stories of suspense and horror	S C
Fukuda, A. The Prey	Fic
Gaiman, N. Coraline	Fic
Garner, E. Contaminated	Fic
Gilman, C. Professor Gargoyle	Fic
Gothic!	S C
Grant, M. Hunger	Fic
Half-minute horrors	S C
Henderson, J. Vampire rising	Fic
Henderson, J. Voice of the undead	Fic

How to feel good. Mangan, T.   **305.23**

How to get rich [series]

How to get rich in the California Gold Rush **979.4**

Olson, T. How to get rich on the Oregon Trail **978**

How to get rich in the California Gold Rush. **979.4**

How to get rich on a Texas cattle drive. Olson, T. **978**

How to get rich on the Oregon Trail. Olson, T. **978**

How to get suspended and influence people. Selzer, A.   **Fic**

How to harness solar power for your home. Bearce, S.   **621.47**

How to help: a guide to giving back [series]

O'Neal, C. Volunteering in your school   **361.3**

O'Neal, C. Ways to help in your community **361.3**

Reusser, K. Celebrities giving back   **361.7**

Saul, L. Ways to help disadvantaged youth **362.7**

How to improve at [series]

McMillan, S. How to improve at drawing **741.2**

How to improve at drawing. McMillan, S. **741.2**

How to make a bird. Murray, M.   **Fic**

How to prepare for the SSAT/ISEE, Secondary School Admissions Test/Independent School Entrance Exam. Elliott, K.   **373.1**

How to raise and keep a dragon. Nigg, J.   **Fic**

How to raise monarch butterflies. Pasternak, C.   **595.78**

How to ruin a summer vacation. Elkeles, S.   **Fic**

How to ruin my teenage life. Elkeles, S.   **Fic**

How to ruin your boyfriend's reputation. Elkeles, S.   **Fic**

How to save a life. Zarr, S.   **Fic**

How to say no to drugs. Kreske, D. P.   **362.29**

How to speak cat. Whitehead, S.   **636.8**

How to speak dog. Whitehead, S.   **636.7**

How to steal a car. Hautman, P.   **Fic**

How to steal a dog. O'Connor, B.   **Fic**

HOW TO STUDY *See* Study skills

How to survive anything. Buchholz, R.   **646.7**

How to survive in Antarctica. Bledsoe, L. J.   **998**

How to survive middle school. Gephart, D.   **Fic**

How to talk to an autistic kid.   **616.85**

How to use waste energy to heat and light your home. O'Neal, C.   **621.1**

How to use wind power to light and heat your home. O'Neal, C.   **621.31**

How to write your life story. Fletcher, R.   **808**

How video game designers use math. Egan, J. **794.8**

How we know what we know about our changing climate. Cherry, L.   **363.7**

How weird is it. Hillman, B.   **500**

How writers work. Fletcher, R.   **808**

How-to-do-it manuals for librarians [series]

Alcorn, L. E. Wireless networking   **025.04**

Alire, C. Serving Latino communities   **027.6**

Curzon, S. C. Managing change   **025.1**

Gorman, M. Connecting young adults and librar-

ies   **027.62**

Halsted, D. D. Disaster planning   **025.8**

Imhoff, K. R. Library contests   **021.7**

Martin, B. S. Fundamentals of school library media management   **025.1**

Martin, H. J. Serving lesbian, gay, bisexual, transgender, and questioning teens   **027.62**

Tallman, J. I. Making the writing and research connection with the I-search process   **025.5**

HOW-TO-STOP-SMOKING PROGRAMS *See* Smoking cessation programs

Howard, Ellen

The crimson cap   **Fic**

Howard, Helen

Living as a refugee in America   **305.23**

Howard, Todd

(ed) Mark Twain   **818**

Howe, Ian

Jennings, M. Soccer step-by-step   **796.334**

Howe, James, 1946-

(ed) 13   **S C**

Addie on the inside   **Fic**

(ed) The Color of absence   **813**

Howe, J. Addie on the inside   **Fic**

The misfits   **Fic**

Totally Joe   **Fic**

Howe, Peter

Waggit again   **Fic**

Waggit's tale   **Fic**

Howe, Samuel Gridley, 1801-1876

About

Alexander, S. H. She touched the world: Laura Bridgman, deaf-blind pioneer   **92**

Howe, William Howe, 5th Viscount, 1729-1814

About

Murphy, J. The crossing   **973.3**

Howell, Brian

Sports   **796**

Howell, Troy

The dragon of Cripple Creek   **Fic**

Howes, Kelly King

The roaring twenties almanac and primary sources   **973.91**

Howl's moving castle. Jones, D. W.   **Fic**

Howland, Leila

Nantucket blue   **Fic**

Howling at the moon. Etingoff, K.   **398**

Howse, Jennifer

The Civil War   **973.7**

HPV. Parks, P. J.   **362.1**

Hrdlitschka, Shelley

Allegra   **Fic**

Sister wife   **Fic**

Hsüan-tsang, ca. 596-664

About

Galloway, P. Adventures on the ancient Silk

I

I am (not) the walrus. Briant, E.   **Fic**

I am a SEAL Team Six warrior. Templin, S. **359.009**

I am Mordred. Springer, N.   **Fic**

I am Morgan le Fay. Springer, N.   **Fic**

I am not Joey Pigza. Gantos, J.   **Fic**

I am phoenix: poems for two voices. Fleischman, P.   **811**

I am Rembrandt's daughter. Cullen, L.   **Fic**

I am Scout: the biography of Harper Lee. Shields, C. J.   **92**

I am the cheese. Cormier, R.   **Fic**

I am the darker brother.   **811**

I and I. Medina, T.   **92**

I can't keep my own secrets.   **808.8**

I did it without thinking. Hugel, B.   **155.5**

I don't want to be crazy. Schutz, S.   **92**

I feel a little jumpy around you.   **808.81**

I found a dead bird. Thornhill, J.   **306.9**

I found it on the Internet. Harris, F. J.   **025.042**

I have lived a thousand years. Bitton-Jackson, L.   **940.53**

I have the right to be a child.   **323.3**

I heard God talking to me. Spires, E.   **811**

I kissed a zombie, and I liked it. Selzer, A.   **Fic**

I know what you did last summer. Duncan, L.   **Fic**

I love him to pieces.   **741.5**

--I never saw another butterfly-- Volavkova, H. **741.9**

I once was a monkey. Lee, J. M.   **294.3**

I put a spell on you. Selzer, A.   **Fic**

I shall wear midnight. Pratchett, T.   **Fic**

I survived the Battle of Gettysburg, 1863. Tarshis, L.   **E**

I wanna be your shoebox. Garcia, C.   **Fic**

I want to live. Lugovskaia, N.   **92**

I was dreaming to come to America.   **304.8**

I was Jane Austen's best friend. Harrison, C.   **Fic**

I will plant you a lilac tree. Hillman, L.   **940.53**

I wouldn't thank you for a valentine.   **808.81**

I'll ask you three times, are you ok? Nye, N. S.   **92**

I'll be there. Sloan, H. G.   **Fic**

I'll get there, it better be worth the trip. Donovan, J.   **Fic**

I'll pass for your comrade. Silvey, A.   **973.7**

I'm a vegetarian. Schwartz, E.   **613.2**

I'm not her. Gurtler, J.   **Fic**

I, Coriander. Gardner, S.   **Fic**

I, Emma Freke. Atkinson, E. J.   **Fic**

I, Q.: book one, Independence Hall. Smith, R.   **Fic**

I, robot. Asimov, I.   **S C**

I, too, sing America.   **811**

I. Q.: book two, The White House. Smith, R.   **Fic**

I.M. Pei. Slavicek, L. C.   **92**

I.M. Pei. Rubalcaba, J.   **92**

Ibbitson, John

   The Landing   **Fic**

Ibbotson, Eva

The beasts of Clawstone Castle   **Fic**

The dragonfly pool   **Fic**

The Ogre of Oglefort   **Fic**

One dog and his boy   **Fic**

The star of Kazan   **Fic**

Ibn al-Haytham. Steffens, B.   **92**

Ice. Durst, S. B.   **Fic**

ICE

   See also Cold; Frost; Physical geography; Water

ICE

   Berlatsky, N. Water and ice   **551.4**

   Glaciers, sea ice, and ice formation   **551.3**

   Pringle, L. Ice!   **621.5**

ICE -- FICTION

   Kirby, M. J. Icefall   **Fic**

Ice age Neanderthals. Stefoff, R.   **599.93**

Ice claw. Gilman, D.   **Fic**

The **ice** cream con. Docherty, J.   **Fic**

ICE CREAM, ICES, ETC.

   See also Desserts; Frozen foods

ICE FISHING

   See also Fishing; Winter sports

Ice hockey. Sharp, A. W.   **796.962**

ICE HOCKEY *See* Hockey

Ice island. Shahan, S.   **Fic**

ICE MUMMIES

   Deem, J. M. Bodies from the ice   **393**

Ice scientist. Latta, S. L.   **998**

ICE SKATERS

   Aldridge, R. Apolo Anton Ohno   **92**

   Koestler-Grack, R. A. Michelle Kwan   **92**

ICE SKATING

   McDougall, C. Figure skating   **796.91**

ICE SKATING

   See also Winter sports

ICE SKATING -- BIOGRAPHY

   Aldridge, R. Apolo Anton Ohno   **92**

   Koestler-Grack, R. A. Michelle Kwan   **92**

ICE SKATING -- FICTION

   Messner, K. Sugar and ice   **Fic**

ICE SKATING -- GRAPHIC NOVELS

   Nakajo, H. Sugar Princess volume 1: skating to win   **741.5**

ICE SPORTS *See* Winter sports

Ice time. McKinley, M.   **796.962**

Ice! Pringle, L.   **621.5**

Iceberg right ahead! McPherson, S. S.   **910.4**

ICEBERGS

   See also Ice; Ocean; Physical geography

ICEBOATS

   See also Boats and boating

The **icebound** land. Flanagan, J.   **Fic**

Icecore. Whyman, M.   **Fic**

Icefall. Kirby, M. J.   **Fic**

Icefire. D'Lacey, C.   **Fic**

Indie girl. Daswani, K.   Fic
INDIGENOUS PEOPLES -- AMERICA *See* Native Americans
INDIGENOUS PEOPLES -- FICTION
    Khoury, J. Origin   Fic
INDIGESTION
    See also Digestion
The **indigo** king. Owen, J. A.   Fic
The **indigo** notebook. Resau, L.   Fic
Indigo's star. McKay, H.   Fic
INDIVIDUALISM
    Orwell, G. Nineteen eighty-four   Fic
INDIVIDUALISM
    See also Economics; Equality; Political science; Sociology
INDIVIDUALISM -- FICTION
    Austen, C. All good children   Fic
    Philbin, J. The daughters take the stage   Fic
    Wolitzer, M. The fingertips of Duncan Dorfman Fic
INDIVIDUALITY
    Spinelli, J. Stargirl   Fic
    Voigt, C. It's not easy being bad   Fic
INDIVIDUALITY
    See also Consciousness; Psychology
INDIVIDUALITY -- FICTION
    Spinelli, J. Jake and Lily   Fic
Indiviglio, Frank
    The everything aquarium book   639.34
Indonesia. Cooper, R.   959.8
INDONESIA
    Cooper, R. Indonesia   959.8
INDONESIA -- FICTION
    Fama, E. Overboard   Fic
INDONESIA -- HISTORY
    Cooper, R. Indonesia   959.8
INDONESIA
    Cooper, R. Indonesia   959.8
INDONESIAN COOKING
    Cornell, K. A. Cooking the Indonesian way 641.5
    Reusser, K. Recipe and craft guide to Indonesia   641.5
INDOOR AIR POLLUTION
    See also Air pollution
INDOOR GAMES
    See also Games
INDOOR GARDENING
    See also Gardening
Indovino, Shaina C.
    (jt. auth) Docalavich, H. Czech Republic 943.710
    (jt. auth) Docalavich, H. Denmark   948.9
    (jt. auth) Docalavich, H. The Netherlands 949.2
    (jt. auth) Docalavich, H. Poland   943.8
    (jt. auth) Docalavich, H. Sweden   948.5
    (jt. auth) Etingoff, K. Greece   949.5
    (jt. auth) Etingoff, K. Portugal   946.9
    Austria   943.6

Belgium   949.304
Dracula and beyond   791.43
France   944
Germany   943
Italy   945
Spain   946
Transylvania and beyond   398
United Kingdom   941
INDUCED ABORTION *See* Abortion
INDUCTION MOTORS *See* Electric motors
INDUSTRIAL ACCIDENTS
    Kops, D. The Great Molasses Flood   363.17
    Scott, E. Buried alive!   363.11
INDUSTRIAL ACCIDENTS -- MASSACHU-SETTS -- BOSTON -- HISTORY -- 20TH CENTURY
    Kops, D. The Great Molasses Flood   363.17
INDUSTRIAL ARBITRATION
    See also Industrial relations; Labor; Labor disputes; Labor unions; Negotiation
INDUSTRIAL ARCHEOLOGY
    See also Archeology; Industries -- History
INDUSTRIAL ARTS
    See also Handicraft
INDUSTRIAL BUILDINGS
    See also Buildings
INDUSTRIAL BUILDINGS -- DESIGN AND CONSTRUCTION
    See also Architecture; Building
INDUSTRIAL CHEMISTRY
    See also Chemistry; Technology
INDUSTRIAL DESIGN
    Arato, R. Design it!   745.2
    Oxlade, C. Gadgets and games   688.7
    Welsbacher, A. Earth-friendly design   745.2
INDUSTRIAL DESIGNERS
    Tiger, C. Isamu Noguchi   92
INDUSTRIAL DISASTERS *See* Industrial accidents
INDUSTRIAL EQUIPMENT
    See also Machinery
INDUSTRIAL INJURIES *See* Industrial accidents
INDUSTRIAL MATERIALS *See* Materials
INDUSTRIAL MOBILIZATION
    See also Economic policy; Military art and science; War -- Economic aspects
INDUSTRIAL PLANTS *See* Factories
INDUSTRIAL POLICY -- UNITED STATES
    Bezdecheck, B. Bailout!   338.6
INDUSTRIAL RESEARCH
    See also Research
The **Industrial** Revolution. Staton, H. N. 330.973
The **Industrial** Revolution. Mooney, C.   330.9
The **industrial** revolution. Arnold, J. R.   330.9
INDUSTRIAL REVOLUTION
    See also Economic conditions; Industries --

Wildavsky, R. The secret of Rover   **Fic**
Williams, A. The deep freeze of Bartholomew Tullock   **Fic**

INVENTIONS -- HISTORY
Cole, D. J. Encyclopedia of modern everyday inventions   **609**
Diagram Group Historical inventions on file   **609**
Ferris, J. Ideas that changed the world   **609**
Jedicke, P. Great inventions of the 20th century **609**
Landau, E. The history of everyday life   **609**
Marshall Cavendish Corporation Inventors and inventions   **609**
Robinson, J. Inventions   **609**
Rossi, A. Bright ideas   **609**
Tomecek, S. What a great idea!   **609**
Ye The Chinese thought of it   **609**

INVENTIONS -- HISTORY -- 20TH CENTURY
Cole, D. J. Encyclopedia of modern everyday inventions   **609**

INVENTIONS -- HISTORY
Wulffson, D. L. Toys!   **688.7**

INVENTIONS
Currie, S. African American inventors   **500**
Stronger Than Steel   **595.4**

INVENTIONS -- UNITED STATES -- HISTORY
Currie, S. African American inventors   **500**
Thimmesh, C. Girls think of everything   **920**
Inventions and investigations. Solway, A.   **600**
Inventions that shaped the world [series]
Kummer, P. K. The calendar   **529**
Kummer, P. K. The telephone   **621.385**
Trueit, T. S. Gunpowder   **623.4**

INVENTORS
Aaseng, N. Construction: building the impossible   **624**
Adler, D. A. B. Franklin, printer   **973.3**
Baxter, R. Illuminated progress   **92**
Burgan, M. Nikola Tesla   **92**
Carlson, L. M. Thomas Edison for kids   **92**
Carson, M. K. Alexander Graham Bell   **92**
Carson, M. K. The Wright Brothers for kids **629.13**
Coe, L. The telegraph   **621.383**
Collins, M. Airborne: a photobiography of Wilbur and Orville Wright   **92**
Crompton, S. The Wright brothers   **92**
Dash, J. A dangerous engine   **92**
Fleming, C. Ben Franklin's almanac   **92**
Freedman, R. Out of darkness: the story of Louis Braille   **92**
Freedman, R. The Wright brothers: how they invented the airplane   **92**
Gifford, C. 10 inventors who changed the world **920**
Herweck, D. Robert Fulton   **92**
Jarrow, G. Lincoln's flying spies   **973.7**
Lagos, A. The sons of liberty 2   **741.5**
Marshall Cavendish Corporation Inventors and inventions   **609**

Matsen, B. The incredible record-setting deep-sea dive of the bathysphere   **551.46**
McElligott, M. Benjamin Franklinstein lives! **Fic**
Miller, B. M. Benjamin Franklin, American genius   **92**
Outman, J. L. Industrial Revolution: biographies   **330**
Philosophy, invention, and engineering   **920**
Pierce, M. A. Robert Fulton and the development of the steamboat   **92**
Sandler, M. W. Secret subway   **388.4**
Schraff, A. E. Ellen Ochoa   **92**
Skelton, M. Endymion Spring   **Fic**
Solway, A. Inventions and investigations   **600**
Sonneborn, L. The electric light   **621.32**
Thimmesh, C. Girls think of everything   **920**
Tucker, T. Brainstorm!   **609.2**
Watson, G. Edison's gold   **Fic**
Weyn, S. Distant waves   **Fic**
Woodruff, E. Fearless   **Fic**
Woodruff, E. George Washington's spy   **Fic**
Woodside, M. Thomas A. Edison   **92**
Worek, M. The Nobel Prize   **001.4**
Zannos, S. Guglielmo Marconi and the story of radio waves   **92**

INVENTORS -- BIOGRAPHY
Outman, J. L. Industrial Revolution: biographies   **330**
Tucker, T. Brainstorm!   **609.2**

INVENTORS -- FICTION
Evans, L. Horten's miraculous mechanisms   **Fic**

INVENTORS
Arato, R. Design it!   **745.2**

INVENTORS -- UNITED STATES -- BIOGRAPHY
Blumenthal, K. Steve Jobs   **621.39**

INVENTORS -- UNITED STATES -- BIOGRAPHY
Adler, D. A. B. Franklin, printer   **973.3**
Blumenthal, K. Steve Jobs   **621.39**
Freedman, R. Becoming Ben Franklin   **973.309**
Yount, L. Nikola Tesla   **621.309**
Inventors and inventions. Marshall Cavendish Corporation   **609**

INVENTORY CONTROL
See also Management; Retail trade

INVERTEBRATES
Meinkoth, N. A. The Audubon Society field guide to North American seashore creatures   **592**
Silverstein, A. Dung beetles, slugs, leeches, and more   **590**

INVERTEBRATES
See also Animals

Parker, S. Sponges, jellyfish & other simple animals   **592**

Jaramillo, Ann
  La linea   Fic
Jarrell, Jill S.
  (jt. auth) Cannon, T. C. Cooler than fiction 027.62
Jarrow, Gail
  The amazing Harry Kellar   793.809
Jarrow, Gail
  Lincoln's flying spies   973.7
  The printer's trial   345
  Robert H. Jackson   92
Jars of glass. Barkley, B.   Fic
Jarzab, Anna
  The opposite of hallelujah   Fic
Jarzab, Anna
  All unquiet things   Fic
JASON (GREEK MYTHOLOGY) -- FICTION
  Friesner, E. M. Nobody's prize   Fic
Jason's gold. Hobbs, W.   Fic
Jasper Dash and the flame-pits of Delaware. Anderson, M. T.   Fic
Jasper Jones. Silvey, C.   Fic
Jasper, Richard P.
  Halsted, D. D. Disaster planning   025.8
Jastrzembski, Joseph C.
  The Apache wars   970.004
JATAKA STORIES
  Lee, J. M. I once was a monkey   294.3
JATAKA STORIES, ENGLISH
  Lee, J. M. I once was a monkey   294.3
JAVELIN THROWERS
  Lobby, M. Babe Didrikson Zaharias   92
  Van Natta, D. Wonder girl   92
Jay-Z. Spilsbury, R.   92
Jay-Z, 1969-
About
  Spilsbury, R. Jay-Z   92
Jazmin's notebook. Grimes, N.   Fic
Jazz. Handyside, C.   781.65
JAZZ
  Townley, R. Sky   Fic
JAZZ -- HISTORY AND CRITICISM
  Kallen, S. A. The history of jazz   781.65
JAZZ -- HISTORY AND CRITICISM
  Kallen, S. A. The history of jazz   781.65
JAZZ
  Nelson, M. Sweethearts of rhythm   811
Jazz A-B-Z. Marsalis, W.   781.65
JAZZ MUSIC
  Gourse, L. Sophisticated ladies   920
  Handyside, C. Jazz   781.65
  Kallen, S. A. The history of jazz   781.65
  Lynette, R. Miles Davis   788.9
  Marsalis, W. Jazz A-B-Z   781.65
JAZZ MUSIC
  See also Music
JAZZ MUSIC -- FICTION

Volponi, P. Hurricane song   Fic
Weatherford, C. B. Becoming Billie Holiday   Fic
JAZZ MUSIC -- HISTORY AND CRITICISM
  Batten, J. Oscar Peterson   786.2
JAZZ MUSIC
  Roberts, R. Scott Joplin   780.92
JAZZ MUSIC -- POETRY
  Nelson, M. Sweethearts of rhythm   811
JAZZ MUSICIANS -- BIOGRAPHY
  Boone, M. Dizzy Gillespie   788.9
  Rice, E. Charlie Parker   788.7
JAZZ MUSICIANS -- FICTION
  Townley, R. Sky   Fic
JAZZ MUSICIANS
  Marsalis, W. Jazz A-B-Z   781.65
JAZZ MUSICIANS -- UNITED STATES -- BIOGRAPHY
  Boone, M. Dizzy Gillespie   788.9
  Golio, G. Spirit seeker   788.7
  Lynette, R. Miles Davis   788.9
  Mattern, J. Benny Goodman   781.650
  Orr, T. Louis Armstrong   781.650
  Rice, E. Charlie Parker   788.7
JAZZ MUSICIANS -- UNITED STATES
  Orr, T. Miles Davis   788.9
Jealousy. St. Crow, L.   Fic
JEALOUSY
  DeFelice, C. C. The ghost and Mrs. Hobbs   Fic
JEALOUSY
  See also Emotions
JEALOUSY -- FICTION
  Anderson, J. L. Tiger Lily   Fic
Jean-Michel Cousteau presents [series]
  Hall, H. A charm of dolphins   599.5
  Hunt, J. P. A band of bears   599.78
  Leon, V. A pod of killer whales   599.5
JEANS (CLOTHING)
  Brashares, A. The sisterhood of the traveling pants   Fic
  Kyi, T. L. The blue jean book   391
  Warwick, E. Injeanuity   746
Jedicke, Peter
  Great inventions of the 20th century   609
  Great moments in space exploration   629.4
Jeff Bezos. Scally, R.   92
Jeff Bezos. Garty, J.   380.1
Jeff Bezos. Robinson, T.   92
Jeff Corwin: a wild life. Corwin, J.   92
Jefferson family
About
  Lanier, S. Jefferson's children   973.4
Jefferson's children. Lanier, S.   973.4
Jefferson's sons. Bradley, K. B.   Fic
Jefferson, Thomas, 1743-1826
About
  Bradley, K. B. Jefferson's sons   Fic

Joyce, Graham, 1954-
The exchange   Fic

Joyce, Jaime
Bullet proof!   363.2

Joyce, Marilyn Z.
Tallman, J. I. Making the writing and research connection with the I-search process   025.5

Joyful noise: poems for two voices. Fleischman, P.   811

Jozefowicz, Chris
Video game developer   794.8

Juan Seguin. Chemerka, W. R.   976.4

Juárez, Benito, 1806-1872
About
Stein, R. C. Benito Juarez and the French intervention   92

Juby, Susan
Another kind of cowboy   Fic
Getting the girl   Fic

Judaism. Rosinsky, N. M.   296
Judaism. Morrison, M. A.   296
Judaism. Ehrlich, C. S.   296

JUDAISM
See also Religions

Judaism. Keene, M.   296

JUDAISM
Buxbaum, S. M. Jewish faith in America   296
Ehrlich, C. S. Judaism   296
Keene, M. Judaism   296
Morrison, M. A. Judaism   296
Osborne, M. P. One world, many religions   200
Rosinsky, N. M. Judaism   296

JUDAISM -- DICTIONARIES
The Oxford dictionary of the Jewish religion 296.03

JUDAISM -- ENCYCLOPEDIAS
The Oxford dictionary of the Jewish religion 296.03

JUDAISM -- RELATIONS -- CHRISTIANITY
See also Christianity and other religions; Judaism

JUDAISM -- RELATIONS -- CHRISTIANITY -- FICTION
Sanders, S. Rachel's secret   Fic

JUDAISM -- RELATIONS -- ISLAM
See also Islam; Judaism

JUDAISM -- UNITED STATES -- HISTORY
Buxbaum, S. M. Jewish faith in America   296

JUDGES
Abrams, D. Sandra Day O'Connor   92
Branscomb, L. W. Earl Warren   92
Crowe, C. Thurgood Marshall   92
Gitlin, M. Sonia Sotomayor   92
Jarrow, G. Robert H. Jackson   92
Kennedy, J. F. Profiles in courage   920
McElroy, L. T. Sonia Sotomayor   92

JUDGES
See also Lawyers

JUDGES -- BIOGRAPHY
The Supreme Court justices   347.73

JUDGES -- UNITED STATES -- BIOGRAPHY
The Supreme Court justices   347.73

JUDGMENT DAY
See also End of the world; Second Advent

Judo. Mason, P.   796.815

JUDO
See also Martial arts; Self-defense

JUDO
Ellis, C. Judo and jujitsu   796.8
Inman, R. The judo handbook   796.8
Mason, P. Judo   796.815

Judo and jujitsu. Ellis, C.   796.8
The **judo** handbook. Inman, R.   796.8

Judson, Karen
Animal testing   179
Resolving conflicts   303.6

Juettner, Bonnie
Acne   616.5
Blackmail and bribery   364.16
Diet and disease   613.2

JUGGLING
See also Amusements; Tricks

Juggling fire. Bell, J.   Fic

JUJITSU *See* Jiu-jitsu

Jukes, Mavis
Growing up: it's a girl thing   612.6
The guy book   305.235

Julia Alvarez. Aykroyd, C.   92
Julia Child. Abrams, D.   92
Julia Child, chef. Abrams, D.   641.509
The **Julian** game. Griffin, A.   Fic

Julian, Percy L., 1899-1975
About
Stille, D. R. Percy Lavon Julian   92

JULIET (FICTITIOUS CHARACTER) -- FICTION
Coville, B. William Shakespeare's Romeo and Juliet   822.3

The **Juliet** club. Harper, S.   Fic
Juliet Dove, Queen of Love. Coville, B.   Fic
Julius Caesar. Galford, E.   92
Julius Caesar. McKeown, A.   822.3

Julius, Edward H.
Arithmetricks   513

The **jumbo** book of art. Luxbacher, I.   702.8
Jump. Carbone, E.   Fic
Jump into the sky. Pearsall, S.   Fic
Jump ship to freedom. Collier, J. L.   Fic
Jumped. Williams-Garcia, R.   Fic
Jumping spiders. Markle, S.   595.4

JUMPING SPIDERS
Markle, S. Jumping spiders   595.4

Jumping the scratch. Weeks, S.   Fic

Jun Lim

Justice league unlimited [series]

Beechen, A. Justice League Unlimited: the ties that bind **741.5**

Justice League Unlimited: the ties that bind. Beechen, A. **741.5**

JUSTICE, ADMINISTRATION OF

Jacobs, T. A. They broke the law, you be the judge **345**

Wormser, R. Defending the accused **345**

JUSTICE, ADMINISTRATION OF *See* Administration of justice

Justin Bieber. Yasuda, A. **92**

Justin Bieber: first step 2 forever. Bieber, J. **92**

JUVENILE COURTS

Cohen, L. The Gault case and young people's rights **345**

Jacobs, T. A. They broke the law, you be the judge **345**

JUVENILE DELINQUENCY

Kuklin, S. No choirboy **364.66**

See also Crime; Social problems

JUVENILE DELINQUENCY -- FICTION

Griffin, C. J. Nowhere to run **Fic**

Rapp, A. The children and the wolves **Fic**

JUVENILE DELINQUENTS

Jacobs, T. A. They broke the law, you be the judge **345**

JUVENILE DELINQUENTS *See* Juvenile delinquency

Kuklin, S. No choirboy **364.66**

JUVENILE DELINQUENTS -- REHABILITATION

Mikaelsen, B. Touching Spirit Bear **Fic**

JUVENILE DELINQUENTS -- UNITED STATES

Jacobs, T. A. They broke the law, you be the judge **345**

JUVENILE DETENTION HOMES -- FICTION

Cummings, P. The journey back **Fic**

JUVENILE JUSTICE, ADMINISTRATION OF

Kuklin, S. No choirboy **364.66**

JUVENILE JUSTICE, ADMINISTRATION OF -- UNITED STATES

Jacobs, T. A. They broke the law, you be the judge **345**

JUVENILE PROSTITUTION

See also Juvenile delinquency; Prostitution

JUVENILE PROSTITUTION -- FICTION

Leavitt, M. My book of life by Angel **Fic**

The **Juvie** three. Korman, G. **Fic**

Jyotirmayee Mohapatra. Woog, A. **92**

K

K-9 police units. Stewart, G. **363.2**

Kaboom! Richardson, G. **500**

KABUKI

Hoobler, D. The ghost in the Tokaido Inn **Fic**

Kacer, Kathy

Hiding Edith **940.53**

We Are Their Voice **940.53**

Kade, Stacey

The ghost and the goth **Fic**

Queen of the dead **Fic**

Kadohata, Cynthia

Cracker! **Fic**

Kira-Kira **Fic**

A million shades of gray **Fic**

Outside beauty **Fic**

The thing about luck **Fic**

Weedflower **Fic**

Kadziolka, Jan

Poland **943.8**

Kagawa, Julie

The Eternity Cure **Fic**

The immortal rules **Fic**

Kagayame, Johnny

Discovering the construct of time **529**

Kagda, Falaq

Algeria **965**

Hong Kong **951.25**

Kagda, Sakina

Lithuania **947.93**

Kahlo, Frida, 1907-1954

About

Bernier-Grand, C. Frida **811**

Hillstrom, L. Frida Kahlo **92**

Kai's journey to Gold Mountain. Currier, K. S. **Fic**

Kajder, Sara B.

Bringing the outside in **028.5**

KAKAPO

Montgomery, S. Kakapo rescue **639.9**

Kakapo rescue. Montgomery, S. **639.9**

Kaleidoscope eyes. Bryant, J. **Fic**

Kallen, Stuart A.

The aftermath of the Sandinista Revolution **972.85**

Che Guevara **980.03**

Claude Monet **92**

Crop circles **001.9**

Elizabethan England **942.05**

The history of classical music **781.6**

The history of country music **781.642**

The history of jazz **781.65**

The history of rock and roll **781.66**

The instruments of music **784.19**

Marcus Garvey and the Back to Africa Movement **92**

Pablo Picasso **92**

Pharaohs of Egypt **932.01**

Photography **770**

Renewable energy research **333.79**

Rigoberta Menchu, Indian rights activist **92**

Shamans **201**

Shinto **299.5**

Kemer, Eric
  Gardner, R. Easy genius science projects with temperature and heat   **536**

Kempe, Margery, b. ca. 1373
        About
  Barnhouse, R. The book of the maidservant   **Fic**

Kempe, Margery, b. ca. 1373 -- Fiction
        About
  Barnhouse, R. The book of the maidservant   **Fic**

Kendall, Martha E.
  Keat, N. Alive in the killing fields   **92**

Kendo. Ellis, C.   **796.8**

KENDO
  Ellis, C. Kendo   **796.8**

Kennedy through the lens. Sandler, M. W.   **92**

Kennedy's last days. O'Reilly, B.   **973.922**

Kennedy, Edward Moore, 1932-2009
        About
  Sapet, K. Ted Kennedy   **92**

Kennedy, James
  The Order of Odd-Fish   **Fic**

Kennedy, John E.
  Puppet planet   **791.5**

Kennedy, John F.
  Profiles in courage   **920**

Kennedy, John F.
        About
  Cooper, I. Jack   **973**
  Heiligman, D. High hopes   **92**
  O'Reilly, B. Kennedy's last days   **973.922**
  Sandler, M. W. Kennedy through the lens   **92**
  Stockland, P. M. The assassination of John F. Kennedy   **973.922**

Kennedy, Kerry
  Speak truth to power   **920**

Kennedy, Michael
  Bourne, J. The concise Oxford dictionary of music   **780**

Kennedy, Mike
  Stewart, M. Goal!: the fire and fury of soccer's greatest moment   **796.334**
  Stewart, M. Score!   **796.962**
  Stewart, M. Swish   **796.323**
  Stewart, M. Touchdown   **796.332**

Kennedy, Robert F., 1925-1968
        About
  Aronson, M. Robert F. Kennedy   **92**

KENNEWICK MAN
  Kirkpatrick, K. Mysterious bones   **979.7**
  Owsley, D. W. Their skeletons speak   **970.01**

Kenney, Karen Latchana
  (jt. auth) Frederick, S. Strength training for teen athletes   **613.7**
  Cool costumes   **792**
  Cool hip-hop music   **781.66**
  Cool makeup   **792**

Cool productions   **792**
Cool rock music   **781.66**
Cool scripts & acting   **792**
Cool sets & props   **792**
Cool special effects   **792**
Korematsu v. the United States   **341.6**
Skiing & snowboarding   **796.93**

Kenschaft, Lori
  Lydia Maria Child   **303.48**

Kensuke's kingdom. Morpurgo, M.   **Fic**

Kent, Deborah
  Animal helpers for the disabled   **636.088**
  Athletes with disabilities   **371.9**
  Hawaii   **996.9**
  Idaho   **979.6**
  Mexico   **972**
  New Hampshire   **974.2**
  New Jersey   **974.9**
  Oregon   **979.5**
  Snake pits, talking cures, & magic bullets   **616.89**
  The tragic history of the Japanese-American internment camps   **940.53**
  Utah   **979.2**
  Virginia   **975.5**
  Washington, D.C.   **975.3**

Kent, Evelyn Julia
  Schloss, E. Eva's story   **92**

Kent, Rose
  Kimchi & calamari   **Fic**

Kent, Trilby
  Medina Hill   **Fic**
  Stones for my father   **Fic**

Kent, Zachary
  Connecticut   **974.6**

Kentucky. Santella, A.   **976.9**

Kentucky. Barrett, T.   **976.9**

Kenya. Bowden, R.   **967.62**

Kenya in pictures. Broberg, C.   **967.62**

KENYAN COOKING
  Sheen, B. Foods of Kenya   **641.5**

Keoke, Emory Dean
  American Indian contributions to the world   **970.004**

Kephart, Beth
  Dangerous neighbors   **Fic**
  Dr. Radway's Sarsaparilla Resolvent   **Fic**
  The heart is not a size   **Fic**
  House of Dance   **Fic**
  Nothing but ghosts   **Fic**
  Undercover   **Fic**
  You are my only   **Fic**

Kepler and the laws of planetary motion. Hasan, H.   **92**

Kepler's dream. Bell, J.   **Fic**

Kepler, Johannes, 1571-1630
        About
  Bell, J. Kepler's dream   **Fic**

Leeds, C. The unfortunate son   **Fic**
McDonald, I. Be my enemy   **Fic**
Rapp, A. The children and the wolves   **Fic**
Schlitz, L. A. Splendors and glooms   **Fic**
KIDNAPPING VICTIMS -- FICTION
Balliett, B. Hold fast   **Fic**
KIDNEYS
The kidneys and the renal system   **616.6**
KIDNEYS -- DISEASES
The kidneys and the renal system   **616.6**
The **kidneys** and the renal system.   **616.6**
Kids at work. Freedman, R.   **331.3**
The **Kids** Can Press jumbo book of gardening. Morris, K.   **635**
Kids growing up without a home. Fields, J.   **362.5**
Kids knit! Bradberry, S.   **746.43**
Kids make history. Buckley, S.   **973**
Kids of Kabul. Ellis, D.   **305.235**
Kids on strike! Bartoletti, S. C.   **331.892**
Kids weaving. Swett, S.   **746.41**
Kids who rule. Cotter, C.   **920**
Kids' crafts [series]
Davis, J. Crochet   **746.43**
The **kids'** guide to balloon twisting. Trusty, B.   **745.594**
The **kids'** guide to building cool stuff. Bell-Rehwoldt, S.   **745.5**
The **kids'** guide to classic games. Bell-Rehwoldt, S.   **790.1**
The **kids'** guide to jumping rope. Bell-Rehwoldt, S.   **796.2**
The **kids'** guide to paper airplanes. Harbo, C. L.   **745.592**
The **kids'** guide to working out conflicts. Drew, N.   **303.6**
Kids' guides [series]
Bell-Rehwoldt, S. The kids' guide to building cool stuff   **745.5**
Bell-Rehwoldt, S. The kids' guide to classic games   **790.1**
Bell-Rehwoldt, S. The kids' guide to jumping rope   **796.2**
Harbo, C. L. The kids' guide to paper airplanes   **745.592**
Trusty, B. The kids' guide to balloon twisting   **745.594**
Kiernan, Denise
(jt. auth) D'Agnese, J. Signing their rights away   **920**
Signing our lives away   **920**
Kiesbye, Stefan
(ed) Cheating   **179**
The **Kiesha'ra** [series]
Atwater-Rhodes, A. Snakecharm   **Fic**
Kiki Strike. Miller, K.   **Fic**
Kiki Strike: inside the shadow city. Miller, K.   **Fic**

Kiki Strike: the Empress's tomb. Miller, K.   **Fic**
The **kill** order. Dashner, J.   **Fic**
Killer Pizza. Taylor, G.   **Fic**
Killer Pizza: the slice. Taylor, G.   **Fic**
Killer rocks from outer space. Koppes, S. N.   **523.5**
Killer whales. Gish, M.   **599.5**
The **killer's** cousin. Werlin, N.   **Fic**
Killing Mr. Griffin. Duncan, L.   **Fic**
Kilworth, Garry
Attica   **Fic**
Kim. Helfand, L.   **741.5**
Kim Jong Il. Wyborny, S.   **921**
Kim, Derek Kirk
Good as Lily   **741.5**
Kim, Doug
About
Major, J. S. Caravan to America   **745**
Kim, Jong Il, 1942-2011
About
Wyborny, S. Kim Jong Il   **921**
Kim, Melissa
Learning about the endocrine and reproductive systems   **612.4**
Kim, Susan
City of spies   **741.5**
Kimball, Chad T.
(ed) Child and youth security sourcebook   **362.7**
Kimchi & calamari. Kent, R.   **Fic**
Kimmel, Elizabeth Cody
Boy on the lion throne   **92**
Ladies first   **920**
The look-it-up book of explorers   **920**
The reinvention of Moxie Roosevelt   **Fic**
Kimmel, Eric A.
Wonders and miracles   **296.4**
Kimmel, J. L.
(jt. auth) Ceccarelli, D. The Yawning Rabbit River Chronicle   **Fic**
Kinard, Kami
The Boy Project   **Fic**
Kincher, Jonni
Psychology for kids vol. 1: 40 fun tests that help you learn about yourself   **150**
Psychology for kids vol. 2: 40 fun experiments that help you learn about others   **150**
Kind. Black, H.   **741.5**
The **kind** of friends we used to be. Dowell, F. O. **Fic**
KINDERGARTEN
See also Elementary education; Schools
Kindl, Patrice
Keeping the castle   **Fic**
The **kindling.** Bell, B.   **Fic**
Kindred. Stein, T.   **Fic**
Kindred souls. MacLachlan, P.   **FIC**
Kindschi, Tara
4-H guide to raising chickens   **636.5**

Knowles, Laura
  (ed) Ancient treasures   930.1

Knowlton, MaryLee
  Albania   949.65
  Macedonia   949.7
  Turkmenistan   958.5

Knox, Elizabeth
  Dreamhunter   Fic
  Dreamquake   Fic
  Mortal fire   Fic

Knucklehead. Scieszka, J.   92

Knudsen, Michelle
  The dragon of Trelian   Fic
  The princess of Trelian   Fic

Knudsen, Shannon
  Fairies and elves   398

Knutsson, Catherine
  Shadows cast by stars   Fic

Kobe Bryant. Thornley, S.   796.323

Kochel, Marcia Agness
  Baxter, K. A. Gotcha again for guys!   028.5
  Baxter, K. A. Gotcha good!   028.5

KODOMO
      See also Manga

Koehl, Mimi, 1948-
        About
  Parks, D. Nature's machines   92

Koellhoffer, Tara
  Ecstasy and other club drugs   362.29
  Inhalants and solvents   362.29
  Prozac and other antidepressants   615

Koelling, Holly
  (ed) Best books for young adults   028.1
  Classic connections   027.62

Koertge, Ronald
  Now playing   Fic
  Shakespeare makes the playoffs   Fic
  Stoner & Spaz   Fic
  Strays   Fic

Koestler-Grack, Rachel A.
  Annie Oakley   92
  Elie Wiesel   92
  Ferdinand Magellan   92
  The Johnstown flood of 1889   974.8
  Marie Curie   92
  Michelle Kwan   92
  Sir Ernest Shackleton   92

Koh, Magdalene
  Kagda, F. Hong Kong   951.25

Kohl, Victoria
  Chaikin, A. Mission control, this is Apollo   629.45

Koja, Kathe
  Buddha boy   Fic
  Headlong   Fic
  Kissing the bee   Fic

Kolencik, Patricia Liotta

Bernadowski, C. Research-based reading strategies in the library for adolescent learners   372.4

KOMODO DRAGON
  Gish, M. Komodo dragons   597.95
Komodo dragons. Gish, M.   597.95

Konigsberg, Bill
  Openly straight   Fic

Konigsburg, E. L.
  The mysterious edge of the heroic world   Fic
  The outcasts of 19 Schuyler Place   Fic
  Silent to the bone   Fic
  The view from Saturday   Fic

Konomi, Takeshi
  The Prince of Tennis, Vol. 1   741.5

Koopmans, Andy
  Rwanda   967.571

Koppes, Steven N.
  Killer rocks from outer space   523.5

Kops, Deborah
  The Great Molasses Flood   363.17
  Palenque   972
  Racial profiling   363.2

Kor, Eva Mozes
  Surviving the Angel of Death   92

Kor, Eva Mozes, 1935-
        About
  Kor, E. M. Surviving the Angel of Death   92

Koran
  The meaning of the glorious Koran   297.1

KOREA (NORTH)
  Senker, C. North Korea and South Korea   951.9

KOREA (SOUTH)
  Senker, C. North Korea and South Korea   951.9

KOREA -- HISTORY -- JAPANESE OCCUPATION, 1910-1945 -- FICTION
  Park, L. S. When my name was Keoko   Fic
Korean Americans. Thomas, W. D.   305.8

KOREAN AMERICANS
  Thomas, W. D. Korean Americans   305.8

KOREAN AMERICANS -- BIOGRAPHY
  Tiger, C. Margaret Cho   92

KOREAN AMERICANS -- FICTION
  Hautman, P. Doppelganger   Fic
  Kent, R. Kimchi & calamari   Fic
  Na, A. A step from heaven   Fic
  Na, A. Wait for me   Fic
  Park, L. S. Archer's quest   Fic
  Park, L. S. Project Mulberry   Fic
  Son, J. Finding my hat   Fic
  Williams, L. E. Slant   Fic
  Yoo, D. The detention club   Fic
  Yoo, P. Good enough   Fic

KOREAN COOKING
  Sheen, B. Foods of Korea   641.5
The **Korean** War. Santella, A.   951.9
The **Korean** War. Reece, R.   951.9

Oprah Winfrey 92
Stephenie Meyer 92
Vera Wang 92
Krokos, Dan
False memory Fic
The Kronos Chronicles [series]
Rutkoski, M. The Cabinet of Wonders Fic
Rutkoski, M. The Celestial Globe Fic
Rutkoski, M. The Jewel of the Kalderash Fic
Krueger, Susan Heidi
The tempest 822.3
Krul, J. T.
Kreisberg, A. Green Arrow and Black Canary: five
stages 741.5
Krull, Kathleen
Albert Einstein 92
Charles Darwin 92
Isaac Newton 92
A kid's guide to America's Bill of Rights 342
Leonardo da Vinci 92
Lives of extraordinary women 920
Lives of the presidents 920
Lives of the writers 809
Marie Curie 92
Lives of the writers 809
KU KLUX KLAN
Bartoletti, S. C. They called themselves the
K.K.K. 322.4
Hesse, K. Witness Fic
Kublai Khan, 1216-1294
About
McCaughrean, G. The kite rider Fic
Yang, D. J. Daughter of Xanadu Fic
Kublai Khan, 1216-1294 -- Fiction
About
McCaughrean, G. The kite rider Fic
Yang, D. J. Daughter of Xanadu Fic
Kuhlman, Evan
The last invisible boy Fic
Kuhn, Betsy
Angels of mercy 940.54
The race for space 629.45
Kuklin, Susan
No choirboy 364.66
Kummer, Patricia K.
The calendar 529
The food of Thailand 394.1
The Great Barrier Reef 578.7
The Great Lakes 977
North Korea 951.93
The telephone 621.385
Schwabacher, M. Minnesota 977.6
Shirley, D. Mississippi 976.2
KUNG FU
See also Martial arts
Kunkel, Dennis

Latta, S. L. The good, the bad, the slimy 579
Siy, A. Sneeze! 612.2
Kunkel, Dennis
About
Kramer, S. Hidden worlds: looking through a scientist's microscope 502.8
Kunzel, Bonnie Lendermon
The teen-centered book club 027.62
Kupesic, Rajka
The white ballets 792.8
Kupperberg, Paul
The influenza pandemic of 1918-1919 614.5
Kurilla, Renee
Emerson, S. Zebrafish 741.5
Peter H. Reynolds and FableVision present Zebrafish 741.5
Kurlansky, Mark, 1948-
The world without fish 333.95
Kurt Cobain. Burlingame, J. 92
Kurtis, Bill
Garner, J. We interrupt this broadcast 070.1
Kurtti, Jeff
Schumacher, T. L. How does the show go on? 792
Kurtz, Chris
The adventures of a South Pole pig Fic
Kushner, Ellen
(ed) Welcome to Bordertown 808
Kushner, Jill Menkes
Who on earth is Dian Fossey? 92
Kuskowski, Alex
Cool relaxing 613.7
Kusky, Timothy M.
Tsunamis 551.46
Kusugak, Michael
About
Ellis, S. From reader to writer 028
Kuwait. O'Shea, M. 953.67
KUWAIT -- DESCRIPTION AND TRAVEL
Tracy, K. We visit Kuwait 953.67
Kwan, Michelle
About
Koestler-Grack, R. A. Michelle Kwan 92
KWANZAA
See also Holidays
Kwasney, Michelle D.
Itch Fic
Kwolek, Stephanie L., 1923-
About
Thimmesh, C. Girls think of everything 920
Kyi, Tanya Lloyd
The blue jean book 391
Kyle's island. Derby, S. Fic
Kynaston, Suzanne
Ward, P. Bears of the world 599.78
Kyrgyzstan. King, D. C. 958.4
Kyvelos, Peter

Latham, Donna
Backyard Biology   570.78

Latham, Donna
Amazing biome projects you can build yourself **577**
Ecology   **577**

Latham, Irene
Leaving Gee's Bend   Fic

Latif, Zawiah Abdul
Gish, S. Ethiopia   963
Hassig, S. M. Somalia   967.73
Heale, J. Madagascar   969.1
Kagda, F. Algeria   965
Kagda, S. Lithuania   947.93
Levy, P. Sudan   962.4
Sheehan, S. Lebanon   956.92

Latimer, Jonathan P.
Backyard birds   598
Birds of prey   598.9
Caterpillars   595.7
Songbirds   598

LATIN AMERICA -- POLITICS AND GOVERN-MENT
See also Politics

Latin America and the Caribbean. Solway, A. **780.9**

LATIN AMERICAN ART
Makosz, R. Latino arts and their influence on the United States   **700**

LATIN AMERICAN ART
See also Art

LATIN AMERICAN LITERATURE
See also Literature

LATIN AMERICAN LITERATURE -- BIBLIOG-RAPHY
Schon, I. Recommended books in Spanish for children and young adults, 2004-2008   **011.6**

LATIN AMERICANS -- CULTURAL ASSIMILA-TION -- FICTION
Ada, A. F. Yes! we are Latinos   Fic

LATIN AMERICANS -- SOCIAL LIFE AND CUSTOMS
Sanna, E. Latino folklore and culture   398.2

LATIN AMERICANS -- UNITED STATES -- FICTION
Ada, A. F. Yes! we are Latinos   Fic

LATIN LANGUAGE -- DICTIONARIES
Simpson, D. P. Cassell's Latin dictionary   473

LATIN LITERATURE
See also Literature

The **Latin** music scene. Tsoukanelis, E. A. **780.89**

Latino American history [series]
Doak, R. S. Struggling to become American **305.8**

Latino arts and their influence on the United States. Makosz, R.   **700**

LATINO AUTHORS
Amend, A. Hispanic-American writers   810

Latino biography library [series]

Schraff, A. E. Ellen Ochoa   92
Warrick, K. C. Sandra Cisneros   92

Latino folklore and culture. Sanna, E.   **398.2**

LATINOS (U.S.)
Cruz, B. Triumphs and struggles for Latino civil rights   323.1
Doak, R. S. Struggling to become American 305.8
Growing up Latino   810
Hernandez, R. E. The Civil War, 1840s-1890s 973.7
Otfinoski, S. The new republic: 1760-1840s 973.3
Wachale! poetry and prose on growing up Latino in America   810

LATINOS (U.S.)
See also Ethnic groups

Latno, Mark
The paper boomerang book   745.54

Latta, Sara L.
The good, the bad, the slimy   579
Ice scientist   998
Lava scientist   551.2

LATTER-DAY SAINTS *See* Church of Jesus Christ of Latter-day Saints

Lau, Ruth
Berg, E. Senegal   966.3

Laubach, Christyna M.
Raptor! a kid's guide to birds of prey   598

Laubach, Rene
Laubach, C. M. Raptor! a kid's guide to birds of prey   598

Laugh & learn [series]
Fox, J. S. Get organized without losing it   371.3

The **laugh** stand. Cleary, B. P.   817

Laugh till you cry. Nixon, J. L.   Fic

Laughing out loud, I fly. Herrera, J. F.   811

Laughlin, Rosemary
The Ludlow massacre of 1913-14   331.8
The Pullman strike of 1894   331.8

LAUGHTER
See also Emotions

Laughton, Timothy
Exploring the life, myth, and art of the Maya **972.81**

Laura Ingalls Wilder. Anderson, W. T.   813
Laura Ingalls Wilder. Berne, E. C.   92
Laura Ingalls Wilder. Sickels, A.   92

Laure, Jason
Altman, L. J. Arkansas   976.7
Blauer, E. Mali   966.2
Blauer, E. Mauritania   966.1
McDaniel, M. New Mexico   972

Lauren Yanofsky hates the holocaust. Lieberman, L.   Fic

Lauren, Ralph
About
Mattern, J. Ralph Lauren   92

Laurence Yep. Marcovitz, H.   92

Laurie Halse Anderson. Glenn, W. J.   92

Ford, E. What you must think of me   **616.85**

Lies. Grant, M.   **Fic**

The **lies** that bind. Roecker, L.   **Fic**

Liesl & Po. Oliver, L.   **Fic**

Lieurance, Suzanne

   The locket   **Fic**

Life. Fredericks, M.   **Fic**

LIFE (BIOLOGY)

   McManus, L. Cell systems   **570**

   Somervill, B. A. Animal cells and life processes   **571.6**

LIFE (BIOLOGY)

   Winston, R. Life as we know it   **570**

     See also Biology

LIFE -- ORIGIN

   Herbst, J. Germ theory   **616**

   Solway, A. Why is there life on Earth?   **576.8**

LIFE -- ORIGIN

     See also Evolution

LIFE AFTER DEATH *See* Future life; Immortality

Life along the ancient Nile. Whiting, J.   **932.01**

The **life** and death of Crazy Horse. Freedman,
R.   **978**

The **life** and times of Buddha. Gedney, M.   **294.3**

The **life** and times of Father Jacques Marquette.
Harkins, S. S.   **92**

The **life** and times of Rosa Parks. Tracy, K.   **92**

Life as we knew it. Pfeffer, S. B.   **Fic**

Life as we know it. Winston, R.   **570**

Life balance [series]

   Andrews, L. W. Emotional intelligence   **152.4**

   Andrews, L. W. Meditation   **158**

   Landau, E. Date violence   **362.88**

Life cycles. Spilsbury, R.   **591.56**

LIFE CYCLES *See* Life cycles (Biology)

LIFE CYCLES (BIOLOGY)

   Spilsbury, R. Life cycles   **591.56**

LIFE CYCLES (BIOLOGY)

   Thornhill, J. I found a dead bird   **306.9**

     See also Biology; Cycles; Life (Biology)

Life happens next. Trueman, T.   **Fic**

LIFE HISTORIES *See* Biography

Life in ancient Egypt [series]

   Hinds, K. Religion   **299**

LIFE IN LITERATURE

   Bookmarked   **809**

Life in the Australian Outback. Einfeld, J.   **994**

Life in the desert. Fridell, R.   **577.5**

Life in the Medieval Muslim world [series]

   Hinds, K. Faith   **297**

   Hinds, K. The palace   **909.07**

Life in the sea [series]

   Walker, P. The continental shelf   **578.7**

   Walker, P. The coral reef   **577.7**

   Walker, P. The open ocean   **578.7**

Life in the temperate grasslands. Toupin, L.   **577.4**

Life in the tropical forests. Tocci, S.   **577.3**

A **life** in the wild. Turner, P. S.   **92**

Life in Victorian England [series]

   Schomp, V. The church   **274**

   Schomp, V. Victoria and her court   **941.081**

Life is fine. Whittenberg, A.   **Fic**

Life is funny. Frank, E. R.   **Fic**

Life is tough. Bilz, R. L.   **028.5**

Life of a soldier in Washington's army. Stewart,
G.   **973.3**

The **life** of glass. Cantor, J.   **Fic**

The life of plants [series]

   Spilsbury, R. Plant growth   **571.8**

   Spilsbury, R. Plant habitats   **581.7**

   Spilsbury, R. Plant reproduction   **575.6**

The **life** of rice. Sobol, R.   **633.1**

Life on earth--and beyond. Turner, P. S.   **576.8**

Life on Mars: tales from the new frontier.   **S C**

LIFE ON OTHER PLANETS

   Berkowitz, J. Out of this world   **576.8**

   Bortz, A. B. Astrobiology   **576.8**

   Scott, E. Mars and the search for life   **576.8**

   Skurzynski, G. Are we alone?   **576.8**

   Solway, A. Why is there life on Earth?   **576.8**

   Turner, P. S. Life on earth--and beyond   **576.8**

   Wittenstein, V. O. Planet hunter   **523.2**

LIFE ON OTHER PLANETS

     See also Astronomy; Planets; Universe

LIFE ON OTHER PLANETS -- FICTION

   DiTerlizzi, T. A hero for WondLa   **Fic**

Life on the edge. Winner, C.   **578.7**

Life portraits [series]

   Koestler-Grack, R. A. Elie Wiesel   **92**

   Piddock, C. Rachel Carson   **92**

Life processes [series]

   Spilsbury, R. Life cycles   **591.56**

LIFE SAVING *See* Lifesaving

Life science in depth [series]

   Fullick, A. Adaptation and competition   **578.4**

Life sciences.   **920**

LIFE SCIENCES

   Life sciences   **920**

LIFE SCIENCES

     See also Science

LIFE SCIENCES ETHICS *See* Bioethics

LIFE SKILLS

   Bostick, N. Managing Money   **332**

   Buchholz, R. How to survive anything   **646.7**

   Ehrman, M. K. Taking a stand   **646.7**

   Erlbach, A. The middle school survival guide   **373.1**

   Fox, J. S. Get organized without losing it   **371.3**

   Jeffrie, S. The girls' book of glamour   **646.7**

   Mangan, T. How to feel good   **305.23**

   Morgenstern, J. Organizing from the inside out for
teens   **646.7**

Looking at maps. Taylor, B.   912
Looking at pictures. Richardson, J.   750.1
Looking at settlements. Anderson, J.   307
Looking back. Lowry, L.   813
Looking for Lucy Buick. Murphy, R.   Fic
Looking for Marco Polo. Armstrong, A.   Fic
Looking for seabirds. Webb, S.   598
Looks. George, M.   Fic
Loos, Pamela
   A reader's guide to Amy Tan's The joy luck club   813
   A reader's guide to Lorraine Hansberry's A raisin in
     the sun   812
Loose threads. Grover, L. A.   811
Lopez, Diana
   Ask my mood ring how I feel   Fic
   Confetti girl   Fic
Lopez, Jose Javier
   Puerto Rico   972.95
LORAN
     See also Navigation
Lorbiecki, Marybeth
   Prairie dogs   599.3
Lord Loss. Shan, D.   Fic
The **lord** of Opium. Farmer, N.   Fic
Lord of the deep. Salisbury, G.   Fic
Lord of the flies. Golding, W.   Fic
The **lord** of the rings. Tolkien, J. R. R.   Fic
Lord Sunday. Nix, G.   Fic
Lord, Cynthia
   Rules   Fic
   Touch blue   Fic
Lorinc, John
   Cities   307.7
Los Angeles Police Department. Worth, R.   363.2
Losing Faith. Jaden, D.   Fic
Losing is not an option: stories. Wallace, R.   S C
Losing someone you love. Phillips, T. A.   155.9
Loss. Kessler, J.   Fic
LOSS (PSYCHOLOGY)
   The Color of absence   813
   Hantman, C. 30 days to getting over the dork you
     used to call your boyfriend   158
   Myers, E. When will I stop hurting?   155.9
   Van Leeuwen, J. Lucy was there--   Fic
   What have you lost?   808.81
LOSS (PSYCHOLOGY)
     See also Psychology
LOSS (PSYCHOLOGY) -- FICTION
   Baskin, N. R. All we know of love   Fic
   Cooper, I. Angel in my pocket   Fic
   Galante, C. The summer of May   Fic
   Johnson, J. J. The theory of everything   Fic
   Kephart, B. Nothing but ghosts   Fic
   Key, W. Fourmile   Fic
   A monster calls   Fic
   Pennypacker, S.   The summer of the gypsy

   moths   Fic
   Ransom, C. Rebel McKenzie   Fic
   Schindler, H. Playing hurt   Fic
   Stein, T. High dive   Fic
LOSS (PSYCHOLOGY) -- POETRY
   What have you lost?   808.81
LOSS (PSYCHOLOGY) IN ADOLESCENCE
   Myers, E. When will I stop hurting?   155.9
Lost. Davies, J.   Fic
Lost. Prineas, S.   Fic
Lost journals of Ven Polypheme [series]
   Haydon, E. The Thief Queen's daughter   Fic
Lost & found. Tan, S.   S C
LOST AND FOUND POSSESSIONS -- FICTION
   Booraem, E. Small persons with wings   Fic
   Chari, S. Vanished   Fic
   Huntley, A. The everafter   Fic
   Korman, G. Zoobreak   Fic
   Springer, N. The case of the peculiar pink fan   Fic
LOST ARCHITECTURE
     See also Architecture
The **lost** art. Morden, S.   Fic
Lost boy. Newbery, L.   Fic
Lost boy, lost girl. Dau, J. B.   962.4
Lost childhood. Layson, A. H.   92
Lost cities. Barber, N.   930.1
The **lost** city of Faar. MacHale, D. J.   Fic
The **lost** conspiracy. Hardinge, F.   Fic
The **lost** crown. Miller, S.   Fic
The **lost** garden. Yep, L.   979.4
The **lost** garden. Yep, L.   979.4
Lost Goat Lane. Jordan, R.   Fic
The **lost** heiress. Fisher, C.   Fic
The **lost** hero. Riordan, R.   Fic
Lost in the river of grass. Rorby, G.   Fic
The **lost** island of Tamarind. Aguiar, N.   Fic
Lost sight. Markle, S.   617.7
The **lost** stories. Flanagan, J.   S C
Lost time. Schmid, S. M.   Fic
The **lost** train of thought. Hulme, J.   Fic
Lost treasure of the Inca. Lourie, P.   986.6
The **lost** treasure of Tuckernuck. Fairlie, E.   Fic
LOST TRIBES OF ISRAEL
     See also Jews
Lost voices. Porter, S.   Fic
The **lost** warrior. Hunter, E.   741.5
The **lost** years of Merlin. Barron, T. A.   Fic
Losure, Mary
   The Fairy Ring, or, Elsie and Frances Fool the
     World   398
Lottridge, Celia Barker
   The listening tree   Fic
   Stories from Adam and Eve to Ezekiel   220.9
   Stories from the life of Jesus   232.9
Lou Gehrig. Buckley, J.   92
The **loud** silence of Francine Green. Cushman,

LUMINESCENCE
> *See also* Light; Radiation

LUMINESCENCE
Sitarski, A. Cold light   572

LUNAR BASES
> *See also* Civil engineering; Life support systems (Space environment)

LUNAR ECLIPSES
> *See also* Astronomy

LUNAR EXPEDITIONS *See* Space flight to the moon

LUNAR GEOLOGY
> *See also* Astrogeology

LUNAR PROBES
> *See also* Space probes

The **lunatic's** curse. Higgins, F. E.   Fic

Lunch with Lenin and other stories. Ellis, D.   S C

Lunch-box dream. Abbott, T.   Fic

LUNCHEONS
Rau, D. M. Teen guide to fast, delicious lunches   641.5

LUNCHEONS
> *See also* Cooking; Menus

LUNCHROOMS *See* Restaurants

LUNG CANCER
> *See also* Cancer; Lungs -- Diseases

Lunge-Larsen, Lise
Gifts from the gods   401

LUNGS -- DISEASES
Blank, A. Invincible microbe   616.9

LUNGS -- DISEASES
> *See also* Diseases

Luper, Eric
Bug boy   Fic

Lupica, Mike
The batboy   Fic
The big field   Fic
Heat   Fic
Heat   Fic
Hero   Fic
Miracle on 49th Street   Fic
Play Makers   Fic
Summer ball   Fic

Lurie, April
The latent powers of Dylan Fontaine   Fic

Lush. Friend, N.   Fic

Lushington, Nolan
Libraries designed for kids   025.1

Lusted, Marcia Amidon
The capture and killing of Osama bin Laden   958.1
The Chernobyl Disaster   363.1
Entertainment   791
Poverty   362.5
Social networking: MySpace, Facebook, & Twitter   302.3
The Three Mile Island nuclear disaster   363.1

Lutes, Jason
Houdini: the handcuff king   741.5

Lutz, Richard A.
> About

Mallory, K. Diving to a deep-sea volcano   551.46

Luv ya bunches. Myracle, L.   Fic

Luxbacher, Irene
The jumbo book of art   702.8

Luxembourg. Sheehan, P.   949.35

Luxenberg, Alan
Radical Islam   297

Ly, Many
Roots and wings   Fic

Lyddie. Paterson, K.   Fic

Lydia Maria Child. Kenschaft, L.   303.48

Lye, Keith
Campbell, R. Atlas of Asia   950

Lyga, Barry
Archvillain   Fic
The astonishing adventures of Fanboy & Goth Girl   Fic
Goth girl rising   Fic
Hero-type   Fic
Mangaman   741.5
Wolverine: worst day ever   741.5

LYME DISEASE
> *See also* Diseases

LYMPHATIC SYSTEM
> *See also* Physiology

LYMPHATIC SYSTEM
Gold, J. C. Learning about the circulatory and lymphatic systems   612.1

LYMPHATICS
Gold, J. C. Learning about the circulatory and lymphatic systems   612.1

The Lynburn legacy [series]
Brennan, S. R. Unspoken   Fic

Lynch, Chris, 1962-
Angry young man   Fic
The Big Game of Everything   Fic
Casualties of war   Fic
Hothouse   Fic
Inexcusable   Fic
Pieces   Fic

Lynch, Patricia Ann
African mythology, A to Z   299.6

Lynch, Wayne
Arctic   998
The Everglades   508
Rocky Mountains   577.4
Sonoran Desert   577.5

LYNCHING
Aretha, D. The murder of Emmett Till   364.152
Coleman, W. Racism on trial   345
Crowe, C. Getting away with murder: the true story of the Emmett Till case   364.152

Manet, Édouard, 1832-1883
About
Spence, D. Manet 92
MANGA
Arai, K. Beauty Pop, Vol. 1 **741.5**
Ebine, K. Gandhi: a manga biography **92**
Hotta, Y. Hikaru No Go, Volume 1 **741.5**
Igarashi, D. Children of the sea, vol. 1 **741.5**
Konomi, T. The Prince of Tennis, Vol. 1 **741.5**
Nakajo, H. Sugar Princess volume 1: skating to win **741.5**
Sakura, K. Dragon drive. Vol. 1, D-break **741.5**
Shimura Takako Wandering son **Fic**
Toriyama, A. Cowa! **741.5**
MANGA
See also Graphic novels
MANGA -- DRAWING
Hart, C. Manga for the beginner **741.5**
Hart, C. Manga mania romance **741.5**
Nagatomo, H. Draw your own Manga **741.5**
MANGA -- STUDY AND TEACHING
Brenner, R. E. Understanding manga and anime **025.2**
Manga for the beginner. Hart, C. **741.5**
Manga mania romance. Hart, C. **741.5**
Manga Shakespeare [series]
Appignanesi, R. As you like it **741.5**
Appignanesi, R. Hamlet **741.5**
Appignanesi, R. A midsummer night's dream **741.5**
Appignanesi, R. Romeo and Juliet **741.5**
Appignanesi, R. The tempest **741.5**
The merchant of Venice **741.5**
Twelfth night **741.5**
Manga touch. Pearce, J. **Fic**
Mangaman. **741.5**
Mangan, Tricia
How to feel good **305.23**
Manganese. Beatty, R. **546**
MANGANESE
Beatty, R. Manganese **546**
Mangled by a hurricane! Aronin, M. **551.55**
A **mango-shaped** space. Mass, W. **Fic**
Mangum, Lisa
After hello **Fic**
The **Manhattan** Project. Vander Hook, S. **355.8**
MANIA See Manic-depressive illness
Maniac Magee. Spinelli, J. **Fic**
MANIC DEPRESSION See Manic-depressive illness
MANIC-DEPRESSIVE ILLNESS
Meisel, A. Investigating depression and bipolar disorder **616.89**
Mooney, C. Mood disorders **616.85**
Silverstein, A. The depression and bipolar disorder update **616.89**
MANIC-DEPRESSIVE ILLNESS

See also Affective disorders; Mental illness
MANIC-DEPRESSIVE ILLNESS -- FICTION
Leal, A. H. A finders-keepers place **Fic**
Michaels, R. Nobel genes **Fic**
Mills, C. One square inch **Fic**
Turner, A. W. Father of lies **Fic**
MANIC-DEPRESSIVE PSYCHOSES See Manic-depressive illness
MANIC-DEPRESSIVE PSYCHOSIS See Manic-depressive illness
MANIKINS (FASHION MODELS) See Fashion models
Manipulating light. Stille, D. R. **535**
Manitoba. Laws, G. D. **971**
Manivong, Laura
Escaping the tiger **Fic**
Mankell, Henning
A bridge to the stars **Fic**
Shadows in the twilight **Fic**
When the snow fell **Fic**
Mankiller, Wilma
About
Krull, K. Lives of extraordinary women **920**
Sonneborn, L. Wilma Mankiller **92**
Manmade disasters [series]
Mayell, M. Tragedies of space exploration **363.1**
Mann, Bethany
Hines-Stephens, S. Show off **790.1**
Mann, Charles C.
Before Columbus **970.01**
Mann, Elizabeth
Statue of Liberty **974.7**
Mann, Elizabeth
Hoover Dam **627**
The Parthenon **726**
The Roman Colosseum **937**
Statue of Liberty **974.7**
Taj Mahal **954**
Tikal **972.81**
Mann, Gurinder Singh
Buddhists, Hindus, and Sikhs in America **294**
Mann, Jonathan H.
(ed) The Election of 2000 and the administration of George W. Bush **324**
Mann, Michael E., 1965-
(ed) Berlatsky, N. Water and ice **551.4**
Henningfeld, D. A. Health and disease **363.7**
MANNED SPACE FLIGHT
Holden, H. M. The coolest job in the universe **629.44**
MANNED SPACE FLIGHT See Space flight
MANNED SPACE FLIGHT -- HISTORY
Richie, J. Space flight **629**
MANNEQUINS (FASHION MODELS) See Fashion models
MANNERS See Courtesy; Etiquette

McNeese, Tim
The abolitionist movement — 973.7
The Alamo — 976.4
Civil War battles — 973.7
The Civil War era, 1851-1865 — 973.7
Civil War leaders — 973.7
Colonial America, 1543-1763 — 973.2
The Donner Party — 979.4
Early national America, 1790-1850 — 973.4
The fascinating history of American Indians — 970.004
The Gilded Age and Progressivism, 1891-1913 — 973.8
The Great Depression, 1929-1940 — 973.917
Isabel Allende — 92
Jorge Luis Borges — 92
Modern America, 1964-present — 973.92
Reconstruction — 973.8
Revolutionary America, 1764-1789 — 973.3
The rise and fall of American slavery — 326
Salvador Dali — 92
Tito Puente — 92

McNicholas, June
Rats — 636.9

McNicoll, Sylvia
Last chance for Paris — Fic

McNish, Cliff
Angel — Fic
The silver child — Fic
Silver City — Fic
Silver world — Fic

McPhee, Marc E.
Farmer, L. S. J. Neal-Schuman technology management handbook for school library media centers — 025.1

McPhee, Peter
New blood — Fic

McPherson, James M.
Fields of fury — 973.7

McPherson, Stephanie Sammartino
Iceberg right ahead! — 910.4
Stressed out in school? — 371.7

McQuade, Samuel C.
(jt. auth) Gentry, S. E. Living with the Internet — 303.48

McQuein, Josin L.
Arclight — Fic

McQuerry, Maureen Doyle
The Peculiars — Fic

McQuinn, Anna
McQuinn, C. Ireland — 941.5

McQuinn, Colm
Ireland — 941.5

McRobbie, David
A whole lot of Wayne — S C

McVay, Charles Butler, III
About
Nelson, P. Left for dead — 940.54

McWhorter, Diane
A dream of freedom — 323.1

McWilliams, Kelly
Doormat — Fic

Me & death. Scrimger, R. — Fic
Me & Earl & the dying girl. Andrews, J. — Fic
Me and my feelings. Guarino, R. — 152.4

MÉTIS -- FICTION
Erdrich, L. Chickadee — Fic
Me, the missing, and the dead. Valentine, J. — Fic

Mead, Alice
Dawn and dusk — Fic
Swimming to America — Fic

Mead, Margaret, 1901-1978
About
Mark, J. T. Margaret Mead — 306

Mead, Wendy
Bennett, C. Montana — 978.6
McDaniel, M. Arizona — 979.1
The alternative rock scene — 781.66
Stefoff, R. Utah — 979.2

MEADOW ECOLOGY
Martin, P. A. F. Prairies, fields, and meadows — 577.4

MEAL PLANNING See Menus; Nutrition

MEALS ON WHEELS PROGRAMS
See also Food relief

MEANING (PHILOSOPHY) -- FICTION
Nothing — Fic
The meaning of the glorious Koran. Koran — 297.1

Means, A. L.
A student's guide to George Orwell — 828

Meanwhile. Shiga, J. — 741.5

Measure up! [series]
Sullivan, N. Area, distance, and volume — 516
Sullivan, N. Speed — 531
Sullivan, N. Temperature — 536
Sullivan, N. Time — 529
Sullivan, N. Weight — 530

MEASUREMENT
Ball, J. Why pi — 530.8
Gardner, R. Ace your math and measuring science project — 530.8
Sullivan, N. Area, distance, and volume — 516
Sullivan, N. Speed — 531

MEASUREMENT
See also Mathematics

MEASURES See Weights and measures

MEASURING INSTRUMENTS
See also Measurement; Weights and measures

Measuring the Earth. Gow, M. — 92

MEAT
Llewellyn, C. Cooking with meat and fish — 641.6
Watson, S. Mystery meat — 613.2

MEAT

Forler, N. Winterberries and apple blossoms **811**

The **Menominee.** Bial, R. **977.4**

MENOMINEE INDIANS

Bial, R. The Menominee **977.4**

Menon, Sujatha

Discover snakes **597.96**

MENSTRUATION

Gravelle, K. The period book **612.6**

Jukes, M. Growing up: it's a girl thing **612.6**

MENSTRUATION

See also Reproduction

MENSTRUATION -- FICTION

Don't cramp my style **S C**

MENSURATION

Ball, J. Why pi **530.8**

Gardner, R. Ace your math and measuring science project **530.8**

MENTAL ARITHMETIC

See also Arithmetic

MENTAL DEPRESSION *See* Depression (Psychology)

MENTAL DISEASES *See* Abnormal psychology; Mental illness

Mental disorders. Farrell, C. **362.1**

MENTAL HEALING

See also Alternative medicine

MENTAL HEALTH

Mental health information for teens **616.89**

MENTAL HEALTH

See also Happiness; Health

Mental health information for teens. **616.89**

MENTAL HEALTH LAWS -- UNITED STATES

Houser, A. Tragedy in Tucson **364.152**

MENTAL HEALTH SERVICES

See also Medical care

MENTAL HOSPITALS *See* Psychiatric hospitals

MENTAL HYGIENE *See* Mental health

MENTAL ILLNESS

Farrell, C. Mental disorders **362.1**

Kent, D. Snake pits, talking cures, & magic bullets **616.89**

Mental illness: opposing viewpoints **362.2**

White, R. Memories of Summer **Fic**

MENTAL ILLNESS

See also Abnormal psychology; Diseases

MENTAL ILLNESS -- FICTION

Collomore, A. The ruining **Fic**

Halpern, J. Have a nice day **Fic**

Vaught, S. Freaks like us **Fic**

MENTAL ILLNESS -- GRAPHIC NOVELS

White, T. How I made it to eighteen **741.5**

MENTAL ILLNESS -- HISTORY

Kent, D. Snake pits, talking cures, & magic bullets **616.89**

MENTAL ILLNESS -- PHYSIOLOGICAL ASPECTS

See also Physiology

Mental illness: opposing viewpoints. **362.2**

MENTAL PATIENTS *See* Mentally ill

MENTAL STRESS *See* Stress (Psychology)

MENTAL SUGGESTION

See also Mind and body; Parapsychology; Subconsciousness

MENTAL TESTS *See* Intelligence tests; Psychological tests

MENTALLY DEPRESSED *See* Depression (Psychology)

MENTALLY DERANGED *See* Mentally ill

MENTALLY HANDICAPPED

Couwenhoven, T. The boys' guide to growing up **613**

MENTALLY HANDICAPPED

See also Handicapped

MENTALLY HANDICAPPED -- FICTION

Hooper, M. Fallen Grace **Fic**

Lowry, L. The silent boy **Fic**

Mackall, D. D. The silence of murder **Fic**

Magnin, J. Carrying Mason **Fic**

Martin, A. M. A corner of the universe **Fic**

Nolan, H. A face in every window **Fic**

Nuzum, K. A. A small white scar **Fic**

Sturtevant, K. The brothers story **Fic**

Williams, M. Now is the time for running **Fic**

Wood, J. R. The man who loved clowns **Fic**

MENTALLY HANDICAPPED CHILDREN

See also Child psychiatry; Handicapped children; Mentally handicapped

MENTALLY HANDICAPPED CHILDREN -- FICTION

Hamilton, K. R. In the forests of the night **Fic**

Hamilton, K. R. Tyger tyger **Fic**

Sturtevant, K. The brothers story **Fic**

MENTALLY ILL

Binstock, M. Nourishment **92**

Monaque, M. Trouble in my head **616.85**

Patterson, J. Med head **92**

MENTALLY ILL

See also Sick

MENTALLY ILL -- FICTION

Graves, K. The orphan of Awkward Falls **Fic**

Michaels, R. Nobel genes **Fic**

Trueman, T. Inside out **Fic**

White, R. Memories of Summer **Fic**

MENTORING

See also Counseling

MENTORING -- FICTION

McMullan, M. Cashay **Fic**

Myers, W. D. Kick **Fic**

MENUS

See also Cooking; Diet

Menzel, Peter

What the world eats **641.3**

Mercado, Nancy E.
(ed) Baseball crazy: ten short stories that cover all the bases **S C**
(ed) Every man for himself **S C**

Mercator, Gerardus, 1512-1594
About
Heinrichs, A. Gerardus Mercator **92**

MERCENARY SOLDIERS
See also Military personnel; Soldiers

MERCENARY SOLDIERS -- FICTION
Taylor, L. Silksinger **Fic**

Mercer, Bobby
The flying machine book **745.592**
Newcomb, R. Smash it! crash it! launch it! **507.8**

Mercer, Bobby

MERCHANDISING *See* Marketing; Retail trade

MERCHANT MARINE
See also Maritime law; Sailors; Ships; Transportation
The **merchant** of death. MacHale, D. J. **Fic**
The **merchant** of Venice. Hinds, G. **741.5**
The **merchant** of Venice. **741.5**
The **merchant's** daughter. Dickerson, M. **Fic**

MERCHANTS
See also Businesspeople

Mercian triology [series]
Wignall, K. J. Blood **Fic**

Mercury. Watt, S. **546**
Mercury. Larson, H. **741.5**

MERCURY
See also Chemical elements; Metals
Mercury. Colligan, L. H. **523.4**

MERCURY
Watt, S. Mercury **546**

MERCURY (PLANET)
See also Planets

MERCY KILLING *See* Euthanasia

Meridian. Kizer, A. **Fic**

Merino, Noel
Smoking **362.29**
Vaccines **615**

Merlin. Yolen, J. **Fic**

Merlin [series]
Barron, T. A. The book of magic **Fic**

MERLIN (LEGENDARY CHARACTER)
Barron, T. A. The book of magic **Fic**
Barron, T. A. The fires of Merlin **Fic**
Barron, T. A. The lost years of Merlin **Fic**
Barron, T. A. The mirror of Merlin **Fic**
Barron, T. A. The seven songs of Merlin **Fic**
Barron, T. A. The wings of Merlin **Fic**
McKenzie, N. Guinevere's gamble **Fic**
Service, P. F. Tomorrow's magic **Fic**
Service, P. F. Yesterday's magic **Fic**
Yolen, J. Hobby **813**
Yolen, J. Merlin **Fic**

Yolen, J. Passager **813**

MERLIN (LEGENDARY CHARACTER) -- GRAPHIC NOVELS
Excalibur **741.5**

Merlin's dragon. Barron, T. A. **Fic**

Merlin's dragon [series]
Barron, T. A. Doomraga's revenge **Fic**
Barron, T. A. Merlin's dragon **Fic**
Barron, T. A. Ultimate magic **Fic**

The **mermaid** of Warsaw. Monte, R. **398.2**
Mermaid Park. Mayall, B. **Fic**
The **mermaid's** mirror. Madigan, L. K. **Fic**

MERMAIDS
McKinley, R. Water: tales of elemental spirits **S C**

MERMAIDS AND MERMEN
See also Mythical animals

MERMAIDS AND MERMEN -- FICTION
Appelt, K. Keeper **Fic**
Deebs, T. Tempest rising **Fic**
Dunmore, H. The deep **Fic**
Dunmore, H. Ingo **Fic**
Dunmore, H. Tide knot **Fic**
Madigan, L. K. The mermaid's mirror **Fic**
McKinley, R. Water: tales of elemental spirits **S C**
Meyer, K. The water mirror **Fic**
Nielson, S. A. Forbidden sea **Fic**
Porter, S. Lost voices **Fic**

Merman, Ethel, 1908 or 9-1984
About
Orgill, R. Shout, sister, shout! **920**

MERMEN
McKinley, R. Water: tales of elemental spirits **S C**

Merrell, Billy
(ed) The Full spectrum **306.76**

The **Merriam-Webster** dictionary of synonyms and antonyms. **423**

Merriam-Webster Inc.
(comp) Merriam-Webster's visual dictionary **423**

Merriam-Webster's school thesaurus. **423**
Merriam-Webster's visual dictionary. **423**

Merrill, Jean
The pushcart war **Fic**

Merrill, Martha
McCain, M. M. Dictionary for school library media specialists **020**

The **merry** adventures of Robin Hood. Pyle, H. **398.2**

Meshbesher, Wendy
Hartman, E. Changing life on Earth **576.8**
Hartman, E. Climate change **551.6**
Hartman, E. Fossil fuels **333.8**
Hartman, E. Light and sound **530**
Hartman, E. Mission to Mars **629.45**
Hartman, E. Science ethics and controversies **174**

Mesopotamia and the Bible lands. Morris, N. **935**
Mesopotamians. Kerrigan, M. **935**

Living with depression   616.85

Miller, Arthur, 1915-2005

          About

  Andersen, R. Arthur Miller   92

  Dunkleberger, A. A student's guide to Arthur Miller   812

Miller, Brandon Marie

  Benjamin Franklin, American genius   92

  George Washington for kids   92

  Good women of a well-blessed land   305.4

  Thomas Jefferson for kids   92

  Women of the frontier   978

Miller, Calvin Craig

  A. Philip Randolph and the African American labor movement   92

  Backlash   305.8

  Che Guevara   92

  No easy answers   92

  Reggae poet: the story of Bob Marley   92

Miller, Calvin Craig, 1954-

  (jt. auth) Miller, C. C. Backlash   305.8

Miller, Debra A.

  (ed) Factory farming   179

  (ed) The green movement   333.72

  Energy production and alternative energy   333.79

  Garbage and recycling   363.7

  Hurricane Katrina   363.34

  Organic foods   641.3

  Pandemics   614.4

  Political corruption   364.1

Miller, Donalyn

  The book whisperer   372.6

Miller, Donna P.

  Crash course in teen services   027.62

Miller, Heather

  Smoking   616.86

Miller, James

  (ed) The Complete history of American slavery   326

Miller, Jeanne

  Food science   641.3

Miller, Karen

  (ed) Male and female roles: opposing viewpoints   305.3

  (ed) Race relations: opposing viewpoints   305.8

Miller, Kirsten

  All you desire   Fic

  The eternal ones   Fic

  Kiki Strike: inside the shadow city   Fic

  Kiki Strike: the Empress's tomb   Fic

Miller, Lee

  Roanoke   975.6

Miller, Linda L.

  Baumbach, D. Less is more   025.2

Miller, Malinda

  Green construction   690

  Modern mechanics   629.28

The pharmaceutical industry   615

Tomorrow's teachers   371.1

Tomorrow's transportation   363.7

Miller, Mara

  Hurricane Katrina strikes the Gulf Coast   363.34

  School desegregation and the story of the Little Rock Nine   379

Miller, Mary

  Zeinert, K. The brave women of the Gulf Wars   956.7

Miller, Ron

  Earth and the moon   525

  The elements   546

  Is the end of the world near?   001.9

  Jupiter   523.45

  Mars   523.4

  Robot explorers   629.43

  Rockets   621.43

  Satellites   629.44

  Saturn   523.46

  Seven wonders beyond the solar system   523.8

  Seven wonders of the gas giants and their moons   523.4

  Seven wonders of the rocky planets and their moons   523.4

  Space exploration   629.4

  Special effects   778.5

Miller, Sara Swan

  Seahorses, pipefishes, and their kin   597

  Secret lives of burrowing beasts   591.7

  Secret lives of cave creatures   591.7

  Secret lives of deep-sea creatures   591.7

  Secret lives of seashell dwellers   594

  Secret lives of soil creatures   591.7

  Woodpeckers, toucans, and their kin   598

Miller, Sarah

  The lost crown   Fic

  Miss Spitfire   Fic

Miller, Steve

  Dinosaurs: how to draw thunder lizards and other prehistoric beasts   743

Miller, Terry

  D-Day   940.54

Miller-Lachmann, Lyn

  (ed) Once upon a cuento   S C

Miller-Schroeder, Patricia

  Boreal forests   577.3

Millet, Lydia

  The fires beneath the sea   Fic

Millicent Min, girl genius. Yee, L.   Fic

The **million** dollar shot. Gutman, D.   Fic

A **million** miles from Boston. Day, K.   Fic

A **million** shades of gray. Kadohata, C.   Fic

MILLS

    See also Manufactures; Technology

Mills, Andrea

Hammer of witches   **Fic**

Mlynowski, Sarah
Gimme a call   **Fic**
See Jane write   **808.3**
Ten things we did (and probably shouldn't have) **Fic**

MOBILE HOMES
    See also Housing
Mobile platforms. Wilkinson, C.   **004**

MOBILES (SCULPTURE)
    See also Kinetic sculpture; Sculpture
Mobley, Jeannie
Katerina's wish   **Fic**
MOBS See Crowds; Riots
Moccasin thunder.   **S C**
Mochizuki, Ken
Beacon Hill boys   **Fic**

MOCK-HEROIC LITERATURE
    See also Literature; Wit and humor
Mockingjay. Collins, S.   **Fic**
MODEL AIRPLANES See Airplanes -- Models
MODEL MAKING See Models and modelmaking
MODELING
Beker, J. Strutting it!   **659.1**
MODELING
    See also Clay; Sculpture
MODELMAKING See Models and modelmaking
MODELS See Artists' models; Fashion models;
    Mathematical models; Models and modelmaking
MODELS (PERSONS)
Todd, A. M. Tyra Banks   **92**
MODELS (PERSONS) See Artists' models; Fash-
ion models
MODELS AND MODEL MAKING See Models
and modelmaking
MODELS AND MODELMAKING
Mercer, B. The flying machine book   **745.592**
Thomson, R. Toys and models   **745.592**
MODELS AND MODELMAKING
    See also Handicraft; Miniature objects
Models don't eat chocolate cookies. Dionne, E. **Fic**
Modern Africa. Bowden, R.   **960**
Modern America, 1964-present. McNeese,
T.   **973.92**
MODERN ART
Claybourne, A. Surrealism   **709.04**
Modern astronomy. Yount, L.   **520**
MODERN CIVILIZATION
    See also Civilization
Modern dance. Solway, A.   **792.8**
MODERN DANCE
Freedman, R. Martha Graham, a dancer's life **792.8**
Solway, A. Modern dance   **792.8**
MODERN DANCE
    See also Dance
The **modern** feminist movement. Gorman, J.
L.   **305.4**

Modern genetics. Yount, L.   **576.5**
MODERN GREEK LITERATURE
    See also Literature
MODERN HISTORY
Finger, B. 13 photos children should know   **770**
Sutherland, J. The ten-year century   **973.93**
MODERN HISTORY
    See also World history
Modern humans. Stefoff, R.   **599.93**
The Modern Library classics [series]
Twain, M. The prince and the pauper   **Fic**
MODERN LITERATURE See Literature; Mod-
ernism in literature
Modern marine science. Yount, L.   **551.46**
Modern mechanics. Miller, M.   **629.28**
Modern Mexico. Stein, R. C.   **972.08**
Modern Muslim societies.   **297**
Modern peacemakers [series]
Slavicek, L. C. Mother Teresa   **92**
MODERN PHILOSOPHY
    See also Philosophy
Modern robotics. Henderson, H.   **629.8**
Modern world cultures [series]
Desaulniers, K. L. Northern America   **970**
Gritzner, J. A. North Africa and the Middle East **956**
Leppman, E. J. Australia and the Pacific   **994**
Oppong, J. R. Africa South of the Sahara   **967**
Phillips, D. A. Southeast Asia   **959**
Modern world leaders [series]
Abrams, D. Nicolas Sarkozy   **92**
Reed, J. The Saudi royal family   **920**
Renehan, E. J. Pope John Paul II   **92**
Shields, C. J. Vladimir Putin   **92**
Modern world nations [series]
Cooper, C. W. Ukraine   **947.7**
Gillespie, C. A. New Zealand   **993**
Lopez, J. J. Puerto Rico   **972.95**
Phillips, D. A. Bangladesh   **954.92**
Phillips, D. A. Thailand   **959.3**
Zeigler, D. J. Israel   **956.94**
MODERNISM (AESTHETICS)
    See also Aesthetics
MODERNISM IN ARCHITECTURE
    See also Architecture; Modernism (Aesthet-
ics)
MODERNISM IN ART
    See also Art; Modernism (Aesthetics)
MODERNISM IN LITERATURE
    See also Literature; Modernism (Aesthetics)
MODERNISM IN SCULPTURE
    See also Modernism (Aesthetics); Sculpture
MODERNIZATION (SOCIOLOGY)
    See also Social change
Mofford, Juliet Haines
Recipe and craft guide to Japan   **641.5**
Recipe and craft guide to the Caribbean   **641.5**

Spence, D. Monet   92

MONETARY UNIONS
   See also Money

Money. Cribb, J.   332.4

MONEY
   See also Economics; Exchange; Finance

MONEY
   Chatzky, J. Not your parents' money book   332.024
   Cribb, J. Money   332.4
   Hall, A. Show me the money   332.024
   Hlinka, M. Follow Your Money   330
   Hollander, B. Money matters   330
   Simons, R. All about money   332.4
   Thompson, H. Investing money   332.6

Money matters. Hollander, B.   330
The **money** pit mystery. Walters, E.   Fic
Money run. Heath, J.   Fic

MONEY SUPPLY
   See also Money

MONEY-MAKING PROJECTS FOR CHILDREN
   Bielagus, P. G. Quick cash for teens   658.1
   Bochner, A. B. The new totally awesome business book for kids (and their parents)   658

MONEY-MAKING PROJECTS FOR CHILDREN
   See also Business enterprises

MONEY-MAKING PROJECTS FOR CHILDREN -- FICTION
   Ransom, C. Rebel McKenzie   Fic

MONEYMAKING PROJECTS FOR CHILDREN *See* Money-making projects for children

Mongolia. Pang   951.7
Mongols. Helget, N.   950

MONGOLS
   Demi Genghis Khan   92
   Helget, N. Mongols   950
   McCaughrean, G. The kite rider   Fic
   Nardo, D. Genghis Khan and the Mongol Empire   950

MONGOLS -- HISTORY
   Helget, N. Mongols   950

MONGOLS -- WARFARE
   Helget, N. Mongols   950

MONGOOSES
   Somervill, B. A. Small Indian Mongoose   599.74

Monitor lizard. Somervill, B. A.   597.95
Monkey High!: vol. 1. Akira, S.   741.5
Monkeys. Zabludoff, M.   599.8

MONKEYS
   Zabludoff, M. Monkeys   599.8

MONKEYS
   See also Primates

MONKEYS -- BEHAVIOR
   See also Animal behavior

MONKEYS -- FICTION

Tashjian, J. My life as a stuntboy   Fic

MONKS
   Goldberg, E. A. Grigory Rasputin   92

MONKS -- FICTION
   Thompson, R. City of cannibals   Fic

Monnin, Katie
   Teaching graphic novels   372.6

Monninger, Joseph
   Finding somewhere   Fic
   Hippie chick   Fic
   Wish   Fic

MONOGRAPHIC SERIES -- BIBLIOGRAPHY
   Thomas, R. L. Popular series fiction for middle school and teen readers   016

MONOLOGUES
   Actor's choice   808.82
   The Book of monologues for aspiring actors   808.82
   Great monologues for young actors   808.82
   Lamedman, D. The ultimate audition book for teens   792
   Millennium monologs   792
   New audition scenes and monologs from contemporary playwrights   808.82
   Schlitz, L. A. Good masters! Sweet ladies!   940.1
   Shakespeare, W. One hundred and eleven Shakespeare monologues   822.3
   Surface, M. H. More short scenes and monologues for middle school students   808.82
   Surface, M. H. Short scenes and monologues for middle school actors   808.82
   Voices in first person   S C

MONONUCLEOSIS -- FICTION
   Weissman, E. B. The short seller   Fic

MONOPOLIES
   See also Commerce; Economics

MONORAIL RAILROADS
   See also Railroads

MONOTHEISM
   See also Religion; Theism

The **Monroe** doctrine. Renehan, E. J.   327

MONROE DOCTRINE
   Renehan, E. J. The Monroe doctrine   327

MONROE DOCTRINE
   See also International relations; Intervention (International law); United States -- Foreign relations

Monroe, James, 1758-1831
      About
   Naden, C. J. James Monroe   92

Monroe, Judy
   The Susan B. Anthony women's voting rights trial   324.6

Monroy, Manuel
   Delano, P. When I was a boy Neruda called me Policarpo   92

MONSOONS

The snake scientist   597.96

The tarantula scientist   595.4

A **month** of Sundays. White, R.   Fic

The **monthly** sky guide. Ridpath, I.   523.802

MONTHS

     See also Calendars; Chronology

MONTHS -- POETRY

     Forler, N. Winterberries and apple blossoms   811

Montmorency. Updale, E.   Fic

Montmorency and the assassins. Updale, E.   Fic

Montmorency on the rocks. Updale, E.   Fic

Montmorency's revenge. Updale, E.   Fic

Monumental milestones [series]

     Gibson, K. B. The Obama view   92

     Torres, J. A. Disaster in the Indian Ocean, Tsunami 2004   909.83

     Tracy, K. The Clinton view   92

Monumental verses. Lewis, J. P.   811

MONUMENTS

     See also Architecture; Sculpture

MONUMENTS -- POETRY

     Lewis, J. P. Monumental verses   811

MOOD (PSYCHOLOGY)

     See also Psychology

Mood disorders. Mooney, C.   616.85

Moodie, Craig

     Into the trap   Fic

Moog, Robert

About

     VanHecke, S. Raggin', jazzin', rockin'   784.19

The **moon.** Carlowicz, M. J.   523.3

MOON

     See also Astronomy; Solar system

The **moon.** Simon, S.   523.3

Moon & sun [series]

     Lisle, H. The Ruby Key   Fic

     Lisle, H. The silver door   Fic

MOON -- EXPLORATION

     See also Space flight to the moon

MOON -- FICTION

     Hickam, H. H. Crater   Fic

     Hickam, H. Crescent   Fic

     Lin, G. Starry River of the Sky   Fic

MOON -- MAPS

     See also Maps

The **moon** and I. Byars, B. C.   813

The **moon** and more. Dessen, S.   Fic

Moon landing. Platt, R.   629.45

The **moon** over High Street. Babbitt, N.   Fic

Moon over Manifest. Vanderpool, C.   Fic

MOON ROCKS

     See also Lunar geology; Petrology

Moon without magic. Tunnell, M. O.   Fic

MOON WORSHIP

     See also Religion

MOON, VOYAGES TO See Space flight to the moon

Moon: science, history, and mystery. Ross, S.   629.45

Moonbird. Hoose, P.   598.072

Mooney, Bel

     (ed) You never did learn to knock   S C

Mooney, Carla

     Amazing Africa   960

     Explorers of the New World   970.01

     George Washington   92

     Junk food junkies   613.2

     Mood disorders   616.85

     Oil spills and offshore drilling   333.8

     Online predators   004.6

     Pilotless planes   623.7

     The Industrial Revolution   330.9

Mooney, Maggie

     Benjamin, M. Nobel's women of peace   920

Moonglass. Kirby, J.   Fic

Moonrunner. Thomason, M.   Fic

Moonshadow. Higgins, S.   Fic

Moonshadow [series]

     Higgins, S. The nightmare ninja   Fic

Moonshine express. Norville, R.   Fic

MOONSHINING -- FICTION

     Norville, R. Moonshine express   Fic

The **moorchild.** McGraw, E. J.   Fic

Moore, Ann

About

     Thimmesh, C. Girls think of everything   920

Moore, Carley

     The stalker chronicles   Fic

Moore, Charles, 1931-2010

About

     Nardo, D. Birmingham 1963   323.1

Moore, Christopher, 1957-

     From then to now   909

Moore, Derrick

     Always upbeat / All that   Fic

Moore, Inga

     Burnett, F. H. The secret garden   Fic

Moore, Kate

     The Battle of Britain   940.54

Moore, Perry

     Hero   Fic

Moore, Peter

     Red moon rising   Fic

Moore, Peter D.

     Wetlands   578.7

Moore, Sarah W.

     The rap scene   781.66

Moore, Stephanie Perry

     (jt. auth) Moore, D. Always upbeat / All that   Fic

Moore, Wes

     Discovering Wes Moore   975.2

Moore, Wes, 1975- --- Childhood and youth

Kinney, J. The wimpy kid movie diary   **791.43**

O'Brien, L. Lights, camera, action!   **791.43**

MOTION PICTURES -- PRODUCTION AND DIRECTION -- FICTION

Crawford, B. Carter's big break   **Fic**

Doctorow, C. Pirate cinema   **Fic**

Kidd, R. The year of the bomb   **Fic**

Pauley, K. Cat Girl's day off   **Fic**

Shan, D. Slawter   **Fic**

MOTION PICTURES -- PRODUCTION AND DIRECTION -- FICTION.

Selzer, A. Pirates of the retail wasteland   **Fic**

MOTION PICTURES AND CHILDREN

See also Children; Motion pictures

MOTION PICTURES IN EDUCATION

See also Audiovisual education; Motion pictures; Teaching -- Aids and devices

MOTION.

Nardo, D. Force and motion   **531**

Motivating readers in the middle grades. Collins, J.   **028.5**

MOTIVATION (PSYCHOLOGY)

Bachel, B. K. What do you really want?   **153.8**

MOTIVATION (PSYCHOLOGY)

See also Psychology

MOTOR CARS *See* Automobiles

MOTOR CYCLES *See* Motorcycles

MOTOR VEHICLE INDUSTRY *See* Automobile industry

MOTORBOATS

See also Boats and boating

MOTORBOATS -- MODELS

Gabrielson, C. Kinetic contraptions   **621.46**

MOTORBOATS -- MODELS

See also Models and modelmaking

MOTORCYCLES

Amado, E. High riders, saints and death cars **709.2**

Smedman, L. From boneshakers to choppers   **629.227**

Woods, B. Hottest motorcycles   **629.227**

MOTORCYCLES

See also Bicycles

MOTORCYCLES -- HISTORY

Smedman, L. From boneshakers to choppers   **629.227**

MOTORCYCLING

See also Cycling

MOTORS *See* Electric motors; Engines

Moulton, Courtney Allison

Angelfire   **Fic**

Mouly, Francoise

The TOON treasury of classic children's comics   **741.5**

MOUNDS AND MOUND BUILDERS

See also Archeology; Burial; Tombs

MOUNT EVEREST (CHINA AND NEPAL)

See also Mountains

MOUNT EVEREST (CHINA AND NEPAL)

Bodden, V. To the top of Mount Everest   **796.522**

MOUNT RAINIER (WASH.)

See also Mountains

MOUNTAIN ANIMALS

See also Animals

MOUNTAIN BIKES

See also All terrain vehicles; Bicycles

MOUNTAIN BIKING

See also Cycling

MOUNTAIN BIKING -- FICTION

Davis, R. F. Chasing AllieCat   **Fic**

MOUNTAIN CLIMBING *See* Mountaineering

MOUNTAIN ECOLOGY

Lynch, W. Rocky Mountains   **577.4**

MOUNTAIN ECOLOGY

See also Ecology

MOUNTAIN LIFE

See also Country life

MOUNTAIN LIFE -- FICTION

Donaldson, J. On Viney's mountain   **Fic**

Dowell, F. O. Dovey Coe   **Fic**

Hemingway, E. M. Road to Tater Hill   **Fic**

Mordecai, M. Blue Mountain trouble   **Fic**

MOUNTAIN LIFE -- NORTH CAROLINA

Dowell, F. O. Dovey Coe   **Fic**

MOUNTAIN PLANTS

See also Plant ecology; Plants

Mountain pose. Wilson, N. H.   **Fic**

Mountain solo. Ingold, J.   **Fic**

MOUNTAINEERING

Brennan, K. Sir Edmund Hillary, modern day explorer   **796.52**

Cleare, J. Epic climbs   **796.52**

Crompton, S. Sir Edmund Hillary   **92**

Elish, D. Edmund Hillary   **92**

Helfand, L. Conquering Everest   **741.5**

Skreslet, L. To the top of Everest   **796.52**

Wurdinger, S. D. Rock climbing   **796.52**

MOUNTAINEERING

See also Outdoor life

MOUNTAINEERING -- EVEREST, MOUNT (CHINA AND NEPAL) -- HISTORY

Bodden, V. To the top of Mount Everest   **796.522**

MOUNTAINEERING -- FICTION

Birdseye, T. Storm Mountain   **Fic**

Carbone, E. Jump   **Fic**

Patneaude, D. A piece of the sky   **Fic**

Smith, R. Peak   **Fic**

MOUNTAINEERING

Skreslet, L. To the top of Everest   **796.52**

MOUNTAINEERING -- MOUNT EVEREST (CHINA AND NEPAL)

Taylor-Butler, C. Sacred mountain   **954.9**

MOUNTAINEERS

The **murder** of Emmett Till. Robson, D. **364.152**

The **murder** of Emmett Till. Aretha, D. **364.152**

MURDER TRIALS *See* Trials (Homicide)

MURDER VICTIMS

Aretha, D. The murder of Emmett Till **364.152**

Crowe, C. Getting away with murder: the true story of the Emmett Till case **364.152**

Fireside, B. J. The trial of the police officers in the shooting death of Amadou Diallo **345**

Haugen, B. The Black Dahlia **364.152**

Kushner, J. M. Who on earth is Dian Fossey? **92**

Nelson, M. A wreath for Emmett Till **811**

Neri, G. Yummy **741.5**

Robson, D. The murder of Emmett Till **364.152**

Wright, S. Simeon's story **305.8**

MURDERERS

Coleman, W. Racism on trial **345**

Giblin, J. Good brother, bad brother **92**

Swanson, J. L. Chasing Lincoln's killer **92**

Worth, R. Massacre at Virginia Tech **364.152**

MURDERERS -- NEW YORK (STATE) -- BIOG-RAPHY

Behnke, A. M. Death of a dreamer **782.421**

Murdoch, David Hamilton

North American Indian **970.004**

Murdock, Catherine Gilbert

Dairy Queen **Fic**

Front and center **Fic**

The off season **Fic**

Princess Ben **Fic**

Wisdom's kiss **Fic**

Murdock, James R.

Martin, H. J. Serving lesbian, gay, bisexual, trans-gender, and questioning teens **027.62**

Murie, Margaret E., 1902-2003

About

Byrnes, P. Environmental pioneers **363.7**

Murie, Olaus Johan, 1889-1963

About

Byrnes, P. Environmental pioneers **363.7**

Murphy, Alexa Gordon

Chico Mendes **92**

Murphy, Bruce

(ed) Benet's reader's encyclopedia **803**

Murphy, Claire Rudolf

Daughters of the desert **220.9**

Free radical **Fic**

Murphy, Glenn

How loud can you burp? **502**

Why is snot green **500**

Murphy, Jim

(jt. auth) Blank, A. Invincible microbe **616.9**

The giant and how he humbugged America **974.7**

Murphy, Jim

Across America on an emigrant train **385**

An American plague **614.5**

The boys' war **973.7**

The crossing **973.3**

Gone a-whaling **306.3**

The great fire **977.3**

The long road to Gettysburg **973.7**

The real Benedict Arnold **92**

A savage thunder **973.7**

Truce **940.4**

A young patriot **973.3**

Murphy, Larry

African-American faith in America **200**

Murphy, Rita

Bird **Fic**

Looking for Lucy Buick **Fic**

Murray, Craig

Sexpectations **613.96**

Murray, Elizabeth A.

Death **616.07**

Murray, Jocelyn

Africa **960**

Murray, Kirsty

The secret life of Maeve Lee Kwong **Fic**

Murray, Martine

How to make a bird **Fic**

MUSCLE STRENGTH

Frederick, S. Strength training for teen athletes **613.7**

Muscles. Colligan, L. H. **612.7**

MUSCLES

See also Musculoskeletal system

MUSCLES

Brynie, F. H. 101 questions about muscles to stretch your mind and flex your brain **612.7**

Colligan, L. H. Muscles **612.7**

MUSCULAR SYSTEM

Parker, S. The skeleton and muscles **612.7**

MUSCULAR SYSTEM *See* Musculoskeletal system

MUSCULOSKELETAL SYSTEM

Gold, S. D. Learning about the musculoskeletal system and the skin **612.7**

Parker, S. The skeleton and muscles **612.7**

MUSCULOSKELETAL SYSTEM

See also Anatomy; Physiology

MUSEUM ADMINISTRATORS

Bausum, A. Dragon bones and dinosaur eggs: a photobiography of Roy Chapman Andrews **92**

Marcovitz, H. Pat Mora **92**

Schyffert, B. U. The man who went to the far side of the moon: the story of Apollo 11 astronaut Michael Collins **92**

Tyson, N. D. G. The Pluto files **523.4**

The **museum** of Mary Child. Golds, C. **Fic**

Museum of thieves. Tanner, L. **Fic**

MUSEUMS -- FICTION

Golds, C. The museum of Mary Child **Fic**

(ed) Religion in America: opposing viewpoints **200.9**

Mussi, Sarah

The door of no return **Fic**

Must love black. McClymer, K. **Fic**

MUTATION (BIOLOGY) *See* Evolution; Variation (Biology)

MUTATION (BIOLOGY) -- FICTION

Reeve, P. Scrivener's moon **Fic**

MUTISM, ELECTIVE

Konigsburg, E. L. Silent to the bone **Fic**

MUTUAL FUNDS

See also Investments

MUTUALISM (BIOLOGY) *See* Symbiosis

Má»¥hammad, d. 632

About

Demi Muhammad **297**

My America. **811**

My anxious mind. Tompkins, M. A. **616.85**

My big mouth. Hannan, P. **Fic**

My black me. **811**

My bonny light horseman. Meyer, L. A. **Fic**

My book of life by Angel. Leavitt, M. **Fic**

My boyfriend bites. Jolley, D. **741.5**

My boyfriend is a monster [series]

I love him to pieces **741.5**

Jolley, D. My boyfriend bites **741.5**

Storrie, P. D. Made for each other **741.5**

My bridges of hope. Bitton-Jackson, L. **940.53**

My brother Abe. Mazer, H. **Fic**

My brother Sam is dead. Collier, J. L. **Fic**

My brother's book. **808**

My brother's keeper. McCormick, P. **Fic**

My brother's shadow. SchrÃ¶der, M. **Fic**

My brother, my sister, and I. Watkins, Y. K. **Fic**

My childhood under fire. Halilbegovich, N. **949.7**

My contract with Henry. Vaupel, R. **Fic**

My dad's a punk. **S C**

My Daniel. Conrad, P. **Fic**

My fake boyfriend is better than yours. Springer, K. **Fic**

My favorite band does not exist. Jeschonek, R. T. **Fic**

My future career [series]

McAlpine, M. Working in music and dance **780**

McAlpine, M. Working with animals **636**

McAlpine, M. Working with children **362.7**

My Havana. Wells, R. **Fic**

My heartbeat. Freymann-Weyr, G. **Fic**

My kind of sad. Scowen, K. **616.85**

My last skirt. Durrant, L. **Fic**

My letter to the world and other poems. **811**

My life as a book. **Fic**

My life as a stuntboy. Tashjian, J. **Fic**

My life in black and white. Friend, N. **Fic**

My life in dog years. Paulsen, G. **813**

My life in pink and green. Greenwald, L. **Fic**

My life the musical. Wood, M. **Fic**

My life undecided. Brody, J. **Fic**

My life with the Lincolns. Brandeis, G. **Fic**

My life, the theater, and other tragedies. Zadoff, A. **Fic**

My misadventures as a teenage rock star. Raskin, J. **Fic**

My most excellent year. Kluger, S. **Fic**

My mother the cheerleader. Sharenow, R. **Fic**

My name is Mina. Almond, D. **Fic**

My name is not easy. Edwardson, D. D. **Fic**

My name is Parvana. Ellis, D. **Fic**

My name is Sally Little Song. Woods, B. **Fic**

My one hundred adventures. Horvath, P. **Fic**

My Own Revolution. Marsden, C. **Fic**

My parent has cancer and it really sucks. Silver, M. **616.99**

My perfect life. Sheldon, D. **Fic**

My sister lives on the mantelpiece. Pitcher, A. **Fic**

My swordhand is singing. Sedgwick, M. **Fic**

My two moms. Littlefield, B. **306.874**

My very unfairy tale life. Staniszewski, A. **Fic**

MYANMAR

O'Keefe, S. Champion of freedom **959.105**

MYCOLOGY *See* Fungi

Myers, Anna

Assassin **Fic**

The grave robber's secret **Fic**

Spy! **Fic**

Time of the witches **Fic**

Tulsa burning **Fic**

Wart **Fic**

Myers, Edward

Storyteller **Fic**

When will I stop hurting? **155.9**

Myers, Jill J.

Responding to cyber bullying **371.5**

Myers, Walter Dean, 1937-

Amiri & Odette **Fic**

Antarctica **998**

A star is born **Fic**

Bad boy **813**

Carmen **Fic**

Carmen **Fic**

The Cruisers: checkmate **Fic**

The Cruisers: checkmate **Fic**

The Cruisers **Fic**

The Cruisers **Fic**

Darius & Twig **Fic**

(jt. auth) Dial, C. Fallen angels **Fic**

Dope sick **Fic**

Game **Fic**

The greatest: Muhammad Ali **92**

Harlem summer **Fic**

Harlem **811**

Here in Harlem	811
Hoops	Fic
Just write	808.02
Kick	Fic
Kick	Fic
Lawrence, J. The great migration	759.13
Lockdown	Fic
Monster	Fic
Oh, Snap!	Fic
145th Street	S C
Riot	Fic
Scorpions	Fic
Slam!	Fic
Street love	Fic
Sunrise over Fallujah	Fic
Sunrise over Fallujah	Fic
USS Constellation	359.8
What they found	S C

Myers, Walter Dean, 1937-
About

Myers, W. D. Bad boy	813
Sickels, A. Walter Dean Myers	92
Marler, M. D. Walter Dean Myers	813

Myklusch, Matt

Jack Blank and the Imagine Nation	Fic
The secret war	Fic

Myracle, Lauren

Eleven	Fic
Luv ya bunches	Fic
Peace, love, and baby ducks	Fic
Thirteen	Fic
Thirteen plus one	Fic
Twelve	Fic
Violet in bloom	Fic

Myron, Vicki

Dewey the library cat	636.8

MYSPACE (WEB SITE)

See also Social networking; Web sites

MYSTERIES See Mysteries and miracle plays; Mystery and detective plays; Mystery fiction; Mystery films; Mystery radio programs; Mystery television programs

MYSTERIES AND MIRACLE PLAYS

See also Bible plays; English drama; Pageants; Religious drama; Theater

The **mysteries** of Beethoven's hair. Martin, R.	92
Mysteries of the mummy kids. Halls, K. M.	393

Mysteries unwrapped [series]

Bardhan-Quallen, S. The real monsters	001.9
Wetzel, C. Haunted U.S.A.	133.1

The mysterious & unknown [series]

Kallen, S. A. Crop circles	001.9
Kallen, S. A. Werewolves	398
Stewart, G. UFOs	001.9

The **mysterious** Benedict Society. Stewart, T. L.	Fic
The **mysterious** Benedict Society and the perilous	
journey. Stewart, T. L.	Fic
The **mysterious** Benedict Society and the prisoner's	
dilemma. Stewart, T. L.	Fic
Mysterious bones. Kirkpatrick, K.	979.7
The **mysterious** case of the Allbright Academy. Stanley, D.	Fic
The **mysterious** edge of the heroic world. Konigsburg, E. L.	Fic
The **mysterious** matter of I.M. Fine. Stanley, D.	Fic
Mysterious messages. Blackwood, G. L.	652
The **mysterious** universe. Jackson, E. B.	523.8

MYSTERY AND DETECTIVE STORIES

Balliett, B. Hold fast	Fic
Barnholdt, L. Girl meets ghost	Fic
Baucom, I. Through the skylight	Fic
Bell, J. Kepler's dream	Fic
Berk, J. Guy Langman, crime scene procrastinator	Fic
Brennan, J. H. The secret prophecy	Fic
Carey, B. Poison most vial	Fic
Coben, H. Seconds away	Fic
Cox, S. The Dead Girls Detective Agency	Fic
DeFelice, C. C. The ghost and Mrs. Hobbs	Fic
DeFelice, C. C. The ghost of Cutler Creek	Fic
Draanen, W. v. Sammy Keyes and the hotel thief	Fic
Draanen, W. v. Sammy Keyes and the search for Snake Eyes	Fic
Fairlie, E. The lost treasure of Tuckernuck	Fic
Frazier, A. The mastermind plot	Fic
Goeglein, T. M. Cold fury	Fic
Hoobler, D. The demon in the teahouse	Fic
Hoobler, D. The ghost in the Tokaido Inn	Fic
Klise, K. Letters from camp	Fic
Lacey, J. Island of Thieves	Fic
Lane, A. Black ice	Fic
Lane, A. Rebel fire	Fic
Lawrence, C. The case of the deadly desperados	Fic
Lawrence, C. P.K. Pinkerton and the petrified man	Fic
Littke, L. Lake of secrets	Fic
MacColl, M. Nobody's secret	Fic
Patron, S. Behind the masks	Fic
Pauley, K. Cat Girl's day off	Fic
Pullman, P. Two crafty criminals!	Fic
Renn, D. Tokyo heist	Fic
The secrets of Shakespeare's grave	Fic
Shoemaker, T. Back before dark	Fic
Stanley, D. The mysterious matter of I.M. Fine	Fic
Stewart, T. L. The extraordinary education of Nicholas Benedict	Fic
Turnage, S. Three times lucky	Fic
Van Draanen, W. Sammy Keyes and the showdown in Sin City	Fic
Vande Velde, V. Magic can be murder	Fic

Fairlie, E. The lost treasure of Tuckernuck Fic
Feinstein, J. Change up Fic
Feinstein, J. Cover-up Fic
Feinstein, J. Last shot Fic
Feinstein, J. The rivalry Fic
Feinstein, J. Vanishing act Fic
Ferraiolo, J. D. The big splash Fic
Ford, J. C. The morgue and me Fic
Frazier, A. The mastermind plot Fic
Frazier, A. The midnight tunnel Fic
Fusilli, J. Marley Z and the bloodstained violin Fic
Gibbs, S. Belly up Fic
Gilman, D. Blood sun Fic
Gilman, D. Ice claw Fic
Grabenstein, C. The black heart crypt Fic
Grant, V. Quid pro quo Fic
Grant, V. Res judicata Fic
Graves, K. The orphan of Awkward Falls Fic
Grisham, J. Theodore Boone: kid lawyer Fic
Hahn, M. D. Mister Death's blue-eyed girls Fic
Haines, K. M. The girl is murder Fic
Haines, K. M. The girl is trouble Fic
Hamilton, V. The house of Dies Drear Fic
Harrison, M. 13 treasures Fic
Harvey, A. Haunting Violet Fic
Hautman, P. Doppelganger Fic
Hautman, P. Skullduggery Fic
Hautman, P. Snatched Fic
Healey, K. The shattering Fic
Higgins, F. E. The Eyeball Collector Fic
Hilmo, T. With a name like Love Fic
Hoobler, D. The demon in the teahouse Fic
Hoobler, D. The ghost in the Tokaido Inn Fic
Hoobler, D. Seven paths to death Fic
Hoobler, D. The sword that cut the burning grass Fic
Horowitz, A. The Falcon's Malteser Fic
Horowitz, A. The Greek who stole Christmas Fic
Horowitz, A. Public enemy number two Fic
Horowitz, A. South by southeast Fic
Horowitz, A. Three of diamonds Fic
Ibbotson, E. The star of Kazan Fic
Jarzab, A. All unquiet things Fic
Jinks, C. The abused werewolf rescue group Fic
Jinks, C. The reformed vampire support group Fic
Johnson, M. The madness underneath Fic
Juby, S. Getting the girl Fic
Kelsey, M. A recipe 4 robbery Fic
Kirby, J. Golden Fic
Konigsburg, E. L. Silent to the bone Fic
Lane, A. Black ice Fic
Lane, A. Rebel fire Fic
Lawrence, C. The case of the deadly desperados Fic
Lawrence, C. P.K. Pinkerton and the petrified man Fic

Lawrence, I. The seance Fic
Leck, J. The adventures of Jack Lime Fic
Lee, Y. S. The body at the tower Fic
Lee, Y. S. A spy in the house Fic
Leonard, J. P. Cold case Fic
Levine, G. C. A tale of Two Castles Fic
Littke, L. Lake of secrets Fic
MacColl, M. Nobody's secret Fic
MacDonald, B. The secret of the sealed room Fic
MacDonald, B. Wicked Will Fic
Mack, T. The fall of the Amazing Zalindas Fic
Mack, T. The mystery of the conjured man Fic
Mackall, D. D. The silence of murder Fic
Madison, B. Lulu Dark and the summer of the Fox Fic
Margolis, L. Girl's best friend Fic
Matthews, T. L. Danger in the dark Fic
Matthews, T. L. Frame-up on the Bowery Fic
Matthews, T. L. Shots at sea Fic
McClintock, N. Masked Fic
McLoughlin, J. At Yellow Lake Fic
McMann, L. Cryer's Cross Fic
McNamee, G. Acceleration Fic
Miller, K. Kiki Strike: inside the shadow city Fic
Miller, K. Kiki Strike: the Empress's tomb Fic
Mills, R. Charlie's key Fic
Morton-Shaw, C. The hunt for the seventh Fic
Mulligan, A. Trash Fic
Nayeri, D. Straw house, Wood house, Brick house, Blow S C
Newbery, L. Lost boy Fic
Nixon, J. L. Nightmare Fic
Osterlund, A. Aurelia Fic
Park, L. S. Trust no one Fic
Parker, R. B. The Edenville Owls Fic
Patron, S. Behind the masks Fic
Pauley, K. Cat Girl's day off Fic
Peacock, S. Death in the air Fic
Peacock, S. The dragon turn Fic
Peacock, S. Eye of the crow Fic
Peacock, S. The secret fiend Fic
Peacock, S. Vanishing girl Fic
Perez, M. Dead is a killer tune Fic
Poblocki, D. The nightmarys Fic
Pullman, P. Two crafty criminals! Fic
Reichs, K. J. Virals Fic
Renn, D. Tokyo heist Fic
Roecker, L. The Liar Society Fic
Runholt, S. Adventure at Simba Hill Fic
Runholt, S. The mystery of the third Lucretia Fic
Runholt, S. Rescuing Seneca Crane Fic
Ryan, A. K. Spark Fic
Schlitz, L. A. Splendors and glooms Fic
Schrefer, E. The deadly sister Fic
The secrets of Shakespeare's grave Fic
Selfors, S. Smells like treasure Fic

Nelson, Marilyn
Alexander, E. Miss Crandall's School for Young Ladies and Little Misses of Color **811**
Carver, a life in poems **811**
Fortune's bones **811**
The freedom business **811**
Sweethearts of rhythm **811**
A wreath for Emmett Till **811**
Nelson, Nina
Bringing the boy home **Fic**
Nelson, Pete
Left for dead **940.54**
Nelson, R. A.
Days of Little Texas **Fic**
Nelson, Richard E.
Galas, J. C. The power to prevent suicide **362.28**
Nelson, S. D.
Black Elk's vision **92**
Nelson, Sara Kirsten
Stay safe! **613.6**
Nelson, Scott Reynolds
Ain't nothing but a man **92**
Nelson, Sheila
In defense of our country **362.87**
The psychology of our dark side **398**
Nelson, Theresa
Ruby electric **Fic**
Nemeth, Sally
The heights, the depths, and everything in between **Fic**
NEO-IMPRESSIONISM (ART) See Impressionism (Art)
NEON GENESIS EVANGELION (FICTIONAL ROBOT)
See also Fictional robots; Manga; Mecha
NEOPAGANISM
See also Religions
NEPHEWS -- FICTION
Ransom, C. Rebel McKenzie **Fic**
NEPHILA MACULATA
Stronger Than Steel **595.4**
Neptune. Sherman, J. **523.4**
NEPTUNE (PLANET)
See also Planets
The **Neptune** Project. Holyoke, P. **Fic**
Neptune's children. Dobkin, B. **Fic**
Neri, G.
Ghetto cowboy **Fic**
Neri, Greg
Neri, G. Ghetto cowboy **Fic**
Chess rumble **Fic**
Yummy **741.5**
Neruda, Pablo, 1904-1973
About
Delano, P. When I was a boy Neruda called me Policarpo **92**

Ryan, P. M. The dreamer **Fic**
NERVES
See also Nervous system
NERVOUS SYSTEM
Gold, M. V. Learning about the nervous system **612.8**
Morgan, J. Cells of the nervous system **611**
Simon, S. The brain **612.8**
NERVOUS SYSTEM
See also Anatomy; Physiology
NERVOUS SYSTEM -- DISEASES
See also Diseases
Ness, Patrick, 1971-
A monster calls **Fic**
The Ask and the Answer **Fic**
The knife of never letting go **Fic**
Monsters of men **Fic**
NEST BUILDING
See also Animal behavior; Animals -- Habitations
The **Netherlands.** Docalavich, H. **949.2**
NETHERLANDS
Docalavich, H. The Netherlands **949.2**
Nettleton, Pamela Hill
William Shakespeare **822.3**
Netzley, Patricia D.
Civil War **973.7**
The Greenhaven encyclopedia of ancient Egypt **932**
Neuburger, Emily K.
Juster, N. The annotated Phantom tollbooth **813**
A Caldecott celebration **741.6**
(ed) The wand in the word **813**
Neumeier, Rachel
The City in the Lake **Fic**
The Floating Islands **Fic**
NEURASTHENIA
See also Mental illness
NEUROLOGY See Nervous system
NEUROSCIENCES
See also Medicine
NEUTRON BOMB
See also Bombs; Neutron weapons
NEUTRON WEAPONS
See also Nuclear weapons
NEUTRONS
See also Atoms; Particles (Nuclear physics)
Nevada. Stefoff, R. **979.3**
Nevada. Heinrichs, A. **979.3**
Never cry werewolf. Davis, H. **Fic**
Never say die. Hobbs, W. **Fic**
Never say genius. Gutman, D. **Fic**
Never sit down in a hoopskirt and other things I learned in Southern belle hell. Rumley, C. **Fic**
Never to forget: the Jews of the Holocaust. Meltzer, M. **940.53**
The **never** war. MacHale, D. J. **Fic**

Nevermore. Lange, K. E.   92

NEW AGE MOVEMENT

> *See also* Cults; Occultism; Social movements

The **New** American Bible. Bible   220.5

New Americans [series]

Gustaitis, J. A. Chinese Americans   305.8

Keedle, J. Americans from the Caribbean and Central America   305.8

Keedle, J. Mexican Americans   305.8

Keedle, J. West African Americans   305.8

Park, K. Americans from India and other South Asian countries   305.8

Thomas, W. D. Korean Americans   305.8

Wachtel, A. Southeast Asian Americans   305.8

Weiss, G. G. Americans from Russia and Eastern Europe   305.8

The **new** and improved Vivien Leigh Reid. Collins, Y.   Fic

New audition scenes and monologs from contemporary playwrights.   808.82

New blood. McPhee, P.   Fic

The **new** book of popular science.   503

New boy. Houston, J.   Fic

NEW BUSINESS ENTERPRISES

Hollander, B. G. The next big thing   004.068

NEW BUSINESS ENTERPRISES

> *See also* Business enterprises

New careers for the 21st century: finding your role in the global renewal [series]

Flath, C. 21st-century counselors   362.2

Flath, C. Careers in green energy   333.79

Flath, C. Freelance and technical writers   808

Flath, C. Media in the 21st century   741.6

Flath, C. Social workers   361.3

Flath, C. Therapy jobs in educational settings   371.7

Flath, C. Tomorrow's enterprising scientists   004

Miller, M. Green construction   690

Miller, M. Modern mechanics   629.28

Miller, M. The pharmaceutical industry   615

Miller, M. Tomorrow's teachers   371.1

Miller, M. Tomorrow's transportation   363.7

Strange, C. Environmental science & protection   333.72

Strange, C. Medical technicians   610.28

Strange, C. Physicians assistants & nurses   610.73

The **new** cultural atlas of Egypt.   932

The **new** cultural atlas of the Greek world.   938

A **new** deal for women. Coster, P.   305.4

NEW DEAL, 1933-1939

Bolden, T. FDR's alphabet soup   973.917

Collier, C. Progressivism, the Great Depression, and the New Deal, 1901 to 1941   973.91

Lindop, E. America in the 1930s   973.917

NEW DEAL, 1933-1939 -- SOURCES

McElvaine, R. S. The Depression and New Deal   973.91

New elements. Yannuzzi, D. A.   92

New found land. Wolf, A.   Fic

New France, 1534-1763. Worth, R.   971.01

A **new** generation of warriors. Whiting, J.   796.8

New Hampshire. Otfinoski, S.   974.2

New Hampshire. Kent, D.   974.2

New Hampshire, 1603-1776. Auden, S.   974.2

NEW HAVEN AND NORTHAMPTON CANAL (CONN. AND MASS.)

Hurst, C. O. Through the lock   Fic

The new immigrants [series]

Horst, H. A. Jamaican Americans   305.8

Radzilowski, J. Ukrainian Americans   305.8

Rangaswamy, P. Indian Americans   305.8

Schroeder, M. J. Mexican Americans   305.8

New Jersey. Kent, D.   974.9

New Jersey. Moragne, W.   974.9

New Jersey 1609-1776. Doak, R. S.   974.9

The **new** Jerusalem Bible. Bible   220.5

New kid, new scene. Glasser, D.   373.1

New Mexico. Burgan, M.   978.9

New Mexico. McDaniel, M.   972

New moon. Meyer, S.   Fic

NEW NEGRO MOVEMENT *See* Harlem Renaissance

The **new** policeman. Thompson, K.   Fic

NEW PRODUCTS

Hollander, B. G. The next big thing   004.068

NEW PRODUCTS

> *See also* Commercial products; Industrial research; Marketing

The **New** Republic (1763-1815) Stanley, G. E.   973.2

The **new** republic: 1760-1840s. Otfinoski, S.   973.3

New research techniques. Randolph, R. P.   001.4

New Spain: 1600-1760s. Hernandez, R. E.   973.1

New technology [series]

Graham, I. Forensic technology   363.2

Graham, I. Robot technology   629.8

Oxlade, C. Gaming technology   794.8

Ross, S. Sports technology   688.7

New Testament miracles. Connolly, S.   226

The **new** totally awesome business book for kids (and their parents) Bochner, A. B.   658

The **new** totally awesome money book for kids (and their parents) Bochner, R.   332.024

The **new** way things work. Macaulay, D.   600

The **new** weapons of the world encyclopedia. Diagram Group   623.4

NEW WORDS

> *See also* Vocabulary

NEW YEAR

Batmanglij, N. Happy Nowruz   641.5

NEW YEAR

> *See also* Holidays

NEW YEAR -- FICTION

Draanen, W. v. Sammy Keyes and the curse of

Next to Mexico. Nails, J. — Fic

NEZ PERCE INDIANS

Biskup, A. Thunder rolling down the mountain — 92

Freedman, R. Indian chiefs — 970.004

Hopping, L. J. Chief Joseph — 92

NEZ PERCE INDIANS -- FICTION

O'Dell, S. Thunder rolling in the mountains — Fic

Nezahualcôyotl, King of Texcoco, 1402-1472

About

Serrano, F. The poet king of Tezcoco — 92

The **NFL**. Sommers, M. A. — 362.29

NgCheong-Lum, Roseline

Eritrea — 963.5

Maldives — 954.9

Tahiti — 996

Nguyen, Duy

Monster origami — 736

Origami birds — 736

Zombigami — 736

Nibley, Lydia

Martin, R. The mysteries of Beethoven's hair — 92

Nicaragua. Kott, J. — 972.85

Nicholas II, Emperor of Russia, 1868-1918 -- Fiction

About

Miller, S. The lost crown — Fic

Nicholls, Sally

Season of secrets — Fic

Ways to live forever — Fic

Nichols, Beverly

Managing curriculum and assessment — 375

Nichols, Janet

Messed up — Fic

Nichols, Travis

Punk rock etiquette — 781.66

Nicholson, William

Jango — Fic

Noman — Fic

Seeker — Fic

Nick McIver time adventure [series]

Bell, T. Nick of time — Fic

Nick of time. Bell, T. — Fic

Nicola, Christos

Taylor, P. L. The secret of Priest's Grotto — 940.53

Nicolas Sarkozy. Abrams, D. — 92

Nicotine. Price, S. — 616.86

Nicotine and tobacco. Naff, C. F. — 362.29

NICOTINE HABIT *See* Tobacco habit

Niehaus, Theodore F.

A field guide to Pacific states wildflowers — 582.13

Niels Bohr. Spangenburg, R. — 92

Nielsen, Jennifer A.

Elliot and the Yeti threat — Fic

Nielsen, Susin

Dear George Clooney — Fic

The reluctant journal of Henry K. Larsen — Fic

Word nerd — Fic

Nielson, Sheila A.

Forbidden sea — Fic

Nieuwenhuizen, Agnes

Right book, right time — 011.6

Nigeria. Giles, B. — 966.9

Nigeria. Walker, I. — 966.9

NIGERIANS -- ENGLAND -- LONDON

Naidoo, B. The other side of truth — Fic

NIGERIANS -- ENGLAND -- LONDON -- FICTION

Naidoo, B. The other side of truth — Fic

Nigg, Joe

How to raise and keep a dragon — Fic

Wonder beasts — 398.24

NIGHT

See also Chronology; Time

NIGHT -- FICTION

Abrahams, P. Up all night — S C

Night fires. Stanley, G. E. — Fic

Night hoops. Deuker, C. — Fic

Night of the howling dogs. Salisbury, G. — Fic

Night of the soul-stealer. Delaney, J. — Fic

Night road. Jenkins, A. M. — Fic

Night runner. Turner, M. — Fic

Night runner [series]

Turner, M. End of days — Fic

The **night** tourist. Marsh, K. — Fic

Night wings. Bruchac, J. — Fic

Nightingale, Florence, 1820-1910

About

Dunlap, S. In the shadow of the lamp — Fic

Dunlap, S. In the shadow of the lamp — Fic

Springer, N. The case of the cryptic crinoline — Fic

Springer, N. The case of the cryptic crinoline — Fic

Nightjohn. Paulsen, G. — Fic

Nightmare. Nixon, J. L. — Fic

The **nightmare** garden. Kittredge, C. — Fic

The **nightmare** ninja. Higgins, S. — Fic

Nightmare plagues [series]

Aronin, M. Tuberculosis — 616.9

Person, S. Bubonic plague — 614.5

Person, S. Malaria — 614.5

Reingold, A. Smallpox — 614.5

Rudolph, J. The flu of 1918 — 614.5

The **nightmarys**. Poblocki, D. — Fic

Nightrise. Horowitz, A. — Fic

Nightshade. Wood, M. — Fic

The **Nightshade chronicles** [series]

Wagner, H. The white assassin — Fic

Nightshade City. Wagner, H. — Fic

Nightspell. Cypess, L. — Fic

NightWatch: a practical guide to viewing the universe. — 520

Nikola Tesla. Burgan, M. — 92

Nikola Tesla. Yount, L. — 621.309

The **Nile.** Heinrichs, A. 962

Nilsen, Alleen Pace
Literature for today's young adults 028.5
Names and naming in young adult literature 813

Nilsen, Don L. F.
Nilsen, A. P. Names and naming in young adult literature 813

Nimmo, Jenny
Charlie Bone and the beast Fic
Charlie Bone and the castle of mirrors Fic
Charlie Bone and the hidden king Fic
Charlie Bone and the invisible boy Fic
Charlie Bone and the Red Knight Fic
Charlie Bone and the shadow Fic
Charlie Bone and the time twister Fic
Emlyn's moon Fic
Midnight for Charlie Bone Fic
The snow spider Fic

Nimr, Sonia
Laird, E. A little piece of ground Fic

The **nine** lives of Travis Keating. MacLean, J. Fic
The **nine** pound hammer. Bemis, J. C. Fic
Nineteen eighty-four. Orwell, G. Fic

NINETEEN FIFTIES
Gourley, C. Gidgets and women warriors 305.4

NINETEEN SIXTIES
Hill, L. C. America dreaming 303.4
Gourley, C. Gidgets and women warriors 305.4
Kaufman, M. T. 1968 909.82

NINETEEN SIXTY-EIGHT, A.D.
Kaufman, M. T. 1968 909.82

NINJA -- FICTION
Bradford, C. Young samurai: the way of the sword Fic
Higgins, S. Moonshadow Fic
Higgins, S. The nightmare ninja Fic
Lake, N. Blood ninja II: the revenge of Lord Oda Fic

Nintendo. Firestone, M. 338.7
The **Ninth** Amendment. Furgang, K. 342
Ninth Ward. Rhodes, J. P. Fic

NITROGEN
See also Gases

Nix Minus One. MacLean, J. Fic

Nix, Garth
Nix, G. Troubletwisters Fic
Abhorsen Fic
Across the wall S C
Drowned Wednesday Fic
Grim Tuesday Fic
Lady Friday Fic
Lirael, daughter of the Clayr Fic
Lord Sunday Fic
Mister Monday Fic
Sabriel Fic
Shade's children Fic

Sir Thursday Fic
Superior Saturday Fic

Nix, Garth, 1963-
Troubletwisters Fic

Nixon, Joan Lowery
The haunting Fic
Laugh till you cry Fic
Nightmare Fic

Nixon, Richard M. (Richard Milhous), 1913-1994
About
Aronson, B. Richard M. Nixon 92
Barron, R. Richard Nixon 92
Stefoff, R. U.S. v. Nixon 342

Niz, Xavier
Samurai 952

No castles here. Bauer, A. C. E. Fic
No choirboy. Kuklin, S. 364.66
No compromise: the story of Harvey Milk. Aretha, D. 92
No cream puffs. Day, K. Fic
No crystal stair. Fic
No easy answers. Miller, C. C. 92
No god but God. Aslan, R. 297
No laughter here. Williams-Garcia, R. Fic
No moon. Watts, I. N. Fic
No more butts. Esherick, J. 616.86
No more dead dogs. Korman, G. Fic
No ordinary day. Ellis, D. Fic
No passengers beyond this point. Choldenko, G. Fic
No problem! Watanabe, K. 153.4
No school library left behind. Harvey, C. A. 025.1
No shelter here. Laidlaw, R. 636.7
No such thing as dragons. Reeve, P. Fic
No such thing as the real world. Na, A. S C
Noah Barleywater runs away. Boyne, J.

NOAH'S ARK -- FICTION
McCaughrean, G. Not the end of the world Fic

The **Nobel** book of answers. 001.4
Nobel genes. Michaels, R. Fic

NOBEL LAUREATES FOR CHEMISTRY
Atkins, J. Borrowed names 811
Hager, T. Linus Pauling and the chemistry of life 540

NOBEL LAUREATES FOR ECONOMIC SCIENCES
Crain, C. D. Milton Friedman 92

NOBEL LAUREATES FOR LITERATURE
Bell, T. Nick of time Fic
Crayton, L. A. A student's guide to Toni Morrison 813
Darraj, S. M. Gabriel Garcia Marquez 92
Delano, P. When I was a boy Neruda called me Policarpo 92
Hermann, S. A student's guide to Eugene O'Neill 812
McArthur, D. A student's guide to William

Norwich, Grace

Mar, J. The body book for boys   612.6

Nory Ryan's song. Giff, P. R.   Fic

NOSE

Ear, nose, and throat   617.5

Larsen, C. S. Crust and spray   612.8

Not a drop to drink. Burgan, M.   363.6

Not the end of the world. McCaughrean, G.   Fic

Not your parents' money book. Chatzky, J. 332.024

Not your typical book about the environment.
Kelsey, E.   333.72

Notable Americans [series]

Barron, R. Richard Nixon   92

Young, J. C. Dwight D. Eisenhower   973.921

NOTE-TAKING

Green, J. Write it down   371.3

Notes from a liar and her dog. Choldenko, G.   Fic

Notes from a totally lame vampire. Collins, T.   Fic

Notes from the dog. Paulsen, G.   Fic

Notes from the midnight driver. Sonnenblick, J. Fic

Nothing.   Fic

Nothing but ghosts. Kephart, B.   Fic

Nothing but the truth. Avi   Fic

Nothing here but stones. Oswald, N.   Fic

Nothing special. Herbach, G.   Fic

The **notorious** Benedict Arnold. Sheinkin, S.   92

Nouraee, Andisheh

(jt. auth) Anderson, J. L. Americapedia   320

Nourishment. Binstock, M.   92

Nouvian, Claire

(ed) The Deep   591.7

Novak, Amy

Glenn Beck   320.52

**NOVÉ MĚSTO NAD METUJI (CZECH REPUB-
LIC) -- BIOGRAPHY**

Levine, K. Hana's suitcase   940.53

NOVELETTES

Cisneros, S. The house on Mango Street   Fic

London, J. The call of the wild   Fic

Stevenson, R. L. The strange case of Dr. Jekyll and
Mr. Hyde   Fic

NOVELISTS

See also Authors

**NOVELISTS, AMERICAN -- 20TH CENTURY
-- BIOGRAPHY**

Hickam, H. H. The Coalwood way   813

**NOVELISTS, AMERICAN -- 20TH CENTURY
-- BIOGRAPHY**

Kramer, B. Toni Morrison   813

NOVELISTS, ENGLISH

Reef, C. Jane Austen   92

NOVELS IN LETTERS *See* Epistolary fiction

NOVELS IN VERSE

Agard, J. The young inferno   Fic

Applegate, K. Home of the brave   Fic

Bingham, K. Shark girl   Fic

Bryant, J. Kaleidoscope eyes   Fic

Bryant, J. Ringside, 1925   Fic

Burg, A. E. All the broken pieces   Fic

Chaltas, T. Because I am furniture   Fic

Cheng, A. Brushing Mom's hair   Fic

Creech, S. Hate that cat   Fic

Crossan, S. The Weight of Water   Fic

Engle, M. Firefly letters   Fic

Engle, M. Hurricane dancers   Fic

Engle, M. The surrender tree   811

Engle, M. Tropical secrets   Fic

Engle, M. The wild book   Fic

Fehler, G. Beanball   Fic

Frost, H. The braid   Fic

Frost, H. Crossing stones   Fic

Frost, H. Diamond Willow   Fic

Frost, H. Hidden   Fic

Grimes, N. Dark sons   Fic

Grimes, N. A girl named Mister   Fic

Grimes, N. Planet Middle School   Fic

Hemphill, S. Sisters of glass   Fic

Hemphill, S. Wicked girls   Fic

Hesse, K. Out of the dust   Fic

Hesse, K. Witness   Fic

Howe, J. Addie on the inside   Fic

Koertge, R. Shakespeare makes the playoffs   Fic

Lai, T. Inside out and back again   Fic

Leavitt, M. My book of life by Angel   Fic

LeZotte, A. C. T4   Fic

Macdonald, M. Odette's secrets   Fic

MacLean, J. Nix Minus One   Fic

Marcus, K. Exposed   Fic

Myers, W. D. Amiri & Odette   Fic

Myers, W. D. Street love   Fic

Ostlere, C. Karma   Fic

Richards, J. Three rivers rising   Fic

Rose, C. S. May B.   Fic

Saller, C. F. Eddie's war   Fic

Schroeder, L. Chasing Brooklyn   Fic

Smith, H. A. Keeping the night watch   Fic

Smith, H. A. The way a door closes   Fic

Sones, S. What my mother doesn't know   Fic

Thompson, H. The language inside   Fic

Thompson, H. Orchards   Fic

Tregay, S. Love and leftovers   Fic

Turner, A. W. Hard hit   Fic

Wayland, A. H. Girl coming in for a landing   811

Weatherford, C. B. Becoming Billie Holiday   Fic

Weston, R. P. Zorgamazoo   Fic

Williams, C. L. Glimpse   Fic

Wolf, A. The watch that ends the night   Fic

Wolff, V. E. Make lemonade   Fic

Wolff, V. E. This full house   Fic

Wolff, V. E. True believer   Fic

Woodson, J. Locomotion   Fic

Yeomans, E. Rubber houses   Fic

See also Mental health; Physical therapy; Physically handicapped -- Rehabilitation; Therapeutics

OCCUPATIONS

Farrell, C. Green jobs   **331.7**

Occupational outlook handbook 2013-2014 **331.120**

United States/Dept. of Labor   Young person's occupational outlook handbook   **331.7**

OCCUPATIONS -- ENCYCLOPEDIAS

J.G. Ferguson Publishing Company Encyclopedia of careers and vocational guidance   **331.7**

OCCUPIED TERRITORY *See* Military occupation

OCCUPY PROTEST MOVEMENTS

See also Demonstrations; Protest movements

Ocean.   **591.77**

OCEAN

See also Earth; Physical geography; Water

OCEAN

Bodden, V. To the ocean deep   **551.46**

Carson, R. The sea around us   **551.46**

Day, T. Oceans   **551.46**

Desonie, D. Oceans   **551.46**

Knowles, J. Jacques Cousteau   **92**

McMillan, B. Oceans   **551.46**

Ocean   **591.77**

Oceans   **551.46**

Olmstead, K. A. Jacques Cousteau   **92**

Rizzo, J. Oceans   **551.46**

Simon, S. Seymour Simon's extreme oceans **551.46**

Turner, P. S. Prowling the seas   **591.7**

Woodward, J. Creatures of the deep   **591.7**

Young, K. R. Across the wide ocean   **623.89**

OCEAN -- FICTION

Holyoke, P. The Neptune Project   **Fic**

OCEAN -- GRAPHIC NOVELS

Igarashi, D. Children of the sea, vol. 1   **741.5**

An **ocean** apart, a world away. Namioka, L.   **Fic**

OCEAN BOTTOM

Aleshire, P. Ocean ridges and trenches   **551.46**

Johnson, R. L. Journey into the deep   **591.7**

Lindop, L. Venturing the deep sea   **551.46**

Mallory, K. Diving to a deep-sea volcano   **551.46**

Matsen, B. The incredible record-setting deep-sea dive of the bathysphere   **551.46**

OCEAN BOTTOM

See also Ocean; Submarine geology

OCEAN CURRENTS

Burns, L. G. Tracking trash   **551.46**

OCEAN CURRENTS

See also Navigation; Ocean

Ocean drifters. Kirby, R. R.   **578.7**

OCEAN ENERGY RESOURCES

See also Energy resources; Marine resources; Ocean engineering

OCEAN ENGINEERING

See also Engineering; Marine resources; Oceanography

OCEAN FLOOR *See* Ocean bottom

OCEAN LIFE *See* Marine biology

Ocean liners. Zimmermann, K. R.   **387.2**

OCEAN LINERS

Zimmermann, K. R. Ocean liners   **387.2**

OCEAN LINERS

See also Ships

OCEAN POLLUTION *See* Marine pollution

Ocean ridges and trenches. Aleshire, P.   **551.46**

OCEAN ROUTES *See* Trade routes

OCEAN TRAVEL

Paulsen, G. Caught by the sea   **818**

Zimmermann, K. R. Ocean liners   **387.2**

OCEAN TRAVEL

See also Transportation; Travel; Voyages and travels

OCEAN TRAVEL -- FICTION

Matthews, T. L. Shots at sea   **Fic**

OCEAN WAVES

See also Ocean; Waves

Ocean wildlife. Vogel, C. G.   **591.7**

OCEANIA -- DISCOVERY AND EXPLORATION

Lawlor, L. Magnificent voyage   **910.4**

OCEANOGRAPHERS

Burns, L. G. Tracking trash   **551.46**

Hodgkins, F. Champions of the ocean   **920**

Knowles, J. Jacques Cousteau   **92**

Olmstead, K. A. Jacques Cousteau   **92**

OCEANOGRAPHIC RESEARCH *See* Oceanography -- Research

OCEANOGRAPHIC SUBMERSIBLES

Mallory, K. Diving to a deep-sea volcano   **551.46**

OCEANOGRAPHY

Basher, S. Oceans   **551.46**

Day, T. Oceans   **551.46**

Desonie, D. Oceans   **551.46**

Desonie, D. Oceans   **551.46**

Hodgkins, F. Champions of the ocean   **920**

Olmstead, K. A. Jacques Cousteau   **92**

Walker, P. The open ocean   **578.7**

Yount, L. Modern marine science   **551.46**

OCEANOGRAPHY

See also Earth sciences

OCEANOGRAPHY -- RESEARCH

Hague, B. Alien deep   **551.2**

OCEANOGRAPHY -- RESEARCH

See also Research

OCEANOLOGY *See* Oceanography

Oceans. Basher, S.   **551.46**

Oceans. Rizzo, J.   **551.46**

Oceans. Desonie, D.   **551.46**

Oceans. Day, T.   **551.46**

Oceans. McMillan, B.   **551.46**

OCEANS *See* Ocean

Oceans. 551.46

Ochoa, Ellen, 1958-

About

Schraff, A. E. Ellen Ochoa 92

Ochoa, George

(ed) American history on file 973

Atlas of Hispanic-American history 305.8

Octavia Boone's big questions about life, the universe, and everything. Rupp, R. Fic

Odd girl in. Whittemore, J. Fic

Odd man out. Ellis, S. Fic

The **Odd** Squad. Fry, M. Fic

Oddballs. Sleator, W. S C

Odden, Allan R.

Improving student learning when budgets are tight 371.2

Oddest of all. Coville, B. S C

ODDITIES *See* Curiosities and wonders

Odessa again. Reinhardt, D. Fic

Odette's secrets. Macdonald, M. Fic

Odysseus. McCaughrean, G. 292

ODYSSEUS (GREEK MYTHOLOGY)

Chwast, S. The odyssey 741.5

Hamilton, E. Mythology 292

Lister, R. The odyssey 883

McCaughrean, G. Odysseus 292

McCaughrean, G. Odysseus 292

Osborne, M. P. Return to Ithaca 883

Osborne, M. P. Return to Ithaca 883

Osborne, M. P. The gray-eyed goddess 883

Osborne, M. P. The land of the dead 883

Osborne, M. P. The land of the dead 883

Osborne, M. P. The one-eyed giant 883

Osborne, M. P. The one-eyed giant 883

ODYSSEUS (GREEK MYTHOLOGY) -- FICTION

Barrett, T. King of Ithaka Fic

Geras, A. Ithaka Fic

The **Odyssey.** Hinds, G. 741.5

The **odyssey.** Lister, R. 883

The **Odyssey.** Odyssey 883

Odyssey

The Odyssey 883

The **odyssey.** Chwast, S. 741.5

The **Odyssey.** Ita, S. 741.5

Oeming, Michael Avon

Glass, B. J. L. The mice templar, volume one: the prophecy 741.5

The **off** season. Murdock, C. G. Fic

Off the map. Clark, W. 917

Off to war. Ellis, D. 303.6

Off-color. McDonald, J. Fic

OFFENSES AGAINST PROPERTY

See also Crime; Criminal law

OFFENSES AGAINST PUBLIC SAFETY

See also Crime; Criminal law

OFFENSES AGAINST THE PERSON

See also Crime; Criminal law

Offermann, Andrea

Appelbaum, S. The Shepherd of Weeds Fic

Milford, K. The Boneshaker Fic

OFFICE BUILDINGS

See also Buildings

OFFICE SUPPLY INDUSTRY EXECUTIVES

Thimmesh, C. Girls think of everything 920

The **official** YALSA awards guidebook. 011.6

OFFSHORE OIL WELL DRILLING

Marcovitz, H. Is offshore oil drilling worth the risks? 363.7

Mooney, C. Oil spills and offshore drilling 333.8

OFFSHORE OIL WELL DRILLING

See also Ocean engineering; Offshore oil industry; Oil well drilling

OFFSHORE WATER POLLUTION *See* Marine pollution

Ogawa, Narumi

Mr. Funky's super crochet wonderful 746.43

OGLALA INDIANS

Freedman, R. Indian chiefs 970.004

Freedman, R. The life and death of Crazy Horse 978

Nelson, S. D. Black Elk's vision 92

OGLALA INDIANS -- KINGS AND RULERS -- BIOGRAPHY

Sanford, W. R. Oglala Lakota Chief Red Cloud 978.004

Sanford, W. R. Oglala Sioux Chief Crazy Horse 978.004

OGLALA INDIANS -- WARS

Sanford, W. R. Oglala Lakota Chief Red Cloud 978.004

Oglala Lakota Chief Red Cloud. Sanford, W. R. 978.004

Oglala Sioux Chief Crazy Horse. Sanford, W. R. 978.004

The **Ogre** of Oglefort. Ibbotson, E. Fic

Oh my godmother [series]

Brauner, B. The glitter trap Fic

Oh my gods! Bryant, M. E. 292

Oh, rats! Marrin, A. 599.35

Oh, Snap! Myers, W. D. Fic

Oh. My. Gods. Childs, T. L. Fic

Ohio. Sherrow, V. 977.1

Ohio. Stille, D. R. 977.1

OHIO -- ANTIQUITIES

See also Antiquities

OHIO -- BIOGRAPHY

See also Biography

OHIO -- CHURCH HISTORY

See also Church history

OHIO -- CIVILIZATION

See also Civilization

Olson, Arielle North
  Ask the bones: scary stories from around the world   **398.2**
  More bones   **398.2**
Olson, Gretchen
  Call me Hope   **Fic**
Olson, Kay Melchisedech
  The D.B. Cooper hijacking   **364.1**
Olson, Tod
  How to get rich in the California Gold Rush   **979.4**
  How to get rich on a Texas cattle drive   **978**
  How to get rich on the Oregon Trail   **978**
Olwell, Robert
  Doak, R. S. South Carolina, 1540-1776   **975.7**
Olympians [series]
  O'Connor, G. Athena   **741.5**
  O'Connor, G. Hades   **398.209**
  O'Connor, G. Hera: the goddess and her glory   **741.5**
  O'Connor, G. Zeus   **741.5**
OLYMPIC ATHLETES
  Burford, M. Grace, gold and glory   **796.440**
  Cantor, G. Usain Bolt   **796.42**
  Uschan, M. V. Apolo Anton Ohno   **796.91**
OLYMPIC ATHLETES
  See also Athletes
OLYMPIC GAMES
  Bobrick, B. A passion for victory: the story of the Olympics in ancient and early modern times **796.4**
  Butterfield, M. Events   **796.48**
  Butterfield, M. History   **796.48**
  Butterfield, M. Scandals   **796.48**
  Hotchkiss, R. The matchless six   **796.48**
  Macy, S. Freeze frame   **796.98**
  Macy, S. Swifter, higher, stronger   **796.48**
OLYMPIC GAMES
  See also Athletics; Contests; Games; Sports
OLYMPIC GAMES (9TH: 1928: AMSTERDAM, NETHERLANDS)
  Hotchkiss, R. The matchless six   **796.48**
OLYMPIC GAMES, 1972 (MUNICH, GER.)
  Farrell, C. Terror at the Munich Olympics **796.48**
OLYMPIC GAMES, 1996 (ATLANTA, GA.)
  See also Olympic games
OLYMPIC GAMES, 2012 (LONDON, ENG-LAND)
  See also Olympic games
Olympic National Park. Jankowski, S.   **979.7**
OLYMPIC NATIONAL PARK (WASH.)
  Jankowski, S. Olympic National Park   **979.7**
OLYMPICS
  Bobrick, B. A passion for victory: the story of the Olympics in ancient and early modern times **796.4**
OLYMPICS *See* Olympic games
The Olympics [series]
  Butterfield, M. Events   **796.48**

  Butterfield, M. History   **796.48**
  Butterfield, M. Scandals   **796.48**
OMAN -- DESCRIPTION AND TRAVEL
  Ejaz, K. We visit Oman   **953.53**
Omidyar, Pierre
  About
  Gitlin, M. eBay   **338.7**
The omnivore's dilemma. Pollan, M.   **338.1**
Omololu, Cynthia Jaynes
  Dirty little secrets   **Fic**
On my honor. Bauer, M. D.   **Fic**
On my journey now. Giovanni, N.   **782.25**
On parade. Laidlaw, R.   **791.8**
On rough seas. Hull, N. L.   **Fic**
On the Blue Comet. Wells, R.   **Fic**
On the fringe.   **S C**
On the radar: sports [series]
  Eason, S. Free running   **613.7**
On the rocks. Aretha, D.   **362.292**
On the Texas trail of Cabeza de Vaca. Lourie, P. **92**
On the volcano. Nelson, J.   **Fic**
On the wings of heroes. Peck, R.   **Fic**
On thin ice. Bastedo, J.   **Fic**
On Viney's mountain. Donaldson, J.   **Fic**
Onassis, Jacqueline Kennedy, 1929-1994 -- Fiction
  About
  Axelrod, A. Your friend in fashion, Abby Shapiro   **Fic**
Once. Gleitzman, M.   **Fic**
Once a witch. MacCullough, C.   **Fic**
The **once** and future king. White, T. H.   **Fic**
Once upon a cuento.   **S C**
Once upon a time in the North. Pullman, P.   **Fic**
Once was lost. Zarr, S.   **Fic**
ONE ACT PLAYS
  Acting out   **812**
The **one** and only Ivan. Applegate, K.   **Fic**
One crazy summer. Williams-Garcia, R.   **Fic**
One dog and his boy. Ibbotson, E.   **Fic**
One fat summer. Lipsyte, R.   **Fic**
One for the Murphys. Hunt, L. M.   **Fic**
One good punch. Wallace, R.   **Fic**
One hundred and eleven Shakespeare monologues. Shakespeare, W.   **822.3**
One kingdom. Noyes, D.   **590**
One million things [series]
  Woodward, J. Planet Earth   **550**
The **one** o'clock chop. Fletcher, R.   **Fic**
One of the survivors. Shaw, S.   **Fic**
ONE PARENT FAMILY *See* Single-parent families
One peace. Wilson, J.   **305.23**
One square inch. Mills, C.   **Fic**
One Step at a Time. Skrypuch, M. F.   **618.927**
One true friend. Hansen, J.   **Fic**
One white dolphin.   **Fic**

Africa: opposing viewpoints   **960**

America's prisons: opposing viewpoints   **365**

The death penalty: opposing viewpoints   **364.66**

Discrimination: opposing viewpoints   **305.8**

Domestic violence: opposing viewpoints   **362.82**

Endangered oceans: opposing viewpoints   **333.95**

Endangered species: opposing viewpoints   **578.68**

The environment: opposing viewpoints   **363.7**

Epidemics: opposing viewpoints   **614.4**

Euthanasia: opposing viewpoints   **179.7**

Global warming: opposing viewpoints   **363.7**

The Homeless: opposing viewpoints   **362.5**

The Internet: opposing viewpoints   **303.4**

Israel: opposing viewpoints   **956.94**

Male and female roles: opposing viewpoints   **305.3**

Mass media: opposing viewpoints   **302.23**

Media violence: opposing viewpoints   **363.3**

Mental illness: opposing viewpoints   **362.2**

The Middle East: opposing viewpoints   **956**

Paranormal phenomena: opposing viewpoints   **133**

Pollution: opposing viewpoints   **363.7**

Pornography: opposing viewpoints   **363.4**

Race relations: opposing viewpoints   **305.8**

Religion in America: opposing viewpoints   **200.9**

Suicide: opposing viewpoints   **362.28**

Terminal illness: opposing viewpoints   **362.1**

Terrorism   **363.32**

Tobacco and smoking: opposing viewpoints   **362.29**

War: opposing viewpoints   **355**

The **opposite** of hallelujah. Jarzab, A.   **Fic**

Oprah Winfrey. Krohn, K. E.   **92**

Oprah Winfrey. Cooper, I.   **92**

OPTICAL ILLUSIONS

Jarrow, G. The amazing Harry Kellar   **793.809**

Vry, S. Trick of the eye   **152.14**

Wick, W. Walter Wick's optical tricks   **152.14**

OPTICAL ILLUSIONS

    See also Hallucinations and illusions; Psychophysiology; Vision

OPTICS

    See also Physics

The **oracle** betrayed. Fisher, C.   **Fic**

Oracle prophecies [series]

Fisher, C. Day of the scarab   **Fic**

Fisher, C. The oracle betrayed   **Fic**

Fisher, C. The sphere of secrets   **Fic**

ORACLES

    See also Occultism

ORAL HISTORY

    See also History

ORANGUTAN

Russon, A. E. Orangutans: wizards of the rainforest   **599.8**

Orangutans: wizards of the rainforest. Russon, A. E.   **599.8**

ORATIONS *See* Speeches

ORATORS

Shecter, V. A. Cleopatra's moon   **Fic**

ORATORY *See* Public speaking

Orb weavers. Markle, S.   **595.4**

ORBITAL LABORATORIES *See* Space stations

ORBITAL RENDEZVOUS (SPACE FLIGHT)

    See also Space flight; Space stations; Space vehicles

ORBITING VEHICLES *See* Artificial satellites; Space stations

Orca currents [series]

Butcher, K. Cheat   **Fic**

Peterson, L. J. Beyond repair   **Fic**

Walters, E. Special Edward   **Fic**

Watson, C. Benched   **Fic**

Orca soundings [series]

McClintock, N. Masked   **Fic**

Rodman, S. Infiltration   **Fic**

Schwartz, E. Cellular   **Fic**

Tullson, D. Riley Park   **Fic**

Van Tol, A. Knifepoint   **Fic**

Yee, P. Learning to fly   **Fic**

Orca sports [series]

Muller, R. D. Squeeze   **Fic**

Ross, J. The drop   **Fic**

Stevenson, R. H. Dead in the water   **Fic**

Thomas, E. Boarder patrol   **Fic**

Orchards. Thompson, H.   **Fic**

ORCHESTRA

Ganeri, A. The young person's guide to the orchestra   **784.2**

ORCHESTRAL MUSIC

    See also Instrumental music; Music; Orchestra

The **Order** of Odd-Fish. Kennedy, J.   **Fic**

ORDERLINESS

Morgenstern, J. Organizing from the inside out for teens   **646.7**

Ordinary miracles. Aspin, D.   **S C**

ORDNANCE

    See also Military art and science

ORDNANCE -- HISTORY

Collier, J. L. Gunpowder and weaponry   **623.4**

ORE DEPOSITS

    See also Geology

Oregon. Kent, D.   **979.5**

OREGON TRAIL

Dallas, S. The quilt walk   **Fic**

Olson, T. How to get rich on the Oregon Trail   **978**

OREGON TRAIL

    See also Overland journeys to the Pacific; United States

Orenstein, Denise Gosliner

The secret twin   **Fic**

Unseen companion   **Fic**

ORES

See also Minerals

ORGAN MUSIC

    See also Church music; Instrumental music; Music

Organ transplants. Campbell, A.   **617.9**

Organ transplants. Schwartz, T. P.   **617.9**

ORGAN TRANSPLANTS *See* Transplantation of organs, tissues, etc.

ORGANIC AGRICULTURE *See* Organic farming

ORGANIC CHEMISTRY

    Gardner, R. Organic chemistry science fair projects   **547**

ORGANIC CHEMISTRY

    See also Chemistry

Organic chemistry science fair projects. Gardner, R.   **547**

ORGANIC COMPOUNDS

    See also Chemicals; Organic chemistry

ORGANIC FARMING

    Organic food and farming   **641.3**

    Rau, D. M. Going organic   **613.2**

ORGANIC FARMING

    See also Agriculture

Organic food and farming.   **641.3**

Organic foods. Miller, D. A.   **641.3**

ORGANIC GARDENING

    See also Gardening; Horticulture

ORGANIC WASTE AS FUEL *See* Waste products as fuel

ORGANICALLY GROWN FOODS *See* Natural foods

ORGANICULTURE *See* Organic farming; Organic gardening

ORGANIZATION OFFICIALS

    Brimner, L. D. Black & white   **323.1**

    Byrnes, P. Environmental pioneers   **363.7**

    Pinkney, A. D. Let it shine   **920**

Organizational storytelling for librarians. Marek, K.   **025.1**

ORGANIZED CRIME

    Korman, G. Son of the mob   **Fic**

ORGANIZED CRIME

    See also Crime

ORGANIZED CRIME -- FICTION

    Black, H. Black heart   **Fic**

ORGANIZED LABOR *See* Labor unions

Organizing from the inside out for teens. Morgenstern, J.   **646.7**

ORGANS (MUSICAL INSTRUMENTS)

    See also Musical instruments

ORGANS, ARTIFICIAL *See* Artificial organs

Orgill, Roxane

    Shout, sister, shout!   **920**

ORIENT *See* Asia; East Asia; Middle East

ORIENTAL ARCHITECTURE *See* Asian architecture

ORIENTEERING

    Champion, N. Finding your way   **613.6**

ORIENTEERING

    See also Hiking; Racing; Running; Sports

ORIGAMI

    Boursin, D. Easy origami   **736**

    Henry, S. Paper folding   **736**

    Krier, A. K. Totally cool origami animals   **736**

    Nguyen, D. Monster origami   **736**

    Nguyen, D. Origami birds   **736**

    Nguyen, D. Zombigami   **736**

    Stern, J. Jewish holiday origami   **736**

    Temko, F. Origami holiday decorations for Christmas, Hanukkah, and Kwanzaa   **736**

ORIGAMI

    See also Paper crafts

ORIGAMI -- FICTION

    Angleberger, T. Darth Paper strikes back   **Fic**

Origami birds. Nguyen, D.   **736**

Origami holiday decorations for Christmas, Hanukkah, and Kwanzaa. Temko, F.   **736**

Origin. Leone, B.   **92**

Origin. Khoury, J.   **Fic**

ORIGIN OF MAN *See* Human origins

ORIGIN OF SPECIES *See* Evolution

The **Originals.** Patrick, C.   **Fic**

Origins. Thompson, K.   **Fic**

The **origins** of the Holocaust. Downing, D.   **940.53**

ORINOCO RIVER REGION (VENEZUELA AND COLOMBIA)

    Montgomery, S. Encantado   **599.53**

Orlev, Uri

    Run, boy, run   **Fic**

    The song of the whales   **Fic**

Cornerstones of freedom [series]

    Benoit, P. September 11 we will never forget   **973.931**

ORNITHOLOGISTS

    Sherman, P. John James Audubon   **92**

ORPHAN DRUGS

    See also Drugs

The **orphan** of Awkward Falls. Graves, K.   **Fic**

Orphan of destiny. Spradlin, M. P.   **Fic**

Orphan train rider. Warren, A.   **362.7**

ORPHAN TRAINS

    Warren, A. We rode the orphan trains   **362.73**

ORPHANAGES

    Reef, C. Alone in the world   **362.7**

ORPHANAGES

    See also Charities; Children -- Institutional care

ORPHANAGES -- FICTION

    Barnaby, H. Wonder show   **Fic**

    Reef, C. Alone in the world   **362.7**

    Stewart, T. L. The extraordinary education of Nicholas Benedict   **Fic**

PANICS (FINANCE) *See* Financial crises

PANTHEISM

    See also Philosophy; Religion

The **Pantheon.** DuTemple, L. A.   726

Pantheon fairy tale & folklore library [series]

    African folktales   398.2

PANTOMIMES

    See also Acting; Amateur theater; Drama; Theater

Paolini, Christopher

    Brisingr   Fic

    Eldest   Fic

    Eragon   Fic

Paolini, Christopher
About

    Bankston, J. Christopher Paolini   92

PAPACY

    See also Catholic Church; Church history

Papademetriou, Lisa

    Drop   Fic

    M or F?   Fic

PAPAL VISITS

    See also Voyages and travels

Paper. Morris, N.   676

PAPER

    Knapp, B. J. Materials science   620.1

    Morris, N. Paper   676

PAPER

    See also Fibers

PAPER AIRPLANES

    Mercer, B. The flying machine book   745.592

PAPER AIRPLANES *See* Airplanes -- Models

Paper airplanes: Captain, level 4. Harbo, C. L.   745.592

Paper airplanes: Copilot, level 2. Harbo, C. L.   745.592

Paper airplanes: Flight school, level 1. Harbo, C. L.   745.592

Paper airplanes: Pilot, level 3. Harbo, C. L. 745.592

The **paper** boomerang book. Latno, M.   745.54

PAPER CRAFTS

    Boursin, D. Easy origami   736

    Castleforte, B. Papertoy monsters   745.592

    Diehn, G. Making books that fly, fold, wrap, hide, pop up, twist, and turn   745.54

    Dobson, C. Wind power   333.9

    Harbo, C. L. The kids' guide to paper airplanes   745.592

    Harbo, C. L. Paper airplanes: Captain, level 4   745.592

    Harbo, C. L. Paper airplanes: Copilot, level 2   745.592

    Harbo, C. L. Paper airplanes: Flight school, level 1   745.592

    Harbo, C. L. Paper airplanes: Pilot, level 3 745.592

    Henry, S. Paper folding   736

    Latno, M. The paper boomerang book   **745.54**

    Torres, L. Rock your party   **745.54**

PAPER CRAFTS

    See also Handicraft

Paper folding. Henry, S.   736

PAPER FOLDING *See* Origami; Paper crafts

PAPER MONEY

    See also Money

PAPER SCULPTURE *See* Paper crafts

Paper son. James, H. F.   Fic

PAPER WORK *See* Paper crafts

PAPERBACK BOOKS

    See also Books; Editions

Paperboy. Vawter, V.   Fic

PAPERHANGING

    See also Interior design

PAPERMAKING

    See also Manufactures; Paper

Papertoy monsters. Castleforte, B.   745.592

PAPIER-MÂCHÉ *See* Paper crafts

PAPILLOMAVIRUSES

    Parks, P. J. HPV   362.1

Paprocki, Sherry Beck

    Bob Marley   92

    Diana, Princess of Wales   92

    Ellen Degeneres   92

Papua New Guinea. Gascoigne, I.   995.3

Paquette, Ammi-Joan

    Nowhere girl   Fic

Paquette, Penny Hutchins

    Learning disabilities   371.9

PARACHUTE TROOPS

    Stone, T. L. Courage has no color, the true story of the Triple Nickles   940.54

PARACHUTE TROOPS

    See also Military aeronautics; Parachutes

PARACHUTES

    See also Aeronautics

PARADES

    See also Festivals; Pageants

Paradise. Alexander, J. S.   Fic

PARADISE

    See also Future life

Paradise red. Grant, K. M.   Fic

Paraguay. Jermyn, L.   989.2

PARALLEL UNIVERSES -- FICTION

    Lipsyte, R. The twinning project   Fic

PARALYSIS, CEREBRAL *See* Cerebral palsy

PARANORMAL FICTION

    Stiefvater, M. The raven boys   Fic

PARANORMAL PHENOMENA *See* Parapsychology

Paranormal phenomena: opposing viewpoints. **133**

Paranormalcy. White, K.   Fic

PARAPROFESSIONALS

    See also Occupations; Professions

Passion blue. Strauss, V.   **Fic**

A **passion** for print. Mahood, K.   **027.62**

A **passion** for victory: the story of the Olympics in ancient and early modern times. Bobrick, B. **796.4**

PASSION PLAYS

    See also Bible plays; Mysteries and miracle plays; Religious drama; Theater

PASSIONS *See* Emotions

PASSIVE RESISTANCE

  O'Brien, A. S. After Gandhi   **303.6**

  Wilkinson, P. Gandhi   **92**

PASSIVE RESISTANCE

  O'Brien, A. S. After Gandhi   **303.6**

PASSIVE RESISTANCE

    See also Resistance to government

PASSOVER

  Kimmel, E. A. Wonders and miracles   **296.4**

PASSOVER

    See also Jewish holidays

Past perfect. Sales, L.   **Fic**

Past perfect, present tense: new and collected stories. Peck, R.   **S C**

PASTEL DRAWING

    See also Drawing

Pasternak, Carol

  How to raise monarch butterflies   **595.78**

Pasteur, Louis, 1822-1895

    About

  Hyde, N. What is germ theory?   **615**

  Miles, L. Louis Pasteur   **509.2**

  Robbins, L. E. Louis Pasteur   **92**

  Zamosky, L. Louis Pasteur   **92**

PASTIMES *See* Amusements; Games; Recreation

PASTORAL PEOPLES *See* Nomads

PASTORAL POETRY

    See also Poetry

PASTORS *See* Clergy; Priests

PASTRY

    See also Baking; Cooking

PASTURES

    See also Agriculture; Land use

Pastworld. Beck, I.   **Fic**

Pat Mora. Marcovitz, H.   **92**

Pateman, Robert

  Bolivia   **984**

PATENT MEDICINES *See* Nonprescription drugs

Patent, Dorothy Hinshaw

  The horse and the Plains indians   **978**

Patent, Dorothy Hinshaw

  Munoz, W. Plants on the trail with Lewis and Clark   **581**

  Animals on the trail with Lewis and Clark   **917**

  Shaping the earth   **550**

PATENTS

    See also Manufactures

Paterson, Katherine

Bread and roses, too   **Fic**

Bridge to Terabithia   **Fic**

The day of the pelican   **Fic**

The great Gilly Hopkins   **Fic**

Jacob have I loved   **Fic**

Jip   **Fic**

Lyddie   **Fic**

Park's quest   **Fic**

Preacher's boy   **Fic**

The same stuff as stars   **Fic**

Paterson, Katherine

    About

  Bankston, J. Katherine Paterson   **92**

  Ellis, S. From reader to writer   **028**

  McGinty, A. B. Katherine Paterson   **92**

Pathfinder. Card, O. S.   **Fic**

PATHOLOGY

    See also Medicine

PATIENCE

    See also Human behavior; Virtue

Patients' rights. Naden, C. J.   **362.1**

Patneaude, David

  A piece of the sky   **Fic**

  Thin wood walls   **Fic**

Paton Walsh, Jill

  A parcel of patterns   **Fic**

Paton, Alan

  Cry, the beloved country   **Fic**

Patrick, Cat

  Forgotten   **Fic**

  The Originals   **Fic**

  Revived   **Fic**

Patrick, Danica, 1982-

    About

  Sirvaitis, K. Danica Patrick   **92**

Patrick, John J.

  The Bill of Rights   **342**

Patriotic holidays of the United States. Henderson, H.   **394.26**

PATRIOTIC POETRY

    See also Poetry

PATRIOTIC SONGS *See* National songs

PATRIOTISM

  Henderson, H. Patriotic holidays of the United States   **394.26**

PATRIOTISM

    See also Citizenship; Human behavior; Loyalty

PATRIOTISM -- FICTION

  Erskine, K. Quaking   **Fic**

  Lyga, B. Hero-type   **Fic**

The **patron** saint of butterflies. Galante, C.   **Fic**

Patron, Susan

  Behind the masks   **Fic**

PATRONS OF THE ARTS

  Atkins, J. Borrowed names   **811**

PLAGUE
See also Communicable diseases; Epidemics
PLAGUE
Cunningham, K. The bubonic plague — 614.5
Cunningham, K. Plague — 614.5
Nardo, D. The Black Death — 614.5
Person, S. Bubonic plague — 614.5
Slavicek, L. C. The Black Death — 614.5
Zahler, D. The Black Death — 614.5
PLAGUE -- ENGLAND
Blackwood, G. L. Shakespeare's scribe — Fic
PLAGUE -- FICTION
Kessler, J. Loss — Fic
Knutsson, C. Shadows cast by stars — Fic
PLAGUE -- HISTORY
Currie, S. The black death — 614.5
A **plague** year. Bloor, E. — Fic
The **Plain** Janes. Castellucci, C. — 741.5
Plain Janes [series]
Castellucci, C. Janes in love — 741.5
Plain Kate. Bow, E. — Fic
The **Plains** Indian wars 1864-1890. Langley, A. — 978.004
Plaisted, Caroline
Boy talk — 612.6
Plan B. Simon, C. — Fic
Planck, Max, 1858-1947
About
Weir, J. Max Planck — 92
PLANE CRASHES *See* Aircraft accidents
PLANE GEOMETRY
See also Geometry
PLANE TRIGONOMETRY *See* Trigonometry
Planesrunner. McDonald, I. — Fic
Planet Earth. Gilpin, D. — 550
Planet Earth. Reilly, K. M. — 333.72
Planet Earth. Woodward, J. — 550
Planet Earth science fair projects. Gardner, R. — 507.8
Planet girl [series]
Birkemoe, K. Strike a pose — 613.7
Roderick, S. Centsibility — 332.024
Warwick, E. Everywear — 745.5
Warwick, E. Injeanuity — 746
Planet hunter. Wittenstein, V. O. — 523.2
Planet Middle School. Grimes, N. — Fic
The **planet** of Junior Brown. Hamilton, V. — Fic
Planet SOS [series]
Bailey, G. Changing climate — 551.6
Bailey, G. Farming for the future — 630
Bailey, G. Fragile planet — 363.34
Bailey, G. Out of energy — 333.79
Planet under pressure [series]
Mason, P. Poverty — 362.5
PLANETARIUMS
See also Astronomy
PLANETOIDS *See* Asteroids

Planetology. Jones, T. D. — 523.4
PLANETOLOGY
Jones, T. D. Planetology — 523.4
PLANETS
Aguilar, D. A. 13 planets — 523.2
Jones, T. D. Planetology — 523.4
Miller, R. Seven wonders of the gas giants and their moons — 523.4
Miller, R. Seven wonders of the rocky planets and their moons — 523.4
Scott, E. When is a planet not a planet? — 523.4
PLANETS
See also Astronomy; Solar system
PLANETS -- EXPLORATION
See also Outer space -- Exploration
PLANETS -- GEOLOGY
Jones, T. D. Planetology — 523.4
Planets, stars, and galaxies. Aguilar, D. A. — 520
PLANKTON
Cerullo, M. M. Sea soup: zooplankton — 592
PLANNED COMMUNITIES
See also City planning
PLANNED PARENTHOOD *See* Birth control
Planning for a sustainable future. Belmont, H. — 338.9
PLANNING, LIBRARY
Bolan, K. Teen spaces — 022
Curzon, S. C. Managing change — 025.1
PLANS *See* Geometrical drawing; Map drawing; Maps; Mechanical drawing
Plant and animal science fair projects. Calhoun, Y. — 570.7
Plant biotechnology. Hopkins, W. G. — 630
PLANT BIOTECHNOLOGY
Hopkins, W. G. Plant biotechnology — 630
PLANT BREEDING
See also Agriculture; Breeding; Horticulture
Plant cells and life processes. Somervill, B. A. — 571.6
PLANT COLLECTING -- HISTORY
Silvey, A. The plant hunters — 580.75
PLANT COLLECTING -- WEST (U.S.) -- HISTORY -- 19TH CENTURY
Munoz, W. Plants on the trail with Lewis and Clark — 581
PLANT COLLECTORS -- BIOGRAPHY
Silvey, A. The plant hunters — 580.75
PLANT CONSERVATION
See also Conservation of natural resources; Economic botany; Endangered species; Nature conservation
PLANT DEFENSES
See also Plant ecology
PLANT DISEASES
See also Agricultural pests; Diseases; Fungi
Plant diversity. Gibson, J. P. — 580
PLANT DIVERSITY
Gibson, J. P. Plant diversity — 580

PLASTICS

Finkelstein, N. H. Plastics   **620.1**

Goodstein, M. Plastics and polymers science fair projects   **540.7**

Knapp, B. J. Materials science   **620.1**

Morris, N. Plastics   **668.4**

Plastics and polymers science fair projects. Goodstein, M.   **540.7**

PLASTICS CRAFT

See also Handicraft

Plate tectonics. Stille, D. R.   **551.1**

PLATE TECTONICS

Hanson, E. A. Canyons   **551.4**

Plate tectonics, volcanoes, and earthquakes   **551**

Saunders, C. What is the theory of plate tectonics?   **551.1**

Silverstein, A. Plate tectonics   **551.1**

Snedden, R. Earth's shifting surface   **551.1**

Stille, D. R. Plate tectonics   **551.1**

Plate tectonics. Silverstein, A.   **551.1**

Plate tectonics, volcanoes, and earthquakes.   **551**

Plath, Sylvia -- Poetry

About

Hemphill, S. Your own, Sylvia   **811**

Platt, Chris

Astra   Fic

Platt, Randall Beth

Hellie Jondoe   Fic

Platt, Richard

Moon landing   **629.45**

New York City   **974.7**

They wore what?!   **391**

PLAY

See also Recreation

PLAY -- FICTION

Spinelli, J. Hokey Pokey   Fic

Play Makers. Lupica, M.   Fic

Player's ruse. Bell, H.   Fic

Playground. 50 Cent (Musician)   Fic

PLAYGROUNDS

See also Recreation; Sports facilities

Playing hurt. Schindler, H.   Fic

Playing safe, eating right. Orr, T.   **613**

Playing with fire. Landy, D.   Fic

Playing with matches. Katcher, B.   Fic

PLAYS *See* Drama -- Collections; One act plays

PLAYS -- COLLECTIONS

Theatre for young audiences   **812**

PLAYS FOR CHILDREN *See* Children's plays

PLAYS FOR LIBRARY PRESENTATION

Black, A. N. Readers theatre for middle school boys   **812**

PLAYWRIGHTS *See* Dramatists

PLEASURE

See also Emotions; Joy and sorrow; Senses and sensation

The **pledge.** Derting, K.   Fic

PLEISTOCENE-HOLOCENE BOUNDARY

Holmes, T. Early humans   **599.93**

Plessy v. Ferguson. Axelrod-Contrada, J.   **342**

Plessy v. Ferguson. Anderson, W.   **342**

Plessy, Homer

About

Anderson, W. Plessy v. Ferguson   **342**

Plessy, Homer

About

Axelrod-Contrada, J. Plessy v. Ferguson   **342**

Pliny

Moser, B. Ashen sky   **937**

PLOT-YOUR-OWN STORIES

See also Children's literature; Fiction; Literary recreations

Plum, Amy

Die for me   Fic

Plum-Ucci, Carol

Celebrate Diwali   **294.5**

Plumber. Gregory, J.   **696**

PLUMBING

Gregory, J. Plumber   **696**

PLUMBING

See also Building

Plumley, Amie Petronis

Sewing school   **646.2**

Plunked. Northrop, M.   Fic

PLURALISM (SOCIAL SCIENCES)

See also Culture

PLUTO (DWARF PLANET)

See also Planets

The **Pluto** files. Tyson, N. D. G.   **523.4**

PLYMOUTH (MASS.) -- BIOGRAPHY

Doherty, K. William Bradford   **974.4**

The **Plymouth** Colony and the Pilgrim adventure in American history. Edwards, J.   **974.4**

PLYWOOD

See also Wood

PNEUMATICS

See also Physics

PNEUMONIA

See also Lungs -- Diseases

POACHING -- FICTION

Fletcher, S. Ancient, strange, and lovely   Fic

Poblocki, Dan

The nightmarys   Fic

The stone child   Fic

Pobst, Sandy

Animals on the edge   **578.68**

Virginia, 1607-1776   **975.5**

Pocahontas. Jones, V. G.   **92**

Pocahontas, d. 1617

About

Jones, V. G. Pocahontas   **92**

POCASSET INDIANS

Wooten, S. M. Robert Frost　　　92
Yu Chun Little Green　　　951.05
POETS
　　See also Authors
POETS -- FICTION
　Leal, A. H. Also known as Harper　　Fic
　MacColl, M. Nobody's secret　　Fic
　Rue, G. Brand new Emily　　Fic
　Williams-Garcia, R. One crazy summer　Fic
POETS -- GRAPHIC NOVELS
　Weing, D. Set to sea　　741.5
POETS, AMERICAN
　Angelou, M. Maya Angelou　　811
　Aykroyd, C. Julia Alvarez　　92
　Caravantes, P. Deep woods　　92
　The Invisible ladder　　811
　Kerley, B. Walt Whitman　　92
　Marcovitz, H. Pat Mora　　92
　Meltzer, M. Emily Dickinson　　92
　Meltzer, M. Walt Whitman　　811
　Reef, C. E. E. Cummings　　92
　Reef, C. Walt Whitman　　811
　Wooten, S. M. Robert Frost　　92
POETS, AMERICAN -- 19TH CENTURY -- BI-
OGRAPHY
　Meltzer, M. Walt Whitman　　811
POETS, CHILEAN
　Delano, P. When I was a boy Neruda called me
　Policarpo　　92
POETS, ENGLISH
　Bedard, M. William Blake　　92
Pohlen, Jerome
　Albert Einstein and relativity for kids　530.092
Point blank. Horowitz, A.　　Fic
Point blank: the graphic novel. Horowitz, A.　741.5
Point-counterpoint [series]
　Marzilli, A. Election reform　　324.6
　Marzilli, A. Stem cell research and cloning　174.2
Poison. Zinn, B.　　Fic
Poison. Wooding, C.　　Fic
The **poison** diaries. Wood, M.　　Fic
The poison diaries [series]
　Wood, M. Nightshade　　Fic
Poison frogs and other amphibians. Solway,
A.　　597.87
Poison Ivy. Koss, A. G.　　Fic
Poison most vial. Carey, B.　　Fic
The **poisoned** house. Ford, M.　　Fic
POISONOUS ANIMALS
　Frogs!　　597.8
　Singer, M. Venom　　591.6
POISONOUS ANIMALS
　　See also Animals; Dangerous animals; Eco-
　nomic zoology; Poisons and poisoning
POISONOUS ANIMALS
　Singer, M. Venom　　591.6

POISONOUS GASES
　　See also Gases; Poisons and poisoning
POISONOUS GASES -- WAR USE *See* Chemical
　warfare
POISONOUS PLANTS
　　See also Economic botany; Plants; Poisons
　and poisoning
POISONS AND POISONING
　　See also Accidents; Hazardous substances;
　Homicide; Medical jurisprudence
POISONS AND POISONING -- FICTION
　Appelbaum, S. The Hollow Bettle　　Fic
　Appelbaum, S. The Shepherd of Weeds　Fic
　Appelbaum, S. The Tasters Guild　　Fic
　Wood, M. Nightshade　　Fic
　Wood, M. The poison diaries　　Fic
The Poisons of Caux [series]
　Appelbaum, S. The Hollow Bettle　　Fic
　Appelbaum, S. The Shepherd of Weeds　Fic
　Appelbaum, S. The Tasters Guild　　Fic
A **Poke** in the I.　　811
POKER -- FICTION
　Full house　　S C
　Hautman, P. All-in　　Fic
　Volponi, P. The hand you're dealt　　Fic
Polak, Monique
　The middle of everywhere　　Fic
　What world is left　　Fic
Poland. Deckker, Z.　　943.8
Poland. Kadziolka, J.　　943.8
Poland. Docalavich, H.　　943.8
POLAND
　Docalavich, H. Poland　　943.8
POLAR BEAR
　Lockwood, S. Polar Bears　　599.78
　Ovsyanikov, N. Polar bears　　599.78
POLAR BEAR -- FICTION
　Bastedo, J. On thin ice　　Fic
　Durst, S. B. Ice　　Fic
POLAR BEAR -- RUSSIA (FEDERATION) --
WRANGEL ISLAND
　Ovsyanikov, N. Polar bears　　599.78
Polar Bears. Lockwood, S.　　599.78
Polar bears. Ovsyanikov, N.　　599.78
POLAR EXPEDITIONS *See* Antarctica -- Explo-
　ration; Arctic regions -- Exploration; Scientific
　expeditions
Polar explorations. Nardo, D.　　910.911
POLAR REGIONS -- EXPLORATION
　Nardo, D. Polar explorations　　910.911
Polar worlds. Wade, R.　　998
Polcovar, Jane
　Rosalind Franklin and the structure of life　92
Police. Mezzanotte, J.　　363.2
POLICE
　Busby, C. The year we disappeared　　92

Katz, S. M. Against all odds **363.32**
Newton, M. Bomb squad **363.2**
Newton, M. SWAT teams **363.2**
POLICE
    See also Administration of criminal justice; Law enforcement
POLICE -- CALIFORNIA -- LOS ANGELES -- FICTION
Dial, C. Fallen angels **Fic**
POLICE -- COMPLAINTS AGAINST *See* Police brutality; Police corruption
POLICE -- FICTION
Myers, W. D. Kick **Fic**
Pierce, T. Bloodhound **Fic**
Pierce, T. Mastiff **Fic**
Pierce, T. Terrier **Fic**
White, K. Paranormalcy **Fic**
POLICE -- HISTORY -- 20TH CENTURY
Samuels, C. Spying and security **940.54**
POLICE -- LOS ANGELES (CALIF.)
Worth, R. Los Angeles Police Department **363.2**
POLICE -- NEW YORK (N.Y.)
Evans, C. New York Police Department **363.2**
Police brutality. Stewart, G. **363.2**
POLICE BRUTALITY
Fireside, B. J. The trial of the police officers in the shooting death of Amadou Diallo **345**
Stewart, G. Police brutality **363.2**
POLICE BRUTALITY
    See also Police
POLICE BRUTALITY -- FICTION
Kephart, B. Dr. Radway's Sarsaparilla Resolvent **Fic**
POLICE BRUTALITY -- NEW YORK (STATE) -- NEW YORK
Fireside, B. J. The trial of the police officers in the shooting death of Amadou Diallo **345**
POLICE CORRUPTION
    See also Misconduct in office; Police
POLICE CORRUPTION -- FICTION
Dial, C. Fallen angels **Fic**
POLICE CRUELTY *See* Police brutality
Police lab. Owen, D. **363.2**
POLICE OFFICERS *See* Police
POLICE OFFICIALS
Brimner, L. D. Black & white **323.1**
Rosenberg, A. The Civil War **920**
POLICE REPRESSION *See* Police brutality
POLICE VIOLENCE *See* Police brutality
POLICEMEN *See* Police
POLICEWOMEN
    See also Police; Women
POLICEWOMEN -- FICTION
Dial, C. Fallen angels **Fic**
POLIOMYELITIS
Skrypuch, M. F. One Step at a Time **618.927**

POLIOMYELITIS
    See also Diseases
POLIOMYELITIS -- FICTION
Durbin, W. The Winter War **Fic**
Lasky, K. Chasing Orion **Fic**
Lawrence, I. The giant-slayer **Fic**
Tooke, W. King of the mound **Fic**
POLIOMYELITIS VACCINE
Sherrow, V. Jonas Salk **92**
POLIOMYELITIS VACCINE
    See also Vaccination
POLISH AMERICANS
Cushman, K. Rodzina **Fic**
POLISH AMERICANS -- FICTION
Cushman, K. Rodzina **Fic**
Friesner, E. M. Threads and flames **Fic**
Sternberg, L. The case against my brother **Fic**
Polisner, Gae
The pull of gravity **Fic**
POLITENESS *See* Courtesy; Etiquette
POLITICAL ACTIVISTS
Brave Bird, M. Lakota woman **92**
Chemerka, W. R. Juan Seguin **976.4**
Levinson, C. Y. We've got a job **323.119**
O'Keefe, S. Champion of freedom **959.105**
POLITICAL ACTIVISTS -- BIOGRAPHY
O'Brien, A. S. After Gandhi **303.6**
POLITICAL ACTIVISTS -- FICTION
Nye, N. S. Going going **Fic**
SchrÃ¶der, M. My brother's shadow **Fic**
Tashjian, J. Larry and the meaning of life **Fic**
Political advocacy for school librarians. Schuckett, S. **027.8**
POLITICAL AND SOCIAL PHILOSOPHERS
Rossig, W. Karl Marx **92**
Scott, M. The magician **Fic**
Scott, M. The sorceress **Fic**
Scott, M. The warlock **Fic**
POLITICAL ATROCITIES -- CAMBODIA
Sonneborn, L. The Khmer Rouge **959.604**
POLITICAL CAMPAIGNS *See* Politics
Political corruption. Miller, D. A. **364.1**
POLITICAL CORRUPTION
    See also Conflict of interests; Political crimes and offenses; Political ethics; Politics
POLITICAL CORRUPTION
Miller, D. A. Political corruption **364.1**
POLITICAL CORRUPTION -- FICTION
Mulligan, A. Trash **Fic**
Singer, N. Gem X **Fic**
POLITICAL CRIMES AND OFFENSES
    See also Criminal law; Political ethics; Subversive activities
POLITICAL DEFECTORS *See* Defectors
POLITICAL ECONOMY *See* Economics
POLITICAL ETHICS

The humming room	Fic

POTTERS

See also Artists

POTTERY

Park, L. S. A single shard — Fic

POTTERY

See also Ceramics; Clay industry; Decoration and ornament; Decorative arts; Tableware

POTTERY -- FICTION

Park, L. S. A single shard — Fic

POULTRY

See also Birds; Domestic animals

Pouy, Jean-Bernard

The big book of dummies, rebels and other geniuses — 920

Poverty. Senker, C. — 362.5

Poverty. Lusted, M. A. — 362.5

Poverty. Gifford, C. — 362.5

Poverty. — 362.5

POVERTY

See also Economic conditions; Social problems

POVERTY

Chambers, C. Living as a child laborer — 331.3

Gifford, C. Poverty — 362.5

Inner-city poverty — 362.5

Kowalski, K. M. Poverty in America — 362.5

Lusted, M. A. Poverty — 362.5

Mason, P. Poverty — 362.5

Poverty — 362.5

Senker, C. Poverty and hunger — 362.5

Senker, C. Poverty — 362.5

Tejubehan (Singer) Drawing from the City — 745

Poverty. Mason, P. — 362.5

POVERTY -- FICTION

Avi Traitor's gate — Fic

Brown, D. The train jumper — Fic

Cullen, L. I am Rembrandt's daughter — Fic

Cushman, K. Alchemy and Meggy Swann — Fic

Ellis, D. No ordinary day — Fic

Hirsch, O. Darius Bell and the glitter pool — Fic

Hooper, M. Fallen Grace — Fic

Kephart, B. The heart is not a size — Fic

Madden, K. Gentle's Holler — Fic

Madden, K. Jessie's mountain — Fic

Madden, K. Louisiana's song — Fic

Mulligan, A. Trash — Fic

Newton, R. Runner — Fic

Qamar, A. Beneath my mother's feet — Fic

Shulman, M. Scrawl — Fic

Steinbeck, J. The pearl — Fic

Stellings, C. The contest — Fic

Strasser, T. If I grow up — Fic

Uchida, Y. The best bad thing — Fic

Wolff, V. E. Make lemonade — Fic

Wolff, V. E. True believer — Fic

POVERTY -- UNITED STATES

Inner-city poverty — 362.5

Kowalski, K. M. Poverty in America — 362.5

Poverty and hunger. Senker, C. — 362.5

Poverty in America. Kowalski, K. M. — 362.5

Powder monkey. Dowswell, P. — Fic

POWDER, SMOKELESS *See* Gunpowder

Powell, Anton

Ancient Greece — 938

Powell, Ben

Skateboarding skills — 796.22

Stock, C. Skateboarding step-by-step — 796.22

Powell, Colin L., 1937-
About
Shichtman, S. H. Colin Powell — 92

Vander Hook, S. Colin Powell — 92

Powell, Jillian

Alcohol and drug abuse — 362.29

Explaining cystic fibrosis — 616.3

Self-harm and suicide — 616.85

Powell, Laura

Burn mark — Fic

The game of triumphs — Fic

The Master of Misrule — Fic

Powell, Martin

The seven voyages of Sinbad — 741.5

Powell, Randy

Swiss mist — Fic

Three clams and an oyster — Fic

Powell, Ransom J., 1849-1899
About
Wisler, G. C. Red Cap — Fic

Powell, Ransom J., 1849-1899 -- Fiction
About
Wisler, G. C. Red Cap — Fic

Power. Ravilious, K. — 179

The **power** of one. Fradin, J. B. — 323

The **power** of reading. Krashen, S. D. — 028.5

POWER PLANTS, HYDROELECTRIC *See* Hydroelectric power plants

POWER PLANTS, NUCLEAR *See* Nuclear power plants

POWER POLITICS *See* Balance of power; Cold war

Power research tools. Valenza, J. K. — 001.4

POWER RESOURCES *See* Energy resources

POWER RESOURCESE

Gunderson, J. The energy dilemma — 333.79

Rau, D. M. Alternative energy beyond fossil fuels — 333.79

POWER RESOURCES CONSERVATION *See* Energy conservation

Power Scott, Jennifer

Green careers — 333.72

POWER SUPPLY *See* Energy resources

The **power** to prevent suicide. Galas, J. C. — 362.28

Senker, C. Privacy and surveillance   **323.44**

PRIVATE EYE STORIES *See* Mystery and detective plays; Mystery fiction; Mystery films; Mystery radio programs; Mystery television programs

PRIVATE INVESTIGATORS -- ENGLAND -- FICTION

Doyle, A. C. S. The adventures and the memoirs of Sherlock Holmes   **Fic**

Private Peaceful. Morpurgo, M.   **Fic**

PRIVATE SCHOOLS

Independent school libraries   **025.1**

PRIVATE SCHOOLS

See also Schools

PRIVATE SCHOOLS -- DIRECTORIES

The Handbook of private schools   **370.2**

PRIVATE SCHOOLS -- FICTION

Fisher, C. Darkwater   **Fic**

Stiefvater, M. The raven boys   **Fic**

Wells, R. Feedback   **Fic**

The **private** thoughts of Amelia E. Rye. Shimko, B.   **Fic**

PRIVATEERING

See also International law; Naval art and science; Naval history; Pirates

PRIZE FIGHTING *See* Boxing

PRO-CHOICE ACTIVISTS

Gold, S. D. Roe v. Wade   **344**

PRO-CHOICE MOVEMENT

See also Social movements

PRO-LIFE MOVEMENT

See also Social movements

PROBABILITIES

See also Algebra; Logic; Mathematics; Statistics

The **probability** of miracles. Wunder, W.   **Fic**

Probably still Nick Swansen. Wolff, V. E.   **Fic**

Probably the world's best story about a dog and the girl who loved me. Smith, D. J.   **Fic**

PROBATION

See also Corrections; Criminal law; Prisons; Punishment; Reformatories; Social case work

PROBIOTICS

See also Dietary supplements; Microorganisms

PROBLEM CHILDREN

McIntyre, T. The behavior survival guide for kids   **158**

PROBLEM DRINKING *See* Alcoholism

PROBLEM SOLVING

Jones, J. B. Bouncing back   **158**

Watanabe, K. No problem!   **153.4**

Wingard-Nelson, R. Graphing and probability word problems   **519.2**

PROBLEM SOLVING

See also Psychology

PROBLEM SOLVING -- FICTION

Mister Max   **Fic**

PROCEDURE MANUALS

Gorman, M. Connecting young adults and libraries   **027.62**

Miller, D. P. Crash course in teen services   **027.62**

Stephens, C. G. Library 101   **027.8**

PRODUCT LIFE CYCLE

Oxlade, C. Gadgets and games   **688.7**

PRODUCTION *See* Economics; Industries

PRODUCTS, AGRICULTURAL *See* Farm produce

PROFESSIONAL ETHICS

See also Ethics

PROFESSIONAL SPORTS

See also Sports

Professional wrestling. Freedman, J.   **362.29**

PROFESSIONS

See also Occupations; Self-employed

Professor Gargoyle. Gilman, C.   **Fic**

PROFESSORS *See* Educators; Teachers

Profiles [series]

Byrnes, P. Environmental pioneers   **363.7**

Rosenberg, A. The Civil War   **920**

Profiles in American history [series]

Harkins, S. S. The life and times of Father Jacques Marquette   **92**

Tracy, K. The life and times of Rosa Parks   **92**

Profiles in courage. Kennedy, J. F.   **920**

Profiles in economics [series]

Crain, C. D. Adam Smith   **92**

Crain, C. D. John Maynard Keynes   **92**

Crain, C. D. Milton Friedman   **92**

Rossig, W. Karl Marx   **92**

Profiles in fashion [series]

Branscomb, L. W. Marc Jacobs   **92**

Freistadt, M. Kate Spade   **92**

Petrillo, L. Vera Wang   **92**

Sapet, K. Jimmy Choo   **92**

Profiles in mathematics [series]

Corrigan, J. Alan Turing   **92**

Profiles in science [series]

Baxter, R. Ernest Rutherford and the birth of the atomic age   **530.092**

Baxter, R. Illuminated progress   **92**

Baxter, R. Skeptical chemist   **92**

Fox, M. V. Scheduling the heavens   **92**

Leone, B. Origin   **92**

Steffens, B. Ibn al-Haytham   **92**

Yannuzzi, D. A. New elements   **92**

PROFIT

See also Business; Capital; Economics; Wealth

PROGRAM PLANNING -- HANDBOOKS, MANUALS, ETC.

Heath, A. Windows on the world   **394.2**

Langemack, C. The author event primer   **021.2**

Quick, Barbara
  A golden web   Fic
Quick, Matthew
  Sorta like a rockstar   Fic
Quicksand.   616.97
Quicksand pony. Lester, A.   Fic
Quicksilver. Spinner, S.   Fic
QUICKSILVER See Mercury
Quid pro quo. Grant, V.   Fic
The Quillan games. MacHale, D. J.   Fic
Quilt of states. Yorinks, A.   973
The quilt walk. Dallas, S.   Fic
QUILTING
    See also Needlework; Sewing
QUILTING -- FICTION
  Dallas, S. The quilt walk   Fic
QUILTMAKERS
  Warren, A. Pioneer girl   92
QUILTS
    See also Interior design
QUILTS -- FICTION
  Dallas, S. The quilt walk   Fic
QUINCEANERA (SOCIAL CUSTOM) -- FICTION
  Adler, E. Sweet 15   Fic
  Alegria, M. Estrella's quinceanera   Fic
  Chambers, V. Fifteen candles   Fic
Quinlan, Susan E.
  The case of the monkeys that fell from the trees   577.3
Quinn, Jason
  Steve Jobs   338.46
Quinn, Patricia O.
  Attention, girls!   616.85
Quintana of Charyn. Marchetta, M.   Fic
Quintero, Sofia
  Efrain's secret   Fic
QUIT-SMOKING PROGRAMS See Smoking cessation programs
Quiver. Spinner, S.   Fic
QUIZZES See Questions and answers
QUOTATIONS
  Alcorn, S. A gift of days   808.88
  Hudson, W. Powerful words   081
  O'Brien, G. Bartlett's familiar quotations   808.88
  Spinelli, E. Today I will   808.8
QUOTATIONS, ENGLISH
  O'Brien, G. Bartlett's familiar quotations   808.88
The Qur'an. Abdel Haleem, M. A. S.   297.122
QUR'AN
    See also Islam; Sacred books

R

R my name is Rachel. Giff, P. R.   Fic
RÉSUMÉS (EMPLOYMENT)
    See also Applications for positions; Job hunt-ing

R.L. Stine. Marcovitz, H.   92
Raabe, Michelle
  Hemophilia   616.1
Raatma, Lucia
  Citizenship   323.609
  Green living   333.72
  Islam   297
  Michigan   977.4
  Safety in your neighborhood   613.6
  Shirley Chisholm   92
  The Underground Railroad   973.7
Rabbat, Suzy
  Find your way online   025.04
  Using digital images   775
RABBIS
  Grimberg, T. Out of line   92
RABBIS
    See also Clergy; Judaism
RABBITS
  Jennings, R. W. Orwell's luck   Fic
RABBITS
    See also Mammals
RABBITS -- FICTION
  Adams, R. Watership Down   Fic
  Jennings, R. W. Orwell's luck   Fic
  Zuckerman, L. A taste for rabbit   Fic
Rabey, Melissa
  Historical fiction for teens   016
RABIES
    See also Communicable diseases
Rabiger, Joanna
  Daily prison life   365
Rabin, Staton
  Black powder   Fic
RACCOONS
  Read, T. C. Exploring the world of raccoons   599.74
RACCOONS -- FICTION
  Appelt, K. The true blue scouts of Sugarman Swamp   Fic
RACE AWARENESS
    See also Race relations
RACE DISCRIMINATION
  Cooper, J. Season of rage   323.1
  Racial discrimination   342
RACE DISCRIMINATION
    See also Discrimination; Race relations; Racism; Social problems
The race for space. Kuhn, B.   629.45
RACE PREJUDICE See Racism
RACE PROBLEMS See Race relations
RACE RELATIONS
  Bolden, T. Tell all the children our story   305.8
RACE RELATIONS -- FICTION
  Rhodes, J. P. Sugar   Fic
  Vawter, V. Paperboy   Fic

Race relations: opposing viewpoints.   305.8
The **race** to save the Lord God Bird. Hoose, P.
M.   598
RACETRACKS (HORSE RACING)
Tate, N. Behind the scenes: the racehorse   798.4
Rachael Ray. Abrams, D.   92
Rachel Carson. Piddock, C.   92
Rachel Spinelli punched me in the face. Acampora,
P.   Fic
Rachel's secret. Sanders, S.   Fic
RACIAL BALANCE IN SCHOOLS *See* School
integration; Segregation in education
RACIAL BIAS *See* Racism
Racial discrimination.   342
RACIAL DISCRIMINATION *See* Race discrimi-
nation
RACIAL INTEGRATION *See* Race relations
RACIAL INTERMARRIAGE *See* Interracial mar-
riage
Racial profiling. Kops, D.   363.2
RACIAL PROFILING
Kops, D. Racial profiling   363.2
Orr, T. Racial profiling   363.2
Racial profiling. Orr, T.   363.2
**RACIAL PROFILING IN LAW ENFORCE-
MENT**
Kops, D. Racial profiling   363.2
Orr, T. Racial profiling   363.2
**RACIAL PROFILING IN LAW ENFORCE-
MENT**
See also Law enforcement; Race discrimina-
tion
RACIALLY MIXED PEOPLE
Abramson, J. Obama   92
Brewster, H. The other Mozart   92
Burgan, M. Barack Obama   92
Fields, J. Multiracial families   306.8
Gibson, K. B. The Obama view   92
It's not all black and white   305.8
Krensky, S. Barack Obama   92
Lanier, S. Jefferson's children   973.4
Obama, B. Dreams from my father   92
Schwartz, V. F. Send one angel down   Fic
Thomas, G. E. Yes we can: a biography of Barack
Obama   92
Warren, A. Escape from Saigon   92
RACIALLY MIXED PEOPLE
See also Ethnic groups
RACIALLY MIXED PEOPLE -- FICTION
Hopkinson, N. The Chaos   Fic
Lawrence, C. The case of the deadly despera-
dos   Fic
Taylor, M. D. The land   Fic
**RACIALLY MIXED PEOPLE -- GRAPHIC
NOVELS**
Tamaki, M. Emiko superstar   741.5

**RACIALLY MIXED PEOPLE -- UNITED
STATES -- BIOGRAPHY**
Zeiger, J. Barack Obama   973.932
**RACIALLY MIXED PEOPLE -- UNITED
STATES -- BIOGRAPHY**
Zeiger, J. Barack Obama   973.932
**RACIALLY MIXED PEOPLE -- UNITED
STATES -- GENEALOGY**
Lanier, S. Jefferson's children   973.4
**RACIALLY MIXED PEOPLE -- UNITED
STATES -- INTERVIEWS**
Lanier, S. Jefferson's children   973.4
RACING
See also Sports
RACING -- FICTION
Stiefvater, M. The Scorpio Races   Fic
Racing the moon. Armstrong, A.   Fic
Racing to freedom [series]
Hart, A. Gabriel's horses   Fic
Hart, A. Gabriel's triumph   Fic
RACISM
Bartoletti, S. C. They called themselves the
K.K.K.   322.4
Crowe, C. Getting away with murder: the true story
of the Emmett Till case   364.152
Robson, D. The murder of Emmett Till   364.152
Rodger, M. Racism and prejudice   305.8
Sanna, E. We shall all be free   305.8
Wright, S. Simeon's story   305.8
RACISM
See also Attitude (Psychology); Prejudices;
Race awareness; Race relations
RACISM -- FICTION
Crowe, C. Mississippi trial, 1955   Fic
Magoon, K. Fire in the streets   Fic
RACISM -- HISTORY
Miller, C. C. Backlash   305.8
RACISM
Brimner, L. D. Birmingham Sunday   323.1
RACISM -- UNITED STATES
Bartoletti, S. C. They called themselves the
K.K.K.   322.4
Racism and prejudice. Rodger, M.   305.8
RACISM IN SPORTS -- UNITED STATES
Stanton, T. Hank Aaron and the home run that
changed America   92
Racism on trial. Coleman, W.   345
RACKETEERING
See also Crime; Organized crime
RACQUETBALL
See also Ball games; Sports
Raczka, Bob
Before they were famous   704
Name that style   709
Unlikely pairs   750
RADAR

Rafferty, John P.

(ed) Glaciers, sea ice, and ice formation   **551.3**

(ed) Plate tectonics, volcanoes, and earthquakes **551**

The **raft.** Bodeen, S. A.   **Fic**

Rafter, Dan

Atlas   **741.5**

RAFTING (SPORTS) -- FICTION

Woods, R. The hero   **Fic**

RAGE *See* Anger

Rage of the fallen. Delaney, J.   **Fic**

Rage within. Roberts, J.   **Fic**

Raggin', jazzin', rockin' VanHecke, S.   **784.19**

Raicht, Mike

Dezago, T. Spider-man: Spidey strikes back Vol. 1 digest   **741.5**

Raiders' ransom. Diamand, E.   **Fic**

Raiders' ransom [series]

Diamand, E. Flood and fire   **Fic**

RAILROAD ACCIDENTS

See also Accidents; Disasters

RAILROAD CONSTRUCTION *See* Railroad engineering

RAILROAD CONSTRUCTION WORKERS -- HISTORY -- 19TH CENTURY

Barter, J. A worker on the transcontinental railroad   **331.7**

RAILROAD CONSTRUCTION WORKERS -- UNITED STATES -- HISTORY -- 19TH CENTURY

Barter, J. A worker on the transcontinental railroad   **331.7**

Perl, L. To the Golden Mountain   **305.8**

RAILROAD ENGINEERING

Barter, J. A worker on the transcontinental railroad   **331.7**

RAILROAD ENGINEERING

See also Civil engineering; Engineering; Railroads

RAILROAD WORKERS

Anderson, W. Brown v. Board of Education   **344**

Fleischman, J. Phineas Gage: a gruesome but true story about brain science   **362.1**

Gold, S. D. Brown v. Board of Education   **344**

Nelson, S. R. Ain't nothing but a man   **92**

RAILROADS

Collier, C. Indians, cowboys, and farmers and the battle for the Great Plains, 1865-1910   **978**

Haugen, B. The Great Train Robbery   **364.1**

McMahon, P. Ultimate trains   **385**

Zimmermann, K. R. All aboard!   **385**

RAILROADS

See also Transportation

RAILROADS -- FICTION

Miéville, C. Railsea   **Fic**

RAILROADS -- HISTORY

Barter, J. A worker on the transcontinental railroad   **331.7**

Gimpel, D. The transcontinental railroad   **385**

Landau, E. The transcontinental railroad   **385**

Laughlin, R. The Pullman strike of 1894   **331.8**

Murphy, J. Across America on an emigrant train   **385**

Nelson, S. R. Ain't nothing but a man   **92**

Renehan, E. J. The Transcontinental Railroad **385**

RAILROADS -- MODELS

See also Models and modelmaking

RAILROADS -- PASSENGER-CARS

Zimmermann, K. R. All aboard!   **385**

RAILROADS -- STATISTICS

See also Statistics

RAILROADS -- UNITED STATES

Best shot in the West   **978**

Murphy, J. Across America on an emigrant train   **385**

RAILROADS -- UNITED STATES -- HISTORY -- 19TH CENTURY

Barter, J. A worker on the transcontinental railroad   **331.7**

Railsback, Lisa

Noonie's masterpiece   **Fic**

Railsea. Miéville, C.   **Fic**

RAILWAYS *See* Railroads

RAIN -- FICTION

Scaletta, K. Mudville   **Fic**

RAIN FOREST ANIMALS

Jackson, T. Tropical forests   **577.34**

RAIN FOREST CONSERVATION

Littlewood, A. Rain forest destruction   **333.75**

Rain forest destruction. Littlewood, A.   **333.75**

RAIN FOREST ECOLOGY

Berkenkamp, L. Discover the Amazon   **981**

Greenaway, T. Jungle   **577.3**

Jackson, K. Rain forests   **577.3**

Jackson, T. Tropical forests   **577.34**

Lasky, K. The most beautiful roof in the world **577.3**

Littlewood, A. Rain forest destruction   **333.75**

McAllister, I. Salmon bears   **599.78**

McAllister, I. The sea wolves   **599.77**

Quinlan, S. E. The case of the monkeys that fell from the trees   **577.3**

Sobol, R. Breakfast in the rainforest   **599.8**

Tocci, S. Life in the tropical forests   **577.3**

RAIN FOREST ECOLOGY

See also Ecology

Rain forests. Vogt, R. C.   **577.3**

RAIN FORESTS

See also Forests and forestry

RAIN FORESTS

Heinrichs, A. The Amazon rain forest   **981**

Jackson, K. Rain forests   **577.3**

Jackson, T. Tropical forests   **577.34**

Littlewood, A. Rain forest destruction   **333.75**

Murphy, A. G. Chico Mendes   **92**

Vogt, R. C. Rain forests   **577.3**

Welsbacher, A. Protecting Earth's rain forests **577.3**

Rain forests. Jackson, K.   **577.3**

RAIN FORESTS -- FICTION

Gilman, D. Blood sun   **Fic**

Khoury, J. Origin   **Fic**

Nelson, N. Bringing the boy home   **Fic**

Rain is not my Indian name. Smith, C. L.   **Fic**

RAINBOW

     See also Meteorology

Rainbow family collections. Naidoo, J. C.   **028.1**

The **rainbow** people. Yep, L.   **398.2**

Rainey, Ma, 1886-1939

     About

Orgill, R. Shout, sister, shout!   **920**

RAINFORESTS *See* Rain forests

Rainis, Kenneth G.

Gardner, R. Ace your animal science project **590.7**

Gardner, R. Ace your chemistry science project   **540.7**

Blood & DNA evidence   **363.2**

Cell and microbe science fair projects   **571.6**

Forgery   **363.2**

Hair, clothing and tire track evidence   **363.2**

Rainmaker. Jackson, A.   **Fic**

Raintree fusion [series]

Hall, M. Skin deep   **612.7**

Raising the flag. Burgan, M.   **940.54**

Raising voices. Sima, J.   **027.62**

Rajtar, Steve

United States holidays and observances   **394.26**

Raleigh, Walter Sir, 1552?-1618

     About

Aronson, M. Sir Walter Ralegh and the quest for El Dorado   **942.05**

Raleigh, Walter Sir, 1552?-1618 -- Fiction

     About

Klein, L. M. Cate of the Lost Colony   **Fic**

RALLIES (PROTEST) *See* Demonstrations

Rallison, Janette

Just one wish   **Fic**

Ralph Lauren. Mattern, J.   **92**

Ralph Masiello's ancient Egypt drawing book. Masiello, R.   **743**

Ralston, Birgitta

Snow play   **796**

Ram-Prasad, Chakravarthi

Exploring the life, myth, and art of India   **954**

RAMADAN

Jeffrey, L. S. Celebrate Ramadan   **297.3**

RAMADAN -- FICTION

Robert, N. B. Boy vs. girl   **Fic**

The **Ramayana** and Hinduism. Ganeri, A.   **294.5**

Ramen, Catherine

Carson, B. Understanding your right to freedom

from searches   **323.44**

Ramen, Fred

Albucasis (Abu al-Qasim al-Zahrawi)   **92**

Ramirez, Manny, 1972-

     About

Friedman, I. C. Manny Ramirez   **92**

Ramm, David

Rich, M. World authors, 2000-2005   **920.003**

The **Ramones.** Bowe, B. J.   **781.66**

Rampersad, Arnold

(ed) African American Poetry   **811.008**

Rampersad, Arnold

(ed) Hughes, L. Langston Hughes   **811**

Ramses II. Fitzgerald, S. J.   **92**

Ramses II, King of Egypt

     About

Fitzgerald, S. J. Ramses II   **92**

RANCH LIFE

Freedman, R. In the days of the vaqueros   **636.2**

Steele, C. Cattle ranching in the American West **636**

RANCH LIFE

     See also Farm life; Frontier and pioneer life

RANCH LIFE -- FICTION

Amateau, G. A certain strain of peculiar   **Fic**

Brennan, C. House of the star   **Fic**

Enderle, D. Crosswire   **Fic**

Horvath, P. Northward to the moon   **Fic**

Law, I. Scumble   **Fic**

Parry, R. Heart of a shepherd   **Fic**

Smiley, J. The Georges and the Jewels   **Fic**

Smiley, J. A good horse   **Fic**

Smiley, J. True Blue   **Fic**

Stanley, D. Saving Sky   **Fic**

Steinbeck, J. The red pony   **Fic**

Waters, Z. C. Blood moon rider   **Fic**

RANCH LIFE -- SOUTHWEST, NEW -- HISTORY

Freedman, R. In the days of the vaqueros   **636.2**

RANCH LIFE -- WEST (U.S.)

Branzei, S. Cowgirls   **920.720**

RANCHERS -- TEXAS -- BIOGRAPHY

Henrietta King, la patrona   **976.4**

Rand, Casey

DNA and heredity   **572.8**

Glass squid and other spectacular squid   **594**

Graphing sports   **796**

Human reproduction   **612.6**

Randall, Thomas

Dreams of the dead   **Fic**

Spirits of the Noh   **Fic**

Randolph, Asa Philip, 1889-1979

     About

Miller, C. C. A. Philip Randolph and the African American labor movement   **92**

Randolph, Ryan P.

New research techniques   **001.4**

The **Random** House book of poetry for children. 811

Random House Webster's American Sign Language dictionary: unabridged. Costello, E. **419**

Random House Webster's unabridged dictionary. **423**

Rangaswamy, Padma
Indian Americans **305.8**

Ranger's apprentice [series]
Flanagan, J. The battle for Skandia **Fic**
Flanagan, J. The burning bridge **Fic**
Flanagan, J. The emperor of Nihon-Ja **Fic**
Flanagan, J. Erak's ransom **Fic**
Flanagan, J. Halt's peril **Fic**
Flanagan, J. The icebound land **Fic**
Flanagan, J. The kings of Clonmel **Fic**
Flanagan, J. The lost stories **S C**
Flanagan, J. The ruins of Gorlan **Fic**
Flanagan, J. The siege of Macindaw **Fic**
Flanagan, J. The sorcerer of the north **Fic**

RANK *See* Social classes

Rankin, Jeannette, 1880-1973
About
Krull, K. Lives of extraordinary women **920**

Rankin, Kenrya
Start it up **338**

Rankin, Virginia
The thoughtful researcher **027.62**

Ransford, Sandy
The Kingfisher illustrated horse & pony encyclopedia **636.1**

Ransom, Candice F.
Maggie L. Walker **92**
Rebel McKenzie **Fic**
Scrapbooking just for you! **745.593**

Ransome, Arthur, 1884-1967
About
Ellis, S. From reader to writer **028**

RAP MUSIC
Gaines, A. The hip-hop scene **781.66**
Golus, C. Tupac Shakur **92**
Harris, A. R. Tupac Shakur **92**
Moore, S. W. The rap scene **781.66**
Sanna, E. Hip-hop: a short history **781.66**

RAP MUSIC
See also African American music; Popular music

RAP MUSIC -- FICTION
McDonald, J. Harlem Hustle **Fic**

RAP MUSICIANS
Spilsbury, R. Jay-Z **92**

RAP MUSICIANS -- UNITED STATES -- BIOGRAPHY
Spilsbury, R. Jay-Z **92**

The **rap** scene. Moore, S. W. **781.66**

RAP SONGS *See* Rap music

RAPE

Kaminker, L. Everything you need to know about dealing with sexual assault **364.1**
Simons, R. Gender danger **362.88**
Strong at the heart **362.7**

RAPE
See also Offenses against the person; Sex crimes

RAPE -- FICTION
Grace, A. In too deep **Fic**

RAPE -- UNITED STATES
Kaminker, L. Everything you need to know about dealing with sexual assault **364.1**

Rapp, Adam
The children and the wolves **Fic**

Rapp, Valerie
Protecting Earth's air quality **363.7**
Protecting Earth's land **333.72**

Rappaport, Doreen
John's secret dreams **92**

Rappaport, Doreen, 1939-
Beyond courage **940.53**

Rapparlie, Leslie
Wurdinger, S. D. Kayaking **797.1**
Wurdinger, S. D. Rock climbing **796.52**

RAPPING (MUSIC) *See* Rap music

Rappoport, Ken
Alex Rodriguez **796.357**
Derek Jeter **796.357**
Peyton Manning **796.332**

Raptor! a kid's guide to birds of prey. Laubach, C. M. **598**

RAPTOREX
See also Dinosaurs

Rapture of the deep. Meyer, L. A. **Fic**

Rapunzel and other magic fairy tales. **398.2**

Rapunzel's revenge. Hale, D. **741.5**

RARE AMPHIBIANS
Reptiles and amphibians **333.95**

RARE ANIMALS
Mills, A. Animals like us **333.95**

RARE ANIMALS
See also Animals

RARE BOOKS
See also Books

RARE MAMMALS -- NORTHERN HEMISPHERE
Mammals of the Northern Hemisphere **599.168**

RARE PLANTS
See also Plants

RARE REPTILES
Reptiles and amphibians **333.95**

Rasamandala Das
Hinduism **294.5**

Rascal. Wells, K. **Fic**

Raskin, Joyce
My misadventures as a teenage rock star **Fic**

Read, Tracy C.
  Exploring the world of raccoons   **599.74**
The **read-aloud** handbook. Trelease, J.   **028.5**
READER GUIDANCE
  Booth, H. Serving teens through readers' advisory   **028.5**
READER SERVICES (LIBRARIES) *See* Library services
A **reader's** guide to Amy Tan's The joy luck club. Loos, P.   **813**
A **reader's** guide to Chinua Achebe's Things fall apart. Shea, G.   **823**
A **reader's** guide to Gary Soto's Taking sides. Jones, J.   **813**
A **reader's** guide to Lorraine Hansberry's A raisin in the sun. Loos, P.   **812**
A **reader's** guide to Marjane Satrapi's Persepolis. Schroeder, H. L.   **813**
A **reader's** guide to Richard Wright's Black boy. Hinds, M. J.   **813**
A **reader's** guide to Zora Neale Hurston's Their eyes were watching god. Litwin, L. B.   **813**
READERS AND LIBRARIES *See* Library services
Readers theatre [series]
  Black, A. N. Readers theatre for middle school boys   **812**
Readers theatre for middle school boys. Black, A. N.   **812**
The **readers'** advisory guide to graphic novels. Goldsmith, F.   **025.2**
READERS' THEATER
  Black, A. N. Readers theatre for middle school boys   **812**
READERS' THEATER
  See also Theater
READINESS FOR SCHOOL
  See also Elementary education; Preschool education
READING
  Bacon, P. S. 100+ literacy lifesavers   **428**
  Bernadowski, C. Research-based reading strategies in the library for adolescent learners   **372.4**
  Into focus   **028.1**
  Kajder, S. B. Bringing the outside in   **028.5**
  Krashen, S. D. The power of reading   **028.5**
  Ostenson, J. W. Integrating young adult literature through the common core standards   **418**
READING
  See also Language arts
READING (MIDDLE SCHOOL)
  Into focus   **028.1**
READING (MIDDLE SCHOOL) -- ABILITY TESTING
  Fuhrken, C. What every middle school teacher needs to know about reading tests (from someone

who has written them)   **428**
READING (MIDDLE SCHOOL) -- HANDBOOKS, MANUALS, ETC
  Into focus   **028.1**
READING (MIDDLE SCHOOL) -- UNITED STATES
  Keane, N. J. Booktalking across the curriculum: the middle years   **028.5**
  Sullivan, E. T. Reaching reluctant young adult readers   **028.5**
READING (SECONDARY)
  Ostenson, J. W. Integrating young adult literature through the common core standards   **418**
READING -- FICTION
  Castan, M. Fighting for Dontae   **Fic**
  Charlie Joe Jackson's guide to summer vacation **Fic**
READING -- PHONETIC METHOD
  See also English language -- Pronunciation; Reading
READING -- SEX DIFFERENCES
  Sullivan, M. Connecting boys with books 2 **028.5**
READING -- STUDY AND TEACHING *See* Reading
READING COMPREHENSION
  Grimes, S. Reading is our business   **027.8**
  Moreillon, J. Collaborative strategies for teaching reading comprehension   **372.4**
READING COMPREHENSION
  See also Psychology of learning; Reading; Verbal learning
READING DISABILITY
  See also Learning disabilities; Reading
READING INTERESTS
  Knowles, E. Boys and literacy   **028.5**
  Zbaracki, M. D. Best books for boys   **028.5**
READING INTERESTS *See* Books and reading
READING INTERESTS OF CHILDREN *See* Children -- Books and reading
Reading is our business. Grimes, S.   **027.8**
READING MATERIALS
  See also Children's literature
READING PROMOTION
  Bromann, J. Booktalking that works   **028.5**
  Ray, V. L. School wide book events   **027.8**
  Sullivan, M. Connecting boys with books 2 **028.5**
READING PROMOTION -- UNITED STATES
  Sullivan, E. T. Reaching reluctant young adult readers   **028.5**
READING READINESS
  See also Reading
Ready to make music [series]
  Landau, E. Are the drums for you?   **786.9**
  Landau, E. Is singing for you?   **783**
  Landau, E. Is the flute for you?   **788**
  Landau, E. Is the guitar for you?   **787.87**
  Landau, E. Is the trumpet for you?   **788**

REFERENCE BOOKS

See also Bibliography; Books; Books and reading

REFERENCE BOOKS -- BIBLIOGRAPHY

REFERENCE BOOKS -- REVIEWS

REFERENCE SERVICES (LIBRARIES)

Fisher, C. The dark city	Fic
Fisher, C. The hidden Coronet	Fic
Fisher, C. The lost heiress	Fic
Fisher, C. The Margrave	Fic

RELICS

Murphy, J. The giant and how he humbugged America **974.7**

RELICS AND RELIQUARIES See Relics

RELIEF WORKERS

Park, L. S. A long walk to water **Fic**

RELIEF, PUBLIC See Public welfare

Religion. Langley, M. **200**

Religion. Hinds, K. **299**

RELIGION

Baldwin, J. Go tell it on the mountain **Fic**

Langley, M. Religion **200**

RELIGION -- FICTION

Adams, S. J. Sparks **Fic**

Agell, C. Shift **Fic**

Blume, J. Are you there God?, it's me, Margaret **Fic**

Bunce, E. C. Star crossed **Fic**

Card, O. S. A war of gifts **Fic**

Epstein, R. God is in the pancakes **Fic**

Hautman, P. Godless **Fic**

Hautman, P. The obsidian blade **Fic**

Levitin, S. Strange relations **Fic**

Mills, S. The viper within **Fic**

Rich, N. Alis **Fic**

Rupp, R. Octavia Boone's big questions about life, the universe, and everything **Fic**

Rylant, C. A fine white dust **Fic**

Woodson, J. Feathers **Fic**

RELIGION -- GOVERNMENT POLICY See Church and state

RELIGION -- HISTORY -- CHRONOLOGY

National Geographic concise history of world religions **200**

RELIGION -- POLITICAL ASPECTS See Religion and politics

RELIGION AND ART See Art and religion

RELIGION AND ETHICS

National Geographic concise history of world religions **200**

Religion and modern culture [series]

McIntosh, K. When religion & politics mix **201**

RELIGION AND POLITICS

McIntosh, K. When religion & politics mix **201**

Shapera, P. M. Iran's religious leaders **955**

RELIGION AND POLITICS

See also Politics; Religion

RELIGION AND SCIENCE

See also Religion; Science

RELIGION AND SCIENCE -- FICTION

Morden, S. The lost art **Fic**

RELIGION AND SOCIOLOGY

See also Religion; Sociology

RELIGION AND STATE See Church and state

Religion in America: opposing viewpoints. **200.9**

Religion in American life [series]

Bushman, C. L. Mormons in America **289.3**

Mann, G. S. Buddhists, Hindus, and Sikhs in America **294**

Martin, J. Native American religion **299.7**

Noll, M. A. Protestants in America **280**

Stein, S. J. Alternative American religions **209**

Women and American religion **200.9**

RELIGION IN LITERATURE

See also Literature; Religion

RELIGION IN THE PUBLIC SCHOOLS

Mountjoy, S. Engel v. Vitale **344**

RELIGION IN THE PUBLIC SCHOOLS

See also Church and education; Church and state; Public schools; Religious education

RELIGIONS

Breuilly, E. Religions of the world **200**

Buller, L. A faith like mine **200**

Osborne, M. P. One world, many religions **200**

Sanna, E. Gay believers **306.76**

What do you believe? **200**

RELIGIONS

See also Civilization

RELIGIONS -- ENCYCLOPEDIAS

National Geographic concise history of world religions **200**

RELIGIONS -- HISTORY

National Geographic concise history of world religions **200**

RELIGIONS

Osborne, M. P. One world, many religions **200**

RELIGIONS -- POLITICAL ASPECTS See Religion and politics

Religions of the world. Breuilly, E. **200**

Religions of the world [series]

Ganeri, A. Buddhism **294.3**

Kallen, S. A. Shinto **299.5**

Keene, M. Judaism **296**

Rasamandala Das Hinduism **294.5**

Self, D. Christianity **230**

Taylor, R. L. Confucianism **299**

RELIGIOUS AND ECCLESIASTICAL INSTITUTIONS See Religious institutions

RELIGIOUS ART

Fischer, C. In the beginning: the art of Genesis **222**

RELIGIOUS ART

See also Art

RELIGIOUS ART AND SYMBOLISM See Religious art

RELIGIOUS AWAKENING

See also Religion

RELIGIOUS BIOGRAPHY

See also Biography

RELIGIOUS COMMUNITIES

Stewart, S. Growing up in religious communities   **305**

RELIGIOUS CULTS *See* Cults

RELIGIOUS DENOMINATIONS *See* Sects

RELIGIOUS EDUCATION

    See also Education; Religion

RELIGIOUS FESTIVALS *See* Religious holidays

RELIGIOUS FREEDOM *See* Freedom of religion

Religious fundamentalism. Fridell, R.   **200.9**

RELIGIOUS FUNDAMENTALISM

    Fridell, R. Religious fundamentalism   **200.9**

    Marsico, K. The Texas polygamist raid   **364.1**

RELIGIOUS FUNDAMENTALISM

    See also Religion

RELIGIOUS GRAPHIC NOVELS

    See also Graphic novels

RELIGIOUS HISTORY *See* Church history

RELIGIOUS HOLIDAYS

    Breuilly, E. Festivals of the world   **394.26**

    Hackney Blackwell, A. Lent, Yom Kippur, and other Atonement days   **200**

RELIGIOUS HOLIDAYS

    See also Holidays; Rites and ceremonies

RELIGIOUS INSTITUTIONS

    National Geographic concise history of world religions   **200**

RELIGIOUS INSTITUTIONS

    See also Associations; Religion

RELIGIOUS LEADERS

    Stille, D. R. Anne Hutchinson   **92**

RELIGIOUS LIBERTY *See* Freedom of religion

RELIGIOUS LIFE

    See also Religion

RELIGIOUS LIFE (CHRISTIAN) *See* Christian life

RELIGIOUS LIFE -- FICTION

    Barnhouse, R. The book of the maidservant   **Fic**

    Hoffman, M. The falconer's knot   **Fic**

RELIGIOUS LITERATURE

    See also Literature

RELIGIOUS ORGANIZATIONS *See* Religious institutions

RELIGIOUS PAINTING *See* Religious art

RELIGIOUS PERSECUTION *See* Persecution

RELIGIOUS POETRY

    Spires, E. I heard God talking to me   **811**

    Yolen, J. Sacred places   **811**

RELIGIOUS POETRY

    See also Poetry; Religious literature

RELIGIOUS REFUGEES

    See also Refugees

RELIGIOUS SCULPTURE *See* Religious art

RELIGIOUS SUMMER SCHOOLS

    See also Schools; Summer schools

RELIGIOUS TOLERANCE

    See also Toleration

Relin, David Oliver

    Mortenson, G. Three cups of tea   **371.82**

RELOCATION OF JAPANESE AMERICANS, 1942-1945 *See* Japanese Americans -- Evacuation and relocation, 1942-1945

The **reluctant** assassin. Colfer, E.   **Fic**

The **reluctant** journal of Henry K. Larsen. Nielsen, S.   **Fic**

Reluctantly Alice. Naylor, P. R.   **Fic**

Remarkable. Foley, L. K.   **FIC**

The **remarkable** journey of Prince Jen. Alexander, L.   **Fic**

Remarkable journeys: the story of Jules Verne. Schoell, W.   **843**

Remarkable people [series]

    Goldsworthy, S. Steve Jobs   **92**

    Rose, S. Aung San Suu Kyi   **92**

    Yasuda, A. Justin Bieber   **92**

    Yasuda, A. Lebron James   **92**

    Yasuda, A. Miranda Cosgrove   **92**

The **remarkable,** rough-riding life of Theodore Roosevelt and the rise of empire America. Harness, C.   **92**

REMARRIAGE -- FICTION

    Allison, J. Gilda Joyce, psychic investigator: the bones of the holy   **Fic**

    Brooks, B. What hearts   **Fic**

    Collins, Y. The new and improved Vivien Leigh Reid   **Fic**

    Friend, N. Bounce   **Fic**

    Konigsburg, E. L. Silent to the bone   **Fic**

    Margolis, L. Girls acting catty   **Fic**

    Myers, A. Wart   **Fic**

    Reinhardt, D. Odessa again   **Fic**

    Rowen, M. Reign or shine   **Fic**

    Smith, R. I. Q.: book two, The White House   **Fic**

    Suma, N. R. Dani noir   **Fic**

    Vail, R. Kiss me again   **Fic**

Rembrandt. Roberts, R.   **92**

Rembrandt Harmenszoon van Rijn, 1606-1669

About

    Cullen, L. I am Rembrandt's daughter   **Fic**

    Roberts, R. Rembrandt   **92**

Remember as you pass me by. Perez, L. K.   **Fic**

Remember D-day. Drez, R. J.   **940.54**

Remember Little Bighorn. Walker, P. R.   **973.8**

Remember Little Rock. Walker, P. R.   **379**

Remember not to forget. Finkelstein, N. H.   **940.53**

Remember Pearl Harbor. Allen, T. B.   **940.54**

Remember the Alamo. Walker, P. R.   **976.4**

Remember the bridge. Weatherford, C. B.   **811**

Remember Valley Forge. Allen, T. B.   **973.3**

Remembering Raquel. Vande Velde, V.   **Fic**

reMIND. Brubaker, J.   **741.5**

The **reminder.** Michaels, R.   **Fic**

Remote control. Heath, J.   **Fic**

REMOTE SENSING

    See also Aerial photography

The **Renaissance.** Spilsbury, R.   **709.02**

RENAISSANCE

    See also Civilization

The **Renaissance.** Claybourne, A.   **940.2**

The **Renaissance.** Currie, S.   **940.2**

RENAISSANCE

  Anderson, M. Amazing Leonardo da Vinci inventions you can build yourself   **92**

  Barter, J. A Renaissance painter's studio   **759**

  Claybourne, A. The Renaissance   **940.2**

  Currie, S. The Renaissance   **940.2**

  Dawson, I. Renaissance medicine   **610**

  Elliott, L. Exploration in the Renaissance   **910**

  Elliott, L. The Renaissance in Europe   **940.2**

  Encyclopedia of women in the Renaissance   **940.2**

  Grant, N. Renaissance Europe   **940.2**

  Hinds, K. Everyday life in the Renaissance   **940.2**

  Krull, K. Leonardo da Vinci   **92**

  Mullins, L. Science in the Renaissance   **509**

  Phillips, J. Leonardo da Vinci   **92**

  Spilsbury, R. The Renaissance   **709.02**

  Stanley, D. Michelangelo   **92**

RENAISSANCE -- FICTION

  Avi Midnight magic   **Fic**

  Beaufrand, M. J. Primavera   **Fic**

  Hoffman, M. The falconer's knot   **Fic**

  Marsh, K. Jepp, who defied the stars   **Fic**

  Napoli, D. J. The smile   **Fic**

RENAISSANCE -- ITALY -- FLORENCE

Renaissance painter's studio. Barter, J.   **759**

Renaissance Europe. Grant, N.   **940.2**

The **Renaissance** in Europe. Elliott, L.   **940.2**

Renaissance medicine. Dawson, I.   **610**

A **Renaissance** painter's studio. Barter, J.   **759**

Renaissance scientists [series]

  Boerst, W. J. Isaac Newton   **92**

  Boerst, W. J. Johannes Kepler   **520**

  Boerst, W. J. Tycho Brahe   **92**

The **rendering.** Naftali, J.   **Fic**

Renegade Magic. Burgis, S.   **Fic**

Renehan, Edward J.

  The Monroe doctrine   **327**

  Pope John Paul II   **92**

  The Transcontinental Railroad   **385**

  The Treaty of Paris   **973.3**

Renewable energy research. Kallen, S. A.   **333.79**

RENEWABLE ENERGY RESOURCES

  Bailey, G. Out of energy   **333.79**

  Brezina, C. Jobs in sustainable energy   **333.79**

  Caduto, M. J. Catch the wind, harness the sun   **333.79**

  Currie, S. Hydropower   **333.91**

  Flath, C. Careers in green energy   **333.79**

  Fridell, R. Earth-friendly energy   **333.79**

  Friedman, L. S. Energy alternatives   **333.79**

  Kallen, S. A. Renewable energy research   **333.79**

  Laidlaw, J. A. Cities   **307.7**

  Laidlaw, J. A. Energy   **333.79**

  Leardi, J. Making cities green   **333.72**

  Miller, D. A. Energy production and alternative energy   **333.79**

  O'Neal, C. How to use wind power to light and heat your home   **621.31**

  Rau, D. M. Alternative energy beyond fossil fuels   **333.79**

  Rigsby, M. Doable renewables   **333.79**

  Sobey, E. Solar cell and renewable energy experiments   **333.79**

  Solway, A. Renewable energy sources   **333.79**

  Thaddeus, E. Powering the future   **333.79**

RENEWABLE ENERGY RESOURCES

    See also Energy resources

Renewable energy sources. Solway, A.   **333.79**

Rengel, Marian

  Daly, K. N. Greek and Roman mythology, A to Z   **292**

  Daly, K. N. Norse mythology A to Z   **293**

Renier, Aaron

  The Unsinkable Walker Bean   **741.5**

Renn, Diana

  Tokyo heist   **Fic**

Rennison, Louise

  Withering tights   **Fic**

Reno v. ACLU. Axelrod-Contrada, J.   **344**

Renoir. Spence, D.   **92**

RENOWN *See* Fame

Repka, Janice

  The clueless girl's guide to being a genius   **Fic**

Replay. Creech, S.   **Fic**

Repman, Judi

  (ed) School library management   **025.1**

REPORT WRITING

  Cefrey, H. Researching people, places, and events   **001.4**

  Cornwall, P. Put it all together   **808**

  Fogarty, M. Grammar girl presents the ultimate writing guide for students   **428**

  Janeczko, P. B. Writing winning reports and essays   **808**

  Tallman, J. I. Making the writing and research connection with the I-search process   **025.5**

  Valenza, J. K. Power research tools   **001.4**

REPORT WRITING

    See also Authorship

REPORT WRITING -- STUDY AND TEACHING

  Valenza, J. K. Power research tools   **001.4**

REPORTERS AND REPORTING

    See also Journalism; Newspapers

REPORTERS AND REPORTING -- FICTION

Rhinoceroses. Gish, M.   599.66

Rhode Island. Burgan, M.   974.5

Rhode Island. Klein, T.   974.5

Rhodes, Jewell Parker

Ninth Ward   Fic

Sugar   Fic

Rhodes-Courter, Ashley Marie

Three little words   92

Rhodes-Courter, Ashley Marie

About

Rhodes-Courter, A. M. Three little words   92

Rhuday-Perkovich, Olugbemisola

8th grade superzero   Fic

RHYME

    See also Poetics; Versification

Rhyme, meter, and other word music. Fandel, J.   808.1

RHYMES *See* Limericks; Nonsense verses; Nursery rhymes; Poetry -- Collections

RHYTHM

    See also Aesthetics; Poetics

RHYTHM AND BLUES MUSIC

Handyside, C. Soul and R&B   781.644

RHYTHM AND BLUES MUSIC -- HISTORY AND CRITICISM

Mendelson, A. A. American R & B   781.644

Rhythm and folklore. Sapet, K.   92

Riahi, Sep

Maydell, N. Extraordinary women from the Muslim world   920

RIBBON WORK

    See also Handicraft

Ribeiro, Myra

The assassination of Medgar Evers   976.2

RIBONUCLEIC ACID *See* RNA

RIBOSE NUCLEIC ACID *See* RNA

Ricciuti, Edward R.

Federal Bureau of Investigation   363.2

RICE

Sobol, R. The life of rice   633.1

Rice, Barry A.

Growing carnivorous plants   635.9

Rice, Condoleezza, 1954-

Condoleezza Rice   92

Hubbard-Brown, J. Condoleezza Rice   92

Rice, C. Condoleezza Rice   92

Rice, David

Crazy loco   S C

Rice, Earle

Adolf Hitler and Nazi Germany   92

Canaletto   92

Charlie Parker   788.7

RICH

    See also Social classes

Rich, Mari

World authors, 2000-2005   920.003

Rich, Naomi

Alis   Fic

Rich, Susan

(ed) Half-minute horrors   S C

Richard Feynman. Henderson, H.   92

Richard Francis Burton. Young, S.   92

Richard I, King of England, 1157-1199

About

Crompton, S. The Third Crusade   956

Richard III, King of England, 1452-1485 -- Fiction

About

Haddix, M. P. Sent   Fic

Richard M. Nixon. Aronson, B.   92

Richard Nixon. Barron, R.   92

Richard Peck. Gallo, D. R.   813

Richard Peck. Campbell, K.   92

Richard Peck. Sickels, A.   92

Richard Wright. Levy, D.   92

Richards, Jame

Three rivers rising   Fic

Richards, Jasmine

The book of wonders   Fic

Richards, Justin

Higgins, J. Death run   Fic

Higgins, J. First strike   Fic

Higgins, J. Sharp shot   Fic

Higgins, J. Sure fire   Fic

Richardson, Gillian

10 plants that shook the world   630.9

Kaboom!   500

Richardson, Joy

Looking at pictures   750.1

Richardson, Kim

(jt. auth) Meissner, D. Call of the Klondike   904

Richardson, Will

Blogs, wikis, podcasts, and other powerful Web tools for classrooms   371.3

Richelieu, Armand Jean du Plessis, Cardinal, duc de, 1585-1642 -- Fiction

About

Gibbs, S. The last musketeer   Fic

Richie, Jason

Space flight   629

Richter, Conrad

The light in the forest   Fic

Richter, John J.

Zeller, B. Lincoln in 3-D   92

Richter, Jutta

Beyond the station lies the sea   Fic

Riddell, Chris

Stewart, P. The curse of the night wolf   Fic

Stewart, P. Legion of the Dead   Fic

Stewart, P. Phantom of Blood Alley   Fic

Stewart, P. Return of the emerald skull   Fic

The riddle of the Rosetta Stone. Giblin, J.   493

RIDDLES

The **ring** of Solomon. Stroud, J. Fic

Ringside, 1925. Bryant, J. Fic

Riordan, Rick
 (jt. auth) Collar, O. The Red Pyramid 741.5
 The battle of the Labyrinth Fic
 The lightning thief Fic
 The lost hero Fic
 The Serpent's Shadow Fic
 The throne of fire Fic

Riordan, Rick
 (jt. auth) Collar, O. The Red Pyramid 741.5
 The battle of the Labyrinth Fic
 The last Olympian Fic
 The lightning thief Fic
 The lost hero Fic
 The maze of bones Fic
 The Sea of Monsters Fic
 The son of Neptune Fic
 The throne of fire Fic
 The Titan's curse Fic
 Vespers rising Fic
 Venditti, R. The lightning thief: the graphic novel 741.5

Riot. Myers, W. D. Fic

RIOT CONTROL
 See also Crowds; Riots

RIOTS
 Mara, W. Civil unrest in the 1960s 303.6

RIOTS
 See also Crime; Freedom of assembly; Offenses against public safety

RIOTS -- FICTION
 Myers, A. Tulsa burning Fic
 Myers, W. D. Riot Fic

RIOTS -- UNITED STATES
 Miller, C. C. Backlash 305.8

RIOTS -- UNITED STATES -- HISTORY -- 20TH CENTURY
 Miller, C. C. Backlash 305.8

Rip tide. Falls, K. Fic

RIPOFFS *See* Fraud

Ripple. Hubbard, A. Fic

Riptide. Scheibe, L. Fic

The **rise** and fall of American slavery. McNeese, T. 326

The **rise** and fall of Mount Majestic. Trafton, J. Fic

The **rise** and fall of Senator Joe McCarthy. Giblin, J. C. 92

Rise of a hero. Bell, H. Fic

The **rise** of Jim Crow. Haskins, J. 305.8

The **rise** of the cities, 1820-1920. Collier, C. 307.76

Rise of the huntress. Fic

The **Rise** of the Soviet Union. 947.084

Rise of the thinking machines. VanVoorst, J. 629.8

The **rise** of the wolf. Jobling, C. Fic

The **rising** star of Rusty Nail. Blume, L. M. M. Fic

Rising storm. Hunter, E. Fic

RISK
 See also Economics

RISK-TAKING (PSYCHOLOGY)
 Braun, L. W. Risky business 027.62
 Hugel, B. I did it without thinking 155.5

RISK-TAKING (PSYCHOLOGY)
 See also Psychology

Risky business. Braun, L. W. 027.62

Rissa Bartholomew's declaration of independence. Comerford, L. B. Fic

Ritchie, Donald A.
 Our Constitution 342

The **rites** & wrongs of Janice Wills. Pearson, J. Fic

Ritschel, John
 The kickboxing handbook 796.8

Ritter, John H.
 The boy who saved baseball Fic
 Choosing up sides Fic
 The desperado who stole baseball Fic

The **rivalry.** Feinstein, J. Fic

Rivals. Green, T. Fic

The **river.** Beaufrand, M. J. Fic

The **river.** Paulsen, G. Fic

The **river** between us. Peck, R. Fic

RIVER DOLPHINS
 Montgomery, S. Encantado 599.53

RIVER ECOLOGY
 Lynette, R. River food chains 577.6

RIVER ECOLOGY
 See also Ecology

River food chains. Lynette, R. 577.6

River of dreams. Talbott, H. 974.7

River of words. 808.81

RIVER POLLUTION *See* Water pollution

River roads west. Roop, P. 386

River secrets. Hale, S. Fic

Rivera, Diego, 1886-1957
    About
 Bernier-Grand, C. T. Diego 811
 Hillstrom, K. Diego Rivera 92
 Rubin, S. G. Diego Rivera 759.972

Rivers. Burnham, L. 551.48

RIVERS
 See also Physical geography; Water; Waterways

RIVERS
 Burnham, L. Rivers 551.48
 Roop, P. River roads west 386

RIVERS -- FICTION
 Ceccarelli, D. The Yawning Rabbit River Chronicle Fic

Rivers of fire. Carman, P. Fic

The **Rivers** of Zadaa. MacHale, D. J. Fic

Rizal, José 1861-1896
    About

ROCK AND ROLL MUSIC *See* Rock music

The **rock** and the river. Magoon, K.   **Fic**

Rock band [series]

  Witmer, S. Bookings & gigs   **781.66**

  Witmer, S. Drums, keyboards, and other instruments   **786**

  Witmer, S. Guitars & bass   **787.87**

  Witmer, S. History of rock bands   **781.66**

  Witmer, S. Managing your band   **781.66**

  Witmer, S. Recording   **781.66**

  Witmer, S. The show   **781.66**

  Witmer, S. Songwriting   **782.42**

Rock climbing. Wurdinger, S. D.   **796.52**

ROCK CLIMBING *See* Mountaineering

ROCK DRAWINGS, PAINTINGS, AND ENGRAVINGS

    See also Archeology; Prehistoric art

ROCK MUSIC

  George-Warren, H. Shake, rattle, & roll   **781.66**

  Goodmark, R. Girls rock   **781.66**

  Handyside, C. Rock   **781.66**

  Kallen, S. A. The history of rock and roll   **781.66**

  Kenney, K. L. Cool rock music   **781.66**

  Mead, W. The alternative rock scene   **781.66**

  Nichols, T. Punk rock etiquette   **781.66**

  Tanner, M. Flat-out rock   **781.66**

  Witmer, S. Bookings & gigs   **781.66**

  Witmer, S. Drums, keyboards, and other instruments   **786**

  Witmer, S. Guitars & bass   **787.87**

  Witmer, S. Managing your band   **781.66**

  Witmer, S. Recording   **781.66**

  Witmer, S. The show   **781.66**

  Witmer, S. Songwriting   **782.42**

ROCK MUSIC

    See also Music; Popular music

ROCK MUSIC -- ENCYCLOPEDIAS

  The Rolling Stone encyclopedia of rock & roll   **781.66**

ROCK MUSIC -- FICTION

  Briant, E. I am (not) the walrus   **Fic**

ROCK MUSIC -- GRAPHIC NOVELS

  Emerson, S. Zebrafish   **741.5**

ROCK MUSIC -- HISTORY AND CRITICISM

  Kallen, S. A. The history of rock and roll   **781.66**

  Witmer, S. History of rock bands   **781.66**

ROCK MUSICIANS

  Aberback, B. Black Sabbath   **781.66**

  Anderson, J. J. John Lennon   **92**

  Bowe, B. J. The Ramones   **781.66**

  Burlingame, J. Aerosmith   **781.66**

  Burlingame, J. John Lennon   **92**

  Burlingame, J. Kurt Cobain   **92**

  Collins, T. Elvis   **92**

  Gelfand, D. E. Jimi Hendrix   **92**

  Golio, G. Jimi: sounds like a rainbow: a story of young Jimi Hendrix

  Hampton, W. Elvis Presley   **92**

  Micklos, J. Elvis Presley   **92**

  Partridge, E. John Lennon   **92**

  Pratt, M. Michael Jackson   **92**

  Rappaport, D. John's secret dreams   **92**

  Roberts, J. The Beatles   **781.66**

  Slavicek, L. C. Carlos Santana   **92**

  Spitz, B. Yeah! yeah! yeah!   **920**

  Willett, E. Jimi Hendrix   **92**

ROCK MUSICIANS -- BIOGRAPHY

  George-Warren, H. Shake, rattle, & roll   **781.66**

ROCK MUSICIANS -- ENGLAND -- BIOGRAPHY

  Behnke, A. M. Death of a dreamer   **782.421**

ROCK MUSICIANS -- ENGLAND -- BIOGRAPHY

  Behnke, A. M. Death of a dreamer   **782.421**

ROCK MUSICIANS -- FICTION

  Farrar, J. Rules to rock by   **Fic**

  John, A. Five flavors of dumb   **Fic**

  Scott, M. Freefall   **Fic**

ROCK MUSICIANS -- POLITICAL ACTIVITY

  Behnke, A. M. Death of a dreamer   **782.421**

ROCK SPRINGS MASSACRE, ROCK SPRINGS, WYO., 1885

  Yep, L. The traitor   **Fic**

Rock your . . . [series]

  Torres, L. Rock your party   **745.54**

  Torres, L. Rock your room   **746**

  Torres, L. Rock your school stuff   **745.5**

  Torres, L. Rock your wardrobe   **646.4**

Rock your party. Torres, L.   **745.54**

Rock your room. Torres, L.   **746**

Rock your school stuff. Torres, L.   **745.5**

Rock your wardrobe. Torres, L.   **646.4**

Rockefeller, John D. (John Davison), 1839-1937

About

  Segall, G. John D. Rockefeller   **338.7**

Rocket boys. Hickam, H. H.   **629.1**

ROCKET FLIGHT *See* Space flight

ROCKET PLANES

    See also High speed aeronautics; Space vehicles

ROCKETRY

  Miller, R. Rockets   **621.43**

  Otfinoski, S. Rockets   **621.43**

  Skurzynski, G. This is rocket science   **629.4**

ROCKETRY

    See also Aeronautics; Astronautics

Rockets. Otfinoski, S.   **621.43**

Rockets. Miller, R.   **621.43**

ROCKETS (AERONAUTICS)

  Miller, R. Rockets   **621.43**

  Otfinoski, S. Rockets   **621.43**

ROCKETS (AERONAUTICS)

Rosen, Renee

Every crooked pot — Fic

Rosenberg, Aaron

The Civil War — 920

Rosenberg, Liz

(ed) The Invisible ladder — 811

(ed) Light-gathering poems — 808.81

Rosenthal, Beth

(ed) Bullying — 302.3

Rosenthal, Joe, 1911-2006

About

Bradley, J. Flags of our fathers — 940.54

Burgan, M. Raising the flag — 940.54

Rosenwald, Laurie

All the wrong people have self esteem — 646.7

ROSES

See also Flowers

ROSETTA STONE

See also Hieroglyphics

ROSH HA-SHANAH

See also Jewish holidays

Rosie and Mrs. America. Gourley, C. — 305.4

Rosie O'Donnell's crafty U. O'Donnell, R. — 745.5

Rosie the riveter. Colman, P. — 331.4

Rosinsky, Natalie M.

Ancient China — 931

Graphic content! — 741.5

Hinduism — 294.5

Judaism — 296

Write your own biography — 808

Write your own fairy tale — 808.3

Write your own graphic novel — 741.5

Write your own myth — 808.3

Write your own tall tale — 808.3

Rosoff, Meg

There is no dog — Fic

Ross, Edmund Gibson, 1826-1907

About

Kennedy, J. F. Profiles in courage — 920

Ross, Elizabeth

Belle epoque — Fic

Ross, Jeff

The drop — Fic

Ross, Kathy

Earth-friendly crafts — 745.5

Ross, Stewart

Into the unknown — 910.4

Hiroshima — 940.54

Moon: science, history, and mystery — 629.45

Pearl Harbor — 940.54

Sports technology — 688.7

Ross, Val

The road to there — 912

You can't read this — 028

Ross-Stroud, Catherine

Janet McDonald — 813

Rossetti, Rinsai

The girl with borrowed wings — Fic

Rossi, Ann

Bright ideas — 609

Rossi, Veronica

Under the never sky — Fic

Rossig, Wolfgang

Karl Marx — 92

Roten, Lindsay Grace

Webb, L. S. Holidays of the world cookbook for students — 641.5

Webb, L. S. The multicultural cookbook for students — 641.5

Roth, Rita

The story road to literacy — 372.6

Roth, Terri

About

Carson, M. K. Emi and the rhino scientist — 599.66

Rothman, Julia

Farm anatomy — 630

Rottman, Gordon L.

The most daring raid of the Civil War — 973.7

Rottman, S. L.

Out of the blue — Fic

The **rottweiler**. Biniok, J. — 636.7

ROUTES OF TRADE See Trade routes

ROVING VEHICLES (ASTRONAUTICS)

Rusch, E. The mighty Mars rovers — 523.43

Siy, A. Cars on Mars — 629.43

Rowan Hood returns. Springer, N. — Fic

Rowan Hood, outlaw girl of Sherwood Forest. Springer, N. — Fic

Rowell, Rebecca

YouTube — 006.7

Rowell, Victoria

Tag, toss & run — 790.1

Rowen, Michelle

Reign check — Fic

Reign or shine — Fic

ROWING

See also Athletics; Boats and boating; Exercise; Sports; Water sports

Rowland-Warne, L.

Costume — 391

Rowling, J. K., 1965-

Harry Potter and the deathly hallows — Fic

Harry Potter and the Chamber of Secrets — Fic

Harry Potter and the Goblet of Fire — Fic

Harry Potter and the Half-blood Prince — Fic

Harry Potter and the Order of the Phoenix — Fic

Harry Potter and the prisoner of Azkaban — Fic

Harry Potter and the Sorcerer's Stone — Fic

The tales of Beedle the Bard — S C

Rowling, J. K., 1965-

About

Colbert, D. The magical worlds of Harry Potter — 823

Rules. Lord, C.   **Fic**

The **rules** for disappearing. Elston, A.   **Fic**

The **rules** of survival. Werlin, N.   **Fic**

Rules of the game. Maddox, M.   **811**

The **rules** of the universe by Austin W. Hale. Vaupel, R.   **Fic**

The **rules** to be cool. Dougherty, K.   **395.1**

Rules to rock by. Farrar, J.   **Fic**

Rumble & spew. Donovan, S.   **612.3**

Rumford, James
   Beowulf   **398.2**

Rumi. Demi   **92**

Rumley, Crickett
   Never sit down in a hoopskirt and other things I learned in Southern belle hell   **Fic**

RUMOR -- FICTION
   Grace, A. In too deep   **Fic**

Rump. Shurtliff, L.   **Fic**

Run wild! Danks, F.   **790.1**

Run, boy, run. Orlev, U.   **Fic**

Runaway. Draanen, W. v.   **Fic**

Runaway. Cabot, M.   **Fic**

RUNAWAY ADULTS
   See also Desertion and nonsupport; Missing persons

RUNAWAY CHILDREN
   See also Children; Homeless persons; Missing children

RUNAWAY CHILDREN -- FICTION
   Barnaby, H. Wonder show   **Fic**
   Cushman, K. Will Sparrow's road   **Fic**
   The **runaway** dragon. Coombs, K.   **Fic**
   Runaway girl: the artist Louise Bourgeois. Greenberg, J.   **92**
   The **runaway** princess. Coombs, K.   **Fic**

RUNAWAY SLAVES *See* Fugitive slaves

RUNAWAY TEENAGERS
   See also Homeless persons; Missing persons; Teenagers

RUNAWAY TEENAGERS -- FICTION
   Doctorow, C. Pirate cinema   **Fic**
   Leavitt, M. My book of life by Angel   **Fic**
   Rush, J. Altered   **Fic**

RUNAWAYS
   Tocher, T. Chief Sunrise, John McGraw, and me   **Fic**
   Whelan, G. Chu Ju's house   **Fic**

RUNAWAYS -- FICTION
   Armistead, C. Being Henry David   **Fic**
   Barnaby, H. Wonder show   **Fic**
   Cushman, K. Will Sparrow's road   **Fic**
   Leavitt, M. My book of life by Angel   **Fic**
   Ross, E. Belle epoque   **Fic**
   Rush, J. Altered   **Fic**

Runemarks. Harris, J.   **Fic**

Runholt, Susan

Adventure at Simba Hill   **Fic**

The mystery of the third Lucretia   **Fic**

Rescuing Seneca Crane   **Fic**

Runner. Newton, R.   **Fic**

RUNNERS (ATHLETES)
   Anderson, J. J. Wilma Rudolph   **92**
   Burlingame, J. Jesse Owens   **92**
   Gigliotti, J. Jesse Owens   **92**
   McDougall, C. Jesse Owens   **92**

RUNNING
   Eason, S. Free running   **613.7**

RUNNING
   See also Track athletics

RUNNING -- FICTION
   Childs, T. L. Oh. My. Gods.   **Fic**
   Messner, K. The brilliant fall of Gianna Z   **Fic**
   Myers, W. D. Darius & Twig   **Fic**
   Newton, R. Runner   **Fic**
   Van Draanen, W. The running dream   **Fic**
   The **running** dream. Van Draanen, W.   **Fic**
   Running loose. Crutcher, C.   **Fic**
   Running on the cracks. Donaldson, J.   **Fic**

Runyon, Brent
   The burn journals   **92**
   Surface tension   **Fic**

Runyon, Brent

About

   Runyon, B. The burn journals   **92**

Rupp, Rebecca
   After Eli   **Fic**
   Octavia Boone's big questions about life, the universe, and everything   **Fic**

RURAL LIFE *See* Country life; Farm life; Outdoor life

RURAL SCHOOLS
   See also Public schools; Schools

RURAL-URBAN MIGRATION *See* Internal migration

RURAL-URBAN MIGRATION -- UNITED STATES -- HISTORY -- 20TH CENTURY
   Harris, L. L. The great migration north, 1910-1970   **307.2**

Rusch, Elizabeth
   Eruption!   **363.34**
   The mighty Mars rovers   **523.43**

Rush, Jennifer
   Altered   **Fic**

Russell Simmons. Lommel, C.   **92**

Russell Simmons. Baughan, B.   **92**

Russell, Carrie
   Complete copyright for K-12 librarians and educators   **346.730**

Russell, Christopher
   Dogboy   **Fic**

Russell, Henry
   Germany   **943**

Space exploration, Primary sources   629.4

SABBATH

See also Judaism

Sabbeth, Carol

Monet and the impressionists for kids   759.05

Van Gogh and the Post-Impressionists for kids   759.05

SABIN VACCINE *See* Poliomyelitis vaccine

SABOTAGE

See also Offenses against public safety; Strikes; Subversive activities; Terrorism

Sabotaged. Haddix, M. P.   Fic

Sabriel. Nix, G.   Fic

Sabuda, Robert

Sharks and other sea monsters   560

Sacagawea. Green, C. R.   978.004

Sacagawea. Berne, E. C.   92

Sacagawea. Crosby, M. T.   92

Sacagawea, b. 1786

About

Berne, E. C. Sacagawea   92

Crosby, M. T. Sacagawea   92

Green, C. R. Sacagawea   978.004

O'Dell, S. Streams to the river, river to the sea   Fic

Saccardi, Marianne

Books that teach kids to write   028.5

Sachar, Louis

The cardturner   Fic

Holes   Fic

Small steps   Fic

SACRED ART *See* Religious art

Sacred mountain. Taylor-Butler, C.   954.9

Sacred places. Yolen, J.   811

Sacred scars. Duey, K.   Fic

Sacred texts [series]

Brown, A. The Bible and Christianity   220

Ganeri, A. The Ramayana and Hinduism   294.5

The **sacrifice.** Duble, K. B.   Fic

Sadek, Ademola O.

(jt. auth) Indovino, S. C. Italy   945

Saenz, Benjamin Alire

He forgot to say good-bye   Fic

SAFARIS

See also Adventure and adventurers; Outdoor recreation; Scientific expeditions; Travel

Safe. Shaw, S.   Fic

Safe house. Heneghan, J.   Fic

SAFE SEX IN AIDS PREVENTION

See also AIDS (Disease) -- Prevention; Sexual hygiene

Safe social networking. Schwartz, H. E.   302.302

Safekeeping. Hesse, K.   Fic

SAFETY EDUCATION

Child and youth security sourcebook   362.7

Doeden, M. Safety smarts   613.608

Nelson, S. K. Stay safe!   613.6

Raatma, L. Safety in your neighborhood   613.6

Safety in your neighborhood. Raatma, L.   613.6

Safety smarts. Doeden, M.   613.608

Safford, Barbara Ripp

Guide to reference materials for school library media centers   011.6

Saffy's angel. McKay, H.   Fic

Safire, William

(comp) Lend me your ears   808.85

Saga. Kostick, C.   Fic

Saga of the Sioux. Zimmerman, D. J.   970.004

SAGAS

See also Folklore; Literature; Old Norse literature; Scandinavian literature

Sage, Angie

Darke   Fic

Flyte   Fic

Magyk   Fic

The Magykal papers   Fic

Physik   Fic

Queste   Fic

Syren   Fic

The **Sahara.** Heinrichs, A.   966

Sahwira. Marsden, C.   Fic

Sailing. Storey, R.   797.1

SAILING

Storey, R. Sailing   797.1

SAILING

See also Ships; Water sports

SAILING -- FICTION

Appelt, K. Keeper   Fic

Bukiet, M. J. Undertown   Fic

Herlong, M. The great wide sea   Fic

Stevenson, R. H. Dead in the water   Fic

Welsh, M. L. Heart of stone   Fic

Welsh, M. L. Mistress of the Storm   Fic

Sailing the unknown.   Fic

SAILORS

Kraske, R. Marooned   92

Llanas, S. G. Women of the U.S. Navy   359

SAILORS

See also Military personnel; Naval art and science; Navies

SAILORS -- FICTION

Russell, K. Chasing the Nightbird   Fic

SAILORS -- FICTION *See* Sea stories

SAILORS' LIFE *See* Sailors; Seafaring life

Saint Lucia. Orr, T.   972.98

SAINT PETERSBURG (RUSSIA) -- HISTORY -- SIEGE, 1941-1944 -- FICTION

Whelan, G. Burying the sun   Fic

SAINT PETERSBURG (RUSSIA) -- SIEGE, 1941-1944 -- FICTION

Whelan, G. Burying the sun   Fic

Saint training. Fixmer, E.   Fic

Saint-Exupery, Antoine de, 1900-1944

SASQUATCH

Ape-men   001.9

SASQUATCH

See also Monsters; Mythical animals

SASQUATCH -- GRAPHIC NOVELS

TenNapel, D. R. Flink   741.5

Satanta, Kiowa Chief, 1820-1878

About

Freedman, R. Indian chiefs   970.004

Satch & me. Gutman, D.   Fic

Satchel Paige. Sturm, J.   741.5

SATELLITE COMMUNICATION SYSTEMS

See Artificial satellites in telecommunication

Satellites. Miller, R.   629.44

Satellites. Johnson, R. L.   629.46

SATELLITES, ARTIFICIAL *See* Artificial satellites

SATIRE

Adams, D. The hitchhiker's guide to the galaxy   Fic

Adams, D. Life, the universe, and everything   Fic

Adams, D. The restaurant at the end of the universe   Fic

Adams, D. So long, and thanks for all the fish   Fic

Anderson, M. T. Feed   Fic

The hobbit   Fic

Huxley, A. Brave new world   Fic

Orwell, G. Nineteen eighty-four   Fic

SATIRE

See also Literature; Rhetoric; Wit and humor

SATIRE, AMERICAN *See* American satire

SATIRICAL FICTION

Adams, D. Mostly harmless   Fic

SATIRISTS

Caravantes, P. A great and sublime fool   92

Diorio, M. A. L. A student's guide to Mark Twain   813

Ellis, S. From reader to writer   028

Fleischman, S. The trouble begins at 8   92

Hamilton, J. C. S. Lewis   92

Houle, M. M. Mark Twain   92

Mark Twain   818

Sonneborn, L. Mark Twain   92

Satrapi, Marjane, 1969-

About

Schroeder, H. L. A reader's guide to Marjane Satrapi's Persepolis   813

Sattler, Helen Roney

The book of North American owls   598.9

Saturday night dirt. Weaver, W.   Fic

Saturn. Miller, R.   523.46

Saturn. Hicks, T. A.   523.4

SATURN (PLANET)

See also Planets

SAUCERS, FLYING *See* Unidentified flying objects

SAUCES

See also Cooking

SAUDI ARABIA

Tracy, K. We visit Saudi Arabia   953.8

The **Saudi** royal family. Reed, J.   920

SAUK INDIANS

Bowes, J. P. Black Hawk and the War of 1832 973.5

Saul, Laya

Ways to help after a natural disaster   363.34

Ways to help disadvantaged youth   362.7

We visit Israel   956.94

Saunders, Barbara R.

Ivan Pavlov   92

Saunders, Craig

What is the theory of plate tectonics?   551.1

Saunders, Kate

Beswitched   Fic

The Whizz Pop Chocolate Shop   Fic

Saunders, N.

Who invented the periodic table?   546

SAUSAGES

Watson, S. Mystery meat   613.2

Sauvant, Henriette

(ed) Rapunzel and other magic fairy tales   398.2

The **savage**. Almond, D.   Fic

The **savage** damsel and the dwarf. Morris, G.   Fic

A **savage** thunder. Murphy, J.   973.7

Saval, Malina

The secret lives of boys   155.5

Savannas. Toupin, L.   577.4

Save the Earth science experiments. Harris, E. S.   507.8

The **saver**. Ravel, E.   Fic

Saving. Morrison, J.   332.024

SAVING AND INVESTMENT

Healey, A. Making the trade   332.6

Morrison, J. Saving   332.024

Thompson, H. Investing money   332.6

SAVING AND INVESTMENT

See also Capital; Economics; Personal finance; Wealth

SAVING AND THRIFT *See* Saving and investment

Saving birds. Salmansohn, P.   333.95

Saving children from the Holocaust. Byers, A.   940.53

Saving endangered species [series]

Feinstein, S. The chimpanzee   599.8

Saving Juliet. Selfors, S.   Fic

Saving manatees. Swinburne, S. R.   599.5

Saving our living Earth [series]

Fridell, R. Earth-friendly energy   333.79

Fridell, R. Protecting Earth's water supply   363.7

Johnson, R. L. Understanding global warming   363.7

Rapp, V. Protecting Earth's air quality   363.7

Rapp, V. Protecting Earth's land   333.72

Welsbacher, A. Earth-friendly design   745.2

SCHOOL SPORTS -- UNITED STATES -- RULES

Diagram Group Sports rules on file   **796**

SCHOOL STORIES

Abdel-Fattah, R. Does my head look big in this? **Fic**

Abdel-Fattah, R. Ten things I hate about me   **Fic**

Abrahams, P. Reality check   **Fic**

Ackley, A. Sign language   **Fic**

Adler, E. Sweet 15   **Fic**

Alender, K. Bad girls don't die   **Fic**

Alexie, S. The absolutely true diary of a part-time Indian   **Fic**

Allison, J. Gilda Joyce: the Ladies of the Lake **Fic**

Alvarez, J. How Tia Lola learned to teach   **Fic**

Amato, M. Invisible lines   **Fic**

Anderson, K. D. Kiss & Make Up   **Fic**

Anderson, L. H. Speak   **Fic**

Angleberger, T. Darth Paper strikes back   **Fic**

Appelt, K. Kissing Tennessee and other stories from the Stardust Dance   **S C**

Archer, J. Through her eyes   **Fic**

Armstrong, K. The gathering   **Fic**

Ashby, A. Fairy bad day   **Fic**

Ashby, A. Zombie queen of Newbury High   **Fic**

Asher, J. The future of us   **Fic**

Asher, J. Thirteen reasons why   **Fic**

Atkins, C. Alt ed   **Fic**

Atkinson, E. From Alice to Zen and everyone in between   **Fic**

Avi Nothing but the truth   **Fic**

Ayres, K. Macaroni boy   **Fic**

Balliett, B. The Wright 3   **Fic**

Bancks, T. Mac Slater hunts the cool   **Fic**

Baratz-Logsted, L. Crazy beautiful   **Fic**

Barnes, J. L. The Squad: perfect cover   **Fic**

Barnes, J. The Squad: killer spirit   **Fic**

Barnholdt, L. Sometimes it happens   **Fic**

Baskin, N. R. Anything but typical   **Fic**

Basye, D. E. Heck   **Fic**

Bates, M. Awkward   **Fic**

Bauer, A. C. E. Come Fall   **Fic**

Bauer, J. Peeled   **Fic**

Beil, M. D. The Red Blazer Girls: the ring of Rocamadour   **Fic**

Beil, M. The Red Blazer Girls: the mistaken masterpiece   **Fic**

Bennett, O. The Allegra Biscotti collection   **Fic**

Benoit, C. You   **Fic**

Benway, R. The extraordinary secrets of April, May and June   **Fic**

Berk, J. The dark days of Hamburger Halpin **Fic**

Bigelow, L. J. Starting from here   **Fic**

Block, F. L. The waters & the wild   **Fic**

Bloor, E. London calling   **Fic**

Bloor, E. A plague year   **Fic**

Boie, K. The princess trap   **Fic**

Boyd, M. Will   **Fic**

Brande, R. Evolution, me, & other freaks of nature   **Fic**

Brande, R. Fat Cat   **Fic**

Brennan, S. R. Team Human   **Fic**

Brewer, H. The chronicles of Vladimir Tod: eighth grade bites   **Fic**

Brewer, H. The chronicles of Vladimir Tod: ninth grade slays   **Fic**

Brewer, H. Eleventh grade burns   **Fic**

Brewer, H. Tenth grade bleeds   **Fic**

Brian, K. Geek magnet   **Fic**

Brody, J. My life undecided   **Fic**

Budhos, M. Ask me no questions   **Fic**

Burton, R. Leaving Jetty Road   **Fic**

Butcher, K. Cheat   **Fic**

Butler, D. H. The truth about Truman School   **Fic**

Buyea, R. Because of Mr. Terupt   **Fic**

Buyea, R. Mr. Terupt falls again   **Fic**

Calloway, C. Confessions of a First Daughter   **Fic**

Carriger, G. Etiquette & espionage   **Fic**

Carter, A. R. Love, football, and other contact sports   **S C**

Carvell, M. Sweetgrass basket   **Fic**

Carvell, M. Who will tell my brother?   **Fic**

Castan, M. The price of loyalty   **Fic**

Castellucci, C. Rose sees red   **Fic**

Castle, J. The beginning of after   **Fic**

Chaltas, T. Because I am furniture   **Fic**

Chapman, L. Flawless   **Fic**

Chatterton, M. The Brain finds a leg   **Fic**

Cheva, C. DupliKate   **Fic**

Childs, T. L. Oh. My. Gods.   **Fic**

Clark, C. G. Secrets of Greymoor   **Fic**

Cleary, B. Dear Mr. Henshaw   **Fic**

Coben, H. Shelter   **Fic**

Cody, M. Powerless   **Fic**

Colasanti, S. So much closer   **Fic**

Colasanti, S. Something like fate   **Fic**

Collins, T. Notes from a totally lame vampire **Fic**

Comerford, L. B. Rissa Bartholomew's declaration of independence   **Fic**

Cooney, C. B. Code orange   **Fic**

Cooper, I. Angel in my pocket   **Fic**

Cormier, R. Beyond the chocolate war   **Fic**

Cormier, R. The chocolate war   **Fic**

Cornered   **Fic**

Corrigan, E. Accomplice   **Fic**

Coy, J. Box out   **Fic**

Coy, J. Crackback   **Fic**

Coy, J. Love of the game   **Fic**

Crawford, B. Carter finally gets it   **Fic**

Creech, S. Bloomability   **Fic**

Creech, S. Hate that cat   **Fic**

Creech, S. Love that dog   **Fic**

Crewe, M. Give up the ghost   **Fic**

Crutcher, C. Deadline   **Fic**

Crutcher, C. Ironman	**Fic**	Gantos, J. Heads or tails	**Fic**
Crutcher, C. Running loose	**Fic**	Gantos, J. Jack on the tracks	**Fic**
Crutcher, C. Whale talk	**Fic**	Gantos, J. Joey Pigza swallowed the key	**Fic**
Cummings, P. Blindsided	**Fic**	Garcia, K. Beautiful creatures	**Fic**
Cushman, K. The loud silence of Francine Green	**Fic**	Garden, N. Endgame	**Fic**
		Gensler, S. The revenant	**Fic**
Daly, C. Flirt Club	**Fic**	George, M. Looks	**Fic**
Daneshvari, G. Class is not dismissed!	**Fic**	Gephart, D. How to survive middle school	**Fic**
Daneshvari, G. School of Fear	**Fic**	Gilman, C. Professor Gargoyle	**Fic**
Danziger, P. The cat ate my gymsuit	**Fic**	Gorman, C. Games	**Fic**
De Goldi, K. The 10 p.m. question	**Fic**	Gosselink, J. The defense of Thaddeus A. Ledbetter	**Fic**
De Lint, C. The blue girl	**Fic**	Grabenstein, C. The smoky corridor	**Fic**
Delsol, W. Frost	**Fic**	Gratz, A. Samurai shortstop	**Fic**
Delsol, W. Stork	**Fic**	Green, T. Baseball great	**Fic**
Derting, K. Desires of the dead	**Fic**	Greenwald, T. Charlie Joe Jackson's guide to not reading	**Fic**
Despain, B. The dark Divine	**Fic**	Griffin, A. The Julian game	**Fic**
Dessen, S. 1. What happened to goodbye	**Fic**	Griffin, C. J. Nowhere to run	**Fic**
Deuker, C. Gym candy	**Fic**	Grimes, N. Bronx masquerade	**Fic**
Deuker, C. High heat	**Fic**	Grimes, N. Planet Middle School	**Fic**
Deuker, C. Painting the black	**Fic**	Hagerup, K. Markus and the girls	**Fic**
Deuker, C. Payback time	**Fic**	Han, J. Shug	**Fic**
DeVillers, J. Lynn Visible	**Fic**	Hannan, P. My big mouth	**Fic**
Dionne, E. The total tragedy of a girl named Hamlet	**Fic**	Hannigan, K. True (. . . sort of)	**Fic**
Dowell, F. O. R. Ten miles past normal	**Fic**	Hansen, J. The gift-giver	**Fic**
Dowell, F. O. The kind of friends we used to be	**Fic**	Hautman, P. The big crunch	**Fic**
Draanen, W. v. Sammy Keyes and the wedding crasher	**Fic**	Hautman, P. Blank confession	**Fic**
Drama	**741.5**	Hawkins, R. Hex Hall	**Fic**
Draper, S. M. The Battle of Jericho	**Fic**	Heldring, T. Roy Morelli steps up to the plate	**Fic**
Draper, S. M. Fire from the rock	**Fic**	Henderson, J. Vampire rising	**Fic**
Draper, S. M. Just another hero	**Fic**	Henderson, J. Voice of the undead	**Fic**
Draper, S. M. November blues	**Fic**	Higgins, M. G. Bi-Normal	**Fic**
Duey, K. Sacred scars	**Fic**	Hiranandani, V. The whole story of half a girl	**Fic**
Duncan, L. Killing Mr. Griffin	**Fic**	Hodkin, M. The unbecoming of Mara Dyer	**Fic**
Edwardson, D. D. My name is not easy	**Fic**	Holm, J. L. Middle school is worse than meatloaf	**Fic**
Ellis, A. D. This is what I did	**Fic**	Holmes, S. L. Operation Yes	**Fic**
Ellis, D. Bifocal	**Fic**	Houston, J. New boy	**Fic**
Ellsworth, L. Unforgettable	**Fic**	Houtman, J. The reinvention of Edison Thomas	**Fic**
Emond, S. Happyface	**Fic**	Howe, J. Addie on the inside	**Fic**
Erskine, K. Quaking	**Fic**	Howe, J. The misfits	**Fic**
Fehler, G. Beanball	**Fic**	Hrdlitschka, S. Allegra	**Fic**
Ferraiolo, J. D. The big splash	**Fic**	Hurley, T. Ghostgirl	**Fic**
Finneyfrock, K. The sweet revenge of Celia Door	**Fic**	Ibbotson, E. The dragonfly pool	**Fic**
Fitzgerald, D. Soccer chick rules	**Fic**	Jaden, D. Losing Faith	**Fic**
Fixmer, E. Saint training	**Fic**	Jarzab, A. All unquiet things	**Fic**
Flake, S. G. The broken bike boy and the Queen of 33rd Street	**Fic**	Jenkins, A. M. Repossessed	**Fic**
Flake, S. G. The skin I'm in	**Fic**	Jinks, C. Evil genius	**Fic**
Forester, V. The girl who could fly	**Fic**	Johnson, M. The name of the star	**Fic**
Fredericks, M. Head games	**Fic**	Johnson, M. Scarlett fever	**Fic**
Fredericks, M. Love	**Fic**	Jones, T. L. Finding my place	**Fic**
Freitas, D. The possibilities of sainthood	**Fic**	Jones, T. L. Silhouetted by the blue	**Fic**
Fusilli, J. Marley Z and the bloodstained violin	**Fic**	Jones, T. L. Standing against the wind	**Fic**
Gale, E. K. The Bully Book	**Fic**	Jordan, R. The goatnappers	**Fic**
		Juby, S. Getting the girl	**Fic**

Neff, H. H. The fiend and the forge   **Fic**
Neff, H. H. The hound of Rowan   **Fic**
Neff, H. H. The second siege   **Fic**
Nelson, B. Destroy all cars   **Fic**
Nichols, J. Messed up   **Fic**
Nimmo, J. Charlie Bone and the beast   **Fic**
Nimmo, J. Charlie Bone and the castle of mirrors   **Fic**
Nimmo, J. Charlie Bone and the hidden king   **Fic**
Nimmo, J. Charlie Bone and the invisible boy   **Fic**
Nimmo, J. Charlie Bone and the Red Knight   **Fic**
Nimmo, J. Charlie Bone and the shadow   **Fic**
Nimmo, J. Charlie Bone and the time twister   **Fic**
Nimmo, J. Midnight for Charlie Bone   **Fic**
Nixon, J. L. Laugh till you cry   **Fic**
Nolan, H. Crazy   **Fic**
Northrop, M. Trapped   **Fic**
Nothing   **Fic**
Oates, J. C. Big Mouth & Ugly Girl   **Fic**
O'Connell, T. True love, the sphinx, and other unsolvable riddles **Fic**
O'Connor, B. Fame and glory in Freedom, Georgia   **Fic**
O'Dell, K. Agnes Parker . . . girl in progress   **Fic**
O'Dell, K. Agnes Parker . . . keeping cool in middle school **Fic**
Okimoto, J. D. Maya and the cotton candy boy   **Fic**
Omololu, C. J. Dirty little secrets   **Fic**
Ostow, M. So punk rock (and other ways to disappoint your mother) **Fic**
Padian, M. Brett McCarthy: work in progress   **Fic**
Patrick, C. Forgotten   **Fic**
Paulsen, G. Liar, liar   **Fic**
Paulsen, G. The Schernoff discoveries   **Fic**
Paulsen, G. Vote   **Fic**
Pearce, J. As you wish   **Fic**
Pearsall, S. All of the above   **Fic**
Pearson, J. The rites & wrongs of Janice Wills   **Fic**
Perez, M. Dead is a state of mind   **Fic**
Perez, M. Dead is just a rumor   **Fic**
Perez, M. Dead is not an option   **Fic**
Perez, M. Dead is the new black   **Fic**
Perkins, S. Anna and the French kiss   **Fic**
Peters, J. A. Define normal   **Fic**
Petrucha, S. The Rule of Won   **Fic**
Philbin, J. The daughters   **Fic**
Philbin, J. The daughters break the rules   **Fic**
Philbin, J. The daughters take the stage   **Fic**
Pike, A. Illusions   **Fic**
Pinkney, A. D. With the might of angels   **Fic**
Pixley, M. Freak   **Fic**
Preller, J. Bystander   **Fic**
Prose, F. After   **Fic**
Prose, F. Touch   **Fic**
Quick, M. Sorta like a rockstar   **Fic**
Quintero, S. Efrain's secret   **Fic**

Raf, M. The symptoms of my insanity   **Fic**
Railsback, L. Noonie's masterpiece   **Fic**
Randall, T. Dreams of the dead   **Fic**
Randall, T. Spirits of the Noh   **Fic**
Ray, D. Ghost girl   **Fic**
Ray, D. Here lies Linc   **Fic**
Rees, D. C. Vampire High   **Fic**
Rees, D. Vampire High: sophomore year   **Fic**
Repka, J. The clueless girl's guide to being a genius **Fic**
Rhuday-Perkovich, O. 8th grade superzero   **Fic**
Roecker, L. The Liar Society   **Fic**
Roecker, L. The lies that bind   **Fic**
Rowen, M. Reign check   **Fic**
Rowen, M. Reign or shine   **Fic**
Ruby, L. Bad apple   **Fic**
Rue, G. Brand new Emily   **Fic**
Rupp, R. Octavia Boone's big questions about life, the universe, and everything **Fic**
Russell, R. Dead rules   **Fic**
Rylander, C. The fourth stall   **Fic**
Saldin, E. The girls of No Return   **Fic**
Sandell, L. A. A map of the known world   **Fic**
Saunders, K. Beswitched   **Fic**
Schmatz, P. Bluefish   **Fic**
Schmidt, G. D. The Wednesday wars   **Fic**
Schneider, R. Knightley Academy   **Fic**
Schneider, R. The secret prince   **Fic**
Schreiber, E. Vampire kisses 7: Love bites   **Fic**
Schreiber, E. Vampire kisses 8: cryptic cravings   **Fic**
Schumacher, J. Black box   **Fic**
Scott, E. Perfect you   **Fic**
Selfors, S. Coffeehouse angel   **Fic**
Selzer, A. How to get suspended and influence people **Fic**
Selzer, A. I put a spell on you   **Fic**
Shanahan, L. The sweet, terrible, glorious year I truly, completely lost it **Fic**
Shaw, S. One of the survivors   **Fic**
Sheldon, D. The crazy things girls do for love   **Fic**
Sheldon, D. My perfect life   **Fic**
Sherman, D. The BEDMAS conspiracy   **Fic**
Sherman, D. The Magic Mirror of the Mermaid Queen   **Fic**
Shreve, S. The lovely shoes   **Fic**
Shulman, M. Scrawl   **Fic**
Shulman, P. Enthusiasm   **Fic**
Shusterman, N. Antsy does time   **Fic**
Simon, C. Plan B   **Fic**
Singleton, L. J. Dead girl walking   **Fic**
Sitomer, A. L. The downside of being up   **Fic**
Slade, A. G. Jolted   **Fic**
Sones, S. What my girlfriend doesn't know   **Fic**
Sonnenblick, J. After ever after   **Fic**
Sonnenblick, J. Zen and the art of faking it   **Fic**
Soto, G. Accidental love   **Fic**

Crilley, M. Miki Falls, Book One: Spring   **741.5**

Hicks, F. E. The war at Ellsmere   **741.5**

Tamaki, M. Skim   **741.5**

SCHOOL STORIES -- FICTION

Barnholdt, L. Girl meets ghost   **Fic**

Benway, R. Also known as   **Fic**

Booraem, E. Texting the underworld   **Fic**

Crawford, B. Carter's unfocused, one-track mind   **Fic**

Crossan, S. The Weight of Water   **Fic**

Fry, M. The Odd Squad   **Fic**

Kinney, J. Diary of a wimpy kid   **Fic**

Kinney, J. The third wheel   **Fic**

The mighty Quinn   **Fic**

Stemple, A. B.U.G.   **Fic**

Wells, R. Feedback   **Fic**

The **school** story. Clements, A.   **Fic**

SCHOOL SUPERINTENDENTS AND PRINCIPALS

McGhee, M. W. The principal's guide to a powerful library media program   **025.1**

SCHOOL SUPERINTENDENTS AND PRINCIPALS

See also Schools -- Administration

SCHOOL SUPERVISION

See also Schools -- Administration; Teaching

School survival. Gagliardi, T.   **373.1**

School survival. Tym, K.   **371.8**

SCHOOL TEACHING *See* Teaching

SCHOOL VERSE *See* Children's writings

School violence. Parks, P. J.   **371.7**

SCHOOL VIOLENCE

Child and youth security sourcebook   **362.7**

Hester, J. P. Public school safety   **371.7**

Myers, J. J. Responding to cyber bullying   **371.5**

Parks, P. J. School violence   **371.7**

Simons, R. Students in danger   **371.7**

Worth, R. Massacre at Virginia Tech   **364.152**

SCHOOL VIOLENCE

See also Juvenile delinquency; Violence

SCHOOL VIOLENCE -- FICTION

Prose, F. After   **Fic**

SCHOOL VIOLENCE

Schier, H. The causes of school violence   **371.7**

SCHOOL VIOLENCE -- UNITED STATES

Hester, J. P. Public school safety   **371.7**

Schier, H. The causes of school violence   **371.7**

SCHOOL VIOLENCE -- UNITED STATES -- PREVENTION

Hester, J. P. Public school safety   **371.7**

School wide book events. Ray, V. L.   **027.8**

School's out - forever. Patterson, J.   **Fic**

SCHOOL-AGE FATHERS *See* Teenage fathers

SCHOOL-AGE MOTHERS *See* Teenage mothers

Schooled. Korman, G.   **Fic**

SCHOOLGIRLS -- ILLINOIS -- CHICAGO -- DIARIES

Morrison, J. W. Home front girl   **977.3**

SCHOOLS

Erlbach, A. The middle school survival guide **373.1**

Fields, T. After the death of Anna Gonzales   **811**

On the fringe   **S C**

Tym, K. School survival   **371.8**

SCHOOLS -- ADMINISTRATION

Cahill, S. LGBT youth in America's schools **371.826**

Odden, A. R. Improving student learning when budgets are tight   **371.2**

SCHOOLS -- AFGHANISTAN

Mortenson, G. Three cups of tea   **371.82**

SCHOOLS -- CENTRALIZATION

See also Schools -- Administration

SCHOOLS -- DECENTRALIZATION

See also Schools -- Administration

SCHOOLS -- EQUIPMENT AND SUPPLIES

Torres, L. Rock your school stuff   **745.5**

SCHOOLS -- FICTION *See* School stories

SCHOOLS -- FICTION.

Selzer, A. Pirates of the retail wasteland   **Fic**

SCHOOLS -- FINANCE

Odden, A. R. Improving student learning when budgets are tight   **371.2**

SCHOOLS -- GRAPHIC NOVELS

Robbins, T. The drained brains caper   **741.5**

SCHOOLS -- FICTION

Rowling, J. K. Harry Potter and the Goblet of Fire   **Fic**

SCHOOLS -- MANAGEMENT AND ORGANIZATION *See* Schools -- Administration

SCHOOLS -- PAKISTAN

Mortenson, G. Three cups of tea   **371.82**

SCHOOLS -- POETRY

Alexander, E. Miss Crandall's School for Young Ladies and Little Misses of Color   **811**

George, K. O. Swimming upstream   **811**

Lewis, J. P. Countdown to summer   **811**

Wayland, A. H. Girl coming in for a landing   **811**

SCHOOLS AND LIBRARIES *See* Libraries and schools

Schorer, Suki

Put your best foot forward   **792.8**

Schouten, Peter

Long, J. A. Feathered dinosaurs   **567.9**

Schraff, Anne E.

A boy called Twister   **Fic**

Ellen Ochoa   **92**

Ida B. Wells-Barnett   **92**

Schrag, Ariel

(ed) Stuck in the middle   **741.5**

Schram, Peninnah

(ed) Oberman, S. Solomon and the ant   **398.2**

Schreck, Karen

Verne, J. 20,000 leagues under the sea   **Fic**
   See also Adventure and adventurers; Adventure fiction; Fiction

SEA STORIES -- GRAPHIC NOVELS

Weing, D. Set to sea   **741.5**

SEA TRAVEL *See* Ocean travel

Sea turtles. Lockwood, S.   **597.92**

SEA TURTLES

Lockwood, S. Sea turtles   **597.92**

SEA URCHINS

Gilpin, D. Starfish, urchins & other echinoderms   **593**

SEA WATER

   See also Water

SEA WATER CONVERSION

   See also Water purification

The **sea** wolves. Golden, C.   **Fic**

The **sea** wolves. McAllister, I.   **599.77**

SEA-SHORE *See* Seashore

SEAFARING LIFE

   See also Adventure and adventurers; Manners and customs; Voyages and travels

SEAFARING LIFE -- FICTION

Bunting, E. The pirate captain's daughter   **Fic**
Conly, J. L. Murder afloat   **Fic**
Duble, K. B. Quest   **Fic**
Flanagan, J. The hunters   **Fic**
Flanagan, J. The invaders   **Fic**
Frazier, A. Everlasting   **Fic**
Frederick, H. V. The voyage of Patience Goodspeed   **Fic**
Golding, J. Cat o' nine tails   **Fic**
Lawlor, L. Dead reckoning   **Fic**
Lawrence, I. The buccaneers
Meyer, L. A. Bloody Jack   **Fic**
Meyer, L. A. In the belly of The Bloodhound   **Fic**
Meyer, L. A. The mark of the golden dragon   **Fic**
Meyer, L. A. Rapture of the deep   **Fic**
Meyer, L. A. Under the Jolly Roger   **Fic**
Meyer, L. A. Viva Jacquelina!   **Fic**
Meyer, L. A. The wake of the Lorelei Lee   **Fic**
Pignat, C. Wild geese   **Fic**
Somper, J. Empire of night   **Fic**

SEAFARING LIFE -- GRAPHIC NOVELS

Weing, D. Set to sea   **741.5**

SEAFOOD

Llewellyn, C. Cooking with meat and fish   **641.6**

SEAFOOD

   See also Food; Marine resources

Seahorses, pipefishes, and their kin. Miller, S. S.   **597**

SEALS (ANIMALS)

   See also Mammals; Marine mammals

SEALS (ANIMALS) -- FICTION

Brooks, L. Selkie girl   **Fic**

SEALS (NUMISMATICS)

Shearer, B. F. State names, seals, flags, and symbols   **929.9**
   See also Heraldry; History; Inscriptions; Numismatics

SEAMANSHIP *See* Navigation

SEAMEN *See* Sailors

Sean Griswold's head. Leavitt, L.   **Fic**

The **seance.** Lawrence, I.   **Fic**

Search and destroy. Hughes, D.   **Fic**

SEARCH AND RESCUE OPERATIONS *See* Rescue work

SEARCH DOGS

   See also Working dogs

SEARCH ENGINES *See* Web search engines

Search for the golden moon bear. Montgomery, S.   **599.78**

The **search** for the Red Dragon. Owen, J. A.   **Fic**

The **search** for WondLa. DiTerlizzi, T.   **Fic**

SEARCHES AND SEIZURES

Carson, B. Understanding your right to freedom from searches   **323.44**
Galiano, D. The Fourth Amendment   **345**

Searching for dragons. Wrede, P. C.   **Fic**

SEARCHING THE INTERNET *See* Internet searching

Sears list of subject headings.   **025.4**

SEAS

   See also Earth; Physical geography; Water

Seashore. Parker, S.   **577.7**

SEASHORE

Carson, R. The edge of the sea   **577.7**
Parker, S. Seashore   **577.7**

SEASHORE -- FICTION

One white dolphin   **Fic**

SEASHORE ECOLOGY

   See also Ecology

SEASIDE RESORTS -- FICTION

Hocking, A. Wake   **Fic**
A **season** of gifts. Peck, R.   **Fic**
Season of ice. Les Becquets, D.   **Fic**
Season of rage. Cooper, J.   **323.1**
Season of secrets. Nicholls, S.   **Fic**

SEASONS

Art, H. W. Woodswalk   **508**

SEASONS

   See also Astronomy; Climate; Meteorology

SEATTLE (WASH.) -- FICTION

John, A. Five flavors of dumb   **Fic**
Renn, D. Tokyo heist   **Fic**
Trueman, T. Life happens next   **Fic**

SEAWEEDS *See* Algae

Seba, Jaime

Coming out   **306.76**
Gallup guides for youth facing persistent prejudice   **306.76**
Gay characters in theatre, movies, and television: new roles, new attitudes   **791.43**

Miller, R. Seven wonders of the rocky planets and their moons **523.4**

Woods, M. Seven wonders of Ancient Asia **950**

Seven wonders beyond the solar system. Miller, R. **523.8**

Seven wonders of Ancient Asia. Woods, M. **950**

Seven wonders of space phenomena. Ward, D. J. **520**

Seven wonders of space technology. Bortz, A. B. **629.4**

Seven wonders of the gas giants and their moons. Miller, R. **523.4**

Seven wonders of the rocky planets and their moons. Miller, R. **523.4**

The **Seventh** Amendment. Furgang, K. **347**

Severance, John B.

Thomas Jefferson **973.4**

Winston Churchill **941.084**

SEVERE STORMS

Evans, B. It's raining fish and spiders **551.6**

Sew teen. Zent, S. **646.4**

SEWAGE DISPOSAL

See also Public health; Refuse and refuse disposal

Sewall, May Wright, 1844-1920

About

Boomhower, R. E. Fighting for equality **92**

Seward, Pat

Morocco **964**

SEWERAGE

Macaulay, D. Underground **624**

SEWERAGE

See also House drainage; Municipal engineering; Plumbing; Sanitary engineering

SEWERAGE -- FICTION

Bukiet, M. J. Undertown **Fic**

SEWERS *See* Sewerage

SEWING

Plumley, A. P. Sewing school **646.2**

Warwick, E. Injeanuity **746**

Zent, S. Sew teen **646.4**

Sewing school. Plumley, A. P. **646.2**

SEX

See also Human behavior

SEX -- PHYSIOLOGICAL ASPECTS

See also Biology

SEX -- PSYCHOLOGICAL ASPECTS

See also Psychology

SEX CRIMES

Simons, R. Gender danger **362.88**

SEX CRIMES

See also Crime; Sex

SEX DISCRIMINATION

Blumenthal, K. Let me play **796**

Gold, S. D. Roberts v. Jaycees **342**

Stone, T. L. Almost astronauts **629.45**

See also Discrimination; Sexism

SEX DISCRIMINATION AGAINST WOMEN

Stone, T. L. Almost astronauts **629.45**

SEX EDUCATION

Bailey, J. Sex, puberty, and all that stuff **612.6**

Bell, R. Changing bodies, changing lives **613.9**

Brynie, F. H. 101 questions about reproduction **612.6**

Cole, J. Asking about sex & growing up **613.9**

Forssberg, M. Sex for guys **306.7**

Harris, R. H. It's perfectly normal **613.9**

Jukes, M. The guy book **305.235**

Madaras, L. The what's happening to my body? book for boys **612.6**

Madaras, L. The what's happening to my body? book for girls **612.6**

McCoy, K. The teenage body book **613**

Murray, C. Sexpectations **613.96**

Rand, C. Human reproduction **612.6**

Sexual health information for teens **613.9**

Sex for guys. Forssberg, M. **306.7**

SEX IN MASS MEDIA

See also Mass media

SEX IN POPULAR CULTURE

See also Popular culture

SEX INSTRUCTION *See* Sex education

SEX INSTRUCTION FOR BOYS

Jukes, M. The guy book **305.235**

SEX INSTRUCTION FOR BOYS

Jukes, M. The guy book **305.235**

SEX INSTRUCTION FOR CHILDREN WITH MENTAL DISABILITIES

Couwenhoven, T. The boys' guide to growing up **613**

SEX INSTRUCTION FOR TEENAGERS

Jukes, M. The guy book **305.235**

SEX INSTRUCTION FOR YOUTH

McCoy, K. The teenage body book **613**

SEX ORGANS *See* Reproductive system

SEX PRESELECTION

See also Reproduction

SEX REASSIGNMENT SURGERY

See also Surgery

SEX REASSIGNMENT SURGERY -- FICTION

Farizan, S. If you could be mine **Fic**

SEX ROLE

The Full spectrum **306.76**

Macy, S. Wheels of change **796.6**

Male and female roles: opposing viewpoints **305.3**

SEX ROLE *See* Gender role

SEX ROLE -- GRAPHIC NOVELS

Shimura Takako Wandering son **Fic**

Sex, brains, and video games. Burek Pierce, J. **027.62**

Sex, puberty, and all that stuff. Bailey, J. **612.6**

SEXISM

See also Attitude (Psychology); Prejudices

Sexpectations. Murray, C. **613.96**

SEXUAL ABUSE *See* Child sexual abuse; Sex crimes; Sexual harassment

SEXUAL ASSAULT *See* Rape

SEXUAL BEHAVIOR

Harris, A. R. Do you love me? **613.9**

SEXUAL BEHAVIOR IN ANIMALS

See also Animal behavior; Sex -- Physiological aspects

SEXUAL CRIMES *See* Sex crimes

SEXUAL ETHICS

See also Ethics

SEXUAL HARASSMENT

Strauss, S. L. Sexual harassment and bullying **302.34**

SEXUAL HARASSMENT -- PREVENTION

Strauss, S. L. Sexual harassment and bullying **302.34**

Sexual harassment and bullying. Strauss, S. L. **302.34**

SEXUAL HARASSMENT IN EDUCATION

Strauss, S. L. Sexual harassment and bullying **302.34**

Sexual health information for teens. **613.9**

SEXUAL HYGIENE

Murray, C. Sexpectations **613.96**

SEXUAL HYGIENE

See also Hygiene

SEXUAL IDENTITY *See* Gender role

SEXUAL MINORITIES -- CIVIL RIGHTS -- ARIZONA -- TUCSON

Hernandez, D. They call me a hero **979.1**

SEXUAL MINORITIES -- CIVIL RIGHTS -- UNITED STATES

Seba, J. Gallup guides for youth facing persistent prejudice **306.76**

SEXUAL MINORITIES -- EDUCATION

Cahill, S. LGBT youth in America's schools **371.826**

SEXUAL MINORITIES -- BIBLIOGRAPHY

Naidoo, J. C. Rainbow family collections **028.1**

SEXUAL MINORITIES IN LITERATURE

Naidoo, J. C. Rainbow family collections **028.1**

SEXUAL OFFENSES *See* Sex crimes

SEXUAL ORIENTATION

The Full spectrum **306.76**

Sexuality and teens. Feinstein, S. **306.7**

SEXUALLY ABUSED CHILDREN *See* Child sexual abuse

Sexually transmitted diseases. Dougherty, T. **616.95**

Sexually transmitted diseases. Currie-McGhee, L. K. **614.5**

SEXUALLY TRANSMITTED DISEASES

Collins, N. Frequently asked questions about STDs **616.95**

Currie-McGhee, L. K. Sexually transmitted diseases **614.5**

Dougherty, T. Sexually transmitted diseases **616.95**

Yancey, D. STDs **616.95**

SEXUALLY TRANSMITTED DISEASES

See also Communicable diseases

SEXUALLY TRANSMITTED DISEASES

Collins, N. Frequently asked questions about STDs **616.95**

SEXUALLY TRANSMITTED DISEASES -- MISCELLANEA

Collins, N. Frequently asked questions about STDs **616.95**

SEXUALLY TRANSMITTED DISEASES -- PREVENTION

See also Sexual hygiene

Seymour Simon's extreme oceans. Simon, S. **551.46**

Sfar, Joann

Dungeon Vol. 1: Duck Heart **741.5**

The little prince **741.5**

SHAANXI SHENG (CHINA) -- ANTIQUITIES

O'Connor, J. The emperor's silent army **931**

Shabanu. Staples, S. F. **Fic**

Shackleton's stowaway. McKernan, V. **Fic**

Shackleton, Ernest Henry Sir, 1874-1922

About

Armstrong, J. Shipwreck at the bottom of the world **919.8**

Johnson, K. The Endurance expedition **998**

Johnson, R. L. Ernest Shackleton **92**

Koestler-Grack, R. A. Sir Ernest Shackleton **92**

McKernan, V. Shackleton's stowaway **Fic**

Shade's children. Nix, G. **Fic**

SHADES AND SHADOWS

See also Drawing

Shades of London [series]

Johnson, M. The madness underneath **Fic**

Shadow. Moss, J. **Fic**

Shadow and bone. Bardugo, L. **Fic**

Shadow children [series]

Haddix, M. P. Among the enemy **Fic**

The **shadow** door. Bannister (Person) **741.5**

The **shadow** dragons. Owen, J. A. **Fic**

The **shadow** hunt. Langrish, K. **Fic**

The **shadow** of Malabron. Wharton, T. **Fic**

Shadow of the dragon [series]

O'Hearn, K. Elspeth **Fic**

O'Hearn, K. Kira **Fic**

Shadow on the mountain. Preus, M. **Fic**

Shadow on the sun. Gill, D. M. **Fic**

SHADOW PANTOMIMES AND PLAYS

See also Amateur theater; Pantomimes; Puppets and puppet plays; Shadow pictures; Theater

SHADOW PICTURES

See also Amusements

The **Shadow** Project. Brennan, H. **Fic**

The **shadow** society. Rutkoski, M. **Fic**

The **shadow** speaker. Okorafor, N. **Fic**

The **Shadow** Spies. Bannister (Person)   **741.5**
Shadow wolf. Lasky, K.   **Fic**
Shadowcry. Burtenshaw, J.   **Fic**
Shadoweyes.   **741.5**
Shadowfell. Marillier, J.   **Fic**
The **Shadowing:** Hunted. Slater, A.   **Fic**
SHADOWPACT (FICTIONAL CHARACTERS)
   See also Fictional characters; Superheroes
Shadows cast by stars. Knutsson, C.   **Fic**
Shadows in the twilight. Mankell, H.   **Fic**
The **shadows** of Ghadames. Stolz, J.   **Fic**
Shahan, Sherry
  Death mountain   **Fic**
  Ice island   **Fic**
Shake, rattle, & roll. George-Warren, H.   **781.66**
SHAKERS -- FICTION
  Durrant, L. Imperfections   **Fic**
  Peck, R. N. A day no pigs would die   **Fic**
Shakespeare explained [series]
  Krueger, S. H. The tempest   **822.3**
  Mussari, M. Othello   **822.3**
Shakespeare kids. Cox, C.   **792.9**
Shakespeare makes the playoffs. Koertge, R.   **Fic**
The **Shakespeare** stealer. Blackwood, G. L.   **Fic**
Shakespeare stories [I]-II. Garfield, L.   **822.3**
Shakespeare's scribe. Blackwood, G. L.   **Fic**
Shakespeare's secret. Broach, E.   **Fic**
Shakespeare's spy. Blackwood, G. L.   **Fic**
Shakespeare, William, 1564-1616
About
  Aliki William Shakespeare & the Globe   **792.09**
  All the world's a stage   **Fic**
  Appignanesi, R. As you like it   **741.5**
  Appignanesi, R. Hamlet   **741.5**
  Appignanesi, R. Romeo and Juliet   **741.5**
  Blackwood, G. L. Shakespeare's scribe   **Fic**
  Blackwood, G. L. The Shakespeare stealer   **Fic**
  Coville, B. William Shakespeare's A midsummer night's dream   **822.3**
  Coville, B. William Shakespeare's Romeo and Juliet   **822.3**
  Cox, C. Shakespeare kids   **792.9**
  Harper, S. The Juliet club   **Fic**
  Henry V   **741.5**
  Hinds, G. King Lear   **741.5**
  Klein, L. M. Lady Macbeth's daughter   **Fic**
  Krueger, S. H. The tempest   **822.3**
  Lives of the writers   **809**
  Macbeth   **741.5**
  MacDonald, B. Wicked Will   **Fic**
  McDermott, K. William Shakespeare   **822.3**
  The merchant of Venice   **741.5**
  Mussari, M. Othello   **822.3**
  Nettleton, P. H. William Shakespeare   **822.3**
  One hundred and eleven Shakespeare monologues   **822.3**

Packer, T. Tales from Shakespeare   **822.3**
Raum, E. Twenty-first-century Shakespeare   **822.3**
Rees, C. The fool's girl   **Fic**
Schmidt, G. D. The Wednesday wars   **Fic**
Selfors, S. Saving Juliet   **Fic**
Twelfth night   **741.5**
Sobran, J. A midsummer night's dream   **822.3**
Hinds, G. The merchant of Venice   **741.5**
McKeown, A. Julius Caesar   **822.3**
Appignanesi, R. The tempest   **741.5**
Appignanesi, R. A midsummer night's dream   **741.5**
Cooper, S. King of shadows   **Fic**
Stanley, D. Bard of Avon: the story of William Shakespeare   **822.3**
Garfield, L. Shakespeare stories [I]-II   **822.3**
SHAKESPEARE, WILLIAM, 1564-1616 -- ALLUSIONS
  See also Allusions
SHAKESPEARE, WILLIAM, 1564-1616 -- AUTHORSHIP
  See also Authorship
SHAKESPEARE, WILLIAM, 1564-1616 -- DICTIONARIES
  See also Encyclopedias and dictionaries
SHAKESPEARE, WILLIAM, 1564-1616 -- ETHICS
  See also Ethics
SHAKESPEARE, WILLIAM, 1564-1616 -- PORTRAITS
  See also Portraits
SHAKESPEARE, WILLIAM, 1564-1616 -- PSYCHOLOGY
  See also Psychology
SHAKESPEARE, WILLIAM, 1564-1616 -- QUOTATIONS
  See also Quotations
SHAKESPEARE, WILLIAM, 1564-1616 -- RELIGION
  See also Religion
SHAKESPEARE, WILLIAM, 1564-1616 -- STAGE HISTORY
  See also Theater
Shakespeare, William, 1564-1616 -- Adaptations
About
  Appignanesi, R. A midsummer night's dream   **741.5**
  Appignanesi, R. As you like it   **741.5**
  Appignanesi, R. Hamlet   **741.5**
  Appignanesi, R. Romeo and Juliet   **741.5**
  Appignanesi, R. The tempest   **741.5**
  Coville, B. William Shakespeare's A midsummer night's dream   **822.3**
  Coville, B. William Shakespeare's Romeo and Juliet   **822.3**
  Garfield, L. Shakespeare stories [I]-II   **822.3**
  Henry V   **741.5**
  Hinds, G. King Lear   **741.5**

Hinds, G. The merchant of Venice   741.5
Macbeth   741.5
McKeown, A. Julius Caesar   822.3
The merchant of Venice   741.5
Packer, T. Tales from Shakespeare   822.3
Twelfth night   741.5

Shakespeare, William, 1564-1616 -- Criticism

About

Krueger, S. H. The tempest   822.3
Mussari, M. Othello   822.3
Sobran, J. A midsummer night's dream   822.3

Shakespeare, William, 1564-1616 -- Fiction

About

All the world's a stage   Fic
Blackwood, G. L. Shakespeare's scribe   Fic
Blackwood, G. L. The Shakespeare stealer   Fic
Cooper, S. King of shadows   Fic
Harper, S. The Juliet club   Fic
Klein, L. M. Lady Macbeth's daughter   Fic
MacDonald, B. Wicked Will   Fic
Rees, C. The fool's girl   Fic
Schmidt, G. D. The Wednesday wars   Fic
The secrets of Shakespeare's grave   Fic
Selfors, S. Saving Juliet   Fic

Shakespeare, William, 1564-1616 -- Study and teaching

About

Cox, C. Shakespeare kids   792.9

Shakespeare, William, 1564-1616 -- Work -- Henry V

About

Henry V   741.5

Shakespeare, William, 1564-1616 -- Work -- MacBeth

About

Macbeth   741.5

Shakespeare, William, 1564-1616 -- Work -- Merchant of Venice

About

The merchant of Venice   741.5

Shakespeare, William, 1564-1616 -- Work -- Twelfth night

About

Twelfth night   741.5
Shaking the foundation. Johnson, S. A.   576.8
Shakur, Tupac

About

Golus, C. Tupac Shakur   92
Harris, A. R. Tupac Shakur   92
Woodson, J. After Tupac and D Foster   Fic
SHAMANISM
Kallen, S. A. Shamans   201
   See also Religions
Shamans. Kallen, S. A.   201
SHAMANS
Nelson, S. D. Black Elk's vision   92

SHAMANS -- FICTION
Friesner, E. Spirit's princess   Fic
SHAME
   See also Emotions
Shan, Darren
Bec   Fic
Blood beast   Fic
Dark calling   Fic
Death's Shadow   Fic
Demon apocalypse   Fic
Demon thief   Fic
Lord Loss   Fic
Slawter   Fic
Wolf Island   Fic
Shanahan, Lisa
The sweet, terrible, glorious year I truly, completely lost it   Fic
Shandler, Sara
Ophelia speaks   305.235
Shange, Ntozake
Freedom's a-callin' me   811
We troubled the waters   811
Shanghai shadows. Ruby, L.   Fic
SHAPE
   See also Concepts; Geometry; Perception
Shapera, Paul M.
Iran's religious leaders   955
Shapers of America [series]
Crosby, M. T. Sacagawea   92
Shapeshifter. Bennett, H.   Fic
Shapeshifters.   292
SHAPESHIFTING -- FICTION
Armstrong, K. L. Loki's wolves   Fic
Bell, H. Traitor's son   Fic
Rossetti, R. The girl with borrowed wings   Fic
Shaping modern science [series]
Cohen, M. What is cell theory?   571.6
Hyde, N. What is germ theory?   615
McLean, A. What is atomic theory?   539.7
O'Leary, D. What are Newton's laws of motion?   531
Saunders, C. What is the theory of plate tectonics?   551.1
Walker, R. What is the theory of evolution?   576.8
Shaping the earth. Patent, D. H.   550
Shapiro, Ouisie
Bullying and me   302.3
Shards and Ashes.   S C
SHARED HOUSING
   See also Housing
Sharenow, Rob
The Berlin Boxing Club   Fic
Sharenow, R. The Berlin Boxing Club   Fic
My mother the cheerleader   Fic
SHARES OF STOCK *See* Stocks
Shark. Macquitty, M.   597.3

Shark girl. Bingham, K.   Fic
Shark life. Benchley, P.   597
Sharks.   597.3
SHARKS
  Benchley, P. Shark life   597
  Capuzzo, M. Close to shore   597
  Cerullo, M. M. The truth about great white sharks   597
  Hamilton, S. L. Eaten by a shark   597
  Mallory, K. Swimming with hammerhead sharks   597.3
  Sharks   597.3
Sharks & boys. Tracy, K.   Fic
SHARKS -- FICTION
  Monninger, J. Wish   Fic
SHARKS
  Macquitty, M. Shark   597.3
Sharks and other sea monsters. Sabuda, R.   560
Sharon Creech. Baptiste, T.   92
Sharon Creech. Tighe, M. A.   813
Sharon Creech. Carroll, P. S.   813
Sharon M. Draper. Hinton, K.   813
Sharp shot. Higgins, J.   Fic
Sharp, Anne Wallace
  A dream deferred   323.1
  Ice hockey   796.962
  Malcolm X and Black pride   92
  Separate but equal   379
Sharp, S. Pearl
  The slave trade and the middle passage   326
Sharrar, Jack F.
  (ed) Great monologues for young actors   808.82
  (ed) Great scenes for young actors from the stage   808.82
Shattered bones. Markle, S.   617.1
Shattered youth in Nazi Germany. Altman, L. J.   940.53
Shattered: stories of children and war.   S C
The **shattering.** Healey, K.   Fic
Shaughnessy, Edward L.
  Exploring the life, myth, and art of ancient China   931
Shaw, Daniel
  (jt. auth) Keithley, M. Eco-tracking   577
Shaw, Elizabeth M.
  (ed) Brannen, D. E. Supreme Court drama   347
Shaw, Liane
  Fostergirls   Fic
Shaw, Susan
  One of the survivors   Fic
  Safe   Fic
  Tunnel vision   Fic
SHAWNEE INDIANS
  Zimmerman, D. J. Tecumseh   92
She dared. Butts, E.   920
She said/she saw. McClintock, N.   Fic

She touched the world: Laura Bridgman, deaf-blind pioneer. Alexander, S. H.   92
She's all that! Bryant, M. E.   292
Shea, George
  A reader's guide to Chinua Achebe's Things fall apart   823
Shea, Kitty
  Teens in Canada   971
Shea, Therese
  The robotics club   629.8
  The Sixth Amendment   345
Shearer, Barbara Smith
  Shearer, B. F. State names, seals, flags, and symbols   929.9
Shearer, Benjamin F.
  State names, seals, flags, and symbols   929.9
Sheba, Queen of
About
  Lucks, N. Queen of Sheba   92
Shecter, Vicky Alvear
  Cleopatra rules!   92
  Cleopatra's moon   Fic
Sheehan, Anna
  A long, long sleep
Sheehan, Patricia
  Cote d'Ivoire   966.68
  Luxembourg   949.35
Sheehan, Sean
  Angola   967.3
  Auschwitz   940.53
  Cameroon   967.11
  Cuba   972.91
  Endangered species   333.95
  Jamaica   972.92
  Lebanon   956.92
  Malta   945.8
  Trinidad & Tobago   972.983
  Why did the Holocaust happen?   940.53
Sheen, Barbara
  Foods of Chile   641.5
  Foods of Cuba   641.5
  Foods of Egypt   641.5
  Foods of Ireland   641.5
  Foods of Kenya   641.5
  Foods of Korea   641.5
  Foods of Peru   641.5
  MRSA   616.9
  Prostate cancer   616.99
SHEEP
See also Domestic animals; Mammals
Sheinkin, Steve
  Bomb   623.4
  Lincoln's Grave Robbers   973.709
  The notorious Benedict Arnold   92
  Which way to the wild West?   978
Sheinmel, Alyssa B.

SHOJO-AI

> *See also* Manga

SHONA (AFRICAN PEOPLE)

Hall, M. Great Zimbabwe   **968.91**

SHONEN MANGA

Hotta, Y. Hikaru No Go, Volume 1   **741.5**

Konomi, T. The Prince of Tennis, Vol. 1   **741.5**

Sakura, K. Dragon drive. Vol. 1, D-break   **741.5**

SHONEN MANGA

> *See also* Manga

SHONEN-AI

> *See also* Manga

Shooting star. McKissack, F.   **Fic**

SHOOTING STARS *See* Meteors

Shooting the moon. Dowell, F. O.   **Fic**

Shooting video to make learning fun. Green, J. **778.5**

SHOOTINGS IN SCHOOLS *See* School shootings

SHOPPERS' GUIDES *See* Consumer education; Shopping

SHOPPING CENTERS AND MALLS

> *See also* Commercial buildings; Retail trade

SHOPPING CENTERS AND MALLS -- FICTION

Esckilsen, E. E. The last mall rat   **Fic**

Mass, W. Heaven looks a lot like the mall   **Fic**

Short. Schwartz, J.   **612.6**

SHORT FILMS

> *See also* Motion pictures

SHORT PLAYS *See* One act plays

Short scenes and monologues for middle school actors. Surface, M. H.   **808.82**

The **short** seller. Weissman, E. B.   **Fic**

SHORT STORIES

13   **S C**

666: the number of the beast   **S C**

Abrahams, P. Up all night   **S C**

Alexander, L. The foundling and other tales of Prydain   **S C**

American eyes   **S C**

Amnesty International Free?: stories about human rights   **S C**

Appelt, K. Kissing Tennessee and other stories from the Stardust Dance   **S C**

Asimov, I. I, robot   **S C**

Aspin, D. Ordinary miracles   **S C**

The August House book of scary stories   **398.2**

Avi Strange happenings   **S C**

Avi What do fish have to do with anything? and other stories   **S C**

Baseball crazy: ten short stories that cover all the bases   **S C**

The beastly bride   **S C**

Best shorts   **S C**

Brooks, B. All that remains   **Fic**

Carter, A. R. Love, football, and other contact sports   **S C**

The chronicles of Harris Burdick   **S C**

Cleavage   **S C**

The Color of absence   **813**

Compestine, Y. C. A banquet for hungry ghosts **S C**

Cornered   **Fic**

Corsets & clockwork   **S C**

Coville, B. Oddest of all   **S C**

Cowboy stories   **S C**

The Coyote Road   **808.8**

Crutcher, C. Athletic shorts   **S C**

Dahl, R. Skin and other stories   **S C**

Dare to be scared   **S C**

Del Negro, J. Passion and poison   **S C**

Delacre, L. Salsa stories   **S C**

Delaney, J. The Spook's tale and other horrors **S C**

Destination unexpected: short stories   **S C**

Does this book make me look fat?   **S C**

Don't cramp my style   **S C**

Ellis, D. Lunch with Lenin and other stories   **S C**

Enthralled   **S C**

Estevis, A. Down Garrapata road   **S C**

Every man for himself   **S C**

Explorer   **Fic**

Face relations   **S C**

Fear: 13 stories of suspense and horror   **S C**

Firebirds   **S C**

Firebirds rising   **S C**

Firebirds soaring   **S C**

Flake, S. G. Who am I without him?   **S C**

Flake, S. G. You don't even know me   **808.8**

Flanagan, J. The lost stories   **S C**

Fleischman, P. Graven images   **S C**

Friends   **S C**

Full house   **S C**

Gaiman, N. M is for magic   **S C**

Gallo, D. R. Owning it   **S C**

Geektastic   **S C**

Give me shelter   **S C**

Gothic!   **S C**

Growing up Latino   **810**

Guys read: funny business   **S C**

Hague, M. The Book of dragons   **808.83**

Half-human   **S C**

Half-minute horrors   **S C**

Hearne, B. G. The canine connection: stories about dogs and people   **S C**

Holt, K. W. Part of me   **S C**

Horowitz, A. Horowitz horror   **S C**

Horowitz, A. More Horowitz horror   **S C**

Join in   **813**

Kiss me deadly   **S C**

Lay-ups and long shots   **S C**

Le Guin, U. K. Tales from Earthsea   **S C**

Leaving home: stories   **808.8**

Lester, J. Long journey home: stories from black

SHORT STORIES -- BY INDIVIDUAL AUTHORS

Spinelli, J. The library card   S C

Tan, S. Lost & found   S C

Tan, S. Tales from outer suburbia   S C

Taylor, L. Lips touch   S C

Vande Velde, V. All Hallows' Eve   S C

SHORT STORIES -- COLLECTIONS

Tomo   S C

Under the moons of Mars   Fic

SHORT STORIES -- COLLECTIONS

Abrahams, P. Up all night   S C

Amnesty International Free?: stories about human rights   S C

Baseball crazy: ten short stories that cover all the bases   S C

The beastly bride   S C

Cleavage   S C

Does this book make me look fat?   S C

Every man for himself   S C

Firebirds rising   S C

Firebirds soaring   S C

Friends   S C

Full house   S C

Gallo, D. R. Owning it   S C

Geektastic   S C

Guys read: funny business   S C

Hague, M. The Book of dragons   808.83

Half-minute horrors   S C

Join in   813

Kiss me deadly   S C

Life on Mars: tales from the new frontier   S C

Magic in the mirrorstone   S C

Moccasin thunder   S C

Na, A. No such thing as the real world   S C

Noyes, D. The restless dead   S C

Our White House   975.3

Outside rules   S C

Pierce, T. Young warriors   S C

Sideshow   S C

This family is driving me crazy   S C

Ultimate sports   813

What are you afraid of?   S C

You don't have a clue   S C

SHORT STORIES, AMERICAN

The Color of absence   813

McKinley, R. Water: tales of elemental spirits   S C

Places I never meant to be   813

Under the moons of Mars   Fic

SHORT STORIES, ENGLISH

Dahl, R. Skin and other stories   S C

McKinley, R. Water: tales of elemental spirits   S C

SHORT STORY

See also Authorship; Fiction; Literature

SHORT STORY WRITERS

Abrams, D. Anthony Horowitz   92

Abrams, D. Ernest J. Gaines   92

Avi The man who was Poe   813

Bankston, J. Ray Bradbury   92

Blasingame, J. B. Gary Paulsen   813

Bledsoe, L. J. How to survive in Antarctica   998

Brown, J. K. Ursula K. Le Guin   92

Caravantes, P. A great and sublime fool   92

Caravantes, P. Writing is my business   92

Cook, J. Natural writer: a story about Marjorie Kinnan Rawlings   813

Cooling, W. D is for Dahl   823

Dahl, R. Boy: tales of childhood   92

Dahl, R. More about Boy   92

Darraj, S. M. Gabriel Garcia Marquez   92

Delano, P. When I was a boy Neruda called me Policarpo   92

Diorio, M. A. L. A student's guide to Mark Twain   813

Ellis, S. From reader to writer   028

Fleischman, S. The trouble begins at 8   92

Fritz, J. Harriet Beecher Stowe and the Beecher preachers   813

Gill, D. M. Graham Salisbury   92

Golden, C. The wild   Fic

Grant, A. Robert Louis Stevenson's Kidnapped   741.5

Grant, A. Robert Louis Stevenson's Strange case of Dr. Jekyll and Mr. Hyde   741.5

Hart, J. Native son: the story of Richard Wright   92

Hinds, M. J. A reader's guide to Richard Wright's Black boy   813

Hinton, K. Angela Johnson   813

Hoppa, J. Isaac Asimov   92

Houle, M. M. Mark Twain   92

Klimowski, A. Dr. Jekyll and Mr. Hyde   741.5

Lange, K. E. Nevermore   92

Latham, D. David Almond   823

Lazo, C. E. F. Scott Fitzgerald   813

Levy, D. Richard Wright   92

Litwin, L. B. A reader's guide to Zora Neale Hurston's Their eyes were watching god   813

Litwin, L. B. Zora Neale Hurston   92

Loos, P. A reader's guide to Amy Tan's The joy luck club   813

Lyons, M. E. Sorrow's kitchen   92

Macdonald, F. Kidnapped   741.5

Madden, K. Harper Lee   92

Marcovitz, H. Scott O'Dell   92

Mark Twain   818

McArthur, D. A student's guide to Edgar Allan Poe   813

McArthur, D. A student's guide to William Faulkner   813

McClellan, M. Madeleine L'Engle   813

McNeese, T. Jorge Luis Borges   92

Meltzer, M. Edgar Allan Poe   92

Meltzer, M. Nathaniel Hawthorne   92

Meltzer, M. Willa Cather   92

Murphy, J. Across America on an emigrant train **385**

Mussari, M. Amy Tan **92**

Mussari, M. Haruki Murakami **92**

O'Keefe, S. From China to America **92**

Paulsen, G. Caught by the sea **818**

Paulsen, G. Guts **813**

Paulsen, G. How Angel Peterson got his name **813**

Paulsen, G. My life in dog years **813**

Paulsen, G. Woodsong **796.5**

Pingelton, T. J. A student's guide to Ernest Hemingway **813**

Poe, E. A. The raven and other poems **741.5**

Raven, N. Bram Stoker's Dracula **741.5**

Reef, C. Ernest Hemingway **92**

Russell, P. C. Coraline **741.5**

Sapet, K. Rhythm and folklore **92**

Shea, G. A reader's guide to Chinua Achebe's Things fall apart **823**

Shields, C. J. I am Scout: the biography of Harper Lee **92**

Sonneborn, L. Mark Twain **92**

Stefoff, R. Stephen King **92**

Stefoff, R. Jack London **813**

Thomas, J. C. The skull talks back and other haunting tales **398.2**

Tyson, E. S. Orson Scott Card **813**

Varmer, H. Hans Christian Andersen **92**

Warrick, K. C. Sandra Cisneros **92**

Whitelaw, N. Dark dreams **92**

Whiting, J. Ernest Hemingway **92**

Wooldridge, C. N. The brave escape of Edith Wharton **92**

Yu Chun Little Green **951.05**

Short, Elizabeth, 1924-1947
About
Haugen, B. The Black Dahlia **364.152**

Shortelle, Dennis
Gardner, R. Slam dunk! science projects with basketball **530**

The **Shoshone.** Bial, R. **970.004**

SHOSHONE INDIANS
Berne, E. C. Sacagawea **92**
Freedman, R. Indian chiefs **970.004**

SHOSHONI INDIANS
Bial, R. The Shoshone **970.004**
Crosby, M. T. Sacagawea **92**
Freedman, R. Indian chiefs **970.004**

SHOSHONI INDIANS -- BIOGRAPHY
Green, C. R. Sacagawea **978.004**

SHOSHONI INDIANS -- HISTORY
Bial, R. The Shoshone **970.004**

SHOSHONI INDIANS -- SOCIAL LIFE AND CUSTOMS
Bial, R. The Shoshone **970.004**

SHOSHONI WOMEN -- BIOGRAPHY

Green, C. R. Sacagawea **978.004**

Shot down. Mary-Todd, J. **Fic**

SHOTGUNS
See also Firearms

Shots at sea. Matthews, T. L. **Fic**

Should drilling be permitted in the Arctic National Wildlife Refuge? **333.95**

Shout, sister, shout! Orgill, R. **920**

The **show.** Witmer, S. **781.66**

Show me America [series]
Worth, R. George Catlin **92**

Show me the money. Hall, A. **332.024**

Show off. Hines-Stephens, S. **790.1**

SHOW WINDOWS
See also Advertising; Decoration and ornament; Windows

Showalter, Gena
Intertwined **Fic**

SHOWERS (PARTIES)
See also Parties

SHOWING OFF
See also Human behavior

Shreve, Susan
The lovely shoes **Fic**

SHRINES
Yolen, J. Sacred places **811**

SHRUBLAND ECOLOGY
Burnie, D. Shrublands **577.3**

Shrublands. Burnie, D. **577.3**

SHRUBLANDS
Burnie, D. Shrublands **577.3**

SHRUBS
See also Plants; Trees

Shug. Han, J. **Fic**

Shugo chara! Momo no Tane **741.5**

Shulman, Mark
Scrawl **Fic**

Shulman, Polly
Enthusiasm **Fic**
The Grimm Legacy **Fic**
The Wells Bequest **Fic**

Shurtliff, Liesl
Rump **Fic**

Shusterman, Neal, 1962-
Shusterman, N. Unwind **Fic**
Antsy does time **Fic**
Bruiser **Fic**
Darkness creeping **S C**
Downsiders **Fic**
Everfound **Fic**
Everlost **Fic**
Everwild **Fic**
Full tilt **Fic**
The Schwa was here **Fic**
UnWholly **Fic**
Unwind **Fic**

Shut up! Reynolds, M.   Fic

Shute, Carolyn
  (ed) Best shorts   S C

Shuter, Jane
  Ancient China   931
  Resistance to the Nazis   943.086

Shutout. Halpin, B.   Fic

Shuttlesworth, Fred L., 1922-2011
                    About
  Brimner, L. D. Black & white   323.1

SHYNESS
        See also Emotions

SHYNESS -- FICTION
  Crowley, C. A little wanting song   Fic
  Markus and Diana

SIAMESE TWINS -- FICTION
  Orenstein, D. G. The secret twin   Fic

Siberell, Anne
  Bravo! brava! a night at the opera   782.1

SIBLING RIVALRY
        See also Child psychology; Siblings
The sibling slam book.   306.8

SIBLINGS
  The sibling slam book   306.8
  Skotko, B. Fasten your seatbelt   616.85
  Winchester, E. Sisters and brothers   306.8

SIBLINGS
        See also Family

SIBLINGS -- FICTION
  Armstrong, A. Racing the moon   Fic
  Cotler, S. Cheesie Mack is cool in a duel   Fic
  Gewirtz, A. R. Zebra forest   Fic
  Knowles, J. See you at Harry's   Fic
  Myers, W. D. A star is born   Fic
  Sullivan, M. Dear Blue Sky   Fic

SIBLINGS -- FICTION
  Hopkinson, N. The Chaos   Fic
  Pennypacker, S.   The summer of the gypsy
    moths   Fic

SIBLINGS OF PRESIDENTS
  Aronson, M. Robert F. Kennedy   92
  Sapet, K. Ted Kennedy   92

Sibyl-Anne vs. Ratticus. Macherot, R.   741.5

SICK
  Gunther, J. Death be not proud   92
        See also Handicapped

SICK -- FICTION
  Christopher, L. Flyaway   Fic

SICK -- PRAYERS
        See also Prayers

Sickels, Amy
  Laura Ingalls Wilder   92
  Mythmaker: the story of J.K. Rowling   92
  Richard Peck   92
  Walter Dean Myers   92

SICKLE CELL ANEMIA

Jones, P. Sickle cell disease   616.1

Sickle cell disease. Jones, P.   616.1

SICKNESS See Diseases

Sid Fleischman. Freedman, J.   92

Siddell, Thomas
  Gunnerkrigg Court: orientation   741.5
  Gunnerkrigg Court: research   741.5

Side by side.   808.81

Side effects. Koss, A. G.   Fic

Sidekicks. Ferraiolo, J. D.   Fic

Sideshow.   S C

SIDESHOWS -- FICTION
  Barnaby, H. Wonder show   Fic

Sidman, Joyce
  The world according to dog   810

Siebert, Charles
  (jt. auth)   Baker, M.   The secret world of
    whales   599.5

Siegal, Aranka
  Memories of Babi   92
  Upon the head of the goat: a childhood in Hungary,
    1939-1944   92

Siegal, Aranka
                    About
  Siegal, A. Memories of Babi   92
  Siegal, A. Upon the head of the goat: a childhood in
    Hungary, 1939-1944   92

Siege. Durman, L.   355.4

Siege and storm. Bardugo, L.   Fic

The siege of Macindaw. Flanagan, J.   Fic

SIEGE WARFARE
  Durman, L. Siege   355.4

Siegelson, Kim L.
  Honey Bea   Fic

SIEGES
  Durman, L. Siege   355.4

Sieges that changed the world [series]
  McNeese, T. The Alamo   976.4

Sierra Club
  Hart, J. Walking softly in the wilderness   796.51

Sierra Club outdoor adventure guide [series]
  Hart, J. Walking softly in the wilderness   796.51

Sierra Leone. LeVert, S.   966.4

Sierra Leone. Hasday, J. L.   966.4

Sigerman, Harriet
  Elizabeth Cady Stanton   305.42

The sight. Hunter, E.   Fic

SIGHT See Vision

Sight. Vrettos, A. M.   Fic

SIGHT SAVING BOOKS See Large print books

Sign language. Ackley, A.   Fic

SIGN LANGUAGE
  Butterworth, R. R. The Perigee visual dictionary of
    signing   419
  Sternberg, M. L. A. American Sign Language   419
  Warner, P. Signing fun   419

SINGERS -- FICTION
Curry, J. L. The Black Canary   **Fic**
Dolamore, J. Magic under glass   **Fic**
Fienberg, A. Number 8   **Fic**
Harmel, K. When you wish   **Fic**
Ortiz Cofer, J. If I could fly   **Fic**
Philbin, J. The daughters take the stage   **Fic**
Supplee, S. Somebody everybody listens to   **Fic**
Weatherford, C. B. Becoming Billie Holiday   **Fic**

SINGERS -- UNITED STATES -- BIOGRAPHY
Cartlidge, C. Jennifer Hudson   **782.421**

Singh, Nikky-Guninder Kaur
Sikhism   **294.6**

Singing. Fishkin, R. L.   **783**

SINGING
See also Music

SINGING
Fishkin, R. L. Singing   **783**
Landau, E. Is singing for you?   **783**

SINGING -- FICTION
Crossley-Holland, K. Crossing to Paradise   **Fic**
Levine, G. C. Fairest   **Fic**
Porter, S. Lost voices   **Fic**
Singing for Mrs. Pettigrew. Morpurgo, M.   **S C**

SINGING GAMES
See also Games

Singing hands. Ray, D.   **Fic**
Singing the Dogstar blues. Goodman, A.   **Fic**

SINGLE PARENT FAMILY *See* Single-parent families

SINGLE PARENT FAMILY -- FICTION
Acampora, P. Rachel Spinelli punched me in the face   **Fic**
Amato, M. Invisible lines   **Fic**
Atkinson, E. J. I, Emma Freke   **Fic**
Barrow, R. G. Saving Zasha   **Fic**
Bateson, C. Magenta McPhee   **Fic**
Bauer, J. Close to famous   **Fic**
Birdsall, J. The Penderwicks   **Fic**
Bodeen, S. A. The gardener   **Fic**
Day, K. A million miles from Boston   **Fic**
Dee, B. Just another day in my insanely real life   **Fic**
Galante, C. Willowood   **Fic**
Herrick, S. By the river   **Fic**
Horvath, P. My one hundred adventures   **Fic**
Joyce, G. The exchange   **Fic**
Leal, A. H. Also known as Harper   **Fic**
Leal, A. H. A finders-keepers place   **Fic**
Lynch, C. Angry young man   **Fic**
Maldonado, T. Secret Saturdays   **Fic**
Mankell, H. When the snow fell   **Fic**
McDonald, J. Off-color   **Fic**
Philbin, J. The daughters break the rules   **Fic**
Rapp, A. The children and the wolves   **Fic**
Reinhardt, D. The summer I learned to fly   **Fic**
Resau, L. The indigo notebook   **Fic**

Resau, L. The ruby notebook   **Fic**
Sanders, S. L. Gray baby   **Fic**
Stein, T. High dive   **Fic**
Tubb, K. O. Selling hope   **Fic**
Valentine, J. Me, the missing, and the dead   **Fic**
Wolff, V. E. True believer   **Fic**
Wright, B. Putting makeup on the fat boy   **Fic**
A **single** shard. Park, L. S.   **Fic**

SINGLE WOMEN
See also Single people; Women

SINGLE-PARENT FAMILIES
Wolff, V. E. True believer   **Fic**

SINGLE-PARENT FAMILIES
See also Family

SINGLE-PARENT FAMILIES -- FICTION
Gantos, J. Joey Pigza swallowed the key   **Fic**
Lean, S. A dog called Homeless   **Fic**
Patrick, C. The Originals   **Fic**

SINGLE-SEX SCHOOLS
See also Schools

Singleton, Linda Joy
Dead girl dancing   **Fic**
Dead girl in love   **Fic**
Dead girl walking   **Fic**

SINGULARITIES (MATHEMATICS)
See also Geometry

Singularity. Sleator, W.   **Fic**

SINO-JAPANESE CONFLICT, 1937-1945 -- FICTION
Alban, A. Anya's war   **Fic**

Sioras, Efstathia
Czech Republic   **943.7**

Sir Charlie. Fleischman, S.   **92**
Sir Edmund Hillary. Crompton, S.   **92**
Sir Edmund Hillary, modern day explorer. Brennan, K.   **796.52**
Sir Ernest Shackleton. Koestler-Grack, R. A.   **92**
Sir Francis Drake. Lace, W. W.   **92**
Sir Gawain and the Green Knight. Morpurgo, M.   **398.2**
Sir John Hargrave's mischief maker's manual. Hargrave, J.   **818**
Sir Thursday. Nix, G.   **Fic**
Sir Walter Ralegh and the quest for El Dorado. Aronson, M.   **942.05**
The **sirens.** Orr, T.   **398.2**

SIRENS (MYTHOLOGY)
Orr, T. The sirens   **398.2**

SIRENS (MYTHOLOGY) -- FICTION
Hocking, A. Wake   **Fic**

Sirimarco, Elizabeth
American voices from the civil rights movement   **323.1**
American voices from the time of slavery   **326**

SIRIUS
See also Stars

The clones   Fic
The revolt   Fic
Sweat and blood   331.8
This is rocket science   629.4
The Virtual War   Fic
Sky. Townley, R.   Fic
SKY
> *See also* Astronomy; Atmosphere

Sky chasers [series]
Ryan, A. K. Glow   Fic
The **sky** inside. Dunkle, C. B.   Fic
Sky sailors. Bristow, D.   910.4
The **sky's** the limit. Thimmesh, C.   500.8
Skybreaker. Oppel, K.   Fic
Skygazers. Greathouse, L. E.   920
Skyscrapers. Oxlade, C.   720
SKYSCRAPERS
Barker, G. P. Incredible skyscrapers   720
Macaulay, D. Building big   720
Macaulay, D. Unbuilding   690
Oxlade, C. Skyscrapers   720
Stern, S. L. Building greenscrapers   720
Weitzman, D. Skywalkers   682
> *See also* Buildings

SKYSCRAPERS -- EARTHQUAKE EFFECTS
> *See also* Buildings -- Earthquake effects; Earthquakes

SKYSCRAPERS -- HISTORY
Weitzman, D. Skywalkers   682
Skywalkers. Weitzman, D.   682
Slade, Arthur G.
The dark deeps   Fic
Empire of ruins   Fic
Jolted   Fic
Slade, A. The hunchback assignments   Fic
Slade, Suzanne
Basketball   796.323
Slaight, Craig
(ed) Great monologues for young actors   808.82
(ed) Great scenes for young actors from the stage   808.82
Slam dunk! science projects with basketball. Gardner, R.   530
Slam! Myers, W. D.   Fic
Slammed by a tsunami! Aronin, M.   551.46
Slant. Williams, L. E.   Fic
Slate, Barbara
You can do a graphic novel   741.5
Slated. Terry, T.   Fic
Slater, Adam
The Shadowing: Hunted   Fic
SLAVE INSURRECTIONS
Edwards, J. Abolitionists and slave resistance   326
Eskridge, A. E. Slave uprisings and runaways   326
SLAVE INSURRECTIONS -- UNITED STATES -- HISTORY

Edwards, J. Abolitionists and slave resistance   326
SLAVE INSURRECTIONS -- UNITED STATES
Eskridge, A. E. Slave uprisings and runaways   326
SLAVE LABOR
Bales, K. Slavery today   306
Slave life on the plantation. Worth, R.   326
SLAVE NARRATIVES
> *See also* Autobiography; Slavery

Slave spirituals and the Jubilee Singers. Cooper, M. L.   782.421
SLAVE TRADE
Clifford, B. Real pirates   910.4
Grayson, R. The Amistad   326
Nardo, D. The Atlantic slave trade   326
Sharp, S. P. The slave trade and the middle passage   326
Thomas, V. M. Lest we forget   326
Worth, R. The slave trade in America   326
SLAVE TRADE
> *See also* International law; Slavery

SLAVE TRADE -- AFRICA -- HISTORY
Worth, R. The slave trade in America   326
SLAVE TRADE -- FICTION
McKissack, P. C. Nzingha, warrior queen of Matamba   Fic
SLAVE TRADE -- HISTORY
Worth, R. The slave trade in America   326
SLAVE TRADE -- UNITED STATES -- HISTORY
Worth, R. The slave trade in America   326
The **slave** trade and the middle passage. Sharp, S. P.   326
The **slave** trade in America. Worth, R.   326
Slave uprisings and runaways. Eskridge, A. E.   326
SLAVEHOLDERS
Cloud Tapper, S. Voices from slavery's past   326
SLAVEHOLDERS -- UNITED STATES -- BIOGRAPHY
Cloud Tapper, S. Voices from slavery's past   326
Slavery. Grant, R.   326
SLAVERY
Africa to America   973
Aronson, M. Sugar changed the world   664
Bales, K. Slavery today   306
Eskridge, A. E. Slave uprisings and runaways   326
Gann, M. Five thousand years of slavery   326
Grant, R. Slavery   326
Hahn, M. D. Promises to the dead   Fic
Nardo, D. The Atlantic slave trade   326
Schwartz, V. F. Send one angel down   Fic
Sharp, S. P. The slave trade and the middle passage   326
Slavery.   326
SLAVERY -- EMANCIPATION *See* Slaves -- Emancipation
SLAVERY -- FICTION
Anderson, L. H. Chains   Fic

Ralston, B. Snow play   **796**

SNOW -- FICTION

Delsol, W. Frost   **Fic**

Snow baby. Kirkpatrick, K. A.   **92**

SNOW BOARDING *See* Snowboarding

Snow bound. Mazer, H.   **Fic**

Snow falling in spring. Moying Li   **92**

Snow in Summer. Yolen, J.   **Fic**

SNOW LEOPARD

Montgomery, S. Saving the ghost of the mountain   **599.75**

Snow play. Ralston, B.   **796**

SNOW SKIING *See* Skiing

The **snow** spider. Nimmo, J.   **Fic**

Snow, Alan

Here be monsters!   **Fic**

Snow, Carol

Snap   **Fic**

Switch   **Fic**

Snow, fire, sword. Masson, S.   **Fic**

Snow, Maya

Chasing the secret   **Fic**

Journey through fire   **Fic**

Sisters of the sword   **Fic**

Snow, Tamie

Tiny yarn animals   **746.43**

Snowball launchers, giant-pumpkin growers, and other cool contraptions. Fox, T.   **745.5**

Snowboarding. Schwartz, H. E.   **796.93**

SNOWBOARDING

See also Winter sports

Kenney, K. L. Skiing & snowboarding   **796.93**

Schwartz, H. E. Snowboarding   **796.93**

SNOWBOARDING -- FICTION

Ross, J. The drop   **Fic**

Thomas, E. Boarder patrol   **Fic**

Snowmobile racers. Woods, B.   **796.94**

SNOWMOBILES

Woods, B. Snowmobile racers   **796.94**

Snyder, Carrie L.

(ed) Euthanasia: opposing viewpoints   **179.7**

Snyder, Grace, 1882-1982

About

Warren, A. Pioneer girl   **92**

Snyder, Laurel

Any which wall   **Fic**

Snyder, Trish

Alligator & crocodile rescue   **597.98**

Snyder, Zilpha Keatley

The magic nation thing   **Fic**

William S. and the great escape   **Fic**

William's midsummer dreams   **Fic**

So far from the bamboo grove. Watkins, Y. K.   **Fic**

So hard to say. Sanchez, A.   **Fic**

So long, and thanks for all the fish. Adams, D.   **Fic**

So much closer. Colasanti, S.   **Fic**

So punk rock (and other ways to disappoint your mother) Ostow, M.   **Fic**

So silver bright. Mantchev, L.   **Fic**

So totally Emily Ebers. Yee, L.   **Fic**

So yesterday. Westerfeld, S.   **Fic**

So you wanna be a superstar?   **792.602**

SOAP SCULPTURE

See also Modeling; Sculpture

Sobel, David

What's the catch?   **153.8**

Sobey, Ed

Electric motor experiments   **621**

Radio-controlled car experiments   **796.1**

Robot experiments   **629.8**

Solar cell and renewable energy experiments **333.79**

Sobol, Richard

Breakfast in the rainforest   **599.8**

The life of rice   **633.1**

Sobran, Joseph

A midsummer night's dream   **822.3**

Soccer. Kassouf, J.   **796.334**

Soccer. Kelley, K. C.   **796.334**

SOCCER

See also Ball games; Football; Sports

SOCCER

Bazemore, S. Soccer: how it works   **796.334**

Crisfield, D. Winning soccer for girls   **796.334**

Gifford, C. Soccer   **796.334**

Goodstein, M. Goal! science projects with soccer   **507.8**

Hornby, H. Soccer   **796.334**

Jennings, M. Soccer step-by-step   **796.334**

Kassouf, J. Soccer   **796.334**

Kelley, K. C. Soccer   **796.334**

Stewart, M. Goal!: the fire and fury of soccer's greatest moment   **796.334**

Soccer. Hornby, H.   **796.334**

Soccer. Gifford, C.   **796.334**

SOCCER -- BIOGRAPHY

Buckley, J. Pele   **92**

SOCCER -- ENCYCLOPEDIAS

Gifford, C. The Kingfisher soccer encyclopedia   **796.334**

SOCCER -- FICTION

Aronson, S. Beyond lucky   **Fic**

Bloor, E. Tangerine   **Fic**

Choat, B. Soccerland   **Fic**

Fitzgerald, D. Soccer chick rules   **Fic**

Halpin, B. Shutout   **Fic**

Myers, W. D. Kick   **Fic**

Walliams, D. The boy in the dress   **Fic**

Williams, M. Now is the time for running   **Fic**

Soccer chick rules. Fitzgerald, D.   **Fic**

SOCCER COACHES

St. John, W. Outcasts united   **796.334**

SOCIALIZATION

Tym, K. School survival 371.8

See also Acculturation; Child rearing; Education; Sociology

SOCIALLY HANDICAPPED

See also Handicapped; Social adjustment

SOCIALLY HANDICAPPED CHILDREN

See also Handicapped children; Socially handicapped

Society & class. Bingham, J. 704.9

SOCIETY IN ART

Bingham, J. Society & class 704.9

The **Society** of Dread. Dakin, G. Fic

SOCIETY OF FRIENDS

Mierka, G. A. Nathanael Greene 92

SOCIETY OF FRIENDS -- FICTION

Erskine, K. Quaking Fic

The **Society** of Unrelenting Vigilance. Dakin, G. Fic

SOCIOLOGISTS

Bolden, T. W.E.B. Du Bois 92

Hinman, B. A stranger in my own house 92

Whiting, J. W.E.B. Du Bois 92

SOCIOLOGY, URBAN *See* Urban sociology

Socrates. Jun Lim 183

Socrates

About

Jun Lim Socrates 183

SOD HOUSES -- FICTION

MacLachlan, P. Kindred souls Fic

Sodium. O'Daly, A. 546

SODIUM

O'Daly, A. Sodium 546

SOFT TOY MAKING

See also Sewing; Toy making

Softball. Gitlin, M. 796.357

SOFTBALL

See also Ball games; Baseball; Sports

Gitlin, M. Softball 796.357

Gola, M. Winning softball for girls 796.357

SOFTBALL -- FICTION

Mackey, W. K. Throwing like a girl Fic

The **softer** side of hip-hop. Haskins-Bookser, L. 811

SOFTWARE ENGINEERS

Freese, S. M. Craigslist 381

Gitlin, M. eBay 338.7

Soil. Gardner, R. 631.4

Soil. Cunningham, K. 333.7

SOIL CONSERVATION

Cunningham, K. Soil 333.7

See also Conservation of natural resources; Environmental protection

SOIL ECOLOGY

Miller, S. S. Secret lives of soil creatures 591.7

See also Ecology; Soils

SOIL FERTILITY *See* Soils

SOIL MICROBIOLOGY

See also Microbiology; Sanitary engineering

SOILS

Cunningham, K. Soil 333.7

Gardner, R. Soil 631.4

See also Agriculture; Economic geology

Sojourner Truth. Horn, G. M. 305.5

Sojourner Truth. Butler, M. G. 92

Solar cell and renewable energy experiments. Sobey, E. 333.79

SOLAR ECLIPSES

See also Astronomy

SOLAR ECLIPSES -- FICTION

Mass, W. Every soul a star Fic

SOLAR ENERGY

Bearce, S. How to harness solar power for your home 621.47

Walker, N. Harnessing power from the sun 621.47

See also Energy resources; Renewable energy resources; Solar radiation; Sun

SOLAR ENGINES

See also Engines; Solar energy

SOLAR HEATING

See also Heating; Solar energy

SOLAR PHYSICS *See* Sun

SOLAR POWER *See* Solar energy

SOLAR RADIATION

See also Meteorology; Space environment

Solar system. Greathouse, L. E. 523.2

SOLAR SYSTEM

See also Astronomy; Stars

Carson, M. K. Exploring the solar system 523.2

SOLDERING

See also Metals; Metalwork

Soldier bear. Tak, B. D. Fic

Soldier boys. Hughes, D. Fic

Soldier X. Wulffson, D. L. Fic

Soldier's courage: the story of Stephen Crane. Lukes, B. L. 813

Soldier's heart. Paulsen, G. Fic

Soldier's secret. Klass, S. S. Fic

Soldiers. Samuels, C. 940.54

SOLDIERS

See also Armies; Military personnel

Haney, E. L. Inside Delta Force 356

Murphy, J. A young patriot 973.3

Nelson, S. In defense of our country 362.87

Park, L. The Spartan hoplites 938

Smithson, R. Ghosts of war 956.7

Sullivan, G. Knockout!: a photobiography of boxer Joe Louis 92

Watkins, S. R. The diary of Sam Watkins, a confederate soldier 973.7

Zenatti, V. When I was a soldier 92

SOLDIERS -- FICTION

Lynch, C. Casualties of war Fic

SOLDIERS -- HISTORY -- 20TH CENTURY

Jewish holiday origami 736

Stern, Rebecca

(ed) Breakfast on Mars and 37 Other delectable Essays 372.62

Stern, Sam

Real food, real fast 641.5

Sam Stern's get cooking 641.5

Stern, Steven L.

Building greenscrapers 720

Stern, Susan

Stern, S. Real food, real fast 641.5

Sternberg, Libby

The case against my brother Fic

Sternberg, Martin L. A.

American Sign Language 419

Sterngass, Jon

John Brown 92

Same sex marriage 306.84

Steroids 362.29

Steroids. Schaefer, A. 362.29

Steroids. LeVert, S. 362.29

Steroids. Sterngass, J. 362.29

STEROIDS

See also Biochemistry; Drugs

Freedman, J. Professional wrestling 362.29

LeVert, S. The facts about steroids 362.29

LeVert, S. Steroids 362.29

Porterfield, J. Doping 362.29

Porterfield, J. Major League Baseball 362.29

Schaefer, A. Steroids 362.29

Sommers, A. L. College athletics 362.29

Sommers, M. A. The NFL 362.29

Sterngass, J. Steroids 362.29

West, K. Steroids and other performance-enhancing drugs 362.29

STEROIDS -- FICTION

Deuker, C. Gym candy Fic

Mackel, K. Boost Fic

McKissack, F. Shooting star Fic

Steroids and other performance-enhancing drugs. West, K. 362.29

Steve and Bindi Irwin. Breguet, A. 92

Steve Jobs. Blumenthal, K. 621.39

Steve Jobs. Goldsworthy, S. 92

Steve Jobs. Quinn, J. 338.46

Steven Caney's ultimate building book. Caney, S. 624

Stevenson, Robert Louis, 1850-1894

About

Ellis, S. From reader to writer 028

Grant, A. Robert Louis Stevenson's Kidnapped 741.5

Grant, A. Robert Louis Stevenson's Strange case of Dr. Jekyll and Mr. Hyde 741.5

Klimowski, A. Dr. Jekyll and Mr. Hyde 741.5

Lives of the writers 809

Macdonald, F. Kidnapped 741.5

Murphy, J. Across America on an emigrant train 385

Stevenson, Robin

Dead in the water Fic

Escape velocity Fic

Liars and fools Fic

Out of order Fic

Stevermer, Caroline

Magic below stairs Fic

Wrede, P. C. The mislaid magician, or, ten years after Fic

Wrede, P. C. Sorcery and Cecelia, or, The enchanted chocolate pot Fic

Stewart, Alex

Dragonwood Fic

Stewart, Brian A.

Murray, J. Africa 960

Stewart, Gail

Anorexia 616.85

Bombings 363.2

Bulimia 616.85

Catastrophe in southern Asia 909.83

Human rights in the Middle East 323

K-9 police units 363.2

Life of a soldier in Washington's army 973.3

Police brutality 363.2

Trolls 398.2

UFOs 001.9

Vampires: do they exist? 398

Stewart, Jennifer Mackey

Mackey, B. A librarian's guide to cultivating an elementary school garden 372

Stewart, Mark

Blizzards and winter storms 551.55

Goal!: the fire and fury of soccer's greatest moment 796.334

The Indian Removal Act 973.5

Score! 796.962

Swish 796.323

Touchdown 796.332

Stewart, Melissa

Cell biology 571.6

Inside Earthquakes 551.2

Inside lightning 551.56

Inside Volcanoes 551.2

Stewart, Paul

The curse of the night wolf Fic

Legion of the Dead Fic

Phantom of Blood Alley Fic

Return of the emerald skull Fic

Stewart, Sheila

Growing up in religious communities 305

A house between homes 362.7

What is a family? 306.8

When Daddy hit Mommy 362.82

Stewart, Trenton Lee

The extraordinary education of Nicholas Benedict **Fic**

The mysterious Benedict Society **Fic**

The mysterious Benedict Society and the perilous journey **Fic**

The mysterious Benedict Society and the prisoner's dilemma **Fic**

Stickman Odyssey. Ford, C. **741.5**

Sticks and stones. Bazelon, E. **302.34**

Stieff, Barbara

Earth, sea, sun, and sky **704.9**

Stiefvater, Maggie

The raven boys **Fic**

The Scorpio Races **Fic**

Stiekel, Bettina

(ed) The Nobel book of answers **001.4**

Stier, Catherine

The terrible secrets of the Tell-All Club **Fic**

Still star-crossed. Taub, M. **Fic**

STILL-LIFE PAINTING

See also Painting

Stille, Darlene R., 1942-

Anne Hutchinson **92**

Architects of the Holocaust **940.53**

Erosion **551.3**

Great shakes **551.2**

The greenhouse effect **363.7**

Indiana **977.2**

The journals of Lewis and Clark **917.804**

Manipulating light **535**

Nature interrupted **577**

North Dakota **978.4**

Ohio **977.1**

Percy Lavon Julian **92**

Plate tectonics **551.1**

Puerto Rico **972.95**

Waves **531**

Stimola, Aubrey

Cell biology **571.6**

STIMULANTS

Warburton, L. Amphetamines and other stimulants **362.29**

See also Drugs; Psychotropic drugs

Stine, R. L.

(comp) Beware! **808.8**

(ed) Fear: 13 stories of suspense and horror **S C**

Stine, R. L., 1943-

About

Marcovitz, H. R.L. Stine **92**

Stink City. Jennings, R. W. **Fic**

A **stir** of bones. Hoffman, N. K. **Fic**

STOCK CAR RACING

See also Automobile racing

STOCK EXCHANGE See Stock exchanges

STOCK EXCHANGE CRASHES See Financial crises

STOCK EXCHANGES

Connolly, S. The stock market **332.6**

Furgang, K. How the stock market works **332.6**

Healey, A. Making the trade **332.6**

Thompson, H. Understanding the stock market **332.6**

The **stock** market. Connolly, S. **332.6**

STOCK MARKET See Stock exchanges

The **Stock** Market Crash of 1929. Lange, B. **330.9**

STOCK MARKET CRASH, 1929

Blumenthal, K. Six days in October **332.64**

Doak, R. S. Black Tuesday **330.9**

Grant, R. G. Why did the Great Depression happen? **330.9**

Lange, B. The Stock Market Crash of 1929 **330.9**

STOCK MARKET PANICS See Financial crises

STOCK PRICE INDEXES

See also Prices

STOCK RAISING See Livestock industry

Stock, Charlotte

Skateboarding step-by-step **796.22**

Stockland, Patricia M.

The assassination of John F. Kennedy **973.922**

STOCKS

Connolly, S. The stock market **332.6**

Furgang, K. How the stock market works **332.6**

STOCKS -- FICTION

Weissman, E. B. The short seller **Fic**

Stofan, Ellen Renee

Jones, T. D. Planetology **523.4**

Stoffels, Karlijn

Heartsinger **Fic**

Stohl, Margaret

(jt. auth) Garcia, K. Beautiful creatures **Fic**

Garcia, K. Beautiful darkness **Fic**

STOICS

See also Ancient philosophy; Ethics

Stoker, Bram

Raven, N. Bram Stoker's Dracula **741.5**

Stoker, Bram, 1847-1912 -- Adaptations

About

Raven, N. Bram Stoker's Dracula **741.5**

Stokes beginner's guide to bats. Williams, K. **599.4**

Stokes, John

Students on strike **379**

Stokes, Mark

Colon cancer **616.99**

Prostate cancer **616.99**

Stolarz, Laurie Faria

Black is for beginnings **741.5**

Stolen. Vande Velde, V. **Fic**

Stolen hearts. Foley, R. **741.5**

Stolen magic. Burgis, S. **Fic**

Stolen nights. Maizel, R. **Fic**

The **stolen** one. Crowley, S.   **Fic**

Stolz, Joelle

    The shadows of Ghadames   **Fic**

STOMACH

    See also Anatomy

STONE AGE

    See also Civilization

The **stone** child. Poblocki, D.   **Fic**

A **stone** in my hand. Clinton, C.   **Fic**

The **stone** light. Meyer, K.   **Fic**

Stone, Biz

About

    Smith, C. Twitter   **92**

Stone, Lynn M.

    Box turtles   **597.92**

Stone, Phoebe

    The boy on Cinnamon Street   **Fic**

    Deep down popular   **Fic**

    Romeo blue   **Fic**

    The Romeo and Juliet code   **Fic**

Stone, Tamara Ireland

    Time between us   **Fic**

Stone, Tanya Lee

    Almost astronauts   **629.45**

    Courage has no color, the true story of the Triple Nickles   **940.54**

    Ella Fitzgerald   **92**

    The good, the bad, and the Barbie   **688.7**

Stoneheart. Fletcher, C.   **Fic**

Stoneheart trilogy [series]

    Fletcher, C. Ironhand   **Fic**

    Fletcher, C. Silvertongue   **Fic**

    Fletcher, C. Stoneheart   **Fic**

Stoner & Spaz. Koertge, R.   **Fic**

Stones for my father. Kent, T.   **Fic**

Stones in water. Napoli, D. J.   **Fic**

Stonewall Hinkleman and the Battle of Bull Run. Hemphill, M.   **Fic**

STONEWARE *See* Pottery

Stop pretending. Sones, S.   **Fic**

STORAGE IN THE HOME

    Walsh, P. It's all too much, so get it together   **640**

STORES

    See also Commercial buildings; Retail trade

Storey, Rita

    Sailing   **797.1**

STORIES *See* Anecdotes; Bible stories; Fairy tales; Fiction; Legends; Romances; Short stories; Stories in rhyme; Stories without words; Storytelling

STORIES FOR CHILDREN *See* Children's stories

Stories for young people [series]

    Mark Twain   **S C**

    Poe, E. A. Edgar Allan Poe   **S C**

Stories from Adam and Eve to Ezekiel. Lottridge, C.

B.   **220.9**

Stories from the Billabong. Marshall, J. V.   **398.2**

Stories from the life of Jesus. Lottridge, C. B.   **232.9**

Stories in art [series]

    Harris, N. Mosaics   **738.5**

    Harris, N. Wall paintings   **751.7**

The **stories** of the Mona Lisa. Barsony, P.   **759.06**

STORIES WITHOUT WORDS

    Tan, S. The arrival   **741.5**

       See also Picture books for children

STORIES, PLOTS, ETC.

       See also Literature

Stork. Delsol, W.   **Fic**

Stork, Francisco X.

    The last summer of the death warriors   **Fic**

    Marcelo in the real world   **Fic**

The **storm** before Atlanta. Schwabach, K.   **Fic**

STORM CHASERS -- FICTION

    Smith, R. Eruption   **Fic**

The **storm** in the barn. Phelan, M.   **741.5**

Storm Mountain. Birdseye, T.   **Fic**

Storm runners. Smith, R.   **Fic**

Storm runners [series]

    Smith, R. Eruption   **Fic**

    Smith, R. The surge   **Fic**

Storm scientist. Gaffney, T. R.   **551.5**

The **storm** thief. Wooding, C.   **Fic**

Storm warning. Park, L. S.   **Fic**

STORM: The Black Sphere. Young, E. L.   **Fic**

STORM: the ghost machine. Young, E. L.   **Fic**

STORM: The Infinity Code. Young, E. L.   **Fic**

Stormbreaker. Horowitz, A.   **Fic**

Stormbreaker: the graphic novel. Horowitz, A.   **741.5**

Storming the tulips. Sanders, R.   **940.53**

STORMS

    Challoner, J. Hurricane & tornado   **551.55**

    Harris, C. Wild weather   **551.55**

    Longshore, D. Encyclopedia of hurricanes, typhoons, and cyclones   **551.55**

    Royston, A. Storms!   **551.55**

    Stewart, M. Blizzards and winter storms   **551.55**

    Treaster, J. B. Hurricane force   **551.55**

       See also Meteorology; Natural disasters; Weather

STORMS -- FICTION

    Maguire, G. What-the-Dickens   **Fic**

    Smith, R. The surge   **Fic**

STORMS

    Treaster, J. B. Hurricane force   **551.55**

Storms! Royston, A.   **551.55**

Storrie, Paul D.

    Beechen, A. Justice League Unlimited: the ties that bind   **741.5**

    Beowulf   **741.5**

    Made for each other   **741.5**

The **story** of Britain from the Norman Conquest to the European Union. Dillon, P. **941**

The **story** of Cirrus Flux. Skelton, M. **Fic**

The **story** of eBay. Gilbert, S. **381**

The **story** of King Arthur and his knights. Pyle, H. **398.2**

The story of Mexico [series]

  Stein, R. C. Ancient Mexico **972**

  Stein, R. C. Benito Juarez and the French intervention **92**

  Stein, R. C. Cortes and the Spanish Conquest **972**

  Stein, R. C. Emiliano Zapata and the Mexican Revolution **92**

  Stein, R. C. The Mexican Revolution **972**

  Stein, R. C. The Mexican War of Independence **972**

  Stein, R. C. The Mexican-American War **973.6**

  Stein, R. C. Modern Mexico **972.08**

The **story** of my life. Keller, H. **92**

Story of science [series]

  Hakim, J. The story of science: Aristotle leads the way **509**

  Hakim, J. The story of science: Einstein adds a new dimension **509**

  Hakim, J. The story of science: Newton at the center **509**

The **story** of science: Aristotle leads the way. Hakim, J. **509**

The **story** of science: Einstein adds a new dimension. Hakim, J. **509**

The **story** of science: Newton at the center. Hakim, J. **509**

The **story** of Sir Launcelot and his companions. Pyle, H. **398.2**

The **story** of the champions of the Round Table. Pyle, H. **398.2**

The **story** of the Grail and the passing of Arthur. Pyle, H. **398.2**

The **story** of the NFL. Gilbert, S. **796.332**

The **story** of Wal-Mart. Gilbert, S. **381**

The **story** of writing. Donoughue, C. **411**

Story painter: the life of Jacob Lawrence. Duggleby, J. **759.13**

The **story** road to literacy. Roth, R. **372.6**

Storyteller. Giff, P. R. **Fic**

Storyteller. Myers, E. **Fic**

The **storyteller's** secrets. Mitton, T. **398.2**

STORYTELLERS

  Bruchac, J. Bowman's store **92**

  Weber, E. N. R. Rattlesnake Mesa **92**

STORYTELLING

  The August House book of scary stories **398.2**

  Danks, F. Run wild! **790.1**

  Hamilton, M. Children tell stories **372.6**

  Hostmeyer, P. Storytelling and QAR strategies **372.6**

  Literacy development in the storytelling classroom **372.6**

  Marek, K. Organizational storytelling for librarians **025.1**

  Pellowski, A. The storytelling handbook **372.64**

  Reid, R. What's black and white and Reid all over? **027.62**

  Sima, J. Raising voices **027.62**

STORYTELLING

  See also Children's literature

STORYTELLING -- FICTION

  Lin, G. Starry River of the Sky **Fic**

  Mlawski, S. Hammer of witches **Fic**

STORYTELLING

  Pellowski, A. The storytelling handbook **372.64**

STORYTELLING -- UNITED STATES

  Reid, R. What's black and white and Reid all over? **027.62**

Storytelling and QAR strategies. Hostmeyer, P. **372.6**

The **storytelling** handbook. Pellowski, A. **372.64**

Stotan! Crutcher, C. **Fic**

Stott, Carole

  Space exploration **629.4**

Stotts, Stuart

  We shall overcome **782.42**

Stout, Glenn

  Yes she can! **920**

Stout, Harry S.

  (ed) Noll, M. A. Protestants in America **280**

  (ed) Women and American religion **200.9**

Stover, Lois T.

  Jacqueline Woodson **813**

STOWAWAYS

  Jacques, B. The angel's command **Fic**

Stowe, Harriet Beecher, 1811-1896

About

  Fritz, J. Harriet Beecher Stowe and the Beecher preachers **813**

Stoyles, Pennie

  The A-Z of health **616**

Strahan, Jonathan

  (ed) Life on Mars: tales from the new frontier **S C**

  (ed) Under my hat **S C**

Straight talk about . . . [series]

  Rodger, M. Racism and prejudice **305.8**

  Wilkins, J. Date rape **362.883**

STRAIN (PSYCHOLOGY) *See* Stress (Psychology)

Strange angels. St. Crow, L. **Fic**

Strange animals. Matthews, R. **001.9**

The **strange** case of Dr. Jekyll and Mr. Hyde. Stevenson, R. L. **Fic**

Strange creatures: the story of Mary Shelley. Wells, C. **92**

Strange happenings. Avi **S C**

Strange new species. Kelsey, E. **578**

Strange relations. Levitin, S. **Fic**

Strange, Cordelia
Environmental science & protection **333.72**
Medical technicians **610.28**
Physicians assistants & nurses **610.73**
A **stranger** in my own house. Hinman, B. **92**
Stranger with my face. Duncan, L. **Fic**
STRANGERS AND CHILDREN *See* Children
  and strangers
Strapp, James
Science and technology **609**
Strasser, Todd
Boot camp **Fic**
Can't get there from here **Fic**
Famous **Fic**
If I grow up **Fic**
STRATEGIC MATERIALS *See* Materials
Strategies for evaluation. Wilson, D. **370.15**
STRATEGY
  See also Military art and science; Naval art
  and science
STRATIGRAPHIC GEOLOGY
Gallant, R. A. History **551.7**
  See also Geology
Stratton, Allan
Borderline **Fic**
Chanda's secrets **Fic**
Chanda's wars **Fic**
Straub, Deborah Gillan
(ed) U-X-L Asian American voices **815**
Strauss, Susan L.
Sexual harassment and bullying **302.34**
Strauss, Victoria
Passion blue **Fic**
Straw house, Wood house, Brick house, Blow.
Nayeri, D. **S C**
Stray. Goldblatt, S. **Fic**
Strays. Koertge, R. **Fic**
STREAM ANIMALS
  See also Animals; Rivers
STREAM ECOLOGY
  See also Ecology; Freshwater ecology
Streams to the river, river to the sea. O'Dell, S. **Fic**
STREET ART
  See also Art
STREET CHILDREN -- FICTION
Armistead, C. Being Henry David **Fic**
Pyron, B. The dogs of winter **Fic**
STREET CLEANING
  See also Cleaning; Municipal engineering;
  Public health; Roads; Sanitary engineering;
  Streets
STREET GANGS *See* Gangs
STREET LIFE
  See also City and town life
Street love. Myers, W. D. **Fic**

STREET MUSICIANS -- FICTION
Brouwer, S. Devil's pass **Fic**
STREET PEOPLE *See* Homeless persons
STREET RAILROADS
  See also Local transit; Railroads
A **street** through time. Millard, A. **936**
STREETS
  See also Cities and towns; Civil engineering;
  Transportation
Streiffert, Kristi
Kott, J. Nicaragua **972.85**
Streissguth, Thomas
(ed) Custer's last stand **973.8**
(ed) The Rise of the Soviet Union **947.084**
Clay v. United States and how Muhammad Ali
  fought the draft **343**
Extreme weather **551.5**
Strength in numbers. Senker, C. **305.4**
STRENGTH TRAINING *See* Weight lifting
Strength training for teen athletes. Frederick,
S. **613.7**
STRESS (PHYSIOLOGY)
  See also Adaptation (Biology); Physiology
STRESS (PSYCHOLOGY)
Bingham, J. Stress and depression **616.85**
De la Bedoyere, C. Balancing work and play **155.9**
Donovan, S. Keep your cool! **616.85**
Fox, A. Too stressed to think? **158**
Harmon, D. Frequently asked questions about
  overscheduling and stress **155.9**
Hyde, M. O. Stress 101 **616.85**
McPherson, S. S. Stressed out in school? **371.7**
Reber, D. Chill **613**
Stress information for teens **616.9**
  See also Mental health; Psychology
Stress 101. Hyde, M. O. **616.85**
Stress and depression. Bingham, J. **616.85**
Stress information for teens. **616.9**
STRESS MANAGEMENT
  See also Health
STRESS MANAGEMENT FOR TEENAGERS
Stress information for teens **616.9**
Stressed out in school? McPherson, S. S. **371.7**
STRETCHING EXERCISES
  See also Exercise
Strickland, Brad
The house where nobody lived **Fic**
John Bellairs's Lewis Barnavelt in The whistle, the
  grave, and the ghost **Fic**
The sign of the sinister sorcerer **Fic**
Strider. Cleary, B. **Fic**
Strike a pose. Birkemoe, K. **613.7**
STRIKES
Baker, J. The Bread and Roses strike of 1912 **331.8**
Bartoletti, S. C. Kids on strike! **331.892**
Laughlin, R. The Ludlow massacre of 1913-

ers.   **810.9**

Student's Encyclopedia of Great American Writers. Crumbley, P.   **810.9**

A **student's** guide to Arthur Miller. Dunkleberger, A.   **812**

A **student's** guide to Edgar Allan Poe. McArthur, D.   **813**

A **student's** guide to Emily Dickinson. Borus, A.   **811**

A **student's** guide to Ernest Hemingway. Pingelton, T. J.   **813**

A **student's** guide to Eugene O'Neill. Hermann, S.   **812**

A **student's** guide to George Orwell. Means, A. L.   **828**

A **student's** guide to Herman Melville. Diorio, M. A. L.   **813**

A **student's** guide to Mark Twain. Diorio, M. A. L.   **813**

A **student's** guide to Robert Frost. Kirk, C. A. **811**

A **student's** guide to Toni Morrison. Crayton, L. A.   **813**

A **student's** guide to William Faulkner. McArthur, D.   **813**

STUDENTS

Alexander, S. H. She touched the world: Laura Bridgman, deaf-blind pioneer   **92**

Binstock, M. Nourishment   **92**

Dau, J. B. Lost boy, lost girl   **962.4**

The diary of Ma Yan   **951.05**

Glasser, D. New kid, new scene   **373.1**

Kowalski, K. M. The Earls case and the student drug testing debate   **344**

McPherson, S. S. Stressed out in school?   **371.7**

Nelson, P. Left for dead   **940.54**

Thimmesh, C. Girls think of everything   **920**

Tougas, S. Little Rock girl 1957   **379**

Worth, R. Massacre at Virginia Tech   **364.152**

STUDENTS -- CIVIL RIGHTS

Student drug testing   **371.7**

STUDENTS -- GRADING AND MARKING See
Grading and marking (Education)

STUDENTS -- LAW AND LEGISLATION

Gold, S. D. Vernonia School District v. Acton **344**

Kowalski, K. M. The Earls case and the student drug testing debate   **344**

Phillips, T. A. Hazelwood v. Kuhlmeier and the school newspaper censorship debate   **342**

STUDENTS -- LIBRARY SERVICES
See also Libraries and schools; Library services; School libraries

STUDENTS -- POLITICAL ACTIVITY
See also Political participation; Youth movement

Students in danger. Simons, R.   **371.7**

Students on strike. Stokes, J.   **379**

STUDENTS' SONGS
See also Songs

STUDENTS, FOREIGN -- FICTION
Delsol, W. Flock   **Fic**

STUDY GUIDES FOR EXAMINATIONS See
Examinations -- Study guides

STUDY METHODS See Study skills

STUDY SKILLS
Fox, J. S. Get organized without losing it   **371.3**

Greenberg, M. Painless study techniques   **371.3**

STUDY SKILLS
See also Education; Life skills; Teaching

Stung. Wiggins, B.   **Fic**

STUNT FLYING -- FICTION
Tashjian, J. My life as a stuntboy   **Fic**

STUNT PERFORMERS
See also Actors

Stupid fast. Herbach, G.   **Fic**

Sturm, James

Satchel Paige   **741.5**

STUTTERING -- FICTION
Vawter, V. Paperboy   **Fic**

Stuyvesant High School (New York, N.Y.)

With their eyes   **812**

STYLE IN DRESS See Clothing and dress; Costume; Fashion

STYLE MANIKINS See Fashion models

SUBCONSCIOUSNESS
See also Parapsychology; Psychology

SUBCULTURE See Counter culture

SUBJECT DICTIONARIES See Encyclopedias and dictionaries

SUBJECT HEADINGS
Sears list of subject headings   **025.4**

SUBJECT HEADINGS
See also Cataloging; Indexes; Subject catalogs

SUBMARINE BOATS See Submarines

SUBMARINE CABLES
See also Telecommunication; Telegraph

SUBMARINE EXPLORATION See Underwater exploration

SUBMARINE GEOLOGY
See also Geology; Oceanography

SUBMARINE MEDICINE
See also Medicine

SUBMARINE OIL WELL DRILLING See Offshore oil well drilling

SUBMARINE TOPOGRAPHY
Lindop, L. Venturing the deep sea   **551.46**

SUBMARINE WARFARE
See also Naval art and science; War

Submarines. Stefoff, R.   **623.82**

SUBMARINES
Stefoff, R. Submarines   **623.82**

Walker, S. M. Secrets of a Civil War submarine   973.7

SUBMARINES

See also Ships; Submarine warfare; Submersibles; Warships

SUBMARINES (SHIPS)

Verne, J. 20,000 leagues under the sea   Fic

SUBMARINES -- FICTION

Verne, J. 20,000 leagues under the sea   Fic

SUBMERSIBLES

See also Vehicles

SUBSISTENCE ECONOMY

See also Cost and standard of living

SUBSTANCE ABUSE -- ENCYCLOPEDIAS

Drugs, alcohol, and tobacco   362.29

SUBTERFUGE *See* Deception

The **subtle** knife. Pullman, P.   Fic

SUBTRACTION

See also Arithmetic

The **suburb** beyond the stars. Anderson, M. T.   Fic

SUBURBAN ANIMALS -- MONITORING -- CITIZEN PARTICIPATION

Burns, L. G. Citizen scientists   590.72

SUBURBAN ANIMALS -- RESEARCH -- CITIZEN PARTICIPATION

Burns, L. G. Citizen scientists   590.72

SUBURBAN AREAS *See* Suburbs

SUBURBAN LIFE

See also Suburbs

SUBURBAN LIFE -- FICTION

Tan, S. Tales from outer suburbia   S C

SUBURBS

Burns, L. G. Citizen scientists   590.72

SUBURBS

See also Cities and towns -- Growth; City planning; Metropolitan areas

SUBURBS AND ENVIRONS *See* Suburbs

SUBWAYS

Macaulay, D. Underground   624

Reis, R. A. The New York City subway system   388.4

Sandler, M. W. Secret subway   388.4

SUBWAYS

See also Local transit; Railroads

SUBWAYS -- FICTION

Shusterman, N. Downsiders   Fic

SUBWAYS -- NEW YORK (N.Y.)

Sandler, M. W. Secret subway   388.4

SUBWAYS -- NEW YORK (STATE) -- NEW YORK

Shusterman, N. Downsiders   Fic

SUCCESS

Bachel, B. K. What do you really want?   153.8

SUCCESS IN BUSINESS

Spilsbury, R. Jay-Z   92

Such wicked intent. Oppel, K.   Fic

Suciu, Peter

Gerardi, D. Careers in the computer game industry   794.8

Suck it up. Meehl, B.   Fic

Sudan. Levy, P.   962.4

SUDAN -- HISTORY -- DARFUR CONFLICT, 2003-

Steele, P. Sudan, Darfur and the nomadic conflicts   962.4

Sudan in our world. Brownlie, A.   962.4

Sudan, Darfur and the nomadic conflicts. Steele, P.   962.4

Suddenly in the depths of the forest. Oz, A.   Fic

Suellentrop, Tricia

Gorman, M. Connecting young adults and libraries   027.62

SUFFRAGE

See also Citizenship; Constitutional law; Democracy; Elections; Political science

SUFFRAGETTES *See* Suffragists

SUFFRAGISTS

Boomhower, R. E. Fighting for equality   92

Colman, P. Elizabeth Cady Stanton and Susan B. Anthony   92

Goldsmith, B. Z. Dr. Mary Edwards Walker   92

Havelin, K. Victoria Woodhull   92

Kenschaft, L. Lydia Maria Child   303.48

Krull, K. Lives of extraordinary women   920

Monroe, J. The Susan B. Anthony women's voting rights trial   324.6

Mosley, S. The suffragists in literature for youth 016

Norgren, J. Belva Lockwood   92

Sigerman, H. Elizabeth Cady Stanton   305.42

Todd, A. M. Susan B. Anthony   92

See also Reformers

SUFFRAGISTS -- UNITED STATES -- HISTORY

Hollihan, K. L. Rightfully ours   324.6

The **suffragists** in literature for youth. Mosley, S.   016

Sugar. Rhodes, J. P.   Fic

SUGAR

Furgang, A. Salty and sugary snacks   613.2

SUGAR

See also Food

SUGAR -- HISTORY

Aronson, M. Sugar changed the world   664

Sugar and ice. Messner, K.   Fic

Sugar changed the world. Aronson, M.   664

SUGAR GLIDER

Boruchowitz, D. E. Sugar gliders   636.935

Sugar gliders. Boruchowitz, D. E.   636.935

SUGAR GLIDERS AS PETS

Boruchowitz, D. E. Sugar gliders   636.935

Sugar Princess volume 1: skating to win. Nakajo, H.   741.5

SUGAR TRADE

Aronson, M. Sugar changed the world   664

Crewe, M. The lives we lost — **Fic**
Dashner, J. The kill order — **Fic**
Fukuda, A. The Prey — **Fic**
Mary-Todd, J. Shot down — **Fic**
Shusterman, N. UnWholly — **Fic**

SURVIVALISM
  See also Social movements
Survive alive [series]
  Champion, N. Finding food and water — **613.6**
  Champion, N. Finding your way — **613.6**
  Champion, N. Fire and cooking — **796.54**
  Champion, N. In an emergency — **613.6**
  Champion, N. Making shelter — **613.6**
Surviving Antarctica. White, A. — **Fic**
Surviving divorce. Trueit, T. S. — **306.89**
Surviving extreme sports. Hile, L. — **796**
Surviving Hitler. Warren, A. — **940.53**
Surviving Southside [series]
  Fontes, J. Benito runs — **Fic**
  Simon, C. Plan B — **Fic**
  Weyn, S. Recruited — **Fic**
Surviving the Angel of Death. Kor, E. M. — **92**
Surviving the Applewhites. Tolan, S. S. — **Fic**
Surviving the wilderness. Hurley, M. — **613.6**
Survivor kid. Long, D. — **613.6**
Survivors: ordinary people, extraordinary circumstances [series]
  Nelson, S. In defense of our country — **362.87**
  Sanna, E. Nature's wrath — **363.34**
  Sanna, E. We shall all be free — **305.8**
  Simons, R. Gender danger — **362.88**
  Simons, R. Students in danger — **371.7**
  Simons, R. Survival skills — **155.9**
Susan B. Anthony. Todd, A. M. — **92**
The **Susan** B. Anthony women's voting rights trial. Monroe, J. — **324.6**

SUSPENSE FICTION
  Cross, J. Tempest — **Fic**
  Wasserman, R. The book of blood and shadow — **Fic**
SUSPENSE NOVELS *See* Adventure fiction; Mystery fiction; Romantic suspense novels
SUSTAINABLE AGRICULTURE
  See also Agriculture
  Apte, S. Eating green — **630**
  Johanson, P. Jobs in sustainable agriculture — **630**
  Pollan, M. The omnivore's dilemma — **338.1**
SUSTAINABLE ARCHITECTURE
  Farrell, C. Build it green — **720**
  Laidlaw, J. A. Cities — **307.7**
  Miller, M. Green construction — **690**
  Somervill, B. A. Green general contractor — **690**
  Stern, S. L. Building greenscrapers — **720**
  See also Architecture
SUSTAINABLE FARMING *See* Sustainable agriculture
SUSTAINABLE LIVING

Kelsey, E. Not your typical book about the environment — **333.72**
Sustaining our environment [series]
  Bellamy, R. Population growth — **304.6**
  Bellamy, R. Tourism — **363.7**
  Bellamy, R. Waste and pollution — **363.7**
  Laidlaw, J. A. Cities — **307.7**
  Laidlaw, J. A. Energy — **333.79**
  Laidlaw, J. A. Water — **333.91**
Sutcliff, Rosemary
  Sword song — **Fic**
Sutherland, James
  Ronald Reagan — **92**
  The ten-year century — **973.93**
Sutton, Roger
  A family of readers — **809**
Suvanjieff, Ivan
  Engle, D. PeaceJam — **303.6**
Suzanna Snow mysteries [series]
  Frazier, A. The mastermind plot — **Fic**
Suzuki, David T.
  You are the Earth — **577**
Swain, Gwenyth
  World War I — **940.3**
SWAMP ANIMALS
  See also Animals
SWAMP ANIMALS -- FICTION
  Appelt, K. The true blue scouts of Sugarman Swamp — **Fic**
SWAMP ECOLOGY
  See also Ecology; Wetland ecology
SWAMPS
  See also Wetlands
SWAMPS -- FICTION
  Appelt, K. The true blue scouts of Sugarman Swamp — **Fic**
The **swan** kingdom. Marriott, Z. — **Fic**
The **swan** maiden. Tomlinson, H. — **Fic**
Swans. Helget, N. L. — **598**
SWANS
  Helget, N. L. Swans — **598**
SWANS -- FICTION
  Christopher, L. Flyaway — **Fic**
Swanson, James L.
  Bloody times — **973.7**
  Chasing Lincoln's killer — **92**
Swarmed by bees. Hamilton, S. L. — **595.7**
SWASHBUCKLERS *See* Adventure fiction; Adventure films
SWAT teams. Newton, M. — **363.2**
Sweat and blood. Skurzynski, G. — **331.8**
Sweat, Eddie, 1939-1998
  About
  Scanlan, L. The big red horse — **798.4**
Sweden. Phillips, C. — **948.5**
Sweden. Docalavich, H. — **948.5**

SYMBOLISM IN LITERATURE
See also Literature; Symbolism

Symes, R. F.
Rocks & minerals   **552**

SYMPATHY
See also Conduct of life; Emotions

The **symptoms** of my insanity. Raf, M.   **Fic**

SYNAGOGUES
See also Buildings; Religious institutions; Temples

SYNCHRONIZED SWIMMING
See also Swimming

SYNESTHESIA -- FICTION
Ellsworth, L. Unforgettable   **Fic**
Mass, W. A mango-shaped space   **Fic**
Parkinson, S. Blue like Friday   **Fic**

SYNTHESIZER MUSIC *See* Electronic music

SYNTHETIC DRUGS OF ABUSE *See* Designer drugs

SYNTHETIC FABRICS
See also Fabrics; Synthetic products

SYNTHETIC RUBBER
See also Plastics; Synthetic products

SYPHILIS
Uschan, M. V. Forty years of medical racism **174.2**

SYPHILIS
See also Sexually transmitted diseases

Syren. Sage, A.   **Fic**
Syria. Gelfand, D. E.   **956.91**

SYRIA
Gelfand, D. E. Syria   **956.91**

SYRUPS
See also Sugar

SYSTEM THEORY
See also Science

SYSTEMS ENGINEERING
See also Automation; Cybernetics; Engineering; Industrial design; System analysis; System theory

Szpirglas, Jeff
You just can't help it!   **599.9**

Szulhan, Rebecca
Contemporary achievements   **305.8**

Szumski, Bonnie
(jt. auth) Karson, J. Are cell phones dangerous?   **615.9**
(jt. auth) Karson, J. Is medical marijuana necessary?   **615.7**

Szynkowski, Liz
Ferry, S. Yukon Territory   **971**

T

T-Minus: the race to the moon. Ottaviani, J. **629.45**
T-SHIRTS
See also Clothing and dress

T. rex and the great extinction. Bacchin, M.   **567.9**

T4. LeZotte, A. C.   **Fic**
Tabak, John
A look at Neptune   **523.4**
TABLE ETIQUETTE
See also Eating customs; Etiquette
TABLE TENNIS
See also Ball games
Tabletop scientist [series]
Parker, S. The science of air   **533**
Parker, S. The science of water   **532**
Tackach, James
The abolition of American slavery   **326**
TACTICS
See also Military art and science; Strategy
Tadjo, Veronique
Talking drums   **808**
TADPOLES *See* Frogs
Tae kwon do. Haney-Withrow, A.   **796.8**
TAE KWON DO
Haney-Withrow, A. Tae kwon do   **796.8**
Pawlett, M. The tae kwon do handbook   **796.8**
TAE KWON DO
See also Karate; Martial arts; Self-defense
The **tae** kwon do handbook. Pawlett, M.   **796.8**
Taft, Robert A., 1889-1953
     About
Kennedy, J. F. Profiles in courage   **920**
Tag, toss & run. Rowell, V.   **790.1**
Tahiti. NgCheong-Lum, R.   **996**
TAI CHI
Jennings, M. Tai chi step-by-step   **613.7**
TAI CHI
See also Exercise; Martial arts
Tai chi step-by-step. Jennings, M.   **613.7**
TAI JI QUAN *See* Tai chi
TAICHI *See* Tai chi
TAILORING
See also Clothing and dress; Clothing industry
TAINO INDIANS -- FICTION
Dorris, M. Morning Girl   **Fic**
Tait, Noel
Insects & spiders   **595.7**
The **Taj** Mahal. DuTemple, L. A.   **726**
Taj Mahal. Arnold, C.   **954**
Taj Mahal. Mann, E.   **954**
TAJ MAHAL (AGRA, INDIA)
Arnold, C. Taj Mahal   **954**
DuTemple, L. A. The Taj Mahal   **726**
Mann, E. Taj Mahal   **954**
Tajikistan. Abazov, R.   **958.6**
Tak, Bibi Dumon
Soldier bear   **Fic**
Takako, Shimura
(jt. auth) Shimura Takako Wandering son   **Fic**
Take a stand! Golus, C.   **302.3**

Take control of Asperger's syndrome. Price, J. **616.85**

Take control of OCD. Zucker, B. **616.85**

Take me to the river. Hobbs, W. **Fic**

Take me with you. Marsden, C. **Fic**

Take-off! Bolden, T. **784.4**

Taken. McClintock, N. **Fic**

Taken. Bloor, E. **Fic**

Taking a stand. Ehrman, M. K. **646.7**

Taking sides. Soto, G. **Fic**

Takio, vol. 1. Bendis, B. M. **741.5**

Tal, Eve
Cursing Columbus **Fic**
Double crossing **Fic**

Talbott, Hudson
River of dreams **974.7**

A tale dark & Grimm. Gidwitz, A. **Fic**

A tale of Two Castles. Levine, G. C. **Fic**

The talent thief. Williams, A. **Fic**

TALES
Helbig, A. Myths and hero tales **398.2**
San Souci, R. A terrifying taste of short & shivery **398.2**
Schwartz, H. The day the Rabbi disappeared: Jewish holiday tales of magic **398.2**

TALES See Fables; Fairy tales; Folklore; Legends

TALES -- AFRICA
Bryan, A. Ashley Bryan's African tales, uh-huh **398.2**

TALES -- CHINA
Krasno, R. Cloud weavers **398.2**

TALES -- NEW YORK (STATE)
Martin, R. The world before this one **398.2**

Tales from Earthsea. Le Guin, U. K. **S C**

Tales from India. Gavin, J. **398.2**

Tales from outer suburbia. Tan, S. **S C**

Tales from Shakespeare. Packer, T. **822.3**

Tales from the Brothers Grimm and the Sisters Weird. Vande Velde, V. **398**

Tales from the five kingdoms [series]
The flight of dragons **Fic**
French, V. The bag of bones **Fic**
French, V. The heart of glass **Fic**
The robe of skulls **Fic**

The tales of Beedle the Bard. Rowling, J. K. **S C**

Tales of Famous Animals. **590.92**

Tales of invention [series]
Spilsbury, R. The telephone **621.385**

Tales of terror. Poe, E. A. **S C**

Tales of the cryptids. Halls, K. M. **001.9**

Tales out of the school library. Bush, G. **027.8**

TALISMANS -- FICTION
Strauss, V. Passion blue **Fic**

TALK SHOW HOSTS
Abrams, D. Rachael Ray **92**
Cooper, I. Oprah Winfrey **92**

Krohn, K. E. Oprah Winfrey **92**
Paprocki, S. B. Ellen Degeneres **92**
Petrillo, L. Isaac Mizrahi **92**
Todd, A. M. Tyra Banks **92**

Talk that talk: an anthology of African-American storytelling. **398.2**

Talking about your weight. Edwards, H. **613.2**

TALKING BOOKS See Audiobooks

Talking drums. Tadjo, V. **808**

Talking leaves. **S C**

Talking to dragons. Wrede, P. C. **Fic**

The tall Mexican: the life of Hank Aguirre, all-star pitcher, businessman, humanitarian. Copley, B. **92**

Tall story. Gourlay, C. **Fic**

TALL TALES
San Souci, R. Cut from the same cloth **398.2**

TALL TALES
See also Folklore; Legends; Wit and humor

TALL TALES -- AUTHORSHIP
Rosinsky, N. M. Write your own tall tale **808.3**

TALL TALES
San Souci, R. Cut from the same cloth **398.2**

Tallman, Julie I.
Making the writing and research connection with the I-search process **025.5**

TALMUD
See also Hebrew literature; Jewish literature; Judaism

TAM LIN (LEGENDARY CHARACTER)
McNaughton, J. An earthly knight **Fic**

Tamaki, Mariko
Emiko superstar **741.5**
Skim **741.5**

Tamar. Peet, M. **Fic**

Tamez, Modesto
Bazin, M. Math and science across cultures **510**

Tamora Pierce. Dailey, D. **92**

Tan, Amy

About
Loos, P. A reader's guide to Amy Tan's The joy luck club **813**
Mussari, M. Amy Tan **92**
O'Keefe, S. From China to America **92**

Tan, Chung Lee
Finland **948.97**

Tan, Shaun
The arrival **741.5**
The bird king **741.6**
Lost & found **S C**
Tales from outer suburbia **S C**

Tan, Shaun -- Notebooks, sketchbooks, etc
About
Tan, S. The bird king **741.6**

Tanaka, Shelley
Augustyn, F. Footnotes **792.8**
Amelia Earhart **92**

Jocelyn, M. Mable Riley   **Fic**
Miller, S. Miss Spitfire   **Fic**
Myers, A. Spy!   **Fic**
Parker, R. B. The Edenville Owls   **Fic**
Peck, R. The teacher's funeral   **Fic**
Ray, D. Ghost girl   **Fic**
Repka, J. The clueless girl's guide to being a genius   **Fic**
Schmatz, P. Bluefish   **Fic**
Volponi, P. The hand you're dealt   **Fic**
Winters, B. H. The secret life of Ms. Finkleman **Fic**

TEACHERS -- FICTION
Gilman, C. Professor Gargoyle   **Fic**

TEACHERS -- PRACTICE TEACHING *See* Student teaching

TEACHERS -- TRAINING
Brooks-Young, S. Teaching with the tools kids really use   **372**

TEACHERS -- TRAINING
    See also Education -- Study and teaching; Teaching

TEACHERS -- UNITED STATES -- HAND-BOOKS, MANUALS, ETC
Crews, K. D. Copyright law for librarians and educators   **346.04**

TEACHERS COLLEGES
    See also Colleges and universities; Education -- Study and teaching

TEACHERS OF THE BLIND
Alexander, S. H. She touched the world: Laura Bridgman, deaf-blind pioneer   **92**
Delano, M. F. Helen's eyes   **92**
Freedman, R. Out of darkness: the story of Louis Braille   **92**

TEACHERS OF THE DEAF
Carson, M. K. Alexander Graham Bell   **92**
Delano, M. F. Helen's eyes   **92**

TEACHING
Hauser, P. C. How deaf children learn   **371.91**
McAlpine, M. Working with children   **362.7**
McKeown, R. Into the classroom   **370.71**
Miller, M. Tomorrow's teachers   **371.1**

TEACHING -- AIDS AND DEVICES
Richardson, W. Blogs, wikis, podcasts, and other powerful Web tools for classrooms   **371.3**

TEACHING -- DATA PROCESSING *See* Computer-assisted instruction

Teaching banned books. Scales, P. R.   **098**
Teaching Generation M.   **027.62**
Teaching graphic novels. Monnin, K.   **372.6**
Teaching literacy skills to adolescents using Coretta Scott King Award winners. Bernadowski, C. **372.4**

TEACHING TEAMS
Bacon, P. S. 100+ literacy lifesavers   **428**
Harada, V. H. Inquiry learning through librarian-teacher partnerships   **371.1**

TEACHING TEAMS
    See also Teaching

TEACHING TEAMS -- UNITED STATES
Harada, V. H. Inquiry learning through librarian-teacher partnerships   **371.1**
Teaching with the tools kids really use. Brooks-Young, S.   **372**

TEACHING, FREEDOM OF *See* Academic freedom

Teague, Mark
The doom machine   **Fic**
Team moon. Thimmesh, C.   **629.45**
Team Green science projects [series]
Gardner, R. Air   **533**
Gardner, R. Earth's cycles   **550**
Gardner, R. Energy   **333.79**
Gardner, R. Recycle   **628.4**
Gardner, R. Soil   **631.4**
Gardner, R. Water   **551.48**
Team Human. Brennan, S. R.   **Fic**
TEAM TEACHING *See* Teaching teams
Team up online. Pascaretti, V.   **025.04**

TEAMS IN THE WORKPLACE
    See also Social groups; Work environment
The **Teapot** Dome Scandal. Davis, B. J.   **973.91**

TEAPOT DOME SCANDAL, 1921-1924
Davis, B. J. The Teapot Dome Scandal   **973.91**

TEAROOMS
    See also Restaurants; Tea industry

TEASING
Howe, J. The misfits   **Fic**

TEASING
    See also Aggressiveness (Psychology); Interpersonal relations

Tebbetts, Chris
Middle school, the worst years of my life   **Fic**
Papademetriou, L. M or F?   **Fic**
The **tech-savvy** booktalker. Keane, N. J.   **021.7**
Techies [series]
Ehrenhaft, D. Larry Ellison   **338.7**
Ehrenhaft, D. Marc Andreessen   **338.7**

TECHNICAL EDUCATION
    See also Education; Higher education; Technology

TECHNICAL WRITING
Flath, C. Freelance and technical writers   **808**
    See also Authorship; Technology -- Language
Technically, it's not my fault. Grandits, J.   **811**

TECHNOLOGICAL CHANGE *See* Technological innovations

TECHNOLOGICAL INNOVATIONS
Gifford, C. Cool tech   **537.5**
Harris, A. R. Txt me l8r   **303.4**
Hughes, S. Case closed?   **902**
Lee, D. Biomimicry   **608**
    See also Inventions; Technology

THERMOMETERS

> *See also* Heat; Meteorological instruments

THERMOMETRY *See* Thermometers

Therrien, Patricia

> An enemy within   362.196

THESAURI *See* Subject headings

THESEUS (GREEK MYTHOLOGY)

> Hamilton, E. Mythology   292

**THESEUS (GREEK MYTHOLOGY) -- FIC-
TION**

> Barrett, T. Dark of the moon   Fic

They broke the law, you be the judge. Jacobs, T.
A.   345

They call me a hero. Hernandez, D.   979.1

They called themselves the K.K.K. Bartoletti, S.
C.   322.4

They came from below. Nelson, B.   Fic

They had a dream. Archer, J.   323.1

They suck, they bite, they eat, they kill. Bodart, J.
R.   813

They wore what?! Platt, R.   391

The **thief.** Turner, M. W.   Fic

Thief eyes. Simner, J. L.   Fic

The **Thief** Queen's daughter. Haydon, E.   Fic

Thieret, John W.

> National Audubon Society field guide to North
> American wildflowers: eastern region   582.13

THIEVES

> Blackwood, G. L. Highwaymen   364.15
> Blackwood, G. L. Outlaws   364.15
> Haugen, B. The Great Train Robbery   364.1
>   *See also* Criminals

THIEVES -- FICTION

> Heath, J. Money run   Fic
> Patron, S. Behind the masks   Fic

THIEVES -- POETRY

> Noyes, A. The highwayman   821

Thieves like us. Cole, S.   Fic

Thieves till we die. Cole, S.   Fic

Thimmesh, Catherine

> Girls think of everything   920
> Lucy long ago   599.93
> The sky's the limit   500.8
> Team moon   629.45

Thin wood walls. Patneaude, D.   Fic

The **thing** about luck. Kadohata, C.   Fic

The **things** a brother knows. Reinhardt, D.   Fic

Things hoped for. Clements, A.   Fic

Things I have to tell you.   810

Things not seen. Clements, A.   Fic

Things that are. Clements, A.   Fic

Think again. Lawson, J.   811

Think green, take action. Kriesberg, D. A.   333.72

The **Third** Amendment. Porterfield, J.   342

The **Third** Crusade. Crompton, S.   956

THIRD PARTIES (UNITED STATES POLITICS)

> *See also* Political parties; United States -- Pol-
> itics and government

The **third** wheel. Kinney, J.   Fic

Thirteen. Myracle, L.   Fic

Thirteen plus one. Myracle, L.   Fic

Thirteen reasons why. Asher, J.   Fic

The **thirteenth** child. Wrede, P. C.   Fic

The **thirteenth** princess. Zahler, D.   Fic

This child, every child.   305.23

This dark endeavor. Oppel, K.   Fic

This family is driving me crazy.   S C

This full house. Wolff, V. E.   Fic

This is my life. Wadham, R.   016

This is not a test. Summers, C.   Fic

This is PUSH.   S C

This is rocket science. Skurzynski, G.   629.4

This is so not happening. Scott, K.   Fic

This is what I did. Ellis, A. D.   Fic

This journal belongs to Ratchet. Cavanaugh, N.
J.   Fic

This land was made for you and me. Partridge, E.   92

This means war! Wittlinger, E.   Fic

This our dark country. Reef, C.   966.62

This thing called the future. Powers, J. L.   Fic

This world we live in. Pfeffer, S. B.   Fic

Thisdale, Francois

> Pinsker, M. In the days of sand and stars   296.1

Thomas A. Edison. Woodside, M.   92

Thomas Edison for kids. Carlson, L. M.   92

Thomas Jefferson. Whitelaw, N.   973.4

Thomas Jefferson. Severance, J. B.   973.4

Thomas Jefferson for kids. Miller, B. M.   92

Thomas, Erin

> Boarder patrol   Fic

Thomas, Garen Eileen

> Yes we can: a biography of Barack Obama   92

Thomas, George H.

> **About**
> Bobrick, B. The Battle of Nashville   973.7

Thomas, Jens

> The noble gases   546
> Silicon   546

Thomas, Joyce Carol

> (ed) Linda Brown, you are not alone   323.1
> The skull talks back and other haunting tales   398.2

Thomas, Keltie

> Bear rescue   599.78
> How basketball works   796.323

Thomas, Rebecca L.

> Popular series fiction for middle school and teen
> readers   016

Thomas, Valerie

> **About**
> Thimmesh, C. Girls think of everything   920

Thomas, Velma Maia

> Lest we forget   326

Thomas, Vivien T., 1910-1985
About
Yount, L. Alfred Blalock, Helen Taussig, and Vivien Thomas   **617.4**

Thomas, William David
Korean Americans   **305.8**
Marine biologist   **578.7**

Thomason, Mark
Moonrunner   Fic

Thompson, Bill
The young birder's guide to birds of eastern North America   **598**

Thompson, Helen
Cost of living   **339.4**
Investing money   **332.6**
Understanding the stock market   **332.6**

Thompson, Holly
The language inside   Fic
Orchards   Fic
(ed) Tomo   S C

Thompson, Kate
The last of the High Kings   Fic
The new policeman   Fic
Origins   Fic
The white horse trick   Fic

Thompson, Paul B.
The devil's door   Fic

Thompson, Ricki
City of cannibals   Fic

Thoms, Annie
(ed) With their eyes   **812**

Thomson, Jamie
Dark Lord, the early years   Fic

Thomson, Neil
Thomson, R. Toys and models   **745.592**

Thomson, Ruth
Terezin   **940.53**
Toys and models   **745.592**

Thomson, Sarah L.
Mortenson, G. Three cups of tea   **371.82**
The secret of the Rose   Fic
Watanabe, K. No problem!   **153.4**

THOR (NORSE DEITY)
See also Gods and goddesses

Thor, Annika
A faraway island   Fic
The lily pond   Fic
Thor, the mighty avenger, v.1. Langridge, R. **741.5**

Thoreau, Henry David, 1817-1862
About
Armistead, C. Being Henry David   Fic
Hausman, G. A mind with wings   Fic
Kirk, A. Understanding Thoreau's Civil disobedience   **814**
McCurdy, M. Walden then & now   **818**
Meltzer, M. Henry David Thoreau   **92**

Tashjian, J. Larry and the meaning of life   Fic
Vaupel, R. My contract with Henry   Fic

Thorn, John
First pitch   **796.357**

Thornhill, Jan
I found a dead bird   **306.9**
Who wants pizza?   **641.3**

Thornley, Stew
Kevin Garnett   **796.323**
Kobe Bryant   **796.323**
Tim Duncan   **796.323**

Thornton, Denise
Living with cancer   **616.99**
Physical disabilities   **362.4**

Thorpe, Jim, 1888-1953
About
Bruchac, J. Jim Thorpe   **92**
Gutman, D. Jim & me   Fic
Labrecque, E. Jim Thorpe   **92**
Schuman, M. Jim Thorpe   **92**

Thorpe, Yvonne
Canoeing and kayaking   **797.1**
Those amazing musical instruments. Helsby, G.   **784.19**

THOUGHT AND THINKING
See also Educational psychology; Psychology
THOUGHT AND THINKING -- FICTION
Hulme, J. The lost train of thought   Fic
The **thought** of high windows. Kositsky, L.   Fic
The **thoughtful** researcher. Rankin, V.   **027.62**
A **thousand** never evers. Burg, S.   Fic
A **thousand** peaks. Liu Siyu   **895.1**
A **thousand** years of pirates. Gilkerson, W.   **910.4**
Threads and flames. Friesner, E. M.   Fic
THREATENED SPECIES *See* Endangered species
THREE (THE NUMBER)
See also Numbers
Three across. Finkelstein, N. H.   **629.13**
Three black swans. Cooney, C. B.   Fic
Three clams and an oyster. Powell, R.   Fic
Three cups of tea. Mortenson, G.   **371.82**
THREE DIMENSIONAL PHOTOGRAPHY
Zeller, B. Lincoln in 3-D   **92**
See also Photography
Three little words. Rhodes-Courter, A. M.   **92**
The **Three** Mile Island nuclear disaster. Lusted, M. A.   **363.1**
The **three** musketeers. Dumas, A.   Fic
Three of diamonds. Horowitz, A.   Fic
Three rivers rising. Richards, J.   Fic
THREE STOOGES FILMS
See also Comedy films; Motion pictures
Three times lucky. Turnage, S.   Fic
Three wishes. Ellis, D.   **956.94**
Three-quarters dead. Peck, R.   Fic
THRIFT *See* Saving and investment

To the moon. Bodden, V.   **629.45**

To the mountaintop! Hunter-Gault, C.   **070.92**

To the ocean deep. Bodden, V.   **551.46**

To the South Pole. Bodden, V.   **919.8**

To the top of Everest. Skreslet, L.   **796.52**

To the top of Mount Everest. Bodden, V.   **796.522**

To the young writer. Nuwer, H.   **808**

TOADS

Beltz, E. Frogs: inside their remarkable world **597.8**

Somervill, B. A. Cane toad   **597.8**

TOADS -- FICTION

Williams, L. A. The witches' kitchen   **Fic**

Toads and diamonds. Tomlinson, H.   **Fic**

TOADSTOOLS *See* Mushrooms

TOASTS

> *See also* Epigrams; Speeches

TOBACCO

Hyde, M. O. Smoking 101   **616.86**

LeVert, S. The facts about nicotine   **362.29**

TOBACCO

> *See also* Plants

TOBACCO -- PRODUCTS LIABILITY -- UNIT-ED STATES

Sergis, D. K. Cipollone v. Liggett Group   **346.03**

Tobacco and smoking: opposing viewpoints. **362.29**

TOBACCO HABIT

Hunter, D. Born to smoke   **616.86**

Merino, N. Smoking   **362.29**

Miller, H. Smoking   **616.86**

Naff, C. F. Nicotine and tobacco   **362.29**

Price, S. Nicotine   **616.86**

Tobacco and smoking: opposing viewpoints **362.29**

Tobacco information for teens   **362.29**

TOBACCO HABIT

> *See also* Habit; Smoking

TOBACCO HABIT -- ENCYCLOPEDIAS

Drugs, alcohol, and tobacco   **362.29**

TOBACCO INDUSTRY

Sergis, D. K. Cipollone v. Liggett Group   **346.03**

Tobacco and smoking: opposing viewpoints **362.29**

Tobacco information for teens.   **362.29**

TOBACCO PIPES

> *See also* Smoking

Tobacco: the deadly drug [series]

Esherick, J. No more butts   **616.86**

Hunter, D. Born to smoke   **616.86**

Toby alone. Fombelle, T. d.   **Fic**

Toby and the secrets of the tree. Fombelle, T. d. **Fic**

Tocci, Salvatore

Gardner, R. Ace your chemistry science project   **540.7**

Gardner, R. Ace your ecology and environmental science project   **577**

Gardner, R. Ace your exercise and nutrition science project: great science fair ideas   **613**

Gardner, R. Ace your food science project   **664**

Gardner, R. Ace your weather science project **551.5**

The chaparral   **577.3**

Life in the tropical forests   **577.3**

Tocher, Timothy

Bill Pennant, Babe Ruth, and me   **Fic**

Chief Sunrise, John McGraw, and me   **Fic**

Today [series]

Ponsford, S. The European Union today   **341.242**

Today I will. Spinelli, E.   **808.8**

Today the world is watching you. Magoon, K.   **379**

Today's writers and their works [series]

Axelrod-Contrada, J. Isabel Allende   **92**

Mussari, M. Amy Tan   **92**

Mussari, M. Haruki Murakami   **92**

Stefoff, R. Stephen King   **92**

Todd, Anne M.

Susan B. Anthony   **92**

Tyra Banks   **92**

Vera Wang   **92**

Todd, Mark

(ed) The Pain tree, and other teenage angst-ridden poetry   **811**

Whatcha mean, what's a zine?   **070.5**

Todd, Pamela

The blind faith hotel   **Fic**

TODD, SWEENEY (LEGENDARY CHARAC-TER) -- FICTION

Pratchett, T. Dodger   **Fic**

Todras, Ellen H.

Explorers, trappers, and pioneers   **911**

Toft, Di

The twilight circus   **Fic**

Wolven   **Fic**

TOILET TRAINING

> *See also* Child rearing

TOILETRIES

> *See also* Personal grooming

TOILETS

Albee, S. Poop happened!   **363.7**

Toksvig, Sandi

Hitler's canary   **Fic**

TOKYO (JAPAN) -- FICTION

Renn, D. Tokyo heist   **Fic**

Tokyo heist. Renn, D.   **Fic**

Tolan, Stephanie S.

Surviving the Applewhites   **Fic**

TOLERANCE *See* Toleration

TOLERATION

Webber, D. Totally tolerant   **303.3**

TOLERATION

> *See also* Interpersonal relations

TOLERATION -- FICTION

McKay, S. E. Enemy territory   **Fic**

Toliver, Wendy

Lifted   **Fic**

Tolkien, J. R. R. (John Ronald Reuel), 1892-1973

Dixon, C. Hobbit: an illustrated edition of the fantasy classic   **741.5**

The hobbit   **Fic**

The hobbit, or, There and back again   **Fic**

The lord of the rings   **Fic**

The hobbit   **Fic**

Tolkien, J. R. R. (John Ronald Reuel), 1892-1973

About

Ellis, S. From reader to writer   **028**

Neimark, A. E. Myth maker: J.R.R. Tolkien   **828**

Willett, E. J.R.R. Tolkien   **92**

Tom Thumb. Sullivan, G.   **92**

Tom Thumb, 1838-1883

About

Sullivan, G. Tom Thumb   **92**

Tom Trueheart and the Land of Dark Stories. Beck, I.   **Fic**

TOMATOES -- FICTION

Walters, E. Splat!   **Fic**

Tomb explorers. Barber, N.   **930.1**

TOMBS

See also Archeology; Architecture; Burial; Monuments; Shrines

Barber, N. Tomb explorers   **930.1**

The **Tombs** of Atuan. Le Guin, U. K.   **Fic**

Tomecek, Steve

Animal communication   **591.59**

Art & architecture   **701**

Electromagnetism, and how it works   **537**

Music   **781.2**

Tools and machines   **621.9**

What a great idea!   **609**

Tomlinson, Heather

Aurelie   **Fic**

The swan maiden   **Fic**

Toads and diamonds   **Fic**

Tomljanovic, Tatiana

Borrowing   **332.7**

Tommaso, Rich

Sturm, J. Satchel Paige   **741.5**

Tommysaurus Rex. TenNapel, D. R.   **741.5**

Tomo.   **S C**

Tomorrow's enterprising scientists. Flath, C.   **004**

Tomorrow's magic. Service, P. F.   **Fic**

Tomorrow's teachers. Miller, M.   **371.1**

Tomorrow's transportation. Miller, M.   **363.7**

Tomorrow, the river. Gray, D. E.   **Fic**

Tomorrow, when the war began. Marsden, J.   **Fic**

Tompkins, Michael A.

My anxious mind   **616.85**

TONGUE TWISTERS

See also Children's poetry; Folklore; Nonsense verses

Toni Morrison. Kramer, B.   **813**

Toning for teens. Vedral, J. L.   **613.7**

Toning the sweep. Johnson, A.   **Fic**

Too stressed to think? Fox, A.   **158**

Tooke, Wes

King of the mound   **Fic**

TOOLS

Tomecek, S. Tools and machines   **621.9**

Tools and machines. Tomecek, S.   **621.9**

The **TOON** treasury of classic children's comics.   **741.5**

Tooth and claw. Lewin, T.   **590**

Top 50 reasons to care about elephants. Firestone, M.   **599.67**

Top 50 reasons to care about endangered animals [series]

Barker, D. Top 50 reasons to care about great apes   **599.8**

Christopherson, S. C. Top 50 reasons to care about whales and dolphins   **599.5**

Firestone, M. Top 50 reasons to care about elephants   **599.67**

Firestone, M. Top 50 reasons to care about giant pandas   **599.78**

Firestone, M. Top 50 reasons to care about rhinos   **599.66**

Firestone, M. Top 50 reasons to care about tigers   **599.75**

Top 50 reasons to care about giant pandas. Firestone, M.   **599.78**

Top 50 reasons to care about great apes. Barker, D.   **599.8**

Top 50 reasons to care about rhinos. Firestone, M.   **599.66**

Top 50 reasons to care about tigers. Firestone, M.   **599.75**

Top 50 reasons to care about whales and dolphins. Christopherson, S. C.   **599.5**

TOPOGRAPHICAL DRAWING

See also Drawing; Surveying

TOPOLOGY

See also Geometry; Set theory

The **Torah:** the five books of Moses. Bible/O.T./Pentateuch   **222**

Torched. Henry, A.   **Fic**

TORIES, AMERICAN *See* American Loyalists

Toriyama, Akira

Cowa!   **741.5**

Torn. O'Rourke, E.   **Fic**

Torn. Haddix, M. P.   **Fic**

Torn to pieces. McDonnell, M.   **Fic**

Tornado! Fradin, D. B.   **551.55**

Tornadoes. Prokos, A.   **551.55**

Tornadoes. Silverstein, A.   **551.55**

Tornadoes. Ceban, B. J.   **551.55**

Tornadoes. Simon, S.   **551.55**

TORNADOES

Carson, M. K. Inside tornadoes   **551.55**

Ceban, B. J. Tornadoes   **551.55**

da   **741.5**

Tremendous tunnels. Graham, I.   **624.1**

TRENT AFFAIR, 1861

> *See also* United States -- History -- 1861-1865, Civil War

TRENTON (N.J.), BATTLE OF, 1776

Murphy, J. The crossing   **973.3**

TRENTON, BATTLE OF, 1776

Murphy, J. The crossing   **973.3**

Trexler, Sally

Berger, P. Choosing Web 2.0 tools for learning and teaching in a digital world   **025.04**

TRIAL BY JURY *See* Jury

The **trial** of the police officers in the shooting death of Amadou Diallo. Fireside, B. J.   **345**

The **trial** of the Scottsboro boys. Aretha, D.   **345**

TRIALS

Aaseng, N. You are the juror   **345**

Aretha, D. The trial of the Scottsboro boys   **345**

Fireside, B. J. The trial of the police officers in the shooting death of Amadou Diallo   **345**

Jarrow, G. The printer's trial   **345**

Pellowski, M. The terrorist trial of the 1993 bombing of the World Trade Center   **974.7**

Sergis, D. K. Cipollone v. Liggett Group   **346.03**

Sorensen, L. The Scottsboro Boys Trial   **345**

TRIALS (ABORTION) -- UNITED STATES

Gold, S. D. Roe v. Wade   **344**

TRIALS (CONSPIRACY)

Pellowski, M. The terrorist trial of the 1993 bombing of the World Trade Center   **974.7**

TRIALS (HOMICIDE)

Coleman, W. Racism on trial   **345**

Crowe, C. Getting away with murder: the true story of the Emmett Till case   **364.152**

Pellowski, M. The O.J. Simpson murder trial   **345**

Wright, S. Simeon's story   **305.8**

TRIALS (HOMICIDE)

> *See also* Homicide; Trials

TRIALS (MANSLAUGHTER) -- NEW YORK (STATE) -- NEW YORK

Fireside, B. J. The trial of the police officers in the shooting death of Amadou Diallo   **345**

TRIALS (MURDER) *See* Trials (Homicide)

TRIALS (MURDER) -- CALIFORNIA -- LOS ANGELES

Pellowski, M. The O.J. Simpson murder trial   **345**

TRIALS (MUTINY) -- UNITED STATES

Hulm, D. United States v. the Amistad   **326**

TRIALS (NAVAL OFFENSES) -- UNITED STATES

Nelson, P. Left for dead   **940.54**

TRIALS (PRODUCTS LIABILITY) -- UNITED STATES

Sergis, D. K. Cipollone v. Liggett Group   **346.03**

TRIALS (RAPE) -- ALABAMA -- SCOTTSBORO

Cates, D. The Scottsboro boys   **345**

Sorensen, L. The Scottsboro Boys Trial   **345**

TRIALS (TERRORISM)

Pellowski, M. The terrorist trial of the 1993 bombing of the World Trade Center   **974.7**

TRIALS (TERRORISM) -- UNITED STATES -- NEW YORK (STATE) -- NEW YORK

Pellowski, M. The terrorist trial of the 1993 bombing of the World Trade Center   **974.7**

TRIALS -- FICTION

Hemphill, S. Wicked girls   **Fic**

Myers, A. Time of the witches   **Fic**

Myers, W. D. Monster   **Fic**

Thompson, P. B. The devil's door   **Fic**

TRIALS -- HISTORY

Margulies, P. The devil on trial   **345.73**

TRIALS -- UNITED STATES

Margulies, P. The devil on trial   **345.73**

TRIANGLE

> *See also* Geometry; Shape

Triangle Shirtwaist Factory fire. Houle, M. M. **974.7**

The **Triangle** Shirtwaist Factory fire. Marsico, K.   **974.7**

The **Triangle** Shirtwaist Factory fire. Getzinger, D.   **974.7**

TRIASSIC PERIOD

Bonner, H. When dinos dawned, mammals got munched, and Pterosaurs took flight   **567.9**

TRIATHLETES

Whitfield, S. Simon says gold: Simon Whitfield's pursuit of athletic excellence   **92**

TRIATHLON

> *See also* Sports

TRIATHLON -- FICTION

Crutcher, C. Ironman   **Fic**

TRIBAL LEADERS

Hinds, K. Huns   **936**

Price, S. Attila the Hun   **92**

TRIBES

> *See also* Clans; Family

TRICERATOPS

> *See also* Dinosaurs

Trick of the eye. Vry, S.   **152.14**

TRICKS

> *See also* Amusements

Trickster's choice. Pierce, T.   **Fic**

Trickster's girl. Bell, H.   **Fic**

Trickster: Native American tales.   **398.2**

TRICYCLES

> *See also* Vehicles

Trigiani, Adriana

Viola in reel life   **Fic**

Viola in the spotlight   **Fic**

TRIGONOMETRY

Wingard-Nelson, R. Trigonometry smarts!   **516.2**

> *See also* Geometry; Mathematics

Yancey, D. Tuberculosis   **616.2**

Tuberculosis. Yancey, D.   **616.2**

TUBERCULOSIS -- FICTION

Hayles, M. Breathing room   Fic

Hitchcock, S. The ballad of Jessie Pearl   Fic

TUBERCULOSIS -- VACCINATION

See also Vaccination

Tubman, Harriet, 1820?-1913

About

Adler, D. A. Harriet Tubman and the Underground
Railroad   **973.7**

Allen, T. B. Harriet Tubman, secret agent   **92**

Krull, K. Lives of extraordinary women   **920**

Pinkney, A. D. Let it shine   **920**

Sawyer, K. K. Harriet Tubman   **92**

Tuccillo, Diane

Teen-centered library service   **027.62**

Tucker, Sophie, 1884-1966

About

Orgill, R. Shout, sister, shout!   **920**

Tucker, Tom

Brainstorm!   **609.2**

TUGBOATS

See also Boats and boating

Tukey, Paul

(jt. auth) Rowell, V. Tag, toss & run   **790.1**

Tulloch, Coral

Antarctica   **998**

Tullson, Diane

Riley Park   Fic

Tulsa burning. Myers, A.   Fic

Tundra. Warhol, T.   **577.5**

TUNDRA ECOLOGY

Warhol, T. Tundra   **577.5**

Woodford, C. Arctic tundra and polar deserts   577

See also Ecology

Tungsten. Turrell, K.   **546**

TUNGSTEN

Turrell, K. Tungsten   **546**

Tunis, Edwin

Frontier living   **978**

Tunisia. Brown, R. V.   **961.1**

Tunnel vision. Shaw, S.   Fic

Tunnell, Michael

Candy bomber   **92**

Moon without magic   Fic

Wishing moon   Fic

Tunnell, M. Candy bomber   **92**

Tunnels. Gordon, R.   Fic

TUNNELS

See also Civil engineering

Graham, I. Tremendous tunnels   **624.1**

Macaulay, D. Building big   **720**

Tupac Shakur. Harris, A. R.   **92**

Tupac Shakur. Golus, C.   **92**

TURBINES

See also Engines; Hydraulic machinery

Turbulent planet [series]

Colson, M. Forest furnace   **634.9**

Turck, Mary

Freedom song   **323.1**

Turing, Alan Mathison, 1912-1954

About

Corrigan, J. Alan Turing   **92**

Henderson, H. Alan Turing   **92**

Turkey. Shields, S. D.   **956.1**

TURKEY -- ANTIQUITIES

See also Antiquities

TURKEY -- DESCRIPTION AND TRAVEL

LaRoche, A. We visit Turkey   **956.1**

TURKEYS

See also Birds; Poultry

Turkmenistan. Knowlton, M.   **958.5**

Turnage, Sheila

Three times lucky   Fic

Turnbull, Ann

Greek myths   **292**

Turnbull, Stephen R.

The most daring raid of the samurai   **952**

TURNCOATS See Defectors

Turner, Alan

National Geographic prehistoric mammals   **569**

Turner, Ann Warren

Father of lies   Fic

Hard hit   Fic

Turner, Barry

(ed) The Statesman's Yearbook 2014   **330**

Turner, Glennette Tilley

Fort Mose   **975.9**

Turner, Kate

Australia   **994**

Turner, Max

End of days   Fic

Night runner   Fic

Turner, Megan Whalen

A conspiracy of kings   Fic

The King of Attolia   Fic

The Queen of Attolia   Fic

The thief   Fic

Turner, Pamela S.

The frog scientist   **597.8**

A life in the wild   **92**

Life on earth--and beyond   **576.8**

Project Seahorse   **597**

Prowling the seas   **591.7**

Turner, Sharon

Find your style and knit it too   **746.43**

Turner, Tracey

Horne, R. 101 things you wish you'd invented--and
some you wish no one had   **609**

World of the weird   **031**

Turney, Jon

TYPHOID FEVER
> *See also* Diseases

TYPHOID FEVER -- FICTION
Chibbaro, J. Deadly   Fic

Typhoid Mary, d. 1938
> **About**
Chibbaro, J. Deadly   Fic

TYPHOONS
Longshore, D. Encyclopedia of hurricanes, typhoons, and cyclones   551.55

TYPHOONS
> *See also* Cyclones; Storms; Winds

TYPHOONS -- ENCYCLOPEDIAS
Longshore, D. Encyclopedia of hurricanes, typhoons, and cyclones   551.55

TYPOLOGY (PSYCHOLOGY)
> *See also* Personality; Psychology; Temperament

Tyra Banks. Todd, A. M.   92

TYRANNOSAURUS REX
> *See also* Dinosaurs

Tyranny. Fairfield, L.   741.5

Tyson, Edith S.
Orson Scott Card   813

Tyson, Neil De Grasse
The Pluto files   523.4

Tzu-hsi, Empress dowager of China, 1835-1908
> **About**
Krull, K. Lives of extraordinary women   920

U

U-X-L Asian American voices.   815
U-X-L encyclopedia of biomes.   577.8
U-X-L encyclopedia of world mythology.   201

The U.S. Armed Forces and military careers [series]
Gray, J. S. The U.S. Coast Guard and military careers   359.9

The **U.S.** Coast Guard and military careers. Gray, J. S.   359.9

U.S. Department of Labor
(comp) Occupational outlook handbook 2013-2014   331.120

U.S. involvement in Vietnam. Gitlin, M.   959.704
U.S. marshals. Newton, M.   363.2
U.S. v. Eichman. Fridell, R.   342
U.S. v. Nixon. Stefoff, R.   342

Uchida, Yoshiko
The best bad thing   Fic
A jar of dreams   Fic
Journey to Topaz   Fic

Udvardy, Miklos D. F.
National Audubon Society field guide to North American birds, Western region   598

Uehashi, Nahoko
Moribito   Fic

Moribito II   Fic
UFOs. Stewart, G.   001.9
UFOS *See* Unidentified flying objects
Uganda. Barlas, R.   967.61
Uglies. Westerfeld, S.   Fic
Uglies.   741.5
Uglies. Westerfeld, S.   Fic
Uh huh!: the story of Ray Charles. Duggleby, J.   92

UIGHUR (TURKIC PEOPLE) -- FICTION
La Valley, J. The Vine basket   Fic

Ukraine. Cooper, C. W.   947.7
Ukraine. Bassis, V.   947.7
Ukrainian Americans. Radzilowski, J.   305.8

UKRAINIAN AMERICANS
Radzilowski, J. Ukrainian Americans   305.8

The ultimate 10. Natural disasters [series]
Prokos, A. Tornadoes   551.55
Ryback, C. Hurricanes   551.55
Stewart, M. Blizzards and winter storms   551.55

The **ultimate** audition book for teens. Lamedman, D.   792
The **ultimate** dinopedia. Lessem, D.   567.9
Ultimate field trip 5. Goodman, S.   629.45
Ultimate guide to baseball. Buckley, J.   796.357
Ultimate guide to football. Buckley, J.   796.332
The **ultimate** guide to your microscope. Levine, S.   502.8
Ultimate magic. Barron, T. A.   Fic
Ultimate sports.   813
Ultimate trains. McMahon, P.   385
The **ultimate** weapon. Sullivan, E. T.   355.8

ULTRASONICS
> *See also* Sound

Uluru, Australia's Aboriginal heart. Arnold, C.   994

Umansky, Kaye
Solomon Snow and the stolen jewel   Fic

UMBRELLAS AND PARASOLS
> *See also* Clothing and dress

Umubyeyi, Jeanne d'Arc, 1986-
> **About**
Jansen, H. Over a thousand hills I walk with you   Fic

Un Lun Dun. Mieville, C.   Fic
The **un-forgotten** coat. Cottrell Boyce, F.   Fic
The **unbecoming** of Mara Dyer. Hodkin, M.   Fic
Unbored. Glenn, J.   790
Unbound and unbroken: the story of Frederick Douglass. Esty, A.   92
Unbuilding. Macaulay, D.   690

Uncharted, unexplored and unexplained [series]
Conley, K. A. Joseph Priestley and the discovery of oxygen   92
Zannos, S. Guglielmo Marconi and the story of radio waves   92

Uncle Montague's tales of terror. Priestley, C.   S C
Uncle Remus, the complete tales. Lester, J.   398.2

UNITED STATES -- POLITICS AND GOVERNMENT -- 1865-1933 -- SOURCES

Telgen, D. The Gilded Age   973.8

UNITED STATES -- POLITICS AND GOVERNMENT -- GRAPHIC NOVELS

L'Engle, M. A wrinkle in time   741.5

UNITED STATES -- POPULATION

     See also Population

UNITED STATES -- PRESIDENTS *See* Presidents -- United States

UNITED STATES -- RACE RELATIONS

Osborne, L. B. Miles to go for freedom   305.896

UNITED STATES -- RACE RELATIONS

     See also Race relations

UNITED STATES -- RACE RELATIONS -- HISTORY

Miller, C. C. Backlash   305.8

Mullenbach, C. Double victory   940.53

UNITED STATES -- RELIGION

     See also Religion

UNITED STATES -- SOCIAL CONDITIONS -- TO 1865 -- FICTION

Woodruff, E. Dear Austin   Fic

UNITED STATES -- SOCIAL LIFE AND CUSTOMS -- HISTORY

Bowers, R. Superman versus the Ku Klux Klan   741.5

DiPiazza, F. D. Friend me!   302.3

UNITED STATES -- STATISTICS

     See also Statistics

UNITED STATES -- WORLD WAR, 1939-1945

     See World War, 1939-1945 -- United States

The **United** States Constitution. Vile, J. R.   342

The **United** States cookbook. D'Amico, J.   641.59

The **United** States enters the world stage: from the Alaska Purchase through World War I, 1867-1919. Collier, C.   973.8

United States holidays and observances. Rajtar, S.   394.26

United States Holocaust Memorial Museum

Volavkova, H. --I never saw another butterfly--   741.9

The **United** States in the Cold War: 1945-1989. Collier, C.   327

UNITED STATES MILITARY ACADEMY

     See also Colleges and universities

United States presidents [series]

Allen, M. G. Calvin Coolidge   973.91

United States v. Amistad. Gold, S. D.   326

United States v. the Amistad. Hulm, D.   326

UNITED STATES. ARMY

     See also Armies; Military history; United States -- Armed forces

UNITED STATES. ARMY -- BIOGRAPHY

     See also Biography

UNITED STATES. ARMY -- MILITARY LIFE

     See also Military personnel; Soldiers

UNITED STATES. ARMY -- OFFICERS

     See also Military personnel; Soldiers

UNITED STATES. ARMY -- PARACHUTE TROOPS

     See also Parachute troops

UNITED STATES. ARMY -- SONGS

     See also Songs

UNITED STATES. NAVY -- BIOGRAPHY

     See also Biography

UNITED STATES. NAVY -- OFFICERS

     See also Military personnel

UNITED STATES. SUPREME COURT -- BIOGRAPHY

     See also Biography

UNITED STATES/BIOGRAPHY/DICTIONARIES

Rubel, D. Scholastic encyclopedia of the presidents and their times   973

UNITED STEELWORKERS OF AMERICA

     See also Labor unions

UNIVERSAL HISTORY *See* World history

Universe.   523.1

The **universe.** Silverstein, A.   520

UNIVERSE

A black hole is not a hole   523.8

Silverstein, A. The universe   520

Universe   523.1

Ward, D. J. Seven wonders of space phenomena   520

UNIVERSITIES *See* Colleges and universities

UNIVERSITIES AND COLLEGES *See* Colleges and universities

UNIVERSITIES AND COLLEGES -- FICTION

Charbonneau, J. The Testing   Fic

Cooney, C. B. Janie face to face   Fic

UNIVERSITY EXTENSION

     See also Colleges and universities; Distance education; Higher education

The **unknowns.** Carey, B.   Fic

The unladylike adventures of Kat Stephenson [series]

Burgis, S. Kat, incorrigible   Fic

Burgis, S. Renegade Magic   Fic

An **unlikely** friendship. Rinaldi, A.   Fic

Unlikely pairs. Raczka, B.   750

Unlucky charms. Rex, A.   Fic

UNMARRIED COUPLES

     See also Lifestyles; Shared housing

UNMARRIED FATHERS

     See also Fathers; Single parents

UNMARRIED PARENTS *See* Unmarried fathers; Unmarried mothers

The **unnameables.** Booraem, E.   Fic

Unnatural creatures.   S C

Unraveling freedom. Bausum, A.   940.3

Unseen companion. Orenstein, D. G.   **Fic**

The **unseen** guest.   **Fic**

The **Unsinkable** Walker Bean. Renier, A.   **741.5**

Unsolved history [series]
    Blackwood, G. L. Enigmatic events   **904**
    Blackwood, G. L. Legends or lies?   **398.2**

UNSOLVED MYSTERIES
    Cryptic Canada   **971.1**

Unsolved: what really happened to Amelia Earhart?
    Micklos, J.   **92**

The **unspoken.** Fahy, T. R.   **Fic**

Unspoken. Brennan, S. R.   **Fic**

UNWED MOTHERS See Unmarried mothers

UnWholly. Shusterman, N.   **Fic**

Unwind. Shusterman, N.   **Fic**

Up all night. Abrahams, P.   **S C**

Up before daybreak. Hopkinson, D.   **331.7**

Up close [series]
    Aronson, M. Bill Gates   **92**
    Aronson, M. Robert F. Kennedy   **92**
    Bardhan-Quallen, S. Jane Goodall   **92**
    Bolden, T. W.E.B. Du Bois   **92**
    Cooper, I. Oprah Winfrey   **92**
    Cooper, M. L. Theodore Roosevelt   **92**
    Crowe, C. Thurgood Marshall   **92**
    Hampton, W. Babe Ruth   **92**
    Hampton, W. Elvis Presley   **92**
    Madden, K. Harper Lee   **92**
    Stone, T. L. Ella Fitzgerald   **92**
    Sutherland, J. Ronald Reagan   **92**

Up from slavery. Washington, B. T.   **92**

Updale, Eleanor
    Montmorency   **Fic**
    Montmorency and the assassins   **Fic**
    Montmorency on the rocks   **Fic**
    Montmorency's revenge   **Fic**

UPHOLSTERY
    See also Interior design

Upjohn, Rebecca
    The secret of the village fool   **Fic**

Upon the head of the goat: a childhood in Hungary, 1939-1944. Siegal, A.   **92**

UPPER ATMOSPHERE
    See also Atmosphere

UPPER CLASS
    See also Social classes

Uprising. Haddix, M. P.   **Fic**

The **upstairs** room. Reiss, J.   **92**

URANIUM
    See also Chemical elements

Uranus. Sherman, J.   **523.4**

URANUS (PLANET)
    See also Planets

URBAN AGRICULTURE
    See also Agriculture

URBAN ANIMALS

Read, N. City critters   **591.75**

URBAN AREAS See Cities and towns; Metropolitan areas

URBAN DEVELOPMENT See Cities and towns -- Growth; City planning; Urbanization

URBAN ECOLOGY
    Laidlaw, J. A. Cities   **307.7**
    Leardi, J. Making cities green   **333.72**
    Read, N. City critters   **591.75**
    See also Cities and towns; Ecology

URBAN ECOLOGY (SOCIOLOGY)
    Spilsbury, R. Towns and cities   **307.76**

URBAN ENVIRONMENT See Urban ecology

URBAN FOLKLORE
    See also Folklore

URBAN FORESTRY
    See also Forests and forestry

URBAN HOMESTEADING
    See also Houses -- Buying and selling; Housing; Urban renewal

URBAN HOUSING See Housing

URBAN LIFE See City and town life

URBAN PLANNERS
    Lang, G. Genius of common sense   **92**

URBAN PLANNING See City planning

URBAN POLICY
    See also City and town life; Economic policy; Social policy; Urban sociology

URBAN POOR -- UNITED STATES
    Inner-city poverty   **362.5**

URBAN RENEWAL
    See also Metropolitan areas; Urban sociology

URBAN SCHOOLS
    See also Schools
    Lang, G. Genius of common sense   **92**
    Swift, R. Gangs   **364.1**

Urban teens in the library.   **027.62**

Urban underground [series]
    Schraff, A. E. A boy called Twister   **Fic**

Urban warfare. McIntosh, J. S.   **355.4**

URBAN WARFARE
    McIntosh, J. S. Urban warfare   **355.4**

Urban, Linda
    The center of everything   **Fic**

URBAN-RURAL MIGRATION See Internal migration

URBANIZATION
    Lorinc, J. Cities   **307.7**

URBANIZATION
    See also Cities and towns; Rural sociology; Social change; Social conditions; Urban sociology

URBANIZATION -- UNITED STATES -- HISTORY
    Collier, C. The rise of the cities, 1820-1920 **307.76**

URINARY ORGANS

disorders (and their parents) **618.92**

Verhoeven, Rian

Rol, R. v. d. Anne Frank, beyond the diary **940.53**

Vermeer, Johannes, 1632-1675 -- Fiction
About
Balliett, B. Chasing Vermeer **Fic**

Vermont. Heinrichs, A. **974.3**

Verne, Jules, 1828-1905

20,000 leagues under the sea **Fic**

Macdonald, F. Journey to the Center of the Earth **741.5**

Schoell, W. Remarkable journeys: the story of Jules Verne **843**

Vernick, Audrey

Water balloon **Fic**

Vernick, Shirley Reva

The blood lie **Fic**

Vernonia School District v. Acton. Gold, S. D. **344**

VERONA (ITALY) -- FICTION

Coville, B. William Shakespeare's Romeo and Juliet **822.3**

Versace. Davis, D. K. **92**

Versace, Gianni, 1946-1997
About
Davis, D. K. Versace **92**

VERSIFICATION

See also Authorship; Poetics; Rhythm

VERTEBRATES

Holmes, T. The first vertebrates **567**

VERTEBRATES

See also Animals

A **very** fine line. Johnston, J. **Fic**

Vescia, Monique

Rauf, D. Computer game designer **794.8**

Vespers rising. Riordan, R. **Fic**

The **vespertine.** Mitchell, S. **Fic**

Vespucci, Amerigo, 1451-1512
About
Fritz, J. Around the world in a hundred years **910.92**

Vessel. Durst, S. B. **Fic**

VESSELS (SHIPS) *See* Ships

VESTA (ROMAN DEITY)

See also Gods and goddesses

VETERANS

Haney, E. L. Inside Delta Force **356**

VETERANS

See also Military art and science; Veterans

VETERANS -- EMPLOYMENT

See also Employment

VETERANS -- FICTION

Lerangis, P. Somebody, please tell me who I am

VETERANS DAY

See also Holidays

VETERINARIANS

Jackson, D. M. ER vets **636.089**

VETERINARY EMERGENCIES

Jackson, D. M. ER vets **636.089**

VETERINARY MEDICINE

See also Medicine

Jackson, D. M. ER vets **636.089**

VETERINARY MEDICINE -- FICTION

Wilson, D. L. Firehorse **Fic**

VIADUCTS *See* Bridges

VIBRATION

See also Mechanics; Sound

VICE

See also Conduct of life; Ethics; Human behavior

VICE-PRESIDENTS

Adams, J. John Adams the writer **92**

Allen, M. G. Calvin Coolidge **973.91**

Aronson, B. Richard M. Nixon **92**

Baptiste, T. Al Gore **92**

Barron, R. Richard Nixon **92**

Cooper, M. L. Theodore Roosevelt **92**

Driver, S. S. Understanding the Declaration of Independence **973.3**

Elish, D. Theodore Roosevelt **92**

Fitzpatrick, B. Theodore Roosevelt **92**

Fritz, J. Bully for you, Teddy Roosevelt! **92**

Gold, S. D. Lyndon B. Johnson **92**

Gottfried, T. Millard Fillmore **92**

Harness, C. The remarkable, rough-riding life of Theodore Roosevelt and the rise of empire America **92**

Hollihan, K. L. Theodore Roosevelt for kids **92**

Kraft, B. H. Theodore Roosevelt **973.91**

Lanier, S. Jefferson's children **973.4**

Miller, B. M. Thomas Jefferson for kids **92**

Sergis, D. K. Bush v. Gore **342**

Severance, J. B. Thomas Jefferson **973.4**

St. George, J. The duel: the parallel lives of Alexander Hamilton and Aaron Burr **92**

Stefoff, R. U.S. v. Nixon **342**

Whitelaw, N. Thomas Jefferson **973.4**

Young, J. C. Joe Biden **92**

See also Presidents

VICE-PRESIDENTS -- UNITED STATES

Baptiste, T. Al Gore **92**

Young, J. C. Joe Biden **92**

Vicious. **302.34**

Vickers, Tanya M.

Teen science fair sourcebook **507.8**

Vicodin, OxyContin, and other pain relievers. Breguet, A. **362.29**

VICTIMS OF CRIMES

See also Crime

Victoria and her court. Schomp, V. **941.081**

Victoria Woodhull. Havelin, K. **92**

Victoria, Queen of Great Britain, 1819-1901
About
Deedy, C. A. The Cheshire Cheese cat **Fic**

Vrettos, Adrienne Maria
Sight   Fic
Skin   Fic
Vry, Silke
Paul Klee for children   759.949
Trick of the eye   152.14

W

W.A.R.P. [series]
Colfer, E. The reluctant assassin   Fic
W.E.B. Du Bois. Whiting, J.   92
W.E.B. Du Bois. Bolden, T.   92
Wachale! poetry and prose on growing up Latino in America.   810
Wachtel, Alan
September 11   973.931
Southeast Asian Americans   305.8
Wade, Henry, 1914-2001
About
Gold, S. D. Roe v. Wade   344
Wade, Mary Dodson
Henrietta King, la patrona   976.4
Wade, Rosalyn
Polar worlds   998
Wadham, Rachel
(jt. auth) Ostenson, J. W. Integrating young adult literature through the common core standards   418
This is my life   016
Wadsworth, Ginger
First Girl Scout   369.463
John Burroughs   508
WAGE-PRICE POLICY
    See also Inflation (Finance); Prices; Salaries, wages, etc.
The **wager.** Napoli, D. J.   Fic
Waggit again. Howe, P.   Fic
Waggit's tale. Howe, P.   Fic
Waging peace. Caravantes, P.   92
Wagner, Heather Lehr
The Algerian war   965
Hernan Cortes   92
The Iranian Revolution   955
Spies in the Civil War   973.7
Wagner, Hilary
Nightshade City   Fic
The white assassin   Fic
Wagner, Honus, 1874-1955 -- Fiction
About
Gutman, D. Honus & me   Fic
Wagner, Viqi
(ed) Endangered species: opposing viewpoints   578.68
WAGON TRAINS -- FICTION
Dallas, S. The quilt walk   Fic
Wague Diakite, Baba
A gift from childhood   92

Wagué Diakité, Baba
About
Wague Diakite, B. A gift from childhood   92
Wahls, Zach
About
Littlefield, B. My two moms   306.874
Wahls, Zach, 1991-
(jt. auth) Littlefield, B. My two moms   306.874
Wainwright, Louie L.
About
Fridell, R. Gideon v. Wainwright   345
Wait for me. Na, A.   Fic
Wait till Helen comes. Hahn, M. D.   Fic
Waite, Michael P.
The witches of Dredmoore Hollow   Fic
Waiting for no one. Brenna, B.   Fic
Waiting for normal. Connor, L.   Fic
Waiting to forget. Welch, S. K.   Fic
Wake. Hocking, A.   Fic
Wake. McMann, L.   Fic
The **wake** of the Lorelei Lee. Meyer, L. A.   Fic
Wake up our souls. Bolden, T.   704
Wakefield, Ruth
About
Thimmesh, C. Girls think of everything   920
The **waking** [series]
Randall, T. Dreams of the dead   Fic
Randall, T. Spirits of the Noh   Fic
Walden then & now. McCurdy, M.   818
Walden, Mark
Dreadnought   Fic
Escape velocity   Fic
H.I.V.E   Fic
H.I.V.E.: the Overlord protocol   Fic
Waldman, Carl
Encyclopedia of Native American tribes   970.004
Waldman, Neil
Out of the shadows   92
Voyages   92
Waldman, Neil, 1947-
About
Waldman, N. Out of the shadows   92
Waldorf, Heather
Tripping   Fic
Waldron, Melanie
Scotland   941.1
Wales. Hestler, A.   942.9
WALES -- HISTORY -- FICTION
Coats, J. A. The wicked and the just   Fic
Walk across the sea. Fletcher, S.   Fic
Walk softly, Rachel. Banks, K.   Fic
Walk two moons. Creech, S.   Fic
Walker, A'Lelia, 1885-1931 -- Poetry
About
Atkins, J. Borrowed names   811
Walker, Denise

Saunders, C. What is the theory of plate tectonics? **551.1**

Weigel, Marlene

(ed) U-X-L encyclopedia of biomes **577.8**

Weighing in. Favor, L. J. **613.2**

Weighing in. Favor, L. J. **613.2**

Weight. Sullivan, N. **530**

WEIGHT

See also Physics

WEIGHT CONTROL See Weight loss

WEIGHT LIFTING

See also Athletics; Exercise

Frederick, S. Strength training for teen athletes **613.7**

WEIGHT LOSS

Dieting **613.2**

Edwards, H. Talking about your weight **613.2**

Favor, L. J. Weighing in **613.2**

Heller, T. Overweight **613.2**

Hidalgo-Robert, A. Fat no more **616.85**

Smolin, L. A. Nutrition and weight management **613.2**

Zahensky, B. A. Diet fads **613.2**

WEIGHT LOSS -- FICTION

Lipsyte, R. One fat summer **Fic**

Zarr, S. Sweethearts **Fic**

WEIGHT LOSS -- PERSONAL NARRATIVES

Hidalgo-Robert, A. Fat no more **616.85**

The **Weight** of Water. Crossan, S. **Fic**

WEIGHT TRAINING See Weight lifting

WEIGHTLIFTING See Weight lifting

WEIGHTS AND MEASURES

See also Physics

Gardner, R. Ace your math and measuring science project **530.8**

Sullivan, N. Weight **530**

Weihs, Jean

(ed) Cataloging correctly for kids **025.3**

Wein, Elizabeth E.

The empty kingdom **Fic**

The lion hunter **Fic**

Weinberg, Leonard

What is terrorism? **303.6**

Weiner, Roberta

Arnold, J. R. The industrial revolution **330.9**

Weing, Drew

Set to sea **741.5**

Weingarten, Lynn

Wherever Nina lies **Fic**

Weinick, Suzanne

Increasing your tweets, likes, and ratings **658.8**

Weinman, Brad

Neimark, A. E. Myth maker: J.R.R. Tolkien **828**

Weinstein, Bruce D.

Is it still cheating if I don't get caught? **170**

Weinstein, Lauren

Girl stories **741.5**

Weir, Jane

Matter **530**

Max Planck **92**

Weir, William

Border patrol **363.2**

Weird meat-eating plants. Aaseng, N. **583**

Weird U.S. Lake, M. **973**

Weird weather. Evans, K. **363.7**

Weird zone. **796.1**

Weird zone [series]

Weird zone **796.1**

Weiss, Gail Garfinkel

Americans from Russia and Eastern Europe **305.8**

Weiss, Helen S.

(ed) This family is driving me crazy **S**

Weiss, M. Jerry

(ed) This family is driving me crazy **S C**

Weiss, Mitch

Hamilton, M. Children tell stories **372.6**

Weissman, Elissa Brent

The short seller **Fic**

The trouble with Mark Hopper **Fic**

Weitzman, David

Pharaoh's boat **932**

Skywalkers **682**

Weitzman, D. Skywalkers **682**

Welch, Janet

Lerch, M. T. Serving homeschooled teens and their parents **027.6**

Welch, Rollie James

A core collection for young adults **011.6**

The guy-friendly YA library **027.62**

Welch, Sheila Kelly

Waiting to forget **Fic**

Welcome to Bordertown. **808**

Welden, Amelie

(jt. auth) McCann, M. R. Girls who rocked the world **920.72**

WELDERS

Anderson, W. Brown v. Board of Education **344**

Gold, S. D. Brown v. Board of Education **344**

WELFARE AGENCIES See Charities

WELFARE REFORM See Public welfare

WELFARE STATE

See also Economic policy; Public welfare; Social policy; State, The

WELFARE WORK See Charities; Social work

WELFARE, PUBLIC See Public welfare

The **well.** Taylor, M. D. **Fic**

The **well** between the worlds. Llewellyn, S. **Fic**

WELL DRILLING, OIL See Oil well drilling

The **Wells** Bequest. Shulman, P. **Fic**

Wells, Catherine

Strange creatures: the story of Mary Shelley **92**

Wells, H. G.

The war of the worlds   **Fic**

Wells, H. G. (Herbert George), 1866-1946

About

Geary, R. The invisible man   **741.5**

Abrams, D. H.G. Wells   **92**

Palma, F. J. The map of the sky   **Fic**

Wells, Ken

Rascal   **Fic**

Wells, Robison

Feedback   **Fic**

Variant   **Fic**

Wells, Rosemary

Mary on horseback   **92**

My Havana   **Fic**

On the Blue Comet   **Fic**

Red moon at Sharpsburg   **Fic**

Wells-Cole, Catherine

Charles Dickens   **823**

Welsbacher, Anne

Earth-friendly design   **745.2**

Protecting Earth's rain forests   **577.3**

Welsh, M. L.

Heart of stone   **Fic**

Mistress of the Storm   **Fic**

Weltig, Matthew Scott

The aftermath of the Anglo-Zulu war   **968**

Welton, Jude

Henri Matisse   **92**

Welty, Tara

Jane Goodall   **92**

Wenzel, Angela

13 art mysteries children should know   **759.2**

13 artists children should know   **709**

13 paintings children should know   **750**

13 sculptures children should know   **731**

The **werewolf.** Hirschmann, K.   **398.24**

Werewolves. Kallen, S. A.   **398**

WEREWOLVES

See also Folklore

Bennett, A. Ancient werewolves and vampires   **398.2**

Bennett, A. Global legends and lore   **398.2**

Etingoff, K. Howling at the moon   **398**

Etingoff, K. The science of the beast   **398**

Hirschmann, K. The werewolf   **398.24**

Indovino, S. C. Dracula and beyond   **791.43**

Indovino, S. C. Transylvania and beyond   **398**

Kallen, S. A. Werewolves   **398**

Martin, N. Fighting the fangs   **398**

Nelson, S. The psychology of our dark side   **398**

Sanna, E. Pop monsters   **398**

Valentino, S. How to be a werewolf   **398.2**

WEREWOLVES -- FICTION

Armstrong, K. The reckoning   **Fic**

Davis, H. Never cry werewolf   **Fic**

Jinks, C. The abused werewolf rescue group   **Fic**

Jobling, C. The rise of the wolf   **Fic**

Meyer, S. Breaking dawn   **Fic**

Meyer, S. Eclipse   **Fic**

Moore, P. Red moon rising   **Fic**

Perez, M. Dead is a state of mind   **Fic**

Perez, M. Dead is just a rumor   **Fic**

Shan, D. Blood beast   **Fic**

Shan, D. Dark calling   **Fic**

Shan, D. Death's Shadow   **Fic**

Shan, D. Demon apocalypse   **Fic**

Showalter, G. Intertwined   **Fic**

St. Crow, L. Betrayals   **Fic**

St. Crow, L. Defiance   **Fic**

St. Crow, L. Jealousy   **Fic**

St. Crow, L. Strange angels   **Fic**

Stewart, P. The curse of the night wolf   **Fic**

Toft, D. The twilight circus   **Fic**

Toft, D. Wolven   **Fic**

Wereworld [series]

Jobling, C. The rise of the wolf   **Fic**

Werker, Kim P.

Get hooked   **746.43**

Get hooked again   **746.43**

Werlin, Nancy

Double helix   **Fic**

Extraordinary   **Fic**

Impossible   **Fic**

The killer's cousin   **Fic**

The rules of survival   **Fic**

Wesson, Lindsey Patrick

Green reads   **016**

WEST (U.S.) -- DESCRIPTION AND TRAVEL

Munoz, W. Plants on the trail with Lewis and Clark   **581**

Patent, D. H. Animals on the trail with Lewis and Clark   **917**

Stille, D. R. The journals of Lewis and Clark   **917.804**

WEST (U.S.) -- DISCOVERY AND EXPLORATION

Bodden, V. Through the American West   **917.804**

Green, C. R. Zebulon Pike   **978**

Hirschfelder, A. B. Photo odyssey: Solomon Carvalho's remarkable Western adventure, 1853-54   **917**

WEST (U.S.) -- HISTORY

See also United States -- History

WEST (U.S.) -- HISTORY -- GRAPHIC NOVELS

Best shot in the West   **978**

WEST (U.S.) IN ART

Reich, S. Painting the wild frontier: the art and adventures of George Catlin   **92**

West African Americans. Keedle, J.   **305.8**

West African kingdoms. Haywood, J.   **966**

WEST INDIAN AMERICANS

Horst, H. A. Jamaican Americans   **305.8**

All my noble dreams and then what happens **Fic**
Burying the sun **Fic**
Chu Ju's house **Fic**
The Disappeared **Fic**
Goodbye, Vietnam **Fic**
Homeless bird **Fic**
Listening for lions **Fic**
The locked garden **Fic**
See what I see **Fic**
Small acts of amazing courage **Fic**
When a friend dies. Gootman, M. E. **155.9**
When Daddy hit Mommy. Stewart, S. **362.82**
When dinos dawned, mammals got munched, and Pterosaurs took flight. Bonner, H. **567.9**
When elephants fight. Walters, E. **920**
When I crossed No-Bob. McMullan, M. **Fic**
When I grow up. Loy, J. **331.702**
When I was a boy Neruda called me Policarpo. Delano, P. **92**
When I was a soldier. Zenatti, V. **92**
When I was Joe. David, K. **Fic**
When is a planet not a planet? Scott, E. **523.4**
When life stinks. Piquemal, M. **158**
When love comes to town. Lennon, T. **Fic**
When Molly was a Harvey Girl. Wood, F. **Fic**
When my name was Keoko. Park, L. S. **Fic**
When nothing matters anymore. Cobain, B. **616.85**
When Ratboy lived next door. Woodworth, C. **Fic**
When religion & politics mix. McIntosh, K. **201**
When the black girl sings. Wright, B. **Fic**
When the children marched. Mayer, R. H. **323.1**
When the snow fell. Mankell, H. **Fic**
When the Tripods came. Christopher, J. **Fic**
When the whistle blows. Slayton, F. C. **Fic**
When we wake. Healey, K. **Fic**
When will I stop hurting? Myers, E. **155.9**
When you reach me. Stead, R. **Fic**
When you wish. Harmel, K. **Fic**
When you wish upon a rat. McCarthy, M. **Fic**
When Zachary Beaver came to town. Holt, K. W. **Fic**
Where do you stay? Cheng, A. **Fic**
Where I belong. Cross, G. **Fic**
Where I want to be. Griffin, A. **Fic**
Where she went. Forman, G. **Fic**
Where the ground meets the sky. Davies, J. **Fic**
Where the lillies bloom. Cleaver, V. **Fic**
Where the mountain meets the moon. Lin, G. **Fic**
Where the red fern grows. Rawls, W. **Fic**
Where the sidewalk ends. Silverstein, S. **811**
Where the streets had a name. Abdel-Fattah, R. **Fic**
Where we are, what we see. **808**
Wherever Nina lies. Weingarten, L. **Fic**
Which way to the wild West? Sheinkin, S. **978**
While he was away. Schreck, K. **Fic**
While I live. Marsden, J. **Fic**

The **whipping** boy. Fleischman, S. **Fic**
Whipple, Laura
  If the shoe fits **811**
Whirlwind. Klass, D. **Fic**
The **whirlwind.** Matas, C. **Fic**
The **Whisper.** Clayton, E. **Fic**
Whisper and shout. **811**
WHISTLE BLOWING
  See also Political corruption; Public interest
Whitaker, Alecia
  The queen of Kentucky **Fic**
Whitaker, John O.
  National Audubon Society field guide to North American mammals **599**
The **white** assassin. Wagner, H. **Fic**
The **white** ballets. Kupesic, R. **792.8**
The **white** cat. Black, H. **Fic**
The **White** City. Bemis, J. C. **Fic**
WHITE COLLAR CRIMES
  See also Crime
  Juettner, B. Blackmail and bribery **364.16**
White crow. Sedgwick, M. **Fic**
White Fang. London, J. **Fic**
The **white** giraffe. St. John, L. **Fic**
White girl. Olsen, S. **Fic**
White heat. Grant, K. M. **Fic**
The **white** horse trick. Thompson, K. **Fic**
White House autumn. White, E. E. **Fic**
White House kids. **973.09**
The **White** Mountains. Christopher, J. **Fic**
White sands, red menace. Klages, E. **Fic**
WHITE SUPREMACIST MOVEMENTS *See* White supremacy movements
WHITE SUPREMACISTS
  Coleman, W. Racism on trial **345**
WHITE SUPREMACY MOVEMENTS
  Bartoletti, S. C. They called themselves the K.K.K. **322.4**
  Roleff, T. L. Hate groups **364.1**
WHITE SUPREMACY MOVEMENTS
  See also Race relations; Racism; Social movements
White, Amy Brecount
  Forget-her-nots **Fic**
White, Andrea
  Surviving Antarctica **Fic**
  Window boy **Fic**
  Windows on the world **Fic**
White, E. B.
  About
  Lives of the writers **809**
White, Ellen Emerson
  Long live the queen **Fic**
  Long may she reign **Fic**
  The President's daughter **Fic**
  White House autumn **Fic**

Wittenstein, Vicki Oransky
Planet hunter — 523.2

Witter, Bret
Myron, V. Dewey the library cat — 636.8

Wittlinger, Ellen
Hard love — Fic
Love & lies — Fic
Parrotfish — Fic
This means war! — Fic
Zigzag — Fic

Wittmann, Kelly
Botswana — 968.83

WIVES
See also Family; Marriage; Married people; Women

The **wizard** heir. Chima, C. W. — Fic
A **wizard** of Earthsea. Le Guin, U. K. — Fic
The **Wizard** of Rondo. Rodda, E. — Fic

WIZARDS -- FICTION
Barron, T. A. The fires of Merlin — Fic
Chima, C. W. The Crimson Crown — Fic
Mlawski, S. Hammer of witches — Fic
Rowling, J. K. Harry Potter and the Goblet of Fire — Fic

Wizards and witches. Kerns, A. — 133.4
Woe is I Jr. O'Conner, P. T. — 428

Woelfle, Gretchen
All the world's a stage — Fic
The wind at work — 621.4

Wohlenhaus, Kim
(ed) Asthma information for teens — 616.2

Wojciechowski, Tadeusz
Kadziolka, J. Poland — 943.8

Wojtanik, Andrew, 1989-
The National Geographic Bee ultimate fact book — 910

WOK COOKING
See also Cooking

Wolf brother. Paver, M. — Fic
Wolf Island. Shan, D. — Fic
Wolf mark. Bruchac, J. — Fic
Wolf spiders. Markle, S. — 595.4
The **Wolf** Tree. Bemis, J. C. — Fic

Wolf, Allan
Holbrook, S. More than friends — 811
Immersed in verse — 808.1
New found land — Fic
The watch that ends the night — Fic

Wolf, Joan M.
Someone named Eva — Fic

Wolf, Laurie Goldrich
Recyclo-gami — 745.5

Wolf, Sallie
The robin makes a laughing sound — 598

Wolf, Shelby A.
(ed) Handbook of research on children's and young adult literature — 028.5

Wolfe, Brad
(ed) Breakfast on Mars and 37 Other delectable Essays — 372.62

Wolfe, Brian
Extreme face painting — 745.5

Wolfe, Lois
Stokes, J. Students on strike — 379

Wolfe, Nick
Wolfe, B. Extreme face painting — 745.5

Wolff, Virginia Euwer
Make lemonade — Fic
The Mozart season — Fic
Probably still Nick Swansen — Fic
This full house — Fic
True believer — Fic

Wolff, Virginia Euwer
About
Reid, S. E. Virginia Euwer Wolff — 813

Wolfgang Amadeus Mozart. Riggs, K. — 92

Wolfson, Jill
Home, and other big, fat lies — Fic
What I call life — Fic

Wolitzer, Meg
The fingertips of Duncan Dorfman — Fic

Wollard, Kathy
How come? in the neighborhood — 500

Wollman, Jessica
Switched — Fic

Wolny, Philip
Chemical reactions — 541
Waterfowl — 799.2

Wolven. Toft, D. — Fic
Wolverine. Manning, M. K. — 741.5

WOLVERINE (FICTIONAL CHARACTER)
Lyga, B. Wolverine: worst day ever — 741.5
Manning, M. K. Wolverine — 741.5
Wolverine: worst day ever. Lyga, B. — 741.5

WOLVES
Imbriaco, A. The red wolf — 599.77
McAllister, I. The sea wolves — 599.77

WOLVES -- FICTION
The unseen guest — Fic

Wolves of the Beyond [series]
Lasky, K. Frost wolf — Fic
Lasky, K. Lone wolf — Fic
Lasky, K. Shadow wolf — Fic
Lasky, K. Watch wolf — Fic

The **wolves** of Willoughby Chase. Aiken, J. — Fic
Wolves, boys, & other things that might kill me. Chandler, K. — Fic

WOMAN See Women
WOMEN
Branzei, S. Adventurers — 920.72
Green, M. Y. A strong right arm: the story of Mamie Peanut Johnson — 92

Roberts, J. Tiger Woods 92

Woodside, Martin
  Thomas A. Edison 92

Woodson, Jacqueline
About
  Hinton, K. Jacqueline Woodson 92
  Stover, L. T. Jacqueline Woodson 813

Woodson, Jacqueline
  After Tupac and D Foster Fic
  Feathers Fic
  From the notebooks of Melanin Sun Fic
  Hush Fic
  If you come softly Fic
  Lena Fic
  Locomotion Fic
  Peace, Locomotion Fic

Woodsong. Paulsen, G. 796.5

Woodswalk. Art, H. W. 508

Woodward, Joe
  Ross, S. Pearl Harbor 940.54

Woodward, John
  (ed) Conserving the environment 333.7
  3-D dinosaur 567.9
  Creatures of the deep 591.7
  Malam, J. Dinosaur atlas 567.9
  Ocean 591.77
  Planet Earth 550
  Water 553.7

WOODWORK
  See also Architecture -- Details; Decorative arts; Wood

WOODWORK -- FICTION
  Giff, P. R. Eleven Fic

WOODWORKING MACHINERY
  See also Machinery

Woodworth, Chris
  Double-click for trouble Fic
  When Ratboy lived next door Fic

Woog, Adam
  The bionic hand 617
  The Emancipation Proclamation 973.7
  Food myths and facts 613.2
  Jacques Cartier 92
  Jyotirmayee Mohapatra 92
  Mark Zuckerberg, Facebook creator 92
  Ray Charles and the birth of soul 92
  SCRATCHbot 629.8
  Vampires in the movies 791.43

WOOL
  See also Animal products; Fabrics; Fibers

Wooldridge, Connie Nordhielm
  The brave escape of Edith Wharton 92

Woolf, Alex
  The Arab-Israeli War since 1948 956.04
  Buildings 690
  Death and disease 610

Finding an identity 305.4

Woolley, John T.
  (ed) The presidency A to Z 973.09

Woolls, E. Blanche
  The school library media manager 027.8

Woon, Yvonne
  Dead beautiful Fic

Wooster, Robert
  (ed) Encyclopedia of Native American wars and warfare 970.004

Wooten, Sara McIntosh
  Robert Frost 92

Worcester v. Georgia. Gold, S. D. 342

Worcester, Samuel Austin, 1798-1859
About
  Gold, S. D. Worcester v. Georgia 342

WORD GAMES
  See also Games; Literary recreations
  Cleary, B. P. The laugh stand 817

Word histories and mysteries. 422

Word nerd. Nielsen, S. Fic

WORD PROBLEMS (MATHEMATICS)
  See also Mathematics

WORD RECOGNITION
  See also Reading; Vocabulary

WORD SKILLS
  See also Reading

The **word** snoop. Dubosarsky, U. 420

WORDLESS STORIES See Stories without words

WORDS See Vocabulary; Word skills

Words in the dust. Reedy, T. Fic

The **words** of Martin Luther King, Jr. King, M. L. 323.1

Words of the ancient Romans. Nardo, D. 937

Words set me free. Cline-Ransome, L. 973.8

Words that changed the world [series]
  Driver, S. S. Understanding the Declaration of Independence 973.3
  Kirk, A. Understanding Thoreau's Civil disobedience 814
  Macgillivray, A. Understanding Rachel Carson's Silent Spring 363.7

Words with wings. 811

Wordsworth, William
  William Wordsworth 821

Worek, Michael
  The Nobel Prize 001.4

WORK
  Fischer, J. Earning money 650.1

WORK -- SONGS
  Yolen, J. Apple for the teacher 782.42

WORK AND FAMILY
  See also Family; Work

WORK ENVIRONMENT
  See also Environment; Work

WORK ETHIC

See also Ethics; Work

WORK STOPPAGES *See* Strikes

A **worker** on the transcontinental railroad. Barter, J.   **331.7**

WORKERS *See* Employees; Labor; Working class

WORKERS' COMPENSATION

    See also Accident insurance; Health insurance; Social security

WORKING ANIMALS

    See also Animals; Domestic animals; Economic zoology

    Kent, D. Animal helpers for the disabled   **636.088**

Working animals [series]

    Grayson, R. Military   **355.4**

    Grayson, R. Performers   **791.8**

    Grayson, R. Transportation   **636.088**

    Martin, C. Farming   **636**

    Martin, C. Helpers   **362.4**

    Mezzanotte, J. Police   **363.2**

WORKING CHILDREN *See* Child labor

WORKING CLASS

    See also Social classes

    Hopkinson, D. Up before daybreak   **331.7**

    Skurzynski, G. Sweat and blood   **331.8**

WORKING CLASSES *See* Working class

WORKING DOGS

    See also Dogs; Working animals

    Gorrell, G. K. Working like a dog   **636.7**

    Stewart, G. K-9 police units   **363.2**

Working in music and dance. McAlpine, M.   **780**

Working life [series]

    Barter, J. A Renaissance painter's studio   **759**

    Barter, J. A worker on the transcontinental railroad   **331.7**

    Currie, S. An actor on the Elizabethan stage **792.09**

    Uschan, M. V. The cavalry during the Civil War   **973.7**

Working like a dog. Gorrell, G. K.   **636.7**

Working with animals. McAlpine, M.   **636**

Working with children. McAlpine, M.   **362.7**

Workman, James G.

    Water   **363.6**

Workman, Ross

    (jt. auth) Myers, W. D. Kick   **Fic**

The **world** according to dog. Sidman, J.   **810**

The **world** almanac and book of facts 2013.   **030**

The **World** almanac for kids.   **031.02**

World Almanac Library of the Holocaust [series]

    Downing, D. The origins of the Holocaust   **940.53**

World art & culture [series]

    Bingham, J. African art & culture   **709**

    Bingham, J. Indian art & culture   **709**

    January, B. Native American art & culture   **704**

    Khanduri, K. Japanese art & culture   **709**

    Lewis, E. Mexican art & culture   **709**

World authors, 2000-2005. Rich, M.   **920.003**

A **world** away. Grossman, N.   **Fic**

The **world** before this one. Martin, R.   **398.2**

The **World** Book Encyclopedia.   **031**

The **World** Book encyclopedia.   **031**

World Book Inc.

    (comp) The World Book Encyclopedia   **031**

    The World Book Encyclopedia   **031**

World commodities [series]

    Chapman, G. Coffee   **641.3**

The **world** cookbook for students. Jacob, J.   **641.5**

World crafts and recipes [series]

    Ejaz, K. Recipe and craft guide to India   **641.5**

    LaRoche, A. Recipe and craft guide to France **641.5**

    Mattern, J. Recipe and craft guide to China **641.5**

    Mofford, J. H. Recipe and craft guide to Japan   **641.5**

    Mofford, J. H. Recipe and craft guide to the Caribbean   **641.5**

    Reusser, K. Recipe and craft guide to Indonesia   **641.5**

WORLD CUP (SOCCER)

    See also Soccer; Sports tournaments

WORLD ECONOMICS *See* Commercial geography; Commercial policy; Economic conditions; International competition

World economy explained [series]

    Connolly, S. Banks and banking   **332.1**

    Connolly, S. The stock market   **332.6**

The **world** encyclopedia of Christmas. Bowler, G.   **394.26**

The **world** famous Miles City Bucking Horse Sale. Collard III, S. B.   **791.8**

World folklore series

    English folktales   **398.2**

WORLD HISTORY

    Adams, S. The Kingfisher atlas of world history   **909**

    Aronson, M. Sugar changed the world   **664**

    Christie, P. The curse of Akkad   **551.6**

    Eamer, C. Traitors' Gate and other doorways to the past   **909**

    From then to now   **909**

    Knight, J. Middle ages: almanac   **909.07**

    Lifelines in world history   **920.003**

    National Geographic concise history of world religions   **200**

World history [series]

    Brownell, R. American counterculture of the 1960s   **306**

    Corrick, J. A. The Louisiana Purchase   **973.4**

    George, C. Maya civilization   **972**

    Nardo, D. Aztec civilization   **972**

    Nardo, D. The Black Death   **614.5**

    Nardo, D. The European colonization of Africa **960**

    Nardo, D. Genghis Khan and the Mongol Empire   **950**